PRESENTED TO:

BY:

DATE

NOTES

NOTES

NOTES

NOTES

NOTES

NOTES

NOTES

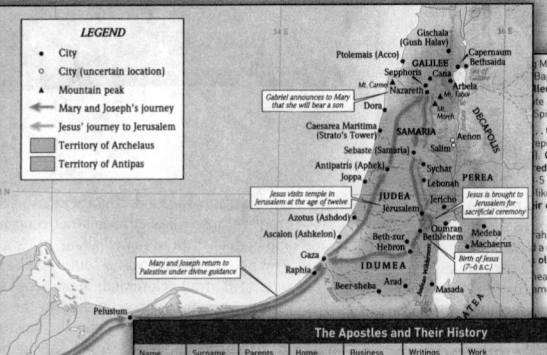

LEGEND

- ● City
- ○ City (uncertain location)
- ▲ Mountain peak
- ← Mary and Joseph's journey
- ← Jesus' journey to Jerusalem
- Territory of Archelaus
- Territory of Antipas

Gabriel announces to Mary that she will bear a son

Jesus visits temple in Jerusalem at the age of twelve

Mary and Joseph return to Palestine under divine guidance

Jesus is brought to Jerusalem for sacrificial ceremony

Birth of Jesus (7–6 B.C.)

... Messiah. **Never drink wine or beer** indicates ... Baptist was under a lifelong Nazirite vow (Nm ... lled with the Holy Spirit . . . in his mother's ... te at verse 41. On the meaning of being filled ... Spirit, see Eph 5:18.

... to the Lord their God speaks of conversion, ... repentance, which John the Baptist preached ... . Go before Him . . . to make ready for the ... red people echoes the essence of the proph- ... 5 (see Lk 3:4-6). Malachi 4:5-6 prophesied ... like figure would come and turn the hearts of ... ir children. That new "Elijah" would be John ...

... aham (Gn 15:8) and Sarah (Gn 18:10-15), ... a difficult time believing God would fulfill His ... old age.

... eans "[mighty] man of God." He is one of only ... med in Scripture. The other is Michael (Dn ...

the Judean hill country, not far from Jerusalem (v. 39).

1:24-25 Elizabeth withdrew **and kept herself in seclusion for five months** after she miraculously **conceived.** Why did she do this? Some speculate that she feared miscarrying during the early months of pregnancy. More likely she recognized that her unusual pregnancy would draw unwelcome attention if it became widely known. Better to have a restful start to a pregnancy that came so late in life.

1:26-38 Here the announcement of Jesus' coming birth is told from Mary's perspective. Matthew gives it from Joseph's vantage point (Mt 1:18-23).

1:26 In the **sixth month** of Elizabeth's pregnancy, **Gabriel,** the same angel who had appeared to Zechariah previously

parthenos

Greek Pronunciation	[pahr THEHN ahss]
HCSB Translation	virgin
Uses in Luke's Gospel	2
Uses in the NT	15
Focus passage	Luke 1:27,34

In the Greek NT, *parthenos* (*virgin*) connotes an unmarried female virgin of marriageable age. Once, the term refers to a male *virgin* (Rv 14:4). Both Matthew and Luke acknowledge that Mary was a *parthenos* at the time she conceived Jesus (Mt 1:20,23; Lk 1:27,34), and Matthew indicates that she remained a virgin while she carried the child to term (Mt 1:25). Both books mention the salvific significance of Jesus' birth (Mt 1:21; Lk 1:31-32). However, Matthew alone indicates the prophetic significance of Jesus' birth by a virgin (Mt 1:23). According to Matthew, Mary was the fulfillment of a prophecy given through the prophet Isaiah, who described a virgin (Is 7:14, *parthenos* occurs here in the Greek OT) who would give birth to a child to be named Immanuel. Matthew applies this prophecy to Messiah's birth.

... 's pronounce- ... nt and unable ... The day these ... at John's birth ...

... ariah to come ... use he did not ... rendered him ... pronounce the ... pon the crowd. ... because they ... signs he made ...

... week at a time, ...

The Apostles and Their History

Name	Surname	Parents	Home	Business	Writings	Work	Death
Simon	Peter or Cephas = Rock	Jonah	Early life: Bethsaida. Later: Capernaum	Fisherman	1 & 2 Peter	Peter may have ministered in the provinces of Pontus, Galatia, Cappadocia; Asia; perhaps in Corinth, and finally in Rome.	According to tradition, attested by Tertullian and Origin, Peter was crucified "with his head downwards" in Rome. The date of his death is likely between A.D. 64–68.
Andrew = manhood or valor		Jonah	Early life: Bethsaida. Later: Capernaum	Fisherman		Uncertain but tradition says he ministered in Cappadocia, Galatia, Bithynia; later in the Sythian deserts, Byzantium and finally in Thrace, Macedonia, Thessaly, and Achaia.	The traditional view is that he was crucified at Patrae in Achaia by order of the Roman governor Ageas.
James the greater or the elder	Boanerges or Sons of Thunder	Zebedee and Salome	Bethsaida, Capernaum, and Jerusalem	Fisherman		Preached in Jerusalem and Judea	Beheaded by Herod in A.D. 62 or 66 at Jerusalem.
John, the beloved disciple	Boanerges or Sons of Thunder	Zebedee and Salome	Bethsaida, Capernaum, and Jerusalem	Fisherman	Gospel, three epistles, and Revelation	Labored among the churches of Asia Minor, especially in Ephesus	Banished to Patmos A.D. 95. Recalled, died a natural death.
James the less		Alphaeus and Mary	Galilee			Preached in Judea and Egypt	According to tradition, he was martyred in Egypt.
Judas (not Iscariot)	Same as Thaddaeus and Lebbaeus	James	Galilee			Preached in Mesopotamia and Armenia	Was martyred in present day Iran and buried near Tabriz.

Luke 2:11   1734

for look, I proclaim to you good news of great joy that will be for all the people:[A] [11] Today a Savior,[a] who is •Messiah[b] the Lord,[c] was born for you in the city of David. [12] This will be the sign for you:[d] You will find a baby wrapped snugly in cloth and lying in a feeding trough."

[13] Suddenly there was a multitude of the heavenly host with the angel, praising God and saying:

[14]   Glory to God in the highest heaven,[e]
     and peace on earth[f] to people
     He favors![B,C,g]

[15] When the angels had left them and returned to heaven, the shepherds said to one another, "Let's go straight to Bethlehem and see what has happened, which the Lord has made known to us."

[16] They hurried off and found both Mary and Joseph, and the baby who was lying in the feeding trough. [17] After seeing them, they reported the message they were told about this child, [18] and all who heard it were amazed at what the shepherds said to them. [19] But Mary was treasuring up all these things[h] and meditating on them. [20] The shep-

herds returned, glorifying and praising God[i] for all they had seen and heard, just as they had been told.

The Circumcision and Presentation of Jesus

[21] When the eight days were completed for His circumcision,[j] He was named Jesus[k]—the name given by the angel before He was conceived.[E] [22] And when the days of their purification according to the law of Moses were finished,[l] they brought Him up to Jerusalem to present Him to the Lord [23] (just as it is written in the law of the Lord: **Every firstborn male[F] will be dedicated[G] to the Lord[H,m]) [24] and to offer a sacrifice (according to what is stated in the law of the Lord: **a pair of turtledoves or two young pigeons[I,n]).

Simeon's Prophetic Praise

[25] There was a man in Jerusalem whose name was Simeon. This man was righteous and devout,[o] looking forward to Israel's consolation,[J,p] and the Holy Spirit was on him. [26] It had been revealed to him by the Holy Spirit[q] that he would not see death before he saw the Lord's Messiah.[r] [27] Guided by the Spirit, he en-

Cross-references:
a 2:11 Mt 1:21; Jn 4:42; Ac 5:31
b Mt 1:16; 16:16,20; Jn 11:27
c Lk 1:43; Ac 2:36; 10:36
d 2:12 1Sm 2:34; 2Kg 19:29; 20:8-9; Is 7:11,14
e 2:14 Mt 21:9; Lk 19:38
f Lk 12:51
g Lk 3:22; Eph 1:9; Php 2:13
h 2:19 Lk 2:51
i 2:20 Mt 9:8
j 2:21 Lk 1:59
k Lk 1:31
l 2:22 Lv 12:6-8
m 2:23 Ex 13:2,12
n 2:24 Lv 5:11; 12:8
o 2:25 Lk 1:6
p Mk 15:43; Lk 2:38; 23:51
q 2:26 Mt 2:12
r Ps 89:48; Jn 8:51; Heb 11:5

The Dedication to Theophilus

1 Many have undertaken to compile a narrative about the events that have been fulfilled^A among us,^{a 2} just as the original eyewitnesses^b and servants of the word^c handed them down to us. ³ It also seemed good to me, since I have carefully investigated everything from the very first, to write to you in an orderly sequence, most honorable^d Theophilus,^{e 4} so that you may know the certainty of the things about which you have been instructed.^{B,f}

Gabriel Predicts John's Birth

⁵ In the days of King •Herod^g of Judea, there was a priest of Abijah's division^{C,h} named Zechariah. His wife was from the daughters of Aaron, and her name was Elizabeth. ⁶ Both were righteous in God's sight,ⁱ living without blame^j according to all the commands and re-

quirements of the Lord. ⁷ But they had no children^D because Elizabeth could not conceive,^E and both of them were well along in years.^F

⁸ When his division was on duty^k and he was serving as priest before God, ⁹ it happened that he was chosen by lot, according to the custom of the priesthood, to enter the sanctuary of the Lord and burn incense.^{l 10} At the hour of incense the whole assembly of the people was praying outside. ¹¹ An angel of the Lord^m appeared to him, standing to the right of the altar of incense. ¹² When Zechariah saw him, he was startled and overcome with fear.^{G 13} But the angel said to him:

> Do not be afraid,ⁿ Zechariah,
> because your prayer has been heard.
> Your wife Elizabeth will bear you a son,
> and you will name him John.^o

^a1:1 Rm 4:21; 14:5; Col 2:2; 4:12; 1Th 1:5; 2Tm 4:17; Heb 6:11; 10:22 ^b1:2 Jn 15:27; Ac 1:21; 2Pt 1:16; 1Jn 1:1 ^cAc 26:16; 1Co 4:1; Heb 2:3 ^d1:3 Ac 23:26; 24:3; 26:25 ^eAc 1:1 ^f1:4 Ac 18:25; Rm 2:18; 1Co 14:19; Gl 6:6 ^g1:5 Mt 2:1 ^h1Ch 24:10 ⁱ1:6 Gn 7:1; Ac 2:25; 8:21 ^jPhp 2:15; 3:6; 1Th 3:13 ^k1:8 1Ch 24:19; 2Ch 8:14; 31:2 ^l1:9 Ex 30:7-8 ^m1:11 Mt 2:13-14; 28:2; Lk 2:9; Ac 5:19; 8:26; 12:7 ⁿ1:13 Gn 15:1; Mt 14:27; Lk 1:30 ^oGn 16:11; 17:19; Lk 1:60,63

A1:1 Or *events that have been accomplished,* or *events most surely believed* **B**1:4 Or *informed* **C**1:5 One of the 24 divisions of priests appointed by David for temple service; 1Ch 24:10 **D**1:7 Lit *child* **E**1:7 Lit *Elizabeth was sterile or barren* **F**1:7 Lit *in their days* **G**1:12 Lit *and fear fell on him*

1:1-4 Using elegant Greek, Luke began his **narrative about the events** of Jesus' life and ministry with a formal preface. This was a common practice in historical works of Luke's era. His prologue: (1) acknowledged previous treatments of the subject, (2) stated his methodology, (3) identified the recipient, and (4) articulated his purpose in writing.

1:1 Many have undertaken to compile a narrative means that a number of others had previously written about the life and works of Jesus. This may include the Gospels of Mark and Matthew since they preceded Luke's writing. **Events . . . fulfilled among us** speaks of how Jesus fulfilled many OT prophecies (see note at 24:44-45).

1:2 Original eyewitnesses included Mary, the mother of Jesus, about whom Luke wrote more than any other NT author. Mary may have still been alive when Luke wrote his Gospel. **Servants of the word** refers to the apostles of Jesus but may also include His brothers, James and Jude. Tradition says both brothers wrote NT books.

1:3 It also seemed good to me does not mean that Luke found the previous narratives (v. 1) to be erroneous or inadequate. Rather, he wrote his Gospel to complement what was already written. **Carefully investigated everything from the very first** means Luke studied the life and ministry of Jesus in meticulous detail ("carefully") and with comprehensive scope ("everything"), including many aspects related to the births of John the Baptist and Jesus ("from the very first") that are not found in the other Gospels. **Orderly sequence** does not mean strict chronological sequence, but in an orderly manner, whether chronological (generally) or topical. On **most honorable Theophilus,** see Introduction.

1:4 Luke's stated purpose in writing his Gospel was to provide historical **certainty** and theological clarity for Theophilus in regard to what he had been taught (**instructed**) about Jesus.

1:5 King Herod the Great was an Idumean appointed by the Roman emperor who ruled from 37-4 B.C. His realm covered not only **Judea,** but also Samaria, Galilee, and parts of Perea and Syria. **In the days of** indicates that the events

that immediately follow probably occurred in 7-6 B.C. The priesthood of Israel was made up of 24 divisions, including the house of Abijah (1Ch 24:10). **Daughters of Aaron** reveals that **Elizabeth** and her husband **Zechariah** were from priestly families. It is also the first instance of Luke's regular emphasis on the vital role that women played throughout Jesus' life.

1:6-7 The words **righteous . . . living without blame** refers to consistent obedience to God's **commands and requirements,** but more foundationally to living by faith. This is how Abraham was justified in **God's sight** (Gn 15:6; Gl 3:6-7,9). Like Abraham and Sarah, despite their godliness, Zechariah and Elizabeth **had no children** and were **well along in years** (past the age of child-bearing). It was considered a curse from God for a woman to be unable to bear children (see note at vv. 24-25).

1:8-9 Twice a year the priestly **division** of Abijah (see note at v. 5) was **on duty** at the Jerusalem temple for a week. Out of hundreds of priests in his division, Zechariah was **chosen** by the casting of a **lot** (see notes at Pr 16:33; Ac 1:24-26) to **burn incense** on the altar in front of the holy of holies (**the sanctuary**), a privileged duty that a priest could perform only once in his life. In fact, many never enjoyed this privilege because the lot never fell to them.

1:10 The **hour of incense** occurred at 9:00 a.m. and 3:00 p.m. daily. The presence of a sizeable **assembly of the people** makes it more likely that this incident took place in the afternoon.

1:11-12 On **an angel of the Lord,** see note at verse 19. To be **overcome with fear** upon seeing an angel is common in Luke (v. 29; 2:9) and elsewhere in Scripture (Jdg 6:22-23; Dn 8:16-17).

1:13 Your prayer may refer to Zechariah and Elizabeth praying to have a child (**your wife . . . will bear you a son**), or it could have been the prayer a priest was to offer at the altar for the redemption of Israel. **John** means "the Lord is gracious."

1:14-15 Joy is the prevailing mood of the first two chapters

Features of the HCSB Study Bible

The HCSB was undertaken as a translation that strongly supports Bible study. In the *HCSB Study Bible*, the Scripture is primary. All features and tools are designed to help you understand the Scripture and be transformed by it.

Two kinds of HCSB notes enable you to see for yourself how the translation was derived. When translators do their work, they begin with several possible translations that reflect the original language. **①ALTERNATE TRANSLATIONS** marked by *Or*. See some of the options HCSB translators considered. A second kind of note marks **②LITERAL TRANSLATIONS**. They are indicated by *Lit*. HCSB aims to be as literal as possible. Where a literal translation doesn't conform to good English style, HCSB translators find a way to render the expression that optimizes accuracy and readability. The *Lit* feature enables you to see the literal translation for yourself and compare it with the what the HCSB translators view as the most accurate translation of the sentence or phrase.

Other Features of the HCSB Study Bible

③CROSS REFERENCES point to other Bible passages that are related to the text on which you are focusing.

④STUDY NOTES provide historical, cultural, linguistic, and biblical information that enhances your understanding of a given passage. Words in bold are directly from the Scripture text.

⑤BULLET POINTS indicate key words for which definitions are provided in the section beginning on p. 2231.

⑥BOLDED TEXT IN THE NEW TESTAMENT are words quoted directly from the Old Testament.

⑦MAPS illuminate the Bible text by showing it's geographical context.

⑧CHARTS organize information in a way that enables the reader to grasp important connections quickly.

⑨WORD STUDIES enable the reader to see a key word and the family of words to which it is related. It also shows a range of expression in which that word functions.

⑩ILLUSTRATIONS recreate architectural structures that were part of the landscape in which the Bible was written. Being able to visualize these structures provides a context in which to read and study passages of Scripture. Both the writer of the passage and many of his first readers knew these structures first hand.

⑪PHOTOS, like Illustrations and Maps, provide visual context known by the biblical writers and many of their first readers. Being able to see the context is a significant aid to comprehension. Both Cyril of Jerusalem (A.D. 315-86) and Jerome (340-420) called the land of the Bible "the Fifth Gospel." Experiencing the land by photos enriches one's reading and understanding of the Bible.

⑫INTRODUCTIONS give overviews of books by providing information on **Circumstances of Writing** including **Author & Background**, **Message and Purpose**, **Contribution to the Bible**, **Structure**, and **Outline**.

⑬TIMELINES place the book in a chronological framework of biblical events (black font) and events of world history (brown font).

⑭ESSAYS give in-depth coverage to major biblical/theological issues.

Introduction to the HCSB Study Bible

The Christian religion rests fundamentally on the belief that God has chosen to reveal Himself to a human race that is estranged from Him. God has done this not only through miraculous signs, sweeping acts of providence, and the life and works of Jesus Christ, but through 66 writings collectively known as the Bible. These books are taken to be nothing less than authoritative communications from God, given through human authors who were led by the Holy Spirit to write down what God would have us know. Among other things, we learn in the Bible that God is the sovereign Creator of all reality. No corner of the universe is outside His rule. We learn that God is love, that His character is steadfast for eternity, that He is in all ways holy, and that He alone is worthy of praise and glory. We also learn that we are sinners in need of reconciliation with God, and that this reconciliation comes only through faith in God's Son who paid our sin debt on the cross.

Since the Bible conveys such serious matters as these, we must be careful to understand its teachings properly. To misunderstand or misapply the Bible can lead to serious error. Now more than ever, the church is gifted with a multitude of teachers who are equipped to provide tools that help readers comprehend the Bible and apply it to their lives. The *HCSB Study Bible* represents the work of more than a hundred scholars who have devoted their lives to living and teaching the truths of Scripture. They come from different denominations and diverse backgrounds. Since its release in 2004, readers have recognized the Holman Christian Standard Bible as a multi-denominational effort, reflecting the very best in updated Bible translation scholarship. We have taken the same approach in the *HCSB Study Bible*. Our contributors reflect a broad sampling of evangelical scholars whose ministries are based at seminaries, colleges, and churches.

The goal of each tool in this study Bible, whether study notes, essays, book introductions, maps, charts, or the online study component (hcsbstudybible.com), is to serve the text of Scripture by bringing to light facts that aid comprehension. As servants to the text, the study tools are designed to keep the focus on Scripture and never on the tools themselves. Practically speaking this approach is demonstrated by the fact that the text of Scripture is never positioned beneath a study tool. The uppermost feature on any given page is the text of Scripture itself. Theologically speaking our text-centric approach is reflected in the fact that each of our contributors honors the Bible as God's inspired and inerrant Word.

Some of the study notes and essays in this study Bible will encourage you and provide answers to questions you have long pondered. Others will surprise you with information you could not have anticipated and prompt you to ask new questions. Still others will challenge you, possibly even provoke you, as you are presented with information that invites you to question your preconceived notions or settled opinions. In all cases our aim is to provide you with tools for engaging God's Word on a deeper level, which leads to life transformation and true knowledge of God. We endeavor to be even-handed on controversial issues. To help achieve this, each note and essay has been pored over by a team of theological editors. In some cases we will adopt positions that are hotly debated, but we always land in a place that is well represented among biblically committed scholars and that seeks to honor the intentions of God's Word.

Our hope is that, in conjunction with other fine study tools that are available, you will use the *HCSB Study Bible* to deepen your walk with the God who has graciously revealed Himself in the Bible.

Jeremy Royal Howard
General Editor

Books of the Bible

Arranged Alphabetically

Additional Features

Table of Contents

Books of the Bible

OLD TESTAMENT

The *HCSB Study Bible* was produced with the assistance of Peachtree Editorial Services. Typesetting was provided by TF Designs.

Styles	ISBN
Hardcover	978-1-5864-0506-9
Black Bonded	978-1-5864-0505-2
Black Bonded Indexed	978-1-5864-0504-5
Black Genuine	978-1-5864-0508-3
Black Genuine Indexed	978-1-5864-0507-6
Black/Gray Simulated	978-1-5864-0502-1
Black/Gray Simulated Indexed	978-1-4336-0123-1
Brown/Tan Simulated	978-1-5864-0503-8
Brown/Tan Simulated Indexed	978-1-4336-0122-4
Black Premium Cowhide	978-1-5864-0457-4

220.52 BIBLE

Printed in the United States of America
1 2 3 4 5 6 13 12 11 10
RRD

HCSB
STUDY BIBLE
Holman Christian Standard Bible

GOD'S WORD *for* LIFE

HCSB

HOLMAN
BIBLE PUBLISHERS

Nashville, Tennessee

HCSB
STUDY BIBLE
Holman Christian Standard Bible

ᴬ10:17 Other mss read *The Seventy-two* ᴮ10:20 Lit *don't rejoice in this, that* ᶜ10:21 Other mss read *Jesus* ᴰ10:21 Other mss omit *Holy* ᴱ10:21 Or *thank, or confess* ᶠ10:21 Lit *was well-pleasing in Your sight* ᴳ10:22 Other mss read *And turning to the disciples, He said, "Everything has*

gospel message. In some sense, the present tense aspects of **the kingdom of God** were present in the preaching of the gospel and the healing ministry delegated by Jesus to the 70.

10:10–11 On wiping dust off the feet, see note at 9:3-5. On **the kingdom of God has come near**, see note at vv. 8-9.

10:12 That day is the day of judgment. **Sodom** was destroyed by the Lord because of its sin (Gn 19:23).

10:13-14 Chorazin and **Bethsaida** were towns in Galilee near Capernaum. **Tyre** and **Sidon** were Gentile cities in Phoenicia on the Mediterranean coast northwest of Galilee. **Sackcloth and ashes** were worn by those in mourning, sometimes as an expression of repentance from sin (Neh 9:1; Jnh 3:5).

10:15 Jesus spent more time in ministry in **Capernaum** than anywhere else in Galilee. Yet, in their arrogance (**exalted to heaven**), the people of this city rejected Jesus and, as a result of their unbelief, would be sent to **Hades** (death, the realm of death or punishment beyond the grave).

10:16 The principle here is that rejection of the disciples is ultimately rejection of God the Father (**the One who sent Me**), for the Father sent the Son and the Son in turn sent out the 70 disciples to preach and heal (vv. 1,9). Since they were commissioned by Christ, to listen to the 70 was like listening to Jesus Himself. Likewise, to reject the 70 was to reject Jesus. Finally, to reject Jesus was to reject God the Father.

10:17-20 Part of the healing that **the Seventy** disciples performed (v. 9) had to do with casting out **demons**. The phrase **Satan fall from heaven** is probably an echo of Ezk 28:16-17, speaking of the initial judgment upon the Devil after he rebelled against God. This passage speaks of a further defeat suffered by Satan as Jesus' disciples were victorious in ministry over the power of the enemy (Satan), symbolized

here by **snakes and scorpions**. As awesome as the power to cast out demons was, it was even more significant that the disciples' **names** were written in the listing of the elect of God—the Lamb's book of life **in heaven** (see Rv 13:8).

10:21-22 The mention of the **Holy Spirit** here is part of Luke's emphasis on the Spirit. The **wise** and **learned** people of the area had rejected the ministry of the 70 disciples, but the insignificant and children (**infants**) had accepted their message. This was part of the plan of God. In His **good pleasure** (see Eph 1:3-11), these things were hidden (Gk *apokrupto*, "to keep secret") from some and revealed to others. It is

The old Roman road from Jerusalem to Jericho was legendary for the dangers it posed to first-century travelers. The road is part of the precipitous drop from the east side of the Mount of Olives down to the Jordan Valley. A Roman aqueduct that is still used today is in the lower portion of the photo.

⑪ **PHOTOS**

⑩ **ILLUSTRATIONS**

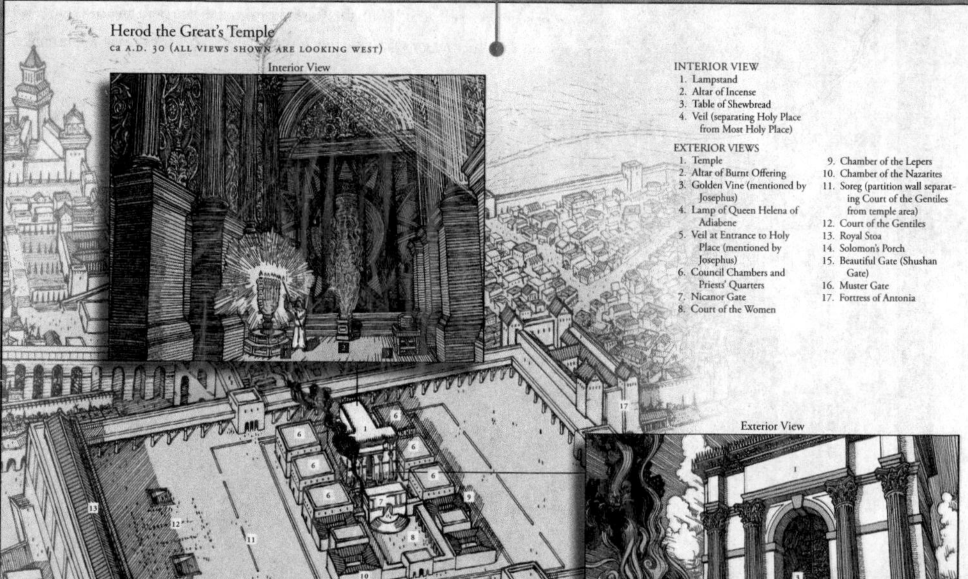

Herod the Great's Temple
ca A.D. 30 (ALL VIEWS SHOWN ARE LOOKING WEST)

Interior View

Exterior View

INTERIOR VIEW
1. Lampstand
2. Altar of Incense
3. Table of Shewbread
4. Veil (separating Holy Place from Most Holy Place)

EXTERIOR VIEWS
1. Temple
2. Altar of Burnt Offering
3. Golden Vine (mentioned by Josephus)
4. Lamp of Queen Helena of Adiabene
5. Veil at Entrance to Holy Place (mentioned by Josephus)
6. Council Chambers and Priests' Quarters
7. Nicanor Gate
8. Court of the Women
9. Chamber of the Lepers
10. Chamber of the Nazarites
11. Soreg (partition wall separating Court of the Gentiles from temple area)
12. Court of the Gentiles
13. Royal Stoa
14. Solomon's Porch
15. Beautiful Gate (Shushan Gate)
16. Muster Gate
17. Fortress of Antonia

Circumstances of Writing

Author: The author of the Third Gospel is not named. Considerable evidence points to Luke as its author. Much of that proof is found in the book of Acts, which identifies itself as a sequel to Luke (Ac 1:1-3). A major line of evidence has to do with the so-called "we" sections of the book (Ac 16:10-17; 20:5-15; 21:1-18; 27:1-37; 28:1-16). Most of Acts is narrated in third-person plural ("they," "them"), but some later sections having to do with the ministry of the apostle Paul unexpectedly shift to first-person plural ("we," "us"). This indicates that the author had joined the apostle Paul for the events recorded in those passages. Since there are no "we" passages in the Gospel of Luke, that fits with the author stating that he used eyewitness testimony to the life of Jesus (1:2), indicating he was not such an eyewitness himself.

Among Paul's well-known coworkers, the most likely candidate is Luke, the doctor (see Phm 24; Col 4:14). That is also the unanimous testimony of the earliest Christian writers (e.g., Justin Martyr, the Muratorian Canon, and Tertullian). Since Luke is not named among the workers who were "of the circumcision" (i.e., a Jew; Col 4:11), he was almost certainly a Gentile. That explains the healthy emphasis on Gentiles in Luke (6:17; 7:1-10). Luke also reflects an interest in medical matters (e.g., 4:38; 14:2).

Background: Traditionally, the Gospel of Luke is believed to have been written after both Matthew and Mark. Those who date Matthew and Mark in the 60s or 70s of the first century A.D. have tended to push the dating of Luke back to the 70s or 80s.

Since Luke wrote both the Third Gospel and the book of Acts (Ac 1:1-3), it is relevant to consider the dating of both books together. The events at the end of Acts occurred around A.D. 62–63. That is the earliest point at which Acts could have been written. If Acts was written in the early 60s from Rome, where Paul was imprisoned for two years (Ac 28:30), the Third Gospel could date from an earlier stage of that period of imprisonment. The other reasonable possibility is during Paul's earlier two-year imprisonment in Caesarea

50 B.C.

Augustus Caesar's reign begins. March 15, 44 B.C.

Roman Senate declares Herod king of the Jews. 39 B.C.

Herod assumes possession of the domain to which he had been named earlier 37 B.C.

Herod begins thorough expansion of the temple in Jerusalem in 20 B.C. The inner sanctuary was completed in 1 ½ years and the rest of the temple was finished in A.D. 63, only seven years before it was destroyed.

Imperial census in territory governed by Herod 6 to 4 B.C.

5 B.C.–A.D. 9

Jesus' birth 5 B.C.

Eclipse of the moon just prior to Herod's death March 12/13, 4 B.C.

Passover celebrated just after Herod's death April 11, 4 B.C.

Herod's sons, Herod Phillip, Herod Antipas, and Archelaus divide Palestine and rule three territories under the aegis of Rome 4 B.C.

Jesus travels with His parents from Nazareth to Jerusalem for the Passover Festival A.D. 9

(Ac 24:27). From that location, Luke would have been able to travel and interview the eyewitnesses to Jesus' life and ministry who were still alive.

The Third Gospel is addressed to "most honorable Theophilus" (Lk 1:3), about whom nothing else is known other than that he is also the recipient of the book of Acts (Ac 1:1). The Greek name Theophilus means "lover of God" or "friend of God" and implies that he was a Gentile, probably Greek. He seems to have been a relatively new believer, recently instructed about Jesus and the Christian faith (Lk 1:4). The title "most honorable" indicates that, at the least, he was a person of high standing and financial substance. It may also reflect that he was an official with some governmental authority and power.

Message and Purpose

The Gospel of Luke is a carefully researched (1:3), selective presentation of the person and life of Jesus Christ, designed to strengthen the faith of believers (1:3-4) and to challenge the misconceptions of unbelievers, especially those from a Greek background. Its portrait of Jesus is well-balanced, skillfully emphasizing His divinity and perfect humanity.

Contribution to the Bible

Nearly 60 percent of the material in the Gospel of Luke is u[...]
Scripture would not know if the Third Gospel were not in [...]
portions are: (1) much of the material in Luke 1–2 about the [...]
biblical material on Jesus' childhood and pre-ministry adul[...]
38) that is significantly different from the one in Matthew 1[...]
Jesus' journey to Jerusalem (9:51–19:44), (5) a considerably [...]
(21:5-38) from the Olivet Discourse in Matthew 24–25 and [...]
the post-resurrection appearances, including the Emmaus [...]
mission, and the only description in the Gospels of Jesus' as[...]

A.D. 10–30

Caiaphas is high priest. 18–36

Pontius Pilate is prefect of Judea. 26–36

John the Baptist's ministry begins. 29

Jesus' baptism 29

Jesus' wilderness temptations 29

Jesus' call of His first disciples 29

The first Passover of Jesus' ministry, an occasion on which it was said that the temple (inner sanctuary) had stood for 46 years 30

Jesus goes from Judea to Galilee when he learns of John the Baptist's death. 30

⑭ ESSAYS

Christ in the Old Testament

Craig Blaising

In Luke 24 Jesus showed Himself alive to His disciples and explained that the [...] indeed much else in His life, were predicted in Scripture. Verse 27 states: "T[...] and all the Prophets, He interpreted for them the things concerning Him[...] Then in verse 44, He told them "that everything written about Me in the Law o[...] the Psalms must be fulfilled."

In the preaching of the apostles in Acts, the evidence given in the Gospels [...] Testament, many (OT) texts are applied to Jesus. This practice likely reflects J[...] how the OT relates to Him. Furthermore, because themes are repeated and d[...] application of a particular text to Jesus is suggestive of other texts that relate t[...] this way we can see a rich portrait of OT patterns, types, allusions, and predicti[...] Person and Work of Christ.

From beginning to end the OT exudes an expectation that someone is coming. [...] "seed" of the woman who comes to crush the tempter's head (Gn 3:15). To Abrah[...] that through his "offspring" blessing or curse would come to all nations (Gn 12:[...] descendants of Abraham many patterns and types pointed to a Coming One. I[...] 15:3-6; 17:19), was offered to God as a sacrifice but was redeemed by a substi[...] raised up to bless all peoples, was first rejected by his brothers but later was soug[...] (Gn 37; 41-48; 50:15-21). Judah offered himself in place of his brother and rece[...] and the obedience of all peoples (Gn 49:1,9-12). Moses failed to enter the pro[...] works, but it was said that a prophet like him would arise in the future (Dt 18:15[...] Judah, was raised up by God to deliver and shepherd Israel. God made a covena[...] and seat him on his throne, establishing his kingdom forever (2Sm 7:8-17; 1Ch [...] Father, and he would be His son (2Sm 7:14).

The covenant with David is the key to messianic prophecy. It incorporates [...] coming king, such as Balaam's prophecy that a star would arise from Jacob an[...] 24:15-19; cf. 23:24; 24:7-9), plus it serves as the basis for later prophecies suc[...] who establishes the throne of David forever with peace, justice, and righteou[...] "shoot . . . from the stump of Jesse" upon whom the Spirit rests and who de[...] peace, righteousness, and extends the knowledge of God to the entire earth; Jer[...] righteous "Branch" of David who will reign with justice and wisdom; and Zech[...] righteous king, bringing salvation, speaking peace to the nations and ruling fro[...] David's experiences of suffering, deliverance, and exaltation become type[...]

Contributors

Editorial Staff

General Editors

Edwin A. Blum
Executive Editor, *Holman Christian Standard Bible*
Th.D., Dallas Theological Seminary
D.Th., University of Basel

Jeremy Royal Howard
Managing Acquisitions Editor for Bibles, Reference
   Books, and Commentaries
B&H Publishing Group
Ph.D., Southern Baptist Theological Seminary

Associate Editors

Steve Bond
Executive Editor for Bibles, Reference Books, and
   Commentaries
B&H Publishing Group
Ph.D., Vanderbilt University

E. Ray Clendenen
Senior Acquisitions Editor for Bibles, Reference
   Books, and Commentaries
B&H Publishing Group
Ph.D., University of Texas at Arlington

David K. Stabnow
Editor for Bibles, Reference Books, and
   Commentaries
B&H Publishing Group
Ph.D., Westminster Theological Seminary

Study Note Contributors

The Study Notes in the HCSB Study Bible have gone through numerous levels of editorial review and revision. The Notes as they now appear often differ from the Notes as originally submitted by the contributors. In some few cases, the final form of the Notes may express views that the contributors did not set out to discuss or endorse.

Genesis
Robert D. Bergen
Hannibal-LaGrange College
Ph.D., Southwestern Baptist Theological Seminary

Exodus
Dorian G. Coover-Cox
Dallas Theological Seminary
Ph.D., Dallas Theological Seminary

Leviticus
Kenneth A. Mathews
Beeson Divinity School
Ph.D., The University of Michigan

Tiberius Rata
Grace Theological Seminary
Ph.D., Trinity Evangelical Divinity School

Numbers
R. Dennis Cole
New Orleans Baptist Theological Seminary
Ph.D., New Orleans Baptist Theological Seminary

Deuteronomy
Eugene H. Merrill
Dallas Theological Seminary
Ph.D., Columbia University

Joshua
Richard S. Hess
Denver Seminary
Ph.D., Hebrew Union College

Judges
Iain M. Duguid
Grove City College
Ph.D., Cambridge University

Ruth
Iain M. Duguid
Grove City College
Ph.D., Cambridge University

1,2 Samuel
Bryan E. Beyer
Columbia International University Seminary
Ph.D., Hebrew Union College

1,2 Kings
Andrew C. Bowling
John Brown University
Ph.D., Brandeis University

1,2 Chronicles
Winfried Corduan
Taylor University (Emeritus)
Ph.D., Rice University

Ezra
Carl R. Anderson
Trinity Fellowship Church, Richardson, Texas
Ph.D., Dallas Theological Seminary

Nehemiah
Carl R. Anderson
Trinity Fellowship Church, Richardson, Texas
Ph.D., Dallas Theological Seminary

Esther
Carl R. Anderson
Trinity Fellowship Church, Richardson, Texas
Ph.D., Dallas Theological Seminary

Job
Richard D. Patterson
Liberty University (Emeritus)
Ph.D., University of California, Los Angeles

Psalms
Kevin R. Warstler
Criswell College
Ph.D., Dallas Theological Seminary

Sherri L. Klouda
Taylor University
Ph.D., Southwestern Baptist Theological Seminary

Proverbs
David K. Stabnow
B&H Publishing Group
Ph.D., Westminster Theological Seminary

Ecclesiastes
Duane A. Garrett
Southern Baptist Theological Seminary
Ph.D., Baylor University

Song of Songs
Craig Glickman
Attorney, Dallas, TX
D.Th., University of Basel

Isaiah
Tremper Longman III
Westmont College
Ph.D., Yale University

Jeremiah
Walter C. Kaiser
Gordon-Conwell Theological Seminary
Ph.D., Brandeis University

Lamentations
Walter C. Kaiser
Gordon-Conwell Theological Seminary
Ph.D., Brandeis University

Ezekiel
Mark F. Rooker
Southeastern Baptist Theological Seminary
Ph.D., Brandeis University

Daniel
Michael Rydelnick
Moody Bible Institute
D. Miss., Trinity Evangelical Divinity School

Hosea
E. Ray Clendenen
B&H Publishing Group
Ph.D., University of Texas at Arlington

Joel
Shawn C. Madden
Southeastern Baptist Theological Seminary
Ph.D., University of Texas at Arlington

Amos
Duane A. Garrett
Southern Baptist Theological Seminary
Ph.D., Baylor University

Obadiah
Gregory W. Parsons
Baptist Missionary Association Theological Seminary
Th.D., Dallas Theological Seminary

Jonah
Joe Sprinkle
Crossroads College
Ph.D., Hebrew Union College–Jewish Institute of Religion

Micah
Kevin Peacock
Canadian Southern Baptist Seminary
Ph.D., Southwestern Baptist Theological Seminary

Nahum
Gregory W. Parsons
Baptist Missionary Association Theological Seminary
Th.D., Dallas Theological Seminary

Habakkuk
Joe Sprinkle
Crossroads College
Ph.D., Hebrew Union College–Jewish Institute of Religion

Zephaniah
Gregory W. Parsons
Baptist Missionary Association Theological Seminary
Th.D., Dallas Theological Seminary

Haggai
Gregory W. Parsons
Baptist Missionary Association Theological Seminary
Th.D., Dallas Theological Seminary

Zechariah
D. Brent Sandy
Grace College and Theological Seminary
Ph.D., Duke University

Malachi
E. Ray Clendenen
B&H Publishing Group
Ph.D., University of Texas at Arlington

Matthew
Charles L. Quarles
Louisiana College
Ph.D., Mid-America Baptist Theological Seminary

Mark
Ross H. McLaren
LifeWay Christian Resources
D.Min., Vanderbilt Divinity School

Luke
A. Boyd Luter
Comal Country Church, New Braunfels, TX
Ph.D., Dallas Theological Seminary

John
Andreas J. Köstenberger
Southeastern Baptist Theological Seminary
Ph.D., Trinity Evangelical Divinity School

Acts
Stanley E. Porter
McMaster Divinity College, Ontario
Ph.D., University of Sheffield

Romans
Edwin A. Blum
B&H Publishing Group
D.Th., University of Basel

1 Corinthians
F. Alan Tomlinson
Midwestern Baptist Theological Seminary
Ph.D., Southern Baptist Theological Seminary

2 Corinthians
Kendell H. Easley
Union University
Ph.D., Southwestern Baptist Theological Seminary

Galatians
A. Boyd Luter
Comal Country Church, New Braunfels, TX
Ph.D., Dallas Theological Seminary

Ephesians
David S. Dockery
Union University
Ph.D., University of Texas at Arlington

Philippians
Richard R. Melick, Jr.
Golden Gate Baptist Theological Seminary
Ph.D., Southwestern Baptist Theological Seminary

Colossians
Andreas J. Köstenberger
Southeastern Baptist Theological Seminary
Ph.D., Trinity Evangelical Divinity School

1,2 Thessalonians
James F. Davis
Capital Bible Seminary
Ph.D., Dallas Theological Seminary

1,2 Timothy, Titus
Ray Van Neste
Union University
Ph.D., University of Aberdeen

Philemon
Murray J. Harris
Trinity Evangelical Divinity School (Emeritus)
Ph.D., University of Manchester

Hebrews
Malcolm B. Yarnell III
Southwestern Baptist Theological Seminary
D. Phil., University of Oxford

James
R. Gregg Watson
Golden Gate Baptist Theological Seminary
Ph.D., Southwestern Baptist Theological Seminary

1,2 Peter
Terry L. Wilder
Southwestern Baptist Theological Seminary
Ph.D., University of Aberdeen

1,2,3 John
Robert W. Yarbrough
Trinity Evangelical Divinity School
Ph.D., University of Aberdeen

Jude
Terry L. Wilder
Southwestern Baptist Theological Seminary
Ph.D., University of Aberdeen

Revelation
A. Boyd Luter
Comal Country Church, New Braunfels, TX
Ph.D., Dallas Theological Seminary

Essay Contributors

List of
Maps, Illustrations, and Charts

MAPS

ILLUSTRATIONS

CHARTS

List of
Hebrew Word Studies

List of
Greek Word Studies

Commonly Used Abbreviations in the HCSB

A.D.	In the year of our Lord	Lat	Latin
aka	also known as	Lit/lit	Literally/literally
alt	alternate	LXX	Septuagint—an ancient transla-
a.m.	from midnight until noon		tion of the Old Testament
Ant.	Antiquities—a history of the Jew-		into Greek
	ish people by Josephus	MT	Masoretic Text
Aq	Aquila	NT	New Testament
Aram	Aramaic	ms(s)	manuscript(s)
B.C.	before Christ	OT	Old Testament
c.	century	p., pp.	page, pages
ca	circa	p.m.	from noon until midnight
chap(s).	chapter(s)	pl	plural
cp.	compare	Ps(s)	Psalm(s)
d.	died	Sam	Samaritan Pentateuch
DSS	Dead Sea Scrolls	sg	singular
e.g.	for example	Sym	Symmachus
Eng	English	Syr	Syriac
esp.	especially	Tg	Targum
etc.	etcetera	Theod	Theodotian
ff.	following	v., vv.	verse, verses
Gk	Greek	Vg	Vulgate—an ancient translation
Hb	Hebrew		of the Bible into Latin
i.e.	that is	vol(s).	volume(s)
Jer	Latin translation of Psalms by	vs.	versus
	Jerome	x	times

Plan of Salvation

What do you understand it takes for a person to go to heaven?
Consider how the Bible answers this question: It's a matter of **FAITH**:

F IS FOR FORGIVENESS

We cannot have eternal life and heaven without God's forgiveness.

—Read Ephesians 1:7a

A IS FOR AVAILABLE

Forgiveness is available. It is—

- Available for all   —Read John 3:16
- But not automatic   —Read Matthew 7:21a

I IS FOR IMPOSSIBLE

It is impossible for God to allow sin into heaven.

- Because of who He is: God is loving and just
  His judgment is against sin   —Read James 2:13a
- Because of who we are:
  Every person is a sinner   —Read Romans 3:23

But how can a sinful person enter heaven, when God allows no sin?

T IS FOR TURN

Turn means to repent.

- Turn from something—sin and self   —Read Luke 13:3b
- Turn to Someone; trust Christ only   —Read Romans 10:9

H IS FOR HEAVEN

Heaven is eternal life.

- Here   —Read John 10:10b
- Hereafter   —Read John 14:3

How can a person have God's forgiveness, heaven and eternal life, and Jesus as personal Savior and Lord? By trusting in Christ and asking Him for forgiveness. Take the step of faith described by another meaning of FAITH: Forsaking All, I Trust Him.

PRAYER:

Lord Jesus, I know I am a sinner and have displeased You in many ways. I believe You died for my sin and only through faith in Your death and resurrection can I be forgiven.

I want to turn from my sin and ask You to come into my life as my Savior and Lord. From this day on, I will follow You by living a life that pleases You. Thank You, Lord Jesus, for saving me. Amen.

After you have received Jesus Christ into your life, tell a Christian friend about this important decision you have made. Follow Christ in believer's baptism and church membership. Grow in your faith and enjoy new friends in Christ by becoming part of His church. There, you'll find others who will love and support you.

Introduction to the
Holman Christian Standard Bible®

The Bible is God's revelation to man. It is the only book that gives us accurate information about God, man's need, and God's provision for that need. It provides us with guidance for life and tells us how to receive eternal life. The Bible can do these things because it is God's inspired Word, inerrant in the original manuscripts.

The Bible describes God's dealings with the ancient Jewish people and the early Christian church. It tells us about the great gift of God's Son, Jesus Christ, who fulfilled Jewish prophecies of the Messiah. It tells us about the salvation He accomplished through His death on the cross, His triumph over death in the resurrection, and His promised return to earth. It is the only book that gives us reliable information about the future, about what will happen to us when we die, and about where history is headed.

Bible translation is both a science and an art. It is a bridge that brings God's Word from the ancient world to the world today. In dependence on God to accomplish this sacred task, Holman Bible Publishers presents the Holman Christian Standard Bible, an English translation of God's Word.

Textual base of the HCSB

The textual base for the New Testament [NT] is the Nestle-Aland *Novum Testamentum Graece*, 27th edition, and the United Bible Societies' *Greek New Testament*, 4th corrected edition. The text for the Old Testament [OT] is the *Biblia Hebraica Stuttgartensia,* 5th edition.

Where there are significant differences among Hebrew [Hb] and Aramaic [Aram] manuscripts of the OT or among Greek [Gk] manuscripts of the NT, the translators have followed what they believe is the original reading and have indicated the main alternative(s) in footnotes. The HCSB uses the traditional verse divisions found in most Protestant Bibles.

Goals of this translation

- to provide English-speaking people across the world with an accurate, readable Bible in contemporary English

- to equip serious Bible students with an accurate translation for personal study, private devotions, and memorization

- to give those who love God's Word a text that has numerous reader helps, is visually attractive on the page, and is appealing when heard

- to affirm the authority of Scripture as God's Word and to champion its absolute truth against social or cultural agendas that would compromise its accuracy

- to continue making improvements to the translation in each printing

The name Holman Christian Standard Bible captures these goals: *Holman* Bible Publishers presents a *Bible* translation, for *Christian* and English-speaking communities, which will be a *standard* in Bible translations for years to come.

Why is there a need for another English translation of the Bible?

There are several good reasons why Holman Bible publishers invested its resources in a modern language translation of the Bible:

1. <u>Each generation needs a fresh translation of the Bible in its own language.</u>

The Bible is the world's most important book, confronting each individual and each culture with issues that affect life, both now and forever. Since each new generation must be introduced to God's Word in its own language, there will always be a need for new translations such as the HCSB. The majority of Bible translations on the market today are revisions of translations from previous generations. The HCSB is a new translation for today's generation.

2. <u>English, one of the world's greatest languages, is rapidly changing, and Bible translations must keep in step with those changes.</u>

English is the first truly global language in history. It is the language of education, business, medicine, travel, research, and the Internet. More than 1.3 billion people around the world speak or read English as a primary or secondary language. The HCSB seeks to serve many of those people with a translation they can easily use and understand.

English is also the world's most rapidly changing language. The HCSB seeks to reflect recent changes in English by using modern punctuation, formatting, and vocabulary, while avoiding slang, regionalisms, or changes made specifically for the sake of political or social agendas. Modern linguistic and semantic advances have been incorporated into the HCSB, including modern grammar.

3. <u>Rapid advances in biblical research provide new data for Bible translators.</u>

This has been called the "information age," a term that accurately describes the field of biblical research. Never before in history has there been as much information about the Bible as there is today—from archaeological discoveries to analysis of ancient manuscripts to years of study and statistical research on individual Bible books. Translations made as recently as the late 20th century do not reflect many of these advances in biblical research. The HCSB translators have taken into consideration as much of this new data as possible.

4. <u>Advances in computer technology have opened a new door for Bible translation.</u>

The HCSB has used computer technology and telecommunications in its creation perhaps more than any Bible translation in history. Electronic mail was used daily and sometimes hourly for communication and transmission of manuscripts. An advanced Bible software program, Accordance®, was used to create and revise the translation at each step in its production. A developmental copy of the translation itself was used within Accordance to facilitate crosschecking during the translation process—something never done before with a Bible translation.

Translation philosophy of the HCSB

Most discussions of Bible translations speak of two opposite approaches: formal equivalence and dynamic equivalence. Although this terminology is meaningful, Bible translations cannot be neatly sorted into these two categories any more than people can be neatly sorted into two cat-

egories according to height or weight. Holman Bible Publishers is convinced there is room for another category of translation philosophy that capitalizes on the strengths of the other two.

1.   Formal Equivalence

Often called "word-for-word" (or "literal") translation, the principle of formal equivalence seeks as nearly as possible to preserve the structure of the original language. It seeks to represent each word of the original text with an exact equivalent word in the translation so that the reader can see word for word what the original human author wrote. The merits of this approach include its consistency with the conviction that the Holy Spirit did inspire the very words of Scripture in the original manuscripts. It also provides the English Bible student some access to the structure of the text in the original language. Formal equivalence can achieve accuracy to the degree that English has an exact equivalent for each word and that the grammatical patterns of the original language can be reproduced in understandable English. However, it can sometimes result in awkward, if not incomprehensible, English or in a misunderstanding of the author's intent. The literal rendering of ancient idioms is especially difficult.

2.   Dynamic or Functional Equivalence

Often called "thought-for-thought" translation, the principle of dynamic equivalence rejects as misguided the desire to preserve the structure of the original language. It proceeds by distinguishing the meaning of a text from its form and then translating the meaning so that it makes the same impact on modern readers that the ancient text made on its original readers. Strengths of this approach include a high degree of clarity and readability, especially in places where the original is difficult to render word for word. It also acknowledges that accurate and effective translation requires interpretation. However, the meaning of a text cannot always be neatly separated from its form, nor can it always be precisely determined. A biblical author may have intended multiple meanings. In striving for readability, dynamic equivalence also sometimes overlooks some of the less prominent elements of meaning. Furthermore, lack of formal correspondence to the original makes it difficult to verify accuracy and thus can affect the usefulness of the translation for in-depth Bible study.

3.   Optimal Equivalence

In practice, translations are seldom if ever purely formal or dynamic but favor one theory of Bible translation or the other to varying degrees. Optimal equivalence as a translation philosophy recognizes that form cannot be neatly separated from meaning and should not be changed (for example, nouns to verbs or third person "they" to second person "you") unless comprehension demands it. The primary goal of translation is to convey the sense of the original with as much clarity as the original text and the translation language permit. Optimal equivalence appreciates the goals of formal equivalence but also recognizes its limitations. Optimal equivalence starts with an exhaustive analysis of the text at every level (word, phrase, clause, sentence, discourse) in the original language to determine its original meaning and intention (or purpose). Then relying on the latest and best language tools and experts, the nearest corresponding semantic and linguistic equivalents are used to convey as much of the information and intention of the original text with as much clarity and readability as possible. This process assures the maximum transfer of both the words and thoughts contained in the original. The HCSB uses optimal equivalence as its translation philosophy. When a literal translation meets these criteria, it is used. When clarity and readability demand an idiomatic translation,

the reader can still access the form of the original text by means of a footnote with the abbreviation "Lit."

The gender language policy in Bible translation

Some people today ignore the Bible's teachings on distinctive roles of men and women in family and church and have an agenda to eliminate those distinctions in every arena of life. These people have begun a program to engineer the removal of a perceived male bias in the English language. The targets of this program have been such traditional linguistic practices as the generic use of "man" or "men" as well as "he," "him," and "his."

A group of Bible scholars, translators, and other evangelical leaders met in 1997 to respond to this issue as it affects Bible translation. This group produced the "Guidelines for Translation of Gender-Related Language in Scripture" (adopted May 27, 1997 and revised Sept. 9, 1997). The HCSB was produced in accordance with these guidelines.

The goal of the translators has not been to promote a cultural ideology but to faithfully translate the Bible. While the HCSB avoids using "man" or "he" unnecessarily, the translation does not restructure sentences to avoid them when they are in the text. For example, the translators have not changed "him" to "you" or to "them," neither have they avoided other masculine words such as "father" or "son" by translating them in generic terms such as "parent" or "child."

History of the HCSB

After several years of preliminary development, Holman Bible Publishers, the oldest Bible publisher in America, assembled an international, interdenominational team of 100 scholars, editors, stylists, and proofreaders, all of whom were committed to biblical inerrancy. Outside consultants and reviewers contributed valuable suggestions from their areas of expertise. An executive team then edited, polished, and reviewed the final manuscripts.

Traditional features found in the HCSB

In keeping with a long line of Bible publications, the HCSB has retained a number of features found in traditional Bibles:

1. Traditional theological vocabulary (such as justification, sanctification, redemption, etc.) has been retained since such terms have no translation equivalent that adequately communicates their exact meaning.
2. Traditional spellings of names and places found in most Bibles have been used to make the HCSB compatible with most Bible study tools.
3. Some editions of the HCSB will print the words of Christ in red letters to help readers easily locate the spoken words of the Lord Jesus Christ.
4. Nouns and personal pronouns that clearly refer to any person of the Trinity are capitalized.
5. Descriptive headings, printed above each section of Scripture, help readers quickly identify the contents of that section.
6. Two common forms of punctuation are used in the HCSB to help with clarity and ease of reading: an em dash (—) is used to indicate sudden breaks in thought or to help clarify long or difficult sentences. Parentheses are used infrequently to indicate words that are parenthetical in the original languages.

How certain names and terms are translated

1. The names of God

The HCSB OT consistently translates the Hebrew names for God as follows:

HCSB English:	Hebrew original:
God	*Elohim*
LORD	*YHWH (Yahweh)*
Lord	*Adonai*
Lord GOD	*Adonai Yahweh*
LORD of Hosts	*Yahweh Sabaoth*
God Almighty	*El Shaddai*

However, the HCSB OT uses Yahweh, the personal name of God in Hebrew, when a biblical text emphasizes Yahweh as a name: "His name is Yahweh" (Ps 68:4). Yahweh is also used in places of His self-identification as in "I am Yahweh" (Is 42:8). Yahweh is used more often in the HCSB than in most Bible translations because the word LORD in English is a title of God and does not accurately convey to modern readers the emphasis on God's personal name in the original Hebrew.

2. The uses of Christ and Messiah

The HCSB translates the Greek word *Christos* ("anointed one") as either "Christ" or "Messiah" based on its use in different NT contexts. The first use of "Messiah" in each chapter is also marked with a bullet referring readers to the Bullet Note at the back of most editions.

3. Place names

In the original text of the Bible, particularly in the OT, a number of well-known places have names different from the ones familiar to contemporary readers. For example, "the Euphrates" often appears in the original text simply as "the River." In cases like this, the HCSB uses the modern name, "the Euphrates River," in the text without a footnote.

4. Substitution of words in sentences

A literal translation of the biblical text sometimes violates standard rules of English grammar, such as the agreement of subject and verb or person and number. In order to conform to standard usage, the HCSB has often made these kinds of grammatical constructions agree in English without footnotes.

In addition, the Greek or Hebrew texts sometimes seem redundant or ambiguous by repeating nouns where modern writing substitutes pronouns or by using pronouns where we would supply nouns for clarity and good style. When a literal translation of the original would make the English unclear, the HCSB sometimes changes a pronoun to its corresponding noun or a noun

to its corresponding pronoun without a footnote. For example, Jn 1:42 reads: "And he brought Simon to Jesus . . ." The original Greek of this sentence reads: "And he brought him to Jesus."

Special formatting features

The HCSB has several distinctive formatting features:

1. OT passages quoted in the NT are set in boldface type. OT quotes consisting of two or more lines are block-indented.
2. In dialogue, a new paragraph is used for each new speaker as in most modern publications.
3. Many passages, such as 1Co 13, have been formatted as dynamic prose (separate block-indented lines like poetry) for ease in reading and comprehension. Special block-indented formatting has also been used extensively in both the OT and NT to increase readability and clarity in lists, series, genealogies, and other parallel or repetitive texts.
4. Almost every Bible breaks lines in poetry using automatic typesetting programs with the result that words are haphazardly turned over to the next line. In the HCSB, special attention has been given to break every line in poetry and dynamic prose so that awkward or unsightly word wraps are avoided and complete units of thought turn over to the next line. The result is a Bible page that is much more readable and pleasing to the eye.
5. Certain foreign, geographical, cultural, or ancient words are preceded by a superscripted bullet (• *Abba*) at their first occurrence in each chapter. These words are listed in alphabetical order at the back of the Bible under the heading HCSB Bullet Notes.
6. Italics are used in the text for a transliteration of Greek and Hebrew words (*"Hosanna!"* in Jn 12:13) and in footnotes for direct quotations from the biblical text and for words in the original languages (the footnote at Jn 1:1 reads: "The *Word* (Gk *Logos*) is a title for Jesus . . .").
7. Since the majority of English readers do not need to have numbers and fractions spelled out in the text, the HCSB uses a similar style to that of modern newspapers in using Arabic numerals for the numbers 10 and above and in fractions, except in a few cases, such as when a number begins a sentence.

Footnotes

Footnotes are used to show readers how the original biblical language has been understood in the HCSB.

1. <u>OT Textual Footnotes</u>

OT textual notes show important differences among Hebrew manuscripts and among ancient OT versions, such as the Septuagint and the Vulgate. See the list of abbreviations on page xii for a list of other ancient versions used.

Some OT textual notes (like NT textual notes) give only an alternate textual reading. However, other OT textual notes also give the support for the reading chosen by the editors as well as for the alternate textual reading. For example, the HCSB text of Ps 12:7 reads:

You will protect us[a] from this generation forever.

The textual footnote for this verse reads:

[a]**12:7** Some Hb mss, LXX; other Hb mss read *him*

The textual note in this example means that there are two different readings found in the Hebrew manuscripts: some manuscripts read *us* and others read *him*. The HCSB translators chose the reading *us*, which is also found in the Septuagint (LXX), and placed the other Hebrew reading *him* in the footnote.

Two other kinds of OT textual notes are:

Alt Hb tradition reads _____	a variation given by scribes in the Hebrew manuscript tradition (known as *Kethiv/Qere* readings)
Hb uncertain	when it is uncertain what the original Hebrew text was

2. NT Textual Footnotes

NT textual notes indicate significant differences among Greek manuscripts (mss) and are normally indicated in one of three ways:

Other mss read _____

Other mss add _____

Other mss omit _____

In the NT, some textual footnotes that use the word "add" or "omit" also have large square brackets before and after the corresponding verses in the biblical text. Examples of this use of square brackets are Mk 16:9-20, Jn 5:3-4, and Jn 7:53–8:11.

3. Other Kinds of Footnotes

Lit _____	a more literal rendering in English of the Hebrew, Aramaic, or Greek text
Or _____	an alternate or less likely English translation of the same Hebrew, Aramaic, or Greek text
=	an abbreviation for "it means" or "it is equivalent to"
Hb, Aram, Gk	the actual Hebrew, Aramaic, or Greek word is given using equivalent English letters
Hb obscure	the existing Hebrew text is especially difficult to translate
emend(ed) to _____	the original Hebrew text is so difficult to translate that competent scholars have conjectured or inferred a restoration of the original text based on the context, probable root meanings of the words, and uses in comparative languages

In some editions of the HCSB, additional footnotes clarify the meaning of certain biblical texts or explain biblical history, persons, customs, places, activities, and measurements. Cross-references are given for parallel passages or passages with similar wording, and in the NT, for passages quoted from the OT.

How to Read and Study the Bible

George H. Guthrie

The Bible is unique among the books of the world. Its "release date" is centuries old, yet it still dominates the best-seller lists, confronting moderns with messages as fresh as today's news headlines. At times the Bible is so crystal clear that a child can understand it, yet its difficulties can humble the most learned of scholars. Diverse in theme and literary genres, it conveys a unified story, a message that climaxes in the person and work of Jesus Christ. It was delivered through human writers, yet it truly is God's Word. The Bible can seem as familiar as a walk next door, or as foreign as a distant country.

This article aims to help you hear from God through daily interaction with the Bible. Hearing God in the pages of the Bible takes time and effort; spiritual listening is a skill that we continue to develop all of our lives. Hearing someone well can be challenging when we move across cultural lines, and, in fact, reading the Bible is very much a cross-cultural conversation, since God gave His Word in places, times, and circumstances very much removed from our own.

Why Spend Time in the Bible?

Perhaps your past has been marked by starts and stops in reading the Bible, and you are wondering whether you have the discipline to engage the Bible consistently. Well, join the club. Most of us have struggled with the discipline of Bible reading and study. So is it worth giving consistent Bible reading and study another try, or a first try? Most believers know intuitively that it is.

This is *God's* Word. The God who spoke the world into being has spoken His truth about life through the Bible, so that we might know what He intends for this world and how we might live for His fame. He calls us to be "Word people," people who are countercultural in the ways we approach life. Thus the Bible serves as the foundation for understanding who we are and what we should be doing in this world.

In the next few pages I offer a number of suggestions that you can start applying daily in less time than it takes you to watch a sitcom on TV.

Begin with the Heart

In the parable of the seeds and soils (Mk 4:3-20), Jesus used a word picture to describe the different levels of receptivity people have toward God's Word. He tells of a farmer broadcasting seed along the edge of a field. Some seeds fall on the hard-packed path beside the field; some fall on rocky ground that has little topsoil; some fall in the weeds; and some fall in fertile soil that offers a good environment for growth. The various places they fall provide images of the human heart as it is confronted with God's Word.

Some people have hearts that are hard-packed, like a frequented footpath. God's Word does not get through to these hearts. Others have shallow hearts that seem open to God's Word. The Word comes and they respond, but the moment things get tough, the pressures of life override the principles of God's Word, and the spiritual life withers. A third type of person engages God's Word at a deeper level, but worries and desire for worldly things squeeze out the Word, choking it from the person's life. Finally, there are those who receive the Word with a heart like a well-tilled field. This is the picture of a person fully receptive to God's Word, and God's Word brings exponential growth to their spiritual life.

Which pattern of response describes the condition of your heart today? Perhaps you have never committed to following Christ as Lord of your life. I encourage you to talk to a Christian or a minister whom you trust and ask them about following Christ as Lord. First Corinthians 2:14 tells us that a person who is not a Christ-follower cannot engage spiritual truth in a way that is life-changing, so this would be the beginning place for you. Turn to Christ, asking Him to bring His good news to life in you.

Or, perhaps you have committed your life to follow Christ, but your heart is not very receptive

to God's Word at this time. You may be plagued by a heart that is consumed with worry or material things. Sin and self-absorption can eat the heart out of your Bible study. Begin your path back to healthy relationship with God by crying out to Him right now, asking Him to forgive you for your hard-heartedness, expressing your desire to hear and live His Word.

Motivations

Once our hearts are receptive to the Word, we can hear the motivations offered us in Scripture. Among other motives, we read the Bible . . .

* to experience consistent joy (Ps 119:111)
* to sort out our thoughts and motivations (Heb 4:12)
* to guard ourselves from sin and error (Eph 6:11-17; 1Pt 2:1-2)
* to know God in a personal relationship (1Co 1:21; Gl 4:8-9; 1Tm 4:16)
* to know truth and think clearly about what God says is valuable (2Pt 1:21)
* to be built up as a community with other believers (Ac 20:32; Eph 4:14-16)
* to reject conformity to the world as we renew our minds (Rm 12:1-2; 1Pt 2:1-2)
* to experience God's freedom, grace, peace, and hope (Jn 8:32; Rm 15:4; 2Pt 1:2)
* to live well for God, expressing our love for Him (Jn 14:23-24; Rm 12:2; 1Th 4:1-8)
* to minister to Christ-followers and to those who have yet to respond to the gospel, experiencing God's approval for work well done (Jos 1:8; 2Tm 2:15; 3:16-17)

12 Practical Suggestions for Reading Well

We want to approach our reading of the Bible in a way that will lead to a fulfilling, faithful, and fruitful pattern of life. Below are a dozen suggestions to make your Bible reading more effective and fulfilling.

Read the Bible prayerfully: Engaging the Bible regularly is a spiritual exercise, and you need spiritual power and discernment to do it well. As you begin your Bible reading, ask God for a receptive and disciplined heart, ask Him to speak to you through the Word, and use the passages you read as providing you with thoughts and words you can use as you pray to God.

Read expectantly and joyfully: As you pray over your Bible reading, also read it expecting to hear from God, being joyful and thankful for what you find in the Scriptures. Allow the "music" of the Word to give you joy in your walk with God.

Meditate on what you are reading: To meditate means to mentally "chew" on what we are reading, to think about what the passage means as well as its implications for belief and practice. Just as food chewed and swallowed too quickly gives indigestion, so we will not be able to digest our Bible readings unless we slow down and consider the "meat" we find there.

Read for transformation: The Bible is not meant merely to inform—it is meant to transform us in accordance with God's truth (Rm 12:1-2). Therefore, read with expectation that you will hear from the Lord. Be thinking about ways to apply God's truth to your life as you read.

Read with perseverance. Commit yourself to being consistent for the next 10 to 12 weeks, which is about how long it takes to form a long-term habit. As you are faithful with your Bible reading and begin to see it make a difference in your life, you will begin to hunger for your time in the Word.

Be realistic about the goals you set, and have a good plan: If you take just 20 to 30 minutes per day, you can read through the whole Bible in a year. In just 10 to 15 minutes per day, you can read through the whole Bible in two years. The key is not volume but consistency and a clear plan.

Set aside a consistent time and place to read and study the Bible: Make it a time and place that guards you from distractions and allows you to be consistent, missing no more than a handful of times per month. When you do miss a day, just pick back up the next day.

Read with a few good tools at hand: Along with this study Bible, have a good Bible dictionary

on hand. These typically provide outlines and message summaries of each book of the Bible, plus quick entries on theological, historical, and cultural elements.

Read with a pen in hand: Underline key passages and make notes in the margins as you read. As the saying goes, the lightest ink is stronger than the strongest memory. If you prefer a keyboard to an ink pen, store your notes on your computer.

Read in light of the immediate context: Not only do we need the "big picture" of the Bible's overarching story, we also need the "little picture" of the immediate context. So read with an awareness of where you are in the development of a particular book.

Do your Bible reading and study as part of a community: It helps if you have family or friends who also are reading the Bible, for they can encourage you and discuss the Bible with you. Become part of a community of Christians, a church, so you can have a place to celebrate what you are learning, to pose questions that come up in your study, and to use your spiritual gifts in ministering to others.

Read in light of the overarching story of the Bible: Reading the Bible is much more meaningful if you read it in light of its overarching story. As you read, notice great interwoven themes such as how creation in Genesis 1–2 relates to creation themes in Psalm 8, Isaiah 65:17-25, John 1, Romans 8:19-22, and Revelation 21. Read book introductions in your study Bible, noting where each book fits in the overall development of God's story. That story can be outlined in three great Acts.

ACT 1: God's Plan for All People
(Genesis 1—11)

    Creation: The God of All of Life

    Fall: Rejecting God's Vision for Life

    Flood: God Judges and Makes a Covenant to Preserve Life

ACT 2: God's Covenant People
(Genesis 12—Malachi 4:6) (2081–420? B.C.)

    The People: God Calls a Covenant People (2081 B.C.)

    Deliverance: God Rescues His People (1446 B.C.)

    The Sinai Covenant & Law: God Embraces and Instructs His People (1446 B.C.)

    The Land: God's Place for his People (1406 B.C.)

    Kings and Prophets: God Shapes a Kingdom People (1050 B.C.)

    Kings and Prophets: God Divides the Kingdom People (931 B.C.)

    Kings and Prophets: The Southern Kingdom as God's People (931–586 B.C.)

    Exile: God Disciplines His People (586–538 B.C.)

    Return: God Delivers His People Again (538 B.C.)

ACT 3: God's New Covenant People
(Matthew—Revelation) (5 B.C. – ?)

    Christ's Coming: God's True King Arrives (5 B.C.–A.D. 33)

    Christ's Ministry: God's True King Manifests His Kingdom (A.D. 29–33)

    Christ's Deliverance of His People: God's Work Through Death, Resurrection, and Enthronement of His King (A.D. 33)

    Christ's Church: God's People Advance the Kingdom (A.D. 33–?)

    Christ's Second Coming and Reign: God's Future for the Kingdom

Going Deeper: The Basics of Sound Bible Study

Think for a moment about a trip you have taken. You left home, traveled to your destination, and had various memorable experiences. Perhaps you experienced a culture different from your own and found that the greater the cultural differences between home and destination, the greater the effort needed to communicate and to learn in your new environment. Yet you persevered, experienced new people and places, and were enriched by it all.

The Bible is God's Word to us; we are not simply "reading someone else's mail." Yet, Bible study can be like taking a trip to another culture. The language at times seems foreign. You might have difficulty finding your way around the history or the literature. You see new things that are beautiful or even strange. You then gather up what you have gained from your study time and hopefully you grow by the experience.

Since reading the Bible is a crosscultural experience, we need a vehicle that can take us to where we can hear what God is saying to us through those experiences, and I suggest that the right vehicle is *a sound process of listening to the text of Scripture*. Through a sound process of Bible reading, we see "the sights" God wants us to see. We learn to navigate the unfamiliar territories of biblical history and literature, read the "road signs" that mark the main points to which we must pay attention, and understand the language of the Bible.

After we have lived in the world of the biblical text for a while and become familiar with what is going on there, persevering through challenges and hearing what God wants us to hear, we then "travel back home" to our life contexts, bringing with us changed hearts and minds. The vehicle that can bring us home is *discerning the principles and significance* of what we have encountered in the Bible and then finding specific ways to apply God's truth to our lives.

Using this word picture, let's look at five main stages for doing a more thorough study of a Bible passage.

FIVE STAGES OF THOROUGH BIBLE STUDY				
1	2	3	4	5
PACK YOUR BAGS	READ THE MAPS	READ THE ROAD SIGNS	LEARN TO SPEAK LIKE A LOCAL	HEAD HOME
Choose a passage	Study the broad historical context of the book	Read the passage in several translations	Choose key words to study	Identify the main points and principles of the passage
Gather your tools	Study the literary genre	Look for key dynamics in the passage	Consult word study tools	Identify how these address original and modern contexts
Pray	Study the immediate literary context of the passage	Make a provisional outline of the passage	Consult a concordance	Make specific application for your own life

Stage 1: Pack Your Bags

One of the most important aspects of a trip is what happens *before* the trip. Preparation and packing can make all the difference.

Choose a Passage: Just as when traveling you need to start out with a destination in mind, when studying the Bible you must first decide what specific passage you will address. Be sure to choose a passage that you can cover well in your designated period of time. For instance, if you are doing a detailed study of a passage from one of Paul's letters, four to seven verses (e.g., 2Co

2:14-17) are plenty to tackle in one session. If you have a longer passage you want to study (e.g., all of Romans 8), break it down into smaller segments and study the whole of the chapter over an extended period of time. Trying to study too large a section all at once will lead to frustration. However, if you are studying a section of biblical narrative, your passage can be longer since narratives do not depend on detailed argumentation.

As you attempt to do Bible study over the coming weeks, you will get a sense of how much ground you can cover in a week's time. Over time you will become more familiar with your tools and processes, allowing you to study more efficiently. But remember, just as you would not want to hurry past important historical sites just to get to the end of a trip, the key in Bible study is not speed but rather an approach that takes you deeper into God's Word and transforms you in the process.

Gather Your Tools: In addition to this study Bible, which includes a variety of features to take you deeper into the Word, it helps to have several types of translation on hand. Some translations are more "formal," following the patterns of the original words as closely as possible, even if the results are not always readily understandable to modern readers. Others are more "functional," trying to communicate the author's meaning even if that means departing from the exact pattern of words in the passage. Still other translations attempt to strike a balance between these two approaches, which is the tactic taken in the HCSB.

A strong Bible dictionary has much to offer, including an outline and introduction to each book of the Bible, plus entries on people, places, culture, theological issues, and key events mentioned in the Bible. It is also helpful to have dictionaries specifically covering the original languages of the Old and New Testaments. These show you the range of possible meanings a given word can have. There are many Bible study software programs available. Some may be had for free on the Internet. While the Internet can be an amazing resource for Bible study, not all Web sites are created equal. Therefore, do your best to assess the quality of the site. You might ask a minister or mature Christian to help you discern a site's trustworthiness. Also, while free Internet sites can be helpful, they often use outdated tools that are public domain. These tools still have value but need to be used in conjunction with tools based on recent study by evangelical scholars.

The best Bible commentaries provide a treasure trove of information, including an introduction to the book, an outline of the book, theological reflection, deep word studies, thoughtful interpretive insights, and application. Ask a trusted Christian or minister to help you evaluate the usefulness, trustworthiness, and accessibility of the commentaries that are available.

Pray: Once you have chosen your passage and gathered your tools, begin your time of study with prayer. You might begin by praying something like this:

> Lord, thank You for Your Word. I pray that You will give me the discipline to study this passage carefully. Please also give me the discernment to understand the details. Lord, please guide me by Your Spirit and lead me into Your truth. I am committed to applying what I find here, and I pray that You will change me by Your Word, bringing my life in line with Your will and ways of thinking. Thank You for this time.

Stage 2: Read the Maps

Maps are vital to navigation—you must know where you are to understand how to get to where you want to go. In Bible study, knowledge of the historical and literary contexts provides orientation. Like maps, they give us the layout of the biblical "neighborhood." The historical context can give us a clearer backdrop in terms of historical events or cultural dynamics of the time, and the literary context can help us understand how these words function, given where the author placed them in the book.

The Broad Historical Context of the Book: In studying the historical context of a book, you want to understand the following facts:

- Who authored the book?
- Who were the original recipients?
- Where were the author and the recipients located?
- When was the book written?
- What is the purpose of the book?

You can find this kind of information in the book introductions in this study Bible. You can also find it in Bible dictionaries, commentaries, and Bible handbooks. The *Holman Bible Handbook*, for instance, gives general background information on the city of Philippi and the church there, including the following:

> The Letter to the Philippians was written while the apostle Paul was in prison probably from Rome about A.D. 62, though we cannot know for sure. Other possible locations for the writing of the letter could have been Ephesus or Caesarea (sometime between A.D. 54 and 62).

The Literary Genre: Another aspect of the context of a passage has to do with "genre," or the kind of literature with which we are dealing. The kind of literature of a given passage will determine how we approach the text and what kind of questions we might ask of it. If I pick up a novel, I understand that its purpose is not primarily to communicate historical facts. If, however, I read a book detailing the history of America, the purpose is to communicate and interpret historical facts.

Different parts of the Bible reflect different literary genres and, therefore, are intended to accomplish different purposes and must be interpreted by different rules. Our goal with each is to understand what God intends to communicate through the human author, but to do so we must understand how the author intended his writing to communicate with his original audience.

This brings us to vital questions we must ask of the text. For narrative literature, for instance, we want to ask, "What is the significance of this part of the story? How does it fit into the grand story of God in the Scriptures?" The biblical authors had much material from which to choose, and they chose to include the stories they did for a reason.

Psalms and other poetic literature, on the other hand, often communicate emotions expressed in worship. These might include celebration, thanksgiving, sadness, reflection, or anger. Therefore, an important interpretive key when studying a psalm is to ask, "What is the emotion expressed?" and "How is the emotion being expressed?" The Psalms often use figurative language, for instance.

Finally, proverbs are meant to communicate general guidelines for living. Consider the following passage from Proverbs 4:10-12:

> Listen, my son. Accept my words, and you will live many years. I am teaching you the way of wisdom; I am guiding you on straight paths. When you walk, your steps will not be hindered; when you run, you will not stumble.

Some mistakenly take this passage as a promise that an obedient child will be guaranteed a long life free of impediments. There are many wonderful promises in Scripture that are intended to give comfort and hope to God's people, but neither the human author nor the Divine Author intended for proverbs to be promises. This proverb is saying, in effect, that the best way for a child to live is by seeking out wisdom; this is the path of success in life, and, generally speaking, will lead to a long and effective life.

The Immediate Context of the Passage: By the immediate literary context we mean how the passage under consideration fits into the overall development of the book. Words need a context to have a specific meaning. Think about the English word "hand." It has more than a dozen possible meanings. It can be used for your physical hand, "give him a hand" (meaning either "applause" or "help"), the hand of a clock, etc. Yet, you normally have no trouble following the

meaning of the word in specific contexts. Someone might say, "I cut my hand with a knife," and you know they are not talking about the "hand" on a wall clock.

In the same way, the words of the Bible often could be understood to mean different things, but the authors used their words to communicate in specific contexts. So reading a Bible passage in its correct context is foundational for understanding what a given word means. One way to identify the context is to track the themes in a section of Scripture. Write in the margins the main topics covered, and constantly reflect on these as you progress through the passage.

When we consider the immediate context in a narrative passage, we are looking for any aspect of a historical situation indicated by the passage itself. What do we mean by the immediate historical situation? In studying the story of Elijah and the prophets of Baal in 1 Kings 18:1-46, for example, the immediate historical situation has to do with Ahab as king of Israel, a time of punishing drought, Elijah the prophet, and the location of Mount Carmel. The historical situation of the book as a whole, on the other hand, would have to do with when and why 1 Kings was written and the fact that the book spans from the reign of Solomon down through the death of the wicked king Ahab.

Stage 3: Read the Road Signs Carefully

When you travel, it is critical that you read the road signs well. As we study the Bible, there are many clues to the author's intentions built right into any given passage. So, one important aspect of Bible study is slowing down and reading the passage carefully.

When you are driving down a road at 65 miles per hour, how many roadside details do you catch? Not many. You might be able to *see* interesting objects on roadside, but they blur and then fade quickly as you speed by.

Many of us are "drive by" readers of Scripture, never slowing down to explore and enjoy the details of God's Word; consequently there is much that we miss in the process. Choose to slow down and read with care. Read a passage repeatedly if you sense you've yet to catch all the elements. One way to ensure that you are reading slowly enough to catch the details is to underline key phrases or words, or write notes in the margin.

Read the Passage in Several Translations: Doing a comparison of modern English Bible translations can be a helpful way to highlight key interpretive issues in a passage. Why? Because translation, by its nature, requires interpretation. With almost any verse of Scripture, translators have to choose, given the context and grammatical constructions, between various possible word meanings. Therefore, the differences reflected in the various translations represent various interpretations of the passage.

Look for Key Dynamics in the Passage: Now read through your chosen passage again in your main translation. Look for the features listed below and circle, underline, or highlight them, perhaps using different color pens. This exercise will give you a much clearer picture of the passage. Common features to look for include:

* *Subject*—who or what is the passage focusing on?
* *Verb*—is it a statement, an exhortation, a question or answer, an action, explanation, or illustration?
* *Conjunctions*—and, but, or, so, for, both . . . and, neither . . . nor, either . . . or, not only . . . but also
* *Time*—after, before, when, while, since, until
* *Cause*—because, since, in order that, so that
* *Condition*—if, in case, even if, unless
* *Concession*—although, even though, whereas
* *Means*—how is the action accomplished?
* *Agent*—who does the action?
* *Result*—what is accomplished?

- *Purpose*—why was the action done?

When reading narrative material, identify the following:

- *Introduction and Conclusion*—the author often tips off the intended impact of a narrative in his introduction and conclusion
- *Setting*—details on place, time (historical era and duration of the event), and social situation (who is involved?)
- *Character Information*—identify the protagonist and antagonist, note prevailing emotions and actions, and pay close attention to dialogue and character descriptions
- *Narrative Dynamics*—identify the conflict, its escalation, and eventual resolution
- *Teaching Forms and Figures of Speech*—look for the presence of allusions to or quotations of the Old Testament, plus figures of speech such as hyperbole, simile, metaphor, riddle, pun, parable, object lesson, illustration, parabolic act, paradox, irony, amen formula, and prophecy

Don't get overwhelmed with searching for these dynamics. Take a few at a time, reading the passage with those dynamics in mind. Then read again, looking for a few more of the dynamics listed above. "Filtering" the passage in this way will give you great insight into the passage. If when reading the passage you see just two or three features that you had not seen before, you are making progress!

Make a Provisional Outline of the Passage: The outline is provisional since you still have a good bit of study to do on the passage. However, it is helpful to make a tentative outline at this point to begin to assess the general structure of the passage.

Stage 4: Learn to Speak Like a Local

One of the most interesting aspects of traveling has to do with learning how people in different places use words. For instance, the German phrase "Guten Tag" literally means "good day," yet it is normally used as a greeting only in the afternoon, and thus is equivalent to an English speaker saying, "good afternoon."

To understand the biblical text, we need to have an accurate understanding of *how* words are used. Word meanings are determined by the contexts in which they are used. When studying a word in the biblical text we want to (a) know the possible meanings for that word in the ancient world, (b) determine, based on the context, which meaning the author most likely intended, and (c) see whether insight on an author's use can be gained by noting how the same word is used elsewhere in the Bible.

Choose Key Words to Study: Identify key words in the passage. These may be terms that are repeated, terms that are unclear or puzzling, or terms that seem to be theologically important.

Consult Word Study Tools: Get at the Hebrew or Greek words behind our English translations by using an exhaustive concordance, Bible software programs, or various types of expository dictionaries. Once you have accessed the range of possible meanings for the Hebrew or Greek word, consider those possible meanings in the context of the passage you are studying. This gives you a look at the various nuances of the Greek or Hebrew word behind the translation you are using, deepening your understanding of what the biblical author might have been trying to say.

This is also an excellent point in your Bible study to consult good commentaries. They will discuss the key words of the passage against the backdrop of literary context, background issues, the author's theology, and other factors.

Consult a Concordance: You can use a concordance to look for other uses of the same Hebrew or Greek term you are studying. Identify places where the word is used similarly to the way it is used in the passage you are studying. Such cross references can provide you with greater understanding of the passage on which you are doing your word studies.

Word studies can be very helpful, but they can also be abused, and there are word study fallacies we want to avoid. A few of the most common fallacies include:

- *Cross reference fallacy*—Insisting that a word as used in one passage must be used the same way in another passage, simply because the same word is being used.
- *Root fallacy*—Insisting that a word's true meaning is tied to its root meanings, or the parts of the word. But this is not always how language works.
- *Multiple meanings fallacy*—Insisting that all the possible meanings of a word occur in a given use in a particular passage. Most of the time, an author had a particular meaning in mind.

Stage 5: Head Home

As with any trip, there comes a time to travel home. Bible study is analogous in that applying the Bible to our lives is "bringing it home." We were never meant to read and study the Bible simply to learn a list of facts. Rather, we were meant to experience transformation by the Word (Rm 12:1-2), and transformation takes place as we embrace the Word, applying it to our everyday lives. Commenting on the command to love one's neighbor, James says:

> What good is it, my brothers, if someone says he has faith but does not have works? Can his faith save him? If a brother or sister is without clothes and lacks daily food and one of you says to them, "Go in peace, keep warm, and eat well," but you don't give them what the body needs, what good is it? In the same way faith, if it doesn't have works, is dead by itself (Jms 2:14-17).

Faith without deeds, without application, is dead. James was addressing those who had disconnected belief in the Christian life from active obedience.

At times the application may be a right belief, the adjusting of one's understanding to fit what God says is true. At other times, application might be to worship God. Often application will involve active obedience that puts into practice what has been learned. But the movement from understanding the Word to its application in obedience is nonnegotiable from the Bible's standpoint.

How then can we apply the things we learn in the Bible to our lives in responsible ways?

Identify the main points and principles of the passage: What truth claims is the Scripture passage making? Identify them. Search for the principles as well. A principle is a "universal truth" that applies in all places at all times.

Identify how these address original and modern contexts: Notice how the principle is applied to the situation dealt with in your passage and think through parallel situations in your life.

Make specific applications to your life: Work at moving beyond vague generalities like, "I need to love people more!" Write down *who* you need to love and *how* you need to express love to them. As noted above, applications might be an *action* to do (e.g., "wash the dishes"). Yet, they could also involve the change of a belief, or even to respond to God's Word by worshiping Him.

A Simple Plan

I hope you have enjoyed the "trip" as we have discussed how to read and study the Bible more effectively. Begin your new commitment with a definite reading plan. Commit to taking 15-30 minutes per day, and read through the Bible over the next year or two. Take one or two longer blocks of time per week to study the Bible in greater depth.

Bible reading and study can give us great joy and fulfillment as we open our lives to God's Word. May you be blessed as you pursue being a "Word person" led by the Spirit, transformed by the Scriptures, and effective in advancing God's agendas in the world.

The Origin, Transmission, and Canonization of the Old Testament Books

Jeremy Royal Howard

The term *canon* is used to describe the list of books approved for inclusion in the Bible. It stems from a Greek word meaning "rod," as in a straight stick that serves as a standard for measuring. Hence, to speak of the biblical canon is to speak of authoritative books, given by God, the teachings of which define correct belief and practice. Obviously, only books inspired by God should be received as canonical. The Bible before you includes 39 books in the Old Testament (OT). Are these the right books? Who wrote them? What were their sources of information? These questions are asked by friends and foes of biblical faith. The present essay will touch on such issues with an aim to bolster Christian confidence in the OT.

Sources for the Earliest Histories

Genesis chapters 1-11 are referred to as "primeval history" because they cover events that occurred far back in the shadows of earliest time. Genesis chapters 12-50 are in turn called "patriarchal history" since they recount the lives of Israel's founding fathers from Abraham down to Joseph. From the creation of the world to Joseph's establishment in Egypt, all the events retold in Genesis occurred long before Moses was born. This is significant because the Bible and long-standing Jewish tradition assert that Moses wrote the first five books of the Bible (the Pentateuch). Most likely he composed them between 1440 and 1400 B.C. while he and the Israelites sojourned outside Canaan. Many events in Exodus through Deuteronomy coincided with Moses' lifetime, and so he authored these largely as an eyewitness. But what about Genesis? How did Moses know details about events and people that preceded him by many centuries?

Some suggest Moses knew the ancient histories because God revealed them to him supernaturally. In this scenario, God's inspiration of Moses would include God supplying Moses with historical details about far gone people, places, times, and even conversations— information Moses would not have known had God not told him. This possibility cannot be ruled out in principle since God is capable of working such miracles, but careful analysis reveals the Pentateuch nowhere hints that the historical narratives were given to Moses in this manner. For instance, Genesis never says anything like, "The word of the Lord came to Moses, saying, 'This is the history of Abraham.'" Instead, the Genesis narratives about Abraham and other historical figures read like straightforward accounts that have been handed down in the usual way: through oral and written records, with the oral records presumably originating soon after the events occurred. In this case, we would add that God superintended the transmission of the early oral and written accounts so that Moses received reliable histories worthy of inclusion in Genesis.

That Moses possibly used such sources may seem surprising at first. People often assume the Bible is the product of divine dictation, but it is more accurate to view Bible composition as having involved both supernatural and natural means, with the result that the original Bible manuscripts were fully reliable and stemmed simultaneously from divine inspiration as well as regular human approaches to writing. This model is supported by Luke 1:1-4, where Luke says he did a lot of research before writing his Gospel. A similar example is found in Numbers 21:14, where a quote is lifted from the now lost "Book of the Lord's Wars." From these examples we see that Bible writers were free to draw reliable historical data from non-biblical sources. Thus it seems Moses was able to write about historical events that occurred long before his birth by drawing upon information found in pre-existing sources, all while God's Spirit inspired him in penning Genesis.

How did these written sources come down to Moses? For the primeval history, it is reasonable to suggest that from earliest times people passed down carefully preserved oral accounts about key events and significant persons. Later, when elementary writing arose, many of these would

have been committed to writing. The transfer to written format may have happened earlier than is commonly supposed. Rudimentary alphabets are known to have circulated in the early second millennium B.C., and with the discovery of the Palermo Stone we have solid evidence that the Egyptians wrote detailed historical records (in hieroglyphic text) at least as far back as 2600 B.C., a time that predated Moses by over 1,100 years. The rich details inscribed on the Palermo Stone reach back toward the very dawn of Egypt, naming kings from 3100 B.C. and even earlier. In light of this example it is fitting to suppose that key remembrances of early human history were preserved and passed down to later generations.

That the very earliest writings have not survived to our day is no surprise, for they would have been rare to begin with and would have perished long ago as the acids of time worked their destruction. But they survived long enough to bequeath vital facts to later societies who learned to write the histories in more permanent formats. Some of the greatest modern archeological digs have uncovered ancient nonbiblical texts that resemble the biblical accounts of Noah's flood and the Tower of Babel. These texts date from 1600 B.C. and earlier, and in broad strokes they corroborate Genesis. Their points of departure from Genesis may reflect corruptions that slipped in as cultures pulled farther and farther away from knowledge of God. By contrast, people who kept alive a faith like Noah's preserved the stories uncorrupted, and it is these accounts that came down to men like Moses in later generations.

As for the patriarchal histories, it goes without saying that men such as Abraham would pass down close accounts of their remarkable experiences with God. Once God interrupted Abraham's life and promised to create a nation through him, he knew his life was unique. This heritage was repeatedly confirmed to his descendants as God kept up His habit of revealing Himself and confirming His covenant of blessing. Somewhere down the line Abraham's descendants began writing down these stories. This may have begun most earnestly with Joseph, the son of Israel who became a great political figure in Egypt. Writing was a very old art in Egypt by the time Joseph ascended to power. Having achieved a royal-like status and having married a well-placed Egyptian, Joseph and his family would have had every opportunity to learn the Egyptian writing craft. As a chief bearer of Abraham's lineage, Joseph would have been keen to preserve the family traditions and the link to the one true God.

In the years after Joseph's death, the Hebrews grew in number but came to be suppressed by the Egyptians. This suppression highlighted the need to preserve the histories. One theory holds that one of the Israelite families, possibly the Levites, became the official preservers of the old stories. If so, these materials would have been available to Moses (a Levite) when he became leader of the Hebrews. This inheritance, plus God's commission of Moses and the fact that he was raised and educated in Pharaoh's household, put Moses in a fine position to write an early history of humankind from the Hebrew perspective. A possible exception would be the portions of the creation accounts (Genesis 1-2) that could not stem from human eyewitness testimony. These accounts bear close resemblance to visionary revelations that were later given to prophets such as Isaiah and Ezekiel, as well as John in the book of Revelation. Hence, it is plausible to suggest that God gave Moses a revelatory vision for the first two chapters of Genesis. But in his writings generally, whether he was making use of oral accounts, written histories, or relying on God's Spirit for the unveiling of the creation accounts, Moses often wrote more than he knew. In other words, Moses could not plumb the depths of everything he wrote, for an Author greater than he breathed profundity and prophecy into the works of his pen.

Who Wrote the Books and When?

The OT books do not have copyright dates on them, and few of them explicitly identify their author. Nevertheless, by aid of biblical testimony and Jewish history we know the approximate time at which the books were composed. We also know in many cases who the author was or who was likely to have been chiefly responsible for a book's content. For thousands of years

Sources and Authorship for Genesis

PRIMEVAL AND PATRIARCHAL ERAS

Theologically significant events occurring from creation to roughly 1800 BC.

ORAL HISTORIES OF THESE ERAS

Oral histories arose among early peoples who sought to preserve knowledge of key events. In the Patriarchal Age, Abraham and his descendants would have taken great care to pass down knowledge of God, His covenant promises, and key events in the lives of the Hebrew clan. God's sovereign Spirit ensured that these histories were uncorrupted by error.

EARLY WRITTEN RECORDS OF THESE ERAS

When elementary alphabets were invented, oral histories were set down in writing. Under God's guidance the biblical patriarchs would have taken great care to pass down accounts of their dealings with God. Through men such as Joseph, these records came down to Moses.

MOSES

Drawing from the reliable histories available to him, and guided by God, Moses infallibly wrote a theologically driven early history of earth in the book of Genesis.

MINOR EDITING

Done under the care of God's providence in the centuries after Moses wrote Genesis, mindful priests updated the text without modifying its meaning. This helped keep the text accessible to later generations of Hebrews, whose language and life situations differed significantly from those of Moses and the era about which he wrote.

DIVINE INSPIRATION

God commissioned Moses to write, guided his search through the histories, and supernaturally guided every word he wrote

GOD'S SPIRIT GUIDING THE PROCESS

now scholarly people of faith have studied the matter and have concluded that the OT books and their earliest recipients have reliably portrayed the authorship and dates for the sacred writings, yet today critics say the books were written many hundreds of years *after* the dates and authors traditionally assigned to them. For instance, it is claimed that the Pentateuch was actually written nearly 1,000 years after Moses. In its extreme version, this theory even says men such as Moses and Abraham never existed; they and their histories were allegedly invented by priests who sought to provide hope-inspiring stories during the tough years when the Hebrews were exiled in Babylon in the sixth century B.C.

Such theories are chiefly built on the slim supports of (1) skepticism, which presupposes that God does not exist and/or that the Bible is just a human book, and (2) the occasional anachronisms scattered throughout the early portions of the OT. Skepticism is itself a faith of sorts, for the assertions that God does not exist or did not inspire the Bible if He does exist cannot be proven from the data at hand. Ironically skeptics, who insist we should form beliefs only on the basis of evidence, contradict their own mantra. But what about the anachronisms found in the OT? It is true that the Pentateuch occasionally includes such things as place names or vocabulary that did not belong to the era described. In other words, some of these only came into usage hundreds of years after men like Abraham died. Skeptics take this as proof that the books (and all the stories they contain) originated much later than popularly believed, and that the priests who invented these stories occasionally slipped up and placed contemporary names and words into ancient settings.

But this radical theory is firmly against the evidence. In reality, the early OT books consistently bear the mark of ancient contexts—contexts that suit times long before national Israel arose. For instance, the laws, customs, and political situations described in the Pentateuch fit very naturally with the second millennium B.C. and earlier. This is proven by the discovery of many nonbiblical texts and artifacts from that era. It is unlikely that unethical priests a thousand years or more removed from the historical situations described in the Pentateuch could have gotten things so right. Also, the concerns that dominated the Hebrew mindset during the Babylonian exile are not addressed by the Pentateuch. Hence, how could priests hope to encourage their downtrodden fellow Hebrews in Babylon by inventing stories that bore no semblance to their situation? Further, it is unimaginable that the mass of Hebrews would fall for such a ruse, choose to base their entire worldview on false histories passed off on them by a band of inventive clergymen, and then succeed in selling the hoax to their children for generations to come.

So what should we conclude about the anachronisms? Simply this: in the years after the Pentateuch was written, inevitable changes in place names, vocabulary, and political situations made these old books harder to comprehend. To alleviate this problem, priestly guardians of the sacred oracles updated the texts at key junctures to reflect contemporary word usage and geopolitical situations. Such changes as these (e.g., Jdg 1:10; 1Sm 9:9) would have been undertaken soberly and with great care to preserve the meaning and intention of the holy text. Thus, under strict guidelines the books underwent helpful editing, with the result that the texts remained accessible with the passage of time.

On the whole, however, virtually all the scribes who ever touched the sacred scrolls did so only to read them or copy them word for word. Literary copying was an important skill in the ancient world since there was no means of rapid duplication, such as modern printing presses or photocopiers. Believing that the writings in their care were authoritative and inspired by God, the Hebrew scribes took exceptional care when copying the scrolls.

In conclusion, we can be confident in the traditional beliefs about the date and authorship of the OT books. We can also rest assured that the books were carefully copied and preserved, and that all editorial updates of the books were done in a strictly conservative fashion.

Do We Have the Right Books?

Are the 39 books of our OT really the ones God meant for us to revere? The first step to answering this question is to address the issue of collection: who was it that originally collected the sacred writings together? Solid evidence indicates that the priests undertook this duty. In Deuteronomy 31:24-26, Moses commanded that the book of the law be kept with the ark of the covenant, where the Ten Commandments were stored. This put Moses' writings at the very center of Jewish religious life just as soon as they were complete. Further, in Deuteronomy 4:2 we read the command to preserve the commandments of God faithfully. Taken together, these passages indicate that the priests were to keep charge of God's written revelations, and that these were to be safeguarded against perversion.

Since Moses was the author of the earliest biblical books, and since Moses himself charged the priests with the duties to store and protect God's words, the high value of identifying, collecting, and protecting the sacred writings was established when the Pentateuch originated. When other prophets and holy men arose in Israel subsequent to Moses and were given revelations by God, their teachings (whether written by them or by their close associates) would have been gathered quickly by the community of the faithful. At some later point the books came to be stored at the Jerusalem temple. We know this because in a time of national backsliding the unused books collected dust in the temple's storerooms (2Kg 22:8-13). At a much later time in history the books were still kept in the temple, for Josephus (a reputable Jewish historian) received the Scriptures from his Roman benefactors who had sacked the temple in A.D. 70.

We have seen that the Jews identified, collected, and preserved the sacred writings as a matter of course. Next we must ask if or when they believed the production of sacred writings had ceased. Josephus is helpful for elucidating this matter. He tells us (*Against Apion* 1.37-43) that the Jews widely recognized that the succession of the prophets ended in the time of Artaxerxes, when Latter Prophets such as Haggai and Malachi fell silent and left no successors. Hence, says Josephus, books written after about 400 B.C. were not regarded as Scripture even if they were valuable on other terms. In 164 B.C. Judas Maccabaeus reconsolidated the Scriptures in the temple after the fires of the Antiochene persecution died out, and it appears that the scrolls were harbored there in a long stretch of safety that did not end until the abovementioned Roman aggressions. There can be no doubt of the identity of the Scriptures held at the temple throughout this time: there were 22 books (or 24, depending on how they were divided and counted), and they were lumped into three major divisions: the Law (Pentateuch), the Prophets, and the Writings. Though we divide them into 39 books rather than 22 or 24, the Protestant OT canon is identical to those books that were safeguarded at the temple before the time of Christ. The two most significant religious bodies in Israel (Pharisees and Sadducees) both accepted this body of books as the canon of Scripture, though one often hears it mistakenly asserted that the Sadducees accepted only the Pentateuch.

What about the books of the Apocrypha? This is a diverse set of books—most of which were written between 200 B.C. and early in the first century A.D.—that treat various aspects of Jewish religious and national life in the Intertestamental period, which ranged from 400 B.C. to the time of Christ. They offer important windows into the Jewish context, and many Jews of that time regarded them as valuable religious literature. However, they were never received as Scripture by mainstream Judaism, and even fringe groups such as the Essenes reckoned them valuable but *not* scriptural. The books of the Apocrypha were never stored in the temple, a sure sign that they were not thought to be inspired by God.

This is not to say there were no struggles among the Jews about the identity of the canon. In fact, five of the books that were counted as canonical had a hard time winning unilateral acceptance. The books of Proverbs, Ecclesiastes, Esther, Song of Songs, and Ezekiel were subjected to scrutiny because they seemed secular in outlook or else promoted teachings that initially seemed inconsistent with the Pentateuch. Jewish leaders debated the merits of these

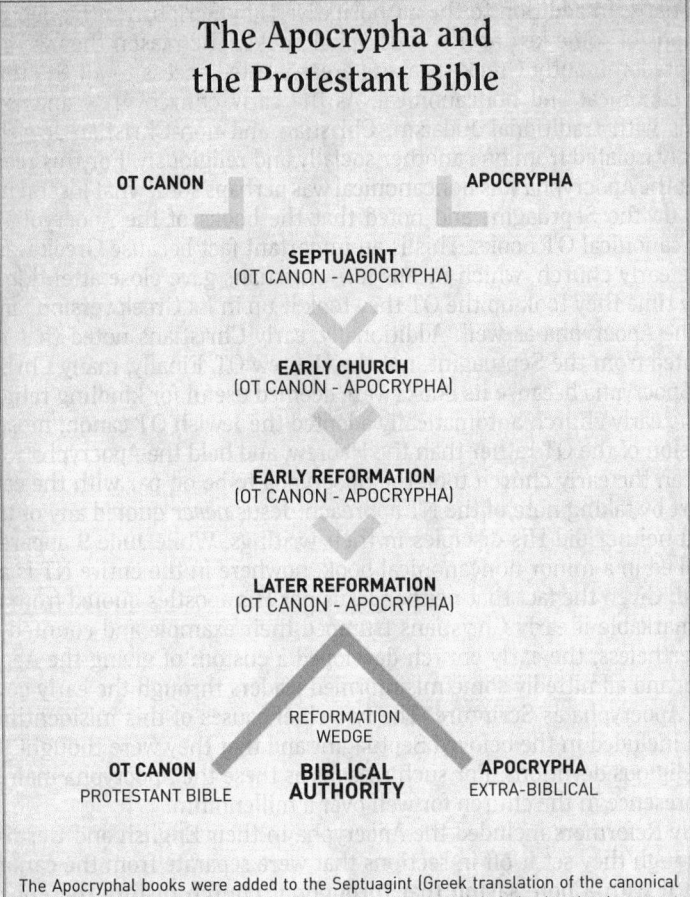

The Apocrypha and the Protestant Bible

OT CANON   **APOCRYPHA**

SEPTUAGINT
(OT CANON - APOCRYPHA)

EARLY CHURCH
(OT CANON - APOCRYPHA)

EARLY REFORMATION
(OT CANON - APOCRYPHA)

LATER REFORMATION
(OT CANON - APOCRYPHA)

REFORMATION
WEDGE

OT CANON   **BIBLICAL**   **APOCRYPHA**
PROTESTANT BIBLE   **AUTHORITY**   EXTRA-BIBLICAL

The Apocryphal books were added to the Septuagint (Greek translation of the canonical OT) because Greek-speaking Jews wanted access to Jewish holy books plus important nonbiblical books. The Early Church widely used the Septuagint, and though the Apocrypha was rarely (and *mistakenly*) equated with inspired Scripture, it was rightly deemed a valuable collection of historical books. Seeing the need to clarify the status of the Apocrypha, the Reformers elected to separate it from the canonical books. Thus the Apocrypha came to be excluded from Protestant Bibles

books from time to time, as Christian leaders would do in the centuries to come, but all in all their status in the canon was well established.

Following Jesus' example, early Christians adopted the Jewish consensus on the OT canon. During His ministry Jesus showed that He was in line with the standard Jewish assessment of the canon by quoting from all three divisions of the OT. Furthermore, He demonstrated that the OT included many prophecies and veiled allusions to Himself, the Messiah. Thus, Christians learned to read the Jewish holy books with a view to seeing Jesus in them. In fact, for the first few decades of the church the majority of Christians had little access to the New Testament (NT) writings that were starting to emerge. The OT was the only Bible many of them knew, and they valued it greatly as they read it from a Christ-centered vantage point. Interestingly, they tended to hold the Apocrypha in high esteem as well—higher than most Jews did, in fact. A little background information helps us understand how this situation arose.

Several centuries before Christ the Jews living in Alexandria commissioned a Greek translation of the Hebrew OT. They did this because they increasingly spoke and read Greek rather than Hebrew. Known as the Septuagint, this Greek translation was the Bible of choice for many Jews

and early Christians. In addition to the authoritative Holy Scriptures, the Septuagint included Greek translations of some key Jewish apocryphal books. The reason they were added is clear: Jews living in predominantly Greek-speaking areas wanted access to all the important Jewish writings, both canonical and noncanonical. As the early church grew and experienced ever greater tensions with traditional Judaism, Christian and non-Christian Jewish communities were increasingly isolated from one another socially and religiously. For this reason, the Jewish assessment that the Apocrypha was noncanonical was perhaps somewhat lost on many Christians as they picked up the Septuagint and noted that the books of the Apocrypha were included along with the canonical OT books. This is an important fact because Greek was the dominant language of the early church, which means few Christians gave close attention to the Hebrew OT. Thus, every time they took up the OT they took it up in its Greek version, and in doing this they took up the Apocrypha as well. Additionally, early Christians noted that the NT authors most often quoted from the Septuagint, not the Hebrew OT. Finally, many Christians had high regard for the Apocrypha because its books were deemed useful for kindling religious affections. In summary, the early church automatically adopted the Jewish OT canon, most often read the Septuagint version of the OT rather than the Hebrew, and held the Apocrypha to be valuable.

Does this mean the early church took the Apocrypha to be on par with the canonical books? It is best to start by taking note of the NT approach. Jesus *never* quoted any of the books of the Apocrypha, and neither did His disciples in their writings. While Jude 9 apparently alludes to an event described in a minor noncanonical book, nowhere in the entire NT is any book of the Apocrypha cited. Given the fact that neither Jesus nor His apostles quoted from the Apocrypha, it would be remarkable if early Christians trumped their example and counted these books as Scripture. Nevertheless, the early church developed a custom of giving the Apocrypha a place in religious life, and admittedly some misinformed leaders through the early centuries seemed to think of the Apocrypha as Scripture. The two chief causes of this misidentification are that the books were included in the beloved Septuagint and that they were thought to be genuinely conducive to religious devotions. For such reasons as these the Apocrypha maintained a steady but unofficial presence in the church for well over a millennium.

Even the early Reformers included the Apocrypha in their English and German translations of the Bible, though they set it off in sections that were separate from the canonical OT books and introduced it with a note saying that throughout church history the Apocrypha had not been received as Scripture. Thus the Reformers initially kept alive the old tradition of packing the Apocrypha into the Bible, though as in a seatless balcony reserved for bystanders. As they continued to debate Roman Catholic leaders over the proper bases for doctrinal formation, the Reformers eventually concluded that for the sake of clarity the Apocrypha should be dropped altogether from the Bible. As inheritors of the Reformation movement, Protestant Bibles today exclude the Apocrypha, signifying that while those books may be useful, they are nonbiblical.

Conclusion

We have solid reasons for believing that the OT books include only true history and that they were written by men who were appointed by God to deliver Spirit-inspired writings to humanity. Further, it is clear that the Jews of old received these books with awe and a sense of responsibility. Hence, the sacred books were identified, collected, preserved, and transmitted through the generations by men approved for such high tasks. The 39 books of the Protestant OT are assuredly the books God would have us venerate as scriptural. The books of the Apocrypha are valuable (indeed, more valuable than most Protestants realize), but should be consulted for their historical value and not for instruction in doctrine or religious practice.

Old Testament

Genesis

Introduction

The book of Genesis is the great book of beginnings in the Bible. True to the meanings of its Hebrew and Greek names (Hb *bere'shith,* "In Beginning" [based on 1:1]; Gk *Geneseos,* "Of Birth" [based on 2:4]), Genesis permits us to view the beginning of a multitude of realities that shape our daily existence: the creation of the universe and the planet earth; the origins of plant and animal life; and the origins of human beings, marriage, families, nations, industry, artistic expression, religious ritual, prophecy, sin, law, crime, conflict, punishment, and death.

Circumstances of Writing

Author: Since pre-Christian times authorship of the Torah, the five books that include the book of Genesis, has been attributed to Moses, an enormously influential Israelite leader from the second millennium B.C. with an aristocratic Egyptian background. Even though Genesis is technically anonymous, both the Old and New Testaments unanimously recognize Moses as the Torah's author (Jos 8:35; 23:6; 1Kg 2:3; 8:9; 2Kg 14:6; 23:25; 2Ch 23:18; 25:4; 30:16; 34:14; 35:12; Ezr 3:2; 6:18; Neh 8:1; 9:14; Dn 9:11,13; Mal 4:4; Mk 12:19,26; Lk 2:22; 20:28; 24:44; Jn 1:17,45; 7:19; Ac 13:39; 15:21; 28:23; Rm 10:5; 1Co 9:9; Heb 10:28). At the same time, evidence in Genesis suggests that minor editorial changes dating to ancient times have been inserted into the text. Examples include the mention of "Dan" (14:14), a city that was not named until the days of the judges (Jdg 18:29), and the use of a phrase that assumed the existence of Israelite kings (Gn 36:31).

Background: The Torah (a Hebrew term for law) was seen as one unit until at least the second century B.C. Sometime prior to the birth of Christ, the Torah was divided into five separate books, later referred to as the Pentateuch (literally, five vessels). Genesis, the first book of the Torah, provides both the universal history of humankind and the patriarchal history of the nation of Israel. The first section (chaps. 1–11) is a general history commonly called the "primeval history," showing how all humanity descended from one couple and became sinners. The second section (chaps. 12–50) is a more specific history commonly referred to as the "patriarchal history," focusing on the covenant God made with Abraham and his descendants: Isaac, Jacob, and Jacob's 12 sons. Genesis unfolds God's plan to bless and redeem humanity through Abraham's descendants. The book concludes with the events that led to the Israelites being in the land of Egypt.

Message and Purpose

Creation: God is the sovereign Lord and Creator of all things. God created everything out of nothing. No pre-existent material existed. He is the Creator, not a craftsman. This indicates that He has infinite power and perfect control over everything. He is separate from the created order, and no part of creation is to be consid-

2100 B.C.		2000 B.C.	
Job 2100?–1900?	**Abraham** 2166–1991	**Isaac** 2066–1886	**Jacob** 2006–1859
11th Dynasty of Egypt **2134–1991**	3rd Dynasty of Ur **2113–2006**		12th Dynasty of Egypt **1991–1786**

Abraham moves from Haran to Canaan. 2091	Contraceptives developed in Egypt 2000
Destruction of Sodom and Gomorrah 2085	Chinese create first zoo, Park of Intelligence. 2000
God's covenant with Abraham 2081?	Babylonians and Egyptians divide days into hours, minutes, and seconds. 2000
Earliest pottery in South America 2200	
Construction of Ziggurat at Ur in Sumer 2100	Mesopotamians learn to solve quadratic equations. 2000
	Code of medical ethics, Mesopotamia 2000
	Courier systems of communication developed in both China and Egypt 2000

ered an extension of God. All that God created is good, because He is a good and majestic God. God is Lord, maintaining sovereignty and involvement with His creation. God's control over human history is so complete that even the worst of human deeds can be turned to serve His benevolent purposes (50:20).

Human life: Adam and Eve were created in the image of God, unique from the rest of creation, to have fellowship with Him. Humans are a paradox. On the one hand, people are the capstone of all God's creation, created in God's image (1:26-27) and possessing Godlike authority over all the created order within their realm (1:28-29; 9:1-3). On the other hand, they are sinners—beings who have used their God-given resources and abilities in ways that violate God's laws (2:17; 3:6) and hurt other people (3:8-11; 6:5,11-12). Even so, during their lifetime God expects people to follow His laws (4:7), and He blesses those who live according to His ways (6:8-9; 39:2,21). God wants to work through individuals to bring a blessing to every human life (18:18; 22:18; 26:4). Nevertheless, Genesis teaches that because of sin all human beings must die (2:17; 3:19; 5:5,8,11). Since all human life is created in the image of God, there is no person or class of humans superior to others. Humanity was created to live in community. The most fundamental unit of community is the family: a husband and wife (male and female) with children.

Sin: Evil and sin did not originate with God. Adam and Eve were created innocent and with the capacity to make choices. Sin entered the world at a specific place and time in history. Adam and Eve chose freely to disobey God, fell from innocence, and lost their freedom. Their sinful nature has passed to every other human being. Sin resulted in death, both physical and spiritual. Sin has led to a world of pain and struggle.

Covenant: Genesis is a narrative of relationships, and certainly relationships grounded in covenants with God. These covenants provide a unifying principle for understanding the whole of Scripture and define the relationship between God and man. The heart of that relationship is found in the phrase, "They will be My people, and I will be their God" (Jr 32:38; cp. Gn 17:7-8; Ex 6:6-7; Lv 26:12; Dt 4:20; Jr 11:4; Ezk 11:20). God's covenant with Abraham is a major event both in Genesis and throughout the Bible. God called Abraham out

---

1900 B.C.   1800 B.C.

Joseph 1915–1805

Jacob wrestles with God. 1903?   Amorite Ascendancy 1894–1595

Potter's wheel introduced to Crete 1900   Musical theory, Mesopotamia 1800

Use of the sail in the Aegean 1900   Multiplication tables, Mesopotamia 1800

First Chinese city founded at Erlitou on   Babylonians develop catalog of stars and
  Yellow River 1900   planets. 1800

Egyptian town of El Lahun gives evidence of town Book of the Dead, Egypt 1800
  planning with streets at right angles. 1900
                                                  Horses introduced in Egypt 1800
Mesopotamian mathematicians discover what later
  came to be called the Pythagorean theorem. 1900 Wooden plows, Scandinavia 1800

Khnumhotep II, an architect of Pharoah
  Amenemhet II, develops encryption. 1900

of Ur to go to Canaan, promising to make him a great nation which in turn would bless all nations (Gn 12:1-3). God repeats His oath in Genesis 22:18, adding further that it would be through Abraham's seed that all nations would someday be blessed. Paul applies the singular noun "seed" as a reference to Christ (Gl 3:16). It is through Christ, Abraham's prophesied descendant, that the blessings of the Abrahamic Covenant would come to every nation.

Contribution to the Bible

Genesis lays the groundwork for everything else we read and experience in Scripture. Through Genesis we understand where we came from, how we got in the fallen state we are in, and the beginnings of God's gracious work on our behalf. Genesis unfolds God's original purpose for humanity.

Genesis provides the foundation from which we understand God's covenant with Israel that was established with the giving of the Law. For the Israelite community, the stories of the origins of humanity, sin, and the covenant relationship with God helped them understand why God gave them the Law.

Structure

Genesis is chiefly a narrative. From a narrative standpoint, God is the only true hero of the Bible, and the book of Genesis has the distinct privilege of introducing Him. God is the first subject of a verb in the book and is mentioned more frequently than any other character in the Bible. The content of the first 11 chapters is distinct from the patriarchal stories in chapters 12–50. The primary literary device is the catchphrase "these are the family records." The phrase is broader in meaning than simply "generation," and refers more to a narrative account. This was a common practice in ancient Near East writings. This phrase also serves as a link between the key person in the previous narrative and the one anticipated in the next section. Genesis could be described as historical genealogy, which ties together creation and human history in one continuum.

Outline

I. Creation of Heaven and Earth (1:1–2:3)
    A. Creator and creation (1:1-2)
    B. Six days of creation (1:3-31)
    C. Seventh day—day of consecration (2:1-3)

II. The Human Family In and Outside the Garden (2:4–4:26)
    A. The man and woman in the garden (2:4-25)
    B. The man and woman expelled from the garden (3:1-24)
    C. Adam and Eve's family outside the garden (4:1-26)

III. Adam's Family Line (5:1–6:8)
    A. Introduction: Creation and blessing (5:1-2)
    B. "Image of God" from Adam to Noah (5:3-32)
    C. Conclusion: Procreation and perversion (6:1-8)

IV. Noah and His Family (6:9–9:29)
    A. Righteous Noah and the corrupt world (6:9-12)
    B. Coming judgment but the ark of promise (6:13–7:10)
    C. Worldwide flood of judgment (7:11-24)
    D. God's remembrance and rescue of Noah (8:1-14)

XI. Jacob's Family: Joseph and His Brothers (37:2–50:26)
  A. The early days of Joseph (37:2-36)
  B. Judah and Tamar (38:1-30)
  C. Joseph in Egypt (39:1-23)
  D. Joseph, savior of Egypt (40:1–41:57)
  E. The brothers' journeys to Egypt (42:1–43:34)
  F. Joseph tests the brothers (44:1-34)
  G. Joseph reveals his identity (45:1-28)
  H. Jacob's migration to Egypt (46:1-27)
  I. Joseph, savior of the family (46:28–47:12)
  J. Joseph's administration in Egypt (47:13-31)
  K. Jacob's blessings (48:1–49:28)
  L. The death and burial of Jacob (49:29–50:14)
  M. The final days of Joseph (50:15-26)

The Creation

1 In the beginning[a] God created the heavens and the earth.[A,b]

[2] Now the earth was[B] formless and empty,[c] darkness covered the surface of the watery depths, and the Spirit of God was hovering over the surface of the waters.[d] [3] Then God said, "Let there be light,"[e] and there was light. [4] God saw that the light was good, and God separated the light from the darkness. [5] God called the light "day," and He called the darkness "night." Evening came and then morning: the first day.

[6] Then God said, "Let there be an expanse[C] between the waters, separating water from water."[f] [7] So God made the expanse and separated the water under the expanse from the water above the expanse.[g] And it was so. [8] God called the expanse "sky."[D] Evening came and then morning: the second day.

[9] Then God said, "Let the water under the sky be gathered into one place,[h] and let the dry land appear." And it was so. [10] God called the dry land "earth," and He called the gathering of the water "seas." And God saw that it was good. [11] Then God said, "Let the earth

[a]1:1 Ps 90:2; 102:12; Is 40:21; Jn 1:1-3; Eph 3:21
[b]Neh 9:6; Is 40:12-14; 43:7; Jr 10:12-16; Am 4:13; Rm 1:25; 1Co 11:9; Col 1:16; Rv 4:11
[c]1:2 Jr 4:23
[d]Jb 26:13; 33:4; Ps 33:6; 104:30
[e]1:3 2Co 4:6
[f]1:6 Is 44:24; Jr 10:12
[g]1:7 Ps 148:4
[h]1:9 Jb 38:8-11; Ps 33:7; 136:6; Jr 5:22; 2Pt 3:5

[A]1:1 Or *created the universe*   [B]1:1-2 Or *When God began to create the sky and the earth,* [2] *the earth was*   [C]1:6 The Hb word for *expanse* is from a root meaning "to spread out, stamp, beat firmly," which suggests something like a dome; Jb 37:16-18; Is 40:22.   [D]1:8 Or *"heavens"*

1:1 This opening verse of the Bible, seven words in the Hebrew, establishes seven key truths upon which the rest of the Bible is based.

First, God exists. The essential first step in pleasing God is recognizing His existence (Heb 11:6). Second, God existed before there was a universe and will exist after the universe perishes (Heb 1:10-12). Third, God is the main character in the Bible. He is the subject of the first verb in the Bible (in fact, He is the subject of more verbs than any other character) and performs a wider variety of activities than any other being in the Bible. Fourth, as Creator God has done what no human being could ever do; in its active form the Hebrew verb *bara'*, meaning "to create," never has a human subject. Thus *bara'* signifies a work that is uniquely God's. Fifth, God is mysterious; though the Hebrew word for God is plural, the verb form of which "God" is the subject is singular. This is perhaps a subtle allusion to God's Trinitarian nature: He is three divine persons in one divine essence. Sixth, God is the Creator of heaven and earth. He doesn't just modify pre-existing matter but calls matter into being out of nothing (Ps 33:6,9; Heb 11:3). Seventh, God is not dependent on the universe, but the universe is totally dependent on God (Heb 1:3).

1:2 Bible translations since the time of the Septuagint, the translation of the OT into Greek (ca 175 B.C.), have rendered the first Hebrew verb in this verse as **was**. However, in an effort to explain the origins of evil and/or find biblical evidence for an old earth, some Bible scholars have suggested that this verb should be translated as "became." Citing evidence in Is 14:12-21 and Ezk 28:12-19, they believe a time gap, possibly a vast one, exists between the first two verses of the Bible, during which Satan led a rebellion in heaven against God. This allows interpreters to suggest that the early earth was **formless and empty** because Satan's rebellion marred God's good creation. However, the construction of this sentence in the original Hebrew favors the traditional translation ("was" rather than "became").

The sense of verse 2 is that God created the earth "formless and empty" as an unfinished and unfilled state. Working through an orderly process over a period of six days, God formed (days 1-3) and filled (days 4-6) His created handiwork. The "forming" was accomplished by means of three acts of separating or sorting various elements of creation from one another. The "filling" was carried out through five acts of populating the newly created domains. **Watery depths**, a single word in Hebrew, suggests an original state of creation that was shapeless as liquid water. The Hebrew verb translated **was hovering**, used also in Dt 32:11, suggests that the Spirit of God was watching over His creation just as a bird watches over its young.

1:3 A foundational teaching of the Bible is that God speaks and does so with universe-changing authority. The command in this verse is just two words in Hebrew.

1:4 Another basic truth of the Bible is that **God saw**; this means He is fully aware of His creation. Later writers directly declared that God is aware of events occurring throughout the earth (2Ch 16:9; Zch 4:10). The term **good**, used here for the first of seven times in this chapter, to evaluate God's creative work, can be used to express both high quality and moral excellence. The physical universe is a good place because God made it. God found satisfaction in His labor. This first instance where **God separated** created the twin realms of light and darkness, day and night. God's activity in the material world parallels the role He also performs in the moral universe, that of the righteous Judge distinguishing between those who live in moral light and those who do not (1Th 5:5).

1:5 In ancient Israel, the act of naming an object, place, or person indicated that you held control over it (35:10; 41:45; Nm 32:42; Dt 3:14; Jos 19:47; 2Kg 23:34; 24:17). When God named the light and the darkness, He asserted His lordship and control over all of time. **Evening came**. In ancient Israelite and modern Jewish tradition, sundown is the transition point from one day to the next.

1:6 Based on a verb that can refer to covering something with a thin sheet of metal (Nm 16:39; Is 40:19), the noun **expanse** always refers to the vast spread of the open sky.

1:7 God's second act of separation was to divide atmospheric water from terrestrial water. Thus He began the process of giving form to the material world. The clause **it was so**, found six times in this chapter, emphasizes God's absolute power over creation.

1:8 **Sky** can refer to the earth's atmospheric envelope (v. 20), outer space (v. 15), or "heaven," the spiritual realm where God lives (Ps 11:4).

1:9 God's third and final act of separation created oceans and continents.

1:10 In His third and final act of naming, God demonstrated His authority over all of the earth. This contrasts with what Israel's polytheistic neighbors believed about the range of divine powers. Their gods were not all-powerful, but instead exercised authority over a limited territory. The God of Genesis 1 holds dominion over everything at all times and in all places.

1:11 In preparation for the rise of animal and human life, God provided an abundant supply of food. The consistent biblical teaching is that "like begets like" (Lk 6:44; Jms

produce vegetation: seed-bearing plants and fruit trees on the earth bearing fruit with seed in it according to their kinds." ª And it was so. ¹²The earth produced vegetation: seed-bearing plants according to their kinds and trees bearing fruit with seed in it according to their kinds. And God saw that it was good. ¹³Evening came and then morning: the third day.

¹⁴Then God said, "Let there be lights in the expanse of the sky to separate the day from the night. They will serve as signs ᵇ for festivals ᴬ and for days and years. ᶜ ¹⁵They will be lights in the expanse of the sky to provide light on the earth." And it was so. ¹⁶God made the two great lights—the greater light to have dominion over the day and the lesser light to have dominion over the night—as well as the stars. ᵈ ¹⁷God placed them in the expanse of the sky to provide light on the earth, ¹⁸to dominate the day and the night, and to separate light from darkness. ᵉ And God saw that it was good. ¹⁹Evening came and then morning: the fourth day.

²⁰Then God said, "Let the water swarm with ᴮ living creatures, and let birds fly above the earth across the expanse of the sky." ²¹So God created the large sea-creatures ᶜ and every living creature that moves and swarms in the water, ᶠ according to their kinds. He also created every winged bird according to its kind. And God saw that it was good. ²²So God blessed them, "Be fruitful, multiply, and fill the waters of the seas, and let the birds multiply on the earth." ᵍ ²³Evening came and then morning: the fifth day.

²⁴Then God said, "Let the earth produce living creatures according to their kinds: livestock, creatures that crawl, and the wildlife of the earth according to their kinds." And it was so. ²⁵So God made the wildlife of the earth according to their kinds, the livestock according to their kinds, and creatures that crawl on the ground according to their kinds. And God saw that it was good.

²⁶Then God said, "Let Us ʰ make man in Our image, according to Our likeness. ᶦ They will

ª1:11 Ps 65:9-13; 104:14
ᵇ1:14 Jr 10:2
ᶜPs 104:19
ᵈ1:16 Dt 4:19; Ps 136:7-9; Is 40:26
ᵉ1:18 Jr 31:35
ᶠ1:21 Ps 104:25-28
ᵍ1:22 Gn 8:17; 9:1
ʰ1:26 Gn 3:22; 11:7
ᶦGn 5:1,3; 9:6; Rm 8:29; 1Co 11:7; 15:49; 2Co 3:18; 4:4; Eph 4:24; Col 1:15; Jms 3:9

ᴬ1:14 Or for the appointed times　ᴮ1:20 Lit with swarms of　ᶜ1:21 Or created sea monsters

3:12]; Gn 1:11-12 establish that principle for plant life. While five of the six days contain at least one act of creation evaluated as good, only the third and sixth days have this statement more than once.

1:14-15 The events of day four complement those of day one, filling the day and night with finished forms of light. The various **lights**, or "light-giving objects," were worshiped as gods in the cultures that surrounded ancient Israel. In Genesis, however, the sun, moon, and stars are portrayed as servants of God that would fulfill three roles: separating the newly created realms of **day** and **night**; marking time so that those who worshiped the Creator could keep their appointed **festivals** (cp. Lv 23:4,44); and providing **light on the earth**.

1:20 The fifth day's events complement those of day two, filling the newly formed heavenly domains above and the watery regions below.

yom

Hebrew Pronunciation	[YOHM]
HCSB Translation	day, time
Uses in Genesis	152
Uses in the OT	2,301
Focus passage	Genesis 1:5,8,13-14,16,18-19,23,31

Yom means day, the Hebrew day lasting from one evening to the next (Gn 1:5). Yom describes a working day (Ex 20:9) or day of the month (Zch 1:7). It indicates a time (Pr 24:10) or occasion (Nm 10:10). In the day often appears as when (Zch 8:9). The plural can represent age (Jb 32:7), lifetime (Jos 24:31), or reign (Is 1:1). The plural denotes a number of days (Neh 1:4), a time period (Lv 25:8), some time (Gn 40:4), a year (Lv 25:29), or years (Ex 2:11). With the definite article yom suggests today (Dt 4:39), now (Neh 1:6), whenever (1Sm 1:4), one day (Jb 1:6), or by day (Neh 4:22). Yom could characterize a particular event such as the day of Jezreel (Hs 1:11). Similarly, the Day/day of Yahweh, or the LORD, is a time or day that belongs to the Lord in a special way (Zph 1:14).

1:21 The reuse of the verb **created** (Hb bara'; cp. v. 1) emphasizes God's authority over **the large sea-creatures**. This point was especially significant to the ancient Israelites, whose neighbors worshiped Rahab, a mythical sea monster.

1:22 The first of three blessings God pronounced in the creation narrative occurred when **God blessed** the water animals and birds. This blessing is similar to the one for persons, but lacks the commands to "subdue" and "rule" (v. 28).

1:26 God's use of plural pronouns (**Us ... Our ... Our**) to refer to Himself has raised many questions (3:22; 11:7; Is 6:8). At least five different suggestions have been put forward to explain them: they may be references to (1) the Trinity, (2) God and His angels, (3) God and creation, (4) God's majesty as expressed by a literary device known as the "plural of majesty," or (5) a polytheistic view of God. Since the Bible teaches elsewhere that there is only one God (Dt 6:4; Mk 12:29; 1Co 8:4), the fifth option is not tenable.

The two Hebrew words translated as **image** and **likeness** are often understood as having the same meaning. But some interpreters suggest that "image" refers to the ability to reason, with "likeness" referring to the spiritual dimension. What exactly is the "image" of God? Since the Bible teaches that God is Spirit (Jn 4:24), many commentators believe it refers to the non-material aspects of a person—our moral sensibilities, intellectual abilities, will, and emotions. Based on God's commands in Gn 1:28, others have suggested that it consists of the role humans are to play on earth—their rulership over the planet and its resources, and secondarily the physical, mental, and spiritual abilities that enable them to fulfill that role. The NT teaches that Christians will someday bear the image of Christ (1Co 15:49; 1Jn 3:2).

1:27 The creation of humanity is the crowning event of chapter 1, as shown by the fact that **created** is repeated three times. The verb "created" (Hb bara') is the same one used in 1:1, referring to a kind of creative activity that only God

rule the fish of the sea, the birds of the sky, the livestock, all the earth, [A] and the creatures that crawl [B] on the earth." [a]

27 So God created man in His own image;
He created him in the image of God;
He created them male and female. [b]

28 God blessed them, and God said to them, "Be fruitful, multiply, fill the earth, [c] and subdue it. Rule the fish of the sea, the birds of the sky, and every creature that crawls [c] on the earth." 29 God also said, "Look, I have given you every seed-bearing plant on the surface of the entire earth and every tree whose fruit contains seed. This food will be for you, [d] 30 for all the wildlife of the earth, for every bird of the sky, and for every creature that crawls on the earth—everything having the breath of life in it. I have given every green plant for food." [e] And it was so. 31 God saw all that He had made, and it was very good. [f] Evening came and then morning: the sixth day.

*1:26 Gn 9:2; Ps 8:6-8; Jms 3:7 *1:27 Gn 5:2; Mt 19:4; Mk 10:6 *1:28 Gn 9:1,7 *1:29 Gn 9:3; Ps 104:14-15; 136:25; 145:15-16 *1:30 Ps 147:9 *1:31 1Tm 4:4 *2:1 Neh 9:6; Ps 33:6; Is 34:4; 45:12 *2:2 Ex 20:8-11; 31:17; Dt 5:12-14; Heb 4:4 *2:3 Ex 31:17 *Ex 20:11; 31:17; Ps 121:2 *2:4 Gn 5:1; 6:9; 10:1; 11:10,27; 25:12,19; 36:1,9; 37:2 *2:5 Gn 1:11-12 *2:7 Gn 3:19,23; 18:27; Ps 103:14; Ec 12:7; 1Co 15:47 *Gn 7:22; Jb 33:4; Is 2:22 *1Co 15:45

2 So the heavens and the earth and everything in them [D] were completed. [g] 2 By the seventh [E] day God completed His work that He had done, and He rested [F] on the seventh day from all His work that He had done. [h] 3 God blessed the seventh day and declared it holy, for on it He rested [i] from His work of creation. [G,i]

Man and Woman in the Garden

4 These are the records [k] of the heavens and the earth, concerning their creation at the time [H] that the Lord God made the earth and the heavens. 5 No shrub of the field [l] had yet grown on the land, [I] and no plant of the field had yet sprouted, for the Lord God had not made it rain on the land, and there was no man to work the ground. 6 But water would come out of the ground and water the entire surface of the land. 7 Then the Lord God formed the man out of the dust from the ground [m] and breathed the breath of life into his nostrils, [n] and the man became a living being. [o]

[A]1:26 Syr reads *sky, and over every animal of the land* [B]1:26 Lit *scurry* [C]1:28 Lit *and all scurrying animals that scurry* [D]2:1 Lit *and all their host* [E]2:2 Sam, LXX, Syr read *sixth* [F]2:2 Or *ceased* [G]2:3 Lit *work that God created to make* [H]2:4 Lit *creation on the day* [I]2:5 Or *earth*

can do. The term "man" (Hb *'adam*) is used elsewhere in the Hebrew Bible to refer to humanity in general, not just males (7:21); all people, both male and female, are created **in the image of God** (cp. Jms 3:9). People are the only beings that are created in the image of God (Gn 9:3-6). The Bible never lumps people into the category of animals. Instead, it separates the creation of people from all other beings and attributes the most privileged roles in creation to humans alone.

1:28 In this the longest of the five blessings found in the account of creation, **God** gave humanity five different commands. Implicit in the first three commands is God's blessing on the institutions of marriage and the family. The final two commands, to **subdue** the earth and **rule** the animal kingdom, express God's blessing on the use of the planet's renewable and nonrenewable natural resources. Of course, only the wise use of these resources permits people to fulfill God's command to fill the earth. A similar command to the survivors of the flood is shorter, having only the first three verbs in it (9:1).

1:29 After the flood in Noah's day, God issued additional dietary guidelines that expanded humanity's permitted food sources beyond plants and trees to include meats (9:3).

1:30 The Bible does not address the issue of diet for carnivorous and insect-eating animals.

1:31 This is the seventh, final, and most elaborate use of the word **good** in the account of the seven days of creation.

2:1 This verse serves as a complement to 1:1. Together, the two set the first six days of creation apart from the sacred seventh day.

2:2 This is the first use of the number seven in the Bible, a number that will play an especially significant role in the religious and social life of ancient Israel (4:15; 7:2-4,10; 21:28-31; 29:18-20). On the seventh day God **rested**, thus setting an example for people—who are made in His im-

age—to follow (Ex 20:8-11; Dt 5:12-14). Though God rested **from all His work that He had done**, this is not to say that God has abandoned the universe. In the NT Jesus affirmed that God is still at work in the world, even on the Sabbath (Jn 5:16-17).

2:3 This is the only instance during the creation process when God **blessed** a unit of time. The term **holy** is applied in the Bible to something set aside for service to God.

2:4 The Hebrew word *toledoth*, translated here as **records**, is used 11 times in the book of Genesis to introduce new units of material (5:1; 6:9; 10:1; 11:10,27; 25:12,19; 36:1,9; 37:2). Here it introduces a detailed elaboration of some key aspects of the creation account that opens the book of Genesis (1:1–2:3). Special emphasis is placed on the events of day six. Verse 4 includes the first use of God's personal name, rendered in English as the Lord, the most commonly used noun in the OT. The Hebrew spelling is transliterated as "YHWH," a word Jews considered so sacred that they would not permit themselves to pronounce it. Its accurate pronunciation is thus unknown, though common suggestions include "Jehovah" and "Yahweh."

2:6 This source of water, a bountiful blessing that provided moisture for **the entire surface of the land** in the time of human innocence, later became a source of judgment on humanity's sin (7:11).

2:7 The Hebrew verb translated here as **formed** is used elsewhere in the Bible to describe the potter's profession (Jr 18:4; Zch 11:13); God acts here as the divine potter, skillfully fashioning **man out of the dust from the ground**. But the Bible makes it very clear that people are more than just material beings. It was only when God **breathed** into the man's **nostrils** the **breath of life** that Adam became alive. God is Spirit (Jn 4:24); thus, when God breathed into him, Adam and all later human beings became a unique mix of the physical and the spiritual. The Hebrew phrase translated as

The Uniqueness of the Genesis Creation Story

Kenneth Mathews

While there are many similarities between parts of Genesis and ancient Near Eastern (ANE) myths, there are also fundamental differences. These are seen especially in the significantly different views of the Creator and creation. Five features in particular distinguish the biblical creation account and perspective. So distinctive theologically is the biblical teaching from that of Israel's neighbors that it is best explained as the result of divine revelation, not the imagination or "religious genius" of the biblical author.

The Identity of God

The basic identity of God as revealed in Genesis is distinct from all other ANE conceptions. The Lord God did not have an origin and did not have a female counterpart. In fact, Genesis does not present any kind of theogony (origin of the gods). God simply always existed. The concept of fertility was a common explanation among the ancients for how the world was created. It was believed that gods and goddesses joined in sexual union and thus produced the world, just as man and woman can come together to create a child. Israel's God, however, was revealed to be asexual, neither male nor female. According to other ANE religions the world (or parts of it, like the sun) was a divine "Thou," whereas in Genesis the world was revealed to be an "it," a non-supernatural reality brought into existence by a supernatural God.

No Rival Gods

While polytheistic views dominated the ANE, Genesis revealed that God has no divine rivals. A common explanation for creation among the ancients was that an epic battle had raged between creator gods and anti-creation deities. Ultimately, the creator god overcame the anti-creation forces/gods, in some cases using the slain bodies of their enemies to make the stuff of the world. In Genesis there is no rival opposing the Creator. All creation obeyed the voice of God, as expressed in the recurring phrase, "and it was so" (1:7).

Creation out of Nothing

In Genesis the Creator by inherent authority as Sovereign Lord spoke creation into a functional, well-ordered existence. There was no eternal pre-created matter, such as was believed in the ancient myths. Genesis says God spoke all things into origination. This does not mean He uttered words that possessed inherent magical powers. Rather, the irrevocable power of God's creation words was grounded in the authority of God Himself. Unlike the nature deities whose existence was limited to the world system, God existed before creation and above creation. Also, creation was not the emanation of divine person or power. It was separate from Him, a new reality subject to His will.

The Value of Humanity

In Genesis the Creator bestowed special value on humanity. Human beings in the ANE view were not indispensable to the operation of the world, whereas in Genesis they were essential as its chief caretakers. The Lord blessed humanity, assigning man and woman the responsibility to propagate and to rule over the earth (1:26-28). ANE myths explained the purpose of humanity as servants who met the servile interests of the gods. The Bible elevates the person and role of humans who were "crowned . . . with glory and honor" (Ps 8:5), made in the divine image. God prepared the resplendent Garden of Eden for humanity, giving humanity meaningful work and purpose (Gn 2:8-18). Also, Genesis presents the first humanity as individuals who were the progenitors of the human race.

The Sabbath

In Genesis the Creator provided the seventh day as a holy day of rest and celebration (2:1-3), which was later memorialized in Israel's Sabbath (Ex 20:8-11). The Sabbath was unique to Israel, not tied to the movement of the stars, such as in the ancient preoccupation with astrology. The Lord was revealed as Master of the material universe *and* of time. All creation was invited to join in the knowledge of God and in the worship of Him as Creator and Sustainer of all things.

⁸The Lord God planted a garden in Eden, in the east,ᵃ and there He placed the man He had formed. ⁹The Lord God caused to grow out of the ground every tree pleasing in appearance and good for food, including the tree of life in the middle of the garden,ᵇ as well as the tree of the knowledge of good and evil.ᶜ

¹⁰A river wentᴬ out from Eden to water the garden. From there it divided and became the source of four rivers.ᴮ ¹¹The name of the first is Pishon, which flows through the entire land of Havilah,ᶜ,ᵈ where there is gold. ¹²Gold from that land is pure;ᴰ bdelliumᴱ and onyxᶠ are also there. ¹³The name of the second river is Gihon, which flows through the entire land of ˙Cush. ¹⁴The name of the third river is the Tigrisᵉ which runs east of Assyria. And the fourth river is the Euphrates.ᶠ

¹⁵The Lord God took the man and placed him in the garden of Eden to work it and watch over it. ¹⁶And the Lord God commanded the man, "You are free to eat from any tree of the garden,ᵍ ¹⁷but you must not eatᴳ from the tree of the knowledge of good and evil, for on the day you eat from it, you will certainly die."ʰ ¹⁸Then the Lord God said, "It is not good for the man to be alone. I will make a helper as his complement."ⁱ ¹⁹So the Lord God formed out of the ground every wild animal and every bird of the sky, and brought each to the man to see what he would call it.ʲ And whatever the man called a living creature, that was its name. ²⁰The man gave names to all the livestock, to the birds of the sky, and to every wild animal; but for the manᴴ no helper was found as his complement. ²¹So the Lord God caused a deep sleep to come over the man,ᵏ and he slept. God took one of his ribs and closed the

---

ᵃ2:8 Gn 13:10; Is 51:3; Ezk 28:13; 31:8; Jl 2:3 ᵇ2:9 Gn 3:22; Rv 2:7; 22:2,14 ᶜPr 3:18 ᵈ2:11 Gn 10:7,29; 25:18; 1Sm 15:7 ᵉ2:14 Dn 10:4 ᶠGn 15:18 ᵍ2:16 Gn 3:1-2 ʰ2:17 Gn 3:5; Dt 30:15,19-20; Rm 6:23; 1Tm 5:6; Jms 1:15 ⁱ2:18 Pr 31:11-12; 1Co 11:9; 1Tm 2:13 ʲ2:19 Ps 8:6 ᵏ2:21 Gn 15:12

ᴬ2:10 Or goes   ᴮ2:10 Lit became four heads   ᶜ2:11 Or of the Havilah   ᴰ2:12 Lit good   ᴱ2:12 A yellowish, transparent gum resin   ᶠ2:12 Identity of this precious stone uncertain   ᴳ2:17 Lit eat from it   ᴴ2:20 Or for Adam

---

living being is used elsewhere in Genesis to describe other types of living beings (1:20,24,30; 9:12,15-16). Nevertheless, humans are considered to be in a class by themselves since they alone are made in God's image.

2:8 The location of **Eden** is unknown; suggestions include Armenia, Iraq, Africa, and Arabia. Changes in geography caused by the flood in Noah's day (7:11) make it unlikely that Eden will ever be discovered. The Hebrew word "Eden" literally means "pleasantness."

2:9 God's concern for beauty is seen in the fact that the trees He caused to grow were **pleasing in appearance**. The Lord's love of beauty will later be extended to Israel's religion, which will make use of furnishings fashioned by expert craftsmen using expensive materials (Ex 25–40). Of course, God's beautiful created works were also practical, being **good for food**.

2:10 The abundance of the waters supplied in the garden of Eden is indicated by the fact that it served as the headwaters for **four rivers**.

2:11 The location of the **Pishon** river is unknown. A land known as **Havilah** existed in the region of the Arabian peninsula at a later point in time (1Sm 15:7), but the preflood land may have represented a different locale.

2:13 The locations of the **Gihon** river and **Cush** are unknown. A later Cush was located in the region of modern Ethiopia and Sudan (Est 1:1).

2:14 The **Tigris** and **Euphrates** rivers, as well as **Assyria**, probably correspond to geographical features associated with modern Iraq.

2:15 The Hebrew word translated as **placed** literally means, "caused to rest"; this pre-sin state of rest anticipates the "rest" ("relief"; 5:29) that would again come to humanity because of righteous Noah, as well as the rest that God would again give Israel following its episode of calf worship (Ex 32:1-21; 33:14). As a being created in God's image, Adam, like God, was to be a worker. Without the taint of sin, **work** was an undiluted blessing. The verb translated here as "work" literally means "serve." Adam's second task in the garden was to **watch over it**. The verb is used

elsewhere to refer to the action of God toward His people (Ps 121:3-4) or the work of a military guard (Sg 5:7).

2:16 The seriousness of God's order is reflected in the fact that it is introduced by a two-verb phrase in Hebrew, rendered simply as **commanded** in the HCSB. This formula was used frequently to express royal decrees (1Sm 18:22; 2Sm 18:5). God gave Adam both freedom and limits. The God-given freedoms vastly outnumbered the limitations. After all, Adam was **free to eat from any tree of the garden** except one.

2:17 The only limit God placed on Adam was eating **from the tree of the knowledge of good and evil**, which apparently imparted divine wisdom (3:22). Eating the forbidden fruit represented Adam's rejection of God as the source of divine wisdom and his choice to pursue wisdom apart from God. God's penalty for disobedience was stated especially forcefully in the original language, with a two-verb construction, "dying you shall die" (**you will certainly die**). Death would certainly come to Adam and all humanity after him; but the death that God warned about would be more than physical (3:19). Besides severing the cord of life, sin would shatter the harmonious relationship that existed between Adam and his environment (3:17-18), his wife (3:16), and God.

2:18 The theme of God providing for Adam's needs (see note at v. 8) is picked up again here, as God declared that Adam's being alone is **not good**. God created the man with a need to relate to one **as his complement**, and now God will meet that need.

2:19 Like man, animals were **formed out of the ground**, but they did not receive the breath of life from God (v. 7) nor the image of God. By giving names to the animals, Adam showed that he ruled the animals and that he perceived the nature of each animal (see note at 1:5).

2:20 Adam's understanding of the nature of the animals he named only highlighted the differences that existed between him and the rest of God's creatures: **no helper was found as his complement**.

2:21 At what must have been a moment of loneliness in Adam's life, God stepped in to create one who would perfectly meet Adam's need. Because **God took one of his ribs** to use as His raw material, the woman would correspond

flesh at that place. [22]Then the Lord God made the rib He had taken from the man into a woman and brought her to the man. [a] [23]And the man said:

This one, at last, is bone of my bone
and flesh of my flesh;
this one will be called "woman,"
for she was taken from man. [b]

[24]This is why a man leaves his father and mother and bonds with his wife, and they become one flesh. [c] [25]Both the man and his wife were naked, yet felt no shame.

The Temptation and the Fall

3 Now the serpent was the most cunning of all the wild animals that the Lord God had made. He said to the woman, "Did God really say,

'You can't eat from any tree in the garden'?" [d] [2]The woman said to the serpent, "We may eat the fruit from the trees in the garden. [3]But about the fruit of the tree in the middle of the garden, God said, 'You must not eat it or touch it, or you will die.'" [e] [4]"No! You will not die," the serpent said to the woman. [f] [5]"In fact, God knows that when[A] you eat it your eyes will be opened and you will be like God,[B] knowing good and evil." [6]Then the woman saw that the tree was good for food and delightful to look at, and that it was desirable for obtaining wisdom. So she took some of its fruit and ate it; she also gave some to her husband, who was with her, and he ate it. [g] [7]Then the eyes of both of them were opened, and they knew they were naked; so they sewed fig leaves together and made loincloths for themselves.

Cross references (center column):
[a]2:22 1Co 11:8,12
[b]2:23 Eph 5:28-30
[c]2:24 Mal 2:15; Mt 19:5; Mk 10:7-8; 1Co 6:16; Eph 5:31
[d]3:1 Mt 10:16; 2Co 11:3; Rv 12:9; 20:2
[e]3:3 Gn 2:17
[f]3:4 Jn 8:44
[g]3:6 1Tm 2:14; Jms 1:14-15; 1Jn 2:16

[A]3:5 Lit on the day   [B]3:5 Or gods, or divine beings

---

perfectly—though not identically—to Adam. Like Adam, the woman possessed God's image. The fact that she was not taken either from the man's head or his foot may suggest that the woman was not to rule over the man (1Co 11:3), nor the man to oppress the woman (1Pt 3:7).

2:23 Adam's first recorded words express his delight with God's handiwork and his recognition of the unique suitability of God's last recorded creation in the creation accounts. As with no other piece of divine craftsmanship, this one was singularly suited for the man, being **bone of** his **bone** and **flesh of** his **flesh**. Adam expresses dominion by choosing a name for God's final created being, but the name he chose suggests that he viewed her as his equal. The Hebrew term 'ishshah, **woman**, identifies her as the feminine complement to 'ish, the man.

2:24 God's timeless design for marriage is declared here. The **one flesh** relationship certainly involves sexual union, but also includes a husband and wife coming together in spiritual, mental, and emotional harmony.

2:25 Because the devastating effects of sin had not yet rav-

'ishshah

Hebrew Pronunciation	[eesh SHAH]
HCSB Translation	woman
Uses in Genesis	152
Uses in the OT	781
Focus passage	Genesis 2:22-25

'Ishshah may not be related to a Hebrew word for man in Gn 2:22-25 that looks and sounds like it ('iysh). 'Ishshah resembles a word for woman in several Semitic languages, and may derive from a verb meaning "be weak" that could also lie behind 'enosh, "man" (2 Sm 12:15). The phrase born of woman (Jb 14:1) points to mankind's weaknesses. 'Ishshah has two basic meanings, woman and wife. Both ideas are present in the word's first occurrences (Gn 2:22-25). 'Ishshah connotes fiancée or bride (Dt 22:24; 24:5). It signifies woman without implying marriage (Ec 7:28). "The way of women" is a euphemism for menstruation (Gn 31:35). Sometimes 'ishshah describes a kind of woman, like a prophetess (Jdg 4:4). Fearful soldiers are compared to women (Nah 3:13). 'Ishshah functions as a feminine distributive meaning each, referring to women (Ru 1:8), animals, or even things. "Each to each" appears as together (Ex 26:5).

aged nature or humanity, there was no need for clothing. Adam and Eve could live without the barriers needed to shield them from their environment and each other without a sense of shame. Later, in the time of the patriarchs and kings, clothing was associated with dignity. Accordingly, prisoners of war were not permitted to wear any clothing, slaves wore very little clothing, and higher social classes wore more clothing than anyone else in society.

3:3 The woman's claim that God said, **You must not . . . touch** the tree, **or you will die**, goes beyond anything recorded in God's instructions to Adam. Therefore it seems that Adam had given his wife an additional command beyond what God said, or else Eve herself exaggerated the command as Satan tempted her to view God as selfish and overly restrictive. If Adam added to God's command, he almost certainly had a good motive—after all, if Eve never touched the tree, she certainly wouldn't eat its fruit. However, the sad truth is that when people add to the word of God, they create confusion and trouble.

3:4-5 The serpent, recognizing the woman's confusion, found a point of attack. Knowing that the woman would **not die** by merely touching the fruit, he boldly contradicted what she had reported to be God's command. He then skillfully lied (Jn 8:44) by distorting God's word (Mt 4:6), implying that God had prohibited people from eating the fruit only to keep them from becoming as knowledgeable as He. The woman was now fully deceived (1Tm 2:14).

3:6 Since the woman did not die when she touched the fruit—in contradiction to what she had thought God said (v. 3.)—she **ate it**. Though Adam was **with her** at the time, he did nothing to stop her. Perhaps he wanted to eat of it as much as the woman did, but fearing the consequences, used his wife as a "guinea pig" to make sure it would not cause instant death.

3:7 As the serpent had indicated, **the eyes of both of them were opened, and they knew**, but instead of producing godlike power, the knowledge brought only a sense of human inadequacy, fear, and shame.

3:9 God took the initiative in reaching out to sinful humanity. This pattern—humanity sinning, then God seeking out sinners—becomes the primary theme of the rest of the Bible. Its ultimate expression is found in Jesus Christ, who came to seek and to save people alienated from God because

Sin's Consequences

⁸Then the man and his wife heard the sound of the Lᴏʀᴅ God walking in the garden at the time of the evening breeze,ᴬ and they hid themselves from the Lᴏʀᴅ God among the trees of the garden.ᵃ ⁹So the Lᴏʀᴅ God called out to the man and said to him, "Where are you?"

¹⁰And he said, "I heard Youᴮ in the garden and I was afraid because I was naked, so I hid."

¹¹Then He asked, "Who told you that you were naked? Did you eat from the tree that I commanded you not to eat from?"

¹²Then the man replied,ᵇ "The woman You gave to be with me—she gave me some fruit from the tree, and I ate."

¹³So the Lᴏʀᴅ God asked the woman, "What is this you have done?"

And the woman said, "It was the serpent. He deceived me, and I ate."ᶜ

¹⁴Then the Lᴏʀᴅ God said to the serpent:

ᵃ3:8 Jb 34:22-23
ᵇ3:12 Jb 31:33; Pr 28:13
ᶜ3:13 Rm 7:11; 2Co 11:3; 1Tm 2:14
ᵈ3:14 Is 65:25; Mc 7:17
ᵉ3:15 Heb 2:14; 1Jn 3:8
ᶠ3:16 Jn 16:21; 1Tm 2:15
ᵍGn 4:7

Because you have done this,
you are cursed more than
    any livestock
and more than any wild animal.
You will move on your belly
and eat dust all the days
    of your life. ᵈ
¹⁵ I will put hostility between you
    and the woman,
and between your •seed and her seed.
He will strike your head,
and you will strike his heel. ᵉ

¹⁶He said to the woman:

I will intensify your labor pains;
you will bear children in anguish. ᶠ
Your desireᵍ will be for your husband,
yet he will rule over you.

¹⁷And He said to Adam, "Because you lis-tened to your wife's voice and ate from the

---

ᴬ3:8 Lit at the wind of the day   ᴮ3:10 Lit the sound of You

---

of their sin (Lk 19:10); in Him God once again walked on the earth in search of sinners. The all-knowing God asked Adam, **Where are you?** for Adam's benefit, to encourage Adam to face his sin.

3:10 When Adam **heard** God, he **was afraid**. Rather than walking with God as righteous men of later generations would do (Enoch, 5:22; Noah, 6:9), Adam **hid** from Him.

3:11 Through the use of two direct questions God brought Adam to accountability for his sin. God does not overlook sin, but He can be gently firm in confronting it.

3:12 Adam answered neither of God's questions. Instead he sought to shift the blame for his sin first to **the woman**, and then to God.

3:13 The woman passed the blame to **the serpent** and ad-mitted that prior to eating, she was **deceived** (1Tm 2:14).

3:14 Though accountability began with God's confrontation

nachash

Hebrew Pronunciation	[nah KHASH]
HCSB Translation	serpent, snake
Uses in Genesis	6
Uses in the OT	31
Focus passage	Genesis 3:1-2,4,13-14

Although *nachash* is the most prevalent of eight OT terms for *snake* (Nm 21:6), the usage is broader than that. The *nachash* in Gn 3:1,14 was the shrewdest animal and did not crawl on its belly before the curse. The *nachash* Leviathan was a *sea monster* (Is 27:1), and there were other *sea serpents* (Am 9:3). Associated with *nachash* are slithering motion (Pr 30:19), flying (Is 14:29), sudden attack (Gn 49:17), poisonous venom (Ps 58:4), sharp bite (Ps 140:3), hissing (Jr 46:22), eggs (Is 14:29), and licking of dust (Gn 3:14; Mc 7:17). Five times *nachash* occurs with words meaning "viper." The Middle East has large desert areas that are habitats for *serpents*. The *serpent* of Genesis 3, an enemy of man linked with evil, is particularly identified with Satan in Rv 12:9, where he is also called a *"dragon,"* based on the Greek *drakon*, which can mean *"serpent."*

of Adam, judgment began with the **serpent**. Because of the serpent's key role (being used of Satan) in bringing sin into the human experience, it would be permanently consigned to the position of ultimate shame, under the foot. Just as conquered kings were made to lie on the ground under the foot of their conquerors (Jos 10:24), so now the serpent would live under the feet of humanity.

3:15 **Hostility** between the first woman and the serpent would be passed on to future generations. This verse is known in Christendom as the *protoevangelium*, or "first good news," because it is the first foretelling of the gospel of Jesus Christ. Using an emphatic Hebrew construction, God announced here that a male descendant—**He**—would someday deal the serpent (meaning Satan) a fatal blow. The NT writers under-stood Jesus Christ to have fulfilled this prophecy (Heb 2:14; 1Jn 3:8). In an extended sense, the NT also indicates that God would work through the church—those indwelt by the Spirit of Christ—to destroy the works of the devil (Rm 16:20). The assertion that the snake would only strike his opponent's **heel** (as opposed to **head**) suggests that the devil will be de-feated in the ensuing struggle (Rv 2:2,7-10).

3:16 Even though the woman had been deceived into eating the forbidden fruit, she was still held accountable for her act. Notably, however, the word "cursed" is not contained in God's words to her (vv. 14,16). Two penalties were im-posed; both struck at the heart of a woman's roles in life. More than would have been the case had sin not entered creation, bearing children would add to the sum of **anguish** in the universe (God said he would **intensify**, not originate, woman's **labor pains**). Marriage would also be marred; though the woman's **desire** would be for her **husband**, sin would mar God's plan for marriage and create tormenting inequality and subjugation. The latter is a description of the ravaging effect of sin on a husband-wife relationship, not a prescription for abusing one's wife. The NT teaches that marriage should reflect the relationship of Christ with the church (Eph 5:24-25) and be characterized by a husband's understanding of and respect for his wife (1Pt 3:7).

3:17 Because Adam **listened to** and obeyed his **wife's voice** in preference to what God **commanded** (2:17), a curse would

tree about which I commanded you, 'Do not eat from it':

The ground is cursed because of you. [a]
You will eat from it by means of
    painful labor [A]
all the days of your life.

18 It will produce thorns and thistles
    for you,
and you will eat the plants
    of the field. [b]

19 You will eat bread [B] by the sweat
    of your brow
until you return to the ground, [c]
since you were taken from it.
For you are dust,
and you will return to dust."

20 Adam named his wife Eve [c] because she was the mother of all the living. 21 The LORD God made clothing out of skins for Adam and his wife, and He clothed them.

22 The LORD God said, "Since man has become like one of Us, knowing good and evil, he must not reach out, take from the tree of life, eat, and live forever." [d] 23 So the LORD God sent him away from the garden of Eden to work the ground from which he was taken. 24 He drove man out and stationed the *cherubim and the flaming, whirling sword east of the garden of Eden to guard the way to the tree of life. [e]

Cain Murders Abel

4 Adam was intimate with his wife Eve, and she conceived and gave birth to Cain. She said, "I have had a male child with the LORD's help." [D] 2 Then she also gave birth to his brother Abel. Now Abel became a shepherd of flocks, but Cain worked the ground. 3 In the course of time Cain presented some of the land's produce as an offering to the LORD. [f] 4 And Abel also presented an offering—some of the firstborn of his flock and their fat portions. [g] The LORD had regard for Abel and his offering, [h] 5 but He did not have regard for Cain and his offering. Cain was furious, and he looked despondent. [E]

a 3:17 Gn 5:29; Rm 8:20-22; Heb 6:8
b 3:18 Gn 2:5
c 3:19 Ps 90:3; 104:29; Ec 12:7
d 3:22 Gn 2:9; Rv 2:7
e 3:24 Ex 25:18-22; Ps 104:4; Ezk 10:1-20; Heb 1:7
f 4:3 Ex 23:19; 34:26; Neh 10:35
g 4:4 Ex 13:12; Nm 18:17; Pr 3:9
h Heb 11:4

A 3:17 Lit it through pain   B 3:19 Or food   C 3:20 Lit Living, or Life   D 4:1 Lit the LORD   E 4:5 Lit and his face fell

strike at the heart of a fundamental relationship in his life as well. Adam's relationship with the ground would now be forever damaged by sin. **All the days** of his **life** he would experience **painful labor** (cp. the woman's labor pains, v. 16) as he worked to bring forth the fruit of the earth.

3:18 Prior to the first couple's sins God is only recorded as having put trees in the garden (2:8-9); now there would also be **thorns and thistles**. Prior to sin, humanity had only to reach up to get food; now they would have to bend their backs to gather **plants of the field**.

3:19 The simple plucking of fruit in order to **eat** food (lit "**bread**") would now be replaced by backbreaking labor and **the sweat** of the **brow**. Working daily in the soil, Adam would be continually reminded that he was **dust** and that he would **return to dust**.

3:20 The new name Adam gave his wife emphasizes the woman's life-giving role that counteracts the curse of sin, which is death. Yet the divine order calls for a reciprocity exhibited in male servant leadership and female submission, both of which are modeled in Jesus Himself.

3:21 By making **clothing out of skins**, the LORD **God** graciously provided for humanity's need in a way superior to what Adam and Eve had done with fig leaves. The use of animal skins anticipates the OT system of animal sacrifices (Lv 1; 3–7; Nm 15:1-31). In the NT, the apostle Paul spoke of a day when God would clothe His people with immortality (1Co 15:53-54; 2Co 5:4), thus providing the complete undoing of the curse of humanity's sin.

3:22 Because of sin, people now knew **good and evil** experientially. Since the gift of life was directly tied to obedience, man's sin meant that the penalty of death must be enforced.

3:23 As the Hebrew text ironically expresses it, **the LORD God sent** Adam **from the garden** so that he would not send forth ("reach out"; v. 22) his hand for the garden's fruit.

3:24 Following their sin, the first couple went **east**, a direction associated with departure from God in numerous biblical examples. Other instances of eastward movement in Genesis include Cain's journeys after judgment (4:16), humanity's migration toward Babylon (11:2), and the migration of Keturah's sons (25:6). **Cherubim** are used as an artistic motif in the tabernacle (Ex 25:18-22; 26:1) and are also mentioned in Ezekiel 10 and 11. The ironies continue as the man who was once commanded to "watch over" the garden (Gn 2:15) is now guarded from the garden.

4:1 Adam and **Eve** now begin to fulfill God's original command to them, to "be fruitful" and "multiply" (1:28). Eve, whose name means "Life," now becomes the life-giver. Eve knew that the child was more than the result of her and her husband's love; it came into being **with the LORD's help**. A wordplay in the Hebrew suggests that the name **Cain** (qayin) came from the verb "had" (qaniti) in Eve's comment, **I have had a male child**.

4:2 The name **Abel** means "Breath"; the term is used elsewhere in the OT to refer to that which passes away quickly and is unsubstantial (Ps 62:10; Ec 1:2).

4:3 Cain's sacrifice marks the first mention of **an offering to the LORD** in the Bible. The Hebrew term used here suggests a freewill gift given to an authority.

4:5 Ironically, the first recorded offering given to God was also the first one rejected by Him. Since cereal offerings were authorized in the law of Moses, the fact that Cain's offering was of vegetation rather than an animal is not why God **did not have regard** for it. Cain's **furious** reaction suggests that the offering was rejected because of sin in his heart, not the nature of his offering. See note at verse 7.

4:7 The Bible makes it clear that God had rejected Cain's offering because of Cain's wicked lifestyle (1Jn 3:12). The animal-like description of sin as **crouching** is reused in 49:9 to describe a lion. The parallel use of **desire** in this verse and 3:16 suggests that sin wishes to be as intimate with humanity as a woman is with her husband. The only way to avoid this is to be its master, not its companion.

⁶Then the LORD said to Cain, "Why are you furious?ᵃ And why do you look despondent?ᴬ ⁷If you do what is right, won't you be accepted? But if you do not do what is right, sin is crouching at the door. Its desire is for you, but you must rule over it."ᵇ

⁸Cain said to his brother Abel, "Let's go out to the field."ᴮ And while they were in the field, Cain attacked his brother Abel and killed him.ᶜ

⁹Then the LORD said to Cain, "Where is your brother Abel?"

"I don't know," he replied. "Am I my brother's guardian?"

¹⁰Then He said, "What have you done? Your brother's blood cries out to Me from the ground!ᵈ ¹¹So now you are cursed, alienated, from the ground that opened its mouth to receive your brother's blood you have shed.ᶜ ¹²If you work the ground, it will never again give you its yield. You will be a restless wanderer on the earth."ᵉ

¹³But Cain answered the LORD, "My punishmentᴰ is too great to bear! ¹⁴Since You are banishing me today from the soil, and I must hide myself from Your presence and become a restless wanderer on the earth, whoever finds me will kill me."ᶠ

¹⁵Then the LORD replied to him, "In that case,ᴱ whoever kills Cain will suffer vengeance seven times over."ᶠ And He placed a markᵍ on Cain so that whoever found him would not kill him. ¹⁶Then Cain went out from the LORD's presence and lived in the land of Nod, east of Eden.

The Line of Cain

¹⁷Cain was intimate with his wife, and she conceived and gave birth to Enoch. Then Cain became the builder of a city, and he named the city Enoch after his son. ¹⁸Irad was born to Enoch, Irad fathered Mehujael, Mehujael fathered Methushael, and Methushael fathered Lamech. ¹⁹Lamech took two wives for himself, one named Adah and the other named Zillah.

ᵃ4:6 Jnh 4:4
ᵇ4:7 Gn 3:16
ᶜ4:8 Mt 23:35; Lk 11:51; 1Jn 3:12-15; Jd 11
ᵈ4:10 Nm 35:33; Dt 21:1-9; Heb 12:24; Rv 6:9-10
ᵉ4:12 Dt 28:16-18; Is 26:21
ᶠ4:14 Nm 35:26-27
ᵍ4:15 Ex 9:4; Ezk 9:4,6; Rv 13:16-17

ᴬ4:6 Lit why has your face fallen   ᴮ4:8 Sam, LXX, Syr, Vg; MT omits Let's go out to the field   ᶜ4:11 Lit blood from your hand   ᴰ4:13 Or sin   ᴱ4:15 LXX, Syr, Vg read Not so!   ᶠ4:15 Or suffer severely

---

4:8 In a move that demonstrates premeditation, Cain led Abel **to the field** and **attacked** him in a place where there were no human witnesses. Though the blood of animals had been shed prior to this (v. 4), Cain's killing of his brother brought about the first death of a human being. The curse of human death pronounced against Adam (2:17; 3:19) had now been realized.

4:9 God's use of questions with guilty sinners continues here (v. 6; cp. 3:9-13). By claiming he did not know where his brother was, Cain added lying to his sin of murder. God once made Adam a guardian (Hb shamar) of the garden (2:15). Cain now asked if he was to be his **brother's guardian** (Hb shamar). The Bible's answer to Cain's question is yes (Lv 19:18; Mt 22:39; Gl 5:14).

4:10 Unlike his father Adam (3:12), Cain never confessed his guilt, even though God directly confronted him with his sin. Though Abel never spoke in the preceding narrative, his **blood** now cried out **from the ground**.

4:11 God's judgment began with a curse whose wording in the Hebrew parallels the curse placed on the snake. This is particularly fitting since both were liars and murderers (Jn 8:44). It is possible to translate God's statement here as "You are more cursed than the ground." The curse against a murderer is repeated in the law of Moses (Dt 27:24).

4:12 Cain's punishment destroyed his livelihood as a farmer and turned him into a **restless wanderer**.

4:13 Cain's response has several possible English renderings. The HCSB—which reflects the unrepentant attitude Cain showed earlier—expresses Cain's anguish, but no remorse. The Septuagint and Martin Luther translated it as, "My sin is too great to be forgiven," while early rabbis took it as a question: "Is my sin too great to forgive?" In view of Cain's previous and later actions, the HCSB's translation (**my punishment is too great to bear!**) seems best.

4:14 Just as his father Adam had been driven out (Hb garash) of the garden, Cain noted that God was **banishing** (Hb garash) him **from the soil**. Since he would **hide** himself (or

possibly, "be hidden") from God's protective **presence**, he feared that other descendants of Adam and Eve (5:4) would **kill** him to avenge Abel's murder.

4:15 True to His compassionate and forgiving nature (Ex 34:6-7), God made two provisions for Cain in order to protect him despite his sin.

4:16 Cain's departure **from the LORD's presence** was both physical and spiritual (Jnh 1:3,10). "Nod" means "Wandering." **The land of Nod** is never again mentioned in the Bible. Perhaps the phrase simply referred to any location in which Cain resided. The notation that Cain departed to live **east of Eden** identifies him with other sinners who also moved east (see note at 3:24).

4:17 The parallel tracks of Adam's and Cain's lives—sin, judgment by God, banishment, and eastward movement—continue with the notation that after these things **Cain was intimate with his wife** (cp. v. 1). In spite of his grave sin, Cain still fulfilled the divine command to be fruitful and multiply (1:28). On the other hand, Cain's efforts to become **the builder of a city** were one more expression of disobedience to God, for God had ordained Cain to be a wanderer (v. 12). The city of **Enoch** is not mentioned elsewhere in the Bible, and its location is unknown.

Cain's genealogy in verses 17-24 has similarities with Seth's genealogy (5:3-32). Two of the names in both lines are identical (Enoch, Lamech) and others are similar (Cain/Kenan; Methushael/Methuselah). In addition, the seventh member of both genealogies (Cain's Lamech, Seth's Enoch) are given special emphasis, and both conclude with a person who has three named sons. Notable differences exist as well: Seth's genealogy is longer and contains lifespan details, but it omits any mention of occupations or wives' names.

4:18 Three individuals here—**Irad . . . Mehujael**, and **Methushael**—are mentioned in the Bible only in this verse.

4:19 More details are provided in this genealogical section for **Lamech**, the seventh member of Adam's line through

20 Adah bore Jabal; he was the father of the no-madic herdsmen. A 21 His brother was named Jubal; he was the father of all who play the lyre and the flute. 22 Zillah bore Tubal-cain, who made all kinds of bronze and iron tools. Tubal-cain's sister was Naamah.

23 Lamech said to his wives:

Adah and Zillah, hear my voice;
wives of Lamech, pay attention
  to my words.
For I killed a man for wounding me,
a young man for striking me.
24   If Cain is to be avenged
    seven times over,
    then for Lamech it will be
    seventy-seven times!

25 Adam was intimate with his wife again,

and she gave birth to a son and named him Seth, for she said, "God has given B me an-other child in place of Abel, since Cain killed him." 26 A son was born to Seth a also, and he named him Enosh. At that time people began to call on the name of •Yahweh. b

The Line of Seth

5 These are the family c records c of the de-scendants of Adam. On the day that God created man, D He made him in the likeness of God; 2 He created them male and female. When they were created, He blessed them and called them man. D

3 Adam was 130 years old when he fathered a son in his likeness, according to his image, and named him Seth. 4 Adam lived 800 years after the birth of Seth, and he fathered other

a 4:26 Lk 3:38
b Gn 12:8; 26:25;
1Kg 18:24; Ps
116:17; Jl 2:32;
Zph 3:9; 1Co 1:2
c 5:1 Gn 2:4

A 4:20 Lit *the dweller of tent and livestock*   B 4:25 The Hb word for given sounds like the name "Seth."   C 5:1 Lit *written family*   D 5:1,2 Or *Adam*

Cain, than for any other. His three named sons made crucial contributions to human culture. However, the de-scription of Lamech's life paints a troubling picture of an individual who lacked respect for marriage or human life. By taking **two wives for himself** Lamech became the first polygamist, a violation of God's intentions for marriage (2:22; Mk 10:6-8).

4:20 Jabal brought about key advances in the profession of **the nomadic herdsmen**—those who cared for sheep, goats, and cattle (Hb *miqneh*). This represents an advance beyond what Abel had done since he is only known to have tended sheep and goats (v. 2; Hb *tso'n*).

4:21 Jubal advanced civilization in the area of the musical arts, playing a key role in developing two of the most im-portant musical instruments of the ancient world, **the lyre and the flute**.

4:22 Tubal-cain's metallurgical advances in creating **bronze** (made by combining copper and tin) and smelting **iron** would prove crucial for crafting **tools** and weapons.

4:23 Lamech's so-called "Song of the Sword," the longest recorded speech by a human being to this point in the Bible (21 Hebrew words), represents the dark climax of the Cain-ite genealogy. His level of retaliation against **a man** and **a young man** goes far beyond the biblical limits (Ex 21:23-25), and his boast of killing for vengeance foreshadows the con-ditions that led to the flood in Noah's day (Gn 6:11).

4:24 Using twisted logic, Lamech seemed to suggest that God would provide him with greater protection than He did **Cain** since he had killed double the number of men.

4:25 The name **Seth** (Hb *sheth*) is a wordplay on the verb translated **has given** (Hb *shath*). Once again (v. 1), Eve rec-ognized God as the ultimate source of her offspring. The expectation that Seth would be more righteous than Cain is established by Eve's statement that **God** gave him to her **in place of** Abel. In fact, the family line that ultimately pro-duced Jesus is traceable through Seth (Lk 3:38).

4:26 The name **Enosh**, like the name Adam, means "hu-manity." In a very real sense Enosh's birth marks a new and brighter beginning for humanity, as **people** now **began**

to call on the name of Yahweh. Yahweh is God's personal name (Ex 3:15).

5:1 This is the second of eleven *toledoth* sections in Genesis (2:4; 6:9; 10:1; 11:10,27; 25:12,19; 36:1,9; 37:2). The Hebrew term *toledoth* ("family records") refers to "those who were given birth." Each section contains genealogical informa-tion and/or accounts regarding the descendants of the people or things named in the section title.

Only the Sethite genealogy is called **the family records of the descendants of Adam**, even though Cain's descendants are equally related. The reason for this is undoubtedly the contrasting descendants within the brothers' genealogies; only offspring in Seth's line are noted as being righteous. In this genealogy, emphasis is given to the fact that Adam was created in God's **likeness**, a characteristic that would be passed along to future generations (v. 3).

5:2 Key themes of chapter 1 are repeated and extended in the Sethite genealogy: (1) God created both **male and fe-male**, thus making it possible for humanity to fulfill the di-vine mandate to create offspring; (2) people, though made in God's image, are not God; **they were created**; (3) human-ity has been specially **blessed** by God; and (4) humanity is under God's authority, as demonstrated by the fact that God assigned them the name **man**.

5:3 Adam's role in Seth's life both compares and contrasts with God's role with Adam. Whereas God "created" Adam, Adam **fathered** Seth. Whereas Adam was made in God's image, Seth was made in Adam's **image**. Like God, Adam **named** the one he was responsible for bringing into being.

5:4 The phrase **fathered other sons and daughters** is re-peated 10 times in the Sethite genealogy, but it never oc-curs in the Cainite genealogy. The clear implication is that the line of Seth more faithfully fulfilled God's command to be fruitful and multiply (1:28).

5:5 Only three individuals are said to have lived longer than Adam's **930 years**. They are Noah (950), Jared (962) and Methuselah (969). The notation that **he died** empha-sizes the solemn truth of God's curse following Adam's sin (3:19). The fact that it is repeated seven other times

sons and daughters. ⁵So Adam's life lasted 930 years; then he died.

⁶Seth was 105 years old when he fathered Enosh. ⁷Seth lived 807 years after the birth of Enosh, and he fathered other sons and daughters. ⁸So Seth's life lasted 912 years; then he died.

⁹Enosh was 90 years old when he fathered Kenan. ¹⁰Enosh lived 815 years after the birth of Kenan, and he fathered other sons and daughters. ¹¹So Enosh's life lasted 905 years; then he died.

¹²Kenan was 70 years old when he fathered Mahalalel. ¹³Kenan lived 840 years after the birth of Mahalalel, and he fathered other sons and daughters. ¹⁴So Kenan's life lasted 910 years; then he died.

¹⁵Mahalalel was 65 years old when he fathered Jared. ¹⁶Mahalalel lived 830 years after the birth of Jared, and he fathered other sons and daughters. ¹⁷So Mahalalel's life lasted 895 years; then he died.

¹⁸Jared was 162 years old when he fathered Enoch. ¹⁹Jared lived 800 years after the birth of Enoch, and he fathered other sons and daughters. ²⁰So Jared's life lasted 962 years; then he died.

²¹Enoch was 65 years old when he fathered Methuselah. ²²And after the birth of Methuselah, Enoch walked with God*a* 300 years and fathered other sons and daughters. ²³So Enoch's life lasted 365 years. ²⁴Enoch walked with God; then he was not there because God took him. *b*

²⁵Methuselah was 187 years old when he fathered Lamech. ²⁶Methuselah lived 782 years after the birth of Lamech, and he fathered other sons and daughters. ²⁷So Methuselah's life lasted 969 years; then he died.

²⁸Lamech was 182 years old when he fathered a son. ²⁹And he named him Noah,*A* saying, "This one will bring us relief from the agonizing labor of our hands, caused by the ground the Lord has cursed."*c* ³⁰Lamech lived 595 years after Noah's birth, and he fathered other sons and daughters. ³¹So Lamech's life lasted 777 years; then he died.

³²Noah was 500 years old, and he fathered Shem, Ham, and Japheth.

*a*5:22 Gn 6:9; 17:1; 24:40; 48:15; Mc 6:8; Mal 2:6; 1Th 2:12
*b*5:24 2Kg 2:11; Heb 11:5
*c*5:29 Gn 3:17-19; 4:11

A5:29 In Hb, the name Noah sounds like the phrase "bring us relief."

---

in this chapter demonstrates the lasting consequences of Adam's sin.

5:9 The name **Kenan** (Hb *qeynan*) is closely linked to Cain (Hb *qayin*), and may mean "Metalworker."

5:12 The name **Mahalalel** may mean "One who praises God."

5:18 The name **Enoch** means "Dedication."

5:21 Enoch, as the seventh member of the Sethite genealogy, is given special emphasis. The name **Methuselah** may mean either "Man of the Spear" or "Man of Shelah."

5:22 Enoch's life stands in stark contrast to Lamech, the seventh member of Cain's line. Whereas Lamech was notorious for his immorality and violence, **Enoch walked with God**, much as Adam must have done before his sin in the garden (3:8) and as Noah did later (6:9). The phrase "walked with God" suggests living a life consistent with God's will as well as experiencing fellowship with Him. Perhaps it was Enoch's entrance into parenthood with **the birth of Methuselah** that inspired him to take his relationship with God seriously. Imagine the level of spiritual maturity Enoch must have attained after **300 years** of living wholeheartedly for God! Jude 14 indicates that Enoch was a prophet.

5:24 The description of Enoch's life differs from the others in two remarkable ways. First, his righteousness is highlighted through the double notation that **Enoch walked with God**. Second, the description of the end of his life is mysterious: **he was not there because God took him**. The NT confirms the meaning of this phrase: "Enoch was taken away so that he did not experience death" (Heb 11:5). Enoch's experience, like Elijah's later (2Kg 2:11), anticipates an experience reserved for Christians living at the end of time (1Co 15:51-55; 1Th 4:17).

5:27 Methuselah's **969 years** marks him as the oldest person in the Bible. Ancient genealogies commonly attribute long life spans to people. While the Bible's numbers are exceptionally large compared to modern life spans, they seem much more credible than those found in the Sumerian king list, which states that one individual reached the age of 72,000!

5:29 The Lamech of the Sethite genealogy (v. 28) stands in sharp contrast to the Lamech of the Cainite genealogy. Both Lamechs are the only individuals in their respective genealogies to have quotations attributed to them, but Cain's Lamech spoke of murder and vengeance (4:23-24), while the Lamech in this chapter spoke words of hope and deliverance. The name **Noah** means "Rest/Relief." Prophetically, Lamech declared that the son born to him would live up to his name: he would **bring . . . relief** to humanity **from the agonizing labor** that had resulted from Adam's sin. The verb "relief" is more commonly translated "comfort."

5:31 A final point of comparison between the Cainite and Sethite Lamechs is the use of sevens. The first Lamech mentioned Cain's sevenfold curse and pronounced a 77-fold curse on anyone who would bring death to him, while Seth's Lamech lived **777 years** before death came to him. For the numbers-conscious original audience, the author's inclusion of a figure consisting of three sevens would have trumped the first Cain's numbers, and would have added a sense of completeness and perfection to the portrait of this man's life.

5:32 The mention of **Noah** at the end of the Sethite genealogy serves as both a conclusion to this section of Genesis and a subtle introduction of the central human character in its next major section. A similar technique will be used in the case of Terah and Abraham (cp. 5:32 and 6:9 with 11:26-27).

Sons of God and Daughters of Men

6 When mankind began to multiply on the earth and daughters were born to them, [2] the sons of God[a] saw that the daughters of mankind were beautiful, and they took any they chose as wives[A] for themselves. [b] [3] And the LORD said, "My Spirit will not remain[B] with[c] mankind forever,[c] because they are corrupt. [D,d] Their days will be 120 years." [4] The Nephilim[E] were on the earth both in those days and af-

terward, when the sons of God came to the daughters of mankind, who bore children to them. They were the powerful men of old, the famous men.

Judgment Decreed

[5] When the LORD saw that man's wickedness was widespread on the earth and that every scheme his mind thought of was nothing but evil all the time,[e] [6] the LORD regretted that He had made man on the earth,[f] and

[a]6:2 Jb 1:6; 2:1; 38:7
[b]1Pt 3:19-20; Jd 6
[c]6:3 Gl 5:16-17; 1Pt 3:20
[d]Ps 78:39
[e]6:5 Gn 8:21; Ps 14:1-3; Pr 6:18; Mt 15:19; Rm 1:28-32
[f]6:6 Nm 23:19; 1Sm 15:11,29; 2Sm 24:16; Jl 2:13

A 6:2 Or women   B 6:3 Or strive   C 6:3 Or in   D 6:3 Lit flesh   E 6:4 Possibly means "fallen ones"; traditionally, "giants"; Nm 13:31-33

6:1-4 The first four verses of this chapter serve as a transition introducing the account of God's greatest act of nature-based judgment on sinful humanity. Positively, these opening verses demonstrate humanity's faithfulness in fulfilling God's command to "multiply on the earth" (1:28). This brief portion of Genesis is one of the most controversial sections of the entire Bible. Major disagreements surround each of these verses. Careful study of the Hebrew text does not end the debates; if anything, it only sharpens them. The controversies are listed below.

6:2 This verse begins to build the case that there was something terribly wrong about the way in which God's command to multiply was being fulfilled. Using language that parallels the sequence leading to humanity's first sin in the garden (3:6), the **sons of God** first **saw** something that they thought was good, and then **took** what they desired **for themselves**.

Controversy surrounds the phrase "the sons of God." Three different basic positions have been staked out regarding the identity of these "sons." They have been understood as heavenly beings (an ancient Jewish position, still accepted by many today), as kings or men of high social status, and as men from the godly family line of Seth.

Favoring their identity as heavenly beings—likely angels—is the fact that elsewhere in the OT the phrase "sons of God" refers only to heavenly creatures (Jb 1:6; 2:1; 38:7) and that the NT refers to fallen angels (2Pt 2:4; Jd 6). Those who accept this view hold that the sin that prompted God's anger in this passage was a violation of Gn 2:24, brought about by sexual relations between human and angelic beings, resulting in the creation of the Nephilim. But this view has its difficulties. For instance, Jesus indicated that angels do not marry (Mt 22:30) and Paul used the phrase "sons of God" to refer to godly people, not angels (Gl 3:26).

The view that the "sons of God" are kings or aristocrats is supported by the fact that the common Hebrew word for God is sometimes applied to persons who have great social power (Ps 82:6-7; Jn 10:34-35). Advocates of this position say that the "daughters of mankind" were people of lower social status. Thus the passage is thought to indicate possible abuse of lower class women by licentious men of privilege. Interpreters who take this view do not necessarily connect the Nephilim with these marriages.

The third position is the most popular view among evangelical Christians. It assumes that the "sons of God" were descendants of godly Seth, while the "daughters of mankind" were descendants of ungodly Cain. Assuming the descendants of both men kept true to the moral examples set by their respective forefathers, the union of these two spiritually incompatible lines was contradictory to God's will (2Co 6:14) and resulted in the total corruption of humanity, represented by the Nephilim.

6:3 The meaning of this verse is one of the most disputed in

the Bible: Is it about God shortening humanity's life spans, or about God setting a time for the universal flood? There is no general agreement as to its meaning, and so the various Bible translations reflect translators' differing viewpoints. Accordingly, disagreement exists among translators regarding the reference to **Spirit**; some understand the Hebrew word to refer to the animating force present in living beings—thus rendering it "spirit" (KJV)—while many others, such as the HCSB, understand it to refer to the Holy Spirit. Closely related to this issue is the appropriate translation of the phrase rendered in the HCSB as **remain with**. Significant variations include "abide in" (ESV) and "contend with" (NIV). Complicating the issue still further is the Hebrew word *basar*, which is normally translated "flesh" (KJV) but which can be taken figuratively to refer to that which is **corrupt**.

6:4 Two major questions arise in this verse: who are the **Nephilim** and what if anything is the connection of the Nephilim to the **sons of God** and the **daughters of mankind**? The word "Nephilim" is actually a transliteration—not a translation—of the Hebrew word; translated, it means "fallen ones," a phrase that could mean morally or physically degraded individuals, or possibly angels who fell from heaven (Is 14:12).

In spite of its literal meaning, many versions (e.g., KJV, NLT) have followed the Septuagint in translating it as "giants," a guess seemingly based on the mention of Nephilim in Nm 13:33. This proposal appears unlikely, however, since no Nephilim would have survived the flood (Gn 7:22-23) and thus could not have lived during the postflood events narrated in Numbers. Plus the Nephilim are never mentioned as one of the groups to be wiped out by the Israelites when they entered Canaan. Their mention in Numbers 13 probably came from the lips of a fear-crazed spy who misinterpreted what he had seen in Canaan.

Were the Nephilim products of the marriages between the sons of God and the daughters of mankind (v. 2)? Possibly, but in the Hebrew text there is no explicit connection between them. Moreover, the fact that **they were on the earth . . . in those days**, i.e., before and during the sinful unions, leads some to suggest that their origins are elsewhere. Whatever their ancestry, as **powerful** and **famous** men they played a significant role in preflood society.

6:5 God, who alone can observe both people's outward actions (Jb 34:21) and their thoughts (1Sm 16:7), **saw** what was visible—**that man's wickedness was widespread**—and what was invisible—**that every scheme his mind thought of was nothing but evil all the time**. The word translated "mind" is literally "heart," reflecting the ancient conception that this organ was the seat of the intellect, emotion, and will.

6:6 For the first time in the Bible, **the LORD regretted** something **that He had made**. However, His regret did not stem from something He had done wrong, but rather what humanity was doing wrong. The fact that people had be-

He was grieved in His heart. ⁷Then the LORD said, "I will wipe off from the face of the earth mankind, whom I created, together with the animals, creatures that crawl, and birds of the sky—for I regret that I made them." ⁸Noah, however, found favor in the sight of the LORD.ᵃ

God Warns Noah

⁹These are the family recordsᵇ of Noah. Noah was a righteous man,ᶜ blameless among his contemporaries;ᵈ Noah walked with God.ᵉ ¹⁰And Noah fathered three sons: Shem, Ham, and Japheth.

¹¹Now the earth was corrupt in God's sight, and the earth was filled with wickedness.ᴬ

¹²God saw how corrupt the earth was, for every creature had corrupted its way on the earth.ᶠ ¹³Then God said to Noah, "I have decided to put an end to every creature, for the earth is filled with wickednessᴬ because of them; therefore I am going to destroy them along with the earth.

¹⁴"Make yourself an ark of gopherᴮ wood. Make rooms in the ark, and cover it with pitch inside and outside. ¹⁵This is how you are to make it: The ark will be 450 feet long, 75 feet wide, and 45 feet high.ᶜ ¹⁶You are to make a roof,ᴰ finishing the sides of the ark to within 18 inchesᴱ of the roof. You are to put a door in the side of the ark. Make it with lower, middle, and upper decks.

Cross-references (center column):
ᵃ6:8 Gn 19:19; Ex 33:17; Lk 1:30
ᵇ6:9 Gn 2:4
ᶜPs 37:39; 2Pt 2:5
ᵈGn 17:1; Dt 18:13; Jb 1:1
ᵉGn 5:22
ᶠ6:12 Jb 22:15-17; Ps 14:2-3; 53:2-3

Ꭺ6:11,13 Or *injustice* Ᏼ6:14 Unknown species of tree; perhaps pine or cypress ᶜ6:15 Or *300 cubits long, 50 cubits wide, and 30 cubits high* ᴰ6:16 Or *window*, or *hatch*; Hb uncertain ᴱ6:16 Lit *to a cubit*

---

come totally preoccupied with evil **grieved** Him **in His heart**, much as Israel's sin would later grieve Him (Ps 78:40-41; Is 63:10).

6:7 Humanity was created to obey, worship, and fellowship with God. However, the magnitude of people's sin had progressively increased from that of eating forbidden fruit (3:6), to murder (4:8), to polygamy and multiple murders (4:23), and finally to worldwide preoccupation with evil (6:6). God's patience had come to an end, and the curse pronounced against Adam would now be amplified in a single catastrophic act. Since humanity was the capstone of God's creation, the elimination of people would take away any need for the ecological support system that sustained them; therefore it was expedient to destroy **the animals, creatures that crawl, and birds** as well. Even as Adam's sin had caused him to lose the garden of Eden and Cain's sin drove him from the soil, the sins of humanity would now cause them to lose the earth.

6:8 This contrast to the rest of humanity anticipates Noah's contrasting destiny. The word **favor** means undeserved blessing given by a powerful being to one who is less powerful. Noah did not earn his salvation, but his life did

demonstrate that he possessed saving faith (Heb 11:7). A wordplay exists in Hebrew between the words "Noah" and "favor," as both contain the same two consonants but use them in reverse order: n-ch/ch-n.

6:9 **The family records of Noah** is the third of eleven (Hb) *toledoth* sections in Genesis (2:4; 5:1; 10:1; 11:10,27; 25:12,19; 36:1,9; 37:2).

6:11-12 Within these two verses three different forms of the verb **corrupt** are used to describe what humanity had done to itself and the world in Noah's day. The Hebrew word translated "corrupt" means "to bring to ruin, to destroy."

6:13 For the first time in the Bible—but by no means the last (18:17; Am 3:7)—God is shown expressing to one person what His intentions were for others. Noah is thus established as a prophet, a role which he would faithfully fulfill (2Pt 2:5). As indicated first in Gn 6:5-7, God would **put an end to every creature . . . because of** human sin. But judgment would not be limited to people; God would also **destroy . . . the earth**. Sadly, one of the victims of human sin is the earth on which we live (Lv 26:18-20; Is 24:4-7; Jr 12:11; Hs 4:1-3).

6:14 Because of God's grace (v. 8) and Noah's relationship with God (v. 9), Noah and his family would be saved in an **ark**, along with the land and air animals. The term "ark" is used only in the Noah account and the story of Moses' early childhood (Ex 2:3); as used in the Bible it refers to a watertight vessel used to preserve human life from impending disaster. **Gopher** is the transliteration of a Hebrew word whose meaning is unknown; gopher wood may be pine or cypress.

6:15 Noah was **to make** the ark rectangular and barge-like in shape, six times longer than it was wide, and ten times longer than it was high. These ratios have been used to produce seaworthy craft for centuries. In the Hebrew text the measurements are expressed as "cubits," a cubit being the length from a person's elbow to the end of the fully extended middle finger—about 18 inches. The **450**-foot length made the ark the largest ship known to be constructed in ancient times. The ark was to contain an unspecified number of rooms—literally, "nests"—and was to have two layers of pitch, (that is, asphalt or bitumen) painted over the boards.

6:16 The Hebrew word translated **roof** occurs only here, and its meaning is unknown; other possible translations include

---

tamiym

Hebrew Pronunciation	[tah MEEM]
HCSB Translation	blameless, mature, perfect
Uses in Genesis	2
Uses in the OT	91
Focus passage	Genesis 6:9

Tamiym, an adjective from *tamam*, "be complete," has both physical and spiritual significance. Fifty-one occurrences describe animals as *unblemished* (Ex 12:5) or *without blemish*, thus qualified to be sacrificial victims. Related ideas are *entire* (Lv 3:9), *complete* (Lv 23:15), *healthy* (Pr 1:12), *whole* (Ezk 15:5), and *full* (Lv 25:30). A frequent spiritual meaning is *blameless, devout,* or *upright* (Gn 6:9; 17:1; Jb 12:4). A synonym is *yashar* ("upright"; Pr 2:21). This is God's standard for human behavior (Dt 18:13) echoed in the NT by the word translated "*perfect*" (*teleios*) in Mt 5:48. *Tamiym* means *perfect* when describing God's ways, knowledge, or word (Dt 32:4; 2Sm 22:31; Jb 37:16). He can make our way *perfect* (2Sm 22:33). *Tamiym* can function nominatively as *integrity* or *sincerity* (Jos 24:14; Am 5:10), and adverbially as *honestly* (Jdg 9:16). Once it seems to mean the *right decision* (1Sm 14:41).

¹⁷"Understand that I am bringing a flood —floodwaters on the earth*ᵃ* to destroy every creature under heaven with the breath of life in it. Everything on earth will die. ¹⁸But I will establish My covenant with you,*ᵇ* and you will enter the ark with your sons, your wife, and your sons' wives. ¹⁹You are also to bring into the ark two of all the living creatures, male and female, to keep them alive with you. ²⁰Two of everything—from the birds according to their kinds, from the livestock according to their kinds, and from the animals that crawl on the ground according to their kinds—will come to you so that you can keep them alive. ²¹Take with you every kind of food that is eaten; gather it as food for you and for them."

ᵃ6:17 Gn 7:4; 2Pt 2:5
ᵇ6:18 Gn 9:9-16; 17:7
ᶜ6:22 Gn 7:5
ᵈ7:1 Mt 24:38-39; Lk 17:26-27; Heb 11:7
ᵉ7:2 Gn 8:20; Lv 11:1-31; Dt 14:3-20

²²And Noah did this. He did everything that God had commanded him. *ᶜ*

Entering the Ark

7 Then the LORD said to Noah, "Enter the ark, you and all your household, for I have seen that you alone are righteous before Me in this generation. *ᵈ* ²You are to take with you seven pairs, a male and its female, of all the •clean animals, *ᵉ* and two of the animals that are not clean, a male and its female, ³and seven pairs, male and female, of the birds of the sky—in order to keep •offspring alive on the face of the whole earth. ⁴Seven days from now I will make it rain on the earth 40 days and 40 nights, and I will wipe off from the face

---

"window" or "hatch." If the term means "roof," then the text probably indicates that it was to extend **18 inches** over the sides of the boat. If the term means "window," then it refers to an 18-inch high gap separating the four sides of the boat from its roof.

6:17 Only after He commanded Noah to make the ark did God tell him why it was to be built: God was **bringing a flood**—a term used only in connection with the massive, all-destroying flood in Noah's day. **Everything on earth will die**. The biblical language here and elsewhere in Genesis 6–8 most naturally indicates that Noah's flood covered the entire globe. The apostle Peter seems to affirm this (2Pt 2:5; 3:6). That the flood was global has been the dominant Christian understanding throughout history and remains so today. Defenders of this view offer models to explain the flood's impact on the geological column. They also tackle questions such as how much water was required to flood the entire globe. If geography today reflects preflood geography, scientists estimate that Earth would have needed four times the current quantity of water for the flood to cover the highest mountains (Gn 7:19-20). In this light some defenders of a global flood have suggested that preflood geography differed from today's geography. Specifically, they suggest that Earth's landscape was flatter in the preflood era, thus requiring less water to flood, and that the violent flood created many of today's geographical and geological features. Others take a different approach, sug-

gesting that pre- and postflood geography is largely the same, that the flood did indeed require a greater quantity of water than is now present on Earth, and that by an unknown mechanism Earth's quantity of water has greatly diminished after the flood.

Citing the flexible application of some terms used to describe the flood (e.g., *kol ha'arets* is rendered as "the whole earth" in 7:3 but legitimately can refer to limited areas of land), the inclusion of details that could indicate a regional flood (e.g., the dove returning with a "plucked olive leaf" in her beak just as soon as the waters subsided despite the fact that low-lying areas where olive trees grow would have been fully submerged for roughly a year, 8:11), and the difficulty of finding traces of a global flood in earth's geological record, some evangelicals conclude that Noah's flood covered only that portion of the earth that was inhabited by humans. In this view the flood destroyed all humans except the persons on Noah's ark, but did not need to cover the whole globe in order to do so.

6:18 The term **covenant** refers to a binding, formal agreement between two parties—a sort of treaty, pact, or contract.

6:19 God's preservation of Noah meant that the ecological support network of animals would still be needed. Consequently, Noah was to **bring into the ark** one **male** and one **female** of **all the living creatures**. Representatives of all vulnerable species were to be preserved.

A reconstruction of the ark Noah built. The dimensions of the ark made it eminently seaworthy. The vessel in the *Epic of Gilgamesh*, an account of a flood that has some parallels to Noah's, is a cube. Such a vessel would have rolled over at the slightest disturbance.

of the earth every living thing I have made." ⁵And Noah did everything that the LORD commanded him.ᵃ

⁶Noah was 600 years old when the flood came and water covered the earth. ⁷So Noah, his sons, his wife, and his sons' wives entered the ark because of the waters of the flood. ⁸From the clean animals, *unclean animals, birds, and every creature that crawls on the ground, ⁹two of each, male and female, entered the ark with Noah, just as God had commanded him. ¹⁰Seven days later the waters of the flood came on the earth.

The Flood

¹¹In the six hundredth year of Noah's life, in the second month, on the seventeenth day of the month, on that day all the sources of the watery depths burst open,ᵇ the floodgates of the sky were opened,ᶜ ¹²and the rain fell on the earth 40 days and 40 nights. ¹³On that

ᵃ7:5 Gn 6:22
ᵇ7:11 Gn 8:2; Pr 8:28; Am 9:6
ᶜ2Kg 7:19; Ps 78:23; Is 24:18; Mal 3:10

same day Noah along with his sons Shem, Ham, and Japheth, Noah's wife, and his three sons' wives entered the ark with him. ¹⁴They entered it with all the wildlife according to their kinds, all livestock according to their kinds, the creatures that crawl on the earth according to their kinds, all birds, every fowl, and everything with wings according to their kinds. ¹⁵Two of all flesh that has the breath of life in it entered the ark with Noah. ¹⁶Those that entered, male and female of all flesh, entered just as God had commanded him. Then the LORD shut him in.

¹⁷The flood continued for 40 days on the earth; the waters increased and lifted up the ark so that it rose above the earth. ¹⁸The waters surged and increased greatly on the earth, and the ark floated on the surface of the water. ¹⁹Then the waters surged even higher on the earth, and all the high mountains under the whole sky were covered. ²⁰The mountains

6:20 Noah would not have to go on safaris to collect the various animals. They would **come to** him so he could **keep them alive**. On at least three other occasions in the Bible God directed animals to come to people (Ex 16:13; Nm 11:31; 1Kg 17:2-6).

6:22 As other heroic men of the Bible would do in later times—Moses and Aaron (Ex 7:6), Aaron's sons (Lv 8:36), Joshua (Jos 11:9), Gideon (Jdg 6:27), Samuel (1Sm 16:4), David (2Sm 5:25), and Elijah (1Kg 17:5)—Noah **did everything that God had commanded him**. An undetermined amount of time passed between this verse and the previous verses in this chapter. Certainly the construction of the ark would have been a lengthy endeavor.

7:1 Following the ark's completion, **the LORD** gave **Noah** the order to begin the complex process of boarding the craft. Because of Noah's **righteous** walk with God he and his **household** would be saved. The concept of sparing many because of the righteousness of a few occurs elsewhere in the Bible (18:24-32).

7:2-3 While one male and one female of every species of air and land animal were to be taken aboard the ark, **all the clean animals**—both those of the land and among the **birds of the sky**—were to have **seven pairs** of males and females onboard. The concept of clean animals is explained elsewhere in the Torah (Lv 11:1-46); essentially, these were animals that were fit for human consumption and could be offered as sacrifices to God. On the meaning of **the whole earth**, see note at 6:17.

7:4 The advance warning God gives Noah here about the onset of rain was necessary, for it almost certainly would have taken seven days to finish boarding the ark. Loading, securing, and tending to the dietary needs of all the wild animals onboard the three-story barge-like structure was a complicated and dangerous task.

Here rain was the mechanism for the deadly act of judgment that would **wipe off from the face of the earth every living thing**. Elsewhere in the OT God caused burning sulfur (19:24) and hailstones (Ex 9:18,23) to "rain" from

the sky as a mechanism of judgment against sinners. The rains would continue unabated for **40 days and 40 nights**. The number 40 played a significant role throughout the OT: Isaac and Esau were 40 when they married (25:20; 26:34), Moses was on Mount Sinai 40 days and nights receiving the law from God (Ex 24:18; 34:28; Dt 9:11,18,25), Israel spent 40 years in the wilderness following their disobedience (Nm 32:13), the Philistines oppressed Israel for 40 years (Jdg 13:1), and several kings and judges ruled over Israel for 40 years (Othniel, Jdg 3:11; Deborah, Jdg 5:31; Gideon, Jdg 8:28; Eli, 1Sm 4:8; David, 2Sm 5:4; Solomon, 1Kg 11:42; Joash, 2Kg 12:1; Saul, Ac 13:21).

7:6 Noah's age at the onset of the flood—**600 years**—will be used to indicate the duration of the flood (8:13). No other human being after Noah will be said to live to this age. On the scope of the flood, see note at 6:17.

7:10 **Seven days later**, exactly when God said it would occur, the **waters of the flood** began.

7:11 Water came from two different sources—one below and one above. Exactly what is meant by **all the sources of the watery depths** is unknown; the phrase appears to refer to a massive outflow of pressurized water from underground sources that **burst** out of the ground with devastating effect. No known phenomenon in nature today corresponds to this description.

7:12 Exactly as God had indicated (v. 4), **the rain fell on the earth 40 days and 40 nights**. God's word to Noah is once again shown to be trustworthy.

7:13-15 The **same day** that **Noah** completed the task of loading **the ark**—that is, the seventh day (v. 10) after God's command was given—**Noah** and his family **entered the ark**.

7:16 **Shut him in**—No details are given to explain how God performed the supernatural act of shutting Noah in. This divine act highlights the truth found elsewhere in the Bible: "Salvation is from the LORD" (Jnh 2:9).

7:19-20 **More than 20 feet** is literally 22.5 feet or 15 cubits. For more on the scope of Noah's flood, see note at 6:17.

were covered as the waters surged above them more than 20 feet.[A] [21]Every creature perished—those that crawl on the earth, birds, livestock, wildlife, and those that swarm[B] on the earth, as well as all mankind. [22]Everything with the breath of the spirit of life in its nostrils[a]—everything on dry land died. [23]He wiped out every living thing that was on the surface of the ground, from mankind to livestock, to creatures that crawl, to the birds of the sky, and they were wiped off the earth. Only Noah was left, and those that were with him in the ark.[b] [24]And the waters surged on the earth 150 days.

The Flood Recedes

8 God remembered Noah,[c] as well as all the wildlife and all the livestock that were with him in the ark. God caused a wind[C] to pass over the earth,[d] and the water began to subside. [2]The sources of the watery depths and the floodgates of the sky were closed, and the rain from the sky stopped.[e] [3]The water steadily

receded from the earth, and by the end of 150 days the waters had decreased significantly.[f] [4]The ark came to rest in the seventh month, on the seventeenth day of the month, on the mountains of Ararat.[D,g]

[5]The waters continued to recede until the tenth month; in the tenth month, on the first day of the month, the tops of the mountains were visible. [6]After 40 days Noah opened the window of the ark that he had made, [7]and he sent out a raven. It went back and forth until the waters had dried up from the earth. [8]Then he sent out a dove to see whether the water on the earth's surface had gone down, [9]but the dove found no resting place for her foot. She returned to him in the ark because water covered the surface of the whole earth. He reached out and brought her into the ark to himself. [10]So Noah waited seven more days and sent out the dove from the ark again. [11]When the dove came to him at evening, there was a plucked olive leaf in her beak. So Noah knew that the water on the earth's surface

Cross references (center column):
[a]7:22 Gn 2:7
[b]7:23 1Pt 3:20; 2Pt 2:5
[c]8:1 Gn 19:29; Ex 2:24; 1Sm 1:19; Ps 105:42
[d]Ex 14:21; Ps 29:10; Is 44:27; Nah 1:4
[e]8:2 Gn 7:11
[f]8:3 Gn 7:24
[g]8:4 2Kg 19:37; Is 37:38; Jr 51:27

[A]7:20 Lit *surged 15 cubits*   [B]7:21 Lit *all the swarming swarms*   [C]8:1 Or *spirit*; Gn 1:2   [D]8:4 Turkey or Armenia

7:21 Through the use of expanded restatement the author brings the detailed account of the flood's destruction to a climax.

7:22 For dramatic effect a second expanded expression of the flood's destructive effects immediately follows the one in the previous verse.

7:23 The overpowering presentation of death is contrasted with Noah's preservation.

7:24 Though the text does not explicitly say so, the total of 150 days seems to include the 40 days of rain (see note at v. 12). The Hebrew word translated as **surged** emphasizes the power of the waters.

8:1 Remembered does not suggest that God had ever forgotten about Noah; when used of God, "remember" suggests the initiation of a miraculous, saving act of God. Other instances of God "remembering" as the first step in providing divine help for His people include His intervention in the lives of Lot (19:29), Rachel (30:22), and the Israelites in Egypt (Ex 2:24). Using language that reflects God's initial act of creating the universe (Gn 1:2), God caused (Hb) *ruach*—"Spirit" or **wind**—to pass over the waters of **the earth**. Immediately the **water began to subside**.

8:2 Following the 150 days of ever-surging waters, a turnabout occurred: all **the sources of** water (from above and below) **stopped** and the water began to subside. The initial downpour ended after 40 days and nights (7:12), so presumably the rains that are said to have ceased in the present verse were only sporadic showers.

8:3 Just as the flood had increased upon the earth for 150 days, so it **steadily receded from the earth** for **150 days**, until the levels had **decreased significantly**.

8:4 Exactly five months after the flood had begun (7:11), **the ark came to rest . . . on the mountains of Ararat**—modern Turkey or Armenia.

8:6 This is the only mention of a **window** (Hb *hallon*) in the ark. Noah opened the window to determine the earth's readiness to receive the ark's cargo of people and animals.

8:7 Rabbis have suggested that Noah first **sent out a raven**, a ritually unclean bird, because it was expendable. The fact that **it went back and forth** from the ark means that it could find no suitable habitat.

8:8 Perhaps simultaneous with the release of the raven or soon thereafter, Noah **sent out a dove**. Since the dove ate seed and insects, it would provide a useful indication of **whether the water on the earth's surface had gone down**.

8:9 Though the ark was now resting on Ararat (v. 4) and mountaintops were visible (v. 5), the waters had not yet receded enough for the dove to find a **resting place for her foot**.

8:10-11 When the dove returned to Noah from its second foray with an **olive leaf**, this confirmed that the lower elevations (where olive trees grow) were now above water. Inspired by this passage, the image of a dove with an olive branch in its mouth has become a universal symbol of peace.

8:12 When Noah sent the dove out a third time and it **did not return**, it was clear that life-sustaining conditions now existed at the earth's more temperate, lower elevations.

A reproduction of tablet eleven of the *Epic of Gilgamesh*, a Babylonian account of the great flood.

had gone down. ¹²After he had waited another seven days, he sent out the dove, but she did not return to him again. ¹³In the six hundred and first year,ᴬ in the first month, on the first day of the month, the water that had covered the earth was dried up. Then Noah removed the ark's cover and saw that the surface of the ground was drying. ¹⁴By the twenty-seventh day of the second month, the earth was dry.

The Lord's Promise

¹⁵Then God spoke to Noah, ¹⁶"Come out of the ark, you, your wife, your sons, and your sons' wives with you. ¹⁷Bring out all the living creaturesᴮ that are with you—birds, livestock, those that crawl on the ground—and they will spread over the earth and be fruitful and multiply on the earth."ᵃ ¹⁸So Noah, along with his sons, his wife, and his sons' wives, came out. ¹⁹All wildlife, all livestock, every bird, and every creature that crawls on the earth came out of the ark by their groups.

²⁰Then Noah built an altar to the Lord. He took some of every kind of •clean animal and every kind of clean bird and offered •burnt of-

ferings on the altar. ²¹When the Lord smelled the pleasing aroma,ᵇ He said to Himself, "I will never again curse the groundᶜ because of man, even though man's inclination is evil from his youth.ᵈ And I will never again strike down every living thing as I have done.ᵉ

²² As long as the earth endures,
    seedtime and harvest, cold and heat,
    summer and winter, and day and night
    will not cease."ᶠ

God's Covenant with Noah

9 God blessed Noah and his sons and said to them, "Be fruitful and multiply and fill the earth.ᵍ ²The fear and terror of you will be in every living creature on the earth, every bird of the sky, every creature that crawls on the ground, and all the fish of the sea. They are placed under your authority.ᶜ ³Every living creature will be food for you;ʰ as I gave the green plants, I have given you everything.ⁱ ⁴However, you must not eat meat with its lifeblood in it.ʲ ⁵I will require the life of every animalᵏ and every man for your life and

Cross references (center column)

ᵃ8:17 Gn 1:22,28; 9:1
ᵇ8:21 Ex 29:18; Lv 1:9; Ezk 16:19; 20:41; 2Co 2:15; Eph 5:2; Php 4:18
ᶜGn 3:17; 5:29; 6:7; Is 54:9
ᵈGn 6:5; Ps 51:5; Jr 17:9; Rm 1:21; 3:23; Eph 2:1-3
ᵉGn 9:11,15
ᶠ8:22 Jr 33:20,25
ᵍ9:1 Gn 1:28; 8:17; 9:7; 35:11
ʰ9:3 Dt 12:15; 1Tm 4:3-4
ⁱ9:1-3 Gn 1:28-30
ʲ9:4 Lv 3:17; 7:20; 17:10-16; 19:26; Dt 12:16,23; 15:23; 1Sm 14:34; Ac 15:20,29
ᵏ9:5 Ex 21:28

ᴬ8:13 = of Noah's life   ᴮ8:17 Lit *creatures of all flesh*   ᶜ9:2 Lit *are given in your hand*

8:13-14 On Noah's six hundred and first birthday he **removed the ark's cover** and confirmed what the dove had indicated—that the plains beneath the mountain range were **drying**. Some 57 days (one 29.5-day cycle of the moon plus 27 days) later, **the earth was dry**.

8:15-16 Perhaps this is the first time that God had spoken to Noah since before the flood; during the entire year of the catastrophic flood there is no record that God communicated directly with the patriarch or his family. What faith Noah demonstrated during that terrifying time in the ark's dark interior!

8:20 Noah's first act following his departure from the ark was to worship God by giving a burnt offering. Since **every kind of clean animal** and **bird**—that is, one of every mammal that chewed the cud and possessed split hoofs, as well as one representative of every kind of bird that did not eat carrion—was offered, it must have been an impressive sacrifice.

8:21 Using anthropomorphic language—words that describe God's actions in human terms—the text notes that **the Lord smelled the pleasing aroma**. The phrase means that God accepted Noah's sacrifice. Elsewhere in the Torah, God's refusal to smell a sacrifice meant His rejection of the offering (Lv 26:31). Acceptable offerings in other parts of the Bible are said to have a pleasing aroma (Ex 29:25; Lv 1:9; 2:2; 3:16; Nm 18:17). Following Noah's sacrifice the Lord made a solemn promise **never again** to **curse the ground** as He had done following Adam's sin (Gn 3:17; 5:29). Almost with a sense of resignation, God noted that **man's inclination** was **evil from his youth** (Ps 14:1; Rm 3:9,23). Yet in spite of humanity's sinful nature, God's grace and love would prevail: He would **never again** destroy all life as He had done in Noah's day.

8:22 The terrifying chaos of the flood would give way to the predictable, comforting rhythms of life—the **harvest**, the seasons, **day and night**—for **as long as the earth endures**.

9:1-2 This blessing fortifies the parallels between Noah and Adam (1:28), as both blessings began with the command to **be fruitful and multiply and fill the earth**. However, in Noah's day the blessing is altered. Mankind is still to take dominion over creation (1:28), but due to the presence of sin, the harmony that existed in the garden of Eden had forever ended; now animals are filled with **the fear and terror** of humans. Terrorized animals can be dangerous; even so, God **placed** the animals **under** people's **authority**, ensuring that humans would prevail over the animal kingdom.

9:3 The original dietary regulations given to Adam and Eve (1:29) were now expanded. Animal proteins would join **green plants** within the human diet. The phrase referring to animal food sources can be translated literally as "every creeping/gliding animal" and would normally be understood to refer to smaller animals on land or sea, but it is usually understood here to mean **every living creature**. Israelites would later be limited to eating only clean animals (Lv 11).

9:4 Though meat would be permissible as food, blood would not. God required Noah and his offspring to drain the **lifeblood** from any animal before eating it. This guideline would be expanded and clarified in Israel's Sinai law code (Lv 7:26-27; 17:10-14; 19:26; Dt 12:16,24; 15:23). To avoid offending Jewish Christians, first-century Christian Gentiles were also encouraged not to eat blood (Ac 15:20,29).

9:5-6 Because **God made man in his image**, the taking of a human life by either an animal or another person was not treated like the death of an animal. **Every animal** and **every man** who killed another human being was to have its own **blood . . . shed by man** as a just punishment. This verse establishes that unauthorized taking of a human life is a capital offense and implicitly authorizes properly credentialed authorities to execute murderers. Other verses in the law of Moses reinforced this concept (Ex 20:13; 21:23; Dt 19:21).

The Historical Reliability of the Old Testament

Kenneth A. Kitchen

"Reliability" is the quality of being dependable and truthful. Is the Old Testament (OT) reliable in what it says about God's dealings with humanity in the Ancient Near East? Discoveries from that early world often illustrate the factual reality of OT history.

Primeval History

Shared memories represent one proof of the reliability of the OT. Far antiquity saw the passing of countless human generations, but they kept a living memory of momentous events. For instance, other cultures told stories that are strikingly similar to Noah's Flood. This is indirect proof for the reliability of the OT. The Genesis schema of documenting creation and listing two sets of eight or ten representative generations living before and after the Flood also finds commonality in ancient Sumerian and Babylonian literature. This demonstrates that the OT fits the literary forms and practices of the era it documents. Finally, long lives like Methuselah's 969 years are no bar to personal historicity; ancient Sumerian documents maintain that king (En)-me-bara-gisi reigned for 900 years. The 900-year reign is not credible, but king (En)-me-bara-gisi was not fictional. He is known to be historical because archaeologists have discovered inscriptions bearing his name. It was a widespread ancient convention to "stretch" spans of true events and ages of people that hailed from primeval times.

Patriarchal History

With Abraham we enter the era of the patriarchs (ca 2000–1600 B.C.). Historical records are more plentiful from this point on in history. The patriarchs herded sheep and cattle, ranging from Ur (modern Iraq) down to Egypt. Data from Ur during this era record large flocks of sheep, which fits with OT depictions. Archives from Mari mention Haran, where Abraham once lived. From the time of Abraham down to Jacob, Canaan was a land of independent "city-states" like Shechem, (Jeru)salem, and Gerar. These population centers were sustained by pastures, frequented by local herdsmen and visitors like Abraham and his descendants (Gn 37:12-13). Egyptian "execration-texts" provide extrabiblical evidence of this practice. The war between

the Canaanite kings and eastern rulers from Babylonia (Shinar, Ellasar—see Gn 14) and Iranian Elam is true to this period. The Mari archives verify that this was the only period in which Elam's forces reached so far west and when many war alliances flourished. Patriarchal customs involving things like marriage and covenant-formation reflect this period, as does the sum of 20 shekels paid to purchase Joseph (Gn 37:28). Egyptian details mentioned in the OT (personal names, deadly famines, the practice of "reading" dreams, etc.) match what is learned about Egypt from other ancient sources.

In Egypt the enslaved Hebrews labored to build cities such as Rameses and Pithom. One view is that this took place under Ramesses II (1279–1213 B.C.). Another view is that the exodus took place around 1446 B.C. Archaeology reveals that Rameses included chariotry-stables (see Ex 14:25). During the exodus from Egypt, God led the Hebrews not by the nearby northern route to Canaan (cp. Ex 13:17-18), which was infested with Egyptian military stations, but by Mount Sinai, which was safely south of Egyptian control.

The Merenptah Stele (left) dates to the late 13th century B.C. Pharaoh Merenptah (1212-1203 B.C.) memorializes his victories against Libya and in Canaan on this granite stele. Outside the Bible, this is the earliest reference to Israel to date: "Israel is laid waste, its seed is not." The Merenptah Stele was discovered in 1896 by Flanders Petrie at Thebes and is currently in the Cairo Museum, Egypt.

The covenant Moses mediated between God and Israel at Mount Sinai includes features (historical introduction, identification of witnesses, the naming of covenant blessings and curses) that reflect known usage in the fourteenth and thirteenth centuries B.C., and the Tabernacle (Ex 25:9; 26:1ff) echoes a long regional tradition (ca 2800–1000 B.C.) of building sacred tents and sanctuaries. By 1209 B.C., tribal Israel was already in Canaan. Extrabiblical proof for this is found on Pharaoh Merenptah's Victory Stele.

Historical Israel

After the troubled times of the judges, Saul, David, and Solomon ruled Israel. "The House of David" is named on an Aramean stele from Dan, and likewise on the stele of Mesha king of Moab. Less than 50 years after David, the place-name "Heights of Davit" (Egyptians used *t* for final *d*) is included in the geographic list of Palestine drawn up for Shoshenq I ("Shishak" ca 924 B.C.). The design of Solomon's temple reflected trends that were current in neighboring Syria, though the temple's décor was modest by comparison. Solomon's wisdom-writings fit his epoch in format and content.

After Solomon's death (930 B.C.), Israel and Judah split into two kingdoms. The Assyrians advanced southward and came into repeated contact with Hebrew rulers. Thus Ahab and Jehu of Israel are mentioned in texts of Shalmaneser III, while his successors mention Jehoash, Menahem, Pekah, and Hoshea. We have Hebrew seals identifying servants of Jeroboam II and Hoshea. From Judah, Jotham, Ahaz, and Hezekiah are included on official seal-impressions, while Assyrian records name (Jeho)-ahaz, Hezekiah, and Manasseh. All these kings appear in the same sequence and epochs in both biblical and Assyrian records.

Mesha of Moab left a stele mentioning Omri and Ahab of Israel. In turn, the narratives in Kings and Chronicles mention, in correct periods and order, the following kings of Egypt: Shoshenq I [Shishak], Osorkon IV [So], Taharqa [Tirhakah], Necho (II), and Hophra. Also mentioned are Assyrian rulers Tiglath-pileser III, Shalmaneser (V), Sargon (II), Sennacherib, and Esar-haddon. Finally, the Babylonian rulers Merodach-baladan (II), Nebuchadrezzar (II), and Evil-Merodach are named. Various events are documented in both biblical and external sources through 200 years for Israel and 340 years for Judah. The falls of Samaria (722/720 B.C.) and Judah (605–597 B.C.) are mentioned in Assyrian and Babylonian chronicles respectively.

We have discovered ration-tablets from Babylon for the banished Judean king Jehoiachin and his family for 594–570 B.C. The well-documented Persian triumph in 539 B.C. enabled many exiles to return to Judah and rebuild Jerusalem and its temple, just as the OT says. Other biblical figures now verified through archaeological discoveries include: Sanballat I of Samaria from Aramaic papyri; the later family of Tobiah of Ammon from tombs at Iraq al-Amir; and Gashmu/Geshem as an Arabian king in Qedar, from a bowl belonging to his son Qaynu.

The historicity of the OT should be taken seriously. As for the OT text itself, the Dead Sea Scrolls (ca 150 B.C.–A.D. 70) provide good evidence of a carefully transmitted core-text tradition through almost a thousand years down to the Masoretic scribes (ca eighth–tenth centuries A.D.) Thus, the basic text of OT Scripture can be established as essentially soundly transmitted, and the evidence shows that the form and content of the OT fit with known literary and cultural realities of the Ancient Near East. For more, see K. A. Kitchen, *On the Reliability of the Old Testament*.

The House of David Inscription is the earliest reference to David outside the Bible. This inscription was part of a victory monument erected by an Aramaean king in the 9th century B.C. He celebrates victories over a "king of Israel" and a king of the "House of David"—a reference to Judah. This artifact was discovered in 1994 at Tell Dan in Northern Israel. It resides currently in the Israel Museum, Jerusalem.

your blood. I will require the life of each man's brother for a man's life. [a]

⁶ Whoever sheds man's blood,
his blood will be shed by man, [b]
for God made man in His image. [c]

⁷But you, be fruitful and multiply; spread out over the earth and multiply on it." [d]

⁸Then God said to Noah and his sons with him, ⁹"Understand that I am confirming My covenant [e] with you and your descendants after you, ¹⁰and with every living creature that is with you—birds, livestock, and all wildlife of the earth that are with you—all the animals of the earth that came out of the ark. ¹¹I confirm My covenant with you that never again will every creature be wiped out by the waters of a flood; there will never again be a flood to destroy the earth." [f]

¹²And God said, "This is the sign of the covenant [g] I am making between Me and you and every living creature with you, a covenant for all future generations: ¹³I have placed My bow in the clouds, [h] and it will be a sign of the covenant between Me and the earth. ¹⁴Whenever I form clouds over the earth and the bow

appears in the clouds, ¹⁵I will remember My covenant [i] between Me and you and all the living creatures: ^A water will never again become a flood to destroy every creature. ¹⁶The bow will be in the clouds, and I will look at it and remember the everlasting covenant [j] between God and all the living creatures ^B on earth." ¹⁷God said to Noah, "This is the sign of the covenant that I have confirmed between Me and every creature on earth."

Prophecies about Noah's Family

¹⁸Noah's sons who came out of the ark were Shem, Ham, and Japheth. Ham was the father of Canaan. ¹⁹These three were Noah's sons, and from them the whole earth was populated. [k]

²⁰Noah, a man of the soil, was the first to plant ^C a vineyard. ²¹He drank some of the wine, became drunk, and uncovered himself inside his tent. ²²Ham, the father of Canaan, saw his father naked and told his two brothers outside. [l] ²³Then Shem and Japheth took a cloak and placed it over both their shoulders, and walking backward, they covered their father's nakedness. Their faces were turned away, and they did not see their father naked. ²⁴When Noah awoke from his drinking and

---

Cross references (center column):

[a] 9:5 Gn 4:2,8
[b] 9:6 Ex 21:12-14; Lv 24:17; Nm 35:33; Mt 26:52
[c] Gn 1:26-27
[d] 9:7 Gn 1:28
[e] 9:9 Gn 6:18; 8:22; 17:2; Ex 6:4; 19:5; Lv 26:9
[f] 9:11 Is 54:9-10
[g] 9:12 Gn 17:11
[h] 9:13 Ezk 1:28; Rv 4:3; 10:1
[i] 9:15 Lv 26:42,45; Dt 7:9; 1Kg 8:23; Ezk 16:60
[j] 9:16 Gn 17:13; 2Sm 23:5; 1Ch 16:17; Is 24:5
[k] 9:19 Gn 9:1,7; 10:32; 1Ch 1:4
[l] 9:22 Lm 4:21; Hab 2:15

---

^A9:15 Lit and creatures of all flesh   ^B9:16 Lit creatures of all flesh   ^C9:20 Or Noah began to be a farmer and planted

---

No such law exists for the killing of animals; the Bible consistently teaches that human beings are of superior worth to animals.

9:7 God's blessing of humanity in Noah's day begins (v. 2) and ends with the command to **be fruitful and multiply**. This repetition underscores the sacredness and desirability of human reproduction within God's plan.

9:8-11 These verses are the formal conclusion of the covenant first mentioned in 6:18. The initial expression of the covenant unconditionally offered safety in the ark to Noah's family and many classes of animals. In the style of a royal grant or unilateral agreement, this portion of the Noahic covenant unconditionally promises that **there will never again be a flood** of the same destructive scale as Noah's flood.

9:12-17 Accompanying the covenant was a tangible confirmation of the agreement between God **and the earth** that would continue **for all future generations**: God's **bow in the clouds** represented His promise that He would **never again** send **a flood to destroy every creature**. From this point forward the rainbow would have profound significance as an affirmation of God's grace and peace. Elsewhere in the Bible the rainbow is associated with the presence of God or His angelic representative (Ezk 1:28; Rv 4:3; 10:1). This covenant is one of three in the Bible that were accompanied by a sign; the other signs were circumcision (Gn 17:11) and the Sabbath (Ex 31:16-17).

9:18-19 Beginning with repeated material (5:32; 6:10), the writer launches into a new narrative designed to prepare readers for God's judgment on the nation of Canaan. The familiar genealogy is extended with the note that **Ham was the father of Canaan**. At the same time verse 19 prepares readers for chapter 10.

9:20 The parallels continue between Noah and Adam as **Noah** is now shown to be a farmer (lit **man of the soil** [Hb 'adamah]) in the new world prepared for him by God.

9:21 As Adam had sinned through the consumption of fruit (3:6), so Noah **drank some of the wine** and **became drunk**. After sin entered the world, shattering innocence, nakedness was associated with shame (cp. 2:25; 3:10). In this case Noah brought the shame on himself through his sinful drunkenness. A minimum of two years must have elapsed between verses 20 and 21 since grapevines must grow that long before they can produce grapes.

9:22 A parent's sin often becomes a child's stumbling block (Ex 34:7). In this case, Ham dishonored his father and thus sinned (Ex 20:12; Dt 5:16) in two ways: First, he dishonored his father by staring at his nakedness (Hab 2:15). Second, he increased both his sin and his father's shame by reporting his father's condition to others. Later, the law stipulated curses for dishonoring a parent (Ex 21:17; Dt 27:16).

9:23 **Shem and Japheth** demonstrated their nobler natures by reacting to their father's condition far differently from Ham. First, they did not look upon their father's shameful condition. Second, **they covered their father's nakedness**, thus ending his shame. Their action parallels God's clothing of Adam following Adam's sin (3:21).

9:24-27 When Noah **learned what his youngest son had done**, he placed the curse on Ham's son, **Canaan**, who would **be the lowest of slaves to his brothers**, that is, the slave of the descendants of Shem and Japheth. This curse on Canaan had prophetic implications. In later centuries the Canaanites, the descendants of Canaan, were pressed into slavery by the Israelites (Jos 17:13; Jdg 1:28-35; 1Kg 9:20-21). This curse does not refer to the descendants of Ham who settled in Africa.

learned what his youngest son had done to him, ²⁵ he said:

Canaan will be cursed. ^a
He will be the lowest of slaves
to his brothers. ^b

²⁶ He also said:

Praise the LORD, the God of Shem;
Canaan will be ^A his slave.
²⁷ God will extend ^B Japheth;
he will dwell in the tents of Shem;
Canaan will be his slave.

²⁸ Now Noah lived 350 years after the flood. ²⁹ So Noah's life lasted 950 years; then he died.

^a9:25 Dt 27:16
^bJos 9:23; Jdg 1:28; 1Kg 9:20-21
^c10:1 Gn 2:4
^d10:2-5 1Ch 1:5-7; Ezk 38:1-6
^e10:4 1Kg 10:22; Is 2:16
^f10:6-7 1Ch 1:8-10

The Table of Nations

10 These are the family records ^c of Noah's sons, Shem, Ham, and Japheth. They also had sons after the flood.

² Japheth's sons: ^d Gomer, Magog, Madai, Javan, Tubal, Meshech, and Tiras. ³ Gomer's sons: Ashkenaz, Riphath, and Togarmah. ⁴ And Javan's sons: Elishah, Tarshish, ^e Kittim, and Dodanim. ^{C 5} The coastland peoples spread out into their lands. These are Japheth's sons by their clans, in their nations. Each group had its own language.

⁶ Ham's sons: ^f Cush, Egypt, Put, and Canaan. ⁷ Cush's sons: Seba, Havilah, Sabtah, Raamah, and Sabteca. And Raamah's sons: Sheba and Dedan.

^A9:26 As a prophecy; others interpret the verbs in vv. 26-27 as a wish or prayer: *let Canaan be . . .* ^B9:27 In Hb, the name Japheth sounds like the word "extend." ^C10:4 Some Hb mss, Sam, LXX read *Rodanim;* 1Ch 1:7

9:28-29 Noah's **950 years** mark him as the third-oldest human being in biblical history, behind Methuselah (969 years) and Jared (962 years).

10:1 **The family records of Noah's sons** is the fourth of eleven (Hb) *toledoth* sections in Genesis (2:4; 5:1; 6:9; 11:10,27; 25:12,19; 36:1,9; 37:2). The purpose of this section is twofold: to show that Noah's sons fulfilled the command to be fruitful, multiply, and spread out over the earth (9:7), and to distinguish the "unchosen" lines of Noah's descendants (the Japhethites and Hamites) from the line that would be both the recipient and the agent of God's special blessing to the rest of humanity (the Shemites). Genesis 10:1-32 list a total of 70 descendants in the family lines of **Shem, Ham, and**

Japheth. Seventy, a multiple of two numbers which suggest completeness (7, the number of days of creation week; 10, the number of fingers), would have suggested to ancient Israelites a satisfying completeness to the quantity of persons and nations that came into being after the flood.

10:2-5 Fourteen of **Japheth's** descendants are listed here. **Coastland peoples** refers to people living in areas reachable by ship, especially in the Mediterranean basin. The fact that **each group had its own language** suggests that this listing refers to the situation after the Tower of Babylon event (11:1-9).

10:6-7 Thirty of **Ham's** descendants are included in this list. The geographic or ethnic identifications of most of the

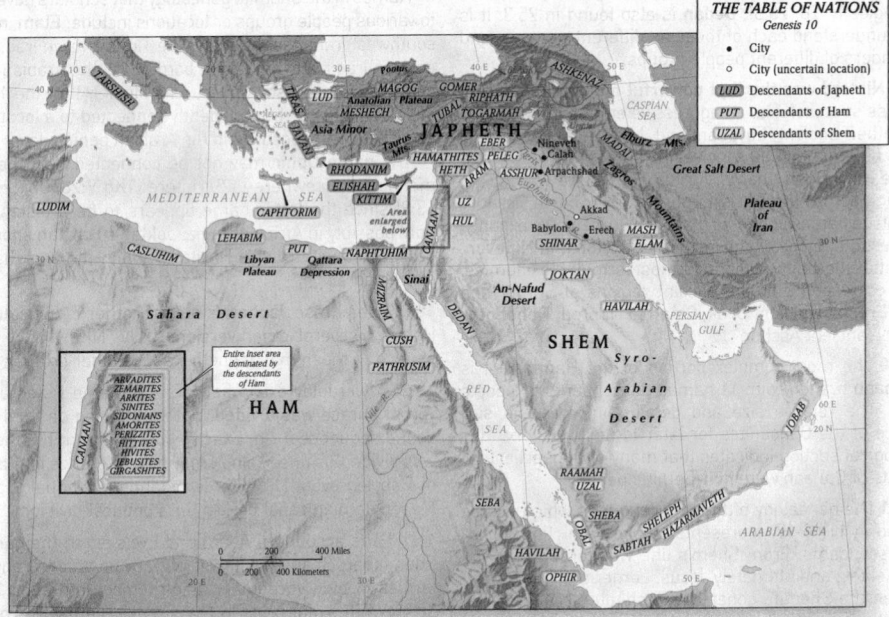

The Table of Nations shows that the Bible is firmly based on historical events. It provides the historical context for understanding Abraham, whose family became a nation through whom God would bless all peoples of the earth.

[8]Cush fathered Nimrod, who was the first powerful man on earth. [9]He was a powerful hunter in the sight of the LORD. That is why it is said, "Like Nimrod, a powerful hunter in the sight of the LORD." [10]His kingdom started with Babylon,[a] Erech,[A] Accad,[B] and Calneh,[C] in the land of •Shinar.[D,b] [11]From that land he went to Assyria[c] and built Nineveh, Rehoboth-ir, Calah, [12]and Resen, between Nineveh and the great city Calah.

[13]Mizraim[E,d] fathered Ludim, Anamim, Lehabim, Naphtuhim, [14]Pathrusim, Casluhim (the Philistines came from them), and Caphtorim.[e]

[15]Canaan fathered Sidon his firstborn, then Heth, [16]the Jebusites, the Amorites, the Girgashites,[f] [17]the Hivites, the Arkites, the Sinites, [18]the Arvadites, the Zemarites, and the Hamathites. Afterward the Canaanite clans scattered. [19]The Canaanite border went from Sidon going toward Gerar as far as Gaza, and going toward Sodom, Gomorrah, Admah, and Zeboiim as far as Lasha.

[20]These are Ham's sons, by their clans, according to their languages, in their own lands and their nations.

[21]And Shem, Japheth's older brother, also had sons. Shem was the father of all the sons of Eber.[g] [22]Shem's sons[h] were Elam, Asshur,[F] Arpachshad, Lud, and Aram.

[23]Aram's sons: Uz, Hul, Gether, and Mash.

[24]Arpachshad fathered[G] Shelah,[i] and Shelah fathered Eber. [25]Eber had two sons. One was named Peleg, for during his days the earth was divided;[j] his brother was named Joktan. [26]And Joktan fathered Almodad, Sheleph, Hazarmaveth, Jerah, [27]Hadoram, Uzal, Diklah, [28]Obal, Abimael, Sheba, [29]Ophir, Havilah, and Jobab. All these were Joktan's sons. [30]Their settlements extended from Mesha to Sephar, the eastern hill country.

[31]These are Shem's sons by their clans, according to their languages, in their lands and their nations.

[32]These are the clans of Noah's sons, according to their family records, in their nations. The nations on earth spread out from these after the flood.[k]

The Tower of Babylon

11 At one time the whole earth had the same language and vocabulary.[H] [2]As

a10:10 Gn 11:9
bGn 11:2; 14:1
c10:11 Mc 5:6
d10:13-18 1Ch 1:11-16
e10:14 Jr 47:4; Am 9:7
f10:16 Gn 15:19-21
g10:21 Gn 11:13-14
h10:22-29 1Ch 1:17-23
i10:24 Gn 11:12; Lk 3:35
j10:25 Gn 11:8; Ps 55:9
k10:32 Gn 9:19

A10:10 Or *Uruk*   **B**10:10 Or *Akkad*   **C**10:10 Or *and all of them*   **D**10:10 Or *in Babylonia*   **E**10:13 = Egypt   **F**10:22 Or *Assyria*   **G**10:24 LXX reads *fathered Cainan, and Cainan fathered*; Gn 11:12-13; Lk 3:35-36   **H**11:1 Lit *one lip and the same words*

---

names have been lost in history, but they are associated with regions in Africa and Arabia. **Havilah** probably refers to a different geographic region than the Havilah of 2:11. Three different persons by the name of **Seba** are listed in Genesis genealogies (v. 28; 25:3); **Dedan** is also found in 25:3. It is best to understand each of these as different persons, and the founders of different people groups.

10:8-12 **Nimrod was the first powerful man on earth,** that is, he was successful as an aggressive empire builder. Like many other ancient Egyptian and Mesopotamian kings, he was also famous as **a powerful hunter**. Nimrod's origins are from **Cush**, that is, Africa; his empire was Asian, stretching across the Tigris-Euphrates river basin. The order of place names suggests that Nimrod's empire expanded from south to north, and included **Babylon** and **Nineveh**, the capital cities of two of Israel's most formidable enemies. **Shinar** corresponds to the ancient regions of Sumer and Akkad; **Erech** to ancient Uruk; **Calah** to Nimrod; **Rehoboth-ir** may be ancient Asshur.

10:15-20 The most complex portion of the Hamite list is the **Canaan** branch, with 11 named descendants or people groups. The relative size and detail reinforces the significance of the Canaanites for later Israelite history. This genealogical section indicates that many of the earliest inhabitants of Canaan were non-Semitic peoples.

10:21-31 The genealogy of **Shem**, portions of which will be repeated in 11:10-17, represents the "chosen" line of Noah's descendants. From Shem's line will come Abraham, the Israelites, and ultimately Jesus. Larger and more complex than the Shemite genealogy in chapter 11 (26 names vs. 12), this presentation differs from the other, mainly in that it includes the "unchosen" branches of Shem's lineage, especially that of **Joktan** with his 13 sons. The mention of **all the sons of Eber** brings attention to the point in Shem's

line where the "chosen" branch splits from the rest of the family. The word "Hebrew" is often understood to be derived from Eber's name.

Names in the Shemite genealogy that scholars have linked to various people groups or locations include: **Elam**, modern southwest Iran; **Asshur**, along the Tigris river in Iraq; **Aram**, eastern Iraq near the Iranian border; **Uz**, the Arabian peninsula or Edom; **Mash**, central Asia Minor. All of the 13 sons of Joktan that can be confidently connected to a location are associated with locations in the Arabian peninsula.

The name **Ophir** may not be connected with the Ophir mentioned elsewhere in Scripture (1Kg 9:28; Jb 22:24; Ps 45:9) since the latter name appears to be a distant location, possibly in Africa or India. Joktan's **Havilah** should not be equated with Cush's Havilah, though the two share the same name.

10:21 The phrase **Japheth's older brother** is difficult in the Hebrew: several other versions (KJV, NKJV, NIV) understand it to mean that Japheth was the older brother.

10:25 A wordplay exists between the name **Peleg** and the verbal phrase **was divided**. Both are based on the Hebrew sound sequence *p-l-g*. Exactly what is meant by "the earth was divided" is uncertain. It may be a reference to the Tower of Babylon event (11:9), a devastating earthquake, a large Mesopotamian canal project, or a political division.

11:1-9 The account of Adam and Eve's sin in the garden of Eden (chap. 3) and the Tower of Babylon share many similarities in plot, vocabulary, and theme. Both show people acting with sinful pride to try to make themselves godlike, and both show God expelling sinners from their homes as punishment for their sin.

11:1 The Tower of Babylon incident occurred earlier than at

people[A] migrated from the east,[B] they found a valley in the land of *Shinar and settled there.[a] ³They said to each other, "Come, let us make oven-fired bricks." They used brick for stone and asphalt for mortar.[b] ⁴And they said, "Come, let us build ourselves a city and a tower with its top in the sky.[c] Let us make a name for ourselves; otherwise, we will be scattered over the face of the whole earth."

⁵Then the LORD came down[d] to look over the city and the tower that the *men were building. ⁶The LORD said, "If they have begun to do this as one people all having the same language, then nothing they plan to do will be impossible for them. ⁷Come, let Us go down there and confuse[c] their language[D] so that they will not understand one another's speech."[E] ⁸So from there the LORD scattered them over the face of the whole earth,[e] and they stopped building the city. ⁹Therefore its

name is called Babylon,[F,f] for there the LORD confused the language of the whole earth, and from there the LORD scattered them over the face of the whole earth.

From Shem to Abram

¹⁰These are the family records[g] of Shem. Shem lived 100 years and fathered Arpachshad two years after the flood. ¹¹After he fathered Arpachshad, Shem lived 500 years and fathered other sons and daughters. ¹²Arpachshad lived 35 years[G] and fathered Shelah. ¹³After he fathered Shelah, Arpachshad lived 403 years and fathered other sons and daughters. ¹⁴Shelah lived 30 years and fathered Eber. ¹⁵After he fathered Eber, Shelah lived 403 years and fathered other sons and daughters. ¹⁶Eber lived 34 years and fathered Peleg. ¹⁷After he fathered Peleg, Eber lived 430 years and fathered other sons and daughters. ¹⁸Peleg

Cross-references:
[a]11:2 Gn 10:10; 14:1; Dn 1:2
[b]11:3 Gn 14:10; Ex 2:3
[c]11:4 Dt 1:28; 9:1; Ps 107:26
[d]11:5 Gn 18:21; Ex 3:8; 19:11,18,20
[e]11:8 Gn 11:4; Ps 92:9; Lk 1:51
[f]11:9 Gn 10:10
[g]11:10 Gn 2:4; 11:27

[A]11:2 Lit *they*   [B]11:2 Or *migrated eastward*   [C]11:7 Or *confound*   [D]11:7 Lit *lip*   [E]11:7 Lit *understand each man the lip of his companion*   [F]11:9 In Hb, the name Babylon sounds like the word "confuse."   [G]11:12-13 LXX reads *years and fathered Cainan.* [13] *After he fathered Cainan, Arphachshad lived 430 years and fathered other sons and daughters, and he died. Cainan lived 130 years and fathered Shelah. After he fathered Shelah, Cainan lived 330 years and fathered other sons and daughters, and he died*; Gn 10:24; Lk 3:35-36

---

least some of the events of chapter 10 since **the whole earth** still **had the same language and vocabulary** (10:5,20,31).

11:2 The land of Shinar corresponds to ancient Babylonia and includes the region of the cities of Babylon, Erech, Accad, and Calneh (10:10). On "from the east," see textual footnote.

11:3 Unlike the original readers' homeland of Israel, with its extensive quantity of limestone building material, the people of Babylonia used **oven-fired bricks**. Archaeological excavations have confirmed that ancient inhabitants of the land used **asphalt for mortar**.

11:4 The people's pride and ambition is expressed in three different ways: (1) the fivefold use of the first-person pronouns—**us** (twice), **ourselves** (twice), and **we**; (2) their desire to **build . . . a tower** into **the sky**, thus giving them access to "the heavens," the domain of God; and (3) their attempt at self-glorification—**let us make a name for ourselves**. Because they did it to avoid being **scattered over the face of the whole earth**, all their efforts amounted to a rebellion against God and His command to fill the earth (9:1).

11:5 In spite of their best efforts to elevate themselves to God's domain, the Lord still had to come **down to look over the city and the tower**. Human attempts to achieve glory, which belongs to God alone, always fall pitifully short.

11:6 God's concern that **nothing** the people might **plan to do** would **be impossible for them** does not express a divine fear that humans might someday become as powerful as God. Rather, it conveys dismay that people, unchecked, would undertake extraordinary deeds of evil and defiance.

11:7 On God's reference to Himself as **Us**, see note at 1:26. Perhaps the most dramatic Hebrew wordplay in the Tower of Babylon episode involves the deliberate reversal of sounds between verses 3 and 7. Human beings created brick—a word which contains the sound sequence *l-b-n* in Hebrew—to rebel against God. In response God created confusion—a Hebrew word containing *n-b-l*—to reverse the evil human plot.

11:9 Most English versions refer to "Babel" here, but this is the same Hebrew word translated "Babylon" throughout the OT. The connection between the words **Babylon** and **confused** (Hb *babel* and *balal*) constitute another of the many wordplays in this chapter. The Lord's action had two positive outcomes: first, because it **confused the language of the whole earth**, it ended the possibility of large-scale evil ventures; second, it caused humanity to scatter **over the face of the whole earth**, thus bringing people into compliance with God's command to fill the earth (9:1).

11:10-26 The family records of Shem constitute the fifth of eleven (Hb) *toledoth* sections in Genesis (2:4; 5:1; 6:9; 10:1; 11:27; 25:12,19; 36:1,9; 37:2). Whereas the previous *toledoth* section ("the family records of Noah's sons," 10:1–11:9) presented Noah's "unchosen" descendants, this one traces the "chosen" offspring.

This genealogical table, which partially repeats information provided in 10:21-25, connects Noah's son Shem to Abram/Abraham. Though this list contains fewer names (12 vs. 26) than the genealogy in chapter 10, it traces out more generations (10 vs. 6) and includes chronological data as well. Its style links it with the genealogy in chapter 5, which also traces the "chosen" line and contains 10 generations. Whereas chapter 5 stretches from Adam to Noah (the preflood world), this table connects Seth to Abram/Abraham (the postflood world).

11:12 Departing from the Hebrew text, both Lk 3:35-36 and the septuagintal version of this verse indicate that Arpachshad's actual son was Cainan. Because the inspired NT author confirms the Septuagint's reading, Cainan should be accepted as Arpachshad's son. Thus it is best to accept Arpachshad as Shelah's father in an indirect sense, and to view the Hebrew version here as a stylized genealogy shaped for thematic purposes. A similar technique appears to have been used by Matthew in his presentation of Jesus' genealogy in Matthew 1.

11:17 Eber lived a total of 464 years. This distinguishes him

lived 30 years and fathered Reu. ¹⁹After he fathered Reu, Peleg lived 209 years and fathered other sons and daughters. ²⁰Reu lived 32 years and fathered Serug. ²¹After he fathered Serug, Reu lived 207 years and fathered other sons and daughters. ²²Serug lived 30 years and fathered Nahor. ²³After he fathered Nahor, Serug lived 200 years and fathered other sons and daughters. ²⁴Nahor lived 29 years and fathered Terah. ª ²⁵After he fathered Terah, Nahor lived 119 years and fathered other sons and daughters. ²⁶Terah lived 70 years and fathered Abram, Nahor, and Haran.

²⁷These are the family records of Terah. Terah fathered Abram, Nahor, and Haran, and Haran fathered Lot. ²⁸Haran died in his native land, in Ur of the Chaldeans, during his father Terah's lifetime. ²⁹Abram and Nahor took wives: Abram's wife was named Sarai,ᵇ and Nahor's wife was named Milcah.ᶜ She was the daughter of Haran, the father of both Milcah and Iscah. ³⁰Sarai was unable to conceive;ᵈ she did not have a child.

³¹Terah took his son Abram, his grandson Lot (Haran's son), and his daughter-in-law Sarai, his son Abram's wife, and they set out together from Ur of the Chaldeansᵉ to go to the land of Canaan. But when they came to Haran, they settled there. ³²Terah lived 205 years and died in Haran.

ª11:24 Jos 24:2
ᵇ11:29 Gn 17:15;
20:12
ᶜGn 22:20,23;
24:15
ᵈ11:30 Gn 25:21;
29:31; Ex 23:26;
Jdg 13:2-3; 1Sm
2:5; Jb 24:21; Is
54:1; Lk 1:36;
23:29; Gl 4:27;
Heb 11:11
ᵉ11:31 Gn 15:7;
Neh 9:7; Ac 7:4
ᶠ12:1 Gn 15:7; Ac
7:3; Heb 11:8
ᵍ12:2 Gn 17:4-6;
18:18; 46:3; Dt
26:5
ʰGn 22:17
ⁱZch 8:13
ʲ12:3 Gn 27:29;
Nm 24:9
ᵏGn 18:18; 26:4;
28:14; Ac 3:25;
Gl 3:8
ˡ12:4 Gn
11:27,31
ᵐ12:6 Gn 35:4;
Dt 11:30; Heb
11:9
ⁿ12:7 Gn 13:15;
Ex 33:1; Ps
105:9-12; Ac 7:5;
Gl 3:16

The Call of Abram

12 The LORD said to Abram:

Go out from your land,
    your relatives,
    and your father's house
    to the land that I will show you.ᶠ
² I will make you into a great nation,ᵍ
    I will bless you,ʰ
    I will make your name great,
    and you will be a blessing.ᴬⁱ
³ I will bless those who bless you,
    I will curse those who treat you
        with contempt,ʲ
    and all the peoplesᴮ on earth
    will be blessedᶜ through you. ᴰ,ᵏ

⁴So Abram went, as the LORD had told him, and Lot went with him. Abram was 75 years old when he left Haran.ˡ ⁵He took his wife Sarai, his nephew Lot, all the possessions they had accumulated, and the people he had acquired in Haran, and they set out for the land of Canaan. When they came to the land of Canaan, ⁶Abram passed through the land to the site of Shechem,ᵐ at the oak of Moreh. At that time the Canaanites were in the land. ⁷Then the LORD appeared to Abram and said, "I will give this land to your •offspring."ⁿ So he built an altar there to the LORD who had appeared

---

ᴬ12:2 Or *great. Be a blessing!*   ᴮ12:3 Lit *clans*   ᶜ12:3 Or *will find blessing*   ᴰ12:3 Or *will bless themselves by you*

---

as the oldest living person in the Bible who was born after the flood.

11:27 The family records of Terah is the sixth of eleven (Hb) *toledoth* sections in Genesis (2:4; 5:1; 6:9; 10:1; 11:10; 25:12,19; 36:1,9; 37:2). Far more than a simple genealogical table, this section stretches across parts of 15 chapters and includes a rich supply of information about the life of Terah's most famous son, **Abram** (later called Abraham). In the Hebrew, the spelling of the personal name **Haran** differs from the place name Haran (v. 31).

11:29 Nahor's wife . . . Milcah eventually produced eight sons (22:20-23); her most famous son Bethuel became the father-in-law of Abraham's son Isaac (25:20).

11:30 In contrast to Milcah, **Sarai** (later called Sarah) **was unable to conceive**. This painful fact is emphasized by the biblical writer restating the fact: **she did not have a child**. God's provision of an heir for Abraham in spite of Sarah's barrenness is a major theme in the narratives that follow (15:2-4; 17:15-21; 21:10).

12:1-3 According to Ac 7:2, **The LORD** spoke **to Abram** while he was still in Mesopotamia (Gn 11:31). God gave Abram a one-verb command with four aspects to it. Abram was to **go out from** (1) his **land**, (2) his **relatives**, and (3) his **father's house**, (4) **to a land** chosen by God. Obedience to God often means leaving one thing in order to receive something else even better.

12:4 Having migrated with his father's household from Ur (11:31), Abram stayed an uncertain amount of time in Haran. Since Terah lived 145 years after the birth of Abram (11:26,32) and **Abram was 75 years old when he left Haran**, Abram literally fulfilled the command to leave his father's house (v. 1).

12:5 Abram was apparently his nephew Lot's protector since Lot's father had died in Ur (11:28). The group's journey to **Canaan** was about 450 miles.

12:6 Shechem is in north central Israel on the slope of Mount Ebal. Abram's grandson Jacob would live for a time in this region as well (33:18-19). Later, Abram's great grandson Joseph would be buried there (Jos 24:32). The **Canaanites** were a distinct cultural group (Gn 15:21), but the term "Canaanite" is also an umbrella term for many different people groups who were living in the region, including the Hittites, Amorites, Perizzites, Girgashites, Hivites, and Jebusites.

12:7 This is the first of three times Scripture indicates that the Lord physically **appeared to Abram** (cp. 17:1; 18:1). The Lord's promise to **give the land** of Canaan to Abram's **offspring** is the single most repeated affirmation in the Torah. At least 37 references are made to it in the books of Moses. The **altar** Abram **built** at Shechem is the first of four he is said to have built; others were set up between Bethel and Ai (v. 8), at Hebron (13:18), and at Mt. Moriah (22:9).

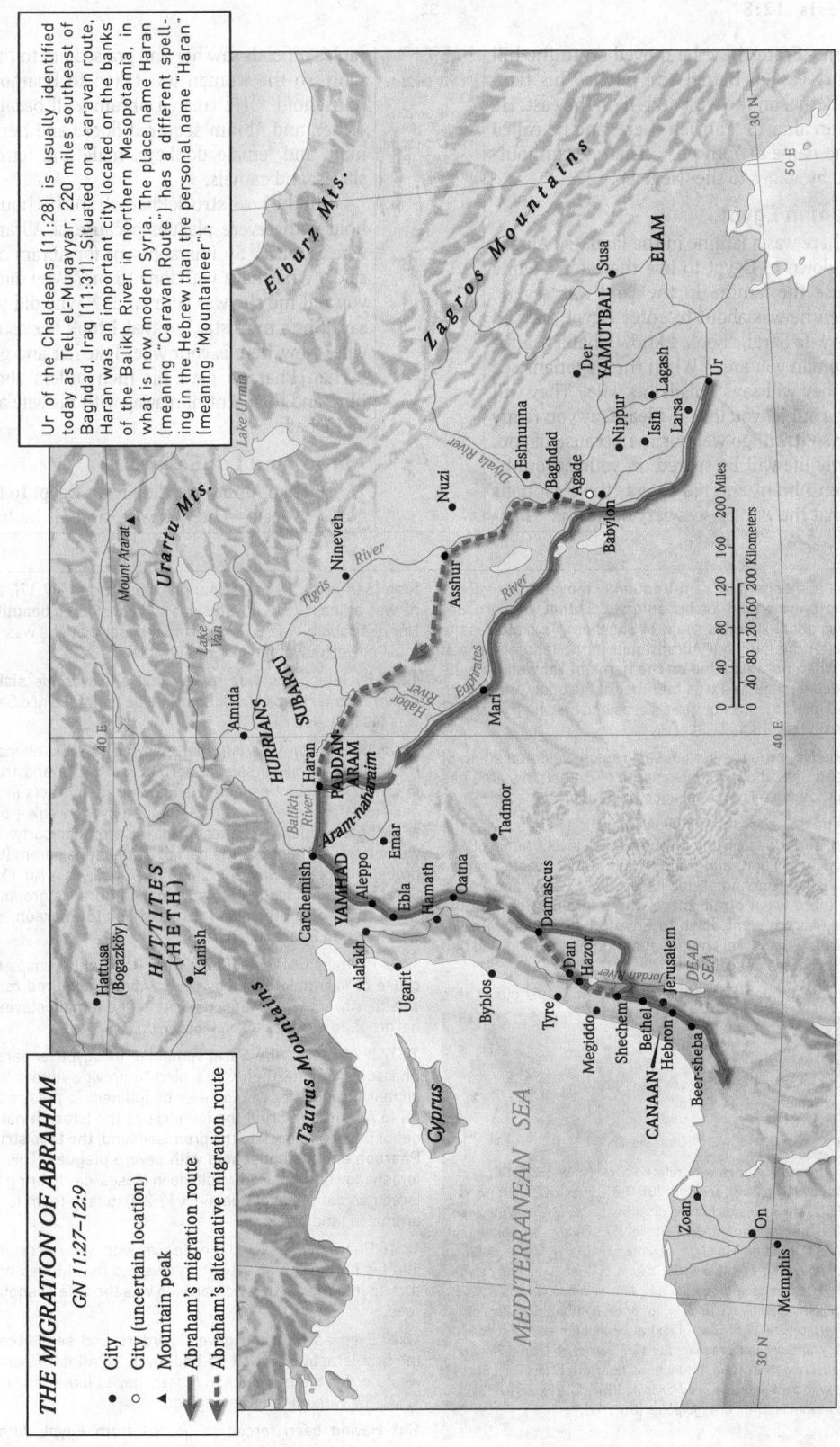

THE MIGRATION OF ABRAHAM
GN 11:27–12:9

- ● City
- ○ City (uncertain location)
- ▲ Mountain peak
- ⬇ Abraham's migration route
- ⇣ Abraham's alternative migration route

Ur of the Chaldeans (11:28) is usually identified today as Tell el-Muqayyar, 220 miles southeast of Baghdad, Iraq (11:31). Situated on a caravan route, Haran was an important city located on the banks of the Balikh River in northern Mesopotamia, in what is now modern Syria. The place name Haran (meaning "Caravan Route") has a different spelling in the Hebrew than the personal name "Haran" (meaning "Mountaineer").

MEDITERRANEAN SEA

DEAD SEA

Cyprus

Taurus Mountains

Zagros Mountains

Elburz Mts.

Urartu Mts.

Mount Ararat ▲

Lake Van

Lake Urmia

HITTITES (HETH)
- Hattusa (Bogazköy)
- Kanish

- Ugarit
- Alalakh
- Carchemish
- Byblos

YAMHAD
- Aleppo
- Emar
- Ebla
- Hamath
- Qatna

Aram-naharaim

PADDAN ARAM
- Haran

HURRIANS

SUBARTU

Balikh River
Habor River
Euphrates River
Tigris River
Djala River

- Amida
- Nineveh
- Asshur
- Nuzi
- Mari
- Tadmor
- Damascus

- Tyre
- Dan
- Hazor
- Megiddo
- Shechem
- Bethel
- Jerusalem
- Hebron
- Beersheba

CANAAN

Jordan River

- Eshnunna
- Baghdad
- Agade
- Babylon
- Nippur
- Isin
- Lagash
- Larsa
- Ur
- Der
- Susa

YAMUTBAL

ELAM

- Zoan
- On
- Memphis

30 N

40 E

50 E

40 E

30 N

50 E

0   40   80   120   160   200 Miles
0   40 80 120 160 200 Kilometers

to him. [8]From there he moved on to the hill country east of Bethel and pitched his tent, with Bethel on the west and Ai on the east. He built an altar to *Yahweh there, and he called on the name of Yahweh.[a] [9]Then Abram journeyed by stages to the *Negev.

Abram in Egypt

[10]There was a famine in the land,[b] so Abram went down to Egypt to live there for a while because the famine in the land was severe. [11]When he was about to enter Egypt, he said to his wife Sarai, "Look, I know what a beautiful woman you are. [12]When the Egyptians see you, they will say, 'This is his wife.' They will kill me but let you live.[c] [13]Please say you're my sister so it will go well for me because of you, and my life will be spared on your account." [14]When Abram entered Egypt, the Egyptians saw that the woman was very beautiful. [15]Pha-

raoh's officials saw her and praised her to Pharaoh, so the woman was taken to Pharaoh's household. [16]He treated Abram well because of her, and Abram acquired flocks and herds, male and female donkeys, male and female slaves, and camels.

[17]But the LORD struck Pharaoh and his household with severe plagues because of Abram's wife Sarai.[d] [18]So Pharaoh sent for Abram and said, "What have you done to me? Why didn't you tell me she was your wife? [19]Why did you say, 'She's my sister,' so that I took her as my wife? Now, here is your wife. Take her and go!" [20]Then Pharaoh gave his men orders about him, and they sent him away with his wife and all he had.

Abram and Lot Separate

13 Then Abram went up from Egypt to the *Negev[e]—he, his wife, and all he had,

Cross-references (margin)
[a]12:8 Gn 4:26; 21:33
[b]12:10 Gn 26:1; 43:1
[c]12:12 Gn 20:1-18; 26:6-11
[d]12:17 Gn 20:18; 1Ch 16:21; Ps 105:14
[e]13:1 Gn 12:9

12:8 As a shepherd, Abram frequently **moved** to new locations to provide food for his animals. **Bethel**, modern Beitin, was about 20 miles south of Shechem. This **altar** is the second of the four that Abram built in the land of Canaan (v. 7). When Abram **called on the name of Yahweh** here, he identified himself as a true member of the godly line of Seth (4:26). This is the first of three occasions on which Abram is said to do this (13:4; 21:3).

12:9 The **Negev** is the semidesert region west and south of the Dead Sea. About 50 miles south of Bethel, this area has been inhabited by nomads since ancient times.

12:10 The only river that flowed year-round in Israel was the Jordan, and it was completely below sea level (minus 686 ft. at its highest point, and minus 1300 at its lowest). Canaan relied heavily on rainfall for its drinking water and crops. When there was no rain **there was a famine**. To avoid the famine, **Abram went down to Egypt**, the location with the best water supply. This meant abandoning the land God had promised to his descendants.

12:11 Even though **Sarai** was at least 65 years old at this

zera

Hebrew Pronunciation	[ZEH ra]
HCSB Translation	seed, offspring
Uses in Genesis	59
Uses in the OT	229
Focus passage	Genesis 12:7

Zera' appears 15 times with related *zara'* (*sow*; Ex 23:10). *Zera'* means seed (Nm 24:7), *seedtime* (Gn 8:22), *crop* (Dt 22:9), or *grain* (Is 23:3). *Zera'* indicates human or animal *seed* (Jr 31:27), *semen* (Lv 22:4), or *offspring* (Gn 3:15). It signifies *child* (Gn 4:25) or *son* (1Sm 1:11), *children* (Gn 46:6), *descendants* (Ps 18:50), *heirs* (2Kg 11:1), *family* (1Kg 11:14), a nation's *kindred* (Est 10:3), and *people* (Is 61:9). It connotes *brood* (Is 1:4), *line* or *bloodline* (Gn 19:32), *lineage* (Nm 16:40), *race* (Is 57:4), or *ancestry* (Ezr 2:59). *Zera'* implies *fertile* (Ezk 17:5). *Zara'* (56x) also denotes *sowed seed* (Gn 26:12), *plant*, *become pregnant* (Lv 12:2), *conceive* (Nm 5:28), and *have offspring* (Nah 1:14). It functions figuratively (Hs 8:7). Participles with *zera'* indicate *seed-bearing* (Gn 1:12,29). *Zerua'* (3x) is *sowing*, what is *sown*, or *vegetables* (Dn 1:12).

time (Sarai was 10 years younger than Abram [17:17], and he was at least 75 [v. 4]), she was still considered **beautiful**. Her desirability was due in part to the fact that she was the most powerful woman in a wealthy clan.

12:13 By telling his wife to **say** that she was his **sister**, Abram was technically asking her to be truthful since Sarai was his half sister (20:12).

12:15 Since Abram's group had many people and animals, they had to be given special permission to live and trade in Egypt. Important economic and political contracts in the ancient world were sometimes finalized by the weaker party giving a woman to the leader of the stronger party. The woman would then become part of the leader's harem (this probably explains why Solomon had 700 wives, 1Kg 11:3). Sarai was the most desirable woman in Abram's group, so when **Pharaoh's officials . . . praised her to Pharaoh**, she **was taken to Pharaoh's** harem.

12:16 Perhaps because of gifts from Pharaoh, perhaps because of favorable business deals, **Abram acquired** much wealth. Abram would later use one of the **female slaves** in his group to produce a son (16:1-4,15).

12:17 If **Abram's wife Sarai** remained in Egypt as part of Pharaoh's harem, then God's plan to provide Abram with an heir through her would never be fulfilled. To restore Sarai to Abram and bring the founders of the Israelite nation out of Egypt and back to the promised land, **the LORD struck Pharaoh and his household with severe plagues**. This act foreshadowed what God would do in Moses' day to bring the Israelites out of Egypt again (Ex 12:29), to take them to the promised land.

12:18 Pharaoh connected the plagues with Sarai's entrance into his harem. An investigation revealed that he had been tricked into marrying a woman who was the **wife** of another man.

12:20 Even as **Pharaoh gave . . . orders** and **sent** Abram, the first Israelite, and **all he had away**, so a later Pharaoh would order the Israelites in Moses' day to leave Egypt (Ex 12:31-32) with all their belongings.

13:1 Having been forced to go out **from Egypt**, Abram

and Lot with him. ²Abram was very rich^A in livestock, silver, and gold. ³He went by stages from the Negev to Bethel, to the place between Bethel and Ai where his tent had formerly been, ⁴to the site where he had built the altar. And Abram called on the name of •Yahweh there.ᵃ

⁵Now Lot, who was traveling with Abram, also had flocks, herds, and tents. ⁶But the land was unable to support them as long as they stayed together, for they had so many possessions that they could not stay together,ᵇ ⁷and there was quarreling between the herdsmen of Abram's livestock and the herdsmen of Lot's livestock.ᶜ At that time the Canaanites and the Perizzites were living in the land.ᵈ

⁸Then Abram said to Lot, "Please, let's not have quarreling between you and me, or between your herdsmen and my herdsmen, since we are relatives.ᴮ ⁹Isn't the whole land before you? Separate from me: if you go to the left, I will go to the right; if you go to the right, I will go to the left."

¹⁰Lot looked out and saw that the entire Jordan Valleyᵉ as far asᶜ Zoarᶠ was well watered everywhere like the Lord's gardenᵍ and the land of Egypt. This was before the Lord destroyed Sodom and Gomorrah.ʰ ¹¹So Lot chose the entire Jordan Valley for himself. Then Lot journeyed eastward, and they separated from each other. ¹²Abram lived in the land of Canaan, but Lot lived in the cities of the valley and set up his tent near Sodom. ¹³Now the men of Sodom were evil, sinning greatlyᴰ against the Lord.ⁱ

¹⁴After Lot had separated from him, the Lord said to Abram, "Look from the place where you are. Look north and south, east and west,ʲ ¹⁵for I will give you and your •offspring forever all the land that you see.ᵏ ¹⁶I will make your offspring like the dust of the earth,ˡ so that if anyone could count the dust of the earth, then your offspring could be counted. ¹⁷Get up and walk around the land, through its length and width, for I will give it to you."

¹⁸So Abram moved his tent and went to live near the oaks of Mamre at Hebron,ᵐ where he built an altar to the Lord.

Cross references (center column):

ᵃ13:4 Gn 12:7,8
ᵇ13:6 Gn 36:7
ᶜ13:7 Gn 26:20
ᵈGn 12:6; 15:20-21
ᵉ13:10 Gn 19:17-29
ᶠGn 14:2,8; Dt 34:3
ᵍGn 2:8-10
ʰGn 19:24-25
ⁱ13:13 Gn 18:20; Ezk 16:49; 2Pt 2:7-8
ʲ13:14 Gn 28:14
ᵏ13:15 Gn 12:7; 15:18; 17:8; 24:7; 26:4; 28:13; 35:12; Dt 34:4; 2Ch 20:7; Ac 7:5
ˡ13:16 Gn 16:10; 28:14; Nm 23:10
ᵐ13:18 Gn 14:13; 18:1; 23:17-19

---

^A13:2 Lit *heavy*   ^B13:8 Lit *brothers*   ^C13:10 Lit *Valley as you go to*   ^D13:13 Lit *evil and sinful*

---

returned to the **Negev**, the last place he had lived in the promised land (12:9) before his departure to Africa.

13:3 Abram moved northward **to Bethel**, an area of Canaan with greater rainfall—and thus more vegetation—than **the Negev**. This move was probably necessary in order to feed the large flocks of Abram and his nephew Lot.

13:4 Abram's physical return to the place where God first spoke to him in the promised land was paralleled by a spiritual recommitment of his life to God. For the first time since he left Canaan for Egypt, **Abram called on the name of Yahweh**.

13:6 Especially during the dry summer months, **the land** around Bethel and Ai was too dry for such a large number of flocks and people. To remain in the area, Abram and Lot would have to separate.

13:7 With limited natural resources, **quarreling** between **Abram's** and **Lot's herdsmen** was inevitable.

13:8 Abram defused a tense situation that had soured the relationship **between** himself and his nephew, and between their **herdsmen**. Since they were **relatives** and were surrounded by people groups that had no reason to be friendly to them, it was important that they work out a compromise.

13:9 Abram realized the only way to end the dispute was for them to **separate**. As senior member and head of the clan, he should have been the one to select the region in which he would live. But Abram graciously handed the choice over to Lot, allowing his nephew to lay claim to the most desirable spot in **the whole land**.

13:10 Thinking especially of his flocks' need for water and pasture, Lot was particularly interested in the southern end of the **Jordan Valley**, an area that **was well-watered everywhere**. So well off was this region **before the Lord destroyed Sodom and Gomorrah**, two prominent cities located there (19:24-25), that it was reputed to be as lush as **the Lord's garden**—or the garden of Eden (2:9-10). The

name **Zoar** anticipates the events of 19:20-22; the name of the village at this time was Bela (14:2).

13:11 To the careful reader, Lot's journey **eastward** has some troubling implications. Other situations in the early chapters of Genesis in which the "east" is mentioned as a destination include those of Adam and Eve following their sin in Eden (3:24), Cain following his judgment (4:16), and sinful humanity prior to the Tower of Babylon incident (11:2).

13:12 Lot apparently lived a transitional existence, living **in the cities of the valley** while also maintaining a **tent** camp **near Sodom** in order to maintain his flocks.

13:13 The **evil** state of **the men of Sodom** and how they were **sinning greatly against the Lord** will be addressed further in 18:20-19:25.

13:14-15 When Abram gave parts of Canaan to Lot in the land-for-peace deal, it threatened to undo God's earlier promise to Abram (12:7), but God's promises could not be thwarted by Abram's actions. In spite of Abram's commitment to Lot, the Lord Himself would give Abram **all the land** that he could **see** in every direction. What is more, Canaan would also belong to Abram's **offspring forever**. Lot's offspring would not be left landless, however. His sons—Moab and Ben-Ammi (19:37-38)—would become the founders of Moab and Ammon, nations east of the land promised to Abram.

13:16 In addition to land, the Lord also promised Abram **offspring** too numerous to **be counted**. Since Abram was more than 75 years old and still childless at the time the Lord spoke these words, this divine pledge was particularly amazing.

13:17-18 Perhaps as a test of Abram's faith, the Lord issued two commands. With them came a reaffirmation of the promise first uttered when Abram arrived in the promised land (12:7). Immediately after God's command to **walk around the land, through its length and width,**

Abram Rescues Lot

14 In those days Amraphel king of *Shinar,ᵃ Arioch king of Ellasar, Chedorlaomer king of Elam,ᴬ,ᵇ and Tidalᴮ king of Goiimᶜ² waged war against Bera king of Sodom, Birsha king of Gomorrah, Shinab king of Admah, and Shemeber king of Zeboiim,ᶜ as well as the king of Bela (that is, Zoarᵈ). ³All of these came as allies to the Valley of Siddim (that is, the Dead Seaᵉ). ⁴They were subject to Chedorlaomer for 12 years, but in the thirteenth year they rebelled. ⁵In the fourteenth year Chedorlaomer and the kings who were with him came and defeated the Rephaimᶠ in Ashteroth-karnaim, the Zuzim in Ham,ᵍ the Emim in Shaveh-kiriathaim, ⁶and the Horitesʰ in the mountains of Seir, as far as El-paranⁱ by the wilderness. ⁷Then they came back to invade En-mishpat (that is, Kadeshʲ), and they defeated all the territory of the Amalekites, as well as the Amorites who lived in Hazazon-tamar.ᵏ

⁸Then the king of Sodom, the king of Gomorrah, the king of Admah, the king of Zeboiim, and the king of Bela (that is, Zoar) went out and lined up for battle in the Valley of Siddim ⁹against Chedorlaomer king of Elam, Tidal king of Goiim, Amraphel king of Shinar, and Arioch king of Ellasar—four kings against five. ¹⁰Now the Valley of Siddim contained many asphalt pits, and as the kings of Sodom and Gomorrah fled, some fell into them,ᴰ but the rest fled to the mountains.ˡ ¹¹The four kings took all the goods of Sodom and Gomorrah and all their food and went on. ¹²They also took Abram's nephew Lot and his possessions, for he was living in Sodom,ᵐ and they went on.

¹³One of the survivors came and told Abram the Hebrew,ⁿ who lived near the oaks belonging to Mamre the Amorite, the brother of Eshcol and the brother of Aner. They were bound by a treaty withᴱ Abram. ¹⁴When Abram heard that his relative had been taken prisoner, he assembledᶠ his 318 trained men, born in his household,ᵒ and they went in pursuit as far as Dan.ᵖ ¹⁵And he and his servants deployed against them by night, attacked them, and pursued them as far as Hobah to the north of Damascus. ¹⁶He brought back all the goods and also his relative Lot and his goods, as well as the women and the other people.

ᵃ14:1 Gn 10:10; 11:2
ᵇGn 10:22; Is 11:11; Dn 8:2
ᶜ14:2 Hs 11:8
ᵈGn 19:22-23
ᵉ14:3 Nm 34:12; Dt 3:17; Jos 3:16
ᶠ14:5 Gn 15:20; Dt 2:11,20-21; 3:11,13; Jos 12:4
ᵍDt 1:4; Jos 9:10
ʰ14:6 Gn 36:20; Dt 2:12,22
ⁱGn 21:21; Nm 10:12
ʲ14:7 Nm 13:26
ᵏ2Ch 20:2
ˡ14:10 Gn 19:17
ᵐ14:12 Gn 13:12
ⁿ14:13 Gn 39:14; 40:15
ᵒ14:14 Gn 12:5; 15:3; 17:27; Ec 2:7
ᵖDt 34:1; Jdg 18:29; 1Kg 15:20

ᴬ14:1 A region in southwest Iran   ᴮ14:1 The name Tidal may be related to the Hittite royal name *Tudhaliya*.   ᶜ14:1 Or *nations*
ᴰ14:10 Sam, LXX; MT reads *fell there*   ᴱ14:13 Lit *were possessors of a covenant of*   ᶠ14:14 Sam; MT reads *poured out*

Abram went to live near the oaks of Mamre, a site about two miles north of **Hebron**. Hebron became the primary residence of Abram and later, his son Isaac (18:1; 23:2; 35:27; 37:14).

14:1 The prosperity of the lower Jordan River Valley attracted not only Lot, but it also got the attention of four Asian kings hundreds of miles to the north and east. While scholars cannot match the names here with the names of the kings found in nonbiblical sources, the following observations have been made: **Chedorlaomer** = the Elamite name "Kutir" + a deity name; **Arioch** = the name "Arriwuk/Arriyuk" found at Mari; **Tidal** = the Hittite name "Tudkhalia." The name **Amraphel** seems to be a Semitic name. **Shinar** (Babylonia) is in modern Iraq; **Elam** is in modern southwest Iran; **Ellasar** and **Goiim** are unknown locations.

14:2 The north Asian kings probably **waged war** against the peoples of the southern Jordan Valley in order to control a trade route (the King's Highway in the area of modern Jordan) as well as the food supply. The food produced there would have been particularly useful for armies marching to Egypt or fighting other nations in the region.

14:3 The **Valley of Siddim** is mentioned in the Bible only in this narrative.

14:4 For **12 years** the five kings of the southern Jordan Valley **were subject to** (lit "served") **Chedorlaomer**; that is, they sent a portion of their annual income to him.

14:5-7 Chedorlaomer could not mount an immediate military response to the regional rebellion. But having assembled a coalition of kings by the following spring, he led the troops southward down the King's Highway to subjugate the rebellious city-states. Among those conquered were **Ashteroth-karnaim** (modern Tell Ashtarah in Syria), **Ham . . . Shaveh-kiriathaim** (probably near the ancient Moabite city

of Kiriathaim, Jr 48:1), and **El-paran** (in ancient Edom). He then went to **En-mishpat . . . Kadesh** in the northern Sinai desert and **Hazazon-tamar** (En-gedi, 2Ch 20:2).

14:10 The battlefield, with its **many asphalt pits**, proved to be more dangerous than the enemy. The literal reading of the Hebrew text states, "The kings of Sodom and Gomorrah fled and fell there"—implying that the two kings fell into the asphalt pits.

14:13 **One of the survivors** (lit "the escapee") came to Abram's camp, some 17 miles west of the Dead Sea. In that semidesert region Abram had established **a treaty** with some Amorites who gave him permission to encamp in the shade of **the oaks belonging to Mamre**.

14:14 When the survivor informed Abram that Lot had been taken prisoner, the elderly clan leader hastily **assembled his 318 trained men**—his adult male slaves—and headed 120 miles north **as far as Dan** in **pursuit** of his nephew's captors. The use of the name "Dan"—and not "Laish"—suggests that this verse was edited to include the updated name sometime during or after the period of the judges (Jdg 18:29).

14:15 Mounting a nighttime surprise attack, Abram gave his outnumbered troops the advantage. Caught off guard, the coalition of invaders fled headlong on a caravan route **as far as Hobah to the north of Damascus**.

14:16 In their hasty retreat the invaders abandoned the loot and captives they had taken from Canaan.

14:17 The **king of Sodom**, who apparently survived his fall into the asphalt pit (v. 10), met Abram's triumphant group **in the valley of Shaveh**, probably located just east of Jerusalem.

14:18 **Melchizedek**, whose name means "king of righteousness" (Heb 7:2), held two titles: he was **king of Salem** (lit-

Melchizedek's Blessing

[17] After Abram returned from defeating Chedorlaomer and the kings who were with him, the king of Sodom went out to meet him in the Valley of Shaveh (that is, the King's Valley [a]). [18] Then Melchizedek, king of Salem, [A,b] brought out bread and wine; he was a priest to God 'Most High. [c] [19] He blessed him and said:

> Abram is blessed by God Most High,
>   Creator [B] of heaven and earth,
> [20] and I give praise to [c] God Most High
>   who has handed over your enemies
>   to you.

And Abram gave him a tenth of everything. [d]

Cross references (center column):
[a] 14:17 2Sm 18:18
[b] 14:18 Ps 110:4; Heb 5:6; 7:1
[c] Ps 57:2
[d] 14:20 Heb 7:4
[e] 15:1 1Sm 15:10; 2Sm 7:4; 1Kg 6:11; Is 38:4; Jr 1:2

[21] Then the king of Sodom said to Abram, "Give me the people, but take the possessions for yourself."

[22] But Abram said to the king of Sodom, "I have raised my hand in an oath to 'Yahweh, God Most High, Creator of heaven and earth, [23] that I will not take a thread or sandal strap or anything that belongs to you, so you can never say, 'I made Abram rich.' [24] I will take nothing [D] except what the servants have eaten. But as for the share of the men who came with me—Aner, Eshcol, and Mamre—they can take their share."

The Abrahamic Covenant

15 After these events, the word of the Lord came [e] to Abram in a vision:

[A] 14:18 = Jerusalem   [B] 14:19 Or *Possessor*   [C] 14:20 Or *and blessed be*   [D] 14:24 Lit *Nothing to me*

---

erally, "King of Peace")—Salem being another name for nearby Jerusalem—and **priest to God Most High**. Abram considered Melchizedek, who is the first person in the Bible to be called a priest, to be a priest of Yahweh, since he equated the title "God Most High" with **Yahweh** (v. 22). The writer of Hebrews drew significant parallels between Melchizedek and Jesus Christ (Heb 5:6; 7:1-28). Jesus is the ultimate king of righteousness and peace, and the ideal high priest who offered up the ultimate sacrifice that sufficed for all time for the sins of the whole world.

14:19 When Melchizedek **blessed** Abram, he was performing what would become a major traditional function of priests (Nm 6:23; Dt 10:8). Abram was blessed in the name of **God Most High** (Hb *'el 'elyon*), whom he confessed to be **Creator of heaven and earth** (1:1).

14:20 In a construction that paralleled his blessing to Abram, Melchizedek also "blessed" (give praise to) **God Most High** because of the saving acts He had performed. The priest

subtly reminded Abram that his recent victory was really God's work; God had **handed over** the **enemies** to Abram. The first recorded act of tithing took place here as **Abram gave** the priest **a tenth** of the booty he had acquired from the Mesopotamian kings. Abram's tithe anticipates Israel's tithe to God (Lv 27:30-32; Nm 18:21-30; Mt 23:23).

14:21 The **king of Sodom** then ordered Abram to hand over the liberated captives, including citizens of the king's city. As payment for his military efforts, however, the king gave Abram the recaptured **possessions**, a term which can refer to livestock as well as objects.

14:22-23 With Melchizedek king of Salem, who worshiped God, Abram was cooperative (vv. 18-20); but when the Canaanite king of Sodom told him to **take the possessions**, he refused. Abram would not let the king diminish God's glory by taking credit for Abram's prosperity.

15:1 Abram's role as a prophet (20:7) is shown here. Visions were one of two standard means (the other was dreams) by

Paintings from the tomb of Knumhotep found in the noblemen cemetery of Beni-Hasan, a village on the east bank of the Nile River about 130 miles south of Cairo. The paintings date from the Middle Kingdom of Egypt (ca 1099 B.C.) and show a group of 37 Asiatics as they enter Egypt. This painting provides us with an idea of how Abraham might have dressed.

Do not be afraid,[a] Abram.
I am your shield;[b]
your reward will be very great.

[2] But Abram said, "Lord GOD, what can You give me, since I am childless and the heir of my house is Eliezer of Damascus?"[A] [3] Abram continued, "Look, You have given me no •offspring, so a slave born in[B] my house will be my heir."

[4] Now the word of the LORD came to him: "This one will not be your heir; instead, one who comes from your own body[c] will be your heir." [5] He took him outside and said, "Look at the sky and count the stars, if you are able to count them." Then He said to him, "Your offspring will be that numerous."[c]

[6] Abram believed the LORD, and He credited it to him as righteousness.[d]

[7] He also said to him, "I am •Yahweh who brought you from Ur of the Chaldeans to give you this land to possess."[e]

[8] But he said, "Lord GOD, how can I know[f] that I will possess it?"

[9] He said to him, "Bring Me a three-year-old cow, a three-year-old female goat, a three-year-old ram, a turtledove, and a young pigeon."

[10] So he brought all these to Him, split them down the middle, and laid the pieces opposite each other, but he did not cut up the birds.[g] [11] Birds of prey came down on the carcasses, but Abram drove them away. [12] As the sun was setting, a deep sleep[h] fell on Abram, and suddenly great terror and darkness descended on him.

[13] Then the LORD said to Abram,[i] "Know this for certain: Your offspring will be foreigners[j] in a land that does not belong to them; they will be enslaved and oppressed[D] 400 years.[k] [14] However, I will judge the nation they serve,[l] and afterward they will go out with many possessions.[m] [15] But you will go to your fathers in peace and be buried at a ripe old age.[n] [16] In the fourth generation they will return here,

---

a15:1 Gn 26:24; Is 41:10; Jr 30:10; Lk 1:13,30
bDt 33:29; 2Sm 22:3,31; Ps 3:3; 7:10
c15:5 Gn 22:17; 26:4; Ex 32:13; Dt 1:10; 10:22; 1Ch 27:23; Rm 4:18; Heb 11:12
d15:6 Rm 4:3,9,22; Gl 3:6; Jms 2:23
e15:7 Gn 11:31; 12:1; Neh 9:7-8; Ac 7:2-4
f15:8 Jdg 6:17; 2Kg 20:8; Ps 86:17; Is 7:11-13; Lk 1:18
g15:10 Lv 1:17
h15:12 Gn 2:21
i15:13-14 Ac 7:6-7
j15:13 Ex 22:21; 23:9
kEx 12:40; Gl 3:17
l15:14 Ex 6:6; 7:4; 12:12
mEx 3:22
n15:15 Gn 25:8; 47:30

A15:2 Hb obscure   B15:3 Lit a son of   C15:4 Lit loins   D15:13 Lit will serve them and they will oppress them

---

which the Lord revealed His word to people (Nm 12:6). The only other patriarch who is said to have received a vision was Jacob (Gn 46:2). The vision's content included a command (**Do not be afraid**), an assurance (**I am your shield**), and a promise (**your reward will be very great**). Though Abram turned down a reward from the king of Sodom, the Lord would reward him richly.

15:2-3 Neither God's protection nor His reward seemed important to elderly Abram since all his goods would go to **Eliezer of Damascus**, a **slave born in** his **house**. Engaging in something of a "pity party," Abram made seven references to himself (in the Hb) in the space of 22 Hebrew words and twice utters the complaint that he was **childless**.

15:4-5 Ignoring Abram's apparent lack of gratitude, **the LORD** gave Abram one of the great promises of the Bible; the elderly patriarch would produce an **heir . . . from** his **own body**. God then made the breathtaking promise that Abram's **offspring** would **be as numerous as the stars**.

15:6 Old and childless, **Abram believed the LORD**, that is, he affirmed that God is dependable. God **credited it to him as righteousness**, that is, He judged or accounted that Abram measured up to the standard, conformed to the norm. Abram's faith and God's gracious response to it served as a paradigm of the Christian experience in three different NT books (Rm 4:3; Gl 3:6; Jms 2:23).

15:7 For the third time in Abram's life (12:1; 13:14-17) **Yahweh** addressed the issue of land. Here Yahweh linked His name and His past leadership in Abram's life to the promise of land. He reminded Abram that the same God who had faithfully brought him out of **Ur of the Chaldeans** would just as surely give him **this land to possess**.

15:8 Abram, the shrewd businessman who had once dealt with earth's mightiest human—the pharaoh of Egypt (12:14-19)—now negotiated with the **Lord GOD**. How can he be assured of God's promise? Verse 9 provides the answer.

15:9 God provided assurance in the form of a solemn commitment ceremony. The **cow . . . female goat**, and **ram** were mammals later authorized for sacrifice in the law of Moses; however, this is the only time that three-year-olds—specimens in the prime of their lives—were used. Turtledoves and young pigeons were permitted for certain Israelite sacrifices (Lv 5:7). The ceremony here differs from other sacred rituals in the OT involving animals in that no animal parts were burned.

15:10 In an act unparalleled in the OT, Abram **split** the animals **down the middle, and laid the pieces opposite each other**, creating a clear central lane flanked by the carcass portions. The birds, being smaller, were **not cut up**; probably, one was placed on each site of this lane.

15:12 Since days were reckoned in that culture from sunset to sunset, the events of verses 12-21 occurred at the end of the day that began in verse 1. Abram's **deep sleep** (Hb *tardemah*) recalls the one Adam experienced when the Lord created Eve (2:21).

15:13-16 Here the LORD revealed **to Abram** the prophet (20:7) an outline of the events of Genesis 46 through Exodus 13. Like Abram himself, his promised **offspring** would live as **foreigners** (Hb *ger*; Gn 23:4, "resident alien"). The **land that** did not **belong to them** was Egypt, where they would **be enslaved and oppressed** (Ex 1:11-14) for approximately **400 years** (more precisely, 430 years; Ex 12:40). God would **judge the nation they** served through a series of ten miraculous plagues (Ex 7:14-12:30), after which they would **go out with many possessions** (Ex 12:35-36). Though Abram would not live to see these events, he would **go to** his **fathers in peace**—die a peaceful death—and **be buried** at the **ripe old age** of 175 (25:7). Abram's descendants would **return** to the land in **the fourth generation**, that is, after four hundred years in Egypt; in this case, each generation seems to be one hundred years, Abram's age when Isaac was born (21:5).

The Lord also hinted regarding the purpose of the return of Abram's descendants to the promised land. In large part

for the iniquity of the Amorites has not yet reached its full measure."[A,a]

[17] When the sun had set and it was dark, a smoking fire pot and a flaming torch appeared and passed between the divided animals. [18] On that day the LORD made a covenant with Abram, saying, "I give this land to your offspring,[b] from the brook of Egypt[c] to the Euphrates River:[B] [19] the land of the Kenites, Kenizzites, Kadmonites, [20] Hittites, Perizzites, Rephaim, [21] Amorites, Canaanites, Girgashites, and Jebusites."

Hagar and Ishmael

16 Abram's wife Sarai had not borne any children for him, but she owned an Egyptian slave named Hagar. [2] Sarai said to Abram, "Since the LORD has prevented me from bearing children, go to my slave; perhaps through her I can build a family." And Abram agreed to what Sarai said.[C] [3] So Abram's wife Sarai took Hagar, her Egyptian slave, and gave her to her husband Abram as a wife for him. This happened after Abram had lived in

a15:16 Lv 18:24-28; Dn 8:23; Mt 23:32; 1Th 2:16
b15:18 Gn 12:7; 13:15; 17:8; 24:7; 26:4; Nm 34:2; Dt 34:4; Jos 21:43; Neh 9:8; Ac 7:5
cEx 23:31; Nm 34:1-15; Dt 1:7-8; 2Kg 24:7
d16:5 Gn 31:49; Jos 22:25; 1Sm 24:12
e16:7 Gn 22:11; Ex 3:2; Nm 22:22; Jdg 2:1; 2Sm 24:16; 1Kg 19:7; 2Kg 19:35; Ps 34:7

the land of Canaan 10 years. [4] He slept with[D] Hagar, and she became pregnant. When she realized that she was pregnant, she treated her mistress with contempt. [5] Then Sarai said to Abram, "You are responsible for my suffering![E] I put my slave in your arms,[F] and ever since she saw that she was pregnant, she has treated me with contempt. May the LORD judge between me and you."[d]

[6] Abram replied to Sarai, "Here, your slave is in your hands; do whatever you want with her." Then Sarai mistreated her so much that she ran away from her.

[7] The Angel of the LORD[e] found her by a spring of water in the wilderness, the spring on the way to Shur. [8] He said, "Hagar, slave of Sarai, where have you come from and where are you going?"

She replied, "I'm running away from my mistress Sarai."

[9] Then the Angel of the LORD said to her, "You must go back to your mistress and submit to her mistreatment."[G] [10] The Angel of the LORD also said to her, "I will greatly multiply

---

A15:16 Lit Amorites is not yet complete　B15:18 Lit the great river, the river Euphrates　C16:2 Lit Abram listened to the voice of Sarai　D16:4 Lit He came to　E16:5 Or May my suffering be on you　F16:5 Lit bosom　G16:9 Lit to mistreatment under her hand

---

Israel's return to Canaan would bring God's judgment on **the iniquity of the Amorites**.

15:17 When **the sun had set** the Lord climaxed the mystery by causing **a smoking fire pot and a flaming torch** to appear and pass **between the divided animals**. Both elements symbolized essential aspects of God; the smoke perhaps representing divine inscrutability, and the flame God's power. By going between the divided carcasses, the Lord was solemnly obligating Himself to fulfill the terms of the covenant—symbolically indicating that He would Himself be split asunder if He failed to carry out His promises.

15:18-21 The second explicit covenant in the Bible between God and a person (9:9-17) is established here with Abram, obliging God to provide the patriarch with **offspring** and a geographic inheritance for them that began in the south with **the brook of Egypt** (either the Wadi el 'Arish or the Shihor River—the easternmost branch of the Nile in Egypt's delta region) and extended as far north as **the Euphrates River**. The list of 10 different people groups here is the longest list of Canaan's inhabitants in the Torah. This is the only list to include the **Kenites, Kenizzites**, and **Kadmonites**; the Kenites and Kenizzites were probably groups living in the Negev that coexisted peacefully with the Israelites (Nm 32:12; Jdg 1:16). Perhaps the Kadmonites were the same as the Qedemites, a desert-dwelling enemy of Israel (Jdg 6:33).

16:1 The issue of providing an heir from Abram's own body (cp. 15:3-4) reappears. Abram's wife, **Sarai**, was now 75 years old and well past her childbearing years. However, she did own **an Egyptian slave named Hagar**, probably acquired when she lived in Egypt (12:16).

16:2-3 Sarai faced a dilemma. On the one hand, **the LORD** had **prevented** her—Abram's only wife—**from bearing children**.

On the other hand, the Lord promised that her husband would become a father. To "fix" the problem, she ordered her husband to **go to** her **slave**—quite possibly a teenager—and try to **build a family** through her. Abram, now 85, **agreed**. Sarai likely intended to use Hagar as a surrogate mother, and then adopt the child as her own. In offering something that was tempting but not appropriate **to her husband**, Sarai was imitating Eve's fateful actions in the garden of Eden (3:6).

16:4 The young slave girl found herself carrying the child of the most important man in the clan—something Sarai had never done. As a result, Hagar **treated her mistress with contempt**.

16:5 Sarai, whose inadequacies were highlighted with Hagar's pregnancy, now found her own **suffering** unbearable. Abram had caused the pregnancy, thus he was **responsible** for Sarai's **slave** girl looking down on her. Sarai called on **the LORD** to hold Abram accountable for her humiliation and pain.

16:6 Though Hagar was now his wife (v. 3), Abram relinquished his rights to her. Hagar was once again no more than Sarai's **slave**.

16:7-8 Hagar could run away from Sarai, but not from **the Angel of the LORD**. He **found** her at a spring on a road leading **to Shur** and Egypt, where she might have been able to get assistance from passing caravans. Hagar, like many runaways, could say where she was from, but ignored the question of where she was going.

16:9-10 **The Angel of the LORD** directed Hagar to **go back** and **submit** to Sarai. The true source of Hagar's problems was her own bad attitude, not her owner. By obeying the Angel's divine guidance, she and her **offspring** would receive a tremendous blessing. God's promise to **multiply** her

your •offspring,ª and they will be too many to count."

¹¹Then the Angel of the Lᴏʀᴅ said to her:

> You have conceived and will have a son.
> You will name him Ishmael,ᴬ
> for the Lᴏʀᴅ has heard
> your cry of affliction.
>
> ¹² This man will be like a wild donkey.
> His hand will be against everyone,
> and everyone's hand will be
>   against him;
> he will live at odds withᴮ all
>   his brothers.ᵇ

¹³So she called the Lᴏʀᴅ who spoke to her: The God Who Sees,ᶜ for she said, "In this place, have I actually seenᶜ the One who sees

me?"ᴰ ¹⁴That is why she named the spring, "A Well of the Living One Who Sees Me."ᴱ It is located between Kadesh and Bered.

¹⁵So Hagar gave birth to Abram's son, and Abram gave the name Ishmael to the son Hagar had. ¹⁶Abram was 86 years old when Hagar bore Ishmael to him.

Covenant Circumcision

17 When Abram was 99 years old, the Lᴏʀᴅ appeared to him, saying, "I am •God Almighty.ᵈ Live in My presence and be blameless.ᵉ ²I will establish My covenant between Me and you, and I will multiply you greatly."

³Then Abram fell facedown and God spoke with him: ⁴"As for Me, My covenant is with you: you will become the father of many nations.ᶠ

Side notes:
ª16:10 Gn 15:5; 17:2; 26:24; Lv 26:9; Dt 7:13; 30:5; Ps 107:38
ᵇ16:12 Gn 25:18
ᶜ16:13 Gn 32:30; Ex 33:23; Ps 139:1-12
ᵈ17:1 Gn 28:3; 35:11; Ex 6:3
ᵉGn 6:9; Ps 15:2; Lk 1:6

ᴬ16:11 = God Hears　ᴮ16:12 Or *live away from*　ᶜ16:13 Lit *her: You God Who Sees*　ᴰ16:13 Hb obscure　ᴱ16:14 Or *Beer-lahai-roi*
ᶠ17:4 Abraham was the father of the Israelites, Ishmaelites, Edomites, and Midianites. Spiritually, he is the father of all believers; Gl 3:7,29.

---

descendants both paralleled and enhanced the promise given to Abram (15:5).

16:11-12 This is the final and longest of three consecutive speeches by **the Angel** to Hagar. Hagar is told that she **will have a son**, the more prestigious gender of offspring for a woman in the ancient Near East to bear. She is directed to **name** her son **Ishmael** ("God hears"), in recognition of the fact that **the Lᴏʀᴅ . . . heard** her **cry of affliction**. In the climactic final quatrain, character and destiny are presented: the boy will live outside of cultured society like **a wild donkey . . . at odds with all his brothers**.

16:13-14 In wonder-filled recognition of God's intervention in her life, Hagar gave **the Lᴏʀᴅ** the title "**The God Who Sees**" (or "The God Who Sees Me"). She is thus the only person in the Bible who is said to have renamed Yahweh. The Asian custom of naming/renaming someone was always associated with the possession of authority over the one being named. To rename God would normally be considered blasphemous. Perhaps Hagar's lack of restraint in renaming the Lord was due to the fact that she was quite young and was a spiritually uninformed Egyptian slave.

16:15-16 Exactly as the Angel of the Lord had promised, Hagar **gave birth** to a **son**. The fact that **Abram**, the 86-year-old clan leader, **gave the name Ishmael to the son** indicates that he allowed the young slave girl to tell him her story, and he believed it.

17:1 Thirteen years after Ishmael's birth, **the Lᴏʀᴅ appeared to** Abram for the second time (12:7). In contrast to Hagar naming the Lord (16:13), here the Lord gives Himself a name: "El Shaddai," the meaning of which is unknown, though it is translated as **God Almighty**, based on a tradition going back more than two thousand years. For more, see note at Ex 6:2-3. In commanding Abram to **live in My presence and be blameless**, God told Abram to live like Enoch and Noah (Gn 5:24; 6:9).

17:2 As Abram obeyed the Lord, God promised him two things: first, He would **establish** His **covenant** with Abram and second, God would **multiply** the patriarch **greatly**. Proof that the Lord kept the latter promise is found in Ex 1:7, which speaks of the Israelites' fruitfulness and repeats the phrase found elsewhere in the Torah only here.

17:3 Falling **facedown** was Abram's sign of respect for a superior.

17:4-8 This section contains the fullest presentation of God's covenant with Abram. Eight different aspects of the covenant are presented in these verses. Most of these promises are not new, but nowhere else are they put together in one place. The new aspect is where God changed the patriarch's

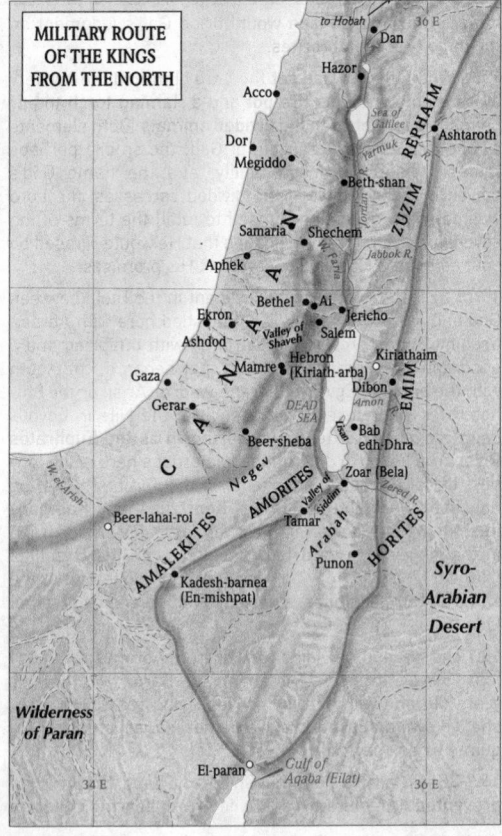

MILITARY ROUTE
OF THE KINGS
FROM THE NORTH

⁵Your name will no longer be Abram,ᴬ but your name will be Abraham,ᴮ for I will make you the father of many nations.ᵃ ⁶I will make you extremely fruitful and will make nations and kings come from you. ⁷I will keep My covenant between Me and you, and your future •offspring throughout their generations, as an everlasting covenantᵇ to be your God and the God of your offspring after you.ᶜ ⁸And to you and your future offspringᵈ I will give the land where you are residing—all the land of Canaan—as an eternal possession,ᵉ and I will be their God."

⁹God also said to Abraham, "As for you, you and your offspring after you throughout their generations are to keep My covenant. ¹⁰This is My covenant, which you are to keep, between Me and you and your offspring after you: Every one of your males must be circumcised. ¹¹You must circumcise the flesh of your foreskin to serve as a sign of the covenant between Me and you. ᶜ,ᶠ ¹²Throughout your generations, every male among you at eight days old is to be circumcised. ᵍ This includes a slave born in your house and one purchased with money from any foreigner. The one who is not your offspring, ¹³a slave born in your house, as well as one•purchased with money, must be circumcised. My covenant will be marked in your flesh as an everlasting covenant. ¹⁴If any male is not circumcised in the flesh of his foreskin, that man will be cut off from his people; he has broken My covenant."

¹⁵God said to Abraham, "As for your wife Sarai, do not call her Sarai, for Sarahᴰ will be her name. ¹⁶I will bless her; indeed, I will give you a son by her. ʰ I will bless her, and she will produce nations; kings of peoples will come from her."

¹⁷Abraham fell facedown. Then he laughedⁱ and said to himself, "Can a child be born to a hundred-year-old man? Can Sarah, a ninety-year-old woman, give birth?" ¹⁸So Abraham said to God, "If only Ishmael were acceptable to You!"ᴱ

¹⁹But God said, "No. Your wife Sarah will bear you a son, and you will name him Isaac.ᶠ I will confirm My covenant with him as an everlasting covenant for his future offspring. ²⁰As for Ishmael, I have heard you. I will certainly bless him; I will make him fruitful and will multiply him greatly. He will father 12 tribal leaders,ʲ and I will make him into a great nation. ²¹But I will confirm My covenant with Isaac, whom Sarah will bear to you at this time next year."ᵏ ²²When He finished talking with him, God withdrewᴳ from Abraham.ˡ

ᵃ17:5 Gn 35:11; 48:19; Rm 4:11-12,16-18
ᵇ17:7 Gn 9:16
ᶜEx 6:7; Lv 11:45; 26:12,45; Dt 29:13; Heb 11:16; Rv 21:7
ᵈ17:8 Gl 3:16
ᵉGn 48:4; Ac 7:5
ᶠ17:11 Ex 12:48; Dt 10:16; Ac 7:8; Rm 4:11
ᵍ17:12 Lv 12:3; Lk 1:59; 2:21; Php 3:5
ʰ17:16 Gn 18:10
ⁱ17:17 Gn 21:6-7; Rm 4:19
ʲ17:20 Gn 25:13-16
ᵏ17:21 Gn 18:10,14; 21:1
ˡ17:22 Gn 35:13

ᴬ17:5 = The Father Is Exalted   ᴮ17:5 = Father of a Multitude   ᶜ17:11 You in v. 11 is pl.   ᴰ17:15 = Princess   ᴱ17:18 Lit Ishmael would live in Your sight   ᶠ17:19 = He Laughs   ᴳ17:22 Lit went up, or ascended

---

name, thus indicating His authority over him: instead of **Abram** ("Exalted Father"), his new **name** would be **Abraham** ("Father of a Multitude").

17:9-14 God now placed one final covenant-related demand on **Abraham** and his **offspring**: circumcision. This surgical removal of the **foreskin** of the penis was typically done with a razor-sharp flint knife (Jos 5:2-3). On new-borns it was performed when the boy was **eight days old**; no form of female circumcision was authorized. This surrender of the first portion of the bodily instrument used to fulfill God's first command to humanity ("Be fruitful and multiply," Gn 1:28) symbolized the individual's willingness to submit all of himself to God and to all of His covenant commands.

The fact that **every male among** them was to be circumcised had a leveling effect within the Israelite community; whether wealthy or poor, master or **slave**, all shared a common experience and a common mark. All were equal before God. So vital was the acceptance of the sign on the body that anyone who lacked it was to be **cut off from his people** because he had **broken** the **covenant**.

17:15-16 The Lord decreed that Abraham's **wife Sarai** was now to receive the name **Sarah** ("Princess," which is an alternate form of Sarai). This "princess" would be given the privilege of producing **nations; kings of peoples** would **come from her**. During the OT period at least four nations came from Sarah's womb: Israel, Judah, Edom, and the Amalekites. Over Israel and Judah collectively a total of 41 kings reigned. Sarah is the only woman in the OT whom the Lord specifically indicated He would **bless**.

17:19-22 Undaunted by Abraham's well-intended suggestion regarding Ishmael, God reaffirmed that **Sarah** would **bear** him **a son** who, appropriately, would be named **Isaac**—"He Laughs." With Isaac God would confirm **an everlasting covenant**—the Abrahamic covenant—that would continue with **future offspring**. Lesser promises were made for **Ishmael**. Though no covenant would be established with him,

---

'achuzzah

Hebrew Pronunciation	[a khooz ZAH]
HCSB Translation	possession
Uses in Genesis	9
Uses in the OT	66
Focus passage	Genesis 17:8

'Achuzzah generally refers to real estate, but can refer to other forms of property such as slaves (Lv 25:45). A common translation of the word is property. The noun derives from the verb 'achaz, meaning to grasp or take hold of. The first and most common OT use of the noun is for land promised by God to Abraham and his descendants (Gn 17:8). Most occurrences of 'achuzzah are in the Pentateuch, Joshua, and Ezekiel 44-48, where this topic is in the forefront. A number of times the word refers to a burial plot (Gn 23:4); these burial plots served the patriarchs as a foretaste of the eventual possession of Canaan by their descendants. The word is often associated with another noun translated as "inheritance" (nachalah), since the Israelites' land was God's gracious gift to be handed down from generation to generation (Nm 32:32).

²³ Then Abraham took his son Ishmael and all the slaves born in his house or purchased with his money—every male among the members of Abraham's household—and he circumcised the flesh of their foreskin on that very day, just as God had said to him. ²⁴ Abraham was 99 years old when the flesh of his foreskin was circumcised, ²⁵ and his son Ishmael was 13 years old when the flesh of his foreskin was circumcised. ²⁶ On that same day Abraham and his son Ishmael were circumcised. ²⁷ And all the men of his household—both slaves born in his house and those purchased with money from a foreigner—were circumcised with him.

Abraham's Three Visitors

18 Then the LORD appeared to Abraham at the oaks of Mamre ᵃ while he was sitting in the entrance of his tent during the heat of the day. ² He looked up, and he saw three men standing near him. ᵇ When he saw them, he ran from the entrance of the tent to meet them and bowed to the ground. ³ Then he said, "My lord, ᴬ if I have found favor in your sight, please do not go on past your servant. ⁴ Let a little water be brought, that you may wash your feet and rest yourselves under the tree. ⁵ I will bring a bit of bread so that you may strengthen yourselves. ᴮ This is why you have passed your servant's way. Later, you can continue on."

"Yes," they replied, "do as you have said."

⁶ So Abraham hurried into the tent and said to Sarah, "Quick! Knead three measures ᶜ of fine flour and make bread." ᴰ ⁷ Meanwhile, Abraham ran to the herd and got a tender, choice calf. He gave it to a young man, who hurried to prepare it. ⁸ Then Abraham took curds ᴱ and milk, and the calf that he had prepared, and set them before the men. He served ᶠ them as they ate under the tree.

Sarah Laughs

⁹ "Where is your wife Sarah?" they asked him.

"There, in the tent," he answered.

¹⁰ The LORD said, "I will certainly come back to you in about a year's time, and your wife Sarah will have a son!" ᶜ Now Sarah was listening at the entrance of the tent behind him. ¹¹ Abraham and Sarah were old and getting on in years. ᴳ Sarah had passed the age of childbearing. ᴴ,ᵈ ¹² So she laughed to herself:

ᵃ18:1 Gn 13:18; 14:13; 23:17-19
ᵇ18:2 Gn 18:16,22; 19:1; 32:24; Jos 5:13; Jdg 13:6-11; Heb 13:2
ᶜ18:10 Gn 17:10; 21:1; Rm 9:9
ᵈ18:11 Gn 17:17; Rm 4:19; Heb 11:11-12

ᴬ18:3 Or My Lord, or The Lord   ᴮ18:5 Lit may sustain your heart   ᶜ18:6 Lit three seahs; about 21 quarts   ᴰ18:6 A round, thin, unleavened bread   ᴱ18:8 Or butter   ᶠ18:8 Lit was standing by   ᴳ18:11 Lit days   ᴴ18:11 Lit The way of women had ceased for Sarah

---

God would **bless** Ishmael, enabling him to fulfill humanity's basic command to be **fruitful** and **multiply . . . greatly** (1:28; 9:1,7). No kings were promised in Ishmael's lineage, but from him would come **12 tribal leaders** (25:13-16), and his offspring would become **a great nation**.

The Lord's amazing final statement named the child not yet conceived, confirmed a binding relationship between God and that son, and then set a date when the boy would be born to 90-year-old Sarah. Dramatically, God then "ascended above" (HCSB, **withdrew from**) Abraham.

17:23-27 Promptly after the Lord ascended, Abraham **circumcised** himself and all the males in his **household**. With the sign of the covenant now on his body, Abraham was qualified to father the covenant child.

18:1 For the third time in Abraham's life **the LORD appeared to** him (12:7; 17:1). **Mamre**, near Hebron, was Abraham's preferred abode in Canaan (13:18; 14:13). This divine encounter must have taken place within three months after the events of the previous chapter (see note at 18:9-10).

18:2-8 Abraham is presented as the ideal host. He sees **three men**—actually God and two angels (19:1)—to whom he eagerly extended greeting and showed proper respect by calling them "my lords" (Hb 'adonai; a term that can refer to God) and bowing **to the ground**. Then he provided water, rest, and a feast that included **bread** baked from 21 quarts of **flour**. Abraham's behavior shows him to be a better host than Lot (19:1-3).

18:9-10 In keeping with western Asian customs still practiced in traditional Muslim culture today, the host's wife was not permitted to be in the presence of male visitors. But since her tent walls were thin and the conversation was interesting, **Sarah was listening** to every word. During or after the meal the Lord confirmed the promise made in 17:21, that **in about a year's time . . . Sarah** would already have given birth to **a son**. This promise was fulfilled (21:1-2).

18:11-15 For the sixth time in the Abraham narratives the writer emphasizes the advanced ages of Abraham and Sarah (12:4; 16:16; 17:1,17,24). Sarah's laughter expressed her skepticism, but the Lord, who heard her laugh and knew her heart, reminded Abraham and Sarah through the use

mul

Hebrew Pronunciation	[MOOL]
HCSB Translation	circumcise, cut off
Uses in Genesis	17
Uses in the OT	35
Focus passage	Genesis 17:10-14,23-27

The Egyptians, Edomites, Ammonites, Moabites, Arabs, and Phoenicians practiced *circumcision* (Jr 9:25-26), but normally on adolescents. God made it the sign of His eternal covenant with Abraham, to be kept by all generations of His male descendants. Any man not *circumcised* would be *cut off* from the community (Gn 17:11-14). *Circumcision* was to be done on the eighth day of life if possible (Gn 21:4; Lv 12:3). Jacob's sons made it a condition of intermarriage with other people groups (Gn 34:15). Later, slaves and foreign residents had to undergo *circumcision* to celebrate the Passover (Ex 12:44,48). Flint knives were initially the instrument (Jos 5:2). *Mul* eventually acquired a metaphorical sense of loyalty. *Circumcised* hearts contrast with being stiff-necked (Dt 10:16). By removing the foreskin of their hearts, Israelites *circumcised* themselves to the Lord (Jr 4:4).

"After I have become shriveled up and my lord is old, will I have delight?"[a]

[13]But the LORD asked Abraham, "Why did Sarah laugh, saying, 'Can I really have a baby when I'm old?' [14]Is anything impossible for the LORD?[b] At the appointed time I will come back to you, and in about a year she will have a son."

[15]Sarah denied it. "I did not laugh," she said, because she was afraid.

But He replied, "No, you did laugh."

Abraham's Plea for Sodom

[16]The men got up from there and looked out over Sodom, and Abraham was walking with them to see them off. [17]Then the LORD said, "Should I hide what I am about to do from Abraham?[c] [18]Abraham is to become a great and powerful nation, and all the nations of the earth will be blessed through him.[d] [19]For I have chosen[A] him so that he will command his children and his house after him to keep the way of the LORD by doing what is right and just. This is how the LORD will fulfill to Abraham what He promised him." [20]Then the LORD said, "The outcry against Sodom and Gomorrah is immense, and their sin is extremely serious. [21]I will go down[e] to see if what they have done justifies the cry that has come up to Me. If not, I will find out."

[22]The men turned from there and went toward Sodom[f] while Abraham remained standing before the LORD.[B] [23]Abraham stepped forward and said, "Will You really sweep away the righteous with the wicked?[g] [24]What if there are 50 righteous people in the city? Will You really sweep it away instead of spar-

[a]18:12 Gn 17:17; Lk 1:18; 1Pt 3:6
[b]18:14 Jb 34:10; Jr 32:17,27; Mt 19:26; Mk 10:27; Lk 1:37; 18:27; Heb 6:18
[c]18:17 Am 3:7
[d]18:18 Gn 12:3; 26:4; Gl 3:8
[e]18:21 Gn 11:5; Ex 3:8; Ps 14:2
[f]18:22 Gn 19:1
[g]18:23 Ex 23:7; Nm 16:22; 2Sm 24:17; Ps 11:4-7
[h]18:25 Dt 1:16-17; 32:4; Jb 8:3,20; Ps 58:11; 94:2; Is 3:10-11; Rm 3:5-6
[i]18:26 Jr 5:1
[j]18:32 Jdg 6:39

ing the place for the sake of the 50 righteous people who are in it? [25]You could not possibly do such a thing: to kill the righteous with the wicked, treating the righteous and the wicked alike. You could not possibly do that! Won't the Judge of all the earth do what is just?"[h]

[26]The LORD said, "If I find 50 righteous people in the city of Sodom, I will spare the whole place for their sake."[i]

[27]Then Abraham answered, "Since I have ventured to speak to the Lord—even though I am dust and ashes— [28]suppose the 50 righteous lack five. Will you destroy the whole city for lack of five?"

He replied, "I will not destroy it if I find 45 there."

[29]Then he spoke to Him again, "Suppose 40 are found there?"

He answered, "I will not do it on account of 40."

[30]Then he said, "Let the Lord not be angry, and I will speak further. Suppose 30 are found there?"

He answered, "I will not do it if I find 30 there."

[31]Then he said, "Since I have ventured to speak to the Lord, suppose 20 are found there?"

He replied, "I will not destroy it on account of 20."

[32]Then he said, "Let the Lord not be angry, and I will speak one more time.[j] Suppose 10 are found there?"

He answered, "I will not destroy it on account of 10." [33]When the LORD had finished speaking with Abraham, He departed, and Abraham returned to his place.

[A]18:19 Lit known   [B]18:22 Ancient Jewish tradition reads while the LORD remained standing before Abraham

---

of a rhetorical question that nothing is **impossible for the LORD**.

18:16-19 The Lord and the two angels—referred to here as **the men** because of their man-like appearance—headed in the direction of **Sodom**, Lot's home since 13:12. The exact location of Sodom is unknown, but it, along with Gomorrah and Zoar, were in the area of the Dead Sea. **Abraham**, the ideal host, accompanied **them to see them off**. Treating Abraham like a prophet (20:7), **the LORD** did not want to **hide . . . from** him what He intended to do to the place where his nephew lived. God gave two reasons for revealing His plans to the patriarch: the fact that Abraham had been chosen to become a **great . . . nation** through whom **all the nations of the earth** would **be blessed**, and the fact that God "knew" (HCSB), **chosen**—that is, had a personal relationship with) Abraham to establish a people who would **keep the way of the LORD**.

18:20-21 The Lord would investigate **Sodom and Gomorrah** for two reasons: **the outcry** coming from their victims was **immense**, and the cities' **sin** was **extremely serious**. According to Ezk 16:49-50, the sins of Sodom and Gomor-

rah included self-centered pride, neglect of the poor and needy, and doing unnamed detestable things. According to Gn 19:5-9, one of the "detestable things" was attempted homosexual gang rape. Through His appointed representatives the Lord would experience **what** justified **the cry** that had **come up to** Him.

18:22-32 This passage is one of the three greatest illustrations of petitionary prayer in the OT (cp. Ex 32:11-14; Am 7:1-6). Abraham got the Lord to agree to spare Sodom if six successively smaller totals of **righteous people** could be found within **the city**. Clearly evident in the section are Abraham's respect for God (exemplified by him **standing before the LORD**, v. 22; cp. v. 27), his confidence in God's power and justice (vv. 23,25), and the patriarch's compassionate concern for Lot and the other inhabitants of Sodom. At the same time the Lord's extravagant mercy is seen in His willingness to spare the entire city **on account of 10** righteous people who lived there.

18:33 The Lord did not accompany the angels. His destination remains a mysterious part of the narrative.

The Destruction of Sodom and Gomorrah

19 The two angels entered Sodom[a] in the evening as Lot was sitting at Sodom's ·gate. When Lot saw them, he got up to meet them. He bowed with his face to the ground [2] and said, "My lords, turn aside to your servant's house, wash your feet, and spend the night. Then you can get up early and go on your way."

"No," they said. "We would rather spend the night in the square." [3] But he urged them so strongly that they followed him and went into his house. He prepared a feast and baked unleavened bread for them, and they ate.

[4] Before they went to bed, the men of the city of Sodom, both young and old, the whole population, surrounded the house. [5] They called out to Lot and said, "Where are the men who came to you tonight? Send them out to us so we can have sex with them!"[b]

[6] Lot went out to them at the entrance and shut the door behind him. [7] He said, "Don't do this evil, my brothers. [8] Look, I've got two daughters who haven't had sexual relations with a man.[c] I'll bring them out to you, and you can do whatever you want[A] to them. However, don't do anything to these men, because they have come under the protection of my roof."

[9] "Get out of the way!" they said, adding, "This one came here as a foreigner, but he's acting like a judge![d] Now we'll do more harm to you than to them." They put pressure on Lot and came up to break down the door. [10] But the angels[B] reached out, brought Lot into the house with them, and shut the door. [11] They struck the men who were at the entrance of the house, both young and old, with a blinding light so that they were unable to find the entrance.[e]

[12] Then the angels[B] said to Lot, "Do you have anyone else here: a son-in-law, your sons and daughters, or anyone else in the city who belongs to you? Get them out of this place, [13] for we are about to destroy this place because the outcry against its people is so great before the LORD, that the LORD has sent us to destroy it."[f]

[14] So Lot went out and spoke to his sons-in-law, who were going to marry[c] his daughters. "Get up," he said. "Get out of this place, for the LORD is about to destroy the city!"[g] But his sons-in-law thought he was joking.

[15] At daybreak the angels urged Lot on: "Get up! Take your wife and your two daughters who are here, or you will be swept away in the punishment[D] of the city." [16] But he hesitated. Because of the LORD's compassion for him, the men grabbed his hand, his wife's hand, and

Cross references:
[a]19:1 Gn 18:2,22
[b]19:5 Lv 18:22; Jdg 19:22
[c]19:8 Jdg 19:24
[d]19:9 Ex 2:14
[e]19:11 Dt 28:28-29; 2Kg 6:18; Ac 13:11
[f]19:13 Gn 18:20-21; Ex 3:7; 22:23; 1Sm 9:16; Jb 27:9
[g]19:14 Nm 16:21,26,45; Jr 51:6; Rv 18:4

[A]19:8 Lit *do what is good in your eyes*   [B]19:10,12 Lit *men*   [C]19:14 Lit *take*   [D]19:15 Or *iniquity*, or *guilt*

19:1-3 Lot's position at the **gate** may indicate that he was accorded a spot of honor with the elders of the city (Pr 31:23). Like Abraham in Genesis 18, Lot also played the role of gracious host to divine beings in human form, though in a lesser way. Whereas Abraham met with three divine guests, including the Lord, Lot met with **two angels**. Abraham "ran" to greet his guests and prepared a lavish meal; by contrast, Lot only **got up to meet them**, and prepared a **feast** that consisted only of **unleavened bread**.

19:4-5 Though it was the custom to go **to bed** soon after the evening meal, the ritual was interrupted by **the men of the city** demanding sex, justifying the immense outcry raised earlier against the city (18:20-21).

19:6-8 Ancient Asian hospitality customs made Lot responsible for his visitors' safety while **under the protection of** his **roof**—no matter what the cost. Accordingly, he put himself at risk by facing the mob and warning them that their intentions were **evil**. Failing in his appeal to their higher moral instincts, Lot then put his family at risk, offering up his **two** virgin **daughters** to satisfy the rabble's sexual desires. Lot's daughters would soon get even with their father for his repulsive offer by making him a victim of disgusting sexual misconduct (vv. 32-36).

19:9-11 Enraged because Lot had declared homosexual rape to be evil, the mob condemned him for **acting like a judge**. Sinners rarely appreciate having a cherished sin condemned.

19:12-14 Parallels exist between Noah and Lot. Both were

righteous men (6:9; 2Pt 2:7), both were warned that **the LORD** was **about to destroy** entire civilizations for their great sin (6:13), and the families of both were included in God's salvation. Because the **outcry against** Sodom had been confirmed, the angels, as God's servants (Heb 1:7),

gadal

Hebrew Pronunciation	[gah DAHL]
HCSB Translation	be great, grow
Uses in Genesis	14
Uses in the OT	117
Focus passage	Genesis 19:13,19

Gadal is related to *gadol*, and means *be great* (Gn 19:13). It denotes *grow*, *grow up*, and *mature*. It implies *be magnified* or *exalted*. Someone is *powerful* or *valuable*; something is *intense* or *magnificent*. People *become rich* or *are wealthy*. With comparative words *gadal* means *surpass*. The intensive denotes *make great*, *exalt*, *honor*, or *promote*. It denotes *raising*, *caring for*, or *training* youth. One *makes* or *lets grow*. One *proclaims greatness* or *thinks highly* of someone. An intensive passive verb means *nurtured*. The causative means *make great* or *large* and describes *exalting*, *increasing*, *magnifying*, or *enlarging something*. It appears as *show great* kindness or *give great* wisdom. It means *do great* or *catastrophic* things and connotes *boast*, *boastfully mock*, or *threaten*. One is *arrogant* or *acts arrogantly*. He *rises up* against. He *exalts* or *magnifies* himself, *appears superior*, or *triumphs*. Additionally, the reflexive means *display greatness*.

the hands of his two daughters. Then they brought him out and left him outside the city.

¹⁷As soon as the angels got them outside, one of them^A said, "Run for your lives! Don't look back and don't stop anywhere on the plain! Run to the mountains, or you will be swept away!"

¹⁸But Lot said to them, "No, my lords^B—please. ¹⁹Your servant has indeed found favor in your sight, and you have shown me great kindness by saving my life. But I can't run to the mountains; the disaster will overtake me, and I will die. ²⁰Look, this town is close enough for me to run to. It is a small place. Please let me go there—it's only a small place, isn't it?—so that I can survive."

²¹And he said to him, "All right,^C I'll grant your request^D about this matter too and will not demolish the town you mentioned. ²²Hurry up! Run there, for I cannot do anything until you get there." Therefore the name of the city is Zoar.^{E,a}

²³The sun had risen over the land when Lot reached Zoar. ²⁴Then out of the sky the Lord

^a19:22 Gn 14:2
^b19:24 Dt 29:23; Ps 11:6; Is 13:19; Jr 20:16; Ezk 16:49-50; Lk 17:28-29; 2Pt 2:6-8; Jd 7
^c19:26 Lk 17:32
^d19:27 Gn 18:22

rained burning sulfur on Sodom and Gomorrah from the Lord.^b ²⁵He demolished these cities, the entire plain, all the inhabitants of the cities, and whatever grew on the ground. ²⁶But his wife looked back and became a pillar of salt.^c

²⁷Early in the morning Abraham went to the place where he had stood before the Lord.^d ²⁸He looked down toward Sodom and Gomorrah and all the land of the plain, and he saw that smoke was going up from the land like the smoke of a furnace. ²⁹So it was, when God destroyed the cities of the plain, He remembered Abraham and brought Lot out of the middle of the upheaval when He demolished the cities where Lot had lived.

The Origin of Moab and Ammon

³⁰Lot departed from Zoar and lived in the mountains along with his two daughters, because he was afraid to live in Zoar. Instead, he and his two daughters lived in a cave. ³¹Then the firstborn said to the younger, "Our father is old, and there is no man in the land to sleep with us as is the custom of all the land. ³²Come,

^A19:17 LXX, Syr, Vg read *outside, they*   ^B19:18 Or *My Lord,* or *My lords*   ^C19:21 Or *Look!*   ^D19:21 Lit *I will lift up your face*
^E19:22 In Hb, the name Zoar is related to the phrase "small place" in v. 20; its original name was Bela; Gn 14:2.

had to **destroy** the **place** as God had directed. The men who had entered into binding agreements to marry Lot's virgin

Both of Lot's daughters became pregnant (19:36), resulting in the births of Moab, whose name sounds like the Hebrew phrase "From Father," and Ben-ammi, "Son of My People." Moab was father of the Moabites and Ben-ammi was father of the Ammonites. Many of Israel's neighbors who lived to the east, including the Edomites (from the line of Esau), were distant relatives.

daughters proved themselves unworthy of salvation because they rejected Lot's message.

19:15-22 Lot and his family apparently disbelieved the angels' warnings as well, because the next morning they were still in **the city**. The family was literally saved **because of the Lord's compassion** as the angels **grabbed the hands of** each family member. Like Abraham (18:23-32), Lot negotiated a deal with God to save his life. As with Abraham, God graciously granted the **request** and spared a wicked village for the sake of the righteous people in it. Prior to this time **Zoar** (lit "Small") was named Bela (14:2).

19:23-25 The **Lord rained burning sulfur** (lit "sulfur and fire"). As in Noah's day, the fatal instrument of judgment against sinners came **out of the sky**. No natural explanation (e.g., volcano) is suggested, only a supernatural one: it came **from the Lord**. Perhaps the asphalt pits (14:10) were ignited, adding to the destruction.

19:26 The disobedience of Lot's **wife** brought about one of the most mysterious deaths in the Bible as she **became a pillar of salt**—perhaps becoming permanently entombed in one of the many halite formations in this region.

19:27-29 The destruction was so complete that thick **smoke** like that of a **furnace** was still billowing up 24 hours later. Nevertheless, Lot had been saved because God **remembered Abraham** and acted in consideration of His covenantal relationship with him (18:19).

19:30-38 The **cave** where Lot and his daughters moved to was probably east of the Dead Sea. Isolation and their knowledge of the detestable ways of the men of the region convinced Lot's daughters that there was **no man in the land to sleep with** them (i.e., to make them pregnant). Consequently, they schemed to "give life to seed from our father" (**preserve our father's line**).

let's get our father to drink wine so that we can sleep with him and preserve our father's line." [33] So they got their father to drink wine that night, and the firstborn came and slept with her father; he did not know when she lay down or when she got up.

[34] The next day the firstborn said to the younger, "Look, I slept with my father last night. Let's get him to drink wine again tonight so you can go sleep with him and we can preserve our father's line." [35] That night they again got their father to drink wine, and the younger went and slept with him; he did not know when she lay down or when she got up.

[36] So both of Lot's daughters became pregnant by their father. [37] The firstborn gave birth to a son and named him Moab. [A] He is the father of the Moabites of today. [a] [38] The younger also gave birth to a son, and she named him Ben-ammi. [B] He is the father of the Ammonites of today. [b]

Sarah Rescued from Abimelech

20 From there Abraham traveled to the region of the *Negev and settled between Kadesh and Shur. While he lived in Gerar, [c] [2] Abraham said about his wife Sarah, "She is my sister." [d] So Abimelech king of Gerar had Sarah brought to him.

[3] But God came to Abimelech in a dream by night and said to him, "You are about to die because of the woman you have taken, for she is a married woman." [c]

[4] Now Abimelech had not approached her, so he said, "Lord, would You destroy a nation even though it is innocent? [5] Didn't he himself say to me, 'She is my sister'? And she herself said, 'He is my brother.' I did this with a clear conscience [D] and *clean [E] hands."

[6] Then God said to him in the dream, "Yes, I know that you did this with a clear conscience. [F] I have also kept you from sinning against Me. Therefore I have not let you touch her. [7] Now return the man's wife, for he is a prophet, [e] and he will pray for you and you

[a]19:37 Dt 2:9
[b]19:38 Dt 2:19
[c]20:1 Gn 26:1,6
[d]20:2 Gn 12:13; 26:7
[e]20:7 1Sm 7:5; 2Kg 5:11; Jb 42:8
[f]20:9 Gn 12:19; 26:9
[g]20:11 Neh 5:15; Pr 16:6
[h]20:13 Gn 12:1
[i]Gn 12:13; 20:5
[j]20:15 Gn 13:9; 34:10; 47:6
[k]20:17 Nm 12:13; 21:7; Jms 5:16
[l]21:1 Gn 17:16; 18:10; Gl 4:23

will live. But if you do not return her, know that you will certainly die, you and all who are yours."

[8] Early in the morning Abimelech got up, called all his servants together, and personally [G] told them all these things, and the men were terrified.

[9] Then Abimelech called Abraham in and said to him, "What have you done to us? How did I sin against you that you have brought such enormous *guilt on me and on my kingdom? You have done things to me that should never be done." [f] [10] Abimelech also said to Abraham, "What did you intend when you did this thing?"

[11] Abraham replied, "I thought, 'There is absolutely no *fear of God in this place. [g] They will kill me because of my wife.' [12] Besides, she really is my sister, the daughter of my father though not the daughter of my mother, and she became my wife. [13] So when God had me wander from my father's house, [h] I said to her: Show your loyalty to me wherever we go and say about me: 'He's my brother.'" [i]

[14] Then Abimelech took sheep and cattle and male and female slaves, gave them to Abraham, and returned his wife Sarah to him. [15] Abimelech said, "Look, my land is before you. [j] Settle wherever you want." [H] [16] And he said to Sarah, "Look, I am giving your brother 1,000 pieces of silver. It is a verification of your honor [I] to all who are with you. You are fully vindicated."

[17] Then Abraham prayed to God, [k] and God healed Abimelech, his wife, and his female slaves so that they could bear children, [18] for the LORD had completely closed all the wombs in Abimelech's household on account of Sarah, Abraham's wife.

The Birth of Isaac

21 The LORD came to Sarah as He had said, and the LORD did for Sarah what He had promised. [l] [2] Sarah became pregnant and bore a son to Abraham in his old age, at the

[A]19:37 = From My Father   [B]19:38 = Son of My People   [C]20:3 Lit is possessed by a husband   [D]20:5 Lit with integrity of my heart   [E]20:5 Lit cleanness of my   [F]20:6 Lit with integrity of your heart   [G]20:8 Lit in their ears   [H]20:15 Lit Settle in the good in your eyes   [I]20:16 Lit a covering of the eyes

This passage does not explicitly condemn drunkenness or incest; it doesn't have to. Every Israelite reader would have known these were sins to be avoided, because two of Israel's most troublesome enemies were spawned as a result of Lot's drunken actions.

20:1-2 Abraham traveled from Mamre to Gerar, a Philistine settlement west of the Dead Sea between Kadesh and Shur, perhaps to get farther away from the devastated area where Sodom had been. Then, less than three months after God had promised that Sarah would bear Abraham a son (18:10), the patriarch gave his wife to Abimelech! Abraham

had previously told pharaoh that his wife was his sister (12:12-15); later his son would try the same trick (26:7).

20:3-8 God in His mercy intervened to keep His promise regarding Sarah (18:10) from being destroyed by Abraham's foolish act. In addition to warning Abimelech that Sarah was married, the Lord had also created a health crisis in his household, causing all the other women to become temporarily sterile (v. 18). Because Abimelech had acted with a clear conscience and clean hands—despite accepting Sarah into his harem—God would not destroy Gerar's governmental leadership and thus undermine the nation.

appointed time God had told him.[a] [3]Abraham
named his son who was born to him—the
one Sarah bore to him—Isaac.[b] [4]When his
son Isaac was eight days old, Abraham circumcised him, as God had commanded him.[c]
[5]Abraham was 100 years old when his son
Isaac was born to him.[d]

[6]Sarah said, "God has made me laugh, and
everyone who hears will laugh with me."[A,e]
[7]She also said, "Who would have told Abraham that Sarah would nurse children? Yet I
have borne a son for him[B] in his old age."

Hagar and Ishmael Sent Away

[8]The child grew and was weaned, and
Abraham held a great feast on the day Isaac
was weaned. [9]But Sarah saw the son mocking[C]—the one Hagar the Egyptian had borne
to Abraham.[f] [10]So she said to Abraham, "Drive
out this slave with her son, for the son of
this slave will not be a coheir with my son
Isaac!"[g]

[11]Now this was a very difficult thing for[D]
Abraham because of his son. [12]But God said
to Abraham, "Do not be concerned[E] about
the boy and your slave. Whatever Sarah says
to you, listen to her, because your •offspring
will be traced through Isaac.[h] [13]But I will also
make a nation of the slave's son[i] because he is
your offspring."

[14]Early in the morning Abraham got up,
took bread and a waterskin, put them on
Hagar's shoulders, and sent her and the boy
away.[F] She left and wandered in the Wilderness of Beer-sheba. [15]When the water in the
skin was gone, she left the boy under one of
the bushes. [16]Then she went and sat down
nearby, about a bowshot away, for she said, "I
can't bear to watch the boy die!" So as she sat
nearby, she[G] wept loudly.[j]

[17]God heard the voice of the boy, and the[H]
angel of God called to Hagar from heaven and
said to her, "What's wrong, Hagar? Don't be
afraid, for God has heard the voice of the boy
from the place where he is. [18]Get up, help the
boy up, and support him, for I will make him
a great nation." [19]Then God opened her eyes,[k]
and she saw a well of water. So she went and
filled the waterskin and gave the boy a drink.
[20]God was with the boy, and he grew; he settled in the wilderness and became an archer.
[21]He settled in the Wilderness of Paran, and
his mother got a wife for him from the land
of Egypt.

Abraham's Covenant with Abimelech

[22]At that time Abimelech, accompanied by
Phicol the commander of his army,[l] said to
Abraham, "God is with you in everything you
do.[m] [23]Swear to me by God here and now, that
you will not break an agreement with me or
with my children and descendants. As I have
been loyal to you, so you will be loyal to me
and to the country where you are a foreign
resident."

[a]21:2 Gn 17:21; 18:10,14; Heb 11:11
[b]21:3 Gn 17:19
[c]21:4 Gn 17:10, 12; Ac 7:8
[d]21:5 Gn 17:1, 17; Rm 4:19
[e]21:6 Gn 18:12-15
[f]21:9 Gn 16:1,15; Gl 4:29
[g]21:10 Gl 4:30
[h]21:12 Rm 9:7; Heb 11:18
[i]21:13 Gn 16:10; 21:18; 25:12-18
[j]21:16 Jr 6:26; Am 8:10
[k]21:19 Nm 22:31; 2Kg 6:17-18,20; Lk 24:16,31
[l]21:22 Gn 20:2; 26:1,26
[m]Gn 26:28

[A]21:6 Isaac = He laughs; Gn 17:19 [B]21:7 Sam, Tg Jonathan; MT omits *him* [C]21:9 LXX, Vg add *Isaac her son* [D]21:11 Lit *was very bad in the eyes of* [E]21:12 Lit *Let it not be bad in your eyes* [F]21:14 To "send away" a woman = divorce her; Dt 24:1. To "send away" a slave = free her; Dt 15:13. [G]21:16 LXX reads *the boy* [H]21:17 Or *an*

Abraham is the first person to be called a **prophet** in the OT, though Enoch, who lived before him, is called a prophet in the NT (Jd 14). As Abraham's intercession with God had saved Lot's life (Gn 18:23-32; 19:29), so now his prayer for Abimelech would save his life.

21:5 Though **Abraham was 100 years old** at Isaac's birth, at least four preflood patriarchs had fathered children when they were older than he (5:6,18,25,28).

21:8-10 The Bible does not indicate Isaac's age when he **was weaned**. In some cultures children receive nourishment from their mother into their fifth year; beyond age two this provides comfort more than nourishment. When the day came for Isaac to be weaned, **Abraham held a great feast** to assist the child psychologically in taking this step. During the party, however, Ishmael was **mocking** Isaac. The apostle Paul understood this to mean he was persecuting Isaac (Gl 4:29). "**Drive out**" (Hb *garash*) is the same term used to describe the expulsions of Adam and Cain following their sins (3:24; 4:14).

21:11-13 It was **a very difficult thing for Abraham** (lit "it was very bad in Abraham's eyes") to expel his firstborn son from the household. However, God's guidance and comforting assurances enabled Abraham to do the right thing. Because Ishmael was Abraham's **offspring**, God would not allow the child to die in the wilderness; instead, God would **make** him **a nation**. And though Isaac was not Abraham's firstborn, the patriarch's **offspring** would be **traced through** his lineage.

21:14-19 Abraham's love and concern for Hagar and Ishmael are reflected in his diligence—getting up **early** and giving them provisions. The banished pair wandered in **the Wilderness of Beer-sheba**, an area some 20 miles west of the southern end of the Dead Sea. When Hagar and Ishmael ran out of water, Ishmael almost died, perhaps of heatstroke. Overwhelmed with grief, Hagar placed him in the shadow of **one of the bushes** and then went about **a bowshot away**—just far enough to avoid hearing his **voice** as he lay dying. Though Hagar may not have known that where there is large vegetation in a desert there is also a high water table, **God opened her eyes** to the fact that **a well of water** was nearby. God had providentially directed her wanderings and given her a demonstration of His faithfulness.

21:20-21 Honoring His promises to Abraham (v. 13; 17:20) and Hagar (21:18), God protected Ishmael, who eventually settled in **the Wilderness of Paran**, west of the Gulf of Aqaba in the northern Sinai Desert. Hagar, who was herself an Egyptian (16:3), got her son an Egyptian wife. Ishmael would produce 12 sons (25:13-15).

21:22-24 Isaac's miraculous birth and the success of Abraham's prayer (20:17) convinced **Abimelech** that God was

²⁴And Abraham said, "I swear it." ²⁵But Abraham complained to Abimelech because of the water well that Abimelech's servants had seized.ᵃ

²⁶Abimelech replied, "I don't know who did this thing. You didn't report anything to me, so I hadn't heard about it until today."

²⁷Abraham took sheep and cattleᴬ and gave them to Abimelech, and the two of them made a covenant.ᵇ ²⁸Abraham separated seven ewe lambs from the flock. ²⁹And Abimelech said to Abraham, "Why have you separated these seven ewe lambs?"

³⁰He replied, "You are to accept the seven ewe lambs from my hand so that this actᴮ will serve as my witness that I dug this well." ³¹Therefore that place was called Beer-shebaᶜ,ᶜ because it was there that the two of them swore an oath. ³²After they had made a covenant at Beer-sheba, Abimelech and Phicol, the commander of his army, left and returned to the land of the Philistines.

³³Abraham planted a tamarisk tree in Beersheba, and there he called on the name of •Yahweh, the Everlasting God.ᵈ ³⁴And Abraham lived as a foreigner in the land of the Philistines for many days.

The Sacrifice of Isaac

22 After these things God tested Abrahamᵉ and said to him, "Abraham!"

"Here I am," he answered.

²"Take your son," He said, "your only son Isaac, whom you love,ᶠ go to the land of Moriah,ᵍ and offer him there as a •burnt offering on one of the mountains I will tell you about."

³So Abraham got up early in the morning,ʰ saddled his donkey, and took with him two of his young men and his son Isaac. He split wood for a burnt offering and set out to go to the place God had told him about. ⁴On the third dayⁱ Abraham looked up and saw the place in the distance. ⁵Then Abraham said to his young men, "Stay here with the donkey. The boy and I will go over there to worship; then we'll come back to you." ⁶Abraham took the wood for the burnt offering and laid it on his son Isaac.ʲ In his hand he took the fire

Cross references (center column)
ᵃ21:25 Gn 26:15,18,20-22
ᵇ21:27 Gn 26:31
ᶜ21:31 Gn 26:33
ᵈ21:33 Ps 45:6; 48:14; 90:2; 93:2; Is 40:28; Jr 10:10; Rm 16:26; Heb 13:8
ᵉ22:1 Dt 8:2,16; 1Co 10:13; Heb 11:17; Jms 1:12-14; 1Pt 1:6-7
ᶠ22:2 Gn 22:12,16; Jr 6:26; Am 8:10; Mk 12:6; Lk 7:12; Jn 3:16; 1Jn 4:9
ᵍ2Ch 3:1
ʰ22:3 Jos 3:1
ⁱ22:4 Ex 19:11,16; Jos 9:17; Jdg 20:30; 2Sm 1:2; 1Kg 12:12; 2Kg 20:5; Est 5:1; Hs 6:2; Mt 17:23
ʲ22:6 Jn 19:17

ᴬ21:27 A covenant or treaty was regularly ratified by animal sacrifice (Gn 8:20–9:9; 15:9-17; Ex 24:8) and often involved an exchange of gifts (1Kg 15:19; Hs 12:1). The animals here could serve both purposes. ᴮ21:30 Lit *that it* ᶜ21:31 = Well of the Oath, or Seven Wells

---

with the patriarch **in everything**. Fearing that Abraham, who had hundreds of trained fighters in his camp (14:14), might mount a successful attack on Gerar, Abimelech and his military commander Phicol asked Abraham to **swear** that he would never **break an agreement** of peace with their community. Abraham calmed their fears by making an oath of peace.

21:25-32 Having relieved their worries about war, the patriarch then expressed his own concerns about water rights. Though Abimelech's group had wronged the patriarch, Abraham gave **sheep and cattle** to Abimelech as part of a formal **covenant**. This gift, reminiscent of Abimelech's gift to Abraham earlier (20:14), was probably used in part for the animal sacrifices offered up when a covenant was established. Abimelech's acceptance of the additional gift of **seven ewe lambs** obligated him to recognize that the **well** that Abraham's men had **dug** would not be seized. The name **Beer-sheba** is a wordplay, meaning both "Well of Oath" and "Well of Seven."

21:33-34 In recognition of God's good gifts, including a son who would carry the bloodline forward into the future, **Abraham planted a tamarisk tree**, a tree with many branches and small leaves, growing 20 to 30 feet high. He also worshiped **Yahweh** as **the Everlasting God** (Hb *'el 'olam*) in recognition of the perpetuity of God's promises to Abraham.

22:1-2 Abraham's ultimate test of obedience to God is described in 22:1-19, a section known in the Hebrew tradition as the *Akedah* (lit "the binding," v. 9). The Hebrew verb *nissah*, translated as **tested**, means "to prove the quality of," not "to entice to do wrong." God used this event to affirm the sterling character of Abraham's faith by giving him the incredibly difficult task of sacrificing his son Isaac in **the land of Moriah**, i.e., the Jerusalem area (2Ch 3:1). Pagans in Canaan during the OT period regularly practiced child sacrifice by making them pass through the fire (2Kg 16:3) to give them as food to their gods (Ezk 23:37). With this command God was asking Abraham to demonstrate that he was as committed to the Lord God as pagans were to their gods.

22:3-4 Confirmation of Abraham's amazing trust in God is found first in the fact that he was up before sunrise (**early in the morning**) the next day to begin the journey. His diligence in going **to the place God had told him about** contrasts sharply with Jonah's actions (Jnh 1:3). Traveling from

nissah

Hebrew Pronunciation	[nis SAH]
HCSB Translation	test
Uses in Genesis	1
Uses in the OT	36
Focus passage	Genesis 22:1

The verb *nissah* describes *testing* that one gives oneself (Ec 2:1), other people (1Kg 10:1), or various aspects of life (Ec 7:23). Most OT usage depicts either God's *testing* of man or the reverse. Man's *testing* of God is almost always due to lack of faith. People forget what God has already done for them (Ps 95:9). They are complaining, rebellious, provocative, and full of excessive desires (Ex 17:2; Ps 78:17-18,41,56). God forbade Israel to *test* Him this way (Dt 6:16). God, in contrast, *tested* Israel for the purpose of advancing its welfare (Dt 8:16). He *tested* the Israelites to see what was in their hearts (2Ch 32:31), whether they would obey (Ex 16:4) and love (Dt 13:3) Him. So the psalmist invites God to *test* him (Ps 26:2). Passive-reflexive verbs mean *attempt* (Dt 4:34), *try* (Jb 4:2), *venture* (Dt 28:56), or *be used to* (1Sm 17:39).

and the sacrificial knife, [A] and the two of them walked on together.

[7] Then Isaac spoke to his father Abraham and said, "My father."

And he replied, "Here I am, my son."

Isaac said, "The fire and the wood are here, but where is the lamb for the burnt offering?"

[8] Abraham answered, "God Himself will provide [B,a] the lamb for the burnt offering, my son." Then the two of them walked on together.

[9] When they arrived at the place that God had told him about, Abraham built the altar there and arranged the wood. He bound his son Isaac [c] and placed him on the altar [b] on top of the wood. [10] Then Abraham reached out and took the knife to slaughter his son.

[11] But the Angel of the Lord called to him from heaven and said, "Abraham, Abraham!"

He replied, "Here I am."

[12] Then He said, "Do not lay a hand on the boy or do anything to him. For now I know that you •fear God, since you have not withheld your only son from Me." [c] [13] Abraham looked up and saw a ram [D] caught in the thicket by its horns. So Abraham went and took the ram and offered it as a burnt offering in place of his son. [14] And Abraham named that place The Lord Will Provide, [E] so today it is said: "It will be provided [F] on the Lord's mountain."

[15] Then the Angel of the Lord called to Abra-

ham a second time from heaven [16] and said, "By Myself I have sworn," [d] this is the Lord's declaration: "Because you have done this thing and have not withheld your only son, [G] [17] I will indeed bless you [e] and make your •offspring as numerous as the stars of the sky [f] and the sand on the seashore. [g] Your offspring will possess the gates of their enemies. [h] [18] And all the nations of the earth will be blessed [H] by your offspring [i] because you have obeyed My command."

[19] Abraham went back to his young men, and they got up and went together to Beer-sheba. And Abraham settled in Beer-sheba.

Rebekah's Family

[20] Now after these things Abraham was told, "Milcah also has borne sons to your brother Nahor: [j] [21] Uz his firstborn, his brother Buz, Kemuel the father of Aram, [22] Chesed, Hazo, Pildash, Jidlaph, and Bethuel." [23] And Bethuel fathered Rebekah. [k] Milcah bore these eight to Nahor, Abraham's brother. [24] His concubine, whose name was Reumah, also bore Tebah, Gaham, Tahash, and Maacah.

Sarah's Burial

23 Now Sarah lived 127 years; these were all the years of her life. [2] Sarah died in Kiriath-arba (that is, Hebron [l]) in the land

[a] 22:8 Gn 22:14
[b] 22:9 Heb 11:17; Jms 2:21
[c] 22:12 Rm 8:32
[d] 22:16 Ps 105:9; Lk 1:73; Heb 6:13
[e] 22:17 Heb 6:14
[f] Gn 15:5; 26:4; Jr 33:22; Heb 11:12
[g] Gn 13:16; 32:12
[h] Gn 24:60
[i] 22:18 Gn 12:3; 26:4; Ac 3:25; Gl 3:8
[j] 22:20 Gn 11:29
[k] 22:23 Gn 24:15
[l] 23:2 Gn 35:27; Jos 14:15; 15:13; 21:11; Jdg 1:10

[A] 22:6 The same word is used in Jdg 19:29 and Pr 30:14.   [B] 22:8 Lit see   [C] 22:9 Or *Isaac hand and foot*   [D] 22:13 Some Hb mss, Sam, LXX, Syr, Tg; other Hb mss read *saw behind him a ram*   [E] 22:14 Or *Yahweh-yireh*   [F] 22:14 Or *He will be seen*   [G] 22:16 Sam, LXX, Syr, Vg add *from Me*   [H] 22:18 Or *will bless themselves,* or *will find blessing*

Beer-sheba, it was not until **the third day** that Abraham reached the Jerusalem area.

22:5-8 Evidence that Abraham believed God could raise Isaac from the dead (Heb 11:17-18) is found in his comment, **we'll come back**. Abraham carried the most dangerous elements of the sacrifice—**the fire and the sacrificial knife**—himself, perhaps as a sign of his protective love for Isaac. Ignorant of God's command and surprised that his father would forget the most important element in an animal sacrifice, Isaac asked Abraham where **the lamb** (Hb *seh* also means "sheep") was. Abraham's faith-filled response was that **God Himself** would **provide the lamb** ("sheep").

22:9-10 Abraham followed the standard procedure for a burnt offering involving a living being. In describing his preparation, the Bible emphasizes only Abraham's systematic acts of obedience, omitting any mention of Abraham's or Isaac's feelings.

22:11-12 Just before the knife was put to Isaac's neck, **the Angel of the Lord** spared **him**. The patriarch had passed the test, providing experiential evidence that he feared **God** more than he loved his **only son**.

22:13-14 Exactly as Abraham had predicted (v. 8), God had miraculously provided a sheep—and the most prized variety, **a ram**. To memorialize the event Abraham named that place **The Lord Will Provide** (Hb *yahweh yir'eh*).

22:15-18 As the **Angel** (meaning "Messenger") **of the Lord** who had the Lord's authority, the divine emissary delivered a second message (v. 12), this one in the first person. Because Abraham had passed the "priorities test" by obeying God and not withholding his **only son**, the Lord would **indeed bless** him with offspring, victory, land, and goodwill. Since there is nothing greater, God swears by Himself (cp. Ex 32:13; Is 45:23; Jr 22:5; 49:13). Ironically, since Abraham was willing to accept the loss of his covenant offspring, God would make those **offspring as numerous as the stars of the sky and the sand on the seashore**. They would **possess** the fortified city entrance **gates**—and thus the cities—**of their enemies**, a promise of both military victory and expanded territory. But more than being feared as conquerors, Abraham's offspring would be recognized as a fountainhead of blessing for **all the nations of the earth**.

22:20-24 Genesis next presents the offspring of Abraham's **brother Nahor** through his wife **Milcah** and his concubine **Reumah**. This brief section prepares the reader for the events of chapter 24 by introducing **Bethuel** and identifying him as the father of **Rebekah**, Isaac's future wife.

23:1-2 Indicative of Sarah's importance is the fact that she is the only woman in the Bible whose age at the time of her death is reported. **Kiriath-arba** ("City of Four") was the name for the city later known as **Hebron**.

of Canaan, and Abraham went to mourn for Sarah and to weep for her.

³Then Abraham got up from beside his dead wife and spoke to the Hittites:[A] ⁴“I am a foreign resident among you.[a] Give me a burial site among you so that I can bury my dead.”[B,b]

⁵The Hittites replied to Abraham,[C] ⁶“Listen to us, lord.[D] You are God's chosen one[E] among us. Bury your dead in our finest burial place.[F] None of us will withhold from you his burial place for burying your dead.”

⁷Then Abraham rose and bowed down to the Hittites, the people of the land. ⁸He said to them, “If you are willing for me to bury my dead, listen to me and ask Ephron son of Zohar on my behalf ⁹to give me the cave of Machpelah that belongs to him; it is at the end of his field. Let him give it to me in your presence, for the full price, as a burial place.”

¹⁰Ephron was sitting among the Hittites. So in the presence[G] of all the Hittites who came to the •gate of his city,[c] Ephron the Hittite answered Abraham: ¹¹“No, my lord. Listen to me. I give you the field, and I give you the cave that is in it. I give it to you in the presence[H] of my people. Bury your dead.”

¹²Abraham bowed down to the people of the land ¹³and said to Ephron in the presence[G] of the people of the land, “Please listen to me.

Let me pay the price of the field. Accept it from me, and let me bury my dead there.”

¹⁴Ephron answered Abraham and said to him, ¹⁵“My lord, listen to me. Land worth 400 •shekels of silver[d]—what is that between you and me? Bury your dead.” ¹⁶Abraham agreed with Ephron, and Abraham weighed out to Ephron the silver that he had agreed to in the presence[G] of the Hittites: 400 shekels of silver at the current commercial rate.[e] ¹⁷So Ephron's field[f] at Machpelah near Mamre—the field with its cave and all the trees anywhere within the boundaries of the field—became ¹⁸Abraham's possession in the presence of all the Hittites who came to the gate of his city. ¹⁹After this, Abraham buried his wife Sarah in the cave of the field at Machpelah near Mamre (that is, Hebron) in the land of Canaan. ²⁰The field with its cave passed from the Hittites to Abraham[g] as a burial place.

A Wife for Isaac

24 Abraham was now old, getting on in years,[i,h] and the LORD had blessed him in everything. ²Abraham said to his servant, the elder of his household who managed all he owned, “Place your hand under my thigh,[i] ³and I will have you swear by the LORD, God of heaven and God of earth, that you will not take a wife for my son from the daughters of

Cross references (center column)
[a]23:4 Gn 17:8; Lv 25:23; 1Ch 29:15; Ps 39:12; 105:12; Heb 11:9,13
[b]Gn 49:30; Ac 7:16
[c]23:10 Gn 34:20,24; Ru 4:1
[d]23:15 Ex 30:13; Ezk 45:12
[e]23:16 Jr 32:9; Zch 11:12
[f]23:17 Gn 25:9; 49:29–32; 50:13
[g]23:20 Jr 32:10–14
[h]24:1 Gn 18:11; Jos 13:1; 23:1–2; 1Kg 1:1
[i]24:2 Gn 47:29; Ex 1:5

[A]23:3 Or sons of Heth; also in vv. 5,7,10,16,18,20   [B]23:4 Lit dead from before me   [C]23:5 Lit Abraham, saying to him   [D]23:6 Lit my lord   [E]23:6 Or prince of God, or mighty prince   [F]23:6 Or finest graves   [G]23:10,13,16 Lit ears   [H]23:11 Lit in the eyes of the sons   [i]24:1 Lit days

---

23:3-6 When a family member died in Abraham's culture, the survivors were obliged to preserve the deceased's bones, ideally in a cave where all other family members could later have their remains preserved. Abraham owned no land in Canaan, so he had to obtain **a burial site** from the Hittites to bury Sarah. Like the Philistines earlier (21:22), the Hittites recognized that Abraham was **God's chosen one among** them. Perhaps in order to guarantee the favor of Abraham's God, they offered Abraham the right to use the region's **finest burial place**.

23:7-11 In the market square at the **gate of** Kiriath-arba, Abraham showed his respect for the Hittites, placing his head at the level of their feet. The patriarch was wealthy and highly respected, but he played the role of one who was unworthy to speak to the landowner whose property he desired. Accordingly, he asked the Hittites to **ask Ephron** on his **behalf** for the right to purchase **the cave of Machpelah**. Though Abraham was a skilled bargainer (18:23-32), he offered to pay **the full price** for the property. This gesture signaled respect for the Hittites and the desire to avoid undignified haggling. Matching Abraham's decorum, **Ephron the Hittite** spoke directly to Abraham and offered to **give** him not only **the cave**, but also **the field**.

23:12-18 With both parties in agreement, Abraham **bowed** again respectfully and repeated his willingness to **pay the** full **price of the field**—even though he did not yet know how much that would be. Four hundred **shekels of silver**—perhaps the price of eight healthy adult male slaves (Lv 27:3)—

may or may not have been a reasonable valuation. Either way, **Abraham agreed** to the price. The amount represented a weight that in Moses' time equaled 10 pounds; we do not know how much it was at the Hittites' **commercial rate**. The piece of land was particularly valuable because it contained both a **cave** and **trees**.

23:19-20 Following the successful negotiations, **Abraham buried his wife Sarah in the cave . . . at Machpelah**. Others who would be buried there included Abraham, Isaac, Rebekah, Leah, and Jacob (49:31; 50:13).

24:1-9 Abraham, now 140 years of age, had been **blessed** by **the LORD** in everything, but one thing was missing—a worthy wife for his 40-year-old son to insure the continuance of the covenant line. Based on his experience with the inhabitants of Canaan—whether the Sodomites or the Philistines—Abraham did not want Isaac to marry a woman **from the daughters of the Canaanites**. Instead, she must come from his relatives hundreds of miles away in northwest Mesopotamia. Abraham himself was too old to make the journey back, so he summoned his most trusted **servant**, perhaps Eliezer (15:2), to fulfill the task. Finding the right wife for Isaac required divine help, so Abraham had his servant take an oath **by the LORD, God of heaven and God of earth**, and also to **place** his **hand under** Abraham's **thigh**, the bodily zone associated with Abraham's posterity.

This act symbolically underscored the importance of the task for Abraham's future and that of his clan. With great

the Canaanites among whom I live, [a] [4]but will go to my land and my family to take a wife for my son Isaac."

[5]The servant said to him, "Suppose the woman is unwilling to follow me to this land? Should I have your son go back to the land you came from?"

[6]Abraham answered him, "Make sure that you don't take my son back there. [7]The LORD, the God of heaven, [b] who took me from my father's house and from my native land, [c] who spoke to me and swore to me, 'I will give this land to your •offspring' [d]—He will send His angel before you, [e] and you can take a wife for my son from there. [8]If the woman is unwilling to follow you, then you are free from this oath to me, [f] but don't let my son go back there."

[9]So the servant placed his hand under his master Abraham's thigh and swore an oath to him concerning this matter.

[10]The servant took 10 of his master's camels and departed with all kinds of his master's goods in hand. Then he set out for Nahor's town Aram-naharaim. [11]He made the camels kneel beside a well of water outside the town at evening. This was the time when the women went out to draw water.

[12]"LORD, God of my master Abraham," he prayed, "give me success today, [g] and show kindness to my master Abraham. [13]I am standing here [h] at the spring where the daughters of the men of the town are coming out to draw water. [14]Let the girl to whom I say, 'Please lower your water jug so that I may drink,' and who responds, 'Drink, and I'll water your camels also'—let her be the one You have appointed for Your servant Isaac. By this

I will know that You have shown kindness to my master."

[15]Before he had finished speaking, there was Rebekah—daughter of Bethuel son of Milcah, [i] the wife of Abraham's brother Nahor—coming with a jug on her shoulder. [16]Now the girl was very beautiful, [j] a young woman who had not known a man intimately. She went down to the spring, filled her jug, and came up. [17]Then the servant ran to meet her and said, "Please let me have a little water from your jug."

[18]She replied, "Drink, my lord." She quickly lowered her jug to her hand and gave him a drink. [19]When she had finished giving him a drink, she said, "I'll also draw water for your camels until they have had enough to drink." [A] [20]She quickly emptied her jug into the trough and hurried to the well again to draw water. She drew water for all his camels [21]while the man silently watched her to see whether or not the LORD had made his journey a success.

[22]After the camels had finished drinking, the man took a gold ring weighing half a •shekel, and for her wrists two bracelets weighing 10 shekels of gold. [23]"Whose daughter are you?" he asked. "Please tell me, is there room in your father's house for us to spend the night?"

[24]She answered him, "I am the daughter of Bethuel son of Milcah, whom she bore to Nahor." [25]She also said to him, "We have plenty of straw and feed and a place to spend the night."

[26]Then the man bowed down, worshiped the LORD, [k] [27]and said, "Praise the LORD, the God of my master Abraham, who has not withheld His kindness and faithfulness from my master. [l]

Cross references:
[a] 24:3 Gn 26:34,35; 27:46; Dt 7:3; 2Co 6:14
[b] 24:7 2Ch 36:23; Ezr 1:2
[c] Gn 12:1
[d] Gn 12:7; 13:15; 15:18; Ex 32:13
[e] Gn 16:7; 21:17; 22:11; Ex 23:20,23
[f] 24:8 Jos 2:17-20
[g] 24:12 Gn 27:20
[h] 24:13-14 Gn 24:43-44
[i] 24:15 Gn 11:29; 22:23
[j] 24:16 Gn 12:11; 26:7; 29:17
[k] 24:26 Ex 4:31
[l] 24:27 Ru 2:20; Ezr 9:9; Neh 9:17

[A]24:19 Lit *they are finished drinking*

---

faith and prophetic insight the patriarch promised that God would **send His angel before** the servant so that he could **take a wife for** Isaac from the clan. As part of the concern for his posterity, Abraham also warned his servant not to let Isaac abandon the promised land—and with it God's covenant—by going **back there** himself to Aram-naharaim.

24:10-11 The chief **servant** and several other slaves (v. 32) took **goods** reflective of Abraham's wealth, which could be used to pay the bride price for Isaac's wife. The journey from Beer-sheba to **Aram-naharaim**—located somewhere in northwest Mesopotamia—could have taken a couple of weeks. The **town of Nahor** could mean that Nahor was the name of the village or that it was Nahor's hometown. Nahor was the name of Abraham's brother and grandfather (11:25-26), thus suggesting that this village was populated by Abraham's relatives.

24:12-14 Being in the ancestral village at the best time and spot to interact with eligible girls, the servant still needed divine help to accomplish his task. He had faith that God had **appointed** a worthy young woman from this area to marry **Isaac** and would show **kindness to** his **master**. He prayed

to the Lord, suggesting a test of hospitality and service. A thirsty camel can drink as much as 30 gallons of water in 15 minutes. Since 10 camels accompanied the servant (v. 10), it is possible that the young woman would have had to draw 300 hundred gallons of water (equal to 2,500 lbs) from the spring to pass the servant's test.

24:15-22 Before the servant **finished speaking**, God more than answered his prayer (Is 65:24) with the arrival of **Rebekah**. Not only was she the granddaughter of **Abraham's brother Nahor** and a virgin, but she was also **very beautiful**. With courtesy and enthusiasm she passed the servant's test. As a generous reward for her selfless act, the servant gave Rebekah a **gold** nose **ring** (Hb *nezem*) and two gold bracelets weighing **10 shekels** (four ounces).

24:23-27 The servant received the best possible answers to two more questions: Rebekah was indeed **the daughter** of Abraham's nephew **Bethuel**, and the men and their camels could **spend the night** with her family. Overwhelmed with gratitude, the servant **bowed down, worshiped the LORD**, and praised Him for His acts of **kindness** (Hb *chesed*; "covenant faithfulness") **and faithfulness**.

As for me, the LORD has led me on the journey to the house of my master's relatives."

[28] The girl ran and told her mother's household about these things. [29] Now Rebekah had a brother named Laban,[a] and Laban ran out to the man at the spring. [30] As soon as he had seen the ring and the bracelets on his sister's wrists, and when he had heard his sister Rebekah's words—"The man said this to me!"—he went to the man. He was standing there by the camels at the spring.

[31] Laban said, "Come, you who are blessed by the LORD.[b] Why are you standing out here? I have prepared the house and a place for the camels." [32] So the man came to the house, and the camels were unloaded.[c] Straw and feed were given to the camels, and water was brought to wash his feet and the feet of the men with him.

[33] A meal was set before him, but he said, "I will not eat until I have said what I have to say."

So Laban said, "Please speak."

[34] "I am Abraham's servant," he said. [35] "The LORD has greatly blessed my master, and he has become rich. He has given him sheep and cattle, silver and gold, male and female slaves, and camels and donkeys. [36] Sarah, my master's wife, bore a son to my master in her[A] old age,[d] and he has given him everything he owns.[e] [37] My master put me under this oath: 'You will not take a wife for my son from the daughters of the Canaanites in whose land I live [38] but will go to my father's household and to my family to take a wife for my son.' [39] But I said to my master, 'Suppose the woman will not come back with me?' [40] He said to me, 'The LORD before whom I have walked[f] will send His angel with you and make your journey a success, and you will take a wife for my son from my family and from my father's household. [41] Then you will be free from my oath if you go to my family and they do not give her to you—you will be free from my oath.'

[42] "Today when I came to the spring, I prayed: LORD, God of my master Abraham, if only You will make my journey successful! [43] I am standing here at a spring. Let the virgin who comes out to draw water, and I say to her: Please let me drink a little water from your jug, [44] and who responds to me, 'Drink, and I'll draw water for your camels also'—let her be the woman the LORD has appointed for my master's son.

[45] "Before I had finished praying silently,[g] there was Rebekah coming with her jug on her shoulder, and she went down to the spring and drew water. So I said to her: Please let me have a drink. [46] She quickly lowered her jug from her shoulder and said, 'Drink, and I'll water your camels also.' So I drank, and she also watered the camels. [47] Then I asked her: Whose daughter are you? She responded, 'The daughter of Bethuel son of Nahor, whom Milcah bore to him.' So I put the ring on her nose[h] and the bracelets on her wrists. [48] Then I bowed down, worshiped the LORD, and praised the LORD, the God of my master Abraham, who guided me on the right way to take the granddaughter of my master's brother for his son. [49] Now, if you are going to show kindness and faithfulness to my master,[i] tell me; if not, tell me, and I will go elsewhere."[B]

[50] Laban and Bethuel answered, "This is from the LORD; we have no choice in the matter.[C,j] [51] Rebekah is here in front of you. Take her and go, and let her be a wife for your master's son, just as the LORD has spoken."

[52] When Abraham's servant heard their words, he bowed to the ground before the LORD. [53] Then he brought out objects of silver and gold, and garments, and gave them to Rebekah. He also gave precious gifts to her brother and her mother. [54] Then he and the men with him ate and drank and spent the night.

When they got up in the morning, he said, "Send me to my master."

---

a24:29 Gn 25:20; 28:2; 29:5
b24:31 Gn 26:29; Jdg 17:2; Ru 3:10
c24:32 Gn 43:24; Jdg 19:21
d24:36 Gn 21:2
eGn 25:5
f24:40 Gn 17:1; 1Sm 2:30; 1Kg 2:4; 8:23; 2Kg 20:3; Ps 116:9
g24:45 1Sm 1:13
h24:47 Ezk 16:11-12
i24:49 Gn 47:29; Jos 2:14
j24:50 Gn 31:24,29; 2Sm 13:22

A24:36 Sam, LXX read his   B24:49 Lit go to the right or to the left   C24:50 Lit we cannot say to you anything bad or good

24:28-33 The generosity of Abraham's servant generated a response in kind from Rebekah's **mother's household**. The level of hospitality provided by Rebekah and her family rivals the hospitality Abraham showed his visitors in 18:3-8.

24:34-49 In the longest recorded speech by a slave in the OT (238 words in the Hebrew), **Abraham's servant** recounted in detail three relevant matters: how **the LORD** had **greatly blessed** Abraham, why a young woman was needed from Bethuel's **household**, and how God had revealed that He had **appointed** Rebekah for his **master's son**. Then the servant gave them the opportunity **to show kindness and faithfulness** to Abraham by permitting Rebekah to accompany him back to his master's household.

24:50-53 When **Laban and Bethuel**—the ruling adult males in the clan—were presented with evidence that **the LORD** had **spoken** and had selected Rebekah for Isaac, they released her to **be a wife** for Abraham's **son**. As the bride price the servant then presented **gifts to Rebekah . . . her brother, and her mother**.

24:54-61 The next **morning**, Abraham's servant asked Bethuel **not** to **delay** the return to Abraham, even though it was customary to spend several days with the wife's family members (Jdg 19:8-10). Rebekah's statement, **I will go**, expressed her willingness to leave immediately, not her acceptance of the marriage arrangement—that was already settled. As a wedding gift the family gave Rebekah **the one**

⁵⁵ But her brother and mother said, "Let the girl stay with us for about 10 days. ᴬ Then she ᴮ can go."

⁵⁶ But he responded to them, "Do not delay me, since the Lᴏʀᴅ has made my journey a success. Send me away so that I may go to my master."

⁵⁷ So they said, "Let's call the girl and ask her opinion." ᶜ

⁵⁸ They called Rebekah and said to her, "Will you go with this man?"

She replied, "I will go." ⁵⁹ So they sent away their sister Rebekah with the one who had nursed and raised her, ᴰ,ᵃ and Abraham's servant and his men.

⁶⁰ They blessed Rebekah, saying to her:

Our sister, may you become
thousands upon ten thousands. ᵇ
May your offspring possess
the gates of their ᴱ enemies. ᶜ

⁶¹ Then Rebekah and her female servants got up, mounted the camels, and followed the man. So the servant took Rebekah and left. ⁶² Now Isaac was returning from Beer-lahai-roi, ᶠ,ᵈ for he was living in the •Negev region. ⁶³ In the early evening Isaac went out to walk ᴳ in the field, and looking up he saw camels coming. ⁶⁴ Rebekah looked up, and when she saw Isaac, she got down from her camel ⁶⁵ and asked the servant, "Who is that man in the field coming to meet us?"

The servant answered, "It is my master." So she took her veil and covered herself. ⁶⁶ Then the servant told Isaac everything he had done.

⁶⁷ And Isaac brought her into the tent of his mother Sarah and took Rebekah to be his wife. Isaac loved her, and he was comforted after his mother's death. ᵉ

Abraham's Other Wife and Sons

25 Now Abraham had taken another wife, whose name was Keturah, ᶠ ² and she bore him Zimran, Jokshan, Medan, Midian, Ishbak, and Shuah. ³ Jokshan fathered Sheba and Dedan. Dedan's sons were the Asshurim, Letushim, and Leummim. ⁴ And Midian's sons were Ephah, Epher, Hanoch, Abida, and Eldaah. All these were sons of Keturah. ⁵ Abraham gave everything he owned to Isaac. ᵍ ⁶ And Abraham gave gifts to the sons of his concubines, but while he was still alive he sent them eastward, away from his son Isaac, to the land of the East. ʰ

Abraham's Death

⁷ This is the length of Abraham's life: ᴴ 175 years. ⁸ He took his last breath and died at a ripe old age, ⁱ old and contented, ⁱ and he was gathered to his people. ʲ ⁹ His sons Isaac and Ishmael buried him in the cave of Machpelah ᵏ near Mamre, in the field of Ephron son of Zohar the Hittite. ¹⁰ This was the field that Abraham bought from the Hittites. ˡ Abraham was buried there with his wife Sarah. ¹¹ After Abraham's death, God blessed his son Isaac, who lived near Beer-lahai-roi. ᵐ

Ishmael's Family Records

¹² These are the family records ⁿ of Abraham's son Ishmael, ᵒ whom Hagar the Egyptian,

Cross references (center column)

ᵃ24:59 Gn 35:8
ᵇ24:60 Gn 17:16
ᶜGn 22:17
ᵈ24:62 Gn 16:14; 25:11
ᵉ24:67 Gn 23:1-2
ᶠ25:1-4 1Ch 1:32-33
ᵍ25:5 Gn 24:35-36
ʰ25:6 Gn 21:14
ⁱ25:8 Gn 15:15; 47:8-9
ʲGn 25:17; 35:29; 49:29,33
ᵏ25:9 Gn 23:17-18; 49:29-30; 50:13
ˡ25:10 Gn 23:16; 50:13
ᵐ25:11 Gn 16:14; 24:62
ⁿ25:12 Gn 2:4; 25:19
ᵒ25:12-16 1Ch 1:29-31

ᴬ24:55 Lit *us a few days or 10*   ᴮ24:55 Or *you*   ᶜ24:57 Lit *mouth*   ᴰ24:59 Lit *with her wet nurse;* Gn 35:8   ᴱ24:60 Lit *his*
ᶠ24:62 = A Well of the Living One Who Sees Me   ᴳ24:63 Or *pray,* or *meditate;* Hb obscure   ᴴ25:7 Lit *And these are the days of the years of the lives of Abraham that he lived*   ⁱ25:8 Sam, LXX, Syr read *full of days*

---

who had nursed her, a beloved slave named Deborah (35:8) who attended to her for many years. The clan also gave her a prophetic blessing, commending both fruitfulness and victory for her offspring.

24:62-66 After a journey of hundreds of miles on camelback, the caravan returned to Isaac's home. Rebekah **saw Isaac** for the first time on the day she married him. As was apparently the custom on the wedding day, Rebekah **covered herself** with a **veil** before meeting her husband. Before presenting Rebekah to Isaac, Abraham's servant told Isaac **everything he had done** and what God had done for him.

24:67 As part of the marital ritual Isaac brought Rebekah **into** what had been his mother Sarah's **tent**. This would now become her home, which marked her as the clan matriarch, the most powerful woman in the group. There Isaac and Rebekah consummated the marriage. Having waited 40 years to marry, **Isaac loved** his wife deeply, and was finally **comforted after his mother's death**, which had occurred three years earlier (17:17; 23:1; 25:20).

25:1-4 Probably after Sarah's death **Abraham took another**

wife with concubine status, **Keturah**. In partial fulfillment of God's promise that he would have descendants as numerous as the stars (15:5; 22:17), Abraham fathered six additional sons.

25:5-6 Abraham was generous to Isaac because Keturah, like Hagar, was a concubine; she and her sons had less status than Sarah and Isaac. Accordingly, Abraham only **gave gifts** to Keturah's sons, while he gave Isaac **everything he owned**. Because God had given the land of Canaan only to Isaac's descendants, Abraham sent Keturah's sons **eastward** to the Arabian peninsula.

25:7-10 Abraham lived some 37 years after Sarah's death and died at the age of **175**. The biblical writer's comment that Abraham **was gathered to his people** hints at the Israelites' early belief in an afterlife. The patriarch's two oldest sons **Isaac** (now 75; see 21:5) and **Ishmael** (now 89; see 16:16) took the responsibility of burying their father.

25:12-18 The family records of Abraham's son Ishmael, the seventh of the eleven (Hb) *toledoth* sections of Genesis (see note at 5:1), complement the family records of Abraham's

Sarah's slave, bore to Abraham. [13] These are the names of Ishmael's sons; their names according to the family records are: Nebaioth, Ishmael's firstborn, then Kedar, Adbeel, Mibsam, [14] Mishma, Dumah, Massa, [15] Hadad, Tema, Jetur, Naphish, and Kedemah. [16] These are Ishmael's sons, and these are their names by their villages and encampments: 12 leaders [A,a] of their clans. [B] [17] This is the length [C] of Ishmael's life: 137 years. He took his last breath and died, and was gathered to his people. [18] And they [D] settled from Havilah to Shur, which is opposite Egypt as you go toward Asshur. He [E] lived in opposition to [F] all his brothers. [b]

The Birth of Jacob and Esau

[19] These are the family records of Isaac son of Abraham. Abraham fathered Isaac. [c] [20] Isaac was 40 years old when he took as his wife Rebekah [d] daughter of Bethuel the Aramean from Paddan-aram [e] and sister of Laban the Aramean. [f] [21] Isaac prayed to the LORD on behalf of his wife because she was childless. [g] The LORD heard his prayer, and his wife Rebekah conceived. [h] [22] But the children inside her struggled with each other, and she said, "Why is this happening to me?" [G] So she went to inquire of the LORD. [i] [23] And the LORD said to her:

> Two nations are in your womb;
> two people will come from you
>   and be separated.
> One people will be stronger
>   than the other, [j]
> and the older will serve
>   the younger. [k]

[24] When her time came to give birth, there

were indeed twins in her womb. [25] The first one came out red-looking, [H] covered with hair [I] like a fur coat, and they named him Esau. [I] [26] After this, his brother came out grasping Esau's heel with his hand. [m] So he was named Jacob. [J,n] Isaac was 60 years old when they were born.

Esau Sells His Birthright

[27] When the boys grew up, Esau became an expert hunter, an outdoorsman, [K] but Jacob was a quiet man who stayed at home. [L] [28] Isaac loved Esau because he had a taste for wild game, but Rebekah loved Jacob. [o]

[29] Once when Jacob was cooking a stew, Esau came in from the field exhausted. [30] He said to Jacob, "Let me eat some of that red stuff, because I'm exhausted." That is why he was also named Edom. [M]

[31] Jacob replied, "First sell me your birthright."

[32] "Look," said Esau, "I'm about to die, so what good is a birthright to me?"

[33] Jacob said, "Swear to me first." So he swore to Jacob and sold his birthright to him. [34] Then Jacob gave bread and lentil stew to Esau; he ate, drank, got up, and went away. So Esau despised his birthright. [p]

The Promise Reaffirmed to Isaac

26 There was another famine in the land in addition to the one that had occurred in Abraham's time. [q] And Isaac went to Abimelech, king of the Philistines, at Gerar. [r] [2] The LORD appeared to him and said, "Do not go down to Egypt. Live in the land that I tell

Cross references (center column)

a 25:16 Gn 17:20
b 25:18 Gn 16:12
c 25:19 Mt 1:2
d 25:20 Gn 24:15,29,67
e 25:22 Gn 22:23
f Gn 24:29
g 25:21 Gn 11:30; 29:31; Ex 23:26; Jdg 13:2-3; 1Sm 2:5; Jb 24:21; Is 54:1; Lk 1:36; 23:29; Gl 4:27; Heb 11:11
h 1Sm 1:17; 1Ch 5:20; 2Ch 33:13; Ezr 8:23; Ps 127:3; Rm 9:10
i 25:22 1Sm 9:9; 10:22
j 25:23 2Sm 8:14; Ob 18-21
k Gn 27:29; Mal 1:2-3; Rm 9:12
l 25:25 Gn 27:11,16,23
m 25:26 Hs 12:3
n Gn 27:36
o 25:28 Gn 27:4-9
p 25:34 Heb 12:16-17
q 26:1 Gn 12:10
r Gn 20:2

Text notes

A 25:16 Or chieftains B 25:16 Or peoples C 25:17 Lit And these are the years D 25:18 LXX, Vg read he E 25:18 = Ishmael and his descendants F 25:18 Or He settled down alongside of G 25:22 Lit If thus, why this I H 25:25 In Hb, the word red-looking sounds like "Edom"; Gn 32:3. I 25:25 In Hb, the word hair sounds like "Seir"; Gn 32:3. J 25:26 = He Grasps the Heel K 25:27 Lit a man of the field L 25:27 Lit man living in tents M 25:30 = Red

Study notes

son Isaac (25:19). The lesser status of Ishmael's family line compared to Isaac's is reflected in the section's relatively small size (7 verses vs. 364 verses) and the notation that Ishmael's mother **Hagar** was the **slave** of Isaac's mother Sarah.

Ishmael fathered 12 sons, all of whom became **leaders of their clans**. **Their villages and encampments** stretched **from Havilah to Shur**—the region between the modern Suez canal and the Wadi el-Arish. Later their settlements, the best known of which was **Kedar**, would extend into the northwest Arabian Peninsula; these would be involved in incense trade. During his **137 years**, Ishmael would also father two daughters, Mahalath and Basemath (28:9; 36:3). In keeping with the prophetic word (16:12), Ishmael **lived in opposition to all his brothers**.

25:19 The family records of Isaac son of Abraham, the eighth of the eleven (Hb) *toledoth* sections in Genesis (see note at 5:1), extend from 25:19 through 35:29.

25:27-28 The differences between Esau and Jacob, already apparent at birth, became more pronounced as **the boys grew up**. Esau was a rough-and-tumble **hunter** and **outdoorsman** (lit "man of rural regions"); Jacob was **quiet** and **stayed at home** (lit "dweller in tents"). The differences between the boys highlighted a division between the parents: **Isaac**, something of an outdoorsman himself (24:63), **loved** his rugged son **Esau**, while **Rebekah loved** her more domestic son **Jacob**, even teaching him how to cook.

25:29-34 Esau's impatient, appetite-driven life contrasted sharply with Jacob's shrewd, calculating character. Esau willingly traded his **birthright**—the right of the firstborn son to a double portion (or perhaps two-thirds) of the inheritance (Dt 21:17)—for the chance to **eat some . . . red stuff**. Because of his fateful decision, Esau picked up the alternate name **Edom** ("Red"), which would be carried by the people group stemming from him (32:3). And because Jacob had made him **swear** to **sell** his birthright, the decision could not be undone.

you about; [3]stay in this land as a foreigner, and I will be with you and bless you.[a] For I will give all these lands to you and your *offspring,[b] and I will confirm the oath that I swore to your father Abraham.[c] [4]I will make your offspring as numerous as the stars of the sky, I will give your offspring all these lands, and all the nations of the earth will be blessed[A] by your offspring,[d] [5]because Abraham listened to My voice and kept My mandate, My commands, My statutes, and My instructions."[e] [6]So Isaac settled in Gerar.

Isaac's Deception

[7]When the men of the place asked about his wife, he said, "She is my sister,"[f] for he was afraid to say "my wife," thinking,[g] "The men of the place will kill me on account of Rebekah, for she is a beautiful woman."[h] [8]When Isaac had been there for some time, Abimelech king of the Philistines looked down from the window and was surprised to see[B] Isaac caressing his wife Rebekah.

[9]Abimelech sent for Isaac and said, "So she is really your wife! How could you say, 'She is my sister'?"

Isaac answered him, "Because I thought I might die on account of her."

[10]Then Abimelech said, "What is this you've done to us? One of the people could easily have slept with your wife, and you would have brought *guilt on us."[i] [11]So Abimelech warned all the people with these words: "Whoever harms this man or his wife will certainly die."

Conflicts over Wells

[12]Isaac sowed seed in that land, and in that year he reaped[C] a hundred times what was

sown. The Lord blessed him,[j] [13]and the man became rich and kept getting richer until he was very wealthy. [14]He had flocks of sheep, herds of cattle, and many slaves, and the Philistines were envious of him. [15]The Philistines stopped up all the wells that his father's slaves had dug in the days of his father Abraham,[k] filling them with dirt. [16]And Abimelech said to Isaac, "Leave us, for you are much too powerful for us."[D]

[17]So Isaac left there, camped in the Valley of Gerar, and lived there. [18]Isaac reopened the water wells that had been dug in the days of his father Abraham and that the Philistines had stopped up after Abraham died. He gave them the same names his father had given them. [19]Then Isaac's slaves dug in the valley and found a well of spring[E] water there. [20]But the herdsmen of Gerar quarreled with Isaac's herdsmen and said, "The water is ours!" So he named the well Quarrel[F] because they quarreled with him.[l] [21]Then they dug another well and quarreled over that one also, so he named it Hostility.[G] [22]He moved from there and dug another, and they did not quarrel over it. He named it Open Spaces[H] and said, "For now the Lord has made room for us, and we will be fruitful in the land."

The Lord Appears to Isaac

[23]From there he went up to Beer-sheba, [24]and the Lord appeared to him that night and said, "I am the God of your father Abraham.[m] Do not be afraid, for I am with you.[n] I will bless you and multiply your offspring because of My servant Abraham."

[25]So he built an altar there,[o] called on the

[a] 26:3 Gn 12:2; 26:24; 28:15; 31:3
[b] Gn 12:7; 13:15; 15:18
[c] Gn 22:16-18; Ps 105:9
[d] 26:4 Gn 12:3; 18:18; Ac 3:25; Gl 3:8
[e] 26:5 Lv 18:30; Dt 11:1
[f] 26:7 Gn 12:13; 20:5
[g] Pr 29:25
[h] Gn 24:16
[i] 26:10 Gn 20:8-10
[j] 26:12 Gn 24:1,35
[k] 26:15 Gn 21:30
[l] 26:20 Gn 21:25
[m] 26:24 Gn 17:7-8; 24:12; Ex 3:6; Ac 7:32
[n] Gn 21:17; Ex 20:20; 2Kg 6:16; Is 41:10; 43:1,5
[o] 26:25 Gn 8:20; 12:7; 13:18; 35:7; Ex 17:15; Jos 8:30

[A]26:4 Or will bless themselves   [B]26:8 Or and he looked and behold—   [C]26:12 Lit found   [D]26:16 Or are more numerous than we are   [E]26:19 Lit living   [F]26:20 Or Esek   [G]26:21 Or Sitnah   [H]26:22 Or Rehoboth

---

26:1-6 Isaac and his clan experienced the second recorded famine of the Bible (12:10). To avoid the effects of the famine, Isaac sought refuge in the region where his father had once lived (20:1). The **Abimelech** mentioned here may or may not be the same one with whom Abraham negotiated a treaty (21:27). The name may have been given to each succeeding king within a dynastic family. Isaac must have been tempted to leave the famine-ravaged land and **go down to** well-watered **Egypt** as his father had done (12:10), but **the Lord** warned him **not** to do this. To inherit the promises of **offspring**, land, and blessing that God had given Abraham, Isaac had to **stay in** the **land as a foreigner**.

26:7-11 Isaac would have had to negotiate with the Philistines to enjoy certain privileges among them. As a result he might have to provide a wife for someone's harem. If the person asked for Rebekah (and she was, after all, the most important female in the clan and **a beautiful woman**), Isaac might be killed if he refused. Thus Isaac, like Abraham before him (12:13; 20:2), told outsiders that his wife was his **sister**. Isaac's lie was uncovered when he was caught **caressing** (lit

"laughing/playing with") **Rebekah**. **Abimelech**, as the supreme authority in the region, **sent for Isaac** and demanded an explanation. Isaac patterned his defense after his father's (20:11); he feared he **might die on account of** his wife.

26:12-22 Because **the Lord blessed him**, Isaac enjoyed amazing success as a farmer, achieving the highest level of agricultural productivity recorded in the Bible (cp. Mt 13:8). The Philistines viewed Isaac as a rich foreigner with a reputation for trickery, and they wanted him off their land. Isaac complied, moving to the nearby **Valley of Gerar**, reopening old wells that had been filled with dirt and having his slaves dig three new ones to accommodate his increased herds and flocks without threatening the Philistines. However, as in the days of Abraham (Gn 21:25) the contentious Philistines claimed the rights to the first two wells, giving rise to the names "Esek" (**Quarrel**) and "Sitnah" (**Hostility**). When at last the Philistines **did not quarrel** over a well, Isaac rejoiced and **named** the well "Rehoboth" (**Open Spaces**).

26:23-25 Isaac's clan moved about 25 miles southeast to **Beer-sheba**, where his father had once lived (21:31). There

name of *Yahweh, and pitched his tent there. Isaac's slaves also dug a well there. ᵃ

Covenant with Abimelech

²⁶ Now Abimelech came to him from Gerar with Ahuzzath his adviser and Phicol the commander of his army. ᵇ ²⁷ Isaac said to them, "Why have you come to me? You hated me and sent me away from you."

²⁸ They replied, "We have clearly seen how the LORD has been with you. We think there should be an oath between two parties—between us and you. Let us make a covenant with you: ²⁹ You will not harm us, just as we have not harmed you but have only done what was good to you, sending you away in peace. You are now blessed by the LORD." ᶜ

³⁰ So he prepared a banquet for them, and they ate and drank. ³¹ They got up early in the morning and swore an oath to each other. ᴬ,ᵈ Then Isaac sent them on their way, and they left him in peace. ³² On that same day Isaac's slaves came to tell him about the well they had dug, saying to him, "We have found water!" ᵉ ³³ He called it Sheba. ᴮ Therefore the name of the city is Beer-sheba ᶜ,ᶠ to this day.

Esau's Wives

³⁴ When Esau was 40 years old, he took as his wives Judith daughter of Beeri the Hittite, and Basemath daughter of Elon the Hittite. ᵍ ³⁵ They made life bitter ᴰ for Isaac and Rebekah. ʰ

The Stolen Blessing

27 When Isaac was old and his eyes were so weak that he could not see, ⁱ he called his older son Esau and said to him, "My son."

And he answered, "Here I am."

² He said, "Look, I am old and do not know the day of my death. ³ Take your hunting gear, your quiver and bow, and go out in the field to hunt some game for me. ʲ ⁴ Then make me a delicious meal that I love and bring it to me to eat, so that I can bless you before I die." ᵏ

⁵ Now Rebekah was listening to what Isaac said to his son Esau. So while Esau went to the field to hunt some game to bring in, ⁶ Rebekah said to her son Jacob, "Listen! I heard your father talking with your brother Esau. He said, ⁷ 'Bring me the game and make a delicious meal for me to eat so that I can bless you in the LORD's presence before I die.' ⁸ Now obey every order I give you, my son. ⁹ Go to the flock and bring me two choice young goats, and I will make them into a delicious meal for your father—the kind he loves. ¹⁰ Then take it to your father to eat so that he may bless you before he dies."

¹¹ Jacob answered Rebekah his mother, "Look, my brother Esau is a hairy man, but I am a man with smooth skin. ˡ ¹² Suppose my father touches me. Then I will be revealed to him as a deceiver and bring a curse rather than a blessing on myself."

¹³ His mother said to him, "Your curse be on me, my son. Just obey me and go get them for me."

¹⁴ So he went and got the goats and brought them to his mother, and his mother made the delicious food his father loved. ¹⁵ Then Rebekah took the best clothes of her older son Esau, which were in the house, and had her younger son Jacob wear them. ¹⁶ She put the skins of the young goats on his hands and the smooth

Cross references
ᵃ26:25 Gn 26:32
ᵇ26:26 Gn 21:22
ᶜ26:29 Gn 24:31; Ps 115:15
ᵈ26:31 Gn 21:31
ᵉ26:32 Gn 26:19
ᶠ26:33 Gn 21:30-31
ᵍ26:34 Gn 28:9; 36:2-3
ʰ26:35 Gn 27:46
ⁱ27:1 Gn 48:10; 1Sm 3:2
ʲ27:3 Gn 25:27-28
ᵏ27:4 Gn 27:19,25,31; 48:9,15-16; Dt 33:1; Heb 11:20
ˡ27:11 Gn 25:25

A 26:31 Lit *swore, each man to his brother*   **B** 26:33 Or *Shibah*   **C** 26:33 = Well of the Oath   **D** 26:35 Lit *And they became bitterness of spirit*

---

the LORD appeared to Isaac and reassured him at a time when the Philistines were making trouble. The Lord was with Isaac to **bless** him and **multiply** his **offspring**, in keeping with God's promises to **Abraham** (15:5; 17:2; 22:17). Isaac was the third patriarch to build **an altar** (besides Noah, 8:20; and Abraham, 12:7-8; 13:18; 22:9).

26:26-29 As with Abraham (21:22-23), God's blessing was clearly present on Isaac's life. The Philistine leaders believed that to oppose Isaac was to invite disaster from God and reprisals from members of Isaac's clan who felt they had been wronged. Thus they wanted to **make a covenant** with him.

26:30-33 Isaac's preparation of a **banquet** signified his acceptance of the treaty, which became official the next day when the parties **swore an oath** of non-aggression. That same day Isaac's slaves reported success in digging a fifth well, this one named **Sheba** (Hb *shiva'h*; "Seven"), similar to the Hebrew word for oath (*shevua'*) and confirming Abraham's name for Beer-sheba (21:31).

26:34-35 Esau married at the same age his father had

(25:20). His marriages to two pagan Hittites, **Judith** ("Praise") and **Basemath** ("Balsam/Spice"), expressed more of his animal-like nature (see note at 25:27-28). Esau's wives **made life bitter for Isaac and Rebekah**, most likely by being contentious about Jacob's favored status.

27:1-4 Isaac was now over 100 years old (see 25:26; 26:34). Though he would live to 180—at least 20 years beyond this point (35:28)—Isaac may have been sick at the time, since his vision was obviously poor and he was so concerned to bless **his older son Esau** before he died. The blessing given by a clan patriarch to his heir was of great significance since it formally conferred the right to rule over the clan following the patriarch's death. As with covenant-making (26:28-30), a patriarchal blessing was accompanied by a delicious meal.

27:5-17 Following Near Eastern tradition (18:9-10), Rebekah could not be in the immediate company of males—even family members—who were conducting business. However, she was **listening** to the men from nearby. After learning of Isaac's intentions for Esau, Rebekah came up with a

part of his neck. ¹⁷Then she handed the delicious food and the bread she had made to her son Jacob.

¹⁸When he came to his father, he said, "My father."

And he answered, "Here I am. Who are you, my son?"

¹⁹Jacob replied to his father, "I am Esau, your firstborn. I have done as you told me. Please sit up and eat some of my game so that you may bless me."

²⁰But Isaac said to his son, "How did you ever find it so quickly, my son?"

He replied, "Because the LORD your God worked it out for me."

²¹Then Isaac said to Jacob, "Please come closer so I can touch you, my son. Are you really my son Esau or not?"

²²So Jacob came closer to his father Isaac. When he touched him, he said, "The voice is the voice of Jacob, but the hands are the hands of Esau." ²³He did not recognize him, because his hands were hairy like those of his brother Esau; so he blessed him. ²⁴Again he asked, "Are you really my son Esau?"

And he replied, "I am."

²⁵Then he said, "Serve me, and let me eat some of my son's game so that I can bless you." Jacob brought it to him, and he ate; he brought him wine, and he drank.

²⁶Then his father Isaac said to him, "Please come closer and kiss me, my son." ²⁷So he came closer and kissed him. When Isaac smelled^A his clothes, he blessed him and said:

> Ah, the smell of my son
> is like the smell of a field
> that the LORD has blessed.
> ²⁸ May God give to you—
> from the dew of the sky^a
> and from the richness of the land^b—
> an abundance of grain and new wine. ^c

Cross references (center column):
a 27:28 Gn 27:39; Dt 32:2; 33:13,28; 2Sm 1:21; Pr 3:20; Is 18:4; Hs 14:5; Hg 1:10; Zch 8:12
bNm 18:12
cDt 7:13; Jl 2:19
d 27:29 Gn 25:23; Is 45:14; 49:7,23; 60:12-14
eGn 12:3; Nm 24:9
f27:34 Heb 12:17
g27:36 Gn 25:26,32-34

²⁹ May peoples serve you^d
and nations bow down to you.
Be master over your brothers;
may your mother's sons bow down
to you.
Those who curse you will be cursed,
and those who bless you
will be blessed. ^e

³⁰As soon as Isaac had finished blessing Jacob and Jacob had left the presence of his father Isaac, his brother Esau arrived from the hunt. ³¹He had also made some delicious food and brought it to his father. Then he said to his father, "Let my father get up and eat some of his son's game, so that you may bless me."

³²But his father Isaac said to him, "Who are you?"

He answered, "I am Esau your firstborn son."

³³Isaac began to tremble uncontrollably. "Who was it then," he said, "who hunted game and brought it to me? I ate it all before you came in, and I blessed him. Indeed, he will be blessed!"

³⁴When Esau heard his father's words, he cried out with a loud and bitter cry and said to his father, "Bless me too, my father!" ^f

³⁵But he replied, "Your brother came deceitfully and took your blessing."

³⁶So he said, "Isn't he rightly named Jacob? ^B,g For he has cheated me twice now. He took my birthright, and look, now he has taken my blessing." Then he asked, "Haven't you saved a blessing for me?"

³⁷But Isaac answered Esau: "Look, I have made him a master over you, have given him all of his relatives as his servants, and have sustained him with grain and new wine. What then can I do for you, my son?"

³⁸Esau said to his father, "Do you only have

---

^A27:27 Lit *smelled the smell of*   ^B27:36 = He Grasps the Heel

---

scheme to overturn the plans. Perhaps she did it because she remembered the decades-old prophecy about Jacob dominating his older brother (25:23).

With this the Bible paints a picture of a troubled family: Rebekah using **her son** (not "their son") to destroy her husband's plans, and Jacob agreeing to lie to his father and cheat his brother. A curse of an unexpected sort did result for both Jacob and Rebekah: their scheme forced Jacob to leave his father and mother (28:5), and the Bible gives no indication that Rebekah ever saw her favorite son again.

27:18-27a Isaac was blind, but he could still use his other senses in addition to his reasoning. To overcome this, Jacob used at least five different things to deceive his father: goatskins to make his **hands** seem rough and **hairy** (v. 23), the cooked goat his mother prepared (v. 25), his

brother's **clothes** in order to smell like Esau (v. 27), alcohol to impair his father's judgment (v. 25), and blatant lies (vv. 19,20,24). Jacob's craftiness paid off since his father **blessed him.**

27:27b-29 Isaac's blessing included four elements: agricultural prosperity (v. 28)—even as He had done for Isaac (26:12); international respect and success (27:29); a command directing Jacob to **be master over** the entire clan; and the transference of the protective provision of cursing and blessing that God had once given Jacob's grandfather Abraham (12:3).

27:31-38 Esau apparently had to awaken his blind father, who was confused at first, but **began to tremble uncontrollably** when he realized he had given someone other than Esau the right to rule the clan. Esau complained that Jacob had now **cheated** him **twice**, first gaining the double portion

one blessing, my father? Bless me too, my father!" And Esau wept loudly. [A]

³⁹ Then his father Isaac answered him:

> Look, your dwelling place will be
> away from the richness of the land,
> away from the dew of the sky above.
> ⁴⁰ You will live by your sword,
> and you will serve your brother.
> But when you rebel, [B]
> you will break his yoke
> from your neck.

Esau's Anger

⁴¹ Esau held a grudge against Jacob because of the blessing his father had given him. And Esau determined in his heart: "The days of mourning for my father are approaching; then I will kill my brother Jacob."

⁴² When the words of her older son Esau were reported to Rebekah, she summoned her younger son Jacob and said to him, "Listen, your brother Esau is consoling himself by planning to kill you. ⁴³ So now, my son, listen to me. Flee at once to my brother Laban in Haran, ⁴⁴ and stay with him for a few days until your brother's anger subsides— ⁴⁵ until your brother's rage turns away from you and he forgets what you have done to him. Then I will send for you and bring you back from there. Why should I lose you both in one day?"

⁴⁶ So Rebekah said to Isaac, "I'm sick of my life because of these Hittite women. [a] If Jacob marries a Hittite woman like one of them, [c] what good is my life?" [b]

Jacob's Departure

28 Isaac summoned Jacob, blessed him, and commanded him: "Don't take a wife from the Canaanite women. ² Go at once to Paddan-aram, to the house of Bethuel, your mother's father. Marry one of the daughters of Laban, your mother's brother. ³ May ·God Almighty bless you and make you fruitful and multiply you[c] so that you become an assembly of peoples. [d] ⁴ May God give you and your ·offspring the blessing of Abraham[e] so that you may possess the land where you live as a foreigner, the land God gave to Abraham."[f] ⁵ So Isaac sent Jacob to Paddan-aram, to Laban son of Bethuel the Aramean, the brother of Rebekah, the mother of Jacob and Esau.

⁶ Esau noticed that Isaac blessed Jacob and sent him to Paddan-aram to get a wife there. When he blessed him, Isaac commanded Jacob, "Do not marry a Canaanite woman." ⁷ And Jacob listened to his father and mother and went to Paddan-aram. ⁸ Esau realized that his father Isaac disapproved of the Canaanite women,[g] ⁹ so Esau went to Ishmael and married, in addition to his other wives, Mahalath daughter of Ishmael, Abraham's son. She was the sister of Nebaioth.

[a]27:46 Gn 26:34-35; 28:8
[b]Gn 24:3
[c]28:3 Gn 1:28
[d]Gn 48:4
[e]28:4 Gn 12:1-3
[f]Gn 12:7; 15:18
[g]28:8 Gn 24:3; 26:34-35; 27:46

[A]27:38 Lit *Esau lifted up his voice and wept*   [B]27:40 Hb obscure   [C]27:46 Lit *of these daughters of the land*

---

of inheritance (25:31-33), and now the clan's headship. **Jacob** (Hb *ya'aqov*), whose name sounds similar to words meaning "deceitfulness" (Hb *'aqevah*) and "to supplant/replace" (Hb *'aqav*), had lived up to his name. Having lost every desirable blessing, Esau begged his father to find some way to **bless** him, **too**.

27:39-40 Isaac's response to Esau was much shorter than Jacob's blessing (21 vs. 34 Hebrew words), and was more of an "anti-blessing." Creating an ironic wordplay with phrases from Jacob's blessing (v. 28), Isaac stated that Esau would live **away from the richness of the land** and **from the dew of the sky**. Jacob would "be master" (v. 29), but Esau would **serve**. Living a life of violence by the **sword**, Esau's only consolation was that he would someday **break** Jacob's **yoke from** his **neck**.

27:41-46 For a second time in this chapter, Rebekah intervened to change Jacob's destiny. Her latest plan was for Jacob to **stay with** his uncle Laban **in Haran**—hundreds of miles away—until Esau's **anger** subsided. Otherwise, she feared, she would **lose** both her sons **in one day**—Jacob by murder, Esau by capital punishment (9:6). The **few days**, however, turned out to be more than 20 years (31:38)!

28:1-2 As with Abraham in the previous generation, Isaac was concerned that his youngest son not **take a wife from the Canaanite women** (lit "daughters of Canaan"; cp. 24:3).

28:3-5 Before Jacob's departure Isaac extended to him two major covenant blessings: offspring and land. The bless-

ing of being **fruitful** was previously given to Adam (1:28), Noah and his sons (9:1,7), Abraham (17:6), and Ishmael (17:20). Isaac invoked it using the name "El Shaddai" (**God Almighty**), a name first revealed to Abraham (17:1; see note there). The second blessing was possession of **the land God gave to Abraham**, a blessing that only God could give. Hav-

---

'erets

Hebrew Pronunciation	[EHR ehtz]
HCSB Translation	land
Uses in Genesis	311
Uses in the OT	2,505
Focus passage	Genesis 28:4,12-14

'Erets is one of the most common and flexible OT nouns, whose meanings seem derived from the idea of *land* (Gn 2:5). Often it refers to nations such as the *land of Israel*. *'Erets* denotes *area, region, homeland, country,* or *earth,* the latter often in conjunction with "heaven" to represent the whole world (Gn 1:1; 20:1; 21:23; 30:25; 34:1). *'Erets* means *district* (1Ch 13:2). It is *soil* (Lv 27:30) or *dirt* (Jr 17:13) but may suggest the *land's produce* (Lv 27:30). *'Erets* can involve *distance* (Gn 35:16), the *surface of the ground* (Jdg 6:37), or *private property* (Gn 23:15). *'Erets* indicates *earth* (Ps 66:4) or *world* (Gn 41:57) as the inhabitants of the *earth.* It describes the depths of the *earth* (Is 44:23) and, with modifiers, the *underworld* (Ezk 26:20). "People of the *land*" can connote *common people* (Lv 4:27). "Field of the *land*" indicates *open fields* (Lv 25:31).

Jacob at Bethel

[10]Jacob left Beer-sheba and went toward Haran. [11]He reached a certain place and spent the night there because the sun had set. He took one of the stones from the place, put it there at his head, and lay down in that place. [12]And he dreamed: [a] A stairway was set on the ground with its top reaching heaven, and God's angels were going up and down on it.[b] [13]•Yahweh was standing there beside him,[A] saying, "I am Yahweh, [c] the God of your father Abraham and the God of Isaac. I will give you and your offspring the land that you are now sleeping on. [14]Your offspring will be like the dust of the earth,[d] and you will spread out toward the west, the east, the north, and the south. All the peoples on earth will be blessed through you and your offspring.[e] [15]Look, I am with you and will watch over you wherever you go. I will bring you back to this land,[f] for I will not leave you until I have done what I have promised you."

[16]When Jacob awoke from his sleep, he said, "Surely the LORD is in this place, and I did not know it."[g] [17]He was afraid and said, "What an awesome place this is! This is none other than the house of God. This is the gate of heaven."

[18]Early in the morning Jacob took the stone that was near his head and set it up as a marker. He poured oil on top of it [19]and named the place Bethel,[B] though previously the city was named Luz.[h] [20]Then Jacob made a vow:[i] "If God will be with me and watch over me on this journey, if He provides me with food to eat and clothing to wear, [21]and if I return safely to my father's house, [j] then the LORD will be my God. [k] [22]This stone that I have set up as a marker will be God's house, and I will give to You a tenth of all that You give me."[l]

Jacob Meets Rachel

29 Jacob resumed his journey[c] and went to the eastern country.[D,m] [2]He looked and saw a well in a field. Three flocks of sheep were lying there beside it because the sheep were watered from this well. A large stone covered the opening of the well. [3]When all the flocks[E] were gathered there, the shepherds would roll the stone from the opening of the well and water the sheep. The stone was then placed back on the well's opening.

[4]Jacob asked the men at the well, "My brothers! Where are you from?"

"We're from Haran," they answered.

[5]"Do you know Laban grandson of Nahor?" Jacob asked them.

They answered, "We know him."

[6]"Is he well?" Jacob asked.

"Yes," they said, "and here is his daughter Rachel, coming with his sheep."

[7]Then Jacob said, "Look, it is still broad daylight. It's not time for the animals to be gathered. Water the flock, then go out and let them graze."

[8]But they replied, "We can't until all the flocks have been gathered and the stone is rolled from the well's opening. Then we will water the sheep."

[9]While he was still speaking with them, Rachel came with her father's sheep, for she was a shepherdess. [10]As soon as Jacob saw his uncle Laban's daughter Rachel with his sheep,[F] he went up and rolled the stone from

---

a 28:12 Gn 41:1; Nm 12:6; Jb 33:15-16
b Jn 1:51
c 28:13 Gn 15:7; Ex 6:8
d 28:14 Gn 13:16
e Gn 12:3
f 28:15 Gn 48:21; Dt 30:3; 1Kg 8:34; Zph 3:20
g 28:16 Ex 3:4-6; Jos 5:13-15; Ps 139:7-12
h 28:19 Gn 35:6; 48:3; Jdg 1:23,26
i 28:20 Gn 31:13
j 28:21 Gn 33:18; Jdg 11:31; 2Sm 15:7-9
k Dt 26:17
l 28:22 Gn 14:20; Lv 27:30; Dt 14:22
m 29:1 Nm 23:7; Jdg 6:3

[A]28:13 Or *there above it*   [B]28:19 = House of God   [C]29:1 Lit *Jacob picked up his feet*   [D]29:1 Lit *the land of the children of the east*   [E]29:3 Sam, some LXX mss read *flocks and the shepherds*   [F]29:10 Lit *with the sheep of Laban his mother's brother*

---

ing received these blessings, Jacob left for his mother's ancestral home of **Paddan-aram**.

28:6-9 When **Esau noticed** that **his father Isaac disapproved** of the two **Canaanite women** he had married (26:34), he did not divorce them. Instead he added to them, taking his cousin **Mahalath daughter of Ishmael** as a third wife. Mahalath was also known as Basemath (36:3). Mahalath's brother **Nebaioth** was Ishmael's firstborn son (1Ch 1:29).

28:10-15 **Jacob** started northward on the approximately 500-mile journey to **Haran**. At the end of one of his first days he stopped in central Palestine and camped outdoors. That night God appeared to him. Perhaps the **stairway** (a better translation than "ladder") **he dreamed** of was a supernatural version of humanity's Tower of Babylon (11:4), with **God's angels**—and not sinful humans—using it to commute from heaven to earth. In the dream **Yahweh** transferred to Jacob all the essential elements of the promises given originally to Abraham and Isaac.

Key features from Abraham's era include: the gift of land (12:7; 13:17); the promise of offspring as numerous as the **dust of the earth** (cp. 13:16); and peoples being blessed through Jacob and his **offspring** (cp. 12:3; 18:18). As with his father Isaac, God promised He would be with him wherever he went (26:24) and bring him back to the promised land.

28:16-19 No other person in the OT is recorded as anointing a sacred stone; Jacob would do it twice (35:14). Jacob renamed the site **Bethel** ("House of God"), a name that would be retained throughout Israelite history (Jdg 1:23; Neh 11:31).

28:20-22 Jacob is the only patriarch to make **a vow**. Though his words can appear selfish, the vow may simply contain a request that God would carry out the implications of the promises made in verse 15. Years later Jacob would confess that God had indeed kept the terms of His promises (35:3).

29:1-6 Jacob arrived at Haran after an unspecified amount of time, stopping at **a well** just outside the town. The well was covered with **a large stone** to protect it from unauthorized use and wild animals.

29:7-12 Foreshadowing his exceptional shepherding skills (30:29-30), Jacob instructed the local shepherds on how to

the opening and watered his uncle Laban's sheep. [11] Then Jacob kissed Rachel and wept loudly. [A] [12] He told Rachel that he was her father's relative, Rebekah's son. She ran and told her father.

Jacob Deceived

[13] When Laban heard the news about his sister's son Jacob, he ran to meet him, hugged him, and kissed him. Then he took him to his house, and Jacob told him all that had happened.

[14] Laban said to him, "Yes, you are my own flesh and blood." [B,a]

After Jacob had stayed with him a month, [15] Laban said to him, "Just because you're my relative, should you work for me for nothing? Tell me what your wages should be."

[16] Now Laban had two daughters: the older was named Leah, and the younger was named Rachel. [17] Leah had ordinary [C] eyes, but Rachel was shapely and beautiful. [18] Jacob loved Rachel, so he answered Laban, "I'll work for you seven years for your younger daughter Rachel." [b]

[19] Laban replied, "Better that I give her to you than to some other man. Stay with me." [20] So Jacob worked seven years for Rachel, and they seemed like only a few days to him because of his love for her.

[21] Then Jacob said to Laban, "Give me my wife, for my time is completed. I want to sleep with [D] her." [22] So Laban invited all the men of the place to a feast. [23] That evening, Laban took his daughter Leah and gave her to Jacob, and he slept with her. [24] And Laban gave his slave Zilpah to his daughter Leah as her slave.

[a]29:14 Gn 2:23; 37:27; Jdg 9:2; 2Sm 5:1; 19:12-13; 1Ch 11:1
[b]29:18 Gn 30:26; 31:41; Hs 12:12
[c]29:30 Gn 31:41
[d]29:31 Gn 25:28; Dt 21:15-16; 22:13; 24:3; Lk 14:26; 16:13
[e]Gn 30:22
[f]Gn 11:30; 25:21; Jdg 13:2-3; 1Sm 2:5; Lk 1:36
[g]29:32 Gn 31:42; Ex 3:7; 4:31; Dt 26:7
[h]29:35 Gn 49:8; Mt 1:2

[25] When morning came, there was Leah! So he said to Laban, "What is this you have done to me? Wasn't it for Rachel that I worked for you? Why have you deceived me?"

[26] Laban answered, "It is not the custom in this place to give the younger daughter in marriage before the firstborn. [27] Complete this week of wedding celebration, and we will also give you this younger one in return for working yet another seven years for me."

[28] And Jacob did just that. He finished the week of celebration, and Laban gave him his daughter Rachel as his wife. [29] And Laban gave his slave Bilhah to his daughter Rachel as her slave. [30] Jacob slept with Rachel also, and indeed, he loved Rachel more than Leah. And he worked for Laban another seven years. [c]

Jacob's Sons

[31] When the LORD saw that Leah was unloved, [d] He opened her womb; [e] but Rachel was unable to conceive. [f] [32] Leah conceived, gave birth to a son, and named him Reuben, [E] for she said, "The LORD has seen my affliction; [g] surely my husband will love me now."

[33] She conceived again, gave birth to a son, and said, "The LORD heard that I am unloved and has given me this son also." So she named him Simeon. [F]

[34] She conceived again, gave birth to a son, and said, "At last, my husband will become attached to me because I have borne three sons for him." Therefore he was named Levi. [G]

[35] And she conceived again, gave birth to a son, and said, "This time I will praise the LORD." Therefore she named him Judah. [H,h] Then Leah stopped having children.

[A]29:11 Lit and he lifted his voice and wept   [B]29:14 Lit my bone and my flesh   [C]29:17 Lit tender   [D]29:21 Lit to go to   [E]29:32 = See, a Son; in Hb, the name Reuben sounds like "has seen my affliction."   [F]29:33 In Hb, the name Simeon sounds like "has heard."   [G]29:34 In Hb, the name Levi sounds like "attached to."   [H]29:35 In Hb, the name Judah sounds like "praise."

---

do their job properly. The apparent laziness of the shepherds—or weakness—is suggested by their unwillingness to remove the stone from the top of the well.

Jacob's actions contrasted sharply with those of the local shepherds. Inspired by the appearance of **Rachel**, Jacob **rolled the** heavy **stone** from the well's **opening** all by himself. His act of watering **his uncle Laban's sheep** is reminiscent of his mother's act of watering Abraham's camels years earlier (24:20). Rachel is the first **shepherdess** of the Bible (cp. Ex 2:16); the task of shepherding flocks was usually given to men. The first mention in the Bible of a man kissing a woman occurs in Gn 29:11; such actions were not normally performed in public.

29:13-20 In the ancient Near East, a male kissing another male in greeting signified acceptance of and respect for the other person (27:27; 45:15; Ex 18:7; 1Sm 10:1). Laban called Jacob **my own flesh and blood** and gave him the right to stay in the home permanently. Jacob was neither a son nor a slave, so it was appropriate to work out a suitable arrangement that compensated Laban for his provisions and

Jacob for his labor. It was not appropriate for Jacob to work **for nothing**, so it was agreed that Jacob would work for **seven years** for the right to marry **Rachel**.

This arrangement is reminiscent of a provision in the law of Moses that permitted certain slaves to work seven years for their freedom (Ex 21:2). Men did not buy wives in the strict sense of the word; however, they did customarily pay a bride-price (Gn 34:12; Ex 22:17; 1Sm 18:25) to their future wife's family to compensate them for the care and protection provided to the woman prior to her marriage.

29:21-23 Jacob, now almost 50 years old (25:24-26; 26:34-35; 27:46) after working for Laban seven years, informed Laban that it was time for him to **sleep with** Rachel. Arranging a weeklong wedding **feast**, Laban proceeded to cheat the family member who had cheated other people in the past (27:12-25,36). Instead of the expected younger daughter Rachel, Laban **gave** Leah **to Jacob**. In the darkness of the **evening** and with his bride concealed behind a veil (24:65), Jacob did not realize what had been done to him. Accordingly, he **slept with** Leah.

30 When Rachel saw that she was not bearing Jacob any children, she envied her sister. "Give me sons, or I will die!"[a] she said to Jacob.

[2] Jacob became angry with Rachel and said, "Am I in God's place, who has withheld children[A] from you?"

[3] Then she said, "Here is my slave Bilhah. Go sleep with her, and she'll bear children for me[B,b] so that through her I too can build a family." [4] So Rachel gave her slave Bilhah to Jacob as a wife, and he slept with her. [5] Bilhah conceived and bore Jacob a son. [6] Rachel said, "God has vindicated me; yes, He has heard me and given me a son," and she named him Dan.[c]

[7] Rachel's slave Bilhah conceived again and bore Jacob a second son. [8] Rachel said, "In my wrestlings with God,[D] I have wrestled with my sister and won," and she named him Naphtali.[E]

[9] When Leah saw that she had stopped having children, she took her slave Zilpah and gave her to Jacob as a wife. [10] Leah's slave Zil-pah bore Jacob a son. [11] Then Leah said, "What good fortune!"[F] and she named him Gad. [G]

[12] When Leah's slave Zilpah bore Jacob a second son, [13] Leah said, "I am happy that the women call me happy,"[c] so she named him Asher.[H]

[14] Reuben went out during the wheat harvest and found some mandrakes in the field.[d] When he brought them to his mother Leah, Rachel asked, "Please give me some of your son's mandrakes."

[15] But Leah replied to her, "Isn't it enough that you have taken my husband? Now you also want to take my son's mandrakes?"

"Well," Rachel said, "you can sleep with him tonight in exchange for your son's mandrakes."

[16] When Jacob came in from the field that evening, Leah went out to meet him and said, "You must come with me, for I have hired you with my son's mandrakes." So Jacob slept with her that night.

[17] God listened to Leah, and she conceived

---

*a*30:1 1Sm 1:5-6   *b*30:3 Gn 50:23   *c*30:13 Lk 1:48   *d*30:14 Sg 7:13

A30:2 Lit *the fruit of the womb*   B30:3 Lit *bear on my knees*   C30:6 In Hb, the name Dan sounds like "has vindicated," or "has judged."   D30:8 Or *With mighty wrestlings*   E30:8 In Hb, the name Naphtali sounds like "my wrestling."   F30:11 Alt Hb tradition, LXX, Vg read *Good fortune has come*   G30:11 = Good Fortune   H30:13 = Happy

---

29:31-35 The Lord, who had seen and provided for Hagar previously in her time of need (16:13-14), now **saw that Leah was unloved** (lit "hated") and **opened her womb.** In a society where a woman's prestige depended almost entirely on her success in bearing sons, the Lord gave Leah four sons before she temporarily (31:17) **stopped having children.** Three themes are present in Leah's remarks: her conviction that God provided these children in response to her **affliction** and **unloved** condition, her hope that the births would cause her **husband** to **love** her, and her **praise** to **the Lord** for what He had done. The explanations connected with each son's name are not linguistic etymologies, but explanations of wordplays.

30:1-8 Rachel's extreme unhappiness created serious tensions in the marriage. Jacob reminded her that it was God, not he, who has **withheld children** (lit "fruit of a womb") from her. Partial relief came through the practice of surrogate motherhood as Rachel gave Jacob her **slave Bilhah** so she could **bear children** "upon [Rachel's] knees" (**for me**). The phrase suggests that the adoption process involved placing the newborn child on the adopting mother's knees (50:23). When Bilhah gave birth to **Dan**, Rachel felt that God had **vindicated** her. When Bilhah **conceived again** and gave birth to **a second son**, Rachel, who had frankly struggled in her relationships with God and Leah, felt that she had finally prevailed and **won.** Accordingly, she named her second adoptive son **Naphtali.**

30:9-13 Leah, who had once used her fertility to try to win her husband's love, now resorted to the desperate act of giving **her slave** to **Jacob as a** surrogate **wife** to produce additional sons, **Gad** and **Asher.** Leah signaled their adoption by being the one who named them.

30:14-21 During the late springtime **harvest,** Leah's oldest son Reuben found some wild **mandrakes.** A plant possessing tuberous roots resembling human torsos, the mandrake was thought to enhance one's sexual powers and fertility. Leah, still lonely and desperate for her husband's affection, bartered some of the mandrakes with Jacob's favorite wife Rachel for the right to sleep with Jacob for a night. Because **God listened to Leah**—and not because of the mandrakes—

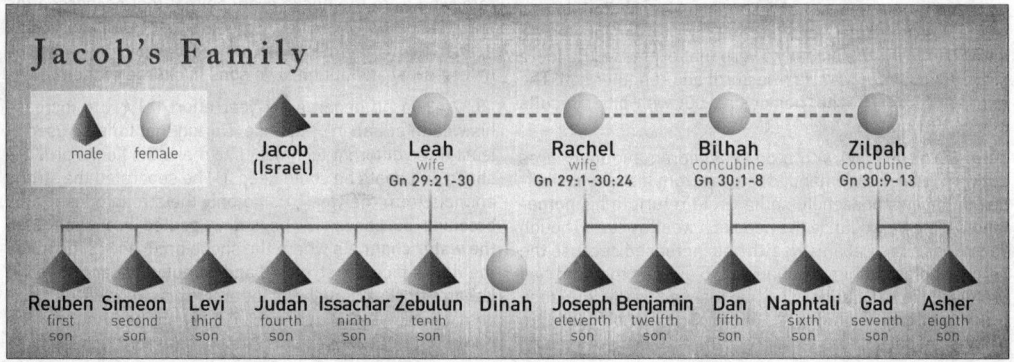

Jacob's Family

and bore Jacob a fifth son. [18]Leah said, "God has rewarded me for giving my slave to my husband," and she named him Issachar.[A]

[19]Then Leah conceived again and bore Jacob a sixth son. [20]"God has given me a good gift," Leah said. "This time my husband will honor me because I have borne six sons for him," and she named him Zebulun.[B] [21]Later, Leah bore a daughter and named her Dinah.

[22]Then God remembered Rachel. He listened to her and opened her womb.[a] [23]She conceived and bore a son, and said, "God has taken away my shame."[b] [24]She named him Joseph:[C] "May the LORD add another son to me."[c]

Jacob's Flocks Multiply

[25]After Rachel gave birth to Joseph, Jacob said to Laban, "Send me on my way so that I can return to my homeland. [26]Give me my wives and my children that I have worked for, and let me go.[d] You know how hard I have worked for you."

[27]But Laban said to him, "If I have found favor in your sight, stay. I have learned by ·divination that the LORD has blessed me because of you." [28]Then Laban said, "Name your wages, and I will pay them."[e]

[29]So Jacob said to him, "You know what I have done for you and your herds.[f] [30]For you had very little before I came, but now your wealth has increased. The LORD has blessed you because of me. And now, when will I also do something for my own family?"

[31]Laban asked, "What should I give you?"

And Jacob said, "You don't need to give me anything. If you do this one thing for me, I will continue to shepherd and keep your flock. [32]Let me go through all your sheep today and remove every sheep that is speckled or spotted, every dark-colored sheep among the lambs, and the spotted and speckled among the female goats. Such will be my wages. [33]In the future when you come to check on my wages, my honesty will testify for me. If I have any female goats that are not speckled or spotted, or any lambs that are not black, they will be considered stolen."

[34]"Good," said Laban. "Let it be as you have said."

[35]That day Laban removed the streaked and spotted male goats and all the speckled and spotted female goats—every one that had any white on it—and every dark-colored one among the lambs, and he placed his sons in charge of them. [36]He put a three-day journey between himself and Jacob. Jacob, meanwhile, was shepherding the rest of Laban's flock.

[37]Jacob then took branches of fresh poplar, almond, and plane wood, and peeled the bark, exposing white stripes on the branches. [38]He set the peeled branches in the troughs in front of the sheep—in the water channels where the sheep came to drink. And the sheep bred when they came to drink. [39]The flocks bred in front of the branches and bore streaked, speckled, and spotted young.[g] [40]Jacob separated the lambs and made the flocks face the streaked and the completely dark sheep in Laban's flocks. Then he set his own stock apart and didn't put them with Laban's sheep.

[41]Whenever the stronger of the flock were breeding, Jacob placed the branches in the

---

[a]30:22 Gn 29:31
[b]30:23 Is 4:1; Lk 1:25
[c]30:24 Gn 35:17
[d]30:26 Gn 29:18,20,27; Hs 12:12
[e]30:28 Gn 29:15; 31:7,41
[f]30:29 Gn 31:6,38-40
[g]30:39 Gn 31:10-12

[A]30:18 In Hb, the name Issachar sounds like "reward."   [B]30:20 In Hb, the name Zebulun sounds like "honored."   [C]30:24 = He Adds

---

she **conceived and bore** a fifth son, **Issachar**. When Leah **bore Jacob a sixth son . . . Zebulun**—her last—she gave **God** the credit. Jacob's only named daughter, **Dinah**, would play a tragic role in chapter 34.

30:22-24 For the third time in Genesis **God** is said to have **remembered** someone (cp. 8:1; 19:21), an event that always indicates the onset of a beneficial act by God. In this case He gave Rachel her firstborn **son . . . Joseph**, whose name (Hb *yoseph*) is actually a verb that expressed Rachel's prayerful hopes—"May He [the Lord] add" another son. The Lord would give Rachel her desire, but with bitter results (35:16-19).

30:25-36 Jacob, now with a dozen children and four wives but very little else, demanded release from his responsibilities in Laban's household so he could return to his **homeland**, where he would be the head of a wealthy clan. Though Jacob was poor, Laban's **wealth** had **increased** because **the LORD** had **blessed** him through Jacob, just as the Lord had promised (28:14). Laban, who had **learned by** the forbidden practice of **divination** (Lv 19:26) that God had **blessed** him **because of** Jacob, realized the great advantages of keeping Jacob around, so he offered to **pay** Jacob whatever **wages** his son-in-law would **name**.

Jacob asked for two things: the right to **continue to shepherd** Laban's **flock**, and all of Laban's sheep and goats that had rare and unusual markings. Laban readily agreed to the terms and virtually assured Jacob's financial failure by removing from the flocks every animal that possessed the traits Jacob had specified. To guarantee that Jacob could not use them, he drove them **a three-day journey**—40 to 50 miles—away and put **his** own **sons in charge of them**.

30:37-43 Jacob began a six-year effort (31:41) to increase his wealth at Laban's expense. During that time he used at least three different techniques to make the flocks produce sheep and goats he could keep: (1) he separated the strong animals from the weak, using only the strong ones for his breeding purposes; (2) he **set . . . peeled branches . . . in the water channels** where the sheep bred; and (3) he **made the flocks face the streaked and completely dark sheep in Laban's flocks**. Though the latter two practices have no scientific value, God Himself (31:7-8,42) and the Angel of the Lord (31:11-12) caused Jacob to become **very rich**.

troughs, in full view of the flocks, and they would breed in front of the branches. [42]As for the weaklings of the flocks, he did not put out the branches. So it turned out that the weak sheep belonged to Laban and the stronger ones to Jacob. [43]And the man became very rich.[A] He had many flocks, male and female slaves, and camels and donkeys.[a]

Jacob Separates from Laban

31 Now Jacob heard what Laban's sons were saying: "Jacob has taken all that was our father's and has built this wealth from what belonged to our father." [2]And Jacob saw from Laban's face that his attitude toward him was not the same.

[3]Then the LORD said to him, "Go back to the land of your fathers and to your family, and I will be with you."[b]

[4]Jacob had Rachel and Leah called to the field where his flocks were. [5]He said to them, "I can see from your father's face that his attitude toward me is not the same, but the God of my father has been with me. [6]You know that I've worked hard[B] for your father[c] [7]and that he has cheated me and changed my wages 10 times. But God has not let him harm me. [8]If he said, 'The spotted sheep will be your wages,' then all the sheep were born spotted. If he said, 'The streaked sheep will be your wages,' then all the sheep were born streaked.[d] [9]God has taken away your father's herds and given them to me.

[10]"When the flocks were breeding, I saw in a dream that the streaked, spotted, and speckled males were mating with the females. [11]In that dream the Angel of God said to me, 'Jacob!' and I said, 'Here I am.' [12]And He said, 'Look up and see: all the males that are mating with

the flocks are streaked, spotted, and speckled, for I have seen all that Laban has been doing to you.[e] [13]I am the God of Bethel, where you poured oil on the stone marker and made a solemn vow to Me.[f] Get up, leave this land, and return to your native land.'"

[14]Then Rachel and Leah answered him, "Do we have any portion or inheritance in our father's household? [15]Are we not regarded by him as outsiders? For he has sold us[g] and has certainly spent our money. [16]In fact, all the wealth that God has taken away from our father belongs to us and to our children. So do whatever God has said to you."

[17]Then Jacob got up and put his children and wives on the camels. [18]He took all the livestock and possessions he had acquired in Paddan-aram, and he drove his herds to go to the land of his father Isaac in Canaan. [19]When Laban had gone to shear his sheep, Rachel stole her father's household idols.[h] [20]And Jacob deceived[c] Laban the Aramean, not telling him that he was fleeing. [21]He fled with all his possessions, crossed the Euphrates, and headed for[D] the hill country of Gilead.

Laban Overtakes Jacob

[22]On the third day Laban was told that Jacob had fled. [23]So he took his relatives with him, pursued Jacob for seven days, and overtook him at Mount Gilead. [24]But God came to Laban the Aramean in a dream at night. "Watch yourself!" God warned him. "Don't say anything to Jacob, either good or bad."[i]

[25]When Laban overtook Jacob, Jacob had pitched his tent in the hill country, and Laban and his brothers also pitched their tents in the hill country of Gilead. [26]Then Laban said to Jacob, "What have you done? You have deceived

*a*30:43 Gn 12:16; 13:2; 24:35; 26:13-14; 30:30
*b*31:3 Gn 28:15; 32:10
*c*31:6 Gn 30:29
*d*31:8 Gn 30:32
*e*31:12 Gn 30:37-40; Ex 3:7
*f*31:13 Gn 28:18-19
*g*31:15 Gn 29:19-30
*h*31:19 Jdg 17:5; 1Sm 15:23; 19:13; Ezk 21:21; Hs 3:4; Zch 10:2
*i*31:24 Gn 24:50; 31:29; 2Sm 13:22

A30:43 Lit *The man spread out very much, very much*   **B**31:6 Lit *worked with all my strength*   **C**31:20 Lit *And he stole the heart of*
D31:21 Lit *and set his face to*

31:1-3 Jacob's overwhelming success created deep resentment in **Laban's sons**; their father's loss meant less inheritance for them. It also changed Laban's **attitude** to the point where Jacob no longer felt welcome. As the situation deteriorated, **the LORD** gave Jacob a command and a promise: he was to return to his clan and to the land promised to his grandfather (12:7), armed with the assurance that the Lord would **be with** him.

31:4-16 Jacob presented Rachel and Leah with three reasons for making a major move away from the only home they had ever known to a land they had never even seen: (1) their father Laban had an unfavorable **attitude toward** Jacob; (2) Laban was unethical in business, having **cheated** Jacob and **changed** his **wages 10 times**—almost every time a new generation of sheep and goats was born (there would have been about 14 breeding cycles for sheep in six years); and (3) most important of all, the God who had **taken** their **father's herds and given them** to Jacob had now ordered him to **return to** his **native . . . land**. **Rachel and Leah** were

agreeable to the idea, since their father had treated them like "foreigners" (**outsiders**).

31:17-21 Jacob now began the journey back to **the land of his father Isaac**. Though he had left 20 years earlier alone and with no possessions, he now returned with a family and an abundance of property. Even as Jacob "stole the heart of" (**deceived**) Laban by leaving secretly, his wife **Rachel** had also stolen **her father's household idols** (Hb *teraphim*). The group **crossed the Euphrates** in what is now Syria, then **headed** south for **Gilead** (part of modern Jordan).

31:22-30 Learning of Jacob's secret departure, Laban gathered a posse and set out to catch the group. Laban intended to harm Jacob, probably because he believed Jacob had **stolen** his household **gods**, but **the God of** Jacob's **father** kept the promise of protection made 20 years earlier (28:15), and **warned** Laban **in a dream** not to harm Jacob. Laban was frustrated not only because he had lost his household gods, but because he had no opportunity to **kiss**

me and taken my daughters away like prisoners of war! [27] Why did you secretly flee from me, deceive me, and not tell me? I would have sent you away with joy and singing, with tambourines and lyres, [28] but you didn't even let me kiss my grandchildren and my daughters. You have acted foolishly. [29] I could do you great harm, but last night the God of your father said to me: 'Watch yourself. Don't say anything to Jacob, either good or bad.' [30] Now you have gone off because you long for your father—but why have you stolen my gods?" [a]

[31] Jacob answered, "I was afraid, for I thought you would take your daughters from me by force. [32] If you find your gods with anyone here, he will not live! [b] Before our relatives, point out anything that is yours and take it." Jacob did not know that Rachel had stolen the idols.

[33] So Laban went into Jacob's tent, then Leah's tent, and then the tents of the two female slaves, but he found nothing. Then he left Leah's tent and entered Rachel's. [34] Now Rachel had taken Laban's household idols, put them in the saddlebag of the camel, and sat on them. Laban searched the whole tent but found nothing.

[35] She said to her father, "Sir, don't be angry that I cannot stand up in your presence; [c] I am having my period." So Laban searched, but could not find the household idols.

Jacob's Covenant with Laban

[36] Then Jacob became incensed and brought charges against Laban. "What is my crime?" he said to Laban. "What is my sin, that you have pursued me? [37] You've searched all my possessions! Have you found anything of yours? Put it here before my relatives and yours, and let them decide between the two of us. [38] I've been with you these 20 years. Your ewes and female

goats have not miscarried, and I have not eaten the rams from your flock. [39] I did not bring you any of the flock torn by wild beasts; I myself bore the loss. You demanded payment from me for what was stolen by day or by night. [40] There I was—the heat consumed me by day and the frost by night, and sleep fled from my eyes. [41] For 20 years I have worked in your household—14 years for your two daughters and six years for your flocks [d]—and you have changed my wages 10 times! [42] If the God of my father, the God of Abraham, the Fear of Isaac, had not been with me, certainly now you would have sent me off empty-handed. But God has seen my affliction and my hard work, [A] and He issued His verdict last night."

[43] Then Laban answered Jacob, "The daughters are my daughters; the sons, my sons; and the flocks, my flocks! Everything you see is mine! But what can I do today for these daughters of mine or for the children they have borne? [44] Come now, let's make a covenant, you and I. [e] Let it be a witness between the two of us."

[45] So Jacob picked out a stone and set it up as a marker. [f] [46] Then Jacob said to his relatives, "Gather stones." And they took stones and made a mound, then ate there by the mound. [47] Laban named the mound Jegar-sahadutha, but Jacob named it Galeed. [B]

[48] Then Laban said, "This mound is a witness between you and me today." Therefore the place was called Galeed [49] and also Mizpah, [C,g] for he said, "May the LORD watch between you and me when we are out of each other's sight. [50] If you mistreat my daughters or take other wives, though no one is with us, understand that God will be a witness between you and me." [h] [51] Laban also said to Jacob, "Look at this mound and the marker I have set up between you and me. [52] This mound is a witness and

[a]31:30 Gn 31:19; Jos 24:2; Jdg 18:24
[b]31:32 Gn 44:9
[c]31:35 Lv 19:32
[d]31:41 Gn 29:27,30
[e]31:44 Gn 21:27,32; 26:28
[f]31:45 Jos 24:26-27
[g]31:49 Jdg 11:29; 1Sm 7:5-6
[h]31:50 Jdg 11:10; 1Sm 12:5; Jb 16:19; Jr 42:5; Mc 1:2

[A]31:42 Lit and the work of my hands   [B]31:47 Jegar-sahadutha is Aram, and Galeed is Hb; both names = Mound of Witness
[C]31:49 = Watchtower

---

his **grandchildren and . . . daughters** good-bye and send the group off **with** a joyful celebration.

31:31-35 Jacob was apparently afraid that Laban would treat him as a slave and take his wives away **by force** (Ex 21:3-4). Ignorant of what his favorite wife Rachel had done, Jacob promised death for the person possessing Laban's household **gods**. As shrewd and deceptive as her father Laban, Rachel prevented him from checking the saddlebags by claiming she was **having** her monthly **period**. During that phase of a woman's monthly cycle, anything she sat on became ceremonially unclean and was not to be touched by others (Lv 15:26).

31:36-43 Jacob unleashed a torrent of pent-up anger at **Laban**, noting seven ways in which he had helped his father-in-law and labored selflessly on his behalf. Then Jacob

confessed that Yahweh, **the God of** his grandfather **Abraham**, alternately known as **the Fear of Isaac** (the only use of this term in the Bible), saw Jacob's **affliction**, protected him from financial ruin, and **issued** a **verdict** on his behalf. In response, Laban expressed his disgust by insisting that **everything** Jacob had was rightfully his.

31:44-55 To end the dispute, Laban proposed that he and Jacob **make a covenant** that would bring peace and a separation between the Israelite (Jacob's) and the Aramean (Laban's) branches of the Terah clan. In classic ancient Near Eastern treaty tradition, the covenant-making event consisted of building a sacred stone and a mound (**Jegar-sahadutha**, or **Galeed** ["Mound of Witness"]), the calling of witnesses (the covenant itself, the **marker**, and the **mound**), a preliminary ceremonial meal, expression of the covenant

the marker is a witness that I will not pass beyond this mound to you, and you will not pass beyond this mound and this marker to do me harm. [53]The God of Abraham, and the gods[a] of Nahor—the gods of their father[A]—will judge between us." And Jacob swore by the Fear of his father Isaac. [54]Then Jacob offered a sacrifice on the mountain and invited his relatives to eat a meal. So they ate a meal and spent the night on the mountain. [55B]Laban got up early in the morning, kissed his grandchildren and daughters, and blessed them. Then Laban left to return home.

Preparing to Meet Esau

32 Jacob went on his way, and God's angels met him.[b] [2]When he saw them, Jacob said, "This is God's camp." So he called that place Mahanaim.[C,c]

[3]Jacob sent messengers ahead of him to his brother Esau in the land of Seir, the country of Edom. [4]He commanded them, "You are to say to my lord Esau, 'This is what your servant Jacob says. I have been staying with Laban and have been delayed until now. [5]I have oxen, donkeys, flocks, male and female slaves. I have sent this message to inform my lord, in order to seek your favor.'"[d]

[6]When the messengers returned to Jacob, they said, "We went to your brother Esau; he is coming to meet you—and he has 400 men with him."[e] [7]Jacob was greatly afraid and distressed; he divided the people with him into two camps, along with the flocks, cattle, and camels. [8]He thought, "If Esau comes to one camp and attacks it, the remaining one can escape."[f]

[9]Then Jacob said, "God of my father Abraham and God of my father Isaac,[g] the LORD who said to me, 'Go back to your land and to your family, and I will cause you to prosper,'[h]

a 31:53 Jos 24:2
b 32:1 Ps 91:9-11
c 32:2 Jos 21:38; 2Sm 2:8; 17:24,27; 1Kg 2:8
d 32:5 Gn 33:8,15
e 32:6 Gn 33:1
f 32:8 Gn 27:41
g 32:9 Gn 28:13; 31:42,53
h Gn 31:3,13
i 32:12 Gn 28:13-15
j 32:13 Gn 43:11
k 32:22 Dt 2:37; 3:16; Jos 12:2

[10]I am unworthy of all the kindness and faithfulness You have shown Your servant. Indeed, I crossed over this Jordan with my staff, and now I have become two camps. [11]Please rescue me from the hand of my brother Esau, for I am afraid of him; otherwise, he may come and attack me, the mothers, and their children. [12]You have said, 'I will cause you to prosper, and I will make your •offspring like the sand of the sea, which cannot be counted.'"[i]

[13]He spent the night there and took part of what he had brought with him as a gift for his brother Esau:[j] [14]200 female goats, 20 male goats, 200 ewes, 20 rams, [15]30 milk camels with their young, 40 cows, 10 bulls, 20 female donkeys, and 10 male donkeys. [16]He entrusted them to his slaves as separate herds and said to them, "Go on ahead of me, and leave some distance between the herds."

[17]And he told the first one: "When my brother Esau meets you and asks, 'Who do you belong to? Where are you going? And whose animals are these ahead of you?' [18]then tell him, 'They belong to your servant Jacob. They are a gift sent to my lord Esau. And look, he is behind us.'"

[19]He also told the second one, the third, and everyone who was walking behind the animals, "Say the same thing to Esau when you find him. [20]You are also to say, 'Look, your servant Jacob is right behind us.'" For he thought, "I want to appease Esau with the gift that is going ahead of me. After that, I can face him, and perhaps he will forgive me."

[21]So the gift was sent on ahead of him while he remained in the camp that night. [22]During the night Jacob got up and took his two wives, his two female slaves, and his 11 sons, and crossed the ford of Jabbok.[k] [23]He took them and sent them across the stream, along with all his possessions.

A31:53 Two Hb mss, LXX omit *the gods of their father*   B31:55 Gn 32:1 in Hb   C32:2 = Two Camps

---

terms, invocation of deities that would oversee the covenant (**the God of Abraham, and the gods of Nahor**), and a concluding ceremonial meal.

32:1-2 For the second time while on a journey, Jacob saw **God's angels** (cp. 28:12). As before, he named the place where he encountered them. In this case he **called** it **Mahanaim**, "Two Camps," probably in recognition of the fact that both people and angels were at the same location.

32:3-12 Remembering Esau's death threats from 20 years earlier (27:41-42), Jacob now made a special effort to gain Esau's favor with the assistance of messengers. The first prong of his strategy was verbal: Jacob had the messengers call Esau **lord** and himself **your servant**, thus honoring Esau's position as firstborn—even though he had previously taken Esau's birthright and blessing. Jacob also

made sure he was the first to initiate contact between the brothers, **in order to seek** Esau's **favor**.

To prepare for the coming confrontation with his brother Jacob did two things: first, **he divided** his group in two so at least some of his people could **escape** if necessary; second, he offered a prayer with three elements: an admission that he was **unworthy of** the many blessings God had given him, a prayer for **rescue**, and a reminder of God's promises to **prosper** and multiply Jacob.

32:13-21 Jacob, who had been so adept at taking from others in the past, now arranged to give a generous **gift** to **his brother Esau**. Only after Esau had received all the gifts would Jacob meet him.

32:22-23 As a final measure of self-protection that **night**, Jacob put one more barrier between himself and Esau, moving his family and possessions across the **Jabbok**, a

Jacob Wrestles with an Angel

24 Jacob was left alone, and a man wrestled with him until daybreak.[a] 25 When the man saw that He could not defeat him, He struck Jacob's hip socket as they wrestled and dislocated his hip. 26 Then He said to Jacob, "Let Me go, for it is daybreak."

But Jacob said, "I will not let You go unless You bless me."

27 "What is your name?" the man asked.

"Jacob," he replied.

28 "Your name will no longer be Jacob,"[b] He said. "It will be Israel[A] because you have struggled with God[c] and with men and have prevailed."

29 Then Jacob asked Him, "Please tell me Your name."

But He answered, "Why do you ask My name?"[d] And He blessed him there.

30 Jacob then named the place Peniel,[B] "For I have seen God face to face," he said, "and I have been delivered."[e] 31 The sun shone on him as he passed by Penuel[C,f]—limping be-

cause of his hip. 32 That is why, to this day, the Israelites don't eat the thigh muscle that is at the hip socket: because He struck Jacob's hip socket at the thigh muscle.[D]

Jacob Meets Esau

33 Now Jacob looked up and saw Esau coming toward him with 400 men. So he divided the children among Leah, Rachel, and the two female slaves. 2 He put the female slaves and their children first, Leah and her children next, and Rachel and Joseph last. 3 He himself went on ahead and bowed to the ground[g] seven times until he approached his brother.

4 But Esau ran to meet him, hugged him, threw his arms around him, and kissed him. Then they wept.[h] 5 When Esau looked up and saw the women and children, he asked, "Who are these with you?"

He answered, "The children God has graciously given your servant."[i] 6 Then the female slaves and their children approached him and bowed down. 7 Leah and her children also ap-

Cross references
a 32:24 Hs 12:3-4
b 32:28 Gn 35:10; 2Kg 17:34
c Hs 12:3-4
d 32:29 Jdg 13:18
e 32:30 Gn 16:13; Ex 24:10-11; 33:20; Nm 12:8; Jdg 6:22; 13:22
f 32:31 Jdg 8:8
g 33:3 Gn 18:2; 42:6; 43:26
h 33:4 Gn 44:14
i 33:5 Gn 48:9; Ps 127:3; Is 8:18

A 32:28 In Hb, the name Israel sounds like "he struggled (with) God."   B 32:30 = Face of God   C 32:31 Variant of Peniel   D 32:32 Or tendon

---

westward-flowing tributary emptying into the Jordan River 15 miles north of the Dead Sea. Perhaps Jacob believed that Esau would have compassion on his **wives** and children, and so end his pursuit.

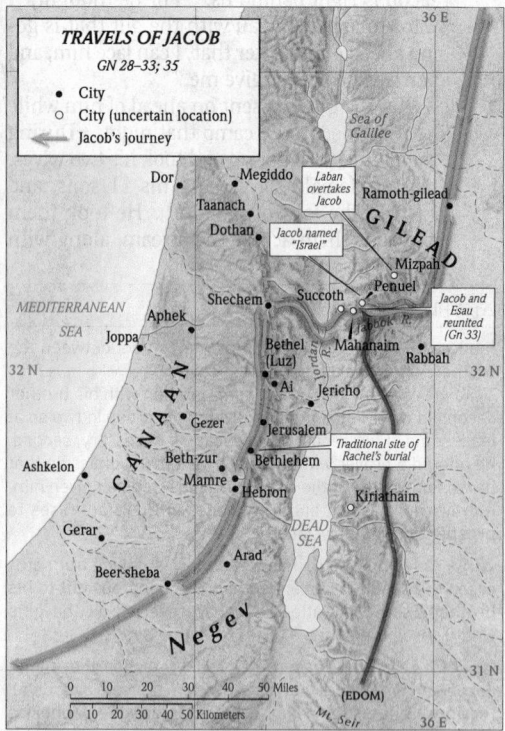

TRAVELS OF JACOB
GN 28–33; 35
- City
- City (uncertain location)
- Jacob's journey

36 E
Sea of Galilee
Dor
Megiddo
Laban overtakes Jacob
Ramoth-gilead
Taanach
GILEAD
Dothan
Jacob named "Israel"
Mizpah
MEDITERRANEAN SEA
Shechem
Succoth
Penuel
Jacob and Esau reunited (Gn 33)
Aphek
Joppa
Bethel (Luz)
Mahanaim
Rabbah
32 N
Ai
Jericho
32 N
Gezer
Jerusalem
Traditional site of Rachel's burial
Ashkelon
Beth-zur
Bethlehem
Mamre
Hebron
Kiriathaim
Gerar
DEAD SEA
Arad
Beer-sheba
Negev
0 10 20 30 40 50 Miles
0 10 20 30 40 50 Kilometers
(EDOM)
Mt. Seir
31 N
36 E

32:24-30 Now Jacob experienced his third and final encounter with God while on a journey (cp. v. 1; 27:12-15). **A man**, understood by later Israelites to be God or an angel possessing the authority of God (Hs 12:3-4), **wrestled with** the elderly patriarch **until daybreak**. The fight ended when the divine being **dislocated** Jacob's hip. Jacob, injured but still unwilling to release his grip on the being, demanded that He **bless** him. Asserting His authority over Jacob (see note at Gn 1:5), the man changed Jacob's name to **Israel** (Hb yisra'el), linking the name with the fact that the patriarch had **struggled** (Hb sarah) **with God** (Hb 'el), as well as **with men**, and had **prevailed**.

Jacob was the third person to be renamed by God, joining Abraham and Sarah (17:5,15). The patriarch's inferior status is reflected in the fact that, unlike the divine being, who asked for Jacob's name and got it, Jacob was unable to learn the being's name. The renamed man now renamed the place **Peniel**—or **Penuel**—lit "the face of God," because he had **seen God face to face** and yet was spared from death.

33:1-3 Following his transforming encounter with God, Jacob went from hiding behind his wives and children (32:22-23) to boldly taking the lead in protecting his family. In his encounter with **Esau** and his **400 men**, Jacob **went on ahead** of the group, arranging his family behind him according to their status. In a display of respect unparalleled in the Bible, Jacob **bowed** down to Esau **seven times** as he approached.

33:4-11 Even as Jacob had been changed the previous night, it seems that Esau had changed too. Perhaps he had been warned by God not to harm Jacob, even as other adversaries of the patriarchs had been before (20:3-7; 31:24). The once-estranged brothers **hugged . . . kissed**, and **wept** together in gracious reunion—a scene that anticipated a reunion between estranged brothers in the next generation (45:14-15). Esau, who had three wives and five sons (36:2-5), inquired about Jacob's family. Each of the mothers ap-

proached and bowed down, and then Joseph and Rachel approached and bowed down.

[8] So Esau said, "What do you mean by this whole procession[A] I met?"[a]

"To find favor with you, my lord,"[b] he answered.

[9] "I have enough, my brother," Esau replied. "Keep what you have."

[10] But Jacob said, "No, please! If I have found favor with you, take this gift from my hand. For indeed, I have seen your face, and it is like seeing God's face, since you have accepted me. [11] Please take my present that was brought to you, because God has been gracious to me and I have everything I need." So Jacob urged him until he accepted.

[12] Then Esau said, "Let's move on, and I'll go ahead of you."

[13] Jacob replied, "My lord knows that the children are weak, and I have nursing sheep and cattle. If they are driven hard for one day, the whole herd will die. [14] Let my lord go ahead of his servant. I will continue on slowly, at a pace suited to the livestock and the children, until I come to my lord at Seir."

[15] Esau said, "Let me leave some of my people with you."

But he replied, "Why do that? Please indulge me,[B] my lord."[c]

[16] That day Esau started on his way back to Seir, [17] but Jacob went on to Succoth. He built a house for himself and stalls for his livestock; that is why the place was called Succoth.[C,d]

[18] After Jacob came from Paddan-aram, he arrived safely[e] at Shechem[f] in the land of Canaan and camped in front of the city. [19] He purchased a section of the field where he had pitched his tent from the sons of Hamor, Shechem's father, for 100 *qesitahs*.[D,g] [20] And he set up an altar there and called it "God, the God of Israel."[E]

Dinah Defiled

34 Dinah, Leah's daughter[h] whom she bore to Jacob, went out to see some of the young women of the area. [2] When Shechem son of Hamor the Hivite, a prince of the region, saw her, he took her and raped her. [3] He became infatuated with Dinah, daughter of Jacob. He loved the young girl and spoke tenderly to her.[F] [4] "Get me this girl as a wife,"[i] he told his father Hamor.

[5] Jacob heard that Shechem had defiled his daughter Dinah, but since his sons were with his livestock in the field, he remained silent until they returned. [6] Meanwhile, Shechem's father Hamor came to speak with Jacob. [7] Jacob's sons returned from the field when they heard about the incident and were deeply grieved and angry. For Shechem had committed an outrage against Israel by raping Jacob's daughter,[j] and such a thing should not be done.

[8] Hamor said to Jacob's sons, "My son Shechem is strongly attracted to your[G] daughter. Please give her to him as a wife. [9] Intermarry with us; give your daughters to us, and take

Cross references (center column)
[a]33:8 Gn 32:13-16
[b]Gn 32:5
[c]33:15 Gn 34:11; 47:25; Ru 2:13
[d]33:17 Jos 13:27; Jdg 8:5; Ps 60:6
[e]33:18 Gn 28:21
[f]Jos 24:1; Jdg 9:1; Ps 60:6; Ac 7:16
[g]33:19 Jos 24:32; Jn 4:5
[h]34:1 Gn 30:21
[i]34:4 Jdg 14:2
[j]34:7 Dt 22:20-30; Jdg 20:6; 2Sm 13:12

[A]33:8 Lit *camp*   [B]33:15 Lit *May I find favor in your eyes*   [C]33:17 = Stalls or Huts   [D]33:19 The value of this currency is unknown. [E]33:20 Or El-Elohe-Israel   [F]34:3 Lit *spoke to her heart*   [G]34:8 The Hb word for "your" is pl, showing that Hamor is speaking to Jacob and his sons.

---

proached Esau with **their children** and respectfully **bowed down**. The fact that **Joseph** was the only named son in the group and was mentioned ahead of his mother foreshadows his leading role in later narratives.

Though Esau encouraged Jacob to keep what animals he had earlier sent ahead, Jacob insisted that Esau **take** the **gift** as a confirmation that the younger brother had **found favor with** him.

33:12-15 To compensate Jacob for his generous gift, Esau offered to provide companionship ("let *us* go"; **let's move on**), leadership (**I'll go ahead**), and—with the assistance of his 400 men—protection to Jacob's group for the remainder of the journey. Jacob, who had just escaped from 20 years of oppression from a troublesome relative, respectfully declined the offer, calling his brother **my lord**, but suggesting that he needed to travel alone.

33:16-17 Esau went south **to Seir**, a forested mountainous region east of the Dead Sea, while Jacob's group traveled a few miles north to settle at **Succoth** (Hb for "Temporary Shelters"; **stalls**), named for the temporary facilities Jacob constructed **for his livestock**. The Bible does not indicate that Jacob and Esau met again until they buried their father many years later (35:29).

33:18-20 Jacob's journey ended when he **arrived safely** at

Shechem, where his grandfather Abraham had first lived when he entered Canaan (12:6). Jacob intended to live permanently in the land promised to him by God (28:13), so he **purchased a section** of land in front of Shechem from **the sons of Hamor**, including his son Shechem, whose name matched the city's name. The price of **100 qesitahs** represents an unknown quantity; one suggestion is that a *qesitah* represented the value of one lamb. True to the seminomadic heritage of his grandfather and father (12:8; 26:25), Jacob lived in a **tent**. Like Abraham and Isaac before him (12:8; 13:18; 22:9; 26:25), Jacob also **set up an altar**, naming it **God, the God of Israel**.

34:1-7 Perhaps **Dinah** was seeking some female companionship since she was the only daughter in her large family. Shechem, one of the previous owners of the property on which Dinah now lived, **saw her**, forcefully **took her**, and then **raped** ("humbled") **her**. The fact that **he loved** her, **spoke tenderly to her**, and even ordered his father to **get** that **girl** for him to take **as a wife** suggests that Shechem was following Hivite customs in his treatment of Dinah, though what he did **should not be done** in Israelite society. Jacob delayed responding to Shechem, probably because he knew there was nothing he could do alone.

34:8-12 **Hamor**, a prince, had the right to negotiate treaties

our daughters for yourselves. ¹⁰Live with us. The land is before you. Settle here, move about, and acquire property in it."

¹¹Then Shechem said to Dinah's father and brothers, "Grant me this favor,ᴬ and I'll give you whatever you say. ¹²Demand of me a high compensationᴮ and gift; I'll give you whatever you ask me. Just give the girl to be my wife!"

¹³But Jacob's sons answered Shechem and his father Hamor deceitfully because he had defiled their sister Dinah. ¹⁴"We cannot do this thing," they said to them. "Giving our sister to an uncircumcised man is a disgrace to us. ¹⁵We will agree with you only on this condition: if all your males are circumcised as we are.ᵃ ¹⁶Then we will give you our daughters, take your daughters for ourselves, live with you, and become one people. ¹⁷But if you will not listen to us and be circumcised, then we will take our daughter and go."

¹⁸Their words seemed good to Hamor and his son Shechem. ¹⁹The young man did not delay doing this, because he was delighted with Jacob's daughter. Now he was the most important in all his father's house. ²⁰So Hamor and his son Shechem went to the •gate of their cityᵇ and spoke to the men there.

²¹"These men are peaceful toward us," they said. "Let them live in our land and move about in it, for indeed, the region is large enough for them. Let us take their daughters as our wives and give our daughters to them. ²²But the men will agree to live with us and

a 34:15 Gn 17:23-27
b 34:20 Ru 4:1; 2Sm 15:2
c 34:24 Gn 23:10
d 34:25 Gn 49:5-7
e 34:30 Jos 7:25
f Ex 5:21; 1Sm 13:4; 2Sm 10:6
g Gn 13:7; 34:2
h Gn 46:26-27; Dt 4:27; 1Ch 16:19; Ps 105:12
i 35:1 Gn 28:19

be one people only on this condition: if all our men are circumcised as they are. ²³Won't their livestock, their possessions, and all their animals become ours? Only let us agree with them, and they will live with us."

²⁴All the able-bodied menᶜ,ᶜ listened to Hamor and his son Shechem, and all the able-bodied menᴰ were circumcised. ²⁵On the third day, when they were still in pain, two of Jacob's sons, Simeon and Levi,ᵈ Dinah's brothers, took their swords, went into the unsuspecting city, and killed every male. ²⁶They killed Hamor and his son Shechem with their swords, took Dinah from Shechem's house, and went away. ²⁷Jacob's other sons came to the slaughter and plundered the city because their sister had been defiled. ²⁸They took their sheep, cattle, donkeys, and whatever was in the city and in the field. ²⁹They captured all their possessions, children, and wives and plundered everything in the houses.

³⁰Then Jacob said to Simeon and Levi, "You have brought trouble on me,ᵉ making me odious to the inhabitants of the land,ᶠ the Canaanites and the Perizzites.ᵍ We are few in number; if they unite against me and attack me, I and my household will be destroyed."ʰ ³¹But they answered, "Should he have treated our sister like a prostitute?"

Return to Bethel

35 God said to Jacob, "Get up! Go to Bethel and settle there.ⁱ Build an altar there

---

ᴬ 34:11 Lit *May I find favor in your eyes*   ᴮ 34:12 Or *bride-price*, or *betrothal present*   ᶜ 34:24 Lit *All who went out of the city gate*   ᴰ 34:24 Lit *all the males who went out of the city gate*

---

with Jacob, who was now a landowner in the region. Jacob had been trustworthy in past business deals (33:19), so Hamor negotiated in good faith to build closer ties with Jacob and his **sons**. As a "member of the family" through intermarriage, Jacob would be able to **move about** with fewer restrictions and **acquire** additional **property**.

34:13-18 By answering the Hivite leaders **deceitfully**, Jacob's older sons proved that they could behave as wickedly toward outsiders as Hamor's son, Shechem, had done. Ironically, a later generation of Hivites would practice deception to join their peoples with the Hebrews (Jos 9:3-15). In an outrageous misuse of the sacred rite of circumcision (Gn 17:9-14), **Jacob's sons** stated that they could only **give** their **daughters**—and their sister Dinah—away in marriage to men who had been **circumcised**. Men of many different cultures in the biblical world besides the Israelites practiced circumcision, including the Egyptians, Edomites, Moabites, and Ammonites (Jr 9:25-26), and the idea **seemed good** to **Hamor** and **Shechem** as well.

34:19-24 As the future prince over the region, Shechem had great influence over the citizens of the village bearing his name. Meeting with the men at **the gate of their city**, where people gathered to share news and consider proposals, Shechem and Hamor provided the men with four reasons to establish a treaty with Jacob's sons, ratifying it with circumcision. Shechem convinced **all the able-bodied men** of the village, and they **were circumcised**.

34:25-29 While the men of Shechem **were still in pain**, immobilized and recovering from the removal of their foreskins with flint knives, they were murdered by **Simeon** and **Levi**, two of Jacob's four sons who had the same mother (Leah) as Dinah. After killing **Shechem**, they **took Dinah from** his house; she had been brought there after Shechem's circumcision. When Jacob's **other** adult **sons**—Joseph was probably not among them—learned of it, they **plundered the city**, using the excuse that **their sister had been defiled**. The Hivite **children** and **wives** they stole would possibly have been sold to slave traders (37:27-28).

34:30-31 Upon learning of the outrageous actions of **Simeon** and **Levi**, Jacob condemned them. Their actions had not only brought death to the Hivites, they had **brought trouble on** their father as well. Jacob's reputation for being a man of peace (v. 21) had now been destroyed. The clan, now marked as murderers, would have to live in fear that **the Canaanites and the Perizzites** would attack and kill them. Simeon and Levi would later be cursed by their father (49:5-7) because of their horrific crime. Their only defense was that Shechem had **treated** their **sister like a prostitute**—a criminal act, to be sure, but not one that was

to the God who appeared to you when you fled from your brother Esau."[a]

[2] So Jacob said to his family and all who were with him, "Get rid of the foreign gods that are among you.[b] Purify yourselves and change your clothes.[c] [3] We must get up and go to Bethel. I will build an altar there to the God who answered me in my day of distress.[d] He has been with me everywhere I have gone."[e]

[4] Then they gave Jacob all their foreign gods and their earrings, and Jacob hid them under the oak near Shechem. [5] When they set out, a terror from God came over the cities around them, and they did not pursue Jacob's sons.[f] [6] So Jacob and all who were with him came to Luz (that is, Bethel[g]) in the land of Canaan. [7] Jacob built an altar there and called the place God of Bethel[A] because it was there that God had revealed Himself to him when he was fleeing from his brother.

[8] Deborah, the one who had nursed and raised Rebekah,[B,h] died and was buried under the oak south of Bethel. So Jacob named it Oak of Weeping.[C]

[9] God appeared to Jacob again after he re-turned from Paddan-aram, and He blessed him. [10] God said to him:

> Your name is Jacob;
> you will no longer be named Jacob,
> but your name will be Israel.[i]

So He named him Israel. [11] God also said to him:

> I am *God Almighty.[j]
> Be fruitful and multiply.[k]
> A nation, indeed an assembly of nations,
> will come from you,[l]
> and kings will descend from you[D,m]
> [12] I will give to you the land
> that I gave to Abraham and Isaac.[n]
> And I will give the land
> to your future descendants.

[13] Then God withdrew[E,o] from him at the place where He had spoken to him.

[14] Jacob set up a marker at the place where He had spoken to him—a stone marker. He poured a drink offering on it and anointed it with oil.[p] [15] Jacob named the place where God had spoken with him Bethel.

Cross references (center column):

[a] 35:1 Gn 27:43
[b] 35:2 Gn 31:19; Jos 24:23; 1Sm 7:3
[c] 35:2 Ex 19:10
[d] 35:3 1Sm 7:9; 2Sm 24:25; Jb 12:4; Ps 20:1; 34:4
[e] Gn 28:10-22
[f] 35:5 Ex 23:27
[g] 35:6 Gn 28:19; 48:3
[h] 35:8 Gn 24:59
[i] 35:10 Gn 17:5; 32:28
[j] 35:11 Gn 17:1; 28:3; Ex 6:3
[k] Gn 9:1,7
[l] Gn 48:4
[m] Gn 17:6,16; 36:31
[n] 35:12 Gn 12:7; 13:15; 26:3-4; 28:13; Ex 32:13
[o] 35:13 Gn 17:22; 18:33
[p] 35:14 Gn 28:18-19; 31:45

[A] 35:7 Or *El-bethel*   [B] 35:8 Lit *Deborah, Rebekah's wet nurse*; Gn 24:59   [C] 35:8 Or *Allon-bacuth*   [D] 35:11 Lit *will come from your loins*   [E] 35:13 Lit *went up*

---

considered punishable by death in the Torah (Ex 22:16-17; Dt 22:28-29).

35:1-5 In his time of trouble **God** called **Jacob** back to **Bethel**, the spot where he had first met God. There Jacob was to **build** a more formal **altar** to **God** than the marker he had left there 20 years earlier (28:22). God's command in Gn 35:1 represents the only time in Genesis that He ordered an altar be built. The patriarch ordered **his family and all who were with him** to prepare themselves for an encounter with the living God.

This preparation involved three things: first, getting **rid of the foreign gods** among them. Laban's household idols (31:19) as well as possible Hivite idols acquired in the raid on Shechem (34:29) were among the items that Jacob buried **under the oak near Shechem**. Second, the people were to **purify** themselves, a command that normally involved washing the body and clothing (Ex 19:10; 30:19-21; Lv 16:26), as well as avoidance of sexual contact since seminal emissions created temporary ritual uncleanness (Lv 15:16-18). Purification would especially have been necessary because of Dinah's defilement and the touching of human corpses (Nm 19:11-12). Third, they were to **change** their **clothes** (Lv 6:10-11). Having purified themselves, they experienced God's protection on their journey to Bethel. **Jacob's sons** were marked for death by the Canaanites in the region, but **God** sent **a terror** on the nearby inhabitants, and no one pursued the clan.

35:6-8 At **Bethel**, known to the Canaanites as **Luz**, Jacob built "El-bethel" (**God of Bethel**), his second named altar (33:20). Rebekah's nurse **Deborah** (see 24:59 and note at 24:54-61), a woman who probably was like a beloved second mother to Jacob, **died** at Bethel. Her death, along with Isaac's in verse 28, marked the passing of a generation.

35:9-15 God's final recorded words to Jacob came as He spoke to him for the second time (cp. v. 1) since the patriarch returned **from Paddan-aram**. In this proclamation the Lord revealed Himself as **God Almighty** (Hb "*El Shaddai*"), a name for God revealed first to Abraham (17:1; see note there) and later known to Isaac (28:3). The 26 Hebrew words in God's speech reaffirm promises previously made to Jacob (cp. 28:13).

At the same time God **blessed** Jacob with words that enlarged previously given promises. The blessing previously given to Adam, Noah, and Noah's sons (1:28; 9:1)—**be fruitful and multiply**—was now extended to Jacob. For the first

---

'El Shaddai

Hebrew Pronunciation	[ALE shad EYE]
HCSB Translation	God Almighty
Uses in Genesis	5
Uses in the OT	7
Focus passage	Genesis 35:11

God called Himself '*El Shaddai* when addressing Abram and Jacob, but after He explained the name Yahweh to Moses (Ex 6:3), '*El Shaddai* hardly appears—just once in Ezekiel 10:5. Yet *Shaddai* occurs 48 times, once or twice in Numbers, Ruth, Isaiah, Ezekiel, Psalms, and Joel, and 31 times in Job, perhaps suggesting that Job is an early book. '*El* was a Semitic word for "god" but could designate the high god, as in the ancient city-state Ugarit. The sense of *Shaddai* is uncertain but was probably linked with an Akkadian word for mountain—the gods were pictured as living on mountains. Modern versions that translate '*El Shaddai* as *God Almighty* follow the Septuagint and Vulgate. *Shaddai* alone may be a shortened form of '*El Shaddai*, for '*El* and *Shaddai* are separated in Gn 49:25; Nm 24:4,16; and 20 times in Job.

Rachel's Death

[16]They set out from Bethel. When they were still some distance from Ephrath, Rachel began to give birth, and her labor was difficult. [17]During her difficult labor, the midwife said to her, "Don't be afraid, for you have another son."[a] [18]With her last breath—for she was dying—she named him Ben-oni,[A] but his father called him Benjamin.[B] [19]So Rachel died and was buried on the way to Ephrath (that is, Bethlehem[b]). [20]Jacob set up a marker on her grave; it is the marker at Rachel's grave to this day.

Israel's Sons

[21]Israel set out again and pitched his tent beyond the Tower of Eder.[c] [22]While Israel was living in that region, Reuben went in and slept with his father's concubine Bilhah, and Israel heard about it.[c]

Jacob had 12 sons:[d]

23   Leah's sons were Reuben
      (Jacob's firstborn),
      Simeon, Levi, Judah,
      Issachar, and Zebulun.
24   Rachel's sons were
      Joseph and Benjamin.
25   The sons of Rachel's slave Bilhah
      were Dan and Naphtali.
26   The sons of Leah's slave Zilpah
      were Gad and Asher.

These are the sons of Jacob, who were born to him in Paddan-aram.

Isaac's Death

[27]Jacob came to his father Isaac at Mamre[e] in Kiriath-arba (that is, Hebron[f]), where Abraham and Isaac had stayed. [28]Isaac lived 180 years. [29]He took his last breath and died, and was gathered to his people,[g] old and full of days. His sons Esau and Jacob buried him.

Esau's Family

36 These are the family records[h] of Esau (that is, Edom[i]). [2]Esau took his wives from the Canaanite women: Adah daughter of Elon the Hittite,[j] Oholibamah daughter of Anah and granddaughter[D] of Zibeon the Hivite, [3]and Basemath daughter of Ishmael and sister of Nebaioth.[k] [4]Adah bore Eliphaz to Esau, Basemath bore Reuel, [5]and Oholibamah bore Jeush, Jalam, and Korah. These were Esau's sons, who were born to him in the land of Canaan.

[6]Esau took his wives, sons, daughters, and all the people of his household, as well as his herds, all his livestock, and all the property he had acquired in Canaan; he went to a land away from his brother Jacob. [7]For their possessions were too many for them to live together,[l] and because of their herds, the land where they stayed could not support them.[m] [8]So Esau (that is, Edom) lived in the mountains of Seir.[n]

[9]These are the family records of Esau, father of the Edomites in the mountains of Seir.

10   These are the names of Esau's sons:[o]
      Eliphaz son of Esau's wife Adah,

Cross-reference notes (center column)

[a]35:17 Gn 30:24
[b]35:19 Mc 5:2;
[c]35:22 Gn 49:3-4
[d]35:22-26 1Ch 2:1-2
[e]35:27 Gn 13:18; 18:1; 23:19
[f]Jos 14:15
[g]35:29 Gn 25:8,17; 49:33; Nm 20:24,26; Dt 32:50
[h]36:1 Gn 2:4; 36:9
[i]Gn 25:30
[j]36:2 Gn 26:34
[k]36:3 Gn 28:9
[l]36:7 Gn 13:6
[m]Gn 17:8; Heb 11:9
[n]36:8 Dt 2:5
[o]36:10-14 1Ch 1:35-37

[A]35:18 = Son of My Sorrow   [B]35:18 = Son of the Right Hand   [C]35:21 Or beyond Migdal-eder   [D]36:2 Sam, LXX read Anah son

---

time also it is stated that **kings** and **an assembly of nations** would come from the patriarch. After the revelatory words **God** "went up" (**withdrew**) from **the place**. To memorialize the event and bring closure to his vow to make Yahweh his God (28:21), Jacob set up **a stone marker**, pouring **a drink offering on it** (2Sm 23:16) and anointing it with **oil**.

35:16-20 While Jacob's clan was making a 15-mile journey **to Ephrath, Rachel**—now pregnant with her second child—**began to give birth**. As her **son** was being born she apparently began bleeding uncontrollably, an occurrence that kills about 1 out of every 200 mothers in many African nations even today. Before she died **she named** her son **Ben-oni**, meaning "Son of My Sorrow." However, to make sure that his wife's dying gift to him would be properly remembered, Jacob renamed the child **Benjamin**, meaning "Right-hand Son," the most honored son. Jacob also **set up a marker** at Rachel's burial site in the Bethlehem area. Visitors to Israel today can still visit the traditional site of her grave.

35:21-22 The disgusting character of another of Jacob's sons—this time his firstborn **Reuben**—was revealed **beyond the Tower of Eder**, a spot probably situated southwest of Bethlehem. Reuben **slept with Bilhah**, the mother of his half brothers Dan and Naphtali. By doing this Reuben was asserting his right to take his father's place as leader of the group (2Sm 12:8,11; 16:21-22) and perhaps seeking revenge

for Jacob's shunning of his mother Leah. His father learned of it and later cursed Reuben because of it (Gn 49:3-4).

35:23-26 With Benjamin's birth Jacob's set of offspring was now complete. This section lists the patriarch's **12 sons** during his time in **Paddan-aram** and, in Benjamin's case, following his return to Canaan. The sons are listed according to their mothers, not their birth order; the mothers are listed chronologically in the order of their connection with Jacob.

35:27-29 Jacob moved his family to stay with **his father Isaac**, who was living near the family burial cave at **Mamre** in the vicinity of **Hebron**. Isaac would live for many years, dying at the age of **180** and being buried by **Esau and Jacob** in the cave of Machpelah (49:31).

36:1-8 The family records of Esau, the ninth and shortest of the eleven (Hb) toledoth sections in Genesis (see note at 5:1), consists only of 36:1-8. This section complements the toledoth section of verses 9-43, which also contains family records of Esau, in that this emphasizes the "Canaan" portion of Esau's life. Esau, whose nickname was **Edom** (cp. 25:30), moved his family and property to Edom, whose primary feature is **the mountains of Seir**.

36:9 The family records of Esau, father of the Edomites, the tenth of the (Hb) toledoth sections in Genesis (see note at 5:1),

and Reuel son of Esau's wife Basemath.

[a]36:20-28 Gn 14:6; Dt 2:12,22; 1Ch 1:38-42
[b]36:31-43 Gn 17:6,16; 35:11; 1Ch 1:43-54

11 The sons of Eliphaz were
Teman, Omar, Zepho, Gatam,
and Kenaz.
12 Timna, a concubine of Esau's son
Eliphaz,
bore Amalek to Eliphaz.
These were the sons of Esau's wife
Adah.

13 These are Reuel's sons:
Nahath, Zerah, Shammah, and Mizzah.
These were the sons of Esau's wife
Basemath.

14 These are the sons of Esau's wife
Oholibamah
daughter of Anah and granddaughter[A]
of Zibeon:
She bore Jeush, Jalam, and Korah
to Edom.

15 These are the chiefs of Esau's sons:
the sons of Eliphaz, Esau's firstborn:
Chiefs Teman, Omar, Zepho, Kenaz,
16 Korah,[B] Gatam, and Amalek.
These are the chiefs of Eliphaz
in the land of Edom.
These are the sons of Adah.

17 These are the sons of Reuel, Esau's son:
Chiefs Nahath, Zerah, Shammah,
and Mizzah.
These are the chiefs of Reuel
in the land of Edom.
These are the sons of Esau's wife
Basemath.

18 These are the sons of Esau's wife
Oholibamah:
Chiefs Jeush, Jalam, and Korah.
These are the chiefs of Esau's wife
Oholibamah
daughter of Anah.

19 These are the sons of Esau
(that is, Edom),
and these are their chiefs.

Seir's Family
20 These are the sons of Seir the Horite,[a]
the inhabitants of the land:
Lotan, Shobal, Zibeon, Anah,
21 Dishon, Ezer, and Dishan.
These are the chiefs of the Horites,
the sons of Seir, in the land of Edom.
22 The sons of Lotan were Hori
and Heman.
Timna was Lotan's sister.
23 These are Shobal's sons:
Alvan, Manahath, Ebal, Shepho,
and Onam.
24 These are Zibeon's sons:
Aiah and Anah.
This was the Anah who found
the hot springs[c] in the wilderness
while he was pasturing the donkeys
of his father Zibeon.
25 These are the children of Anah:
Dishon and Oholibamah
daughter of Anah.
26 These are Dishon's sons:
Hemdan, Eshban, Ithran, and Cheran.
27 These are Ezer's sons:
Bilhan, Zaavan, and Akan.
28 These are Dishan's sons: Uz and Aran.

29 These are the chiefs of the Horites:
Chiefs Lotan, Shobal, Zibeon, Anah,
30 Dishon, Ezer, and Dishan.
These are the chiefs of the Horites,
according to their divisions, in the land
of Seir.

Rulers of Edom
31 These are the kings who ruled
in the land of Edom[b]

[A]36:14 Sam, LXX read *Anah son*   [B]36:16 Sam omits *Korah*   [C]36:24 Syr, Vg; Tg reads *the mules*; Hb obscure

---

consists of 36:9-43. This section, which repeats the genealogical information of verses 1-5, differs from the previous (Hb) *toledoth* unit in that it provides five major subsections that focus on historical and genealogical details relevant to Edom.

36:10-14 These verses contain the first of five subsections found in the second Esau (Hb) *toledoth*, and it expands on verses 4-5. This section supplements previous materials with a listing of six sons born to Adah's son **Eliphaz** and four sons descending from Basemath's son **Reuel**. **Teman** ("South") is the namesake of an important region in southern Edom (Jr 49:20; Ob 9) associated with wisdom (Jr 49:7). **Timna** was the daughter of Seir the Horite (vv. 20-22); thus, her son **Amalek** provides an important genealogical link between the Edomites and the Horites.

36:15-19 The second of the four Esau-related subsections

contains **the chiefs of Esau's sons**, listing all of Esau's sons and grandsons in verses 10-14, but adding a seventh son, **Korah**, to the listing of Eliphaz's sons. The term translated as "chiefs" (Hb *'alluph*) refers to the leader of a familial unit or of a geographical region.

36:20-30 The third of the final Esau (Hb) *toledoth* comprises the sons and chiefs of **Seir the Horite**, the father of Eliphaz's concubine **Timna**.

36:31-39 The fourth subsection of the second Esau (Hb) *toledoth* lists eight consecutive **kings who ruled in the land of Edom** prior to the days of King Saul, i.e., before 1050 B.C. Its inclusion demonstrates the fulfillment of God's promise to Abraham (17:6). The observation that no kings **ruled over the Israelites**, a nation that did not yet formally exist, suggests that this list was compiled no earlier than the days of King David. The parallel passage in 1Ch 1:43-50 differs from

before any king ruled
   over the Israelites:

32 Bela son of Beor ruled in Edom;
the name of his city was Dinhabah.

33 When Bela died, Jobab son of Zerah
from Bozrah became king
in his place.

34 When Jobab died, Husham
from the land of the Temanites
became king in his place.

35 When Husham died, Hadad
son of Bedad became king
in his place.
He defeated Midian in the field
of Moab;
the name of his city was Avith.

36 When Hadad died, Samlah
from Masrekah became king
in his place.

37 When Samlah died, Shaul
from Rehoboth on the
Euphrates River became king
in his place.

38 When Shaul died, Baal-hanan
son of Achbor became king
in his place.

39 When Baal-hanan son of Achbor died,
Hadar^A became king in his place.
His city was Pau, and his wife's name
was Mehetabel
daughter of Matred daughter
of Me-zahab.

40 These are the names of Esau's chiefs,
according to their families
   and their localities,
by their names:
Chiefs Timna, Alvah, Jetheth,

41 Oholibamah, Elah, Pinon,

42 Kenaz, Teman, Mibzar,

43 Magdiel, and Iram.
These are Edom's chiefs,

according to their settlements
   in the land they possessed.
Esau^B was father of the Edomites.

Joseph's Dreams

37 Jacob lived in the land where his father had stayed, the land of Canaan.^a ²These are the family records of Jacob.

At 17 years of age, Joseph tended sheep with his brothers. The young man was working with the sons of Bilhah and Zilpah, his father's wives,^b and he brought a bad report about them to their father.^c ³Now Israel loved Joseph more than his other sons because Joseph was a son born to him in his old age,^d and he made a robe of many colors^C for him. ⁴When his brothers saw that their father loved him more than all his brothers, they hated him and could not bring themselves to speak peaceably to him.

⁵Then Joseph had a dream. When he told it to his brothers, they hated him even more. ⁶He said to them, "Listen to this dream I had: ⁷There we were, binding sheaves of grain in the field. Suddenly my sheaf stood up, and your sheaves gathered around it and bowed down to my sheaf."^e

⁸"Are you really going to reign over us?" his brothers asked him. "Are you really going to rule us?" So they hated him even more because of his dream and what he had said.

⁹Then he had another dream and told it to his brothers. "Look," he said, "I had another dream, and this time the sun, moon, and 11 stars were bowing down to me."

¹⁰He told his father and brothers, but his father rebuked him. "What kind of dream is this that you have had?" he said. "Are your mother and brothers and I going to come and bow down to the ground before you?" ¹¹His brothers were jealous of him,^f but his father kept the matter in mind.^g

a 37:1 Gn 26:3
b 37:2 Gn 30:1-13
c 1Sm 2:22-24
d 37:3 Gn 44:20
e 37:7 Gn 42:6,9; 43:26; 44:14
f 37:11 Ac 7:9
g Dn 7:28; Lk 2:19,51

---

^A 36:39 Many Hb mss, Sam, Syr read *Hadad*   ^B 36:43 Lit *He Esau*   ^C 37:3 Or *robe with long sleeves*

---

this only in the spelling of the name Hadar (**Hadad**) and the name of Hadar's royal city **Pau** (Pai).

36:40-43 The fifth and final subsection of the second Esau (Hb) *toledoth* consists of a list of 11 of **Esau's chiefs** who ruled over various portions of the land of Edom. This list appears in abbreviated form in 1Ch 1:51b-54.

37:1 In contrast to Esau, who left the land promised to Abraham's descendants, **Jacob** remained in **the land of Canaan**, demonstrating Jacob's acceptance of God's gift of the land to him and his descendants (35:12).

37:2-4 The family records of Jacob, which extend through the end of the book, constitute the eleventh and last of the (Hb) *toledoth* sections in Genesis (see note at 5:1). The account begins with a description of 17-year-old **Joseph**, the central human figure in this section; he is the subject of

more than 200 verbs within the narrative framework of the final 14 chapters of Genesis. These opening verses continue the troubled portrait of Jacob's sons begun in chapter 35, as **the sons of Bilhah and Zilpah**—Dan, Naphtali, Gad, and Asher—misbehaved. Jacob's unequal treatment of his sons (cp. 25:28) aroused great jealousy, so that Joseph's brothers **hated** him. The **robe of many colors** probably marked Joseph as Jacob's chosen successor for clan leadership, especially since he was the firstborn of Rachel, the only woman Jacob had ever intended to marry.

37:5-11 Like his father Jacob (28:12-15; 31:10-13), **Joseph** received two dreams from God during his lifetime. Both portrayed Joseph as gaining a position of supremacy in his family, though the symbols differed greatly. The first dream used an agricultural image (v. 7). The second, more important and wider in scope than the first, was astronomical (vv.

Joseph Sold into Slavery

¹²His brothers had gone to pasture their father's flocks at Shechem. ¹³Israel said to Joseph, "Your brothers, you know, are pasturing the flocks at Shechem. Get ready. I'm sending you to them."

"I'm ready," Joseph replied.

¹⁴Then Israel said to him, "Go and see how your brothers and the flocks are doing, and bring word back to me." So he sent him from the Valley of Hebron,ᵃ and he went to Shechem.

¹⁵A man found him there, wandering in the field, and asked him, "What are you looking for?"

¹⁶"I'm looking for my brothers," Joseph said. "Can you tell me where they are pasturing their flocks?"

¹⁷"They've moved on from here," the man said. "I heard them say, 'Let's go to Dothan.'"ᵇ So Joseph set out after his brothers and found them at Dothan.

¹⁸They saw him in the distance, and before he had reached them, they plotted to kill him.ᶜ ¹⁹They said to one another, "Here comes that dreamer!ᴬ ²⁰Come on, let's kill him and throw him into one of the pits. We can say that a vicious animal ate him. Then we'll see what becomes of his dreams!"

²¹When Reuben heard this, he tried to save him from them.ᴮ He said, "Let's not take his life."ᵈ ²²Reuben also said to them, "Don't shed blood. Throw him into this pit in the wilderness, but don't lay a hand on him"—intending to rescue him from their hands and return him to his father.

²³When Joseph came to his brothers, they stripped off his robe, the robe of many colors that he had on. ²⁴Then they took him and threw him into the pit. The pit was empty; there was no water in it.

²⁵Then they sat down to eat a meal.ᵉ They looked up, and there was a caravan of Ishmaelites coming from Gilead.ᶠ Their camels were carrying aromatic gum, balsam, and resin, going down to Egypt.ᵍ

²⁶Then Judah said to his brothers, "What do we gain if we kill our brother and cover up his blood? ²⁷Come, let's sell him to the Ishmaelites and not lay a hand on him, for he is our brother, our own flesh," and they agreed. ²⁸When Midianiteʰ traders passed by, his brothers pulled Joseph out of the pit and sold him for 20 pieces of silver to the Ishmaelites, who took Joseph to Egypt.ⁱ

²⁹When Reuben returned to the pit and saw that Joseph was not there, he tore his clothes.ʲ ³⁰He went back to his brothers and said, "The boy is gone! What am I going to do?"ᶜ ³¹So they took Joseph's robe, slaughtered a young goat, and dipped the robe in its blood. ³²They sent the robe of many colors to their father and said, "We found this. Examine it. Is it your son's robe or not?"

³³His father recognized it. "It is my son's robe," he said. "A vicious animal has devoured him. Joseph has been torn to pieces!"ᵏ ³⁴Then Jacob tore his clothes, put •sackcloth around his waist, and mourned for his son many days. ³⁵All his sons and daughters tried to comfort him, but he refused to be comforted. "No," he said. "I will go down to •Sheol to my son, mourning." And his father wept for him.

ᵃ37:14 Gn 13:18; 35:27
ᵇ37:17 2Kg 6:13
ᶜ37:18 Ps 31:13; 37:12,32; Mk 14:1; Jn 11:53; Ac 23:12
ᵈ37:21 Gn 42:22
ᵉ37:25 Gn 42:21
ᶠGn 39:1
ᵍGn 43:11; Jr 8:22; 46:11
ʰ37:28 Dt 25:5,7; Jdg 8:22-24; Mt 22:24; Mk 12:19; Lk 20:28
ⁱGn 45:4-5; Ps 105:17; Ac 7:9
ʲ37:29 Gn 44:13; Nm 14:6; 2Sm 1:11; 3:31; Jb 1:20
ᵏ37:33 Gn 44:28

ᴬ37:19 Lit comes the lord of the dreams   ᴮ37:21 Lit their hands   ᶜ37:30 Lit And I, where am I going

---

9-10). The pairing of dreams with a shared meaning meant that God would certainly make the events happen (41:32). Ancient interpreters suggested that the moon signified Bilhah since Joseph's mother Rachel was dead at this time (35:19).

37:12-17 Israel (i.e., Jacob) made his teenage son **Joseph** a supervisor over his brothers. Joseph, who had earlier given a bad report about his older brothers, was once again called upon to report how they were doing. Joseph traveled about 50 miles north **to Shechem**. Learning that his brothers had moved on, he finally found them at **Dothan**, some 15 miles farther north.

37:18-24 Joseph's older brothers, all of whom hated him and were violent men (34:27-29) or even murderers (34:25-26), immediately **plotted to kill him,** calling him "the lord of the dreams" **(that dreamer).** Being skilled at deception as well (34:13), the brothers also concocted the lie that **a vicious animal ate him.** They **threw him into** a dry cistern designed to store water for the flocks.

37:25-28 The fact that Joseph's brothers **sat down to eat a meal** soon after they disposed of him reveals how bra-

zenly sinful they were. Later Joseph would be free while the brothers were in prison (42:17). But on this day the brothers saw **a caravan of Ishmaelites** traveling south on the main road leading from Egypt to Damascus. **Judah** convinced seven of his brothers that it was more profitable to **sell** Joseph as a slave than to **kill** him. According to 42:21, Joseph pleaded with his brothers, but to no avail. They sold him for **20 pieces of silver,** the standard price for a teenage male slave (Lv 27:5). **Midianite** is another designation for Ishmaelites in this narrative. Mention of the descendants of Ishmael (21:9-13) and Midian (25:1-6) call to mind the kind of sibling rivalry that is taking place here again.

37:29-35 As the oldest of the brothers, **Reuben** felt responsible for Joseph's safety. He had not been present when his brothers decided to sell Joseph. He was shocked and dismayed when he discovered what had happened. In a traditional ancient Near Eastern show of grief, he **tore his clothes.**

Jacob naturally concluded that **a vicious animal** had **torn** Joseph **to pieces.** Joseph had been Jacob's favorite son (v. 4), and Jacob's mother Rachel had recently died tragically. Thus when confronted with this evidence, **he refused to be comforted,** expressing instead the desire to **go down to**

³⁶Meanwhile, the Midianites sold Joseph in Egypt to Potiphar, an officer of Pharaoh and the captain of the guard.

Judah and Tamar

38 At that time Judah left his brothers and settled near an Adullamite ᵃ named Hirah. ²There Judah saw the daughter of a Canaanite named Shua; he took her as a wife and slept with her. ³She conceived and gave birth to a son, and he named him Er.ᵇ ⁴She conceived again, gave birth to a son, and named him Onan. ⁵She gave birth to another son and named him Shelah. It was at Chezib thatᴬ,ᴮ she gave birth to him.

⁶Judah got a wife for Er, his firstborn, and her name was Tamar. ⁷Now Er, Judah's firstborn, was evil in the Lᴏʀᴅ's sight, and the Lᴏʀᴅ put him to death.ᶜ ⁸Then Judah said to Onan, "Sleep with your brother's wife. Perform your duty as her brother-in-lawᵈ and produce ⸱offspring for your brother."ᵉ ⁹But Onan knew that the offspring would not be his, so whenever he slept with his brother's wife, he released his semen on the ground so that he would not produce offspring for his brother. ¹⁰What he did was evil in the Lᴏʀᴅ's sight, so He put him to death also.

¹¹Then Judah said to his daughter-in-law Tamar, "Remain a widow in your father's house until my son Shelah grows up."ᶠ For he thought, "He might die too, like his brothers." So Tamar went to live in her father's house.

¹²After a long time ᶜ Judah's wife, the daughter of Shua, died. When Judah had finished mourning, he and his friend Hirah the Adullamite went up to Timnahᵍ to the sheepshearers. ¹³Tamar was told, "Your father-in-law is going up to Timnah to shear his sheep." ¹⁴So she took off her widow's clothes, veiled her face,ʰ covered herself, and sat at the entrance to Enaim,ᴰ which is on the way to Timnah. For she saw that, though Shelah had grown up, she had not been given to him as a wife. ¹⁵When Judah saw her, he thought she was a prostitute, for she had covered her face.

¹⁶He went over to her and said, "Come, let me sleep with you," for he did not know that she was his daughter-in-law.ⁱ

She said, "What will you give me for sleeping with me?"

¹⁷"I will send you a young goat from my flock," he replied.

But she said, "Only if you leave something with me until you send it."

¹⁸"What should I give you?" he asked.

She answered, "Your signet ring, your cord, and the staff in your hand." So he gave them to her and slept with her, and she got pregnant by him. ¹⁹She got up and left, then removed her veil and put her widow's clothes back on.

ᵃ38:1 Jos 15:35; 1Sm 22:1
ᵇ38:3 Gn 46:12; Nm 26:19
ᶜ38:7 1Ch 2:3
ᵈ38:8 Dt 25:5-10
ᵉMt 22:24
ᶠ38:11 Ru 1:12-13
ᵍ38:12 Jos 15:10,57
ʰ38:14 Gn 24:65
ⁱ38:16 Lv 18:15

ᴬ38:5 LXX reads *She was at Chezib when*   ᴮ38:5 Or *He was at Chezib when*   ᶜ38:12 Lit *And there were many days*   ᴰ38:14 Or *sat by the mouth of the springs*

Sheol—the traditional term for the place of the dead—to be with his **son**.

37:36 Even as Jacob mourned his son's death, Joseph—very much alive—was taken to Egypt and **sold** to **Potiphar**, a prestigious military officer in the court **of Pharaoh**.

38:1-5 Judah's departure while Jacob grieved may have been motivated by a combination of intense guilt feelings and anger at his brothers. Continuing the dark picture of Jacob's sons begun in chapter 36, Judah rejected the covenant family's marriage tradition (24:3; 28:1) and took **the daughter of a Canaanite** as **a wife**. The couple conceived three sons, **Er** ("Watchful"), **Onan** ("Strength/Vigorous"), and **Shelah** ("Drawn Out [from the Womb]").

38:6-11 In keeping with ancient Near Eastern tradition, **Judah got a wife for** his son **Er** (24:2-4; Ex 2:21; Jdg 4:1-3). The absence of any ethnic identification for Er's wife **Tamar** ("Palm Tree") may mean she was not a Canaanite. Because Er **was evil in the Lᴏʀᴅ's sight**, the Lᴏʀᴅ **put him to death**. God's judgment on sinners is not always immediate but there are cases in both the OT and the NT, and presumably throughout history, when God brings justice swiftly (6:5-7; 19:13; Ac 5:4; 1Co 11:29-31). Er died before fathering any children, and ancient Near Eastern custom required the childless widow's **brother-in-law** to marry her and produce **offspring** who would be counted as the dead male's heir (Dt 25:5-6).

Onan, however, realized **that the offspring would not be his**, so he took a course of action known as onanism (named after Onan's actions here) to prevent conception. Onan's motive **was evil in the Lᴏʀᴅ's sight**, and so God killed him also. With two sons having died while married to Tamar, Judah feared that Shelah **might die too** if he fulfilled the responsibility to his sister-in-law. Consequently Judah sent her away to live **in her father's house**, with the deceptive excuse that Shelah was not old enough.

38:12-19 Even after **Shelah had grown up** and was eligible for marriage, Tamar remained a widow. In the meantime, **Judah's wife** had **died**. Having been deceived by Judah earlier, Tamar cunningly set about to deceive her father-in-law (cp. 27:15,27). In order to get Judah to fulfill his family's obligation to produce an heir for Er and remove the stigma of her childlessness, Tamar apparently knew her father-in-law's immoral character. So she **took off her widow's clothes** (signs of mourning), **veiled her face**, positioned herself alone by **Enaim** ("Two Springs") where she knew Judah would pass, and played the role of a roadside cult prostitute.

Though sexual relations with a daughter-in-law were prohibited in the Israelite law that was written centuries later (Lv 18:15), Judah did not recognize her and so propositioned her. As proof of his willingness to pay once he had money in hand, Judah had to give Tamar his "cylinder seal" (**signet ring**), among other items. Having achieved her objective by getting pregnant, Tamar returned home and **put her widow's clothes back on** for the time being.

²⁰ When Judah sent the young goat by his friend the Adullamite in order to get back the items he had left with the woman, he could not find her. ²¹ He asked the men of the place, "Where is the cult prostitute who was beside the road at Enaim?"

"There has been no cult prostitute here," they answered.

²² So the Adullamite returned to Judah, saying, "I couldn't find her, and furthermore, the men of the place said, 'There has been no cult prostitute here.'"

²³ Judah replied, "Let her keep the items for herself; otherwise we will become a laughingstock. After all, I did send this young goat, but you couldn't find her."

²⁴ About three months later Judah was told, "Your daughter-in-law, Tamar, has been acting like a prostitute, and now she is pregnant."

"Bring her out!" Judah said. "Let her be burned to death!"^a

²⁵ As she was being brought out, she sent her father-in-law this message: "I am pregnant by the man to whom these items belong." And she added, "Examine them. Whose signet ring, cord, and staff are these?"

²⁶ Judah recognized them and said, "She is more in the right^A than I,^b since I did not give her to my son Shelah." And he did not know her intimately again.

²⁷ When the time came for her to give birth, there were twins in her womb. ²⁸ As she was giving birth, one of them put out his hand, and the midwife took it and tied a scarlet thread around it, announcing, "This one came out first." ²⁹ But then he pulled his hand back, and his brother came out. Then she said, "You have broken out first!" So he was named Perez.^{B, c} ³⁰ Then his brother, who had the scarlet thread tied to his hand, came out, and was named Zerah.^C

Joseph in Potiphar's House

39 Now Joseph had been taken to Egypt. An Egyptian named Potiphar, an officer of Pharaoh and the captain of the guard, bought him from the Ishmaelites^d who had brought him there. ² The LORD was with Joseph,^e and he became a successful man, serving^D in the household of his Egyptian master. ³ When his master saw that the LORD was with him and that the LORD made everything he did successful,^f ⁴ Joseph found favor in his master's sight^g and became his personal attendant. Potiphar also put him in charge of his household and placed all that he owned under his authority.^E ⁵ From the time that he put him in charge of his household and of all that he owned, the LORD blessed the Egyptian's house because of Joseph.^h The LORD's blessing was on all that he owned, in his house and in his fields. ⁶ He left all that he owned under Joseph's authority;^F he did not concern himself with anything except the food he ate.

Now Joseph was well-built and handsome.ⁱ ⁷ After some time^G his master's wife looked longingly at Joseph and said, "Sleep with me." ⁸ But he refused. "Look," he said to his

^a38:24 Lv 20:14
^b38:26 1Sm 24:17
^c38:29 Gn 46:12; Nm 26:20; 1Ch 2:4; Mt 1:3
^d39:1 Gn 37:25,28,36; Ps 105:17
^e39:2 Gn 39:3,21,23; Ac 7:9
^f39:3 Ps 1:3
^g39:4 Gn 18:3; 19:19; 33:10
^h39:5 Gn 30:27
ⁱ39:6 Gn 29:17; 1Sm 16:12

^A38:26 Or *more righteous*   ^B38:29 = Breaking Out   ^C38:30 = Brightness of Sunrise; perhaps related to the scarlet thread
^D39:2 Lit *and he was*   ^E39:4 Lit *owned in his hand*   ^F39:6 Lit *owned in Joseph's hand*   ^G39:7 Lit *And after these things*

38:20-23 Keeping his promise, **Judah sent** Hirah (v. 1) to Tamar with a **young goat** to **get back** his possessions. When Hirah returned **to Judah** without recovering Judah's possessions, Judah recognized he had been outwitted by the prostitute since his credentials represented his honor and were thus more valuable than a young goat. He attempted to minimize the humiliation by giving up on the search and thus telling no one else what had happened.

38:24-26 Three months after the fateful encounter **Judah** was informed that his **daughter-in-law** was **pregnant**. Since she had an obligation to remain chaste and available for marriage to Shelah, Shelah's father ordered that she be **burned to death**—a penalty that in later times was reserved for depraved sexual sins in the law of Moses (Lv 20:14; 21:9). Before she could be executed, however, Tamar informed her would-be executioners that she was **pregnant by the man** whose "cylinder seal" (**signet ring**) she possessed. Confronted by indisputable evidence of his responsibility for Tamar's pregnancy, Judah admitted that **she** was **more . . . right** than he; he had wronged her by denying her the right to marry his **son Shelah**.

38:27-30 Six months later it was discovered that Tamar was carrying **twins in** her **womb**; the language mirrors that of Jacob and Esau's birth (25:24). The birth was a complicated one, as one of the babies stuck **his hand**—not his head, as is normal—out the birth canal. The child **pulled his hand back** inside the mother.

As it turned out, **his brother** actually **came out** first, earning himself not only the rights of the firstborn but also the name **Perez** ("Bursting Forth/Breach"). **His brother**, born belatedly with the **scarlet thread** still **tied to his hand**, received the name **Zerah** ("Dawning/Shining"). Perez would later be mentioned as an ancestor of both David (Ru 4:12,18) and Jesus (Mt 1:3).

39:1 This verse, which retraces details presented in 37:36, returns the storyline to **Joseph**. The terms Midianites and **Ishmaelites** are used interchangeably by the writer (37:28,36; see note at 37:25-28).

39:2-6 Because **the LORD** is God over the whole earth (1Ch 29:11; Ps 47:2; 83:18; 97:9), He **was with Joseph** even in Egypt. God's active presence in Joseph's life made him **successful**. Potiphar noticed the teenage Hebrew slave's remarkable effectiveness, and as a result Joseph not only **found favor** with him, but was put in charge of Potiphar's entire **household** as well. With Joseph in charge, **the LORD's blessing** extended to all that Potiphar **owned**.

39:7-10 In contrast to his brother Judah, who sacrificed his honor for the pleasure of a prostitute (38:15-16), Joseph

master's wife, "with me here my master does not concern himself with anything in his house, and he has put all that he owns under my authority.[A] [9]No one in this house is greater than I am. He has withheld nothing from me except you, because you are his wife. So how could I do such a great evil and sin against God?"[a]

[10]Although she spoke to Joseph day after day, he refused[B] to go to bed with her.[c] [11]Now one day he went into the house to do his work, and none of the household servants were there.[D] [12]She grabbed him by his garment and said, "Sleep with me!" But leaving his garment in her hand, he escaped and ran outside. [13]When she saw that he had left his garment with her and had run outside, [14]she called the household servants. "Look," she said to them, "my husband brought a Hebrew man to make fools of us. He came to me so he could sleep with me, and I screamed as loud as I could. [15]When he heard me screaming for help,[E] he left his garment with me and ran outside."

[16]She put Joseph's garment beside her until his master came home. [17]Then she told him the same story: "The Hebrew slave you brought to us came to make a fool of me, [18]but when I screamed for help,[F] he left his garment with me and ran outside."

[19]When his master heard the story his wife told him—"These are the things your slave did to me"—he was furious [20]and had him thrown into prison,[b] where the king's prisoners were confined. So Joseph was there in prison.

Joseph in Prison

[21]But the LORD was with Joseph and extended kindness to him.[c] He granted him favor in the eyes of the prison warden.[d] [22]The warden put all the prisoners who were in the prison under Joseph's authority,[G] and he was responsible for everything that was done there. [23]The warden did not bother with anything under Joseph's authority,[H] because the LORD was with him, and the LORD made everything that he did successful.[e]

Joseph Interprets Two Prisoners' Dreams

40 After this, the Egyptian king's cupbearer[f] and baker offended their master, the king of Egypt. [2]Pharaoh was angry with his two officers, the chief cupbearer and the chief baker, [3]and put them in custody in the house of the captain of the guard[g] in the prison where Joseph was confined. [4]The captain of the guard assigned Joseph to them, and he became their personal attendant. And they were in custody for some time.[I]

[5]The Egyptian king's cupbearer and baker,

[a]39:9 Gn 20:6; 42:18; 2Sm 12:13; Ps 51:4; Pr 6:29
[b]39:20 Gn 40:3; Ps 105:18
[c]39:21 Gn 39:2; Ps 105:19; Ac 7:9
[d]Ex 3:21; 11:3; 12:36
[e]39:23 Gn 39:2-3
[f]40:1 Neh 1:11
[g]40:3 Gn 39:20

[A]39:8 Lit owns in my hand   [B]39:10 Lit did not listen to her   [C]39:10 Lit refused to lie beside her, to be with her   [D]39:11 Lit there in the house   [E]39:15 Lit me raise my voice and scream   [F]39:18 Lit I raised my voice and screamed   [G]39:22 Lit prison in the hand of Joseph   [H]39:23 Lit anything in his hand   [I]40:4 Lit custody days

---

refused the advances of his master's wife. To commit adultery would have been **a great evil** and a **sin against God** (cp. Ex 20:14). Potiphar's wife persisted, telling Joseph **day after day** to "lie beside her" (**go to bed with her**).

39:11-15 When the subtle approach failed to seduce Joseph, Potiphar's wife resorted to a more direct method. Finding—or perhaps creating—a situation where **none of the household servants** except Joseph was in the house, she grabbed Joseph **by his garment** and ordered him to **sleep with her**. In a courageous display of godly self-control, Joseph resisted, **escaped and ran outside, leaving his garment in her hand**. This is the second time that a woman used the personal effects of one of Jacob's sons (cp. Judah, 38:25) to get the upper hand in a situation where they would otherwise have been put to death. Potiphar's wife then lied **to the household servants**, playing upon the other slaves' jealousy that had been inflamed when Potiphar placed the Hebrew young man over them as their boss. The presence of Joseph's **garment** seemed like circumstantial evidence for her false claim.

39:16-20 When Potiphar's wife repeated the story to her husband, she framed the lie in a way that placed the blame squarely on him. Her story made Potiphar **furious**. Without investigating the truth of her claims, Potiphar declared Joseph guilty. But instead of killing him, he **had him thrown into prison** (lit "the round house"). Why? Ancient Jewish opinion held that Potiphar's wife intervened because she hoped to take advantage of Joseph later. Perhaps this is true. It is also possible that Potiphar already distrusted his wife and thus doubted the truth of her story.

39:21-23 The LORD, who is present in Sheol (Ps 139:8), was also **with Joseph** in prison. God, who is rich in "faithful love" (**kindness**; Hb chesed; see Ex 34:7), demonstrated His love by granting Joseph **favor in the eyes of the prison warden**. For the third time in his life (cp. v. 4; Gn 37:14), Joseph was given authority over his peers—in this case, **all the prisoners who were in the prison**. Mirroring Potiphar's level of confidence in Joseph, the warden did not "see anything in his hand" (**bother with anything under Joseph's authority**) because **the LORD** caused everything Joseph did to be **successful** (Hb matsliach; cp. Ps 1:3 "prospers").

40:1-4 After Joseph had been imprisoned for a number of years and was now 28 years old (41:1,46), Pharaoh "became furious" (**was angry**; Hb qatsaph) with two high-ranking officials (Hb saris), **the chief cupbearer and the chief baker**. Though Potiphar was also a "captain of the guard," this detention center was apparently located in someone else's house since it was the same location **where Joseph was confined**. Because of their high rank, the cupbearer and baker were given certain privileges even in prison: Joseph, as a young Hebrew slave, was assigned as **their personal attendant**. The officials stayed in prison for "days" (**some time**).

40:5-8 During their confinement the royal cupbearer and baker **each had a dream** during **the same night**—the third and fourth non-Israelites to have dreams with divinely inspired meanings (cp. Abimelech, 20:3; Laban, 31:24). When they awoke the men were **distraught** (lit their "faces were bad") because there was no professional Egyptian dream

who were confined in the prison, each had a dream. Both had a dream on the same night, and each dream had its own meaning. ⁶When Joseph came to them in the morning, he saw that they looked distraught. ⁷So he asked Pharaoh's officers who were in custody with him in his master's house, "Why do you look so sad today?" ᵃ

⁸"We had dreams," they said to him, "but there is no one to interpret them."

Then Joseph said to them, "Don't interpretations belong to God? Tell me your dreams." ᵇ

⁹So the chief cupbearer told his dream to Joseph: "In my dream there was a vine in front of me. ¹⁰On the vine were three branches. As soon as it budded, its blossoms came out and its clusters ripened into grapes. ¹¹Pharaoh's cup was in my hand, and I took the grapes, squeezed them into Pharaoh's cup, and placed the cup in Pharaoh's hand."

¹²"This is its interpretation,"ᶜ Joseph said to him. "The three branches are three days. ¹³In just three days Pharaoh will lift up your headᵈ and restore you to your position. You will put Pharaoh's cup in his hand the way you used to when you were his cupbearer. ¹⁴But when all goes well for you, remember that I was with you. Please show kindness to me by mentioning me to Pharaoh, and get me out of this prison. ¹⁵For I was kidnapped from the land of the

Hebrews,ᵉ and even here I have done nothing that they should put me in the dungeon."ᶠ

¹⁶When the chief baker saw that the interpretation was positive, he said to Joseph, "I also had a dream. Three baskets of white bread were on my head. ¹⁷In the top basket were all sorts of baked goods for Pharaoh, but the birds were eating them out of the basket on my head."

¹⁸"This is its interpretation," Joseph replied. "The three baskets are three days. ¹⁹In just three days Pharaoh will lift up your head—from off you—and hang you on a tree.ᴬ Then the birds will eat the flesh from your body."ᴮ

²⁰On the third day, which was Pharaoh's birthday, he gave a feast for all his servants. He lifted up the heads of the chief cupbearer and the chief baker.ᵍ ²¹Pharaoh restored the chief cupbearer to his position as cupbearer, and he placed the cup in Pharaoh's hand. ²²But Pharaoh hangedᶜ the chief baker, just as Joseph had explained to them. ²³Yet the chief cupbearer did not remember Joseph; he forgot him.ʰ

Joseph Interprets Pharaoh's Dreams

41 Two years later Pharaoh had a dream: He was standing beside the Nile,ⁱ ²when seven healthy-looking, well-fed cows came up from the Nile and began to graze among the

ᵃ40:7 Neh 2:2
ᵇ40:8 Dn 2:11,20-24
ᶜ40:12 Gn 41:12; Dn 2:36
ᵈ40:13 Gn 40:19-22
ᵉ40:15 Gn 37:28
ᶠGn 39:20
ᵍ40:20 2Kg 25:27; Jr 52:31; Mt 14:6
ʰ40:23 Ec 9:15-16
ⁱ41:1-7 Gn 41:17-23

ᴬ40:19 Or *and impale you on a pole*   ᴮ40:19 Lit *eat your flesh from upon you*   ᶜ40:22 Or *impaled*

interpreter present. Joseph told them that accurate **interpretations belong to God**. And since the Lord was with Joseph even in prison (39:2,21,23), the men were directed to tell their dreams to him.

40:9-15 The chief cupbearer, who was an adviser and security officer for Pharaoh, was the first to tell **his dream to Joseph**. While aspects of the dream seemed to portray something positive—**blossoms . . . grapes**, placing **the cup**

chalam

Hebrew Pronunciation	[khah LAM]
HCSB Translation	dream
Uses in Genesis	14
Uses in the OT	29
Focus passage	Genesis 40:5,8

The word *dream* is a translation of a Hebrew verb *(chalam)*, a Hebrew noun *(chalom*; 65x), and an Aramaic noun *(chelem)* in Daniel (22x). *Dreams* are of great importance in the Bible. While six passages can refer to ordinary *dreams* (e.g., Jb 7:14), the rest pertain to *dreams* that are or claim to be supernatural in origin. This does not imply that most *dreams* are supernatural, but *dreams* are used as an avenue of communication between God and humans. God may appear in the *dream* (Gn 28:12-15) or may disclose His message through symbols that the dreamer or another person must interpret (Dn 2:4). Occasionally an angel will interpret a *dream* (Dn 7:16). God regularly used *dreams* to give revelation to His prophets (Nm 12:6). A *dream* could consist of several visions, or scenes (Dn 7:1-2,7,13).

in Pharaoh's hand—other aspects were doubtful, particularly the **three branches**. Joseph explained that the branches represented the next **three days**, after which Pharaoh would **lift** the cupbearer's **head** (or release him from prison; cp. 2Kg 25:27) and **restore** him to his **position**. Confident that the interpretation was accurate, Joseph pleaded for the cupbearer to **remember** him, mention him to Pharaoh, and arrange to get him out of prison. Joseph's release was a matter of simple justice since he had **done nothing** to deserve imprisonment.

40:16-19 Heartened by Joseph's positive interpretation of the cupbearer's dream, the **chief baker** shared his **dream**. As with the previous dream, this one contained ambiguous elements—particularly the **three baskets of white bread** and the **birds**—that needed a clear interpretation. This time the meaning was a dark one: Pharaoh would release the chief baker from prison and **hang** him **on a tree** (or possibly "impale" him "on wood"). The birds eating white bread symbolized the birds that would eat the baker's body.

40:20-22 Consistent with the dreams' divinely inspired interpretations, the two officials were released from prison three days later, on the festive occasion of **Pharaoh's birthday**. The "birthday" could either refer to Pharaoh's physical birth or to his accession day, the day he became king and thus was believed to have become a son of the Egyptian god Horus. Just as Joseph had foretold, Pharaoh **restored the chief cupbearer** to his previous position, but **hanged the chief baker**.

41:1-7 Pharaoh, the most powerful man in the world of his day, was also the Egyptian who received dreams from God that were far-reaching in their implications. His two

reeds. ³After them, seven other cows, sickly and thin, came up from the Nile and stood beside those cows along the bank of the Nile. ⁴The sickly, thin cows ate the healthy, well-fed cows. Then Pharaoh woke up. ⁵He fell asleep and dreamed a second time: Seven heads of grain, plump and ripe, came up on one stalk. ⁶After them, seven heads of grain, thin and scorched by the east wind, sprouted up. ⁷The thin heads of grain swallowed up the seven plump, ripe ones. Then Pharaoh woke up, and it was only a dream.

⁸When morning came, he was troubled,ᵃ so he summoned all the magicians of Egypt and all its wise men.ᵇ Pharaoh told them his dreams, but no one could interpret them for him.

⁹Then the chief cupbearer said to Pharaoh, "Today I remember my faults. ¹⁰Pharaoh had been angry with his servants, and he put me and the chief baker in the custody of the captain of the guard. ¹¹He and I had dreams on the same night; each dream had its own meaning. ¹²Now a young Hebrew, a slave of the captain of the guards, was with us there. We told him our dreams, he interpreted our dreams for us, and each had its own interpretation. ¹³It turned out just the way he interpreted them to us: I was restored to my position, and the other man was hanged."ᶜ

¹⁴Then Pharaoh sent for Joseph, and they quickly brought him from the dungeon.ᵈ He shaved, changed his clothes, and went to Pharaoh.ᵉ

¹⁵Pharaoh said to Joseph, "I have had a dream, and no one can interpret it. But I have heard it said about you that you can hear a dream and interpret it."ᶠ

¹⁶"I am not able to,"ᵍ Joseph answered Pharaoh. "It is God who will give Pharaoh a favorable answer."ᴬ,ʰ

¹⁷So Pharaoh said to Joseph: "In my dream I was standing on the bank of the Nile, ¹⁸when seven well-fed, healthy-looking cows came up from the Nile and began to graze among the reeds. ¹⁹After them, seven other cows—ugly, very sickly, and thin—came up. I've never seen such ugly ones as these in all the land of Egypt. ²⁰Then the thin, ugly cows ate the first seven well-fed cows. ²¹When they had devoured them, you could not tell that they had devoured them; their appearance was as bad as it had been before. Then I woke up. ²²In my dream I had also seen seven heads of grain, plump and ripe, coming up on one stalk. ²³After them, seven heads of grain—withered, thin, and scorched by the east wind—sprouted up. ²⁴The thin heads of grain swallowed the seven plump ones. I told this to the magicians, but no one can tell me what it means."ⁱ

²⁵Then Joseph said to Pharaoh, "Pharaoh's dreams mean the same thing. God has revealed to Pharaoh what He is about to do.ʲ ²⁶The seven good cows are seven years, and the seven ripe heads are seven years. The dreams mean the same thing. ²⁷The seven thin, ugly cows that came up after them are seven years, and the seven worthless, scorched heads of grain are seven years of famine.ᵏ ²⁸"It is just as I told Pharaoh: God has shown Pharaoh what He is about to do. ²⁹Seven ᴮ years of great abundance are coming throughout the land of Egypt. ³⁰After them, seven years of famine will take place, and all the abundance in the land of Egypt will be forgotten. The famine will devastate the land.ˡ ³¹The abundance in the land will not be remembered because of the famine that follows it, for the famine will be very severe. ³²Since the dream

ᵃ41:8 Dn 2:1,3
ᵇEx 7:11,22; Dn 1:20; 2:2
ᶜ41:13 Gn 40:1-22
ᵈ41:14 Ps 105:20
ᵉDn 2:25
ᶠ41:15 Dn 5:16
ᵍ41:16 Dn 2:30
ʰGn 40:8; Dn 2:22,28,47
ⁱ41:24 Is 8:19; Dn 4:7
ʲ41:25 Dn 2:28-29,45; Rv 4:1
ᵏ41:27 2Kg 8:1
ˡ41:30 Gn 41:54,56; 47:13; Ps 105:16

ᴬ41:16 Or *"God will answer Pharaoh with peace of mind."* ᴮ41:29 Lit *Look! Seven*

---

dreams, both on the same night, had essentially identical plots, though the images were different. Both had 14 items, seven **healthy** and seven **thin** and **sickly**. In both dreams the seven healthy things appeared first, only to be consumed by the afflicted ones. Both were symbolic since they contained features not found in the real world.

41:8-14 These dreams clearly indicated trouble, but exactly what trouble was the question. To unravel the mystery, Pharaoh **summoned all the** court **magicians**, who would have received instruction from ancient Egyptian scrolls of dream interpretation; some of these ancient scrolls, dating to the Twelfth Dynasty (1973-1786 B.C.), have been recovered by archaeologists. Pharaoh also summoned all of Egypt's **wise men** to assist in the critical task of discerning the dreams' meanings. However, **no one could interpret** the dreams satisfactorily.

The crisis caused **the chief cupbearer** to remember how Joseph had accurately interpreted two mysterious dreams

two years earlier. Desperate for insight into his own dreams, Pharaoh immediately **sent for Joseph**. Prior to entering the royal court he had to be **shaved**—probably both his beard and scalp—and he put on **clothes** made of linen, as was appropriate for the Egyptian court. Joseph's change in appearance mirrored the change that was about to occur in his career.

41:15-16 Fluent in the Egyptian language after 13 years in the land, Joseph listened intently as Pharaoh described his problem. With humility Joseph confessed to Pharaoh that he was unable to interpret the dreams, but confidently added that his **God** would **give Pharaoh** the information he desired.

41:17-24 As Pharaoh repeated his account of the dreams, he added that the **ugly cows** still appeared wasted after they had eaten the healthy ones.

41:25-32 Joseph prefaced his interpretation with three im-

was given twice to Pharaoh, it means that the matter has been determined by God, and He will carry it out soon.

[33] "So now, let Pharaoh look for a discerning and wise man and set him over the land of Egypt. [34] Let Pharaoh do this: Let him appoint overseers over the land and take a fifth of the harvest of the land of Egypt during the seven years of abundance. [35] Let them gather all the excess food during these good years that are coming. Under Pharaoh's authority, store the grain in the cities, so they may preserve it as food. [36] The food will be a reserve for the land during the seven years of famine that will take place in the land of Egypt. Then the country will not be wiped out by the famine."

Joseph Exalted

[37] The proposal pleased Pharaoh and all his servants. [38] Then Pharaoh said to his servants, "Can we find anyone like this, a man who has God's spirit[A] in him?"[a] [39] So Pharaoh said to Joseph, "Since God has made all this known to you, there is no one as intelligent and wise as you are. [40] You will be over my house, and all my people will obey your commands. [B,b] Only with regard to the throne will I be greater than you." [41] Pharaoh also said to Joseph, "See, I am placing you over all the land of Egypt." [42] Pharaoh removed his signet ring from his hand and put it on Joseph's hand, clothed him with fine linen garments, and placed a gold chain around his neck.[c] [43] He had Joseph ride in his second chariot, and servants called out before him, "Abrek!"[C] So he placed him over all the land of Egypt. [44] Pharaoh said to Joseph, "I am Pharaoh, but no one will be able to raise his hand or foot in all the land of Egypt without your permission." [45] Pharaoh gave Joseph the name Zaphenath-paneah and gave him a wife, Asenath daughter of Potiphera, priest at

[a]41:38 Jb 32:8; Dn 4:8,9,18; 5:11,14
[b]41:40 Ps 105:21; Ac 7:10
[c]41:42 Est 3:10; 8:2; Dn 5:7,16,29
[d]41:50 Gn 46:20; 48:5
[e]41:57 Gn 12:10

On. [D] And Joseph went throughout[E] the land of Egypt.

Joseph's Administration

[46] Joseph was 30 years old when he entered the service of Pharaoh king of Egypt. Joseph left Pharaoh's presence and traveled throughout the land of Egypt.

[47] During the seven years of abundance the land produced outstanding harvests. [48] Joseph gathered all the excess food in the land of Egypt during the seven years and put it in the cities. He put the food in every city from the fields around it. [49] So Joseph stored up grain in such abundance—like the sand of the sea—that he stopped measuring it because it was beyond measure.

[50] Two sons were born to Joseph before the years of famine arrived.[d] Asenath daughter of Potiphera, priest at On,[D] bore them to him. [51] Joseph named the firstborn Manasseh, meaning, "God has made me forget all my hardship in my father's house." [52] And the second son he named Ephraim, meaning, "God has made me fruitful in the land of my affliction."

[53] Then the seven years of abundance in the land of Egypt came to an end, [54] and the seven years of famine began, just as Joseph had said. There was famine in every country, but throughout the land of Egypt there was food. [55] Extreme hunger came to all the land of Egypt, and the people cried out to Pharaoh for food. Pharaoh told all Egypt, "Go to Joseph and do whatever he tells you." [56] Because the famine had spread across the whole country, Joseph opened up all the storehouses and sold grain to the Egyptians, for the famine was severe in the land of Egypt. [57] Every nation came to Joseph in Egypt to buy grain, for the famine was severe in every land.[e]

A41:38 Or the spirit of the gods, or a god's spirit   B41:40 Lit will kiss your mouth   C41:43 Perhaps an Egyptian word meaning "Attention" or a Hb word meaning "Kneel."   D41:45,50 Or Heliopolis   E41:45 Or Joseph gained authority over

---

portant insights: first, Pharaoh actually had only one dream (lit "Pharaoh's dream is one"), though it **was given twice** using different symbols. Second, the dream's source was the one true **God** (lit "the God"). Third, it revealed what God was **about to do**.

41:33-36 Joseph advised Pharaoh to take four steps in preparation for the upcoming 14-year cycle of events in order to create a food reserve for the **seven years of famine**.

41:37-46 Joseph's insight into the dream, along with his ability to devise such an **intelligent** plan, convinced Pharaoh that Joseph had **God's spirit in him**. Pharaoh gave Joseph the Egyptian name **Zaphenath-paneah** ("Then God Said, 'Let Him Live'") and a wife of high social status. **Asenath** ("She Who Belongs to the Goddess Neith") was the **daughter of Potiphera**, a **priest at On** (Heliopolis), the prestigious religious center of solar worship in ancient Egypt.

Joseph, who was now **30 years old**, had been transformed by God in 13 years from an imprisoned foreign slave to the world's second most powerful man. He who had spent years in prison now went **throughout the land of Egypt** overseeing a project that would save the lives of untold thousands.

41:47-52 In addition to God's blessing on the harvests, God blessed Joseph's personal life with two sons. Manasseh's name reflected the fact that **God** had helped Joseph forget his **hardship** both in Egypt and in his **father's house**, with its sordid background of rape (34:2), murder (34:25-26), incest (35:22), deception (34:13), and betrayal (37:28). Ephraim's name confessed that **God** had **made** Joseph **fruitful** in a land where he had once been treated as a despised felon.

41:53-57 As Joseph, guided by God's revelation, had said, after **seven years of abundance** famine struck **every country** in the region, even beyond Egypt's borders. Pharaoh

Joseph's Brothers in Egypt

42 When Jacob learned that there was grain in Egypt,ᵃ he said to his sons, "Why do you keep looking at each other? ²Listen," he went on, "I have heard there is grain in Egypt. Go down there and buy some for us so that we will live and not die."ᵇ ³So 10 of Joseph's brothers went down to buy grain from Egypt. ⁴But Jacob did not send Joseph's brother Benjamin with his brothers, for he thought, "Something might happen to him."

⁵The sons of Israel were among those who came to buy grain, for the famine was in the land of Canaan. ⁶Joseph was in charge of the country; he sold grain to all its people. His brothers came and bowed down before him with their faces to the ground.ᶜ ⁷When Joseph saw his brothers, he recognized them, but he treated them like strangers and spoke harshly to them.

"Where do you come from?" he asked.

"From the land of Canaan to buy food," they replied.

⁸Although Joseph recognized his brothers, they did not recognize him. ⁹Joseph remembered his dreams about themᵈ and said to them, "You are spies. You have come to see the weaknessᴬ of the land."

¹⁰"No, my lord. Your servants have come to buy food," they said. ¹¹"We are all sons of one man. We are honest; your servants are not spies."

¹²"No," he said to them. "You have come to see the weakness of the land."

¹³But they replied, "We, your servants, were 12 brothers, the sons of one man in the land of Canaan. The youngest is nowᴮ with our father, and one is no longer living."

¹⁴Then Joseph said to them, "I have spoken:ᶜ 'You are spies!' ¹⁵This is how you will be tested: As surely as Pharaoh lives, you will not leave this place unless your youngest brother comes here. ¹⁶Send one from among you to get your brother. The rest of you will be imprisoned so that your words can be tested to see if they are true. If they are not, then as surely as Pharaoh lives, you are spies!" ¹⁷So Joseph imprisoned them together for three days.

¹⁸On the third day Joseph said to them, "I 'fear God'ᵉ—do this and you will live. ¹⁹If you are honest, let one of youᴰ be confined to the guardhouse, while the rest of you go and take grain to relieve the hunger of your households. ²⁰Bring your youngest brother to me so that your words can be confirmed; then you won't die." And they consented to this.

²¹Then they said to each other, "Obviously, we are being punished for what we did to our brother. We saw his deep distress when he

---

ᵃ42:1 Ac 7:12
ᵇ42:2 Gn 43:8
ᶜ42:6 Gn 37:7-10; 41:43; Is 60:14
ᵈ42:9 Gn 37:5-11
ᵉ42:18 Gn 39:9; Lv 25:43; Neh 5:15

ᴬ42:9 Lit *nakedness*   ᴮ42:13 Or *today*   ᶜ42:14 Lit *"That which I spoke to you saying*   ᴰ42:19 Lit *your brothers*

---

directed the people to **go to Joseph**, who **sold grain to the Egyptians** to preserve the lives of his adopted countrymen. However, as other nations learned of Egypt's food supply, the whole affected part of the world also **came to Joseph**. As it would for thousands of years beyond this point, Egypt proved to be the breadbasket for the Mediterranean world.

42:1-38 In many ways this chapter reuses the elements of chapters 37–38. Members of Jacob's clan go to Egypt, are unjustly accused of a crime they did not commit, one (Simeon) is imprisoned under false pretenses, several of the brothers acquire silver after consigning a brother to live in Egypt, the (supposed) eldest living son of Rachel is forced to go to Egypt, and Jacob is made to grieve over Rachel's son.

42:1-5 News of Egypt's willingness to sell **grain** to outsiders reached Jacob. Since he was the patriarch and chief decision maker of the clan, it was Jacob's responsibility to look out for the clan's welfare. He had the right to order the rest of the adult males to **go down** to Egypt to **buy** grain. In a virtual replay of chapter 37, Jacob sent **10 of Joseph's brothers** out to do the family's work, but he spared a son of his beloved late wife Rachel (**Benjamin**). Jacob's sons joined a stream of others who **came** to Egypt **to buy grain**.

42:6-13 Since **Joseph was in charge** of selling **grain** to all the people of Egypt, his first responsibility was to meet the needs of his own people. Nevertheless, he did permit sales to non-Egyptians who posed no threat to Egypt. When Joseph's older **brothers . . . bowed down before him with their faces to the ground**, they fulfilled Joseph's prophetic dreams (37:7,9). Joseph had not seen his brothers for 20

years, yet **he recognized them** immediately. But the brothers did not recognize him; as a top Egyptian official Joseph had no hair on his head, wore eye makeup and expensive clothing, and spoke fluent Egyptian.

Joseph remembered his dreams about his brothers and their treacherous actions against him, so he devised a test to see if they had changed during the past two decades: he accused them of being **spies** sent to identify **the weakness of the land** (lit "the nakedness of the land"). They immediately denied the charges, supporting their claim by telling him they were **all sons of one man**—members of a single clan, not a large coalition of enemies poised to strike Egypt. Furthermore, it was a relatively small clan, with only **12 brothers** (by comparison, Gideon had 70 sons, Jdg 9:2), and one of them was **no longer living**.

42:14-20 As part of his test Joseph threatened to keep nine of the brothers imprisoned, letting **one** return to Canaan and come back with their **youngest brother** Benjamin. To give all 10 of them a small taste of what they had made him experience, Joseph had them **imprisoned** for **three days**. After their initial "shock probation" Joseph softened his initial conditions, requiring that only **one of** them **be confined to the guardhouse** while the rest returned to Jacob. Before leaving, however, **they consented** to bring Benjamin back to Egypt. Joseph probably made them do this to make sure they would not do to Benjamin what they had done to him.

42:21-26 The brothers' harsh treatment in Egypt—the land where they had once sent Joseph—as well as the stiff demands placed on them made it plain to them that

pleaded with us, but we would not listen. That is why this trouble has come to us."[a]

[22]But Reuben replied: "Didn't I tell you not to harm the boy?[b] But you wouldn't listen. Now we must account for his blood!"[A]

[23]They did not realize that Joseph understood them, since there was an interpreter between them. [24]He turned away from them and wept. Then he turned back and spoke to them. He took Simeon from them and had him bound before their eyes. [25]Joseph then gave orders to fill their containers with grain, return each man's money to his sack, and give them provisions for their journey. This order was carried out. [26]They loaded the grain on their donkeys and left there.

The Brothers Return Home

[27]At the place where they lodged for the night, one of them opened his sack to get feed for his donkey, and he saw his money there at the top of the bag. [28]He said to his brothers, "My money has been returned! It's here in my bag." Their hearts sank. Trembling, they turned to one another and said, "What is this that God has done to us?"

[29]When they reached their father Jacob in the land of Canaan, they told him all that had happened to them: [30]"The man who is the lord of the country spoke harshly to us and accused us of spying on the country. [31]But we told him: We are honest and not spies. [32]We were 12 brothers, sons of the same[B] father. One is no longer living, and the youngest is now[c] with our father in the land of Canaan.

[33]The man who is the lord of the country said to us, 'This is how I will know if you are honest: Leave one brother with me, take food to relieve the hunger of your households, and go. [34]Bring back your youngest brother to me, and I will know that you are not spies but honest men. I will then give your brother back to you, and you can trade in the country.'"

[35]As they began emptying their sacks, there in each man's sack was his bag of money! When they and their father saw their bags of money, they were afraid.

[36]Their father Jacob said to them, "You have deprived me of my sons. Joseph is gone and Simeon is gone. Now you want to take Benjamin. Everything happens to me!"

[37]Then Reuben said to his father, "You can kill my two sons if I don't bring him back to you. Put him in my care,[D] and I will return him to you."

[38]But Jacob answered, "My son will not go down with you, for his brother is dead and he alone is left.[c] If anything happens to him on your journey, you will bring my gray hairs down to *Sheol in sorrow."[d]

Decision to Return to Egypt

43 Now the famine in the land was severe.[e] [2]When they had used up the grain they had brought back from Egypt, their father said to them, "Go back and buy us some food."

[3]But Judah said to him, "The man specifically warned us: 'You will not see me again unless your brother is with you.' [4]If you will

[a]42:21 Gn 37:26-28
[b]42:22 Gn 37:22
[c]42:38 Gn 37:33-34; 42:13; 44:27-28
[d]Gn 44:29
[e]43:1 Gn 12:10; 41:56-57; 47:20

[A]42:22 Lit *Even his blood is being sought*   [B]42:32 Lit *of our*   [C]42:32 Or *today*   [D]42:37 Lit *hand*

they were **being punished** for what they had done **to** their **brother** 20 years earlier. **Reuben**, eldest of the group and the one who had kept Joseph from being killed by his brothers (37:22), interpreted the current events as a divine accounting for Joseph's **blood**, i.e., his death. Reuben's earlier defense of Joseph and his current rebuke of his brothers may explain why second-born **Simeon** was detained instead of Reuben.

Joseph, whose heart—but not his outward appearance—had been softened toward his brothers by Reuben's comments, understood the words the brothers spoke in Hebrew, **turned away from** his brothers, **and wept**. After dismissing his brothers Joseph compassionately provided them not only with **grain** for the family, but returned **each man's money to his sack** and gave them food **for their journey**. Joseph's act of kindness was probably also meant to test the brothers' character; if they were honest they would return the money.

42:27-35 Joseph's brothers, who had once traded Joseph's life for money, now felt their hearts "depart" (**sank**) when they received this money from him. Worried that they would be pursued as criminals, they trembled in fear of what **God** had **done to** them. Upon their return home Jacob was greeted by only nine sons. The matter worsened when he

was told that the brothers were **accused** of **spying**, and the clan could get Simeon **back** and **trade** for additional food in Egypt only if the men brought back their **youngest brother** Benjamin. Everyone became even more afraid when they found **bags of money** in **each man's sack**; now all nine brothers could be imprisoned as thieves if they ever returned to Egypt.

42:36-38 Reduced to despair by his sons' report, Jacob responded by saying, **everything happens to me**! Perhaps Jacob even doubted God's repeated promise to bless him (32:39; 35:9). His adamant refusal to let Benjamin **go down** with his brothers to Egypt was understandable but irrational, since it meant that the entire clan would die of starvation. **Reuben**, who had once saved Joseph's life (37:22), now stepped forward to save the clan. He countered his father's fears of losing Benjamin by offering to experience the loss of two of his four sons (Ex 6:14) if anything happened to him in a return trip to Egypt. If Benjamin died, Reuben would experience a proportionately worse fate than his father. However, Reuben's argument had no effect on Jacob; if Jacob's son should die, it would not make him feel better to kill two of his grandchildren as well.

43:1-10 Two years into **the famine** (cp. 45:6), Jacob's family **had used up the grain** purchased by the brothers in Egypt.

send our brother with us, we will go down and buy food for you. ⁵But if you will not send him, we will not go, for the man said to us, 'You will not see me again unless your brother is with you.'"ᵃ

⁶"Why did you cause me so much trouble?" Israel asked. "Why did you tell the man that you had another brother?"

⁷They answered, "The man kept asking about us and our family: 'Is your father still alive? Do you have another brother?' And we answered him accordingly. How could we know that he would say, 'Bring your brother here'?"

⁸Then Judah said to his father Israel, "Send the boy with me. We will be on our way so that we may live and not die—neither we, nor you, nor our children. ⁹I will be responsible for him. You can hold me personally accountable!ᴬ If I do not bring him back to you and set him before you, I will be •guilty before you forever.ᵇ ¹⁰If we had not wasted time, we could have come back twice by now."

¹¹Then their father Israel said to them, "If it must be so, then do this: Put some of the best products of the land in your packs and take them down to the man as a gift—some balsam and some honey, aromatic gum and resin, pistachios and almonds.ᶜ ¹²Take twice as much money with you. Return the money that was returned to you in the top of your bags. Perhaps it was a mistake. ¹³Take your brother also, and go back at once to the man. ¹⁴May •God Almighty cause the man to be merciful to you so that he will release your other brother and Benjamin to you. As for me, if I am deprived of my sons, then I am deprived."ᵈ

The Return to Egypt

¹⁵The men took this gift, double the amount

ᵃ43:5 Gn 42:18-20; 44:23
ᵇ43:9 Gn 42:37; 44:32
ᶜ43:11 Gn 37:25; Jr 8:22; Ezk 27:17
ᵈ43:14 Gn 42:36
ᵉ43:21 Gn 42:27,35
ᶠ43:24 Gn 18:4; 19:2; 24:32

of money, and Benjamin. They made their way down to Egypt and stood before Joseph.

¹⁶When Joseph saw Benjamin with them, he said to his steward,ᴮ "Take the men to my house. Slaughter an animal and prepare it, for they will eat with me at noon." ¹⁷The man did as Joseph had said and brought them to Joseph's house.

¹⁸But the men were afraid because they were taken to Joseph's house. They said, "We have been brought here because of the money that was returned in our bags the first time. They intend to overpower us, seize us, make us slaves, and take our donkeys." ¹⁹So they approached Joseph's stewardᶜ and spoke to him at the doorway of the house.

²⁰They said, "Sir, we really did come down here the first time only to buy food. ²¹When we came to the place where we lodged for the night and opened our bags of grain, each one's money was at the top of his bag!ᵉ It was the full amount of our money, and we have brought it back with us. ²²We have brought additional money with us to buy food. We don't know who put our money in the bags."

²³Then the steward said, "May you be well. Don't be afraid. Your God and the God of your father must have put treasure in your bags. I received your money." Then he brought Simeon out to them. ²⁴The steward brought the men into Joseph's house, gave them water to wash their feet,ᶠ and got feed for their donkeys. ²⁵Since the men had heard that they were going to eat a meal there, they prepared their gift for Joseph's arrival at noon. ²⁶When Joseph came home, they brought him the gift they had carried into the house, and they bowed to the ground before him.

²⁷He asked if they were well, and he said, "How is your elderly father that you told me about? Is he still alive?"

ᴬ43:9 Lit *can seek him from my hand*   ᴮ43:16 Lit *to the one who was over his house*   ᶜ43:19 Lit *approached the one who was over the house*

Jacob, as clan head, ordered nine of his sons to go back to Egypt and **buy** more **food**. Judah, Jacob's fourth-born but still the most trusted of his older sons (34:30; 35:22), reminded his father that he must send Benjamin to Egypt in order for the family to buy food. In response Jacob, who was known for his deceptions (27:12-27), accused his sons (**you** [v. 6] is pl.) of causing **much trouble** by telling the Egyptian the truth. Judah finally convinced his father to let his sons go by using two things. First, his father's own words: they must go **so that we may live and not die** (cp. 42:2), and second, his willingness to have Jacob **hold** him **personally accountable** for Benjamin's well-being.

43:11-14 Jacob realized he had to send Benjamin to Egypt, but to increase the likelihood that his beloved son of Rachel would return safely, he directed his sons to give the Egyptian **some of the best products** associated with the land of Ca-

naan. Hoping that his sons had not actually stolen the money, Jacob had them return the original money, taking **twice as much money** as before. Finally, they were to travel with their brother Benjamin, accompanied by a prayer that **God Almighty** would secure the release of Simeon **and Benjamin**.

43:15-24 When the men returned to Joseph in Egypt, they were brought to Joseph's own house. They feared they were about to be arrested and made **slaves** as punishment for taking their original grain money back to Canaan, but Joseph's **steward** informed them that he had already **received** their **money**. All seemed well as **Simeon** was brought out of prison to them, and they were given a traditional sign of hospitality—water to wash their feet (18:4; 19:2).

43:25-28 Learning that they were to eat the noon meal—the first meal of the day—with Joseph, the brothers **prepared**

²⁸They answered, "Your servant our father is well. He is still alive." And they bowed down to honor him.

²⁹When he looked up and saw his brother Benjamin, his mother's son, he asked, "Is this your youngest brother that you told me about?" Then he said, "May God be gracious to you, my son." ³⁰Joseph hurried out because he was overcome with emotion for his brother, and he was about to weep. He went into an inner room to weep. ³¹Then he washed his face and came out. Regaining his composure,^a he said, "Serve the meal."

³²They served him by himself, his brothers by themselves, and the Egyptians who were eating with him by themselves, because Egyptians could not eat with Hebrews, since that is abhorrent to them.^{b 33}They were seated before him in order by age, from the firstborn to the youngest. The men looked at each other in astonishment. ³⁴Portions were served to them from Joseph's table, and Benjamin's portion was five times larger than any of theirs.^c They drank, and they got intoxicated with Joseph.

Joseph's Final Test

44 Then Joseph commanded his steward: "Fill the men's bags with as much food

*a*43:31 Gn 45:1
*b*43:32 Gn 46:34; Ex 8:26
*c*43:34 Gn 35:24; 45:22
*d*44:1 Gn 42:25
*e*44:5 Gn 30:27; 44:15; Lv 19:26; Dt 18:10-14
*f*44:9 Gn 31:32

as they can carry, and put each one's money at the top of his bag.^{d 2}Put my cup, the silver one, at the top of the youngest one's bag, along with his grain money." So he did as Joseph told him.

³At morning light, the men were sent off with their donkeys. ⁴They had not gone very far from the city when Joseph said to his steward, "Get up. Pursue the men, and when you overtake them, say to them, 'Why have you repaid evil for good?^{A 5}Isn't this the cup that my master drinks from and uses for •divination?^e What you have done is wrong!'"

⁶When he overtook them, he said these words to them. ⁷They said to him, "Why does my lord say these things? Your servants could not possibly do such a thing. ⁸We even brought back to you from the land of Canaan the money we found at the top of our bags. How could we steal gold and silver from your master's house? ⁹If any of us is ^Bfound to have it, he must die, and we also will become my lord's slaves."^f

¹⁰The steward replied, "What you have said is right, but only the one who is found to have it will be my slave, and the rest of you will be blameless."

¹¹So each one quickly lowered his sack to

A44:4 LXX adds *Why have you stolen my silver cup?*   **B**44:9 Lit *If your servants are*

---

the food **gift** (v. 11) and then humbly presented it to Joseph (cp. 37:7,9). Then the powerful Egyptian asked them about their **elderly father**, eliciting a polite response and a second bowing to the ground.

43:29-31 Joseph confirmed the identity of **his brother Benjamin, his mother's** only other son and therefore his only full brother. Joseph's blessing on Benjamin in the name of **God** was the first time Joseph blessed one of his brothers. Though Joseph had been filled with emotion in the presence of his brothers earlier (42:24), the

yakal

Hebrew Pronunciation	[yah KAL]
HCSB Translation	be able, prevail, defeat
Uses in Genesis	22
Uses in the OT	193
Focus passage	Genesis 44:1,22,26

Yakal indicates *capability* and regularly takes a complementary infinitive: someone *is able* to stand (1Sm 6:20). It appears as *can* (Gn 44:1) or *could* (Jdg 2:14). It frequently takes the negative, perhaps as *cannot. Yakal* sometimes involves lack of permission: *may not* (Dt 24:4), *must not* (Dt 22:3), or *are not* (Dt 16:5) to do something. *Yakal* also signifies *prevail* (Jr 5:22). It connotes *win* (Gn 30:8), *defeat* (Gn 32:25), *conquer* (Ob 7), *overcome* (Jr 15:20), and *triumph over* (Ps 13:4). Twice *yakal* implies not *daring* (Lm 4:14) to act. It means *be capable of* (Hs 8:5). *Yakal* may imply other words: God *can do* anything (Jb 42:2), Job *could not do* these things (Jb 31:23). The psalmist *is unable to reach* certain knowledge (Ps 139:6); he *cannot tolerate* evil people (Ps 101:5). *Yakal* may suggest that action *does no* good (Is 16:12).

sight of Benjamin overwhelmed him. To retain his dignity he quickly **went into an inner room to weep**. The fact that as an Egyptian official he was wearing eye makeup was probably in part why he **washed his face** before returning to the room.

43:32-34 Because of racial and cultural prejudice, the meal was served at two different tables. Food was first brought to Joseph and the rest of **the Egyptians**, who ate at one table, then portions were brought to the table of the Hebrews. As an indication of respect for seniority among these non-Egyptians, the brothers were seated **from the firstborn to the youngest**—a fact that created **astonishment** among them since it would have required a detailed knowledge of the family. Perhaps as a further test of the brothers, **Benjamin's portion was five times larger than any of** the other brothers'. Joseph may have made sure they **got intoxicated** to loosen the brothers' self-restraint; if they harbored any jealousy or hatred toward Benjamin, Rachel's son, it would be more likely to show.

44:2 Joseph secretly put in place the ultimate test of his older brothers, ordering the steward to put Joseph's ceremonial silver **cup . . . at the top** of Benjamin's bag. By watching the other brothers' response to Benjamin's trouble, Joseph would be able to observe firsthand the other brothers' true character.

44:3-13 Joseph then ordered **his steward** to **overtake** the small caravan. Armed with a scripted accusation regarding the ceremonial **cup**, the steward confronted the group. Joseph mentions **divination** as part of the ploy to make the brothers think this is a very valuable cup; there is no evidence that he actually practiced divination. At a later time,

the ground and opened it. ¹²The steward searched, beginning with the oldest and ending with the youngest, and the cup was found in Benjamin's sack. ¹³Then they tore their clothes,ᵃ and each one loaded his donkey and returned to the city.

¹⁴When Judah and his brothers reached Joseph's house, he was still there. They fell to the ground before him.ᵇ ¹⁵"What is this you have done?" Joseph said to them. "Didn't you know that a man like me could uncover the truth by divination?"

¹⁶"What can we say to my lord?" Judah replied. "How can we plead? How can we justify ourselves? God has exposed your servants' iniquity. We are now my lord's slaves—both we and the one in whose possession the cup was found."

¹⁷Then Joseph said, "I swear that I will not do this. The man in whose possession the cup was found will be my slave. The rest of you can go in peace to your father."

Judah's Plea for Benjamin

¹⁸But Judah approached him and said, "Sir, please let your servant speak personally to my lord.ᴬ Do not be angry with your servant, for you are like Pharaoh.ᶜ ¹⁹My lord asked his servants, 'Do you have a father or a brother?' ²⁰and we answered my lord, 'We have an elderly father and a younger brother, the child of his old age.ᵈ The boy's brother is dead. He is the only one of his mother's sons left, and his father loves him.' ²¹Then you said to your servants, 'Bring him to me so that I can see him.'ᵉ ²²But we said to my lord, 'The boy cannot leave his father. If he were to leave, his

father would die.' ²³Then you said to your servants, 'If your younger brother does not come down with you, you will not see me again.'ᶠ

²⁴"This is what happened when we went back to your servant my father: We reported your words to him. ²⁵But our father said, 'Go again, and buy us some food.'ᵍ ²⁶We told him, 'We cannot go down unless our younger brother goes with us. So if our younger brother isn't with us, we cannot see the man.' ²⁷Your servant my father said to us, 'You know that my wife bore me two sons. ²⁸One left—I said that he must have been torn to pieces—and I have never seen him again.ʰ ²⁹If you also take this one from me and anything happens to him, you will bring my gray hairs down to •Sheol in sorrow.'ⁱ

³⁰"So if I come to your servant my father and the boy is not with us—his life is wrapped up with the boy's life— ³¹when he sees that the boy is not with us, he will die. Then your servants will have brought the gray hairs of your servant our father down to Sheol in sorrow. ³²Your servant became accountable to my father for the boy, saying, 'If I do not return him to you, I will always bear the •guilt for sinning against you, my father.'ʲ ³³Now please let your servant remain here as my lord's slave, in place of the boy. Let him go back with his brothers. ³⁴For how can I go back to my father without the boy? I could not bear to see the grief that would overwhelm my father."

Joseph Reveals His Identity

45 Joseph could no longer keep his composure in front of all his attendants,ᴮ so he called out, "Send everyone away from

ᵃ44:13 Gn 37:29
ᵇ44:14 Gn 37:7-10; 42:6; 43:26-28
ᶜ44:18 Gn 37:7-8; 41:40-44
ᵈ44:20 Gn 37:3; 43:8; 44:30
ᵉ44:21 Gn 42:15,20
ᶠ44:23 Gn 43:3,5
ᵍ44:25 Gn 43:2
ʰ44:28 Gn 37:31-35
ⁱ44:29 Gn 42:38
ʲ44:32 Gn 43:9

ᴬ44:18 Lit *speak a word in my lord's ears*   ᴮ45:1 Lit *all those standing about him*

---

divination was officially prohibited for Israelites in the law (Lv 19:26; Dt 18:10).

The brothers responded with disbelief and disavowal to the steward's accusation. Quickly mounting a defense, they first provided evidence of their honesty: they had **brought back the money** found in their **bags** after the first journey. Next they proposed a harsh punishment for any of their number caught with the bowl—**he must die.** Finally, they offered the remaining 10 of their group as lifelong **slaves.**

Rejecting their excessive offer, the steward indicated that only the guilty party would become his slave. Though the steward gave the innocent brothers permission to return home, they all **returned to the city** in a show of solidarity with Benjamin.

44:14-17 Jacob's most trusted son, Judah (see note at 43:1-10), spoke for the group. Bowing **to the ground before** Joseph (cp. 37:7,9), Judah confessed that **God had exposed** the men's **iniquity**—a reference to the sins against Joseph more than 20 years earlier (37:18-28). Second, Judah maintained the group's solidarity by indicating that all the brothers, not just Benjamin, would become **my lord's slaves.**

Joseph's immediate rejection of the offer would have added more tension to the situation.

44:18-29 Judah's speech, the longest in the Bible by any of Jacob's sons (218 Hebrew words), marks the turning point in the relationship between Joseph and his brothers. In a display of great humility, Judah referred to Joseph on seven occasions as **my lord,** and on 12 occasions referred to himself and members of his clan as **your servants.** After a representation of three contentious conversations—one that the brothers had had with Joseph (vv. 19-23; 42:13-20) and two involving Jacob (vv. 25-29; 42:38; 43:2-7)—Judah said that his father would die of grief if anything happened to Benjamin.

44:30-34 Judah had once separated his father Jacob from a son of Rachel by making Joseph a slave in Egypt (37:26-27). To save the life of the clan he had voluntarily made himself **accountable** to his **father** for the well-being of Benjamin, Rachel's only other son besides Joseph (43:8-9). Now Benjamin, like his older brother Joseph, was on the verge of being made a slave in Egypt. Knowing that he would always **bear the guilt for sinning against** his **father** if Benjamin did

me!" No one was with him when he revealed his identity to his brothers. [a] [2] But he wept so loudly that the Egyptians heard it, and also Pharaoh's household heard it. [3] Joseph said to his brothers, "I am Joseph! Is my father still living?" But they could not answer him because they were terrified in his presence.

[4] Then Joseph said to his brothers, "Please, come near me," and they came near. "I am Joseph, your brother," he said, "the one you sold into Egypt. [b] [5] And now don't be worried or angry with yourselves for selling me here, because God sent me ahead of you to preserve life. [c] [6] For the famine has been in the land these two years, and there will be five more years without plowing or harvesting. [7] God sent me ahead of you to establish you as a remnant within the land and to keep you alive by a great deliverance. [A] [8] Therefore it was not you who sent me here, but God. He has made me a father to Pharaoh, lord of his entire household, and ruler over all the land of Egypt.

[9] "Return quickly to my father and say to him, 'This is what your son Joseph says: "God has made me lord of all Egypt. Come down to me without delay. [10] You can settle in the land of Goshen [d] and be near me—you, your children, and grandchildren, your sheep, cattle, and all you have. [11] There I will sustain you, for there will be five more years of famine. Otherwise, you, your household, and everything you have will become destitute."' [e] [12] Look! Your eyes and my brother Benjamin's eyes

can see that it is I, Joseph, who am [B] speaking to you. [13] Tell my father about all my glory in Egypt and about all you have seen. And bring my father here quickly." [f]

[14] Then Joseph threw his arms around Benjamin and wept, and Benjamin wept on his shoulder. [15] Joseph kissed each of his brothers as he wept, [C] and afterward his brothers talked with him.

The Return for Jacob

[16] When the news reached Pharaoh's palace, "Joseph's brothers have come," Pharaoh and his servants were pleased. [17] Pharaoh said to Joseph, "Tell your brothers, 'Do this: Load your animals and go on back to the land of Canaan. [18] Get your father and your families, and come back to me. I will give you the best of the land of Egypt, and you can eat from the richness of the land.' [19] You are also commanded, 'Do this: Take wagons from the land of Egypt for your young children and your wives and bring your father here. [g] [20] Do not be concerned about your belongings, for the best of all the land of Egypt is yours.'" [h]

[21] The sons of Israel did this. Joseph gave them wagons as Pharaoh had commanded, and he gave them provisions for the journey. [22] He gave each of the brothers changes of clothes, [i] but he gave Benjamin 300 pieces of silver and five changes of clothes. [j] [23] He sent his father the following: 10 donkeys carrying the best products of Egypt and 10 female donkeys carrying

Cross references (center column)

[a] 45:1 Ac 7:13
[b] 45:4 Gn 37:18-36
[c] 45:5 Gn 45:7-8; 50:20; Ps 105:17
[d] 45:10 Gn 46:34; 47:1,4,6,11,27; 50:8; Ex 8:22; Jos 10:41
[e] 45:11 Gn 47:12; 50:21
[f] 45:13 Ac 7:14
[g] 45:19 Gn 46:5
[h] 45:20 Dt 32:9-14
[i] 45:22 2Kg 5:5
[j] Gn 43:34

[A] 45:7 Or keep alive for you many survivors   [B] 45:12 Lit that my mouth is   [C] 45:15 Lit brothers, and he wept over them

---

not return home, Judah volunteered to **remain** in Egypt as Joseph's **slave**.

45:1-4 Joseph was overwhelmed by Judah's words. Not wishing to lose his dignity before his Egyptian attendants, he ordered everyone but his brothers out of the room. Joseph then released more than 20 years of pent-up emotions, weeping **so loudly that the Egyptians** outside the room **heard it**. Joseph's revelation of his true identity—undoubtedly spoken in Hebrew, not Egyptian—so **terrified** his brothers that they could not **answer** his question about his father's well-being. Violating protocol, Joseph ordered brothers to **come near** to him so he could speak to them more intimately, this time explicitly identifying himself.

45:5-8 These verses stand as the theological high point of the account of Joseph's life (chaps. 37–50) and one of the most eloquent affirmations in the Bible regarding God's sovereignty in human events. With amazing spiritual maturity Joseph confessed that God had worked beyond the foul intentions of his older brothers to accomplish two vital things: **to preserve life** through Joseph's leadership leading up to and during the seven-year famine, and **to establish** Israel **as a remnant** "on the earth" (**within the land**). The word "remnant" is an important term used to refer to Israel as the people group who would pass along God's blessings throughout the generations (Ezr 9:8; Is 10:20; 28:5; Jr 23:3). Three times Joseph affirmed that it was **God**—not his brothers—who had sent him to Egypt.

Therefore the brothers did not need to **be worried or angry** with themselves. Indeed, God had made Joseph **a father**— a top-level adviser—to Pharaoh, and a **ruler over all the land of Egypt**.

45:9-15 Joseph, who had once presented a plan to Pharaoh to save Egypt, now offered a plan to his brothers to save Israel's clan by moving them to Egypt to live in **Goshen** during the five more years of famine that were to come. Goshen was a region in the eastern portion of Egypt's Nile Delta and was also known as "the land of Rameses" (47:11). The brothers, who were still having trouble believing that Joseph was not only alive but a ruler in Egypt, watched as Joseph **threw his arms around Benjamin and wept**. To their amazement, he also **kissed each of his brothers** who had once plotted to kill him.

45:16-20 Affirming the commands Joseph had given, Pharaoh told him to have his brothers load their animals with food, **go on back** to Jacob in **Canaan**, and then return with their families. New to the set of instructions was Pharaoh's provision of **wagons from the land of Egypt** to transport the weaker members of the clan down to Egypt, the promise that Joseph's family could live in **the best of the land of Egypt**, and that they would be permitted to **eat the richness** ("the fat") **of the land**.

45:21-24 Joseph supplied his brothers with generous **provisions for the journey** back to Canaan, as well as items for

grain, food, and provisions for his father on the journey. [24] So Joseph sent his brothers on their way, and as they were leaving, he said to them, "Don't argue on the way."

[25] So they went up from Egypt and came to their father Jacob in the land of Canaan. [26] They said, "Joseph is still alive, and he is ruler over all the land of Egypt!" Jacob was stunned,[A] for he did not believe them. [27] But when they told Jacob all that Joseph had said to them, and when he saw the wagons that Joseph had sent to transport him, the spirit of their father Jacob revived.

[28] Then Israel said, "Enough! My son Joseph is still alive. I will go to see him before I die."

Jacob Leaves for Egypt

46 Israel set out with all that he had and came to Beer-sheba,[a] and he offered sacrifices to the God of his father Isaac. [2] That night God spoke to Israel in a vision:[b] "Jacob, Jacob!" He said.

And Jacob replied, "Here I am."

[3] God said, "I am God, the God of your father. Do not be afraid to go down to Egypt, for I will make you into a great nation there.[c] [4] I will go down with you to Egypt, and I will also bring you back.[d] Joseph will put his hands on your eyes."[B,e]

[5] Jacob left Beer-sheba. The sons of Israel took their father Jacob in the wagons Pharaoh had sent to carry him,[f] along with their children and their wives. [6] They also took their cattle and possessions they had acquired in the land of Canaan. Then Jacob and all his children went with him to Egypt.[g] [7] His sons and grandsons, his daughters and granddaughters, indeed all his •offspring, he brought with him to Egypt.

Cross references

[a]46:1 Gn 21:14; 28:10; Jos 15:28; Jdg 20:1; 2Sm 24:7; 1Kg 19:3
[b]46:2 Gn 15:1; Jb 33:14-15
[c]46:3 Gn 12:2; 15:13-14; 35:11; Ex 1:7,9; Dt 26:5
[d]46:4 Gn 15:16; 28:15; 48:21; 50:24; Ex 3:8
[e]Gn 50:1
[f]46:5 Gn 45:19,21
[g]46:6 Dt 26:5; Jos 24:4; Ps 105:23; Is 52:4; Ac 7:15
[h]46:8-27 Ex 1:1-5; Nm 26:4-5
[i]46:9 Ex 6:14
[j]46:10 Ex 6:15
[k]46:11 Ex 6:16; 1Ch 6:16
[l]46:12 Gn 38:29; 1Ch 2:5
[m]46:13 1Ch 7:1
[n]46:17 1Ch 7:30-31

Jacob's Family

[8] These are the names of the Israelites, Jacob and his sons, who went to Egypt:[h]

Jacob's firstborn: Reuben.
[9] Reuben's sons:[i] Hanoch, Pallu, Hezron, and Carmi.
[10] Simeon's sons:[j] Jemuel, Jamin, Ohad, Jachin, Zohar, and Shaul, the son of a Canaanite woman.
[11] Levi's sons:[k] Gershon, Kohath, and Merari.
[12] Judah's sons: Er, Onan, Shelah, Perez, and Zerah; but Er and Onan died in the land of Canaan.
Perez's sons:[l] Hezron and Hamul.
[13] Issachar's sons:[m] Tola, Puvah,[C] Jashub,[D] and Shimron.
[14] Zebulun's sons: Sered, Elon, and Jahleel.
[15] These were Leah's sons born to Jacob in Paddan-aram, as well as his daughter Dinah. The total number of persons:[E] 33.
[16] Gad's sons: Ziphion, Haggi, Shuni, Ezbon, Eri, Arodi, and Areli.
[17] Asher's sons:[n] Imnah, Ishvah, Ishvi, Beriah, and their sister Serah.
Beriah's sons were Heber and Malchiel.
[18] These were the sons of Zilpah—whom Laban gave to his daughter Leah—that she bore to Jacob: 16 persons.
[19] The sons of Jacob's wife Rachel: Joseph and Benjamin.
[20] Manasseh and Ephraim were born to Joseph in the land of Egypt.

[A]45:26 Lit *Jacob's heart was numb*   [B]46:4 = Joseph will close your eyes after you die   [C]46:13 Sam, Syr read *Puah*; 1Ch 7:1
[D]46:13 Sam, LXX; MT reads *Iob*   [E]46:15 Lit *All persons his sons and his daughters*

---

the clan's return to Egypt. The translation of Joseph's final command (**Don't argue**) is uncertain and may also mean "Don't fear" or "Don't take undue risks."

45:25-28 Jacob experienced a storm of emotion when the group returned from Egypt. Initially he experienced relief, as all 11 brothers came back to him. "His heart went numb" (**was stunned**) when he was told that Joseph was still alive. Jacob agreed to **go to see him** before he died. God's promise of blessing to Jacob (32:29; 35:9) had proven true.

46:1-4 Jacob, referred to here by his covenant name **Israel**, had God speak to him **in a vision**, the first vision granted to a patriarch since the days of Abraham (15:1). Calling the elderly patriarch's name twice—a practice in the Bible reserved for special revelatory moments (cp. 22:1; Ex 3:4)—**God, the God of** Jacob's **father** made four important remarks to Jacob. First, He commanded Jacob not to be afraid to go down to Egypt, because He would **go down with** him. Second, He affirmed the generations-old promise to make Abraham's family line—represented through Jacob— **a great nation**, even in Egypt. Third, He promised to **bring**

Israel's descendants **back**. Finally, God promised that Jacob's beloved son Joseph would **put his hands on** the patriarch's **eyes**—i.e., be present at Jacob's death.

46:5-7 Encouraged by God's words, Jacob/Israel left **Beersheba** in one of **the wagons Pharaoh had sent** for the two-hundred-plus-mile journey.

46:8-27 Not counting Jacob or his four wives, the list of those **who went to Egypt** contains the names of 71 people descended from Jacob/Israel. Since the list contains 71 descendants, the significance of the numbers 66 and 70 are debated. The total of 66 may be based on the fact that Jacob's daughter Dinah was not included, **Er and Onan died** before they could **come to Egypt** (38:7,10), and **Manasseh and Ephraim were born** in Egypt (41:50-52). Perhaps Dinah was not counted because she produced no children. Acts 7:14, reflecting the Septuagint, states 75 people went to Egypt; this number includes five more of Joseph's descendants: three grandsons and two great-grandsons (Nm 26:29,35-36).

46:28-30 As the group made its way to **Goshen**, Jacob sent

They were born to him by Asenath daughter of Potiphera, a priest at On. [A]

21 Benjamin's sons: [a] Bela, Becher, Ashbel, Gera, Naaman, Ehi, Rosh, Muppim, Huppim, and Ard.

22 These were Rachel's sons who were born to Jacob: 14 persons.

23 Dan's son: [B] Hushim.

24 Naphtali's sons: [b] Jahzeel, Guni, Jezer, and Shillem.

25 These were the sons of Bilhah, whom Laban gave to his daughter Rachel. [c] She bore to Jacob: seven persons.

26 The total number of persons belonging to Jacob—

his direct descendants, [c] not including the wives of Jacob's sons—who came to Egypt: 66.

27 And Joseph's sons who were born to him in Egypt: two persons. All those of Jacob's household who had come to Egypt: 70 [D] persons. [d]

Jacob Arrives in Egypt

28 Now Jacob had sent Judah ahead of him to Joseph to prepare for his arrival [E] at Goshen. [e] When they came to the land of Goshen, 29 Joseph hitched the horses to his chariot and went up to Goshen to meet his father Israel. Joseph presented himself to him, threw his arms around him, and wept for a long time. [f] 30 Then Israel said to Joseph, "At last I can

[a] 46:21 Nm 26:38-40; 1Ch 7:6-12; 8:1 [b] 46:24 1Ch 7:13 [c] 46:25 Gn 29:29; 30:5-8 [d] 46:27 Ex 1:5; Dt 10:22; Ac 7:14 [e] 46:28 Gn 45:10 [f] 46:29 Gn 45:14

[A] 46:20 Or *Heliopolis*   [B] 46:23 Alt Hb tradition reads *sons*   [C] 46:26 Lit *Jacob who came out from his loins*   [D] 46:27 LXX reads *75*; Ac 7:14   [E] 46:28 Lit *to give directions before him*

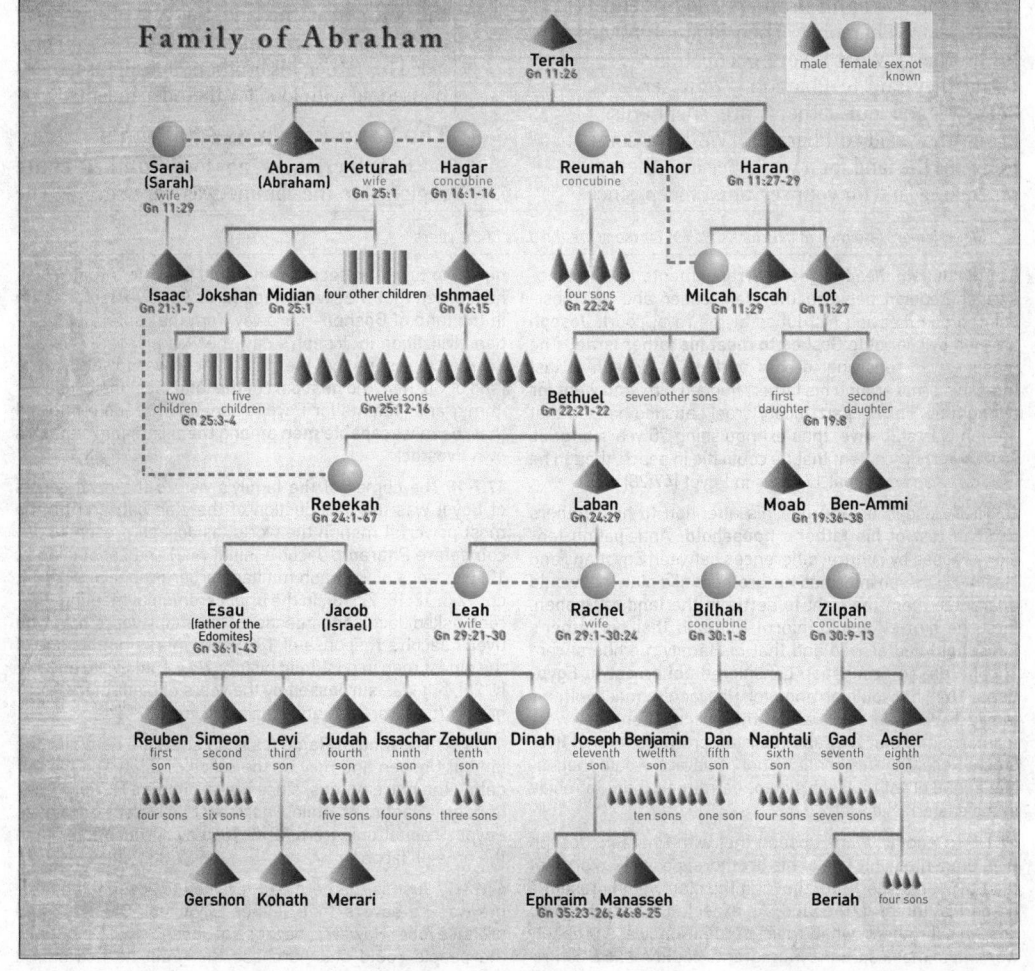

Family of Abraham

male   female   sex not known

Terah   Gn 11:26

Sarai (Sarah) wife Gn 11:29   Abram (Abraham)   Keturah wife Gn 25:1   Hagar concubine Gn 16:1-16   Reumah concubine   Nahor   Haran Gn 11:27-29

Isaac Gn 21:1-7   Jokshan Gn 25:1   Midian Gn 25:1   four other children   Ishmael Gn 16:15   four sons Gn 22:24   Milcah Gn 11:29   Iscah   Lot Gn 11:27

two children   five children Gn 25:3-4   twelve sons Gn 25:12-16   Bethuel Gn 22:21-22   seven other sons   first daughter   second daughter Gn 19:8

Rebekah Gn 24:1-67   Laban Gn 24:29   Moab   Ben-Ammi Gn 19:36-38

Esau (father of the Edomites) Gn 36:1-43   Jacob (Israel)   Leah wife Gn 29:21-30   Rachel wife Gn 29:1-30:24   Bilhah concubine Gn 30:1-8   Zilpah concubine Gn 30:9-13

Reuben first son   Simeon second son   Levi third son   Judah fourth son   Issachar ninth son   Zebulun tenth son   Dinah   Joseph eleventh son   Benjamin twelfth son   Dan fifth son   Naphtali sixth son   Gad seventh son   Asher eighth son

four sons   six sons   five sons   four sons   three sons   ten sons   one son   four sons   seven sons

Gershon   Kohath   Merari   Ephraim   Manasseh Gn 35:23-26; 46:8-25   Beriah   four sons

die, now that I have seen your face and know you are still alive!"

[31] Joseph said to his brothers and to his father's household, "I will go up and inform Pharaoh, telling him: My brothers and my father's household, who were in the land of Canaan, have come to me.[a] [32] The men are shepherds; they also raise livestock. They have brought their sheep and cattle and all that they have. [33] When Pharaoh addresses you and asks, 'What is your occupation?' [34] you are to say, 'Your servants, both we and our fathers, have raised livestock[A] from our youth until now.' Then you will be allowed to settle in the land of Goshen, since all shepherds are abhorrent to Egyptians."[b]

Pharaoh Welcomes Jacob

47 So Joseph went and informed Pharaoh: "My father and my brothers, with their sheep and cattle and all that they own, have come from the land of Canaan and are now in the land of Goshen."[c]

[2] He took five of his brothers and presented them before Pharaoh.[d] [3] Then Pharaoh asked his brothers, "What is your occupation?"

And they said to Pharaoh, "Your servants, both we and our fathers, are shepherds."[e] [4] Then they said to Pharaoh, "We have come to live in the land for a while because there is no grazing land for your servants' sheep, since

the famine in the land of Canaan has been severe. [f] So now, please let your servants settle in the land of Goshen."

[5] Then Pharaoh said to Joseph, "Now that your father and brothers have come to you, [6] the land of Egypt is open before you; settle your father and brothers in the best part of the land. [g] They can live in the land of Goshen. If you know of any capable men among them, put them in charge of my livestock."[h]

[7] Joseph then brought his father Jacob and presented him before Pharaoh, and Jacob blessed Pharaoh. [8] Then Pharaoh said to Jacob, "How many years have you lived?"[B]

[9] Jacob said to Pharaoh, "My pilgrimage[i] has lasted 130 years. My years have been few and hard,[j] and they have not surpassed the years of my fathers during their pilgrimages."[k] [10] So Jacob blessed Pharaoh and departed from Pharaoh's presence.

[11] Then Joseph settled his father and brothers in the land of Egypt and gave them property in the best part of the land, the land of Rameses,[l] as Pharaoh had commanded. [12] And Joseph provided his father, his brothers, and all his father's household with food for their dependents.[m]

The Land Becomes Pharaoh's

[13] But there was no food in that entire region, for the famine was very severe. The

Cross-references

[a]46:31 Gn 47:1
[b]46:34 Gn 43:32; Ex 8:26
[c]47:1 Gn 45:10; 46:28
[d]47:2 Ac 7:13
[e]47:3 Gn 46:32-34
[f]47:4 Gn 15:13; Dt 26:5
[g]47:6 Gn 45:10,18; 47:11
[h]Ex 18:21,25; 1Kg 11:28; Pr 22:29
[i]47:9 1Ch 29:15; Ps 39:12; 119:19,54; Heb 11:9,13
[j]Jb 14:1; Ps 39:4-5; Jms 4:14
[k]Gn 11:32; 25:7; 35:28
[l]47:11 Gn 45:10; Ex 1:11; 12:37
[m]47:12 Gn 45:11; 50:21

A46:34 Lit *fathers, are men of livestock*   B47:8 Lit *many are the days of the years*

---

his son **Judah** ahead to make arrangements for the long-awaited reunion between the clan leader and his most-beloved son. Leaving his duties at the royal court, **Joseph** traveled by chariot to Goshen **to meet his father Israel**. The meeting was satisfying to both parties, as Joseph at last threw his arms around his father, hugged him, **and wept for a long time**. For his part Jacob/Israel satisfied himself that Joseph was **still alive**, thus extinguishing 20 years of grief. Jacob was now content that he could **die** in peace, though he would live an additional 17 years in Egypt (47:28).

46:31-34 Joseph now turned his attention to his brothers and the rest of **his father's household**. Anticipating tensions caused by cultural differences between Egyptians and Hebrews, Joseph informed his brothers of a plan that would guarantee them the right to **settle in the land of Goshen**. First, he himself would inform Pharaoh that his **father's household** had arrived and that his family members were **shepherds**, an occupation considered **abhorrent to Egyptians**. Then he would arrange for Pharaoh to meet with his family. If Pharoah asked about their occupation, they were to inform him that they and their fathers were men of **livestock**. Receiving this confirmation, Pharaoh would then issue a land grant to Jacob's clan, permitting them to reside in the eastern Nile Delta.

47:1-6 True to his word, Joseph met with Pharaoh. Joseph then presented only **five of his brothers**, possibly to prevent the Egyptian leader from thinking the clan would present a numerical threat to the land. As expected, Pharaoh asked Joseph's brothers what their **occupation** was, probably wanting to make sure the immigrants could make a contri-

bution to Egyptian society and would pose no threat. When he learned that they were **shepherds** who wanted to **settle in the land of Goshen**—far away from the centers of Egyptian civilization in Joseph's day—he was pleased. Pharaoh decreed to Joseph that the clan of Jacob was to settle in the land of Goshen, the **best part of the land**. Seeking to use the immigrants' talents for Egypt's benefit, Pharaoh requested that the most **capable men among them** care for Pharaoh's own **livestock**.

47:7-10 The climax of the family's visit to the royal courts of Egypt was the introduction of the clan patriarch to the most powerful man in the world, as Joseph presented Jacob **before Pharaoh**. Jacob's initial (v. 7) and concluding (v. 10) blessings of Pharaoh fulfilled earlier prophecies (28:14; cp. 12:3; 18:18; 22:18). In the brief ceremonial meeting Pharaoh asked Jacob one question: **How many years have you lived?** Jacob's response of **130 years** marks him as one of the oldest men in postflood history. He would live to age 147 (v. 28), but was **surpassed** by the years of his **fathers** Abraham (175 years; 25:7) and Isaac (180 years; 35:28).

47:11-12 **The land of Rameses** is an alternate name for the land of Goshen and may be the result of a later scribe updating the place names, since the city named Pi-Ramesses (modern Qantir, 65 miles northeast of Cairo) served as Egypt's capital only from 1295–1065 b.c.—much later than the time of Jacob.

47:13-17 Just as the Lord had revealed to Joseph, the **famine** was so **severe** that neither **Egypt** nor **Canaan** could produce **food**. However, because of Joseph's wise planning, the people could still purchase the grain he had stored

land of Egypt and the land of Canaan were exhausted by the famine. [14] Joseph collected all the money to be found in the land of Egypt and the land of Canaan in exchange for the grain they were purchasing, and he brought the money to Pharaoh's palace. [a] [15] When the money from the land of Egypt and the land of Canaan was gone, all the Egyptians came to Joseph and said, "Give us food. Why should we die here in front of you? The money is gone!"

[16] But Joseph said, "Give me your livestock. Since the money is gone, I will give you food in exchange for your livestock." [17] So they brought their livestock to Joseph, and he gave them food in exchange for the horses, the herds of sheep, the herds of cattle, and the donkeys. That year he provided them with food in exchange for all their livestock.

[18] When that year was over, they came the next year and said to him, "We cannot hide from our lord that the money is gone and that all our livestock belongs to our lord. There is nothing left for our lord except our bodies and our land. [19] Why should we die here in front of you—both us and our land? Buy us and our land in exchange for food. Then we with our land will become Pharaoh's slaves. Give us seed so that we can live and not die, and so that the land won't become desolate."

[20] In this way, Joseph acquired all the land in Egypt for Pharaoh, because every Egyptian sold his field since the famine was so severe for them. The land became Pharaoh's, [21] and Joseph moved the people to the cities [A] from one end of Egypt to the other. [22] The only land he didn't acquire was the priests' portion, for it was given to them by Pharaoh. They lived off [B] the rations Pharaoh had given them; therefore they did not sell their land.

[23] Then Joseph said to the people, "Understand today that I have acquired you and your land for Pharaoh. Here is seed for you. Sow it in the land. [24] At harvest, you are to give a fifth of it to Pharaoh, [b] and four-fifths will be yours as seed for the field and as food for yourselves, your households, and your dependents."

[25] And they said, "You have saved our lives. We have found favor in our lord's eyes and will be Pharaoh's slaves." [26] So Joseph made it a law, still in effect today in the land of Egypt, that a fifth of the produce belongs to Pharaoh. Only the priests' land does not belong to Pharaoh.

Israel Settles in Goshen

[27] Israel settled in the land of Egypt, in the region of Goshen. They acquired property in it and became fruitful and very numerous. [c] [28] Now Jacob lived in the land of Egypt 17 years, and his life span was 147 years. [29] When the time drew near for him to die, [d] he called his son Joseph and said to him, "If I have found favor in your eyes, put your hand under

Cross references (center column):
[a] 47:14 Gn 41:56
[b] 47:24 Gn 41:34
[c] 47:27 Gn 17:6; 26:4; 35:11; Ex 1:7; Dt 26:5; Ac 7:17
[d] 47:29 Dt 31:14; 1Kg 2:1

A 47:21 Sam, LXX, Vg read *and he made the people servants*   **B** 47:22 Lit *They ate*

up. But as the famine progressed, the region's inhabitants spent all their money. Joseph therefore authorized a barter system to trade **livestock** for food.

47:18-22 Consistent with cultures throughout Asia and Africa at that time, the Egyptians asked their government to **buy** them as slaves once all their resources were exhausted. Slavery was a universal practice in the region, and even impoverished Israelites were permitted to sell themselves as slaves during the OT period (Lv 25:39-43). Such slavery was often temporary, and might be terminated when the debt was paid (Dt 15:12).

Joseph accepted their offer. Members of the Egyptian priesthood were exempted from the land contract since the land was **given to them by Pharaoh**. The Hebrew text, unlike the Septuagint, suggests that Joseph took the additional step of relocating **the people to the cities** during the famine; if the Hebrew text represents the accurate reading, perhaps Joseph adopted this policy in order to make the food distribution program more efficient.

47:23-26 Though the citizens gave up ownership of their land, Joseph permitted them to continue working their old fields. The requirement to **give a fifth** of their produce to **Pharaoh** was far less than the two-thirds to one-half rate that eighteenth-century B.C. Iraqi farmers paid Hammurabi after expenses. Egypt's citizens gratefully accepted Joseph's program. Joseph's policies produced such a stable society that they remained **in effect** in the days of the biblical writer hundreds of years later.

47:27 While the Egyptians were losing their possessions, land, and freedom because of the famine, the clan of **Israel/ Jacob** prospered. The contrast at this point between Egypt and Israel could hardly be more complete, though the situation would be reversed later (Ex 1:8-11).

47:28-31 As Jacob's death approached, he called for **his son Joseph** (cp. 46:4) and made him swear a solemn oath while

parah

Hebrew Pronunciation	[pah RAH]
HCSB Translation	*be fruitful*
Uses in Genesis	15
Uses in the OT	29
Focus passage	Genesis 47:27

Parah means *be fruitful* (Gn 1:22) or *sprout* (Is 45:8). In some verses the sense is to have *plenty of fruit* (Is 17:6; 32:12). *Parah* refers to many offspring or descendants, appearing as *become numerous* (Ex 23:30) or *increase* (Jr 3:16). This sense was applied to a mother with numerous children (Ps 128:3). It regularly stands alongside other verbs with similar meanings. Exodus 1:7 lists four in a row to emphasize that God blessed Israel as He originally intended to bless creation (Gn 1:22,28). In 15 verses *parah* occurs together with *ravah* meaning *fruitful and multiply*. Israelites linked the two verbs (Gn 28:3) in imitation of the Lord's repeatedly stressed intention for His creation (e.g., Gn 8:17; Lv 26:9; Ezk 36:11). Participles denote *fruitful* or *bearing fruit* (Dt 29:18). Causative verbs indicate *make fruitful* (Ps 105:24).

my thigh[a] and promise me that you will deal with me in kindness and faithfulness.[b] Do not bury me in Egypt. [30]When I rest with my fathers, carry me away from Egypt and bury me in their burial place."[c]

Joseph answered, "I will do what you have asked."

[31]And Jacob said, "Swear to me." So Joseph swore to him. Then Israel bowed in thanks at the head of his bed.[A,d]

Jacob Blesses Ephraim and Manasseh

48 Some time after this, Joseph was told, "Your father is weaker." So he set out with his two sons, Manasseh and Ephraim. [2]When Jacob was told, "Your son Joseph has come to you," Israel summoned his strength and sat up in bed.

[3]Jacob said to Joseph, "'God Almighty[e] appeared to me at Luz[f] in the land of Canaan and blessed me. [4]He said to me, 'I will make you fruitful and numerous; I will make many nations come from you, and I will give this land as an eternal possession[g] to your future descendants.'[h] [5]Your two sons[i] born to you in the land of Egypt before I came to you in Egypt are now mine.[j] Ephraim and Manasseh belong to me just as Reuben and Simeon do. [6]Children born to you after them will be yours and will be recorded under the names of their brothers with regard to their inheritance. [7]When I was returning from Paddan, to my sorrow Rachel died along the way,[k] some distance from Ephrath in the land of Canaan. I buried her there along the way to Ephrath," (that is, Bethlehem).

[8]When Israel saw Joseph's sons, he said, "Who are these?"

[9]And Joseph said to his father, "They are my sons God has given me here."

So Jacob said, "Bring them to me and I will bless them."[l] [10]Now his eyesight was poor because of old age; he could hardly[B] see.[m] Joseph brought them to him, and he kissed and embraced them.[n] [11]Israel said to Joseph, "I never expected to see your face again, but now God has even let me see your •offspring." [12]Then Joseph took them from his father's knees and bowed with his face to the ground.[o]

Ephraim's Greater Blessing

[13]Then Joseph took them both—with his right hand Ephraim toward Israel's left, and with his left hand Manasseh toward Israel's right—and brought them to Israel. [14]But Israel stretched out his right hand and put it on the head of Ephraim, the younger, and crossing his hands, put his left on Manasseh's head, although Manasseh was the firstborn.[p] [15]Then he blessed Joseph and said:

> The God before whom my fathers
> Abraham and Isaac walked,[q]
> the God who has been my shepherd[r]
> all my life to this day,
> [16] the Angel who has redeemed me
> from all harm[s]—
> may He bless these boys.
> And may they be called by my name
> and the names of my fathers Abraham
> and Isaac,[t]
> and may they grow to be numerous
> within the land.

Cross references (center column)

[a]47:29 Gn 24:2
[b]Gn 24:49
[c]47:30 Gn 23:17-20; 25:9-10; 35:29; 49:29-32; 50:5,13; Ac 7:15-16
[d]47:31 Gn 48:2; 1Kg 1:47; Heb 11:21
[e]48:3 Gn 17:1
[f]Gn 28:13,19; 35:6,9
[g]48:4 Gn 17:8
[h]Gn 35:9-12
[i]48:5 Gn 41:50-52; 46:20
[j]Jos 13:7; 14:4; 17:17
[k]48:7 Gn 35:9-19
[l]48:9 Gn 27:4; 49:25-26; Heb 11:21
[m]48:10 Gn 27:1
[n]Gn 27:27
[o]48:12 Gn 18:2; 24:52; 33:3; 42:6; 43:26; Ex 34:8
[p]48:14 Gn 25:23; 27:18-30
[q]48:15 Gn 17:1; 24:40
[r]Gn 49:24; Ps 23:1; Jr 31:10
[s]48:16 Gn 28:13-15; 31:11; Is 63:9; Ac 7:35
[t]Dt 28:10; 2Ch 7:14; Is 4:1; 43:1; 48:1

[A]47:31 Or Israel worshiped while leaning on the top of his staff   [B]48:10 Lit he was not able to

---

his **hand** was **under** Jacob's **thigh**, an act that expressed great trust and accompanied only the most serious requests (cp. 24:2-4). Jacob asked that his son not bury him in Egypt, but rather that he be buried in the promised land **with** his **fathers . . . in their burial place** near Hebron in the cave at Machpelah (23:19; 25:9; 35:27-29; 50:13).

48:1-7 Joseph, accompanied by his two eldest sons, visited Jacob again. Summoning his strength on this last day of his life, Jacob **sat up in bed** and spoke with Joseph of how **God Almighty** (El Shaddai; see note at 17:1) gave a second revelation to him at Bethel, more than 50 years earlier (35:9-12). Recounting God's promise to make him **fruitful and numerous**, Jacob now became even more fruitful by adopting Manasseh and Ephraim, counting them as his primary heirs (1Ch 5:1). Ephraim and Manasseh would receive the blessings of the first- and second-born, instead of **Reuben and Simeon**, who had previously dishonored Jacob (Gn 34:25-30).

Any other sons born to Joseph would be **recorded under the names** of their older brothers, and their inheritance would be split with the sons of Ephraim and Manasseh. All of Jacob's **descendants** would receive the land of Canaan **as an eternal possession**. The mention of **Rachel** references the events associated with Benjamin's birth (35:16-20).

48:9-12 Jacob used his last measure of strength to **bless** his sons, beginning with the two newly adopted ones. Before blessing them, Jacob **kissed and embraced them** (cp. 27:26-27). Though his **eyesight was poor** because of old age (cp. 27:1), God let him see once more not only Joseph but also his **offspring**.

48:13-16 Joseph presented **Ephraim** (at **his right hand** side) and **Manasseh** (at **his left hand** side) to Jacob in hopes that Jacob would reach out with his right hand and confer the greater blessing on the elder son, Manasseh, who was standing to Joseph's left. But Jacob crossed his arms and put **his right hand . . . on the head of Ephraim, the younger**, thus symbolically conferring the greater blessing on him. Jacob then **blessed Joseph**, but because his two hands were on Joseph's sons, it was they who received the blessing. Calling on the God of his fathers **Abraham and Isaac**, who had been his **shepherd** (cp. Ps 23:1; 80:1; Ezk 34:11-12; Jn 10:11) all his life, Jacob's requests on behalf of Ephraim and Manasseh included that they would be called by the names of Jacob, **Abraham and Isaac**, that is, that they would identify with God's covenant people, not with Egyptian culture and religion.

48:17-20 Frustrated because it seemed that his blind fa-

¹⁷ When Joseph saw that his father had placed his right hand on Ephraim's head, he thought it was a mistake ^A and took his father's hand to move it from Ephraim's head to Manasseh's. ¹⁸ Joseph said to his father, "Not that way, my father! This one is the firstborn. Put your right hand on his head."

¹⁹ But his father refused and said, "I know, my son, I know! He too will become a tribe, ^B and he too will be great; nevertheless, his younger brother will be greater than he, and his offspring will become a populous nation." ^C ²⁰ So he blessed them that day with these words:

> The nation Israel will invoke blessings
>> by you, saying,
> "May God make you like Ephraim
>> and Manasseh,"
> putting Ephraim before Manasseh.

²¹ Then Israel said to Joseph, "Look, I am about to die, but God will be with you and will bring you back to the land of your fathers. ^a ²² Over and above what I am giving your brothers, I am giving you the one mountain slope ^D that I took from the hand of the Amorites with my sword and bow." ^b

Jacob's Last Words

49 Then Jacob called his sons and said, "Gather around, and I will tell you what will happen to you in the days to come. ^{E,c}

²   Come together and listen,
>> sons of Jacob;
> listen to your father Israel:

³   Reuben, you are my firstborn, ^d
> my strength and the firstfruits
>> of my virility, ^e
> excelling in prominence,
>> excelling in power.
⁴   Turbulent as water, you will
>> no longer excel,
> because you got into your father's bed ^f
> and you defiled it—he ^F got
>> into my bed.

⁵   Simeon and Levi are brothers;
> their knives are vicious weapons. ^g
⁶   May I never enter their council;
> may I never join their assembly.
> For in their anger they kill men,
> and on a whim they hamstring oxen.
⁷   Their anger is cursed, for it is strong,
> and their fury, for it is cruel!
> I will disperse them throughout Jacob
> and scatter them throughout Israel. ^h

⁸   Judah, your brothers will praise you. ⁱ
> Your hand will be on the necks
>> of your enemies;
> your father's sons will bow down
>> to you. ^j
⁹   Judah is a young lion ^k—
> my son, you return from the kill.
> He crouches; he lies down like a lion
> or a lioness—who dares to rouse him?
¹⁰   The scepter will not depart from Judah
> or the staff from between his feet
> until He whose right it is comes ^{G,l}
> and the obedience of the peoples
>> belongs to Him. ^m

Cross references

^a48:21 Gn 46:4; 50:24 ^b48:22 Gn 34:25-29; Jos 24:32; Jn 4:5 ^c49:1 Nm 24:14; Dt 4:30; 31:29; Is 2:2; Jr 23:20; Dn 2:28; 10:14; Hs 3:5 ^d49:3 Gn 29:32 ^eDt 21:17 ^f49:4 Gn 35:22 ^g49:5 Gn 34:25,30 ^h49:7 Ex 32:28; Nm 3:5-13; Dt 33:10; Jos 19:1-9; 1Ch 4:24-39; 2Ch 34:6; Neh 11:25-28 ⁱ49:8 Gn 29:35 ^jGn 27:29; 1Ch 5:2 ^k49:9 Nm 24:9; Ezk 19:5-7; Mc 5:8; Rv 5:5 ^l49:10 Nm 2:9; 10:14; 24:17; Jdg 1:1-2; Ps 60:7; 108:8; Ezk 21:27 ^mPs 2:6-9; 72:8-11; Is 42:1,4; 49:6

Footnotes

^A48:17 Or *he was displeased*; lit *head, it was ba in his eyes*   ^B48:19 Lit *people*   ^C48:19 Or *a multitude of nations*; lit *a fullness of nations*   ^D48:22 Or *Shechem*, Joseph's burial place; lit *one shoulder*   ^E49:1 Or *in the last days*   ^F49:4 LXX, Syr, Tg read *you*   ^G49:10 Or *until tribute comes to him*, or *until Shiloh comes*, or *until He comes to Shiloh*

---

ther had made a mistake, Joseph **took his father's hand to move it from Ephraim's head**. Emboldened by prophetic insight, however, Jacob refused to move his hands, because by God's own hand Ephraim's blessings were ordained to exceed Manasseh's. Manasseh would become a **tribe**, but **his younger brother** Ephraim would become something more—**a populous nation**. Even so, both would be blessed so richly that in the future Israel would **invoke blessings by** asking God to make someone like Ephraim and Manasseh. The placement of Ephraim's name before Manasseh's foreshadowed his later superiority. Because of Ephraim's leading position in later Israelite history, prophets often referred to the entire northern kingdom of Israel as Ephraim (Is 7:5; Jr 31:20; Ezk 37:16; Hs 5:13; Zch 10:7).

48:21-22 Jacob promised Joseph that God would be with him (39:2,21,23) and would **bring** him **back to the land of his fathers**, i.e., Canaan (50:25; Ex 13:19; Jos 24:32; Ac 7:14-16).

49:1-2 As he spoke his dying words, Jacob was essentially blind (48:10), but he retained a clear prophetic insight of **the days to come** (lit "in the last days"; cp. Nm 24:14; Dt 31:2; Is 2:2).

49:3-27 Jacob's prophetic words to his 12 sons were delivered in three units: those delivered to (1) the sons of Leah (vv. 3-15); (2) the sons of the concubines Bilhah and Zilpah (vv. 16-21); and (3) the sons of Rachel (vv. 22-27).

49:3-4 As the oldest son in a Semitic family **Reuben** was poised to lead the clan when his father died. However, Reuben lost his rights as firstborn because he had intimate relations with Jacob's wife Bilhah (35:22). Ephraim would take his place.

49:5-7 **Simeon and Levi** are grouped together because **in their anger** they conspired together to **kill** the **men** of Shechem, even hamstringing the **oxen** after seizing them (34:25-29). Their out-of-control anger at Dinah's rape (34:2) cost them the full measure of their inheritance. Historically, Simeon's land allotment was shared with Judah (Jos 19:9), and the Levites were never given a region to call their own; they had to live in other tribes' cities (Jos 14:3-4).

49:8-12 **Judah**, Jacob's fourth-born son received the second-longest of the blessings, behind Joseph's (55 vs. 61

¹¹ He ties his donkey to a vine,
and the colt of his donkey
   to the choice vine.
He washes his clothes in wine
and his robes in the blood of grapes.
¹² His eyes are darker than wine,
and his teeth are whiter than milk.

¹³ Zebulun will live by the seashore
and will be a harbor for ships,
and his territory will be next to Sidon. ^a

¹⁴ Issachar is a strong donkey
lying down between the saddlebags. ^A
¹⁵ He saw that his resting place was good
and that the land was pleasant,
so he leaned his shoulder to bear
   a load
and became a forced laborer. ^b

¹⁶ Dan will judge his people ^c
as one of the tribes of Israel.
¹⁷ He will be a snake by the road,
a viper beside the path,
that bites the horses' heels
so that its rider falls backward.

¹⁸ I wait for Your salvation, LORD.

¹⁹ Gad will be attacked by raiders,
but he will attack their heels. ^d

²⁰ Asher's ^B food will be rich,
and he will produce royal delicacies. ^e

²¹ Naphtali is a doe set free
that bears beautiful fawns. ^f

²² Joseph is a fruitful vine,
a fruitful vine beside a spring;
its branches ^c climb over the wall. ^D
²³ The archers attacked him,
shot at him, and were hostile
   toward him.
²⁴ Yet his bow remained steady,
and his strong ^E arms were made agile
by the hands of the Mighty One
   of Jacob, ^g
by the name of ^F the Shepherd, ^h
   the Rock of Israel, ⁱ
²⁵ by the God of your father
   who helps you,
and by the •Almighty who blesses you
with blessings of the heavens above,
blessings of the deep that lies below,
and blessings of the breasts
   and the womb.
²⁶ The blessings of your father excel
the blessings of my ancestors ^G
and ^H the bounty of the eternal hills. ^{D,j}
May they rest on the head of Joseph,

^a49:13 Dt 33:19; Jos 19:10-16 ^b49:15 Jdg 5:15-16 ^c49:16 Dt 33:22; Jdg 13:2,25; 18:25-27 ^d49:19 Dt 33:20; 1Ch 5:18-22; Jr 49:1 ^e49:20 Dt 33:24-25; Jos 19:24-31; Jdg 5:17; 1Kg 4:7 ^f49:21 Jos 19:32-39 ^g49:24 Gn 31:42; Ps 132:2,5; Is 1:24; 49:26 ^hGn 48:15; Ps 23:1; Jr 31:10 ⁱPs 118:22; Is 28:16; 1Pt 2:6-8 ^j49:26 Dt 33:15-16

Hebrew words). **The scepter** and **staff**—symbols of kingship in ancient Israel—foretold the establishment of the Davidic dynasty as Israel's kings (2Sm 7:8-16). As reflected in the passage, the **He** and **Him** of verse 10b have been understood for thousands of years as messianic references (Ezk 21:27) and, for Christians, a prophecy of Jesus' coming.

49:13 Though the territorial allotment of Zebulun, Jacob's tenth-born son, was landlocked (Jos 19:10-16), Jacob's mention of **a harbor for ships** may refer to the prosperity of the sea trade associated with the Mediterranean coastal city of **Sidon**. Alternatively, Jacob may have referred to Zebulun's territorial division that was later mentioned in Ezk 48:26.

49:14-15 Jacob's ninth-born son **Issachar** was prophetically compared to **a strong donkey** situated between two **saddlebags**. Though the descendants of Issachar would live in a land that **was pleasant** (Jos 19:17-22), they would be compelled to do the work of a **forced laborer**—probably a reference to the oppression this tribe suffered at the hands of their own leaders and foreign invaders.

49:16-18 Jacob used a wordplay to describe the key positive action associated with his fifth-born son: **Dan will judge** (Hb dan yadin; "the judging one will judge")—a possible prophetic reference to Samson's work (Jdg 15:20). Dan was compared to **a snake**, the enemy of humanity in the garden of Eden. The comparison is to an animal with venom so poisonous that it could kill **horses**. This contrast between images foreshadows the checkered history of the tribe of Dan. On the one hand, it was the second most populous tribe (Nm 2:26);

on the other hand, it could not defeat the Canaanite inhabitants in its territory and so abandoned its allotment (Jos 19:47). Though Samson led Israel for 20 years, the Danites also played a leading role in encouraging idolatry in Israel (Jdg 18:14-27; 1Kg 12:28-30).

49:19 Gad, Jacob's seventh-born son, was once associated with good fortune (30:11). However, in an involved wordplay (Hb gad gedud yegudennu) Jacob prophesied that **Gad** would **be attacked by raiders**, a reference to its vulnerability based on the location of its land allotment east of the Jordan River. But Jacob praised the tenacity of the Gadites because they would not give up but rather **attack** the **heels** of their oppressors.

49:20 Asher, Jacob's eighth-born, was prophetically foreseen to enjoy prosperity that, associated with its coastal land allotment, would **produce royal delicacies** supporting Israel's prosperity.

49:21 Jacob's sixth-born son, **Naphtali**, whose descendants would live just west of the Sea of Galilee, was foreseen to produce a people who would be free and populous, like a **doe** that **bears beautiful fawns**. Naphtali's freedom may have been realized historically by the fact that its tribal territory had no northern boundary—the tribe was free to expand its holdings to whatever extent it was able to do so.

49:22-26 Jacob's longest blessing (61 Hebrew words) was associated with **Joseph**, Rachel's firstborn son (his eleventh son). This section contains the largest number and variety of references to God (five: **Mighty One of Jacob . . . Shepherd . . . Rock of Israel . . . God of your father . . . Almighty**)

on the crown of the prince
    of his brothers.

[27] Benjamin is a wolf; he tears his prey.
In the morning he devours the prey,
    and in the evening he divides
      the plunder."[a]

[28] These are the tribes of Israel, 12 in all, and this was what their father said to them. He blessed them, and he blessed each one with a suitable blessing.

Jacob's Burial Instructions

[29] Then he commanded them: "I am about to be gathered to my people.[b] Bury me with my fathers[c] in the cave in the field of Ephron the Hittite.[d] [30] The cave is in the field of Machpelah near Mamre, in the land of Canaan. This is the field Abraham purchased from Ephron the Hittite as a burial site.[e] [31] Abraham and his wife Sarah are buried there,[f] Isaac and his wife Rebekah are buried there,[g] and I buried Leah

[a]49:27 Jdg 5:14; 20:21; 1Sm 14:47-48
[b]49:29 Gn 25:8
[c]Gn 47:30
[d]Gn 23:16-20; 50:13
[e]49:30 Gn 23:3-20
[f]49:31 Gn 23:19; 25:9
[g]Gn 35:29
[h]Gn 48:7
[i]50:3 Gn 50:10; Nm 20:29; Dt 34:8
[j]50:5 Gn 47:29-31
[k]2Ch 16:14; Is 22:16; Mt 27:60

there.[h] [32] The field and the cave in it were purchased from the Hittites." [33] When Jacob had finished instructing his sons, he drew his feet into the bed and died. He was gathered to his people.

Jacob's Burial

50 Then Joseph, leaning over his father's face, wept and kissed him. [2] He commanded his servants who were physicians to embalm his father. So they embalmed Israel. [3] They took 40 days to complete this, for embalming takes that long, and the Egyptians mourned for him 70 days.[i]

[4] When the days of mourning were over, Joseph said to Pharaoh's household, "If I have found favor with you, please tell[A] Pharaoh that [5] my father made me take an oath,[j] saying, 'I am about to die. You must bury me there in the tomb that I made for myself in the land of Canaan.'[k] Now let me go and bury my father. Then I will return."

[A]50:4 Lit *please speak in the ears of*

---

and the greatest number of references to "blessing" (six: one verb, five nouns). Joseph alone is termed **the prince of his brothers** and is the one who uniquely receives from God both **blessings of the heavens above, blessings of the deep**, and **blessings of** numerous offspring.

49:27 Jacob's final prophetic blessing was reserved for his last-born son **Benjamin**. Metaphorically compared to a **wolf**, Jacob identified him as one who **tears** and **devours** prey and **divides the plunder**. Benjamin's descendants were thus characterized as dangerous fighters, but also as ones who would provide benefits for others. Benjamin's fighting skills were most clearly seen in the sordid events of Jdg 20:14-25, but more positively in the capable military leadership of Saul and Jonathan (1Sm 11:4-11; 14:1-23,47-48). Benjamin was the fifth of the sons to be prophetically compared to an animal (also Judah: lion; Issachar: donkey; Dan: snake; Naphtali: deer).

49:28 Jacob's 12 prophetic blessings were for **the tribes of Israel** founded by his sons/grandsons. Each **blessing** would prove **suitable** to later historical realities.

49:29-33 The dying patriarch emphasized two matters in his final words: where he was to be buried, and with whom he was to be buried. The burial site was in Canaan, two miles north of Hebron and some 17 miles west of the Dead Sea. Wishing to reestablish family solidarity in death, Jacob asked to be buried with his grandparents **Abraham and his wife Sarah**, his parents **Isaac and his wife Rebekah**, and his first wife **Leah**.

His last request made and his strength now spent, Jacob **drew his feet into the bed**, lay down, **and died**. At death Jacob was spiritually **gathered to his people**; as his sons fulfilled his request, his physical remains would soon be gathered to those of his ancestors. Jacob, who had spent 17 years in Egypt (47:28), outlived the famine by approximately 12 years.

50:1-3 Joseph, who was physically closest to his father at the moment of his death, "fell upon" (**leaning over**) his **father's face, wept and kissed him**. The usual Hebrew

custom was to practice same-day burial without embalming; however, embalming was necessary to prepare Jacob's body for the journey to Canaan. Egyptian embalming, which **took 40 days to complete**, was normally a religious practice performed by priests to prepare the person for the afterlife; the fact that Joseph used physicians rather than priests to perform the task may suggest that he had rejected Egyptian afterlife beliefs and wished to avoid giving a different impression.

The **70 days** of mourning probably reflected Egyptian customs associated with the deaths of particularly important individuals; normal Hebrew mourning periods were either seven days (1Sm 31:13) or 30 days (one lunar cycle; Dt 34:8).

50:4-9 When the 70 **days of mourning were over**, Joseph went to **Pharaoh's household**, asking permission to bury his father in **the land of Canaan**. Joseph probably had

bakah

Hebrew Pronunciation	[bah KAH]
HCSB Translation	weep
Uses in Genesis	16
Uses in the OT	114
Focus passage	Genesis 50:1,3,17

The root behind *bakah* means *weep* in all Semitic languages. *Bakah* also suggests *mourn* (Lv 10:6), *cry* (Nm 11:4), and *lament* (Ps 78:64). *Bakah* is often vocal, involving loud (2Sm 15:23) or bitter (Ezr 10:1) *weeping*. There is mention of tears (1Sm 1:10), and fasting that accompanies *weeping* (2Sm 1:12). *Weeping* was natural during days of mourning (Gn 50:3) but also signaled complaining (Nm 11:4), repentance (2Ch 34:27), infatuation (Gn 29:11), or reunion (Gn 33:4). *Weeping* is contrasted with laughing (Ec 3:4). The inner being *weeps* (Jr 13:17). *Bekiy* is *weeping* (Dt 34:8), sometimes as the object of *bakah* (Jdg 21:2). Once it signifies *tears* (Ps 102:9), and once the *flowing* of a stream (Jb 28:11). So *bakah* apparently implied *tears*. *Bekiyt* is *mourning* (Gn 50:4). *Bakut* (Gn 35:8), *bekeh* (Ezr 10:1), and the proper name Bochim (*bokiym*; Jdg 2:5) all imply *weeping*.

[6]So Pharaoh said, "Go and bury your father in keeping with your oath."

[7]Then Joseph went to bury his father, and all Pharaoh's servants, the elders of his household, and all the elders of the land of Egypt went with him, [8]along with all Joseph's household, his brothers, and his father's household. Only their children, their sheep, and their cattle were left in the land of Goshen. [9]Horses and chariots went up with him; it was a very impressive procession. [10]When they reached the threshing floor of Atad, which is across the Jordan, they lamented and wept loudly, and Joseph mourned seven days for his father. [11]When the Canaanite inhabitants of the land saw the mourning at the threshing floor of Atad, they said, "This is a solemn mourning on the part of the Egyptians." Therefore the place is named Abel-mizraim.[A] It is across the Jordan.

[12]So Jacob's sons did for him what he had commanded them. [13]They carried him to the land of Canaan and buried him in the cave at Machpelah in the field near Mamre, which Abraham had purchased as a burial site from Ephron the Hittite.[a] [14]After Joseph buried his father, he returned to Egypt with his brothers and all who had gone with him to bury his father.

Joseph's Kindness

[15]When Joseph's brothers saw that their father was dead, they said to one another, "If Joseph is holding a grudge against us, he will certainly repay us for all the suffering we caused him."[b]

[16]So they sent this message to Joseph, "Before he died your father gave a command: [17]'Say this to Joseph: Please forgive your brothers' transgression and their sin—the suffering they caused you.' Therefore, please forgive the transgression of the servants of the God of your father." Joseph wept[c] when their message came to him. [18]Then his brothers also came to him, bowed down before him, and said, "We are your slaves!"

[19]But Joseph said to them, "Don't be afraid. Am I in the place of God?[d] [20]You planned evil against me; God planned it for good to bring about the present result—the survival of many people.[e] [21]Therefore don't be afraid. I will take care of you and your little ones."[f] And he comforted them and spoke kindly to them. [B]

Joseph's Death

[22]Joseph and his father's household remained in Egypt. Joseph lived 110 years. [23]He saw Ephraim's sons to the third generation;[g] the sons of Manasseh's son Machir were recognized by[C,D] Joseph.[h]

[24]Joseph said to his brothers, "I am about to die,[i] but God will certainly come to your aid and bring you up from this land to the land

Cross references
[a]50:13 Gn 23:16-20
[b]50:15 Gn 37:28; 42:21-22
[c]50:17 Gn 43:30; 46:29; 50:1
[d]50:19 Gn 3:5
[e]50:20 Gn 45:7; Rm 8:28
[f]50:21 Gn 45:11; 47:12
[g]50:23 Jb 42:16; Ps 128:6
[h]Gn 30:3
[i]50:24 Gn 48:21; Ex 3:16-17; Heb 11:22

A 50:11 = Mourning of Egypt   B 50:21 Lit *spoke to their hearts*   C 50:23 Lit *were born on the knees of*   D 50:23 Referring to a ritual of adoption or of legitimation; Gn 30:3

---

reduced access to Pharaoh by now, which was about 12 years after the famine ended and the crisis Joseph had handled so well was long past. Even so, Pharaoh granted him permission to go and bury his father, thus fulfilling the oath Joseph had made to his dying father (47:29-31).

As a sign of Pharaoh's continuing gratitude for Joseph's work, he permitted **all his servants, the elders of his household, and all the elders of the land of Egypt**—a considerable number of high-ranking Egyptian politicians—to accompany all the adult members of the clan of Jacob on the journey to Canaan. **Horses and chariots**, prestigious transportation used only by members of the Egyptian aristocracy, were part of **a very impressive procession** to Canaan.

50:10-14 When the group crossed the Jordan River into Canaan, they camped at the open, level **threshing floor of Atad** and went through a Hebrew mourning ritual. The presence of a large number of Egyptians publicly displaying solemn mourning so impressed the local **Canaanite inhabitants** that they renamed the place **Abel-mizraim** ("The Meadow of Egypt"), a wordplay on a Semitic word for weeping (*'ebel*). Proceeding westward to the cave at Machpelah two miles north of Hebron, **Joseph buried his father**, thus fulfilling what his father had commanded Joseph and his brothers to do.

50:15-21 With Jacob now dead, Joseph's older brothers feared for their lives and hoped the words spoken by Jacob **before he died** would protect them from Joseph's wrath. They were so afraid of Joseph that they did not dare at first to come to him personally; instead they only

sent a **message** entreating him to **forgive** his **brothers'** "rebellion" (**transgression**) and **sin**, especially since they were "slaves" (**servants**) **of the God of your father**—that is, they worshiped the same God that Joseph did. Perhaps the reason the brothers came to Joseph was that they heard he had **wept** when he received their message. To maximize their chances of survival they **bowed down before him** (cp. 37:7,9) and offered themselves as his personal **slaves**.

Joseph refused their offer. They were slaves of God, not of him, and he would not put himself **in the place of God** to make them his slaves. He admitted that his older brothers **planned evil against** him, but with great spiritual insight he also confessed that **God planned it for good to bring about . . . the survival of many people** (see note at 45:5-8). God had transformed the soot of human sin into a diamond of divine blessing (Rm 8:28; 1Pt 2:24). Far from being embittered, Joseph was emboldened to take care of the very ones who had tried to kill him, along with their **little ones**. He **spoke kindly to them** (lit "spoke upon their heart"; cp. Is 40:2) and **comforted them**.

50:22-23 God's blessing on Joseph's life is apparent as he **lived 110 years**, 93 of them in Egypt and 80 of them as a ruler in Egypt. He lived to see **the third generation** of descendants through **Ephraim**, a phrase that could refer either to great-grandsons or great-great-grandsons. A further sign of God's blessing was the fact that Gilead (Nm 26:29) and other great-grandsons by Machir son of Manasseh "were

He promised Abraham,[a] Isaac,[b] and Jacob."[c] [26] Joseph died at the age of 110. They embalmed him and placed him in a coffin in Egypt.
[25] So Joseph made the sons of Israel take an oath: "When God comes to your aid, you are to carry my bones up from here."[d]

[a]50:24 Gn 13:15-17; 15:7-8
[b]Gn 26:3
[c]Gn 28:13; 35:12
[d]50:25 Ex 13:19

---

born on the knees of Joseph," that is, they were ritually adopted by him (Gn 30:3; Ru 4:16).

50:24-26 As **Joseph** was **about to die**, some 54 years after his father Jacob's death, he called **his brothers** to him for one last time and gave them two prophetic promises. First, that God would **certainly come to** the **aid** of their descendants. Second, that God would indeed bring their descendants up from Egypt **to the land He promised Abraham, Isaac, and Jacob** (12:7; 13:15,17; 15:7,18; 24:7; 26:3; 28:13).

After **Joseph died**, he was **embalmed**—one of only two persons in the Bible said to have been embalmed (also Jacob; see v. 2 and note at vv. 1-3). His preserved body was then **placed . . . in a coffin**, awaiting a future day when it was to be carried by Moses and the Israelites to the promised land (Ex 13:19; Jos 24:32).

The Nile is the basis of Egypt's very life and wealth. It is the only river to flow northwards across the Sahara. Egypt was unique as an agricultural community in not being dependent on rainfall. The secret was the black silt deposited on the fields by the annual flood caused when the Blue Nile was swollen by the run-off from the winter rains in Ethiopia. This silt was remarkably fertile. Irrigation waters, raised laboriously from the river, let the Egyptians produce many varieties of crops in large quantities (Gn 42:1-2; Nm 11:5). If the winter rains failed, the consequent small or nonexistent inundation resulted in disastrous famine: some are recorded as lasting over a number of years (Gn 41). This photo shows the striking contrast between the ribbon of land in which the rich silt was deposited annually and the desert-like land in the background.

Exodus

The title "Exodus" is an anglicized version of a Greek word that means "departure" in recognition of one of the book's major events—the departure of God's people from Egypt. Exodus could be considered the central book in the Old Testament because it records God's act of saving the Israelites and establishing them as a covenant community, a nation chosen to serve and represent Him. Exodus describes: the enslavement and oppression of the Israelites; the preparation and call of Moses; the conflict between Yahweh the God of Israel and the gods of Egypt (represented by Pharaoh); the exodus of the Israelites; their establishment as a nation in covenant with the Lord; their rebellion; and the Lord's provision for their ongoing relationship, symbolized by His presence at the tabernacle that they built for Him.

The Sphinx and Pyramids at Giza in Egypt

Circumstances of Writing

Author: The book of Exodus does not state who its author was. It does refer to occasions when Moses made a written record of events that took place and what God had said (17:14; 24:4,7; 34:27-28). The book also contains references to preserving and passing on information. Along with the other four books of the Pentateuch, it has long been considered to be primarily the work of Moses. Moses could have written Exodus at any time during a 40-year time span: after the Israelites finished constructing and dedicating the tabernacle at Mount Sinai, at the start of their second year after leaving Egypt (1445 B.C.), and before his death in the land of Moab (about 1406 B.C.).

Background: Exodus picks up where the Genesis narrative ended with the death of Joseph around 1805 B.C. It quickly moves us forward almost 300 years to a time when the circumstances of Jacob's descendants had changed in Egypt. The Israelites were serving as slaves during Egypt's Eighteenth Dynasty, probably under the pharaohs Thutmose and Amenhotep II. The Hebrew slaves experienced a miraculous deliverance by God's hand through His servant-leader Moses. The Israelite slavery ended in 1446 B.C. The book of Exodus records the events surrounding the exodus from Egypt and the Israelites' first year in the wilderness, including the giving of the law.

The date of the exodus is disputed, but biblical evidence favors 1446 B.C. First Kings 6:1 states that the exodus occurred 480 years before Solomon's fourth year as king, established by biblical data combined with Assyrian chronology to be 966 B.C. In Judges 11:26, Jephthah said that Israel had been living in regions of Palestine for 300 years. Jephthah lived around 1100 B.C., thus dating the end of the wilderness journey around 1400 B.C.

Message and Purpose

The book of Exodus shows God at work with the goal of having such close fellowship with people that He is described as dwelling among them. He rescued the Israelites in order to make Himself known, not only by the exercise of His power but also through an ongoing covenant relationship based on His capacity for patience,

---

3000 B.C.

1700 B.C.

Edwin Smith Surgical Papyrus dating to 1550 is the earliest known surgical treatise; it is a copy of a much older Egyptian document (3000–2500).

Hammurabi develops the first legal code in Mesopotamia. 1792–1750

Hyksos rule Egypt. 1710–1570

Body armor is used in China. 1700

Minoans develop a system for running water. 1700

Underground ice houses, Kingdom of Mari, northwest Iraq 1700

Cookbook, Mesopotamia 1700

Linear A script comes into use on Crete 1700

Egyptians show proficiency in geometry including a formula for calculating the volume of a truncated pyramid. Sources: The Moscow Papyrus and the Rhind Papyrus. 1700

grace, and forgiveness. The record of what the Lord did for the Israelites provided grounds for them to recognize Him as their God who deserved their complete loyalty and obedience. This record would make clear to the Israelites their identity as God's people and would continue the display of His glorious identity.

Exodus conveys four strong messages:

1. *The LORD God:* God revealed Himself to Moses and Israel as Yahweh, "I Am Who I Am." This covenant name for God carries profound meaning and affirms the power, authority, and eternal nature of God.

2. *Redemption:* The Israelites prayed for deliverance and God responded. God worked through His servant-leader Moses, but He did it in such a miraculous way that it was obvious that God was at work. The Israelites could not save themselves; it was all the work of God. The Passover was established to serve as an annual reminder of God's work on their behalf.

3. *Law:* The law of God is encapsulated in the Ten Commandments, God's absolutes for spiritual and moral living. The law is divided into two sections: the civil law—the rules that govern life in the community—and the ceremonial law—the patterns for worship and building the tabernacle.

4. *Tabernacle:* God gave specific instructions on how the tabernacle was to be built, but its significance is in what it represented—God dwelling among His people. He was specifically understood to dwell in the holy of holies, inaccessible to the normal Israelite. The tabernacle points ahead to the moment when Christ removed the veil of separation, giving all believers access to God. In the NT, believers become the tabernacle, for God doesn't just dwell *among* His people; He dwells *in* them.

Contribution to the Bible

Exodus provides the high point of redemptive history in the OT. Many patterns and concepts from Exodus receive attention, further development, and fulfillment elsewhere in Scripture, especially in the past, present, and future work of the Lord Jesus. These include rescue from oppression, provision of sustenance, God's

---

1600 B.C.

Aaron 1529–1409?   **Moses** 1526–1406

1445 B.C.

Joshua 1490?–1380?

Volcanic island of Thera (Santorini) erupts with massive environmental consequences felt as far as the British Isles and North America. 1600

Chocolate originates in northern Honduras. 1600

Children's swings invented; Crete 1600

Linear B script comes into use on Crete. 1600

War chariot used in Egypt 1600

18th Dynasty of Egypt, includes Thutmose and Amenhotep, traditionally the pharaohs of oppression 1570–1303

Egyptians develop effective pharmaceutical compounds. 1500

Shoes worn in Mesopotamia 1500

Plows made of bronze developed in Vietnam 1500

Bellows are used in making glass and in metallurgy. 1500

Exodus and defeat of Pharaoh at the Red Sea 1446

Passover instituted 1446

God's covenant at Sinai 1446

Tabernacle built and dedicated 1445

faithfulness to His promises, the self-revelation of God, knowledge of God resulting from His actions, the presence of God, His glory, efforts required to preserve the knowledge of God, a new identity for people that is based on God's actions, provision for worship, provision for life in community, connection between the reputation of God and His relationship with a group of people, obedience and rebellion, intercession, and gracious forgiveness.

Structure

Exodus is considered a part of the Law, but it is more historical narrative than law. The book is structured around the life and travels of Moses. Sandwiched between the narratives of chapters 1–18 and 32–40 are the establishment of the covenant (chaps. 19–24) and the laws related to the tabernacle and priesthood.

Outline

I. Oppression of God's People in Egypt (1:1–11:10)
   A. Egyptian slavery (1:1-22)
   B. Preparation of the deliverer (2:1–4:31)
   C. Struggles with the oppressor (5:1–11:10)

II. Deliverance of God's People from Egypt (12:1–14:31)
   A. Redemption by blood (12:1-51)
   B. Redemption by divine miracles (13:1–14:31)

III. Education of God's People in the Wilderness (15:1–18:27)
   A. Israel's song of victory (15:1-21)
   B. Testing and trials (15:22–17:16)
   C. Shared leadership under Moses (18:1-27)

IV. Consecration of God's People at Sinai (19:1–34:35)
   A. Acceptance of the law (19:1–31:18)
   B. Breaking of the law (32:1-35)
   C. Restoration of the law (33:1–34:35)

V. Worship of God's People in the Tabernacle (35:1–40:38)
   A. Gifts and workmen for the tabernacle (35:1-35)
   B. Construction and furnishings of the tabernacle (36:1–39:43)
   C. Filling of the tabernacle with God's glory (40:1-38)

Israel Oppressed in Egypt

1 These are the names of the sons of Israel who came to Egypt with Jacob; each came with his family:[a]

2 Reuben, Simeon, Levi, and Judah;
3 Issachar, Zebulun, and Benjamin;
4 Dan and Naphtali; Gad and Asher.

5 The total number of Jacob's descendants[A] was 70;[B,b] Joseph was already in Egypt.

6 Then Joseph and all his brothers and all that generation died.[c] 7 But the Israelites were fruitful, increased rapidly, multiplied, and became extremely numerous[d] so that the land was filled with them.

8 A new king, who had not known Joseph, came to power in Egypt. 9 He said to his people, "Look, the Israelite people are more numerous and powerful than we are.[e] 10 Let us deal

shrewdly with them; otherwise they will multiply further, and if war breaks out, they may join our enemies, fight against us, and leave the country."[f] 11 So the Egyptians assigned taskmasters over the Israelites to oppress them with forced labor.[g] They built Pithom and Rameses as supply cities[h] for Pharaoh. 12 But the more they oppressed them, the more they multiplied and spread so that the Egyptians came to dread[c] the Israelites. 13 They worked the Israelites ruthlessly[i] 14 and made their lives bitter with difficult labor in brick and mortar and in all kinds of fieldwork. They ruthlessly imposed all this work on them.[j]

15 Then the king of Egypt said to the Hebrew midwives, one of whom was named Shiphrah and the other Puah, 16 "When you help the Hebrew women give birth, observe them as they deliver.[D] If the child is a son, kill him, but if

Cross references:
a 1:1 Gn 46:8
b 1:5 Gn 46:26-27; Dt 10:22
c 1:6 Gn 50:26
d 1:7 Gn 12:2; 46:3; Dt 26:5; Ac 7:17
e 1:9 Ps 105:24
f 1:10 Ps 83:3-4; Ac 7:19
g 1:11 Gn 15:13; Ex 2:11; 3:7; 5:4-5; 6:6; Dt 26:6
h Gn 47:11; 1Kg 9:19; 2Ch 8:4
i 1:13 Dt 4:20
j 1:14 Ex 2:23; Nm 20:15; Ac 7:19

A 1:5 Lit *of people issuing from Jacob's loins*   B 1:5 LXX, DSS read *75*; Gn 46:27; Ac 7:14   C 1:12 Or *Egyptians loathed*   D 1:16 Lit *birth, look at the stones*

1:1-7 These verses summarize Gn 37–50, which describe in full how Jacob's family arrived in Egypt, the welcome they received, and the deaths of **Jacob** and **Joseph**. The list of sons (vv. 2-4) does not follow chronological order. It begins with Leah's six sons, then Rachel's younger son, Benjamin. Rachel's older son, Joseph, had come to Egypt first, before Jacob and the rest. The names continue with the two sons of Rachel's maid and finally the two sons of Leah's maid. Without mentioning the mothers, the arrangement of the list reflects family tensions.

1:5 Two other Scripture passages also say that the number who went to Egypt was **70** (Gn 46:27; Dt 10:22). The Septuagint (at Gn 46:27 and Ex 1:5 but not Dt 10:22), two Qumran manuscripts of Exodus, and Ac 7:14 all mention 75. The Septuagint of Gn 46:20 lists five sons and grandsons of Ephraim and Manasseh. These go unmentioned in the Hebrew text and therefore account for the different totals.

1:7 Verses 7, 12, and 20 use several terms to talk about the multiplication of the Israelites. These terms also appear repeatedly in God's creation and flood mandates (Gn 1:20-22,28; 9:1,7) and in promises He made to the patriarchs (Gn 17:2,6,20; 18:18; 26:4,24; 28:14; 35:11). Any Egyptian king who feared and opposed the growth of the Israelite population was opposing the purposes of the Lord.

1:8-22 These unsuccessful attempts to **deal shrewdly** with the Israelites seem to escalate in desperation and decline in shrewdness. The king of Egypt never reexamined his assumptions; he only tried new methods.

1:8 One plausible explanation of Egyptian and Israelite connections contends that Joseph came to Egypt when the native Egyptian 12th Dynasty ruled in the Middle Kingdom era. Years later, Semitic foreigners known as "Hyksos" took over much of Egypt until the time of Kamose, who reasserted Egyptian rule. The **new king** is not named in Exodus, nor is any other Egyptian king, but perhaps he was a Hyksos ruler without concern for the rights granted to the Israelites by an earlier regime. Another suggestion is that the "new king" was Ahmose, who followed his brother Kamose as ruler, reigned about 25 years, completed the restoration of Egyptian rule, and founded Dynasty 18 and the New King-

dom era, a period when Egypt exerted a powerful presence in the ancient Near East. Any 18th Dynasty king might have been wary of the Israelites if he associated them with foreigners such as the ousted Hyksos.

1:9 This is the first time **the Israelite people** are called a "people." They came to Egypt as an extended family, but now Pharaoh compared their numbers with his own. This exaggeration indicates Pharaoh's eagerness to convince his courtiers that they must take decisive action.

1:10 Pharaoh's concerns are ironic in view of the Lord's later statement that if the Israelites faced war on the way to Canaan, they would flee back to Egypt for safety (13:17).

1:11 Supply cities held agricultural produce and other useful items as part of the king's strategic oversight of the country (Gn 41:35; 1Kg 9:15-19).

1:12 The Moabites shared with the Egyptians this **dread** of the Israelites when they saw how numerous they were (Nm 22:3). Pharaoh's scheme resulted in more Israelites and more fear among the Egyptians, not less of both as he had intended.

1:13-14 Five forms of the same Hebrew word are translated here with forms of "work" or "labor." (A different word for **labor** is in v. 11.) The repetition drives home what the Egyptians were doing, and also prepares for making a comparison, since the same word can refer to service in worship. The Lord would give the Israelites new work of a different sort (3:12; 4:23; 7:16,26; 8:1). Elsewhere forms of the word translated **bitter** describe situations of severe hardship and loss (Ru 1:13,20; 1Sm 30:6; 2Kg 4:27; Is 22:4).

1:15 In this book that takes a profound interest in identities, ironically the king is nameless, but the midwives who honored God are named. Verse 15 begins with the introduction to the king's speech, but then it is as if the king could not speak until the midwives were identified. The delay is more obvious in Hebrew since verse 16 starts over with the same statement **the king . . . said** that starts verse 15.

1:16 Observe them as they deliver is literally "look at the stones," a term referring here to the genitals. The orders

it's a daughter, she may live." [17] The Hebrew midwives, however, •feared God[a] and did not do as the king of Egypt had told them;[b] they let the boys live. [18] So the king of Egypt summoned the midwives and asked them, "Why have you done this and let the boys live?"

[19] The midwives said to Pharaoh, "The Hebrew women are not like the Egyptian women, for they are vigorous and give birth before a midwife can get to them."[c]

[20] So God was good to the midwives,[d] and the people multiplied and became very numerous. [21] Since the midwives feared God, He gave them families.[e] [22] Pharaoh then commanded all his people: "You must throw every son born to the Hebrews[A] into the Nile, but let every daughter live."[f]

Moses' Birth and Adoption

2 Now a man from the family of Levi married a Levite woman.[g] [2] The woman became pregnant and gave birth to a son; when she saw that he was beautiful,[B] she hid him for three months.[h] [3] But when she could no longer hide him, she got a papyrus basket for him and coated it with asphalt and pitch.

She placed the child in it and set it among the reeds by the bank of the Nile. [4] Then his sister[i] stood at a distance in order to see what would happen to him.

[5] Pharaoh's daughter went down to bathe at the Nile while her servant girls walked along the riverbank. Seeing the basket among the reeds, she sent her slave girl to get it. [6] When she opened it, she saw the child—a little boy, crying. She felt sorry for him and said, "This is one of the Hebrew boys."

[7] Then his sister said to Pharaoh's daughter, "Should I go and call a woman from the Hebrews to nurse the boy for you?"

[8] "Go," Pharaoh's daughter told her. So the girl went and called the boy's mother. [9] Then Pharaoh's daughter said to her, "Take this child and nurse him for me, and I will pay your wages." So the woman took the boy and nursed him. [10] When the child grew older, she brought him to Pharaoh's daughter, and he became her son. She named him Moses, "Because," she said, "I drew him out of the water."[c]

Moses in Midian

[11] Years later,[D] after Moses had grown up,

*a*1:17 Ex 1:21; Pr 16:6
*b*Dn 3:16-18; Ac 4:18-20; 5:29
*c*1:19 Jos 2:4; 2Sm 17:20
*d*1:20 Pr 11:18; Is 3:10
*e*1:21 1Sm 2:35; 2Sm 7:11,27; 1Kg 11:38; Ps 127:1
*f*1:22 Gn 41:1; Ac 7:19
*g*2:1 Ex 6:20; Nm 26:59; 1Ch 23:14
*h*2:2 Ac 7:20; Heb 11:23
*i*2:4 Ex 15:20; Nm 26:59

A1:22 Sam, LXX, Tg; MT omits *to the Hebrews*   **B**2:2 Or *healthy*   **C**2:10 The name Moses sounds like "drawing out" in Hb and "born" in Egyptian.   **D**2:11 Lit *And it was in those days*

---

are clear; the midwives must kill Israelite sons and let the daughters live.

1:17 By letting the boys live, the midwives showed that they **feared God** rather than Pharaoh (Pss 96; 112; Pr 1:7; 3:7; Ac 4:19; 5:29).

1:18-20 True or not, the midwives' excuse about the superior ability of **Hebrew women** must have been believable, since Pharaoh did not pursue the matter further.

1:22 When Pharaoh **commanded all his people**, his desperate desire to kill Israelites came out into the open.

2:1-10 The story of how this unnamed baby was protected during dangerous and uncertain times adds to the suspense and indicates the child's important future role. Its close-up depiction of Pharaoh's oppression in one family helps communicate how all the Israelites needed deliverance. It also raises sympathy for the rescued infant and causes us to wonder what he will be like as both a child of slaves and the adopted son of a princess.

2:1 The genealogy of Aaron and Moses names Amram and Jochebed as the parents (6:20; Nm 26:59). Moses' **Levite** heritage is appropriate, considering his later responsibilities in instituting national worship, since the tribe of Levi was set apart for priestly service (chaps. 28-29; Nm 1:47-54; 3:5-13; 8:5-26).

2:2 Readers in cultures that prize superficial attractiveness may wonder if the mother would have cared for the baby if he had been homely. Her reaction is probably better understood against a background of high infant mortality. The mother recognized that, except for the decree of Pharaoh, this baby would surely live and thrive. Also, the broadly positive adjective translated **beautiful** is often translated

"good" and could describe such varied items as a calf (Gn 18:7), houses (Dt 8:12), a tree (2Kg 3:19), land (Ex 3:8), a method of operating (Ex 18:7), or what is morally right (Ps 14:1; 34:8). The combination of "saw" and "good" in Exodus 2 echoes its use in Genesis 1. Hebrews 11:23 refers to hiding this child as an exercise of faith by his parents. No doubt they were both involved, though the narrative focuses on what the mother and sister did.

2:3 Asphalt and pitch made the basket waterproof; even full-sized boats could be similarly sealed (Is 18:2).

2:4 His sister was Miriam (15:20; Nm 26:59). If a baby was found, people might look around for the mother, but a small girl would attract little attention and could report to her mother or, better yet, think quickly and offer the services of her mother.

2:5-6 The wording in Hebrew tracks the movements of **Pharaoh's daughter** more closely than the English wording can easily do, helping reflect her important status.

2:10 During the New Kingdom era, Egypt would bring foreign boys to court to train them for service in Egyptian territories. The actions of Pharaoh's daughter continue the undermining of his plans by women, though he considered daughters safe enough to let them live (1:16,22). Moses' name had significance for both Egyptian and Hebrew hearers. In an Egyptian name like Thutmose, *mose* is related to an Egyptian verb meaning "bear, produce, bring forth" and a noun meaning "child," while Thut/Thoth was a god; so "Thutmose" and similar names celebrated a connection between the birth of a child and an Egyptian god. Pharaoh's daughter named **Moses** in a way that suited Egyptian naming patterns and commemorated her action in saving his life, celebrating his connection with her. The name calls

he went out to his own people[A] and observed their forced labor.[a] He saw an Egyptian beating a Hebrew, one of his people. [12]Looking all around and seeing no one, he struck the Egyptian dead and hid him in the sand. [13]The next day he went out and saw two Hebrews fighting. He asked the one in the wrong, "Why are you attacking your neighbor?"[B]

[14]"Who made you a leader and judge over us?" the man replied. "Are you planning to kill me as you killed the Egyptian?"

Then Moses became afraid and thought: What I did is certainly known. [15]When Pharaoh heard about this, he tried to kill Moses. But Moses fled from Pharaoh and went to live in the land of Midian,[b] and sat down by a well.[c]

[16]Now the priest of Midian[d] had seven daughters. They came to draw water and filled the troughs to water their father's flock. [17]Then some shepherds arrived and drove them away, but Moses came to their rescue and watered

their flock. [18]When they returned to their father Reuel[C,e] he asked, "Why have you come back so quickly today?"

[19]They answered, "An Egyptian rescued us from the shepherds. He even drew water for us and watered the flock."

[20]"So where is he?" he asked his daughters. "Why then did you leave the man behind? Invite him to eat dinner."

[21]Moses agreed to stay with the man, and he gave his daughter Zipporah[f] to Moses in marriage. [22]She gave birth to a son whom he named Gershom, for he said, "I have been a foreigner[g] in a foreign land."[D]

[23]After a long time, the king of Egypt died. The Israelites groaned because of their difficult labor, and they cried out;[h] and their cry for help ascended to God because of the difficult labor. [24]So God heard their groaning, and He remembered[i] His covenant with Abraham, Isaac, and Jacob.[j] [25]God saw the Israelites, and He took notice.[k]

Cross references:
[a]2:11 Ex 1:11; Ac 7:23; Heb 11:24-26
[b]2:15 Ac 7:29; Heb 11:27
[c]Gn 24:11; 29:2
[d]2:16 Ex 3:1; 1Sm 9:11
[e]2:18 Ex 3:1; 4:18; Nm 10:29
[f]2:21 Ex 4:25; 18:2
[g]2:22 Ex 18:3-4; Ac 7:29; Heb 11:13
[h]2:23 Ex 3:7,9; Dt 26:7; Jms 5:4
[i]2:24 Gn 9:15; Ex 6:5; 1Ch 16:15; Ps 105:8; 106:45; 111:4
[j]Ps 22:23; Lk 1:33,55
[k]2:25 Ex 3:7; 4:31; Lk 1:25

[A]2:11 Lit *his brothers*   [B]2:13 Or *fellow Hebrew*   [C]2:18 Jethro's clan or last name was Reuel; Ex 3:1.   [D]2:22 In Hb the name Gershom sounds like the phrase "a stranger there."

---

to mind a verb meaning "draw out" (2Sm 22:17; Ps 18:16), which to Hebrew readers must have sounded appropriate for the person who led the Israelites out of Egypt. This child's name seems more appropriate than Pharaoh or his daughter could have thought.

2:12 Moses' caution indicates that his action was deliberate. **Struck** translates the same root word as "beating" (v. 11) and "attacking" (v. 13). In other words, the Egyptian was striking a Hebrew man, a Hebrew man struck another Hebrew, and Moses struck the Egyptian but with a different outcome. **Hid** translates a word used sometimes in contexts involving burying something (Gn 35:4; Jos 2:6; 7:21); it is different from the word used in verses 2 and 3 about Moses' mother hiding him.

2:13-14 Moses expressed surprise that the **two Hebrews** were **fighting**. This incident is evidence that the Israelites' deliverance from Egypt exemplifies God's loyalty and grace; it did not take place because they were all fine, deserving people.

2:15 The **land of Midian** included territory in modern Saudi Arabia, on the east of the Gulf of Aqaba. The Sinai Peninsula to the west would not have been far enough from Pharaoh to be safe, since Egypt had mining interests in the Sinai and it was under Egyptian military control. When he **sat down by a well** as a newcomer, Moses positioned himself to meet people, as had Abraham's servant when he met Rebekah, and as Jacob had done when he met Rachel (Gn 24:11-14; 29:1-6).

2:16 The **priest of Midian**, the father of **seven daughters**, was called Reuel (v. 18; Nm 10:29), Hobab (Jdg 4:11), and most often Jethro (Ex 3:1; 4:18; 18:1-12). Other men with more than one name include Jacob (Gn 32:28; 46:2; 48:2; 49:2), Gideon (Jdg 7:1; 8:35), and Solomon (2Sm 12:24-25). Midianites were descendants of Abraham through his wife Keturah (Gn 25:1-2). Because of this connection, perhaps Jethro led others in worship of the God of Abraham and Isaac, as did Melchizedek (Gn 14:18-20). The Midianites as a whole seem to have

been nomadic desert dwellers who were later enemies of Israel (Gn 37:28,36; Nm 22:4,7; 25:1-18; 31:1-20; Jos 13:21; Jdg 6-8; 9:17; Ps 83:9; Is 9:4; 10:26; 60:6).

2:17-19 Again Moses came to the defense of someone, but this time it had nothing to do with the Israelites or their plight. He rescued a bunch of shepherd girls from what seems to have been a common annoyance, and they thought he was **an Egyptian**. Moses' identity continued to be an issue.

2:22 The name **Gershom** reflected the son's status as an alien in both Egypt and Midian.

2:23-24 The word for **groaning** describes a man with broken arms in Ezk 30:24. Four different words for the Israelite outcry and four words for God's response combine to make a weighty statement of desperation and response. The formality in Hebrew is enhanced by the unusual repetition of the word **God** as the subject of each verb in verse 24, which also underscores God's superiority and sovereignty: God **heard** . . . God **remembered** . . . God **saw** . . . God **took notice**. God's remembering is more than mental awareness; it implies action in keeping with His covenant promises (Gn 8:1; 19:29; 30:22; Lv 26:42-45; Ps 105:8; 106:44-46; Jr 14:21; Am 1:9). The command to "remember" the Sabbath Day is parallel to the command to "keep" the Sabbath (Ex 20:8; Dt 5:12).

"Took notice" (**heard**) translates a verb often translated "know" or "knew" (1:8; 5:2; 6:3,7; 7:5; 16:12; 18:11), which like "remember" typically involves more than awareness of information. Here it carries the thought of having regard for something or someone and of exercising personal concern (Ps 31:7; 37:18; 144:3; Hs 13:4). Because God knew their situation and took action, the Israelites and others would come to know Him in a new way. This verse assumes that readers are familiar with the promises that God had made and confirmed by covenants with Abraham, Isaac, and Jacob (Gn 12:1-3,7; 13:14-17; 15:1-21; 17:1-21; 18:17-19; 21:12-13; 22:15-18; 28:3-4,10-22; 32:9-12; 35:9-15; 46:1-4; 48:3-4,15-16; 50:24-25).

Moses and the Burning Bush

3 Meanwhile, Moses was shepherding the flock of his father-in-law Jethro,[A] the priest of Midian. He led the flock to the far side of the wilderness and came to Horeb,[B] the mountain of God.[a] [2] Then the Angel of the LORD appeared to him in a flame of fire within a bush.[b] As Moses looked, he saw that the bush was on fire but was not consumed. [3] So Moses thought: I must go over and look at this remarkable sight. Why isn't the bush burning up?

[4] When the LORD saw that he had gone over to look, God called out to him from the bush, "Moses, Moses!"

"Here I am," he answered.

[5] "Do not come closer," He said. "Remove the sandals from your feet, for the place where you are standing is holy ground."[c] [6] Then He continued, "I am the God of your father,[C] the God of Abraham, the God of Isaac, and the

God of Jacob."[d] Moses hid his face because he was afraid to look at God.

[7] Then the LORD said, "I have observed the misery of My people in Egypt, and have heard them crying out[e] because of their oppressors, and I know about their sufferings. [8] I have come down to rescue them from the power of the Egyptians and to bring them from that land to a good and spacious land, a land flowing with milk and honey[f]—the territory of the Canaanites, Hittites, Amorites, Perizzites, Hivites, and Jebusites.[g] [9] The Israelites' cry for help has come to Me, and I have also seen the way the Egyptians are oppressing[h] them. [10] Therefore, go. I am sending you to Pharaoh so that you may lead My people, the Israelites, out of Egypt."

[11] But Moses asked God, "Who am I[i] that I should go to Pharaoh and that I should bring the Israelites out of Egypt?"

[12] He answered, "I will certainly be with you,[j]

Cross references

[a]3:1 Ex 2:18; 18:5; 1Kg 19:8
[b]3:2 Dt 33:16; Ac 7:30
[c]3:5 Jos 5:15; Ac 7:33
[d]3:6 Gn 28:13; Mt 22:32; Mk 12:26; Lk 20:37; Ac 7:32
[e]3:7 Ex 2:23-25; Neh 9:9; Ps 106:44
[f]3:8 Gn 50:24; Ex 6:6
[g]Gn 15:18-21; Ex 3:17; 13:5; Dt 1:25; Jr 11:5; Ezk 20:6
[h]3:9 Ex 1:14; 2:23
[i]3:11 Ex 6:12; 1Sm 18:18
[j]3:12 Gn 31:3; Jos 1:5; Rm 8:31

[A]3:1 Moses' father-in-law's first name was Jethro; Ex 2:18.   [B]3:1 = Desolation; another name for Mount Sinai; Dt 4:10,15; 18:16; Mal 4:4   [C]3:6 Sam, some LXX mss read *fathers*; Ac 7:32

3:1 Many ancient gods were associated with a mountain where they were believed to live. The Lord was by no means limited to this mountain, however, as His actions at other mountains and other places make clear (e.g., Gn 22:14; 1Kg 18:20-45; 2Kg 6:17; Is 2:3; Ezk 28:14,16; Zch 8:3).

3:2-3 The **Angel of the LORD** was active in Genesis to inform, rebuke, protect, and provide guidance and success (Gn 16:7-11; 21:17; 22:11,15; 24:7,40; 31:11). The account in Exodus 3 describes the following conversation as directly between the Lord and Moses, without concern for how the event occurred. **Fire** is frequently associated with special displays of God's presence (Ex 13:21-22; 19:18; 40:38; Dt 4:11-24,33-36; Jdg 6:21; 13:20; 1Kg 18:24,38; 2Ch 7:1-3; Ps 18:8,12-13; 50:3; 97:1-5; Is 66:15-16; Dn 7:9).

3:6 The possibility of danger implicit in human contact with God is reflected throughout Scripture (19:21-24; 24:11; 33:20-23; Gn 32:30; Jdg 13:20-23; Is 6:5; Ac 9:3-9; 1Tm 6:15-16; Rv 19:11-21). This place was holy, not because of any quality intrinsic to it, but because of God's presence and activity. The tabernacle would be a place set apart by the Lord's presence (Ex 29:43-44). To stay at a distance and remove footwear was then and is now in many cultures a sign of respect and humility. The Lord's self-identification, which began, **I am the God of your father**, connected this event with the past both by naming the patriarchs and by the wording of the statement (Gn 15:7; 17:1; 26:24; 28:13; 31:13; 35:11; 46:3). It also had the ring of a formal pronouncement by a king (Gn 41:44).

3:8 In Egypt the Israelite flocks were limited to the region of Goshen (see Gn 46:32-34). By comparison, the new land would be **spacious . . . flowing with milk and honey**—resentful Levites later used this phrase to describe Egypt (Nm 16:12-14). In the land of Canaan, such abundance depended on rain. The word for honey may also describe a sweet syrup made from boiling dates, grapes, and other fruit.

3:11-12 Moses' question—**Who am I?**—reminds us of the question one of the Hebrews asked Moses in 2:14: "Who are you?" The answer to these questions has nothing to do with Moses' upbringing or abilities. The Lord's promise to Moses, **I will certainly be with you**, depends for its value on who the Lord is; it matters that He is present because He is willing and able to act. This promise gave Moses grounds for authority that was missing earlier (2:11-15) and continues the important theme of God's personal involvement in the lives of His people (Gn 28:15; 31:3; 46:4; 48:21; Ex 33:14-16; Nm 14:43; Jos 1:9; Zch 8:23; Mt 28:20; Jn 14:16; Heb 13:5). To **worship God** with all the Israelites at the **mountain** where God and Moses were speaking would be a sign for Moses because he would be able to look back and know that this worship was possible only because of what the Lord had done (Ex 18:1-12; 24:1-11).

3:13-15 God's statement is worded with a finality that sometimes appears at the end of a conversation, typically to put an end to debate without volunteering information, like Pilate's statement, "What I have written, I have written" (Jn 19:22; also Gn 43:14; Ex 16:23; 33:19; 2Sm 15:20; Est 4:16; Jr 15:1-2). The statements containing **I AM** (v. 14) use the

---

'ehyeh 'asher 'ehyeh

Hebrew Pronunciation	[eh YEH ah SHEHR eh YEH]
HCSB Translation	I AM WHO I AM
Uses in Exodus	1
Uses in the OT	1
Focus Passage	Exodus 3:14

'Ehyeh 'asher 'ehyeh is God's statement as He revealed His preferred form of address to be Yahweh (Ex 3:14-16). 'Ehyeh is the first person form of the Hb verb meaning "to be." God may have spoken 'ehyeh 'asher 'ehyeh as a name in answer to Moses' request in verse 13, but He certainly reduced the words to the name 'Ehyeh, or I AM in verse 14. Yahweh seems to be an ancient form of the third person form of "to be." The third person may have been most suitable for Israelites considering their God. Some scholars interpret Yahweh as a causative form like "He Causes To Be," but 'ehyeh 'asher 'ehyeh favors a meaning like "He Is." Such a translation agrees with the NT portrayal of Christ as the eternally present One (Jn 8:56). I AM WHO I AM suggests God's sovereign freedom to be what He chooses to be.

and this will be the sign to you that I have sent you: when you bring the people out of Egypt, you will all worship[A] God at this mountain."

[13] Then Moses asked God, "If I go to the Israelites and say to them: The God of your fathers has sent me to you, and they ask me, 'What is His name?' what should I tell them?"

[14] God replied to Moses, "I AM WHO I AM.[B,a] This is what you are to say to the Israelites: I AM has sent me to you." [15] God also said to Moses, "Say this to the Israelites: •Yahweh, the God of your fathers, the God of Abraham, the God of Isaac, and the God of Jacob, has sent me to you. This is My name forever;[b] this is how I am to be remembered in every generation.

[16] "Go and assemble the elders of Israel and say to them: Yahweh, the God of your fathers, the God of Abraham, Isaac, and Jacob, has appeared to me and said: I have paid close attention to you and to what has been done to you in Egypt.[c] [17] And I have promised you that I will bring you up from the misery of Egypt[d] to the land of the Canaanites, Hittites, Amorites, Perizzites, Hivites, and Jebusites—a land

flowing with milk and honey. [18] They will listen to what you say. Then you, along with the elders of Israel, must go to the king of Egypt and say to him: Yahweh, the God of the Hebrews, has met with us. Now please let us go on a three-day trip into the wilderness so that we may sacrifice to Yahweh our God.[e]

[19] "However, I know that the king of Egypt will not allow you to go, unless he is forced by a strong hand.[f] [20] I will stretch out My hand and strike Egypt with all My miracles that I will perform in it. After that, he will let you go.[g] [21] And I will give these people such favor in the sight of the Egyptians that when you go, you will not go empty-handed.[h] [22] Each woman will ask her neighbor and any woman staying in her house for silver and gold jewelry, and clothing, and you will put them on your sons and daughters. So you will plunder the Egyptians."[i]

Miraculous Signs for Moses

4 Then Moses answered, "What if they won't believe me and will not obey me but say, 'The LORD did not appear[j] to you'?"

Cross references:
a3:14 Ex 6:3; Ps 68:4; Jn 8:58; Heb 13:8; Rv 1:4; 4:8
b3:15 Ps 102:12; 135:13; Hs 12:5
c3:16 Ex 4:29; Lk 1:68
d3:17 Gn 15:16; Jos 24:11
e3:18 Ex 4:31; 5:1; Nm 23:3-4,15-16
f3:19 Ex 5:2; 6:1
g3:20 Ex 6:6; 9:15; 12:31; Dt 6:22; Neh 9:10
h3:21 Ex 11:3; 12:36
i3:22 Gn 15:14; Ex 11:2; Ezk 39:10
j4:1 Ex 3:18; 6:30

A3:12 Or serve   B3:14 Or I AM BECAUSE I AM, or I WILL BE WHO I WILL BE

---

same Hebrew verb that God's promise, "I will certainly be with you," does in verse 12 (and also 4:12,15).

The wordplay with the verb makes it especially prominent and recalls the promise, as if to remind Moses, "The one who promises to be with you is the one who sends you." Since Hebrew verbs gather much of their temporal meaning from their contexts, the same form can indicate present or future or both at once, depending on the situation. Here the promises in 3:12; 4:12,15 are oriented to the future; so though "will" is appropriate in English, it does not exclude God's presence with Moses at the time they were speaking. Nor does the English present tense "am" in 3:14 exclude the future.

3:16 The name **Yahweh** is connected etymologically with the Hebrew verb "to be" that appears so prominently in

Yahweh

Hebrew Pronunciation	[YAH weh]
HCSB Translation	LORD, Yahweh
Uses in Exodus	398
Uses in the OT	6,828
Focus Passage	Exodus 3:15

God told Moses, "I AM WHO I AM." Moses was to tell Israel, "I AM has sent me to you" (Ex 3:14). Then God replaced I AM with "Yahweh, the God of your fathers, the God of Abraham, the God of Isaac, and the God of Jacob . . . This is My name forever" (Ex 3:15). Yahweh is probably a third person singular equivalent of I AM. Its pronunciation was almost lost because Jews considered it so holy that they replaced its vowels with those of other divine names. Yahweh communicates God's commitment to deliver Israel in ways that reveal His character. God did not reveal this name to the patriarchs (Ex 6:3), but Yahweh occurs in Genesis dialogue (Gn 14:22). Either the meaning was previously unknown, its significance had not been fully appreciated, or Genesis reflects later language. Moses' mother Jochebed might have a shortened form of Yahweh in her name (Jo-) if the name follows later practice.

verses 12,14. Yahweh was no stranger. He was the God of their fathers: Abraham, Isaac, and Jacob. Four hundred years in Egypt had not annulled the promises made to them and their offspring (2:24). He now sent Moses to their descendants, the Israelites. If the Israelites wanted to know who He was, they needed to look at what He had done. When the present translation uses the word LORD (with large and small capital letters), it is representing the Hebrew name that can also be transliterated "Yahweh."

3:18 A three-day trip . . . so that we may sacrifice was a reasonable request, since other slave groups in Egypt received permission for similar journeys to worship their gods. Something about Israelite sacrifices was abhorrent to the Egyptians (8:26); a three-day trip into the wilderness would get them well out of sight.

3:20 The two clauses **I will stretch out My hand** and **he will let you go** both use a form of the same Hebrew verb, making tight connection between cause and effect. When God's hand goes to work, the Israelites will go out of Egypt. The contest would be between the hand of the Lord and the "power [lit "hand"] of the Egyptians" as personified by Pharaoh (v. 8).

3:21-22 Gifts of **silver** and **gold** would fulfill what the Lord had told Abram (Gn 15:14), repeating the pattern of Abram's own departure from Egypt with wealth that had been handed to him (Gn 12:16,20; cp. Gn 20:14,16). The word translated **plunder** has a parallel use in 2Ch 20:25 to describe plundering corpses on a battlefield. Its use in Ex 3:22 and 12:36 may be an intentional overstatement. It contributes to showing the nature of the Lord's victory over Egypt, which may be why 3:22 particularly mentions that Israelite women—noncombatants ordinarily—would be doing the asking. In 11:2 and 12:35 men also participate.

4:1-9 These three signs the Lord gave Moses pertain to areas of common human vulnerability—attack by other creatures, illness, and the need for water—all of which are under the sovereign power of the Lord. The signs begin a

² The Lᴏʀᴅ asked him, "What is that in your hand?"

"A staff," he replied.

³ Then He said, "Throw it on the ground." He threw it on the ground, and it became a snake. Moses ran from it, ⁴ but the Lᴏʀᴅ told him, "Stretch out your hand and grab it by the tail." So he stretched out his hand and caught it, and it became a staff in his hand. ⁵ "This will take place," He continued, "so they will believe that ˙Yahweh, the God of their fathers, the God of Abraham, the God of Isaac, and the God of Jacob, has appeared to you."ᵃ

⁶ In addition the Lᴏʀᴅ said to him, "Put your hand inside your cloak." So he put his hand inside his cloak, and when he took it out, his hand was diseased, white as snow.ᴬ,ᵇ ⁷ Then He said, "Put your hand back inside your cloak." He put his hand back inside his cloak, and when he took it out,ᴮ it had again become like the rest of his skin.ᶜ ⁸ "If they will not believe you and will not respond to the evidence of the first sign, they may believe the evidence of the second sign. ⁹ And if they don't believe even these two signs or listen to what you say, take some water from the Nile and pour it on the dry ground. The water you take from the Nile will become blood on the ground."ᵈ

¹⁰ But Moses replied to the Lᴏʀᴅ, "Please, Lord, I have never been eloquent—either in the past or recently or since You have been speaking to Your servantᶜ—because I am slow and hesitant in speech."ᴰ,ᵉ

¹¹ Yahweh said to him, "Who made the human mouth? Who makes him mute or deaf, seeing or blind? Is it not I, Yahweh?ᶠ ¹² Now go! I will helpᴱ you speak and I will teach you what to say."ᵍ

¹³ Moses said, "Please, Lord, send someone else."ᶠ

¹⁴ Then the Lᴏʀᴅ's anger burned against Moses, and He said, "Isn't Aaron the Levite your brother? I know that he can speak well. And also, he is on his way now to meet you. He will rejoice when he sees you. ¹⁵ You will speak with him and tell him what to say.ʰ I will helpᴳ both you and him to speak and will teach you both what to do. ¹⁶ He will speak to the people for you. He will be your spokesman, and you will serve as God to him. ¹⁷ And take this staff in your hand that you will perform the signs with."ⁱ

Moses' Return to Egypt

¹⁸ Then Moses went back to his father-in-law Jethro and said to him, "Please let me return to my relatives in Egypt and see if they are still living."

Cross references:
ᵃ4:1-5 Ex 3:6,15; 4:17,20; 19:9
ᵇ4:6 Nm 12:10; 2Kg 5:27
ᶜ4:7 Nm 12:13-14; Dt 32:39; 2Kg 5:14
ᵈ4:9 Ex 7:19
ᵉ4:10 Ex 6:12; Jr 1:6
ᶠ4:11 Ps 94:9
ᵍ4:12 Is 50:4; Jr 1:9; Mt 10:19-20; Mk 13:11; Lk 12:11-12; 21:14-15
ʰ4:15 Ex 7:1-2; Nm 23:5,12,16
ⁱ4:17 Ex 4:2; 7:15

ᴬ4:6 A reference to whiteness or flakiness of the skin   ᴮ4:7 Lit *out of his cloak*   ᶜ4:10 = Moses   ᴰ4:10 Lit *heavy of mouth and heavy of tongue*   ᴱ4:12 Lit *will be with you*   ᶠ4:13 Lit *send by the hand of whom You will send*   ᴳ4:15 Lit *be with*

---

pattern in Exodus of actions that are intended to prompt faith and obedience.

4:3-4 Moses ordinarily would have used his **staff** to defend himself and his flock from snakes; now his staff became a **snake**. Speculation that the command to catch the snake **by the tail** rather than some other method required more faith from Moses, and that the writer of Exodus was unfamiliar with snakes is unnecessary. As Moses reached out, the tail would have been closest to him and, in fact, snakes are often picked up tail first.

4:6-7 Traditionally and in many translations, Moses' disease has been called leprosy, though the Hebrew term used here covers a variety of severe afflictions, even problems found in garments and buildings (Lv 13-14; Nm 12:10; Dt 24:8-9; 2Kg 5; 2Ch 26:19-21). The descriptions in Leviticus do not match the symptoms of leprosy, a condition also called Hansen's disease that is caused by bacteria.

4:10-12 Moses' next objection that he was **slow . . . in speech** returned to the problem of his personal identity and unsuitability (2:14; 3:11), as if God were dependent on him. God's answer returned attention to who He is and what He would do.

4:10 Moses began by saying he was not **eloquent** (lit "I am not a man of words"). Ironically, Moses used 21 Hebrew words arranged in somewhat complicated expressions to say that he could not speak well. He used a figure of speech referring to his mouth and tongue as "heavy" (lit "I am heavy of mouth and heavy of tongue"). The word for "heavy" also describes ears that do not hear (Is 6:10; 59:1; Zch 7:11) and eyes that do not see (Gn 48:10). One might think of a tool

that is too heavy to be used easily and so impedes the efforts that it ought to make easier.

4:11 The Lord answered by arguing from the greater to the lesser, implying that the Creator of all can deal with the problem of one. His rhetorical questions invited Moses to think and recognize that he was making a mistake by not viewing the situation from God's point of view.

4:12 The Lord's command and statement amount to a repeat of His promise to be with Moses (3:12). He applies it specifically to the problem of speaking, saying literally, "I will be with your mouth."

4:14-16 I will help both you and him repeats again His promise to be with Moses and applies it to Aaron as well. To help them speak well, God promised (lit), "I will be with your mouth and with his mouth." The promise that God would teach Moses and Aaron what to say and do has NT parallels (Lk 12:11-12; Jn 14:26). The working relationship that the Lord described for Aaron and Moses was analogous to that of a prophet with God. **He will be your spokesman** (lit "he will be a mouth for you"), and Moses would be like God for Aaron in telling him what to say to the people. Moses had complained of having a defective mouth; he would now have a new one to use.

4:19 This verse resumes God's instruction to Moses (3:10) and adds some reassuring information.

4:20 This is the first mention of Moses' two **sons**. Gershom was named in 2:22. The name of the second was Eliezer (18:3).

4:21-22 This introductory summary is matched by the simi-

Jethro said to Moses, "Go in peace." [19]Now in Midian the LORD told Moses, "Return to Egypt, for all the men who wanted to kill you are dead."[a] [20]So Moses took his wife and sons, put them on a donkey, and returned to the land of Egypt. And Moses took God's staff[b] in his hand.

[21]The LORD instructed Moses, "When you go back to Egypt, make sure you do all the wonders before Pharaoh that I have put within your power. But I will harden his heart[A,c] so that he won't let the people go. [22]Then you will say to Pharaoh: This is what Yahweh says: Israel is My firstborn son.[d] [23]I told you: Let My son go so that he may worship Me, but you refused to let him go. Now I will kill your firstborn son!"[e] [24]On the trip, at an overnight campsite, it happened that the LORD confronted him and sought to put him to death. [25]So Zipporah took a flint, cut off her son's foreskin, and threw it at Moses' feet.[B] Then she said, "You are a bridegroom of blood to me!"[f] [26]So He

let him alone. At that time she said, "You are a bridegroom of blood," referring to the circumcision.[c]

Reunion of Moses and Aaron

[27]Now the LORD had said to Aaron, "Go and meet Moses in the wilderness." So he went and met him at the mountain of God and kissed him.[g] [28]Moses told Aaron everything the LORD had sent him to say, and about all the signs He had commanded him to do. [29]Then Moses and Aaron went and assembled all the elders of the Israelites. [30]Aaron repeated everything the LORD had said to Moses and performed the signs before the people. [31]The people believed, and when they heard that the LORD had paid attention[h] to them and that He had seen their misery,[i] they bowed down and worshiped.

Moses Confronts Pharaoh

5 Later, Moses and Aaron went in and said to Pharaoh, "This is what •Yahweh, the God of Israel, says: Let My people go, so that

---

a 4:19 Ex 2:15,23; Mt 2:20
b 4:20 Ex 17:9; Nm 20:8-9
c 4:21 Ex 7:13; 9:12,35; 14:8; Dt 2:30; Jos 11:20; Is 63:17; Jn 12:40; Rm 9:18
d 4:22 Is 63:16; 64:8; Jr 31:9; Hs 11:1; Rm 9:4
e 4:23 Ex 11:5; 12:29
f 4:25 Gn 17:14; Jos 5:2-3
g 4:27 Ex 3:1; 4:14
h 4:31 Ex 2:25; 3:7,18; 4:8-9
i Gn 24:26; 1Ch 29:20

A 4:21 Or *will make him stubborn*   B 4:25 Some interpret "feet" as a euphemism for genitals.   C 4:25-26 Zipporah appeased God on Moses' behalf by circumcising Gershom.

---

lar concluding statement in 11:9-10 that "Moses and Aaron did all these wonders before Pharaoh." So the signs Moses had been given and the use of the staff would apply to both the Israelites (4:1-9) and to Pharaoh to authenticate Moses' message, although **all the wonders** would include the plagues Moses would announce as well. God informed Moses here not of what he was to say initially to Pharaoh but of the final result. In order to free Yahweh's **firstborn son**, Pharaoh's **firstborn son** would have to die (11:4-8).

When He presented the matter as a formal declaration (**This is what Yahweh says**), the Lord framed the message as a demand from a king to an underling. In the language of ancient treaties and letters, when a king declared that someone was his son, respect for the superior rank and authority of the "father" was called for. Yahweh was claiming that He, and not Pharaoh, had authority over Israel. Yahweh was also demanding that Pharaoh show proper respect to Yahweh by treating His "son" with respect. Everyone understood that failure to comply would call for severe penalties.

Such a demand to submit to the Lord would go entirely against the grain of Egyptian culture and beliefs about Pharaoh as a deity and the only king—inferior to no one. Making matters worse, Israel was being claimed as the "firstborn," a position of privilege which ancient families that was obtained through birth order or by appointment (Gn 25:21-36; Dt 21:16-17; 1Ch 5:1-2; 26:10; Ps 89:27). In short, Pharaoh was informed that he was merely a vassal ruling a second-rate nation and must answer to Yahweh.

Exodus uses three different Hebrew words for **harden** to describe what the Lord and Pharaoh himself did to his heart. The word here is especially associated with strength. Depending on the context, it could have a positive meaning (courage, steadfastness, Ps 27:14; 31:24) or a negative meaning (stubbornness, obstinacy, Ezk 2:4). When the Lord hardened hearts, it was a matter of executing judgment against confirmed rebels, not people who otherwise wanted to serve the Lord (Dt 2:30; Jos 11:20; Is 6:9-10; 63:17). It meant that Pharaoh would not listen and obey but would demonstrate that he deserved God's judgment.

The hardening of Pharaoh's heart was especially appropriate as an attack on Egyptian beliefs. Egyptians valued a "hard heart," since it was needed after death during judgment to testify on behalf of the dead individual rather than to admit wrongdoing. This terminology was also used to describe the ideal man in public life, who because of his "hard heart" would always appear firm and unshaken. When Pharaoh's heart becomes hard in Exodus, however, he is not cool and in command, and the truth about his character becomes known.

4:24-26 Perhaps the statement that the Lord **sought to put him to death** expressed how the circumstances appeared to Moses and Zipporah. It was apparent to Zipporah what had to be done, and nothing is said about what would have happened if she had failed to act. **Circumcision** was performed in Egypt when boys were 14 years of age. However, circumcision on the eighth day had been commanded of Abraham as the sign of God's covenant (Gn 17:1-14; 21:4). Moses' failure to circumcise his son shows that Moses had not been acting like a member of the covenant community, a serious offense. In contrast with the custom in Egypt—where a boy's circumcision was associated with coming into manhood—performing circumcision on the eighth day of an infant's life would naturally have involved his mother, who would closely care for the infant. So every Israelite wife and mother of a son would have thus been reminded of the covenant between God and Israel. Now because Moses had neglected the circumcision of at least one of his sons, **Zipporah** suddenly was involved. If Moses was to speak for Abraham's God, who was in the process of keeping His covenant promises, Moses needed to observe the sign of that covenant.

4:28 This summary parallels the one in 18:8.

4:31 The Israelites responded to Aaron and Moses with belief and worship, rather than with the skepticism that Moses had expected (3:13). This was a sign of God's faithfulness to His chosen servant.

5:1 Subservient groups in Egypt were allowed time off to worship their gods, but the way that **Moses and Aaron**

they may hold a festival for Me in the wilderness."[a]

[2] But Pharaoh responded, "Who is Yahweh that I should obey Him by letting Israel go? I do not know anything about Yahweh, and besides, I will not let Israel go."[b]

[3] Then they answered, "The God of the Hebrews has met with us. Please let us go on a three-day trip into the wilderness so that we may sacrifice to Yahweh our God, or else He may strike us with plague or sword."

[4] The king of Egypt said to them, "Moses and Aaron, why are you causing the people to neglect their work? Get to your work!" [5] Pharaoh also said, "Look, the people of the land are so numerous, and you would stop them from working."[c]

Further Oppression of Israel

[6] That day Pharaoh commanded the overseers[d] of the people as well as their foremen: [7] "Don't continue to supply the people with straw for making bricks, as before. They must go and gather straw for themselves. [8] But require the same quota of bricks from them as they were making before; do not reduce it. For they are slackers—that is why they are crying out,[e] 'Let us go and sacrifice to our God.' [9] Impose heavier work on the men. Then they will be occupied with it and not pay attention to deceptive words."

[10] So the overseers and foremen of the people went out and said to them, "This is what Pharaoh says:[f] 'I am not giving you straw. [11] Go get

straw yourselves wherever you can find it, but there will be no reduction at all in your workload.'" [12] So the people scattered throughout the land of Egypt to gather stubble for straw. [13] The overseers insisted, "Finish your assigned work each day, just as you did when straw was provided." [14] Then the Israelite foremen, whom Pharaoh's slave drivers had set over the people, were beaten[g] and asked, "Why haven't you finished making your prescribed number of bricks yesterday or today, as you did before?"

[15] So the Israelite foremen went in and cried for help to Pharaoh: "Why are you treating your servants this way? [16] No straw has been given to your servants, yet they say to us, 'Make bricks!' Look, your servants are being beaten, but it is your own people who are at fault."

[17] But he said, "You are slackers. Slackers! That is why you are saying, 'Let us go sacrifice to the LORD.' [18] Now get to work. No straw will be given to you, but you must produce the same quantity of bricks."

[19] The Israelite foremen saw that they were in trouble when they were told, "You cannot reduce your daily quota of bricks." [20] When they left Pharaoh, they confronted Moses and Aaron, who stood waiting to meet them.

[21] "May the LORD take note of you and judge," they said to them, "because you have made us reek in front of Pharaoh and his officials—putting a sword in their hand to kill us!"[h]

[22] So Moses went back to the LORD and asked,

Cross references (center column):
5:1 Ex 3:18; 10:9
5:2 Ex 3:19; 2Kg 18:35; Jb 21:15
5:3-5 Ex 1:7,9,11; 3:18
5:6 Ex 1:1; 3:7
5:8 Ex 2:23; 3:7; 5:15
5:10 Ex 4:22; 5:1
5:14 Is 10:24
5:21 Gn 34:30; Ex 6:9; 14:11

---

spoke for the Lord told their hearers that this message was a command from Pharaoh's superior.

5:2 Pharaoh intended his question as an insult, not as a request for information (like the question asked about Moses' identity and authority in 2:14). Proverbs 30:9 describes the question, "Who is the Lord?" as that of a self-satisfied person who is denying God's providence. Pharaoh's assertion **I do not know anything about Yahweh** continues the insult and makes no admission of ignorance. Pharaoh would have believed the answer to his rhetorical question to be "Yahweh is certainly no one that I need to recognize or obey." Pharaoh was rejecting Yahweh's position of superiority. A right knowledge of and respect for the identity of the Lord is central to the issue of whether or not to obey Him (cp. Jn 8:48-55); the events recorded in the book of Exodus answer Pharaoh's question about who the Lord is for the benefit of the Israelites (Ex 6:7), the Egyptians (7:5), onlookers (18:11; Jos 2:8-11; Jdg 2:2-11; 1Sm 4:7-8; 6:6), and subsequent readers (Ps 105; Is 63:7-14), providing ample grounds for obedience.

5:3 Concern over consequences for failure to obey the Lord gave Pharaoh another indication that He was someone to be reckoned with and that Israelite allegiance must ultimately be to Him rather than to Pharaoh (Is 8:11-13; Jr 1:17). The

Lord had authority to command and power to enforce that Pharaoh did not have.

5:19 Repeated mention of the **daily quota** (lit "the requirement/amount of a day in its day") from 5:13 helps convey the oppressiveness of the situation: the Egyptians made demands and kept account of what the Israelites did every day.

5:20 The sight of Moses and Aaron standing on the outside, waiting to hear what had happened, only to be scolded by the foremen, further shows them as having little or no power.

5:21 Earlier when Moses intervened in a fight between Israelites, one of them challenged his right to act as a **judge** and accused Moses of intending to kill him (2:14). Now the foremen called on the Lord to judge Moses. They were not expecting freedom at this point. Their hopes for restoring the status quo had just been crushed, so much so that they considered Moses responsible for their impending death. They believed Moses had made the Israelites so offensive to the Egyptians (**you have made us reek**) that they would want to kill the Israelites. Their comment also shows that the Israelite foremen already knew that the Lord had the right and the ability to act as the ultimate Judge in the situation.

5:22-23 The foremen hoped to gain favor with Pharaoh by

"Lord, why have You caused trouble for this people? And why did You ever send me?[a] [23] Ever since I went in to Pharaoh to speak in Your name he has caused trouble for this people, and You haven't delivered Your people at all." [1] But the LORD replied to Moses, "Now you are going to see what I will do to Pharaoh: he will let them go because of My strong hand; he will drive them out of his land because of My strong hand."[b]

God Promises Freedom

[2] Then God spoke to Moses, telling him, "I am •Yahweh. [3] I appeared to Abraham, Isaac, and Jacob as •God Almighty, but I did not reveal My name Yahweh to them.[c] [4] I also established My covenant with them to give them the land of Canaan, the land they lived in as

foreigners.[d] [5] Furthermore, I have heard the groaning of the Israelites, whom the Egyptians are forcing to work as slaves, and I have remembered[e] My covenant.

[6] "Therefore tell the Israelites: I am Yahweh, and I will deliver you from the forced labor of the Egyptians and free you from slavery to them. I will redeem you with an outstretched arm[f] and great acts of judgment. [7] I will take you as My people,[g] and I will be your God. You will know[h] that I am Yahweh your God, who delivered you from the forced labor of the Egyptians. [8] I will bring you to the land that I swore[A,i] to give to Abraham, Isaac, and Jacob, and I will give it to you as a possession. I am Yahweh." [9] Moses told this to the Israelites, but they did not listen[j] to him because of their broken spirit and hard labor.

[a]5:22 Nm 11:11; Jr 4:10
[b]6:1 Ex 3:19; 12:31,33,39
[c]6:3 Gn 17:1; Ex 3:14; Ps 68:4; 83:18; Jn 8:58
[d]6:4 Gn 15:18; 28:4
[e]6:5 Gn 9:15; Ex 2:24; 1Ch 16:15; Ps 105:8; 106:45; 111:4
[f]6:6 Ex 3:17; Dt 7:8; 26:8; 1Ch 17:21
[g]6:7 Dt 4:20; 2Sm 7:24
[h]Ex 16:12; 29:45; Is 41:20; Rv 21:7
[i]6:8 Gn 14:22; 15:18; 26:3
[j]6:9 Ex 5:21; Ac 7:25

A6:8 Lit raised My hand

blaming others for the trouble. They still saw their welfare as under his control. When he spoke to the Lord, Moses boldly blamed both the Lord and Pharaoh (**You caused trouble** and **he has caused trouble**) for worsening conditions and asserted that the Lord had done nothing to rescue His people. Obedience of the Lord's commands by Moses and Aaron and the elders had led to trouble rather than immediate ease.

6:1 The Hebrew wording does not include the pronoun **My** to specify that the **strong hand** must be that of the Lord rather than Pharaoh, but this impetus has been mentioned in 3:19-20.

6:2-3 A variety of attempts have been made to derive English renderings other than (or more precise than) **God Almighty** for the Hebrew name El Shaddai, based on proposed etymological connections with words in Hebrew or in other Semitic languages. But as with many names, usage provides the best insights into its significance. Among these are references to the exercise of authoritative power, discernment, justice, chastening, protection or destruction, provision of blessings, and the hearing of prayer. "Shaddai" appears most often in the book of Job (Jb 5:17; 6:4,14; 8:3,5; 11:7; 13:3; 21:15; 33:4; 34:12; 37:23; 40:2, among others], and the combination with El is prominent in Genesis as a name for God in His dealings with the patriarchs (Gn 17:1; 28:3; 35:11; 43:14; 48:3). Naomi used the name Shaddai in her complaint against God (Ru 1:20-21), and it appears also in Nm 24:4,16; Ps 68:14; 91:1; Is 13:6; Ezk 1:24; 10:5; Jl 1:15. The rendering of "Shaddai" with "Almighty" is traceable to Greek translations done before the time of Christ (pantokrator) and to the Vulgate (Omnipotens). Meanwhile, the word "El" is associated with a Hebrew word for strength, and forms of it appear widely in ancient Semitic languages to refer to deity.

"El" is a generic word for deity—a classifying word—while "Yahweh" is a personal name. Because the name Yahweh is used in Genesis, even frequently in quoted speech (Gn 9:26; 15:2,7-8; 16:5; 18:4; 19:13-14; 21:33; 22:14,17; 24:27-56; 26:28-29; 27:20,27; 28:13), scholars have debated about what is meant when in Ex 6:3 God says, **I did not reveal My name Yahweh** to Abraham, Isaac, and Jacob. Since the name Yahweh was well known by the time Genesis was written, some have proposed its usage in Genesis is anachronistic but compatible with common literary practice—

much like a modern historian might tell the story of a king's early years using the throne name that he later adopted at his coronation.

Or it may be that Ex 6:3 is not indicating that the name "Yahweh" was previously unknown among the Israelites but rather that now the Israelites would see the truth of the name's meaning displayed before them. They would come to know by experience Yahweh as their covenant-keeping God. This has parallels in Is 52:6 and Jr 16:21, which look forward to future occasions when people will personally experience His actions that fill His name with meaning (Is 64:2; Ezk 39:7).

It is also possible to translate God's words as "Did I not reveal My name Yahweh?" (cp. 2Sam 23:5; Ps 105:28). This rendering would relieve the present difficulty, but few translations have thought it the most accurate rendering.

For God to recall to Moses the name El Shaddai, a deeply meaningful name from the experiences of the patriarchs, while also referring to Himself as Yahweh, is part of emphasizing the continuity between God's promises to the patriarchs and what He was doing for Israel through Moses.

6:5 I have remembered is a way of saying that He was about to act in accordance with His covenant with the ancestors (Ps 98:1-3; 109:14-16; 115:12; Jr 14:21; Am 1:9).

6:6-8 God's message for the Israelites put emphasis at the beginning, middle, and end on His identity: **I am Yahweh.** Freeing Israel from Egypt would be part of a permanent relationship between the Lord and the Israelites. By what He did, the Israelites would come to **know** from experience who He is, and their own identity as His people would be established and displayed.

Both the Lord and the Israelites would be known as a result of what the Lord would do: **deliver you from the forced labor** (lit, and perhaps easier to visualize, "bring you out from under the burdensome labor"), **free you . . . redeem you . . . take you as My people . . . bring you to the land,** and **give it to you.** That the Lord would be known as a result of what He did continues the theme of action leading to knowledge (see 4:1-9), which is repeated frequently throughout Exodus and serves as one of the book's unifying elements (7:5,17; 8:10,22; 9:14,29; 10:2; 11:7; 14:4,18; 16:6,12; 18:11; 29:46; 31:13; 33:13,16).

¹⁰Then the Lord spoke to Moses, ¹¹"Go and tell Pharaoh king of Egypt to let the Israelites go from his land."

¹²But Moses said in the Lord's presence: "If the Israelites will not listen to me, then how will Pharaoh listen to me, since I am such a poor speaker?"^A,a ¹³Then the Lord spoke to Moses and Aaron and gave them commands concerning both the Israelites and Pharaoh king of Egypt to bring the Israelites out of the land of Egypt.

Genealogy of Moses and Aaron

¹⁴These are the heads of their fathers' families:

The sons of Reuben,^b the firstborn
    of Israel:
Hanoch and Pallu, Hezron and Carmi.
These are the clans of Reuben.

¹⁵ The sons of Simeon:^c
Jemuel, Jamin, Ohad, Jachin,
Zohar, and Shaul, the son
    of a Canaanite woman.
These are the clans of Simeon.

¹⁶ These are the names of the sons
    of Levi
according to their genealogy:
Gershon, Kohath, and Merari.^d
Levi lived 137 years.
¹⁷ The sons of Gershon:

Libni and Shimei, by their clans.
¹⁸ The sons of Kohath:
Amram, Izhar, Hebron, and Uzziel.
Kohath lived 133 years.
¹⁹ The sons of Merari:
Mahli and Mushi.
These are the clans of the Levites^e
according to their genealogy.
²⁰ Amram married his father's sister
    Jochebed,
and she bore him Aaron
    and Moses.^f
Amram lived 137 years.
²¹ The sons of Izhar:^g
Korah, Nepheg, and Zichri.
²² The sons of Uzziel:
Mishael, Elzaphan,^h and Sithri.
²³ Aaron married Elisheba,
daughter of Amminadab^i and sister
    of Nahshon.
She bore him Nadab and Abihu, Eleazar
    and Ithamar.^j
²⁴ The sons of Korah:^k
Assir, Elkanah, and Abiasaph.
These are the clans of the Korahites.
²⁵ Aaron's son Eleazar married
one of the daughters of Putiel
and she bore him Phinehas.^l
These are the heads of the Levite
    families by their clans.

²⁶It was this Aaron and Moses whom the

---

^a6:12 Ex 4:10; 6:30; Jr 1:6
^b6:14 Gn 46:9; 1Ch 5:3
^c6:15 Gn 46:10; 1Ch 4:24
^d6:16 Gn 46:11; Nm 3:17
^e6:17-19 Nm 3:18-20; 1Ch 6:17-19; 23:21
^f6:20 Ex 2:1-2; Nm 26:59
^g6:21 Nm 16:1; 1Ch 6:37-38
^h6:22 Lv 10:4; Nm 3:30
^i6:23 Ru 4:19-20; 1Ch 2:10; Mt 1:4
^j Lv 10:1; Nm 3:2; 26:60
^k6:24 Nm 26:11; 1Ch 6:22-23,37
^l6:25 Nm 25:7,11; Jos 24:33; Ps 106:30

6:6 The references to **forced labor** in verses 6 and 7 translate the same Hebrew word that was heard twice when Pharaoh complained that Moses and Aaron were stopping the Israelites "from working" (5:5) and told them to get back to their "labors" (5:4); it is also used at the start of the oppression (1:11; cp. 2:11). The Lord would oppose Pharaoh and his plans and would be successful where Moses was not, despite how it might appear at first.

The promise **I will redeem you** uses a legal term that pictures the Lord's action as that of a close relative who protected a family member or recovered property that belonged to someone in the extended family (Lv 25; 27; Dt 19; Jr 32:6-15). Boaz did this for Naomi and Ruth (Ru 3:2,9-13; 4:1-17). Such things were a matter of special interest to the Lord, who gained the reputation as Redeemer supreme (Pr 23:10-11; Is 41:14; 44:6; Jr 31:9-11). For the Lord to speak of Himself as redeeming the Israelites by means of His **outstretched arm** clarified the nature of the conflict with Pharaoh. In Egyptian art and literature, Pharaoh was pictured in battle gear with his arm stretched out as a way of showing how powerful he was. Along with the "strong hand" (v. 1), the "outstretched arm" was a frequently used figure in references to what the Lord did at the time of the exodus (Dt 4:34; 5:15; 7:19; 9:29; 11:2; 2Kg 17:36; Ps 136:12; Jr 32:21).

In a later prophecy about the future defeat of Egypt, Pharaoh's arms are broken (Ezk 30:20-26), and in a terrible reversal of the exodus, the Lord's hand and arm are turned against Judah (Jr 21:5), but when restoration is

prophesied, the strong hand and outstretched arm of the Lord are again at work on behalf of His people (Ezk 20:33-34). The Lord's **great acts of judgment** (cp. Ex 7:4) would include action taken against the gods of Egypt (12:12; Nm 33:4). Ezekiel 14:21 also uses this term and defines the judgments planned there as including losses in war ("the sword"), famine, dangerous animals, and plagues, all sent as Israel's punishment for idolatry (cp. Ezk 5:17).

6:10-12 Regardless of the rejections Moses had received, the Lord instructed him to try again. Not even the Israelites had listened to him; why should Pharaoh? Moses' self-deprecating **I am such a poor speaker** is (lit) "I am uncircumcised of lips." The term "uncircumcised" is used elsewhere of ears that could not listen (Jr 6:10) as well as being a derogatory description of the enemies of Israel (Jdg 14:3; 15:18; 1Sm 14:6; Jr 9:26; Ezk 28:10).

6:13-7:6 This genealogy could theoretically have been placed in a different location that would have required less effort and repetition. Here it interrupts the conversation between the Lord and Moses and creates suspense by forcing readers to wait for the answer that Moses presumably received immediately. In answer to questions raised in chapters 2-6 about the identity and abilities of Moses, it supplies a formal identification of Moses and Aaron that 6:13,26-27, and 7:6 make even more formal.

6:16-25 This family would be important to the institution of worship at the tabernacle in the wilderness, since Aaron

LORD told, "Bring the Israelites out of the land of Egypt according to their divisions."[a] [27] Moses and Aaron were the ones who spoke to Pharaoh king of Egypt in order to bring the Israelites out of Egypt.

Moses and Aaron before Pharaoh

[28] On the day the LORD spoke to Moses in the land of Egypt, [29] He said to him, "I am Yahweh;[b] tell Pharaoh king of Egypt everything I am telling you."

[30] But Moses replied in the LORD's presence, "Since I am such a poor speaker,[A,c] how will Pharaoh listen to me?"

7 The LORD answered Moses, "See, I have made you like God to Pharaoh, and Aaron your brother will be your prophet. [2] You must say whatever I command you; then Aaron your brother must declare it to Pharaoh so that he will let the Israelites go from his land. [3] But I will harden Pharaoh's heart[d] and multiply My signs and wonders in the land of Egypt. [4] Pharaoh will not listen to you, but I will put My hand on Egypt and bring the divisions of My people the Israelites out of the land of Egypt by great acts of judgment. [5] The Egyptians will know that I am •Yahweh[e] when I stretch out My hand[f] against Egypt, and bring out the Israelites from among them."

[6] So Moses and Aaron did this; they did just as the LORD commanded them. [7] Moses was 80 years old[g] and Aaron 83 when they spoke to Pharaoh.

[8] The LORD said to Moses and Aaron, [9] "When Pharaoh tells you, 'Perform a miracle,' tell Aaron, 'Take your staff and throw it down before Pharaoh. It will become a serpent.'"[h] [10] So Moses and Aaron went in to Pharaoh and did just as the LORD had commanded. Aaron threw down his staff before Pharaoh and his officials, and it became a serpent. [11] But then Pharaoh called the wise men and sorcerers—the magicians[i] of Egypt, and they also did the same thing by their occult practices.[j] [12] Each one threw down his staff, and it became a serpent. But Aaron's staff swallowed their staffs. [13] However, Pharaoh's heart hardened,[k] and he did not listen to them, as the LORD had said.

The First Plague: Water Turned to Blood

[14] Then the LORD said to Moses, "Pharaoh's

Cross references
[a] 6:26 Ex 7:4; 12:17,51; Nm 33:1
[b] 6:29 Ex 6:11; 7:2
[c] 6:30 Ex 4:10; 6:12
[d] 7:3 Ex 4:21
[e] 7:5 Ex 7:17; 8:19,22; 14:4,18
[f] Ex 3:20; 6:6
[g] 7:7 Dt 29:5; 31:2; 34:7; Ac 7:23,30
[h] 7:9 Ex 4:2; Is 7:11; Jn 2:18; 6:30
[i] 7:11 Gn 41:8; 2Tm 3:8
[j] Ex 7:22; 8:7,18
[k] 7:13 Ex 4:21; 7:22; 8:15,19,32; 9:7,12,34; 10:1,20,27; 11:10; 14:8

[A] 6:30 Lit I have uncircumcised lips

---

and his sons and finally one line of his sons (Nm 25:1-18) would be designated as priests. Moses' sons are not mentioned.

6:26 According to their divisions uses a military term to speak of the Israelites leaving in an orderly fashion. The same word is used in 7:4, and it sometimes refers to "armies" (1Kg 2:5; 2Kg 5:1; Is 34:2).

7:3-5 God promised to **harden Pharaoh's heart** (cp. 4:21), this time using a word that also describes the oppression that Pharaoh inflicted on the Israelites. Pharaoh had made their slavery "difficult" or "hard" (1:14; 6:9; Dt 26:6), and in return, his heart would become "hard." This way it would be clear that when the Israelites left Egypt it was not because of the persuasiveness of Moses or the wise leadership of Pharaoh. Earlier the Lord had said that as a result of His actions, the Israelites would know Him as Yahweh their God (Ex 6:7). Now He said that also **the Egyptians will know that I am Yahweh** by the way He would bring the Israelites out of Egypt. This continues and expands the theme of action leading to knowledge of the Lord (see note at 6:6-8).

7:6 The formal notice that Moses and Aaron **did just as the LORD commanded them** introduces a refrain with later parallels, especially in the account of the construction of the tabernacle (vv. 10,20; 12:28,50; 38:22; 39:1,32,42-43; 40:16).

7:8-13 Miracle in verse 9 represents the singular form of the same word translated "wonders" in verse 3. But seeing this wonder did Pharaoh no good, since he did not respond with faith and obedience (Heb 3:13–4:6). A **staff** (sometimes called a scepter) as a symbol of power and authority has had widespread currency (Ps 110:2; Is 10:5,24; 14:5; Ezk 19:10-14). Both staffs and serpents were prominent in Egyptian art. The kings of Egypt are also pictured wearing crowns that display a menacing cobra as a symbol of protection for the king and danger for his enemies, so that all would respect his commands.

7:9 The term translated **serpent** here and in verses 10 and 12 is a different Hebrew word than in 4:3. Since it is sometimes used to refer to large water creatures (Is 27:1; Ezk 29:3; 32:2), its appearance here may emphasize the size and frightening effect of the snakes in the contest.

7:11-12 Pharaoh summoned **the wise men and sorcerers**, functionaries who were present in other ancient royal courts (Gn 41:8,24; Is 19:11-13; Jr 27:9; Dn 1:20; 2:2,10,27). To have them as part of the retinue at his command was another evidence of Pharaoh's power. These men used **occult practices** to demonstrate their power and that of Pharaoh by duplicating what Moses and Aaron did when they simply obeyed the Lord (cp. 1Kg 18:25-39). Israel was unique among ancient Near Eastern cultures in that all forms of occult activity were outlawed because the people of God were to trust Him and His provisions for their security (Lv 19:26-31; Dt 18:9-14; 2Kg 21:1-12; Is 8:13-22; 47:9-15). Even if someone could produce a miracle, if the message that person brought led away from loyalty to the Lord, the Israelites must not listen (Dt 13:1-4; Mt 7:21-23; 24:24).

7:13 This verse uses the word for **hardened** associated with strength and firmness (as in 4:21) to describe **Pharaoh's heart**. King Josiah exemplifies the opposite condition, when his heart is described as "tender" (or soft) and he listened humbly to the Lord's words (2Kg 22:19).

7:14–11:10 The ten plagues described in this section are in three groups of three plagues each, plus one last climactic plague—the death of the firstborn. Elsewhere the pattern of three plus a fourth appears in contexts that emphasize thorough observation and completeness of reckoning (Pr 30:15-31; Am 1:3–2:8). Each plague that has an announcement comes with the same command: **Let My people go, so**

heart is hard: he refuses to let the people go. [a]
¹⁵ Go to Pharaoh in the morning. When you see him walking out to the water, stand ready to meet him by the bank of the Nile. Take in your hand the staff that turned into a snake.[a] ¹⁶ Tell him: Yahweh, the God of the Hebrews, has sent me to tell you: Let My people go, so that they may worship[A] Me in the wilderness, but so far you have not listened. ¹⁷ This is what Yahweh says: Here is how you will know that I am Yahweh. Watch. I will strike the water in the Nile with the staff in my hand, and it will turn to blood. ¹⁸ The fish in the Nile will die, the river will stink, and the Egyptians will be unable to drink water from it."

ᵃ7:14-15 Ex 4:2-3; 8:15; 10:1,20,27
ᵇ7:19 Ex 8:5-6,16-17; 9:22; 10:12,21; 14:21,26
ᶜ7:20 Ex 17:5; Ps 78:44; 105:29

¹⁹ So the Lord said to Moses, "Tell Aaron: Take your staff and stretch out your hand[b] over the waters of Egypt—over their rivers, canals,[B] ponds, and all their water reservoirs—and they will become blood. There will be blood throughout the land of Egypt, even in wooden and stone containers."

²⁰ Moses and Aaron did just as the Lord had commanded; in the sight of Pharaoh and his officials, he raised the staff and struck the water in the Nile, and all the water in the Nile was turned to blood.[c] ²¹ The fish in the Nile died, and the river smelled so bad the Egyptians could not drink water from it. There was blood throughout the land of Egypt.

[A]7:16 Or serve; Ex 4:23   [B]7:19 The Hb word refers specifically to the various branches and canals of the Nile River; Ex 8:5.

that they may worship Me (v. 16; 8:1,20; 9:1,13; 10:3). The exception is the tenth plague. There Moses informed Pharaoh that after this last plague, Pharaoh's own people would come to Moses to beg the Israelites to leave Egypt (11:8).

In each group of plagues, Moses brings the announcement of the first one to Pharaoh when meeting him "in the morning" (7:15; cp. 8:20; 9:13). The second plague of each group is announced in the palace, when Moses "went in to Pharaoh" (10:3; cp. 8:1; 9:1). After each of the nine plagues comes a notice about the condition of Pharaoh's heart (7:22-23; 8:15,19,32; 9:7,12,35; 10:20,27).

The orderliness and consistency of the Lord and Moses as the contest progresses contrast with the vacillation in Pharaoh's personal behavior (expressing regret, offering concessions and taking them back, angry outbursts) and the growing chaos in the realm in which he was thought responsible to maintain order. Throughout, Moses did what the Lord told him to do, while Pharaoh did the opposite, just as God had foretold; the implication is that the Lord is sovereign in human affairs. The plagues involved natural elements and events that were familiar to Egyptians—water, frogs, insects, east and west winds, storms, diseases, darkness—but they were not merely natural. The Lord, to and through Moses and Aaron, foretold the timing, intensity, and extent of the plagues, which set them apart from mere natural disasters. For example, hordes of locusts have come to portions of Egypt intermittently throughout history, but not to the extent reported in Exodus and not in the wake of the series of disasters that struck Egypt then. Likewise, all firstborn humans die, but they do not die all at once and to the exclusion of other humans. The Lord also announced the purpose of the plagues, explaining that they were intended to reveal His identity, to make Him known to a wide audience (6:1,7; 7:5,17; 8:10,22; 9:14-16,29; 10:2; 11:7). Note the gradual increase in seriousness and the gradual defeat of the magicians (7:12; 8:18-19; 9:11).

Attempts have been made to identify each of the plagues as an attack on one of the many Egyptian gods. Such equivalence is not required, however, for the events to show the futility of Egyptian beliefs, the powerlessness of Egyptian deities, and the necessity of allegiance to Yahweh. The events in Exodus as a whole reveal Him to be trustworthy. The contest with Pharaoh displays the Lord's sovereignty over an array of natural elements necessary for human life and over the inner workings of a man whom Egyptians believed to be a god but who was in fact just an ordinary human king (Ezr 6:22; Pr 21:1).

7:14 The word **hard** (lit "heavy") represents a Hebrew figure of speech. In English to have a "heavy heart" typically means to be troubled or sad. But the Hebrew term for "heavy" could describe a mouth and tongue that did not speak well (4:10), eyes that did not see (Gn 48:10), and ears that did not hear (Is 6:10; 59:1; Zch 7:11). In both Egyptian and Hebrew, the heart (like the mind)—as the center of mental, emotional, and volitional activity—was supposed to listen and respond appropriately (Dt 30:17; 1Kg 3:9; Solomon asked to be given "a hearing heart"). Pharaoh was failing to respond as he ought.

Pharaoh's "heavy" heart registered another problem, because according to Egyptian beliefs, gods would weigh a person's heart after death to determine his destiny in the afterlife. If it was heavy by comparison with a feather, a symbol for wisdom, then a fierce god stood by to devour the individual. Elsewhere in the OT sin is spoken of as heavy and as making the heart heavy (Gn 18:20; Ps 38:4; Is 1:4; 24:20), and the Lord is the One who weighs hearts, which makes Him the ultimate Judge of all, including Pharaoh and other kings (1Sm 2:3; Pr 16:2; 21:2; 24:12; Dn 5:25-28).

The Lord's assessment of Pharaoh was also important because Pharaoh and his heart were thought to be responsible for maintaining order throughout Egypt. Order was thought to be the essential expression of wisdom (in contrast to the essence of wisdom in Ps 111:10; Pr 1:7; 9:10; 15:33; Dn 2:20). During the plagues Pharaoh could not maintain order; he failed by both the Lord's standards and his own.

7:17-18 Suggestions about why Pharaoh was expected to go out in the morning to the river (8:20) include the possibility of a worship ritual, something about his personal habits, or to measure the river's depth and reach during its flood stage. It is unclear whether the river became actual **blood**, or whether it was so polluted that the word "blood" would best describe how it looked. The Hebrew word is related to the word for the color red and is sometimes used to describe something that had the appearance of blood but was not literal blood (Gn 49:11; Dt 32:14; 2Kg 3:22; Jl 2:31). Either way, it caused the **fish** to **die**, the water to **stink**, and people to need something else to **drink**. Pharaoh had used the Nile to bring death to Israelite babies, but now it would be a source of death rather than life for Egyptians, and Pharaoh could do nothing about it.

7:21 The Israelite foremen had complained that Moses had made them reek to Pharaoh (same Hb verb as in v. 18; 5:21), but now there was something that truly stank—**the Nile**.

²² But the magicians of Egypt did the same thing by their occult practices. So Pharaoh's heart hardened, and he would not listen to them, as the LORD had said. ²³ Pharaoh turned around, went into his palace, and didn't even take this to heart. ²⁴ All the Egyptians dug around the Nile for water to drink because they could not drink the water from the river. ²⁵ Seven days passed after the LORD struck the Nile.

The Second Plague: Frogs

8 ᴬ Then the LORD said to Moses, "Go in to Pharaoh and tell him: This is what •Yahweh says: Let My people go, so that they may worship Me.ᵃ ² But if you refuse to let them go, then I will plague all your territory with frogs.ᵇ ³ The Nile will swarm with frogs; they will come up and go into your palace, into your bedroom and on your bed, into the houses of your officials and your people, and into your ovens and kneading bowls. ⁴ The frogs will come up on you, your people, and all your officials."

⁵ᴮ The LORD then said to Moses, "Tell Aaron: Stretch out your hand with your staff over the rivers, canals, and ponds, and cause the frogs to come up onto the land of Egypt."ᶜ ⁶ When Aaron stretched out his hand over the waters of Egypt, the frogsᵈ came up and covered the land of Egypt. ⁷ But the magicians did the same thing by their occult practices and brought frogs up onto the land of Egypt.

⁸ Pharaoh summoned Moses and Aaron and said, "Askᵉ Yahweh to remove the frogs from me and my people. Then I will let the people go and they can sacrifice to Yahweh."

⁹ Moses said to Pharaoh, "You make the choice rather than me. When should I ask on behalf of you, your officials, and your people, that the frogs be taken away from you and your houses, and remain only in the Nile?"

ᵃ8:1 Ex 3:12,18; 4:23
ᵇ8:2 Ex 7:14; 9:2; Rv 16:13
ᶜ8:3-5 Ex 7:19; 10:6
ᵈ8:6 Ps 78:45; 105:30
ᵉ8:8 Ex 8:28; 9:28; 10:17
ᶠ8:10 Ex 9:14; Dt 33:26; 2Sm 7:22; 1Ch 17:20; Is 46:9; Jr 10:6-7
ᵍ8:15 Ex 7:4; Ec 8:11
ʰ8:18 Ex 7:11; 9:11; Dn 5:8
ⁱ8:19 Ps 8:3; Lk 11:20
ʲ8:20 Ex 2:5; 7:15; 8:1; 9:13

¹⁰ "Tomorrow," he answered.

Moses replied, "As you have said, so you may know there is no one like Yahweh our God,ᶠ ¹¹ the frogs will go away from you, your houses, your officials, and your people. The frogs will remain only in the Nile." ¹² After Moses and Aaron went out from Pharaoh, Moses cried out to the LORD for help concerning the frogs that He had brought againstᶜ Pharaoh. ¹³ The LORD did as Moses had said: the frogs in the houses, courtyards, and fields died. ¹⁴ They piled them in countless heaps, and there was a terrible odor in the land. ¹⁵ But when Pharaoh saw there was relief, he hardened his heartᵍ and would not listen to them, as the LORD had said.

The Third Plague: Gnats

¹⁶ Then the LORD said to Moses, "Tell Aaron: Stretch out your staff and strike the dust of the earth, and it will become gnatsᴰ throughout the land of Egypt." ¹⁷ And they did this. Aaron stretched out his hand with his staff, and when he struck the dust of the earth, gnats were on man and beast. All the dust of the earth became gnats throughout the land of Egypt. ¹⁸ The magicians tried to produce gnats using their occult practices, but they could not. The gnats remained on man and beast.ʰ

¹⁹ "This is the finger of God,"ⁱ the magicians said to Pharaoh. But Pharaoh's heart hardened, and he would not listen to them, as the LORD had said.

The Fourth Plague: Swarms of Flies

²⁰ The LORD said to Moses, "Get up early in the morning and present yourself to Pharaoh when you see him going out to the water. Tell him: This is what Yahweh says: Let My people go, so that they may worshipᴱ Me.ʲ ²¹ But if you will not let My people go, then I will send

---

ᴬ8:1 Ex 7:26 in Hb   ᴮ8:5 Ex 8:1 in Hb   ᶜ8:12 Or *frogs, as he had agreed with*   ᴰ8:16 Perhaps sand fleas or mosquitoes
ᴱ8:20 Or *serve*

7:25 The Lord striking the Nile had been symbolized and enacted when Aaron struck it with his staff (v. 20).

8:8 Pharaoh's request put Moses in a situation similar to that of Abraham in Gn 20:7,17; both were called prophets, both prayed for a foreign ruler, and the Lord answered both with relief (Ex 7:1; 8:13-14). The wording of Pharaoh's request shows that he understood what had happened and what he ought to do.

8:9-10 The opportunity for Pharaoh to choose the time would show that the end of the plague was under the Lord's control. Unless Pharaoh's answer, **Tomorrow**, was idiomatic for "immediately," or "as soon as possible," his **choice** postponed the end of the plague until the next day. The response to Moses' prayer pointed to the Lord's incomparability; He could start and stop this plague at will.

8:15 This is the first instance of Pharaoh making his heart "heavy" himself (cp. 7:14), but it is matched by the notice in

7:23 that he failed to "take to heart" the first plague. References to Pharaoh's hardening his own heart, in the sense of making it "heavy" and so inoperative, also include 8:32; 9:34.

8:16-19 Researchers have debated about exactly what kind of troublesome insects these were: **gnats**, fleas, mosquitoes, or ticks. When they found they could not duplicate the plague, Pharaoh's magicians declared, **This is the finger of God** (cp. 31:18; Dt 9:10; Ps 8:3). Yet, by their description, this disaster required the action of just a finger of the God who had said He would put His hand into Egypt. After the magicians' admission, Goshen began to be excluded from the plagues beginning with the fourth, making it irrefutable that the God of the Hebrews was responsible since He spared His own people.

8:21 The use of two somewhat rhyming forms of a Hebrew word for **send** marks the cause-and-effect connection that Pharaoh needed to recognize. An idea of the tone may be

swarms of flies^A against you, your officials, your people, and your houses. The Egyptians' houses will swarm with flies, and so will the land where they live.^B ²²But on that day I will give special treatment to the land of Goshen, where My people are living;^a no flies will be there. This way you will know that I, •Yahweh, am in the land. ²³I will make a distinction^C between My people and your people. This sign will take place tomorrow."

²⁴And the LORD did this. Thick swarms of flies went into Pharaoh's palace and his officials' houses. Throughout Egypt the land was ruined because of the swarms of flies.^b ²⁵Then Pharaoh summoned Moses and Aaron and said, "Go sacrifice to your God within the country."

²⁶But Moses said, "It would not be right^D to do that, because what we will sacrifice to the LORD our God is detestable to the Egyptians.^c If we sacrifice what the Egyptians detest in front of them, won't they stone us? ²⁷We must go a distance of three days into the wilderness and sacrifice to the LORD our God as He instructs us."

²⁸Pharaoh responded, "I will let you go and sacrifice to the LORD your God in the wilderness, but don't go very far. Make an appeal^d for me."

²⁹"As soon as I leave you," Moses said, "I will appeal to the LORD, and tomorrow the swarms of flies will depart from Pharaoh, his officials,

a8:22 Ex 9:4,6; 10:23; 11:7
b8:24 Ps 78:45; 105:31
c8:26 Gn 43:32; 46:34
d8:28 Ex 8:8; 9:28; 1Kg 13:6
e9:1-5 Ex 7:4,16; 8:1-2,22; 11:7
f9:6 Ex 9:19; Ps 78:50
g9:7 Ex 7:14; 8:32

and his people. But Pharaoh must not act deceptively again by refusing to let the people go and sacrifice to the LORD." ³⁰Then Moses left Pharaoh's presence and appealed to the LORD. ³¹The LORD did as Moses had said: He removed the swarms of flies from Pharaoh, his officials, and his people; not one was left. ³²But Pharaoh hardened his heart this time also and did not let the people go.

The Fifth Plague: Death of Livestock

9 Then the LORD said to Moses, "Go in to Pharaoh and say to him: This is what •Yahweh, the God of the Hebrews, says: Let My people go, so that they may worship Me. ²But if you refuse to let them go and keep holding them, ³then the LORD's hand will bring a severe plague against your livestock in the field—the horses, donkeys, camels, herds, and flocks. ⁴But the LORD will make a distinction between the livestock of Israel and the livestock of Egypt, so that nothing of all that the Israelites own will die." ⁵And the LORD set a time, saying, "Tomorrow the LORD will do this thing in the land."^e ⁶The LORD did this the next day. All the Egyptian livestock died,^f but none among the Israelite livestock died. ⁷Pharaoh sent messengers who saw that not a single one of the Israelite livestock was dead. But Pharaoh's heart was hardened,^g and he did not let the people go.

---

^A8:21 Or insects   ^B8:21 Lit are   ^C8:23 LXX, Syr, Vg; MT reads will place deliverance   ^D8:26 Or allowable

indicated by a rendering such as, "If you won't send out, I will send in."

8:22-23 During the fourth plague and others to follow, the Lord would distinguish His people from Pharaoh's people in order to give knowledge of His sovereign presence. This new element and the use of two forms of the word "send" in verse 21 help to highlight the conflict and contrast between the Lord and Pharaoh. It would be clear that Pharaoh was unable to protect his people. **Goshen** was in northeastern Egypt, possibly near Wadi Tumilat, and had excellent pasture for sheep and goats (Gn 45:10; 46:34; 47:4,6).

8:24-28 The rare word translated **swarms of flies** does not specify a particular insect and may indicate a mixture. Pharaoh's stipulations in verses 25 and 28 show that he still thought he was in charge and could assert his authority. His **don't go very far** uses an emphatic construction and the kind of negative command that only someone of superior status could issue. The word Moses used for **detest** is the same one that Gn 43:32 and 46:34 use to talk about the Egyptians' refusal to eat with Joseph's Hebrew brothers, that is, the Egyptian scorn for shepherds. Apparently Pharaoh could admit that Moses was right about the clash of cultures. Pharaoh would let the Israelites go and sacrifice in the wilderness, but his quick command—**make an appeal for me**—just two words in Hebrew, shows what he was primarily interested in.

8:29 Jacob used the word translated here **act deceptively** to describe how Laban had cheated him when he kept changing Jacob's pay (Gn 31:7). The Lord did not owe Pharaoh warnings or rebukes. Each rebuke and each warning of an impending plague gave Pharaoh an opportunity to change course.

9:2 The phrase **holding them** uses a form of the same verb that 4:4 uses where Moses "caught" the snake. To speak of Pharaoh holding on to the Israelites fits scenes in Egyptian art that depict the king as a warrior with one hand grasping a captive by the hair and the other holding a club ready to strike him.

9:3 Plague five is in keeping with the Lord's earlier announcements that He would put His hand into Egypt and extend His hand against Egypt (3:20; 7:4-5).

9:5-7 The word for **time** is used later in Exodus to speak of the appointments that the Lord set for the Israelites as occasions to gather for worship (13:10; 23:15; 34:18). Again a distinction was made; no Israelite livestock died, which Pharaoh knew both from the plague announcement and from checking afterward, but he did not benefit from the information that he gathered. Verse 7 highlights Pharaoh's contradictory behavior by using two forms of the Hebrew word for "send"; he sent to find out about Israelite livestock but would not send the Israelites out of Egypt. Later events (vv. 19-25) indicate that **all the Egyptian livestock** is

The Sixth Plague: Boils

[8]Then the LORD said to Moses and Aaron, "Take handfuls of furnace soot, and Moses is to throw it toward heaven in the sight of Pharaoh. [9]It will become fine dust over the entire land of Egypt. It will become festering boils[a] on man and beast throughout the land of Egypt." [10]So they took furnace soot and stood before Pharaoh. Moses threw it toward heaven, and it became festering boils on man and beast. [11]The magicians could not stand before Moses because of the boils, for the boils were on the magicians as well as on all the Egyptians.[b] [12]But the LORD hardened Pharaoh's heart[c] and he did not listen to them, as the LORD had told Moses.

The Seventh Plague: Hail

[13]Then the LORD said to Moses, "Get up early in the morning and present yourself to Pharaoh. Tell him: This is what Yahweh, the God of the Hebrews says: Let My people go, so that they may worship Me. [14]Otherwise, I am going to send all My plagues against you,[A] your officials, and your people. Then you will know there is no one like Me in all the earth. [15]By now I could have stretched out My hand and struck you and your people with a plague, and you would have been obliterated from the earth.[d] [16]However, I have let you live for this purpose: to show you My power[e] and to make My name known in all the earth. [17]You are still acting arrogantly against[B] My people

by not letting them go. [18]Tomorrow at this time I will rain down the worst hail[f] that has ever occurred in Egypt from the day it was founded until now. [19]Therefore give orders to bring your livestock and all that you have in the field into shelters. Every person and animal that is in the field and not brought inside will die when the hail falls on them." [20]Those among Pharaoh's officials who ·feared the word of the LORD made their servants and livestock flee to shelters, [21]but those who didn't take the LORD's word seriously left their servants and livestock in the field.

[22]Then the LORD said to Moses, "Stretch out your hand toward heaven and let there be hail throughout the land of Egypt—on man and beast and every plant of the field in the land of Egypt." [23]So Moses stretched out his staff toward heaven, and the LORD sent thunder and hail.[g] Lightning struck the earth, and the LORD rained hail on the land of Egypt. [24]The hail, with lightning flashing through it, was so severe that nothing like it had occurred in the land of Egypt since it had become a nation. [25]Throughout the land of Egypt, the hail struck down everything in the field, both man and beast. The hail beat down every plant of the field and shattered every tree in the field. [26]The only place it didn't hail was in the land of Goshen where the Israelites were.[h]

[27]Pharaoh sent for Moses and Aaron. "I have sinned this time," he said to them. "Yahweh is the Righteous[i] One, and I and my people are

---

[a]9:9 Dt 28:27; Rv 16:2
[b]9:11 Ex 8:18; 2Tm 3:9
[c]9:12 Ex 4:21; 7:22
[d]9:15 Ex 3:20; 8:10,20
[e]9:16 Ex 14:17; Pr 16:4; Rm 9:17
[f]9:18 Jos 10:11; Jb 38:22; Ps 18:12; Is 28:2; 30:30; Ezk 13:11; 38:22
[g]9:23 Ps 78:47-48; 105:32; 148:8; Rv 8:7; 11:19; 16:21
[h]9:26 Ex 8:22; 9:4,6; 11:7; 12:13; Is 32:18
[i]9:27 Ex 10:16; 2Ch 12:6; Ps 129:4; 145:17; Lm 1:18

[A]9:14 Lit your heart   [B]9:17 Or still obstructing

---

meant to be taken as (a) an intentional hyperbole or general statement, with exceptions being minor enough not to matter, or (b) that it refers to most of the varieties mentioned in verse 3, or (c) that animals not "in the field" (v. 3) were spared, or (d) that enough time passed for Egyptians to acquire more animals.

9:8 Furnace soot may have been readily available from brick kilns, which would have offered a measure of poetic justice, though soot from a smelting furnace or lime kiln would also have sufficed.

9:9 Festering boils and specifically Egyptian boils were infamous enough to be included among the covenant curses in Dt 28:27,35.

9:10-11 Moses and Aaron **stood before Pharaoh**, but **the magicians could not stand before Moses**. This turnabout of wording enhances the status of Moses by putting him in the position of "holding court." The magicians were finished and are not mentioned again in Exodus.

9:12 This is the first *instance* in which **the LORD hardened Pharaoh's heart**. Earlier notices have mentioned his heart's condition (7:13,22; 8:19) or recorded that Pharaoh did the hardening (8:15,32), although the first *reference* to the Lord's hardening Pharaoh's heart is in 4:21.

9:13-17 The Lord could easily have destroyed Pharaoh and

his people without plagues or the hardening of Pharaoh's heart (cp. Dn 2:20-21), but these events were designed to show the Lord's incomparability (**there is no one like Me in all the earth**). Thus God now made for Himself the claim that Moses made for Him earlier (8:10). The Lord described Pharaoh as **still acting arrogantly**. Such statements might seem arrogant and egotistical, but taking Exodus as a whole, they demonstrate the truthfulness of the claims and show that the Lord is just and compassionate. Throughout the conflict with Pharaoh, the Lord was demonstrating His right to rule while calling for allegiance and obedience.

9:19 Previous plagues did not include direct commands about how to avoid damage. The outcome for obedience and disobedience before the seventh plague should have helped prompt obedience when the last plague came with its commands about preparing.

9:20-21 Some officials **feared the word of the LORD**. Others **didn't take the LORD's word seriously** (lit, anyone "who did not set his heart to the Lord's word"). A person who fears the Lord and His word takes them seriously—giving attention and credence—leading to appropriate action (cp. 1:17,21).

9:27-28 When Pharaoh said, **I have sinned**, he may have been admitting to being merely "at fault," or "in the wrong,"

the •guilty ones. 28 Make an appeal to Yahweh. There has been enough of God's thunder and hail. I will let you go;*a* you don't need to stay any longer."

29 Moses said to him, "When I have left the city, I will extend my hands*b* to Yahweh. The thunder will cease, and there will be no more hail, so that you may know the earth*c* belongs to Yahweh. 30 But as for you and your officials, I know that you still do not fear Yahweh our God."

31 The flax and the barley were destroyed because the barley was ripe*A* and the flax was budding,*d* 32 but the wheat and the spelt were not destroyed since they are later crops.*B*

33 Moses went out from Pharaoh and the city, and extended his hands to the LORD. Then the thunder and hail ceased, and rain no longer poured down on the land. 34 When Pharaoh saw that the rain, hail, and thunder had ceased, he sinned again and hardened his heart, he and his officials. 35 So Pharaoh's heart hardened, and he did not let the Israelites go, as the LORD had said through Moses.

The Eighth Plague: Locusts

10 Then the LORD said to Moses, "Go to Pharaoh, for I have hardened his heart and the hearts of his officials so that I may do these miraculous signs of Mine among

*a*9:28 Ex 8:8; 10:17
*b*9:29 1Kg 8:22,38; Ps 143:6; Is 1:15
*c*Ps 24:1; 1Co 10:26
*d*9:31 Ru 1:22; 2:23
*e*10:1 Ex 4:21; 7:4,13
*f*10:2 Ex 13:8,14; Dt 4:9; 6:20-22; Ps 44:1; 78:5-7; Jl 1:3
*g*10:3 1Kg 21:29; Jms 4:10; 1Pt 5:6
*h*10:4 Pr 30:27; Rv 9:3
*i*10:5 Ex 9:32; Jl 1:4
*j*10:7 Ex 23:33; Jos 23:13; 1Sm 18:21; Ec 7:26

them,*C,e* 2 and so that you may tell*D* your son and grandson*f* how severely I dealt with the Egyptians and performed miraculous signs among them, and you will know that I am •Yahweh."

3 So Moses and Aaron went in to Pharaoh and told him, "This is what Yahweh, the God of the Hebrews, says: How long will you refuse to humble yourself before Me? Let My people go, that they may worship Me.*g* 4 But if you refuse to let My people go, then tomorrow I will bring locusts*h* into your territory. 5 They will cover the surface of the land so that no one will be able to see the land. They will eat the remainder left*i* to you that escaped the hail; they will eat every tree you have growing in the fields. 6 They will fill your houses, all your officials' houses, and the houses of all the Egyptians—something your fathers and ancestors never saw since the time they occupied the land until today." Then he turned and left Pharaoh's presence.

7 Pharaoh's officials asked him, "How long must this man be a snare*j* to us? Let the men go, so that they may worship Yahweh their God. Don't you realize yet that Egypt is devastated?"

8 So Moses and Aaron were brought back to Pharaoh. "Go, worship Yahweh your God,"

A9:31 Lit *was ears of grain*   **B**9:32 Lit *are late*   **C**10:1 Lit *Mine in his midst*   **D**10:2 Lit *tell in the ears of*

---

using the word translated "sinned" in a way similar to its use in 5:16.

9:29 Extending **hands** was a gesture associated with prayer and a sign of need and dependence (1Kg 8:22,38,54; Jr 4:31). Again God's action was meant to provide knowledge. The seventh plague added significance to the Lord's name by showing His ownership of and sovereignty over the entire earth, not just a portion as with many pagan gods.

9:30 Moses pointed Pharaoh to the source of Egypt's problems (cp. 7:16; 8:29).

9:31-32 The description of the crops when the seventh plague hit indicates that people might have held out hope for a good harvest, but the locusts of the eighth plague would soon devour them.

9:34 Here the word for **sinned** gets its full force and perhaps a touch of irony (cp. v. 27; 5:16).

9:34–10:1 These verses contain three references to the hardening of Pharaoh's heart following the plague of hail. The first reference names Pharaoh as the agent (**he . . . hardened his heart**), and it says that his officials did the same. The second names no agent and simply describes the condition (**Pharaoh's heart hardened**). The third names the Lord as the agent (**I have hardened his heart and the hearts of his officials**). The first (9:34) and third (10:1) use the same verb. So it seems that both Pharaoh and the Lord are responsible for the condition that the second reference describes without naming an agent. Other similar descriptions may likewise leave room for both the Lord and Pharaoh to be involved. Later some Philistines commented on

the hardening of hearts that took place in Egypt and spoke of the Egyptians and Pharaoh as responsible (1Sm 6:7).

10:1-2 This prologue to the plague of locusts introduces the topic of provisions for remembering and recording what the Lord had done for them (12:14-27,42-49; 13:1-16; 16:33-34; 17:14-16). The hardening of Egyptian hearts was the occasion for **miraculous signs** that the Israelites should recount to succeeding generations so they would know who the Lord is (Ps 111:4-6).

10:3-7 This is the first time Moses and Aaron deliver the plague announcement and then leave, showing the Lord's control of events and revealing to readers what will happen.

10:3 The correct answer to Moses' and Aaron's question should have been, "No longer." Pharaoh was refusing to humble himself. Would he like to avoid plagues? Yes. Humble himself? No.

10:4 **Locusts** are still dreaded in Africa. The eighth plague would bring the worst visitation of locusts ever in Egypt.

10:7 **Pharaoh's officials** blamed Moses for the problem. Their second rhetorical question drew attention to what Pharaoh did not "know," that is, to recognize and respond appropriately. **Realize** translates the word usually rendered "know" (1:8; 5:2). The officials were convinced that more trouble was coming.

10:8-11 In an attempt to forestall the plague of locusts, Moses and Aaron were brought back to Pharaoh, who immediately began an argument over who should go. Moses' list included everyone and everything they owned, since the

Pharaoh said. "But exactly who will be going?"

⁹Moses replied, "We will go with our young and our old; we will go with our sons and daughters and with our flocks and herds because we must hold Yahweh's festival."ᵃ

¹⁰He said to them, "May Yahweh be with you if I ever let you and your families go!ᴬ Look out—you are planning evil. ¹¹No, only the men may go and worship Yahweh, for that is what you have been asking for." And they were driven from Pharaoh's presence.

¹²The LORD then said to Moses, "Stretch out your hand over the land of Egypt and the locusts will come up over it and eat every plant in the land, everything that the hail left." ¹³So Moses stretched out his staff over the land of Egypt, and the LORD sent an east wind over the land all that day and through the night. By morning the east wind had brought in the locusts. ¹⁴The locusts went up over the entire land of Egypt and settled on the whole territory of Egypt. Never before had there been such a large number of locusts, and there never will be again.ᵇ ¹⁵They covered the surface of the whole land so that the land was black, and they consumed all the plants on the ground and all the fruit on the trees that the hail had left. Nothing green was left on the trees or the plants in the field throughout the land of Egypt.ᶜ

¹⁶Pharaoh urgently sent for Moses and Aaron and said, "I have sinned against Yahweh your God and against you. ¹⁷Please forgive my sin once more and make an appeal to Yahweh your God, so that He will take this death away

ᵃ10:8-9 Ex 5:1; 8:8
ᵇ10:14 Ps 78:46; 105:34; Jl 2:2
ᶜ10:15 Ex 10:5; Ps 105:35
ᵈ10:16-18 Ex 8:8,30; 9:27
ᵉ10:19 Ex 13:18; 15:4,22; 23:31; Nm 14:25; 21:4; 33:10-11
ᶠ10:20 Ex 4:21; 11:10
ᵍ10:22-23 Ex 8:22; Ps 105:28
ʰ10:27 Ex 4:21; 10:20

from me." ¹⁸Moses left Pharaoh's presence and appealed to the LORD.ᵈ ¹⁹Then the LORD changed the wind to a strong westᴮ wind, and it carried off the locusts and blew them into the •Red Sea.ᵉ Not a single locust was left in all the territory of Egypt. ²⁰But the LORD hardened Pharaoh's heart,ᶠ and he did not let the Israelites go.

The Ninth Plague: Darkness

²¹Then the LORD said to Moses, "Stretch out your hand toward heaven, and there will be darkness over the land of Egypt, a darkness that can be felt." ²²So Moses stretched out his hand toward heaven, and there was thick darkness throughout the land of Egypt for three days. ²³One person could not see another, and for three days they did not move from where they were. Yet all the Israelites had light where they lived.ᵍ

²⁴Pharaoh summoned Moses and said, "Go, worship Yahweh. Even your families may go with you; only your flocks and herds must stay behind."

²⁵Moses responded, "You must also let us haveᶜ sacrifices and •burnt offerings to prepare for Yahweh our God. ²⁶Even our livestock must go with us; not a hoof will be left behind because we will take some of them to worship Yahweh our God. We will not know what we will use to worship Yahweh until we get there."

²⁷But the LORD hardened Pharaoh's heart,ʰ and he was unwilling to let them go. ²⁸Pharaoh said to him, "Leave me! Make sure you never see my face again, for on the day you see my face, you will die."

ᴬ10:10 Pharaoh's reply is sarcastic. ᴮ10:19 Lit sea ᶜ10:25 Lit also give in our hand

entire nation belonged to the Lord. **You are planning evil** translates a terse phrase with no verb, literally, "evil [is] opposite your face." The word translated "evil" often refers to calamity or disaster; so it may be that Pharaoh referred to the trouble that the Israelites would experience if they continued to annoy him with talk of leaving—"Look out, you are about to be in trouble from me; it's right in front of you!" Or he may have been saying that what they were contemplating was bad, evil from his point of view. Pharaoh considered both the journey and the reason for it unimportant. To him, going off to worship Yahweh was just something that Moses and Aaron had contrived.

10:16-20 Monarchs cultivate the image of serenity and control. Pharaoh's hurry to call Moses and Aaron back, his longer confession, and his request for relief from the plague show its impact on him. Unlike before, in the aftermath of this plague, Moses said nothing to Pharaoh.

10:19 The Hebrew name for **the Red Sea**, yam suph, is used here for the first time. It is also applied to what is now called the Gulf of Aqaba or Gulf of Eilat, the branch of the Red Sea that extends east of the Sinai Peninsula and west of the Arabian Peninsula (1Kg 9:26). The translation "Reed Sea"

or "Sea of Reeds" that is sometimes suggested recognizes that the word suph means "reed" or "reeds," as in Ex 2:3,5 and Is 19:6. The name "Red Sea" reflects ancient Greek usage, which included the Gulf of Suez, the Gulf of Aqaba, the Arabian Sea, and the Persian Gulf under the Greek equivalent of "Red Sea" (eruthra thalassey).

10:21-23 Darkness seems appropriate as an attack on the Egyptian king, since Pharaoh was believed to be the son of Egypt's chief god, the sun-god Re. It is also part of later judgment pronounced against Egypt (Ezk 32:7-8). Pharaoh had refused to allow a three-day journey for the Israelites, and now, ironically, Pharaoh's people were surrounded by darkness and unable to go anywhere for **three days**, while the Lord's people had **light** for their activities. An unusually severe sandstorm could have been the plague that the Lord used to impose darkness on Egypt.

10:24 Pharaoh's restriction of the movement of the **flocks and herds** of the Israelites showed that he was still unwilling to submit to the Lord.

10:28-29 Make sure you never see my face again has to do with initiating a formal appearance before Pharaoh, not a

²⁹"As you have said," Moses replied, "I will never see your face again."ᵃ

The Tenth Plague: Death of the Firstborn

11 The Lord saidᴬ to Moses, "I will bring one more plague on Pharaoh and on Egypt. After that, he will let you go from here. When he lets you go,ᴮ he will drive you out of here. ²Now announce to the people that both men and women should ask their neighbors for silver and gold jewelry." ³The Lᴏʀᴅ gaveᶜ the people favor in the sight of the Egyptians. And the man Moses was highly regardedᴰ in the land of Egypt byᴱ Pharaoh's officials and the people.ᵇ

⁴So Moses said, "This is what •Yahweh says: 'About midnight I will go throughout Egypt, ⁵and every firstborn male in the land of Egypt will die, from the firstborn of Pharaoh who sits on his throne to the firstborn of the servant girl who is behind the millstones, as well as every firstborn of the livestock. ⁶Then there

*a*10:29 Heb 11:27
*b*11:1-3 Ex 3:21-22; 12:35-36
*c*11:8 Ex 12:3; Am 5:17
*d*11:9 Ex 3:19; 7:4; 10:1
*e*11:10 Ex 4:21; 10:20,27

will be a great cry of anguish through all the land of Egypt such as never was before, or ever will be again. ⁷But against all the Israelites, whether man or beast, not even a dog will snarl,ᶠ so that you may know that Yahweh makes a distinction between Egypt and Israel. ⁸All these officials of yours will come down to me and bow before me, saying: Leave, you and all the people who follow you.ᴳ After that, I will leave.'" And he left Pharaoh's presence in fierce anger.ᶜ

⁹The Lᴏʀᴅ said to Moses, "Pharaoh will not listenᵈ to you, so that My wonders may be multiplied in the land of Egypt." ¹⁰Moses and Aaron did all these wonders before Pharaoh, but the Lᴏʀᴅ hardened Pharaoh's heart,ᵉ and he would not let the Israelites go out of his land.

Instructions for the Passover

12 The Lᴏʀᴅ said to Moses and Aaron in the land of Egypt: ²"This month is to be the beginning of months for you; it is the

ᴬ11:1 Or had said   ᴮ11:1 Or go, it will be finished—   ᶜ11:3 Or had given   ᴰ11:3 Lit was very great   ᴱ11:3 Or in the eyes of
ᶠ11:7 Lit point its tongue   ᴳ11:8 Lit people at your feet

casual sighting (cp. 23:17; 34:23; 2Sm 14:23-33). Moses did see Pharaoh again secretly (Ex 12:31). Moses' words in verse 29 may also mean "I will not keep seeing you" rather than **I will never see your face again**. The words Moses delivered to Pharaoh in 11:4-8 may have been uttered during the encounter in 10:24-29 (translating the speech verb in 11:1 as "had said"). The angry exchange between Pharaoh and Moses shows that they agreed on one thing—that Moses' series of announcements and demands was finished. There would be no more bargaining. For Pharaoh to threaten to kill the messenger of the Lord shows that he still disrespected them both.

11:1-3 The notice that **the Lᴏʀᴅ gave the people favor** with the Egyptians and that **Moses was highly regarded** by them summarizes opinions that were unexpected and different from those of Pharaoh. He wasn't shaping the Egyptians' opinions to the degree that a king would like to do. Meanwhile, the inner workings of Pharaoh's people, like his own heart, were accessible to the Lord.

11:2-5 The instructions to request **silver** and **gold** and the announcement that the **firstborn** of **Egypt** would die return to matters that the Lord had told Moses about much earlier (3:19-22; 4:21-23). Events were taking place according to God's plan.

11:5 The servant girl who is behind the millstones refers to someone grinding grain by pushing the top stone over the lower one.

11:6 A great cry of anguish corresponds to the cry of the oppressed Israelites in 3:7,9.

11:8 Moses' **anger** is unusual, since during the cycle of plagues nothing is said about his feelings. Moses expressed anger on behalf of the Lord, who had been angry when Moses repeatedly objected to obeying (4:14). The notice of anger contributes to recognizing that Moses, although he knew about the hardening of Pharaoh's heart, considered him accountable for his actions. By the end of

the tenth plague, Moses would in a sense be in the position of Pharaoh, with Pharaoh's officials bowing as supplicants to Moses.

12:1–13:16 Chapters 12–13 are arranged topically in a way that intersperses long sections of instruction with short sections that describe events taking place. With earlier plagues, the report of the plague follows immediately after its announcement. Not so with the tenth. Instructions to Moses and Aaron and then to the Israelites about how to observe **the Lᴏʀᴅ's Passover** (12:11) postpone the report of the plague's enactment (12:29-42). Some of the instructions that stand before the report of the plague and of the Israelite departure are ones that the Israelites would have needed at the time in order to prepare. Some instructions would be of use only in later years, but they are prominent among the instructions before the event. The report of the exodus (12:29-42) is followed by further instructions for future celebrations (12:43-49) and a short summary of the first Passover observance and the exodus (12:50-51).

Another section of instructions for the future follows. It involves dedication of the firstborn and observing the feast of unleavened bread (13:1-16) before the account returns to the unfolding events of the exodus (13:17–14:31). People usually wait to make plans for commemorating an event until after the event has occurred, but here the Israelites were still in Egypt (12:1). The attention given to future celebrations in these preparatory chapters highlights the event's certainty and importance as well as the authority of the Lord, who would give the Israelites cause for celebration.

12:2 Because of what the Lord was about to do in the current month, the Israelites were to consider it the first month of their year (**the beginning of months**). Its Canaanite name was Abib and its Babylonian name was Nisan (13:4). This lunar month overlaps with portions of the solar months of March and April.

12:3 To select **an animal of the flock** four days in advance

first month of your year.*ᵃ* ³Tell the whole community of Israel that on the tenth day of this month they must each select an animal of the flock according to their fathers' households, one animal per household. ⁴If the household is too small for a whole animal, that person and the neighbor nearest his house are to select one based on the combined number of people; you should apportion the animal according to what each personᴬ will eat. ⁵You must have an unblemishedᵇ animal, a year-old male; you may take it from either the sheep or the goats. ⁶You are to keep it until the fourteenth day of this month; then the whole assembly of the community of Israel will slaughter the animals at twilight.ᶜ ⁷They must take some of the blood and put it on the two doorposts and the lintel of the houses where they eat them. ⁸They are to eat the meat that night; they should eat it, roasted over the fire along with unleavened bread and bitter herbs.ᵈ ⁹Do not eat any of it raw or cooked in boilingᴮ water, but only roastedᵉ over fire—its head as well as its legs and inner organs. ¹⁰Do not let any of it remain until morning;ᶠ you must burn up any part of it that does remain before morning. ¹¹Here is how you must eat it: you must be dressed for travel,ᶜ your sandals on your feet, and your staff in your hand. You are to eat it in a hurry; it is the Lᴏʀᴅ's •Passover.ᵍ

¹²"I will pass throughʰ the land of Egypt on that night and strike every firstborn male in the land of Egypt, both man and beast. I am •Yahweh; I will execute judgments against all the gods of Egypt.ⁱ ¹³The blood on the houses where you are staying will be a distinguishing mark for you; when I see the blood, I will pass over you. No plague will be among you to destroy you when I strike the land of Egypt.

¹⁴"This day is to be a memorial for you, and you must celebrate it as a festival to the Lᴏʀᴅ. You are to celebrate it throughout your generations as a permanent statute.ʲ ¹⁵You must eat unleavened bread for seven days. On the first day you must remove yeastᵏ from your houses. Whoever eats what is leavened from the first day through the seventh day must be cut offˡ from Israel. ¹⁶You are to hold a sacred assemblyᵐ on the first day and another sacred assembly on the seventh day. No work may be done on those days except for preparing what people need to eat—you may do only that.

¹⁷"You are to observe the Festival of •Unleavened Bread because on this very day I brought your divisions out of the land of Egypt.ⁿ You must observe this day throughout your generations as a permanent statute. ¹⁸You are to eat unleavened bread in the first month,ᵒ from the evening of the fourteenth day of the month until the evening of the twenty-first day. ¹⁹Yeast must not be found in your houses for seven days. If anyone eats something leavened, that person, whether a foreign resident or native of the land, must be cut off from the community of Israel. ²⁰Do not eat anything leavened; eat unleavened bread in all your homes."ᴰ

²¹Then Moses summoned all the elders of Israel and said to them, "Go, select an animal from the flock according to your families,

---

ᵃ12:2 Ex 13:4; 23:15; 34:18; Dt 16:1 ᵇ12:5 Lv 22:19-21; Mal 1:8,14 ᶜ12:6 Lv 23:5; Nm 9:3; Dt 16:6 ᵈ12:8 Ex 34:25; Nm 9:11; Dt 16:3; 1Co 5:8 ᵉ12:9 Dt 16:7; 2Ch 35:13 ᶠ12:10 Ex 23:18; 34:25 ᵍ12:11 Ex 12:27; Dt 16:5 ʰ12:12 Ex 11:4-5; Am 5:17 ⁱEx 6:2; Nm 33:4 ʲ12:14 Ex 12:17,43; 13:9-10; 2Kg 23:21 ᵏ12:15 Ex 13:6-7; 23:15; 34:18; Lv 23:6; Dt 16:3,8 ˡGn 17:14; Nm 9:13 ᵐ12:16 Lv 23:7-8; Nm 28:18,25 ⁿ12:17 Ex 12:41,51; 13:3 ᵒ12:18 Lv 23:5-8; Nm 28:16-25

ᴬ12:4 Or household ᴮ12:9 Or or boiled at all in ᶜ12:11 Lit it: with your loins girded ᴰ12:20 Or settlements

would give opportunity to observe it for defects. But more importantly, early selection would draw attention to what was ahead. Just enough should be prepared for the people who would eat together.

12:8-10 The **meat** must be eaten immediately, and anything left must be burned and not left to ordinary uses the next morning. That it must be **roasted** whole also fits the need for special treatment of this animal, whose blood above the doorway and on the side posts identified the inhabitants of the house; they were people who took the Lord's commands seriously (9:20-21).

12:11-12 The declarations **it is the Lᴏʀᴅ's Passover** and **I am Yahweh** reinforce the truth that what was happening centered on God's identity and His self-revelatory actions (6:2-8,29; 7:5,17, etc.). In this instance He exercised His ability and right to **execute judgments**, as He had said He would do (cp. 6:6; 7:4), even **against all the gods of Egypt**.

12:15-20 Eating **unleavened bread** would remind the Israelites of their rapid departure from Egypt that did not allow time for a leavening agent to make the bread rise (v. 39). Those who ate leavened bread showed disdain for what the Lord had done in founding Israel as a nation and were subject to either banishment (Nm 19:13) or the death penalty, which was meted out to intentionally defiant lawbreakers in Nm 15:22-31 and carried out by human or divine agency (Ex 31:14; Lv 20:1-24).

pesach

Hebrew Pronunciation	[peh SAHKH]
HCSB Translation	Passover
Uses in Exodus	6
Uses in the OT	49
Focus Passages	Exodus 12:11,21,27,43,48

The first occurrence of *pesach* (Ex 12:11) refers either to the *Passover lamb* (Ex 12:21) or the *Passover Festival* (Ex 12:48). Exodus 12 explains both. *Pesach* usually refers to the festival, but the reference to the *Passover lamb* occurs before and after the exile (Dt 16:2; Ezr 6:20), as well as into the NT era (1Co 5:7). The plural of *pesach* indicates the *Passover lambs* needed for the nation (2Ch 35:6). People "slaughtered" (2Ch 35:1) and "ate" (2Ch 30:18) the lamb while "observing" the festival (2Ch 35:1). *Pesach* seems related to the verb *pasach* ("pass over") in Ex 12:13,23,27. God mercifully *passes over* the people, doors, and houses. The verb can imply sparing (Is 31:5).

and slaughter the Passover animal.[a] [22]Take a cluster of hyssop, dip it in the blood[b] that is in the basin, and brush the lintel and the two doorposts with some of the blood in the basin. None of you may go out the door of his house until morning. [23]When the LORD passes through to strike Egypt and sees the blood on the lintel and the two doorposts, He will pass over the door and not let the destroyer enter your houses to strike you.[c]

[24]"Keep this command permanently as a statute for you and your descendants. [25]When you enter the land that the LORD will give you as He promised, you are to observe this ritual. [26]When your children[d] ask you, 'What does this ritual mean to you?' [27]you are to reply, 'It is the Passover sacrifice[e] to the LORD, for He passed over the houses of the Israelites in Egypt when He struck the Egyptians and spared our homes.'" So the people bowed down and worshiped. [28]Then the Israelites went and did this; they did just as the LORD had commanded Moses and Aaron.

The Exodus

[29]Now at midnight the LORD struck every firstborn male in the land of Egypt, from the firstborn of Pharaoh who sat on his throne to the firstborn of the prisoner who was in the dungeon, and every firstborn of the livestock.[f] [30]During the night Pharaoh got up, he along with all his officials and all the Egyptians, and there was a loud wailing[g] throughout Egypt because there wasn't a house without someone dead. [31]He summoned Moses and Aaron during the night and said, "Get up, leave my people, both you and the Israelites, and go, worship Yahweh as you have asked. [32]Take even your flocks and your herds as you asked and leave, and also bless me."

[33]Now the Egyptians pressured the people in order to send them quickly out of the country, for they said, "We're all going to die!"[h] [34]So the people took their dough before it was leavened, with their kneading bowls wrapped up in their clothes on their shoulders.

[35]The Israelites acted on Moses' word and asked the Egyptians for silver and gold jewelry and for clothing.[i] [36]And the LORD gave the people such favor in the Egyptians' sight that they gave them what they requested. In this way they plundered the Egyptians.

[37]The Israelites traveled from Rameses to

[a] 12:21 Ex 12:3; Mk 14:12-16
[b] 12:22 Ex 12:7; Heb 11:28
[c] 12:23 Ezk 9:6; 1Co 10:10; Rv 7:3
[d] 12:26 Ex 10:2; 13:8,14; Dt 6:20; 32:7; Jos 4:6,21; Ps 78:3-6
[e] 12:27 Ex 4:31; 12:11
[f] 12:29 Ex 4:23; 11:4; Nm 8:17; 33:4; Ps 78:51; 135:8
[g] 12:30 Ex 11:6; Am 5:17
[h] 12:33 Ex 11:8; Ps 105:38
[i] 12:35 Gn 15:14; Ex 3:21; Ps 105:37

12:23 The descriptions of the death of the firstborn say nothing more about **the destroyer**, nor do they indicate how the humans or animals died. The Lord's sovereign activity was the issue, and He presented Himself as bringing about the deaths. He also referred to the plague as destroying (v. 13), in an expression that uses a Hebrew word closely related to the one here translated "destroyer." Elsewhere an angel from the Lord is described using the Hebrew word for "the destroyer" in a situation that involved a deadly plague (2Sm 24:16). David chose "plague" because it would allow him to "fall into the LORD's hands" (2Sm 24:14). Angels came to destroy Sodom and Gomorrah (Gn 19:13), while He was repeatedly credited with destroying the cities (Gn 13:10; 18:22–19:14,24-25).

12:24-27 The Lord expected the Israelites to teach their **children** about Him in the process of regularly celebrating what He had done for them (10:2; 13:8-9,14-15).

12:29 The prisoner who was in the dungeon was another person opposite Pharaoh in social standing, like "the servant girl who is behind the millstones" (11:5). Mention of both extremes encompassed all people in between.

12:31-32 Pharaoh had one last encounter with **Moses and Aaron**. He had declared that Moses would die if they met again, but he could not keep that resolve. Instead he capitulated and gave unconditional release of all the Israelites to go and worship, but he himself made no mention of worshiping the Lord (cp. 2Kg 5:17-18). Pharaoh's desire for blessing recalls earlier dealings of Egyptians and others with God's people that show things could have been far different for him (Gn 12:3; 21:22-24; 26:28-31; 39:5; 47:7,10).

12:33 We're all going to die! is the last recorded statement to Moses by ordinary Egyptians. It uses just two words in Hebrew and assesses the situation without any pretense, the expectation being that all the Egyptians were about to die if the Israelites stayed any longer in Egypt.

12:35-36 These verses describe what the statements in 3:21-22 and 11:2-3 had looked toward.

12:37 Rameses and **Succoth** are thought to have been in eastern Egypt (1:11), with Succoth east of Rameses in an area that the ancient Egyptians called Tjeku. This was at the eastern end of the Wadi Tumilat and contained fortifications because the area was a trade route with access to the Sinai

---

matstsah

Hebrew Pronunciation	[mah TSAH]
HCSB Translation	unleavened bread, unleavened
Uses in Exodus	16
Uses in the OT	53
Focus Passages	Exodus 12:8,15,17-18,20,39

Matstsah, or matzo, is a flat bread, cake, or wafer baked quickly from flour and water in dough prepared without yeast (Lv 10:12). People could make it when there was no time to be more elaborate (Gn 19:3; Jdg 6:19; 1Sm 28:24). Israelites ate unleavened bread under such conditions at the exodus (Ex 12:39). God required unleavened bread, or "bread of hardship," at the Passover to remind the Israelites that they left Egypt hurriedly (Ex 12:8; Dt 16:3). The Passover together with the Festival of Unleavened Bread celebrated over the next seven days could both be called the Festival of Unleavened Bread (2Ch 8:13). Unleavened bread was also necessary for the consecration of priests, the dedication of Nazirites, the grain offering, and the fellowship sacrifice (Ex 29:2; Lv 2:4-5; 7:11-12; Nm 6:15). A part of it was burned on the altar, with the priests eating the rest (Lv 6:15-16; 10:12).

Succoth,ᵃ about 600,000ᵇ soldiers on foot, besides their families. ³⁸An ethnically diverse crowd also went up with them, along with a huge number of livestock, both flocks and herds. ³⁹The people baked the dough they had brought out of Egypt into unleavened loaves, since it had no yeast; for when they had been drivenᶜ out of Egypt they could not delay and had not prepared any provisions for themselves.

⁴⁰The time that the Israelites lived in EgyptᴬÂ was 430 years.ᵈ ⁴¹At the end of 430 years, on that same day, all the Lᴏʀᴅ's divisions went out from the land of Egypt. ⁴²It was a night of vigil in honor of the Lᴏʀᴅ, because He would bring them out of the land of Egypt. This same night is in honor of the Lᴏʀᴅ, a night vigil for all the Israelites throughout their generations.ᵉ

Passover Instruction

⁴³The Lᴏʀᴅ said to Moses and Aaron, "This is the statute of the Passover: no foreigner may eat it. ⁴⁴But any slave a man has purchased may eat it, after you have circumcised him. ⁴⁵A temporary resident or hired hand may not eat the Passover.ᶠ ⁴⁶It is to be eaten in one house. You may not take any of the meat outside the house, and you may not break any of its bones.ᵍ ⁴⁷The whole community of Israel must celebrateᴮ it. ⁴⁸If a foreigner resides with you and wants to celebrate the Lᴏʀᴅ's Pass-

over, every male in his household must be circumcised, and then he may participate;ᶜ he will become like a native of the land. But no uncircumcised person may eat it. ⁴⁹The same law will apply to both the native and the foreignerʰ who resides among you."

⁵⁰Then all the Israelites did this; they did just as the Lᴏʀᴅ had commanded Moses and Aaron. ⁵¹On that same day the Lᴏʀᴅ brought the Israelites out of the land of Egypt according to their divisions.ⁱ

13 The Lᴏʀᴅ spoke to Moses: ²"Consecrate every firstborn maleʲ to Me, the firstborn from every womb among the Israelites, both man and domestic animal; it is Mine."

³Then Moses said to the people, "Remember this day when you came out of Egypt, out of the place of slavery, for the Lᴏʀᴅ brought you out of here by the strength of His hand. Nothing leavened may be eaten.ᵏ ⁴Today, in the month of Abib,ᴰˡ you are leaving. ⁵When the Lᴏʀᴅ brings you into the land of the Canaanites, Hittites, Amorites, Hivites, and Jebusites,ᴱ which He swore to your fathers that He would give you, a land flowing with milk and honey,ᵐ you must carry out this ritual in this month.ⁿ ⁶For seven days you must eat unleavened bread, and on the seventh day there is to be a festival to the Lᴏʀᴅ. ⁷Unleavened bread is to be eaten for those seven days. Nothing leavened may be found among you, and no

---

ᵃ 12:37Gn 47:11; Nm 33:3,5 ᵇEx 38:26; Nm 1:46; 11:21 ᶜ 12:39Ex 6:1; 12:33 ᵈ 12:40Gn 15:13-16; Ac 7:6; Gl 3:17 ᵉ 12:42Ex 13:10; Dt 16:1,6 ᶠ 12:43-45Gn 17:11-13; Lv 22:10; Nm 9:14 ᵍ 12:46Nm 9:12; Ps 34:20; Jn 19:33,36 ʰ 12:49Nm 9:14; 15:15-16,19; Gl 3:28 ⁱ 12:51Ex 6:26; 12:41 ʲ 13:2Ex 13:12-13,15; 22:29-30; Nm 3:13; Dt 15:9; Lk 2:23 ᵏ 13:3Ex 6:1; 12:8,42; Dt 16:3 ˡ 13:4Ex 12:2; 23:15; 34:18; Dt 16:1 ᵐ 13:5Ex 3:8; 33:3; Nm 16:14; Jos 5:6; Jr 32:22 ⁿEx 6:8; 12:25

ᴬ 12:40LXX, Sam add *and in Canaan* ᴮ 12:47Lit *do* ᶜ 12:48Lit *may come near to do it* ᴰ 13:4March–April; called Nisan in the post-exilic period; Neh 2:1; Est 3:7 ᴱ 13:5DSS, Sam, LXX, Syr add *Girgashites* and *Perizzites*; Jos 3:10

Peninsula. The large number of people who left Egypt contrasts with the small number who had entered it (1:1-5).

12:38 The **ethnically diverse crowd** may have included other laborers who saw an opportunity to escape from Egyptian servitude, but who had not necessarily come to faith in Yahweh (Nm 11:4).

12:40-41 Starting from 966 B.C., when Solomon began to build the temple, and adding 480 years (1Kg 6:1) yields 1446 B.C. for the date of the exodus. Adding **430 years** to that brings Jacob to Egypt in 1876 B.C., during the Egyptian Middle Kingdom era.

12:43-49Passover was a family event for those who belonged to the covenant community of Israel, to whom circumcision was the sign of the covenant that God was in the process of fulfilling (2:24; Gn 17:9-13). **The whole community of Israel must celebrate** the Passover, and one law would apply to anyone who was part of the covenant community, whether by birth (and membership in a family through purchase) or by choice of affiliation. A woman's participation would normally depend on her family connections.

13:1-16 In addition to having the Passover Feast and Festival of Unleavened Bread, the Israelites would memorialize what the Lord had done for them when they set apart, or consecrated, the firstborn males of both humans and animals. In future years the Israelites were to reenact certain events of the exodus. They would eat a meal like their

last one in Egypt, and they would eat unleavened bread, as they had done in the early days of their journey out of Egypt (12:39). Because the Lord had distinguished and redeemed Israel, His firstborn, they would redeem their firstborn sons (4:22-23; 6:6; 15:13; 22:29-31; 34:18-20; Dt 7:8; 9:26). All these people, animals, and events were built into Israelite life as reminders of the Lord's identity. He was known from His actions, and He gave meaning to the lives of His people (cp. Ti 2:14).

13:2 Elsewhere the Lord explained that He had consecrated **every firstborn male** of Israel as belonging to Him when He struck down the firstborn of Egypt (Nm 3:13; 8:17). The significance of Israel's firstborn sons and animals was tied to what the Lord had done and said rather than to anything special about them.

13:3 The theme of God's strong **hand** comes up repeatedly in instructions about the celebration (vv. 9,14,16; cp. 32:11) and uses forms of the Hebrew word for "strong" or "strength" that describe the hardening of Pharaoh's heart by strengthening his resolve and making him more firmly determined (7:13,22; 8:19; 9:35; 10:22,27; 11:10; 14:4,8,17). What had seemed impossible to Egyptian observers had happened (3:19; 5:22–6:1). The might of Pharaoh had been crushed by the strong hand of the Lord.

13:5 On the groups in Canaan that the Israelites would drive out, see 3:7-8; Dt 7:1.

yeast may be found among you in all your territory. [8] On that day explain to your son, 'This is because of what the LORD did for me when I came out of Egypt.'[a] [9] Let it serve as a sign for you on your hand and as a reminder on your forehead,[A,b] so that the LORD's instruction may be in your mouth; for the LORD brought you out of Egypt with a strong hand. [10] Keep this statute at its appointed time from year to year.

[11] "When the LORD brings you into the land of the Canaanites, as He swore to you and your fathers, and gives it to you, [12] you are to present to the LORD every firstborn male of the womb. All firstborn offspring of the livestock you own that are males will be the LORD's. [13] You must redeem every firstborn of a donkey with a flock animal, but if you do not redeem it, break its neck. However, you must redeem every firstborn among your sons.[c]

[14] "In the future, when your son[d] asks you,

[a]13:8 Ex 12:26-27; 3:14
[b]13:9 Ex 13:16; Dt 6:8; 11:18
[c]13:13 Ex 34:20; Nm 3:46-47; 18:15
[d]13:14 Ex 12:26-27; Dt 6:20
[e]13:15-16 Ex 12:29; 13:9
[f]13:17 Ex 14:11; Nm 14:1-4; Dt 17:16

'What does this mean?' say to him, 'By the strength of His hand the LORD brought us out of Egypt, out of the place of slavery. [15] When Pharaoh stubbornly refused to let us go, the LORD killed every firstborn male in the land of Egypt, from the firstborn of man to the firstborn of livestock. That is why I sacrifice to the LORD all the firstborn of the womb that are males, but I redeem all the firstborn of my sons.' [16] So let it be a sign on your hand and a symbol[B] on your forehead, for the LORD brought us out of Egypt by the strength of His hand."[e]

The Route of the Exodus

[17] When Pharaoh let the people go, God did not lead them along the road to the land of the Philistines, even though it was nearby; for God said, "The people will change their minds and return to Egypt if they face war."[f] [18] So He led the people around toward the •Red Sea along

13:9 That the LORD's instruction may be in your mouth emphasizes that the Israelites would accept, meditate on, and do what the Lord prescribed (Dt 30:14; Jos 1:8; Ps 1:2; Is 59:21). In the context of teaching children, it also describes what the Israelites should know well and talk about to remind themselves and one another (Dt 6:6-8). The effect of what the Lord had done should be as great as if it all were displayed on each person's **hand** (easy for the person to see) and **forehead** (easy for others to see). When that was the case, the individual would readily speak of what the Lord had said, meditate on it, and act accordingly (Ps 50:16; 119:46-48; Mal 2:7).

13:12 The command **you are to present to the LORD** uses a verb that refers elsewhere to transferring property (Gn 32:16; Nm 27:7-8; 2Sm 3:10; Is 45:14). It is not normally used to describe offerings to the Lord, but it does occur prominently in references to the pagan practice, forbidden

bekor

Hebrew Pronunciation	[beh KOHR]
HCSB Translation	firstborn
Uses in Exodus	20
Uses in the OT	120
Focus Passages	Exodus 13:2,13,15

Babylonian (eighteenth century B.C.) and Assyrian (fourteenth and fifteenth century B.C.) inheritance laws usually gave the *firstborn* son a portion twice as big as the other sons. This was true in Israel (Dt 21:15-17). The *firstborn* son was prized (Mc 6:7; Zch 12:10) because he embodied the father's strength (Gn 49:3). *Bekor* is used entirely with reference to males. *Bekor* could also indicate status since Israel was God's *firstborn* son among the nations (Ex 4:22-23). God judged the *firstborn* in Egypt for Egypt's mistreatment of His *firstborn*. He then claimed the Israelite *firstborn*, whether man or beast (Nm 3:13). He took the Levites in place of the *firstborn*, but *firstborn* sons and the *firstborn* among unclean animals had to be monetarily redeemed (Nm 3:41; 18:15). The *firstborn* of the flock and herd became sacrifices (Lv 27:26; Dt 15:19). Later the Davidic king was God's *firstborn* among earth's kings (Ps 89:27).

to Israel, of killing and burning children as sacrifices (Lv 18:21; Dt 18:10; 2Kg 16:3; 17:17; 21:6; 23:10; Jr 32:35; Ezk 16:21). Its use in Ex 13:12 ("pass something over to"/"convey over to") recalls its use in describing the actions of the Lord, who "passed through" Egypt (12:12,23). What He had done must shape what His people would do.

13:13 Redemption brought an animal or person back into its original or ordinary use (Lv 25:23-28). Donkeys could not be sacrificed, so a **donkey** firstborn should be redeemed for normal use by giving a sheep or goat in its place. A human firstborn must be redeemed (Nm 18:15-16). The Lord's requirement of redemption for a human firstborn contrasted with the practices of pagan worshipers who killed children in rituals designed to curry favor with their gods.

13:17 The Lord could have taken His people safely on any route He wished. The choice of route here and the comment on it offer insight into the thinking of both the Lord and the Israelites. The Lord knew the Israelites better than Pharaoh, who considered them a military threat (1:10). It balances reports that the Israelites worshiped and obeyed (12:27-28,35,50-51) and foreshadows their upcoming behavior (14:10-12; 16:2-3). In the process of the exodus, God anticipated the thinking of both the Israelites and the Egyptians and put it to His own use (14:3).

Like His choice to keep Pharaoh alive (9:13-16), this choice of route displays who the Lord is. As a result of it, the Israelites would watch the Lord fight for them (14:13-14). They would experience His care and His willingness to work in spite of their frailties (Ps 103:13-14). Archaeologists have found that Egypt had heavy fortifications along the northern route close to the Mediterranean coast. Though that route would have taken the Israelites by the most direct path to Canaan, through Philistine territory, it would have presented extreme danger and constant opposition. The **Philistines** came to the western coast of the Mediterranean from islands in the Aegean Sea and would later be frequent foes of Israel. Egyptian or Philistine opposition would have been daunting to the Israelites at this time (cp. 6:9).

13:18 The road of the wilderness would take Israel east into the Sinai Peninsula, to the Wilderness of Shur (15:22; cp.

the road of the wilderness. And the Israelites left the land of Egypt in battle formation.[a]

[19] Moses took the bones of Joseph[b] with him, because Joseph had made the Israelites swear a solemn oath, saying, "God will certainly come to your aid; then you must take my bones with you from this place."

[20] They set out from Succoth and camped at Etham on the edge of the wilderness. [21] The LORD went ahead of them in a pillar of cloud[c] to lead them on their way during the day and in a pillar of fire to give them light at night, so that they could travel day or night. [22] The pillar of cloud by day and the pillar of fire by night never left its place in front of the people.

14 Then the LORD spoke to Moses: [2] "Tell the Israelites to turn back and camp in front of Pi-hahiroth, between Migdol and the sea; you must camp in front of Baal-zephon, facing it by the sea.[d] [3] Pharaoh will say of the Israelites: They are wandering around the land in confusion; the wilderness has boxed them in. [4] I will harden Pharaoh's heart so that he will pursue them. Then I will receive glory by means of Pharaoh and all his army, and the Egyptians will know that I am *Yahweh." So the Israelites did this.[e]

The Egyptian Pursuit

[5] When the king of Egypt was told that the people had fled, Pharaoh and his officials changed their minds about the people and said: "What have we done? We have released Israel from serving us." [6] So he got his chariot ready and took his troops[A] with him; [7] he took 600 of the best chariots and all the rest of the chariots of Egypt, with officers in each one. [8] The LORD hardened the heart of Pharaoh king of Egypt, and he pursued the Israelites, who were going out triumphantly.[B,f] [9] The Egyptians—all Pharaoh's horses and chariots, his horsemen,[c] and his army—chased[g] after them and caught up with them as they camped by the sea beside Pi-hahiroth, in front of Baal-zephon.

[10] As Pharaoh approached, the Israelites looked up and saw the Egyptians coming after them. Then the Israelites were terrified and cried out[h] to the LORD for help. [11] They said to Moses: "Is it because there are no graves in Egypt that you took us to die in the wilderness? What have you done to us by bringing us out of Egypt? [12] Isn't this what we told you in Egypt: Leave us alone so that we may serve the Egyptians? It would have been better for

---

[a] 13:18 Ex 14:2; Nm 33:6; Jos 1:14
[b] 13:19 Gn 50:25; Jos 24:32; Ac 7:16; Heb 11:22
[c] 13:21 Ex 14:19; Nm 9:15-16; Dt 1:33; Neh 9:12; Ps 78:14; 99:7; Is 4:5; 1Co 10:1
[d] 14:2 Ex 13:18; Nm 33:7; Jr 44:1
[e] 14:4 Ex 4:21; 7:5; Rm 9:17,22-23
[f] 14:8 Ex 6:1; 13:9; Nm 33:3; Ac 13:17
[g] 14:9 Ex 15:9; Jos 24:6
[h] 14:10 Jos 24:7; Neh 9:9; Ps 34:17

A 14:6 Lit people   **B** 14:8 Lit with a raised hand   **C** 14:9 Or chariot drivers

---

1Sm 15:7). "Wilderness" describes uninhabited areas with varying amounts of water and pasturage, depending on the area and the time of year. The description of the Israelites leaving **in battle formation** uses a rare word (Jos 1:14; 4:12; Jdg 7:11) and seems contrary to the Lord's assessment. Perhaps there is irony to be recognized in the discrepancy between outward and inward readiness.

13:19 God was doing exactly what **Joseph** had said He would do (3:16; 4:31; Gn 50:24-25).

13:21-22 The Lord had promised to accompany Moses as he confronted Pharaoh (3:12; 4:12,15). Now He signified His presence with the Israelites by means of a **pillar of cloud** and a **pillar of fire**. Sometimes it would descend and show that the Lord was talking with Moses (33:9; Nm 12:5; Dt 31:15); even other peoples heard about it (Nm 14:14).

14:2 The Lord led the Israelites to where they could be trapped between the sea and the Egyptian army. The name **Pi-hahiroth** may mean "Mouth of the Canal." The remnants of an ancient canal have been found east of Wadi Tumilat, a route into the Sinai Peninsula. **Migdol** means "Tower" or "Watchtower." **Baal-zephon**, "lord of the north," incorporates the name of a Canaanite god important to seafarers.

14:3 Pharaoh's assumption that the Israelites were lost grew from his low opinion of them and their God (5:2,8; 10:10). He was not counting on the Lord's planning or the fiery and cloudy pillar that gave evidence of His presence.

14:4 The Hebrew word translated **glory** (related to the idea of being heavy) is related to one of the words describing Pharaoh's "hardened" heart (8:15,32; 9:7,34; 10:1). The Lord would receive glory from Pharaoh's refusal to give glory.

14:5 The Israelites' actions appeared to evidence fear, which fit the Egyptian opinion of them better than the triumph

described in verse 8. The word translated **fled** indicates they had cleared out entirely, as did Moses after killing the Egyptian (2:15, in contrast with the word used in 4:3 and 14:25,27 for escaping immediate peril). It is typically used of people who were emigrating in order to escape the reach of a powerful person (Gn 16:6,8; 31:21-22; 1Sm 19:12,18; 21:10; 27:4; 1Kg 11:17,23,40). The Egyptians began to focus on their loss—**we have released Israel from serving us**—plus the change in the situation of the Israelites. The Egyptian magicians had failed, but to this point the Egyptian army had not had an opportunity to act. With the Israelites wandering around and seemingly boxed in (v. 3), certainly some slaves, livestock, and wealth could be recovered or destroyed (15:9).

14:6-7 To people on foot, **chariots** and horses would have seemed as terrifying as armored tanks (see v. 10 and note there). Egypt took pride in its chariots, portraying them in art meant to display Egyptian power.

14:8 Going out triumphantly gives a glimpse into the Israelites' frame of mind (Nm 33:3). Having been urged to leave Egypt, they had received valuables to take with them, and they were gladly going; they had no reason to look over their shoulders in fear.

14:10 Verses 5-9 provided a panoramic perspective. The perspective switches here to that of the Israelites, using a word that older translations render "and behold," which Hebrew authors could use to make a rapid switch in perspective and give readers a momentary share in the experience of someone in the story. When the Egyptian army suddenly appeared, the Israelites' eyes became wide with terror.

14:11-12 Egypt had been preoccupied for centuries with

us to serve the Egyptians than to die in the wilderness."[a]

[13] But Moses said to the people, "Don't be afraid. Stand firm and see[b] the LORD's salvation He will provide for you today; for the Egyptians you see today, you will never see again. [14] The LORD will fight for you; you must be quiet."[c]

Escape through the Red Sea

[15] The LORD said to Moses, "Why are you crying out to Me? Tell the Israelites to break camp. [16] As for you, lift up your staff, stretch out your hand over the sea, and divide it so that the Israelites can go through the sea on dry ground.[d] [17] I am going to harden the hearts of the Egyptians so that they will go in after them, and I will receive glory by means of Pharaoh, all his army, and his chariots and horsemen. [18] The Egyptians will know that I am Yahweh when I receive glory through Pharaoh, his chariots, and his horsemen."

[19] Then the Angel of God,[e] who was going in front of the Israelite forces, moved and went behind them. The pillar of cloud moved from in front of them and stood behind them.[f] [20] It came between the Egyptian and Israelite forces. The cloud was there in the darkness, yet it lit up the night.[A] So neither group came near the other all night long.

[21] Then Moses stretched out his hand over the sea. The LORD drove the sea back with a powerful east wind all that night and turned the sea into dry land. So the waters were divided,[g] [22] and the Israelites went through the sea on dry ground, with the waters like a wall to them on their right and their left.[h]

[23] The Egyptians set out in pursuit—all Pharaoh's horses, his chariots, and his horsemen—and went into the sea after them. [24] Then during the morning watch, the LORD looked down on the Egyptian forces from the pillar of fire[i] and cloud, and threw them into confusion. [25] He caused their chariot wheels to swerve[B,C] and made them drive[D] with difficulty. "Let's get away from Israel," the Egyptians said, "because Yahweh is fighting for them against Egypt!"

[26] Then the LORD said to Moses, "Stretch out your hand over the sea so that the waters may come back on the Egyptians, on their chariots and horsemen." [27] So Moses stretched out his hand over the sea, and at daybreak the sea returned to its normal depth. While the Egyptians were trying to escape from it, the LORD threw them into the sea.[j] [28] The waters came back and covered the chariots[k] and horsemen, the entire army of Pharaoh, that had gone after them into the sea. None of them survived. [29] But the Israelites had walked through the sea on dry ground, with the waters like a wall

---

Cross references (center column):

[a]14:12 Ex 5:21; Ps 106:7-8
[b]14:13 Gn 15:1; 46:3; Ex 20:20; 2Ch 20:15,17; Is 41:10
[c]14:14 Ex 14:25; Dt 1:30; 3:22; Jos 10:14; 2Ch 20:29; Is 30:15
[d]14:16 Ex 4:17; Nm 20:8-9; Is 10:26
[e]14:19 Ex 23:20,23; 32:34; 33:2
[f]Ex 13:21; Is 63:9
[g]14:21 Ex 15:8; Jos 3:16; Neh 9:11; Ps 74:13; 114:3,5; Is 63:12-13
[h]14:22 Ex 15:19; Ps 66:6; Is 63:13; Hab 3:10; 1Co 10:1; Heb 11:29
[i]14:24 Ex 13:21; Nm 14:14; Neh 9:12
[j]14:27 Ex 5:1,7; Jos 4:18; Ps 78:53; Heb 11:29
[k]14:28 Ps 106:11; Heb 3:8,13

[A]14:20 Perhaps the cloud brought darkness to the Egyptians but light to the Israelites; Ex 10:22-23; Ps 105:39.   [B]14:25 Sam, LXX, Syr read *He bound their chariot wheels*   [C]14:25 Or *fall off*   [D]14:25 Or *and they drove them*

---

death, mummification, and the building of elaborate graves, some of which the Israelites themselves may have been forced to help construct. Terror turned Israelite elation and triumph into sarcasm and accusation. They considered Moses responsible for their impending doom, and themselves helpless victims. Their assessment gave no thought to any third option besides death or servitude in Egypt. By not considering the Lord's involvement, the Israelites resembled faithless Pharaoh.

14:13-14 The command **Don't be afraid**, given as a word from the Lord to His people or an affirmation of confidence before battle, has many parallels (Nm 21:34; Dt 1:21,29; 3:2,22; Jos 8:1; 10:8,25; 2Ch 20:15,17; 32:7; Neh 4:14). Moses gave no defense of himself but focused instead on what the Lord would accomplish. The words **salvation** (here and Ex 15:2; Hb *yeshu'ah*) and "saved" (14:30) mark the instructions for the encounter with Egyptian forces, its summary, and its celebration. The "save" word group in Hebrew (the root *yasha'*) was applied in a variety of situations, often military ones, so that salvation took the form of victory (Dt 20:1-4; Jdg 10:12-14; 2Kg 19:32-35; Ps 3) or rescue (Ex 2:17). An earlier pharaoh was afraid that the Israelites might fight against Egypt (1:10), but something greater happened—the Lord fought for Israel and against Egypt (14:14,25).

14:19-20 The **Angel of God** and the **pillar of cloud** may have looked familiar to Moses, for he saw the Angel and the fire when God commissioned him to return to Egypt (3:2; Nm 20:16; Dt 31:15). Besides showing the way to go, day

or night, the pillar of cloud prevented a clash between the **Egyptian and Israelite forces**.

14:21-28 Parallels exist between the plague of locusts and the overthrow of the Egyptians: Moses' outstretched **hand** (cp. v. 21; 10:12), the **east wind** (cp. v. 21; 10:13), morning initiation (v. 24; 10:13), use of the Hebrew word translated "sent" (10:13) and **drive** (v. 25), drowning in the sea (vv. 27-28; 10:19), and the observation that **none of them survived** (cp. v. 28; 10:19). It was no more difficult for the Lord to defeat Pharaoh and his army than to dispense with a horde of insects.

14:22 The **waters like a wall** on both sides forced the Egyptians to follow straight ahead and protected the Israelites from a flanking attack.

14:24-25 The night hours were divided into three "watches": the first watch (Lm 2:19) being the beginning of the night, perhaps roughly 6:00–10:00 p.m., the second watch (Jdg 7:19) being the middle of the night, perhaps about 10:00 p.m.–2:00 a.m., and **the morning watch** or end of the night, roughly 2:00–6:00 a.m. The Lord observed the Egyptians from His superior vantage point (cp. Dt 26:15; Ps 14:2; 53:2; 85:11; 102:19). With His accurate reconnaissance, God threw the Egyptians **into confusion**. This is a weapon He used on a number of occasions (23:27; Jos 10:10; 1Sm 5:9,11; 7:10; cp. 2Kg 7:6-7). Now the Lord, rather than the Israelites whom an earlier Egyptian king had feared (Ex 1:10), was the one who fought against Egypt, and the Egyptians themselves announced the fact.

to them on their right and their left. [30]That day the LORD saved Israel from the power of the Egyptians, and Israel saw the Egyptians dead on the seashore. [31]When Israel saw the great power that the LORD used against the Egyptians, the people *feared the LORD and believed[a] in Him and in His servant Moses.

Israel's Song

15 Then Moses and the Israelites sang this song to the LORD. They said:

I will sing to the LORD,
for He is highly exalted;
He has thrown the horse
and its rider into the sea.
[2] The LORD is my strength and my song;[A]
He has become my salvation.[b]
This is my God, and I will praise Him,
my father's God, and I will exalt Him.[c]
[3] The LORD is a warrior;[d]
*Yahweh is His name.[e]

[4] He threw Pharaoh's chariots
and his army into the sea;
the elite of his officers
were drowned in the *Red Sea.[f]
[5] The floods covered them;
they sank to the depths like a stone.[g]
[6] LORD, Your right hand is glorious
in power.

LORD, Your right hand shattered
the enemy.[h]
[7] You overthrew Your adversaries
by Your great majesty.
You unleashed Your burning wrath;
it consumed them like stubble.[i]
[8] The waters heaped up[j] at the blast
of Your nostrils;
the currents stood firm like a dam.
The watery depths congealed
in the heart of the sea.
[9] The enemy said:
"I will pursue, I will overtake,
I will divide the spoil.[k]
My desire will be gratified
at their expense.
I will draw my sword;
my hand will destroy[B] them."
[10] But You blew with Your breath,
and the sea covered them.
They sank like lead
in the mighty waters.

[11] LORD, who is like You
among the gods?
Who is like You, glorious
in holiness,[l]
revered with praises,
performing wonders?[m]
[12] You stretched out Your right hand,

Cross-references (center column)

[a]14:31 Ps 106:12; Jn 2:11
[b]15:2 Ps 18:2; 59:17; Is 12:2; Hab 3:18
[c]Gn 28:21; Ex 3:6,15,18; Is 25:1
[d]15:3 Ps 24:8; Rv 19:11
[e]Ex 6:3; Ps 83:18
[f]15:4 Ex 13:18; 15:22; 23:31
[g]15:5 Ex 14:28; 15:10; Neh 9:11
[h]15:6 Ps 118:15-16
[i]15:7 Dt 33:26; Is 5:24
[j]15:8 Ex 14:21; Ps 78:13
[k]15:9 Ex 14:9; Jdg 5:30; Is 53:12
[l]15:11 Dt 3:24; 1Kg 8:23
[m]Ps 77:14; Is 6:3; Rv 4:8

[A]15:2 Or might   [B]15:9 Or conquer

14:30-31 These verses summarize the completeness of the Lord's victory by using many terms that the speakers have used earlier, mostly in the near context. Instead of dying (vv. 11-12), the Israelites **saw the Egyptians dead**. **The LORD saved Israel from the power** [lit "hand"] **of the Egyptians** (cp. 3:8; 18:10; Dt 7:8; 2Kg 17:7). The assertion that **Israel saw the great power** [lit "hand"] **that the LORD used** continues the theme of the Lord's action as an exercise of His hand (Ex 3:20; 7:4-5; 9:3,15; 13:3,9,14,16) in contest with the hand of Pharaoh and the Egyptians, and it uses the verb that Moses used in 14:13 (cp. vv. 5,11). **The people feared the LORD,** and this is what Pharaoh had failed to do (1:17,21; 9:20-21,30). The mention of Moses as the Lord's **servant** gives a subtle reminder that an alternative to serving Egypt was available to the Israelites (cp. v. 12) and accords Moses the highest of titles in the hierarchy of the Lord's society and the one by which Moses was called many times (Nm 12:7-8; Dt 34:5; Jos 1:1,7,13,15; cp. Gn 26:24; 2Sm 3:18; Is 41:8; Rm 1:1; Rv 19:10).

15:1-18 This poetic rehearsal of the exodus event demonstrates a technique found in extrabiblical ancient Near Eastern literature as well as elsewhere in the OT (Dt 32–33; 2Sm 1:17-27; 22:1-23:7), particularly the song of Deborah (Jdg 5). Other poetic reflections on the exodus include Pss 77; 78; 105; 106; Is 63:7-14. The introduction of this song conveys a change of atmosphere and highlights the importance of the occasion. While the prose account speaks *about* the Lord, the song speaks *to* the Lord and is more personal. Since Moses had complained about being inarticulate, it is something of a surprise as well. It also contrasts with the grumbling and skepticism that often typified the Israelites.

The vivid and prosodic language of poetry can invite readers to use their imaginations to view the same event in multiple ways. For example, the song celebrates that the Lord threw horse and rider into the sea (Ex 15:1), He threw Pharaoh's chariots and army into the sea (v. 4), His "right hand shattered the enemy" (v. 6), He overthrew His enemies by virtue of His majesty (v. 7), and He unleashed His wrath (v. 7). These and other descriptions of the same victory help readers to enter into the experience and celebrate the events.

15:1 Other victories of the Israelites were also celebrated with singing and dancing (Jdg 5; 11:34; 1Sm 18:6-7; Jr 31:4).

15:2-3 This is my God affirms the Lord's objective that the Israelites would know Him as their God (6:7). Israel had not selected Him; rather He had shown Himself to be their God based on His actions. **My father's God** ties this event to the covenant relationship between the Lord and the patriarchs (2:24; 3:6). **Yahweh is His name** celebrates that His reputation was growing.

15:7 Stubble recalls how the Egyptians had troubled the Israelites over obtaining straw for bricks, forcing them to scrabble about for "stubble" (5:12). Now the Egyptians had been reduced to stubble.

15:11 The truth of God's unequaled power is one of the lessons of the plagues (8:10; 9:14; Dt 4:39; Ps 86:3-10; 96:4-5; 135:5,15-17).

15:12 The earth swallowed them is a poetic way of saying that they died (Ps 63:9; 71:20; Pr 1:12; Jnh 2:6).

and the earth swallowed them.

13 You will lead the people
You have redeemed
with Your faithful love;
You will guide them
to Your holy dwelling
with Your strength.ᵃ

14 When the peoples hear,
they will shudder;
anguish will seize the inhabitants
of Philistia.

15 Then the chiefs of Edom will be
terrified;ᵇ
trembling will seize the leaders
of Moab;
the inhabitants of Canaan will panic;

16 and terrorᶜ and dread will fall on them.
They will be as stillᴬ as a stone
because of Your powerful arm
until Your people pass by, LORD,
until the people whom You purchasedᴮ
pass by.ᵈ

17 You will bring them in and plant them
on the mountain of Your possession;ᵉ
LORD, You have prepared the place
for Your dwelling;
Lord,ᶜ Your hands have established
the sanctuary.

18 The LORD will reignᶠ forever and ever!

19 When Pharaoh's horses with his chariots

and horsemen went into the sea, the LORD brought the waters of the sea back over them. But the Israelites walked through the sea on dry ground. 20 Then Miriam the prophetess,ᵍ Aaron's sister, took a tambourine in her hand, and all the women followed her with their tambourines and danced.ʰ 21 Miriam sang to them:

Sing to the LORD,
for He is highly exalted;
He has thrown the horse
and its rider into the sea.

Water Provided

22 Then Moses led Israel on from the Red Sea, and they went out to the Wilderness of Shur. They journeyed for three days in the wilderness without finding water. 23 They came to Marah, but they could not drink the water at Marah because it was bitter—that is why it was named Marah.ᴰ 24 The people grumbled to Moses, "What are we going to drink?"ⁱ 25 So he cried out to the LORD, and the LORD showed him a tree. When he threw it into the water, the water became drinkable.

He made a statute and ordinance for them at Marah and He tested them there.ʲ 26 He said, "If you will carefully obey Yahweh your God, do what is right in His eyes, pay attention to His commands, and keep all His statutes, I will not inflict any illnesses on you that I

ᵃ15:13 Ps 77:15,20; 78:54
ᵇ15:15 Gn 36:15,40; Nm 22:3; Dt 2:4; Jos 5:1
ᶜ15:16 Ex 23:27; Jos 2:9
ᵈ1Sm 25:37; Ps 74:2; 1Pt 2:9
ᵉ15:17 Ps 44:2; 78:54
ᶠ15:18 Ps 10:16; 29:10; Is 57:15
ᵍ15:20 Nm 26:59; Jdg 4:4
ʰJdg 11:34; 1Sm 18:6; Ps 150:4
ⁱ15:23-24 Ex 16:2; Nm 33:8
ʲ15:25 Ex 14:10; Dt 8:2,16; Jdg 2:22; 3:1,4; 2Kg 2:21; Ps 66:10

ᴬ15:16 Or silent   ᴮ15:16 Or created   ᶜ15:17 Some Hb mss, DSS, Sam, Tg read LORD   ᴰ15:23 = bitter or bitterness

---

15:13 The word translated **faithful love** refers to displays of loyalty and kind provisions of help between family members or friends, often in situations where the needy party would have no legal right to the assistance (20:6; 34:6-7 contain the other uses of the word in Exodus; cp. Ru 1:8; 2:20; 3:10; 1Sm 20:8; 2Sm 9:1).

15:14-16 As He intended, the Lord was becoming widely known (cp. 9:16; 18:11; 32:12). The nations are listed in the order Israel would encounter them during the exodus: first the people of **Philistia**, then those in **Edom** (descended from Esau), **Moab** (descended from Lot), and **Canaan** (descended from Ham's son Canaan). The idea that God **purchased** or redeemed Israel is also found elsewhere (see Ps 74:2; Is 11:11, where "recover" translates the same verb). The verb is often used of buying a slave (Gn 39:1; Ex 21:2) or land (Gn 47:20; 2Sm 24:21).

15:17 Earlier in Exodus the land was described as spacious and fertile, as well as occupied by other nations (3:8,17; 13:5); the song describes it in ways that imply privilege and fellowship. In short, the Lord was taking the Israelites to be at home with Him (cp. Jn 14:1-3).

15:20 Moses and Aaron were already familiar with the work of prophets and prophecy (4:14-16; 6:30–7:2). Their sister **Miriam** shared in the work (6:20; Nm 12:1-15; 26:59; cp. Jdg 4:4; 2Kg 22:12-20; Neh 6:14; Is 8:3; Ezk 13; Jl 2:28-29).

15:21 The last lines of the song repeat the first, except that the first is a declaration of resolve to praise and the last is

a command, an exhortation to praise. The song was sung antiphonally (cp. Ps 136).

15:22–17:26 In this section, the primary conflict is no longer the Lord and Moses versus Pharaoh and the Egyptians, but the Lord and Moses versus the Israelites, who still tended to look back to Egypt for provision (13:17; 17:3). The Lord graciously showed them that when it came to matters basic to survival, He was capable of sustaining them.

15:22-27 The account of water provided at **Marah** introduces themes prominent in the accounts of Israel's time in the wilderness: grumbling, testing, and the need for attention and obedience to the Lord's commands.

15:22 **The Wilderness of Shur**, in the Sinai Peninsula, has been mentioned in connection with Hagar (Gn 16:7-14) and Abraham (Gn 20:1). Since "Shur" means "wall," this area may have received its name by being associated with fortifications protecting Egypt's eastern border and referred to in Egyptian records as the "Wall of the Ruler."

15:24 The word translated **grumbled** signals a hostile question and is used mostly to describe the Israelites' rebellious complaining (chaps. 15–17; Nm 14–17).

15:25-26 The word translated **tested** is used once before in the Pentateuch when the Lord tested Abraham by commanding him to sacrifice Isaac (Gn 22:1-2). The changing of bitter water recalls when God did the opposite to Egypt's water (Ex 7:17-24; cp. 23:25). At issue in the call for

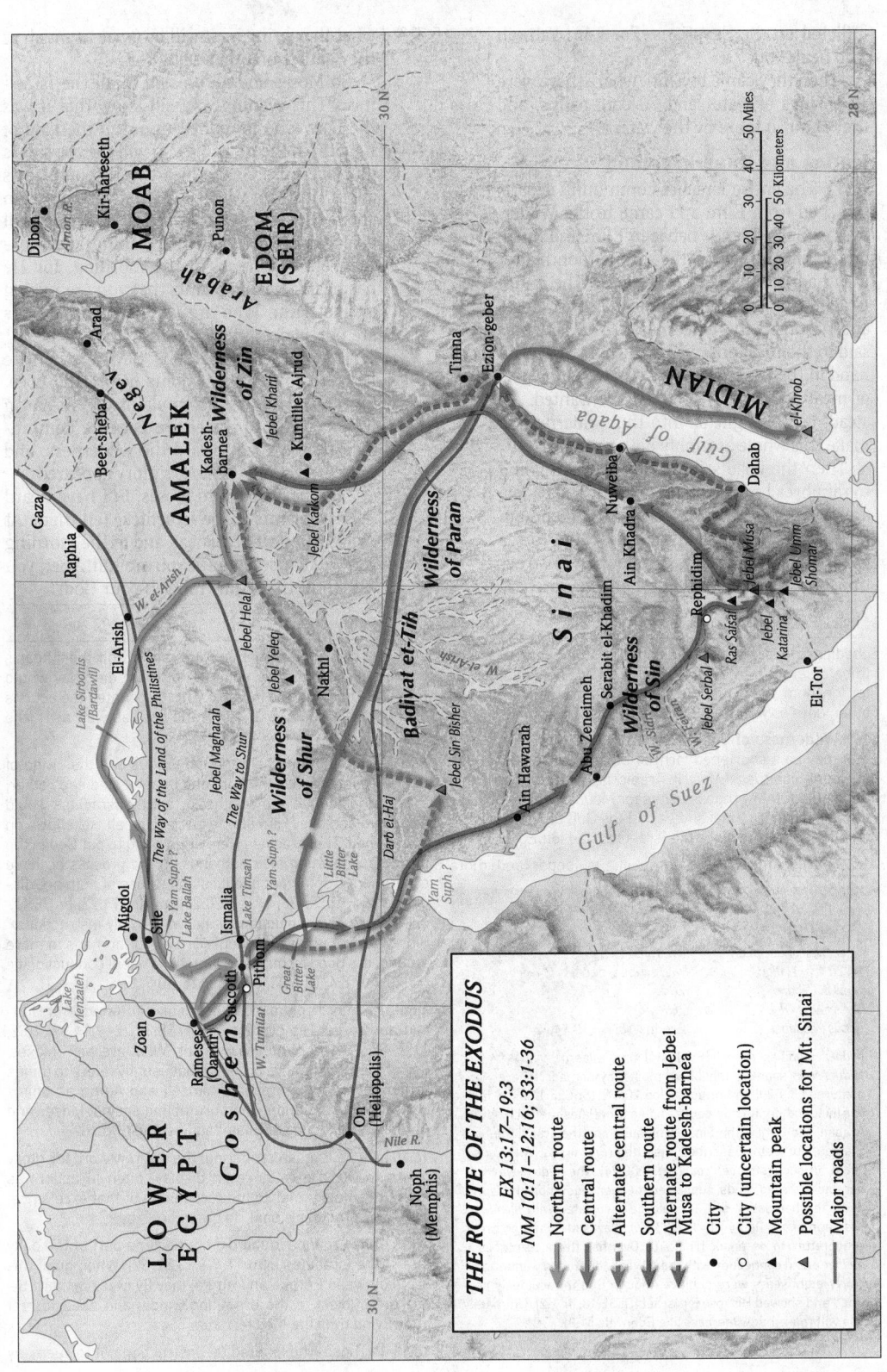

THE ROUTE OF THE EXODUS

EX 13:17–19:3
NM 10:11–12:16; 33:1–36

Northern route
Central route
Alternate central route
Southern route
Alternate route from Jebel
Musa to Kadesh-barnea

• City
○ City (uncertain location)
▲ Mountain peak
▲ Possible locations for Mt. Sinai
— Major roads

LOWER EGYPT
Goshen
MOAB
EDOM (SEIR)
MIDIAN
Sinai
AMALEK
Negev
Wilderness of Zin
Wilderness of Paran
Wilderness of Shur
Wilderness of Sin
Badiyat et-Tih

Dibon
Kir-hareseth
Punon
Arad
Beer-sheba
Gaza
Raphia
El-Arish
Kadesh-barnea
Timna
Ezion-geber
Dahab
el-Khrob
Nuweiba
Ain Khadra
Rephidim
El-Tor
Serabit el-Khadim
Abu Zeneimeh
Ain Hawarah
Nakhl
Migdol
Sile
Ismailia
Pithom
Succoth
Rameses (Qantir)
Zoan
On (Heliopolis)
Noph (Memphis)

Jebel Kharif
Kuntillet Ajrud
Jebel Kakom
Jebel Helal
Jebel Yeleq
Jebel Magharah
Jebel Sin Bisher
Jebel Musa
Jebel Umm Shomar
Jebel Katarina
Jebel Serbal
Ras Safsaf

Gulf of Aqaba
Gulf of Suez
Arabah
Lake Sirbonis (Bardawil)
Lake Menzaleh
Lake Ballah
Lake Timsah
Little Bitter Lake
Great Bitter Lake
Nile R.
Amon R.
W. el-Arish
W. Tumilat
W. el-Arish
W. Sidri Feiran
Yam Suph ?
Darb el-Hai

The Way of the Land of the Philistines
The Way to Shur

50 Miles
50 Kilometers

30 N
28 N
30 N

inflicted on the Egyptians. For I am Yahweh who heals you."[a]

[27] Then they came to Elim, where there were 12 springs of water and 70 date palms, and they camped there by the waters.

Manna and Quail Provided

16 The entire Israelite community departed from Elim and came to the Wilderness of Sin, which is between Elim and Sinai, on the fifteenth day of the second month after they had left the land of Egypt.[b] [2] The entire Israelite community grumbled[c] against Moses and Aaron in the wilderness. [3] The Israelites said to them, "If only we had died by the LORD's hand in the land of Egypt, when we sat by pots of meat and ate all the bread we wanted. Instead, you brought us into this wilderness to make this whole assembly die of hunger!"[d]

[4] Then the LORD said to Moses, "I am going to rain bread from heaven for you. The people are to go out each day and gather enough for that day. This way I will test them to see whether or not they will follow My instructions.[e] [5] On the sixth day, when they prepare what they bring in, it will be twice as much as they gather on other days."[A]

[6] So Moses and Aaron said to all the Israelites: "This evening you will know that it was the LORD who brought you out of the land of Egypt;[f] [7] in the morning you will see the LORD's glory because He has heard your complaints about Him. For who are we that you complain about us?"[g] [8] Moses continued, "The LORD will give you meat to eat this evening and more than enough bread in the morning, for He has heard the complaints that you are raising against Him. Who are we? Your complaints are not against us but against the LORD."[h]

[9] Then Moses told Aaron, "Say to the entire Israelite community, 'Come before the LORD, for He has heard your complaints.'" [10] As Aaron was speaking to the entire Israelite community, they turned toward the wilderness, and there in a cloud the LORD's glory appeared.[i]

[11] The LORD spoke to Moses, [12] "I have heard the complaints of the Israelites. Tell them: At twilight you will eat meat, and in the morning you will eat bread until you are full. Then you will know that I am *Yahweh your God."

Cross references (center column)

[a] 15:26 Ex 23:25; Dt 7:12,15; 28:27,60; Ps 103:3
[b] 16:1 Nm 33:10-11
[c] 16:2 Ex 15:24; 1Co 10:10
[d] 16:3 Nm 11:4-5; Lm 4:9
[e] 16:4 Dt 8:2; Jn 6:31
[f] 16:6 Ex 6:7; Nm 16:28-30
[g] 16:7 Nm 14:27; 16:11; Is 35:2; 40:5
[h] 16:8 1Sm 8:7; Lk 10:16; Rm 13:2
[i] 16:10 Ex 13:21-22; Nm 16:19; 1Kg 8:10

[A] 16:5 Lit as gathering day to day

---

obedience was Israel's distinct identity; they were supposed to be different from Egypt. The Lord had "healed" the water for them and would provide healing for the Israelites in other ways as well (Dt 32:39; 2Kg 2:21-22; Ezk 47:8-9).

16:1 **Wilderness of Sin** uses a transliterated Hebrew word that may be a shortened form of **Sinai**. The traditional site of Mount Sinai, *Jebel Musa* in Arabic, is in the southern Sinai Peninsula. Other proposed sites for Mount Sinai are in central and northern Sinai and east of the Gulf of Aqaba. Only a month had passed since the Israelites had left Egypt.

16:2-3 This time Israel's complaint is longer and more

midbar

Hebrew Pronunciation	[midh BAHR]
HCSB Translation	wilderness, desert
Uses in Exodus	26
Uses in the OT	269
Focus Passages	Exodus 16:1-3,10,14,32

Midbar signifies *desert* (Ex 16:14) and *wilderness* (Gn 14:16). *Midbar* was sparsely inhabited, mostly by nomads. There were pastures (Jl 1:20) and refuges (Jdg 20:47; 1Sm 23:14). The *midbar* included dry terrain south and east of Palestine such as the Arabah, the Negev, the Sinai Peninsula, and the Transjordanian Plateau, but it also described unsettled rural areas. With *sadeh*, "field," it suggests *open country* (Jos 8:24). The *midbar* was vulnerable to strong winds, supported meager vegetation and fauna, and often had saline soil. It could be associated with *formlessness* and *chaos* (Is 34:11; Jr 4:23-26). Devastated settled areas could return to *wasteland* (Jr 12:10). Over half the occurrences of *midbar* are in connection with the 40 years of exodus wanderings. Thirty-eight years were punitive, though God miraculously provided and showed His love for Israel (Dt 32:10; Jr 2:2). Ultimately "He will make her *wilderness* like Eden" (Is 51:3).

hostile. The people's memory was short and their hearts ungrateful. If God were going to let them die, they would rather He had done so in Egypt. This discounted the actions of the **LORD's hand** for them in the past as well as in the future (cp. 2Sm 24:13-14,17).

16:4 During the time between the exodus and the giving of the covenant at Sinai, the Lord and Israel tested each other, the Lord looking to see whether or not the Israelites would trust Him and obey Him after experiencing all His efforts on their behalf. The Israelites were attempting to put God in the position of meeting *their* demands. In the process of these experiments, dominant qualities and values of both are displayed (v. 4; 15:25-26; 17:2,7; 20:20; cp. Nm 14:22; Ps 78:17-22). **Follow My instructions** is lit "walk in My instructions." Since walking is the most common way for humans to move around, it is good terminology for talking about conduct of life (18:20; Lv 18:4; Dt 5:33; 8:6; Pr 1:15; 10:9; Eph 2:10; 4:1).

16:6-8 The Lord continued to act to give knowledge of Himself and reveal His glory (6:6; 7:17; 8:10,22; 9:14,29; 10:2; 11:7; 14:4,17-18). **Who are we** is lit "What are we?" Moses' use of the interrogative pronoun that usually refers to things rather than people presents himself and Aaron as unimportant in the situation. Their grumbling against Moses and Aaron was in fact a complaint against the Lord.

16:10 Like its English rendering, the Hebrew word for **glory** refers to God's excellence on display, often in action, as here. It can also refer to the recognition of that excellence, as when someone is said "to give glory."

16:13 Unlike manna, **quail** did not become part of the daily fare of the Israelites (Nm 11:4-6,13,31-32). When quail migrate between Europe and Africa, they fly over northern Sinai, are subject to the prevailing winds, and need to rest after flying over the Mediterranean Sea.

16:18-19 Those who ignored the instruction not to keep any

¹³So at evening quail[a] came and covered the camp. In the morning there was a layer of dew all around the camp. ¹⁴When the layer of dew evaporated, there were fine flakes on the desert surface, as fine as frost on the ground. ¹⁵When the Israelites saw it, they asked one another, "What is it?" because they didn't know what it was.

Moses told them, "It is the bread the LORD has given you to eat.[b] ¹⁶This is what the LORD has commanded: 'Gather as much of it as each person needs to eat. You may take two quarts[A] per individual, according to the number of people each of you has in his tent.'"

¹⁷So the Israelites did this. Some gathered a lot, some a little. ¹⁸When they measured it by quarts,[B] the person who gathered a lot had no surplus, and the person who gathered a little had no shortage. Each gathered as much as he needed to eat.[c] ¹⁹Moses said to them, "No one is to let any of it remain until morning." ²⁰But they didn't listen to Moses; some people left part of it until morning, and it bred worms and smelled. Therefore Moses was angry with them.

²¹They gathered it every morning. Each gathered as much as he needed to eat, but when the sun grew hot, it melted. ²²On the sixth day they gathered twice as much food, four quarts[C] apiece, and all the leaders of the community came and reported this to Moses. ²³He told them, "This is what the LORD has said: 'Tomorrow is a day of complete rest, a holy Sabbath[d] to the LORD. Bake what you want to bake, and boil what you want to boil, and set aside everything left over to be kept until morning.'"

²⁴So they set it aside until morning as Moses commanded, and it didn't smell or have any maggots in it. ²⁵"Eat it today," Moses said, "because today is a Sabbath to the LORD. Today you won't find any in the field. ²⁶For six days you may gather it, but on the seventh day, the Sabbath, there will be none."

²⁷Yet on the seventh day some of the people went out to gather, but they did not find any. ²⁸Then the LORD said to Moses, "How long will you[D] refuse to keep My commands[e] and instructions? ²⁹Understand that the LORD has given you the Sabbath; therefore on the sixth day He will give you two days' worth of bread. Each of you stay where you are; no one is to leave his place on the seventh day." ³⁰So the people rested on the seventh day.

³¹The house of Israel named the substance manna.[E,f] It resembled coriander seed, was white, and tasted like wafers made with honey. ³²Moses said, "This is what the LORD has commanded: 'Two quarts[F] of it are to be preserved throughout your generations, so that they may see the bread I fed you in the wilderness when I brought you out of the land of Egypt.'"

³³Moses told Aaron, "Take a container and put two quarts[G] of manna in it. Then place it before the LORD to be preserved throughout your generations." ³⁴As the LORD commanded Moses, Aaron placed it before the •testimony[g] to be preserved.

³⁵The Israelites ate manna for 40 years, until they came to an inhabited land. They ate manna until they reached the border of the land of Canaan.[h] ³⁶(Two quarts are[H] a tenth of an ephah.)

Water from the Rock

17 The entire Israelite community left the Wilderness of Sin, moving from one

[a] 16:13 Nm 11:9,31; Ps 78:27-28; 105:40 [b] 16:15 Ex 16:4; Jn 6:31 [c] 16:18 2Co 8:15 [d] 16:23 Gn 2:3; Ex 20:8; 31:15; 35:3; Lv 23:3 [e] 16:28 2Kg 17:14; Ps 78:10 [f] 16:31 Ex 16:14; Nm 11:7; Dt 8:3 [g] 16:34 Ex 25:16,21; 27:21; 40:20; Nm 17:10 [h] 16:35 Jos 5:12; Neh 9:20-21; Jn 6:31,49

[A] 16:16 Lit an omer   [B] 16:18 Lit by an omer   [C] 16:22 Lit two omers   [D] 16:28 The Hb word for you is pl, referring to the whole nation.   [E] 16:31 = what?; Ex 16:15   [F] 16:32 Lit A full omer   [G] 16:33 Lit a full omer   [H] 16:36 Lit The omer is

of the manna overnight presumably went without enough to eat. They failed to enjoy the Lord's provision because of their distrust.

16:23-26 Sabbath is an anglicized form of the Hebrew word shabbath, associated with a verb meaning "cease, stop, rest" (v. 30; 5:5; 31:12-17; Gn 8:22).

16:28 The rhetorical question expresses the Lord's displeasure and returns to the theme of testing for obedience (v. 4; 15:25-26). The Israelites' refusal to keep the Lord's commands put them in the company of Pharaoh, who refused to humble himself (4:23; 7:14; 10:3; cp. Dt 8:16).

16:29 Pharaoh had refused to give the Israelites any days of rest, and he had withheld the straw needed for their work. But the Lord provided a day of rest each week and the food the Israelites needed for that day of rest.

16:31-36 The name **manna** is the anglicized form of the Hebrew word man (interrogative "What?"), which partially echoes the question in verse 15, (Hb) man hu'; "What is it?" No naturally occurring substance matches the description, constancy, and duration of manna well enough to account for it. The **testimony** is a shortened form of "the ark of the testimony," the box that would later contain the Ten Commandments and would testify about the covenant the Lord had given Israel (25:16,21; 26:33; 30:36; 31:18; Nm 17:1-10). The construction of the ark is described in Ex 37:1-9, so it was not built until after 16:33-34. God continued sending the manna until the day after the Israelites first ate food grown in their new land (Jos 5:12). So Moses' instructions to Aaron here could have been given any time after the tabernacle was built.

16:36 The measure of about **two quarts** (Hb 'omer) appears only in Exodus 16. Apparently the **ephah** remained in use longer than the 'omer. The passing of a generation or a change in region can make such explanations helpful.

17:1-7 At Rephidim the Israelites complained about lack of

place to the next according to the Lord's command. They camped at Rephidim, but there was no water for the people to drink.[a] [2] So the people complained to Moses, "Give us water to drink."

"Why are you complaining to me?" Moses replied to them. "Why are you testing[b] the Lord?"

[3] But the people thirsted there for water, and grumbled against Moses. They said, "Why did you ever bring us out of Egypt to kill us and our children and our livestock with thirst?"[c]

[4] Then Moses cried out to the Lord, "What should I do with these people? In a little while they will stone me!"[d]

[5] The Lord answered Moses, "Go on ahead of the people and take some of the elders of Israel with you. Take the staff you struck the Nile with in your hand and go. [6] I am going to stand there in front of you on the rock at Horeb; when you hit the rock, water[e] will come out of it and the people will drink." Moses did this in the sight of the elders of Israel. [7] He named the place Massah[A] and Meribah[B,f] because the Israelites complained, and because they tested the Lord, saying, "Is the Lord among us or not?"

The Amalekites Attack

[8] At Rephidim, Amalek[C,g] came and fought against Israel. [9] Moses said to Joshua,[h] "Select some men for us and go fight against Amalek. Tomorrow I will stand on the hilltop with God's staff in my hand."

[10] Joshua did as Moses had told him, and fought against Amalek, while Moses, Aaron, and Hur went up to the top of the hill. [11] While Moses held up his hand,[D] Israel prevailed, but whenever he put his hand[D] down, Amalek prevailed.[i] [12] When Moses' hands grew heavy, they took a stone and put it under him, and he sat down on it. Then Aaron and Hur supported his hands, one on one side and one on the other so that his hands remained steady until the sun went down. [13] So Joshua defeated Amalek and his army[E] with the sword.

[14] The Lord then said to Moses, "Write this down on a scroll as a reminder and recite it to Joshua: I will completely blot out the memory of Amalek under heaven."[j]

[15] And Moses built an altar[k] and named it, "The Lord Is My Banner."[F] [16] He said, "Indeed, my hand is lifted up toward[G] the Lord's throne. The Lord will be at war with Amalek from generation to generation."

[a]17:1 Ex 16:1; Nm 33:12,14
[b]17:2 Nm 20:3; Dt 6:16; Ps 78:18,41; 1Co 10:9
[c]17:3 Ex 15:24; 16:2,7-8; Nm 14:2,27,29,36; 16:11
[d]17:4 Nm 14:10; 1Sm 30:6; Jn 8:59; 10:31
[e]17:6 Ex 20:10-11; Ps 114:8; 1Co 10:9
[f]17:7 Nm 20:13,24; Ps 81:7; 95:8
[g]17:8 Gn 36:12; Nm 13:29; 24:20; Dt 25:17; Jdg 3:13; 6:3; 10:12; 1Sm 14:48
[h]17:9 Ex 24:13; 32:17; 33:11; Ac 7:45
[i]17:11 Ex 24:14; Jms 5:16
[j]17:14 Ex 34:27; Dt 25:17-19; 1Sm 15:3
[k]17:15 Ex 20:24-26; 24:4; Jdg 6:24

[A]17:7 = testing   [B]17:7 = arguing   [C]17:8 A semi-nomadic people descended from Amalek, a grandson of Esau; Gn 36:12   [D]17:11 Sam, LXX, Syr, Tg, Vg read hands   [E]17:13 Or people   [F]17:15 Or Yahweh-nissi   [G]17:16 Or hand was on, or hand was against; Hb obscure

water, but again the core issue was their mistrust of the Lord. The level of their hostility continued to increase.

17:2-3 The verb translated **complained** here and in verse 7 has not been used before in Exodus. It and a closely related noun describe disputes like the one between Jacob and Laban (Gn 13:7-8; 26:20-21; 31:36). Later in Exodus they describe interpersonal conflict that might lead to blows between two men (Ex 21:18) or to formal legal proceedings (23:2; cp. Dt 17:8; 25:1). By continuing to accuse Moses, the Israelites were **testing the Lord**.

17:5 The instruction to **take some of the elders** fits the thought that the Israelite "complaining" had become a quasi-official legal case. The mention of striking the **Nile** indicates that while Moses might have been unpopular, he was still designated to represent the Lord and lead the Israelites.

17:6 Moses pointed back to this and similar events in Dt 8:15. The apostle Paul considered **the rock** here to be a significant sign pointing to Christ (1Co 10:4). The Lord is referred to in the OT as "the Rock" (Dt 32:4,15,18,30; 1Sm 2:2). God could also bring fire out of rock (Jdg 6:21).

17:7 To remind everyone of conduct to be avoided in light of God's presence and provision, Moses renamed the place. The name **Massah** is closely related to the verb translated "tested," and the name **Meribah** is cognate to the verb translated **complained** (see Ps 95:8-9). So the new name was something like "Testing and Complaint" or "Quarrelsome Trial." The Israelites' question expressed their impatience with what they considered unsatisfactory performance.

17:8 Deuteronomy 25:18 describes how **Amalek** preyed on the weakest among the Israelites. Amalekites troubled Israel intermittently for many years (Nm 14:40-45; Jdg 3:12-13; 6:3-6; 7:12; 10:12; 1Sm 14:47-48; 15:1-33; 27:8; 30:1-18; 2Sm 1:1-16; 1Ch 4:43).

17:9-11 Raising the **staff** in this case likely symbolized God's exercise of power (v. 11; 7:20; 14:16,21,26-27). **Joshua** would go on to serve Moses and succeed him as leader of the Israelites (24:13; Nm 27:18-23; Jos 1:1-9). **Hur** is best known for his part in this event and for Moses trusting him to help the Israelites when Moses was away (24:14).

17:12 The weakness of Moses showed that he was not the source of the victory.

17:14-15 The **scroll** could be a kind of diary from which Moses would write the book of Exodus. It is clear that knowledge of the Lord by means of His actions must be preserved. The sort of **Banner** that Moses referred to was commonly hoisted high on a pole as a rallying point or signal. The image asserts Moses' intention to orient his life and actions according to the Lord's direction.

17:16 Moses' testimony of faith here conveys far more than first appears. Moses' uplifted hand may seem small and insignificant, but it symbolizes all that is implied by the **Lord's throne**. The solemn affirmation that follows offered reassurance to the Israelites and a warning to the Amalekites and others like them that the Lord would be at enmity with predators who attacked the Israelites. It confirmed the promise made in verse 14—retribution against Amalek would be complete and lasting.

18:1-27 The events in this chapter mark a turning point in

Jethro's Visit

18 Moses' father-in-law Jethro, the priest of Midian,[a] heard about everything that God had done for Moses and His people Israel, and how the LORD had brought Israel out of Egypt.

[2] Now Jethro, Moses' father-in-law, had taken in Zipporah,[b] Moses' wife, after he had sent her back, [3] along with her two sons, one of whom was named Gershom (because Moses had said, "I have been a foreigner in a foreign land")[A,c] [4] and the other Eliezer (because he had said, "The God of my father was my helper and delivered me from Pharaoh's sword").[B]

[5] Moses' father-in-law Jethro, along with Moses' wife and sons, came to him in the wilderness where he was camped at the mountain of God.[d] [6] He sent word to Moses, "I, your father-in-law Jethro, am coming to you with your wife and her two sons."

[7] So Moses went out to meet his father-in-law, bowed down,[e] and then kissed him. They asked each other how they had been[C] and went into the tent. [8] Moses recounted to his father-in-law all that the LORD had done to Pharaoh and the Egyptians for Israel's sake, all the hardships that confronted them on the way, and how the LORD delivered them.[f]

[9] Jethro rejoiced over all the good things the LORD had done for Israel when He rescued them from the power of the Egyptians. [10] "Praise the LORD,"[g] Jethro exclaimed, "who

rescued you from Pharaoh and the power of the Egyptians and snatched the people from the power of the Egyptians. [11] Now I know that •Yahweh is greater than all gods, because He did wonders when the Egyptians acted arrogantly against Israel."[D,h]

[12] Then Jethro, Moses' father-in-law, brought a •burnt offering and sacrifices to God, and Aaron came with all the elders of Israel to eat a meal with Moses' father-in-law in God's presence.

[13] The next day Moses sat down to judge the people, and they stood around Moses from morning until evening. [14] When Moses' father-in-law saw everything he was doing for them he asked, "What is this thing you're doing for the people? Why are you alone sitting as judge, while all the people stand around you from morning until evening?"

[15] Moses replied to his father-in-law, "Because the people come to me to inquire of God. [16] Whenever they have a dispute, it comes to me, and I make a decision between one man and another. I teach them God's statutes and laws."[i]

[17] "What you're doing is not good," Moses' father-in-law said to him. [18] "You will certainly wear out both yourself and these people who are with you, because the task is too heavy for you. You can't do it alone.[j] [19] Now listen to me; I will give you some advice, and God be with you. You be the one to represent the people before God and bring their cases to Him.

a18:1 Ex 2:16,18; 3:1
b18:2 Ex 2:21; 4:25
c18:3 Ex 2:22; 4:20; Ac 7:29
d18:4-5 Ex 3:1; 1Ch 23:15
e18:7 Gn 29:13; Ex 18:2
f18:8 Ex 15:6,16; Ps 81:7
g18:10 Gn 14:20; 2Sm 18:28
h18:11 2Ch 2:5; Lk 1:51
i18:15-16 Ex 24:14; Lv 24:12; Nm 15:34; Dt 17:8
j18:18 Ex 3:12; 4:16; Nm 27:5

A18:3 In Hb the name Gershom sounds like the phrase "a stranger there." **B**18:4 = My God Is Help **C**18:7 Lit other about well-being **D**18:11 Hb obscure

the book of Exodus. The first half looks back at what had happened and describes responses to it, while the second half looks ahead by showing the need for the Israelites to be organized to conduct life with one another as a nation. At the end of Exodus 18, Moses and Jethro part company, but Nm 10:11,29-32 indicates that Moses' father-in-law was with the Israelites when they left Mount Sinai after the events in chapters 19–40 had taken place.

18:1-2 Earlier mentions of **Jethro** and **Zipporah** are in 2:18-21; 3:1; 4:18-26. Nothing is said about when or why Moses had sent his family to stay with Jethro.

18:3-4 Gershom was introduced in 2:22. He was no longer an alien in Egypt or a fugitive in Midian. **Eliezer** is mentioned here for the first time, perhaps because now his name has even more to commemorate, since the Lord had repeatedly helped Moses and had delivered him from two pharaohs who wanted to kill him.

18:5 Moses was back at the place where the Lord had first spoken to him from the burning bush (3:1-4).

18:6-7 These details present **Jethro** and **Moses** as men of rank and dignity. Previously Moses took polite leave of Jethro (4:18-19); now Moses was the host. Jethro showed deference by announcing his coming, and Moses showed deference by coming to **meet** him and by bowing. All this

shows who Moses had become and portrays Jethro as a person qualified to offer advice.

18:10-11 The references to rescue from the **power of the Egyptians** continue the use of "hand" in Hebrew as a prominent means by which power is displayed. God had become known through His rescue of Israel from Egypt (6:7; 9:14; 14:18; 16:12). The breadth of the word translated **know** could mean that Jethro was previously unconvinced of the Lord's superiority, or that he was simply declaring a new awareness from experience. Either way, he was convinced and glad to say so. Jethro's response contrasts with that of Pharaoh and exemplifies how the Israelites and the readers of Exodus should respond to learning about who the Lord is from His actions.

18:12 Recognition of the Lord and His actions led to worship, a fulfillment of the sign that He gave Moses at the burning bush (3:12). A **burnt offering** was consumed by fire, and parts of **sacrifices** were burned, but most was roasted and eaten by people present to worship and celebrate (Lv 1:2-17; 3:1-17; 7:11-18).

18:13-26 This section answers the Israelite who asked Moses, "Who made you a leader and judge over us?" (2:14). In a sense, it also answers Moses' questions and misgivings about his ability (3:11; 4:10-13; 6:12,30).

18:19-20 Jethro was thinking of conflicts between Israelites

²⁰Instruct them about the statutes and laws, and teach them the way to live and what they must do.^a ²¹But you should select from all the people able men, God-fearing, trustworthy, and hating bribes.^b Place them over the people as commanders of thousands, hundreds, fifties, and tens.^c ²²They should judge the people at all times. Then they can bring you every important case but judge every minor case themselves. In this way you will lighten your load,^A and they will bear it with you.^d ²³If you do this, and God so directs you, you will be able to endure, and also all these people will be able to go home satisfied."^B

²⁴Moses listened to his father-in-law and did everything he said. ²⁵So Moses chose able men from all Israel and made them leaders over the people as commanders of thousands,

a 18:20 Dt 1:18; 5:1; Ps 143:8
b 18:21 Ex 18:8; Dt 16:19; Ac 6:3
c Dt 1:15; 2Ch 19:5-10
d 18:22 Lv 24:11; Nm 11:17; Dt 1:17
e 18:25-27 Ex 18:22; Nm 10:29-30; Dt 1:15
f 19:2 Ex 3:1; 17:1,8
g 19:3 Ex 3:4; Ac 7:38

hundreds, fifties, and tens. ²⁶They judged the people at all times; they would bring the hard cases to Moses, but they would judge every minor case themselves.

²⁷Then Moses said good-bye to his father-in-law, and he journeyed to his own land.^e

Israel at Sinai

19 In the third month, on the same day of the month that the Israelites had left the land of Egypt, they entered the Wilderness of Sinai. ²After they departed from Rephidim, they entered the Wilderness of Sinai and camped in the wilderness, and Israel camped there in front of the mountain.^f

³Moses went up the mountain to God, and the LORD called^g to him from the mountain: "This is what you must say to the house of Ja-

^A18:22 Lit *lighten from on you*   ^B18:23 Lit *go to their place in peace*

when he said that Moses should **bring their cases to Him**, but a far more serious case was ahead (32:30-35; 34:9).

18:21 The word translated **commanders** is the plural of the one translated in 2:14 as "leader." It is used repeatedly in 18:21,25 (lit "officials of thousands, officials of hundreds," etc.). This tends to strengthen the tie with the question about Moses' status in 2:14. Jethro's list of qualifications for leadership requires qualities of character, belief, and behavior rather than age, wealth, or family position (Dt 1:13,16-17; 2Ch 19:6-7,9-10).

18:23 The verb rendered **endure** can also mean "stand." It repeats the Hebrew verb for "stand/endure" from the descriptions in verses 13 and 14 of the people standing around Moses waiting for him to hear their cases. If Moses followed Jethro's advice, the people would not have to "stand around" so much and Moses would be able to "stand" the work.

19:3–24:11 This section describes events surrounding the making of the covenant between the Lord and Israel, using practices and terms familiar in the culture. When a powerful king (the suzerain) would send a treaty to a less powerful king (the vassal) informing him and his people of the suzerain's intention to rule them, the treaty contained: (1) formal self-identification of the more powerful ruler; (2) a review of the history between the parties as grounds for issuing and accepting the covenant; (3) the requirement of loyalty to the suzerain; (4) stipulations regulating future conduct of the vassal; (5) positive and negative consequences for obedience or disobedience; and (6) instructions for copying, storing, and publicly reading the covenant.

The Mosaic covenant with its laws was given to people who had expressed belief in the Lord (14:31)—people already rescued from Egypt. Its purpose was not to provide a means for people to initiate or merit a relationship with the Lord. Rather, the covenant was a means of communicating what Israel should do as a people who already belonged to Him. The covenant was tied to what the Lord had already done for the Israelites. This was the reason why it was appropriate for them to keep it.

For its contents and system of values the covenant was further tied to what the Lord had done and would continue to do in the expression of His own character—for example, out of His concern for justice and His concern for weaker members of society. It contains some individual regulations

that were shared with extrabiblical law codes and wisdom literature. In the covenant the Lord issued, these laws exist in a framework that ties them to the task of displaying the character of the Lord. Even as the actions of the Lord Himself had revealed who He is, so the actions of His people were to display His character.

Other law codes (like that of the Babylonian king Hammurabi) were the pronouncements of a human king and might be offered to a deity to show that the king deserved the deity's approval and support. Israel's laws came from their God with the recognition that people who claimed the Lord as God should resemble Him in their dealings. This was part of the benefit of belonging to Him, not a means of acquiring this status (Dt 10:12-13).

19:3-6 God's program for the future of Israel is the next step in the outworking of His plan in bringing Israel out of Egypt (6:7; Lv 26:12; Dt 29:9-13).

19:3 One purpose for Moses making three trips **up the mountain** and back (vv. 3,7-8,14,20,25) was to clarify visually the unique role and privileges he was granted. The people

segullah

Hebrew Pronunciation	[seh gool LAH]
HCSB Translation	special possession, treasure
Uses in Exodus	1
Uses in the OT	8
Focus Passage	Exodus 19:5

Extrabiblical evidence confirms that *segullah* denotes acquired property, a reserve set aside as a personal *possession*. Six of the biblical references describe Israel's people as God's chosen ("My own") *possession* (Ex 19:5) or *treasured possession* (Ps 135:4). The other two concern the *treasures* of human kings. David consecrated *segullah*, or *personal treasures*, for building the temple, encouraging others to do likewise (1Ch 29:3,6-8). Solomon mentioned "the *treasure* of kings and provinces" that he had accumulated (Ec 2:8). Although God owns all nations, He uniquely acquired Israel by His initiatives with that people (Ex 19:4-5). But fulfillment of the potential in this acquisition was conditioned on Israel's obedience to Him. At the close of the OT God asserted His intent to make Israel His *special possession* in the "Day of the LORD" through His compassion (Mal 3:17; 4:5). First Peter 2:9 cites Ex 19:5 as having a fulfillment in the church.

cob, and explain to the Israelites: ⁴'You have seen what I did to the Egyptians and how I carried you on eagles' wings and brought you to Me.ᵃ ⁵Now if you will listen to Me and carefully keep My covenant,ᵇ you will be My own possessionᶜ out of all the peoples, although all the earth is Mine, ⁶and you will be My kingdom of priests and My holy nation.'ᵈ These are the words that you are to say to the Israelites."

⁷After Moses came back, he summoned the elders of the people and set before them all these words that the LORD had commanded him. ⁸Then all the people responded together,

ᵃ19:4 Dt 29:2;
Is 63:9
ᵇ19:5 Ex 15:26;
Dt 5:2
ᶜDt 7:6; 14:2;
26:18; Ps 135:4;
Ti 2:14
ᵈ19:6 Dt 26:19;
Is 62:12; 1Pt
2:5,9
ᵉ19:8 Ex 24:3,7;
Dt 5:27
ᶠ19:9 Ex 24:15-
16; Mt 17:5
ᵍDt 4:12,36; Jn
12:29
ʰ19:10 Gn 35:2;
Lv 11:44-45; Heb
10:22
ⁱ19:11 Ex 19:16;
34:5

"We will do all that the LORD has spoken."ᵉ So Moses brought the people's words back to the LORD.

⁹The LORD said to Moses, "I am going to come to you in a dense cloud,ᶠ so that the people will hear when I speakᵍ with you and will always believe you." Then Moses reported the people's words to the LORD. ¹⁰And the LORD told Moses, "Go to the people and consecrate them today and tomorrow. They must wash their clothesʰ ¹¹and be prepared by the third day, for on the third day the LORD will come down on Mount Sinai in the sight of all the people.ⁱ ¹²Put boundaries for the people all

---

needed to acknowledge his authority as God's representative and the importance of his message.

19:4 The Lord's past provision should be the basis for Israel's future decisions. The mention of being carried **on eagles' wings** implied a comparison between the Lord's bringing Israel out of Egypt and eagles that sometimes carried their young on their backs (Dt 32:10-11). Eagles were also noted for their speed, long flights, and high nests (2Sm 1:23; Is 40:31; Jr 4:13; 49:16; Ob 4).

19:5 The Lord wanted Israel to be known by what He had done as well as by what they would do. **My own possession** uses a word that is sometimes translated "treasure." David used it to speak of his "personal treasures of gold and silver" that he had set aside for building the temple (1Ch 29:3). In extrabiblical literature a king sometimes used a closely related word to speak positively of a vassal with whom he had a good relationship and where a king advertised himself on his royal seal as the treasured possession of a certain god.

19:6 The ideas of priesthood and holiness go together, since special requirements marked priests as set apart for special service that benefited others (Lv 21). The tasks of priests included helping people offer sacrifices to God, according to the need or condition of the person (Lv 1–7). Priests acted as judges, both in matters of ritual purity and in civil controversies (Lv 13–14; Dt 17:9; 21:5), and they taught God's law (Lv 10:11; Mal 2:7-9). These tasks pointed to the work of Israel among the nations. As the priesthood

in Israel was to the nation as a whole, so Israel should be to the other nations; as Israelite priests had unique requirements, duties, and privileges among the Israelites, so Israel would have unique requirements, duties, and privileges among the nations (Lv 20:22-26; Dt 4:5-8; 14:21; 26:17-19; Is 2:1-5).

19:9-25 The preparations for a meeting between the Lord and the Israelites continue the extended metaphor that compares the Lord to a great king issuing a covenant to his vassal. The Lord had chosen to come to Mount Sinai in a way designed to reveal His presence and to communicate with the Israelites, making it "private property," where no one should expect to wander in and out oblivious to the wishes of the owner. For as long as the Lord visited that place, it was holy ground, an extension of His royal court. Coming there required a royal summons. It was not a casual meeting of equals.

19:9 This statement of God's intention increases the gravity of future failures by the people to believe Moses.

19:10 The requirements to be purified and to wear clean **clothes** involved everyone in the preparation. When Pharaoh summoned him, Joseph likewise changed his clothes before appearing at court (Gn 41:14; cp. Gn 35:2; Nm 8:7; Rv 22:14).

19:12 Refusal to observe **boundaries** was a sign of disrespect. Those who violated the warning would die. Such was

Rocky pathway down from Jebel Musa, the traditional site of Mount Sinai

around the mountain and say: Be careful that you don't go up on the mountain or touch its base. Anyone who touches the mountain will be put to death.[a] [13]No hand may touch him; instead he will be stoned or shot with arrows. No animal or man will live. When the ram's horn sounds a long blast, they may go up the mountain."

[14]Then Moses came down from the mountain to the people and consecrated them, and they washed their clothes. [15]He said to the people, "Be prepared by the third day. Do not have sexual relations with women."

[16]On the third day, when morning came, there was thunder and lightning, a thick cloud on the mountain, and a loud trumpet sound, so that all the people in the camp shuddered. [17]Then Moses brought the people out of the camp to meet God, and they stood at the foot of the mountain. [18]Mount Sinai was completely enveloped in smoke because the LORD came down on it in fire.[b] Its smoke went up like the smoke of a furnace,[c] and the whole mountain shook violently.[d] [19]As the sound of the trumpet grew louder and louder, Moses spoke and God answered him in the thunder.[e]

ᵃ19:12 Heb 12:20
ᵇ19:18 Ex 3:2; 24:17; Dt 4:11; 2Ch 7:1
ᶜPs 144:5; Rv 15:8
ᵈJdg 5:5; Ps 68:7; Jr 4:24; Heb 12:26
ᵉ19:19 Neh 9:13; Ps 81:7
ᶠ19:21 Ex 3:5; 1Sm 6:19
ᵍ19:22 Lv 10:3; 2Sm 6:7-8
ʰ20:2 Ex 13:3; Hs 13:4

[20]The LORD came down on Mount Sinai at the top of the mountain. Then the LORD summoned Moses to the top of the mountain, and he went up. [21]The LORD directed Moses, "Go down and warn the people not to break through to see the LORD; otherwise many of them will die.[f] [22]Even the priests who come near the LORD must purify themselves or the LORD will break out in anger against them."[g]

[23]But Moses responded to the LORD, "The people cannot come up Mount Sinai, since You warned us: Put a boundary around the mountain and consider it holy." [24]And the LORD replied to him, "Go down and come back with Aaron. But the priests and the people must not break through to come up to the LORD, or He will break out in anger against them." [25]So Moses went down to the people and told them.

The Ten Commandments

20 Then God spoke all these words:

[2] I am the LORD your God, who brought you out of the land of Egypt, out of the place of slavery.[h]

---

the case even with merely human kings whose sanctity and security measures had been violated (Est 4:11).

19:15 Abstaining from sex would prevent contact with semen, which caused ritual uncleanness (Lv 15:16-18). Considering the pagan practice of mixing sexual activity with religious rituals, this prohibition may also have contributed to separating such practices from worship of the Lord. If nothing else, it marked a life change and redirection of attention for the Israelites (cp. 1Co 7:5).

19:16-17 All these phenomena are associated with occasions when God revealed His presence (40:34; Jdg 5:4-5; 1Kg 19:11-12; Ps 18:6-15; Is 29:6; 30:30; 64:1-3; Rv 4:1,5).

19:18 Like the smoke of a furnace uses the word for furnace that also appears in 9:8,10. Its only other use is to describe the source of the smoke compared with what came from the ruins of Sodom and Gomorrah (Gn 19:28). The **whole mountain shook violently** uses the same Hebrew verb as the statement that "all the people in the camp shuddered" (v. 16).

19:21 Moses' warning **not . . . to see the LORD** on penalty of death shows God's concern to protect the Israelites and to reveal to them His awesome, personal reality. He cannot be treated as an object of curiosity that one might walk up to, examine at will, and then walk away from without personal engagement.

19:22 Some interpreters think reference to **priests** here and in verse 24 is anachronistic, since Aaron and his sons were appointed as priests at a later time (28:1; 40:12-15). Based on ancient practices, however, it would have been normal for selected Israelites to have functioned as priests even before the formal appointment of the Aaronic priesthood. Knowledge of sacrifices, intercession, consecration, and priestly activities is taken for granted throughout Genesis and Exodus (cp. Gn 14:18-20). In later years disobedient Israelites appointed priests to suit their own purposes (Jdg 17:1-5; 1Kg 13:33).

20:1-17 Hebrew has two forms of negative commands. One is used for specific, immediate situations, and the other, used here, is for general prohibitions. The idea is "Don't ever . . ." It is used by a superior to an inferior but not the reverse. The eight negative commands and two positive commands (vv. 8,12) became known as the Ten Commandments (lit "the ten words"; 34:28; Dt 4:13; 10:4), or the Decalogue (from Gk for "ten words," *deka + logoi*). They provide basic principles that laid the foundation for the other rules and regulations for ancient Israel.

For example, God's delivery of the Israelites out of slavery in Egypt influenced stipulations about how slaves should be treated (Ex 20:1; 21:2-11). The prohibition against murder made a distinction between premeditated murder and manslaughter (20:13; 21:12-14). They were the commands written on the stone tablets and stored in the ark of the covenant to be kept in the most holy part of the tabernacle (34:28; Dt 4:13; 9:10-11; 10:4-5). The importance of these commandments is further indicated by their repetition in Dt 5:6-21 and elsewhere (Mt 19:18; Mk 10:19; Lk 18:20). The first four commands (Ex 20:2-11) focus on loyalty to the Lord, while the last six (vv. 12-17) focus on dealings between humans.

20:2 To start with self-identification, as **the LORD** does here, was normal for a covenant document sent from a king and for royal proclamations and inscriptions. Delivering the Israelites had become part of His identity, what people should think of when His name was mentioned. In the ancient Near East, Israel's system of laws was unique in that it came from God and obedience or disobedience was oriented toward God; elsewhere rulers might present laws to a deity for approval, but the laws themselves were not given by the deity. In Israel, lawbreaking was first of all an offense against the Lord, not just a disruption of order or an offense against other people.

20:4-6 Not to make an **idol** ran counter to every instinct of

³ Do not have other gods besides Me.ᵃ
⁴ Do not make an idolᵇ for yourself, whether in the shape of anything in the heavens above or on the earth below or in the waters under the earth. ⁵You must not bow down to them or worship them; for I, the Lᴏʀᴅ your God, am a jealous God,ᶜ punishing the children for the fathers' sin, to the third and fourth generationsᵈ of those who hate Me, ⁶but showing faithful love to a thousand generations of those who love Me and keep My commands.ᵉ

⁷ Do not misuse the name of the Lᴏʀᴅ your God, because the Lᴏʀᴅ will not leave anyone unpunished who misuses His name.ᶠ
⁸ Remember the Sabbath day, to keep it holy:ᵍ ⁹You are to labor six days and do all your work,ʰ ¹⁰but the seventh day is a Sabbath to the Lᴏʀᴅ your God. You must not do any work—you, your son or daughter, your male or female slave, your livestock, or the foreigner who is within your gates.ⁱ ¹¹For the Lᴏʀᴅ made the heavens and the earth, the sea, and

Cross-reference column:
ᵃ20:3 Dt 6:14; Jr 35:15
ᵇ20:4 Lv 26:1; Dt 27:15
ᶜ20:5 Ex 34:14; Dt 4:24; Is 44:15,19
ᵈNm 14:18; Ps 79:8; Jr 32:18
ᵉ20:6 Dt 7:9
ᶠ20:7 Lv 19:12; Mt 5:33
ᵍ20:8 Ex 31:13-16; Lv 26:2
ʰ20:9 Ex 34:21; Lk 13:14
ⁱ20:10 Gn 2:2-3; Neh 13:16-19

---

ancient Near Eastern cultures, but to do so is an affront to **a jealous God**. God is concerned to protect the integrity of His relationship with His people (34:14). If the Israelites made idols to worship, it would be an act of hatred, disloyalty, and repudiation. When the Lord made Himself known to the Israelites, they did not see any form (Dt 4:10-20). The best way to know and worship Him was to recall what He had already done and said and to be alert to trust Him and see what He would do in the future.

Punishing the children for the fathers' sin involved penalties for successive generations who continued to commit the sins they learned from their fathers. This did not mean that in a court case a son would have to suffer the penalty for his father's crime (Dt 24:16), nor that individual standing or fellowship with God was determined by the behavior of one's parents (Jr 31:29-30; Ezk 18:1-32). It meant the excuse, "They don't know any better; it's how they were raised," doesn't work with God. But the Lord's **faithful love** would far exceed His judgment (**to a thousand generations**; Lv 26:39-45; Is 65:6-7; Jr 11:9-12; 32:17-19; Dn 9:8-16).

20:7 In ancient times misusing **the name of the Lᴏʀᴅ** could have meant failing to fulfill a sworn oath or making an oath with the intention of deceiving someone. Those who swore an oath in the Lord's name called on Him to bring punishment if they did not keep the promise or tell the truth (Gn 24:3; Lv 19:12; Jos 2:12). Those who might do this would cause the Lord's reputation to suffer, while acting as if His presence as a witness were not important (Dt 6:13-14; 10:20; Is 48:1-11; Jr 4:2; 12:16; Zph 1:14). To swear by the Lord's name was an affirmation of allegiance to Him that required appropriate action (Jos 23:6-8). By extension, this command would also apply when a person attached the Lord's name to an activity contrary to His character or will, resulting in certain punishment (cp. Ps 50:16-23; Jr 14:14-16). In a sense, misusing the Lord's name misrepresented His character, purposes, and actions revealed to the people of Israel and amounted to lying about who God is.

20:8-11 The **Sabbath**, introduced with the giving of manna (16:22-30; the term "Sabbath" being related to the Hb verb

---

THE TEN COMMANDMENTS				
Commandment	Passage	Related OT Passages	Related NT Passages	Jesus' Teachings
Do not have other gods besides Me.	Ex 20:3; Dt 5:7	Ex 20:23; 34:14; Dt 6:4,13-14; 2Kg 17:35; Ps 81:9; Jr 25:6; 35:15	Ac 5:29	Mt 4:10; 6:33; 22:37-40
Do not make an idol for yourself.	Ex 20:4-6; Dt 5:8-10	Ex 32:8; 34:17; Lv 19:4; 26:1; Dt 4:15-20; 7:25; 32:21; Ps 115:4-7; Is 44:12-20	Ac 17:29-31; 1Co 8:4-6,10-13; Col 3:5; 1Jn 5:21	Mt 6:24; Lk 16:13
Do not misuse the name of the Lᴏʀᴅ your God.	Ex 20:7; Dt 5:11	Ex 22:28; Lv 18:21; 19:12; 22:2; 24:16; Ezk 39:7	Jms 5:12	Mt 5:33-37; 6:9; 23:16-22
Remember the Sabbath day, to keep it holy.	Ex 20:8-11; Dt 5:12-15	Gn 2:3; Ex 16:23-30; 31:13-16; 35:2-3; Lv 19:30; Is 56:2; Jr 17:21-27	Heb 10:25	Mt 12:1-13; Mk 2:23-27; 3:1-6; Lk 6:1-11
Honor your father and your mother.	Ex 20:12; Dt 5:16	Ex 21:17; Lv 19:3; Dt 21:18-21; 27:16; Pr 6:20	Eph 6:1-3; Col 3:20	Mt 15:4-6; 19:19; Mk 7:9-13; Lk 18:20
Do not murder.	Ex 20:13; Dt 5:17	Gn 9:6; Lv 24:17; Nm 35:33	Rm 13:9-10; Jms 2:11	Mt 5:21-24; 19:18; Mk 10:19; Lk 18:20
Do not commit adultery.	Ex 20:14; Dt 5:18	Lv 18:20; 20:10; Nm 5:12-31; Dt 22:22; Pr 6:29,32	Rm 13:9-10; Heb 13:4	Mt 5:27-30; 19:18; Mk 10:19; Lk 18:20
Do not steal.	Ex 20:15; Dt 5:19	Lv 19:11,13; Ezk 18:7	Eph 4:28; Jms 5:4	Mt 19:18; Mk 10:19; Lk 18:20
Do not give false testimony.	Ex 20:16; Dt 5:20	Ex 23:1,7; Lv 19:11; Ps 15:2; 101:5; Pr 10:18; Jr 9:3-5; Zch 8:16	Eph 4:25,31; Col 3:9; Ti 3:2	Mt 5:37; 19:18; Mk 10:19; Lk 18:20
Do not covet.	Ex 20:17; Dt 5:21	Dt 7:25; Jb 31:24-28; Ps 62:10	Rm 7:7; 13:9; Eph 5:3-5; Heb 13:5; Jms 4:1-2	Lk 12:15-34

everything in them in six days; then He rested on the seventh day. Therefore the Lord blessed the Sabbath day and declared it holy.

12 Honor your father and your mother[a] so that you may have a long life in the land that the Lord your God is giving you.

13 Do not murder.[b]

14 Do not commit adultery.[c]

15 Do not steal.[d]

16 Do not give false testimony against your neighbor.[e]

17 Do not covet your neighbor's house. Do not covet your neighbor's wife, his male or female slave, his ox or donkey, or anything that belongs to your neighbor.[f]

The People's Reaction

18 All the people witnessed[A] the thunder and lightning, the sound of the trumpet, and the mountain surrounded by smoke. When the people saw it[B] they trembled and stood at a distance.[g] 19 "You speak to us, and we will listen," they said to Moses, "but don't let God speak to us, or we will die."[h]

20 Moses responded to the people, "Don't be afraid, for God has come to test you, so that you will ·fear Him and will not[c] sin."[i] 21 And

the people remained standing at a distance as Moses approached the thick darkness where God was.[j]

Moses Receives Additional Laws

22 Then the Lord told Moses, "This is what you are to say to the Israelites: You have seen that I have spoken to you from heaven.[k] 23 You must not make gods of silver to rival Me; you must not make gods of gold for yourselves.[D,l]

24 "You must make an earthen altar for Me and sacrifice on it your ·burnt offerings and ·fellowship offerings, your sheep and goats, as well as your cattle. I will come to you and bless you in every place where I cause My name to be remembered.[m] 25 If you make a stone altar for Me, you must not build it out of cut stones. If you use your chisel on it, you will defile it.[n] 26 You must not go up to My altar on steps, so that your nakedness is not exposed on it.

21 "These are the ordinances that you must set before them:

Laws about Slaves

2 "When you buy a Hebrew slave, he is to serve for six years; then in the seventh he is to leave as a free man[E] without paying anything.[o] 3 If he arrives alone, he is to leave alone; if he

Cross-references (center column)

a 20:12 Lv 19:3; Mt 15:4; Mk 7:10; Lk 18:20; Eph 6:2
b 20:13 Mt 5:21; Rm 13:9
c 20:14 Dt 5:18; Mt 5:27
d 20:15 Lv 19:11; Mt 19:18
e 20:16 Ex 23:1
f 20:17 Dt 5:21; Mt 5:28; Lk 12:15; Rm 7:7; 13:9; Eph 5:3,5; Heb 13:5
g 20:18 Ex 19:18; Heb 12:18
h 20:19 Dt 5:25,27; Gl 3:19
i 20:20 Dt 13:3; Pr 16:6; Is 8:13
j 20:21 Ex 19:16; Dt 5:22
k 20:22 Dt 4:36; Neh 9:13
l 20:23 Ex 20:3; 32:4
m 20:24 Gn 12:2; Dt 12:5; 16:6,11; 1Kg 9:3; 2Ch 6:6
n 20:25 Dt 27:5-6; Jos 8:31
o 21:2 Dt 4:14; Jr 34:14

A 20:18 Lit saw   B 20:18 Sam, LXX, Syr, Tg, Vg read smoking; the people (or they) were afraid   C 20:20 Lit that the fear of Him may be in you, and you do not   D 20:23 Hb obscure   E 21:2 Lit to go forth

---

meaning "to cease"), would be a perpetual institution, not just a day to observe while receiving manna in the wilderness. It would serve as a reminder of the Mosaic or Sinai covenant. In Exodus it comes up for discussion again in 23:12; 31:12-17; 35:1-3. Verses 8 and 11 use forms of the same Hebrew verb qadash, "keep/declare holy," to speak of consecrating the Sabbath. The Lord had set this day apart (declared it holy), so the Israelites should treat it as such. The list in verse 10 makes the Sabbath command particularly directed to adults who had children and were wealthy enough to own slaves and livestock. If it applied to these people—the ones with the most influence in a community—it would apply to everyone.

20:12 A stubborn and rebellious son who refused other discipline could be taken before the elders for judgment (Dt 21:18-21; cp. Lv 19:3). Eli's sons showed contempt for their father and for the Lord, who brought them death as a result (1Sm 2:12-17,22-25,29-30). The respect and kindness that Ruth and Boaz showed for Naomi and that Joseph showed for Jacob provide positive examples (cp. Pr 1:8; 19:26; 20:20; 23:22; 28:24; 30:17]. Long life may refer to the tenure of the nation in the land. Failure to honor parents was one of the sins that Ezekiel listed in a description of the people of Jerusalem before the city was destroyed (Ezk 22:7; cp. Mc 7:6). Long life for individuals is also possible and is mentioned elsewhere as an outcome from the Lord for loyal obedience (Ex 23:26).

20:13 The word translated murder is not a general word for "killing," and it is not used for killing animals or for killing humans in war or legal execution. Cities of refuge were designated so that anyone who killed another person could run to these cities to avoid being killed in revenge. This also

meant that a case of homicide could be properly investigated to determine whether the killing was accidental or premeditated (21:12-14; Nm 35; Dt 19; Jos 20).

20:17 This command addresses the inner life, the source of wrong actions including murder, adultery, and stealing.

20:18-21 In the same breath Moses told the people not to fear (Don't be afraid) but to fear (lit "so that the fear of Him will be before your face"). They should not fear that God might capriciously exterminate them. Nevertheless, the purpose of the frightening display is that they might recognize God's power, His presence, and His holiness and be motivated to avoid sin and consequent judgment.

20:22–23:19 This section includes laws that were similar to those of other ancient cultures—which we know from ancient documents—altered and put into a context of motivation based on the Lord's actions, character, requirements, and oversight.

20:22-23 Obedience to the instructions in verses 22-26 would have distinguished Israelite worship from the pagan worship around them.

20:24-26 Mention of places where the Lord would come and bless the Israelites provided a reminder that, unlike pagan gods, the Lord must not be considered limited to Mount Sinai or any other locality. If they obeyed Him, they would enjoy God's blessings wherever they were.

21:2-6 These rules for Hebrew slaves applied to both males and females, according to Dt 15:12-17 (cp. Ex 21:20,26-27,32; Jr 34:13-16). An Israelite might choose to go into slavery to pay restitution for theft, to repay another debt, or to obtain food and shelter in hard times. On penalty of death, Ex 21:16 rules out kidnapping and forcing an Israelite

arrives with^A a wife, his wife is to leave with him. ⁴If his master gives him a wife and she bears him sons or daughters, the wife and her children belong to her master, and the man must leave alone.

⁵"But if the slave declares: 'I love my master, my wife, and my children; I do not want to leave as a free man,'^a ⁶his master is to bring him to the judges^B and then bring him to the door or doorpost. His master must pierce his ear with an awl, and he will serve his master for life.

⁷"When a man sells his daughter as a slave,^C she is not to leave as the male slaves do.^b ⁸If she is displeasing to her master, who chose her for himself, then he must let her be redeemed. He has no right to sell her to foreigners because he has acted treacherously toward her. ⁹Or if he chooses her for his son, he must deal with her according to the customary treatment of daughters. ¹⁰If he takes an additional wife, he must not reduce the food, clothing, or marital rights of the first wife.^c ¹¹And if he does not do these three things for her, she may leave free of charge, without any exchange of money.^D

Laws about Personal Injury

¹²"Whoever strikes a person so that he dies must be put to death.^d ¹³But if he didn't intend any harm,^E and yet God caused it to happen by his hand, I will appoint a place for you where he may flee.^e ¹⁴If a person schemes and willfully^F acts against his neighbor to murder him, you must take him from My altar to be put to death.^f

¹⁵"Whoever strikes his father or his mother must be put to death.

¹⁶"Whoever kidnaps a person must be put to death, whether he sells him or the person is found in his possession.^g

¹⁷"Whoever curses his father or his mother must be put to death.^h

¹⁸"When men quarrel and one strikes the other with a stone or his fist, and the injured man does not die but is confined to bed, ¹⁹if he can later get up and walk around outside leaning on his staff, then the one who struck him will be exempt from punishment. Nevertheless, he must pay for his lost work time^G and provide for his complete recovery.

²⁰"When a man strikes his male or female slave with a rod, and the slave dies under his abuse,^H the owner must be punished.^I ²¹However, if the slave can stand up after a day or two, the owner should not be punished^J because he is his owner's property.^K,i

²²"When men get in a fight and hit a pregnant woman so that her children are born prematurely^L but there is no injury, the one who hit her must be fined as the woman's husband demands^j from him, and he must pay according to judicial assessment. ²³If there is an injury, then you must give life for life, ²⁴eye for eye, tooth for tooth,^k hand for hand, foot for foot, ²⁵burn for burn, bruise for bruise, wound for wound.

²⁶"When a man strikes the eye of his male or female slave and destroys it, he must let the slave go free in compensation for his eye. ²⁷If

Cross references (center column)

^a 21:5 Dt 15:16-17
^b 21:7 Neh 5:5
^c 21:10 1Co 7:5
^d 21:12 Gn 9:6; Mt 26:52
^e 21:13 Nm 35:11,22-25; Dt 19:2-5; Jos 20:2-9; 1Sm 24:4,10,18
^f 21:14 Dt 19:11-12; 1Kg 2:28-34
^g 21:16 Gn 37:28; Ex 22:4; Dt 24:7
^h 21:17 Lv 20:9; Mt 15:4; Mk 7:10
^i 21:21 Lv 25:44-46
^j 21:22 Ex 21:30; Dt 22:18-19
^k 21:24 Lv 24:20; Dt 19:21; Mt 5:38

---

^A 21:3 Lit he is the husband of   ^B 21:6 Or to God; that is, to His sanctuary or court   ^C 21:7 Or concubine   ^D 21:11 She doesn't have to pay any redemption price.   ^E 21:13 Lit he was not lying in wait   ^F 21:14 Or maliciously   ^G 21:19 Lit his inactivity   ^H 21:20 Lit hand   ^I 21:20 Or must suffer vengeance   ^J 21:21 Or not suffer vengeance   ^K 21:21 Lit money   ^L 21:22 Either a live birth or a miscarriage

---

into slavery. And while the life of slaves might be difficult, there were penalties for mistreatment (vv. 20-21,26-27) and slaves who ran away were not to be returned to their masters (Dt 23:15-16).

21:7-11 These verses deal with the status and rights of a woman who had been sold with the expectation of becoming a kind of second-class wife, somewhat like Hagar, Bilhah, and Zilpah, who bore children for Abraham and Jacob.

21:14 You must take him from My altar pictures the murderer as having come to the sanctuary for protection. But even the Lord's altar provided no asylum for a person who planned a murder (cp. 1Kg 1:50-53; 2:28-34). This is a reminder that the Lord's sacred spaces and objects are not endowed with power that could be manipulated apart from Him.

21:16 Under this statement, what Joseph's brothers did to him (Gn 37:27-28) was a death-penalty offense.

21:20-21 If a slave died from being beaten, the death would be avenged by death (vv. 12-14). If the slave lived but sustained permanent injury, he or she would go free (vv. 26-27). A later death might be from another cause than the owner's action; so the owner should not die. **Because he**

is his owner's property adopts a pragmatic stance and assumes that the owner had shown regard for potential monetary loss and had not intended to kill or permanently injure the slave.

21:22-25 A fine was to be assessed for a blow that caused premature delivery. The only other uses of the word translated "injury" here occurs in Gn 42:4,38, where the harm that Jacob feared was that Benjamin might die. The series that begins with **life for life** seems to have been a formula that might be repeated partly or in full, even in situations like blasphemy, where physical harm was not an issue (Lv 24:17-21; Dt 19:16-21). The formula called for proportionate punishment rather than a process of escalating violence between individuals or families (in contrast to the attitude of Lamech in Gn 4:23-24). Considering pregnancy as a special complication implies concern for the infant. Certain other deaths incurred financial penalties (Ex 21:28-32). The case assumed that even unintentional injury must be remedied, while Exodus 1-2 with its portrayal of intentional injury to infants stands in the background of this passage.

21:26-27 Laws protecting slaves are not found in other ancient Near Eastern law collections.

he knocks out the tooth of his male or female slave, he must let the slave go free in compensation for his tooth.

²⁸ "When an ox[A] gores a man or a woman to death, the ox must be stoned,[a] and its meat may not be eaten, but the ox's owner is innocent. ²⁹ However, if the ox was in the habit of goring, and its owner has been warned yet does not restrain it, and it kills a man or a woman, the ox must be stoned, and its owner must also be put to death. ³⁰ If instead a ransom[b] is demanded of him, he can pay a redemption price for his life in the full amount demanded from him. ³¹ If it gores a son or a daughter, he is to be dealt with according to this same law. ³² If the ox gores a male or female slave, he must give 30 •shekels[c] of silver[B] to the slave's master, and the ox must be stoned.

³³ "When a man uncovers a pit or digs a pit, and does not cover it, and an ox or a donkey falls into it, ³⁴ the owner of the pit must give compensation; he must pay money to its owner, but the dead animal will become his.

³⁵ "When a man's ox injures his neighbor's ox and it dies, they must sell the live ox and divide its proceeds; they must also divide the dead animal. ³⁶ If, however, it is known that the ox was in the habit of goring, yet its owner has not restrained it, he must compensate fully, ox for ox; the dead animal will become his.

Laws about Theft

22 [c] "When a man steals an ox or a sheep and butchers it or sells it, he must repay[d] five cattle for the ox or four sheep for the sheep. ²D If a thief is caught in the act of breaking in, and he is beaten to death, no one

---

*a*21:28 Gn 9:5
*b*21:30 Nm 35:31
*c*21:32 Zch 11:12; Mt 26:15; 27:3,9
*d*22:1 2Sm 12:6; Pr 6:31; Lk 19:8
*e*22:2 Nm 35:27; Mt 24:43
*f*22:3 Ex 21:2,16
*g*22:8 Dt 17:8-9

---

is •guilty of bloodshed.[e] ³ But if this happens after sunrise,[E] there is guilt of bloodshed. A thief must make full restitution. If he is unable, he is to be sold because of his theft.[f] ⁴ If what was stolen—whether ox, donkey, or sheep—is actually found alive in his possession, he must repay double.

Laws about Crop Protection

⁵ "When a man lets a field or vineyard be grazed in, and then allows his animals to go and graze in someone else's field, he must repay[F] with the best of his own field or vineyard.

⁶ "When a fire gets out of control, spreads to thornbushes, and consumes stacks of cut grain, standing grain, or a field, the one who started the fire must make full restitution for what was burned.

Laws about Personal Property

⁷ "When a man gives his neighbor money or goods to keep, but they are stolen from that person's house, the thief, if caught, must repay double. ⁸ If the thief is not caught, the owner of the house must present himself to the judges[G] to determine[H] whether or not he has taken his neighbor's property.[g] ⁹ In any case of wrongdoing involving an ox, a donkey, a sheep, a garment, or anything else lost, and someone claims, 'That's mine,'[I] the case between the two parties is to come before the judges.[J] The one the judges condemn[K] must repay double to his neighbor.

¹⁰ "When a man gives his neighbor a donkey, an ox, a sheep, or any other animal to care for, but it dies, is injured, or is stolen, while

---

A21:28 Or *a bull, or a steer*   B21:32 About 1 pound of silver   C22:1 Ex 21:37 in Hb   D22:2 Ex 22:1 in Hb   E22:3 Lit *if the sun has risen over him*   F22:5 LXX adds *from his field according to its produce. But if someone lets his animals graze an entire field, he must repay*; DSS, Sam also support this reading.   G22:8 Or *to God*   H22:8 LXX, Tg, Vg read *swear*   I22:9 Lit *That is it*   J22:9 Or *before God*   K22:9 Or *one whom God condemns*

21:28-32 Stoning was a form of public execution and not the ordinary way to slaughter an animal (Dt 13:10; 17:5; Jos 7:25; 1Kg 21:13). If the owner's negligence caused the death, he too must die or pay a ransom for his life. The possibility of a ransom implies that the owner was less directly responsible for the person's death than in cases of murder (Ex 21:12,20,23; Nm 35:31). This value placed on human life over animals fits with God's earlier statement, "I will require the life of every animal and every man for your life and your blood" because humans are made in God's image (Gn 9:5-6). Other ancient Near Eastern laws treat these situations strictly as monetary matters. In case a child died, the stipulation that the negligent owner was **to be dealt with according to this same law** treated the lives of children as valuable and protected the negligent owner's child, whose life was forfeited in some ancient law codes.

21:35-36 Unlike the death of a human, the death of an **ox** was a monetary matter. When the matter was unforeseeable, the owners of both oxen bore the loss equally.

22:2-4 The difference in responses to burglary at different times rests on the concern that the owners' lives might be at stake, especially if the break-in took place at night. During the day they could recognize the thief and know whether or not this was a dangerous intruder (cp. Jr 2:26,34-35). Even the life of a thief was valued; he could not be sold as a slave or be killed in revenge.

22:8-9 In these verses, **the judges** translates the Hebrew word *elohim*, which usually refers to "God" or to "gods." Here it refers to superiors in the society, or judges, rather than a superior being, or God (cp. 1Sm 2:25, where Yahweh is distinguished from judges in a dispute between humans). In verse 9, the verb translated **condemn** is plural, which is appropriate for **judges**. The noun translated **wrongdoing** and its related verb are used in both political and private situations in which a breach of trust, violation of an agreement, disloyalty, or treachery were involved (23:21; Gn 31:36; 50:17; 1Kg 12:19; 2Kg 1:1; Pr 28:24; Is 1:2).

no one is watching, ¹¹ there must be an oath before the Lord between the two of them to determine whether or not he has taken his neighbor's property. Its owner must accept the oath, and the other man does not have to make restitution. ¹² But if, in fact, the animal was stolen from his custody, he must make restitution to its owner.ᵃ ¹³ If it was actually torn apart by a wild animal, he is to bring it as evidence; he does not have to make restitution for the torn carcass.

¹⁴ "When a man borrows an animal from his neighbor, and it is injured or dies while its owner is not there with it, the man must make full restitution. ¹⁵ If its owner is there with it, the man does not have to make restitution. If it was rented, the loss is covered byᴬ its rental price.

Laws about Seduction

¹⁶ "If a man seduces a virgin who is not engaged, and he has sexual relations with her, he must certainly pay the bridal price for her to be his wife. ¹⁷ If her father absolutely refuses to give her to him, he must pay an amount in silver equal to the bridal price for virgins.ᵇ

Capital Offenses

¹⁸ "You must not allow a sorceressᶜ to live.

¹⁹ "Whoever has sexual intercourse with an animalᵈ must be put to death.

²⁰ "Whoever sacrifices to any gods, except the Lord alone, is to be ˙set apart for destruction.ᵉ

Laws Protecting the Vulnerable

²¹ "You must not exploit a foreign residentᶠ

or oppress him, since you were foreigners in the land of Egypt.

²² "You must not mistreat any widow or fatherless child.ᵍ ²³ If you do mistreat them, they will no doubt cry to Me, and I will certainly hear their cry.ʰ ²⁴ My anger will burn, and I will kill you with the sword; then your wives will be widows and your children fatherless.ⁱ

²⁵ "If you lend money to My people, to the poor person among you, you must not be like a moneylender to him; you must not charge him interest.ʲ

²⁶ "If you ever take your neighbor's cloak as collateral, return it to him before sunset. ²⁷ For it is his only covering; it is the clothing for his body.ᴮ What will he sleep in? And if he cries out to Me, I will listen because I am compassionate.ᵏ

Respect for God

²⁸ "You must not blaspheme Godᶜ or curse a leader among your people.ˡ

²⁹ "You must not hold back offeringsᵐ from your harvest or your vats. Give Me the firstborn of your sons. ³⁰ Do the same with your cattle and your flock. Let them stay with their mothers for seven days, but on the eighth day you are to give them to Me.ⁿ

³¹ "Be My holy people. You must not eat the meat of a mauled animalᵒ found in the field; throw it to the dogs.

Laws about Honesty and Justice

23 "You must not spread a false report. Do not joinᴰ the wicked to be a malicious witness.ᵖ

ᵃ22:11-12 Gn 31:39; Heb 6:16
ᵇ22:16-17 Gn 34:12; Dt 22:28-29
ᶜ22:18 Lv 20:27; Dt 18:11; 1Sm 28:3
ᵈ22:19 Lv 18:23; 20:15; Dt 27:21
ᵉ22:20 Dt 17:2-5
ᶠ22:21 Lv 19:33; Dt 10:19
ᵍ22:22 Dt 24:17; Jms 1:27
ʰ22:23 Ps 18:6; Lk 18:7
ⁱ22:24 Ps 69:4; 109:9
ʲ22:25 Lv 25:36-37; Dt 23:20; Ps 15:5
ᵏ22:26-27 Ex 34:6; Dt 24:6
ˡ22:28 Ec 10:20; Ac 23:5
ᵐ22:29 Ex 13:2; 23:16
ⁿ22:30 Lv 22:27; Dt 15:19
ᵒ22:31 Ex 19:2; Ezk 4:14
ᵖ23:1 Ps 35:11; 101:5; Ac 6:11

ᴬ22:15 Lit rented, it comes with   ᴮ22:27 Lit skin   ᶜ22:28 Or judges   ᴰ23:1 Lit join hands with

---

22:11 For examples of **an oath before the Lord**, see 1Sm 20:42; 2Sm 21:7; 1Kg 2:42-43.

22:16-17 The verb rendered **seduces** expresses the idea of persuading or enticing someone, often used negatively in the case of a gullible individual (Jdg 14:15; 16:5; Pr 1:10; 16:29). "Makes a fool of" would be another possible translation. Payment of a **bridal price** to the girl's father was a widely established ancient custom. The payment eventually should become her possession (Gn 31:14-15; 34:12). If a man had sexual intercourse with a woman to whom he was not engaged, he was required to pay the bridal price and marry her.

22:18 This prohibition represents one of several that outlawed all forms of occult activity (Lv 19:26-31; Dt 18:9-14). The three violations in Ex 22:18-20 would be more of a temptation once the Israelites reached the land of Canaan (23:32-33; Lv 18:1-5,23-30; 20:15-26,23-27; Dt 18:14-15).

22:20 The kind of **sacrifices** mentioned here involved fellowship between the deity and the worshiper. The Israelites must be loyal to and have fellowship with **the Lord alone**.

22:21-26 The Israelites were to remember who they were and their mistreatment in Egypt, and they were to remember

that the Lord would take action on behalf of the powerless and vulnerable members of society. The word translated **oppress** in verse 21 and 23:9 is used in 3:9 to describe what prompted the Israelites to call out for help. They needed to avoid putting themselves in the position of the Egyptians. The mention of **collateral** consisting of a garment needed for warmth at night shows that the loan involved helping a poverty-stricken person survive. No luxury or business venture is in view.

22:28 Respect for God displayed in behavior toward others is an issue in the verses that precede and follow this one. Respect for a **leader** is included, perhaps in both halves of the verse, if the Hebrew word elohim has the same reference to "judges" that it seems to have in verses 8-9.

22:31 Be My holy people recalls the fuller description of the Lord's vision for Israel in 19:4-6 but is expressed more personally by listing individual choices. Leviticus provides further directions about what the Israelites could eat (Lv 17:12-15).

23:1-9 These verses touch on every economic status or personal feeling that might tempt someone to treat another unjustly. Favoritism either to the poor or to the rich is ruled

²"You must not follow a crowd in wrongdoing. Do not testify in a lawsuit and go along with a crowd to pervert justice.ᵃ ³Do not show favoritism to a poor person in his lawsuit.

⁴"If you come across your enemy's stray ox or donkey, you must return it to him.

⁵"If you see the donkey of someone who hates you lying helpless under its load, and you want to refrain from helping it, you must help with it.ᴬ,ᵇ

⁶"You must not deny justice to a poor person among you in his lawsuit. ⁷Stay far away from a false accusation. Do not kill the innocent and the just, because I will not justify the •guilty.ᶜ ⁸You must not take a bribe,ᵈ for a bribe blinds the clear-sighted and corrupts the wordsᴮ of the righteous. ⁹You must not oppress a foreign resident;ᵉ you yourselves know how it feels to be a foreigner because you were foreigners in the land of Egypt.

Sabbaths and Festivals

¹⁰"Sow your land for six years and gather its produce.ᶠ ¹¹But during the seventh year you are to let it rest and leave it uncultivated,

ᵃ23:2 Dt 16:19; 24:17; 27:19
ᵇ23:5 Dt 22:1,4; Rm 12:20
ᶜ23:6–7 Ec 5:8; Eph 4:25
ᵈ23:8 Dt 10:17; 16:19; Pr 15:27
ᵉ23:9 Ex 22:21
ᶠ23:10 Lv 25:3-4
ᵍ23:12 Ex 20:9
ʰ23:13 Dt 4:9; Jos 23:7; Hs 2:17; 1Tm 4:16
ⁱ23:14 Ex 34:23; Dt 16:16
ʲ23:15 Ex 12:15; 34:20
ᵏ23:16 Ex 34:22; Lv 23:39; Dt 16:13

so that the poor among your people may eat from it and the wild animals may consume what they leave. Do the same with your vineyard and your olive grove.

¹²"Do your workᵍ for six days but rest on the seventh day so that your ox and your donkey may rest, and the son of your female slave as well as the foreign resident may be refreshed.

¹³"Pay strict attention to everything I have said to you. You must not invoke the names of other gods; they must not be heard on your lips.ᶜ,ʰ

¹⁴"Celebrate a festival in My honor three times a year.ⁱ ¹⁵Observe the Festival of •Unleavened Bread. As I commanded you, you are to eat unleavened bread for seven days at the appointed time in the month of Abib,ᴰ because you came out of Egypt in that month. No one is to appear before Me empty-handed.ʲ ¹⁶Also observe the Festival of Harvestᴱ with the •firstfruits of your produce from what you sow in the field, and observe the Festival of Ingatheringᶠ,ᵏ at the end of the year, when you gather your produceᴳ from the field. ¹⁷Three

ᴬ23:5 Or load, you must refrain from leaving it to him; you must set it free with him   ᴮ23:8 Or and subverts the cause   ᶜ23:13 Lit mouth   ᴰ23:15 March–April; called Nisan in the post-exilic period; Neh 2:1; Est 3:7   ᴱ23:16 The Festival of Harvest is called Festival of Weeks elsewhere; Ex 34:22. In the NT it is called Pentecost; Ac 2:1.   ᶠ23:16 The Festival of Ingathering is called Festival of Booths elsewhere; Lv 23:34-36.   ᴳ23:16 Lit labors

out (Lv 19:15). Even in private matters involving the need of an enemy, an Israelite must not only return straying livestock but also render aid on the spot (Lv 19:15-18; Mt 5:43-48; Rm 12:17-21).

23:6-9 As in 22:21-26, the Israelites must remember who they were and what it was like as foreigners, and they must consider who the Lord is in His support of justice. The warning in 23:7 not to execute an innocent person comes with a reason: **because I will not justify the guilty**. This may refer to God ultimately bringing to justice a guilty person who may slip through the court when judges take care not to execute an innocent person. Or it may refer to God bring-

ing to justice any witness or judge who contributes to the execution of an innocent person. Either way, the Lord declared His concern for maintaining justice (Dt 10:17; 16:18-20; 2Ch 19:6-7; Jr 22:3; 1Pt 1:15-17). With these things in mind, the Israelites must support justice equally for the poor, the rich, and foreigners.

23:10-19 The section on Sabbaths and festivals has as its unifying thread inclusion of matters with agricultural connections, even the prohibition against invoking other gods. The Israelites would find it easy to mimic surrounding cultures that called on other gods in hopes of improving the fertility of their crops and flocks.

23:10-11 The Lord's provision for His people from year to year would be like His provision of manna from day to day; there would be sufficient left over for the seventh day and for the **seventh year** so that everyone could eat without constant labor.

23:12 The two animals and two sorts of people here are illustrative and not an exhaustive list of who would **rest** and **be refreshed** (cp. 20:10).

23:13 This verse does not mean an Israelite must never pronounce the name of a false god, since the names of some pagan gods are included in Scripture. Rather, it is a prohibition of calling on any other god for guidance, help, thanksgiving, or praise.

23:14-17 The **Festival of Unleavened Bread** took place near the start of the barley harvest; the **Festival of Harvest** took place at the time of the wheat harvest; and the **Festival of Ingathering** celebrated the completion of all the harvesting, including grapes and olives. Bringing **firstfruits**, the first items harvested, expressed gratitude for the harvest as coming from the Lord and faith that He would supply

chag

Hebrew Pronunciation	[KHAG]
HCSB Translation	festival, feast
Uses in Exodus	12
Uses in the OT	62
Focus Passages	Exodus 23:15-16,18

Chag denotes *festival* (Ex 32:5) and regularly represents one of the three annual *festivals* that required all Israelite men to come to Jerusalem: Unleavened Bread, Weeks, and Booths (Dt 16:16). For many this would involve a trip, and a related Arabic word that has come into English as *hajj* meaning "pilgrimage." *Chag* first signifies a *festival* that Israel would hold after making a trip (Ex 10:9), but not every *chag* involved traveling. *Chag* also connotes feasts (Am 5:21) or *festival sacrifices* (Mal 2:3). It derives from the verb *chagag* (16x), which appears eight times with *chag* as *celebrate a festival* (Nm 29:12) or something *as a festival* (Ex 12:14). *Chagag* alone means *hold* or *celebrate a festival* (Ex 5:1; 23:14) and describes non-Israelites *celebrating* (1Sm 30:16).

times a year all your males are to appear before the Lord God.

[a]"You must not offer the blood of My sacrifices with anything leavened. The fat of My festival offering must not remain until morning.[a]

[b]"Bring the best of the firstfruits of your land to the house of the LORD your God.

"You must not boil a young goat in its mother's milk.[b]

Promises and Warnings

[20]"I am going to send an angel[c] before you to protect you on the way and bring you to the place I have prepared. [21]Be attentive to him and listen to his voice. Do not defy[A] him, because he will not forgive your acts of rebellion, for My name is in him.[d] [22]But if you will carefully obey him and do everything I say, then I will be an enemy[e] to your enemies and a foe to your foes. [23]For My angel will go before you and bring you to the land of the Amorites, Hittites, Perizzites, Canaanites, Hivites,

---

Marginal references:
a23:18 Ex 34:25; Dt 16:4
b23:19 Ex 22:29; 26:2,10; Dt 14:21
c23:20 Ex 14:19; 15:16-17; 23:23; 32:34; 33:2
d23:21 Nm 14:11; Dt 18:19; Ps 78:40,56
e23:22 Gn 12:3; Dt 30:7; Jr 30:20
f23:23 Ex 23:20; Jos 24:8
g23:24 Ex 20:5; 34:13; Nm 33:52; Dt 12:30
h23:25 Ex 15:26; Dt 6:13; 7:15; 28:5,8; Mt 4:10
i23:26 Dt 7:14; Jb 5:26; Mal 3:11
j23:27 Dt 2:25; 7:23
k23:28 Dt 7:20; Jos 24:12

---

and Jebusites, and I will wipe them out.[f] [24]You must not bow down to their gods or worship them. Do not imitate their practices. Instead, demolish them[B] and smash their sacred pillars to pieces.[g] [25]Worship the LORD your God, and He[c] will bless your bread and your water. I will remove illnesses from you.[h] [26]No woman will miscarry or be childless in your land. I will give you the full number of your days.[i]

[27]"I will cause the people ahead of you to feel terror[D] and throw into confusion[j] all the nations you come to. I will make all your enemies turn their backs to you in retreat. [28]I will send the hornet[E,k] in front of you, and it will drive the Hivites, Canaanites, and Hittites away from you. [29]I will not drive them out ahead of you in a single year; otherwise, the land would become desolate, and wild animals would multiply against you. [30]I will drive them out little by little ahead of you until you have become numerous[F] and take possession of the

---

A23:21 Or *embitter*   B23:24 Probably the idols   C23:25 LXX, Vg read *I*   D23:27 Lit *will send terror of Me ahead of you*   E23:28 Or *send panic*   F23:30 Lit *fruitful*

---

the remainder of the harvest (Dt 26:1-11). The name **Lord God** emphasizes His sovereignty and could also be rendered "the Sovereign (or "Master"), Yahweh." Any ancient king who did not receive the prescribed tribute at the appropriate times would conclude that his vassal was plotting rebellion (1Kg 12:16-19; Ezr 4:8-24). In the ancient Near East, the appearance of **all your males** would demonstrate the loyalty or rebellion of those with potential for military service.

23:18-19 Based on 34:25, the sacrifice and **festival offering** is the Passover lamb, which was sacrificed, roasted, and eaten on the eve of the week of the Festival of Unleavened Bread. All leaven was to be dispensed with before the Passover lamb was offered (Dt 16:2-4). Regulations in Leviticus prohibit eating specified portions of fat from sacrificed animals (Lv 3:16-17; 7:25); the fat and anything else left from the Passover lamb was to be burned (Ex 12:10). The prohibition about boiling **a young goat in its mother's milk** is repeated in 34:26 and Dt 14:21. It may have been connected with the Festival of Ingathering, since goats gave birth around that time, or it may have referred to a pagan custom of unknown significance.

23:20-23 The Lord's sending of **an angel** (cp. 13:21; 14:19) continues the picture of Israel's relationship with the Lord as that of a vassal with a suzerain. The vassal must understand that the envoy came with the king's authority behind him (**My name is in Him**).

23:24 Sacred pillars could be set up as monuments for various purposes (24:4; Gn 28:18,22; 31:13,45,51-52; 35:20; Lv 26:1; Is 19:19).

23:25 The Lord had already shown His ability in the areas of **bread . . . water**, and **illnesses** (cp. 15:22-26; 16:4-5; 17:1-7).

23:26 The Lord referred to provision and preservation of life at both ends of the spectrum—for infants and the elderly—having already spoken about what was needed in between (vv. 22,25). He was concerned about all aspects of life.

23:27-30 While the military battles of Joshua may be more typical of the era of conquest in Canaan, this passage focuses on what might be called psychological warfare and

on the departure of the previous inhabitants. The Lord may have intended to use a plague of hornets to **drive . . . out** the groups living in the land (Dt 7:20; Jos 24:12). It may also be a figure of speech referring to the image of people running away from a place as if chased by swarming hornets (cp. Dt 1:44; Ps 118:12; Is 7:18-19).

Because of the **terror** and **confusion** that the Lord would instigate (Jos 2:9-11; 1Sm 5:6-8,11-12), many people would leave gradually rather than stay to engage in combat. Joshua noted that the Israelites had taken possession of cities, olive groves, and vineyards that they did not build or plant (Dt 6:10-11; Jos 24:11-13). It seems that major portions of the land were intact and not destroyed by protracted warfare. **I will cause the people ahead of you to feel terror** is literally, "My terror I will send before you." God may be interpreted as either the source or the object of the terror. In the events that followed, both took place; the Lord caused fear/confusion and was also the object of fear as His reputation spread. Rahab's report in Jos 2:9 of what was

garash

Hebrew Pronunciation	[gah RASH]
HCSB Translation	drive out, banish
Uses in Exodus	12
Uses in the OT	48
Focus Passage	Exodus 23:28-31

Garash has related words in Ugaritic and Moabite. It means *drive* (Jdg 9:41), *drive out* (Gn 3:24), or *drive away* (Ex 2:17). It connotes *banish* (Gn 4:14), *force out* (Mc 2:9), and *expel* (Jb 30:5). *Garash* usually involves *driving out* of a location, but can indicate *loss of a ministry position* (1Kg 2:27). It suggests *rejection* and often is accomplished through military force. The passive participle was standard terminology for *divorced woman* (Lv 21:14). Three times *garash*, either as a homonym or a variant of *drive out*, characterizes water as *tossing*, *churning up*, or *surging* (Is 57:20; Am 8:8).

land. [31] I will set your borders from the *Red Sea to the Mediterranean Sea,[A] and from the wilderness to the Euphrates River.[B] For I will place the inhabitants of the land under your control, and you will drive them out ahead of you.[a] [32] You must not make a covenant[b] with them or their gods. [33] They must not remain in your land, or else they will make you sin against Me. If you worship their gods, it will be a snare for you."[c]

The Covenant Ceremony

24 Then He said to Moses, "Go up to the LORD, you and Aaron, Nadab, and Abihu, and 70 of Israel's elders,[d] and bow in worship at a distance. [2] Moses alone is to approach the LORD, but the others are not to approach, and the people are not to go up with him."

[3] Moses came and told the people all the commands of the LORD and all the ordinances. Then all the people responded with a single voice, "We will do everything that the LORD

has commanded."[e] [4] And Moses wrote[f] down all the words of the LORD. He rose early the next morning and set up an altar and 12 pillars for the 12 tribes of Israel at the base of the mountain. [5] Then he sent out young Israelite men, and they offered *burnt offerings and sacrificed bulls as *fellowship offerings to the LORD. [6] Moses took half the blood and set it in basins; the other half of the blood he sprinkled on the altar. [7] He then took the covenant scroll and read it aloud to the people. They responded, "We will do and obey everything that the LORD has commanded."

[8] Moses took the blood, sprinkled it on the people, and said, "This is the blood of the covenant that the LORD has made with you concerning all these words."[g]

[9] Then Moses went up with Aaron, Nadab, and Abihu, and 70 of Israel's elders, [10] and they saw[h] the God of Israel. Beneath His feet was something like a pavement made of sapphire[c] stone, as clear as the sky itself.[i] [11] God did not

Reference column:
[a]23:31 Gn 15:18; Dt 11:24; Jos 21:44; 1Kg 4:21
[b]23:32 Ex 34:12,15; Dt 7:2
[c]23:33 Dt 7:16; Ps 106:36
[d]24:1 Ex 6:23; Lv 10:1-2; Nm 11:16
[e]24:3 Ex 19:8; Dt 5:27
[f]24:4 Gn 28:18; Dt 31:9
[g]24:6-8 Heb 9:18-20; 1Pt 1:2
[h]24:10 Jn 1:18; 1Jn 4:12
[i]Ezk 1:26; Mt 17:2; Rv 4:3

[A]23:31 Lit the Sea of the Philistines   [B]23:31 Lit the River   [C]24:10 Or lapis lazuli

---

happening among people in Canaan uses the same rare word for terror or dread as does Ex 15:16.

23:30-31 I will drive them out and **you will drive them out** assumes the involvement of both divine and human effort. **Borders from the Red Sea** refers to the portion of the Red Sea known as the Gulf of Aqaba (cp. 1Kg 9:26). **The Mediterranean Sea**, as it is called now, is in Hebrew literally "the sea of the Philistines," since they lived along the coast (cp. 13:17).

23:33 It will be a snare for you uses the word that 10:7 used to express what Pharaoh's men thought about Moses as they surveyed the damage caused by the plagues. Snares were naturally associated with death (1Sm 18:21; Ps 18:5; Pr 13:14; 14:27; 18:7). Idolatry as a snare to the Israelites pictured serious trouble, not a minor inconvenience (Ex 34:12; Dt 7:16; Jos 23:13; Jdg 2:3; Ps 106:36).

24:1-2 The ceremonies in chapter 24 are the climax of preparations and instructions in chapters 19-23. The arrangements of people and spaces at the mountain parallel those at the tabernacle, with areas that admitted everyone who was properly prepared, initial boundaries past which designated people could go (Moses, Aaron, Nadab, Abihu, **70** elders, priests, and Levites) and further boundaries past which only one representative could go (Moses and the high priest). Nadab and Abihu were two of Aaron's sons (6:23; Lv 10:1-5). To **bow in worship at a distance** fits ancient customs that called for bowing in full-length prostration at various points when approaching a person to whom one showed great respect (Gn 33:3). While only Moses could approach closely, Aaron and the elders could come near enough to participate in the ways that Ex 24:9-11 describes.

24:3 All the commands may refer specifically to the Ten Commandments (20:1-17), and **the ordinances** to additional commands given in 20:22-23:33.

24:4 The **12 pillars** represented the people as silent witnesses to their participation and agreement, like the ones built by Jacob and Laban (Gn 31:44-53) and by Joshua (Jos 24:24-27).

24:5-8 Burnt offerings were burned entirely, except for the

animal hides, and they showed total dedication to the Lord. **Fellowship offerings** were primarily cooked and eaten by the worshipers, symbolizing that the people and the Lord, who had invited them, were at peace with one another. It was normal for covenant-making to include a meal, as in the case of the parity treaty between Isaac and Abimelech (Gn 26:26-31; cp. Gn 31:43-54). The shedding of blood when making a covenant reminded everyone of the covenant's seriousness and the penalties for breaking it (Jr 34:18-20). The sprinkling of blood marked the altar and the people as associated with the covenant sacrifices. And because this covenant was with God, the shed blood was also a provision for atonement and forgiveness, life for life (Lv 4:13-20; 17:1-16; Heb 9:13-22).

In addition to telling the people what the Lord commanded (v. 3), Moses read aloud **the covenant scroll** before he sprinkled them with blood, so they knew exactly what responsibili-

---

mitswah

Hebrew Pronunciation	[mits VAH]
HCSB Translation	command, commandment
Uses in Exodus	4
Uses in the OT	184
Focus Passage	Exodus 24:12

Mitswah is an important OT legal term that retains its importance in current Judaism. *Mitswah* derives from the verb *tsiwwah*, meaning *command*, *direct*, or *appoint*. *Mitswah* has the force of a *duty* or *obligation* to the recipient. God gave such *commands* to Abraham (Gn 26:5). There are 613 divine *commandments* in the Law, and most other OT occurrences of the word refer back to these. But in Jr 32:11, *mitswah* indicates *terms* of a deed of purchase. The word can also refer to *commands* from a forefather (Jr 35:14) or father (Pr 6:20). It can be man-made *rules* (Is 29:13), a divine *decree* (Mal 2:1), or a royal *command* (2Kg 18:36). *Mitswah* can indicate self-imposed *duties* (Neh 10:32). Psalm 119 focuses on God's *commandments*. *Mitswah* is a key term in Deuteronomy 28 and Leviticus 26, which give blessings or curses as the consequences of one's response to God's *commandments*.

harm^A the Israelite nobles; they saw^a Him, and they ate and drank.

^12 The LORD said to Moses, "Come up to Me on the mountain and stay there so that I may give you the stone tablets^b with the law and commandments I have written for their instruction."

^13 So Moses arose with his assistant Joshua and went up the mountain of God.^c ^14 He told the elders, "Wait here for us until we return to you. Aaron and Hur are here with you. Whoever has a dispute should go to them." ^15 When Moses went up the mountain, the cloud^d covered it. ^16 The glory of the LORD settled on Mount Sinai, and the cloud covered it for six days. On the seventh day He called to Moses from the cloud.^e ^17 The appearance of the LORD's glory to the Israelites was like a consuming fire^f on the mountaintop. ^18 Moses entered the cloud as he

went up the mountain, and he remained on the mountain 40 days and 40 nights.^g

Offerings to Build the Tabernacle

25 The LORD spoke to Moses: ^2 "Tell the Israelites to take an offering for Me. You are to take My offering from everyone who is willing to give.^h ^3 This is the offering you are to receive from them: gold, silver, and bronze; ^4 blue, purple, and scarlet yarn; fine linen and goat hair; ^5 ram skins dyed red^i and manatee skins;^B acacia wood; ^6 oil^j for the light; spices for the anointing oil and for the fragrant incense; ^7 and onyx^C along with other gemstones for mounting on the •ephod and breastpiece.^D,k

^8 "They are to make a sanctuary^l for Me so that I may dwell^m among them. ^9 You must make it according to all that I show you—the pattern^n of the tabernacle as well as the pattern of all its furnishings.

Cross references (center column)

^a24:11 Gn 32:30; Ex 19:21
^b24:12 Ex 32:15; Dt 5:22
^c24:13 Ex 3:1; 17:9
^d24:15 Ex 19:9; Mt 17:5
^e24:16 Ex 16:10
^f24:17 Ex 3:2; Dt 4:36; Heb 12:18,29
^g24:18 Ex 34:28; Dt 9:9
^h25:2 Ex 35:5,21; 1Ch 29:5; Ezr 2:68; Neh 11:2; 2Co 8:12; 9:7
^i25:5 Ex 26:14; 35:7,23; 36:19; 39:34
^j25:6 Ex 27:20; 30:23-24
^k25:7 Ex 28:4,6-15
^l25:8 Ex 36:1-5; Heb 9:12
^m Ex 29:45; 1Kg 6:13; 2Co 6:16; Rv 21:3
^n25:9 Ex 25:40; 26:30; Ac 7:44; Heb 8:2,5

---

^A24:11 Lit *not stretch out His hand against*   ^B25:5 Or *and dolphin skins,* or *and fine leather;* Hb obscure   ^C25:7 Or *carnelian*
^D25:7 Traditionally, *breastplate*

---

ties they were agreeing to fulfill. To read a covenant aloud in the hearing of the vassal was another part of the process.

24:10-11 The description of what Moses and the Israelite leaders saw when they approached **the God of Israel** must employ comparisons. It was **something like a pavement made of sapphire stone**, and it had a clarity like that of **the sky**. It was similar to, but beyond anything people knew of (likewise in v. 17). The description is further limited in that it offers the point of view of someone face down and able to see only what was **beneath His feet**. The mention that **God did not harm the Israelite nobles** (lit "stretch out His hand") reflects ancient customs that gave kings the ability to call for a subject's removal or death with just a hand gesture. Instead, He received them with favor.

24:12 **The stone tablets** are also mentioned in 31:18, forming a frame around the instructions for building the tabernacle in chapters 25–31.

24:13-15 The departure of **Moses** and **Joshua** parallels that of Abraham and Isaac (Gn 22). In both cases the older man left instructions, and the younger man required an explanation of events from the older man. That the Israelites began worshiping the golden calf (Ex 32) rather than waiting as instructed showed that they failed to match either the faithfulness of Abraham or even of his servants. Meanwhile, Moses and Joshua in a sense continued the legacy of Abraham and Isaac's faithful worship.

25:1–31:17 These chapters contain instructions for the tabernacle and its furnishings and the clothing for priests that the Israelites were to make. Much of the information is repeated in chapters 35–40, which report the tabernacle's construction. It would have been possible to put all the necessary details about the tabernacle in the report about its construction and go almost immediately from the events at the end of chapter 24 to the events surrounding worship of the golden calf in chapter 32. The attention to detail in chapters 25–31 slows the account, forcing readers to wait for what happens next. It also highlights the catastrophe of worshiping the golden calf against a background of concern for proper worship. It is ironic that while the Lord gave instructions for correct worship, the Israelites were doing it their own way.

25:1 The statement **The LORD spoke to Moses** divides chapters 25–31 into seven unequal segments, ending with instructions about the Sabbath, as if to show a connection between creation and this new building where God would meet with human beings (25:1; 30:11,17,22,34; 31:1,12; cp. Rv 21:1-3). Recording the instructions as they came in the voice of the Lord Himself, rather than in a narrative summary, helps reinforce God's personal interest in these matters and His personal offense at the worship of the golden calf.

25:2 This offering would be the result of internal compulsion and not external—as with taxes or public pressure. The willingness of the people extended so far that the workmen had more than enough materials (36:3-7).

25:7 The **ephod and breastpiece** are described more fully in chapter 28, along with other priestly garments.

25:8 For the Israelites **to make a sanctuary for** the Lord to **dwell** in continues the theme of His presence with His people and His goal in bringing them out of Egypt—to make Himself known as their God, and to give them a unique identity as His people (6:6-7; 19:4-6; 29:43-46). The word translated "dwell" is rendered "settled" in the statement that "the glory of the Lord settled on Mount Sinai" in 24:16. It is closely associated with the word "shekinah," used in postbiblical discussions of the Lord's presence. It is also connected by sound and concept with the Greek verb in Jn 1:14 that is translated "took up residence." By commissioning the building of the tabernacle, a portable worship center, the Lord showed that He intended to live among the Israelites more closely than when meeting with them on Mount Sinai.

Returning to the suzerain-vassal comparison, the suzerain would customarily live far from the vassal, using his collected tribute exclusively for his own enjoyment. The best a vassal nation could hope for was that their suzerain would provide security and predictable levies of tribute rather than sporadic, devastating raids. The Lord, however, was talking to Moses about residing among the Israelites as His own people.

25:9 Attempts to imagine or to build a replica of the **tabernacle** and its furnishings can only proceed with the disadvantage of not having seen what the Lord showed

The Ark

[10] "They are to make an ark[a] of acacia wood, 45 inches long, 27 inches wide, and 27 inches high.[A] [11]Overlay it with pure gold; overlay it both inside and out. Also make a gold molding all around it. [12]Cast four gold rings for it and place them on its four feet, two rings on one side and two rings on the other side. [13]Make poles of acacia wood and overlay them with gold. [14]Insert the poles into the rings on the sides of the ark in order to carry the ark with them. [15]The poles are to remain in the rings of the ark; they must not be removed from it. [16]Put the tablets of the •testimony that I will give you into the ark.[b] [17]Make a •mercy seat[c] of pure gold, 45 inches long and 27 inches wide.[B] [18]Make two •cherubim of gold; make them of hammered work at the two ends of the mercy seat. [19]Make one cherub at one end and one cherub at the other end. At its two ends, make the cherubim of one piece with the mercy seat. [20]The cherubim are to have wings spread out above, covering[d] the mercy seat with their wings, and are to face one another. The faces of the cherubim should be toward the mercy seat. [21]Set the mercy seat on top of the ark and put the testimony that I will give you into the ark.[e] [22]I will meet with you there above the mercy seat, between the two cherubim[f] that are over the ark of the testimony; I will speak with you from there about all that I command you regarding the Israelites.

The Table

[23]"You are to construct a table[g] of acacia wood, 36 inches long, 18 inches wide, and 27 inches high.[C] [24]Overlay it with pure gold and make a gold molding all around it. [25]Make

[a]25:10 Ex 37:1,3-4; Dt 10:3; Heb 9:4
[b]25:16 Ex 16:34; Dt 31:26; 1Kg 8:9
[c]25:17 Ex 37:6; Rm 3:25; Heb 9:5
[d]25:20 1Kg 8:7; 1Ch 28:18; Heb 9:5
[e]25:21 Ex 25:16; 26:34
[f]25:22 Nm 7:89; 1Sm 4:4; 2Sm 6:2; 2Kg 19:15; Ps 80:1; Is 37:16
[g]25:23 Ex 37:10; 1Kg 7:48; 2Ch 4:8; Heb 9:2

[A]25:10 Lit two and a half cubits its length, one and a half cubits its width, and one and a half cubits its height   [B]25:17 Lit two and a half cubits its length, one and a half cubits its width   [C]25:23 Lit two cubits its length, one cubit its width, and one and a half cubits its height

---

Moses, in addition to difficulties posed by rare words describing unfamiliar items. The tabernacle itself and a complete description of all its details were not what subsequent generations needed.

25:10-22 The **ark**, a rectangular wooden box covered inside and out with gold, sat in the most sacred area in the tabernacle. It symbolized the Lord's presence with the Israelites in at least three ways: (1) It was a repository for the stone tablets given to Moses, which were a witness, or **testimony** to the requirements the Israelites had agreed to. (2) On the annual Day of Atonement, the high priest sprinkled blood on the **mercy seat**, the ark's cover, in keeping with the Lord's provision for dealing with the sins of the people (Lv 16:13-15,29-34). (3) The ark was also where the Lord met with Moses and spoke with him (Nm 7:89). This was in keeping with His earlier assurance of His presence with Moses (Ex 3:11-12; 4:11-15).

25:10 Many measurements for the tabernacle and its furnishings used a unit called *ammah* in Hebrew, traditionally rendered "cubit," an anglicized version of the Latin *cubitus*. The Hebrew word also meant "forearm," and an *ammah* measured from the tip of a man's fingers to his elbow, roughly 18 inches. The HCSB makes the conversions to English measures.

25:16 Recording a covenant on tablets and placing them in a sanctuary in the presence of a deity were common practices for preserving covenants. Certain Hittite covenant documents mention doing this.

25:18 The cover of the ark was to be decorated with two **cherubim**. Elsewhere the Lord is spoken of as enthroned

Reconstruction of the ark of the covenant drawn in Egyptian style, reflecting the influence of 400 years of bondage in Egypt. The mysterious origin of the ark is seen by contrasting the two accounts of how it was made in the Pentateuch. The more elaborate account of the manufacture and ornamentation of the ark by the craftsman Bezalel appears in Ex 25:10-22; 31:2,7; 35:30-35; 37:1-9. It was planned during Moses' first sojourn on Sinai and built after the tabernacle specifications had been communicated and completed. The other account is found in Dt 10:1-5. After the sin of the golden calf and the breaking of the original Decalogue tablets, Moses made a plain box of acacia wood as a container to receive the new tables of the law. A very ancient poem, the "Song of the Ark" in Nm 10:35-36, sheds some light on the function of the ark in the wanderings in the wilderness.

a three-inch[A] frame all around it and make a gold molding for it all around its frame. [26] Make four gold rings for it, and attach the rings to the four corners at its four legs. [27] The rings should be next to the frame as holders for the poles to carry the table. [28] Make the poles of acacia wood and overlay them with gold, and the table can be carried by them. [29] You are also to make its plates[a] and cups, as well as its pitchers and bowls for pouring •drink offerings. Make them out of pure gold. [30] Put the •bread of the Presence[b] on the table before Me at all times.

The Lampstand

[31] "You[c] are to make a lampstand[d] out of pure, hammered gold. It is to be made of one piece: its base and shaft, its ornamental cups, and its calyxes[B] and petals. [32] Six branches are to extend from its sides, three branches of the lampstand from one side and three branches of the lampstand from the other side. [33] There are to be three cups shaped like almond blossoms, each with a calyx and petals, on the first branch, and three cups shaped like almond blossoms, each with a calyx and petals, on the next branch. It is to be this way for the six branches that extend from the lampstand. [34] There are to be four cups shaped like almond blossoms on the lampstand shaft along with

its calyxes and petals. [35] For the six branches that extend from the lampstand, a calyx must be under the first pair of branches from it, a calyx under the second pair of branches from it, and a calyx under the third pair of branches from it. [36] Their calyxes and branches are to be of one piece.[C] All of it is to be a single hammered piece of pure gold.

[37] "Make seven lamps[e] on it. Its lamps are to be set up so they illuminate the area in front of it. [38] Its snuffers and firepans must be of pure gold. [39] The lampstand[D] with all these utensils is to be made from 75 pounds[E] of pure gold. [40] Be careful to make them according to the pattern[f] you have been shown on the mountain.

The Tabernacle

26 "You[g] are to construct the tabernacle itself with 10 curtains. You must make them of finely spun linen, and blue, purple, and scarlet yarn, with a design of •cherubim worked into them. [2] The length of each curtain should be 42 feet,[F] and the width of each curtain six feet;[G] all the curtains are to have the same measurements. [3] Five of the curtains should be joined together, and the other five curtains joined together. [4] Make loops of blue yarn on the edge of the last curtain[H] in the first set, and do the same on the edge of the

[a]25:29 Ex 37:16; Nm 4:7
[b]25:30 Ex 35:13; 39:36; 40:23; Lv 24:5-9; Nm 4:7
[c]25:31-39 Ex 37:17-24
[d]25:31 1Kg 7:49; Zch 4:2; Heb 9:2; Rv 1:12
[e]25:37 Ex 27:21; 37:23; Lv 24:3-4; Nm 8:2; 2Ch 13:11
[f]25:40 Ex 26:30; Nm 8:4; 1Ch 28:11,19; Ac 7:44; Heb 8:5
[g]26:1-37 Ex 36:8-38

A25:25 Lit *Make it a handbreadth*   B25:31 = the outer covering of a flower   C25:36 Lit *piece with it*   D25:39 Lit *It*   E25:39 Lit *a talent*   F26:2 Lit *28 cubits*   G26:2 Lit *four cubits*   H26:4 Lit *the one curtain on the end*

---

above the cherubim, so that the ark was His footstool (1Sm 4:4; 2Sm 6:2; 2Kg 19:15; Ps 99:1,5; 132:7). "Cherubim" is the plural for "cherub," and both are anglicized Hebrew words. Winged beings of this sort were commissioned "to guard the way to the tree of life" (Gn 3:24), and they were described by the prophet Ezekiel, who saw them transporting God's throne (Ezk 10).

25:29 To present **drink offerings**, a priest would pour out a liquid—wine, for example—to be burned along with certain animal sacrifices (29:40-41; Lv 23:9-13).

25:30 The **bread of the Presence** consisted of 12 loaves made with fine flour and arranged in two rows on the gold-covered table located just outside the most holy area of the tabernacle (Lv 24:5-9). Unlike foodstuffs that were placed in pagan temples for the gods to eat, this bread was for the Israelite priests to eat as a symbolic provision for them from the Lord's table.

25:31-37 The highly decorated **lampstand** (Hb *menorah*) resembled the almond tree, noted for its early blossoming. The Hebrew word for "almond" is associated with a verb that means "watch over" or "keep watch," so that almond blossoms seem an appropriate decoration for an item that enhanced visibility. Aaron's staff was made of almond wood (Nm 17:8). In Jr 1:11-12 it is a symbol of God watching over His word to accomplish His purpose.

26:1-14 The tabernacle proper was made with four layers; the first of **finely spun linen**, the second of woven **goat hair**,

the third of leather made from **ram skins dyed red**, and the fourth another kind of leather whose source is uncertain. The word used for it appears also in Ezk 16:10 to describe material for special sandals. The translation **manatee skins**

mishkan

Hebrew Pronunciation	[mish KAN]
HCSB Translation	tabernacle, dwelling
Uses in Exodus	58
Uses in the OT	139
Focus Passages	Exodus 26:1,6-7,12-13,15

Mishkan, from *shakan* ("dwell"), describes human *dwellings* (Nm 16:24) or the divine *dwelling place* (Ps 43:3). Commonly these are tents (Nm 24:5), and *mishkan* is sometimes translated *tent* (Sg 1:8; Ezk 25:4). *Mishkan* occurs with *'ohel*, "tent," in 73 verses. *Mishkan* can suggest *home* (Jr 51:30), a permanent structure (Is 32:18). *Mishkan* can connote a *crypt* (Is 22:16), salt flats as an animal's *dwelling* (Jb 39:6), or *territories* as dwelling places (Hab 1:6). Exodus 25-40 describes the tabernacle (Ex 26:6) built as God's *residence* (Lv 26:11), also called the "tent of meeting." This structure as the *mishkan* can be distinguished from its top, called a "tent" (Ex 26:7), and its "courtyard" (Ex 38:31). *Mishkan* also characterized the *temple* (Ps 43:3; 74:7), and most references to *mishkan* concern either the *tabernacle* or the *temple*. God will again establish His *mishkan* among Israel (Ezk 37:26-27) at the end of the age.

outermost curtain in the second set. ⁵ Make 50 loops on the one curtain and make 50 loops on the edge of the curtain in the second set, so that the loops line up together. ⁶ Also make 50 gold clasps and join the curtains together with the clasps, so that the tabernacle may be a single unit.

⁷ "You are to make curtains of goat hair for a tent over the tabernacle; make 11 of these curtains. ⁸ The length of each curtain should be 45 feet^A and the width of each curtain six feet.^B All 11 curtains are to have the same measurements. ⁹ Join five of the curtains by themselves, and the other six curtains by themselves. Then fold the sixth curtain double at the front of the tent. ¹⁰ Make 50 loops on the edge of the one curtain, the outermost in the first set, and make 50 loops on the edge of the corresponding curtain of the second set. ¹¹ Make 50 bronze clasps; put the clasps through the loops and join the tent together so that it is a single unit. ¹² As for the flap that is left over from the tent curtains, the leftover half curtain is to hang down over the back of the tabernacle. ¹³ The half yard^C on one side and the half yard^D on the other of what is left over along the length of the tent curtains should be hanging down over the sides of the tabernacle on either side to cover it. ¹⁴ Make a covering for the tent from ram skins dyed red^a and a covering of manatee skins^E on top of that.

¹⁵ "You are to make upright planks^F of acacia wood^b for the tabernacle. ¹⁶ The length of each plank is to be 15 feet,^G and the width of each plank 27 inches.^H ¹⁷ Each plank must be connected together with two tenons. Do the same for all the planks of the tabernacle. ¹⁸ Make the planks for the tabernacle as follows: 20 planks for the south side, ¹⁹ and make 40 silver bases

^a26:14 Ex 25:5; 35:7; 36:19; 39:34; Nm 4:25
^b26:15 Ex 25:28; 26:37; 27:1,6; 30:1,5; 35:33; 36:20; 37:15; 38:6
^c26:30 Ex 25:9,40; Ac 7:44; Heb 8:5
^d26:31 Ex 36:35; 2Ch 3:14; Mt 27:51; Heb 9:3
^e26:33 Ex 25:16; 40:21; Lv 16:2; Heb 9:2
^f26:34 Ex 25:21; 40:20; Heb 9:5

under the 20 planks, two bases under the first plank for its two tenons, and two bases under the next plank for its two tenons; ²⁰ 20 planks for the second side of the tabernacle, the north side, ²¹ along with their 40 silver bases, two bases under the first plank and two bases under each plank; ²² and make six planks for the west side of the tabernacle. ²³ Make two additional planks for the two back corners of the tabernacle. ²⁴ They are to be paired at the bottom, and joined together^I at the top in a single ring. So it should be for both of them; they will serve as the two corners. ²⁵ There are to be eight planks with their silver bases: 16 bases; two bases under the first plank and two bases under each plank.

²⁶ "You are to make five crossbars of acacia wood for the planks on one side of the tabernacle, ²⁷ five crossbars for the planks on the other side of the tabernacle, and five crossbars for the planks of the back side of the tabernacle on the west. ²⁸ The central crossbar is to run through the middle of the planks from one end to the other. ²⁹ Then overlay the planks with gold, and make their rings of gold as the holders for the crossbars. Also overlay the crossbars with gold. ³⁰ You are to set up the tabernacle according to the plan for it that you have been shown on the mountain.^c

³¹ "You are to make a veil of blue, purple, and scarlet yarn, and finely spun linen with a design of cherubim worked into it.^d ³² Hang it on four gold-plated posts of acacia wood that have gold hooks and that stand on four silver bases. ³³ Hang the veil under the clasps^J and bring the ark of the •testimony there behind the veil, so the veil will make a separation for you between the holy place^e and the most holy place. ³⁴ Put the •mercy seat on the ark of the testimony in the most holy place.^f ³⁵ Place the

---

^A26:8 Lit 30 cubits ^B26:8 Lit four cubits ^C26:13 Lit The cubit ^D26:13 Lit the cubit ^E26:14 Or of dolphin skins, or of fine leather; Hb obscure ^F26:15 Or frames, or beams ^G26:16 Lit 10 cubits ^H26:16 Lit a cubit and a half ^I26:24 Lit and together they are to be complete ^J26:33 The clasps that join the 10 curtains of the tabernacle; Ex 26:6

---

depends on the similarity in sound of the Hebrew term to an Arabic word for a marine mammal native to the Red Sea. Another possibility is that the Hebrew word is a borrowed Egyptian word for "leather."

26:15-25 The tabernacle would be oriented with its open side to the east, its short wall on the west, and its long walls on the north and south. See the reconstruction of the tabernacle and its court on page 145.

26:31-35 The veil (Hb paroketh) is a term used only of this curtain that divides the two halves of the tabernacle proper. The outer room, **the holy place**, would contain **the table** and **the lampstand** described in chapter 25. The inner room, **the most holy place**, would contain **the ark** and its cover, **the mercy seat**.

26:36-37 The **entrance** to the holy place, on the east side

of the tabernacle, would have a woven linen **screen** of the same fine material as the veil, but with no mention of the cherubim design.

27:1 The **altar** (also called "the bronze altar"; see 38:30; 39:39) would sit outside the sanctuary or tabernacle proper in the middle of the courtyard square in front of the holy place. It was massive in size; a man of average height standing beside it would barely be able to look over it. Anything burning on it would be at about eye level or higher.

27:2 Discoveries by archaeologists indicate that **horns** were typical of stone altars. The incense altar would also have horns (30:1-2), which may have been symbols of strength. Psalm 118:27 mentions using ropes to tie a sacrifice to the altar's horns. Blood was put on the horns of both the altar of burnt offering and the incense altar (Ex 29:12; 30:10; Lv 4:7,18,25,30,34; 8:15; 9:9; 16:18). A person seeking refuge in

table outside the veil and the lampstand on the south side of the tabernacle, opposite the table; put the table on the north side.[a]

[36]"For the entrance to the tent you are to make a screen embroidered with blue, purple, and scarlet yarn, and finely spun linen. [37]Make five posts of acacia wood for the screen and overlay them with gold; their hooks are to be gold, and you are to cast five bronze bases for them.

The Altar of Burnt Offering

27 "You[b] are to construct the altar of acacia wood. The altar must be square, 7½ feet long, and 7½ feet wide;[A] it must be 4½ feet high.[B] [2]Make horns for it on its four corners; the horns are to be of one piece.[C] Overlay it with bronze.[c] [3]Make its pots for removing ashes, and its shovels, basins, meat forks, and firepans; make all its utensils of bronze. [4]Construct a grate for it of bronze mesh, and make four bronze rings on the mesh at its four corners. [5]Set it below, under the altar's ledge,[D] so that the mesh comes halfway up[E] the altar. [6]Then make poles for the altar, poles of acacia wood, and overlay them with bronze. [7]The

[a] 26:35 Ex 40:22,24; Heb 9:2
[b] 27:1-8 Ex 38:1-7; Ezk 43:13
[c] 27:2 Nm 16:38; Ps 118:27
[d] 27:8 Ex 25:40; 26:30
[e] 27:9-19 Ex 38:9-20

poles are to be inserted into the rings so that the poles are on two sides of the altar when it is carried. [8]Construct the altar with boards so that it is hollow. They are to make it just as it was shown to you on the mountain.[d]

The Courtyard

[9]"You[e] are to make the courtyard for the tabernacle. Make the hangings on the south of the courtyard out of finely spun linen, 150 feet[F] long on that side. [10]There are to be 20 posts and 20 bronze bases. The hooks and bands[G] of the posts must be silver. [11]Then make the hangings on the north side 150 feet[H] long. There are to be 20 posts and 20 bronze bases. The hooks and bands[G] of the posts must be silver. [12]Make the hangings of the courtyard on the west side 75 feet[I] long, including their 10 posts and 10 bases. [13]Make the hangings of the courtyard on the east side toward the sunrise 75 feet.[I] [14]Make the hangings on one side of the gate 22½ feet,[J] including their three posts and their three bases. [15]And make the hangings on the other side 22½ feet,[K] including their three posts and their three bases. [16]The gate of the courtyard is to have a thirty-

---

---

hope of avoiding death would grasp the horns on the altar for burnt offerings (1Kg 1:50-51; 2:28).

27:8 Since the altar was **hollow**, which helped make it portable, it could be filled with stones and earth each time the tabernacle was rebuilt (cp. 20:24).

27:9-18 The **courtyard for the tabernacle** would be enclosed by a fence seven and a half feet high made with linen cloth hung from posts at seven-and-a-half-foot intervals. Like the tabernacle proper, it would open to the east.

Reconstruction of the tabernacle and its court (26:1-35). The tabernacle was always set up to face east, so this view is from the northeast.

foot[A] screen[a] embroidered with blue, purple, and scarlet yarn, and finely spun linen. It is to have four posts including their four bases.

[17]"All the posts around the courtyard are to be banded with silver and have silver hooks and bronze bases. [18]The length of the courtyard is to be 150 feet, the width 75 feet at each end, and the height 7½ feet,[B] all of it made of finely spun linen. The bases of the posts must be bronze. [19]All the tools of the tabernacle for every use and all its tent pegs as well as all the tent pegs of the courtyard are to be made of bronze.

The Lampstand Oil

[20]"You are to command the Israelites to bring you pure oil from crushed olives for the light, in order to keep the lamp burning continually. [21]In the tent of meeting outside the veil that is in front of the •testimony,[b] Aaron and his sons are to tend the lamp[c] from evening until morning before the LORD. This is to be a permanent statute[d] for the Israelites throughout their generations.

The Priestly Garments

28 "Have your brother Aaron, with his sons, come to you from the Israelites to serve Me as priest—Aaron, his sons Nadab and Abihu, Eleazar and Ithamar.[e] [2]Make holy garments[f] for your brother Aaron, for glory and beauty. [3]You are to instruct all the skilled craftsmen,[C,g] whom I have filled with a spirit of wisdom, to make Aaron's garments for consecrating him to serve Me as priest. [4]These are the garments that they must make: a breastpiece, an •ephod, a robe,

a specially woven tunic,[D] a turban, and a sash. They are to make holy garments for your brother Aaron and his sons so that they may serve Me as priests. [5]They should use[E] gold; blue, purple, and scarlet yarn; and fine linen.

The Ephod

[6]"They[h] are to make the ephod of finely spun linen embroidered with gold, and with blue, purple, and scarlet yarn. [7]It must have two shoulder pieces attached to its two edges so that it can be joined together. [8]The artistically woven waistband that is on the ephod[F] must be of one piece,[G] according to the same workmanship of gold, of blue, purple, and scarlet yarn, and of finely spun linen.

[9]"Take two onyx stones and engrave on them the names of Israel's sons: [10]six of their names on the first stone and the remaining six names on the second stone, in the order of their birth. [11]Engrave the two stones with the names of Israel's sons as a gem cutter engraves a seal. Mount them, surrounded with gold filigree settings. [12]Fasten both stones on the shoulder pieces of the ephod as memorial stones for the Israelites. Aaron will carry their names on his two shoulders before the LORD as a reminder.[i] [13]Fashion gold filigree settings [14]and two chains of pure gold; you will make them of braided cord work, and attach the cord chains to the settings.

The Breastpiece

[15]"You[j] are to make an embroidered breastpiece for making decisions.[H] Make it with the same workmanship as the ephod; make it of

---

[a]27:16 Ex 35:17; 38:18; 39:40; 40:8,33; Nm 3:26; 4:26
[b]27:21 Ex 30:8; 1Sm 3:3; 2Ch 13:11
[c]Ex 26:31,33; 28:43
[d]Ex 29:9; Lv 3:17; 16:34; Nm 18:23; 19:21
[e]28:1 Nm 18:7; Ps 99:6; Heb 5:1
[f]28:2 Ex 29:5,9; 31:10; 39:1-2; Lv 8:7,30; Nm 20:26,28
[g]28:3 Ex 31:6; 35:25; 36:1
[h]28:6-12 Ex 39:2-7; Lv 8:7
[i]28:12 Ex 28:29; Jos 4:7; Zch 6:14
[j]28:15-28 Ex 39:8-21

[A]27:16 Lit *twenty-cubit*   [B]27:18 Lit *be 100 by the cubit, and the width 50 by 50, and the height five cubits*   [C]28:3 Lit *all wise of heart*   [D]28:4 Hb obscure   [E]28:5 Lit *receive*   [F]28:8 Lit *waistband of its ephod, which is on it*   [G]28:8 Lit *piece with the ephod*   [H]28:15 Used for determining God's will; Nm 27:21

27:20-21 This variety of **pure oil from crushed olives** (crushed and pressed rather than ground in a mill) would give bright light with little smoke. Mention of **Aaron and his sons**, who would **tend the lamp**, prepares for the start of a lengthy section (chaps. 28–29) that describes preparations for their service. The tabernacle is called **the tent of meeting** in view of the Lord's intention to meet with His people there (25:22; 29:42-43; 30:6,36).

28:1-2 The **holy garments** of Aaron and his sons marked them as the Lord's priests. The Lord's directions provided clothing and food for those who served in His presence (29:28), in contrast with certain pagan rituals, which focused on clothing and feeding idol gods. The phrase **for glory and beauty** indicates that the priestly garments were much more than utilitarian. They resembled other elements of the tabernacle complex, which featured fine fabrics, colorful designs, precious metals, and specialized workmanship, as appropriate for honoring the Lord, who would reside there. **Nadab and Abihu** accompanied their father and the Israelite elders who were privileged to take part in the covenant ceremony on Mount Sinai (24:1-11). Their sudden

deaths are recorded in Lv 10:1-7. **Eleazar** followed Aaron as high priest (Nm 20:28). **Ithamar** directed the Levites, who made an inventory of materials used in constructing the tabernacle (Ex 38:21).

28:3 The men and women who would make the priestly **garments** would use abilities that God gave them. In contrast with Pharaoh, whose heart was characteristically "hard" in rebellion toward the Lord, these people were "wise of heart" and were **filled with a spirit of wisdom**. Wisdom in this case would display itself in both willingness and skill to do the needed work.

28:6 The word **ephod** is a transliterated Hebrew word referring to a vest-like garment worn by the high priest.

28:11-12 A **seal** would stamp a distinctive impression into wax or clay, or leave an identifying pattern of ink and act like a signature (cp. Gn 38:18; 1Kg 21:8; Jr 22:24). Exodus 28:12 does not specify who should be reminded by the stones or for what purpose. Previously in Exodus both the Lord and the Israelites received impetus to remember (2:24; 3:15; 6:5; 12:14; 13:9; 17:14).

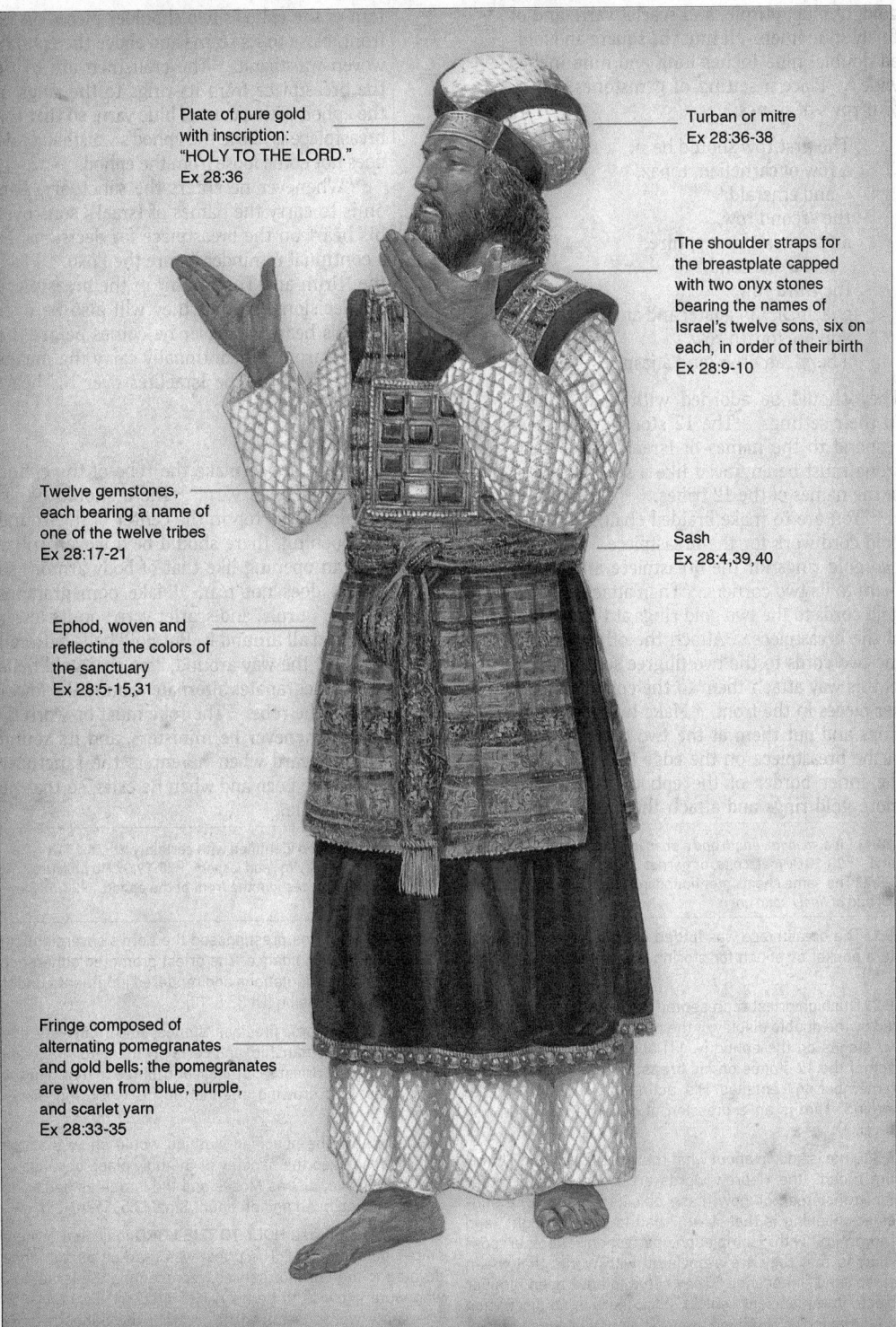

Plate of pure gold
with inscription:
"HOLY TO THE LORD."
Ex 28:36

Turban or mitre
Ex 28:36-38

The shoulder straps for
the breastplate capped
with two onyx stones
bearing the names of
Israel's twelve sons, six on
each, in order of their birth
Ex 28:9-10

Twelve gemstones,
each bearing a name of
one of the twelve tribes
Ex 28:17-21

Sash
Ex 28:4,39,40

Ephod, woven and
reflecting the colors of
the sanctuary
Ex 28:5-15,31

Fringe composed of
alternating pomegranates
and gold bells; the pomegranates
are woven from blue, purple,
and scarlet yarn
Ex 28:33-35

Artist's rendition of the high priest's garments (28:1-38)

gold, of blue, purple, and scarlet yarn, and of finely spun linen. [16]It must be square and folded double, nine inches long and nine inches wide.[A] [17]Place a setting of gemstones[B] on it, four rows of stones:

> The first row should be
> a row of carnelian, topaz,
> and emerald;[C]
> [18] the second row,
> a turquoise,[D] a sapphire,[E]
> and a diamond;[F]
> [19] the third row,
> a jacinth,[G] an agate, and an amethyst;
> [20] and the fourth row,
> a beryl, an onyx, and a jasper.

They should be adorned with gold filigree in their settings. [21]The 12 stones are to correspond to the names of Israel's sons. Each stone must be engraved like a seal, with one of the names of the 12 tribes.

[22]"You are to make braided chains[H] of pure gold cord work for the breastpiece. [23]Fashion two gold rings for the breastpiece and attach them to its two corners. [24]Then attach the two gold cords to the two gold rings at the corners of the breastpiece. [25]Attach the other ends of the two cords to the two filigree settings, and in this way attach them to the ephod's shoulder pieces in the front. [26]Make two other gold rings and put them at the two other corners of the breastpiece on the edge that is next to the inner border of the ephod. [27]Make two more gold rings and attach them to the bot-

a 28:30 Lv 8:8; Nm 27:21; Dt 33:8; Ezr 2:63; Neh 7:65 *b* 28:31-40 Ex 39:22-31

tom of the ephod's two shoulder pieces on its front, close to its seam,[I] and above the ephod's woven waistband. [28]The craftsmen are to tie the breastpiece from its rings to the rings of the ephod with a cord of blue yarn, so that the breastpiece is above the ephod's waistband and does not come loose from the ephod.

[29]"Whenever he enters the sanctuary, Aaron is to carry the names of Israel's sons over his heart on the breastpiece for decisions, as a continual reminder before the LORD. [30]Place the •Urim and Thummim[a] in the breastpiece for decisions, so that they will also be over Aaron's heart whenever he comes before the LORD. Aaron will continually carry the means of decisions for the Israelites over his heart before the LORD.

The Robe

[31]"You[b] are to make the robe of the ephod entirely of blue yarn. [32]There should be an opening at its top in the center of it. Around the opening, there should be a woven collar with an opening like that of body armor[G] so that it does not tear. [33]Make pomegranates of blue, purple, and scarlet yarn[J] on its lower hem and all around it. Put gold bells between them all the way around, [34]so that gold bells and pomegranates alternate around the lower hem of the robe. [35]The robe must be worn by Aaron whenever he ministers, and its sound will be heard when he enters the sanctuary before the LORD and when he exits, so that he does not die.

[A]28:16 Lit *a span its length and a span its width*   [B]28:17 Many of these stones cannot be identified with certainty.   [C]28:17 Or *beryl*   [D]28:18 Or *malachite, or garnet*   [E]28:18 Or *lapis lazuli*   [F]28:18 Hb obscure; LXX, Vg read *jasper*   [G]28:19,32 Hb obscure   [H]28:22 The same chains mentioned in v. 14   [I]28:27 The place where the shoulder pieces join the front of the ephod   [J]28:33 Sam, LXX add *of finely spun linen*

28:16 The breastpiece was **folded double**, it seems, to create a pocket or pouch for storing the Urim and Thummim (v. 30).

28:29 The high priest represented the Israelites, as symbolized by the double display of the names of each tribe on the two stones on the ephod (v. 11) and also by the name on each of the 12 stones on his **breastpiece**. Since the Lord's "remembering" entailed His acting (2:24-25; 3:7-10), to "remind" Him is an expression of dependence, faith, and prayer.

28:30 Little is known about what the words **Urim and Thummim** meant (the Hebrew words are transliterated rather than translated), or how these objects worked. One suggested meaning is that "Urim" had to do with "light" and "Thummim" with "completion, perfection." Another possibility is that they are associated with words that mean "curse" and "innocence." They seem to have been familiar objects in the ancient context since there is no discussion about making or obtaining them. Their use included receiving direction from the Lord for decisions (Nm 27:18-21; 1Sm 28:5-6). For the high priest to carry into the presence of the Lord both the names of the tribes and items used in

rendering decisions presupposed the Lord's sovereignty in these quests for guidance. The priest promoted adherence to the covenant stipulations and rendered judgments under the Lord's supervision (Dt 33:8-10).

28:33-34 The colors, precious stones, fine materials and specialized workmanship, and certainly the bells that went into making the priest's clothing contributed to marking the high priest and drawing attention to his work and movements.

28:35 To wear the specified clothing would show that the priest recognized the sanctity of the holy place because of God's presence, just as Moses and the Israelites had to do at the burning bush and at Mount Sinai (3:5; 19:10-24).

28:36-37 The phrase **HOLY TO THE LORD** indicated ownership—"belonging to." The priest was marked as someone devoted to the Lord for service, representing the Israelites, who were likewise to be holy (19:5-6; 22:31; Lv 11:44-45). The same words are used to describe the Sabbath in Ex 31:15 where it is translated, "dedicated to the LORD" (cp. Ezr 8:28; Jr 2:2-3; Zch 14:20-21).

28:38 In place of and as representatives of the rest of the

The Turban

[36]"You are to make a pure gold medallion and engrave it, like the engraving of a seal:[a]

HOLY TO THE LORD.

[37]Fasten it to a cord of blue yarn so it can be placed on the turban; the medallion is to be on the front of the turban. [38]It will be on Aaron's forehead so that Aaron may bear the •guilt[b] connected with the holy offerings that the Israelites consecrate as all their holy gifts. It is always to be on his forehead, so that they may find acceptance with the LORD.

Other Priestly Garments

[39]"You are to weave the tunic from fine linen, make a turban of fine linen, and make an embroidered sash. [40]Make tunics, sashes, and headbands for Aaron's sons to give them glory and beauty.[c] [41]Put these on your brother Aaron and his sons; then anoint,[d] ordain,[A] and consecrate[e] them, so that they may serve Me as priests. [42]Make them linen undergarments[f] to cover their naked bodies; they must extend from the waist[B] to the thighs. [43]These must be worn by Aaron and his sons whenever they enter the tent of meeting or approach the altar to minister in the sanctuary area, so that they do not incur guilt[g] and die. This is to be a permanent statute[h] for Aaron and for his future descendants.

Instructions about Consecration

29 "This is what you are to do for them to consecrate them to serve Me as priests.

[a] 28:36 Lv 8:9; Zch 14:20
[b] 28:38 Lv 10:17; 22:16; Nm 18:1; Is 53:11; Ezk 4:4-6; Jn 1:29; Heb 9:28; 1Pt 2:24
[c] 28:40 Ex 39:41; Ezk 44:17-18
[d] 28:41 Ex 29:7; 30:30; 40:15; Lv 10:7
[e] Ex 29:9; Heb 7:28
[f] 28:42 Lv 6:10; 16:4; Ezk 44:18
[g] 28:43 Ex 20:26; Lv 5:1,17; 20:19
[h] Ex 27:21; Lv 17:7
[i] 29:2 Lv 2:4; 6:19-23
[j] 29:4 Ex 40:12; Lv 8:6; Heb 10:22
[k] 29:5 Ex 28:2,8; Lv 8:7
[l] 29:6; Ex 28:36-37; Lv 8:9
[m] 29:7 Ex 30:25; Lv 8:12; 10:7; 21:10; Nm 35:25
[n] 29:9 Ex 28:41; Nm 18:7
[o] 29:10 Lv 1:4; 8:14
[p] 29:12 Ex 27:2; Lv 8:15
[q] 29:13 Lv 3:3-4
[r] 29:14 Lv 4:11-12,21; Heb 13:11

Take a young bull and two unblemished rams, [2]with unleavened bread, unleavened cakes mixed with oil, and unleavened wafers coated with oil. Make them out of fine wheat flour,[i] [3]put them in a basket, and bring them in the basket, along with the bull and two rams. [4]Bring Aaron and his sons to the entrance to the tent of meeting and wash them with water.[j] [5]Then take the garments and clothe Aaron with the tunic, the robe for the •ephod, the ephod itself, and the breastpiece; fasten the ephod on him with its woven waistband.[k] [6]Put the turban on his head and place the holy diadem[l] on the turban. [7]Take the anointing oil, pour it on his head, and anoint[m] him. [8]You must also bring his sons and clothe them with tunics. [9]Tie the sashes on Aaron and his sons and fasten headbands on them. The priesthood is to be theirs by a permanent statute. This is the way you will ordain Aaron and[c] his sons.[n]

[10]"You are to bring the bull to the front of the tent of meeting, and Aaron and his sons must lay their hands on the bull's head.[o] [11]Slaughter the bull before the LORD at the entrance to the tent of meeting. [12]Take some of the bull's blood and apply it to the horns[p] of the altar with your finger; then pour out all the rest of the blood at the base of the altar. [13]Take all the fat[q] that covers the entrails, the fatty lobe of the liver, and the two kidneys with the fat on them, and burn them on the altar. [14]But burn up the bull's flesh, its hide, and its dung outside the camp;[r] it is a •sin offering.

[A]28:41 Lit anoint them, fill their hand   [B]28:42 Lit loins   [C]29:9 Lit you will fill the hand of Aaron and the hand of; Ex 29:23-24

Israelites, Aaron and his sons were responsible to care for the tabernacle and present offerings there (Nm 17:12–18:7). The high priest would **bear the guilt** (or suffer the consequences) associated with failure to observe the requirements of holiness (cp. v. 43). In that process the people needed a high priest marked by holiness to offer acceptable sacrifices to the Lord (Heb 7:25-28).

28:41 Ceremonial anointing involved pouring oil on a person to designate the start of a new role in life. Among those anointed were priests, kings, and prophets (30:30; Jdg 9:8; 1Sm 9:16; 1Kg 19:16). Objects also could be anointed to set them apart for holy uses (Ex 29:36; 40:9-11).

29:1 The word **unblemished** applies also to the **young bull** (Lv 22:19-21; Dt 17:1).

29:4-9 Leviticus 8 describes the ceremony enacted in the tabernacle. Much later in Israel's history, the prophet Zechariah looked forward to a time when the Lord would graciously restore His people and reclothe their high priest (Zch 2:10–3:5).

29:6 **Holy diadem** is another term for the engraved gold plate described in 28:36-37 (cp. 39:30).

29:7 Instructions for making the fragrant **anointing oil** appear in 30:22-25.

29:10 Aaron and his sons would associate themselves with **the bull** by putting their hands on it, transferring their guilt to receive atonement and forgiveness as the bull was offered up (Lv 4:4,15,24,29,33). The bull would be sacrificed as a substitute for the people; they must do likewise with two rams (Ex 29:15,19; cp. Lv 16:21; Nm 8:10; 27:18-23).

29:12-13 The use of **blood** reflects its significance as essential to life and to God's provision of a substitute whose life was lost on behalf of the worshiper (Lv 17:11). Certain portions of the animal's **fat** were to be burned as a way of offering what was best to the Lord. While the blood symbolized life, the fat symbolized abundance and was characteristic of an animal that had been well fed and cared for; it was considered the finest part (Gn 4:4; 45:18, "richness"; Ezk 34:3). The **kidneys** were associated with the inner life of a person, along with the heart (Ps 7:10; 73:21; Jr 17:10; 20:12). Perhaps separating the kidneys signified the examination and dedication of the offerer at that level.

29:14 The various kinds of **sin offering** and their circumstances are described in Lv 4:1–5:13. Sometimes called a purification offering, its purpose was to atone for sin or ceremonial uncleanness in order to restore communion. Most of the animal had to be burned **outside the camp** (cp. Heb 13:11-12).

¹⁵"Take one ram, and Aaron and his sons are to lay their hands on the ram's head.ᵃ ¹⁶You are to slaughter the ram, take its blood, and sprinkle it on all sides of the altar. ¹⁷Cut the ram into pieces. Wash its entrails and shanks, and place them with its head and its pieces on the altar. ¹⁸Then burn the whole ram on the altar; it is a •burnt offering to the Lᴏʀᴅ. It is a pleasing aroma,ᵇ a fire offering to the Lᴏʀᴅ.

¹⁹"You are to take the second ram, and Aaron and his sons must lay their hands on the ram's head.ᶜ ²⁰Slaughter the ram, take some of its blood, and put it on Aaron's right earlobe, on his sons' right earlobes, on the thumbs of their right hands, and on the big toes of their right feet. Sprinkle the remaining blood on all sides of the altar. ²¹Take some of the blood that is on the altar and some of the anointing oil,ᵈ and sprinkle them on Aaron and his garments, as well as on his sons and their garments. In this way, he and his garments will become holy, as well as his sons and their garments.

²²"Take the fat from the ram, the fat tail, the fat covering the entrails, the fatty lobe of the liver, the two kidneys and the fat on them, and the right thigh (since this is a ram for ordinationᴬ); ²³take one loaf of bread, one cake of bread made with oil, and one wafer from the basket of unleavened bread that is before the Lᴏʀᴅ; ²⁴and put all of them in the hands of Aaron and hisᴮ sons and wave them as a presentation offering before the Lᴏʀᴅ.ᵉ ²⁵Take them from their hands and burn them on the altar on top of the burnt offering, as a pleasing aroma before the Lᴏʀᴅ; it is a fire offering to the Lᴏʀᴅ.

²⁶"Take the breast from the ram of Aaron's ordination and wave it as a presentation offering before the Lᴏʀᴅ; it is to be your por-

tion.ᶠ ²⁷Consecrate for Aaron and his sonsᵍ the breast of the presentation offering that is waved and the thigh of the contribution that is lifted up from the ram of ordination. ²⁸This will belong to Aaron and his sons as a regular portion from the Israelites, for it is a contribution. It will be the Israelites' contribution from their •fellowship sacrifices, their contribution to the Lᴏʀᴅ.

²⁹"The holy garments that belong to Aaron are to belong to his sons after him, so that they can be anointed and ordainedᶜ in them.ʰ ³⁰Any priest who is one of his sons and who succeeds him and enters the tent of meeting to minister in the sanctuary must wear them for seven days.ⁱ

³¹"You are to take the ram of ordination and boil its flesh in a holy place. ³²Aaron and his sons are to eat the meat of the ram and the bread that is in the basket at the entrance to the tent of meeting.ʲ ³³They must eat those things by which •atonement was made at the time of their ordinationᴰ and consecration. An unauthorized person must not eatᵏ them, for these things are holy. ³⁴If any of the meat of ordination or any of the bread is left until morning, burn up what is left over. It must not be eaten because it is holy.

³⁵"This is what you are to do for Aaron and his sons based on all I have commanded you. Take seven days to ordain them. ³⁶Sacrifice a bull as a sin offering each day for atonement. Purifyᴱ the altar when you make atonement for it, and anoint it in order to consecrate it.ˡ ³⁷For seven days you must make atonement for the altar and consecrate it. The altar will become especially holy; whatever touches the altar will become holy.ᵐ

³⁸"This is what you are to offer regularly on the altar every day: two year-old lambs.ⁿ ³⁹In

ᵃ29:15 Lv 1:4; 8:18
ᵇ29:18 Gn 8:21; Ex 29:25
ᶜ29:19 Ex 29:3; Lv 8:22
ᵈ29:21 Ex 30:25,31; Heb 9:22
ᵉ29:23-24 Lv 7:30; 8:22
ᶠ29:26 Lv 7:3; 8:29
ᵍ29:27 Lv 7:31,34; Nm 18:11,18; Dt 18:3
ʰ29:29 Nm 18:8; 20:26,28
ⁱ29:30 Lv 8:35; Nm 20:28
ʲ29:31-32 Lv 8:31; Mt 12:4
ᵏ29:33 Lv 10:14-15,17; 22:10
ˡ29:36 Ex 40:10; Heb 10:11
ᵐ29:37 Ex 30:29; Mt 23:19
ⁿ29:38 Nm 28:3; 1Ch 16:40; Ezr 3:3; Dn 12:11

ᴬ29:22 The priest would normally receive the right thigh to be eaten, but here it is burned; Lv 7:32-34.   ᴮ29:24 Lit in the hands of his   ᶜ29:29 Lit him for anointing in them and for filling their hand   ᴰ29:33 Lit made to fill their hand   ᴱ29:36 Or Make a sin offering on

29:18 The first ram was given as a **burnt offering**. It went up in smoke as a gift in tribute to God by means of fire, making it **a fire offering**. That it would make **a pleasing aroma** signified God's acceptance of the offering and the worshiper (Lv 1).

29:20-21 No reason is given for placing **blood** on the **right earlobes . . . thumbs**, and **toes**. A person who came for ceremonial cleansing after recovering from a skin disease received the same treatment with both blood and oil (Lv 14:14-18). The outcome of the marking of both priests and garments was holiness; they would be clearly set apart for service to the Lord.

29:22-25 The sacrifice of the second **ram** is one of the "fellowship sacrifices" (Lv 3; 7:11-21). It celebrated communion with God with ceremonies including a shared meal. The ram's designation as **a ram for ordination** explains why the

right thigh was to be burned rather than eaten, as was normal for fellowship sacrifices. The words "ordination" and "ordain" reflect the idiomatic Hebrew expression that reads literally, "to fill the hand of someone." By placing items in the hands of Aaron and his sons and then waving and burning the items, Moses would act out the filling of the hands of the new priests. It would become their work to present to the Lord the offerings that the Israelites would bring.

29:26-28 **It is to be your portion** specifies that this time Moses would receive **the breast** because he was the officiating priest. On later occasions it would go to Aaron or his sons (Lv 7:34-36).

29:38-42 After the instructions for the seven-day consecration of Aaron and his sons and of the altar in verses 1-37, instructions for regular sacrifices to be offered on normal days are presented.

the morning offer one lamb, and at twilight
offer the other lamb.[a] 40 With the first lamb offer two quarts[A] of fine flour mixed with one
quart[B] of oil from crushed olives, and a •drink
offering of one quart[B] of wine. 41 You are to offer the second lamb at twilight. Offer a •grain
offering and a drink offering with it, like the
one in the morning, as a pleasing aroma, a fire
offering to the LORD. 42 This will be a regular
burnt offering throughout your generations
at the entrance to the tent of meeting before
the LORD, where I will meet you[C] to speak
with you.[b] 43 I will also meet with the Israelites there, and that place will be consecrated
by My glory.[c] 44 I will consecrate the tent of
meeting and the altar; I will also consecrate
Aaron and his sons to serve Me as priests. 45 I
will dwell[d] among the Israelites and be their
God.[e] 46 And they will know that I am •Yahweh
their God, who brought them out of the land
of Egypt, so that I might dwell among them. I
am Yahweh their God.[f]

The Incense Altar

30 "You are to make an altar for the
burning of incense; make it of acacia
wood.[g] 2 It must be square, 18 inches long and
18 inches wide;[D] it must be 36 inches high.[E]
Its horns must be of one piece.[F] 3 Overlay its
top, all around its sides, and its horns with
pure gold; make a gold molding all around it.
4 Make two gold rings for it under the molding on two of its sides; put these on opposite
sides of it to be holders for the poles to carry
it with. 5 Make the poles of acacia wood and
overlay them with gold.
6 "You are to place the altar in front of the
veil by the ark of the •testimony—in front
of the •mercy seat that is over the testimony—where I will meet with you. 7 Aaron must
burn fragrant incense on it; he must burn
it every morning when he tends the lamps.[h]
8 When Aaron sets up the lamps at twilight, he
must burn incense. There is to be an incense
offering before the LORD throughout your generations. 9 You must not offer unauthorized incense on it,[i] or a •burnt or •grain offering; you
are not to pour a •drink offering on it.
10 "Once a year Aaron is to perform the
purification rite[G] on the horns of the altar.
Throughout your generations he is to perform
the purification rite[G] for[H] it once a year, with
the blood of the •sin offering for •atonement.[j]
The altar is especially holy to the LORD."

The Atonement Money

11 The LORD spoke to Moses: 12 "When you
take a census[k] of the Israelites to register them,
each of the men must pay a ransom[l] for himself to the LORD as they are registered. Then no
plague[m] will come on them as they are registered. 13 Everyone who is registered must pay
half a •shekel[I] according to the sanctuary shekel (20 *gerahs* to the shekel). This half shekel is
a contribution to the LORD.[n] 14 Each man who is
registered, 20 years old or more, must give this
contribution to the LORD. 15 The wealthy may
not give more and the poor may not give less[o]
than half a shekel when giving the contribution to the LORD to atone for[J] your lives. 16 Take
the atonement money[K] from the Israelites and
use it for the service of the tent of meeting. It
will serve as a reminder for the Israelites before
the LORD to atone for[J] your lives."[p]

The Bronze Basin

17 The LORD spoke to Moses: 18 "Make a bronze
basin[q] for washing and a bronze stand for it. Set

[a] 29:39 1Kg 18:29,36; 2Kg 16:15; Ezr 9:4-5; Ps 141:2; Ezk 46:13-15
[b] 29:42 Ex 25:22; 30:8
[c] 29:43 1Kg 8:11; 2Ch 5:14; Ezk 43:5; Hg 2:7,9
[d] 29:45 Zch 2:10; Jn 14:17
[e] Ex 25:8; Lv 26:12
[f] 29:46 Ex 20:2
[g] 30:1 Ex 37:25; Rv 8:3
[h] 30:7 Ex 27:21; 1Sm 2:28; 1Ch 23:13; Lk 1:9
[i] 30:9 Lv 10:1
[j] 30:10 Lv 16:18
[k] 30:12 Nm 1:2; 2Sm 24:2
[l] Nm 31:50; Mt 20:28
[m] Ex 12:13; 2Sm 24:13,21,25
[n] 30:13 Ex 38:26; Nm 3:47; Mt 17:24
[o] 30:15 Pr 22:2; Eph 6:9
[p] 30:16 Ex 38:25-28; Nm 16:40
[q] 30:18 Ex 38:8; 40:7,30; 1Kg 7:38

[A] 29:40 Lit *offer a tenth* [B] 29:40 Lit *a fourth of a hin* [C] 29:42 = Moses [D] 30:2 Lit *one cubit its length and one cubit its width* [E] 30:2 Lit *wide; and two cubits its height* [F] 30:2 Lit *piece with it* [G] 30:10 Or *to make atonement* [H] 30:10 Or *on* [I] 30:13 About 2/5 of an ounce of silver [J] 30:15,16 Or *to ransom* [K] 30:16 Lit *the silver of the atonement*

29:43-46 The most important consecrations would be accomplished not by the Israelites but by the Lord. Their priests and ceremonies would have significance because of Yahweh's presence. The display of His **glory** would then extend from victory over Pharaoh (14:4,17-18) to provision for the Israelites in the wilderness (16:7,10), to making a covenant with them (24:16-17), and then to this tent they would build.

He would be with them to act on their behalf, as when He answered Moses' objections by promising to be with him (3:12; 4:12,15). In this place He would continue the pattern of action leading to knowledge of His identity: **They will know that I am Yahweh their God** (cp. 6:7; 7:17; 8:10,22; 9:14,29; 10:2; 11:7; 14:4,18; 16:6,12). This is the last and climactic divine statement in Exodus of God's revelatory purpose. But all this would be jeopardized by the Israelites' actions in chapter 32.

30:1 **Incense** is a picture of prayer (Ps 141:2; Rv 5:8; 8:3-4).

30:9 The other offerings mentioned were to be made outside the holy place, at the altar for burnt offerings.

30:10 To **perform the purification rite** (or "make atonement") involved putting blood on the horns of the incense altar on the Day of Atonement (Lv 16:16-20).

30:12-16 The motive for taking a **census** was typically military (Nm 1:2-3,20-45; Jdg 20:2,15-17). The need to **pay a ransom**, also called a **contribution**, of half a shekel each in order to avert a **plague** reminded everyone that the nation as a whole and its citizens belonged to the Lord. Their preservation depended ultimately on Him, not their military strength, wealth, or poverty (12:13; 15:26; 17:8-16; Nm 8:19).

30:13 At the time of Moses, a **shekel** was a measure of weight. Coins of various weights, including the shekel, came into being centuries later. Measuring **according to the sanctuary** may mean that this weight was different from the

it between the tent of meeting and the altar, and put water in it. ¹⁹Aaron and his sons must wash their hands and feet from the basin. ²⁰Whenever they enter the tent of meeting or approach the altar to minister by burning up an offering to the LORD, they must wash with water so that they will not die. ²¹They must wash their hands and feet so that they will not die; this is to be a permanent statute[a] for them, for Aaron and his descendants throughout their generations."

The Anointing Oil

²²The LORD spoke to Moses: ²³"Take for yourself the finest spices:[b] 12½ pounds[A] of liquid myrrh, half as much (6¼ pounds[B]) of fragrant cinnamon, 6¼ pounds[B] of fragrant cane, ²⁴12½ pounds[A] of cassia (by the sanctuary shekel), and one gallon[c] of olive oil.[c] ²⁵Prepare from these a holy anointing oil, a scented blend, the work of a perfumer; it will be holy anointing oil.[d]

²⁶"With it you are to anoint[e] the tent of meeting, the ark of the testimony, ²⁷the table with all its utensils, the lampstand with its utensils, the altar of incense, ²⁸the altar of burnt offering with all its utensils, and the basin with its stand. ²⁹Consecrate them and they will be especially holy. Whatever touches them will be consecrated. ³⁰Anoint Aaron and his sons and consecrate[f] them to serve Me as priests.

³¹"Tell the Israelites: This will be My holy anointing oil throughout your generations. ³²It must not be used for ordinary anointing on a person's body, and you must not make anything like it using its formula. It is holy, and it must be holy to you. ³³Anyone who blends something like it or puts some of it on an unauthorized person must be cut off[g] from his people."

The Sacred Incense

³⁴The LORD said to Moses: "Take fragrant spices: stacte, onycha, and galbanum; the

a 30:21 Ex 27:21; 28:43
b 30:23 Sg 4:14; Ezk 27:22
c 30:24 Ex 29:40; Ps 45:8
d 30:25 Ex 37:29; Nm 35:25
e 30:26 Ex 40:9; Lv 8:10; Nm 7:1
f 30:30 Ex 29:7; Lv 8:12,30
g 30:33 Gn 17:14; Ex 30:38
h 30:36 Ex 29:37; Lv 2:3
i 31:2 Ex 35:30; 36:1; 1Ch 2:20
j 31:3 Ex 35:31; 1Kg 7:14
k 31:7 Ex 36:8-38; 37:1-6
l 31:8-11 Ex 30:25,31,34; 37:10-29; 38:1,8; 39:1,41

spices and pure frankincense are to be in equal measures. ³⁵Prepare expertly blended incense from these; it is to be seasoned with salt, pure and holy. ³⁶Grind some of it into a fine powder and put some in front of the testimony in the tent of meeting, where I will meet with you. It must be especially holy[h] to you. ³⁷As for the incense you are making, you must not make any for yourselves using its formula. It is to be regarded by you as sacred to the LORD. ³⁸Anyone who makes something like it to smell its fragrance must be cut off from his people."

God's Provision of the Skilled Workers

31 The LORD also spoke to Moses: ²"Look, I have appointed by name Bezalel[i] son of Uri, son of Hur, of the tribe of Judah. ³I have filled him with God's Spirit, with wisdom, understanding, and ability in every craft[j] ⁴to design artistic works in gold, silver, and bronze, ⁵to cut gemstones for mounting, and to carve wood for work in every craft. ⁶I have also selected Oholiab[D] son of Ahisamach, of the tribe of Dan, to be with him. I have placed wisdom within every skilled craftsman[E] in order to make all that I have commanded you: ⁷the tent of meeting, the ark of the •testimony, the •mercy seat that is on top of it, and all the other furnishings of the tent[k]— ⁸the table with its utensils, the pure gold lampstand with all its utensils, the altar of incense, ⁹the altar of •burnt offering with all its utensils, the basin with its stand— ¹⁰the specially woven[F] garments, both the holy garments for Aaron the priest and the garments for his sons to serve as priests, ¹¹the anointing oil, and the fragrant incense for the sanctuary. They must make them according to all that I have commanded you."[l]

Observing the Sabbath

¹²The LORD said to Moses: ¹³"Tell the Israelites: You must observe My Sabbaths, for it is

A30:23,24 Lit 500 (shekels)   B30:23 Lit 250 (shekels)   C30:24 Lit a hin   D31:6 LXX, Syr read Eliab   E31:6 Lit every person skilled of heart   F31:10 Hb obscure

one commonly used in scales (Gn 23:16) or that the sanctuary was the center for a system of standardizing weights.

30:22-38 The oil and incense for the tabernacle required costly ingredients (some coming from a great distance) and expert knowledge to compound them properly. **Myrrh** came from the sap of a tree found in Arabia and Ethiopia. **Cinnamon** came from the bark of a tree grown in Ceylon and Malaysia. **Cassia** may have come from a type of tree bark. **Stacte** is a transliterated Greek term used for different varieties of tree and plant sap. **Onycha**, based on an Arabic word, may have come from a type of mollusk. **Galbanum** came from the sap of a plant grown in Afghanistan and Persia. **Frankincense** also came from sap and could be imported from Arabia or Ethiopia.

31:1-6 The Israelites would construct the tabernacle and its furnishings by using a wide variety of skills that the Lord had supplied to the builders. Their calling and enabling came from the Lord by His Spirit. The terms for **wisdom, understanding, and ability** appear also in Pr 2:6. Like other matters in Exodus, these abilities to make beautiful objects involved the person's "heart." **Every skilled craftsman** is more literally "everyone wise of heart," which helps in recognizing that "wise" and "wisdom" in Proverbs refer to skills for living in relationships with other people and with God, even as wisdom here shows itself as skills needed for building the tabernacle. The Lord provided what people needed to make things that would be valuable to Him and to other people. A fuller description appears in Ex 35:4–36:7.

a sign between Me and you throughout your generations, so that you will know that I am •Yahweh who sets you apart.[a] [14]Observe the Sabbath, for it is holy to you. Whoever profanes it must be put to death. If anyone does work on it, that person must be cut off from his people.[b] [15]Work may be done for six days, but on the seventh day there must be a Sabbath of complete rest,[c] dedicated to the LORD. Anyone who does work on the Sabbath day must be put to death. [16]The Israelites must observe the Sabbath, celebrating it throughout their generations as a perpetual covenant. [17]It is a sign forever between Me and the Israelites, for in six days the LORD made the heavens and the earth, but on the seventh day He rested and was refreshed."

The Two Stone Tablets

[18]When He finished speaking with Moses on Mount Sinai, He gave him the two tablets of the testimony, stone tablets inscribed by the finger of God.[d]

Cross references (center column)
[a] 31:13 Lv 19:3,30; Ezk 20:12,20
[b] 31:14 Nm 15:35
[c] 31:15 Gn 2:2; Ex 16:23; 20:9
[d] 31:18 Ex 24:12; 32:15-16; Dt 4:13; 5:22; 2Co 3:3
[e] 32:1 Ex 13:21; 24:18; Dt 9:9; Ac 7:40
[f] 32:2 Ex 35:22; Jdg 8:24-27
[g] 32:4 Dt 9:16; Jdg 17:3-4; 1Kg 12:28; Neh 9:18; Ps 106:19; Ac 7:41
[h] 32:5 Lv 23:2,37; 2Kg 10:20

The Gold Calf

32 When the people saw that Moses delayed in coming down from the mountain, they gathered around Aaron and said to him, "Come, make us a god[A] who will go before us because this Moses, the man who brought us up from the land of Egypt—we don't know what has happened to him!"[e] [2]Then Aaron replied to them, "Take off the gold rings[f] that are on the ears of your wives, your sons, and your daughters and bring them to me." [3]So all the people took off the gold rings that were on their ears and brought them to Aaron. [4]He took the gold from their hands, fashioned it with an engraving tool, and made it into an image of a calf.

Then they said, "Israel, this is your God,[B] who brought you up from the land of Egypt!"[g]

[5]When Aaron saw this, he built an altar before it; then he made an announcement: "There will be a festival[h] to the LORD tomorrow." [6]Early the next morning they arose, offered •burnt offerings, and presented •fellowship offerings.

[A]32:1 Or *us gods*   [B]32:4 Or *Israel, this is your god,* or *Israel, these are your gods*

31:12-13 Here again action leads to knowledge (see notes at 4:1-9; 6:2-8], but this time it is what the Israelites must do—**observe My Sabbaths**—that will lead to knowing the identity of the Lord and of themselves. The term translated **sets you apart** can also be translated "consecrates you" or "sanctifies you." The Israelites were to have a unique identity, distinct from other nations and closely associated with the Lord.

31:14-15 Anyone who **profaned** the Sabbath by working was in willful rebellion against the Lord. They refused to recognize His past provisions or to trust Him for present and future provisions.

31:16-17 To **observe the Sabbath** would be **a sign forever** of

shabbath

Hebrew Pronunciation	[shah BAT]
HCSB Translation	Sabbath
Uses in Exodus	15
Uses in the OT	111
Focus Passage	Exodus 31:13-16

Shabbath, related to the verb *shavath* ("cease, rest"], designates the day in the week when work must *cease*. There is no clear parallel for the *Sabbath* in surrounding cultures. God first mentioned *shabbath* shortly before giving the Mosaic law, as if to anticipate it (Ex 16:23-29). The *Sabbath* became the fourth and most elaborated of the Ten Commandments (Ex 20:8-11). God associated *shabbath* with His sanctification of the week's seventh day when He *ceased* His work of creation. He later gave His deliverance of Israel from Egyptian slavery as a motive for keeping the *Sabbath* (Dt 5:15). Even slaves and animals were to *rest* that day (Ex 20:10). The *Sabbath* was a sign of God's covenant with Israel, so that they might know He set them apart as holy (Ex 31:13). Consequently, the penalty for breaking the *Sabbath* was death (Ex 31:14). Related *shabbaton* (11x) means *complete rest* (Ex 31:15).

the covenant between the Lord and the Israelites, reminding them of the Lord's provision as the One who had **made the heavens and the earth** and as the One who had made Israel a new nation (16:24-30; 20:8-11). As part of their loyalty to the Lord, their Sovereign, the Israelites could participate in the rest that He enjoyed.

31:18 The **two tablets of the testimony** contained the Ten Commandments and were to be placed inside the ark in the most holy place in the tabernacle to remind the people of the covenant that the Israelites had promised to keep (25:16).

32:1 **When the people saw that Moses delayed in coming down** presents the situation from the viewpoint of the people. The preceding verse about the Lord having finished speaking and having given Moses the tablets, plus 24:14,18, indicates that their notion was mistaken. Moses could not have returned sooner; he had been summoned by the sovereign Lord and could leave only when dismissed. Their way of speaking about **this Moses, the man who brought us up from . . . Egypt**, gives insight into their ungrateful attitude. What they said was insulting to Moses and also to the Lord, since it ignored His involvement. It matched their earlier complaints (14:11-12; 16:2-3,6-8; 17:3). The assumption seems to be that Moses (not to mention Joshua) had abandoned them.

32:2-6 While Moses was viewing patterns and receiving detailed instructions about building the tabernacle and its furnishings, and about consecrating Aaron as priest of the Lord, Aaron made a golden calf, set up an altar, and began making sacrifices on it. To worship a calf fit well with both Egyptian and Canaanite practices, in which the calf was a symbol of strength and fertility.

32:5 Perhaps Aaron's declaration attempted to put a better face on the situation with a version of the theory that the end justified the means. But the **festival** could never be in honor of the Lord when the method it used defied Him.

The people sat down to eat and drink, then got up to play.ᵃ

⁷The LORD spoke to Moses: "Go down at once! For your people you brought up from the land of Egypt have acted corruptly.ᵇ ⁸They have quickly turned from the way I commanded them; they have made for themselves an image of a calf. They have bowed down to it, sacrificed to it, and said, 'Israel, this is your God,ᴬ who brought you up from the land of Egypt.'ᶜ ⁹The LORD also said to Moses: "I have seen this people, and they are indeed a stiff-neckedᵈ people. ¹⁰Now leave Me alone, so that My anger can burn against them and I can destroy them. Then I will make you into a great nation."ᵉ

¹¹But Moses interceded with the LORD his God: "LORD, why does Your anger burn against Your people You brought out of the land of Egypt with great power and a strong hand? ¹²Why should the Egyptians say, 'He brought them out with an evil intent to kill them in the mountains and wipe them off the face of the earth'? Turn from Your great anger and relent concerning this disaster planned for Your people.ᶠ ¹³Remember Your servants Abraham, Isaac, and Israel—You swore to them by Your very selfᵍ and declared, 'I will make your •offspring as numerous as the stars of the sky and will give your offspring all this land that I have promised, and they will inherit it forever.'ʰ ¹⁴So the LORD relentedⁱ concerning the disaster He said He would bring on His people.

¹⁵Then Moses turned and went down the mountain with the two tablets of the •testimony in his hands. They were inscribed on both sides—inscribed front and back. ¹⁶The tablets were the work of God, and the writing was God's writing, engraved on the tablets.ʲ

¹⁷When Joshua heard the sound of the people as they shouted, he said to Moses, "There is a sound of war in the camp."

¹⁸But Moses replied:

It's not the sound of a victory cry
and not the sound of a cry of defeat;
I hear the sound of singing!

¹⁹As he approached the camp and saw the calf and the dancing, Moses became enraged and threw the tablets out of his hands, smashing them at the base of the mountain. ²⁰Then he took the calf they had made, burned it up, and ground it to powder. He scattered the powder over the surface of the water and forced the Israelites to drink the water.

²¹Then Moses asked Aaron, "What did these people do to you that you have led them into such a grave sin?"

²²"Don't be enraged, my lord," Aaron replied. "You yourself know that the people are intent on evil.ᵏ ²³They said to me, 'Make us a godᴮ who will go before us because this Moses, the man who brought us up from the land of Egypt—we don't know what has happened to him!' ²⁴So I said to them, 'Whoever has gold, take it off,' and they gave it to me. When I threw it into the fire, out came this calf!"

ᵃ32:6 Nm 25:2; 1Co 10:7
ᵇ32:7 Gn 6:11-12; Dt 9:12
ᶜ32:8 Ex 20:3-4,23; 34:15; Dt 32:17; 1Kg 12:28
ᵈ32:9 Ex 33:3,5; 34:9; 2Ch 30:8; Is 48:4; Ac 7:51
ᵉ32:10 Ex 22:24; Nm 14:12; Dt 9:14
ᶠ32:11-12 Nm 14:13-16; Dt 9:18,26-29
ᵍ32:13 Gn 22:16-18; Heb 6:13
ʰGn 12:7; 13:15; 15:7,18; 26:4; 35:11-12
ⁱ32:14 2Sm 24:16; Ps 106:45
ʲ32:15-16 Ex 31:18; Dt 9:15
ᵏ32:19-22 Gn 20:9; 26:10; Ex 14:11; Dt 9:16-17,21

ᴬ32:8 Or *Israel, this is your god*, or *Israel, these are your gods*   ᴮ32:23 Or *us gods*

32:7 The word translated **acted corruptly** indicates total ruin, as in 8:24; Gn 6:12-13; 19:13; Jr 12:10; 13:7. The word "corrupt" describes something irrevocably spoiled in such a way that it is no longer of any use.

32:9-14 During the plagues against Egypt, Moses frequently prayed on behalf of Pharaoh and the Egyptians. Now Moses prayed for the Israelites (vv. 30-32; 33:12-16; 34:8-9). That the Lord told Moses about the situation and did not immediately destroy the Israelites left the door open for Moses to pray for them and for the Lord to relent (unlike Jr 15:1). As He would Himself proclaim, compassion, grace, and the capacity to forgive are among God's most prominent characteristics (Ex 34:6-7; cp. Jnh 3:9-10; 4:2). Earlier the Lord had needed to persuade Moses to accept His plans; now Moses uses the Lord's own words to persuade Him to have mercy on His people. This displayed the depth of the victory that the Lord had won in Moses' heart.

32:11-12 The same terms describe the anger of both the Lord and Moses (vv. 10-11,19,22). Moses agreed with the Lord's assessment that the Israelites were stubbornly rebellious ("stiff-necked," v. 9; 33:3,5; 34:9) and called what they had done "grave sin" (v. 31). "To what end? For what purpose?" is the point of both questions (cp. Gn 25:32; 27:45-46; Dt 5:24; Jdg 15:10; Ru 1:11).

32:15-16 This lengthy description of the **two tablets** reinforces their importance and underscores the statement Moses made by smashing them.

32:17 No one had told **Joshua** what was happening in the Israelite **camp**. His concerned but erroneous explanation conveyed how bad things had gotten. Even war would be better than what was happening. It also provides a brief glimpse into Joshua's character as an innocent man who cared about the people; he was unaware of the terrible events that had taken place.

32:20 Drinking **water** containing the ground-up golden **calf** meant that whatever was left of the calf would become nothing but human waste. Similarities exist between this action by Moses and the trial of a woman accused of adultery (Nm 5:11-31).

32:21-22 This attempt to deflect blame shows that Aaron knew that making the calf was wrong.

32:23-24 Aaron's account minimizes his participation by leaving out much of what he did and by describing the calf as a surprise.

32:25-29 The phrasing of Moses' order to **kill** was a forceful way to rule out sparing anyone based on a personal connection, no matter how close. The Levites must have

25 Moses saw that the people were out of control, for Aaron had let them get out of control, resulting in weakness before their enemies.A 26 And Moses stood at the camp's entrance and said, "Whoever is for the LORD, come to me." And all the Levites gathered around him. 27 He told them, "This is what the LORD, the God of Israel, says, 'Every man fasten his sword to his side; go back and forth through the camp from entrance to entrance, and each of you kill his brother, his friend, and his neighbor.'"a 28 The Levites did as Moses commanded, and about 3,000 men fell dead that day among the people. 29 Afterward Moses said, "Today you have been dedicatedB to the LORD, since each man went against his son and his brother. Therefore you have brought a blessing on yourselves today."b

30 The following day Moses said to the people, "You have committed a grave sin. Now I will go up to the LORD; perhaps I will be able to atone for your sin."c

31 So Moses returned to the LORD and said, "Oh, these people have committed a grave sin; they have made a god of gold for themselves.d 32 Now if You would only forgive their sin. But if not, please erase me from the book You have written."e

33 The LORD replied to Moses: "I will erase whoever has sinned against Me from My book.f 34 Now go, lead the people to the place I told you about; see, My angel will go before you. But on the day I settle accounts, I will hold them accountable for their sin."g 35 And the LORD inflicted a plague on the people for what they did with the calf Aaron had made.

The Tent Outside the Camp

33 The LORD spoke to Moses: "Go, leave here, you and the people you brought up from the land of Egypt, to the land I promised to Abraham, Isaac, and Jacob, saying: I will give it to your *offspring.h 2 I will send an angel ahead of you and will drive out the Canaanites, Amorites, Hittites, Perizzites,C Hivites, and Jebusites.i 3 Go up to a land flowing with milk and honey. But I will not go with you because you are a stiff-necked people; otherwise, I might destroy you on the way."j 4 When the people heard this bad news, they mourned and didn't put on their jewelry.k

5 For the LORD said to Moses: "Tell the Israelites: You are a stiff-necked people. If I went with you for a single moment, I would destroy you. Now take off your jewelry, and I will decide what to do with you." 6 So the Israelites remained stripped of their jewelry from Mount Horeb onward.

a32:27 Nm 25:5; Dt 33:9
b32:29 Nm 25:11-13; Zch 13:3
c32:30 1Sm 12:20; 2Sm 16:12
d32:31 Ex 20:23; Dt 9:18
e32:32 Ps 69:28; Dn 12:1; Rm 9:3; Php 4:3; Rv 3:5; 21:27
f32:33 Dt 29:20; Ps 9:5
g32:34 Dt 32:35; Rm 2:5-6
h33:1 Gn 12:7; Ex 32:7
i33:2 Ex 32:34; Jos 24:11
j33:3 Ex 3:8; 32:9; Nm 16:21,45
k33:4 Nm 14:39; Ezk 24:17,23

A32:25 Hb obscure; Or *resulting in derision*   B32:29 Text emended; MT reads *Today dedicate yourselves*; LXX, Vg read *Today you have dedicated yourselves*   C33:2 Sam, LXX add *Girgashites*

killed known leaders of the rebellion but not all of the participants, since later events show that not all guilty parties died at this point.

32:30-33 Throughout Scripture, it is clear that consequences for sin in general come in stages and with varying degrees of severity, giving people an opportunity to repent (cp. 2Pt 2:9). Moses knew that although the Israelites as a nation had not been destroyed (Ex 32:9-14), the matter of consequences from their sin with the golden calf was not yet settled. Perhaps Moses intended to offer himself as a substitute for the people since sacrifices were normally offered when people sought atonement (Lv 16:6,11,17,24; Ezk 45:17). In any case, by requesting to die if the people died, Moses identified himself with them and refused to be the start of a "great nation" to replace them (Ex 32:10). His reference to erasure from **the book You have written**, that lists those who were alive on earth, implies a comparison between God's actions and that of a person who kept and consulted written records, such as census lists used for collecting taxes or for military conscriptions (cp. Ezr 2:62; Ps 69:28; Jr 22:30; Ezk 13:9).

32:34 The **angel** was first mentioned in 3:2 and would be a topic of further discussion between the Lord and Moses (23:20,23; 32:34; 33:2).

33:1-5 The instruction to set out for the land promised to Israel, in terms similar to those used before the golden calf incident (13:21-22; 14:19), might suggest that all was well. The Lord even said that He would **drive out** the land's current inhabitants. He added, however, that He would not go

among the Israelites. This amounted to saying that there would be no use for the tabernacle to be built, since it was intended as the dwelling of the Lord among His people (29:45-46). Earlier the Israelites had questioned whether the Lord was among them (17:7), and now He assured them that He would not be.

33:6 The verb translated **stripped** recalls 3:22 and 12:36,

qasheh

Hebrew Pronunciation	[kah SHEH]
HCSB Translation	harsh, stiff, hard
Uses in Exodus	7
Uses in the OT	36
Focus Passages	Exodus 33:3,5

Qasheh describes *difficult* or *hard* labor (Ex 1:14; 6:9), *fierce* battles (2Sm 2:17), *harsh* masters (Is 19:4), and *severe* storms (Is 27:8). Eight times it indicates "*stiff-necked*" (Dt 9:6). *Qasheh* suggests *unrelenting* love (Sg 8:6), *troubling* visions (Is 21:2), *obstinate* ways (Jdg 2:19), and *broken* hearts (1Sm 1:15). Adverbially, it connotes *harshly* (Gn 42:30). Nominally, it is *hardship* or *bad news* (1Kg 14:6). *Qasheh* derives from *qashah* (30x), be *severe* (1Sm 5:7), *harsh* (2Sm 19:43), *difficult* (Dt 1:17), *cruel* (Gn 49:7), or a *hardship* (Dt 15:18). The passive participle connotes *dejected* (Is 8:21). Causative and intensive forms imply *harden* (Ex 7:3). The causative is *treat harshly* (Jb 39:16), *oppose* (Jb 9:4), *make stubborn* (Dt 2:30), or *stubbornly refuse* (Ex 13:15). To "*stiffen the neck*" (Neh 9:29) appears as *be stiff-necked* (Dt 10:16) or *become obstinate* (Jr 7:26). *Qeshiy* signifies *stubbornness* (Dt 9:27).

[7]Now Moses took a tent and set it up outside the camp, far away from the camp; he called it the tent of meeting. Anyone who wanted to consult the Lord would go to the tent of meeting that was outside the camp.[a] [8]Whenever Moses went out to the tent, all the people would stand up, each one at the door of his tent, and they would watch Moses until he entered the tent. [9]When Moses entered the tent, the pillar of cloud would come down and remain at the entrance to the tent, and the Lord would speak with Moses.[b] [10]As all the people saw the pillar of cloud remaining at the entrance to the tent, they would stand up, then bow in worship, each one at the door of his tent. [11]The Lord spoke with Moses face to face, just as a man speaks with his friend. Then Moses would return to the camp, but his assistant, the young man Joshua son of Nun, would not leave the inside of the tent.[c]

The Lord's Glory

[12]Moses said to the Lord, "Look, You have told me, 'Lead this people up,' but You have not let me know whom You will send with me. You said, 'I know you by name,[d] and you have also found favor in My sight.' [13]Now if I have indeed found favor in Your sight, please teach me Your ways,[e] and I will know You and find favor in Your sight. Now consider that this nation is Your people."[f]

[14]Then He replied, "My presence will go with you, and I will give you rest."[g]

[15]"If Your presence does not go," Moses responded to Him, "don't make us go up from here. [16]How will it be known that I and Your people have found favor in Your sight unless You go with us? I and Your people will be distinguished by this from all the other people on the face of the earth."[h]

[17]The Lord answered Moses, "I will do this very thing you have asked, for you have found favor in My sight, and I know you by name."

[18]Then Moses said, "Please, let me see Your glory."[i]

[19]He said, "I will cause all My goodness to pass in front of you, and I will proclaim the name •Yahweh before you. I will be gracious to whom I will be gracious, and I will have compassion on whom I will have compassion."[j] [20]But He answered, "You cannot see My face, for no one can see[k] Me and live." [21]The Lord said, "Here is a place near Me. You are

Cross References

a 33:7 Ex 29:42-43; Dt 4:29
b 33:9 Ex 13:21; 31:18; Ps 99:7
c 33:11 Ex 24:13; Nm 12:8; Dt 34:10
d 33:12 Ex 32:34; Jn 10:14-15; 2Tm 2:19
e 33:13 Ps 25:4; 86:11; 119:33
f Ex 34:9; Dt 9:26,29
g 33:14 Jos 21:44; 22:4; Is 63:9
h 33:16 Ex 34:10; Nm 14:14
i 33:18 Ex 33:20; 1Tm 6:16
j 33:19 Rm 9:15
k 33:20 Gn 32:30; Is 6:5

Notes

which use a form of the same Hebrew verb to speak of the Egyptians being "plundered" when they gave gold and silver items to the Israelites. The disobedience of the Israelites made them like the Egyptians in worship and now in the loss of their ornaments.

33:7-11 The tent **far away from the camp** contrasts with the splendid tabernacle that had been intended for the middle of the camp. At the same time, the tent's location kept open the possibility of further consideration on all sides without immediate danger to the Israelites. The description of the close access that Moses enjoyed provides a background for his further requests. Moses, more than anyone else, knew what the Israelites were in danger of losing.

33:12 Moses' polite objection, **You have not let me know whom You will send with me**, returns to issues that the Lord and Moses discussed at the beginning of Moses' mission. The Lord had assured Moses that He would go with him (3:12; 4:12,15; cp. 10:10). Now rather than asking the Lord to send whomever He wished, so long as it was someone else (4:13), Moses insisted that the Lord should go with him and with the Israelites as His people.

33:13 Throughout the conflict with Pharaoh, the events in the wilderness, and the explanation of the tabernacle, the Lord spoke of actions designed to make Himself known by revealing who He is. In addition, Moses' desire to **know** the Lord contrasts with Pharaoh's boast about not knowing the Lord and not listening to Him (5:2).

33:14 The phrase **I will give you rest** may be short for "rest from your enemies." It probably refers to security for the Israelites in their new land (Dt 3:20; 12:9-10; 25:19; Jos 1:13,15; 21:44; 22:4; 23:1; 2Sm 7:1,11). This continues the presentation of the Lord as the One who gave His people rest, both from danger and from labor (Ex 16:21-30; 20:8-

11; 23:10-12), by His presence and provision (Mt 11:28-29; 28:20; Heb 13:5).

33:15-16 Moses knew that the Israelites' entering and possessing the land of Canaan would not by itself set them apart from other nations. All the nations had land (Dt 2:5,9,19-22), but they did not have the covenant relationship with the Lord that He had initiated with the Israelites (Ex 3:9-10; 4:22-23; 19:4-6). Only if Yahweh went with them would the Israelites have a distinct identity as His special people. The word for **distinguished** or "make a distinction" is the relatively rare word the Lord had used earlier when He spoke about the identity of His people (8:22; 9:4; 11:7; cp. Ps 4:3).

33:17 The agreement—**I will do this very thing you have asked**—was a display of the Lord's **favor**, or grace, already extended to Moses, who was interceding for the Israelites on that basis rather than on the basis of their merits (vv. 12-13,16; cp. Dt 7:7; 9:4-6).

33:19 With these words regarding His grace and compassion, Yahweh tied the continued existence of Israel and of any individual within the nation to God's capacity for and right to show favor even to those who deserved disfavor. Moses himself had provoked the Lord's anger and had been in danger of dying, though not for the same reason (4:14,24-26; cp. 32:10-11); but Moses had also been shown the Lord's favor (33:12-13,17). The Lord's words about grace and compassion would have been encouraging in view of His earlier words, "On the day I settle accounts, I will hold them accountable for their sin" (32:34).

33:20-23 Scripture often speaks of the potential danger of an encounter with God (3:6; 24:9-11; Gn 28:12-17; 32:30; Nm 17:12-13; Jdg 6:22-24; 13:22; 2Sm 6:6-7; 1Kg 19:11-13; Ps 76:7; 103:3; Is 2:10; 6:1-5; cp. Jn 1:18; 14:8-9; 1Tm 6:16).

to stand on the rock, [22]and when My glory passes by, I will put you in the crevice of the rock and cover you with My hand until I have passed by.[a] [23]Then I will take My hand away, and you will see My back, but My face will not be seen."

New Stone Tablets

34 The Lord said to Moses, "Cut two stone tablets like the first ones, and I will write on them the words that were on the first tablets, which you broke.[b] [2]Be prepared by morning. Come up Mount Sinai in the morning and stand before Me on the mountaintop. [3]No one may go up with you; in fact, no one must be seen anywhere on the mountain. Even the flocks and herds are not to graze in front of that mountain."[c]

[4]Moses cut two stone tablets like the first ones. He got up early in the morning, and taking the two stone tablets in his hand, he climbed Mount Sinai, just as the Lord had commanded him.

[5]The Lord came down in a cloud, stood with him there, and proclaimed His name •Yahweh. [6]Then the Lord passed in front of him and proclaimed:

Yahweh—Yahweh is a compassionate and gracious God, slow to anger and rich in faithful love and truth,[d] [7]maintaining faithful love to a thousand generations, forgiving wrongdoing, rebellion, and sin.[e] But He will not leave the •guilty[f] unpunished, bringing the consequences of the fathers' wrongdoing on the children and grandchildren to the third and fourth generation.

[8]Moses immediately bowed down to the ground and worshiped. [9]Then he said, "My Lord, if I have indeed found favor in Your sight, my Lord, please go with us. Even though this is a stiff-necked people, forgive our wrongdoing and sin, and accept us as Your own possession."[g]

Covenant Obligations

[10]And the Lord responded: "Look, I am making a covenant. I will perform wonders in the presence of all your people[A] that have never been done[B] in all the earth or in any nation. All the people you live among will see the Lord's work, for what I am doing with you is awe-inspiring.[h] [11]Observe what I command you today. I am going to drive out before you the Amorites, Canaanites, Hittites, Perizzites, Hivites,[c] and Jebusites. [12]Be careful not to make a treaty with the inhabitants of the land that you are going to enter; otherwise, they will become a snare among you.[i] [13]Instead, you must tear down their altars, smash their sacred pillars, and chop down their •Asherah poles.[j] [14]You are never to bow down to another god because Yahweh, being jealous[k] by nature,[D] is a jealous God.

[15]"Do not make a treaty with the inhabitants of the land, or else when they prostitute themselves with their gods and sacrifice to their gods, they will invite you, and you will eat their sacrifices.[l] [16]Then you will take some of their daughters as brides for your sons. Their daughters will prostitute themselves with their gods and cause your sons to prostitute themselves with their gods.[m]

[17]"Do not make cast images[n] of gods for yourselves.

Cross references
a33:22 Ps 91:1,4; Is 2:21
b34:1 Ex 32:19; 34:28; Dt 10:2,4
c34:2-3 Ex 19:12-13,20-21
d34:6 Nm 14:18; Neh 9:17; Ps 86:15; 103:8; 108:4; Jl 2:13; Rm 2:4
e34:7 Ex 20:6; Ps 103:3; 130:4; Dn 9:9; 1Jn 1:9
fJos 24:19; Jb 10:14; Nah 1:3
g34:9 Ex 33:15-16; Ps 33:12; 94:14
h34:10 Dt 4:32; 5:2; Ps 77:14; 145:6
i34:11-12 Ex 23:32-33; 33:2
j34:13 Ex 23:24; Dt 12:3; 2Kg 18:4; 2Ch 34:3-4
k34:14 Ex 20:3,5; Dt 4:24
l34:15 Nm 25:2; Jdg 2:17; 1Co 8:4,7,10
m34:16 Dt 7:3; 1Kg 11:2,4; Ezr 9:2; Neh 13:25
n34:17 Ex 32:8; Lv 19:14

A34:10 Lit in all nations   B34:10 Lit created   C34:11 DSS, Sam, LXX add Girgashites   D34:14 Lit Yahweh—His name is Jealous, or Yahweh is jealous for His name, He

---

If a person survived the contact, it was because of the Lord's restraint, often in the form of a specific provision. The description of the Lord's provision for Moses presents Moses as so small and the Lord as so great that protecting Moses would be like the action of a man who could cover a little opening with his hand while walking past it. Of the Hebrew words for **hand**, the one used here refers to the palm of the hand (Ex 3:20; 5:21).

The contrast between seeing God's **face** and His **back** is figurative for full and partial revelation. "Face" is used as a way of referring to a person himself (vv. 14-15; Dt 4:37, "presence" = "face"; 2Sm 17:11, "personally" = "your face"), since the face displayed the attitudes of a person (Ps 102:2; Pr 16:15; 21:29).

34:6-7 Rather than providing a new visual description (in contrast with chaps. 3; 13-14; 19-20; 24), the account of the Lord's display of His glory this time offers His list of a series of invisible qualities. The Lord has the capacity to be **compassionate and gracious**, to be **slow to anger**, and to forgive, in addition to exacting punishment (cp. Nm

14:18; Neh 9:17; Ps 86:15; 103:6-14; 145:8; Jl 2:13-14; Jnh 4:2; Nah 1:3).

34:9 Nowhere in Moses' prayers for the Israelites did he point to their repentance or promise any improvement; their future would depend on the Lord's ongoing **favor**, forgiveness, and faithfulness.

34:14 The phrase translated **being jealous by nature** is (lit) "Yahweh jealous His name." It reflects the close connection between traits of character and the concept of name or reputation. It can also be rendered, "His name is Jealous" or "Yahweh is jealous for His name." It is a forceful assertion that the Lord zealously protects the integrity of His relationships (cp. 20:5; Dt 4:24; 5:9; 6:15; Jos 24:19; Nah 1:2).

34:15-16 The derogatory way of referring to pagan worship and to the Israelites' possible participation in it shows that it was wrong for both (Nm 25:1-13). The Lord was the only God who anyone ought to worship, but the Israelites were especially accountable to Him because of their covenant relationship with Him (Ex 34:10).

[18] "Observe the Festival of *Unleavened Bread. You are to eat unleavened bread for seven days at the appointed time in the month of Abib[A] as I commanded you. For you came out of Egypt in the month of Abib.[a]

[19] "The firstborn[b] male from every womb belongs to Me, including all your male[B,C] livestock, the firstborn of cattle or sheep. [20] You must redeem the firstborn of a donkey with a sheep, but if you do not redeem it, break its neck.[c] You must redeem all the firstborn of your sons. No one is to appear before Me empty-handed.

[21] "You are to labor six days but you must rest[d] on the seventh day; you must even rest during plowing and harvesting times.

[22] "Observe the Festival of Weeks with the *firstfruits of the wheat harvest, and the Festival of Ingathering[D] at the turn of the agricultural year. [23] Three times a year[e] all your males are to appear before the Lord God, the God of Israel. [24] For I will drive out nations[f] before you and enlarge your territory.[g] No one will covet your land when you go up three times a year to appear before the Lord your God.

[25] "Do not present[E] the blood for My sacrifice with anything leavened. The sacrifice of the *Passover Festival must not remain until morning.[h]

[26] "Bring the best firstfruits[i] of your land to the house of the Lord your God.

"You must not boil a young goat in its mother's milk."

[27] The Lord also said to Moses, "Write[j] down these words, for I have made a covenant with you and with Israel based on these words." [28] Moses was there with the Lord 40 days and 40 nights; he did not eat bread or drink water. He wrote the Ten Commandments,[k] the words of the covenant, on the tablets.

Moses' Radiant Face

[29] As Moses descended from Mount Sinai—with the two tablets of the *testimony in his hands as he descended the mountain—he

did not realize that the skin of his face shone as a result of his speaking with the Lord.[F,f] [30] When Aaron and all the Israelites saw Moses, the skin of his face shone![m] They were afraid to come near him. [31] But Moses called out to them, so Aaron and all the leaders of the community returned to him, and Moses spoke to them. [32] Afterward all the Israelites came near, and he commanded them to do everything the Lord had told him on Mount Sinai. [33] When Moses had finished speaking with them, he put a veil over his face. [34] But whenever Moses went before the Lord to speak with Him, he would remove the veil until he came out. After he came out, he would tell the Israelites what he had been commanded,[n] [35] and the Israelites would see that Moses' face[G] was radiant. Then Moses would put the veil over his face again until he went to speak with the Lord.

The Sabbath Command

35 Moses assembled the entire Israelite community and said to them, "These are the things that the Lord has commanded you to do:[o] [2] For six days work is to be done, but on the seventh day you are to have a holy day, a Sabbath[p] of complete rest to the Lord. Anyone who does work on it must be executed. [3] Do not light a fire in any of your homes on the Sabbath day."[q]

Building the Tabernacle

[4] Then Moses said to the entire Israelite community, "This is what the Lord has commanded: [5] Take[r] up an offering among you for the Lord. Let everyone whose heart is willing bring this as the Lord's offering: gold, silver, and bronze; [6] blue, purple, and scarlet yarn; fine linen and goat hair; [7] ram skins dyed red and manatee skins;[H] acacia wood; [8] oil for the light; spices for the anointing oil and for the fragrant incense; [9] and onyx with gemstones to mount on the *ephod and breastpiece.

[10] "Let all the skilled craftsmen[i] among you

[a] 34:18 Ex 12:15; 13:4
[b] 34:19 Ex 13:2; 22:29
[c] 34:20 Ex 13:13,15; 23:15; Dt 16:16
[d] 34:21 Ex 20:9; Lk 13:14
[e] 34:23 Ex 23:14
[f] 34:24 Ex 33:2; Ps 78:55
[g] Dt 12:20; 19:8
[h] 34:25 Ex 12:10; 23:18
[i] 34:26 Ex 23:19; Dt 26:2
[j] 34:27 Ex 17:14; 24:4
[k] 34:28 Ex 24:18; 31:18; Dt 4:13; 10:2,4
[l] 34:29 Ex 32:15
[m] 34:30 Ps 34:5; Mt 17:2; 2Co 3:7,13
[n] 34:34 Ex 24:3; 2Co 3:13-16
[o] 35:1 Ex 34:32
[p] 35:2 Ex 20:9; Lv 23:3
[q] 35:3 Ex 16:23
[r] 35:5-9 Ex 25:2-7

[A]34:18 March–April; called Nisan in the post-exilic period; Neh 2:1; Est 3:7 [B]34:19 LXX, Theod, Vg, Tg read *males* [C]34:19 Hb obscure [D]34:22 The Festival of Ingathering is called Festival of Booths elsewhere; Lv 23:34-36. [E]34:25 Lit *slaughter* [F]34:29 Lit *with Him* [G]34:35 Lit *see Moses' face, that the skin of his face* [H]35:7 Or *and dolphin skins,* or *and fine leather;* Hb obscure [I]35:10 Lit *the skilled of heart*

34:33-35 The **veil** that Moses put over his **face** was like the boundaries placed around Mount Sinai (19:21-22; 20:18-19), like the veil that hung between the holy place and the most holy place (26:31-33), and like the Lord's hand placed over the rocky crevice where Moses was hidden (33:20-23). All were gracious provisions to protect people from casual and deadly exposure to the glory of God. The shining (**Moses' face was radiant**) and the veil demonstrate the success of Moses' intercession; the Lord had agreed to go with the Israelites in such a gracious way that they could safely

see His glory among them, despite their stiff-necked frailty (cp. 2Co 3:13-14).

35:4-36:6 This section describes the preparation of materials and workers needed to build the tabernacle. The people who brought the prized and costly materials contributed them willingly (35:5,21-22,29; 36:2-3,5). They also worked willingly (35:26; 36:2), using God-given skills in design, execution, and teaching (35:30-36:2). They had both the will and the skills needed for the work that the Lord had commanded (35:4,10,28; 36:1,4; cp. Eph 2:8-10).

come and make everything that the LORD has commanded:[a] [11] the tabernacle—its tent and covering, its clasps and planks, its crossbars, its posts and bases; [12] the ark with its poles, the *mercy seat, and the veil for the screen; [13] the table with its poles, all its utensils, and the *bread of the Presence; [14] the lampstand for light with its utensils and lamps as well as the oil for the light; [15] the altar of incense with its poles; the anointing oil and the fragrant incense; the entryway screen for the entrance to the tabernacle; [16] the altar of *burnt offering with its bronze grate, its poles, and all its utensils; the basin with its stand; [17] the hangings of the courtyard, its posts and bases, and the screen for the gate of the courtyard; [18] the tent pegs for the tabernacle and the tent pegs for the courtyard, along with their ropes; [19] and the specially woven[A] garments for ministering in the sanctuary—the holy garments for Aaron the priest and the garments for his sons to serve as priests."[b]

[20] Then the entire Israelite community left Moses' presence. [21] Everyone whose heart was moved and whose spirit prompted him came and brought an offering to the LORD for the work on the tent of meeting, for all its services, and for the holy garments.[c] [22] Both men and women came; all who had willing hearts brought brooches, earrings, rings, necklaces, and all kinds of gold jewelry—everyone who waved a presentation offering of gold to the LORD. [23] Everyone who had in his possession blue, purple, or scarlet yarn,[d] fine linen or goat hair, ram skins dyed red or manatee skins,[B] brought them. [24] Everyone making an offering

of silver or bronze brought it as a contribution to the LORD. Everyone who possessed acacia wood useful for any task in the work brought it. [25] Every skilled[c] woman[e] spun yarn with her hands and brought it: blue, purple, and scarlet yarn, and fine linen. [26] And all the women whose hearts were moved spun the goat hair by virtue of their skill. [27] The leaders[f] brought onyx and gemstones to mount on the ephod and breastpiece, [28] as well as the spice[g] and oil for the light, for the anointing oil, and for the fragrant incense. [29] So the Israelites brought a freewill offering to the LORD, all the men and women whose hearts prompted them to bring something for all the work that the LORD, through Moses, had commanded to be done.[h]

Bezalel and Oholiab

[30] Moses[i] then said to the Israelites: "Look, the LORD has appointed by name Bezalel son of Uri, son of Hur, of the tribe of Judah. [31] He has filled him with God's Spirit, with wisdom, understanding, and ability in every kind of craft [32] to design artistic works in gold, silver, and bronze, [33] to cut gemstones for mounting, and to carve wood for work in every kind of artistic craft. [34] He has also given both him and Oholiab son of Ahisamach, of the tribe of Dan, the ability to teach others. [35] He has filled them with skill[D] to do all the work[j] of a gem cutter; a designer; an embroiderer in blue, purple, and scarlet yarn and fine linen; and a weaver. They can do every kind of craft and design artistic designs. [1] Bezalel, Oholiab, and all the skilled[c] people are to work based on everything the LORD has commanded. The LORD

36

[a]35:10 Ex 31:6
[b]35:11-19 Ex 24:5-6; 25:10,23,30-31; 26:1-2; 27:1,9; 30:1,25,34; 31:10; 39:1,41; Lv 24:5-6; Nm 4:5
[c]35:21 Ex 36:2
[d]35:23 1Ch 29:8
[e]35:25 Ex 28:3
[f]35:27 1Ch 29:6; Ezr 2:68
[g]35:28 Ex 30:23
[h]35:29 Ex 35:21; 36:3; 1Ch 29:9
[i]35:30-34 Ex 31:1-6; 2Ch 2:14
[j]35:35 Ex 31:3,6; 1Kg 7:14

[A]35:19 Hb obscure   [B]35:23 Or *or dolphin skins,* or *or fine leather;* Hb obscure   [C]35:25; 36:1 Lit *wise of heart*   [D]35:35 Lit *with wisdom of heart*

At the start of Exodus the Israelites were oppressed slaves forced to make mud bricks and build cities to suit Pharaoh. He considered the Israelites to be seditious and lazy, so he refused to supply enough straw for their work. Now the Israelites could willingly participate in building a structure for the glory of God for which He had provided the necessary materials and even skills for the workers.

35:31 Because the Lord had called Bezalel and **filled him with God's Spirit,** he would be able to do with excellence what the Lord had commanded (Nm 11:17; Dt 34:9; Jdg 3:10; 6:14-16,34).

35:34–36:1 The **ability to teach others** attributed to Bezalel and Oholiab is described as both a matter of the "heart" and a work of God in them. The idiomatic Hebrew expression says, "And He has put in his heart to teach," referring first to Bezalel, who is mentioned before Oholiab. Moses added that the Lord had **filled them with skill.** He further described Bezalel, Oholiab, and the other workers—all those who were "wise/skillful of heart"—as people "in whom the Lord has put wisdom/skill and understanding." This is why

chashav

Hebrew Pronunciation	[khah SHAV]
HCSB Translation	plan, consider, design
Uses in Exodus	13
Uses in the OT	124
Focus Passages	Exodus 35:32,35

Chashav is *think* (Ps 40:17), *consider* (Ps 77:5), or *intend* (1Sm 18:25), then *plan* (Jr 18:8) or *devise* (Mc 2:3). It is *credit* (Gn 15:6), *charge with* (Ps 32:2), *value,* or *regard* (Is 53:3-4). People *invent* (Am 6:5), *contrive* (Ps 35:20), or *design* (Ex 31:4). The participle denotes *designer* (Ex 38:23). Passives include *be counted* (Ps 44:22), *considered* (Neh 13:13), *regarded* (Gn 31:15), *credited* (Lv 7:18), or *classified* (Lv 25:31). Intensives signify *calculate* (Lv 25:27), *require an accounting* (2Kg 12:15), *plot* (Hs 7:15), *scheme* (Pr 24:8), or *threaten* (Jnh 1:4). The reflexive is *consider oneself* (Nm 23:9). The related noun *machashavah* occurs with *chashav* 18 times as *make plots* (Dn 11:25), *execute designs* (2Ch 2:14), *devise plans* (Ezk 38:10) or *strategies* (Jr 49:20), and *skillfully designed* (2Ch 26:15). *Machashavah* is also *scheme* (Gn 6:5), *thought* (Is 55:7), *purpose* (Jr 51:29), and *artistic* (Ex 35:33).

has given them wisdom and understanding to know how to do all the work of constructing the sanctuary."[a]

[2] So Moses summoned Bezalel, Oholiab, and every skilled[A] person in whose heart the LORD had placed wisdom, everyone whose heart moved him,[b] to come to the work and do it. [3] They took from Moses' presence all the contributions that the Israelites had brought for the task of making the sanctuary. Meanwhile, the people continued to bring freewill offerings morning after morning.

[4] Then all the craftsmen who were doing all the work for the sanctuary came one by one from the work they were doing [5] and said to Moses, "The people are bringing more than is needed[c] for the construction of the work the LORD commanded to be done."

[6] After Moses gave an order, they sent a proclamation throughout the camp: "Let no man or woman make anything else as an offering for the sanctuary." So the people stopped. [7] The materials were sufficient for them to do all the work. There was more than enough.

Building the Tabernacle

[8] All[d] the skilled craftsmen[B] among those doing the work made the tabernacle with 10 curtains. Bezalel made them of finely spun linen, as well as blue, purple, and scarlet yarn, with a design of *cherubim worked into them. [9] The length of each curtain was 42 feet,[C] and the width of each curtain six feet;[D] all the curtains had the same measurements. [10] He joined five of the curtains to each other, and the other five curtains he joined to each other. [11] He made loops of blue yarn on the edge of the last curtain in the first set and did the same on the edge of the outermost curtain in the second set. [12] He made 50 loops on the one curtain and 50 loops on the edge of the curtain in the second set, so that the loops lined up with each other. [13] He also made 50 gold clasps and joined the curtains to each other, so that the tabernacle became a single unit.

[14] He made curtains of goat hair for a tent over the tabernacle; he made 11 of them. [15] The length of each curtain was 45 feet,[E] and the width of each curtain six feet.[D] All 11 curtains had the same measurements. [16] He joined five of the curtains together, and the other six together. [17] He made 50 loops on the edge of the outermost curtain in the first set and 50 loops on the edge of the corresponding curtain in the second set. [18] He made 50 bronze clasps to join the tent together as a single unit. [19] He also made a covering for the tent from ram skins dyed red and a covering of manatee skins[F] on top of it.

[20] He[e] made upright planks[G] of acacia wood for the tabernacle. [21] The length of each plank was 15 feet,[H] and the width of each was 27 inches.[I] [22] There were two tenons connected to each other for each plank. He did the same for all the planks of the tabernacle. [23] He made planks for the tabernacle as follows: 20 for the south side, [24] and he made 40 silver bases to put under the 20 planks, two bases under the first plank for its two tenons, and two bases under each of the following planks for their two tenons; [25] for the second side of the tabernacle, the north side, he made 20 planks, [26] with their 40 silver bases, two bases under the first plank and two bases under each of the following ones; [27] and for the west side of the tabernacle he made six planks. [28] He also made two additional planks for the two back corners of the tabernacle. [29] They were paired at the bottom and joined together[J] at the[K] top in a single ring. This is what he did with both of them for the two corners. [30] So there were eight planks with their 16 silver bases, two bases under each one.

[31] He made five crossbars of acacia wood for the planks on one side of the tabernacle, [32] five crossbars for the planks on the other side of the tabernacle, and five crossbars for those at the back of the tabernacle on the west. [33] He made the central crossbar run through the middle of the planks from one end to the other. [34] He overlaid them with gold and made their

---

[a] 36:1 Ex 25:8; 28:3; 31:6; 35:10,35
[b] 36:2 Ex 25:2; 35:21,26; 1Ch 29:5
[c] 36:5 2Ch 31:10; 2Co 8:2-3
[d] 36:8-19 Ex 26:1-14
[e] 36:20-34 Ex 25:5; 26:15-29

[A] 36:2 Lit wise of heart [B] 36:8 Lit the wise of heart [C] 36:9 Lit 28 cubits [D] 36:9,15 Lit four cubits [E] 36:15 Lit 30 cubits [F] 36:19 Or of dolphin skins, or of fine leather; Hb obscure [G] 36:20 Or made frames [H] 36:21 Lit 10 cubits [I] 36:21 Lit a cubit and a half [J] 36:29 Lit and together they are to be complete [K] 36:29 Lit its

---

they would **know how to do all the work of constructing the sanctuary**.

36:2 This verse, with verse 1 and 35:35, speaks of the Lord providing wisdom and skill to those who would build the tabernacle. The **heart**, or inner core, of a person was spoken of as central to both willingness and skillfulness to do **work** in service to the Lord, even as it was spoken of as central to Pharaoh's rebellion.

36:7 In Egypt, the Israelites lacked straw for making bricks

for Pharaoh (5:6-18). Now, thanks to the Lord's action on their behalf, **there was more than enough** of the silver, gold, and other beautiful materials that they would use to build a dwelling for the Lord.

36:8–40:33 Repeating the Lord's instructions to Moses in describing the construction of the tabernacle emphasized the people's commitment to making everything according to the Lord's specifications and completing the work as He commanded (see note at 25:1–31:17).

rings out of gold as holders for the crossbars. He also overlaid the crossbars with gold.

³⁵Then*ᵃ* he made the veil with blue, purple, and scarlet yarn, and finely spun linen. He made it with a design of cherubim worked into it. ³⁶He made four posts of acacia wood for it and overlaid them with gold; their hooks were of gold. And he cast four silver bases for the posts.

³⁷He made a screen embroidered with blue, purple, and scarlet yarn, and finely spun linen for the entrance to the tent, ³⁸together with its five posts and their hooks. He overlaid the tops of the posts and their bands with gold, but their five bases were bronze.

Making the Ark

37 Bezalel*ᵇ* made the ark of acacia wood, 45 inches long, 27 inches wide, and 27 inches high.ᴬ ²He overlaid it with pure gold inside and out and made a gold molding all around it. ³He cast four gold rings for it, for its four feet, two rings on one side and two rings on the other side. ⁴He made poles of acacia wood and overlaid them with gold. ⁵He inserted the poles into the rings on the sides of the ark for carrying the ark.

⁶He made a •mercy seat of pure gold, 45 inches long and 27 inches wide.ᴮ ⁷He made two •cherubim of gold; he made them of hammered work at the two ends of the mercy seat, ⁸one cherub at one end and one cherub at the other end. At each end, he made a cherub of one piece with the mercy seat. ⁹They had wings spread out. They faced each other and covered the mercy seat with their wings. The faces of the cherubim were looking toward the mercy seat.

Making the Table

¹⁰He*ᶜ* constructed the table of acacia wood, 36 inches long, 18 inches wide, and 27 inches high.ᶜ ¹¹He overlaid it with pure gold and made a gold molding all around it. ¹²He made a three-inchᴰ frame all around it and made a gold molding all around its frame. ¹³He cast four gold rings for it and attached the rings to the four corners at its four legs. ¹⁴The rings were next to the frame as holders for the poles to carry the table. ¹⁵He made the poles for carrying the table from acacia wood and overlaid them with gold. ¹⁶He also made the utensils that would be on the table out of pure gold: its

*ᵃ*36:35-38 Ex 26:31-37
*ᵇ*37:1-9 Ex 25:10-20
*ᶜ*37:10-16 Ex 25:23-29
*ᵈ*37:17-24 Ex 25:31-39
*ᵉ*37:25-28 Ex 30:1-5
*ᶠ*37:29 Ex 30:23-24,34-35
*ᵍ*38:1-7 Ex 27:1-8

plates and cups, as well as its bowls and pitchers for pouring •drink offerings.

Making the Lampstand

¹⁷Then*ᵈ* he made the lampstand out of pure hammered gold. He made it all of one piece: its base and shaft, its ornamental cups, and its calyxesᴱ and petals. ¹⁸Six branches extended from its sides, three branches of the lampstand from one side and three branches of the lampstand from the other side. ¹⁹There were three cups shaped like almond blossoms, each with a calyx and petals, on the first branch, and three cups shaped like almond blossoms, each with a calyx and petals, on the next branch. It was this way for the six branches that extended from the lampstand. ²⁰On the lampstand shaft there were four cups shaped like almond blossoms with its calyxes and petals. ²¹For the six branches that extended from it, a calyx was under the first pair of branches from it, a calyx under the second pair of branches from it, and a calyx under the third pair of branches from it. ²²Their calyxes and branches were of one piece.ᶠ All of it was a single hammered piece of pure gold. ²³He also made its seven lamps, snuffers, and firepans of pure gold. ²⁴He made it and all its utensils of 75 poundsᴳ of pure gold.

Making the Altar of Incense

²⁵He*ᵉ* made the altar of incense out of acacia wood. It was square, 18 inches long and 18 inches wide; it was 36 inches high.ᴴ Its horns were of one piece.ᶠ ²⁶He overlaid it, its top, all around its sides, and its horns with pure gold. Then he made a gold molding all around it. ²⁷He made two gold rings for it under the molding on two of its sides; he put these on opposite sides of it to be holders for the poles to carry it with. ²⁸He made the poles of acacia wood and overlaid them with gold.

²⁹He also made the holy anointing oil and the pure, fragrant, and expertly blended incense.*ᶠ*

Making the Altar of Burnt Offering

38 Bezalel*ᵍ* constructed the altar of •burnt offering from acacia wood. It was square, 7¹/₂ feet long and 7¹/₂ feet wide,ᴵ and was 4¹/₂ feetᴶ high. ²He made horns for it on its four corners; the horns were of one piece.ᶠ Then he overlaid it with bronze.

³He made all the altar's utensils: the pots,

ᴬ37:1 Lit *two and a half cubits its length, one and a half cubits its width, and one and a half cubits its height*   ᴮ37:6 Lit *two and a half cubits its length and one and a half cubits its width*   ᶜ37:10 Lit *two cubits its length, one cubit its width, and one and a half cubits its height*   ᴰ37:12 Lit *a handbreadth*   ᴱ37:17 = the outer covering of a flower   ᶠ37:22,25; 38:2 Lit *piece with it*   ᴳ37:24 Lit *a talent*   ᴴ37:25 Lit *a cubit its length, a cubit its width, and two cubits its height*   ᴵ38:1 Lit *five cubits its length and five cubits its width*   ᴶ38:1 Lit *three cubits*

shovels, basins, meat forks, and firepans; he made all its utensils of bronze. [4] He constructed for the altar a grate of bronze mesh under its ledge,[A] halfway up from the bottom. [5] At the four corners of the bronze grate he cast four rings as holders for the poles. [6] Also, he made the poles of acacia wood and overlaid them with bronze. [7] Then he inserted the poles into the rings on the sides of the altar in order to carry it with them. He constructed the altar with boards so that it was hollow.

Making the Bronze Basin

[8] He made the bronze basin and its stand from the bronze mirrors of the women who served at the entrance to the tent of meeting.[a]

Making the Courtyard

[9] Then[b] he made the courtyard. The hangings on the south side of the courtyard were of finely spun linen, 150 feet in length,[B] [10] including their 20 posts and 20 bronze bases. The hooks and bands[c] of the posts were silver. [11] The hangings on the north side were also 150 feet in length,[B] including their 20 posts and 20 bronze bases. The hooks and bands[c] of the posts were silver. [12] The hangings on the west side were 75 feet in length,[D] including their 10 posts and 10 bases. The hooks and bands of the posts were silver. [13] The hangings on the east toward the sunrise were also 75 feet in length.[D] [14] The hangings on one side of the gate were 22½ feet,[E] including their three posts and three bases. [15] It was the same for the other side. The hangings were 22½ feet,[E] including their three posts and three bases on both sides of the courtyard gate. [16] All the hangings around the courtyard were of finely spun linen. [17] The bases for the posts were bronze; the hooks and bands[c] of the posts were silver; and the plating for the tops of the posts was silver. All the posts of the courtyard were banded with silver.

[18] The screen for the gate of the courtyard

[a]38:8 Ex 30:18; 1Sm 2:22
[b]38:9-20 Ex 27:9-19
[c]38:21 Nm 1:50,53; 9:15; 10:11; 17:7-8; 2Ch 24:6; Ac 7:44
[d]Nm 4:28,33
[e]38:24 Ex 30:13; Lv 27:25; Nm 3:47; 18:16
[f]38:26-27 Ex 26:19,21,25,32; 30:13; Nm 1:46

was embroidered with blue, purple, and scarlet yarn, and finely spun linen. It was 30 feet[F] long, and like the hangings of the courtyard, 7½ feet[G] high.[H] [19] It had four posts, including their four bronze bases. Their hooks were silver, and the bands[c] as well as the plating of their tops were silver. [20] All the tent pegs for the tabernacle and for the surrounding courtyard were bronze.

Inventory of Materials

[21] This is the inventory for the tabernacle, the tabernacle of the *testimony,[c] that was recorded at Moses' command. It was the work of the Levites under the direction of[I] Ithamar son of Aaron the priest.[d] [22] Bezalel son of Uri, son of Hur, of the tribe of Judah, made everything that the LORD commanded Moses. [23] With him was Oholiab son of Ahisamach, of the tribe of Dan, a gem cutter, a designer, and an embroiderer with blue, purple, and scarlet yarn, and fine linen.

[24] All the gold of the presentation offering that was used for the project in all the work on the sanctuary, was 2,193 pounds,[J] according to the sanctuary *shekel.[e] [25] The silver from those of the community who were registered was 7,544 pounds,[K] according to the sanctuary shekel— [26] ⅖ of an ounce[L] per man, that is, half a shekel according to the sanctuary shekel, from everyone 20 years old or more who had crossed over to the registered group, 603,550 men. [27] There were 7,500 pounds[M] of silver used to cast the bases of the sanctuary and the bases of the veil—100 bases from 7,500 pounds,[M] 75 pounds[N] for each base.[f] [28] With the remaining 44 pounds[o] he made the hooks for the posts, overlaid their tops, and supplied bands[c] for them.

[29] The bronze of the presentation offering totaled 5,310 pounds.[P] [30] He made with it the bases for the entrance to the tent of meeting, the bronze altar and its bronze grate, all the utensils for the altar, [31] the bases for the surrounding courtyard, the bases for the gate of

[A]38:4 Or rim   [B]38:9,11 Lit 100 cubits   [C]38:10,11,17,19,28 Or connecting rods   [D]38:12,13 Lit 50 cubits   [E]38:14,15 Lit 15 cubits   [F]38:18 Lit 20 cubits   [G]38:18 Lit five cubits   [H]38:18 Lit high in width   [I]38:21 Lit Levites by the hand of   [J]38:24 Lit 29 talents and 730 shekels   [K]38:25 Lit 100 talents and 1,775 shekels   [L]38:26 Lit a beka   [M]38:27 Lit 100 talents   [N]38:27 Lit one talent   [O]38:28 Lit 1,775 (shekels)   [P]38:29 Lit 70 talents and 2,400 shekels

38:8 Since the instructions for the tabernacle do not refer to **the women who served at the entrance to the tent of meeting**, little is known about them beyond this mention (cp. 1Sm 2:22-25). The Hebrew verb that describes their service is somewhat rare; a related noun and this verb also describe service by Levites at the tabernacle (Nm 4:23; 8:24). Its connections with military service give it overtones of organization and service in the sense of being "on duty" (2Kg 25:19). A letter written in the mid-fourteenth century B.C. indirectly shows the value of this donation; the letter

mentions a shipment of mirrors from Egypt to the king of Babylon.

38:21 **The inventory** was appropriate even when supplies were plentiful. It promoted order, showed concern for conservation rather than waste or theft, and let people know what had been accomplished with their offerings. Similar accountings are known from Egyptian records.

38:26 Each man moved from one group to another when he had paid his **half a shekel** (30:11-16).

the courtyard, all the tent pegs for the tabernacle, and all the tent pegs for the surrounding courtyard.

Making the Priestly Garments

39 They made specially woven[A] garments for ministry in the sanctuary, and the holy garments for Aaron from the blue, purple, and scarlet yarn, just as the LORD had commanded Moses.[a]

Making the Ephod

[2] Bezalel[b] made the *ephod of gold, of blue, purple, and scarlet yarn, and of finely spun linen. [3] They hammered out thin sheets of gold, and he[B] cut threads from them to interweave with the blue, purple, and scarlet yarn, and the fine linen in a skillful design. [4] They made shoulder pieces for attaching it; it was joined together at its two edges. [5] The artistically woven waistband that was on the ephod was of one piece with the ephod, according to the same workmanship of gold, of blue, purple, and scarlet yarn, and of finely spun linen, just as the LORD had commanded Moses.

[6] Then they mounted the onyx stones surrounded with gold filigree settings, engraved with the names of Israel's sons as a gem cutter engraves a seal. [7] He fastened them on the shoulder pieces of the ephod as memorial stones for the Israelites, just as the LORD had commanded Moses.

Making the Breastpiece

[8] He[c] also made the embroidered breastpiece with the same workmanship as the ephod of gold, of blue, purple, and scarlet yarn, and of finely spun linen. [9] They made the breastpiece square and folded double, nine inches long and nine inches wide.[C] [10] They mounted four rows of gemstones[D] on it. The first row was a row of carnelian, topaz, and emerald;[E] [11] the second row, a turquoise,[F] a sapphire,[G] and a diamond;[H] [12] the third row, a jacinth,[A] an agate, and an amethyst; [13] and the fourth row, a beryl, an onyx, and a jasper. They were surrounded with gold filigree in their settings. [14] The 12 stones corresponded to the names of Israel's sons. Each stone was engraved like a seal with one of the names of the 12 tribes.

[a]39:1 Ex 28:2,4; 31:10; 35:19,23; 39:41
[b]39:2-7 Ex 28:6-12
[c]39:8-21 Ex 28:15-28
[d]39:22-26 Ex 28:31-34
[e]39:28 Ex 28:39,42; Ezk 44:18

[15] They made braided chains of pure gold cord for the breastpiece. [16] They also fashioned two gold filigree settings and two gold rings and attached the two rings to its two corners. [17] Then they attached the two gold cords to the two gold rings on the corners of the breastpiece. [18] They attached the other ends of the two cords to the two filigree settings and, in this way, attached them to the ephod's shoulder pieces in front. [19] They made two other gold rings and put them at the two other corners of the breastpiece on the edge that is next to the inner border of the ephod. [20] They made two more gold rings and attached them to the bottom of the ephod's two shoulder pieces on its front, close to its seam,[I] above the ephod's woven waistband. [21] Then they tied the breastpiece from its rings to the rings of the ephod with a cord of blue yarn, so that the breastpiece was above the ephod's waistband and did not come loose from the ephod. They did just as the LORD had commanded Moses.

Making the Robe

[22] They[d] made the woven robe of the ephod entirely of blue yarn. [23] There was an opening in the center of the robe like that of body armor[K] with a collar around the opening so that it would not tear. [24] They made pomegranates of finely spun blue, purple, and scarlet yarn[J] on the lower hem of the robe. [25] They made bells of pure gold and attached the bells between the pomegranates, all around the hem of the robe between the pomegranates, [26] a bell and a pomegranate alternating all around the lower hem of the robe[K] to be worn for ministry. They made it just as the LORD had commanded Moses.

The Other Priestly Garments

[27] They made the tunics of fine woven linen for Aaron and his sons. [28] They also made the turban and the ornate headbands[L] of fine linen, the undergarments,[e] [29] and the sash of finely spun linen of embroidered blue, purple, and scarlet yarn. They did just as the LORD had commanded Moses.

Making the Holy Diadem

[30] They also made a medallion, the holy

A39:1,12,23 Hb obscure   B39:3 Sam, Syr, Tg read *they*   C39:9 Lit *a span its length and a span its width*   D39:10 Many of these stones cannot be identified with certainty.   E39:10 Or *beryl*   F39:11 Or *malachite, or garnet*   G39:11 Or *lapis lazuli*   H39:11 Hb uncertain; LXX, Vg read *jasper*   I39:20 The place where the shoulder pieces join the front of the ephod   J39:24 Sam, LXX, Vg add *and linen*   K39:26 Lit *bell and pomegranate, bell and pomegranate, on the hem of the robe around*   L39:28 Lit *and the headdresses of headbands*

39:30-31 As the final item in the record of construction (in contrast to its position toward the middle of the record of building instructions listed earlier), the inscription of the high priest's headdress serves as a kind of finishing label for everything the artisans had made, all marked as belonging to the Lord.

diadem, out of pure gold and wrote on it an inscription like the engraving on a seal:[a]

HOLY TO THE LORD.

[31] Then they attached a cord of blue yarn to it in order to mount it on the turban, just as the LORD had commanded Moses.

Moses' Inspection of the Tabernacle

[32] So all the work for the tabernacle, the tent of meeting, was finished. The Israelites did everything just as the LORD had commanded Moses.[b] [33] Then they brought the tabernacle to Moses: the tent with all its furnishings, its clasps, its planks, its crossbars, and its posts and bases; [34] the covering of ram skins dyed red and the covering of manatee skins;[A] the veil for the screen; [35] the ark of the *testimony with its poles and the *mercy seat; [36] the table, all its utensils, and the *bread of the Presence; [37] the pure gold lampstand, with its lamps arranged and all its utensils, as well as the oil for the light; [38] the gold altar; the anointing oil; the fragrant incense; the screen for the entrance to the tent; [39] the bronze altar with its bronze grate, its poles, and all its utensils; the basin with its stand; [40] the hangings of the courtyard, its posts and bases, the screen for the gate of the courtyard, its ropes and tent pegs, and all the equipment for the service of the tabernacle, the tent of meeting; [41] and the specially woven[B] garments for ministering in the sanctuary, the holy garments for Aaron the priest and the garments for his sons

to serve as priests. [42] The Israelites had done all the work according to everything the LORD had commanded Moses.[c] [43] Moses inspected all the work they had accomplished. They had done just as the LORD commanded. Then Moses blessed them.[d]

Setting up the Tabernacle

40 The LORD spoke to Moses: [2] "You are to set up the tabernacle, the tent of meeting, on the first day of the first month.[C,e] [3] Put the ark[f] of the *testimony there and screen off the ark with the veil. [4] Then bring in the table and lay out its arrangement; also bring in the lampstand and set up its lamps. [5] Place the gold altar for incense in front of the ark of the testimony. Put up the screen for the entrance to the tabernacle. [6] Position the altar of burnt offering in front of the entrance to the tabernacle, the tent of meeting. [7] Place the basin[g] between the tent of meeting and the altar, and put water in it. [8] Assemble the surrounding courtyard and hang the screen for the gate of the courtyard.

[9] "Take the anointing oil and anoint[h] the tabernacle and everything in it; consecrate it along with all its furnishings so that it will be holy. [10] Anoint the altar of burnt offering and all its utensils; consecrate the altar so that it will be especially holy. [11] Anoint the basin and its stand and consecrate it.

[12] "Then bring Aaron and his sons to the entrance to the tent of meeting and wash them with water.[i] [13] Clothe Aaron with the holy garments,[j] anoint him, and consecrate him, so

[a]39:30 Ex 28:36-37; 29:6
[b]39:32 Ex 25:40; 39:42-43
[c]39:33-42 Ex 25:31; 27:9-15; 30:3; 35:10
[d]39:43 Lv 9:22-23; Nm 6:23-27; Jos 22:6; 2Sm 6:18; 1Kg 8:14; 2Ch 30:27
[e]40:2 Ex 12:12; 13:4; 26:30
[f]40:3 Ex 26:33; 40:21; Nm 4:5
[g]40:7 Ex 30:18; 40:30
[h]40:9 Ex 30:26; Lv 8:10
[i]40:12 Lv 8:1-3
[j]40:13 Ex 28:41

39:32-43 Several terms and concepts here, especially in verse 43, recall the completion of creation. Both the Lord and Moses completed **work**, saw **all the work they had accomplished**, and pronounced a blessing (Gn 1:22,28,31; 2:1-2; 5:2). Earlier in Exodus, Pharaoh begged for a blessing from Moses (12:32). Now the workers who had built the tabernacle received his blessing, as had the Levites who showed loyalty to the Lord (32:29; cp. 20:24; 23:25).

39:38 The **gold altar** was the altar for incense (30:1-5).

39:39 The **bronze altar** was the altar for burnt offerings (27:1-6).

40:2 **The first day of the first month**, in other words New Year's day, was appropriate for inaugurating use of the new structure. Since the Israelites had left Egypt at the middle of the first month of the year (12:1-11), the tabernacle was to be erected two weeks before the first anniversary of their exodus, at the start of the month that marked the beginning of their second year of freedom (40:17), and nine months after their arrival at Mount Sinai (19:1).

40:12-15 A full description of installing Aaron and his sons as priests appears in Leviticus 8–9.

mizbeach

Hebrew Pronunciation	[miz BAY akh]
HCSB Translation	altar
Uses in Exodus	59
Uses in the OT	403
Focus Passages	Exodus 40:5-6,10,26,29-30,32-33

Mizbeach is related to the verb *zavach* ("sacrifice") and the noun *zevach* ("sacrifice"). Use of *altars* to present sacrifices to God is as ancient as Noah (Gn 8:20). Abraham, Isaac, and Jacob built *altars* at places where God manifested Himself to them in some way. Exodus 20:24-26 gives instructions for building "an earthen *altar* for Me . . . in every place where I cause My name to be remembered." Forbidden is the use of cutting tools on a stone *altar*, and steps are also disallowed. The tabernacle and sanctuary had more elaborate *altars* of two types. The outdoor sacrificial *altar* was large and bronze-plated. It probably required a ramp to mount and there were horns at its four corners. The indoor incense *altar* was small and gold-plated. Ezekiel pictures an indoor *altar* that was made of wood (Ezk 41:22). At least one biblical *altar* is purely memorial (Jos 22:21-29). The tabernacle and sanctuary *altars* were portable.

that he can serve Me as a priest. ¹⁴Have his sons come forward and clothe them in tunics. ¹⁵Anoint them just as you anointed their father, so that they may also serve Me as priests. Their anointing will serve to inaugurate a permanent priesthood for them throughout their generations."ᵃ

¹⁶Moses did everything just as the Lord had commanded him. ¹⁷The tabernacle was set up in the first month of the second year, on the first day of the month.ᴬ,ᵇ ¹⁸Moses set up the tabernacle: he laid its bases, positioned its planks, inserted its crossbars, and set up its posts. ¹⁹Then he spread the tent over the tabernacle and put the covering of the tent on top of it, just as the Lord had commanded Moses.

²⁰Moses took the testimonyᶜ and placed it in the ark, and attached the poles to the ark. He set the •mercy seat on top of the ark. ²¹He brought the ark into the tabernacle, put up the veil for the screen, and screened off the ark of the testimony, just as the Lord had commanded him.

²²Moses placed the table in the tent of meeting on the north side of the tabernacle, outside the veil. ²³He arranged the bread on it before the Lord, just as the Lord had commanded him. ²⁴He also put the lampstand in the tent of meeting opposite the table on the south side of the tabernacle ²⁵and set up the lamps before the Lord, just as the Lord had commanded him.

²⁶Moses also installed the gold altar in the tent of meeting, in front of the veil, ²⁷and burned fragrant incense on it, just as the Lord

had commanded him. ²⁸He put up the screen at the entrance to the tabernacle. ²⁹Then he placed the altar of burnt offering at the entrance to the tabernacle, the tent of meeting, and offered the •burnt offering and the •grain offering on it, just as the Lord had commanded him.

³⁰He set the basin between the tent of meeting and the altar and put water in it for washing. ³¹Moses, Aaron, and his sons washed their hands and feet from it. ³²They washed whenever they came to the tent of meeting and approached the altar, just as the Lord had commanded Moses.

³³Next Moses set up the surrounding courtyard for the tabernacle and the altar and hung a screen for the gate of the courtyard. So Moses finished the work.ᵈ

The Lord's Glory

³⁴The cloud covered the tent of meeting, and the glory of the Lord filled the tabernacle.ᵉ ³⁵Moses was unable to enter the tent of meeting because the cloud rested on it, and the glory of the Lord filled the tabernacle.

³⁶The Israelites set out whenever the cloud was taken up from the tabernacle throughout all the stages of their journey.ᶠ ³⁷If the cloud was not taken up, they did not set out until the day it was taken up.ᵍ ³⁸For the cloud of the Lord was over the tabernacle by day, and there was a fire inside the cloud by night, visible to the entire house of Israel throughout all the stages of their journey.

ᵃ40:15 Ex 29:9; Nm 25:13
ᵇ40:17 Ex 40:2; Nm 7:1
ᶜ40:20 Ex 16:34; 25:16
ᵈ40:21-33 Ex 25:37; 26:33,35-36; 27:9,16; 29:38; 30:5-7,19-20; 40:1-7
ᵉ40:34 Lv 16:2; Nm 9:15; 1Kg 8:10-11; 2Ch 5:13-14; 7:2; Is 6:4; Hg 2:7,9; Rv 15:8
ᶠ40:36 Nm 9:17; Neh 9:19
ᵍ40:37 Nm 9:19-22

ᴬ40:17 DSS, Sam, LXX add *of their coming out of Egypt*

40:17 The **first month of the second year** refers to the start of the Israelites' second year after they had left Egypt.

40:34-35 This visible display, in the form of a **cloud**, showed that the Lord was consecrating the tabernacle by His presence, as He had promised (25:8; 29:44-46). What He had described to Moses before the Israelites made the golden calf was taking place on the basis of the Lord's character and Moses' intercession. The Lord was revealing Himself to His redeemed people at this meeting place (1Kg 8:10-

11,56-60; 9:3; Mt 17:1-8; Mk 9:2-8; Lk 9:28-36; Jn 1:14,18; 2Co 3:18; 4:6; Eph 1:17-18; Rv 21:3).

40:36-38 Exodus ends with a summary of what was ahead. The Lord guided the Israelites on **their journey** by means of the movement of the **cloud**, as He had done before their sin with the golden calf. Now the cloud that the Israelites had seen above Mount Sinai was associated with the **tabernacle**, a portable dwelling place for the Lord. He would dwell among His covenant people on their way to the land that He had promised them.

Leviticus

The book's name comes from the Septuagint (the Greek translation of the Old Testament): "relating to the Levites." This third section of the Pentateuch deals primarily with the duties of the priests and the service of the tabernacle, but it contains other laws as well. Leviticus gives us regulations for worship, laws on ceremonial cleanness, moral laws, and holy days.

Jebel Musa, on the Arabian Peninsula, is the traditional location of Mount Sinai, where God delivered the Ten Commandments to Moses.

Circumstances of Writing

Author: Although the book of Leviticus is technically anonymous, the evidence from the Bible and from Jewish and Christian traditions attributes it to the lawgiver, Moses (cp. 18:5 with Rm 10:5). Moses was the chief recipient of God's revelation in the book of Leviticus (1:1; 4:1). Elsewhere, Moses is said to have written down revelation that he received (Ex 24:4; 34:28; Mk 10:4-5; 12:19; Jn 1:45; 5:46). The author of Leviticus was someone well acquainted with the events in the book, and he was knowledgeable of the Sinai Wilderness, making him most likely a firsthand witness.

Background: About one year passed from the time Israel arrived at Sinai until they departed (Ex 19:1; Nm 10:11). During that time, Moses received the covenant from the Lord, erected the tabernacle (Ex 40:17), and received all the instructions in Leviticus and in the early chapters of Numbers. This block of material is the continuous narrative extending from Exodus 19 through Leviticus to Numbers 10:11. Since these events occurred in just one year and yet received the largest amount of space in the books from Exodus through Deuteronomy, Moses showed the special importance of the Sinai revelation to the writing of the Pentateuch. The repeated expression "The LORD spoke to Moses" throughout Leviticus leaves no doubt that its instructions were of divine origin, not the creation of Moses (Lv 1:1; 27:1).

Message and Purpose

The message and purpose of Leviticus must be studied in the context of the redemption of Israel from Egypt (Ex 12), the covenant made with Israel (Ex 20–24), and the building of the tent of meeting, or the tabernacle (Ex 25–40). The Lord dwelt among Israel symbolically in the tent of meeting, which stood in the center of the camp's tribal arrangement. In order for the Lord to reside with Israel, it was imperative that the people maintain a holy character and ethical behavior (Lv 11:44-45; 19:2; Dt 23:14; 1Pt 1:15-16). The decrees in Leviticus instructed the people in regulating this holy relationship through atonement and ritual cleansing. The sacrifices, the ordination of the holy priests, the purity laws, and the code for holy living made the benevolence of

---

1550 B.C.

1500 B.C.

Moses 1526–1406

Aaron 1529–1409?

Hyksos rule Egypt **1710–1570**

Egyptians find a way to create lubricants that last and do not burn off. **1500**

18th Dynasty of Egypt **1570–1303**
(includes Thutmose and Amenhotep; traditionally the pharaohs of oppression)

Clay tablet map of the Babylonian city of Nippur **1500**

Battle of Megiddo between Egyptian forces of Pharaoh Thutmose III and a Kadesh alliance, reestablishing Egyptian hegemony in the Levant **1479**

Queen Makare Hatshepsut, daughter of Thutmose I, reigned in Egypt during a period of peace and prosperity. **1479–1457**

the Lord a reality through the forgiveness of sin and ceremonial purification. The purpose of Leviticus was to instruct Israel in holiness so that the Lord might abide among them and bless them. Five key words capture the message of Leviticus:

Holiness: The chief idea in Leviticus is the holiness of God. The priests were to teach the people to differentiate "between the holy and the common, and the clean and the unclean" (10:10). "Holy" describes special persons (priests), places (tents), or things (offerings) that are captivated by or share in God's holy presence. Thus the holiness of everything and everyone is contingent upon the Holy One who alone is inherently holy. Anything that compromises this exclusive relationship profanes (treats as common) the person or thing and thereby offends God, who is apart and "who sets . . . apart" (makes holy; 22:16).

Clean: "Clean" and "unclean" are ritual terms that pertain to physical substances. Any item that was a departure from its normal state was unclean. This included certain foods, skin diseases, bodily emissions, and contamination. Consequently, rites of purgation ("cleansing") were a feature of daily life and a constant reminder of the inadequacy of the people to maintain their relationship with God apart from His provision.

Sacrifice: The sacrifices were holy gifts presented to the Lord. They also made atonement and provided stipends for the priests and communal meals. The three voluntary offerings were the burnt, grain, and fellowship sacrifices; the required offerings were the sin and restitution offerings. Special, additional instructions for sacrifices applied to special events.

Atonement: The term "to atone, make atonement" (Hb *kipper*) means "to reconcile two estranged parties"; theologically, God is the aggrieved party and must be appeased by the offender (26:14-45). The Lord provided the means by which the affront could be remedied and forgiven (4:20; 19:22). Genuine remorse and confession of sin were required (5:5; 16:21; 26:40-42), not just ritual performance (Hs 6:6; Mc 6:8; Mt 9:13).

Priests: The Lord appointed only Aaron and his sons as priests to serve in His house (8:30; cp. Ex 28:1,41);

1400 B.C.   1350 B.C.

Joshua 1490?–1380?

The exodus and defeat of Pharaoh at the Red Sea. 1446

Passover instituted 1446

God's covenant at Sinai 1446

Tabernacle built and dedicated 1445

Events in Leviticus 1445

Exploration of Canaan by 12 spies 1445

Musical notation, Ugarit 1400

Water clocks invented 1400

Bronze hand mirrors taken from Egypt by Hebrew women 1446

the Levites were the priests' assistants in caring for the tabernacle (Nm 8:13,19,22). It was the priest who made atonement on the guilty person's behalf (Lv 4:20) as well as for himself (16:6,24). Their role of protecting the holiness of God, the sanctity of the tent, and the Israelite people is illustrated by the intercessory action of Aaron, who "stood between the dead and the living" (Nm 16:48).

Contribution to the Bible

Leviticus is often neglected because Christians have misunderstood its message and purpose. This was not true of Jesus, who designated "love your neighbor as yourself" (19:18) as the second greatest commandment (Mt 22:39). The apostle Paul considered these words the summation of the Mosaic commandments (Rm 13:9; Gl 5:14; cp. Jms 2:8). The writer of Hebrews relied on the images of Leviticus in describing the person and role of Jesus Christ: sacrifice, the priesthood, and the Day of Atonement (Heb 4:14–10:18). Studying Leviticus gives us a deeper devotion to Jesus Christ, a stronger worship of God, and a better understanding of daily Christian living.

Structure

Leviticus is primarily a collection of laws, with a little historical narrative. The laws contained in Leviticus can be divided into two groups. First are the commands, or apodictic law. These are both positive commands ("You must . . .") and negative commands ("You must not . . ."). The second type of law is casuistic law. These are case laws using an example of what to do if such-and-such happened ("If a man . . ."). Some scholars seek to divide the laws further into civil laws, moral laws, and ceremonial laws, but there is no evidence that the Israelites made such a distinction.

Outline

I. Laws on Sacrifices and the Priesthood (1:1–7:38)
   A. Instructions on different offerings (1:1–6:7)
   B. Regulations for the priests (6:8–7:38)

II. Ordination and Ministry of the Priests (8:1–10:20)
   A. Consecration of Aaron (8:1-36)
   B. Dedication of the tabernacle (9:1-24)
   C. Warning about immoral priests (10:1-20)

III. Laws on Purity (11:1–16:34)
   A. Clean and unclean animals (11:1-47)
   B. Purification for uncleanness (12:1–15:33)
   C. Regulations for the Day of Atonement (16:1-34)

IV. God's Requirements for Holiness (17:1–27:34)
   A. Reverence for blood (17:1-16)
   B. Obedience to the Lord's commands (18:1–22:33)
   C. Appropriate worship (23:1–26:46)
   D. Making and keeping vows (27:1-34)

The Burnt Offering

1 Then the LORD summoned Moses[a] and spoke to him from the tent of meeting:[b] [2]"Speak to the Israelites and tell them: When any of you brings an offering to the LORD from the livestock, you[A] may bring your offering from the herd or the flock.

[3]"If his gift is a •burnt offering[c] from the herd, he is to bring an unblemished male.[d] He must bring it to the entrance to the tent of meeting so that he[B] may be accepted by the LORD.[e] [4]He is to lay his hand on[f] the head of the burnt offering so it can be accepted[g] on his behalf to make •atonement for him.[h] [5]He is to slaughter the bull before the LORD; Aaron's sons the priests[i] are to present the blood[j] and sprinkle it[k] on all sides of the altar that is at the entrance to the tent of meeting. [6]Then he must skin the burnt offering[l] and cut it into pieces.[C] [7]The sons of Aaron the priest will prepare a fire on the altar and arrange wood on the fire. [8]Aaron's sons the priests are to arrange the pieces, the head, and the suet[m] on top of the burning wood on the altar. [9]The offerer must wash its entrails[n] and shanks[o] with water. Then the priest will burn all of it on the altar as a burnt offering, a fire offering[p] of a pleasing aroma[q] to the LORD.

[10]"But if his gift for a burnt offering is from the flock, from sheep or goats,[r] he is to present an unblemished male. [11]He will slaughter it on the north side of the altar before the

Cross references

[a] 1:1 Ps 77:20; Mt 8:4; Heb 3:2
[b] Ex 27:21
[c] 1:3 Gn 22:2; Lv 3:5
[d] Ex 29:1
[e] Lv 19:5; Heb 9:14; 1Pt 1:19
[f] 1:4 Ex 29:10; Lv 3:2; 8:14,18,22; 16:21; Nm 8:10,12
[g] Gn 33:10; Lv 7:18; 19:7; 22:23,25,27
[h] Ex 30:15
[i] 1:5 Lv 4:16
[j] Heb 9:12
[k] Ex 24:6; 29:16,20
[l] 1:6 Lv 7:8; 9:11; 2Ch 29:34
[m] 1:8 Lv 1:12; 8:20
[n] 1:9 Ex 12:9; 29:13,22;
[o] Ex 12:9; 29:17; Lv 1:13; 4:11; 8:21; 9:14; Am 3:12
[p] Dt 18:1
[q] Lv 2:2; 23:13
[r] 1:10 Lv 4:23
Lv 1:13; 3:3

A 1:2 Or LORD, from the livestock you   **B** 1:3 Or it   **C** 1:6 Lit its pieces

---

1:1 The **tent of meeting** refers to the tabernacle tent erected under Moses' supervision at Sinai (Ex 40), not the temporary tent used only for communication (Ex 33:7). Moses must have stood outside the tent (Ex 40:34-35), although later he with Aaron would enter once again (Lv 9:23). The period from the building of the structure to the departure from Sinai was about 48 days (Ex 40:2; Nm 10:11), which included all the events of Leviticus and the preparations for departure in Nm 1:1–10:10.

1:2 Brings (Hb *qarav*) **an offering** (Hb *qorban*) is technical jargon describing any gift presented to the Lord ("Corban" in Mk 7:11). **Livestock** (Hb *behemah*) is the general term for domesticated cattle and sheep, as distinguished from the birds (v. 14).

1:3 The **burnt offering** (Hb *'olah*) is the first of the five regular offerings: burnt, grain, fellowship, sin, and restitution. The first three offerings were voluntary gifts and the last two were required. The burnt offering was for the general (nonspecific) sinfulness of the offerer. The term *'olah* means "an ascending" (Hb *'alah*; "to ascend"), referring probably to the rising smoke of the burning animal. The burnt offering was also known as the "whole burnt offering" because it was totally consumed on the altar (v. 9), except the hide (7:8), expressing the person's total dedication to God. Since it was so commonly associated with the altar of sacrifice, the altar itself was sometimes called "the altar of burnt offering" (4:7).

    He . . . he refers to the layman, not the priests, who are identified as "Aaron's sons" (vv. 5,7,11). The **unblemished male** from cattle was considered culturally as the most valued and thus appropriate as the most costly offering made to God (22:22-24; Mal 1:13-14; 1Pt 1:19). **He may be accepted** can also be translated "it may be accepted," indicating the animal, not the offerer (see NIV, NLT, NJB). "Accepted" (Hb *ratson*) means divine favor, indicating that the person received forgiveness (v. 4).

1:4 By laying **his hand on the head**, the layperson symbolically transferred guilt or identified with the fate of the victim (16:21). The result was **to make atonement** (Hb *kapper*), which meant appeasement (propitiation) with God (Gn 32:20) by removing (expiation) sin and impurities (Day of Atonement, Lv 16:30; 23:28; "propitiation," Rm 3:25; Heb 9:25).

1:5 The offerer himself slit the bull's throat (2Kg 10:7; Tal-

mud), and the priest sprinkled the **blood . . . on all sides of the altar**, signifying that the animal's life belonged to God. **Before the LORD** identified multiple locations: the entrance to the courtyard (4:4,14), the altar area inside the courtyard (4:18), the curtain inside the tent that separated the holy place from the most holy place where the altar of incense stood (4:6-7), and the furniture in the holy place (24:3,6).

1:6 The skinning provided the gift of the hide for the priest (7:8).

1:9 Washing the internal organs and **shanks** (lower back legs) removed filth, making the sacrifice ritually fit for God. A **fire offering** is the traditional translation, but it may be generally "a food offering." **Pleasing aroma** is a frequent expression meaning the Lord accepted the gift (vv. 13,17; Gn 8:21; Ex 29:18); fragrant incense (Ex 30:7; Lv 4:7; 16:12) explains the agreeable smell that masked the odor of the burning corpse. The Greek translation of the OT *(osme euodias)* also describes the sacrifice of Christ (Eph 5:2) and Christian giving (Php 4:18).

1:11 Sheep were the most common burnt offering. The **north side of the altar** was especially for the flock (also

---

qarav

Hebrew Pronunciation	[khah RAV]
HCSB Translation	draw near, present
Uses in Leviticus	102
Uses in the OT	280
Focus Passages	Leviticus 1:5,10,13-14

Qarav, related to *qorban* (offering), means draw (come, go, be) near (Gn 47:29). People come (forward, closer, here). They get close, step in, advance, approach, or reach. *Qarav* denotes take place (Is 5:19), consult (1Sm 14:36), and support (1Kg 2:7). People are about to act (Gn 12:11) and are sexually intimate (Dt 22:14). Intensive verbs mean join (Ezk 37:17) and draw (Hs 7:6). People submit cases (Is 41:21). Causative verbs signify bring (near, forward), present, offer, or have/let come (near, forward). They imply join or invite (Jr 30:21). *Qarov* (75x) means near (Nm 24:17), close, approaching, soon, brief, almost, or just. It connotes relative or neighbor. *Qarev* (12x) involves being about to (Dt 20:3), coming (near, closer), approaching, or drawing near. *Qerav* (9x) is battle (Zch 14:3), war, or warfare. *Qirvah* is nearness (Is 58:2) or presence.

Lord. Aaron's sons the priests will sprinkle its blood against the altar on all sides. [12]He will cut the animal into pieces[A] with its head and its suet, and the priest will arrange them on top of the burning wood on the altar. [13]But he is to wash the entrails and shanks with water. The priest will then present all of it and burn it on the altar; it is a burnt offering, a fire offering of a pleasing aroma to the Lord.

[14]"If his gift to the Lord is a burnt offering of birds,[a] he is to present his offering from the turtledoves[b] or young pigeons.[B,c] [15]Then the priest must bring it to the altar, and must twist off its head and burn it on the altar; its blood should be drained at the side of the altar. [16]He will remove its digestive tract,[c] cutting off the tail feathers, and throw it on the east side of the altar at the place for ashes.[d] [17]He will tear it open by its wings without dividing the bird.[e] Then the priest is to burn it on the altar on top of the burning wood. It is a burnt offering, a fire offering of a pleasing aroma to the Lord.

The Grain Offering

2 "When anyone presents a •grain offering[f] as a gift to the Lord, his gift must consist of fine flour.[D,g] He is to pour olive oil[h] on it, put frankincense on it,[E,i] [2]and bring it to Aaron's sons the priests. The priest will take a handful of fine flour and oil from it, along with all its frankincense, and will burn this memorial

portion[j] of it on the altar, a fire offering of a pleasing aroma to the Lord. [3]But the rest of the grain offering will belong to Aaron and his sons; it is the holiest part[k] of the fire offerings to the Lord.

[4]"When you present a grain offering baked in an oven, it must be made of fine flour, either unleavened cakes[l] mixed with oil or unleavened wafers[m] coated with oil. [5]If your gift is a grain offering prepared on a griddle,[n] it must be unleavened bread[o] made of fine flour mixed with oil. [6]Break it into pieces and pour oil on it; it is a grain offering. [7]If your gift is a grain offering prepared in a pan,[p] it must be made of fine flour with oil. [8]When you bring[F] to the Lord the grain offering made in any of these ways, it is to be presented to the priest, and he will take it to the altar. [9]The priest will remove the memorial portion[G] from the grain offering and burn it on the altar, a fire offering of a pleasing aroma to the Lord. [10]But the rest of the grain offering will belong to Aaron and his sons;[q] it is the holiest part of the fire offerings to the Lord.

[11]"No grain offering that you present to the Lord is to be made with yeast, for you are not to burn[H] any yeast[r] or honey[s] as a fire offering to the Lord. [12]You may present them to the Lord as an offering of •firstfruits,[t] but they are not to be offered on the altar as a pleasing aroma. [13]You are to season each of your grain offerings with salt; you must not omit from

a1:14 Gn 40:17; Lv 17:13
b Gn 15:9; Lv 1:14; 5:7,11; 12:6,8; 14:22,30; 15:14,29; Nm 6:10; Ps 74:19; Sg 2:12; Jr 8:7
c Gn 8:8-12; Lv 5:7,11
d 1:16 Lv 4:12; 6:10-11; 1Kg 13:3,5; Jr 31:40
e 1:17 Gn 15:9-10
f 2:1 Ex 40:29
g Gn 18:6; Ex 29:2,40; Lv 2:1-7
h Gn 28:18; 35:14
i Ex 30:34
j 2:2 Lv 2:9,16; 5:12; 6:8; 24:7; Nm 5:26; Ac 10:4
k 2:3 Lv 14:13
l 2:4 Ex 29:2
m Ex 29:2,23; Lv 7:12; 8:26; Nm 6:15,19; 1Ch 23:29
n 2:5 Lv 6:14; 7:9; 1Ch 23:29; Ezk 4:3
o Ex 12:8; Mt 16:6,11-12; 1Co 5:6-8
p 2:7 Lv 7:9
q 2:10 Lv 7:9-10
r 2:11 Ex 12:14
s Jdg 14:8
t 2:12 Gn 49:3; Ex 23:16,19

A1:12 Lit *its pieces*   B1:14 Or *or pigeons*   C1:16 Or *its crop*, or *its crissum*   D2:1 = wheat flour; Ex 29:2   E2:1 DSS, Sam, LXX add *it is a grain offering*   F2:8 DSS, LXX read *When he brings*   G2:9 Lit *portion of it*   H2:11 Some Hb mss, Sam, LXX, Tg read *present*

---

sin offering, 4:24,29,33), perhaps because less space was needed for them than cattle, which were slaughtered "before the Lord," that is, on the larger east side facing the entrance to the tent of meeting (1:5).

1:14 Easily domesticated, numerous, and affordable for the poor, these two species of **birds** were common offerings (5:7; 12:8; 14:21-22; cp. Gn 15:9). Mary offered birds at Jesus' birth for her purification (Lk 2:22-24).

1:15-17 The **blood** was too meager to be caught in a receptacle; nevertheless, proper disposal (i.e., squeezing it out, Jdg 6:38) was necessary to show that the life belonged to God (Lv 17:10-17). The **place for ashes** (lit "fat" because of animal fat deposits) was east of the altar; a priest cleaned off the altar each morning and took the ash heap outside the camp to purge the refuse from God's sight (6:10-11).

2:1 By the **grain offering** (or cereal offering) the worshiper acknowledged God as the source of provision and prosperity. The Hebrew word *minchah* has the general meaning of **gift** (cp. Gn 32:13) and could refer to grain or animal offerings (Gn 4:3-5), or "sacrifices" in general (Is 19:21); it has the technical sense of "grain" offering in cultic texts. It was grain derived from wheat that produced a **fine**, white **flour** (Ex 29:2). This offering could be offered in raw, cooked, ground (into flour), and baked forms. Typically, it accompanied animal offerings (Lv 7:12-13; 14:20; Nm 28:4-15), but it could be presented independently (Lv 5:11; 7:12-14). For

the very poor it was offered in place of a bird offering (5:11). The priests relied largely on grain offerings for their daily sustenance (2:3,10).

Frankincense, a white resin of pleasant fragrance, was widely valued in the ancient world (Mt 2:11). Tabernacle worship required its pure form in the incense for anointing (Ex 30:34) and the bread loaves (Lv 24:7). Although frankincense typically accompanied grain offerings, it was specifically prohibited in cases of offerings for sin and jealousy (5:11; Nm 5:15). Its association with joy may explain its customary use (Sg 3:6; 4:14; Is 60:6; Jr 17:26).

2:2 The **memorial portion**, given to God, was a representative handful of the treated flour and all of the frankincense (v. 16).

2:3,10 What the priests, as consecrated persons (lit "holy of holies," i.e., "especially holy," Ex 30:29), consumed was considered **the holiest part** (lit "holy of holies"); only a ritually clean priest could eat the holiest part and only in a ritually clean place (probably near the altar).

2:11 Yeast had a corrupting influence and thus could symbolize evil (Mk 8:15; 1Co 5:8). Perhaps **honey** was prohibited because it was used in pagan rites.

2:13-14 Yeast and honey could be offered as **firstfruits** although not burned on the altar (23:17). Firstfruits, the first portion of the harvest, were viewed as the choice part that

your grain offering the salt of the covenant[a] with your God. You are to present salt[A] with each of your offerings.

[14]"If you present a grain offering of firstfruits to the LORD, you must present fresh heads of grain, crushed kernels, roasted on the fire, for your grain offering of firstfruits. [15]You are to put oil and frankincense on it; it is a grain offering. [16]The priest will then burn some of its crushed kernels and oil with all its frankincense as a fire offering to the LORD.

The Fellowship Offering

3 "If his offering is a *fellowship sacrifice,[b] and he is presenting an animal from the herd, whether male or female, he must present one without blemish[c] before the LORD. [2]He is to lay his hand on the head of his offering and slaughter it at the entrance to the tent of meeting. Then Aaron's sons the priests will sprinkle the blood on all sides of the altar.[d] [3]He will present part of the fellowship sacrifice as a fire offering to the LORD: the fat[e] surrounding the entrails,[f] all the fat that is on the entrails, [4]and the two kidneys[g] with the fat on them at the loins; he will also remove the fatty lobe of the liver[h] with the kidneys. [5]Aaron's sons will burn it on the altar along with the *burnt offering[i] that is on the burning wood, a fire offering of a pleasing aroma to the LORD.

[6]"If his offering as a fellowship sacrifice to the LORD is from the flock, he must present a

male or female without blemish. [7]If he is presenting a lamb for his offering, he is to present it before the LORD. [8]He must lay his hand on the head of his offering, then slaughter it before the tent of meeting. Aaron's sons will sprinkle its blood on all sides of the altar. [9]He will then present part of the fellowship sacrifice as a fire offering to the LORD consisting of its fat and the entire fat tail,[j] which he is to remove close to the backbone. He will also remove the fat surrounding the entrails,[k] all the fat on the entrails, [10]the two kidneys with the fat on them at the loins, and the fatty lobe of the liver above the kidneys. [11]Then the priest will burn the food on the altar,[l] as a fire offering to the LORD.

[12]"If his offering is a goat,[m] he is to present it before the LORD. [13]He must lay his hand on its head and slaughter it before the tent of meeting. Aaron's sons will sprinkle[B] its blood on all sides of the altar. [14]He will present part of his offering as a fire offering to the LORD: the fat surrounding the entrails, all the fat that is on the entrails, [15]and the two kidneys with the fat on them at the loins; he will also remove the fatty lobe of the liver with the kidneys. [16]Then the priest will burn the food on the altar, as a fire offering for a pleasing aroma.[C]

"All fat belongs to the LORD. [17]This is a permanent statute[n] throughout your generations, wherever you live: you must not eat any fat or any blood."[o]

Cross references
[a] 2:13 Ex 19:5; Nm 18:19; 2Ch 13:5
[b] 3:1 Lv 7:11
[c] Ex 29:1
[d] 3:2 Lv 1:5
[e] 3:3 Ex 23:18; 29:13,22
[f] Ex 12:9
[g] 3:4 Lv 7:4
[h] Lv 9:10
[i] 3:5 Lv 1:3-4
[j] 3:9 Ex 29:22; Lv 7:3; 8:25; 9:19
[k] Lv 1:9
[l] 3:11 Lv 3:16; 21:6,8,17,21-22; 22:25; 26:5; Nm 28:24
[m] 3:12 Lv 4:23
[n] 3:17 Ex 28:43; Lv 11:46
[o] Lv 7:26; 17:10,14; 19:26; Dt 12:16,23; 15:23

A 2:13 Salt, used as a preservative, is a symbol of the permanence of the covenant.   B 3:13 Or *dash*   C 3:16 Sam, LXX add *to the LORD*

---

belonged to God as the source of all blessing (Festival of Harvest, 23:10; Ex 23:16; 34:26; 1Co 15:20). The permanent quality of **salt** indicates the eternality of the relationship between the Lord and His people (Nm 18:19). **Fresh heads** describes the first ripening sheaves, indicating the best produce (Ex 23:19). The general principle was to give the Lord the first and the best of a person's livelihood (2Co 8:5; 9:7).

3:1 The three kinds of **fellowship offering** were thanksgiving, votive, and freewill (7:11-21). The fellowship offering signified communion between the worshiper and God (9:18,21; 23:19; Nm 6:18) because it was the only sacrifice in which the worshiper ate the shared meal with the priests (Lv 7:31-35). Guests of the offerer—including his household, Levites, and the poor—were part of the communal meal (Dt 12:7,12,18; 26:12-13; Ps 22:25-26). Shared meals characterized the life of the early church (Ac 2:46). That the daily burnt offering preceded the fellowship offering conveyed the importance of atonement as the basis for fellowship with God (Lv 3:5; 6:12), which Christ provided for the church (Rm 5:1; 1Jn 1:3). Because the fellowship offering required a valuable contribution by the worshiper, it is also vital for fellowship with Christ (Php 3:10; 2Tm 1:8; 1Pt 4:13).

3:3-4 The rationale for restricting the **fat** is not stated, except that the fat was the prerogative of God (Is 43:24; Ezk 44:7). The fat was considered the best part of an animal (Gn

4:4; 45:18; Is 34:6) and was associated with robust power (2Sm 1:22; Is 10:27). Fat was especially associated with the fellowship offering (1Kg 8:64; 2Ch 7:7). Figuratively, the **kidneys** conveyed a person's feelings and inner thoughts (often parallels "heart," Ps 73:21), and both the **liver** and kidneys were vital to physical life (Jb 16:13; Pr 7:23).

3:9 The **entire fat tail** refers to the broad-tail sheep whose tail was reputed to be a heavy fat organ weighing from five to fifteen pounds (*Herodotus*; Geikie, ca 1887).

3:11 Identifying the animal sacrifice as a **food** offering occurs here in connection with the fellowship offering that could be eaten (v. 16; 21:8; Nm 28:2). Since the Hebrews did not conceive of God as fed by the sacrifice (Ps 50:12-13), the offering requires a different explanation, perhaps as a metaphorical allusion to the worshiper sharing in a meal with the Lord.

3:12 The **goat** is distinguished from the sheep (unlike the burnt offering, 1:10) because of the special feature of the fat in sheep.

3:16b-17 Belongs to the LORD applies to the **fat** that was removed from a sacrifice at the altar (Ezk 44:7) and not necessarily the fat of animals for the common table. The fat of nonsacrificed animals and birds could be eaten but never the blood (Lv 7:22-27; Dt 12:15-16,20-24; 32:14). **Permanent statute** and **wherever you live** show that there were no exceptions to the command. On blood, see notes at 17:10-11.

The Sin Offering

4 Then the LORD spoke to Moses: ²"Tell the Israelites: When someone sins unintentionally[a] against any of the LORD's commands and does anything prohibited by them—

³"If the anointed priest[A,b] sins, bringing •guilt[c] on the people, he is to present to the LORD a young, unblemished[d] bull as a •sin[B] offering[e] for the sin he has committed. ⁴He must bring the bull to the entrance to the tent of meeting before the LORD, lay his hand on the bull's head, and slaughter it before the LORD. ⁵The anointed priest must then take some of the bull's blood and bring it into the tent of meeting. ⁶The priest is to dip his finger in the blood and sprinkle some of it seven times[f] before the LORD in front of the veil[g] of the sanctuary.[h] ⁷The priest must apply some of the blood to the horns of the altar of fragrant incense[i] that is before the LORD in the tent of meeting. He must pour out the rest of the bull's blood at the base of the altar of burnt

Marginal references:
a 4:2 Nm 15:22,24
b 4:3 Lv 4:16; 6:15
c Lv 6:5,7; 22:16
d Ex 29:1
e Ex 29:14
f 4:6 Lv 16:14
g Mk 15:38; Lk 23:45
h Ex 15:17; Lv 10:4
i 4:7 Ex 30:27

A 4:3 Probably the high priest; Lv 6:22   B 4:3 Or *purification*

4:2 Sins committed **unintentionally** (Hb *shegagah*) are inadvertent transgressions committed through ignorance or neglect, not premeditated, defiant sins. Although all **sins** are serious, requiring the cost of a substitutionary death, the sins and impurities were atoned for by the sin offering. Compare 5:1-5a for examples of unplanned sins.

4:3 Anointed priest refers to the high priest (6:22; 21:10; Ex 29:7). As the representative of the people before God, his sin—which was probably some inadvertent error in carrying out prescribed rituals—would also impact the purity of the people. **A young, unblemished bull** refers to its pristine, vital youth, but the Hebrew phrase may also mean a bull taken from the herd—a domesticated specimen. The traditional translation **sin offering** is better understood as "purification offering" since it involved the ritual removal of impurities and provided forgiveness (Milgrom). The Hebrew noun (*chatta'th*) is related to the verb meaning "to purify," that is, "to decontaminate" (*chitte*'; e.g., Ezk 43:19-23). The sin offering also dealt with the offerer's sin (Lv 4:20; 5:13).

The instructions for the sin offering (4:1-5:13) consisted of two parts: the general instructions (4:1-35) and the appendix naming special circumstances (5:1-13). The sin offering addressed the consequences of sin, which always rendered the sanctuary and its furnishings unclean, meaning that the relationship between the worshiper and God had been impaired, making it unacceptable for the worshiper to access the sanctuary and receive God's forgiveness. The sin offering removed the corrupting effects of sin, which permitted the remorseful sinner not only to receive forgiveness but to have the assurance of acceptance with God. For this reason, the ritual included the application of blood to the sanctuary furnishings, not to the person (4:5-7,16-18,25,30,34).

The importance of the sin offering is validated by its role in the everyday lives of individuals and its use at special times in the community, such as the ordination of Aaron to the priesthood (chap. 8) and significant annual festivals (Passover, Ex 12:11-27; Day of Atonement, Lv 16:3; Booths, Nm 29:16).

The sin offering varied according to the progressive degrees of responsibility: the high priest (Lv 4:3-12), the congregation collectively (vv. 13-21), the ruler (vv. 22-26), and the individual layperson (vv. 27-35). The underlying principle is that although all sin is contaminating, the sins of leadership (priest, king) and the congregation have greater impact than the individual transgressor. The variation in the cost of the sacrifice and the placement of blood on the sanctuary furnishings reflected this same principle. The reason was the infiltration of sin and impurities inside the tent. Thus, the more profound the impact of the sin, the farther into the tent the blood was applied, that is, the closer to the presence of the Lord as symbolized by the ark. In all cases, however, the remaining blood was poured at the base of the altar in the courtyard, symbolizing that the life of the victim belonged to God (vv. 7,18,25,30,34; 5:9). Another distinction was that for the priest's and the congregation's sins, the animal's carcass must be butchered into parts and burned (4:8-12,19-21), while for the leader and individual, a portion of the offering was assigned to the priest, who could eat it as a sign of divine acceptance of the worshiper (5:13; 6:26).

4:4 Lay his hand indicates an identification of the person with the sacrificial animal that served as his substitute (see note at 1:4).

4:6 Seven indicates the thoroughness of the purging; this number occurs also in the accounts of the ordination rite (8:11), purification of lepers (14:7), the Day of Atonement (16:14,19), and the ceremony of the red heifer (Nm 19:4). On **before the LORD**, see note at 1:5. The **veil** (Hb *paroketh*) was the curtain that separated the holy place from the most holy place inside the tent canopy (Ex 26:33). The sin offering on the Day of Atonement had the sprinkling inside the veil before the mercy seat, whereas here the priest could go no farther than **in front of** the veil. It may be that the veil represented the whole sanctuary (16:16), guaranteeing that the entire tabernacle was thus purged. Another possibility is that the veil represented the mercy seat (Hb *kapporeth*) of the ark, which the priest could not approach except on the annual Day of Atonement.

4:7 The priest **must apply** (Hb *natan*) the blood by smearing rather than sprinkling (Hb *nazah*) it; the **altar of fragrant incense** refers to the golden altar before the dividing curtain inside the tent canopy that Aaron lit each morning and evening (Ex 30:7-8). Only priests could offer the incense (2Ch 26:18). The word **incense** (Hb *qetoreth*) is related to the Hebrew word that means "to produce smoke by burning up" (*qatar*). The altar symbolized intercessory prayer (Ps 141:2; Rv 5:8; 8:3-4). Thus by decontaminating this altar, the prayers of the priest and people could be received by the Lord. The fragrance refers to a unique blend of spices that made a special perfume used in the tabernacle (Ex 30:34-38). Compare its distinctive use on the Day of Atonement (Lv 16:12).

The four **horns**, one protruding from each of the altar's four corners (Ex 30:1-6; 38:2), conveyed the power of a formidable animal (Dt 33:17) and thus the efficacy (strength, e.g., 1Sm 2:10; Am 3:14) of the altar's purpose. The disposal of the remaining blood **at the base of the** (courtyard's) **altar**, around which a trench probably ran (1Kg 18:32), occurred only for the sin offering of the five offerings detailed in Leviticus 1-7, and also during the special ordination rites of Aaron's priesthood (9:9; Ex 29:12). The blood, as the symbol of life, belonged solely to God and could not be used for any other purpose.

offering[a] that is at the entrance to the tent of meeting. [8]He is to remove all the fat from the bull of the sin offering: the fat surrounding the entrails, all the fat that is on the entrails, [9]and the two kidneys with the fat on them at the loins. He will also remove the fatty lobe of the liver with the kidneys, [10]just as the fat is removed from the ox of the *fellowship sacrifice.[b] The priest is to burn them on the altar of burnt offering. [11]But the hide[c] of the bull and all its flesh, with its head and shanks, and its entrails and dung— [12]all the rest of the bull—he must bring to a ceremonially *clean place[d] outside the camp[e] to the ash heap, and must burn it on a wood fire. It is to be burned at the ash heap.

[13]"Now if the whole community of Israel[f] errs,[g] and the matter escapes the notice of the assembly,[h] so that they violate any of the Lord's commands and incur guilt[i] by doing what is prohibited, [14]then the assembly must present a young bull as a sin offering. When the sin they have committed in regard to the command becomes known, they are to bring it before the tent of meeting. [15]The elders[j] of the community are to lay their hands on the bull's head before the Lord and it is to be slaughtered before the Lord. [16]The anointed priest will bring some of the bull's blood into the tent of meeting. [17]The priest is to dip his finger in the blood and sprinkle it seven times before the Lord in front of the veil. [18]He is to apply some of the blood to the horns of the al-

tar that is before the Lord in the tent of meeting. He must pour out the rest of the blood at the base of the altar of burnt offering that is at the entrance to the tent of meeting. [19]He is to remove all the fat from it and burn it on the altar. [20]He is to offer this bull just as he did with the bull in the sin offering; he will offer it the same way. So the priest will make *atonement[k] on their behalf, and they will be forgiven.[l] [21]Then he will bring the bull outside the camp[m] and burn it just as he burned the first bull. It is the sin offering for the assembly.

[22]"When a leader[A,n] sins and unintentionally violates any of the commands of the Lord his God by doing what is prohibited, and incurs guilt, [23]or someone informs him about the sin he has committed, he is to bring an unblemished male goat[o] as his offering. [24]He is to lay his hand on the head of the goat and slaughter it at the place where the *burnt offering[p] is slaughtered before the Lord. It is a sin offering.[q] [25]Then the priest must take some of the blood from the sin offering with his finger and apply it to the horns of the altar of burnt offering.[r] The rest of its blood he must pour out at the base of the altar of burnt offering. [26]He must burn all its fat on the altar, like the fat of the fellowship sacrifice. In this way the priest will make atonement on his behalf for that person's sin, and he will be forgiven.

[27]"Now if any of the common people[B] sins unintentionally by violating one of the Lord's

[a]4:7 Ex 3:5; 35:16
[b]4:8-10 Lv 7:11
[c]4:11 Lv 7:8
[d]4:12 Lv 6:4; 10:14; Nm 19:9
[e]Lv 8:17; Heb 13:11-13
[f]4:13 Ex 12:47
[g]Nm 15:22
[h]Ex 16:3; Lv 4:21; Nm 10:7; 15:15; 20:6,10
[i]Nm 5:6; Ps 68:21
[j]4:15 Ex 18:12
[k]4:20 Ex 30:15
[l]Lv 5:16; 6:7
[m]4:21 Lv 8:17
[n]4:22 Ex 34:31
[o]4:23 Lv 9:3; 16:5; 23:19; Nm 7:16-82
[p]4:24 Gn 22:2; Ex 20:24; Lv 3:5
[q]Ex 29:14
[r]4:25 Lv 5:9

A4:22 Or ruler   B4:27 Lit the people of the land

4:8-12 For the burning of the **fat**, compare the fellowship offering (3:3-4,9,16-17). The precise instructions for the bull's parts were necessary since the meat of a sin offering taken from the flock could be eaten by the priest (6:26). Any sin offering whose blood was taken into the tent (6:30), such as prescribed for the priest and the congregation (4:5,16; 16:24), could not be eaten. A distinguishing feature of the sin offering was that the bull's remaining parts were taken **to a ceremonially clean place outside the camp** (also Day of Atonement, 16:27) where they were burned. But the burnt offering required the burning of the whole animal on the altar (except the hide). The disposal site for the bull's remaining parts had to be ritually clean, unpolluted by unclean persons or defiled by human refuse (13:46; Nm 5:3; Dt 23:10,13). The phrase **ash heap** occurs only here, describing the place where the remaining parts were burned (6:11-12; Jr 31:40; Ezk 43:21).

4:13 The priest who carried out the offering on his own behalf (16:11) now did so for the congregation. The word **errs** (Hb shegag) refers to unintended transgressions (cp. v. 2). This sort of sin escaped **notice** (Hb 'alam), hidden at the time of the trespass, but was perceived later. The priest's sin imposing "guilt" on the congregation (v. 3) may indicate that the congregation's **guilt** was related to the error committed by the priest, which the assembly obeyed.

4:15 **Before the Lord** is equivalent to "before the tent of meeting" (v. 14; cp. v. 4). The passage does not specify who **slaughtered** the sin offering, although the priest did so on the Day of Atonement (16:15).

4:20 This is the first occurrence in Leviticus of the word **forgiven** (Hb salach; cp. vv. 26,31,35; 5:10,13,16,18; 6:7; 19:22); the Hebrew passive form of the verb implies that it is God alone who can forgive sin.

4:22 A **leader** (Hb nasi') was a ruler over a tribe (Gn 25:16; Ex 34:31). The expression **the Lord his God** is often used of a significant leader (Moses, Ex 32:11; king, Dt 17:18-19; priest and Levite, Dt 18:6-7).

4:24 **The burnt offering** was **slaughtered** north of the altar (see note at 1:11). The declaration that it **is a sin offering** was a reminder that this rite should not be confused with the burnt offering.

4:25 The blood remained outside the tent and was applied to the courtyard's **altar of burnt offering** for its purgation (Ex 29:38-42; on the altar's construction, see Ex 27:1-8). On **horns of the altar**, see note at verse 7.

4:27-35 The individual was permitted to offer a female goat or female sheep.

4:27 **Common people** renders (lit) "people of the land," meaning anyone who was not the high priest or an official.

commands, does what is prohibited, and incurs guilt, ²⁸or if someone informs him about the sin he has committed, then he is to bring an unblemished female goat as his offering for the sin that he has committed. ²⁹He is to lay his hand on the head of the sin offering and slaughter it at the place of the burnt offering. ³⁰Then the priest must take some of its blood with his finger and apply it to the horns of the altar of burnt offering. He must pour out the rest of its blood at the base of the altar. ³¹He is to remove all its fat just as the fat is removed from the fellowship sacrifice. The priest is to burn it on the altar as a pleasing aroma to the LORD. In this way the priest will make atonement on his behalf, and he will be forgiven.

³²"Or if the offering that he brings as a sin offering is a lamb,^a he is to bring an unblemished female. ³³He is to lay his hand on the head of the sin offering and slaughter it as a

^a4:32 Lv 9:3
^b5:1 Gn 4:13; Ex 20:5; Lv 16:21-22; Nm 5:15,31; Dt 19:15

sin offering at the place where the burnt offering is slaughtered. ³⁴Then the priest must take some of the blood of the sin offering with his finger and apply it to the horns of the altar of burnt offering. He must pour out the rest of its blood at the base of the altar. ³⁵He is to remove all its fat just as the fat of the lamb is removed from the fellowship sacrifice. The priest will burn it on the altar along with the fire offerings to the LORD. In this way the priest will make atonement on his behalf for the sin he has committed, and he will be forgiven.

Cases Requiring Sin Offerings

5 "When someone sins in any of these ways:

If he has seen, heard, or known about something he has witnessed, and did not respond to a public call to testify, he is responsible for his sin.^b

---

4:31 Divine acceptance shown by the catchphrase **pleasing aroma** occurs only here in chapter 4, and it is assumed for the previous procedures for the sin offering (see note at 1:9).

5:1-13 The remaining instructions for the sin offering provide four case examples (vv. 1-4) and the ritual procedure required (vv. 5-6), including special directives for the poor (vv. 5-13).

5:1-4 The four cases involve those who failed to testify in court (v. 1); those who became unclean through contact with an unclean animal (v. 2) or an unclean person (v. 3); and those who uttered an oath rashly (v. 4). The first and fourth of these cases of sin pertained to an oath, and the second and third cases regarded ceremonial uncleanness. One suggestion for why these four cases are treated as a separate category is that the person remained in his guilt for a prolonged time before he confessed (Milgrom, 1:310-13).

5:1 A **public call to testify** (lit "voice of an oath") indicates a judicial matter in which formal testimony is requested of those who have knowledge to contribute to a court proceeding. Typically, with an oath came a divine curse against someone who failed in his oath; in this case, the implied curse was that the person's failure made him answerable to God (Pr 29:24). The sinner felt guilty and he openly confessed his sin (Lv 5:5); this indicates that he had genuine remorse. Precisely why he failed to testify was left open to a number of possible scenarios, including complicity in the crime, neglect, or forgetfulness. The absence of the qualification "unintentional" (cp. 4:2) in the verse may mean that the sin could have been deliberate. The sin, however, could qualify for purging since the wrong was not as severe as the crime of bearing false witness and since the person showed remorse.

SACRIFICIAL SYSTEM			
NAME	**REFERENCE**	**ELEMENTS**	**SIGNIFICANCE**
Burnt Offering	Lv 1; 6:8-13	Bull, ram, male goat, male dove, or young pigeon without blemish. (Always male animals, but species of animal varied according to individual's economic status.)	Voluntary. Signifies propitiation for sin and complete surrender, devotion, and commitment to God.
Grain Offering. Also called Meal or Tribute Offering	Lv 2; 6:14-23	Grain, flour, or bread (always unleavened) made with olive oil and salt; or incense.	Voluntary. Signifies thanksgiving for first-fruits.
Fellowship Offering. Also called Peace Offering, which includes: (1) Thank Offering, (2) Vow Offering, and (3) Freewill Offering	(1) Lv 3; 7:11-36; 22:17-30; 27	Any animal without blemish. (Species of animal varied according to individual's economic status.) (1) Can be grain offering.	Voluntary. Symbolizes fellowship with God. (1) Signifies thankfulness for a specific blessing; (2) offers a ritual expression of a vow; and (3) symbolizes general thankfulness (to be brought to one of three required religious services).
Sin Offering	Lv 4:1-5:13; 6:24-30; 12:6-8	Male or female animal without blemish—as follows: bull for high priest or congregation; male goat for king; female goat or lamb for common person; dove or pigeon for slightly poor; tenth of an ephah of flour for the very poor.	Mandatory. Made by one who had sinned unintentionally or was unclean in order to attain purification.
Guilt Offering	Lv 5:14-6:7; 7:1-6; 14:12-18	Ram or lamb without blemish.	Mandatory. Made by a person who had either deprived another of his rights or had desecrated something holy. Made by lepers for purification.

² Or if someone touches anything *unclean[a]—a carcass of an unclean wild animal,[b] or unclean livestock, or an unclean swarming creature[A,c]—without being aware of it, he is unclean and *guilty.[d] ³ Or if he touches human uncleanness[e]—any uncleanness by which one can become defiled[f]—without being aware of it, but later recognizes it, he is guilty. ⁴ Or if someone swears rashly[g] to do what is good or evil—concerning anything a person may speak rashly in an oath—without being aware of it, but later recognizes it, he incurs guilt in such an instance.[B]

⁵ If someone incurs guilt in one of these cases, he is to confess[h] he has committed that sin. ⁶ He must bring his restitution[i] for the sin he has committed to the LORD: a female lamb or goat from the flock as a *sin offering. In this way the priest will make *atonement[j] on his behalf for his sin.

⁷ "But if he cannot afford an animal from the flock, then he may bring to the LORD two turtledoves or two young pigeons[k] as restitution for his sin—one as a sin offering and the other as a *burnt offering. ⁸ He is to bring them to the priest, who will first present the one for the sin offering. He must twist its head at the back of the neck without severing it.[l] ⁹ Then he will sprinkle some of the blood of the sin offering on the side of the altar, while the rest of the blood is to be drained out at the base of the altar;[m] it is a sin offering. ¹⁰ He must prepare the second bird as a burnt offering according to the regulation.[n] In this way the priest will make atonement on his behalf for the sin he has committed, and he will be forgiven.

¹¹ "But if he cannot afford[c] two turtledoves or two young pigeons,[o] he may bring two quarts[D] of fine[E] flour[F,p] as an offering for his sin. He must not put olive oil or frankincense on it, for it is a sin offering. ¹² He is to bring it to the priest, who will take a handful from it as its memorial portion[q] and burn it on the altar along with the fire offerings to the LORD; it is a sin offering. ¹³ In this way the priest will

Cross references (margin):
- a 5:2 Lv 11:4; Nm 19:13
- b Lv 26:6
- c Lv 11:24-40; Dt 14:8
- d Nm 5:6; Ps 68:21
- e 5:3 Lv 14:19
- f Lv 11:24
- g 5:4 Ps 106:33; Pr 12:18
- h 5:5 Lv 16:21
- i 5:6 Lv 14:12
- j Ex 30:15
- k 5:7 Lv 1:14
- l 5:8 Gn 15:10; Lv 1:15,17
- m 5:9 Lv 4:25,30
- n 5:10 Lv 1:14-17
- o 5:11 Lk 2:24
- p Lv 2:1
- q 5:12 Lv 2:2

A 5:2 Perhaps a fish, insect, rodent, or reptile; Gn 1:20; Lv 11:20-23,29-31   B 5:4 Lit in one of such things   C 5:11 Lit if his hand is not sufficient for   D 5:11 Lit one-tenth of an ephah   E 5:11 Or wheat; Ex 29:2   F 5:11 Lit flour as a sin offering

---

5:2 The possibility of touching an unclean creature was always a threat (11:24-28,35-40), and therefore it was common that a person might forget it or postpone the purification rite. For the **unclean swarming creature**, see the specifics in chapter 11.

5:3 For the purity laws that designate **human uncleanness**, see chapters 12–15; 17:15-16; 18:19; cp. 1Sm 20:26; Ezk 22:10.

5:4 Rashly (Hb bata') describes hurtful, hastily spoken words (Ps 106:33; Pr 12:18); here it indicates a careless **oath**, made regardless of whether it was virtuous or not. The oath was forgotten; it either could not be or should not be realized. Typically, an unfulfilled oath included a divine punishment. Even failure to fulfill an oath with an evil purpose resulted in personal guilt, because God required His people to speak truthful words, just as He is truthful (2Sm 22:31; Is 40:8; Rm 3:4). Because of the seriousness of this sin, oaths should be made only after careful thought (Nm 30:2; Dt 23:21-22; Ec 5:4-5).

5:5-6 Two measures were required of the offender for any of these four crimes. The root word for **confess** (Hb yadah) can also mean "praise aloud" (Ps 7:17), indicating that confession involved declaring one's sin publicly (Lv 16:21; 26:40; Nm 5:6-7; 1Jn 1:9). The **restitution** (Hb 'asham) compensation was an animal offering; the word can mean "guilt" (4:13). It is the word for "the restitution offering" (traditionally "guilt" or "trespass" offering) in 5:14–6:7.

5:7 On birds as a substitute offering, see note at 1:14.

5:8 Two birds were necessary since the regular **sin offering** required two acts (4:6-10): (1) the disposal of the blood and (2) the burning of its internal organs and fat. The sin offering granted cleansing and acceptance with God, which was necessary before the burnt offering (indicating devotion) was appropriate.

5:11 Although the **sin offering** presented by the very poor was similar to the grain offering by the use of wheat flour, it is identified as a sin offering, not a grain offering ("a fire offering," 2:16). Oil and incense that characterized the grain offering (see note at 2:1) were omitted from the sin offering since these elements signified the joy of worship. The amount of **flour** was small enough that the very poor could afford it. Rich (e.g., a leader) and poor alike were guilty of sin, but by God's gracious provision, all could be purified.

5:12 The burning of the **memorial portion** (cp. 2:2) corresponded to the burning of the sacrificial animal's entrails in the regular offering procedure.

5:13 The remainder of the flour customarily belonged to the

---

chatta'th

Hebrew Pronunciation	[khat TAT]
HCSB Translation	sin, sin offering
Uses in Leviticus	82
Uses in the OT	298
Focus Passage	Leviticus 5:6-13

Chatta'th, related to the verb chata' (sin), indicates sin as behavior (Gn 50:17) or thoughts (Pr 21:4). Sin afflicts everyone (Pr 20:9). Whether conscious (Jb 34:37) or unconscious (Nm 15:24), it contrasts with righteousness (Pr 14:34). Scripture considers God the chief victim, and idolatry was one of the gravest sins (1Sm 15:23; 1Kg 16:13; Jr 16:10-18). Chatta'th specifies sin's guilt (Jr 17:1) or its punishment (Zch 14:19). God instituted sacrifice as a means to forgive sin (Lv 4:27-31), and chatta'th denotes sin offering (Ex 29:14). Chatta'th implies purification from ceremonial impurity (Nm 8:7). Chete' (34x) means sin (Nm 27:3), offense, fault (Gn 41:9), guilt (Lv 19:17), consequences of sin (Lv 24:15), or punishment (Lm 3:39). Adjectival chatta' (19x) indicates sinning (Gn 13:13) or sinner (Is 33:14). Chata'ah (8x) is sin (Ex 32:21), guilt, or sin offering (Ps 40:6).

make atonement on his behalf concerning the sin he has committed in any of these cases, and he will be forgiven. The rest will belong to the priest, like the *grain offering."[a]

The Restitution Offering

[14] Then the Lord spoke to Moses: [15] "If someone offends[b] by sinning unintentionally[c] in regard to any of the Lord's holy things,[A] he must bring his *restitution offering to the Lord: an unblemished ram from the flock (based on your assessment of its value in silver *shekels, according to the sanctuary shekel[d]) as a restitution offering. [16] He must make restitution[e] for his sin regarding any holy[f] thing, adding a fifth of its value to it,[g] and give it to the priest. Then the priest will make atonement on his behalf with the ram of the restitution offering, and he will be forgiven.[h]

[17] "If someone sins and without knowing it violates any of the Lord's commands concerning anything prohibited, he bears the consequences of his guilt. [18] He must bring an unblemished ram from the flock according to your assessment of its value as a restitu-

tion offering to the priest. Then the priest will make atonement on his behalf for the error he has committed unintentionally, and he will be forgiven. [19] It is a restitution offering; he is indeed guilty before the Lord."

6 [B] The Lord spoke to Moses: [2] "When someone sins and offends the Lord by deceiving[i] his neighbor in regard to a deposit,[j] a security,[C] or a robbery;[k] or defrauds[l] his neighbor; [3] or finds something lost and lies about it;[m] or swears falsely[n] about any of the sinful things a person may do— [4] once he has sinned[o] and acknowledged his *guilt[p]—he must return what he stole or defrauded, or the deposit entrusted to him, or the lost item he found, [5] or anything else about which he swore falsely. He must make full restitution for it and add a fifth of its value to it.[q] He is to pay it to its owner on the day he acknowledges his guilt.[r] [6] Then he must bring his *restitution offering[s] to the Lord: an unblemished[t] ram from the flock according to your assessment of its value as a restitution offering to the priest. [7] In this way the priest will make *atonement on his behalf before the

Cross references (center column):
- [a]5:13 Lv 2:3,10
- [b]5:15 Dt 32:51
- [c]Nm 15:24
- [d]Lv 27:3; Nm 3:47
- [e]5:16 Lv 14:12; 24:18
- [f]Lv 25:12
- [g]Lv 27:13
- [h]Lv 4:20,26, 31,35; 6:7
- [i]6:2 Lv 19:11
- [j]Ex 22:7-13
- [k]Is 61:8; Ezk 22:29
- [l]Dt 24:14
- [m]6:3 Ex 23:4; Dt 22:1-3
- [n]Ex 22:11; Lv 19:12
- [o]6:4 Gn 44:32; Jdg 10:10; Neh 1:6; Ps 39:1; Is 1:4
- [p]Lv 4:3
- [q]6:5 Lv 27:13
- [r]6:4-5 Ex 22:9-12; 23:4-5; Dt 22:13; Mt 5:23-24; Lk 19:8-9
- [s]6:6 Lv 14:12
- [t]Ex 29:1

[A]5:15 Things dedicated to the Lord such as tabernacle furnishings, priestly portions of the sacrifices, tenths, firstfruits, and firstborn livestock   [B]6:1 Lv 5:20 in Hb   [C]6:2 Or an investment

---

officiating **priest** (cp. 6:26); although this was a minimal amount, its consumption by the priest symbolized to the poor that his offering had been accepted by God and that he had received forgiveness. It was the grace of the Lord, not the value of the offering, that procured forgiveness.

5:14–6:7 The **restitution offering** (5:15), traditionally translated "trespass" or "guilt" offering, remedied the sins defrauding God's "holy things" (5:14-19) or defrauding a person, which involved offending the Lord through a false oath (6:1-7). This offering addressed the damage of depriving someone of his rightful due, and thus monetary reparations were required. The word "restitution" (Hb *asham*) refers to the crime (6:5,7, "guilt") as well as the offering (6:6, "restitution offering"). The precise shade of meaning for the word "guilt" is uncertain, meaning either the fact of guilt or the feelings of guilt.

The offering involved an assessment by the priest of the damages plus a surcharge payment of 20 percent. The restitution ritual varied for compensating damages against God and against a person. In addition to those listed here, the offering was required for the purification of a leper (14:12), payment for a sexual crime against a slave woman (19:20), and the purification ritual of a Nazirite (Nm 6:12).

5:15 The term **offends** (Hb *ma'al*) means "acts treacherously," which can describe sacrilege against God (Jos 7:1) or betrayal of another person (Nm 5:6). On sins committed **unintentionally**, see note at 4:2. **Holy things** refer broadly to any of those things that were consecrated to the Lord, such as unlawfully eating food dedicated to the Lord (22:14) and a Nazirite who became defiled (Nm 6:9-12). The ritual required compensation to **the Lord** by bringing the sacrificial animal to His representative, the priest. The ritual was like the sin offering (4:1–5:13; 7:7). The offender slaughtered the sacrificial animal at the main altar; the priest sprinkled blood on all its sides and burned up the fat, leaving the

meat for the officiating priest to eat (7:2-7). The restitution offering included additional steps. The offender had to pay back for the damages, as evaluated by the priest (27:12), according to the standard **sanctuary shekel** (27:3), with an additional 20 percent charge (5:16).

5:16 The payment was **to the priest** since the offense was against the Lord. On the word **forgiven**, see note at 4:20.

5:17 The second case was a transgression in which the person had desecrated something holy (**without knowing it**). This distinguished the restitution offering from the sin offering, which described an offender who later came to realize his crime (4:2,22,27).

5:19 Before the Lord here means "against the Lord."

6:1 The third case was a breach of trust that involved the misappropriation of another person's property. Since it most likely involved an oath in the Lord's name, the crime also ultimately offended the Lord. If the defrauded person was dead and a relative could not be repaid, then the priest as the representative of God received the compensation (Nm 5:5-10). Sin against a neighbor was considered a sin against the Lord (Ex 20:16; Lv 19:18; Mt 22:39).

6:2-3 Six examples are listed: the illegal withholding of another's property received through (1) a deposit given for safekeeping; (2) an investment made in a business; (3) theft; (4) property falsely acquired through defrauding a neighbor; (5) keeping lost property; and (6) swearing against a neighbor falsely.

6:5 On the day shows the immediate effect of the guilty conscience of the offender whose restitution demonstrated genuine remorse. Numbers 5:7 requires the offender to confess his sin.

6:7 The Suffering Servant, our Lord Jesus Christ, was the ultimate "restitution offering" (Is 53:10) that provided full

LORD, and he will be forgiven for anything he may have done to incur guilt."[a]

The Burnt Offering

[8A] The LORD spoke to Moses: [9] "Command Aaron and his sons: This is the law of the •burnt offering; the burnt offering itself must remain on the altar's hearth all night until morning, while the fire of the altar is kept burning on it. [10] The priest is to put on his linen robe and linen undergarments.[B,b] He is to remove the ashes of the burnt offering the fire has consumed on the altar, and place them beside the altar. [11] Then he must take off his garments, put on other clothes,[c] and bring the ashes outside the camp to a ceremonially •clean place. [12] The fire on the altar is to be kept burning; it must not go out. Every morning the priest will burn wood on the fire. He is to arrange the burnt offering on the fire and burn the fat portions from the •fellowship offerings[d] on it. [13] Fire must be kept burning on the altar continually; it must not go out.

The Grain Offering

[14] "Now this is the law of the •grain offering:[e] Aaron's sons will present it before the LORD in front of the altar. [15] The priest is to remove a handful of fine flour and olive oil from the grain offering, with all the frankincense that is on the offering, and burn its memorial portion on the altar as a pleasing aroma to the LORD. [16] Aaron and his sons may eat the rest of it.[f] It is to be eaten in the form of unleavened bread[g] in a holy place;[h] they are to eat it in the courtyard[i] of the tent of meeting. [17] It must not be baked with yeast; I have assigned it as their portion[j] from My fire offerings.[k] It is especially holy, like the •sin offering[l] and the restitution offering. [18] Any male among Aaron's descendants[m] may eat it. It is a permanent portion[C,n] throughout your generations from the fire offerings to the LORD. Anything that touches the offerings will become holy."[o]

[19] The LORD spoke to Moses: [20] "This is the offering that Aaron and his sons must present to the LORD on the day that he is anointed: two quarts[D] of fine flour as a regular[E] grain offering, half of it in the morning and half in the evening. [21] It is to be prepared with oil on a griddle; you are to bring it well-kneaded. You must present it as a grain offering of baked pieces,[F] a pleasing aroma to the LORD. [22] The priest, who is one of Aaron's sons and will be anointed to take his place, is to prepare it. It must be completely burned as a permanent portion for the LORD. [23] Every grain offering

Cross references (center column)

[a]6:7 Lv 5:10,13,18
[b]6:10 Ex 28:42-43; Lv 16:4; Ezk 44:17-19
[c]6:11 Lv 16:23; Ezk 42:14; 44:19
[d]6:12 Lv 1:2; 7:11
[e]6:14-18 Lv 2:1-16
[f]6:16 1Co 9:13
[g]Ex 12:8; 1Co 5:8
[h]Lv 16:24
[i]Ex 27:9
[j]6:17 Lv 6:10; Nm 18:20; 31:36; Dt 10:9; 12:12
[k]Dt 18:1
[l]Ex 29:14
[m]6:18 Lv 21:18-23
[n]Lv 7:34; Heb 13:10
[o]Ex 29:37; Lk 11:2

[A]6:8 Lv 6:1 in Hb   [B]6:10 Lit undergarments on his flesh   [C]6:18 Or statute   [D]6:20 Lit a tenth of an ephah   [E]6:20 Daily   [F]6:21 Hb obscure

---

forgiveness. Because of sin against the Lord and their neighbors, people have a debt to God, but Jesus has made the ransom payment (Mk 10:45). Restitution must precede the act of worship (Mt 5:23-26).

6:8-7:38 The previous descriptions of the five offerings were addressed primarily to everyday Israelites, but these regulations are directed primarily to the priests. Also, instructions on the procedure for the restitution offering appear for the first time (7:1-7).

6:8-13 On the **burnt offering**, see note at 1:3.

6:9 The daily burnt offering (Ex 29:42-43; Nm 28:3,6,10), known as the *tamid* ("continually," Lv 6:13), provided for the meat to roast **all night until morning**; the phrase **kept burning** describes the perpetual flame on the altar (vv. 12-13). The eternal flame came from the Lord (see note at 9:24), indicating perpetual cleansing and intercession.

6:10-11 Special holy garments were required of the priest (Ex 28:42-43) when handling the **ashes** in the sacred courtyard. **Other clothes** were appropriate since the priest left the sacred precinct; yet, even outside, the ashes were to remain in a **ceremonially clean place**, or the designated "ash heap" (4:12).

6:14-23 This passage probably describes the layperson's private grain offering, although it may refer to the daily grain offering of Israel presented by the priest that accompanied the daily burnt offering. On the private **grain offering**, see 2:1-16 and note at 2:1; on the daily offering, compare Ex 29:40-41; Nm 28:4-8.

6:14 The word **law** (Hb torah) can mean "instruction."

6:15 On the **memorial portion**, see note at 2:2.

6:16-17 Only the priests were qualified to eat the remainder of the sacrifice, which they ate in the **courtyard** (2:11). In the NT, the same principle applied to Christian leaders who received their livelihood from the gifts of the parishioners (1Co 9:14; 1Tm 5:17-18).

6:17 **Especially holy** (Hb qodesh qadashim) refers to the offerings from which the priests received their sustenance (vv. 25-26; 2:3; 7:1,6; Nm 18:8-10); therefore, these sacrifices could only be consumed in the sanctuary courtyard.

6:18 The **permanent portion** identified this food as one of many divine gifts for the service of the priests (v. 29; 7:6,34; 24:9; Nm 18). **Anything . . . will become holy** describes the resulting state of someone who handled the grain or meat (in the case of an animal offering) or something that came into contact with it (for other occasions, see Ex 29:37; Nm 16:37-38; cp. the opposite state, Lv 11:24 and see note at Hg 2:13).

6:19-23 The daily grain offering of the high priest had its beginning with the ordination service of **Aaron and his sons** (8:1-8; Ex 29:1-9).

6:20 The amount corresponded to the daily **grain offering** of Israel (Ex 29:40; Nm 28:5) and the sin offering of the very poor (Lv 5:11). It was offered twice per day by the high priest.

6:22-23 The successor to Aaron as high priest would make the offering at the altar. The burning of the entire offering indicated that the priest could not benefit from the offering made for himself; this was a perpetual reminder to the

for a priest will be a whole burnt offering;[a] it is not to be eaten."

The Sin Offering

[24] The LORD spoke to Moses: [25] "Tell Aaron and his sons: This is the law of the sin offering.[b] The sin offering is most holy and must be slaughtered before the LORD at the place where the burnt offering is slaughtered. [26] The priest who offers it as a sin offering is to eat it. It must be eaten in a holy place,[c] in the courtyard of the tent of meeting. [27] Anything that touches its flesh will become holy, and if any of its blood spatters on a garment, then you must wash that garment[A] in a holy place. [28] A clay pot in which the sin offering is boiled must be broken; if it is boiled in a bronze vessel, it must be scoured and rinsed with water. [29] Any male among the priests may eat it; it is especially holy. [30] But no sin offering may be eaten if its blood has been brought into the tent of meeting to make atonement in the holy place; it must be burned up.

The Restitution Offering

7 "Now this is the law of the •restitution offering;[d] it is especially holy. [2] The restitution offering must be slaughtered at the place where the •burnt offering[e] is slaughtered, and the priest is to sprinkle its blood on all sides of the altar. [3] The offerer must present all the fat from it: the fat tail,[f] the fat surrounding the entrails,[B] [4] and the two kidneys with the fat on them at the loins; he will also remove the fatty lobe of the liver[g] with the kidneys. [5] The priest will burn them on the altar as a fire offering[h] to the LORD; it is a restitution offering. [6] Any male among the priests may eat it.[i] It is to be eaten in a holy place;[j] it is especially holy.[k]

[7] "The restitution offering is like the •sin offering;[l] the law is the same for both. It belongs to the priest[m] who makes •atonement[n] with it. [8] As for the priest who presents someone's burnt offering, the hide of the burnt offering he has presented belongs to him; it is the priest's. [9] Any •grain offering[o] that is baked in an oven or prepared in a pan or on a griddle belongs to the priest who presents it; it is his. [10] But any grain offering, whether dry or mixed with oil, belongs equally[C] to all of Aaron's sons.

The Fellowship Sacrifice

[11] "Now this is the law of the •fellowship sacrifice[p] that someone may present to the LORD:

[a]6:23 Dt 13:17; 33:10; 1Sm 7:9; Ps 51:19
[b]6:25 Ex 29:14
[c]6:26 Lv 16:24; 1Co 9:13
[d]7:1 Lv 14:12-13
[e]7:2 Gn 22:2; Lv 3:5; Nm 6:11; Jos 8:31; 1Ch 16:1; Ps 20:3; Mc 6:6
[f]7:3 Lv 3:9
[g]7:4 Lv 9:10
[h]7:5 Dt 18:1
[i]7:6 1Co 9:13
[j]Lv 16:24
[k]Lv 14:13
[l]7:7 Ex 29:14
[m]Lv 14:13
[n]Ex 30:15
[o]7:9 Ex 40:29
[p]7:11 Lv 3:1,3,6,9

A6:27 Lit wash what it spattered on   B7:3 LXX, Sam add and all the fat that is on the entrails; Lv 3:3,9,14; 4:8   C7:10 Lit oil, will be a man like his brother

priest and congregation that he must be dedicated totally to the Lord. These twice-daily offerings contrast with the high priesthood of Jesus, who offered the perfect sacrifice of Himself for all time (Heb 7:27).

6:24-30 The purpose of this segment was to protect the holiness of the offering and to warn those who might desecrate the meat through unlawful consumption. On the sin offering, see chapter 4.

6:25 Most holy (or "especially holy"; see v. 29) indicates that the priest was the recipient of the meat. The place for slaughter of the sacrificial animal must be on the north side of the altar, just as with animals from the flock (1:11; 4:24,29,33).

6:26 The officiating priest must consume the meat, showing divine acceptance of the gift, but he could share it with other priests (v. 29; see note at v. 30). The location was in the courtyard of the tent of meeting (cp. v. 16), meaning that the meat was not taken home for family members to eat.

6:27 Since this offering was holy, anything the meat touched would become holy. The priest became holy through contact with the sacrifice. Special cautions were in order for the animal's disposal since it was for the forgiveness of sin. Inevitably, blood splattered on the priest's clothes when he sprinkled the blood on the altar (4:6,17; 5:9; 16:14-15,19); the cleaning of the garments must be in a holy place, which was inside the courtyard. On the blood of Christ, see 1Pt 1:19 and note there.

6:28 Since a clay pot used in this sacrifice was made of porous material that absorbed the animal's blood, it could not be used again, but a bronze pot could be scrubbed clean and reused.

6:30 The exception to the priestly consumption of the offering was that a priest could not benefit from a sin offering given for himself. When the priest took the blood inside the sacred tent, or the holy place, that was the sin offering to atone for the sins of the priest and the congregation (cp. 4:5,16). The animal was therefore burned up on the ash heap (4:12,21).

7:1 On especially holy, see note at 6:25.

7:2 The blood sprinkled on all sides of the altar was also part of the rituals for the burnt and fellowship offerings (1:11; 3:2,8,13) but not the sin offering (see note at 6:25).

7:3-7 These instructions are similar to those for the sin offering (4:1-35; 6:25-30).

7:8 The gift of the hide to the officiating priest of the burnt offering is new information, not mentioned in chapter 1; the skin of the sin offering was burned (4:11).

7:9-10 The officiating priest received his due, but provision of grain was designated for all the priests, whether they officiated at offerings or not. This included priests with physical defects (2:3; 6:18,29; 22:21-22).

7:11-21 Three subtypes made up the fellowship sacrifice: thanksgiving (vv. 12-15), vow, and freewill offerings (vv. 16-18). Since the fellowship offering was voluntary and it was shared with family and guests, the offering demonstrated the generosity of the giver, who made his offering as an expression of praise. On the fellowship sacrifice, see chapter 3.

¹² If he presents it for thanksgiving, in addition to the thanksgiving sacrifice,^{A,a} he is to present unleavened cakes^b mixed with olive oil, unleavened wafers^c coated with oil, and well-kneaded cakes of fine flour mixed with oil. ¹³ He is to present as his offering cakes of leavened bread^B with his thanksgiving sacrifice of fellowship. ¹⁴ From the cakes he must present one portion of each offering as a contribution^d to the Lord. It will belong to the priest who sprinkles the blood of the fellowship offering; it is his. ¹⁵ The meat of his thanksgiving sacrifice of fellowship must be eaten on the day he offers it;^e he may not leave any of it until morning.^f

¹⁶ "If the sacrifice he offers is a vow^{C,g} or a freewill offering,^{D,h} it is to be eaten on the day he presents his sacrifice, and what is left over may be eaten on the next day. ¹⁷ But what remains of the sacrificial meat by the third day must be burned up.ⁱ ¹⁸ If any of the meat of his fellowship sacrifice is eaten on the third day, it will not be accepted.^j It will not be credited to the one who presents it; it is re-

pulsive.^k The person who eats any of it will be responsible for his sin.^E

¹⁹ "Meat that touches anything •unclean must not be eaten; it is to be burned up. Everyone who is •clean may eat any other meat. ²⁰ But the one who eats meat from the Lord's fellowship sacrifice while he is unclean,^F that person must be cut off from his people.^l ²¹ If someone touches anything unclean, whether human uncleanness, an unclean animal, or any unclean, detestable^{G,m} creature, and eats meat from the Lord's fellowship sacrifice, that person must be cut off from his people."

Fat and Blood Prohibited

²² The Lord spoke to Moses: ²³ "Tell the Israelites: You are not to eat any fatⁿ of an ox, a sheep, or a goat. ²⁴ The fat of an animal that dies naturally or is mauled by wild beasts^{H,o} may be used for any purpose, but you must not eat it.^p ²⁵ If anyone eats animal fat from a fire offering presented to the Lord, the person who eats it must be cut off from his people.

^a7:12 Lv 22:29
^bEx 12:8
^cLv 2:4
^d7:14 Ex 36:3
^e7:15 Lv 22:30
^fEx 12:10; 34:25; Lv 19:5-8; Dt 16:4
^g7:16 Lv 27:8
^hEx 35:29
ⁱ7:17 Lv 19:6
^j7:18 Lv 1:4
^kLv 19:7; Is 65:4; Ezk 4:14
^l7:20 Gn 17:14; Lv 7:27; 19:8; Nm 9:13
^m7:21 Lv 11:10-13,20,23,41-42; Is 66:17; Ezk 8:10
ⁿ7:23 Lv 3:16-17
^o7:24 Lv 17:15; 22:8
^pEx 22:31; Lv 3:17; 17:15; 22:8; Dt 14:21; Ezk 4:14; 44:31

---

^A7:12 The thanksgiving sacrifice is the first of three kinds of fellowship sacrifices. It was given to express gratitude to God (Jr 33:11) in circumstances such as answered prayer (Ps 50:14-15) or safe travel (Ps 107:22-25).   ^B7:13 Although yeast was prohibited from being burned on the altar (Lv 2:11), leavened bread could still be an offering (Lv 23:17-20) to be eaten by the priests and their families.   ^C7:16 The vow offering, the second category of fellowship sacrifice, was brought as an expression of gratitude to fulfill a vow; Gn 28:20; 2Sm 15:7-8; Pr 7:14.   ^D7:16 The freewill offering, the third category of fellowship sacrifice, was a voluntary expression of gratitude toward God for any reason; Dt 16:10; Ps 54:6.   ^E7:18 Or will bear his guilt   ^F7:20 Lit while his uncleanness is upon him   ^G7:21 Some Hb mss, Sam, Syr, Tg read swarming   ^H7:24 Lit fat of a carcass or the fat of a mauled beast

---

7:12-13 Thanksgiving (Hb *todah*) offerings were typically associated with a song of joy (Neh 12:27; Ps 42:14; 50:14; 69:30; 100:1; 116:17). This was the Israelite's response to answered prayer and a proclamation to others of God's goodness; the worshiper in similar fashion was generous toward others by sharing his meal with guests. A grain offering of three bread products accompanied the thanksgiving animal (chap. 3). One of the cakes had to be made of yeast (**leavened bread**), a departure from the typical practice. The inclusion of yeast was appropriate since this sacrifice was an offering of joy.

7:14 The bread offering belonged to the officiating priest of the **blood** sacrifice who represented its acceptance by the Lord. **Contribution** (Hb *terumah*), traditionally known as the "heave offering," was not necessarily lifted up in the ritual. It is related to the word "to remove" (Hb *herim*), which describes a dedicatory portion that was set aside especially for the Lord (2:9; 6:15). It probably means a dedicated "gift" made to the Lord.

7:15 Eating the offering **on the day he offers it** showed its special holiness; any delay removed the offering from the act of sacrifice and increased the possibility of its defilement. The participants in the communal meal witnessed the immediate acceptance of the offering by the Lord through eating the freshly roasted meat.

7:16-17 The **vow** offering was a grateful response to the completion of a vow, and the **freewill offering** was a general expression of joyful thanksgiving by the worshiper. The freewill gift was often given in conjunction with the establishment of community worship (Ex 35:29; Nm 29:39; 1Ch

29:6; Ezr 2:68). The psalmist depicted them as offerings of praise (Ps 54:6; 119:108).

7:18 The word **credited** (Hb *chashav*) refers to the act of counting or evaluating (25:27). If the meat was not eaten or burned up within the required time, the offering was **repulsive**, meaning tainted and desecrated (19:7; Ezk 4:14).

7:19 The general principle regarding the purity of the **meat** was the threat of defilement through contact. The **clean** must eat only clean meat, or the consequences were severe.

7:20-21 If the person who ate this sacrifice was ceremonially unclean, he was **cut off**, which meant either excommunicated from worship (22:3) or premature death by the intervention of God (17:4). This stern warning was given because of the communal nature of the fellowship offerings. First Corinthians 11:27-32 contains a similar warning against those who took the Lord's Supper unworthily. The categories of defilement are **human . . . animal**, and **detestable creature** (Hb *sheqets*), which is the same term that designated unclean food (11:10; 20:25) or an idol (Dt 7:26).

7:22-27 An offering's **fat** and **blood** belonged to the Lord, and they could not be eaten (3:17; 17:6). The fat was the best portion, and the blood represented the life of the animal that had been surrendered to God. The blood was to be properly drained from the sacrifice before the meat was eaten (Dt 12:23; cp. Ac 15:29).

7:24 Animal **fat** that came from a source other than a sacrifice could be used for household purposes (e.g., oil), but

²⁶Wherever you live, you must not eat the blood^a of any bird or animal. ²⁷Whoever eats any blood, that person must be cut off from his people."

The Portion for the Priests

²⁸The LORD spoke to Moses: ²⁹"Tell the Israelites: The one who presents a fellowship sacrifice to the LORD must bring an offering to the LORD from his sacrifice. ³⁰His own hands will bring the fire offerings to the LORD. He will bring the fat together with the breast. The breast is to be waved as a presentation offering^b before the LORD. ³¹The priest is to burn the fat on the altar, but the breast belongs to Aaron and his sons. ³²You are to give the right thigh^c to the priest as a contribution from your fellowship sacrifices. ³³The son of Aaron who presents the blood of the fellowship offering and the fat will have the right thigh as a portion. ³⁴I have taken from the Israelites the breast of the presentation offering and the thigh of the contribution from their fellowship sacrifices, and have assigned them to Aaron the priest and his sons as a permanent portion^{A,d} from the Israelites."

³⁵This is the portion from the fire offerings to the LORD for Aaron and his sons^e since the day they were presented to serve the LORD as priests. ³⁶The LORD commanded this to be given to them by the Israelites on the day He

anointed them.^f It is a permanent portion^A throughout their generations.

³⁷This is the law for the burnt offering, the grain offering, the sin offering, the restitution offering, the ordination offering,^g and the fellowship sacrifice, ³⁸which the LORD commanded Moses on Mount Sinai^h on the day He^B commanded the Israelites to present their offerings to the LORD in the Wilderness of Sinai.ⁱ

Ordination of Aaron and His Sons

8 The LORD spoke to Moses: ²"Take Aaron, his sons with him, the garments, the anointing oil,^j the bull of the *sin^C offering, the two rams, and the basket^k of unleavened bread, ³and assemble the whole community^l at the entrance to the tent of meeting." ⁴So Moses did as the LORD commanded him, and the community assembled at the entrance to the tent of meeting. ⁵Moses said to them, "This is what the LORD has commanded to be done."

⁶Then Moses presented Aaron and his sons and washed them with water. ⁷He put the tunic on Aaron, wrapped the sash around him, clothed him with the robe, and put the *ephod^m on him. He put the woven band of the ephod around him and fastened it to him. ⁸Then he put the breastpiece on him and placed the *Urim and Thummimⁿ into the breastpiece. ⁹He also put the turban^o on his head and placed the gold medallion, the

Cross references (center column)

^a7:26 Gn 9:3-4; Lv 17:10-12; Dt 12:16,23
^b7:30 Ex 29:24
^c7:32 Ex 29:22; Lv 8:25-26; 9:21; Nm 18:18
^d7:34 Ex 29:28; 30:21; Lv 6:11,15; 10:15; 24:9; Nm 18:8,11,19; Jr 5:22
^e7:35 Mt 10:10; 1Co 9:13-14; 1Tm 5:17-18
^f7:36 Ex 40:13-15; Lv 8:12,30
^g7:37 Lv 8:22
^h7:38 Ex 34:2
ⁱEx 31:18; 34:32; Lv 26:46; Neh 9:13
^j8:2 Ex 29:7
^kGn 40:16
^l8:3 Ex 12:47
^m8:7 Ex 28:4
ⁿ8:8 Ex 28:30; Nm 27:21; Dt 33:8; 1Sm 28:6; Ezr 2:63; Neh 7:65
^o8:9 Lv 16:4

---

^A7:34,36 Or statute   ^B7:38 Or he   ^C8:2 Or purification

---

the blood from an animal could never be eaten (3:16-17; 17:13).

7:26 Wherever you live refers to any domestic dwelling place, setting apart the people's homes from the sanctuary (3:17; 23:3,21; Ex 12:20; Nm 35:29).

7:28-36 After detailing the procedure about the laity and the disposal of the bread and meat, the passage focuses on the portions of the fellowship offering presented to the Lord—that which belonged to the priests.

7:30-31 His own hands refers to the individual layperson, emphasizing that the gift came voluntarily from the owner. Since the **fat** belonged to the Lord, it must be burned up, and the **breast** was given to the priests collectively, symbolizing that the sacrifice had been accepted by the Lord. The expression **waved as a presentation offering**, traditionally known as the "wave offering," describes the (Hb) tenuphah offering (v. 34; 8:27; 9:21; 10:14-15; Ex 29:24; 35:22). Rather than waving the offering, the worshiper presented it as a dedicatory gift ("elevation offering") to the Lord. This symbolized the transfer of the gift portion from the owner's possession (Milgrom, 1:475).

7:32-33 The officiating priest received the **right thigh** (cp. Nm 18:18-19) as a **contribution** (Hb terumah; see note at v. 14). The breast and thigh were meaty portions that provided a regular stipend for the priestly families, showing the

generosity of the Lord. The owner first burned the fat on the altar to the Lord. Then the owner apportioned the meat as a gift from the Lord to His servants, His priests.

7:35-36 The distribution of portions of offerings to the priests began with the ordination of Aaron and his sons (8:25-28; Ex 29:22-26).

7:37-38 This summary statement points back to the setting described in 1:1.

8:2 Take Aaron begins the installation service that was prescribed in Exodus 29. Just as Aaron was a mediator for the nation, Israel was to function as priest to the nations (Ex 19:5-6). Christians serve as witnesses to the priesthood of the perfect high priest, Jesus (Heb 7:1-28; 1Pt 2:5,9).

8:3 The service was a public installation to assure the community of the legitimacy of the Aaronic priesthood.

8:6 Aaron underwent a ceremonial washing to show the moral purity required of priests (1Pt 3:21).

8:7-9 The outfitting of the priests in sacred garments gave them "glory and beauty" in the eyes of the congregation (Ex 28:2,40). Although the brightly colored garments symbolized the mediation of the nation in the presence of the Lord, the priesthood of Jesus is not accompanied by a dress code; His mediation is in His personhood as the perfect God-man who reigns with the Father (1Tm 2:5-6; Heb 1:4; 4:14; 6:20).

holy diadem, on the front of the turban, as the LORD had commanded Moses.[a]

[10] Then Moses took the anointing oil and anointed the tabernacle and everything in it to consecrate[b] them. [11] He sprinkled some of the oil on the altar seven times, anointing the altar with all its utensils, and the basin with its stand, to consecrate them.[c] [12] He poured some of the anointing oil on Aaron's head and anointed and consecrated him.[d] [13] Then Moses presented Aaron's sons, clothed them with tunics, wrapped sashes around them, and fastened headbands on them, as the LORD had commanded Moses.

[14] Then he brought the bull near for the sin offering, and Aaron and his sons laid their hands on the head of the bull for the sin offering. [15] Then Moses slaughtered it,[A] took the blood, and applied it with his finger to the horns of the altar on all sides, purifying[e] the altar. He poured out the blood at the base of the altar and consecrated it so that •atonement can be made on it.[B,f] [16] Moses took all the fat that was on the entrails, the fatty lobe of the liver, and the two kidneys[g] with their fat, and he burned them on the altar.[h] [17] He burned up the bull with its hide, flesh, and dung outside the camp,[i] as the LORD had commanded Moses.

[18] Then he presented the ram for the •burnt offering, and Aaron and his sons laid their hands on the head of the ram. [19] Moses slaughtered it and[c] sprinkled the blood on all sides of the altar. [20] Moses cut the ram into pieces and burned the head, the pieces, and the suet,[j] [21] but he washed the entrails and shanks with water. He then burned the entire ram on the altar. It was a burnt offering for a pleasing

aroma, a fire offering to the LORD as He had commanded Moses.

[22] Next he presented the second ram, the ram of ordination,[k] and Aaron and his sons laid their hands on the head of the ram. [23] Moses slaughtered it,[D] took some of its blood, and put it on Aaron's right earlobe, on the thumb of his right hand, and on the big toe of his right foot.[l] [24] Moses also presented Aaron's sons and put some of the blood on their right earlobes, on the thumbs of their right hands, and on the big toes of their right feet. Then Moses sprinkled the blood on all sides of the altar. [25] He took the fat—the fat tail,[m] all the fat that was on the entrails, the fatty lobe of the liver, and the two kidneys with their fat—as well as the right thigh. [26] From the basket of unleavened bread that was before the LORD he took one cake of unleavened bread, one cake of bread made with oil, and one wafer, and placed them on the fat portions and the right thigh.[n] [27] He put all these in the hands of Aaron and his sons and waved them before the LORD as a presentation offering. [28] Then Moses took them from their hands and burned them on the altar with the burnt offering. This was an ordination offering for a pleasing aroma, a fire offering to the LORD. [29] He also took the breast and waved it before the LORD as a presentation offering; it was Moses' portion of the ordination ram as the LORD had commanded him.

[30] Then Moses took some of the anointing oil and some of the blood that was on the altar and sprinkled them on Aaron and his garments, as well as on his sons and their garments. In this way he consecrated Aaron

a 8:1-9 Ex 28:1-43; 29:1-8; 39:1-31
b 8:10 Ex 19:10,14,23; 20:11
c 8:10-11 Ex 30:18-28; 38:8; 40:7-11
d 8:12 Ex 29:7; 30:30; Lv 21:10-12
e 8:15 Ex 29:36; Lv 14:49,52; Nm 19:19; Ps 51:7; Ezk 43:22-23; 45:18
f 8:14-15 Ex 29:10-12,36-37; Lv 4:7
g 8:16 Lv 7:4
h Ex 29:13; Lv 4:7-10
i 8:17 Ex 29:14; 33:7; Lv 4:12,21; 6:4; 9:11; 10:4-5; 13:46; 14:3; 16:27; 17:3; 24:14,23
j 8:20 Lv 1:8
k 8:22 Ex 29:22,26-34; Lv 7:37; 8:28-33
l 8:23 Ex 29:20; Lv 14:14,17,25,28
m 8:25 Lv 3:9
n 8:26 Ex 29:3,23; Lv 7:32; Nm 6:15-19

A 8:14-15 Or offering, and he slaughtered it. [15] Then Moses   B 8:15 Or it by making •atonement for it   C 8:18-19 Or ram, [19] and he slaughtered it. Moses   D 8:22-23 Or ram, [23] and he slaughtered it. Moses

---

8:10-13 The holiness of God demanded a consecration of the place, items, and persons who ministered before the Lord. This was satisfied by Christ through His perfect offering and as the perfect offerer (Heb 7:26; 9:11-12). Christians are anointed by a spiritual anointing (2Co 1:21-22; 1Jn 2:20). **All its utensils** refers to the items that enabled the carrying out of the offerings, such as forks, firepans, and the tabernacle furniture (Ex 27:3).

8:14-17 The priests made **atonement** for their own sins before they could mediate for the people. The death of an animal was necessary, but this could not take away the sins of the people (Heb 5:3; 9:22; 10:4). The death of Jesus Christ alone achieved complete atonement (2Co 5:21; Col 1:20). The High Priest Jesus had no need to make atonement for His own sins since He was without sin (Heb 4:15; 5:9-10; 7:26-27; 10:11-12).

8:18-21 The complete incineration of the **ram** indicated the total dedication of the priests to the Lord's service.

8:22-30 The application of the blood from the "ram of or-

dination" to the priests' extremities symbolized the total cleansing of the priests. The ear indicated hearing the confessions of the people, the hand represented the touching and handling of the offerings, and the foot represented the holy courtyard and tent in which they served.

8:25-29 Moses placed the **unleavened bread** in the hands of Aaron and his sons to lift it up as a gesture of presentation to the Lord. Moses retrieved the presentation offering and burned it on the altar that was still smoking from the incineration of the first ram offering. Moses took the **breast** for himself as the officiating priest and made it his presentation offering (7:31).

8:30 The Hebrew term for **consecrated** (Hb qaddesh) refers to select persons, places, or things that were designated exclusively for the Lord's service (Ex 29:21; Heb 10:22). The public nature of this rite gave the congregation confidence in the effectiveness of the Aaronic household. Christians can have greater confidence in their acceptance by the Lord through Jesus Christ (Eph 3:12).

and his garments, as well as his sons and their garments.ᵃ

³¹ Moses said to Aaron and his sons, "Boil the meat at the entrance to the tent of meeting and eat it there with the bread that is in the basket for the ordination offering as I commanded:ᴬ Aaron and his sons are to eat it.ᵇ ³² You must burn up what remains of the meat and bread.ᶜ ³³ You must not go outside the entrance to the tent of meeting for seven days, until the time your days of ordination are completed, because it will take seven days to ordain you.ᴮ ³⁴ The LORD commanded what has been done today in order to make atonement for you.ᵈ ³⁵ You must remain at the entrance to the tent of meeting day and night for seven days and keep the LORD's chargeᵉ so that you will not die,ᶠ for this is what I was commanded." ³⁶ So Aaron and his sons did ev-

erything the LORD had commanded through Moses.

The Priestly Ministry Inaugurated

9 On the eighth day Moses summoned Aaron, his sons, and the elders of Israel.ᵍ ² He said to Aaron, "Take a young bull for a •sinᶜ offering and a ram for a •burnt offering, both without blemish,ʰ and present them before the LORD. ³ And tell the Israelites:ᴰ Take a male goat for a sin offering; a calf and a lamb, male yearlings without blemish, for a burnt offering; ⁴ an ox and a ram for a •fellowship offering to sacrifice before the LORD; and a •grain offering mixed with oil. For today the LORD is going to appearⁱ to you."

⁵ They brought what Moses had commanded to the front of the tent of meeting, and the whole community came forward and stood before the LORD. ⁶ Moses said, "This is

ᵃ8:30 Ex 29:21; Is 6:6-7; Heb 10:22
ᵇ8:31 Lv 6:16,18; 10:12; 1Co 9:13-14
ᶜ8:32 Ex 29:34
ᵈ8:33-34 Ex 29:35-37; Heb 7:28
ᵉ8:35 Gn 26:5
ᶠLv 10:1-2
ᵍ9:1 Ex 18:12
ʰ9:2 Ex 29:1
ⁱ9:4 Gn 35:9

ᴬ8:31 LXX, Syr, Tg read was commanded; Ex 29:31-32   ᴮ8:33 Lit because he will fill your hands for seven days   ᶜ9:2 Or purification   ᴰ9:3 Sam, LXX read elders of Israel

---

8:31-32 The **ordination** meal was also public and was consumed by the priests to indicate the divine approval of their offerings and to symbolize their fellowship with the Lord. To avoid any polluting effect and to prevent its consumption by an unlawful person, the remainder of the meal was burned up on the same day (7:15).

8:33-36 The number **seven** symbolized the completion of the ritual's purpose. Since the ordination rite was about consecration, the priests could not leave the sacred grounds during the ordination week. Although the priests enjoyed the privileges of service, the gravity of their responsibility put them at risk if they offended the holiness of God (10:1-2; 1Sm 2:12-17). Christian leaders, whether lay or clergy, have a special accountability before the Lord and the church (1Tm 1:7; 4:14-16; 2Tm 1:6; Jms 3:1).

9:1-24 Verses 6 and 23 are the only ones in Leviticus that in-

•olah

Hebrew Pronunciation	[oh LAH]
HCSB Translation	burnt offering
Uses in Leviticus	62
Uses in the OT	286
Focus Passage	Leviticus 9:2-3,7,12-14,16-17,22,24

'Olah always signifies burnt offering and is the first kind of Israelite offering described in detail (Lv 1:3-17). 'Olah could be a participle of the verb rise up ('alah), and speculation occurs whether what rises is the smoke and fire, the aroma, or the animal onto the altar. However, the verb in a causative form ("to offer up") regularly has 'olah as object, suggesting an offering of sacrifice to God (Gn 8:20; 22:2). Its burning was a form of presentation. The 'olah was unique in being entirely consumed by altar fire, yet its preparation involved removing the animal's skin, which the officiating priest could keep (Lv 7:8). The offerer put his hand on the victim in apparent identification with it. The 'olah could express joy (1Sm 6:14-15), accompany petition (Jr 14:12), or seek atonement (Lv 1:4). God permitted poor people to present birds as burnt offerings (Lv 5:7; 12:8).

clude the word "glory." The purpose of the inaugural act of worship was to recognize the presence of the Lord among His people, symbolized by the fiery glory of the Lord in the tent of meeting. This exhibition gave the congregation assurance of His favor. Christians can have confidence in the acceptance of their worship through the certainty of Christ's cleansing blood that makes full atonement. The call to worship (vv. 1-6) was followed by the ritual cleansing of the priests (vv. 7-14) and of the people (vv. 15-21). The conclusion was the act of worship (vv. 22-24).

9:1 On the **eighth day** after the seven days of ordination (8:33; Ex 29:35), the divine call to worship began a new creative act. All the events of this first communal service occurred on this one day. Worship begins at the initiation of the Lord, who directs the proper protocol for acceptable worship. The **elders** represented the congregation, although the entire congregation approached the tent of meeting (v. 5).

9:2 Aaron and his sons had to present a **sin offering** (4:1-5:13) and a **burnt offering** (1:3-17), although they had undergone seven days of consecration. This demonstrated their constant need for atonement before they officiated as mediators.

9:3-5 Aaron's giving directions to the congregation elevated him in their eyes. Four of the five offerings described in chapters 1-7 were called for; the exception, the guilt offering, involved restitution and was a private, individual ceremony. The purpose of the instructions was to prepare for the appearance of the "glory of the Lord" (v. 6). The word "appear" (Hb ra'ah) occurs three times (vv. 4,6,23); the "appearance" was a visible manifestation of the presence of the Lord. This theophany, an outward manifestation of the invisible God, involved a light or fire (Ex 3:2). The fiery presence of the Lord was an echo of God's coming to Moses at Sinai (Ex 19:18), making the portable tent another "Sinai." Christians look to Jesus' incarnation as the presence of the Lord (Jn 1:14). Through His atonement they receive the glory of the Lord by faith (Jn 17:22-24; Rm 8:30; 1Pt 1:7).

what the LORD commanded you to do, that the glory of the LORD[a] may appear to you." [7] Then Moses said to Aaron, "Approach the altar and sacrifice your sin offering and your burnt offering; make *atonement for yourself and the people.[A,b] Sacrifice the people's offering and make atonement for them, as the LORD commanded."

[8] So Aaron approached the altar and slaughtered the calf as a sin offering for himself. [9] Aaron's sons brought the blood to him, and he dipped his finger in the blood and applied it to the horns of the altar. He poured out the blood at the base of the altar. [10] He burned the fat, the kidneys, and the fatty lobe of the liver from the sin offering on the altar, as the LORD had commanded Moses. [11] He burned up the flesh and the hide[c] outside the camp.[d]

[12] Then he slaughtered the burnt offering. Aaron's sons brought him the blood, and he sprinkled it on all sides of the altar. [13] They brought him the burnt offering piece by piece, along with the head, and he burned them on the altar. [14] He washed the entrails and the shanks and burned them with the burnt offering on the altar.

[15] Aaron presented the people's offering. He took the male goat for the people's sin offering, slaughtered it, and made a sin offering with it as he did before. [16] He presented the burnt offering and sacrificed it according to

the regulation.[e] [17] Next he presented the grain offering, took a handful of it, and burned it on the altar in addition to the morning burnt offering.[f]

[18] Finally, he slaughtered the ox and the ram as the people's fellowship sacrifice. Aaron's sons brought him the blood, and he sprinkled it on all sides of the altar. [19] They also brought the fat portions from the ox and the ram—the fat tail, the fat surrounding the entrails, the kidneys, and the fatty lobe of the liver— [20] and placed these on the breasts. Aaron burned the fat portions on the altar, [21] but he waved the breasts[g] and the right thigh as a presentation offering[h] before the LORD, as Moses had commanded.[B]

[22] Aaron lifted up his hands toward the people and blessed[i] them. He came down after sacrificing the sin offering, the burnt offering, and the fellowship offering. [23] Moses and Aaron then entered the tent of meeting. When they came out, they blessed the people, and the glory of the LORD appeared to all the people. [24] Fire came from the LORD and consumed[j] the burnt offering and the fat portions on the altar. And when all the people saw it, they shouted[k] and fell facedown on the ground.[l]

Nadab and Abihu

10 Aaron's sons Nadab[m] and Abihu[n] each took his own firepan,[o] put fire in it,

Cross-references (center column):
[a]9:6 Ex 40:34; Lk 9:32
[b]9:7 Heb 5:1-3; 7:26-27
[c]9:11 Lv 7:8
[d]Ex 29:14; Lv 4:8-10,12,21; 8:17; 16:27
[e]9:16 Lk 18:26
[f]9:17 Ex 29:38-42; Lv 2:2
[g]9:21 Ex 29:26-27; Lv 7:30-34; 8:26; 10:14-15; Nm 6:20; 18:18
[h]Ex 29:24
[i]9:22 Gn 14:19; Nm 6:24-26
[j]9:24 1Kg 18:38-39; 2Ch 7:1
[k]Ps 35:27; Is 12:6; 24:14
[l]Nm 16:4
[m]10:1 Ex 6:23; 28:1; Nm 3:2,4; 26:60-61; 1Ch 6:3
[n]Ex 24:1
[o]Ex 27:3; 38:3; 1Kg 7:50; 2Kg 25:15; Jr 52:19

[A]9:7 LXX reads *and your household*   [B]9:21 Some Hb mss, LXX, Sam read *as the LORD commanded Moses*

9:6 The fullest disclosure of the Lord was the human incarnation of Jesus Christ, whose death and resurrection demonstrated **the glory of the LORD** (Rm 6:4; Heb 2:9). Christians participate in the glory of the Lord (2Co 4:17; 1Pt 5:10).

9:7-14 After the gathering of the elements of worship, the priests first received the rites of cleansing and dedication.

9:8-11 When Aaron went **outside the camp**, this was the first time he had left the sanctuary since his seven-day ordination. The incineration of the sacrificial animal demonstrated that the officiating priest could not benefit from the offering made for his own sins (8:17). Another variation from the regular sin offering was that the **blood** was not taken inside the tent.

9:12-14 No mention is made of the calf's hide (7:8), which apparently was burned up (8:17; 9:11).

9:15-16 By offering a **male goat** in accordance with the **regulation** of the sin offering for a leader, the animal represented the elders, and by proxy, the entire community (4:22-23).

9:17-21 The priests continued to represent the entire community by carrying out the **grain** and **fellowship** offerings that were typically offered by an individual Israelite. For the procedures of the two offerings, see chapters 2–3.

9:22 When Aaron **lifted up his hands**, it showed that he invoked the Lord (1Kg 8:22; Ps 28:2). Prayer for blessing was

the duty of the priestly order (Dt 10:8; 21:5). On the traditional priestly blessing, see Nm 6:24-26 and notes there.

9:23 The entrance into **the tent** by Moses and Aaron confirmed the legitimacy of the newly ordained Aaron, who would enter the holy place every day from then on (Ex 29:42-44; 30:7-8). Moses entered the cloud when God descended on Mount Sinai (Ex 24:18; cp. Lk 9:34). His entrance now signaled the imminent presence of the Lord. Christians receive and declare the imminent relationship with God through Christ (2Co 5:18-20; Col 1:20).

9:24 The fiery blast probably came out of the tent from the most holy place and incinerated the remains of the smoldering offerings. The God who revealed Himself at Sinai was now the God of the tent who dwelt in their midst (Ex 24:17; 2Ch 7:3). The Hebrew words for **saw** (*wayyar'*) and **shouted** (*wayyaronnu*) may be a pun on "appeared" (*wayyera'*; v. 23). The response of the people exhibited their joy and humility (cp. 2Ch 7:1-3). "Shouted" (Hb *ranan*) means to give a ringing cry aloud (Jr 31:7), and **fell facedown** (Hb *naphal*) also describes later reactions to the fiery demonstrations of the Lord (Jdg 13:20; 2Ch 7:3; cp. Nm 16:22; 20:6; Mt 17:6).

10:1 Nadab was the firstborn of Aaron, and presumably **Abihu** was his second born (Ex 6:23). **Firepan** (Hb *machtah*) describes a hand-held censer used to transport live coals from one place to another (16:12; Nm 16:17-18,46). The **incense** (Hb *qetoreth*) may have been from the altar of incense (Ex 30:1-10) or from another unnamed source

placed incense on it,[a] and presented unauthorized[b] fire before the Lord, which He had not commanded them to do. [2] Then fire came from the Lord[c] and burned them to death before the Lord.[d] [3] So Moses said to Aaron, "This is what the Lord meant when He said:

I will show My holiness[A,e]
to those who are near Me,[f]
and I will reveal My glory[B,g]
before all the people."

But Aaron remained silent.

[4] Moses summoned Mishael and Elzaphan,[h] sons of Aaron's uncle Uzziel,[i] and said to them, "Come here and carry your relatives away from the front of the sanctuary to a place outside the camp."[j] [5] So they came forward and carried them in their tunics outside the camp, as Moses had said.

[6] Then Moses said to Aaron and his sons Eleazar and Ithamar,[k] "Do not let your hair hang loose[l] and do not tear your garments,[m] or else you will die, and the Lord will become angry[n] with the whole community. However, your brothers, the whole house of Israel, may mourn[o] over that tragedy when the Lord sent the fire. [7] You must not go outside the entrance to the tent of meeting or you will die, for the Lord's anointing oil[p] is on you." So they did as Moses said.

Regulations for Priests

[8] The Lord spoke to Aaron: [9] "You and your sons are not to drink wine[q] or beer[r] when you enter the tent of meeting, or else you will die;

Cross references

[a]10:1 Ex 30:7-9; Lv 16:12; Nm 16:17,46
[b]Ex 30:9; Nm 3:4; 26:61; Jr 2:25; 3:13; Hs 5:7
[c]10:2 Gn 4:14
[d]Nm 26:61; Dt 4:24; 2Sm 6:7
[e]10:3 Nm 20:13; Ezk 20:41; 28:22,25; 36:23; 38:16; 39:27
[f]Dt 30:14; Heb 7:19
[g]Ex 14:4,17-18; Is 26:15; Ezk 28:22; 39:13; Hg 1:8
[h]10:4 Ex 6:22
[i]Nm 3:19
[j]Lv 8:17; Heb 13:11-13
[k]10:6 Ex 6:23
[l]Lv 13:45; 21:10; Nm 5:18; Jdg 5:2
[m]Lv 21:10; Mk 14:63
[n]Ex 16:20
[o]Gn 37:34
[p]10:7 Ex 29:7; Lv 21:12
[q]10:9 Gn 9:21
[r]Nm 6:3-4; Dt 7:13; 11:14; Jdg 13:4; Pr 20:1; Ezk 44:21; Dn 1:3-16; 10:3; Am 2:12; Mk 4:23-25; Lk 1:15; Jn 2:1-11; Rm 14:21; 1Tm 3:3,8

[A]10:3 Or will be treated as holy   [B]10:3 Or will be glorified

(Nm 16:6,17-18). The location **before the Lord** may refer to the bronze altar in the courtyard (1:5) or inside the tent in the holy place (4:4). The word **unauthorized** (Hb *zarah*) translates the adjective "strange, foreign," meaning that the fire came from some place other than the altar of the sanctuary (16:12; Nm 16:46). The crime of Aaron's sons was not the incense (Ex 30:9) but the fire that came from some place other than the legitimate source.

10:2 The phrase **fire came from the Lord and burned** is the same Hebrew expression as that in 9:24 (cp. Nm 16:35) in which the fire that consumed the offerings on the altar came from the Lord Himself (the most holy place). It inaugurated the altar's perpetual fire that was to be maintained indefinitely (Lv 6:12-13) by the priests, making it the legitimate source for all future offerings and the burning of incense.

10:3 God's immediate lethal response displayed His **holiness to those who are near Me**, the officiating priests. The incident especially illustrates the failure of the priests to

zar

Hebrew Pronunciation	[ZARR]
HCSB Translation	strange, foreign, unauthorized
Uses in Leviticus	4
Uses in the OT	70
Focus Passage	Leviticus 10:1

Zar occurs nominally (56x) and adjectivally (14x). It describes *unauthorized* incense or people in the Lord's sanctuary (Ex 29:33; 30:9). God had not given orders or freedom for Nadab and Abihu's incense burning (Lv 10:1). The noun mostly designates non-Israelite *strangers* or *foreigners* (Lm 5:2), who may be seen as *foes* (Is 29:5) or *barbarians* (Is 25:5). It implies *someone unknown* (Pr 11:15) or *outside* a family (Lv 22:13). *Zar* suggests *someone else* (1Kg 3:18). It refers to plants as *exotic* (Is 17:10), children as *illegitimate* (Hs 5:7), and behavior as *strange* (Is 28:21) or *alien* (Hs 8:12). *Zar* connotes what is *forbidden* (Pr 5:3). Related *zur* (6x) means *go astray* (Ps 58:3). It is "turn from" as *abandon* (Jb 19:13) or *satisfy* (Ps 78:30). Passive-reflexives denote *be estranged* (Ezk 14:5) or *turn one's* back (Is 1:4). The causative passive participle means *stranger* (Ps 69:8).

distinguish between the "holy" and the "common" (v. 10). **Reveal My glory** parallels "show My holiness," indicating that the display of the fiery glory (9:23-24) exhibited the holy demands of God for proper worship; the objective was to instruct **all the people** in the holiness of God (v. 11). Aaron's silence reflected his discernment that mourning rites in the sacred sanctuary were inappropriate (v. 6).

10:4 Mishael and **Elzaphan** were Aaron and Moses' cousins (Ex 6:16-22), making them Levites—and thus responsible for the purity of the sanctuary—but not priests. They could remove the bodies of Nadab and Abihu without offending God (Nm 3:5-10; 18:2-6). **Front of the sanctuary** describes the courtyard's altar area (v. 18). The Hebrew term for **come here** (*qarav*) echoes the same word describing an illicit offering ("presented" in v. 1 and "approach" in 9:7). The priestly function is described as those who are "near" (Hb *qarov*) God (10:3).

10:6 Eleazar and **Ithamar** (Ex 28:1) replaced their deceased brothers (Nm 3:4), and Eleazar later succeeded Aaron as high priest (Dt 10:6). Eleazar's descendant Zadok ultimately displaced the priestly family of Abiathar, a descendant of Ithamar (1Kg 2:27, 35). Disheveled **hair** and torn **garments** (Gn 37:34) were part of mourning rites (Lv 13:45; 21:10). By desecrating the holy sanctuary through mourning, the priests risked death and bringing guilt on the **whole community**. If the priests compromised the holiness of God and were disqualified to make atonement, the community would not be protected from divine wrath. Although Aaron and his sons could not mourn, the community (**brothers**) could fulfill their obligation.

10:7 Priests bearing holy **anointing oil** (cp. 8:12) would defile themselves if they left the holy precinct for mourning rites during the time of their consecration (21:10-12).

10:8 Only here in Leviticus does Aaron alone receive a direct word from the Lord (cp. Ex 4:27; Nm 18:1,8). God usually addressed Aaron and Moses as a team (Lv 13:1).

10:9 Libations accompanied offerings (23:13; Nm 28:7,14), and through tithes wine was provided the priests (Nm 18:12; Dt 14:23). During their performance of priestly functions, the priests were not allowed to drink **wine or beer** so they would be clear-headed in making judgments and

this is a permanent statute[a] throughout your generations. [10]You must distinguish[b] between the holy and the common,[c] and the *clean and the *unclean,[d] [11]and teach the Israelites all the statutes[e] that the Lord has given to them through Moses."

[12]Moses spoke to Aaron and his remaining sons, Eleazar and Ithamar: "Take the *grain offering that is left over from the fire offerings[f] to the Lord, and eat it prepared without yeast beside the altar, because it is especially holy. [13]You must eat it in a holy place because it is your portion[A] and your sons' from the fire offerings to the Lord, for this is what I was commanded. [14]But you and your sons and your daughters may eat the breast of the presentation offering and the thigh of the contribution in any ceremonially clean place, because these portions have been assigned to you and your children from the Israelites' *fellowship sacrifices. [15]They are to bring the thigh of the contribution and the breast of the presentation offering, together with the offerings of fat portions made by fire, to wave as a presentation offering before the Lord. It will belong

permanently[g] to you and your children, as the Lord commanded."

[16]Later, Moses inquired about the male goat of the *sin offering, but it had already been burned up. He was angry with Eleazar and Ithamar, Aaron's surviving sons, and asked, [17]"Why didn't you eat the sin offering in the sanctuary area?[h] For it is especially holy, and He has assigned it to you to take away the *guilt[i] of the community[j] and make *atonement for them before the Lord. [18]Since its blood was not brought inside the sanctuary, you should have eaten it in the sanctuary area, as I commanded."[k]

[19]But Aaron replied to Moses, "See, today they presented their sin offering and their *burnt offering before the Lord. Since these things have happened to me, if I had eaten the sin offering today, would it have been acceptable in the Lord's sight?" [20]When Moses heard this, it was acceptable to him.[B]

Clean and Unclean Land Animals

11 The Lord spoke to Moses and Aaron: [2]"Tell the Israelites: You may eat[l] all

[a]10:9 Ex 28:43; Lv 11:46 [b]10:10 Lv 20:25 [c]Ezk 22:26; 42:20; 44:23; 48:15; Ac 10:28 [d]Lv 11:4; Nm 19:13 [e]10:11 Gn 47:2 [f]10:12 Dt 18:1 [g]10:15 Ex 29:28; 30:21; Lv 6:11,15; 24:9; Nm 18:8,11,19; Jr 5:22 [h]10:17 Lv 6:26,29 [i]Nm 5:31 [j]Ex 28:38; Hs 14:2; Jn 1:29 [k]10:18 Lv 6:26,29-30 [l]11:2 Lv 11:1-23; Dt 14:3-21; Dn 1:3-16; Ac 10:9-16; 11:3; Rm 14:2; Gl 2:11-14

[A]10:13 Or statute   [B]10:20 Lit acceptable in his sight

carrying out their duties in the sanctuary (v. 10). The abuse of alcohol by priests rendered their service useless (Is 28:7ff).

10:10 The assignment for the priests was cultic—distinguishing between the holy and the ordinary—and pedagogical—instructing the congregation in cultic matters (Ezk 22:26). **Distinguish** (from Hb badal; "to separate, divide") meant differentiating the distinctive from the commonplace, such as edible animals from prohibited animals (11:47; 20:25). The **holy** (Hb qodesh) versus the **common** (Hb chol) refers to anything or anyone that was dedicated to the Lord and His service as opposed to that which was for normal use. **Clean** (Hb tahor) and **unclean** (Hb tame') refer to matters pertaining to the physical existence of the people, especially foods (chap. 11; Dt 14) and persons (Lv 12–15; Nm 5:2-4).

10:11 The term **teach** (Hb yarah) means "to instruct" but it can also mean "to determine" (14:57). The instruction was intended to enable the people to discern the proper conduct in cultic matters and everyday activities. The Levites in general and the priests in particular were to direct the people in the ways commanded by the Lord (Dt 17:9-11; 33:10; Ezk 44:23-24). A statute (Hb choq) was a divine enactment that must be kept (Lv 19:37; 26:46).

10:12 For the portion of the **grain offering** belonging to the priests, see 2:10; 6:15-18; 7:9-10; 21:22.

10:13 The word **portion** (Hb choq), meaning that which was owed to him, is the same as "statute" in verse 11. Moses emphasized that the command came from the Lord, not by his authority.

10:14-15 For the **breast** and **thigh** belonging to the priestly families, see 7:31-34; Nm 18:18-19; the priestly portion of the fellowship offerings could be eaten in their homes (Lv 22:10-13; Nm 18:11).

10:16-18 Moses complained that Aaron's sons had failed

to eat the consecration portions of the **sin offering** as prescribed by the Lord. By their failure to perform the proper ritual ceremony, the guilt of the community remained. The Hebrew phrase translated **inquired** (darosh darash) can be rendered "diligently inquired," reflecting the urgency of Moses' concern for proper observance. For instructions on the priestly consumption of the sin offering, see 6:26,29-30.

10:19 Aaron had to determine whether the desecration by Nadab and Abihu made the **sin offering** portions inappropriate for priestly consumption. Rather than run the risk of defiling the sanctuary further, Aaron chose to burn up the entire goat.

10:20 A wordplay on **acceptable** (Hb yatav), which describes the divine approval in verse 19, also describes Moses' acceptance of the explanation; Moses accepted the determination of Aaron according to verse 10.

11:1–15:33 By observing the purity laws, the Israelites would live and prosper by God's presence and blessing.

11:1-47 This chapter includes two separate listings of clean and unclean creatures (vv. 1-23; vv. 41-45); the identity of many of the animals is uncertain. If the food laws were observed by the Israelites, the holiness of God would extend from the sanctuary to their homes, ensuring His continued presence.

Although there may have been some hygienic benefit derived from keeping the food laws, the prohibited creatures were not consistently unhealthy for human consumption. More likely, these laws reflected the distinctive types at creation (Gn 1:26) and thereby taught the Israelites that there was an ordained pattern of conformity. The instructions showed the Israelites that they must conform to their creation as a holy people, avoiding assimilation with their pagan neighbors by adopting their domestic habits.

The food laws that once separated the Israelites and the nations are not binding on modern believers (Ac 10:11-16;

these kinds of land animals.[a] [3] You may eat any animal with divided hooves and that chews the cud. [4] But among the ones that chew the cud or have divided hooves you are not to eat these:

the camel,[b] though it chews the cud, does not have divided hooves—it is 'unclean for you;

[5] the hyrax,[A,c] though it chews the cud, does not have hooves—it is unclean for you;

[6] the hare, though it chews the cud, does not have hooves—it is unclean for you;

[7] the pig, though it has divided hooves, does not chew the cud—it is unclean for you.

[8] Do not eat any of their meat or touch their carcasses—they are unclean for you.[d]

Clean and Unclean Aquatic Animals

[9] "This is what you may eat from all that is in the water: You may eat everything in the water that has fins and scales, whether in the seas or streams. [10] But these are to be detestable to you: everything in the seas or streams that does not have fins and scales among all the swarming things and other living creatures[e] in the water. [11] They are to remain detestable to you; you must not eat any of their meat, and you must detest their carcasses. [12] Everything in the water that does not have fins and scales will be detestable to you.

Unclean Birds

[13] "You are to detest these birds. They must not be eaten because they are detestable:

the eagle,[B,f] the bearded[c] vulture, the black vulture,[D] [14] the kite,[E] any kind of falcon,[F,g]

[a]11:2 Dt 14:4-21; Ac 10:9-16; Rm 14:14
[b]11:4 Gn 24:64; 31:34; Dt 14:7; Jr 2:23; Mt 19:24; 23:24; Mk 10:25; Lk 18:25
[c]11:5 Dt 14:7; Ps 104:18; Pr 30:26
[d]11:8 Lv 7:21; 11:24-27; Is 52:11; 2Co 6:17
[e]11:10 Gn 1:20; 2:19; Lv 11:46
[f]11:13 Dt 14:12; 28:49; 32:11; Pr 23:5; Is 40:31
[g]11:14 Dt 14:13; Jb 28:7
[h]11:16 Dt 14:15; Jb 39:26
[i]11:17 Dt 14:16
[j]11:18 Dt 14:17; Ps 102:6; Is 34:11; Zph 2:14
[k]11:22 Dt 28:38
[l]11:24 Ezk 22:3-4; 23:17; 44:25; Mc 2:10; Hg 2:13
[m]11:25 Lv 16:28; 17:15-16; 22:6; Nm 19:7-10
[n]11:27 Rv 18:2
[o]11:29 Ex 8:3

[15] every kind of raven, [16] the ostrich,[G] the short-eared owl,[H] the gull,[I] any kind of hawk,[h]

[17] the little[J] owl, the cormorant,[K] the long-eared owl,[L,i]

[18] the white[M] owl, the desert owl,[N,j] the osprey,[O] [19] the stork,[P] any kind of heron,[Q] the hoopoe, and the bat.

Clean and Unclean Flying Insects

[20] "All winged insects that walk on all fours are to be detestable to you. [21] But you may eat these kinds of all the winged insects that walk on all fours: those that have jointed legs above their feet for hopping on the ground. [22] You may eat these:

any kind of locust,[k] katydid, cricket, and grasshopper.

[23] All other winged insects that have four feet are to be detestable to you.

Purification after Touching Dead Animals

[24] "These will make you unclean. Whoever touches their carcasses will be unclean[l] until evening, [25] and whoever carries any of their carcasses must wash his clothes and will be unclean until evening.[m] [26] All animals that have hooves but do not have a divided hoof and do not chew the cud are unclean for you. Whoever touches them becomes unclean. [27] All the four-footed animals[n] that walk on their paws are unclean for you. Whoever touches their carcasses will be unclean until evening, [28] and anyone who carries their carcasses must wash his clothes and will be unclean until evening. They are unclean for you.

[29] "These creatures that swarm[o] on the ground are unclean for you:

[A]11:5 A rabbit-like animal   [B]11:13 Or griffon-vulture   [C]11:13 Or black   [D]11:13 Or the osprey, or the bearded vulture   [E]11:14 Or hawk   [F]11:14 Or buzzards, or hawks   [G]11:16 Or eagle owl   [H]11:16 Or the night hawk, or the screech owl   [I]11:16 Or long-eared owl   [J]11:17 Or tawny   [K]11:17 Or fisher owl, or pelican   [L]11:17 Or the ibis   [M]11:18 Or little   [N]11:18 Or the pelican, or the horned owl   [O]11:18 Or Egyptian vulture   [P]11:19 Or heron   [Q]11:19 Or cormorant, or hawk

---

Col 2:16), but the underlying principle remains true: all that a Christian does must be for the glory of God (1Co 10:31). Consecrated Christian living arises from the inner person who is redeemed, not from physical things (Mk 7:18-23; Rm 14:17-18). Christians must exercise spiritual maturity in choosing food and drink (Rm 14; 1Co 8; 10:23) and in associating with others (1Co 5:11; 2Co 6:14).

11:1 The Lord included **Aaron** as the recipient of the purity instructions (chaps. 11–15) since they were primarily a priestly responsibility (10:10-11; 13:1; 14:33; 15:1).

11:9-12 The unacceptable sea creatures were designated **detestable** (Hb sheqets) three times (vv. 10,11,12). Although there is no specific prohibition against touching them or warning of ritual uncleanness by consumption, as "detest-

able" creatures these prohibitions may be assumed.

11:13-19 These birds may have been outlawed because they are scavengers.

11:24-25 Defilement occurred by touching **carcasses** or by transporting them. When transporting them, the clothing of the person was defiled by contact and required laundering. All corpses conveyed uncleanness through touch (22:4; Nm 5:2). For consecrated persons, just being in the presence of a dead body resulted in defilement (Lv 21:11; Nm 6:6; Hg 2:13). The duration of uncleanness stretched until sunset, which concluded a day (Dt 22:26; Jos 8:29).

11:27 Four-footed animals that walked on **paws** (lit "palms"), such as dogs and cats, were considered unclean.

the weasel,^A the mouse,^a any kind of large lizard,^B

30 the gecko, the monitor lizard,^C the common lizard,^D the skink,^E and the chameleon.^F

^31 These are unclean for you among all the swarming creatures. Whoever touches them when they are dead will be unclean until evening. ^32 When any one of them dies and falls on anything it becomes unclean—any item of wood, clothing, leather, •sackcloth,^b or any implement used for work. It is to be rinsed with water and will remain unclean until evening; then it will be •clean. ^33 If any of them falls into any clay pot, everything in it will become unclean; you must break it. ^34 Any edible food^c coming into contact with that unclean water will become unclean, and any drinkable liquid in any container will become unclean. ^35 Anything one of their carcasses falls on will become unclean. If it is an oven or stove, it must be smashed; it is unclean and will remain unclean for you. ^36 A spring or cistern containing water will remain clean, but someone who touches a carcass in it will become unclean. ^37 If one of their carcasses falls on any seed that is to be sown, it is clean; ^38 but if water has been put on the seed and one of their carcasses falls on it, it is unclean for you.

^39 "If one of the animals that you use for food dies,^G anyone who touches its carcass will be

^a 11:29 1Sm 6:4-5,11,18; Is 66:17
^b 11:32 Gn 37:34
^c 11:34 Lv 26:5
^d 11:44 Nm 15:41
^e Ex 19:22; Lv 20:7; Nm 11:18; Ezk 38:23
^f Lv 19:2; 20:7,26; 1Pt 1:16
^g 11:45 Ex 6:7; 20:2; Lv 25:38, 42; 26:13,45
^h Lv 21:8
^i 11:47 Lv 26:6

unclean until evening. ^40 Anyone who eats some of its carcass must wash his clothes and will be unclean until evening. Anyone who carries its carcass must wash his clothes and will be unclean until evening.

Unclean Swarming Creatures

^41 "All the creatures that swarm on the earth are detestable; they must not be eaten. ^42 Do not eat any of the creatures that swarm on the earth, anything that moves on its belly or walks on all fours or on many feet,^H for they are detestable. ^43 Do not become contaminated by any creature that swarms; do not become unclean or defiled by them. ^44 For I am •Yahweh your God,^d so you must consecrate yourselves^e and be holy because I am holy.^f You must not defile yourselves by any swarming creature that crawls on the ground. ^45 For I am Yahweh, who brought you up from the land of Egypt to be your God,^g so you must be holy because I am holy.^h

^46 "This is the law concerning animals, birds, all living creatures that move in the water, and all creatures that swarm on the ground, ^47 in order to distinguish between the unclean and the clean, between the animals^i that may be eaten and those that may not be eaten."

Purification after Childbirth

12 The LORD spoke to Moses: ^2 "Tell the Israelites: When a woman becomes

---

^A 11:29 Or mole rat, or rat   ^B 11:29 Or of thorn-tailed or dabb lizard, or of crocodile   ^C 11:30 Or the spotted lizard, or the chameleon
^D 11:30 Or the gecko, or the newt, or the salamander   ^E 11:30 Or sand lizard, or newt, or snail   ^F 11:30 Or salamander, or mole
^G 11:39 Dies of itself or by predators; this does not apply to animals slaughtered for food.   ^H 11:42 Lit fours, to anything multiplying pairs of feet

11:29-38 Carcasses of creatures **that swarm on the ground** (such as insects) conveyed defilement through direct contact or indirectly to persons who handled inanimate things which had already come into contact with the dead creatures. Since a **clay pot** absorbed the liquid polluted by a carcass, it must be thrown away; food or drink touched secondarily by the contaminated water in the pot was unclean. Two exceptions pertained to water: the water of a reservoir from which a carcass was retrieved remained clean, probably because of the ritual significance of water for purification; and **seed** already germinated by **water** was **unclean**.

11:39-40 Animals that had been killed by wild animals or that had died by natural means—that is, not slaughtered for food—could be eaten, but they still conveyed uncleanness (17:15; they were prohibited for a priest, 22:8). The cleansing rite demanded more of the person who had longer contact with a corpse. This involved the laundering of clothes for those who ate or transported the animal.

11:44-45 Since the Lord had made the Israelites uniquely His by delivering them from **the land of Egypt**, they must be **holy** as He is holy (Ex 19:2). It was necessary that the people maintain their ritual cleanness in everyday activities as well as in sanctuary worship. The food offered to the Lord in worship involved the partaking of portions by the priests and the people. For God to continue His presence among

the people, they must practice the same measure of holiness in their homes. Since it was inevitable that the people became unclean, they **must consecrate** themselves by undergoing these cleansing procedures.

11:46-47 The purpose was to **distinguish** (Hb badal) what could be lawfully consumed; the same root term occurs in 10:10 and means "set apart" in 20:24. The ultimate rationale was theological: because the Lord is holy, the people had to express holiness by their behavior (19:2; 20:7,26).

12:1-8 The newborn child of a mother was not impure, since the male child was circumcised on the eighth day while the mother was in isolation. That circumcision was a part of her duty showed the mother's valued contribution to the community. She was the vehicle of God's blessing of children within the covenant commitment of the Israelites to God (Gn 17). Children were considered a gift from God; the woman was not ritually defiled when she was pregnant. The impurity resulted from blood and fluids that are a part of the birth process (Lv 12:4-5,7). Men also underwent separation and ritual reintegration due to bodily discharges (15:2-18).

The message of these restrictions is that a person's spiritual relationship is more important than physical attributes (Ross, Holiness, 264). Jesus healed a woman who endured constant hemorrhaging, showing His power to cleanse physically and spiritually (Mk 5:25-34). Although the physical

pregnant and gives birth to a male child,*a* she will be ˚unclean seven days, as she is during the days of her menstrual impurity.*b* ³The flesh of his foreskin*c* must be circumcised*d* on the eighth day.*e* ⁴She will continue in purification*f* from her bleeding*g* for 33 days. She must not touch any holy thing or go into the sanctuary until completing her days of purification. ⁵But if she gives birth to a female child, she will be unclean for two weeks as she is during her menstrual impurity. She will continue in purification from her bleeding for 66 days.

⁶"When her days of purification are complete, whether for a son or daughter, she is to bring to the priest at the entrance to the tent of meeting a year-old male lamb for a ˚burnt offering, and a young pigeon or a turtledove for a ˚sin*A* offering. ⁷He will present them before the LORD and make ˚atonement on her behalf; she will be ˚clean from her discharge of blood. This is the law for a woman giving birth, whether

to a male or female. ⁸But if she doesn't have sufficient means*B,h* for a sheep, she may take two turtledoves or two young pigeons,*i* one for a burnt offering and the other for a sin*A* offering. Then the priest will make atonement on her behalf, and she will be clean."

Skin Diseases

13 The LORD spoke to Moses and Aaron: ² "When a person has a swelling,*c* scab,*D* or spot on the skin of his body, and it becomes a disease on the skin*j* of his body, he is to be brought to Aaron the priest or to one of his sons, the priests. ³The priest will examine the infection*k* on the skin of his body. If the hair in the infection has turned white and the infection appears to be deeper than the skin of his body, it is a skin disease. After the priest examines him, he must pronounce him ˚unclean. ⁴But if the spot on the skin of his body is white and does not appear to be deeper than the skin,

*a*12:2 Lv 10:14
*b*Lv 15:19
*c*12:3 Ex 4:25
*d*Gn 34:14
*e*Gn 17:12-13; 21:4; Lk 2:21; Gl 3:5; 5:6; 6:15
*f*12:4 Lv 14:2
*g*Lk 8:43
*h*12:8 Lv 14:21
*i*Lk 2:24
*j*13:2 Lv 14:3,7,32,44,54-57; Dt 24:8; 2Kg 5:3,6-7,27; 2Ch 26:19
*k*13:3 Ex 11:1; Dt 17:8; 21:5; Is 53:8

A12:6,8 Or *purification*   **B**12:8 Lit *if her hand cannot obtain what is sufficient*   **C**13:2 Or *discoloration*   **D**13:2 Or *rash,* or *eruption*

---

body was created good, Christians must subject their physical life to the greater good of the kingdom of God (Rm 12:1; 1Co 6:13; Php 3:19-21). Jesus Christ is the perfect High Priest and pure sacrifice (Heb 7:26). By His blood Christians receive His purity and holiness (Heb 13:12; 1Jn 3:3). This was true also of Mary, the mother of Jesus, whose flow of blood and physical impurities after childbirth symbolized her more serious spiritual defilement that was finally and fully cleansed through the blood of her son, Jesus.

12:2 Although the text does not say that anyone who came into contact with a woman after childbirth became unclean, the parallel instructions about menstruation and any other discharge of blood made this explicit (15:25-30). Her domestic duties would defile the home and members of her family through touch.

12:3 On circumcision, compare Gn 17:10-11; on the **eighth day**, compare Lk 1:59; 2:21; Php 3:5.

nega'

Hebrew Pronunciation	[neh GAH]
HCSB Translation	disease, affliction, plague
Uses in Leviticus	61
Uses in the OT	78
Focus Passage	Leviticus 13:2-6,9,12-13,17,20

Nega' derives from *naga'*, a verb that basically means *touch* but often indicates infliction of a painful blow. The noun implies a negative touch, either an *affliction* sent by God, a *diseased* condition of skin, a *contamination* of clothing or housing, or a *physical assault*. God may send a *plague* (Gn 12:17). *Nega'* denotes *skin disease* when combined with another word that by itself can mean skin disease or leprosy (*tsara'ath*; Lv 13:3). In these cases *nega'* may emphasize the *affliction* or *divine stroke* that the disease represents. *Nega'* alone can mean a person's *infection* (Lv 13:6) or the *contamination* of objects (13:49); with a definite article it sometimes refers to the *infected person* (13:4). Each individual knows his *afflictions* (1Kg 8:38). Victims of *assault* (Dt 17:8) go to court for redress, probably for *blows* they have suffered (2Sm 7:14). The Suffering Servant bore a *nega'* that mankind deserved (Is 53:8).

12:5 The rationale for doubling the period of isolation for the birth of a **female child** was not a matter of gender bias since the purification rite was the same for the male child. Possibly the circumstance of both a mother and a daughter (a future mother) doubled the period of time.

12:6-7 The **sin offering** is better understood as a "purification offering," since no sin was committed by the mother or child. The mother was in a state of ritual uncleanness because of the **discharge of blood**.

12:8 The grace of the Lord provided a concession for the poor (5:7,11; cp. Lk 2:22-24); it was the willing spirit of the worshiper that was foremost, not the value of the gift.

13:1–14:32 The instructions on physical purity emphasize the holiness of God and the necessity of purity in every aspect of our relationship with Him. In order for God's covenant people to enter the tabernacle—that is, enter into the place for worship and fellowship with Him—their bodies had to be free from skin disease. The priests diagnosed the disease and isolated the sick person. But God in His grace provided for the restoration of the isolated party after healing occurred. A restored person could return to the community of the faithful.

13:1 God addressed both Moses and Aaron in verse 1; 11:1; 14:33; and 15:1 (cp. 10:8).

13:2 The Hebrew word for "skin disease" (*tsara'ath*) was translated into the Greek as *lepra* and transliterated as such into Latin. Thus most English translations render the word as "leprosy." The Hebrew word, however, is a generic term that refers to changes in the surface of the human skin and is best translated as **a disease on the skin**; it can also indicate fungus or mildew (v. 47; 14:34). During the postexilic period, rabbis identified 72 types of skin disease.

13:3-8 Two different types of problems are described here. One can be classified as minor because the disorder was not severe and the isolation was not long, but in the second type, the infinitive absolute in verse 7 indicates that the infection had spread drastically. The ritual period of **seven days** is predominant in Leviticus (8:33; 12:2; 14:8; 15:13,28,

and the hair in it has not turned white, the priest must quarantine the infected person for seven days.[a] [5]The priest will then reexamine him on the seventh day. If he sees that the infection remains unchanged and has not spread on the skin, the priest must quarantine him for another seven days. [6]The priest will examine him again on the seventh day. If the infection has faded and has not spread on the skin, the priest is to pronounce him *clean;[b] it is a scab. The person is to wash his clothes and will become clean. [7]But if the scab spreads further on his skin after he has presented himself to the priest for his cleansing,[c] he must present himself again to the priest. [8]The priest will examine him, and if the scab has spread on the skin, then the priest must pronounce him unclean; he has a skin disease.

[9]"When a skin disease develops on a person, he is to be brought to the priest. [10]The priest will examine him. If there is a white swelling on the skin that has turned the hair white, and there is a patch of raw flesh in the swelling, [11]it is a chronic disease on the skin of his body, and the priest must pronounce him unclean.[d] He need not quarantine him, for he is unclean. [12]But if the skin disease breaks out all over the skin so that it covers all the skin of the infected person from his head to his feet so far as the priest can see, [13]the priest will look, and if the skin disease has covered his entire body, he is to pronounce the infected person clean.[e] Since he has turned totally white, he is clean. [14]But whenever raw flesh appears on him, he will be unclean. [15]When the priest examines the raw flesh, he must pronounce him unclean. Raw flesh is unclean; it is a skin disease. [16]But if the raw flesh changes[A] and[B] turns white, he must go to the priest. [17]The priest will examine him, and if the infection has turned white, the priest must pronounce the infected person clean; he is clean.

[18]"When a boil appears on the skin[f] of one's body[g] and it heals, [19]and a white swelling or a reddish-white spot develops where the boil was, the person must present himself to the priest. [20]The priest will make an examination, and if the spot seems to be beneath the skin and

a 13:4 Nm 12:14-15; 2Kg 15:5
b 13:6 Nm 8:6-7; Ps 51:2; Ezk 24:13
c 13:7 Lv 14:2
d 13:11 Lv 11:4
e 13:13 Lv 10:10
f 13:18 Lv 13:2
g Ex 9:9-11; Dt 28:27,35; Jb 2:7
h 13:30 Lv 13:2
i 13:33 Gn 41:14; Lv 14:8-9; 21:5; Nm 6:9,18-19; Dt 21:12; Jdg 16:17,19,22

the hair in it has turned white, the priest must pronounce him unclean; it is a skin disease that has broken out in the boil. [21]But when the priest examines it, if there is no white hair in it, and it is not beneath the skin but is faded, the priest must quarantine him seven days. [22]If it spreads further on the skin, the priest must pronounce him unclean; it is an infection. [23]But if the spot remains where it is and does not spread, it is only the scar from the boil. The priest is to pronounce him clean.

[24]"When there is a burn on the skin of one's body produced by fire, and the patch made raw by the burn becomes reddish-white or white, [25]the priest is to examine it. If the hair in the spot has turned white and the spot appears to be deeper than the skin, it is a skin disease that has broken out in the burn. The priest must pronounce him unclean; it is a skin disease. [26]But when the priest examines it, if there is no white hair in the spot and it is not beneath the skin but is faded, the priest must quarantine him seven days. [27]The priest will reexamine him on the seventh day. If it has spread further on the skin, the priest must pronounce him unclean; it is a skin disease. [28]But if the spot has remained where it was and has not spread on the skin but is faded, it is the swelling from the burn. The priest is to pronounce him clean, for it is only the scar from the burn.

[29]"When a man or woman has an infection on the head or chin, [30]the priest must examine the infection. If it appears to be deeper than the skin,[h] and the hair in it is yellow and sparse, the priest must pronounce the person unclean. It is a scaly outbreak,[c] a skin disease of the head or chin. [31]When the priest examines the scaly infection, if it does not appear to be deeper than the skin, and there is no black hair in it, the priest must quarantine the person with the scaly infection for seven days. [32]The priest will reexamine the infection on the seventh day. If the scaly outbreak has not spread and there is no yellow hair in it and it does not appear to be deeper than the skin, [33]the person must shave himself[i] but not shave the scaly area. Then the priest must quarantine the person who has the scaly

---

A 13:16 Or recedes   B 13:16 Or flesh again   C 13:30 Or is scall; Hb obscure

---

23:6; 25:4). The number seven and its derivatives occur 176 times in Leviticus. The number seven symbolizes fullness, perfection, or completion. Later rabbis suggested that the person being isolated was banished outside the camp or city, while others suggested that it was in special quarters, as in the case of King Uzziah (1Kg 15:5; 2Ch 26:21).

13:9,11,15 The **chronic disease on the skin** involved the presence of raw flesh rendering a person unclean. The Hebrew word tsara'ath appears 35 times in the OT, but only six times

outside of Leviticus (Dt 24:8; 2Kg 5:3,6-7,27; 2Ch 26:19). A person is pronounced **unclean** seven times in chapter 13 (vv. 11,15,36,44,46,51,55).

13:25 The skin condition described here could be identified as psoriasis.

13:30 The term **scaly outbreak** appears only in this pericope of the Bible (vv. 30-37; 14:54). It refers to a skin disease that appeared on a person's **head or chin**.

outbreak for another seven days. ³⁴ The priest will examine the scaly outbreak on the seventh day, and if it has not spread on the skin and does not appear to be deeper than the skin, the priest is to pronounce the person clean. He is to wash his clothes, and he will be clean. ³⁵ But if the scaly outbreak spreads further on the skin after his cleansing, ³⁶ the priest is to examine the person. If the scaly outbreak has spread on the skin, the priest does not need to look for yellow hair; the person is unclean. ³⁷ But if as far as he can see, the scaly outbreak remains unchanged and black hair has grown in it, then it has healed; he is clean. The priest is to pronounce the person clean.

³⁸ "When a man or a woman has white spots on the skin of the body, ³⁹ the priest is to make an examination. If the spots on the skin of the body are dull white, it is only a rashᴬ that has broken out on the skin; the person is clean.

⁴⁰ "If a man loses the hair of his head, he is bald,ᵃ but he is clean. ⁴¹ Or if he loses the hair at his hairline, he is bald on his forehead, but he is clean. ⁴² But if there is a reddish-white infection on the bald head or forehead, it is a skin disease breaking out on his head or forehead.ᵇ ⁴³ The priest is to examine him, and if the swelling of the infection on his bald head or forehead is reddish-white, like the appearance of a skin disease on his body, ⁴⁴ the man is afflicted with a skin disease;ᶜ he is unclean. The priest must pronounce him unclean; the infection is on his head.

⁴⁵ "The person afflicted with an infectious skin disease is to have his clothes tornᵈ and his hair hanging loose, and he must cover his mouthᵉ and cry out, 'Unclean, unclean!' ⁴⁶ He will remain unclean as long as he has the infection; he is unclean. He must live alone in a place outside the camp.ᶠ

Contaminated Fabrics

⁴⁷ "If a fabric is contaminated with mildew—in wool or linen fabric, ⁴⁸ in the warp or woof of linen or wool, or in leather or anything made of leather— ⁴⁹ and if the contamination is green or red in the fabric, the leather, the

ᵃ13:40 2Kg 2:23
ᵇ13:42 2Ch 26:19-20
ᶜ13:44 Ex 4:6; Lv 14:2-3; 22:4; Nm 5:2; 12:10
ᵈ13:45 Lv 10:6; 21:10
ᵉEzk 24:17,22; Mc 3:7
ᶠ13:46 Nm 5:1-4; 8:17; 12:14-15
ᵍ13:51 Lv 11:24; 15:10-12,21-27; Hg 2:12-13
ʰ13:59 Lv 10:10-11
ⁱ14:2 Lv 11:46
ʲLv 12:4-5; Nm 6:9; Ezk 44:26
ᵏLv 4:16
ˡ14:3 Lv 8:17
ᵐLv 13:2-3

warp, the woof, or any leather article, it is a mildew contamination and is to be shown to the priest. ⁵⁰ The priest is to examine the contamination and quarantine the contaminated fabric for seven days. ⁵¹ The priest is to reexamine the contamination on the seventh day. If it has spread in the fabric, the warp, the woof, or the leather, regardless of how it is used, the contamination is harmful mildew; it is unclean.ᵍ ⁵² He is to burn the fabric, the warp or woof in wool or linen, or any leather article, which is contaminated. Since it is harmful mildew it must be burned up.

⁵³ "When the priest examines it, if the contamination has not spread in the fabric, the warp or woof, or any leather article, ⁵⁴ the priest is to order whatever is contaminated to be washed and quarantined for another seven days. ⁵⁵ After it has been washed, the priest is to reexamine the contamination. If the appearance of the contaminated article has not changed, it is unclean. Even though the contamination has not spread, you must burn up the fabric. It is a fungusᴬ on the front or back of the fabric.

⁵⁶ "If the priest examines it, and the contamination has faded after it has been washed, he must cut the contaminated section out of the fabric, the leather, or the warp or woof. ⁵⁷ But if it reappears in the fabric, the warp or woof, or any leather article, it has broken out again. You must burn up whatever is contaminated. ⁵⁸ But if the contamination disappears from the fabric, the warp or woof, or any leather article, which have been washed, it is to be washed again, and it will be clean.

⁵⁹ "This is the law concerning a mildew contamination in wool or linen fabric, warp or woof, or any leather article, in order to pronounce it clean or unclean."ʰ

Cleansing of Skin Diseases

14 The Lᴏʀᴅ spoke to Moses: ² "This is the lawⁱ concerning the person afflicted with a skin disease on the day of his cleansing.ʲ He is to be brought to the priest,ᵏ ³ who will go outside the campˡ and examine him.ᵐ

ᴬ13:39,55 Hb obscure

13:45-46 The person rendered **unclean** was relegated to life outside the community until healed. The **torn clothes** were a sign of mourning, while the crying out was a warning to those who were ceremonially clean. This practice was still observed during Jesus' time, when 10 men with serious skin diseases stood at a distance from the community and were asked by Jesus to show themselves to the priest after He had healed them (Lk 17:11-14).

13:47-59 As with contagious skin diseases, so also with **mildew** or fungus; no spreadable **contamination** of fabric or

leather was permitted to undermine the ceremonial cleanliness of the community.

14:1-32 God, in His grace, provided for the restoration of the person rendered unclean by a skin disease. The priests did not cure the person affected. They only diagnosed the disease and helped with the religious rituals subsequent to a person's healing. Chapter 14 points to the grace of God, who made provision for the people affected by disease to return to the community of the faithful.

14:3 The examination of the person afflicted with a skin dis-

If the skin disease has disappeared from the afflicted person,^A ^4the priest will order that two live •clean birds,^a cedar wood,^b scarlet^c yarn, and hyssop^d be brought for the one who is to be cleansed. ^5Then the priest will order that one of the birds be slaughtered over fresh water in a clay pot. ^6He is to take the live bird together with the cedar wood, scarlet yarn, and hyssop, and dip them all into the blood of the bird that was slaughtered over the fresh water. ^7He will then sprinkle the blood seven times on the one who is to be cleansed from the skin disease. He is to pronounce him clean and release the live bird over the open countryside.^e ^8The one who is to be cleansed must wash his clothes, shave off all his hair, and bathe with water; he is clean. Afterward he may enter the camp, but he must remain outside his tent for seven days. ^9He is to shave off all his hair again on the seventh day: his head, his beard, his eyebrows, and the rest of his hair. He is to wash his clothes and bathe himself with water; he is clean.

^10"On the eighth day he must take two unblemished^f male lambs, an unblemished year-old ewe lamb, a •grain offering of three quarts^B of fine flour mixed with olive oil, and one-third of a quart^C of olive oil. ^11The priest who performs the cleansing will place the person who is to be cleansed, together with these offerings, before the Lord at the entrance to the tent of meeting. ^12The priest is to take one male lamb

and present it as a •restitution offering,^g along with the one-third quart^C of olive oil, and he must wave them as a presentation offering^h before the Lord. ^13He is to slaughter the male lamb at the place in the sanctuary area where the •sin offering^i and •burnt offering^j are slaughtered,^k for like the sin offering, the restitution offering belongs to the priest;^l it is especially holy.^m ^14The priest is to take some of the blood from the restitution offering and put it on the lobe of the right ear of the one to be cleansed, on the thumb of his right hand, and on the big toe of his right foot.^n ^15Then the priest will take some of the one-third quart^C of olive oil and pour it into his left palm. ^16The priest will dip his right finger into the oil in his left palm and sprinkle some of the oil with his finger seven times before the Lord. ^17From the oil remaining in his palm the priest will put some on the lobe of the right ear of the one to be cleansed, on the thumb of his right hand, and on the big toe of his right foot, on top of the blood of the restitution offering.^o ^18What is left of the oil in the priest's palm he is to put on the head of the one to be cleansed. In this way the priest will make •atonement for him before the Lord. ^19The priest must sacrifice the sin offering and make atonement for the one to be cleansed from his uncleanness.^p Afterward he will slaughter the burnt offering. ^20The priest is to offer the burnt offering and the

---

^a14:4 Gn 40:17
^b Jdg 9:15; 2Sm 5:11; 7:2,7; 1Kg 5:13; 6:9-10; Ps 29:5; Sg 1:17; 8:9; Am 2:9; Zch 11:1-2
^c Ex 25:4; Nm 4:8; 19:6
^d Ex 12:22
^e 14:7 Lv 14:53; 16:21-22
^f 14:10 Ex 29:1
^g 14:12 Lv 5:6-19
^h Ex 29:24
^i 14:13 Ex 29:14
^j Gn 22:2; Lv 3:5; Nm 6:11; Jos 8:31; 1Ch 16:1; Ps 20:3; Mc 6:6
^k Lv 1:11; 6:25; 7:2
^l Lv 7:7
^m Lv 2:3; 6:10; 7:1,6; 10:12; 24:9; 27:28
^n 14:14 Ex 29:20; Lv 8:23-24; 14:25,28
^o 14:17 Lv 14:14
^p 14:19 Lv 5:3

---

^A14:3 Lit the person afflicted with skin disease   ^B14:10 Lit three-tenths; probably 3/10 of an ephah   ^C14:10,12,15 Lit one log

---

ease had to be done **outside the camp** in case the disease had not healed completely. The camp was a place of great ritual significance in Leviticus because it was the place where the tent of meeting was located. People or things rendered unclean had to be taken outside the camp—a place where ashes were dumped (4:12,21; 6:11; 8:17; 9:11; 16:27), corpses were buried (10:4-5), illegitimate sacrifices were offered (17:3), blasphemers were executed (24:14,23), and people with skin diseases were banished. Hebrews 13:11-13 declares that Jesus suffered outside the gate.

14:4 Although the person was healed, he had to go through a cleansing ritual that involved animal sacrifice. The **scarlet yarn** was a woolen yarn colored with a crimson-scarlet dye made from the kermes or cochineal scale insects. The plant known as **hyssop** had a good absorbing quality, was abundant in Israel, and was associated with purification (Ps 51:7).

14:7 The **release** of a **live bird over the open countryside** could be a parallel to the Day of Atonement rite of releasing the scapegoat (16:21-22), or it could represent the releasing of the healed person from the chains of death and being allowed to live freely in the community.

14:10 The healed person was allowed in the camp on the **eighth day**, which marked a new beginning, and it has special significance in Leviticus. It is generally associated

with rest and celebration (vv. 10,23; 9:1; 12:3; 15:14,29; 22:27; 23:36,39).

14:11-13 A **restitution offering** was necessary because the person afflicted was absent from the community and was separated from God by not being allowed in the **sanctuary**. This offering was unique in that it was the only blood sacrifice in which the entire animal had to undergo the **wave** rite (see note at 7:30-31). Because the blood of the lamb was crucial for this offering, a person could not commute this sacrifice with money (1Pt 1:19-20).

14:14 The placing of blood on the healed person's extremities symbolized that his entire being—his **ear . . . hand**, and **foot**—must be consecrated to God. The ears were important because people confessed their sin to the priest. The hands and the feet were part of the important rituals performed at the tabernacle (8:23-24).

14:18-20 The priest must also bring a **burnt offering** in order to make **atonement** for the person who had been healed. The verb "to atone for" can mean "to wipe away," "to purge," "to purify," or "to make atonement." As a result, the healed person would be pronounced **clean** and thus forgiven, ready to enter God's presence with confidence. The concept is important to the sacrificial theology of Leviticus because atonement cleansed a person from all sins, known and unknown. The language used affirms that physical impurity was purified while moral impurity had to be forgiven.

grain offering on the altar. The priest will make atonement for him, and he will be clean.[a]

[21]"But if he is poor[b] and cannot afford these,[A,c] he is to take one male lamb for a restitution offering to be waved in order to make atonement for him, along with two quarts[B] of fine flour mixed with olive oil for a grain offering, one-third of a quart[C] of olive oil, [22]and two turtledoves or two young pigeons, whatever he can afford,[D] one to be a sin offering and the other a burnt offering. [23]On the eighth day he is to bring these things for his cleansing to the priest at the entrance to the tent of meeting before the Lord. [24]The priest will take the male lamb for the restitution offering and the one-third quart[C] of olive oil, and wave them as a presentation offering before the Lord. [25]After he slaughters the male lamb for the restitution offering, the priest is to take some of the blood of the restitution offering and put it on the right earlobe of the one to be cleansed, on the thumb of his right hand, and on the big toe of his right foot. [26]Then the priest will pour some of the oil into his left palm. [27]With his right finger the priest will sprinkle some of the oil in his left palm seven times before the Lord. [28]The priest will also put some of the oil in his palm on the right earlobe of the one to be cleansed, on the thumb of his right hand, and on the big toe of his right foot, on the same place as the blood of the restitution offering. [29]What is left of the oil in the priest's palm he is to put on the head of the one to be cleansed to make atonement for him before the Lord.[d] [30]He must then sacrifice one type of what he can afford,[E] either the turtledoves or young pigeons, [31]one as a sin offering and the other as a burnt offering, sacrificing what he can afford[F,G] together with the grain offering. In this way the priest will make atonement before the Lord for the one to be cleansed. [32]This is the law for someone who has[H] a skin disease and cannot afford[I] the cost of his cleansing."

Cleansing of Contaminated Objects

[33]The Lord spoke to Moses and Aaron: [34]"When you enter the land of Canaan[e] that I am giving you as a possession,[f] and I place

a mildew contamination in a house in the land you possess,[J] [35]the owner of the house is to come and tell the priest: Something like mildew contamination has appeared[K] in my house. [36]The priest must order them to clear the house before he enters to examine the contamination, so that nothing in the house becomes •unclean. Afterward the priest will come to examine the house. [37]He will examine it, and if the contamination in the walls of the house consists of green or red indentations[L] that appear to be beneath the surface of the wall, [38]the priest is to go outside the house to its doorway and quarantine the house for seven days. [39]The priest is to return on the seventh day and examine it. If the contamination has spread on the walls of the house, [40]the priest must order that the stones with the contamination be pulled out and thrown into an unclean place outside the city. [41]He is to have the inside of the house completely scraped, and the plaster[M] that is scraped off must be dumped in an unclean place outside the city. [42]Then they must take different stones to replace the former ones and take additional plaster[M] to replaster the house.

[43]"If the contamination reappears in the house after the stones have been pulled out, and after the house has been scraped and replastered, [44]the priest must come and examine it. If the contamination has spread in the house, it is harmful mildew; the house is unclean. [45]It must be torn down with its stones, its beams, and all its plaster, and taken outside the city to an unclean place. [46]Whoever enters the house during any of the days the priest quarantines it will be unclean until evening. [47]Whoever lies down in the house is to wash his clothes, and whoever eats in it is to wash his clothes.

[48]"But when the priest comes and examines it, if the contamination has not spread in the house after it was replastered, he is to pronounce the house clean because the contamination has disappeared.[N] [49]He is to take two birds, cedar wood, scarlet yarn, and hyssop to purify the house, [50]and he is to slaughter one of the birds over a clay pot containing

[a] 14:20 Mt 8:1-4; Mk 1:21-44; Lk 5:12-14
[b] 14:21 Am 5:11
[c] Lv 5:7-13; 12:8
[d] 14:29 Lv 14:18
[e] 14:34 Gn 37:1
[f] Gn 17:8; 23:4; 36:43; 47:11; 48:4; 49:30; 50:13; Dt 32:49; Jos 21:12,41

A 14:21 Lit and his hand is not   B 14:21 Lit him, and one-tenth; probably 1/10 of an ephah   C 14:21,24 Lit one log   D 14:22 Lit pigeons, for which his hand is sufficient   E 14:30 Lit of that for which his hand is sufficient   F 14:31 LXX, Syr, Vg omit what he can afford   G 14:31 Lit sacrificing that for which his hand is sufficient   H 14:32 Lit someone on whom there is   I 14:32 Lit disease whose hand is not sufficient for   J 14:34 Lit land of your possession   K 14:35 Lit appeared to me   L 14:37 Or eruptions; Hb obscure   M 14:41,42 Lit dust   N 14:48 Lit healed

14:21-32 In His grace, God provided concessions for the **poor** (Ex 22:25; 23:11; Dt 15:4).

14:33-53 As with mildew in fabric in 13:47-59, **mildew** in a **house** would compromise the ceremonial cleanness of the community and therefore was not allowed. Because it could

spread, it was thoroughly eradicated (vv. 43-45). The ceremony for purifying a building with mildew was similar to that for a person with a skin disease, except that there was no restitution offering or sin offering for the building since it only had to be declared clean; it did not have to be prepared for communion with God.

fresh water. [51]He will take the cedar wood, the hyssop, the scarlet yarn, and the live bird, dip them in the blood of the slaughtered bird and the fresh water, and sprinkle the house seven times. [52]He will purify the house with the blood of the bird, the fresh water, the live bird, the cedar wood, the hyssop, and the scarlet yarn. [53]Then he is to release the live bird into the open countryside[a] outside the city. In this way he will make atonement for the house, and it will be clean.

[54]"This is the law for any skin disease or mildew, for a scaly outbreak,[A] [55]for mildew in clothing or on a house, [56]and for a swelling, scab, or spot, [57]to determine when something is unclean or clean. This is the law regarding skin disease and mildew."

Bodily Discharges

15 The LORD spoke to Moses and Aaron: [2]"Speak to the Israelites and tell them: When any man has a discharge[b] from his body, he is •unclean. [3]This is uncleanness of his discharge: Whether his body secretes the discharge or retains it, he is unclean. All the days that his body secretes or retains anything because of his discharge,[B] he is unclean.[C] [4]Any bed the man with the discharge lies on will be unclean, and any furniture he sits on will be unclean. [5]Anyone who touches his bed is to wash his clothes and bathe with water, and he will remain unclean until evening. [6]Whoever sits on furniture that the man with the discharge was sitting on is to wash his clothes and bathe with water, and he will remain unclean until evening. [7]Whoever touches the body of the man with a discharge is to wash his clothes and bathe with water, and he will remain unclean until evening. [8]If the man with the discharge spits on anyone who is •clean, he is to wash his clothes and bathe with water, and he

will remain unclean until evening. [9]Any saddle the man with the discharge rides on will be unclean.[c] [10]Whoever touches anything that was under him will be unclean until evening, and whoever carries such things is to wash his clothes and bathe with water, and he will remain unclean until evening. [11]If the man with the discharge touches anyone without first rinsing his hands in water,[d] the person who was touched is to wash his clothes and bathe with water, and he will remain unclean until evening. [12]Any clay pot that the man with the discharge touches must be broken, while any wooden utensil must be rinsed with water.[e]

[13]"When the man with the discharge has been cured of it, he is to count seven days for his cleansing, wash his clothes, and bathe his body in fresh water; he will be clean. [14]He must take two turtledoves or two young pigeons on the eighth day, come before the LORD at the entrance to the tent of meeting, and give them to the priest. [15]The priest is to sacrifice them, one as a •sin offering and the other as a •burnt offering.[f] In this way the priest will make •atonement for him before the LORD because of his discharge.

[16]"When a man has an emission of semen,[g] he is to bathe himself completely with water, and he will remain unclean until evening. [17]Any clothing or leather on which there is an emission of semen must be washed with water, and it will remain unclean until evening. [18]If a man sleeps with a woman and has an emission of semen, both of them are to bathe with water, and they will remain unclean until evening.[h]

[19]"When a woman has a discharge, and it consists of blood from her body, she will be unclean because of her menstruation[i] for seven days. Everyone who touches her will be unclean until evening. [20]Anything she lies

---

[a]14:53 Lv 14:7
[b]15:2 Lv 15:33; 22:4; Nm 5:2; 2Sm 3:29
[c]15:9 Gn 31:34-35
[d]15:11 Ex 30:19; Mt 15:2; Mk 7:3
[e]15:12 Lv 6:28; 11:33
[f]15:15 Gn 22:2; Lv 3:5; Nm 6:11; Jos 8:31; 1Ch 16:1; Ps 20:3; Mc 6:6
[g]15:16 Lv 15:32; 19:20; 22:4; Nm 5:13
[h]15:18 2Sm 11:2-4
[i]15:19 Lv 12:2,5; 18:19; Ezk 22:10; 36:17

15:2-3 The word **body** here is a euphemism for the male genitalia. The word **discharge** occurs only in Leviticus. It probably refers to some chronic infection in men. The adjective **unclean** is used 25 times in Leviticus, and it can refer to either an ethical or a religious impurity.

15:7-12 In His grace, God made provision for the purification of affected people or objects.

15:8 Spitting was a gesture of extreme contempt, and it pointed not just to the outside uncleanness but to the man's wicked heart.

15:13 The fact that an unclean man could be **cured** of the **discharge** points to the fact that the discharge refers to a medical condition.

15:14-15 The **sin offering** removed the impurity while the **burnt offering** restored the man to the Israelite commu-

nity. The animals needed for these offerings are the least costly, **two turtledoves or two young pigeons** (1:14; 5:11; 12:8; 14:22,30; Lk 2:24).

15:16-18 The phrase **emission of semen** can refer to a nocturnal ejaculation (vv. 16-17) as well as ejaculation in sexual intercourse (v. 18). This passage does not suggest that God considered sex sinful. Rather, God gave laws to ensure that sex must not be part of the sanctuary rites. These laws were a clear contrast with the ancient Near Eastern religions that portrayed gods and goddesses engaging in sexual relations and their followers imitating them as part of pagan temple worship.

15:19 The word **body** here is a euphemism for the female genitalia.

15:20 The idea that **menstruation** rendered a woman

on during her menstruation will become unclean, and anything she sits on will become unclean. [21]Everyone who touches her bed is to wash his clothes and bathe with water, and he will remain unclean until evening. [22]Everyone who touches any furniture she was sitting on is to wash his clothes and bathe with water, and he will remain unclean until evening. [23]If discharge is on the bed or the furniture she was sitting on, when he touches it he will be unclean until evening. [24]If a man sleeps with her, and blood from her menstruation gets on him, he will be unclean for seven days, and every bed he lies on will become unclean.[a]

[25]"When a woman has a discharge of her blood for many days, though it is not the time of her menstruation, or if she has a discharge beyond her period, she will be unclean all the days of her unclean discharge, as she is during the days of her menstruation. [26]Any bed she lies on during the days of her discharge will be like her bed during menstrual impurity; any furniture she sits on will be unclean as in her menstrual period. [27]Everyone who touches them will be unclean; he must wash his clothes and bathe with water, and he will remain unclean until evening. [28]When she is cured of her discharge, she is to count seven days, and after that she will be clean.[b] [29]On the eighth day she must take two turtledoves or two young pigeons and bring them to the priest at the entrance to the tent of meeting. [30]The priest is to sacrifice one as a sin offering and the other as a burnt offering. In this way the priest will make atonement for her before the LORD because of her unclean discharge.

[31]"You must keep the Israelites from their uncleanness, so that they do not die by defiling My tabernacle[c] that is among them. [32]This is the law for someone with a discharge: a man who has an emission of semen, becoming unclean by it; [33]a woman who is in her menstrual period; anyone who has a discharge, whether male or female; and a man who sleeps with an unclean woman."

The Day of Atonement

16 The LORD spoke to Moses after the death of two of Aaron's sons when they approached the presence[d] of[A] the LORD and died.[e] [2]The LORD said to Moses: "Tell your brother Aaron that he may not come whenever he wants into the holy place[f] behind the veil[g] in front of the •mercy seat[h] on the ark or else he will die, because I appear in the cloud[i] above the mercy seat.[j]

[3]"Aaron is to enter the most holy place[k] in this way: with a young bull for a •sin offering and a ram for a •burnt offering.[l] [4]He is to wear a holy linen tunic, and linen undergarments are to be on his body. He must tie a linen sash around him and wrap his head with a linen turban.[m] These are holy garments; he must bathe his body with water before he wears them. [5]He is to take from the Israelite community two male goats for a sin offering and one ram for a burnt offering.[n]

[6]"Aaron will present the bull for his sin offering and make •atonement for himself and his household. [7]Next he will take the two goats and place them before the LORD at the entrance to the tent of meeting. [8]After Aaron casts lots[o]

Cross references

[a] 15:24 Lv 18:19; 20:18; Ezk 18:6
[b] 15:28 Lv 15:13; Mt 9:20-22
[c] 15:31 Ex 25:9; Nm 5:2-3
[d] 16:1 Gn 4:14
[e] Lv 10:1-2
[f] 16:2 Heb 6:19
[g] Mk 15:38
[h] Ex 31:7
[i] Ex 16:10
[j] Nm 7:89; 16:42; 1Kg 8:10-12; Heb 9:5
[k] 16:3 Lv 4:1-15; Heb 9:7,24-25
[l] Gn 22:2; Lv 3:5; Nm 6:11; Jos 8:31; 1Ch 16:1; Ps 20:3; Mc 6:6
[m] 16:4 Ex 28:42-43; Lv 6:10; 8:7-8; Ezk 44:17-19
[n] 16:5 Lv 4:23-24; 8:18-21; 9:15
[o] 16:8 Nm 26:55

[A] 16:1 LXX, Tg, Syr, Vg read *they brought strange fire before*; Nm 3:4

---

unclean was a common conception throughout the ancient Near East. Both the Egyptians and the Persians thought of menstruation as cultic uncleanness.

15:25 This **discharge** refers to a chronic condition that is not related to menstruation.

15:31 The verb **keep** comes from the Hebrew root *nazar*, which means "to refrain, to be a Nazirite." Here it conveys the idea that the Israelites were to refrain from being unclean so they could enter God's sanctuary. **Defiling** the sanctuary was grounds for the death penalty.

16:1-34 In His mercy and grace, God provided the Day of Atonement as a sacred time in which the high priest cleansed the sanctuary and made atonement for the sins of the people.

16:1 The sanctuary was polluted because of the actions of **two of Aaron's sons**, Nadab and Abihu (10:1-2). Chapter 16 is in part a response to their sinful actions.

16:2 The **holy place** refers to the holy of holies (vv. 16-17,20,23,27,33]. The **mercy seat** was the place of atonement and was made of a solid gold slab that covered the ark of the covenant. The Septuagint (LXX) translates this word as

"instrument of propitiation." The **cloud** is not the cloud of smoke from the incense; it is the divine cloud representing God's presence that descended on the tabernacle as a sign that Israel was to make camp (Ex 40:34-35) and that rested on the ark when God spoke to Moses (Ex 25:22; Nm 7:89).

16:4 The high priest wore the **garments** of an ordinary priest, indicating that he must be humble, free of all pretense. The garments were classified as **holy**, and thus set apart exclusively for the high priest. The high priest would **bathe** his body twice (vv. 4,26), and he would wash his hands and feet each time he entered the tabernacle or officiated at the altar (v. 24; Ex 30:19).

16:6 Atonement was made for the high priest and his **household** before he could bring the sacrifice for the nation. The word "household" refers to family and the line of subsequent high priests.

16:8 Three different interpretations have been proposed for the meaning of **azazel**, a word that occurs only in chapter 16. The LXX translates it as "the one carrying away evil," from which we got the term "scapegoat." The second view was developed by later rabbis who suggested that azazel means "a rough and difficult place" and that it represented

for the two goats, one lot for the LORD and the other for azazel,[A,a] [9]he is to present the goat chosen by lot for the LORD and sacrifice it as a sin offering.[b] [10]But the goat chosen by lot for azazel[A] is to be presented alive before the LORD to make purification with it by sending it into the wilderness[c] for azazel.

[11]"When Aaron presents the bull for his sin offering and makes atonement for himself and his household, he will slaughter the bull for his sin offering. [12]Then he must take a firepan full of fiery coals from the altar before the LORD and two handfuls of finely ground fragrant incense,[d] and bring them inside the veil.[e] [13]He is to put the incense on the fire before the LORD, so that the cloud[f] of incense covers the mercy seat that is over the *testimony,[g] or else he will die.[h] [14]He is to take some of the bull's blood[i] and sprinkle it with his finger against the east side of the mercy seat; then he will sprinkle some of the blood with his finger before the mercy seat seven times.[j]

[15]"When he slaughters the male goat for the people's sin offering and brings its blood inside the veil, he must do the same with its blood as he did with the bull's blood: he is to sprinkle it against the mercy seat and in front of it. [16]He will purify the most holy place in this way for all their sins because of the Israelites' impurities and rebellious acts.[k] He will do the same for the tent of meeting that remains among them, because it is surrounded by their impurities. [17]No one may be in the tent of meeting from the time he enters to make atonement in the most holy place until he leaves after he has made atonement for himself, his household, and the whole assembly of Israel.[l] [18]Then he will go out to the altar that is before the LORD and make atonement for it. He is to take

some of the bull's blood and some of the goat's blood and put it on the horns on all sides of the altar. [19]He is to sprinkle some of the blood on it with his finger seven times to cleanse and set it apart[m] from the Israelites' impurities.[n]

[20]"When he has finished purifying the most holy place, the tent of meeting, and the altar, he is to present the live male goat. [21]Aaron will lay both his hands on the head of the live goat and confess[o] over it all the Israelites' wrongdoings[p] and rebellious acts—all their sins.[q] He is to put them on the goat's head and send it away into the wilderness[r] by the man appointed for the task.[B] [22]The goat will carry on it all their wrongdoings into a desolate land,[s] and he will release it there.

[23]"Then Aaron is to enter the tent of meeting, take off the linen garments[t] he wore when he entered the most holy place, and leave them there. [24]He will bathe his body with water in a holy place[u] and put on his clothes.[v] Then he must go out and sacrifice his burnt offering and the people's burnt offering; he will make atonement for himself and for the people. [25]He is to burn the fat of the sin offering on the altar. [26]The man who released the goat for azazel[A] is to wash his clothes and bathe his body with water; afterward he may reenter the camp. [27]The bull for the sin offering and the goat for the sin offering, whose blood was brought into the most holy place to make atonement, must be brought outside the camp[w] and their hide,[x] flesh, and dung burned up.[y] [28]The one who burns them is to wash his clothes and bathe himself with water; afterward he may reenter the camp.

[29]"This is to be a permanent statute[z] for you: In the seventh month, on the tenth day of the

---

[a]16:8 Lv 16:26
[b]16:9 Nm 29:11
[c]16:10 Gn 14:6
[d]16:12 Nm 7:14
[e]Mk 15:38
[f]16:13 Ex 16:10
[g]Ex 31:18
[h]Lv 10:1; Nm 16:46-48; Ps 141:2; Rv 8:3-5
[i]16:14 Heb 9:22
[j]Lv 4:6; Heb 9:4-5
[k]16:16 Ex 22:9
[l]16:17 1Tm 2:5; Heb 9:7
[m]16:19 Lv 8:10
[n]16:17-19 Heb 9:11-14
[o]16:21 Lv 5:5; 26:40; Nm 5:7; 2Ch 30:22; Neh 1:6; 9:2; Dn 9:4,20
[p]Lv 5:1
[q]Ezr 10:1; Neh 9:2-3; Dn 9:20; 2Co 5:21; Jms 5:16; 1Jn 1:9
[r]Lv 14:7
[s]16:22 Ps 103:12; Is 53:4,6,11-12; Jn 1:29; Heb 9:28; 1Pt 2:24; 1Jn 3:5
[t]16:23 Lv 6:11
[u]16:24 Ex 29:31; Lv 6:16,26-27; 7:6; 10:13; 24:9; Ec 8:10; Ezk 42:13
[v]Lv 8:6-9
[w]16:27 Lv 8:17
[x]Lv 7:8
[y]Lv 4:11-12; Heb 13:11-12
[z]16:29 Ex 28:43; Lv 11:46

[A]16:8,10,26 Perhaps a term that means "for the goat that departs", or "for removal", or "for a rough, difficult place", or "for a goat demon"; Hb obscure   [B]16:21 Lit *wilderness in the hand of a ready man*

---

the goat's destination. The third view suggests that the word is the name of a demon that inhabited the desert. Later Jewish interpreters identified azazel with Azael, whom legend identified as the leader of the fallen angels. The first interpretation seems to best fit the context of chapter 16 where the goat is sent away into the wilderness.

16:11 The first phase of purification took place through the blood-sprinkling rituals. The **sin offering**—for intentional or inadvertent sins—appears first in chapter 4.

16:12-14 The **fragrant incense** had a very practical purpose since the blood on the mercy seat would produce an unpleasant odor. The incense included spices such as stacte, onycha, and galbanum mixed with pure frankincense (Ex 30:34-35).

16:16 The atoning blood would purify the people of their sin and rebellion. This definitely points toward Christ, whose blood provides for the purification of all sin (Heb 9:24-28).

16:20-28 The second phase of purification occurred through the removal of the scapegoat. The author of Hebrews drew a parallel to this ritual when he affirmed that Christ offered Himself as a sin offering once and for all (Heb 10:10). Jesus is also compared to the scapegoat because He also "suffered outside the gate, so that He might sanctify the people by His own blood" (Heb 13:12). The fact that Jesus took our sins upon Himself is also affirmed in Is 53:5-6; 2Co 5:21; Gl 3:13; and 1Pt 2:24. From a symbolic perspective, when Jesus died on the cross, the curtain that divided the holy of holies from the holy place was torn from top to bottom (Mt 27:51; Mk 15:38; Lk 23:45), signaling access to God by all people through Christ's atoning act on our behalf.

16:29 The Day of Atonement (Hb *yom kippur*) was an annual ceremony held on the tenth day of Tishri (September/October). **Self-denial** is usually associated with fasting and prayer (Is 58:3,5). The Targum adds that the people should abstain from "food and drink, from the enjoyment of the

month you are to practice self-denial[A,a] and do no work,[b] both the native and the foreigner[c] who resides among you. [30]Atonement will be made for you on this day to cleanse you,[d] and you will be *clean from all your sins before the Lord. [31]It is a Sabbath[e] of complete rest for you,[f] and you must practice self-denial; it is a permanent statute. [32]The priest who is anointed and ordained[B,g] to serve as high priest[h] in place of his father will make atonement. He will put on the linen garments, the holy garments, [33]and purify the most holy place. He will purify the tent of meeting and the altar and will make atonement for the priests and all the people of the assembly. [34]This is to be a permanent statute for you, to make atonement for the Israelites once a year[i] because of all their sins." And all this was done as the Lord commanded Moses.

Forbidden Sacrifices

17 The Lord spoke to Moses: [2]"Speak to Aaron, his sons, and all the Israelites and tell them: This is what the Lord has commanded: [3]Anyone from the house of Israel who slaughters[j] an ox, sheep, or goat in the camp, or slaughters it outside the camp, [4]instead of bringing it to the entrance to the tent

of meeting to present it as an offering to the Lord before His tabernacle—that person will be considered *guilty.[C,k] He has shed blood[l] and must be cut off from his people.[m] [5]This is so the Israelites will bring to the Lord the sacrifices[n] they have been offering in the open country. They are to bring them to the priest at the entrance to the tent of meeting and offer them as *fellowship sacrifices[o] to the Lord. [6]The priest will then sprinkle the blood on the Lord's altar at the entrance to the tent of meeting and burn the fat as a pleasing aroma to the Lord. [7]They must no longer offer their sacrifices to the goat-demons[p] that they have prostituted[q] themselves with. This will be a permanent statute[r] for them throughout their generations.

[8]"Say to them: Anyone from the house of Israel or from the foreigners[s] who live among them who offers a *burnt offering or a sacrifice [9]but does not bring it to the entrance to the tent of meeting to sacrifice it to the Lord, that person must be cut off from his people.

Eating Blood and Carcasses Prohibited

[10]"Anyone from the house of Israel or from the foreigners who live among them who eats

Cross references (center column)

a 16:29 Lv 23:27-32; Nm 29:7; Ps 35:13; Is 58:3,5; Dn 10:12
b Ex 12:16; Lv 23:3,28,31; Nm 29:7; Jr 17:22
c Ex 12:49; Lv 17:15; 18:26
d 16:30 Lv 13:6
e 16:31 Gn 2:2
f Ex 16:23; 31:15; 35:2; Lv 23:3,24,32,39; 25:4-5
g 16:32 Ex 29:33
h Lv 8:12,33
i 16:34 Heb 9:7
j 17:3 Dt 12:5-21
k 17:4 Ex 22:1; Lv 20:9; Nm 35:27; Dt 19:10; Ps 55:23; Is 33:15
l Gn 9:6
m Nm 9:13
n 17:5 Gn 46:1; Ex 34:25
o Lv 7:11
p 17:7 2Ch 11:15; Is 13:21; 34:14
q Dt 22:21
r Gn 26:5; Ex 12:14; Lv 3:17; Nm 9:3; Dt 6:2; 8:11
s 17:8 Gn 19:9; Ex 2:22

A 16:29 Traditionally, fasting, abstinence from sex, and refraining from personal grooming   B 16:32 Lit and will fill his hand
C 17:4 Lit tabernacle—blood will be charged against that person

---

baths and anointing, from wearing shoes, and from marital intercourse." Today, yom kippur is generally celebrated as a day of confession of sin and asking for forgiveness. Readings from Leviticus are included in this celebration, one of the most important holy days in Judaism.

17:1-16 This chapter introduces what is known as the Holiness Code, laws that call the people to live holy lives before a holy God.

kaphar

Hebrew Pronunciation	[kah PHAR]
HCSB Translation	cover, make atonement, purge
Uses in Leviticus	49
Uses in the OT	102
Focus Passage	Leviticus 16:29-34

Akkadian and Arabic cognates mean wipe on, wipe away, or cover. Kaphar as cover occurs with kopher, asphalt, in Gn 6:14. Elsewhere kaphar uses other conjugations with different meanings. The intensive verb means make/provide atonement (Ex 29:36), atone for (Ps 65:3), wipe out (1Sm 3:14), or wipe away (Dn 9:24). It suggests appease (Gn 32:20), ward off (Is 47:11), or forgive (Dt 21:8). It denotes make purification or purify (Lv 16:10,16). Passive forms also indicate be purged (Is 27:9), dissolved (Is 28:18), or absolved of responsibility (Dt 21:8). Some verbs connote ransom and could possibly derive from a homonym kopher, ransom. But this connotation could have developed secondarily because cleansing so often came through substitutionary sacrifice. Capporeth (27x) indicates mercy seat (Lv 16:13), the place of atonement. Kippuriym (8x) is atonement (Lv 25:9).

17:3-4 The verb slaughter is a technical term for all sacrificial slaughter (1:5; 3:8; 4:29,33; 7:2). It does not refer to the killing of animals in general. This was not a command prohibiting nonsacrificial slaughter or hunting (Dt 12:20-25). The seriousness of the offense can be seen in the phrase be cut off, an expression that always refers to the death penalty when used in the context of punishment (vv. 9,10,14; 7:20-21,25,27; 18:29; 19:8; 20:3; 22:3). In broader OT context, to be cut off designated the judgment of a person who offended God or the community of the faithful. The ostracized person was usually removed or expelled, and in extreme cases, killed.

17:7-9 In their wilderness wandering, the Israelites resorted to worshiping goat-demons, which could refer to demons in the form of goats that haunted the wilderness (Is 13:21; 34:14). Unfaithfulness toward Yahweh was often depicted as prostitution, so the reference here does not suggest that the Israelites were worshiping Canaanite fertility gods (Jr 2-3; Ezk 16; 23; Hs 1-3). God in His grace also included foreigners who lived among the covenant people; they had to observe the commandment not to worship other gods (vv. 8,10,12-13,15). The expression burnt offering or a sacrifice (Nm 15:3; Dt 12:6; 1Sm 15:22; 2Kg 5:17; Is 43:23) is a figure of speech called a merism, and it points to all sacrifices. The law's intent was to ban all sacrifices offered to any god other than Yahweh.

17:10 The prohibition against eating blood pertains to both sacrificial and nonsacrificial animals and is mentioned in other parts of the Torah (3:17; 7:26-27; Gn 9:4; Dt 12:16,23-25). The expression I will turn against is literally "I will set My face against." It points to God's decision not just

any blood,[a] I will turn[A] against that person who eats blood and cut him off from his people. [11]For the life of a creature is in the blood, and I have appointed it to you to make •atonement on the altar for[B] your lives, since it is the lifeblood that makes atonement.[b] [12]Therefore I say to the Israelites: None of you and no foreigner who lives among you may eat blood.

[13]"Any Israelite or foreigner living among them, who hunts[c] down a wild animal or bird that may be eaten must drain its blood[d] and cover it with dirt. [14]Since the life of every creature is its blood, I have told the Israelites: You must not eat the blood of any creature,[e] because the life of every creature is its blood; whoever eats it must be cut off.

[15]"Every person, whether the native or the foreigner,[f] who eats an animal that died a natural death or was mauled by wild beasts[g] is to wash his clothes and bathe with water, and he will remain •unclean until evening; then he will be •clean. [16]But if he does not wash his clothes and bathe himself, he will bear his punishment."

Prohibited Pagan Practices

18 [1]•Yahweh spoke to Moses: [2]"Speak to the Israelites and tell them: I am Yahweh your God.[h] [3]Do not follow the practices of the

land of Egypt,[i] where you used to live, or follow the practices of the land of Canaan,[j] where I am bringing you. You must not follow their customs.[k] [4]You are to practice My ordinances[l] and you are to keep My statutes[m] by following them; I am Yahweh your God. [5]Keep My statutes and ordinances; a person will live[n] if he does them.[o] I am Yahweh.

[6]"You are not to come near[p] any close relative[C] for sexual intercourse;[q] I am Yahweh. [7]You are not to shame your father[r] by having sex with your mother. She is your mother; you must not have sexual intercourse with her. [8]You are not to have sex with your father's wife;[s] it will shame your father.[t] [9]You are not to have sexual intercourse with your sister, either your father's daughter or your mother's,[u] whether born at home or born elsewhere. You are not to have sex with her. [10]You are not to have sexual intercourse with your son's daughter or your daughter's daughter, because it will shame your family.[D] [11]You are not to have sexual intercourse with your father's wife's daughter,[E] who is adopted by[F] your father; she is your sister. [12]You are not

Cross references (center column):

[a]17:10 Gn 9:4; Lv 3:17
[b]17:11 Mt 26:28; Mk 14:24; Rm 3:25; 5:9; Eph 1:7; Col 1:14,20; Heb 13:12; 1Jn 1:7; Rv 1:5
[c]17:13 Gn 25:27
[d]Ex 29:12; Lv 17:4; Dt 12:16,24; 15:23; Ezk 24:7
[e]17:14 Lv 3:17
[f]17:15 Lv 16:29
[g]Ex 22:31; Lv 7:24; 22:8; Dt 14:21
[h]18:2 Nm 15:41
[i]18:3 Lv 11:45; 19:34,36
[j]Dt 18:9-12
[k]Ex 23:24; Lv 18:24-30; 2Kg 17:7-8
[l]18:4 Lv 18:26; Nm 29:18; Jos 6:15; Ezr 3:4; Jb 9:19; Ps 119:13; Is 1:17; Ezk 18:5
[m]Lv 7:7
[n]18:5 Dt 4:1; Neh 9:29; Ezk 20:13,21,25; 33:12; Rm 7:10; Php 1:21
[o]Dt 6:24; Pr 6:23; Lk 10:26-28; Rm 7:10; 10:5; Gl 3:12
[p]18:6 Gn 20:4
[q]1Tm 4:3
[r]18:7 Ezk 22:10
[s]18:8 Gn 35:22; 49:4; Lv 20:11; 2Sm 16:21-22; Am 2:7; 1Co 5:1
[t]Lv 20:11
[u]18:9 Lv 20:17; Dt 27:22; 2Sm 13:11-14; Ezk 22:11

[A]17:10 Lit will set My face   [B]17:11 Or to ransom   [C]18:6 Lit any flesh of his flesh   [D]18:10 Lit because they are your nakedness
[E]18:11 This must refer to a daughter from a previous marriage.   [F]18:11 Lit daughter, a relative of

---

to oppose those who disobey the law, but it suggests that He would destroy those who committed such lawlessness (20:3; 26:17; Ezk 14:8; 15:7).

17:11 The concept that **the life** was **in the blood** goes back to creation (Gn 2:7; 7:22). Here Yahweh gave a rationale for the law—that the blood is the life, and God has designed the blood for **atonement**. Eating blood would profane something that God had sanctified or set apart for the sanctuary. The NT clearly teaches that Jesus' blood serves as atonement for the sin of humanity (Heb 9:24-26).

18:1-30 The ancient Near Eastern world had many pagan practices that included incest, adultery, bestiality, homosexuality, and child sacrifice. God made it clear that the covenant community must not adopt such practices.

18:3 **Egypt** was known for its licentiousness and for condoning intrafamily practices such as father-daughter, brother-sister, aunt-nephew, and uncle-niece marriages. **Canaan** was identified with homosexuality (Gn 19:5-8) and bestiality. Seven times Israel is warned not to behave like those living in Canaan (Lv 18:3,24,26-27,29-30). Six times the expression **I am Yahweh** appears in chapter 18 as the motive for observing the law (vv. 2,4,5,6,21,30). The formula "I am Yahweh your God" appears in the context of God's redeeming Israel from Egypt (11:45; 19:34,36; 23:43; 25:38,55; 26:13,45; Ex 6:7; Nm 15:41). In this context, the formula shows that these statutes were God's commandments and not human conventions.

18:6 The expression **close relative** (lit "flesh of his flesh") designates all close blood relatives, such as father, mother, brother, sister, son, daughter, and grandchild (vv. 12-13; 20:19; 21:2-3). Sexual intercourse with **any** close relative—

even those who are not specifically mentioned in the list—is prohibited.

18:7 This prohibition is repeated because of the possibility of double incest—with the **father** and with the **mother**.

18:9,11 Marriage with one's half **sister** (Gn 20:12) was not prohibited before the Mosaic covenant at Sinai. Brother-sister marriages were commonplace in Egypt, Phoenicia, and pre-Islamic Arabia.

18:12-14 While sexual intercourse between aunts and

dam

Hebrew Pronunciation	[DAHM]
HCSB Translation	blood
Uses in Leviticus	88
Uses in the OT	361
Focus Passage	Leviticus 17:4,6,10-14

The word for blood is ancient and much the same in every Semitic language. Dam can have the same meanings in the singular or plural, although some phrases are set. The OT uses blood of men, animals, and birds, but not fish. Blood could symbolize life itself (Dt 12:23) and so was important in sacrificial ritual. Dam can be translated life (Ps 72:14) but more commonly might be translated death (Ps 30:9). Dam especially connotes violent death in the phrase "to shed blood" (Gn 9:6). A "man of blood" is a murderer (2Sm 16:7). Dam sometimes has the meanings bloodshed (Ex 22:2) or bloodguilt (Is 4:4). Fat and blood are treated separately from the rest of the animal in sacrificial rituals (Lv 1:11; 3:17). Wine can be called (lit) "blood of grapes" (Dt 32:14), and blood is compared to wine (Is 49:26).

to have sexual intercourse with your father's sister;[a] she is your father's close relative. [13]You are not to have sexual intercourse with your mother's sister,[b] for she is your mother's close relative. [14]You are not to shame your father's brother by coming near his wife to have sexual intercourse; she is your aunt.[c] [15]You are not to have sexual intercourse with your daughter-in-law.[d] She is your son's wife; you are not to have sex with her. [16]You are not to have sexual intercourse with your brother's wife; it will shame your brother.[e] [17]You are not to have sexual intercourse with a woman and her daughter.[f] You are not to marry her son's daughter or her daughter's daughter and have sex with her. They are close relatives; it is depraved.[g] [18]You are not to marry a woman as a rival to her sister and have sexual intercourse with her during her sister's lifetime.[h]

[19]"You are not to come near[i] a woman dur-

ing her menstrual impurity to have sexual intercourse with her.[j] [20]You are not to have sexual intercourse with[A] your neighbor's wife, defiling yourself with her.[k]

[21]"You are not to make any of your children pass through the fire to *Molech.[l] Do not profane the name[m] of your God; I am Yahweh. [22]You are not to sleep with a man as with a woman;[n] it is detestable.[o] [23]You are not to have sexual intercourse with[B] any animal, defiling yourself with it; a woman is not to present herself to an animal to mate with it;[p] it is a perversion.

[24]"Do not defile yourselves by any of these practices, for the nations I am driving out before you have defiled themselves by all these things. [25]The land has become defiled, so I am punishing it for its sin, and the land will vomit out its inhabitants.[q] [26]But you are to keep My

[a]18:12 Ex 6:20
[b]18:13 Lv 20:19
[c]18:14 Lv 20:20
[d]18:15 Gn 38:16; Lv 20:12; Ezk 22:11
[e]18:16 Lv 20:21; Dt 25:5-10; Mt 14:3-4; Mk 6:18
[f]18:17 Lv 20:14; Dt 27:23; Am 2:7
[g]Lv 19:29
[h]18:18 Gn 29:21-28
[i]18:19 Gn 20:4
[j]Lv 15:19-24; 20:18; Ezk 18:6
[k]18:20 Ex 20:14; Lv 20:10; Nm 5:11-31; Dt 22:22; 1Co 6:9; Heb 13:4
[l]18:21 Lv 20:2-5; Dt 18:10; 1Kg 11:7; 2Kg 23:10; Jr 32:35; Ac 7:43
[m]Ex 20:7; Lv 20:3; Jn 10:25
[n]18:22 Gn 19:5; Lv 20:13; Dt 23:18; Rm 1:26-27; 1Co 6:9-11; Gl 5:21; 1Tm 1:10; Rv 21:8
[o]Gn 46:34
[p]18:23 Ex 22:19
[q]18:25 Nm 35:33-34; Dt 9:4; Ezr 9:11; Is 24:5-6; Jr 2:7; Ezk 36:1

[A]18:20 Lit *to give your emission of semen to*   [B]18:23 Lit *to give your emission to*

nephews was forbidden, unions between uncles and nieces were permitted (Jos 15:17; Jdg 1:13). Later, marriages between uncles and nieces were forbidden in both the Qumran (11QT 66:16-17) and Christian communities.

18:15 The prohibition of a sexual relationship with one's **daughter-in-law** extends to a person who is divorced or widowed, even though this practice was common in the ancient Near East.

18:16 John the Baptist used this law to rebuke Herod for marrying his brother's wife (Mt 14:4; Mk 6:18). This law was in effect only if the **brother** was alive. If the brother died, the law of levirate marriage, which was instituted in Dt 25:5-9, would go into effect.

18:17 Orgies involving a woman and her daughter were clas-

tame'

Hebrew Pronunciation	[tah MAY]
HCSB Translation	be unclean, defiled, declare unclean
Uses in Leviticus	85
Uses in the OT	162
Focus Passage	Leviticus 18:20,23-25,27-28,30

Tame' indicates *being/becoming* (ceremonially) *unclean* (Nm 19:7) or *defiled* (Ezk 22:3) by things like skin disease (Lv 13:3), abnormal or sexual bodily discharges (Lv 15:4,16), touching dead animals or people (Lv 11:24; Nm 19:11), and giving birth (Lv 12:2). People *defiled themselves* (Lv 18:20). Things and people could *become unclean* by secondary or tertiary contact (Lv 11:34; 15:5). *Uncleanness* is contrasted with God's holiness (Lv 11:43-44). *Tame'* involved *defiling* through rape (Gn 34:5), adultery, bestiality, consulting mediums (Lv 19:31), Baal worship (Jr 2:23), and sacrificing children to idols (Lv 20:3). *Defiled* things included God's name (Ezk 43:8), the sanctuary, houses (Lv 14:36), land, and even pagans (Lv 18:24-25). The intensive verb denotes *declare* or *make unclean* (Lv 13:11; Nm 35:34) or *defile* (Lv 15:31; 2Kg 23:8). The adjective *tame'* (88x) means *unclean, defiled, impure,* or *pagan* (Am 7:17). The noun *tum'ah* (36x) refers to *uncleanness* (Lv 5:3), *impurity,* or *defilement.*

sified as **depraved**, a legal term that was also used for incest (20:14), rape (Jdg 20:6), and prostitution (Lv 19:29; Ezk 16:27). Orgies of any type were prohibited and were seen as paganistic, profane acts.

18:19 Self-control was one of the concepts God was trying to teach His people. Refraining from sex during a woman's **menstrual impurity** was meant to keep the other person ceremonially clean (15:19-24). The apostle Paul listed self-control as part of the fruit of the Spirit (Gl 5:22-23).

18:20 This prohibition restates the seventh of the Ten Commandments (Ex 20:14; Dt 5:18), and it refers to sexual intercourse with a married or engaged person.

18:21 Child sacrifice practiced as worship of **Molech** was common among the Canaanites. The name Molech appears five times in Leviticus (v. 21; 20:2,3,4,5), and it refers to the god of the Ammonites. Human sacrifice was practiced in Israel only by corrupt rulers (1Kg 11:7; 2Kg 23:10; Jr 32:35). The expression **pass through the fire** indicates that the child was probably burned to honor Molech in a pagan ritual. This practice was labeled as **profane** by God.

18:22 Homosexuality is clearly prohibited throughout the Bible (20:13; Rm 1:27; 1Co 6:9). The Sodomites were destroyed because of their sodomy (Gn 19:5), and the men of Gibeah were destroyed following their homosexual rampage (Jdg 19:22). Male prostitution was practiced as part of a fertility ritual because pagans deified not just gods but sex as well; ironically, male and female shrine prostitutes were called literally "holy ones" (Dt 23:17). Homosexuality is called **detestable** because it is against God's order of creation and against His laws pertaining to the covenant community. The word occurs 116 times in the OT in contexts addressing idolatry, magic, transvestism, and defective sacrifice.

18:23 Just like homosexuality, bestiality was prohibited in the Bible under all circumstances. This act was classified as **a perversion**, a violation of the divine order.

18:24-30 The punishment for these **detestable things** was the death penalty. When the covenant community profaned

statutes and ordinances. You must not commit any of these detestable things—not the native or the foreigner who lives among you. [27] For the men who were in the land prior to you have committed all these detestable things, and the land has become defiled. [28] If you defile the land, it will vomit[a] you out as it has vomited out the nations that were before you. [29] Any person who does any of these detestable practices must be cut off from his people. [30] You must keep My instruction to not do any of the detestable customs[b] that were practiced before you, so that you do not defile yourselves by them; I am Yahweh your God."

Laws of Holiness

19 The LORD spoke to Moses: [2] "Speak to the entire Israelite community and tell them: Be holy[c] because I, •Yahweh your God, am holy.[d]

[3] "Each of you is to respect his mother and father.[e] You are to keep My Sabbaths; I am Yahweh your God. [4] Do not turn to idols[f] or make cast images[g] of gods for yourselves;[h] I am Yahweh your God.

[5] "When you offer a •fellowship sacrifice to the LORD, sacrifice it so that you may be accepted. [6] It is to be eaten on the day you sacrifice it or on the next day, but what remains on the third day must be burned up.[i] [7] If any is eaten on the third day, it is a repulsive thing;

it will not be accepted.[j] [8] Anyone who eats it will bear his punishment, for he has profaned what is holy to the LORD. That person must be cut off from his people.[k]

[9] "When you reap the harvest of your land, you are not to reap to the very edge of your field or gather the gleanings[l] of your harvest. [10] You must not strip your vineyard bare or gather its fallen grapes. Leave them for the poor[m] and the foreign resident;[n] I am Yahweh your God.

[11] "You must not steal.[o] You must not act deceptively[p] or lie[q] to one another. [12] You must not swear falsely by My name, profaning the name of your God;[r] I am Yahweh.

[13] "You must not oppress[s] your neighbor or rob[t] him. The wages due a hired hand[u] must not remain with you until morning. [14] You must not curse the deaf or put a stumbling block in front of the blind,[v] but you are to •fear your God;[w] I am Yahweh.[x]

[15] "You must not act unjustly[y] when deciding a case. Do not be partial[z] to the poor or give preference to the rich;[aa] judge your neighbor fairly. [16] You must not go about spreading slander[ab] among your people; you must not jeopardize[A] your neighbor's life; I am Yahweh.

[17] "You must not harbor hatred against your

Cross references (center column)
[a]18:28 Lv 20:22; Dt 8:20
[b]18:30 Lv 7:7
[c]19:2 Ex 19:5-6
[d]Lv 11:44; 21:8
[e]19:3 Ex 20:12; 21:15
[f]19:4 Lv 26:1
[g]Nm 33:52
[h]Ex 20:3,23; 32:31; Dt 4:15-16
[i]19:6 Lv 7:17
[j]19:7 Lv 1:4
[k]19:7-8 Lv 7:18,20
[l]19:9 Lv 23:22; Dt 24:19-22; Ru 2:2-7,15-19,23; Is 17:5
[m]19:10 Dt 15:11
[n]Ex 2:22; Dt 24:20-21; Is 17:5-6; 24:13
[o]19:11 Ex 20:15; 22:1; Rm 13:9; Eph 4:28
[p]Pr 30:9; Is 30:9; 59:13; Jr 5:12; Hs 4:2; 7:3; 9:2; 10:13; Nah 3:1; Hab 3:17; Zch 13:4
[q]Gn 21:23; Ex 20:16; 1Sm 15:29; Ps 44:18; 89:34; Is 63:8; Eph 4:25
[r]19:12 Ex 20:7; Lv 18:21; 20:3; Mal 3:5; Jms 5:12
[s]19:13 Dt 24:14
[t]Dt 28:29
[u]Ex 12:45; 22:14; Lv 22:10; 25:6,40,50,53;
Is 7:20; Jr 46:21; Ezk 18:7; Mal 3:5; Jms 5:4
[v]19:14 Ex 4:11; Dt 27:18
[w]Ps 147:11; Pr 1:7; Ac 10:2; Rv 14:7
[x]Ex 31:13
[y]19:15 Dt 25:16
[z]Ex 23:2-3; Dt 1:17; Jms 2:9
[aa]Gn 24:35; Jb 34:19
[ab]19:16 Ps 15:3; Jr 6:28; 9:4; Lk 6:22; 2Co 6:8; 12:20; Eph 4:31; Col 3:8; Ti 3:2; 1Pt 2:1; 4:4; Rv 2:9

A19:16 Lit *not stand against*

God's name by following pagan practices, it was not just a mistake, it was a grave **sin**, an abomination, and something that defiled the community. The fact that the laws of chapter 18 begin and end with the statement **I am Yahweh your God** shows the seriousness of these laws.

19:1-37 All commandments from the Decalogue are reasserted here. The covenant community must live a holy life demonstrated through worship, integrity, justice, and love.

Ten Commandments (Ex 20:2-17)	Leviticus
1-2	19:4
3	19:12
4	19:3b
5	19:3a
6	19:16b
7	19:29
8	19:11a
9	19:16a
10	19:18

19:2 This is the only time where God tells Moses to speak directly to the **entire Israelite community**. The imperative **be holy** (11:44; 20:7,26) and the reason for the people's holiness—**because I, Yahweh your God, am holy**—are the

main message of this chapter as well as the theme of the entire book of Leviticus. This idea was repeated by Jesus in the Sermon on the Mount when He told His disciples to "be perfect . . . as your heavenly Father is perfect" (Mt 5:48).

19:3 The placement of the **mother** before the **father** is unusual in the male-oriented Israelite society. Greek, Syriac, and Aramaic translations reverse the order to harmonize it with the Decalogue.

19:4 The expressions "I am Yahweh" and **I am Yahweh your God** (vv. 2-4,10-12,14,16,18,25,28,31-32,34,36-37) emphasize that God is the author of these holiness laws as well as the rationale for them.

19:9-10 God in His grace made provision for **the poor and the foreign resident**. Boaz obeyed this commandment when Ruth was allowed to glean after the reapers (Ru 2:8-9). Jesus repeatedly taught His disciples to care for the poor (Mt 19:21; Mk 12:42-43; Lk 4:18; 6:20; 11:41; 12:33; 14:13).

19:14 The command against abusing **the deaf** and **the blind** can be applied concerning any handicapped or disadvantaged people. The imperative **you are to fear your God** serves as the rationale for the law because, unlike the deaf and the blind, God can see and hear everything we do. Outside the Bible, laws protecting disabled people were conspicuously absent in the ancient Near East.

19:15 The law against acting **unjustly** is directed not at judges (Dt 1:16; 16:18) but at the people in general, since

brother.[A,a] Rebuke your neighbor directly, and you will not incur •guilt because of him.[b] [18] Do not take revenge[c] or bear a grudge against members of your community, but love your neighbor as yourself;[d] I am Yahweh.

[19] "You are to keep My statutes. You must not crossbreed two different kinds of your livestock, sow your fields with two kinds of seed, or put on a garment made of two kinds of material.[e]

[20] "If a man has sexual intercourse with a woman who is a slave designated for another man, but she has not been redeemed[f] or given her freedom, there must be punishment.[B] They are not to be put to death, because she had not been freed. [21] However, he must bring a ram as his •restitution offering to the LORD at the entrance to the tent of meeting.[g] [22] The priest will make •atonement on his behalf before the LORD with the ram of the restitution offering for the sin he has committed, and he will be forgiven for the sin he committed.

[23] "When you come into the land and plant any kind of tree for food, you are to consider the fruit forbidden.[C] It will be forbidden to you for three years; it is not to be eaten. [24] In the fourth year all its fruit must be consecrated as a praise offering[h] to the LORD. [25] But in the

fifth year you may eat its fruit. In this way its yield will increase for you;[i] I am Yahweh your God.

[26] "You are not to eat anything with blood in it.[D,j] You are not to practice •divination[k] or sorcery.[l] [27] You are not to cut off the hair at the sides of your head or mar the edge of your beard.[m] [28] You are not to make gashes on your bodies for the dead[n] or put tattoo marks on yourselves; I am Yahweh.

[29] "Do not debase[E,o] your daughter by making her a prostitute,[p] or the land will be prostituted and filled with depravity. [30] You must keep My Sabbaths and revere My sanctuary;[q] I am Yahweh.

[31] "Do not turn to mediums[F,r] or consult spiritists,[G,s] or you will be defiled by them; I am Yahweh your God.

[32] "You are to rise in the presence of the elderly and honor the old.[t] Fear your God; I am Yahweh.

[33] "When a foreigner lives with you in your land, you must not oppress[u] him. [34] You must regard the foreigner who lives with you as the native-born among you. You are to love him

Cross references (center column):

[a]19:17 2Th 3:15; 1Jn 2:9,11; 3:15; 4:20
[b]Pr 9:8; 27:5; Ezk 3:18; Mt 18:15; Gl 6:1
[c]19:18 Dt 32:35; Pr 20:22; Rm 12:17,19; Heb 10:30; Rv 19:2
[d]Pr 17:17; Mt 5:43; 22:39; Mk 12:31; Lk 10:27; Rm 13:9; Gl 5:14; Jms 2:8
[e]19:19 Dt 22:9-11
[f]19:20 Ex 6:6; 21:7-11; Lv 27:29; Dt 22:23-27
[g]19:21 Ex 27:21
[h]19:24 Jdg 9:27
[i]19:25 Lv 25:18-22
[j]19:26 Gn 9:4; Lv 3:17; 17:10-12; 1Sm 14:32-35; Ezk 33:25
[k]1Kg 20:33
[l]Dt 18:10,14; Jdg 9:37; 2Kg 21:6; 2Ch 33:6; Is 2:6; 57:3; Jr 27:9
[m]19:27 Lv 21:5; Dt 14:1; 2Sm 10:4-5; Jr 41:5; 48:37; Ezk 5:1-5; 44:20
[n]19:28 1Kg 18:28; Jr 16:6; 41:5; 47:5; 48:37
[o]19:29 Lv 21:12
[p]Ex 34:31; Lv 21:9; Dt 23:17-18
[q]19:30 Ex 15:17; Lv 20:3; 26:2; Nm 19:20
[r]19:31 Lv 20:6
[s]Dt 18:11; Ac 16:16
[t]19:32 Jb 12:12; 32:4; Pr 23:22; Lm 5:12; 1Tm 5:1
[u]19:33 Dt 23:16

[A]19:17 Or your fellow Israelite   [B]19:20 Or compensation   [C]19:23 Lit uncircumcised   [D]19:26 Or anything over its blood   [E]19:29 Lit profane   [F]19:31 Or spirits of the dead   [G]19:31 Or familiar spirits

---

any Israelite could be a juror and stand in judgment of his **neighbor** (Ru 4).

19:17 One way to show love for a **neighbor** is to **rebuke** him when he does wrong. New Testament leaders were commanded to rebuke those whom they served (1Tm 5:20; 2Tm 4:2; Ti 1:9,13; 2:15).

19:18 The importance of the command to **love your neighbor as yourself** was affirmed by Jesus and the apostle Paul; it also shows continuity between the OT and the NT (Mt 22:39-40; Rm 13:9).

19:20-22 Having **sexual intercourse with a woman who is a slave** was a sin, and this is why a **restitution offering** had to be made, though the death penalty was not required. The man alone was guilty since the female slave was not required to bring the guilt offering. This law protected vulnerable female slaves who did not have the social power and economic clout that free men had.

19:23-25 This law dealing with horticultural holiness was intended for the benefit of the Israelites. The prohibition from eating the **fruit** of a newly planted fruit **tree** may have had to do with the fact that the fruit did not taste good in the first **three years**. Because the firstfruits belonged to God (Nm 18:12-17), the fruit of the fourth year was **consecrated** to God as **a praise offering** in which the covenant community recognized that God was the One who gave them the good things the earth produced. Following this law would result in an **increase** of production.

19:26 **Divination** involved trying to determine the future by such devices as casting lots, using arrows, or looking at liquids or entrails. **Sorcery** involved interpreting natural phenomena such as clouds or stars, or communicating with the spirits of the dead. Both of these practices were common in the ancient Near East, but they were denounced in the Bible because they were an attempt to undermine God's sovereignty. God, when He chose to, revealed the future through His servants, the prophets.

19:27 In Israel **hair** was the sign of a person's strength and beauty. To this day orthodox Jews keep this law because the **beard** was a symbol of manhood. To **mar the edge of** the beard may have been a pagan practice that Israel was forbidden to emulate. In later Israelite culture, shaving was considered disgraceful (2Sm 10:4-5; Is 7:20).

19:28 Because the body is God's creation, it was to be kept whole (1Co 6:8-20). The pagan custom of gashing the body as a sign of mourning was prohibited (Dt 14:1; Jr 16:6; 41:5; 47:5; 48:37). Painting one's body (**tattoo marks**) was also a custom that denoted belonging to a pagan cult, or it was done to ward off spirits of the dead.

19:31 In the ancient Near East, necromancy, or communication with the dead, was sought through **mediums** or **spiritists**, but God's law ruled against such pagan practice (1Sm 28).

19:32 Respect for the **elderly** is God's rule not just in the Jewish culture, but universally (Pr 16:31; 20:29).

19:35-36 The holiness laws must also permeate business dealings. The way a person buys and sells is an indication of his obedience to God. Honesty was a sign of wise living (Pr 11:1; 16:11; 20:10,23).

20:1-27 The laws in this chapter are similar to those in

as yourself,[a] for you were foreigners in the land of Egypt;[b] I am Yahweh your God.

[35] "You must not be unfair[c] in measurements of length, weight, or volume. [36] You are to have honest balances,[d] honest weights, an honest dry measure,[A] and an honest liquid measure;[B,e] I am Yahweh your God, who brought you out of the land of Egypt. [37] You must keep all My statutes and all My ordinances and do them; I am Yahweh."

Molech Worship and Spiritism

20 The LORD spoke to Moses: [2] "Say to the Israelites: Any Israelite or foreigner living in Israel who gives any of his children to *Molech[f] must be put to death; the people of the country are to stone him.[g] [3] I will turn[C] against that man and cut him off from his people, because he gave his *offspring to Molech, defiling My sanctuary[h] and profaning My holy name.[i] [4] But if the people of the country look the other way when that man[D] gives any of his children to Molech, and do not put him to death, [5] then I will turn[C] against that man and his family, and cut off from their people both him and all who follow[E] him in prostituting[j] themselves with Molech.

[6] "Whoever turns to mediums[F,k] or spiritists[G] and prostitutes himself with them, I will turn[C] against that person and cut him off from his people. [7] Consecrate yourselves and be holy, for I am *Yahweh your God. [8] Keep My statutes and do them; I am Yahweh who sets you apart.

Family and Sexual Offenses

[9] "If anyone curses his father or mother, he must be put to death.[l] He has cursed his father or mother; his blood is on his own hands.[H]

[10] If a man commits adultery[m] with a married woman—if he commits adultery with his neighbor's wife—both the adulterer and the adulteress must be put to death. [11] If a man sleeps with his father's wife, he has shamed his father.[n] Both of them must be put to death; their blood is on their own hands.[I] [12] If a man sleeps with his daughter-in-law,[o] both of them must be put to death. They have acted perversely; their blood is on their own hands.[I] [13] If a man sleeps with a man as with a woman,[p] they have both committed a detestable thing.[q] They must be put to death; their blood is on their own hands.[I] [14] If a man marries a woman and her mother,[r] it is depraved. Both he and they must be burned with fire,[s] so that there will be no depravity among you. [15] If a man has sexual intercourse with[J] an animal, he must be put to death; you are also to kill the animal. [16] If a woman comes near any animal and mates with it, you are to kill the woman and the animal.[t] They must be put to death; their own blood is on them. [17] If a man marries his sister,[u] whether his father's daughter or his mother's daughter, and they have sexual relations,[K,v] it is a disgrace.[w] They must be cut off publicly from their people. He has had sexual intercourse with his sister; he will bear his punishment. [18] If a man sleeps with a menstruating woman and has sexual intercourse with her, he has exposed the source of her flow, and she has uncovered the source of her blood.[x] Both of them must be cut off from their people. [19] You must not have sexual intercourse with your mother's sister or your father's sister,[y] for it is exposing one's own blood relative; both people will bear their punishment. [20] If a man sleeps with his aunt, he has shamed his uncle;[z] they will bear their

Cross references (center column)
[a]19:34 Lv 19:18
[b]Ex 23:9; Lv 18:3; Dt 10:19; 23:7
[c]19:35 Dt 25:16
[d]19:36 Hs 12:8; Am 8:5; Mc 6:11
[e]Dt 25:13-16; Pr 16:11; Ezk 45:10
[f]20:2 Lv 18:21; Dt 18:10; 2Kg 23:10; Ac 7:43
[g]Lv 24:14; Nm 15:35-36; Dt 17:2-7; 21:21; Jos 7:25
[h]20:3 Ex 15:17
[i]Lv 18:21; 19:12; 22:2,32; Jr 34:16; Ezk 36:20; 39:7; Am 2:7
[j]20:5 Dt 22:21
[k]20:6 Lv 19:31; 20:27; Dt 18:11; 1Sm 28:3,7-9; 2Kg 21:6; 23:24; 1Ch 10:13; 2Ch 33:6; Is 8:19; 19:3; 29:4
[l]20:9 Ex 21:17; Dt 21:18-21; 27:16; Pr 20:20; 30:11; Mt 15:4; Mk 7:10
[m]20:10 Ex 20:14; Dt 5:18; 22:22; 31:16; Pr 6:32; Mal 3:5; Mt 5:27-28,32; 19:9,18
[n]20:11 Lv 18:8; Dt 22:30; 27:20; 1Co 5:1
[o]20:12 Gn 38:16; Lv 18:15; Ezk 22:11
[p]20:13 Gn 19:5
[q]Gn 46:34
[r]20:14 Lv 18:17
[s]Gn 38:24; Lv 18:22; 21:9; Jdg 14:15; Rv 17:16
[t]20:15-16 Ex 22:19
[u]20:17 Lv 18:13
[v]Lv 18:9
[w]Lv 19:29
[x]20:18 Lv 18:19
[y]20:19 Ex 6:20; Lv 18:12-13
[z]20:20 Lv 18:14

[A]19:36 Lit *honest ephah*; an *ephah* is a dry measure of grain equivalent to about 23 quarts.   [B]19:36 Lit *honest hin*; a *hin* is a liquid measure of about 1 gallon.   [C]20:3,5,6 Lit *will set My face*   [D]20:4 Lit *country ever close their eyes from that man when he*   [E]20:5 Lit *prostitute themselves with*   [F]20:6 Or *spirits of the dead*   [G]20:6 Or *familiar spirits*   [H]20:9 Lit *on him*   [I]20:11,12,13 Lit *on them*   [J]20:15 Lit *man gives his emission to*   [K]20:17 Lit *and he sees her nakedness and she sees his nakedness*

---

chapter 18 except that here the penalties for disobedience are attached to the laws forbidding Molech worship, pagan religious practices, and sexual offenses.

20:2 **Death** by stoning was also applied to blasphemers (24:16; 1Kg 21:9-14), sorcerers (Lv 20:27), Sabbath violators (Nm 15:35-36), idolaters (Dt 13:6-10; 17:3-5), rebellious children (Dt 21:18-21), adulterers (Ezk 16:35-40; 23:43-47), a bride who did not disclose she was not a virgin (Dt 22:23-24), a man and a betrothed woman who engaged in consensual sex (Dt 22:24), and those who did not destroy things that had been placed under a divine ban (Jos 7:1,25).

20:9 The fact that both parents are mentioned promotes the value of women in a traditional patriarchal society. The curse against one's parents carried the **death** penalty (Ex 21:17; Dt 21:18-21; Pr 20:20; Mt 15:4; Mk 7:10).

20:17-19 The punishment for lesser offenses was being **cut off publicly from their people**. In some instances God Himself carried out this punishment (vv. 3,5-6; 17:10), in which He excommunicated the offenders from their relatives (7:20-21,25,27; 17:4,9-10; 18:29; 19:8; 20:3,5-6; 23:29).

20:20-21 Lesser violations were punished with childlessness. The presence of children was depicted in the Bible as divine reward (Ps 127:3). To be barren was regarded as shameful (Gn 16:2; 25:21; 30:1; 1Sm 1:5-11). Barrenness as punishment for sexual offenses was not a new judgment (Gn 20:17-18; Nm 5:22,27), but not all cases of barrenness were punishment for sin. Sarah, Rachel, and Hannah in the OT, and Elizabeth in the NT are examples of barrenness, but nowhere does Scripture indicate that their barrenness was punishment for sin.

•guilt and die childless. 21 If a man marries his
brother's wife, it is impurity.[a] He has shamed
his brother;[b] they will be childless.

Holiness in the Land

22 "You are to keep all My statutes and all
My ordinances, and do them, so that the land
where I am bringing you to live will not vomit
you out.[c] 23 You must not follow the statutes
of the nations I am driving out before you,
for they did all these things, and I abhorred
them.[d] 24 And I promised you: You will inherit
their land, since I will give it to you to possess,
a land flowing with milk and honey.[e] I
am Yahweh your God who set you apart from
the peoples. 25 Therefore you must distinguish
the •clean animal from the •unclean one,
and the unclean bird from the clean one. Do
not become contaminated[f] by any land animal,
bird, or whatever crawls on the ground; I
have set these apart as unclean for you.[g] 26 You
are to be holy to Me because I, Yahweh, am
holy, and I have set you apart from the nations
to be Mine.[h]

27 A man or a woman who is[A] a medium or a
spiritist must be put to death. They are to be
stoned; their blood is on their own hands."[B]

The Holiness of the Priests

21 The LORD said to Moses: "Speak to Aaron's
sons, the priests, and tell them:
A priest is not to make himself ceremonially
•unclean for a dead person among his relatives,[i]
2 except for his immediate family: his
mother, father, son, daughter, or brother. 3 He
may make himself unclean for his young unmarried
sister in his immediate family. 4 He is
not to make himself unclean for those related
to him by marriage[C] and so defile himself.

5 "Priests may not make bald spots on their
heads, shave the edge of their beards, or make
gashes on their bodies.[j] 6 They are to be holy to
their God and not profane the name of their
God.[k] For they present the fire offerings to
•Yahweh, the food of their God, and they must
be holy. 7 They are not to marry a woman defiled
by prostitution.[D,l] They are not to marry
one divorced[m] by her husband, for the priest
is holy to his God. 8 You are to consider him
holy since he presents the food of your God.
He will be holy to you because I, Yahweh who
sets you apart, am holy. 9 If a priest's daughter
defiles herself by promiscuity,[E,n] she defiles
her father; she must be burned up.[o]

10 "The priest who is highest among his
brothers, who has had the anointing oil poured
on his head and has been ordained[F] to wear
the garments, must not dishevel his hair[G] or
tear his garments.[p] 11 He must not go near any
dead person or make himself unclean even for
his father or mother.[q] 12 He must not leave the
sanctuary or he will desecrate the sanctuary of
his God, for the consecration of the anointing
oil of his God is on him;[r] I am Yahweh.

13 "He is to marry a woman who is a virgin.
14 He is not to marry a widow,[s] a divorced
woman,[t] or one defiled by prostitution. He
is to marry a virgin from his own people,
15 so that he does not corrupt his bloodline[H]
among his people, for I am Yahweh who sets
him apart."

Physical Defects and Priests

16 The LORD spoke to Moses: 17 "Tell Aaron:

[a] 20:21 Mk 6:18 [b] Lv 18:16 [c] 20:22 Lv 18:25 [d] 20:23 Ex 23:24; Lv 18:3 [e] 20:24 Ex 3:8; 13:5; Nm 14:8; 16:13-14 [f] 20:25 Dt 7:26 [g] Lv 11:1-47 [h] 20:26 Ex 19:5-6; Lv 11:44-45; Is 1:4; 6:3 [i] 21:1 Nm 5:2-3; 6:6; 19:11-13; 31:19; Ezk 44:25 [j] 21:5 Lv 19:27-28 [k] 21:6 Ex 20:7; Lv 20:3; Jn 10:25 [l] 21:7 Gn 34:31 [m] Dt 22:19,29; 24:1,3; Mal 2:16; Mt 1:19; 5:31-32; 19:3-9 [n] 21:9 Dt 22:21 [o] Gn 38:24; Lv 20:14; Jdg 15:6; Rv 17:16 [p] 21:10 Lv 10:6; Ezk 44:20; Mk 14:63 [q] 21:11 Ezk 44:25 [r] 21:12 Lv 10:7 [s] 21:14 Ex 22:22 [t] Lv 21:7; 22:13; Nm 30:10; Ezk 44:22

[A] 20:27 Lit *is in them* [B] 20:27 Lit *on them* [C] 21:4 Lit *unclean a husband among his people* [D] 21:7 Or *a prostitute* or *a defiled woman* [E] 21:9 Or *prostitution* [F] 21:10 Lit *and one has filled his hand* [G] 21:10 Or *not uncover his head* [H] 21:15 Lit *not profane his seed*

21:1-24 The standard of holiness was set higher for the priests. While all Israelites were part of the "holy nation" (Ex 19:5-6), the leaders were held to a higher standard in matters such as mourning, marriage, and family. This concept parallels the NT where church leaders such as elders, bishops, and deacons are held to higher standards (Jms 3:1).

21:1-2 Priests were forbidden from defiling themselves by touching a **dead person** except in the case of a close relative. This law was a polemic against the cult of the dead, which was widespread in the ancient Near East. The Egyptians were so preoccupied with death that their pharaohs would spend years preparing their pyramid tombs.

21:4-5 Since contact with the dead defiled a person (Nm 19:11-22), **priests** could not even prepare their wives for burial because they were not blood relatives. The priest was also forbidden to follow the mourning laws of the Canaanites, who would mutilate their **bodies** to show their sorrow and pain as well as to venerate the dead.

21:7 In the ancient Near East, there were two types of prostitutes. Common prostitutes were sexually loose and were paid for their services. Cult prostitutes, on the other hand, committed sexual acts as worship to pagan gods. The prohibition against marrying a **divorced** woman carried over into the NT rules about elders and deacons (1Tm 3; Ti 1:5-9).

21:9 Because the family in Israel was a solid unit, the activity of each member reflected on the others. Since cremation was not an accepted practice in Israel, the punishment for this filial **promiscuity** was probably death by stoning, after which the body was **burned up**.

21:16-23 A **priest** in Israel had to be in good physical condition and without **physical defect**. While the text lists 12 blemishes that would prevent a person from serving as a priest, later rabbis expanded the list of blemishes to 142. The NT does not address physical requirements but only spiritual qualifications for ministers. While some cultures today still hold to the OT requirements for ministers, the Levitical law does not carry over to the NT, and it is not binding on the church.

None of your descendants throughout your generations who has a physical defect[a] is to come near to present the food[b] of his God. [18] No man who has any defect is to come near: no man who is blind, lame, facially disfigured, or deformed; [19] no man who has a broken foot or hand, [20] or who is a hunchback or a dwarf,[A,c] or who has an eye defect, a festering rash, scabs,[d] or a crushed testicle.[e] [21] No descendant of Aaron the priest who has a defect is to come near to present the fire offerings to the LORD. He has a defect and is not to come near to present the food of his God. [22] He may eat the food of his God from what is especially holy as well as from what is holy. [23] But because he has a defect, he must not go near the curtain[f] or approach the altar. He is not to desecrate My sanctuaries, for I am Yahweh who sets them apart."[g] [24] Moses said this to Aaron and his sons and to all the Israelites.

[a]21:17 Nm 19:2
[b]Lv 3:11
[c]21:20 Gn 41:3-4,6-7,23-24; Ex 16:14; Lv 13:30; 16:12; 1Kg 19:12; Is 29:5; 40:15,22
[d]Lv 22:22
[e]21:18-20 Lv 22:24; Dt 23:1
[f]21:23 Mk 15:38; Heb 6:19
[g]Ex 31:13; Lv 20:8; 21:8,15; 22:9,16,32; Ezk 20:12

[A]21:20 Or or emaciated

PRIESTS IN THE OLD TESTAMENT
(Listed alphabetically)

NAME	REFERENCE	IDENTIFICATION
Aaron	Ex 28–29	Older brother of Moses; first high priest of Israel
Abiathar	1Sm 22:20-23; 2Sm 20:25	Son of Ahimelech who escaped the slayings at Nob
Abihu	See Nadab and Abihu	
Ahimelech	1Sm 21–22	Led a priestly community at Nob; killed by Saul for befriending David
Amariah	2Ch 19:11	High priest during the reign of Jehoshaphat
Amaziah	Am 7:10-17	Evil priest of Bethel; confronted Amos the prophet
Azariah	2Ch 26:16-20	High priest who stood against Uzziah when the ruler began to act as a prophet
Eleazar and Ithamar	Lv 10:6; Nm 20:26	Godly sons of Aaron; Eleazar—Israel's second high priest
Eli	1Sm 1–4	Descendant of Ithamar; raised Samuel at Shiloh
Eliashib	Neh 3:1; 13:4-5	High priest during the reign of Josiah
Elishama and Jehoram	2Ch 17:7-9	Teaching priests during the reign of Jehoshaphat
Ezra	Ezr 7–10; Neh 8	Scribe, teacher, and priest during the rebuilding of Jerusalem
Hilkiah	2Kg 22–23	High priest during the reign of Josiah
Hophni and Phinehas	1Sm 2:12-36	Evil sons of Eli
Ithamar	See Eleazar and Ithamar	
Jahaziel	2Ch 20:14-17	Levite who assured Jehoshaphat of deliverance from an enemy
Jehoiada	2Kg 11–12	High priest who saved Joash from Queen Athaliah's purge
Jehoram	See Elishama and Jehoram	
Joshua	Hg 1:1,12; Zch 3	First high priest after the Babylonian captivity
Nadab and Abihu	Lv 10:1-2	Evil sons of Aaron
Pashhur	Jr 20:1-6	False priest who persecuted the prophet Jeremiah
Phinehas	(1) Nm 25:7-13 (2) See Hophni and Phinehas	(1) Son of Eleazar; Israel's third high priest whose zeal for pure worship stopped a plague
Shelemiah	Neh 13:13	Priest during the time of Nehemiah; was in charge of administrating storehouses
Uriah	2Kg 16:10-16	Priest who built pagan altar for evil King Ahaz
Zadok	2Sm 15; 1Kg 1	High priest during the reign of David and Solomon

Priests and Their Food

22 The LORD spoke to Moses: 2“Tell Aaron
and his sons to deal respectfully with
the holy offerings of the Israelites that they
have consecrated to Me, so they do not profane
My holy name;[a] I am •Yahweh. 3Say to them:
If any man from any of your descendants
throughout your generations is in a state of
uncleanness yet approaches the holy offerings
that the Israelites consecrate to the LORD, that
person will be cut off from My presence; I am
Yahweh. 4No man of Aaron’s descendants who
has a skin disease[A] or a discharge is to eat from
the holy offerings until he is •clean. Whoever
touches anything made •unclean by a dead
person or by a man who has an emission of
semen, 5or whoever touches any swarming
creature that makes him unclean or any person who makes him unclean—whatever his
uncleanness— 6the man who touches any of
these will remain unclean until evening[b] and
is not to eat from the holy offerings unless he
has bathed his body with water. 7When the
sun has set, he will become clean, and then
he may eat from the holy offerings, for that
is his food.[c] 8He must not eat an animal that
died naturally or was mauled by wild beasts,[B,d]
making himself unclean by it; I am Yahweh.
9They must keep My instruction,[e] or they will
be •guilty and die because they profane it; I am
Yahweh who sets them apart.
10“No one outside a priest’s family[C,f] is to eat
the holy offering. A foreigner staying with a
priest or a hired hand is not to eat the holy
offering. 11But if a priest purchases someone
with his money, that person may eat it, and
those born in his house may eat his food. 12If
the priest’s daughter is married to a man outside a priest’s family,[D] she is not to eat from
the holy contributions.[E] 13But if the priest’s
daughter becomes widowed or divorced, has
no children, and returns to her father’s house
as in her youth, she may share her father’s
food. But no outsider may share it. 14If anyone
eats a holy offering in error,[g] he must add a
fifth to its value and give the holy offering to
the priest.[h] 15The priests must not profane the
holy offerings the Israelites give to the LORD
16by letting the people eat their holy offerings
and having them bear the penalty of restitution.[i] For I am Yahweh who sets them apart.”

Acceptable Sacrifices

17The LORD spoke to Moses: 18“Speak to Aaron, his sons, and all the Israelites and tell
them: Any man of the house of Israel or of the
foreign residents[j] in Israel who presents his
offering[k]—whether they present freewill gifts
or payment of vows to the LORD as •burnt offerings— 19must offer an unblemished male[l]
from the cattle, sheep, or goats in order for
you to be accepted. 20You are not to present
anything that has a defect, because it will not
be accepted on your behalf.
21“When a man presents a •fellowship sacrifice to the LORD to fulfill a vow or as a freewill offering from the herd or flock, it has
to be unblemished to be acceptable; there
must be no defect in it. 22You are not to present any animal to the LORD that is blind,
injured, maimed, or has a running sore, festering rash,[m] or scabs; you may not put any
of them on the altar as a fire offering to the
LORD.[n] 23You may sacrifice as a freewill offering any animal from the herd or flock that has
an elongated or stunted limb, but it is not acceptable as a vow offering. 24You are not to
present to the LORD anything that has bruised,
crushed, torn, or severed testicles;[o] you must
not sacrifice them in your land. 25Neither you
nor[F] a foreigner are to present food to your
God from any of these animals. They will not
be accepted for you because they are deformed
and have a defect.”[p]
26The LORD spoke to Moses: 27“When an ox,
sheep, or goat is born, it must remain with[G] its
mother for seven days; from the eighth day[q]
on, it will be acceptable as a gift, a fire offering
to the LORD. 28But you are not to slaughter an
animal from the herd or flock on the same day

a 22:2 Ex 20:7; Jn 10:25
b 22:6 Lv 11:24-28,31-32,39-40
c 22:7 Lv 6:16-18,29; 7:7-10,32-36; 26:5
d 22:8 Ex 22:31; Lv 7:24; 17:15; Ezk 44:31
e 22:9 Gn 26:5; Lv 18:30
f 22:10 Ex 29:33; Nm 3:10; 18:4,7
g 22:14 Nm 15:22,24
h Lv 5:14-16
i 22:16 Lv 14:12
j 22:18 Ex 2:22
k Lv 1:2
l 22:19 Ex 29:1
m 22:22 Dt 28:27; 2Sm 23:38; 1Ch 11:40; Jr 31:39
n Lv 21:18-20; Is 28:20
o 22:24 Lv 21:20
p 22:25 Mal 1:14
q 22:27 Ex 22:30

A 22:4 Or *has leprosy* or *scale disease* B 22:8 Lit *eat a carcass or a mauled beast* C 22:10 Lit *No stranger* D 22:12 Lit *man, a stranger* E 22:12 Lit *the contribution of holy offerings* F 22:25 Lit *nor from the hand of* G 22:27 Lit *under*

22:1-33 Since the priests led in corporate worship, they had to be ceremonially pure. The sacrifices they brought also had to be unblemished in order to be acceptable to the Lord.

22:4-5 The impurities that rendered a priest **unclean** are listed in descending order of severity. During the time of Jesus, the religious leaders were angry that Jesus touched what would render Him as unclean, but when Jesus touched an unclean person, that person became clean.

22:11 This law was consistent with the instruction given to Abraham to circumcise purchased slaves (Gn 17:12-13), thus making them part of the covenant community.

22:19 The word **unblemished** comes from a term that means "to be complete, perfect." It conveys the idea that sacrifices must be without flaw. During the Second Temple period, the prophet Malachi spoke against the people's bringing defective animals as sacrifices (Mal 1:8-14). The NT teaches that the covenant community must bring their best to God (2Co 8–9; Eph 5:2; Php 4:10-20; Heb 13:15-16; 1Pt 2:5). The ultimate perfect sacrifice was Jesus, the Messiah, through whose atoning death believers are forgiven of sin and granted eternal life (Jn 1:29; 1Pt 1:19; Rv 7:9; 12:11).

as its young.[a] 29 When you sacrifice a thank offering[b] to the LORD, sacrifice it so that you may
be accepted. 30 It is to be eaten on the same
day.[c] Do not let any of it remain until morning; I am Yahweh.
31 "You are to keep My commands and do
them; I am Yahweh. 32 You must not profane
My holy name; I must be treated as holy[d]
among the Israelites. I am Yahweh who sets
you apart, 33 the One who brought you out of
the land of Egypt to be your God; I am Yahweh."

Holy Days

23 The LORD spoke to Moses: 2 "Speak to
the Israelites and tell them: These are
My appointed times,[e] the times of the LORD
that you will proclaim as sacred assemblies.[f]
3 "Work may be done for six days, but on
the seventh day there must be a Sabbath of
complete rest,[g] a sacred assembly. You are not
to do any work; it is a Sabbath[h] to the LORD
wherever you live.
4 "These are the LORD's appointed times, the
sacred assemblies you are to proclaim at their
appointed times. 5 The •Passover[i] to the LORD
comes in the first month, at twilight on the
fourteenth day of the month. 6 The Festival of
•Unleavened Bread[j] to the LORD is on the fifteenth day of the same month. For seven days
you must eat unleavened bread. 7 On the first
day you are to hold a sacred assembly; you are
not to do any daily work. 8 You are to present a
fire offering to the LORD for seven days. On the
seventh day there will be a sacred assembly;
you must not do any daily work."
9 The LORD spoke to Moses: 10 "Speak to the
Israelites and tell them: When you enter the
land I am giving you and reap its harvest,[A] you
are to bring the first sheaf of your harvest to the

[a] 22:28 Ex 23:19; Dt 22:6-7
[b] 22:29 Lv 7:12-15; 2Ch 29:31; 33:16; Ps 56:13; Jr 17:26; 33:11; Am 4:5
[c] 22:30 Ex 34:25; Lv 7:15; 19:6-7
[d] 22:32 Lv 19:12; 21:6-8,23; 22:2; Lk 11:2
[e] 23:2 Lv 23:37,44; Nm 10:10; 2Ch 2:3; Ezr 3:5
[f] Ex 12:16; Lv 23:21,24,27,35-37; Nm 28:18,25-26; 29:1,7,12
[g] 23:3 Ex 31:15; 35:2; Lv 16:31; 23:32; 25:4
[h] Gn 2:2-3
[i] 23:5 Ex 12:11
[j] 23:6 Ex 12:17

[A] 23:10 = the barley harvest

23:1-44 God set aside a sacred period that included festivals and holy days to give the covenant community rest from everyday life. These special days would also help them remember His acts of creation, deliverance, protection, and provision.

23:2 The expression **sacred assemblies** occurs 11 times in chapter 23 (vv. 2,3,4,7,8,21,24,27,35,36,37) and 8 times elsewhere in the Torah (Ex 12:16; Nm 28:18,25,26; 29:1,7,12). A sacred assembly was a time during which the people were to lay aside their usual work to focus on the worship of Yahweh. The eight days that were designated sacred assemblies were the first and seventh days of Unleavened Bread (Lv 23:7-8), the Festival of Weeks (v. 21), the first day of the seventh month (v. 24), the Day of Atonement (v. 27), the first and eighth days of Booths (vv. 35-36), and the Sabbath.

23:3 The **Sabbath** is the only holy day commanded in the Ten Commandments (Ex 20:8-11) and the only commandment grounded in creation (Ex 20:11). Examples of **work** mentioned in the Torah are plowing and reaping (Ex 34:21), kindling fire (Ex 35:3), and gathering wood (Nm 15:32-36). Work that was prohibited elsewhere in the OT includes trade (Am 8:5) and carrying burdens (Jr 17:21-27). The Hebrew verb *shavath* means "to rest" or "to cease," and it is the root on which the word "Sabbath" was formed. Jesus affirmed that He is "Lord of the Sabbath" (Mt 12:8) and that "it is lawful to do what is good on the Sabbath" (Mt 12:12). The book of Hebrews also speaks of a spiritual rest into which the community of faith enters through Jesus Christ (Heb 3–4). Just as the rainbow was the sign of the covenant with Noah and circumcision was the sign of the Abrahamic covenant, the Sabbath served as the sign of the Mosaic covenant.

qodesh

Hebrew Pronunciation	[koh DESH]
HCSB Translation	sacred, holy, sanctuary
Uses in Leviticus	92
Uses in the OT	470
Focus Passage	Leviticus 23:2-4,7-8,20-21,24,27,35-37

This noun regularly functions adjectivally as *holy, sacred, dedicated*, or *consecrated* (Ex 3:5; 12:16; 31:15; Lv 19:24). It denotes *sanctuary* (Ex 28:29) or various parts such as *holy place, sanctuary area*, or *most holy place* (Ex 26:33; 28:43; Lv 16:6). *Qodesh* occurs twice in a row to indicate superlatives: *most holy place, especially holy*, and *holiest part* (Ex 26:34; 30:10; Lv 2:3). Singular uses suggest *holiness, what is holy*, or *holy portion* (Ex 15:11; Lv 19:8; Nm 6:20). With numbers *qodesh* connotes *holy ones* (Dt 33:2). Plurals can signify *holy offerings, gifts, things*, or *objects* (Ex 28:38; Lv 5:15; Nm 4:16). Implicit in *qodesh* are concepts of *separateness* and *consecration* (Ezk 42:20). *Holiness* is associated with *glory* and commands respect or awe (Ex 15:11). God is *holy* as separated from sin. *Holy* things and people belong to God, being set apart from common use (Ex 39:30) for His *consecrated* purposes (Lv 10:17).

23:5 The **Passover** was celebrated in the first month, Abib (later called Nisan; March-April). Further instructions about Passover were given in Exodus 12, before the Israelites were delivered by God's mighty hand. It was during the Passover Festival that Jesus was crucified, signaling that He was the unblemished lamb that was sacrificed for all humanity (Is 53:5-6; Heb 8–10; 1Pt 1:18-19).

23:6 The Festival of Unleavened Bread began on the fifteenth day of Abib and was a reminder of the haste with which the Hebrews left Egypt (Ex 12). The word "festival" designates the event as a pilgrimage, and it could not be celebrated at home. The unleavened bread was usually in the form of small round wafers baked from new grain without leaven (Lv 2:4). Over time leaven came to signify corruption. Thus, the festival was intended to remind the covenant community that they were supposed to purge corruption as they celebrated redemption (1Co 5:8). By the first century A.D., the Passover and Unleavened Bread festivals were celebrated at the same time (Mk 14:1,12; Lk 22:1,7), although Passover was also treated as part of the pilgrimage during the reign of King Hezekiah (2Ch 30:1).

23:9-12 The Feast of Firstfruits occurred during the week of Unleavened Bread and was both commemorative and prophetic. During this feast the Israelites were to show their gratitude to God for His provision. The community of faith

priest. [11] He will wave the sheaf before the LORD so that you may be accepted; the priest is to wave it on the day after the Sabbath. [12] On the day you wave the sheaf, you are to offer a year-old male lamb[A] without blemish[a] as a *burnt offering to the LORD. [13] Its *grain offering is to be four quarts[B] of fine flour mixed with oil as a fire offering to the LORD, a pleasing aroma, and its *drink offering will be one quart[C] of wine. [14] You must not eat bread, roasted grain, or any new grain[D] until this very day, and until you have brought the offering to your God. This is to be a permanent statute throughout your generations wherever you live.

[15] "You are to count seven[E] complete weeks[F,b] starting from the day after the Sabbath, the day you brought the sheaf of the presentation offering.[c] [16] You are to count 50 days until the day after the seventh Sabbath and then present an offering of new grain[G] to the LORD. [17] Bring two loaves of bread from your settlements as a presentation offering, each of them made from four quarts[B] of fine flour, baked

with yeast, as *firstfruits[d] to the LORD. [18] You are to present with the bread seven unblemished male lambs a year old, one young bull, and two rams. They will be a burnt offering to the LORD, with their grain offerings and drink offerings, a fire offering of a pleasing aroma to the LORD. [19] You are also to prepare one male goat as a *sin offering, and two male lambs a year old as a *fellowship sacrifice. [20] The priest will wave the lambs with the bread of firstfruits as a presentation offering before the LORD; the bread and the two lambs will be holy to the LORD for the priest. [21] On that same day you are to make a proclamation and hold a sacred assembly. You are not to do any daily work. This is to be a permanent statute wherever you live throughout your generations. [22] When you reap the harvest of your land, you are not to reap all the way to the edge of your field or gather the gleanings of your harvest. Leave them for the poor and the foreign resident;[e] I am *Yahweh your God."

[23] The LORD spoke to Moses: [24] "Tell the Isra-

[a]23:12 Ex 29:1
[b]23:15 Ex 34:22; Nm 28:26; Dt 16:10; Ac 2:1
[c]Ex 29:24
[d]23:17 Lv 2:12; 1Co 15:20; Rv 14:4
[e]23:22 Ex 2:22; Lv 19:9-10; Ac 6:1; 11:29

[A]23:12 Or *a male lamb in its first year*   [B]23:13,17 Lit *two-tenths of an ephah*   [C]23:13 Lit *one-fourth of a hin*   [D]23:14 Grain or bread from the new harvest   [E]23:15 Lit *count; they will be seven*   [F]23:15 Or *Sabbaths*   [G]23:16 = the wheat harvest; Ex 34:22

---

was to acknowledge God's provision by giving Him the **first** of their income. The waving of the **sheaf** was to be an outward sign of an inward attitude; therefore it was accompanied by the bringing of sacrifices. The people could only eat from the fruit of the land after they acknowledged God as its source. The prophetic element of this feast was fulfilled in the risen Jesus Christ, who is the firstfruits of those believers who have died (1Co 15:20).

23:15-22 The word "Pentecost" comes from the Greek. It means "fiftieth," and it concluded the period of **seven weeks** that began during Passover. Originally the Festival

of Weeks was for the wheat harvest (Ex 34:22), but later it was tied with the events on Sinai. During this feast the Jews were supposed to show gratitude for God's provisions by bringing gifts (Lv 23:15-17), by setting aside times for worship (vv. 18-21), and by making provision for the **poor**. God's concern for the poor is evident throughout the OT, and He always makes provision for their well-being (v. 22; 19:10, 25:35; Ex 23:11; Dt 15:4; Ru 2). The Jews were celebrating this pilgrimage feast when the Holy Spirit came upon those gathered in Jerusalem (Ac 2).

23:23-25 What later became known as the Festival of Trum-

JEWISH FEASTS AND FESTIVALS				
NAME	**MONTH**	**DATE**	**REFERENCE**	**SIGNIFICANCE**
Passover	Nisan	(Mar./Apr.): 14-21	Ex 12:2-20; Lv 23:5	Commemorates God's deliverance of Israel out of Egypt.
Festival of Unleavened Bread	Nisan	(Mar./Apr.): 15-21	Lv 23:6-8	Commemorates God's deliverance of Israel out of Egypt. Includes a Day of Firstfruits for the barley harvest.
Festival of Harvest, or Weeks (Pentecost)	Sivan	(May/June): 6 (seven weeks after Passover)	Ex 23:16; 34:22; Lv 23:15-21	Commemorates the giving of the law at Mount Sinai. Includes a Day of Firstfruits for the wheat harvest.
Festival of Trumpets (Rosh Hashanah)	Tishri	(Sept./Oct.): 1	Lv 23:23-25; Nm 29:1-6	Day of the blowing of the trumpets to signal the beginning of the civil new year.
Day of Atonement (Yom Kippur)	Tishri	(Sept./Oct.): 10	Ex 30:10; Lv 23:26-33;	On this day the high priest makes atonement for the nation's sin. Also a day of fasting.
Festival of Booths, or Tabernacles (Sukkot)	Tishri	(Sept./Oct.): 15-21	Lv 23:33-43; Nm 29:12-39; Dt 16:13	Commemorates the forty years of wilderness wandering.
Festival of Dedication, or Festival of Lights (Hanukkah)	Kislev and Tebeth	(Nov./Dec.): 25-30; and Tebeth (Dec./Jan.): 1-2	Jn 10:22	Commemorates the purification of the temple by Judas Maccabeus in 164 B.C.
Feast of Purim, or Esther	Adar	(Feb./Mar.): 14	Est 9	Commemorates the deliverance of the Jewish people in the days of Esther.

elites: In the seventh month, on the first day of the month, you are to have a day of complete rest, commemoration, and joyful shouting[A,a]—a sacred assembly.[b] 25 You must not do any daily work, but you must present a fire offering to the LORD."

26 The LORD again spoke to Moses: 27 "The tenth day of this seventh month is the Day of •Atonement.[c] You are to hold a sacred assembly and practice self-denial;[B,d] you are to present a fire offering to the LORD. 28 On this particular day you are not to do any work, for it is a Day of Atonement to make atonement for yourselves before the LORD your God. 29 If any person does not practice self-denial on this particular day, he must be cut off from his people. 30 I will destroy among his people anyone who does any work on this same day. 31 You are not to do any work. This is a permanent statute throughout your generations wherever you live. 32 It will be a Sabbath of complete rest for you, and you must practice self-denial. You are to observe your Sabbath from the evening of the ninth day of the month until the following evening."

33 The LORD spoke to Moses: 34 "Tell the Israelites: The Festival of Booths[C,e] to the LORD begins on the fifteenth day of this seventh month and continues for seven days. 35 There is to be a sacred assembly on the first day; you are not to do any daily work. 36 You are to present a fire offering to the LORD for seven days. On the eighth day you are to hold a sacred assembly and present a fire offering to the LORD. It is a solemn gathering;[f] you are not to do any daily work.

37 "These are the LORD's appointed times that you are to proclaim as sacred assemblies for presenting fire offerings to the LORD, burnt offerings and grain offerings, sacrifices and drink offerings, each on its designated day. 38 These are in addition to the offerings for the LORD's Sabbaths, your gifts, all your vow offerings, and all your freewill offerings that you give to the LORD.

39 "You are to celebrate the LORD's festival on the fifteenth day of the seventh month for seven days after you have gathered the produce of the land. There will be complete rest on the first day and complete rest on the eighth day. 40 On the first day you are to take the product[g] of majestic trees—palm fronds,[h] boughs of leafy trees,[i] and willows of the brook[j]—and rejoice before the LORD your God for seven days. 41 You are to celebrate it as a festival to the LORD seven days each year. This is a permanent statute for you throughout your generations; you must celebrate it in the seventh month. 42 You are to live in booths[k] for seven days. All the native-born of Israel must live in booths, 43 so that your generations may know that I made the Israelites live in booths when I brought them out of the land of Egypt; I am Yahweh your God." 44 So Moses declared the LORD's appointed times to the Israelites.

Tabernacle Oil and Bread

24 The LORD spoke to Moses: 2 "Command the Israelites to bring you pure oil from crushed olives for the light, in order to keep the lamp burning continually.[l] 3 Aaron is to tend it continually from evening until morning before the LORD outside the veil[m] of the •testimony[n] in the tent of meeting. This is a permanent statute throughout your generations. 4 He must continually tend the lamps on the pure gold lampstand in the LORD's presence.[o]

a 23:24 Lv 25:9; Nm 5:15
b Nm 29:1; Ps 81:3
c 23:27 Ex 30:10; Lv 16:29-30; 25:9; Nm 29:7-11
d Ac 27:9
e 23:34 Ex 23:16; Jn 7:37
f 23:36 Nm 29:35
g 23:40 Gn 1:11
h Ex 15:27; Nm 33:9; Jdg 4:5; Neh 8:15; Ps 92:12; Sg 7:8-9; Jl 1:12; Rv 7:9
i Neh 8:15; Ezk 6:13; 20:28
j Jb 40:22; Is 44:4
k 23:42 Gn 33:17; Dt 16:13,16; 31:10; Neh 8:14-17; Am 9:11; Jnh 4:5
l 24:2 Ex 25:37
m 24:3 Mk 15:38; Heb 6:19
n Ex 31:18
o 24:4 Gn 4:14; Ex 25:31; 37:17; Zch 4:2

A 23:24 Or *blast*; traditionally trumpet blasts B 23:27 Traditionally, fasting, abstinence from sex, and refraining from personal grooming C 23:34 Or *Feast of Tabernacles*

pets was observed in the seventh month of Tishri, when the Israelites celebrated the end of the harvest. During the postexilic time, this day became the Jewish New Year (Rosh Hashanah). The words **joyful shouting** mean a shout or a blast; it refers to the sound of the trumpet that reminded the Israelites to assemble in God's presence for spiritual service. Trumpet blasts are important in the end time when events surrounding Christ's second coming will be preceded by angels blowing trumpets (Rv 8:7-8,10,12; 9:1,13-14; 10:7; 11:15).

23:27 The **Day of Atonement** was to be celebrated during the tenth day of Tishri. Details on the celebration of this day are outlined in chapter 16. In contrast to the other feasts, this was to be a day of fasting in which the people exercised **self-denial** and expressed remorse over personal and corporate sin.

23:33-34 The **Festival of Booths** or Tabernacles began on Tishri 15. It was primarily a thanksgiving festival showing gratitude for God's provision (Ex 34:22) and closing out the agricultural year. The booths (Hb *succoth*) were also a reminder that the Israelites lived in tents during the 40-year journey from Egypt to the promised land (Lv 23:42-43). The Festival of Booths was observed during the monarchy period as well as the postexilic period (2Ch 8:13; Ezr 3:4; Zch 14:16,18-19) and during the early church period.

23:40 Booths is the only festival where the Israelites are commanded to **rejoice before the LORD** (cp. Dt 12:10-12; Php 4:4).

24:4 The **lampstand** was the seven-branched menorah that lighted the holy place of the tabernacle (Ex 25:31-40). The light represented the presence of God with His people. In the Bible, light also represents God or His Word (Ps 27:1; 36:9; 119:105). Jesus' affirmation that He was the light of the world was a polemic against those who put their faith in a menorah that was only the symbol of a greater reality (Jn 8:12; 9:5).

⁵"Take fine flour and bake it into 12 loaves;ᵃ each loaf is to be made with four quarts.ᴬ ⁶Arrange them in two rows, six to a row, on the pure gold tableᵇ before the Lᴏʀᴅ. ⁷Place pure frankincenseᶜ near each row, so that it may serve as a memorial portionᵈ for the bread and a fire offeringᵉ to the Lᴏʀᴅ. ⁸The bread is to be set out before the Lᴏʀᴅ every Sabbath day as a perpetual covenantᶠ obligation on the part of the Israelites. ⁹It belongs to Aaron and his sons, who are to eat it in a holy place, for it is the holiest portion for him from the fire offerings to the Lᴏʀᴅ; this is a permanent rule."

A Case of Blasphemy

¹⁰Now the son of an Israelite mother and an Egyptian father wasᴮ among the Israelites. A fight broke out in the camp between the Israelite woman's son and an Israelite man. ¹¹Her son cursed and blasphemed the Name,ᵍ and they brought him to Moses. (His mother's name was Shelomith, a daughter of Dibri of the tribe of Dan.ʰ) ¹²They put him in custodyⁱ until the Lᴏʀᴅ's decisionʲ could be made clear to them.

¹³Then the Lᴏʀᴅ spoke to Moses: ¹⁴"Bring the one who has cursed to the outside of the camp and have all who heard him lay their hands on his head; then have the whole community stone him.ᵏ ¹⁵And tell the Israelites: If anyone curses his God, he will bear the consequences of his sin. ¹⁶Whoever blasphemes the name of •Yahweh is to be put to death;ˡ the whole community must stone him. If he blasphemes the Name, he is to be put to death, whether the foreign resident or the native.

¹⁷"If a man kills anyone, he must be put to death.ᵐ ¹⁸Whoever kills an animal is to make restitution for it, life for life. ¹⁹If any man inflicts a permanent injury on his neighbor, whatever he has done is to be done to him: ²⁰fracture for fracture, eye for eye, tooth for tooth. Whatever injury he inflicted on the person, the same is to be inflicted on him.ⁿ ²¹Whoever kills an animal is to make restitution for it, but whoever kills a person is to be put to death.ᵒ ²²You are to have the same law for the foreign resident and the native, because I am Yahweh your God."

²³After Moses spoke to the Israelites, they brought the one who had cursed to the outside of the camp and stoned him. So the Israelites did as the Lᴏʀᴅ had commanded Moses.

Sabbath Years and Jubilee

25 The Lᴏʀᴅ spoke to Moses on Mount Sinai: ²"Speak to the Israelites and tell them: When you enter the land I am giving you, the land will observe a Sabbath to the Lᴏʀᴅ. ³You may sow your field for six years, and you may prune your vineyard and gather its produce for six years. ⁴But there will be a Sabbath of complete restᵖ for the land in the seventh year, a Sabbath to the Lᴏʀᴅ: you are not to sow your field or prune your vineyard. ⁵You are not to reap what grows by itself from your crop, or harvest the grapes of your untended vines. It must be a year of complete rest for the land. ⁶Whatever the land produces during the Sabbath year can be food for you—for yourself, your male or female slave, and the hired hand or foreigner who stays with you. ⁷All of its growth may serve as food for your livestock and the wild animals in your land.

⁸"You are to count seven sabbatical years, seven times seven years, so that the time period of the seven sabbatical years amounts to 49. ⁹Then you are to sound a trumpet loudly

---

ᵃ24:5 Ex 25:30
ᵇ24:6 Ex 25:23; Heb 9:2
ᶜ24:7 Ex 30:34
ᵈLv 2:2
ᵉDt 18:1
ᶠ24:8 Ex 19:5
ᵍ24:11 Ex 20:7; Lv 24:16; Nm 15:30; 1Sm 3:13; Neh 9:18
ʰGn 49:16
ⁱ24:12 Gn 40:3-7; 41:10; 42:17
ʲNm 3:39; 15:32-36
ᵏ24:14 Lv 20:2,27; 24:16,23; Nm 14:10; 15:35-36; Dt 21:21; Jos 7:25; 1Kg 12:18; Ezk 16:40; 23:47; Jn 10:33
ˡ24:16 Ex 20:7; 22:28; 1Kg 21:10,13; Jn 8:59; 19:7; 2Tm 2:19
ᵐ24:17 Gn 9:5-6; Ex 20:13; 21:12-14; Nm 35:30-31
ⁿ24:19-20 Ex 21:24; Dt 19:21; Mt 5:38-39; 7:12
ᵒ24:21 Nm 35:30-33
ᵖ25:4 Lv 16:31

ᴬ24:5 Lit two-tenths of an ephah   ᴮ24:10 Lit went out

24:5-7 The **12 loaves** of bread were called "the bread of the Presence" (Ex 25:30). They were a constant reminder of God's provision for the Israelites every day and especially during the wilderness period. The 12 loaves represented the 12 tribes of Israel, pointing to the totality of God's provision. Jesus affirmed that He was the Bread of Life (Jn 6:33,35,48,51), satisfying the spiritual hunger of humanity.

24:11 To blaspheme the name of God was to blaspheme God Himself, just as to praise His name was to praise Him. Jews stopped using the name of Yahweh because they thought it too sacred. When they referred to God, they called him **the Name**.

24:16 The punishment for blasphemy was the **death** penalty by stoning, a punishment used also for those who worshiped Molech (20:2).

24:20 The **eye for eye, tooth for tooth** principle was a figurative way of pointing to God's justice to show that the pun-

ishment should fit the crime. The principle of punishing an offender with the same injury that he had inflicted is called (Lat) *lex talionis*. Quoting this verse, Jesus raised the bar in His teaching on turning the other cheek (Mt 5:38-42), the offering of forgiveness instead of retribution.

25:4 The expression **a Sabbath of complete rest** occurs only with the sabbatical year, the Sabbath (23:3) and the Day of Atonement (23:32). These are the only times in which abstinence from all work was prescribed.

25:8 The number seven is sacred, so the expression **seven times seven years** points to a most sacred time which ushered in the Year of Jubilee. While amnesties in the ancient Near East occurred at the discretion of a particular king or ruler, in Israel the Year of Jubilee was fixed and ordained by God, who did not leave it to human discretion. This assured that Jubilee would be observed.

25:10 Israel was asked to **consecrate** or sanctify only the Sabbath (Ex 20:8,11; Dt 5:12; Jr 17:22,24,27; Ezk 20:20; 44:24)

in the seventh month, on the tenth day of the month; you will sound it throughout your land on the Day of *Atonement.ᵃ ¹⁰You are to consecrate the fiftieth year and proclaim freedom in the land for all its inhabitants. It will be your Jubilee,ᵇ when each of you is to return to his property and each of you to his clan. ¹¹The fiftieth year will be your Jubilee; you are not to sow, reap what grows by itself, or harvest its untended vines. ¹²It is to be holy to you because it is the Jubilee; you may only eat its produce directly from the field.

¹³"In this Year of Jubilee, each of you will return to his property. ¹⁴If you make a sale to your neighbor or a purchase from him, do not cheatᶜ one another. ¹⁵You are to make the purchase from your neighbor based on the number of years since the last Jubilee. He is to sell to you based on the number of remaining harvest years. ¹⁶You are to increase its price in proportion to a greater amount of years, and decrease its price in proportion to a lesser amount of years, because what he is selling to you is a number of harvests. ¹⁷You are not to cheat one another, but *fear your God, for I am *Yahweh your God.

¹⁸"You are to keep My statutes and ordinances and carefully observe them, so that you may live securely in the land.ᵈ ¹⁹Then the land will yield its fruit, so that you can eat, be satisfied, and live securely in the land. ²⁰If you wonder: 'What will we eat in the seventh year if we don't sow or gather our produce?' ²¹I will appoint My blessing for you in the sixth year, so that it will produce a crop sufficient for three years. ²²When you sow in the eighth year, you will be eating from the previous harvest. You will be eating this until the ninth year when its harvest comes in.

²³"The land is not to be permanently sold because it is Mine, and you are only foreigners and temporary residents on My land.ᴬ,ᵉ ²⁴You are to allow the redemption of any land you occupy. ²⁵If your brother becomes destitute and sells part of his property, his nearest rela-

ᵃ25:9 Lv 23:27
ᵇ25:10 Lv 27:17-24; Nm 36:4; Dt 15:1
ᶜ25:14 Dt 23:16
ᵈ25:18 Lv 18:4-5,26; 19:37; 20:8,22; 26:3-5
ᵉ25:23 1Ch 29:15; Heb 11:13
ᶠ25:32 Nm 35:1-8; Dt 18:1-2; 19:2-9; Jos 21; 1Ch 6:54-81
ᵍ25:36 Ex 22:25; Dt 23:19-20; Ezk 22:12

tive may come and redeem what his brother has sold. ²⁶If a man has no *family redeemer, but he prospersᴮ and obtains enough to redeem his land, ²⁷he may calculate the years since its sale, repay the balance to the man he sold it to, and return to his property. ²⁸But if he cannot obtain enough to repay him, what he sold will remain in the possession of its purchaser until the Year of Jubilee. It is to be released at the Jubilee, so that he may return to his property.

²⁹"If a man sells a residence in a walled city, his right of redemption will last until a year has passed after its sale; his right of redemption will last a year. ³⁰If it is not redeemed by the end of a full year, then the house in the walled city is permanently transferred to its purchaser throughout his generations. It is not to be released on the Jubilee. ³¹But houses in villages that have no walls around them are to be classified as open fields. The right to redeem such houses stays in effect, and they are to be released at the Jubilee.

³²"Concerning the Levitical cities,ᶠ the Levites always have the right to redeem houses in the cities they possess. ³³Whatever property one of the Levites can redeemᶜ—a house sold in a city they possess—must be released at the Jubilee, because the houses in the Levitical cities are their possession among the Israelites. ³⁴The open pastureland around their cities may not be sold, for it is their permanent possession.

³⁵"If your brother becomes destitute and cannot sustain himself amongᴰ you, you are to support him as a foreigner or temporary resident, so that he can continue to live among you. ³⁶Do not profit or take interest from him,ᵍ but fear your God and let your brother live among you. ³⁷You are not to lend him your silver with interest or sell him your food for profit. ³⁸I am Yahweh your God, who brought you out of the land of Egypt to give you the land of Canaan and to be your God.

³⁹"If your brother among you becomes

ᴬ25:23 Lit *residents with Me*   ᴮ25:26 Lit *but his hand reaches*   ᶜ25:33 Hb obscure   ᴰ25:35 Lit *and his hand falters with*

and the Year of **Jubilee**. The verb "to consecrate" may be translated, "to sanctify" or "to treat as holy."

25:23 **The land** refers to the promised land. The notion of God's ownership of the land occurs throughout the OT (Ex 15:17; Ps 10:16; 85:1; Is 14:2,25; Jr 2:7; Ezk 36:5; 38:16; Hs 9:3).

25:25 In order to keep **property** in the family, a well-off **relative**, known as a family redeemer, was allowed to buy it. This law was applied when Ruth was redeemed by Boaz after her closest family redeemer refused to marry her.

25:32-34 Even though the **Levites** were not allotted permanent property in the promised land (Nm 18:23; 26:62),

they were provided permanent residences and pastureland. These consisted of 48 towns and their surrounding fields (Nm 35:1-8). Sacred cities similar to these Levitical cities have been found in Ugarit and Mesopotamia.

25:35-38 A **destitute** Israelite who became impoverished was supposed to be supported (strengthened) by his fellow Israelites, who were not allowed to **profit** from the needs of the poor. The text implies that if a person took advantage of his impoverished brother, he did not **fear . . . God**.

25:39-55 God provided for the poor who had to sell themselves as indentured servants. However, slavery was only a temporary condition, and the law prohibited harsh treatment

destitute and sells himself to you,[a] you must not force him to do slave labor. [40]Let him stay with you as a hired hand or temporary resident; he may work for you until the Year of Jubilee. [41]Then he and his children are to be released from you, and he may return to his clan and his ancestral property.[b] [42]They are not to be sold as slaves,[A] because they are My slaves that I brought out of the land of Egypt. [43]You are not to rule over them harshly[c] but fear your God. [44]Your male and female slaves are to be from the nations around you; you may purchase male and female slaves. [45]You may also purchase them from the foreigners staying with you, or from their families living among you—those born in your land. These may become your property. [46]You may leave them to your sons after you to inherit as property; you can make them slaves for life. But concerning your brothers, the Israelites, you must not rule over one another harshly.

[47]"If a foreigner or temporary resident living among you prospers, but your brother living near him becomes destitute and sells himself to the foreigner living among you, or to a member of the foreigner's clan, [48]he has the right of redemption after he has been sold. One of his brothers may redeem him. [49]His uncle or cousin may redeem him, or any of his close relatives from his clan may redeem him. If he prospers, he may redeem himself. [50]The one who purchased him is to calculate the time from the year he sold himself to him until the Year of Jubilee. The price of his sale will be determined by the number of years. It will be set for him like the daily wages of a hired hand. [51]If many years are still left, he must pay his redemption price in proportion to them based on his purchase price. [52]If only a few years remain until the Year of Jubilee, he will calculate and pay the price of his redemption in proportion to his remaining years. [53]He will stay with him like a man

hired year by year. A foreign owner is not to rule over him harshly in your sight. [54]If he is not redeemed in any of these ways, he and his children are to be released at the Year of Jubilee. [55]For the Israelites are My slaves.[d] They are My slaves that I brought out of the land of Egypt; I am Yahweh your God.

Covenant Blessings and Discipline

26 "Do not make idols for yourselves,[e] set up a carved image or sacred pillar for yourselves, or place a sculpted stone in your land to bow down to it, for I am *Yahweh your God. [2]You must keep My Sabbaths and revere My sanctuary;[f] I am Yahweh.

[3]"If you follow My statutes and faithfully observe My commands, [4]I will give you rain at the right time, and the land will yield its produce, and the trees of the field will bear their fruit. [5]Your threshing will continue until grape harvest, and the grape harvest will continue until sowing time; you will have plenty of food to eat and live securely in your land.[g] [6]I will give peace to the land, and you will lie down with nothing to frighten you. I will remove dangerous animals from the land, and no sword will pass through your land.[h] [7]You will pursue your enemies, and they will fall before you by the sword. [8]Five of you will pursue 100, and 100 of you will pursue 10,000; your enemies will fall before you by the sword.[i]

[9]"I will turn to you, make you fruitful and multiply you, and confirm My covenant with you. [10]You will eat the old grain of the previous year and will clear out the old to make room for the new. [11]I will place My residence[B] among you, and I will not reject you.[j] [12]I will walk among you and be your God, and you will be My people.[k] [13]I am Yahweh your God, who brought you out of the land of Egypt, so that you would no longer be their slaves. I broke the bars of your yoke[l] and enabled you to live in freedom.[c]

---

a 25:39 2Kg 4:1; Neh 5:5; Is 50:1; Mt 18:25
b 25:41 Ex 21:3-6
c 25:43 Ex 1:13-14
d 25:55 Ex 4:10
e 26:1 Ex 20:3-4; Ps 81:9
f 26:2 Ex 15:17; Lv 19:30; Ezk 20:13,16,21; 23:38
g 26:3-5 Lv 25:18-19; Dt 28:1-2,12; Is 30:21-23; Am 9:13
h 26:6 Jr 30:10; Ezk 34:25,28; Mc 4:4
i 26:7-8 Dt 3:22; 32:30; Jos 10:19; 23:3,10
j 26:11 Ex 25:8; 29:45-46; Lv 26:44; 1Kg 6:13
k 26:12 Jr 7:23; Lk 1:68; 2Co 6:16; Rv 21:3
l 26:13 Ex 6:6-7; Is 9:4; Jr 5:5; 28:10-11

A 25:42 Lit sold with a sale of a slave   B 26:11 Or tabernacle   C 26:13 Lit to walk uprightly

---

and provided for release in the **Year of Jubilee**. Proslavery movements in recent history have misused passages in Leviticus by ignoring their provisions and limitations.

26:2 The verb **keep** refers to the detailed observation of the commandments. The expression **you must keep My Sabbaths** occurs four times (v. 2; 19:3,30; Ex 31:13), and it is an allusion to the Fourth Commandment about keeping and sanctifying the Sabbath.

26:4 In Hebrew the word **rain** is in the plural. It refers to the two rainy periods that occurred in autumn and spring (Dt 11:14; Jr 5:24; Jl 2:23).

26:8 The 1 to 20 and 1 to 100 proportions point to the mi-

raculous victories over their **enemies** with which God would reward His people if they obeyed His commandments.

26:11 The promise of divine fellowship is rendered by the phrase, **I will place My residence among you**. The "residence" is literally a "tabernacle." This is a direct parallel to Jn 1:14, where John affirmed that Jesus, the Word, became flesh and "took up residence" or "tabernacled" among us.

26:13 The **bars of your yoke** were a reminder of the Egyptian bondage from which God delivered the Israelites. Here Israel is pictured as an animal held down by a heavy yoke. Later Jesus invited humanity to take His light yoke and partake of His rest (Mt 11:28-30).

¹⁴"But if you do not obey Me and observe all these commands— ¹⁵if you reject My statutes and despise My ordinances, and do not observe all My commands—and break My covenant, ¹⁶then I will do this to you: I will bring terror[a] on you—wasting disease and fever that will cause your eyes to fail and your life to ebb away. You will sow your seed in vain because your enemies will eat it. ¹⁷I will turn[A] against you, so that you will be defeated by your enemies. Those who hate you will rule over you, and you will flee even though no one is pursuing you.[b]

¹⁸"But if after these things you will not obey Me, I will proceed to discipline you seven times for your sins.[c] ¹⁹I will break down your strong pride. I will make your sky like iron and your land like bronze, ²⁰and your strength will be used up for nothing.[d] Your land will not yield its produce, and the trees of the land will not bear their fruit.

²¹"If you act with hostility toward Me and are unwilling to obey Me, I will multiply your plagues seven times for your sins.[e] ²²I will send wild animals against you that will deprive you of your children, ravage your livestock, and reduce your numbers until your roads are deserted.[f]

²³"If in spite of these things you do not accept My discipline, but act with hostility toward Me, ²⁴then I will act with hostility toward you; I also will strike you seven times for your sins. ²⁵I will bring a sword against you[g] to execute the vengeance of the covenant. Though you withdraw into your cities, I will send a pestilence among you, and you will be delivered into enemy hands. ²⁶When I cut off your supply of bread, 10 women will bake your bread in a single oven and ration out your bread by weight, so that you will eat but not be satisfied.[h]

²⁷"And if in spite of this you do not obey Me but act with hostility toward Me, ²⁸I will act with furious hostility toward you; I will also discipline you seven times for your sins. ²⁹You will eat the flesh of your sons; you will eat the flesh of your daughters.[i] ³⁰I will destroy your •high places, cut down your incense altars, and heap your dead bodies on the lifeless bodies of your idols;[j] I will reject you. ³¹I will reduce your cities to ruins and devastate your sanctuaries. I will not smell the pleasing aroma of your sacrifices.[k] ³²I also will devastate the land, so that your enemies who come to live there will be appalled by it. ³³But I will scatter you among the nations, and I will draw a sword to chase after you. So your land will become desolate, and your cities will become ruins.

³⁴"Then the land will make up for its Sabbath years during the time it lies desolate, while you are in the land of your enemies. At that time the land will rest and make up for its Sabbaths. ³⁵As long as it lies desolate, it will have the rest it did not have during your Sabbaths when you lived there.

³⁶"I will put anxiety in the hearts of those of you who survive in the lands of their enemies. The sound of a wind-driven leaf will put them to flight, and they will flee as one flees from a sword, and fall though no one is pursuing them. ³⁷They will stumble over one another as if fleeing from a sword though no one is pursuing them. You will not be able to stand against your enemies. ³⁸You will perish among the nations; the land of your enemies will devour you. ³⁹Those[B] who survive in the lands of your enemies will waste away because of their sin; they will also waste away because of their fathers' sins along with theirs.

⁴⁰"But if they will confess their sin and the sin of their fathers—their unfaithfulness that

---

a 26:16 Ps 78:33; Is 65:23; Jr 15:8
b 26:17 Ex 12:23; Dt 28:25
c 26:18 Gn 4:15,24; Heb 12:4-11
d 26:20 Dt 28:23; Am 4:7-8
e 26:21 Gn 4:15,24
f 26:22 Dt 32:24; Jdg 5:6; Is 33:8; Lm 1:1-4; Ezk 14:15; Zch 7:14
g 26:25 Ezk 14:21
h 26:26 Is 3:1; Ezk 4:16; 14:13; Am 4:6; Mc 6:14
i 26:29 Dt 28:53-57; 2Kg 6:28-29; Jr 19:9; Lm 4:10; Mc 3:2-3
j 26:30 Gn 31:19; Ezk 6:3-6
k 26:31 Gn 8:21; 1Sm 26:19; Am 5:21-22

A 26:17 Lit *will set My face*   B 26:39 Lit *Those of you*

26:14-17 The five sets of curses that begin in verse 14 are presented as punishment for disobedience of God's **commands . . . statutes . . . ordinances**, and **covenant**. These curses match the five sets of blessings in verses 3-13. The curses increase in severity with a persistent refusal to repent. The Lord would **turn against** His people only after they defiantly turned against Him.

26:18-20 The number **seven** associated with the **discipline** for **sins** is not to be taken literally, but it is used figuratively to mean "many times" or "thoroughly." It could be an allusion to the Sabbaths not kept by the Israelites (v. 34).

26:22 Because Yahweh is the God of all creation, He can also sovereignly use **wild animals** to punish His people. The outbreak of wild animals is frequently regarded as punishment for sin (Dt 32:24; 2Kg 2:24; 17:25; Is 13:21-22).

26:29 This curse was fulfilled when the Syrian king

Ben-Hadad besieged Samaria, the capital of the northern kingdom of Israel (2Kg 6:24-29).

26:31 The expression **I will not smell the pleasing aroma of your sacrifices** refers to the fact that God would not accept His people's sacrifices, and thus He was rejecting them. Sacrifices without obedience are meaningless (1Sm 15:22).

26:33 The Hebrew verb *zarâ*, translated here as **scatter**, can also be translated "winnow." In the mind of the Jews it would trigger the image of wicked people being blown away like chaff (Ps 1:4). This is an obvious reference to God's ultimate rejection of the errant Jews—the exile.

26:34-35 This curse anticipates Israel's failure to keep the **Sabbath years**. The Chronicler fused this verse with Jeremiah's prophecy that the exile would last 70 years (2Ch 36:21; cp. Jr 25:11; 29:10).

26:40-41 The expression **but if** indicates a turning point and

they practiced against Me, and how they acted with hostility toward Me, ⁴¹and I acted with hostility toward them and brought them into the land of their enemies—and if their uncircumcised hearts will be humbled,ᵃ and if they will pay the penalty for their sin, ⁴²then I will remember My covenant with Jacob. I will also remember My covenant with Isaac and My covenant with Abraham, and I will remember the land. ⁴³For the land abandoned by them will make up for its Sabbaths by lying desolate without the people, while they pay the penalty for their sin, because they rejected My ordinances and abhorred My statutes. ⁴⁴Yet in spite of this, while they are in the land of their enemies, I will not reject or abhor them so as to destroy them and break My covenant with them, since I am Yahweh their God.ᵇ ⁴⁵For their sake I will remember the covenant with their fathers, whom I brought out of the land of Egypt in the sight of the nations to be their God; I am Yahweh."

⁴⁶These are the statutes, ordinances, and laws the LORD established between Himself and the Israelites through Moses on Mount Sinai.

Funding the Sanctuary

27 The LORD spoke to Moses: ²"Speak to the Israelites and tell them: When someone makes a special vowᶜ to the LORD that involves the assessment of people, ³if the assessment concerns a male from 20 to 60 years old, your assessment is 50 silver *shekelsᵈ measured by the standard sanctuary shekel.ᵉ ⁴If the person is a female, your assessment is 30 shekels.ᶠ ⁵If the person is from five to 20 years old, your assessment for a male is 20 shekelsᵍ and for a female 10 shekels. ⁶If the person is from one month to five years old, your assessment for a male is five silver shekels,ʰ and for a female your assessment is three shekels of silver. ⁷If the person is 60 years or more, your assessment is 15 shekels for a male and 10 shekels for a female. ⁸But if one is too poor to pay the assessment, he must present the person before the priest and the priest will set a value for him. The priest will set a value for him ac-

cording to what the one making the vow can afford.

⁹"If the vow involves one of the animals that may be brought as an offering to the LORD, any of these he gives to the LORD will be holy. ¹⁰He may not replace it or make a substitution for it, either good for bad, or bad for good.ⁱ But if he does substitute one animal for another, both that animal and its substitute will be holy.

¹¹"If the vow involves any of the *unclean animals that may not be brought as an offering to the LORD, the animal must be presented before the priest. ¹²The priest will set its value, whether high or low; the price will be set as the priest makes the assessment for you. ¹³If the one who brought it decides to redeem it, he must add a fifth to theᴬ assessed value.ʲ

¹⁴"When a man consecrates his house as holy to the LORD, the priest will assess its value, whether high or low. The price will stand just as the priest assesses it. ¹⁵But if the one who consecrated his house redeems it, he must add a fifth to theᴬ assessed value, and it will be his.ᵏ

¹⁶"If a man consecrates to the LORD any part of a field that he possesses, your assessment of value will be proportional to the seed needed to sow it, at the rate of 50 silver shekels for every five bushelsᴮ of barley seed.ᶜ ¹⁷If he consecrates his field during the Year of Jubilee,ˡ the price will stand according to your assessment. ¹⁸But if he consecrates his field after the Jubilee, the priest will calculate the price for him in proportion to the years left until the next Year of Jubilee, so that your assessment will be reduced. ¹⁹If the one who consecrated the field decides to redeem it, he must add a fifth to theᴬ assessed value, and the field will transfer back to him. ²⁰But if he does not redeem the field or if he has sold it to another man, it is no longer redeemable. ²¹When the field is released in the Jubilee, it will be holy to the LORD like a field permanently set apart; it becomes the priest's property.

²²"If a person consecrates to the LORD a field he has purchased that is not part of his inherited landholding, ²³then the priest will calculate for him the amount of theᴬ assessment up

ᵃ 26:41 Dt 30:6; Jr 4:4; 9:25; Ezk 44:7,9
ᵇ 26:44 Gn 17:8; Ezk 36:22; Hs 11:8-9; Zch 10:9
ᶜ 27:2 Lv 27:8
ᵈ 27:3 2Kg 15:20
ᵉ Ex 30:13; Lv 5:15; 27:25; Nm 3:47
ᶠ 27:4 Ex 21:32
ᵍ 27:5 Gn 37:28
ʰ 27:6 Nm 3:46-47; 18:15-16
ⁱ 27:10 Mal 1:8
ʲ 27:13 Gn 47:24; Lv 5:16; 6:5
ᵏ 27:14-15 Lv 25:29-31
ˡ 27:17 Lv 25:10

---

involves a note of hope. The promised restoration is contingent upon the people's confession of **sin** and their humility. The verb translated **humbled** is literally "to bring to one's knees."

26:44 The purifying agent will be the exile, not the flood that destroyed the earth during the time of Noah (Gn 6; 9). The great judgments of wars and famines in Revelation 6–19 have

their original setting in Leviticus 26 and Deuteronomy 28. As in OT times, the NT believer must repent or be judged.

27:2-3 People who were dedicated by vow to the Lord's service could be redeemed through a sum of money established by God or the priest. Hannah promised Samuel to the Lord (1Sm 1:11), but if she had wanted to keep the child, God would have allowed her to take him back through mon-

to the Year of Jubilee, and the person will pay the assessed value on that day as a holy offering to the Lord. [24]In the Year of Jubilee the field will return to the one he bought it from,[a] the original owner. [25]All your assessed values will be measured by the standard sanctuary shekel, 20 *gerahs* to the shekel.[b]

[26]"But no one can consecrate a firstborn of the livestock, whether an animal from the herd or flock, to the Lord, because a firstborn already belongs to the Lord.[c] [27]If it is one of the unclean livestock, it must be ransomed according to your assessment by adding a fifth of its value to it. If it is not redeemed, it can be sold according to your assessment.[d]

[28]"Nothing that a man permanently sets apart to the Lord from all he owns, whether a person, an animal, or his inherited landhold-

ing, can be sold or redeemed; everything set apart is especially holy to the Lord. [29]No person who has been set apart for destruction is to be ransomed; he must be put to death.[e]

[30]"Every tenth of the land's produce, grain from the soil or fruit from the trees, belongs to the Lord;[f] it is holy to the Lord. [31]If a man decides to redeem any part of this tenth, he must add a fifth to its value. [32]Every tenth animal from the herd or flock, which passes under the shepherd's rod,[g] will be holy to the Lord. [33]He is not to inspect whether it is good or bad, and he is not to make a substitution for it. But if he does make a substitution, both the animal and its substitute will be holy;[h] they cannot be redeemed."[i]

[34]These are the commands the Lord gave Moses for the Israelites on Mount Sinai.[j]

Cross references:
[a] 27:24 Lv 25:28
[b] 27:25 Ex 30:13; Nm 18:16; Ezk 45:12
[c] 27:26 Ex 13:2, 15; 34:19; Nm 18:15
[d] 27:27 Ex 13:13; 34:20
[e] 27:29 Nm 21:1-3; 31:7,13-17; Jos 6:17; 1Sm 15:17-33
[f] 27:30 Nm 18:21-32; Dt 14:22-29; Neh 10:37-39
[g] 27:32 Gn 28:22; 2Ch 31:6; Jr 33:13
[h] 27:33 Lv 12:4; 25:12
[i] Lv 27:10
[j] 27:34 Nm 36:13

etary redemption. The Bible also affirms that the Nazirites made vows that included people (Nm 6).

27:26 No one could **consecrate a firstborn**, because he already belonged **to the Lord** (Ex 13:2; 34:19-20).

27:28-29 The penalty for disobeying God's law regarding things **set apart . . . to the Lord** was death. It is possible that Ananias and Sapphira in the early church were guilty of breaking this law as well as lying to the Holy Spirit (Ac 5:1-11).

27:30 The tithe is not a human invention but a divine com-

mand. The first time the tithe is mentioned in the Bible was when Abram gave a tenth of what he had to Melchizedek (Gn 14:20). The Israelites are told to tithe from their **land's produce** (cp. Dt 14:22-24). During the monarchy, the tithe was important because it provided the capital necessary for the day-to-day operation of the temple. The giving of the tithe was revived by Nehemiah during the postexilic era since it seems that the practice had been ignored (Neh 13:10-13,37-38). Through the prophet Malachi, God rebuked the people for robbing God by not bringing their tithes to the temple (Mal 3:8-10).

Numbers

Introduction

The English title "Numbers" derives from the Septuagint name "Arithmoi," based on the two military censuses in chapters 1 and 26. The Hebrew title, *Bemidbar*, "In the Wilderness," describes the geographical setting of much of the book—from the Wilderness of Sinai to the arid Plains of Moab, across the Jordan River from Jericho.

The Book of Numbers opens at Mount Sinai and ends at Mount Nebo. Here is a view of the promised land as seen from Mount Nebo about 12 miles east of the mouth of the Jordan River. Nebo rises over 4,000 feet above the Dead Sea and gives an excellent view of the southwest, west, and as far north as Mount Hermon. Israel captured the area around Mount Nebo as they marched toward Canaan. They camped in the area of Mount Nebo opposite Jericho when the Balaam incident occurred (Nm 22–24).

Circumstances of Writing

Author: Christian scholars have traditionally held that Moses was the author of the Pentateuch, which includes the book of Numbers. As with the other books in the Pentateuch, Numbers is anonymous, but Moses is a central character throughout. Moses kept a journal (33:2), and the phrase "The LORD spoke to Moses" is used 31 times. It is possible that a few portions were later added by scribes, such as the reference to Moses' humility (12:3) and the reference to the "Book of the LORD's Wars" (21:14). Moses remains the primary writer.

Background: Numbers continues the historical narrative begun in Exodus. It picks up one month after the close of Exodus (Ex 40:2; Nm 1:1), which is about one year after the Israelites' departure from Egypt. Numbers covers the remaining 39 years of the Israelites' stay in the wilderness, from Sinai to Kadesh, and finally to the plains on the eastern side of the Jordan River.

Message and Purpose

Sovereignty of God: The principal character in the book of Numbers is Yahweh, the God of Israel. He is sovereign over the affairs of all peoples from all nations. Even Balaam, a sorcerer opposed to the ways of God, could be made into an instrument for accomplishing His purposes. God would accomplish His will even when His people rebelled, as in the rejection of the promised land in chapters 13–14; in the end He kept His promise to Abraham by achieving this goal in the next generation of Israelites.

Presence of God: God's presence is exemplified in the pillar of fire by night and the pillar of cloud by day, by the ark of the covenant that represents the throne of His presence among humanity, and by the mobile sanctuary which demonstrates that the God of Israel cannot be confined to a territory, region, or city, much less a sanctuary of any kind.

Purity and Holiness of God: God is holy and pure, and He requires such behavior from those who claim Him as their God. This is a central theme of the Pentateuch and the book of Numbers.

1525 B.C.

1500 B.C.

Aaron 1529–1409?

Moses 1526–1406

Hittite Ascendancy 1600–1200

Glass bottles are first used in Egypt. 1500

Kassite Ascendancy 1595–1174

Copper trumpet is developed in Egypt. 1500

18th Dynasty 1570–1303 (includes Thutmose and Amenhotep; traditionally the pharaohs of oppression)

Hatshepsut, female pharaoh in Egypt 1490

The first well-documented battle in history. Pharaoh Thutmose III defeats an alliance of enemies at Megiddo. 1469

God and Revelation: The revelatory terminology of "the Lᴏʀᴅ spoke to Moses" provides the framework for the structure of the book. Moses is the primary human agent of revelation. Numbers presents God as One who is able to accomplish His revelatory will even through a donkey or a reluctant pagan diviner.

Promise and Fulfillment: God promised Abram that He would produce a great nation through him (Gn 12:2) and give his descendants the land of the Canaanites and Amorites (Gn 15:1,8-21; 17:8). The two censuses show God's fulfillment of the first promise. The granting of territory to two and one-half tribes in Transjordan is the beginning of the land fulfillment. God proved Himself faithful to that second promise by bringing it to fruition for the second generation (Nm 15:1-21; 27:1-23; 36:1-12).

Uniqueness and Exclusivity of God: The God of Israel is the one true God, and therefore He is worthy of humanity's exclusive devotion. He cannot tolerate the worship of other deities, the elements, and forces of His creation. He is beyond human reason to comprehend and incomparable to human character (23:19). All images of deity were forbidden by Israelite law along with unauthorized worship centers, cultic instruments, and certain worship styles. All such forms of idolatry were to be removed from the land, lest Israel lapse into such transgression and suffer punishment.

Celebration in Worship: The dual themes of celebration and worship are delineated from the initial chapters of Numbers, which depict Israel in harmonious devotion to Yahweh (chaps. 1–7), to the promise of an abundance of crops in the land, which would be brought to Yahweh in sacrifices and offerings when the people inherited their tribal territories (15:1-21; 28:1–29:40). Interspersed throughout the book are several songs, including the "Song of the Cloud" (9:17-23) and the "Battle Song of the Ark" (10:35-36). The parameters of faithful worship for the sojourning Israelites are also delineated through several negative circumstances, including their failure to keep the Passover (9:13), the breaking of the Sabbath (15:32-41), and the judgment against unfaithful priests or their supporters (chaps. 16–17). Worship and celebration of the God of Israel are not limited to Israelites. Several passages state that there is one law for the Israelites and foreigners.

1450 B.C.   1400 B.C.

Joshua 1490?–1380?

Passover instituted 1446

The exodus and defeat of Pharaoh at the Red Sea. 1446

The Ten Commandments given at Mount Sinai 1446

Tabernacle built and dedicated 1445

Exploration of Canaan by 12 spies 1445

Events in Leviticus 1445

Events in Numbers 1445–1407

Events in Deuteronomy 1406

Events in Joshua 1406–1380?

The Egyptians develop a water clock, a container into which water dripped at a constant rate indicating the amount of time that had elapsed by reference to marks on the container into which the water flowed. This device had an advantage over the sundial in being able to tell time at night. 1400

Foreigners could celebrate the Passover if they wanted to identify with Israel in its devotion to Yahweh, the one true God, but they had to abide by His instructions and precepts (9:14).

Contribution to the Bible

Numbers shows us how God responded to the unbelief of the Israelites. There are consequences to our disobedience, but God's grace remains and His redemptive plan and desire for us will not be stopped. The book of Numbers underscores for us the importance of obedience in the life of a Christian, and Paul reminded us of the value of learning from the way God has worked in the past (Rm 15:4; 1Co 10:6,11).

Structure

Numbers reflects the challenging message of faithfulness. The book consists of seven cycles of material, with the repetition of the following types of material: (1) a statement of the historical setting, (2) reference to the 12 tribes of Israel and their respective leaders, (3) matters related to the priests and Levites, and (4) laws for defining the nature of the faithful community.

This book of the Law is primarily narrative with portions of case law interwoven into a vibrant literary fabric.

Outline

I. First Census and Consecration of Israel at Sinai (1:1–6:27)
   A. Numbering and arrangement of the people (1:1–2:34)
   B. Choosing of the Levites (3:1–4:49)
   C. Cleansing and blessing of the people (5:1–6:27)

II. Preparation for Departure to the Promised Land (7:1–10:36)
   A. Gifts of the tribal leaders (7:1-89)
   B. Consecration of the Levites (8:1-26)
   C. Observance of the Passover (9:1-14)
   D. Movement of the camp (9:15–10:36)

III. From Mount Sinai to Kadesh (11:1–15:41)
   A. Disobedience of the people (11:1–14:45)
   B. Miscellaneous instructions and laws (15:1-41)

IV. Rebellion Against Aaron's Priesthood (16:1–19:22)
   A. Judgment of Korah, Dathan, and Abiram (16:1–17:13)
   B. Duties and revenues of priests and Levites (18:1-32)
   C. Ordinance of the red cow (19:1-22)

V. From Kadesh to the Plains of Moab (20:1–25:18)
   A. Rebellion and judgment of Moses and Aaron (20:1-29)
   B. Judgment and healing by snakes (21:1-35)
   C. Balaam's efforts to curse Israel (22:1–24:25)
   D. Campaign of Phinehas against idolatry (25:1-18)

VI. Second Census and Preparation of the New Generation (26:1–30:16)
   A. Another counting of Israel (26:1-65)
   B. Inheritance for Zelophehad's daughters (27:1-23)
   C. Instructions to the new generation (28:1–30:16)

The Census of Israel

1 The LORD spoke to Moses in the tent of meeting in the Wilderness of Sinai, on the first day of the second month of the second year[a] after Israel's departure from the land of Egypt: [2]"Take a census[b] of the entire Israelite community by their clans and their ancestral houses, counting the names of every male one by one. [3]You and Aaron are to register those who are 20 years old or more by their military divisions—everyone who can serve in Israel's army.[A] [4]A man from each tribe is to be with you, each one the head of his ancestral house.[c] [5]These are the names of the men who are to assist you:

Elizur son of Shedeur from Reuben;
[6] Shelumiel son of Zurishaddai
    from Simeon;
[7] Nahshon son of Amminadab
    from Judah;
[8] Nethanel son of Zuar from Issachar;
[9] Eliab son of Helon from Zebulun;
[10] from the sons of Joseph:
Elishama son of Ammihud
    from Ephraim,
Gamaliel son of Pedahzur
    from Manasseh;
[11] Abidan son of Gideoni from Benjamin;
[12] Ahiezer son of Ammishaddai
    from Dan;

[a]1:1 Ex 12:40-41; 19:1; 40:17
[b]1:2 Ex 30:11-16; Nm 26:2
[c]1:4 Nm 1:16; Jos 22:14
[d]1:20 Gn 29:32; 49:3-4; 1Ch 5:1
[e]1:22 Gn 29:33; 42:14-24; 49:5-7

[13] Pagiel son of Ochran from Asher;
[14] Eliasaph son of Deuel[B] from Gad;
[15] Ahira son of Enan from Naphtali.

[16]These are the men called from the community; they are leaders of their ancestral tribes, the heads of Israel's clans."

[17]So Moses and Aaron took these men who had been designated by name, [18]and they assembled the whole community on the first day of the second month. They recorded their ancestry by their clans and their ancestral houses, counting one by one the names of those 20 years old or more, [19]just as the LORD commanded Moses. He registered them in the Wilderness of Sinai:

[20]The descendants of Reuben,[d] the first-born of Israel: according to their family records by their clans and their ancestral houses, counting one by one the names of every male 20 years old or more, everyone who could serve in the army, [21]those registered for the tribe of Reuben numbered 46,500.

[22]The descendants of Simeon:[e] according to their family records by their clans and their ancestral houses, those registered counting one by one the names of every male 20 years old or more, everyone who could serve in the army, [23]those regis-

---

[A]1:3 Lit everyone going out to war in Israel   [B]1:14 LXX, Syr read Reuel

---

1:1 The LORD spoke to Moses is a key phrase in the book of Numbers. It is best understood as a statement of divine revelation and instruction. Many of the approximately 65 uses of this phrase are complemented by a statement that the recipient of the instruction did exactly what the Lord commanded. Church tradition from the fourth century A.D. places Mount Sinai in the south central mountains of the Sinai Peninsula at Jebel Musa ("Mount of Moses"). Other mountains suggested included Jebel Sin Bisher in west central Sinai, and Jebel Helal in northeast Sinai. The **tent of meeting** was the place of divine disclosure that housed the ark of the covenant and other cultic and historical items. The mobile shrine (tabernacle) had just been constructed one month before (7:1, Ex 40:17). **First day of the second month** indicates that the first 10 chapters of Numbers are not set forth chronologically but theologically. The military conscription census took place two weeks after the Passover described in 9:1-14.

1:2 Take a census translates the phrase "lift up the heads" ("skulls"), a phrase used in ancient Near Eastern military conscription texts. The patriarchal leaders of the 12 tribes of Israel were enlisted to stand and report to Moses and Aaron the count of the able-bodied militia of age 20 and upward.

1:5-15 The names of the leaders of the 12 tribes are listed with their lineage by tribe and by their fathers. Through **Nahshon** of Judah came the lineage of Boaz, who married Ruth and fathered the Davidic ancestry (Ru 4:20-22),

and hence the messianic line of Jesus Christ (Mt 1:4-16; Lk 3:23-33). Elishama's grandson was Joshua son of Nun, the successor to Moses and leader of the Israelites in the conquest account.

1:17-19 The central theme of the book of Numbers is indicated here by the leaders who followed the Lord's instructions in taking the census in verses 1-4: they did **just as the LORD commanded Moses**. This phraseology occurs more than 20 times in the book.

1:20-43 The census of the militia of Israel was taken by patriarchal tribe, **according to their family records**. Here is a comparative list of the censuses taken in chapters 1 and 26. The latter was taken of the second generation after the first had refused to enter the promised land.

Tribe	First Census	Second Census
Reuben	46,500	43,730
Simeon	59,300	22,200
Gad	45,650	40,500
Judah	74,600	76,500
Issachar	54,400	64,300
Zebulun	57,400	60,500
Ephraim	40,500	32,500
Manasseh	32,200	52,700
Benjamin	35,400	45,600
Dan	62,700	64,400
Asher	41,500	53,400
Naphtali	53,400	45,400
TOTAL	603,550	601,730

tered for the tribe of Simeon numbered 59,300.

²⁴ The descendants of Gad:ᵃ according to their family records by their clans and their ancestral houses, counting the names of those 20 years old or more, everyone who could serve in the army, ²⁵ those registered for the tribe of Gad numbered 45,650.

²⁶ The descendants of Judah:ᵇ according to their family records by their clans and their ancestral houses, counting the names of those 20 years old or more, everyone who could serve in the army, ²⁷ those registered for the tribe of Judah numbered 74,600.

²⁸ The descendants of Issachar:ᶜ according to their family records by their clans and their ancestral houses, counting the names of those 20 years old or more, everyone who could serve in the army, ²⁹ those registered for the tribe of Issachar numbered 54,400.

³⁰ The descendants of Zebulun:ᵈ according to their family records by their clans and their ancestral houses, counting the names of those 20 years old or more, everyone who could serve in the army, ³¹ those registered for the tribe of Zebulun numbered 57,400.

³² The descendants of Joseph:ᵉ

The descendants of Ephraim:ᶠ according to their family records by their clans and their ancestral houses, counting the names of those 20 years old or more, everyone who could serve in the army, ³³ those registered for the tribe of Ephraim numbered 40,500.

³⁴ The descendants of Manasseh:ᵍ according to their family records by their clans and their ancestral houses, counting the names of those 20 years old or more, everyone who could serve in the army,

ᵃ1:24 Gn 30:11; 49:19
ᵇ1:26 Gn 29:35; 49:8-12; Mt 1:2-3; Rv 5:5
ᶜ1:28 Gn 30:18; 49:14-15
ᵈ1:30 Gn 30:20; 49:13
ᵉ1:32 Gn 30:22-24; 49:22-26
ᶠGn 46:20; 48:13-20
ᵍ1:34 Gn 46:20; 48:13-20
ʰ1:36 Gn 35:18; 49:27
ⁱ1:38 Gn 30:6; 49:16-17
ʲ1:40 Gn 30:13; 49:20
ᵏ1:42 Gn 30:8; 49:21
ˡ1:46 Ex 12:37; Nm 26:51

³⁵ those registered for the tribe of Manasseh numbered 32,200.

³⁶ The descendants of Benjamin:ʰ according to their family records by their clans and their ancestral houses, counting the names of those 20 years old or more, everyone who could serve in the army, ³⁷ those registered for the tribe of Benjamin numbered 35,400.

³⁸ The descendants of Dan:ⁱ according to their family records by their clans and their ancestral houses, counting the names of those 20 years old or more, everyone who could serve in the army, ³⁹ those registered for the tribe of Dan numbered 62,700.

⁴⁰ The descendants of Asher:ʲ according to their family records by their clans and their ancestral houses, counting the names of those 20 years old or more, everyone who could serve in the army, ⁴¹ those registered for the tribe of Asher numbered 41,500.

⁴² The descendants of Naphtali:ᵏ according to their family records by their clans and their ancestral houses, counting the names of those 20 years old or more, everyone who could serve in the army, ⁴³ those registered for the tribe of Naphtali numbered 53,400.

⁴⁴ These are the men Moses and Aaron registered, with the assistance of the 12 leaders of Israel; each represented his ancestral house. ⁴⁵ So all the Israelites 20 years old or more, everyone who could serve in Israel's army, were registered by their ancestral houses. ⁴⁶ All those registered numbered 603,550.ˡ

Duties of the Levites

⁴⁷ But the Levites were not registered with them by their ancestral tribe. ⁴⁸ For the LORD had told Moses: ⁴⁹ "Do not register or take a census of the tribe of Levi with the other Israelites. ⁵⁰ Appoint the Levites over the

---

1:44-46 The total of **603,550** is consistent with the round number 600,000 in 11:21 and Ex 12:37. Some scholars reduce this number by reinterpreting the Hebrew word 'eleph to mean "clan" instead of "thousand," but the way the 12 subtotals add up to the grand total does not support that interpretation. Some suggest that the actual numbers were multiplied by 10 as a rhetorical device to bring glory to God, which may have been acceptable in that culture but does not sit well with modern notions of accurate reporting (see note at 3:43). According to the second census in chapter 26, the total militia prospects decreased by only 1,820 (three percent) during 40 years in the wilderness (see note at 26:51).

1:47-53 Based on the Levites' zealous actions in defense of the faith in the golden calf incident (Ex 32:26-29), this tribe was granted the privilege of servicing the **tabernacle** and assisting the Aaronic priests. Though the **Levites** were not technically priests—that position was restricted to descendants of Aaron of the tribe of Levi—they performed duties similar to those in the priestly circles of ancient Ugarit, Mari, Emar, Assyria, and Babylon.

tabernacle of the •testimony, all its furnishings, and everything in it. They are to transport the tabernacle and all its articles, take care of it, and camp around it. ⁵¹Whenever the tabernacle is to move, the Levites are to take it down, and whenever it is to stop at a campsite, the Levites are to set it up. Any unauthorized person who comes near it must be put to death.ᵃ

⁵²"The Israelites are to camp by their military divisions, each man with his encampment and under his banner. ⁵³The Levites are to camp around the tabernacle of the testimony and watch over it, so that no wrath will fall on the Israelite community."ᵇ ⁵⁴The Israelites did everything just as the LORD had commanded Moses.

Organization of the Camps

2 The LORD spoke to Moses and Aaron: ²"The Israelites are to camp under their respective banners beside the flags of their ancestral houses. They are to camp around the tent of meeting at a distance from it:

³Judah's military divisions will camp on

ᵃ1:51 Nm 3:10,38; 8:19; 18:7
ᵇ1:53 Nm 3:7; 18:4-5; 1Ch 23:32; Ezk 44:15-16

the east side toward the sunrise under their banner. The leader of the descendants of Judah is Nahshon son of Amminadab. ⁴His military division numbers 74,600. ⁵The tribe of Issachar will camp next to it. The leader of the Issacharites is Nethanel son of Zuar. ⁶His military division numbers 54,400. ⁷The tribe of Zebulun will be next. The leader of the Zebulunites is Eliab son of Helon. ⁸His military division numbers 57,400. ⁹The total number in their military divisions who belong to Judah's encampment is 186,400; they will move out first.

¹⁰Reuben's military divisions will camp on the south side under their banner. The leader of the Reubenites is Elizur son of Shedeur. ¹¹His military division numbers 46,500. ¹²The tribe of Simeon will camp next to it. The leader of the Simeonites is Shelumiel son of Zurishaddai. ¹³His military division numbers 59,300. ¹⁴The tribe of Gad will be next. The leader of the Gadites is Eliasaph son of Deuel.ᴬ ¹⁵His

ᴬ2:14 Some Hb mss, Sam, Vg; other Hb mss read *Reuel*

2:1-2 The members of each tribe were given a designated area to pitch their tents around the tabernacle. The Hebrew terms *degel* ("standard") and *'ototh* ("banners, signs") refer to a flag or placard with an insignia or color scheme to represent the given tribe. **At a distance** describes the safety zone around the tabernacle. The Levites served as guardians to prevent defilement of the sacred space and to keep anyone from experiencing God's punishment for coming too close to the tabernacle.

2:3-31 Just as wonder and beauty are reflected in the order of creation in Genesis 1, so the unity and symmetry of the sacred assembly of Israel evoke splendor and awe.

2:3 **Judah's military divisions** were given a positional priority, leading the camps of Issachar and Zebulun on the **east side** of the camp. The inner circle contained Aaronic priests. This was the place to which all Israelites brought their sacrifices and offerings for presentation to the priests. Typically

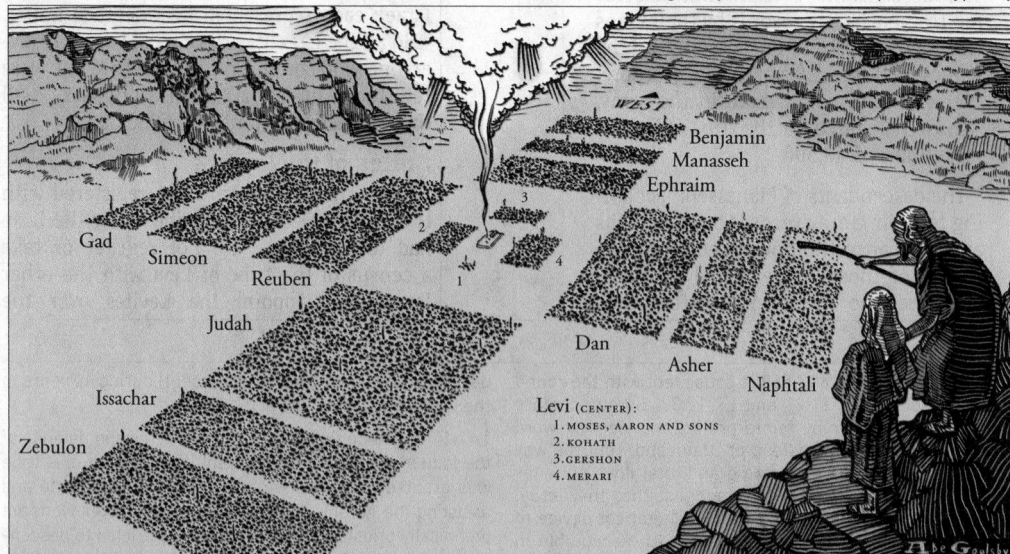

WEST

Benjamin
Manasseh
Ephraim

Gad
Simeon
Reuben
Judah
Dan
Asher
Naphtali
Issachar
Zebulon

Levi (CENTER):
1. MOSES, AARON AND SONS
2. KOHATH
3. GERSHON
4. MERARI

The Lord prescribed a specific arrangement for the Israelites to camp in the wilderness around the tent of meeting (2:1-34).

military division numbers 45,650. ¹⁶ The total number in their military divisions who belong to Reuben's encampment is 151,450; they will move out second.

¹⁷ The tent of meeting is to move out with the Levites' camp, which is in the middle of the camps. They are to move out just as they camp, each in his place,ᴬ with their banners.

¹⁸ Ephraim's military divisions will camp on the west side under their banner. The leader of the Ephraimites is Elishama son of Ammihud. ¹⁹ His military division numbers 40,500. ²⁰ The tribe of Manasseh will be next to it. The leader of the Manassites is Gamaliel son of Pedahzur. ²¹ His military division numbers 32,200. ²² The tribe of Benjamin will be next. The leader of the Benjaminites is Abidan son of Gideoni. ²³ His military division numbers 35,400. ²⁴ The total in their military divisions who belong to Ephraim's encampment number 108,100; they will move out third.

²⁵ Dan's military divisions will camp on the north side under their banner. The leader of the Danites is Ahiezer son of Ammishaddai. ²⁶ His military division numbers 62,700. ²⁷ The tribe of Asher will camp next to it. The leader of the Asherites is Pagiel son of Ochran. ²⁸ His military division numbers 41,500. ²⁹ The tribe of Naphtali will be next. The leader of the Naphtalites is Ahira son of Enan. ³⁰ His military division numbers 53,400. ³¹ The total number who belong to Dan's en-

ᵃ2:33 Nm 1:49
ᵇ2:34 Nm 10:10-28
ᶜ3:1 Ex 19:3
ᵈ3:4 Lv 10:1-2
ᵉLv 10:6; Nm 4:16,28,33
ᶠ3:8 Nm 1:50,53

campment is 157,600; they are to move out last, with their banners."

³² These are the Israelites registered by their ancestral houses. The total number in the camps by their military divisions is 603,550. ³³ But the Levites were not registered among the Israelites, just as the LORD had commanded Moses.ᵃ

³⁴ The Israelites did everything the LORD commanded Moses; they camped by their banners in this way and moved out the same way, each man by his clan and by his ancestral house.ᵇ

Aaron's Sons and the Levites

3 These are the family records of Aaron and Moses at the time the LORD spoke with Moses on Mount Sinai.ᶜ ² These are the names of Aaron's sons: Nadab, the firstborn, and Abihu, Eleazar, and Ithamar. ³ These are the names of Aaron's sons, the anointed priests, who were ordained to serve as priests. ⁴ But Nadab and Abihu died in the LORD's presence when they presented unauthorized fireᵈ before the LORD in the Wilderness of Sinai, and they had no sons. So Eleazar and Ithamar served as priests under the direction of Aaron their father.ᵉ

⁵ The LORD spoke to Moses: ⁶ "Bring the tribe of Levi near and present them to Aaron the priest to assist him. ⁷ They are to perform duties forᴮ him and the entire community before the tent of meeting by attending to the service of the tabernacle. ⁸ They are to take care ofᴮ all the furnishings of the tent of meetingᶠ and perform duties forᶜ the Israelites by attending to the service of the tabernacle. ⁹ Assign the Levites to Aaron and his sons; they have been assigned exclusively to himᴰ from the

---

ᴬ2:17 Lit *each on his hand*   ᴮ3:7,8 Or *to guard*   ᶜ3:8 Or *and guard*   ᴰ3:9 Some Hb mss, LXX, Sam read *Me*; Nm 8:16

in the ancient Near East, the firstborn offspring were given special privileges, but in Israelite history the supplanting of the firstborn is a prominent theme (e.g., Jacob over Esau; Gn 25:23,29-34).

2:32-33 The total of **603,550** equals that of 1:46, and the exclusion of the **Levites** is likewise repeated. Repetition is a common practice in Hebrew narrative, showing consistency and development in the broader narrative.

3:1-3 Within the cultural framework of the ancient Near East, genealogical **records** (Hb *toledoth*; see note at Gn 5:1) served several purposes: (1) to provide historical connection to a pivotal point in the past; (2) to preserve familial community and organization within the larger societal structure; (3) to justify one's position within the societal structure by providing a historical precedent from within one's family line; and (4) to provide future generations with a source of pride. Moses used his records of the census to substantiate his and Aaron's authority.

3:4 Nadab and Abihu suffered the judgment of death (Lv 10:1-2) by offering an unholy censer of incense (by fire). No improper or innovative cultic acts were allowed in the service of the tabernacle. This reminder of their death warned future generations of priests against attempting improper ritual. **Eleazar** would succeed his father in the high priest position following Aaron's death in the region of Moab, across the Jordan River from the promised land (20:23-29; 33:38-39).

3:5-6 The language of God's instruction to Moses is that of an animal sacrifice formally brought before a priest. Hence the Levites were brought and set apart before the high priest Aaron to serve God's people.

3:7-8 The duties of the Levites on behalf of the **entire community** included daily maintenance to ensure the ceremonial purity of the sacrificial implements and curtains of the tabernacle furnishings that only they were allowed to touch.

Israelites.[a] [10] You are to appoint Aaron and his sons to carry out their priestly responsibilities, but any unauthorized person who comes near the sanctuary must be put to death."[b]

[11] The LORD spoke to Moses: [12] "See, I have taken the Levites from the Israelites in place of every firstborn Israelite from the womb.[c] The Levites belong to Me, [13] because every firstborn belongs to Me. At the time I struck down every firstborn in the land of Egypt,[d] I consecrated every firstborn in Israel to Myself, both man and animal. They are Mine; I am •Yahweh."[e]

The Levitical Census

[14] The LORD spoke to Moses in the Wilderness of Sinai: [15] "Register the Levites by their ancestral houses and their clans. You are to register every male one month old or more." [16] So Moses registered them in obedience to the LORD as he had been commanded:

[17] These were Levi's sons by name: Gershon, Kohath, and Merari. [18] These were the names of Gershon's sons by their clans: Libni and Shimei. [19] Kohath's sons by their clans were Amram, Izhar, Hebron, and Uzziel. [20] Merari's sons by their clans were Mahli and Mushi. These were the Levite clans by their ancestral houses.[f]

[21] The Libnite clan and the Shimeite clan came from Gershon; these were the Gershonite clans. [22] Those registered, count-

ing every male one month old or more, numbered 7,500. [23] The Gershonite clans camped behind the tabernacle on the west side,[g] [24] and the leader of the Gershonite family was Eliasaph son of Lael. [25] The Gershonites' duties[h] at the tent of meeting involved the tabernacle, the tent, its covering, the screen for the entrance to the tent of meeting,[i] [26] the hangings of the courtyard, the screen for the entrance[j] to the courtyard that surrounds the tabernacle and the altar, and the tent ropes—all the work relating to these.

[27] The Amramite clan, the Izharite clan, the Hebronite clan, and the Uzzielite clan came from Kohath; these were the Kohathites. [28] Counting every male one month old or more, there were 8,600[A] responsible for the duties of[B] the sanctuary. [29] The clans of the Kohathites camped on the south side of the tabernacle,[k] [30] and the leader of the family of the Kohathite clans was Elizaphan son of Uzziel. [31] Their duties involved the ark, the table, the lampstand, the altars, the sanctuary utensils that were used with these, and the screen[C,l]—and all the work relating to them.[m] [32] The chief of the Levite leaders was Eleazar[n] son of Aaron the priest; he had oversight of those responsible for the duties of[B] the sanctuary.

[33] The Mahlite clan and the Mushite clan

Cross references (center column)

a3:9 Nm 8:16, 19,22; 18:6
b3:10 Nm 1:51; 3:38; 8:19; 18:7
c3:12 Ex 13:1-2; Nm 8:16-18
d3:13 Ex 13:15-16
e Ex 3:14-16; 6:6-7; Nm 3:41,45
f3:17-20 Ex 6:17-19; 1Ch 6:1,16,20-29
g3:23 Nm 2:18-24
h3:25-26 Nm 4:24-26
i3:25 Ex 26:7,14,36-37; 35:11,15
j3:26 Ex 27:9-19; 35:17-18; 38:9-31
k3:29 Nm 2:10-16
l3:31 Ex 35:12
m Ex 25:10-27:21
n3:32 Ex 6:23-25; 28:1; Lv 10:6,12,16; Nm 3:2,4

A3:28 LXX reads *8,300*　B3:28,32 Or *for guarding*　C3:31 The screen between the most holy place and the holy place; Ex 35:12

3:10 The presence of God was symbolized by the ark of the covenant within the holy of holies. This area was protected by the priests on one level and by the Levites on the next. The Levites functioned as a lightning rod for the fiery wrath of God against potential encroachment of the holy place. Improper service by priests or their assistants was punishable by death.

3:11-12 In place of every firstborn of the Israelite families, the Levites served as a substitutionary living sacrifice before God for sacred service on behalf of the people of the other 12 tribes. The firstborn males of the Israelite families were to be presented to God through the agency of the priests (Ex 13:2,11-16; 22:29-30; 34:19-20). The firstborn were God's sole possession based on the redemption-of-the-firstborn principle. "Redemption" finds a parallel in the Babylonian term *padu*, a form of monetary payment to transfer property from one party to another. An indentured servant could gain his freedom through monetary or property transfer, performance of a period of servitude, or a general cancellation of the debt by the owner.

3:13 The price of the Israelite redemption in the exodus was the death of the **firstborn** of **Egypt**, from Pharaoh to the slave, as well as the firstborn of all Egyptian animals.

3:14-16 The census of the **Levites** was separated from the militia (1:17-46). They were exempt from military service.

They served as support personnel who carried the sacred vessels and sounded the trumpets during the various stages of the battle. Note the role of Phinehas in the Midianite campaign (31:6). The census of the militia numbered those 20 years of age and older, but the Levites were counted for the purpose of the firstborn redemption beginning at age **one month**. This ensured that there were enough Levites to approximate the number of the firstborn of the other 12 tribes.

3:21-26 The **tabernacle** was composed of 10 curtains of finely twisted blue, purple, and scarlet linen, each 42 ft. x 6 ft., with cherubim symbols woven into them (Ex 26:1-6). The **tent** was made from 11 curtains of goat hair, 45 ft. x 6 ft., with additional coverings of dyed red ram skins and hides of manatees (Ex 26:7-14).

3:27-32 The **Kohathite** clan was assigned the tasks of guarding and transporting the sacred tabernacle furnishings, including the **ark** of the covenant. They did not actually handle these items; this was done by the priests, who wrapped the implements and then handed them over to the Kohathites for transport.

3:33-36 The **clan** of **Merari** were the caretakers and transporters of the equipment needed to erect and dismantle the tabernacle. By the time of the Davidic monarchy, the three

came from Merari; these were the Merarite clans. [34] Those registered, counting every male one month old or more, numbered 6,200. [35] The leader of the family of the Merarite clans was Zuriel son of Abihail; they camped on the north side of the tabernacle.[a] [36] The assigned duties of Merari's descendants involved the tabernacle's supports, crossbars, posts, bases, all its equipment, and all the work related to these,[b] [37] in addition to the posts of the surrounding courtyard with their bases, tent pegs, and ropes.

[38] Moses, Aaron, and his sons, who performed the duties of[A] the sanctuary as a service on behalf of the Israelites, camped in front of the tabernacle on the east,[c] in front of the tent of meeting toward the sunrise. Any unauthorized person who came near it was to be put to death.[d]

[39] The total number of all the Levite males one month old or more that Moses and Aaron[B] registered by their clans at the LORD's command was 22,000.

Redemption of the Firstborn

[40] The LORD told Moses: "Register every firstborn male of the Israelites[e] one month old or more, and list their names. [41] You are to take the Levites for Me—I am Yahweh—in place of every firstborn among the Israelites, and the Levites' cattle in place of every firstborn among the Israelites' cattle." [42] So Moses registered every firstborn among the Israelites, as the LORD commanded him. [43] The total num-

[a] 3:35 Nm 2:25-31
[b] 3:36-37 Ex 35:1-13; Nm 4:31-32
[c] 3:38 Nm 2:3-9
[d] Nm 1:51; 3:10; 8:19; 18:7
[e] 3:40 Ex 13:1-2; Nm 8:16-18
[f] 3:45 Nm 3:13,41; 10:10; 15:40-41
[g] 3:47 Nm 18:16
[h] 4:2 Ex 6:16,18; Nm 3:27-31; 1Ch 6:22-28
[i] 4:4 Nm 3:30-31; 4:15-19
[j] 4:5 Ex 25:10-22; 26:31-33

ber of the firstborn males one month old or more listed by name was 22,273.

[44] The LORD spoke to Moses again: [45] "Take the Levites in place of every firstborn among the Israelites, and the Levites' cattle in place of their cattle. The Levites belong to Me; I am Yahweh.[f] [46] As the redemption price for the 273 firstborn Israelites who outnumber the Levites, [47] collect five ·shekels for each person, according to the standard sanctuary shekel—20 gerahs to the shekel.[g] [48] Give the money to Aaron and his sons as the redemption price for those who are in excess among the Israelites."

[49] So Moses collected the redemption money from those in excess of the ones redeemed by the Levites. [50] He collected the money from the firstborn Israelites: 1,365 shekels[c] measured by the standard sanctuary shekel. [51] He gave the redemption money to Aaron and his sons in obedience to the LORD, just as the LORD commanded Moses.

Duties of the Kohathites

4 The LORD spoke to Moses and Aaron: [2] "Among the Levites, take a census of the Kohathites[h] by their clans and their ancestral houses, [3] men from 30 years old to 50 years old—everyone who is qualified[D] to do work at the tent of meeting.

[4] "The service of the Kohathites at the tent of meeting concerns the most holy objects.[i] [5] Whenever the camp is about to move on, Aaron and his sons are to go in, take down the screening veil, and cover the ark of the ·testimony with it.[j] [6] They are to place over this

---

[A] 3:38 Or who guarded   [B] 3:39 Some Hb mss, Sam, Syr omit and Aaron   [C] 3:50 Over 34 pounds of silver   [D] 4:3 Lit everyone entering the service

---

clans of Levites also served as musicians for the sanctuary service (1Ch 6:31-48).

3:39 The **Levite** total of **22,000** does not match the sum of the clans at 22,300, which would have made the five-shekel ransom price unnecessary. Most scholars emend the Kohathite total to 8,300 in line with the Lucianic recension of the Septuagint Greek translation, resulting in the 22,000 total.

3:40-51 The excess number of Israelite males was to be redeemed by five shekels, which amounted to 2.1 ounces of silver according to the 20-gerah **sanctuary shekel**. The **redemption** price for each man in the Israelite militia was one-half shekel (Ex 30:11-16). These funds provided support for the service of the tent of meeting. Five shekels was the standard **price** of a slave, and six months of wages for the average day laborer. In Leviticus the redemption rate was five shekels for a small male child, and 50 shekels for an adult male (Lv 27:1-8). The substitutionary aspect of the ransom price theme in the Pentateuch has its ultimate fulfillment in the work of Jesus Christ as the paschal lamb and the final sacrifice for sin—a lamb without blemish (1Pt 1:18-19).

3:43 The census figure of **22,273** presents a practical problem. If there were only that many **firstborn** among the 603,550 **males**, then each firstborn had an average of 26 brothers—an incredible birthrate not substantiated in the Bible or elsewhere. R. B. Allen attempts to solve the problem by contending that the author employed hyperbolic language, exaggerating the actual number of 60,355 by a factor of ten, yielding 603,550. Such tactics were common in ancient literature and were considered a meaningful use of symbolic or sacred numbers (e.g., seven, ten, etc.). Another solution is to identify the 22,273 as only those firstborn males who were born during the year and a half between the exodus and the census since the total number of firstborn among the 603,550 would have been much higher.

4:4 The **most holy objects** were the ark of the covenant, the bronze laver, the seven-tiered menorah, and other implements of the tabernacle.

4:5-6 When the pillar of cloud moved out from one campsite to the next, the Aaronic priests would dismantle the tabernacle and prepare each part for the journey. The **screening veil** of scarlet, blue, and purple that separated the holy of holies from the outer court was used in the covering of the **ark of**

a covering made of manatee skin,^A spread a solid blue cloth on top, and insert its poles.^a

^7"They are to spread a blue cloth over the table of the Presence and place the plates and cups on it, as well as the bowls and pitchers for the •drink offering. The regular bread offering is to be on it.^b ^8They are to spread a scarlet cloth over them, cover them with a covering made of manatee skin,^A and insert the poles in the table.^c

^9"They are to take a blue cloth and cover the lampstand^d used for light, with its lamps, snuffers, and firepans,^e as well as its jars of oil by which they service it. ^10Then they must place it with all its utensils inside a covering made of manatee skin^A and put them on the carrying frame.

^11"They are to spread a blue cloth over the gold altar,^f cover it with a covering made of manatee skin,^A and insert its poles.^g ^12They are to take all the serving utensils they use in the sanctuary, place them in a blue cloth, cover them with a covering made of manatee skin,^A and put them on a carrying frame.

^13"They are to remove the ashes from the bronze altar, spread a purple cloth over it, ^14and place all the equipment on it that they use in serving: the firepans, meat forks, shovels, and basins—all the equipment of the altar.^h They are to spread a covering made of manatee skin^A over it and insert its poles.^B,i

^15"Aaron and his sons are to finish covering the holy objects and all their equipment whenever the camp is to move on. The Kohathites will come and carry them, but they are not to touch the holy objects or they will die.^j These are the transportation duties of the Kohathites regarding the tent of meeting.

^16"Eleazar, son of Aaron the priest, has oversight of the lamp oil,^k the fragrant incense,^l the daily •grain offering,^m and the anointing oil.^n He has oversight of the entire tabernacle

and everything in it, the holy objects and their utensils."^C

^17 Then the LORD spoke to Moses and Aaron: ^18 "Do not allow the Kohathite tribal clans to be wiped out from the Levites. ^19 Do this for them so that they may live and not die when they come near the most holy objects:^o Aaron and his sons are to go in and assign each man his task and transportation duty. ^20 The Kohathites are not to go in and look at the holy objects, even for a moment,^D or they will die."

Duties of the Gershonites

^21 The LORD spoke to Moses: ^22 "Take a census of the Gershonites^p also, by their ancestral houses and their clans. ^23 Register men from 30 years old to 50 years old, everyone who is qualified to perform service, to do work at the tent of meeting. ^24 This is the service of the Gershonite clans regarding work and transportation duties: ^25 They are to transport the tabernacle curtains,^q the tent of meeting with its covering and the covering made of manatee skin^A on top of it, the screen for the entrance to the tent of meeting, ^26 the hangings of the courtyard, the screen for the entrance at the gate of the courtyard that surrounds the tabernacle and the altar, along with their ropes and all the equipment for their service. They will carry out everything that needs to be done with these items.

^27 "All the service of the Gershonites, all their transportation duties and all their other work, is to be done at the command of Aaron and his sons; you are to assign to them all that they are responsible to carry. ^28 This is the service of the Gershonite clans at the tent of meeting, and their duties will be under the direction of Ithamar son of Aaron the priest.

Duties of the Merarites

^29 "As for the Merarites, you are to regis-

^a4:6 Ex 25:13-15
^b4:7 Ex 25:30; Lv 24:5-9
^c4:8 Ex 25:26-28
^d4:9 Ex 25:31-35; 26:35; 37:17-20
^eEx 25:38; 37:23; Nm 4:14
^f4:11 Ex 30:1-3; 31:8; 39:38; 40:5,26
^gEx 30:4; 35:15
^h4:14 Ex 27:3; 38:3; Nm 7:13-8:4
^iEx 27:7
^j4:15 Nm 1:51; 4:20; 8:19; 18:7
^k4:16 Ex 25:6; 27:20; Lv 4:2
^lEx 25:6; 30:7; Lv 4:7
^mLv 6:20-22
^nEx 25:6; 29:7,21; Lv 8:2,10,12,30
^o4:19 Nm 3:31; 4:4
^p4:22 Nm 3:17,21-26
^q4:25 Ex 26:1-13; 36:8-17

---

^A4:6,8,10,11,12,14,25 Or of dolphin skin, or of fine leather; Hb obscure   ^B4:14 Sam, LXX add They are to take a purple cloth and cover the wash basin and its base. They are to place them in a covering made of manatee skin and put them on the carrying frame.   ^C4:16 Or the sanctuary and its furnishings   ^D4:20 Or at the covering of the holy objects

---

the testimony. It was then wrapped in yellow-orange skins of the **manatee** (aka dugong, sea cow) for protection during the transport from one camp to the next. A final covering of royal purple cloth completed the preparation process.

4:7-8 The 12 loaves, representing the 12 tribes of Israel, were replaced weekly on the Sabbath and were symbolic of God's presence and constant provision for His people (Ex 24:5-9).

4:20 Violation of the Holiness Code, even for the Kohathites, was punishable by death.

4:21-28 See Ex 26:1-14,36-37 for a detailed description of the tabernacle curtains and other items.

4:34-49 This section summarizes the census of the three clans of the Levites.

Levite Clan	Age 1 Month+	Age 30-50
Kohathite	8,300	2,750
Gershon	7,500	2,630
Merari	6,200	3,200
TOTAL	22,000	8,580

5:2 These people were not banished, but sent outside the sacred area so the holy place would not be defiled. The unclean were quarantined on the outer perimeter of the camp. Leviticus 13-14 describes the process of purification by which people could be restored to the camp of the holy.

ter them by their clans[a] and their ancestral houses. [30]Register men from 30 years old to 50 years old, everyone who is qualified to do the work of the tent of meeting. [31]This is what they are responsible to carry as the whole of their service at the tent of meeting: the supports of the tabernacle, with its crossbars, posts, and bases, [32]the posts of the surrounding courtyard with their bases, tent pegs, and ropes, including all their equipment and all the work related to them. You are to assign by name the items that they are responsible to carry. [33]This is the service of the Merarite clans regarding all their work at the tent of meeting, under the direction of Ithamar son of Aaron the priest."

Census of the Levites

[34]So Moses, Aaron, and the leaders of the community registered the Kohathites by their clans and their ancestral houses, [35]men from 30 years old to 50 years old, everyone who was qualified for work at the tent of meeting. [36]The men registered by their clans numbered 2,750. [37]These were the registered men of the Kohathite clans, everyone who could serve at the tent of meeting. Moses and Aaron registered them at the LORD's command through Moses.

[38]The Gershonites were registered by their clans and their ancestral houses, [39]men from 30 years old to 50 years old, everyone who was qualified for work at the tent of meeting. [40]The men registered by their clans and their ancestral houses numbered 2,630. [41]These were the registered men of the Gershonite clans. At the LORD's command Moses and Aaron registered everyone who could serve at the tent of meeting.

[42]The men of the Merarite clans were registered by their clans and their ancestral houses, [43]those from 30 years old to 50 years old, everyone who was qualified for work at the tent of meeting. [44]The men registered by their clans numbered 3,200. [45]These were the registered men of the Merarite clans; Moses

and Aaron registered them at the LORD's command through Moses.

[46]Moses, Aaron, and the leaders of Israel registered all the Levites by their clans and their ancestral houses, [47]from 30 years old to 50 years old, everyone who was qualified to do the work of serving at the tent of meeting and transporting it. [48]Their registered men numbered 8,580. [49]At the LORD's command they were registered under the direction of Moses, each one according to his work and transportation duty, and his assignment was as the LORD commanded Moses.

Isolation of the Unclean

5 The LORD instructed Moses: [2]"Command the Israelites to send away anyone from the camp who is afflicted with a skin disease, anyone who has a bodily discharge, or anyone who is defiled because of a corpse.[b] [3]You must send away both male or female; send them outside the camp, so that they will not defile their camps where I dwell among them." [4]The Israelites did this, sending them outside the camp. The Israelites did as the LORD instructed Moses.

Compensation for Wrongdoing

[5]The LORD spoke to Moses: [6]"Tell the Israelites: When a man or woman commits any sin against another, that person acts unfaithfully toward the LORD and is •guilty. [7]The person is to confess the sin he has committed. He is to pay full compensation, add a fifth of its value to it, and give it to the individual he has wronged.[c] [8]But if that individual has no relative[d] to receive compensation,[A] the compensation goes to the LORD for the priest, along with the •atonement ram by which the priest will make atonement for the guilty person.[e] [9]Every holy contribution the Israelites present to the priest will be his.[f] [10]Each one's holy contribution is his to give; what each one gives to the priest will be his."

The Jealousy Ritual

[11]The LORD spoke to Moses: [12]"Speak to the Israelites and tell them: If any man's wife goes

Marginal cross-references:
[a]4:29 Ex 6:16,19; Nm 3:17,33-37
[b]5:2 Lv 14:2-3; 15:2; 22:4; Nm 9:6-7
[c]5:7 Lv 6:1-5
[d]5:8 Lv 25:25,48-49; Jr 32:7
[e]Lv 6:6-7
[f]5:9 Ex 25:2-3; 29:27-28; Lv 7:14,32,34

[A]5:8 If the individual has died

Skin diseases ranged from abscesses or eczema to perhaps Hansen's disease (leprosy), though some scholars reject the inclusion of Hansen's disease in the OT restrictions. Bodily discharges refer to those emitted by male and female sexual organs (cp. Lv 15). Contact with a dead animal rendered a person impure for a day, but pollution by contact with a human corpse made him unclean for a week.

5:3 As with most OT laws, **both male or female** were on equal status regarding ritual purity, except for those things which were unique to one gender.

5:5-10 **When a man or woman commits any sin against another** addressed purity in interpersonal relationships as part of the Hebrew *'asham* ("restitution offering") legislation of Lv 6:1-7. Damage to property, fraud, or false statements affected the well-being of the community of faith and had to be dealt with forthrightly. Human relationship and a restitution of value were essential for maintaining harmony and holiness in the community.

5:12-14 Probably no case study in pentateuchal law has so many conditional clauses. **If any man's wife was**

astray, is unfaithful to him, [13] and sleeps with another,[A] but it is concealed from her husband, and she is undetected, even though she has defiled herself, since there is no witness against her, and she wasn't caught in the act; [14] and if a feeling of jealousy comes over the husband and he becomes jealous because of his wife who has defiled herself—or if a feeling of jealousy comes over him and he becomes jealous of her though she has not defiled herself— [15] then the man is to bring his wife to the priest. He is also to bring an offering for her of two quarts[B] of barley flour. He is not to pour oil over it or put frankincense on it because it is a *grain offering of jealousy, a grain offering for remembrance that brings sin to mind.

[16] "The priest is to bring her forward and have her stand before the LORD. [17] Then the priest is to take holy water in a clay bowl, and take some of the dust from the tabernacle floor and put it in the water. [18] After the priest has the woman stand before the LORD, he is to let down her hair[C] and place in her hands the grain offering for remembrance, which is the grain offering of jealousy. The priest is to hold the bitter water that brings a curse. [19] The priest will require the woman to take an oath and will say to her, 'If no man has slept with you, if you have not gone astray and become defiled while under your husband's authority, be unaffected by this bitter water that brings a curse. [20] But if you have gone astray while under your husband's authority, if you have defiled yourself and a man other than your husband has slept with you'— [21] at this point the priest must make the woman take the oath with the sworn curse, and he is to say to her—'May the LORD make you into an object of your people's cursing and swearing when

[a]6:2 Jdg 13:5,7; 16:17; Am 2:11-12

He makes your thigh[D] shrivel and your belly swell. [E] [22] May this water that brings a curse enter your stomach, causing your belly to swell and your thigh to shrivel.'

"And the woman must reply, ''Amen, Amen.'

[23] "Then the priest is to write these curses on a scroll and wash them off into the bitter water. [24] He will require the woman to drink the bitter water that brings a curse, and it will enter her and cause bitter suffering. [25] The priest is to take the grain offering of jealousy from the woman's hand, wave the offering before the LORD, and bring it to the altar. [26] The priest is to take a handful of the grain offering as a memorial portion and burn it on the altar. Then he will require the woman to drink the water.

[27] "When he makes her drink the water, if she has defiled herself and been unfaithful to her husband, the water that brings a curse will enter her and cause bitter suffering; her belly will swell, and her thigh will shrivel. She will become a curse among her people. [28] But if the woman has not defiled herself and is pure, she will be unaffected and will be able to conceive children.

[29] "This is the law regarding jealousy when a wife goes astray and defiles herself while under her husband's authority, [30] or when a feeling of jealousy comes over a husband and he becomes jealous of his wife. He is to have the woman stand before the LORD, and the priest will apply this entire ritual to her. [31] The husband will be free of guilt, but that woman will bear the consequences of her guilt."

The Nazirite Vow

6 The LORD instructed Moses: [2] "Speak to the Israelites and tell them: When a man or woman makes a special vow, a Nazirite vow,[a] to consecrate himself to[F] the LORD, [3] he is to

---

[A]5:13 Lit and man lies with her and has an emission of semen   [B]5:15 Lit a tenth of an ephah   [C]5:18 Or to uncover her head   [D]5:21-22 Possibly a euphemism for the reproductive organs   [E]5:21 Or flood   [F]6:2 Or vow, to live as a Nazirite for

---

apprehended in the act of adultery, her act was punishable by death along with the adulterous male partner (Lv 20:10). The ritual outlined here put the matter in the hands of God (who sees and knows all) when adultery was suspected but not proven by human witnesses. The woman would not be stoned if the community followed this legislation. Throughout the book of Numbers special attention is given to matters related to women, including women's property rights (Nm 27:1-11; 36:1-12) and women's vows (30:3-16; including female Nazirites in 6:2).

5:15-16 The woman suspected of adultery would be brought before the **priest** at the entrance of the tabernacle. The woman was to **stand before the LORD**, who would act as her judge.

5:18 To **let down her hair** was a sign of mourning or disgrace (Lv 10:6, 13:45; 21:10).

5:19-22 The extended oath of imprecation took place at the entrance to the sanctuary before God and the priest. The mixture of holy water and dust from the tabernacle floor (v. 16) became either a purification tonic if the woman was innocent or a curse that left her barren for life.

5:23-28 In the solemn ceremony, the woman drank the potion and the results were left to God. Perhaps there was only a slight possibility that the punishment would happen. A jealous husband, having no more than a hunch of evidence against his wife, subjected her to a test in which the prospects of punishment were very limited. God is the only infallible judge.

6:1 After two chapters of Levitical and priestly instructions (chaps. 3-4), and a series of community purity laws in chapter 5, the Nazirite legislation defines an additional level of service for the laity in the community of faith.

abstain[A] from wine and beer.[a] He must not drink vinegar made from wine or from beer. He must not drink any grape juice or eat fresh grapes or raisins. He is not to eat anything produced by the grapevine, from seeds to skin,[B] during his vow.

[5]"You must not cut his hair[c] throughout the time of his vow of consecration. He must be holy until the time is completed during which he consecrates himself to the Lord; he is to let the hair of his head grow long. He must not go near a dead body during the time he consecrates himself to the Lord.[b] He is not to defile himself for his father or mother, or his brother or sister, when they die, because the hair consecrated to his God is on his head. [8]He is holy to the Lord[c] during the time of consecration.

[9]"If someone suddenly dies near him, defiling his consecrated head of hair, he must shave his head on the day of his purification; he is to shave it on the seventh day.[d] [10]On the eighth day he is to bring two turtledoves or two young pigeons to the priest at the entrance to the tent of meeting.[e] [11]The priest is to offer one as a *sin offering and the other as a *burnt offering[f] to make *atonement on behalf of the Nazirite, since he sinned because of the corpse. On that day he must consecrate[D] his head again.[g] [12]He is to rededicate his time of consecration to the Lord and to bring a year-old male lamb as a *restitution offering.[h] But do not count the previous period, because his consecrated hair became defiled.

[13]"This is the law of the Nazirite: On the day his time of consecration is completed, he

must be brought to the entrance to the tent of meeting.[i] [14]He is to present an offering to the Lord[j] of one unblemished year-old male lamb as a burnt offering, one unblemished year-old female lamb as a sin offering, one unblemished ram as a *fellowship offering,[k] [15]along with their *grain offerings and *drink offerings,[l] and a basket of unleavened cakes made from fine flour mixed with oil, and unleavened wafers coated with oil.[m]

[16]"The priest is to present these before the Lord and sacrifice the Nazirite's sin offering and burnt offering. [17]He will also offer the ram as a fellowship sacrifice to the Lord, together with the basket of unleavened bread. Then the priest will offer the accompanying grain offering and drink offering.

[18]"The Nazirite is to shave his consecrated head at the entrance to the tent of meeting, take the hair from his head, and put it on the fire under the fellowship sacrifice. [19]The priest is to take the boiled shoulder from the ram, one unleavened cake from the basket, and one unleavened wafer, and put them into the hands[n] of the Nazirite after he has shaved his consecrated head. [20]The priest is to wave them as a presentation offering before the Lord.[o] It is a holy portion for the priest, in addition to the breast of the presentation offering and the thigh of the contribution.[p] After that, the Nazirite may drink wine.

[21]"This is the ritual of the Nazirite who vows his offering to the Lord for his consecration,[q] in addition to whatever else he can afford; he must fulfill whatever vow he makes in keeping with the ritual for his consecration."

---

[a]6:3 Jdg 13:4,7,14
[b]6:6 Nm 19:11-16
[c]6:8 Nm 6:5; Dt 7:6; 14:2,21; 26:19; 2Ch 35:3
[d]6:9 Nm 19:11
[e]6:10 Ex 29:42-43; Lv 5:7; Nm 6:18
[f]6:11 Lv 1:14-17; 5:7-10
[g]Lv 15:13-15
[h]6:12 Lv 5:14-19; 7:1-6
[i]6:13 Lv 14:11; Nm 8:9
[j]6:14 Ac 21:24
[k]Lv 1:10-13; 3:1-5; 4:32-35
[l]6:15 Ex 29:40-41; Lv 23:12-13,18; Nm 15:1-12
[m]Ex 29:2; Lv 2:4-11; 7:12
[n]6:19 Ex 29:24; Lv 2:4-11
[o]6:20 Ex 29:25-27
[p]Ex 25:2-3; 29:27-28; Lv 7:14,32,34
[q]6:21 Ac 21:24

A6:3 In Hb, the words Nazirite, consecrate, and abstain are related and involve the idea of separation.   B6:4 Or from unripe grapes to hulls   C6:5 Lit A razor is not to pass over his head   D6:11 Lit set apart

6:2 Unlike the priestly and Levitical service, which was limited to males of a certain age and ancestral heritage, the **Nazirite vow** was a special dedicatory service for the Lord that was open to females. Though only Aaronic priests were permitted to conduct cultic ritual in the tabernacle, any person could dedicate his or her life in service to the Lord for a specific period of time. Samson was dedicated as a Nazirite for the purpose of delivering Israel from Philistine oppression (Jdg 13:2-4). The mothers of Samson and Samuel took Nazirite vows during their time of barrenness.

6:3-4 The Nazirite vow involved total restriction from the vineyard and any of its products. This was more stringent than the restriction of priests from consuming **wine** during their time of ritual service. The vineyard denoted a sedentary lifestyle that often lost its perspective of total devotion to the Lord. Note the example of the Rechabites in Jeremiah 35 (see notes at Jr 35:2 and Jr 35:6-11). **Beer** translates a Hebrew term traditionally translated "strong drink," derived from the verb shakar, "to be drunk." The distillation process, which leads to a higher alcoholic content than can be achieved via mere fermentation, was unknown until the ninth century A.D. Thus the ancients were unable to make

beverages that are as potent as the "strong drinks" that have been available since medieval times. For this reason the HCSB translators reason that "beer" is a more accurate translation since it has a lower alcohol percentage than the "strong drink" that results from distillation.

6:5-6 The uncut **hair** would be an outward symbol to others of the Nazirite dedication. Refraining from coming near the **dead** or participating in the burial ritual would be a reminder to that person's family that he had been totally dedicated to the Lord.

6:9-12 Closeness to a dead body, a major contaminant mentioned in 5:2, could happen accidentally while a person was sleeping in his tent when an elderly relative died. If the vineyard and razor restrictions were deliberately broken, the vow was automatically ended. See chapter 19 for detailed legislation on cleansing from contamination by a corpse.

6:13-20 The concluding ceremony of the **Nazirite** vow involved each of these sacrificial offerings: (1) a **burnt offering** (Hb 'olah) for consecration, (2) a **sin offering** (Hb chatta'ath) for purification, and (3) a **fellowship offering** (Hb shelomim) for celebration.

The Priestly Blessing

[22] The LORD spoke to Moses: [23] "Tell Aaron and his sons how you are to bless the Israelites. Say to them:

[24]   May *Yahweh bless you
        and protect you;[a]

[25]   may Yahweh make His face shine
        on you
        and be gracious to you;[b]

[26]   may Yahweh look with favor on you[A]
        and give you peace.[B,c]

[27] In this way they will pronounce My name over[c] the Israelites, and I will bless them."

Offerings from the Leaders

7 On the day Moses finished setting up the tabernacle,[d] he anointed and consecrated it and all its furnishings, along with the altar and all its utensils. After he anointed and consecrated these things, [2] the leaders of Israel, the heads of their ancestral houses, presented an offering. They were the tribal leaders who supervised the registration.[e] [3] They brought as their offering before the LORD six covered carts and 12 oxen, a cart from every two leaders and an ox from each one, and presented them in front of the tabernacle.

[4] The LORD said to Moses, [5] "Accept these from them to be used in the work of the tent of meeting, and give this offering to the Le-

vites, to each division according to their service."

[6] So Moses took the carts and oxen and gave them to the Levites. [7] He gave the Gershonites two carts and four oxen corresponding to their service,[f] [8] and gave the Merarites four carts and eight oxen corresponding to their service,[g] under the direction of Ithamar son of Aaron the priest. [9] But he did not give any to the Kohathites, since their responsibility was service related to the holy objects[h] carried on their shoulders.[i]

[10] The leaders also presented the dedication gift for the altar when it was anointed.[j] The leaders presented their offerings in front of the altar. [11] The LORD told Moses, "Each day have one leader present his offering for the dedication of the altar."[k]

[12] The one who presented his offering on the first day was Nahshon son of Amminadab[l] from the tribe of Judah. [13] His offering was one silver dish weighing 3¼ pounds[D] and one silver basin weighing 1¾ pounds,[E] measured by the standard sanctuary *shekel, both of them full of fine flour mixed with oil for a *grain offering;[m] [14] one gold bowl weighing four ounces,[F] full of incense; [15] one young bull, one ram, and one male lamb a year old, for a *burnt offering;[n] [16] one male goat for a *sin offering;[o] [17] and two bulls, five rams, five male breeding goats, and five

---

[a]6:24 Ps 121:4,7; 128:5; 134:3
[b]6:25 Ps 67:1; 80:3; 89:15; 119:135
[c]6:26 Ps 4:6; 147:14
[d]7:1 Ex 39:32; 40:17; Nm 9:15
[e]7:2 Nm 1:4-16
[f]7:7 Nm 4:23-28,32
[g]7:8 Nm 3:36-37; 4:30-33
[h]7:9 Nm 4:4-16
[i]Nm 3:28-31; 4:4-20
[j]7:10 Nm 7:11, 84,88; 1Kg 8:62-64; 2Ch 7:4-9; Neh 12:27
[k]7:11 Ex 40:10
[l]7:12 Nm 1:7; 2:3; 10:14
[m]7:13 Lv 2:1-2; 6:14-18
[n]7:15 Lv 1:1-13; 6:8-13
[o]7:16 Lv 4:1-5:13; 6:24-30; Nm 28:11-15

A6:26 Lit LORD lift His face to you   B6:26 Or prosperity   C6:27 Or put My name on   D7:13 Lit dish, 130 its shekel-weight   E7:13 Lit 70 shekels   F7:14 Lit 10 (shekels)

6:22-27 The priestly blessing concludes the first section of the book of Numbers.

6:23 Blessing was invoking the power of God on behalf of the people of God (**bless the Israelites**). This blessing would bring such things as numerous descendants, a fruitful land, good health, long life, deliverance from danger and oppression, protection from one's enemies, and God's abiding presence. As the recipient of God's blessing, Israel was to bless the nations (Gn 12:3) as His instrument, serving as a light to the entire world and pointing the nations to the one true God.

6:24 God's protection of Israel had been demonstrated by their deliverance from Egypt. The prayer calls for that protection to continue.

6:25 The **face** reflected the righteous character of God. **Be gracious to you** evoked God's favor, which was beyond measure. God's grace would be exemplified when God brought the second generation into the promised land after the rejection of that gift by the generation delivered from Egypt.

6:26 Look with favor on you and give you peace expresses God's grace and beneficence. Favor is the directing of one's full attention toward the needs and desires of another person. The smile of God on the community of faith would bring

peace as His covenant mercy came to fruition in the life of the community.

6:27 The **name** of God is a reflection of the fullness of His character. When Jesus spoke of coming in the name of the Father (Jn 5:43; 10:25), He was evoking the fullness of God's character upon His public ministry.

7:1 The historical setting of the construction of the tabernacle (Ex 40:17) is the first day of the first month of the second year, nearly a year after the exodus from Egypt.

7:12-83 Each of the 12 tribal representatives presented the given number of items for use in the Israelite celebration. The repetition in this passage highlights the fact that every tribe participated in the ritual celebrations and had an equal role in the religious practices. A people in communion with God were ready to worship together and experience His abiding presence. The order of the offerings from each of the tribal representatives follows an administrative-list pattern of the ancient Near East. The normal sequence for Israelite relations with God is: (1) consecration/whole burnt offering for sanctification, (2) purification/sin offering to atone for a broken relationship with God, and (3) peace/thanksgiving offering for the celebration of the relationship with God. Only the restitution offering is not mentioned in this context of consecration and celebration.

male lambs a year old, for the *fellowship sacrifice.ᵃ This was the offering of Nahshon son of Amminadab.

¹⁸On the second day Nethanel son of Zuar,ᵇ leader of Issachar, presented an offering. ¹⁹As his offering, he presented one silver dish weighing 3¹/₄ poundsᴬ and one silver basin weighing 1³/₄ pounds,ᴮ measured by the standard sanctuary shekel, both of them full of fine flour mixed with oil for a grain offering; ²⁰one gold bowl weighing four ounces,ᶜ full of incense; ²¹one young bull, one ram, and one male lamb a year old, for a burnt offering; ²²one male goat for a sin offering; ²³and two bulls, five rams, five male breeding goats, and five male lambs a year old, for the fellowship sacrifice. This was the offering of Nethanel son of Zuar.

²⁴On the third day Eliab son of Helon,ᶜ leader of the Zebulunites, presented an offering. ²⁵His offering was one silver dish weighing 3¹/₄ poundsᴬ and one silver basin weighing 1³/₄ pounds,ᴮ measured by the standard sanctuary shekel, both of them full of fine flour mixed with oil for a grain offering; ²⁶one gold bowl weighing four ounces,ᶜ full of incense; ²⁷one young bull, one ram, and one male lamb a year old, for a burnt offering; ²⁸one male goat for a sin offering; ²⁹and two bulls, five rams, five male breeding goats, and five male lambs a year old, for the fellowship sacrifice. This was the offering of Eliab son of Helon.

³⁰On the fourth day Elizur son of Shedeur,ᵈ leader of the Reubenites, presented an offering. ³¹His offering was one silver dish weighing 3¹/₄ poundsᴬ and one silver basin weighing 1³/₄ pounds,ᴮ measured by the standard sanctuary shekel, both of them full of fine flour mixed with oil for a grain offering; ³²one gold bowl weighing four ounces,ᶜ full of incense; ³³one young bull, one ram, and one male lamb a year old, for a burnt offering; ³⁴one male goat for a sin offering; ³⁵and two bulls, five rams, five male breeding goats, and five male lambs a year old, for the fellowship sacrifice. This was the offering of Elizur son of Shedeur.

³⁶On the fifth day Shelumiel son of Zurishaddai,ᵉ leader of the Simeonites, pre-

ᵃ7:17 Lv 3:1-17; 7:11-21
ᵇ7:18 Nm 1:8; 2:5; 10:15
ᶜ7:24 Nm 1:9; 2:7; 10:16
ᵈ7:30 Nm 1:5; 2:10; 10:18
ᵉ7:36 Nm 1:6; 2:12; 10:19
ᶠ7:42 Nm 1:14; 2:14; 10:20
ᵍ7:48 Nm 1:10; 2:18; 10:22
ʰ7:54 Nm 1:10; 2:20; 10:23

sented an offering. ³⁷His offering was one silver dish weighing 3¹/₄ poundsᴬ and one silver basin weighing 1³/₄ pounds,ᴮ measured by the standard sanctuary shekel, both of them full of fine flour mixed with oil for a grain offering; ³⁸one gold bowl weighing four ounces,ᶜ full of incense; ³⁹one young bull, one ram, and one male lamb a year old, for a burnt offering; ⁴⁰one male goat for a sin offering; ⁴¹and two bulls, five rams, five male breeding goats, and five male lambs a year old, for the fellowship sacrifice. This was the offering of Shelumiel son of Zurishaddai.

⁴²On the sixth day Eliasaph son of Deuel,ᴰ,ᶠ leader of the Gadites, presented an offering. ⁴³His offering was one silver dish weighing 3¹/₄ poundsᴬ and one silver basin weighing 1³/₄ pounds,ᴮ measured by the standard sanctuary shekel, both of them full of fine flour mixed with oil for a grain offering; ⁴⁴one gold bowl weighing four ounces,ᶜ full of incense; ⁴⁵one young bull, one ram, and one male lamb a year old, for a burnt offering; ⁴⁶one male goat for a sin offering; ⁴⁷and two bulls, five rams, five male breeding goats, and five male lambs a year old, for the fellowship sacrifice. This was the offering of Eliasaph son of Deuel.ᴰ

⁴⁸On the seventh day Elishama son of Ammihud,ᵍ leader of the Ephraimites, presented an offering. ⁴⁹His offering was one silver dish weighing 3¹/₄ poundsᴬ and one silver basin weighing 1³/₄ pounds,ᴮ measured by the standard sanctuary shekel, both of them full of fine flour mixed with oil for a grain offering; ⁵⁰one gold bowl weighing four ounces,ᶜ full of incense; ⁵¹one young bull, one ram, and one male lamb a year old, for a burnt offering; ⁵²one male goat for a sin offering; ⁵³and two bulls, five rams, five male breeding goats, and five male lambs a year old, for the fellowship sacrifice. This was the offering of Elishama son of Ammihud.

⁵⁴On the eighth day Gamaliel son of Pedahzur,ʰ leader of the Manassites, presented an offering. ⁵⁵His offering was one silver dish weighing 3¹/₄ poundsᴬ and one silver basin weighing 1³/₄ pounds,ᴮ measured by the standard sanctuary shekel, both of them full of fine flour mixed with oil for a

ᴬ7:19,25,31,37,43,49,55 Lit *dish, 130 its shekel-weight*   ᴮ7:19,25,31,37,43,49,55 Lit *70 shekels*   ᶜ7:20,26,32,38,44,50, Lit *10* (shekels)   ᴰ7:42,47 LXX, Syr read *Reuel*

grain offering; [56] one gold bowl weighing four ounces,[A] full of incense; [57] one young bull, one ram, and one male lamb a year old, for a burnt offering; [58] one male goat for a sin offering; [59] and two bulls, five rams, five male breeding goats, and five male lambs a year old, for the fellowship sacrifice. This was the offering of Gamaliel son of Pedahzur.

[60] On the ninth day Abidan son of Gideoni,[a] leader of the Benjaminites, presented an offering. [61] His offering was one silver dish weighing 3¹⁄₄ pounds[B] and one silver basin weighing 1³⁄₄ pounds,[C] measured by the standard sanctuary shekel, both of them full of fine flour mixed with oil for a grain offering; [62] one gold bowl weighing four ounces,[A] full of incense; [63] one young bull, one ram, and one male lamb a year old, for a burnt offering; [64] one male goat for a sin offering; [65] and two bulls, five rams, five male breeding goats, and five male lambs a year old, for the fellowship sacrifice. This was the offering of Abidan son of Gideoni.

[66] On the tenth day Ahiezer son of Ammishaddai,[b] leader of the Danites, presented an offering. [67] His offering was one silver dish weighing 3¹⁄₄ pounds[B] and one silver basin weighing 1³⁄₄ pounds,[C] measured by the standard sanctuary shekel, both of them full of fine flour mixed with oil for a grain offering; [68] one gold bowl weighing four ounces,[A] full of incense; [69] one young bull, one ram, and one male lamb a year old, for a burnt offering; [70] one male goat for a sin offering; [71] and two bulls, five rams, five male breeding goats, and five male lambs a year old, for the fellowship sacrifice. This was the offering of Ahiezer son of Ammishaddai.

[72] On the eleventh day Pagiel son of Ochran,[c] leader of the Asherites, presented an offering. [73] His offering was one silver dish weighing 3¹⁄₄ pounds[B] and one silver basin weighing 1³⁄₄ pounds,[C] measured by the standard sanctuary shekel, both of them full of fine flour mixed with oil for a grain offering; [74] one gold bowl weighing

[a] 7:60 Nm 1:11; 2:22; 10:24
[b] 7:66 Nm 1:12; 2:25; 10:25
[c] 7:72 Nm 1:13; 2:27; 10:26
[d] 7:78 Nm 1:15; 2:29; 10:27
[e] 7:84 Nm 7:1,10
[f] 7:87 Lv 1:1-13; 6:8-13
[g] Lv 4:22-26; 6:24-30; Nm 28:11-15
[h] 7:88 Lv 3:1-17; 7:11-21
[i] 7:89 Nm 12:8
[j] Ex 25:10-22; 37:1-9; 1Kg 6:25

four ounces,[A] full of incense; [75] one young bull, one ram, and one male lamb a year old, for a burnt offering; [76] one male goat for a sin offering; [77] and two bulls, five rams, five male breeding goats, and five male lambs a year old, for the fellowship sacrifice. This was the offering of Pagiel son of Ochran.

[78] On the twelfth day Ahira son of Enan,[d] leader of the Naphtalites, presented an offering. [79] His offering was one silver dish weighing 3¹⁄₄ pounds[B] and one silver basin weighing 1³⁄₄ pounds,[C] measured by the standard sanctuary shekel, both of them full of fine flour mixed with oil for a grain offering; [80] one gold bowl weighing four ounces,[A] full of incense; [81] one young bull, one ram, and one male lamb a year old, for a burnt offering; [82] one male goat for a sin offering; [83] and two bulls, five rams, five male breeding goats, and five male lambs a year old, for the fellowship sacrifice. This was the offering of Ahira son of Enan.

[84] This was the dedication gift from the leaders of Israel for the altar when it was anointed:[e] 12 silver dishes, 12 silver basins, and 12 gold bowls. [85] Each silver dish weighed 3¹⁄₄ pounds,[D] and each basin 1³⁄₄ pounds.[E] The total weight of the silver articles was 60 pounds[F] measured by the standard sanctuary shekel. [86] The 12 gold bowls full of incense each weighed four ounces[A] measured by the standard sanctuary shekel. The total weight of the gold bowls was three pounds.[G] [87] All the livestock for the burnt offering[f] totaled 12 bulls, 12 rams, and 12 male lambs a year old, with their grain offerings, and 12 male goats for the sin offering.[g] [88] All the livestock for the fellowship sacrifice[h] totaled 24 bulls, 60 rams, 60 male breeding goats, and 60 male lambs a year old. This was the dedication gift for the altar after it was anointed.

[89] When Moses entered the tent of meeting to speak with the LORD, he heard the voice speaking to him[i] from above the *mercy seat that was on the ark of the *testimony, from between the two *cherubim.[j] He spoke to him that way.

[A] 7:56,62,68,74,80,86 Lit 10 (shekels)   [B] 7:61,67,73,79 Lit dish, 130 its shekel-weight   [C] 7:61,67,73,79 Lit 70 shekels   [D] 7:85 Lit 130 (shekels)   [E] 7:85 Lit 70 (shekels)   [F] 7:85 Lit 2,400 (shekels)   [G] 7:86 Lit 120 (shekels)

7:84-89 This passage fulfills the promise of Ex 25:22. The tent of meeting, where Moses had sought revelation from God, had formerly been located outside the camp, but with the tabernacle construction completed, it was placed within the area of the ark of the covenant. Moses could not enter the tent immediately after its construction because of the smoke from the cloud of the Lord that had descended (Ex 40:34-38), but now with the dedication of the tabernacle

The Lighting in the Tabernacle

8 The Lord spoke to Moses: [2]"Speak to Aaron and tell him: When you set up the lamps, the seven lamps are to give light in front of the lampstand." [3]So Aaron did this; he set up its lamps to give light in front of the lampstand just as the Lord had commanded Moses. [4]This is the way the lampstand was made: it was a hammered work of gold, hammered from its base to its flower petals. The lampstand was made according to the pattern the Lord had shown Moses.[a]

Consecration of the Levites

[5]The Lord spoke to Moses: [6]"Take the Levites from among the Israelites and ceremonially cleanse them. [7]This is what you must do to them for their purification: Sprinkle them with the purification water.[b] Have them shave their entire bodies and wash their clothes, and so purify themselves.[c]

[8]"They are to take a young bull and its •grain offering of fine flour mixed with oil, and you are to take a second young bull for a •sin offering. [9]Bring the Levites before the tent of meeting and assemble the entire Israelite community.[d] [10]Then present the Levites before the Lord, and have the Israelites lay their hands on them. [11]Aaron is to present the Levites before the Lord as a presentation offering from the Israelites, so that they may perform the Lord's work.[e] [12]Next the Levites are to lay their hands on the heads of the bulls. Sacrifice one as a sin offering and the other as a •burnt offering to the Lord, to make •atonement for the Levites.[f]

[13]"You are to have the Levites stand before Aaron and his sons, and you are to present them before the Lord as a presentation of-

[a] 8:2-4 Ex 25:31-40
[b] 8:7 Lv 14:51; Nm 19:7,13,17,20; Heb 9:13,23
[c] Lv 8:1-6; 14:8-9; Nm 6:19
[d] 8:9 Ex 29:4; Lv 8:1-6
[e] 8:11 Nm 1:50,53; 3:6-7
[f] 8:12 Lv 1:3-5; 4:3-4
[g] 8:14 Nm 3:12,45; 16:8-9
[h] 8:15 Ex 29:26-27; Lv 8:26-29; Nm 6:20
[i] 8:16 Nm 3:9; 18:6
[j] Ex 13:2,12,15; Nm 3:12,41-45
[k] 8:17 Ex 13:1-2,11-12,15-16
[l] 8:19 Nm 1:51,53; 16:1-3,32-50; 18:1-7
[m] 8:24 Nm 4:3,23,30

fering. [14]In this way you are to separate the Levites from the rest of the Israelites so that the Levites will belong to Me.[g] [15]After that the Levites may come to serve at the tent of meeting, once you have ceremonially cleansed them and presented them as a presentation offering.[h] [16]For they have been exclusively assigned to Me from the Israelites.[i] I have taken them for Myself in place of all who come first from the womb, every Israelite firstborn.[j] [17]For every firstborn among the Israelites is Mine, both man and animal. I consecrated them to Myself[k] on the day I struck down every firstborn in the land of Egypt. [18]But I have taken the Levites in place of every firstborn among the Israelites. [19]From the Israelites, I have given the Levites exclusively to Aaron and his sons to perform the work for the Israelites at the tent of meeting and to make atonement on their behalf, so that no plague will come against the Israelites when they approach the sanctuary."[l]

[20]Moses, Aaron, and the entire Israelite community did this to the Levites. The Israelites did everything to them the Lord commanded Moses regarding the Levites. [21]The Levites purified themselves and washed their clothes; then Aaron presented[A] them before the Lord as a presentation offering. Aaron also made atonement for them to ceremonially cleanse them. [22]After that, the Levites came to do their work at the tent of meeting in the presence of Aaron and his sons. So they did to them as the Lord had commanded Moses concerning the Levites.

[23]The Lord spoke to Moses: [24]"In regard to the Levites: From 25 years old or more, a man enters the service in the work at the tent of meeting.[m] [25]But at 50 years old he is to retire

[A]8:21 Lit waved

implements and sacrifices, he could once more seek counsel from God.

8:1-4 The **lampstand**, or menorah, mentioned in 3:31 and 4:9, was a symbol of God's presence and glory. Instructions for construction of the tabernacle were provided in Ex 25:31-40; 37:17-24. The verses are included here as part of the celebration and dedication of the tabernacle and its implements for worship.

8:5-7 The **purification** process involved three steps: (1) sprinkling the Levites with special **purification water**, probably taken from the bronze basin in the outer court of the tabernacle; (2) shaving their entire **bodies**, as the Nazirite would do if the vow were broken (6:9,18); and (3) washing their **clothes** (19:8; Lv 16:26,28).

8:8-12 Two **bulls** were sacrificed in the ceremony after the Levites had laid their **hands** on the bulls' heads as a symbol of substitutionary identification in the atonement process. The order of **sin offering** and then **burnt offering**

follows the delineation in Leviticus, the first for ceremonial purification and the second for consecration.

8:13-14 The Levites were to **stand** before the Aaronic priests and the congregation of Israelites as an offering for sanctuary service. This **presentation offering** is sometimes called a "wave" or "elevation" offering, but here it functioned as a communion offering of celebration for the dedication of the **Levites** for tabernacle service.

8:15-19 The **Levites** served as assistants to the Aaronic priests, transporting and maintaining sanctuary structures and implements. They also served as guardians against encroachment upon the holiness of the sanctuary. The substitutionary role of the Levites for the firstborn of Israel is reiterated here (3:40-45; Ex 13:11-16), with emphasis on the exodus event as the historical precedent for this legislation.

8:23-26 The addendum to the dedication of the **Levites** cites their retirement age as 50 and their minimum age of service as 25 **years**, whereas 4:3 suggests a minimum age of

from his service in the work and no longer serve. [26]He may assist his brothers to fulfill responsibilities[A] at the tent of meeting,[a] but he must not do the work. This is how you are to deal with the Levites regarding their duties."

The Second Passover

9 In the first month of the second year after their departure from the land of Egypt, the LORD told Moses in the Wilderness of Sinai:[b] [2]"The Israelites are to observe the *Passover at its appointed time.[c] [3]You must observe it at its appointed time on the fourteenth day of this month at twilight; you are to observe it according to all its statutes and ordinances."[d] [4]So Moses told the Israelites to observe the Passover, [5]and they observed it in the first month on the fourteenth day at twilight in the Wilderness of Sinai. The Israelites did everything as the LORD had commanded Moses.

[6]But there were some men who were *unclean because of a human corpse, so they could not observe the Passover on that day.[e] These men came before Moses and Aaron the same day [7]and said to him, "We are unclean because of a human corpse. Why should we be excluded from presenting the LORD's offering at its appointed time with the other Israelites?"

[8]Moses replied to them, "Wait here until I hear what the LORD commands for you."

[9]Then the LORD spoke to Moses: [10]"Tell the Israelites: When any one of you or your descendants is unclean because of a corpse[f] or is on a distant journey, he may still observe the Passover to the LORD. [11]Such people are to observe it in the second month, on the fourteenth day at twilight. They are to eat the animal with unleavened bread and bitter herbs;[g] [12]they may not leave any of it until morning or break any of its bones.[h] They must observe the Passover according to all its statutes.

[13]"But the man who is ceremonially *clean, is not on a journey, and yet fails to observe the Passover is to be cut off from his people, because he did not present the LORD's offering at its appointed time. That man will bear the consequences of his sin.

[14]"If a foreigner resides with you and wants to observe the Passover to the LORD,[i] he is to do so according to the Passover statute and its ordinances. You are to apply the same statute to both the foreign resident and the native of the land."[j]

Guidance by the Cloud

[15]On the day the tabernacle was set up, the cloud covered the tabernacle, the tent of the *testimony,[k] and it appeared like fire above the tabernacle from evening until

Cross references (center column):
[a] 8:26 Nm 3:7-8
[b] 9:1 Ex 19:1-2; Nm 1:1; 3:4,14
[c] 9:2 Ex 13:10; 23:15
[d] 9:3 Ex 12:2-27; Lv 23:4-8; Nm 28:16-25; Dt 16:1-8
[e] 9:6 2Ch 30:3
[f] 9:10 Lv 21:1-3; Nm 5:2; 6:6-12
[g] 9:11 Ex 12:8,15; Dt 16:3-4,8
[h] 9:12 Ex 12:10,46; Ps 34:20; Jn 19:36
[i] 9:14 Ex 12:48
[j] Ex 12:49; Lv 24:22; Nm 15:14-16
[k] 9:15 Ex 40:17, 34; Nm 7:1

[A]8:26 Or *to keep guard*

30. Some scholars attempt to resolve the inconsistency by suggesting that the Levites may have served a five-year apprenticeship beginning at age 25. Others suggest that the age minimum was raised as a result of the deaths of Nadab and Abihu (Lv 10:1-3). During the latter part of David's reign two different censuses were taken of the Levites who were 30 and above and those who were 20 and above (1Ch 23:2-5,24-27). Later, in the days of Hezekiah, another Levitical census was taken for those at least 20 years of age (2Ch 31:17).

9:1 In the first month of the second year after the exodus, the Israelites celebrated their second Passover at Mount Sinai, just two days after the receiving of the tribal offerings (7:12-88), and two weeks before the first military census (1:2-44).

9:2-4 The Israelites were instructed to **observe the Passover at its appointed time** as outlined in Ex 12:12-40. The original Passover lasted only one evening as the Israelites departed from Egypt in haste, but later guidelines dictated that this celebration last for one week, beginning on 14 Abib (later called Nisan). Participants were required to be in a state of ceremonial purity in order to join in the celebration.

9:5-7 Biblical case law arose out of circumstances experienced by the community of faith. Questions of obedience to the commands of God were posed to the leading interpreter of the law, such as the high priest, another priest, or a Levite, who would then seek God's will in the matter.

9:8-13 The legislation of verses 10-13 probably served as the historical precedent for the second month **Passover** in the late eighth century B.C., during the reign of King Hezekiah (2Ch 30:1-27), after the king had led the people to destroy pagan worship centers in and around Jerusalem. That celebration lasted the full week in accordance with the normal Passover, or unleavened bread sequence (Ex 12:14-20; 23:15), although chapter 9 does not contain stipulations for the week-long celebration of the Festival of **Unleavened Bread** in the **second month**. That legislation probably arose in the planning of the great celebration of King Hezekiah's era.

9:14 Israelite law gave considerable attention to the status of resident aliens who identified with the Israelite religion. The same law applied to the native Israelite and to the **foreigner**. Note the cases in 15:14-16 and Ex 12:49. Second Chronicles 30:25 also notes that sojourners came to celebrate Passover in the days of King Hezekiah from all the former tribal territories of Israel as well as Judah. This would have included many people who had been deported by the Assyrians from Babylon, Cuthah, and other countries (2Kg 17:24). Anyone who wanted to identify with the Israelite community of faith and who was willing to submit to the Lord's laws and statues was permitted to do so.

9:15 The chronological sequence returns to that of 7:1 and Ex 40:17, the day when the tabernacle construction was completed—on the first day of the first month of year two. See note at Nm 7:1.

morning. ¹⁶It remained that way continuously: the cloud would cover it,ᴬ appearing like fire at night.ᵃ ¹⁷Whenever the cloud was lifted up above the tent, the Israelites would set out; at the place where the cloud stopped, there the Israelites camped.ᵇ ¹⁸At the LORD's command the Israelites set out, and at the LORD's command they camped. As long as the cloud stayed over the tabernacle, they camped.

¹⁹Even when the cloud stayed over the tabernacle many days, the Israelites carried out the LORD's requirement and did not set out. ²⁰Sometimes the cloud remained over the tabernacle for only a few days. They would camp at the LORD's command and set out at the LORD's command. ²¹Sometimes the cloud remained only from evening until morning; when the cloud lifted in the morning, they set out. Or if it remained a day and a night, they moved out when the cloud lifted. ²²Whether it was two days, a month, or longer,ᴮ the Israelites camped and did not set out as long as the cloud stayed over the tabernacle. But when it was lifted, they set out. ²³They camped at the LORD's command, and they set out at the LORD's command. They carried out the LORD's requirement according to His command through Moses.

Two Silver Trumpets

10 The LORD spoke to Moses: ²"Make two trumpets of hammered silver to summon the communityᶜ and have the camps set

out. ³When both are sounded in long blasts, the entire community is to gather before you at the entrance to the tent of meeting. ⁴However, if one is sounded, only the leaders, the heads of Israel's clans,ᵈ are to gather before you.

⁵"When you sound short blasts, the camps pitched on the eastᵉ are to set out. ⁶When you sound short blasts a second time, the camps pitched on the southᶠ are to set out. Short blasts are to be sounded for them to set out. ⁷When calling the assembly together, you are to sound long blasts, not short ones. ⁸The sons of Aaron, the priests, are to sound the trumpets. Your use of these is a permanent statute throughout your generations.

⁹"When you enter into battle in your land against an adversary who is attacking you, sound short blasts on the trumpets, and you will be remembered before the LORD your God and be delivered from your enemies.ᵍ ¹⁰You are to sound the trumpets over your •burnt offerings and your •fellowship sacrifices and on your joyous occasions, your appointed festivals, and the beginning of each of your months. They will serve as a reminder for you before your God: I am •Yahweh your God."ʰ

From Sinai to Paran

¹¹During the second year, in the second month on the twentieth day of the month, the cloud was lifted up above the tabernacle of the •testimony. ¹²The Israelites traveled on

a 9:16 Ex 13:21-22; 40:38
b 9:17 Ex 40:36-38; Nm 10:11,33-34
c 10:2 Jl 2:15-16
d 10:4 Nm 1:5-16
e 10:5 Nm 2:3-9; 10:14-16
f 10:6 Nm 2:10-16; 10:18-20
g 10:9 Dt 20:4; 2Ch 13:12; Ps 18:3
h 10:10 Ex 6:7; Lv 18:2,4,30; 19:2-4

ᴬ9:16 LXX, Vg, Syr, Tg read *it by day*   ᴮ9:22 Or *a year*

9:17-23 The poetic structure of verse 17 hints that this section was originally a song that was sung during the wilderness journey. The song's refrain occurs in verse 18, perhaps to be translated,

At the word of the LORD they set out,
    the children of Israel,
and at the word of the LORD they **camped**;
    all the days that it dwelt,
the cloud upon the **tabernacle**, they camped.

This "Song of the Journey" set the stage for the actual departure from Mount Sinai in 10:11-36. The same sequence of marching and camping recurs in chapter 33. The NT also depicts God's presence in the imagery of the cloud, as in the transfiguration of Jesus (Mk 9:7; Lk 9:34) and at His ascension (Ac 1:9).

9:19-22 The periodic movement of God's presence from one campsite to the next varied from a day to several months— perhaps a year or more at Kadesh-barnea after the people refused to enter the promised land (13:25–14:38).

10:2 The **two trumpets of hammered silver** were different from the ram's horn (Hb *shofar*). The shofar announced the Day of Atonement (Lv 25:9), and it was used in the march around Jericho at the beginning of the conquest of the promised land (Jos 6:2-21). The distinctive pitch of the silver trumpets summoned the people to march through the

wilderness. It was also blown by the priest Phinehas in the battle against Midian (Nm 31:6).

10:5-6 After the Lord moved His presence in the cloud, the priests would sound the trumpets in sequence and at varying duration, and possibly differing pitch, to signal the people of Israel to follow the Lord's leading.

10:11-13 The twentieth of the month was less than a week after the unclean persons were able to celebrate Passover on the fourteenth of the **second month** (cp. 9:8-13). This was also about a month after the week-long Passover described in 9:1-14 (cp. Ex 13:6). After spending 11 months in the Sinai Wilderness, the Lord would now begin to lead the people to His intended destination—the promised land. Again the Israelites are described as faithfully following the Lord's command through Moses, in the language of the "Song of the Journey" (Nm 9:17-23).

10:12 The geographical parameters of this initial movement are the Sinai and Paran deserts. The Israelites camped at Taberah (11:3), Kibroth-hattavah (11:34-35), and Hazeroth (12:16) on their way to the **Wilderness of Paran**. Paran was west of Midian, east of Egypt, extending northward from some point north or northeast of Mount Sinai, northward toward Kadesh-barnea, and eastward to the Arabah. The text shifts from the Paran Wilderness region (13:26) to a more specific context, in a literary style similar to the listing of the itinerary of the spies (13:21) and later the rebellion

from the Wilderness of Sinai, moving from one place to the next[a] until the cloud stopped in the Wilderness of Paran.[b] [13]They set out for the first time according to the LORD's command through Moses.[c]

[14]The military divisions of the camp of Judah with their banner set out first, and Nahshon son of Amminadab[d] was over Judah's divisions. [15]Nethanel son of Zuar[e] was over the division of the Issachar tribe, [16]and Eliab son of Helon was over the division of the Zebulun tribe. [17]The tabernacle was then taken down, and the Gershonites and the Merarites set out, transporting the tabernacle.

[18]The military divisions of the camp of Reuben with their banner set out, and Elizur son of Shedeur was over Reuben's division. [19]Shelumiel son of Zurishaddai[f] was over the division of Simeon's tribe, [20]and Eliasaph son of Deuel was over the division of the tribe of Gad. [21]The Kohathites then set out, transporting the holy objects;[g] the tabernacle was to be set up before their arrival.

[22]Next the military divisions of the camp of Ephraim with their banner set out, and Elishama son of Ammihud[h] was over Ephraim's division. [23]Gamaliel son of Pedahzur was over the division of the tribe of Manasseh, [24]and Abidan son of Gideoni was over the division of the tribe of Benjamin.

[25]The military divisions of the camp of Dan with their banner set out, serving as rear guard for all the camps, and Ahiezer son of Ammishaddai[i] was over Dan's division. [26]Pagiel son of Ochran was over the division of the tribe of

Asher, [27]and Ahira son of Enan was over the division of the tribe of Naphtali. [28]This was the order of march for the Israelites by their military divisions as they set out.

[29]Moses said to Hobab, son of Moses' father-in-law[A] Reuel[Bj] the Midianite: "We're setting out for the place the LORD promised: 'I will give it to you.'[k] Come with us, and we will treat you well, for the LORD has promised good things to Israel."[l]

[30]But he replied to him, "I don't want to go. Instead, I will go to my own land and my relatives."

[31]"Please don't leave us," Moses said, "since you know where we should camp in the wilderness, and you can serve as our eyes. [32]If you come with us, whatever good the LORD does for us we will do for you."[m]

[33]They set out from the mountain of the LORD on a three-day journey with the ark of the LORD's covenant traveling ahead of them for those three days to seek a resting place for them.[n] [34]Meanwhile, the cloud of the LORD was over them by day when they set out from the camp.

[35]Whenever the ark set out, Moses would say:

Arise, LORD!
Let Your enemies be scattered,
and those who hate You flee
    from Your presence.[o]

[36]When it came to rest, he would say:

Return, LORD,
to the countless thousands of Israel.[p]

Cross references

[a]10:12 Ex 17:1; 19:1; Nm 1:1
[b]Gn 21:21; Nm 12:16; 13:3,26; 1Sm 25:1
[c]10:13 Nm 9:18-23
[d]10:14 Nm 1:7; 2:3; 7:12; 1Ch 2:10
[e]10:15 Nm 1:8; 2:5; 7:18
[f]10:19 Nm 1:6; 2:12; 7:36
[g]10:21 Nm 3:27-31; 4:2-4,15,18-20
[h]10:22 Nm 1:10; 2:18; 7:48
[i]10:25 Nm 1:12; 2:25; 7:66
[j]10:29 Ex 2:16-18; 3:1; 4:18; Jdg 4:11
[k]Gn 12:7; 13:14-17; 15:7; Ac 7:5
[l]Ex 18:9
[m]10:32 Jdg 1:16; 4:11
[n]10:33 Dt 1:33
[o]10:35 Ps 68:1
[p]10:36 Gn 15:5; Dt 1:8,10

[A]10:29 Or said to Hobab's brother-in-law   [B]10:29 = Jethro; Ex 2:16-18; 3:1; 4:18

---

of Moses (20:1-13; 27:14). Paran's relationship to Midian is confirmed later in history when the Edomite king Hadad fled from Solomon to Egypt through Midian and Paran (1Kg 11:18).

10:14-28 The orderly departure from Mount Sinai of the priests, Levites, and 12 tribes follows the pattern of the encampment detailed in 2:1-3:38, with **Judah** led by **Nahshon** setting out first (v. 14). The tribal leaders who assisted Moses and Aaron in taking the military census (1:5-15) are those who led their respective groups at the beginning of the victory march to the promised land. Order, harmony, and faithfulness marked the beginning of the wilderness journey.

10:29-32 Moses noted twice that **the LORD has promised good things to Israel**, and twice Moses promised Hobab that the goodness would be apportioned to him as well if he would help guide them through the wilderness. Who was this Hobab son of Reuel? The dual names Reuel (Ex 2:18) and Jethro (Ex 3:1) in reference to Moses' in-laws are perhaps references to two generation of this Midianite clan, since the Hebrew term can mean "father-in-law," "brother-in-law," or just "in-law." Thus the patriarchal clan leader was probably named "Reuel" (taking "father" as "grandfa-

ther" which is common in the Hebrew Bible) and the actual father-in-law of Moses was named Jethro. Others suggest Jethro and Reuel are the same person, since dual names are commonly reflected in Bronze Age texts. The blessing of God was fulfilled for Hobab and his Kenite clan in Jdg 1:16.

Did Moses show a lack of faith by asking his brother-in-law to serve as a guide in the wilderness? The text does not even hint at this suggestion, since the focus is on the involvement of Hobab as a potential recipient of the covenant blessings of Israel. Instead, the idea of shared leadership is emphasized in which Moses was the interpreter of God's direction as revealed through the cloud in the wilderness. Hobab would provide valuable support in the desert setting known by the Midianites.

10:33-36 The "Battle Song of the Ark" (vv. 35-36) is preceded by a dual chronological marker about the first stage in the movement of the Lord's cloud. A **three-day journey** would mean a distance of about 35 to 45 miles, based on travel rates mentioned in military annals of the pharaohs of Egypt. On the journey the **cloud**, symbolizing God's presence and leadership (9:15-23), preceded them at a distance though still covering them for protection. **The ark of the LORD's covenant**, the symbolic throne of God in king-to-servant rela-

Complaints about Hardship

11 Now the people began complaining openly before[A] the LORD about hardship. When the LORD heard, His anger burned,[a] and fire[b] from the LORD blazed among them and consumed the outskirts of the camp. Then the people cried out to Moses, and he prayed to the LORD, and the fire died down. So that place was named Taberah,[B,c] because the LORD's fire had blazed among them.

Complaints about Food

Contemptible people[c] among them[d] had a strong craving[e] for other food. The Israelites cried again and said, "Who will feed us meat? We remember the free fish we ate in Egypt,[f] along with the cucumbers, melons, leeks, onions, and garlic. But now our appetite is gone;[D] there's nothing to look at but this manna!"

The manna[g] resembled coriander seed, and its appearance was like that of bdellium.[E] The people walked around and gathered it. They ground it on a pair of grinding stones or crushed it in a mortar, then boiled it in a cooking pot and shaped it into cakes. It tasted like a pastry cooked with the finest oil. When the dew fell on the camp at night, the manna would fall with it.[h]

Moses heard the people, family after family, crying at the entrance of their tents. The LORD was very angry;[i] Moses was also provoked.[F] So Moses asked the LORD, "Why have You brought such trouble on Your servant? Why are You angry with me, and why do You burden me with all these people?[j] Did I conceive all these people? Did I give them birth so You should tell me, 'Carry them at your breast, as a nursing woman carries a baby,'[k] to the land that You[G] swore to give their fathers?[l] Where can I get meat to give all these people? For they are crying to me: 'Give us meat to eat!' I can't carry all these people by myself. They are too much for me. If You are going to treat me like this, please kill me right now.[m] If You are pleased with me,[n] don't let me see my misery[H] anymore."

a 11:1 Ex 22:24; 32:10-11; Nm 11:1,33; 32:13; Dt 6:15
b 1Kg 18:38; 19:12; Is 66:16
c 11:3 Dt 9:22
d 11:4 Ex 12:38
e Nm 11:34; Ps 78:29-31; 106:14-15; 1Co 10:5-6
f 11:5 Ex 16:3
g 11:7 Ex 16:4-35; Dt 8:3,16; Jos 5:12; Neh 9:20; Ps 78:24; Jn 6:48-51; Rv 2:17
h 11:9 Ex 16:13-14
i 11:10 Ex 22:24; 32:10-11; Nm 11:1,33; 32:13; Dt 6:15
j 11:11 Ex 5:22; Dt 1:9-13
k 11:12 Is 40:11; 66:11-12
l Gn 12:7; 26:3-4; Nm 14:16,23; Dt 6:10,23
m 11:15 Ex 32:32; Jb 6:9; 7:15-16
n Gn 6:8; Ex 33:12-17; Ru 2:2,10,13

A 11:1 Lit in the ears of   B 11:3 = blaze   C 11:4 Or The mixed multitude; Hb obscure   D 11:6 Or our lives are wasting away, or our throat is dry   E 11:7 A yellowish, transparent gum resin   F 11:10 Lit and it was evil in the eyes of Moses   G 11:12 One Hb ms, Sam, LXX, Syr, Tg read I   H 11:15 Ancient Jewish tradition reads Your misery

tionship with Israel, led the way for the people. The three-day journey is reminiscent of Moses' request to Pharaoh to allow the Israelites to journey three days into the wilderness to worship the Lord.

11:1-3 These verses establish the complaint pattern of later narratives (chaps. 11–25): (1) complaint, (2) divine punishment, and (3) naming the place after some aspect of the event. Hence, the "fiery" judgment of God led to the place being named Taberah, or "blaze."

11:1 The **complaining** Israelites and others were literally grumbling evil (Hb ra') in the ears of God. In his dialogue with Hobab, Moses had spoken three times about the promise of God's goodness (Hb tov, yatav), but the people began a continuous protest against God. Good and evil are

charah

Hebrew Pronunciation	khah RAH
HCSB Translation	burn, be angry
Uses in Numbers	11
Uses in the OT	93
Focus Passage	Numbers 11:1,10,33

Charah has 'ap ("anger, nose") as subject 55 times so that anger burns (Jb 19:11), and people become incensed (Nm 22:22), enraged (Ex 32:19), or infuriated (2Sm 12:5). God's anger burns and He sends literal fire (Nm 11:1). Charah alone denotes be angry or incensed (Gn 18:30; 31:36). This anger can be against someone (1Ch 13:10). Charah connotes burning with anxiety, being agitated (Ps 37:1) or worrying (Pr 24:19). People burn with zeal when competing or excelling (Jr 12:5; 22:15). Once charah appears as diligently to modify another verb (Neh 3:20). Charah in Scripture most often refers to God who is angry at human sins. Charon (41x) occurs 34 times with 'ap as burning anger (Nm 25:4). Charon suggests wrath (Ezk 7:12), burning (Ps 58:9), anger, fury, and burning wrath. Choriy (6x) with 'ap suggests outburst of (fierce, burning) anger (Dt 29:24; Is 7:4; Lm 2:3).

purposefully contrasted in these two chapters to begin the cycles of rebellion that dominate chapters 11–25. This form of judgment parallels what was meted out against Nadab and Abihu (Lv 10:1-3), though that fire came from the midst of the tabernacle.

11:4 Contemptible people were a mixed crowd of Israelites who were descendants of Jacob and others who had left Egypt in the exodus. The text contrasts with two parallel events in Ex 16:1-36 and 18:13-27, drawing new perspectives on the themes of God's provision for the people and the matter of leadership on the human level. The human response factor has deteriorated in the current context. In Exodus 16 God supplied needed food, but in Numbers 11 the people complained about God's provision.

11:5 The people's complaint is summarized in the words, **We remember the free fish we ate in Egypt**. This amounted to calling the evil of the Egyptian oppression "good" and God's good provision in the wilderness "evil." Insatiable human lust, whatever the object of desire, will lead to a life of bondage.

11:7 The phrase **the manna resembled coriander seed** is one of the few descriptions of the wilderness diet. This description was inserted to refute the people's complaints. Precise identification of manna is somewhat tentative. But manna's association with coriander seed is probably an indicator of its taste, since the seed was used for flavoring. The comparison of manna to **bdellium** indicates a yellow-white aromatic resin similar to a by-product of the tamarisk tree found in northern Arabia.

11:10-15 The effect of the discontentment throughout the camp drew the attention of Moses and God. Though he was angry with the people, Moses approached God with respect, asserting that he could not carry **all these people by myself**. Moses also declared, **If You are going to treat me like this, please kill me right now**. The words of his

Seventy Elders Anointed

[16] The LORD answered Moses, "Bring Me 70 men from Israel known to you as elders and officers of the people. Take them to the tent of meeting and have them stand there with you. [17] Then I will come down and speak with you there. I will take some of the Spirit who is on you and put the Spirit on them.[a] They will help you bear the burden of the people, so that you do not have to bear it by yourself.[b]

[18] "Tell the people: Purify yourselves in readiness for tomorrow, and you will eat meat because you cried before the LORD: 'Who will feed us meat? We really had it good in Egypt.' The LORD will give you meat and you will eat. [19] You will eat, not for one day, or two days, or five days, or 10 days, or 20 days, [20] but for a whole month—until it comes out of your nostrils and becomes nauseating to you—because you have rejected the LORD who is among you, and cried to Him: 'Why did we ever leave Egypt?'"[c]

[21] But Moses replied, "I'm in the middle of a people with 600,000 foot soldiers,[d] yet You say, 'I will give them meat, and they will eat for a month.' [22] If flocks and herds were slaughtered for them, would they have enough? Or if all the fish in the sea were caught for them, would they have enough?"[e]

[23] The LORD answered Moses, "Is the LORD's power limited?[A,f] You will see whether or not what I have promised will happen to you."

[24] Moses went out and told the people the words of the LORD. He brought 70 men from the elders of the people and had them stand around the tent. [25] Then the LORD descended in the cloud and spoke to him.[g] He took some of the Spirit that was on Moses and placed the Spirit on the 70 elders. As the Spirit rested on them, they prophesied,[h] but they never did it again. [26] Two men had remained in the camp, one named Eldad and the other Medad; the Spirit rested on them—they were among those listed, but had not gone out to the tent—and they prophesied in the camp. [27] A young man ran and reported to Moses, "Eldad and Medad are prophesying in the camp."

[28] Joshua son of Nun, assistant to Moses since his youth,[B] responded, "Moses, my lord, stop them!"

[29] But Moses asked him, "Are you jealous on my account?[i] If only all the LORD's people were prophets and the LORD would place His Spirit on them!" [30] Then Moses returned to the camp along with the elders of Israel.

Quail in the Camp

[31] A wind sent by the LORD[j] came up and blew quail in from the sea; it dropped them at the camp all around, three feet[C] off[D] the ground, about a day's journey in every direction.[k] [32] The

---

Cross-references

[a] 11:17 2Kg 2:9,15
[b] Ex 18:18; Dt 1:9-13; Ac 6:1-6
[c] 11:20 Ex 17:3
[d] 11:21 Ex 12:37; Nm 1:45-46; 2:32; 26:51
[e] 11:22 Mt 15:33; Mk 6:37; 8:4
[f] 11:23 Jb 38:1-42:6; Is 50:2; 59:1
[g] 11:25 Ex 19:9; 33:9-10; Nm 12:5-8
[h] 1Sm 10:6-10; 19:20-24; Is 63:11; Jl 2:28
[i] 11:29 Nm 12:2; 16:3
[j] 11:31 Ex 14:21
[k] Ex 16:12-13; Ps 78:26-28

A 11:23 Lit LORD's arm too short   B 11:28 LXX, some Sam mss read Moses, from his chosen ones   C 11:31 Lit two cubits   D 11:31 Or on, or above

---

misery-filled complaint bordered on rebellion, as this section prepares the reader for the rebellion of Moses and Aaron in chapter 20. Moses is the focal person in the first cycle of rebellion (chaps. 11–15); Aaron is the main leader in the second cycle; and in the third cycle, both men rebel, leaving God to raise up a new temporary spokesman, Balaam.

11:16 The term for "officers" (Hb shoterim) also denotes scribes, whom R. K. Harrison has suggested were responsible for the writing and collecting of documents that would eventually become the Pentateuch. The **tent of meeting** was the place of revelation and mediation, two aspects of the relationship between God and His people.

11:17 The possession of the **Spirit** of God that had been exclusively on Moses would now be distributed to the 70 elders, giving them a spiritual dimension that would set them apart from the administrative and judicial appointees of Ex 18:25-26. The work of the Spirit of God would enable the elders and officers to carry out the tasks of teaching, judging, and leading the Israelites through the wilderness. God ratified the 70 registered elders by placing His Spirit on them, even two who had remained in the camp. Later in Numbers, Balaam also received the Spirit of prophecy from God (24:2).

11:18 **Purify yourselves** refers to the process of consecration through the bathing of body and clothes that was used to prepare people to receive a theophany—a manifestation of God's presence.

11:19-20 God declared to the Israelites that they would **eat . . . for a whole month**. The supply of quail in Ex 16:13 was in response to a need for food in the first wilderness journey before reaching Mount Sinai. This request arose out of rebellious discontentment with the continuous provision of manna that God had made.

11:25 That God **took some of the Spirit that was on Moses** and placed it on the Israelite elders did not diminish the Spirit that was on Moses. This miracle provided the necessary power and wisdom to those who functioned on behalf of God and under the direction of Moses.

11:26 Two elders, **Eldad** and **Medad**, who had not attended the presentation ceremony, prophesied in the same manner as the other elders, demonstrating that God's Spirit cannot be confined to any space or time.

11:31-32 In a manner similar to the **wind** that blew back the waters of the Red Sea in the exodus event, a divinely driven wind brought a large quantity of **quail** across the camp. Arabs in the early twentieth century are known to have captured between one and two million quail during the autumn bird migration. The extraordinary quantity of quail was swept in from the sea, probably from the Gulf of Aqaba (Elath) if the wind were from the east, and then downward toward the encampment of Israel.

11:33 The **severe plague** sent upon the people might have been food poisoning due to the time the quail meat remained in the sun without proper processing and drying.

people were up all that day and night and all the next day gathering the quail—the one who took the least gathered 50 bushels[A]—and they spread them out all around the camp.[B,a]

[33] While the meat was still between their teeth, before it was chewed, the LORD's anger burned[b] against the people, and the LORD struck them with a very severe plague.[c] [34] So they named that place Kibroth-hattaavah,[C] because there they buried the people who had craved the meat.

[35] From Kibroth-hattaavah the people moved on to Hazeroth[D,d] and remained there.

Miriam and Aaron Rebel

[12] Miriam[e] and Aaron criticized Moses because of the *Cushite[E,F] woman he married (for he had married a Cushite woman). [2] They said, "Does the LORD speak only through Moses? Does He not also speak through us?" And the LORD heard it. [3] Moses was a very humble man, more so than any man on the face of the earth.

[4] Suddenly the LORD said to Moses, Aaron, and Miriam, "You three come out to the tent of meeting." So the three of them went out. [5] Then the LORD descended in a pillar of cloud,[f] stood at the entrance to the tent, and summoned Aaron and Miriam. When the two of them came forward, [6] He said:

"Listen to what I say:
If there is a prophet among you
from the LORD,

I make Myself known to him
in a vision;[g]
I speak with him in a dream.
[7] Not so with My servant Moses;
he is faithful in[G] all My household.[h]
[8] I speak with him[i] directly,[H]
openly, and not in riddles;
he sees the form of the LORD.[j]

So why were you not afraid to speak against My servant Moses?" [9] The LORD's anger burned against them,[k] and He left.

[10] As the cloud moved away from the tent, Miriam's skin suddenly became diseased, as white as snow. When Aaron turned toward her, he saw that she was diseased [11] and said to Moses, "My lord, please don't hold against us this sin we have so foolishly committed. [12] Please don't let her be like a dead baby[l] whose flesh is half eaten away when he comes out of his mother's womb."

[13] Then Moses cried out to the LORD, "God, please heal her!"[l]

[14] The LORD answered Moses, "If her father had merely spit in her face, wouldn't she remain in disgrace for seven days? Let her be confined outside the camp[m] for seven days;[n] after that she may be brought back in." [15] So Miriam was confined outside the camp for seven days, and the people did not move on until Miriam was brought back in.[o] [16] After that, the people set out from Hazeroth and camped in the Wilderness of Paran.

Cross references:
a 11:32 2Sm 17:19; Ezk 26:5,14
b 11:33 Ex 22:24; 32:10-11; Nm 11:1,10; 32:13; Dt 6:15
c Ps 78:29-31; 106:14-15
d 11:35 Nm 12:16; 33:16-17
e 12:1 Ex 15:20-21; Nm 20:1; 26:59; Dt 24:9
f 12:5 Dt 31:15
g 12:6 1Sm 3:15; Ezk 1:1; Dn 10:7-8,16; Rv 1:10-12
h 12:7 Heb 3:2,5
i 12:8 Ex 33:11; Nm 7:89; Jdg 6:22
j 1Co 13:12
k 12:9 Ex 22:24; 32:10-11; Nm 11:1,10,33; 32:13; Dt 6:15
l 12:13 Gn 20:17; Ex 15:26; Lv 14:3; Dt 32:39
m 12:14 Lv 13:46; Nm 5:1-4; 2Kg 15:5
n Lv 13:4
o 12:15 Lv 14:2,8

A 11:32 Lit 10 homers   B 11:32 To dry or cure the meat; 2Sm 17:19; Ezk 26:5,14   C 11:34 = Graves of Craving   D 11:35 = settlements; Nm 12:16; 33:16-17   E 12:1 LXX reads Ethiopian   F 12:1 = Sudan and Ethiopia   G 12:7 Or is entrusted with   H 12:8 Lit mouth to mouth   I 12:12 Ancient Jewish tradition reads baby who comes out of our mother's womb and our flesh is half eaten away.

Even if there are natural explanations, the ultimate cause was **the LORD's anger**.

11:34 The blessing turned to craving, and the craving to disease and death, leading to the naming of the location **Kibroth-hattaavah** ("Graves of Craving").

12:1 The supposed reason for the complaint of **Miriam and Aaron** against Moses was his marriage to a **Cushite woman**, though the real reason was Moses' authority as God's primary spokesman. Explanations for the Cushite identity include: (1) she was Moses' second wife of Cushite origin (Nubian = modern Ethiopian or Sudanese), whom Moses perhaps had married while Zipporah was back in Midian visiting her father Jethro; (2) perhaps Zipporah (a Midianite) had died and Moses had recently remarried; and (3) Zipporah and the Cushite woman are one and the same.

12:2 The terminology and the context suggest that Aaron and Miriam were challenging Moses' prophetic position as the primary recipient of revelation from God. The ethnic issue was a smokescreen for the real challenge—Moses' divinely appointed position of leadership. Miriam and Aaron are both spoken of in a prophetic sense in the OT (Ex 4:14-15; 15:20-21; Mc 6:4).

12:4-5 the **pillar of cloud** descended to provide the personal encounter for divine disclosure.

12:7 Being called **My servant** by the Lord and a **faithful** prophet placed Moses in the category of Abraham (Gn 26:24) and the "servant" in the Servant Songs of Isaiah (Is 42–53).

12:8 God declared of Moses, **I speak with him directly, openly.** Some translations have "face to face" (Hb _peh 'el peh_), but Moses could not look upon God's face (Ex 33:11,20-23). Only Jesus Christ could truly look upon the face of the Father (Jn 6:44-51). The expression denotes the direct method by which the will of God was communicated through the words of Moses, which could legitimately be translated "mouth to mouth," since out of the mouth of a person echoes his character (Mt 12:34).

12:9-13 The description of Miriam's disease as **white as snow** like a stillborn **baby** suggests a variety of ailments ranging from skin cancer to psoriasis, or perhaps even modern leprosy, Hansen's disease. All of these would render her unclean according to Levitical law (Lv 13–14). Both Aaron and Moses expressed their love and concern for their sister in their desperate pleas on her behalf.

12:14-15 The **seven days** of separation after healing follows the Levitical law consistently, and the purification process described in Lv 14:1-32 is assumed here.

12:16 The location of **Hazeroth** in the **Wilderness of Paran** is viewed in the context of the summary statement in

Scouting Out Canaan

13 The LORD spoke to Moses: [2] "Send men to scout out the land of Canaan[a] I am giving to the Israelites. Send one man who is a leader among them from each of their ancestral tribes." [3] Moses sent them from the Wilderness of Paran at the LORD's command. All the men were leaders in Israel.[b] [4] These were their names:

Shammua son of Zaccur from the tribe of Reuben;

[5] Shaphat son of Hori from the tribe of Simeon;

[6] Caleb[c] son of Jephunneh from the tribe of Judah;

[7] Igal son of Joseph from the tribe of Issachar;

[8] Hoshea son of Nun[d] from the tribe of Ephraim;

[9] Palti son of Raphu from the tribe of Benjamin;

[10] Gaddiel son of Sodi from the tribe of Zebulun;

[11] Gaddi son of Susi from the tribe of Manasseh (from the tribe of Joseph);

[12] Ammiel son of Gemalli from the tribe of Dan;

[13] Sethur son of Michael from the tribe of Asher;

[14] Nahbi son of Vophsi from the tribe of Naphtali;

[15] Geuel son of Machi from the tribe of Gad.

[16] These were the names of the men Moses sent to scout out the land, and Moses renamed Hoshea son of Nun, Joshua.

[17] When Moses sent them to scout out the land of Canaan, he told them, "Go up this way to the *Negev, then go up into the hill country. [18] See what the land is like, and whether the people who live there are strong or weak, few or many. [19] Is the land they live in good[e] or bad? Are the cities they live in encampments or fortifications?[f] [20] Is the land fertile or unproductive?[g] Are there trees in it or not? Be coura-

Cross references
a13:2 Dt 1:22-26
b13:3 Ex 18:25-26; Dt 1:13-18
c13:6 Nm 14:6,24,30,38; 26:65
d13:8 Ex 33:11; Nm 14:30,38; 27:18-23
e13:19 Nm 14:7; Dt 1:25
f Dt 1:28; 3:5; 9:1; Jos 14:12
g13:20 Neh 9:25,35; Is 30:23; Ezk 34:14,20

10:12—that the people journeyed from Sinai to the Paran Wilderness in the first phase of the journey to the promised land. The Paran Wilderness is a broad area of northeastern Sinai, bordered on the northeast by the Zin Wilderness within which Kadesh-barnea is located (cp. 33:15-37).

13:1–14:45 The climax to the first cycle of rebellions is the refusal of the people to enter the promised land. The people adopted the majority report of 10 of 12 spies—that the inhabitants of the land and their fortified cities were too

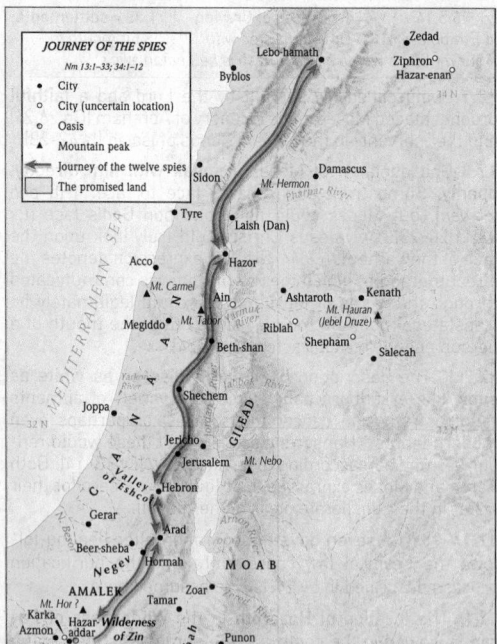

JOURNEY OF THE SPIES
Nm 13:1–33; 34:1–12
- • City
- ○ City (uncertain location)
- ○ Oasis
- ▲ Mountain peak
- ← Journey of the twelve spies
- ☐ The promised land

strong for them to conquer. The rejection of the land was a rejection of God and His blessings.

13:1 The book of Numbers says **the LORD** instructed Moses to send out the spies, but Dt 1:22-23 suggests that Moses sent the scouts at the request of the people. As with many OT historical events, the human and the divine involvements go hand in hand.

13:2 The mission of these spies was to **scout out the land**. The list of scouts from the 12 tribes (vv. 4-15) introduces a different, presumably younger, group from the elder patriarchal leaders who had led in taking the military census in chapter 1.

13:3 The geographical designations in the chapter move from the broader context of the **Wilderness of Paran** to the more specific citation of Kadesh (-barnea) in the Zin Wilderness (33:36-37), the starting point of their exploration (v. 21). The Zin Wilderness is defined by the desert drainage basin of the Nahal Zin, a subsection of the Paran Wilderness. The Nahal Zin today is viewed as portions of Sinai and the Negev in modern Israel.

13:4-14 The list of these scouts contains a number of unusual names, rarely appearing again in the OT, with the exception of Joshua and Caleb. This gives an indication of the early date of the composition of Numbers, contrary to critics who propose that it was written in the postexilic period, 539–332 B.C.

13:17-20 Moses' question **Is the land . . . good or bad?** builds upon the good-versus-evil theme presented in 10:29-33 and 11:1. The parenthetic note about the season of the **first ripe grapes** places the exploration of Canaan in August or early September, several months after the departure from Mount Sinai in early spring.

13:17 The **Negev** in the OT refers to the region south of Hebron, but north of the Zin Wilderness. In modern Israel "Negev" refers to the region from the Beer-sheba-Arad line southward to Eilat on the Gulf of Aqaba.

geous. Bring back some fruit from the land." It was the season for the first ripe grapes.*

²¹ So they went up and scouted out the land from the Wilderness of Zin^A as far as Rehob^B near the entrance to Hamath.^C ²² They went up through the Negev and came to Hebron, where Ahiman, Sheshai, and Talmai, the descendants of Anak,^b were living. Hebron was built seven years before Zoan^c in Egypt. ²³ When they came to the Valley of Eshcol,^d they cut down a branch with a single cluster of grapes, which was carried on a pole by two men. They also took some pomegranates and figs.^e ²⁴ That place was called the Valley of Eshcol^D because of the cluster of grapes the Israelites cut there. ²⁵ At the end of 40 days^f they returned from scouting out the land.

*13:20 Nm 13:23
*13:22 Nm 13:28,33; Dt 1:28; 2:10-11,21
*Ps 78:12; Is 19:11; 30:4; Ezk 30:14
*13:23 Nm 32:9; Dt 1:24
*Nm 20:5; Dt 8:8
*13:25 Nm 14:33-34; 32:13; Ps 95:10
*13:26 Nm 32:9; Dt 1:24-25
*13:27 Ex 3:8; Lv 20:24; Nm 14:8; 16:13-14
*13:28 Dt 1:28; 3:5; 9:1; Jos 14:12
*Nm 13:22,33; Dt 1:28; 2:10-11,21
*13:29 Ex 17:8-16; Nm 14:25,43,45; Dt 25:17-19

Report about Canaan

²⁶ The men went back to Moses, Aaron, and the entire Israelite community in the Wilderness of Paran at Kadesh. They brought back a report for them and the whole community, and they showed them the fruit of the land.^g ²⁷ They reported to Moses: "We went into the land where you sent us. Indeed it is flowing with milk and honey,^h and here is some of its fruit. ²⁸ However, the people living in the land are strong, and the cities are large and fortified.^i We also saw the descendants of Anak^j there. ²⁹ The Amalekites^k are living in the land of the Negev; the Hittites, Jebusites, and Amorites live in the hill country; and the Canaanites live by the sea and along the Jordan."

^A13:21 Southern border of the promised land   ^B13:21 Northern border of the promised land   ^C13:21 Or *near Lebo-hamath*
^D13:24 = cluster

13:21 The scouts explored the land from the **Wilderness of Zin as far as Rehob near the entrance to Hamath**. Parallel to the later description of the land as extending from Dan (in the north) to Beersheba (in the south), these parameters reverse the order and extend the distance from south of Beersheba to Rehob of Lebo-Hamath in southeastern Lebanon, somewhat north of Tel Dan. Lebo is recounted as a city on the northern border of the promised land (34:7-8) and later of the Israelite kingdom of David and Solomon (1Kg 8:65).

13:22 Hebron is said to have been fortified **seven years before Zoan**, which was in the eastern Nile Delta, about 100 miles northeast of Cairo. The Egyptian name for Zoan is *Dja'net*, which was pronounced by the Greeks as *Tanis*. It is associated with the site known as Tel el-Daba. The names of the three clans of the Anakim reflect Semitic background for these giant individuals.

13:23 The Hebrew word *'eshcol* means "a cluster of grapes," and hence **Valley of Eshcol** reflects the productivity of the vineyards in the valley, which is located west of Hebron. Ripe **pomegranates and figs** suggest a date of late August or early September for this exploration of Canaan.

13:25 The scouts' **40 days** of exploring the land matches the approximate time it would have taken for the 350 to 400-mile journey on foot, based upon the 12 to 15 miles per day average recounted in the annals of the Egyptian military campaigns of Thutmose III (1504-1450 B.C.) and Ramesses II (1290-1225 B.C.).

13:26 The Israelite scouts had departed from the **Paran** Desert area and had worked their way north into the Negev and through what would later be Judah and Israel. The Israelites meanwhile continued their journey to the oasis of **Kadesh**-barnea, presumed to be the area of Quseima, at the headwaters of the wilderness basin of the Nahal Zin.

13:27 The report of the scouts began on the positive side with the demonstration of the fruitfulness of the promised land. **Milk and honey** became the classic description of the abundance of natural flora and fauna of the land of Canaan (Ex 3:8,17; 13:5; 33:3; Lv 20:24; Dt 6:3; 11:9). This assessment is echoed in the Egyptian travel account "The Story of Sinuhe" in which the princely emissary described the land of Yaa and its abundant produce.

13:28-29 The tenor of the report quickly changed to a negative assessment of the possibility of conquering the heavily fortified cities and the numerous inhabitants, which they claimed included giants. The problem was that the people focused on their own strength rather than the power of God. The point of the later victories over the Midianites, Amorites, and Canaanites was to demonstrate God's strength. The power of Israel was never in her armies. Victory came at the hands of the Lord of Hosts. Recent discoveries that confirm the biblical data suggest a complex composite of ethnic groups living in the land of Canaan during the Late Bronze (1550-1200 B.C.) and Iron 1 (1200-1000 B.C.) ages.

The **Amalekites** were a semi-nomadic tribe from the region of Edom that ranged throughout the southern Levant, from northern Sinai to the hill country of Samaria. Hormah (Tel Masos in the Negev) may have been one of their cities (14:45).

The **Hittites**, known from the patriarchal period (Gn 23:3-20), were from the central highlands; they originated in eastern Anatolia around the third millennium B.C. The Hittite Empire flourished in the late Bronze Age (1550-1200 B.C.). Centered at Hattusa, it extended from central Anatolia to the upper Euphrates River and to the northern Levant.

The **Jebusites** were a non-Semitic clan who lived in Jerusalem during the middle Bronze through Iron 1 periods (2000-1000 B.C.), and who remained in control of the city until the time of the Davidic conquests (2Sm 5:6-9). They are unknown outside the Bible, though the city of Jerusalem is mentioned in the cuneiform documents from Tel Amarna from the late Bronze Age (1550-1200 B.C.). Scholars have suggested they may have been a subclan of the Perizzites or related to the Hurrians. The Table of Nations lists the Jebusites as descendants of Canaan (Gn 10:16).

The Semitic **Amorites** lived in the hill country of the central and southern Levant. The term "Amorite" can refer to a number of inhabitants of areas known today as Syria, Lebanon, Jordan, Israel, and Palestine. It may also refer more specifically to ethnic descendants of Canaan as delineated in Gn 10:16. They were referred to as the *Amurru* ("Amorites" or "westerners") in Akkadian records at Mari and the *Martu* in Sumerian texts of the third and second millennia B.C. Egyptian records describe their territory as extending from the Negev to the heights of Lebanon.

The **Canaanites** emerged in the middle Bronze Age

³⁰Then Caleb[a] quieted the people in the presence of Moses and said, "We must go up and take possession of the land because we can certainly conquer it!"

³¹But the men who had gone up with him responded, "We can't go up against the people because they are stronger than we are!" ³²So they gave a negative report to the Israelites about the land they had scouted: "The land we passed through to explore is one that devours its inhabitants, and all the people we saw in it are men of great size. ³³We even saw the Nephilim[A,b] there—the descendants of Anak come from the Nephilim![c] To ourselves we seemed like grasshoppers, and we must have seemed the same to them."

Israel's Refusal to Enter Canaan

14 Then the whole community broke into loud cries, and the people wept that night. ²All the Israelites complained about Moses and Aaron,[d] and the whole community told them, "If only we had died in the land of Egypt, or if only we had died in this wilderness! ³Why is the LORD bringing us into this land to die by the sword? Our wives and little children will become plunder.[e] Wouldn't it be

[a]13:30 Nm 14:6,24,30,38; 26:65
[b]13:33 Gn 6:4
[c]Dt 2:10-11,20-21
[d]14:2 Ex 16:2,7-8; 17:3; Nm 14:27; 16:11,41; Ps 59:15
[e]14:3 Gn 34:29; Nm 14:31
[f]Nm 11:5; Dt 17:16; Neh 9:17; Ac 7:39
[g]14:7 Ex 3:8; Nm 13:27; Dt 1:25; 3:25
[h]14:8 Ex 3:8; Lv 20:24; Nm 13:17; 16:13-14
[i]14:9 Nm 14:3
[j]Ps 17:8; 36:7; 57:1; 63:7; 91:1; Is 49:2; 51:16
[k]14:10 Ex 17:4; Mt 23:37

better for us to go back to Egypt?"[f] ⁴So they said to one another, "Let's appoint a leader and go back to Egypt."

⁵Then Moses and Aaron fell down with their faces to the ground in front of the whole assembly of the Israelite community. ⁶Joshua son of Nun and Caleb son of Jephunneh, who were among those who scouted out the land, tore their clothes ⁷and said to the entire Israelite community: "The land we passed through and explored is an extremely good land.[g] ⁸If the LORD is pleased with us, He will bring us into this land, a land flowing with milk and honey,[h] and give it to us. ⁹Only don't rebel against the LORD, and don't be afraid of the people of the land, for we will devour them.[i] Their protection[j] has been removed from them, and the LORD is with us. Don't be afraid of them!"

¹⁰While the whole community threatened to stone them,[k] the glory of the LORD appeared to all the Israelites at the tent of meeting.

God's Judgment of Israel's Rebellion

¹¹The LORD said to Moses, "How long will these people despise Me? How long will they not trust in Me despite all the signs I have

---

[A]13:33 Possibly means fallen ones; traditionally, "giants"; Gn 6:4

(2000–1550 B.C.) in the southern Levant (Gn 12:6) and continued to be a significant percentage of the population into the late Bronze Age (1550–1200 B.C.) and Iron 1 Age (1200–1000 B.C.). The land of Canaan was controlled by Egypt under the Eighteenth (Empire Kingdom, 1570–1400 B.C.) and Nineteenth (Ramesside, 1302–1175 B.C.) dynasties. The region extended along the Mediterranean Sea from the Wadi el-'Arish to Lebo-hamath in Lebanon, and inland to the Jordan Valley region. The designation of "Canaan" may derive from the Akkadian word meaning "red purple," based on the production of red-to-purple dyes produced from the abundant murex shells along the Lebanese coast. Other scholars point to the Semitic root *k-n-'* meaning "to bend, be subdued." The earliest reference to "Canaan" comes from the eighteenth century B.C. in Mari.

13:30 **Caleb** was the first to counter the objections of the majority of the scouts. The name Caleb means "dog," and it serves as an example of the danger of reading too much into the meaning of biblical names.

13:32 The **negative report** was circulated by word of mouth. The grumbling grew into greater discontent as the scouts exaggerated the stature and strength of their enemies.

13:33 The reference to the descendants of Anak as **Nephilim** was designed to instill fear in the hearts of the Israelites. The Nephilim, "fallen ones" ("giants" in the LXX), are noted in Gn 6:4 as the offspring of the "sons of God" ("angelic beings" or "divine warriors") and the "daughters of men." The Nephilim were of large stature, but they all would have been destroyed in Noah's flood (Gn 6:11ff), so it is best to conclude that the frightened spies gave an exaggerated report. **Grasshoppers** were the smallest of edible creatures permitted for Israelite consumption (Lv 11:22).

14:1-4 The grumbling rebellion against God and His gift of

the land reached a climax when the Israelite congregation moaned, **If only we had died in the land of Egypt**. Persons in fear and depression focus on the negative side of events and circumstances rather than turn their hearts and minds to God, the source of hope and deliverance.

14:3 The outcry of the people turned to the potential loss of their **wives and little children**. This heightened the drastic nature of the complaint.

14:4 The rebellion turned to the rejection of God's chosen and faithful leaders: Moses, Aaron, Caleb, and later Joshua.

14:5-9 Moses and Aaron **fell down with their faces to the ground** in humble submission before God at the entrance to the tabernacle where the people had gathered. At the same time they were bowing before the rebellious Israelites, propitiating God on their behalf. The faithful scouts Joshua and Caleb **tore their clothes** as a symbol of mourning and disdain for the defiant Israelites and their humiliated leaders. The tearing of one's garments was a gesture of mourning for the dead, for expressing lament over disease or plague, and for introducing a prophetic lament of judgment against an individual or nation.

14:10 God's dramatic intervention in the history of His people is integral to fulfilling His promise to bless His people. Here, as in 12:5; 16:19; Ex 14:19, the dynamic work of God demonstrates how He will intervene in history when the survival of His people is at stake. The theophany of the cloud/fiery pillar became even clearer to the Israelites as they grumbled against God.

14:11-12 The miraculous **signs** the Israelites had experienced in their deliverance from Egypt and their wandering in the wilderness were all forgotten. God threatened to de-

performed among them?[a] [12]I will strike them with a plague and destroy them. Then I will make you into a greater and mightier nation than they are."[b]

[13]But Moses replied to the LORD, "The Egyptians will hear about it, for by Your strength You brought up this people from them. [14]They will tell it to the inhabitants of this land.[c] They have heard that You, LORD, are among these people, how You, LORD, are seen face to face, how Your cloud stands over them, and how You go before them in a pillar of cloud by day and in a pillar of fire by night.[d] [15]If You kill this people with a single blow,[A,e] the nations that have heard of Your fame[f] will declare, [16]'Since the LORD wasn't able to bring this people into the land He swore to give them,[g] He has slaughtered them in the wilderness.'[h]

[17]"So now, may my Lord's power be magnified just as You have spoken: [18]The LORD is slow to anger and rich in faithful love,[i] forgiving wrongdoing and rebellion.[j] But He will not leave the •guilty unpunished,[k] bringing the consequences of the fathers' wrongdoing on the children to the third and fourth generation.[l] [19]Please pardon the wrongdoing of this people, in keeping with the greatness of Your faithful love,[m] just as You have forgiven them from Egypt until now."

[20]The LORD responded, "I have pardoned them as you requested. [21]Yet as surely as I live and as the whole earth is filled with the LORD's glory,[n] [22]none of the men who have seen My glory and the signs I performed in Egypt and in the wilderness, and have tested Me these 10 times and did not obey Me, [23]will ever see the land I swore to give their fathers.[o] None of those who have despised Me[p] will see it. [24]But since My servant Caleb has a different spirit and has followed Me completely, I will bring him into the land where he has gone, and his descendants will inherit it.[q] [25]Since the Amalekites and Canaanites are living in the lowlands,[B] turn back tomorrow and head for the wilderness in the direction of the •Red Sea."[r]

[26]Then the LORD spoke to Moses and Aaron: [27]"How long must I endure this evil community that keeps complaining about Me? I have heard the Israelites' complaints that they make against Me.[s] [28]Tell them: As surely as I

---

[a]14:11 Ex 4:1-12:31; 14:11,21-22; Nm 14:22
[b]14:12 Gn 12:2; Ex 32:10
[c]14:14 Ex 15:13-15; Dt 2:25
[d]Ex 13:21-22; Nm 9:16-17; Dt 1:33
[e]14:15 Ex 32:9-12
[f]Dt 2:25; Jos 2:10; 9:9; Is 66:19; Hab 3:2
[g]14:16 Gn 12:7; 13:14-17; 15:7; Ac 7:5
[h]Dt 9:28
[i]14:18 Neh 9:17; Ps 86:5,15; 103:8; 145:8; Jl 2:13; Jnh 4:2
[j]Ezr 9:13; Ps 78:38; 85:2; Is 43:25; 44:22
[k]Pr 11:21; Jr 25:29; Nah 1:3
[l]Ex 20:5; 34:6-7; Dt 5:9; Jr 32:18
[m]14:19 Ex 34:9; Ps 25:11; 86:5; Jl 2:13
[n]14:21 Ps 72:19; Hab 2:14
[o]14:23 Gn 12:7; 13:14-17; 15:7; Ac 7:5
[p]Nm 14:11; Dt 31:20; Ps 74:18 [q]14:24 Jos 14:6-15; Jdg 1:10-12,20 [r]14:25 Nm 21:4; Dt 1:40; 2:1 [s]14:27 Ex 16:2,7-8; 17:3; Nm 14:29,36; 16:11, 41; Dt 1:27

[A]14:15 Lit people as one man   [B]14:25 Lit valley

---

stroy the Israelites and start over with a new people through Moses.

14:13-16 Moses intervened on behalf of a rebellious nation with an appeal to God's reputation among the nations (**the Egyptians will hear about it**) and to the power of God to fulfill His promises. God's glory was at stake in this crisis.

14:14 Most translations have **face to face** (lit "eye to eye,"), but neither Israel nor Moses could look upon God's face (Ex 33:11,20-23). The expression denotes the method by which the will of God was communicated directly through the words of Moses. The "face" of God was His continual presence in the pillar of cloud by day and the pillar of fire by night.

14:17-18 Slow to anger describes God's longsuffering character. He was willing to endure the rebellion of the people for an extended period of time and to respond to their waywardness with grace and faithfulness. Later in Israelite history, the prophets responded to Israel's idolatrous practices of adopting Canaanite gods and goddesses in worship and practicing injustice against their own people by declaring that God's longsuffering would soon come to an end. His judgment was imminent and came to pass in the Assyrian and Babylonian invasions of Israel and Judah in the eighth and sixth centuries B.C.

Rich in faithful love describes God's lovingkindness and covenant loyalty to the descendants of Abraham, Isaac, and Jacob. But in spite of His love, His justice and righteousness would not allow him to **leave the guilty unpunished**. Moses' understanding of the balance between the love of God and His righteous judgment came through his close relationship with God.

The phrase **bringing the consequences of the fathers' wrongdoing on the children** meant that stemming the tide of sinfulness within the family structure often took many generations. God does not cause one's descendants to suffer because of the sins of their fathers (Dt 24:16; Ezk 18; see note at Ex 20:4-6), but He does punish children who keep doing the same sorts of sins as their parents. This passage set the stage for the words of the Shema (Dt 6:4-9), which instructed parents to set an example in the worship of God in the context of the family.

14:19 Please pardon was Moses' way of asking God to show the Israelites His merciful love instead of His righteous judgment.

14:20-23 God's reputation would be preserved through the meting out of His judgment against the disobedient first-generation leaders, and His mercy would be extended to the generation that followed. In refusing to enter the promised land, the older generation had rejected an essential part of their covenant relationship with God that was set forth in the Abrahamic covenant (Gn 12:1-3,7; 13:14-18; 15:18-21; 17:7-8).

14:24 Caleb, the faithful scout from the tribe of Judah, would join Hoshea (Joshua) of Ephraim as one of only two exceptions to God's judgment against the 10 scouts who had issued the majority report (v. 30). Thus the passage echoes the theme of the book of Numbers—that those who followed God's instructions faithfully would experience the fullness of God's blessing in the promised land.

14:25 The **wilderness in the direction of the Red Sea** was the line of the trade route that connected to Ezion-geber on the Gulf of Aqaba/Elath from Kadesh-barnea through the Zin Wilderness and the southern Arabah. Though Red Sea can be translated "Reed Sea," the terminology refers to the eastern arm of the Red Sea known as the Gulf of Aqaba (1Kg 9:26-28).

14:28 As surely as I live is the language of the court as

live," this is the LORD's declaration, "I will do to you exactly as I heard you say. [29] Your corpses will fall in this wilderness—all of you who were registered in the census, the entire number of you 20 years old or more[a]—because you have complained about Me. [30] I swear that none of you will enter the land I promised[A] to settle you in, except Caleb son of Jephunneh and Joshua son of Nun. [31] I will bring your children whom you said would become plunder[b] into the land you rejected, and they will enjoy it.[c] [32] But as for you, your corpses will fall in this wilderness. [33] Your children will be shepherds in the wilderness for 40 years and bear the penalty for your acts of unfaithfulness until all your corpses lie scattered in the wilderness. [34] You will bear the consequences of your sins 40 years based on the number of the 40 days that you scouted the land, a year for each day.[B,d] You will know My displeasure.[c] [35] I, *Yahweh, have spoken. I swear that I will do this to the entire evil community that has conspired against Me.[e] They will come to an end in the wilderness, and there they will die."[f]

[36] So the men Moses sent to scout out the land, and who returned and incited the entire community to complain about him by spreading a negative report about the land— [37] those men who spread the negative report about the land were struck down by the LORD. [38] Only Joshua son of Nun and Caleb son of Jephunneh remained alive of those men who went to scout out the land.

Israel Routed

[39] When Moses reported these words to all the Israelites, the people were overcome with grief. [40] They got up early the next morning and went up the ridge of the hill country, saying, "Let's go to the place the LORD promised, for we were wrong."[g]

[41] But Moses responded, "Why are you going against the LORD's command? It won't succeed. [42] Don't go, because the LORD is not among you and you will be defeated by your enemies. [43] The Amalekites and Canaanites are right in front of you, and you will fall by the sword. The LORD won't be with you, since you have turned from following Him."

[44] But they dared to go up the ridge of the hill country, even though the ark of the LORD's covenant and Moses did not leave the camp. [45] Then the Amalekites and Canaanites who lived in that part of the hill country came down, attacked them, and routed them as far as Hormah.[h]

Laws about Offerings

15 The LORD instructed Moses: [2] "Speak to the Israelites and tell them: When you enter the land I am giving you to settle in, [3] and you make a fire offering to the LORD from the herd or flock—either a *burnt offering or a sacrifice, to fulfill a vow,[i] or as a freewill offering, or at your appointed festivals—to produce a pleasing aroma for the LORD, [4] the one presenting his offering to the LORD must also present a *grain offering of two quarts[D] of fine flour mixed with a quart[E] of oil. [5] Prepare a quart[E] of wine as a *drink offering with the burnt offering or sacrifice of each lamb.

[6] "If you prepare a grain offering with a ram, it must be four quarts[F] of fine flour mixed

a14:29 Nm 1:3
b14:31 Nm 14:3
c Dt 1:39
d14:34 Nm 13:25; 32:13; Dt 2:14; Ps 95:10; Ezk 4:6
e14:35 Nm 16:11; 27:3; Ps 2:1-3
f Nm 14:30; 26:64-65; 1Co 10:5
g14:40 Dt 1:41-44
h14:45 Nm 21:3; Jdg 1:17
i15:3 Lv 22:21; 27:2; Nm 15:8

A14:30 Lit I raised My hand   B14:34 Lit a day for the year, a day for the year   C14:34 Or My opposition   D15:4 Lit a tenth (of an ephah]   E15:4,5 Lit a fourth hin   F15:6 Lit two-tenths (of an ephah)

Yahweh, God of Israel, took an oath on His own honor and announced the verdict against the guilty spies. Punishment would be dispensed in a slow and methodical manner. See the similar statement in verse 35.

14:34 A form of talionic justice (judgment equal to the crime, "an eye for an eye") was announced: **40 days** of spying, which led to the negative report, would be matched by **40 years** of wandering, with an effective death sentence on the first generation of Israelite leaders and militia.

14:43 Any attempt to launch out in conquest of the land without the Lord's blessing would be futile. Deliberate disobedience to God's command not to attack the Canaanites would meet with resounding defeat.

14:45 The city of **Hormah** has been identified tentatively with Tel Masos in the Beer-sheba Valley region. Hormah is also mentioned in the Execration Texts of middle Bronze Age Egypt.

15:1-41 This chapter consists of three units that address important matters issuing from the rebellious acts in chapters 11-14: land, sinfulness, and the need to remember God and His revelation.

15:2 **When you enter the land** clearly implies that God would bring the second generation into the land He had promised Abraham and Moses.

15:3-9 A **fire offering** presented in celebration stands in contrast to the destructive fire of God depicted in 11:1-4. The book of Leviticus focuses on the animal sacrifices and the manner in which they were offered, while Numbers 15 and 28-29 emphasize the produce of the land—grain, oil, and wine—that the Lord would provide for faithful Israel. The consecration offering described in Leviticus 1 in which the entire offering was consumed by fire on the altar is the **burnt offering**. This form of dedication typically followed the sin offering that was given to restore one's relationship with God through atonement and purification. The **sacrifice, to fulfill a vow** and the **fellowship offering** were forms of communion offering, designed to celebrate the relationship with God among the community of faith. Out of those blessings the people would bring offerings from the produce of the land in celebration of the Lord's goodness and miraculous

with a third of a gallon[A] of oil. [7]Also present a third of a gallon[A] of wine for a drink offering as a pleasing aroma to the LORD.

[8]"If you prepare a young bull as a burnt offering or as a sacrifice, to fulfill a vow, or as a *fellowship offering to the LORD, [9]a grain offering of six quarts[B] of fine flour mixed with two quarts[C] of oil must be presented with the bull. [10]Also present two quarts[C] of wine as a drink offering. It is a fire offering of pleasing aroma to the LORD. [11]This is to be done for each ox, ram, lamb, or goat. [12]This is how you must prepare each of them, no matter how many.

[13]"Every Israelite is to prepare these things in this way when he presents a fire offering as a pleasing aroma to the LORD. [14]When a foreigner resides with you or someone else is among you and wants to prepare a fire offering as a pleasing aroma to the LORD, he is to do exactly as you do throughout your generations. [15]The assembly is to have the same statute for[D] both you and the foreign resident as a permanent statute throughout your generations. You and the foreigner will be alike before the LORD. [16]The same law and the same ordinance will apply to both you and the foreigner who resides with you."[a]

[17]The LORD instructed Moses: [18]"Speak to the Israelites and tell them: After you enter the land where I am bringing you, [19]you are to offer a contribution to the LORD when you eat from the food of the land. [20]You are to offer a loaf from your first batch of dough[b] as a contribution; offer it just like a contribution from the threshing floor.[c] [21]Throughout your

generations, you are to give the LORD a contribution from the first batch of your dough.

[22]"When you sin unintentionally and do not obey all these commands that the LORD spoke to Moses[d]— [23]all that the LORD has commanded you through Moses, from the day the LORD issued the commands and onward throughout your generations— [24]and if it was done unintentionally without the community's awareness, the entire community is to prepare one young bull for a burnt offering as a pleasing aroma to the LORD, with its grain offering and drink offering according to the regulation, and one male goat as a *sin offering. [25]The priest must then make *atonement for the entire Israelite community so that they may be forgiven, for the sin was unintentional. They are to bring their offering, one made by fire to the LORD, and their sin offering before the LORD for their unintentional sin. [26]The entire Israelite community and the foreigner who resides among them will be forgiven, since it happened to all the people unintentionally.

[27]"If one person sins unintentionally,[e] he is to present a year-old female goat as a sin offering. [28]The priest must then make atonement before the LORD on behalf of the person who acts in error sinning unintentionally, and when he makes atonement for him, he will be forgiven. [29]You are to have the same law for the person who acts in error, whether he is an Israelite or a foreigner who lives among you.

[30]"But the person who acts defiantly,[E] whether native or foreign resident, blasphemes the LORD.[f] That person is to be cut off from his people. [31]He will certainly be cut off, because

---

[a]15:16 Ex 12:19,49; Lv 16:29-31; 17:8-16
[b]15:20 Neh 10:37; Ezk 44:30
[c]Lv 2:14
[d]15:22 Lv 4:2
[e]15:27 Lv 4:27
[f]15:30 2Kg 19:6,22; Is 37:6,23; Ezk 20:27

[A]15:6,7 Lit *a third hin*   [B]15:9 Lit *three-tenths* (of an ephah)   [C]15:9,10 Lit *a half hin*   [D]15:14-15 Sam, LXX read [14] *. . . the LORD, the assembly must do exactly as you do.* [15] *The same statute will apply to . . .*   [E]15:30 Lit *with a high hand*

---

works in history, commemorated in the appointed festivals: Passover, Pentecost, and Booths. Numbers 15:1-21 complements Leviticus 1–3 with details about the amounts and proportions of grain, oil, and wine that were supplements to the normal offerings.

15:14-16 Sacrificial requirements were the same for native Israelites and foreign residents who wanted to identify with the Israelite faith and submit to the authority of the Torah. Faith for Israel was not limited to the descendants of the sons of Jacob. This issue complements the mixed multitude who complained about the food supply in chapter 11, and it also follows the tradition of 9:14 with regard to the **foreigner who resides with you** celebrating Passover; see verses 29-30.

15:17-21 The **first batch of dough**, a form of firstfruits offering, was dedicated to the Lord in celebration of the abundant produce from the land. During the harvest of barley and wheat in the spring—the season of Passover, Unleavened Bread, and Pentecost—the firstfruit grain offering was presented to God. Even the mundane daily practice of kneading dough for making bread was to be a time of worship and celebration of God's goodness (1Co 10:31). Ac-

cording to Nm 18:11-16, all firstfruits and products offered in devotion to the Lord were given to the priests to support their services to the community.

15:22 Unintentional sins included matters in which the individual or community acted unknowingly in breaking a legal stipulation or in failing to perform certain ritual requirements.

15:24 If someone or a group of people sinned **unintentionally without the community's awareness**, the priest was obligated to make a sin offering and a **burnt offering** on behalf of the entire congregation. The requirement for an individual was a year-old female goat for such offenses. Leviticus 4:1–5:19 provides several examples of these unintentional sins.

15:30-31 In the textual backdrop of Israel's rejection of God and the promised land, the matter of willful defiance of God's word is raised. When a person acted **defiantly** in breaking the covenant relationship, that person blasphemed the Lord and defamed His righteous reputation. The penalty was either capital punishment or permanent banishment from the community of faith.

he has despised the LORD's word and broken His command; his *guilt remains on him."

Sabbath Violation

[32] While the Israelites were in the wilderness, they found a man gathering wood on the Sabbath day.[a] [33] Those who found him gathering wood brought him to Moses, Aaron, and the entire community. [34] They placed him in custody because it had not been decided what should be done to him. [35] Then the LORD told Moses, "The man is to be put to death. The entire community is to stone him outside the camp." [36] So the entire community brought him outside the camp and stoned him to death, as the LORD had commanded Moses.

Tassels for Remembrance

[37] The LORD said to Moses, [38] "Speak to the Israelites and tell them that throughout their generations they are to make tassels[b] for the corners of their garments, and put a blue cord on the tassel at each corner. [39] These will serve as tassels for you to look at, so that you may remember all the LORD's commands and obey them and not become unfaithful by following your own heart and your own eyes. [40] This way you will remember and obey all My commands and be holy to your God. [41] I am *Yahweh your God who brought you out of the land of Egypt to be your God; I am Yahweh your God."[c]

[a]15:32 Ex 35:2-3
[b]15:38 Dt 22:12; Mt 23:5
[c]15:41 Ex 29:46; Lv 19:36; 25:38; 26:13
[d]16:1 Ex 6:16-21
[e]Nm 26:9; Dt 11:6; Ps 106:16-18
[f]16:3 Nm 14:14; Ezk 37:26-28
[g]16:5 Ex 40:12-15
[h]16:7 Lv 10:1-2; 16:12
[i]Nm 17:5

Korah Incites Rebellion

16 Now Korah son of Izhar, son of Kohath, son of Levi,[d] with Dathan and Abiram,[e] sons of Eliab, and On son of Peleth, sons of Reuben, took [2] 250 prominent Israelite men who were leaders of the community and representatives in the assembly, and they rebelled against Moses. [3] They came together against Moses and Aaron and told them, "You have gone too far![A] Everyone in the entire community is holy, and the LORD is among them.[f] Why then do you exalt yourselves above the LORD's assembly?"

[4] When Moses heard this, he fell facedown. [5] Then he said to Korah and all his followers, "Tomorrow morning the LORD will reveal who belongs to Him, who is set apart, and the one He will let come near[g] Him. He will let the one He chooses come near Him. [6] Korah, you and all your followers are to do this: take firepans, and tomorrow [7] place fire in them and put incense on them before the LORD.[h] Then the man the LORD chooses will be the one who is set apart.[i] It is you Levites who have gone too far!"[B]

[8] Moses also told Korah, "Now listen, Levites! [9] Isn't it enough for you that the God of Israel has separated you from the Israelite community to bring you near to Himself, to perform the work at the LORD's tabernacle, and to stand

A16:3 Lit Enough of you   B16:7 Lit Enough of you, sons of Levi

15:32-36 The defiant breaking of the law of God is exemplified by an Israelite who performed work on the **Sabbath** by **gathering wood**. No work was permitted on the Sabbath. The Sabbath was called the sign of the covenant, so the breaking of the Sabbath law was considered a rejection of the covenant relationship with God. Capital punishment by stoning for breaking this law seems harsh by modern standards. But at this crucial juncture in Israelite history, a case precedent would be set for dealing with a person who deliberately broke the covenant.

15:38 The instructions in this verse were about the outward symbol for reminding the people of their covenant faith—the blue corded **tassels** attached to the **corners of their garments** (Dt 22:12). This practice was followed in the time of Jesus and remains a tradition among orthodox Jews today.

15:40 The words **This way you will remember and obey all My commands** provide a parallel to the phraseology of chapters 1–10: that the people or Moses did according to all that the Lord commanded.

15:41 The declaration **I am Yahweh your God** resonates with covenant overtones, calling to mind the initial words of Moses' encounter with God in Ex 6:2-8 and the introduction to the Ten Commandments in Ex 20:2.

16:1–19:22 The second cycle of rebellion focuses on a challenge to the Aaronic priesthood. The insurrection resulted in the deaths of the 250 followers of Korah and an additional 14,700 from the plague that followed. This section warns against violation of the holiness of the sanctuary.

16:1 In patriarchal tribal societies in the ancient Near East, the firstborn son often carried on the religious traditions for the family. This could be why **Dathan and Abiram**, who were from the tribe of **Reuben**, the firstborn of Jacob, decided to join the rebellion. But the leader of the insurrection was **Korah**, a Levite from the Kohathite clan. The Kohathites had been granted responsibilities in 3:27-32; 4:1-20, but Korah wanted a higher status (16:8-10).

16:3 Korah's claim that **Everyone in the entire community is holy, and the LORD is among them** had an element of truth, since God had called Israel to be "My kingdom of priests and My holy nation" (Ex 19:6). But that role was based on Israel's faithful obedience to God's revelation. God had ordained Moses and Aaron's exalted positions; they had not assigned themselves these roles.

16:6-7 The **firepans** were pans or shallow bowls with long handles (Lv 10:1) in which the priests carried hot coals upon which incense was sprinkled. Incense enhanced the sweet-smelling aroma of burning sacrifices that ascended into the heavens, symbolically entering into the nostrils of God (Lv 1:9,13,17; 2:2,9; 3:5,16). Moses' words **the man the LORD chooses will be the one who is set apart** set the challenge in the court of God to defend the truly faithful servant.

16:9-10 Korah and the Kohathites had a favored status among the three Levite clans in handling the holy things of the tabernacle (3:27-32), but they desired greater glory for themselves.

16:11-14 The rebels claimed Moses had failed to bring the people to a place of rest and abundance. They would not

before the community to minister to them? [10]He has brought you near, and all your fellow Levites who are with you, but you are seeking the priesthood as well. [11]Therefore, it is you and all your followers who have conspired against the LORD![a] As for Aaron, who is he[A] that you should complain about him?"

[12]Moses sent for Dathan and Abiram, the sons of Eliab, but they said, "We will not come! [13]Is it not enough that you brought us up from a land flowing with milk and honey to kill us in the wilderness? Do you also have to appoint yourself as ruler over us? [14]Furthermore, you didn't bring us to a land flowing with milk and honey or give us an inheritance of fields and vineyards. Will you gouge out the eyes of these men? We will not come!"

[15]Then Moses became angry and said to the LORD, "Don't respect their offering. I have not taken one donkey from them or mistreated a single one of them." [16]So Moses told Korah, "You and all your followers are to appear before the LORD tomorrow—you, they, and Aaron. [17]Each of you is to take his firepan, place incense on it, and present his firepan before the LORD—250 firepans. You and Aaron are each to present your firepan also."

[18]Each man took his firepan, placed fire in it, put incense on it, and stood at the entrance to the tent of meeting along with Moses and Aaron. [19]After Korah assembled the whole community against them at the entrance to the tent of meeting, the glory of the LORD appeared to the whole community. [20]The LORD spoke to Moses and Aaron, [21]"Separate yourselves from this community so I may consume them instantly."[b]

[22]But Moses and Aaron fell facedown and said, "God, God of the spirits[B,c] of all flesh, when one man sins, will You vent Your wrath on the whole community?"[d]

[23]The LORD replied to Moses, [24]"Tell the community: Get away from the dwellings of Korah, Dathan, and Abiram."

[25]Moses got up and went to Dathan and Abiram, and the elders of Israel followed him. [26]He warned the community, "Get away now from the tents of these wicked men. Don't touch anything that belongs to them, or you will be swept away because of all their sins." [27]So they got away from the dwellings of Korah, Dathan, and Abiram. Meanwhile, Dathan and Abiram came out and stood at the entrance of their tents with their wives, children, and infants.

[28]Then Moses said, "This is how you will know that the LORD sent me[e] to do all these things and that it was not of my own will: [29]If these men die naturally as all people would, and suffer the fate of all, then the LORD has not sent me. [30]But if the LORD brings about something unprecedented, and the ground opens its mouth and swallows them along with all that belongs to them so that they go down alive into •Sheol, then you will know that these men have despised the LORD."

[31]Just as he finished speaking all these words, the ground beneath them split open. [32]The earth opened its mouth and swallowed them and their households, all Korah's people,[f] and all their possessions. [33]They went down alive into Sheol with all that belonged to them. The earth closed over them, and they vanished from the assembly. [34]At their cries, all the people of Israel who were around them fled because they thought, "The earth may swallow us too!" [35]Fire also came out from the LORD and consumed the 250 men who were presenting the incense.[g]

[36C] Then the LORD spoke to Moses: [37]"Tell Eleazar son of Aaron the priest to remove the

[a]16:11 Nm 14:35; 27:3; Ps 2:1-3
[b]16:21 Nm 16:45
[c]16:22 Nm 27:16
[d]Gn 18:24-26
[e]16:28 Ex 3:10-12
[f]16:32 Ex 15:12; Nm 26:10
[g]16:35 Gn 19:24; Lv 10:1-2; Nm 11:1; 2Kg 1:10

A 16:11 Or Aaron, what has he done   **B** 16:22 Or breath; Nm 27:16   **C** 16:36 Nm 17:1 in Hb

---

admit that it was their rebellion that had led to the wilderness judgment.

16:19 The **glory of the LORD**, probably manifest as a cloud (v. 42), dramatically intervened in sight of the entire Israelite congregation.

16:22 Only the true servants of God—Moses and Aaron—**fell facedown** and, risking their own lives, appealed to His graciousness so the **whole community** might not suffer His **wrath**. The true servant of God puts the needs of the people before his own welfare.

16:23-33 By God's grace, in response to Moses' and Aaron's plea, only the instigators of the insurrection were consumed.

16:26 The tents, families, and property of the rebellious leaders had effectively been dedicated to destruction (Hb cherem), and anyone who touched any of these things would be swallowed up in the devastation.

16:33-35 The grave (**Sheol**) at this point in Israel's history was perceived to be a shadowy, unknowable realm of the dead, the netherworld of both good and evil where a person was gathered among ancestors at death. In this incident the bodies of the leading rebels, their families, and their possessions plummeted into the gaping abyss. A judgmental **fire . . . consumed the** other 250 insurrectionists. The second census informs us that Korah's fate was the same as that of Dathan and Abiram (26:10). Sheol is described as opening its mouth to receive the dead (Pr 1:12; Is 5:14; Hab 2:5). A similar description is found in the creation myth of Ugarit, where the god Mot received Baal into his mouth like a lamb in the jaws of a lion. In the Pentateuch the realm of Sheol and the dead is under the sovereign power of the God of Israel. Since Moses pronounced the curse before it happened, no one could mistake the judgment as accidental.

16:36-40 Divine instruction (**Then the LORD spoke to Moses**)

firepans from the burning debris, because they are holy, and scatter the fire far away. [38]As for the firepans of those who sinned at the cost of their own lives, make them into hammered sheets as plating for the altar, for they presented them before the LORD, and the firepans are holy. They will be a sign to the Israelites."

[39]So Eleazar the priest took the bronze firepans that those who were burned had presented, and they were hammered into plating for the altar, [40]just as the LORD commanded him through Moses. It was to be a reminder for the Israelites that no unauthorized person outside the lineage of Aaron should approach to offer incense before the LORD[a] and become like Korah and his followers.

[41]The next day the entire Israelite community complained about Moses and Aaron,[b] saying, "You have killed the LORD's people!" [42]When the community assembled against them, Moses and Aaron turned toward the tent of meeting, and suddenly the cloud covered it, and the LORD's glory appeared.

[43]Moses and Aaron went to the front of the tent of meeting, [44]and the LORD said to Moses, [45]"Get away from this community so that I may consume them instantly."[c] But they fell facedown.

[46]Then Moses told Aaron, "Take your firepan, place fire from the altar in it, and add incense. Go quickly to the community and make *atonement for them, because wrath has come from the LORD; the plague has be-

gun." [47]So Aaron took his firepan as Moses had ordered, ran into the middle of the assembly, and saw that the plague had begun among the people. After he added incense, he made atonement for the people. [48]He stood between the dead and the living, and the plague was halted. [49]But those who died from the plague numbered 14,700, in addition to those who died because of the Korah incident. [50]Aaron then returned to Moses at the entrance to the tent of meeting, since the plague had been halted.[d]

Aaron's Staff Chosen

17 [A] The LORD instructed Moses: "Speak to the Israelites and take one staff from them for each ancestral house, 12 staffs from all the leaders of their ancestral houses. Write each man's name on his staff. [3]Write Aaron's name on Levi's staff, because there must be one staff for the head of each ancestral house. [4]Then place them in the tent of meeting in front of the *testimony where I meet with you. [5]The staff of the man I choose will sprout, and I will rid Myself of the Israelites' complaints that they have been making about you."

[6]So Moses spoke to the Israelites, and each of their leaders gave him a staff, one for each of the leaders of their ancestral houses, 12 staffs in all. Aaron's staff was among them. [7]Moses placed the staffs before the LORD in the tent of the testimony.

[8]The next day Moses entered the tent of the testimony and saw that Aaron's staff, rep-

Cross references:
[a]16:40 Ex 28:1; Nm 3:10,38; 18:4,7
[b]16:41 Ex 16:2,7-8; 17:3; Nm 14:27; 17:6; 1Co 10:10
[c]16:45 Nm 16:21
[d]16:47-50 Nm 25:1-9; 2Sm 24:15-25

[A]17:1 Nm 17:16 in Hb

came to the faithful recipient who had followed the Lord's commands throughout this miraculous event. Death can have both contaminating and cleansing effects. Touching and even being in close proximity to the dead could render a person unclean. Yet in the conclusion to this section in chapter 19, impurity from the dead was cleansed with a mixture of holy water and the ashes of a burned red cow. God commanded Moses to **remove the firepans from the burning debris, because they are holy . . . They will be a sign to the Israelites**. The fiery death of the 250 rebellious collaborators brought purification to the bronze censers. Now the raw materials could be used to produce an additional bronze covering for the sacrificial altar.

16:41-50 The lesson of the previous day was soon forgotten as **the entire Israelite community complained about Moses and Aaron**, citing them as the reason for the judgment against the rebellious Korah and his conspirators. God's reaction followed the judgment sequence of the previous day with a call for the people to separate themselves from the insurgents as God's glory descended, lest they be consumed in the judgment. Aaron's **atonement** for the people portrays the concept of propitiatory atonement as he literally stood as the mediator between **the dead and the living** to ward off the wrath of God.

17:2-3 The **staff** was the official symbol of the tribal chief-

tain, which in Babylonia and Egypt often was designed to represent its owner. One word (Hb *matteh*) means both "tribe" and "staff/scepter," and each carried some significance of tribal identity. In this context the names were inscribed for identification. Perhaps the names were those of the patriarchal leaders who took the census of the military in chapter 1. Aaron's name was inscribed on the staff of the tribe of Levi, though Moses was the elder brother.

17:4 The solemnity of the test of leadership was evidenced by the placement of the inscribed staffs **in the tent of meeting in front of the testimony**, where the high priest went once a year on the Day of Atonement to cleanse the holy place because of the sins of the people.

17:8 The fourfold statement of the miraculous produce from Aaron's staff (**sprouted, formed buds, blossomed, and produced almonds**) heightened the drama, with God demonstrating the priority of the Aaronic priesthood. In Jeremiah's call to ministry (Jr 1:4ff), his vision of the budding almond branch demonstrated God's concern that His word and His will be accomplished in the life of the prophet and the nation (Jr 1:11-12). The white blossoms of the budding almond tree were a symbol of holiness and purity that God expected from His faithful priestly servants. The Aaronic priests were to serve as mediators between God and Israel. Holiness and

resenting the house of Levi, had sprouted, formed buds, blossomed, and produced almonds! [9]Moses then brought out all the staffs from the LORD's presence to all the Israelites. They saw them, and each man took his own staff. [10]The LORD told Moses, "Put Aaron's staff back in front of the testimony to be kept as a sign[a] for the rebels, so that you may put an end to their complaints before Me, or else they will die." [11]So Moses did as the LORD commanded him.

[12]Then the Israelites declared to Moses, "Look, we're perishing! We're lost; we're all lost! [13]Anyone who comes near the LORD's tabernacle will die.[b] Will we all perish?"

Provision for the Priesthood

18 The LORD said to Aaron, "You, your sons, and your ancestral house[c] will be responsible for sin against the sanctuary. You and your sons will be responsible for sin involving your priesthood. [2]But also bring your relatives with you from the tribe of Levi, your ancestral tribe, so they may join you and assist you and your sons in front of the tent of the *testimony.[d] [3]They are to perform duties for you and for the whole tent. They must not come near the sanctuary equipment or the altar; otherwise, both they and you will die. [4]They are to join you and guard the tent of meeting, doing all the work at the tent, but no unauthorized person may come near you.

[5]"You are to guard the sanctuary and the altar so that wrath may not fall on the Israelites again.[e] [6]Look, I have selected your fellow Levites from the Israelites as a gift for you,[A] assigned by the LORD to work at the tent of meeting. [7]But you and your sons will carry out your priestly responsibilities for everything concerning the altar and for what is inside the veil, and you will do that work. I am giving you the work of the priesthood as a gift,[B] but an unauthorized person who comes near the sanctuary will be put to death."

Support for the Priests and Levites

[8]Then the LORD spoke to Aaron, "Look, I have put you in charge of the contributions brought to Me. As for all the holy offerings of the Israelites, I have given them to you and your sons as a portion and a permanent statute.[f] [9]A portion of the holiest offerings kept from the fire will be yours; every one of their offerings that they give Me, whether the *grain offering, *sin offering, or *restitution offering will be most holy for you and your sons. [10]You are to eat it as a most holy offering.[c] Every male may eat it; it is to be holy to you.

[11]"The contribution of their gifts also belongs to you. I have given all the Israelites' presentation offerings to you and to your sons and daughters as a permanent statute.[g] Every ceremonially *clean person in your house may eat it. [12]I am giving you all the best of the fresh olive oil, new wine, and grain, which the Israelites give to the LORD as their *firstfruits. [13]The firstfruits of all that is in their land, which they bring to the LORD, belong to you. Every clean person in your house may eat them.

[14]"Everything in Israel that is permanently

Cross references
[a]17:10 Heb 9:4
[b]17:13 Nm 3:10,38; 8:19; 18:7
[c]18:1 Nm 10:21
[d]18:2 Nm 8:5-26
[e]18:5 Nm 1:53; 16; 17:12-13
[f]18:8 Lv 10:12-15; Nm 5:9
[g]18:11 Lv 7:34-36

A18:6 LXX, Syr, Vg omit *for you*   **B**18:7 Or *veil. So you are to perform the service; a gift of your priesthood I grant*   **C**18:10 Or *it in a most holy place*

---

purity were to permeate their words as they taught the people of God the statutes and precepts of the Lord (Lv 10:11).

17:10 After Moses showed the other tribal leaders the collection of tribal staffs, they were able to see God's blessing upon Aaron's staff. Then God told Moses to **put Aaron's staff back in front of the testimony to be kept as a sign**. Moses placed the staff in front of the ark of the covenant as a sign against the rebels that God had indeed chosen the Aaronic line for priestly service. Aaron's priestly line prefigured the high priesthood of Jesus Christ, who exemplified the qualities of purity and holiness in His earthly ministry, who as a priest of a higher order—of Melchizedek—offered Himself as the unblemished paschal lamb for our sins. In light of the priesthood of the believer in Christ, the need for purity and holiness in Christian service is duly emphasized.

17:11 Moses the faithful and humble servant of God carried out the Lord's instructions, even though the opposition again had placed a heavy burden on his shoulders. In the manner of Paul's words in Rm 12:1, Moses offered himself as a living and holy sacrifice in service to God.

18:3-5 The Aaronic priests were camped in front of the entrance to the tabernacle on the east side of the sanctuary.

The three clans of the Levites—Kohathites, Gershonites, and Merarites—were camped on the other three sides. This arrangement provided a physical and spiritual barrier against violation of the holy place. The Levites performed various maintenance and transportation duties for the tabernacle, but only the priests could actually touch the holy furnishings.

18:7 The prohibition against violation of the sanctity of the tabernacle is expressed in verses 3,4,5,7,22, along with the consequences for infringement. Trespassers and irreverent persons would **be put to death**, so that God's wrath might not bring widespread destruction on the nation.

18:8-13 The priests and Levites would not be given territory in the promised land like the other tribes, but their provisions were gifts of tithes and offerings from the people. Portions of all sacrifices but the burnt offerings, which were to be totally consumed by the fire on the altar, were dedicated to the Lord and then provided as gifts for the priests and Levites. Even the priests and Levites were required to tithe their gifts to the Lord (v. 26). This section complements similar allocations described in chapters 3; 4; 8; 35; and Leviticus 8–9.

18:14-20 Based on the principle of Ex 11:1-10 and 13:2-16, Israel was redeemed through the firstborn of Egypt, both

dedicated to the Lord[a] belongs to you. [15]The firstborn of every living thing, man or animal, presented to the Lord belongs to you. But you must certainly redeem the firstborn of man,[b] and redeem the firstborn of an ˚unclean animal. [16]You will pay the redemption price for a month-old male according to your assessment: five ˚shekels of silver by the standard sanctuary shekel, which is 20 *gerahs*.[c]

[17]"However, you must not redeem the firstborn of an ox, a sheep, or a goat; they are holy. You are to sprinkle their blood on the altar and burn their fat as a fire offering for a pleasing aroma to the Lord. [18]But their meat belongs to you. It belongs to you like the breast of the presentation offering and the right thigh.

[19]"I give to you and to your sons and daughters all the holy contributions that the Israelites present to the Lord as a permanent statute. It is a permanent covenant of salt[d] before the Lord for you as well as your ˚offspring."

[20]The Lord told Aaron, "You will not have an inheritance in their land; there will be no portion among them for you. I am your portion and your inheritance among the Israelites.[e]

[21]"Look, I have given the Levites every tenth in Israel as an inheritance in return for the work they do, the work of the tent of meeting. [22]The Israelites must never again come near the tent of meeting, or they will incur ˚guilt and die. [23]The Levites will do the work of the tent of meeting, and they will bear the consequences of their sin. The Levites will not receive an inheritance among the Israelites;[f] this is a permanent statute throughout your generations. [24]For I have given them the tenth that the Israelites present to the Lord as a contribution for their inheritance. That is why I told them that they would not receive an inheritance among the Israelites."

a 18:14 Lv 27:28
b 18:15 Ex 13:11-16
c 18:16 Lv 27:6; Nm 3:46-47
d 18:19 Lv 2:13; 2Ch 13:5
e 18:20 Dt 10:9; Jos 18:7; Ezk 44:28-30
f 18:23 Dt 10:8-9; 18:1-2; Jos 13:14,33
g 18:29 Nm 18:12
h 19:2 Dt 21:3; 1Sm 6:7; Heb 9:13
i 19:6 Lv 14:4-7,49-52; Heb 9:19

[25]The Lord instructed Moses, [26]"Speak to the Levites and tell them: When you receive from the Israelites the tenth that I have given you as your inheritance, you must present part of it as an offering to the Lord—a tenth of the tenth. [27]Your offering will be credited to you as if it were your grain from the threshing floor or the full harvest from the winepress. [28]You are to present an offering to the Lord from every tenth you receive from the Israelites. Give some of it to Aaron the priest as an offering to the Lord. [29]You must present the entire offering due the Lord from all your gifts. The best part of the tenth[g] is to be consecrated.

[30]"Tell them further: Once you have presented the best part of the tenth, and it is credited to you Levites as the produce of the threshing floor or the winepress, [31]then you and your household may eat it anywhere. It is your wage in return for your work at the tent of meeting. [32]You will not incur guilt because of it once you have presented the best part of it, but you must not defile the Israelites' holy offerings, so that you will not die."

Purification Ritual

19 The Lord spoke to Moses and Aaron, [2]"This is the legal statute that the Lord has commanded: Instruct the Israelites to bring you an unblemished red cow that has no defect and has never been yoked.[h] [3]Give it to Eleazar the priest, and he will have it brought outside the camp and slaughtered in his presence. [4]Eleazar the priest is to take some of its blood with his finger and sprinkle it seven times toward the front of the tent of meeting. [5]The cow must be burned in his sight. Its hide, flesh, and blood, are to be burned along with its dung. [6]The priest is to take cedar wood, hyssop, and crimson yarn,[i] and throw

---

human and animal. As the Levites provided redemption for the firstborn of Israel's families (Nm 3:40-51), so **the firstborn of every living thing** was to be presented to the Levites as provisions for them and their families. Since unclean animals could not be consumed, their redemption price was paid in shekels.

18:21-24 The gift of the **tenth** to the **Levites** was new legislation, whereas much of verses 1-20 is a review of existing legislation. This highlights the role of the priests and Levites within the community after the threat to their positions in the Korah rebellion. Tithing one-tenth of one's produce as a gift to the temple and its priesthood was a common practice among various cultures of the ancient Near East. These requirements are anticipatory in that they assumed God's blessing in the land after the conquest.

18:25-31 The Levites in turn were required to present to the Lord **a tenth of the tenth**, and thus participate in the full

cycle of blessings. The **best part of the tenth**, the highest quality from the produce of the flocks and fields, was to be presented to the Aaronic priesthood.

The cycle of blessing begins and ends with the Lord: (1) The Lord instructs His people in the proper sowing and reaping principles. (2) As the people obediently sow and reap, He blesses the community of faith with an abundant harvest of flocks and fields. (3) The firstborn, firstfruits, and first ripe produce are consumed by the priests after portions have been sacrificed to God. (4) Tithes and offerings are also presented to the holy and faithful Levites for their provision, as additional portions are rendered to God. (5) Then the Levites present a best-of-the-best tithe of their received tithes to support the Aaronic priesthood, who then offer additional portions to God in thanksgiving and praise.

19:2-6 The original historical context of the **red cow** ritual was under the auspices of the priesthood of **Eleazar**, while his father Aaron was still alive (his death is cited in 20:22-

them onto the fire where the cow is burning. ⁷Then the priest must wash his clothes and bathe his body in water; after that he may enter the camp, but he will remain ceremonially *unclean until evening. ⁸The one who burned the cow must also wash his clothes and bathe his body in water, and he will remain unclean until evening.

⁹"A man who is *clean is to gather up the cow's ashes and deposit them outside the camp in a ceremonially clean place. The ashes must be kept by the Israelite community for preparing the water to remove impurity; it is a *sin offering.ᵃ ¹⁰Then the one who gathers up the cow's ashes must wash his clothes, and he will remain unclean until evening. This is a permanent statute for the Israelites and for the foreigner who resides among them.

¹¹"The person who touches any human corpse will be unclean for seven days. ¹²He is to purify himself with the waterᴬ on the third day and the seventh day; then he will be clean.ᵇ But if he does not purify himself on the third and seventh days, he will not be clean. ¹³Anyone who touches a body of a person who has died, and does not purify himself, defiles the tabernacle of the LORD. That person will be cut off from Israel. He remains unclean because the water for impurity has not been sprinkled on him, and his uncleanness is still on him.

¹⁴"This is the law when a person dies in a

ᵃ19:9 Lv 4
ᵇ19:12 Nm 31:19
ᶜ19:20 1Co
6:19-20

tent: everyone who enters the tent and everyone who is already in the tent will be unclean for seven days, ¹⁵and any open container without a lid tied on it is unclean. ¹⁶Anyone in the open field who touches a person who has been killed by the sword or has died, or who even touches a human bone, or a grave, will be unclean for seven days. ¹⁷For the purification of the unclean person, they are to take some of the ashes of the burnt sin offering, put them in a jar, and add fresh water to them. ¹⁸A person who is clean is to take hyssop, dip it in the water, and sprinkle the tent, all the furnishings, and the people who were there. He is also to sprinkle the one who touched a bone, a grave, a corpse, or a person who had been killed.

¹⁹"The one who is clean is to sprinkle the unclean person on the third day and the seventh day. After he purifies the unclean person on the seventh day, the one being purified must wash his clothes and bathe in water, and he will be clean by evening. ²⁰But a person who is unclean and does not purify himself, that person will be cut off from the assembly because he has defiled the sanctuary of the LORD.ᶜ The water for impurity has not been sprinkled on him; he is unclean. ²¹This is a permanent statute for them. The person who sprinkles the water for impurity is to wash his clothes, and whoever touches the water for impurity will be unclean until evening. ²²Anything the

---

ᴬ19:12 Or *ashes*; lit *with it*

---

29). The sprinkling of the blood of the slaughtered cow is consistent with other blood rituals in the Pentateuch (Lv 4:6,17; 8:11; 16:14,19). The **unblemished** cow was entirely red—not spotted or mottled.

Since the cow had never been yoked, it was probably young and strong. Elsewhere it was a bull that was sacrificed as a sin offering for the high priest and his family (Lv 4:3-12; 16:6,11), or on behalf of the entire community (Lv 4:13-21). Thus the female is specified here so there would be no confusion of purification agents or rituals. The cow would also offer the maximum yield of purification ashes so the ritual need not be repeated as often. The redness of the cow reflected the color of blood, as did the other sacrificial elements burned with the cow.

The plant species translated **hyssop** was probably not the Greek *hussopos*, but marjoram, sage, or thyme, the leaves of which are very absorbent. Other reddish or colored elements in ritual sanctification included cypress wood, roses, red wine, and cedar sap.

19:7-10 The **priest**, the assistant who **burned the cow**, and the **one who** gathered and stored the **ashes**, were each made unclean by touching this purification (sin) offering—the red cow ashes—but this was a lesser state of uncleanness than what was generated by touching a dead body. The ashes alone caused uncleanness, but when mixed with water they became a purifying agent. This seeming paradox is similar to that of blood that was used for the ultimate

purification of the holy place on the Day of Atonement, yet rendered a person unclean if improperly used or eaten.

19:11-22 Ritual impurity from exposure to the dead required a "sin offering" that was actually a purification. Failure to perform the symbolic cleansings on the **third** and **seventh** days resulted in banishment from the community or death. Contamination could result from several situations: (1) being in or entering a tent where someone had just died, (2) contact with the dead in battle or by accidental proximity, or (3) contact with a grave or its remains. The seven-day period of the impurity was the maximum length for persons who had become unclean through a variety of serious diseases. Other forms of impurity, such as contact with the red cow, rendered a person impure only until sundown.

19:13 The severity of the impurity resulting from touching a corpse is evidenced in the ritual washings administered on the third and seventh days, the potential of defiling the sanctuary from a distance if left unpurified, and the potential penalty of (Hb) *karath*—being **cut off from** the community.

19:21 In future generations (**This is a permanent statute for them**) this purification offering and ritual would be a common purification offering, not only because of the exposure to corpses, but because it was considered acceptable for cleansing other forms of impurity. It often functioned as an instant sin offering in the second temple rituals. In his presentation of the person and work of Jesus Christ as superior to OT ceremonies, the writer of the book of Hebrews

unclean person touches will become unclean, and anyone who touches it will be unclean until evening."

Water from the Rock

20 The entire Israelite community entered the Wilderness of Zin in the first month, and they[A] settled in Kadesh. Miriam[a] died and was buried there.

[2]There was no water for the community, so they assembled against Moses and Aaron. [3]The people quarreled with Moses and said, "If only we had perished when our brothers perished before the Lord.[b] [4]Why have you brought the Lord's assembly into this wilderness for us and our livestock to die here? [5]Why have you led us up from Egypt to bring us to this evil place? It's not a place of grain,

figs, vines, and pomegranates,[c] and there is no water to drink!"

[6]Then Moses and Aaron went from the presence of the assembly to the doorway of the tent of meeting. They fell down with their faces to the ground, and the glory of the Lord appeared to them. [7]The Lord spoke to Moses, [8]"Take the staff[d] and assemble the community. You and your brother Aaron are to speak to the rock while they watch, and it will yield its water. You will bring out water for them from the rock and provide drink for the community and their livestock."

[9]So Moses took the staff from the Lord's presence[e] just as He had commanded him. [10]Moses and Aaron summoned the assembly in front of the rock, and Moses said to them, "Listen, you rebels! Must we bring water out

a 20:1 Ex 15:20-21; Nm 12:1; 26:59; Dt 24:9
b 20:3 Nm 16:31-35,41-50
c 20:5 Ex 13:5; Nm 13:23-27; Dt 8:8
d 20:8 Ex 4:2-5; 17:4-9; Nm 17:8
e 20:9 Nm 17:10

[A]20:1 Lit *the people*

---

combined the ritual of the ashes of the red cow with that of the Day of Atonement in demonstrating the once-and-for-all sufficiency of the blood of Christ in cleansing us from all our sins (Heb 9:11-14).

20:1 The **first month**, Abib (Nisan), in the spring of the fortieth year, brought the conclusion of the punishment of Israel in the wilderness. The chapter begins with the death of **Miriam** and concludes with Aaron's death on the first day of the fifth month of the fortieth year after the exodus (33:38-39). This was the month of the deliverance from Egypt, in which the people should have been celebrating the Passover and the Festival of Unleavened Bread in the promised land. Instead they found themselves back at Kadesh after 40 years. Once more they grumbled about their water supply just as the first generation had done soon after they crossed the Red Sea (Ex 15:23-26; 17:1-7). On Kadesh and the Zin Wilderness, see note at Nm 13:26. Miriam's death is recounted briefly. Its inclusion here provides a clue about the coming sin of Moses and Aaron.

20:2 The grumbling Israelites were now back where they had first received the scouts' report assessing the promised land (13:25-26). Their 10-person majority report had produced a rebellious rejection of the land by the Israelites and the 40-year judgment in the wilderness. Miriam had just died, and Moses and Aaron were aging leaders suffering the loss of their beloved sister, who had rescued the infant Moses from death at the hands of the Egyptians.

20:3-5 The shortage of water led to an insurrection of the Israelites against their leaders. Once more the people claimed that it would have been better to **die** in **Egypt** than to suffer such hardship in that barren wilderness. They preferred bondage, oppression, and death in captivity over their miraculous deliverance, freedom, and provision from the Lord.

20:5 The wilderness around Kadesh was a difficult environment, but the people were responsible for their own predicament because they had refused to enter the land "flowing with milk and honey."

20:8 The **staff** mentioned here was probably the staff of Aaron that had budded, blossomed, and produced almonds to confirm Aaron's priestly authority (see note at 17:8). It was kept before the ark of the testimony as a warning to any fu-

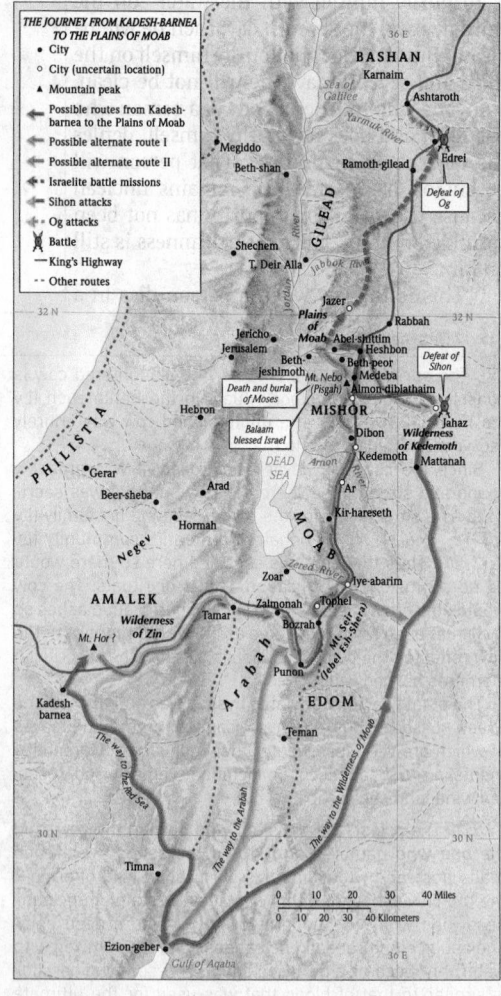

THE JOURNEY FROM KADESH-BARNEA TO THE PLAINS OF MOAB
- • City
- ○ City (uncertain location)
- ▲ Mountain peak
- Possible routes from Kadesh-barnea to the Plains of Moab
- Possible alternate route I
- Possible alternate route II
- Israelite battle missions
- Sihon attacks
- Og attacks
- Battle
- King's Highway
- Other routes

of this rock for you?" ¹¹Then Moses raised his hand and struck the rock twice with his staff, so that a great amount of water gushed out, and the community and their livestock drank.ᵃ

¹²But the Lord said to Moses and Aaron, "Because you did not trust Me to show My holiness in the sight of the Israelites, you will not bring this assembly into the land I have given them."ᵇ ¹³These are the waters of Meribah,ᴬ,ᶜ where the Israelites quarreled with the Lord, and He showed His holiness to them.

Edom Denies Passage

¹⁴Moses sent messengers from Kadesh to the king of Edom, "This is what your brother Israelᵈ says, 'You know all the hardships that have overtaken us. ¹⁵Our fathers went down to Egypt, and we lived in Egypt many years, but the Egyptians treated us and our fathers badly. ¹⁶When we cried out to the Lord, He heard our voice, sent an angel,ᴮ,ᵉ and brought us out of Egypt. Now look, we are in Kadesh,

a city on the border of your territory. ¹⁷Please let us travel through your land. We won't travel through any field or vineyard, or drink any well water. We will travel the King's Highway; we won't turn to the right or the left until we have traveled through your territory.'"ᶠ

¹⁸But Edom answered him, "You must not travel through our land, or we will come out and confront you with the sword."

¹⁹"We will go on the main road," the Israelites replied to them, "and if we or our herds drink your water, we will pay its price.ᵍ There will be no problem; only let us travel through on foot."

²⁰Yet Edom insisted, "You must not travel through." And they came out to confront them with a large force of heavily-armed people.ᶜ ²¹Edom refused to allow Israel to travel through their territory, and Israel turned away from them.

Aaron's Death

²²After they set out from Kadesh, the entire

Cross references
ᵃ 20:11 Ex 17:6; Ps 78:15; 1Co 10:4
ᵇ 20:12 Nm 27:12-14
ᶜ 20:13 Ex 17:7; Nm 27:14; Dt 32:51; Ps 95:8; 106:32
ᵈ 20:14 Gn 25:23-26,30; 36:8
ᵉ 20:16 Ex 3:7-10; 14:19; 23:20
ᶠ 20:17 Nm 21:22; Dt 2:27
ᵍ 20:19 Dt 2:1-7

ᴬ 20:13 = quarreling   ᴮ 20:16 Or *a messenger*   ᶜ 20:20 Lit *with numerous people and a strong hand*

---

ture grumbling rebels (17:10). The water the Lord promised to Moses and Aaron would be more than enough for the people and their animals.

20:9-11 Moses fell into unfaithfulness by unleashing a verbal attack on the rebels and declaring that he and Aaron were about to bring forth water from a rock. Then he **struck the rock twice** instead of speaking to it. He presumed upon the presence of God to respond faithfully and graciously to his rebellious acts.

20:11 When Moses struck the rock, **a great amount of water gushed out**. Geographers and biblical interpreters have written for years of the aquifers beneath portions of the Sinai Peninsula. The several oases such as at Serabit al-Khadem, Ain Hawarah, Ain Khadra, and Ain el-Qudeirat (Kadesh-barnea) provide examples of such abundant water. Nevertheless, provision of water where none had been before was a miracle displaying the grace of God.

20:12 Moses' actions were similar to those of an idolatrous pagan magician who claimed to have god-like powers. Holiness and purity, parallel themes of the book of Numbers, had been violated by Moses and Aaron. The cycles of rebellion now had reached from the general population to its most noble leaders. God punished Moses by declaring that he would **not bring this assembly into the land**.

20:14-17 Moses' message to **the king of Edom** followed classical Hebrew epistolary form and customary protocol of the Bronze and Iron ages. The content had all the earmarks of ancient Near Eastern diplomatic correspondence between nobles delivered by royal messengers.

The mention of the point of origin for the letter at **Kadesh, a city on the border of your territory**, made the king of Edom aware of Israel's immediate need for passage. If this Kadesh is taken to be Kadesh-barnea, and if it lay near the border of Edomite territory, this implies that some of the early tribal Edomites had settled or controlled some areas west of the Arabah. Others believe the phrase means that Israel under Moses was simply approaching the Edom-

ite region. If Edom was transitioning from a seminomadic society to a sedentary culture, "outskirts of your border" would have been rather fluid. Like Israel, the Edomites did not become a formal state in the modern sense until the Iron II period (1000–550 B.C.).

20:17 Moses' request included specifics about how the Israelites would respect Edomite domain if they would grant passage. The seasonal description indicates spring, when grain fields were at or near harvest time and vine dressing for the summer and fall crops had just begun. Thus it was important to assure the Edomites that their crops would not be trampled or scavenged. Water rights also were of great concern, even as they are among the Israelis, Palestinians, and Jordanians today. The Israelites would presumably bring their own water supply from Kadesh during their brief passage of perhaps two days through the Edomite highlands.

The King's Highway was a famous trade route connecting Damascus with Arabia, Sinai, and Egypt through the Transjordan tablelands (Golan, Bashan, Gilead, Ammon, Moab, and Edom) and the southern mountains, paralleling the Arabah on the eastern side. Caravans brought highly prized incense, spices, perfumes, precious jewels, and copper from the Sinai and Paran wilderness sources.

20:19-21 Moses' attempt at diplomatic correspondence carried alternative stipulations, some of which is preserved in the text of verse 19. The suggestion of payment for safe passage was in keeping with ancient Near Eastern protocol, as tolls or tribute were often exacted from trade caravans. The harsh Edomite answer caused bitter feelings between Israel and Edom for centuries.

20:22 The location of **Mount Hor** depends on the route followed by the Israelites. As with Kadesh (v. 16), Mount Hor was on the border with Edom, according to 33:37. The Israelites skirted around the boundaries of the militant Edomites. Suggested mountains have included the traditional Islamic identity of Jebel Nebi Harun ("Mount of the Prophet

Israelite community came to Mount Hor.[a] [23]The LORD said to Moses and Aaron at Mount Hor on the border of the land of Edom, [24]"Aaron will be gathered to his people; he will not enter the land I have given the Israelites, because you both rebelled against My command at the waters of Meribah. [25]Take Aaron and his son Eleazar and bring them up Mount Hor. [26]Remove Aaron's garments and put them on his son Eleazar. Aaron will be gathered to his people and die there."

[27]So Moses did as the LORD commanded, and they climbed Mount Hor in the sight of the whole community. [28]After Moses removed Aaron's garments and put them on his son Eleazar, Aaron died there on top of the mountain. Then Moses and Eleazar came down from the mountain. [29]When the whole community saw that Aaron had passed away, the entire house of Israel mourned for him 30 days.

Canaanite King Defeated

21 When the Canaanite king of Arad,[b] who lived in the *Negev, heard that Israel was coming on the Atharim road, he fought against Israel and captured some prisoners. [2]Then Israel made a vow to the LORD, "If You will deliver this people into our hands, we will *completely destroy their cities."[c] [3]The LORD listened to Israel's request, the Canaanites were defeated, and Israel completely destroyed them and their cities. So they named the place Hormah.[A,d]

Cross references (margin)

[a]20:22 Nm 21:4; 33:37-41; Dt 32:50
[b]21:1 Nm 33:40; Jos 12:14; Jdg 1:16
[c]21:2 Dt 2:34; 13:16-17; Jos 6:18,21
[d]21:3 Nm 14:45; Dt 1:44; Jdg 1:17
[e]21:6 1Co 10:9
[f]21:8 2Kg 18:4; Jn 3:14-15
[g]21:10-11 Nm 33:43-44

The Bronze Snake

[4]Then they set out from Mount Hor by way of the *Red Sea to bypass the land of Edom, but the people[B] became impatient because of the journey. [5]The people spoke against God and Moses: "Why have you led us up from Egypt to die in the wilderness? There is no bread or water, and we detest this wretched food!" [6]Then the LORD sent poisonous[C,D] snakes among the people, and they bit them so that many Israelites died.[e]

[7]The people then came to Moses and said, "We have sinned by speaking against the LORD and against you. Intercede with the LORD so that He will take the snakes away from us." And Moses interceded for the people.

[8]Then the LORD said to Moses, "Make a snake image and mount it on a pole. When anyone who is bitten looks at it, he will recover."[f] [9]So Moses made a bronze snake and mounted it on a pole. Whenever someone was bitten, and he looked at the bronze snake, he recovered.

Journey around Moab

[10]The Israelites set out and camped at Oboth.[g] [11]They set out from Oboth and camped at Iye-abarim in the wilderness that borders Moab on the east. [12]From there they went and camped at Zered Valley. [13]They set out from there and camped on the other side of the Arnon River, in the wilderness that extends from the Amorite border, because the

---

[A]21:3 = destruction   [B]21:4 Lit soul of the people   [C]21:6 LXX reads deadly; Syr reads cruel; Vg reads fiery   [D]21:6 Lit burning

---

Aaron") near Petra; Jebel Medra about six miles northeast of Kadesh; 'Imaret el-Khurisheh about eight miles north of Kadesh; or Jebel Madurah about 15 miles northeast of Kadesh-barnea.

20:25-26 Aaron's death, like the death and burial of Abraham (Gn 25:8), Ishmael (Gn 25:17), Isaac (Gn 35:29), Jacob (Gn 49:29, 33), and then later Moses (Nm 27:13; Dt 32:50), is described as being **gathered to his people**. The phrase conveys the idea of being reunited with one's ancestral families in Sheol, the place of the dead. A person was not to be left unburied or "ungathered" since this was viewed as a disgraceful end of life.

21:1-3 After the death of Aaron, the Israelites set out from Mount Hor to go around Edom along **the Atharim road**. The city of Arad, ruled by the **king of Arad**, cannot be Tel Arad in the eastern Negev since it was unoccupied until the early Israelite monarchy. The Atharim was another trade route leading from Kadesh-barnea to Arad along which the fortresses of Bir Hafir, Oboda, and Aroer were built during the Israelite monarchy.

21:4 The trade route referred to as the **way of the Red Sea** extended from Elath on the eastern finger of the Red Sea in the Gulf of Aqaba northward through the Arabah to the Dead Sea. Hence the desert route would have the Israelites approaching the northern end of the Arabah from the southwest, and then crossing the Arabah between Tamar and Zalmonah.

21:5 For the seventh time, **the people spoke against God and Moses**. Their words were the same monotonous complaint about food and water.

21:6-7 God's judgment against the people came in the form of **poisonous snakes**, likely the carpet viper (Echis carinatus or E. coleratus).

21:8-9 The Lord directed Moses to **make a snake image and mount it on a pole** as an antidote for those who had been bitten by these snakes. Those who looked at this snake image would be healed—by faith in God's provision, not by faith in the graven serpent. Because it was God who graciously did the healing, it was neither idolatry nor magic. John's Gospel cited Jesus' use of this imagery as a metaphor for His crucifixion. Just as those in Moses' time looked upon this snake and were healed, those who look in faith to the Christ who was lifted up on the cross will be healed of their sins. Those who looked upon Him and believed in Him would have eternal life (Jn 3:14-16).

21:10-13 The pattern of the Israelites' journey was from south to north and around the area occupied by the Edomites. They departed from Mount Hor, through Zalmon and Punon, which are not mentioned here but are in Moses' recording of the stages of the journey (33:42). They continued through **Oboth** in the upper Arabah, south of the Dead Sea, to **Iye-abarim**, located near the edge of the Moabite region.

21:14-15 **The Book of the LORD's Wars** was apparently an early source of Israelite documentation of God's victories

Arnon was the Moabite border between Moab and the Amorites. [14]Therefore it is stated in the Book of the LORD's Wars:

> Waheb[A] in Suphah
> and the ravines of the Arnon,
> [15] even the slopes of the ravines
> that extend to the site of Ar[B,a]
> and lie along the border of Moab.

[16]From there they went to Beer,[C] the well the LORD told Moses about, "Gather the people so I may give them water." [17]Then Israel sang this song:

> Spring up, well—sing to it!
> [18] The princes dug the well;
> the nobles of the people hollowed it out
> with a scepter and with their staffs.

They went from the wilderness to Mattanah, [19]from Mattanah to Nahaliel, from Nahaliel to Bamoth, [20]from Bamoth to the valley in the territory of Moab near the Pisgah highlands[D,b] that overlook the wasteland.[E,c]

Amorite Kings Defeated

[21]Israel sent messengers to say to Sihon[d] king of the Amorites: [22]"Let us travel through your land. We won't go into the fields or vineyards. We won't drink any well water. We will travel the King's Highway until we have traveled through your territory."[e] [23]But Sihon would not let Israel travel through his territory. Instead, he gathered his whole army and went out to confront Israel in the wilderness. When he came to Jahaz,[f] he fought against Israel. [24]Israel struck him with the sword and took possession of his land from the Arnon to the Jabbok,[g] but only up to the Ammonite border, because it was fortified.[F,G] [25]Israel took all the cities and lived in all these Amorite cities, including Heshbon and all its villages. [26]Heshbon was the city of Sihon king of the Amorites, who had fought

[a]21:15 Nm 21:28; Dt 2:9,18,29; Is 15:1
[b]21:20 Nm 23:14; Dt 3:17,27; 4:49; 34:1; Jos 12:3; 13:20
[c]Nm 23:28
[d]21:21 Nm 32:33; Dt 1:4; 2:24–4:46
[e]21:22 Nm 20:17; Dt 2:26-33
[f]21:23 Dt 2:32; Jdg 11:20; 1Ch 6:78
[g]21:21-24 Jdg 11:19-22

A21:14 = the source of the Arnon River   B21:15 A city in Moab; Nm 21:28; Dt 2:9,18,29; Is 15:1   C21:16 = well   D21:20 = Moabite mountain plateau; Nm 23:14; Dt 3:17,27; 4:49; 34:1; Jos 12:3; 13:20   E21:20 Or *overlook Jeshimon*   F21:24 LXX reads *was Jazer*   G21:24 Or *was at Az*

on behalf of His people, perhaps in poetic form. This source is otherwise unknown in the OT, though paralleled by the Book of Jashar, cited in Jos 10:13 and 2Sm 1:18. This quotation implies that the original composition was longer. **Waheb in Suphah** is probably the source of the Arnon River. The mention of **ravines** is indicative of the **Arnon** River gorge. **Ar** of **Moab** was a city, probably south of the Arnon River (v. 28; Dt 2:9; Is 15:1).

21:16-20 The epic narrative poem sung by Israel continues the journey motif from this **well** where the Israelites did not complain about a lack of water. They journeyed to the sites of Mattanah ("gift"), Nahaliel ("river of God"), Bamoth ("high places, cultic center"), a valley in the Moabite countryside, and the peak of the **Pisgah** mountains which overlooks the **wasteland**. Translators and commentators alike have faced the problem of whether these are genuine place names or just descriptive terms. The sequence does not contain the usual phraseology of the book of Numbers, "they departed from . . . they camped at . . . ." Poised on top of Mount Nebo in the Pisgah mountains, Moses would be granted a glimpse of the promised land. **Mattanah** has not been identified, though Khirbet el-Medeiyineh (Madaynah) has been suggested. Y. Aharoni identified Iye-abarim (Iyyim) with Khirbet el-Medeiyineh, located about 11 miles northeast of Diban.

Nahaliel has not been located, though this could be a reference to the Wadi Zerqa-ma'in, which flows from the central highlands to the Dead Sea. **Bamoth** has not been identified, though it could have been preserved in the longer form Bamoth-baal (22:41) or Beth-bamoth of the Mesha Inscription. Bamoth was a common place name that was combined with names or titles of deities in the naming of important worship centers among the Canaanites and the Amorites. This Bamoth may have been somewhere near Mount Nebo in the Pisgah range. On a clear winter day from the traditional Mount Nebo, one can see where the Jordan River flows into the Dead Sea, the northern end of the Judean Wilderness and the Jericho oasis. The valley in

verse 20 could be identified with the Wadi 'Ayun Musa, about two miles northeast of the corner of the Dead Sea.

Finally, Aharoni identified **the wasteland** as a place name within Beth-jeshimoth, part of the realm of the Amorites that was conquered by Israel (Jos 12:3). The Way of Beth-jeshimoth descended from Heshbon westward toward the Jordan River.

21:21-22 Moses dispatched diplomatic envoys to **Sihon king of the Amorites** to negotiate rights of passage northward along the King's Highway in the Transjordan highlands and then westward down the hillsides to the shores of the Jordan River. The Amorites were a large ethnic group that formed in upper Mesopotamia near the end of the early Bronze Age, about 2300–2000 B.C. Sometimes the word "Amorite" is used generically in the Bible as a reference to the population of Canaan.

21:23-25 Just as the king of Edom had refused to grant the Israelites passage through his territory, so too **Sihon**, the recent usurper and conqueror of Moab, **would not let Israel travel through his territory**. Perhaps he had heard of the encounter with Edom and thought his response would be treated the same way. But his military's attempt to block the advance of Israel was met with a resounding defeat, a victory that would be remembered throughout Israel's history (Dt 2:26-31; Jos 12:2-5; 13:21; Jdg 11:19-21; 1Kg 4:19, Neh 9:22; Jr 48:45). Biblical and extrabiblical evidence locates **Jahaz** somewhere between Dibon and Madaba. The Amorite kingdom of Sihon seems to have spread from the Arnon to the Jabbok rivers, a north-south length of about 45 to 50 miles, flanked by the fortified towns of the Ammonites on the eastern and northern sides.

21:26-31 Heshbon was the major city of **Sihon** at the time of the Israelite conflicts. S. Horn suggested that the Heshbon of Sihon could have been located at Jalul, or another nearby site. The song declared about the rebuilding of Heshbon, **let it be rebuilt**. The Amorite woe oracle song, which the Israelites adapted for singing about their victory over the

against the former king of Moab and had taken control of all his land as far as the Arnon. [27]Therefore the poets[A] say:

> Come to Heshbon, let it be rebuilt;
> let the city of Sihon be restored.[B]
> [28] For fire came out of Heshbon,
> a flame from the city of Sihon.
> It consumed Ar of Moab,
> the lords of[C] Arnon's heights.
> [29] Woe to you, Moab!
> You have been destroyed,
> people of Chemosh![a]
> He gave up his sons as refugees,
> and his daughters into captivity
> to Sihon the Amorite king.
> [30] We threw them down;
> Heshbon has been destroyed
> as far as Dibon.[D,b]
> We caused desolation as far as Nophah,
> which reaches as far as Medeba.[E,c]

[31]So Israel lived in the Amorites' land. [32]After Moses sent spies to Jazer, Israel captured its villages and drove out the Amorites who were there.

[33]Then they turned and went up the road to Bashan, and Og king of Bashan[d] came out against them with his whole army to do battle at Edrei.[e] [34]But the LORD said to Moses, "Do not fear him, for I have handed him over to you along with his whole army and his land. Do to him as you did to Sihon king of the Amorites, who lived in Heshbon."[f] [35]So they struck him, his sons, and his whole army until no one was left,[F] and they took possession of his land.[g]

Balak Hires Balaam

22 The Israelites traveled on and camped in the plains of Moab near the Jordan across from Jericho. [2]Now Balak[h] son of Zippor saw all that Israel had done to the Amorites. [3]Moab was terrified of the people because they were numerous, and Moab dreaded the Israelites. [4]So the Moabites said to the elders of Midian, "This horde will devour everything

---

Cross-references column:

a 21:27-29 Jdg 11:24; 1Kg 11:7,33; Jr 48:45-47
b 21:30 Nm 32:34; Neh 11:25; Jr 48:18,22
c Jos 13:9,16; 1Ch 19:7; Is 15:2
d 21:33 Nm 32:33; Dt 3:1-13; 4:47
e Dt 3:1,10; Jos 12:4; 13:12,31
f 21:34 Dt 3:2
g 21:35 Ps 135:10-11
h 22:2 Jos 24:9-10; Mc 6:5; Rv 2:14

A 21:27 Lit *ones who speak proverbs*   B 21:27 Or *firmly founded*   C 21:28 LXX reads *Moab, and swallowed*   D 21:30 LXX reads *Their seed will perish from Heshbon*; Vg reads *Their yoke has perished from Heshbon*   E 21:30 LXX reads *Dibon. And their women have further kindled a fire against Moab*; Hb uncertain   F 21:35 Lit *left to him*

---

great conqueror Sihon, denounced the Moabites and their god Chemosh. Portions of this song would be recounted in the prophets' oracles against Moab in the eighth to the sixth centuries B.C., including Is 15:1-14 and Jr 48:1-47.

Chemosh was the patron deity of the Moabites. He is first mentioned among the deities at Ebla about 2600–2250 B.C. and was associated with mud brick production and then later with agricultural production. The worship of Chemosh of Moab was brought into Jerusalem in the tenth century B.C. by King Solomon, who built a temple to Chemosh on the hill opposite that upon which the temple of Yahweh was built early in his reign. Chemosh is mentioned 12 times in the Mesha Stele, including the appellation Ashtar-Chemosh, as the god who enabled Mesha to break the yoke of Israel's domination, recapturing and rebuilding a number of his cities, including Jahaz (v. 23) and Dibon (also Dibon-gad in 33:45-46), Almon-diblathaim (33:46-47), and Medeba (21:30). **Heshbon** is not preserved in the Mesha Inscription, though it remained a vital city during this period in Moab's history.

21:32 Jazer may have come under Amorite dominion in the expansion of Sihon or Og into the Ammonite region. Jazer was both the name of a region (32:1) and its principal city (32:3). The town of Jazer was located in the valley of the Wadi Kefrein, which flows down toward the Jordan River. The city was identified by J. Simons with Khirbet-Gazzir (Jazer), about 10 miles northwest of Amman.

21:33-35 The capital of **Og king of Bashan** was located at Ashtaroth, situated on a northern tributary of the Yarmuk River (Dt 1:4). The battle ensued at **Edrei**, generally associated with modern Der'a on the Syrian-Jordanian border, about 30 miles east of the Sea of Galilee. Later Edrei would be included in the tribal territorial allocation of the Machirites of the eastern half of the tribe of Manasseh (Jos 13:31). Though no other battles in this campaign are recounted in Numbers, 60 cities from the kingdom of Og of Bashan were subjected to the stipulations of holy war (Dt 3:4-6). The key to Israel's success in the battles in Transjordan and in conquest of the promised land across the Jordan River was its dependence on Yahweh and not on its military might.

22:1–24:25 This passage contains the account of Balaam, a renowned pagan divination expert, and his oracles of blessing upon Israel. As the very antithesis of the great prophet Moses, this prophet sought Israel's demise at the bidding of the Moabite king Balak. Instead Balaam was used by God in a manner like Moses to pronounce future divine blessing for Israel. Moses is curiously absent from the story, probably because of his sin of rebellion and irreverence at Meribah (20:2-13). In this section God demonstrated that He can use even a pagan wizard to bring blessing to His people.

22:1 The setting of this story for Israel was the eastern side of the Jordan River. The leading characters Balak and Balaam were situated in the hills of Transjordan, overlooking the Israelite encampment from the southeast. The **plains of Moab** was the broad plain between the Transjordan highlands and the Jordan River, extending about 10 miles from just north of the Dead Sea.

According to an inscription in a temple at Deir 'Alla, Balaam son of Beor, a "seer of the gods," had a frightening night vision that he described while fasting and mourning. He foretold a period of drought and darkness, of mourning and death, in which the natural order of the world was reversed. The sparrow attacks the eagle, the deaf hear things from a distance, and fools have insightful visions. Balaam then implored the goddesses Ashtar (consort of Chemosh in Moab) and Sheger (known from Ugarit and Phoenicia) to bring light, rain, and fertility to the land. Thus the structure at Deir 'Alla and its wall inscriptions may have been built to honor the gods Sheger and Ashtar who once heeded Balaam's plea.

22:2-4 Balak is called **Moab's king**, meaning he was the head of an emerging tribal confederation like similar

around us like an ox eats up the green plants in the field."

Since Balak son of Zippor was Moab's king at that time, [5]he sent messengers to Balaam[a] son of Beor at Pethor, which is by the Euphrates in the land of his people.[A,B] Balak said to him: "Look, a people has come out of Egypt; they cover the surface of the land and are living right across from me. [6]Please come and put a curse on these people for me because they are more powerful than I am. I may be able to defeat them and drive them out of the land, for I know that those you bless are blessed and those you curse are cursed."

[7]The elders of Moab and Midian departed with fees for *divination in hand.[b] They came to Balaam and reported Balak's words to him. [8]He said to them, "Spend the night here, and I will give you the answer the LORD tells me." So the officials of Moab stayed with Balaam.

[9]Then God came to Balaam and asked, "Who are these men with you?"

[10]Balaam replied to God, "Balak son of Zippor, king of Moab, sent this message to me: [11]'Look, a people has come out of Egypt, and they cover the surface of the land. Now come and put a curse on them for me. I may be able to fight against them and drive them away.'"

[12]Then God said to Balaam, "You are not to go with them. You are not to curse this people, for they are blessed."

[13]So Balaam got up the next morning and said to Balak's officials, "Go back to your land, because the LORD has refused to let me go with you."

[14]The officials of Moab arose, returned to Balak, and reported, "Balaam refused to come with us."

[15]Balak sent officials again who were more numerous and higher in rank than the others. [16]They came to Balaam and said to him, "This is what Balak son of Zippor says: 'Let nothing keep you from coming to me, [17]for I will greatly honor you and do whatever you ask me. So please come and put a curse on these people for me!'"

[18]But Balaam responded to the servants of Balak, "If Balak were to give me his house full of silver and gold, I could not go against the command of the LORD my God to do anything small or great. [19]Please stay here overnight as the others did, so that I may find out what else the LORD has to tell me."

[20]God came to Balaam at night and said to him, "Since these men have come to summon you, get up and go with them, but you must only do what I tell you." [21]When he got up in the morning, Balaam saddled his donkey and went with the officials of Moab.

a 22:5 Dt 23:3-5; Jos 24:9-10; Mc 6:5; 2Pt 2:15-16; Jd 11; Rv 2:14
b 22:7 2Pt 2:15; Jd 11

A 22:5 Sam, Vg, Syr read *of the Ammonites*   B 22:5 Or *of the Amawites*

---

groups in Transjordan, such as the Edomites and Ammonites. At various times Moabite territory stretched northward to Heshbon and the surrounding plains, and in this context, the plains just east of the Jordan River opposite the city of Jericho. The Midianites originated in northern Arabia and southern Transjordan. According to Gn 25:1-6, they were descendants of Abraham and his concubine Keturah. Their loose-knit seminomadic culture carried them from Arabia to Sinai and Egypt (Ex 2:15-22; Nm 10:29), and occasionally they made forays into Canaan as traders (Gn 37:25-36) or as marauding invaders (Jdg 6:1-6). A group of Midianite **elders** joined Balak's emissaries in enlisting the services of Balaam to curse Israel.

22:5 Balaam was from the Mesopotamian town of **Pethor**, identified with Pitru, on the Sajur River tributary west of the Euphrates River. The distance from Pethor to Moab would have exceeded 400 miles, making each trip by the emissaries of Balak 25 days each way.

22:6 Balak asked Balaam to **come and put a curse on these people**, referring to the Israelites. Ancient Near Eastern texts recount the power of diviners, magicians, and sorcerers to manipulate the will of the gods through augury, special sacrificial rituals such as ritual dissection, and incantations aimed at blessing or cursing an individual or group, forecasting the future, and advising kings and other leaders.

22:7 Balaam was to be rewarded after fulfilling his cursing of Israel (v. 37; 24:11). Scholars have interpreted the phrase "divination in their hands" (Hb *uqsamim beyadam*) as indi-

cating that they had divination equipment or **fees for divination** in their hands, or as saying that the emissaries of Balak were versed in divination. V. Hurowitz ("The Expression *uqsamin beyadam*") suggests that certain "magical" objects were used in the negotiation process with the recipient of the divination, including clay models of intestinal entrails, livers, or other body parts used in the practice of extispicy, the art of ritual dissection. So what was "in their hands" may have been baked clay models of the entrails predicting Moab's downfall and Israel's ascendancy. These predictions may have alarmed Balak's own trained diviners so much that they sought a person of great renown such as Balaam to curse Israel so Moab would be delivered.

22:9-11 Appearing to **Balaam** in a dream-like manner, **God** began a dialogue with the pagan diviner. In all ancient societies dreams were thought to be a major channel by which deity communicated with humanity.

22:12 God's clear intent was to bless His people as He had promised to do since the call of Abram (Gn 12:1-3).

22:15-21 The attempt at procuring Balaam's service by a second, higher-ranking group of emissaries from Balak was met with a cautious response. The words used in verse 18 indicate that Balaam would become God's spokesman. The terminology of divine speech has now come full circle from Moses to Balaam; Balaam should only "do" (Hb *'asah*) what God "speaks" (Hb *davar*; v. 20). These terms are used together throughout the book of Numbers in the context of the faithful following of the Lord's commands in the

Balaam's Donkey and the Angel

a 22:28 2Pt 2:15-16

[22] But God was incensed that Balaam was going, and the Angel of the LORD took His stand on the path to oppose him. Balaam was riding his donkey, and his two servants were with him. [23] When the donkey saw the Angel of the LORD standing on the path with a drawn sword in His hand, she turned off the path and went into the field. So Balaam hit her to return her to the path. [24] Then the Angel of the LORD stood in a narrow passage between the vineyards, with a stone wall on either side. [25] The donkey saw the Angel of the LORD and pressed herself against the wall, squeezing Balaam's foot against it. So he hit her once again. [26] The Angel of the LORD went ahead and stood in a narrow place where there was no room to turn to the right or the left. [27] When the donkey saw the Angel of the LORD, she crouched down under Balaam. So he became furious and beat the donkey with his stick.

[28] Then the LORD opened the donkey's mouth, and she asked Balaam, "What have I done to you that you have beaten me these three times?"[a]

[29] Balaam answered the donkey, "You made me look like a fool. If I had a sword in my hand, I'd kill you now!"

[30] But the donkey said, "Am I not the donkey you've ridden all your life until today? Have I ever treated you this way before?"

"No," he replied.

[31] Then the LORD opened Balaam's eyes, and he saw the Angel of the LORD standing in the path with a drawn sword in His hand. Balaam knelt and bowed with his face to the ground. [32] The Angel of the LORD asked him, "Why have you beaten your donkey these three times? Look, I came out to oppose you, because what you are doing is evil in My sight. [33] The donkey saw Me and turned away from Me these three times. If she had not turned away from Me, I would have killed you by now and let her live."

[34] Balaam said to the Angel of the LORD, "I have sinned, for I did not know that You were standing in the path to confront me. And now, if it is evil in Your sight, I will go back."

[35] Then the Angel of the LORD said to Balaam, "Go with the men, but you are to say only what I tell you." So Balaam went with Balak's officials.

[36] When Balak heard that Balaam was coming, he went out to meet him at the Moabite city[A] on the Arnon border at the edge of his territory. [37] Balak asked Balaam, "Did I not send you an urgent summons? Why didn't you come to me? Am I really not able to reward you?"

[38] Balaam said to him, "Look, I have come to you, but can I say anything I want? I must speak only the message God puts in my mouth." [39] So Balaam went with Balak, and they came to Kiriath-huzoth.[B] [40] Balak sacrificed cattle and sheep, and sent for Balaam and the officials who were with him.

[41] In the morning, Balak took Balaam and

A 22:36 Or at Ir-moab, or at Ar of Moab   B 22:39 = The City of Streets

---

sequence of God speaking and Moses (or others) doing just what the Lord commanded.

22:22 The Angel of the LORD challenged the commitment of the prophet-diviner to fulfill the task that God had for him. That God would become angry and engage one of his servants on a journey directed by Him is consistent with the challenges presented to Jacob when he was traveling back to Canaan (Gn 32:22-32). This also reminds us of Moses when he was headed to Egypt to challenge the pharaoh (Ex 4:24-26). In both cases these men were reminded that a holy God was in control of the situation, and they were to be faithful in completing their assigned tasks.

22:23-27 The words **when the donkey saw the Angel of the LORD** are filled with irony, especially when used three times in this context. This renowned "seer of the gods" could not see what this lowly donkey saw. Furthermore, this donkey was a female, placing the animal in an even lower status when compared to the relative value and usefulness of male donkeys. Balaam beat her into submission, though she was ultimately more submissive to God than the one whom God was sending to pronounce blessing upon Israel.

22:28 Tales of talking animals were common in ancient literature, and were considered fables that often contained warning, irony, or satire. There are two general interpretations of this event: (1) God literally gave the donkey the power of speech (**the LORD opened the donkey's mouth**), or (2) the donkey's normal braying was heightened to such a degree that it was perceived and interpreted by Balaam in a human manner. R. K. Harrison has suggested, "As the donkey brayed, she conveyed a message of anger and resentment that the seer understood in his mind in a verbal form" (Harrison, *Numbers,* 300).

22:36-38 Balaam's repetition of the words of divine instruction—**I must speak only the message God puts in my mouth** (cp. vv. 20,35)—shows that what is about to come from him is divine revelation. Balaam's ability to influence the coming events was less than that of his donkey.

22:39 Kiriath-huzoth, the "city of plazas" as the name translates, may have been a central market area for the city of Ar in Moab, based on the suggestions of A. Biran, excavator of Tel Dan in northern Israel. Such buildings near the market plaza outside the gates of cities apparently served as offices for the oversight of commercial activity.

22:41 Balaam's sacrificial activity began at **Bamoth-baal** ("the high places of Baal"), a cultic center for the worship of the Semitic deity Baal, the champion of creation in the mythology of Ugarit.

brought him to Bamoth-baal.[A] From there he
saw the outskirts of the people's camp.

Balaam's Oracles

23 Then Balaam said to Balak, "Build me
seven altars here and prepare seven
bulls and seven rams for me." 2 So Balak did as
Balaam directed, and they offered a bull and
a ram on each altar. 3 Balaam said to Balak,
"Stay here by your •burnt offering while I am
gone. Maybe the LORD[B] will meet with me. I
will tell you whatever He reveals to me." So
he went to a barren hill.
4 God[C] met with him and Balaam said to
Him, "I have arranged seven altars and offered a bull and a ram on each altar." 5 Then
the LORD put a message in Balaam's mouth
and said, "Return to Balak and say what I tell
you."
6 So he returned to Balak, who was standing
there by his burnt offering with all the officials of Moab.

Balaam's First Oracle

7 Balaam proclaimed his poem:

Balak brought me from Aram;[a]
the king of Moab,
from the eastern mountains:
"Come, put a curse on Jacob for me;
come, denounce Israel!"[b]
8 How can I curse someone
God has not cursed?
How can I denounce someone the LORD
has not denounced?
9 I see them from the top of rocky cliffs,
and I watch them from the hills.
There is a people living alone;[c]
it does not consider itself
among the nations.
10 Who has counted the dust of Jacob
or numbered the dust clouds[D] of Israel?
Let me die the death of the upright;
let the end of my life be like theirs.

11 "What have you done to me?" Balak asked
Balaam. "I brought you to curse my enemies,
but look, you have only blessed them!"
12 He answered, "Shouldn't I say exactly
what the LORD puts in my mouth?"[d]

Balaam's Second Oracle

13 Then Balak said to him, "Please come with
me to another place where you can see them.
You will only see the outskirts of their camp;
you won't see all of them. From there, put a
curse on them for me." 14 So Balak took him
to Lookout Field[E] on top of Pisgah, built seven
altars, and offered a bull and a ram on each
altar.
15 Balaam said to Balak, "Stay here by your
burnt offering while I seek the LORD over
there."
16 The LORD met with Balaam and put a message in his mouth. Then He said, "Return to
Balak and say what I tell you."
17 So he returned to Balak, who was standing
there by his burnt offering with the officials
of Moab. Balak asked him, "What did the LORD
say?"
18 Balaam proclaimed his poem:

Balak, get up and listen;
son of Zippor, pay attention to what
I say!
19 God is not a man who lies,

[a] 23:7 Dt 23:4
[b] Nm 22:6,17
[c] 23:9 Dt 33:28
[d] 23:12 Nm 22:38

[A] 22:41 = The High Places of Baal [B] 23:3 DSS, LXX, Sam read *Maybe God* [C] 23:4 DSS, Sam read *The Angel of God* [D] 23:10 Or *numbered a fourth* [E] 23:14 Or *to the field of Zophim*

23:1 The preference for performing seven rituals was widespread in the ancient Near East, though multiple altars are not mentioned elsewhere in the OT. The sacrificing of **seven bulls and seven rams** on seven altars parallels a well-known Babylonian text in which Ea, Shamash, and Marduk are worshiped with the ritual libation of blood of seven sheep poured out on seven altars.

23:3 In the ancient Near Eastern context of sacrificial cults, to "stand by one's offering" meant to have a proxy for the offerer. In some settings a high priest of the given deity would make a sacrifice on behalf of the king while the king stood by the offering. Balaam functioned as a priest and diviner in these narratives on behalf of Balak, who "stood by" the offering made on behalf of the Moabite people. Balaam was called to curse Israel to deliver the Moabites from potential enslavement and oppression.

23:7-8 God's hand was upon **Israel** and she could **not** be **cursed**, even by the best divination experts of that time. The God of Israel cannot be manipulated or cajoled into carrying out the desires of kings or diviners. God had promised Abraham that his descendants would become a great nation through which the other nations would be blessed—even Moab and Balaam (Gn 12:1-3; 22:17-18).

23:11-12 The prophet-diviner **Balaam** had become the mouth of God.

23:13-26 From another outpost overlooking the northeastern corner of the Dead Sea and the plains of Moab where Israel was camped, Balaam and Balak repeated the ritual sacrifices of the first encounter. Nothing Balaam could muster could bring any harm to God's people.

23:14 The **Lookout Field on top of Pisgah** was probably so named because of its strategic observation location. Several scholars interpret this location as a known place for observing heavenly omens and making astrological observations. At Pisgah, a prominent peak in the Abarim range, Moses would later commission Joshua (27:12-23), and God would give Moses an overview of the promised land from this spot (Dt 34:1-12).

23:19-20 Unlike the gods of Mesopotamia, who were depicted often as whimsical and easily manipulated through

or a son of man who changes His mind.
Does He speak and not act,
or promise and not fulfill?[a]

20 I have indeed received a command
　to bless;
since He has blessed,[A]
　I cannot change it.
21 He considers no disaster for Jacob;
He sees no trouble for Israel.[B]
The LORD their God is with them,[b]
and there is rejoicing over the King
　among them.
22 God brought them out of Egypt;
He is like the horns of a wild ox
　for them.[C,c]
23 There is no magic curse against Jacob
and no *divination against Israel.
It will now be said about Jacob
　and Israel,
"What great things God has done!"
24 A people rise up like a lioness;
They rouse themselves like a lion.[d]
They will not lie down
　until they devour the prey
and drink the blood of the slain.

25 Then Balak told Balaam, "Don't curse them and don't bless them!"

26 But Balaam answered him, "Didn't I tell you: Whatever the LORD says, I must do?"[e]

Balaam's Third Oracle

27 Again Balak said to Balaam, "Please come. I will take you to another place. Maybe it will be agreeable to God that you can put a curse on them for me there." 28 So Balak took Balaam to the top of Peor, which overlooks the wasteland.[D,f]

29 Balaam told Balak, "Build me seven altars here and prepare seven bulls and seven rams for me."[g] 30 So Balak did as Balaam said and offered a bull and a ram on each altar.

24 Since Balaam saw that it pleased the LORD to bless Israel, he did not go to seek omens as on previous occasions, but turned[E] toward the wilderness. 2 When Balaam looked up and saw Israel encamped tribe by tribe, the Spirit of God[h] came on him, 3 and he proclaimed his poem:

The *oracle of Balaam son of Beor,
　the oracle of the man whose eyes
　　are opened,[F]
4 the oracle of one who hears the sayings
　　of God,
who sees a vision from the *Almighty,[i]
who falls into a trance with his eyes
　uncovered:
5 How beautiful are your tents,
　Jacob,
your dwellings, Israel.
6 They stretch out like river valleys,[G]
like gardens beside a stream,
like aloes the LORD has planted,
like cedars beside the water.
7 Water will flow from his buckets,
and his seed will be
　by abundant water.
His king will be greater than Agag,[H,j]
and his kingdom will be exalted.
8 God brought him out of Egypt;
He is like[i] the horns of a wild ox
　for them.[k]
He will feed on enemy nations
and gnaw their bones;
he will strike them with his arrows.
9 He crouches, he lies down like a lion
or a lioness—who dares
　to rouse him?[l]
Those who bless you will be blessed,
and those who curse you
　will be cursed.[m]

10 Then Balak became furious with Balaam,

a 23:19 1Sm 15:29; Rm 11:29; 2Tm 2:13; Heb 6:17-18
b 23:21 Dt 2:7; 20:1; Jos 1:17; Zph 3:17; Rv 21:3
c 23:22 Nm 24:8
d 23:24 Nm 24:9
e 23:26 Nm 22:38
f 23:28 Nm 21:20
g 23:29 Nm 23:1-2
h 24:2 Ex 35:31; Nm 11:17,25-26,29; 1Sm 10:10
i 24:4 Is 13:6,9; Ezk 30:2-3; Jl 2:1-2,11,31
j 24:7 Ex 17:14-16; 1Sm 15:8-33
k 24:8 Nm 23:22
l 24:9 Gn 49:9; Nm 23:24
m Gn 12:3; 27:29

A 23:20 Sam, LXX read *since I will bless*　B 23:21 Or *not observe sin in Jacob; not see wrongdoing*　C 23:22 Or *Egypt; they have the horns of a wild ox*　D 23:28 Or *overlooks Jeshimon*　E 24:1 Lit *set his face*　F 24:3 LXX reads *true*; Vg reads *closed*　G 24:6 Or *like date palms*　H 24:7 Sam, LXX, Sym, Theod read *Gog*　I 24:8 Or *He has*

---

sorcery and divination, the God of Israel was **not a man who lies . . . who changes His mind**. Balaam could not change what God had instructed him to proclaim—blessing for Israel, God's chosen people.

23:22 Israel's strength was totally in her God, but by His power she was compared to a ravaging **wild ox**. Ancient Near Eastern deities such as El and Baal were often depicted as horned bulls or as humans with the head or horns of a bull.

23:23 Israel did not need augurs, diviners, or magicians; in fact these were condemned and prohibited. Augury included reading cloud patterns, bird movements, and other activities in the skies. Divination included extispicy, the ritual slaughter of animals and the reading of their entrails by hepatoscopy (liver dissection) and colonoscopy (viewing of the intestinal lining). Such practices were not the source

of Israel's defense, nor could such powers be used against God's people. The Lord would use Balaam, a pagan diviner, to bless those he had been called to condemn.

23:25–24:9 After two failed attempts, Balak reeled from the words of Balaam and called for the prophet to refrain from pronouncing a blessing on them. Then Balaam and Balak resorted to a third cultic center, in the heights above **Peor**, overlooking Jeshimon, from which they could see **Israel encamped tribe by tribe** (24:2). The sevenfold ritual is repeated again, without resorting to divination as Balaam had previously done. An ecstatic encounter with the Spirit of God ensued, opening Balaam's **eyes** to a vision of God Almighty. Balaam's utterance forecast the Lord's blessing upon the land with abundance of **water** bringing productivity to the crops, and a powerful kingdom that would surpass that of

struck his hands together, and said to him, "I summoned you to put a curse on my enemies, but instead, you have blessed them these three times. [11] Now go to your home! I said I would reward you richly,[a] but look, the LORD has denied you a reward."

[12] Balaam answered Balak, "Didn't I previously tell the messengers you sent me: [13] If Balak were to give me his house full of silver and gold, I could not go against the LORD's command, to do anything good or bad of my own will? I will say whatever the LORD says.[b] [14] Now I am going back to my people, but first, let me warn you what these people will do to your people in the future."

Balaam's Fourth Oracle

[15] Then he proclaimed his poem:

The oracle of Balaam son of Beor,
the oracle of the man whose eyes
are opened;[A]
[16] the oracle of one who hears the sayings
of God
and has knowledge
from the •Most High,
who sees a vision from the Almighty,
who falls into a trance with his
eyes uncovered:[c]
[17] I see him,[B] but not now;
I perceive him,[B] but not near.

A star will come from Jacob,
and a scepter will arise from Israel.[d]
He will smash the forehead[c] of Moab
and strike down[D] all the Shethites.[E]
[18] Edom will become a possession;
Seir[e] will become a possession
of its enemies,
but Israel will be triumphant.
[19] One who comes from Jacob
will rule;
he will destroy the city's survivors.

[20] Then Balaam saw Amalek and proclaimed his poem:

Amalek was first among the nations,[f]
but his future is destruction.

[21] Next he saw the Kenites and proclaimed his poem:

Your dwelling place is enduring;
your nest is set in the cliffs.
[22] Kain will be destroyed
when Asshur takes you captive.

[23] Once more he proclaimed his poem:

Ah, who can live when God does this?
[24] Ships will come from the coast
of Kittim;[g]
they will afflict Asshur and Eber,[h]
but they too will come to destruction.

Cross references (center column):
[a] 24:11 Nm 22:17
[b] 24:13 Nm 22:18,38
[c] 24:15-16 Nm 24:3-4
[d] 24:17 Gn 49:10; Mt 2:2; Rv 22:16
[e] 24:18 Gn 32:3
[f] 24:20 Ex 17:8-16; 1Sm 15
[g] 24:24 Gn 10:4; Is 23:1,12; Jr 2:10; Dn 11:30
[h] Gn 10:21,24-25; 11:14-27

[A] 24:15 LXX reads *true*; Vg reads *closed*   [B] 24:17 Or *Him*   [C] 24:17 Or *frontiers*   [D] 24:17 Sam reads *and the skulls of*; Jr 48:45   [E] 24:17 Or *Sethites*

---

the forces of **Agag** the Amalekite. But the strength of Israel was in the strength of her God. The Lord's blessing was so powerful that even the most renowned divination expert of the day could not turn it back.

24:15-19 In a visionary encounter similar to that of the third oracle, Balaam uttered predictive prophecy about the distant future of Israel. The **star** and **scepter** are symbols of a glorious and powerful kingdom that would subdue the enemies of Israel, typified as **Moab** and **Edom**. In the early Israelite monarchy, David fulfilled this prophecy by defeating and subjugating both Moab and Edom (2Sm 8:1-12). But as later Israelite kings failed to obey God's instructions and as oppression and exile followed, this passage would be interpreted messianically to refer to a coming glorious king. The model of a just and righteous king was brought to ultimate fulfillment in Jesus' establishment of the kingdom of God.

24:20-24 Three brief oracles about the destiny of other nations conclude the account of Balaam. Critics ascribe these texts to late authors or sources because of their brevity and language. Yet their collective theme is that God would subdue all peoples like Moab who opposed His will and His people. The **Amalekite** people would be subdued under Saul, Samuel, and David. The **Kenites** would be subdued by their neighbors, the northern Sinai tribe of Asshur (Gn 25:3,18—not the same as the later Assyrians). The Kenites were a nomadic clan from the eastern Sinai region whose roots are traced biblically to the descendants of Cain and who are associated with metallurgical craftsmanship (Gn 4:17-24). In Jdg 1:16 the association is made between the Kenites and Moses' Midianite in-laws, Jethro, Reuel, and Hobab, whose descendants settled in the Negev near Arad. Later Kenites lived as far north as the territory of Naphtali. The present text notes a group of Kenites who, like some Midianites, had become enemies of Israel and would eventually be subdued. Then the Asshurite people would in turn be conquered by the **Kittim**, a reference to the Mediterranean peoples such as the Philistines. They too would then see their demise.

The reference to Asshur is probably not to the later Assyrian empire of the ninth to seventh centuries B.C., or even the Middle Assyrian peoples of the late Bronze Age, who seldom ventured west of the Euphrates River. Most associate this citation with the relatively unknown Asshurites, a nomadic group of the Negev region, mentioned in Gn 25:3,18 and Ps 83:8. They were descendants of Abraham and his concubine Keturah. Kittim is one of the ancient terms for Cyprus (Gn 10:4), derived from its major city Kition (thus Kitionites). In several OT passages, the term was used generically for the islands of the Mediterranean and their inhabitants (Jr 2:10; Dn 11:30). The (Hb) *kittiyim* mentioned in the Arad inscriptions were probably Greek and Cypriot mercenaries serving in the Judean army in border fortresses. During the Hellenistic period "Kittim" became a byword for the archenemies of God, a prominent motif in the Qumran scrolls in reference to the Greeks and then the Romans. In the eschatological climax of history, all rebellious nations will bow to the judgment of God.

²⁵Balaam then arose and went back to his homeland, and Balak also went his way.

Israel Worships Baal

25 While Israel was staying in the Acacia Grove,^(A,a) the people began to have sexual relations with the women of Moab. ²The women invited them to the sacrifices for their gods, and the people ate and bowed in worship to their gods.^b ³So Israel aligned itself with •Baal of Peor,^c and the Lord's anger burned against Israel.^d ⁴The Lord said to Moses, "Take all the leaders of the people and execute^B them in broad daylight before the Lord so that His burning anger may turn away from Israel."

⁵So Moses told Israel's judges, "Kill each of the men who aligned themselves with Baal of Peor."

Phinehas Intervenes

⁶An Israelite man came bringing a Midianite woman to his relatives in the sight of Moses and the whole Israelite community while they were weeping at the entrance to the tent of meeting. ⁷When Phinehas son of Eleazar, son of Aaron the priest, saw this, he got up from the assembly, took a spear in his hand, ⁸followed the Israelite man into the tent,^c and drove it through both the Israelite man and the woman—through her belly. Then the plague on the Israelites was stopped, ⁹but those who died in the plague numbered 24,000.^e

¹⁰The Lord spoke to Moses, ¹¹"Phinehas son of Eleazar, son of Aaron the priest, has turned back My wrath from the Israelites because he was zealous among them with My zeal,^(D,f) so that I did not destroy the Israelites in My zeal. ¹²Therefore declare: I grant him My covenant of peace.^g ¹³It will be a covenant of perpetual priesthood for him and his future descendants,^h because he was zealous for his God and made •atonement for the Israelites."

¹⁴The name of the slain Israelite man, who was struck dead with the Midianite woman,

Cross references:
a 25:1 Nm 33:49; Jos 2:1; 3:1; Mc 6:5
b 25:2 Ex 34:15-16; 1Co 10:8; Rv 2:14
c 25:3 Nm 23:28
d Dt 4:3; Ps 106:28-29; Hs 9:10
e 25:9 1Co 10:8
f 25:11 Ex 34:14; Zch 8:2
g 25:12 Is 54:10; Ezk 34:25; 37:26; Mal 2:5
h 25:13 Ex 40:15; Ps 106:30-31

---

^A 25:1 Or *in Shittim*   ^B 25:4 Or *impale*, or *hang*, or *expose*; Hb obscure   ^C 25:8 Perhaps a tent shrine or bridal tent   ^D 25:11 Or *jealousy*

24:25 Balaam began his trek homeward, but as 31:8 suggests, he was killed in the Midianite campaign, having been instrumental in instigating the idolatrous enticement of Israelites in chapter 25.

25:1 The scene moves back from the mountains of Moab to the Israelite camp at **Acacia Grove** in the lower Jordan River Valley. The tenor of the narrative immediately reverts back to rebellious Israel. The placement of the two scenes back-to-back was designed to contrast Balaam's obedience with Israel's sinfulness.

25:2 The chief deity of the Moabites was known as Chemosh (21:29). Worship of Chemosh, Asherah, and others involved sacrificial rituals along with sacrificial meals (communal offerings) celebrating the goodness of the gods. The final step was bowing **in worship**, demonstrating their submission to the gods as servants. In doing this, the idolatrous Israelites were rejecting their exclusive allegiance to the one true God, who could not be portrayed by figurines or other symbols.

25:3 This is the first reference in the OT to the god Baal (**Baal of Peor**), who would become the primary competitor with Yahweh for the devotion of the people of Israel. The historical setting is the late Bronze Age (1550–1200 B.C.), when Baal was emerging as one of the chief deities in Canaan. Numerous cuneiform texts from the excavations of Ugarit reveal that Baal was the agent of the creative order who, with his consort Anath, defeated the forces of evil. The father-god was El, who with his consort Asherah was said to rule the heavens and the earth. The final words of the verse, **and the Lord's anger burned against Israel**, echo the refrain of the first rebellion at Taberah (11:1). God's judgment was about to fall, implying the onset of a plague (25:9).

25:4-5 The Lord instructed Moses, who delegated authority to the righteous **judges** of Israel to **execute** (lit "impale") the leaders of this rebellion immediately to avert any further judgment against the people. These judges were probably those appointed by Moses at the suggestion of his father-in-law Jethro (Ex 18:13-27). The guilty parties were to be executed **before the Lord**, meaning that they were to be rendered unto the Lord to expiate the divine wrath demonstrated in the plague. This was harsh punishment, but the holiness of the community of faith was at stake. If the nation did not remain holy, she would fail like the previous generation that had died in the wilderness.

25:6-7 Phinehas son of Eleazar was Aaron's grandson. He executed a rebellious Israelite who dared to present his Midianite seductress to his family near the entrance of the tabernacle, the place reserved for sacred presentation of offerings to God.

25:8 Phinehas, with his executioner's spear in hand, impaled the man and his mistress together, quite possibly while they were beginning to have sexual relations (v. 1). Like Aaron did in the judgment scene against Korah and his rebellious followers (16:46-50), Phinehas stood in the gap between the living and the dying.

25:10 A shift in the language of divine instruction (**the Lord spoke to Moses**) goes almost unnoticed in the English translation. After Moses and Aaron had rebelled against God in the striking of the rock at Meribah (20:9-13), God merely "said" various things to Moses (Hb *amar*; 20:12,23; 21:8,16,34; 25:4), but now at the conclusion of the rebellion cycles of Numbers, and in the backdrop of Moses and Phinehas faithfully following the Lord's commands, the Lord restored communication with Moses by "speaking" or "instructing" (Hb *dibber*; over 30 times in the first 19 chaps.). Moses was restored to full fellowship with God.

25:11-13 The zeal of Phinehas in defending the faith was rewarded with a divinely ordained relationship. His descendants would serve continuously as high priests (**covenant of perpetual priesthood**) over the nation of Israel. A **covenant of peace** is also mentioned in Is 54:10; Ezk 34:25; 37:26; and Mal 2:5. The recipients of this covenant were assured of God's presence, protection, and provision in times of trouble.

25:14-15 The people killed by Phinehas were from prominent

was Zimri son of Salu, the leader of a Simeonite ancestral house. ¹⁵The name of the slain Midianite woman was Cozbi, the daughter of Zur, a tribal head of an ancestral house in Midian.

Vengeance against the Midianites

¹⁶The LORD told Moses: ¹⁷"Attack the Midianites and strike them dead. ¹⁸For they attacked you with the treachery that they used against you in the Peor incident. They did the same in the case involving their sister Cozbi, daughter of the Midianite leader who was killed the day the plague came at Peor."

The Second Census

26 After the plague, the LORD said to Moses and Eleazar son of Aaron the priest, ²"Take a census of the entire Israelite community by their ancestral houses of those 20 years old or more who can serve in Israel's army."ᵃ

³So Moses and Eleazar the priest said to them in the plains of Moab by the Jordan across from Jericho, ⁴"Take a census of those 20 years old or more, as the LORD had commanded Moses and the Israelites who came out of the land of Egypt."ᵇ

⁵　Reubenᶜ was the firstborn of Israel. Reuben's descendants:

the Hanochite clan from Hanoch;
the Palluite clan from Pallu;
⁶　the Hezronite clan from Hezron;
the Carmite clan from Carmi.
⁷　These were the Reubenite clans, and their registered men numbered 43,730.
⁸　The son of Pallu was Eliab.
⁹　The sons of Eliab were Nemuel, Dathan, and Abiram.
(It was Dathan and Abiram, chosen by the community, who fought against Moses and Aaron; they and Korah's followers fought against the LORD.ᵈ
¹⁰The earth opened its mouth and swallowed them with Korah, when his followers died and the fire consumed 250 men.ᵉ They serve as a warning sign. ¹¹The sons of Korah, however, did not die.)

¹²　Simeon's descendants by their clans:
the Nemuelite clan from Nemuel;ᴬᶠ
the Jaminite clan from Jamin;
the Jachinite clan from Jachin;
¹³　the Zerahite clan from Zerah;
the Shaulite clan from Shaul.
¹⁴　These were the Simeonite clans, numbering 22,200 men.

Cross-references (center column):
ᵃ26:2 Nm 1:2-3
ᵇ26:4 Nm 1
ᶜ26:5 Gn 46:8-27; Ex 6:14-25
ᵈ26:9 Nm 16:1-3
ᵉ26:10 Nm 16:31-35
ᶠ26:12 Gn 46:10; Ex 6:15; 1Ch 4:24

ᴬ26:12 Syr reads *Jemuel* (Gn 46:10; Ex 6:15); 1Ch 4:24 reads *Nemuel*

families, the man being a son of a **Simeonite** leader and the woman being the daughter of **Zur**, a **Midianite** tribal leader. Sinfulness and its judgment are no respecters of persons, whether from the lower classes or the elite.

26:1-2 The Hebrew Bible includes a half verse at 25:19, **after the plague**, as a transition. The Baal-peor incident reminded future Israelite generations of the dangers of intermarriage with those from idolatrous backgrounds who might lead the nation into judgment. This incident served as a case study in God's holiness and righteousness; He would allow no other gods to replace Him in the hearts and minds of His people. The rest of 26:1-2 is very similar to God's command in 1:1-2 mandating the first census.

26:3 The first census took place at the foot of Mount Sinai in the wilderness, the second at the doorway of the promised land, **in the plains of Moab by the Jordan across from Jericho**.

26:5-50 More than 38 years had passed since the first census, but that first generation, which had seen the miraculous power of God in Egypt and in the wilderness, had rejected God by refusing to enter the land, and had suffered the consequences. Yet a connection is made with the first generation through genealogical accounting for each of the 12 tribes—beginning with the descendants of **Reuben**—plus the Levites, in a manner not found in chapter 1. Both oral and written genealogies were maintained during this historical period to connect the past with the present, to trace particular lines of development, and to justify claims to inheritance or leadership. Recounting one's genealogy

was commonplace at the dedication of a newborn child or in the crowning of a king.

The tribes of Simeon (declined by 37,100; v. 12) and Naphtali (declined by 8,000; v. 48) had suffered the greatest losses in their militias during the wilderness era, and the tribe of Simeon would eventually dissipate into Judah within whose territory they were given an allotment. Manasseh (increased by 20,500; v. 29), Asher (increased by 11,900; v. 44), and Issachar (increased by 9,900; v. 23) reaped the most significant increases.

paqad

Hebrew Pronunciation	pah KADH
HCSB Translation	number, appoint, punish, visit
Uses in Numbers	103
Uses in the OT	304
Focus Passage	Numbers 26:7,18,22,25,27

Paqad, whose root occurs in all Semitic languages, has a variety of meanings that may stem from the concept of *paying attention* (Ex 4:31). *Paqad* describes *taking note of* (Jr 15:15) or *taking care of* (2Kg 9:34). *Inspecting* (Jb 7:18), *checking* (1Sm 17:18), or *overseeing* (2Kg 22:5) can determine that something *is missing* (Nm 31:49). *Paqad* involves *counting* (1Sm 11:8) or *recording* (Ex 38:21). One cares for by *storing* (2Kg 5:24) and *depositing* (Jr 36:20), or by *entrusting* (Lv 6:4) and *committing* (1Kg 14:27) something to another. *Attention* comes by *visiting* (Ps 17:3), or by *going to* someone (Is 26:16). Positively, people may *come to the aid of* (Gn 50:24), *appoint* (Nm 1:50), or *put in charge* (Gn 39:4). Negatively, they may *accuse* (2Sm 3:8) or *punish* (Ex 20:5). One may *count* by *calling the roll* (1Sm 14:17) and *mobilizing* troops (Jos 8:10).

15 Gad's descendants by their clans:
the Zephonite clan from Zephon;
the Haggite clan from Haggi;
the Shunite clan from Shuni;
16 the Oznite clan from Ozni;
the Erite clan from Eri;
17 the Arodite clan from Arod;
the Arelite clan from Areli.
18 These were the Gadite clans numbered
by their registered men: 40,500.

19 Judah's sons included Er and Onan,
but they died in the land of Canaan.ᵃ
20 Judah's descendants by their clans:
the Shelanite clan from Shelah;
the Perezite clan from Perez;
the Zerahite clan from Zerah.
21 The descendants of Perez:
the Hezronite clan from Hezron;
the Hamulite clan from Hamul.
22 These were Judah's clans numbered
by their registered men: 76,500.

23 Issachar's descendants by their clans:
the Tolaite clan from Tola;
the Punite clan from Puvah;ᴬ,ᵇ
24 the Jashubite clan from Jashub;
the Shimronite clan from Shimron.
25 These were Issachar's clans numbered
by their registered men: 64,300.

26 Zebulun's descendants by their clans:
the Seredite clan from Sered;
the Elonite clan from Elon;
the Jahleelite clan from Jahleel.
27 These were the Zebulunite
clans numbered by their
registered men: 60,500.

28 Joseph's descendants by their clans
from Manasseh and Ephraim:
29 Manasseh's descendants:
the Machirite clan from Machir.
Machir fathered Gilead;
the Gileadite clan from Gilead.
30 These were Gilead's descendants:
the Iezerite clan from Iezer;
the Helekite clan from Helek;
31 the Asrielite clan from Asriel;
the Shechemite clan from Shechem;
32 the Shemidaite clan from Shemida;
the Hepherite clan from Hepher;
33 Zelophehad son of Hepher had no
sons—only daughters. The names of

ᵃ26:19 Gn 38:3-4,6-11
ᵇ26:23 1Ch 7:1
ᶜ26:33 Nm 27:1-11; Jos 17:3

Zelophehad's daughters were Mahlah,
Noah, Hoglah, Milcah, and Tirzah.ᶜ
34 These were Manasseh's
clans, numbered by their
registered men: 52,700.
35 These were Ephraim's descendants
by their clans:
the Shuthelahite clan from Shuthelah;
the Becherite clan from Becher;
the Tahanite clan from Tahan.
36 These were Shuthelah's descendants:
the Eranite clan from Eran.
37 These were the Ephraimite
clans numbered by their
registered men: 32,500.
These were Joseph's descendants
by their clans.

38 Benjamin's descendants
by their clans:
the Belaite clan from Bela;
the Ashbelite clan from Ashbel;
the Ahiramite clan from Ahiram;
39 the Shuphamite clan from Shupham;ᴮ
the Huphamite clan from Hupham.
40 Bela's descendants from Ard
and Naaman:
the Ardite clan from Ard;
the Naamite clan from Naaman.
41 These were the Benjaminite
clans numbered by their
registered men: 45,600.

42 These were Dan's descendants
by their clans:
the Shuhamite clan from Shuham.
These were the clans of Dan
by their clans.
43 All the Shuhamite clans numbered
by their registered men: 64,400.

44 Asher's descendants by their clans:
the Imnite clan from Imnah;
the Ishvite clan from Ishvi;
the Beriite clan from Beriah.
45 From Beriah's descendants:
the Heberite clan from Heber;
the Malchielite clan from Malchiel.
46 And the name of Asher's daughter
was Serah.
47 These were the Asherite
clans numbered by their
registered men: 53,400.
48 Naphtali's descendants by their clans:

ᴬ26:23 Sam, LXX, Vg, Syr read *Puite clan from Puah*; 1Ch 7:1   ᴮ26:39 Some Hb mss, Sam, LXX, Syr, Tg, Vg; other Hb mss read
Shephupham

the Jahzeelite clan from Jahzeel;
the Gunite clan from Guni;
⁴⁹ the Jezerite clan from Jezer;
the Shillemite clan from Shillem.
⁵⁰ These were the Naphtali
clans numbered by their
registered men: 45,400.

⁵¹ These registered Israelite men
numbered 601,730.

⁵²The LORD spoke to Moses, ⁵³"The land is to be divided among them as an inheritance based on the number of names. ⁵⁴ Increase the inheritance for a large tribe and decrease it for a small one. Each is to be given its inheritance according to those who were registered in it. ⁵⁵ The land must be divided by lot; they will receive an inheritance according to the names of their ancestral tribes. ⁵⁶ Each inheritance will be divided by lot among the larger and smaller tribes."ᵃ

⁵⁷ These were the Levites registered
by their clans:
the Gershonite clan from Gershon;
the Kohathite clan from Kohath;
the Merarite clan from Merari.
⁵⁸ These were the Levite family groups:
the Libnite clan,
the Hebronite clan,
the Mahlite clan,
the Mushite clan,
and the Korahite clan.ᵇ

ᵃ26:56 Nm 33:53-54; 36:2; Jos 18:6-11
ᵇ26:58 Ex 6:21,24; Nm 3:17-20
ᶜ26:61 Lv 10:1-2
ᵈ26:64 Nm 1:17-46; 3:39

Kohath was the ancestor of Amram. ⁵⁹The name of Amram's wife was Jochebed, a descendant of Levi, born to Levi in Egypt. She bore to Amram: Aaron, Moses, and their sister Miriam. ⁶⁰Nadab, Abihu, Eleazar, and Ithamar were born to Aaron, ⁶¹but Nadab and Abihu died when they presented unauthorized fire before the LORD.ᶜ ⁶²Those registered were 23,000, every male one month old or more; they were not registered among the other Israelites, because no inheritance was given to them among the Israelites.

⁶³These were the ones registered by Moses and Eleazar the priest when they registered the Israelites on the plains of Moab by the Jordan across from Jericho. ⁶⁴But among them there was not one of those who had been registered by Moses and Aaron the priest when they registered the Israelites in the Wilderness of Sinai.ᵈ ⁶⁵For the LORD had said to them that they would all die in the wilderness. None of them was left except Caleb son of Jephunneh and Joshua son of Nun.

A Case of Daughters' Inheritance

27 The daughters of Zelophehad approached; Zelophehad was the son of Hepher, son of Gilead, son of Machir, son of Manasseh from the clans of Manasseh, the son of Joseph. These were the names of his daughters: Mahlah, Noah, Hoglah, Milcah, and Tirzah. ² They stood before Moses, Eleazar the priest, the leaders, and the entire community

---

26:51 The number of **registered Israelite men** in the second census came to 601,730. The net decrease from the first census was 1,820 warriors (see note at 1:44-46).

26:53-56 In 33:54 instructions are given for deciding the territorial location for each of the tribes in the midst of a warning about potential idolatry. In 34:1-29 the boundaries of the whole inheritance are outlined. The case of Zelophehad's daughters adds the potential of women's inheritance to the matter of tribal allocations (26:33; 27:1-11; 36:1-12). The allotment would take into consideration tribal populations and the amount of land within a given region (Jos 17:17-18).

26:55 Divided by lot refers to a second principle governing land allocation—providential probability as expressed through a game of chance. The Lord was presumed to oversee the casting of the lots, thereby bringing His decision to pass (Pr 16:33). The casting of lots was a common means of determining the will of God. It was used to choose between the two goats on the Day of Atonement (Lv 16:8), to divide the spoils of war (Ob 11), and to settle political issues (1Sm 10:21).

26:57-62 In a manner similar to the first census, the second numbering of the **Levites** separately from the militia follows the genealogical pattern of verses 5-52. Mention of the deaths of **Nadab and Abihu**, the sons of Aaron who offered **unauthorized fire** on the altar, served as a reminder of the

dangerous task the Levites and priests had in maintaining the holiness of God in the heart of a community with a history of rebellion.

26:65 The census of the second generation militia concludes with a reminder to the people of the consequences of rebellion. The OT theme of the remnant is set forth in the survival of two faithful men—**Caleb** and **Joshua**—out of thousands who died over the 40-year **wilderness** experience. The Numbers theme of the challenge to be faithful in following the Lord's instructions is repeated.

27:1 Only male descendants were registered by patriarchal lineage in the census. According to levirate law, in a case where a man died without a male heir, a male relative would redeem the land to keep it within the clan. This account is an example of case law development early in Israelite history: (1) the specific case was presented to the leaders at the entrance of the tabernacle (vv. 1-4); (2) an appeal was made by the leader to divine legislative authority (v. 5); and (3) a precedent-setting decision was issued, accompanied by principles derived from the case (vv. 6-11).

27:2-3 The **daughters of Zelophehad** were concerned that their family, lacking a male heir, would be passed over and their patriarchal ancestral name would be forgotten. The disappearance of one's family name was a matter of grave concern, often associated with divine judgment that would lead to societal shunning and abandonment (Ru 4:10; Ps

at the entrance to the tent of meeting and said, [3] "Our father died in the wilderness, but he was not among Korah's followers, who gathered together against the LORD.[a] Instead, he died because of his own sin, and he had no sons. [4] Why should the name of our father be taken away from his clan? Since he had no son, give us property among our father's brothers."

[5] Moses brought their case before the LORD, [6] and the LORD answered him, [7] "What Zelophehad's daughters say is correct. You are to give them hereditary property among their father's brothers and transfer their father's inheritance to them.[b] [8] Tell the Israelites: When a man dies without having a son, transfer his inheritance to his daughter. [9] If he has no daughter, give his inheritance to his brothers. [10] If he has no brothers, give his inheritance to his father's brothers. [11] If his father has no brothers, give his inheritance to the nearest relative of his clan, and he will take possession of it. This is to be a statutory ordinance for the Israelites as the LORD commanded Moses."

Joshua Commissioned to Succeed Moses

[12] Then the LORD said to Moses,[c] "Go up this mountain of the Abarim range[A] and see the land that I have given the Israelites. [13] After you have seen it, you will also be gathered to your people, as Aaron your brother was.[d] [14] When the community quarreled in the Wilderness of Zin, both of you rebelled against My command to show My holiness in their sight at the waters." Those were the waters of Meribah[B] of Kadesh in the Wilderness of Zin.[e]

[15] So Moses appealed to the LORD, [16] "May the LORD, the God of the spirits of all flesh,[f] appoint a man over the community [17] who will go out before them and come back in before them,[g] and who will bring them out and bring them in, so that the LORD's community won't be like sheep without a shepherd."[h]

[18] The LORD replied to Moses, "Take Joshua son of Nun, a man who has the Spirit in him, and lay your hands on him.[i] [19] Have him stand before Eleazar the priest and the whole community, and commission[j] him in their sight. [20] Confer some of your authority on him so that the entire Israelite community will obey him. [21] He will stand before Eleazar who will consult the LORD for him with the decision of the •Urim.[k] He and all the Israelites with him, even the entire community, will go out and come back in at his command."

[22] Moses did as the LORD commanded him. He took Joshua, had him stand before Eleazar the priest and the entire community, [23] laid his hands on him, and commissioned him, as the LORD had spoken through Moses.

Cross references
a 27:3 Nm 16:1-3
b 27:7 Jos 17:4
c 27:12-14 Dt 32:48-51
d 27:13 Nm 20:22-29
e 27:14 Nm 20:2-13
f 27:16 Nm 16:22
g 27:17 Jos 14:11; 1Sm 18:13-16; 2Sm 5:2; 11:1; 1Kg 3:7; 2Kg 11:9
h 1Kg 22:17; 2Ch 18:16; Ezk 34:5; Mt 9:36; Mk 6:34
i 27:18 Dt 34:9
j 27:19 Dt 31:14,23; Ps 91:11; Is 10:6
k 27:21 Ex 28:30

A 27:12 = Mount Nebo; Nm 33:47-48; Dt 32:49; Jr 22:20   B 27:14 = quarreling

---

83:4; Jr 11:19). The daughters of Zelophehad sought status and inheritance rights within the Machirite clan of Manasseh. Later the Machirites received an inheritance in the Gilead region of Transjordan (Nm 32:39-42). Similar laws about women's inheritance and property rights existed among various cultures of the ancient Near East.

27:6-11 The decision in the case (**what Zelophehad's daughters say is correct**) set forth in the days of Moses in the second millennium B.C., and fulfilled by Joshua in the land distribution (Jos 17:3-6), was still in force more than 500 years later. The names of two of Manasseh's descendants through Zelophehad, Hoglah and Noah, were preserved as the names of districts or towns in the region of Samaria (within the territory of Manasseh) in the Samaria Ostraca (inscribed potsherds) of the eighth century B.C., at least 200 years before the exile of Judah.

27:12 The **Abarim range** extended from an area northeast of the Dead Sea and then southward along the western edge of the Moabite plateau in Transjordan. The opportunity for Moses to **see the land** of promise from Dan to Zoar took place at Mount Nebo in the heights of Pisgah (Dt 32:49; 34:1).

27:13 Moses was to **be gathered to** his **people**, meaning he was to be buried properly, though not in the family burial site that was typical of this era. The phrase conveys the idea of being reunited with one's ancestral families in Sheol, the place of the dead. To be left unburied or "ungathered" was viewed as disgraceful.

27:14 The Lord had been dishonored at the **waters of Meribah of Kadesh in the Wilderness of Zin** when Moses struck the rock instead of speaking to it. God did provide the needed water for the people, but the action of Israel's leaders was reprimanded (20:9-11).

27:15-17 Moses' words **the God of the spirits of all flesh** speak of God's sovereignty over all humankind. He is the master of the universe who can thwart even the ways of a pagan diviner like Balaam and accomplish His desires for His people. Moses, the elder statesman of Israel, appealed to God the way a humble servant would appear before his master. Moses desired that the newly appointed leader would be just as concerned as he had been for the welfare of the nation (cp. Jesus' compassion in Mt 9:36). The language of going **out** and coming **in** has to do with successfully leading the people in battle. The **shepherd** can also be a military metaphor (1Kg 22:17).

27:18 The phrase **Take Joshua son of Nun, a man who has the Spirit in him** reflects the language of formal appointment. "Take" means to exert authority. It is similar in usage to the way the word is used in the introduction to the Korah rebellion, when the Kohathite leader attempted to usurp the authority of Aaron the high priest. Possession of the Holy Spirit in the OT was for the purpose of carrying out the specific tasks to which a person had been appointed by the Lord.

27:22-23 The formal transfer of leadership from Moses to Joshua begins with a statement about Moses faithfully following the Lord's instruction. The ceremony involved the oversight of the high priest **Eleazar** in the ritual ceremony,

Prescribed Offerings

28 The Lord spoke to Moses, ²"Command the Israelites and say to them: Be sure to present to Me at its appointed time My offering and My food[a] as My fire offering, a pleasing aroma to Me. ³And say to them: This is the fire offering you are to present to the Lord:[b]

Daily Offerings

"Each day present two unblemished year-old male lambs as a regular •burnt offering. ⁴Offer one lamb in the morning and the other lamb at twilight, ⁵along with two quarts[A] of fine flour for a •grain offering mixed with a quart[B] of olive oil from crushed olives.[c] ⁶It is a regular burnt offering established at Mount Sinai for a pleasing aroma, a fire offering to the Lord. ⁷The •drink offering is to be a quart[B] with each lamb. Pour out the offering of beer to the Lord in the sanctuary area. ⁸Offer the second lamb at twilight, along with the same kind of grain offering and drink offering as in the morning. It is a fire offering, a pleasing aroma to the Lord.

Sabbath Offerings

⁹"On the Sabbath day present two unblemished year-old male lambs, four quarts[C] of fine flour mixed with oil as a grain offering, and its drink offering. ¹⁰It is the burnt offering for every Sabbath, in addition to the regular burnt offering and its drink offering.

Monthly Offerings

¹¹"At the beginning of each of your months

ᵃ28:2 Lv 3:11,16; 22:25; Nm 28:24 ᵇ28:3-8 Ex 29:38-41 ᶜ28:5 Ex 27:20; Lv 24:2 ᵈ28:16-17 Ex 12:18; Lv 23:5-6; Ezk 45:21 ᵉ28:18 Ex 12:16; Lv 23:3,7,28; Nm 29:7

present a burnt offering to the Lord: two young bulls, one ram, seven male lambs a year old—all unblemished— ¹²with six quarts[D] of fine flour mixed with oil as a grain offering for each bull, four quarts[C] of fine flour mixed with oil as a grain offering for the ram, ¹³and two quarts[E] of fine flour mixed with oil as a grain offering for each lamb. It is a burnt offering, a pleasing aroma, a fire offering to the Lord. ¹⁴Their drink offerings are to be two quarts[F] of wine with each bull, one and a third quarts[G] with the ram, and one quart[H] with each male lamb. This is the monthly burnt offering for all the months of the year. ¹⁵And one male goat is to be offered as a •sin offering to the Lord, in addition to the regular burnt offering with its drink offering.

Offerings for Passover

¹⁶"The •Passover[d] to the Lord comes in the first month, on the fourteenth day of the month. ¹⁷On the fifteenth day of this month there will be a festival; unleavened bread is to be eaten for seven days. ¹⁸On the first day there is to be a sacred assembly; you are not to do any daily work.[e] ¹⁹Present a fire offering, a burnt offering to the Lord: two young bulls, one ram, and seven male lambs a year old. Your animals are to be unblemished. ²⁰The grain offering with them is to be of fine flour mixed with oil; offer six quarts[D] with each bull and four quarts[C] with the ram. ²¹Offer two quarts[E] with each of the seven lambs ²²and one male goat for a sin offering to make •atonement for yourselves. ²³Offer these with

---

ᴬ28:5 Lit *one-tenth of an ephah* ᴮ28:5,7 Lit *a fourth of a hin* ᶜ28:9,12,20 Lit *two-tenths* (of an ephah) ᴰ28:12,20 Lit *three-tenths* (of an ephah) ᴱ28:13,21 Lit *one-tenth* (of an ephah) ᶠ28:14 Lit *a half hin* ᴳ28:14 Lit *bull, a third hin* ᴴ28:14 Lit *a fourth hin*

---

accompanied by the laying on of **hands** in symbolic transfer of blessing and authority. The parallel passage in Dt 31:1-8,14-29 highlights the placing of the book of the law next to the ark of the covenant. This emphasized the need for faithfulness to the Lord's commands by the Israelites.

28:1-2 The Lord spoke to Moses introduces the divine instruction about the special **fire offering** to be presented to the Lord on the various holy days of the Israelite calendar. God would bless the faithful Israelites with abundance in their fields and flocks in the promised land, so they in turn might celebrate His greatness and goodness in rendering the fruits of their labors.

28:3-8 Every day was holy and thus was to be dedicated to the Lord at the entrance of the tabernacle through the rendering of a **burnt offering**, a sacrifice for consecration of the day. Both in the morning and in the evening a **lamb** was sacrificed on behalf of the nation in a substitutionary identification ritual accomplished by the priest placing his hands on the head of the lamb. As the priest recited special blessings, the life blood of the animal was extracted as the animal was slaughtered. Then the blood was poured out to the Lord around the altar. The sacrifice would be accompanied by its appropriate portion of **grain** and oil, plus a

prescribed amount of **beer** for the **drink offering**—a libation poured over the animal and grain elements as they were roasting on the fire of the sacrificial altar. For "beer" see note at 6:3-4.

28:6 The burnt offering legislation was **established at Mount Sinai for a pleasing aroma** (savory smell) **to the Lord** (Ex 20:24; 29:38-43). The vapors that rose up from the altar depicted God's acceptance of the offering. Only the highest quality, unblemished animals could be presented to the Lord.

28:9-10 The daily burnt offerings of lamb, grain, and liquid libation were doubled on the **Sabbath**.

28:11-15 At the **beginning of each of your months** additional burnt offerings of consecration were made, constituting a grand rite through which the nation paid homage to God as its Creator and Sustainer.

28:16-25 According to Ex 12:8, the foundational **Passover** foods were the Passover lamb, unleavened bread, and bitter herbs. These helped the people remember the events that brought about the redemption of Israel from Egypt. Passover **lambs** were offered as communal sacrifices, with portions consumed by both the priests and the offerers in

the morning burnt offering that is part of the regular burnt offering. ²⁴You are to offer the same food each day for seven days as a fire offering,ᵃ a pleasing aroma to the LORD. It is to be offered with its drink offering and the regular burnt offering. ²⁵On the seventh day you are to hold a sacred assembly; you are not to do any daily work.

Offerings for the Festival of Weeks

²⁶"On the day of ˚firstfruits, you are to hold a sacred assembly when you present an offering of new grain to the LORD at your Festival of Weeks;ᵇ you are not to do any daily work. ²⁷Present a burnt offering for a pleasing aroma to the LORD: two young bulls, one ram, and seven male lambs a year old, ²⁸with their grain offering of fine flour mixed with oil, six quartsᴬ with each bull, four quartsᴮ with the ram, ²⁹and two quartsᶜ with each of the seven lambs, ³⁰and one male goat to make atonement for yourselves. ³¹Offer them with their drink offerings in addition to the regular burnt offering and its grain offering. Your animals are to be unblemished.

Festival of Trumpets Offerings

29 "You are to hold a sacred assembly in the seventh month, on the first day of the month, and you are not to do any daily work.ᶜ This will be a day of joyful shoutingᴰ for you.ᵈ ²Offer a ˚burnt offering as a pleasing aroma to the LORD: one young bull, one ram, seven male lambs a year old—all unblemished— ³with their ˚grain offering of fine flour mixed with oil, six quartsᴬ with the bull, four quartsᴮ with the ram, ⁴and two quartsᶜ with each of the seven male lambs. ⁵Also offer one male goat as a ˚sin offering to make ˚atonement for yourselves. ⁶These are in addition to the monthly and regular burnt offerings with their prescribed grain offerings and ˚drink offerings. They are a pleasing aroma, a fire offering to the LORD.

Offerings for the Day of Atonement

⁷"You are to hold a sacred assembly on the tenth day of this seventh month and practice self-denial;ᴱ,ᵉ you must not do any work. ⁸Present a burnt offering to the LORD, a pleasing aroma: one young bull, one ram, and seven male lambs a year old. All your animals are to be unblemished. ⁹Their grain offering is to be of fine flour mixed with oil, six quartsᴬ with the bull, four quartsᴮ with the ram, ¹⁰and two quartsᶜ with each of the seven lambs. ¹¹Offer one male goat for a sin offering. The regular burnt offering with its grain offering and

ᵃ28:24-25 Lv 23:8
ᵇ28:26 Ex 34:22; Dt 16:9-10
ᶜ29:1 Ex 12:16
ᵈLv 23:23-25
ᵉ29:7 Lv 23:27-28

ᴬ28:28; 29:3,9 Lit three-tenths (of an ephah)   ᴮ28:28; 29:3,9 Lit two-tenths (of an ephah)   ᶜ28:29; 29:4,10 Lit one-tenth (of an ephah)   ᴰ29:1 Or blast; traditionally, trumpet blasts   ᴱ29:7 Traditionally, fasting, abstinence from sex, and refraining from personal grooming

---

the presence of God in the Israelite camp, or later in Jerusalem after the temple was built. **Unleavened bread** was consumed in imitation of the original setting, which Deuteronomy calls the "bread of affliction." The bitter herbs were a reminder of the bitterness of slavery in Egypt. In this passage some elements are added to the celebration: Sabbath designation (meaning no work) for the first and final days of the Festival of Unleavened Bread, complete with a **sacred assembly** at the sanctuary; and additional sacrifices equivalent to those offered on the New Moon (two bulls, one ram, and seven lambs, each accompanied by their appropriate grain/oil and libation offerings). The sacrificial list was completed with the offering of a goat for a **sin offering** on behalf of the people.

28:26-31 The first day of the **Festival of Weeks** (Hb shavuoth) was called the **day of firstfruits**. It was considered a Sabbath, with burnt and sin offerings essentially the same as the New Moon sacrifices. The firstfruits offering of the new grain harvest was included in the ritual practices for the day when the seven weeks after the first sheaf (Lv 23:10) were completed. Sheaves of new barley and wheat were elevated and waved before the Lord in celebration of the gift of the harvest. These were in addition to the prescribed offering of two loaves of leavened bread (Lv 23:15-22; Dt 16:3) given in thanksgiving for the abundance of God's blessing. In the NT, the Festival of Weeks is called Pentecost, based on the Greek pentekoste (fiftieth), since the day is the fiftieth day after the first sheaf.

29:1-38 The beginning of the agricultural year, in the sev-enth month, on the first day, was the beginning of the penitential season. The tenth day of the month was considered the holiest day of the year, the Day of Atonement. Five days later the Festival of Booths began and lasted for a week. In Early Israelite history, the seventh month was known as Ethanim, but when the Jews adopted the Babylonian calendar during the exile, the month was called Tishri.

29:1-6 The collective offerings presented on the **day of joyful shouting** were three bulls, two rams, 16 male lambs, 1.6 bushels of fine flour, and six gallons each of oil and wine. Traditionally, the first of Tishri was called the "day for blowing trumpets" in which the ram's horn (Hb shophar) was sounded rather than the silver trumpets of 10:1-10. The sounding of the ram's horn was a call to repentance. The designation of this day as Rosh Hashanah, "the head of the year," was a late postexilic development in emerging Judaism.

29:7-11 The holiest day of the year required a **sacred assembly** of **self-denial**, and Sabbath restrictions against work as described in Lv 23:16-32. A full description of the activities for the Day of Atonement (Hb yom kippur) is found in Lv 16:1-34, where the focus is upon the unique purification rituals required. The holy of holies was cleansed because of the sins of the people, and azazel (the scapegoat) was led into the wilderness, symbolically carrying the sins of the people away from the camp. Two sin offerings were sacrificed on this day, one parallel to the **sin offering** at the New Moon Festival, and the other on behalf of the people, the blood of which was then used to purify the holy place (Lv 16:15-20).

drink offerings are in addition to the sin offering of atonement.

Offerings for the Festival of Booths

[12] "You are to hold a sacred assembly on the fifteenth day of the seventh month;[a] you must not do any daily work. You are to celebrate a seven-day festival for the LORD. [13] Present a burnt offering, a fire offering as a pleasing aroma to the LORD: 13 young bulls, two rams, and 14 male lambs a year old. They are to be unblemished. [14] Their grain offering is to be of fine flour mixed with oil, six quarts[A] with each of the 13 bulls, four quarts[B] with each of the two rams, [15] and two quarts[C] with each of the 14 lambs. [16] Also offer one male goat as a sin offering. These are in addition to the regular burnt offering with its grain and drink offerings.

[17] "On the second day present 12 young bulls, two rams, and 14 male lambs a year old—all unblemished— [18] with their grain and drink offerings[b] for the bulls, rams, and lambs, in proportion to their number. [19] Also offer one male goat as a sin offering. These are in addition to the regular burnt offering with its grain and drink[D] offerings.

[20] "On the third day present 11 bulls, two rams, 14 male lambs a year old—all unblemished— [21] with their grain and drink offerings for the bulls, rams, and lambs, in proportion to their number. [22] Also offer one male goat as a sin offering. These are in addition to the regular burnt offering with its grain and drink offerings.

[23] "On the fourth day present 10 bulls, two rams, 14 male lambs a year old—all unblemished— [24] with their grain and drink offerings for the bulls, rams, and lambs, in proportion to their number. [25] Also offer one male goat as a sin offering. These are in addition to the

[a]29:12 Lv 23:34-35
[b]29:18 Nm 15:1-12
[c]29:35 Ex 12:16; Lv 23:36

regular burnt offering with its grain and drink offerings.

[26] "On the fifth day present nine bulls, two rams, 14 male lambs a year old—all unblemished— [27] with their grain and drink offerings for the bulls, rams, and lambs, in proportion to their number. [28] Also offer one male goat as a sin offering. These are in addition to the regular burnt offering with its grain and drink offerings.

[29] "On the sixth day present eight bulls, two rams, 14 male lambs a year old—all unblemished— [30] with their grain and drink offerings for the bulls, rams, and lambs, in proportion to their number. [31] Also offer one male goat as a sin offering. These are in addition to the regular burnt offering with its grain and drink[E] offerings.

[32] "On the seventh day present seven bulls, two rams, and 14 male lambs a year old—all unblemished— [33] with their grain and drink offerings for the bulls, rams, and lambs, in proportion to their number. [34] Also offer one male goat as a sin offering. These are in addition to the regular burnt offering with its grain and drink offerings.

[35] "On the eighth day you are to hold a solemn assembly; you are not to do any daily work.[c] [36] Present a burnt offering, a fire offering as a pleasing aroma to the LORD: one bull, one ram, seven male lambs a year old—all unblemished— [37] with their grain and drink offerings for the bulls, rams, and lambs, in proportion to their number. [38] Also offer one male goat as a sin offering. These are in addition to the regular burnt offering with its grain and drink offerings.

[39] "You must offer these to the LORD at your appointed times in addition to your vow and freewill offerings, whether burnt, grain, drink, or •fellowship offerings." [40][F] So Moses

---

[A]29:14 Lit *three-tenths* (of an ephah)   [B]28:14 Lit *two-tenths* (of an ephah)   [C]29:15 Lit *one-tenth* (of an ephah)   [D]29:19 Some Hb mss, Syr, Vg, Sam; other Hb mss, LXX read *and their drink*   [E]29:31 Some Hb mss, Syr, Tg, Vg; other Hb mss, Sam read *and their drink*   [F]29:40 Nm 30:1 in Hb

The acts of self-denial included fasting, leading to the day being called "The Fast" in later Judaism. Other restrictions included any activities that brought comfort and pleasure. The work of Christ on the cross brought fulfillment to the ritual of the Day of Atonement. Functioning as a high priest of a superior order—of Melchizedek (Heb 7:17-28)—Christ offered Himself as a once-for-all, eternal sacrifice (Heb 9:11-28). His work accomplished redemption from sin and cleansed our guilty consciences (Heb 10:19-22).

29:12-38 The longest section of these two chapters is devoted to a description of the daily offerings of the Festival of Booths (or Tabernacles; Hb *sukkoth*). The first day of the festival and the appended eighth day were considered Sabbaths for sacred assembly. The *sukkah* was a hut or tent constructed in imitation of the dwellings of early Israelites

during the wilderness period, when God provided what was needed for protection. In Lv 23:39-43 the Israelites were instructed to erect huts in future generations as a reminder of God's protection and provision in the wilderness. First called the Festival of Ingathering (Ex 23:16), the celebration commemorated God's provision in the fall harvest of the vegetable crops, the vineyards, and finally the olive orchards. The association of Booths with the exodus from Egypt provided a continuation of the salvation/redemption/providence/preservation motifs of Passover, Unleavened Bread, and Pentecost.

29:40 Moses faithfully accomplished the task assigned to him by God as he instructed the Israelite priests on the proper procedure for commemorating and celebrating God's goodness in the holy days of the calendar.

told the Israelites everything the LORD had commanded him.

Regulations about Vows

30 Moses told the leaders of the Israelite tribes, "This is what the LORD has commanded: ²When a man makes a vow to the LORD or swears an oath to put himself under an obligation, he must not break his word; he must do whatever he has promised.ᵃ

³"When a woman in her father's house during her youth makes a vow to the LORD or puts herself under an obligation, ⁴and her father hears about her vow or the obligation she put herself under, and he says nothing to her, all her vows and every obligation she put herself under are binding. ⁵But if her father prohibits her on the day he hears about it, none of her vows and none of the obligations she put herself under are binding. The LORD will absolve her because her father has prohibited her.

⁶"If a woman marries while her vows or the rash commitment she herself made are binding, ⁷and her husband hears about it and says nothing to her when he finds out, her vows are binding, and the obligations she put herself under are binding. ⁸But if her husband prohibits her when he hears about it, he will cancel her vow that is binding or the rash commitment she herself made, and the LORD will forgive her.

⁹"Every vow a widow or divorced woman puts herself under is binding on her.

¹⁰"If a woman in her husband's house has made a vow or put herself under an obligation with an oath, ¹¹and her husband hears about it, says nothing to her, and does not prohibit her, all her vows are binding, and every obligation she put herself under is binding. ¹²But if her husband cancels them on the day he hears about it, nothing that came from her lips, whether her vows or her obligation, is binding. Her husband has canceled them, and the LORD will absolve her. ¹³Her husband may confirm or cancel any vow or any sworn obligation to deny herself. ¹⁴If her husband says nothing at all to her from day to day, he confirms all her vows and obligations, which are binding. He has confirmed them because he said nothing to her when he heard about them. ¹⁵But if he cancels them after he hears about them, he will be responsible for herᴬ commitment."ᴮ

¹⁶These are the statutes that the LORD commanded Moses concerning the relationship between a man and his wife, or between a father and his daughter in his house during her youth.

War with Midian

31 The LORD spoke to Moses, ²"Execute vengeance for the Israelites against the

ᵃ30:2 Mt 5:33

ᴬ30:15 Sam, LXX, some Syr mss read *his*   ᴮ30:15 Or *will bear her guilt*

30:1-16 In this section the legal force of vows and oaths is set forth for both men and women. A vow was a conditional promise, made in the context of petitionary prayer (T. W. Cartledge, *Vows*). The force of women's vows was limited by her male guardian, usually either her father or her husband. If the guardian was passive or assenting, the vows of the woman had the same legal force as a man's vow. The vows of widows and divorced women were also binding. This statute also applied to a woman who was taking a Nazirite vow (6:1-21).

30:1-2 Making vows was voluntary, but any **man** who made a **vow** or swore an **oath** to the Lord was required to fulfill his **obligation**. Vows involved a verbal act of commitment to a task, or to consecration of oneself or property to the Lord. Oral vows were just as binding as formal written documents. To break a vow in which God's name had been evoked was to profane God's name (Lv 27:28-29). Sacrificial offerings were part of the obligation ritual, especially in ancient Israel where oaths were to be made only to God. In the case of the Nazirite vow (Nm 6), the procedure included an oath of abstinence from wine and strong drink, from shaving of the head, and from contamination by a corpse.

30:3-5 If **a woman in her father's house during her youth** had made a vow, the patriarchal headship of her father became the controlling factor. A young female lived under her father's authority until she married (usually in the late teenage years), at which time her husband assumed this responsibility (vv. 6-8).

30:9 In the case of a **widow or divorced woman**, she no longer lived under the patriarchal authority of her father or husband, so she had the same status and responsibility as a man with regard to vows.

30:10-15 In the patriarchal society of ancient Israel, vows could be annulled by the **husband** if they were considered detrimental to the woman, to her husband, or to the husband-wife relationship. Special considerations were given to the circumstances under which the wife took a vow, when the husband was apprised of the commitment, and how he responded to the information. The cases of Hannah (1Sm 1:11) and the mother of Samson (Jdg 13:1-23) are good examples of vow-taking under the condition of childlessness.

31:1-36:13 The final cycle of Numbers completes the challenge to faithfulness as God was preparing Israel to enter the promised land.

31:2 The **Midianites** are an enigmatic people in biblical, historical, and archaeological research. According to Gn 25:1-4, Midian was one of the sons of Abraham through his concubine Keturah. Midianites were allied at times with the Moabites (Gn 36:35; Nm 22:7; 25:6,14-18), the Amalekites (Jdg 6:3; 7:12), and the Ishmaelites (Gn 37:28). The Midianites seem to have been a loosely connected confederation of nomadic and semi-nomadic tribes with origins in northern Saudi Arabia who traveled the regions of the western Sinai Peninsula, southern Jordan, and the Arabah (see notes at Nm 22:2-4 and 25:14).

Midianites. After that, you will be gathered to your people."

³So Moses spoke to the people, "Equip some of your men for war. They will go against Midian to inflict the LORD's vengeance[a] on them. ⁴Send 1,000 men to war from each Israelite tribe." ⁵So 1,000 were recruited from each Israelite tribe out of the thousands[A] in Israel—12,000 equipped for war. ⁶Moses sent 1,000 from each tribe to war. They went with Phinehas son of Eleazar the priest, in whose care were the holy objects and signal trumpets.

⁷They waged war against Midian, as the LORD had commanded Moses, and killed every male. ⁸Along with the others slain by them, they killed the Midianite kings—Evi, Rekem, Zur, Hur, and Reba, the five kings of Midian.[b] They also killed Balaam son of Beor[c] with the sword. ⁹The Israelites took the Midianite women and their children captive, and they plundered all their cattle, flocks, and property.[d] ¹⁰Then they burned all the cities where the Midianites lived, as well as all their encampments, ¹¹and took away all the spoils of war and the captives, both man and beast. ¹²They brought the prisoners, animals, and spoils of war to Moses, Eleazar the priest, and the Israelite community at the camp on the plains of Moab by the Jordan across from Jericho.

¹³Moses, Eleazar the priest, and all the leaders of the community went to meet them outside the camp. ¹⁴But Moses became furious with the officers, the commanders of

thousands and commanders of hundreds, who were returning from the military campaign. ¹⁵"Have[B] you let every female live?" he asked them. ¹⁶"Yet they are the ones who, at Balaam's advice, incited the Israelites to unfaithfulness against the LORD in the Peor incident, so that the plague came against the LORD's community.[e] ¹⁷So now, kill all the male children and kill every woman who has had sexual relations with a man, ¹⁸but keep alive for yourselves all the young females who have not had sexual relations.

¹⁹"You are to remain outside the camp for seven days. All of you and your prisoners who have killed a person or touched the dead are to purify yourselves on the third day and the seventh day. ²⁰Also purify everything: garments, leather goods, things made of goat hair, and every article of wood."[f]

²¹Then Eleazar the priest said to the soldiers who had gone to battle, "This is the legal statute the LORD commanded Moses: ²²Only the gold, silver, bronze, iron, tin, and lead— ²³everything that can withstand fire—you are to pass through fire, and it will be ˙clean. It must still be purified with the purification water.[g] Anything that cannot withstand fire, pass through the water. ²⁴On the seventh day wash your clothes, and you will be clean. After that you may enter the camp."

²⁵The LORD told Moses, ²⁶"You, Eleazar the priest, and the family leaders of the community are to take a count of what was captured, man and beast. ²⁷Then divide the captives

---

Cross references (center column):
[a]31:3 Ps 18:47; 79:10; 94:1; Jr 11:20
[b]31:8 Jos 13:21-22
[c]Nm 22:5–24:25
[d]31:9 Gn 34:28-29; Dt 20:13-14
[e]31:16 Nm 25; Dt 20:18
[f]31:19-20 Lv 11:32; Nm 19:11-20
[g]31:23 Nm 19:1-9,17-20

A31:5 Or *clans*   **B**31:15 Sam, LXX, Syr, Vg read *Why have*

31:3-5 Each of the seven cycles in the book of Numbers begins with a reference to the 12-tribe unity (or disunity in the case of the Korah rebellion, chaps. 16–17), and here **1,000 men . . . from each Israelite tribe** are mustered for battle. Equal participation in the holy war by the tribes parallels their equal contribution of gifts for the tabernacle in chapter 7.

31:6 The model for holy war is presented with the priest **Phinehas** accompanying the 12,000-man army into battle. They carried with them the sanctuary vessels for needed purification rituals and the **trumpets** for sounding battle alerts (10:1-10).

31:8 The five **Midianite kings** defeated in the campaign are listed in the same order in the battle summary of Jos 13:21, where they are called "princes of Sihon." The nature of the political relationships among the Amorites, Moabites, and Midianites remains nebulous. One of these Midianite leaders, **Zur**, was the father of Cozbi, the Midianite woman who was killed by Phinehas along with her Israelite lover Zimri ben Salu (25:14-18).

31:13-24 The purpose of holy war was to eradicate impure elements, whether persons or property, from society. This battle followed on the heels of the idolatrous activity of Baal-peor (chap. 25) that began with unholy **sexual rela-**tions and resulted in the death of thousands of Israelites. It also set the stage for the instructions in 33:50-56 for possessing the promised land by driving out the Canaanites and eradicating the sources of idolatry. Critics suggest this holy war mentality was a development among ancient peoples and not in keeping with God's purpose; but these instructions were specific in time and place at the critical point of the founding of the theocracy of Israel, where their survival as the holy community of faith was at stake.

Numbers 31 is consistent with the instructions given in other pentateuchal passages, including Dt 7:5,24-25; 12:1-12; and 20:16-19 (purging of idolatry) and Dt 21:10-14 (female captives). But the instructions for Israel in the era of Moses and Joshua have been superseded by the law of Christ and the law of love. God still abhors evil in society, and the people of God should be diligent in opposing every expression of evil, but not to the extent of conducting holy war.

31:25 The LORD told Moses is again the language of divine revelation and instruction that anticipates faithful obedience, summarized in verse 31.

31:27-46 These instructions for the distribution of the spoils of war among the community members set the standard for the coming campaigns in the promised land.

between the troops who went out to war and the entire community. ²⁸Set aside a tribute for the Lord from what belongs to the fighting men who went out to war: one out of every 500 humans, cattle, donkeys, sheep, and goats. ²⁹Take the tribute from their half and give it to Eleazar the priest as a contribution to the Lord. ³⁰From the Israelites' half, take one out of every 50 from the people, cattle, donkeys, sheep, and goats, all the livestock, and give them to the Levites who perform the duties ofᴬ the Lord's tabernacle."

³¹So Moses and Eleazar the priest did as the Lord commanded Moses. ³²The captives remaining from the plunder the army had taken totaled:

675,000 sheep and goats,
³³ 72,000 cattle,
³⁴ 61,000 donkeys,
³⁵ and 32,000 people, all the females
who had not had sexual relations
with a man.

³⁶The half portion for those who went out to war numbered:

337,500 sheep and goats,
³⁷ and the tribute to the Lord was 675
from the sheep and goats;
³⁸ from the 36,000 cattle,
the tribute to the Lord was 72;
³⁹ from the 30,500 donkeys,
the tribute to the Lord was 61;
⁴⁰ and from the 16,000 people,
the tribute to the Lord was 32 people.

⁴¹Moses gave the tribute to Eleazar the priest as a contribution for the Lord, as the Lord had commanded Moses.

⁴²From the Israelites' half, which Moses separated from the men who fought, ⁴³the community's half was:

337,500 sheep and goats,
⁴⁴ 36,000 cattle,

ᵃ 31:50 Ex 30:12-16
ᵇ 32:4 Nm 21:24

⁴⁵ 30,500 donkeys,
⁴⁶ and 16,000 people.

⁴⁷Moses took one out of every 50, selected from the people and the livestock of the Israelites' half. He gave them to the Levites who perform the duties of the Lord's tabernacle, as the Lord had commanded him.

⁴⁸The officers who were over the thousands of the army, the commanders of thousands and of hundreds, approached Moses ⁴⁹and told him, "Your servants have taken a census of the fighting men under our command, and not one of us is missing. ⁵⁰So we have presented to the Lord an offering of the gold articles each man found—armlets, bracelets, rings, earrings, and necklaces—to make ˙atonement for ourselves before the Lord."ᵃ

⁵¹Moses and Eleazar the priest received from them all the articles made out of gold. ⁵²All the gold of the contribution they offered to the Lord, from the commanders of thousands and of hundreds, was 420 pounds.ᴮ ⁵³Each of the soldiers had taken plunder for himself. ⁵⁴Moses and Eleazar the priest received the gold from the commanders of thousands and of hundreds and brought it into the tent of meeting as a memorial for the Israelites before the Lord.

Transjordan Settlements

32 The Reubenites and Gadites had a very large number of livestock. When they surveyed the lands of Jazer and Gilead, they saw that the region was a good one for livestock. ²So the Gadites and Reubenites came to Moses, Eleazar the priest, and the leaders of the community and said: ³"The territory of Ataroth, Dibon, Jazer, Nimrah, Heshbon, Elealeh, Sebam,ᶜ Nebo, and Beon, ⁴which the Lord struck downᵇ before the community of Israel, is good land for livestock, and your servants own livestock." ⁵They said, "If we have found favor in your sight, let this land be given to

---

ᴬ31:30 Or *who protect*   ᴮ31:52 Lit *16,750 shekels*   ᶜ32:3 Sam, LXX read *Sibmah* (v. 38); Syr reads *Sebah*

31:47 From the spoils of war **Moses took one out of every 50 . . . of the Israelites' half** and **gave them to the Levites**. The two percent here contrasts with the tradition in Abraham's day, where a tithe of 10 percent was presented to the temple priesthood.

31:50-54 The amount of **gold** offered by Israel's commanders exceeded the minimal requirement of one-half shekel per person by nearly threefold, with the armlets, bracelets, signet rings, earrings, and necklaces totaling 16,750 shekels (6,700 ounces, or nearly **420 pounds**). The leaders gave sacrificially in the spirit of thanksgiving to God.

32:1-5 Having journeyed through the arid regions south of the Arnon River such as Edom and Moab, the **Reubenites and Gadites** observed that the region around **Gilead** was more fertile. The several rivers in the region such as the Yarmuk, Jabesh, and Jabbok, along with the numerous springs, would provide an ample water supply for their needs. The cities named were located in the highland plains of Transjordan on the eastern side of the Dead Sea. The request for territorial allocation east of the Jordan River was made in proper protocol: they presented themselves as servants seeking favor before **Moses, Eleazar . . . and the leaders of the community** (cp. 31:13). Their claim was that since the Lord had provided victory over the Amorites and others, and the land could provide ample pasturage for their **livestock**, they should be allowed to settle there. They

your servants as a possession. Don't make us cross the Jordan."

⁶But Moses asked the Gadites and Reubenites, "Should your brothers go to war while you stay here? ⁷Why are you discouraging^A the Israelites from crossing into the land the Lord has given them? ⁸That's what your fathers did when I sent them from Kadesh-barnea to see the land.ᵃ ⁹After they went up as far as Eshcol Valley and saw the land, they discouraged the Israelites from entering the land the Lord had given them. ¹⁰So the Lord's anger burned that day, and He swore an oath: ¹¹'Because they did not follow Me completely,ᵇ none of the men 20 years old or more who came up from Egypt will see the land I swore to give Abraham, Isaac, and Jacob— ¹²none except Calebᶜ son of Jephunneh the Kenizzite and Joshuaᵈ son of Nun, because they did follow the Lord completely.' ¹³The Lord's anger burned against Israel, and He made them wander in the wilderness 40 years until the whole generation that had done what was evil in the Lord's sight was gone. ¹⁴And here you, a brood of sinners, stand in your fathers' place adding even more to the Lord's burning anger against Israel. ¹⁵If you turn back from following Him, He will once again leave this people in the wilderness, and you will destroy all of them."

¹⁶Then they approached him and said, "We want to build sheepfolds here for our livestock and cities for our dependents. ¹⁷But we will arm ourselves and be ready to go ahead of the Israelites until we have brought them into their place. Meanwhile, our dependents will remain in the fortified cities because of the inhabitants of the land. ¹⁸We will not return to our homes until each of the Israelites has taken possession of his inheritance. ¹⁹Yet we will not have an inheritance with them across

ᵃ 32:8 Nm 13:1-3,32-33
ᵇ 32:11-12 Nm 14:22-24,29-30
ᶜ 32:12 Nm 14:6,24,30,38; 26:65
ᵈ Ex 33:11; Nm 27:18-23
ᵉ 32:24 Nm 30:2; Jos 1:12-18; 4:12
ᶠ 32:29 Jos 22:9

the Jordan and beyond, because our inheritance will be across the Jordan to the east."

²⁰Moses replied to them, "If you do this—if you arm yourselves for battle before the Lord, ²¹and every one of your armed men crosses the Jordan before the Lord until He has driven His enemies from His presence, ²²and the land is subdued before the Lord—afterward you may return and be free from obligation to the Lord and to Israel. And this land will belong to you as a possession before the Lord. ²³But if you don't do this, you will certainly sin against the Lord; be sure your sin will catch up with you. ²⁴Build cities for your dependents and folds for your flocks, but do what you have promised."ᵉ

²⁵The Gadites and Reubenites answered Moses, "Your servants will do just as my lord commands. ²⁶Our little children, wives, livestock, and all our animals will remain here in the cities of Gilead, ²⁷but your servants are equipped for war before the Lord and will go across to the battle as my lord orders."

²⁸So Moses gave orders about them to Eleazar the priest, Joshua son of Nun, and the family leaders of the Israelite tribes. ²⁹Moses told them, "If the Gadites and Reubenites cross the Jordan with you, every man in battle formation before the Lord, and the land is subdued before you, you are to give them the land of Gilead as a possession.ᶠ ³⁰But if they don't go across with you in battle formation, they must accept land in Canaan with you."

³¹The Gadites and Reubenites replied, "What the Lord has spoken to your servants is what we will do. ³²We will cross over in battle formation before the Lord into the land of Canaan, but we will keep our hereditary possession across the Jordan."

³³So Moses gave them—the Gadites, Reubenites, and half the tribe of Manasseh son

---

^A32:7 Lit discouraging the hearts of

added the stipulation that they not be required to **cross the Jordan** River—they did not want to go to war.

32:6 Moses called attention to the real reason why these tribes wanted to settle the Transjordan highlands—they were hesitant about going to **war**. This was a potentially treasonous act against God's plan for the nation. The promised land was across the Jordan River to the west (34:12) and not on the eastern side of the river. Moses realized that their request had all the hallmarks of the great rebellion in which Israel had rejected God's gift of the land. Note the words "discouraging" and "discouraged" in 32:7 and 9.

32:9 On the **Eshcol Valley**, see note at 13:23.

32:16-19 The Reubenites and Gadites pledged their full support for the conquest of the land west of the Jordan River—even to the point of leading the way for the remainder of the tribes (**we will arm ourselves and be ready to go**)—if Moses

would allow them to take their inheritance in Transjordan and permit them to leave their families in the safekeeping of the local towns.

32:20-24 Moses consented to the request of these tribes under both positive (**if you do this**) and negative (**if you don't do this**) stipulations. The covenant between the Gad-Reuben alliance and the other ten tribes had Moses as the mediator, and Yahweh as the witness and guarantor of the commitment made by the two groups.

32:25,31 The **Gadites and Reubenites** ratified the agreement as **servants** of Moses, and ultimately of God.

32:28-32 All treaty arrangements were ratified in the context of the religious assembly and climaxed by rituals overseen by the priests.

32:33-36 The **Gadites** were granted land in the southern part of the territory formerly held by **Sihon king of the Amorites**.

of Joseph—the kingdom of Sihon king of the Amorites and the kingdom of Og king of Bashan, the land including its cities with the territories surrounding them. [34] The Gadites rebuilt Dibon, Ataroth, Aroer, [35] Atroth-shophan, Jazer, Jogbehah, [36] Beth-nimrah, and Beth-haran[a] as fortified cities, and built sheepfolds. [37] The Reubenites rebuilt Heshbon, Elealeh, Kiriathaim, [38] as well as Nebo and Baal-meon (whose names were changed), and Sibmah. They gave names to the cities they rebuilt.

[39] The descendants of Machir[b] son of Manasseh went to Gilead, captured it, and drove out the Amorites who were there. [40] So Moses gave Gilead to the clan of Machir son of Manasseh, and they settled in it. [41] Jair, a descendant of Manasseh, went and captured their villages, which he renamed Jair's Villages.[A,c] [42] Nobah went and captured Kenath with its villages and called it Nobah after his own name.

Wilderness Travels Reviewed

33 These were the stages of the Israelites' journey when they went out of the land of Egypt by their military divisions under the leadership of Moses and Aaron. [2] At the Lord's command, Moses wrote down the starting points for the stages of their journey; these are the stages listed by their starting points:

[3] They departed from Rameses[d] in the first month, on the fifteenth day of the month. On the day after the

*Passover[e] the Israelites went out triumphantly[B,f] in the sight of all the Egyptians. [4] Meanwhile, the Egyptians were burying every firstborn male the Lord had struck down among them, for the Lord had executed judgment against their gods.[g] [5] The Israelites departed from Rameses and camped at Succoth.[h]

[6] They departed from Succoth and camped at Etham,[i] which is on the edge of the wilderness.

[7] They departed from Etham and turned back to Pi-hahiroth, which faces Baal-zephon, and they camped before Migdol.[j]

[8] They departed from Pi-hahiroth[c] and crossed through the middle of the sea[k] into the wilderness. They took a three-day journey into the Wilderness of Etham and camped at Marah.[l]

[9] They departed from Marah and came to Elim.[m] There were 12 springs of water and 70 date palms at Elim, so they camped there.

[10] They departed from Elim and camped by the *Red Sea.

[11] They departed from the Red Sea and camped in the Wilderness of Sin.[n]

[12] They departed from the Wilderness of Sin and camped in Dophkah.

[13] They departed from Dophkah and camped at Alush.

[a] 32:36 Jos 13:27
[b] 32:39 Gn 50:23; Nm 26:29; Jos 17:1,3
[c] 32:41 Dt 3:14; Jos 13:30; 1Kg 4:13; 1Ch 2:23
[d] 33:3 Gn 47:11; Ex 1:11; 12:37
[e] Ex 12:11-48; Lv 23:5; Nm 9:2-14
[f] Ex 14:8
[g] 33:4 Ex 12:12
[h] 33:5 Ex 12:37
[i] 33:6 Ex 13:20
[j] 33:7 Ex 14:2,9; Jr 46:14; Ezk 30:6
[k] 33:8 Ex 14:22-26
[l] Ex 15:23
[m] 33:9 Ex 15:27; 16:1
[n] 33:11 Ex 16:1; 17:1

[A] 32:41 Or *renamed Havvoth-jair*　[B] 33:3 Lit *with a raised hand*; Ex 14:8　[C] 33:8 Some Hb mss, Sam, Syr, Vg; other Hb mss read *from before Hahiroth*

Gad shared its northern border with the half-tribe of Manasseh. The cities listed for Gad in the OT suggest that a narrow strip of land in the Jordan River plain, extending from the Jabbok River to the Sea of Galilee, was to be included in the allocation. **Aroer** (modern 'Ara'ir) was located on the Kings Highway, just north of the Arnon River. The Gadite cities are described in Jos 13:24-28. The allocation to **half the tribe of Manasseh** was generally to the north of the tribe of Gad, extending from the region of Gilead into Bashan and Golan.

32:37-38 The Reubenites were allocated lands and cities south of Gad, especially the cities of **Heshbon** (the former capital of Sihon's Amorite kingdom), **Elealeh, Kiriathaim . . . Nebo**, and **Baal-meon**. Additional cities and territories are described in Jos 13:15-23, including Dibon and Aroer, which were located on the highland plateau just north of the Arnon River Valley.

32:39-42 The Machirite clan of the tribe of **Manasseh** apparently joined in the quest for Transjordan territory after gaining victory over the **Amorites** in the upper and northern Gilead region. The language here closely parallels that of 21:32 and 33:52-54, the model terminology for the conquest of the land. They were to take control of the given territory, drive out the inhabitants, and destroy all sources of false religion.

33:3-10 The pattern of "they **departed** / they **camped**" echoes the pattern of the journey song of 9:18-23, providing conti-

nuity in the literary style of these two sections of the book. The first cycle, **from Rameses** to **the Red Sea**, provides the date and setting of the miraculous and historic deliverance of Israel from bondage in Egypt—highlighting the death of the firstborn in Egypt, which provided redemption for the firstborn Israelites (3:13) and victory over the gods of Egypt.

33:11-17 From **the Wilderness of Sin** to **Hazeroth**, Mount Sinai is not mentioned, though the Sinai Wilderness is included. The details of the year-long stay in the vicinity of the mountain of God are found in Exodus 19–40 and Numbers 1–10. One of the key questions in attempting to locate the sites in the second through fifth cycles is the location of Mount Sinai. Through the centuries more than 20 different mountains have been suggested. These include Jebel Helal in the northeastern Sinai Peninsula near the Way of the Wilderness of Shur (Ex 15:22), Jebel Sin Bisher in the west central region, Jebel Serbal and the traditional Jebel Musa in the southern Sinai region, and Har Karkom in the Paran Wilderness region. Several mountains in northwestern Saudi Arabia have also been proposed, including Jebel el-Lawra, southeast of Aqaba. If the request of Moses before Pharaoh to journey three days into the wilderness to celebrate a festival to the Lord (Ex 8:3) is to be applied to the quest for the mountain's locale, then the sacred summit must be closer to the Egyptian border fortresses than

¹⁴ They departed from Alush and camped at Rephidim,ᵃ where there was no water for the people to drink.ᵇ

¹⁵ They departed from Rephidim and camped in the Wilderness of Sinai.ᶜ

¹⁶ They departed from the Wilderness of Sinai and camped at Kibroth-hattaavah.ᵈ

¹⁷ They departed from Kibroth-hattaavah and camped at Hazeroth.ᵉ

¹⁸ They departed from Hazeroth and camped at Rithmah.

¹⁹ They departed from Rithmah and camped at Rimmon-perez.

²⁰ They departed from Rimmon-perez and camped at Libnah.

²¹ They departed from Libnah and camped at Rissah.

²² They departed from Rissah and camped at Kehelathah.

²³ They departed from Kehelathah and camped at Mount Shepher.

²⁴ They departed from Mount Shepher and camped at Haradah.

²⁵ They departed from Haradah and camped at Makheloth.

²⁶ They departed from Makheloth and camped at Tahath.

²⁷ They departed from Tahath and camped at Terah.

²⁸ They departed from Terah and camped at Mithkah.

²⁹ They departed from Mithkah and camped at Hashmonah.

³⁰ They departed from Hashmonah and camped at Moseroth.

³¹ They departed from Moseroth and camped at Bene-jaakan.ᶠ

³² They departed from Bene-jaakan and camped at Hor-haggidgad.

³³ They departed from Hor-haggidgad and camped at Jotbathah.

³⁴ They departed from Jotbathah and camped at Abronah.

ᵃ33:14 Ex 17:1,8; 19:2
ᵇEx 17:1-7
ᶜ33:15 Ex 19:1-2
ᵈ33:16 Nm 11:34-35; Dt 9:22
ᵉ33:17 Nm 11:35; 12:16; Dt 1:1
ᶠ33:31-33 Dt 10:6-7
ᵍ33:35 Dt 2:8; 1Kg 9:26
ʰ33:36 Nm 10:12
ⁱ33:37 Nm 21:4; 33:37-41; Dt 32:50
ʲ33:38 Nm 20:23-29
ᵏ33:40 Nm 21:1-3
ˡ33:43 Nm 21:10-11
ᵐ33:44 Nm 21:11
ⁿ33:45 Nm 32:34; Neh 11:25; Jr 48:18,22
ᵒ33:46 Jr 48:22
ᵖ33:47 Nm 27:12; Dt 32:49; Jr 22:20
ᵠDt 32:49; 34:1
ʳ33:48 Nm 22:1
ˢ33:49 Jos 12:3; 13:20; Ezk 25:9
ᵗNm 25:1; Jos 2:1; 3:1; Jl 3:18; Mc 6:5

³⁵ They departed from Abronah and camped at Ezion-geber.ᵍ

³⁶ They departed from Ezion-geber and camped in the Wilderness of Zinʰ (that is, Kadesh).

³⁷ They departed from Kadesh and camped at Mount Horⁱ on the edge of the land of Edom. ³⁸ At the Lord's command, Aaron the priest climbed Mount Hor and died there on the first day of the fifth month in the fortieth year after the Israelites went out of the land of Egypt.ʲ ³⁹ Aaron was 123 years old when he died on Mount Hor. ⁴⁰ At that time the Canaanite king of Arad, who lived in the *Negev in the land of Canaan,ᵏ heard the Israelites were coming.

⁴¹ They departed from Mount Hor and camped at Zalmonah.

⁴² They departed from Zalmonah and camped at Punon.

⁴³ They departed from Punon and camped at Oboth.ˡ

⁴⁴ They departed from Oboth and camped at Iye-abarim on the border of Moab.ᵐ

⁴⁵ They departed from Iyimᴬ and camped at Dibon-gad.ⁿ

⁴⁶ They departed from Dibon-gad and camped at Almon-diblathaim.ᵒ

⁴⁷ They departed from Almon-diblathaim and camped in the Abarimᵖ range facing Nebo.ᵠ

⁴⁸ They departed from the Abarim range and camped on the plains of Moab by the Jordan across from Jericho.ʳ ⁴⁹ They camped by the Jordan from Beth-jeshimothˢ to the Acacia Meadowᴮ·ᵗ on the plains of Moab.

Instructions for Occupying Canaan

⁵⁰ The Lord spoke to Moses in the plains of Moab by the Jordan across from Jericho, ⁵¹ "Tell the Israelites: When you cross the

---

ᴬ33:45 A shortened form of Iye-abarim   ᴮ33:49 Or Abel-shittim

---

most of the mountains except Jebel Sin Bisher or perhaps another mountain in western Sinai. The clearest statement regarding this part of the itinerary is found in Dt 1:2, which states that the distance from Horeb (= Sinai) to Kadesh-barnea via Ezion-geber was an 11-day journey, or about 140 to 150 miles.

33:18-31 None of the sites in the third or fourth cycles can be accurately located. Most of them are unknown to the rest of Scripture, later history, and modern historical geographers.

33:32-41 From **Hor-haggidgad** to **Zalmonah**—the fifth cycle includes the death on **Mount Hor** of the first high priest **Aaron**, who like Moses was prohibited from entering

the promised land because of his rebellion "at the waters of Meribah" (20:11-13,23-29). The reference to the **king of Arad** reminds the reader of the victory over the Canaanite armies (21:1-3) that had once defeated Israel soon after the Israelites refused to enter the promised land (14:39-45).

33:42-49 From **Punon** to **the plains of Moab**—the sites mentioned in the sixth cycle are located in the vicinity of the Arabah south of the Dead Sea and in the Transjordan regions of Edom, Moab, and Ammon.

33:50-56 The seventh and final cycle of victory-march stages would begin from the plains of Moab directly opposite

Jordan into the land of Canaan, ⁵²you must drive out all the inhabitants of the land before you, destroy all their stone images*a* and cast images,*b* and demolish all their ˙high places. ⁵³You are to take possession of the land and settle in it because I have given you the land*c* to possess. ⁵⁴You are to receive the land as an inheritance by lot according to your clans. Increase the inheritance for a large clan and decrease it for a small one. Whatever place the lot indicates for someone will be his. You will receive an inheritance according to your ancestral tribes. ⁵⁵But if you don't drive out the inhabitants of the land before you, those you allow to remain will become thorns in your eyes and in your sides; they will harass you in the land where you will live. ⁵⁶And what I had planned to do to them, I will do to you."*d*

Boundaries of the Promised Land

34 The LORD spoke to Moses, ²"Command the Israelites and say to them: When you enter the land of Canaan, it will be allotted to you as an inheritance*A* with these borders:

³Your southern side will be from the Wilderness of Zin along the boundary of Edom. Your southern border on the east will begin at the east end of the Dead Sea.

⁴Your border will turn south of the Ascent of Akrabbim,*B* proceed to Zin, and end south of Kadesh-barnea. It will go to Hazar-addar and proceed to Azmon.*e* ⁵The border will turn from Azmon*f* to the Brook of Egypt,*g* where it will end at the Mediterranean Sea.

⁶Your western border will be the coastline of the Mediterranean Sea; this will be your western border.

⁷This will be your northern border: From the Mediterranean Sea draw a line to Mount Hor;*C,h* ⁸from Mount Hor draw a line to the entrance of Hamath,*D,i* and the border will reach Zedad.*j* ⁹Then the border will go to Ziphron and end at Hazar-enan.*k* This will be your northern border.

¹⁰For your eastern border, draw a line from Hazar-enan to Shepham. ¹¹The border will go down from Shepham to Riblah east of Ain.*l* It will continue down and reach the eastern slope of the Sea of Chinnereth.*E,m* ¹²Then the border will go down to the Jordan and end at the Dead Sea. This will be your land defined by its borders on all sides."

Cross references (center column)

a 33:52 Lv 26:1; Ezk 8:12
b Ex 32:4,8; 34:17; Lv 19:4; Dt 27:15
c 33:53 Gn 12:7; 15:18; 24:7; 35:12
d 33:56 Dt 28:15
e 34:4 Jos 15:3; Jdg 1:36
f 34:4-5 Jos 15:4
g 34:5 Jos 15:47; Is 27:12; Ezk 47:19
h 34:7 Nm 20:22-28; 33:37-56
i 34:8 Nm 13:21; 2Kg 14:25; 2Ch 7:8; Ezk 48:1
j Ezk 47:15
k 34:9 Ezk 47:17; 48:1
l 34:11 Jos 15:32
m Jos 12:3; 13:27; Lk 5:1

A34:2 Lit *inheritance—the land of Canaan*   **B**34:4 Lit *of Scorpions*; Jos 15:3; Jdg 1:36   **C**34:7 In Lebanon; Nm 20:22-28; 33:37-56   **D**34:8 Or *to Lebo-hamath*   **E**34:11 = the Sea of Galilee; Jos 12:3; 13:27; Lk 5:1

---

the city of Jericho. This Canaanite city would become the initial victory for the Israelites when they faithfully followed the Lord's commands to march around the city on successive days (Jos 6).

33:52 These idols were representations of the pagan gods, a record of the perception of reality conceived of by a worshiper or craftsman. **Cast images** were molten forms (Hb *massekoth*) of deities from clay or molten metal such as copper or bronze. **High places** translates the Hebrew *bamoth*, referring to a cultic worship center, which may or may not indicate an elevated site or structure. All forms of local idolatrous worship were to be eradicated from the land, lest the Israelites be tempted to adopt them.

33:55-56 The statement of conditional judgment of Israel gives evidence of the literary and thematic unity of the Pentateuch, paralleling the message of judgment in Lv 26:14-33 and Dt 28:15-68. Just as God intended for Israel to displace (disinherit) the Canaanites, so He could drive the Israelites from the promised land if they did not obey His commands.

34:2 Not "if," but **when** the Israelites entered **the land** promised to Abraham (Gn 15:18-21), Isaac (Gn 26:4), and Jacob (Gn 28:13-14), they were to divide the territory among the 12 tribes according to the need dictated by each tribe's population (Nm 26:52-56). The **borders** of the promised land represented the limits of the land of Canaan during the late Bronze Age (1550–1200 B.C.) and were the ideal setting for the national boundaries.

34:3-5 The **southern side** of the border began with the **Wilderness of Zin**, from which the original scouts returned with their report (13:21). The line extended northeast to

the southern end of the **Dead Sea** (Salt Sea), avoiding the Edomite territory on the west side of the Arabah, and then moved westward from the Wilderness of Zin, gradually turning more northwest. The border ran along the edge of Edomite territory in order to avoid any further conflicts with those who had prohibited passage for the Israelites when they moved into Transjordan. The description continues on a general line south of the **Ascent of Akrabbim** ("Scorpion Ascent") and on through the south side of **Kadesh-barnea** ('Ain Qedeis or 'Ain el-Qudeirat), and extending toward the **Brook of Egypt** (modern Wadi el-Arish) just south of Raphia and the Gaza Strip. The border then followed the brook northwest to the **Mediterranean Sea** (Hazar-addar and Azmon are unknown).

34:6 The **western border** was the natural barrier formed by the "Great Sea," the **Mediterranean**.

34:7-9 The **northern border** reached from the **Mediterranean** toward **Mount Hor**, perhaps today's Jebel Akkar. The northern border town of Hethlon mentioned in Ezk 47:15 is identified with modern Heitela on the lower slope of Jebel Akkar. The **entrance of Hamath** (or Lebo-hamath) is generally identified with modern Lebweh near one of the sources of the Orontes River. Hamath was the northernmost extent of the land surveyed by the 12 Israelite scouts, according to 13:21. It was also the northern boundary of the Israelite kingdom during the monarchy of David and Solomon (1Kg 8:65).

34:10-12 The **eastern border** began with the site of **Hazar-enan**, which has been associated with either the oasis of Qaryatein or modern Hadr in the vicinity of Mount Hermon.

¹³ So Moses commanded the Israelites, "This is the land you are to receive by lot as an inheritance, which the LORD commanded to be given to the nine and a half tribes. ¹⁴ For the tribe of the Reubenites and the tribe of the Gadites have received their inheritance according to their ancestral houses, and half the tribe of Manasseh has received its inheritance. ¹⁵ The two and a half tribes have received their inheritance[a] across the Jordan from Jericho, eastward toward the sunrise."

Leaders for Distributing the Land

¹⁶ The LORD spoke to Moses, ¹⁷ "These are the names of the men who are to distribute the land as an inheritance for you: Eleazar the priest and Joshua son of Nun. ¹⁸ Take one leader from each tribe to distribute the land. ¹⁹ These are the names of the men:

Caleb[b] son of Jephunneh from the tribe of Judah;
²⁰ Shemuel son of Ammihud from the tribe of Simeon;
²¹ Elidad son of Chislon from the tribe of Benjamin;
²² Bukki son of Jogli, a leader from the tribe of Dan;
²³ from the sons of Joseph:
Hanniel son of Ephod, a leader from the tribe of Manasseh,
²⁴ Kemuel son of Shiphtan, a leader from the tribe of Ephraim;
²⁵ Eli-zaphan son of Parnach, a leader from the tribe of Zebulun;
²⁶ Paltiel son of Azzan, a leader from the tribe of Issachar;

[a]34:15 Nm 32:33
[b]34:19 Nm 14:6,24,30,38; 26:65
[c]35:2 Jos 21:2-3
[d]35:6 Dt 19:1-13; Jos 20:7-9
[e]Jos 21:13

²⁷ Ahihud son of Shelomi, a leader from the tribe of Asher;
²⁸ Pedahel son of Ammihud, a leader from the tribe of Naphtali."

²⁹ These are the ones the LORD commanded to distribute the inheritance to the Israelites in the land of Canaan.

Cities for the Levites

35 The LORD again spoke to Moses in the plains of Moab by the Jordan across from Jericho: ²"Command the Israelites to give cities out of their hereditary property for the Levites to live in and pastureland around the cities.[c] ³ The cities will be for them to live in, and their pasturelands will be for their herds, flocks, and all their other animals. ⁴ The pasturelands of the cities you are to give the Levites will extend from the city wall 500 yards[A] on every side. ⁵ Measure 1,000 yards[B] outside the city for the east side, 1,000 yards[B] for the south side, 1,000 yards[B] for the west side, and 1,000 yards[B] for the north side, with the city in the center. This will belong to them as pasturelands for the cities.

⁶ "The cities you give the Levites will include six cities of refuge,[d] which you must provide so that the one who kills someone may flee there; in addition to these, give 42 other cities.[e] ⁷ The total number of cities you give the Levites will be 48, along with their pasturelands. ⁸ Of the cities that you give from the Israelites' territory, you should take more from a larger tribe and less from a smaller one. Each tribe is to give some of its cities to the Levites in proportion to the inheritance it receives."

[A]35:4 Lit *1,000 cubits*   [B]35:5 Lit *2,000 cubits*

The border continued southeast toward **Shepham** (location unknown) and then south toward **Riblah**, then around the east side of **Ain**, and onward to the eastern edge of the Sea of Galilee (**Chinnereth**). The town of Ain ("spring") may be identified with one of the springs that serve as the sources of the Jordan River. The boundary extended to the eastern side of the Huleh (upper Jordan) Valley, descending toward the Sea of Galilee, including a narrow strip of land on the eastern side of the Jordan up to the lower slopes of the Golan Heights. From the Sea of Galilee the eastern border then followed the **Jordan** River down to the Salt Sea (**Dead Sea**), a distance of about 60 miles, though the river itself meanders back and forth over a distance of more than 100 miles.

34:13-15 Moses fulfilled the task given to him, and the responsibility to carry out these instructions would fall on Joshua son of Nun, his successor. The distribution of the land **by lot** and according to the relative size of each of the tribes was completed under Joshua (Jos 13–19). This allotment applied to the nine and one-half tribes who lived on the west side of the Jordan River, whereas the other two and one-half tribes had already received their allotment, according to the description in Nm 32:33-42. The borders reflect the ideal territorial limits for the land of Israel as

outlined by divine instruction, but this was not fully realized until the time of the united monarchy under David and Solomon (2Sm 8:1-18; 10:1-19; 2Ch 18:1–20:3).

34:19-29 Of the original spies sent to assess the land, only **Caleb** remained as a leader of a tribe for the territorial allotments. With the new leadership responsibilities placed on the shoulders of Joshua, his place as the representative for the tribe of Ephraim was assumed by **Kemuel son of Shiphtan**.

35:1 The statement of the geographical setting (**in the plains of Moab**) alerts the reader to the land theme of chapters 26–36.

35:2-3 This special allocation provided lands among the 12 Israelite tribes for the **Levites to live in and pastureland around the cities** for their flocks and herds acquired through the collection of tithes and offerings from the Israelites (18:21-32). From these settlements they and the priests could teach the people the laws of God, a vital concern if the nation was to learn the statutes and precepts of God's law.

35:6-8 Parallel to the encampment of the priests and Levites around the tabernacle during the wilderness journey (chap. 2), the theocratic state organization was such that

LEVITICAL CITIES AND CITIES OF REFUGE
NM 35

- ● Levitical city
- ○ Levitical city (uncertain location)
- ▣ City of refuge
- ● Other city
- ▲ Mountain peak

Sidon

Damascus

Abana River

Mt. Hermon ▲

Litani River

Pharpar River

Kedesh ▣

Lake Huleh

Rehob

Abdon

33 N

ASHER   NAPHTALI   EAST MANASSEH

Mishal

Kishon River

Rimmon

Sea of Galilee

Golan ▣   Ashtaroth

Nahalal   Kartan

Helkath   ZEBULUN   Hammath

Daberath

Jokneam   Kishion   Tabor

ISSACHAR   Jarmuth

Yarmuk River

Taanach

En-gannim

Ramoth-gilead ▣

Ibleam

MEDITERRANEAN SEA

WEST MANASSEH

Jordan River

Shechem ▣

Jabbok River

Mahanaim   AMMON

GAD

Yarkon River

Gath-rimmon

EPHRAIM   Kibzaim

Jazer

32 N   32 N

DAN

Eltekeh   Beth-horon

Gezer   Gibeon   Geba

Gibbethon   Aijalon   Almon   Mephaath

Anathoth   Heshbon

Beth-   Jerusalem   Bezer ▣

shemesh

BENJAMIN   Kedemoth

Libnah

REUBEN

Hebron ▣   Jahaz

JUDAH

Debir

Juttah   DEAD SEA

Holon   Arnon River

Eshtemoa

Gaza   Jattir

N. Besor

Ashan

Eastern Desert

MOAB

SIMEON

Zered River

31 N   31 N

| 0 | 10 | 20 | 30 | 40 Miles |
| 0 | 10 | 20 | 30 | 40 Kilometers |

Arabah   EDOM

35 E   36 E

Cities of Refuge

[9] The LORD said to Moses, [10] "Speak to the Israelites and tell them: When you cross the Jordan into the land of Canaan, [11] designate cities to serve as cities of refuge for you, so that a person who kills someone unintentionally may flee there.[a] [12] You will have the cities as a refuge from the avenger, so that the one who kills someone will not die until he stands trial before the assembly. [13] The cities you select will be your six cities of refuge. [14] Select three cities across the Jordan and three cities in the land of Canaan to be cities of refuge. [15] These six cities will serve as a refuge for the Israelites and for the foreigner or temporary resident among them, so that anyone who kills a person unintentionally may flee there.

[16] "If anyone strikes a person with an iron object and death results, he is a murderer; the murderer must be put to death. [17] If a man has in his hand a stone capable of causing death and strikes another person and he dies, the murderer must be put to death. [18] If a man has in his hand a wooden object capable of causing death and strikes another person and he dies, the murderer must be put to death. [19] The avenger of blood himself is to kill the murderer; when he finds him, he is to kill him. [20] Likewise, if anyone in hatred pushes a person or throws an object at him with malicious intent and he dies, [21] or if in hostility he strikes him with his hand and he dies, the one who struck him must be put to death; he is a murderer. The avenger of blood is to kill the murderer when he finds him.

[22] "But if anyone suddenly pushes a person without hostility or throws any object at him without malicious intent [23] or without looking drops a stone that could kill a person and he dies, but he was not his enemy and wasn't trying to harm him, [24] the assembly is to judge between the slayer and the avenger of blood according to these ordinances. [25] The assembly is to protect the one who kills someone from the hand of the avenger of blood. Then the assembly will return him to the city of refuge he fled to, and he must live there until the death of the high priest who was anointed with the holy oil.[b]

[26] "If the one who kills someone ever goes outside the border of the city of refuge he fled to, [27] and the avenger of blood finds him outside the border of his city of refuge and kills him, the avenger will not be •guilty of bloodshed, [28] for the one who killed a person was supposed to live in his city of refuge until the death of the high priest. Only after the death of the high priest may the one who has killed a person return to the land he possesses. [29] These instructions will be a statutory ordinance for you throughout your generations wherever you live.

[30] "If anyone kills a person, the murderer is to be put to death based on the word of witnesses. But no one is to be put to death based on the testimony of one witness.[c] [31] You are not to accept a ransom for the life of a murderer who is guilty of killing someone; he must be put to death. [32] Neither should you accept a ransom for the person who flees to his city of refuge, allowing him to return and live in the land before the death of the high priest.[A]

[33] "Do not defile the land where you are,[B] for bloodshed defiles the land,[d] and there can be no •atonement for the land because of the blood that is shed on it, except by the blood of the person who shed it. [34] Do not make the land •unclean where you live and where I reside; for I, •Yahweh, reside among the Israelites."

[a]35:11 Dt 4:42; 19:3-4,6; Jos 20:3-6
[b]35:22-25 Ex 21:13
[c]35:30 Dt 17:6; 19:15; Mt 18:16
[d]35:33 Ps 106:38; Is 24:5; Jr 3:9

[A]35:32 Sam, LXX, Syr read high priest   [B]35:33 Sam, LXX, Syr, Vg, Tg read live

---

the Levites provided a visible presence among the 12 tribes to remind them of the need for holiness and righteousness as the people of God.

35:10-15 The **six cities of refuge** were needed in order to maintain purity and order in the community. Three of these cities are delineated later in Jos 20:7-9: Bezer in the Reubenite territory of southern Transjordan, Ramoth in Gilead in the Gadite highlands, and Golan in the Bashan region.

35:16-21 Those deaths involving deliberate use of lethal weapons or deliberate personal assaults were considered murder and therefore not under the guidelines of the cities of refuge. Murderers were to be executed by the **avenger of blood**, a designated kinsman to the deceased. The Hebrew word *go'el* here is the same term used of the family redeemer in Ru 2:20; 4:4,6. He was one who redeemed property or persons from another. The avenger of blood was

a kinsman who redeemed the life of an individual by taking the life of the murderer.

35:22-29 The promised land was to be a holy land, free from the impurity of shed blood. The six cities of refuge provided a sanctuary to protect the lives of those convicted of manslaughter. It also served as the place of banishment for offenders. If a person was placed under the protection of a city of refuge but then decided to leave the city, he could be subject to execution by the blood avenger. City elders were responsible for assessing each case to determine the nature and cause of a person's death. Atonement was offered to the person who had committed manslaughter only through the time of the high priest's death. Thus that person was required to remain inside the city until that time. Murderers who sought refuge in these cities were not protected under the law. Capital punishment for willful death

The Inheritance of Zelophehad's Daughters

a 36:2 Nm 27:1-11
b 36:4 Lv 25:8-55; 27:7-24

36 The family leaders from the clan of the descendants of Gilead—the son of Machir, son of Manasseh—who were from the clans of the sons of Joseph, approached and addressed Moses and the leaders who were over the Israelite families. [2]They said, "•Yahweh commanded my lord to give the land as an inheritance by lot to the Israelites. My lord was further commanded by Yahweh to give our brother Zelophehad's inheritance to his daughters.[a] [3]If they marry any of the men from the other Israelite tribes, their inheritance will be taken away from our fathers' inheritance and added to that of the tribe into which they marry. Therefore, part of our allotted inheritance would be taken away. [4]When the Jubilee[b] comes for the Israelites, their inheritance will be added to that of the tribe into which they marry, and their inheritance will be taken away from the inheritance of our ancestral tribe."

[5]So Moses commanded the Israelites at the word of the Lord, "What the tribe of Joseph's descendants says is right. [6]This is what the Lord has commanded concerning Zelophehad's daughters: They may marry anyone they like provided they marry within a clan of their ancestral tribe. [7]An inheritance belonging to the Israelites must not transfer from tribe to tribe, because each of the Israelites is to retain the inheritance of his ancestral tribe. [8]Any daughter who possesses an inheritance from an Israelite tribe must marry someone from the clan of her ancestral tribe, so that each of the Israelites will possess the inheritance of his fathers. [9]No inheritance is to transfer from one tribe to another, because each of the Israelite tribes is to retain its inheritance."

[10]The daughters of Zelophehad did as the Lord commanded Moses. [11]Mahlah, Tirzah, Hoglah, Milcah, and Noah, the daughters of Zelophehad, married cousins on their father's side. [12]They married men from the clans of the descendants of Manasseh son of Joseph, and their inheritance remained within the tribe of their father's clan.

[13]These are the commands and ordinances the Lord commanded the Israelites through Moses in the plains of Moab by the Jordan across from Jericho.

---

cases was to be carried out by the city after the elders had determined that the death penalty was justified.

36:1-3 Patriarchal leaders of the Machirites of the tribe of **Manasseh** feared that if the women married outside their clan, the land allotment might go to some other tribe or clan. This would upset the balanced distribution called for in 33:54.

36:4 The Year of **Jubilee** occurred every 50 years (Lv 25:13-55), after seven sabbatical years. During Jubilee, property that had been bought and sold among various tribes or clans reverted to its original tribal owner. This custom maintained the balance of land and wealth distribution among the 12 tribes. The law in Leviticus addressed matters of purchased property, but not that of inherited lands. During the Jubilee Year various debts, such as those of indentured slaves, were forgiven and individuals were freed of financial and other obligations in order to rebuild their lives. "Jubilee" is an anglicized word from the Hebrew word *yovel* ("ram's horn"), which was sounded in to usher in the year of celebration, redemption, and restoration.

36:5-9 The adjudication of the case came through the Lord's instruction to Moses that would permit the women to marry the person of their choosing **provided they marry within a clan of their ancestral tribe**. Hence, a loophole from the earlier case was closed.

36:10-12 The faithful adherence to the instruction from the Lord is highlighted as **the daughters of Zelophehad did as the Lord commanded Moses**. These words remind the reader of the central theme of the book of Numbers—faithfulness to the Lord's instruction.

36:13 The conclusion to the book of Numbers summarizes the position of the Israelite nation as it was poised to inherit the promised land. Throughout the book, references to Israel's faithfulness to God have been defined by the phraseology, "[Moses, Israelites, etc.] did just as the Lord had commanded." The laws of Torah and the extensions of case law in various settings of life in the book of Numbers (and the subsequent book of Deuteronomy) must be the foundation of the community of faith as they enter the land of Canaan as the people of God. If they are faithful and obedient, the blessings of the covenant relationship in the inheritance and productivity of the land will be theirs, but if they do not follow the Lord's commands, their lives will be beset by opposition from without—foreign enemy attacks—and from within—plague, civil war, and natural disaster.

Deuteronomy

The title of this book of the Pentateuch, Deuteronomy, comes from the Septuagint (the Greek translation of the Old Testament) and means "second law" or "repetition of the law." The phrase is actually a mistranslation of 17:18, which reads "a copy of this instruction." It is still a fitting title since much of the book contains repetitions of the laws found in Exodus, Leviticus, and Numbers.

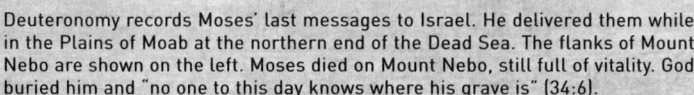

Deuteronomy records Moses' last messages to Israel. He delivered them while in the Plains of Moab at the northern end of the Dead Sea. The flanks of Mount Nebo are shown on the left. Moses died on Mount Nebo, still full of vitality. God buried him and "no one to this day knows where his grave is" (34:6).

Circumstances of Writing

Author: The book itself asserts that Moses is the principle source and author for the material (1:1), as do subsequent OT texts (Jos 1:7-8; 1Kg 2:3; Ezr 3:2) and NT texts (Mt 19:7; Ac 3:22; Rm 10:19). This attribution remained virtually unchallenged until the advent of modern rationalism in the seventeenth and eighteenth centuries, but no arguments advanced by this school of thought have successfully overcome the ancient Mosaic tradition.

Background: The exodus probably occurred in 1446 B.C., whereupon Israel set out for Canaan, the inheritance God had promised His people. Because of their rebellious spirit, the Israelites were forced to wander in the desert for 40 years (2:7) until at last they arrived in Moab, just opposite Jericho (32:49). It was there that Moses put pen to parchment to compose this farewell treatise (31:9,24).

Message and Purpose

Though the initial covenant between the Lord and Israel was made at Sinai, the generation that received it had largely died out in the 38 years since that event. Now the younger generation needed to affirm their commitment to the covenant (4:1-8). Moreover, the transition from a largely nomadic existence in the desert to a sedentary lifestyle in Canaan required a covenant revision and expansion suitable to these new conditions. The purpose of Deuteronomy is to provide guidelines for the new covenant community to enable them to live obediently before God and to carry out His intentions for them. Several themes appear through Deuteronomy:

Nature and character of God: The chief attribute of God is His holiness. With the Shema (6:4), Israel's confession of faith, the holiness and uniqueness of God is emphasized. There is no God but Yahweh. His holiness and righteousness are reflected throughout the moral nature of His law.

Because He is the only God, He is also completely sovereign. God's sovereignty is especially stressed in light

---

1550 B.C.

1500 B.C.

Aaron 1529–1409?

Amenhotep I becomes pharaoh of Egypt **1548**

Egypt's Pharaoh orders midwives to abort Hebrew males at birth. **1548**

Glass invented accidentally in Phoenicia **1530**

Thutmose I becomes pharaoh of Egypt **1528**

Hebrew parents are ordered to throw newborn sons into the Nile. **1528**

Moses 1526–1406

Bronze razors, Scandinavia **1500**

Egyptians develop effective pharmaceutical compounds. **1500**

First tomb in the Valley of the Kings in Egypt **1500**

Cinnamon is exported from Kerala to the Middle East. **1500**

Evidence of gold hammered into foil in South America **1500**

Moses flees Egypt **1487**

of the covenant relationship. Yahweh is Israel's sovereign Lord, and He will not share His sovereignty with another, whether a person or a false god.

Another key attribute of God is His love. His love for His people is seen repeatedly as Deuteronomy recounts the miraculous acts God performed on behalf of His chosen people. God has a purpose for His people, and His loving acts were designed to bring His people in line with His purpose for them. Closely akin to God's love is His graciousness. God did not have to choose Israel. Even when they complained or were disobedient, God exhibited grace though they didn't deserve it.

Covenant relationship: God had entered into a covenant relationship with Israel out of love (7:8). In that covenant as God's people, the Israelites were to reflect their relationship with God by reflecting His character to the nations around them. God's election of them and the gift of land were parts of God's side of the covenant, and obedience and service were the Israelites' part of the covenant. Deuteronomy gives strong words regarding the blessings of living in that covenant.

Faith response of God's people: The Israelites' response to the covenant relationship with God was to live lives—both individually and as a nation—in total commitment to the Lord God. There is no area of life that does not fall under God's sovereign rule. No distinction is made between the religious and the secular, and God expects the highest standards of ethical conduct from His people.

How God's people reflected this would be expressed in obedience to the law. All of the law might be summed up in one command: "Love the LORD your God with all your heart, with all your soul, and with all your strength" (6:5). God's people are to respond not with fearful obedience but with loving obedience. "If you love Me, you will keep My commands" (Jn 14:15). The command to love is grounded in God's love that He demonstrated to them; therefore loving obedience is the natural faith response to a loving God: "We love because He first loved us" (1Jn 4:19).

1450 B.C.   1400 B.C.

Joshua 1490?–1380?

Pictographic writing appears in China 1450

Thutmose III erects numerous obelisks in Egypt, one of which has mistakenly been called "Cleopatra's Needle." The shadow of this obelisk was used to calculate time, seasons, and solstices. 1450

Dogs are domesticated in North America. 1450

Single tube seed drill is developed by the Sumerians. 1450

The exodus and defeat of Pharaoh at the Red Sea 1446

Events in Leviticus 1445

Events in Numbers 1445–1407

Events in Deuteronomy 1406

Miraculous crossing of the Jordan River 1406

Events in Joshua 1406–1380?

Sin and its consequences: In Deuteronomy, sin is presented in the context of the covenant. Failure to follow God's commands would disrupt the covenant relationship, affecting its purity, unity, and witness. Disobedience would lead to cursing. Deuteronomy 27–28 gives strong words about what would happen if the people failed to keep their part of the covenant. The consequences included the loss of the gift of land. Idolatry would lead to death. The nation as a whole would suffer for their disobedience and apostasy. Their history shows that God carried through with the consequences about which He warned Israel.

Contribution to the Bible

Next to the books of Psalms and Isaiah, the NT alludes to Deuteronomy more than any other book in the OT. This is true not only in terms of the sheer number of instances but especially in the passages where theological truth seems most to be at issue. Jesus and the apostles considered Deuteronomy of paramount importance to their own teaching about God and His dealings with His chosen people and humanity at large. Jesus in His temptation quoted the book of Deuteronomy three times against Satan (Mt 4:4-10).

Structure

The style of the book of Deuteronomy appears as a series of repetitious, reminiscent, and even irregular exhortations, which is fitting for a collection of Moses' sermons preparing the people for their move into the promised land. The style is also reflective of the typical suzerain-vassal treaties, which could contain a preamble, historical prologue, main provisions, blessings and curses, and plans for continuing the covenant relationship. The book of Deuteronomy could be considered the constitution for the nation of Israel once it was established in the promised land.

Outline

I. **First Address of Moses (1:1–4:49)**
    A. Preface and historical introduction (1:1-5)
    B. Review of Israel's history (1:6–4:49)

II. **Second Address of Moses (5:1–26:19)**
    A. A series of exhortations (5:1–11:32)
    B. A series of laws and statutes (12:1–21:23)
    C. A series of laws for Israel's social life (22:1–26:19)

III. **Third Address of Moses (27:1–30:20)**
    A. Provision for future renewal of the covenant (27:1-26)
    B. Covenant blessings and curses (28:1–29:15)
    C. Final exhortation to obedience (29:16–30:20)

IV. **Final Days of Moses (31:1–34:12)**
    A. Designation of Moses' successor (31:1-30)
    B. Song of Moses (32:1-52)
    C. Moses' final blessing of Israel (33:1-29)
    D. Death and burial of Moses (34:1-12)

Introduction

1 These are the words Moses spoke to all Israel across the Jordan in the wilderness,[a] in the ˙Arabah opposite Suph,[A] between Paran[b] and Tophel, Laban, Hazeroth,[c] and Di-zahab. [2] It is an eleven-day journey from Horeb to Kadesh-barnea by way of Mount Seir. [3] In the fortieth year, in the eleventh month, on the first of the month, Moses told the Israelites everything the LORD had commanded him to say to them. [4] This was after he had defeated Sihon king of the Amorites, who lived in Heshbon, and Og king of Bashan, who lived in Ashtaroth, at Edrei.[d] [5] Across the Jordan in the land of Moab, Moses began to explain this law, saying:

Departure from Horeb

[6] "The LORD our God spoke to us at Horeb: 'You have stayed at this mountain long enough. [7] Resume your journey and go to the hill country of the Amorites and their neighbors in the Arabah, the hill country, the Judean foothills,[B] the ˙Negev and the sea coast—to the land of the Canaanites and to Lebanon as far as the Euphrates River.[C] [8] See, I have set the land before you. Enter and take possession of the land the LORD swore to give to your fathers[e] Abraham, Isaac, and Jacob and their future descendants.'[f]

Leaders for the Tribes

[9] "I said to you at that time: I can't bear the responsibility for you on my own. [10] The LORD your God has so multiplied you that today you are as numerous as the stars of the sky.[g] [11] May ˙Yahweh, the God of your fathers, increase you a thousand times more, and bless you as He promised you. [12] But how can I bear your troubles, burdens, and disputes by myself? [13] Appoint for yourselves wise, understanding, and respected men from each of your tribes, and I will make them your leaders.'

[14] "You replied to me, 'What you propose to do is good.'

[15] "So I took the leaders of your tribes, wise and respected men, and set them over you as leaders: officials for thousands, hundreds, fifties, and tens, and officers for your tribes. [16] I commanded your judges at that time: Hear the cases between your brothers, and judge rightly between a man and his brother or a foreign resident. [17] Do not show partiality when deciding a case;[h] listen to small and great alike. Do not be intimidated by anyone, for judgment belongs to God.[i] Bring me any case too difficult for you, and I will hear it. [18] At that time I commanded you about all the things you were to do.[j]

Israel's Disobedience at Kadesh-barnea

[19] "We then set out from Horeb and went across all the great and terrible wilderness you saw on the way to the hill country of the Amorites, just as the LORD our God had commanded us. When we reached Kadesh-barnea, [20] I said to you: You have reached the hill country of the Amorites, which the LORD our God is giving us. [21] See, the LORD your God has set the land before you. Go up and take possession of it as Yahweh, the God of your fathers, has told you. Do not be afraid or discouraged.

[22] "Then[k] all of you approached me and said, 'Let's send men ahead of us, so that they may explore the land for us and bring us back a report about the route we should go up and the cities we will come to.' [23] The plan seemed

[a]1:1 Gn 50:10-11; Dt 4:41,46-47; 11:30; Jos 1:14-15
[b]Nm 12:16; Dt 33:2
[c]Nm 11:35
[d]1:4 Nm 21:21-35
[e]1:8 Dt 1:35
[f]Gn 15:18-21; 26:3; 35:12
[g]1:10 Gn 22:17; 26:4; Ex 32:13
[h]1:17 Lv 19:15; Dt 16:19; Pr 24:23
[i]2Ch 19:6
[j]1:9-18 Ex 18:13-26
[k]1:22-46 Nm 13-14

1:1 The reference to Moses being **across the Jordan** is from the perspective of one standing in Canaan to the west. The east side of the river was called Transjordan even by those living there.

1:3 Forty years had passed since Israel's exodus from Egypt. Though the journey from Horeb (Sinai) to Kadesh-barnea was normally 11 days (v. 2), Israel, because of its sin, had spent 40 years on the not-much-longer route from Egypt to Moab (2:7; 8:2,4; Nm 14:33).

1:4 Sihon and **Og** were rulers of kingdoms in Transjordan whose defeat permitted Israel to occupy most of the region, which was later settled by the tribes of Reuben, Gad, and part of Manasseh (Nm 32; Jos 22).

1:7 The Amorites and their neighbors is a way of speaking of all the peoples of Canaan. "Arabah" more technically describes the Great Rift Valley of the Jordan River and the Dead Sea.

1:8 The land the LORD swore to give was part of the covenant in which the Lord called Abraham out of paganism to found a people whom He would use to bless the whole earth (Gn 12:1-3; 15:12-21; 17:8). Israel's impending conquest would be the inheritance God had already allotted to Abraham's descendants.

1:10 Abraham had been promised that his offspring would eventually be innumerable (Gn 15:5). Through the gospel age and the proliferation of the church, this promise now extends to the spiritual descendants of Abraham as well (Rm 4:16-18).

1:15 The adjective **respected** means literally "known." These leaders must have been thoroughly scrutinized and found to be all that they professed to be.

1:17 Do not show partiality is a translation of a phrase that can be rendered, "Do not recognize faces." A judge must not be swayed by friendship or high rank.

1:19 Kadesh-barnea was Israel's main staging area throughout the 40 years of desert sojourn. Known today as ˙Ain Qedeis, this large oasis would have been adequate for hundreds of thousands of Hebrews.

good to me, so I selected 12 men from among you, one man for each tribe. [24] They left and went up into the hill country and came to the Valley of Eshcol, scouting the land. [25] They took some of the fruit from the land in their hands, carried it down to us, and brought us back a report: 'The land the LORD our God is giving us is good.'[a]

[26] "But you were not willing to go up, rebelling against the command of the LORD your God. [27] You grumbled in your tents[b] and said, 'The LORD brought us out of the land of Egypt to deliver us into the hands of the Amorites so they would destroy us, because He hated us. [28] Where can we go? Our brothers have discouraged us,[c] saying: The people are larger and taller than we are; the cities are large, fortified to the heavens.[d] We also saw the descendants of the Anakim[e] there.'

[29] "So I said to you: Don't be terrified or afraid of them![f] [30] The LORD your God who goes before you[g] will fight for you,[h] just as you saw Him do for you in Egypt. [31] And you saw in the wilderness how the LORD your God carried you as a man carries his son all along the way you traveled until you reached this place. [32] But in spite of this you did not trust the LORD your God, [33] who went before you on the journey to seek out a place for you to camp. He went in the fire by night and in the cloud by day to guide you on the road you were to travel.

[34] "When the LORD heard your[A] words, He grew angry and swore an oath: [35] 'None of these men in this evil generation will see the good land I swore to give your fathers,[i] [36] except Caleb the son of Jephunneh. He will see

it, and I will give him and his descendants the land on which he has set foot, because he followed the LORD completely.'

[37] "The LORD was angry with me also because of you and said: 'You will not enter there either.[j] [38] Joshua son of Nun, who attends you, will enter it. Encourage him, for he will enable Israel to inherit it.[k] [39] Your little children, whom you said would be plunder, your sons who[B] don't know good from evil, will enter there. I will give them the land, and they will take possession of it. [40] But you are to turn back and head for the wilderness by way of the •Red Sea.'[l]

[41] "You answered me, 'We have sinned against the LORD. We will go up and fight just as the LORD our God commanded us.' Then each of you put on his weapons of war and thought it would be easy to go up into the hill country.

[42] "But the LORD said to me, 'Tell them: Don't go up and fight, for I am not with you to keep you from being defeated by your enemies.'[m] [43] So I spoke to you, but you didn't listen. You rebelled against the LORD's command and defiantly went up into the hill country. [44] Then the Amorites who lived there came out against you and chased you like a swarm of bees. They routed you from Seir as far as Hormah.[n] [45] When you returned, you wept before the LORD, but He didn't listen to your requests or pay attention to you. [46] For this reason you stayed in Kadesh as long as you did.[c]

Journey past Seir

2 "Then we turned back and headed for the wilderness by way of the •Red Sea, as the

Cross references (center column)

[a]1:25 Dt 8:7
[b]1:27 Ps 106:25
[c]1:28 Jos 14:8
[d]Dt 9:1-2
[e]Dt 2:10; 9:2;
Jos 11:21; 14:12
[f]1:29 Dt 31:6
[g]1:30 Ex 23:23;
32:34; Dt 31:8;
Jdg 4:14; Is
52:12
[h]Ex 14:14; Dt
20:4; Jdg 9:17
[i]1:35 Dt 1:8;
6:18; 10:11;
11:21; 30:20;
31:7,20; Ezk
20:42
[j]1:37 Nm 20:12
[k]1:38 Nm
27:12-21
[l]1:40 Nm 14:25
[m]1:42 Nm 14:42
[n]1:44 Nm 14:45

[A]1:34 Lit *the sound of your*   [B]1:39 Lit *who today*   [C]1:46 Lit *Kadesh for many days, according to the days you stayed*

1:24 The **Valley of Eshcol** was in southern Canaan near Hebron. Its name means "bunch of grapes," from the abundance of this fruit that grew there. Canaan had already been called a "land flowing with milk and honey" (6:3; 11:9; 26:9; cp. Nm 13:27), so this display of grapes reinforced the lushness of the land the Lord had bequeathed to His people Israel (Dt 1:25).

1:28 The description of the cities of Canaan as **fortified to the heavens** came from spies who were afraid to trust God for victory and therefore exaggerated the difficulties involved. Jesus taught that a person of true faith could command mountains (Mk 11:23). The **Anakim**, named for Anak, a descendant of the founder of Hebron (Jos 21:11), were a gigantic people (Nm 13:33), some of whom moved to Philistia and may have been related to Goliath and other giant Philistines (Jos 11:21-22; cp. 1Ch 20:4-8).

1:31 The imagery of God carrying Israel **as a man carries his son** brings to mind Israel's special relationship to the Lord through His covenant with Abraham. Moses demanded Israel's release from Pharaoh because, in God's words, "Israel is My firstborn son" (Ex 4:22; cp. Ex 2:24-25).

1:33 The fire by night and **the cloud by day** are expressions

of the presence of God as He led His people through the wilderness. The fire of God's presence speaks of His visible glory and holiness and recalls His judgment against those who fail to revere Him (4:9-14,24; Nm 11:1-3). The cloud symbolized God's mysteriousness, occasionally overshadowing His brilliance lest it destroy the curious who might try to become too familiar (Ex 19:9-13,16-25; Dt 31:15).

1:37 This curious statement is not Moses' attempt to deflect guilt from himself to the nation. The point was that he as well as the older generation of Israelites would fail to enter the land of promise because all alike were guilty. When the people sinned with regard to their demand for water (the incident in view here; cp. Nm 20:1-8), Moses became angry; this undermined his credibility as a leader (Dt 20:12).

1:39 The **sons who don't know good from evil** were not morally deficient but too young to form moral values (Is 7:16; 8:4). They were innocent and therefore not disqualified from entering the land of promise.

1:44 From Seir as far as Hormah refers to an area just south of the Dead Sea and about 50 miles across. Its residents expelled the Israelites because Israel had attempted to penetrate the area despite God's command not to do so (v. 42).

LORD had told me, and we traveled around the hill country of Seir for many days. ²The LORD then said to me, ³'You've been traveling around this hill country long enough; turn north. ⁴Command the people: You are about to travel through the territory of your brothers, the descendants of Esau, who live in Seir. They will be afraid of you, so you must be very careful. ⁵Don't fight with them, for I will not give you any of their land, not even an inch of it,ᴬ because I have given Esau the hill country of Seir as his possession. ⁶You may purchase food from them with silver, so that you may eat, and buy water from them to drink.ᵃ ⁷For the LORD your God has blessed you in all the work of your hands.ᵇ He has watched over your journey through this immense wilderness. The LORD your God has been with you this past 40 years, and you have lacked nothing.'

Journey past Moab

⁸"So we bypassed our brothers, the descendants of Esau, who live in Seir. We turned away from the ˙Arabah road and from Elath and Ezion-geber. We traveled along the road to the Wilderness of Moab. ⁹The LORD said to me, 'Show no hostility toward Moab, and do not provoke them to battle, for I will not give you any of their land as a possession, since I have given Ar as a possession to the descendants of Lot.'ᶜ

¹⁰The Emim, a great and numerous people as tall as the Anakim, had previously lived there. ¹¹They were also regarded as Rephaim,ᵈ like the Anakim, though the Moabites called them Emim.ᵉ ¹²The Horites had previously lived in

Seir, but the descendants of Esau drove them out, destroying them completelyᴮ and settling in their place, just as Israel did in the land of its possession the LORD gave them.

¹³"The LORD said, 'Now get up and cross the Zered Valley.' So we crossed the Zered Valley.ᶠ ¹⁴The time we spent traveling from Kadesh-barnea until we crossed the Zered Valley was 38 years until the entire generation of fighting men had perished from the camp, as the LORD had sworn to them. ¹⁵Indeed, the LORD's hand was against them, to eliminate them from the camp until they had all perished.

Journey past Ammon

¹⁶"When all the fighting men had died among the people, ¹⁷the LORD spoke to me, ¹⁸'Today you are going to cross the border of Moab at Ar. ¹⁹When you get close to the Ammonites, don't show any hostility to them or fight with them, for I will not give you any of the Ammonites' land as a possession; I have given it as a possession to the descendants of Lot.'ᵍ

²⁰This too used to be regarded as the land of the Rephaim. The Rephaim lived there previously, though the Ammonites called them Zamzummim, ²¹a great and numerous people, tall as the Anakim. The LORD destroyed the Rephaim at the advance of the Ammonites, so that they drove them out and settled in their place. ²²This was just as He had done for the descendants of Esau who lived in Seir, when He destroyed the Horites before them; they drove them out and have lived in their place until now. ²³The Caphtorim, who came

---

Cross references (center column):
ᵃ2:1-6 Nm 20:14-21
ᵇ2:7 Dt 30:9
ᶜ2:9 Gn 19:36-37; 15:20; Jos 13:13;
ᵈ2:11 Gn 14:5; 2Sm 21:15-22
ᵉGn 14:5
ᶠ2:8-13 Nm 21:10-20
ᵍ2:19 Gn 19:36,38

ᴬ2:5 Lit *land as far as the width of a sole of a foot*   ᴮ2:12 Lit *them before them*

2:1 The **Red Sea** mentioned here is not the body of water at the Gulf of Suez crossed by Israel during the exodus, but another arm of that sea between the Sinai Peninsula and Arabia.

2:3 The Israelites had tried to avoid the difficult route through the **hill country** by penetrating Canaan from the south. When that failed they had to go south to the Red Sea, skirt the hill country by hugging the coast, then **turn north** through Edom's interior.

2:4-5 When Israel encountered the Edomites (**the descendants of Esau**), they did not attack them because the Lord had **given . . . the hill country of Seir as his possession**. Thus, Israel was not the only people given a promised land (vv. 9,19; cp. Gn 33:16; 36:1-8). It was Israel's task that was unique and not the fact that God gave them a special place of habitation.

2:8 The **Arabah road** linked the Dead Sea with the Gulf of Aqaba and took its name from the valley that is part of the Great Rift geological fault (1:1).

2:9 The **descendants of Lot** were the Moabites and Ammonites, named for the sons whom Lot fathered by his own daughters following the destruction of Sodom and Gomor-

rah (Gn 19:30-38). Lot was Abraham's nephew, and it was this kinship that permitted **Moab** and Ammon to be treated with such favor. **Ar** was a city just south of the Arnon gorge, but the name here is synonymous with all of Moab.

2:11 The **Rephaim** (and **Anakim**) were a giant race associated not only with Moab (as here) but with Bashan (Jos 12:4) and Ammon (Dt 2:20). Their identification as Anakim locates them also in Canaan, particularly in Philistine areas (Jos 11:21-22; 14:12,15; 15:13-14).

2:12 Esau's clan drove the **Horites** out of Edom, their ancestral land, and settled Edom **in their place** (cp. v. 22; Gn 36:8). This statement was probably added by a later inspired writer, since it speaks of Israel's conquest in the past tense.

2:13 The **Zered Valley**, now known as Wadi el-Hesa, flows from the Edomite hill country into the southeast corner of the Dead Sea.

2:19 Ammon, the brother of Moab—born as the result of incest between Lot and his daughters (v. 9)—was the ancestor of the **Ammonites**.

2:22 See note at verses 4-5.

2:23 The **Caphtorim** appear to be equivalent to the earlier

from Caphtor,[A] destroyed the Avvim, who lived in villages as far as Gaza, and settled in their place.

Defeat of Sihon the Amorite

[24] "The LORD also said, 'Get up, move out, and cross the Arnon Valley. See, I have handed Sihon the Amorite, king of Heshbon, and his land over to you. Begin to take possession of it; engage him in battle. [25] Today I will begin to put the fear and dread of you on the peoples everywhere under heaven. They will hear the report about you, tremble, and be in anguish because of you.'

[26] "So I sent messengers with an offer of peace to Sihon king of Heshbon from the Wilderness of Kedemoth, saying, [27] 'Let us travel through your land; we will keep strictly to the highway. We will not turn to the right or the left.[a] [28] You can sell us food in exchange for silver so we may eat, and give us water for silver so we may drink. Only let us travel through on foot, [29] just as the descendants of Esau who live in Seir did for us, and the Moabites who live in Ar, until we cross the Jordan into the land the LORD our God is giving us.' [30] But Sihon king of Heshbon would not let us travel through his land, for the LORD your God had made his spirit stubborn and his heart obstinate in order to hand him over to you, as has now taken place.

[31] "Then the LORD said to me, 'See, I have begun to give Sihon and his land to you. Begin to take possession of it.' [32] So Sihon and his whole army came out against us for battle at Jahaz. [33] The LORD our God handed him over to us, and we defeated him, his sons, and his whole army. [34] At that time we captured all his cities and •completely destroyed the people of every city, including the women and children. We left no survivors. [35] We took only the

livestock and the spoil from the cities we captured as plunder for ourselves. [36] There was no city that was inaccessible to[B] us, from Aroer on the rim of the Arnon Valley, along with the city in the valley, even as far as Gilead.[b] The LORD our God gave everything to us. [37] But you did not go near the Ammonites' land, all along the bank of the Jabbok River,[c] the cities of the hill country, or any place that the LORD our God had forbidden.[d]

Defeat of Og of Bashan

3 "Then we turned and went up the road to Bashan, and Og king of Bashan[e] came out against us with his whole army to do battle at Edrei.[f] [2] But the LORD said to me, 'Do not fear him, for I have handed him over to you along with his whole army and his land. Do to him as you did to Sihon king of the Amorites,[g] who lived in Heshbon.' [3] So the LORD our God also handed over Og king of Bashan and his whole army to us. We struck him until there was no survivor left. [4] We captured all his cities at that time. There wasn't a city that we didn't take from them: 60 cities, the entire region of Argob, the kingdom of Og in Bashan. [5] All these were fortified with high walls, gates, and bars, besides a large number of rural villages. [6] We •completely destroyed them, as we had done to Sihon king of Heshbon, destroying the men, women, and children of every city. [7] But we took all the livestock and the spoil from the cities as plunder for ourselves.[h]

The Land of the Transjordan Tribes

[8] "At that time we took the land from the two Amorite kings across the Jordan, from the Arnon Valley as far as Mount Hermon, [9] which the Sidonians call Sirion, but the Amorites call Senir, [10] all the cities of the plateau, Gilead, and Bashan as far as Salecah and Edrei,

---

a2:27 Nm 20:17
b2:36 Jos 13:9, 16
c2:37 Nm 21:24; Jos 12:2
d2:24-37 Nm 21:21-31
e3:1 Nm 32:33
f Nm 21:33,35;
Dt 1:4; 3:10; 29:6-7; Jos 12:4; 13:12,31
g3:2 Nm 21:23-26,34
h3:1-7 Nm 21:32-35

A2:23 Probably Crete   B2:36 Or was too high for

Philistines of the patriarchal era (Gn 21:32,34; 26:1,8). They are said to have settled in the vicinity of **Gaza** (Jos 13:3), and elsewhere they are said to have originated in Caphtor, likely the island of Crete (Jr 47:4; Am 9:7; cp. Gn 10:14). Thus, the common argument that considers Philistines in Genesis as anachronistic has no real substance.

2:24 Heshbon, the capital city of King **Sihon the Amorite**, is identified by many scholars with Tell Hesban, near Amman, Jordan. However, this seems unlikely because Hesban is too small to have been a capital and it did not exist as early as the biblical date of the conquest.

2:30 The LORD making Sihon's **spirit stubborn and his heart obstinate** is similar to God's hardening of Pharaoh's heart before the exodus (Ex 9:12; 10:1,20)—an act of God that followed Pharaoh's consistent hardening of his own heart (Ex 8:15,32; 9:34). The hardening in both cases was so God's

deliverance could be seen as a miracle on behalf of His people (Dt 2:30; Ex 7:3-5).

2:34 Sihon's destruction sanctioned by the Lord must be viewed not as a cruel act but as a means of eliminating a hopelessly unrepentant people who, if left alive, would corrupt the Israelites through intermarriage and religious syncretism (7:1-6). In fact, Israel's failure to obey God in this respect brought about precisely this result (1Kg 11:1-6; 2Kg 17:7-17).

3:4 The name **Bashan** (cp. v. 1) is a general term for the whole region north of the Yarmuk River, now the border between Jordan and Syria. **Argob** appears to have been the technical name for the political entity in Bashan over which **Og** was ruler.

3:8-9 Mount Hermon, over 9,000 feet high, is the tallest peak of the Anti-Lebanon range. In a psalm thought to have

cities of Og's kingdom in Bashan.[a] [11](Only Og king of Bashan was left of the remnant of the Rephaim. His bed was made of iron.[A] Isn't it in Rabbah of the Ammonites? It is 13 feet six inches long and six feet wide by a standard measure.[B])

[12]"At that time we took possession of this land.[b] I gave to the Reubenites and Gadites the area extending from Aroer by the Arnon Valley, and half the hill country of Gilead along with its cities. [13]I gave to half the tribe of Manasseh the rest of Gilead and all Bashan, the kingdom of Og. The entire region of Argob, the whole territory of Bashan, used to be called the land of the Rephaim. [14]Jair, a descendant of Manasseh, took over the entire region of Argob as far as the border of the Geshurites and Maacathites. He called Bashan by his own name, Jair's Villages,[c] as it is today. [15]I gave Gilead to Machir, [16]and I gave to the Reubenites and Gadites the area extending from Gilead to the Arnon Valley (the middle of the valley was the border) and up to the Jabbok River, the border of the Ammonites. [17]The ·Arabah and Jordan are also borders from Chinnereth[D] as far as the Sea of the Arabah, the Dead Sea, under the slopes of Pisgah on the east.[c]

[18]"I commanded you at that time: The LORD your God has given you this land to possess. All your fighting men will cross over in battle formation ahead of your brothers the Israelites. [19]But your wives, young children, and livestock—I know that you have a lot of livestock—will remain in the cities I have given you [20]until the LORD gives rest to your brothers as He has to you, and they also take possession of the land the LORD your God is giving them across the Jordan. Then each of you may return to his possession that I have given you.[d]

a 3:10 Jos 13:11
b 3:12 Gn 28:4;
Lv 20:24; Dt 4:5;
6:1; 7:1; 8:1;
12:29; 30:5
c 3:8-17 Nm
32:1-19,33-42;
Jos 12:2-3
d 3:18-20 Nm
32:20-32; Jos
1:14-15
e 3:25 Dt 8:7
f 3:26-27 Nm
20:1-13
g 3:27-28 Nm
27:12-23
h 4:2 Dt 12:32;
Rv 22:18-19
i 4:3 Nm 25:1-9

The Transfer of Israel's Leadership

[21]"I commanded Joshua at that time: Your own eyes have seen everything the LORD your God has done to these two kings. The LORD will do the same to all the kingdoms you are about to enter. [22]Don't be afraid of them, for the LORD your God fights for you.

[23]"At that time I begged the LORD: [24]Lord GOD, You have begun to show Your greatness and power to Your servant, for what god is there in heaven or on earth who can perform deeds and mighty acts like Yours? [25]Please let me cross over and see the beautiful land[e] on the other side of the Jordan, that good hill country and Lebanon.

[26]"But the LORD was angry with me on account of you and would not listen to me. The LORD said to me, 'That's enough! Do not speak to Me again about this matter. [27]Go to the top of Pisgah and look to the west, north, south, and east, and see it with your own eyes, for you will not cross this Jordan.[f] [28]But commission Joshua and encourage and strengthen him, for he will cross over ahead of the people and enable them to inherit this land that you will see.'[g] [29]So we stayed in the valley facing Beth-peor.

Call to Obedience

4 "Now, Israel, listen to the statutes and ordinances I am teaching you to follow, so that you may live, enter, and take possession of the land ·Yahweh, the God of your fathers, is giving you. [2]You must not add anything to what I command you or take anything away from it,[h] so that you may keep the commands of the LORD your God I am giving you. [3]Your eyes have seen what the LORD did at Baal-peor, for the LORD your God destroyed every one of you who followed ·Baal of Peor.[i] [4]But you who have remained faithful[E] to the LORD your God

A 3:11 Or *His sarcophagus was made of basalt*   B 3:11 Lit *Nine cubits its length and four cubits its width, by a man's cubit*   C 3:14 Or *Havvoth-jair*   D 3:17 = the Sea of Galilee; Jos 12:3; 13:27; Lk 5:1   E 4:4 Lit *have held on*

strong literary and conceptual associations with Phoenicia, Hermon is called **Sirion** (Ps 29:6).

3:11 The **iron . . . bed** of Og may in fact have been his sarcophagus. The Hebrew term describing it (*'eres*) should likely be taken figuratively of Og's resting place in death.

3:14-15 The conquest of the region of **Bashan** and part of **Gilead** was accomplished not by **Manasseh** *per se* but by Manassite clans, namely **Jair** and **Machir** (cp. Nm 32:39-42). Jair seems to have been a descendant of Machir (1Ch 2:21-23). In any case, they were not contemporaneous, suggesting that the conquest took a number of years.

3:24 Moses' question was not implying that other gods existed. His point was that the Lord is superior to all gods, real or imaginary, in the polytheistic culture of the time (Is 44:6-20; 45:20-25; Jr 10:11-16).

3:27 Pisgah is the name of a summit in the range of hills in Transjordan called Abarim overlooking the Arabah and the Dead Sea. It lies just north of Mount Nebo, the traditional setting of Moses' vantage point from which he could see the land of Canaan (32:49). Pisgah (now identified as Ras Siyaghah) and Nebo were twin peaks of the same mountain, but it was from Pisgah that the great lawgiver viewed the land he was forbidden to enter (34:1).

4:1 Statutes and ordinances are technical terms referring to elements common to covenant texts. They occur together regularly in Deuteronomy (vv. 5,8,14,45; 5:1,31; 6:1,20; 7:11; 11:1; 12:1) and always to describe the Lord's requirement of His people Israel with whom He had entered into covenant fellowship.

4:3 Baal-peor was the place in Transjordan where Israel

are all alive today. ⁵Look, I have taught you statutes and ordinances as the LORD my God has commanded me, so that you may follow them in the land you are entering to possess. ⁶Carefully follow them, for this will show your wisdom and understanding in the eyes of the peoples. When they hear about all these statutes, they will say, 'This great nation is indeed a wise and understanding people.' ⁷For what great nation is there that has a god near to it as the LORD our God is to us whenever we call to Him? ⁸And what great nation has righteous statutes and ordinances like this entire law I set before you today?

⁹"Only be on your guard and diligently watch yourselves, so that you don't forget the things your eyes have seen and so that they don't slip from your mind as long as you live. Teach them to your children and your grandchildren.ᵃ ¹⁰The day you stood before the LORD your God at Horeb, the LORD said to me, 'Assemble the people before Me, and I will let them hear My words, so that they may learn to ˙fear Me all the days they live on the earth and may instruct their children.' ¹¹You came near and stood at the base of the mountain, a mountain blazing with fire into the heavens and enveloped in a dense, black cloud. ¹²Then the LORD spoke to you from the fire. You kept hearing the sound of the words, but didn't see a form; there was only a voice.ᵇ ¹³He declared His covenantᶜ to you. He commanded you to follow the Ten Commandments, which He wrote on two stone tablets. ¹⁴At that time the

LORD commanded me to teach you statutes and ordinances for you to follow in the land you are about to cross into and possess.

Worshiping the True God

¹⁵"For your own good, be extremely careful—because you did not see any form on the day the LORD spoke to you out of the fire at Horeb— ¹⁶not to act corruptly and make an idol for yourselves in the shape of any figure: a male or female form, ¹⁷or the form of any beast on the earth, any winged creature that flies in the sky, ¹⁸any creature that crawls on the ground, or any fish in the waters under the earth. ¹⁹When you look to the heavens and see the sun, moon, and stars—all the array of heaven—do not be led astray to bow down and worship them. The LORD your God has provided them for all people everywhere under heaven. ²⁰But the LORD selected you and brought you out of Egypt's iron furnace to be a people for His inheritance, as you are today.

²¹"The LORD was angry with me on your account. He swore that I would not cross the Jordan and enter the good landᵈ the LORD your God is giving you as an inheritance.ᵉ ²²I won't be crossing the Jordan because I am going to die in this land. But you are about to cross over and take possession of this good land. ²³Be careful not to forget the covenant of the LORD your God that He made with you, and make an idol for yourselves in the shape of anything He has forbidden you. ²⁴For the

ᵃ4:9-10 Ex 12:26; Dt 6:7,20-25; 11:2-7,18-21; 31:12-13,19-22; 32:46; Jos 4:6,21-22; 8:35
ᵇ4:9-12 Ex 19:10-19; Heb 12:18-19
ᶜ4:13 Dt 31:16
ᵈ4:21 Dt 8:7
ᵉDt 15:4

was first seduced into the licentious worship of the fertility deity **Baal of Peor** (Nm 25:1-9). As a result the Lord commanded Moses to kill all the men who had participated in this sexually perverse paganism.

berith

Hebrew Pronunciation	[beh REET]
HCSB Translation	covenant
Uses in Deuteronomy	27
Uses in the OT	287
Focus Passage	Deuteronomy 4:13,23,31

Berith probably relates to an Akkadian word pointing to covenants (Gn 6:18) as bonds, a fundamental implication being obligation. Berith also denotes treaty (Jos 9:15) or agreement (Is 33:8). People confirmed covenants by oath (Gn 21:22-27); word, testimony, counsel, agreement, and law are associated terms. Covenants initiated relationships implying love, friendship, loyalty, goodness, peace, and brotherhood. People entered covenants by "cutting" (making) them, originally cutting apart animals (Gn 15:9-10; Jr 34:18). "Cut a covenant" appears as form an alliance (Ps 83:5) or cut a deal (Is 28:15). Other ceremonies were sacrifices (Ex 24:3-8), meals (Gn 26:26-31), sharing salt (Lv 2:13), and shaking hands (Ezk 17:18). Covenants were between men, with God, and figuratively with animals (Hs 2:18). God dealt with mankind through two important kinds of covenant, an obligatory one modeled after suzerain-vassal treaties (e.g., Mosaic), and a promissory one comparable to royal grants (e.g., Davidic).

4:7 The reference to the gods of the nations suggests only that the nations believed that those gods existed, though, of course, they did not exist (3:24).

4:13 The **Ten Commandments** were the foundational principles upon which the covenant between the Lord and Israel was based. As with legal texts in general, there must be two copies. Exodus 32:15 points out that each of the **two stone tablets** was written on both sides.

4:15-18 To conceptualize God in a manufactured **form** was to limit His power and glory. To worship idols of other gods was to deny God's uniqueness and sovereignty.

4:20 **Egypt's** description as an **iron furnace** is a metaphor for a smelter or crucible whose function was to melt down metals under such intense heat that all the dross and other impurities were separated from them, leaving them pure and usable (Pr 17:3). The Lord had allowed Israel to suffer in Egypt so they would be better prepared **to be a people for His inheritance** (cp. 1Kg 8:51; Jr 11:4-5; Zch 13:9; Mal 3:3).

4:23-24 God is never envious of anyone or anything, but He emphatically states and defends His right to exclusive worship by His people (6:14-15).

Lord your God is a consuming fire,[a] a jealous God.[b]

[25] "When you have children and grandchildren and have been in the land a long time, and if you act corruptly, make an idol in the form of anything, and do what is evil in the sight of the Lord your God, provoking Him to anger, [26] I call heaven and earth as witnesses against you today that you will quickly perish[c] from the land you are about to cross the Jordan to possess. You will not live long there, but you will certainly be destroyed. [27] The Lord will scatter you among the peoples, and you will be reduced to a few survivors[A] among the nations where the Lord your God will drive you. [28] There you will worship man-made gods of wood and stone, which cannot see, hear, eat, or smell. [29] But from there, you will search for the Lord your God, and you will find Him when you seek Him with all your heart and all your soul.[d] [30] When you are in distress and all these things have happened to you, you will return to the Lord your God in later days and obey Him. [31] He will not leave you, destroy you, or forget the covenant[e] with your fathers that He swore to them by oath, because the Lord your God is a compassionate God.[f]

[32] "Indeed, ask about the earlier days that preceded you, from the day God created man on the earth and from one end of the heavens to the other: Has anything like this great event ever happened, or has anything like it been heard of? [33] Has a people heard God's voice speaking from the fire as you have, and lived? [34] Or has a god attempted to go and take a nation as his own out of another nation, by trials, signs, wonders, and war, by a strong hand and an outstretched arm, by great terrors, as the Lord your God did for you

*a*4:24 Ex 24:17; Dt 9:3; 2Sm 22:9; Is 29:6; 30:27,30; 34:14 *b*4:23–24 Ex 20:5; 34:14; Dt 5:9; 6:15; Jos 24:19; Heb 12:29 *c*4:26 Dt 8:19 *d*4:29 Jr 29:13 *e*4:31 Lv 26:45; Dt 5:3; 7:12; 8:18; 31:20 *f*Ex 34:6 *g*4:35 1Kg 8:60; Is 43:11; 44:8; 45:5-6,18-22; 46:9; Dn 3:29; Jl 2:27; Mk 12:32 *h*4:36 Ex 20:22 *i*Ex 19:18 *j*4:37 Dt 7:6-8; 10:15; 23:5; 33:3; Jr 31:3; Hs 11:1; Mal 1:2 *k*4:38 Lv 20:24 *l*4:41-43 Nm 35:6-15; Dt 19:2-13; Jos 20:7-9

in Egypt before your eyes? [35] You were shown these things so that you would know that the Lord is God; there is no other besides Him.[g] [36] He let you hear His voice from heaven to instruct you.[h] He showed you His great fire on earth, and you heard His words from the fire.[i] [37] Because He loved[j] your fathers, He chose their descendants after them and brought you out of Egypt by His presence and great power, [38] to drive out before you nations greater and stronger than you and to bring you in and give you their land as an inheritance,[k] as is now taking place. [39] Today, recognize and keep in mind that the Lord is God in heaven above and on earth below; there is no other. [40] Keep His statutes and commands, which I am giving you today, so that you and your children after you may prosper and so that you may live long in the land the Lord your God is giving you for all time."

Cities of Refuge

[41] Then Moses set apart three cities across the Jordan to the east. [42] Someone could flee there who committed manslaughter, killing his neighbor accidentally without previously hating him. He could flee to one of these cities and stay alive: [43] Bezer in the wilderness on the plateau land, belonging to the Reubenites; Ramoth in Gilead, belonging to the Gadites; or Golan in Bashan, belonging to the Manassites.[l]

Introduction to the Law

[44] This is the law Moses gave the Israelites. [45] These are the decrees, statutes, and ordinances Moses proclaimed to them after they came out of Egypt, [46] across the Jordan in the valley facing Beth-peor in the land of Sihon

---

[A]4:27 Lit be left few in number

4:26 Since human beings are not qualified to certify the durability and reliability of God's promises, and since no other gods exist to serve as witnesses, Moses invoked **heaven and earth** to serve that function (30:19; 31:28; cp. note at Gn 22:15-18).

4:27 The **peoples** and **nations** most immediately in view are the Assyrians and Babylonians, who took Israel and Judah captive in 722 and 586 B.C., respectively. Since then, Greece, Rome, and other world powers have successively uprooted the Jewish people for various reasons, including their violation of the covenant the Lord made with them (vv. 23,25; cp. 2Kg 17:7-41; 2Ch 36:15-19).

4:29-31 When Israel went into exile they would find the Lord when they sought Him **with all** their **heart** and **soul**. Yet the promise is clear that this would happen, because they would in fact return to the Lord **in later days**. The Lord's promises to His chosen people must come to pass because He has sworn by His own reputation to make it so (30:6-10; Gn 17:3-8; Jr 31:31-34; Ezk 36:24-30; Rm 11:1-2,25-26). He

thus provides the grace by which Israel can believe, repent, and return (Rm 11:28-32).

4:32-34 The **event** in view is the whole complex of God's election of Abraham to establish a nation, the deliverance of that nation from Egyptian bondage (v. 34), His gracious act of making covenant with them (v. 33), and His care for them ever since. This event was unique in the history of the world (cp. 32:9; 33:29).

4:41 Before Moses' death and the conquest of Canaan, he selected **three cities** as places of refuge for people accused but not convicted of manslaughter (19:2-13): one in the territory of Reuben, one in the territory of Gad, and the third in the allotment of Manasseh (4:43).

4:42 **Manslaughter** is qualified here as the killing of a person **accidentally without previously hating him**. If the accused hated the victim, there might be cause to suspect him of premeditated murder, in which case no refuge could suffice. Manslaughter today is defined similarly as accidental or "without malice aforethought."

king of the Amorites. He lived in Heshbon, and Moses and the Israelites defeated him after they came out of Egypt. ⁴⁷They took possession of his land and the land of Og king of Bashan, the two Amorite kings who were across the Jordan to the east, ⁴⁸from Aroer on the rim of the Arnon Valley as far as Mount Sion (that is, Hermon) ⁴⁹and all the •Arabah on the east side of the Jordan as far as the Dead Sea below the slopes of Pisgah.

The Ten Commandments

5 Moses summoned all Israel and said to them, "Israel, listen to the statutes and ordinances I am proclaiming as you hear them today. Learn and follow them carefully. ²The LORD our God made a covenant*ᵃ* with us at Horeb. ³He did not make this covenant with our fathers,*ᵇ* but with all of us who are alive here today. ⁴The LORD spoke to you face to face from the fire on the mountain. ⁵At that time I was standing between the LORD and you to report the word^A of the LORD to you, because you were afraid of the fire and did not go up the mountain. And He said:

⁶ I am the LORD your God,*ᶜ* who brought you out of the land of Egypt, out of the place of slavery.*ᵈ*
⁷ Do not have other gods besides Me.
⁸ Do not make an idol for yourself in the shape of anything in the heavens above or on the earth below or in the waters under the earth. ⁹You must not bow down

to them or worship them, because I, the LORD your God, am a jealous God, punishing the children for the fathers' sin to the third and fourth generations of those who hate Me,*ᵉ* ¹⁰but showing faithful love to a thousand generations of those who love Me and keep My commands.

¹¹ Do not misuse the name*ᶠ* of the LORD your God, because the LORD will not leave anyone unpunished who misuses His name.

¹² Be careful to remember the Sabbath day, to keep it holy as the LORD your God has commanded you. ¹³You are to labor six days and do all your work, ¹⁴but the seventh day is a Sabbath to the LORD your God. You must not do any work—you, your son or daughter, your male or female slave, your ox or donkey, any of your livestock, or the foreigner who lives within your gates, so that your male and female slaves may rest as you do. ¹⁵Remember that you were a slave in the land of Egypt, and the LORD your God brought you out of there with a strong hand and an outstretched arm. That is why the LORD your God has commanded you to keep the Sabbath day.

¹⁶ Honor your father and your mother,*ᵍ* as the LORD your God has commanded you, so that you may live long and so that you may prosper in the land the LORD your God is giving you.*ʰ*

ᵃ5:2 Dt 31:16
ᵇ5:3 Dt 4:31
ᶜ5:6-21 Ex 20:2-17; Dt 8:14
ᵈ5:6 Lv 26:13; Dt 6:12; 8:14; 13:5,10; Jos 24:17; Jr 34:13
ᵉ5:9 Ex 34:7; 7:10; Ezk 18
Nm 14:18; Dt 7:10; Ezk 18
ᶠ5:11 Ex 3:13; 6:3; 33:19
ᵍ5:16-20 Mt 19:18-19; Mk 10:19; Lk 18:20; Rm 13:9
ʰ5:16 Mt 15:4; Mk 7:10; Eph 6:2-3

---

^A5:5 One Hb ms, DSS, Sam, LXX, Syr, Vg read *words*

5:2-3 Though revealed again now in a new, expanded form in Moab, **this covenant** was essentially a restatement of the covenant given 40 years earlier. **Fathers** refer to the patriarchal ancestors beginning with Abram with whom God had made a covenant centuries earlier (Gn 12:1-3; 15:1-21; 17:1-21).

5:7 The phrase **other gods** does not admit their existence but only the fact that the polytheistic worldview was rife in the surrounding cultures of OT Israel (4:7; 1Co 8:4-6).

5:8 The Hebrew term translated **idol** *(pesel)* means "a carved thing." It could, in this context, refer not just to likenesses of pagan gods but to that of the Lord Himself (4:15-16).

5:9-10 To **hate** God in a covenant context means not so much to detest Him with strong emotional overtones as it does to reject Him as a covenant partner. For Israel to **love** God was to choose Him and agree to obey Him (6:4-5; Jn 14:15). Conversely, to hate Him was to disobey Him. When God is the subject, He is said to have loved Israel in the sense that He chose Israel to be His special people (Dt 7:8). The best illustration of love and hate with these nuances is the statement of the Lord, "I loved Jacob, but I hated Esau" (Mal 1:2-3). What clearly is meant is that God had chosen Jacob to inherit the covenant privileges but had not chosen Esau (cp. Gn 25:23; 27:29).

5:11 The Hebrew word behind the term **misuse** bears the literal idea of using **the name of the LORD** in an empty, flippant, or purposeless way. To make light of His name is to denigrate God Himself (12:5).

5:12 To **remember the Sabbath day** is, literally, to set it apart for a special purpose. The emphasis is not so much on remaining inactive on the Sabbath as it is on making it a time of reflection, praise, worship, and service.

5:14 The **seventh day** calls to mind the seventh day of creation by which time all of God's creation work had been accomplished (Gn 2:1-2). The verb used in Genesis is (Hb) *shavath* ("to cease") which lends the nuance of stopping from one thing with the possibility of doing something else, not necessarily an absolute cessation from activity.

5:15 To **remember** in Hebrew idiom carries the sense of deep reflection and meditation on the past, particularly with regard to God's mighty acts of love and grace (7:18; 8:2; 9:7; 15:15; Ps 42:4,6; 77:11; 137:6; Is 46:8; 1Co 11:24-25). In the exodus account, the motive for remembering the Sabbath was that God had ceased His creation work on the seventh day (Ex 20:11). In Deuteronomy, Israel was called on to remember a more recent event, God's mightiest work on their behalf—their redemption from cruel bondage.

5:16 As those created in the image of God and most immediately representing His glory and His authority over them, children must **honor** their **father and** their **mother**. The

¹⁷ Do not murder.ᵃ

¹⁸ Do not commit adultery.ᵇ

¹⁹ Do not steal.

²⁰ Do not give dishonest testimony against your neighbor.ᶜ

²¹ Do not covet your neighbor's wife or desire your neighbor's house, his field, his male or female slave, his ox or donkey, or anything that belongs to your neighbor.ᵈ

The People's Response

²²"The LORD spoke these commands in a loud voice to your entire assembly from the fire, cloud, and thick darkness on the mountain; He added nothing more. He wrote them on two stone tablets and gave them to me. ²³All of you approached me with your tribal leaders and elders when you heard the voice from the darkness and while the mountain was blazing with fire. ²⁴You said, 'Look, the LORD our God has shown us His glory and greatness, and we have heard His voice from the fire. Today we have seen that God speaks with a person, yet he still lives. ²⁵But now, why should we die? This great fire will consume us and we will die if we hear the voice of the LORD our God any longer. ²⁶For who out of all mankind has heard the voice of the living God speaking from the fire, as we have, and lived? ²⁷Go near and lis-

ᵃ 5:17 Mt 5:21; Jms 2:11
ᵇ 5:18 Mt 5:27
ᶜ 5:20 Pr 25:18
ᵈ 5:16–21 Mt 19:18-19; Mk 10:19; Lk 18:20; Rm 13:9
ᵉ 5:22-27 Ex 20:18-21
ᶠ 6:1 Dt 3:12
ᵍ 6:2 Dt 14:23

ten to everything the LORD our God says. Then you can tell us everything the LORD our God tells you; we will listen and obey.'ᵉ

²⁸"The LORD heard yourᴬ words when you spoke to me. He said to me, 'I have heard the words that these people have spoken to you. Everything they have said is right. ²⁹If only they had such a heart to ˙fear Me and keep all My commands always, so that they and their children will prosper forever. ³⁰Go and tell them: Return to your tents. ³¹But you stand here with Me, and I will tell you every command—the statutes and ordinances—you are to teach them, so that they may follow them in the land I am giving them to possess.'

³²"Be careful to do as the LORD your God has commanded you; you are not to turn aside to the right or the left. ³³Follow the whole instruction the LORD your God has commanded you, so that you may live, prosper, and have a long life in the land you will possess.

The Greatest Commandment

6 "This is the command—the statutes and ordinances—the LORD your God has instructed me to teach you, so that you may follow them in the land you are about to enter and possess.ᶠ ²Do this so that you may ˙fearᵍ the LORD your God all the days of your life by

---

ᴬ5:28 Lit the sound of your

---

word "honor" translates a verb meaning literally "regard as weighty." It is associated with the notion that important people are "heavyweights," loaded down with glory and honor. Parents were to be considered as such, heavy with responsibility and privilege of which children must be aware and to which they must submit if they are to be obedient and pleasing to God. The opposite is to dishonor parents by considering them to be nobodies. Exodus 21:17 states that "whoever curses his father or his mother must be put to death." The word "curses" here translates a verb meaning "be light" or "esteem to be light." To honor one's parents is to accord them the highest esteem; to dishonor them is to curse them and regard them with contempt.

5:17 Though a generic term for killing is used here, the intent clearly is to speak of premeditated **murder**. Manslaughter as accidental homicide has already been considered (4:42), and killing by government and other constituted authority was permitted as capital punishment (13:5,9; Ex 21:12,14-17) and in times of war (Dt 7:2; 20:13,17). Murder is heinous because human beings are created in the image of God and their murder, in effect, is a blow against God Himself (Gn 9:5-6).

5:18 Adultery is described in a number of ancient Near Eastern texts as "the great sin," suggesting that even pagans were aware of its seriousness. A common biblical image is marriage as a metaphor for God's relationship to Israel (Ezk 16:8,32; Hs 2:14-16) and for Christ's relationship to the church (Rv 19:7; 21:2,9). In both cases, unfaithfulness on the part of God's people is identical to adultery.

5:20 The Ninth Commandment is most at home in a legal setting where testimony is required of witnesses or other

knowledgeable persons. Since a person accused of a crime could suffer serious penalties or death for his violation of the law, it was essential that the evidence be truthful (cp. 17:6; 19:15-21).

5:21 To **covet** and to **desire** are essentially the same thing, as is seen in Ex 20:17 where the same Hebrew verb is used of both houses and wives. Here the same verb occurs for **wife** and a different verb for everything else. A possible explanation is that in the land of Canaan families would live in close quarters where desire for a neighbor's property might be a more serious temptation.

5:22 The **fire, cloud, and thick darkness** indicated the Lord's transcendent glory. The fire suggested its openness and the cloud and darkness its hiddenness. Were the glory of the Lord to appear in all its brightness, no human could look upon it and live (vv. 25-26; Ex 19:20-22). The **two stone tablets** reflect the ancient Near Eastern custom of making a copy of the covenant texts for each party. One of these was for the Lord and the other for Israel.

5:28-29 Upon receiving the terms of the covenant, the **people** had said, "We will do all that the LORD has spoken" (Ex 19:8). However, the Lord would not be impressed with their verbal commitment but with a **heart to fear** Him and **keep** all His **commands**.

6:1 The term translated **command** is a generic word synonymous with the covenant as a whole, including within it **statutes and ordinances**.

6:2 The **fear** of the Lord is not a condition of terror or foreboding. Rather, it is a profound reverence for God that may, indeed, have overtones or manifestations of fear in the

keeping all His statutes and commands I am giving you, your son, and your grandson, and so that you may have a long life. ³ Listen, Israel, and be careful to follow them, so that you may prosper and multiply greatly, because •Yahweh, the God of your fathers, has promised you a land flowing with milk and honey.ᵃ

⁴ "Listen, Israel: The LORD our God, the LORD is One.ᴬ,ᵇ ⁵ Love the LORD your God with all your heart, with all your soul, and with all your strength.ᶜ ⁶ These words that I am giving you today are to be in your heart.ᵈ ⁷ Repeat them to your children.ᵉ Talk about them when you sit in your house and when you walk along the road, when you lie down and when you get up. ⁸ Bind them as a sign on your hand and let

them be a symbolᴮ on your forehead.ᶜ,ᶠ ⁹ Write them on the doorposts of your house and on your gates.

Remembering God through Obedience

¹⁰ "When the LORD your God brings you into the land He swore to your fathers Abraham, Isaac, and Jacob that He would give you—a land with large and beautiful cities that you did not build, ¹¹ houses full of every good thing that you did not fill them with, wells dug that you did not dig, and vineyards and olive groves that you did not plantᵍ—and when you eat and are satisfied,ʰ ¹² be careful not to forget the LORD who brought you out

ᵃ6:3 Dt 11:9
ᵇ6:4 Mk 12:29,32; Jms 2:19
ᶜ6:5 Mt 22:37; Mk 12:30; Lk 10:27
ᵈ6:6-9 Dt 11:18-20
ᵉ6:7 Dt 4:9-10
ᶠ6:8 Ex 13:16; Dt 11:18
ᵍ6:10-11 Jos 24:13
ʰ6:11 Dt 8:10; Neh 9:25

ᴬ6:4 Or *Yahweh is our God; Yahweh is One*, or *The LORD is our God, the LORD alone*, or *The LORD our God is one LORD*   ᴮ6:8 Or *phylactery*; Mt 23:5   ᶜ6:8 Lit *symbol between your eyes*

---

usual sense (5:5,24-26; Ex 3:6), though that is not the intent here (see word study on *yare'* at Dt 10:12).

6:3 **Milk and honey** were products of the comparatively rich soils of Canaan, but are also metaphorical of the best the **land** had to offer from human labor (milk) and nature (honey). The phrase became a cliché that is likely also a merism, a figure of speech intended to include all things by mentioning two of its parts (11:9; Ex 3:8,17; Nm 13:27).

A Jewish man praying at the Western Wall in Jerusalem. He wears phylacteries that come from a Jewish tradition dating to the 2nd century B.C. They were required to be worn at morning prayers and festivals but not on Sabbaths. A phylactery, or frontlet, is a small black leather (or parchment) case containing four OT Scriptures which is attached to a long single leather strap by a loop, forming two long straps on either side of the loop.

6:4-5 These two verses are commonly known as the Shema (shuh MAH), after the first word of verse 4 in Hebrew. This was considered the greatest commandment; Jesus Christ, when asked which commandment was greatest, cited this passage (Mk 12:28-30). The Shema is the foundational principle for the Ten Commandments, and they in turn contain the essence of God's covenant with Israel. It is divided between a statement asserting the nature of God and one enjoining a certain response to that understanding. He is described as being **One**—of a single essence. Other interpretations are that **the LORD** alone is our God or the Lord our God is one Lord.

6:6 The Shema must be more than a mere abstraction: it must first be deeply ingrained in the **heart** (that is, the mind; v. 5) and then put into action.

6:7 The old adage that "repetition aids learning" is an ancient one as this verse attests. Parents must **repeat** the words of the Shema and the rest of God's instruction to their **children** and not in a hit-or-miss manner. There must be strong intentionality that issues in constant instruction by word and deed **about** devotion to God. By a figure of speech (merism) Moses described the unremitting process of education by speaking in terms of opposites. To **sit** and to **walk** suggest being at rest and being active, that is, in any situation. To **lie down** and to **get up** naturally call to mind nighttime and daytime, that is, *all the time*. The kind of love God requires is one that is full time and under every circumstance. Children must therefore be taught to love Him in the same way.

6:8 Though the command to **bind** the commandments is most likely figurative language, such practices were taken literally in postbiblical Judaism and remain part of contemporary conservative Jewish custom.

6:9 The **doorposts** of Israel's houses and their **gates** must be identified as those dedicated to covenant compliance by the affixing of the law to them as well. Small metal boxes known as (Hb) *mezuzah* are to this day attached to doorways of Jewish homes to signify the commitment of their inhabitants to Judaism. These also contain Scripture portions (vv. 4-9; 11:13-21).

6:10-11 The reference to **cities** Israel **did not build, houses** they **did not fill . . . wells** they **did not dig**, and **vineyards and olive groves** they **did not plant** is significant in terms of the nature of Israel's conquest of Canaan. With few ex-

of the land of Egypt, out of the place of slavery.[a] [13]Fear Yahweh your God, worship Him, and take your oaths in His name.[b] [14]Do not follow other gods, the gods of the peoples around you, [15]for the LORD your God, who is among you, is a jealous God.[c] Otherwise, the LORD your God will become angry with you and wipe you off the face of the earth. [16]Do not test[d] the LORD your God as you tested Him at Massah.[e] [17]Carefully observe the commands of the LORD your God, the decrees and statutes He has commanded you. [18]Do what is right and good in the LORD's sight, so that you may prosper and so that you may enter and possess the good land[f] the LORD your God swore to give your fathers,[g] [19]by driving out all your enemies before you, as the LORD has said.[h]

[20]"When your son asks you in the future, 'What is the meaning of the decrees, statutes, and ordinances, which the LORD our God has commanded you?' [21]tell him, 'We were slaves of Pharaoh in Egypt, but the LORD brought us out of Egypt with a strong hand. [22]Before our eyes the LORD inflicted great and devastating signs and wonders on Egypt, on Pharaoh, and on all his household, [23]but He brought us from there in order to lead us in and give us the

land that He swore to our fathers. [24]The LORD commanded us to follow all these statutes and to fear the LORD our God for our prosperity always and for our preservation, as it is today. [25]Righteousness will be ours if we are careful to follow every one of these commands before the LORD our God, as He has commanded us.'

Israel to Destroy Idolatrous Nations

7 "When the LORD your God brings you into the land[i] you are entering to possess,[j] and He drives out many nations before you—the Hittites, Girgashites, Amorites, Canaanites, Perizzites, Hivites and Jebusites, seven nations more numerous and powerful than you— [2]and when the LORD your God delivers them over to you and you defeat them, you must •completely destroy them. Make no treaty with them and show them no mercy. [3]Do not intermarry with them. Do not give your daughters to their sons or take their daughters for your sons,[k] [4]because they will turn your sons away from Me to worship other gods. Then the LORD's anger will burn against you, and He will swiftly destroy you. [5]Instead, this is what you are to do to them: tear down their altars, smash their sacred pillars, cut

Reference column:

[a] 6:12 Lv 26:13; Dt 5:6; 8:14; 13:5,10; Jos 24:17; Jr 34:13
[b] 6:13 Dt 10:12,20; 13:4; Jos 24:14; 1Sm 12:24; Mt 4:10; Lk 4:8; Rv 14:7
[c] 6:15 Dt 5:9
[d] 6:16 Ex 15:25; 16:4; Nm 14:22; Ps 78:18,41,56; 106:14; Mal 3:15; Mt 4:7; Lk 4:12
[e] Ex 17:1-7; Dt 9:22; 33:8; Ps 95:8-9
[f] 6:18 Dt 8:7
[g] Dt 1:35
[h] 6:19 Ex 34:11
[i] 7:1-5 Ex 23:23-26
[j] 7:1 Dt 3:12
[k] 7:3 Jos 23:12-13; 1Kg 11:12; Ezr 9:12,14

---

ceptions, physical structures and agricultural assets were left intact precisely so Israel could take them over and thus more quickly and easily settle the land (Jos 11:13; 24:13). On the other hand, the wicked Canaanite populations were to be destroyed because they would become a stumbling block to Israel, an influence drawing them away from the Lord and toward idolatry (Dt 7:1-6).

6:16 Massah means "testing" and refers to an episode in Exodus in which Israel, fresh from deliverance from Egypt, demanded that Moses provide them water to drink (Ex 17:1-7). At the Lord's instruction, Moses struck a rock from which water gushed forth. The real issue was not water, however, but Israel's unbelief. The people were testing the Lord to see if He was really among them (Ex 17:7).

6:20 With the passing of time it is difficult to keep fresh the ideas and principles that give birth to movements and institutions. Moses was keenly aware that Israel must never forget its history.

6:24 The reason for remembering the history of God's dealings with His people was so that future generations might understand them (v. 20) and **fear the Lord**. This would ensure **prosperity** from the Lord as well as their **preservation**.

6:25 Absolute **righteousness** cannot be earned by good works but is imparted only by the grace of God through faith (Eph 2:8-9). This fundamental truth is rooted in God's covenant with Abraham, who "believed the LORD and He [God] credited it to him as righteousness" (Gn 15:6). Abraham did nothing but believe, and on that basis alone he was declared righteous (cp. Rm 4:1-3,9-12). In this verse righteousness is associated with obedience to the Lord's **commands**, suggesting, if read in isolation from the rest of Scripture, that

righteousness can be earned. However, reading this verse in the larger context of Deuteronomy (7:7-11; 9:5-6) makes it clear that God's favor is a gift that can't be earned. Having received God's gift, the believer is called to live according to the standard expected of those to whom the covenant has been extended.

7:1 The **seven nations** were the inhabitants of Canaan who in some cases had lived there since the days of Abraham (Gn 12:6; 13:7; 15:21). Their long tenure there had not secured them any claim to the land, however, for in the plan of God Canaan had from ages past been allotted to Abraham and his descendants (Gn 12:1; 13:14-17; 15:18-21). The time had now come to dispossess these people so that Israel, the offspring of Abraham, could take their rightful place.

7:2 Completely destroy translates a Hebrew verb that has the technical meaning of placing someone or something under the ban (charam), an aspect of what may be described as "holy war" or "Yahweh war." This was warfare initiated by **the Lord** to annihilate its targets or bring them into His possession or under His dominion. The religious or theological nature of this kind of war is clear from the presence of the priests and of the ark of the covenant whenever God directed its use (20:1-4; Jos 6:1-5).

7:3-4 Prohibition against intermarriage between Israel and the nations was designed to protect Israel from the **worship** of **other gods**. Alluding to this text, Paul commanded, "Do not be mismatched with unbelievers," and then he made a linkage with idolatry when he asked what agreement Christ can have with Belial or God's sanctuary with idols (2Co 6:14-16).

7:5 Sacred pillars, usually of stone, marked places deemed to be holy because of the appearance there of deity.

down their *Asherah poles,[a] and burn up their carved images. [6]For you are a holy people[b] belonging to the LORD your God. The LORD your God has chosen you to be His own possession[c] out of all the peoples on the face of the earth.

[7]"The LORD was devoted to you and chose you, not because you were more numerous than all peoples, for you were the fewest of all peoples. [8]But because the LORD loved[d] you and kept the oath He swore to your fathers, He brought you out with a strong hand and redeemed[e] you from the place of slavery, from the power of Pharaoh king of Egypt. [9]Know that *Yahweh your God is God, the faithful God who keeps His gracious covenant loyalty for a thousand generations with those who love Him and keep His commands.[f] [10]But He directly pays back[A] and destroys those who hate Him.[g] He will not hesitate to directly pay back[B] the one who hates Him. [11]So keep the command—the statutes and ordinances—that I am giving you to follow today.

[12]"If you listen to and are careful to keep these ordinances, the LORD your God will keep His covenant loyalty with you, as He swore to your fathers.[h] [13]He will love you, bless you, and multiply you. He will bless your descendants,[C,i] and the produce of your land—your grain, new wine, and oil—the young of your herds, and the newborn of your flocks, in the land He swore to your fathers that He would give you. [14]You will be blessed above all peoples; there will be no infertile male or female

among you or your livestock. [15]The LORD will remove all sickness from you; He will not put on you[j] all the terrible diseases of Egypt that you know about, but He will inflict them on all who hate you. [16]You must destroy all the peoples the LORD your God is delivering over to you and not look on them with pity. Do not worship their gods, for that will be a snare to you.

[17]"If you say to yourself, 'These nations are greater than I; how can I drive them out?' [18]do not be afraid of them. Be sure to remember what the LORD your God did to Pharaoh and all Egypt: [19]the great trials that you saw, the signs and wonders, the strong hand and outstretched arm, by which the LORD your God brought you out. The LORD your God will do the same to all the peoples you fear. [20]The LORD your God will also send the hornet against them until all the survivors and those hiding from you perish.[k] [21]Don't be terrified of them, for the LORD your God, a great and awesome God, is among you. [22]The LORD your God will drive out these nations before you little by little. You will not be able to destroy them all at once; otherwise, the wild animals will become too numerous for you.[l] [23]The LORD your God will give them over to you and throw them into great confusion until they are destroyed. [24]He will hand their kings over to you, and you will wipe out their names under heaven. No one will be able to stand against you; you will annihilate them. [25]You must burn up the

Cross references (center column):

[a]7:5 Ex 34:13; Dt 12:2-3
[b]7:6 Dt 14:2,21; 26:19; 28:9
[c]Ex 19:5; Dt 14:2; 26:18-19
[d]7:8 Dt 4:37
[e]Dt 9:26; 15:15; 24:18
[f]7:9 Neh 1:5; Dn 9:4
[g]7:10 Ex 34:6-7
[h]7:12 Dt 4:31
[i]7:13 Dt 28:4
[j]7:15 Ex 15:26; 23:25; Dt 28:27,60
[k]7:20 Ex 23:28; Jos 24:12
[l]7:22 Ex 23:29-30

[A]7:10 Lit *He pays back to their faces*   [B]7:10 Lit *to pay back to their faces*   [C]7:13 Lit *bless the fruit of your womb*

Sometimes they were erected by God's people (Gn 28:18-22; 35:14; Ex 24:4), but usually they were associated with Baal worship (Ex 23:24; 34:13; 2Kg 18:4; 23:14). **Asherah**, the principal goddess of the Canaanite pantheon, was represented sometimes as a living tree (Dt 16:21; Mc 5:14) but most often as a wooden pole (1Kg 14:15,23; 16:33; 2Kg 17:10,16; Is 17:8). Both objects symbolized fertility rites and other rituals of the crudest kind.

7:6 The term **possession** translates a Hebrew noun (*segullah*) that describes an unusually precious treasure. It occurs also in Ex 19:5 upon the Lord's offer of the Mosaic covenant to Israel at Mount Sinai. As Creator He has claim to **all the peoples**, but in line with His purposes to redeem them, He chose only the **holy people** Israel as the vehicle of His saving grace (Rm 9:1-5; 11:28-32).

7:8 God's choice of Israel as "His own possession" (v. 6) was not based on any merit on Israel's part but solely on His love for them (4:37). Their present position as imminent heirs of the land of promise was evidence of His love.

7:9 A thousand generations is a term denoting an immeasurable future and not a specific span of time. The point is that God's **covenant loyalty** is boundless and unending. Though Israel (and mankind in general) might prove to be unfaithful to the Lord, the promises of God to the nation cannot fail to be fulfilled (30:1-10; Jr 31:31-34; Ezk 36:24-32; Rm 11:29).

7:12-15 These blessings do not include the fundamental **covenant** relationship with **the LORD** *per se*. God's promises depended on heeding and being **careful to keep** the covenant **ordinances** (28:1-4; Lv 26:3-13).

7:19 Signs and wonders (words commonly joined in the OT; cp. 4:34; 6:22; 26:8; 29:3; Neh 9:10; Ps 135:9; Dn 6:27) were deeds done by **the LORD** to generate faith on the part of His people and to sustain them in times of doubt, such as the exodus deliverance referred to here (Ex 7:3; 8:23; 10:2; 11:9). Jesus also performed signs and wonders that only the Messiah could accomplish (Jn 2:11; 3:2; 4:54; 6:2,14; cp. Jn 20:30-31). Signs and wonders could also be performed by false prophets, however (Ex 7:11; Dt 13:1-2), so by themselves they did not attest to divine origination.

7:20 The **hornet** is likely a metaphor for military forces (1:44; Is 7:18-19) or other means, natural or otherwise, that **the LORD** would use to drive out the illegal residents of the land.

7:24 The threat to **wipe out** the **names** of Israel's enemies indicates their utter destruction. When the Lord threatened to destroy Israel for worshiping the golden calf, Moses said that if that threat were carried out he would want his name erased from the Lord's book. The Lord answered that only those who sinned against Him would suffer that fate (Ex 32:32-33; Rm 9:3).

7:25-26 The warning not to **covet** went unheeded by Achan,

carved images of their gods. Don't covet the silver and gold on the images and take it for yourself, or else you will be ensnared by it, for it is abhorrent to the LORD your God. [26]You must not bring any abhorrent thing into your house, or you will be •set apart for destruction like it. You are to utterly detest and abhor it, because it is set apart for destruction.

Remember the LORD

8 "You must carefully follow every command I am giving you today, so that you may live and increase, and may enter and take possession of the land[a] the LORD swore to your fathers. [2]Remember that the LORD your God led you on the entire journey these 40 years in the wilderness, so that He might humble you and test you to know what was in your heart, whether or not you would keep His commands. [3]He humbled you by letting you go hungry; then He gave you manna to eat, which you and your fathers had not known, so that you might learn that man does not live on bread alone but on every word that comes from the mouth of the LORD.[b] [4]Your clothing did not wear out, and your feet did not swell these 40 years.[c] [5]Keep in mind that the LORD your God has been disciplining you just as a man disciplines his son. [6]So keep the commands of the LORD your God by walking in His ways and •fearing Him. [7]For the LORD your God is bringing you into a good land,[d] a land with streams of water, springs, and deep water sources, flowing in both valleys and hills; [8]a land of wheat, barley, vines, figs, and pome-

granates; a land of olive oil and honey; [9]a land where you will eat food without shortage, where you will lack nothing; a land whose rocks are iron and from whose hills you will mine copper. [10]When you eat and are full,[e] you will praise the LORD your God for the good land[f] He has given you.

[11]"Be careful that you don't forget the LORD your God by failing to keep His command—the ordinances and statutes—I am giving you today. [12]When you eat and are full, and build beautiful houses to live in, [13]and your herds and flocks grow large, and your silver and gold multiply, and everything else you have increases, [14]be careful that your heart doesn't become proud and you forget the LORD your God who brought you out of the land of Egypt, out of the place of slavery.[g] [15]He led you through the great and terrible wilderness with its poisonous[A] snakes and scorpions, a thirsty land where there was no water. He brought water out of the flint-like rock for you. [16]He fed you in the wilderness with manna[h] that your fathers had not known, in order to humble and test you, so that in the end He might cause you to prosper. [17]You may say to yourself, 'My power and my own ability have gained this wealth for me,' [18]but remember that the LORD your God gives you the power to gain wealth, in order to confirm His covenant He swore to your fathers,[i] as it is today. [19]If you ever forget the LORD your God and go after other gods to worship and bow down to them, I testify against you today that you will perish.[j] [20]Like the nations the LORD is

Cross references:
[a] 8:1 Dt 3:12
[b] 8:3 Mt 4:4; Lk 4:4
[c] 8:4 Dt 29:5; Neh 9:21
[d] 8:7 Ex 3:8; Nm 14:7; Dt 1:25,35; 3:25; 4:21-22; 6:18; 8:10; 9:6; 11:17; Jos 23:16
[e] 8:10 Dt 11:15
[f] Dt 8:7
[g] 8:14 Lv 26:13; Dt 5:6; 6:12; 13:5,10; Jos 24:17; Jr 34:13
[h] 8:16 Ex 16:4
[i] 8:18 Dt 4:31
[j] 8:19 Dt 4:26

[A]8:15 Lit *burning*

who, following the conquest of Jericho, buried stolen silver and gold in his tent (Jos 7:20-23). Because these things had been placed under the ban (the [Hb] *cherem*; cp. Dt 7:2), they should have been turned over as tribute to the Lord. Should any Israelites (like Achan) take such spoils into their houses, the annihilation that often accompanied *cherem* would fall on them. This is the meaning of the phrase **set apart for destruction**.

8:2 The **40**-year **journey . . . in the wilderness** was partly a punishment of Israel for her unwillingness to occupy the land at first (Nm 14:26-35), but it also was a time for the Lord to **humble** and **test** His people to determine the quality of their character and their commitment to obedience. They had tested the Lord and found Him trustworthy (6:16; cp. Ex 17:5-7), but the older generation failed the test and thus were unable to enter the land of promise (Ex 20:20; Dt 1:34-40).

8:3 Manna (cp. Ex 16:31) was a bread-like substance that the Lord miraculously provided His people as a sign of His loving care and, more important, of the fact that Israel must recognize its dependence on Him. When Jesus was tempted by Satan to turn stones into bread, He cited this text to remind the enemy that physical bread lasts for a little while

and has limited value (Mt 4:4). On another occasion He described Himself as the Bread of Life (Jn 6:35).

8:5-6 Israel as God's covenant **son** (cp. Ex 4:22-23) must, like all children, submit to His paternal leadership and care. In biblical imagery, **walking** is a metaphor for pursuing a course of life, while **fearing** suggests a sense of reverence, appreciating the holy and solemn awesomeness of God.

8:11 Forgetting **the LORD** is not simply failing to recall that God exists, but acting as though He does not. It does no good to call Him Lord and refuse to do what He says (Lk 6:46).

8:18 No matter how clever, intelligent, or hard-working a person might be, success flows only from the gracious hand of the Lord (Jms 4:13-16). Israel's prosperity must be interpreted as the fulfillment of ancient promises made to the patriarchal ancestors as part of the covenant blessing the Lord would lavish upon them (Gn 15:14; 17:6; Dt 28:1-6). By blessing them in this manner the Lord would **confirm His covenant** to Israel.

8:19-20 The threat that Israel would **perish** cannot mean utter annihilation because the promise God made to the ancestors was that they would endure forever (Gn 17:7; Ps 105:9-10; Jr 33:25-26; Rm 11:25-32). In light of future

about to destroy before you, you will perish if you do not obey the LORD your God.

Warning against Self-Righteousness

9 "Listen, Israel: Today you are about to cross the Jordan to go and drive out nations greater and stronger than you, with large cities fortified to the heavens.[a] [2]The people are strong and tall, the descendants of the Anakim.[b] You know about them and you have heard it said about them, 'Who can stand up to the sons of Anak?'[c] [3]But understand that today the LORD your God will cross over ahead of you[d] as a consuming fire; He will devastate and subdue them before you. You will drive them out and destroy them swiftly, as the LORD has told you. [4]When the LORD your God drives them out before you, do not say to yourself, 'The LORD brought me in to take possession of this land because of my righteousness.' Instead, the LORD will drive out these nations before you because of their wickedness. [5]You are not going to take possession of their land because of your righteousness or your integrity. Instead, the LORD your God will drive out these nations before you because of their wickedness, in order to keep the promise He swore to your fathers, Abraham, Isaac, and

[a]9:1 Dt 1:28
[b]9:2 Dt 2:10; Jos 11:21; 14:12
[c]Nm 13:22; Jos 15:13-14; 21:11; Jdg 1:20
[d]9:3 Dt 31:3
[e]9:6 Dt 8:7
[f]9:7–10:11 Ex 32-34

Jacob. [6]Understand that the LORD your God is not giving you this good land[e] to possess because of your righteousness, for you are a stiff-necked people.

Israel's Rebellion and Moses' Intercession

[7]"Remember[f] and do not forget how you provoked the LORD your God in the wilderness. You have been rebelling against the LORD from the day you left the land of Egypt until you reached this place. [8]You provoked the LORD at Horeb, and He was angry enough with you to destroy you. [9]When I went up the mountain to receive the stone tablets, the tablets of the covenant the LORD made with you, I stayed on the mountain 40 days and 40 nights. I did not eat bread or drink water. [10]On the day of the assembly the LORD gave me the two stone tablets, inscribed by God's finger. The exact words were on them, which the LORD spoke to you from the fire on the mountain. [11]The LORD gave me the two stone tablets, the tablets of the covenant, at the end of the 40 days and 40 nights.

[12]"The LORD said to me, 'Get up and go down immediately from here. For your people whom you brought out of Egypt have acted

---

events, the perishing of Israel was her exile from the land and the cessation of her self-governance, which ended the dynasty of David. Even that was not complete because a remnant remained in the land (Jos 15:63; 16:10; Jdg 2:20-23).

9:1 The **nations greater and stronger than** Israel are the seven listed in 7:1, all of which were essentially Canaanite by that time. This description is probably hyperbolic to show the impossibility of their being overcome by Israel without God's help. It also recalls the account of the spies who, 40 years earlier, had reported that the cities of Canaan were large and fortified and the people were gigantic (Nm 13:28,33). Joshua and Caleb had said that Israel could still prevail because the Lord would be with them (Nm 13:30; 14:7-8).

9:2 The **Anakim** were a giant people so feared that a proverb arose comparing any difficult situation to that of facing the Anakim. Joshua defeated them later (Jos 11:21-23).

9:3 The depiction of God as **a consuming fire** reflects not only His awesome presence (Ex 19:12-13,18,21; 24:17) but also His role as a warrior leading His hosts in holy war (Ex 15:6-7; Ps 18:7-15; 21:9; 50:3-5; Rv 1:12-16).

9:4 God sometimes saves His own because of their **righteousness** and other times He condemns His enemies because of their **wickedness**. It is important to know the difference and to realize that often what is thought to be a reward for personal righteousness may be God's response to the unrighteousness of others.

9:6 Israel's possession of the **land** would take place not because of her **righteousness**, for, in fact, she was anything but righteous. She was a **stiff-necked people**, a na-

tion like a stubborn ox that would not submit to the yoke and pull its load. Any good thing that came to her from the Lord—including the conquest of Canaan—issued only from the grace of God. The very definition of biblical grace is receiving what one does not deserve. God's bestowal of such grace was based on His election of Israel to be His people and the self-obligation under which He put Himself to fulfill the promises He had made to the patriarchs.

9:8 The provocation **at Horeb** concerned the fabrication of a golden calf by Aaron and many of the people while Moses was receiving the Ten Commandments (Ex 32:1-6). The Lord was so angered by their idolatry that He wanted to **destroy** His people, but He was so committed to them by virtue of the everlasting covenant He had made with Abraham that absolute destruction was unthinkable.

9:10 The reference to **God's finger** is an anthropomorphism, which is the attribution to God of human characteristics. As Jesus told the Samaritan woman: "God is spirit, and those who worship Him must worship in spirit and truth" (Jn 4:24). Having no physical body, "God's finger" must be construed as His direct involvement in the inscription on the **stone tablets**. Inasmuch as He ordinarily revealed Himself through dreams and visions (Nm 12:6), the more immediate process of inscripturation (the writing of Scripture) here is striking.

9:11 The commandments were engraved on **two stone tablets** because each party to a **covenant** must have a copy.

9:12 The **cast image** was in the form of a calf, but it likely was not a pagan deity but an attempt to represent the Lord Himself. Israel was no doubt familiar with the powerful Apis bull of Egyptian mythology and also with El (also called "Bull"), chief of the Canaanite pantheon.

corruptly. They have quickly turned from the way that I commanded them; they have made a cast image for themselves.' [13]The LORD also said to me, 'I have seen this people, and indeed, they are a stiff-necked people. [14]Leave Me alone, and I will destroy them and blot out their name under heaven. Then I will make you into a nation stronger and more numerous than they.'

[15]"So I went back down the mountain, while it was blazing with fire, and the two tablets of the covenant were in my hands. [16]I saw how you had sinned against the LORD your God; you had made a calf image for yourselves. You had quickly turned from the way the LORD had commanded for you. [17]So I took hold of the two tablets and threw them from my hands, shattering them before your eyes. [18]Then I fell down like the first time in the presence of the LORD for 40 days and 40 nights; I did not eat bread or drink water because of all the sin you committed, doing what was evil in the LORD's sight and provoking Him to anger. [19]I was afraid of the fierce anger the LORD had directed against you,[a] because He was about to destroy you. But again the LORD listened to me on that occasion.[b] [20]The LORD was angry enough with Aaron to destroy him. But I prayed for Aaron at that time also. [21]I took the sinful calf you had made, burned it up, and crushed it, thoroughly grinding it to powder as fine as dust. Then I threw it into the stream that came down from the mountain.[c]

[22]"You continued to provoke the LORD at Taberah, Massah, and Kibroth-hattaavah.[d] [23]When the LORD sent you from Kadesh-barnea, He said, 'Go up and possess the land I have given you'; you rebelled against the command of the LORD your God. You did not believe or obey Him.[e] [24]You have been rebelling against the LORD ever since I have[A] known you.[f]

[25]"I fell down in the presence of the LORD 40 days and 40 nights because the LORD had threatened to destroy you. [26]I prayed to the LORD:

Lord GOD, do not annihilate Your people, Your inheritance, whom You redeemed[g] through Your greatness and brought out of Egypt with a strong hand. [27]Remember Your servants Abraham, Isaac, and Jacob. Disregard this people's stubbornness, and their wickedness and sin. [28]Otherwise, those in the land you brought us from will say, 'Because the LORD wasn't able to bring them into the land He had promised them, and because He hated them, He brought them out to kill them in the wilderness.'[h] [29]But they are Your people, Your inheritance, whom You brought out by Your great power and outstretched arm.[i]

The Covenant Renewed

10 "The LORD said to me at that time, 'Cut two stone tablets like the first ones and come to Me on the mountain and make a wooden ark. [2]I will write on the tablets the words that were on the first tablets you broke, and you are to place them in the ark.' [3]So I made an ark of acacia wood, cut two stone tablets like the first ones, and climbed the mountain with the two tablets in my hand. [4]Then

---

Cross references:

[a]9:19 Heb 12:21
[b]Dt 10:10
[c]9:21 Ex 32:20
[d]9:22 Nm 11:1-35; Ex 17:1-7
[e]9:23 Nm 13–14
[f]9:24 Ps 95; 106
[g]9:26 Dt 7:8; 15:15; 24:18
[h]9:28 Nm 14:16
[i]9:29 2Kg 17:36; Neh 1:10; Jr 27:5; 32:17

[A]9:24 Sam, LXX read *since He has*

9:14 The Lord could carry out His threat and still be true to the Abrahamic promise that his seed would never end by preserving Moses. The Exodus narrative records Moses' intercession in response to the threat.

9:17 Moses' **shattering** of the **tablets** was more than an act of justifiable rage. Just as the commandments now lay in a thousand pieces, so Israel had smashed the covenant seemingly beyond repair. It also anticipated the shattering of the calf image to signify the removal of idolatry from the nation (v. 21).

9:19 Moses' acknowledgement that **the Lord listened** to him and averted His intended wrath teaches not only that Moses was a faithful advocate but that God hears the prayers of those who earnestly intercede with Him for others (Jms 5:13-18).

9:21 The disposition of the **sinful calf** revealed the impotence of idols and dramatized how anything that competes for the worship of the true God is to be dealt with. Moses' example had to be repeated many times in Israel's history (1Kg 15:13; 2Kg 11:18; 18:4; 23:4).

9:27 Moses' prayer that the Lord would **remember** His **servants** rose not out of any fear that He would no longer retain them in His consciousness but out of a desire that He would act to keep His covenant promises to them. "Remember" when in reference to God always carries with it an implicit response or action.

9:29 For Israel to be God's **inheritance** meant that they belonged to Him (7:6) and also that He belonged to them, a unique relationship that gave each of them exclusive claims on the other.

10:2 The fact that the new **tablets** had the same **words** as **the first** suggests that Moses was not free to improvise and capture just the essence of their wording. This attention to precise detail lays the foundation for a verbal plenary view of inspiration. God's Word may have come through human instruments, but it was done so without error of the slightest kind (2Tm 3:16-17; 2Pt 1:20-21). The commandments were engraved on two **tablets** because each party to a covenant must have a copy. Both copies were deposited in the **ark** of the covenant (Ex 25:16), probably because it was a location held in common by both parties.

on the day of the assembly, the LORD wrote on the tablets what had been written previously, the Ten Commandments that He had spoken to you on the mountain from the fire. The LORD gave them to me, [5]and I went back down the mountain and placed the tablets in the ark I had made. And they have remained there, as the LORD commanded me."

[6]The Israelites traveled from Beeroth Bene-jaakan[A] to Moserah. Aaron died and was buried there, and Eleazar his son became priest in his place.[a] [7]They traveled from there to Gudgodah, and from Gudgodah to Jotbathah, a land with streams of water.[b]

[8]"At that time the LORD set apart the tribe of Levi[c] to carry the ark of the LORD's covenant, to stand before •Yahweh to serve Him, and to pronounce blessings in His name, as it is today. [9]For this reason, Levi does not have a portion or inheritance like his brothers; the LORD is his inheritance, as the LORD your God told him.[d]

[10]"I stayed on the mountain 40 days and 40 nights like the first time. The LORD also listened to me on this occasion;[e] He agreed not to annihilate you. [11]Then the LORD said to me, 'Get up. Continue your journey ahead of the people, so that they may enter and possess the land I swore to give their fathers.'[f]

What God Requires

[12]"And now, Israel, what does the LORD your God ask of you except to •fear[g] the LORD your God by walking in all His ways, to love Him, and to worship the LORD your God with all your heart and all your soul? [13]Keep the LORD's commands and statutes I am giving you today, for your own good. [14]The heavens, indeed the highest heavens, belong to the LORD your God, as does the earth and everything in it. [15]Yet the LORD was devoted to your fathers and loved them.[h] He chose their descendants after them—He chose you out of all the peoples, as it is today. [16]Therefore, circumcise your hearts[i] and don't be stiff-necked any longer. [17]For the LORD your God is the God of gods and Lord of lords, the great, mighty, and awesome God, showing no partiality and taking no bribe. [18]He executes justice for the fatherless and the widow, and loves the foreigner, giving him food and clothing. [19]You also must love the foreigner, since you were foreigners in the land of Egypt.[j] [20]You are to fear Yahweh your God and worship Him. Remain faithful[B] to Him and take oaths in His name.[k] [21]He is your praise and He is your God, who has done for you these great and awesome works your eyes have seen. [22]Your fathers went down to Egypt, 70 people in all,[l] and now the LORD your

Cross references (center column):
- [a]10:6 Nm 20:22-29
- [b]10:6-7 Nm 33:31-33
- [c]10:8 Ex 32:26-29
- [d]10:9 Lv 25:32-34; Nm 18:20; 26:62; Dt 18:1-2; Jos 13:14,33; Ezk 44:28-30
- [e]10:10 Dt 9:19
- [f]10:11 Dt 1:35
- [g]10:12 Dt 14:23
- [h]10:15 Dt 4:37
- [i]10:16 Jr 4:4; Rm 2:29
- [j]10:19 Lv 19:34
- [k]10:20 Dt 6:13; 13:4
- [l]10:22 Gn 46:27; Ex 1:5

[A]10:6 Or from the wells of Bene-jaakan, or from the wells of the Jaakanites   [B]10:20 Lit Hold on

---

10:6 Like the office of king, that of the priesthood was hereditary. **Aaron** and his sons were selected first, as members of the priestly tribe of Levi (Nm 17:3,8). Two of Aaron's four sons died because of an act of sacrilege (Lv 10:1-5). Of his two surviving sons, **Eleazar** was next in line for the office of chief **priest** (Nm 20:25-26).

10:8-9 All the tribes of Israel except **Levi** received allotments of territory; **the LORD** was Levi's **inheritance**. Levi was to devote itself fully to the service of the Lord, at first in the tabernacle in the wilderness and then in the temple in Jerusalem. This was because of Israel's redemption from Egypt,

which demanded in turn that Israel dedicate to the Lord the firstborn son of every family in lieu of the firstborn who were spared in the tenth plague (Ex 13:1-2,14-16).

10:14-15 The Lord's choice of Israel is a mark of inexplicable and discretionary grace, because Israel had no moral or theological claim to the Lord's favor (7:7-11; Ex 19:5).

10:16 Circumcision was the sign of the Abrahamic covenant, a rite to be followed by all succeeding generations of the faithful (Gn 17:9-14). This symbolized a cutting off of the previous life and a willingness to propagate sons and daughters who would also enter into covenant with the Lord. Circumcision of the flesh alone could not guarantee a right relationship to the Lord because that relationship was one of faith springing from the heart. Moses therefore commanded Israel, **Circumcise your hearts and don't be stiff-necked any longer**, an exhortation picked up in the NT as well (Rm 2:25-29; Col 2:8-15).

10:18-19 The OT is clear that those who take advantage of defenseless people can expect the Lord's swift and severe judgment (24:17-18; Ex 22:21-24; Ps 146:9; Jr 7:3-8). The Israelites were **foreigners** themselves **in the land of Egypt**; those delivered from difficult and oppressive situations should be the first to deal kindly with others in the same circumstances.

10:22 Israel's explosive growth was an overwhelming sign of the Lord's faithfulness to His promises to Abraham (Gn 15:5; Ex 1:1-5). Though comparison to the **stars of the sky** is hyperbolic, so large a population growth within 430 years is miraculous (Ex 12:37,40).

---

yare'

Hebrew Pronunciation	[yah RAY]
HCSB Translation	be afraid, fear, revere
Uses in Deuteronomy	37
Uses in the OT	317
Focus Passage	Deuteronomy 10:12,17,20-21

Yare' denotes be afraid (Gn 3:10) or fear (Ex 1:17). People are cautious (Pr 14:16), intimidated (Neh 6:16), alarmed (Jos 10:2), or fearful (Jr 51:46). They tremble (Ps 33:8) or panic (1Sm 4:7). Combined with the intensive "very," yare' means be terrified (Gn 20:8). Yare' often takes God as object, implying be or stand in awe (Mc 7:17) and be awed (Ps 65:8). People revere (Lv 19:30), are reverent (Ec 8:12), or worship (2Kg 17:7). Children respect parents (Lv 19:3). Passive participles signify remarkable (Ps 139:14), awesome (Dt 7:21), awe-inspiring (Ex 34:10), and revered (Ex 15:11), but can also denote dreadful (Jl 2:11), terrible (Dt 1:19), feared (Is 18:2), and terrifying (Hab 1:7). The intensive verb means make afraid (2Sm 14:15), frighten (2Ch 32:18), or intimidate (Neh 6:9).

God has made you as numerous as the stars of the sky.*ᵃ*

Remember and Obey

11 "Therefore, love the Lᴏʀᴅ your God and always keep His mandate and His statutes, ordinances, and commands. ²You must understand today that it is not your children who experienced or saw the discipline of the Lᴏʀᴅ your God:

His greatness, strong hand, and outstretched arm; ³His signs and the works He did in Egypt to Pharaoh king of Egypt and all his land;*ᵇ* ⁴what He did to Egypt's army, its horses and chariots, when He made the waters of the •Red Sea flow over them as they pursued you, and He destroyed them*ᶜ* completely;^A ⁵what He did to you in the wilderness until you reached this place; ⁶and what He did to Dathan and Abiram, the sons of Eliab the Reubenite, when in the middle of the whole Israelite camp the earth opened its mouth and swallowed them, their households, their tents, and every living thing with them.*ᵈ*

⁷Your own eyes have seen every great work the Lᴏʀᴅ has done.

⁸"Keep every command I am giving you today, so that you may have the strength to cross into and possess the land you are to inherit, ⁹and so that you may live long in the

land the Lᴏʀᴅ swore to your fathers to give them and their descendants, a land flowing with milk and honey.*ᵉ* ¹⁰For the land you are entering to possess is not like the land of Egypt, from which you have come, where you sowed your seed and irrigated by hand^B as in a vegetable garden. ¹¹But the land you are entering to possess is a land of mountains and valleys, watered by rain from the sky. ¹²It is a land the Lᴏʀᴅ your God cares for. He is always watching over it from the beginning to the end of the year.

¹³"If you carefully obey my commands I am giving you today, to love the Lᴏʀᴅ your God and worship Him with all your heart and all your soul, ¹⁴I^C will provide rain for your land in the proper time, the autumn and spring rains,^D and you will harvest your grain, new wine, and oil.*ᶠ* ¹⁵I^C will provide grass in your fields for your livestock. You will eat and be satisfied.*ᵍ* ¹⁶Be careful that you are not enticed to turn aside, worship, and bow down to other gods. ¹⁷Then the Lᴏʀᴅ's anger will burn against you. He will close the sky, and there will be no rain; the land will not yield its produce, and you will perish quickly from the good land*ʰ* the Lᴏʀᴅ is giving you.

¹⁸"Imprint these words of mine on your hearts and minds, bind them as a sign on your hands, and let them be a symbol^E on your foreheads.^F ¹⁹Teach them to your children,*ⁱ*

ᵃ 10:22 Gn 15:5; 22:17; 26:4
ᵇ 11:3 Ex 7–12
ᶜ 11:4 Ex 14
ᵈ 11:6 Nm 16
ᵉ 11:9 Ex 3:17; Lv 20:24; Nm 13:27; Dt 6:3; 26:9,15; 27:3; 31:20; Jos 5:6; Jr 11:5; Ezk 20:6
ᶠ 11:14 Hs 2:22; Jl 2:19,24
ᵍ 11:15 Lv 25:19; Dt 6:11; 8:10; 31:20
ʰ 11:17 Dt 8:7
ⁱ 11:19 Dt 4:9-10

^A 11:4 Lit *to this day*   ^B 11:10 Lit *foot*   ^C 11:14,15 DSS, Sam, LXX read *He*   ^D 11:14 Following the Hb calendar, the early rain came in September/October and the late rain in March/April.   ^E 11:18 Or *phylactery*; Mt 23:5   ^F 11:18 Lit *symbol between your eyes*; Ex 13:16; Dt 6:8

11:1-2 The people had seen and **experienced** the Lord's **discipline** and were therefore without excuse for their waywardness. Their **children**, on the other hand, were not so culpable for they had not seen these things for themselves.

11:3-4 The **signs** and **works** are the plagues the Lord inflicted on **Pharaoh** and **Egypt** and the miracle of drowning their armies in the **Red Sea**. Seeing these proofs of God's power and glory should have instilled such a sense of awe in His people that they could not help but love and serve Him unreservedly, but that was not the case (9:7-24).

11:6 Dathan and **Abiram**, along with Korah the Levite, led a rebellion against Moses and Aaron in the wilderness (Nm 16:1-3). Their sin was more against the Lord than against human authority because they questioned His selection of leaders (Nm 16:8-11). Their rebellion resulted in their destruction and that of their families and properties as well.

11:9-11 The description of Canaan is especially meaningful in comparison to **Egypt**, where rain was scarce and agriculture depended on the annual overflow of the Nile River and irrigation **by hand**. The fact that Canaan was **watered by rain from the sky** insinuates that the rain came from God Himself so that it was He who did the backbreaking work for them. For "hand" (v. 10) the Hebrew has "foot," which may

refer to a primitive foot-operated irrigation pump called in Arabic *shaduf*.

11:13-14 The rainy season in Israel, or early rains, begins in the **autumn**, while **spring** is the time of the late rains. This provision of the Lord for the land indicated His care in "watching over it from the beginning to the end of the year" (v. 12). So important was this agricultural cycle that the Israelites celebrated the new year in the fall.

11:16 The warning not **to turn aside, worship, and bow down to other gods** must be understood in the context of the agricultural motifs just described. Baal, Asherah, Astarte, and other gods and goddesses were thought to generate and sustain life in soil, livestock, and even human beings by their own sexual activity, and they became objects of worship, often through various fertility rites. Moses and the prophets constantly condemned such incursions into paganism (2Kg 17:7-15).

11:17 The **Lᴏʀᴅ's** closing of **the sky** would prove that the gods of the heathen did not exist and that He was the One who created and sustained life.

11:18-20 God's command is a repetition of the instruction given when introducing the Shema (6:4-9; see note at 6:4-5), here clearly showing that all of God's instruction is to be learned and passed along, not just the Shema. **Hearts** is a metaphor for the intellect, and **minds** represents the

talking about them when you sit in your house and when you walk along the road, when you lie down and when you get up. ²⁰ Write them on the doorposts of your house and on your gates,^a ²¹ so that as long as the heavens are above the earth, your days and those of your children may be many in the land the LORD swore to give your fathers.^b ²² For if you carefully observe every one of these commands I am giving you to follow—to love the LORD your God, walk in all His ways, and remain faithful^A to Him— ²³ the LORD will drive out all these nations before you, and you will drive out nations greater and stronger than you are. ²⁴ Every place the sole of your foot treads will be yours.^c Your territory will extend from the wilderness to Lebanon and from the Euphrates River^B to the Mediterranean Sea.^d ²⁵ No one will be able to stand against you; the LORD your God will put fear and dread of you in all the land where you set foot, as He has promised you.^e

A Blessing and a Curse

²⁶ "Look, today I set before you a blessing and a curse:^f ²⁷ there will be a blessing, if you obey the commands of the LORD your God I am giving you today, ²⁸ and a curse, if you do not obey the commands of the LORD your God and you turn aside from the path I command you today by following other gods you have not known. ²⁹ When the LORD your God brings you into the land you are entering to possess, you

are to proclaim the blessing at Mount Gerizim and the curse at Mount Ebal. ³⁰ Aren't these mountains across the Jordan, beyond the western road in the land of the Canaanites, who live in the *Arabah, opposite Gilgal, near the oaks^c of Moreh? ³¹ For you are about to cross the Jordan to enter and take possession of the land the LORD your God is giving you. When you possess it and settle in it, ³² be careful to follow all the statutes and ordinances I set before you today.

The Chosen Place of Worship

12 "Be careful to follow these statutes and ordinances in the land that *Yahweh, the God of your fathers, has given you to possess all the days you live on the earth. ² Destroy completely all the places where the nations that you are driving out worship their gods^g—on the high mountains, on the hills, and under every green tree. ³ Tear down their altars, smash their sacred pillars, burn up their *Asherah poles, cut down the carved images of their gods, and wipe out their names from every^D place. ⁴ Don't worship the LORD your God this way. ⁵ Instead, you must turn to the place Yahweh your God chooses from all your tribes to put His name for His dwelling and go there. ⁶ You are to bring there your *burnt offerings and sacrifices, your tenths and personal contributions,^E your vow offerings and freewill offerings, and the firstborn

^a11:18-20 Dt 6:6-9
^b11:21 Dt 1:35
^c11:24-25 Jos 1:3-5
^d11:24 Gn 15:18-20; Ex 23:31
^e11:25 Dt 2:25
^f11:26 Dt 30:15; Jr 21:8
^g12:2 Ex 23:23-26; 34:13; Dt 7:1-5

---

^A11:22 Lit and hold on   ^B11:24 Some Hb mss, LXX, Tg, Vg read the great river, the river Euphrates   ^C11:30 Sam, LXX, Syr, Aq, Sym read oak; Gn 12:6   ^D12:3 Lit that   ^E12:6 Lit and the contributions from your hands

---

person as a whole being. Together, they are the internalizing of the word of God.

11:21 The phrase **as long as the heavens are above the earth** is a biblical way of expressing the idea of forever. The Lord promised this **land** to the patriarchs on the condition of their obedience and the obedience of their descendants (28:36-37; Gn 17:9-14; Lv 26:14-33).

11:24 Every place the sole of your foot treads is a way of describing conquest and occupation of a territory, usually (but not always) by military might. The image occurs in Gn 13:17 where Abraham was told to "walk around the land, through its length and width," a sign that it would become his as a gift from the Lord. God also told Joshua on the eve of the conquest of Canaan, "I have given you every place where the sole of your foot treads" (Jos 1:3). The area described here is essentially the territory controlled by David (2Sm 8:1-3) and promised in ancient times to Abraham (Gn 15:18-19).

11:26-28 Blessing and curse were essential elements in ancient Near Eastern covenant or treaty texts. Moses, as covenant mediator, set before the people **a blessing and a curse**, the full texts of which he elaborates later on (27:15-28:58). The disobedience mentioned was covenant disloyalty, defined as **following other gods**.

11:29 Mount Gerizim and **Mount Ebal** were twin peaks overshadowing a wide valley in which ancient Shechem (and

modern Nablus) was located. This is where Jacob bought property and dug a well (Gn 33:19-20; Jn 4:6), the very well where Jesus encountered the Samaritan woman and from which she directed His attention to Mount Gerizim, the site of the Samaritan temple (Jn 4:20).

12:2 The **high mountains**, the **hills**, and the **green tree** were sites of pagan worship where the peoples of Canaan built their altars and shrines, though at times they were located even in the valleys (2Kg 23:10; 2Ch 28:3). Groves of trees or even single trees also marked sacred **places** because their luxuriant growth, surrounded by sparse vegetation, symbolized the gods' fertility (1Kg 14:23; 2Kg 16:4; Jr 2:20).

12:3 The **sacred pillars** and **Asherah poles** were stone and wooden columns that represented, respectively, Baal and Asherah, the principal Canaanite fertility deities (7:5).

12:5 Israel must seek Yahweh at **the place** He **chooses** to **put His name**. In the wilderness this was at various altars (Ex 20:24), but once in the land only one central sanctuary would qualify. At first this was Gilgal, then Shechem, then for many years at Shiloh, and finally Jerusalem, the location of Solomon's temple. This place alone came to be recognized as the Lord's **dwelling**, though Solomon himself realized that it could only symbolically be such because in reality even heaven cannot contain the omnipresent God (1Kg 8:27).

12:6 Tenths and personal contributions are essentially

of your herds and flocks. ⁷You will eat there in the presence of the Lord your God and rejoice with your household in everything you do,ᴬ because the Lord your God has blessed you.

⁸"You are not to do as we are doing here today; everyone is doing whatever seems right in his own eyes. ⁹Indeed, you have not yet come into the resting place*ᵃ and the inheritance*ᵇ the Lord your God is giving you. ¹⁰When you cross the Jordan and live in the land the Lord your God is giving you to inherit,*ᶜ and He gives you rest from all the enemies around you and you live in security, ¹¹then Yahweh your God will choose the place to have His name dwell.*ᵈ Bring there everything I command you: your burnt offerings, sacrifices, offerings of the tenth, personal contributions,ᴮ and all your choice offerings you vow to the Lord. ¹²You will rejoice*ᵉ before the Lord your God—you, your sons and daughters, your male and female slaves, and the Levite who is within your gates, since he has no portion or inheritance among you.*ᶠ ¹³Be careful not to offer your burnt offerings in all the sacred places you see. ¹⁴You must offer your burnt offerings only in the place the Lord chooses in one of your tribes, and there you must do everything I command you.

Slaughtering Animals to Eat

¹⁵"But whenever you want, you may slaughter and eat meat within any of your gates,*ᵍ

according to the blessing the Lord your God has given you. Those who are •clean or •unclean may eat it, as they would a gazelle or deer, ¹⁶but you must not eat the blood; pour it on the ground like water.*ʰ ¹⁷Within your gates you may not eat: the tenth of your grain, new wine, or oil; the firstborn of your herd or flock; any of your vow offerings that you pledge; your freewill offerings; or your personal contributions.ᶜ ¹⁸You must eat them in the presence of the Lord your God at the place the Lord your God chooses—you, your son and daughter, your male and female slave, and the Levite who is within your gates. Rejoice before the Lord your God in everything you do,ᴬ ¹⁹and be careful not to neglect the Levite, as long as you live in your land.

²⁰"When the Lord your God enlarges your territory as He has promised you,*ⁱ and you say, 'I want to eat meat' because you have a strong desire to eat meat, you may eat it whenever you want. ²¹If the place where Yahweh your God chooses to put His name is too far from you, you may slaughter any of your herd or flock He has given you, as I have commanded you, and you may eat it within your gates whenever you want. ²²Indeed, you may eat it as the gazelle and deer are eaten; both the clean and the unclean may eat it. ²³But don't eat the blood, since the blood is the life, and you must not eat the life with the meat. ²⁴Do not eat blood; pour it on the ground like water.

*ᵃ12:9 Dt 3:20;
5:14; 25:19;
28:65
*ᵇDt 15:4
*ᶜ12:10 Dt 15:4
*ᵈ12:11 Dt 14:23;
16:2,6,11; 26:2
*ᵉ12:12 Lv 23:40;
Dt 14:26; 16:11-
15; 26:11; 27:7
*ᶠNm 18:20
*ᵍ12:15-16 Dt
15:22-23
*ʰ12:16 Lv
17:10-14
*ⁱ12:20 Ex 34:24

ᴬ12:7,18 Lit you put your hand to   ᴮ12:11 Lit tenth, the contributions from your hands   ᶜ12:17 Lit or the contributions from your hands

---

synonymous, the former being a generic term for mandatory gifts to the Lord and the latter a subset of offerings designated to religious personnel, especially the priests and Levites (Lv 7:32,34). A traditional term for tenths is "tithes." All such gifts must be given to the Lord at the central sanctuary and then redistributed to meet the needs of those who served Him there.

12:7 Those who worship at the central sanctuary must share their freewill offerings (v. 6) with one another **in the presence of the Lord**. Sometimes the Lord Himself was perceived as participating in a common meal with His worshipers. This would, of course, be symbolized by the offerings to Him (Ex 24:5-8,11).

12:8 An individual Israelite doing **whatever seems right in his own eyes** does not mean that religious anarchy prevailed as in the days of the judges (Jdg 21:25). In this context it speaks to the lack of a single central sanctuary site in the wilderness.

12:10-11 The first permanent central **place** of worship was Shiloh, in the center of the land (Jr 7:12). The tabernacle remained there nearly 300 years, from the latter days of Joshua until the early years of the prophet Samuel.

12:13-14 The **sacred places** were pagan shrines as well as local worship centers that at times were perfectly appropriate. The former were taboo under any circumstances (vv. 2-3). The prohibition against the others must be understood

as distinguishing between private worship and the corporate worship of all Israel. The principle behind this whole section of Deuteronomy is the recognition of Israel as a single entity, God's covenant people.

12:15-16 When the community as a whole was not in pilgrimage at the three annual festivals, **slaughter** at a local level for profane purposes was acceptable. Certain other restrictions were lifted when slaughtering for food, including the need for ritual purification and the avoidance of clean game animals (Lv 1:2).

12:17-18 Animals and produce intended for sacrifice only must be offered only in a **place** set apart by the Lord for worship (Ex 20:24). This is clear because the place mentioned here is not described as the place where His name dwells (Dt 12:5). The OT has many examples of local shrines that coexisted with either the tabernacle or the temple and were yet considered legitimate places of worship of the true God (Jdg 6:26; 1Sm 7:17; 1Kg 18:30).

12:21 Religious rites could be carried out apart from the central sanctuary, provided certain requirements, such as the proper disposal of the blood, were carried out (vv. 22-25).

12:23 Blood must not be eaten because **blood is the life**. Since life is regarded as sacred in the Bible (Gn 9:4; Lv 17:11), blood—the most eloquent metaphor for life itself—was also sacred and therefore could not be eaten.

12:24 The rationale for pouring blood **on the ground** seems

²⁵ Do not eat it, so that you and your children after you will prosper, because you will be doing what is right in the LORD's sight.

²⁶ "But you are to take the holy offerings you have and your vow offerings and go to the place the LORD chooses. ²⁷ Present the meat and blood of your burnt offerings on the altar of the LORD your God. The blood of your other sacrifices is to be poured out beside the altar of the LORD your God, but you may eat the meat. ²⁸ Be careful to obey all these things I command you, so that you and your children after you may prosper forever, because you will be doing what is good and right in the sight of the LORD your God.

²⁹ "When the LORD your God annihilates the nations before you,ᵃ which you are entering to take possession of,ᵇ and you drive them out and live in their land, ³⁰ be careful not to be ensnared by their ways after they have been destroyed before you. Do not inquire about their gods, asking, 'How did these nations worship their gods? I'll also do the same.' ³¹ You must not do the same to the LORD your God, because they practice every detestable thing, which the LORD hates, for their gods. They even burn their sons and daughters in the fire to their gods. ³²ᴬ You must be careful

ᵃ12:29 Dt 19:1
ᵇDt 3:12
ᶜ12:32 Dt 4:2; Rv 22:18-19
ᵈ13:4 Dt 10:20
ᵉ13:5 Lv 26:13; Dt 5:6; 6:12; 8:14; 13:10; Jos 24:17; Jr 34:13

to do everything I command you; do not add anything to it or take anything away from it.ᶜ

The False Prophet

13 "If a prophet or someone who has dreams arises among you and proclaims a sign or wonder to you, ² and that sign or wonder he has promised you comes about, but he says, 'Let us follow other gods,' which you have not known, 'and let us worship them,' ³ do not listen to that prophet's words or to that dreamer. For the LORD your God is testing you to know whether you love the LORD your God with all your heart and all your soul. ⁴ You must follow the LORD your God and •fear Him. You must keep His commands and listen to His voice; you must worship Him and remain faithfulᴮ to Him.ᵈ ⁵ That prophet or dreamer must be put to death, because he has urged rebellion against the LORD your God who brought you out of the land of Egypt and redeemed you from the place of slavery,ᵉ to turn you from the way the LORD your God has commanded you to walk. You must purge the evil from you.

Don't Tolerate Idolatry

⁶ "If your brother, the son of your mother,ᶜ or your son or daughter, or the wife you embrace, or your closest friend secretly entices

ᴬ12:32 Dt 13:1 in Hb   ᴮ13:4 Lit and hold on   ᶜ13:6 DSS, Sam, LXX read If the son of your father or the son of your mother

to be that just as man was created from the ground and returns to the ground at death, so blood, the ultimate symbol of life, should also be returned to the earth.

12:27 Burnt offerings is a generic term for sin and trespass offerings and others required to restore fellowship with God. **Other sacrifices** indicate nonexpiatory or propitiatory sacrifices such as fellowship or peace offerings.

12:30 The residual effects of the wicked nations of Canaan would be so powerful that even after their expulsion from the land, the Israelites would be tempted to **inquire about their gods**. The human heart is fickle, always in danger of yielding to a downward pull (Jr 17:9).

12:31 Human sacrifice was part of the ritual of many ancient religions, including those of Canaan and surrounding nations. They believed it had the persuasive power to coerce the gods to a course of action on one's behalf or to avert calamity; therefore the more precious the victim, the more likely the desired response. The unthinkable act of burning **sons and daughters** was associated especially with the Moabite god, Chemosh, and the Ammonite god, Molech (Lv 18:21; 2Kg 3:27). Worse still, Israel at various times permitted or even authorized human sacrifice (Jr 32:35).

13:1 The person who **arises among you** refers to a fellow Israelite. Being the chosen people did not guarantee that none who violated the covenant would ever turn up.

13:2 The genuineness of prophets and dreamers cannot be determined by their ability to perform a **sign or wonder** (cp. 4:34), but by their commitment to the Lord and their faith-

fulness in proclaiming His word. The message must validate the works of signs and wonders, and not the reverse.

13:3 The dreamer's remarkable ability may originate with the Lord Himself **to know whether you love the Lord your God with all your heart and all your soul**. Not all such manifestations are from Satan (though surely some can be; cp. Rv 13:2), for the Lord desires to reveal who truly knows and loves Him that others might know the true character of those whom they are called to follow. The greatest commandment, the Shema (Dt 6:4-9), instructs God's people to "love the LORD your God with all your heart and all your soul," exactly the demand made here. A person can profess that kind of love, but sometimes only severe testing can authenticate the testimony.

13:4 To love the Lord is to **fear Him**, to fear Him is to love Him, and the proof of both is obedience. Jesus linked these together when He said, "If you love Me, you will keep My commands" (Jn 14:15).

13:5 The death sentence for false prophets within Israel reflects the severity of their offense. Acts of treason against human rulers and their governments are commonly capital offenses, how much more when seditious disloyalty is displayed against the King of kings? The first of the Ten Commandments states, "Do not have other gods besides Me" (5:7). Only by such drastic measures would the nation be able to **purge the evil** from its midst.

13:6-8 Loyalty to the Lord outweighs loyalty to any other person, family members included. Jesus made this matter clear when He taught His disciples "the person who loves

you, saying, 'Let us go and worship other gods'—which neither you nor your fathers have known, [7]any of the gods of the peoples around you, near you or far from you, from one end of the earth to the other— [8]you must not yield to him or listen to him. Show him no pity,[A] and do not spare him or shield him. [9]Instead, you must kill him. Your hand is to be the first against him to put him to death, and then the hands of all the people.[a] [10]Stone him to death for trying to turn you away from the LORD your God who brought you out of the land of Egypt, out of the place of slavery. [11]All Israel will hear and be afraid, and they will no longer do anything evil like this among you.[b]

[12]"If[c] you hear it said about one of your cities the LORD your God is giving you to live in, [13]that 'wicked men have sprung up among you, led the inhabitants of their city astray, and said, 'Let us go and worship other gods,' which you have not known, [14]you are to inquire, investigate, and interrogate thoroughly. If the report turns out to be true that this detestable thing has happened among you, [15]you must strike down the inhabitants of that city with the sword. *Completely destroy everyone in it as well as its livestock with the sword. [16]You are to gather all its spoil in the middle of the city square and completely burn up the city and all its spoil for the LORD your God. The city must remain a mound of

*a*13:9 Dt 17:7
*b*13:11 Dt 19:20
*c*13:12-15 Dt 17:2-5
*d*14:1 Ex 4:22-23; Dt 32:6
*e*Lv 19:28
*f*14:2 Ex 19:5; Dt 7:6

ruins forever; it is not to be rebuilt. [17]Nothing *set apart for destruction is to remain in your hand, so that the LORD will turn from His burning anger and grant you mercy, show you compassion, and multiply you as He swore to your fathers. [18]This will occur if you obey the LORD your God, keeping all His commands I am giving you today, doing what is right in the sight of the LORD your God.

Forbidden Practices

14 "You are sons of the LORD your God;[d] do not cut yourselves or make a bald spot on your head[B] on behalf of the dead,[e] [2]for you are a holy people belonging to the LORD your God. The LORD has chosen you to be His own possession[f] out of all the peoples on the face of the earth.

Clean and Unclean Foods

[3]"You must not eat any detestable thing. [4]These are the animals you may eat:

> the ox, the sheep, the goat,
> [5]   the deer, the gazelle, the roe deer,
>   the wild goat, the ibex, the antelope,
>   and the mountain sheep.

[6]You may eat any animal that has hooves divided in two and chews the cud. [7]But among the ones that chew the cud or have divided hooves, you are not to eat these:

[A]13:8 Lit *Your eye must not pity him*   [B]14:1 Or *forehead*

---

father or mother more than Me is not worthy of Me" (Mt 10:37).

13:9 Being **the first** to undertake retribution would likely deter someone from making false accusation and would also underscore the seriousness of the offence. Silence in the face of such egregious violation of covenant would in and of itself suggest implication on the part of the one who refused to testify. Sometimes the cost of loving the Lord might be a willingness to forfeit family in pursuit of a higher good.

13:10-11 The deterrent effect of stoning a covenant traitor to death was to make **all Israel . . . afraid** so that they would **no longer do** such **evil** again. If not immediately and consistently applied, such measures are unlikely to have any good effect.

13:12-13 Unpunished individual apostasy is likely to spread near and far like a disease. If **wicked men** lead **the inhabitants of their city astray**, other individuals or households will become contaminated. Though Israel was God's elect covenant nation, the salvation of a chosen people is no guarantee of the salvation of all its members. As Paul put it, "For not all who are descended from Israel are Israel . . . That is, it is not the children by physical descent who are God's children, but the children of the promise are considered to be the offspring" (Rm 9:6,8).

13:15-16 An Israelite **city** that tolerated apostasy must be burned to the ground like a pagan city (cp. 3:6; 7:2). The point is that rebellion against the Lord is rebellion, no matter its source. To be the chosen nation did not exempt Is-

rael from God's judgment should they violate His covenant requirements. The same was true of a single individual or a family (cp. 13:6-11) such as in the case of Achan, who stole goods from the ruins of Jericho that should have been devoted to the Lord (Jos 7). Furthermore, a city once destroyed as an effect of the ban was under a curse and often was never to be rebuilt. This was true of Jericho (Jos 6:26) and Ai (Jos 8:28).

14:1-2 The Canaanites and other heathen lamented their **dead** in all kinds of physical ways, including pulling out the hair and lacerating the body, perhaps to gain sympathy from the gods and thus a renewed sense of peace and equilibrium (1Kg 18:28; Jr 47:5; Hs 7:14). Israel, however, must not imitate these pagan practices (Lv 19:27-28). Having been **chosen** by God above all nations, they must live to reflect His glory and their own uniqueness as bearers of the covenant.

14:3 A **detestable thing** is anything that the Lord declares to be such, regardless of its nature or character. Whatever God deems to be holy (or acceptable) is, by virtue of His decision, to be viewed as holy. Likewise, what He states to be unholy is unholy because of His having said so.

14:7 The **hare** (similar to rabbits) and **hyrax** (similar to badgers) are not technically ruminants, but the way they chew their food makes it appear that they **chew the cud**. In this and other cases the Bible reflects the prescientific custom of describing or classifying things by their everyday

the camel, the hare, and the hyrax,
though they chew the cud, they do not
   have hooves—
they are *unclean for you;
  8 and the pig, though it has hooves,
   it does not chew the cud—
it is unclean for you.

You must not eat their meat or touch their carcasses.*a*

9"You may eat everything from the water that has fins and scales, 10but you may not eat anything that does not have fins and scales—it is unclean for you.*b*

11"You may eat every *clean bird, 12but these are the ones you may not eat:

   the eagle, the bearded vulture,
   the black vulture, 13the kite,
   any kind of falcon,A
  14 every kind of raven, 15the ostrich,
   the short-eared owl, the gull,
   any kind of hawk,
  16 the little owl, the long-eared owl,
   the white owl, 17the desert owl,
   the osprey, the cormorant, 18the stork,
   any kind of heron,
   the hoopoe, and the bat.B,c

19All winged insects are unclean for you; they may not be eaten. 20But you may eat every clean flying creature.*d*

21"You are not to eat any carcass; you may give it to a temporary resident living within your gates, and he may eat it, or you may sell it to a foreigner. For you are a holy people belonging to the LORD your God. You must not boil a young goat in its mother's milk.

Reference column

a14:4-8 Lv 11:1-8
b14:9-10 Lv 11:9-12
c14:11-18 Lv 11:13-19
d14:19-20 Lv 11:20-23
e14:23 Dt 12:11
fDt 4:10; 6:2; 10:12; 17:19; 31:12-13; Jos 4:24; 24:14; 1Sm 12:14; 2Kg 17:25; Ps 15:4
g14:26-27 Dt 12:12,18-19
h14:28-29 Dt 26:12
i14:29 Dt 30:9
j15:1 Ex 22:25-27; Lv 25

A Tenth for the LORD

22"Each year you are to set aside a tenth of all the produce grown in your fields. 23You are to eat a tenth of your grain, new wine, and oil, and the firstborn of your herd and flock, in the presence of *Yahweh your God at the place where He chooses to have His name dwell,*e* so that you will always learn to *fear*f* the LORD your God. 24But if the distance is too great for you to carry it, since the place where Yahweh your God chooses to put His name is too far away from you and since the LORD your God has blessed you, 25then exchange it for money, take the money in your hand, and go to the place the LORD your God chooses. 26You may spend the money on anything you want: cattle, sheep, wine, beer, or anything you desire. You are to feast there in the presence of the LORD your God and rejoice with your family. 27Do not neglect the Levite within your gates, since he has no portion or inheritance among you.*g*

28"At the end of every three years, bring a tenth of all your produce for that year and store it within your gates. 29Then the Levite, who has no portion or inheritance among you, the foreigner, the fatherless, and the widow within your gates may come, eat, and be satisfied.*h* And the LORD your God will bless you in all the work of your hands that you do.*i*

Debts Canceled

15 "At the end of every seven years you must cancel debts.*j* 2This is how to cancel debt: Every creditor*c* is to cancel what he has lent his neighbor. He is not to collect anything from his neighbor or brother, be-

---

A14:13 Some Hb mss, Sam, LXX; other Hb mss, Vg read *the falcon, the various kinds of kite* B14:5-18 The identification of some of these animals is uncertain. C15:2 Lit *owner of a loan of his hand*

---

appearance and not according to exhaustive testing and observation. Rather than seeking to convey to the Hebrews scientific knowledge that would not be discovered until many centuries later, God simply accommodated their commonplace observations (i.e., that hares seemingly "chew the cud"). Such accommodation is an act of grace and love on God's part, making His revelations comprehensible to the original audience.

14:21 Carcass means any animal that had died naturally. The reason for the prohibition has to do again with the principle of holiness. God's people were strictly forbidden to come in contact with the dead lest they become ritually impure (Lv 11:24-40). By eating a carcass they would compromise their status as **a holy people belonging to the LORD**.

14:22 Paying the **tenth** is not a practice first instituted in the Mosaic law, but one adopted by that law and mandated as part of the regular worship of the Lord. When Abraham returned from his battle with the kings of the east, he paid Melchizedek a tenth of all he had (Gn 14:20). Likewise, Jacob, having encountered God at Bethel, promised Him that if he returned safely from his journey to Haran, he would

render to the Lord a tenth of his possessions (Gn 28:18-22). In the context of the Mosaic covenant, the Lord is viewed as the great King to whom tribute is due (Nm 23:21; 31:28).

14:24-25 Grace even in the midst of apparent legalism in the OT is clearly displayed in this concession to allow certain tithes-givers to offer money instead of animals or produce.

14:26 The practice of buying offerings continued into NT times but came to be abused by money changers who bought low and sold high, turning the sacred precincts of the temple into what Jesus called a "marketplace" (Jn 2:16).

14:28-29 In the absence of a "paid clergy" in ancient Israel, priests and Levites depended on the offerings of the people for their livelihood. Thus, every third year a **tenth** of all the **produce** must be stored up for distribution not only to the **Levite**, but to **the foreigner, the fatherless, and the widow**. The more the people cared for the less fortunate, the more they could expect the blessing of the Lord.

15:1-3 The principle of the Sabbath—that all creation should rest and be rejuvenated on the seventh day—was extended

cause the LORD's release of debts has been pro-claimed. ³You may collect something from a foreigner, but you must forgive whatever your brother owes you.

⁴"There will be no poor among you, how-ever, because the LORD is certain to bless you in the land the LORD your God is giving you to possess as an inheritance[a]— ⁵if only you obey the LORD your God and are careful to follow every one of these commands I am giving you today. ⁶When the LORD your God blesses you as He has promised you, you will lend to many nations but not borrow; you will rule over many nations, but they will not rule over you.

Lending to the Poor

⁷"If there is a poor person among you, one of your brothers within any of your gates in the land the LORD your God is giving you, you must not be hardhearted or tightfisted toward your poor brother. ⁸Instead, you are to open your hand to him and freely loan him enough for whatever need he has. ⁹Be careful that there isn't this wicked thought in your heart, 'The seventh year, the year of canceling debts, is near,' and you are stingy toward your poor brother and give him nothing. He will cry

out to the LORD against you, and you will be •guilty. ¹⁰Give to him, and don't have a stingy heart[A] when you give, and because of this the LORD your God will bless you in all your work and in everything you do.[B] ¹¹For there will never cease to be poor people in the land;[b] that is why I am commanding you, 'You must willingly open your hand to your afflicted and poor brother in your land.'

Release of Slaves

¹²"If your fellow Hebrew, a man or woman, is sold to you and serves you six years, you must set him free in the seventh year.[c] ¹³When you set him free, do not send him away empty-handed. ¹⁴Give generously to him from your flock, your threshing floor, and your wine-press. You are to give him whatever the LORD your God has blessed you with. ¹⁵Remember that you were a slave in the land of Egypt and the LORD your God redeemed[d] you; that is why I am giving you this command today.[e] ¹⁶But if your slave says to you, 'I don't want to leave you,' because he loves you and your family, and is well off with you, ¹⁷take an awl and pierce through his ear into the door, and he will become your slave for life. Also treat your female slave the same way. ¹⁸Do not regard it

ᵃ15:4 Ex 32:13; Lv 20:24; Dt 4:21; 12:10; 16:20; 19:10; 21:23; 24:4; 25:19; 26:1; 29:8; Jos 1:6 ᵇ15:11 Mt 26:11 ᶜ15:12 Jr 34:14 ᵈ15:15 Ex 15:13; Dt 7:8; 9:26; 24:18 ᵉDt 24:18,22

A15:10 Lit *and let not your heart be grudging*   **B**15:10 Lit *you put your hand to*

---

to the seventh year as well. Canceling **debts** on the sab-batical year meant that (1) the borrower who was unable to pay his debt could walk away free of obligation following the seventh year or (2) repayment could not be demanded on the seventh year. On the other hand, a foreigner must pay back his loan entirely. The reason for the sabbatical release was likely related to the remission of Israel's debt to Egypt by the Lord's gracious deliverance in the exodus. Jesus spoke of such grace in His parable of the unforgiving slave who, though having been forgiven of a great debt to his creditor, refused to forgive a small debt owed to him (Mt 18:32-33).

15:4-5 The declaration that **there will be no poor among you** is neither an unqualified assertion nor a prediction. There *should* be no poor because the Lord would abundantly **bless** them **in the land** He was giving them. Due to sin this ideal was never achieved throughout Israel's history and, indeed, Jesus Himself affirmed, "You always have the poor with you" (Mt 26:11; cp. Dt 15:11).

15:9 A **stingy** creditor might be tempted not to lend to his poor brother when **the seventh year** was **near** because he would then have less chance of being repaid (cp. v. 2). Such an attitude, however, is a sin against the Lord.

15:12-14 Not only a debtor but a bondservant must also be relieved of encumbrances in the **seventh year**. According to the Mosaic law, a poor person could indenture himself to a more affluent Israelite in order to work off any indebted-ness (Ex 21:2-11). Unlike the repayment of a monetary debt, which was cancelled after a fixed period (Dt 15:1), a bond servant must work a full **six years** and then be **set . . . free** with a generous spirit and with provisions proportionate to the blessing of the Lord upon the benefactor.

15:15 Referring to the exodus deliverance, Moses provided the motivation or justification for beneficent treatment of the poor debtor. The least a creditor could do was to release his Hebrew brother from his financial bondage and supply him with provisions sufficient for a new start in life. Even the Egyptians had done this much for their departed Hebrew slaves (Ex 12:35-36).

15:17 Release from bondage was not mandatory for bond slaves. Should they love their masters and find life more pleasant and secure in their relationship with them, they were entitled to stay with them (v. 16). Such a commitment was for a lifetime, however, and must be carefully thought out ahead of time. Once the decision was made, the slave submitted to an ordeal in which the master took **an awl** and pierced **through his ear into the door**, thus indicating the slave's desire to become the master's **slave for life**. Be-sides testifying publicly by this act that the slave was com-mitting himself wholly and permanently to his master, the scar he bore would be a reminder to him and others from that time forward that he was no longer his own. Paul may have had this in mind when he said, "I bear on my body scars for the cause of Jesus" (Gl 6:17). That is, his wounds marked him as a slave of Christ for life.

The **female slave** was treated in exactly **the same way**. The same law in Ex 21:6 states that the slave under these circum-stances had to go before the judges to formalize the arrange-ment and then her ear would be bored against the doorpost. The word for judges (Hb *elohim*) usually means "God," so that the doorpost where the ear was pierced may have been at the tabernacle, making the ceremony a religious act.

15:18 **A hired hand** would normally work for hourly wages, while a bond slave could be called upon day and night. For this reason, his or her service was **worth twice the wages**

as a hardship^A when you set him free, because he worked for you six years—worth twice the wages of a hired hand. Then the LORD your God will bless you in everything you do.^a

Consecration of Firstborn Animals

^19 "You must consecrate to the LORD your God every firstborn male produced by your herd and flock.^b You are not to put the firstborn of your oxen to work or shear the firstborn of your flock. ^20 Each year you and your family are to eat it before the LORD your God in the place the LORD chooses. ^21 But if there is a defect in the animal, if it is lame or blind or has any serious defect, you must not sacrifice it to the LORD your God. ^22 Eat it within your gates; both the •unclean person and the •clean may eat it, as though it were a gazelle or deer. ^23 But you must not eat its blood; pour it on the ground like water.^c

The Festival of Passover

16 "Observe the month of Abib^B,d and celebrate the •Passover to the LORD your God, because the LORD your God brought you out of Egypt by night in the month of Abib. ^2 Sacrifice to •Yahweh your God a Passover animal from the herd or flock in the place where the LORD chooses to have His name dwell.^e ^3 You must not eat leavened bread with it. For seven days you are to eat unleavened bread with it, the bread of hardship—because you left the

^a15:12-18 Ex 21:2-11
^b15:19 Lv 23:9-14
^c15:22-23 Dt 12:15-16,22-24
^d16:1-8 Ex 12
^e16:2 Dt 12:11
^f16:9-12 Lv 23:15-21
^g16:11 Lv 23:40; Dt 12:12; 14:26; 26:11; 27:7

land of Egypt in a hurry—so that you may remember for the rest of your life the day you left the land of Egypt. ^4 No yeast is to be found anywhere in your territory for seven days, and none of the meat you sacrifice in the evening of the first day is to remain until morning. ^5 You are not to sacrifice the Passover animal in any of the towns the LORD your God is giving you. ^6 You must only sacrifice the Passover animal at the place where Yahweh your God chooses to have His name dwell. Do this in the evening as the sun sets at the same time of day you departed from Egypt. ^7 You are to cook and eat it in the place the LORD your God chooses, and you are to return to your tents in the morning. ^8 You must eat unleavened bread for six days. On the seventh day there is to be a solemn assembly to the LORD your God, and you must not do any work.

The Festival of Weeks

^9 "You are to count seven weeks, counting the weeks from the time the sickle is first put to the standing grain.^f ^10 You are to celebrate the Festival of Weeks to the LORD your God with a freewill offering that you give in proportion to how the LORD your God has blessed you. ^11 Rejoice^g before Yahweh your God in the place where He chooses to have His name dwell—you, your son and daughter, your male and female slave, the Levite within

---

^A15:18 Lit *Let it not be hard in your sight*   ^B16:1 March–April; called Nisan in the post-exilic period; Neh 2:1; Est 3:7

---

of a hired hand. This fact lends significance to Paul's description of himself as "a slave of Christ Jesus" (Rm 1:1; cp. Php 1:1; Ti 1:1), and it should also enhance the meaning of Christian discipleship. We are not mere hirelings or temporary servants, but slaves with a lifetime commitment.

15:19 In gratitude to the Lord for His preservation of their **firstborn** in Egypt (Ex 12:12-13,29), the Israelites must dedicate them to Him in lifetime service (Ex 13:2). However, they could be redeemed from this service by the payment of a firstborn sacrificial animal (Ex 13:13-16) and, later, by the substitution of a Levite for each firstborn son of Israel (Nm 3:11-13,40-51). Firstborn animals could therefore not be put to the service of the Israelites, but they belonged to the Lord.

15:21 The Lord demands our best in tribute and service. The NT enjoins believers to "present your bodies as a living sacrifice, holy and pleasing to God" (Rm 12:1). This implies the giving of one's total self and all he possesses to serving the Lord.

16:1 The **month of Abib** (meaning "ears of grain"), early in the spring, must be celebrated as the month when the liberating event of the exodus took place. **Passover**, the festival commemorating the deliverance of Israel from the tenth plague, began on the fourteenth day of Abib and continued through the twenty-first as the Festival of Unleavened Bread (Ex 12:17-20).

16:3 The **bread of hardship** symbolized the duress under

which Israel lived as slaves in **Egypt** and also the **hurry** in which they escaped, with the Egyptian army hard on their heels (Ex 12:11,34,39). The people of Israel must eat the unleavened bread as a means of remembering the cost of their redemption. The church also is commanded by the Lord to eat the communion bread and drink the cup "in remembrance" of Him (1Co 11:24-25). This helps the believer to recall the great acts of salvation history and even to reenact and participate in them.

16:5-6 Whereas **sacrifice** in general was permitted at local sites (Ex 20:24-26), three times a year the community—at least males 20 years and older—had to assemble **at the place where Yahweh** chose **to have His name dwell**—the central sanctuary (12:5). When the community as a whole presented the Passover sacrifice, they commemorated God's gracious act of redemption and offered their tribute to Him as a response of worship and thanksgiving.

16:7 To **cook and eat** the Passover sacrifice not only brought the nation together but it also depicted the Lord as the table host. The setting is much the same as the Christian gathering known as the Lord's Supper. Christ is there not as a participant but as an observer and in anticipation of a literal participation in the consummation of the kingdom of God (Lk 22:15-18).

16:10 The **Festival of Weeks**—known to Judaism as (Hb) *Shabuoth* ("weeks") or *Qatsir* ("harvest") and to Christians as Pentecost—was the second of the great pilgrimage festi-

your gates, as well as the foreigner, the fatherless, and the widow among you. [12]Remember that you were slaves in Egypt; carefully follow these statutes.

The Festival of Booths

[13]"You are to celebrate the Festival of Booths for seven days when you have gathered in everything from your threshing floor and winepress.[a] [14]Rejoice during your festival—you, your son and daughter, your male and female slave, as well as the Levite, the foreigner, the fatherless, and the widow within your gates. [15]You are to hold a seven-day festival for the LORD your God in the place He chooses, because the LORD your God will bless you in all your produce and in all the work of your hands,[b] and you will have abundant joy.

[16]"All your males are to appear three times a year[c] before the LORD your God in the place He chooses: at the Festival of •Unleavened Bread, the Festival of Weeks, and the Festival of Booths. No one is to appear before the LORD empty-handed. [17]Everyone must appear with a gift suited to his means, according to the blessing the LORD your God has given you.

Appointing Judges and Officials

[18]"Appoint judges and officials for your tribes in all your towns the LORD your God is giving you. They are to judge the people with righteous judgment. [19]Do not deny justice or show partiality to anyone. Do not accept

a bribe, for it blinds the eyes of the wise and twists the words of the righteous. [20]Pursue justice and justice alone, so that you will live and possess the land the LORD your God is giving you.[d]

Forbidden Worship

[21]"Do not set up an •Asherah of any kind of wood next to the altar you will build for the LORD your God, [22]and do not set up a sacred pillar; the LORD your God hates them.[e]

17 "You must not sacrifice to the LORD your God an ox or sheep with a defect or any serious flaw, for that is detestable to the LORD your God.[f]

The Judicial Procedure for Idolatry

[2]"If[g] a man or woman among you in one of your towns that the LORD your God will give you is discovered doing evil in the sight of the LORD your God and violating His covenant[h] [3]and has gone to worship other gods by bowing down to the sun, moon, or all the stars in the sky—which I have forbidden— [4]and if you are told or hear about it, you must investigate it thoroughly. If the report turns out to be true that this detestable thing has happened in Israel, [5]you must bring out to your •gates that man or woman who has done this evil thing and stone them to death. [6]The one condemned to die is to be executed on the testimony of two or three witnesses. No one is

Cross references (center column)

a 16:13-15 Lv 23:33-43
b 16:15 Dt 30:9
c 16:16 Ex 23:14,17; 34:23-24; 1Kg 9:25; Lk 2:42
d 16:19-20 Ex 23:2-9
e 16:21-22 Dt 7:1-5; 12:2-3
f 17:1 Lv 22:17-25
g 17:2-5 Dt 13:12-15
h 17:2 Dt 31:16

---

vals at the central sanctuary. It celebrated the harvest of the ripened grain 50 days after gathering the firstfruits (v. 9). The selection of the day of Pentecost for the coming of the Holy Spirit on the gathered church at Jerusalem probably was to inaugurate the birth of the church and also to view the firstfruits as having become a ripened body ready for harvest as God's redeemed community (Ac 2:1,36,41).

16:13 After the Israelites left Egypt, for 40 years thereafter they lived in temporary shelters described as "booths," underscoring the transient nature of their journey and their dependence on the Lord for sustenance. Exodus 23:16 refers to this time as the Festival of Ingathering but makes no allusion to the wilderness experience nor does Deuteronomy. Leviticus, however, draws attention to the fact that the Lord "made the Israelites live in booths when [He] brought them out of the land of Egypt" (Lv 23:43). The **Festival of Booths** thus served to remind Israel of its fragile history in the wilderness and to celebrate God's goodness to them in the land and the joy that would result in the crops from the work of their hands.

16:14 The list of persons here characterizes the Festival of Booths not only as a time of feasting and worship, but also an annual opportunity to attend to the needs of some of the lowliest and most neglected of Israel's population.

16:16-17 No one is too poor to give something, and no one is expected to give more than he can. The OT tenth adheres

to this standard and is therefore a measure for NT giving. Jesus illustrated this principle when He drew attention to a poor widow who dropped only two tiny coins into the temple treasury. She had done better than the rich, He said, "for they all gave out of their surplus, but she out of her poverty" (Mk 12:44).

16:18-19 Righteous judgment is the application of the law so as to conform to a set standard determined either by fiat or precedent. In the covenant law, the standard is Torah itself, so any judgment is righteous only to the extent that it conforms to Torah, which itself reflects the just and righteous character of the Lord.

16:21-22 The **Asherah** and **sacred pillar** were cult objects representing the chief goddess and god (Baal) respectively. A hint of syncretism is evident here in that Israel was told not to erect these pagan symbols **next to the altar** of **the LORD**. Recent discoveries in the Negev have confirmed that the Lord was sometimes worshiped along with Asherah, who is even described as His wife.

17:5 To worship false gods was an act of high treason, punishable by **death**. The covenant was founded on the first two commandments—that only the Lord could be worshiped and that images of Him or other gods could not be tolerated.

17:6-7 The stoning of an idolater must take place only after adequate testimony by credible witnesses. A **single witness**

to be executed on the testimony of a single witness. [7] The witnesses' hands are to be the first in putting him to death, and after that, the hands of all the people.[a] You must purge the evil from you.[b]

Difficult Cases

[8] "If a case is too difficult for you—concerning bloodshed,[c] lawsuits,[d] or assaults[e]—cases disputed at your gates,[f] you must go up to the place the LORD your God chooses. [9] You are to go to the Levitical priests and to the judge who presides at that time. Ask, and they will give you a verdict in the case. [10] You must abide by the verdict they give you at the place the LORD chooses. Be careful to do exactly as they instruct you. [11] You must abide by the instruction they give you and the verdict they announce to you. Do not turn to the right or the left from the decision they declare to you. [12] The person who acts arrogantly, refusing to listen either to the priest who stands there serving the LORD your God or to the judge, must die. You must purge the evil from Israel. [13] Then all the people will hear about it, be afraid, and no longer behave arrogantly.

Appointing a King

[14] "When you enter the land the LORD your God is giving you,[g] take possession of it, live

a17:7 Dt 13:9
b1Co 5:13
c17:8 Ex 21:12-14,18-25; Nm 35:9-34; Dt 19:1-13; 25:7
dEx 22:6-14
eEx 21:22-26; Lv 24:19-20
f Dt 21:19; 22:15
g17:14 Dt 26:1
h17:14-15 1Sm 8:4-22
i17:15 Gn 17:6,16; 35:11; Nm 24:17-19
j17:16 1Kg 10:28-29
k17:19 Dt 14:23

in it, and say, 'I will set a king over me like all the nations around me,' [15] you are to appoint over you the king the LORD your God chooses.[h] Appoint a king from your brothers. You are not to set a foreigner over you, or one who is not of your people.[i] [16] However, he must not acquire many horses for himself or send the people back to Egypt to acquire many horses, for the LORD has told you, 'You are never to go back that way again.'[j] [17] He must not acquire many wives for himself so that his heart won't go astray. He must not acquire very large amounts of silver and gold for himself. [18] When he is seated on his royal throne, he is to write a copy of this instruction for himself on a scroll in the presence of the Levitical priests. [19] It is to remain with him, and he is to read from it all the days of his life, so that he may learn to *fear[k] the LORD his God, to observe all the words of this instruction, and to do these statutes. [20] Then his heart will not be exalted above his countrymen, he will not turn from this command to the right or the left, and he and his sons will continue ruling many years[A] over Israel.

Provisions for the Levites

18 "The Levitical priests, the whole tribe of Levi, will have no portion or inheritance with Israel. They will eat the LORD's

---

A17:20 Lit will lengthen days on his kingdom

might have a personal agenda or might have misread what the accused had done. The **two or three** witnesses required must back up their charges by being **the first** in putting the evildoer **to death**, something they would not be likely to do if they harbored any questions about his guilt.

17:8-9 The presence of priests and a judge makes clear that there was no separation between the secular and the sacred and that every violation of the law was a violation of the covenant between the Lord and His people. In the theocracy of OT Israel, sin and crime were one and the same.

17:12 Inasmuch as the **judge** and the **priest** were **serving the LORD**, their judgment was final. This suggests that the verdict was achieved by both wise assessment of the evidence and divine revelation. A "too difficult" case, therefore, was one beyond human capacity to resolve (v. 8). The person acting **arrogantly** against the judgment of the court was in fact acting arrogantly against the Lord and was therefore guilty of a capital offense.

17:14 Israel had lived for more than 400 years under the Egyptian **king**. Though God Himself was now their King, they would want a human king as a means of establishing peace and stability at a time when anarchy might otherwise prevail (cp. Jdg 21:25). The desire for a king would not in itself be wrong, because the Lord had promised Abraham and Sarah that they would produce a line of kings (Gn 17:6,16), and Jacob prophesied that a messianic King would spring from the tribe of Judah (Gn 49:10). At stake here were guidelines by which such future rulers must govern themselves and their people.

17:15 A future **king** of Israel must be a man whom the LORD . . . chooses, and he must not be a **foreigner**. The Lord must make the choice because "man does not see what the LORD sees, for man sees what is visible, but the LORD sees the heart" (1Sm 16:7).

17:16-17 Having been chosen, the future ruler of Israel must adhere to certain standards to assure the success of his reign, placing his confidence in the Lord rather than in **many horses** and armaments (Is 31:1; cp. Ps 20:7). He must also not participate in polygamy because it would lead him into idolatry when he tried to satisfy all his wives' religious preferences (cp. Solomon; 1Kg 11:1-3). Finally, he must resist the urge to accumulate riches because these would likely cause him to depend on his own resources rather than on the Lord (Pr 11:28).

17:18 This instruction refers at least to the book of Deuteronomy and possibly to the entire Pentateuch. Having **a copy** and also writing a copy **in the presence of the Levitical priests** would ingrain the word of God deep within the heart and mind of the king and certify before witnesses that he had made the copy himself.

17:19-20 This admonition to consistent Bible reading is designed to help the reader to **fear the LORD** and to obey all that He commands. Rulers of the OT theocracy (meaning Israel's rulers) in particular needed to be careful to do this so as not to think of themselves as overly **exalted above** their countrymen and to protect themselves against deviating from their covenantal obligations to God. Many of Israel's kings fell short of this ideal, with the result that the

fire offerings; that is their[A,B] inheritance. [2]Although Levi has no inheritance among his brothers, the LORD is his inheritance, as He promised him.[a] [3]This is the priests' share from the people who offer a sacrifice, whether it is an ox, a sheep, or a goat; the priests are to be given the shoulder, jaws, and stomach. [4]You are to give him the •firstfruits of your grain, new wine, and oil, and the first sheared wool of your flock. [5]For •Yahweh your God has chosen him and his sons from all your tribes to stand and minister in His name from now on.[c] [6]When a Levite leaves one of your towns where he lives in Israel and wants to go to the place the LORD chooses, [7]he may serve in the name of Yahweh his God like all his fellow Levites who minister there in the presence of the LORD. [8]They will eat equal portions besides what he has received from the sale of the family estate.[D,b]

Occult Practices versus Prophetic Revelation

[9]"When you enter the land the LORD your God is giving you, do not imitate the de-

testable customs of those nations. [10]No one among you is to make his son or daughter pass through the fire,[E,c] practice •divination, tell fortunes, interpret omens, practice sorcery, [11]cast spells, consult a medium or a familiar spirit, or inquire of the dead.[d] [12]Everyone who does these things is detestable to the LORD, and the LORD your God is driving out the nations before you because of these detestable things. [13]You must be blameless before the LORD your God. [14]Though these nations you are about to drive out listen to fortune-tellers and diviners, the LORD your God has not permitted you to do this.

[15]"The LORD your God will raise up for you a prophet like me from among your own brothers.[e] You must listen to him. [16]This is what you requested from the LORD your God at Horeb on the day of the assembly when you said, 'Let us not continue to hear the voice of the LORD our God or see this great fire any longer, so that we will not die!'[f] [17]Then the LORD said to me, 'They have spoken well. [18]I will raise up for them a prophet like you from among their brothers. I will put My words in his mouth,

[a] 18:2 Nm 18:20
[b] 18:8 Nm 18:8-32
[c] 18:10 Lv 18:21
[d] 18:11 Lv 20:27; Is 8:19
[e] 18:15 Mt 21:11; Lk 2:25-34; 7:16; 24:19; Jn 1:21,25; 4:19; Ac 3:22; 7:37
[f] 18:16 Ex 20:19; Dt 5:23-27

[A] 18:1 LXX; MT reads *his*   [B] 18:1 Or *His*   [C] 18:5 Lit *name all the days*   [D] 18:8 Hb obscure   [E] 18:10 Either a Canaanite cult practice or child sacrifice

---

Davidic line came to an end and would resume only with the reign of Christ, the son of David (Zch 9:9-10; cp. Mt 21:9).

18:1 Part of the promise of the Lord to Abraham was that he and his descendants would inherit a land within which they could discharge their ministry as a people chosen to represent Him to the nations (Gn 12:1-3; 13:14-17). However, the **Levitical priests** would have no such **portion or inheritance** except for the **fire offerings** to be shared with the Lord. In addition, the Levites would be assigned 48 cities throughout the land where they would minister to the local people (v. 6; Nm 35:1-7).

18:2-4 The Lord bestowed an **inheritance** among the other tribes but was Himself the inheritance of Levi. Their office was considered so holy that they could partake of the parts of the sacrifices that otherwise belonged to the Lord but that could not be consumed by the laity. In addition, the people gave them the firstfruits of their produce and livestock since they had no farm lands (Nm 18:1-32).

18:6 Should **a Levite** decide to leave his own town, one of 48 set aside for Levites (cp. v. 1), he could **go to the place the Lord chooses**—the central sanctuary (12:5). This actually happened on a wide scale in late Israelite history but only because many of the Levitical towns had been destroyed in the reformation of King Josiah because of their idolatry (2Kg 23:4-20).

18:8 This passage is somewhat obscure but seems to suggest that Levites did own private properties handed down from father to son. These could be sold, but these added assets should not be used against a Levite to deny him his fair share of the benefits of his office (Nm 5:9-10). One important principle that emerges is that persons in ministry must not be saddled by material things but, at the same

time, must be provided for out of the generosity of God's people.

18:9 Detestable customs refers to anything, especially of a religious nature, that is offensive to the Lord. Israel must not **imitate** these practices that were characteristic of paganism because they had been chosen from among the **nations** to show a better way (Ex 19:5-6; cp. Lv 18:1-5; Dt 7:6).

18:10-11 To **pass through the fire** was to offer human sacrifice. **Divination**, the consulting of natural phenomena such as animal entrails, smoke formations, oil slicks, and the like, was undertaken to determine the plans and purposes of the gods before they happened. A **familiar spirit** is another way of referring to necromancy, the "science" of inquiring of the dead (1Sm 28:3,9; Is 8:19). All such things are essential to religious systems that have no concept of divine revelation. Having no other means of knowing the future, they attempt to elicit this knowledge by forbidden means.

18:12 A major reason for the expulsion and destruction of the Canaanite **nations** is that they practiced **these detestable things** and were therefore likely to infect God's people with their abominable customs (7:4).

18:13 In the context of this verse, to **be blameless before the LORD** was to avoid all the pagan practices outlined in verses 10 and 11. "Blameless" refers not to sinless perfection but to the avoidance of all that the Lord detests.

18:15 In stark contrast to the pagan prophets stood the office of the **prophet** of **the LORD** called and equipped by Him alone. Such spokesmen of God had appeared sporadically throughout Israel's history, including Abraham (Gn 20:7), Miriam the sister of Moses (Ex 15:20), and most prominently, Moses himself (Nm 12:6-8; Dt 34:10).

18:18 The **prophet** like Moses would resemble him in that

and he will tell them everything I command him. [19] I will hold accountable whoever does not listen to My words that he speaks in My name.[a] [20] But the prophet who dares to speak a message in My name that I have not commanded him to speak, or who speaks in the name of other gods—that prophet must die.' [21] You may say to yourself, 'How can we recognize a message the LORD has not spoken?' [22] When a prophet speaks in the LORD's name, and the message does not come true or is not fulfilled, that is a message the LORD has not spoken. The prophet has spoken it presumptuously. Do not be afraid of him.

Cities of Refuge

19 "When the LORD your God annihilates the nations whose land He is giving you,[b] so that you drive them out and live in their cities and houses, [2] you are to set apart three cities for yourselves within the land the LORD your God is giving you to possess.[c] [3] You are to determine the distances[A] and divide the land the LORD your God is granting you as an inheritance into three regions, so that anyone who commits manslaughter can flee to these cities.[B]

[4] "Here is the law concerning a case of someone who kills a person and flees there to save

his life, having killed his neighbor accidentally without previously hating him: [5] If he goes into the forest with his neighbor to cut timber, and his hand swings the ax to chop down a tree, but the blade flies off the handle and strikes his neighbor so that he dies, that person may flee to one of these cities and live. [6] Otherwise, the avenger of blood in the heat of his anger[c] might pursue the one who committed manslaughter, overtake him because the distance is great, and strike him dead. Yet he did not deserve to die,[D] since he did not previously hate his neighbor. [7] This is why I am commanding you to set apart three cities for yourselves. [8] If the LORD your God enlarges your territory as He swore to your fathers, and gives you all the land He promised to give them— [9] provided you keep every one of these commands I am giving you today and follow them, loving the LORD your God and walking in His ways at all times—you are to add three more cities to these three. [10] In this way, innocent blood will not be shed, and you will not become •guilty of bloodshed in the land the LORD your God is giving you as an inheritance.[d] [11] But if someone hates his neighbor, lies in ambush for him, attacks him, and strikes him fatally, and flees to one of these cities, [12] the elders of his city must send for

[a]18:19 Ac 3:23
[b]19:1 Dt 12:29
[c]19:2-13 Nm 35:6-34; Jos 20
[d]19:10 Dt 15:4

A19:3 Or *to prepare the roads*   **B**19:3 Lit *flee there*   **C**19:6 Lit *heart*   **D**19:6 Lit *did not have a judgment of death*

---

he would be an Israelite. He would not conjure up his own message or resort to pagan manipulations but would be a vehicle of divine revelation, speaking only what God put into his mouth (Ex 4:15-16; 7:1-2).

18:19-20 Though this passage has clear messianic overtones (Jn 1:21,25), the admonition about the **prophet**-to-come suggests an order of prophets, primarily the "canonical" prophets, the authors of the various OT Prophetic Books.

18:21-22 The question arises as to how to tell a false prophet from a prophet of the Lord. A fundamental test presented here is that any **prophet** whose **message does not come true or is not fulfilled** has **spoken . . . presumptuously.** He must not be feared because he has no capacity to do harm except as he misleads God's people into error. A classic OT example is Hananiah, who predicted that the Babylonian exile would end in two years rather than the 70 Jeremiah had prophesied (Jr 25:11-12; 28:1-4; 29:10; Dn 9:1-2). Jeremiah confronted him with the truth that the exile would last as long as he had predicted and that Hananiah would never live to see its fulfillment. In fact, Hananiah died the very year of his false message (Jr 28:12-17).

19:1-3 The Israelites must **set apart three cities** of sanctuary or refuge for persons accused of **manslaughter**. These were to be strategically located so that they would be accessible to anyone anywhere in the land. Three cities had already been allotted east of the Jordan River (4:41-43), and there would be a need for three more in Canaan proper. In the event of population growth, three more cities would be added, making nine in all (19:8-9).

19:4-5 Homicide in the OT took many forms, ranging from killing an enemy in war, executing a criminal, and accidental death by manslaughter on one hand, to deliberate and premeditated murder on the other. The first two examples were carried out by the state and obviously were not only permitted but commanded. The present law had to do with an act of homicide whose intentions and circumstances must be determined by a court of law.

19:6 Revenge for murder was not only permitted by the law but fully authorized (Nm 35:16-21). However, it was for malicious murder only and not for accidental homicide as in the present passage. Life is so precious that OT law and custom mandates that its violent destruction must be avenged, especially by the next of kin of the deceased (2Sm 14:1-11).

19:10 The establishment of strategically located cities of refuge would allow accused parties to find safety before unwarranted vengeance could be inflicted. They would preclude **bloodshed in the land the LORD** was giving them. Innocent blood defiled the land so that the land figuratively became hostile toward the guilty person and resisted his attempts to make use of it. When Cain killed Abel, Abel's blood cried out to the Lord from the ground. It would thereafter withhold its yield from Cain (Gn 4:10-12). The soil of Israel would likewise become polluted by the blood of innocent victims (Nm 35:33-34; Dt 19:13).

19:11-12 For the murderer there could be no refuge or safety. Indeed, from the very beginning of human history the penalty for murder was capital punishment by the state. A major stipulation of the covenant with Noah following the flood was,

him, take him from there, and hand him over to the avenger of blood and he will die. ¹³You must not look on him with pity but purge from Israel the guilt of shedding innocent blood, and you will prosper.

Boundary Markers

¹⁴"You must not move your neighbor's boundary marker,ᵃ established at the start in the inheritance you will receive in the land the LORD your God is giving you to possess.

Witnesses in Court

¹⁵"One witness cannot establish any wrongdoing or sin against a person, whatever that person has done.ᵇ A fact must be established by the testimony of two or three witnesses.ᶜ

¹⁶"If a malicious witnessᵈ testifies against someone accusing him of a crime, ¹⁷the two people in the dispute must stand in the presence of the LORD before the priests and judges in authority at that time. ¹⁸The judges are to make a careful investigation, and if the witness turns out to be a liar who has falsely accused his brother, ¹⁹you must do to him as he intended to do to his brother. You must purge the evil from you. ²⁰Then everyone else will hear and be afraid, and they will never again do anything evil like this among you.ᵉ ²¹You must not show pity: life for life, eye for eye, tooth for tooth, hand for hand, and foot for foot.ᶠ

Rules for War

20 "When you go out to war against your enemies and see horses, chariots, and an army larger than yours, do not be afraid of them, for the LORD your God, who brought you out of the land of Egypt,ᵍ is with you. ²When you are about to engage in battle, the priest is to come forward and address the army. ³He is to say to them: 'Listen, Israel: Today you are about to engage in battle with your enemies. Do not be cowardly. Do not be afraid, alarmed, or terrified because of them. ⁴For the LORD your God is the One who goes with you to fight for youʰ against your enemies to give you victory.'

⁵"The officers are to address the army, 'Has any man built a new house and not dedicated it? Let him leave and return home. Otherwise, he may die in battle and another man dedicate it. ⁶Has any man planted a vineyard and not begun to enjoy its fruit?ᴬ Let him leave and return home. Otherwise he may die in battle and another man enjoy its fruit.ᴮ ⁷Has any man become *engaged to a woman and not married her? Let him leave and return home. Otherwise he may die in battle and another man marry her.' ⁸The officers will continue to address the army and say, 'Is there any man who is afraid or cowardly? Let him leave and return home, so that his brothers' hearts won't melt like his own.' ⁹When the officers have finished addressing the army, they will appoint military commanders to lead it.

¹⁰"When you approach a city to fight against it, you must make an offer of peace. ¹¹If it accepts your offer of peace and opens its gates to you, all the people found in it will become forced laborers for you and serve you. ¹²However, if it

ᵃ19:14 Dt 27:17; Pr 22:28; Hs 5:10
ᵇ19:15 Nm 35:30
ᶜMt 18:16; Jn 8:17; 2Co 13:1
ᵈ19:16 Ex 23:1
ᵉ19:20 Dt 13:11
ᶠ19:21 Ex 21:23-25; Lv 24:19-20; Mt 5:38
ᵍ20:1 Dt 1:26-40
ʰ20:4 Ex 14:14; Dt 1:30; Jdg 9:17

ᴬ20:6 Lit *not put it to use*   ᴮ20:6 Lit *man put it to use*

"Whoever sheds man's blood, his blood will be shed by man, for God made man in His image" (Gn 9:6; cp. Dt 5:17).

19:15 To help prevent a miscarriage of justice, the law required **the testimony of two or three witnesses** (cp. 17:6-7).

19:16-20 Should **a malicious witness** turn out to be guilty of perjury, he must suffer the fate intended for the accused. Strict enforcement acts as a deterrent.

19:21 This principle is called (Lat) *lex talionis*, the law of retaliation. An example is the case described in verses 16-19 where a lying witness receives the punishment the accused would have received had he been guilty. There is disagreement as to whether **life for life, eye for eye**, and the rest were to be taken literally or whether the principle was simply that the punishment must fit the crime. The latter seems more likely given other biblical laws that indicate that tit for tat was not always followed (Ex 22:21; Nm 35:31).

20:1-4 War is an unfortunate result of human depravity and in certain forms was sanctioned and even commanded by the Lord in the OT. Deuteronomy pays special attention to the kind traditionally called "holy war" (7:1-6). Primarily conducted against the Canaanite nations, certain forms of **war** could also be waged against more distant nations and still be viewed as holy war. The **enemies** referred to here

were distant ones as verse 15 makes clear. Reference to the LORD as the leader in battle is probably an allusion to the ark of the covenant, the symbol of God's presence with His people, since the priests would have carried it with them (Jos 3:1-4,8,11; 1Sm 4:3; Ps 132:6-10).

20:5-7 Israel had a conscripted army, but there were a number of reasons for deferment, as listed here. The draft law clearly was not rigid and inflexible but revealed sensitivity to human feelings and needs.

20:8 The last reason for deferment affected not just the individual himself but the entire army and is thus separated from the others. Anyone afraid of going to war must be excused because his cowardice would undermine the morale of his fellow soldiers.

20:10-11 Cities outside the areas promised to Israel as an inheritance (cp. v. 15) may be approached with **an offer of peace**, by which is meant terms of surrender, though other cities could not (v. 16). However, even the cities that surrendered peacefully must be reduced to servitude, as illustrated later by Joshua's defeat of the Gibeonites, who professed to be from a distant land (Jos 9:26-27), and by David's treatment of enemies outside Israel (2Sm 8:2,6,14).

20:12-14 Any city that would not surrender could be

does not make peace with you but wages war against you, lay siege to it. [13]When the LORD your God hands it over to you, you must strike down all its males with the sword. [14]But you may take the women, children, animals, and whatever else is in the city—all its spoil—as plunder. You may enjoy the spoil of your enemies that the LORD your God has given you. [15]This is how you are to treat all the cities that are far away from you and are not among the cities of these nations. [16]However, you must not let any living thing survive among the cities of these people the LORD your God is giving you as an inheritance. [17]You must •completely destroy them—the Hittite, Amorite, Canaanite, Perizzite, Hivite, and Jebusite—as the LORD your God has commanded you, [18]so that they won't teach you to do all the detestable things they do for their gods, and you sin against the LORD your God.[a]

[19]"When you lay siege to a city for a long time, fighting against it in order to capture it, you must not destroy its trees by putting an ax to them, because you can get food from them. You must not cut them down. Are trees of the field human, to come under siege by you? [20]But you may destroy the trees that you know do not produce food. You may cut them

a 20:17-18 Dt 7:1-5

down to build siege works against the city that is waging war against you, until it falls.

Unsolved Murders

21 "If a murder victim is found lying in a field in the land the LORD your God is giving you to possess, and it is not known who killed him, [2]your elders and judges must come out and measure the distance from the victim to the nearby cities. [3]The elders of the city nearest to the victim are to get a young cow that has not been yoked or used for work. [4]The elders of that city will bring the cow down to a continually flowing stream, to a place not tilled or sown, and they will break its neck there by the stream. [5]Then the priests, the sons of Levi, will come forward, for •Yahweh your God has chosen them to serve Him and pronounce blessings in His name, and they are to give a ruling in[A] every dispute and case of assault. [6]All the elders of the city nearest to the victim will wash their hands by the stream over the young cow whose neck has been broken. [7]They will declare, 'Our hands did not shed this blood; our eyes did not see it. [8]LORD, forgive Your people Israel You redeemed, and do not hold the shedding of innocent blood against them.' Then they will be absolved of responsibility for bloodshed. [9]You must purge

A 21:5 Lit and according to their mouth will be

plundered and its citizens either killed or taken as prisoners of war. The treatment accorded these distant cities presupposes some kind of provocation against Israel and not likely a desire for Israelite imperialism. David's famous campaign against the Ammonite city of Rabbah is a case in point (2Sm 10:1-19).

20:16-18 Every living thing in the **cities** of Israel's **inheritance** must be put under the *cherem* (Hb; "the ban") and utterly destroyed. This was in line with what the Lord had **commanded** (7:1-6) and with what had already been carried out in Transjordan (Nm 21:24,33-35; cp. Dt 2:31-3:7). Such harsh measures precluded the possibility that these irredeemable inhabitants of Canaan might teach Israel **detestable things**, and Israel might thereby **sin against the LORD**.

20:19-20 Trees which **produce food** must not be cut down, or "killed," during a siege because they are "innocent." The major point in all this is that human beings are different from and privileged beyond all other living things, but this imposes upon them a responsibility to know and serve the Lord with all their being. Failure to do so will result in grievous consequences.

21:1-3 The sense of solidarity among God's people comes to the fore in the case of an anonymous individual who has committed **murder** without witnesses. The city closest to the site will be assumed to have harbored the criminal. This may seem unfair, but the likelihood of the perpetrator being from the closest city in that day of difficult travel was very high.

21:3-7 The ritual that follows was for absolving the community from the sin of only one of its members. A **cow** that had **not been . . . used for work** suggests purity and vitality.

The uncultivated field, like the animal, was full of potential, unlike the victim whose potential had been snuffed out. Next the elders must **break** the cow's **neck** and the priests must **wash their hands**, thus symbolizing their innocence and that of the community. This was no sin offering since no **blood** was **shed**, but it was similar to the rite of breaking the neck of a donkey to be presented as an offering (Ex 13:13), possibly suggesting the fate of the criminal should he ever be apprehended and also of witnesses who failed to come forward.

21:8-9 The testimony of the elders that the people of their

padah

Hebrew Pronunciation	[pah DHAH]
HCSB Translation	redeem, ransom
Uses in Deuteronomy	6
Uses in the OT	60
Focus Passage	Deuteronomy 21:8

Prebiblical Semitic legal use of this root allowed connotations of religion and "setting free." *Padah* indicates change of ownership through payment or substitution. People *redeemed* slave girls to marry them (Lv 19:20). Israel's firstborn had to be *redeemed* (Ex 34:19-20) because God *redeemed* Israel from Egyptian slavery at the cost of Egypt's firstborn (Ex 13:15). God and Israel later recalled this *redemption* (Dt 15:15; 2Sm 7:23). God *redeemed* David from all trouble (2Sm 4:9), and David prayed God would do likewise for Israel (Ps 25:22). Psalmists sought *redemption* from threats like death (Ps 49:7-8,15). *Padah* once describes *redemption* from sin (Ps 130:7-8). Especially when parallel with *ga'al* (also meaning *redeem*), *padah* is translated *ransom* (Hs 13:14).

from yourselves the •guilt of shedding innocent blood, for you will be doing what is right in the LORD's sight.

Fair Treatment of Captured Women

¹⁰"When you go to war against your enemies and the LORD your God hands them over to you and you take some of them prisoner, and ¹¹if you see a beautiful woman among the captives, desire her, and want to take her as your wife, ¹²you are to bring her into your house. She must shave her head, trim her nails, ¹³remove the clothes she was wearing when she was taken prisoner, live in your house, and mourn for her father and mother a full month. After that, you may have sexual relations with her and be her husband, and she will be your wife. ¹⁴Then if you are not satisfied with her, you are to let her go where she wants, but you must not sell her for money or treat her as merchandise,ᴬ because you have humiliated her.

The Right of the Firstborn

¹⁵"If a man has two wives, one loved and the other unloved, and both the loved and the unloved bear him sons, and if the unloved wife has the firstborn son, ¹⁶when that man gives what he has to his sons as an inheritance, he is not to show favoritism to the son of the loved wife as his firstborn over the firstborn of the unloved wife. ¹⁷He must acknowledge the firstborn, the son of the unloved wife, by giving him two sharesᴮ,ᶜ of his estate, for he is the firstfruits of his virility; he has the rights of the firstborn.ᵃ

ᵃ21:15-17 Gn 29:30-33; 49:3
ᵇ21:19 Dt 17:8; 22:15; 25:7
ᶜ21:21 Ex 21:17; Lv 20:9
ᵈ21:23 Gl 3:13
ᵉDt 15:4
ᶠ22:1-3 Ex 23:4

A Rebellious Son

¹⁸"If a man has a stubborn and rebellious son who does not obey his father or mother and doesn't listen to them even after they discipline him, ¹⁹his father and mother must take hold of him and bring him to the elders of his city, to the •gateᵇ of his hometown. ²⁰They will say to the elders of his city, 'This son of ours is stubborn and rebellious; he doesn't obey us. He's a glutton and a drunkard.' ²¹Then all the men of his city will stone him to death.ᶜ You must purge the evil from you, and all Israel will hear and be afraid.

Display of Executed People

²²"If anyone is found guilty of an offense deserving the death penalty and is executed, and you hang his body on a tree, ²³you are not to leave his corpse on the tree overnight but are to bury him that day, for anyone hung on a tree is under God's curse.ᵈ You must not defile the land the LORD your God is giving you as an inheritance.ᵉ

Caring for Your Brother's Property

22 "If you see your brother's ox or sheep straying, you must not ignore it; make sure you return it to your brother. ²If your brother does not live near you or you don't know him, you are to bring the animal to your home to remain with you until your brother comes looking for it; then you can return it to him. ³Do the same for his donkey, his garment, or anything your brother has lost and you have found. You must not ignore it.ᶠ ⁴If you see your brother's donkey or ox fallen

---

ᴬ21:14 Hb obscure   ᴮ21:17 Lit *mouth of two,* or *two mouthfuls*   ᶜ21:17 Or *two-thirds*; the two-thirds interpretation holds that the firstborn son receives two-thirds of the total estate no matter how many sons are in the family.

---

city had neither committed the murder nor witnessed it (v. 7) was followed by an urgent appeal to the Lord that He would not impute to the people collectively the guilt for what only one of them had done.

21:10-14 The fact that female prisoners of war would be taken as wives by Israel does not sanction the practice. The law here was designed to protect the **woman** in such a case. She must be considered as an equal, permitted to display her humiliation by shaving her **head** and trimming her **nails,** and allowed to **mourn for her father and mother a full month.** Only then could her Israelite husband make full claim on her as his **wife.** Further protection was accorded her in the case of divorce.

21:15-17 This law (and perhaps the previous one) regulated the practice of polygamy while, as in the previous example, not endorsing it. Though Israel was the people of God and should have lived out its special relationship reflecting His glory and righteousness, this was often not the case. The law in some cases was thus designed to insure that an imperfect people were kept within certain moral and social boundaries. The present law mandated that a **firstborn son** of an **unloved wife** must receive a **double portion** of the in-

heritance according to what appears to be long-standing custom (Gn 25:31-34; 48:8-22).

21:18-21 Capital punishment for a **rebellious** and drunken **son** may seem unduly harsh, but this behavior was a violation of the commandment to honor one's **father** and **mother** (cp. 5:16). In God's structure of sovereignty, parents represented His authority and therefore showing disobedience to one's parents was showing disobedience of the Lord.

21:22-23 A further humiliation attached to capital punishment was hanging the criminal's corpse from a tree (1Sm 31:10; 2Sm 21:5-6). However, to leave the body on display too long would spread **God's curse** beyond the criminal. The body must therefore be buried before sundown, a practice that continued until the time of Jesus (Gl 3:13).

22:1-4 Brotherly responsibility in Israel was a further application of the principle of oneness inherent in a covenant community. If a person saw a fellow citizen's **ox or sheep straying,** he was obligated to **return it** if the owner was known. Otherwise he must keep it as one of his own until the owner came to claim it. The principle here is that all lands and properties in a sense belonged to all the people

down on the road, you must not ignore it; you must help him lift it up.

Preserving Natural Distinctions

[5]"A woman is not to wear male clothing, and a man is not to put on a woman's garment, for everyone who does these things is detestable to the LORD your God.

[6]"If you come across a bird's nest with chicks or eggs, either in a tree or on the ground along the road, and the mother is sitting on the chicks or eggs, you must not take the mother along with the young. [7]You may take the young for yourself, but be sure to let the mother go free, so that you may prosper and live long. [8]If you build a new house, make a railing around your roof, so that you don't bring bloodguilt on your house if someone falls from it. [9]Do not plant your vineyard with two types of seed; otherwise, the entire harvest, both the crop you plant and the produce of the vineyard, will be defiled. [10]Do not plow with an ox and a donkey together. [11]Do not wear clothes made of both wool and linen.[a] [12]Make tassels on the four corners of the outer garment you wear.[b]

Violations of Proper Sexual Conduct

[13]"If a man marries a woman, has sexual relations with her, and comes to hate her, [14]and accuses her of shameful conduct, and gives her a bad name, saying, 'I married this woman and was intimate with her, but I didn't find any evidence of her virginity,' [15]the young woman's father and mother will take the evidence of her virginity and bring it to the city elders at the *gate.[c] [16]The young woman's father will say to the elders, 'I gave my daughter to this man as a wife, but he hates her. [17]He has accused her of shameful conduct, saying:

"I didn't find any evidence of your daughter's virginity,' but here is the evidence of my daughter's virginity.' They will spread out the cloth before the city elders. [18]Then the elders of that city will take the man and punish him.[d] [19]They will also fine him 100 silver shekels and give them to the young woman's father, because that man gave an Israelite virgin a bad name. She will remain his wife; he cannot divorce her as long as he lives. [20]But if this accusation is true and no evidence of the young woman's virginity is found, [21]they will bring the woman to the door of her father's house, and the men of her city will stone her to death. For she has committed an outrage in Israel by being promiscuous in her father's house. You must purge the evil from you.

[22]"If a man is discovered having sexual relations with another man's wife, both the man who had sex with the woman and the woman must die. You must purge the evil from Israel. [23]If there is a young woman who is a virgin *engaged to a man, and another man encounters her in the city and has sex with her, [24]you must take the two of them out to the gate of that city and stone them to death—the young woman because she did not cry out in the city and the man because he has violated his neighbor's fiancée. You must purge the evil from you. [25]But if the man encounters an engaged woman in the open country, and he seizes and rapes her, only the man who raped her must die. [26]Do nothing to the young woman, because she is not *guilty of an offense deserving death. This case is just like one in which a man attacks his neighbor and murders him. [27]When he found her in the field, the engaged woman cried out, but there was no one to rescue her. [28]If a man

---

collectively as the inheritance of the Lord. The early church adopted this spirit, at least for a time (Ac 4:32).

22:5 For a woman **to wear male clothing** and a man **a woman's garment** (cross-dressing or transvestitism) is wrong because, among other things, it violates the principle of separation that God has built into the created order.

22:6-7 The principle here seems to be that of not mixing life with death. Thus, a **mother** bird, the source of life, must not be taken along with her **chicks** and **eggs** because she would no longer be able to generate new life.

22:9 To plant a **vineyard with two types of seed** makes the point even more clearly that the mixture of unlike things is harmful. Similarly, Israel would be defiled if she mingled with the pagan nations (7:3-4).

22:10 To hitch an **ox and a donkey** up as a team was to invite all kinds of difficulty because of their different natures and habits. Paul chose this law to illustrate how Christians must not marry outside the faith (2Co 6:14-18).

22:13-20 Nowhere was purity of life expected more in ancient Israel than in the realm of sex and marriage, not only because of its inherent rightness but because Israel's relationship to the Lord was often described with the metaphor of marriage (Hs 2:2). The breaking of the covenant that secured marriage was tantamount to divorce brought about by spiritual adultery (Hs 2:3-13). One hundred **shekels** was a considerable amount of money, indicating that damage to the reputation of the girl and her family by false accusations was not to be taken lightly.

22:21-22 The harsh penalty of stoning to death underscores the principle of purity and separation addressed in this section of the book. Israel collectively must be pure before God, with every member of the community responsible for maintaining that holy standard.

22:23-29 If an **engaged . . . virgin** had **sex** with a man **in the city**, it was presumed that she had done so willingly since no one heard her **cry out** in protest. The community must stone him for adultery and her for complicity. If the act took

encounters a young woman, a virgin who is not engaged, takes hold of her and rapes her, and they are discovered, ²⁹the man who raped her must give the young woman's father 50 silver shekels, and she must become his wife because he violated her.ᵃ He cannot divorce her as long as he lives.

³⁰"A man is not to marry his father's wife; he must not violate his father's marriage bed.ᴬ,ᴮ,ᵇ

Exclusion and Inclusion

23 "No man whose testicles have been crushedᶜ or whose penis has been cut off may enter the LORD's assembly. ²No one of illegitimate birth may enter the LORD's assembly; none of his descendants, even to the tenth generation, may enter the LORD's assembly. ³No Ammonite or Moabite may enter the LORD's assembly;ᶜ none of their descendants, even to the tenth generation, may ever enter the LORD's assembly. ⁴This is because they did not meet you with food and water on the journey after you came out of Egypt, and because Balaam son of Beor from Pethor in Aram-naharaim was hired to curse you.ᵈ ⁵Yet the LORD your God would not listen to Balaam, but He turned the curse into a blessing for you because the LORD your God lovesᵉ you.ᶠ ⁶Never seek their peace or prosperity as long as you live. ⁷Do not despise an Edomite, because he is your brother. Do not despise an Egyptian, because you were a foreign resident in his land. ⁸The children born to them in the third generation may enter the LORD's assembly.

Cleanliness of the Camp

⁹"When you are encamped against your enemies, be careful to avoid anything offensive. ¹⁰If there is a man among you who is •unclean because of a bodily emission during the night,

he must go outside the camp; he may not come anywhere inside the camp. ¹¹When evening approaches, he must wash with water, and when the sun sets he may come inside the camp.ᵍ ¹²You must have a place outside the camp and go there to relieve yourself. ¹³You must have a digging tool in your equipment; when you relieve yourself, dig a hole with it and cover up your excrement. ¹⁴For the LORD your God walks throughout your camp to protect you and deliver your enemies to you; so your encampments must be holy. He must not see anything improper among you or He will turn away from you.

Fugitive Slaves

¹⁵"Do not return a slave to his master when he has escaped from his master to you. ¹⁶Let him live among you wherever he wants within your gates. Do not mistreat him.

Cult Prostitution Forbidden

¹⁷"No Israelite woman is to be a cult prostitute, and no Israelite man is to be a cult prostitute. ¹⁸Do not bring a female prostitute's wages or a male prostitute'sᴰ earnings into the house of the LORD your God to fulfill any vow, because both are detestable to the LORD your God.

Interest on Loans

¹⁹"Do not charge your brother interest on money, food, or anything that can earn interest. ²⁰You may charge a foreigner interest, but you must not charge your brother interest, so that the LORD your God may bless you in everything you doᴱ in the land you are entering to possess.ʰ

Keeping Vows

²¹"If you make a vow to the LORD your God,

ᵃ 22:28-29 Ex 22:16-17 ᵇ 22:30 Lv 18:8; 20:10-11 ᶜ 23:3-4 Neh 13:1-2 ᵈ 23:4 Nm 22:5-6 ᵉ 23:5 Dt 4:37 ᶠ Nm 23:11; 24:10 ᵍ 23:11 Lv 15:16-17 ʰ 23:19-20 Ex 22:25

ᴬ 22:30 Dt 23:1 in Hb   ᴮ 22:30 Lit *not uncover the edge of his father's garment*; Ru 3:9; Ezk 16:8   ᶜ 23:1 Lit *man bruised by crushing*
ᴰ 23:18 Lit *a dog's*   ᴱ 23:20 Lit *you put your hand to*

---

place **in the open country**, however, the presumption was that the young woman screamed but **there was no one to rescue her**. She must be exonerated in such a case.

22:30 Father's wife refers to a foster mother. For a man to do such a thing is to be intimate with a woman with whom the father himself has been intimate, thus "exposing his father's nakedness" (a literal rendering; cp. 27:20; Ru 3:9).

23:1-8 Because Israel was to be a pure, undefiled people, certain types of people could not enter **the LORD's assembly**. Such discrimination had nothing to do with inherent worth but served metaphorically to draw attention to the Lord's demand for Israel to be separated from the corrupted and imperfect world around her. In Christ, such disqualifications no longer exist (Gl 3:27-29).

23:9-14 The laws of purity were particularly applicable to holy war in which **God** led His people into battle (7:1-6). Since God is pure and **holy**, He cannot tolerate acts and

conditions that are impure, especially in the context of a religious setting like holy war.

23:15-16 In the context of holy war and Israel's uniqueness, the **slave** here must have **escaped** from a foreign **master**. Contrary to the ordinary practice of repatriating such persons, Israel must show a superior moral code by letting such a slave **live among you wherever he wants**.

23:17-18 A **cult prostitute** was a man or woman engaged in fertility temple rites. This Canaanite practice was taboo to Israel as was the payment of even an ordinary **prostitute's wages** to fulfill a vow made to God. He is not honored by illegitimate expressions of worship but only by obedience (1Sm 15:22-23).

23:21-23 A person could make a **vow to the LORD** in the form of a service to be rendered to Him (Nm 6:2,5,21) or a sacrifice to be offered as an act of worship (Nm 15:8; Dt 12:6; Ps 66:13-14). Though the vow was entered into voluntarily,

do not be slow to keep it, because He will require it of you, and it will be counted against you as sin. [22]But if you refrain from making a vow, it will not be counted against you as sin. [23]Be careful to do whatever comes from your lips, because you have freely vowed what you promised[A] to the LORD your God.[a]

Neighbor's Crops

[24]"When you enter your neighbor's vineyard, you may eat as many grapes as you want until you are full, but you must not put any in your container. [25]When you enter your neighbor's standing grain, you may pluck heads of grain with your hand, but you must not put a sickle to your neighbor's grain.

Marriage and Divorce Laws

24 "If a man marries a woman, but she becomes displeasing to him because he finds something improper about her, he may write her a divorce certificate, hand it to her, and send her away from his house.[b] [2]If after leaving his house she goes and becomes another man's wife, [3]and the second man hates her, writes her a divorce certificate, hands it to her, and sends her away from his house or if he[B] dies, [4]the first husband who sent her away may not marry her again after she has been defiled, because that would be detestable to the LORD. You must not bring *guilt on the land the LORD your God is giving you as an inheritance.[c]

[5]"When a man takes a bride, he must not go out with the army or be liable for any duty. He is free to stay at home for one year, so that he can bring joy to the wife he has married.

Safeguarding Life

[6]"Do not take a pair of millstones or an upper millstone as security for a debt, because that is like taking a life as security.

[7]"If a man is discovered kidnapping[d] one of his Israelite brothers, whether he treats him as a slave or sells him, the kidnapper must die. You must purge the evil from you.

[8]"Be careful in a case of infectious skin disease, following carefully everything the Levitical priests instruct you to do. Be careful to do as I have commanded them. [9]Remember what the LORD your God did to Miriam on the journey after you left Egypt.[e]

Consideration for People in Need

[10]"When you make a loan of any kind to your neighbor, do not enter his house to collect what he offers as security. [11]You must stand outside while the man you are making the loan to brings the security out to you. [12]If he is a poor man, you must not sleep in the garment he has given as security. [13]Be sure to return it[C] to him at sunset. Then he will sleep in it and bless you, and this will be counted as righteousness to you before the LORD your God.[f]

[14]"Do not oppress a hired hand who is poor and needy, whether one of your brothers or one of the foreigners residing within a town[D] in your land. [15]You are to pay him his wages each day before the sun sets, because he is poor and depends on them.[g] Otherwise he will cry out to the LORD against you, and you will be held guilty.

[16]"Fathers are not to be put to death for their children or children for their fathers; each person will be put to death for his own sin.[h] [17]Do not deny justice to a foreigner or fatherless child, and do not take a widow's garment as security. [18]Remember that you were a slave

a23:21-23 Nm 30:2-15; Jb 22:27; Ps 50:14; 56:12; 61:8; Pr 20:25; Ec 5:4-7; Mal 1:14
b24:1 Mt 5:31; 19:7; Mk 10:4
c24:4 Dt 15:4
d24:7 Gn 40:15; Ex 21:16; 22:1; 1Sm 30:2-3,5; 1Tm 1:10
e24:9 Nm 12:1-15; Dt 25:17
f24:12-13 Ex 22:26-27
g24:14-15 Lv 19:13
h24:16 2Kg 14:6; 2Ch 25:4; Ezk 18:20; 33:10-20

A23:23 Lit promised with your mouth   B24:3 Lit if the second man who has taken her as his wife   C24:13 Lit return what he has given as security   D24:14 Lit within the gates

---

refusing to pay it once it was made was to steal from the Lord what was rightfully His.

23:24-25 A person who crossed through a **neighbor's vineyard** or **grain** field could harvest as much as he could gather and hold in his hand. To exceed that would be to take advantage of the neighbor's generosity, and it would be a form of theft. Jesus and His disciples practiced this on the Sabbath with no criticism from the Pharisees except that they were violating the Sabbath (Mk 2:23-28).

24:1-4 The issue here is not divorce *per se* but remarriage following divorce. What the **man** found **improper** is neither clear nor relevant. The point is that if she marries another man and he finds occasion to divorce her, she may not return to her **first husband**. The issue seems to be that marriage to a second husband was a form of adultery. Another consideration is that the prohibition of the first husband taking the woman back would cause husbands to think carefully before enacting a divorce.

24:6 The poor could not be required to promise as collateral items essential to life and well-being. **A pair of millstones** for grinding food must not be demanded **as security** because human **life** depended on them. Taking just the **upper millstone** similarly rendered the pair unusable. There must be mercy as well as justice in applying the law (cp. vv. 12-13).

24:9 The reference to **Miriam** recalls the incident when Aaron and Miriam challenged the God-ordained leadership of Moses. As a result Miriam was struck with a loathsome skin disease (Nm 12:10-12).

24:14-15 An employer must pay wages to the **poor and needy** every day. Otherwise, he would be answerable not to a mere human higher power but to the Lord Himself.

24:16 Though Israelite families were tight knit (Jos 7:24-26), each family member must **be put to death for his own sin**. Jeremiah expanded on this principle when he observed

in Egypt, and the Lord your God redeemed[a] you from there. Therefore I am commanding you to do this.[b]

[19] "When you reap the harvest in your field, and you forget a sheaf in the field, do not go back to get it. It is to be left for the foreigner, the fatherless, and the widow, so that the Lord your God may bless you in all the work of your hands.[c] [20] When you knock down the fruit from your olive tree, you must not go over the branches again. What remains will be for the foreigner, the fatherless, and the widow. [21] When you gather the grapes of your vineyard, you must not glean what is left. What remains will be for the foreigner, the fatherless, and the widow. [22] Remember that you were a slave in the land of Egypt. Therefore I am commanding you to do this.[d]

Fairness and Mercy

25 "If there is a dispute between men, they are to go to court, and the judges will hear their case. They will clear the innocent and condemn the •guilty. [2] If the guilty party deserves to be flogged, the judge will make him lie down and be flogged in his presence with the number of lashes appropriate for his crime. [3] He may be flogged with 40 lashes, but no more. Otherwise, if he is flogged with more lashes than these, your brother will be degraded in your sight.

[4] "Do not muzzle an ox while it treads out grain.[e]

Preserving the Family Line

[5] "When brothers live on the same property[A] and one of them dies without a son, the wife of the dead man may not marry a stranger outside the family. Her brother-in-law is to take

her as his wife, have sexual relations with her, and perform the duty of a brother-in-law for her. [6] The first son she bears will carry on the name of the dead brother, so his name will not be blotted out from Israel.[f] [7] But if the man doesn't want to marry his sister-in-law, she must go to the elders at the city •gate[g] and say, 'My brother-in-law refuses to preserve his brother's name in Israel. He isn't willing to perform the duty of a brother-in-law for me.' [8] The elders of his city will summon him and speak with him. If he persists and says, 'I don't want to marry her,' [9] then his sister-in-law will go up to him in the sight of the elders, remove his sandal from his foot, and spit in his face. Then she will declare, 'This is what is done to a man who will not build up his brother's house.' [10] And his family name in Israel will be called 'The house of the man whose sandal was removed.'[h]

[11] "If two men are fighting with each other, and the wife of one steps in to rescue her husband from the one striking him, and she puts out her hand and grabs his genitals, [12] you are to cut off her hand. You must not show pity.

Honest Weights and Measures

[13] "You must not have two different weights[B] in your bag, one heavy and one light.[i] [14] You must not have two differing dry measures in your house, a larger and a smaller. [15] You must have a full and honest weight, a full and honest dry measure, so that you may live long in the land the Lord your God is giving you. [16] For everyone who does such things and acts unfairly is detestable to the Lord your God.[j]

Revenge on the Amalekites

[17] "Remember what the Amalekites did to you

---

[a] 24:18 Dt 7:8; 9:26; 15:15
[b] Dt 15:15; 24:22
[c] 24:18-19 Ex 23:2-3,6-9; Dt 30:9
[d] 24:19-22 Ex 22:26-27; Lv 19:9-10,13,15
[e] 25:4 1Co 9:9; 1Tm 5:18
[f] 25:5-6 Gn 38:8; Mt 22:24; Mk 12:19; Lk 20:28
[g] 25:7 Dt 17:8; 21:19; 22:15
[h] 25:10 Gn 38; Ru 4:1-12
[i] 25:13 Pr 20:10
[j] 25:16 Lv 19:35-36

A 25:5 Lit *live together*   B 25:13 Lit *have a stone and a stone*

---

that "In those days, it will never again be said: 'The fathers have eaten sour grapes, and the children's teeth are set on edge.' Rather, each will die for his own wrongdoing" (Jr 31:29-30; cp. Ezk 18).

24:19 In the absence of governmental welfare programs in ancient Israel, the wealthy took responsibility for the less fortunate. As an example, if a farmer should **forget a sheaf in the field** he must leave it for the poor and landless to gather (cp. vv. 20-21). A famous illustration of this occurred in the story of Boaz and Ruth. Boaz, realizing he was next of kin to the unsuspecting Ruth, purposefully left scatterings of grain in his fields for her (Ru 2:15-18).

25:3 Limiting the number of **lashes** addresses the fine balance between justice and mercy. The first-century practice of inflicting 39 lashes was to ensure that no more than 40 would accidentally be applied (2Co 11:24).

25:4 Mercy in the application of the law extended even to the treatment of animals, which were to share the fruits of their labor. Paul applied this principle to paying a fair

wage to those engaged in ministry (1Co 9:9-14; cp. 1Tm 5:17-18).

25:5-10 Passing a man's name to future generations was so important that should a man die without a son, his widow must attempt to have a son by one of her brothers-in-law. This was called the levirate custom (from Latin *levir*, "brother-in-law").

25:11-12 Interpreters differ over the meaning of this passage. One possibility is that the woman who forcefully grabbed her husband's opponent by his **genitals** during a fight was to be punished so severely because her act risked emasculating the assailant to the point that he might be unable to sire children.

25:13-16 Differing **weights** and **measures** in this case would constitute theft, the violation of one of the Ten Commandments (5:19).

25:17-19 The **Amalekites** had attacked Israel in the Sinai Desert and consequently had come under God's judgment (Ex 17:8-16). There would be a time of reckoning when Amalek,

on the journey after you left Egypt.[a] [18]They met you along the way and attacked all your stragglers from behind when you were tired and weary. They did not ·fear God. [19]When the LORD your God gives you rest[b] from all the enemies around you in the land the LORD your God is giving you to possess as an inheritance,[c] blot out the memory of Amalek under heaven. Do not forget.[d]

Giving the Firstfruits

26 "When you enter the land the LORD your God is giving you as an inheritance,[e] and you take possession of it and live in it, [2]you must take some of the first of all the land's produce that you harvest from the land ·Yahweh your God is giving you and put it in a container. Then go to the place where the LORD your God chooses to have His name dwell.[f] [3]When you come before the priest who is serving at that time, you must say to him, 'Today I acknowledge to the LORD your[A] God that I have entered the land the LORD swore to our fathers to give us.'

[4]"Then the priest will take the container from your hand and place it before the altar of the LORD your God. [5]You are to respond by saying in the presence of the LORD your God:

My father was a wandering Aramean.[g] He went down to Egypt with a few people and lived there.[h] There he became a great, powerful, and populous nation. [6]But the Egyptians mistreated and afflicted us, and forced us to do hard labor. [7]So we called out to Yahweh, the God of our fathers, and the LORD heard our cry and saw our misery, hardship, and oppression.[i] [8]Then the LORD brought us out of Egypt with a strong hand and an outstretched arm, with terrifying power, and with signs and wonders. [9]He led us to this place and gave us this land, a land flowing with milk and honey.[j] [10]I have

now brought the first of the land's produce that You, LORD, have given me.

You will then place the container before the LORD your God and bow down to Him. [11]You, the Levite, and the foreign resident among you will rejoice[k] in all the good things the LORD your God has given you and your household.

The Tenth in the Third Year

[12]"When you have finished paying all the tenth of your produce in the third year,[l] the year of the tenth, you are to give it to the Levite, the foreigner, the fatherless, and the widow, so that they may eat in your towns and be satisfied. [13]Then you will say in the presence of the LORD your God:

I have taken the consecrated portion out of my house; I have also given it to the Levite, the foreigner, the fatherless, and the widow, according to all the commands You gave me. I have not violated or forgotten Your commands. [14]I have not eaten any of it while in mourning, or removed any of it while ·unclean, or offered any of it for the dead.[m] I have obeyed the LORD my God; I have done all You commanded me. [15]Look down from Your holy dwelling, from heaven, and bless Your people Israel and the land You have given us as You swore to our fathers, a land flowing with milk and honey.

Covenant Summary

[16]"The LORD your God is commanding you this day to follow these statutes and ordinances. You must be careful to follow them with all your heart and all your soul. [17]Today you have affirmed that the LORD is your God and that you will walk in His ways, keep His statutes, commands, and ordinances, and obey Him. [18]And today the LORD has affirmed that you are His special people as He promised you,

---

[a] 25:17 Dt 24:9
[b] 25:19 Dt 3:20; 5:14; 12:9-11; 28:65
[c] Dt 15:4
[d] Ex 17:8-16; 1Sm 15; 30
[e] 26:1 Dt 15:4; 17:14
[f] 26:2 Dt 12:11
[g] 26:5 Gn 28:5
[h] Ex 1:1-3
[i] 26:7 Ex 3:7
[j] 26:9 Dt 11:9; Jr 32:22
[k] 26:11 Lv 23:40; Dt 12:12; 14:26; 16:11; 27:7
[l] 26:12 Dt 14:28-29
[m] 26:14 Jr 16:7; Ezk 24:17; Hs 9:4

[A]26:3 LXX reads *my*

---

like all of the Lord's unrepentant enemies, would come under the destruction of holy war (1Sm 15; cp. Dt 7:1-6).

26:2 The **first . . . produce** is most likely a reference to the Festival of Firstfruits (Gk *Pentecost*), 50 days after the Festival of Passover and Unleavened Bread (cp. Ex 34:26; Lv 23:10). While Israel was in the wilderness they subsisted largely on heavenly manna, but in Canaan they would settle down, plant crops, and live off the produce of the land (Jos 5:10-12). It was fitting then that the people should acknowledge God's goodness by offering Him the first and best of their crops.

26:5-10 Like later church creeds, these verses encapsulate Israel's core beliefs in the form of a resumé of God's mighty acts in history on her behalf (cp. Gn 12:1; 13:14-17; Ex 13:11).

26:12 In the absence of governmental welfare and a paid clergy in OT Israel (cp. 24:19-22), these needy groups must be cared for with the **tenth** of the **produce** given every **third year**. In the other two years, it would be fully given to the Lord.

26:15 To give to poor and dependent persons is to give to the Lord Himself. Having done that, the Israelites could with good cause invoke God's blessing upon the nation.

26:16-19 The bilateral character of the covenant of **these statutes and ordinances** is apparent from the fact that Israel had affirmed that the Lord was their God and the Lord had affirmed in turn that they were His special people (Ex 19:5; cp. Dt 7:6).

that you are to keep all His commands, [19]that He will elevate you to praise, fame, and glory above all the nations He has made, and that you will be a holy people[a] to the LORD your God as He promised."

The Law Written on Stones

27 Moses and the elders of Israel commanded the people, "Keep every command I am giving you today. [2]At the time you cross the Jordan into the land the LORD your God is giving you, you must set up large stones and cover them with plaster.[b] [3]Write all the words of this law on the stones after you cross to enter the land the LORD your God is giving you, a land flowing with milk and honey,[c] as •Yahweh, the God of your fathers, has promised you. [4]When you have crossed the Jordan, you are to set up these stones on Mount Ebal, as I am commanding you today, and you are to cover them with plaster. [5]Build an altar of stones there to the LORD your God—you must not use any iron tool on them.[d] [6]Use uncut stones to build the altar of the LORD your God and offer •burnt offerings to the LORD your God on it. [7]There you are to sacrifice •fellowship offerings, eat, and rejoice in the presence of the LORD your God. [8]Write clearly all the words of this law on the plastered stones."

The Covenant Curses

[9]Moses and the Levitical priests spoke to all

a 26:19 Dt 7:6
b 27:2-8 Jos 8:30-32
c 27:3 Dt 11:9
d 27:5-7 Ex 20:25
e 27:12-13 Dt 11:29-30; Jos 8:33-35

Israel, "Be silent, Israel, and listen! This day you have become the people of the LORD your God. [10]Obey the LORD your God and follow His commands and statutes I am giving you today."

[11]On that day Moses commanded the people, [12]"When you have crossed the Jordan, these tribes will stand on Mount Gerizim to bless the people: Simeon, Levi, Judah, Issachar, Joseph, and Benjamin. [13]And these tribes will stand on Mount Ebal to deliver the curse: Reuben, Gad, Asher, Zebulun, Dan, and Naphtali.[e] [14]The Levites will proclaim in a loud voice to every Israelite:

[15]'The person who makes a carved idol or cast image, which is detestable to the LORD, the work of a craftsman, and sets it up in secret is cursed.'
And all the people will reply, "Amen!'
[16]'The one who dishonors his father or mother is cursed.'
And all the people will say, 'Amen!'
[17]'The one who moves his neighbor's boundary marker is cursed.'
And all the people will say, 'Amen!'
[18]'The one who leads a blind person astray on the road is cursed.'
And all the people will say, 'Amen!'
[19]'The one who denies justice to a foreigner, a fatherless child, or a widow is cursed.'

27:6 The **burnt offerings** provided a means of dealing with sins and trespasses, thus opening the way to fellowship with the Lord. The fellowship offerings were essential to the making and reaffirmation of the covenant relationship (Ex 24:3-8).

27:9 The statement that **this day you have become the people of the LORD your God** does not mean that just now Israel

had entered into that relationship for the first time. It represents a renewal of the covenant by which Israel, in a sense, was becoming the people of the Lord all over again.

27:11-13 Referring again to the upcoming covenant renewal conclave at Shechem (v. 4), Moses instructed the people upon their arrival there to divide into two groups by **tribes**, half on **Mount Gerizim** and half on **Mount Ebal**. Like a great antiphonal chorus, the tribes on Mount Gerizim would shout out the blessings and the tribes on Mount Ebal would shout the curses of the covenant commitments in the hearing of the Levites in the valley below (v. 14).

27:15 The list of curses began with a word of judgment against anyone who made **a carved idol or cast image**, a violation of the Second Commandment (5:8-10). The other curses flowed out of this, though all of them pertained to interpersonal relationships and not directly to a person's relationship to the Lord.

27:16 The word **dishonors** is a translation of a Hebrew verb meaning "to make light of" (5:16). The person who underestimates the role of parents disrespects the honor and glory of God, whom parents represent.

27:17 The sin of moving a **neighbor's boundary marker** was a kind of theft, a violation of the Eighth Commandment, and also it betrayed a lack of satisfaction with what God had allotted a person in life.

27:19 Social justice must be rooted in God's care for

shamar

Hebrew Pronunciation	[shah MAR]
HCSB Translation	keep, watch, guard
Uses in Deuteronomy	73
Uses in the OT	469
Focus passage	Deuteronomy 27:1

Shamar means *keep* (Gn 17:9), *maintain, tend, preserve, continue,* or *guarantee.* It is *watch, observe* (Ezk 43:11), *take note,* or *notice.* It denotes *stand watch, guard* (Gn 3:24), *restrain, safeguard, protect, watch over, care for* (Ex 22:10), *take care of, look after, be in charge of,* or *be responsible for.* People *do, obey, carry out* (Jos 22:3), *fulfill,* or *perform* duties. *Shamar* means *besiege* (2Sm 11:16), *avoid* (Ps 17:4), or *appoint* (2Sm 22:44). One *is devoted to* or *clings to* (Jnh 2:8). Participles signify *watchman, guardian, keeper, spy* (Jdg 1:24), or *sentry.* Passive participles indicate *secured* (2Sm 23:5) or *saved.* Passive-reflexive verbs convey *make/be sure* (Gn 24:6), *pay attention* (Ex 23:13), *calm down,* and *be careful, on guard,* or *kept safe* (Ps 37:28). With other verbs *shamar* implies *carefully* or *exactly* (Nm 23:12). People *spare* life, *follow* instruction, *uphold* justice, *remain* faithful, *harbor* rage, and *accept* rebuke.

And all the people will say, 'Amen!'
²⁰'The one who sleeps with his father's wife is cursed, for he has violated his father's marriage bed.'^A
And all the people will say, 'Amen!'
²¹'The one who has sexual intercourse with any animal is cursed.'
And all the people will say, 'Amen!'
²²'The one who sleeps with his sister, whether his father's daughter or his mother's daughter is cursed.'
And all the people will say, 'Amen!'
²³'The one who sleeps with his mother-in-law is cursed.'
And all the people will say, 'Amen!'
²⁴'The one who secretly kills his neighbor is cursed.'
And all the people will say, 'Amen!'
²⁵'The one who accepts a bribe to kill an innocent person is cursed.'
And all the people will say, 'Amen!'
²⁶'Anyone who does not put the words of this law into practice is cursed.'
And all the people will say, 'Amen!'

Blessings for Obedience

28 "Now if you faithfully obey the LORD your God and are careful to follow all His commands I am giving you today, the LORD your God will put you far above all the nations of the earth.^a ²All these blessings will come and overtake you, because you obey the LORD your God:

Margin references:
^a 28:1-14 Lv 26:3-13
^b 28:4 Dt 7:13
^c 28:9 Dt 7:6
^d 28:12 Dt 30:9

³ You will be blessed in the city
   and blessed in the country.
⁴ Your descendants^B will be blessed,
   and your land's produce,
   and the offspring of your livestock,
   including the young of your herds
   and the newborn of your flocks.^b
⁵ Your basket and kneading bowl
   will be blessed.
⁶ You will be blessed when you come in
   and blessed when you go out.

⁷"The LORD will cause the enemies who rise up against you to be defeated before you. They will march out against you from one direction but flee from you in seven directions. ⁸The LORD will grant you a blessing on your storehouses and on everything you do;^c He will bless you in the land the LORD your God is giving you. ⁹The LORD will establish you as His holy people,^c as He swore to you, if you obey the commands of the LORD your God and walk in His ways. ¹⁰Then all the peoples of the earth will see that you are called by 'Yahweh's name, and they will stand in awe of you. ¹¹The LORD will make you prosper abundantly with children,^D the offspring of your livestock, and your land's produce in the land the LORD swore to your fathers to give you. ¹²The LORD will open for you His abundant storehouse, the sky, to give your land rain in its season and to bless all the work of your hands.^d You will lend to many nations, but you will not bor-

---

^A27:20 Lit *has uncovered the edge of his father's garment*; Ru 3:9; Ezk 16:8   ^B28:4 Lit *The fruit of your womb*   ^C28:8 Lit *you put your hand to*   ^D28:11 Lit *abundantly in the fruit of your womb*

---

vulnerable people in society. The person who denies **justice** to such helpless people goes against the nature of the Lord, who inspired law to regulate such matters (24:17) and who, in the person of Christ, identified with those most in need of justice (Php 2:5-11; cp. 2Co 8:9).

27:20 Father's wife has in mind either one's stepmother or a second wife of one's father (22:30; cp. Lv 18:7-8; 20:11). The father's own shame was at risk when a son had sexual relations with a woman known so intimately by his father.

27:21 Bestiality—**sexual intercourse** with an **animal**—is not only reprehensible, but it goes against God's creation order in which humankind, made in the image of God, is to rule over all other created beings, not to be on the same level with them.

27:22 The **sister** here is a sibling related through polygamy. A **father's daughter** or a **mother's daughter** would thus be a daughter by one's stepmother or stepfather.

27:26 The list of curses is summarized by the warning that covenant violation consisted not only of committing certain misdeeds but failing to observe others. The **law** quoted is the entire book of Deuteronomy and not just this list.

28:2 In an interesting figure of speech, Moses promised that the **blessings** for covenant obedience would not merely lie at hand passively, but with dynamic life and power would **overtake** the obedient person. There is no escaping the

blessings and favor of the Lord when a person is careful to **obey** Him.

28:3 The promise to **be blessed in the city** and **in the country** uses a figure of speech called a "merism," in this case indicating blessing with no geographical limitations. Wherever the obedient person went, God's favor would follow.

28:6 To be blessed **when you come in** and **when you go out** is another merism (v. 3) suggesting no temporal limitation (cp. 6:7). God would bless the obedient all their lives.

28:7 An oncoming enemy moves as a solid phalanx, confident in its own power, but if Israel stayed true to the Lord, that concentrated force would flee from her in disgrace.

28:9 The promise of the Lord here to establish Israel does not mean that they had not previously enjoyed that status. They were already His people by virtue of the Abrahamic covenant and its ratification at Sinai (Gn 17:3-8; cp. Ex 19:4-6). The verb translated **establish** bears the idea of confirming or reaffirming. **Holy** means that Israel was a **people** set apart from all others (Ex 19:6), but it also carries the idea of moral and spiritual purity.

28:10 If Israel obeyed the terms of the covenant, they would then indeed be the kingdom of priests and the holy nation that God created them to be, the means by which God would bless all the nations, as He had promised Abraham (Gn 12:3; 22:18; 26:4).

row. [13]The LORD will make you the head and not the tail; you will only move upward and never downward if you listen to the LORD your God's commands I am giving you today and are careful to follow them. [14]Do not turn aside to the right or the left from all the things I am commanding you today, and do not go after other gods to worship them.

Curses for Disobedience

[15]"But if you do not obey the LORD your God by carefully following all His commands and statutes I am giving you today, all these curses will come and overtake you:[a]

[16] You will be cursed in the city
and cursed in the country.
[17] Your basket and kneading bowl
will be cursed.
[18] Your descendants[A] will be cursed,
and your land's produce,
the young of your herds,
and the newborn of your flocks.
[19] You will be cursed when you come in
and cursed when you go out.

[20]The LORD will send against you curses, confusion, and rebuke in everything you do[B] until you are destroyed and quickly perish, because of the wickedness of your actions in abandoning Me. [21]The LORD will make pestilence cling to you until He has exterminated you from the land you are entering to possess. [22]The LORD will afflict you with wasting disease, fever, inflammation, burning heat, drought,[c] blight, and mildew; these will pur-

sue you until you perish. [23]The sky above you will be bronze, and the earth beneath you iron. [24]The LORD will turn the rain of your land into falling[D] dust; it will descend on you from the sky until you are destroyed. [25]The LORD will cause you to be defeated before your enemies. You will march out against them from one direction but flee from them in seven directions. You will be an object of horror to all the kingdoms of the earth. [26]Your corpses will be food for all the birds of the sky and the wild animals of the land, with no one to scare them away.[b]

[27]"The LORD will afflict you with the boils of Egypt, tumors, a festering rash, and scabies, from which you cannot be cured. [28]The LORD will afflict you with madness, blindness, and mental confusion, [29]so that at noon you will grope as a blind man gropes in the dark.[c] You will not be successful in anything you do. You will only be oppressed and robbed continually, and no one will help you. [30]You will become •engaged to a woman, but another man will rape her. You will build a house but not live in it. You will plant a vineyard but not enjoy its fruit. [31]Your ox will be slaughtered before your eyes, but you will not eat any of it. Your donkey will be taken away from you and not returned to you. Your flock will be given to your enemies, and no one will help you. [32]Your sons and daughters will be given to another people, while your eyes grow weary looking for them every day. But you will be powerless to do anything.[E] [33]A people you don't know

Cross references (margin):
[a]28:15-68 Lv 26:14-46
[b]28:26 Jr 7:33; 16:4
[c]28:28-29 Is 59:9-10

[A]28:18 Lit *The fruit of your womb*   [B]28:20 Lit *you put your hand to*   [C]28:22 Or *sword*   [D]28:24 Lit *powder and*   [E]28:32 Lit *day, and not for power your hand*

28:13 The **head** determines in which direction the whole animal moves while the **tail** just follows along. Israel was brought into being as God's channel of blessing and hope to the world, to be the head of all the nations (Jr 31:7). Should they fail, however, they would become the tail (cp. Dt 28:44).

28:14 The Lord's fundamental requirement was that the Israelites acknowledge only Him as God (5:6-7; cp. 6:4). The greatest possible sin was that they would worship **other gods**. It is fitting that the list of blessings should be climaxed by the injunction to remain faithful to the Lord.

28:15 The **curses** for disobedience were as certain to come as were the blessings for obedience.

28:21 The term translated **pestilence** refers to sickness in general and not to a particular disease. Literal disease did, indeed, afflict Israel from time to time (2Sm 24:13; 1Kg 8:37), but the allusion here to expulsion from the land suggests that pestilence is a metaphor or a means for deportation by enemies (Lv 26:25).

28:23-24 The metaphors of a **bronze** sky and an **iron** earth underscore the severity of the drought referred to in verse 22 (cp. Lv 26:19). The scene is one of absolute hopelessness.

28:25 Disobeying God's covenant would bring such devastation to Israel that the nations would no longer be in awe of her. What should have been a focus of others' admiration and praise would become so disfigured as to elicit nothing but disgust and revulsion (Jr 15:4; 29:18; 34:17).

28:27 Just as the exodus of Israel from Egypt was the sign of God's favor, their covenant failures would initiate a kind of reverse exodus. They would experience the **boils of Egypt** along with a host of other afflictions reminiscent of the ten plagues.

28:29 Continuing the exodus theme, Moses contrasted Israel's experience in Egypt where the Lord was present, with future judgment when the Lord would be absent and **no one** would help them. Unfaithful Israel would be on her own.

28:30 Ordinarily, young men were exempt from military service under certain circumstances (20:5-7). Such gracious provision would someday be taken away in another reversal of fortune, and other calamities listed here would take place as well. The life of disobedience stands in opposition and reversal to life lived in obedience to God's will.

28:33 Oppression by **a people you don't know** was fulfilled a number of times throughout Israel's history, notably in the

will eat your land's produce and everything you have labored for. You will only be oppressed and crushed continually. ³⁴You will be driven mad by what you see. ³⁵The LORD will afflict you with painful and incurable boils on your knees and thighs—from the sole of your foot to the top of your head.ᵃ

³⁶"The LORD will bring you and your king that you have appointed to a nation neither you nor your fathers have known, and there you will worship other gods, of wood and stone. ³⁷You will become an object of horror, scorn, and ridicule among all the peoples where the LORD will drive you.ᵇ

³⁸"You will sow much seed in the field but harvest little, because locusts will devour it. ³⁹You will plant and cultivate vineyards but not drink the wine or gather the grapes, because worms will eat them. ⁴⁰You will have olive trees throughout your territory but not anoint yourself with oil, because your olives will drop off. ⁴¹You will father sons and daughters, but they will not remain yours, because they will be taken prisoner. ⁴²Whirring insects will take possession of all your trees and your land's produce. ⁴³The foreign resident among you will rise higher and higher above you, while you sink lower and lower. ⁴⁴He will lend to you, but you won't lend to him. He will be the head, and you will be the tail.

⁴⁵"All these curses will come, pursue, and overtake you until you are destroyed, since you did not obey the LORD your God and keep the commands and statutes He gave you. ⁴⁶These curses will be a sign and a wonder against you

Cross references:
ᵃ 28:35 Is 1:6
ᵇ 28:37 1Kg 9:7; 2Ch 7:20; Jr 24:9
ᶜ 28:48 Jr 28:13-14
ᵈ 28:53 2Kg 6:25-29; Jr 19:9; Lm 2:20; 4:10

and your descendants forever. ⁴⁷Because you didn't serve the LORD your God with joy and a cheerful heart, even though you had an abundance of everything, ⁴⁸you will serve your enemies the LORD will send against you, in famine, thirst, nakedness, and a lack of everything. He will place an iron yokeᶜ on your neck until He has destroyed you. ⁴⁹The LORD will bring a nation from far away, from the ends of the earth, to swoop down on you like an eagle, a nation whose language you don't understand, ⁵⁰a ruthless nation,ᴬ showing no respect for the old and not sparing the young. ⁵¹They will eat the offspring of your livestock and your land's produce until you are destroyed. They will leave you no grain, new wine, oil, young of your herds, or newborn of your flocks until they cause you to perish. ⁵²They will besiege you within all your gates until your high and fortified walls, that you trust in, come down throughout your land. They will besiege you within all your gates throughout the land the LORD your God has given you.

⁵³"You will eat your children,ᴮ the flesh of your sons and daughters the LORD your God has given youᵈ during the siege and hardship your enemy imposes on you. ⁵⁴The most sensitive and refined man among you will look grudginglyᶜ at his brother, the wife he embraces,ᴰ and the rest of his children, ⁵⁵refusing to share with any of them his children's flesh that he will eat because he has nothing left during the siege and hardship your enemy imposes on you in all your towns. ⁵⁶The most sensitive and refined woman among you, who

ᴬ 28:50 Lit *a nation strong of face*   ᴮ 28:53 Lit *eat the fruit of your womb*   ᶜ 28:54 Lit *you his eye will be evil*   ᴰ 28:54 Lit *wife of his bosom*

days of the judges when foreigners wreaked havoc in Israel and even settled there (Jdg 6:1-6; 8:22).

28:36-37 Foreign occupation was followed by deportation. Moses prophesied that rebellious Israel would be uprooted by the Lord Himself and they and their king would worship other gods in a strange nation neither they nor their fathers had known. This rules out Egypt, of course, which their fathers knew well. History discloses that they ended up in Assyria (2Kg 17:6) and Babylonia (2Kg 24:10-17).

28:44 Rather than being the influential **head** of the nations, as God had intended for Israel to be (v. 13), they would become a powerless **tail** because of their unfaithfulness.

28:46 Usually **a sign and a wonder** indicated the presence and blessing of God (4:34; 7:19; 26:8; Jr 32:21). He performed them to display His incomparable power and glory, especially in the eyes of a doubting world. Jesus performed signs and wonders to validate His ministry and to demonstrate His divine nature (Jn 20:30-31). On the day of Israel's judgment, however, the curses listed in this passage would become signs and wonders not in support of the Lord and His power but as testimony against Israel. When the nations saw His wrath poured out against His own chosen people, they would stand in awe at the fall of a people who had been

greatly blessed. Israel through all the generations to come would be reminded by their disastrous end that disobedience of the Lord's covenant carries a heavy cost.

28:48 An **iron yoke** speaks metaphorically of bondage so severe that it is inescapable. Prisoners of war wore yokes to secure them against escape and to humiliate them. Jeremiah described the Babylonian captivity of Judah as one in which the people would bear the yoke of oppression (Jr 27:7-8) until the Lord broke it (Jr 28:14; 30:8; Ezk 34:27).

28:49-52 The **nation from far away** turned out to be Assyria, as is made clear in light of later biblical events and descriptions. Assyria besieged Samaria, Israel's capital city, for three years until the city was forced to surrender (2Kg 17:5).

28:53-57 The siege of Samaria would be so severe that the people would be forced to resort to cannibalism. Though the horrific behavior described here does not reference the Assyrian siege, an earlier siege under the Arameans resulted in precisely these events (2Kg 6:24-31). Jeremiah also predicted that the citizens of Jerusalem would become just as desperate to survive the siege of that city by the Babylonians in his own time (Jr 19:9), and in fact he lived to see it with his own eyes (Lm 4:10; Ezk 5:10).

would not venture to set the sole of her foot on the ground because of her refinement and sensitivity, will begrudge the husband she embraces, her son, and her daughter, [57]the afterbirth that comes out from between her legs and the children she bears, because she will secretly eat them for lack of anything else during the siege and hardship your enemy imposes on you within your gates.

[58]"If you are not careful to obey all the words of this law, which are written in this scroll, by •fearing this glorious and awesome name—Yahweh, your God— [59]He will bring extraordinary plagues on you and your descendants, severe and lasting plagues, and terrible and chronic sicknesses. [60]He will afflict you again with all the diseases of Egypt, which you dreaded, and they will cling to you. [61]The LORD will also afflict you with every sickness and plague not recorded in the book of this law, until you are destroyed. [62]Though you were as numerous as the stars of the sky, you will be left with only a few people, because you did not obey the LORD your God. [63]Just as the LORD was glad to cause you to prosper and to multiply you, so He will also be glad to cause you to perish and to destroy you. You will be deported from the land you are entering to possess. [64]Then the LORD will scatter you among all peoples from one end of the earth to the other, and there you will worship other gods, of wood and stone, which neither you nor your fathers have known. [65]You will find no peace among those nations, and there will be no resting place[a] for the sole of your foot. There the LORD will give you a trembling

a 28:65 Dt 12:9
b 28:68 Dt 17:16
c 29:1 Dt 31:16
d 29:3 Ex 7:3; Dt 6:22; 7:19; 26:8; 34:11; Neh 9:10; Ps 135:9; Jr 32:20-21
e 29:4 Is 6:9-10; Ezk 12:2; Mt 13:14; Ac 28:26-27; Rm 11:8
f 29:7-8 Nm 21:21-35; 32

heart, failing eyes, and a despondent spirit. [66]Your life will hang in doubt before you. You will be in dread night and day, never certain of survival. [67]In the morning you will say, 'If only it were evening!' and in the evening you will say, 'If only it were morning!'—because of the dread you will have in your heart and because of what you will see. [68]The LORD will take you back in ships to Egypt by a route that I said you would never see again.[b] There you will sell yourselves to your enemies as male and female slaves, but no one will buy you."

Renewing the Covenant

29 [A] These are the words of the covenant[c] the LORD commanded Moses to make with the Israelites in the land of Moab, in addition to the covenant He had made with them at Horeb. [2B] Moses summoned all Israel and said to them, "You have seen with your own eyes everything the LORD did in Egypt to Pharaoh, to all his officials, and to his entire land. [3]You saw with your own eyes the great trials and those great signs and wonders.[d] [4]Yet to this day the LORD has not given you a mind to understand, eyes to see, or ears to hear.[e] [5]I led you 40 years in the wilderness; your clothes and the sandals on your feet did not wear out; [6]you did not eat bread or drink wine or beer—so that you might know that I am •Yahweh your God. [7]When you reached this place, Sihon king of Heshbon and Og king of Bashan came out against us in battle, but we defeated them. [8]We took their land and gave it as an inheritance to the Reubenites, the Gadites, and half the tribe of Manasseh.[f] [9]Therefore,

---

A 29:1 Dt 28:69 in Hb   B 29:2 Dt 29:1 in Hb

28:58 Moses reiterated that all the curses he had listed—concluding with cannibalism, the worst of them all—would come to pass if the people of Israel were **not careful to obey all the words of this law,** specifically those **written in this scroll**—the book of Deuteronomy. It was covenant violation, then, that would be the cause of all of Israel's future judgment should she refuse to repent.

28:60 Reference to the covenant law calls to mind Israel's gracious deliverance from **Egypt** and all its **diseases**. In an ironic twist, Moses declared that Israel's coming judgment would bring the very diseases they had avoided in Egypt.

28:62 Reaching still further back into sacred history, Moses recalled the promise of the Abrahamic covenant that Israel would be **as numerous as the stars of the sky** (cp. 1:10; Gn 15:5; 22:17). That promise too would become inverted, leaving Israel with **only a few people** because they would not obey the Lord.

28:64 The Lord's threat to **scatter** Israel clearly refers to the many times in Israel's future when the people would undergo exile, whether under the Assyrians, Babylonians, Greeks, Romans, or even in the Middle Ages and in modern times. One result of such dislocation would be the tendency

to **worship** foreign **gods** that neither they nor their **fathers** had ever **known** (4:25-31).

28:68 The fact that the Lord would return disobedient Israel **to Egypt** suggests that a reverse of the exodus would take place. Many Israelites did indeed end up in Egypt (Jr 44:11-14,24-30). But the reference to ships and to other deportations (Dt 28:63) leads to the conclusion that Egypt was also a figure of speech—a "synecdoche"—to describe all manner of places of deportation and exile.

29:4 Despite Israel's seeing everything the Lord did in Egypt and in the wilderness (vv. 2-3), He had **not given** them **a mind to understand.** He had not forced them to believe against their will, but He had given them every opportunity and inducement to believe. It is at this point that divine sovereignty and human choices intersect. God makes His truth available to all people, but they can choose to harden themselves against it and thus deny themselves its blessings (Is 6:9-10; Rm 11:8).

29:9 In light of all of God's mighty acts on Israel's behalf (vv. 5-8), He had every right to expect them to **observe** the Deuteronomic **covenant** and thus ensure their success, but human nature being what it is, even miraculous displays

observe the words of this covenant[a] and follow them, so that you will succeed in everything you do.

[10]"All of you are standing today before the LORD your God—your leaders, tribes, elders, officials, all the men of Israel, [11]your children, your wives, and the foreigners in your camps who cut your wood and draw your water— [12]so that you may enter into the covenant of the LORD your God, which He is making with you today, so that you may enter into His oath [13]and so that He may establish you today as His people and He may be your God as He promised you and as He swore to your fathers Abraham, Isaac, and Jacob. [14]I am making this covenant and this oath not only with you, [15]but also with those who are standing here with us today in the presence of the LORD our God and with those who are not here today.

Abandoning the Covenant

[16]"Indeed, you know how we lived in the land of Egypt and passed through the nations where you traveled. [17]You saw their detestable images and idols made of wood, stone, silver, and gold, which were among them. [18]Be sure there is no man, woman, clan, or tribe among you today whose heart turns away from the LORD our God to go and worship the gods of those nations. Be sure there is no root among you bearing poisonous and bitter fruit.[b] [19]When someone hears the words of this oath, he may consider himself exempt,[A] thinking, 'I

a 29:9 Dt 31:16
b 29:18 Heb 12:15
c 29:23 Gn 14:2,8; 19:23-29
d 29:26 Dt 4:19; 1Kg 9:8-9; Jr 22:8-9

will have peace even though I follow my own stubborn heart.' This will lead to the destruction of the well-watered land as well as the dry land. [20]The LORD will not be willing to forgive him. Instead, His anger and jealousy will burn against that person, and every curse written in this scroll will descend on him. The LORD will blot out his name under heaven, [21]and single him out for harm from all the tribes of Israel, according to all the curses of the covenant written in this book of the law.

[22]"Future generations of your children who follow you and the foreigner who comes from a distant country will see the plagues of the land and the sicknesses the LORD has inflicted on it. [23]All its soil will be a burning waste of sulfur and salt, unsown, producing nothing, with no plant growing on it, just like the fall of Sodom and Gomorrah, Admah and Zeboiim, which the LORD demolished in His fierce anger.[c] [24]All the nations will ask, 'Why has the LORD done this to this land? Why this great outburst of anger?' [25]Then people will answer, 'It is because they abandoned the covenant of Yahweh, the God of their fathers, which He had made with them when He brought them out of the land of Egypt. [26]They began to worship other gods, bowing down to gods they had not known—gods that the LORD had not permitted them to worship.[d] [27]Therefore the LORD's anger burned against this land, and He brought every curse written in this book on it. [28]The LORD uprooted them from their land

---

[A]29:19 Lit may bless himself in his heart

of power did not always lead to faith and repentance (Jn 12:37).

29:12 Deuteronomy is a **covenant** renewal document founded on the covenant first made at Mount Sinai. The idea that Israel was now about to **enter into the covenant of the LORD** means, then, that they were renewing the covenant commitment their fathers had made nearly 40 years earlier, assuming its privileges and responsibilities.

29:13 Once Israel had pledged its covenant fidelity, the Lord would reciprocate by establishing Israel as His **people** and Himself as their **God** as **promised** to their forefathers (cp. Gn 17:7; Lv 11:45; 26:12). The verb translated **establish** is a technical term referring to the ratification of an already existing agreement such as this one (8:18; 9:5; Gn 6:18; 9:9; 17:19,21; Ex 6:4;). God had not just introduced a new covenant arrangement with this generation, but had also confirmed one made with the patriarchs and their fathers at Sinai.

29:15 The covenant was being reaffirmed by the Lord not only with Israelites of that generation (v. 14) but **with those who are standing here**—non-Israelite proselytes who had also embraced the God of Israel (cp. v. 11; Ex 12:38). Beyond that, it was being made **with those who are not here today**—the unborn generations who would also need to affirm their commitment to God (4:9).

29:17 The **detestable images and idols** of the nations through which Israel had just traveled (v. 16; Nm 25:1-5) would continue to be a snare to Israel. Sinful human beings prefer gods of their own creation to the living God.

29:18 Because Israel would be attracted to **gods** they could see, they had to avoid the temptation to idolatry. The first two commandments—the heart of covenant confession— called for Israel to acknowledge the existence of **the LORD** as the only god and forbade representing Him or any other deity in visual form. The **root** that Moses warns against here no doubt refers to the concept of idolatry which, if allowed to grow in the human mind and heart, would produce the fruit of idolatrous practice.

29:19 The **well-watered land as well as the dry land** is a proverbial statement suggesting that no person who sins willfully against the covenant can expect to escape the judgment of the Lord, no matter how pious his confessions of faith.

29:20 The fate of a person who sins willfully (lit "with a high hand"; Nm 15:30) is serious indeed—**the LORD will blot out his name under heaven** (cp. 9:14; 25:19; Ex 32:32-33), implying that he would be forgotten by future generations.

29:24-26 When future generations saw the awful destruction of the land and inquired about its cause, the answer would be immediate and clear: **because they abandoned the cov-**

in His anger, rage, and great wrath, and threw them into another land where they are today.' [29]The hidden things belong to the LORD our God, but the revealed things belong to us and our children forever, so that we may follow all the words of this law.

Returning to the LORD

30 "When all these things happen to you—the blessings and curses I have set before you—and you come to your senses while you are in all the nations where the LORD your God has driven you, [2]and you and your children return to the LORD your God and obey Him with all your heart and all your soul by doing[A] everything I am giving you today, [3]then He will restore your fortunes,[B] have compassion on you, and gather you again from all the peoples where the LORD your God has scattered you.[a] [4]Even if your exiles are at the ends of the earth,[c] He will gather you and bring you back from there.[b] [5]The LORD your God will bring you into the land your fathers possessed, and you will take possession of it.[c] He will cause you to prosper and multiply you more than He did your fathers. [6]The LORD your God will circumcise your heart[d] and the hearts of your descendants, and you will love Him with all your heart and all your soul so that you will live. [7]The LORD your God will put all these curses on your enemies who hate and persecute you. [8]Then you will again obey Him and follow all His commands I am giving you today. [9]The LORD your God will make you prosper abundantly in all the work of your

hands[e] with children,[D] the offspring of your livestock, and your land's produce. Indeed, the LORD will again delight in your prosperity, as He delighted in that of your fathers, [10]when you obey the LORD your God by keeping His commands and statutes that are written in this book of the law and return to Him with all your heart and all your soul.

Choose Life

[11]"This command that I give you today is certainly not too difficult or beyond your reach. [12]It is not in heaven so that you have to ask, 'Who will go up to heaven, get it for us, and proclaim it to us so that we may follow it?' [13]And it is not across the sea so that you have to ask, 'Who will cross the sea, get it for us, and proclaim it to us so that we may follow it?' [14]But the message is very near you, in your mouth and in your heart, so that you may follow it.[f] [15]See, today I have set before you life and prosperity, death and adversity.[g] [16]For[E] I am commanding you today to love the LORD your God, to walk in His ways, and to keep His commands, statutes, and ordinances, so that you may live[F] and multiply, and the LORD your God may bless you in the land you are entering to possess. [17]But if your heart turns away and you do not listen and you are led astray to bow down to other gods and worship them, [18]I tell you today that you will certainly perish and will not live long in the land you are entering to possess across the Jordan. [19]I call heaven and earth as witnesses against

[a]30:3 Lv 26:40-45; 1Kg 8:46-50; Jr 29:14
[b]30:4 Neh 1:9
[c]30:5 Dt 3:12
[d]30:6 Dt 10:16; Jr 4:4
[e]30:9 Dt 2:7; 14:29; 16:15; 24:19; 28:12; Ec 5:6; Hg 2:17
[f]30:12-14 Rm 10:6-8
[g]30:15 Dt 11:26; Jr 21:8

[A]30:2 Lit soul according to   [B]30:3 Or will end your captivity   [C]30:4 Lit skies   [D]30:9 Lit hands in the fruit of your womb   [E]30:16 LXX reads If you obey the commands of the LORD your God that   [F]30:16 LXX reads ordinances, then you will live

enant of Yahweh. This most egregious of sins violated the foundational element of the relationship between the Lord and His people—the first two commandments (5:7-8).

29:29 How could the nation continue to exist in light of its promised destruction? The best solution to this apparent contradiction between hidden things belonging to God and revealed things belonging to Israel is to view it as the perception of the other nations. They would observe Israel's outcome and conclude that the covenant relationship had been terminated, but they would be unable to understand that God's word to His people could never be canceled. God would bring His people to repentance so they could enjoy unending fellowship with Him (30:1-10; cp. Jr 31:31-34; Ezk 36:24-38; Rm 11:1-32).

30:1-3 The grammatical structure of this passage suggests that Israel's repentance and return to the Lord would be at His initiative, an act of His grace wherein God's promises and Israel's need to be obedient to the conditions of the covenant would be reconciled—one of the hidden mysteries of the mind of God (29:29).

30:6 The image of circumcising the heart derives from the occasion of Abraham's having been physically circumcised, along with his household, as a sign of his covenant relation-

ship with the Lord (Gn 17:9-14). Jeremiah also spoke of this mark of covenant reality in terms of spiritual circumcision (Jr 4:4; cp. Jr 31:33; Ezk 36:26), and Paul compared it to the new life and relationship to God to be found in Christ (Col 2:11).

30:9 Israel's return to the Lord would bring about a reversal of the curses they had suffered, and they would enjoy the blessings of covenant obedience rather than suffer the consequences of disobedience (28:4).

30:11-14 Lest Israel should protest that the demands of the covenant were too difficult to obey, Moses reminded them that the power to do so resided within them (v. 14). This refers to the revelation of the Lord's mind and purposes to the Israelites at Sinai and now in the plains of Moab. Moses had instructed them about these matters (6:1), and they were to impress them upon their own hearts and souls as well as those of their children (11:18-19). Paul cited this text with reference to the proximity of the gospel and the ease with which it could be understood and appropriated; like the words of the OT covenant, those of the NT message of salvation are ready at hand and made available to all who will believe (Rm 10:6-10).

30:19 In a setting similar to a courtroom, the Lord summoned

you today that I have set before you life and death, blessing and curse. Choose life[a] so that you and your descendants may live, [20]love the LORD your God, obey Him, and remain faithful[A] to Him. For He is your life, and He will prolong your life in the land the LORD swore to give to your fathers[b] Abraham, Isaac, and Jacob."

Joshua Takes Moses' Place

31 Then Moses continued to speak these[B] words to all Israel, [2]saying, "I am now 120 years old; I can no longer act as your leader.[c] The LORD has told me, 'You will not cross this Jordan.'[c] [3]The LORD your God is the One who will cross ahead of you.[d] He will destroy these nations before you, and you will drive them out. Joshua is the one who will cross ahead of you, as the LORD has said.[e] [4]The LORD will deal with them as He did Sihon and Og, the kings of the Amorites, and their land when He destroyed them.[f] [5]The LORD will deliver them over to you, and you must do to them exactly as I have commanded you. [6]Be strong and courageous;[g] don't be terrified or afraid of them. For it is the LORD your God who goes with you;[h] He will not leave you or forsake you."[i]

[7]Moses then summoned Joshua and said to him in the sight of all Israel, "Be strong and courageous, for you will go with[D] this people into the land the LORD swore to give to their fathers.[j] You will enable them to take possession of it. [8]The LORD is the One who will go before you.[k] He will be with you; He will not leave you or forsake you.[l] Do not be afraid or discouraged."

[9]Moses wrote down this law and gave it to the priests, the sons of Levi, who carried the ark of the LORD's covenant, and to all the elders of Israel. [10]Moses commanded them, "At the end of every seven years, at the appointed time in the year of debt cancellation,[m] during the Festival of Booths,[n] [11]when all Israel assembles[E] in the presence of the LORD your God at the place He chooses, you are to read this law aloud before all Israel.[o] [12]Gather the people—men, women, children, and foreigners living within your gates—so that they may listen and learn to 'fear[p] the LORD your God and be careful to follow all the words of this law. [13]Then their children[q] who do not know the law will listen and learn to fear the LORD your God as long as you live in the land you are crossing the Jordan to possess."

[14]The LORD said to Moses, "The time of your death is now approaching. Call Joshua and present yourselves at the tent of meeting so that I may commission him." When Moses and Joshua went and presented themselves at the tent of meeting, [15]the LORD appeared at the tent in a pillar of cloud, and the cloud stood at the entrance to the tent.[r]

[16]The LORD said to Moses, "You are about to rest with your fathers, and these people will soon commit adultery with the foreign gods of the land they are entering. They will abandon Me and break the covenant[s] I have made with them. [17]My anger will burn against them on that day; I will abandon them and hide My face from them so that they will become easy prey.[F] Many troubles and afflictions will come to them. On that day they will say, 'Haven't

---

[a]30:19 Dt 4:1; 5:33; 6:24; 8:1,3; 16:20; 32:46-47
[b]30:20 Dt 1:35
[c]31:2 Dt 3:27
[d]31:3 Dt 9:3
[e]Dt 3:28
[f]31:4 Nm 21:21-35; Dt 29:6
[g]31:6 Dt 31:23; Jos 1:6-7,9,18; 10:25
[h]Dt 1:29; 7:21; 20:3
[i]Heb 13:5
[j]31:7 Dt 1:35; 31:20; Ezk 20:42
[k]31:8 Ex 23:23; 32:34; Dt 1:30; Jdg 4:14; Is 52:12
[l]Jos 1:5; 1Ch 28:20; Heb 13:5
[m]31:10 Dt 15:1-2
[n]Lv 23:34; Dt 16:3
[o]31:10-11 Jr 2:8; Mal 2:1-9
[p]31:12 Dt 14:23
[q]31:13 Dt 4:9-10
[r]31:15 Nm 12:5
[s]31:16 Dt 4:13, 23; 5:2-3; 17:2; 29:1,9-14,21,25

[A]30:20 Lit and hold on   [B]31:1 Some Hb mss, DSS, LXX, Syr, Vg read all these   [C]31:2 Lit no longer go out or come in   [D]31:7 Some Hb mss, Sam, Syr, Vg read you will bring   [E]31:11 Lit comes to appear   [F]31:17 Lit will be for devouring

---

witnesses to His offer to Israel of **life and death**. Since these witnesses must be enduring and objective, He called not on human beings or even angels, but on **heaven and earth** (cp. 4:26; 31:28; 32:1; Is 1:2; Mc 1:2). He appealed for Israel to choose a life of blessed obedience so they and their **descendants** might **live**.

31:1-6 The narrative of Moses' imminent death and the succession of Joshua to leadership is reminiscent of an earlier part of Deuteronomy (3:21-28). It also anticipates the formal call and commissioning of Joshua following Moses' departure (Jos 1:1-9). Human leaders are only God's surrogates and therefore are to be followed only if they are obedient to Him.

31:9 This law is clearly the bulk of the book of Deuteronomy, since chapters 5-28 make up the body of covenant stipulations. Having been written, it must now be preserved for future generations since the covenant was to be kept not only with Moses' immediate hearers but also with their descendants (17:18; 29:10-15).

31:10-11 Because there was only one copy of the law at the

beginning and in light of the limited literacy of the population of Israel at large, Israel had to assemble to hear it read at **the end of every seven years . . . during the Festival of Booths** in the fall of the year at the central sanctuary (12:5,11).

31:12-13 The instruction to the assembly to **follow all the words** of His covenant law and to teach the children formalized the exhortation given previously to obey the stipulations of the covenant and to teach them to their children (6:1-3,6-9).

31:14 The significance of **the tent of meeting**, as the name implies, is that the Lord met there with His servants, especially Moses, on important occasions (Lv 1:1; Nm 7:89; 11:16; 12:4). Joshua's succession to the office held by Moses would be such an occasion, requiring an encounter with the Lord Himself.

31:16 The marriage/**adultery** metaphor describes the **covenant** relationship between the Lord and Israel (Ezk 16:8, 23:36-39; Hs 2:2-13). The worst sin Israel could commit against Him was to acknowledge and worship the **foreign**

these troubles come to us because our God is no longer with us?' [18] I will certainly hide My face on that day because of all the evil they have done by turning to other gods. [19] Therefore write down this song[a] for yourselves and teach it to the Israelites; have them recite it,[A] so that this song may be a witness for Me against the Israelites. [20] When I bring them into the land I swore to give their fathers, a land flowing with milk and honey,[b] they will eat their fill[c] and prosper.[B] They will turn to other gods and worship them, despising Me and breaking My covenant.[d] [21] And when many troubles and afflictions come to them, this song will testify against them, because[c] their descendants will not have forgotten it. For I know what they are prone to do,[D] even before I bring them into the land I swore to give them." [22] So Moses wrote down this song on that day and taught it to the Israelites.

[23] The LORD commissioned Joshua son of Nun, "Be strong and courageous, for you will bring the Israelites into the land I swore to them, and I will be with you."[e]

Moses Warns the People

[24] When Moses had finished writing down on a scroll every single word[E] of this law, [25] he commanded the Levites who carried the ark of the LORD's covenant, [26] "Take this book of the law and place it beside the ark of the covenant of the LORD your God so that it may remain there as a witness against you. [27] For I know how rebellious and stiff-necked you are. If you are rebelling against the LORD now, while I am

[a] 31:19 Dt 32:1-43
[b] 31:20 Dt 11:9
[c] Dt 11:15
[d] Dt 4:31
[e] 31:23 Jos 1:1-9
[f] 31:28 Dt 4:26; 30:19
[g] 31:27-29 Dt 4:25; Jdg 2:6-13
[h] 32:1 Is 1:2

still alive, how much more will you rebel after I am dead! [28] Assemble all your tribal elders and officers before me so that I may speak these words directly to them and call heaven and earth as witnesses against them.[f] [29] For I know that after my death you will become completely corrupt and turn from the path I have commanded you. Disaster will come to you in the future, because you will do what is evil in the LORD's sight, infuriating Him with what your hands have made."[g] [30] Then Moses recited aloud every single word[F] of this song to the entire assembly of Israel:

Song of Moses

32 Pay attention, heavens, and I
will speak;
listen, earth, to the words
of my mouth.[h]
2   Let my teaching fall like rain
and my word settle like dew,
like gentle rain on new grass
and showers on tender plants.
3   For I will proclaim *Yahweh's name.
Declare the greatness of our God!
4   The Rock—His work is perfect;
all His ways are entirely just.
A faithful God, without prejudice,
He is righteous and true.

5   His people have acted corruptly
toward Him;
this is their defect[G]—they are not
His children
but a devious
and crooked generation.

[A] 31:19 Lit Israelites; put it in their mouths   [B] 31:20 Lit be fat   [C] 31:21 Lit because the mouths of   [D] 31:21 Or know the plans they are devising   [E] 31:24 Lit scroll the words to their completion   [F] 31:30 Lit recited the words to their completion   [G] 32:5 Or Him; through their fault; Hb obscure

gods of the pagan nations. Such behavior was a violation of the marriage vows enshrined in the covenant text (27:11-26; Ex 19:8).

31:19 Covenant ceremonies and their reaffirmations required a **witness** who could testify to the legality of what was done and who could bear testimony for or against the covenant partners in the event of a breach of contract by either one (30:19; Ex 24:3-8).

31:20 The need for a song of witness (v. 19) is apparent. The question is not whether Israel would sin but when and what should be done about their sinful behavior. Sadly, Israel's future behavior mirrored that of her past. The song of witness was forever a nagging reminder of her lack of gratitude to God.

31:24 The statement that **Moses** wrote **every single word of this law** attests to the ancient tradition of his authorship of the book of Deuteronomy, the "law" clearly intended here.

31:26 The stone tablets of the Decalogue had already been placed inside the ark of the covenant (Ex 25:16) and now the **book of the law**—no doubt Deuteronomy—must be housed

in the most holy place **beside the ark** (cp. Ex 26:33), which represented the earthly dwelling place of the Lord.

31:28 The Lord now, at the point of covenant renewal, would **call heaven and earth as witnesses against them** (cp. 4:26; 30:19). This is in line with the principle that formal legal matters must be addressed in the presence of at least two witnesses in order for them to be valid (17:6; 19:15).

32:1 Using a figure of speech by which inanimate objects are addressed—"apostrophe"—Moses appealed to the **heavens** and the **earth** to **listen** to the words of his **mouth**—to serve as witnesses to what the Lord was about to say through the song of Moses and to the tacit response of commitment by the nation (31:28).

32:2 Moses' prayer was that Israel would not be like the hardened and thorny soils of Jesus' parable (Mk 4:1-9). Rather, he wanted them to be like **new grass** and **tender plants**.

32:4 The epithet **The Rock** describes the Lord as both (1) a firm and secure foundation upon whom one can build and in whom one can trust for salvation (vv. 15,18,30), and (2) a companion who is able to lead one through the trackless deserts of life (1Co 10:4).

⁶ Is this how you repay the Lord,
  you foolish and senseless people?
  Isn't He your Father and Creator?
  Didn't He make you and sustain you?
⁷ Remember the days of old;
  consider the years long past.
  Ask your father, and he will tell you,
  your elders, and they will teach you.
⁸ When the •Most High gave the nations
    their inheritance^A
  and divided the •human race,^a
  He set the boundaries of the peoples
  according to the number of the people
    of Israel.^B
⁹ But the Lord's portion is His people,
  Jacob, His own inheritance.

¹⁰ He found him in a desolate land,
  in a barren, howling wilderness;
  He surrounded him, cared for him,
  and protected him as the pupil
    of His eye.^b
¹¹ He watches over^c His nest like an eagle
  and hovers over His young;
  He spreads His wings, catches him,
  and lifts him up on His pinions.^c
¹² The Lord alone led him,
  with no help from a foreign god.^D
¹³ He made him ride on the heights
    of the land^d
  and eat the produce of the field.
  He nourished him with honey
    from the rock
  and oil from flint-like rock,

Cross references (center column):
^a 32:8 Gn 11:1-9
^b 32:10 Pr 7:2
^c 32:11 Ex 19:4; Ps 91:4
^d 32:13 Is 58:14
^e 32:15 Is 44:2
^f 32:16 Ps 78:58
^g 32:17 1Co 10:19-20

¹⁴ cream from the herd and milk
    from the flock,
  with the fat of lambs,
  rams from Bashan, and goats,
  with the choicest grains of wheat;
  you drank wine from the finest grapes.^E

¹⁵ Then^F Jeshurun^G,e became fat
    and rebelled—
  you became fat, bloated, and gorged.
  He abandoned the God who made him
  and scorned the Rock of his salvation.
¹⁶ They provoked His jealousy
    with foreign gods;
  they enraged Him
    with detestable practices.^f
¹⁷ They sacrificed to demons, not God,
  to gods they had not known,
  new gods that had just arrived,
  which your fathers did not fear.^g
¹⁸ You ignored the Rock
    who gave you birth;
  you forgot the God who gave birth
    to you.

¹⁹ When the Lord saw this,
    He despised them,
  provoked to anger by His sons
    and daughters.
²⁰ He said: "I will hide My face from them;
  I will see what will become of them,
  for they are a perverse generation—
  unfaithful children.
²¹ They have provoked My jealousy
    with their so-called gods;^H

---

^A32:8 Or *Most High divided the nations*   ^B32:8 One DSS reads *number of the sons of God*; LXX reads *number of the angels of God*   ^C32:11 Or *He stirs up*   ^D32:12 Lit *him, and no foreign god with Him*   ^E32:14 Lit *the blood of grapes*   ^F32:15 DSS, Sam, LXX add *Jacob ate his fill;*   ^G32:15 = Upright One, referring to Israel   ^H32:21 Lit *with no gods*

32:6 The description of the Lord as **Father** (cp. Ps 2:7; 89:26; Is 63:16; 64:8; Jr 3:19) and **Creator** (Gn 14:22; Ec 12:1; Is 27:11; 40:28; 43:15) is rare in the OT, and the two are placed together only here. This combination reminded Israel that He was the God of all creation but also the special Father of His people.

32:8 Israel's special place in the redemptive program of the Lord is clear from the fact that when He **gave the nations their inheritance and divided the human race,** He did so with Israel especially in mind. Their size and location were the fixed points according to which **He set the boundaries of the peoples.** The Table of Nations of Genesis 10 focuses on Shem and his descendants (vv. 21-31), drawing particular attention to Eber, for whom the Hebrews were named (vv. 21,25; cp. 11:14-26). Abram, the ultimate father of Israel, was an Eberite (Hebrew), thus establishing the connection between Israel and Eber, the central individual of the Table of Nations. Israel's role as the nation chosen out of all the others is a major OT theme (7:6-8; Gn 12:1-3; 15:4-5; 17:3-8; Ex 19:4-6).

32:9 What is only hinted at in verse 8 is clear here: Israel is **the Lord's** chosen **people.**

32:10-14 Israel's position as the chosen nation is confirmed by the special care the Lord accorded her, especially in the desert journey out of Egypt. Moses described the Lord's watchcare over Israel as that of an **eagle** protecting his young one in the nest and teaching him to fly. He alone was capable of leading them through the desert until at last they reached the land He had promised to give them (v. 12).

32:15-18 Looking into the future, Moses saw a time when Israel would rebel against the Lord and break the covenant with Him. When they became **fat, bloated, and gorged** with all the blessings of the land (cp. vv. 13-14), they would attribute their prosperity to the **foreign gods,** abandoning the God who made them and the Rock of their salvation (cp. 8:11-20). By their idolatry they would provoke God to jealousy (cp. 5:9). This would include their sacrifice **to demons** and **gods they had not known.** This description of demons provides the theological insight that the pagan gods were in fact fallen angels used by Satan to lead people away from the true God (cp. 1Co 10:20; Rv 9:20). The long history of Israel in the land bears sorrowful testimony to the bleak prospects outlined here by Moses (cp. 2Kg 17:7-17).

32:19-21 Once Israel had lapsed into the idolatry described in verses 15-18, the **Lord** would begin to exert judgment. He threatened to **hide** His **face** from His people, a response

they have enraged Me
with their worthless idols.
So I will provoke their jealousy
with an inferior people;^A
I will enrage them
with a foolish nation.^a
22 For fire has been kindled because of
My anger
and burns to the depths of *Sheol;
it devours the land and its produce,
and scorches the foundations
of the mountains.

23 "I will pile disasters on them;
I will use up My arrows against them.
24 They will be weak from hunger,
ravaged by pestilence and bitter plague;
I will unleash on them wild beasts
with fangs,
as well as venomous snakes that slither
in the dust.
25 Outside, the sword will take
their children,
and inside, there will be terror;
the young man and the young woman
will be killed,
the infant and the gray-haired man.^b

26 "I would have said: I will cut them
to pieces^B
and blot out the memory of them
from mankind,
27 if I had not feared insult
from the enemy,
or feared that these foes
might misunderstand

and say: 'Our own hand has prevailed;
it wasn't the LORD who did all this.'"
28 Israel is a nation lacking sense
with no understanding at all.^C
29 If only they were wise,
they would figure it out;
they would understand their fate.
30 How could one man pursue
a thousand,
or two put ten thousand to flight,
unless their Rock had sold them,
unless the LORD had given them up?
31 But their "rock" is not like our Rock;
even our enemies concede.
32 For their vine is from the vine
of Sodom
and from the fields of Gomorrah.
Their grapes are poisonous;
their clusters are bitter.
33 Their wine is serpents' venom,
the deadly poison of cobras.

34 "Is it not stored up with Me,
sealed up in My vaults?
35 Vengeance^D belongs to Me;
I will repay.^E,c
In time their foot will slip,
for their day of disaster is near,
and their doom is coming quickly."
36 The LORD will indeed vindicate
His people
and have compassion on His servants^d
when He sees that their strength
is gone
and no one is left—slave or free.

reminiscent of His reaction to the worship of the golden calf at Sinai (Ex 32:10,34-35). Like that incident, the sin was rebellion epitomized by the violation of the first two commandments. The NT makes clear that these **inferior people** are the Gentiles whom God would call to Himself through the gospel. Paul quoted this text to say it was God's favor to the nations that would finally awaken Israel to their own disobedience, impelling them to see in Christ their promised Messiah (Rm 10:19-21).

32:22 Sheol refers to the grave, the netherworld, or the place of the departed dead in general. Here it suggests only that there is no place that the burning wrath of God cannot reach.

32:26-27 The Lord declared that if not for His reputation, He would cut Israel to pieces and **blot out the memory of them from mankind**. To do this, however, would allow the enemy to take credit for Israel's failure and punishment rather than attributing it to the Lord. The threat to **blot out** their **memory** recalls Ex 32:32 where Moses said that if the Lord would not forgive His wicked people, he would gladly have his name erased from the book God had written.

32:30 Moses predicted a time when Israel's sin would be

so blatant that they would be delivered over to incredibly powerful armies. Though hyperbole is used to describe the future defeat of Israel by a foreign foe (**one man pursue a thousand**), the fact remains that when God no longer fights for His people and, in fact, fights against them, there is no chance of victory.

32:31 In contrast to the previous scenario, when the Lord fights for His people, they are certain to prevail because the **"rock"** on which the pagans rely does not exist and therefore has no real power.

32:32-33 The **vine**, the **grapes**, and the **wine** are the products of the enemies' "rock" (v. 31)—the pagan fertility gods. The Lord, however, linked these imaginary gods to **Sodom** and **Gomorrah**, the epitome of corruption (Gn 18:20; 19:4-28; Is 1:10; 3:9; Mt 10:15; 11:23-24).

32:34-35 The **vaults** is a figurative image conveying the idea that all judgment originates with God and is stored up until the proper time of its administration. **Vengeance belongs to** God. Only He knows all the facts and only He is absolutely just and righteous (Rm 12:19; Heb 10:30).

32:36 The other side of vengeance on the wicked is

37 He will say: "Where are their gods,
the 'rock' they found refuge in?
38 Who ate the fat of their sacrifices
and drank the wine
of their ˙drink offerings?
Let them rise up and help you;
let it[A] be a shelter for you.
39 See now that I alone am He;
there is no God but Me.[a]
I bring death and I give life;
I wound and I heal.
No one can rescue anyone
from My hand.[b]
40 I raise My hand to heaven and declare:
As surely as I live forever,
41 when I sharpen My flashing sword,
and My hand takes hold of judgment,
I will take vengeance on My adversaries
and repay those who hate Me.
42 I will make My arrows drunk
with blood
while My sword devours flesh—
the blood of the slain and the captives,
the heads of the enemy leaders."[B]

43 Rejoice, you nations,
concerning His people,[C,c]
for He will avenge the blood
of His servants.[D]
He will take vengeance
on His adversaries;[E,d]
He will purify His land and His people.[F]

44 Moses came with Joshua[G] son of Nun and

Cross references (center column):
a 32:39 Is 40:25; 43:11-13; 46:9; Ezk 36:23
b 1Sm 2:6-8
c 32:43 Rm 15:10
d Ps 79:10
e 32:48-51 Nm 27:12-14
f 32:50 Nm 20:22-29
g 32:51-52 Nm 20:2-13
h 33:1-29 Gn 49:1-33

recited all the words of this song in the presence of the people. 45After Moses finished reciting all these words to all Israel, 46he said to them, "Take to heart all these words I am giving as a warning to you today, so that you may command your children to carefully follow all the words of this law. 47For they are not meaningless words to you but they are your life, and by them you will live long in the land you are crossing the Jordan to possess."

Moses' Impending Death

48On that same day the LORD spoke to Moses,[e] 49"Go up Mount Nebo in the Abarim range in the land of Moab, across from Jericho, and view the land of Canaan I am giving the Israelites as a possession. 50Then you will die on the mountain that you go up, and you will be gathered to your people, just as your brother Aaron died on Mount Hor and was gathered to his people.[f] 51For both of you broke faith with Me among the Israelites at the waters of Meribath-kadesh in the Wilderness of Zin by failing to treat Me as holy in their presence. 52Although from a distance you will view the land that I am giving the Israelites, you will not go there."[g]

Moses' Blessings

33 This is the blessing that Moses, the man of God, gave the Israelites before his death.[h] 2He said:

The LORD came from Sinai
and appeared to them from Seir;

A 32:38 Sam, LXX, Tg, Vg read them   B 32:42 Or the long-haired heads of the enemy   C 32:43 LXX reads Rejoice, you heavens, along with Him, and let all the sons of God worship Him; rejoice, you nations, with His people, and let all the angels of God strengthen themselves in Him; DSS read Rejoice, you heavens, along with Him, and let all the angels worship Him; Heb 1:6   D 32:43 DSS, LXX read sons   E 32:43 DSS, LXX add and He will recompense those who hate Him; v. 41   F 32:43 Syr, Tg; DSS, Sam, LXX, Vg read His people's land   G 32:44 LXX, Syr, Vg; MT reads Hoshea; Nm 13:8,16

---

vindication of the righteous. The pledge here is that the Lord will be true to His everlasting covenant promises.

32:37-38 At the same time the Lord rescues them, He will taunt His people by asking where **their gods**, their supposed '**rock**' of **refuge**, have gone. The prophets also taunted idolaters and the gods they worshiped by sarcastically exposing their nonexistence (Is 40:18-20; 44:6-20; Jr 10:1-10).

32:39 The bottom line is that the Lord **alone** is **God**. Surely this puts an end to speculation about other gods and ought to render foolish the devotion that people—especially His own people Israel—pay to them.

32:40-42 Using a figure of speech—"anthropomorphism"—the Lord swears as **heaven** is His witness and as surely as He lives forever that He will execute **judgment** and **vengeance** on His **adversaries** and **the heads of the enemy leaders** who hate Him. The familiar language of the courtroom is used here so Israel can better understand the legal and forensic nature of God's relationship to them and to the nations at large. A second figure of speech—personification—describes the **sword** of the Lord as it **devours flesh** and His **arrows** that are **drunk with blood**. This gruesome

scene reflects the other side of the coin of divine love and grace—holiness and justice.

32:43 When the Lord administers judgment to His adversaries, He will also **avenge . . . His servants** who have been abused. By judging His foes and vindicating Israel, the Lord will **purify His land and His people**.

32:46 The instruction to the people to **take to heart** all the words of Moses' song and to command their children **to carefully follow all the words of this law** (i.e., the book of Deuteronomy) calls to mind the admonitions following the giving of the Ten Commandments (5:32-33) and the Shema (6:4-9). These commands of the Lord must be handed down from one generation to the next.

32:47 Because Israel failed to heed these words of admonition, they were eventually uprooted from the land and forced into exile (2Kg 17:7-17; 2Ch 36:15-19).

32:51 The reason Aaron and Moses were unable to enter the land of promise is that they **broke faith** with the Lord. The verb translated "broke faith" has at its core in this context the idea of covenant treachery or disloyalty. Moses should

He shone on them from Mount Paran
and came with ten thousand
   holy ones,^A
with lightning^B from His right hand^C
   for them.^a
3 Indeed He loves the people.^D,b
   All Your^E holy ones^F are in Your hand,
   and they assemble^G at Your feet.
   Each receives Your words.
4 Moses gave us instruction,
   a possession for the assembly of Jacob.
5 So He became King in Jeshurun^H
   when the leaders of the people gathered
   with the tribes of Israel.

6 Let Reuben live and not die
   though his people become few.^c

7 He said this about Judah:

   LORD, hear Judah's cry and bring him
      to his people.
   He fights for his cause^I
      with his own hands,
   but may You be a help against his foes.

8 He said about Levi:

   Your *Thummim and Urim belong to
      Your faithful one;^J
   You tested him at Massah

and contended with him at the waters
   of Meribah.^d
9 He said about his father and mother,
   "I do not regard them."
   He disregarded his brothers
   and didn't acknowledge his sons,
   for they kept Your word
   and maintained Your covenant.^e
10 They will teach Your ordinances
       to Jacob
   and Your instruction to Israel;^f
   they will set incense before You
   and whole *burnt offerings
       on Your altar.
11 LORD, bless his possessions,^K
   and accept the work of his hands.
   Smash the loins of his adversaries
       and enemies,
   so that they cannot rise again.

12 He said about Benjamin:

   The LORD's beloved rests^L securely
      on Him.
   He^M shields him all day long,
   and he rests on His shoulders.^N

13 He said about Joseph:

   May his land be blessed by the LORD
   with the dew of heaven's bounty
   and the watery depths that lie beneath;^g

Side references:
^a33:2 Jdg 5:4-5; Ps 68:7-8; Hab 3:3
^b33:3 Dt 4:37
^c33:6 Gn 49:3-4; Jdg 5:15-16
^d33:8 Ex 17:1-7; Nm 20:2-13
^e33:9 Ex 32:25-29
^f33:10 Dt 31:9-13
^g33:13 Pr 3:20

---

^A33:2 LXX reads *Mount Paran with ten thousands from Kadesh*   ^B33:2 Or *fiery law*; Hb obscure   ^C33:2 Or *ones, from His southland to the mountain slopes*   ^D33:3 Or *peoples*   ^E33:3 Lit *His, or its*   ^F33:3 Either the saints of Israel or angels   ^G33:3 Hb obscure   ^H33:5 = *Upright One*, referring to Israel   ^I33:7 Or *He contends for them*   ^J33:8 DSS, LXX read *Give to Levi Your Thummim, Your Urim to Your favored one*   ^K33:11 Or *abilities*   ^L33:12 Or *Let the Lord's beloved rest*   ^M33:12 LXX reads *The Most High*   ^N33:12 Or *and He dwells among his mountain slopes*

---

have served as a model of kingdom citizenship in a time of stress, but he failed to do so (Nm 20:1-13).

33:2 The listing of **Sinai . . . Seir,** and **Mount Paran** is an abbreviated itinerary along which the Lord had led His people on their journey from Egypt to the land of promise. The **holy ones** are the angelic hosts that make up His heavenly armies (Ps 68:17). **Lightning** (lit "fiery law") might better be understood as synonymous with holy ones and thus rendered "angels."

33:3 Here **holy ones** is a reference to the **people** of Israel. The Lord led them to the land of promise because He loved them—a key indicator of their covenant relationship with Him (cp. 7:7-11).

33:4 The term **instruction** translates the Hebrew word *torah*. The point is that Israel out of all the nations had been entrusted with God's covenant blessings (14:2,21; Ex 19:4-6).

33:5 **Jeshurun** is a poetic term for Israel (v. 26; 32:15; Is 44:2). Moses' reference to the Lord as **King** in Jeshurun provides a basis for the march of conquest of verse 2. The Lord can exercise such power and glory precisely because He is King (29:10; Ex 19:7-8; 34:31-32).

33:6 Turning to the blessing of the individual tribes, Moses first wished for **Reuben,** the eldest son of Jacob, that he might **live and not die though his people become few.** This partially offsets Jacob's curse against him because of

Reuben's sin involving Jacob's concubine (Gn 49:3-4; cp. Gn 35:22).

33:8 **Levi,** the head of the priestly tribe, was responsible for spiritual leadership. This included determining God's will for them by casting the sacred lots of **Urim** and **Thummim** (Ex 28:15-30; cp. 1Sm 28:6; Ezr 2:63; Neh 7:65). The testing probably refers to the Lord testing Moses the Levite, since otherwise it was the Lord who was being **tested** by Israel and not the other way around (6:16; Ex 17:7; Nm 20:13,24; Ps 95:8-9; 106:32).

33:9 Levi's statement about **his father and mother** probably refers to the impartial attitude of that tribe in punishing Israel for their worship of the golden calf at Sinai (Ex 32:25-29). Thus Levi **kept** the Lord's **word and maintained** His **covenant.**

33:10 Two other privileges reserved only for the Levites were teaching the Lord's **ordinances** (31:9-13; Lv 10:11) and conducting worship.

33:12 The blessing of **Benjamin** also somewhat offsets the last words of Jacob to his sons where he described Benjamin as a wolf who tore his prey (Gn 49:27). Here Benjamin rests on the Lord's **shoulders** much as a shepherd might carry his helpless lambs (Nm 11:12; Ru 4:16; Is 40:11; Jn 10:7-18).

33:13-17 Moses' desire for **Joseph** (the tribes of **Ephraim**

14 with the bountiful harvest from the sun
and the abundant yield of the seasons;
15 with the best products
of the ancient mountains
and the bounty of the eternal hills;
16 with the choice gifts of the land
and everything in it;
and with the favor of Him
who appeared[A] in the burning bush.[a]
May these rest on the head of Joseph,
on the crown of the prince
of his brothers.[b]
17 His firstborn bull has[B] splendor,
and horns like[C] those of a wild ox;
he gores all the peoples with them
to the ends of the earth.
Such are the ten thousands
of Ephraim,
and such are the thousands
of Manasseh.

18 He said about Zebulun:

Rejoice, Zebulun, in your journeys,
and Issachar, in your tents.
19 They summon the peoples
to a mountain;
there they offer acceptable sacrifices.
For they draw from the wealth
of the seas
and the hidden treasures
of the sand.[c]

20 He said about Gad:

The one who enlarges
Gad's territory

will be blessed.
He lies down like a lion
and tears off an arm or even a head.[d]
21 He chose the best part for himself,
because a ruler's portion was assigned
there for him.
He came with the leaders
of the people;
he carried out the LORD's justice
and His ordinances for Israel.[e]

22 He said about Dan:

Dan is a young lion,
leaping out of Bashan.[f]

23 He said about Naphtali:

Naphtali, enjoying approval,
full of the LORD's blessing,
take[D] possession to the west
and the south.

24 He said about Asher:

May Asher[E] be the most blessed
of the sons;
may he be the most favored
among his brothers
and dip his foot in olive oil.[F,g]
25 May the bolts of your gate be iron
and bronze,
and your strength last as long as
you live.

26 There is none like the God
of Jeshurun,[G]
who rides the heavens to your aid,

---

a 33:16 Ex 3:2-4
b Gn 49:26
c 33:18-19 Gn 49:13; Jdg 5:15,18
d 33:20 1Ch 12:8
e 33:20-21 Nm 32:1-38
f 33:22 Jdg 5:17
g 33:24 Gn 49:20
h 33:26 2Sm 22:8-20; Ps 18:7-19

A 33:16 Lit *dwelt*   B 33:17 Some DSS, Sam, LXX, Syr, Vg read *A firstborn bull—he has*   C 33:17 Lit *and his horns are*   D 33:23 Sam, LXX, Syr, Vg, Tg read *he will take*   E 33:24 = Happy or Blessed; Gn 30:13   F 33:24 A symbol for prosperity   G 33:26 = Upright One, referring to Israel

---

and **Manasseh**, Joseph's sons) was primarily for agricultural (vv. 13-16) and military (v. 17) success. The allusion to **Him who appeared in the burning bush** is to place Joseph back at the setting of the covenant God made with Israel and all the promises of His abundant grace associated with it (Ex 3:2-4,16-18).

33:18-19 Zebulun and **Issachar** are linked together as the last two sons of Jacob's wife Leah (Gn 30:18,20) and as neighboring tribes in the area north of the valley of Jezreel. The **mountain** is probably Mount Tabor, the only prominent mountain in their territory. The only reference to Tabor as a place of sacrifice occurs in Hs 5:1; by Hosea's time it was regarded as illegitimate. However, in an earlier time Tabor may have been a place of local worship. Zebulun's border extended as far west as the Mediterranean Sea, and thus its people could **draw from the wealth of the seas and . . . the sand.**

33:20-21 Gad had been described by Jacob as a ferocious warrior who, though attacked by others, would strike back with vengeance (Gn 49:19). Moses viewed the tribe of Gad as one that would seek to enlarge its **territory**, and he blessed anyone who could make that happen. Already in Moses' day

Gad had chosen the fertile land of the northern Transjordan (Nm 32:1-5). Once there, Gad had carved out the largest territory of all the eastern tribes, gaining **a ruler's portion**.

33:22 Jacob depicted **Dan** as a vicious viper that bites horses' heels, throwing their riders to the ground (Gn 49:16-17). Moses compared him to **a young lion, leaping out of Bashan**. Besides affirming the aggressive nature of Dan, the geographical reference to Bashan suggests that the tribe of Dan's occupation of its far northern territory may have originated in Bashan. Dan had been allotted a region near Philistine territory which it was unable to occupy and from which it moved north for more suitable prospects (Jos 19:40-48; Jdg 18:1-29).

33:23 Naphtali settled on the western side of the Sea of Galilee. Jacob said of this son that he "is a doe set free that bears beautiful fawns" (Gn 49:21). Because of the fertile and fruitful nature of the lower Galilee region, Naphtali, Moses said, would enjoy divine **approval**. The spiritual blessing may be seen most fully when Messiah came and spent most of His life and ministry in and about the territory held by Naphtali.

the clouds in His majesty.[h]

27 The God of old is
   your dwelling place,[a]
   and underneath are
   the everlasting arms.
   He drives out the enemy
   before you
   and commands, "Destroy!"

28 So Israel dwells securely;
   Jacob lives untroubled[A,b]
   in a land of grain and new wine;
   even his skies drip with dew.[c]

29 How happy you are, Israel!
   Who is like you,
   a people saved by the LORD?

[a]33:27 Ps 91:9
[b]33:28 Nm 23:9
[c]Dt 8:7-9
[d]33:29 2Sm
22:44-46; Ps
18:43-45
[e]Dt 32:13; Hab
3:19
[f]34:1-4 Dt 3:27

He is the shield that protects you,
   the sword you boast in.
Your enemies will cringe
   before you,[d]
and you will tread
   on their backs.[B,e]

Moses' Death

34 Then Moses went up from the plains of
   Moab to Mount Nebo, to the top of Pisgah,[f] which faces Jericho, and the LORD showed
him all the land: Gilead as far as Dan, [2]all of
Naphtali, the land of Ephraim and Manasseh,
all the land of Judah as far as the Mediterranean[C] Sea, [3]the •Negev, and the region from

---

[A]33:28 Text emended; MT reads *Jacob's fountain is alone*   [B]33:29 Or *high places*   [C]34:2 Lit *Western*

33:24-25 Jacob promised his son Asher that his "food will
be rich, and he will produce royal delicacies" (Gn 49:20).
When Moses prayed, **May Asher be the most blessed of the
sons**, he was probably referring also to material blessings,
particularly to food supplies. This is clear from the desire of
Moses that Asher might **dip his foot in olive oil**. Asher's location on the upper Mediterranean coast, the region of the
modern city of Haifa, accounted for its access to products of
the sea, but the surrounding hills, including Mount Carmel,
also yielded vast quantities of olive oil, as is the case to this
very day. To "dip the foot in olive oil" is a figure of speech
suggesting a luxurious lifestyle.

33:26 Moses concluded the blessing of the tribes by extolling the **God of Jeshurun** (cp. v. 5; 32:15) as the One **who
rides the heavens** on **the clouds in His majesty**. This same
image occurs in ancient Canaanite poetic texts where Baal
is said to ride the clouds, but Moses put to rest the pagan
notions of their God by asserting that it is the God of Israel
who, in fact, is sovereign (Ps 68:4,33; Hab 3:3-15).

33:27-28 The God of history is the God of the present and of
the ages to come, giving Israel security and prosperity.

33:29 In a grand finale, Moses called on **Israel** to recognize

how happy they were—or ought to be. Of all the nations of
the earth, the Lord had **saved** only them in the sense of having called them to be His special possession (7:6; Ex 19:4-
6). They enjoyed His protection as their **shield** and **sword**,
metaphors descriptive of His power and glory (Gn 15:1; Ps
7:10; 18:2; 28:7).

34:1 The Abarim mountain range, east of the Jordan River
just opposite **Jericho**, includes **Mount Nebo** on the western
slope of **Pisgah**. From there it is possible on a clear day
to view all the land of Canaan, including its northernmost
borders at **Gilead** and **Dan**.

34:2 The tribes of **Naphtali . . . Ephraim . . . Manasseh**, and
Judah later occupied the central hill country. Their terri-
tories and even beyond, as far west **as the Mediterranean
Sea**, could be seen from Nebo.

34:3 The rest of the land of Canaan to the south was also
visible from Moses' vantage point. The **Negev** is the vast
desert area south of Judah extending to the Gulf of Aqaba
arm of the Red Sea. The **Valley of Jericho** is another name
for the portion of the Great Rift Valley that includes the
Dead Sea, the southernmost city of which was **Zoar** (cp.
Gn 19:18-26).

A panoramic view from atop Mount Nebo looking toward the Dead Sea. From here Moses looked over into the
promised land.

the Valley of Jericho, the City of Palms, as far as Zoar. ⁴The LORD then said to him, "This is the land I promised Abraham, Isaac, and Jacob, 'I will give it to your descendants.'ᵃ I have let you see it with your own eyes, but you will not cross into it."

⁵So Moses the servant of the LORD died there in the land of Moab, as the LORD had said. ⁶He buried himᴬ in the valleyᵇ in the land of Moab facing Beth-peor, and no one to this day knows where his grave is.ᶜ ⁷Moses was 120 years old when he died; his eyes were not weak, and his vitality had not left him. ⁸The Israelites wept for Moses in the plains of Moab 30 days. Then

the days of weeping and mourning for Moses came to an end.

⁹Joshua son of Nun was filled with the spirit of wisdom because Moses had laid his hands on him. So the Israelites obeyed him and did as the LORD had commanded Moses. ¹⁰No prophet has arisen again in Israel like Moses, whom the LORD knew face to face.ᵈ ¹¹He was unparalleled for all the signs and wonders the LORD sent him to do against the land of Egypt—to Pharaoh, to all his officials, and to all his land, ¹²and for all the mighty acts of power and terrifying deeds that Moses performed in the sight of all Israel.

ᵃ34:4 Gn 12:7; 15:18-20; 26:3; 35:12; Ex 33:1
ᵇ34:6 Nm 21:20
ᶜJd 9
ᵈ34:10 Ex 33:11

ᴬ34:6 Or *He was buried*

34:4 What Moses saw was **the land** God had **promised Abraham, Isaac, and Jacob** hundreds of years earlier as part of the covenant blessing (Gn 12:1; 13:14-17; 15:18-21). Though Moses could see the land with his **own eyes**, he was forbidden access to it because of his sin of dishonoring the Lord in the eyes of the people of Israel (32:51).

34:6 Moses' burial place is unknown today. That was even true "**to this day**," that is, at the time of the final composition of the book of Deuteronomy. Jude referred to the mystery surrounding Moses' burial place, alluding to the dispute of Michael the archangel with the devil about the matter (Jd 9).

34:7 Moses' remarkable **vitality** at the age of **120 years** is mentioned to make the point that he died not of "natural" causes but because he had finished the task of leadership to which God had called him. A person is immortal until God pleases to let his life come to an end.

34:9 **Joshua** had been well schooled to succeed Moses

(3:28; 31:7-8; Nm 27:18-21), but all the training in the world was insufficient without his being **filled with the spirit of wisdom** (cp. Nm 11:17,24-30). When it was apparent to the people that Joshua was adequately prepared for leadership, they **obeyed him . . . as the LORD had commanded Moses**.

34:10 It is impossible to know when the last words of Deuteronomy were penned, but whoever did so remarked that until his day **no prophet . . . like Moses** had **arisen again in Israel**. What set him apart was that he was the only one God communicated with **face to face** (Ex 33:19-23; Nm 12:6-8).

34:11-12 Moses was unique among the prophets also in the number and nature of **the signs and wonders the LORD sent him to do against the land of Egypt** (cp. Ex 4–12). These had the effect of convincing the Egyptians of the mighty **power** of Israel's God (Ex 8:19; 9:27-28; 10:16-17). They were also **performed in the sight of all Israel** to persuade the Lord's own people of His mighty power and glory (Ex 14:31).

Joshua

Introduction

The book of Joshua is named for the most famous member of the Israelites in the generation after the death of Moses. The book describes the history of that generation of Israel who crossed the Jordan River and entered the promised land of Canaan. Their battles and faithfulness have a place among the greatest stories of faith in the Old Testament. Joshua led the people to defeat the adversaries who opposed God's people. He then oversaw the division of the land into the tribal allotments. Finally, Joshua renewed the covenant between the people and God.

The Jordan River was at flood stage when God commanded Joshua to lead the people across. Just as when God opened the Red Sea, He provided a dry path through the Jordan when the priests, bearing the ark of the covenant, touched the edge of the river. This photo of the Jordan taken north of the Sea of Galilee but gives some idea of what the Jordan would have been like facing Jericho. Up until the 1950s, more than 3 billion cubic feet flowed through the southern Jordan annually. With construction of a number of dams on the Jordan north of the Sea of Galilee and on rivers that feed the Jordan, that volume of water has been reduced to 300 million cubic feet a year.

Circumstances of Writing

Author: The author of the book of Joshua is not identified in the Bible and otherwise remains anonymous. If Joshua himself did not originally compose the book that bears his name, then it may be presumed that someone who knew him and his exploits recorded the work. There are numerous references throughout Joshua that suggest a final formation of the book after his lifetime. These include the death of Joshua and descriptions of memorials or names that are said to remain "to this day" (4:9; 5:9; 6:25; 7:26; 8:28-29; 10:27; 13:13; 14:14; 15:63; 16:10; 22:17; 23:8).

Background: The accounts in the book of Joshua occur in the period immediately after Moses' death. This was a new generation, not the one that had left Egypt. The story of Joshua is thus set when the nation of Israel first appeared in the land west of the Jordan River—the land that would bear their name. First Kings 6:1 states that the exodus occurred 480 years before Solomon's fourth year as king (966 B.C.). In Judges 11:26, Jephthah said that Israel had been living in regions of Palestine for 300 years. Jephthah lived around 1100 B.C., thus dating the end of the wilderness journey and the beginning of the conquest around 1400 B.C.

Message and Purpose

Commission of a new leader: Chapter 1 establishes Joshua as divinely appointed leader and as the successor to Moses. God addressed Joshua directly, promising both the land that He promised to Moses (Dt 34:4) and His divine presence (Jos 1:3-5). The commands to be strong and courageous (1:6,7,9) define the mission of Joshua. The miraculous crossing of the Jordan River was God's means of exalting Joshua in the eyes of all Israel (4:14).

Holy War: Joshua's military leadership recurs throughout the first 12 chapters of the book. Its theological dimensions raise questions about the extermination of all people from the land. How could a loving God allow such a slaughter? Appeals to the sovereignty of God and His wrathful judgment may be made. A complemen-

1500 B.C.		1450 B.C.
Aaron 1529–1409?	**Moses** 1526–1406	**Joshua** 1490?–1380?
First alphabet developed in Egypt 1500		Bronze hand mirrors taken from Egypt by Hebrew women 1446
Olmecs settle on the Gulf Coast of Mexico. 1500		The exodus and defeat of Pharaoh at the Red Sea 1446
New Kingdom in Egypt 1500		Exploration of Canaan by the 12 spies 1445
Queen Makare Hatshepsut, daughter of Thutmose I, reigned in Egypt during a period of peace and prosperity. 1483		Hindus perform successful skin grafting and a form of plastic surgery.

tary explanation focuses on the exceptions of Rahab's family and of the Gibeonites, who escaped divine wrath through their confession of faith in Israel's God (2:8-13; 9:9-10,24-25).

Land as an inheritance: Joshua's allocation of the land in chapters 13–21 continued the process already begun by Moses in Transjordan. Insofar as God was giving this land to His people as an inheritance, the tribal allotments take on a covenantal character. This land inheritance formed the material wealth of the families of Israel.

The covenant between God and Israel: The covenant making over which Joshua presided dominates the book. It is explicitly detailed in 8:30-35 and 24:1-28. In both of these sections, Joshua's leadership established Israel in a close relationship with God. God's grace enabled the nation to occupy its land and to worship God alone. The circumcision and Passover celebration in chapter 5, as well as the theological role of the tribal allotments as part of Israel's covenantal inheritance from God, suggest that fulfillment of the covenant is an integral part of the book.

God as holy and as deliverer: The character of God is evident throughout the book, especially in terms of His holiness and His saving acts. Divine holiness occurs in the ceremonies where God separated Israel from the other nations (4:19-24; 5:1-3,13-15; 22:26-27; 24:26-27). The saving acts of God are clearly represented in the military victories of the people.

Contribution to the Bible

Just as Joshua's leadership begins with the death of Moses, so the book of Joshua follows and completes the book of Deuteronomy. Deuteronomy serves as a means by which the new generation of Israelites renewed their covenant with God. The book of Joshua provides the means by which God fulfilled His part of the covenant. God gave them victories, but each victory required a step of faith. God's provision for the people as their leader and guide bore witness to later generations of the divinely willed leadership for Israel, and His gracious gift of the land showed how the people's faithful fulfillment of the covenant could result in abundant blessing.

1425 B.C.   1400 B.C..

Pinnacle of Egyptian prosperity and power under
  Amenhotep III 1417

Events in Deuteronomy 1406

Events in Joshua 1406–1380?

Miraculous crossing of the Jordan River 1406

Destruction of Jericho 1406

Warriors from the north, called Achaians by
  Homer, enter Greece to form foundations of
  Greek civilization. 1400

Multiple cropping within the same year is
  developed in China. 1400

Phoenicians advance open sea transportation
  with ships powered by oars and navigation by
  reference to the stars. 1400

Division of the land into 12 allotments 1385?

Structure

The book of Joshua should be seen as a land grant, similar to the land grants and suzerain treaties of the ancient Near East. The suzerain, who was Israel's God, gave to His people the land that they were meant to receive. There are three major parts to the structure of the land grant.

First is a review of the history and events leading up to the gift of the land. This occurs in chapter 1 and its discussion of what has brought Joshua to this point—the death of Moses. Chapters 2–5 detail the preparation for the acquisition of the gift of the land. Chapters 6–12 describe the battles that were fought as background to the receipt of the land. The second section considers the allotment of the territories to the tribes and families of Israel. The many specific names and towns of this part of the text provide a particularity to the gift that affirms it was an authentic fulfillment of God's promise to His people. The third section is a renewal of the covenant. Here the key parts are the stipulations of the covenant that require loyalty to God alone (24:14-15) and the response of the people that they agree to these demands.

Outline

I. **Preparation for the Land (1:1–5:12)**
   A. Joshua assumes leadership (1:1-18)
   B. Rahab's faith (2:1-24)
   C. Across the Jordan River (3:1–4:24)
   D. Circumcision and Passover (5:1-12)

II. **Victories in the Land (5:13–12:24)**
   A. Success against Jericho (5:13–6:27)
   B. Failure of Achan (7:1-26)
   C. Success against Ai (8:1-29)
   D. Covenant renewal (8:30-35)
   E. Failure of Israel and Gibeon (9:1-27)
   F. Victories in the land (10:1–12:24)

III. **Allotment of the Land (13:1–21:45)**
   A. Remaining lands (13:1-7)
   B. Transjordan's allotment (13:8–14:5)
   C. Judah's allotment (14:6–15:63)
   D. Joseph's allotment (16:1–17:18)
   E. Mapping the remaining land (18:1-10)
   F. Tribal allotments (18:11–19:51)
   G. Cities of refuge (20:1-9)
   H. Cities of the Levites (21:1-42)
   I. God's promises fulfilled (21:43-45)

IV. **Worship of God (22:1–24:33)**
   A. Transjordan and the altar of controversy (22:1-34)
   B. Joshua's farewell address (23:1-16)
   C. Israel's covenant at Shechem (24:1-28)
   D. Joshua and his generation die (24:29-33)

Encouragement of Joshua

1 After the death of Moses[a] the LORD's servant, the LORD spoke to Joshua[A] son of Nun,[b] who had served Moses: [2] "Moses My servant is dead.[c] Now you and all the people prepare to cross over the Jordan[d] to the land I am giving the Israelites. [3] I have given you every place where the sole of your foot treads,[e] just as I promised Moses. [4] Your territory will be from the wilderness and Lebanon[f] to the great Euphrates River—all the land of the Hittites[g]—and west to the Mediterranean Sea.[B,h] [5] No one will be able to stand against you as long as you live.[i] I will be with you, just as I was with Moses. I will not leave you or forsake you.[j]

[6] "Be strong and courageous,[k] for you will distribute the land I swore to their fathers to give them as an inheritance.[l] [7] Above all, be strong and very courageous to carefully observe the whole instruction My servant Moses commanded you.[m] Do not turn from it to the right or the left, so that you will have success wherever you go. [8] This book of instruction must not depart from your mouth;[n] you are to recite[c] it day and night so that you may carefully observe everything written in it. For then you will prosper and succeed in whatever you do.[o] [9] Haven't I commanded you: be strong and courageous?[p] Do not be afraid or discouraged, for the LORD your God is with you wherever you go."

Joshua Prepares the People

[10] Then Joshua commanded the officers of the people: [11] "Go through the camp and tell the people, 'Get provisions ready for yourselves, for within three days you will be crossing the Jordan to go in and take possession of the land the LORD your God is giving you to inherit.'"[q]

Cross references

a1:1 Dt 34:5
b Ex 17:8-13; 33:11; Nm 13:8,16; 14:6-9; 27:18-23; Dt 31:2-8; 1Ch 7:20,27
c1:2 Dt 34:5-8
d Jos 1:11
e1:3-5 Dt 11:24-25
f1:4 Gn 15:18; Nm 34:3
g Gn 10:15; 15:19-21
h Dt 11:24; 1Kg 4:21,24-25; 8:65
i1:5 Dt 7:24
j Dt 31:6-8; Heb 13:5
k1:6 Jos 1:18; 10:25; 1Kg 2:2-3; 1Ch 22:13; 28:20; Ps 27:14; 31:24
l Gn 15:18; Ex 32:13; Dt 15:4
m1:7 Dt 5:32; 20:1-2; 21:1-3
n1:8 Dt 31:24; Jos 8:34
o Dt 29:9; Ps 1:1-3
p1:9 Dt 31:7-8; Jos 10:25
q1:11 Jos 3:2

A1:1 = The LORD Will Save, or The LORD Is Salvation; Joshua is related to the name Jesus. B1:4 Lit and to the Great Sea, the going down of the sun C1:8 Or meditate on

---

1:1 The **death of Moses** created a leadership vacuum. Moses' epithet, **LORD's servant**, was first applied at his death (Dt 34:5) as this epithet would first be applied to Joshua at his death (Jos 24:29). Used rarely in the earlier part of the Bible as an evaluation of a person's life, it became more common and was enhanced by Jesus (Jn 15:15), although Paul retained the title (Rm 1:1). **Joshua son of Nun, who had served Moses**, identifies Joshua as the one who had been with Moses since Exodus 17. That he "served Moses" (cp. Ex 24:13) uses a different term than "LORD's servant."

1:2 God commanded Joshua to prepare the people **to cross over the Jordan**. The key word "cross over" (Hb 'avar) ties this section together. The fact that **all the people** were involved emphasizes the importance of unity among the people of God. God emphasized that the land was something He was **giving the Israelites**; it was God's grace, not the efforts of the Israelites, that provided the land.

1:3 Repeating the emphasis on the land as God's gift, it now included **every place where the sole of your foot treads**. Although the "promised land" is normally understood as something that God promised Abram, Isaac, and Jacob (Gn 12:1-3), here God attached the promise to **Moses**. Deuteronomy 34:4 refers to this promise made to Moses (cp. Ex 3). The extension of Moses' promise to Joshua further establishes him as successor.

1:4 This **wilderness** is not the land of wandering. The term is used in 8:15,20 and 12:8 to describe the area east of Ai and the "desert" region of Judah in the south. It thus designates the southern part of the promised land. **Lebanon** ("white") refers to the mountains north of Israel in the modern land of that name. The **land of the Hittites** seems not to refer to the Hittite Empire of modern Turkey but the Egyptian and later Assyrian usage of this term to describe the region controlled by the Hittites in the western part of modern Syria. These lands and boundaries identify Canaan as it was known both to the Bible (Gn 10:19; Nm 13:17,21-22; 34:3-12) and to Egyptian writers of the second millennium B.C.

1:5 The reference to **as long as you live** looks to the end of Joshua's life, concluding this "Table of Contents" in verses

2-5. The promise **I will not leave you** anticipates the plea of Gibeon in 10:6, "Don't abandon your servants," using the same expression. Likewise the verb **forsake** occurs again in Joshua, in Israel's promise of loyalty to God ("abandon" in 24:16,20). This verse forms a hinge, concluding the previous sections of promises and introducing the next section of responsibilities. God's promise of His presence occurs again in 1:9 and thus provides an "envelope" to 1:6-9. All the responsibilities of these verses depend on God's presence that guarantees the mission's success, just as Christ's presence enables His disciples to achieve their mission (Mt 28:18-20; Mk 16:15,20; Ac 1:8).

1:6 God's command, **Be strong and courageous**, already spoken by Moses to Israel (Dt 31:6), appears three times here (Jos 1:7,9). The expression is used before great undertakings, like David's charge to Solomon to build the temple (1Ch 28:20), King Hezekiah's encouragement to his subjects to withstand the enemy's siege (2Ch 32:7), and Joshua's own charge to Israel to fight (Jos 10:25).

1:7 The word **success** (Hb sakal; cp. "succeed" in v. 8) is found frequently in the Wisdom literature to describe one's mastery of the world and insight into its challenges ("wise" in Pr 1:3). The **whole instruction** (Hb torah) describes God's revelation in the form of the previous books of the law of Moses.

1:8 Two more references to the **instruction** affirm the key importance of God's revelation. Study and learning of it are to form so much a part of one's life that the words are fully obeyed as in Dt 6:6-9. The "frame" of God's promised presence in Jos 1:5,9 indicates that Joshua's success will come because God is with him, enabling him to read and observe God's word (Eph 2:8-10).

1:10 Joshua assumed leadership of the people. These **officers** were equivalent to "foremen" in Egypt (Ex 5:6-19). The title was used for judges and those with other responsibilities (Dt 1:15-18; 20:5-9). They formed a secular or civil counterpart to the priests.

1:11 The expression **go through** uses the key word "cross over" from verse 2. Thus passing through the camp serves as further preparation for **crossing the Jordan**. The

¹²Joshua said to the Reubenites, the Gadites, and half the tribe of Manasseh:[a] ¹³"Remember what Moses the LORD's servant commanded you when he said, 'The LORD your God will give you rest, and He will give you this land.'[b] ¹⁴Your wives, young children, and livestock may remain in the land Moses gave you on this side of the Jordan.[A] But your fighting men must cross over in battle formation[B] ahead of your brothers[c] and help them ¹⁵until the LORD gives your brothers rest, as He has given you, and they too possess the land the LORD your God is giving them. You may then return to the land of your inheritance[c] and take possession of what Moses the LORD's servant[d] gave you on the east side of the Jordan."

¹⁶They answered Joshua, "Everything you have commanded us we will do, and everywhere you send us we will go. ¹⁷We will obey you, just as we obeyed Moses in everything.

Cross references:
a1:12 Nm 32:20-22
b1:13-15 Dt 3:18-20
c1:15 Jos 22:4
dJos 1:1
e1:17 Jos 1:5,9
f1:18 Dt 31:7; Jos 1:6-7,9; 10:25
g2:1 Gn 42:9; Nm 13:2,16-17; Jos 7:2; Jdg 18:2
hHeb 11:31; Jms 2:25

And may the LORD your God be with you, as He was with Moses.[e] ¹⁸Anyone who rebels against your order and does not obey your words in all that you command him, will be put to death. Above all, be strong and courageous!"[f]

Spies Sent to Jericho

2 Joshua son of Nun secretly sent two men as spies[g] from the Acacia Grove,[D] saying, "Go and scout the land, especially Jericho." So they left, and they came to the house of a woman, a prostitute named Rahab,[h] and stayed there.

²The king of Jericho was told, "Look, some of the Israelite men have come here tonight to investigate the land." ³Then the king of Jericho sent word to Rahab and said, "Bring out the men who came to you and entered your house, for they came to investigate the entire land."

⁴But the woman had taken the two men

A1:14 = east of the Jordan River   B1:14 Or *over armed*   C1:14 = fellow Israelites   D2:1 Or *from Shittim*

provisions and the three days recall the previous generation's crossing of the Red Sea where the people had no time for preparation and took unleavened bread (Ex 12–15). This time there will be sufficient time to prepare. The three days may also anticipate the length of time that the spies stayed west of the Jordan River (Jos 2:22).

1:12-18 This latter section seems out of place in the first chapter. Why are the two and one-half tribes singled out for this attention? Joshua needed to be recognized as the leader by all Israel, not just part of it, if he was to fulfill God's plan (v. 2). Reuben, Gad, and the eastern part of Manasseh had already received their land allotment from Moses. They had no incentive to follow Joshua across the Jordan River and risk their lives, unlike their fellow tribes who had yet to take possession of their land. Joshua must persuade these two and one-half tribes to follow him, or Israel would be divided and the mission compromised.

1:13-15 Joshua quoted Moses' word from Dt 3:18-20. The authority who gave these tribes their land east of the Jordan

River did so on the condition that they would follow their fellow tribes across the Jordan River and fight with them. Joshua emphasized the theme of **rest** and how, by crossing over **ahead of your brothers**, these warriors would be in a position to **help them**. These points emphasized the goal of rest for the land and people (11:23; 14:15) and the importance of all Israel working together to achieve the common goal.

1:16-18 This entire statement takes the form of an oath in which promises are made and a curse is invoked upon any who do not carry out their promises.

1:16-17 The affirmation includes three phrases that begin with the words for **everything/everywhere** emphasizing the totality of obedience. The blessing they offered recognized that Joshua had indeed succeeded Moses.

1:18 **Rebels** is used of Israel's rebellion at Kadesh-barnea (Dt 1:26; 9:23), of the nation's history (Dt 9:7,24; 31:27), and of the rebellious son (Dt 21:18-21). All these end in death, as here. The expression **will be put to death** was a legal formula for capital punishment, as found in Ex 21:12 and throughout the Law.

2:1 The term for **spies** comes from the same word as "foot." These "footers" did not always work as spies. In 2Sm 15:10 they announced Absalom as king. Thus they could disseminate information as well as gather it. **Acacia Grove** translates Hebrew *Shittim*, probably a site some miles east of the Jordan River opposite Jericho, and Israel's camp since Nm 25:1. The Hebrew root for Joshua's command, **Go**, is identical to **they left**. Such a response indicates the spies' obedience. Nevertheless, they did not look over the land but went directly to Jericho. Rahab was an innkeeper and prostitute—occupations that are recognized in ancient Near Eastern literature such as the Code of Hammurabi. The presence of an inn at Jericho (Lk 10:30-35) may be explained by its location on the north-south and east-west trade routes. Here the spies could learn about the land and also discover anyone who might be sympathetic.

2:2-3 The story is punctuated by repetitions that emphasize the key points. The first of these is the mission **to investigate the land**. This was told to the king of Jericho who

nuach

Hebrew Pronunciation	[NEW ahkh]
HCSB Translation	rest
Uses in Joshua	9
Uses in the OT	140
Focus Passage	Joshua 1:13,15

Nuach means *rest* (Ex 23:12) or *come to rest* (Gn 8:4). Locusts *settle* (Ex 10:14). *Rest* from enemies means *getting rid of* them (Est 9:16). *Nuach* connotes *wait* (1Sm 25:9), *reside* (Pr 14:33), *remain* (Ps 125:3), *abide* (Ec 7:9), or *be calm* (Is 14:7). Causally, *nuach* signifies *give rest* or *comfort* (Jos 1:13; Pr 29:17). *Nuach* describes *settling* people (Jos 6:23). It means *leave* something (Gn 19:16) or, with a preposition, *leave alone* (Ex 32:10). It suggests *place* (Gn 2:15), *set down* (Jos 4:3), *store* (Dt 14:28), or *deposit* (Nm 19:9). One *lets hands slip* or *rest* (Ec 7:18; 11:6). *Letting rest* conveys *allowing* (Ps 105:14) or *tolerating* (Est 3:8). With objects like wrath or spirit, *nuach* denotes *vent* (Ezk 5:13), *satisfy* (Ezk 16:42), or *pacify* (Zch 6:8). Guards are *stationed* (2Ch 1:14). The infinitive indicates *relief* (Neh 9:28).

and hidden them.ᵃ So she said, "Yes, the men did come to me, but I didn't know where they were from. ⁵At nightfall, when the gate was about to close, the men went out, and I don't know where they were going. Chase after them quickly, and you can catch up with them!" ⁶But she had taken them up to the roof and hidden themᵇ among the stalks of flax that she had arranged on the roof. ⁷The men pursued them along the road to the fords of the Jordan, and as soon as they left to pursue them, the gate was shut.

The Promise to Rahab

⁸Before the men fell asleep, she went up on the roof ⁹and said to them, "I know that the LORD has given you this landᶜ and that the terror of you has fallen on us, and everyone who lives in the land is panicking because of you.ᴬ ¹⁰For we have heard how the LORD dried up the waters of the ˙Red Sea before you when you came out of Egypt,ᵈ and what you did to Sihon and Og, the two Amorite kings you ˙completely destroyedᵉ across the Jordan. ¹¹When

ᵃ2:4 2Sm 17:19
ᵇ2:6 Jms 2:25
ᶜ2:9 Nm 20:24;
Jos 9:24
ᵈ2:10 Ex
14:21-30
ᵉNm 21:23-
30,33-35; Dt
2:32-34; 3:1-3;
Jos 6:21
ᶠ2:11 Jos 5:1;
7:5; Ps 22:14; Is
13:7; 19:1

we heard this, we lost heart, and everyone's courage failedᴮ because of you,ᶠ for the LORD your God is God in heaven above and on earth below. ¹²Now please swear to me by the LORD that you will also show kindness to my family, because I showed kindness to you.ᶜ Give me a sure signᴰ ¹³that you will spare the lives of my father, mother, brothers, sisters, and all who belong to them, and save us from death."

¹⁴The men answered her, "We will give our lives for yours. If you don't report our mission, we will show kindness and faithfulness to you when the LORD gives us the land."

¹⁵Then she let them down by a rope through the window, since she lived in a house that was built into the wall of the city. ¹⁶"Go to the hill country so that the men pursuing you won't find you," she said to them. "Hide yourselves there for three days until they return; afterward, go on your way."

¹⁷The men said to her, "We will be free from this oath you made us swear, ¹⁸unless, when we enter the land, you tie this scarlet cord to the window through which you let us down.

ᴬ2:9 Or *land panics at your approach*   ᴮ2:11 Lit *and spirit no longer remained in anyone*   ᶜ2:12 Lit *to your father's house*   ᴰ2:12 Or *a sign of truth*

---

sent his agents to Rahab's house where they repeated the charge. Known at the highest levels, her actions were high treason in the eyes of the rulers of Jericho.

2:4-5 Rahab's hiding of the spies is mentioned again in verse 6. Rahab denied knowledge about the origin and the destination of the spies. Thus she risked her life, but she also lied. Despite this, Heb 11:31 and Jms 2:25 admire her faith. The text does not condone her act, although there was no other way to save the spies from death. Forgiveness was available with God. The point here is that her words kept the king's men from looking in the house. Repeating information about the **gate** (v. 7) is important because it explains how Rahab's ruse could make sense (the gates were not yet shut when the spies left). Its second mention explains why the spies could no longer leave as they had entered. The shut gates represent the defiance of Jericho, resistant to the movement of God and His people.

2:6 Rahab's hiding of the spies is repeated here from verse 4, delaying explanation of what the spies would actually do, and so heightening the tension.

2:7 The phrase **the road to the fords of the Jordan** informs the reader of how Rahab's ruse worked.

2:9-11 Rahab's **I know** contrasts with her "I didn't know" in verses 4-5. There follows a true confession in place of the former deceit. The phrases **terror of you has fallen on us** and **the land is panicking** repeat the same expressions from Ex 15:15-16. Those predictions looked forward to reactions that Rahab describes having been fulfilled. Confessions of God's gift and sovereignty over heaven and earth begin and end the confession (Jos 2:9a,11b). Situated within these confessions are statements about the fear that has come upon the Canaanites (vv. 9b,11a). All these expressions provide an "envelope" for the central confession of Rahab in verse 10. This confession is based upon the historic acts of God's redemption of Israel at the Red Sea and against Sihon and

Og. As with God's historic act of redemption in the death and resurrection of Jesus Christ, so Rahab's confession of His gracious work in redeeming Israel from Egypt and beyond forms the basis for the salvation faith that she speaks with her mouth and believes in her heart (Rm 10:9).

2:12 Now please introduces Rahab's request with an identical form of words as in 1Sm 24:21 where Saul described God's will for David and then, as here, requested David to spare his family. **Show kindness** is a key expression that also appears when Abraham's servant requested from God direction to find a wife for Isaac (Gn 24:12). In the Decalogue God shows kindness to a thousand generations of those who are faithful to him (Ex 20:6). Here as well the concern is for the preservation of Rahab's family and her descendants. The **sure sign** is the spies' oath to protect Rahab's family.

2:13 Rahab did not ask for her own salvation, but for that of her family.

2:14 The spies acted to guarantee their own protection and thereby ensure the success of their **mission**. The spies were vulnerable and dependent on Rahab.

2:15 The actions described did not occur immediately. How secret would a mission be with the spies on the ground below shouting up to Rahab the negotiations of verses 17-20? That **she let them down by a rope through the window** is a summary that introduces a more detailed description in verses 16-21—a common technique in OT accounts.

2:16 The Jordan River was east of Jericho, but the steep hills that ascended from the Jordan Valley were to the west. The spies could hide there among the many caves and nooks. On the **three days**, see note at 1:11.

2:17-20 The **scarlet cord** at the opening of her house with the family gathered inside is clearly symbolic of the Passover and its placement of blood on the door frames of the house in which the family was preserved from death

Bring your father, mother, brothers, and all your father's family into your house. ¹⁹ If anyone goes out the doors of your house, his blood will be on his own head,ᵃ and we will be innocent. But if anyone with you in the house should be harmed,ᴬ his blood will be on our heads. ²⁰ And if you report our mission, we are free from the oath you made us swear."

²¹ "Let it be as you say," she replied, and she sent them away. After they had gone, she tied the scarlet cord to the window.

²² So the two men went into the hill country and stayed there three days until the pursuers had returned. They searched all along the way, but did not find them. ²³ Then the men returned, came down from the hill country, and crossed the Jordan. They went to Joshua son of Nun and reported everything that had happened to them. ²⁴ They told Joshua, "The LORD has handed over the entire land to us. Everyone who lives in the land is also panicking because of us."ᴮ

Crossing the Jordan

3 Joshua started early the next morning and left the Acacia Groveᶜ with all the Israelites. They went as far as the Jordan and stayed

there before crossing. ² After three days the officers went through the campᵇ ³ and commanded the people: "When you see the ark of the covenant of the LORD your God carried by the Levitical priests,ᶜ you must break camp and follow it. ⁴ But keep a distance of about 1,000 yardsᴰ between yourselves and the ark. Don't go near it, so that you can see the way to go, for you haven't traveled this way before."ᴱ

⁵ Joshua told the people, "Consecrate yourselves,ᵈ because the LORD will do wonders among you tomorrow." ⁶ Then he said to the priests, "Take the ark of the covenant and go on ahead of the people." So they carried the ark of the covenant and went ahead of them.

⁷ The LORD spoke to Joshua: "Today I will begin to exalt you in the sight of all Israel,ᵉ so they will know that I will be with you just as I was with Moses. ⁸ Command the priests carrying the ark of the covenant: When you reach the edge of the waters,ᶠ stand in the Jordan."

⁹ Then Joshua told the Israelites, "Come closer and listen to the words of the LORD your God." ¹⁰ He said: "You will know that the living God is among youᶠ and that He will certainly dispossess before you the Canaanites, Hittites, Hivites, Perizzites, Girgashites, Amorites, and

---

ᵃ2:19 Mt 27:25
ᵇ3:2 Jos 1:11
ᶜ3:3 Dt 31:9
ᵈ3:5 Ex 19:10;
Jos 7:13
ᵉ3:7 Jos 4:14
ᶠ3:10 Dt 5:26

ᴬ2:19 Lit *if a hand should be on him*   ᴮ2:24 Or *also panics at our approach*   ᶜ3:1 Or *left Shittim*   ᴰ3:4 Lit *2,000 cubits*   ᴱ3:4 Lit *yesterday and the day before*   ᶠ3:8 Lit *waters of the Jordan*

(Ex 12:3-13). At the same time that Israel celebrated the Passover in the new land (Jos 5:10-11), Rahab would be joining them in similar actions that would bring about her salvation from Jericho's destruction.

2:24 The spies' report is a summary of what Rahab said, using her words (v. 9). This reiterates the fulfillment of prophecy (Ex 15:15) and the power of God to bring success to Israel. Contrast the majority report of the earlier generation of spies who focused on the obstacles of the land's inhabitants (Nm 13:26-33). The spies here emphasized what God had done. Rahab, though not a leader like Joshua, was able to contribute to the success of Israel. Christians can do the same wherever they are by confessing their faith and acting on it (Jms 2:25-26).

3:1–4:24 These two chapters outline the ceremony of Israel's crossing of the Jordan River. This was not a casual activity but something specifically commanded by God. They illustrate the importance of hearing God's word and responding in faithful obedience (Mt 17:20; Lk 17:6).

3:1 Acacia Grove is the place where Israel had been since Balaam's failed attempt to curse them (Nm 22:1; 25:1). This was some miles from the actual place where they crossed the Jordan River. In the south opposite Jericho, this meandering river was at that time surrounded by thickets, so it was not a place suitable for a stay of any length (Jr 12:5). The key word **crossing** again occurs here (see note at 1:2).

3:2-5 On **the officers**, see note at 1:10. The **ark of the covenant** was the symbol of the presence of God among His people. The considerable distance of **1,000 yards** may suggest the need to remain away from the presence of God, especially as a miracle was happening. This separation

of a holy God from His people occurred at Mount Sinai (Ex 19:10-25). The command to **consecrate yourselves** recalls Ex 19:10-15 where consecration was defined as the washing of clothes and as abstinence from sexual relations. This would allow God to work through the people to accomplish His **wonders**—a term that describes the plagues of Egypt in Ex 3:20 and more general acts in Ex 34:10.

3:6 Joshua's first instructions to the priests appear here. Note that the verse describes their precise obedience to his words.

3:7 God's promise of His presence with Joshua accompanied a promise to **exalt** Joshua (as also Abram in Gn 12:2) as a seal on his leadership over Israel.

3:8 Here is the first example of **the Jordan** River being used as a place where God chose to cleanse and redeem believers. Others included Naaman in 2Kg 5:10-15 and those baptized by John the Baptist (Mt 3:1-6).

3:9 This is Joshua's first speech to the Israelites. His concern that they **come closer and listen** suggests the importance of attention to God and His word.

3:10 The phrase **living God** appears elsewhere only three times in the OT. In Hs 1:10 it is used in the context of the fulfillment of God's promises of an innumerable people who belong to Him. In Ps 42:2 and 84:2 it describes the deepest yearnings of the psalmist, who longed for the presence of God and intimacy with Him. The concern for the presence of God and His fulfillment of His promises for His people are both present here. The **Canaanites, Hittites, Hivites, Perizzites, Girgashites, Amorites, and Jebusites** describe the pre-Israelite inhabitants of the land. "Canaanites" is a general term referring to those living in the land of Canaan,

Jebusites[a] [11]when the ark of the covenant of the Lord of all the earth[b] goes ahead of you into the Jordan. [12]Now choose 12 men from the tribes of Israel, one man for each tribe.[c] [13]When the feet[A] of the priests who carry the ark of the Lord, the Lord of all the earth, come to rest in the Jordan's waters, its waters will be cut off. The water flowing downstream will stand up in a mass."[d]

[14]When the people broke camp to cross the Jordan, the priests carried the ark of the covenant[e] ahead of the people. [15]Now the Jordan overflows its banks throughout the harvest season.[f] But as soon as the priests carrying the ark reached the Jordan, their feet touched the water at its edge [16]and the water flowing downstream stood still, rising up in a mass that extended as far as[B] Adam, a city next to Zarethan. The water flowing downstream into the Sea of the •Arabah[g] (the Dead Sea) was completely cut off, and the people crossed opposite Jericho. [17]The priests carrying the ark of the Lord's covenant stood firmly on dry ground in the middle of the Jordan,[h] while all Israel crossed on dry ground until the entire nation had finished crossing the Jordan.

[a]3:10 Ex 33:2; Dt 7:1
[b]3:11 Zch 6:5
[c]3:12 Jos 4:2
[d]3:13 Ex 15:8
[e]3:14 Ac 7:44-45
[f]3:15 1Ch 12:15; Jr 12:5; 49:19
[g]3:16 Dt 1:1
[h]3:17 Ex 14:29
[i]4:1 Jos 3:17
[j]4:2 Jos 3:12
[k]4:6 Ex 12:26-27; 13:8-9,14; Dt 6:20-24; Jos 4:21-22
[l]4:7 Ex 12:14; Nm 16:40

The Memorial Stones

4 After the entire nation had finished crossing the Jordan,[i] the Lord spoke to Joshua: [2]"Choose 12 men from the people, one man for each tribe,[j] [3]and command them: Take 12 stones from this place in the middle of the Jordan where the priests[c] are standing, carry them with you, and set them down at the place where you spend the night."

[4]So Joshua summoned the 12 men he had selected from the Israelites, one man for each tribe, [5]and said to them, "Go across to the ark of the Lord your God in the middle of the Jordan. Each of you lift a stone onto his shoulder, one for each[D] of the Israelite tribes, [6]so that this will be a sign among you. In the future, when your children ask you, 'What do these stones mean to you?'[k] [7]you should tell them, 'The waters of the Jordan were cut off in front of the ark of the Lord's covenant. When it crossed the Jordan, the Jordan's waters were cut off.' Therefore these stones will always be a memorial for the Israelites."[l]

[8]The Israelites did just as Joshua had commanded them. The 12 men took stones from

---

[A]3:13 Lit soles of the feet   [B]3:16 Alt Hb tradition reads mass at   [C]4:3 Lit feet of the priests   [D]4:5 Lit shoulder according to the number

---

although it may also describe the indigenous peoples of the land.

3:11 The ark's passage, using the key word "cross over" (1:2), demonstrates God's leadership of His people, His presence with them, and His fulfillment of His promises. The **Lord of all the earth** uses a phrase identical to that charged against the spies in 2:3 ("the entire land"). While God is indeed Lord of all the earth, the expression in chapters 2 and 3 focuses on "the whole land" of Canaan.

3:12 The **12 men** introduces a third group in addition to the people who will follow the ark and the priests who will carry it. The purpose of these men is explained in 4:2-3.

3:13 The **mass** of the water is the same term as that used of the waters of the Red Sea in Ex 15:8 and Ps 78:13. God would act for His people when they crossed the Jordan River just as He did with the previous generation at the exodus.

3:15 At spring flood, after the winter rains and during the barley harvest, the **Jordan** River could reach a width in excess of 100 feet and a depth of 10 feet. The **priests** as the leaders of the people were the first to step down into the water. Doing so was a risky activity with the river at flood stage. Carrying the **ark** could easily have caused them to be swept away by the current unless the promised miracle took place.

3:16-17 The town of **Adam** is modern Tell ed-Damiye, about 17 miles north of Jericho. **Zarethan** may be either three or 11 miles north of Adam, depending on which site it is identified with (Tell Umm Hamid or Tell es-Sa'idiyeh). Taking into account the distance from Adam to the **Dead Sea**, this means that approximately 29 percent of the Jordan Valley was affected (R. Hess, *Joshua*, p. 105). Wordplay ties together the actions of the priests and people with God's miracle

of the waters. Thus the same verb (Hb *amad*) describes how the waters **stood still** and how the priests **stood firmly**. The priests stood **on dry ground** while the people crossed **on dry ground**. The water **was completely cut off** (Hb *tammu*) until all Israel **had finished** (Hb *tammu*) **crossing** the river.

4:1 The emphasis on **the entire nation** crossing suggests the importance of the unity pictured here. The term **had finished** could also be interpreted as "were finishing," meaning the crossing and the events of verses 1-5 overlapped. The key word **crossing** (Hb *avar*) occurs four times in this section. See note at 1:2.

4:2 These are the **12 men** selected at 3:12.

4:3 The **12 stones** represent the point of the crossing of the whole nation of Israel, all 12 tribes. This would enable future generations to understand and participate spiritually in the crossing that Joshua and the 12 tribes experienced.

4:6-7 The word **sign** occurs only here in Joshua. In the Pentateuch it is associated with Israel's religious festivals and events, such as Passover (Ex 12:14; 13:9). The explanation given to future generations takes a chiastic form. The outermost phrases designate a sign or **memorial**. Within are lines referring to **these stones** and then how the waters of the Jordan were **cut off**. The central focus is that this occurred when **the ark of the Lord's covenant**, the presence of God, **crossed the Jordan**.

4:8-9 There are three possibilities here. First, Joshua may have set up a separate pile of stones in the middle of the river, which was probably visible during the dry season. Second, Joshua, as leader, was credited with taking the 12 stones out of the river by means of the **12 men** in his employ. The phrase in verse 9 means that **Joshua** commanded the men to **set up 12 stones** *from* the middle of the Jordan.

the middle of the Jordan, one for each[A] of the Israelite tribes, just as the Lord had told Joshua. They carried them to the camp and set them down there. [9]Joshua also set up 12 stones in the middle[B] of the Jordan where the priests[c] who carried the ark of the covenant were standing. The stones are there to this day.[a]

[10]The priests carrying the ark continued standing in the middle of the Jordan until everything was completed that the Lord had commanded Joshua to tell the people, in keeping with all that Moses had commanded Joshua. The people hurried across, [11]and after everyone had finished crossing, the priests with the ark of the Lord crossed in the sight of the people. [12]The Reubenites, Gadites, and half the tribe of Manasseh went in battle formation in front of the Israelites,[b] as Moses had instructed them. [13]About 40,000 equipped for war crossed to the plains of Jericho in the Lord's presence.

[14]On that day the Lord exalted Joshua in the sight of all Israel, and they revered him throughout his life, as they had revered Moses.[c] [15]The Lord told Joshua, [16]"Command the priests who carry the ark of the •testimony[D,d] to come up from the Jordan."

[17]So Joshua commanded the priests, "Come up from the Jordan." [18]When the priests carrying the ark of the Lord's covenant came up

[a]4:9 Jos 6:25
[b]4:12 Nm 32:17
[c]4:14 Jos 3:7
[d]4:16 Ex 25:16
[e]4:22 Jos 3:17
[f]4:23 Ex 14:21
[g]4:24 Ex 9:14-16; 14:31; 1Kg 8:42
[h]Ps 89:13
[i]Ex 14:31
[j]5:1 Nm 13:29
[k]Jos 2:11

from the middle of the Jordan, and their feet[E] stepped out on solid ground, the waters of the Jordan resumed their course, flowing over all the banks as before.

[19]The people came up from the Jordan on the tenth day of the first month,[F] and camped at Gilgal on the eastern limits of Jericho. [20]Then Joshua set up in Gilgal the 12 stones they had taken from the Jordan, [21]and he said to the Israelites, "In the future, when your children ask their fathers, 'What is the meaning of these stones?' [22]you should tell your children, 'Israel crossed the Jordan on dry ground.'[e] [23]For the Lord your God dried up the waters of the Jordan before you until you had crossed over,[f] just as the Lord your God did to the •Red Sea, which He dried up before us until we had crossed over. [24]This is so that all the people of the earth may know[g] that the Lord's hand is mighty,[h] and so that you may always •fear the Lord your God."[i]

Circumcision of the Israelites

5 When all the Amorite kings across the Jordan to the west and all the Canaanite kings near the sea[j] heard how the Lord had dried up the waters of the Jordan before the Israelites until they had crossed over,[k] they lost heart and their courage failed[G] because of the Israelites.

[2]At that time the Lord said to Joshua, "Make

Third, verse 9 might be retrospective—Joshua *had* set up 12 stones in the middle of the Jordan—and the 12 men subsequently picked up those same stones and **set them down** in the camp.

4:12 On these tribes, see note at 1:12-18.

4:13 The troops that crossed entered enemy territory, but they also had established a foothold in the promised land when they arrived west of the Jordan River. This **40,000** represented the best portion of the Transjordanian fighting force that crossed with their kinsmen. According to Nm 26:7,18,34 the total of these two and a half tribes would have been over a hundred thousand (see note at Nm 1:44-46). Perhaps the rest were protecting their land and families.

4:14 That **the Lord exalted Joshua** indicates the fulfillment of 3:8. The connection with Moses is reaffirmed.

4:15-17 The time of the exit from the **Jordan** River, like the time of the entrance into the river, is determined by God.

4:18 The priests' ascent from the river bed brings the miracle to an end. They reversed the procedure by which they began the parting of the waters (3:13-16).

4:19 The **tenth day of the first month** was the day that preparations for the Passover were to be made (Ex 12:2-3). This signals the celebration of chapter 5. **Gilgal,** meaning "circle," could describe any of a variety of sites.

4:20-23 The purpose of the **12 stones** is found in the ques-

tions that the children would ask. The question and the instruction of the next generation about the divine miracles resembles Dt 6:6-9. Questions asked by sons about the significance of the Passover and the exodus are found in the Jewish Passover Seder or liturgy. Their mention here connects this Passover with the events of the crossing of the **Jordan** just as the earlier Passover remembered the crossing of the **Red Sea.**

4:24 The purpose of this miracle is to declare God's might to **all the people of the earth** and to encourage Israel to **always fear the Lord.** Faith and commitment to God is the goal, just as with the miracles of Jesus (Jn 20:30-31).

5:1 The **Amorite kings** dominated the hill country whereas the **Canaanite kings** lived near the Mediterranean Sea. The message that these kings **heard** concerns **how the Lord had dried up the waters of the Jordan,** and it links 4:24 and the statement there. While the effect in chapter 4 was to increase faith, here it had the opposite effect on the enemies. The key word, **crossed over,** again occurs (1:2). That they **lost heart** is literally "their heart melted." This repeats Rahab's description of the Canaanites upon hearing of Israel's victory over Egypt (2:9-11, which also includes the same verb for drying up the Red Sea).

5:2 The command to **circumcise** implies that this generation had not been circumcised (vv. 4-7) and revives **again** this act of covenant making that God began with Abraham

flint knives and circumcise the Israelite men again."[a] [3] So Joshua made flint knives and circumcised the Israelite men at Gibeath-haaraloth.[A] [4] This is the reason Joshua circumcised them: All the people who came out of Egypt who were males—all the men of war—had died in the wilderness along the way after they had come out of Egypt. [5] Though all the people who came out were circumcised, none of the people born in the wilderness along the way were circumcised after they had come out of Egypt. [6] For the Israelites wandered in the wilderness 40 years until all the nation's men of war who came out of Egypt had died off because they did not obey the LORD.[b] So the LORD vowed never to let them see the land He had sworn to their fathers to give us, a land flowing with milk and honey.[c] [7] Joshua raised up their sons in their place; it was these he circumcised. They were still uncircumcised, since they had not been circumcised along the way. [8] After the entire nation had been circumcised, they stayed where they were in the camp until they recovered.[d] [9] The LORD then said to Joshua, "Today I have rolled away the disgrace of Egypt from you." Therefore, that place is called Gilgal[B] to this day.[e]

Food from the Land

[10] While the Israelites camped at Gilgal on

the plains of Jericho, they kept the ˚Passover on the evening of the fourteenth day of the month.[C] [11] The day after Passover they ate unleavened bread and roasted grain from the produce of the land. [12] And the day after they ate from the produce of the land, the manna ceased.[f] Since there was no more manna for the Israelites, they ate from the crops of the land of Canaan that year.

Commander of the LORD's Army

[13] When Joshua was near Jericho, he looked up and saw a man standing in front of him with a drawn sword in His hand.[g] Joshua approached Him and asked, "Are You for us or for our enemies?"

[14] "Neither," He replied. "I have now come as commander of the LORD's army."

Then Joshua bowed with his face to the ground in worship[h] and asked Him, "What does my Lord want to say to His servant?"

[15] The commander of the LORD's army said to Joshua, "Remove the sandals from your feet, for the place where you are standing is holy."[i] And Joshua did so.

The Conquest of Jericho

6 Now Jericho was strongly fortified because of the Israelites—no one leaving or entering. [2] The LORD said to Joshua, "Look, I have handed Jericho, its king, and its fighting

[a]5:2 Gn 17:10-14; Ex 4:24-26; 12:44,48; Lv 12:3
[b]5:6 Dt 2:7,14
[c]Nm 14:23-24; Dt 11:9
[d]5:8 Dt 30:6; Hs 6:1-2
[e]5:9 Jos 6:25
[f]5:12 Ex 16:35; Ps 78:25; Jn 6:48-51
[g]5:13 Gn 18:2; 32:24; Nm 22:31
[h]5:14 Gn 17:3
[i]5:15 Ex 3:5

[A]5:3 Or *The Hill of Foreskins*   [B]5:9 = to roll   [C]5:10 = Nisan (March–April)

(Gn 17). Thus Israel would once again become children of Abraham and heirs of the promised land.

5:3 Gibeath-haaraloth means "the hill of foreskins," an unknown site.

5:4-9 Words and phrases are repeated and interwoven to explain the necessity of this act. A contrast is made repeating the verb "to end, to finish" in verses 6 and 8. Thus the previous generation **died off** (v. 6) while the present generation "finished" being circumcised.

5:5 The generation coming from Egypt had been united in their circumcision. Egyptians also circumcised their males, but as Genesis 17 suggests, the Israelite practice precedes their time in Egypt.

5:9 The wordplay on **Gilgal**, which means "circle" as a noun and "roll" as a verb, refers to rolling away **the disgrace of Egypt**. This was the rebellion of the previous generation of Israel that caused them to die in the desert. Because this current generation had followed the covenant and had been circumcised, they could now enter the promised land and leave behind forever the disgrace of their parents.

5:10 Israel was explicitly commanded to celebrate the **Passover** when the people arrived in the promised land (Ex 13:5). Israel thereby inherited the covenantal promises and blessings that the earlier generation had received when it left Egypt.

5:11 The days of **unleavened bread** follow the Passover (Ex 12:17,20; 23:15; 34:18). The basic food of Canaan was barley that ripened at this time. Manna had been all that the pres-

ent generation of Israel knew. Now they would begin to eat from the food of the new land. Israel enjoyed the fruits of the land where they had arrived as a token of the greater abundance they were to enjoy when the entire land was taken.

5:12 The cessation of **the manna** signaled a new phase in Israel's history. The people were no longer in the wilderness but in their homeland. They began a new life in keeping with the celebration of God's historic acts of redemption. Today this occurs with the new life in Jesus Christ whose death and resurrection bring it about.

5:13 God had promised His presence to Joshua (1:7-9), and here He began to fulfill it. Joshua encountered a man with a **drawn sword**. In Nm 22:23 Balaam's donkey stopped before such a figure.

5:14-15 The man's title **commander of the LORD's army** suggests someone of importance. The relevant question was not whether he was for or against Joshua, but how Joshua regarded him. Joshua bowed to worship. The man's command to remove his sandals evokes God's encounter with Moses at the burning bush (Ex 3:5). God appeared to Joshua before this great challenge to encourage him and to provide directions for what he should do.

6:1 As the gates of Jericho were shut in 2:7, so here the place is similarly described as **strongly fortified**, literally "very much shut." This describes the physical defense, but it also represents a resistance to the plans of God.

6:2 The **king**, as the term is used in contemporary texts, was a military leader responsible to higher authorities such as

men over to you.[a] [3] March around the city with all the men of war, circling the city one time. Do this for six days. [4] Have seven priests carry seven ram's-horn trumpets in front of the ark. But on the seventh day, march around the city seven times, while the priests blow the trumpets.[b] [5] When there is a prolonged blast of the horn and you hear its sound, have all the people give a mighty shout. Then the city wall will collapse, and the people will advance, each man straight ahead."

[6] So Joshua son of Nun summoned the priests and said to them, "Take up the ark of the covenant and have seven priests carry seven trumpets in front of the ark of the LORD." [7] He said to the people, "Move forward, march around the city, and have the armed troops go ahead of the ark of the LORD."

[8] After Joshua had spoken to the people, seven priests carrying seven trumpets before the LORD moved forward and blew the trumpets; the ark of the LORD's covenant followed them. [9] While the trumpets were blowing, the armed troops went in front of the priests who blew the trumpets, and the rear guard

[a]6:2 Dt 7:24
[b]6:4 Ex 19:13; Ps 24:7; Is 18:3; 1Co 15:52; 1Th 4:16; Rv 11:15
[c]6:9 Is 52:12

went behind the ark.[c] [10] But Joshua had commanded the people: "Do not shout or let your voice be heard. Don't let one word come out of your mouth until the time I say, 'Shout!' Then you are to shout." [11] So the ark of the LORD was carried around the city, circling it once. They returned to the camp and spent the night there.[A]

[12] Joshua got up early the next morning. The priests took the ark of the LORD, [13] and the seven priests carrying seven trumpets marched in front of the ark of the LORD. While the trumpets were blowing, the armed troops went in front of them, and the rear guard went behind the ark of the LORD. [14] On the second day they marched around the city once and returned to the camp. They did this for six days.

[15] Early on the seventh day, they started at dawn and marched around the city seven times in the same way. That was the only day they marched around the city seven times. [16] After the seventh time, the priests blew the trumpets, and Joshua said to the people, "Shout! For the LORD has given you the city. [17] But the city and everything in it are •set

---

[A]6:11 Lit at the camp

the leaders of Bethel and Jerusalem. Jericho was situated at the entrance to the roads that ran westward to these towns. God spoke in the past tense as though the victory had already been decided.

6:3-5 These instructions picture a unique ceremony. The ark symbolized the presence of God. The **ram's-horn trumpets** were used for going to war and for the ark (2Sm 6:15; Jr 4:19). The **mighty shout** was used for victory in war and for

Step trench cut by archaeologists into the tel of (OT) Jericho to uncover levels of destruction.

announcing the ark's journey (1Sm 4:5; 2 Ch 13:15). The command to **march around the city** uses the same verb as appears in Ps 48:12 where a pilgrimage was made around Jerusalem to inspect its defenses. In 2Kg 6:14 the king of Aram surrounded Dothan to capture the prophet Elisha. Here at Jericho the march involved a ceremonial inspection of the fort's defenses to note the obstinacy of Jericho and to provide an opportunity for those inside to surrender and open the gates.

The emphasis on **seven times** and seven days coincides with the Feast of Unleavened Bread celebrating God's defeat of the enemies of His people. At the first Passover, Israel marched out of Egypt during this feast. In Numbers 9–10 the nation marched away from Mount Sinai during this feast. Here they would march into the promised land, and then around and through Jericho, **straight ahead**.

6:6-14 The verbs and phrases correspond to those commanded by God in verses 2-5. This suggests a perfect obedience by Joshua. The reference to crossing over (**move forward**) occurs three times, using the same verb as the key term for crossing the Jordan River (1:2).

6:15 The **seventh day** was the number of perfection, and it signaled the conclusion of the Feast of Unleavened Bread.

6:16 The **shout** was a war cry (see note at vv. 3-5).

6:17-25 This account of the destruction of Jericho is interwoven with that of the salvation of Rahab and her household (chap. 2). In this section there are 86 Hebrew words devoted to the salvation of Rahab and 102 words to describe Jericho's destruction (R. Hess, *Joshua*, p. 134). For the author of the book of Joshua, Rahab's salvation is as important as the account of Jericho's fall.

6:17 The city being **set apart to the LORD for destruction** was the complete destruction spoken of by Rahab in 2:10 and commanded by God for the inhabitants of Canaan in

apart to the LORD for destruction. Only Rahab the prostitute and everyone with her in the house will live,ᵃ because she hid the menᴬ we sent. ¹⁸ But keep yourselves from the things set apart, or you will be set apart for destruction. If youᴮ take any of those things, you will set apart the camp of Israel for destruction and bring disaster on it. ¹⁹ For all the silver and gold, and the articles of bronze and iron, are dedicated to the LORD and must go into the LORD's treasury."

²⁰ So the people shouted, and the trumpets sounded. When they heard the blast of the trumpet, the people gave a great shout, and the wall collapsed.ᵇ The people advanced into the city, each man straight ahead, and they captured the city. ²¹ They •completely destroyedᶜ everything in the city with the sword—every man and woman, both young and old, and every ox, sheep, and donkey.

Rahab and Her Family Spared

²² Joshua said to the two men who had scouted the land, "Go to the prostitute's house and bring the woman out of there, and all who are with her, just as you promised her."ᵈ ²³ So the young men who had scouted went in and

ᵃ6:17 Dt 7:2
ᵇ6:20 Heb 11:30
ᶜ6:21 Jos 2:10; 8:26
ᵈ6:22 Jos 2:14
ᵉ6:25 Ex 6:23; Ru 4:21-22; 1Ch 2:10-12; Mt 1:4-5
ᶠJos 4:9; 5:9; 7:26; 14:14; 15:63
ᵍ6:26 1Kg 16:34
ʰ7:1 Lv 6:2; Nm 5:27; 31:16; Dt 32:51; Jos 22:16; Ezr 9:2-4

brought out Rahab and her father, mother, brothers, and all who belonged to her. They brought out her whole family and settled them outside the camp of Israel.

²⁴ They burned up the city and everything in it, but they put the silver and gold and the articles of bronze and iron into the treasury of the LORD's house. ²⁵ However, Joshua spared Rahab the prostitute, her father's household, and all who belonged to her, because she hid the men Joshua had sent to spy on Jericho, and she lives in Israelᵉ to this day.ᶠ

²⁶ At that time Joshua imposed this curse:

> The man who undertakes
> the rebuilding of this city, Jericho,
> is cursed before the LORD.
> He will lay its foundation
> at the cost of his firstborn;
> he will set up its gates
> at the cost of his youngest.ᵍ

²⁷ And the LORD was with Joshua, and his fame spread throughout the land.

Defeat at Ai

7 The Israelites, however, were unfaithfulʰ regarding the things •set apart for

---

ᴬ6:17 Lit *messengers*   ᴮ6:18 LXX reads *you covet and*; Jos 7:21

Dt 20:16-18. There the reason given was so no one in Israel would worship other gods. Elsewhere God's mercy and forgiveness were available up to the moment of judgment (2Ch 7:14; Jr 18:5-10; Jnh 4:11), but after that there was no turning back. Salvation is offered to everyone, but the offer can be rejected and there comes a time when it is too late (2Co 6:2).

6:19 The precious metals were assigned to the Lord's tabernacle treasury because these could not be destroyed by fire.

heriyʼa

Hebrew Pronunciation	[hey REE a]
HCSB Translation	shout
Uses in Joshua	7
Uses in the OT	44
Focus Passage	Joshua 6:5,10,16,20

The verb does not occur in other Semitic languages, except perhaps in later Arabic. *Heriyʼa* means *shout*, with connotation depending on context. It suggests *shout loudly* (Zph 3:14) and *raise a war/battle cry* (2Ch 13:15; Jr 50:15). It implies insulting *shouts* (Jb 30:5) or fearful *crying out* (Jdg 7:21). It connotes *shout triumphantly* or *in triumph* (Ps 95:1-2; Zch 9:9). It conveys *shout for joy* or *joyfully* (Ps 66:1; Is 16:10). With reference to trumpets, *heriyʼa* means *sound the alarm* (Jl 2:1) or *sound short blasts* (Nm 10:7). *Heriyʼa* occurs (6x) with related *teruʼah* (*shout, blast*) as *give/raise a shout* (Jos 6:5; 1Sm 4:5), or *sound a charge* (2Ch 13:12). *Heriyʼa* appears (7x) with nearly synonymous *ranan* ("shout, shout for joy"), but *ranan* does not signify giving *war cries*. *Reʼa* (3x) indicates *shouting* (Ex 32:17) and *thunder* (Jb 36:33), appearing as *loudly* (Mc 4:9).

6:21 The list of people and animals here is not to provide an inventory of who was killed, but to emphasize the obedience of Joshua and the people. Verse 2 may suggest that, with the exception of Rahab and her family, the inhabitants of Jericho were military personnel.

6:25 The salvation of **Rahab** was defined as avoidance of death and as life among the people of God, Israel (cp. Jdg 1:22-26).

6:26 The **curse** imposed by Joshua required that no construction take place on the mound of Jericho. It must remain in ruins as a witness to God's judgment upon the site for its resistance to God. The references to **foundation** and **gates**, and the warning about the loss of the eldest (**firstborn**) and the **youngest** was fulfilled in 1Kg 16:34 when Hiel of Bethel rebuilt Jericho in the ninth century B.C. This is not a curse against those who would disturb burials, which was common in those days, but a consideration of Jericho's symbolism for God's judgment and power.

6:27 God's presence with Joshua fulfilled the divine promises of 1:5-9. The **fame** of Joshua describes his renown at the victory over Jericho. Joshua's success at Jericho, his first battle, demonstrated that he was a powerful figure to be reckoned with.

7:1-26 The story of Achan demonstrates the first breach of purity and wholehearted dedication to God in the Israel of the new generation. When the previous generation of Israel accepted the covenant, and before they sinned, their representatives were able to feast with God (Ex 24:9-11). Their sin with the gold calf compromised that fellowship (Ex 32). This new generation of Israel had just been circumcised and were again enjoying the special blessing of God. Now the people of Israel would again taste the first sin and know its terrible consequences.

destruction. Achan son of Carmi, son of Zabdi, son of Zerah, of the tribe of Judah, took some of what was set apart, and the LORD's anger burned against the Israelites.

²Joshua sent men from Jericho to Ai, which is near Beth-aven,ᵃ east of Bethel, and told them, "Go up and scout the land." So the men went up and scouted Ai.

³After returning to Joshua they reported to him, "Don't send all the people, but send about 2,000 or 3,000ᴬ men to attack Ai. Since the people of Ai are so few, don't wear out all our people there." ⁴So about 3,000 menᴮ went up there, but they fled from the men of Ai.ᵇ ⁵The men of Ai struck down about 36 of them and chased them from outside the gate to the quarries,ᶜ striking them down on the descent. As a result, the people's hearts melted and became like water.ᶜ

⁶Then Joshua tore his clothes and fell before the ark of the LORD with his face to the ground until evening, as did the elders of Israel; they all put dust on their heads. ⁷"Oh, Lord GOD," Joshua said, "why did You ever bring these people across the Jordan to hand us over to the Amorites for our destruction? If only we had been content to remain on the other side of the Jordan! ⁸What can I say, Lord, now that Israel has turned its back and run from its enemies? ⁹When the Canaanites and all who live in the land hear about this, they will surround us and wipe out our name from the earth. Then what will You do about Your great name?"

¹⁰The LORD then said to Joshua, "Stand up! Why are you on the ground?ᴰ ¹¹Israel has sinned. They have violated My covenant that I appointed for them. They have taken some of what was set apart. They have stolen, deceived, and put the things with their own belongings.ᵈ ¹²This is why the Israelites cannot stand against their enemies. They will turn their backs and run from their enemies, because they have been set apart for destruction.ᵉ I will no longer be with you unless you remove from you what is set apart. ¹³"Go and consecrate the people. Tell them to consecrate themselves for tomorrow,ᶠ for

ᵃ7:2 Jos 18:12; 1Sm 13:5; 14:23
ᵇ7:4 Lv 26:17; Dt 28:25
ᶜ7:5 Jos 2:11
ᵈ7:11 Jos 6:18
ᵉ7:12 Nm 14:45; Jdg 2:14
ᶠ7:13 Jos 3:5

ᴬ7:3 Or send two or three military units of   ᴮ7:4 Lit men from the people   ᶜ7:5 Or to Shebarim   ᴰ7:10 Lit Why have you fallen on your face?

7:1 Achan's unfaithfulness (in partaking of **what was set apart**—devoted to destruction at Jericho) resulted in God's anger against the entire nation. The genealogy of five generations, from **Achan** back to **the tribe of Judah**, is the longest in the book of Joshua and emphasizes the connection of Achan with one of the 12 tribes and therefore with the entire tribal nation. As much as Israel benefited by Joshua, it would suffer by Achan (cp. Rm 5:12-21).

7:2 Joshua again sent spies before an assault, as in 2:1. Again there was no condemnation of this move. **Ai**, like Jericho, may have been an outpost guarding **Beth-aven**, **Bethel**, and other towns in the central hill country. It lay on the central road from Jericho westward into the hill country and therefore formed an obstacle to Israel's advance. Most scholars associate Ai with modern et-Tell and Bethel with Beitin. If so, Ai, like Jericho, lacks evidence of occupation during the time of Israel's entry into the land. This supports the interpretation of a makeshift fort for the site at this time. Materials were gathered from earlier walls to build the Ai that Joshua's spies encountered. These associations place Ai one mile southeast of Bethel.

7:3 The report of these spies contrasts with that of chapter 2 and resembles that of Numbers 13. Instead of confessing the promises and acts of God, these spies focused on the strategic details of what appeared to be an easy target. The **2,000 or 3,000 men** may refer to two or three squads, as the same word for "thousand" in Hebrew ('elef) also can mean a squad or company of soldiers. The particular form of the verb **wear out** occurs elsewhere only in Ec 3:10, where it describes a fool who doesn't know the way to town—an apt comment on Joshua 7.

7:5 The **36** who died from the 3,000 or three squads (see note at v. 3) may reflect 12 from each squad and thus prefigure the 12 thousand inhabitants of Ai who would die (8:25). The **quarries** designate some of the steep ravines that break

into the eastern hill country as it descends sharply into the Jordan Valley. In 2:11 and 5:1, the hearts of the Canaanites melted in fear before the accomplishments of Israel and its God. Here the Israelites' **hearts melted**.

7:6 Joshua's actions were those of one in mourning. Only then was **the ark of the LORD** mentioned. Its absence in the opening part of the chapter signifies the absence of God's presence and blessing on what happened.

7:7-8 The wish to remain east of the **Jordan** resembles the report of the first spies sent to Canaan in Nm 14:2-4. In Numbers it was a wish for death or a return to Egypt. Contrast God's promise that Israel's enemies would turn their backs and flee in Ex 23:27 with the fact that Israel had now **turned its back** (lit "the back of its neck") and fled.

7:9 The challenge to God's **great name** recalls Moses' intercession for Israel with the same argument in Nm 14:13-19.

7:11 The key word "cross" of chapters 1–5 (see note at 1:2) recurs here with the meaning, **they have violated My covenant**. Israel had "crossed" God and so could not "cross" over against its enemies as it did at Jericho. Someone had **taken what was set apart**. This violated the general command of Dt 20:16-18 and the specific command of Jos 6:17. By putting these things **with their own belongings**, they had made it impossible to determine the guilty person without divine guidance.

7:12 Joshua was commanded to "stand" in verse 10 as the beginning of Israel's means to overcome the problem that they could not **stand against their enemies**. Here God suggested that, so long as the things devoted for destruction remained in Israel's camp, Israel would be **set apart for destruction**. God would not fight for them or be present with them as He had in 1:5-9.

7:13 For Israel **to consecrate themselves** suggests either that they would examine themselves and their families to

this is what the Lord, the God of Israel, says: There are things that are set apart among you, Israel. You will not be able to stand against your enemies until you remove what is set apart. [14] In the morning you must present yourselves tribe by tribe. The tribe the Lord selects is to come forward clan by clan. The clan the Lord selects is to come forward family by family. The family the Lord selects is to come forward man by man. [15] The one who is caught with the things set apart must be burned,[A] along with everything he has, because he has violated the Lord's covenant and committed an outrage in Israel."[a]

Achan Judged

[16] Joshua got up early the next morning. He had Israel come forward tribe by tribe, and the tribe of Judah was selected. [17] He had the clans of Judah come forward, and the Zerahite clan was selected. He had the Zerahite clan come forward by heads of families,[B] and Zabdi was selected. [18] He then had Zabdi's family come forward man by man, and Achan son of Carmi, son of Zabdi, son of Zerah, of the tribe of Judah, was selected.

[19] So Joshua said to Achan, "My son, give glory to the Lord, the God of Israel,[b] and make a confession to Him.[c] I urge you, tell me what you have done. Don't hide anything from me."

[20] Achan replied to Joshua, "It is true. I have sinned against the Lord, the God of Israel.

[a]7:15 Gn 34:7; Dt 22:21; Jdg 19:23-24; 20:6
[b]7:19 1Sm 6:5; 2Ch 30:22; Jr 13:16; Jn 9:24
[c]7:21 Gn 3:6; 2Sm 12:2-4; 1Jn 2:16
[d]7:24 Jos 15:7
[e]7:25 Jos 6:18
[f]7:26 Jos 6:25; 8:28-29; 10:27; 13:13
[g]8:1 Jos 1:9

This is what I did: [21] When I saw among the spoils a beautiful cloak from Babylon,[D] 200 silver •shekels,[E] and a bar of gold weighing 50 shekels,[F] I coveted them and took them.[c] You can see for yourself. They are concealed in the ground inside my tent, with the money under the cloak." [22] So Joshua sent messengers who ran to the tent, and there was the cloak, concealed in his tent, with the money underneath. [23] They took the things from inside the tent, brought them to Joshua and all the Israelites, and spread them out in the Lord's presence.

[24] Then Joshua and all Israel with him took Achan son of Zerah, the silver, the cloak, and the bar of gold, his sons and daughters, his ox, donkey, and sheep, his tent, and all that he had, and brought them up to the Valley of Achor.[d] [25] Joshua said, "Why have you troubled us?[e] Today the Lord will trouble you!" So all Israel stoned them[G] to death. They burned their bodies,[H] threw stones on them, [26] and raised over him a large pile of rocks that remains to this day.[f] Then the Lord turned from His burning anger. Therefore that place is called the Valley of Achor[I] to this day.

Conquest of Ai

8 The Lord said to Joshua, "Do not be afraid or discouraged.[g] Take the whole military force with you and go attack Ai. Look, I have handed over to you the king of Ai, his people,

---

[A]7:15 Lit burned with fire   [B]7:17 Lit forward man by man   [C]7:19 Or and praise Him   [D]7:21 Lit Shinar   [E]7:21 About 5 pounds of silver   [F]7:21 About 1 pound of gold   [G]7:25 Lit him   [H]7:25 Lit burned them with fire   [I]7:26 Or of Trouble

---

learn who was responsible for the sin, or that they would prepare themselves for an encounter with God the next day.

7:14 The **tribe . . . clan,** and **family** were the basic elements of Israelite society, which could be understood in terms of a greatly extended family. Each larger group would come before God, and He would select the subgroup of the larger component.

7:15 The verdict that the guilty one **must be burned** recalls the burning of the devoted things at Jericho (and the town itself) in 6:24, and it fulfills the command to devote the guilty one to God (Dt 13:15-16).

7:16-18 The text does not describe how each group **was selected,** but the use of the Urim and Thummim (Ex 28:30; Nm 27:21) by the high priest seems a possibility. This may be the same as the casting of lots used in Jos 18:6,8,10.

7:21 Achan's confession, with the emphasis on what he **saw** and how it was **beautiful,** recalls Eve's temptation where she also saw something that was pleasing. Achan **coveted them** and thus violated the Tenth Commandment of the Decalogue (Ex 20:17; Dt 5:21). The words of Achan's admission are recorded because this was necessary for the sin to be dealt with, as in 1Jn 1:9.

7:22 Joshua **sent messengers** to resolve the problem that had begun with his act of sending spies in verse 2.

7:24-26 The destruction of Achan with all his family and possessions contrasts with the salvation of Rahab and all her family in chapter 6. The connection of the family with its representative, for good or for ill, illustrates the key value of the family in the OT. Burning someone to death was rare in Israel (Lv 20:14; 21:9), but it was known as a punishment for this type of wrongdoing in neighboring cultures.

7:25 The references to **trouble** are a wordplay on the name of the Valley of Achor. The same root word is used for this verb and for the name of the valley. The description suggests that first **all Israel stoned** Achan and his family and then they burned the corpses, thereby fulfilling the law.

7:26 The **large pile of rocks** raised over Achan uses the Hebrew word gal, which recalls Gilgal where a pile of rocks had also been raised as a memorial (4:20). God's **burning anger** appeared at the worship of the golden calf (Ex 32:11-12) and at the sin of Baal-peor (Nm 25:4).

8:1 God's words **do not be afraid or discouraged** recall His first charge to Joshua, where they set the stage for His promise of presence and for the miracles that followed (1:9). With **the whole military force,** Israel would again be united (unlike 7:3) and thus their victory was more likely. As with the promise about Jericho (6:2), God's instructions to Joshua began with the promise that victory was already assured.

city, and land.*ᵃ* ² Treat Ai and its king as you did Jericho and its king;*ᵇ* you may plunder its spoil and livestock for yourselves. Set an ambush behind the city."

³ So Joshua and the whole military force set out to attack Ai. Joshua selected 30,000 fighting men and sent them out at night. ⁴ He commanded them: "Pay attention. Lie in ambush behind the city, not too far from it, and all of you be ready.*ᶜ* ⁵ Then I and all the people who are with me will approach the city. When they come out against us as they did the first time, we will flee from them. ⁶ They will come after us until we have drawn them away from the city, for they will say, 'They are fleeing from us as before.' While we are fleeing from them,⁷ you are to come out of your ambush and seize the city, for the Lᴏʀᴅ your God has handed it over to you. ⁸ After taking the city, set it on fire. Follow the Lᴏʀᴅ's command—see that you do as I have ordered you." ⁹ So Joshua sent them out, and they went to the ambush site and waited between Bethel and Ai, to the west of Ai. But he spent that night with the troops.

¹⁰ Joshua started early the next morning and mobilized them. Then he and the elders of Israel led the troops up to Ai. ¹¹ All thoseᴬ who were with him went up and approached the city, arriving opposite Ai, and camped to the north of it, with a valley between them and the city. ¹² Now Joshua had taken about 5,000 men and set them in ambush between Bethel and Ai, to the west of the city. ¹³ The military force was stationed in this way: the mainᴮ camp to the north of the city and its rear guard to the west of the city. And that night Joshua went into the valley.

¹⁴ When the king of Ai saw the Israelites, the men of the city hurried and went out early in the morning so that he and all his people could engage Israel in battle at a suitable place facing the •Arabah. But he did not know there was an ambush waiting for him behind the city. ¹⁵ Joshua and all Israel pretended to be beaten back by them and fled toward the wilderness. ¹⁶ Then all the troops of Ai were summoned to pursue them, and they pursued Joshua and were drawn away from the city. ¹⁷ Not a man was left in Ai or Bethel who did not go out after Israel, leaving the city exposed while they pursued Israel.

¹⁸ Then the Lᴏʀᴅ said to Joshua, "Hold out the sword in your hand toward Ai, for I will hand the city over to you." So Joshua held out his sword toward it. ¹⁹ When he held out his hand, the men in ambush rose quickly from their position. They ran, entered the city, captured it, and immediately set it on fire.

²⁰ The men of Ai turned and looked back, and smoke from the city was rising to the sky! They could not escape in any direction, and the troops who had fled to the wilderness now became the pursuers. ²¹ When Joshua and all Israel saw that the men in ambush had captured the city and that smoke was rising from it, they turned back and struck down the men of Ai. ²² Then men in ambush came out of the city against them, and the men of Ai were trapped between the Israelite forces, some on one side and some on the other. They struck them down until no survivor or fugitive remained, ²³ but they captured the king of Ai alive and brought him to Joshua.

²⁴ When Israel had finished killing everyone

*ᵃ*8:1 Jos 6:2
*ᵇ*8:2 Jos 6:17
*ᶜ*8:4 Jdg 20:29

ᴬ8:11 Lit *the people of war*   ᴮ8:13 Lit *way: all the*

8:2 As with Jericho (6:21), all the people of Ai were to be destroyed. However, here it was possible for Israel to keep the **livestock** for their own use. The change demonstrates that flexibility in the matter of devoting things to God was possible. The use of an **ambush** is a strategy known in the ancient Near East and used more than once in Israel's history (Jdg 9; 20). Its deceptive nature recalls the ruse of Rahab in Jos 2:4-5. The references to the **king** of **Ai** and the **city** might suggest that Ai was not a fort. However, as with Jericho, a "king" could be a military leader rather than an independent sovereign (6:2), and the word for "city" refers to any population center, including a fort (2Sm 5:7).

8:3 Joshua sent the army out **at night** so they would not be detected.

8:4,9 Given the traditional locations of Ai and Bethel (7:2), there is a ravine between them, west of Ai, in which it would be possible for troops to hide and escape notice from either town.

8:8 After capturing Ai, they were to **set it on fire** as they did to Jericho (6:24). Joshua understood this as **the Lᴏʀᴅ's command**, a message he had received directly from God.

8:13 The positions of Joshua's forces were far from the road

they would be expected to approach from, southeast of Ai, providing an additional element of surprise.

8:14-17 The ruse worked as Ai was emptied of its inhabitants. The attack took place **early in the morning** when the advantage would be with Israel's main force because the rising sun would blind the army of Ai as they pursued Joshua's forces eastward.

8:18-19 The **sword** in Joshua's hand symbolized war so that Joshua's action declared the beginning of the hostilities. The sword is also an offensive weapon, indicating the turning point in the battle. Israel moved from the defensive to the offensive when Ai's army experienced the reverse. The ambush accomplished its task without resistance.

8:20-22 As the main body of Israel turned west toward the pursuing army of **Ai**, the warriors of the city were driven back. At that point they saw Ai ablaze and found the ambush moving east **out of the city** and blocking their retreat. Caught between the two forces and despairing at the destruction of their defenses, they were easily defeated and their army was destroyed.

8:23 The capture of the **king of Ai** was a symbolic act, be-

living in Ai who had pursued them into the open country, and when every last one of them had fallen by the sword, all Israel returned to Ai and struck it down with the sword. ²⁵The total of those who fell that day, both men and women, was 12,000—all the people of Ai. ²⁶Joshua did not draw back his hand that was holding the sword until all the inhabitants of Ai were •completely destroyed.ᵃ ²⁷Israel plundered only the cattle and spoil of that city for themselves, according to the Lord's command that He had given Joshua.

²⁸Joshua burned Ai and left it a permanent ruin, desolate to this day.ᵇ ²⁹He hungᴬ the body of the king of Ai on a treeᴮ until evening, and at sunset Joshua commanded that they take his body down from the tree.ᶜ They threw it down at the entrance of the city gate and put a large pile of rocks over it, which remains to this day.

Renewed Commitment to the Law

³⁰At that time Joshua built an altar on Mount Ebalᵈ to the Lord, the God of Israel, ³¹just as Moses the Lord's servant had commanded the Israelites. He built it according to what is written in the book of the law of Moses: an altar of uncut stones on which no iron tool has been used.ᵉ Then they offered •burnt offerings to the Lord and sacrificed •fellowship offerings on it. ³²There on the stones, Joshua

ᵃ8:26 Nm 21:2-3; Dt 2:34; Jos 2:10; 6:21; 10:1,28,35-40; 11:11-12,20-21; 24:20
ᵇ8:28 Dt 13:16; Jos 6:25
ᶜ8:29 Dt 21:21-23
ᵈ8:30 Dt 27:4-6
ᵉ8:31 Dt 27:5-7
ᶠ8:32 Dt 27:2-3
ᵍ8:33 Dt 11:29
ʰDt 27:12-13
ⁱ8:35 Dt 31:12
ʲ9:1 Jos 3:10
ᵏNm 34:6
ˡ9:3 Jos 10:2

copied the law of Moses, which he had written in the presence of the Israelites.ᶠ ³³All Israel, foreigner and citizen alike, with their elders, officers, and judges, stood on either side of the ark of the Lord's covenant facing the Levitical priests who carried it. As Moses the Lord's servant had commanded earlier, half of them were in front of Mount Gerizim and half in front of Mount Ebal,ᵍ to bless the people of Israel.ʰ ³⁴Afterward, Joshua read aloud all the words of the law—the blessings as well as the curses—according to all that is written in the book of the law. ³⁵There was not a word of all that Moses had commanded that Joshua did not read before the entire assembly of Israel, including the women, the little children, and the foreigners who were with them.ⁱ

Deception by Gibeon

9 When all the kings heard about Jericho and Ai, those who were west of the Jordan in the hill country,ʲ in the Judean foothills,ᶜ and all along the coast of the Mediterranean Seaᵏ toward Lebanon—the Hittites, Amorites, Canaanites, Perizzites, Hivites, and Jebusites— ²they formed a unified alliance to fight against Joshua and Israel.

³When the inhabitants of Gibeon heard what Joshua had done to Jericho and Ai,ˡ ⁴they acted deceptively. They gathered provisionsᴰ and took worn-out sacks on their donkeys and

ᴬ8:29 Or impaled ᴮ8:29 Or wooden stake ᶜ9:1 Or the Shephelah ᴰ9:4 Some Hb mss, LXX, Syr, Vg; other Hb mss read They went disguised as ambassadors

cause he had led the defeat of the earlier Israelite army sent out against him. Now his role as a defeated leader contrasted with the victorious role of Joshua.

8:24-27 The destruction of **all the inhabitants of Ai** fulfilled God's clear command in verse 2.

8:27 Joshua followed God's command in verse 2 about the **cattle**.

8:28 The word **Ai** means "ruin." Like Jericho, this defeated city would be a memorial to Israel's victory.

8:29 The focus on the **king of Ai** in chapter 8 corresponds to that of Rahab at the destruction of Jericho in chapter 6. Rahab was delivered from death because of her faith, whereas the king of Ai was put to death because of his antagonism toward Israel. The king of Ai also compares to Achan, as both were executed by Israel. The hanging of his body exposed it to shame. In Israel it was forbidden to allow a body to remain overnight so exposed (Dt 21:23; Jn 19:31).

8:30-31 Joshua's construction of **an altar on Mount Ebal**, north of Shechem, was a fulfillment of what **Moses . . . had commanded** in Dt 27:5. The **burnt offerings** and **fellowship offerings** were the same offerings required in the first law of the altar in Ex 20:24 and in instructions for this gathering on Mount Ebal in Dt 27:6-7.

8:32 Joshua's copying of **the law of Moses** was commanded in Dt 27:3. It resembled the actions of the king who had to make his own copy of the law (Dt 17:18).

8:33 In Dt 27:12-13 half of Israel was to stand **in front of Mount Gerizim** and half **in front of Mount Ebal** in order to pronounce the curses and blessings for obeying or disobeying the covenant. This account in Joshua included the **foreigner** as well as the **citizen**. Thus the entire nation and all who lived with Israel were present and standing around **the ark of the Lord's covenant**.

8:34 In both the writing and reading of the covenant with its **curses** and **blessings** Joshua represented Israel.

8:35 The perfect obedience of Joshua is underscored. Here again, the totality of Israel is emphasized, including **women** and **children** as well as the officers. **Foreigners** were also included.

9:1-2 The phrase **when all the kings heard** is identical to that in 5:1. There the kings heard about God's drying up the Jordan River, and it struck fear in their hearts. In 9:1 the text does not specify what the kings heard, but their reaction is different. Instead of fearing Israel, **they formed a unified alliance** to fight against the nation. What caused this change? It was the defeat of Israel at Ai that gave the Canaanites hope that they could defeat the people of God. The sin of Achan had far-reaching effects just as all sin does (Rm 5:12-14; 8:9-20). If Achan had not sinned, perhaps Israel's advance into the promised land would have been much easier and far less violent.

9:3 The **inhabitants of Gibeon** reacted differently, however. They did not seek to destroy Israel but to join it.

9:4-5 Because Israel had been commanded to destroy all

old wineskins, cracked and mended. [5] They wore old, patched sandals on their feet and threadbare clothing on their bodies. Their entire provision of bread was dry and crumbly. [6] They went to Joshua in the camp at Gilgal and said to him and the men of Israel, "We have come from a distant land. Please make a treaty with us."[a]

[7] The men of Israel replied to the Hivites,[A] "Perhaps you live among us. How can we make a treaty with you?"[b]

[8] They said to Joshua, "We are your servants."

Then Joshua asked them, "Who are you and where do you come from?"

[9] They replied to him, "Your servants have come from a far away land because of the reputation of the LORD your God. For we have heard of His fame, and all that He did in Egypt, [10] and all that He did to the two Amorite kings beyond the Jordan—Sihon king of Heshbon and Og king of Bashan, who was in Ashtaroth. [11] So our elders and all the inhabitants of our land told us, 'Take provisions with you for the journey; go and meet them and say, "We are your servants. Please make a treaty with us."' [12] This bread of ours was warm when we took it from our houses as food on the day we left to come to you. But take a look, it is now dry and crumbly. [13] These wineskins were

new when we filled them, but look, they are cracked. And these clothes and sandals of ours are worn out from the extremely long journey." [14] Then the men of Israel took some of their provisions, but did not seek the LORD's counsel.[c] [15] So Joshua established peace with them and made a treaty to let them live, and the leaders of the community swore an oath to them.[d]

Gibeon's Deception Discovered

[16] Three days after making the treaty with them, they heard that the Gibeonites were their neighbors, living among them. [17] So the Israelites set out and reached the Gibeonite cities on the third day. Now their cities were Gibeon, Chephirah, Beeroth, and Kiriath-jearim.[e] [18] But the Israelites did not attack them, because the leaders of the community had sworn an oath[f] to them by the LORD, the God of Israel. Then the whole community grumbled against the leaders.

[19] All the leaders answered them, "We have sworn an oath to them by the LORD, the God of Israel, and now we cannot touch them. [20] This is how we will treat them: we will let them live, so that no wrath will fall on us because of the oath we swore to them." [21] They also said, "Let them live." So the Gibeonites became woodcutters and water carriers[g] for the

[a]9:6 Jos 5:10
[b]9:7 Ex 23:32; Dt 7:2-5; 20:10-18
[c]9:14 Nm 27:21
[d]9:15 2Sm 21:1-2
[e]9:17 Jos 18:25
[f]9:18 Ps 15:1-4; Ezk 17:16-20
[g]9:21 Dt 29:11

[A]9:7 = the men of Gibeon

---

peoples in Canaan (Dt 20:16-18), Gibeon wanted it to look like they did not live nearby.

9:6 **Gilgal** here may be different from the Gilgal of 4:19-20; and 5:9-10. It was probably located in the hill country, perhaps near Mount Ebal. Gibeon was a city north of Jerusalem in the territory of the tribe of Benjamin, a few hours journey by foot. The word for **treaty** (Hb *berith*) is the same as that for covenant; it recalls the experience of Joshua and the Israelites at Mount Ebal (8:30-35).

9:7 The connection of Gibeon with **the Hivites** implies that this group may have been a recent addition to the region, coming originally from north of Palestine in Syria (see note at 3:10).

9:8 The self-designation by the Gibeonites as Israel's **servants** implies that they accepted a relationship of a vassal nation to the people of God.

9:9-10 The confession of the Gibeonites most closely resembles that of Rahab in 2:9-11. Their expression of faith in God was based on God's historic acts of redemption toward His people. The Gibeonites mentioned the same acts of redemption as Rahab did—the work of God **in Egypt** and against **Sihon** and **Og**.

9:11 The governance of Gibeon by **elders** rather than a king implies a different form of rule than what was common in Canaan at the time, which may have been part of the deception.

9:14 The note that Israel **did not seek the LORD's counsel**,

as well as absence of any mention of Joshua in the initial negotiations, all spell trouble.

9:15 That **Joshua established peace** with the Gibeonites demonstrates his own complicity in the actions. The reference to **peace** and the swearing of **an oath** by **the leaders of the community** bound Israel into a treaty relationship with the Gibeonites that could not be broken.

9:16 The phrase **three days** may suggest a literal three days such as seems to occur in 1:11; 2:16,22, or it may imply an indeterminate period of more than a second day.

9:17 Having discovered the ruse of the Gibeonites, the Israelites set out **on the third day** and reached the Gibeonite cities on that same day. Like Gibeon, **Chephirah, Beeroth, and Kiriath-jearim** lie a few miles north of Jerusalem and close by one another in the territory that would later be assigned to the tribe of Benjamin.

9:18-19 The two references to the oath that the leaders had made surround the statement that the **whole community grumbled against the leaders**. The verb "grumble" refers elsewhere almost exclusively to the complaints of the Israelites against Moses' leadership and against God. Its appearance here may suggest the same negative attitude of Israel as that in the wilderness generation. However, this grumbling against the leaders had a point because the present leadership did not seek God's counsel, and they thereby foolishly bound Israel to a treaty with a Canaanite people group.

whole community, as the leaders had promised them.

²² Joshua summoned the Gibeonites and said to them, "Why did you deceive us by telling us you live far away from us, when in fact you live among us? ²³ Therefore you are cursed and will always be slaves—woodcutters and water carriers for the house of my God."

²⁴ The Gibeonites answered him, "It was clearly communicated to your servants that the Lord your God had commanded His servant Moses to give you all the land and to destroy all the inhabitants of the land before you. We greatly feared for our lives because of you, and that is why we did this. ²⁵ Now we are in your hands. Do to us whatever you think is right."ᴬ ²⁶ This is what Joshua did to them: he delivered them from the hands of the Israelites, and they did not kill them. ²⁷ On that day he made them woodcutters and water carriers—as they are today—for the community

and for the Lord's altar at the place He would choose.ᵃ

The Day the Sun Stood Still

10 Now Adoni-zedek king of Jerusalem heard that Joshua had captured Ai and •completely destroyedᵇ it, treating Ai and its king as he had Jericho and its king, and that the inhabitants of Gibeonᶜ had made peace with Israel and were living among them.ᵈ ² So Adoni-zedek and his people wereᴮ greatly alarmed because Gibeon was a large city like one of the royal cities; it was larger than Ai, and all its men were warriors. ³ Therefore Adoni-zedek king of Jerusalem sent word to Hoham king of Hebron, Piram king of Jarmuth, Japhia king of Lachish, and Debir king of Eglon, saying, ⁴ "Come up and help me. We will attack Gibeon, because they have made peace with Joshua and the Israelites." ⁵ So the five Amorite kings—the kings of Jerusalem, Hebron,

ᵃ9:27 Dt 12:5
ᵇ10:1 Jos 8:26;
10:28,35-40;
11:11-12,20-21;
24:20; Jdg 1:17;
21:11
ᶜJos 8:22
ᵈJos 9:15

ᴬ9:25 Lit *us as is good and as is right in your eyes do*   ᴮ10:2 One Hb ms, Syr, Vg read *So he was*

9:20 The leaders were unwilling to violate their oath and thereby compound their wrongdoing with a second sin.

9:21 Deuteronomy 29:11 implied that aliens living in the land of Israel should fulfill the roles of **woodcutters and water carriers**.

9:22-26 Joshua pronounced a curse against the Gibeonites for causing Israel to disobey God's command to destroy all the inhabitants of Canaan who did not leave the land.

9:27 The deliverance of a people such as the Gibeonites is not unique to Joshua. In the ancient world, many peoples offered themselves as slaves rather than face extinction at the hands of a superior enemy. The establishment of **the Lord's altar at the place He would choose** duplicates Dt 12:5 and the command that Israel should worship God only at the place where He directed they should build an altar.

10:1 Adoni-zedek king of Jerusalem was the leader of the key city in the region of the Gibeonites. The name may mean "my lord is righteous." The second element of the name, (Hb) *tsedeq*, also occurs with Melchizedek king of (Jeru-) Salem in Genesis 14. Some have suggested here a dynastic name that is used of the leader of Jerusalem in succeeding generations.

10:2 Adoni-zedek had heard about Joshua's victory against Ai, and he and **his people were greatly alarmed**. This suggests that things had returned to what they were in 5:1, where all the Canaanites were fearful of Israel. Gibeon lay immediately north of Jerusalem, dominating the plateau and providing key strategic routes to the coastal plain on the west and to the Jordan Valley on the east. Gibeon's defection threatened Jerusalem's trade and contact with the north as well as the west and east. If all the men of Gibeon were **warriors**, this suggests a warlike town whose sole reason for being was to wage war and collect tribute from defeated enemies. If Gibeon joined Israel's side, it could no longer be counted upon to remain loyal to Jerusalem, so it posed a threat.

10:3 The names of the kings of these towns preserve authentic forms and elements of names found in Canaanite

Palestine between 1500 and 1200 B.C. The towns themselves included three (**Hebron . . . Lachish**, and **Eglon**) that formed a line of towns south of Jerusalem and across the entire Judean hill country and desert. The town of **Jarmuth**, probably identified with modern Tel Yarmut, lay to the east of Jerusalem between the Sorek and Elah valleys that stretched east-west and formed major access routes between the coastal plain and the area of Jerusalem.

10:4 This verse recalls the only Canaanite correspondence between Canaanite kings in the Bible. The need to attack Gibeon was based on their peace treaty with Israel. The fact that local towns and cities had their own armies is known from the fourteenth century B.C. Amarna letters, where many of the towns were so defended. These local militias largely disappeared after the rise of the Israelite monarchy.

---

charam

Hebrew Pronunciation	[khah RAM]
HCSB Translation	set apart for destruction, devote, completely destroy
Uses in Joshua	14
Uses in the OT	50
Focus Passage	Joshua 10:1,28,25,27,39-40

Charam, closely associated with God, negatively implies judicial punishment that *sets* people or things *apart for destruction* (Is 34:2). It means *completely destroy* (Nm 21:2) or *annihilate* (Dn 11:44). The context was usually warfare, but such punishment might overtake an individual (Ex 22:20). Positively, Israelites could *permanently set* possessions *apart* to the Lord as holy (Lv 27:28). They *devoted* spoils of war to the Lord (Mc 4:13). The passive may connote *forfeit* (Ezr 10:8). *Cherem* (29x) occurs three times with *charam* (Lv 27:28,29; Jos 6:18). *Cherem* involves *what is devoted* (1Ch 2:7) or *set apart* (Lv 27:29) *for destruction*. Both people (Jos 6:18) and *things* (Jos 7:13) can be *set apart*. *Cherem* signifies *total destruction* (Is 43:28), *curse of destruction* (Zch 14:11), or *curse* (Mal 4:6). It also indicates things, animals, or people *permanently dedicated* (Nm 18:14) or *set apart* (Lv 27:28) to God as holy. These things became the priests' property (Ezk 44:29).

Jarmuth, Lachish, and Eglon—joined forces, advanced with all their armies, besieged Gibeon, and fought against it.

⁶Then the men of Gibeon sent word to Joshua in the camp at Gilgal: "Don't abandon^A your servants. Come quickly and save us! Help us, for all the Amorite kings living in the hill country have joined forces against us." ⁷So Joshua and his whole military force, including all the fighting men, came from Gilgal.^a

⁸The LORD said to Joshua, "Do not be afraid of them,^b for I have handed them over to you. Not one of them will be able to stand against you."

⁹So Joshua caught them by surprise, after marching all night from Gilgal. ¹⁰The LORD threw them into confusion^c before Israel. He defeated them in a great slaughter at Gibeon, chased them through the ascent of Beth-horon, and struck them down as far as Azekah and Makkedah. ¹¹As they fled before Israel, the LORD threw large hailstones on them^d from the sky along the descent of Beth-horon all the way to Azekah, and they died. More of

a10:7 Jos 8:1
b10:8 Jos 1:5
c10:10 Ex 14:24; 23:27; 1Sm 7:10
d10:11 Ps 18:12-14
e10:12 Hab 3:11
f10:14 Ex 14:14,25; Dt 1:30; 3:22; 20:4; Jos 10:42; 23:3,10; 2Ch 20:29; 32:8; Ps 35:1; Zch 14:3

them died from the hail than the Israelites killed with the sword.

¹²On the day the LORD gave the Amorites over to the Israelites, Joshua spoke to the LORD in the presence of Israel:

"Sun,^e stand still over Gibeon,
and moon, over the Valley of Aijalon."
¹³ And the sun stood still
and the moon stopped
until the nation took vengeance
    on its enemies.

Isn't this written in the Book of Jashar?^B

So the sun stopped
in the middle of the sky
and delayed its setting
almost a full day.

¹⁴There has been no day like it before or since, when the LORD listened to the voice of a man, because the LORD fought for Israel.^f ¹⁵Then Joshua and all Israel with him returned to the camp at Gilgal.

Execution of the Five Kings

¹⁶Now the five defeated kings had fled and

A10:6 Lit Don't let your hand go from   B10:13 Or of the Upright

10:6 Gibeon's appeal to Joshua and the Israelites was based on their peace treaty of 9:15. This agreement, while requiring Gibeonites to serve Israel, also assumed that Gibeon would be protected from its enemies by the stronger party, Israel. Such was a common arrangement for suzerain-vassal treaties in the ancient Near East.

10:7-43 This section describes the battle by using a series of perspectives. There is often a summary description, such as here in verses 7-10, followed by more details in the text. The work of God, as Israel's leader in the war, is described first (vv. 11-15). Then there is consideration of the leaders of the enemy coalition (vv. 16-27) and details of battles with the towns in the southern coalition (vv. 28-40). Finally, there is a summary and a note on Israel's return to camp.

10:8 God's admonition to Joshua to not be afraid of them occurred previously in 8:1 in anticipation of the battle and victory over Ai. See also 1:9 and the promise that not one of them will be able to stand against you (cp. 1:5).

10:9 The idea of marching all night was not unprecedented in the ancient world, but it was not common because it could exhaust the soldiers and thus ruin their effectiveness.

10:10 As at the victory against Egypt at the exodus (Ex 14:24), God threw them into confusion before Israel. This tactic is characteristic of God's warfare against His enemies. God was responsible for a great slaughter at Gibeon. He chased the survivors westward through the pass of Beth-horon, the major access route for armies between the plateau of Gibeon and the coastal plain. As they fled westward they would reach Azekah, a site not far from Jarmuth, the hometown of one of the enemy armies. The site of Makkedah (modern Khirbet el-Qom) was close to Hebron, Lachish, and Eglon. Thus the two places represent the final stand of the enemy

armies against Israel's God. Close to their homes, with their backs against the wall, they had nowhere to go.

10:11 The idea that God would use hailstones against Israel's enemy suggests a concern to communicate to Israel and the surrounding peoples that God was sovereign over all things and would even use nature against Israel's enemies.

10:12 Some argue that Joshua in his prayer addressed the sun and moon as deities. This is unlikely in context because in the three previous communications in the chapter (vv. 4, 6, and 8), the addressee is never named in the message itself, but only in the introduction. The same is true here. Instead of addressing the sun and moon as deities, Joshua addressed God and then was given the authority to command the sun and moon. The pass of Beth-horon leads westward into the Valley of Aijalon. It was here that Joshua wished to continue or otherwise to succeed in the battle.

10:13 Here is the confirmation of the preceding verse. Miraculously, the sun and moon ceased in their course across the sky. This enabled Israel to complete its destruction of the enemy. The Book of Jashar is also mentioned in 2Sm 1:18, where it introduces David's eulogy for Saul and Jonathan.

10:14 Verses 11-14 summarize how the LORD fought for Israel. God's part in the miracle was of primary significance. Had He not fought, Israel would not have won. Because He fought, Israel could not lose and needed only to follow up on the victory.

10:15 Israel's return to the camp at Gilgal anticipated the end of the war and the identical conclusion in verse 43. Thus verses 11-15 describe the activity of God as fighting for Israel while the remainder of the chapter focuses on the events of Israel and of its enemies.

10:16 Sometime before the end of the battle with the enemy

hidden themselves in the cave at Makkedah. ¹⁷It was reported to Joshua: "The five kings have been found; they are hiding in the cave at Makkedah."

¹⁸Joshua said, "Roll large stones against the mouth of the cave, and station men by it to guard the kings. ¹⁹But as for the rest of you, don't stay there. Pursue your enemies and attack them from behind. Don't let them enter their cities, for the LORD your God has handed them over to you." ²⁰So Joshua and the Israelites finished inflicting a terrible slaughter on them until they were destroyed, although a few survivors ran away to the fortified cities. ²¹The people returned safely to Joshua in the camp at Makkedah. And no one dared to threaten^A the Israelites.

²²Then Joshua said, "Open the mouth of the cave, and bring those five kings to me out of there." ²³That is what they did. They brought the five kings of Jerusalem, Hebron, Jarmuth, Lachish, and Eglon to Joshua out of the cave. ²⁴When they had brought the kings to him, Joshua summoned all the men of Israel and said to the military commanders who had accompanied him, "Come here and put your feet on the necks of these kings." So the commanders came forward and put their feet on their necks. ²⁵Joshua said to them, "Do not be afraid or discouraged. Be strong and courageous,^a for the LORD will do this to all the enemies you fight."

²⁶After this, Joshua struck them down and executed them. He hung^B their bodies on five trees^c and they were there until evening.^b ²⁷At sunset Joshua commanded that they be taken down from the trees^{C,c} and thrown into the cave where they had hidden. Then large stones were placed against the mouth of the cave, and the stones are there to this day.^d

^a10:25 Dt 31:7; Jos 1:6-7,9,18
^b10:26 Jos 8:29
^c10:27 Dt 21:22-23
^dJos 6:25
^e10:28 Jos 6:21
^f10:29 Jos 21:13
^g10:33 Jos 16:10; Jdg 1:29; 1Kg 9:16-17
^h10:36 Jdg 1:10
ⁱ10:38 Jos 15:15; Jdg 1:11

Conquest of Southern Cities

²⁸On that day Joshua captured Makkedah and struck it down with the sword, including its king. He completely destroyed it^D and everyone in it, leaving no survivors. So he treated the king of Makkedah as he had the king of Jericho.^e

²⁹Joshua and all Israel with him crossed from Makkedah to Libnah and fought against Libnah.^f ³⁰The LORD also handed it and its king over to Israel. He struck it down, putting everyone in it to the sword, and left no survivors in it. He treated Libnah's king as he had the king of Jericho.

³¹From Libnah, Joshua and all Israel with him crossed to Lachish. They laid siege to it and attacked it. ³²The LORD handed Lachish over to Israel, and Joshua captured it on the second day. He struck it down, putting everyone in it to the sword, just as he had done to Libnah. ³³At that time Horam king of Gezer went to help Lachish,^g but Joshua struck him down along with his people, leaving no survivors in it.

³⁴Then Joshua crossed from Lachish to Eglon and all Israel with him. They laid siege to it and attacked it. ³⁵On that day they captured it and struck it down, putting everyone in it to the sword. He completely destroyed it that day, just as he had done to Lachish.

³⁶Next, Joshua and all Israel with him went up from Eglon to Hebron^h and attacked it. ³⁷They captured it and struck down its king, all its villages, and everyone in it with the sword. He left no survivors, just as he had done at Eglon. He completely destroyed Hebron and everyone in it.

³⁸Finally, Joshua turned toward Debirⁱ and attacked it. And all Israel was with him. ³⁹He

---

^A10:21 Lit *No one sharpened his tongue against*   ^B10:26 Or *impaled*   ^C10:26,27 Or *wooden stakes*   ^D10:28 Some Hb mss read *them*

---

armies, the five kings (v. 3) had hidden in **the cave at Makkedah** (v. 10).

10:18-20 When Joshua learned where the kings were hiding, he put a guard on the cave and ordered the army to continue pursuing the enemy so they could not escape to their fortified centers. The note that **a few survivors ran away to the fortified cities** anticipates verses 28-42 and the destruction of the various fortified centers.

10:22-24 Commands given by Joshua in verses 22 and 24a are followed word-for-word in verses 23 and 24b. The Israelite army was in complete unison and obedience to their leader, and a great victory was accomplished.

10:24 The act of the **military commanders** placing their **feet on the necks of these kings** signified the subjugation of the kings and their rule to the army of Israel (Jr 28:14; 30:8; Ezk 21:29).

10:25 Joshua repeated the words of encouragement that God had given to him in 1:5-9.

10:26-27 Joshua's actions toward the kings duplicate those toward the king of Ai (8:29) with execution, hanging on **trees** until sunset, and then "burial" in a **cave** with a pile of **stones** to mark the site.

10:28-40 The capture and destruction of **Makkedah** (v. 28), **Libnah** (vv. 29-30), **Lachish** (vv. 31-33), **Eglon** (vv. 34-35), **Hebron** (vv. 36-37), and **Debir** (vv. 38-39) followed in rapid sequence.

10:33 A fourth town in the sequence, **Gezer**, was not attacked but is mentioned as providing an army to fight against Israel at **Lachish**. The city of Lachish was strategically located. Egyptian inscriptions show that it was probably the base for Egypt's empire in southern Canaan. Its defeat would have been among the most important events of Joshua's entire southern campaign.

captured it—its king and all its villages. They struck them down with the sword and completely destroyed everyone in it, leaving no survivors. He treated Debir and its king as he had treated Hebron and as he had treated Libnah and its king.

⁴⁰ So Joshua conquered the whole region—the hill country, the *Negev, the Judean foothills,ᴬ and the slopes—with all their kings, leaving no survivors. He completely destroyed every living being, as the Lord, the God of Israel, had commanded.ᵃ ⁴¹ Joshua conquered everyone from Kadesh-barnea to Gaza, and all the land of Goshenᵇ as far as Gibeon. ⁴² Joshua captured all these kings and their land in one

ᵃ10:40 Dt 20:16
ᵇ10:41 Jos 15:50
ᶜ11:2 Dt 3:17;
Jos 12:3; 13:27;
19:35; 1Kg
15:20; Mt 14:34;
Lk 5:1

campaign,ᴮ because the Lord, the God of Israel, fought for Israel. ⁴³ Then Joshua returned with all Israel to the camp at Gilgal.

Conquest of Northern Cities

11 When Jabin king of Hazor heard this news, he sent a message to:

Jobab king of Madon,
the kings of Shimron and Achshaph,
² and the kings of the north
in the hill country,
the *Arabah south of Chinnereth,ᶜ
the Judean foothills,ᴬ
and the Slopes of Dorᶜ to the west,
³ the Canaanites in the east and west,

ᴬ10:40; 11:2 Or *the Shephelah* ᴮ10:42 Lit *land at one time* ᶜ11:2 Or *and in Naphoth-dor*

10:40 A summary of the victories by region is presented in this verse. The effect is to describe a complete destruction **leaving no survivors**. This is a stylized, hyperbolic statement celebrating the victorious southern campaign. The reality, however, is that many Canaanites did escape, as will be apparent in chapters 13 and in Judges 1. Here the emphasis is on the obedience of Joshua and Israel in following God's commands from Dt 20:16-18.

10:41 This summary defines all the towns in the south as far north as Gibeon. **Goshen** cannot refer to Egypt but must describe an otherwise unknown region (11:16). In 15:51 the town is associated with a district in the tribe of Judah.

10:43 The return of **all Israel to the camp at Gilgal** signaled the end of the campaign and the peace that resulted so Israel could rest.

11:1 The role of **Jabin king of Hazor** as the leader of the towns of the northern region, corresponded to the king of Jerusalem (10:3) in the south. Situated north of the Sea of Galilee, Hazor was the largest ancient site in Israel. It was the dominant city of the entire land and governed trade to the north where it is mentioned in texts as far away as cities on the Euphrates River. The initial phrase "When Jabin . . . heard" duplicates those in 5:1 and 9:1 and signals that there will be a battle against Israel. **Madon** is unknown.

It may be a variant of Merom, found in the "Waters of Merom" in verses 5 and 7.

Shimron (modern Tel Shimron) was located in the foothills near the western end of the Jezreel Valley. It lay at the southern end of Galilee. **Achshaph** (modern Tell Keisan) was situated to the west in the Acco plain. If Madon/Merom is identified as modern Tel Qarnei Hittin, it lay to the east near the Sea of Galilee. The effect is to identify important sites scattered across the populated areas around the Sea of Galilee to the north and westward along the Jezreel Valley and over to the Acco Plain and the Mediterranean Sea.

11:2 Chinnereth (modern Tel Kinrot) was a site on the northwest end of the Sea of Galilee. Chinnereth was also the name of the sea at that time, so the southern portion of the area could include both the region around the sea and the Jordan Valley farther south. The **Judean foothills** translates "Shephelah," a word meaning only "low hills." Although the Bible often uses this term to describe the western foothills of Judah, here it probably refers to the foothills of Samaria, farther north and more in agreement with this description of lands and towns in the north. The **Slopes of Dor** is a translation of "Naphoth Dor," an otherwise unknown name.

11:3 The **Hivites** were previously associated with Gibeon, but here they are found farther north at the foot of Mount Hermon. The **Jebusites**, often associated with Jerusalem, are

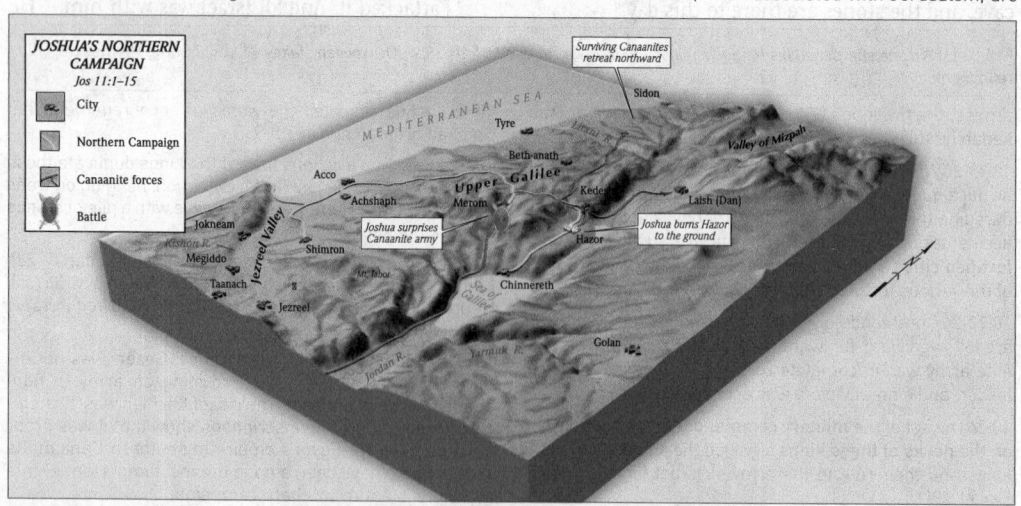

JOSHUA'S NORTHERN CAMPAIGN
Jos 11:1–15

City
Northern Campaign
Canaanite forces
Battle

Surviving Canaanites retreat northward
Sidon
MEDITERRANEAN SEA
Tyre
Beth-anath
Valley of Mizpah
Acco
Upper Galilee
Achshaph
Kedesh
Laish (Dan)
Merom
Jokneam
Jezreel Valley
Joshua surprises Canaanite army
Hazor
Joshua burns Hazor to the ground
Kishon R.
Megiddo
Shimron
Mt. Tabor
Taanach
Sea of Galilee
Chinnereth
Jezreel
Jordan R.
Golan
Yarmuk R.

the Amorites, Hittites, Perizzites,
and Jebusites in the hill country,
and the Hivites at the foot of Hermon
in the land of Mizpah.[a]

[4]They went out with all their armies—a multitude as numerous as the sand on the seashore—along with a vast number of horses and chariots. [5]All these kings joined forces; they came together and camped at the waters of Merom to attack Israel.[b]

[6]The Lord said to Joshua, "Do not be afraid of them, for at this time tomorrow I will cause all of them to be killed before Israel.[c] You are to hamstring their horses and burn up their chariots."[d] [7]So Joshua and his whole military force surprised them at the waters of Merom and attacked them. [8]The Lord handed them over to Israel, and they struck them down, pursuing them as far as Great Sidon and Misrephoth-maim, and to the east as far as the Valley of Mizpeh.[A,e] They struck them down, leaving no survivors. [9]Joshua treated them as the Lord had told him; he hamstrung their horses and burned up their chariots.

[10]At that time Joshua turned back, captured Hazor, and struck down its king with the sword, because Hazor had formerly been the leader of all these kingdoms. [11]They struck down everyone in it with the sword, •completely destroying[f] them; he left no one alive. Then he burned down Hazor.

[12]Joshua captured all these kings and their cities and struck them down with the sword. He completely destroyed them, as Moses the Lord's servant[g] had commanded. [13]However, Israel did not burn any of the cities that stood on their mounds except Hazor, which Joshua burned. [14]The Israelites plundered all the spoils and cattle of these cities for themselves. But they struck down every person with the sword until they had annihilated them, leaving no one alive. [15]Just as the Lord had commanded His servant Moses, Moses commanded Joshua. That is what Joshua did, leaving nothing undone of all that the Lord had commanded Moses.

Summary of Conquests

[16]So Joshua took all this land—the hill country, all the •Negev, all the land of Goshen,[h] the foothills,[B] the Arabah, and the hill country of Israel with its foothills[C]— [17]from Mount Halak,[i] which ascends to Seir, as far

[a]11:3 Jdg 3:3
[b]11:5 Jdg 7:12
[c]11:6 Jos 10:8
[d]2Sm 8:4; Ps 20:7
[e]11:8 Jos 13:6
[f]11:11 Jos 10:1; 24:20; Jdg 1:17; 21:11; 1Sm 15:3; 2Ch 8:8; Jr 25:9
[g]11:12 Dt 20:16-17
[h]11:16 Jos 15:51
[i]11:17 Jos 12:7

[A]11:8 = Mizpah; Jos 11:3; 18:26   [B]11:16 Or the Shephelah   [C]11:16 Or its Shephelah

more generally located in the hill country. Apparently these were people groups who populated more than one location. The reference to **Mizpah** anticipates the Valley of Mizpeh to the east in verse 8. The modern Mount Hermon lies at the southern tip of the Anti-Lebanon range. Mizpeh could refer to the southern end of the Beqa'a Valley where the Litani River flows south and then west to Tyre.

11:4 The huge number of the armies suggests a larger force than that of the southern coalition. As with Tyre (v. 1), these towns and cities tended to be more populous than those mentioned in chapter 10. The **horses and chariots** were the most sophisticated technology available in ancient warfare, used to move archers around the battlefield as a mobile firing platform.

11:5 Although there is a site known as **Merom** in upper Galilee, its location makes it unlikely as a strategic place for a battle. Modern Tel Qarni Hattin near the Horns of Hattin, a site famous for Crusader battles, seems more appropriate as the identification of Merom. It lay in the hills west of the Sea of Galilee and served as a dominating position for trade and armies coming south from Syria and for those coming east from the coast and the Jezreel Plain. The plan of these armies **to attack Israel** suggests that what follows would be a defensive war for Israel.

11:6 God promised to **cause all of them to be killed before Israel**. Again, He did the fighting and Israel reaped the benefits.

11:8 Great Sidon lay at the northwestern corner of Israel. **Misrephoth-maim** may have been at the northeastern end at the valley of the Litani River. Thus the attack began south of the Sea of Galilee and went westward and north to Sidon before turning eastward to Misrephoth-maim, where it turned south along the Valley of Mizpah (v. 3). Twice the text

records how Israel **struck them down** as if to emphasize the complete success of the mission.

11:9 Joshua and Israel obeyed God's commands from verse 6.

11:10 The size and strategic location of **Hazor** made it the most important city in Palestine throughout the second millennium B.C.

11:11-13 Today's ruins in **Hazor** do have a destruction layer from the thirteenth century B.C. This may be the one associated with Joshua (if one accepts a late date for the exodus). The temples of this period were destroyed and the images broken. The destruction layer attests to the burning of the city. No other city in Palestine among those mentioned as destroyed in chapters 1–11 has clear evidence of a burn layer like this during the time of Joshua. This attests to the fact that **Israel did not burn any of the cities . . . except Hazor**.

11:14 The treatment of these captured towns, in which Israel killed all the people but **plundered all the spoils**, resembles that of Ai (8:2,27). Unlike Jericho, at Ai God allowed His people to keep the plunder. Apparently this practice continued elsewhere in the land.

11:15 The battle accounts themselves dramatize the purpose of showing how Joshua and the Israel of his generation were obedient to God's commands. Their faithfulness resulted in God's gift of the land.

11:16 The summary of Israel's battles and victories begins with the regions. Those in the south are followed by those in the north. The **land of Goshen** may refer to the region with the town of that name in 10:41, in Judah (15:51). Perhaps it is a variant for the kingdom of Geshur, north of the Sea of Galilee. However, see note at 13:13.

11:17 The summary turns to the boundaries of the newly

as Baal-gad in the Valley of Lebanon at the foot of Mount Hermon. He captured all their kings and struck them down, putting them to death.[a] [18] Joshua waged war with all these kings for a long time. [19] No city made peace with the Israelites except the Hivites who inhabited Gibeon;[b] all of them were taken in battle. [20] For it was the LORD's intention to harden their hearts, so that they would engage Israel in battle, be completely destroyed without mercy, and be annihilated, just as the LORD had commanded Moses.

[21] At that time Joshua proceeded to exterminate the Anakim[c] from the hill country—Hebron, Debir, Anab—all the hill country of Judah and of Israel. Joshua completely destroyed them with their cities. [22] No Anakim were left in the land of the Israelites, except for some remaining in Gaza, Gath,[d] and Ashdod.

[23] So Joshua took the entire land, in keeping with all that the LORD had told Moses. Joshua then gave it as an inheritance to Israel according to their tribal allotments. After this, the land had rest from war.[e]

Territory East of the Jordan

12 The Israelites struck down the following kings of the land and took possession of their land beyond the Jordan to the east and from the Arnon Valley to Mount Hermon, including all the *Arabah eastward:[f]

[2] Sihon king of the Amorites lived in Heshbon. He ruled over the territory from Aroer[g] on the rim of the Arnon Valley, along the middle of the valley, and half of Gilead up to the Jabbok River (the border of the Ammonites[h]), [3] the Arabah east of the Sea of Chinnereth[A] to the Sea of the Arabah (that is, the Dead Sea), eastward through Beth-jeshimoth[i] and southward[B] below the slopes of Pisgah.[j]

[4] Og[c] king of Bashan, of the remnant of the Rephaim, lived in Ashtaroth and Edrei.[k] [5] He ruled over Mount Hermon, Salecah,

Cross references
[a]11:17 Dt 7:24
[b]11:19 Jos 9:3,7
[c]11:21 Nm 13:22,28,33
[d]11:22 1Sm 17:4
[e]11:23 Jos 14:15; 21:44; 2Ch 14:6; Hs 2:18; Heb 4:8
[f]12:1 Dt 3:8-9
[g]12:2 Dt 2:36
[h]Dt 3:16
[i]12:3 Jos 13:20
[j]Jos 11:2
[k]12:4 Dt 1:4

A 12:3 = the Sea of Galilee   B 12:3 Or *and from Teman*   C 12:4 LXX; MT reads *The territory of Og*

---

acquired land. **Mount Halak** (modern Jebel Halaq) lay midway between Kadesh-barnea and the southern tip of the Dead Sea. It thus defined the southern border with **Seir** (Edom). The precise location of **Baal-gad . . . at the foot of Mount Hermon** is unknown. The **Valley of Lebanon** may refer to the Valley of Mizpah (vv. 3,8; see note at v. 8), or to both it and the Beqaʿa—the entire region between the Lebanon and Anti-Lebanon mountain ranges.

11:19 On **Gibeon**, see notes at chapter 9. **Hivites** first appear in 3:10 and are associated with Gibeon in 9:6-7.

11:20 Exodus 4–14 repeats how God would **harden** the heart of Pharaoh. Here God treated the kings and warriors of Canaan in a similar manner. Thus the reason for the destruction as given here did not lie in other sins of Canaan or in their origins, but in their refusal to recognize Israel's God or to allow Israel access to the land.

11:21 The **Anakim** represent legendary warriors (Dt 2:10-11). By the time of Joshua they had lived for hundreds of years in Palestine, as attested in Egyptian sources. The three Anakim in Jos 14:15 may correspond to the three towns mentioned here, perhaps as rulers. **Anab** may refer to the site of ʿUnnab ets-Tseghur about 15 miles southwest of **Hebron**. With **Debir**, these are all located in southern Palestine. When Joshua **completely destroyed** the three cities, he may have been represented by Caleb (15:14-15).

11:22 The remnants of the **Anakim** in **Gaza, Gath, and Ashdod** anticipate the arrival of the Philistines and the presence of a giant such as Goliath (1Sm 17:4).

11:23 The **inheritance** that Joshua presented to Israel uses a word that occurs in Joshua for the first time, but it will occur dozens of times in the remainder of the book. It serves as a transition from the battles to the division of the inheritance.

12:1-6 A summary review of all the land acquired by Israel begins with the territories east of or "beyond the Jordan." The summary is given in terms of regions, outlined by

towns. The conquest of this region took place while Moses remained alive (Nm 21:21-35).

12:1 The southern part of this section, the **Arnon Valley**, ran from the tableland of Moab westward into the Dead Sea. To the south was territory that belonged to Moab. To the north was the territory allotted Reuben. Gad and Manasseh received lands farther north that reached upward to the modern Golan Heights and to the base of **Mount Hermon**.

12:2-3 The border of the territory ruled by **Sihon** is given in the form of a series of towns. His capital of **Heshbon** was probably not modern Hesban, which was not occupied at that early period. It may be identified with another neighboring site that was inhabited (modern Tell Jalul or Tall al-ʿUmeiri). From the **Arnon Valley** in the south, the territory of Sihon reached to the **Jabbok River** in the north. **Aroer** (modern ʿAraʾir) and **Beth-jeshimoth** (modern Tell ʿAzeimeh) were towns in the area. The **Arabah** was the eastern Jordan Valley extending from the **Sea of Chinnereth** (Sea of Galilee) to the **Sea of the Arabah** (the Dead Sea). The **slopes of Pisgah** represent the descent along the northwestern edge of the plateau of Moab. **Gilead** was apparently bisected by the Jabbok River.

12:4-5 The role of **Og** as the **remnant of the Rephaim** suggests a figure of legendary renown similar to the Anakim of verses 21-22. The towns of **Ashtaroth** (modern Tell ʿAshtarah) and **Edrei** (modern Derʿa) lay near the modern border between northern Jordan and southern Syria. The region of **Bashan** where Og ruled was bordered on the south by the Yarmuk River (the northern border of Sihon's kingdom), on the west by the watercourse Nachal Raqqad, on the north by Mount Hermon, and on the east by Jebel Druze (R. Hess, *Joshua*, pp. 223-224). This makes up the modern southern Hauran. The **Geshurite and Maacathite border** ran along the limits of the kingdoms of Geshur and Maacah east and north of the Sea of Galilee.

12:8 The summary of the regions conquered resembles that already given in 10:40. This is followed by another list of the people groups conquered (3:10; 9:1; 11:3; 12:8).

all Bashan up to the Geshurite and Maacathite border, and half of Gilead to the
border of Sihon, king of Heshbon.[a]

[6] Moses the LORD's servant[b] and the Israelites
struck them[c] down. And Moses the LORD's servant gave their land as an inheritance to the
Reubenites, Gadites, and half the tribe of Manasseh.[d]

Territory West of the Jordan

[7] Joshua and the Israelites struck down the
following kings of the land beyond the Jordan to the west, from Baal-gad in the Valley
of Lebanon to Mount Halak,[e] which ascends
toward Seir (Joshua gave their land as an inheritance to the tribes of Israel according to
their allotments: [8] the hill country, the Judean
foothills,[A] the Arabah, the slopes, the desert,
and the *Negev of the Hittites, Amorites, Canaanites, Perizzites, Hivites, and Jebusites):

[9]	the king of Jericho[f]	one
	the king of Ai,[g] which is next to Bethel	one
[10]	the king of Jerusalem[h]	one
	the king of Hebron	one
[11]	the king of Jarmuth	one
	the king of Lachish	one
[12]	the king of Eglon	one
	the king of Gezer	one
[13]	the king of Debir	one
	the king of Geder	one

[a]12:5 Dt 3:10,14
[b]12:6 Nm 32:33; Dt 3:12
[c]Nm 21:21-35; Dt 2:26–3:11; 29:7; 31:4; Ps 135:11; 136:19-20; Neh 9:22-25
[d]Dt 3:12-17; 29:8
[e]12:7 Jos 11:16-17
[f]12:9 Jos 6:2
[g]Jos 8:29
[h]12:10 Jos 10:23
[i]13:1 Jos 14:10
[j]Ex 23:27-33

[14]	the king of Hormah	one
	the king of Arad	one
[15]	the king of Libnah	one
	the king of Adullam	one
[16]	the king of Makkedah	one
	the king of Bethel	one
[17]	the king of Tappuah	one
	the king of Hepher	one
[18]	the king of Aphek	one
	the king of Lasharon	one
[19]	the king of Madon	one
	the king of Hazor	one
[20]	the king of Shimron-meron	one
	the king of Achshaph	one
[21]	the king of Taanach	one
	the king of Megiddo	one
[22]	the king of Kedesh	one
	the king of Jokneam in Carmel	one
[23]	the king of Dor in Naphath-dor[B]	one
	the king of Goiim in Gilgal[C]	one
[24]	the king of Tirzah	one
	the total number of all kings:	31.

Unconquered Lands

13 Joshua was now old, getting on in years,[i]
and the LORD said to him, "You have become old, getting on in years, but a great deal
of the land remains to be possessed.[j] [2] This is
the land that remains:

All the districts of the Philistines and
the Geshurites: [3] from the Shihor east

[A]12:8 Or the Shephelah   [B]12:23 Or in the Slopes of Dor   [C]12:23 LXX reads Galilee

12:9-24 The 31 **kings** listed cover the entire region, with those in verses 9-16 including the victories in the south described in chapters 6–10; and those in verses 17-24 summarizing the victories in the north as discussed in chapter 11. The structure of this list parallels many itineraries of Egyptian pharaohs that describe their conquests in Canaan between the fifteenth century B.C. and the tenth century B.C. The hieroglyphic writings show individual prisoners, one tied to the next with their hands bound behind them. On the bodies of each of these prisoners is written the name of one of the towns of Canaan. Each of these represents either a town in Canaan that the pharaoh defeated or an army from that town that was defeated. All these elements are found in the Israelite summary. Its resemblance to the Egyptian texts may have been intentional. As Egypt's New Kingdom empire declined and disappeared by 1150 B.C., Israel's presence and increasing power would replace and thus continue the defeat of Egypt, its gods, and its pharaoh. This process began with the plagues and the exodus.

13:1–21:45 Although some of the initial descriptions of the allotments consider regions, most of the divisions of the tribal territories in these chapters appear in two forms of literature: boundary descriptions and town lists. The boundary descriptions normally identify themselves by using the term "border" and verbs such as "turn," "ascend," "descend," "curve" and other terms linking one town or natural feature with another along the line of the border. In defining the lands, God further extended His relationship into the particulars of the blessing of the land that He had given the Israelites.

Town lists also appear in many tribal allotments as towns that belong to a tribe. Sometimes they are subdivided into regions of the tribe. This is true of the lengthiest town list in the allotment—that of Judah in 15:20-63. Such lists are common in administrative texts in the same period. These similarities suggest that this document had the importance and legal force of a treaty. As new towns were founded, they were added to the document throughout Israel's history. This procedure would retain the same boundaries but update the population centers in those tribal areas for as long as Israel possessed them. This was the literary embodiment of the physical witness that made up God's ongoing covenantal gift of the promised land to His people.

13:1 Joshua first appeared in Ex 17:9-13 where he was already the leader of Israel's armies. The chronology of the Pentateuch entails some 40 years of wandering in the wilderness and what Jos 11:18 describes as "a long time" of waging war before Joshua's death. In 24:29 Joshua died at 110. The expression **getting on in years** establishes Joshua as at the end of his active life and military leadership. Here he and Israel transitioned from military activity to allotment of the land. Despite the long list of towns and their kings who were defeated in chapter 12, the Lord confirmed that **a great deal of the land** remained **to be possessed**.

13:2-7 The regions not yet occupied include areas on the

Joshua's Cities of Conquest

CITY	SCRIPTURE	OCCUPANTS	COMMENTS
Gilgal	4:19–5:15	Unoccupied?	No battle; became worship center
Jericho	6:1–27	Canaanites	Rahab spared; oldest walled city; Achan sinned
Ai	7:1–8:29	Amorites	Israel defeated at first for Achan's sin; Ai means "ruin"
Shechem	8:30–35; chap. 24	Hivites (Gn 34); patriarchs	Not conquered; became worship center
Gibeon, Chephirah, Beeroth, Kiriath-jearim	9:1–10:27	Hivites	Entered covenant with Israel to be servants at worship place
Jerusalem	10:1–27	Jebusites	Part of coalition Joshua defeated, but city was not conquered
Hebron	10:1–27,36–37	Amorites, but in patriarchal times Hitites; also home of Anakim (11:21)	Coalition partner whose city was destroyed; patriarchal city (Gn 13:18); given to Caleb (Jos 14:9–13); city of refuge (20:7)
Jarmuth	10:1–27	Amorites	Coalition partner
Lachish	10:1–27,31–32	Amorites	Coalition partner whose city was destroyed
Eglon	10:1–27,34–35	Amorites	Coalition partner whose city was destroyed
Makkedah	10:16–17,28	?	Scene of battle with coalition
Libnah	10:29–30	?	Levitical city (21:13)
Gezer	10:33	Canaanites	Old, large city whose king Joshua defeated; city not occupied (Jdg 1:29); Levitical city (Jos 21:21)
Debir	10:38–39	Amorites; home of Anakim (11:21)	Captured by Joshua and Othniel (15:17); Levitical city (21:15); name of King of Eglon (10:3)
Hazor	11:1–15	Canaanites	Largest city in Canaan; ancient history; head of northern coalition; destroyed by Joshua
Madon	11:1	?	Northern coalition partner Joshua defeated; Greek Septuagint calls it Meron (cp. Waters of Meron)
Shimron	11:1	?	Has various spellings in mss; appears in ancient Egyptian sources

CITY	SCRIPTURE	OCCUPANTS	COMMENTS
Achshaph	11:1	?	Means "place of sorcery"; mentioned in ancient Egyptian sources
Geder	12:13	?	Mystery city unknown elsewhere; sometimes seen as scribe's notation for city of longer name
Hormah	12:14	?	Southern border city (Nm 14:45); defeated by Simeon and Judah (Jdg 1:1, 17)
Arad	12:14	Canaanites	Defeated by Moses (Nm 21:1-3) and named Hormah; occupied by Kenites (Jdg 1:16-17)
Adullam	12:15	?	Patriarchal ties (Gn 38)
Bethel	12:16	?	Strong patriarchal ties (Gn 12; 28; 35); means, "house of God"; associated with Ai (Jos 7:2); Joseph defeated it (Jdg 1:22-25)
Tappuah	12:17	?	Border city between Ephraim and Manasseh (16:8; 17:7-8)
Hepher	12:17	?	Name of a clan in Manasseh (17:1-2; cp. Nm 26:28-37)
Aphek	12:18	?	In ancient Egyptian sources (cp. 1Sm 4; 29)
Lasharon	12:18	?	Unusual Hebrew construction means "of Sharon"; may modify Aphek
Taanach	12:21	Canaanites	In ancient Egyptian sources; Levitical city (21:25); Manasseh could not occupy it (Jdg 1:27)
Megiddo	12:21	Canaanites	Major ancient city guarding military pass; in Egyptian sources; Manasseh could not occupy it (Jdg 1:27)
Kedesh	12:22	?	City of refuge (20:7); Levitical city (21:32); home of Barak (Jdg 4:6)
Jokneam	12:22	?	Also spelled Jokmeam; Levitical city (21:34); in Egyptian sources
Dor	12:23 (cp. 11:2)	Associated with sea peoples	Manasseh could not occupy (17:11-13; Jdg 1:27) in Egyptian records
Goiim in Gilgal	12:23	Name means "nations"	Compare Gn 14:1; uncertain scribal reading in text; appears to be in Galilee
Tirzah	12:24	Canaanite	Ancient city; became capital of Israel (1Kg 15:33); see Sg 6:4

of Egypt to the border of Ekron on the north (considered to be Canaanite territory)—the five Philistine rulers of Gaza, Ashdod, Ashkelon, Gath, and Ekron, as well as the Avvites [4]in the south; all the land of the Canaanites: from Arah of the Sidonians to Aphek and as far as the border of the Amorites; [5]the land of the Gebalites;[a] and all Lebanon east from Baal-gad below Mount Hermon to the entrance of Hamath[A,b]— [6]all the inhabitants of the hill country from Lebanon to Misrephoth-maim,[c] all the Sidonians.

I will drive them out before the Israelites, only distribute the land as an inheritance for Israel, as I have commanded you. [7]Therefore, divide this land as an inheritance to the nine tribes and half the tribe of Manasseh."

The Inheritance East of the Jordan

[8]With the other half of the tribe, the Reubenites and Gadites had received the inheritance Moses gave them beyond the Jordan to the east, just as Moses the LORD's servant had given them:[d]

[9]From Aroer on the rim of the Arnon Valley, along with the city in the middle of the valley,[e] all the Medeba plateau as far as Dibon, [10]and all the cities of Sihon king of the Amorites, who reigned in Heshbon, to the border of the Ammon-

[a]13:5 1Kg 5:18
[b]Jos 12:7
[c]13:6 Jos 11:8
[d]13:8 Jos 12:6
[e]13:9 Dt 2:36; Jos 13:16
[f]13:11 Dt 3:10
[g]13:12 Nm 21:24
[h]13:13 Jos 16:10; 17:12-13; Jdg 1:1–2:5
[i]Jos 6:25
[j]13:14 Nm 18:20; Dt 10:9; 18:1-2; Jos 13:33; 14:3-4; 18:7; 21:1-42
[k]13:18 Nm 21:23
[l]13:19 Nm 32:37

ites; [11]also Gilead[f] and the territory of the Geshurites and Maacathites, all Mount Hermon, and all Bashan to Salecah— [12]the whole kingdom of Og in Bashan, who reigned in Ashtaroth and Edrei; he was one of the remaining Rephaim.

Moses struck them down and drove them out,[g] [13]but the Israelites did not drive out the Geshurites and Maacathites.[h] So Geshur and Maacath live in Israel to this day.[i] [14]He did not give any inheritance to the tribe of Levi. This was its inheritance, just as He had promised: the offerings made by fire to the LORD, the God of Israel.[j]

Reuben's Inheritance

[15]To the tribe of the Reubenites by their clans, Moses gave [16]this as their territory:

From Aroer on the rim of the Arnon Valley, along with the city in the middle of the valley, to the whole plateau as far as[B] Medeba, [17]with Heshbon and all its cities on the plateau—Dibon, Bamoth-baal, Beth-baal-meon, [18]Jahaz, Kedemoth, Mephaath,[k] [19]Kiriathaim, Sibmah, Zereth-shahar on the hill in the valley,[l] [20]Beth-peor, the slopes of Pisgah, and Beth-jeshimoth— [21]all the cities of the plateau, and all the kingdom of Sihon king of the Amorites, who reigned in Heshbon. Moses had killed him and the

---

[A]13:5 Or to Lebo-hamath   [B]13:16 Some Hb mss read plateau near

---

fringes of the promised land. The land of the **Philistines** is described in verse 3. The five towns of the Philistines appear here for the first time. The **Shihor** has been described as the Brook of Egypt (15:4). The word for **rulers** (Hb seren) is a term only applied to Philistines. This may be connected to the Gk tyrannos, with the meaning "tyrant, ruler." The **Avvites** appear as a people living south of the region of the Philistines (Dt 2:23). The **Geshurites** include those inhabiting the region north and east of the Sea of Galilee.

13:4 Arah is not otherwise known, but the region of **the Sidonians** includes coastal areas at the northern end of the region occupied by the 12 tribes. **Aphek** appeared earlier (12:18). It lay on the coastal plain between Joppa and Dor where the plain narrowed and the hill country (**the border of the Amorites**) reached closest to the Mediterranean Sea.

13:5 The **land of the Gebalites** was Byblos, an important coastal city north of Sidon in modern Lebanon. The **entrance of Hamath**, sometimes called Lebo-hamath, is the most northern place described. It is identified with modern Lebweh north of the Beqa'a. For the other place names, see 11:7-8.

13:6 God's promise to **drive ... out** the remaining occupants of the land is followed by a command to distribute the land at this time. The land was not completely conquered, so Israel was still challenged to fulfill the command it had been given.

13:7 The command to **divide this land** is repeated, emphasizing its importance. The **nine tribes and half the tribe of**

Manasseh exclude Reuben, Gad, and the other half of Manasseh, who received an allotment east of the Jordan River.

13:8-33 The territory described in this section is identical to the combined areas controlled by Sihon and Og as described in 12:1-5.

13:9 The text begins in the south along the **Arnon Valley**, the border with Moab. The **Medeba plateau** includes the tableland that rises east of the Dead Sea. **Dibon** is perhaps not modern Tell Dhiban because the archaeological evidence for habitation from this period is lacking. Nevertheless, contemporary Egyptian scribes writing of campaigns in the area knew and identified the city of Dibon.

13:10 The **border of the Ammonites** lay to the east and north of Israel's inheritance and Sihon's previous kingdom. Its capital was Rabbah, modern Amman.

13:13 The presence of **Geshur** and **Maacath** as independent entities is attested during the time of David. He married the daughter of Geshur's king and fathered Absalom (2Sm 3:3).

13:14 In accord with Dt 18:1, the **tribe of Levi** received no inheritance of land. See, however, Jos 21.

13:15-23 Reuben's allotment also began at Aroer on the rim of the Arnon Valley. It is described through a town list (vv. 17-20).

13:21-22 For the deaths of **Evi, Rekem, Zur, Hur . . . Reba**, and **Balaam son of Beor**, see Nm 31:8.

THE TRIBAL ALLOTMENTS
OF ISRAEL

JOSHUA 13:8–19:49

- • City
- ○ City (uncertain location)
- ▲ Mountain peak

35 E
36 E
33 N
32 N
31 N

Sidon
TYRE
Damascus
ARAM
Abana River

Mt. Hermon ▲
Ijon
Pharpar River

Tyre
Litani River
Laish

Beth-anath

Kedesh
Lake Huleh
Yiron
Hazor

ASHER
Merom
NAPHTALI
EAST MANASSEH

Acco
Cabul
Capernaum
Mishal
Aphek
Hannathon
Rimmon
Rakkath
Sea of Galilee
Golan
Ashtaroth
Nahalal
Achshaph
Hammath
Mt. Carmel ▲
ZEBULUN
Chesulloth
Helkath
Daberath
Jabneel
Sarid
Tabor ▲ Mt. Tabor
En-haddah
Yarmuk River
Edrei
Jokneam
Megiddo
Shunem
Endor
Lo-debar
Dor
Jezreel
ISSACHAR
Jarmuth
Ramoth-gilead
Taanach

Beth-shan

En-gannim
Dothan
Ibleam
Jabesh-gilead
WEST MANASSEH
Socoh
Tirzah
Gerasa
Zaphon
Mahanaim
Penuel
AMMON
Mt. Ebal ▲ Shechem
Pirathon
Mt. Gerizim ▲
Janoah
Succoth
Jabbok River
Aphek
Tappuah
Shiloh
GAD
Joppa
Gath-rimmon
Ophrah
Yarkon River
Jehud
Jazer
Lod
Upper
Bethel
Amman
Gittaim
Beth-horon
Mizpah Naaran
Gilgal
Beth-nimrah
Shaalbim
Gibeon
Jericho
Abel-shittim
EPHRAIM
Jabneel
Gezer
Chephirah
Ramah
Heshbon
DAN
Baalath
Gibbethon
Aijalon
Chesalon
Kiriath-jearim
Adummim
Bezer
Ashdod
Ekron
Zorah
Eshtaol
Beth-hoglah
Medeba
Timnah
BENJAMIN
Mt. Nebo ▲
Beth-shemesh
Bethlehem
Ashkelon
Gath
Tekoa
Kedemoth
Mareshah
Beth-zur
REUBEN
Lachish
Hebron
Jahaz
Eglon
DEAD SEA
Dibon
Gaza
Juttah
En-gedi
Aroer
JUDAH
Arnon River
Gerar
Ziklag
Eshtemoa
Bethul
Jattir
Ashan
Arad
MOAB
Sharuhen
Kabzeel
Hormah
Kir-hareseth
Beer-sheba
Baalah
Hazar-shual
SIMEON
Eltolad
Ezem

Jerusalem

MEDITERRANEAN SEA

Jordan River

Aijalon River

N. Besor

W. el-Arish

Zered River

Arabah

Tamar
EDOM

0 10 20 30 40 Miles
0 10 20 30 40 Kilometers

chiefs of Midian—Evi, Rekem, Zur, Hur, and Reba—the princes of Sihon who lived in the land.[a] 22 Along with those the Israelites put to death, they also killed the diviner, Balaam son of Beor, with the sword.

23 The border of the Reubenites was the Jordan and its plain. This was the inheritance of the Reubenites by their clans, with the cities and their villages.

Gad's Inheritance

24 To the tribe of the Gadites by their clans, Moses gave 25 this as their territory:

Jazer and all the cities of Gilead, and half the land of the Ammonites to Aroer, near Rabbah; 26 from Heshbon to Ramath-miz-peh and Betonim, and from Mahanaim to the border of Debir;[A] 27 in the valley:[B] Beth-haram, Beth-nimrah, Succoth, and Zaphon—the rest of the kingdom of Sihon king of Heshbon. Their land also included the Jordan and its territory as far as the edge of the Sea of Chinnereth[C] on the east side of the Jordan.[D]

28 This was the inheritance of the Gadites by their clans, with the cities and their villages.

East Manasseh's Inheritance

29 And to half the tribe of Manasseh, that is, to half the tribe of Manasseh's descendants by their clans, Moses gave 30 this as their territory:

From Mahanaim through all Bashan

—all the kingdom of Og king of Bashan, including all of Jair's Villages[E,b] that are in Bashan—60 cities. 31 But half of Gilead, and Og's royal cities in Bashan—Ashtaroth and Edrei—are for the descendants of Machir son of Manasseh, that is, half the descendants of Machir by their clans.

32 These were the portions Moses gave them on the plains of Moab beyond the Jordan east of Jericho. 33 But Moses did not give a portion to the tribe of Levi. The LORD, the God of Israel, was their inheritance, just as He had promised them.[c]

Israel's Inheritance in Canaan

14 The Israelites received these portions that Eleazar the priest,[d] Joshua son of Nun, and the heads of the families of the Israelite tribes gave them in the land of Canaan.[e] 2 Their inheritance was by lot[f] as the LORD commanded through Moses for the nine and a half tribes, 3 because Moses had given the inheritance to the two and a half tribes beyond the Jordan.[F] But he gave no inheritance among them to the Levites. 4 The descendants of Joseph became two tribes, Manasseh and Ephraim. No portion of the land was given to the Levites except cities to live in, along with pasturelands for their cattle and livestock. 5 So the Israelites did as the LORD commanded Moses,[g] and they divided the land.

Caleb's Inheritance

6 The descendants of Judah approached Joshua at Gilgal, and Caleb son of Jephunneh

[a]13:21 Nm 31:8
[b]13:30 Nm 32:41
[c]13:33 Dt 18:1-2; Jos 13:14
[d]14:1 Nm 34:17-18
[e]Jos 19:51
[f]14:2 Nm 33:54; 34:13
[g]14:5 Nm 35:1-2; Jos 21:2

A 13:26 Or Lidbir, or Lo-debar   B 13:27 = the Jordan River Valley   C 13:27 = the Sea of Galilee   D 13:27 Lit Chinnereth beyond the Jordan to the east   E 13:30 Or all of Havvoth-jair   F 14:3 = east of the Jordan River

13:25 With **Rabbah** (modern Amman) as the Ammonite capital, this allotment took over **half the land of the Ammonites**.

13:26 This verse appears to designate towns along the border of Gad located in the higher plateau region inland toward the desert.

13:27 This verse provides a list of towns in the Jordan Valley extending as far north as the **Sea of Chinnereth** (Galilee). The identification of **Succoth** with modern Tell Deir 'Alla is intriguing in light of verse 22 because at this site in 1967 archaeologists discovered fragmentary texts on white plaster that describe purported visions of Balaam son of Beor.

13:30 **Jair's Villages** numbered **60 cities** (here "city" is a term that can describe a small hamlet). A judge named Jair (Jdg 10:4) had 30 sons who ruled over half of them.

13:31 In 17:1 **Machir son of Manasseh** received **Gilead** and **Bashan** east of the Jordan. The other sons of Manasseh received inheritances west of that river.

13:33 As with the regional summary of verses 8-14, so the summary of specific allotments ends with a note about the absence of **a portion** for **the tribe of Levi**.

14:1 **Eleazar** was the son of Aaron, and his successor as well as the leader of the Levites (Ex 6:23-25; Nm 20:25-28; 26:60; Dt 10:6). He used the Urim (and Thummim) to determine God's will and to allot the tribal lands (Nm 27:19-22; 34:17). The **land of Canaan** implies that the region east of the Jordan River, allotted in the previous chapter, was not part of Canaan.

14:2 The use of the **lot** for the distribution of the land is commanded in Nm 26:55-56; 33:54; 34:13; 36:2. The size of the tribe was also considered (Nm 33:54). The lot was not considered arbitrary but was directed by God (Pr 16:33).

14:3-4 This introduction mentions the absence of Levitical lands twice and explicitly anticipates the allotment of towns to that tribe in chapter 21. The absence of the Levites should reduce the number of eligible tribes to 11, but Joseph's two sons, **Manasseh** and **Ephraim**, each received a tribal inheritance.

the Kenizzite said to him, "You know what the LORD promised Moses the man of God at Kadesh-barnea about you and me.[a] [7]I was 40 years old when Moses the LORD's servant sent me from Kadesh-barnea to scout the land, and I brought back an honest report.[b] [8]My brothers who went with me caused the people's hearts to melt with fear, but I remained loyal to the LORD my God.[c] [9]On that day Moses promised me: 'The land where you have set foot will be an inheritance for you and your descendants forever, because you have remained loyal to the LORD my God.'[d]

[10]"As you see, the LORD has kept me alive these 45 years as He promised,[e] since the LORD spoke this word to Moses while Israel was journeying in the wilderness. Here I am today, 85 years old. [11]I am still as strong today as I was the day Moses sent me out. My strength for battle and for daily tasks[A] is now as it was then.[f] [12]Now give me this hill country the LORD promised me on that day, because you heard then that the Anakim are there, as well as large fortified cities.[g] Perhaps the LORD will be with me and I will drive them out as the LORD promised."

[13]Then Joshua blessed Caleb son of Jephunneh and gave him Hebron as an inheritance.[h] [14]Therefore, Hebron belongs to Caleb son of Jephunneh the Kenizzite as an inheritance to this day,[i] because he remained loyal to the LORD, the God of Israel. [15]Hebron's name used

to be Kiriath-arba; Arba was the greatest man among the Anakim.[j] After this, the land had rest from war.

Judah's Inheritance

15 Now the allotment for the tribe of the descendants of Judah by their clans[k] was in the southernmost region, south to the Wilderness of Zin and over to the border of Edom.

[2]Their southern border began at the tip of the Dead Sea on the south bay[B] [3]and went south of the Ascent of Akrabbim,[C] proceeded to Zin, ascended to the south of Kadesh-barnea, passed Hezron, ascended to Addar, and turned to Karka. [4]It proceeded to Azmon and to the Brook of Egypt and so the border ended at the Mediterranean Sea. This is your[D] southern border.

[5]Now the eastern border was along the Dead Sea to the mouth of the Jordan.[E]

The border on the north side was from the bay of the sea at the mouth of the Jordan. [6]It ascended to Beth-hoglah, proceeded north of Beth-arabah, and ascended to the Stone of Bohan son of Reuben. [7]Then the border ascended to Debir from the Valley of Achor, turning north to the Gilgal that is opposite the Ascent of Adummim, which is south of the ravine. The border

a14:6 Nm 14:24,30
b14:7 Nm 13:1-29
c14:8 Nm 13:30–14:3
d14:9 Dt 1:36
e14:10 Nm 14:30; 26:65; 32:12
f14:11 Dt 34:7
g14:12 Nm 13:28
h14:13-15 Jos 15:13; Jdg 1:10,20
i14:14 Jos 6:25
j14:15 Nm 13:33
k15:1 Nm 34:3

A14:11 Lit *for going out and coming in*   B15:2 Lit *Sea at the tongue that turns southward*   C15:3 Lit *of scorpions*   D15:4 LXX reads *their*   E15:5 = the southern end of the Jordan River at the Dead Sea

14:6 Judah's relative importance, if only because of its larger size than the other tribes, may give it the right to go first. **Caleb** was one of the two spies, along with **Joshua**, who were sent to spy out the promised land and returned with a good report (Nm 13–14). Caleb's designation as a **Kenizzite** is otherwise unattested, but may be related to the name of Caleb's brother, Kenaz (15:17).

14:7 Caleb's age of **40** at the time of the first spying out of the land puts him with the first generation of Israel who left Egypt. He now spoke to the new generation and recounted what they might not know.

14:8 For Israel to **melt with fear** recalls the defeat at the first assault on Ai (7:5). The defeat made Israel "melt with fear," just as the Canaanites had "melted with fear" when they learned of Israel's victories (2:11; 5:1; Ex 15:15).

14:9 See Nm 14:24 and Dt 1:36 for the promise of God to Caleb through **Moses**.

14:10 Caleb's reference to **45 years** suggests that, following the wilderness wanderings of about 40 years, the time spent in the battles of chapters 1–12 amounted to about five years.

14:11 The ongoing **strength** of Caleb despite his old age compares with that of Moses (Dt 34:7). He was still capable of fighting for his land and settling on it.

14:13-14 When the spies searched the land, they traveled its length. However, the description of their activity focused on Hebron and the nearby Valley of Eshcol (Nm 13:22-24). These were located in the southern hill country of Judah. This would have been among the closest major inland towns in Canaan from their base at Kadesh-barnea. Thus the gift of land to **Caleb** involved the area of **Hebron** where he had visited and spent more time than anywhere else (Dt 1:36).

14:15 The note about **Hebron's name** recalls the mighty **Anakim** (11:21) who were there, and it anticipates Caleb's defeat of them in 15:14. **Kiriath-arba** is a second and earlier name for Hebron. The first part of the name means "city." Thus the note suggests the meaning, "city of Arba," where **Arba** is the name of **the greatest man among the Anakim**. This would predate Israel's appearance because none of the Anakim that Caleb fought (15:14) bore this name. The note that **the land had rest from war** indicates success for Caleb.

15:1-12 The account of Caleb in 14:6-15 is a general one in which only one town is mentioned and the occupation of Caleb's inheritance is summarized. The same is true of the first account of Judah's allotment. It describes the contours of the land in terms of its borders, identified mostly by

proceeded to the waters of En-shemesh and ended at En-rogel. [8] From there the border ascended the Valley of Hinnom to the southern Jebusite slope (that is, Jerusalem) and ascended to the top of the hill that faces the Valley of Hinnom on the west, at the northern end of the Valley of Rephaim. [9] From the top of the hill the border curved to the spring of the Waters of Nephtoah, went to the cities of Mount Ephron, and then curved to Baalah (that is, Kiriath-jearim[a]). [10] The border turned westward from Baalah to Mount Seir, went to the northern slope of Mount Jearim (that is, Chesalon), descended to Beth-shemesh, and proceeded to Timnah.[b] [11] Then the border reached to the slope north of Ekron, curved to Shikkeron, proceeded to Mount Baalah, went to Jabneel, and ended at the Mediterranean Sea.

[12] Now the western border was the coastline of the Mediterranean Sea.

This was the boundary of the descendants of Judah around their clans.

Caleb and Othniel

[13] He gave Caleb son of Jephunneh the following portion among the descendants of Judah based on the LORD's instruction to Joshua: Kiriath-arba (that is, Hebron; Arba was the father of Anak). [14] Caleb drove out from there the three sons of Anak: Sheshai, Ahiman, and Talmai, descendants of Anak. [15] From there he marched against the inhabitants of Debir whose name used to be Kiriath-sepher.[c] [16] and Caleb said, "I will give my daughter Achsah as a wife to the one who strikes down and captures Kiriath-sepher." [17] So Othniel[d] son of Caleb's brother, Kenaz, captured it, and Caleb

a15:9 1Ch 13:6
b15:10 Gn 38:13; Jdg 14:1
c15:15-19 Jdg 1:11-15
d15:17 Jdg 3:8-11
e1Sm 17:25
f15:21 Gn 35:21
g15:28 Gn 21:31
h15:31 1Sm 27:6; 30:1
i15:35 1Sm 22:1

gave his daughter Achsah to him as a wife.[e] [18] When she arrived, she persuaded Othniel to ask her father for a field. As she got off her donkey, Caleb asked her, "What do you want?" [19] She replied, "Give me a blessing. Since you have given me land in the *Negev, give me the springs of water also." So he gave her the upper and lower springs.

Judah's Cities

[20] This was the inheritance of the tribe of the descendants of Judah by their clans.

[21] These were the outermost cities of the tribe of the descendants of Judah toward the border of Edom in the Negev: Kabzeel, Eder, Jagur,[f] [22] Kinah, Dimonah, Adadah, [23] Kedesh, Hazor, Ithnan, [24] Ziph, Telem, Bealoth, [25] Hazor-hadattah, Kerioth-hezron (that is, Hazor), [26] Amam, Shema, Moladah, [27] Hazar-gaddah, Heshmon, Beth-pelet, [28] Hazar-shual, Beersheba, Biziothiah,[g] [29] Baalah, Iim, Ezem, [30] Eltolad, Chesil, Hormah, [31] Ziklag, Madmannah, Sansannah,[h] [32] Lebaoth, Shilhim, Ain, and Rimmon—29 cities in all, with their villages.

[33] In the Judean foothills:[A] Eshtaol, Zorah, Ashnah, [34] Zanoah, En-gannim, Tappuah,[B] Enam, [35] Jarmuth, Adullam,[i] Socoh,[C] Azekah, [36] Shaaraim, Adithaim, Gederah, and Gederothaim—14 cities, with their villages; [37] Zenan, Hadashah, Migdal-gad, [38] Dilan, Mizpeh, Jokthe-el, [39] Lachish, Bozkath, Eglon, [40] Cabbon, Lahmam, Chitlish, [41] Gederoth, Bethdagon, Naamah, and Makkedah—16 cities, with their villages; [42] Libnah, Ether, Ashan, [43] Iphtah, Ashnah, Nezib, [44] Keilah, Achzib, and Mareshah—nine cities, with

---

A15:33 Or *the Shephelah*   B15:34 Or *En-gannim-tappuah*   C15:35 Or *Adullam-socoh*

natural formations. The descriptions move counterclockwise beginning with the south border.

15:8 The border arches to the south to go around **Jerusalem**, which at the time was populated by the Jebusites and was not part of Israel.

15:13-19 These verses continue the account of 14:6-15. Here the details appear with the names of specific places within Caleb's inheritance and the bequeathing of these to his children. Thus the general part is followed by the specific part. This anticipates the allotment of **Judah**. Joshua 15:1-12 constituted the general places, describing only the borders of the land. While verses 20-63 will deal with the specific places within those borders. Caleb's allotment represents the premier example of all the allotments of Judah. It is so important because it is the allotment of the most faithful Judahite of his generation. It also describes the acquisition of **Hebron**, David's first capital (2Sm 2:1-11).

15:14 The **three sons of Anak: Sheshai, Ahiman, and Talmai**, whom Caleb drove out, have personal names that are distinctive to the second millennium B.C. and are not found after the tenth century B.C. This suggests that the account in Joshua accurately reflects a second millennium context. The mention of these three names elsewhere (Nm 13:22; Jdg 1:10) suggests that the incident recounted here was well known.

15:17 The capture by **Othniel** of the city of Debir led to his marriage to Caleb's **daughter**. He and the first judge may be one and the same (Jdg 3:9-11). This anticipates David's capture of Jerusalem, where he also started out from Hebron and also offered a reward to the person who succeeded in defeating the enemy (2Sm 5:6-15).

15:18-19 The request of Achsah was to increase her dowry and receive a full inheritance that included the necessary **water** sources for land to be usable in the Judean desert.

their villages; [45]Ekron, with its towns and villages; [46]from Ekron to the sea, all the cities near Ashdod, with their villages; [47]Ashdod, with its towns and villages; Gaza, with its towns and villages, to the Brook of Egypt and the coastline of the Mediterranean Sea.

[48]In the hill country: Shamir, Jattir, Socoh, [49]Dannah, Kiriath-sannah (that is, Debir), [50]Anab, Eshtemoh, Anim, [51]Goshen, Holon, and Giloh—11 cities, with their villages; [52]Arab, Dumah,[A] Eshan, [53]Janim, Beth-tappuah, Aphekah, [54]Humtah, Kiriath-arba (that is, Hebron), and Zior—nine cities, with their villages; [55]Maon, Carmel, Ziph, Juttah, [56]Jezreel, Jokdeam, Zanoah, [57]Kain, Gibeah, and Timnah—10 cities, with their villages; [58]Halhul, Beth-zur, Gedor, [59]Maarath, Beth-anoth, and Eltekon—six cities, with their villages;[B] [60]Kiriath-baal (that is, Kiriath-jearim), and Rabbah—two cities, with their villages.

[61]In the wilderness: Beth-arabah, Middin, Secacah, [62]Nibshan, the City of Salt,[C] and En-gedi—six cities, with their villages.

[63]But the descendants of Judah could not drive

out the Jebusites who lived in Jerusalem.[a] So the Jebusites live in Jerusalem among the descendants of Judah to this day.[b]

Joseph's Inheritance

16 The allotment for the descendants of Joseph[D] went from the Jordan at Jericho to the waters of Jericho on the east, through the wilderness[c] ascending from Jericho into the hill country of Bethel. [2]From Bethel it went to Luz and proceeded to the border of the Archites by Ataroth.[d] [3]It then descended westward to the border of the Japhletites as far as the border of lower Beth-horon, then to Gezer,[e] and ended at the Mediterranean Sea. [4]So Ephraim and Manasseh, the sons of Joseph,[f] received their inheritance.[g]

Ephraim's Inheritance

[5]This was the territory of the descendants of Ephraim by their clans:

The border of their inheritance went from Ataroth-addar[h] on the east of Upper Beth-horon. [6]In the north the border went westward from Michmethath;[i] it turned eastward from Taanath-shiloh

Cross references (center column):
[a]15:63 Jdg 1:21; 2Sm 5:5-9
[b]Jos 6:25; 16:10; 22:17; 23:8-9
[c]16:1 Jos 8:15; 18:12
[d]16:2 Jos 18:13
[e]16:3 Jos 10:33
[f]16:4 Jos 17:14
[g]Gn 48:5-20
[h]16:5 Jos 18:13
[i]16:6 Jos 17:7

A15:52 Some Hb mss read *Rumah* **B**15:59 LXX adds *Tekoa, Ephrathah (that is, Bethlehem), Peor, Etam, Culom, Tatam, Sores, Carem, Gallim, Baither, and Manach—11 cities, with their villages* **C**15:62 Or *Ir-hamelach* **D**16:1 = the tribes of Ephraim and Manasseh

---

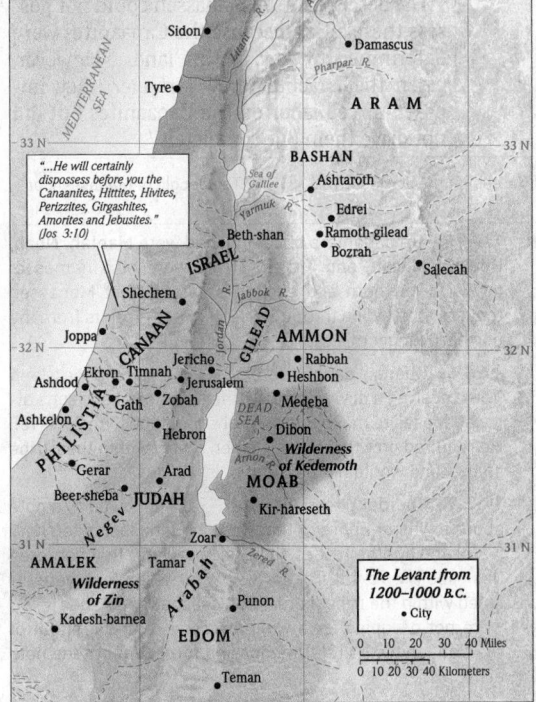

"...He will certainly dispossess before you the Canaanites, Hittites, Hivites, Perizzites, Girgashites, Amorites and Jebusites."
(Jos 3:10)

The Levant from 1200–1000 B.C.
• City

0   10   20   30   40 Miles
0 10 20 30 40 Kilometers

15:20-62 This section contains the most detailed town list of any of the allotments. It reflects the large tract of land given to Judah in comparison with the other tribes. The Hebrew text preserves 11 districts: the **Negev** (vv. 21-32); the western **foothills** with towns in the north (vv. 33-36), the south (vv. 37-41), and the center (vv. 42-44); the coastal plain (vv. 45-47); four regions in the **hill country** (vv. 48-51, vv. 52-54, vv. 55-57, vv. 58-59); a fifth hill country region west of Jerusalem (v. 60); and the Judean **wilderness** (vv. 61-62).

15:63 This note makes explicit what the note at verse 8 suggests—that **Jerusalem** remained unconquered.

16:1-3 These verses describe the southern border of the **Joseph** tribes, that is, the southern boundary of Ephraim.

16:1 The **Jordan at Jericho to the waters of Jericho** may mean "the Jordan River at Jericho which is also called the waters of Jericho," or else "the waters of Jericho" refers to the spring now known as 'Ain es-Sultan.

16:2 The **Archites** are not otherwise known. The Arkites of Gn 10:17 and 1Ch 1:15 are not the same people, as their name is spelled with a Hebrew *qof* instead of a *khet* as here. David's friend Hushai, who brought Absalom's plans to ruin, was called an Archite (2Sm 15:32; 16:16; 17:5,14; 1Ch 27:33).

16:3 The **Japhletites** are otherwise unknown. A Japhlet of the tribe of Asher is mentioned in 1Ch 7:32-33.

and passed it east of Janoah. ⁷From Janoah it descended to Ataroth and Naarah,ᵃ and then reached Jericho and went to the Jordan. ⁸From Tappuah the borderᴬ went westward along the Brook of Kanah and ended at the Mediterranean Sea.ᵇ

This was the inheritance of the tribe of the descendants of Ephraim by their clans, together with ⁹the cities set apart for the descendants of Ephraim within the inheritance of the descendants of Manasseh—all these cities with their villages. ¹⁰But, they did not drive out the Canaanites who lived in Gezer.ᶜ So the Canaanites live in Ephraim to this day,ᵈ but they are forced laborers.

West Manasseh's Inheritance

17 This was the allotment for the tribe of Manassehᵉ as Joseph's firstborn. Gilead and Bashan came to Machir, the firstborn of Manasseh and the father of Gilead, who was a man of war.ᶠ ²So the allotment was for the rest of Manasseh's descendants by their clans, for the sons of Abiezer, Helek, Asriel, Shechem, Hepher, and Shemida. These are the male descendants of Manasseh son of Joseph, by their clans.

³Now Zelophehad son of Hepher, son of Gilead, son of Machir, son of Manasseh, had no sons, only daughters. These are the names of his daughters: Mahlah, Noah, Hoglah, Milcah, and Tirzah.ᵍ ⁴They came before Eleazar the priest, Joshua son of Nun, and the leaders, saying, "The LORD commanded Moses to give us an inheritance among our male relatives."ᴮ So they gave them an inheritance among their father's brothers, in keeping with the LORD's

instruction.ʰ ⁵As a result, 10 tracts fell to Manasseh, besides the land of Gilead and Bashan, which are beyond the Jordan,ᶜ ⁶because Manasseh's daughters received an inheritance among his sons. The land of Gilead belonged to the rest of Manasseh's sons.

⁷The border of Manasseh went from Asher to Michmethath near Shechem. It then went southward toward the inhabitants of En-tappuah. ⁸The region of Tappuah belonged to Manasseh, but Tappuah itself on Manasseh's borderⁱ belonged to the descendants of Ephraim. ⁹From there the border descended to the Brook of Kanah; south of the brook, cities belonged to Ephraim among Manasseh's cities. Manasseh's border was on the north side of the brook and ended at the Mediterranean Sea. ¹⁰Ephraim's territory was to the south and Manasseh's to the north, with the Sea as its border. Theyᴰ reached Asher on the north and Issachar on the east. ¹¹Within Issachar and Asher, Manasseh had Beth-shean with its towns, Ibleam with its towns, and the inhabitants of Dor with its towns;ʲ the inhabitants of En-dor with its towns, the inhabitants of Taanach with its towns, and the inhabitants of Megiddo with its towns—the three cities ofᴱ Naphath.ᵏ

¹²The descendants of Manasseh could not possess these cities, because the Canaanites were determined to stay in this land. ¹³However, when the Israelites grew stronger, they imposed forced labor on the Canaanites but did not drive them out completely.ˡ

ᵃ16:7 1Ch 7:28
ᵇ16:8 Jos 17:8
ᶜ16:10 Jdg 1:29;
1Kg 9:16
ᵈJos 6:25
ᵉ17:1 Gn 41:51;
46:20; 48:18
ᶠ1Ch 28:3
ᵍ17:3 Nm 26:33
ʰ17:4 Nm
27:1-11
ⁱ17:8 Jos 16:8-9
ʲ17:11 1Ch 7:29
ᵏJos 11:2; 12:23
ˡ17:13 Jdg
1:27-28

ᴬ16:8 Ephraim's northern border   ᴮ17:4 Lit *our brothers*   ᶜ17:5 = east of the Jordan River   ᴰ17:10 The people of Manasseh, or Manasseh's borders   ᴱ17:11 LXX, Vg read *the third is*

16:9 Additional towns located in the territory of **Manasseh** were added to the allotment of **Ephraim**.

16:10 As at the end of Judah's allotment (15:63), so at the end of Ephraim's inheritance, there is a note of towns that were not fully conquered. The **forced laborers** (Hb *mas*) identifies a practice used by the Canaanite city-states before the arrival of Israel, and by Solomon for his building activities (1Kg 4:6; 9:21).

17:1 On allotting **Gilead and Bashan** to **Machir**, see 13:29-31. The connection between the Transjordan region and the name of Machir's son, both given as "Gilead," introduces the tendency in Manasseh for town names to follow the names of individuals.

17:2 Several clans in West Manasseh are named in this verse and are also attested as towns in the southern and western parts of West Manasseh's allotment. The names of some of these towns such as **Shechem** appear in the Bible. Others occur on merchandise receipts found in Samaria dating from the eighth century B.C.

17:3 The five daughters of **Zelophehad** were **Mahlah, Noah, Hoglah, Milcah, and Tirzah**. These were also names of towns in northern and eastern areas of West Manasseh that are attested on the eighth century B.C. receipts from the northern kingdom's capital.

17:4-6 Although daughters did not normally inherit land (they received a dowry instead), the absence of any sons allowed Moses to make this special stipulation (Nm 36:1-13). He required only that these women marry within their tribe so the land would not pass out of it.

17:7-13 A border description (vv. 7-9a) is followed by a note about towns of Ephraim that were in **Manasseh's** territory (v. 9b) and by other tribes and bodies of water that bordered this tribe (vv. 9c-10). The towns of Manasseh that were located within the tribal borders of Issachar and Asher (v. 11) were not occupied for a while because of the strength of the Canaanites (v. 12). On imposing **forced labor**, see note at 16:10.

Joseph's Additional Inheritance

[14] Joseph's descendants said to Joshua, "Why did you give us only one tribal allotment[A] as an inheritance? We have many people, because the LORD has been blessing us greatly."

[15] "If you have so many people," Joshua replied to them, "go to the forest and clear an area for yourselves there in the land of the Perizzites and the Rephaim, because Ephraim's hill country is too small for you."

[16] But the descendants of Joseph said, "The hill country is not enough for us, and all the Canaanites who inhabit the valley area have iron chariots, both at Beth-shean with its towns and in the Jezreel Valley."

[17] So Joshua replied to Joseph's family (that is, Ephraim and Manasseh), "You have many people and great strength. You will not have just one allotment, [18] because the hill country will be yours also. It is a forest; clear it and its outlying areas will be yours. You can also drive out the Canaanites, even though they have iron chariots and are strong."

Land Distribution at Shiloh

18 The entire Israelite community assembled at Shiloh[a] where it set up the tent of meeting there; the land had been subdued by them. [2] Seven tribes among the Israelites were left who had not divided up their inheritance. [3] So Joshua said to the Israelites, "How long will you delay going out to take possession of the land that the LORD, the God of your fathers, gave you?[b] [4] Appoint for yourselves three men from each tribe, and I will send them out. They are to go and survey the land, write a description of it for the purpose of their inheritance, and return to me. [5] Then they are to divide it into seven portions. Judah is to remain in its territory in the south and Joseph's family in their[B] territory in the north.[c] [6] When you have written a description of the seven portions of land and brought it to me, I will cast lots for you here in the presence of the LORD our God.[d] [7] But the Levites among you do not get a portion, because their inheritance is the priesthood of the LORD.[e] Gad, Reuben, and half the tribe of Manasseh have taken their inheritance beyond the Jordan to the east, which Moses the LORD's servant gave them."

[8] As the men prepared to go, Joshua commanded them[c] to write down a description of the land, saying, "Go and survey the land, write a description of it, and return to me. I will then cast lots for you here in Shiloh in the presence of the LORD." [9] So the men left, went through the land, and described it by towns in a document of seven sections. They returned to Joshua at the camp in Shiloh. [10] Joshua cast lots for them at Shiloh in the presence of the LORD where he distributed the land to the Israelites according to their divisions.

Cross references
a18:1 Jos 19:51; Jdg 18:31; 1Sm 1:9; 3:3
b18:3 Jdg 18:9
c18:5 Jos 15:1
d18:6 Jos 14:2
e18:7 Jos 13:33

A17:14-17 Lit one lot and one territory   B18:5 = the tribes of Ephraim and Manasseh   C18:8 Lit the ones going around

---

17:14-18 The allocation of additional land was necessary due to the large population among Joseph's descendants who lived in the central hill country of Israel. The **land of the Perizzites and the Rephaim** seems to be identical to the hill country and its forest. In Gn 34:30 the area around Shechem belonged to the Canaanites and Perizzites, thus it may refer to this region of Manasseh. The **Canaanites** in **the valley** had **iron chariots**, which caused the Ephraimites to doubt their ability to conquer them, but Joshua, a man of faith, encouraged them (v. 18; cp. Jdg 1:19; 4:3,13).

18:1-4 This is the first mention of the **tent of meeting** in the book of Joshua. **Shiloh** (modern Khirbet Seilun) lay to the south of Shechem and was situated in the middle of the earliest settlement of Israel in the hill country. It would remain a center for Israel's worship until the time of Samuel (1Sm 1–4). From this secure area, mapmakers were sent out. The proximity to the tent of meeting, the symbol of the presence of God, suggests that all was done in agreement with the Lord's will. The recurrence of the tent of meeting at the end of these allotments (Jos 19:51) implies that God's will was upheld in this activity.

18:5-7 Mention of the five tribes who had already received their inheritance meant that seven tribes remained. Levi, who did not receive such an inheritance, is again mentioned in anticipation of chapter 21.

18:8-10 The ability of these scouts to **write down a descrip-** tion of the land meant that they prepared a document that resembled chapters 18–19 with seven sections, one for each of the remaining tribes. In 7:16-18 **lots** had been used to identify the guilty person and separate him from the rest of Israel. Here they were used to connect each parcel of land with its tribe. The borders probably followed natural

chalaq

Hebrew Pronunciation	[khah LAK]
HCSB Translation	divide, share, apportion
Uses in Joshua	7
Uses in the OT	55
Focus Passage	Joshua 18:2,5,10

Chalaq, a homonym of chalaq meaning "be smooth," denotes divide (Gn 49:27) or share (Pr 17:2). It signifies endow (Jb 39:17), appoint (2Ch 23:18), be a partner (Pr 29:24), or provide (Dt 4:19). Intensives imply divide up (Jl 3:2), disperse (Gn 49:7), allot (Mc 2:4), apportion (Jb 21:17), assign (Neh 9:22), or distribute (Jos 18:10). People allot (give, claim) as a portion (Is 34:17; Jr 37:12). Cheleq (66x) means portion (Gn 31:14), section, or share. It represents fate (Is 17:14), lot (Jb 20:29), or reward (Ec 2:10). It is plot of land (2Kg 9:10), allotted land (Mc 2:4), land, or field (Hs 5:7). It connotes association (Ps 50:18) and what one knows (Jb 32:17). Machalogeth (42x) is division (Neh 11:36), allotment, portion, and tour of duty. Chelqah (23x) indicates field and portion (Dt 33:21), section, plot, piece, or parcel of land. Chaluqqah means distribution (2Ch 35:5).

Benjamin's Inheritance

[11] The lot came up for the tribe of Benjamin's descendants by their clans, and their allotted territory lay between Judah's descendants and Joseph's descendants.

[12] Their border on the north side began at the Jordan, ascended to the slope of Jericho on the north, through the hill country westward, and ended at the wilderness of Beth-aven.[a] [13] From there the border went toward Luz, to the southern slope of Luz (that is, Bethel); it then went down by Ataroth-addar, over the hill south of Lower Beth-horon.[b]

[14] On the west side, from the hill facing Beth-horon on the south, the border curved, turning southward, and ended at Kiriath-baal (that is, Kiriath-jearim), a city of the descendants of Judah. This was the west side of their border.

[15] The south side began at the edge of Kiriath-jearim, and the border extended westward; it went to the spring at the Waters of Nephtoah. [16] The border descended to the foot of the hill that faces the Valley of Hinnom at the northern end of the Valley of Rephaim. It ran down the Valley of Hinnom toward the south Jebusite slope and downward to En-rogel. [17] It curved northward and went to En-shemesh and on to Geliloth, which is opposite the Ascent of Adummim, and continued down to the Stone of Bohan[c] son of Reuben. [18] Then it went north to the slope opposite the Jordan Valley[A,B] and proceeded into the valley.[B] [19] The border continued to the north slope of Beth-hoglah and ended at the northern bay of the Dead Sea, at the southern end of the Jordan. This was the southern border.

[20] The Jordan formed the border on the east side.

This was the inheritance of Benjamin's de-

Column side notes:
a18:12 Jos 16:1
b18:13 Jos 16:3
c18:17 Jos 15:6
d19:2 1Ch 4:28

scendants, by their clans, according to its surrounding borders.

Benjamin's Cities

[21] These were the cities of the tribe of Benjamin's descendants by their clans:

Jericho, Beth-hoglah, Emek-keziz, [22] Beth-arabah, Zemaraim, Bethel, [23] Avvim, Parah, Ophrah, [24] Chephar-ammoni, Ophni, and Geba—12 cities, with their villages; [25] Gibeon, Ramah, Beeroth, [26] Mizpeh,[c] Chephirah, Mozah, [27] Rekem, Irpeel, Taralah, [28] Zela, Haeleph, Jebus[D] (that is, Jerusalem), Gibeah, and Kiriath[E]—14 cities, with their villages.

This was the inheritance for Benjamin's descendants by their clans.

Simeon's Inheritance

19 The second lot came out for Simeon, for the tribe of his descendants by their clans, but their inheritance was within the portion of Judah's descendants. [2] Their inheritance included:

Beer-sheba (or Sheba[d]), Moladah, [3] Hazar-shual, Balah, Ezem, [4] Eltolad, Bethul, Hormah, [5] Ziklag, Beth-marcaboth, Hazar-susah, [6] Beth-lebaoth, and Sharuhen—13 cities, with their villages; [7] Ain, Rimmon, Ether, and Ashan—four cities, with their villages; [8] and all the villages surrounding these cities as far as Baalath-beer (Ramah of the south[F]).

This was the inheritance of the tribe of Simeon's descendants by their clans. [9] The inheritance of Simeon's descendants was within the territory of Judah's descendants, because the share for Judah's descendants was too large for them. So Simeon's descendants received an inheritance within Judah's portion.

Zebulun's Inheritance

[10] The third lot came up for Zebulun's descendants by their clans.

A18:18 LXX reads *went northward to Beth-arabah*   B18:18 Or *the Arabah*   C18:26 = Mizpah; Jos 11:3,8   D18:28 Lit *Jebusite*
E18:28 LXX, Syr read *Kiriath-jearim*   F19:8 Or *the Negev*

---

topographic boundaries that had already been used by Canaanite city-states and their regional control.

18:11-28 Benjamin's allotment includes a boundary description (vv. 11-20) and a town list (vv. 21-28), which took in Jebus/Jerusalem.

19:1-9 The allotment of the tribe of **Simeon** has no boundaries. It is a list of towns (vv. 2-8) located within the southern territory of Judah. This was given to Simeon **because the share for Judah's descendants was too large for them.** The town list subdivides into an eastern (vv. 2-6) and

a western (vv. 7-8) list. This area around the Beer-sheba Valley was already inhabited. Therefore, Simeon's settlement would assist in giving the region an Israelite identity. It would also provide a defense against encroachment by Edomite tribes to the south and east.

19:10-16 The allotment for **Zebulun** consists of a boundary description, beginning with the southern border (vv. 10-11), moving to the eastern border (vv. 12-13), and concluding with the northern boundary (vv. 14-15). The western border is Asher's eastern border. Zebulun lay in the southwest cor-

The territory of their inheritance stretched as far as Sarid; [11] their border went up westward to Maralah, reached Dabbesheth, and met the brook east of Jokneam. [12] From Sarid, it turned east toward the sunrise along the border of Chisloth-tabor, went to Daberath, and went up to Japhia. [13] From there, it went east toward the sunrise to Gath-hepher and to Eth-kazin; it extended to Rimmon, curving around to Neah. [14] The border then circled around Neah on the north to Hannathon and ended at the Valley of Iphtah-el, [15] along with Kattath, Nahalal, Shimron, Idalah, and Bethlehem—12 cities, with their villages.

[16] This was the inheritance of Zebulun's descendants by their clans, these cities, with their villages.

Issachar's Inheritance

[17] The fourth lot came out for the tribe of Issachar's descendants by their clans.

[18] Their territory went to Jezreel, and included Chesulloth, Shunem,[a] [19] Hapharaim, Shion, Anaharath, [20] Rabbith, Kishion, Ebez, [21] Remeth, En-gannim, En-haddah, Beth-pazzez. [22] The border reached Tabor, Shahazumah, and Beth-shemesh, and ended at the Jordan—16 cities, with their villages.

[23] This was the inheritance of the tribe of Issachar's descendants by their clans, the cities, with their villages.

Asher's Inheritance

[24] The fifth lot came out for the tribe of Asher's descendants by their clans.

[25] Their boundary included Helkath, Hali, Beten, Achshaph, [26] Allammelech, Amad, and Mishal and reached westward to Carmel and Shihor-libnath. [27] It turned

a 19:18 1Sm 28:4
b 19:27 1Kg 9:13

eastward to Beth-dagon, passed Zebulun and the Valley of Iphtah-el, north toward Beth-emek and Neiel, and went north to Cabul,[b] [28] Ebron, Rehob, Hammon, and Kanah, as far as Great Sidon. [29] The boundary then turned to Ramah as far as the fortified city of Tyre; it turned back to Hosah and ended at the sea, including Mahalab, Achzib,[A] [30] Ummah, Aphek, and Rehob—22 cities, with their villages.

[31] This was the inheritance of the tribe of Asher's descendants by their clans, these cities with their villages.

Naphtali's Inheritance

[32] The sixth lot came out for Naphtali's descendants by their clans.

[33] Their boundary went from Heleph and from the oak in Zaanannim, including Adami-nekeb and Jabneel, as far as Lakkum, and ended at the Jordan. [34] To the west, the boundary turned to Aznoth-tabor and went from there to Hukkok, reaching Zebulun on the south, Asher on the west, and Judah[B] at the Jordan on the east. [35] The fortified cities were Ziddim, Zer, Hammath, Rakkath, Chinnereth,[C] [36] Adamah, Ramah, Hazor, [37] Kedesh, Edrei, En-hazor, [38] Iron, Migdal-el, Horem, Beth-anath, and Beth-shemesh—19 cities, with their villages.

[39] This was the inheritance of the tribe of Naphtali's descendants by their clans, the cities with their villages.

Dan's Inheritance

[40] The seventh lot came out for the Danite tribe by its clans.

[41] The territory of their inheritance included Zorah, Eshtaol, Ir-shemesh, [42] Shaalabbin, Aijalon, Ithlah, [43] Elon, Timnah, Ekron, [44] Eltekeh, Gibbethon, Baalath, [45] Jehud,

---

A 19:29 Or *sea, in the region of Achzib*   B 19:34 LXX omits *Judah*   C 19:35 A town near the Sea of Galilee

ner of the hills of Galilee, between the Jezreel Valley to the south and the Bet Netofa Valley northward in Galilee.

19:17-23 Issachar's allotment preserves a town list that included **16 cities** in the Jezreel Valley around Mount **Tabor** and those in the southeastern hills of Galilee.

19:24-31 Asher's allotment consists of a boundary list that began in the south (vv. 25-26), turned east along Zebulun (vv. 27-28), and reached north to **Great Sidon** before turning south along the coast (vv. 29-30). **Cabul** and the area around it was later given by Solomon to Hiram king of Tyre in payment for his assistance in constructing the temple of Jerusalem (1Kg 9:11-13).

19:32-39 Naphtali's tribe received the largest area among the seven remaining allotments. However, it was perhaps the worst agriculturally, located in upper Galilee where the heights prevented much cultivation. The southern boundary (vv. 33-34) is supplemented with a town list (vv. 35-38). Its eastern boundaries stretched to the Jordan River and the Sea of Galilee, including the rich and powerful centers of **Chinnereth . . . Kedesh**, and especially **Hazor** (chap. 11).

19:40-48 The territory of the **Danites** consists of a town list including eastern (vv. 41-44) and western towns (vv. 45-47). Its location alongside the Canaanite and Philistine coastal towns threatened its peace and prosperity. Dan lost part or

Bene-berak, Gath-rimmon, ⁴⁶Me-jarkon, and Rakkon, with the territory facing Joppa.

⁴⁷When the territory of the Danites slipped out of their control,ᴬ they went up and fought against Leshem, captured it, and struck it down with the sword. So they took possession of it, lived there, and renamed Leshem afterᴮ their ancestor Dan. ⁴⁸This was the inheritance of the Danite tribe by its clans, these cities with their villages.

Joshua's Inheritance

⁴⁹When they had finished distributing the land into its territories, the Israelites gave Joshua son of Nun an inheritance among them. ⁵⁰By the Lord's command, they gave him the city Timnath-serah in the hill country of Ephraim,ᵃ which he requested. He rebuilt the city and lived in it.

⁵¹These were the portions that Eleazar the priest, Joshua son of Nun, and the heads of the families distributed to the Israelite tribes by lot at Shiloh in the Lord's presence at the entrance to the tent of meeting.ᵇ So they finished dividing up the land.

Cities of Refuge

20 Then the Lord spoke to Joshua, ²"Tell the Israelites: Select your cities of refuge, as I instructed you through Moses,ᶜ ³so that a person who kills someone unintentionally or accidentally may flee there. These will

⁴When someone flees to one of these cities, stands at the entrance of the city ˙gate, and states his case beforeᶜ the elders of that city, they are to bring him into the city and give him a place to live among them.ᵉ ⁵And if the avenger of blood pursues him, they must not hand the one who committed manslaughter over to him, for he killed his neighbor accidentally and did not hate him beforehand. ⁶He is to stay in that city until he stands trial before the assembly and until the death of the high priest serving at that time.ᶠ Then the one who committed manslaughter may return home to his own city from which he fled."

⁷So they designated Kedesh in the hill country of Naphtali in Galilee,ᵍ Shechem in the hill country of Ephraim, and Kiriath-arba (that is, Hebron) in the hill country of Judah.ʰ ⁸Across the Jordan east of Jericho, they selected Bezer on the wilderness plateau from Reuben's tribe, Ramoth in Gilead from Gad's tribe, and Golan in Bashan from Manasseh's tribe.

⁹These are the cities appointed for all the Israelites and foreigners among them,ⁱ so that anyone who kills a person unintentionally may flee there and not die at the hand of the avenger of blood until he stands before the assembly.

Cities of the Levites

21 The heads of the Levite families approached Eleazar the priest, Joshua son

all of this territory (v. 47) and migrated north to the town of **Leshem** which they captured and renamed **Dan** (Jdg 17–18).

19:49-51 As with Caleb, the other faithful spy of the exodus generation, Joshua received a special allotment in his tribal territory—**Timnath-serah** (modern Khirbet Tibnah), southwest of Shechem. As Caleb received the first allotment in the promised land (14:6-15), Joshua received the last. His humility and commitment to complete his God-given responsibilities is evident as he waited until all the other tribes and people had received their inheritance before accepting his own.

20:2 In this chapter some of the land or towns given to Israel are set aside for a specific purpose. On the significance of the **cities of refuge**, see Ex 21:12-14; Nm 35:9-15,22-28; Dt 4:41-43; 19:1-10. These passages indicate that there were to be six towns—three east and three west of the Jordan River.

20:3 Someone who killed another person **unintentionally or accidentally** could find refuge in one of these towns from a form of blood vengeance in which the dead person's nearest kin was to seek the death of the killer in order to remove any blood guilt from their family.

20:4 The **elders of that city** functioned as the judges who heard all important disputes within the community.

20:6 The **trial before the assembly** was presumably a legal trial in his hometown where the killing occurred (Nm 35:22-28). Even if he was acquitted of premeditated murder, he remained in the city of refuge **until the death of the high priest serving at that time**. Presumably the avenger was to accept the high priest's death as a substitute for the guilt incurred by the shedding of innocent blood. The killer was free to return home.

20:7 Three cities of refuge were originally envisioned west of the Jordan River (Nm 35:9-15). Perhaps the size of the population led Joshua and the leadership to appoint six cities and name them here. They were located across the land so that a person was never far from such a place of refuge.

20:8 These cities of refuge located **east** of the **Jordan** River had been designated and named by Moses (Dt 4:41-43).

21:1-42 As Israel was given its inheritance in the preceding chapters, so it now gave back to God some of that inheritance for the use of the Levites. Their responsibility for the holy things of God meant they did not have time for the major occupation of the other Israelites—farming their land. See 1Ch 6:54-81 for a duplicate of this list of cities.

21:1-2 Eleazar at **Shiloh** recalls 18:1-10 and the distribution of the tribal allotments. This would be the Levites' allotment.

of Nun, and the heads of the families of the Israelite tribes. [2]At Shiloh, in the land of Canaan, they told them, "The LORD commanded through Moses that we be given cities to live in, with their pasturelands for our livestock."[a] [3]So the Israelites, by the LORD's command, gave the Levites these cities with their pasturelands from their inheritance.

[4]The lot came out for the Kohathite clans: The Levites who were the descendants of Aaron the priest received 13 cities by lot from the tribes of Judah, Simeon, and Benjamin. [5]The remaining descendants of Kohath[A] received 10 cities by lot from the clans of the tribes of Ephraim, Dan, and half the tribe of Manasseh.

[6]Gershon's descendants received 13 cities by lot from the clans of the tribes of Issachar, Asher, Naphtali, and half the tribe of Manasseh in Bashan.

[7]Merari's descendants received 12 cities for their clans from the tribes of Reuben, Gad, and Zebulun.

[8]The Israelites gave these cities with their pasturelands around them to the Levites by lot, as the LORD had commanded through Moses.

Cities of Aaron's Descendants

[9]The Israelites gave these cities by name from the tribes of the descendants of Judah and Simeon [10]to the descendants of Aaron from the Kohathite clans of the Levites, be-

[a] 21:2 Nm 35:4-5
[b] 21:11 1Ch 6:55
[c] 21:21 Jos 20:7

cause they received the first lot. [11]They gave them Kiriath-arba[b] (that is, Hebron) with its surrounding pasturelands in the hill country of Judah. Arba was the father of Anak. [12]But they gave the fields and villages of the city to Caleb son of Jephunneh as his possession.

[13]They gave to the descendants of Aaron the priest:

Hebron, the city of refuge for the one who commits manslaughter, with its pasturelands, Libnah with its pasturelands, [14]Jattir with its pasturelands, Eshtemoa with its pasturelands, [15]Holon with its pasturelands, Debir with its pasturelands, [16]Ain with its pasturelands, Juttah with its pasturelands, and Beth-shemesh with its pasturelands—nine cities from these two tribes.

[17]From the tribe of Benjamin they gave:

Gibeon with its pasturelands, Geba with its pasturelands, [18]Anathoth with its pasturelands, and Almon with its pasturelands—four cities. [19]All 13 cities with their pasturelands were for the priests, the descendants of Aaron.

Cities of Kohath's Other Descendants

[20]The allotted cities to the remaining clans of Kohath's descendants, who were Levites, came from the tribe of Ephraim. [21]The Israelites gave them:

Shechem,[c] the city of refuge for the one

[A] 21:5 Descendants not in Aaron's priestly line

goral

Hebrew Pronunciation	[goh RAHL]
HCSB Translation	lot
Uses in Joshua	26
Uses in the OT	77
Focus Passages	Joshua 21:4-6,8,10,20,40

The *lot* was an article cast to decipher God's will, since God revealed His plans to Israel that way (Pr 16:33). Other nations also employed the practice (Jnh 1:7). The *lot* was usually used for public decision-making, and various techniques for casting existed. *Lots* could settle disputes (Pr 18:18) or assign goods and services. The *lot* selected arrangements for priestly duties (1Ch 24:5), responsibilities for providing altar firewood (Neh 10:34), and a goat on the Day of Atonement (Lv 16:8-10). Victors cast the *lot* to divide war spoils (Ob 11), so it figured prominently when Joshua distributed tribal lands and assigned Levitical cities (Jos 18–19; 21:4-40). The high priest used special *lots*, the Urim and Thummim, to learn God's will (Ex 28:30). *Goral* may indicate the *allotment* or object *allotted* (Jos 15:1; 21:20). It figuratively indicates one's *lot* (Pr 1:14; Is 17:14) or *destiny* (Dn 12:13) in life.

21:2 The Lord's command **through Moses** about the Levitical cities occurs in Nm 35:1-8, where the towns are not named.

21:4 Those Levites who were **descendants of Aaron the priest** would receive the cities closest to Jerusalem because their responsibilities required them to be close to the temple (Nm 18:1-6). These cities are listed in Jos 21:9-19.

21:5 The **descendants of Kohath**, second son of Levi (Gn 46:11), received their inheritance in the hill country, at that time the location of the ark, for which they were responsible in the wilderness (Nm 3:1; 4:15-20; 7:9). These cities are listed in Jos 21:20-26.

21:6 The **descendants** of Gershon, first son of Levi, had been responsible for the tabernacle's coverings and other textiles (Nm 3:25-26; 4:24-26). They received cities in the northern tribal areas, listed in Jos 21:27-33.

21:7 **Merari's descendants**, from Levi's third son, guarded the tabernacle and transported its frames (Nm 1:47-53; 3:33-37; 4:29-33). They were given the Transjordanian and Zebulun Levitical cities, listed in Jos 21:34-40.

21:9-42 The 48 Levitical cities are listed and subdivided into four groups, with occasional notes. These are further

who commits manslaughter, with its pasturelands in the hill country of Ephraim, Gezer with its pasturelands, ²²Kibzaim with its pasturelands, and Beth-horon with its pasturelands—four cities.

²³From the tribe of Dan they gave:

Elteke with its pasturelands, Gibbethon with its pasturelands, ²⁴Aijalon with its pasturelands, and Gath-rimmon with its pasturelands—four cities.

²⁵From half the tribe of Manasseh they gave:

Taanach with its pasturelands and Gath-rimmonᴬ with its pasturelands—two cities.

²⁶All 10 cities with their pasturelands were for the clans of Kohath's other descendants.

Cities of Gershon's Descendants

²⁷From half the tribe of Manasseh, they gave to the descendants of Gershon,ᵃ who were one of the Levite clans:

Golan, the city of refuge for the one who commits manslaughter, with its pasturelands in Bashan, and Beeshterah with its pasturelands—two cities.

²⁸From the tribe of Issachar they gave:

Kishion with its pasturelands, Daberath with its pasturelands, ²⁹Jarmuth with its pasturelands, and En-gannim with its pasturelands—four cities.

³⁰From the tribe of Asher they gave:

Mishal with its pasturelands, Abdon with its pasturelands, ³¹Helkath with its pasturelands, and Rehob with its pasturelands—four cities.

³²From the tribe of Naphtali they gave:

Kedesh in Galilee, the city of refuge for the one who commits manslaughter, with its pasturelands, Hammoth-dor with its pasturelands, and Kartan with its pasturelands—three cities.

ᵃ21:27 1Ch 6:71
ᵇ21:34 1Ch 6:77
ᶜ21:36-38 Jos 20:8
ᵈ21:41 Nm 35:7
ᵉ21:45 Jos 23:14

³³All 13 cities with their pasturelands were for the Gershonites by their clans.

Cities of Merari's Descendants

³⁴From the tribe of Zebulun, they gave to the clans of the descendants of Merari,ᵇ who were the remaining Levites:

Jokneam with its pasturelands, Kartah with its pasturelands, ³⁵Dimnah with its pasturelands, and Nahalal with its pasturelands—four cities.

³⁶From the tribe of Reuben they gave:

Bezerᶜ with its pasturelands, Jahzahᴮ with its pasturelands, ³⁷Kedemoth with its pasturelands, and Mephaath with its pasturelands—four cities.ᶜ

³⁸From the tribe of Gad they gave:

Ramoth in Gilead, the city of refuge for the one who commits manslaughter, with its pasturelands, Mahanaim with its pasturelands, ³⁹Heshbon with its pasturelands, and Jazer with its pasturelands—four cities in all. ⁴⁰All 12 cities were allotted to the clans of Merari's descendants, the remaining Levite clans.

⁴¹Within the Israelite possession there were 48 cities in all with their pasturelands for the Levites.ᵈ ⁴²Each of these cities had its own surrounding pasturelands; this was true for all the cities.

The Lᴏʀᴅ's Promises Fulfilled

⁴³So the Lᴏʀᴅ gave Israel all the land He had sworn to give their fathers, and they took possession of it and settled there. ⁴⁴The Lᴏʀᴅ gave them rest on every side according to all He had sworn to their fathers. None of their enemies were able to stand against them, for the Lᴏʀᴅ handed over all their enemies to them. ⁴⁵None of the good promises the Lᴏʀᴅ had made to the house of Israel failed. Everything was fulfilled.ᵉ

Eastern Tribes Return Home

22 Joshua summoned the Reubenites, Gadites, and half the tribe of Manasseh ²and told them, "You have done everything

---

ᴬ21:25 Or *Ibleam*   ᴮ21:36 Or *Jahaz*   ᶜ21:36-37 Some Hb mss omit these vv.

subdivided by tribes with numerical totals after each grouping. This is characteristic of a longer town list (15:20-63).

21:43-44 The Lord fulfilled His promises. He **gave Israel** the land He had promised to them and their ancestors (1:3). God also gave the Israelites **rest on every side** just as He had promised (1:13).

21:45 The conclusion that **everything was fulfilled** shows

how God kept His promises and how all the enemies of Israel that they fought against were defeated. Israel did not drive out all the inhabitants of the land, but this was not God's responsibility. He kept His part of the covenant.

22:1-6 These verses bring to fruition 1:12-18 and the promise made by the two and a half tribes from east of the Jordan River to follow Joshua wherever he led. They had been

Moses the LORD's servant commanded you[a] and have obeyed me in everything I commanded you. ³You have not deserted your brothers even once this whole time but have carried out the requirement of the command of the LORD your God. ⁴Now that He has given your brothers rest, just as He promised them, return to your homes in your own land that Moses the LORD's servant gave you across the Jordan. ⁵Only carefully obey the command and instruction that Moses the LORD's servant gave you: to love the LORD your God, walk in all His ways, keep His commands, remain faithful[A] to Him, and serve Him with all your heart and all your soul."[b]

⁶Joshua blessed them and sent them on their way,[c] and they went to their homes. ⁷Moses had given territory to half the tribe of Manasseh in Bashan, but Joshua had given territory to the other half,[B] with their brothers, on the west side of the Jordan.[d] When Joshua sent them to their homes and blessed them, ⁸he said, "Return to your homes with great wealth: a huge number of cattle, and silver, gold, bronze, iron, and a large quantity of clothing. Share the spoil of your enemies with your brothers."[e]

Eastern Tribes Build an Altar

⁹The Reubenites, Gadites, and half the tribe of Manasseh left the Israelites at Shiloh in the land of Canaan to return to their own land of Gilead,[f] which they took possession of according to the LORD's command through Moses. ¹⁰When they came to the region of[C] the Jordan in the land of Canaan, the Reubenites, Gadites, and half the tribe of Manasseh built a large, impressive altar there by the Jordan. ¹¹Then the Israelites heard it said, "Look, the Reubenites, Gadites, and half the tribe

of Manasseh have built an altar on the frontier of the land of Canaan at the region of[D] the Jordan, on the Israelite side." ¹²When the Israelites heard this, the entire Israelite community assembled at Shiloh to go to war against them.[g]

Explanation of the Altar

¹³The Israelites sent Phinehas son of Eleazar the priest to the Reubenites, Gadites, and half the tribe of Manasseh, in the land of Gilead.[h] ¹⁴They sent 10 leaders with him—one family leader for each tribe of Israel. All of them were heads of their families among the clans of Israel.[i] ¹⁵They went to the Reubenites, Gadites, and half the tribe of Manasseh, in the land of Gilead, and told them, ¹⁶"This is what the LORD's entire community says: 'What is this treachery you have committed today against the God of Israel by turning away from the LORD and building an altar for yourselves, so that you are in rebellion against the LORD today? ¹⁷Wasn't the sin of Peor, which brought a plague on the LORD's community, enough for us, so that we have not cleansed ourselves from it even to this day,[j] ¹⁸and now, you would turn away from the LORD? If you rebel against the LORD today, tomorrow He will be angry with the entire community of Israel.[k] ¹⁹But if the land you possess is defiled, cross over to the land the LORD possesses where the LORD's tabernacle stands, and take possession of it among us. But don't rebel against the LORD or against us by building for yourselves an altar other than the altar of the LORD our God. ²⁰Wasn't Achan son of Zerah unfaithful regarding what was •set apart for destruction, bringing wrath on the entire community of Israel? He was not the only one who perished because of his sin.'"[l]

Cross references (center column):
[a] 22:2 Dt 3:18-20
[b] 22:5 Dt 6:5; 10:12-13; 11:13-17
[c] 22:6 Jos 14:13
[d] 22:7 Nm 32:33; Jos 17:5
[e] 22:8 Nm 31:27; 1Sm 30:24
[f] 22:9 Nm 32:1, 26,29
[g] 22:12 Lv 17:8-9; Dt 13:12-15
[h] 22:13 Nm 25:7
[i] 22:14 Nm 1:4, 16
[j] 22:17 Jos 6:25
[k] 22:18 Nm 16:22
[l] 22:20 Jos 7:1-26

[A]22:5 Lit commands, hold on   [B]22:7 Lit to his half   [C]22:10 Or to Geliloth by   [D]22:11 Or at Geliloth by

---

faithful to their oath, so Joshua sent them home with his blessing.

22:5 Joshua dismissed the Transjordanian tribes with one condition: to fully obey God's revealed instruction. To serve God **with all your heart and all your soul** repeats Dt 6:5.

22:8 The people received material blessings even though this was not the main motivation for assisting their fellow tribes.

22:10 The tribes on the eastern side of the Jordan River **built a large, impressive altar** by the river. The altar that these tribes constructed is in Hebrew, mizbeach, a word that means "slaughter." This is what caused the concern of the other tribes: animal sacrifice would take place on this altar.

22:12 Because the altar was beside the Jordan River and

was so large, the ten tribes could probably see it. The rest of Israel assembled against the two and a half tribes to war against them from their base **at Shiloh**.

22:13 How much later this took place is not clear, but **Phinehas son of Eleazar** was now the acting **priest**. He had last appeared in Nm 31:6 where he took articles from the sanctuary into battle.

22:16-19 The 10 representatives of the remaining tribes objected because the altar was considered a competitor to the true **altar of the LORD our God**.

22:17 The **sin of Peor** refers to the time when Israel joined Midian in worshiping the Baal or god of the region of Peor, east of the Jordan River. In Nm 25:1-13 Phinehas executed God's judgment for this sin by killing an Israelite man and a Midianite woman who were engaged in this carnal ritual.

22:20 Mention of **Achan son of Zerah** (8:1-29) explains the

²¹The Reubenites, Gadites, and half the tribe of Manasseh answered the leaders of the Israelite clans, ²²"Yahweh is the God of gods! Yahweh is the God of gods!ᴬ He knows,ᵃ and may Israel also know. Do not spare us today, if it was in rebellion or treachery against the LORD ²³that we have built for ourselves an altar to turn away from Him. May the LORD Himself hold us accountable if we intended to offer •burnt offerings and •grain offerings on it, or to sacrifice •fellowship offerings on it. ²⁴We actually did this from a specific concern that in the future your descendants might say to our descendants, 'What relationship do you have with the LORD, the God of Israel? ²⁵For the LORD has made the Jordan a border between us and you descendants of Reuben and Gad. You have no share in the LORD!' So your descendants may cause our descendants to stop fearing the LORD.

²⁶"Therefore we said: Let us take action and build an altar for ourselves, but not for burnt offering or sacrifice. ²⁷Instead, it is to be a witness between us and you,ᵇ and between the generations after us, so that we may carry out the worship of the LORD in His presence with our burnt offerings, sacrifices, and fellowship offerings.ᶜ Then in the future, your descendants will not be able to say to our descendants, 'You have no share in the LORD!' ²⁸We thought that if they said this to us or to our generations in the future, we would reply: Look at the replica of the LORD's altar that our fathers made, not for burnt offering or sacrifice, but as a witness between us and you. ²⁹We would never rebel against the LORD or turn away from Him today by building an altar for burnt offering, grain offering, or sacrifice, other than the altar of the LORD our God, which is in front of His tabernacle."

ᵃ 22:22 1Kg 8:39
ᵇ 22:27 Gn 31:48;
Jos 24:27
ᶜ Dt 12:6
ᵈ 22:31 Lv
26:11-12
ᵉ 22:33 1Ch
29:20; Dn 2:19;
Lk 2:28
ᶠ 23:2 Jos 24:1
ᵍ 23:3 Jos 10:14

Conflict Resolved

³⁰When Phinehas the priest and the community leaders, the heads of Israel's clans who were with him, heard what the descendants of Reuben, Gad, and Manasseh had to say, they were pleased. ³¹Phinehas son of Eleazar the priest said to the descendants of Reuben, Gad, and Manasseh, "Today we know that the LORD is among us, because you have not committed this treachery against Him.ᵈ As a result, you have delivered the Israelites from the LORD's power."

³²Then Phinehas son of Eleazar the priest and the leaders returned from the Reubenites and Gadites in the land of Gilead to the Israelites in the land of Canaan and brought back a report to them. ³³The Israelites were pleased with the report, and they praised God.ᵉ They spoke no more about going to war against them to ravage the land where the Reubenites and Gadites lived. ³⁴So the Reubenites and Gadites named the altar: Itᴮ is a witness between us that the LORD is God.

Joshua's Farewell Address

23 A long time after the LORD had given Israel rest from all the enemies around them, Joshua was old, getting on in years. ²So Joshua summoned all Israel, including its elders, leaders, judges, and officers,ᶠ and said to them, "I am old, getting on in years, ³and you have seen for yourselves everything the LORD your God did to all these nations on your account, because it was the LORD your God who was fighting for you.ᵍ ⁴See, I have allotted these remaining nations to you as an inheritance for your tribes, including all the nations I have destroyed, from the Jordan westward to the Mediterranean Sea. ⁵The LORD your God will force them back on your account and

ᴬ22:22 Or *The Mighty One, God, the LORD! The Mighty One, God, the LORD!*, or *God, the LORD God! God, the LORD God!*   ᴮ22:34 Some Hb mss, Syr, Tg read *altar Witness because it*

concern of the 10 tribes. They feared that God's judgment for what the Transjordanian tribes had done would also fall on them all.

22:24 The two and a half tribes explained that they had built the altar as a way to maintain the unity of all the tribes in future generations.

22:26,29 Repeatedly the Transjordanian tribes denied any intent to use the altar as a place of sacrifice.

22:27-28 The altar bore **witness** that those on both sides of it worshiped the same God at the same tabernacle. When Abram first came into the promised land, he built altars from north to south as a testimony that the land belonged to God and was His to give to Abram and his descendants (Gn 12:6-8; 13:18). Now the Transjordanian tribes had done the same thing. Although their land was not part of the promised land, they wanted to identify with the God of the prom-

ised land and to show that their land was a place where God was worshiped.

22:34 With the conflict resolved, the **altar** was **named** in recognition of the confession of the Transjordanian tribes.

23:1 The note that **Joshua was old** repeats the words from 13:1, just as the theme of **rest from all the enemies** carries forward the sense of 21:44. Joshua had completed his life's mission.

23:4 The land currently occupied by the **remaining nations** had already been parceled out as **an inheritance**; the Israelites merely had to conquer it with God's help.

23:5 Israel was to remain faithful and watch as God would **force them back on your account**. This is not unlike what had already occurred. Israel had observed God fighting

drive them out before you so that you can take
possession of their land,[a] as the LORD your God
promised you.
6“Be very strong[b] and continue obeying all
that is written in the book of the law of Moses,
so that you do not turn from it to the right
or left 7and so that you do not associate with
these nations remaining among you. Do not
call on the names of their gods or make an
oath to them;[c] do not worship them or bow
down to them. 8Instead, remain faithful to the
LORD your God, as you have done to this day.[d]
9“The LORD has driven out great and powerful nations before you,[e] and no one is able
to stand against you to this day.[f] 10One of you
routed a thousand[g] because the LORD your God
was fighting for you, as He promised.[A,h] 11So
be very diligent to love the LORD your God for
your own well-being. 12For if you turn away
and cling to the rest of these nations remaining among you,[i] and if you intermarry or associate with them[j] and they with you, 13know for
certain that the LORD your God will not continue to drive these nations out before you.
They will become a snare and a trap for you,[k]
a scourge for your sides and thorns in your
eyes, until you disappear from this good land
the LORD your God has given you.
14“I am now going the way of all the earth,[B,l]
and you know with all your heart and all your
soul that none of the good promises the LORD
your God made to you has failed. Everything
was fulfilled for you; not one promise has
failed.[m] 15Since every good thing the LORD
your God promised you has come about, so
He will bring on you every bad thing until He
has annihilated you from this good land the
LORD your God has given you.[n] 16If you break
the covenant of the LORD your God, which He
commanded you, and go and worship other
gods, and bow down to them, the LORD’s anger will burn against you, and you will quickly
disappear from this good land He has given
you.”

Review of Israel’s History

24 Joshua assembled all the tribes of Israel at Shechem[o] and summoned Israel’s
elders, leaders, judges, and officers, and they
presented themselves before God.[p] 2Joshua
said to all the people, “This is what the LORD,
the God of Israel, says: ‘Long ago your ancestors, including Terah,[q] the father of Abraham
and Nahor, lived beyond the Euphrates River
and worshiped other gods. 3But I took your
father Abraham from the region beyond the
Euphrates River, led him throughout the land
of Canaan, and multiplied his descendants.[r] I
gave him Isaac,[s] 4and to Isaac I gave Jacob and
Esau.[t] I gave the hill country of Seir to Esau
as a possession,[u] but Jacob and his sons went
down to Egypt.[v]
5“ ‘Then I sent Moses and Aaron;[w] I plagued

[a] 23:5 Nm 33:53
[b] 23:6 Dt 5:32; Jos 1:7
[c] 23:7 Ex 23:13; Ps 16:4
[d] 23:8 Jos 6:25
[e] 23:9 Ex 23:30
[f] Jos 1:5
[g] 23:10 Jdg 15:15-16
[h] Lv 26:8
[i] 23:12 Ex 34:16
[j] Dt 7:3
[k] 23:13 Ex 23:33; Dt 7:16; Jdg 2:3
[l] 23:14 1Kg 2:2
[m] Jos 21:45
[n] 23:15 Lv 26:14-33; Dt 28:15
[o] 24:1 Gn 12:1-7
[p] Jos 23:2
[q] 24:2 Gn 11:27-32
[r] 24:3 Gn 12:1
[s] Gn 21:3
[t] 24:4 Gn 25:25-26
[u] Gn 36:8; Dt 2:5
[v] Gn 46:6
[w] 24:5 Ex 4:14

[A] 23:10 Lit *promised you* [B] 23:14 = I am going to die

against their enemies and had merely followed after Him to experience the victory.

23:6 The requirement for Israel to continue to enjoy success was that they obey **all that is written in the book of the law of Moses**. This is what Joshua was commanded to do in 1:9-11. His obedience and that of Israel had brought victory.

23:7 The way to obey God is to **worship** Him alone and refuse to be lured into association with other deities or the **nations** who worship them. This was God’s most basic command for Israel (Ex 20:3-6; Dt 5:7-10).

23:10 God wins the victories and enables Israel to succeed.

23:12 This warning against association or intermarriage with other nations is repeated in 24:20.

23:13 Disobedience would result in God withdrawing His strength so that Israel would not fully possess the land. This compromise would lead to **a trap** for Israel and ultimately, in anticipation of the exile centuries later, to the tribes of Israel disappearing from the promised land.

23:14 The **way of all the earth** is death, since everything on earth eventually dies (Ec 9:3; Rm 5:12; Heb 9:27).

23:16 Joshua’s warning, **If you break the covenant**, uses the same verb (Hb *’avar*) as the opening chapters of Joshua where it describes the crossing of the Jordan River (1:2). The same God who enabled Israel to benefit from great miracles can also turn against a faithless nation. The breaking of God’s covenant by worshiping other gods would cause the loss of the **land**.

24:1-27 In this final chapter of the book, Joshua enacted a covenant renewal ceremony with Israel.

24:1 Joshua brought together all the tribes and their leaders to stand before God at **Shechem**, just as he had at Mount Ebal, next to Shechem, in 8:30-35.

24:2a Joshua’s report began by introducing the sovereign **God** who was **LORD** over **Israel** and thus capable of making a covenant with them.

24:2b-13 This is the historical review section of the treaty/covenant. Its purpose is to demonstrate God’s acts of protection and deliverance toward Israel in the past and to motivate Israel to remain faithful to God in the present. Terah, the father of Abraham, lived **beyond the Euphrates River** in Ur and Haran (Gn 11:26-32). Nahor, Terah’s son, also lived in Ur. Their worship of **other gods** is not mentioned in Genesis, but archaeology shows that it was common there.

24:3 The history introduces the manner in which God delivered **Abraham** from the land of many gods and brought him to Canaan.

24:4 Already in the generation of **Jacob and Esau**, God was granting lands to peoples. So He gave **Seir** or Edom to Esau. Since it was not yet time for Jacob to obtain his inheritance, he went south to **Egypt**, away from the land that was to be his (Gn 46:6).

24:5 As God had brought Abraham out of a pagan land (v. 3),

Egypt by what I did there and afterward I brought you out. ⁶When I brought your fathers out of Egypt and you reached the ˙Red Sea,ᵃ the Egyptians pursued your fathers with chariots and horsemen as far as the sea. ⁷Your fathers cried out to the Lᴏʀᴅ, so He put darkness between you and the Egyptians, and brought the sea over them, engulfing them. Your own eyes saw what I did to Egypt. After that, you lived in the wilderness a long time.

⁸"Later, I brought you to the land of the Amorites who lived beyond the Jordan.ᵇ They fought against you, but I handed them over to you. You possessed their land, and I annihilated them before you. ⁹Balak son of Zippor, king of Moab,ᶜ set out to fight against Israel. He sent for Balaam son of Beor to curse you, ¹⁰but I would not listen to Balaam. Instead, he repeatedly blessed you, and I delivered you from his hand.

¹¹"You then crossed the Jordan and came to Jericho.ᵈ The people of Jericho—as well as the Amorites, Perizzites, Canaanites, Hittites, Girgashites, Hivites, and Jebusites—fought against you, but I handed them over to you. ¹²I sent the hornetᴬ,ᵉ ahead of you, and it drove out the two Amorite kingsᶠ before you. It was not by your sword or bow. ¹³I gave you a land you did not labor for, and cities you did not build,ᵍ though you live in them; you are

eating from vineyards and olive groves you did not plant.'

The Covenant Renewal

¹⁴"Therefore, ˙fear the Lᴏʀᴅ and worship Him in sincerity and truth.ʰ Get rid of the gods your fathers worshipedⁱ beyond the Euphrates River and in Egypt, and worship ˙Yahweh. ¹⁵But if it doesn't please you to worship Yahweh, choose for yourselves today the one you will worship: the gods your fathers worshiped beyond the Euphrates River or the gods of the Amorites in whose land you are living.ʲ As for me and my family, we will worship Yahweh."

¹⁶The people replied, "We will certainly not abandon the Lᴏʀᴅ to worship other gods! ¹⁷For the Lᴏʀᴅ our God brought us and our fathers out of the land of Egypt, out of the place of slavery,ᵏ and performed these great signs before our eyes. He also protected us all along the way we went and among all the peoples whose lands we traveled through. ¹⁸The Lᴏʀᴅ drove out before us all the peoples, including the Amorites who lived in the land. We too will worship the Lᴏʀᴅ, because He is our God."

¹⁹But Joshua told the people, "You will not be able to worship Yahweh, because He is a holy God. He is a jealous God;ˡ He will not remove your transgressions and sins.ᵐ ²⁰If you

---

ᵃ24:6 Ex 14:2
ᵇ24:8 Nm 21:21-32
ᶜ24:9 Nm 22:5
ᵈ24:11 Jos 3:14,17
ᵉ24:12 Ex 23:27-28; Dt 7:20
ᶠNm 21:21-35; Dt 2:26–3:11; 29:7
ᵍ24:13 Dt 6:10-11
ʰ24:14 Dt 10:12; 1Sm 12:24
ⁱGn 35:4
ʲ24:15 Jdg 6:10
ᵏ24:17 Lv 26:13; Dt 5:6; 6:12; 8:14; 13:5,10; Jr 34:13
ˡ24:19 Lv 19:2
ᵐEx 23:21

ᴬ24:12 Or *sent terror*

---

so He brought the nation of Israel out of **Egypt** through **Moses and Aaron** and the plagues.

24:6-7 The exodus was another of God's miracles by which He protected His people. Although note is made of how Israel **lived in the wilderness a long time**, no mention is made of their sin. The purpose of this history was not to repeat Israel's failures but to highlight God's successes at preserving the nation in order to encourage them to worship Him.

24:8 The Transjordanian victories against the **Amorites** continue the theme of God's powerful deliverance.

24:9-10 Balaam was mentioned in 13:22 as a sorcerer. Here his being hired by **Balak son of Zippor, king of Moab** to curse Israel was just another opportunity for God to deliver His people.

24:11 And again God **handed . . . over** the nations that the present generation fought (chaps. 6–12). God alone was responsible for the protection and blessing of His people Israel from the very beginning.

24:12 The **hornet** was promised in Ex 23:28 and in Dt 7:20 as the means by which God would drive out the inhabitants of the land. God fulfilled His promise.

24:13 God's gift of **a land you did not labor for, and cities you did not build** recalls His promise to Israel in Dt 6:10-11. That promise was immediately followed by a warning not to forget God and worship other deities.

24:14-15 These are God's demands—the laws or stipulations by which Israel should live. The key is for the people

to choose to **worship** the Lord only. Joshua gave Israel a choice to worship the gods of their ancestors or those of the **Amorites**. He affirmed the God of Israel as his own choice. So if Israel would follow Joshua in peace as they did in war, they must **choose** the true God.

24:19 After the people promised to worship God alone, Joshua warned them that it would be difficult. The people must not choose lightly or in a moment of good feeling about God, **a holy God . . . a jealous God**.

24:20 If the people chose now for God and changed their minds later, God would **completely destroy** them, just as they did their enemies in lands they now inhabited (2:10).

Shechem, viewed from Mount Gerazim, where Joshua placed a standing stone to commemorate the covenant.

abandon the LORD and worship foreign gods, He will turn against you, harm you, and completely destroy[a] you, after He has been good to you."

[21]"No!" the people answered Joshua. "We will worship the LORD."

[22]Joshua then told the people, "You are witnesses against yourselves that you yourselves have chosen to worship Yahweh."

"We are witnesses," they said.

[23]"Then get rid of the foreign gods that are among you and offer your hearts to the LORD, the God of Israel."

[24]So the people said to Joshua, "We will worship the LORD our God and obey Him."

[25]On that day Joshua made a covenant for the people at Shechem and established a statute and ordinance for them. [26]Joshua recorded these things in the book of the law of God;[b] he also took a large stone and set it up there under the oak next to the sanctuary of the LORD. [27]And Joshua said to all the people, "You see this stone—it will be a witness against us,[c] for it has heard all the words the LORD said to us,

and it will be a witness against you, so that you will not deny your God." [28]Then Joshua sent the people away, each to his own inheritance.

Burial of Three Leaders

[29]After these things, the LORD's servant, Joshua son of Nun, died at the age of 110. [30]They buried him in his allotted territory at Timnath-serah, in the hill country of Ephraim[d] north of Mount Gaash. [31]Israel worshiped Yahweh throughout Joshua's lifetime and during the lifetimes of the elders who outlived Joshua[e] and who had experienced all the works Yahweh had done for Israel.

[32]Joseph's bones, which the Israelites had brought up from Egypt,[f] were buried at Shechem in the parcel of land Jacob had purchased from the sons of Hamor, Shechem's father, for 100 qesitahs.[A,g] It was an inheritance for Joseph's descendants.

[33]And Eleazar son of Aaron died, and they buried him at Gibeah,[B] which had been given to his son Phinehas[h] in the hill country of Ephraim.

Cross references (center column):
a 24:20 Jos 10:1; 11:11; Jdg 1:17
b 24:26 Dt 31:24
c 24:27 Jos 22:27,34
d 24:30 Jos 19:49-50
e 24:31 Jdg 2:7
f 24:32 Gn 50:25; Ex 13:19
g Gn 33:19; Jb 42:11
h 24:33 Jos 22:13

A 24:32 The value of this currency is unknown.   B 24:33 = the Hill

---

This warning is the closest chapter 24 comes to pronouncing curses. For a vassal to enter into a treaty obligation and later to break it was considered an act of treason worthy of death. So it is here for Israel.

24:23 Joshua charged Israel to **get rid of the foreign gods that are among you**. The people made their promises, but the report does not indicate that they did away with their gods, unlike their ancestor Jacob. He buried the gods in his possession at Shechem, the same place where his descendants now stood (Gn 35:2-4).

24:26-27 Joshua declared that this covenant would be written **in the book of the law of God**. This suggests that the covenant was preserved in the most sacred and holy place possible. It would never be changed. The **stone** that Joshua erected, like those at the crossing of the Jordan (4:1-7,20-24), would stand as a witness for future generations of all the people agreed to at this place. Israel might be tempted to change, but the stone would always stand as a reminder to the nation of its commitment to the one true God.

24:29-30 These verses are identical to Jdg 2:9-10, where the story of the judges begins as a continuation to that of Joshua and his generation. Joshua is here called **the LORD's servant**. Just like Moses, who was given this name only at his death, Joshua's honor of receiving it indicates a life of faithfulness (1:1; Dt 34:5). The age of Joseph at his death

was also 110 (Gn 50:22,26), which also suggests a life of faithfulness. As Joseph preserved Israel in a time of famine, so Joshua preserved her amid the challenge of taking the land. For Joshua's inheritance and burial site, see note at Jos 19:49-51.

24:31 Despite some uncertainty about their degree of commitment (v. 23), Israel remained faithful to God during the **lifetime** of **Joshua** and **the elders** who had experienced God's miracles and guidance. The following generation would be different as Jdg 2:10-13 attests.

24:32 The mention of Joseph, already hinted at in the age of Joshua's death at 110 (v. 29), is here connected with his **bones** (Gn 50:24-26) and the purchase of the burial place (Gn 33:18-20). This ties together the generation that left the promised land with the one that returned and settled there.

24:33 Both **Eleazar son of Aaron** and **his son Phinehas** had been instrumental in the division of the land (14:1; 17:4; 19:51; 21:1; 22:13,30-32). Eleazar represented the religious leadership of the priesthood. He was of Joshua's generation. Phinehas represented the next generation (he would next appear in Jdg 20:28 in a very different context). Unlike Joshua, whose family is not mentioned and who had no successor in leadership, the priestly line was to continue. It would remain a witness of God to His people, the Israelites.

Judges

Introduction

The book of Judges is the second of the historical books in the Old Testament (Jos–Est). In the Hebrew Bible, these books are called the Former Prophets; the theological and spiritual concerns found in the Pentateuch and the Prophets take precedence over simply recording historical facts. The book derives its name from the Hebrew designation of the principal characters, *shophetim* (2:18), which could also be translated as "governors." These judges were the Lord's agents of deliverance. The Lord is both the central character and the hero of Judges.

Mount Tabor played an important role during the conquest. It served as a boundary point for the tribes of Naphtali, Issachar, and Zebulun (Jos 19), where the tribes worshiped early on (Dt 33:18-19). Barak and Deborah gathered an army at Mount Tabor to defend against Sisera (Jdg 4:6).

Circumstances of Writing

Author: No author is named in the book of Judges, nor is any indication given of the writer or writers who are responsible for it. The three divisions of the book are on a different footing regarding the sources from which they are drawn. The historical introduction presents a form of the traditional narrative of the conquest of Palestine that is parallel to the book of Joshua. The main portion of the book, comprising the narratives of the judges, appears to be based on oral or written traditions of a local observer.

Background: The period of the Israelite judges lay between the conquest of the promised land under Joshua and the rise of the monarchy with Saul and David. The events described are thus to be dated from the end of the fifteenth century B.C. to the latter part of the eleventh century B.C., a period of around 300 years. This was a time of social and religious anarchy, characterized by the repeated refrain, "In those days there was no king in Israel; everyone did whatever he wanted" (17:6; 18:1; 19:1; 21:25).

We cannot ascertain exactly when the book of Judges was composed. The reference in 18:30 to the fate of Dan at "the time of the exile from the land" suggests a date of final editing after the exile of the northern kingdom by Assyria around 722 B.C. Meanwhile, the suggestion that readers could visit the site of Gideon's altar at Ophrah in 6:24 suggests a date prior to the exile of the southern kingdom, Judah, in 586 B.C. Its message would have resonated strongly at several points of Israel's history, and it has been argued that it fits well during the dark days of Manasseh (686–642 B.C.; 2Kg 21:1-18). However, it is not possible to date Judges with precision.

Message and Purpose

The book of Judges chronicles the moral and spiritual descent of Israel from the relative high point at the beginning of the book through a series of downward spirals to the depths of degradation in chapters 17–21. Though God raised up a sequence of deliverers—the judges—they were unable to reverse this trend and some even became part of the problem themselves. By the end of the book, Israel had become as pagan and defiled

---

1400 B.C.   **1300 B.C.**

Joshua 1490?–1380?   **Deborah** 1360?–1300?   **Gideon** 1250?–1175?

Events in Deuteronomy 1406   Division of the land into twelve allotments 1385?

Miraculous crossing of the Jordan River 1406   Deborah and Barak defeat the Canaanites. 1320?

Events in Joshua 1406–1380?   Pharaoh Horemheb creates a river security
                                          unit to board and search boats suspected of
Musical notation, Ugarit 1400   smuggling. 1320

Chopsticks are used in China. 1400   Pharaoh Merneptah (1212–1203) memorializes his
                                          victories against Libya and Canaan on a granite
                                          stele, the so-called Merneptah Stele. This is
                                          the first Egyptian document in which Israel is
                                          mentioned. The Merneptah Stele was discovered
                                          in A.D. 1896 by Flanders Petrie at Thebes.

as the Canaanites they had displaced. If this trend continued, it would only be a matter of time before the land would vomit them out, as it had the Canaanites before them (Lv 18:28).

Human depravity: The book of Judges demonstrates what happens to the Lord's people when everyone does whatever they want. It shows that Israel cannot presume upon God's grace, and neither can we. If we abandon His commandments and pursue the idols of our own imagination, the result will be moral and spiritual chaos. This is where we would all end up if the Lord left us to ourselves.

The grace of God: The book of Judges offers a profound commentary on the grace of God. Left to their own devices, the Israelites would surely have destroyed themselves. Only by the repeated gracious intervention of God did they emerge from the dark premonarchic period as a people and nation distinguishable in lifestyle and beliefs from surrounding pagan groups.

The need for God's leadership: While it is possible that the repeated refrain "there was no king in Israel" (17:6; 18:1; 19:1; 21:25) paints this book as an appeal for a monarchy, it is better to see it as a call to return to God as their King. Rather than lifting up the kings as an ideal above the confusion of this period, the addition of "everyone did whatever he wanted" (17:6; 21:25) reduced the population to the moral and spiritual level of Israel's kings in later years. In other words, rebellion against God is democratized. Israel did not need a king to lead them into sin; they could fall into immorality all on their own. The Israelites had abandoned the God of the covenant to follow the fertility gods of the land. The writer, by exposing this problem, sought to wake up his own generation. This is an appeal to the covenant people to abandon all forms of paganism and return to Yahweh.

Contribution to the Bible

The book of Judges shows us that the nation of Israel survived the dark days of the judges entirely by the grace of God. In mercy He sent oppressors as reminders of their rebellion. In mercy He responded to their cries and

---

1200 B.C.   1100 B.C.

Jephthah 1200?–1150?   **Ruth** 1175?–1125?   **Samson** 1120?–1060?

Events in Judges 1380?–1060?

Gideon defeats Midianites and Amalekites. 1200?

Invasion of the Sea Peoples 1200?

The Phoenicians become the world's first maritime power. 1200

The Phoenicians develop warships with battering rams on the bow. 1200

The Egyptians make several attempts to connect the Nile River with the Red Sea by digging canals. 1200

Jephthah defeats Ammonites and Philistines. 1170?

Ramesses III, Egypt's last great pharaoh, dies. 1166

The Amorite king Nebuchadnezzar captures Babylon. 1124

Body armor made from rhinoceros hide, China 1100

raised up deliverers. Judges also illustrates the fundamental problem of the human heart. When God's people forget His saving acts, they go after other gods. Judges also illustrates the link between spiritual commitments and ethical conduct. In the end the book of Judges illustrates the eternal truth: the Lord will build His kingdom, in spite of our sin and rebellion.

Structure

The book falls into three parts. There is a prologue (1:1–3:6) that deals with the failure of the second generation to press on with the conquest of Canaan. This is followed by a sixfold cycle of sin and salvation (3:7–16:31), which forms the bulk of the book. Finally, there is an appendix (chaps. 17–21) that shows the full effects of total depravity let loose upon the people. This structure demonstrates not only the repetition of patterns of sin and judgment but also negative progress. The midpoint of the narrative is the linked episode involving Gideon and Abimelech, which serves to highlight further the significance of the issue of kingship.

Outline

I. Prologue (1:1–3:6)
   A. Israel's failure to possess the land (1:1-36)
   B. The pattern of sin, judgment, and restoration (2:1–3:6)

II. The Judges (3:7–16:31)
   A. Othniel (3:7-11)
   B. Ehud (3:12-30)
   C. Shamgar (3:31)
   D. Deborah and Barak (4:1–5:31)
   E. Gideon and Abimelech (6:1–9:57)
   F. Tola and Jair (10:1-5)
   G. Jephthah (10:6–12:7)
   H. Ibzan, Elon, and Abdon (12:8-15)
   I. Samson (13:1–16:31)

III. Epilogue (17:1–21:25)
   A. The religious degeneration of Israel (17:1–18:31)
   B. The moral degeneration of Israel (19:1–21:25)

Judah's Leadership against the Canaanites

1 After the death of Joshua,[a] the Israelites inquired of the LORD,[b] "Who will be the first to fight for us against the Canaanites?"

[2] The LORD answered, "Judah[c] is to go.[d] I have handed the land over to him."[e]

[3] Judah said to his brother Simeon, "Come with me to my territory, and let us fight against the Canaanites. I will also go with you to your territory." So Simeon went with him.

[4] When Judah attacked, the LORD handed the Canaanites and Perizzites[f] over to them. They struck down 10,000 men in Bezek. [5] They found Adoni-bezek in Bezek, fought against him, and struck down the Canaanites and Perizzites.

[6] When Adoni-bezek fled, they pursued him, seized him, and cut off his thumbs and big toes.[h] [7] Adoni-bezek said, "Seventy kings with their thumbs and big toes cut off used to pick up scraps[A] under my table. God has repaid me for what I have done." They brought him to Jerusalem, and he died there.

[8] The men of Judah fought against Jerusalem and captured it. They put the city to the sword and set it on fire. [9] Afterward, the men of Judah marched down to fight against the Canaanites who were living in the hill country, the *Negev, and the Judean foothills.[B] [10] Judah also marched against the Canaanites who were living in Hebron[i] (Hebron was formerly named Kiriath-arba[j]). They struck down Sheshai, Ahiman, and Talmai.[k] [11] From there they marched against the residents of Debir[l] (Debir was formerly named Kiriath-sepher).

[12] Caleb[m] said, "Whoever strikes down and captures Kiriath-sepher, I will give my daughter Achsah[n] to him as a wife." [13] So Othniel[o] son of Kenaz, Caleb's youngest brother, captured it, and Caleb gave his daughter Achsah to him as his wife.

[14] When she arrived, she persuaded Othniel[c] to ask her father for a field. As she got off her donkey, Caleb asked her,[D] "What do you want?"

Cross references:
a1:1 Jos 1:1; 24:29-31
bJdg 20:23,27; 1Sm 10:22; 23:2,4; 28:6
c1:2 Gn 29:35; 49:8-12
d1:1-2 Jdg 20:18
e1:2 Gn 35:12; Ex 6:8
f1:4 Gn 13:7; Dt 7:1; Jos 3:10; Ezr 9:1
g1Sm 11:8
h1:6 2Sm 4:12
i1:10 Gn 13:18; 23:2
jGn 23:2; 35:27; Jos 14:15
kNm 13:22; Jos 15:13-14
l1:11 Jos 10:38-39; 11:21; 15:7; 21:15; 1Ch 6:58
m1:12 Nm 13:6,13; 14:6,24,30,38; 26:65; 32:12
n1Ch 2:49
o1:13 Jdg 3:9,11; 1Ch 4:13

A1:7 Lit *toes are gathering*   B1:9 Or *the Shephelah*   C1:14 LXX reads *arrived, he pressured her*   D1:14 LXX reads *... field. She grumbled while on the donkey, and she cried out from the donkey, "Into the southland you sent me out,"* and *Caleb said*

1:1 After the death of Joshua links the book of Judges with the preceding account of the conquest of Canaan in the book of Joshua and sets the agenda for what follows. This is the story of the generations following Joshua's death, who failed to continue the legacy of his faithfulness to the charge Moses gave him. God had commanded His people to destroy the Canaanites during their conquest or the Canaanites would certainly lead the Israelites astray into false worship (Dt 20:16-18). The subsequent story demonstrates the validity of that concern.

1:3 Judah and **Simeon** covenanted together to fight against the Canaanites, providing a positive example of how the tribes could work together to possess the land.

1:4-7 The victory at **Bezek** is a positive beginning that heightens all the more the tragedy of Israel's subsequent failure. Yet the treatment of the leader of the Canaanites, **Adoni-bezek**, injects an ambiguous note into their triumph. The Israelites cut off **his thumbs and big toes**, emphasizing how dramatic a victory the Judahites and Simeonites had won with God's help. Seventy kings could not defeat Adoni-bezek, but the Lord brought him down effortlessly, and even the defeated king recognized God's hand at work. Yet according to the Lord's command in Dt 7:1-2 to destroy completely the Canaanites and Perizzites, Adoni-bezek should have been put to death immediately. Instead, in adopting Adoni-bezek's own strategy of punishment, the Israelites seem to have become exactly like the immoral Canaanites they were supposed to drive out. This sort of failure is a persistent problem throughout the book of Judges.

1:8 The Judahites captured and destroyed **Jerusalem** in accordance with the rules of holy war, but they did not occupy it at this point or, if they did, they were soon driven out again (v. 21; 1Ch 11:4-9).

1:13 Othniel would later become the first of Israel's judges (3:7-11). The story illustrates Othniel's credentials for that position, both as a warrior and through his kinship to **Caleb**, Joshua's faithful companion on the spying trip in Numbers 13-14. Othniel, who was the younger brother or nephew of Caleb, captured Kiriath-sepher (Debir), and thereby gained the right to marry Caleb's daughter, **Achsah**.

1:14-15 Achsah was not only well-connected, she was a woman of faith and spirit. She and her husband had been given **land in the Negev**, the dry southern region of Judah, but they needed water for the land. She therefore sought and received **springs** from her father. Her request, and the faith that drove it, is reminiscent of the daughters of Zelophehad in Numbers 27 who asked for an inheritance in the promised land even though it had not then been won from enemy hands.

lacham

Hebrew Pronunciation	[lah KHAHM]
HCSB Translation	fight, attack, wage war
Uses in Judges	31
Uses in the OT	171
Focus Passage	Judges 1:1,3,5,8-9

Lacham has its greatest use in war narratives and does not appear in Genesis, Leviticus, Ezra, Esther, Ruth, or Ezekiel. It appears in the Wisdom literature only in Psalms (5x), and in the Minor Prophets only in Zechariah. *Lacham* regularly means *fight* (Jdg 1:1) but sometimes *attack* (Jos 10:31) or *wage* (go to, make) *war* (1Kg 14:19). The *fighting* may involve a siege (Jr 32:24). *Lacham* takes prepositions like "with," "against," or "for," and occurs 19 times in the same verse with related *milchamah* ["war," battle"; 1Sm 8:20]. Individuals, peoples, or nations can *fight*. Yahweh also *fights* (Ex 14:14,25) and enlists nature to *fight* (Jdg 5:20). God usually *fought* for Israel but could *fight against* them (Is 63:10) or command others to do so (Jr 34:22). His presence was important for Israelite victory (Dt 1:41-42; 20:4). He will someday *fight* for Israel against all nations (Zch 14:3).

LIMITS OF ISRAELITE
SETTLEMENT AND THE LAND
YET TO BE CONQUERED

JOSHUA 13:1-7; 15:63; 16:10;
17:11-18; JUDGES 1:1–3:6

- • City
- ○ City (uncertain location)
- ◉ City specified by Judges 1 as not
  taken by Israel
- ▲ Mountain peak
- Limit of Israelite control
- Areas yet to be conquered

AMURRU

Zedad

Byblos

Lebo-hamath

Hazar-enan

36 E

34 N

PHOENICIA

Valley of Lebanon

Damascus

Abana River

ARAM

Sidon

Mt.
Hermon

Pharpar River

Ahlab

Laish
(Dan)

MAACAH

Tyre

Litani River

Beth-anath

Kitron

Kedesh

Lake
Huleh

Rehob

Achzib

Beth-shemesh

Hazor

GALILEE

Merom

Acco

Sea of
Galilee

GESHUR

Bashan

Aphik

Golan

Ashtaroth

Nahalal

Mt. Carmel ▲

Shimron

Mt. Tabor ▲

Endor

Jokneam

Jezreel Valley

Yarmuk River

Dor

Megiddo

Taanach

Ramoth-gilead

Ibleam

Beth-shan

GILEAD

MEDITERRANEAN
SEA

Socoh

Jordan River

Jabesh-gilead

Mt. Ebal ▲

Mt. Gerizim ▲ Shechem

Succoth

Mahanaim

Aphek

Tappuah

Jabbok River

AMMON

Joppa

Shiloh

Jazer

Jogbehah

HILL COUNTRY
OF EPHRAIM

Parkon River

Ai

Rabbah
(Amman)

Gezer

Shaalbim

Gibeon

Jericho

Heshbon

Aijalon

Jerusalem
(Jebus)

Bezer

Ashdod

Beth-
shemesh

Mt. Nebo ▲

Medeba

Ekron

Bethlehem

Ashkelon

Gath

Amorites pressure tribe
of Dan near Aijalon
(Jdg 1:34-36)

Eastern
Desert

Lachish

PHILISTIA

Hebron

DEAD
SEA

Dibon

Aroer

Gaza

KENIZZITES

En-gedi

Arnon River

Gerar

Ziklag

JUDAH

KENITES

MOAB

Beer-sheba

Arad

Kir-hareseth

AMALEKITES

Zered River

W. el Arish

31 N

Tamar

EDOM

Wilderness of Zin

Bozrah

0   10   20   30   40   50 Miles

0 10 20 30 40 50 Kilometers

34 E

35 E

36 E

¹⁵She answered him, "Give me a blessing. Since you have given me land in the Negev,ᵃ give me springs of water also." So Caleb gave her both the upper and lower springs.ᴬ,ᵇ

¹⁶The descendants of the Kenite, Moses' father-in-law,ᶜ had gone up with the men of Judah from the City of Palmsᴮ,ᵈ to the Wilderness of Judah, which was in the Negev of Arad.ᵉ They went to live among the people.

¹⁷Judah went with his brother Simeon, struck the Canaanites who were living in Zephath, and •completely destroyed the town. So they named the town Hormah.ᶠ ¹⁸Judah captured Gaza and its territory, Ashkelon and its territory, and Ekron and its territory.ᶜ ¹⁹The Lᴏʀᴅ was withᵍ Judah and enabled them to take possession of the hill country, but they could not drive outʰ the people who were living in the valley because those people had iron chariots.ᴰ,ⁱ

²⁰Judah gave Hebron to Caleb, just as Moses had promised.ʲ Then Caleb drove out the three sons of Anakᵏ who lived there.ᴱ

Benjamin's Failure

²¹At the same time the Benjaminites did not drive out the Jebusites who were living in Jerusalem. The Jebusites have lived among the Benjaminites in Jerusalem to this day.ˡ

Success of the House of Joseph

²²The house of Joseph also attacked Bethel, and the Lᴏʀᴅ was withᵐ them. ²³They sent spies to Bethel (the town was formerly named Luzⁿ). ²⁴The spies saw a man coming out of the town and said to him, "Please show us how to get into town, and we will treat you well."ᵒ ²⁵When he showed them the way into the town, they put the town to the sword but released the man and his entire family. ²⁶Then the man went to the land of the Hittites, built a town, and named it Luz. That is its name to this day.

Failure of the Other Tribes

²⁷At that time Manasseh failed to take possession of Beth-sheanᶠ,ᵖ and its villages,ᴳ or Taanachq and its villages, or the residents of Dorʳ and its villages, or the residents of Ibleamᴴ,ˢ and its villages, or the residents of Megiddoᵗ and its villages; the Canaanites refused to leaveⁱ this land.ᵘ ²⁸When Israel became stronger, they made the Canaanites serve as forced labor but never drove them out completely.ᵛ

²⁹At that time Ephraim failed to drive out the Canaanites who were living in Gezer, so the Canaanites have lived among them in Gezer.ʲ,ʷ

³⁰Zebulun failed to drive out the residents of Kitron or the residents of Nahalol,ˣ so the Canaanites lived among them and served as forced labor.

ᵃ1:15 Gn 12:9; 13:1,3; Nm 13:17,22,29; 2Sm 24:7; Ps 126:4
ᵇ1:11-15 Jos 15:15-19
ᶜ1:16 Ex 2:18; 3:1; 4:18; 18:1-12; Nm 10:29
ᵈDt 34:3; Jdg 3:13; 2Ch 28:15
ᵉNm 21:1; 33:40; Jos 12:14
ᶠ1:17 Nm 21:3; Dt 1:44
ᵍ1:19 Gn 39:2,21; Jos 6:27; Jdg 2:18; 1Sm 18:12
ʰJos 15:63
ⁱJos 17:16,18; Jdg 4:3,13
ʲ1:20 Dt 1:36; Jos 14:9
ᵏNm 13:22
ˡ1:21 Jos 15:63
ᵐ1:22 Gn 39:2,21; Jos 6:27; Jdg 2:18; 1Sm 18:12
ⁿ1:23 Gn 28:19; 35:6; 48:3
ᵒ1:24 Jos 2:12,14; 2Sm 9:1,3,7
ᵖ1:27 Jos 17:11,16; 1Sm 31:10,12; 2Sm 21:12
qJos 21:25; Jdg 5:19
ʳJos 11:2; 12:23; 17:11; 1Kg 4:11
ˢJos 17:11; 2Kg 9:27
ⁱJdg 5:19; 1Kg 9:15; 2Kg 23:29-30
ᵘJdg 1:35; Hs 5:11 ᵛ1:27-28 Jos 17:12-13 ʷ1:29 Jos 16:10
ˣ1:30 Jos 19:15; 21:35

ᴬ1:15 LXX reads give me redemption of water, and Caleb gave her according to her heart the redemption of the upper and the redemption of the lower   ᴮ1:16 = Jericho; Dt 34:3; Jdg 3:13; 2Ch 28:15   ᶜ1:18 LXX reads Judah did not inherit Gaza and its borders nor Ashkelon and its borders nor Ekron and its borders or Azotus and its surrounding lands   ᴰ1:19 LXX reads hill country, for they were not able to drive out the residents of the valley because Rechab separated it   ᴱ1:20 LXX reads And he inherited from there the three cities of the sons of Anak.   ᶠ1:27 LXX reads Beth-shean, which is a Scythian city   ᴳ1:27 LXX reads its villages or the fields around it   ᴴ1:27 LXX reads Balaam   ⁱ1:27 LXX reads Canaanites began to live in   ʲ1:29 LXX reads Gezer, and became forced labor

1:16 The descendants of the Kenite were descended from Jethro, the father-in-law of Moses. They also traveled with the Judahites from Jericho (**the City of Palms**). Far from driving out the inhabitants of the land, they **went to live among the people**.

1:17-20 Initial success on the part of Judah and Simeon was followed by jarring failure. After a string of victories at **Hormah . . . Gaza . . . Ashkelon**, and **Ekron**, Judah took possession of the hill country because the Lord was with them. Yet they were unable to drive out the people living in the valley because they had **iron chariots**. Iron was a relatively new discovery, and the Canaanites had the technological edge. Yet the Lord would prove again and again more than equal to the task of defeating superior forces, even those equipped with chariots (chap. 4; Jos 17:18). Implicit in Judah's failure to conquer the people of the valleys is the removal of the Lord's blessing on their warfare. This stands in stark contrast to Caleb's success at **Hebron** (mentioned already in 1:10), where he defeated the **sons of Anak** who had so terrified his contemporaries in the days of Moses (Nm 13:33).

1:21 Failure after failure is recorded in the subsequent verses. The city of Jerusalem was on the boundary between the territory of Judah and Benjamin; the campaign against it by Judah in verse 8 was only a short-lived success. The Benjaminites come first after Judah in the litany of failure, perhaps foreshadowing their negative role in the final chapters of the book.

1:22-26 The **house of Joseph** (the Ephraimites) had a mixed experience at **Bethel**. The similarities and differences to the assault on Jericho under Joshua are striking (Jos 2; 6). As with Jericho, spies were sent out to explore the city, where they found one of the inhabitants willing to help them, in return for the lives of himself and his family. The city was captured, because **the Lᴏʀᴅ was with them**, but unlike Rahab, the man did not become a member of the covenant community. Instead, he left to recreate his pagan lifestyle in another country.

1:27-33 As the chapter unfolds, conquest is replaced by cohabitation. **Manasseh failed to take possession** of the villages in its territory. Even when the Manassites became stronger than the Canaanites, they failed to drive them out, instead using them as **forced labor**. The same approach was followed by **Ephraim . . . Zebulun . . . Asher**, and **Naphtali**.

³¹Asher failed to drive out the residents of Acco^A or of Sidon, or Ahlab, Achzib, Helbah, Aphik, or Rehob. ³²The Asherites lived among the Canaanites who were living in the land, because they failed to drive them out.

³³Naphtali did not drive out the residents of Beth-shemesh or the residents of Beth-anath. They lived among the Canaanites who were living in the land, but the residents of Beth-shemesh and Beth-anath served as their forced labor.

³⁴The Amorites^a forced the Danites into the hill country and did not allow them to go down into the valley. ³⁵The Amorites refused to leave^B Har-heres, Aijalon,^b and Shaalbim. When the house of Joseph got the upper hand,^c the Amorites^D were made to serve as forced labor. ³⁶The territory of the Amorites extended from the Ascent of Akrabbim,^c that is from Sela^d upward.

Pattern of Sin and Judgment

2 The Angel of the Lord^e went up from Gilgal to Bochim^E and said, "I brought you out of Egypt and led you into the land^f I had promised to your fathers.^g I also said: I will never break My covenant with you. ²You are not to make a covenant^h with the people who are living in this land, and you are to tear down their altars.^F,^i But you have not obeyed Me. What is this you have done? ³Therefore, I now say: I will not drive out these people before you.^j They will be thorns^G,^H in your sides,^k and their gods will be a trap for you."^l ⁴When the Angel of the Lord had spoken these words to all the Israelites, the people wept loudly.

⁵So they named that place Bochim^l and offered sacrifices there to the Lord.

Joshua's Death

⁶Joshua sent the people away, and the Israelites went to take possession of the land, each to his own inheritance.^m ⁷The people worshiped the Lord throughout Joshua's lifetime and during the lifetimes of the elders who outlived^J Joshua. They had seen all the Lord's great works^n He had done for Israel.

⁸Joshua son of Nun, the servant of the Lord, died at the age of 110. ⁹They buried him in the territory of his inheritance, in Timnath-heres, in the hill country of Ephraim,^o north of Mount Gaash. ¹⁰That whole generation was also gathered to their ancestors. After them another generation rose up who did not know the Lord^p or the works He had done for Israel.

¹¹The Israelites did what was evil in the Lord's sight.^q They worshiped the *Baals^r ¹²and abandoned the Lord, the God of their fathers, who had brought them out of Egypt. They went after other gods from the surrounding peoples^s and bowed down to them. They infuriated the Lord,^t ¹³for they abandoned Him and worshiped Baal and the *Ashtoreths.^u

¹⁴The Lord's anger burned against Israel, and He handed them over to marauders who raided them. He sold^v them to^K the enemies around them, and they could no longer resist their enemies. ¹⁵Whenever the Israelites went out, the Lord^L was against them^w and brought

---

Cross references (center column):

ᵃ1:34 Ex 3:8; Nm 13:29; 21:31; Jos 2:10
ᵇ1:35 Jos 10:12; 1Sm 14:31; 1Ch 8:13; 2Ch 28:18
ᶜ1:36 Nm 34:4; Jos 15:3
ᵈ2Kg 14:7; Is 16:1
ᵉ2:1 Gn 22:11; Ex 3:2; Ps 34:7; 35:5-6
ᶠEx 6:8; Nm 14:3,8; Ezk 20:15
ᵍNm 14:23; Dt 6:10,23; 10:11; Jos 1:6
ʰ2:2 Ex 23:32; Dt 7:2
ⁱEx 34:13; Dt 7:5; 12:3; Jdg 6:30-32; 2Ch 34:7
ʲ2:3 Ex 23:29
ᵏNm 33:55
ˡEx 23:33; 34:12; Dt 7:16; Jos 23:13
ᵐ2:6 Dt 9:4; 11:31; Jos 1:11; 18:3; Jdg 18:9; Neh 9:15
ⁿ2:7 Dt 11:7
ᵒ2:9 Jos 19:50; 1Sm 1:1; 14:22; 1Ch 6:67
ᵖ2:10 Ex 5:2; 1Sm 2:12
ᵍ2:11 Nm 32:12; Dt 4:25; 31:29; 1Kg 11:6
ʳJdg 3:7; 8:33; 1Sm 12:10; 2Kg 17:16; Jr 2:23; 9:14
ˢ2:12 Dt 6:14; 13:7
ᵗ1Kg 14:15; 15:30; 2Kg 17:11; 2Ch 28:25
ᵘ2:13 Jdg 10:6; 1Sm 7:3-4; 12:10; 1Kg 11:5,33;
2Kg 23:13 ᵛ2:14 Jdg 3:8; 4:2,9; 10:7; Ps 44:12; Is 50:1; Ezk 30:12; Jl 3:8 ʷ2:15 Dt 2:15

---

^A1:31 LXX reads *Acco, and they became for him forced labor and the residents of Dor*   ^B1:35 Or *Amorites determined to live in*   ^C1:35 Lit *When the hand of the house of Joseph was heavy*   ^D1:35 LXX reads *Joseph became strong on the Amorites, they*   ^E2:1 LXX reads *to the weeping place and to Bethel and to the house of Israel*   ^F2:2 LXX reads *with those lying in wait in this land; neither are you to fall down in worship to their gods, but their carved images you must break to pieces and their altars you must destroy*   ^G2:3 LXX reads *affliction*   ^H2:5 Lit *traps*   ^I2:5 Or *Weeping*   ^J2:7 Lit *extended their days after*   ^K2:14 Lit *into the hand of*   ^L2:15 Lit *the hand of the Lord*

The universality of this failure is underscored by the use of the inclusive title **Israel** in verse 28.

1:34-35 The worst situation of all was that of the **Danites**, who were shut up in the hill country by the **Amorites** who **refused to leave** their cities. Apparently, the inhabitants of the land were more determined to stay there than God's people were to obey the Lord's command to drive them out.

2:1 The **Angel of the Lord** frequently represents God Himself, bringing His word to His people (6:11-24) and protecting them from their enemies (Ex 14:19). The reference to **Gilgal** may be to His previous appearance there to Joshua as commander of the Lord's army (Jos 5:13-15). Now after Israel's inadequate attempts to "go up" (in warfare) against the inhabitants of Canaan, the Angel of the Lord **went up** against them.

2:4-5 The **people wept loudly** and **offered sacrifices**, the outward signs of repentance. They even memorialized their response in the name given to the place, **Bochim** ("weeping"). Yet their actions in the rest of the chapter cast serious doubt on the authenticity of their repentance.

2:6-13 This paragraph is a flashback summarizing the beginning of the book of Judges. **Baal** was the Canaanite god of storm and rain, while Ashtoreth (also known as Astarte) was his consort, the goddess of love and fertility. Both of these deities were worshiped under a variety of local manifestations and were perceived as the key to agricultural success in the land of Canaan.

2:14-15 The consequence of Israel's covenant unfaithfulness was the covenant curse (Dt 28:48). Instead of the Lord fighting for **Israel** and handing their enemies over into their power, the Lord gave them over into the hand of their enemies, and **they suffered greatly**.

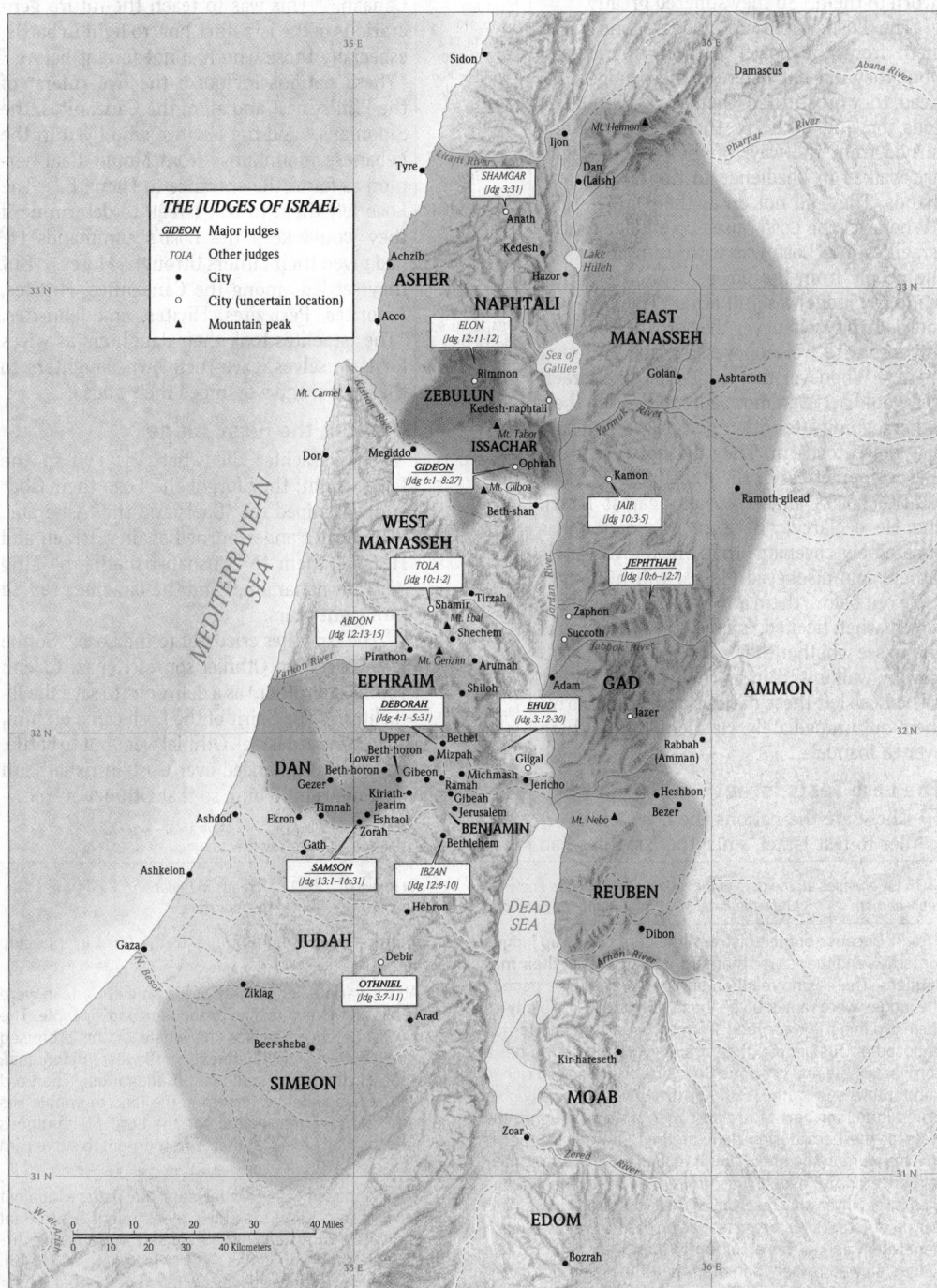

THE JUDGES OF ISRAEL

GIDEON Major judges
TOLA Other judges
● City
○ City (uncertain location)
▲ Mountain peak

Sidon

Damascus

Abana River

35 E

36 E

Mt. Hermon ▲

Ijon

Tyre

Litani River

Dan
(Laish)

Pharpar River

SHAMGAR
(Jdg 3:31)

Anath

Kedesh

Achzib

Lake
Huleh

ASHER

NAPHTALI

Hazor

Acco

ELON
(Jdg 12:11-12)

EAST
MANASSEH

33 N

33 N

Mt. Carmel ▲

Kishon River

Rimmon

Sea of
Galilee

Golan

Ashtaroth

ZEBULUN

Kedesh-naphtali

Yarmuk River

Dor

Megiddo

Mt. Tabor ▲

ISSACHAR

GIDEON
(Jdg 6:1–8:27)

Ophrah

Kamon

Ramoth-gilead

▲ Mt. Gilboa

Beth-shan

JAIR
(Jdg 10:3-5)

MEDITERRANEAN
SEA

WEST
MANASSEH

JEPHTHAH
(Jdg 10:6–12:7)

TOLA
(Jdg 10:1-2)

Tirzah

Shamir

Zaphon

Jordan River

ABDON
(Jdg 12:13-15)

Mt. Ebal ▲
Shechem

Succoth

Jabbok River

Pirathon

Mt. Gerizim ▲

Arumah

GAD

AMMON

Yarkon River

EPHRAIM

Shiloh

Adam

DEBORAH
(Jdg 4:1–5:31)

EHUD
(Jdg 3:12-30)

Jazer

32 N

32 N

Upper
Beth-horon

Bethel

Mizpah

Rabbah
(Amman)

DAN

Lower
Beth-horon

Gibeon

Gilgal

Michmash

Ramah

Jericho

Heshbon

Gezer

Kiriath-
jearim

Gibeah

Bezer

Ashdod

Ekron

Timnah

Eshtaol

Jerusalem

Mt. Nebo ▲

Gath

Zorah

BENJAMIN

REUBEN

Ashkelon

Bethlehem

SAMSON
(Jdg 13:1–16:31)

IBZAN
(Jdg 12:8-10)

Hebron

DEAD
SEA

Gaza

N. Besor

JUDAH

Debir

Arnon River

Dibon

OTHNIEL
(Jdg 3:7-11)

Ziklag

Arad

Kir-hareseth

Beer-sheba

SIMEON

MOAB

W. el-Arish

0   10   20   30   40 Miles

0   10   20   30   40 Kilometers

35 E

Zoar

Zered River

EDOM

36 E

31 N

31 N

Bozrah

disaster on them, just as He had promised and sworn to them.[a] So they suffered greatly.

[16]The LORD raised up[b] judges, who saved them from the power of their marauders, [17]but they did not listen to their judges. Instead, they prostituted[c] themselves with other gods, bowing down to them. They quickly turned from the way[d] of their fathers, who had walked in obedience to the LORD's commands. They did not do as their fathers did. [18]Whenever the LORD raised up a judge for the Israelites, the LORD was with[e] him and saved the people from the power of their enemies while the judge was still alive.[A] The LORD was moved to pity whenever they groaned because of those who were oppressing and afflicting them. [19]Whenever the judge died, the Israelites would act even more corruptly[f] than their fathers, going after other gods to worship and bow down to them. They did not turn from their evil practices or their obstinate[g] ways.

[20]The LORD's anger burned against Israel, and He declared, "Because this nation has violated My covenant[h] that I made with their fathers[i] and disobeyed Me, [21]I will no longer drive out before them any of the nations Joshua left[j] when he died.[k] [22]I did this to test Israel and to see whether they would keep the LORD's way[l] by walking in it, as their fathers had."[m] [23]The LORD left these nations and did not drive them out immediately. He did not hand them over to Joshua.

The LORD Tests Israel

3 These are the nations the LORD left in order to test Israel, since the Israelites had

fought none of these in[B] any of the wars with Canaan.[n] [2]This was to teach the future generations of the Israelites how to fight in battle, especially those who had not fought before.[C] [3]These nations included: the five rulers[o] of the Philistines[p] and all of the Canaanites, the Sidonians,[q] and the Hivites[r] who lived in the Lebanese mountains[D] from Mount Baal-hermon as far as the entrance to Hamath.[E] [4]The LORD left them to test Israel, to determine if they would keep the LORD's commands He had given their fathers through[F] Moses.[s] [5]But they settled among the Canaanites, Hittites, Amorites, Perizzites, Hivites, and Jebusites. [6]The Israelites took their daughters as wives for themselves, gave their own daughters to their sons, and worshiped their gods.[t]

Othniel, the First Judge

[7]The Israelites did what was evil in the LORD's sight; they forgot the LORD their God[u] and worshiped the *Baals and the *Asherahs. [8]The LORD's anger burned against Israel, and He sold them to[G] Cushan-rishathaim[H] king of Aram-naharaim,[I,v] and the Israelites served him eight years.

[9]The Israelites cried out to the LORD.[w] So the LORD raised up Othniel son of Kenaz, Caleb's youngest brother,[x] as a deliverer[y] to save the Israelites. [10]The Spirit of the LORD came on him, and he judged Israel. Othniel went out to battle, and the LORD handed over Cushan-rishathaim king of Aram to him, so that Othniel overpow-

Cross references (center column)

[a]2:15 Lv 26:14-46; Dt 28:15-68 [b]2:16 Jdg 3:9,15; 1Kg 11:14; 14:14 [c]2:17 Dt 4:30; 1Sm 13:6; 30:6; 2Sm 22:7; Jb 20:22; Ps 59:16; Hs 5:15 [d]Ex 32:8; Dt 9:12,16 [e]2:18 Gn 39:2,21; Jos 6:27; 1Sm 18:12 [f]2:19 Gn 6:12; Dt 31:29; Is 1:4 [g]Ex 32:9; Dt 9:6,13; Ezk 2:4 [h]2:20 Jos 7:11,15; 23:16; Jr 34:18; Hs 6:7 [i]Jdg 3:4; 1Kg 8:58; 2Kg 17:13; Ps 78:5; Jr 11:4 [j]2:21 Jos 13:1-7; 23:1-16 [k]Jos 24:29-30 [l]2:22 Gn 18:19; 2Sm 22:22; Ps 138:5 [m]Jos 24:31 [n]3:1 Jos 1-12 [o]3:3 Jos 13:3; 1Sm 5:8,11 [p]Gn 10:14; Ex 13:17 [q]Jos 13:4; 1Kg 5:6; Ezk 32:30 [r]Ex 38:17; Dt 20:17; Jos 9:1,7 [s]3:4 1Kg 8:58; 2Kg 17:13; Ps 78:5; Jr 11:4 [t]3:6 Ex 23:33; Dt 7:16 [u]3:7 Dt 8:11,14,19; 1Sm 12:9; Jr 3:21 [v]3:8 Gn 24:10; Dt 23:3-4; 1Ch 19:6; Ps 60 title [w]3:9 Jdg 3:15; 6:6-7; 10:10 [x]Jdg 1:13 [y]Dt 28:29,31; Jdg 6:36; 1Sm 14:39; Is 19:20; 43:11; Hs 13:4

[A]2:18 Lit enemies all the days of the judge   [B]3:1 Lit had known   [C]3:2 Lit not known it   [D]3:3 LXX reads in Lebanon   [E]3:3 Or as Lebo-hamath   [F]3:4 Lit by the hand of   [G]3:8 Lit into the hand of   [H]3:8 Lit Doubly-Evil   [I]3:8 = Mesopotamia

---

2:16-19 Because of their distress, the Lord **raised up judges** for Israel, and they saved them from **the power of their marauders**. There is no mention of repentance by the people; the judges were raised up as the result of the Lord's **pity** on their groaning. In relenting from the punishment He had imposed on His people, the Lord showed Himself to be "a compassionate and gracious God, slow to anger and rich in faithful love and truth" (Ex 34:6). The judges typically governed Israel (or part of it) and sought to lead them in the ways of the Lord during their lifetime—a ministry that is most evident in the life of the final judge, Samuel. Yet their influence on the people was limited, and after each judge died Israel invariably reverted to their idolatrous ways. This period of Israel's history was a downward spiral, with each generation acting **more corruptly than their fathers**. The judges slowed rather than stemmed the rising tide of iniquity.

2:20-23 It was a mark of the Lord's anger that He no longer referred to Israel as "my people" but as **this nation**. Since they refused to drive out the Canaanites, the Lord would leave the Canaanites among Israel as a **test** of their faithfulness. Each generation would now have to

demonstrate its own faithfulness to the Lord in a hostile environment.

3:1-4 All the various inhabitants of the land of Canaan were intended to serve as a testing ground for God's people. The list in verse 3 encompasses the whole of the promised land: the southwest (**Philistines**), northwest (**Sidonians**), northeast (**Hivites**), and southeast (**Canaanites**). The Lord allowed these peoples to remain in the land to enable His people to learn warfare and to see the Lord's faithfulness first hand, as well as to **test** their commitment to serve Him alone.

3:7-11 The judgeship of **Othniel** sets the pattern against which to compare all of the subsequent judges. Here Baal is linked with his more common consort in Canaanite literature, Asherah, rather than Astarte (see note at 2:6-13). Asherah was a fertility goddess often represented in the form of a tree. As a result of Israel's unfaithfulness, the Lord handed them over into the power of an oppressor, **Cushan-rishathaim** ("Cushan the Doubly Wicked"). The area of Aram of the Two Rivers (v. 8) was north of Israel in Mesopotamia (Gn 24:10). For an Aramean king to oppress the whole land of Israel as far south as Judea was a mark

ered him. [11] Then the land was peaceful[a] 40 years, and Othniel son of Kenaz died.

Ehud

[12] The Israelites again did what was evil in the LORD's sight. He gave Eglon king of Moab[b] power over Israel, because they had done what was evil in the LORD's sight. [13] After Eglon convinced the Ammonites and the Amalekites to join forces with him, he attacked and defeated Israel and took possession of the City of Palms.[A,c] [14] The Israelites served Eglon king of Moab 18 years.

[15] Then the Israelites cried out to the LORD, and He raised up Ehud son of Gera, a left-handed[d] Benjaminite,[B] as a deliverer for them. The Israelites sent him to Eglon king of Moab with tribute[e] money.

[16] Ehud made himself a double-edged sword 18 inches long.[c] He strapped it to his right thigh under his clothes [17] and brought the tribute to Eglon king of Moab, who was an extremely fat man. [18] When Ehud had finished presenting the tribute, he dismissed the people who had carried it. [19] At the carved images near Gilgal he returned and said, "King Eglon, I have a secret message for you." The king called for silence, and all his attendants left him. [20] Then Ehud approached him while he was sitting alone in his room upstairs where it was cool. Ehud said, "I have a word from God for you," and the king stood up from his throne.[D] [21] Ehud[E] reached with his left hand, took the sword from his right thigh, and plunged it into Eglon's belly. [22] Even the handle went in after the blade, and Eglon's fat

*a*3:11 Jdg 3:30; 5:31; 8:28; 2Ch 14:1,5-6 *b*3:12 Nm 22:3; Dt 2:8-9; 32:49 *c*3:13 Dt 34:3; Jdg 1:16; 2Ch 28:15 *d*3:15 Jdg 20:16 *e*2Sm 8:2,6; 2Ch 9:24; 17:11

A3:13 = Jericho; Dt 34:3; Jdg 1:16; 2Ch 28:15   B3:15 = son of the right hand   C3:16 Lit *sword a gomed in length*   D3:20 LXX reads *"A word of my God for you, O king," and Eglon rose up from the throne near him.*   E3:21 LXX reads *It happened that when he rose up, Ehud immediately*

of his military might. After **eight years** of subjugation, Israel cried out to the Lord, who then raised up and empowered Othniel, who as **Caleb's** nephew had the credentials to deliver Israel (vv. 9-10; see note at 1:13). After delivering Israel, Othniel continued to lead them, and Israel was at peace for **40 years**. However, after his death, the cycle of sin and judgment started all over again.

3:12-14 This time the enemy was **Eglon**, the king of **Moab**, with the assistance of the **Ammonites** and **Amalekites**. These tribes lived east of Israel, in Transjordan, so the **City of Palms** (Jericho) would have been a natural base from which to govern their conquered territory. It took longer than during the first cycle for Israel to learn their lesson: they endured **18 years** of suffering before they cried out for release.

3:15-17 When Israel cried to the Lord, He again provided a deliverer, **Ehud**, a **left-handed** man. Left-handedness seems to have been relatively common among Benjamin-

ites (20:15), which is ironic since the name means "son of the right hand." The unusual idiom used here (lit "hindered in the right hand") suggests that left-handedness may have been viewed as a defect, and that Israel's second deliverer lacked the perfect appearance of the first. Ehud also adopted a different approach to delivering Israel, assassinating the oppressor through deceit and cunning rather than engaging in straightforward battle. For that task, he made a relatively short sword and hid it on **his right thigh**, the opposite side from that preferred by a right-handed man. Eglon's name means "calf," a feature that resonates with the emphasis throughout the narrative on his "fatness." This was normally a positive characterization in the OT, where physical size was evidence of great wealth. Together with Eglon's name, however, it marked him out as the fattened calf, ripe for slaughter.

3:18-22 Ehud had been sent to Eglon to deliver Israel's tribute to the oppressor, a task that he completed and then returned to Israelite territory. Significantly, the landmark that

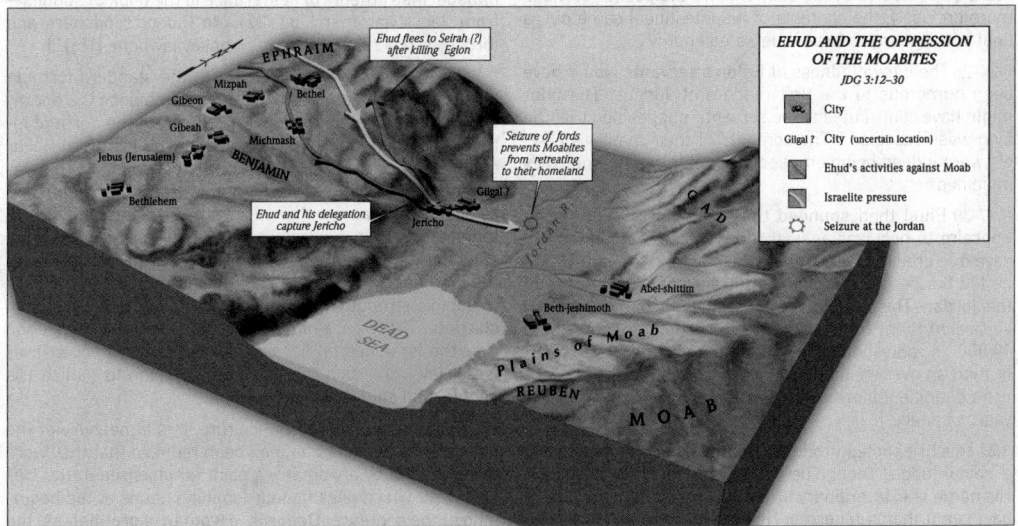

Ehud flees to Seirah (?) after killing Eglon

Seizure of fords prevents Moabites from retreating to their homeland

Ehud and his delegation capture Jericho

EPHRAIM · Mizpah · Gibeon · Bethel · Gibeah · Michmash · Jebus (Jerusalem) · BENJAMIN · Bethlehem · Gilgal ? · Jericho · Jordan R. · GAD · Beth-jeshimoth · Abel-shittim · DEAD SEA · Plains of Moab · REUBEN · MOAB

EHUD AND THE OPPRESSION OF THE MOABITES
JDG 3:12-30

City
Gilgal ?   City (uncertain location)
Ehud's activities against Moab
Israelite pressure
Seizure at the Jordan

closed in over it, so that Ehud did not withdraw the sword from his belly. And Eglon's insides came out. ²³Ehud escaped by way of the porch, closing and locking the doors of the upstairs room behind him.

²⁴Ehud was gone when Eglon's servants came in. They looked and found the doors of the upstairs room locked and thought he was relieving himself^A in the cool room. ²⁵The servants waited until they became worried and saw that he had still not opened the doors of the upstairs room. So they took the key and opened the doors—and there was their lord lying dead on the floor!

²⁶Ehud escaped while the servants waited. He crossed over the Jordan near the carved images and reached Seirah. ²⁷After he arrived, he sounded the ram's horn throughout the hill country of Ephraim. The Israelites came down with him from the hill country, and he became their leader. ²⁸He told them, "Follow me, because the Lord has handed over your enemies, the Moabites, to you." So they followed him, captured the fords of the Jordan leading to Moab, and did not allow anyone to cross over.ª ²⁹At that time they struck down

ª 3:28 Jdg 12:5-6
ᵇ 4:2 Jos 11:1; Ps 83:9
ᶜ 1Sm 12:9
ᵈ Jdg 5:20-30; 1Sm 12:9; Ps 83:9
ᵉ 4:3 Ex 14:10; Nm 12:13; Dt 26:7; Ps 34:17
ᶠ 4:4 Ex 15:20; 2Kg 22:14; Neh 6:14; Is 8:3
ᵍ 4:5 Nm 35:12; 2Ch 19:8; Ps 9:4; 76:8-9; Is 3:13-14; Ezk 44:24

about 10,000 Moabites, all strong and able-bodied men. Not one of them escaped. ³⁰Moab became subject to Israel that day, and the land was peaceful 80 years.

Shamgar

³¹After Ehud, Shamgar son of Anath became judge. He delivered Israel by striking down 600 Philistines with an oxgoad.

Deborah and Barak

4 The Israelites again did what was evil in the sight of the Lord after Ehud had died. ²So the Lord sold them into the hand of Jabinᵇ king of Canaan, who reigned in Hazor.ᶜ The commander of his forces was Siseraᵈ who lived in Harosheth of the Nations.^B ³Then the Israelites cried outᵉ to the Lord, because Jabin had 900 iron chariots, and he harshly oppressed them 20 years.

⁴Deborah, a woman who was a prophetessᶠ and the wife of Lappidoth, was judging Israel at that time. ⁵It was her custom to sit under the palm tree of Deborah between Ramah and Bethel in the hill country of Ephraim, and the Israelites went up to her for judgment.ᵍ

⁶She summoned Barak son of Abinoam from

---

^A 3:24 Lit *was covering his feet*   ^B 4:2 Or *Harosheth-ha-goiim*

---

identified Israelite territory was **the carved images near Gilgal**, a telling pointer to the state of Israelite worship in those days. Ehud then dismissed the rest of his party, returning alone to meet with Eglon. He appealed to Eglon's vanity by claiming **I have a secret message for you**. The Hebrew word translated "message" can also mean "word" or "thing." The original readers would have recognized the nature of the "secret" long before Eglon got the point. Once alone, Ehud delivered God's "message" for Eglon by running him through with the concealed sword. Apparently, Eglon was so fat that the entire 18 inches, including the handle, could be contained by his belly. Eglon's **insides** (or perhaps more precisely, the contents of his intestines) came out, a final humiliation for Israel's defeated enemy.

3:24-26 The dimwittedness of **Eglon's servants** would have been humorous to the first readers of Judges. The odor might have contributed to the servants' supposition that the king was "occupied." The contents of their master's bowels were indeed being emptied, but not in the manner they imagined.

3:27-30 Ehud then **sounded the ram's horn**, summoning **Ephraim** to holy war against the leaderless **Moabites**. He gave due credit to the Lord's involvement in the battle, and he led his people in a successful assault on the **fords of the Jordan**. This would have cut off the Moabite retreat and separated them from any possible reinforcements. **About 10,000 . . . able-bodied . . . Moabites** may be a way of affirming an overwhelming victory, according to the conventions of ancient literature. The result of the victory was **80 years** of peace.

3:31 This brief note introduces **Shamgar**, sometimes called a "minor judge," though never explicitly said to judge Israel. His name is extraordinary on two counts: the form "Shamgar" is not that of a normal Hebrew name, and the ascrip-

tion **son of Anath** suggests that he was (or had been) a follower of Anath, the Canaanite goddess of war. This foreigner apparently delivered Israel by striking down 600 Philistines with an oxgoad. The **Philistines**, or Sea Peoples, were not native to Canaan but arrived there in the twelfth to eleventh centuries B.C. from Anatolia and Crete. From their bases in the coastal plain, the Philistines became an increasing problem for the Israelites as they pressed eastward into the foothills of Israel. An **oxgoad** was a sharp stick up to eight feet long tapering to a sharp point, which may have been tipped with metal (1Sm 13:21). This is the first in a series of unusual instruments of deliverance in the book of Judges—from Jael's hammer (Jdg 4:21), to Gideon's pitchers and torches (7:19-20), to Samson's donkey jawbone (15:15).

4:1-3 A new cycle is introduced with the standard formula of Israelite rebellion (cp. 3:7,12). In this instance the enemy was **Jabin**, a Canaanite king from **Hazor**, in the north of Israel. An earlier Jabin had been defeated by Joshua at Hazor about a century earlier (Jos 11:1-15); this suggests that Jabin may have been a dynastic name. Hazor was destroyed by Joshua, but as was the case with Jerusalem in Jdg 1:8, the destruction did not prevent some form of reoccupation at a later date. Israel's failure to complete the occupation of the land once again came back to haunt them. The source of Jabin's strength, humanly speaking, lay in his **900 iron chariots**. These gave him an enormous technological edge over the Israelites on flat ground. But his real power over Israel lay in the fact that the Lord, seeking to punish His people, had **sold them into** his **hand**.

4:4-5 Given their patriarchal culture, it is a measure of the poor state to which Israel had been reduced that they were being judged by a woman—a point emphasized in the Hebrew text, which piles up four feminine nouns at the beginning of the sentence (**Deborah**, a **woman**, a **prophetess**, the

Kedesh in Naphtali and said to him, "Hasn't the Lord, the God of Israel,[a] commanded you: 'Go, deploy the troops on Mount Tabor,[b] and take with you 10,000 men from the Naphtalites[c] and Zebulunites?[d] [7] Then I will lure Sisera commander of Jabin's forces, his chariots, and his army at the *Wadi Kishon[e] to fight against you, and I will hand him over to you.'"[f]

[8] Barak said to her, "If you will go with me, I will go. But if you will not go with me, I will not go."

[9] "I will go with you," she said, "but you will receive no honor on the road you are about to take, because the Lord will sell Sisera into a woman's hand." So Deborah got up and went with Barak to Kedesh. [10] Barak summoned Zebulun and Naphtali to Kedesh; 10,000 men followed him, and Deborah also went with him.

[11] Now Heber the Kenite had moved away from the Kenites, the sons of Hobab,[g] Moses'

father-in-law,[h] and pitched his tent beside the oak tree of Zaanannim,[i] which was near Kedesh.

[12] It was reported to Sisera that Barak son of Abinoam had gone up Mount Tabor. [13] Sisera summoned all his 900 iron chariots and all the people who were with him from Harosheth of the Nations[A] to the Wadi Kishon. [14] Then Deborah said to Barak, "Move on, for this is the day the Lord has handed Sisera over to you. Hasn't the Lord gone before you?" So Barak came down from Mount Tabor with 10,000 men following him.

[15] The Lord threw Sisera, all his charioteers, and all his army into confusion[j] with the sword before Barak. Sisera left his chariot and fled on foot. [16] Barak pursued the chariots and the army as far as Harosheth of the Nations,[A] and the whole army of Sisera fell by the sword; not a single man was left.

*a*4:6 Ex 5:1; Dt 6:4; Ps 41:13
*b*Jos 19:12,22,34; Ps 89:12
*c*Gn 30:8; 49:21
*d*Gn 30:20; 49:13
*e*4:7 Jdg 5:21; 1Kg 18:40; Ps 83:9
*f*Dt 2:30; Jdg 7:9; 2Sm 5:19; 1Ch 14:10; Is 47:6
*g*4:11 Nm 10:29
*h*Ex 3:1; 4:18; 18:1-27
*i*Jos 19:33
*j*4:15 Ex 14:24; 23:27; Jos 10:10; Ps 18:14; 144:6

A4:13,16 Or *Harosheth-ha-goiim*

---

wife of Lappidoth). She could be found seated **under the palm tree** of Deborah, a location that may reflect a connection with her earlier namesake, Rebekah's nurse (Gn 35:8).

4:6-7 As God's appointed representative, Deborah **summoned Barak** to take the lead in the fighting. She also gave him the Lord's plan of battle, deploying 10,000 men of Naphtali and Zebulun on **Mount Tabor**, a strategic location at the northeast corner of the Jezreel Valley. Further, she assured him of the Lord's victory over Israel's enemies.

4:8-10 Although **Barak's** name means "lightning," his response was slow. Deborah agreed to accompany him to **Kedesh** as a sign that the Lord was indeed with him, and he successfully raised an army of **10,000 men**. As the story unfolds, the men will have less to do with the victory than a single woman.

4:11 What seems at first sight to be an irrelevant note

introduces the key character in what follows. **Heber the Kenite** was one of those Kenites descended from **Moses' father-in-law**, who were mentioned in 1:16 as settling among the people. In keeping with the prominent role of women in this chapter, the key character is not Heber, whom we never meet, but his wife Jael, who has not yet been mentioned.

4:12-16 Sisera responded to Barak's movements by summoning his entire force of 900 iron chariots to the **Wadi Kishon**, the exact place where the Lord had earlier promised to lure him. This was the signal for Israel to prepare for action, a call that significantly came from Deborah rather than Barak. Barak responded to the Lord's call and found that the Lord had gone in front of him, just as He had done with the Egyptian forces at the time of the exodus (Ex 14:24). All that was left for Barak to do was the mopping-up operation.

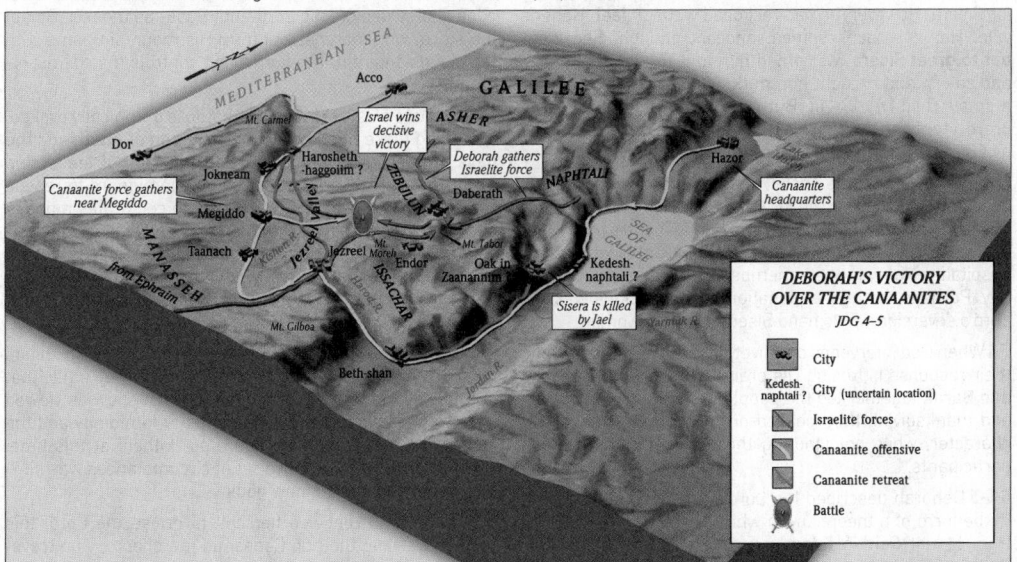

DEBORAH'S VICTORY OVER THE CANAANITES
JDG 4–5

City
City (uncertain location)
Israelite forces
Canaanite offensive
Canaanite retreat
Battle

¹⁷Meanwhile, Sisera had fled on foot to the tent of Jael, the wife of Heber the Kenite, because there was peace between Jabin king of Hazor and the family of Heber the Kenite. ¹⁸Jael went out to greet Sisera and said to him, "Come in, my lord. Come in with me. Don't be afraid." So he went into her tent, and she covered him with a rug. ¹⁹He said to her, "Please give me a little water to drink for I am thirsty." She opened a container of milk, gave him a drink, and covered him again. ²⁰Then he said to her, "Stand at the entrance to the tent. If a man comes and asks you, 'Is there a man here?' say, 'No.'" ²¹While he was sleeping from exhaustion, Heber's wife Jael took a tent peg, grabbed a hammer, and went silently to Sisera. She hammered the peg into his temple and drove it into the ground, and he died.

²²When Barak arrived in pursuit of Sisera, Jael went out to greet him and said to him, "Come and I will show you the man you are looking for." So he went in with her, and there was Sisera lying dead with a tent peg through his temple!

²³That day God subdued Jabin king of Canaan before the Israelites. ²⁴The power of the Israelites continued to increase against Jabin king of Canaan until they destroyed him.

Deborah's Song

5 On that day Deborah and Barak son of Abinoam sang:

2   When the leaders lead^A in Israel,

Cross references (center column):
a 5:4 Gn 14:6; 36:8-9; Dt 2:1
b 2Sm 22:8; Ps 18:7; Is 13:13; Ezk 38:20
c Jb 29:22; Ps 68:8; Pr 5:3; Jl 3:18
d 5:5 Ex 5:1; Dt 6:4; Ps 41:13
e 5:6 Jdg 3:31
f Jdg 4:17-22

when the people volunteer,
praise the LORD.
3   Listen, kings! Pay attention, princes!
I will sing to the LORD;
I will sing praise to the LORD God
of Israel.
4   LORD, when You came from Seir,^a
when You marched from the fields
of Edom,
the earth trembled,^b
the heavens poured^c rain,
and the clouds poured water.
5   The mountains melted before the LORD,
even Sinai^B before the LORD, the God
of Israel.^d

6   In the days of Shamgar^e son of Anath,
in the days of Jael,^f
the main ways were deserted
because travelers kept to the side roads.
7   Villages were deserted,^c
they were deserted in Israel,
until I, Deborah,^D arose,
a mother in Israel.
8   Israel chose new gods,
then war was in the gates.
Not a shield or spear was seen
among 40,000 in Israel.
9   My heart is with the leaders of Israel,
with the volunteers of the people.
Praise the LORD!
10   You who ride on white^c donkeys,
who sit on saddle blankets,

---

^A5:2 Or *the locks of hair are loose*   ^B5:5 Or LORD, *this One of Sinai*   ^C5:7,10 Hb obscure   ^D5:7 Or *you*

4:17-21 Sisera himself **fled on foot**. Since Heber had allied himself to Jabin, his camp should have been a place of safety for Sisera. However, he had reckoned without **Jael**, Heber's wife. Her approach seemed innocent enough. She **went out to greet Sisera**, welcomed him in with words of peace and safety, and brought him **milk**, like a mother caring for a small child (vv. 19-20). But once Sisera fell asleep, Jael drove a **tent peg** through **his temple . . . into the ground**, just as Ehud had driven his dagger into Eglon's belly (3:21).

4:22-24 When **Barak** finally **arrived**, Sisera was already dead. Jael's own rationale for her actions is not clear. Jael's murder of Sisera was in violation of her husband's treaty with Jabin, as well as normal standards of ancient Near Eastern hospitality. Nor was she a member of the Israelite community. Perhaps the only explanation for her actions was the Lord's sovereign will to hand Sisera over to a woman.

5:1 When God intervenes decisively in the lives of His people, their response is to sing His praise (Ex 15). Here **Deborah and Barak** together led the people in a song of celebration and thanksgiving that focused on the Lord as the central character, while not ignoring the heroism of the human participants.

5:4-5 Deborah described the Lord's presence in the battle in the form of a theophany in which the Lord marched out from Mount **Seir** in Edom, bringing a mighty rainstorm.

This storm not only served the practical function of bogging down Sisera's chariots and neutralizing his technological edge, it also depicts the Lord—not Baal—as the true God of the storm who marches out from His mountain home with the clouds and rain. The Lord alone controls the cosmic elements.

5:6 The state of Israel before the battle is graphically evoked. By calling these **the days of Shamgar son of Anath** and **the days of Jael**, Deborah highlighted the lack of leadership at this time. The Lord had to use two foreigners to rescue His people, including one whose name celebrates a pagan goddess. In those days **the main ways were deserted**, either because of fear of attack by bandits or excessive tolls imposed by the Canaanites, pushing what traffic there was onto the hidden trails that only local people knew about.

5:7-8 Life in the unwalled villages became impossible, so they **were deserted**. Only when Deborah arose did things begin to change. She became a **mother in Israel**, a title that not only expresses the respect with which she was viewed as a prophetess, but also highlights her femininity and the absence of a similar male figure as "father" at this time. The reason for this negative set of circumstances was simple: **Israel** had chosen **new gods**.

5:9-11 Deborah renewed her call to praise the Lord, this time addressing the rich Canaanite merchants, who **travel**

and who travel on the road, give praise!

11 Let them tell the righteous acts[a]
of the Lord,
the righteous deeds of His warriors
in Israel,
with the voices of the singers
at the watering places.[A]

Then the Lord's people went down
to the gates.
12 "Awake! Awake, Deborah!
Awake! Awake, sing a song!
Arise, Barak,
and take hold of your captives,
son of Abinoam!"
13 The survivors[b] came down
to the nobles;[c]
the Lord's people came down to me[B]
with the warriors.
14 Those with their roots in Amalek[c] came
from Ephraim;
Benjamin came with your people
after you.
The leaders came down from Machir,[d]
and those who carry a marshal's staff
came from Zebulun.
15 The princes of Issachar were
with Deborah;
Issachar was with Barak.
They set out at his heels[e] in the valley.
There was great searching[D] of heart
among the clans of Reuben.
16 Why did you sit among the sheepfolds
listening to the playing of pipes
for the flocks?
There was great searching of heart
among the clans of Reuben.
17 Gilead[f] remained beyond the Jordan.
Dan, why did you linger at the ships?
Asher remained at the seashore
and stayed in his harbors.

18 Zebulun was a people risking
their lives,
Naphtali also, on the heights
of the battlefield.

19 Kings came and fought.
Then the kings of Canaan fought
at Taanach by the waters of Megiddo,
but they took no spoil of silver.
20 The stars fought from the heavens;
the stars fought with Sisera
from their courses.
21 The river Kishon swept them away,[g]
the ancient river, the river Kishon.
March on, my soul, in strength!
22 The horses' hooves then hammered—
the galloping, galloping
of his[E] stallions.
23 "Curse Meroz," says the Angel
of the Lord,
"Bitterly curse her inhabitants,
for they did not come to help the Lord,
to help the Lord against
the mighty warriors."

24 Jael is most blessed of women,
the wife of Heber the Kenite;
she is most blessed among
tent-dwelling women.
25 He asked for water; she gave him milk.
She brought him curdled milk[h]
in a majestic bowl.
26 She reached for a tent peg,
her right hand, for a workman's mallet.
Then she hammered Sisera—
she crushed his head;
she shattered and pierced his temple.
27 He collapsed, he fell, he lay down
at[F] her feet;
he collapsed, he fell at her feet;
where he collapsed,
there he fell—dead.

a5:11 1Sm 12:7; Ps 103:6; Is 45:24; Mc 6:5 b5:13 Nm 21:35; Dt 2:34; Is 1:9 c5:25; 2Ch 23:20; Neh 3:5; 10:29; Ps 16:3; Jr 14:3; Nah 2:5; 3:18 d5:14 Gn 50:23; Nm 26:29; 32:39-40; Jos 17:1; 2Sm 9:4-5 e5:15 Jdg 4:10 f5:17 Gn 31:25; Nm 32:40; Jdg 10:17-11:11 g5:20-21 Jdg 4:15 h5:25 Gn 18:8; Dt 32:14; 2Sm 17:29; Jb 20:17; 29:6; Pr 30:3; Is 7:15,22

A5:11 Hb obscure B5:13 LXX reads *down for him* C5:14 LXX reads *in the valley* D5:15 Some Hb mss, Syr read *There were great resolves* E5:22 = Sisera's F5:27 Lit *between*

on the road on which the Israelites were afraid to walk. These men were summoned to join the ordinary Israelites in celebrating **the righteous acts of the Lord** and **of His warriors** at the locale for conversation and the sharing of news, **the watering places**. These acts are righteous in the sense that the victory over Sisera vindicated the Lord's power and validated Israel as His chosen people.

5:14-18 The response to God's call to arms shows that Israel was not united. **Ephraim . . . Benjamin . . . Machir** (Manasseh), **Zebulun . . . Issachar**, and **Naphtali** came eagerly, but **Reuben . . . Gilead** (Gad), **Dan**, and **Asher** remained behind.

5:19-21 The climax of the song brings into view the battle itself. Defeating Jabin was in effect a defeat for all the **kings of Canaan**. Earthly kings were no match for the Lord's heavenly host, **the stars** of **the heavens**, who fought on Israel's

side. Divine intervention was evidenced by a sudden storm that swelled the **river Kishon**, normally little more than a brook, into a raging torrent, and made Sisera's horses and chariots useless.

5:23 Meroz cannot be precisely identified. Most likely, they were an Israelite group who had adopted the ways of the Canaanites and remained outside the conflict, thereby earning a **curse** from the **Angel of the Lord**.

5:24-27 The curse on Meroz forms a contrast with the blessing on **Jael**, a non-Israelite who came "to help the Lord against the mighty warriors" (v. 23). She is lauded for her resourcefulness and cunning. A comparison to Eglon's fatal encounter with Ehud is invited by a key comparison: Instead of a left-handed assassin, Jael did her work with **her right hand**. The end result for the oppressor is the

28 Sisera's mother looked
    through the window;
she peered through the lattice,
    crying out:
"Why is his chariot so long in coming?
Why don't I hear the hoofbeats
    of his horses?"[A]

29 Her wisest princesses answer her;
    she even answers herself:[B]

30 "Are they not finding and dividing
    the spoil—
a girl or two for each warrior,
the spoil of colored garments
    for Sisera,
the spoil of an embroidered garment
    or two for my neck?"[C]

31 LORD, may all your enemies perish
    as Sisera did.[D]
But may those who love Him
be like the rising of the sun
    in its strength.

And the land was peaceful 40 years.

Midian Oppresses Israel

6 The Israelites did what was evil in the sight of the LORD. So the LORD handed[a] them over to Midian seven years, [2]and they oppressed Israel.[b] Because of Midian, the Israelites made hiding places[c] for themselves in the mountains, caves, and strongholds.

Cross references (center column):
a6:1 Jos 11:8; Jdg 11:32; 12:3; 13:1; 1Sm 14:10,12
b6:2 Jdg 3:10
c1Sm 23:14,19; 1Ch 11:7; Is 33:16; Jr 48:41
d6:3 Gn 29:1; 1Kg 4:30; Is 11:14
e6:8 Gn 20:7; Ex 7:1; Nm 11:29; 12:6; Dt 18:15,18,20,22; 34:10
fEx 4:22; 5:1; Dt 6:4; Jos 7:13
gEx 13:3,14; 20:2; Dt 5:6; 7:8; Jr 34:13; Mc 6:4
h6:9 Ex 3:9; 1Sm 10:18; Ps 106:42
i6:11 Ex 3:2

[3]Whenever the Israelites planted crops, the Midianites, Amalekites, and the Qedemites[d] came and attacked them. [4]They encamped against them and destroyed the produce of the land, even as far as Gaza. They left nothing for Israel to eat, as well as no sheep, ox or donkey. [5]For the Midianites came with their cattle and their tents like a great swarm of locusts. They and their camels were without number, and they entered the land to waste it. [6]So Israel became poverty-stricken because of Midian, and the Israelites cried out to the LORD.

[7]When the Israelites cried out to Him because of Midian, [8]the LORD sent a prophet[e] to them. He said to them, "This is what the LORD[f] God of Israel says: 'I brought you out of Egypt and out of the place of slavery.[g] [9]I delivered you from the power of Egypt and the power of all who oppressed[h] you. I drove them out before you and gave you their land. [10]I said to you: I am •Yahweh your God. Do not fear the gods of the Amorites whose land you live in. But you did not obey Me.'"

The LORD Calls Gideon

[11]The Angel[E] of the LORD[i] came, and He[F] sat under the oak that was in Ophrah, which belonged to Joash, the Abiezrite. His son Gideon was threshing wheat in the wine vat in order to hide it from the Midianites. [12]Then the Angel of the LORD appeared to him and said: "The LORD is with you, mighty warrior."

A5:28 Lit *Why have the hoofbeats of his chariots delayed*   B5:29 Lit *answers her words*   C5:30 Hb obscure   D5:31 Lit *perish in this way*   E6:11 Or *angel*   F6:11 Or *he*

same—the details of the death repeated with gory redundancy.

5:28-30 From the bloody murder scene, the song moves poignantly to the image of **Sisera's mother**, waiting vainly for his return. Her ladies reassured her that what was delaying her son was just the time involved in **dividing the spoil**. Each soldier would need to select some choice **garments** for themselves and their ladies, and **a girl or two**, or more literally, a "womb or two," highlighting the sexual and reproductive functions the captive women were expected to provide.

5:31 Reinforcing the theme that obedience to the Lord leads to rest and disobedience to death, the final note of the chapter is that **the land was peaceful** (lit "had rest") for **40 years**.

6:1-6 The second main section of the story of the judges, covering the fourth through the sixth major judges (Gideon, Jephthah, Samson), is introduced with a repetition of the rebellion formula from 3:7. The result was predictable: the Lord handed them over to an oppressor. The **Midianites** were semi-nomads who lived in the Sinai Peninsula and western Arabia. They allied themselves with the **Amalekites** and the eastern peoples (**Qedemites**) into a loose confederation. These raiders from the east swept across the country seasonally, plundering it like a **great swarm of locusts**. Although they entered the land from the east,

they traveled as far as **Gaza** on the western coast, leaving nothing behind them. The Israelites were reduced to an animal-like existence in caves, without any livestock of their own.

6:7-10 As in chapter 4, when Israel **cried out** to the Lord, he **sent** them **a prophet**, who used the standard messenger formula, **This is what the LORD God of Israel says**, to identify himself, and then delivered his message. Israel had been disobedient. Calling on the Lord presupposed a relationship with Him as the One who brought them out of Egypt; they could not live on the faith of their fathers if they did not listen to their fathers' God.

6:11-12 The prophetic speech ends abruptly. It is followed neither by repentance nor judgment but, surprisingly, by the provision of another deliverer. The **Angel of the LORD**—the Lord's personal representative who spoke with His full authority—appeared to **Gideon** at **Ophrah**, a town probably located in the Jezreel Valley. Gideon's name means "the one who hacks or cuts down," a fitting name for the man whose first task in the Lord's service would be to cut down Baal's altar. Other aspects of Gideon's demeanor are less promising. In view of the threat of the **Midianites**, he was **threshing wheat** in a **wine vat**, a shallow depression in the rock, a safer location than the more exposed threshing floor. Gideon's natural reserve will emerge again as the narrative unfolds, and it is in sharp contrast to the title given to Gideon by the angel—**mighty warrior**.

¹³ Gideon said to Him, "Please Sir,^A if the Lord is with us, why has all this happened?^B And where are all His wonders that our fathers told us about? They said, 'Hasn't the Lord brought us out of Egypt?' But now the Lord has abandoned us and handed us over to Midian."

¹⁴ The Lord^C turned to him and said, "Go in the strength you have and deliver Israel from the power of Midian. Am I not sending you?"

¹⁵ He said to Him, "Please, Lord, how can I deliver Israel? Look, my family is the weakest in Manasseh, and I am the youngest in my father's house."

¹⁶ "But I will be with you,"^a the Lord said to him. "You will strike Midian down as if it were one man."

¹⁷ Then he said to Him, "If I have found favor in Your sight,^b give me a sign^c that You are speaking with me. ¹⁸ Please do not leave this place until I return to You. Let me bring my gift and set it before You."

And He said, "I will stay until you return."

¹⁹ So Gideon went and prepared a young goat and unleavened bread from a half bushel^D of flour. He placed the meat in a basket and the broth in a pot. He brought them out and offered them to Him under the oak.

²⁰ The Angel of God^d said to him, "Take the meat with the unleavened bread, put it on this stone, and pour the broth on it." And he did so.

²¹ The Angel of the Lord extended the tip of the staff that was in His hand and touched the meat and the unleavened bread. Fire came up from the rock and consumed the meat and the unleavened bread. Then the Angel of the Lord vanished from his sight.

²² When Gideon realized that He was the Angel of the Lord, he said, "Oh no, Lord God!^e I have seen the Angel of the Lord face to face!"^f

²³ But the Lord said to him, "Peace to you. Don't be afraid, for you will not die." ²⁴ So Gideon built an altar to the Lord there and called it Yahweh Shalom.^E It is in Ophrah of the Abiezrites until today.

*a*6:16 Gn 26:3; Ex 3:12 *b*6:17 Gn 6:8; 18:3; Ex 33:12-13; Ru 2:2,10,13; Est 5:8; 7:3 *c*Ex 3:12; 1Sm 10:7,9; Is 7:11,14 *d*6:20 Gn 31:11; Ex 14:19; Jdg 13:6,9; 2Sm 14:17,20; 2Ch 36:16 *e*6:22 Jos 7:7; Jr 1:6; Ezk 4:14 *f*Gn 32:20; Ex 24:10-11; 33:19-23; Jdg 13:21-23; Is 6:5

^A6:13 Lit *Please, my Lord*, or *Please, my lord* ^B6:13 Lit *this found us out* ^C6:14 LXX reads *The Angel of the Lord* ^D6:19 Lit *an ephah* ^E6:24 = The Lord Is Peace

6:13-16 Gideon's response challenged both aspects of the Angel's greeting. First, he cast doubt on the Lord's presence with Israel. The Angel of the Lord did not appear to hear Gideon's objection. Instead, he commissioned him to be the mighty warrior that God had named him. This provoked Gideon to challenge this aspect of the Angel's greeting as well. Gideon claimed that he was doubly unsuited for this task. Yet the rest of the story casts doubt on Gideon's assertions: His father was a substantial landowner in the city, with the resources to build and maintain an altar to Baal, and Gideon was able to call on 10 servants to assist him in pulling down the altar. These were hardly the signs of a man whose family was of no importance. All of Gideon's protestations were useless beside the single fact that the Lord would be with him.

6:17-21 Even with this reassurance, Gideon was not satisfied. The increasing downgrade in the quality of the judges is evident. Othniel, Ehud, and Shamgar obeyed the Lord's call without dissent. Barak placed one stipulation on going—that Deborah would go with him. Gideon was an even more reluctant hero, not content with the assurance that the Lord Himself would go with him. In addition, he demanded a **sign**. He prepared an offering the size of which indicates that this was not just human hospitality but an offering to God. When Gideon brought the elements back, the **Angel of God** graciously condescended to perform the requested sign.

6:22-24 Realizing the true identity of his visitor, Gideon became convinced he was doomed to die (Ex 33:20). Again,

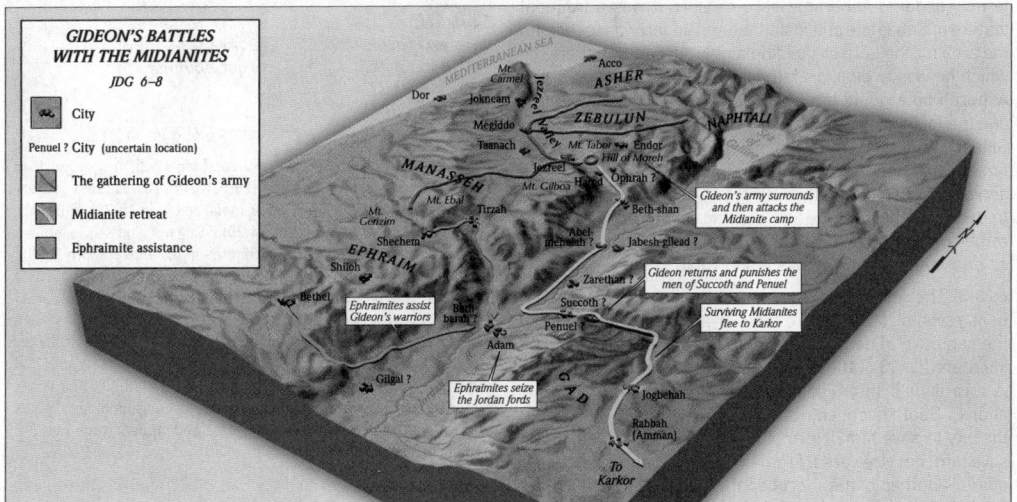

GIDEON'S BATTLES WITH THE MIDIANITES JDG 6–8

Gideon Tears Down a Baal Altar

[25] On that very night the Lord said to him, "Take your father's young bull and a second bull seven years old. Then tear down the altar of *Baal[a] that belongs to your father and cut down the *Asherah pole beside it. [26] Build a well-constructed altar to the Lord your God on the top of this rock.[b] Take the second bull and offer it as a *burnt offering with the wood of the Asherah pole you cut down." [27] So Gideon took 10 of his male servants and did as the Lord had told him. But because he was too afraid of his father's household and the men of the city to do it in the daytime, he did it at night.

[28] When the men of the city got up in the morning, they found Baal's altar torn down, the Asherah pole beside it cut down, and the second bull offered up on the altar that had been built. [29] They said to each other, "Who did this?" After they made a thorough investigation, they said, "Gideon son of Joash did it."

[30] Then the men of the city said to Joash, "Bring out your son. He must die, because he tore down Baal's altar and cut down the Asherah pole beside it."

[31] But Joash said to all who stood against him, "Would you plead Baal's case for him? Would you save him? Whoever pleads his case will be put to death by morning! If he is a god, let him plead his own case because someone tore down his altar." [32] That day, Gideon's father called him Jerubbaal, saying, "Let Baal plead his case with him," because he tore down his altar.

The Sign of the Fleece

[33] All the Midianites, Amalekites, and Qedemites gathered together, crossed over the Jordan, and camped in the Valley of Jezreel.[c] [34] The Spirit of the Lord took control of[A] Gideon, and he blew the ram's horn and the Abiezrites rallied behind him. [35] He sent messengers throughout all of Manasseh, who rallied behind him. He also sent messengers throughout Asher, Zebulun, and Naphtali, who also came to meet him.

[36] Then Gideon said to God, "If You will deliver Israel by my hand, as You said, [37] I will put a fleece of wool here on the threshing floor. If dew is only on the fleece, and all the ground is dry, I will know that You will deliver Israel by my strength, as You said." [38] And that

Marginal cross-references:
a 6:25 Jdg 2:11,13; 10:6; 1Kg 18:21; 2Ch 33:3; Jr 2:23; Zph 1:4
b 6:26 Neh 8:10; Ps 27:1; 37:39; Pr 10:29; Is 17:9-10
c 6:33 Jos 17:16; 1Sm 29:1,11; 1Kg 21:1

A6:34 Lit Lord clothed Himself with; 1Ch 12:18; 2Ch 24:20

---

the Lord spoke to reassure him. This time the Lord's message seems to have been heeded by Gideon, who built an altar to the Lord and named it **Yahweh Shalom**, "the Lord is peace." This altar to the Lord erected by Gideon in Ophrah at the beginning of his service contrasts sharply with the ephod idol that he set up there toward the end of his life (8:27).

6:25-27 Before Gideon could take on the Midianites, he first had to confront the idolatry within his own family by tearing down his father's **altar of Baal** and the **Asherah pole** beside it. An Asherah pole was a stylized tree that represented the fertility goddess Asherah, Baal's consort. It was a frequent feature of Canaanite cult installations. Gideon was to reclaim the area for the Lord by building a new altar to God there, on which he was to offer his **father's . . . bull**. The **wood of the Asherah pole** would provide fuel for the fire, as if to underline the foolishness of worshiping a piece of wood (Is 44:19). Gideon did this at once, though it is clear that his earlier timidity had not disappeared. He gathered 10 of his father's servants to help him, illustrating a trust in numbers rather than trust in the Lord. He also committed this action **at night** rather than in broad daylight because he **was . . . afraid**, so no one would know who was responsible.

6:28-32 The response of the **men of the city** to Gideon's actions reveals clearly where their loyalties lay. They wanted the sentence of death that ought to have been imposed on idolaters (Dt 13:6-10) carried out on Gideon instead. What is surprising is that Gideon's father, **Joash**, who owned this altar to Baal, defended his son. Did Baal need the men of the city to **save him**? Normally, a man expected his god to save him, not vice versa. From this intervention, Gideon acquired another name, **Jerubbaal**, which means "let Baal

contend." Gideon's continued existence was living proof of Baal's inability to defend his honor.

6:33-34 Gideon's initial success was soon followed by a greater challenge. Israel's oppressors crossed over the Jordan River for another seasonal pillaging expedition. **The Spirit of the Lord** enveloped (lit "put on") Gideon, empowering him for action to deliver the Lord's people.

6:36-40 The gathering of the tribes should have been sufficient evidence of God's presence with Gideon, but he

---

za'aq

Hebrew Pronunciation	[zah AK]
HCSB Translation	cry out, summon
Uses in Judges	13
Uses in the OT	74
Focus Passage	Judges 6:6-7,34-35

Za'aq means cry out (Ex 2:23), cry, call (Jdg 12:2), or scream (1Sm 28:12). It may involve weeping (2Sm 13:19). Armies and gatherings are summoned (Jos 8:16) or mobilized (Jdg 18:22). They rally (Jdg 6:34) or assemble (1Sm 14:20). "Cry out and say" signifies issue a decree (Jnh 3:7). Za'aq denotes make appeal (2Sm 19:28). Ze'aqah (18x) means cry (Is 15:5), outcry (Gn 18:20), crying, shout (Ec 9:17), and lamentation (Est 9:31). Tza'aq (55x) sounds like za'aq and denotes cry out (Gn 4:10). Soldiers are summoned (1Sm 13:4), called, called out, or called together (Jdg 10:17). People cry loudly (Is 33:7), call out (Dt 26:7), and appeal (2Kg 8:3). Tse'aqah (21x) means cry, outcry, crying out, and wailing (Ex 12:30). The verbs often describe prayer, imply distress, occur alongside "wail," take their related nouns as objects, and appear together (Ps 107:6,13,19,28).

is what happened. When he got up early in the morning, he squeezed the fleece and wrung dew out of it, filling a bowl with water.

³⁹ Gideon then said to God, "Don't be angry with me; let me speak one more time. Please allow me to make one more test with the fleece. Let it remain dry, and the dew be all over the ground." ⁴⁰ That night God did as Gideon requested: only the fleece was dry, and dew was all over the ground.

God Selects Gideon's Army

7 Jerubbaal (that is, Gideon) and everyone who was with him, got up early and camped beside the spring of Harod. The camp of Midian was north of them, below the hill of Moreh, in the valley. ² The Lᴏʀᴅ said to Gideon, "You have too many people for Me to hand the Midianites over to you,ᴬ or else Israel might brag:ᴮ 'I did it myself.' ³ Now announce in the presence of the people: 'Whoever is fearful and trembling may turn back and leave Mount Gilead.'"ᵃ So 22,000 of the people turned back, but 10,000 remained.

⁴ Then the Lᴏʀᴅ said to Gideon, "There are still too many people. Take them down to the water, and I will test them for you there. If I say to you, 'This one can go with you,' he can go. But if I say about anyone, 'This one cannot

ᵃ7:3 Gn 31:21, 23,25; Dt 3:12

go with you,' he cannot go." ⁵ So he brought the people down to the water, and the Lᴏʀᴅ said to Gideon, "Separate everyone who laps water with his tongue like a dog. Do the same with everyone who kneels to drink." ⁶ The number of those who lapped with their hands to their mouths was 300 men, and all the rest of the people knelt to drink water. ⁷ The Lᴏʀᴅ said to Gideon, "I will deliver you with the 300 men who lapped and hand the Midianites over to you. But everyone else is to go home." ⁸ So Gideon sent all the Israelites to their tents but kept the 300, who tookᶜ the people's provisions and their trumpets. The camp of Midian was below him in the valley.

Gideon Spies on the Midianite Camp

⁹ That night the Lᴏʀᴅ said to him, "Get up and go into the camp, for I have given it into your hand. ¹⁰ But if you are afraid to go to the camp, go with Purah your servant. ¹¹ Listen to what they say, and then you will be strengthened to go to the camp." So he went with Purah his servant to the outpost of the troopsᴰ who were in the camp.

¹² Now the Midianites, Amalekites, and all the Qedemites had settled down in the valley like a swarm of locusts, and their camels were as innumerable as the sand on the seashore.

ᴬ7:2 Lit *them*   ᴮ7:2 Lit *brag against Me*   ᶜ7:8 Lit *took in their hands*   ᴰ7:11 Lit *of those who were arranged in companies of 50*

---

wanted a sign that God would do what He had promised. He doubted that God would deliver Israel by His strength, even though that was what God had promised. As a result, Gideon put God to the test. In the first test, God did as Gideon asked, but it was not enough; Gideon may have thought that it could have been a fluke. So Gideon, showing his timidity, demanded a second test. Displaying great patience, the Lord graciously gave him a confirmatory sign.

7:1-3 Having proven to Gideon's satisfaction that He was present, the Lord emphasized the point that His presence was all Gideon needed. The army was strategically camped at the **spring of Harod**, where water supply would not be an issue. The name of this particular spring means "Spring of Trembling," which describes the state of Gideon's army. Yet from the Lord's perspective, there were **too many people** there. If an army of this size won, even against the innumerable hordes of the Midianites, Israel might be tempted to take credit for the victory. To show that the victory was entirely His, the Lord reduced the size of Gideon's army.

7:4-8 The Lord gave Gideon an additional test to reduce the size of his army further, by taking them **down to the water** to drink. It appears that those chosen scooped water up in their hands and lapped it from there, while those who got down on all fours and drank directly from the river **like a dog** were rejected. Gideon's army now numbered just **300**. Nothing must detract from the truth that the Lord can save as easily by using a few as by using many (1Sm 14:6).

7:9-14 The army was now sufficiently small, so the Lord commanded Gideon to **get up** and begin the action against the camp of the Midianites. Yet instead of immediate action, there was further delay while Gideon's continuing fears

Spring of Harod at Ainharod at the foot of the Gilboa Mountain Range. This is where Gideon's men were tested on how they drank water. This test enabled Gideon to identify those who were qualified to fight against the Midianites (7:4-8).

¹³When Gideon arrived, there was a man telling his friend about a dream. He said, "Listen, I had a dream:ª a loaf of barley bread came tumbling into the Midianite camp, struck a tent, and it fell. The loaf turned the tent upside down so that it collapsed."

¹⁴His friend answered: "This is nothing less than the sword of Gideon son of Joash, the Israelite. God has handed the entire Midianite camp over to him."

Gideon Attacks the Midianites

¹⁵When Gideon heard the account of the dream and its interpretation, he bowed in worship. He returned to Israel's camp and said, "Get up, for the LORD has handed the Midianite camp over to you." ¹⁶Then he divided the 300 men into three companies and gave each of the men a trumpet in one hand and an empty pitcher with a torch inside it in the other.

¹⁷"Watch me," he said,ᴬ "and do the same. When I come to the outpost of the camp, do as I do. ¹⁸When I and everyone with me blow our trumpets, you are also to blow your trumpets all around the camp. Then you will say, 'For •Yahweh and for Gideon!'"

¹⁹Gideon and the 100 men who were with him went to the outpost of the camp at the beginning of the middle watch after the sentries had been stationed. They blew their trumpets and broke the pitchers that were in

ª7:13 Gn 37:5-6,8-10; 40:5,8-9,16; 41; 42:9; Nm 12:6; Dn 1:17
ᵇ7:22 1Kg 4:12; 19:16
ᶜ7:24 Jdg 8:3; Ps 83:11; Is 10:26

their hands. ²⁰The three companies blew their trumpets and shattered their pitchers. They held their torches in their left hands, their trumpetsᴮ in their right hands, and shouted, "A sword for Yahweh and for Gideon!" ²¹Each Israelite took his position around the camp, and the entire Midianite army fled, and cried out as they ran. ²²When Gideon's men blew their 300 trumpets, the LORD set the swords of each man in the army against each other. They fled to Beth-shittah in the direction of Zererah as far as the border of Abel-meholahᵇ near Tabbath. ²³Then the men of Israel were called from Naphtali, Asher, and Manasseh, and they pursued the Midianites.

The Men of Ephraim Join the Battle

²⁴Gideon sent messengers throughout the hill country of Ephraim with this message: "Come down to intercept the Midianites and take control of the watercourses ahead of them as far as Beth-barah and the Jordan." So all the men of Ephraimᶜ were called out, and they took control of the watercourses as far as Beth-barah and the Jordan. ²⁵They captured Oreb and Zeeb, the two princes of Midian; they killed Oreb at the rock of Oreb and Zeeb at the winepress of Zeeb, while they were pursuing the Midianites. They brought the heads of Oreb and Zeeb to Gideon across the Jordan.

8 The men of Ephraim said to him, "Why have you done this to us, not calling us

---

ᴬ7:17 Lit *said to them*   ᴮ7:20 Lit *trumpets to blow*

---

were addressed. The Lord told Gideon that if he was **afraid** to go against the Midianite camp, he should secretly visit it and **listen** to what the Midianites were saying. He crept down to where he could see the **Midianites, Amalekites, and . . . Qedemites** (the "eastern peoples," 6:3) spread out **like a swarm of locusts**, with **innumerable . . . camels**. Visually nothing had changed since the opening verses of chapter 6. Yet what Gideon heard told a different story—God had given members of the enemy force a dream that was utterly demoralizing. It is ironic that the Midianites were quick to grasp the significance of a dream, while Gideon was slow to believe repeated signs and direct messages from the Lord.

7:15-16 Eavesdropping on this conversation at last had the desired effect on Gideon. In response, **he bowed in worship**, acknowledging the truth of the Lord's words, now that he had heard them repeated by pagans. He **returned to Israel's camp** and finally delivered to his men the instruction he had received from the Lord in verse 9. Gideon divided his small army into three divisions and "armed" them with a ram's-horn **trumpet**, an empty **pitcher**, and a **torch**. Clearly, unless the Lord fought for them they would have no chance of victory.

7:17-18 Gideon's earlier hesitancy was now gone. He led his men to the battle, instructing them to follow his example. When they came to the **outpost** at the edge of the Midianite camp, they were to blow their trumpets and to shout as their battle cry, **For Yahweh and for Gideon**. The pairing of the Lord's name with that of Gideon strikes a discordant

note. After all, this was a battle that the Lord had taken great pains to make clear would be won by His might alone, greatly reducing the size of the Israelite army so that they would not be able to boast (v. 3).

7:19-25 The strategy worked out exactly as planned. The **beginning of the middle watch** would be midnight. Gideon's three groups, spread out surrounding the camp, would sound like a much larger army. The element of surprise, combined by a divinely induced fear, sent the Midianites fleeing for their lives and fighting one another in the confusion. The victory was not just the result of successful psychological tactics. It was **the LORD** who **set** the Midianites' **swords . . . against each another**. The surviving Midianites fled toward the Jordan River, though the exact locations of the places mentioned in verse 22 are uncertain.

At this point, with victory assured, Gideon called out the men of **Naphtali, Asher, and Manasseh**—presumably the remainder of his original army of 30,000—to join in the pursuit. He also called out the men of **Ephraim** to seize the fording places over the **Jordan** to cut off any retreat for the remnant of the Midianites. It seems discordant with the spirit of holy war for Gideon to call in reinforcements after the Lord had already won the victory with the smaller force. This was perhaps a sign of Gideon's growing self-confidence. **Oreb and Zeeb** were Midianite **princes**, or military commanders.

8:1-3 With liberation achieved, the cycle normally concludes with a summary statement of peace and harmony during

when you went to fight against the Midianites?" And they argued with him violently.

²So he said to them, "What have I done now compared to you? Is not the gleaning^a of Ephraim better than the vintage^b of Abiezer? ³God handed over to you Oreb and Zeeb, the two princes of Midian. What was I able to do compared to you?" When he said this, their anger against him subsided.

Gideon Pursues the Kings of Midian

⁴Gideon and the 300 men came to the Jordan and crossed it. They were exhausted but still in pursuit. ⁵He said to the men of Succoth,^c "Please give some loaves of bread to the people who are following me,^A because they are exhausted, for I am pursuing Zebah and Zalmunna, the kings of Midian."

⁶But the princes of Succoth asked, "Are^B Zebah and Zalmunna now in your hands that we should give bread to your army?"

⁷Gideon replied, "Very well, when the LORD has handed Zebah and Zalmunna over to me, I will trample^c your flesh on thorns and briers from the wilderness!" ⁸He went from there to Penuel and asked the same thing from them. The men of Penuel^d answered just as the men of Succoth had answered. ⁹He also told the men of Penuel, "When I return in peace, I will tear down this tower!"

¹⁰Now Zebah and Zalmunna were in Karkor, and with them was their army of about 15,000 men, who were all those left of the entire army of the Qedemites. Those who had been killed were 120,000 warriors.^D ¹¹Gideon traveled on the caravan route^E east of Nobah^e and Jogbehah and attacked their army while the army was unsuspecting. ¹²Zebah and Zalmunna fled, and he pursued them. He captured these two kings of Midian and routed the entire army.

¹³Gideon son of Joash returned from the battle by the Ascent of Heres. ¹⁴He captured a youth from the men of Succoth and interrogated him. The youth wrote down for him the names of the 77 princes and elders of Succoth. ¹⁵Then he went to the men of Succoth and said, "Here are Zebah and Zalmunna. You taunted me about them, saying, 'Are^B Zebah and Zalmunna now in your power that we should give bread to your exhausted men?'" ¹⁶So he took the elders of the city, and he took some thorns and briers from the wilderness, and he disciplined the men of Succoth with them. ¹⁷He also tore down the tower of Penuel and killed the men of the city.

¹⁸He asked Zebah and Zalmunna, "What kind of men did you kill at Tabor?"

"They were like you," they said. "Each resembled the son of a king."

---

*a*8:2 Lv 19:9-10; 23:22; Dt 24:19-20; Ru 2
*b*Lv 26:5; Is 24:13; 32:10; Mc 7:1
*c*8:5 Gn 33:17; Jos 13:27; 1Kg 7:46; 2Ch 4:17; Ps 60:6
*d*8:8 Gn 32:31-32; 1Kg 12:25
*e*8:11 Nm 32:42

---

^A8:5 Lit *are at my feet*   ^B8:6,15 Lit *Are the hands of*   ^C8:7 Or *tear*   ^D8:10 Lit *men who drew the sword*   ^E8:11 Lit *on the route of those who live in tents*

---

the judge's lifetime, a summary that is delayed until verse 28. The first complication was a complaint by the Ephraimites that Gideon did not call them out to battle against the Midianites. This is surprising because elsewhere, the problem was persuading the tribes to become involved in conflict, not dissuading them. And since Gideon's task once he assembled his army was to reduce them in size, it is hard to see how the Ephraimites could have played a useful part in the battle. Their complaint shows the weak and fractured nature of the Israelite tribal alliance at this period. Gideon's response was a masterpiece of diplomacy. He downplayed his own standing and role in the victory by saying, **Is not the gleaning** (the grapes left behind after the initial harvesting) **of Ephraim better than the vintage** (the pick of the grapes) **of Abiezer?** Gideon belonged to the clan of Abiezer. Moreover, the Ephraimites achieved the crowning moment of the victory when God handed over to them Oreb and Zeeb, the two princes of Midian. This reply defused the Ephraimites' anger.

8:4-9 It is worth noting that the Lord is no longer mentioned as an active party in what follows. The Midianite kings, **Zebah and Zalmunna**, escaped across the Jordan River. In view of this pursuit, it appears that Gideon was not merely being diplomatic when he compared himself deprecatingly with the Ephraimites. He was angry that God had given Oreb and Zeeb into the hands of the Ephraimites, while he himself had no comparable triumph to show for his efforts. His damaged ego was the driving force behind the fanatical pursuit of the escaped kings. **Succoth** and **Penuel** were

towns in Transjordan under Israelite control. The men of these cities might have been expected to give Gideon aid on his quest, but they refused his appeal for food because they were skeptical of Gideon's ability to thoroughly defeat the Midianites. Gideon took their refusal personally. In contrast to his diplomacy with the Ephraimites, Gideon threatened revenge on those who failed to assist him.

8:10-12 Gideon finally caught up with Zebah and Zalmunna at **Karkor**, about 100 miles east of the Dead Sea. A sizeable remnant of their original army of **120,000 warriors** was with them, numbering around **15,000 men**. Gideon and his force of 300 caught them by surprise, routed them, and captured Zebah and Zalmunna, the two kings of Midian. There is no mention of the Lord's involvement in this battle.

8:13-17 On his return to **Succoth** and **Penuel**, Gideon wasted no time in carrying out his earlier threats. He captured a youth from Succoth, just as he had earlier captured the Midianite kings, and forced him to write down the names of the **elders of Succoth**, whom Gideon then rounded up and thrashed with a switch. Israelites who failed to do Gideon's will were treated as enemies of the state.

8:18-21 Gideon then accused the two Midianite kings, **Zebah and Zalmunna**, of atrocities at Mount **Tabor**, not far from his home in the Jezreel Valley. Their response drew a comparison between Gideon and royalty—probably a desperate attempt at flattery. Gideon replied that the men whom the kings slaughtered were his own close relatives, revealing that the motivation for his pursuit of the Midianites was

¹⁹So he said, "They were my brothers, the sons of my mother! As the LORD lives, if you had let them live, I would not kill you." ²⁰Then he said to Jether, his firstborn, "Get up and kill them." The youth did not draw his sword, for he was afraid because he was still a youth.

²¹Zebah and Zalmunna said, "Get up and kill us yourself, for a man is judged by his strength." So Gideon got up, killed Zebah and Zalmunna, and took the crescent ornaments that were on the necks of their camels.

Gideon's Legacy

²²Then the Israelites said to Gideon, "Rule over us, you as well as your sons and your grandsons, for you delivered us from the power of Midian."

²³But Gideon said to them, "I will not rule over you, and my son will not rule over you; the LORD will rule over you." ²⁴Then he said to them, "Let me make a request of you: Everyone give me an earring from his plunder." Now the enemy had gold earrings because they were Ishmaelites.

²⁵They said, "We agree to give them." So they spread out a mantle, and everyone threw an earring from his plunder on it. ²⁶The weight of the gold earrings he requested was about 43 pounds^A of gold, in addition to the crescent ornaments and ear pendants, the purple garments on the kings of Midian, and the chains on the necks of their camels. ²⁷Gideon made an ephod^a from all this and put it in Ophrah, his hometown. Then all Israel prostituted themselves with it there, and it became a snare to Gideon and his household.

²⁸So Midian was subdued before the Israelites, and they were no longer a threat.^B The land was peaceful 40 years during the days of Gideon. ²⁹Jerubbaal (that is, Gideon) son of Joash went back to live at his house.

³⁰Gideon had 70 sons, his own offspring, since he had many wives. ³¹His concubine who was in Shechem^b also bore him a son, and he named him Abimelech. ³²Then Gideon son of Joash died at a ripe old age and was buried in the tomb of his father Joash in Ophrah of the Abiezrites.

³³When Gideon died, the Israelites turned and prostituted themselves with the *Baals and made Baal-berith^c their god. ³⁴The Israelites did not remember the LORD their God who had delivered them from the power of the enemies around them. ³⁵They did not show kindness^c to the house of Jerubbaal (that is, Gideon) for all the good he had done for Israel.

Abimelech Becomes King

9 Abimelech son of Jerubbaal went to his mother's brothers at Shechem and spoke

Cross references
a 8:27 Ex 25:7; 28:12; 39:12; Jdg 18:14,17-20; 2Sm 6:14; Hs 3:4
b 8:31 Gn 12:6; 37:12-14; Jos 21:22; Ps 60:6; 108:7
c 8:35 Gn 24:12,49; Ex 20:6; 2Sm 22:51; Ps 18:50

---

^A 8:26 Lit *1,700 shekels*   ^B 8:28 Lit *they no longer raised their head*   ^C 8:33 Lit *Baal of the Covenant*, or *Lord of the Covenant*

---

personal vengeance, not obedience to the Lord's call. Gideon instructed his son **Jether** to kill the Midianite kings, but Jether did not do so because **he was afraid**. Gideon's son resembled Gideon himself. Gideon was no longer afraid. He killed Zebah and Zalmunna and took for himself their **crescent** symbols of royalty.

8:22-27 The Israelites recognized the significance of Gideon's behavior. They asked him to **rule over** them as the founder of a dynastic line. Though they carefully avoided the word "king," it is clear that they were offering Gideon that office. The rationale that the people gave is telling: **For you delivered us from the power of Midian**. The Lord's work in raising Gideon as deliverer had become obscured. Gideon's response was orthodox. He replied that neither he nor his sons would rule over them; the Lord would rule over them. Even as he formally refused the status of king, however, he failed to contradict their assertion that it was he who had saved them from the Midianites. He also proceeded to act precisely as a king would. He asked for a royal share of the plunder, **gold earrings** from every man, representing a symbolic token of submission to him. As in Exodus 32, where earrings were used in the making of the golden calf, so Gideon used these earrings to manufacture an idol in the form of an **ephod**, a garment worn by the priests and used as a means of determining God's will. The amount of **gold** suggests that the garment included an idolatrous image. Gideon's intent was to glorify himself, founding his own cult like the Canaanite kings. The result was spiritually disastrous, ensnaring **all Israel** in prostituting themselves.

8:28-32 The narrative ends where it started—at **Ophrah**—

suggesting that nothing had changed. Baal had changed his shape, but the idolatry continued. The oppressive Midianite kings had been replaced by Gideon, who was acting like the worst kind of king. Along with supporting idolatry, Gideon married many wives and had **70 sons**, a family structure forbidden to kings in Dt 17:17. He also intermarried with the local population, taking a concubine from Canaanite **Shechem**, with whom he had a son named **Abimelech**, which literally means "my father is king." Positively, the land was **peaceful 40 years** during Gideon's lifetime, but from this point on in the Judges narrative, Israel never again attained rest. This negative portrayal of kingship suggests that the phrase "In those days there was no king in Israel; everyone did whatever he wanted" (17:6) did not portray an earthly monarchy as the solution to Israel's problems.

8:33-35 After Gideon's death, Israel went from bad to worse and **prostituted themselves** in the worship of the **Baals**. Baal was worshiped in many local manifestations, including **Baal-berith** ("Baal of the covenant"), who was the patron deity of Shechem. It is ironic that in worshiping a god whose name includes the word for "covenant," Israel forgot the covenant faithfulness of their own God, Yahweh, who had delivered them from the power of their enemies. The place where this Baal was worshiped, Shechem, was where the people renewed their covenant with the Lord at the end of the book of Joshua when the people swore never to worship the gods of the land (Jos 24). Nor did they show **kindness** to the house of Gideon after his death. The word "kindness" (Hb *chesed*) is often used in covenantal contexts, and it suggests that Israel forgot Gideon's acts of deliverance as

to them and to all his maternal grandfather's clan, saying, [2]"Please speak in the presence of all the lords of Shechem, 'Is it better for you that 70 men, all the sons of Jerubbaal,[a] rule over you or that one man rule over you?' Remember that I am your own flesh and blood."[A]

[3]His mother's relatives spoke all these words about him in the presence of all the lords of Shechem, and they were favorable to Abimelech, for they said, "He is our brother." [4]So they gave him 70 pieces of silver from the temple of Baal-berith.[B] Abimelech hired worthless and reckless men with this money, and they followed him. [5]He went to his father's house in Ophrah and killed his 70 brothers, the sons of Jerubbaal, on top of a large stone. But Jotham, the youngest son of Jerubbaal, survived, because he hid himself. [6]Then all the lords of Shechem and of Beth-millo gathered together and proceeded to make Abimelech king at the oak of the pillar in Shechem.

Jotham's Parable

[7]When they told Jotham, he climbed to the top of Mount Gerizim,[b] raised his voice, and called to them:

Listen to me, lords of Shechem,
   and may God listen to you:
[8] The trees set out
   to anoint a king over themselves.
They said to the olive tree,
   "Reign over us."

Cross-references
[a]9:2 Jdg 6:32
[b]9:7 Dt 11:29; 27:12; Jos 8:33
[c]9:16 1Sm 12:24; 1Kg 2:4; Ps 111:8; Pr 29:14; Jr 32:41
[d]Jos 24:14; Ps 84:11

[9] But the olive tree said to them,
   "Should I stop giving my oil
   that honors both God and man,
   and rule[c] over the trees?"
[10] Then the trees said to the fig tree,
   "Come and reign over us."
[11] But the fig tree said to them,
   "Should I stop giving
   my sweetness and my good fruit,
   and rule[c] over trees?"
[12] Later, the trees said
      to the grapevine,
   "Come and reign over us."
[13] But the grapevine said to them,
   "Should I stop giving my wine
   that cheers both God and man,
   and rule[c] over trees?"
[14] Finally, all the trees said
      to the bramble,
   "Come and reign over us."
[15] The bramble said to the trees,
   "If you really are anointing me
   as king over you,
   come and find refuge in my shade.
   But if not,
   may fire come out from the bramble
   and consume the cedars of Lebanon."

[16]"Now if you have acted faithfully[c] and honestly[d] in making Abimelech king, if you have done well by Jerubbaal and his family, and if

---

[A]9:2 Lit *your bone and your flesh*   [B]9:4 Lit *Baal of the Covenant*, or *Lord of the Covenant*   [C]9:9,11,13 Lit *and go to sway*

---

swiftly as they forgot the Lord's. The irony of Israel's return to Baal worship is heightened by the use of Gideon's other name, **Jerubbaal**, "let Baal contend."

9:1-6 The account of **Abimelech** is a deviation from the main storyline of the book of Judges, showing the complete Canaanization of the land during this period. Gideon may have formally declined kingship, but Abimelech (whose name means "My father is king") had no such scruples. He went to his mother's family in Shechem, in the center of Israel, and sought the support of **the lords of Shechem** in a coup that would place him on the throne. The principle of dynastic succession that Gideon denied in 8:23 is taken for granted in Abimelech's speech. Either he would rule or the other 70 sons of Gideon would rule. The value of having a relative in power was readily perceived by the lords of Shechem. They gave **70 pieces of silver**, one for each of Gideon's other sons, with which Abimelech hired mercenaries to eliminate his rivals. Israel was so thoroughly corrupt that the money was from a pagan temple and the mercenaries were **worthless and reckless men**. **Beth-millo** may be another way of referring to Shechem's leaders. The location of the coronation may have been the same prominent **oak** where Joshua years before

had set up a pillar as a witness of the people's covenant renewal with God (Jos 24:25-27).

9:7-15 Jotham, the sole son of Gideon to escape the massacre, went to the top of **Mount Gerizim**, which overlooked Shechem. In addition to being a safe place, it was a place with a history. Mount Gerizim and Mount Ebal were the locations where the people of Israel recited the blessings and curses of the covenant when they had first entered the land (Dt 27:12-13). On this occasion, Mount Gerizim would host a curse (Jdg 9:57) rather than a blessing. From the mountain, Jotham proclaimed a *fable*, a story involving plants or animals that teaches a moral lesson. In Jotham's fable, the various trees sought to find a **king**. Each of the first three trees was reluctant to give up its profitable activity in favor of such an unprofitable office. The fourth and final candidate, **the bramble**, had no useful function but was a perpetual nuisance for farmers. But this plant accepted their offer of kingship. He invited the other trees to **come and find refuge in my shade**, though the low spreading bramble provides no real shade. If they would not submit to him, he issued a threat that fiery judgment would come from him and consume the **cedars of Lebanon**, the most exalted of trees.

9:16-21 Jotham himself provided the interpretation of the fable. First, he facetiously wondered whether they had

you have rewarded him appropriately for what he did— [17] for my father fought for you, risked his life, and delivered you from the hand of Midian, [18] and now you have attacked my father's house today, killed his 70 sons on top of a large stone, and made Abimelech, the son of his slave, king over the lords of Shechem 'because he is your brother'— [19] if then you have acted faithfully and honestly with Jerubbaal and his house this day, rejoice in Abimelech and may he also rejoice in you. [20] But if not, may fire come from Abimelech and consume the lords of Shechem and Beth-millo, and may fire come from the lords of Shechem and Beth-millo and consume Abimelech." [21] Then Jotham fled, escaping to Beer, and lived there because of his brother Abimelech.

Abimelech's Punishment

[22] When Abimelech had ruled over Israel three years, [23] God sent an evil spirit[a] between Abimelech and the lords of Shechem. They treated Abimelech deceitfully, [24] so that the crime against the 70 sons of Jerubbaal might come to justice and their blood would be avenged on their brother Abimelech, who killed them, and on the lords of Shechem, who had helped him kill his brothers. [25] The lords of Shechem rebelled against him by putting people on the tops of the mountains to ambush[b] and rob everyone who passed by them on the road. So this was reported to Abimelech.

[26] Gaal son of Ebed came with his brothers and crossed into Shechem, and the lords of Shechem trusted him. [27] So they went out to the countryside and harvested grapes from their vineyards. They trampled the grapes and held a celebration.[c] Then they went to the house of their god, and as they ate and drank, they cursed Abimelech. [28] Gaal son of Ebed said, "Who is Abimelech and who is Shechem that we should serve him? Isn't he the son of

Jerubbaal, and isn't Zebul his officer? You are to serve the men of Hamor, the father of Shechem.[d] Why should we serve Abimelech? [29] If only these people were in my power, I would remove Abimelech." So he said[A] to Abimelech, "Gather your army and come out."

[30] When Zebul, the ruler of the city, heard the words of Gaal son of Ebed, he was angry. [31] So he sent messengers secretly to Abimelech, saying, "Look, Gaal son of Ebed, with his brothers, have come to Shechem and are turning the city against you.[B] [32] Now tonight, you and the people with you are to come wait in ambush in the countryside. [33] Then get up early, and at sunrise charge the city. When he and the people who are with him come out against you, do to him whatever you can."[C] [34] So Abimelech and all the people with him got up at night and waited in ambush for Shechem in four units.

[35] Gaal son of Ebed went out and stood at the entrance of the city gate. Then Abimelech and the people who were with him got up from their ambush. [36] When Gaal saw the people, he said to Zebul, "Look, people are coming down from the mountaintops!" But Zebul said to him, "The shadows of the mountains look like men to you."

[37] Then Gaal spoke again, "Look, people are coming down from the central part of the land,[e] and one unit is coming from the direction of the Diviners' Oak." [38] Zebul replied,[D] "Where is your mouthing off now? You said, 'Who is Abimelech that we should serve him?' Aren't these the people you despised? Now go and fight them!"

[39] So Gaal went out leading the lords of Shechem and fought against Abimelech, [40] but Abimelech pursued him, and Gaal fled before him. Many wounded died[f] as far as the entrance of the gate. [41] Abimelech stayed in Arumah, and Zebul drove Gaal and his brothers from Shechem.

[a]9:23 1Sm 16:14-23; 18:10-12; 19:9; 2Kg 19:7   [b]9:25 Jos 8:2; 1Sm 15:5; 2Ch 20:22; Ezr 8:31; Ps 10:9; Pr 1:11; Jr 9:8   [c]9:27 Lv 19:24; Jdg 21:20-21   [d]9:28 Gn 33:19; 34:2-26; Jos 24:32   [e]9:37 Ezk 38:12   [f]9:40 1Sm 17:52; 2Ch 13:17; Ezk 6:4,7; Dn 11:26

[A]9:29 DSS read *They said*; LXX reads *I would say*   [B]9:31 Hb obscure   [C]9:33 Lit *him as your hand will find*   [D]9:38 Lit *replied to him*

---

acted **faithfully and honestly** (vv. 16-19). Then he invoked a curse that the people would get what they deserve; he also went beyond the fable to make the curse reciprocal: **May fire . . . consume Abimelech**. Jotham then fled, hiding out at a place named **Beer** ("well").

9:22-25 Abimelech's reign lasted only **three years**. The translation **evil spirit** does not necessarily imply demonic activity, since the Hebrew word *ra'ah* can simply mean "bad." The focus is on the fact that God replaced the harmony between Abimelech and the lords of Shechem with a spirit of distrust and disagreement. As a result, the lords of Shechem broke faith with Abimelech by ambushing those who passed by on the roads.

9:26-29 Gaal may have been a Shechemite who had gone

into exile to escape Abimelech. His return was welcomed by the lords of Shechem who **harvested grapes** in order to throw a party for him. The grape harvest was often a time of riotous celebration and drunkenness. On this occasion, after eating and drinking a little too much, the participants **cursed Abimelech**—an action that could incur the death penalty (Ex 22:28; 1Kg 21:13). In a speech whose forthrightness seems emboldened by alcohol, Gaal claimed that if he were king he could do a better job of running Shechem than Abimelech.

9:30-41 Zebul, Abimelech's governor in Shechem, called Gaal's bluff, informing Abimelech of Gaal's insubordination, and forcing Gaal to lead **the lords of Shechem** against Abimelech's army.

⁴²The next day when the people went into the countryside, this was reported to Abimelech. ⁴³He took the people, divided them into three companies, and waited in ambush in the countryside. He looked, and the people were coming out of the city, so he arose against them and struck them down. ⁴⁴Then Abimelech and the units that were with him rushed forward and took their stand at the entrance of the city gate. The other two units rushed against all who were in the countryside and struck them down. ⁴⁵So Abimelech fought against the city that entire day, captured it, and killed the people who were in it. Then he tore down the city and sowed it with salt.

⁴⁶When all the lords of the Tower of Shechem heard, they entered the inner chamberᴬ of the temple of El-berith.ᴮ ⁴⁷Then it was reported to Abimelech that all the lords of the Tower of Shechem had gathered together. ⁴⁸So Abimelech and all the people who were with him went up to Mount Zalmon. Abimelech took his ax in his hand and cut a branch from the trees. He picked up the branch, put it on his shoulder, and said to the people who were with him, "Hurry and do what you have seen me do." ⁴⁹Each person also cut his own branch and followed Abimelech. They put the branches against the inner chamber and set it on fire around the people, and all the people in the Tower of Shechem died—about 1,000 men and women.

⁵⁰Abimelech went to Thebez,ᵃ camped against it, and captured it. ⁵¹There was a strong tower inside the city, and all the men, women, and lords of the city fled there. They locked themselves in and went up to the roof of the tower. ⁵²When Abimelech came to attack the tower, he approached its entrance to

set it on fire. ⁵³But a woman threw the upper portion of a millstone on Abimelech's head and fractured his skull. ⁵⁴He quickly called his armor-bearer and said to him, "Draw your sword and kill me, or they'll say about me, 'A woman killed him.'" So his armor-bearer thrust him through, and he died. ⁵⁵When the Israelites saw that Abimelech was dead, they all went home.

⁵⁶In this way, God turned back on Abimelech the evil that he had done against his father, by killing his 70 brothers. ⁵⁷And God also returned all the evil of the men of Shechem on their heads. So the curse of Jotham son of Jerubbaal came on them.ᵇ

Tola and Jair

10 After Abimelech, Tola son of Puah, son of Dodo became judge and began to deliver Israel. He was from Issachar and lived in Shamir in the hill country of Ephraim. ²Tola judged Israel 23 years and when he died, was buried in Shamir.

³After him came Jair the Gileadite,ᶜ who judged Israel 22 years. ⁴He had 30 sons who rode on 30 donkeys. They had 30 townsᶜ in Gilead, which are called Jair's Villagesᴰ to this day. ⁵When Jair died, he was buried in Kamon.

Israel's Rebellion and Repentance

⁶Then the Israelites again did what was evil in the sight of the Lord.ᵈ They worshiped the •Baals and the •Ashtoreths, the gods of Aram, Sidon, and Moab, and the gods of the Ammonites and the Philistines.ᵉ They abandoned •Yahweh and did not worship Him.ᶠ ⁷So the Lord's anger burned against Israel, and He sold them toᴱ the Philistines and the Ammonites. ⁸They shattered and crushed the Israelites that year,

9:42-49 Abimelech took excessive revenge against Shechem. He massacred the inhabitants of the city and tore down its buildings. He also scattered **salt** over it. Since salt is a preservative, this act symbolized the eternal and unchanging nature of this destruction. Those who escaped fled to the **temple of El-berith** (Baal-berith, Shechem's god). Rather than waste lives in assaulting this stronghold, Abimelech piled wood around it and burned the occupants alive. Fittingly, along with those who financed his original coup, he destroyed the source of the finance, the temple of Baal-berith. The fiery destruction of the lords of Shechem perfectly matched the imagery of Jotham's fable.

9:50-57 Encouraged by his success at Shechem, Abimelech sought to repeat it at **Thebez**, a town not far from Shechem. Instead, he was killed when a **woman** dropped a **millstone** on his head. Like Sisera, he met his end at the hand of a woman, even though his armor bearer struck the final blow.

Abimelech's fire thus consumed himself, as Jotham's curse was fulfilled by the Lord.

10:1-5 After **Abimelech**, there were a pair of minor judges, **Tola** and **Jair**. Both "judged" Israel administratively, like Deborah, without being involved in direct conflict. The description of Tola recalls the days of the good judges. However, **Jair the Gileadite** sounds more like a "minor Gideon," with his **30** pampered **sons**. "Thirty sons" suggests multiple wives, while 30 donkeys and towns implies a tendency to accumulate personal wealth. Like Abimelech, there is no mention that they were raised up by the Lord or empowered for their task by Him. Yet they form part of the total number of 12 judges in the book of Judges. This suggests that they were also part of God's provision for His people.

10:6-9 Israel now plumbed the depths of idolatry, serving no fewer than seven false gods. Seven was the number of completeness, just as there were seven nations listed that Israel needed to drive out of the land of Canaan (Dt 7:1). In

and for 18 years they did the same to all the Israelites who were on the other side of the Jordan[a] in the land of the Amorites[b] in Gilead. [9] The Ammonites also crossed the Jordan to fight against Judah, Benjamin, and the house of Ephraim. Israel was greatly oppressed, [10] so they cried out to the Lord, saying, "We have sinned against You.[c] We have abandoned our God and worshiped the Baals."

[11] The Lord said to the Israelites, "When the Egyptians,[d] Amorites, Ammonites, Philistines, [12] Sidonians, Amalekites, and Maonites[A,e] oppressed you, and you cried out to Me, did I not deliver you from their power? [13] But you have abandoned Me and worshiped other gods. Therefore, I will not deliver you again. [14] Go and cry out to the gods you have chosen.[f] Let them deliver you in the time of your oppression."

[15] But the Israelites said, "We have sinned. Deal with us as You see fit;[B] only deliver us[g] today!" [16] So they got rid of the foreign gods[h] among them and worshiped the Lord,[i] and He became weary[j] of Israel's misery.

[17] The Ammonites were called together, and they camped in Gilead. So the Israelites as-sembled and camped at Mizpah.[k] [18] The rulers[c] of Gilead said to one another, "Which man will lead the fight against the Ammonites? He will be the leader of all the inhabitants of Gilead."

Jephthah Becomes Israel's Leader

11 Jephthah[l] the Gileadite was a great warrior,[m] but he was the son of a prostitute, and Gilead was his father. [2] Gilead's wife bore him sons, and when they grew up, they drove Jephthah out and said to him, "You will have no inheritance in our father's house, because you are the son of another woman." [3] So Jephthah fled from his brothers and lived in the land of Tob.[n] Then some lawless men joined Jephthah and traveled with him.

[4] Some time later, the Ammonites fought against Israel. [5] When the Ammonites made war with Israel, the elders of Gilead went to get Jephthah from the land of Tob. [6] They said to him, "Come, be our commander, and let's fight against the Ammonites."

[7] Jephthah replied to the elders of Gilead, "Didn't you hate me and drive me from my father's house? Why then have you come to me now when you're in trouble?"

[8] They answered Jephthah, "Since that's

Cross references
a10:8 Gn 50:10-11; Dt 1:1,5; 3:8,20,25; Jos 12:17; Jdg 5:17
b Nm 21:31; Jos 24:8; Jdg 11:21; Am 2:10
c10:10 Neh 1:6; Jr 14:20; Dn 9:8
d10:11 Ex 1–15
e10:12 Jos 15:5; 1Sm 23:24-25
f10:14 Dt 32:37-38; Jr 2:28; 11:12
g10:15 1Sm 12:10; 1Ch 16:35; Ps 79:9
h10:16 Gn 35:2; Jos 24:33; 1Sm 7:3; 2Ch 33:15
i Ex 10:7-8; 12:31; Dt 10:12; Jos 24:14-15; 2Ch 30:8
j Nm 21:4; Jdg 16:16; Mc 2:7; Zch 11:8
k10:17 Gn 31:49; Jdg 11:11,34; Hs 5:1
l11:1 1Sm 12:11; Heb 11:32
m Jdg 6:12; Ru 2:1; 1Sm 9:1; 16:18; 1Kg 11:28; 2Kg 5:1
n11:3 2Sm 10:6,8

A 10:12 LXX reads *Midianites*   **B** 10:15 Lit *Do to us what is good in Your eyes*   **C** 10:18 Lit *The people, rulers*

---

accordance with the pattern of Judges 2, **the Lord's anger burned** and He sold them to an oppressor: the **Philistines** occupied the coastal plain west of Israel while the **Ammonites** occupied the Transjordanian region to the east.

Since the Ammonites were the oppressors in the Jephthah narrative (chap. 11) while the Philistines were the enemy with whom Samson had to deal (chaps. 13–16), this description of spiritual unfaithfulness seems to introduce both of these episodes, which may have been contemporaneous. The Lord's anger with Israel was so great that He afflicted them with two oppressors at once. They **crushed** Israel, just as Dt 28:33 had predicted. The initial focus is on the Ammonites, who for 18 years oppressed the Israelites living east of the Jordan River in the land of Gilead. The affliction was not limited to the part of Israel closest to the Ammonite homeland. They went further afield, crossing **the Jordan** and fighting against **Judah, Benjamin, and . . . Ephraim.**

10:10-18 When under pressure, Israel **cried out to the Lord,** confessing their sin of abandoning Him. Before, the Lord had sent a prophet to rebuke them (6:7-10), but this time He confronted them Himself. Though the Israelites called him **our God,** the Lord refused to accept their claim of a relationship to Him. He had in the past delivered them from seven oppressors, a number that matched the number of other gods they had been worshiping (v. 6). Now He would no longer deliver them. If they wanted the Lord to help them in their hour of distress, they should have served Him also in the good times. At this, the Israelites "repented" once more. They **got rid of** their **foreign gods** and **worshiped the Lord.** Was their repentance real, or was it just another attempt to manipulate God into delivering them again? The Lord declared that His patience with Israel's

suffering was exhausted. In the face of their repentance, there was no word of any deliverer to come. The only sound was the impending arrival of the Ammonites camping for war in **Gilead.** Far from receiving a deliverer from the Lord, the Gileadites were left leaderless. As a result, instead of seeking a man empowered by the Spirit of God, they sought to motivate someone—anyone—to step forward with the promise of human reward: leadership over **all the inhabitants of Gilead.**

11:1-3 The candidate that the Gileadites were seeking soon emerged. **Jephthah** is described as a **great warrior,** the same epithet the Angel of the Lord used to address Gideon in 6:12. Yet Jephthah was also a social outcast, **the son of a prostitute.** Driven from his home, Jephthah lived the life of a bandit in the land of **Tob,** where he was joined by **lawless men.** This is the same phrase used to describe Abimelech's mercenaries in 9:4. Jephthah was a man without a home, a family, or a future.

11:4-6 When the **Ammonites** waged war against Israel, the elders of Gilead invited Jephthah to be their commander. There is a parallel between Israel's sudden interest in the Lord when the Ammonites attacked them in chapter 10 and the Gileadites' sudden interest in Jephthah. Both appeals seem prompted by desperation rather than a genuine change of heart. In 10:18 the Gileadites had offered their own citizens the position of leader (Hb *ro'sh*), which implied long-term leadership over the tribe, but they offered to make Jephthah a military **commander** (Hb *qatsin*), which was a lesser position.

11:7-11 Jephthah was not immediately won over by this appeal. Earlier, the leaders of Gilead had been happy to send him elsewhere; now, in their hour of need, they wanted his help. In response, the **elders of Gilead** increased their offer

true, we now turn to you. Come with us, fight the Ammonites, and you will become leader of all the inhabitants of Gilead."

⁹So Jephthah said to them, "If you are bringing me back to fight the Ammonites and the LORD gives them to me, I will be your leader."

¹⁰The elders of Gilead said to Jephthah, "The LORD is our witness if we don't do as you say." ¹¹So Jephthah went with the elders of Gilead. The people put him over themselves as leader and commander, and Jephthah repeated all his terms in the presence of the LORD at Mizpah.

Jephthah Rejects Ammonite Claims

¹²Jephthah sent messengers to the king of the Ammonites, saying, "What do you have against me that you have come to fight against me in my land?"

¹³The king of the Ammonites said to Jephthah's messengers, "When Israel came from Egypt, they seized my land from the Arnon to the Jabbok*ᵃ* and the Jordan. Now restore it peaceably."

¹⁴Jephthah again sent messengers to the king of the Ammonites ¹⁵to tell him, "This is what Jephthah says: Israel did not take away the land of Moab or the land of the Ammonites. ¹⁶But when they came from Egypt, Israel traveled through the wilderness to the •Red Sea and came to Kadesh. ¹⁷Israel sent messengers to the king of Edom, saying, 'Please

ᵃ11:13 Nm 21:24; Dt 2:37; 3:16
ᵇ11:19 Nm 21:25,28,30,34; Dt 3:2,6; Neh 9:22; Is 15:4
ᶜ11:21 Nm 21:24; Dt 4:47; Jos 12:1; Jdg 1:19

let us travel through your land,' but the king of Edom would not listen. They also sent messengers to the king of Moab, but he refused. So Israel stayed in Kadesh.

¹⁸"Then they traveled through the wilderness and around the lands of Edom and Moab. They came to the east side of the land of Moab and camped on the other side of the Arnon but did not enter into the territory of Moab, for the Arnon was the boundary of Moab.

¹⁹"Then Israel sent messengers to Sihon king of the Amorites, king of Heshbon.*ᵇ* Israel said to him, 'Please let us travel through your land to our country,' ²⁰but Sihon would not trust Israel to pass through his territory. Instead, Sihon gathered all his people, camped at Jahaz, and fought with Israel. ²¹Then the LORD God of Israel handed over Sihon and all his people to Israel, and they defeated them. So Israel took possession*ᶜ* of the entire land of the Amorites who lived in that country. ²²They took possession of all the territory of the Amorites from the Arnon to the Jabbok and from the wilderness to the Jordan.

²³"The LORD God of Israel has now driven out the Amorites before His people Israel, and will you now force us out? ²⁴Isn't it true that you may possess whatever your god Chemosh drives out for you, and we may possess everything the LORD our God drives out before us? ²⁵Now are you any better than Balak son

---

to Jephthah, saying they would indeed make him **leader** (Hb ro'sh; v. 8). Jephthah brought the Lord's name into the discussion as he conditionally accepted their offer. The elders of Gilead made a vow in the Lord's presence and made him their **leader and commander**. Both the elders and Jephthah seemed to be using the Lord's name in support of their own interests.

11:12-13 As the new leader, Jephthah acted in king-like fashion, speaking to the king of the Ammonites as an equal and claiming that the land of Gilead was his own personal property (**my land**). The **king of the Ammonites** contested this claim, arguing that the region east of the **Jordan**, from the **Arnon** River in the south to the **Jabbok** River in the north, belonged to him and had been illegally seized **when Israel came from Egypt**. This claim was false. At the time Israel came up from Egypt, the land was occupied by the Amorites, not the Ammonites (Nm 21:21-35).

11:14-22 Negotiations went through another stage, as Jephthah sent more **messengers** to the king. They introduced their communication with the standard royal ambassadorial address, "This is what Jephthah says." They said that the land of Gilead had never belonged either to **Moab**, Ammon's southern neighbor, or to **Ammon**. Rather, when Israel came up out of Egypt, they were careful to respect the territorial boundaries of **Edom** and Moab. But when Sihon king of the Amorites attacked them, they had no choice but to engage him. The Lord then gave Israel Sihon's land, which is the land that the king of the Ammonites had described (vv. 21-22; cp. v. 13).

11:23-27 It was commonly understood in that day that whatever land your god gave you belonged to you. Since **the LORD God of Israel** had driven out the Amorites, it was Israel's to possess. If **Chemosh**, the god of the Ammonites, had real power, he could take the land for them. In this speech, Jephthah seems, either accidentally or deliberately, to have

'avar

Hebrew Pronunciation	[ah VAHR]
HCSB Translation	pass, travel, cross, violate
Uses in Judges	23
Uses in the OT	553
Focus Passage	Judges 11:17,19-20,29,32

'Avar basically means pass, although this idea may not be obvious in translation. Often the word denotes move (Jos 6:7) or go on (Gn 32:16). Borders proceed (Nm 34:4). 'Avar refers to traveling through (Jdg 11:17) and to crossing the Jordan (Dt 9:1). Violate (Jdg 2:20) implies passing limits (Jb 14:5). God passes over sin (Mc 7:18). 'Avar suggests overlook (Pr 19:11), ignore (Is 40:27), or spare (Am 7:8). Water can overwhelm (Nah 1:8) and flood (Is 54:9). To excel (Jr 5:28) is to "pass beyond." 'Avar can indicate sweep through (Is 8:8) or pass through (Lm 3:44), depart (Mc 1:11) or enter (Dt 29:12). The participle refers to passersby (1Kg 9:8), flowing myrrh (Sg 5:5), or drifting chaff (Jr 13:24). 'Avar in the causative can signify remove (Zch 13:2), bring across (Ps 78:13), present (Ex 13:12), or banish (1Kg 15:12). One circulates proclamations (Ezr 10:7) and sounds trumpets (Lv 25:9).

of Zippor, king of Moab? Did he ever contend with Israel or fight against them? ²⁶While Israel lived 300 years in Heshbon and its villages, in Aroer and its villages, and in all the cities that are on the banks of the Arnon, why didn't you take them back at that time? ²⁷I have not sinned against you, but you have wronged me by fighting against me. Let the LORD who is the Judge*ᵃ* decide today between the Israelites and the Ammonites." ²⁸But the king of the Ammonites would not listen to Jephthah's message that he sent him.

Jephthah's Vow and Sacrifice

²⁹The Spirit of the LORD came on Jephthah, who traveled through Gilead and Manasseh, and then through Mizpah of Gilead. He crossed over to the Ammonites from Mizpah

ᵃ11:27 Gn 18:25; Jb 9:15; 23:7; Ps 7:11; 50:6; 75:7; Is 33:22
ᵇ11:30 Gn 28:20; Nm 30:2; 1Sm 1:11
ᶜ11:31 Ps 66:13
ᵈ11:32 Jdg 12:3; 1Sm 14:10
ᵉ11:33 Lv 26:41; Jdg 3:30; 8:28; 1Sm 7:13; 1Ch 20:4; 2Ch 13:18; Ps 106:42
ᶠ11:34 Ex 15:20; 32:19; Jdg 21:21; Sg 6:13

of Gilead. ³⁰Jephthah made this vow*ᵇ* to the LORD: "If You will hand over the Ammonites to me, ³¹whatever comes out of the doors of my house to greet me when I return in peace from the Ammonites will belong to the LORD, and I will offer it as a •burnt offering."*ᶜ*

³²Jephthah crossed over to the Ammonites to fight against them, and the LORD handed them over*ᵈ* to him. ³³He defeated 20 of their cities with a great slaughter from Aroer all the way to the entrance of Minnith and to Abel-keramim. So the Ammonites were subdued*ᵉ* before the Israelites.

³⁴When Jephthah went to his home in Mizpah, there was his daughter, coming out to meet him with tambourines and dancing!*ᶠ* She was his only child; he had no other son

---

confused the deities of Moab and Ammon. Elsewhere in the Bible, Chemosh is the god of Moab, while Molech is the god of Ammon. **Balak** earlier had tried to curse Israel by means of the prophet Balaam, but he was unable to do so (Nm 22–24). The **LORD** would be the ultimate **Judge** of their dispute. At this point diplomacy was over, and the war began.

11:29-33 The **spirit of the LORD came on Jephthah**, empowering him for action. He toured Gilead and Manasseh to muster his troops and headed out against the Ammonites. The Lord in turn gave him victory over the Ammonites, from **Aroer all the way to . . . Minnith and to Abel-keramim**—

three towns that defined the traditional border between Israel and Ammon. In between empowerment and victory, though, there was an intervening episode that undermined Jephthah's triumph. Jephthah sought to ensure the Lord's favor by vowing to sacrifice as a whole burnt offering **whatever** (or whoever) came **out of the doors** of his **house to greet** him after he had won his victory.

It seems probable that Jephthah had a human sacrifice in mind, since animals do not normally come out to greet the returning troops. Just as he confused Chemosh and Molech in the previous section, so now he confused the Lord with Chemosh and Molech. The gods of the Moabites and Am-

Typical Israelite Home of the Iron Age
ca 1300 B.C. — ca 600 B.C.

1. Entrance
2. Central Courtyard
   A. FIREPIT
   B. CISTERN
3. Living Quarters ("LONG ROOM")
4. Storage/Workshop/Kitchen
5. Rooftop (EXTRA AREA FOR EATING, WORKING AND SLEEPING DURING WARM WEATHER)
   C. ROLLER - FOR RECOMPACTING CLAY ROOF FOLLOWING RAIN. MAN SHOWN IS PATCHING ROOF.
6. Animal Pen

5 (UPPER LEVEL)
3 (LOWER LEVEL)

Israelite four-room house. Some interpreters believe Jephthah lived in a four-room house that was common in Israel during the Iron Age. Many such houses had a room for the family's animals. If Jephthah lived in such a house, his vow (11:30) may have been based on the assumption that one of his animals would be the first to greet him when he returned from victory over the Ammonites. For a different view, see the note at 11:29-33.

or daughter besides her. ³⁵When he saw her, he tore his clothes and said, "No! Not my daughter! You have devastated me! You have brought great misery on me.ᴬ I have given my word to the Lᴏʀᴅ and cannot take it back."

³⁶Then she said to him, "My father, you have given your word to the Lᴏʀᴅ. Do to me as you have said, for the Lᴏʀᴅ brought vengeance on your enemies, the Ammonites." ³⁷She also said to her father, "Let me do this one thing: Let me wander two months through the mountains with my friends and mourn my virginity."

³⁸"Go," he said. And he sent her away two months. So she left with her friends and mourned her virginity as she wandered through the mountains. ³⁹At the end of two months, she returned to her father, and he kept the vow he had made about her. And she had never been intimate with a man. Now it became a custom in Israel ⁴⁰that four days each year the young women of Israel would commemorate the daughter of Jephthah the Gileadite.

Conflict with Ephraim

12 The men of Ephraim were called together and crossed the Jordan to Zaphon.ᵃ They said to Jephthah, "Why have you crossed over to fight against the Ammonites

ᵃ12:1 Jos 13:27
ᵇ12:8 Gn 35:19; Ru 1:1-2; Mc 5:2

but didn't call us to go with you? We will burn your house down with you in it!"

²Then Jephthah said to them, "My people and I had a serious conflict with the Ammonites. So I called for you, but you didn't deliver me from their power. ³When I saw that you weren't going to deliver me, I took my life in my own hands and crossed over to the Ammonites, and the Lᴏʀᴅ handed them over to me. Why then have you comeᴮ today to fight against me?"

⁴Then Jephthah gathered all of the men of Gilead. They fought and defeated Ephraim, because Ephraim had said, "You Gileadites are Ephraimite fugitives in the territories of Ephraim and Manasseh." ⁵The Gileadites captured the fords of the Jordan leading to Ephraim. Whenever a fugitive from Ephraim said, "Let me cross over," the Gileadites asked him, "Are you an Ephraimite?" If he answered, "No," ⁶they told him, "Please say Shibboleth." If he said, "Sibboleth," because he could not pronounce it correctly, they seized him and killed him at the fords of the Jordan. At that time 42,000 from Ephraim died.

⁷Jephthah judged Israel six years, and when he died, he was buried in one of the cities of Gilead.ᶜ

Ibzan, Elon, and Abdon

⁸Ibzan, who was from Bethlehem,ᵇ judged

ᴬ11:35 Lit *have been among those who trouble me*   **ᴮ12:3** Lit *come to me*   **ᶜ12:7** LXX reads *in his city in Gilead*

---

monites accepted human burnt offerings as a sign of total dedication (2Kg 3), but such offerings would have delivered Israel anyway, even without Jephthah's rash vow.

11:34-35 After the victory, Jephthah's vow came back to haunt him. The one **coming out to meet him** was **his daughter**, with **tambourines and dancing**, the traditional greeting for a returning hero. She was his only daughter and so sacrificing her left him childless. Jephthah **tore his clothes** and mourned her loss, though his mourning was not so much for her but for himself.

11:36-40 Jephthah's daughter was very different from her father. She had no recriminations for him, only an exhortation to fulfill his vow, just as the Lord had fulfilled the conditions. Unlike Abraham, whose faithfulness to God's demand resulted in a multitude of descendants, Jephthah's "faithfulness" issued in the complete cutting off of his line. That is part of what made the fact that she would die a virgin something to be mourned. She died unfulfilled because she would never get married and have children. Such a fate would normally condemn someone to be numbered among the unremembered in Israel. However, though Jephthah's daughter has no name in the text, the **young women of Israel** honored her memory year after year.

12:1-3 In a replay of the explosive situation that Gideon had faced and successfully defused in chapter 8, the **men of Ephraim** came out and complained to Jephthah about not being invited to the battle against the Ammonites. They

threatened to **burn** his **house down** with him in it. Ironically, in sacrificing his only daughter, Jephthah had already destroyed his own "house." Jephthah claimed that he **called** them and they didn't come **to deliver** him, whereupon he took his life in his hands and the Lord gave the Ammonites into his hands. Jephthah's claim is not confirmed by the text and may be a convenient fabrication. Significantly, he was not willing to place this dispute in the hands of God, as he was with the Ammonites (11:27); the Lord's name appears in Jephthah's argument only as a means of furthering his claims.

12:4-7 Jephthah took action against the Ephraimites because they questioned the legitimacy of Gilead. The illegitimate son who had achieved social acceptability could not tolerate this insult, so he called out the troops once more, this time against a tribe from his own people. There is no mention of the Spirit of the Lord coming on him or giving his enemies into his hand in this conflict. Those who escaped (in a neat twist, the true "fugitives of Ephraim") and attempted to get back across the **Jordan** River to Ephraim were met at the fords with a test question, **Please say Shibboleth**. The Hebrew word *shibboleth* has no clear meaning, but in the Ephraimite dialect, it was apparently pronounced **sibboleth**. In view of this kin-group strife that caused **42,000** deaths, it is not surprising that though **Jephthah judged Israel six years**, there is no mention of the land experiencing any rest during his tenure.

12:8-15 After Jephthah, there were three minor judges, **Ibzan . . . Elon**, and **Abdon**. Ibzan had 30 sons and 30 daughters,

Israel after Jephthah ⁹and had 30 sons. He gave his 30 daughters in marriage to men outside the tribe and brought back 30 wives for his sons from outside the tribe. Ibzan judged Israel seven years, ¹⁰and when he died, he was buried in Bethlehem.

¹¹Elon, who was from Zebulun, judged Israel after Ibzan. He judged Israel 10 years, ¹²and when he died, he was buried in Aijalon in the land of Zebulun.

¹³After Elon, Abdon son of Hillel, who was from Pirathon,ᵃ judged Israel. ¹⁴He had 40 sons and 30 grandsons, who rode on 70 donkeys. Abdon judged Israel eight years, ¹⁵and when he died, he was buried in Pirathon in the land of Ephraim, in the hill country of the Amalekites.ᵇ

Birth of Samson, the Last Judge

13 The Israelites again did what was evil in the LORD's sight,ᶜ so the LORD handed them over to the Philistines 40 years. ²There

was a certain man from Zorah,ᵈ from the family of Dan, whose name was Manoah; his wife was unable to conceive and had no children. ³The Angel of the LORD appeared to the woman and said to her, "It is true that you are unable to conceive and have no children, but you will conceive and give birth to a son. ⁴Now please be careful not to drink wine or beer,ᵉ or to eat anything •unclean;ᶠ ⁵for indeed, you will conceive and give birth to a son. You must never cut his hair,ᴬ because the boy will be a Naziriteᵍ to God from birth, and he will begin to save Israel from the power of the Philistines."

⁶Then the woman went and told her husband, "A man of God came to me. He looked like the awe-inspiring Angel of God. I didn't ask Him where He came from, and He didn't tell me His name. ⁷He said to me, 'You will conceive and give birth to a son. Therefore, do not drink wine or beer, and do not eat

ᵃ12:13 2Sm 23:30; 1Ch 11:31; 27:14
ᵇ12:15 Gn 14:7; Nm 14:45; 2Sm 1:8,13
ᶜ13:1 Jdg 3:12; 4:1; 10:6
ᵈ13:2 Jos 19:42; Jdg 13:25; 16:31; 18:2,8,11
ᵉ13:4 Nm 6:3
ᶠLv 7:19,21; 22:8; Dt 12:22; 14:10; 15:22; Hs 9:3-4
ᵍ13:5 Nm 6:2

ᴬ13:5 Lit And a razor is not to go up on his head

---

in contrast to Jephthah's lost daughter, while Abdon had 40 sons and 30 grandsons, where Jephthah had no grandchildren. They practiced polygamy and acquired wealth (cp. 8:28-32). The summary description of the lives of these judges contrasts with the earlier part of the book. Before Gideon, the cycle concluded with "and the land had rest for __ years." After Gideon, the cycles conclude "and __ judged Israel __ years." In place of saviors, these men were mere office bearers; in place of rest, there was mere stability.

13:1 The story of the final judge, Samson, is introduced with the familiar pattern of doing evil and being handed over to

an enemy for a period of time. Based in the coastal plain, the **Philistines** were constantly seeking to expand their territory into the foothills of Israel. They were already a problem for Israel in 3:31, and they continued to be the chief threat to Israel during the time of Samuel and Saul. There is no mention on this occasion of Israel crying out for deliverance, yet the Lord would still send them a deliverer—of a sort.

13:2-5 The opening of Samson's story, **There was a certain man**, exactly matches that of Samuel, inviting comparison of these two sons born to formerly barren women. The name of his father, **Manoah**, means "rest," which is what Israel

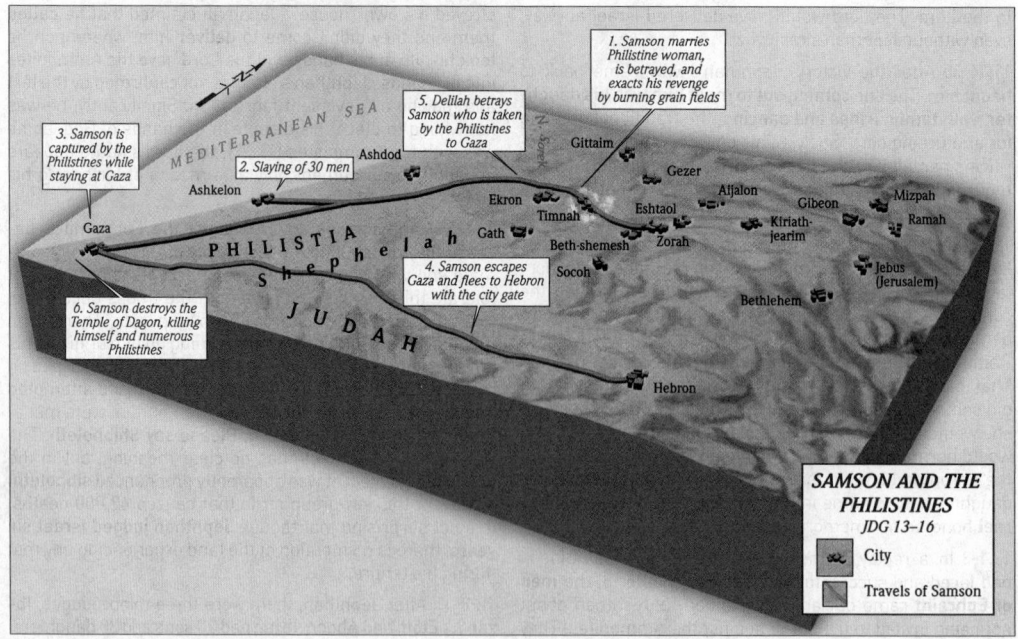

1. Samson marries Philistine woman, is betrayed, and exacts his revenge by burning grain fields
3. Samson is captured by the Philistines while staying at Gaza
5. Delilah betrays Samson who is taken by the Philistines to Gaza
2. Slaying of 30 men
4. Samson escapes Gaza and flees to Hebron with the city gate
6. Samson destroys the Temple of Dagon, killing himself and numerous Philistines

MEDITERRANEAN SEA
Ashdod
Ashkelon
Gaza
PHILISTIA
Shephelah
JUDAH
Gittaim
Gezer
Ekron
Timnah
Gath
Beth-shemesh
Socoh
Eshtaol
Zorah
Aijalon
Kiriath-jearim
Gibeon
Mizpah
Ramah
Jebus (Jerusalem)
Bethlehem
Hebron

SAMSON AND THE PHILISTINES
JDG 13–16
City
Travels of Samson

anything unclean, because the boy will be a Nazirite to God from birth until the day of his death.'"

[8] Manoah prayed[a] to the Lord and said, "Please Lord, let the man of God you sent come again to us and teach us what we should do for the boy who will be born."

[9] God listened[b] to[A] Manoah, and the Angel of God came again to the woman. She was sitting in the field, and her husband Manoah was not with her. [10] The woman ran quickly to her husband and told him, "The man who came to me today has just come back!"

[11] So Manoah got up and followed his wife. When he came to the man, he asked, "Are You the man who spoke to my wife?"

"I am," He said.

[12] Then Manoah asked, "When Your words come true, what will the boy's responsibilities and mission[B] be?"

[13] The Angel of the Lord answered Manoah, "Your wife needs to do everything I told

her. [14] She must not eat anything that comes from the grapevine or drink wine or beer. And she must not eat anything unclean. Your wife must do everything I have commanded her."

[15] "Please stay here," Manoah told Him, "and we will prepare a young goat[c] for You."

[16] The Angel of the Lord said to him, "If I stay, I won't eat your food. But if you want to prepare a *burnt offering, offer it to the Lord." For Manoah did not know He was the Angel of the Lord.

[17] Then Manoah said to Him, "What is Your name, so that we may honor You when Your words come true?"

[18] "Why do you ask My name," the Angel of the Lord asked him, "since it is wonderful."[d]

[19] Manoah took a young goat and a *grain offering and offered them on a rock to the Lord, and He did a wonderful thing[c] while Manoah and his wife were watching. [20] When the flame went up from the altar to the sky, the Angel of the Lord went up in its flame. When Manoah

[a]13:8 Gn 25:21; Ex 10:18; Jb 33:26
[b]13:9 Gn 16:11; Ex 16:8; Dt 1:45; 33:7; Jos 10:14; Ps 27:7
[c]13:15 Gn 18:5
[d]13:18 Gn 32:29

[A]13:9 Lit to the voice of   [B]13:12 Lit work   [C]13:19 LXX reads to the Lord, to the One who works wonders

---

lacked. The description of his wife as **unable to conceive** and having **no children** echoes the description of Sarah in Gn 11:30, raising expectations of a child who would be of great significance for God's plans. Their personal tragedy mirrored the pitiable state of the nation as a whole.

A Nazirite made a vow to abstain from **wine** and other alcoholic beverages, to remain separate from corpses and other sources of defilement, and to leave his hair uncut (Nm 6). Since the dietary restriction **not to . . . eat anything unclean** should have been observed by all Israelites all the time, it suggests that general standards of holiness were low during this period. The baby that she would bear would be called to **begin to save Israel from the power of the Philistines**, though others would finish the work.

The Lord's design for Samson paralleled His design for Israel. Israel was intended to be a holy people, because their Lord was holy (Lv 11:45). Their subsequent history and lack of faithfulness to their calling was matched by Samson's career as he disobeyed every single one of the vows made on his behalf. From the womb on, Samson is a picture of Israel—chosen for holiness, but defiled by his sinful actions.

13:8 The woman's husband, **Manoah**, prayed for a return visit from the angelic figure, presumably so they might receive additional instructions on how to raise this child. In reality, there was nothing more Manoah needed to know. Possibly he was jealous of the fact that the Angel appeared to his wife rather than to him.

13:9-14 God graciously responded to Manoah's request, though it is significant that when the Angel appeared again it was initially to the woman alone. Learning of the appearance, Manoah sought to question the Angel about his identity and the **mission** of the boy. The Angel simply repeated the instructions earlier given to his wife. There was nothing required of Manoah, only of his wife.

13:15-18 Manoah's invitation to a meal may have been an act of hospitality, but the effect of his actions is unwittingly made clear by his words **Please stay here**, which literally meant, "Let us detain you." The Angel declined Manoah's

offer, instead inviting him to present it as a **burnt offering** to the Lord. Manoah asked the Angel's name. Apparently, he was still unable to put the clues together and recognize the Angel of the Lord. The Angel refused to answer his question, affirming that his name was **wonderful**—"extraordinary" or "beyond understanding." In the OT, the Hebrew word translated "wonderful" is almost invariably used to describe God, not human experiences. If the formation of every child in the womb is "wonderful" (Ps 139:14), a work of God, how much more must this be true of a barren woman who would conceive?

13:19-21 Still Manoah failed to grasp the obvious. It was only when the heavenly messenger ascended in the flames going up from the altar that Manoah finally understood who this messenger was.

mal'ak

Hebrew Pronunciation	[mal AHKH]
HCSB Translation	angel, messenger
Uses in Judges	31
Uses in the OT	213
Focus Passage	Judges 13:3,6,9,13,15-18,20-21

Mal'ak refers to divine and human *messengers*. Mal'ak can mean *angel* and *messenger* in the same verse (2Kg 1:3). When indicating a divine manifestation, the phrase "*mal'ak* of the Lord" (58x) is translated *Angel of the Lord* (40x; Ex 3:2) or *Him* (2x). Otherwise the words (14x) imply a regular *angel* (1Kg 19:7). "*Mal'ak of God*" is synonymous with "*mal'ak* of the Lord" (Jdg 13:3,9). It identifies God (Gn 31:11) as One known to Israel (Jdg 13:6). It also indicates ordinary angels (1Sm 29:9). Mal'ak describes God elsewhere according to context (Gn 48:16). It can also describe prophets (Hg 1:13), priests (Mal 2:7), or ordinary messengers (1Sm 23:27). It can mean *envoy* (2Sm 5:11) or *ambassador* (Ezk 17:15). Mal'ak can denote *agents* (1Sm 19:11), even when rendered *men* (Jos 6:17). Winds and divine judgments are figuratively called *messengers* (Ps 78:49; 104:4).

and his wife saw this, they fell facedown on the ground. ²¹The Angel of the LORD did not appear again to Manoah and his wife. Then Manoah realized that it was the Angel of the LORD.

²²"We're going to die," he said to his wife, "because we have seen God!"ᵃ

²³But his wife said to him, "If the LORD had intended to kill us, He wouldn't have accepted the burnt offering and the grain offering from us, and He would not have shown us all these things or spoken to us now like this."

²⁴So the woman gave birth to a son and named him Samson.ᵇ The boy grew,ᶜ and the LORD blessed him. ²⁵Then the Spirit of the LORD began to direct him in the Camp of Dan,ᴬ between Zorah and Eshtaol.ᵈ

Samson's Riddle

14 Samson went down to Timnahᵉ and saw a young Philistine woman there. ²He went back and told his father and his mother: "I have seen a young Philistine woman in Timnah. Now get her for me as a wife."

³But his father and mother said to him, "Can't you findᴮ a young woman among your relatives or among any of our people? Must you go to the uncircumcised Philistines for a wife?"

But Samson told his father, "Get her for me, because I want her."ᶜ ⁴Now his father and

mother did not know this was from the LORD,ᶠ who was seeking an occasion against the Philistines. At that time, the Philistines were ruling over Israel.

⁵Samson went down to Timnah with his father and mother and came to the vineyards of Timnah. Suddenly a young lion came roaring at him, ⁶the Spirit of the LORD took control of ᴰ,ᵍ him, and he tore the lion apart with his bare hands as he might have torn a young goat. But he did not tell his father or mother what he had done. ⁷Then he went and spoke to the woman, because Samson wanted her.ᴱ

⁸After some time, when he returned to get her, he left the road to see the lion's carcass, and there was a swarm of bees with honey in the carcass. ⁹He scooped some honey into his hands and ate it as he went along. When he returned to his father and mother, he gave some to them and they ate it. But he did not tell them that he had scooped the honey from the lion's carcass.ʰ

¹⁰His father went to visit the woman, and Samson prepared a feast there, as young men were accustomed to do. ¹¹When the Philistines saw him, they brought 30 men to accompany him.

¹²"Let me tell you a riddle,"ⁱ Samson said to them. "If you can explain it to me during the seven days of the feast and figure it out, I will

ᵃ13:22 Gn 33:10; Ex 24:10; 33:20; Jdg 6:22; Is 6:5 ᵇ13:24 Heb 11:32 ᶜ1Sm 3:19; Lk 1:80 ᵈ13:25 Jos 15:33; Jdg 16:31; 18:2,8,11; 1Ch 2:53 ᵉ14:1 Jos 15:10; 19:43; 2Ch 28:18 ᶠ14:4 Jos 11:20; 1Kg 12:15; 2Kg 6:33 ᵍ14:6 Jdg 14:19; 15:14; 1Sm 10:6,10; 11:6; 16:13; 18:10 ʰ14:9 Lv 11:27 ⁱ14:12 Nm 12:8; Ps 49:4; Pr 1:6; Ezk 17:2; Dn 8:23

ᴬ13:25 Or in Mahaneh-dan   ᴮ14:3 Lit Is there not   ᶜ14:3 Lit because she is right in my eyes   ᴰ14:6 Lit LORD rushed on   ᴱ14:7 Lit because she was right in the eyes of Samson

13:22-23 Manoah's wife understood God better than her husband. Once he recognized the Angel of the Lord, Manoah thought both he and his wife would **die**. This was indeed the standard penalty for seeing God (Ex 33:20). As Manoah's wife noted, God obviously had other intentions.

13:24-25 So **Samson** was born as a result of the miraculous intervention of God. As he grew, **the Spirit of the LORD began to direct him**. These elements raise the expectation that he would be used by God powerfully to deliver His people—expectations that would be partially fulfilled but mostly unmet in what followed.

14:1-2 After Samson's empowering by the Spirit in 13:25, his next action should have been calling out the Lord's people to battle the Philistines. Instead, he wanted to marry a Philistine woman whom he **saw** in **Timnah**. This city was only six miles west of Zorah, Samson's hometown (13:2), but it was in the hands of the Philistines. To get there involved going **down**, both physically and spiritually.

14:3-4 Samson's parents asked him in vain if there were no women among his relatives whom he could marry. Intermarriage with the Philistines was a denial of Samson's calling as a Nazirite, and his choice of a bride contrasts strongly with the "ideal" wife of Othniel, the first judge, who married Caleb's daughter. Samson said of the woman he "saw" (v. 1), **I want her**, which is literally, "she is right in my eyes." In this he represented Israel, where each citizen "did whatever he wanted" (17:6; 21:25), literally, "what was right in his eyes."

Yet the Lord would use even Samson's sinful desires to accomplish His purposes. The text literally says **his father and his mother did not know that** she **was from the LORD**. This Philistine woman would be the means God would use to stir up Samson to begin a conflict with the Philistines, who were ruling Israel at this time. Again, the absence of any mention of Israel crying out to the Lord is striking.

14:5-6 On another occasion, Samson was going **down to Timnah** with his parents when a **young lion** rushed at him. This attack happened as he came to the **vineyards of Timnah**, an odd place for a Nazirite to be, since he was required to avoid all contact with grape products. The ease with which Samson disposed of the lion raises questions about why he had not yet begun to dispense with the enemies of the Lord—the Philistines.

14:8-9 Some time later, as Samson traveled the same road, he turned aside to see the **lion's carcass**. As a Nazirite, he was supposed to remain distant from corpses, yet here he not only went to see the lion's carcass but also scooped out of it **some honey**. Not only did Samson defile himself, he also defiled his parents by bringing them some of the honey but not informing them of its source. **He gave some to them and they ate it** uses the same vocabulary as when Eve gave Adam the fruit.

14:10-13 Having broken his Nazirite vow by deliberately touching the carcass of the lion, Samson then proceeded to despise it further by hosting a drinking party (the Hebrew

give you 30 linen garments and 30 changes of clothes. [13]But if you can't explain it to me, you must give me 30 linen garments and 30 changes of clothes."

"Tell us your riddle," they replied.[A] "Let's hear it."

[14]So he said to them:

> Out of the eater came something to eat,
> and out of the strong came something sweet.

After three days, they were unable to explain the riddle. [15]On the fourth[B] day they said to Samson's wife, "Persuade your husband to explain the riddle to us, or we will burn you and your father's household to death. Did you invite us here to rob us?"

[16]So Samson's wife came to him, weeping, and said, "You hate me and don't love me![a] You told my people the riddle, but haven't explained it to me."

"Look," he said,[c] "I haven't even explained it to my father or mother, so why should I explain it to you?"

[17]She wept the whole seven days of the feast, and at last, on the seventh day, he explained it to her, because she had nagged him so much. Then she explained it to her people. [18]On the seventh day, before sunset, the men of the city said to him:

> What is sweeter than honey?
> What is stronger than a lion?

a14:16 Jdg 16:15
b15:1 Gn 30:14; Ex 34:22; 1Sm 6:13; 12:17
c15:3 Nm 5:19,28,31; 1Sm 26:9; Jr 2:35
d15:4 Neh 4:3; Ps 63:10; Sg 2:15; Lm 5:18; Ezk 13:4
e15:5 Ex 22:6

So he said to them:

> If you hadn't plowed with
> my young cow,
> you wouldn't know my riddle now!

[19]The Spirit of the LORD took control of him, and he went down to Ashkelon and killed 30 of their men. He stripped them and gave their clothes to those who had explained the riddle. In a rage, Samson returned to his father's house, [20]and his wife was given to one of the men who had accompanied him.

Samson's Revenge

15 Later on, during the wheat harvest,[b] Samson took a young goat as a gift and visited his wife. "I want to go to my wife in her room," he said. But her father would not let him enter.

[2]"I was sure you hated her," her father said, "so I gave her to one of the men who accompanied you. Isn't her younger sister more beautiful than she is? Why not take her instead?"

[3]Samson said to them, "This time I won't be responsible[c] when I harm the Philistines." [4]So he went out and caught 300 foxes.[d] He took torches, turned the foxes tail-to-tail, and put a torch between each pair of tails. [5]Then he ignited the torches and released the foxes into the standing grain of the Philistines. He burned up the piles of grain and the standing grain as well as the vineyards and olive groves.[e]

A14:13 Lit replied to him   B14:15 LXX, Syr; MT reads seventh   C14:16 Lit said to her

---

word "feast" comes from the word "to drink") for his new pagan friends. As the drinking party progressed, Samson proposed a **riddle** that would cost every one of his 30 companions a suit of clothing—an outer garment and a tunic—if they lost and would cost him 30 suits if they were able to solve it before the end of the feast.

14:14-15 Without the interpretive key of Samson's experience with the lion, his riddle was unsolvable. On the fourth day, realizing this, the young men blackmailed Samson's betrothed **wife**. They feared that Samson's riddle would **rob** them or, more precisely, "dispossess" them. The verb "dispossess" is often used of the Israelite conquests in the land, which highlights the Lord's hand in this dispute.

14:16-17 The woman then emotionally blackmailed Samson, claiming that, if he wouldn't tell her the answer to his riddle, then he didn't love her. Their exchange highlights a key issue. She referred to the Philistines as **my people**, while he regarded his parents as the primary circle of his intimacy. They belonged to two different peoples, with naturally opposed loyalties. In the end, under the pressure of her nagging, Samson relented.

14:18-20 The Philistines' answer not only solved Samson's riddle, but spoke of the current situation at the wedding: though Samson had proved himself stronger than a lion, the sweetness of a woman's love was more powerful still. Samson's response is another miniature poem. As well as

a denunciation of their cheating, this reply was also a sharp insult to his Philistine bride. Samson vented his anger by killing 30 Philistines in Ashkelon to acquire the suits of clothing necessary to pay his debt. This act was triggered by the **Spirit of the LORD** rushing on him, which shows that his act of personal vengeance was used by the Lord to begin to execute judgment against the Philistines. Samson returned to his father's house in Zorah, still angry, while his Philistine father-in-law gave his daughter to one of the 30 young men who had been guarding Samson.

15:1-3 Though Samson left Timnah in anger, it was not his intent to call off the wedding. He returned a few weeks later, **during the wheat harvest** in May, with a conventional hospitality gift—**a young goat**—intending to go to his wife's room to consummate the marriage. The father had interpreted Samson's anger as a definitive breach in the relationship, and he had given his daughter to one of the other young men. Nonetheless, he tried to placate Samson by offering him his younger and more attractive daughter. Samson was not so easily pacified. Instead, he vowed to **harm the Philistines**, thus executing the Lord's purpose in 14:4.

15:4-8 Like Gideon, Samson took on the Lord's enemies with an army of **300**, along with some **torches**. His army was made up of **foxes** (or perhaps jackals, which were more common in this area) rather than fellow Israelites because Samson always fought alone. He then fixed burning torches

⁶Then the Philistines asked, "Who did this?"

They were told, "It was Samson, the Timnite's son-in-law, because he has taken Samson's wife and given her to another man." So the Philistines went to her and her father and burned them to death.

⁷Then Samson told them, "Because you did this, I swear that I won't rest until I have taken vengeance on you." ⁸He tore them limb from limbᴬ with a great slaughter, and he went down and stayed in the cave at the rock of Etam.

⁹The Philistines went up, camped in Judah, and raided Lehi. ¹⁰So the men of Judah said, "Why have you attacked us?"

They replied, "We have come to arrest Samson and pay him back for what he did to us."

¹¹Then 3,000 men of Judah went to the cave at the rock of Etam, and they asked Samson, "Don't you realize that the Philistines rule over us?ᵃ What have you done to us?"

"I have done to them what they did to me," he answered.ᴮ

¹²They said to him, "We've come to arrest you and hand you over to the Philistines."

Then Samson told them, "Swear to me that you yourselves won't kill me."

¹³"No," they said,ᶜ "we won't kill you, but we will tie you up securely and hand you over to them." So they tied him up with two new ropesᵇ and led him away from the rock.

ᵃ15:11 Lv 26:25; Dt 28:43; Jdg 13:1; 14:4; Ps 106:40-42
ᵇ15:13 Jdg 16:11-12
ᶜ15:19 Gn 45:27; 1Kg 17:22; 2Kg 13:21; Is 38:16,21; Ezk 37:3,14
ᵈ16:1 Jos 15:47

¹⁴When he came to Lehi, the Philistines came to meet him shouting. The Spirit of the Lord took control ofᴰ him, and the ropes that were on his arms became like burnt flax and his bonds fell off his wrists. ¹⁵He found a fresh jawbone of a donkey, reached out his hand, took it, and killed 1,000 men with it. ¹⁶Then Samson said:

> With the jawbone of a donkey
> I have piled them in a heap.
> With the jawbone of a donkey
> I have killed 1,000 men.

¹⁷When he finished speaking, he threw away the jawbone and named that place Ramath-lehi.ᴱ ¹⁸He became very thirsty and called out to the Lord: "You have accomplished this great victory throughᶠ Your servant. Must I now die of thirst and fall into the hands of the uncircumcised?" ¹⁹So God split a hollow place in the ground at Lehi, and water came out of it. After Samson drank, his strength returned, and he revived.ᶜ That is why he named it En-hakkore,ᴳ which is in Lehi to this day. ²⁰And he judged Israel 20 years in the days of the Philistines.

Samson and Delilah

16 Samson went to Gaza,ᵈ where he saw a prostitute and went to bed with her. ²When the Gazites heard that Samson was there, they surrounded the place and waited

ᴬ15:8 Lit He struck them hip on thigh   ᴮ15:11 Lit answered them   ᶜ15:13 Lit said to him   ᴰ15:14 Lit Lord rushed on
ᴱ15:17 = High Place of the Jawbone   ᶠ15:18 Lit through the hand of   ᴳ15:19 = Spring of the One Who Cried Out

to the animals' tails and sent them among the fields that were ready for harvesting, damaging all of the Philistines' major crops at a crucial point in the agricultural cycle. The Philistines retaliated by burning **Samson's wife** and **her father**, fulfilling the threat they had made earlier (14:15). Samson escalated the cycle of violence by slaughtering another batch of Philistines. The meaning of the idiom, literally, "he struck them hip on thigh" is uncertain, but it clearly reflects a violent manner of death—as in tearing them **limb from limb**.

15:9-11 The **Philistines** then **camped in Judah**. With the other judges, this would have been the cue for the judge to lead out the armies of the Lord against them. However, the Judahites showed no sign of wanting to be delivered. Nor was Samson motivated by a desire to deliver his people; his actions were aimed at gaining revenge for himself.

15:12-17 The Judahites were determined to hand Samson over to the Philistines, as evidence of their good faith submission. Samson, confident in his own strength, was quite content to be handed over. When **the Philistines came to meet him shouting**, their approach was reminiscent of that of the roaring lion in the previous chapter. So too was their fate: Samson seized the **fresh jawbone of a donkey** and promptly dispatched 1,000 of the opposition. The word "fresh" emphasizes Samson's neglect of his Nazirite vows—this time by plundering the corpse of an animal

for his weapon. Samson's response was to give himself all the glory for the slaughter (cp. Gn 4:23). Whereas Deborah's song praised God for giving His people the victory (Jdg 5), Samson's song praised himself for making **a heap** (or "a donkey"; the Hebrew words are identical) out of his enemies. He also renamed the location **Ramath-lehi** ("High Place of the Jawbone") in honor of his feat.

15:18-19 Samson calling **out to the Lord** for a drink is once again a vivid picture of Israel, ascribing his victories to himself and only crying out to the Lord in time of trouble. When he found himself in need, the orthodox vocabulary reasserted itself. He was now "the Lord's servant." When in need, Samson sought the Lord's deliverance, but as soon as the crisis was over, he returned to his old ways. The parallel between Samson and Israel is highlighted by the echoes of Israel's wilderness experience of Exodus 17, where the Lord had made water come out of the rock for His people. Typically, instead of naming the spring that revived him after the Lord, Samson named it after himself, calling it **En-hakkore**, "The Spring of the Caller."

15:20 In this way, Samson **judged Israel 20 years**. Normally this notice comes at the end of the story of a judge. In this case, there is another chapter in the story in which Samson is operating on his own strength, abandoned by God, a tragedy waiting to happen.

16:1-3 The opening verse parallels 14:1. Samson went to a

in ambush for him all that night at the city gate. While they were waiting quietly,^A they said, "Let us wait until dawn; then we will kill him." ³But Samson stayed in bed until midnight when he got up, took hold of the doors of the city gate along with the two gateposts, and pulled them out, bar and all. He put them on his shoulders and took them to the top of the mountain overlooking Hebron.

⁴Some time later, he fell in love with a woman named Delilah, who lived in the Sorek Valley. ⁵The Philistine leaders^a went to her and said, "Persuade him to tell you^B where his great strength comes from, so we can overpower him, tie him up, and make him helpless. Each of us will then give you 1,100 pieces of silver."

⁶So Delilah said to Samson, "Please tell me, where does your great strength come from? How could someone tie you up and make you helpless?"

⁷Samson told her, "If they tie me up with seven fresh bowstrings that have not been dried, I will become weak and be like any other man."

⁸The Philistine leaders brought her seven fresh bowstrings that had not been dried, and she tied him up with them. ⁹While the men in ambush were waiting in her room, she called out to him, "Samson, the Philistines are here!"^C But he snapped the bowstrings as a strand of yarn snaps when it touches fire. The secret of his strength remained unknown.

*a*16:5 Jos 13:3
*b*16:11 Jdg 15:13
*c*16:15 Jdg 14:6
*d*16:17 Nm 6:5; Jdg 13:5

¹⁰Then Delilah said to Samson, "You have mocked me and told me lies! Won't you please tell me how you can be tied up?"

¹¹He told her, "If they tie me up with new ropes that have never been used,^b I will become weak and be like any other man."

¹²Delilah took new ropes, tied him up with them, and shouted, "Samson, the Philistines are here!"^C But while the men in ambush were waiting in her room, he snapped the ropes off his arms like a thread.

¹³Then Delilah said to Samson, "You have mocked me all along and told me lies! Tell me how you can be tied up."

He told her, "If you weave the seven braids on my head with the web of a loom—"^D

¹⁴She fastened the braids with a pin and called to him, "Samson, the Philistines are here!"^C He awoke from his sleep and pulled out the pin, with the loom and the web.

¹⁵"How can you say, 'I love you,'"^c she told him, "when your heart is not with me? This is the third time you have mocked me and not told me what makes your strength so great!"

¹⁶Because she nagged him day after day and pleaded with him until she wore him out,^E ¹⁷he told her the whole truth and said to her, "My hair has never been cut,^F because I am a Nazirite^d to God from birth. If I am shaved, my strength will leave me, and I will become weak and be like any other man."

¹⁸When Delilah realized that he had told

---

^A16:2 Lit *quietly all night*   ^B16:5 Lit *him and see*   ^C16:9,12,14 Lit *are on you*   ^D16:13-14 LXX reads *loom and fasten them with a pin into the wall and I will become weak and be like any other man.* ¹⁴ *And while he was sleeping, Delilah wove the seven braids on his head into the loom.*   ^E16:16 Lit *him and he became short to death*   ^F16:17 Lit *A razor has not gone up on my head*

Philistine town and **saw** a woman. Like the history of Israel, the spiral in Samson's life is downwards. This time he didn't want to marry her, he just wanted to sleep with her. **Gaza** was the most distant city of the Philistines from Samson's home, which symbolizes how far from God Samson had gone. When the Philistines heard that he was there, they surrounded the city and waited for him at the only exit, **the city gate**. Yet such was Samson's enormous strength that the Philistines were unable to trap him. His vast show of strength in uprooting the city gate and carrying it roughly 40 miles uphill to the **mountain overlooking Hebron** heightens the irony of his subsequent weakness in the hands of a woman.

16:4-5 Women were Samson's problem all along, yet his encounter with **Delilah** is the only case where **love** is mentioned. Once again, his heart was set on a Philistine woman. Delilah's name sounds like the Hebrew word for "night," in keeping with the darkness that was about to descend on Samson. The **Philistine leaders**, the rulers of the five city-states that made up that region (1Sm 6:17-18), sought to persuade Delilah to determine the secret of Samson's strength by promising her an enormous sum of money—**1,100 pieces of silver** from each leader. In comparison, the price of an ordinary slave was 30 pieces of silver (Ex 21:32).

16:6-9 Bowstrings were made from the sinews of animals, so **fresh bowstrings** would come directly from an animal's

corpse. As with the earlier incidents with honey from a lion and the jawbone of the donkey, Samson displayed a disdain for his Nazirite vow of separation from corpses. Since seven was seen as the number of completeness in the ancient Near East, the idea of being weakened by seven bowstrings wrongly suggested that the source of Samson's strength lay in magic rather than in the Lord.

16:10-12 This time Samson told Delilah to use **new ropes** to bind him. This was the same technique that the Israelites used to bind Samson in 15:13, so it is no surprise that the attempt was unsuccessful.

16:13-14 The third time Delilah sought the secret of his strength, he told her to **weave . . . seven braids** of his hair into a fabric. This attempt, while also unsuccessful, was more ominous than the previous ones. Not only did Samson point to the connection between his hair and his strength, but the image of a woman standing over a sleeping man with a **pin** in her hands is reminiscent of Jael approaching the sleeping form of Sisera.

16:15-17 Finally Samson told Delilah **the whole truth** (lit "everything of his heart"), that his strength came from his **Nazirite** vow, symbolized by his uncut hair. In fact, this was the only part of his Nazirite vow that he had not yet broken, and this revelation shows how lightly he took it.

16:18-20 Delilah **realized** that this time she had the secret,

her the whole truth, she sent this message to the Philistine leaders: "Come one more time, for he has told me the whole truth." The Philistine leaders came to her and brought the money with them.

[19] Then she let him fall asleep on her lap and called a man to shave off the seven braids on his head. In this way, she made him helpless,[A] and his strength left him. [20] Then she cried, "Samson, the Philistines are here!"[B] When he awoke from his sleep, he said, "I will escape as I did before and shake myself free." But he did not know that the LORD had left him.[a]

Samson's Defeat and Death

[21] The Philistines seized him and gouged out his eyes. They brought him down to Gaza and bound him with bronze shackles, and he was forced to grind grain in the prison. [22] But his hair began to grow back after it had been shaved.

[23] Now the Philistine leaders gathered together to offer a great sacrifice to their god Dagon.[b] They rejoiced and said:

Our god has handed over
our enemy Samson to us.

[24] When the people saw him, they praised their god[c] and said:

Our god has handed over to us

our enemy who destroyed our land
and who multiplied our dead.

[25] When they were drunk,[c] they said, "Bring Samson here to entertain us." So they brought Samson from prison, and he entertained them. They had him stand between the pillars. [26] Samson said to the young man who was leading him by the hand, "Lead me where I can feel the pillars supporting the temple, so I can lean against them." [27] The temple was full of men and women; all the leaders of the Philistines were there, and about 3,000 men and women were on the roof watching Samson entertain them. [28] He called out to the LORD: "Lord GOD, please remember me.[d] Strengthen me, God, just once more. With one act of vengeance, let me pay back the Philistines for my two eyes." [29] Samson took hold of the two middle pillars supporting the temple and leaned against them, one on his right hand and the other on his left. [30] Samson said, "Let me die with the Philistines." He pushed with all his might, and the temple fell on the leaders and all the people in it. And the dead he killed at his death were more than those he had killed in his life.

[31] Then his brothers and his father's family came down, carried him back, and buried him between Zorah and Eshtaol in the tomb

a16:20 Nm 14:9,42-43; Jos 7:12; 1Sm 16:14; 18:12; 28:15-16; 2Ch 15:2
b16:23 Jos 15:41; 19:27; 1Sm 5:2-5,7; 1Ch 10:10
c16:24 Dn 5:4
d16:28 Jr 15:15

A16:19 LXX reads way he began to weaken　B16:20 Lit are on you　C16:25 Or When they were feeling good

so rather than just saying, "The Philistines are here!" (vv. 9,12,14), she actually summoned the Philistine leaders, and they shaved Samson's head. With the final element of his Nazirite vow gone, his power was lost.

16:21-22 Samson was carried off to exile in **Gaza**, the city of his earlier exploits in verses 1-3. His eyes, which had caused so many of his problems, were removed by the Phi-

listines, and his strength was put to work in their service, grinding **grain**. In the midst of his hopeless situation, there was a ray of hope: **his hair began to grow back**.

16:23-27 The name **Dagon** is related to the word for "grain," which suggests an agricultural role for this deity to which the Philistines also ascribed a role in capturing their tormentor, Samson. In fact, Samson's capture was possible only because the Lord had left him (v. 20). As the party progressed, they summoned Samson to entertain them, presumably by being the butt of their mocking humor. In the process, they brought him to the center of the **temple**, whose roof was probably supported by cedar **pillars**.

16:28-31 Samson **called out to the LORD**, just as he had in 15:18, asking the Lord to **remember** him. In the OT, to "remember" means not simply to think about someone but to act on their behalf (see note at Gn 8:1). His motivation was still self-centered: he wanted to pay them back for the loss of his eyes. In the process of destroying the building, he fulfilled his destiny: he began "to save Israel from the power of the Philistines" (Jdg 13:5). Yet the task was left unfinished at his death. His body was retrieved to be buried with his family, but his period of leadership achieved no rest for the people.

17:1-21:25 This last section of the book of Judges stands outside the downward cycles of the middle portion of the book, yet it brings to conclusion two of its central threads: idolatrous worship, which comes to a head at Dan (chaps. 17-18), and sexual immorality, which comes to a head with

pa'am

Hebrew Pronunciation	[PA am]
HCSB Translation	foot, time, step
Uses in Judges	13
Uses in the OT	118
Focus Passage	Judges 16:15,18,20,28

Ugaritic and Punic each had two similar words that seem combined in *pa'am*, which means *foot* (Ex 25:12) and *time* (Gn 29:35). *Pa'am* with the article implies *at last* (Gn 2:23), *one time* (Gn 18:32), *once*, or *this time*. The dual means *twice*, and the plural with numerals means *times*. *Pa'am* implies *occasion* (Dt 9:19), *instant*, or *now* (Pr 7:12). "As *pa'am* by *pa'am*" implies *as on previous occasions* (Nm 24:1), *as before*, or *as usual*. *Pa'am* specifies *hoofbeats* (Jdg 5:28), *human feet* (Is 37:25) or *steps* (Ps 57:6), and *furniture feet* or *corners* (1Kg 7:30). Context suggests *campaign* (Jos 10:42) and *tiers* (1Kg 7:4). The verb *pa'am* (5x) means *direct* (Jdg 13:25). Passive and reflexive forms signify *be disturbed*, *troubled* (Gn 41:8), or *anxious*. *Pa'amon* (7x) means *bell* (Ex 28:33). A common denominator of these words may be striking action.

of his father Manoah. So he judged Israel 20 years.

Micah's Priest

17 There was a man from the hill country of Ephraim named Micah. [2] He said to his mother, "The 1,100 pieces of silver taken from you, and that I heard you utter a curse about—here, I have the silver with me. I took it. So now I return it to you."[A]

Then his mother said, "My son, you are blessed by the LORD!"[a]

[3] He returned the 1,100 pieces of silver to his mother, and his mother said, "I personally consecrate[b] the silver to the LORD for my son's benefit to make a carved image overlaid with silver."[B] [4] So he returned the silver to his mother, and she took five pounds of silver and gave it to a silversmith. He made it into a carved image overlaid with silver,[B] and it was in Micah's house.

[5] This man Micah had a shrine, and he made an *ephod and household idols,[c] and installed one of his sons to be his priest. [6] In those days there was no king in Israel;[d] everyone did whatever he wanted.[C]

[7] There was a young man, a Levite from Bethlehem in Judah, who resided within the clan of Judah.[e] [8] The man left the town of Bethlehem in Judah to settle wherever he could find a place. On his way he came to Micah's home in the hill country of Ephraim.

[9] "Where do you come from?" Micah asked him.

He answered him, "I am a Levite from Bethlehem in Judah, and I'm going to settle wherever I can find a place."

[10] Micah replied,[D] "Stay with me and be my father[f] and priest, and I will give you four ounces of silver a year, along with your clothing and provisions." So the Levite went in [11] and agreed to stay with the man, and the young man became like one of his sons. [12] Micah consecrated the Levite, and the young man became his priest[g] and lived in Micah's house. [13] Then Micah said, "Now I know that the LORD will be good to me, because a Levite has become my priest."

Dan's Invasion and Idolatry

18 In those days, there was no king in Israel,[h] and the Danite tribe was looking for territory to occupy. Up to that time no territory had been captured by them among the tribes of Israel. [2] So the Danites sent out five brave men[i] from all their clans, from Zorah and Eshtaol,[j] to scout[k] out the land and explore it. They told them, "Go and explore the land."

They came to the hill country of Ephraim as

a17:2 Ru 2:20; 1Sm 15:13
b17:3 Lv 22:2-3; 27:14-19; 1Ch 18:11; 26:26-28; 2Ch 30:17
c17:5 Gn 31:19,34-35; Jdg 18:14; 1Sm 19:13; 2Kg 23:24; Hs 3:4
d17:6 Jdg 18:1; 19:1; 21:25
e17:7 Dt 18:6-7
f17:10 Gn 45:8; Jdg 18:19; Jr 3:19
g17:12 Jdg 18:30
h18:1 Jdg 17:6; 19:1; 21:25
i18:2 Dt 3:18; 1Sm 14:52; 18:17; 2Sm 2:7; 13:28; 17:10; 1Kg 1:52; 2Kg 2:16
jJos 19:40-41; Jdg 13:2,25
kNm 13:17; Jos 2:1

A17:2 MT places this sentence at the end of v. 3.   B17:3,4 Or *image and a cast image*   C17:6 Lit *did what was right in his eyes*
D17:10 Lit *replied to him*

Israel's reenactment of the sin (and fall) of Sodom and Gomorrah (chaps. 19–21).

17:1-4 This section begins with **Micah** ("Who is like Yahweh?") confessing to his **mother** that he had stolen from her **1,100 pieces of silver** (a fortune in that time). Fear of the **curse** she had uttered against the thief drove Micah to return it. His mother responded in orthodox fashion: **My son, you are blessed by the LORD.** By this she sought to cancel out the earlier curse. Yet she then consecrated this same silver to the Lord to be made into a **carved image**. In addition, having vowed to dedicate all the silver to the Lord, she only gave **five pounds**, or two hundred shekels, of the silver to the silversmith for the idol.

17:5-6 Centers of personal devotion like Micah's shrine were outlawed in Deuteronomy 12. The ephod is reminiscent of the idol that Gideon constructed at Ophrah (Jdg 8:27). The household idols, or "teraphim," were often associated with divination (Zch 10:2) and were portable objects of veneration throughout the ancient Near East, although their exact form is unknown. Micah also installed **one of his sons to be his priest**, in opposition to the officially authorized Levitical priesthood. In those days **everyone did whatever he wanted** (lit "what was right in his own eyes," a lifestyle exemplified by Samson). The author may have been saying the lawlessness was because **there was no king in Israel**. Alternatively the author—who was writing this much later, and had seen how immorally Israel could function under a wicked king—may have been saying that even without a king to lead them astray, the people behaved atrociously all on their own.

17:7-8 At this point, a **Levite** arrived, a member of the priestly tribe. He was a **young man**, and therefore he would not have been qualified to serve as a priest in the orthodox worship of the Lord, which began at age 30 (Nm 4:3). He was also from **Bethlehem in Judah**, at the opposite end of Israel from Ephraim. The author does not name the young Levite until 18:30 (see note there). According to Dt 18:6-8, Levites who were residing in any of the clans of Israel were allowed to leave their homes and go to the place the Lord had chosen to join in His service there. This Levite, however, was seeking any place that he could find. His behavior is symptomatic of the general tendency in Israel at this time for each man to do "whatever he wanted" (Jdg 17:6).

17:10-13 Seizing the opportunity to have a priest with a legitimate genealogy, Micah engaged this Levite to be his **father and priest**. "Father" is a title of honor that reflects the role of the priest in communicating God's law to Israel (Dt 33:10) and thus shaping their behavior. Instead of the priestly terms of employment prescribed in Numbers 18, Micah promised him his clothing and lodging and four ounces of silver a year, a miserly sum in comparison to the amount of silver that was at his family's disposal (Jdg 18:2). Micah also personally **consecrated** the "priest" to his office (v. 12), emphasizing the Levite's subordinate nature in Micah's household. From Micah's statement in verse 13, it is clear that he viewed this Levite essentially as another idol, an attempted means of ensuring the Lord's blessing upon himself.

18:1-2 During this same period of apostasy, a group of **Danites** were also on the move. Like the Levite in Judges 17,

far as the home of Micah and spent the night there. ³While they were near Micah's home, they recognized the speech of the young Levite. So they went over to him and asked, "Who brought you here? What are you doing in this place? What is keeping you here?" ⁴He told them what Micah had done for him and that he had hired him as his priest.

⁵Then they said to him, "Please inquire of God so we will know if we will have a successful journey."

⁶The priest told them, "Go in peace. The LORD is watching over the journey you are going on."

⁷The five men left and came to Laish. They saw that the people who were there were living securely, in the same way as the Sidonians, quiet and unsuspecting. There was nothing lacking^A in the land and no oppressive ruler. They were far from the Sidonians, having no alliance with anyone.^B

⁸When the men went back to their clans at Zorah and Eshtaol, their people asked them, "What did you find out?"

⁹They answered, "Come on, let's go up against them, for we have seen the land, and it is very good. Why wait? Don't hesitate to go and invade and take possession of the land! ¹⁰When you get there, you will come to an unsuspecting people and a spacious land, for God has handed it over to you. It is a place where nothing on earth is lacking."^a ¹¹Six hundred Danites departed from Zorah and Eshtaol armed with weapons of war. ¹²They went up and camped at Kiriath-jearim^b in Ju-

ᵃ18:10 Dt 8:9
ᵇ18:12 Jos 9:17; 1Ch 13:5-6; 2Ch 1:4; Jr 26:20
ᶜ18:19 Jb 21:5; 29:9; 40:4; Mc 7:16

dah. This is why the place is called the Camp of Dan^C to this day; it is west of Kiriath-jearim. ¹³From there they traveled to the hill country of Ephraim and arrived at Micah's house. ¹⁴The five men who had gone to scout out the land of Laish told their brothers, "Did you know that there are an •ephod, household gods, and a carved image overlaid with silver^D in these houses? Now think about what you should do." ¹⁵So they detoured there and went to the house of the young Levite at the home of Micah and greeted him. ¹⁶The 600 Danite men were standing by the entrance of the gate, armed with their weapons of war. ¹⁷Then the five men who had gone to scout out the land went in and took the carved image overlaid with silver,^D the ephod, and the household idols, while the priest was standing by the entrance of the gate with the 600 men armed with weapons of war.

¹⁸When they entered Micah's house and took the carved image overlaid with silver,^D the ephod, and the household idols, the priest said to them, "What are you doing?"

¹⁹They told him, "Be quiet. Keep your mouth shut.^E,c Come with us and be a father and a priest to us. Is it better for you to be a priest for the house of one person or for you to be a priest for a tribe and family in Israel?" ²⁰So the priest was pleased and took his ephod, household idols, and carved image, and went with the people. ²¹They prepared to leave, putting their small children, livestock, and possessions in front of them.

²²After they were some distance from Micah's

---

^A18:7 Hb obscure   ^B18:7 MT; some LXX mss, Sym, Old Lat, Syr read *Aram*   ^C18:12 Or *called Mahaneh-dan*   ^D18:14,17,18 Or *image, the cast image*   ^E18:19 Lit *Put your hand on your mouth*

---

they were not content with the situation assigned them by the Lord and were looking for something better. They had earlier captured the cities of **Zorah and Eshtaol**, on the border between their territory and that of Judah, but they had been unable to conquer the rest of the territory allotted to them in Jos 19:40-48 (see Jdg 1:34). Instead of seeking the Lord's help in their struggle, they sent out spies in a reenactment of Nm 13–14, seeking a new land for themselves.

18:3-4 The spies came to Micah's house, where they encountered the Levite. Their questions exposed the underlying issue: "What is a Levite doing in a house of idolatry?" The Levite's reply revealed his mercenary motives. Micah **had hired him**, so the Levite was serving **as his priest**.

18:5-7 The spies asked the Levite to inquire of God whether their trip would be successful. It is significant that they used the generic description "God" rather than the personal, covenant name "the Lord." In response, without any effort to consult God, the Levite declared that their journey would be a success, because **the LORD was watching over** them. Since the Lord had assigned the Danites different territory, the Levite was misusing the Lord's name (Ex 20:7) to tell the Danites what they wanted to hear. Indeed, their mission was a success—in their terms. **Laish** was located in a produc-

tive agricultural area at the foot of Mount Hermon. Its inhabitants were **living . . . in the same way as the Sidonians**, which likely means that they viewed themselves as under the protection of Sidon. However, Sidon was a long way off, on the coast near Tyre.

18:8-13 The spies brought home a positive response about their journey, a report that contrasts starkly with that of the majority of the spies about the real promised land (Nm 13–14). Six hundred Danites responded, and they set up a staging post near **Kiriath-jearim**, which became known as the **Camp of Dan**. This was the same place where Samson started out in 13:25, which invites comparison between the Danites' self-centered conquests and those of Samson.

18:14-21 On the way to their new homeland, the Danites visited the home of Micah. The spies reported Micah's idolatry and invited a response. The right response would have been to destroy the idols and the shrine, to root out the sin from their midst. Instead, supported by the **600 men armed with weapons of war**, the spies went into the house and took the carved image, the ephod, and the household idols. When the young Levite objected, they bribed him to join them, offering him the prospect of being **a father and a priest** to an entire tribe rather than a single family. The party then

house, the men who were in the houses near it mobilized and caught up with the Danites. ²³They called to the Danites, who turned to face them, and said to Micah, "What's the matter with you that you mobilized the men?"

²⁴He said, "You took the gods I had made and the priest, and went away. What do I have left? How can you say to me, 'What's the matter with you?'"

²⁵The Danites said to him, "Don't raise your voice against us, or angry men will attack you, and you and your family will lose your lives." ²⁶The Danites went on their way, and Micah turned to go back home, because he saw that they were stronger than he was.

²⁷After they had taken the gods Micah had made and the priest that belonged to him, they went to Laish, to a quiet and unsuspecting people. They killed them with their swords and burned down the city.ᵃ ²⁸There was no one to rescue them because it was far from Sidon and they had no alliance with anyone. It was in a valley that belonged to Beth-rehob. They rebuilt the city and lived in it. ²⁹They named the city Dan, after the name of their ancestor Dan, who was born to Israel. The city was formerly named Laish.

ᵃ18:27 Jdg 1:8,25; 4:15-16
ᵇ18:30 2Kg 15:29
ᶜ19:1 Jdg 17:6; 18:1; 21:25
ᵈ19:3 Gn 34:3; 50:21

³⁰The Danites set up the carved image for themselves. Jonathan son of Gershom, son of Moses,ᴬ and his sons were priests for the Danite tribe until the time of the exile from the land.ᵇ ³¹So they set up for themselves Micah's carved image that he had made, and it was there as long as the house of God was in Shiloh.

Outrage in Benjamin

19 In those days, when there was no king in Israel,ᶜ a Levite living in a remote part of the hill country of Ephraim acquired a woman from Bethlehem in Judah as his concubine. ²But she was unfaithful toᴮ him and left him for her father's house in Bethlehem in Judah. She was there for a period of four months. ³Then her husband got up and went after her to speak kindly to herᶜ,ᵈ and bring her back. He had his servant with him and a pair of donkeys. So she brought him to her father's house, and when the girl's father saw him, he gladly welcomed him. ⁴His father-in-law, the girl's father, detained him, and he stayed with him for three days. They ate, drank, and spent the nights there.

⁵On the fourth day, they got up early in the

ᴬ18:30 Some Hb mss, LXX, Vg; other Hb mss read *Manasseh*   ᴮ19:2 LXX, Vg read *was angry with*   ᶜ19:3 Lit *speak to her heart*

---

formed up for travel again, with the most vulnerable members, the small children and livestock, positioned at the front, in case of reprisals by Micah.

18:22-26 When Micah **mobilized** (lit "cried out") his neighbors and pursued the **Danites**, the Danites asked him why he had done this. "Mobilized" is the same verb used to describe Israel's cry to the Lord when harassed by enemies. Here the Israelites had become their own oppressors. Micah had made his own gods and appointed his own priest, concluding that "Now I know the LORD will be good to me" (17:13). In fact, his gods could be carried off by a passing band of brigands, and the priest he had appointed for money could be lured away by a higher salary. He was left with nothing except his own life, and the Danites were quick to threaten that as well as the lives of his family. The silver he stole at the outset was now stolen from him; his mother's curse in 17:2 was fulfilled.

18:27-29 **Laish** was in a valley that belonged to **Beth-rehob**, a name that links this conquest by the Danites once again with the spying mission of Numbers 13–14, where Rehob was the northern limit of the land (Nm 13:21). They renamed Laish **Dan**, after their ancestor, and established it as the primary center for their idolatrous cult. Later, Jeroboam would locate one of his two golden calves in Dan, continuing the city's tradition of idolatry (1Kg 12:29).

18:30-31 The idol set up by the **Danites** served as a rival for the true worship of God, which was conducted where the ark was, **in Shiloh**. The Levite, introduced in 17:7, is finally named and is revealed to have an illustrious ancestry. He is **Jonathan**, the grandson of **Moses**. Later scribes who wrote out copies of the book of Judges naturally disdained the corrupt "Jonathan" and wished to show that he had greater affinity with the later idolatrous King Manasseh than he

did with Moses. Thus they placed the Hebrew letter *nun* in the middle of the name "Moses," making it read "Manasseh" instead. In this way they passed judgment on the false priest, linking him to evil Manasseh rather than righteous Moses. Since the scribes were careful to superscript the letter *nun* above the rest of the text, making it clear that it was not original to the text, we are not left in doubt that the original reading is "Moses."

Such an idolatrous cult as the Danites, even when served by a priesthood that enjoyed an exalted ancestry, could only have a negative outcome, as the reference to an **exile** makes clear. The mention of the exile suggests that the final editing of Judges occurred some time after the exile of the northern kingdom in 722 B.C.

19:1 The opening line of this chapter anticipates the story's direction. Like the Levite in the last story, this one was living in **the hill country of Ephraim**, and he was connected to **Bethlehem in Judah** (17:7,9), this time through marriage to a **concubine**, a lower-status wife. The Levite is nameless, as is almost every character in this story. This highlights the fact that this episode is not unique but was characteristic of these lawless times.

19:2-4 The Levite's concubine was **unfaithful to him**, a broad term that would cover sexual immorality and more general desertion. There was no provision in ancient Israel for a woman to divorce a man; nevertheless she left him and returned to her father's house. Finally after **four months**, the Levite went to try to persuade her to go back with him. The girl's father was glad to see him and gave him a warm welcome. As was typical in the ancient Near East, the requirements of hospitality took several days of feasting to fulfill.

19:5-9 On the morning of **the fourth day**, the Levite was eager to go on his way, but his host detained him with further

morning and prepared to go, but the girl's father said to his son-in-law, "Have something to eat to keep up your strength[a] and then you can go." [6] So they sat down and the two of them ate and drank together. Then the girl's father said to the man, "Please agree to stay overnight and enjoy yourself."[b] [7] The man got up to go, but his father-in-law persuaded him, so he stayed and spent the night there again. [8] He got up early in the morning of the fifth day to leave, but the girl's father said to him, "Please keep up your strength." So they waited until late afternoon and the two of them ate. [9] The man got up to go with his concubine and his servant, when his father-in-law, the girl's father, said to him, "Look, night is coming. Please spend the night. See, the day is almost over. Spend the night here, enjoy yourself, then you can get up early tomorrow for your journey and go home."

[10] But the man was unwilling to spend the night. He got up, departed, and arrived opposite Jebus (that is, Jerusalem[c]). The man had his two saddled donkeys and his concubine with him. [11] When they were near Jebus and the day was almost gone, the servant[d] said to his master, "Please, why not[A] let us stop at this Jebusite city and spend the night here?"

[12] But his master replied to him, "We will not stop at a foreign city where there are no Israelites. Let's move on to Gibeah."[e] [13] "Come on," he said,[B] "let's try to reach one of these places and spend the night in Gibeah or Ra-

mah." [14] So they continued on their journey, and the sun set as they neared Gibeah in Benjamin. [15] They stopped[c] to go in and spend the night in Gibeah. The Levite went in and sat down in the city square, but no one took them into their home to spend the night.

[16] In the evening, an old man came in from his work in the field. He was from the hill country of Ephraim[f] but was residing in Gibeah, and the men of that place were Benjaminites. [17] When he looked up and saw the traveler in the city square, the old man asked, "Where are you going, and where do you come from?"

[18] He answered him, "We're traveling from Bethlehem in Judah to the remote hill country of Ephraim, where I am from. I went to Bethlehem in Judah, and now I'm going to the house of the LORD.[D] No one has taken me into his home, [19] although we have both straw and feed for our donkeys, and bread and wine for me, your female servant, and the young man with your servant.[E] There is nothing we lack."

[20] "Peace to you," said the old man. "I'll take care of everything you need. Only don't spend the night in the square." [21] So he brought him to his house and fed the donkeys. Then they washed their feet and ate and drank.[g] [22] While they were enjoying themselves, all of a sudden, *perverted men of the city[h] surrounded the house and beat on the door. They said to the old man who was the owner of the house,

---

Cross-references (center column):

[a] 19:5 Gn 18:5
[b] 19:6 Jdg 16:25; 19:22; Ru 3:7; 1Kg 21:7; Est 1:10
[c] 19:10 Jos 18:28; 1Ch 11:4-5
[d] 19:11 Jdg 19:19
[e] 19:12 Jos 18:28; 1Sm 10:26; 22:6; Hs 5:8; 9:9; 10:9
[f] 9:16 Jdg 19:1
[g] 19:21 Gn 24:32-33
[h] 19:22 Gn 19:4-5; Dt 13:13; 1Sm 2:12; 1Kg 21:10; Ezk 16:46-48

A 19:11 Lit Come, please   B 19:13 Lit said to his servant   C 19:15 Lit stopped there   D 19:18 LXX reads to my house   E 19:19 Some Hb mss, Syr, Tg, Vg; other Hb mss read servants

---

offers of hospitality that would have been rude to decline in that culture. As a result, he was persuaded to stay another night. In an almost comic scene, the next day followed an identical pattern, with the host insisting on further hospitality and the Levite seeking to make his departure. In these exchanges, the concubine is nowhere to be seen.

19:10-12 As a result of this profuse hospitality, it was late in the day by the time the Levite and his party got underway. By the time they had arrived at the city of **Jerusalem**, a mere six miles journey from Bethlehem, the day was almost over. The Levite's servant proposed seeking shelter for the night in the city. At this time, Jerusalem was still in the hands of the Jebusites, and the Levite was reluctant to seek hospitality from non-Israelites. The Levite's fear is doubly ironic. First, if the Israelites had pressed forward with the conquest at the outset, Jerusalem would already have been in Israelite hands by this time. Second, the treatment they would experience at the hands of fellow Israelites in Gibeah was to be far worse than anything they could have expected from the Jebusites.

19:13-15 The Levite decided to press on another six miles or so to the Israelite cities of **Gibeah or Ramah**. By the time they reached Gibeah, the sun had already set. They sat down in the **city square** where, according to ancient Near Eastern custom, strangers might expect to receive hospi-

tality. No offers of hospitality were forthcoming, unlike their experience in Bethlehem.

19:16-21 Finally, an **old man** came in from his work. Like the Levite, he was **from the hill country of Ephraim** and merely lived in Gibeah, which perhaps explains his greater hospitality. Custom demanded hospitality should be shown to every stranger, but the Levite would not have been a burdensome guest. He could provide food for his own party and his animals. The Levite's statement that he was going **to the house of the LORD** seems odd in this context, since the temple had not yet been built. Most likely, a scribe misunderstood the final letter in the Hebrew word "my house" as an abbreviation for the name of the Lord. The old man's insistence that they should come to his home and not **spend the night in the square** suggests that he knew things were not as they ought to be in Gibeah. The square, inside the town walls, should have been a safe location.

19:22-24 The echoes of the story of Sodom and Gomorrah in Gn 19 were already present in the preceding verses, in which strangers arrived in the town square in the evening and found lodging with one of the town's inhabitants. These echoes now become a virtual reenactment. The scene of peaceful hospitality was shattered by the arrival of **perverted men** (lit "men of Belial," or "worthless men"; cp. 9:4). The **old man** appealed to them as his **brothers**, but

"Bring out the man who came to your house so we can have sex with him!"

²³The owner of the house went out and said to them, "No, don't do this evil, my brothers. After all, this man has come into my house. Don't do this horrible thing.^a ²⁴Here, let me bring out my virgin daughter^b and the man's concubine now. Use them^c and do whatever you want^A to them. But don't do this horrible thing to this man."

²⁵But the men would not listen to him, so the man seized his concubine and took her outside to them. They raped^B her and abused her all night until morning. At daybreak they let her go. ²⁶Early that morning, the woman made her way back, and as it was getting light, she collapsed at the doorway of the man's house where her master was.

²⁷When her master got up in the morning, opened the doors of the house, and went out to leave on his journey, there was the woman, his concubine, collapsed near the doorway of the house with her hands on the threshold. ²⁸"Get up," he told her. "Let's go." But there was no response.^d So the man put her on his donkey and set out for home.

²⁹When he entered his house, he picked up a knife, took hold of his concubine, cut her into 12 pieces, limb by limb, and then sent her throughout the territory of Israel. ³⁰Everyone who saw it said, "Nothing like this has ever happened or has been seen since the day the Israelites came out of the land of Egypt to this day.^c Think it over, discuss it, and speak up!"

^a19:23 Gn 34:7; Dt 22:21; Jdg 20:6; 2Sm 13:12; Jb 42:8
^b19:24 Gn 19:8
^cJdg 20:5; 2Sm 13:12,14; Lm 5:11
^d19:28 Jdg 20:5
^e20:1 Gn 21:14; 22:19; 1Sm 3:20; 1Kg 4:25
^f1Sm 7:5
^g20:2 1Sm 14:38; Is 19:13
^h20:6 Lv 18:17; 19:29; Ezk 16:27,43; Jr 13:27

War against Benjamin

20 All the Israelites from Dan to Beer-sheba^e and from the land of Gilead came out, and the community assembled as one body before the Lord at Mizpah.^f ²The leaders^g of all the people and of all the tribes of Israel presented themselves in the assembly of God's people: 400,000 armed foot soldiers. ³The Benjaminites heard that the Israelites had gone up to Mizpah.

The Israelites asked, "Tell us, how did this outrage occur?"

⁴The Levite, the husband of the murdered woman, answered: "I went to Gibeah in Benjamin with my concubine to spend the night. ⁵Citizens of Gibeah ganged up on me and surrounded the house at night. They intended to kill me, but they raped my concubine, and she died. ⁶Then I took my concubine and cut her in pieces, and sent her throughout Israel's territory, because they committed a horrible shame^h in Israel. ⁷Look, all of you are Israelites. Give your judgment and verdict here and now."

⁸Then all the people stood united and said, "None of us will go to his tent or return to his house. ⁹Now this is what we will do to Gibeah: we will go against it by lot. ¹⁰We will take 10 men out of every 100 from all the tribes of Israel, and 100 out of every 1,000, and 1,000 out of every 10,000 to get provisions for the people when they go to Gibeah in Benjamin to punish them for all the horror they did in Israel."

---

^A19:24 Lit *do what is good in your eyes*   ^B19:25 Lit *knew*   ^C19:30 LXX reads *day." He commanded the men he sent out, saying, "You will say this to all the men of Israel: Has anything like this happened since the day the Israelites came out of Egypt until this day?*

---

he characterized their request for sex with his male guest as an offense against hospitality and morality. It would be a **horrible thing**, a phrase that characterizes an act that cries out for retributive justice (20:6; Gn 34:7; Dt 22:21). Yet the alternative that the old man proposed is equally abhorrent.

19:25-28 The similarities with the narrative of Sodom and Gomorrah heighten the differences. The perpetrators were not pagans but Israelites. There were no angels to step in and rescue the innocent parties. There was no judgment from heaven at daybreak as with Sodom and Gomorrah. In the morning, the Levite **got up** from his rest and **opened the doors of the house** to leave on his journey, as if nothing had happened the previous night.

19:29-30 There is no mention of the concubine's death in the story, which raises the question of whether she was dead when the Levite found her, or even at the point when he **cut her into 12 pieces**. Her unresponsiveness to his commands suggests she was dead. At the very least, the Levite's action goes against the normal respect shown to a dead body in Israel, carving it up as if it were the carcass of an animal and sending the pieces to the 12 tribes of Israel as a call to arms. The similar passage in 1Sm 11:7, where Saul cut up a pair of oxen into 12 parts and distributed them among the tribes, shows that this act included an implied curse. Those

who failed to respond to the muster could expect to meet a similar fate. Everyone who saw the grisly message agreed that such an outrage demanded a response.

20:1-3 The message conveyed by the carved-up body of the Levite's concubine achieved a remarkable unity among the tribes of Israel. All of the Israelites from the northern border town of **Dan** to the southern border town of **Beer-sheba** came out as one—an achievement that surpassed anything accomplished by the judges raised up by the Lord. Mention of **the land of Gilead** shows that even the Transjordanian tribes responded. A total of **400,000 armed foot soldiers** assembled, a vast army by the standards of the book of Judges. The meeting took place at **Mizpah**, on the border between Benjamin and Ephraim, just north of Jerusalem and only a few miles away from Gibeah. **The Benjaminites**, however, did not take part in this assembly.

20:4-7 The **Levite** presented his own version of the facts to the assembly, carefully leaving out anything that might show him in a bad light. He failed to mention taking his concubine outside, giving her to the men, and then going to bed. Instead, he simply said, **they raped my concubine, and she died**. He termed this act **a horrible shame** in Israel—a gross sin that demanded a response. All the people therefore determined to take united action against Gibeah.

¹¹ So all the men of Israel gathered united against the city. ¹² Then the tribes of Israel sent men throughout the tribe of Benjamin, saying, "What is this outrage that has occurred among you? ¹³ Hand over the •perverted men in Gibeah so we can put them to death and eradicate evil from Israel." But the Benjaminites would not obey their fellow Israelites. ¹⁴ Instead, the Benjaminites gathered together from their cities to Gibeah to go out and fight against the Israelites. ¹⁵ On that day the Benjaminites rallied 26,000 armed men[a] from their cities, besides 700 choice men rallied by the inhabitants of Gibeah. ¹⁶ There were 700 choice men who were left-handed among all these people; all could sling a stone at a hair and not miss.

¹⁷ The Israelites, apart from Benjamin, rallied 400,000 armed men, every one an experienced warrior. ¹⁸ They set out, went to Bethel, and inquired of God.[b] The Israelites asked, "Who is to go first to fight for us against the Benjaminites?"

And the LORD answered, "Judah will be first."

¹⁹ In the morning, the Israelites set out and camped near Gibeah. ²⁰ The men of Israel went out to fight against Benjamin and took their battle positions against Gibeah. ²¹ The Benjaminites came out of Gibeah and slaughtered 22,000 men of Israel on the field that day. ²² But the Israelite army rallied and again took their battle positions in the same place where they positioned themselves on the first day. ²³ They went up, wept[c] before the LORD until evening, and inquired of Him: "Should we again fight against our brothers the Benjaminites?"

And the LORD answered: "Fight against them."

²⁴ On the second day the Israelites advanced against the Benjaminites. ²⁵ That same day the Benjaminites came out from Gibeah to meet them and slaughtered an additional 18,000 Israelites on the field; all were armed men.

²⁶ The whole Israelite army went to Bethel where they wept and sat before the LORD.[d] They fasted that day until evening and offered •burnt offerings and •fellowship offerings to the LORD. ²⁷ Then the Israelites inquired of the LORD. In those days, the ark of the covenant[e] of God was there, ²⁸ and Phinehas son of Eleazar, son of Aaron, was serving before it. The Israelites asked: "Should we again fight against our brothers the Benjaminites or should we stop?"

The LORD answered: "Fight, because I will hand them over to you tomorrow."[f] ²⁹ So Israel set up an ambush[g] around Gibeah. ³⁰ On the third day the Israelites fought against the Benjaminites and took their battle positions against Gibeah as before. ³¹ Then the Benjaminites came out against the people and were drawn away from the city.[h] They began to attack the people as before, killing about 30 men of Israel on the highways, one of which goes

---

Notes

[a]20:15 Nm 1:36-37; 2:23; 26:41
[b]20:18 Nm 27:21; Jdg 18:5; 1Sm 14:37; 1Ch 14:10
[c]20:23 Jos 7:6-7
[d]20:26 Jdg 21:2
[e]20:27 1Sm 4:4; 2Sm 15:24; 1Ch 16:6
[f]20:28 Jdg 7:9
[g]20:29 Jos 8:4
[h]20:31 Jos 8:31

20:12-17 Before engaging in military action, the Israelites sent messengers among the Benjaminites, appealing to them to hand over the guilty men. The **tribe of Benjamin** was more concerned about tribal solidarity than national solidarity or justice, and so the appeal to put these men to death fell on deaf ears. As a result, instead of Israel against Gibeah, the conflict became Israel against Benjamin. The Benjaminites rallied their forces for war—**26,000 armed men**, including 700 from Gibeah. This was a significant army, even if outnumbered by the Israelite's **400,000 . . . experienced** warriors. There was also a special contingent of 700 men who, like the Benjaminite judge Ehud, were **left-handed**, and who were remarkable marksmen, able to hit the smallest of targets with their slings.

20:18-21 The Israelites assembled for war at **Bethel**, northwest of Mizpah, where God had revealed Himself to Jacob (Gn 28). There the Israelites inquired of God not about whether they should fight their brothers, but about who should **go first** against the Benjaminites, and the Lord answered **Judah**. The language is virtually identical to 1:1-2, except here they call on *'Elohim*, the generic Hebrew name of God, rather than Yahweh, the personal, covenant name. The connection to 1:1-2 highlights the fact that the Benjaminites had taken the place of the Canaanites as Israel's enemy. Having shared in the sin of the Canaanites, now they must share in their punishment. Yet when the Israelites went out against the Benjaminites, the Israelites were immediately defeated. The Benjaminites inflicted almost as many casualties on Israel as they had soldiers.

20:22-25 In spite of this initial setback, Israel persisted in the conflict. They sought the Lord again and wept before Him, as they had in 2:4-5. They asked for confirmation of their course: **Should we again fight against our brothers the Benjaminites**? The answer was affirmative, but once again they were defeated by the Benjaminites.

20:26-28 A third time, they went to the Lord. This time, in addition to weeping, they fasted and made **offerings** in recognition that their covenant relationship with God was broken and needed to be restored. They had also apparently brought **the ark** of the Lord from Shiloh, where the tabernacle was at this time, to Bethel, perhaps as a good-luck charm (cp. 1Sm 4). The high priest at this time was **Phinehas**, grandson of Aaron, a detail which suggests that the events described in this chapter took place at an early stage of the period of the judges. The Lord once again responded to their request for guidance, telling Israel that on the next day he would **hand** Benjamin **over** to them.

20:29-35 This time, Israel's strategy was more complex, including a head-on assault, a tactic borrowed from the attack on Ai in Joshua 8. The main battle proceeded **as before**, with the Benjaminites coming out of the city to attack the Israelites and succeeding in inflicting casualties upon them. The Benjaminites believed that another victory lay in front of them. Like Samson, they assumed that nothing

up to Bethel and the other to Gibeah through the open country. ³²The Benjaminites said, "We are defeating them as before."

But the Israelites said, "Let's flee and draw them away from the city to the highways." ³³So all the men of Israel got up from their places and took their battle positions at Baal-tamar, while the Israelites in ambush charged out of their places west of^A Geba.^a ³⁴Then 10,000 choice men from all Israel made a frontal assault against Gibeah, and the battle was fierce, but the Benjaminites did not know that disaster was about to strike them. ³⁵The LORD defeated Benjamin in the presence of Israel, and on that day the Israelites slaughtered 25,100 men of Benjamin; all were armed men. ³⁶Then the Benjaminites realized they had been defeated.

The men of Israel had retreated before Benjamin, because they were confident in the ambush they had set against Gibeah. ³⁷The men in ambush had rushed quickly against Gibeah; they advanced and put the whole city to the sword. ³⁸The men of Israel had a prearranged signal with the men in ambush: when they sent up a great cloud of smoke from the city, ³⁹the men of Israel would return to the battle. When Benjamin had begun to strike them down, killing about 30 men of Israel, they said, "They're defeated before us, just as they were in the first battle."^b ⁴⁰But when the column of smoke began to go up from the city, Benjamin looked behind them, and the whole city was going up in smoke.^B ⁴¹Then the men of Israel returned, and the men of Benjamin were terrified when they realized that disaster had struck them. ⁴²They retreated before the men of Israel toward the wilderness,^c but the battle overtook

them, and those who came out of the cities^c slaughtered those between them. ⁴³They surrounded the Benjaminites, pursued them, and easily overtook them near Gibeah toward the east. ⁴⁴There were 18,000 men who died from Benjamin; all were warriors. ⁴⁵Then Benjamin turned and fled toward the wilderness to the rock of Rimmon,^d and Israel killed 5,000 men on the highways. They overtook them at Gidom and struck 2,000 more dead.

⁴⁶All the Benjaminites who died that day were 25,000 armed men; all were warriors. ⁴⁷But 600 men escaped into the wilderness to the rock of Rimmon and stayed there four months. ⁴⁸The men of Israel turned back against the other Benjaminites and killed them with their swords—the entire city, the animals, and everything that remained. They also burned down all the cities that remained.

Brides for Benjamin

21 The men of Israel had sworn an oath at Mizpah: "None of us will give his daughter to a Benjaminite in marriage."^e ²So the people went to Bethel and sat there before God^f until evening. They wept loudly and bitterly, ³and cried out, "Why, LORD God of Israel, has it occurred^D that one tribe is missing in Israel today?" ⁴The next day the people got up early, built an altar there,^g and offered •burnt offerings and •fellowship offerings. ⁵The Israelites asked, "Who of all the tribes of Israel didn't come to the LORD with the assembly?" For a great oath had been taken that anyone who had not come to the LORD at Mizpah would certainly be put to death.

⁶But the Israelites had compassion on their

a 20:33 Jos 8:19
b 20:39 Jdg 20:32
c 20:42 Jos 8:15,24
d 20:45 Jdg 21:13
e 21:1 Jdg 21:7,18
f 21:2 Jdg 20:26
g 21:4 2Sm 24:25

^A20:33 LXX, Syr, Vg; MT reads places in the plain of, or places in the cave of   ^B20:40 Lit up to the sky   ^C20:42 LXX, Vg read city
^D21:3 Lit has this occurred in Israel

had changed, not knowing that the Lord was about to hand them over to their fate. However, the Israelite strategy was to absorb these losses and retreat before the Benjaminites, drawing them **away from the city**. Once they had successfully lured them away, they took up battle positions at **Baal-tamar**, an otherwise unknown location. Meanwhile, the Israelites who were hidden in ambush emerged, and 10,000 of them assaulted Gibeah. The Benjaminites continued to fight, but they were defeated, and this time the casualties were all on the Benjaminite side.

20:36-41 The **ambush** at **Gibeah** was a complete success, and the **whole city** was put to the sword. A **great cloud of smoke** signaled the Israelites' success and announced the doom of the Benjaminites. Finally, when it was too late, the Benjaminites **realized that disaster had struck them**.

20:42-48 The defeated Benjaminites fled east, toward the wilderness, but there was no escape. Caught between the Israelite army and the troops emerging from Gibeah, Benjamin's army suffered a total of 25,000 casualties (vv. 44-45). A tiny remnant of **600 men** escaped and hid at **the rock**

of Rimmon, where there were many caves in which to hide. Meanwhile, the Israelite army returned to Benjamin and carried out a war of total destruction against its remaining occupants, human and animal, like those waged against the Canaanite population of the land. The tribe of Benjamin was almost completely destroyed.

21:1-9 Before the battle, all the tribes **had sworn an oath** not to allow their **daughters** to marry a **Benjaminite**. Since the Benjaminite women were wiped out in execution of the holy war and only the 600 men of Benjamin were left in the wilderness, it seemed that the tribe was destined for extinction. The seriousness with which Israel viewed their vow against giving their daughters to the Benjaminites is in marked contrast with their failure to remain separate from the Canaanite tribes, as the Lord had demanded. Seeking a solution, **the people went to Bethel**. Again **they wept** and offered **burnt offerings** and **fellowship offerings**, just as in 20:26. However, this time they relied on their own wisdom rather than the wisdom of the Lord. Their solution was to make a scapegoat out of anyone who had failed to show up

brothers, the Benjaminites, and said, "Today a tribe has been cut off from Israel. [7] What should we do about wives for the survivors? We've sworn to the Lord not to give them any of our daughters as wives." [8] They asked, "Which city among the tribes of Israel didn't come to the Lord at Mizpah?" It turned out that no one from Jabesh-gilead had come to the camp and the assembly. [9] For when the people were counted, no one was there from the inhabitants of Jabesh-gilead.

[10] The congregation sent 12,000 brave warriors[A] there and commanded them: "Go and kill the inhabitants of Jabesh-gilead with the sword,[a] including women and children. [11] This is what you should do: •Completely destroy every male, as well as every female who has slept with a man." [12] They found among the inhabitants of Jabesh-gilead 400 young women, who had not had sexual relations with a man, and they brought them to the camp at Shiloh in the land of Canaan.

[13] The whole congregation sent a message of peace[b] to the Benjaminites who were at the rock of Rimmon. [14] Benjamin returned at that time, and Israel gave them the women they had kept alive from Jabesh-gilead. But there were not enough for them.

[15] The people had compassion on Benjamin, because the Lord had made this gap in the tribes of Israel. [16] The elders of the congregation said, "What should we do about wives for those who are left, since the women of Benja-

a21:10 Nm 31:17
b21:13 Dt 20:10
c21:19 Jos 18:1; Jdg 18:31; 1Sm 1:3
d21:21 Ex 15:20; Jdg 11:34
e21:23 Jdg 20:48
f21:25 Jdg 17:6; 18:1; 19:1

min have been destroyed?" [17] They said, "There must be heirs for the survivors of Benjamin, so that a tribe of Israel will not be wiped out. [18] But we can't give them our daughters as wives." For the Israelites had sworn, "Anyone who gives a wife to a Benjaminite is cursed." [19] They also said, "Look, there's an annual festival to the Lord in Shiloh,[c] which is north of Bethel, east of the highway that goes up from Bethel to Shechem, and south of Lebonah."

[20] Then they commanded the Benjaminites: "Go and hide in the vineyards. [21] Watch, and when you see the young women of Shiloh come out to perform the dances,[d] each of you leave the vineyards and catch a wife for yourself from the young women of Shiloh, and go to the land of Benjamin. [22] When their fathers or brothers come to us and protest, we will tell them, 'Show favor to them, since we did not get enough wives for each of them in the battle. You didn't actually give the women to them, so[B] you are not •guilty of breaking your oath.'"

[23] The Benjaminites did this and took the number of women they needed from the dancers they caught. They went back to their own inheritance, rebuilt their cities,[e] and lived in them. [24] At that time, each of the Israelites returned from there to his own tribe and family. Each returned from there to his own inheritance.

[25] In those days there was no king in Israel;[f] everyone did whatever he wanted.[c]

A21:10 Lit *12,000 of their sons of valor*   B21:22 Lit *at this time*   C21:25 Lit *did what was right in his eyes*

---

for the muster at **Mizpah**, when they had taken an oath to impose the death penalty on anyone who refused to fight against the Benjaminites.

21:10-12 No reason is given for the failure of **Jabesh-gilead** to send soldiers, nor were the inhabitants given an opportunity to explain themselves. Instead, a force of **12,000 brave warriors** was sent to wipe out the men of Jabesh-gilead, along with the married women and male children, while sparing the young virgins, who could provide wives for the remaining 600 Benjaminites and thus allow the rest of the Israelites to keep their vow not to give their daughters in marriage. This arrangement provided a solution to their dilemma by means of a cynically selective application of the rules of holy war. The narrator signals his opinion by describing Shiloh as located **in the land of Canaan**. Even though Shiloh had been in Israelite hands for many years, by their behavior the Israelites had demonstrated that they were no better than the people they replaced.

21:13-14 The **whole congregation**, representing all of Israel, sent an offer of **peace** to the Benjaminites, and they returned to the fold. However, the 400 young virgins taken from Jabesh-gilead were not enough to provide wives for the 600 remaining Benjaminites.

21:19-25 The Israelites proposed a second strategy to pro-

vide wives for the Benjaminites, involving the **annual festival to the Lord in Shiloh**. It is not specified which of the three annual festivals is in view here, though the reference to **vineyards** (v. 21) suggests the Feast of Tabernacles. The fact that the Israelites needed detailed directions to find Shiloh (v. 19) suggests that for some time they had not been fulfilling their obligation to appear before the Lord at the tabernacle there three times per year. When the **young women** came out to dance, as would have been typical of such festivals, the Benjaminites would **catch** wives for themselves. This strategy, which resulted in women being taken against their will or the will of their parents, technically absolved the Israelites of breaking their vow not to give their daughters to the Benjaminites. Obviously this came at the cost of still more violence against women. In effect, the elders (Hb *zaqenim*) of Israel proposed a solution similar to that suggested by the old man (Hb *zaqen*) in Gibeah in 19:24, sacrificing virgin daughters for the good of the men.

Then the **Benjaminites** went home and **rebuilt their cities**, a further deviation from the laws of holy war, which specified that the cities that were destroyed should remain in ruins forever (Dt 13:16). These final chapters of the book give graphic demonstration of the depravity that resulted in Israel from the refusal of the people to recognize the Lord as King.

Ruth

The book of Ruth gets its name from one of its principle characters, a Moabite woman named Ruth who was the ancestor of David and Jesus. After reading the book of Judges, which paints a dark and depressing picture of Israel, the reader is relieved to encounter Ruth. Although the book is relatively short, it is rich in examples of kindness, faith, and patience. It is one of the five scrolls that was to be read during the Jewish festivals, in particular the Festival of Weeks.

Field of Boaz near Bethlehem (2:1-3)

Circumstances of Writing

Author: The Talmud attributes the authorship of Ruth to Samuel, but the book itself offers no hint of the identity of its author. We can only speculate about who might have written the book of Ruth, and its provenance and date must be deduced from the internal evidence—language and style, historical allusions, and themes. The genealogy at the end and the explanation of archaic customs requires a date during or later than the reign of King David (1011–971 B.C.), though it could have been written as late as after the exile, when the issue of the inclusion of Gentiles once again became pressing.

Background: The book of Ruth is set "during the time of the judges" (1:1), a period of social and religious disorder when "everyone did whatever he wanted" (Jdg 17:6). Historically, this era bridged the time between the conquest of the land under Joshua and the rise of King David, whose genealogy forms the conclusion of the book. It is not clear exactly when during the time of the judges the book belongs, but it opens with a famine in the land, which may have been the result of Israel's idolatry.

Message and Purpose

Grace: Naomi thought that the Lord's hand of judgment was upon her after she and her husband left the promised land in search of food and married their sons to Moabite women in search of offspring (1:21). She underestimated God's grace. Her daughter-in-law, Ruth the Moabitess, turned out to be the means by which the Lord would meet her needs for food and offspring to carry on the family name. Ruth's choice of a place to glean, which seemed to be a matter of chance, turned out to be a divine appointment with Boaz, the man who would fulfill the role of family redeemer for Naomi and Ruth.

The book of Ruth resembles the parable of the lost son (Lk 15:11-32) in two strands. The family of Elimelech wandered away from the land where the Lord had promised to bless His people in search of fullness. As a result, however, Naomi ended up empty and alone. Yet the Lord's judgment on her was designed to bring her

---

1400 B.C.   **1300 B.C.**

Deborah 1360?–1300?   **Gideon** 1250?–1175?   **Jephthah** 1200?–1150?   **Ruth** 1175?–1125?

Water clocks invented in Egypt **1400**

Division of the land into twelve allotments **1385?**

Events in Judges **1380?–1060?**

Pharaoh Horemheb creates a river security unit to board and search boats suspected of smuggling. **1320**

Deborah and Barak defeat Canaanites **1320?**

Egyptian 19th Dynasty **1303–1200**

Philistine Ascendancy **1300–1000**

Decimal numbers are used in China. **1300**

Signal fires used to communicate across distances by the Greeks **1300**

Battle of Kadesh between Ramesses II of Egypt and Muwatalli, the Hittite king. This may be the first battle in history for which there is sufficient information to understand the tactics of the opposing forces. **1285**

back home and to replace her emptiness with a new fullness. Similarly, the book of Ruth opens with the Lord's people experiencing the trials of the days of the judges, when general disobedience led to famine. Yet the Lord graciously provided food for His hungry people and a king to meet their needs for leadership. These are lessons that speak to us as well. We too have gone astray from the Lord and need to receive His grace and mercy.

God's providence: The genealogy of David at the end of the book shows that the Lord worked through this story to provide for His people's need of a king. Even though the Lord's actions are mainly concealed, there are two specific events attributed directly to Him—providing food for His people (1:6) and conception for Ruth (4:13). In these ways, the Lord provided for all of His people's needs.

Faithful love: The book of Ruth demonstrates how the Lord shows His covenant faithfulness to His undeserving people, often in surprising ways. In the course of the narrative, each of the main characters proved to be a person of extraordinary courage and covenant love (Hb *chesed*; "lovingkindness, faithfulness, loyalty," is the key word in the book: 1:8; 2:20; 3:10). These are people whose spiritual commitment is demonstrated clearly in godly living.

The family redeemer: The book of Ruth provides a great example of a family member who used his power under Jewish law to redeem. Boaz demonstrated one of the duties of the family member—that of marrying the widow of a deceased family member. A correlation is sometimes made between the redemption of Ruth by Boaz and the redemption of sinners by Christ. Because of God's covenant faithfulness, He has provided the Redeemer that we all need in Jesus Christ. Jesus is the true King toward whom the genealogy of David will ultimately extend (Mt 1:5-6), and He is the Redeemer in whom His wandering people find rest. In Him, the Gentiles too are incorporated into the people of God by faith and granted a place in the family of promise.

Contribution to the Bible

Ruth's covenantal faithfulness to Naomi and her God provided a model showing that those who were not ethnic Israelites could be incorporated into the people of God through faith. If Moabites who joined themselves to

---

1200 B.C.   1000 B.C.

Samson 1120?–1060?   **Samuel** 1105–1025   **Saul** 1080–1010   **David** 1050–970

Gideon defeats Midianites and Amalekites 1200?   Samson defeats Philistines 1080?

Lightning rods are used by the Minoans of   Samson destroys Philistine temple 1060?
  Crete. 1200
                                                        Philistines capture ark of the covenant 1055?
Egyptian 20th Dynasty 1200–1085
                                                        The Silk Road in China, the world's longest
The Greek army destroys Troy. 1184   road for 2,000 years 1050

Jephthah defeats Ammonites and
  Philistines 1170?

Events in Ruth 1140?

the Lord could be accepted, there was hope for other Gentiles as well (Is 56:3-7). The book also effectively answered questions that may have been raised over the legitimacy of the Davidic line, given his Moabite roots.

Structure

The book of Ruth is a delightful short story with a classical plot that moves from crisis to complication to resolution. The narrator draws the reader into the minds of the characters (successively Naomi, Ruth, and Boaz), inviting us to identify with their personal anxieties and joys and in the end to celebrate the movement from emptiness and frustration to fulfillment and joy.

Outline

I. Scene 1: Moab (1:1-22)
   A. Elimelech's departure (1:1-5)
   B. Naomi's despair (1:6-13)
   C. Ruth's decision (1:14-22)

II. Scene 2: Fields of Bethlehem (2:1-23)
   A. Ruth meets Boaz (2:1-14)
   B. Boaz provides for Ruth and Naomi (2:15-23)

III. Scene 3: Boaz's Threshing Floor (3:1-18)
   A. Boaz's desire to marry Ruth (3:1-11)
   B. Marriage delayed (3:12-18)

IV. Scene 4: City of Bethlehem (4:1-22)
   A. Boaz marries Ruth (4:1-12)
   B. Ruth gives birth to Obed (4:13-15)
   C. Naomi is blessed with a new family (4:16)
   D. Ruth is an ancestor of David (4:17-22)

Naomi's Family in Moab

1 During the time[A] of the judges,[a] there was a famine in the land.[b] A man left Bethlehem[B,c] in Judah with his wife and two sons to live in the land of Moab for a while. [2]The man's name was Elimelech,[c] and his wife's name was Naomi.[D] The names of his two sons were Mahlon[E] and Chilion.[F] They were Ephrathites[d] from Bethlehem in Judah. They entered the land of Moab and settled there. [3]Naomi's husband Elimelech died, and she was left with her two sons. [4]Her sons took Moabite women as their wives: one was named Orpah and the second was named Ruth. After they lived in Moab about 10 years, [5]both Mahlon and Chilion also died, and Naomi was left without her two children and without her husband.

Ruth's Loyalty to Naomi

[6]She and her daughters-in-law prepared to leave the land of Moab, because she had heard in Moab that the LORD had paid attention to His people's need by providing them food.[e] [7]She left the place where she had been living, accompanied by her two daughters-in-law,

and traveled along the road leading back to the land of Judah.

[8]She said to them, "Each of you go back to your mother's home.[f] May the LORD show faithful love to you as you have shown to the dead and to me. [9]May the LORD enable each of you to find security[g] in the house of your new husband." She kissed them, and they wept loudly.

[10]"No," they said to her. "We will go with you to your people."

[11]But Naomi replied, "Return home, my daughters. Why do you want to go with me? Am I able to have any more sons[G] who could become your husbands?[h] [12]Return home, my daughters. Go on, for I am too old to have another husband. Even if I thought there was still hope for me to have a husband tonight and to bear sons, [13]would you be willing to wait for them to grow up? Would you restrain yourselves from remarrying?[H] No, my daughters, my life is much too bitter for you to share,[i] because the LORD's hand has turned against me."[i] [14]Again they wept loudly, and Orpah kissed her mother-in-law, but Ruth clung

[a]1:1	Jdg 2:16-18
[b]Gn	12:10; 26:1; 43:1; 2Kg 8:1
[c]Jdg	17:7; 19:1
[d]1:2	Gn 35:19; 1Sm 17:12; 1Ch 4:4; Mc 5:2
[e]1:6	Ex 4:31; 1Sm 2:21
[f]1:8	Gn 24:28
[g]1:9	Ru 3:1
[h]1:11	Gn 38:11; Dt 25:5
[i]1:13	Jdg 2:15; Jb 19:21; Ps 32:4; 38:2; 39:10

[A]1:1 Lit *In the days of the judging*   [B]1:1 = House of Bread   [C]1:2 = My God Is King   [D]1:2 = Pleasant   [E]1:2 = Sickly   [F]1:2 = Weak or failing   [G]1:11 Lit *More to me sons in my womb*   [H]1:13 Lit *marrying a man*   [I]1:13 Lit *daughters, for more bitter to me than you*

1:1 During the time of the judges identifies the events of this story as taking place during a time when "everyone did whatever he wanted" (lit "what was right in his own eyes"), when "there was no king in Israel" (Jdg 21:25). During the time of the judges, a **famine in the land** probably would have been part of God's judgment on His people for their apostasy from Him, pursuing the Baals and Ashtoreths (Jdg 2:11-15). This famine even affected **Bethlehem**, whose Hebrew name means "house of bread." As a result, one family from that city did what was right in their own eyes and left the promised land, going to live in the pagan **land of Moab**, where economic prospects seemed brighter. Somewhere along the way, that temporary move turned into a permanent stay.

1:2 Elimelech means "My God is king," which heightens the irony of his behavior in doing "whatever he wanted" because in those days "there was no king in Israel" (Jdg 21:25). His wife's name, **Naomi**, means "Pleasant," which evokes Ps 16:6: "The boundary lines have fallen for me in pleasant places." In contrast, she and her husband were dissatisfied with the boundary lines assigned them by God. The names of their sons, **Mahlon and Chilion**, seem related to words for sickness and mortality.

1:3-5 In the land of Moab, Naomi's husband died and she was **left with her two sons**. The Hebrew verb "left" is related to the word "remnant" and often describes those who survive an outpouring of God's wrath. Her sons then took **Moabite women** as their wives, contrary to the law that forbade marrying women from nations that served other gods (Dt 7:3-4). Moabite women in particular had a reputation for leading Israelites astray after other gods (Nm 25). It must have seemed evident that the hand of the Lord was against Naomi in judgment.

1:6-9 Naomi had little choice but to leave Moab and return

home, a move encouraged by the news that **the LORD** was **providing . . . food** there. This points to repentance on the part of the Hebrews and their restoration. Naomi asked the Lord's blessing upon her daughters-in-law in the form of His **faithful love** (Hb *chesed*). This is a covenantal term that combines love and faithfulness, mercy and grace—all the positive aspects of committed relationship. It is a remarkable request that the Lord's favor should be shown in this way to covenant outsiders like these foreign women. The women were sad to part. They **wept loudly** as they embraced.

1:10-14 Orpah and Ruth repeated their desire to return to Israel with Naomi. Once again, however, Naomi pressed them both to return, on the grounds that the best prospect of remarriage lay among their own people. Naomi assumed that no other family in Bethlehem would be interested in

---

menuchah

Hebrew Pronunciation	[meh noo KHAH]
HCSB Translation	*rest, security*
Uses in Ruth	1
Uses in the OT	21
Focus Passage	Ruth 1:9

Menuchah, from *nuach* (*rest*), denotes *rest* (Jr 45:3). Often *menuchah* signifies *resting place* as a dwelling place: a *homestead* (Is 32:18), *campsite* (Nm 10:33), *temple* (1Ch 28:2), *tribal inheritance* (Gn 49:15), or *nation* (Mc 2:10). *Menuchah* means *home* (Is 66:1). It is *resting place* as a land affected by God's word that comes to rest there (Zch 9:1). *Menuchah* indicates *rest* from enemies (1Ch 22:9), *relief* from anxiety (2Sm 14:17), or familial *security* (Ru 1:9). It functions adjectivally as *quiet* (Ps 23:2) or adverbially as *easily* (Jdg 20:43). A *quartermaster* is a "master of *rest*," supplying troops with physical necessities (Jr 51:59). *Menuchah* describes Canaan as a *restful home* for Israel (Dt 12:9).

to her. [15] Naomi said, "Look, your sister-in-law has gone back to her people and to her god.[A,a] Follow your sister-in-law."

[16] But Ruth replied:

> Do not persuade me to leave you
> or go back and not follow you.
> For wherever you go, I will go,
> and wherever you live, I will live;
> your people will be my people,
> and your God will be my God.
> [17] Where you die, I will die,
> and there I will be buried.
> May •Yahweh punish me,[B,b]
> and do so severely,
> if anything but death separates you
> and me.

[18] When Naomi saw that Ruth was determined to go with her, she stopped trying to persuade her.

[19] The two of them traveled until they came to Bethlehem. When they entered Bethlehem, the whole town was excited about their arrival[C,c] and the local women exclaimed, "Can this be Naomi?"

[20] "Don't call me Naomi. Call me Mara,"[D] she answered,[E] "for the •Almighty[d] has made me very bitter.[e] [21] I went away full, but the LORD has brought me back empty.[f] Why do you call me Naomi, since the LORD has pronounced judgment on[F] me, and the Almighty has afflicted me?"

[22] So Naomi came back from the land of Moab with her daughter-in-law Ruth the Moabitess. They arrived in Bethlehem at the beginning of the barley harvest.[g]

Ruth and Boaz Meet

2 Now Naomi had a relative on her husband's side named Boaz. He was a prominent man of noble character[h] from Elimelech's family.

[2] Ruth the Moabitess asked Naomi, "Will you let me go into the fields and gather fallen grain[i] behind someone who allows me to?"

Naomi answered her, "Go ahead, my daughter." [3] So Ruth left and entered the field to gather grain behind the harvesters. She happened[j] to be in the portion of land belonging to Boaz, who was from Elimelech's family.

[4] Later, when Boaz arrived from Bethlehem, he said to the harvesters, "The LORD be with you."[k]

"The LORD bless you,"[l] they replied.

[5] Boaz asked his servant who was in charge of the harvesters, "Whose young woman is this?"

[6] The servant answered, "She is the young Moabite woman who returned with Naomi from the land of Moab. [7] She asked, 'Will you

---

[a]1:15 Jdg 11:24; 1Kg 11:7; Jr 48:7,13,46
[b]1:17 1Sm 3:17; 2Sm 3:9,35; 1Kg 2:23; 2Kg 6:31
[c]1:19 Mt 21:10
[d]1:20 Gn 49:25; Ex 6:3; Nm 24:4; Jb 6:4
[e]Ex 15:23
[f]1:21 Ru 3:17
[g]1:22 Ex 9:31; Lv 23:10-11
[h]2:1 Ru 1:2
[i]2:2 Lv 19:9-10; 23:22
[j]2:3 Pr 16:33; 20:24
[k]2:4 1Sm 20:13
[l]Nm 6:24

A1:15 Or *gods*   **B**1:17 A solemn oath formula; 1Sm 3:17; 2Sm 3:9,35; 1Kg 2:23; 2Kg 6:31   **C**1:19 Lit *excited because of them*   **D**1:20 = Bitter   **E**1:20 Lit *answered them*   **F**1:21 LXX, Syr, Vg read *has humiliated*

---

marrying Moabite women, and she emphasized the certainty of there being no other children from her own line. She was probably at least 50 years old at this time. Even if she were to have more children at once, by the time they grew up Orpah and Ruth would be too old to have children. Besides, Naomi argued, she was herself under a curse: **the LORD's hand** had **turned against** her. There is no hint of Naomi taking any personal responsibility or expressing repentance for her own actions in leaving the promised land. Convinced by Naomi's arguments, Orpah took her leave of Naomi, but Ruth **clung to her**—the same word used in Gn 2:24 to describe the marriage bond.

1:15-18 The intensity of Naomi's attempts to dissuade her Moabite daughters-in-law from accompanying her back to Bethlehem suggests that she was not completely motivated by concern for their well-being. Their presence would have been a constant and embarrassing reminder of her tragic sojourn in Moab. Yet Ruth was not so easily dissuaded. In a crescendo of commitment, she bound herself to **go** with Naomi and to **live** with her. In fact, she would even **die** and **be buried** where Naomi was—the greatest possible commitment in the ancient world. She sealed her commitment with a self-imprecatory oath, taken in the personal name of Naomi's God, **Yahweh**. Naomi's response to this moving speech was remarkably curt. Literally, the Hebrew in verse 18 says, "She stopped talking to her."

1:19-22 The townswomen's question, **Can this be Naomi?** pointedly and deliberately ignored Ruth's presence. In response, Naomi urged them to rename her **Mara** since the Lord had made her **bitter** rather than "pleasant," which is the meaning of "Naomi." It was at Marah that the Israelites found only bitter water to drink on their way out of Egypt, and so they grumbled against the Lord (Ex 15:23-24). Naomi's heart was similarly turned against the Lord, yet the connection also raised hope that the Lord would heal her bitterness and bring her to a place of rest, just as he did for Israel. Naomi had returned physically to Bethlehem from Moab, but would she similarly return to the Lord in repentance?

2:1-3 The practice of gleaning allowed the poor to go through the fields after the harvesters, picking up the grain that was left behind, along with the grain that landowners were required to leave at the edges of their fields (Lv 19:9-10). The phrase translated **man of noble character** could designate Boaz as possessing wealth and property, but it becomes clear as the story unfolds that Boaz is also a man of integrity. The family connection was unknown to Ruth. Humanly speaking, she just **happened** to end up gleaning in his field, but there are no coincidences in God's program, and this divine appointment proved that the Lord was not against Naomi, as she thought (1:20-21).

2:4-7 Boaz's noble character was displayed in his care for his workers. Even his greeting to them was in the name of the Lord, and he knew them well enough to recognize a stranger in their midst. His question did not seek Ruth's name but her relationships: **Whose young woman is this?** The servant's answer twice highlighted her foreignness. He also offered an unsolicited testimony to her diligent hard work in the hot sun.

let me gather fallen grain among the bundles behind the harvesters?' She came and has remained from early morning until now, except that she rested a little in the shelter."[A]

[8] Then Boaz said to Ruth, "Listen, my daughter.[B] Don't go and gather grain in another field, and don't leave this one, but stay here close to my female servants. [9] See which field they are harvesting, and follow them. Haven't I ordered the young men not to touch you?[C] When you are thirsty, go and drink from the jars the young men have filled."

[10] She bowed with her face to the ground[a] and said to him, "Why are you so kind to notice me, although I am a foreigner?"

[11] Boaz answered her, "Everything you have done for your mother-in-law since your husband's death has been fully reported to me: how you left your father and mother and the land of your birth, and how you came to a people you didn't previously know. [12] May the LORD reward you for what you have done,[b] and may you receive a full reward from the LORD God of Israel, under whose wings you have come for refuge."[c]

[13] "My lord," she said, "you have been so kind to me, for you have comforted and encouraged[D] your slave, although I am not like one of your female servants."

[14] At mealtime Boaz told her, "Come over here and have some bread and dip it in the vinegar sauce." So she sat beside the harvesters, and he offered her roasted grain. She ate and was satisfied and had some left over.

[15] When she got up to gather grain, Boaz ordered his young men, "Let her even gather grain among the bundles, and don't humiliate her. [16] Pull out some stalks from the bundles for her and leave them for her to gather. Don't rebuke her." [17] So Ruth gathered grain in the field until evening. She beat out what she had gathered, and it was about 26 quarts[E] of barley. [18] She picked up the grain and went into the town, where her mother-in-law saw what she had gleaned. Then she brought out what she had left over from her meal and gave it to her.

[19] Then her mother-in-law said to her, "Where did you gather barley today, and where did you work? May the LORD bless the man who noticed you."[d]

Ruth told her mother-in-law about the men she had worked with and said, "The name of the man I worked with today is Boaz."

[20] Then Naomi said to her daughter-in-law, "May he be blessed by the LORD,[e] who has not forsaken his[F] kindness to the living or the dead."[f] Naomi continued, "The man is a close relative. He is one of our *family redeemers."[g]

[21] Ruth the Moabitess said, "He also told me,

Cross-references:
[a] 2:10 1Sm 25:23,41
[b] 2:12 1Sm 24:19
[c] Ru 1:16; Ps 17:8; 36:7; 57:1; 63:7
[d] 2:19 Ps 41:1
[e] 2:20 2Sm 2:5
[f] Ru 1:8
[g] Lv 25:25-26; Ru 3:9,12; 4:1-8,14; Ps 19:14; Is 41:14

[A] 2:7 LXX reads *until evening she has not stopped in the field*; Vg reads *now and she did not return to the house*; Hb uncertain   [B] 2:8 Lit *Haven't you heard, my daughter?*   [C] 2:9 Either sexual or physical harassment   [D] 2:13 Lit *and spoken to the heart of*   [E] 2:17 Lit *about an ephah*   [F] 2:20 Or *His*

2:8-10 Boaz's noble character is again on display in his kind words to Ruth. Gleaning could be dangerous, especially for a young foreign woman, and Boaz issued instructions to ensure her safety. He also allowed her to drink the water his **young men** had brought, saving her the lengthy trip to the well. Ruth's response was to prostrate herself as a mark of respect for a social superior. As a Moabitess, she could easily have been ignored by Boaz, but he had noticed her and shown kindness to her.

2:11-13 The death of a husband exhausted a daughter-in-law's obligations, as Naomi herself had made clear (1:11). Yet Ruth had remained with Naomi, leaving her own land and people, which meant entrusting her future to the favor of the deity of the new land. Boaz asked the Lord, the God of Israel, to **reward** Ruth's faithfulness to Naomi and to shelter her under His protecting **wings**, as a mother bird shelters her young. Ruth responded with an expression of thanks for Boaz's kind and encouraging words to her, even though she had no claim on him, not even that of a maidservant in his employment.

2:14-16 As an impoverished gleaner, Ruth would normally have had little or nothing to eat while out in the fields. Boaz, however, invited her to eat with him and his harvesters. In contrast to Naomi's declaration in 1:21 that she went out full and came back empty, Ruth went out empty and came back full. There is no hint of romantic interest in Boaz's actions. He was simply demonstrating his compassion and generosity to Ruth who, even though a foreigner, was linked

to him through Naomi. He went so far as to instruct his harvesters deliberately to leave some grain for her to pick up, an action that went far beyond the demands of the law of Moses.

2:17-20 The measure of Boaz's generosity and Ruth's hard work is demonstrated in the remarkable quantity of grain that she gathered—an ephah (**about 26 quarts**) of barley. This was enough grain to feed a working man for several weeks. Boaz's generosity was evidence for Naomi that the Lord **has not forsaken his kindness to the living or the dead**. This represents a change in Naomi's attitude toward the Lord from 1:21. The judgment that the family had experienced was not His final word for them.

Family redeemers (Hb *go'el*; v. 20) were relatives who were obliged to buy back family members from debt-slavery or to redeem their field if they had to sell it (Lv 25:25-30). The family redeemer would also receive restitution on behalf of a deceased family member or pursue his killer to ensure that justice was served (Nm 5:8; 35:12). He might also raise up a child for the dead relative in order to maintain the connection between the clan and its hereditary property (Dt 25:5-10), though Boaz had no legal obligation to act in this way.

2:21-23 Naomi's approval of Boaz's invitation for Ruth to remain until the end of the harvest demonstrates a concern for Ruth's safety not evident in verse 2. However, the concern may also reflect Naomi's growing awareness of her own culpability in the fate of her own family. Her earlier

'Stay with my young men until they have finished all of my harvest.'"

²²So Naomi said to her daughter-in-law Ruth, "My daughter, it is good for you to work^A with his female servants, so that nothing will happen to you in another field." ²³Ruth stayed close to Boaz's female servants and gathered grain until the barley and the wheat harvests were finished.^a And she lived with^B her mother-in-law.

Ruth's Appeal to Boaz

3 Ruth's mother-in-law Naomi said to her, "My daughter, shouldn't I find security for you, so that you will be taken care of? ²Now isn't Boaz our relative?^b Haven't you been working with his female servants? This evening he will be winnowing barley on the threshing floor. ³Wash, put on perfumed oil, and wear your best clothes. Go down to the threshing floor, but don't let the man know you are there until he has finished eating and drinking. ⁴When he lies down, notice the place where he's lying, go in and uncover his feet, and lie down. Then he will explain to you what you should do."

⁵So Ruth said to her, "I will do everything you say."^C ⁶She went down to the threshing floor and did everything her mother-in-law

had instructed her. ⁷After Boaz ate, drank, and was in good spirits,^D he went to lie down at the end of the pile of barley. Then she went in secretly, uncovered his feet, and lay down.

⁸At midnight, Boaz was startled, turned over, and there lying at his feet was a woman! ⁹So he asked, "Who are you?"

"I am Ruth, your slave," she replied. "Spread your cloak^E over me,^c for you are a •family redeemer."^d

¹⁰Then he said, "May the LORD bless you,^e my daughter. You have shown more kindness now than before,^F because you have not pursued younger men, whether rich or poor. ¹¹Now don't be afraid, my daughter. I will do for you whatever you say,^G since all the people in my town^H know that you are a woman of noble character.^i ¹²Yes, it is true that I am a family redeemer, but there is a redeemer closer than I am. ¹³Stay here tonight, and in the morning, if he wants to redeem you, that's good.^g Let him redeem you. But if he doesn't want to redeem you, as the LORD lives,^h I will. Now lie down until morning."

¹⁴So she lay down at his feet until morning but got up while it was still dark.^i Then Boaz said, "Don't let it be known that a^j woman came to the threshing floor." ¹⁵And he told Ruth, "Bring the shawl you're wearing and

Cross references (center column)

^a 2:23 Dt 16:9
^b 3:2 Dt 25:5-10
^c 3:9 Ezk 16:8
^d Ru 2:12
^e 3:10 Ru 2:20
^f 3:11 Ru 2:1; Pr 12:4; 31:10
^g 3:13 Dt 25:5; Ru 4:5
^h Jdg 8:19; 1Sm 14:39,45; 19:6; 2Sm 4:9; 12:5; 2Kg 2:2,6

---

^A 2:22 Lit go out   ^B 2:23 Some Hb mss, Vg read she returned to   ^C 3:5 Alt Hb tradition reads say to me   ^D 3:7 Lit and his heart was glad   ^E 3:9 Or Spread the edge of your garment; lit Spread the wing of your garment; Ru 2:12   ^F 3:10 Lit kindness at the last than at the first   ^G 3:11 Some Hb mss, Orig, Syr, Tg, Vg read say to me   ^H 3:11 Lit all the gate of my people   ^I 3:14 Lit up before a man could recognize his companion   ^J 3:14 LXX; MT reads the

---

journey to the fields of Moab was an attempt to glean food "in the field of another" instead of seeking refuge under the wings of the Lord as she should have done. Boaz's generosity may have provided food, but Ruth's need of a home with a husband of her own is still real.

3:1-3 In view of Boaz's relationship to the family and his kindness and generosity thus far to Ruth, perhaps he could be persuaded to take the further step of marriage. At the end of the barley harvest, in late May or June, the barley had to be winnowed, tossed into the air with a fork allowing the wind to carry away the lighter chaff while the heavier grain fell to the ground. At night, someone would guard the grain against being stolen or eaten by animals. Apparently, this was Boaz's night to be on duty. Dressing as Naomi instructed would not only enhance Ruth's attractiveness to Boaz but would symbolize an end to her period of mourning for her husband (2Sm 12:20), signaling her willingness to remarry.

3:4-7 Naomi instructed Ruth to go to Boaz when he was asleep and **uncover his feet**, or, more precisely, "uncover the place of his feet." By this act Ruth was inquiring about Boaz's willingness to fulfill the role of family redeemer, to take her as wife and provide for her (see note at 4:5-8).

3:8-9 Whereas her mother-in-law had anticipated Boaz taking the initiative in the conversation, Ruth responded to Boaz's question about her identity with a clarification of her purpose. She asked him to spread the corner of his robe over her as a symbolic statement of a marriage com-

mitment (Ezk 16:8). The request also involved a wordplay, since **spread your cloak over me** literally means "spread your wing over me," inviting Boaz to become the answer to his own prayer in 2:12 that she might find refuge under the wings of the Lord.

3:10-11 Boaz's first words, **my daughter**, showed he had not been misled by the potential ambiguity of the situation. He declared himself willing to pay the social and financial costs of welcoming this despised outsider into his family. Boaz rightly saw Ruth's proposal as another act of covenant faithfulness (Hb chesed) on Ruth's part. Just as she had left her own household and her own family to be with Naomi, so now she was subordinating her own interests to those of Naomi. In the Hebrew ordering of the OT, the book of Ruth comes immediately after the book of Proverbs, which closes with a description of **a woman of noble character** (Pr 31:10).

3:12-13 Even though Boaz was a near relative of Naomi, there was another who had a prior claim to act as redeemer. Yet Boaz reassured Ruth that, one way or another, she (and Naomi) would be redeemed.

3:14-15 If it became widely known that Ruth had visited Boaz that night, people would wrongly assume that Boaz had taken Ruth as wife or that they were guilty of sexual impropriety. Boaz was unwilling to preempt his close relative who had first right of refusal to Ruth, so getting Ruth home before daylight kept wrong impressions from being formed. To seal his commitment (and perhaps also to provide Ruth

hold it out." When she held it out, he shoveled six measures of barley into her shawl, and she[A] went into the town.

[16] She went to her mother-in-law, Naomi, who asked her, "How did it go,[B] my daughter?"

Then Ruth told her everything the man had done for her. [17] She said, "He gave me these six measures of barley, because he said,[C] 'Don't go back to your mother-in-law empty-handed.'"

[18] Naomi said, "My daughter, wait until you find out how things go, for he won't rest unless he resolves this today."

Ruth and Boaz Marry

4 Boaz went to the •gate of the town[a] and sat down there. Soon the •family redeemer Boaz had spoken about came by. Boaz called him by name and said, "Come[D] over here and sit down." So he went over and sat down. [2] Then Boaz took 10 men of the town's elders[b] and said, "Sit here." And they sat down. [3] He said to the redeemer, "Naomi, who

[a]4:1 Ru 3:11-12; 2Sm 15:2; 18:4,24,33; 19:8; Ps 127:5
[b]4:2 Dt 19:12; 21:3-6; 1Kg 21:8; Pr 31:23
[c]4:3 Lv 25:25
[d]4:5 Gn 38:6-11; Lv 25:23-34; Dt 25:5-10
[e]4:7 Dt 25:8-10

has returned from the land of Moab, is selling a piece of land that belonged to our brother Elimelech.[c] [4] I thought I should inform you:[E] Buy it back in the presence of those seated here and in the presence of the elders of my people. If you want to redeem it, do so. But if you do[F] not want to redeem it, tell me so that I will know, because there isn't anyone other than you to redeem it, and I am next after you."

"I want to redeem it," he answered.

[5] Then Boaz said, "On the day you buy the land from Naomi, you will also acquire[G] Ruth the Moabitess, the wife of the deceased man, to perpetuate the man's name on his property."[d]

[6] The redeemer replied, "I can't redeem it myself, or I will ruin my own inheritance. Take my right of redemption, because I can't redeem it."

[7] At an earlier period in Israel, a man removed his sandal[e] and gave it to the other party in order to make any matter legally binding

---

[A]3:15 Some Hb mss, Aram, Syr, Vg; other Hb mss read he   [B]3:16 Lit Who are you   [C]3:17 Alt Hb tradition, LXX, Syr, Tg read said to me   [D]4:1 Lit Boaz said so-and-so come   [E]4:4 Lit should uncover your ear, saying   [F]4:4 Some Hb mss, LXX, Syr, Vg; other Hb mss read if he does   [G]4:5 Vg; MT reads Naomi and from

---

with an excuse for being out so early), Boaz gave her **six measures of barley**. If the unspecified measures are seahs, then that would be around 80 pounds, an enormous load. Yet the lack of a measure may be intended to focus attention on the number six, which often represents incompleteness in the OT. Even this generous gift is incomplete. Ruth still awaited the final installment of "seed" that would accomplish her rest.

3:16-18 On Ruth's return, Naomi asked her literally, "Who are you, my daughter?" This is the same question that Boaz asked in 3:8. Was Ruth merely an awkward and embarrassing duty to Naomi, or was she the one who would provide Naomi with an enduring place in the genealogies of Israel through the provision of a son? The answer depended on what transpired overnight. This was the real nature of Naomi's question, as evidenced by Ruth's answer.

4:1-2 Boaz immediately **went to the gate of the town**, the place where important legal and social matters were transacted in the presence of the town elders. When Boaz summoned the other redeemer, he literally said, Come over here (Hb) poloni 'almoni, a rhyming phrase equivalent to our "Mr. So-and-So." Boaz gathered a quorum of 10 **elders** as official witnesses.

4:3-4 As a widow Naomi could not sell Elimelech's land; however, she could assign someone else the right to use that land until the next Jubilee Year. Rather than have control over the land go (or remain) outside the family, Boaz requested an intervention in the spirit of the family redeemer laws to **buy . . . back** the use of the land. Since "Mr. So-and-So" was the primary relative entitled to **redeem** that property, Boaz was bringing the matter to his attention. If he did not redeem the property, Boaz himself was willing to act.

4:5-8 Along with the financial cost of redeeming the land, there was a social cost. The transaction also included a commitment to marry **Ruth the Moabitess** and thereby to

seek **to perpetuate the** dead **man's name on his property**. This is a reference back to the practice of levirate marriage in Dt 25:5-10, by which the brother of a man who died without male offspring was required to marry his widow and raise up a family in the name of the dead man. In this case, there was no legal obligation on either "Mr. So-and-So" or on Boaz, yet Boaz asserted a moral obligation to do so. At this, "Mr. So-and-So" backed away from his earlier enthusiasm. Ironically, his concern to protect his own name rather than committing to raise up heirs to the name of Elimelech led to him being left nameless. In seeking to serve self first, he inadvertently undermined his best interests. It is instead Boaz whose name would become famous (Ru 4:11) in Bethlehem. His decision was confirmed by a legal gesture that was archaic even at the time of the writing of the

ga'al

Hebrew Pronunciation	[gah AHL]
HCSB Translation	redeem, avenge
Uses in Ruth	22
Uses in the OT	104
Focus Passage	Ruth 4:1,3-4,6,8,14

Ga'al occurs only in biblically related usage. The original sense may have been "restore, repair." Once ga'al implies reclaim (Jb 3:5). Four times each it is parallel with padah ("ransom"; Jr 31:11) or yasha' ("save"; Ps 106:10). A legal duty to redeem fell on relatives (Lv 25:49), and participles connote relative (Nm 5:8) or kinsman (1Kg 16:11). Land, houses, livestock, and people could be redeemed from another's possession by payment (Lv 25:25; 27:28). Avengers of blood were relatives responsible to slay murderers of family members (Nm 35:19,21). God is the Redeemer (Is 49:26), rescuing people from slavery (Ex 6:6), transgressions (Is 44:22), harm (Gn 48:16), enemies (Ps 107:2), captivity (Is 43:14), and death (Hs 13:14). Ga'al with ge'ullah (14x) suggests take the right of redemption (Ru 4:6).

concerning the right of redemption or the exchange of property. This was the method of legally binding a transaction in Israel.

[8] So the redeemer removed his sandal and said to Boaz, "Buy back the property yourself."

[9] Boaz said to the elders and all the people, "You are witnesses today that I am buying from Naomi everything that belonged to Elimelech, Chilion, and Mahlon. [10] I will also acquire Ruth the Moabitess, Mahlon's widow, as my wife, to perpetuate the deceased man's name on his property, so that his name will not disappear among his relatives or from the gate of his home. You are witnesses today."

[11] The elders and all the people who were at the gate said, "We are witnesses. May the LORD make the woman who is entering your house like Rachel and Leah,[a] who together built the house of Israel. May you be powerful in Ephrathah and famous in Bethlehem. [12] May your house become like the house of Perez, the son Tamar bore to Judah,[b] because of the offspring the LORD will give you by this young woman."

[13] Boaz took Ruth and she became his wife. When he was intimate with her, the LORD en-

abled her to conceive, and she gave birth to a son. [14] Then the women said to Naomi, "Praise the LORD, who has not left you without a family redeemer today. May his name become well known in Israel. [15] He will renew your life and sustain you in your old age. Indeed, your daughter-in-law, who loves you and is better to you than seven sons,[c] has given birth to him." [16] Naomi took the child, placed him on her lap, and took care of him. [17] The neighbor women said, "A son has been born to Naomi," and they named him Obed.[A] He was the father of Jesse, the father of David.

David's Genealogy from Judah's Son

[18] Now this is the genealogy of Perez:

Perez fathered Hezron.
[19] Hezron fathered Ram,[B] who fathered Amminadab.
[20] Amminadab fathered Nahshon, who fathered Salmon.
[21] Salmon fathered Boaz, who fathered Obed.
[22] And Obed fathered Jesse, who fathered David.[d]

a4:11 Gn 29:25-30; 35:16-18 b4:12 Gn 38; 46:12; Ru 4:18 c4:15 Ru 1:16-17; 2:11-12 d4:18-22 Mt 1:3-6

A4:17 = Servant   B4:19 LXX reads *Aram*; Mt 1:3-4

book—the removal of a **sandal**, which was given to the other party.

4:9-12 By receiving the sandal, Boaz committed himself to redeem Naomi's property, to marry Ruth, and to perpetuate the names of **Elimelech** and **Mahlon** on their patrimony. The blessing of the **elders** (vv. 11-12) may simply have been conventional for married couples in Bethlehem, but it had a greater significance for Boaz and Ruth. Through Ruth, Boaz would indeed become famous and have his name remembered in Bethlehem. The link with **Perez, the son Tamar bore to Judah**, invites a comparison and contrast between Ruth and Tamar, two foreign women who became part of Judah's genealogy through very different means.

4:13-17 Although for 10 years in Moab, Ruth had been unable to bear a son for Mahlon, through the Lord's direct intervention she immediately conceived and bore a son for Boaz. The child would be a comfort for Naomi in her **old age** (lit "would sustain her grey hair"); he would be her family

redeemer who would provide for her needs in her declining years. He was named **Obed**, a short form of Obadiah, which means "servant of the LORD." Though no one could bring back Naomi's husband or sons, now she had a daughter-in-law whom all recognized as **better to you than seven sons**—an astonishing accolade in the ancient world.

4:18-22 The story concludes with a linear genealogy linking the child, **Obed**, backwards and forwards. It traces his roots back to **Perez**, the child born in Genesis 38 out of the dubious relationship between Judah and a foreign woman, Tamar. It also traces his progeny on to King **David**, who is highlighted not simply because he was a great king but also because he was the Lord's answer for the anarchy of the days of the judges, in which this story took place (1:1). The genealogy thus shows us that the Lord had been pursuing bigger plans than just bringing together two worthy individuals or restoring the emptiness of a Judean widow. Their story formed part of the bigger plan to provide the Redeemer, Christ Jesus, whom Israel needed.

Family of David

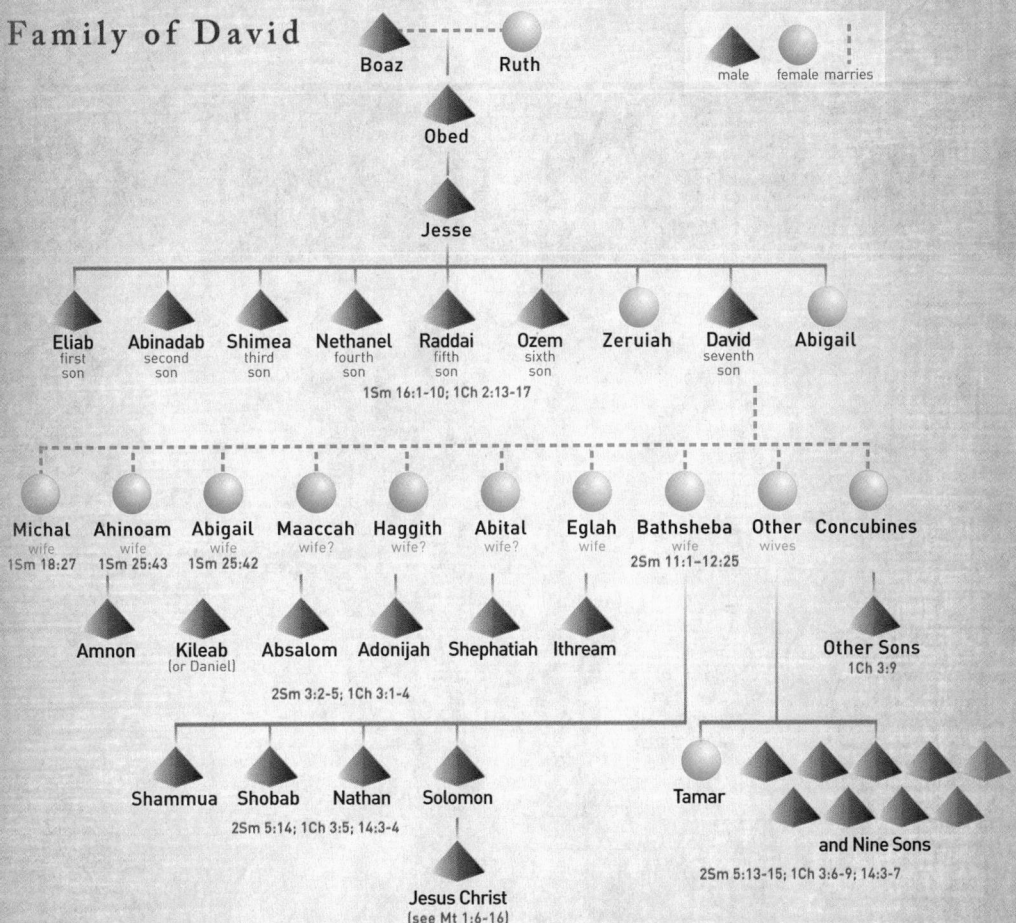

Boaz · **Ruth**

male   female marries

Obed

Jesse

| Eliab first son | Abinadab second son | Shimea third son | Nethanel fourth son | Raddai fifth son | Ozem sixth son | Zeruiah | David seventh son | Abigail |

1Sm 16:1-10; 1Ch 2:13-17

Michal wife 1Sm 18:27 · **Ahinoam** wife 1Sm 25:43 · **Abigail** wife 1Sm 25:42 · **Maacah** wife? · **Haggith** wife? · **Abital** wife? · **Eglah** wife · **Bathsheba** wife 2Sm 11:1–12:25 · **Other** wives · **Concubines**

Amnon   **Kileab** (or Daniel)   **Absalom**   **Adonijah**   **Shephatiah**   **Ithream**

Other Sons 1Ch 3:9

2Sm 3:2-5; 1Ch 3:1-4

Shammua   **Shobab**   **Nathan**   **Solomon**

2Sm 5:14; 1Ch 3:5; 14:3-4

Tamar   **and Nine Sons**

2Sm 5:13-15; 1Ch 3:6-9; 14:3-7

Jesus Christ (see Mt 1:6-16)

1 Samuel

The books of 1 and 2 Samuel highlight a significant
transition time in Israel's history. As 1 Samuel begins,
Israel is a loosely organized tribal league living under poor
spiritual leadership. God's plan for His people nonetheless
continued as He raised up Samuel to guide Israel's
transition from a theocracy to a monarchy. Saul's kingship
constitutes the remainder of 1 Samuel, while David's
kingship is largely the focus of 2 Samuel.

Valley of Elah where David killed the Philistine, Goliath (1Sm 17:2,19)

Circumstances of Writing

Author: Early tradition suggests 1 and 2 Samuel were originally one book. Some scholars believe Samuel was largely responsible for the material up to 1 Samuel 25, and that the prophets Nathan and Gad gave significant input to the rest (based on 1Ch 29:29). This proposal, however, must remain speculative because the books name no authors. First Samuel 27:6 suggests the book was not completed until perhaps a few generations after the division of the kingdom around 930 B.C.

Background: After Israel's conquest of the land during the days of Joshua, Israel entered a time of apostasy. The book of Judges describes recurrences of a cycle with predictable phases. First, the people sinned against the Lord and fell into idolatry. Second, the Lord raised up an adversary to afflict them and turn them back to Him. Third, the people cried out to the Lord in repentance. Fourth, the Lord brought deliverance for them through a judge whom He raised up. The book of Judges' famous verse, "In those days there was no king in Israel; everyone did whatever he wanted" (Jdg 21:25), aptly describes the period. The book of 1 Samuel picks up the historical record toward the end of those stormy days.

Message and Purpose

Leadership: The books of 1 and 2 Samuel provide numerous examples of good and bad leadership. When leaders focused their attention on the Lord and saw their leadership roles as instruments for His glory, they flourished; when they abandoned the Lord and used their offices for their own gain, they failed. The lives of Eli and his sons, plus the lives of Samuel, Saul, David, and others consistently illustrate these principles.

God's sovereignty: The books of 1 and 2 Samuel highlight God's provision at Israel's every turn. He provided good spiritual leadership through Samuel, and He provided Israel its first king, though kingship was not His perfect will for His people at that time. He provided His people the leaders and resources they needed to defeat their enemies and to live out His purpose in the land, though both people and leaders often failed Him.

1200 B.C.   **1100 B.C.**

Samson 1120?–1060?   **Samuel** 1105?–1025?   **Saul** 1080?–1010   **David** 1050?–970

The Olmec civilization flourishes in Central America, establishing a foundation for subsequent civilizations in the Americas. 1200

The process of iron smelting developed in Armenia 1200–1000

The city of Troy falls to the Greeks after a ten-year siege. 1184

World's first recorded labor strike, Thebes, Egypt 1170

Events in Ruth 1140?

Botanical gardens developed by Assyrians during the reign of Tiglath-pileser I 1114–976

Events in 1 Samuel 1105?–1010

Chou-pei, one of China's early mathematical works 1105

Saul anointed king 1050

Iron technology advances throughout India. 1000

The Chinese store ice for use in refrigeration. 1000

Oats are cultivated in central Europe. 1000

Sin's consequences: The books of 1 and 2 Samuel take sin seriously, describing in detail the awful consequences of sin—even forgiven sin. Saul's disobedience of God led to his estrangement from his son Jonathan and from David, and ultimately led to his death in battle. David's sin with Bathsheba, though forgiven, brought consequences that haunted David the rest of his life.

Covenant: The books of 1 and 2 Samuel describe God's relationship with His covenant people and His faithful response to the terms of that covenant. The Lord also established a special covenant with David, a covenant that ultimately would find its fulfillment in the Lord Jesus Christ.

Contribution to the Bible

The books of 1 and 2 Samuel describe Israel's transition from a loosely organized tribal league under God (a theocracy) to centralized leadership under a king who answered to God (a monarchy). Samuel's life and ministry greatly shaped this period of restructuring as he consistently pointed people back to God.

Saul's rule highlighted the dangers to which the Israelites fell victim as they clamored for a king to lead them. Samuel's warnings fell on deaf ears (1Sm 8:10-20) because God's people were intent on becoming like the nations around them. In the end, they got exactly what they asked for, but they paid a terrible price. Saul's life stands as a warning to trust God's timing for life's provisions.

David's rule testified to the amazing works the Lord could and would do through a life yielded to Him. Israel's second king seemed quite aware of God's blessing on his life and displayed a tender heart toward the things of God (2Sm 5:12; 7:1-2; 22:1-51; 23:1-7). Later generations would receive blessing because of David's life (Is 37:35). God's special covenant with David (2Sm 7:1-29) found its ultimate fulfillment in Jesus, the son of David (Lk 1:32-33). The consequences of David's sin with Bathsheba, however, stand as a warning to all who experience sin's attraction. God holds His children accountable for their actions, and even forgiven sin can have terrible consequences.

1000 B.C.		900 B.C.	
Bathsheba 1025?–960?	**Solomon** 990?–931	**Rehoboam** 971–913	**Jeroboam** 971?–909
Egyptian 21st Dynasty 1085–945	Events in 2 Samuel 1010–970	The Kingdom divides. 931?	
David becomes king of Judah. 1010	Events in 1 Chronicles 1010–970	Israel: The Northern Kingdom 931–722	
David becomes king over all Israel. 1003	Absalom's revolt 975?	Judah: The Southern Kingdom 931–586	
David conquers Jerusalem. 1000?	Solomon becomes king. 970		
David moves the ark of the covenant to Jerusalem. 1000?	Solomon begins construction of the temple in Jerusalem. 966	Celts migrate across Europe and begin to settle in Britain. 900	
The Incas preserve potatoes by freezing them in the snow. 1000	The temple dedicated 959	Etruscans emigrate from Lydia to Italy as a result of an extended famine. 900	
	Ascendancy of Neo-Assyrian Empire 950		

Structure

The first seven chapters of 1 Samuel describe Samuel's birth, call, and initial ministry among the Israelites. Chapter 8 is a major turning point as the people ask for a king to rule them "the same as all the other nations have" (1Sm 8:5). Chapters 9–12 then describe Saul's selection—at God's direction, yet not His perfect will for the time (1Sm 12:16-18).

First Samuel 13–31 describes Saul's victories and failures. Saul was a king with great physical stature and military skill (1Sm 14:47-52), but his heart was not one with the Lord (1Sm 13:14). His unwillingness to obey the Lord's commands ultimately outweighed his accomplishments, and chapters 16–31 describe his reign's downward spiral. During this time God raised up David and was preparing him for the day he would succeed Saul—a fact Saul gradually realized (1Sm 15:28; 24:20-21; 28:17).

Second Samuel 1–4 describes the struggle for Israel's throne that began with Saul's death. David was anointed king by the men of Judah (2Sm 2:4), but Abner anointed Ish-bosheth, Saul's oldest surviving son, as king over Israel (2Sm 2:8-9). A two-year civil war resulted in Ish-bosheth's death and in David's becoming king over all Israel.

Second Samuel 5–24 presents highlights of David's reign. God established a special covenant with David, promising to establish the throne of his kingdom forever (2Sm 7:1-29). David's sin with Bathsheba, however, brought disastrous consequences to his reign and became a turning point in 2 Samuel. In the end, David's repentance confirmed his designation as a man after God's heart, but his sin showed that even the king is not above God's laws.

Outline of 1 Samuel

I. Samuel's Ministry (1:1–12:25)
   A. Samuel's birth and call (1:1–3:21)
   B. The ark narrative (4:1–7:17)
   C. The people ask for a king (8:1–12:25)

II. Saul's Reign (13:1–31:13)
   A. Saul's battles with the Philistines (13:1–14:52)
   B. Saul's failure against the Amalekites (15:1–35)
   C. David's selection as Saul's successor (16:1–23)
   D. David's victory over Goliath (17:1–58)
   E. David's struggles with Saul (18:1–26:25)
   F. Saul's reign ends (27:1–31:13)

Hannah's Vow

1 There was a man from Ramathaim-zo-phim[a] in[A] the hill country of Ephraim.[b] His name was Elkanah[c] son of Jeroham, son of Elihu, son of Tohu, son of Zuph, an Ephraimite. [2] He had two wives,[d] the first named Hannah[e] and the second Peninnah. Peninnah had children, but Hannah was childless. [3] This man would go up from his town every year[f] to worship and to sacrifice[g] to the Lord of *Hosts at Shiloh,[h] where Eli's two sons, Hophni and Phinehas, were the Lord's priests.

[4] Whenever Elkanah offered a sacrifice, he always gave portions of the meat[i] to his wife Peninnah and to each of her sons and daughters. [5] But he gave a double[B] portion[j] to Hannah, for he loved her even though the Lord had kept her from conceiving. [6] Her rival would taunt her severely just to provoke her, because the Lord had kept Hannah from conceiving. [7] Whenever she went up to the Lord's house,[k] her rival taunted her in this way every year. Hannah wept and would not eat. [8] "Hannah, why are you crying?" her husband Elkanah asked. "Why won't you eat? Why are you troubled? Am I not better to you than 10 sons?"[l]

[9] Hannah got up after they ate and drank at Shiloh.[C] Eli the priest was sitting on a chair by the doorpost of the Lord's tabernacle.[m] [10] Deeply hurt, Hannah prayed to the Lord and wept with many tears.[n] [11] Making a vow,[o] she pleaded, "Lord of Hosts, if You will take notice of Your servant's affliction,[p] remember and not forget me, and give Your servant a son,[D] I will give him to the Lord all the days of his life, and his hair will never be cut."[E,q]

[12] While she continued praying in the Lord's presence, Eli watched her lips. [13] Hannah was praying silently,[F,r] and though her lips were moving, her voice could not be heard. Eli thought she was drunk [14] and scolded her, "How long are you going to be drunk?[s] Get rid of your wine!"

[15] "No, my lord," Hannah replied. "I am a woman with a broken heart. I haven't had any wine or beer; I've been pouring out my heart before the Lord.[t] [16] Don't think of me as a wicked woman;[u] I've been praying from the depth of my anguish and resentment."[v]

[17] Eli responded, "Go in peace,[w] and may the God of Israel grant the petition you've requested from Him."[x]

[18] "May your servant find favor with you,"[y] she replied. Then Hannah went on her way; she ate and no longer looked despondent.[G,z]

Samuel's Birth and Dedication

[19] The next morning Elkanah and Hannah got up early to bow in worship before the Lord. Afterward, they returned home to Ramah.[aa] Then Elkanah was intimate with his wife Hannah, and the Lord remembered her.[ab] [20] After some time,[H] Hannah conceived and gave birth to a son. She named him Samuel,[I] because she said, "I requested him from the Lord."

[21] When Elkanah and all his household went

a1:1 1Sm 1:19
bJos 17:14-18; Jdg 17:1
c1Ch 6:22-28, 33-38
d1:2 Dt 21:15-17
eLk 2:36
f1:3 Ex 34:23; Dt 16:16; Lk 2:41
gEx 23:14-17
hJos 18:1
i1:4 Dt 12:17-18
j1:5 Gn 43:34; 48:22
k1:7 Jos 18:1
l1:8 Ru 4:15
m1:9 1Sm 3:3
n1:10 1Sm 30:6; 2Kg 4:27
o1:11 Nm 30:6-11
pGn 29:32
qNm 6:5; Jdg 13:5; 16:7
r1:13 Gn 24:42-45
s1:14 Ac 2:4,13
t1:15 Ps 62:8
u1:16 1Sm 2:12
vLk 6:45
w1:17 1Sm 25:35; 2Kg 5:19; Mk 5:34
xRu 2:13
y1:18 Ru 2:13
zRm 15:13
aa1:19 1Sm 1:1; 2:11
ab Gn 8:1; 30:22; 1Sm 1:11

A1:1 Or from Ramathaim, a Zuphite from   B1:5 Or gave only one; Hb obscure   C1:9 LXX adds and presented herself before the Lord
D1:11 Lit a seed of men   E1:11 Lit and no razor will go up on his head   F1:13 Lit praying to her heart   G1:18 Lit and her face was not to
her again   H1:20 Lit In the turning of the days   I1:20 In Hb, the name Samuel sounds like the phrase "requested from God."

1:1 The exact location of **Ramathaim-zophim** is not known, but it is distinct from Ramah, located in the tribal territory of Benjamin (v. 19). It probably designates Elkanah's ancestral home. The name **Elkanah** means "God has acquired." **Ephraimite** denotes Elkanah's place of residence, not his tribal background, which was that of Levi (1Ch 6:25-28).

1:2 The name **Hannah** means "grace." She was **childless**, a condition often viewed with disfavor or even anguish (Gn 16:4-5; 30:1; Lk 1:24-25).

1:3 **Shiloh** was centrally located about 30 miles north of Jerusalem. It was the place from which Joshua divided the land among the tribes (Jos 18:1-10).

1:5 The **double portion** was the amount of the inheritance the firstborn received (Dt 21:17). Here it probably denotes Elkanah's special love for Hannah. The words **the Lord had kept her from conceiving** is literally, "Yahweh had closed her womb" (cp. v. 6).

1:6 The rivalry between Hannah and Peninnah finds parallels in the accounts of Sarah and Hagar (Gn 16:4-5) and Leah and Rachel (Gn 30:14-16).

1:10 The words **deeply hurt** can be more literally rendered

"bitter of soul," using the same Hebrew word that Naomi used (mara; Ru 1:20).

1:11 If God would give Hannah **a son**, she vowed to give him back to God according to the law of the Nazirite (Nm 6:1-21).

1:12-14 **Eli** misread Hannah's anguish as drunkenness and **scolded her** for her apparent disregard of the holy place.

1:15-16 Hannah immediately clarified the situation with Eli. The **depth** (lit "abundance") of Hannah's **anguish and resentment** over her situation had come to the surface.

1:18 The Hebrew word for **favor** with which Hannah replied was a shortened form of her own name.

1:19 **Ramah** lay along the major north-south highway five miles north of Jerusalem in the territory of Benjamin. The tender words **the Lord remembered her** remind the reader that ultimately it is God who brings new life within the womb. In the OT to "remember" means not simply to think about someone but to act on their behalf (see note at Gn 8:1).

1:20 The name **Samuel** may be a wordplay meaning "requested from God." A second possibility is the meaning "heard by God."

1:21 The expression **annual sacrifice** literally means

up to make the annual sacrifice[a] and his vow offering to the LORD, [22]Hannah did not go and explained to her husband, "After the child is weaned, I'll take him to appear in the LORD's presence[b] and to stay there permanently."[c]

[23]Her husband Elkanah replied, "Do what you think is best,[A,d] and stay here until you've weaned him. May the LORD confirm your[B] word."[e] So Hannah stayed there and nursed her son until she weaned him. [24]When she had weaned him, she took him with her to Shiloh, as well as a three-year-old bull,[C] half a bushel[D] of flour, and a jar of wine.[f] Though the boy was still young,[E] she took him to the LORD's house at Shiloh.[g] [25]Then they slaughtered the bull and brought the boy to Eli.

[26]"Please, my lord," she said, "as sure as you live,[h] my lord, I am the woman who stood here beside you praying to the LORD. [27]I prayed for this boy,[i] and since the LORD gave me what I asked Him for,[j] [28]I now give the boy to the LORD. For as long as he lives, he is given to the LORD."[k] Then he[F] bowed in worship to the LORD there.[G]

Hannah's Triumphant Prayer

2 Hannah prayed:[l]

My heart rejoices in the LORD;[m]
my •horn is lifted up by the LORD.

My mouth boasts over my enemies,
because I rejoice in Your salvation.[n]
[2] There is no one holy like the LORD.[o]
There is no one besides You![p]
And there is no rock like our God.[q]
[3] Do not boast so proudly,
or let arrogant words come out of
your mouth,
for the LORD is a God of knowledge,
and actions are weighed by Him.[r]
[4] The bows of the warriors are broken,[s]
but the feeble are clothed
with strength.[t]
[5] Those who are full hire themselves out
for food,
but those who are starving hunger
no more.
The woman who is childless gives birth
to seven,[u]
but the woman with many sons
pines away.[v]
[6] The LORD brings death and gives life;[w]
He sends some to •Sheol, and He raises
others up.[x]
[7] The LORD brings poverty and gives
wealth;[y]
He humbles and He exalts.[z]
[8] He raises the poor from the dust[aa]
and lifts the needy from the garbage pile.[ab]

Cross references

[a]1:21 Dt 12:11; 1Sm 1:3
[b]1:22 Lk 2:22
[c]1Sm 1:11,28
[d]1:23 Nm 30:10-11
[e]Nm 30:13
[f]1:24 Nm 15:9-10
[g]Jos 18:1; 1Sm 4:3-4
[h]1:26 2Kg 2:2,4,6
[i]1:27 1Sm 1:11-13
[j]1Sm 1:17,20
[k]1:28 1Sm 1:11
[l]2:1 Ps 72:20; Hab 3:1; Lk 1:46-55
[m]Ps 75:4-5,10; 92:10
[n]Is 12:2-3
[o]2:2 Ex 15:11
[p]2Sm 22:32
[q]2Sm 7:22; Ps 18:31
[r]2:3 Pr 16:2; 24:12
[s]2:4 Ps 37:15; 46:9
[t]Ps 18:39; Heb 11:32-34
[u]2:5 Ru 4:15; Ps 113:9
[v]Jr 15:9
[w]2:6 Dt 32:39
[x]Is 26:19
[y]2:7 Dt 8:17-18
[z]Jb 15:11; Jms 4:10
[aa]Jb 42:10-12; Ps 75:7
[ab]2Sm 7:8; Dn 2:48; Jms 2:5

[A]1:23 Lit what is good in your eyes   [B]1:23 DSS, LXX, Syr; MT reads His   [C]1:24 DSS, LXX, Syr; MT reads Shiloh with three bulls   [D]1:24 Lit bull and an ephah   [E]1:24 Lit And the youth was a youth   [F]1:28 DSS read she; some Hb mss, Syr, Vg read they   [G]1:28 LXX reads Then she left him there before the LORD

"sacrifice of the days" and probably designates one of the three required festivals—Passover, the Festival of Weeks, or the Festival of Booths (Dt 16:16). The word **vow** may denote a separate vow that Elkanah had made, or perhaps it designates Hannah's vow that Elkanah then shared with her when he heard of it (Nm 30:10-15).

1:22 The apocryphal book of 2 Maccabees (7:27) suggests Israelite children were **weaned** at around age three, a custom not unusual in societies where homes lacked running water and where the purity of drinking water was difficult to maintain.

1:23 The Hebrew verb translated **confirm** literally means "cause to stand." **Elkanah** wanted God's blessing to remain on the young boy Samuel.

1:24 The Masoretic Text, overall the most reliable Hebrew manuscript tradition, reads "three bulls" here. The HCSB adopted **three-year-old bull** because of the reference to a single bull in verse 25 and because of the testimony of other early manuscripts. If the Masoretic Text is correct, however, it may be that the one bull constituted Elkanah's sacrifice of thanksgiving for Samuel's birth, while the other two were part of his usual sacrifice, and hence were not mentioned in verse 25.

1:25 On **bull**, see note at verse 24.

1:26-27 Hannah thought it important to testify to Eli, Israel's high priest, how God had answered her prayer.

1:28 The Hebrew words translated **give** and **given** are related to the Hebrew word for "requested," which also has to

do with the meaning of Samuel's name (v. 20). They literally mean "to give over" or "to grant" what was requested. Hannah had received the son she requested; she now grants him to **the LORD** for His service.

2:1 A **lifted up** horn provides a picture of a proud animal with its head held high. **Enemies** may allude to Peninnah (1:6-7) and perhaps to others who had spoken cruelly to Hannah during her time of barrenness.

2:2 The twofold occurrence of **no one** emphasizes God's uniqueness. **Rock** denotes an immovable, jutting cliff, not a mere stone. This word commonly occurs in the Bible to describe God's support and defense of His people (Ps 18:2; 95:1; Is 44:8).

2:3 **Arrogant words** might come from people who did not realize God's ways were higher than theirs (Is 55:8-9).

2:4 **Warriors are broken . . . feeble are clothed**. These images are not surprising from God's perspective, where poor become rich and rich become poor (2Co 8:9; Jms 2:5), the first become last and the last first (Mt 19:30; 20:16), and those who seek to save their lives lose them while others who willingly lose their lives gain life (Lk 9:24-25).

2:5 **Full . . . starving . . . childless . . . many sons**. As in verse 4, life often brings unexpected turnabouts, especially since the Lord can intervene to overrule the expected.

2:6-7 God is sovereign; nothing happens apart from His control.

2:8 The argument of this verse is from the greater to the

He seats them with noblemen[a]
and gives them a throne of honor.[A]
For the foundations of the earth
     are the LORD's;[b]
He has set the world on them.[c]

9 He guards the steps[B]
     of His faithful ones,[d]
but the wicked perish in darkness,[e]
for a man does not prevail by his own
     strength.[f]

10 Those who oppose the LORD
     will be shattered;[C,g]
He will thunder in the heavens
     against them.[h]
The LORD will judge the ends
     of the earth.[i]
He will give power to His king;
He will lift up the horn
     of His anointed.[j]

11 Elkanah went home to Ramah,[k] but the boy served the LORD in the presence of Eli the priest.[l]

Eli's Family Judged

12 Eli's sons were ·wicked men;[m] they had no regard for the LORD[n] 13 or for the priests' share of the sacrifices from the people. When any man offered a sacrifice, the priest's servant would come with a three-pronged meat fork while the meat was boiling 14 and plunge it into the container or kettle or cauldron or cooking pot.[o] The priest would claim for himself whatever the meat fork brought up. This is the way they treated all the Israelites who came there to Shiloh. 15 Even before the fat was burned,[p] the priest's servant would come and say to the man who was sacrificing, "Give the priest some meat to roast, because he won't accept boiled meat from you—only raw." 16 If that man said to him, "The fat must be burned first; then you can take whatever you want for yourself,"[q] the servant would reply, "No, I insist that you hand it over right now. If you don't, I'll take it by force!" 17 So the servants' sin was very severe in the presence of the LORD, because they treated the LORD's offering with contempt.[r]

18 The boy Samuel served in the LORD's presence[s] and wore a linen ephod.[t] 19 Each year his mother made him a little robe[u] and took it to him when she went with her husband to offer the annual sacrifice.[v] 20 Eli would bless Elkanah and his wife:[w] "May the LORD give you children by this woman in place of the one she[D] has given to the LORD."[x] Then they would go home.

21 The LORD paid attention to Hannah's need,[y] and she conceived and gave birth to three sons and two daughters. Meanwhile, the boy Samuel grew up in the presence of the LORD.[z]

Cross references

a 2:8 Jb 36:7
b Jb 38:4-6; Ps 75:3
c Ps 113:7-8
d 2:9 Ps 91:11-12; 1Pt 1:5
e Mt 8:12
f Ps 33:16-17
g 2:10 Ps 2:9
h 1Sm 7:10; Ps 18:13-14
i Ps 96:13; 98:9
j 1Sm 2:35; 12:3; 16:6; Ps 89:24
k 2:11 1Sm 1:1,19
l 1Sm 1:28; 2:18; 3:1
m 2:12 1Sm 1:15
n Jr 2:8; 9:3,6
o 2:14 Lv 7:29-34
p 2:15 Lv 3:3-5,16
q 2:16 Lv 7:25
r 2:17 Mal 2:7-9
s 2:18 1Sm 2:11; 3:1
t 1Sm 2:28
u 2:19 Ex 28:31
v 1Sm 1:3,21
w 2:20 Lk 2:34
x 1Sm 1:11,22,28
y 2:21 Gn 21:1
z 1Sm 2:26; 3:19-21; Lk 2:40

Textual notes

A 2:8 DSS, LXX add *He gives the vow of the one who makes a vow and He blesses the years of the just*   B 2:9 Lit feet   C 2:10 DSS, LXX read *The LORD shatters those who dispute with Him*   D 2:20 DSS; MT reads *he*

Study notes

lesser; if God controls the earth's **foundations**, He controls the status of its citizens.

2:9 The Lord not only sees people's actions, but He knows **His faithful ones** (cp. Nah 1:7) and the hearts of the **wicked**, and He blesses or judges them accordingly.

2:10 The Hebrew word behind **oppose** has a legal connotation; no one has a case against **the LORD**. The mention of God's **king** and **His anointed** may anticipate the establishment of the kingship in Israel. Some interpreters have suggested that Hannah spoke prophetically of God's everlasting kingdom under the Messiah.

2:11 The term **served** is not used of slaves, and it often denotes a higher level of service (Jos 1:1), including priestly service (Dt 10:8; 1Kg 8:11).

2:12 The phrase **wicked men** means literally "sons of worthlessness." The expression commonly denotes morally corrupt individuals; Hannah used the feminine form of the expression as she implored Eli not to consider her a daughter of worthlessness (1:16). **Had no regard for** means literally "did not know."

2:13-14 The priests' **share of the sacrifices** was specifically prescribed in the law of Moses (Lv 7:32-34). A **three-pronged meat fork** was nowhere stipulated; rather, Eli's sons were making their own rules for sacrifice, presumably to secure more for themselves.

2:15-16 The **fat** was the Lord's portion of the sacrifice (Lv 3:3-5). The text implies Eli's sons were also eating the fat of the sacrificial animals. The warning that **the fat must be burned first**—a warning that went unheeded—indicates the common people had a greater moral conscience than Eli's sons did.

2:17 The Hebrew verb translated **treated . . . with contempt** indicates strong displeasure or disdain; it also would later describe David's sin with Bathsheba (2Sm 12:14). It is often translated "despise" (Nm 14:11; Is 1:4; 5:24).

2:18 On **served**, see note at verse 11. Samuel's **linen ephod** was a vest-like garment that priests or the high priest wore (Ex 28:6-13). It contained special embroidery and 12 stones as a visible reminder of Israel's 12 tribes.

2:19 The **little robe** that Hannah made for Samuel may be linked with the one prescribed for the priests (Ex 28:31; Lv 8:7). Samuel was gone from Hannah's home but not from her heart.

2:20 The **one she has given** is literally "request she requested" or "grant she granted" (cp. 1:28), and it reinforces the special nature of Samuel's birth and dedication.

2:21 The Lord **paid attention to Hannah's need** is literally "Yahweh visited Hannah." The same Hebrew expression occurs in reference to Abraham's wife Sarah when she conceived Isaac, another child of promise (Gn 21:1). Hannah is abundantly blessed, but her **three sons and two daughters** are nonetheless contrasted with **the boy Samuel**, who **grew up in the presence of the LORD**.

²²Now Eli was very old. He heard about everything his sons were doing to all Israel[a] and how they were sleeping with the women who served at the entrance to the tent of meeting.[b] ²³He said to them, "Why are you doing these things? I have heard about your evil actions from all these people. ²⁴No, my sons, the report I hear from the LORD's people is not good. ²⁵If a man sins against another man, God can intercede for him, but if a man sins against the LORD, who can intercede for him?"[c] But they would not listen to their father, since the LORD intended to kill them.[d] ²⁶By contrast, the boy Samuel grew in stature and in favor with the LORD and with men.[e]

²⁷A man of God came to Eli and said to him,[f] "This is what the LORD says: 'Didn't I reveal Myself to your ancestral house when it was in Egypt and belonged to Pharaoh's palace?[g] ²⁸Out of all the tribes of Israel, I selected your house[A] to be priests, to offer sacrifices on My altar, to burn incense, and to wear an •ephod in My presence.[h] I also gave your house all the Israelite fire offerings. ²⁹Why, then, do all of you despise My sacrifices and offerings that I require at the place of worship?[i] You have honored your sons more than Me,[j] by making yourselves fat with the best part of all of the offerings of My people Israel.'

³⁰"Therefore, this is the declaration of the LORD, the God of Israel:

'Although I said
    your family and your ancestral house
    would walk before Me forever,[k]

the LORD now says, "No longer!"
I will honor those who honor Me,[l]
    but those who despise Me
        will be disgraced.[m]

³¹"'Look, the days are coming when I will cut off your strength and the strength of your ancestral family, so that none in your family will reach old age.[n] ³²You will see distress in the place of worship,[o] in spite of all that is good in Israel, and no one in your family will ever again reach old age.[p] ³³Any man from your family I do not cut off from My altar will bring grief[B] and sadness to you. All your descendants will die violently.[C,D] ³⁴This will be the sign that will come to you concerning your two sons Hophni and Phinehas:[q] both of them will die on the same day.[r]

³⁵"'Then I will raise up a faithful priest[s] for Myself. He will do whatever is in My heart and mind. I will establish a lasting dynasty for him,[t] and he will walk before My anointed one for all time.[u] ³⁶Anyone who is left in your family will come and bow down to him for a piece of silver or a loaf of bread. He will say: Please appoint me to some priestly office so I can have a piece of bread to eat.'"

Samuel's Call

3 The boy Samuel served the LORD in Eli's presence.[v] In those days the word of the LORD was rare and prophetic visions were not widespread.[w]

²One day Eli, whose eyesight was failing,[x] was lying in his room. ³Before the lamp of God had gone out,[y] Samuel was lying down in

---

Cross references (center column):

[a]2:22 1Sm 2:13-17
[b]Ex 38:8
[c]2:25 Nm 15:30-31; Heb 10:26-27
[d]Ex 5:2; 14:17-18; Jos 11:18-20
[e]2:26 Lk 2:52
[f]2:27 Dt 33:1; Jdg 13:6
[g]Ex 4:14-16; 12:1,43
[h]2:28 Ex 28:1-4
[i]2:29 Dt 12:5-7
[j]Mt 10:37
[k]2:30 Ex 29:9; 40:12-15; Nm 25:10-13
[l]Ps 50:23
[m]1Kg 2:26-27
[n]2:31 1Sm 4:11-18; 22:17-20
[o]2:32 1Kg 2:26-27
[p]Zch 8:4
[q]2:34 1Sm 10:7-9; 1Kg 13:3
[r]1Sm 4:11
[s]2:35 1Sm 3:20
[t]1Sm 8:3-5; 1Kg 11:38
[u]1Sm 10:9-10; 12:3; 16:13
[v]3:1 1Sm 2:11,18
[w]Ps 74:9; Ezk 7:26; Am 8:11-12
[x]3:2 1Sm 4:15
[y]3:3 Ex 27:20-21

[A]2:28 Lit *selected him*   [B]2:33 Lit *grief to your eyes*   [C]2:33 DSS, LXX read *die by the sword of men*   [D]2:33 Lit *die men*

2:22 The words **very old** probably hint at Eli's lack of strength to stop his sons from their sins, which the text now mentions also included sexual immorality.

2:25 In a dispute between two men, **God might intercede**, but if someone's sin was directly **against the LORD**, no intercession was possible—only condemnation. The words **since the LORD intended to kill them** reveal that much like Pharaoh in Moses' day (Ex 4:21; 5:2; 7:13), the persistent unbelief of Hophni and Phinehas led to God's giving them over to judgment.

2:26 The phrase **grew in stature and in favor with the LORD and with men** is strikingly similar to the description of Jesus as a child (Lk 2:52).

2:27 **Ancestral house . . . in Egypt** recalls God's choice of Aaron (Ex 4:14-16).

2:28 The responsibilities listed were strictly limited to the **priests**, whom the law of Moses designated as the sons of Aaron (Ex 28:1-5; Lv 8–9).

2:30 With the words **no longer**, God indicated that He had not set aside His promise to Aaron's line. The words **I will honor those who honor Me** reveal that God had judged Eli's house unfit to serve as priests among Aaron's sons.

2:31-32 God in His grace did not destroy Eli's house, but drastically reduced its **strength**.

2:34 As the chief sinners, **Hophni and Phinehas** would be the first to **die**—and **on the same day**.

2:35 Some suggest Samuel is intended by the phrase **a faithful priest**, but Samuel did not have a **lasting dynasty** (8:1-5). The term may denote the priestly line of Zadok, who eventually succeeded Eli's line (1Kg 2:27), or any and all priests who followed the Lord faithfully. **My anointed one** designates the line of David, for whom God also built a lasting dynasty (2Sm 7:11-16).

2:36 This verse suggests that Eli's descendants would not even partake of the sacrificial portions reserved for the priests (Lv 2:3; 5:13; 7:7-10).

3:1 On **served**, see note at 2:11. **Prophetic visions were not widespread** because of the general corruption of the time. God might withhold His **word** from people who showed by their conduct they did not want to receive it.

3:3 The **lamp of God** was to burn from evening until morning (Ex 27:21), so the wording suggests a time just before dawn.

the tabernacle of the LORD, where the ark of God was located.

⁴Then the LORD called Samuel,ᴬ and he answered, "Here I am." ⁵He ran to Eli and said, "Here I am; you called me."

"I didn't call," Eli replied. "Go back and lie down." So he went and lay down.

⁶Once again the LORD called, "Samuel!"

Samuel got up, went to Eli, and said, "Here I am; you called me."

"I didn't call, my son," he replied. "Go back and lie down."

⁷Now Samuel had not yet experienced the LORD, because the word of the LORD had not yet been revealed to him. ⁸Once again, for the third time, the LORD called Samuel. He got up, went to Eli, and said, "Here I am; you called me."

Then Eli understood that the LORD was calling the boy. ⁹He told Samuel, "Go and lie down. If He calls you, say, 'Speak, LORD, for Your servant is listening.'" So Samuel went and lay down in his place.

¹⁰The LORD came, stood there, and called as before, "Samuel, Samuel!"

Samuel responded, "Speak, for Your servant is listening."

¹¹The LORD said to Samuel, "I am about to do something in Israel that everyone who hears about it will shudder.ᵃ ¹²On that day I will carry out against Eli everything I said about his family, from beginning to end.ᵇ ¹³I told him that I am going to judge his family forever because of the iniquity he knows about: his

ᵃ3:11 2Kg 21:12; Jr 19:3
ᵇ3:12 1Sm 2:27-36
ᶜ3:13 Dt 17:12; 21:18
ᵈ3:14 Lv 15:31; Is 22:14
ᵉ3:17 2Sm 3:35
ᶠ3:18 Ex 34:5-7; Lv 10:3; Jb 2:10; Is 39:8
ᵍ3:19 1Sm 2:21
ʰGn 21:22; 28:15
ⁱ1Sm 9:6
ʲ3:20 1Sm 2:35
ᵏ3:21 1Sm 3:10
ˡ4:1 1Sm 7:12
ᵐJos 12:18; 1Sm 29:1

sons are defiling the sanctuary,ᴮ and he has not stopped them.ᶜ ¹⁴Therefore, I have sworn to Eli's family: The iniquity of Eli's family will never be wiped out by either sacrifice or offering."ᵈ

¹⁵Samuel lay down until the morning; then he opened the doors of the LORD's house. He was afraid to tell Eli the vision, ¹⁶but Eli called him and said, "Samuel, my son."

"Here I am," answered Samuel.

¹⁷"What was the message He gave you?" Eli asked. "Don't hide it from me. May God punish you and do so severely if you hide anything from me that He told you."ᵉ ¹⁸So Samuel told him everything and did not hide anything from him. Eli responded, "He is the LORD. He will do what He thinks is good."ᶜ,ᶠ

¹⁹Samuel grew,ᵍ and the LORD was with him,ʰ and He fulfilled everything Samuel prophesied.ᴰ,ⁱ ²⁰All Israel from Dan to Beer-sheba knew that Samuel was a confirmed prophet of the LORD.ʲ ²¹The LORD continued to appear in Shiloh, because there He revealed Himself to Samuel by His word.ᵏ ¹And Samuel's words came to all Israel.

The Ark Captured by the Philistines

Israel went out to meet the Philistines in battle andᴱ camped at Ebenezerˡ while the Philistines camped at Aphek.ᵐ ²The Philistines lined up in battle formation against Israel, and as the battle intensified, Israel was defeated by the Philistines, who struck down about 4,000 men on the battlefield.

ᴬ3:4 DSS, LXX read called, "Samuel! Samuel!" ᴮ3:13 Ancient Jewish tradition, LXX, Old Lat read are cursing God ᶜ3:18 Lit what is good in His eyes ᴰ3:19 Lit He let no words fall to the ground ᴱ4:1 LXX reads In those days the Philistines gathered together to fight against Israel, and Israel went out to engage them in battle. They

---

3:4-6 When **the LORD called Samuel**, the youth confused the voice with that of **Eli**.

3:7 The text now gives a reason why Samuel did not recognize God's call—no prior vision or voice had come to him.

3:8 After the **third time**, Eli surmised that Samuel might be hearing God's voice. Perhaps no one else was present in the tabernacle complex.

3:9 Eli's suggested words to Samuel, **Speak, LORD, for Your servant is listening**, provide a model prayer for those who seek to follow God's will.

3:10 The twofold **Samuel, Samuel** may indicate urgency, as it did with Abraham on Mount Moriah (Gn 22:11), with Moses at the burning bush (Ex 3:4), or with Saul of Tarsus on the road to Damascus (Ac 9:4).

3:11 The phrase **everyone who hears about it will shudder** means literally "the two ears of everyone who hears about it will tingle (or ring or quiver)," indicating a response to a horrific report (2Kg 21:12; Jr 19:3).

3:13 Eli did try to stop **his sons** (2:23-25), but apparently his words came after he had let their abuses continue too long.

3:14 The phrase **wiped out** might be translated "atoned for."

3:15 Samuel **was afraid to tell Eli the vision**, probably because Eli had served as Samuel's guardian and mentor and Samuel did not want to bring him bad news.

3:16-17 Eli's words sound harsh, but they were probably intended to encourage Samuel to share the full details of his revelation. This was the standard form of an oath (cp. 2Sm 3:35).

3:18 The Lord's word to **Samuel** confirmed the earlier word that **Eli** had received from the man of God (2:27-36).

3:20 The cities of **Dan** and **Beer-sheba** essentially marked the northern and southern borders of Israel, respectively, spanning a distance of about 110 miles (2Sm 3:10; 24:2).

3:21 Samuel had demonstrated a willingness to receive and follow God's word, so **the LORD continued to appear in Shiloh**, whereas He had not done so during the unfaithfulness of Eli's day (v. 1).

4:1 The **Philistines** migrated to the Judean coastline during the twelfth century B.C. and began threatening Israel during the days of the judges (chaps. 13–16). The Israelites **camped**

³When the troops returned to the camp, the elders of Israel asked, "Why did the Lord let us be defeated today by the Philistines?ᵃ Let's bring the ark of the Lord's covenant from Shiloh. Then itᴬ will go with us and save us from the hand of our enemies."ᵇ ⁴So the people sent men to Shiloh to bring back the ark of the covenant of the Lord of •Hosts, who dwells between the •cherubim.ᶜ Eli's two sons, Hophni and Phinehas, were there with the ark of the covenant of God. ⁵When the ark of the covenant of the Lord entered the camp, all the Israelites raised such a loud shout that the ground shook.ᵈ

⁶The Philistines heard the sound of the war cry and asked, "What's this loud shout in the Hebrews' camp?" When the Philistines discovered that the ark of the Lord had entered the camp, ⁷they panicked. "The gods have entered their camp!" they said. "Woe to us, nothing like this has happened before.ᴮ ⁸Woe to us, who will rescue us from the hand of these magnificent gods? These are the gods that slaughtered the Egyptians with all kinds of plagues in the wilderness. ⁹Show some courage and be men, Philistines!ᵉ Otherwise, you'll serve the Hebrews just as they served you.ᶠ Now be men and fight!"

¹⁰So the Philistines fought, and Israel was defeated,ᵍ and each man fled to his tent.ʰ The slaughter was severe—30,000 of the Israelite foot soldiers fell. ¹¹The ark of God was captured, and Eli's two sons, Hophni and Phinehas, died.ⁱ

Eli's Death and Ichabod's Birth

¹²That same day, a Benjaminite man ranʲ from the battle and came to Shiloh. His clothes were torn,ᵏ and there was dirt on his head. ¹³When he arrived, there was Eli sitting on his chair beside the road watching,ˡ because he was anxious about the ark of God. When the man entered the city to give a report, the entire city cried out.

¹⁴Eli heard the outcry and asked, "Why this commotion?" The man quickly came and reported to Eli. ¹⁵At that time Eli was 98 years old, and his gaze was fixedᶜ because he couldn't see.ᵐ

¹⁶The man said to Eli, "I'm the one who came from the battle.ᴰ I fled from there today."

"What happened, my son?"ⁿ Eli asked.

¹⁷The messenger answered, "Israel has fled from the Philistines, and also there was a great slaughter among the people. Your two sons, Hophni and Phinehas, are both dead, and the ark of God has been captured." ¹⁸When he mentioned the ark of God, Eli fell backward off the chair by the city gate,ᵒ and since he was old and heavy, his neck broke and he died. Eli had judged Israel 40 years.

¹⁹Eli's daughter-in-law, the wife of Phinehas, was pregnant and about to give birth. When she heard the news about the capture of God's ark and the deaths of her father-in-law and her husband, she collapsed and gave birth because her labor pains came on her. ²⁰As she was dying,ᴱ the women taking care of her said, "Don't be afraid. You've given

---

ᵃ 4:3 Jos 7:7-8
ᵇ Nm 10:35; Jos 6:6
ᶜ 4:4 Ex 25:22; Nm 7:89
ᵈ 4:5 Jos 6:5,20
ᵉ 4:9 1Co 16:13
ᶠ Jdg 13:1; 1Sm 14:21
ᵍ 4:10 Dt 28:15,25; 1Sm 4:2
ʰ 2Sm 18:17; 2Kg 14:12
ⁱ 4:11 1Sm 2:34; Ps 78:56-64
ʲ 4:12 Jos 7:22; 1Sm 8:11
ᵏ Jos 7:6; 2Sm 1:2; 15:32; Neh 9:1
ˡ 4:13 1Sm 1:9; 4:18
ᵐ 4:15 1Kg 14:4
ⁿ 4:16 2Sm 1:4
ᵒ 4:18 1Sm 4:13

ᴬ 4:3 Or He   ᴮ 4:7 Lit yesterday or the day before   ᶜ 4:15 Lit his eyes stood; 1Kg 14:4   ᴰ 4:16 LXX reads camp   ᴱ 4:20 LXX reads And in her time of delivery, she was about to die

---

at Ebenezer about 20 miles west of Shiloh, while the Philistines **camped at Aphek** across the plain to the west. Israel's enemies had pushed far north from their home along Israel's southern coastline and now threatened the central territory.

4:3 Why did the Lord **let us be defeated**? is literally "Why did the Lord strike us?" The people associated **the ark of the Lord's covenant** (Ex 25:10-22) with God's presence, and they assumed taking the ark into battle would guarantee victory over their **enemies**. This is the equivalent of trying to manipulate God through a magical talisman.

4:4 The phrase **dwells between the cherubim** is a reference to God's dwelling in the cloud over the mercy seat of the **ark** (Lv 16:2). Ironically, despite their priestly office, **Hophni and Phinehas** were probably the two least worthy individuals to carry the ark.

4:5 The **loud shout** as the **ark . . . entered the camp** further emphasizes the Israelites' incorrect association of God's presence with the ark. God's blessing did not automatically come because of the ark's presence.

4:7 The gods have may possibly be translated "God has." Either way, the Philistines feared for their lives.

4:8 The Philistines either incorrectly assumed the Israelites worshiped many **gods**, or they had seen Israel's idolatry and drawn that conclusion.

4:9 Show some courage is literally "strengthen yourselves." The language may suggest the Philistines currently had control over the Israelites and feared losing it.

4:12 A **Benjaminite** was a man from the tribal territory of Benjamin to the south. Shiloh was part of Ephraim's territory. **Clothes were torn . . . dirt on his head** were expressions of mourning (2Sm 1:2).

4:13 "Keeping vigil" might be a better translation than **watching** since Eli was now blind (v. 15). The Hebrew word translated **cried out** always has a negative connotation, as does the related word "outcry" in the next verse.

4:14 In his haste, this man had run by Israel's former high priest. Now he returned to report to **Eli** and apprise him of the battle.

4:16 The words **I'm the one** suggest the man was a designated messenger to bring the news of the battle (v. 17; cp. 2Sm 18:19-23).

4:19 Eli's **daughter-in-law, the wife of Phinehas**, had lost three family members—her **father-in-law . . . husband**, and brother-in-law—and that news, coupled with the news

birth to a son!"[a] But she did not respond or pay attention. [21]She named the boy Ichabod,[A] saying, "The glory has departed from Israel,"[b] referring to the capture of the ark of God[c] and to the deaths of her father-in-law and her husband. [22]"The glory has departed from Israel," she said, "because the ark of God has been captured."

The Ark in Philistine Hands

5 After the Philistines had captured the ark of God, they took it from Ebenezer[d] to Ashdod,[e] [2]brought it into the temple of Dagon[B,f] and placed it next to his statue.[C] [3]When the people of Ashdod got up early the next morning, there was Dagon, fallen with his face to the ground before the ark of the LORD.[g] So they took Dagon and returned him to his place. [4]But when they got up early the next morning, there was Dagon, fallen with his face to the ground before the ark of the LORD. This time, both Dagon's head and the palms of his hands were broken off and lying on the threshold. Only Dagon's torso remained.[D] [5]That is why, to this day, the priests of Dagon and everyone who enters the temple of Dagon in Ashdod do not step on Dagon's threshold.

[6]The LORD's hand was heavy on the people of Ashdod,[h] terrorizing[i] and afflicting the people of Ashdod and its territory with tumors.[E,F,j] [7]When the men of Ashdod saw what

was happening, they said, "The ark of Israel's God must not stay here with us, because His hand is strongly against us and our god Dagon." [8]So they called all the Philistine rulers together[k] and asked, "What should we do with the ark of Israel's God?"

"The ark of Israel's God should be moved to Gath," they replied. So the men of Ashdod moved the ark. [9]After they had moved it, the LORD's hand was against the city of Gath,[l] causing a great panic. He afflicted the men of the city, from the youngest to the oldest, with an outbreak of tumors.[m]

[10]The Gittites then sent the ark of God to Ekron, but when it got there, the Ekronites cried out, "They've moved the ark of Israel's God to us to kill us and our people!"[G] [11]The Ekronites called all the Philistine rulers together.[n] They said, "Send the ark of Israel's God away. It must return to its place so it won't kill us and our people!"[H] For the fear of death pervaded the city; God's hand was oppressing them.[o] [12]The men who did not die were afflicted with tumors, and the outcry of the city went up to heaven.[p]

The Return of the Ark

6 When the ark of the LORD had been in the land of the Philistines for seven months, [2]the Philistines summoned the priests and the diviners[q] and pleaded, "What should we

[a]4:20 Gn 35:16-19
[b]4:21 Ps 26:8; Jr 2:11
[c]1Sm 4:11
[d]5:1 1Sm 4:1; 7:12
[e]Jos 13:3
[f]5:2 Jdg 16:23-24; 1Ch 10:8-10
[g]5:3 Is 46:1-9
[h]5:6 Ex 9:3; 1Sm 5:7,11
[i]1Sm 6:5
[j]Dt 28:27; Ps 78:66
[k]5:8 1Sm 5:11; 29:6-11
[l]5:9 1Sm 5:11; 7:13
[m]1Sm 5:6
[n]5:11 1Sm 5:8
[o]1Sm 5:6,9
[p]5:12 Ex 12:30
[q]6:2 Gn 41:8; Ex 7:11; Is 2:6

[A]4:21 = Where is Glory? [B]5:2 A Philistine god of the sea, grain, or storm [C]5:2 Lit to Dagon [D]5:4 LXX; Hb reads Only Dagon remained on it [E]5:6 LXX adds He brought up mice against them, and they swarmed in their ships. Then mice went up into the land and there was a mortal panic in the city. [F]5:6 Perhaps bubonic plague [G]5:10 DSS, LXX read Why have you moved . . . people? [H]5:11 DSS, LXX read Why don't you return it to . . . people?

of the **capture of God's ark,** suddenly brought her **labor pains.**

4:21 Ichabod means "where is the glory?" with the clear implication, as she then said, that **the glory has departed from Israel.**

4:22 The wife of Phinehas incorrectly associated God's glorious presence with the presence of **the ark of God.** However, she was right in the sense that she believed life apart from God's presence was not worth living.

5:1 The trip **from Ebenezer to Ashdod** was about 19 miles. Ashdod—along with Ashkelon, Ekron, Gaza, and Gath—was one of Philistia's five major cities.

5:2 Dagon was originally an agricultural and/or storm god of Canaan and Mesopotamia, but the Philistines made him head of their pantheon. Perhaps the Philistines thought they should place the ark **next to his statue** as a symbolic gesture of Dagon's defeat of the Lord in battle.

5:4 Dagon's head and the **palms of his hands** were **broken off** (lit "cut off"), suggesting Dagon's fall was no accident. The positioning of head and palms **on the threshold** nearby also ruled out an accident.

5:5 From then on the **priests of Dagon** and all his worshipers avoided stepping on Dagon's **threshold**—a threshold that marked the place of his defeat before God.

5:6 The Lord now oppressed **the people of Ashdod,** plaguing them as He had plagued the Egyptians (4:8). **Tumors** (Dt 28:27) probably describe symptoms of bubonic plague, a disease spread by rodents (1Sm 6:4). Others believe the term describes boils or hemorrhoids.

5:8 Perhaps **Gath,** located more than 20 miles away at the mouth of the Elah Valley, was on friendlier terms with Israel (21:10; 27:3; 2Sm 15:18; 1Kg 2:39), prompting relocation of the **ark.**

5:9 The Philistines' plan failed as God then brought the **tumors to Gath.**

5:10 The Philistine citizens of **Ekron,** located 10 miles north of Gath, **cried out** (see note at 4:13) in fear of their lives when the **ark of . . . God** came to their city.

5:12 On **outcry,** see note at 4:13.

6:1 The allusion to **seven months** dates the battle that resulted in the ark's capture to around late October, since the wheat harvest (v. 13) typically occurred around late May.

6:2 Priests and . . . diviners represented the Philistines' religious authorities. Diviners were prohibited by the law of Moses (Dt 18:10,14) because they attempted to discern the will of the divine apart from the methods God had prescribed.

do with the ark of the LORD? Tell us how we can send it back to its place."

[3] They replied, "If you send the ark of Israel's God away, you must not send it without an offering.[a] You must send back a restitution offering to Him,[b] and you will be healed. Then the reason His hand hasn't been removed from you will be revealed."[A]

[4] They asked, "What restitution offering should we send back to Him?"

And they answered, "Five gold tumors and five gold mice[c] corresponding to the number of Philistine rulers,[d] since there was one plague for both you[B] and your rulers. [5] Make images of your tumors and of your mice that are destroying the land. Give glory to Israel's God,[e] and perhaps He will stop oppressing you,[C,f] your gods, and your land.[g] [6] Why harden your hearts as the Egyptians and Pharaoh hardened theirs?[h] When He afflicted them, didn't they send Israel away, and Israel left?[i]

[7] "Now then, prepare one new cart and two milk cows that have never been yoked.[j] Hitch the cows to the cart, but take their calves away and pen them up. [8] Take the ark of the LORD, place it on the cart, and put the gold objects that you're sending Him as a restitution offering in a box[k] beside the ark.[l] Send it off and let it go its way. [9] Then watch: If it goes up the road to its homeland toward Beth-shemesh,[m] it is the LORD who has made this terrible trouble for us. However, if it doesn't, we will know that it was not His hand that punished[n] us—it was just something that happened to us by chance."

[10] The men did this: They took two milk cows, hitched them to the cart, and confined their calves in the pen. [11] Then they put the ark of the LORD on the cart, along with the box containing the gold mice and the images of their tumors. [12] The cows went straight up the road to Beth-shemesh.[o] They stayed on that one highway,[p] lowing as they went; they never strayed to the right or to the left. The Philistine rulers were walking behind them to the territory of Beth-shemesh.

[13] The people of Beth-shemesh were harvesting wheat in the valley, and when they looked up and saw the ark, they were overjoyed to see it. [14] The cart came to the field of Joshua of Beth-shemesh and stopped there near a large rock. The people of the city chopped up the cart and offered the cows as a *burnt offering to the LORD.[q] [15] The Levites[r] removed the ark of the LORD, along with the box containing the gold objects, and placed them on the large rock. That day the men of Beth-shemesh offered burnt offerings and made sacrifices to the LORD. [16] When the five Philistine rulers[s] observed this, they returned to Ekron that same day.

[17] As a restitution offering to the LORD, the Philistines had sent back one gold tumor for each city:[t] Ashdod, Gaza, Ashkelon, Gath, and Ekron. [18] The number of gold mice also corresponded to the number of Philistine cities of the five rulers, the fortified cities and the outlying villages.[u] The large rock[D,v] on which the ark of the LORD was placed is in the field of Joshua of Beth-shemesh to this day.

[19] God struck down the men of Beth-she-

Cross references (center column):

[a] 6:3 Dt 16:16
[b] Lv 5:15-16
[c] 6:4 1Sm 5:6,9,12; 6:17
[d] Jos 13:3; Jdg 3:3; 1Sm 6:17-18
[e] 6:5 Jos 7:19; Is 42:2
[f] 1Sm 5:6,11
[g] 1Sm 5:3-4,7
[h] 6:6 Ex 8:15,32; 9:34
[i] Ex 4:21; 12:31
[j] 6:7 Nm 19:2
[k] 6:8 1Sm 6:4-5
[l] 1Sm 6:3
[m] 6:9 Jos 15:10
[n] 1Sm 6:3
[o] 6:12 1Sm 6:9
[p] Nm 20:19
[q] 6:14 1Kg 19:21
[r] 6:15 Nm 4:1-33
[s] 6:16 Jos 13:3
[t] 6:17 1Sm 6:4
[u] 6:18 Dt 3:5
[v] 1Sm 6:14-15

[A]6:3 DSS, LXX read healed, and an atonement shall be made for you. Shouldn't His hand be removed from you?　[B]6:4 Some Hb mss, LXX; other Hb mss read them　[C]6:5 Lit will lighten the heaviness of His hand from you　[D]6:18 Some Hb mss, DSS, LXX, Tg; other Hb mss read meadow

6:3 A **restitution offering** applied to situations where holy things (here the ark) became defiled (Lv 5:15).

6:4 The **five gold tumors** and **five gold mice** do not correspond to the items the law of Moses required for guilt offerings (Lv 5:14–6:7). However, fashioning an offering in the shape of the thing from which a people wanted to be delivered is well attested in the ancient world (Nm 21:6-9).

6:6 The Philistines knew Israel's history and what God had done in Egypt (4:8). They were determined to learn their spiritual lesson quicker than the **Egyptians** had.

6:7-8 The Philistines put forth this one final test with a **cart** and two **cows** to make sure the plagues had come from the Lord's hand. Nonetheless, they were certain they needed to **send** the **ark of the LORD** away. Untrained cows would not normally know how to work together to pull a cart on a road, and they would not normally leave their **calves** behind, so when that's what happened, they knew it was from God.

6:9 **Beth-shemesh** lay in the Sorek Valley a short distance from Timnah, which was controlled by the Philistines (Jdg 14:1).

6:12 The text emphasizes how the cows' path left no room for doubt about God's guidance. **The Philistine rulers** followed the cart to **the territory of Beth-shemesh**, which probably marked the beginning of Israelite-controlled land.

6:13 Harvesting **wheat** was typically done around late May. The Festival of Weeks, called shavu'oth in Hebrew (Nm 28:26-31; Dt 16:16), marked this time of ingathering and included Pentecost (Lv 23:15-16; Ac 2:1).

6:14 The text does not suggest that the people sinned in offering the cows as a **burnt offering**, though such offerings normally required a male without blemish (Lv 1).

6:15 Beth-shemesh was a city appointed for **the Levites** (Jos 21:16).

6:16 The **five Philistine rulers** recognized God's hand in their troubles of the past seven months. They returned to **Ekron**, where presumably they reported what had happened.

6:17-18 On the **Philistine cities**, see note at 5:1. The expression **to this day** refers to the time 1 Samuel was written, probably early in the days of the divided kingdom.

6:19 The Hebrew words translated **out of 50,000 men** do not occur in many early manuscripts, and Beth-shemesh could

mesh because they looked inside the ark of the Lord.[A,a] He struck down 70 men out of 50,000 men.[B] The people mourned because the Lord struck them with a great slaughter. [20] The men of Beth-shemesh asked, "Who is able to stand in the presence of this holy Lord God?[b] Who should the ark go to from here?"

[21] They sent messengers to the residents of Kiriath-jearim,[c] saying, "The Philistines have returned the ark of the Lord. Come down and get it."[C]

7 So the men of Kiriath-jearim came for the ark of the Lord and took it to Abinadab's house on the hill.[d] They consecrated his son Eleazar to take care of it.

Victory at Mizpah

[2] Time went by until 20 years had passed since the ark had been taken to Kiriath-jearim. Then the whole house of Israel began to seek the Lord. [3] Samuel told them, "If you[e] are returning to the Lord[f] with all your heart,[g] get rid of the foreign gods[h] and the •Ashtoreths that are among you, dedicate yourselves to[D] the Lord, and worship only Him.[i] Then He will rescue you from the hand of the Philistines."

[4] So the Israelites removed the •Baals and the Ashtoreths[j] and only worshiped the Lord.

[5] Samuel said, "Gather all Israel at Mizpah,[k] and I will pray to the Lord on your behalf."[l] [6] When they gathered at Mizpah, they drew water and poured it out in the Lord's presence.[m] They fasted that day,[n] and there they confessed, "We have sinned against the Lord."[o] And Samuel judged the Israelites at Mizpah.

[7] When the Philistines heard that the Israelites had gathered at Mizpah, their rulers marched up toward Israel. When the Israelites heard about it, they were afraid because of the Philistines. [8] The Israelites said to Samuel, "Don't stop crying out to the Lord our God for us, so that He will save us from the hand of the Philistines."

[9] Then Samuel took a young lamb[p] and offered it as a whole •burnt offering to the Lord. He cried out to the Lord on behalf of Israel, and the Lord answered him.[q] [10] Samuel was offering the burnt offering as the Philistines drew near to fight against Israel. The Lord thundered loudly[r] against the Philistines that day and threw them into such confusion that they fled before Israel.[s] [11] Then the men of

Cross references (center column):

[a]6:19 Nm 4:15-20; 2Sm 6:7
[b]6:20 Nm 17:13; Ps 76:7; Ezk 44:9-16
[c]6:21 Jos 9:17; 15:9,60
[d]7:1 2Sm 6:3-4
[e]7:3 Ex 20:3
[f]Dt 13:4; 1Ch 19:3
[g]Dt 6:5; 30:10; Jl 2:12-14
[h]Jos 24:14,23; Jdg 10:16
[i]Dt 6:13; Mt 4:10
[j]7:4 Jdg 2:13
[k]7:5 Jdg 20:1
[l]1Sm 8:6; 12:17,19,23
[m]7:6 1Sm 1:15; Ps 62:8; Lm 2:19
[n]Lv 16:29; Neh 9:1
[o]Jdg 10:10
[p]7:9 Lv 22:27
[q]Ps 99:6; Jr 15:1
[r]7:10 1Sm 2:10; 2Sm 22:14
[s]Ex 23:27; Jos 10:10; Jdg 4:15

A6:19 LXX reads *But the sons of Jeconiah did not rejoice with the men of Beth-shemesh when they saw the ark of the Lord.*
B6:19 Some Hb mss, Josephus read *70 men*; other Hb mss read *50,070 men*   C6:21 Lit *and bring it up to you*   D7:3 Lit *you and set your hearts on*

---

not have supported such a large population. The reading **70 men**, on the other hand, is undisputed. The phrase **looked inside the ark** may also be translated "looked at the ark" in the sense of unholy staring or gazing. The Levites should have covered the ark as soon as possible and treated it more reverently.

6:20 The **men of Beth-shemesh** realized their own unholiness **in the presence of** the **holy Lord God**. The Philistines had sent the ark away; the citizens of Beth-shemesh now determined to do the same.

6:21 Kiriath-jearim was a city in Judah's territory about 15 miles to the east. Sending the **ark** there instead of to Shiloh suggests the Philistines may have overrun Shiloh after they captured the ark. Archaeological evidence indicates the city was destroyed about this time.

7:1 Eleazar was a common priestly name (Ex 6:23; 1Ch 9:20; 23:21; Ezr 8:33), and the verb **consecrated** also may hint at the family's Levitical connection.

7:2 The verb translated **seek** contains the connotation of mourning. Genuine heartfelt repentance seems to have arrived at last.

7:3 Samuel instructed the people to demonstrate the genuineness of their repentant words (the Hb word translated **returning** carries the idea of repentance) with action. **Foreign gods** certainly included Baal, chief of the Canaanite gods and a constant object of worship during Israel's days of compromise (Jdg 2:11; 3:7). **Ashtoreths** were representations of Baal's consort.

7:4 Removal of **the Baals and the Ashtoreths** must have required some time—though certainly not 20 years, the period of spiritual dormancy following the ark's return (v. 2).

7:5 Samuel took an active role in confirming Israel's rededication to God. **Mizpah** was located seven miles north of Jerusalem; during the judges period, the tribes had gathered there for intertribal war against Benjamin (Jdg 20:1). Some interpreters have identified the site with modern Nebi Samwil, approximately five miles northwest of Jerusalem. The site afforded Israel the opportunity to renew the covenant and to prepare for war with the Philistines.

7:6 The phrase **drew water and poured it out** is probably a symbolic allusion to the people's hearts being poured out like water before the Lord (2Sm 14:14; Lm 2:19). The phrase **Samuel judged the Israelites at Mizpah** shows that he was acting more prominently than he had before.

7:7 The **Philistines heard** of Israel's gathering and appear to have understood it as preparation for war, because their **rulers marched up toward Israel**.

7:8 The Israelites' impassioned request to **Samuel** reveals the level of trust they had in his spiritual leadership.

7:9 Samuel **cried out to the Lord**, who **answered** his prayer by bringing Israel deliverance.

7:10 The phrase **as the Philistines drew near** suggests urgency; **Samuel** raced to offer the sacrifice as the enemy approached, knowing that God's favor was essential for victory. **The Lord . . . threw them into . . . confusion** as He had done with His enemies in other battles (Ex 14:24; Jos 10:10). That **they fled** (lit "were struck down") **before Israel** highlights the Philistines' defeat.

7:11 The exact site of **Beth-car** is unknown; the Israelites probably chased the Philistines back down the ridge route toward Philistine territory (v. 7).

Israel charged out of Mizpah and pursued the Philistines striking them down all the way to a place below Beth-car. [12]Afterward, Samuel took a stone and set it upright[a] between Mizpah and Shen. He named it Ebenezer,[A] explaining, "The LORD has helped us to this point." [13]So the Philistines were subdued[b] and[B] did not invade Israel's territory again.[c] The LORD's hand was against the Philistines all of Samuel's life. [14]The cities from Ekron to Gath, which they had taken from Israel, were restored; Israel even rescued their surrounding territories from Philistine control. There was also peace between Israel and the Amorites.

[15]Samuel judged Israel throughout his life.[d] [16]Every year he would go on a circuit to Bethel, Gilgal, and Mizpah and would judge Israel at all these locations. [17]Then he would return to Ramah[e] because his home was there, he judged Israel there, and he built an altar to the LORD there.

Israel's Demand for a King

8 When Samuel grew old, he appointed his sons as judges over Israel.[f] [2]His firstborn son's name was Joel and his second was Abijah. They were judges in Beer-sheba.[g] [3]However, his sons did not walk in his ways—they turned toward dishonest gain, took bribes, and perverted justice.[h]

[4]So all the elders of Israel gathered together and went to Samuel at Ramah.[i] [5]They said to him, "Look, you are old, and your sons do not follow your example. Therefore, appoint a king to judge us the same as all the other nations have."[j]

[6]When they said, "Give us a king to judge us," Samuel considered their demand sinful, so he prayed to the LORD. [7]But the LORD told him, "Listen to the people and everything they say to you. They have not rejected you; they have rejected Me as their king.[k] [8]They are doing the same thing to you that they have done to Me,[c] since the day I brought them out of Egypt until this day, abandoning Me and worshiping other gods. [9]Listen to them, but you must solemnly warn them[l] and tell them about the rights of the king who will rule over them."

[10]Samuel told all the LORD's words to the people who were asking him for a king. [11]He said, "These are the rights of the king who will rule over you: He will take your sons and put them to his use in his chariots, on his horses, or running in front of his chariots. [12]He can appoint them for his use as commanders of thousands or commanders of fifties,[m] to plow his ground or reap his harvest, or to make his weapons of war or the equipment for his chariots. [13]He can take your daughters to become

---

Cross references:
a 7:12 Jos 4:9
b 7:13 Jdg 13:1-15
c 1Sm 13:5
d 7:15 1Sm 7:6; 12:11
e 7:17 1Sm 1:1,19; 2:11
f 8:1 Dt 16:18-19
g 8:2 Gn 22:19; 1Kg 19:3; Am 5:5
h 8:3 Ex 23:1-9
i 8:4 1Sm 7:17
j 8:5 Dt 17:14-15
k 8:7 Ex 16:8; 1Sm 10:19
l 8:9 Ezk 3:18
m 8:12 Nm 31:14; 1Sm 22:7

A7:12 = Stone of Help   B7:13 LXX reads *The LORD humbled the Philistines and they*   C8:8 LXX; MT omits *to Me*

7:12 The location of **Shen** (lit "the tooth," perhaps referring to some sharp crag or cliff) is unknown. **Ebenezer** (Hb "stone of help") marks the extent of the Israelite victory and is a different place from the site of Israel's earlier encampment (4:1).

7:14 Such cities as **Ekron** and **Gath** were open to attack because they lay along Israelite-Philistine border territory. **Amorites** probably denotes Canaanite remnant populations in the land.

7:15 Samuel judged Israel throughout his life, though his ministry seemed to decline somewhat (at his own initiative) following the appointment of Saul as Israel's king (chap. 12).

7:16 The cities of **Bethel, Gilgal, and Mizpah** lay in the territory of Benjamin. Bethel's location is identified with modern Ramallah north of Jerusalem. Gilgal sat in the Jordan Valley near Jericho and was Israel's base camp during the days of Joshua's conquest (Jos 4:19). On Mizpah, see note at 1Sm 7:5.

7:17 The name **Ramah** is preserved in the name el-Aram, an Arab village located on the site of ancient Ramah five miles north of Jerusalem. Samuel's establishment of **an altar to the LORD** further suggests Shiloh had been destroyed. Deuteronomy 12:13-14 had warned against building local altars.

8:2 The sons' location in **Beer-sheba** at Israel's southern edge suggests Samuel did not intend to abdicate his role in Ramah just because he had appointed his sons.

8:5 The elders still appreciated Samuel's leadership; in fact, they wanted him to **appoint a king** for Israel. However, Samuel was **old** and they knew they could not count on his

leadership much longer. The words **as all the other nations** contradicted God's desire that Israel be distinct (Lv 20:26; Dt 4:6-8), though the law of Moses did allow for the establishment of a king (Dt 17:14-20).

8:6 Samuel probably **considered their demand sinful** because it appeared motivated by a desire to conform to the pattern of other nations. Nonetheless, **he prayed** for the Lord's answer.

8:7 Samuel felt personal hurt and rejection because of the people's desire for a king, but God informed him the issue was much deeper.

8:8 Israel's rejection of Samuel's leadership was the logical outcome of centuries of the nation's rejection of God's leadership. They didn't want God to rule them, so they wouldn't want God's servant to rule them.

8:9 The words **solemnly warn** could also be translated "strongly testify"; they sound a somber note in the midst of a message of acquiescence. Explaining the **rights of the king** denotes a challenge to count the high cost the kingship would bring the people.

8:11 On **rights of the king**, see note at verse 9. **Chariots** is actually singular both times, suggesting the duties mentioned in this verse pertain more to the king's personal honor guard.

8:12 The king would also need a strong military, and he would draft into service the sons of his subjects.

8:13 Daughters likewise would assume roles, oftentimes demeaning, that would support the royal lifestyle.

perfumers, cooks, and bakers. [14] He can take your best fields, vineyards, and olive orchards and give them to his servants.[a] [15] He can take a tenth of your grain and your vineyards and give them to his officials and servants. [16] He can take your male servants, your female servants, your best young men,[A] and your donkeys and use them for his work. [17] He can take a tenth of your flocks, and you yourselves can become his servants. [18] When that day comes, you will cry out because of the king you've chosen for yourselves,[b] but the LORD won't answer you on that day."[c]

[19] The people refused to listen to Samuel. "No!" they said. "We must have a king over us. [20] Then we'll be like all the other nations: our king will judge us, go out before us,[d] and fight our battles."

[21] Samuel listened to all the people's words and then repeated them to the LORD.[B] [22] "Listen to them," the LORD told Samuel. "Appoint a king for them."[e]

Then Samuel told the men of Israel, "Each of you, go back to your city."

Saul Anointed King

9 There was an influential man of Benjamin named Kish[f] son of Abiel, son of Zeror, son of Becorath, son of Aphiah, son of a Benjaminite. [2] He had a son named Saul, an impressive young man.[g] There was no one more impressive among the Israelites than he. He stood a head taller than anyone else.[C,h]

[3] One day the donkeys of Saul's father Kish wandered off. Kish said to his son Saul, "Take one of the attendants with you and go look for the donkeys." [4] Saul and his attendant went through the hill country of Ephraim[i] and then through the region of Shalishah,[j] but they didn't find them. They went through the region of Shaalim[k]—nothing. Then they went through the Benjaminite region but still didn't find them.

[5] When they came to the land of Zuph,[l] Saul said to the attendant who was with him, "Come on, let's go back, or my father will stop worrying about the donkeys and start worrying about us."[m]

[6] "Look," the attendant said, "there's a man of God[n] in this city who is highly respected; everything he says is sure to come true.[o] Let's go there now. Maybe he'll tell us which way we should go."[p]

[7] "Suppose we do go," Saul said to his attendant, "what do we take the man? The food from our packs is gone, and there's no gift to take to the man of God.[q] What do we have?"

[8] The attendant answered Saul: "Here, I have a piece[D] of silver. I'll give it to the man of God, and he will tell us our way."

---

a 8:14 1Kg 21:7; Ezk 46:18
b 8:18 Is 8:21
c Pr 1:25-28; Mc 3:4
d 8:20 Nm 27:17; 1Sm 18:13; 2Ch 1:10
e 8:22 1Sm 8:7
f 9:1 1Sm 14:51; 1Ch 9:36-39
g 9:2 1Sm 10:24
h 1Sm 10:23
i 9:4 Jos 24:33
j 2Kg 4:42
k Jos 19:42
l 9:5 1Sm 1:1
m 1Sm 10:2
n 9:6 Dt 33:1; 2Kg 5:8
o 1Sm 3:19
p Gn 24:42
q 9:7 1Kg 14:3; 2Kg 5:15; 8:8-9; Ezk 13:19

A 8:16 LXX reads *best cattle* B 8:21 Lit *them in the LORD's ears* C 9:2 Lit *From his shoulder and up higher than any of the people*
D 9:8 Lit *a quarter of a shekel*

8:14 Subjects could expect to lose some of their assets to support the king's **servants**.

8:15 The law of Moses commanded tithes to support the priests and Levites, but a king would demand that much or more to meet his needs.

8:16 The king would want the best of human resources to accomplish **his work** (e.g., his various building projects), and he would take what he wanted.

8:17 The king's additional desire for a tenth of the people's **flocks** would impact the shepherds of the land as well as the farmers (v. 15). The heavy burden the people would have to bear to support the monarchy might well leave them feeling like **servants** instead of citizens.

8:18 On **cry out**, see note at 4:13.

8:19 **To listen to** could be translated "to obey." The people had heard Samuel's words, but they would not heed them. They were determined to **have a king**.

8:20 The words **like all the other nations** (see note at v. 5) again sound ominous. Furthermore, the people's expectation of their leader was too grandiose—they thought a king would do everything for them. They saw the potential benefit, but they had not counted the cost.

8:22 The Lord told Samuel to **appoint a king** over the people. The Lord's judge and prophet instructed everyone to return home to wait for God's leading on the matter.

9:1 The men in Saul's genealogy are not widely attested or known in Scripture apart from their relationship to Saul. Nonetheless, the careful way the text traces the family tree through five generations suggests Saul came from an **influential** family in the tribe of Benjamin, Saul's comment in verse 21 notwithstanding.

9:2 As someone who **stood a head taller than anyone else**, Saul looked **impressive**—seemingly good leadership material according to human perception.

9:4 The **hill country of Ephraim** lay north of Benjamin and boasted fertile ground. **Shalishah** and **Shaalim** were districts northeast of Gibeah.

9:5 **Zuph** lay about five miles north of Gibeah, Saul's hometown.

9:6 The **man of God** was Samuel, though the text does not reveal this until verse 14. Saul's **attendant** described him as **highly respected** (lit "honored") and as one whose word consistently proved **true**. The text may subtly suggest that Saul really did not know about Samuel, whereas his attendant and all Israel did. Some interpreters identify the **city** as Ramah, but this is uncertain.

9:7-8 Saul felt it inappropriate to approach **the man of God** without a **gift**. After all, the prophet's good counsel might result in the discovery of the lost donkeys, leading to his father's financial gain. Or perhaps Saul thought Samuel might expect a reward. At any rate, **the attendant** offered his own **piece of silver** (lit "quarter of a shekel").

⁹Formerly in Israel, a man who was going to inquire of God would say, "Come, let's go to the seer," for the prophet of today was formerly called the seer.ᵃ

¹⁰"Good," Saul replied to his attendant. "Come on, let's go." So they went to the city where the man of God was. ¹¹As they were climbing the hill to the city, they found some young women coming out to draw waterᵇ and asked, "Is the seer here?"

¹²The women answered, "Yes, he is ahead of you. Hurry, he just now came to the city, because there's a sacrificeᶜ for the people at the •high placeᵈ today. ¹³If you go quickly, you can catch up with him before he goes to the high place to eat. The people won't eat until he comes because he must bless the sacrifice; after that, the guests can eat. Go up immediately—you can find him now." ¹⁴So they went up toward the city.

Saul and his attendant were entering the city when they saw Samuel coming toward them on his way to the high place. ¹⁵Now the day before Saul's arrival, the LORD had informed Samuel,ᴬ,ᵉ ¹⁶"At this time tomorrow I will send you a man from the land of Benjamin. Anoint him ruler over My people Israel.ᶠ

He will save them from the hand of the Philistines because I have seen the affliction of My people,ᵍ for their cry has come to Me." ¹⁷When Samuel saw Saul, the LORD told him, "Here is the man I told you about;ʰ he will rule over My people."

¹⁸Saul approached Samuel in the gate area and asked, "Would you please tell me where the seer's house is?"

¹⁹"I am the seer," Samuel answered.ᴮ "Go up ahead of me to the high place and eat with me today. When I send you off in the morning, I'll tell you everything that's in your heart. ²⁰As for the donkeys that wandered away from you three days ago,ⁱ don't worry about them because they've been found. And who does all Israel desireʲ but you and all your father's family?"

²¹Saul responded, "Am I not a Benjaminiteᵏ from the smallest of Israel's tribes and isn't my clan the least important of all the clans of the Benjaminite tribe?ˡ So why have you said something like this to me?"

²²Samuel took Saul and his attendant, brought them to the banquet hall, and gave them a place at the head of the 30ᶜ or so men who had been invited. ²³Then Samuel said to

ᵃ9:9 2Sm 24:11; 1Ch 9:22; 26:28; Is 30:10 ᵇ9:11 Gn 24:15; 29:9; Ex 2:16 ᶜ9:12 Nm 28:11-15 ᵈ1Sm 7:17; 10:5 ᵉ9:15 1Sm 15:1; Ac 13:21 ᶠ9:16 1Sm 10:1 ᵍEx 3:7,9 ʰ9:17 1Sm 16:12 ⁱ9:20 1Sm 9:3 ʲ1Sm 8:5; 12:13 ᵏ9:21 1Sm 15:17 ˡJdg 20:46-48

ᴬ9:15 Lit had uncovered Samuel's ear, saying   ᴮ9:19 Lit answered Saul   ᶜ9:22 LXX reads 70

9:9 Seer (Hb ro'eh) describes a person who sees the things of God; **prophet** (Hb navi') means "called one" (i.e., by God). The text clarifies that the term "prophet" eventually replaced "seer," but the two terms described the same office.

9:11 Social customs restricted the amount of public contact between men and **women**; however, such a question was appropriate. The meeting of the women as they were **coming out to draw water** suggests a late afternoon or early evening time.

9:12 The women suggested the men **hurry** because of the impending **sacrifice** that Samuel would oversee. (Some interpreters see a connection between the **high place** and the altar Samuel built in 7:17.) Saul and his attendant would want to meet Samuel before the beginning of that ceremony.

9:13 Blessing the **sacrifice** was part of Samuel's priestly role.

9:14 The phrase **entering the city** is literally "coming into the midst of the city." The language may suggest Saul and his attendant were already inside the city rather than at the gate (v. 18) when **they saw Samuel coming**.

9:15 The word **informed** is literally "uncovered the ear," a common idiomatic expression (20:12, "tell"; 2Sm 7:27, "revealed").

9:16 Anointing depicted setting someone apart for God's appointed service, especially kings (10:1; 16:13), priests (Lv 4:3), and prophets (1Kg 19:16). **Ruler** was an early term used to describe Saul (10:1), David (13:14), and Solomon (1Kg 1:34), though it also denoted others in authority (1Ch 9:11; 2Ch 31:13, "chief official"). The phrases **I have seen the affliction of My people** and **their cry has come to Me** recall God's remembrance of Israel in bondage in Egypt, just before He used Moses to free them (Ex 2:25; 3:7).

These phrases suggest God was beginning another day of redemption.

9:17 The Hebrew verb behind **rule** normally means "restrain" or "retain," and it may hint at the future negative consequences of Saul's kingship. Others suggest the term may imply Saul would gather a fairly scattered and disjointed group of Israelites into a nation.

9:18 Saul approached Samuel but did not recognize him, as his question reveals. The text may again provide a hint at the negative direction Saul's kingdom would take. All Israel knew Samuel was a prophet of the Lord (3:20), but Saul didn't even recognize him.

9:19 Go up ahead of me was a way of showing honor and respect. **Everything that's in your heart** was probably much more than Saul anticipated hearing; he had just wanted to see Samuel to inquire about the lost donkeys.

9:20 Who does all Israel desire but you may also be translated, "For whom is every desired thing in Israel? Is it not for you?" (The Hb word here translated "desire" is translated "treasures" in Hg 2:7.)

9:21 Whichever rendering is best in verse 20, the language was far more affirming than Saul anticipated. **Smallest of Israel's tribes** well described Benjamin, which occupied a relatively small territory and furthermore faced potential extinction after war with Israel's other tribes in the days of the judges (Jdg 21:1-3). **Least important** also may mean "smallest in size"; this may be the better sense in light of verse 1.

9:22 The **banquet hall** was probably a room connected with the high place for sacrificial meals.

9:23 At Samuel's direction, the cook had set aside a choice **portion of meat** for a guest whom **Samuel** would designate.

the cook, "Get the portion of meat that I gave you and told you to set aside."

²⁴ The cook picked up the thigh[a] and what was attached to it and set it before Saul. Then Samuel said, "Notice that the reserved piece is set before you. Eat it because it was saved for you for this solemn event at the time I said, 'I've invited the people.'" So Saul ate with Samuel that day. ²⁵ Afterward, they went down from the high place to the city, and Samuel spoke with Saul on the roof.[A,b]

²⁶ They got up early, and just before dawn, Samuel called to Saul on the roof, "Get up, and I'll send you on your way!" Saul got up, and both he and Samuel went outside. ²⁷ As they were going down to the edge of the city, Samuel said to Saul, "Tell the attendant to go on ahead of us, but you stay for a while, and I'll reveal the word of God to you." So the attendant went on.

10 Samuel took the flask of oil,[c] poured it out on Saul's head,[d] kissed him, and said, "Hasn't the LORD anointed you[e] ruler over His inheritance?[B,f] ² Today when you leave me, you'll find two men at Rachel's Grave[g] at Zelzah in the land of Benjamin. They will say to you, 'The donkeys you went looking for have been found,[h] and now your father has stopped being concerned about the donkeys and is worried about you, asking: What should I do about my son?'

³ "You will proceed from there until you come to the oak of Tabor.[i] Three men going up to God at Bethel[j] will meet you there, one bringing three goats, one bringing three loaves of bread, and one bringing a skin of wine. ⁴ They will ask how you are and give you two loaves[c] of bread, which you will accept from them.

⁵ "After that you will come to the Hill of God[D,k] where there are Philistine garrisons.[E] When you arrive at the city, you will meet a group of prophets[l] coming down from the •high place prophesying.[m] They will be preceded by harps, tambourines, flutes, and lyres. ⁶ The Spirit of the LORD will control you,[n] you will prophesy with them,[o] and you will be transformed into a different person.[p] ⁷ When these signs have happened to you, do whatever your circumstances require[F,q] because God is with you. ⁸ Afterward, go ahead of me to Gilgal. I will come to you to offer •burnt offerings and to sacrifice •fellowship offerings. Wait seven days until I come to you and show you what to do."

⁹ When Saul turned around[G] to leave Samuel, God changed his heart,[H] and all the signs came about that day. ¹⁰ When Saul and his attendant arrived at Gibeah, a group of prophets

---

[a]9:24 Ex 29:22,27; Lv 7:32-33; Nm 18:18
[b]9:25 Dt 22:8; Ac 10:9
[c]10:1 Ex 30:23-33; 1Sm 16:13; 2Kg 9:3,6
[d]2Kg 9:1-3
[e]1Sm 16:13; 26:9; 2Sm 1:14
[f]Dt 32:9; Ps 78:71
[g]10:2 Gn 35:19-20
[h]1Sm 9:3-5
[i]10:3 Gn 35:8
[j]Gn 28:19; 35:1,3,7
[k]10:5 1Sm 13:2-3
[l]1Sm 19:20; 2Kg 2:3,5,15
[m]2Kg 3:15; 1Ch 25:1-6
[n]10:6 Nm 11:25,29; Jdg 14:6
[o]Ec 9:10
[p]1Sm 19:23-24
[q]10:7 Jos 1:5

[A]9:25 LXX reads city. They prepared a bed for Saul on the roof, and he slept.   [B]10:1 LXX adds And you will reign over the LORD's people, and you will save them from the hand of their enemies all around. And this is the sign to you that the LORD has anointed you ruler over his inheritance.   [C]10:4 DSS, LXX read wave offerings   [D]10:5 Or to Gibeath-elohim   [E]10:5 Or governors   [F]10:7 Lit do for yourself whatever your hand finds   [G]10:9 Lit turned his shoulder   [H]10:9 Lit God turned to him another heart

---

9:24 The Hebrew term behind **thigh** also means "leg," and either way would constitute a large, choice portion of meat.

9:25 Presumably this was the home where Samuel was staying. The **roof** was typically flat, and it was a place where people could enjoy cool evening breezes. The subject of conversation is not known. The LXX adds the words "they prepared a bed for Saul on the roof, and he slept," a natural thing for a host to arrange for his guest.

9:26 Samuel would **send** his guests **on** their **way,** probably with a blessing.

9:27 As the three walked together to **the edge of the city,** Samuel revealed to Saul that he had a particular message for him. Perhaps Saul anticipated some sort of prophetic send-off in light of Samuel's words in verse 19.

10:1 The act of anointing Saul with **oil** was anticipated in 9:16. The rhetorical question **hasn't the LORD anointed you** implies an affirmative answer. For other examples of such questions, see Ex 4:14; Jos 1:9. On **ruler,** see note at 9:16.

10:2 Samuel provided Saul a series of signs that would help Saul validate in his own mind that God had indeed chosen him to lead Israel. **Rachel's Grave** seems to have been located near the border of Ephraim. Based on a misunderstanding of Gn 35:19, a Crusader tradition located the tomb near Bethlehem, where a shrine is dedicated to her.

10:3 The site of the **oak of Tabor** is uncertain, except that it was near **Bethel** in Benjamin. **Going up to God** probably is a reference to Bethel as the place where God appeared to Jacob (Gn 28:15), and hence a religious shrine where others hoped to meet Him as well.

10:5 The **Hill of God** (Hb giv'ath ha-'elohim) is probably Gibeah, Saul's hometown and eventually his capital city (v. 10). The presence of **Philistine garrisons** meant Israel's enemies were encroaching seriously on Israel's territory. If the Philistines controlled Benjamin, they could cut off Israel's communication between north and south and seriously restrict a major access route to the Mediterranean coast.

10:6 **Control you** could be translated "rush upon you," a meaning that might better fit the context. **Transformed** aptly describes a life God has changed (Rm 12:2).

10:7 Samuel's words **do whatever your circumstances require** indicate that when the **signs** came true, Saul would know what to do (Mk 13:11).

10:8 **Gilgal** lay in the Jordan Valley near Jericho. It was the site of Israel's base camp during the days of the conquest (Jos 4:19). Later it became a place where illicit sacrifice was offered (Am 4:4; 5:5).

10:9 The words **God changed his heart** demonstrate the beginning of God fulfilling Samuel's prophetic word. The confirmation of **all the signs . . . that day** further emphasize the truth of Samuel's word to Saul.

10:10 On **the Spirit of God took control of him,** see note at verse 6.

met him. Then the Spirit of God took control of him, and he prophesied along with them. [11]Everyone who knew him previously and saw him prophesy with the prophets asked each other, "What has happened to the son of Kish? Is Saul also among the prophets?"[a]

[12]Then a man who was from there asked, "And who is their father?"[b]

As a result, "Is Saul also among the prophets?" became a popular saying. [13]Then Saul finished prophesying and went to the high place.

[14]Saul's uncle[c] asked him and his attendant, "Where did you go?"

"To look for the donkeys," Saul answered. "When we saw they weren't there, we went to Samuel."[d]

[15]"Tell me," Saul's uncle asked, "what did Samuel say to you?"

[16]Saul told him, "He assured us the donkeys had been found." However, Saul did not tell him what Samuel had said about the matter of kingship.

Saul Received as King

[17]Samuel summoned the people to the Lord at Mizpah[e] [18]and said to the Israelites, "This is what the Lord, the God of Israel, says:[f] 'I brought Israel out of Egypt, and I rescued you from the power of the Egyptians and all the kingdoms that were oppressing you.' [19]But today you have rejected your God,[g] who saves you from all your troubles and afflictions. You said to Him, 'You[A] must set a king over us.'[h] Now therefore present yourselves before the Lord by your tribes and clans."[i]

[20]Samuel had all the tribes of Israel come forward, and the tribe of Benjamin was selected. [21]Then he had the tribe of Benjamin come forward by its clans, and the Matrite clan was selected.[B] Finally, Saul son of Kish was selected.[j] But when they searched for him, they could not find him. [22]They again inquired of the Lord,[k] "Has the man come here yet?"

The Lord replied, "There he is, hidden among the supplies."

[23]They ran and got him from there. When he stood among the people, he stood a head taller than anyone else.[C,l] [24]Samuel said to all the people, "Do you see the one the Lord has chosen?[m] There is no one like him among the entire population."

And all the people shouted,[D] "Long live the king!"[n]

[25]Samuel proclaimed to the people the rights of kingship.[o] He wrote them on a scroll,

[a]10:11 1Sm 19:24; Am 7:14-15; Mt 13:54-57
[b]10:12 Gn 45:8; Jdg 17:10
[c]10:14 1Sm 14:50
[d]1Sm 9:4-6
[e]10:17 1Sm 7:5
[f]10:18 Jdg 6:8-9
[g]10:19 1Sm 8:6-7
[h]1Sm 8:19
[i]Jos 7:14-18; 24:1; Pr 16:33
[j]10:20-21 Jos 7:16-18
[k]10:22 Ex 28:30; Nm 27:21; 1Sm 23:2,4,9-11
[l]10:23 1Sm 9:2
[m]10:24 Dt 17:15; 2Sm 21:6
[n]1Kg 1:25,34,39
[o]10:25 1Sm 8:11-17

[A]10:19 Some Hb mss, LXX, Syr, Vg read You said, 'No, you . . .   [B]10:21 LXX adds And he had the Matrite clan come forward, man by man.   [C]10:23 Lit people, and he was higher than any of the people from his shoulder and up   [D]10:24 LXX reads acknowledged and said

---

10:11 The phrase **everyone who knew him previously** describes the citizens of Gibeah, probably Saul's family and friends. Their question, **Is Saul also among the prophets?** reflects their amazement, since they had never known him to prophesy before.

10:12 The unnamed man's question, **And who is their father?** reminded those who were puzzled by Saul's prophesying that it was God, not man, who determined who would be His prophet. The Spirit of God empowered the prophets (including Saul) for their ministry; their ancestry was irrelevant.

10:13 The **high place** was the place of worship from which the band of prophets had just come (v. 5).

10:14 Saul's **uncle** may be Ner (14:50), father of Abner, who later became Saul's general, but the text does not say for sure.

10:15-16 Saul was reluctant to share Samuel's words **about the matter of kingship** when he first returned home. Perhaps he felt relatives and friends would have a harder time believing he would be their new leader.

10:17 On **Mizpah**, see note at 7:5.

10:18 Samuel did not bring his own words, but the words of God. **I brought Israel out of Egypt** recalled God's dramatic deliverance of His people through the exodus (Ex 14). **The kingdoms that were oppressing you** described many peoples or nations that Israel encountered on the way to Canaan, plus all the enemies who continued to challenge Israel's right to the land.

10:19 Samuel suggested the people's request for **a king** was really a rejection of God's faithful care in favor of a human leader. The law of Moses established the terms for choosing a king (Dt 17:14-20), but Samuel's speech made it clear the people had sinned by asking for one at this time in their history. His command **present yourselves** called the people to stand together **before the Lord** so He could reveal His choice for Israel's leader.

10:20-21 These verses probably describe the casting of lots. God's guidance of the process would verify to the people and again to Saul His choice for Israel's king.

10:22 Interpreters generally believe the question, **Has the man come here yet?** was a request for Saul's whereabouts. Others suggest the phrase be translated, "Is anyone else here?" **Hidden among the supplies** probably suggests a place at the perimeter. Saul had been hesitant to reveal his destiny to his own uncle (v. 16), and now he appeared slow to accept the responsibility of the kingship.

10:23 On **stood a head taller than anyone else**, see note at 9:2. On the other hand, taller people were often viewed elsewhere in Scripture as threats (17:4-5; Nm 13:28).

10:24 At least according to the standards for kingship the nation entertained, Saul seemed like the right choice. The people's enthusiastic, **Long live the king!** signified the instant acceptance Saul received from many.

10:25 The phrase **rights of kingship** recalled Samuel's warning to the people about the cost of having a king (8:11-18). Samuel **wrote them on a scroll** as a lasting testimony or covenant between the people and Saul. Placing the scroll **in the presence of the Lord** meant in the tabernacle (Ex 40:20; Dt 31:26; Jos 24:26), which emphasized God's oversight of

which he placed in the presence of the LORD.^a Then Samuel sent all the people away, each to his home.

²⁶Saul also went to his home in Gibeah,^b and brave men whose hearts God had touched went with him. ²⁷But some *wicked men said, "How can this guy save us?" They despised him and did not bring him a gift,^c but Saul said nothing.^{A,B}

Saul's Deliverance of Jabesh-gilead

11 Nahash^{C,d} the Ammonite came up and laid siege to Jabesh-gilead.^e All the men of Jabesh said to him, "Make a treaty^f with us, and we will serve you."

²Nahash the Ammonite replied, "I'll make one with you on this condition: that I gouge out everyone's right eye^g and humiliate all Israel."^h

³"Don't do anything to us for seven days," the elders of Jabesh said to him, "and let us

send messengers throughout the territory of Israel. If no one saves us, we will surrender to you."

⁴When the messengers came to Gibeah,ⁱ Saul's hometown, and told the terms to^D the people, all wept aloud.^j ⁵Just then Saul was coming in from the field behind his oxen. "What's the matter with the people? Why are they weeping?" Saul inquired, and they repeated to him the words of the men from Jabesh.

⁶When Saul heard these words, the Spirit of God suddenly took control of him,^k and his anger burned furiously. ⁷He took a team of oxen, cut them in pieces,^l and sent them throughout the land of Israel by messengers who said, "This is what will be done to the ox of anyone who doesn't march behind Saul and Samuel."^m As a result, the terror of the LORD fell on the people, and they went out united.ⁿ

⁸Saul counted them at Bezek.^o There were

Cross-references (center column)

^a10:25 Dt 17:18-20
^b10:26 1Sm 11:4; 15:34
^c10:27 1Kg 10:25; 2Ch 17:5
^d11:1 1Sm 12:12
^e1Sm 12:12; 31:11
^f1Kg 20:34; Ezk 17:13
^g11:2 Nm 16:14
^h1Sm 17:26; Ps 44:13
ⁱ11:4 1Sm 10:26; 15:34
^jGn 27:38; Jdg 2:4
^k11:6 Jdg 14:6; 1Sm 10:10
^l11:7 Jdg 19:29
^mJdg 21:5,8,10
ⁿJdg 20:1
^o11:8 Jdg 1:5

A10:27 DSS add *Nahash king of the Ammonites had been severely oppressing the Gadites and Reubenites. He gouged out the right eye of each of them and brought fear and trembling on Israel. Of the Israelites beyond the Jordan none remained whose right eye Nahash, king of the Ammonites, had not gouged out. But there were 7,000 men who had escaped from the Ammonites and entered Jabesh-gilead.* **B**10:27 Lit *gift, and he was like a mute person* **C**11:1 DSS, LXX read *About a month later, Nahash* **D**11:4 Lit *in the ears of*

---

the process; He would hold Israel accountable for this decision.

10:26 Saul's hometown, **Gibeah**, then became Israel's capital. **Brave men whose hearts God had touched** were the beginning of Saul's army; the Lord was providing Saul the resources he needed to rule Israel.

10:27 The expression **wicked men** also describes Hophni and Phinehas (2:12). Although the text condemns their attitude, these individuals doubted Saul's abilities—probably because he appeared too timid to accept the kingship (10:22-23). They **did not bring him a gift** as custom dictated when approaching the king. The phrase **Saul said nothing** is literally "Saul was as one deaf," suggesting he chose to pretend his critics' objections had not been voiced. Others would remember the negative comments, however (11:12).

---

beliyya'al

Hebrew Pronunciation	[beh liy YAH al]
HCSB Translation	worthless, wicked, destruction
Uses in 1 Samuel	6
Uses in the OT	27
Focus Passage	1 Samuel 10:27

Beliyya'al, a strongly derogatory noun, may be formed from *beliy* (*not*) and *ya'al* (*profit*). It is sometimes used alone, meaning *the wicked* (2Sm 23:6). It later became the devil's name *Belial* (2Co 6:15). *Beliyya'al* modifies *ben* ("son"; 9x) and *'iysh* ("man"; 5x), both phrases occurring synonymously in 1Kg 21:13. *Beliyya'al* describes *worthless* (Jb 34:18), *wicked* (1Sm 2:12), and *perverted* (Jdg 19:22) men. A "son/daughter of *beliyya'al*" is a *worthless fool* (1Sm 25:17) or *wicked woman* (1Sm 1:16). Such people are like thorns (2Sm 23:6), rebellious (2Ch 13:7) false accusers (1Kg 21:10) who lie (Pr 6:12), encourage idolatry (Dt 13:13), and plot evil against God (Nah 1:11). *Beliyya'al* with *davar* ("word, thing") implies *wicked thought* (Dt 15:9), *anything worthless* (Ps 101:3), or *lethal poison* (Ps 41:8).

11:1 Nahash the Ammonite controlled Ammon east of Israel beyond the Jordan River. He later may have been on friendlier terms with David than he was with Saul (2Sm 10:1-2), although David controlled his territory (2Sm 8:11-12). **Jabesh-gilead** was located about 20 miles south of the Sea of Galilee and just east of the Jordan River. Thus, Nahash's incursion went deep into Israelite territory. Nonetheless, the city's citizens asked Nahash to offer terms of peace, which might include taxation or tribute paid at designated intervals.

11:2 Nahash's proposal that he **gouge out everyone's right eye** would allow Jabesh-gilead's citizens to see to function for daily tasks, but with their depth perception ruined by the loss of an eye, they would be at a great disadvantage in combat.

11:3 Nahash, of course, had everything to lose and nothing to gain by granting the **elders'** request for **seven days** to **send messengers**. Perhaps out of foolishness or arrogance, he did so.

11:5 Saul had been named king, but the monarchy may still have been in its formational period, so he was farming.

11:6 On **the Spirit of God suddenly took control of him**, see note at 10:6. This was the second such experience for Israel's new king (10:10).

11:7 Saul's **team of oxen** became part of his stern admonition for the Israelites to rally behind their new king against the Ammonites (cp. note at Jdg 19:29-30). His strategy worked; the Israelites went out **united** because **the terror of the LORD** came upon them. The mention of **Saul and Samuel** together reflects Samuel's continuing leadership role during the new monarchy.

11:8 Bezek was located in Manasseh west of the Jordan River, about 10 miles west of Jabesh-gilead (Jdg 1:4). The distinction between **Israelites** and the **men from Judah** may reflect the existence of a separation between the two

300,000[A,a] Israelites and 30,000[B] men from Judah. [9]He told the messengers who had come, "Tell this to the men of Jabesh-gilead: 'Deliverance will be yours tomorrow by the time the sun is hot.'" So the messengers told the men of Jabesh, and they rejoiced.

[10]Then the men of Jabesh said to Nahash, "Tomorrow we will come out, and you can do whatever you want[c] to us."

[11]The next day Saul organized the troops into three divisions.[b] During the morning watch, they invaded the Ammonite camp and slaughtered them until the heat of the day. There were survivors, but they were so scattered that no two of them were left together.

Saul's Confirmation as King

[12]Afterward, the people said to Samuel, "Who said that Saul should not[D] reign over us?[c] Give us those men so we can kill them!"[d] [13]But Saul ordered, "No one will be executed this day, for today the LORD has provided deliverance in Israel."[e]

[14]Then Samuel said to the people, "Come, let's go to Gilgal, so we can renew the kingship there." [15]So all the people went to Gilgal, and there in the LORD's presence[f] they made Saul king. There they sacrificed •fellowship offerings[g] in the LORD's presence, and Saul and all the men of Israel greatly rejoiced.

Samuel's Final Public Speech

12 Then Samuel said to all Israel, "I have carefully listened to everything you said to me and placed a king over you.[h] [2]Now you can see that the king is leading you. As for me, I'm old and gray, and my sons are here with you. I have led you from my youth until today. [3]Here I am. Bring charges against me before the LORD and His anointed: Whose ox or donkey have I taken?[i] Whom have I wronged or mistreated? From whose hand have I taken a bribe to overlook something?[E,F,j] I will return it to you."

[4]"You haven't wronged us, you haven't mistreated us, and you haven't taken anything from anyone's hand," they responded.

[5]He said to them, "The LORD is a witness against you, and His anointed is a witness today that you haven't found anything[k] in my hand."[l]

"He is a witness," they said.

[6]Then Samuel said to the people, "The LORD, who appointed Moses and Aaron[m] and who brought your ancestors up from the land of Egypt, is a witness.[G] [7]Now present yourselves,

Cross-references (center column)

[a]11:8 Jdg 20:2
[b]11:11 Jdg 7:16
[c]11:12 1Sm 10:27
[d]Lk 19:27
[e]11:13 Ex 14:13; 1Sm 19:5
[f]11:15 1Sm 10:17
[g]1Sm 10:8
[h]12:1 1Sm 8:5-22
[i]12:3 Ex 20:17; Nm 16:15
[j]Dt 16:19
[k]12:5 Ac 23:9; 24:20
[l]Ex 22:4
[m]12:6 Ex 6:26

[A]11:8 LXX reads 600,000   [B]11:8 DSS, LXX read 70,000   [C]11:10 Lit do what is good in your eyes   [D]11:12 Some Hb mss, LXX; other Hb mss omit not   [E]12:3 LXX reads bribe or a pair of shoes? Testify against me.   [F]12:3 Lit bribe and will hide my eyes with it?
[G]12:6 LXX; MT omits is a witness

---

groups that would later become formalized after Solomon's death (1Kg 12).

11:9 The phrase **the time the sun is hot** refers to noon.

11:10 The **men of Jabesh** now delivered false information to **Nahash**, promising to **come out** (surrender) to him the next day. The information may have given the Ammonite king and his army a false confidence; consequently, they were unprepared for Saul's surprise attack (v. 11).

11:11 **Three divisions** allowed Saul to attack **the Ammonite camp** from three directions at once. The invasion occurred **during the morning watch**—just before sunrise, surprising and scattering the Ammonite forces.

11:12 In the aftermath of an incredible victory that confirmed Saul's call as king, **the people** asked Samuel to help round up and execute those who had doubted God's choice of Saul as king.

11:13 Saul's order that **no one . . . be executed** refocused the people's attention on the Lord's victory rather than on the evil of Saul's detractors.

11:14 Samuel instructed **the people** to go to **Gilgal** (see notes at 7:16 and 10:8) to reconfirm Saul as king, now that he had demonstrated God's hand on him through the victory over Ammon. This time, no doubt remained—Saul was God's choice.

11:15 The people confirmed Saul again as king. **Fellowship offerings** (sometimes translated "peace offerings") were appropriate for occasions of thankfulness (Lv 7:11-15).

12:1 Samuel spoke **to all Israel**, that is, to all who gathered at Gilgal. In light of Israel's **king** now being in place and Samuel's advancing age, God's prophet may have decided this was the time to begin wrapping up his leadership. At the same time, Samuel's speech was powerful, calling Israel to remember its past failures and to live in light of God's covenant in the days ahead.

12:2 Samuel's tenure of service had begun when he was a boy serving Eli (1:24-28). Now Saul was doing (**leading**) what Samuel had done (**led**). The kingship was in place and would bring a new and more comprehensive administration than Israel had known under Samuel's leadership.

12:3 Samuel called the people to bring before God and the new king any complaint about Samuel's lack of integrity. Samuel wished to settle all his wrongs publicly, with God and Saul as his witnesses, before all the people.

12:4 The people's reply concerning Samuel provides believers a standard for which we can strive as we seek to finish our lives faithful to the Lord.

12:5 The people's reply, **He is a witness**, expressed their agreement with Samuel's statement.

12:6 Samuel's identification of **the LORD** as the one who appointed Moses and Aaron and **brought your ancestors up from the land of Egypt** reminded the people of God's central role in making them the people they were.

12:7 Samuel's command **present yourselves** is the same command he gave the people in 10:19, when they gathered to see God's choice for king. This time Samuel wanted to declare to them **all the righteous acts** God had performed in their lives personally and in the lives of their **ancestors**.

so I may confront you before the LORD about all the righteous acts He has done for you and your ancestors.

[8]"When Jacob went to Egypt,[A] your ancestors cried out to the LORD,[a] and He sent them Moses and Aaron, who led your ancestors out of Egypt and settled them in this place.[b] [9]But they forgot the LORD their God, so He handed them over to Sisera[c] commander of the army of Hazor, to the Philistines, and to the king of Moab.[d] These enemies fought against them. [10]Then they cried out to the LORD and said, 'We have sinned, for we abandoned the LORD and worshiped the •Baals and the •Ashtoreths. Now deliver us from the power of our enemies,[e] and we will serve You.' [11]So the LORD sent Jerubbaal,[f] Barak,[B,g] Jephthah,[h] and Samuel.[i] He rescued you from the power of the enemies around you, and you lived securely. [12]But when you saw that Nahash king of the Ammonites was coming against you, you said to me, 'No, we must have a king rule over us'—even though the LORD your God is your king.

[13]"Now here is the king you've chosen,[j] the one you requested.[k] Look, this is the king

the LORD has placed over you. [14]If you •fear the LORD,[l] worship and obey Him, and if you don't rebel against the LORD's command, then both you and the king who rules over you will follow the LORD your God. [15]However, if you disobey the LORD[m] and rebel against His command, the LORD's hand will be against you[n] and against your ancestors.[C,o]

[16]"Now, therefore, present yourselves and see this great thing that the LORD will do before your eyes.[p] [17]Isn't the wheat harvest today?[q] I will call on the LORD and He will send thunder and rain, so that you will know and see what a great evil you committed in the LORD's sight by requesting a king for yourselves."[r] [18]Samuel called on the LORD, and on that day the LORD sent thunder and rain. As a result, all the people greatly feared the LORD and Samuel.[s]

[19]They pleaded with Samuel, "Pray to the LORD your God for your servants,[t] so we won't die! For we have added to all our sins the evil of requesting a king for ourselves."[u]

[20]Samuel replied, "Don't be afraid. Even though you have committed all this evil, don't turn away from following the LORD.[v] Instead, worship the LORD with all your heart. [21]Don't

Cross references:
[a]12:8 Ex 2:23-25
[b]Ex 3:1-10
[c]12:9 Jdg 4:1-2
[d]Jdg 2:11-15
[e]12:10 Jdg 2:18
[f]12:11 Jdg 6:11-12,32
[g]Jdg 4:6; 11:1
[h]Jdg 11:1
[i]1Sm 7:10-14
[j]12:13 1Sm 10:24
[k]1Sm 8:5; Hs 13:11
[l]12:14 Jos 24:14
[m]12:15 Jos 24:20; Is 1:20
[n]1Sm 5:9
[o]Lv 26:14-33; Jos 24:14-27
[p]12:16 Ex 14:13
[q]12:17 Pr 26:1
[r]1Sm 8:7
[s]12:18 Ex 9:23-25,31; 1Kg 18:37-39; Pr 26:1
[t]12:19 Ex 9:28; Jr 15:1
[u]1Sm 17:20
[v]12:20 Dt 11:16

[A]12:8 LXX reads *When Jacob and his sons went to Egypt and Egypt humbled them*   [B]12:11 LXX, Syr; MT reads *Bedan*; Jdg 4:6; Heb 11:32   [C]12:15 LXX reads *your king*

12:8 Over four centuries separated Jacob's trip to Egypt and the exodus. In the end, after Moses and Aaron died, God **settled them** in the promised land. As they considered the awesome truth of this one verse, the Israelites should have realized that God was their all-sufficient King. But Samuel had much more history to recount.

12:9 The period of the judges saw Israel repeat a four-stage cycle: sin, suffering, supplication, and salvation. The people sinned, then suffered at the hands of their enemies for a time: Deborah's and Barak's army battled **Sisera** (Jdg 4–5), Samson battled **the Philistines** (Jdg 13–16), and Ehud battled **Moab** (Jdg 3:15-30).

12:10 The third of the four stages (see note at v. 9) involved supplication as the people confessed their sin. They agreed to lay aside **the Baals and the Ashtoreths** (see note at 7:3) so they might **serve** the Lord alone.

12:11 Samuel recited some of the judges whom God had used to bring salvation, the fourth stage in the cycle (see note at v. 9). The Lord also used others, but Samuel mentioned these four leaders (including himself) to drive home his point. God faithfully defended His people whenever they followed Him fully.

12:12 Samuel rebuked the people for desiring a human **king**. When **Nahash** threatened them, they forgot the Lord's past acts of deliverance and clamored to be like the other nations.

12:13 The words **the king you've chosen, the one you requested** emphasize that ultimately Saul was the people's choice. **The Lord** guided the process and put him in command, but only in response to the people's denial of His kingship.

12:14 To **fear the Lord** includes an attitude of reverence and

awe toward God. **Worship** literally means "serve" in this verse.

12:16 On **present yourselves**, see note at verse 7. The Lord was about to perform a heavenly sign to confirm that the people had sinned grievously by asking for a king.

12:17 The **wheat harvest** normally occurred around late May, and it was officially marked by the Festival of Weeks (Hb *shavu'oth*; Nm 28:26-31). **Thunder and rain** normally do not come in Israel from about late April to sometime in October. Their coming would function as a sign of **a great evil** the people had **committed . . . by requesting a king**.

12:18 The Israelites realized the miraculous nature of what was happening and **greatly feared** the Lord and Samuel. Such an amazing sign could only mean they had offended God.

12:19 The people **pleaded with Samuel** because he was clearly God's representative. The words **we have added to all our sins** seem to indicate a certain depth of repentance, to which Samuel responded in the next verse.

12:20 Samuel agreed the people had **committed . . . evil** by asking for a king. However, what was done was done, and now a king was God's will for Israel. The commands **don't be afraid** and **don't turn away** emphasize immediacy. The people *were* afraid and *were* considering turning away in light of God's judgment. Rather than fear or flight, Samuel instructed, they should **worship** (or "serve") **the Lord** wholeheartedly.

12:21 In the command, **Don't turn away** is different in structure from the command in verse 20. Here it emphasizes a general prohibition—"Don't ever turn away." The Hebrew word translated **worthless things** and **worthless** is *tohu* (Gn 1:2, "formless") and here probably designates the

turn away to follow worthless[A] things that can't profit or deliver you; they are worthless.[a] [22] The Lord will not abandon His people,[b] because of His great name and because He has determined to make you His own people.[c]

[23] "As for me, I vow that I will not sin against the Lord by ceasing to pray for you.[d] I will teach you the good and right way. [24] Above all, fear the Lord and worship Him faithfully with all your heart; consider the great things He has done for you.[e] [25] However, if you continue to do what is evil, both you and your king will be swept away."[f]

Saul's Failure

13 Saul was 30 years[B] old when he became king, and he reigned 42 years[C] over Israel.[D] [2] He chose 3,000 men from Israel for himself: 2,000 were with Saul at Michmash[g] and in Bethel's hill country, and 1,000 were with Jonathan in Gibeah[h] of Benjamin. He sent the rest of the troops away, each to his own tent.

[3] Jonathan attacked the Philistine garrison[E,i] that was in Geba,[j] and the Philistines heard about it. So Saul blew the ram's horn through-

out the land[k] saying, "Let the Hebrews hear!"[F,l] [4] And all Israel heard the news, "Saul has attacked the Philistine garrison,[E] and Israel is now repulsive to the Philistines." Then the troops were summoned to join Saul at Gilgal.

[5] The Philistines also gathered to fight against Israel: 3,000[G] chariots, 6,000 horsemen, and troops as numerous as the sand on the seashore.[m] They went up and camped at Michmash, east of Beth-aven.[H,n] [6] The men of Israel saw that they were in trouble because the troops were in a difficult situation. They hid in caves, thickets, among rocks, and in holes and cisterns.[o] [7] Some Hebrews even crossed the Jordan to the land of Gad and Gilead.

Saul, however, was still at Gilgal, and all his troops were gripped with fear. [8] He waited seven days for the appointed time that Samuel had set,[p] but Samuel didn't come to Gilgal, and the troops were deserting him. [9] So Saul said, "Bring me the •burnt offering and the •fellowship offerings." Then he offered the burnt offering.

[10] Just as he finished offering the burnt of-

---

a12:21 Is 44:9-20; Jr 2:8,11; Hab 2:18
b12:22 Jos 7:9; Ezk 36:22-28
cDt 7:6-9; 1Pt 2:9
d12:23 Nm 21:7; 1Sm 7:5-9; Rm 1:9-10
e12:24 Dt 10:21; Ps 103:2-14
f12:25 2Kg 17:6-7
g13:2 1Sm 14:31
h1Sm 10:26
i13:3 1Sm 10:5
j1Sm 13:16; 14:5
kJdg 3:27; 6:34
lNm 10:9; Jdg 3:27; 6:34
m13:5 Jos 11:4
n1Sm 14:23
o13:6 Jdg 6:2
p13:8 1Sm 10:8

A12:21 LXX reads *away after empty*   B13:1 Some LXX mss; MT reads *was one year*   C13:1 Text emended; MT reads *two years*   D13:1 Some LXX mss omit v. 1   E13:3,4 Or *governor*   F13:3 LXX reads *The slaves have revolted*   G13:5 One LXX ms, Syr; MT reads 30,000   H13:5 LXX reads *Michmash, opposite Beth-horon to the south*

---

worthlessness of following false gods. False gods are likened to "emptiness" in Is 41:29, and "nothing" in Is 44:9.

12:22 God's honor was at stake because He had entered into covenant with the Israelites and **determined** to **make** them **His own people**. He would keep His word so the whole world might know His faithful and gracious character.

12:23 The words **I vow** could also be translated "far be it from me." Samuel's assurance to the people was expressed in the strongest terms. Samuel had been the people's shepherd leader, and **ceasing to pray** on their behalf was sin in his eyes.

12:24 Samuel's concluding words summarized commands he already had given the people. Remembering God's past faithfulness would guide them in living for Him in the present and into the future.

12:25 Disastrous consequences awaited both ruler and people if they persisted in doing **evil**. God's covenant with His people might continue, but a rebellious generation could not presume on His blessing.

13:1 Ancient manuscripts differ on exactly how many years Saul reigned. Based on a comparison of these manuscripts and Ac 13:21, where Paul gives the round number of 40 years, **42 years** seems the most likely.

13:2 Israel's new king began to establish a standing military presence for his kingdom. In light of the army's larger size mentioned earlier (11:8), the **3,000 men from Israel** may have represented an elite fighting force to protect the king and local interests. **Michmash** lay about four and one-half miles northeast of **Gibeah of Benjamin**, Saul's hometown and new capital. **Bethel's hill country** describes the rugged terrain around the ancient site of Jacob's dream (Gn 28:10-

22). **Jonathan** was one of Saul's sons who would befriend David and become significant later in the narrative (18:1-3; 19:1-3; 20:1-42; 23:16-18].

13:3 The presence of a **Philistine garrison . . . in Geba** less than three miles from Gibeah posed a significant threat to Israel's heartland and to Saul's kingdom. News of their defeat at the hands of **Jonathan** quickly reached the coast, and Saul blew the **ram's horn** to alert Israel that a larger battle was certainly coming.

13:4 More **troops** joined the king at **Gilgal** (see notes at 7:16 and 10:8) to ready themselves for a **Philistine** counter offensive.

13:5 The **Philistines** responded with **chariots** and **horsemen**. Saul's departure from **Michmash** (vv. 1-4) left the area open for his enemies again.

13:6 The men of Israel . . . were in trouble. The Philistines controlled the high ground—a clear military advantage. Further, their push to Michmash meant they controlled much of the central Benjamin plateau, effectively cutting Israel in half and limiting Saul's access to the coast. Saul's decision to retreat to Gilgal gave his enemies control of this region; the situation was indeed serious.

13:7 Many of Saul's citizens even **crossed the Jordan** River and moved northward **to the land of Gad and Gilead**. They calculated that the Philistines would be content with the territory west of the Jordan River.

13:8 Samuel had told Saul to wait **seven days** at **Gilgal** at which time he would come and provide further instructions (10:8). Saul, however, looked around and saw the troops were **deserting him** as morale weakened.

13:9 Saul **offered the burnt offering** himself—a task Sam-

fering, Samuel arrived. So Saul went out to greet him, [11] and Samuel asked, "What have you done?"

Saul answered, "When I saw that the troops were deserting me and you didn't come within the appointed days and the Philistines were gathering at Michmash, [12] I thought: The Philistines will now descend on me at Gilgal, and I haven't sought the Lord's favor. So I forced myself to offer the burnt offering."

[13] Samuel said to Saul, "You have been foolish.[a] You have not kept the command which the Lord your God gave you.[b] It was at this time that the Lord would have permanently established your reign over Israel,[c] [14] but now your reign will not endure.[d] The Lord has found a man loyal to Him,[A,e] and the Lord has appointed him as ruler over His people, because you have not done what the Lord commanded." [15] Then Samuel went[B] from Gilgal to Gibeah in Benjamin. Saul registered the troops who were with him, about 600 men.

[16] Saul, his son Jonathan, and the troops who were with them were staying in Geba[f] of Benjamin, and the Philistines were camped at Michmash. [17] Raiding parties[g] went out from the Philistine camp in three divisions. One division headed toward the Ophrah[h] road leading to the land of Shual. [18] The next divi-

sion headed toward the Beth-horon[i] road, and the last division headed down the border road that looks out over the Valley of Zeboim[j] toward the wilderness.

[19] No blacksmith could be found in all the land of Israel,[k] because the Philistines had said, "Otherwise, the Hebrews will make swords or spears." [20] So all the Israelites went to the Philistines to sharpen their plows, mattocks, axes, and sickles.[C] [21] The price was two-thirds of a •shekel[D] for plows and mattocks, and one-third of a shekel for pitchforks and axes, and for putting a point on an oxgoad. [22] So on the day of battle not a sword or spear could be found in the hand of any of the troops who were with Saul[l] and Jonathan; only Saul and his son Jonathan had weapons.

Jonathan's Victory over the Philistines

14 [23] Now a Philistine garrison[m] took control of the pass at Michmash. [1] That same day Saul's son Jonathan said to the attendant who carried his weapons, "Come on, let's cross over to the Philistine garrison on the other side." However, he did not tell his father.

[2] Saul was staying under the pomegranate tree in Migron[n] on the outskirts of Gibeah.[E,o]

Cross references (center column):
[a]13:13 2Ch 16:9
[b]1Sm 15:22,28
[c]1Sm 1:22
[d]13:14 1Sm 15:28
[e]1Sm 16:7; Ac 13:22
[f]13:16 1Sm 13:2-3
[g]13:17 1Sm 14:15
[h]Jos 18:23
[i]13:18 Jos 18:13-14
[j]Neh 11:34
[k]13:19 Jdg 5:8; 2Kg 24:14
[l]13:22 Jdg 5:8
[m]13:23 1Sm 14:1; 2Sm 23:14
[n]14:2 Is 10:28
[o]1Sm 13:15-16

A13:14 Lit *man according to His heart*   B13:15 LXX reads *Samuel left Gilgal and went on his way, and the rest of the people followed Saul to join the people in his army. They went*   C13:20 LXX; MT reads *plowshares*   D13:21 Lit *of a pim*; about 1/4 ounce of silver   E14:2 LXX reads *on top of the hill*

---

uel should have done as Israel's priest. Years later, King Uzziah also would usurp the priest's duties and receive God's judgment for his act (2Ch 26:16-21).

13:11 Samuel's ominous question **What have you done?** recalls God's questions to Eve and to Cain (Gn 3:13; 4:10) as well as the sailors' terrified question to Jonah (Jnh 1:10).

13:12 Saul rightly estimated the seriousness of the Philistine threat. If they reached **Gilgal**, they would control territory from the Mediterranean Sea to the Jordan River. However, **the Lord's favor** did not come through sacrifice but through faithfulness, a fact Samuel would later drive home to Saul (15:22).

13:13 Foolish is a word that also would describe later kings who failed to put their trust in the Lord (2Sm 24:10; 2Ch 16:9).

13:14 God's purposes would continue for Israel despite Saul's failures because the Lord had **found a man loyal to Him**. The phrase **the Lord has appointed him as ruler** indicates how from God's perspective, His work was already moving ahead and was as good as done, even though David would not become king for several years.

13:15 From **Gilgal to Gibeah** was a distance of about 15 miles upward—a gain in elevation of about 3,000 feet. Meanwhile, only **600 men** (cp. v. 2) remained with the king.

13:16 On **Geba of Benjamin**, see note at verse 3. Only about two miles separated Saul's forces from **the Philistines . . . at Michmash**.

13:17-18 Raiding parties secured the access roads to Michmash. The **Ophrah road** ran northwest of Michmash. **Beth-horon** lay to the west, an important ridge route toward the coast. The **Valley of Zeboim** was located to the east **toward the wilderness** region leading to the Jordan Valley.

13:19 The presence of Philistine-imposed restrictions on metalworking, which limited weapons to those made of wood or stone, shows the extent of their domination in Israel's heartland.

13:20-21 The Philistines also controlled the maintenance of the Israelites' farming tools and charged the people high prices.

13:22 The phrase **only Saul and his son Jonathan had weapons** paints a dismal picture of Israel's situation. The people desperately needed good leadership to answer the Philistine challenge.

13:23 Controlling **the pass at Michmash** cut off Israel's advance northward toward that city. A large group of Philistines controlled territory only a few miles from Saul's capital.

14:1 This chapter begins to show a consistent contrast between Saul and his **son Jonathan**. To this point, Saul had largely retreated from the Philistines, but Jonathan decided to challenge them.

14:2 The exact location of the **pomegranate tree in Migron on the outskirts of Gibeah** is unknown. Perhaps Saul's palace had not yet been established. Assuming Saul stationed

The troops with him numbered about 600.[a] [3] Ahijah,[b] who was wearing an •ephod,[c] was also there. He was the son of Ahitub, the brother of Ichabod[d] son of Phinehas, son of Eli the Lord's priest at Shiloh.[e] But the troops did not know that Jonathan had left.

[4] There were sharp columns[A] of rock on both sides of the pass[f] that Jonathan intended to cross to reach the Philistine garrison. One was named Bozez and the other Seneh; [5] one stood to the north in front of Michmash and the other to the south in front of Geba. [6] Jonathan said to the attendant who carried his weapons, "Come on, let's cross over to the garrison of these uncircumcised men.[g] Perhaps the Lord will help us. Nothing can keep the Lord from saving, whether by many or by few."[h]

[7] His armor-bearer responded, "Do what is in your heart. You choose. I'm right here with you whatever you decide."

[8] "All right," Jonathan replied, "we'll cross over to the men and then let them see us. [9] If they say, 'Wait until we reach you,' then we will stay where we are and not go up to them. [10] But if they say, 'Come on up,' then we'll go up, because the Lord has handed them over to us—that will be our sign."

[11] They let themselves be seen by the Philistine garrison, and the Philistines said, "Look, the Hebrews are coming out of the holes where they've been hiding!" [12] The men of the garrison called to Jonathan and his armor-

bearer. "Come on up, and we'll teach you a lesson!" they said.

"Follow me," Jonathan told his armor-bearer, "for the Lord has handed them over to Israel."[i] [13] Jonathan climbed up using his hands and feet, with his armor-bearer behind him. Jonathan cut them down, and his armor-bearer followed and finished them off. [14] In that first assault Jonathan and his armor-bearer struck down about 20 men in a half-acre field.

A Defeat for the Philistines

[15] Terror spread through the Philistine camp and the open fields to all the troops. Even the garrison and the raiding parties[j] were terrified. The earth shook,[k] and terror spread from God.[B,l] [16] When Saul's watchmen in Gibeah of Benjamin looked, they saw the panicking troops scattering in every direction. [17] So Saul said to the troops with him, "Call the roll and determine who has left us." They called the roll and saw that Jonathan and his armor-bearer were gone.

[18] Saul told Ahijah, "Bring the ark of God," for it was with the Israelites[C] at that time. [19] While Saul spoke to the priest,[m] the panic in the Philistine camp increased in intensity. So Saul said to the priest, "Stop what you're doing."[D]

[20] Saul and all the troops with him assembled and marched to the battle, and there, the Philistines were fighting against each other in

[a]14:2 1Sm 13:15	
[b]14:3 1Sm 22:9-12,20	
[c]1Sm 2:28	
[d]1Sm 4:21	
[e]1Sm 1:3	
[f]14:4 1Sm 13:23	
[g]14:6 1Sm 17:26,36; Jr 9:25-26	
[h]Jdg 7:4-7	
[i]14:12 2Sm 5:24	
[j]14:15 1Sm 13:17-18	
[k]1Sm 7:10	
[l]2Kg 7:6	
[m]14:19 Nm 27:21	

[A]14:4 Lit *There was a tooth*   [B]14:15 Or *and a great terror spread Israel*   [C]14:18 LXX reads *"Bring the ephod." For he wore the ephod before*   [D]14:19 Lit *Withdraw your hand*

his **troops** on Gibeah's north side, he was about an hour's march away from the Philistines at Geba.

14:3 Ahijah, a descendant of **Eli,** was present, wearing his priestly **ephod** (Ex 28:4). Thus, God's counsel was available if Saul was willing to ask for it.

14:4 This verse identifies a portion of the Wadi Suweinit south of Michmash. The meanings of **Bozez** and **Seneh** are uncertain.

14:6 With his words, **Nothing can keep the Lord from saving,** Jonathan demonstrated faith beyond that of his father, who remained at Gibeah with about 600 men (v. 2).

14:8-10 Jonathan proposed they **cross over** into the Philistines' view and seek a **sign** from **the Lord.** An invitation to **come on up** to the Philistines' location may have indicated they did not have the courage to relinquish the high ground to fight against only two Israelites.

14:11 The phrase **the Hebrews are coming out of the holes where they've been hiding** is probably a sarcastic statement mocking the Israelites' weakened position.

14:12 We'll teach you a lesson is literally "we'll make something known to you." The HCSB translation captures the sense of the Philistines' challenge. Jonathan, however, who had entrusted even the Philistines' words into the Lord's

hand, had the confirming sign he needed that victory was his to claim.

14:13 The two Israelites were vulnerable to Philistine attack as they climbed to the Philistines' position. Probably the overconfident Philistines feared little.

14:14 Jonathan's success in the **first assault** indicated God's hand.

14:15 Terror spread as news of the assault came from the survivors. **Terror . . . from God** came upon them, meaning the Philistines may have feared they had come too far inland and incurred the wrath of the Israelites' God as they had done when they captured the ark (5:6-12).

14:17 Taking an account of those present by calling **the roll** would help Saul know if Israelite troops might have been responsible for the Philistine retreat.

14:18 Saul apparently intended to inquire of the Lord about what was happening in the Philistine camp by conferring with the priests who carried **the ark of God**.

14:19 Stop what you're doing is literally "Withdraw your hand." Saul decided he might lose the opportunity to rout the Philistines if he delayed, and he told the priest to stop inquiring of the Lord. Perhaps the Lord had already revealed His will for Saul through **the panic in the Philistine**

great confusion!*a* 21 There were Hebrews from the area who had gone earlier into the camp to join the Philistines, but even they joined the Israelites*b* who were with Saul and Jonathan. 22 When all the Israelite men who had been hiding in the hill country of Ephraim*c* heard that the Philistines were fleeing, they also joined Saul and Jonathan in the battle. 23 So the Lord saved Israel that day.*d*

Saul's Rash Oath

The battle extended beyond Beth-aven, 24 and the men of Israel were worn out that day, for Saul had*A* placed the troops under an oath:*e* "The man who eats food before evening, before I have taken vengeance on my enemies is cursed." So none of the troops tasted any food.

25 Everyone*B* went into the forest, and there was honey on the ground. 26 When the troops entered the forest, they saw the flow of honey, but none of them ate any of it*c* because they feared the oath. 27 However, Jonathan had not heard his father make the troops swear the oath. He reached out with the end of the staff he was carrying and dipped it into the honeycomb.*f* When he ate the honey,*D* he had renewed energy.*g* 28 Then, one of the troops said, "Your father made the troops solemnly swear, 'The man who eats food today is cursed,' and the troops are exhausted."

*a*14:20 Jdg 7:22; 2Ch 20:23
*b*14:21 1Sm 29:4
*c*14:22 1Sm 13:6
*d*14:23 Ex 14:30
*e*14:24 Jos 6:26
*f*14:27 1Sm 14:43
*g*1Sm 30:12
*h*14:29 1Kg 18:17-18
*i*14:31 1Sm 14:5
*j*Jos 10:12
*k*14:32 1Sm 15:19
*l*14:33 Gn 9:4; Lv 17:10-12
*m*14:35 1Sm 7:12,17

29 Jonathan replied, "My father has brought trouble to the land.*h* Just look at how I have renewed energy because I tasted a little honey. 30 How much better if the troops had eaten freely today from the plunder they took from their enemies! Then the slaughter of the Philistines would have been much greater."

31 The Israelites struck down the Philistines that day from Michmash*i* all the way to Aijalon.*j* Since the Israelites were completely exhausted, 32 they rushed to the plunder,*k* took sheep, cattle, and calves, slaughtered them on the ground, and ate meat with the blood still in it. 33 Some reported to Saul: "Look, the troops are sinning against the Lord by eating meat with the blood still in it."*l*

Saul said, "You have been unfaithful. Roll a large stone over here at once." 34 He then said, "Go among the troops and say to them, 'Each man must bring me his ox or his sheep. Do the slaughtering here and then you can eat. Don't sin against the Lord by eating meat with the blood in it.'" So every one of the troops brought his ox that night and slaughtered it there. 35 Then Saul built an altar to the Lord; it was the first time he had built an altar to the Lord.*m*

36 Saul said, "Let's go down after the Philistines tonight and plunder them until morning. Don't let even one remain!"

---

*A*14:24 LXX adds *committed a great act of ignorance and*   *B*14:25 Lit *All the land*   *C*14:26 Lit *but there was none who raised his hand to his mouth*   *D*14:27 Lit *he returned his hand to his mouth*

camp. Another possibility is that the text reveals yet another example of Saul's refusal to follow the Lord's guidance.

14:21 The Philistines' incursion into Israel had led many **Israelites** to defect to the Philistines, but now the defectors switched back as they sensed the Philistine panic. Their doing so meant the Philistines now found themselves on the battlefield with Israelites of whose allegiance they were unsure. They would not make the mistake of joining forces with any Israelites again (29:2-11).

14:22 The **hill country of Ephraim** lay directly north of the central Benjamin plateau where the **battle** was occurring.

14:23 After giving many details about human participants in the battle, the text gives God, not Saul, credit for the incredible victory. The Philistines fled **beyond Beth-aven** (Bethel) as they tried to get back westward across the plateau to the Aijalon Valley (v. 31), which led to their coastal home.

14:24 Many have questioned the wisdom of Saul's placing his **troops under an oath**. Going into battle did not require abstinence from food; perhaps Saul thought such a vow would secure the Lord's favor. Consequently, however, **the men of Israel were worn out** because they had eaten nothing to sustain them while expending much energy.

14:26 The **flow of honey** probably originated from broken nests of wild bees.

14:27 Saul may have made the troops **swear the oath** by having them respond "Amen!" to his statement (v. 24; cp. Dt 27:15). However, **Jonathan had not heard** the oath and

therefore **ate the honey** (lit "put his hand to his mouth") and **had renewed energy** (lit "his eyes brightened").

14:29 The Hebrew word behind **trouble** (Hb *'akar*) was used of Achan, the man who kept some of Jericho's spoil for himself and brought trouble to Israel during Joshua's time (Jos 7:25-26). **Jonathan** suggested his **father** the king had likewise hurt Israel's cause. On **I have renewed energy**, see note at verse 27.

14:31 From **Michmash . . . to Aijalon** was a distance of about 15 miles, stretching from one side of the central Benjamin plateau to the other. **That day** may hint that as the day ended, the people were free from Saul's rash vow (v. 24).

14:32 Sheep, cattle, and calves were clean animals according to the Mosaic law (Lv 11:3-8), but the law also prohibited eating **meat with the blood still in it** (Lv 17:10-14).

14:33-34 To Saul's credit, he acted to prevent people from sinning against the Lord by **eating meat with the blood still in it**.

14:35 The law of Moses normally condemned such an **altar** (Dt 12:13-14), though Samuel also had built one (1Sm 7:17). Perhaps Saul's altar was intended only to commemorate the Lord's victory.

14:36 The elevation dropped **down** over 2,000 feet from the central Benjamin plateau to the Philistine coastal cities. Saul suggested the people continue pursuing their enemies through the night and bring complete destruction on them,

"Do whatever you want,"[A] the troops replied.

But the priest[a] said, "We must consult God here."[b]

[37] So Saul inquired of God,[c] "Should I go after the Philistines? Will You hand them over to Israel?" But God did not answer him that day.[d]

[38] Saul said, "All you leaders of the troops, come here. Let us investigate how this sin has occurred today. [39] As surely as the LORD lives who saves Israel, even if it is because of my son Jonathan, he must die!" Not one of the troops answered him.

[40] So he said to all Israel, "You will be on one side, and I and my son Jonathan will be on the other side."

And the troops replied, "Do whatever you want."[A]

[41] So Saul said to the LORD, "God of Israel, give us the right decision."[B,e] Jonathan and Saul were selected, and the troops were cleared of the charge.

[42] Then Saul said, "Cast the lot between me and my son Jonathan," and Jonathan was selected. [43] Saul commanded him, "Tell me what you did."[f]

Jonathan told him, "I tasted a little honey[g] with the end of the staff I was carrying. I am ready to die!"

[44] Saul declared to him, "May God punish me and do so severely[h] if you do not die, Jonathan!"

[45] But the people said to Saul, "Must Jonathan die, who accomplished such a great deliverance for Israel? No, as the LORD lives, not a hair of his head will fall to the ground,[i] for he worked with God's help today."[j] So the people redeemed Jonathan, and he did not die. [46] Then Saul gave up the pursuit of the Philistines, and the Philistines returned to their own territory.

Summary of Saul's Kingship

[47] When Saul assumed the kingship over Israel, he fought against all his enemies in every direction: against Moab, the Ammonites,[k] Edom, the kings of Zobah,[l] and the Philistines. Wherever he turned, he caused havoc.[C] [48] He fought bravely, defeated the Amalekites,[m] and delivered Israel from the hand of those who plundered them.

[49] Saul's sons[n] were Jonathan, Ishvi, and Malchishua. The names of his two daughters were: Merab,[o] his firstborn, and Michal,[p] the younger. [50] The name of Saul's wife was Ahinoam daughter of Ahimaaz. The name of the commander of his army was Abner son of Saul's uncle Ner.[q] [51] Saul's father was Kish.[r] Abner's father was Ner son of Abiel.

Reference notes: [a]14:36 1Sm 14:3,18-19 [b]Jdg 18:5-6 [c]14:37 1Sm 10:22 [d]1Sm 28:6 [e]14:41 Ac 1:24 [f]14:43 Jos 7:19 [g]1Sm 14:27 [h]14:44 1Sm 25:22 [i]14:45 2Sm 14:11; 1Kg 1:52; Ac 27:34 [j]Jn 3:21 [k]14:47 1Sm 11:1-13 [l]2Sm 8:3-10 [m]14:48 1Sm 15:3,7 [n]14:49 1Sm 31:2; 1Ch 10:2 [o]1Sm 18:17-19 [p]1Sm 18:20,27; 19:12; 2Sm 6:20-23 [q]14:50 2Sm 2:8 [r]14:51 1Sm 9:1,21

A14:36,40 Lit Do what is good in your eyes   B14:41 LXX reads Israel, why have You not answered Your servant today? If the unrighteousness is in me or in my son Jonathan, Lord God of Israel, give Urim; but if the guilt is in Your people Israel, give Thummim."   C14:47 LXX reads he was victorious

an idea his army supported. Saul's **priest**, however, suggested they should **consult God** before proceeding.

14:37 God not answering suggests three responses were possible when someone inquired of the Lord—yes, no, or silence (28:6).

14:38 Saul was convinced that **sin** was present in the camp and that it was preventing the divine answer.

14:39 Saul swore an oath that the guilty party **must die**. Not one of his warriors **answered him**, although many knew who had violated Saul's curse.

14:40 Saul's first step was to determine if the blame for God's silence lay with his house or with someone in his army.

14:41 Jonathan and Saul were selected shows that Saul now knew one of them was responsible.

14:42 Jonathan was selected, and so Saul now knew his son Jonathan was the cause of God's silence.

14:43 Jonathan had not promised to fast that day, but as he confessed eating, he willingly offered to place himself under his father's oath and suffer the consequences.

14:44 With the words **May God punish me . . . severely**, Saul invoked a curse on himself if Jonathan did not die.

14:45 The people insisted Jonathan should not die when God had brought **such a great deliverance for Israel** through him. Saul had not uttered his original oath with divine authority, and Jonathan had not violated it anyway since he had not heard it. Saul's rash curse and oath had put him in a

difficult situation—either he would have to execute his son, or he would have to go back on his oath (this is comparable to Jephthah in the chaotic period of the judges; Jdg 11:29-40). He gave in to the people's wishes and ignored his oath (cp. "the people" in 1Sm 15:24, "the troops" in 13:11; 15:21, and "his servants" in 28:23). This whole episode (14:23-46) points up Saul's impulsiveness and lack of discernment. The reader may be grateful that innocent Jonathan did not die because of Saul's foolish vow, but it is clear that Israel's king is a man of shifting and defective moral character.

14:46 This period of quiet between Israel and the Philistines would not last (v. 52; 28:1).

14:47 Moab lay to Israel's southeast, east of the Dead Sea. The **Ammonites** were east of the Jordan River to Israel's east and northeast. **Edom** was located south of the Dead Sea. **Zobah** was an Aramean city-state in Syria. The verse suggests that at least for a time, Saul secured all Israel's borders.

14:48 The **Amalekites** were a nomadic group known for their marauding bands (15:2-3; 30:1-2; Ex 17:8-15).

14:49-50 Two other members of Saul's family besides Jonathan would figure prominently in biblical history: **Michal** (18:20-29; 19:11-17; 25:44; 2Sm 3:13-16; 6:16,20-23) and **Abner** (2Sm 2:8-9; 3:6-27).

14:52 The constancy of the Philistine threat required that Saul maintain the strongest army he could muster, just as Samuel had warned a king would do (8:11).

[52]The conflict with the Philistines was fierce all of Saul's days, so whenever Saul noticed any strong or brave man, he enlisted him.[a]

Saul Rejected as King

15 Samuel told Saul, "The LORD sent me to anoint you as king over His people Israel.[b] Now, listen to the words of the LORD. [2]This is what the LORD of •Hosts says: 'I witnessed[A] what the Amalekites did to the Israelites when they opposed them along the way as they were coming out of Egypt.[c] [3]Now go and attack the Amalekites and •completely destroy everything they have.[d] Do not spare them. Kill men and women, children and infants, oxen and sheep, camels and donkeys.'"[e]

[4]Then Saul summoned the troops and counted them at Telaim: 200,000 foot soldiers and 10,000 men from Judah. [5]Saul came to the city of Amalek and set up an ambush in the •wadi. [6]He warned the Kenites,[f] "Since you showed kindness to all the Israelites when they came out of Egypt,[g] go on and leave! Get away from the Amalekites, or I'll sweep you away with them." So the Kenites withdrew from the Amalekites.

[7]Then Saul struck down the Amalekites[h] from Havilah[i] all the way to Shur,[j] which is next to Egypt. [8]He captured Agag[k] king of Amalek alive, but he completely destroyed all the rest of the people with the sword.[l] [9]Saul and the troops spared Agag, and the best of the sheep, cattle, and choice animals,[B] as well as the young rams and the best of everything else. They were not willing to destroy them, but they did destroy all the worthless and unwanted things.

[10]Then the word of the LORD came to Samuel, [11]"I regret that I made Saul king,[m] for he has turned away from following Me and has not carried out My instructions."[n] So Samuel became angry and cried out to the LORD all night.[o]

[12]Early in the morning Samuel got up to confront Saul, but it was reported to Samuel,

Cross references (center column):
[a]14:52 1Sm 8:11
[b]15:1 1Sm 9:16
[c]15:2 Ex 17:8-16; Nm 24:20; Dt 25:17-19
[d]15:3 Nm 24:20; Dt 20:16-18
[e]Jos 6:17-21; 1Sm 22:19
[f]15:6 Jdg 1:16; 4:11
[g]Ex 18:9-10; Nm 10:29-32
[h]15:7 1Sm 14:48
[i]Gn 16:7; 25:17-18
[j]Ex 15:22; 1Sm 27:8
[k]15:8 Nm 24:7; Est 3:1
[l]1Sm 27:8; 30:1; 2Sm 8:12
[m]15:11 Gn 6:6-7; Ex 32:14; 2Sm 24:16
[n]1Kg 9:6-7
[o]Ex 32:11-13; Lk 6:12

[A]15:2 LXX reads *I will avenge*   [B]15:9 Lit *and the second*

15:1 Saul's power and purpose lay in God's anointing; **Israel was His people**, not Saul's. Therefore, Saul needed to heed the divine instructions that Samuel now was giving him.

15:2 On the **Amalekites**, see note at 14:48. Exodus 17:8-16 records Israel's initial victory over Amalek under Joshua's leadership. At that time, God promised to oppose the Amalekites continually.

15:3 The phrase **destroy everything they have** describes the practice of the ban, wherein Israel would destroy everything in a town that had breath, including humans and animals. God had authority over when all life began and ended. In the battle of Jericho (Jos 6:17-21), the plunder went into the Lord's treasury; at other times, the people were allowed to keep it (Jos 8:27).

15:4 **Telaim** was probably located in the Negev of Judah (Jos 15:21-24). The **men from Judah** are again listed separately (see note at 11:8).

15:5 The **city of Amalek** may designate the place the Amalekites were living rather than a city, since the group was nomadic.

15:6 Saul's warning to the **Kenites** rewarded earlier friendly terms with them (Jdg 1:16; 4:11). The **kindness to all the Israelites** is only mentioned here, but clearly this was part of Israel's memory in a land where people had long memories (2Ch 20:10-11).

15:7 This extensive campaign covered a broad region, from Arabia almost to Egypt's border, whose inhabitants included many descendants of Ishmael (Gn 25:18).

15:8 The phrase **captured Agag . . . alive** hints at Saul's coming disobedience to what God had commanded (v. 3).

15:9 The Hebrew text emphasizes that **Saul** was the one primarily responsible for sparing **Agag**. The people also **spared . . . the best of everything else**, another violation of God's command (v. 3). Of course, destroying **all the worthless and unwanted things** was no great sacrifice.

15:11 The verb **regret** with God as its subject occurs only here and in Gn 6:7, where it denotes God's regrets over making humanity and His ultimate decision to bring the great flood. In both cases, people made wrong moral choices, and God's foreknowledge meant He knew what people would do. Nonetheless, it pained Him to see the disobedience come to pass. The word translated **turned away** commonly means "repent" when it speaks of turning away from sin, but here it describes Saul's conscious decision to cease **following** the Lord. **Samuel** was frustrated by Saul's failing kingship, particularly as he remembered he had anointed him (10:1). Saul had indeed turned out to be a king just like the ones of "all the other nations" (8:5,20), but the people had persisted in their request despite his sober warnings (8:11-18). On **cried out**, see note at 4:13.

15:12 Perhaps God had told Samuel to get up **early** during Samuel's intense prayer the previous night (v. 11). Ironically, **Saul** had gone to **Carmel**, a town about seven miles south of Hebron in Judah's hill country (Jos 15:55), to

---

nacham

Hebrew Pronunciation	[nah KHAHM]
HCSB Translation	relent, comfort, repent
Uses in 1 Samuel	4
Uses in the OT	108
Focus Passage	1 Samuel 15:11,29,35

Nacham means *change one's mind* (Ex 13:17). God regrets (Gn 6:6) or relents (1Ch 21:15). Sinners *repent* (Jr 31:19). One *takes words back* (Ps 110:4). *Nacham* often entails reaching a positive condition; one *finishes mourning* (Gn 38:12), *is moved to pity* (Jdg 2:18), or *is satisfied* (Is 57:6). *Nacham* implies *having* (Jdg 21:6) or *showing* (Jr 15:6) compassion. Intensive forms denote *console* (2Sm 10:2), *comfort* (Gn 37:35), or *bring relief* (Gn 5:29). Intensive participles suggest *comforters* (Ps 69:20) or *men with condolences* (2Sm 10:3). Reflexive-passive verbs signify *console oneself* (Gn 27:42), *find comfort* (Ps 119:52), *be appeased* (Ezk 5:13), or *have compassion* (Dt 32:36). God does not *change His mind* (Nm 23:19).

"Saul went to Carmel[a] where he set up a monument for himself. Then he turned around and went down to Gilgal."[b] [13]When Samuel came to him, Saul said, "May the Lord bless you.[c] I have carried out the Lord's instructions."

[14]Samuel replied, "Then what is this sound of sheep[A] and cattle I hear?"

[15]Saul answered, "The troops brought them from the Amalekites and spared the best sheep and cattle in order to offer a sacrifice to the Lord your God,[d] but the rest we destroyed."[e]

[16]"Stop!" exclaimed Samuel. "Let me tell you what the Lord said to me last night."

"Tell me," he replied.

[17]Samuel continued, "Although you once considered yourself unimportant,[f] have you not become the leader of the tribes of Israel? The Lord anointed you king over Israel [18]and then sent you on a mission and said: 'Go and completely destroy the sinful Amalekites. Fight against them until you have annihilated them.' [19]So why didn't you obey the Lord? Why did you rush on the plunder[g] and do what was evil in the Lord's sight?"

[20]"But I did obey the Lord!" Saul answered.[B] "I went on the mission the Lord gave me: I brought back Agag, king of Amalek, and I completely destroyed the Amalekites. [21]The troops took sheep and cattle from the plunder—the best of what

was *set apart for destruction—to sacrifice to the Lord your God at Gilgal."[h]

[22]Then Samuel said:

Does the Lord[i] take pleasure
   in *burnt offerings and sacrifices
as much as in obeying the Lord?
Look: to obey is better than sacrifice,
to pay attention is better than the fat
   of rams.[j]
[23]For rebellion is like the sin
   of *divination,[k]
and defiance is like wickedness[l]
   and idolatry.
Because you have rejected the word
   of the Lord,
He has rejected you as king.[m]

[24]Saul answered Samuel, "I have sinned.[n] I have transgressed the Lord's command[o] and your words. Because I was afraid of the people, I obeyed them. [25]Now therefore, please forgive my sin[p] and return with me so I can worship the Lord."

[26]Samuel replied to Saul, "I will not return with you. Because you rejected the word of the Lord,[q] the Lord has rejected you from being king over Israel." [27]When Samuel turned to go, Saul grabbed the hem of his robe, and it tore. [28]Samuel said to him, "The Lord has torn

---

Cross references (center column):
[a]15:12 Jos 15:55; 1Sm 25:2
[b]1Sm 13:13-14
[c]15:13 Gn 14:19; 2Sm 2:5
[d]15:15 Gn 3:12-13
[e]15:14-15 Ex 32:21-24
[f]15:17 1Sm 9:21
[g]15:19 1Sm 14:32
[h]15:21 Ex 32:22-23
[i]15:22 Ps 40:6-8; 51:16-17; Is 1:11-15; Mc 6:6-8
[j]Heb 10:5-7
[k]15:23 Dt 18:10
[l]Gn 31:19,34
[m]1Sm 8:7
[n]15:24 Nm 22:34; 2Sm 12:13; Ps 51:3-4
[o]Pr 29:25; Is 51:12-13
[p]15:25 Ex 10:17
[q]15:26 1Sm 13:14; 16:1

---

erect **a monument for himself**. This monument presumably would remind the Carmelites of the peace that came to their region because of Saul's victory over Amalek. **Gilgal** had great historical significance (see notes at 7:16 and 10:8); it lay about 15 miles east of Gibeah, Saul's capital.

15:13 On **I have carried out the Lord's instructions**, see note at verse 11. God did not share Saul's perspective on this matter.

15:14 The **sound of sheep and cattle** was proof that Saul had failed to execute God's command.

15:15 Saul's reference to **the Lord your God** (not "my God" or "our God") sounds an ominous tone but aptly fits the situation because Saul did not appear to have much of a relationship with the Lord.

15:16 Stop!—The prophet had had enough of Saul's excuses and cut him off, an action most subjects would not dare take with their king.

15:17 God had taken Saul from relatively **unimportant** status as a common citizen (cp. Saul's own words in 9:21) to **king over Israel**. The word **you** is emphasized in the text with respect to Saul to heighten the intensity of Samuel's words.

15:18 On **completely destroy**, see note at verse 3. The presence of any survivors (in this case, King Agag and the best of the flocks and herds) was a violation of God's command.

15:19 The verbal idea in the phrase **rush on the plunder** is related to the word for "bird of prey," in this case swooping down on the spoils of war.

15:20 Saul's own description of his actions condemned

him because he admitted to sparing **Agag** and to putting to death only **the Amalekites** and not their domesticated property as God had commanded (v. 3).

15:21 Sacrifice . . . at Gilgal would not substitute for obedience on Saul's part; further, God had already claimed the animals and given orders for their destruction (vv. 2-3). On **the Lord your God**, see note at verse 15.

15:22 Samuel's words **to obey is better than sacrifice** drove home the point that partial obedience of God was really disobedience, and full obedience of God mattered more than any human-concocted alternatives.

15:23 The Mosaic law prohibited **divination**, the attempt to tap into demonic powers (Dt 18:10,14). Samuel compared both rebellion and **defiance** (lit "pushing back," here, at God) as just as wicked. In its basic sense, **idolatry** is exalting something or someone (including one's own will) above God.

15:24 Saul's half-hearted repentance came only after it was too late, since Samuel had already pronounced the Lord's verdict. Saul feared **the people** more than he feared God.

15:25 Saul wanted Samuel's forgiveness and the endorsement of his kingship that Samuel's staying with him would bring.

15:26 Samuel truly sought God's will for his life; consequently, he could not support Saul's kingship **over Israel**.

15:27 The words **Saul grabbed the hem** of Samuel's **robe** may suggest that Saul had been kneeling before Samuel.

15:28 The words **has given it to your neighbor** suggest that in God's mind the transfer of power to Israel's new king

the kingship of Israel away from you today*a* and has given it to your neighbor who is better than you.*b* ²⁹ Furthermore, the Eternal One of Israel*c* does not lie or change His mind, for He is not man who changes his mind."*d*

³⁰ Saul said, "I have sinned. Please honor me*e* now before the elders of my people and before Israel. Come back with me so I can bow in worship to the Lord your God."*f* ³¹ Then Samuel went back, following Saul, and Saul bowed down to the Lord.

³² Samuel said, "Bring me Agag king of Amalek."

Agag came to him trembling,*A* for he thought, "Certainly the bitterness of death has come."*B,C*

³³ Samuel declared:

As your sword has made women
    childless,
    so your mother will be childless
    among women.*g*

Then he hacked Agag to pieces before the Lord at Gilgal.

³⁴ Samuel went to Ramah,*h* and Saul went up to his home in Gibeah*i* of Saul. ³⁵ Even to the day of his death, Samuel never again visited Saul.*j* Samuel mourned for Saul,*k* and the

Lord regretted He had made Saul king over Israel.

Samuel Anoints David

16 The Lord said to Samuel, "How long are you going to mourn for Saul,*l* since I have rejected him as king over Israel?*m* Fill your horn with oil*n* and go. I am sending you to Jesse of Bethlehem*o* because I have selected a king from his sons."

² Samuel asked, "How can I go? Saul will hear about it and kill me!"

The Lord answered, "Take a young cow with you and say, 'I have come to sacrifice to the Lord.'*p* ³ Then invite Jesse to the sacrifice, and I will let you know what you are to do.*q* You are to anoint for Me the one I indicate to you."*r*

⁴ Samuel did what the Lord directed and went to Bethlehem.*s* When the elders of the town met him, they trembled*D* and asked, "Do*E* you come in peace?"*t*

⁵ "In peace," he replied. "I've come to sacrifice to the Lord. Consecrate yourselves*u* and come with me to the sacrifice."*F* Then he consecrated Jesse and his sons and invited them to the sacrifice. ⁶ When they arrived, Samuel saw Eliab*v* and said, "Certainly the Lord's anointed one is here before Him."

Cross references (center column)
*a*15:28 1Sm 28:17-18
*b*15:27-28 1Kg 11:30-36
*c*15:29 1Ch 29:11; Ps 18:1-2
*d*Nm 23:19; Ezk 24:14
*e*15:30 Jn 12:43
*f*Is 29:13
*g*15:33 Gn 9:6; Jdg 1:7; Mt 7:2
*h*15:34 1Sm 7:17
*i*1Sm 11:4
*j*15:35 1Sm 19:24
*k*1Sm 16:1
*l*16:1 1Sm 15:35
*m*1Sm 13:13-14; 15:23
*n*1Sm 9:16; 10:1; 2Kg 9:1
*o*Ru 4:17-22
*p*16:2 1Sm 20:29
*q*16:3 Ex 4:15; Ac 9:6
*r*Dt 17:14-15; 1Sm 9:16
*s*16:4 Gn 48:7; Lk 2:4
*t*1Kg 2:13; 2Kg 9:22; 1Ch 12:17-18
*u*16:5 Gn 35:2; Ex 19:10
*v*16:6 1Sm 17:13

---

was already accomplished, but Samuel would not learn the identity of the next king until chapter 16.

15:29 God's eternal, constant character can be trusted. The word translated **change His mind** occurs in a totally different sense in verse 11 ("regret"). The Lord had expressed regret over Saul's failures, but He would not change His verdict about Saul's kingship.

15:30 Saul confessed his sin a second time. Note again the words **the Lord your God** (see note at v. 15).

15:31 Saul's persistence paid off as **Samuel went back** and helped the king save face before his troops.

15:32 The Hebrew word behind **trembling** is obscure and may also mean "in bonds" or "confidently." **Certainly the bitterness of death has come** may also be translated "Certainly the bitterness of death has turned aside" and if so, may represent Agag's attempt to keep Samuel from killing him. Context suggests the HCSB rendering is correct.

15:33 The prophet, not Saul, now finished God's command. The Hebrew verb translated **hacked . . . to pieces** is *shasaph,* the sound of a whirring sword.

15:34 The two leaders, Samuel and Saul, parted company once and for all, even though their two cities were only two miles apart.

15:35 **Samuel never again visited Saul** is literally "Samuel did not again see Saul." Technically, Samuel did see Saul, but it was not a prearranged official visit (19:24). The words **the Lord regretted He had made Saul king** (see note at 15:11) highlight the seriousness with which God takes the failures of His leaders (2Sm 11:27; 12:7-12; Heb 13:7).

16:1 How much time had passed since the end of chapter 15 is unknown. At any rate, God wanted to move ahead with His plan. The command **Fill your horn with oil** meant God had someone in mind for Samuel to anoint as king. **Jesse** appears here for the first time in the book. His connection with **Bethlehem** is spelled out in the book of Ruth (Ru 4:17,22).

16:2 Samuel had told Saul that God had rejected his kingship and had chosen another to lead Israel. Consequently, Samuel's travels would be of great interest to Saul. Samuel feared Saul would consider it treason if Samuel anointed another man as king. **A young cow** might be sacrificed in a region where an unsolved murder had occurred (Dt 21:1-9). It is also possible that bringing a **sacrifice to the Lord** merely provided a pretext for Samuel to hide the primary purpose of his journey.

16:3 The presence of **Jesse** was crucial since one of his sons was to succeed Saul.

16:4 The trembling of the **elders of the town** may indicate they feared Saul's wrath if they gave support to Samuel.

16:5 **Consecrate** means to set oneself apart to God. It involved entering into ritual cleanness. No set "consecration checklist" appears in Scripture, though bathing, putting on clean garments, avoiding contact with a dead body, and suspension of sexual relations are mentioned in various consecration contexts. **He consecrated Jesse and his sons** probably means Samuel oversaw their consecration at their home.

16:6 Jesse's son **Eliab** later served in Saul's army (17:13,28); he apparently looked like kingly material.

[7]But the Lord said to Samuel, "Do not look at his appearance or his stature, because I have rejected him. Man does not see what the Lord sees,[A] for man sees what is visible,[B] but the Lord sees the heart."[a]

[8]Jesse called Abinadab[b] and presented him to Samuel. "The Lord hasn't chosen this one either," Samuel said. [9]Then Jesse presented Shammah,[c] but Samuel said, "The Lord hasn't chosen this one either." [10]After Jesse presented seven of his sons to him, Samuel told Jesse, "The Lord hasn't chosen any of these." [11]Samuel asked him, "Are these all the sons you have?"

"There is still the youngest,"[d] he answered, "but right now he's tending the sheep." Samuel told Jesse, "Send for him. We won't sit down to eat until he gets here." [12]So Jesse sent for him. He had beautiful eyes and a healthy,[c] handsome appearance.[e]

Then the Lord said, "Anoint him, for he is the one."[f] [13]So Samuel took the horn of oil, anointed him[g] in the presence of his brothers, and the Spirit of the Lord took control of David from that day forward.[h] Then Samuel set out and went to Ramah.

David in Saul's Court

[14]Now the Spirit of the Lord had left Saul,[i] and an evil spirit sent from the Lord began to torment him, [15]so Saul's servants said to him, "You see that an evil spirit from God is tormenting you. [16]Let our lord command your servants here in your presence to look for someone who knows how to play the lyre. Whenever the evil spirit from God troubles you, that person can play the lyre, and you will feel better."[j]

[17]Then Saul commanded his servants, "Find me someone who plays well and bring him to me."

[18]One of the young men answered, "I have seen a son of Jesse of Bethlehem who knows how to play the lyre. He is also a valiant man,[k] a warrior, eloquent, handsome, and the Lord is with him."[l]

[19]Then Saul dispatched messengers to Jesse and said, "Send me your son David, who is with the sheep." [20]So Jesse took a donkey loaded with bread, a skin of wine, and one young goat and sent them by his son David to Saul.[m] [21]When David came to Saul[n] and entered his service, Saul admired him greatly, and David became his armor-bearer. [22]Then Saul sent word to Jesse: "Let David remain in my service, for I am pleased with him." [23]Whenever the spirit from God troubled Saul,[o] David would pick up his lyre and play, and Saul would then be relieved, feel better, and the evil spirit would leave him.

David versus Goliath

17 The Philistines[p] gathered their forces for war at Socoh in Judah and camped

Cross references (center column)

[a]16:7 1Kg 8:39; Jr 17:10; Lk 16:15; Jn 2:24-25
[b]16:8 1Sm 17:13
[c]16:9 1Sm 17:13
[d]16:11 1Sm 17:12; 2Sm 13:3
[e]16:12 1Sm 17:42
[f]1Sm 9:17
[g]16:13 1Sm 10:1
[h]Ps 51:10-12; Ezk 36:27; Ac 2:1-17
[i]16:14 1Sm 11:6; 18:12; 28:15
[j]16:16 1Sm 18:10; 19:9; 2Kg 3:15
[k]16:18 1Sm 17:32-36
[l]1Sm 3:19; 18:12-14
[m]16:20 1Sm 10:4,27; Pr 18:16
[n]16:21 Gn 41:46; Pr 22:29
[o]16:23 1Sm 16:14-16
[p]17:1 1Sm 13:5

A16:7 LXX reads *God does not see as a man sees*   **B**16:7 Lit *what is of the eyes*   **C**16:12 Or *ruddy*

16:7 Saul also had **appearance** and **stature**, but he had proved unworthy.

16:8-9 Jesse's sons **Abinadab** and **Shammah** also served in Saul's army (17:13).

16:11 The task of **tending the sheep** often fell to **the youngest**. In Bedouin cultures, such work was often the task of young girls (Gn 29:9), but David's sister Zeruiah (1Ch 2:16) is not mentioned in the narrative.

16:12 The Hebrew word behind **healthy** is related to the word for "red" and may describe either David's reddish-toned hair or skin. **Beautiful eyes and a . . . handsome appearance** might help a king's credibility, but ultimately God looks at the heart.

16:13 Despite God's choice of **David** through Samuel, apparently at least Eliab doubted David's heart (17:28). It is also possible that Samuel did not reveal to David's **brothers** the mission to which God was calling David. The Spirit of the Lord **took control of David** just as He had done with Saul earlier (10:6,10; 11:6), empowering David for God's service. Samuel's route from Bethlehem to **Ramah** would have normally taken him directly past or through Gibeah.

16:14 The theological difficulty of the expression **evil spirit . . . from the Lord** may be resolved in one of two ways. God may have intended the evil spirit as redemptive—designed to turn Saul to repentance. Or God may have intended the evil spirit as His instrument of judgment against the rebellious king. God is completely righteous, hates evil, and never does anything unjust, yet He makes use of demons (against their evil intention) to accomplish His good purposes (cp. Jb 1:6-12).

16:18 One of the **young men** of Saul's court apparently knew David well, because he described several good qualities beyond David's musical skill. **Warrior** may be anticipatory (suggesting David seemed to have the qualities that would make a good warrior) since it does not seem that at this stage of life David was accustomed to fighting in battle (17:14-15). **The Lord is with him** describes David's spiritual qualifications, which would prove important as the drama unfolded.

16:20 The items **donkey . . . bread . . . wine**, and **goat** were either Jesse's gift to **Saul** or a contribution to David's sustenance in the royal court. No biblical evidence indicates when Saul initiated a national tax system for providing the palace's needs, but such taxes are assumed in 17:25.

16:21 David became King Saul's **armor-bearer**, a position that would keep him closer to Saul, who **admired** (lit "loved") **him greatly**.

16:23 Being close to Saul also meant David could **pick up his lyre** quickly and play if the king felt **troubled**. Meanwhile, God was continuing to prepare David for the day he would become king.

17:1-2 The heartland of Benjamin and Judah was approach-

between Socoh[a] and Azekah[b] in Ephes-dammim.[c] [2]Saul and the men of Israel gathered and camped in the Valley of Elah;[d] then they lined up in battle formation to face the Philistines.

[3]The Philistines were standing on one hill, and the Israelites were standing on another hill with a ravine between them. [4]Then a champion named Goliath, from Gath,[e] came out from the Philistine camp. He was nine feet, nine inches tall[A,B] [5]and wore a bronze helmet[c] and bronze scale armor that weighed 125 pounds.[D] [6]There was bronze armor on his shins, and a bronze sword[f] was slung between his shoulders. [7]His spear shaft[g] was like a weaver's beam, and the iron point of his spear weighed 15 pounds.[E] In addition, a shield-bearer[h] was walking in front of him.

[8]He stood and shouted to the Israelite battle formations: "Why do you come out to line up in battle formation?" He asked them, "Am I not a Philistine and are you not servants of Saul?[i] Choose one of your men and have him come down against me. [9]If he wins in a fight against me and kills me, we will be your servants. But if I win against him and kill him,

then you will be our servants and serve us."[j] [10]Then the Philistine said, "I defy the ranks of Israel today.[k] Send me a man so we can fight each other!" [11]When Saul and all Israel heard these words from the Philistine, they lost their courage and were terrified.

[12]Now David was the son of the Ephrathite[l] from Bethlehem of Judah named Jesse. Jesse had eight sons[m] and during Saul's reign was already an old man. [13]Jesse's three oldest sons had followed Saul to the war, and their names[n] were Eliab, the firstborn, Abinadab, the next, and Shammah, the third, [14]and David was the youngest.[o] The three oldest had followed Saul, [15]but David kept going back and forth from Saul[p] to tend his father's flock in Bethlehem.

[16]Every morning and evening for 40 days the Philistine came forward and took his stand. [17]One day Jesse had told his son David: "Take this half-bushel[F] of roasted grain along with these 10 loaves of bread[q] for your brothers and hurry to their camp. [18]Also take these 10 portions of cheese to the field commander.[G] Check on the welfare of your brothers[r] and bring a confirmation from them. [19]They are

Cross references
[a]17:1 2Ch 28:18
[b]Jos 10:10
[c]1Ch 11:13
[d]17:2 1Sm 21:9
[e]17:4 2Sm 21:18-22; 1Ch 20:4-8
[f]17:6 1Sm 17:45
[g]17:2 2Sm 21:19; 1Ch 11:23
[h]1Sm 17:41
[i]17:8 1Sm 8:17
[j]17:8-9 2Sm 2:12-16
[k]17:10 1Sm 17:26,36,45
[l]17:12 Gn 35:19
[m]1Sm 16:10-11; 1Ch 2:13-15
[n]17:13 1Sm 16:6,8-9
[o]17:14 1Sm 16:11
[p]17:15 1Sm 16:21-23
[q]17:17 1Sm 25:18
[r]17:18 Gn 37:13-14

[A]17:4 DSS, LXX read four cubits and a span   [B]17:4 Lit was six cubits and a span   [C]17:5 Lit helmet on his head   [D]17:5 Lit 5,000 shekels   [E]17:7 Lit 600 shekels   [F]17:17 Lit this ephah   [G]17:18 Lit the leader of 1,000

---

able from the coast through six valleys. The **Philistines** already had come up the Aijalon Valley (13:23). During the days of Samson (Jdg 13–16), they had come up the Sorek Valley. Now they were coming up the **Valley of Elah** and already controlled **Socoh** and **Azekah**. If they got much farther up the hill country, they could come up the ridge route into the hill country and threaten Bethlehem, Hebron, and Saul's capital, Gibeah. The situation was desperate for Saul and his army.

17:3 The word translated "valley" in verse 2 designates a broad, flat valley. The word translated **ravine** denotes a narrower, more sharply defined valley or wadi. Today, the valley pinches in a bit east of Socoh, perhaps marking the site of the ancient conflict.

17:4 Recent archaeological finds at Tel es-Safi, the site of ancient **Gath**, confirm that the name **Goliath** was used among the Philistines around this period. Two other early manuscripts (LXX, DSS) state that Goliath was "six feet, nine inches tall." However, the description of Goliath's combat gear appears to support the larger height of **nine feet, nine inches tall**. At either height, Goliath would have towered over the much smaller Israelites.

17:5-7 The sheer spectacle of Goliath's **armor** and weapons frightened the Israelite army. At the same time, their weight would have restricted Goliath's agility. He probably assumed he would not have a prolonged fight with anyone.

17:8-9 Goliath challenged and taunted the Israelites. With his words **Choose one of your men**, Goliath suggested representative combat—the army of the losing combatant would become **servants** of the army of the victorious combatant.

17:10 The Hebrew word translated **defy** first came from Goliath's mouth, but it occurs four other times in the account

(vv. 25,26,36,45), with the last three emphasizing Goliath's mocking of God's honor.

17:11 The Israelites needed their leader to articulate a plan of response, but King Saul had none.

17:12 The feminine name Ephrath(ah) occurs in Judah's genealogical lists, and her son Hur is called Bethlehem's father (1Ch 2:19; 4:4). First Chronicles 2:13 says seven rather than **eight sons**, but perhaps one died at an early age and therefore was not noted by the Chronicler.

17:13 Eliab . . . Abinadab, and **Shammah** were the three sons of Jesse other than David mentioned by name in the account of Samuel's anointing of David. If the Philistines made their way up the Valley of Elah, Bethlehem would soon face attack, so these men were defending their own homeland.

17:14 The text's second mention of the fact that **David was the youngest** (16:11) highlights how God's choice often overrides human logic.

17:15 David's primary role was tending **his father's flock in Bethlehem** about 15 miles east of the battle site, but he **kept going back and forth** to take his brothers food and to update his father on the battle.

17:16 Such a long standoff period as **40 days** would cause problems if it came at a time when fighting men needed to be home working their land.

17:17 Families of soldiers normally provided their sustenance on the battlefields.

17:18 Field commander is literally "commander of the thousand." **Confirmation** probably refers to a report from David's **brothers**.

17:19 Jesse's words to David suggest either that this was

with Saul and all the men of Israel in the Valley of Elah fighting with the Philistines."

[20] So David got up early in the morning, left the flock with someone to keep it, loaded up, and set out as Jesse had instructed him.

He arrived at the perimeter of the camp[a] as the army was marching out to its battle formation shouting their battle cry. [21] Israel and the Philistines lined up in battle formation facing each other. [22] David left his supplies in the care of the quartermaster[b] and ran to the battle line. When he arrived, he asked his brothers how they were. [23] While he was speaking with them, suddenly the champion named Goliath, the Philistine from Gath, came forward from the Philistine battle line and shouted his usual words,[c] which David heard. [24] When all the Israelite men saw Goliath, they retreated from him terrified.

[25] Previously, an Israelite man had declared: "Do you see this man who keeps coming out? He comes to defy Israel. The king will make the man who kills him very rich and will give him his daughter.[d] The king will also make the household of that man's father exempt from paying taxes in Israel."[e]

[26] David spoke to the men who were standing with him: "What will be done for the man who kills that Philistine and removes this disgrace from Israel?[f] Just who is this uncircumcised Philistine[g] that he should defy the armies[h] of the living God?"[i]

[27] The people told him about the offer, concluding, "That is what will be done for the man who kills him."[i]

[28] David's oldest brother Eliab listened as he spoke to the men, and became angry with him.[k] "Why did you come down here?" he asked. "Who did you leave those few sheep with in the wilderness? I know your arrogance and your evil heart—you came down to see the battle!"

[29] "What have I done now?" protested David. "It was just a question." [30] Then he turned from those beside him to others in front of him and asked about the offer. The people gave him the same answer as before.[l]

[31] What David said was overheard and reported to Saul, so he had David brought to him. [32] David said to Saul, "Don't let anyone be discouraged by[A] him;[m] your servant will go[n] and fight this Philistine!"

[33] But Saul replied, "You can't go fight this Philistine. You're just a youth, and he's been a warrior since he was young."

[34] David answered Saul: "Your servant has been tending his father's sheep. Whenever a lion or a bear came and carried off a lamb from the flock, [35] I went after it, struck it down, and rescued the lamb from its mouth.[o] If it reared up against me, I would grab it by its fur,[B] strike it down, and kill it. [36] Your servant has killed lions and bears; this uncircumcised Philistine will be like one of them, for he has defied the armies of the living God." [37] Then David said, "The Lord who rescued me from the paw of

---

[a]17:20 1Sm 26:5,7
[b]17:22 Jdg 18:21; Is 10:28
[c]17:23 1Sm 17:8-10
[d]17:25 Jos 15:16
[e]1Sm 8:11
[f]17:26 1Sm 11:2
[g]1Sm 14:6; 17:36; Jr 9:25-26
[h]1Sm 17:10
[i]Dt 5:26; 2Kg 19:4
[i]17:27 1Sm 17:25
[k]17:28 Gn 37:4,8-36
[l]17:30 1Sm 17:26-27
[m]17:32 Dt 20:1-4
[n]1Sm 16:18
[o]17:35 Am 3:12

[A]17:32 Lit *let a man's heart fall over*　[B]17:35 LXX reads *throat*; lit *beard*

David's first trip to look after his brothers (unlikely in view of v. 15) or that David had been keeping the sheep outside Bethlehem and had just returned when Jesse sent him to Saul's camp.

17:20 David must have **left** very **early** in order to have made the 15-mile journey in time to see **the army . . . marching out**.

17:21 It appeared perhaps another day of standoff with the giant Goliath was forthcoming.

17:23 **Came forward** is literally "was going up." The expression may suggest **Goliath** approached a bit closer than before, actually coming part way up the ravine (v. 3). **David heard** Goliath's taunts—a subtle turning point in the account.

17:25 The victorious warrior would become Saul's son-in-law (18:18,23) and would enjoy privileges as part of the royal family.

17:26 David's words indicate he had not heard the announcement from Saul's assistant (v. 25). The word **disgrace** is related to **defy** (vv. 10,25-26,36). **Uncircumcised** denotes someone outside God's covenant. David saw the threat as not merely political (cp. v. 8) but theological. **The armies of the living God**, ironically, were terrified, but to David God's honor was at stake.

17:28 **Eliab**, along with his brothers Abinadab and Shammah, were serving in Saul's army (vv. 13-14). Eliab misread

the intentions of his brother David and **became angry**—thus confirming for the reader God's rejection of him as a possible successor of Saul (16:6-7).

17:31 King Saul apparently heard of David's question and David's interest in the reward for fighting Goliath and summoned the young man.

17:32 David's words **your servant** was a polite way of referring to oneself before a superior (vv. 34,36; 2Sm 7:19-20).

17:33 Saul rejected David's bold offer because David was just a **youth**, and because Goliath had been in training as a warrior from his youth.

17:34 Wild animals such as a lion or a bear were always threats to **a lamb from the flock**, and the shepherd's fighting ability was the lamb's only defense.

17:36 **Lions and bears** (lit "the lion and the bear") probably best gives the sense of the translation. David was probably describing his various encounters with wild animals rather than identifying two specific incidents. **This uncircumcised Philistine** would suffer the same fate as these animals for his defiance of the Lord (see note at v. 26).

17:37 The word **rescued** is the same word that appeared in verse 35; David rescued the sheep, and God rescued him. Now, God would rescue His flock Israel. Encouraged by David's faith, Saul found the courage to invoke God's name in the blessing, **May the Lord be with you.**

the lion and the paw of the bear will rescue me from the hand of this Philistine."[a]

Saul said to David, "Go, and may the LORD be with you."[b]

[38] Then Saul had his own military clothes put on David. He put a bronze helmet on David's head and had him put on armor. [39] David strapped his sword on over the military clothes and tried to walk, but he was not used to them. "I can't walk in these," David said to Saul, "I'm not used to them." So David took them off. [40] Instead, he took his staff in his hand[c] and chose five smooth stones from the •wadi and put them in the pouch, in his shepherd's bag. Then, with his sling in his hand, he approached the Philistine.

[41] The Philistine came closer and closer to David, with the shield-bearer in front of him. [42] When the Philistine looked and saw David, he despised him[d] because he was just a youth, healthy[A,e] and handsome. [43] He said to David, "Am I a dog[f] that you come against me with sticks?"[B] Then he cursed David by his gods.[g] [44] "Come here," the Philistine called to David, "and I'll give your flesh to the birds of the sky and the wild beasts!"[h]

[45] David said to the Philistine: "You come against me with a dagger, spear, and sword, but I come against you in the name of •Yahweh of •Hosts, the God of Israel's armies—you have defied Him.[i] [46] Today, the LORD will hand you over to me. Today, I'll strike you down, cut your head off, and give the corpses[C] of the Philistine camp to the birds of the sky and the creatures of the earth. Then all the world will know that Israel has a God,[j] [47] and this whole assembly will know that it is not by sword or by spear that the LORD saves,[k] for the battle is the LORD's.[l] He will hand you over to us."

[48] When the Philistine started forward to attack him, David ran quickly to the battle line to meet the Philistine.[m] [49] David put his hand in the bag, took out a stone, slung it, and hit the Philistine on his forehead. The stone sank into his forehead, and he fell on his face to the ground. [50] David defeated the Philistine with a sling and a stone. Even though David had no sword, he struck down the Philistine and killed him. [51] David ran and stood over him. He grabbed the Philistine's sword,[n] pulled it from its sheath, and used it to kill him. Then he cut off his head. When the Philistines saw

Cross references:
[a] 17:37 2Tm 4:17-18
[b] 1Sm 20:13
[c] 17:40 Jdg 20:16
[d] 17:42 Pr 16:18
[e] 1Sm 16:12
[f] 17:43 1Sm 24:14
[g] 1Kg 20:10
[h] 17:44 1Sm 17:46
[i] 17:45 2Ch 32:7-8; Ps 124:8; Heb 11:34
[j] 17:46 1Kg 18:36; 2Kg 19:19; Is 37:20
[k] 17:47 Hs 1:7
[l] Ex 14:13-14; Ps 33:16-22; 44:4-8
[m] 17:48 Ps 27:3
[n] 17:51 1Sm 21:9

[A] 17:42 Or *ruddy*   [B] 17:43 Some LXX mss add *and stones?" And David said, "No! Worse than a dog!"*   [C] 17:46 LXX reads *give your limbs and the limbs*

17:38-39 Saul brought **his own military clothes** for **David** to wear, a fact that suggests that although he was the youngest, David may not have been smaller than the king. David tried on the **bronze helmet** and other **armor**, but he was not accustomed to wearing them, so he **took them off**. Ironically, it would not be the last time David wore a king's clothes.

17:40 Rather than wearing royal armor, David took weapons with which he was most familiar. The **five smooth stones** he chose would have been roughly the size of tennis balls and would fly straighter than jagged stones. As a shepherd, he had likely become proficient with **his sling**, which would also enable him to attack Goliath from a distance instead of in close combat, where the giant would have a big advantage.

17:42 Goliath saw David as an unfit challenge to his skill as a warrior. He was **just a youth**, and his features did not show that he had battle experience.

17:43 Goliath began his psychological warfare ("trash talk") against David by suggesting the staff David carried was fit only to beat **a dog**. The statement **he cursed David by his gods** further slants the account toward describing a battle between the gods of the Philistines and the God of Israel rather than just a battle between two men.

17:45 David's response to Goliath highlights the contrast in battle strategy. The Philistine relied on his **dagger, spear, and sword** (or sword, spear, and javelin), but David fought **in the name of** (as the representative of and with the authority of) **Yahweh of Hosts**, who was the God of Israel's armies. Goliath had **defied Him**, but now the Lord would triumph over him through His servant.

17:46 Hand you over to me is literally "shut you into my hand," or leave no way of escape. David's reference to the **Philistine camp** meant the outcome of their personal battle would have implications for the Philistine army. **Birds of the sky and the creatures of the earth** mimicked Goliath's mocking taunt (v. 44). David insisted that when victory was his, all the world would know that **Israel** had a **God** mighty enough to rescue in seemingly impossible situations. David's concern was that the nations would also know the power of Yahweh.

17:47 This whole assembly probably designates Israel's army, but it may include all who were present that day. David testified that the Lord saves, but not **by sword or by spear**. Since **the battle** was His, He would fight and win His way.

17:49 After a lengthy anticipation of the battle in the narrative, the battle was over almost as soon as it began. The words **fell on his face** describe Goliath falling face-forward. The force of the stone's impact likely rocked him backward initially, but then he either lurched forward again to complete his fall or spun around face first as he continued to fall back (away from David) **to the ground**.

17:50 This emphasizes the unlikelihood of David's victory, which gives glory to God. **And killed him** is a summary statement of the whole event. David landed the actual death blow not with a stone but with Goliath's own sword (v. 51).

17:51 Goliath was badly wounded but was yet living when David reached him. Unwilling to stop short of finishing his task, David used Goliath's own sword to **kill him** and **cut off his head**. Seeing that their official representative in this death match was dead, the Philistines turned and **ran** back down the valley toward Gath.

that their hero was dead, they ran.ᵃ ⁵²The men of Israel and Judah rallied, shouting their battle cry, and chased the Philistines to the entrance of the valley and to the gates of Ekron.ᴬ,ᵇ Philistine bodies were strewn all along the Shaaraim roadᶜ to Gath and Ekron.

⁵³When the Israelites returned from the pursuit of the Philistines, they plundered their camps. ⁵⁴David took Goliath'sᴮ head and brought it to Jerusalem, but he put Goliath's weapons in his own tent.

⁵⁵Whenᶜ Saul had seen David going out to confront the Philistine, he asked Abner the commander of the army, "Whose son is this youth, Abner?"ᵈ

"My king, as surely as you live, I don't know," Abner replied.

⁵⁶The king said, "Find out whose son this young man is!"

⁵⁷When David returned from killing the Philistine, Abner took him and brought him before Saul with the Philistine's head still in his hand.ᵉ ⁵⁸Saul said to him, "Whose son are you, young man?"

"The son of your servant Jesse of Bethlehem,"ᶠ David answered.

David's Success

18 When David had finished speaking with Saul, Jonathan committed himself to David, and loved him as much as he loved himself.ᵍ ²Saul kept David with him from that day on and did not let him return to his father's house.

³Jonathan made a covenant with Davidʰ because he loved him as much as himself. ⁴Then Jonathan removed the robe he was wearing and gave it to David,ⁱ along with his military tunic, his sword, his bow, and his belt.

⁵David marched out with the army and was successful in everything Saul sent him to do. Saul put him in command of the soldiers, which pleased all the people and Saul's servants as well.

⁶As the troops were coming back, when David was returning from killing the Philistine, the women came out from all the cities of Israel to meet King Saul,ʲ singing and dancing with tambourines, with shouts of joy, and with three-stringed instruments. ⁷As they celebrated, the women sang:

Saul has killed his thousands,
but David his tens of thousands.ᵏ

Cross-references:
ᵃ17:51 Heb 11:34
ᵇ17:52 Jos 15:11
ᶜJos 15:36
ᵈ17:55 1Sm 16:17-22; 17:25
ᵉ17:57 1Sm 17:54
ᶠ17:58 1Sm 17:12
ᵍ18:1 1Sm 20:17; 2Sm 1:26
ʰ18:3 1Sm 20:8,16; 23:18
ⁱ18:4 Gn 41:42
ʲ18:6 Ex 15:20-21; Jdg 11:34
ᵏ18:7 1Sm 21:11; 29:5

A17:52 LXX reads *Ashkelon*   B17:54 Lit *the Philistine's*   C17:55 LXX omits 1Sm 17:55–18:5

17:52 On **the men of Israel and Judah**, see note at 11:8. Inspired by the Lord's victory through David, Israel's army pursued the Philistines all the way **to the gates of Ekron**, a leading Philistine city (5:1,10) over 10 miles away. **The Shaaraim road** runs north to south right next to Azekah (v. 1); as panic set in, the Philistines tried every avenue possible to escape the Israelites.

17:54 Why David took **Goliath's head** to **Jerusalem** is unclear, since Jerusalem was controlled by the Jebusites at the time. One possibility is that David intended it to frighten the Jebusites and other enemies of Israel. Another is that Jerusalem was a central place where even non-Jebusites could come to divide, barter, and display the spoils of war. A third possibility is that the text was recording what David ultimately did with Goliath's head years later when David conquered Jerusalem (2Sm 5:7), though 17:57 may weigh against this suggestion. See R. D. Bergen, *1, 2 Samuel* for further commentary on options. The giant's sword ended up at the city of Nob, from which David retrieved it years later (1Sm 21:8-9).

17:55 Either Saul's busy schedule, coupled with his torment from the evil spirit (16:14), resulted in his not recognizing David as his personal lyre player (16:15-23), or Saul knew David but did not know who his father was (see note at 17:58).

17:57 A comparison of the details of this verse with those of verse 54 does not require the meeting of **Saul** and **David** to have been in Jerusalem, though nothing precludes this possibility.

17:58 Perhaps the king asked for clarification of David's identity so he could reward **Jesse** with tax-exempt status as he had promised to whoever defeated Goliath (v. 25).

18:1 Jonathan committed himself to David is literally "Jonathan's life was bound together with David's." The same expression occurs in Gn 44:30 in reference to Jacob and his son, Benjamin. Both David and Jonathan were valiant warriors who had taken stands of faith against incredible opposition (1Sm 14:6-14; 17:31-51), so it is not surprising they would become close friends. **As much as he loved himself** could also be translated "as much as he loved his own life." The phrase is repeated in verse 3 and 20:17.

18:2 Before the victory over the Philistines, David would sometimes **return to his father's house** in Bethlehem to look after family matters. Now, the king wanted David to remain constantly **with him**.

18:3 On **he loved him as much as himself**, see note at verse 1.

18:4 The covenant between Jonathan and David may have included the giving of special gifts to David, the new warrior hero. David thus secured not only Goliath's sword (17:54), but the **robe . . . military tunic . . . sword . . . bow**, and **belt** of Israel's prince, showing that God was preparing him for his royal role.

18:5 David enjoyed success with the army wherever **Saul sent him**, so the king made him head of the army. The expression **Saul's servants** probably designate either the king's military officers or his closest advisers.

18:6 The phrase **David was returning from killing the Philistine** probably refers to a later time of battle than David's original battle with Goliath because verse 5 mentions David's promotion, implying some passage of time. Earlier traditions of **women . . . singing and dancing** to celebrate military victories were well known (Ex 15:21; Jdg 5:1-31). The cities of Israel were safe from the Philistine threat, and that was reason to celebrate.

18:7 The words **Saul has killed his thousands, but David**

8 Saul was furious and resented this song.[A] "They credited tens of thousands to David," he complained, "but they only credited me with thousands. What more can he have but the kingdom?"[a] 9 So Saul watched David jealously from that day forward.

Saul Attempts to Kill David

10 The next day an evil spirit sent from God took control of Saul,[b] and he began to rave[B] inside the palace. David was playing the lyre as usual,[c] but Saul was holding a spear,[d] 11 and he threw it, thinking, "I'll pin David to the wall."[e] But David got away from him twice.

12 Saul was afraid of David,[f] because the LORD was with David[g] but had left Saul.[h] 13 Therefore, Saul reassigned David and made him commander over 1,000 men. David led the troops[i] 14 and continued to be successful in all his activities because the LORD was with him.[j] 15 When Saul observed that David was very successful, he dreaded him. 16 But all Israel and Judah loved David[k] because he was leading their troops. 17 Saul told David, "Here is my oldest daughter Merab. I'll give her to you as a wife,[l] if you will be a warrior for me and fight the LORD's battles."[m] But Saul was thinking, "My hand doesn't need to be against him; let the hand of the Philistines be against him."[n]

18 Then David responded, "Who am I,[o] and what is my family or my father's clan in Israel that I should become the king's son-in-law?" 19 When it was time to give Saul's daughter Merab to David, she was given to Adriel the Meholathite as a wife.[p]

David's Marriage to Michal

20 Now Saul's daughter Michal[q] loved David, and when it was reported to Saul, it pleased him.[C] 21 "I'll give her to him," Saul thought. "She'll be a trap for him, and the hand of the Philistines will be against him."[r] So Saul said to David a second time, "You can now be my son-in-law."[s]

22 Saul then ordered his servants, "Speak to David in private and tell him, 'Look, the king is pleased with you, and all his servants love you. Therefore, you should become the king's son-in-law.'"

23 Saul's servants reported these words directly to David,[D] but he replied, "Is it trivial in your sight to become the king's son-in-law? I am a poor man who is common."[t]

24 The servants reported back to Saul, "These are the words David spoke."

Cross references

a 18:8 1Sm 15:28; 24:20
b 18:10 1Sm 16:14; 19:9
c 1Sm 16:23
d 1Sm 19:9
e 18:11 1Sm 19:10; 20:33
f 18:12 1Sm 18:15,29
g 1Sm 16:13,18
h 1Sm 16:14; 17:36,47; 2Sm 5:2
i 18:13 2Sm 5:2
j 18:14 1Sm 3:19; 16:18
k 18:16 1Sm 18:5
l 18:17 1Sm 17:25
m Nm 21:14; 1Sm 17:36-37; 25:28
n 1Sm 18:21; 18:25
o 18:18 1Sm 9:21; 18:23; 2Sm 7:18
p 18:19 Jdg 7:22; 2Sm 21:8; 1Kg 19:16
q 18:20 1Sm 18:28
r 18:21 1Sm 18:17
s 1Sm 18:20
t 18:23 Gn 29:20; 34:12

A 18:8 Lit furious; this saying was evil in his eyes   B 18:10 Or prophesy   C 18:20 Lit Saul, the thing was right in his eyes   D 18:23 Lit words in David's ears

---

his tens of thousands are the only ones preserved from the women's singing. They were not necessarily contrasting Saul's conquests with David's and exalting David over Saul. The Hebrew word translated "but" also may mean "and," and the words "thousands" and "ten thousands" occur elsewhere as a word pair in poetry (Dt 32:30; Ps 91:7; Mc 6:7). In fact, the women may have intended to praise Saul by what they affirmed about David—the king had made an excellent choice by naming David his commander.

18:8 Whatever the women intended by their song, Saul **resented** what he perceived as their lower assessment of his fighting ability. Perhaps Saul also remembered Samuel's words about God already having chosen his successor (13:14; 15:28). Saul's words, **What more can he have but the kingdom?** reveal the depth of his suspicion.

18:9 The Hebrew word for **jealously** is related to the word for "eye" and suggests that Saul kept a close eye on David **from that day forward**.

18:10 On **evil spirit sent from God**, see note at 16:14. The Hebrew term translated **rave** literally means "prophesy," but the word also is used of false prophets (1Kg 18:29; 22:10). In this context it may refer more to Saul's excited, agitated state. Jeremiah 29:26 may also denote this latter sense.

18:11 The evil spirit's influence, combined with Saul's jealousy, may have led him to hurl his spear. The allusion to David's twofold escape suggests he remained after Saul's first throw, perhaps to reason with the king and help him through his tormented state.

18:13 **Saul reassigned David** to military duty to get him out of his presence.

18:15 Saul's fear of David increased in proportion to David's successes.

18:16 The fact that **all Israel and Judah** (see note at 11:8) **loved David** put Saul in a more difficult position, since the people would not understand why Saul removed someone as effective as David.

18:17 Saul tried a new strategy to rid himself of David. He proposed that David marry Saul's **oldest daughter Merab** in exchange for David's increased role as a **warrior**. Saul knew David's chances of death increased the more time he spent in war; perhaps **the Philistines** would kill him and end Saul's problem.

18:18 David's reluctance came from his recognition of his lower social standing in comparison to Saul's more influential background (9:1).

18:19 Merab eventually married and had five sons, all of whom the Gibeonites later put to death because of Saul's sin against them (2Sm 21:8-9).

18:20 **Michal**, another daughter of Saul, **loved David**. The text may imply that Merab, by contrast, had no feelings for David.

18:21 Perhaps Saul thought Michal would be a **trap** because she might distract David's attention from his military duties, or that the bride price Saul intended to request (v. 25) would put David in a life-threatening situation. Yet another possibility is that Saul thought Michal would lead David away from the Lord. First Samuel 19:13 has been cited to support this, but the context is uncertain.

18:23 David again protested becoming **the king's son-in-law** by pointing out his humble ancestry (v. 18).

²⁵Then Saul replied, "Say this to David: 'The king desires no other bride-price*a* except 100 Philistine foreskins, to take revenge on his enemies.'"*b* Actually, Saul intended to cause David's death at the hands of the Philistines.*c* ²⁶When the servants reported these terms to David, he was pleased*A* to become the king's son-in-law. Before the wedding day arrived,*B* ²⁷David and his men went out and killed 200*c* Philistines. He brought their foreskins and presented them as full payment to the king to become his son-in-law. Then Saul gave his daughter Michal to David as his wife.*d* ²⁸Saul realized that the LORD was with David and that his daughter Michal loved him, ²⁹and he became even more afraid of David. As a result, Saul was David's enemy from then on. ³⁰Every time the Philistine commanders came out to fight,*e* David was more successful than all of Saul's officers.*f* So his name became well known.

David Delivered from Saul

19 Saul ordered his son Jonathan and all his servants to kill David.*g* But Saul's son Jonathan liked David very much,*h* ²so he told him: "My father Saul intends to kill you. Be on your guard in the morning and hide in a secret place and stay there. ³I'll go out and stand beside my father in the field where you are and talk to him about you. When I see what he says, I'll tell you."*i* ⁴Jonathan spoke well of David to his father Saul. He said to him: "The king should not sin against his servant David.*j* He hasn't sinned against you; in fact, his actions have been a great advantage to you. ⁵He took his life in his hands when he struck down the Philistine,*k* and the LORD brought about a great victory for all Israel.*l* You saw it and rejoiced, so why would you sin against innocent blood by killing David for no reason?"*m* ⁶Saul listened to Jonathan's advice and swore an oath: "As surely as the LORD lives, David will not be killed." ⁷So Jonathan summoned David and told him all these words. Then Jonathan brought David to Saul, and he served him as he did before.*n* ⁸When war broke out again, David went out and fought against the Philistines. He defeated them with such a great force that they fled from him. ⁹Now an evil spirit sent from the LORD*o* came on Saul as he was sitting in his palace holding a spear.*p* David was playing the lyre,*q* ¹⁰and Saul tried to pin David to the wall with the spear.*r* As the spear struck the wall, David eluded Saul, ran away, and escaped that night. ¹¹Saul sent agents to David's house to watch for him and kill him in the morning.*s* But

Cross references (center column):
*a*18:25 Gn 34:12; Ex 22:17
*b*1Sm 14:24
*c*1Sm 18:17
*d*18:27 2Sm 3:14
*e*18:30 2Sm 11:1
*f*1Sm 18:5
*g*19:1 1Sm 18:8-9
*h*1Sm 18:1-3
*i*19:3 1Sm 20:32-33
*j*19:4 Gn 44:22; Pr 17:13; Jr 18:20
*k*19:5 1Sm 17:42-51
*l*1Sm 11:13
*m*Dt 19:10-13; 1Sm 20:32
*n*19:7 1Sm 16:21; 18:2,10,13
*o*19:9 1Sm 16:14; 18:10-11
*p*1Sm 18:10
*q*1Sm 16:14-16; 18:10
*r*19:10 1Sm 18:11; 20:33
*s*19:11 Ps 59 title

A18:26 Lit *David, it was right in David's eyes*   **B**18:26 Lit *And the days were not full*   **C**18:27 LXX reads *100*

18:25 To pay the bride price David had to kill **100 Philistines**.

18:26 David was **pleased** (lit "it was right in David's eyes") that Saul would put character and valor above ancestral bloodline. **Before the wedding day arrived** (lit "The days were not full") is perhaps a reference to the time Saul had given David to secure the bride price.

18:27 David and his men secured twice the **payment** required—further evidence of David's desire to please Saul regardless of the risk.

18:28 Saul **realized** (lit "Saul saw and knew") too late what perhaps he should have realized earlier (vv. 13-14)—**the LORD was with David**. Further, perhaps Saul had anticipated Michal's loyalties would remain with him, her father, but now he saw that Michal **loved** David. Through David's friendship with Jonathan (vv. 1-3) and now through his marriage to Michal, he was firmly established as part of the royal family.

18:29 Tragically, jealousy and Saul's tormented spirit nullified any family bond or loyalty his son-in-law David showed him.

18:30 Saul's **officers** certainly included some of Saul's relatives (7:55), thus heightening the tension between David and Saul. As David's **name** became **well known**, many people probably began to speculate that he would become Saul's successor.

19:2 Jonathan made sure David knew about Saul's plan.

Ironically, Jonathan, as King Saul's oldest son, had the most to gain by David's death.

19:3 If David did not overhear the conversation between Jonathan and Saul from his hiding place, Jonathan would inform him later.

19:4-5 **Jonathan spoke well of David** and suggested that his father Saul should spare him for three reasons. First, David was innocent of any sin against Saul. Second, the Lord had used David to bring **a great victory for all Israel**. Third, killing David for no reason would make Saul guilty of shedding **innocent blood**.

19:6 The phrase **As surely as the LORD lives** was a common way of introducing an oath (1Kg 17:1).

19:7 It is not clear whether the expression **served him as he did before** denotes David's lyre-playing or leading the military. Perhaps both are intended since both appear in the immediate context (vv. 8-9).

19:9 Holding a **spear** while **sitting in his palace** may suggest Saul's extreme paranoia. David was **playing the lyre** to soothe Saul's tormented mind (16:23).

19:10 **David eluded Saul . . . and escaped**, perhaps because he was more wary after the previous incident (18:10-11). He did not provide the king a second opportunity to strike him down, but fled to his home.

19:11 Michal discovered her father's intentions to murder David and **warned** him that delay in fleeing would bring his death.

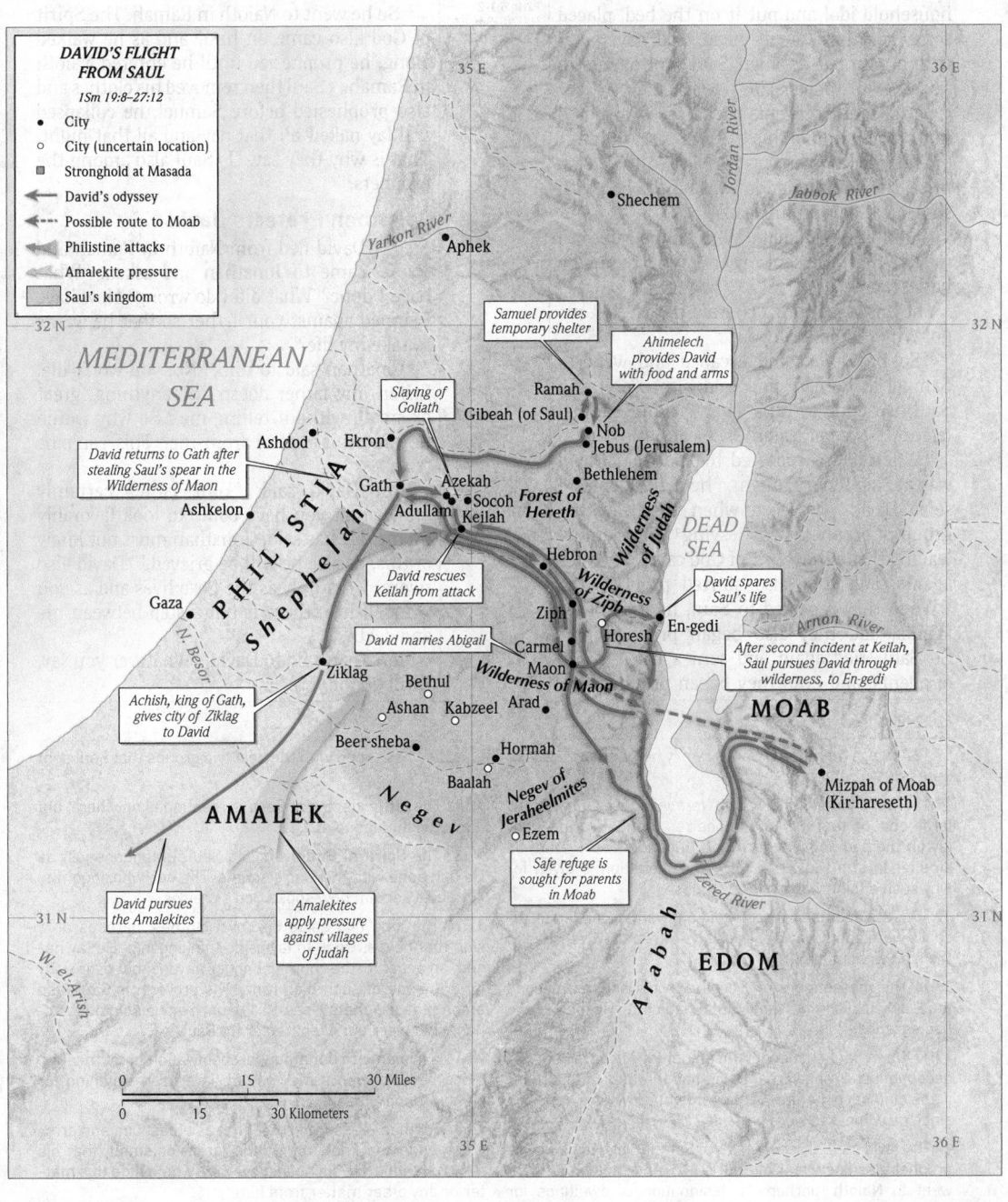

DAVID'S FLIGHT FROM SAUL
1Sm 19:8–27:12

- ● City
- ○ City (uncertain location)
- ■ Stronghold at Masada
- ← David's odyssey
- ◀--- Possible route to Moab
- ◀ Philistine attacks
- ◀ Amalekite pressure
- ▭ Saul's kingdom

MEDITERRANEAN SEA

Jordan River

Jabbok River

Yarkon River

Shechem

Aphek

32 N   32 N

Samuel provides temporary shelter

Ahimelech provides David with food and arms

Ramah

Slaying of Goliath

Gibeah (of Saul)

David returns to Gath after stealing Saul's spear in the Wilderness of Maon

Ashdod   Ekron

Nob

Jebus (Jerusalem)

Gath   Azekah

Bethlehem

Ashkelon   Adullam   Socoh   Forest of Hereth

Keilah

PHILISTIA

Shephelah

Hebron

Wilderness of Judah

David rescues Keilah from attack

DEAD SEA

Gaza

David marries Abigail

Ziph   Wilderness of Ziph

David spares Saul's life

N. Besor

Horesh   En-gedi

Arnon River

Ziklag

Carmel

After second incident at Keilah, Saul pursues David through wilderness, to En-gedi

Achish, king of Gath, gives city of Ziklag to David

Maon   Wilderness of Maon

Bethul   Ashan   Kabzeel   Arad

MOAB

Beer-sheba

Hormah

Baalah   Negev of Jeraheelmites

Mizpah of Moab (Kir-hareseth)

AMALEK   **Negev**

Ezem

Safe refuge is sought for parents in Moab

Zered River

31 N   31 N

David pursues the Amalekites

Amalekites apply pressure against villages of Judah

Arabah

EDOM

W. el-Arish

0   15   30 Miles

0   15   30 Kilometers

35 E   36 E

his wife Michal[a] warned David, "If you don't escape tonight, you will be dead tomorrow!" [12] So she lowered David from the window, and he fled and escaped.[b] [13] Then Michal took the household idol and put it on the bed, placed some goat hair on its head, and covered it with a garment. [14] When Saul sent agents to seize David, Michal said, "He's sick."[c]

[15] Saul sent the agents back to see David and said, "Bring him on his bed so I can kill him." [16] When the messengers arrived, to their surprise, the household idol was on the bed with some goat hair on its head.

[17] Saul asked Michal, "Why did you deceive me like this? You sent my enemy away, and he has escaped!"

She answered him, "He said to me, 'Let me go! Why should I kill you?'"

[18] So David fled and escaped and went to Samuel at Ramah[d] and told him everything Saul had done to him. Then he and Samuel left and stayed at Naioth.[e]

[19] When it was reported to Saul that David was at Naioth in Ramah, [20] he sent agents to seize David.[f] However, when they saw the group of prophets prophesying[g] with Samuel leading them, the Spirit of God came on Saul's agents, and they also started prophesying. [21] When they reported to Saul, he sent other agents, and they also began prophesying.[h] So Saul tried again and sent a third group of agents, and even they began prophesying.

[22] Then Saul himself went to Ramah. He came to the large cistern at Secu, looked around, and asked, "Where are Samuel and David?"

"At Naioth in Ramah," someone said.

[23] So he went to Naioth in Ramah. The Spirit of God also came on him,[i] and as he walked along, he prophesied until he entered Naioth in Ramah. [24] Saul then removed his clothes and also prophesied before Samuel; he collapsed and lay naked[j] all that day and all that night. That is why they say, "Is Saul also among the prophets?"[k]

Jonathan Protects David

20 David fled from Naioth in Ramah and came to Jonathan and asked, "What have I done?[l] What did I do wrong? How have I sinned against your father so that he wants to take my life?"

[2] Jonathan said to him, "No, you won't die. Listen, my father doesn't do anything, great or small, without telling me.[A] So why would he hide this matter from me? This can't be true."

[3] But David said, "Your father certainly knows that you have come to look favorably on me. He has said, 'Jonathan must not know of this, or else he will be grieved.'" David also swore, "As surely as the LORD lives and as you yourself live, there is but a step between me and death."[m]

[4] Jonathan said to David, "Whatever you say, I will do for you."

Cross references
a19:11 1Sm 18:20
b19:12 Jos 2:15; Ac 9:23-25
c19:14 Jos 2:5
d19:18 1Sm 7:17
e2Kg 6:1-2
f19:20 1Sm 19:11; Jn 7:32
g1Sm 10:5-6,10
h19:21 Nm 11:25
i19:23 1Sm 10:10
j19:24 Is 20:2; Mc 1:8
k19:20-24 1Sm 10:5-13
l20:1 1Sm 24:9
m20:3 1Sm 25:26; 2Kg 2:6

A20:2 Lit without uncovering my ear

19:12 Again, a member of Saul's family helped David escape Saul's death sentence.

19:13 The **household idol** (Hb *teraphim*) was apparently large enough that it would appear as though David's body lay **on the bed** under a **garment**. Such idols also could be smaller in size (Gn 31:19,34). No explanation is given for why such a thing was in David's house.

19:15 Saul's **agents** apparently did not want to challenge Michal's word about David's illness (v. 14), so they returned to the king without him.

19:16 The **messengers** arrived at David's house a second time, only to discover what Michal had done. By then, David had escaped.

19:17 When Saul challenged his daughter **Michal** about her deception, she replied that David had threatened to **kill** her if she did not cooperate. Saul could not prove she was lying since no witnesses were present.

19:18 David fled three miles to **Samuel at Ramah**. The prophet also knew fear of Saul (16:2), and the two of them went to **Naioth**, perhaps a designation of dwellings for prophets in Ramah (vv. 19,22).

19:20 As the king's **agents** encountered a **group of prophets** prophesying with Samuel, God's divine touch overrode their human intentions and they also started **prophesying**.

This also happened with the next two groups that Saul sent (v. 21).

19:22 The **large cistern at Secu** is mentioned only here, but it may be alluded to in 9:11.

19:23 The **Spirit of God** overruled Saul's intentions just as He had done with the king's agents. The one who sought to kill God's servant now spoke God's praises.

19:24 The king laid aside his royal **clothes**, perhaps as a sign that he was soon to lay aside the kingship. He **lay naked**, an act of further humiliation for anyone, but especially for someone of such high rank. The proverb, **Is Saul also among the prophets?** (see 10:11), once again pointed to actions that were out of character for Saul.

20:1 David **came to Jonathan**, probably at a secret meeting place because Saul's men would have been watching for David around Gibeah.

20:2 Jonathan reassured David that as eldest son and army commander he knew everything, **great or small**, that his father planned. He did not believe Saul would **hide this matter** or any other matter from him.

20:3 David, however, had keener insight into the situation. Saul knew about Jonathan's and David's covenant and friendship. David suspected the king did not want Jonathan to **be grieved** by the struggle between him and David,

5 So David told him, "Look, tomorrow is the
New Moon,[a] and I'm supposed to sit down and
eat with the king.[b] Instead, let me go, and
I'll hide in the field until the third night.[c] 6 If
your father misses me at all, say, 'David urgently requested my permission to quickly go
to his town Bethlehem[d] for an annual sacrifice[e] there involving the whole clan.' 7 If he
says, 'Good,' then your servant is safe, but if
he becomes angry, you will know he has evil
intentions. 8 Deal faithfully with your servant,
for you have brought me into a covenant with
you before the LORD.[f] If I have done anything
wrong,[g] then kill me yourself; why take me to
your father?"
9 "No!" Jonathan responded. "If I ever find
out my father has evil intentions against you,
wouldn't I tell you about it?"
10 So David asked Jonathan, "Who will tell
me if your father answers you harshly?"
11 He answered David, "Come on, let's go out
to the field." So both of them went out to the
field. 12 "By the LORD, the God of Israel, I will
sound out my father by this time tomorrow or
the next day. If I find out that he is favorable
toward you, will I not send for you and tell
you?[A] 13 If my father intends to bring evil on
you, may God punish Jonathan and do so severely[h] if I do not tell you[B] and send you away
so you may go in peace. May the LORD be with
you,[i] just as He was with my father. 14 If I continue to live, treat me with the LORD's faithful
love, but if I die, 15 don't ever withdraw your
faithful love from my household—not even
when the LORD cuts off every one of David's
enemies from the face of the earth."[j] 16 Then
Jonathan made a covenant with the house of
David,[k] saying, "May the LORD hold David's enemies accountable."[C,l] 17 Jonathan once again
swore to David[D] in his love for him, because
he loved him as he loved himself.[m]
18 Then Jonathan said to him, "Tomorrow
is the New Moon;[n] you'll be missed because
your seat will be empty. 19 The following day
hurry down and go to the place where you hid
on the day this incident began and stay beside the rock Ezel. 20 I will shoot three arrows
beside it as if I'm aiming at a target. 21 Then
I will send the young man and say, 'Go and
find the arrows!' Now, if I expressly say to the
young man, 'Look, the arrows are on this side
of you—get them,' then come, because as the
LORD lives, it is safe for you and there is no
problem. 22 But if I say this to the youth: 'Look,
the arrows are beyond you!'[o] then go, for the
LORD is sending you away. 23 As for the matter
you and I have spoken about,[p] the LORD will be
a witness[E] between you and me forever."[q] 24 So
David hid in the field.
At the New Moon, the king sat down to eat

[a] 20:5 Nm 10:10; 28:11-15; Am 8:5
[b] 1Sm 20:24,27
[c] 1Sm 19:2
[d] 20:6 1Sm 17:58
[e] Dt 12:5
[f] 20:8 1Sm 18:3; 20:16; 23:18
[g] 2Sm 14:32
[h] 20:13 Ru 1:17; 1Sm 3:17
[i] 1Sm 18:12
[j] 20:15 2Sm 9:1
[k] 20:16 1Sm 18:3; 23:18
[l] Dt 23:21
[m] 20:17 1Sm 18:1
[n] 20:18 Nm 10:10
[o] 20:22 1Sm 20:37
[p] 20:23 1Sm 20:14-15
[q] Gn 31:49,53

A 20:12 Lit *and uncover your ear* B 20:13 Lit *will uncover your ears* C 20:16 Lit *LORD require it from the hand of David's enemies*
D 20:17 LXX; MT reads *Jonathan once again made David swear* E 20:23 LXX; MT omits *a witness*

though in the end Jonathan would be (v. 34). Yet, David knew he was potentially close to **death** if Saul could capture him.

20:5 The **New Moon** refers to a monthly festival (Nm 28:11-15) commemorated by the blowing of trumpets (Nm 10:10). David knew Saul would expect his presence at the meal, but he did not want to risk his life by coming to the palace until he knew Saul's intentions.

20:6 Jonathan would tell his father why David was not there if Saul asked about David's absence. The **annual sacrifice** to which Jonathan referred could have been some kind of offering **the whole clan** had determined to offer.

20:7 David trusted that God could reveal Saul's heart through the king's response to Jonathan's words.

20:8 David reminded Jonathan of the **covenant** they had made **before the LORD**. David's passionate request **If I have done anything wrong, then kill me yourself** revealed the depth of his desire for integrity.

20:9 The text emphasizes Jonathan's loyalty to his friend David despite the fact that with David dead, Jonathan would most likely succeed Saul as king.

20:11 The two men probably went **out to the field** so no one would overhear their plan.

20:12-13 Jonathan swore an oath and invited God's punishment on himself if he did not report to David everything Saul intended to do. Jonathan's words of blessing, **May the LORD be with you**, affirm what the text has revealed—that God was with David (16:13,18; 18:12,28). Jonathan's words **as He was with my father** suggest he knew the Lord's Spirit had departed from Saul (16:14).

20:15 Jonathan asked David never to **withdraw** his **faithful love** from his house. Many new kings ordered the death of the former king's family to eliminate contenders for the throne. The Lord might judge **every one of David's enemies**, but David had nothing to fear from Jonathan. After Jonathan's death, David honored Jonathan's request (2Sm 9).

20:16 Jonathan now established a **covenant with the house of David**, not with David alone. God Himself would hold David's enemies accountable for their actions against His chosen servant.

20:17 On **he loved him as he loved himself**, see note at 18:1.

20:19 The Hebrew word translated **rock** also means "stone," but **Ezel**, though unknown outside this verse, was large enough to be known and to have its own name.

20:21-22 Jonathan proposed code language to alert David about Saul's intentions. Calling the **young man** back toward Jonathan to retrieve the three arrows meant that all was **safe**. Telling him to seek the arrows **beyond** him meant David should flee at once.

20:23 Jonathan invoked the Lord's oversight on his and David's agreement and their relationship.

the meal. ²⁵He sat at his usual place on the seat by the wall. Jonathan sat facing him^A and Abner took his place beside Saul, but David's place was empty.ᵃ ²⁶Saul did not say anything that day because he thought, "Something unexpected has happened; he must be ceremonially ˙unclean—yes, that's it, he is unclean."ᵇ

²⁷However, the day after the New Moon, the second day, David's place was still empty, and Saul asked his son Jonathan, "Why didn't Jesse's son come to the meal either yesterday or today?"

²⁸Jonathan answered, "David asked for my permission to go to Bethlehem.ᶜ ²⁹He said, 'Please let me go because our clan is holding a sacrifice in the town, and my brother has told me to be there. So now, if you are pleased with me, let me go so I can see my brothers.' That's why he didn't come to the king's table."

³⁰Then Saul became angry with Jonathan and shouted, "You son of a perverse and rebellious woman! Don't I know that you are siding with Jesse's son to your own shame and to the disgrace of your mother?ᴮ ³¹Every day Jesse's son lives on earth you and your kingship are not secure. Now send for him and bring him to me—he deserves to die."ᵈ

³²Jonathan answered his father back: "Why is he to be killed? What has he done?"ᵉ

³³Then Saul threw his spear at Jonathan to kill him,ᶠ so he knew that his father was determined to kill David.ᵍ ³⁴He got up from the

table in fierce anger and did not eat any food that second day of the New Moon, for he was grieved because of his father's shameful behavior toward David.

³⁵In the morning Jonathan went out to the field for the appointed meeting with David. A small young man was with him. ³⁶He said to the young man, "Run and find the arrows I'm shooting."ʰ As the young man ran, Jonathan shot an arrow beyond him. ³⁷He came to the location of the arrow that Jonathan had shot, but Jonathan called to him and said, "The arrow is beyond you, isn't it?"ⁱ ³⁸Then Jonathan called to him, "Hurry up and don't stop!" Jonathan's young man picked up the arrow and returned to his master. ³⁹He did not know anything; only Jonathan and David knew the arrangement. ⁴⁰Then Jonathan gave his equipment to the young man who was with him and said, "Go, take it back to the city."

⁴¹When the young man had gone, David got up from the south side of the stone Ezel, fell with his face to the ground, and bowed three times.ʲ Then he and Jonathan kissed each other and wept with each other, though David wept more.ᵏ

⁴²Jonathan then said to David, "Go in the assurance the two of us pledged in the name of the LORD when we said: The LORD will be a witness between you and me and between my offspring and your offspring forever."ᶜ·ˡ Then David left, and Jonathan went into the city.

ᵃ20:25 1Sm 20:18
ᵇ20:26 Lv 7:20-21; Nm 10:10
ᶜ20:28 1Sm 20:6
ᵈ20:31 2Sm 12:5
ᵉ20:32 1Sm 19:5
ᶠ20:33 1Sm 18:11; 19:10
ᵍ1Sm 20:7
ʰ20:36 1Sm 20:20-21
ⁱ20:37 1Sm 20:22
ʲ20:41 Gn 42:6
ᵏ1Sm 18:3
ˡ20:42 1Sm 20:15-23

---

^A20:25 Text emended; MT reads *Jonathan got up*   ^B20:30 Lit *your mother's genitals*   ^C20:42 The last sentence of v. 42 is 1Sm 21:1 in Hb.

20:25 Saul's **seat by the wall** offered greater security since no one could approach him from behind.

20:26 Saul's assumption that David was **ceremonially unclean** rested on his knowledge of David's faith, which would have prohibited him from partaking of the meal (Lv 7:20-21).

20:27 Saul became suspicious on **the second day**, when uncleanness would not have required David's absence.

20:28-29 Jonathan explained David's absence along the basic lines the two of them had agreed on (v. 6).

20:30 Saul's words, **son of a perverse and rebellious woman**, were an insult to Jonathan by defaming the character of his mother Ahinoam (14:50).

20:31 Saul's reference to **your kingship** reveals that he intended for Jonathan to succeed him, despite Samuel's pronouncement against his house (13:13-14). **Send for him and bring him to me** indicated Saul believed Jonathan knew David's whereabouts.

20:32 Jonathan cared about justice, not about the personal gain his father suggested might be in store for him. He would show loyalty to David, no matter what.

20:33 Saul **threw his spear at Jonathan** because he had sided with the king's enemy.

20:34 Jonathan was angry and sad over what had happened. It was **his father's shameful behavior toward David** that pained Jonathan more than having to dodge his father's spear.

20:37-38 Jonathan's words, **The arrow is beyond you**, signaled trouble for David (v. 22). He knew that David needed to flee as quickly as possible.

20:40 Though the coded signal had been sent and Jonathan could have departed, perhaps he could not bear to leave without talking with David first, so he sent the **young man** away. The yearning for a personal farewell led them to abandon the caution afforded them by their system of signals.

20:41 David's position shows the **stone Ezel** probably lay south of Gibeah, so that when Jonathan came out with his servant, they would not immediately see him. David **bowed three times** as a sign of his respect and admiration for Jonathan, and they **kissed each other**—a common sign of greeting and farewell among close friends in that culture. They wept because both sensed they might not see each other again.

20:42 **Go in the assurance** is literally "Go in peace." Jonathan could say this to David because of what they pledged in the name of the Lord—on His authority and with Him as a witness. The two of them would always remain friends,

David Flees to Nob

21 David went to Ahimelech[a] the priest at Nob.[b] Ahimelech was afraid to meet David, so he said to him, "Why are you alone and no one is with you?"

[2]David answered Ahimelech the priest, "The king gave me a mission, but he told me, 'Don't let anyone know anything about the mission I'm sending you on or what I have ordered you to do.' I have stationed my young men at a certain place. [3]Now what do you have on hand? Give me five loaves of bread or whatever can be found."

[4]The priest told him, "There is no ordinary bread on hand. However, there is consecrated bread,[c] but the young men may eat it[A] only if they have kept themselves from women."[d]

[5]David answered him, "I swear that women are being kept from us, as always when I go out to battle.[e] The young men's bodies[B] are consecrated[f] even on an ordinary mission, so of course their bodies are consecrated today." [6]So the priest gave him the consecrated bread,[g] for there was no bread there except the •bread of the Presence[h] that had been removed from the presence of the LORD. When the bread was removed, it had been replaced with warm bread.

[7]One of Saul's servants, detained before the LORD, was there that day. His name was Doeg the Edomite,[i] chief of Saul's shepherds.

[a]21:1 1Sm 14:3; Mk 2:26
[b]1Sm 22:19
[c]21:4 Ex 25:30; Lv 24:5-9; Mt 12:3-4
[d]Ex 19:15
[e]21:5 2Sm 11:11
[f]1Th 4:4
[g]21:6 Mt 12:3-4; Mk 2:25
[h]Lv 24:5-9
[i]21:7 1Sm 22:9; Ps 52 title
[j]21:9 1Sm 17:51
[k]21:10 Ps 56 title
[l]21:11 1Sm 18:7; 29:5
[m]21:13 Ps 34 title

[8]David said to Ahimelech, "Do you have a spear or sword on hand? I didn't even bring my sword or my weapons since the king's mission was urgent."

[9]The priest replied, "The sword of Goliath the Philistine,[j] whom you killed in the Valley of Elah, is here, wrapped in a cloth behind the •ephod. If you want to take it for yourself, then take it, for there isn't another one here."

"There's none like it!" David said. "Give it to me."

David Flees to Gath

[10]David fled that day from Saul's presence and went to King Achish of Gath.[k] [11]But Achish's servants said to him, "Isn't this David, the king of the land? Don't they sing about him during their dances:

Saul has killed his thousands,
but David his tens of thousands?"[l]

[12]David took this to heart[c] and became very afraid of King Achish of Gath, [13]so he pretended to be insane in their presence.[m] He acted like a madman around them,[D] scribbling[E] on the doors of the gate and letting saliva run down his beard.

[14]"Look! You can see the man is crazy," Achish said to his servants. "Why did you bring him to me? [15]Do I have such a shortage of crazy people that you brought this one

---

[A]21:4 DSS; MT omits *may eat it*   [B]21:5 Lit *vessels*   [C]21:12 Lit *David placed these words in his heart*   [D]21:13 Lit *madman in their hand*   [E]21:13 LXX reads *drumming*

---

and they would do all they could to ensure their friendship extended to their **offspring**. David then left, heading southward (21:1), while Jonathan went into the city, where soon he would have to face his father again.

21:1 Ahimelech is mentioned for the first time here; some identify him with Ahijah (14:3). **Nob** lay approximately two miles south of Gibeah. Ahimelech was **afraid**, probably because he had heard of Saul's pursuit of David, a fact that would explain his questioning of David.

21:2 Though David said that the king had given him **a mission**, Saul in fact had not. David did not want to reveal his real circumstances to Ahimelech, lest Saul accuse the priest of aiding a fugitive (22:13).

21:4 Consecrated bread, also known as the bread of the Presence (v. 6), came from the tabernacle, where 12 loaves representing Israel's 12 tribes were exchanged weekly (Lv 24:5-9). Normally only priests ate this bread, but Ahimelech was willing to share it with ordinary soldiers if they were not ceremonially unclean due to sexual relations (Lv 15:18).

21:6 Jesus referred to this account in condemning the religious leaders for their rigid interpretation of the Mosaic law (Mt 12:1-4).

21:7 Perhaps **Doeg the Edomite** was a captive servant of Saul after Saul's campaign against Edom (14:47). The words **detained before the LORD** may mean Doeg lingered at the tabernacle to offer further sacrifices and prayers; other

interpreters have suggested he was paying some form of penance or facing punishment for an offense.

21:9 The text does not explain how **the sword of Goliath** ended up in the tabernacle when David had earlier put it in his own tent (17:54). Perhaps David later had dedicated it to the Lord as some kind of offering.

21:10 The leading Philistine city, **Gath**, was located at the mouth of the Valley of Elah (17:1). **King Achish** ruled there, seemingly as chief among the Philistine lords (27:2-7; 29:2-4). David probably **fled** from Saul by going westward into the Sorek Valley to Beth-shemesh (6:9,12-13), then along a diagonal highway that connected Judah's valleys to Azekah (17:1), from whence he could proceed down the Valley of Elah.

21:11 Achish's servants were aware of David's fame among his own people, and they reported it to him. The **tens of thousands** David had killed included many Philistines.

21:12 David became **afraid** when he realized how much the Philistines knew about him.

21:13 In the ancient world, insane people were considered afflicted by the gods and generally left alone. David's letting **saliva run down his beard** brought further disgrace and confirmation of his affliction to Achish (Nm 12:14; Dt 25:9; Jb 17:6; 30:10).

21:15 Achish's statement **Do I have . . . a shortage of crazy people** probably was intended sarcastically, though other

to act crazy around me? Is this one going to come into my house?"[a]

Saul's Increasing Paranoia

22 So David left Gath and took refuge in the cave of Adullam.[b] When David's brothers and his father's whole family heard, they went down and joined him there. [2] In addition, every man who was desperate, in debt, or discontented rallied around him, and he became their leader. About 400 men were with him.[c]

[3] From there David went to Mizpeh of Moab where he said to the king of Moab, "Please let my father and mother stay with you until I know what God will do for me." [4] So he left them in the care of the king of Moab, and they stayed with him the whole time David was in the stronghold.

[5] Then the prophet Gad[d] said to David, "Don't stay in the stronghold. Leave and return to the land of Judah." So David left and went to the forest of Hereth.

[6] Saul heard that David and his men had been discovered. At that time Saul was in Gibeah, sitting under the tamarisk tree[e] at the •high place. His spear was in his hand, and all his servants were standing around him. [7] Saul said to his servants, "Listen, men of Benjamin: Is Jesse's son going to give all of you fields and vineyards? Do you think he'll make all of you commanders of thousands and commanders of hundreds?[f] [8] That's why all of you have conspired against me! Nobody tells me[A] when my

own son makes a covenant with Jesse's son.[g] None of you cares about me[h] or tells me[B] that my son has stirred up my own servant to wait in ambush for me, as is the case today."

[9] Then Doeg the Edomite,[i] who was in charge of Saul's servants, answered: "I saw Jesse's son come to Ahimelech son of Ahitub at Nob.[j] [10] Ahimelech inquired of the LORD for him[k] and gave him provisions.[l] He also gave him the sword of Goliath the Philistine."[m]

Slaughter of the Priests

[11] The king sent messengers to summon Ahimelech the priest, son of Ahitub, and his father's whole family, who were priests in Nob. All of them came to the king. [12] Then Saul said, "Listen, son of Ahitub!"

"I'm at your service,[n] my lord," he said.

[13] Saul asked him, "Why did you and Jesse's son conspire against me? You gave him bread and a sword and inquired of God for him, so he could rise up against me and wait in ambush, as is the case today."[o]

[14] Ahimelech replied to the king: "Who among all your servants is as faithful as David?[p] He is the king's son-in-law, captain of your bodyguard, and honored in your house. [15] Was today the first time I inquired of God for him?[q] Of course not! Please don't let the king make an accusation against your servant or any of my father's household, for your servant didn't have any idea[c] about all this."

[16] But the king said, "You will die, Ahimelech—you and your father's whole family!"

[a]21:13-15 Ps 34 title
[b]22:1 Pss 57, 142 titles
[c]22:2 1Sm 23:13; 25:13
[d]22:5 1Ch 21:9; 29:29; 2Ch 29:25
[e]22:6 Jdg 4:5; 1Sm 14:2
[f]22:7 1Sm 8:12
[g]22:8 1Sm 18:3; 20:16
[h]1Sm 23:21
[i]22:9 Ps 52 title
[j]1Sm 21:1; Ps 52 title
[k]22:10 1Sm 10:22
[l]1Sm 21:6,9
[m]1Sm 21:2-9
[n]22:12 1Sm 3:4-6; 2Sm 1:7
[o]22:13 1Sm 22:8
[p]22:14 1Sm 19:4-5
[q]22:15 2Sm 5:19,23

[A]22:8 Lit *No one uncovers my ear*   [B]22:8 Lit *or uncovers my ear*   [C]22:15 Lit *didn't know a thing, small or large*

---

people with unusual physical features were also associated with Gath (17:4; 2Sm 21:20).

22:1 Adullam was located east of Socoh (17:1) approximately 10 miles into the Valley of Elah. David's retreat thus moved him back into Saul's territory. Probably David's brothers and his father's family met him in the **cave** because they feared Saul's reprisal against them.

22:2 Discontentment with the status quo under Saul influenced many people to join forces with David.

22:3 The exact location of **Mizpeh of Moab** is unknown, though the book of Ruth documents David's ancestral connections there (Ru 4:17-22).

22:4 The **king of Moab** may have been gracious to David because of his ancestral connections (Ru 1:4; 4:17-22) and as a favor to another enemy of Saul. **The stronghold** probably designates Mizpeh of Moab (v. 3), since the next verse suggests it was not in Judah.

22:5 Gad had contact with David at key points in his life (2Sm 24:11-14; 1Ch 29:29). **Land of Judah** probably designates Judah's hill country, since Adullam was also part of Judah.

22:7 Saul's rhetorical questions challenged his closest soldiers' loyalty. They should not think that David, a member of the tribe of Judah, would reward them with positions of power and authority if he took the kingship.

22:8 The king's words **my son has stirred up my own servant to wait in ambush for me** could not have been further from the truth; Jonathan, though he loved David, would later die fighting alongside his father (31:2).

22:9 Doeg the Edomite (21:7) now revealed he had seen David at **Nob**.

22:10 The earlier account of David and Ahimelech (21:1-9) does not say that **Ahimelech inquired of the LORD** for him, though verse 15 suggests he did.

22:13 Saul's question assumed that Ahimelech was guilty of conspiracy. The king made no attempt to investigate the matter thoroughly.

22:14 Ahimelech's rhetorical question to the king implied no one was **as faithful as David**, a suggestion Saul already had heard from Jonathan (19:4-5) and did not want to hear again.

22:15 David regularly **inquired of God** through His prophets and priests, while Saul did not. Ahimelech claimed he **didn't have any idea** about David's alleged conspiracy against the king (21:1-2,8). David would have kept Ahimelech ignorant of the real purpose of his visit so the priest could claim ignorance.

22:16 Saul ignored Ahimelech's words and passed the death

[17] Then the king ordered the guards standing by him, "Turn and kill the priests of the LORD[a] because they sided with David. For they knew he was fleeing, but they didn't tell me."[A] But the king's servants would not lift a hand to execute the priests of the LORD.

[18] So the king said to Doeg, "Go and execute the priests!" So Doeg the Edomite went and executed the priests himself. On that day, he killed 85 men[b] who wore linen •ephods.[c] [19] He also struck down Nob, the city of the priests, with the sword—both men and women, children and infants, oxen, donkeys, and sheep.[d]

[20] However, one of the sons of Ahimelech son of Ahitub escaped. His name was Abiathar,[e] and he fled to David.[f] [21] Abiathar told David that Saul had killed the priests of the LORD. [22] Then David said to Abiathar, "I knew that Doeg the Edomite[g] was there that day and that he was sure to report to Saul. I myself am responsible for[B] the lives of everyone in your father's family. [23] Stay with me. Don't be afraid, for the one who wants to take my life wants to take your life.[h] You will be safe with me."

Deliverance at Keilah

23 It was reported to David: "Look, the Philistines are fighting against Keilah[i] and raiding the threshing floors."

[2] So David inquired of the LORD:[j] "Should I launch an attack against these Philistines?"

The LORD answered David, "Launch an attack against the Philistines and rescue Keilah."

[3] But David's men said to him, "Look, we're afraid here in Judah; how much more if we go to Keilah against the Philistine forces!"

[4] Once again, David inquired of the LORD, and the LORD answered him: "Go at once to Keilah, for I will hand the Philistines over to you."[k] [5] Then David and his men went to Keilah, fought against the Philistines, drove their livestock away, and inflicted heavy losses on them. So David rescued the inhabitants of Keilah. [6] Abiathar son of Ahimelech fled to David at Keilah, and he brought an •ephod with him.

[7] When it was reported to Saul that David had gone to Keilah, he said, "God has handed him over to me, for he has trapped himself by entering a town with barred gates." [8] Then Saul summoned all the troops to go to war at Keilah and besiege David and his men.

[9] When David learned that Saul was plotting evil against him, he said to Abiathar the priest,[l] "Bring the ephod."[m]

[10] Then David said, "LORD God of Israel, Your servant has heard that Saul intends to come to Keilah and destroy the town because of me. [11] Will the citizens of Keilah hand me over to him? Will Saul come down as Your servant has heard? LORD God of Israel, please tell Your servant."

The LORD answered, "He will come down."

[12] Then David asked, "Will the citizens of Keilah hand me and my men over to Saul?"

"They will,"[n] the LORD responded.

Cross references
a22:17 2Kg 10:25; 2Ch 12:10
b22:18 1Sm 2:31
cEx 28:4; 1Sm 2:28
d22:19 1Sm 2:18
e22:20 1Sm 23:9; 30:7; 2Sm 2:1; 1Kg 2:26-27
f1Sm 2:33
g22:22 1Sm 21:7
h22:23 1Kg 2:26
i23:1 Jos 15:44;
j23:2 1Sm 23:4,6,9-12; 2Sm 5:19,23
k23:4 Jos 8:7; Jdg 7:7
l23:9 1Sm 22:20
m1Sm 23:6; 30:7
n23:12 Jdg 15:10-13; 1Sm 23:20

A22:17 Lit didn't uncover my ear   B22:22 LXX, Syr, Vg; MT reads I myself turn in

sentence on the priest's entire household, a decree that further revealed his obsession to kill David.

22:17 Even **the king's servants**—probably his most trusted soldiers—**would not . . . execute the priests** because it was unclear if they were guilty of anything worthy of death.

22:18-19 Eighty-five priests died, along with every other living thing in Nob, because of Saul's misguided wrath.

22:20 **Abiathar** may have caught up with David at Keilah (23:6). He would later serve as priest before David (2Sm 20:25), though he did side with Adonijah, David's oldest son, when Adonijah tried to take the throne without David's blessing (1Kg 1:7; 2:26-27).

22:22 David had his suspicions that **Doeg** would **report to Saul** about David's visit to Nob, but had failed to deal with Doeg when he had the opportunity.

22:23 David suggested that he and Abiathar could trust each other because they had a common enemy (Saul) from whom they needed to protect themselves. Thus David aligned himself with the priests of the Lord, even as Saul further alienated himself from God.

23:1 **Keilah** was a town of Judah located about two miles south of Adullam. **Raiding the threshing floors** meant the **Philistines** were waiting until Keilah's citizens had harvested and threshed their grain, then they stole it from them.

23:2-4 God's instructions to **launch an attack against the Philistines** seemed too dangerous to David's men, who apparently felt that having one enemy, Saul, was risky enough. David's second inquiry confirmed God's command to rescue Keilah. **Go at once** is literally "Arise, go down," indicating David was probably still at the forest of Hereth (22:5) or even higher into the Judean hill country.

23:5 David and his men **drove their livestock away** to keep the cattle from eating all the grain on the threshing floors or to keep the **Philistines** from using them to carry off Israelite plunder.

23:6 On Abiathar's relationship to David, see note at 22:20.

23:7 Saul saw an opportunity to kill David because the town's **barred gates** would prevent his escape.

23:8 Saul's strategy was probably to **besiege** Keilah in the hope that its citizens would hand David over to them to avoid destruction (v. 12).

23:9 David wanted to inquire of the Lord again by consulting the **ephod**.

23:10 Saul had already destroyed one town because of David (22:19), so David thought he might destroy another.

23:11-12 Through David's inquiry, the Lord warned him that **the citizens of Keilah** would deliver him **over to Saul**, just as Saul had calculated (v. 8).

[13] So David and his men, numbering about 600,[a] left Keilah at once and moved from place to place.[b] When it was reported to Saul that David had escaped from Keilah, he called off the expedition. [14] David then stayed in the wilderness strongholds and in the hill country of the Wilderness of Ziph.[c] Saul searched for him every day, but God did not hand David over to him.[d]

A Renewed Covenant

[15] David was in the Wilderness of Ziph in Horesh when he saw that Saul had come out to take his life. [16] Then Saul's son Jonathan came to David in Horesh and encouraged him in his faith in God,[e] [17] saying, "Don't be afraid, for my father Saul will never lay a hand on you. You yourself will be king over Israel,[f] and I'll be your second-in-command. Even my father Saul knows it is true."[g] [18] Then the two of them made a covenant in the LORD's presence.[h] Afterward, David remained in Horesh, while Jonathan went home.

David's Narrow Escape

[19] Some Ziphites[i] came up to Saul at Gibeah and said, "David is[A] hiding among us in the strongholds in Horesh on the hill of Hachilah south of Jeshimon. [20] Now, whenever the king wants to come down, let him come down. Our part will be to hand him over to the king."[j]

[21] "May you be blessed by the LORD," replied Saul, "for you have taken pity on me.[k] [22] Go and check again. Investigate and watch carefully where he goes[B] and who has seen him there; they tell me he is extremely cunning. [23] Look and find out all the places where he hides. Then come back to me with accurate information, and I'll go with you. If it turns out he really is in the region, I'll search for him among all the clans[c] of Judah." [24] So they went to Ziph ahead of Saul.

Now David and his men were in the wilderness near Maon[l] in the •Arabah south of Jeshimon, [25] and Saul and his men went to look for him. When David was told about it, he went down to the rock and stayed in the Wilderness of Maon. Saul heard of this and pursued David there.

[26] Saul went along one side of the mountain and David and his men went along the other side. Even though David was hurrying to get away from Saul, Saul and his men were closing in on David and his men to capture them.[m] [27] Then a messenger came to Saul saying, "Come quickly, because the Philistines have raided the land!" [28] So Saul broke off his pursuit of David and went to engage the Philistines. Therefore, that place was named the Rock of Separation. [29][D] From there David went up and stayed in the strongholds of En-gedi.[n]

David Spares Saul

24 When Saul returned from pursuing the Philistines,[o] he was told, "David

---

Cross references (center column):

[a] 23:13 1Sm 22:2; 25:13
[b] 2Sm 15:20
[c] 23:14 Jos 15:55; 2Ch 11:8
[d] Ps 32:7
[e] 23:16 1Sm 30:6
[f] 23:17 1Sm 16:1-13; 24:20-22
[g] 1Sm 20:31
[h] 23:18 1Sm 18:3; 20:12-17; 20:42
[i] 23:19 1Sm 26:1; Ps 54 title
[j] 23:20 1Sm 23:12
[k] 23:21 1Sm 22:8
[l] 23:24 Jos 15:55; 1Sm 25:2
[m] 23:26 Ps 17:9
[n] 23:29 Jos 15:62; 2Ch 20:2
[o] 24:1 1Sm 23:28-29

[A] 23:19 Lit *Is David not . . . Jeshimon?*   [B] 23:22 Lit *watch his place where his foot will be*   [C] 23:23 Or *thousands*   [D] 23:29 1Sm 24:1 in Hb

---

23:13 The number of David's sympathizers had grown by 50 percent (22:2). Perhaps Saul **called off the expedition** because he was reluctant to conduct a lengthy military campaign in Judah, David's own tribal territory.

23:14 The **Wilderness of Ziph** (Jos 15:55) was located about four and one-half miles southeast of Hebron, deep in Judah's hill country. **Wilderness strongholds** offered David high vantage points from which his watchmen could detect Saul's approach.

23:15 Horesh means "wooded height," but its exact location is unknown.

23:16 Somehow, perhaps through Saul's intelligence reports, Jonathan knew David's whereabouts. Jonathan **came to David** and **encouraged him in his faith** (lit "strengthened his hand") **in God**.

23:17 Jonathan's words were partly correct, because David would indeed be **king over Israel**. Jonathan, despite his humble willingness, would never become David's **second-in-command** because he would die in battle (31:2). Jonathan also suggested that his **father Saul** knew David would succeed him, a fact that would have made Saul's mental state all the more painful (24:20-21).

23:18 David and Jonathan **made a covenant** again, as they had done before (18:3; 20:14-16).

23:19-20 The **Ziphites** informed Saul of David's position in their territory and offered to **hand him over to the king**. Perhaps these Judahites feared Saul might do to them what he had done at Nob (22:18-19) and what he had considered doing at Keilah (23:7-8).

23:23 Saul apparently was willing to hunt David **among all the clans of Judah** if the Ziphites gave him information specific enough that Saul did not have to wage a long, protracted battle with his own people.

23:24 David and his men had moved **near Maon** about five miles south. **Arabah** means a desert or wilderness area with sparse vegetation, yet enough to sustain those accustomed to the life of a shepherd.

23:25 Rock denotes a large rock formation, perhaps a large cliff.

23:26 David may have hurried because he was outnumbered. On the other hand, he was Israel's most skilled warrior and he occupied the advantageous high ground. Perhaps David and his men were trying to avoid a bloody civil war.

23:28 Saul's desire to pursue David deep into the Judean wilderness gave the **Philistines** the opportunity to push into Israel's heartland again. Israel's enemies were capitalizing on Saul's internal troubles.

23:29 Located about 15 miles northeast of the Wilderness of Maon near the Dead Sea's north-south midpoint, **En-gedi** provided David's men with shelter and spring water.

is in the wilderness near En-gedi."[a] 2So Saul
took 3,000 of Israel's choice men[b] and went
to look for David and his men in front of the
Rocks of the Wild Goats. 3When Saul came
to the sheep pens along the road, a cave was
there, and he went in to relieve himself.[A,c] David and his men were staying in the back of
the cave,[d] 4so they said to him, "Look, this is
the day the LORD told you about: 'I will hand
your enemy over to you so you can do to him
whatever you desire.'" Then David got up and
secretly cut off the corner of Saul's robe.
5Afterward, David's conscience bothered[B,e]
him because he had cut off the corner of
Saul's robe.[C] 6He said to his men, "I swear before the LORD: I would never do such a thing to
my lord, the LORD's anointed.[f] I will never lift
my hand against him, since he is the LORD's
anointed."[g] 7With these words David persuaded[D] his men, and he did not let them rise up
against Saul.
Then Saul left the cave and went on his way.
8After that, David got up, went out of the cave,
and called to Saul, "My lord the king!" When
Saul looked behind him, David bowed to the
ground in homage.[h] 9David said to Saul, "Why
do you listen to the words of people who say,
'Look, David intends to harm you'? 10You can
see with your own eyes that the LORD handed
you over to me today in the cave.[i] Someone
advised me to kill you,[j] but I[E,F] took pity on
you and said: I won't lift my hand against my
lord, since he is the LORD's anointed. 11See,
my father![k] Look at the corner of your robe
in my hand, for I cut it off, but I didn't kill
you. Look and recognize that there is no evil
or rebellion in me. I haven't sinned against
you even though you are hunting me down
to take my life.[l]
12"May the LORD judge between you and me,
and may the LORD take vengeance on you for
me, but my hand will never be against you.[m]
13As the old proverb says, 'Wickedness comes
from wicked people.'[n] My hand will never be
against you. 14Who has the king of Israel come
after? What are you chasing after? A dead dog?
A flea?[o] 15May the LORD be judge and decide
between you and me. May He take notice and
plead my case and deliver[G] me from you."[p]
16When David finished saying these things
to him, Saul replied, "Is that your voice, David my son?"[q] Then Saul wept aloud 17and said
to David, "You are more righteous than I, for
you have done what is good to me though I
have done what is evil to you.[r] 18You yourself
have told me today what good you did for me:
when the LORD handed me over to you, you
didn't kill me.[s] 19When a man finds his enemy,
does he let him go unharmed?[H,t] May the LORD
repay you with good for what you've done for
me today.
20"Now I know for certain you will be king,
and the kingdom of Israel will be established[I]
in your hand.[u] 21Therefore swear to me by the
LORD that you will not cut off my descendants
or wipe out my name from my father's family."[v] 22So David swore to Saul. Then Saul went
back home, and David and his men went up to
the stronghold.[w]

David, Nabal, and Abigail

25 Samuel died,[x] and all Israel assembled
to mourn for him,[y] and they buried

[a]24:1 1Sm 23:19 [b]24:2 1Sm 13:2; 26:2 [c]24:3 Jdg 3:24 [d]Pss 57, 142 titles [e]24:5 2Sm 24:10 [f]24:6 1Sm 26:9-11 [g]1Sm 10:1 [h]24:8 1Sm 25:23-24; 1Kg 1:31 [i]24:10 Ps 7:3-4 [j]1Sm 24:4 [k]24:11 2Kg 5:13 [l]1Sm 23:14,23; 26:20 [m]24:12 1Sm 26:10-11,23 [n]24:13 Mt 7:16-20; Lk 6:43-45 [o]24:14 1Sm 26:20; 2Sm 9:8 [p]24:15 Ps 35:1 [q]24:16 1Sm 26:17 [r]24:17 1Sm 26:21 [s]24:18 1Sm 26:23 [t]24:19 1Sm 23:17; Pr 16:29 [u]24:20 1Sm 13:14; 16:1-13 [v]24:21 Gn 21:23; 1Sm 20:14-17; 2Sm 21:6-8 [w]24:22 1Sm 23:29 [x]25:1 1Sm 28:3 [y]Dt 34:8

[A]24:3 Lit *to cover his feet* [B]24:5 Lit *David's heart struck* [C]24:5 Some Hb mss, LXX, Syr, Vg; other Hb mss omit *robe* [D]24:7 Or *restrained* [E]24:10 LXX, Syr, Tg; MT reads *she* or *it* [F]24:10 Or *my eye* [G]24:15 Lit *render a verdict for* [H]24:19 Lit *go on a good way* [I]24:20 Or *will flourish*

24:1 The phrase **returned from pursuing the Philistines** probably means Saul pushed them back down into their territory and secured Israel's border again.

24:4 David **cut off the corner of Saul's robe**. This proved he was so close that he could have killed the king.

24:5-6 David immediately regretted his action against the king. Saul was still his **lord** and was still **the LORD's anointed**, although he had lost the presence of the Lord (16:14).

24:10 David encouraged the king to consider his action in sparing his life rather than relying on what others were saying about him.

24:11 With his words **my father**, David even appealed to his son-in-law relationship with Saul. He contrasted his own lack of **evil or rebellion** against the king with the king's ruthless campaign against him.

24:12 David invited **the LORD** to **judge** Saul and once again pledged he would not retaliate against Saul.

24:13 David cited what was probably a well-known saying at the time—**Wickedness comes from wicked people** (cp. Pr 18:3)—to illustrate he was not wicked because he had spared Saul's life when he could have killed him.

24:14 By comparing himself to **a dead dog** or **a flea**, David suggested that Saul was squandering precious manpower and resources. David was not worth going after since he was a loyal subject.

24:16 At David's words **Saul wept aloud** with tears of repentance, but his repentance would be short-lived (26:1-2).

24:20 Saul confessed full knowledge of God's plan. Samuel had told him part of it earlier (13:14; 15:26-28), and Saul now realized that David would succeed him.

24:21 Saul asked David not to **cut off** his **descendants** or **wipe out** his **name**. Succeeding kings often did this to eliminate potential rivals or family reprisals (1Kg 15:29; 16:11).

24:22 **David swore to Saul** as the king had requested in an attempt to prove his loyalty yet again.

25:1 Samuel's death marked the end of a significant era for

him by his home in Ramah.[a] David then went down to the Wilderness of Paran.[A,b]

[2] A man in Maon[c] had a business in Carmel;[d] he was a very rich man with 3,000 sheep and 1,000 goats and was shearing his sheep in Carmel. [3] The man's name was Nabal, and his wife's name, Abigail. The woman was intelligent and beautiful, but the man, a Calebite,[e] was harsh and evil in his dealings.

[4] While David was in the wilderness, he heard that Nabal was shearing sheep, [5] so David sent 10 young men instructing them, "Go up to Carmel, and when you come to Nabal, greet him in my name.[B] [6] Then say this: 'Long life to you,[C] and peace to you, to your family, and to all that is yours.[f] [7] I hear that you are shearing.[D] When your shepherds were with us, we did not harass them, and nothing of theirs was missing the whole time they were in Carmel.[g] [8] Ask your young men, and they will tell you. So let my young men find favor with you, for we have come on a feast[E] day.[h] Please give whatever you can afford to your servants and to your son David.'"

[9] David's young men went and said all these things to Nabal on David's behalf,[F] and they waited.[G] [10] Nabal asked them, "Who is David?[i] Who is Jesse's son? Many slaves these days are running away from their masters. [11] Am I supposed to take my bread, my water, and my meat that I butchered for my shearers and give them to these men? I don't know where they are from."

[12] David's men retraced their steps. When they returned to him, they reported all these words. [13] He said to his men, "All of you, put on your swords!" So David and all his men put on their swords. About 400 men followed David while 200 stayed with the supplies.[j]

[14] One of Nabal's young men informed Abigail, Nabal's wife: "Look, David sent messengers from the wilderness to greet our master,[k] but he yelled at them. [15] The men treated us well. When we were in the field, we weren't harassed[l] and nothing of ours was missing the whole time we were living among them. [16] They were a wall around us, both day and night,[m] the entire time we were herding the sheep. [17] Now consider carefully what you must do, because there is certain to be trouble for our master and his entire family. He is such a worthless fool nobody can talk to him!"

[18] Abigail hurried, taking 200 loaves of bread, two skins of wine, five butchered sheep, a bushel[H] of roasted grain, 100 clusters of raisins, and 200 cakes of pressed figs, and loaded them on donkeys.[n] [19] Then she said to her male servants, "Go ahead of me. I will be right be-

---

[a] 25:1 2Kg 21:18; 2Ch 33:20
[b] Gn 21:21; Nm 10:12; 13:3
[c] 25:2 1Sm 23:24
[d] Jos 15:55
[e] 25:3 Jos 15:13; 1Sm 30:14
[f] 25:6 1Ch 12:18
[g] 25:7 1Sm 23:24-25; 25:15-16
[h] 25:8 Neh 8:10-12
[i] 25:10 Jdg 9:28
[j] 25:13 1Sm 23:13; 30:9-10
[k] 25:14 1Sm 13:10; 15:13
[l] 25:15 1Sm 25:7,21
[m] 25:16 Ex 14:22
[n] 25:18 2Sm 16:1; 1Ch 12:40

[A] 25:1 LXX reads to Maon   [B] 25:5 Or Nabal, and ask him for peace   [C] 25:6 Lit To life   [D] 25:7 Lit you have shearers   [E] 25:8 Lit good   [F] 25:9 Lit name   [G] 25:9 LXX reads and he became arrogant   [H] 25:18 Lit sheep, five seahs

---

all Israel. His faithful leadership helped the nation make the transition from theocracy to monarchy. The **Wilderness of Paran** (Gn 21:21; Nm 10:12; 13:3) lay beyond Judah's southern edge.

25:2-3 **Maon** and **Carmel** were only about a mile apart on the edge of the Judean wilderness. **Nabal** was descended from Caleb, a friend of Joshua (Nm 13:6; Jos 14:6-14).

'adon

Hebrew Pronunciation	[ah DOAN]
HCSB Translation	lord, Lord
Uses in 1 Samuel	38
Uses in the OT	335
Focus Passage	1 Samuel 25:10,14,17,24-31,41

'Adon may derive from a word meaning "father" and is related to the Greek deity Adonis. In the OT, it refers to human lords of all kinds about 300 times and to the divine Lord about 30 times. This count excludes the divine name 'Adonai, which is a special development of the word 'adon, although it is also translated "Lord." 'Adon is also commonly translated master (Gn 24:9) and can be sir (Gn 31:35). It is especially frequent as a title of respect for people in the phrase my lord (Ex 32:22). 'Adon can refer to other positions of authority such as owner (1Kg 16:24), supervisor (Neh 3:5), or husband (Am 4:1). It sometimes appears in the plural of majesty in relation to God (Neh 8:10), and in compound names for God. The phrases Lord of all the earth (Jos 3:11) and Lord of lords (Dt 10:17) reflect 'adon.

25:4 **Shearing sheep** was normally a festive occasion (Gn 38:12) since wool was a valuable commodity (2Kg 3:4).

25:7-8 David reminded Nabal of a time when he and his men provided protection for Nabal's livestock. David now asked Nabal to return the favor and provide him and his men with **whatever** he could **afford** from his profits.

25:10-11 Nabal's response was arrogant and insulting. He compared David to a runaway slave, insinuating that he was a nobody who was running from Saul.

25:13 David planned to execute vengeance on Nabal with his soldiers.

25:14 **One of Nabal's young men** realized the folly of Nabal's action and told **Abigail**, Nabal's wife, about her husband's offensive action toward David.

25:17 The words **consider carefully what you must do** from Nabal's employees show they had probably come to Abigail on other occasions to cover Nabal's bad decisions. They would not have referred to him as **such a worthless fool** unless he had a history of poor judgment.

25:18 The provisions listed represented a sizable and thoughtful gift, though it would not have been enough to sustain 600 men and their families.

25:19 Abigail's **servants** would run ahead to David and tell him that she was bringing provisions for his men.

25:20 Since Abigail descended through **a mountain pass hidden from view**, she may have thought it all the more important to let David know she was coming.

hind you."[a] But she did not tell her husband Nabal.

[20] As she rode the donkey down a mountain pass hidden from view, she saw David and his men coming toward her and met them. [21] David had just said, "I guarded everything that belonged to this man in the wilderness for nothing. He was not missing anything, yet he paid me back evil for good. [22] May God punish me[A] and do so severely[b] if I let any of his men[B] survive until morning."[c]

[23] When Abigail saw David, she quickly got off the donkey and fell with her face to the ground in front of David.[d] [24] She fell at his feet and said, "The •guilt is mine, my lord, but please let your servant speak to you directly. Listen to the words of your servant. [25] My lord should pay no attention to this worthless man Nabal, for he lives up to his name:[C] His name is Nabal,[D] and stupidity is all he knows.[E] I, your servant, didn't see my lord's young men whom you sent. [26] Now my lord, as surely as the LORD lives and as you yourself live, it is the LORD who kept you from participating in bloodshed and avenging yourself[e] by your own hand. May your enemies and those who want trouble for my lord be like Nabal.[f] [27] Accept this gift[g] your servant has brought to my lord, and let it be given to the young men who follow my lord. [28] Please forgive your servant's offense,[h] for the LORD is certain to make a lasting dynasty for my lord[i] because he fights the LORD's battles.[j] Throughout your life, may evil[F] not be found in you.[k]

[29] "When someone pursues you and attempts to take your life, my lord's life will be tucked safely in the place[G] where the LORD your God protects the living. However, He will fling away your enemies' lives like stones from a sling.[l] [30] When the LORD does for my lord all the good He promised and appoints you ruler over Israel,[m] [31] there will not be remorse or a troubled conscience for my lord because of needless bloodshed or my lord's revenge. And when the LORD does good things for my lord, may you remember me your servant."[n]

[32] Then David said to Abigail, "Praise to the LORD God of Israel,[o] who sent you to meet me today! [33] Your discernment is blessed, and you are blessed. Today you kept me from participating in bloodshed and avenging myself by my own hand.[p] [34] Otherwise, as surely as the LORD God of Israel lives, who prevented me from harming you, if you had not come quickly to meet me, Nabal wouldn't have had any men[H] left by morning light." [35] Then David accepted what she had brought him and said, "Go home in peace.[q] See, I have heard what you said and have granted your request."[r]

[36] Then Abigail went to Nabal, and there he was in his house, holding a feast fit for a king.[s] Nabal was in a good mood[i] and very drunk, so she didn't say anything[J] to him[t] until morning light.

[37] In the morning when Nabal sobered up,[K] his wife told him about these events. Then he had a seizure[L] and became paralyzed.[M] [38] About 10 days later, the LORD struck Nabal dead.[u]

a 25:19 Gn 32:16,20
b 25:22 1Sm 3:17; 20:13
c 1Kg 14:10
d 25:23 1Sm 20:41
e 25:26 Heb 10:30
f 2Sm 18:32
g 25:27 Gn 33:11; 1Sm 30:26
h 25:28 1Sm 25:24
i 1Sm 2:35; 22:14; 2Sm 7:11,16
j 1Sm 18:17
k 1Sm 24:11; Ps 7:3
l 25:29 Jr 10:18
m 25:30 1Sm 13:14
n 25:31 Gn 40:14; 1Sm 25:30
o 25:32 Ex 18:10
p 25:33 1Sm 25:26
q 25:35 1Sm 20:42; 2Kg 5:19
r Gn 19:21
s 25:36 2Sm 13:23
t 1Sm 25:19
u 25:38 1Sm 26:10

A 25:22 LXX; MT reads *David's enemies*　B 25:22 Lit *of those of his who are urinating against the wall*　C 25:25 Lit *for as is his name is, so he is*　D 25:25 = Fool　E 25:25 Lit *and foolishness is with him*　F 25:28 Or *trouble*　G 25:29 Lit *bundle*　H 25:34 Lit *had anyone urinating against a wall*　I 25:36 Lit *Nabal's heart was good on him*　J 25:36 Lit *anything small or great*　K 25:37 Lit *when the wine was gone out of Nabal*　L 25:37 Lit *Then his heart died within him*　M 25:37 Lit *became a stone*

25:21-22 David was so disgusted with Nabal that he did not even mention his name. He referred to him as **this man**, a translation of one Hebrew syllable *(zeh)*. When David expected gratitude and hospitality, he received insults. Consequently, David had vowed to kill all the men in Nabal's household.

25:23 Abigail bowed to **David**, treating him as a superior and humbling herself before him. Ironically, David had earlier humbled himself before Nabal (v. 8) but to no avail.

25:25-26 Though Abigail referred to her husband as **worthless**, she interceded with David to save his life. She suggested she was the Lord's agent in heading off needless **bloodshed**, the act of which might bring guilt on David and serious damage to his reputation in Israel.

25:28 The expression **your servant's offense** refers to Abigail, not to Nabal, and it designates a serious transgression. Again, she took responsibility for Nabal's sin even as she spoke of what she saw as David's future—**a lasting dynasty**. Perhaps Abigail implied **the Lord's battles** should not include a skirmish with Nabal.

25:29 Some interpreters believe the expression **tucked safely in the place** may designate the Book of Life (Php 4:3;

Rv 3:5; 22:19), but the expression at least denotes God's sovereign protection of His righteous ones. The imagery of God flinging away David's enemies **like stones from a sling** was well chosen in light of David's use of a sling against Goliath (17:49-51).

25:31 Abigail didn't want David to suffer **remorse or a troubled conscience** after he became king because he had slaughtered Nabal's household needlessly. The words **remember me your servant** must have seemed a bit peculiar to David since Abigail was married, but time would prove her words true (v. 39).

25:32-35 David confirmed Abigail's role as God's instrument of deliverance for her husband and her household. He told her, **I have . . . granted your request** (lit "I have lifted up your face").

25:36 Nabal's drunken state showed that he had no idea how much danger he faced barring Abigail's intervention. The phrase **until morning light** refers to the time by which he and his servants would have been killed (v. 34).

25:37 Nabal **had a seizure and became paralyzed** is literally "His heart died within him and he became a stone."

³⁹When David heard that Nabal was dead, he said, "Praise the Lord who championed my cause against Nabal's insults^a and restrained His servant from doing evil.^b The Lord brought Nabal's evil deeds back on his own head."^c

Then David sent messengers to speak to Abigail about marrying him. ⁴⁰When David's servants came to Abigail at Carmel, they said to her, "David sent us to bring you to him as a wife."

⁴¹She stood up, then bowed her face to the ground^d and said, "Here I am, your servant, to wash the feet of my lord's servants."^{e 42}Then Abigail got up quickly, and with her five female servants accompanying her, rode on the donkey following David's messengers.^f And so she became his wife.

⁴³David also married Ahinoam of Jezreel,^g and the two of them became his wives. ⁴⁴But Saul gave his daughter Michal, David's wife, to Palti^h son of Laish, who was from Gallim.ⁱ

David Again Spares Saul

26 Then the Ziphites came to Saul at Gibeah saying, "David is hiding on the hill of Hachilah opposite Jeshimon."^{j 2}So Saul, accompanied by 3,000 of the choice men of Israel,^k went to the Wilderness of Ziph to search for David there. ³Saul camped beside the road at the hill of Hachilah^l opposite Jeshimon. David was living in the wilderness and discovered Saul had come there after him.^{m 4}So David sent out spies and knew for certain that Saul had come. ⁵Immediately, David went to the place where Saul had camped. He saw the place where Saul and Abner son of Ner,ⁿ the general of his army, were lying down. Saul was lying inside the inner circle of the camp with the troops camped around him. ⁶Then David asked Ahimelech the Hittite^o and Joab's brother Abishai^p son of Zeruiah, "Who will go with me into the camp^q to Saul?"

"I'll go with you," answered Abishai.

⁷That night, David and Abishai came to the troops, and Saul was lying there asleep in the inner circle of the camp with his spear stuck in the ground by his head. Abner and the troops were lying around him. ⁸Then Abishai said to David, "Today God has handed your enemy over to you. Let me thrust the spear through him into the ground just once. I won't have to strike him twice!"

⁹But David said to Abishai, "Don't destroy him, for who can lift a hand against the Lord's anointed and be blameless?"^{r 10}David added, "As the Lord lives, the Lord will certainly strike him down:^s either his day will come and he will die, or he will go into battle and perish. ¹¹However, because of the Lord, I will never lift my hand against the Lord's anointed.^t Instead, take the spear and the water jug by his head, and let's go."

¹²So David took the spear and the water jug by Saul's head, and they went their way. No one saw them, no one knew, and no one woke up; they all remained asleep because a deep

^a25:39 1Sm 24:15
^b1Sm 25:26,34
^c2Sm 3:28-29
^d25:41 1Sm 25:23
^eMk 1:7
^f25:42 Gn 24:61-67
^g25:43 Jos 15:56
^h25:44 1Sm 18:27; 2Sm 3:14-15
ⁱIs 10:30
^j26:1 1Sm 23:19; Ps 54 title
^k26:2 1Sm 13:2; 24:2
^l26:3 1Sm 24:3
^m1Sm 23:15
ⁿ26:5 1Sm 14:50-51; 17:55
^o26:6 Gn 26:34; Jos 3:10; 1Kg 10:29; 2Kg 7:6
^p1Ch 2:15-16
^qJdg 7:10-11
^r26:9 1Sm 10:1; 24:6-7; 2Sm 1:14,16
^s26:10 1Sm 25:26,38
^t26:11 Dt 32:35; 1Sm 24:6; 25:39; Rm 12:19

25:39 David praised the Lord for two things: (1) intervening for him, and (2) protecting him **from doing evil**. In the final analysis, God brought judgment against Nabal.

25:40 Some interpreters believe David was playing the role of the family redeemer to Abigail (Dt 25:5-6), though the text does not suggest this and biblical genealogical lists (1Ch 2:3-17; 4:15-20) do not support it.

25:41 Abigail's humble response was typical of her culture, though she fully expected David to take her as his wife, not as someone to **wash the feet** of his **servants**.

25:42 Marrying Abigail gave David control of a sizable estate in Judah and gained him valuable resources for his cause.

25:43 The biblical text says about **Ahinoam of Jezreel** only that she bore Amnon, David's firstborn (2Sm 3:2). Jezreel probably designates the Judahite city (Jos 15:56), not the more famous city in the Jezreel Valley.

25:44 The text does not clarify whether Saul gave his daughter **Michal**, who was already **David's wife** (18:27), to another man at her request or as punishment for her support of David against her father (19:12).

26:1 The **Ziphites** (see note at 23:19) **came to Saul at Gibeah** with a report that David had returned to his earlier hiding place in Judah.

26:3 If Saul was on the **hill of Hachilah**, it would mean he had chosen high ground for his camp, which provided him better protection.

26:5 David's **place** designates a safe vantage point (probably higher—see note at v. 6) from which David could see Saul and Abner **inside the inner circle of the camp**.

26:6 **Ahimelech** is described as a **Hittite** (i.e., foreigner), but his name is Hebrew or at least related to Hebrew. **Joab's brother Abishai** is introduced here; he would play an active role in David's kingship (2Sm 10:10; 18:2-3; 23:18). **Go** is literally "go down," implying David was at a higher point than Saul and thus at an advantage.

26:8 **Abishai** must have whispered to David since he stood with him in the midst of Saul's army (but see 26:12).

26:9 On **lift a hand against the Lord's anointed**, see note at 24:6.

26:10 David was content to leave Saul's life in the Lord's hands, a lesson that had just been reinforced in his dealings with Nabal (25:39).

26:11 The **spear** and the **water jug** would provide evidence that David had been close enough to kill Saul.

26:12 This **deep sleep from the Lord** was His specific intervention so He could teach Saul a further lesson about David's loyalty.

26:13 The words **on top of the mountain at a distance**

sleep from the LORD[a] came over them. [13]David crossed to the other side and stood on top of the mountain at a distance; there was a considerable space between them. [14]Then David shouted to the troops and to Abner son of Ner: "Aren't you going to answer, Abner?"

"Who are you who calls to the king?" Abner asked.

[15]David called to Abner, "You're a man, aren't you? Who in Israel is your equal? So why didn't you protect your lord the king when one of the people came to destroy him? [16]What you have done is not good. As the LORD lives, all of you deserve to die since you didn't protect your lord, the LORD's anointed.[b] Now look around; where are the king's spear and water jug that were by his head?"

[17]Saul recognized David's voice and asked, "Is that your voice, my son David?"[c]

"It is my voice, my lord and king," David said. [18]Then he continued, "Why is my lord pursuing his servant? What have I done? What evil is in my hand?[d] [19]Now, may my lord the king please hear the words of his servant: If it is the LORD who has incited you against me,[e] then may He accept an offering.[f] But if it is people,[g] may they be cursed in the presence of the LORD, for today they have driven me away from sharing in the inheritance of the LORD saying,[h] 'Go and worship other gods.' [20]So don't let my blood fall to the ground far from the LORD's presence, for the king of Israel has come out to search for a flea,[i] like one who pursues a partridge in the mountains."

[21]Saul responded, "I have sinned.[j] Come

back, my son David, I will never harm you again because today you considered my life precious. I have been a fool! I've committed a grave error."

[22]David answered, "Here is the king's spear; have one of the young men come over and get it. [23]May the LORD repay every man for his righteousness[k] and his loyalty. I wasn't willing to lift my hand against the LORD's anointed, even though the LORD handed you over to me today.[l] [24]Just as I considered your life valuable today, so may the LORD consider my life valuable[m] and rescue me from all trouble."[n]

[25]Saul said to him, "You are blessed, my son David. You will certainly do great things and will also prevail."[o] Then David went on his way, and Saul returned home.[p]

David Flees to Ziklag

27 David said to himself, "One of these days I'll be swept away by Saul. There is nothing better for me than to escape immediately to the land of the Philistines.[q] Then Saul will stop searching for me everywhere in Israel, and I'll escape from him." [2]So David set out with his 600 men[r] and went to Achish son of Maoch,[s] the king of Gath. [3]David and his men stayed with Achish in Gath. Each man had his family with him,[t] and David had his two wives: Ahinoam of Jezreel and Abigail of Carmel,[u] Nabal's widow. [4]When it was reported to Saul that David had fled to Gath, he no longer searched for him.

[5]Now David said to Achish, "If I have found favor with you, let me be given a place in one

[a]26:12 Gn 2:21; 15:12
[b]26:16 1Sm 20:31
[c]26:17 1Sm 24:16; 26:21,25
[d]26:18 1Sm 24:11
[e]26:19 2Sm 16:11
[f]Gn 8:21
[g]1Sm 24:9
[h]Jos 22:25-27
[i]26:20 1Sm 24:14
[j]26:21 1Sm 15:24,30; 24:17
[k]26:23 1Sm 24:19
[l]1Sm 24:10-12; 26:10-11
[m]26:24 1Sm 18:30
[n]Ps 54:7
[o]26:25 1Sm 24:19
[p]1Sm 24:22
[q]27:1 1Sm 26:19
[r]27:2 1Sm 25:13
[s]1Sm 2:10; 1Kg 2:39
[t]27:3 1Sm 30:3; 2Sm 2:3
[u]1Sm 25:42-44

means this was a safe distance from Saul, but it provided good acoustics so David could call to the king.

26:15 The phrase **one of the people came to destroy him** may refer to Abishai, who wanted to destroy Saul (v. 8), or hypothetically to **David** himself, who could have destroyed Saul as he stood over him.

26:19 David could identify only two sources of Saul's desire to kill him—**the Lord** or the **people**. If the Lord, David wanted Saul to allow him to sacrifice a freewill **offering** to restore the broken fellowship between himself, God, and Saul. But if people had falsely accused him, David called on them to **be cursed**. Their false accusations had the effect of driving David away from **the inheritance of the Lord**, treating him as if he were not an Israelite.

26:20 David compared himself to a **flea** or a **partridge** (see note at 24:14) to suggest Saul's pursuit of him was a waste of resources.

26:21 Saul's words sounded repentant, but Saul's past actions raised serious doubts in David's mind about their genuineness.

26:22 David's suggestion that **one of the young men** of Saul retrieve the **king's spear** was a tactful way of saying he was not returning with Saul.

26:23-24 David called on the Lord to **repay** those involved (especially him and Saul) as God saw their hearts. David didn't ask for Saul to consider his **life valuable**; he asked for the Lord to do so.

26:25 Saul's words appear to be an admission that God had **great things** in store for his son-in-law. The two went on their way, having spoken the last words they would ever say to each other.

27:2 On **600 men**, see note at 23:13. This number did not include the men's families, who traveled with them (27:3). David earlier had feared **Achish** (21:10-15), but now he determined to join him. On **Gath**, see note at 21:10.

27:3 Achish granted **David and his men** refuge in accord with the principle, "The enemy of my enemy is my friend." On **Ahinoam**, see note at 25:43. On **Abigail**, see various notes at 25:14-42.

27:5 David's request that he receive **one of the outlying towns** may have helped Achish's reputation with his own people, since some Philistines may have wondered why their king harbored a noted Israelite warrior in Gath, **the royal city**. David probably also desired the safety that a little distance from the Philistine capital provided.

of the outlying towns, so I can live there. Why should your servant live in the royal city with you?" [6] That day Achish gave Ziklag[a] to him, and it still belongs to the kings of Judah today. [7] The time that David stayed in the Philistine territory amounted to a year and four months.[b]

[8] David and his men went up and raided the Geshurites,[c] the Girzites,[A] and the Amalekites.[d] From ancient times they had been the inhabitants of the region through Shur[e] as far as the land of Egypt. [9] Whenever David attacked the land, he did not leave a single person alive, either man or woman, but he took flocks, herds, donkeys, camels, and clothing.[f] Then he came back to Achish, [10] who inquired, "Where did you raid today?"[B,g]

David replied, "The south country of Judah," "The south country of the Jerahmeelites,"[h] or "Against the south country of the Kenites."[i]

[11] David did not let a man or woman live to be brought to Gath, for he said, "Or they will inform on us and say, 'This is what David did.'" This was David's custom during the whole time he stayed in the Philistine territory. [12] So Achish trusted David, thinking, "Since he has made himself detestable to his people Israel, he will be my servant forever."

Saul and the Medium

28 At that time, the Philistines[j] brought their military units together into one army to fight against Israel. So Achish said to David, "You know, of course, that you and your men must march out in the army[c] with me."

[2] David replied to Achish, "Good, you will find out what your servant can do."

So Achish said to David, "Very well, I will appoint you as my permanent bodyguard."[k]

[3] By this time Samuel had died,[l] and all Israel had mourned for him and buried him in Ramah, his city,[m] and Saul had removed the mediums and spiritists from the land.[n] [4] The Philistines came together and camped at Shunem. So Saul gathered all Israel, and they camped at Gilboa. [5] When Saul saw the Philistine camp, he was afraid and trembled violently. [6] He inquired of the LORD, but the LORD did not answer him in dreams or by the *Urim or by the prophets.[o] [7] Saul then said to his servants, "Find me a woman who is a medium, so I can go and consult her."

His servants replied, "There is a woman at En-dor[p] who is a medium."[q]

[8] Saul disguised himself[r] by putting on different clothes and set out with two of his men. They came to the woman at night, and Saul said, "Consult a spirit for me.[s] Bring up for me the one I tell you."[t]

[9] But the woman said to him, "You surely know what Saul has done,[u] how he has killed the mediums and spiritists in the land. Why are you setting a trap for me to get me killed?"

Cross references:
[a]27:6 Jos 15:31; 19:5; Neh 11:28
[b]27:7 1Sm 29:1-11
[c]27:8 Jos 13:2,13
[d]Ex 17:8; 1Sm 15:7-8
[e]Ex 15:22
[f]27:9 1Sm 15:3; Jb 1:3
[g]27:10 1Sm 23:27
[h]1Sm 30:29; 1Ch 2:9,25
[i]Jdg 1:16; 4:11
[j]28:1 1Sm 29:1
[k]28:2 1Sm 1:22,28
[l]28:3 1Sm 25:1
[m]1Sm 7:17
[n]Lv 19:31; 20:27; Dt 18:10-11
[o]28:6 Ex 28:30; Nm 27:21; 1Kg 3:5
[p]28:7 Jos 17:1; Ps 83:10
[q]Ac 16:16
[r]28:8 2Ch 18:29; 35:21-22
[s]Is 8:19
[t]Dt 18:10-11
[u]28:9 1Sm 28:3

A27:8 Alt Hb tradition reads *Gezerites*   B27:10 Some Hb mss, Syr, Tg; LXX, Vg, DSS read *Against whom did you raid today?*
C28:1 DSS, LXX read *battle*

27:6 The city of **Ziklag** was located approximately 25 miles southwest of Gath. It originally was allotted to both the tribes of Simeon (Jos 19:5) and Judah (Jos 15:31), but Israel never conquered it. Now Ziklag came under Israelite control without a fight. The phrase **it still belongs to the kings of Judah today** designates the time of the writing of the books of 1 and 2 Samuel (see note at 6:17-18).

27:7 Many scholars have dated the time designated by **a year and four months** to around 1012 B.C.

27:8 The **Geshurites** (Jos 13:1-2), **the Girzites, and the Amalekites** (Ex 17:15-16; Dt 25:17-19) were three non-Israelite groups under God's sentence of judgment. The Girzites occupied territory that overlapped with the promised land.

27:9 David's action against these groups fulfilled God's earlier command to Israel during the days of Joshua to wipe out the land's evil inhabitants (Jos 13:1-7). It also left no witnesses who could relay word to **Achish** (v. 11).

27:10 David's claim to have raided **the south country of Judah** was technically correct, and he did fight people in the region of the **Jerahmeelites** and **Kenites**, two Judahite clans. Achish thought David meant he had destroyed many Israelites in the process.

27:12 Though Achish **trusted David** and assumed he would be Achish's **servant forever**, David was actually eliminating future rivals in Judah's territory.

28:1 Achish's words to David present a serious tension in the narrative. If David's forces were to **march** with the **Philistines**, he would end up fighting against his own people as he fought against Saul's army.

28:3 The law of Moses prohibited consulting with **mediums and spiritists** (Lv 19:31; 20:27; Dt 18:10-11), so Saul's effort to rid the land of them was commendable.

28:4 The Philistines camped at **Shunem** deep into the Jezreel Valley at the foot of Mount Moreh. Saul camped at **Gilboa** at the valley's southeastern edge, a vantage point from which he could observe the enemy army.

28:5 Jonathan, Saul's son, knew the Lord was not limited by the size of Israel's army (14:6), but Saul **trembled violently** when he saw the numbers in the **Philistine camp**.

28:6 Saul **inquired of the LORD** for direction. Urim (lit "lights") denoted the device the priest used for discerning God's will (Ex 28:30; Nm 27:21), but Saul may not have had that available to him since Abiathar had taken the ephod to David (23:6). **The prophets** likewise gave Saul no answer, perhaps because Saul had cut himself off from them through his clash with Samuel (15:34-35).

28:7 Desperate to find spiritual guidance of any kind about war with the Philistines, Saul turned to the very avenue he knew was wrong and had tried to destroy. Traveling to **Endor** would present some risk, since it lay about six miles northeast and two miles beyond the Philistine camp.

¹⁰Then Saul swore to her by the LORD: "As surely as the LORD lives, nothing bad will happen to you because of this."

¹¹"Who is it that you want me to bring up for you?" the woman asked.

"Bring up Samuel for me," he answered.

¹²When the woman saw Samuel, she screamed, and then she asked Saul, "Why did you deceive me? You are Saul!"

¹³But the king said to her, "Don't be afraid. What do you see?"

"I see a spirit form[A] coming up out of the earth," the woman answered.

¹⁴Then Saul asked her, "What does he look like?"

"An old man is coming up," she replied. "He's wearing a robe."[a] Then Saul knew that it was Samuel, and he bowed his face to the ground and paid homage.[b]

¹⁵"Why have you disturbed me by bringing me up?" Samuel asked Saul.

"I'm in serious trouble," replied Saul. "The Philistines are fighting against me and God has turned away from me.[c] He doesn't answer me anymore,[d] either through the prophets or in dreams. So I've called on you to tell me what I should do."

¹⁶Samuel answered, "Since the LORD has turned away from you and has become your enemy, why are you asking me? ¹⁷The LORD has done[B] exactly what He said through me: The LORD has torn the kingship out of your hand and given it to your neighbor David.[e] ¹⁸You did not obey the LORD and did not carry out His burning anger against Amalek;[f] therefore the LORD has done this to you today. ¹⁹The LORD will also hand Israel over to the Philistines along with you. Tomorrow you and your sons will be with me,[C,g] and the LORD will hand Israel's army over to the Philistines."

²⁰Immediately, Saul fell flat on the ground. He was terrified by Samuel's words and was also weak because he hadn't had any food all day and all night. ²¹The woman came over to Saul, and she saw that he was terrified and said to him, "Look, your servant has obeyed you. I took my life in my hands[h] and did what you told me to do. ²²Now please listen to your servant. Let me set some food in front of you. Eat and it will give you strength so you can go on your way."

²³He refused, saying, "I won't eat," but when his servants and the woman urged him, he listened to them.[i] He got up off the ground and sat on the bed.[j]

²⁴The woman had a fattened calf at her house, and she quickly slaughtered it.[k] She also took flour, kneaded it, and baked unleavened bread. ²⁵She served it to Saul and his servants, and they ate. Afterward, they got up and left that night.

Philistines Reject David

29 The Philistines[l] brought all their military units together at Aphek[m] while

Cross references (center column)

a28:14 1Sm 15:27
b1Sm 24:8
c28:15 1Sm 16:13-14; 18:12
d1Sm 28:6
e28:17 1Sm 15:28
f28:18 1Sm 15:1-9
g28:19 1Sm 31:2; Jb 3:17-19
h28:21 1Sm 19:5
i28:23 2Kg 5:13
jEst 1:6; Ezk 23:41
k28:24 Gn 18:6-7
l29:1 1Sm 28:1-2
mJos 12:18; 1Sm 4:1

A28:13 Or a god, or a divine being　　B28:17 Some Hb, some LXX mss, Vg read done to you　　C28:19 LXX reads sons will fall

28:8 Saul disguised himself to avoid being recognized by Philistines who might be patrolling the valley. Traveling with only **two of his men** put the king in a high-risk situation, but they also looked less "official" than a large group.

28:9 The medium knew about Saul's cleansing Israel of spiritism and suspected the king of **setting a trap** for her.

28:10 The king **swore** that she would suffer no harm—an oath by the very LORD who condemned divination.

28:12 The text suggests that the spirit of **Samuel** actually appeared and alluded to events in which Samuel had participated (vv. 15-19); the tone of his speech sounds just like Samuel. Perhaps the woman recognized **Saul** in the light of Samuel's appearance, or perhaps the king pulled back his hood to look closer at the spirit who appeared before them.

28:16 Since Samuel was the Lord's servant and spoke as God's representative, it didn't make sense for Saul to ask for guidance from Samuel since God had refused to answer him. In the next three verses, however, Samuel would give Saul his answer, though it wasn't the answer Saul wanted to hear.

28:17 The spirit of Samuel specifically named Saul's successor as **David**, whereas before he had only alluded to him (13:14; 15:28).

28:18 The words of Samuel's spirit, **You did not obey the Lord**, is a reference to 15:1-3,7-9—Saul's miserable failure

regarding **Amalek**, whom God had commanded Saul to destroy.

28:19 The nation's defeat would come at God's hands. The words of Samuel's spirit, **you and your sons will be with me**, was an unmistakable verdict of death on Saul and his house.

28:20 The content of **Samuel's words**, along with Saul's weariness from traveling six miles, the stress of impending battle, and his fasting **all day and all night** (cp. 14:24,28), left the king totally exhausted.

28:23 Saul's initial refusal to **eat** may have been because he did not wish to break his vow of fasting (cp. 14:24), but the people around him prevailed upon him to take some nourishment (see note at 14:45).

28:24 A **fattened calf** was a very nice dinner in a land where meat was not eaten very often. **Unleavened bread** could be prepared quickly (Ex 12:34).

28:25 The six-mile return journey would bring more stress on Saul, and he would also get little rest to prepare for the battle the next day.

29:1 The text now flashes back to 28:1-2, a time prior to the armies gathering at Shunem and Gilboa (28:4). **Aphek** was located along the Yarkon River; it marked the site where the **Philistines** had gathered years earlier to fight Israel during the days of Eli the high priest (4:1). The **spring in Jezreel**

Israel was camped by the spring in Jezreel.[a] 2 As the Philistine leaders were passing in review with their units of hundreds and thousands, David and his men[b] were passing in review behind them with Achish. 3 Then the Philistine commanders asked, "What are these Hebrews doing here?"

Achish answered the Philistine commanders, "That is David, servant of King Saul of Israel. He has been with me a considerable period of time.[A] From the day he defected until today, I've found no fault with him."[c]

4 The Philistine commanders, however, were enraged with Achish and told him, "Send that man back and let him return to the place you assigned him.[d] He must not go down with us into battle only to become our adversary during the battle.[e] What better way could he regain his master's favor than with the heads of our men? 5 Isn't this the David they sing about during their dances:

Saul has killed his thousands,
but David his tens of thousands?"[f]

6 So Achish summoned David and told him, "As the LORD lives, you are an honorable man. I think it is good[B] to have you working[C] with me in the camp, because I have found no fault in you from the day you came to me until today.[g] But the leaders don't think you are reliable. 7 Now go back quietly and you won't be doing anything the Philistine leaders think is wrong."

8 "But what have I done?"[h] David replied to Achish. "From the first day I was with you until today, what have you found against your servant to keep me from going along to fight against the enemies of my lord the king?"

9 Achish answered David, "I'm convinced that you are as reliable as the Angel of God.[i] But the Philistine commanders have said, 'He must not go into battle with us.'[j] 10 So get up early in the morning, you and your masters' servants who came with you.[D,k] When you've all gotten up early, go as soon as it's light." 11 So David and his men got up early in the morning to return to the land of the Philistines. And the Philistines went up to Jezreel.

David's Defeat of the Amalekites

30 David and his men[l] arrived in Ziklag[m] on the third day. The Amalekites[n] had raided the •Negev and attacked and burned down Ziklag. 2 They also had kidnapped the women and everyone[E] in it from the youngest to the oldest. They had killed no one but had carried them off[o] as they went on their way.

3 When David and his men arrived at the town, they found it burned down. Their wives, sons, and daughters had been kidnapped. 4 David and the troops with him wept loudly until they had no strength left to weep. 5 David's two wives,[p] Ahinoam the Jezreelite and Abigail the widow of Nabal the Carmelite, had also been kidnapped. 6 David was in a difficult position because the troops talked about stoning him,[q]

Cross references (side column)
a 29:1 1Kg 18:19; 21:1; 2Kg 9:30
b 29:2 1Sm 28:1-2
c 29:3 1Sm 27:4-12
d 29:4 1Sm 27:6
e 1Sm 14:21
f 29:5 1Sm 18:7; 21:11
g 29:6 1Sm 27:8-12; 29:3
h 29:8 1Sm 27:10-12
i 29:9 2Sm 14:17,20; 19:27
j 1Sm 29:4
k 29:10 1Ch 12:19,22
l 30:1-18 Gn 14:1-16
m 30:1 1Sm 27:6,8
n 1Sm 15:7; 27:8-10
o 30:2 1Sm 27:11
p 30:5 1Sm 25:42-43
q 30:6 Ex 17:4

A 29:3 Hb obscure   B 29:6 Lit *It was good in my eyes*   C 29:6 Lit *you going out and coming in*   D 29:10 LXX adds *and go to the place I appointed you to. Don't take this evil matter to heart, for you are good before me.*   E 30:2 LXX; MT omits *and everyone*

---

probably refers to a spring in the valley near the town. By camping at Jezreel, Israel gave the Philistines full access to the valley where Philistine chariots would be more effective.

29:2 David and his men joined **Achish** and the **Philistine leaders** as they prepared for battle. David's position **behind them** meant that if he turned traitor, Philistine forces could be trapped between Saul and David (vv. 4-5).

29:3 In response to the concerns of the **Philistine commanders**, Achish affirmed David's loyalty to him during the **considerable period of time** (16 months, 27:7) that David had served him.

29:4 The **Philistine commanders** refused to accept Achish's explanation. If David should become their **adversary** during the battle, they could suffer heavy casualties. They also suspected that David, as one of Saul's former generals, might choose just such a time to **regain his master's favor**. The words **heads of our men** may recall the Goliath episode (17:51).

29:6 With his words, **as the LORD lives**, Achish recognized the power of God in David's life.

29:7 The **Philistine leaders** were not ready to kill David and his men, but they couldn't bring themselves to trust him in a battle against his own people.

29:9 Achish affirmed his faith in David, but he felt compelled to follow the counsel of his **Philistine commanders**.

29:10 Achish commanded David to leave **early in the morning** so he wouldn't hinder the Philistine advance northward. **Your master's servants** designated David's men who had defected from Saul to David.

29:11 David's departure providentially prevented him from participating in the battle that would claim Saul's life. Meanwhile, the **Philistines went up to Jezreel** (perhaps a reference to the valley rather than the town), where they soon would face off against Saul.

30:1 On **Ziklag**, see note at 27:6. The town was still under Philistine control (29:11). The **Amalekites** whom Saul should have destroyed (15:1-3) had raided the **Negev** (the southern region) and **burned** the city **down**.

30:2 Though Saul had nearly destroyed the Amalekites (15:7-9), they did not retaliate in kind. Rather, they **kidnapped the women and everyone** in the city.

30:5 David's **two wives** did not escape the Amalekite attack, so he shared personally in the grief that others experienced.

30:6 The pain the troops felt over the loss of **their sons and daughters** led some to blame David for their troubles. Nonetheless, David **found strength** (lit "strengthened him-

for they were all very bitter over the loss of their sons and daughters. But David found strength in the Lord his God.[a]

[7] David said to Abiathar the priest, son of Ahimelech, "Bring me the •ephod."[b] So Abiathar brought it to him, [8] and David asked the Lord:[c] "Should I pursue these raiders? Will I overtake them?"[d]

The Lord replied to him, "Pursue them, for you will certainly overtake them and rescue the people."[e]

[9] David and the 600 men with him[f] went as far as the •Wadi Besor, where 200 men who were to remain behind would stop.[g] [10] They stopped because they were too exhausted to cross the Wadi Besor. David and 400 of the men continued in pursuit.

[11] They found an Egyptian in the open country and brought him to David. They gave him some bread to eat and water to drink. [12] Then they gave him some pressed figs and two clusters of raisins. After he ate he revived,[h] for he hadn't eaten food or drunk water for three days and three nights.

[13] Then David said to him, "Who do you belong to? Where are you from?"

"I'm an Egyptian, the slave of an Amalekite man," he said. "My master abandoned me when I got sick three days ago. [14] We raided the south country of the Cherethites,[i] the territory of Judah, and the south country of Caleb,[j] and we burned down Ziklag."[k]

[15] David then asked him, "Will you lead me to these raiders?"

He said, "Swear to me by God that you won't kill me or turn me over to my master, and I will lead you to them."

[16] So he led him, and there were the Amalekites, spread out over the entire area, eating, drinking, and celebrating because of the great amount of plunder[l] they had taken from the land of the Philistines and the land of Judah. [17] David slaughtered them from twilight until the evening of the next day.[m] None of them escaped, except 400 young men who got on camels and fled.[n]

[18] David recovered everything the Amalekites had taken; he also rescued his two wives. [19] Nothing of theirs was missing from the youngest to the oldest, including the sons and daughters, of all the plunder the Amalekites had taken. David got everything back.[o] [20] He took all the sheep and cattle, which were driven ahead of the other livestock, and the people shouted, "This is David's plunder!"[p]

[21] When David came to the 200 men who had been too exhausted to go with him and had been left at the Wadi Besor,[q] they came out to meet him and to meet the troops with him. When David approached the men, he greeted them, [22] but all the corrupt and •worthless men among those who had gone with David argued, "Because they didn't go with us, we will not give any of the plunder we recovered to them except for each man's wife and children. They may take them and go."

[23] But David said, "My brothers, you must not do this with what the Lord has given us.

a 30:6 1Sm 23:16; Ps 18:2; 27:14
b 30:7 1Sm 23:6-9
c 30:8 1Sm 23:2,4
d Ex 15:9
e 1Sm 30:18
f 30:9 1Sm 27:2
g 1Sm 30:21
h 30:12 Jdg 15:19
i 30:14 1Sm 30:16; 2Sm 8:18; Ezk 25:16
j Jos 14:13; 21:11-12
k 1Sm 30:1
l 30:16 1Sm 30:14
m 30:17 1Sm 11:11
n Jdg 7:12; 1Sm 15:3
o 30:19 1Sm 30:8
p 30:20 1Sm 30:26-31
q 30:21 1Sm 30:9-10

self") **in the Lord his God**, a testimony to his faith in difficult times.

30:7 David summoned **Abiathar the priest** to inquire of the Lord through the **ephod** (see note at 14:3).

30:9 The **Wadi Besor** lay about 15 miles south of Ziklag.

30:10 A third of David's warriors were **too exhausted** to continue farther because of: (1) their 55-mile journey from Aphek to Ziklag over three days (29:11–30:1), (2) the emotional pain of seeing Ziklag destroyed and their families gone, and (3) the 15-mile trek from Ziklag to the **Wadi Besor**.

30:14 The **Cherethites** lived along the coast near the Philistines (Ezk 25:16). The **south country of Caleb** denoted the region around Hebron (Jos 14:13-14; 15:13-15). The words **we burned down Ziklag** implicated the Egyptian in the battle; at the same time, it provided David a potential opportunity.

30:15 David asked whether the man now had more loyalty to those who had saved his life than to those who had left him for dead. The man's reply shows he realized he was in a difficult situation. He had implicated himself in the battle at Ziklag, so he wanted some assurance that David would not cast him aside as his master had.

30:16 The language emphasizes how the **Amalekites** were not expecting any kind of retaliation from either the **Philistines** or **Judah**, but they underestimated David's resolve.

30:17 Despite the long journey David and his men had undertaken, they received renewed energy from finding their families alive and from discovering the Amalekites so vulnerable.

30:18-19 The Lord's hand on David's army was evident as David **recovered everything the Amalekites had taken**, including all the people.

30:20 The phrase **all the sheep and cattle** designates additional animals not part of the people's assets at Ziklag, since it was called **David's plunder**.

30:21 On the **200** exhausted **men**, see note at verse 10.

30:22 Normally the victorious soldiers would divide the spoils of the battle. Some of those who had fought did not want to share **any of the plunder** with those who were too tired to proceed past the Wadi Besor.

30:23 David's reply revealed his character. He emphasized that the Lord had **protected** them and brought the victory. Who could have imagined the rescue of absolutely everything they lost with no loss of life?

He protected us and handed over to us the raiders who came against us. ²⁴Who can agree to your proposal? The share of the one who goes into battle is to be the same as the share of the one who remains with the supplies. They will share equally."ª ²⁵And it has been so from that day forward. David established this policy as a law and an ordinance for Israel and it continues to this very day.

²⁶When David came to Ziklag, he sent some of the plunder to his friends, the elders of Judah, saying, "Here is a gift for you^b from the plunder of the LORD's enemies."^c ²⁷He sent gifts to those in Bethel,^d in Ramoth of the Negev,^e and in Jattir;^f ²⁸to those in Aroer,^g in Siphmoth,^h and in Eshtemoa;ⁱ ²⁹to those in Racal, in the towns of the Jerahmeelites,^j and in the towns of the Kenites;^k ³⁰to those in Hormah,^l in Bor-ashan,^m and in Athach; ³¹to those in Hebron,ⁿ and to those in all the places where David and his men had roamed.^o

The Death of Saul and His Sons

31 The Philistines fought against Israel,^p and Israel's men fled from them. Many were killed on Mount Gilboa.^q ²The Philistines overtook Saul and his sons and killed his sons, Jonathan, Abinadab, and Malchishua. ³When the battle intensified against Saul,^r the archers caught up with him and severely wounded him.^A ⁴Then Saul said to his armor-bearer,^s "Draw your sword and run me through with it, or these uncircumcised men^t will come and run me through and torture me." But his armor-bearer would not do it because he was terrified. Then Saul took his sword and fell on it.^u ⁵When his armor-bearer saw that Saul was dead, he also fell on his own sword and died with him. ⁶So on that day, Saul died together with his three sons, his armor-bearer, and all his men.

⁷When the men of Israel on the other side of the valley and on the other side of the Jordan saw that Israel's men had run away and that Saul and his sons were dead, they abandoned the cities and fled. So the Philistines came and settled in them.

⁸The next day when the Philistines came to strip the dead, they found Saul and his three sons dead on Mount Gilboa. ⁹They cut off Saul's head, stripped off his armor, and sent messengers throughout the land of the

Cross references
^a30:24 Nm 31:25-27; Jos 22:8
^b30:26 1Sm 25:27
^c1Sm 18:17; 25:28
^d30:27 Jos 15:30; 19:4
^eJos 19:8
^fJos 15:48; 21:14
^g30:28 1Ch 11:44
^h1Ch 27:27
ⁱJos 15:50
^j30:29 1Sm 27:10
^k1Sm 15:6
^l30:30 Jos 12:14; 15:30; 19:4
^mJos 15:42; 19:7
ⁿ30:31 Nm 13:22; Jos 14:13-15; 21:11-13
^o1Sm 23:22
^p31:1-13 2Sm 1:12; 1Ch 10:1-12
^q31:1 1Sm 28:4
^r31:3 2Sm 1:6
^s31:4 Jdg 9:54
^tJdg 14:3
^u2Sm 1:6,10

30:24 David's insistence that warriors and keepers of the supplies would **share equally** in the spoils parallels the concept of the unity of the body of Christ described in the NT (Rm 12:3-8).

30:25 David's decision about the equitable distribution of plunder became **a law and an ordinance** for future generations. The specific mention of **Israel** anticipates David's reign over the entire country. On **to this very day**, see note at 6:17-18.

30:26 The plunder of the LORD's enemies came most recently from the Amalekites, but it may have included property that **the elders of Judah** would recognize as formerly taken from them in Amalekite raids.

30:27 The exact location of most of the places in Judah mentioned in verses 27-31 is uncertain. **Ramoth of the Negev** is mentioned in Jos 19:8. **Jattir** was a Levitical city (Jos 21:14), designated for the Levites with its surrounding pasture lands.

30:28 Eshtemoa was also a Levitical city (Jos 21:14).

30:29 The **Jerahmeelites** and **Kenites** lived in the areas where David had fought and destroyed Israel's enemies (27:10).

30:30 Hormah was a place that the Israelites had fought and conquered at least three times (Nm 21:3; Jos 12:14; Jdg 1:17).

30:31 Hebron, Judah's natural capital, lay about 19 miles south of Jerusalem in the Judean hill country. Hebron was conquered by Caleb during Joshua's time (Jos 14:13-14), and it became both a Levitical city (Jos 21:13) and a city of refuge (Jos 20:7). After Saul's death, the city became David's capital for seven and one-half years (2Sm 5:5).

31:1 The account now shifts to the Jezreel Valley. **Israel's men fled from them**; that is, Israel lost the battle (4:17). On **Mount Gilboa**, see note at 28:4.

31:2 Kings and princes normally shielded themselves from the risks associated with the battlefield (2Sm 18:2-4; 21:15-17), but in this battle, **the Philistines overtook Saul and his sons**.

31:3 Archers provided the advantage of inflicting potentially fatal injuries from a distance; raining arrows on Saul's position proved effective.

31:4 Saul feared the Philistines would capture him alive and perhaps treat him as they had treated Samson in the judges period (Jdg 16:21). Saul's **armor-bearer**, however, was paralyzed with fear and could not bring himself to obey the king's request (**run me through**). So Saul took his own sword and **fell on it**. On the discrepancy between these words and 2Sm 1:6-10, see the notes at those verses.

31:7 News of the Philistine victory spread quickly throughout the region. Israelites living **on the other side of the valley . . . abandoned the cities**, as did those directly down the Harod Valley (also called the Beth-shan Valley) and beyond the **Jordan** River. The Philistine settlements in this region marked the enemy's deepest penetration into Israel's heartland, but after David became king, he subdued them and restricted them to the Judean coastal region.

31:8 Part of plundering the enemy involved returning to **strip the dead** of their valuables. The Philistine victory had been so complete that no Israelites had dared try to rescue the bodies of **Saul and his three sons**.

31:9 First Chronicles 10:10 notes that Saul's head was placed in the temple of Dagon, perhaps at Ashdod (1Sm 5:1-2), symbolizing Dagon's victory over Israel's king.

Philistines to spread the good news[a] in the temples of their idols[b] and among the people. [10]Then they put his armor in the temple of the •Ashtoreths[c] and hung his body[d] on the wall of Beth-shan.[e]

[11]When the residents of Jabesh-gilead[f] heard what the Philistines had done to Saul, [12]all their brave men[g] set out, journeyed all night,

and retrieved the body of Saul and the bodies of his sons from the wall of Beth-shan. When they arrived at Jabesh, they burned the bodies there.[h] [13]Afterward, they took their bones and buried them under the tamarisk tree[i] in Jabesh[j] and fasted seven days.

---

[a] 31:9 2Sm 1:20
[b] Jdg 16:23-24
[c] 31:10 Jdg 2:13; 1Sm 7:3
[d] 1Sm 31:12; 2Sm 21:14
[e] Jos 17:11
[f] 31:11 1Sm 11:1-13
[g] 31:12 2Sm 2:4-7
[h] 2Ch 16:14

[i] 31:13 1Sm 22:6　[j] 2Sm 2:4-7; 21:12-14

31:10 Ashtoreths designated images of the Canaanite goddess Ashtoreth, consort of Baal (7:3-4; 12:10). **Beth-shan** was an Israelite city at the mouth of the valley near the Jordan River, probably abandoned by the Israelites in the wake of the Philistine victory (v. 7).

31:11 Jabesh-gilead was a city east of the Jordan River whose citizens **Saul** rescued from Nahash, king of Ammon (11:1-11).

31:12 Retrieving **the body of Saul and the bodies of his sons** would have been risky since the Philistines occupied the valley, but Jabesh-gilead's **brave men** did so—probably under cover of darkness. **At Jabesh, they burned the bodies**, not to ashes, but on a funeral pyre to remove the flesh, probably to protect them from further abuse by wild animals. They had not been able to repay the king for saving them during his life, but they would do what they could now to honor his memory.

31:13 Fasting was a sign of mourning out of deep respect for Saul and his sons.

Mount Gilboa (31:8)

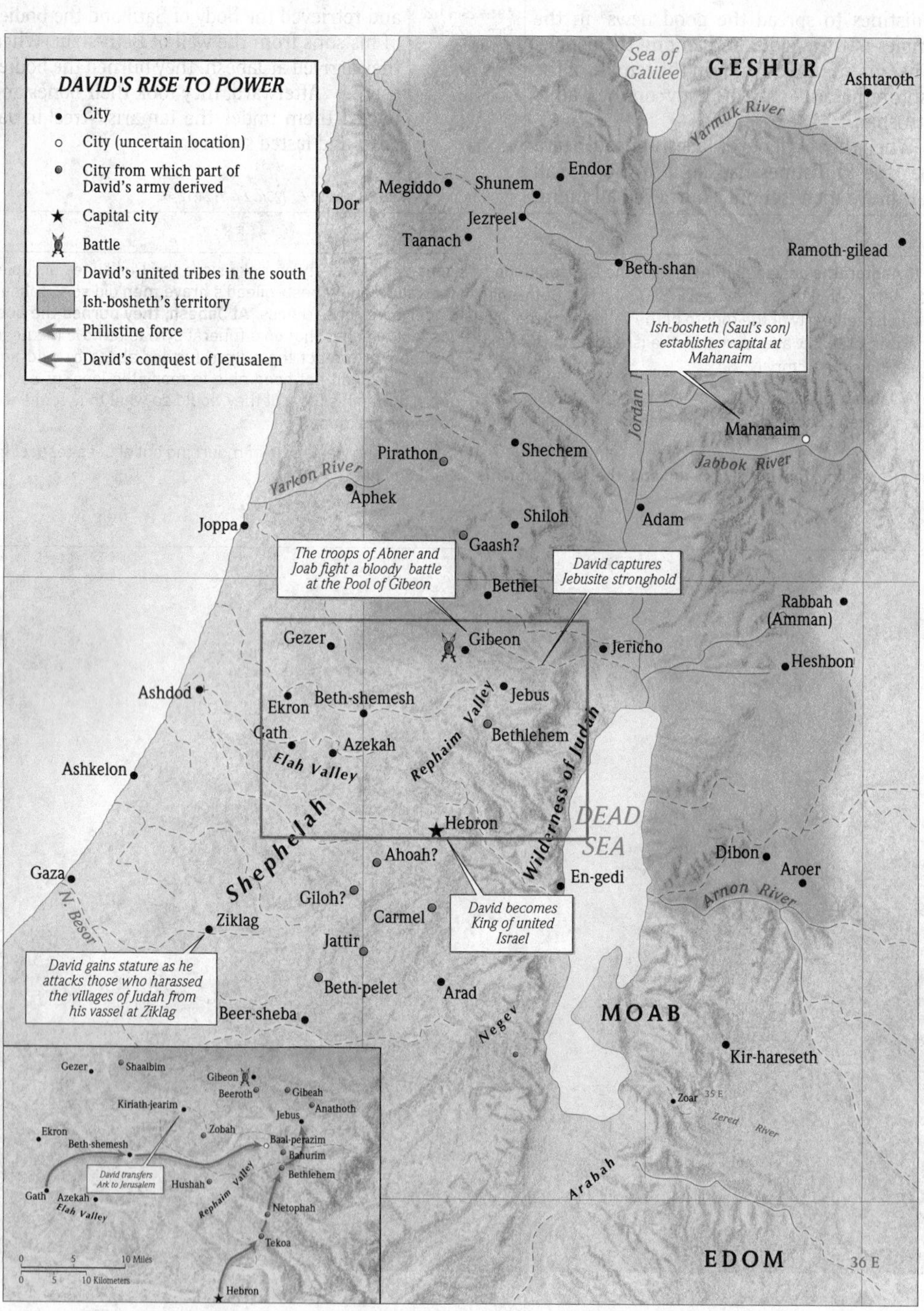

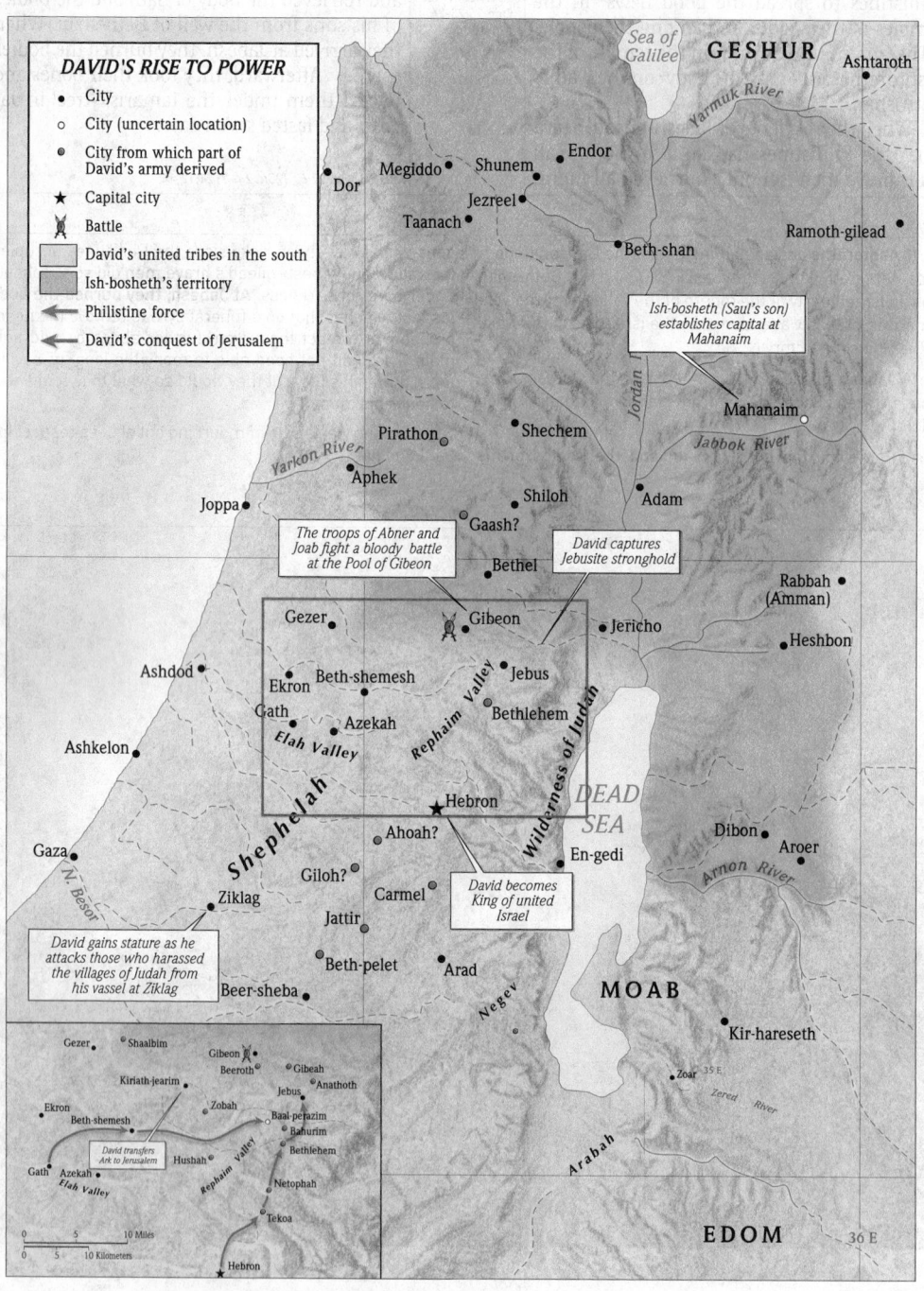

DAVID'S RISE TO POWER
City
City (uncertain location)
City from which part of David's army derived
Capital city
Battle
David's united tribes in the south
Ish-bosheth's territory
Philistine force
David's conquest of Jerusalem
Sea of Galilee
GESHUR
Ashtaroth
Yarmuk River
Dor
Megiddo
Shunem
Endor
Jezreel
Taanach
Beth-shan
Ramoth-gilead
Ish-bosheth (Saul's son) establishes capital at Mahanaim
Jordan R
Mahanaim
Jabbok River
Pirathon
Shechem
Yarkon River
Aphek
Joppa
Shiloh
Adam
Gaash?
The troops of Abner and Joab fight a bloody battle at the Pool of Gibeon
David captures Jebusite stronghold
Bethel
Rabbah (Amman)
Gezer
Gibeon
Jericho
Heshbon
Ashdod
Jebus
Ekron
Beth-shemesh
Rephaim Valley
Bethlehem
Gath
Azekah
Elah Valley
Wilderness of Judah
Ashkelon
DEAD SEA
Shephelah
Hebron
Ahoah?
Dibon
Aroer
Gaza
Giloh?
En-gedi
Arnon River
N. Besor
Ziklag
Carmel
David becomes King of united Israel
Jattir
David gains stature as he attacks those who harassed the villages of Judah from his vassel at Ziklag
Beth-pelet
Arad
Beer-sheba
MOAB
Negev
Kir-hareseth
Zoar
35 E
Zered River
Arabah
EDOM
36 E
Gezer
Shaalbim
Gibeon
Beeroth
Gibeah
Kiriath-jearim
Anathoth
Jebus
Zobah
Ekron
Beth-shemesh
Baal-perazim
Bahurim
David transfers Ark to Jerusalem
Hushah
Bethlehem
Gath
Azekah
Elah Valley
Rephaim Valley
Netophah
Tekoa
0 5 10 Miles
0 5 10 Kilometers
Hebron

2 Samuel

Introduction

See the Introduction to 1 Samuel for the introductory material.

Outline of 2 Samuel

Responses to Saul's Death

1 After the death of Saul,[a] David returned from defeating the Amalekites[b] and stayed at Ziklag two days. ²On the third day a man with torn clothes and dust on his head[c] came from Saul's camp. When he came to David, he fell to the ground and paid homage. ³David asked him, "Where have you come from?"

He replied to him, "I've escaped from the Israelite camp."

⁴"What was the outcome? Tell me," David asked him.

"The troops fled from the battle," he answered. "Many of the troops have fallen and are dead. Also, Saul and his son Jonathan are dead."[d]

⁵David asked the young man who had brought him the report, "How do you know Saul and his son Jonathan are dead?"

⁶"I happened to be on Mount Gilboa,"[e] he replied, "and there was Saul, leaning on his spear. At that very moment the chariots and the cavalry were closing in on him. ⁷When he turned around and saw me, he called out to me, so I answered: I'm at your service. ⁸He asked me, 'Who are you?' I told him: I'm an Amalekite.[f] ⁹Then he begged me, 'Stand over me and kill me, for I'm mortally wounded,[A] but my life still lingers.'[g] ¹⁰So I stood over him and killed him because I knew that after he had fallen he couldn't survive. I took the crown that was on his head and the armband that was on his arm, and I've brought them here to my lord."

¹¹Then David took hold of his clothes and tore them,[h] and all the men with him did the same. ¹²They mourned, wept, and fasted until the evening[i] for those who died by the sword—for Saul, his son Jonathan, the Lᴏʀᴅ's people, and the house of Israel.

¹³David inquired of the young man who had brought him the report, "Where are you from?"

"I'm the son of a foreigner," he said. "I'm an Amalekite."

¹⁴David questioned him, "How is it that you were not afraid to lift your hand to destroy the Lᴏʀᴅ's anointed?"[j] ¹⁵Then David summoned one of his servants and said, "Come here and

a1:1	1Sm 31:1-5
b1Sm 30:1-20	
c1:2	Jos 7:6; 1Sm 4:12
d1:4	1Sm 31:6
e1:6-10	1Sm 31:1-5; 1Ch 10:1-6
f1:8	Gn 36:12,16; Ex 17:8-16; Nm 24:20; Dt 25:19; 1Sm 15:1-34; 30:1-20; 1Ch 1:36
g1:9	Jdg 9:54
h1:11	Jos 7:6; 2Sm 3:31; 13:31
i1:12	2Sm 3:35
j1:14	1Sm 24:6; 26:6-12; 31:4

ᴬ1:9 LXX reads *for terrible darkness has taken hold of me*

1:1 The historical account of the first kings of Israel continues following the description of **the death of Saul** in 1Sm 31. No doubt David and his men needed some rest, so they **stayed at Ziklag**. In addition, Ziklag needed to be rebuilt (1Sm 30:1).

1:2 By **the third day**, Saul had been dead a few days, but David had been occupied elsewhere. **Torn clothes and dust on his head** were signs of mourning, so David immediately knew bad news was forthcoming.

1:4 The words **the troops fled** indicate that Israel had lost the battle (1Sm 4:17; 17:24; 31:1). **Saul and ... Jonathan are dead** was terrible news, but also news that required further verification.

1:6 **Mount Gilboa** was the site of the battle, so the messenger's word placed him at the scene. **Saul, leaning on his spear** gives the sense that an eyewitness was speaking. The mention of **chariots and ... cavalry** was consistent with Philistine warfare, especially in a valley where the chariots had plenty of room to maneuver.

1:8 Ironically, the man was an **Amalekite**, part of the group Saul had been commanded to destroy (1Sm 15:1-3).

1:9 Saul's alleged words could square with the circumstances of 1Sm 31:3-4; see the next note.

1:10 With his words **I stood over him and killed him**, the Amalekite claimed responsibility for killing King Saul. Further, the man's possession of Saul's **crown** and **armband** provided proof of the Amalekite's presence at Gilboa and that Saul was dead. Two possibilities exist on harmonizing this verse with 1Sm 31:4. The first is to assume Saul fell on his sword, did not die immediately, and so asked the Amalekite to help bring about a quicker death. The second and more likely is that the Amalekite arrived on the scene after Saul had died but before the Philistines arrived. He saw an opportunity to receive a reward from David, so he took the

crown and armband to David and lied about the way Saul died. Perhaps David detected the Amalekite's deceit, which in part would explain his command in verse 15.

1:11-12 Throughout his life, David had remained as loyal as possible to Saul's house. The king of **Israel** lay dead, so David and all with him **mourned, wept, and fasted**.

1:14 David's reference to Saul as **the Lᴏʀᴅ's anointed** (1Sm 24:6) highlights the respect he had for God's hand on his former king, despite the struggles he had experienced with Saul.

1:15-16 By ordering the Amalekite's death, David further distanced himself from participation in or endorsement of Saul's death.

1:17 The lengthiest example of a **lament** in the Bible is the

meshiyach

Hebrew Pronunciation	[meh SHEE akh]
HCSB Translation	anointed
Uses in 2 Samuel	5
Uses in the OT	38
Focus Passage	2 Samuel 1:14,16

Meshiyach, from *mashach* (anoint; 70x) describes somebody *anointed* to serve God, usually kings (1Sm 10:1), prophets (1Kg 19:16), or priests (Ex 28:41). *Meshiyach* figuratively designates patriarchs as specially chosen (Ps 105:15). Cyrus was *God's anointed* because of his role in delivering Israel from Babylonian captivity (Is 45:1). All priests were *anointed* (Ex 29:21), but the specially anointed high priest was called the *anointed* priest (Lv 4:3). The king of Israel is often called the Lᴏʀᴅ's *anointed* (2Sm 1:14). After David, *meshiyach* indicates Davidic kings (Ps 18:50). *Meshiyach* identifies God's *Anointed One*, Christ, in Ps 2:2, according to Ac 4:26. *Meshiyach* is transliterated *Messiah* in Dn 9:25-26.

kill him!" The servant struck him, and he died.ᵃ ¹⁶For David had said to the Amalekite, "Your blood is on your own headᵇ because your own mouth testified against you by saying, 'I killed the LORD's anointed.'"

¹⁷David sang the following lamentᶜ for Saul and his son Jonathan, ¹⁸and he ordered that the Judahites be taught The Song of the Bow. It is written in the Book of Jashar:ᴬ,ᵈ

> ¹⁹ The splendor of Israel lies slain
>   on your heights.
>   How the mighty have fallen!
> ²⁰ Do not tell it in Gath,
>   don't announce it in the marketplaces
>   of Ashkelon,
>   or the daughters of the Philistines
>   will rejoice,ᵉ
>   and the daughters of the uncircumcised
>   will gloat.
> ²¹ Mountains of Gilboa,
>   let no dew or rain be on you,
>   or fields of offerings,ᴮ
>   for there the shield of the mighty
>   was defiledᶠ—
>   the shield of Saul, no longer anointed
>   with oil.ᵍ
> ²² Jonathan's bow never retreated,
>   Saul's sword never returned
>   unstained,ᶜ
>   from the blood of the slain,

> from the bodies of the mighty.
> ²³ Saul and Jonathan,
>   loved and delightful,
>   they were not parted in life or in death.
>   They were swifter than eagles,
>   stronger than lions.
> ²⁴ Daughters of Israel, weep for Saul,
>   who clothed you in scarlet,
>   with luxurious things,
>   who decked your garments
>   with gold ornaments.ʰ
> ²⁵ How the mighty have fallen in the thick
>   of battle!
>   Jonathan lies slain on your heights.
> ²⁶ I grieve for you, Jonathan, my brother.
>   You were such a friend to me.
>   Your love for me was more wonderful
>   than the love of women.ⁱ
> ²⁷ How the mighty have fallen
>   and the weapons of war have perished!

David, King of Judah

2 Some time later, David inquired of the LORD:ʲ "Should I go to one of the towns of Judah?"

The LORD answered him, "Go."

Then David asked, "Where should I go?"

"To Hebron,"ᵏ the LORD replied.

²So David went there with his two wives, Ahinoam the Jezreelite and Abigail, the widow of Nabal the Carmelite.ˡ ³In addition, David

Cross references (center column):
ᵃ1:15 2Sm 4:10
ᵇ1:16 Jos 2:19; Mt 27:24-25; Ac 18:5-6
ᶜ1:17 2Sm 3:33; 2Ch 35:24-25
ᵈ1:18 Jos 10:12-13
ᵉ1:20 1Sm 31:8-9
ᶠ1:21 1Sm 31:4
ᵍ1Sm 10:1
ʰ1:24 Ezk 16:1-11
ⁱ1:26 1Sm 18:1-3
ʲ2:1 1Sm 23:1-12
ᵏ1Sm 30:26-31; 2Sm 2:11; 5:5; 1Kg 2:11; 1Ch 3:4; 29:27
ˡ2:2 1Sm 25:42-43

ᴬ1:18 Or of the Upright   ᴮ1:21 LXX reads firstfruits   ᶜ1:22 Lit empty

---

book of Lamentations, though many psalms also are so classified (Pss 3; 22; 137).

1:18 David commanded that Judahites everywhere should learn this lament. Such an order provided further indication of the depth of his sorrow and the respect he had for Saul and Jonathan. The **Book of Jashar** (or "Book of the Upright") is also mentioned in Jos 10:13. It has never been discovered, but it appears to have been a collection of some of God's great works among His people.

1:19 Splendor also may be translated as "gazelle," describing Saul as a majestic animal. Gazelles often inhabited the **heights**, so the image fits well.

1:20 David did not want Israel's enemies to **rejoice**, but they were already doing so (1Sm 31:9). **Gath** and **Ashkelon** were two leading Philistine cities (see note at 1Sm 5:1).

1:21 David called to the **mountains of Gilboa**, the site of Saul's death, to participate in the mourning by lacking **dew** and **rain**, two kinds of moisture much more common in the north where Gilboa was located rather than in the south where David was. The Hebrew seems to reflect the depth of David's extreme emotion. The phrase **the shield of Saul, no longer anointed with oil** perhaps indicates the cleaning and polishing of Saul's weapons. The concept of anointing was fitting for Saul, God's anointed one.

1:22 David praised the king and prince for their bravery and lack of retreat in the face of serious danger.

1:23 David also praised the relationship that **Saul and Jon-**athan had. First Samuel reveals Jonathan's strained relationship with his father, as Jonathan tried to be both a loyal son to Saul and a loyal friend to David. David affirmed the mutual commitment of Saul and Jonathan in that they died fighting beside each other.

1:24 The phrase **clothed you in scarlet** shows that Saul's military victories had provided stability and perhaps even prosperous times for many Israelites.

1:26 David called Jonathan his **brother** and **friend**. His relationship with Jonathan included a covenant bond of deep mutual respect and loyalty (1Sm 18:1-3; 20:13-17; 23:16-18). As leading men of society, they had much in common and developed a deep relationship that David considered **more wonderful than the love of women**. The text does not suggest that David had a homosexual relationship with Jonathan or that David had a poor relationship with his wives. Rather, it speaks to an unbreakable friendship bond between men that has been witnessed countless times and in countless cultures throughout history.

2:1 David **inquired of the LORD** as he often did to determine God's will for his life (1Sm 23:2,9-12; 30:7-8). **Hebron** was Judah's natural capital, located about 19 miles south of Jerusalem high in the hill country.

2:2 Ahinoam and **Abigail** remained with David, though Saul had given Michal, David's first wife, to another man (1Sm 25:44).

2:3 The men who were with David had come from many places (1Sm 22:2), but most were probably from Judah. Set-

brought the men who were with him, each one with his household, and they settled in the towns near Hebron.ᵃ ⁴Then the men of Judah came, and there they anointed David king over the house of Judah.ᵇ They told David: "It was the men of Jabesh-gilead who buried Saul."ᶜ

⁵David sent messengers to the men of Jabesh-gilead and said to them, "The Lᴏʀᴅ bless you, because you have shown this kindness to Saul your lord when you buried him. ⁶Now, may the Lᴏʀᴅ show kindness and faithfulness to you, and I will also show the same goodness to you because you have done this deed. ⁷Therefore, be strong and courageous, for though Saul your lord is dead, the house of Judah has anointed me king over them."

⁸Abner son of Ner, commander of Saul's army,ᵈ took Saul's son Ish-bosheth^{A,B} and moved him to Mahanaim. ⁹He made him king over Gilead, Asher, Jezreel, Ephraim, Benjamin—over all Israel. ¹⁰Saul's son Ish-bosheth was 40 years old when he began his reign over Israel; he ruled for two years. The house of Judah, however, followed David. ¹¹The length of time that David was king in Hebron over the house of Judah was seven years and six months.ᵉ

¹²Abner son of Ner and soldiers of Ish-bosheth

son of Saul marched out from Mahanaim to Gibeon. ¹³So Joab son of Zeruiah and David's soldiers marched out and met them by the pool of Gibeon.ᶠ The two groups took up positions on opposite sides of the pool.

¹⁴Then Abner said to Joab, "Let's have the young men get up and compete in front of us."

"Let them get up," Joab replied.

¹⁵So they got up and were counted off—12 for Benjamin and Ish-bosheth son of Saul, and 12 from David's soldiers. ¹⁶Then each man grabbed his opponent by the head and thrust his sword into his opponent's side so that they all died together. So this place, which is in Gibeon, is named Field of Blades.ᶜ

¹⁷The battle that day was extremely fierce, and Abner and the men of Israel were defeated by David's soldiers. ¹⁸The three sons of Zeruiah were there: Joab, Abishai, and Asahel.ᵍ Asahel was a fast runner, like one of the wild gazelles.ʰ ¹⁹He chased Abner and did not turn to the right or the left in his pursuit of him. ²⁰Abner glanced back and said, "Is that you, Asahel?"

"Yes it is," Asahel replied.

²¹Abner said to him, "Turn to your right or left, seize one of the young soldiers, and take whatever you can get from him." But Asahel

Cross references (center column):
ᵃ2:3 1Sm 27:2-3; 30:9; 1Ch 12:1,23-37
ᵇ2:4 1Sm 16:13; 2Sm 5:3-5
ᶜ1Sm 31:11-13
ᵈ2:8 1Sm 14:50
ᵉ2:11 2Sm 5:5; 1Kg 2:11
ᶠ2:13 Jr 41:11-12
ᵍ2:18 1Ch 2:16
ʰ1Ch 12:8; Sg 8:14

---

^A2:8 Some LXX mss read *Ishbaal*; 1Ch 8:33; 9:39   ^B2:8 = Man of Shame   ^C2:16 Or *Helkath-hazzurim*

---

tling them **in the towns near Hebron** meant David would have many loyal citizens nearby.

2:4 The **men of Judah** recognized God's hand on David and anointed him **king over the house of Judah**—over his own tribe only. At this time, David heard how the men of Jabesh-gilead had **buried Saul**.

2:5-6 David informed the citizens of **Jabesh-gilead** that they had done well with their special **kindness to Saul**. David wanted them to know he did not count their loyalty to Saul as disloyalty to him.

2:7 David probably wanted to be sure people outside **Judah** heard he was now **king** over his own tribe. Perhaps they would then conclude the next logical step was to anoint him king over all Israel.

2:8 **Abner**, Saul's relative and general, had survived the battle at Gilboa. **Saul's son Ish-bosheth** was probably the oldest surviving son (1Sm 31:2). The exact location of **Mahanaim** is uncertain, but Jos 21:38 designates it as a Levitical city east of the Jordan River (Gn 32:2).

2:9 **Gilead** designated the north-central region of Transjordan. The territory of **Asher** lay along Israel's northwestern Mediterranean coastline. **Jezreel** probably denotes the valley rather than the city. **Ephraim** and **Benjamin** were centrally located with Ephraim above Benjamin; Benjamin was Saul's tribe (1Sm 9:1). **All Israel** means everything but Judah in light of verse 4.

2:10 Ish-bosheth's **reign** of **two years** provides a hint about the length of the period of transition between Saul's death and David's assumption of the kingship over all Israel.

2:11 After **seven years and six months**, David would move his capital to Jerusalem, where he would reign for 33 years (5:5).

2:12 **Gibeon** lay in the territory of Benjamin about 23 miles north of Hebron.

2:13 David's general **Joab** wanted to keep Ish-bosheth's army out of Judah. The **pool of Gibeon** probably denotes a large reservoir near the spring outside the city.

2:14 The purpose of the deadly competition between the 24 representatives of the two armies is uncertain. Some have suggested a kind of representative combat as in the David and Goliath account (1Sm 17:8-10); others believe it was to give the Lord a way to show which army He favored.

2:16 The seemingly synchronized death of all 24 soldiers at once heightened tensions between the armies and foreshadowed the toll the civil war would take on the Israelite population.

2:17 The **battle** referred to in this verse apparently began immediately after the stalemate of the contest in verses 14-16.

2:18 **Zeruiah** was David's sister (1Ch 2:16), so **Joab, Abishai, and Asahel** were David's nephews who served in his army.

2:19 Asahel **chased Abner** because he saw an opportunity to strike down the leader of the opposition forces. Both men appear to have been on foot.

2:21 Abner hoped to deter **Asahel** with the possibility of obtaining easy spoil from **one of the young soldiers** of lesser skill whom he might kill more easily.

would not stop chasing him. ²²Once again, Abner warned Asahel, "Stop chasing me. Why should I strike you to the ground? How could I ever look your brother Joab in the face?"*a*

²³But Asahel refused to turn away, so Abner hit him in the stomach with the end of his spear. The spear went through his body, and he fell and died right there. When all who came to the place where Asahel had fallen and died, they stopped, ²⁴but Joab and Abishai pursued Abner. By sunset, they had gone as far as the hill of Ammah, which is opposite Giah on the way to the wilderness of Gibeon.

²⁵The Benjaminites rallied to Abner; they formed a single unit and took their stand on top of a hill. ²⁶Then Abner called out to Joab: "Must the sword devour forever? Don't you realize this will only end in bitterness? How long before you tell the troops to stop pursuing their brothers?"

²⁷"As God lives," Joab replied, "if you had not spoken up, the troops wouldn't have stopped pursuing their brothers until morning."*b* ²⁸Then Joab blew the ram's horn, and all the troops stopped; they no longer pursued Israel or continued to fight. ²⁹So Abner and his men marched through the ˙Arabah all that night. They crossed the Jordan, marched all morning,ᴬ and arrived at Mahanaim.*c*

³⁰When Joab had turned back from pursuing Abner, he gathered all the troops. In addition to Asahel, 19 of David's soldiers were missing, ³¹but they had killed 360 of the Benjaminites and Abner's men. ³²Afterward, they carried

*a*2:22 2Sm 3:27
*b*2:27 2Sm 2:14
*c*2:29 2Sm 2:8
*d*3:2 1Sm 25:42-43
*e*3:3 1Sm 27:8; 2Sm 13:37-38; 14:32; 15:8
*f*3:4 1Kg 1:5
*g*3:5 1Ch 3:1-5
*h*3:6 2Sm 2:8-9
*i*3:7 2Sm 21:8-10

Asahel to his father's tomb in Bethlehem and buried him. Then Joab and his men marched all night and reached Hebron at dawn.

Civil War

3 The war between the house of Saul and the house of David was long and drawn out, with David growing stronger and the house of Saul becoming weaker.

²Sons were born to David in Hebron:

> his firstborn was Amnon,
> by Ahinoam*d* the Jezreelite;
> ³ his second was Chileab,
> by Abigail, the widow of Nabal
>   the Carmelite;
> the third was Absalom,
> son of Maacah the daughter
>   of King Talmai of Geshur;*e*
> ⁴ the fourth was Adonijah,*f*
> son of Haggith;
> the fifth was Shephatiah,
> son of Abital;
> ⁵ the sixth was Ithream,
> by David's wife Eglah.

These were born to David in Hebron.*g*

⁶During the war between the house of Saul and the house of David, Abner kept acquiring more power in the house of Saul.*h* ⁷Now Saul had a concubine whose name was Rizpah*i* daughter of Aiah, and Ish-bosheth questioned Abner, "Why did you sleep with my father's concubine?"

⁸Abner was very angry about Ish-bosheth's

ᴬ2:29 Or *marched through the Bithron*

2:22 Abner's words, **Stop chasing me**, suggest that **Asahel** was gaining on him. Abner probably was better armed and more experienced in fighting than Asahel.

2:23 The **end of his spear** may designate the butt end, since it may have been sharpened to stick in the ground (1Sm 26:7). Or **Abner** may have turned the spear around and thrust it back at **Asahel**.

2:24 The **hill of Ammah** is an unknown site east of Gibeon.

2:25 The **top of a hill** was more easily defended.

2:26 Abner's questions to **Joab** challenged him to consider the high price of a civil war in Israel. During the days of the judges, another civil war almost resulted in Benjamin's extermination (Jdg 20:46–21:3).

2:28 The blowing of a **ram's horn** was a signal to gather the troops—in this case, to stop fighting (18:16; 20:22).

2:29 Abner and **his men** then retreated across the Jordan River and northward about 30 miles to **Mahanaim** (v. 8).

2:30-31 The differences in the number of casualties (**19 of David's soldiers ... 360 of the Benjaminites and Abner's men**) reveal the overwhelming victory David's forces achieved and suggest God's favor on David.

2:32 **Bethlehem** lay approximately 10 miles south of the bat-

tle site. From there to **Hebron** was another 14 miles along the highway.

3:1 The phrase **long and drawn out** suggests the struggle between David and Saul's son lasted awhile, probably at least two years (2:10).

3:2 **Amnon** would prove a tragic figure later (13:1-29).

3:3 **Absalom** would later die in an attempt to seize his father's throne (15:1–18:33). The reference to his mother as **the daughter of King Talmai of Geshur**, a Aramean city-state near the Sea of Galilee, suggests a marriage alliance between David and Talmai to strengthen David's position in the north.

3:4 **Adonijah** would later try to assume the throne, but Solomon would succeed David as king (1Kg 1:5-40).

3:6 Ish-bosheth naturally gave his leading general, **Abner**, a lot of authority. The text may indicate that Abner's intentions were to seize the kingship.

3:7 Having sexual relations with a woman of the harem was obviously the unique privilege of the king and could have been perceived as an attempt by **Abner** to usurp the kingship (2Kg 12:8; 16:20-22).

3:8 Abner's response does not indicate whether he actually was guilty. He may have been shocked by Ish-bosheth's

accusation. "Am I a dog's head[A,a] who belongs to Judah?" he asked. "All this time I've been loyal to the house of your father Saul, to his brothers, and to his friends and haven't handed you over to David, but now you accuse me of wrongdoing with this woman! [9]May God punish Abner and do so severely if I don't do for David what the LORD swore to him: [10]to transfer the kingdom from the house of Saul and establish the throne of David over Israel and Judah[b] from Dan to Beer-sheba." [11]Ish-bosheth could not answer Abner because he was afraid of him.

[12]Abner sent messengers as his representatives to say to David, "Whose land is it? Make your covenant with me, and you can be certain I am on your side to hand all Israel over to you."

[13]David replied, "Good, I will make a covenant with you. However, there's one thing I require of you: Do not appear before me unless you bring Saul's daughter Michal[c] here when you come to see me."

[14]Then David sent messengers to say to Ish-bosheth son of Saul, "Give me back my wife, Michal. I was *engaged to her for the price of 100 Philistine foreskins."[d]

[15]So Ish-bosheth sent someone to take her away from her husband, Paltiel son of Laish.[e] [16]Her husband followed her, weeping all the way to Bahurim. Abner said to him, "Go back." So he went back.

The Assassination of Abner

[17]Abner conferred with the elders of Israel: "In the past you wanted David to be king over you. [18]Now take action, because the LORD has spoken concerning David: 'Through My servant David I will save My people Israel from the power of the Philistines and the power of all Israel's enemies.'"

[19]Abner also informed the Benjaminites and went to Hebron to inform David about all that was agreed on by Israel and the whole house of Benjamin.[f] [20]When Abner and 20 men came to David at Hebron, David held a banquet for him and his men.

[21]Abner said to David, "Let me now go and I

Cross references
[a]3:8 Ex 22:31; 1Sm 17:43; 24:14; 2Sm 9:8; 16:9
[b]3:10 1Sm 15:28; 16:1-13; 28:17; 1Ch 12:23
[c]3:13 1Sm 14:49
[d]3:14 1Sm 18:20-27
[e]3:15 1Sm 25:44
[f]3:19 1Ch 12:29

[A]3:8 = a despised person

---

suggestion of disloyalty after all he had done to support Ish-bosheth's kingship. On the other hand, he may have felt Ish-bosheth should have overlooked his indiscretion with Saul's concubine in light of his loyalty to Ish-bosheth in every other way.

3:9 Ironically, **Abner** was well aware of God's promise to **David**, yet he had been advancing Ish-bosheth's cause.

3:10 The two cities, **Dan** and **Beer-sheba**, essentially marked the northern and southern borders of Israel, respectively, spanning a distance of about 110 miles (24:2; 1Sm 3:20). Abner thus envisioned the entire nation unified under **the throne of David**.

3:12 Abner **sent messengers . . . to David** because he would have wanted to make sure David accepted him. He did not want to be taken prisoner or executed.

tov

Hebrew Pronunciation	[TOVE]
HCSB Translation	good, fine
Uses in 2 Samuel	18
Uses in the OT	490
Focus Passage	2 Samuel 3:13

The noun and adjective *tov* denotes *good* (Gn 1:4), *kind* (1Kg 12:7), *fair* (1Kg 2:38), *right* (Neh 5:9), or *pleasant* (2Sm 19:35). *Tov* describes *fine* (2Ch 3:5) or *pure* (Gn 2:12) commodities. *Tov* connotes *goodness* (Ps 23:6), *bounty* (Jr 5:25), *well-being* (Ps 119:122), *advantage* (1Sm 19:4), or *prosperity* (Dt 30:9). *Tov* can imply *well* (1Sm 25:15). What is "not *good*" is *wrong* or *unfair* (Pr 20:23; Is 65:2). *Tov* encompasses *better* (Gn 29:19) or *best* (1Sm 1:23). "What is *good* in the eyes of" can signify *whatever you want* (Gn 16:6). "Seeing *good*" is *enjoying* (Ec 3:13); "being *good*" indicates *going well* (Ec 8:12). "*Good* day" suggests *feast day* (1Sm 25:8) or *holiday* (Est 8:17). *Tov* means *pleasing* (Ec 2:26), *favorable* (2Ch 18:12), *gracious* (Ezr 7:9), *happy* (2Ch 7:10), or *beautiful* (Dt 8:12).

3:13 Saul's daughter Michal was David's first wife (1Sm 18:27) whom Saul took away and gave to Paltiel son of Laish after David became a fugitive (1Sm 25:44). By getting her back, David also would reestablish himself as a legitimate relative and heir to Saul's throne. David had never divorced Michal, so she rightfully belonged with him.

3:14-15 Ish-bosheth's compliance with David's demand further highlights his weakness. Perhaps with Abner having deserted to David's side, Ish-bosheth lacked any real power and was trying to ensure that David didn't kill him after becoming king (1Sm 24:20-21).

3:16 Paltiel, Michal's **husband** of several years, was perhaps the one who along with Michal suffered the most through this ordeal. **Bahurim** was located near the Benjamin-Judah border. Abner was probably an imposing military man, so when he bluntly told Paltiel to **go back**, Paltiel was intimidated into obeying despite his broken heart.

3:17 Abner's words, **In the past you wanted David**, to the **elders** of Israel seem to reflect earlier sentiments that may have arisen during days of discontentment with Saul's leadership.

3:18 With his words **the LORD has spoken**, Abner appealed to the promise of the heavenly King to confirm David as Israel's new king. The **Philistines** continued to be a threat to Israel during these uncertain days of civil war; the nation desperately needed unifying leadership.

3:19 Abner also **informed the Benjaminites** because Saul had come from them. David wanted the support of these citizens as much or more than any other, and he wanted to accomplish as much as he could through diplomacy rather than war.

3:21 Abner was ready to coordinate final plans among the northern tribes to **gather all Israel** to David. Once they made a **covenant** ratifying his rule over them, David would control the entire nation.

will gather all Israel to my lord the king. They will make a covenant with you,[a] and you will rule over all you desire." So David dismissed Abner, and he went in peace.

[22] Just then David's soldiers and Joab returned from a raid and brought a large amount of plundered goods with them. Abner was not with David in Hebron because David had dismissed him, and he had gone in peace. [23] When Joab and all his army arrived, Joab was informed, "Abner son of Ner came to see the king, the king dismissed him, and he went in peace."

[24] Joab went to the king and said, "What have you done? Look here, Abner came to you. Why did you dismiss him? Now he's getting away. [25] You know that Abner son of Ner came to deceive you and to find out about your activities and everything you're doing." [26] Then Joab left David and sent messengers after Abner. They brought him back from the well[A] of Sirah, but David was unaware of it. [27] When Abner returned to Hebron, Joab pulled him aside to the middle of the gateway, as if to speak to him privately, and there Joab stabbed him in the stomach. So Abner died in revenge for the death of Asahel,[B] Joab's brother.[b]

[28] David heard about it later and said: "I and my kingdom are forever innocent before the LORD concerning the blood of Abner son of Ner. [29] May it hang over Joab's head and his

father's whole house, and may the house of Joab never be without someone who has a discharge or a skin disease,[c] or a man who can only work a spindle,[c] or someone who falls by the sword or starves." [30] Joab and his brother Abishai killed Abner because he had put their brother Asahel to death in the battle at Gibeon.[d]

[31] David then ordered Joab and all the people who were with him, "Tear your clothes, put on •sackcloth,[e] and mourn over Abner." And King David walked behind the funeral procession.[D]

[32] When they buried Abner in Hebron, the king wept aloud at Abner's tomb. All the people wept, [33] and the king sang a lament for Abner:[f]

> Should Abner die as a fool dies?
> [34] Your hands were not bound,
>   your feet not placed in bronze shackles.
> You fell like one who falls victim
>   to criminals.

And all the people wept over him even more.

[35] Then they came to urge David to eat bread while it was still day, but David took an oath: "May God punish me and do so severely if I taste bread or anything else before sunset!"[g] [36] All the people took note of this, and it pleased them. In fact, everything the king did pleased them. [37] On that day all the troops and

a 3:21 2Sm 3:12
b 3:27 2Sm 2:23;
1Kg 2:5,32
c 3:29 Lv 14:2-8
d 3:30 2Sm 2:23
e 3:31 Gn 37:34;
Jos 7:6
f 3:33 2Sm 1:17;
2Ch 35:25
g 3:35 2Sm 12:17

A 3:26 Or cistern　　B 3:27 Lit And he died for the blood of Asahel　　C 3:29 LXX reads who uses a crutch　　D 3:31 Or the bier; lit the bed

---

3:22 A **raid** of foreign populations living close to Judah would yield plunder that would help fund ongoing operations (see note at 4:2).

3:24 Joab expressed his shock (**What have you done?**) when he heard that David had let the man who used to be his enemy's general leave in peace.

3:25 Joab was certain Abner's motives were impure. It appears Joab's motives were to protect David's interests, though he may have been protecting his own as well since Abner would have been a potential rival to Joab as David's leading general.

3:26 The **well of Sirah** was a site about two miles northwest of Hebron.

3:27 Joab **stabbed him** [Abner] **in the stomach** just as Abner had done to **Asahel**, Joab's brother (2:23). Joab may have decided he knew better than David how to handle Saul's former general. If Joab's intentions were to exact revenge for Abner's self-defense slaying of Asahel, he might have needed to submit to the decision of the elders of **Hebron**, which was a city of refuge (Jos 20:7).

3:28 David heard about what Joab had done, and he distanced himself from any blame for Abner's death.

3:29 With his words **May it hang over Joab's head**, David pronounced a series of curses that might fall on his general for his injustice. At the same time, he did not take Joab's life because many people may have felt that Joab's actions were justified, and because Joab was his nephew.

3:30 Perhaps **Abishai** led the delegation that summoned **Abner** back to Hebron, thus serving as Joab's co-conspirator. Abner had killed Asahel in legitimate **battle**, but Joab killed Abner in a time of peace (1Kg 2:5).

3:31-32 David's public participation in Abner's stately funeral would further distance him from blame for Abner's death. He is also called **King David** for the first time here. Abner's burial in **Hebron** may have been David's way of honoring Abner by treating him as one of David's own tribe members. The king **wept aloud**, something kings did not normally do.

3:33-34 David took his mourning for Abner even further when he **sang a lament**. He alluded to Abner's killers (Joab and Abishai) as **criminals**.

3:35 David determined that he would fast the rest of the day in mourning for Abner. His taking of an **oath** emphasized his determination to honor Abner in this way.

3:36 David's integrity with regard to Abner and with regard to his oaths **pleased** the people. Ironically, Saul had sought to please the people but went back on his oaths and pleased neither the people nor God (see note at 1Sm 14:45).

3:37-38 David's actions persuaded **all the troops and all Israel** of his innocence in Abner's death. His designation of Abner as **a great leader** may have been the king's way of showing he could forgive those Israelites who had challenged his kingship if they were now willing to submit to him.

all Israel were convinced that the king had no part in the killing of Abner son of Ner.

[38] Then the king said to his soldiers, "You must know that a great leader has fallen in Israel today. [39] As for me, even though I am the anointed king, I have little power today. These men, the sons of Zeruiah, are too fierce for me.[a] May the LORD repay the evildoer according to his evil!"[b]

The Assassination of Ish-bosheth

4 When Saul's son Ish-bosheth heard that Abner had died in Hebron, his courage failed, and all Israel was dismayed. [2] Saul's son had two men who were leaders of raiding parties: one named Baanah and the other Rechab, sons of Rimmon the Beerothite of the Benjaminites. Beeroth is also considered part of Benjamin, [3] and the Beerothites fled to Gittaim and still live there as foreigners to this very day.

[4] Saul's son Jonathan had a son whose feet were crippled. He was five years old when the report about Saul and Jonathan came from Jezreel. The one who had nursed him[A] picked him up and fled, but as she was hurrying to flee, he fell and became lame. His name was Mephibosheth.[c]

[5] Rechab and Baanah, the sons of Rimmon the Beerothite, set out and arrived at Ish-bosheth's house during the heat of the day while the king was taking his midday nap. [6] They entered the interior of the house as if to get wheat and stabbed him in the stomach. Then Rechab and his brother Baanah escaped. [7] They had entered the house while

Ish-bosheth was lying on his bed in his bedroom and stabbed and killed him. Then they beheaded him, took his head, and traveled by way of the •Arabah[d] all night. [8] They brought Ish-bosheth's head to David at Hebron and said to the king, "Here's the head of Ish-bosheth son of Saul, your enemy who intended to take your life. Today the LORD has granted vengeance to my lord the king against Saul and his offspring."

[9] But David answered Rechab and his brother Baanah, sons of Rimmon the Beerothite, "As the LORD lives, the One who has redeemed my life from every distress,[e] [10] when the person told me, 'Look, Saul is dead,' he thought he was a bearer of good news, but I seized him and put him to death at Ziklag.[f] That was my reward to him for his news! [11] How much more when wicked men kill a righteous man in his own house on his own bed! So now, should I not require his blood from your hands and wipe you off the earth?"[g]

[12] So David gave orders to the young men, and they killed Rechab and Baanah. They cut off their hands and feet and hung their bodies by the pool in Hebron, but they took Ish-bosheth's head and buried it in Abner's tomb in Hebron.[h]

David, King of Israel

5 All the tribes of Israel came to David at Hebron[i] and said, "Here we are, your own flesh and blood.[B,j] [2] Even while Saul was king over us, you were the one who led us out to battle and brought us back.[k] The LORD also

Cross references (center column)

[a]3:39 2Sm 16:10; 19:22
[b]Ps 28:4; 2Tm 4:14
[c]4:4 2Sm 9:3-7
[d]4:7 Dt 1:1
[e]4:9 1Kg 1:29
[f]4:10 2Sm 1:2-15
[g]4:11 Gn 9:5-6
[h]4:12 2Sm 3:32
[i]5:1-3 1Ch 11:1-3
[j]5:1 Gn 29:14
[k]5:2 1Sm 18:5,12-16

[A]4:4 Lit His nurse   [B]5:1 Lit your bone and flesh

3:39 Up to this point David had been anointed as king over Judah only (2:1-4); perhaps he intended his words **I am the anointed king** to further ingrain this idea in the minds of others as well. At the same time, he considered his position weak in contrast to the **fierce** nature of Joab and Abishai, the **sons of Zeruiah**.

4:1 News of Abner's death reached **Ish-bosheth**, whose **courage failed** because Ish-bosheth had now lost his strongest general. Probably **all Israel** who had supported him were **dismayed** because they feared reprisal following a victory by David that now appeared certain.

4:2 As **leaders of raiding parties**, Baanah and Rechab performed a role for Ish-bosheth that was similar to what Abishai and Joab did for David (3:22).

4:4 **Mephibosheth**, a **son** of **Jonathan**, would find favor with David during David's reign (9:1-10).

4:6 These two men entered the **interior** of Ish-bosheth's **house**, something that might not have been unusual for trusted officers (v. 2).

4:7 Baanah and Rechab **beheaded** Ish-bosheth because they wanted proof of his death for David. **By way of the Arabah**

took them through the Jordan Valley, the quickest and most direct route to Hebron about 50 miles southwest. They hoped they might receive a reward for eliminating David's rival.

4:8 With their words, **Today the LORD has granted vengeance**, Baanah and Rechab credited God with their act of murder.

4:10 David reminded the two assassins of the death of the Amalekite messenger who claimed to have killed King **Saul** (1:6-10).

4:11 David contrasted the character of Baanah and Rechab with Ish-bosheth, whom he called **a righteous man**. The words **in his own house on his own bed** suggested they had committed a cowardly, cold-blooded act (cp. 3:26-30).

4:12 David commanded his men to **cut off** the **hands** that had committed the murder and **feet** that had run to bring the news of the murder to David. **Ish-bosheth's head** was placed in **Abner's tomb** in **Hebron**, uniting him with family in death but also perhaps subtly identifying him with Judah (3:32).

5:1 Representatives of **all the tribes** then **came to David at Hebron**. They were not his **own flesh and blood** as much as the Judahites were (19:41-43), but they were Israelites just like him.

said to you, 'You will shepherd My people Israel and be ruler over Israel.'"

³So all the elders of Israel came to the king at Hebron. King David made a covenant with them*a* at Hebron in the Lord's presence, and they anointed David king over Israel.

⁴David was 30 years old when he began his reign;*b* he reigned 40 years. ⁵In Hebron he reigned over Judah seven years and six months, and in Jerusalem he reigned 33 years over all Israel and Judah.

⁶The king and his men marched to Jerusalem against the Jebusites*c* who inhabited the land. The Jebusites had said to David: "You will never get in here. Even the blind and lame can repel you;" thinking, "David can't get in here."

⁷Yet David did capture the stronghold of *Zion, that is, the city of David.*d* ⁸He said that day, "Whoever attacks the Jebusites must go through the water shaft to reach the lame and the blind who are despised by David."*A* For

*a*5:3 2Sm 3:12-13,21
*b*5:4-5 1Kg 2:11; 1Ch 29:26-27
*c*5:6 Jos 15:63; Jdg 1:21
*d*5:7 Lk 2:4
*e*5:10 2Sm 3:1
*f*1Ch 11:9
*g*5:11 1Kg 5:1,10,18
*h*5:14 Lk 3:31
*i*5:11-16 1Ch 3:5-8; 14:1-7

this reason it is said, "The blind and the lame will never enter the house."*B*

⁹David took up residence in the stronghold, which he named the city of David. He built it up all the way around from the supporting terraces inward. ¹⁰David became more and more powerful,*e* and the Lord God of *Hosts was with him.*f* ¹¹King Hiram of Tyre sent envoys to David; he also sent cedar logs, carpenters, and stonemasons,*g* and they built a palace for David. ¹²Then David knew that the Lord had established him as king over Israel and had exalted his kingdom for the sake of His people Israel.

¹³After he arrived from Hebron, David took more concubines and wives from Jerusalem, and more sons and daughters were born to him. ¹⁴These are the names of those born to him in Jerusalem: Shammua, Shobab, Nathan,*h* Solomon, ¹⁵Ibhar, Elishua, Nepheg, Japhia, ¹⁶Elishama, Eliada, and Eliphelet.*i*

¹⁷When the Philistines heard that David had

---

*A*5:8 Alt Hb tradition, LXX, Tg, Syr read *who despise David*　*B*5:8 Or *temple*, or *palace*

5:3 In the Lord's presence (lit "before Yahweh") further confirmed God's blessing over David's reign.

5:5 The mention of **Jerusalem** anticipates David's conquest of the city and his making it his capital (vv. 6-9).

Some view David's moving Israel's capital from Hebron to Jerusalem as the most important geographical decision in the Bible. Shown here is Warren's Shaft, a channel through which water came into the fortified Jebusite citadel from the Gihon Spring (2Sm 5:8). This shaft was discovered in 1867 by Sir Charles Warren, a British Army officer and archaeologist.

5:6 The **Jebusites** had held at least a district of Jerusalem since the days of Joshua (Jos 15:63), and they thought their city was invincible.

5:7 Zion was a poetic name for Jerusalem; its exact meaning is unknown. The size of Jebusite Jerusalem was only about 12 acres (David subsequently expanded it somewhat), with a population estimated at around 1,500. Nonetheless, the city would serve the king well.

5:8 Water shaft may designate an almost 50-foot vertical shaft (today called "Warren's Shaft" after Charles Warren who discovered it) cut through rock from the Gihon Spring, Jerusalem's main water source. David's reference to **the blind and the lame** should be understood as a mocking taunt of the Jebusites who were not, in fact, able to defend their city.

5:9 Archaeological excavations have revealed some of David's **supporting terraces** on the city's eastern slope. David's choice of Jerusalem as his capital was a strategic move. It was more centrally located than Hebron, and it was located in Benjamin, the tribe of Saul. The northern tribes probably applauded this move because it promoted healing and unity among the tribes following the bitter civil war.

5:10 The phrase **the Lord God of Hosts was with him** shows that Yahweh was the true source of David's power and greatness.

5:11 King Hiram of Tyre, the leader of a wealthy Phoenician port city, sought to placate David through building assistance. He would later partner with David's son, Solomon, in the building of Israel's temple (1Kg 5:1-12).

5:12 David had a clear understanding that he was playing the role for which God had prepared him **for the sake of . . . Israel**.

5:13-16 Of the **sons . . . born to** David in **Jerusalem**, only **Solomon** would later play a role in the biblical account (12:24-25; 1Kg 1:33-40).

5:17 The **Philistines heard** about David's unification of **Israel**; now he stood as their enemy. They marched against

been anointed king over Israel,[a] they all went in search of David, but he heard about it and went down to the stronghold.[b] [18] So the Philistines came and spread out in the Valley of Rephaim.

[19] Then David inquired of the Lord:[c] "Should I go to war against the Philistines? Will you hand them over to me?"

The Lord replied to David, "Go, for I will certainly hand the Philistines over to you."

[20] So David went to Baal-perazim and defeated them there and said, "Like a bursting flood, the Lord has burst out against my enemies before me."[d] Therefore, he named that place the Lord Bursts Out.[A] [21] The Philistines abandoned their idols there, and David and his men carried them off.

[22] The Philistines came up again and spread out in the Valley of Rephaim. [23] So David inquired of the Lord, and He answered, "Do not make a frontal assault. Circle around behind them and attack them opposite the balsam trees. [24] When you hear the sound of marching in the tops of the balsam trees, act decisively, for then the Lord will have marched out ahead of you to attack the camp of the Philistines."[e] [25] So David did exactly as the Lord commanded him, and he struck down the Philistines all the way from Geba to Gezer.

a5:17-25 1Ch 14:8-17
b5:17 1Sm 22:4-5; 2Sm 23:14
c5:19 2Sm 2:1
d5:20 Is 28:21
e5:24 2Kg 7:6
f6:1 2Sm 10:9; 1Ch 19:10
g6:2-11 1Ch 13:6-14
h6:2 Ex 25:22; 1Sm 4:4
i6:3 1Ch 15:2,12-15
j6:5 Ps 150:3-5
k6:7 Ex 25:14; Nm 4:5,15,20
l1Sm 6:19-20

David Moves the Ark

6 David again assembled all the choice men in Israel,[f] 30,000. [2] He and all his troops set out[g] to bring the ark of God from Baale-judah.[B] The ark is called by the Name, the name of •Yahweh of •Hosts who dwells between the •cherubim.[h] [3] They set the ark of God on a new cart and transported it from Abinadab's house, which was on the hill. Uzzah and Ahio,[c] sons of Abinadab, were guiding the cart[i] [4] and brought it with the ark of God from Abinadab's house on the hill. Ahio walked in front of the ark. [5] David and the whole house of Israel were celebrating before the Lord with all kinds of fir wood instruments,[D] lyres, harps, tambourines, sistrums,[E] and cymbals.[j]

[6] When they came to Nacon's threshing floor, Uzzah reached out to the ark of God and took hold of it because the oxen had stumbled. [7] Then the Lord's anger burned against Uzzah,[k] and God struck him dead on the spot for his irreverence,[l] and he died there next to the ark of God. [8] David was angry because of the Lord's outburst against Uzzah, so he named that place an Outburst Against Uzzah,[F] as it is today. [9] David feared the Lord that day and said, "How can the ark of the Lord ever come to me?" [10] So he was not willing to

---

A5:20 Or Baal-perazim; 2Sm 6:8; 1Ch 13:11   B6:2 = Kiriath-jearim in 1Sm 7:1; 1Ch 13:6; 2Ch 1:4   C6:3 Or and his brothers
D6:5 DSS, LXX read with tuned instruments with strength, with songs; 1Ch 13:8   E6:5 = an Egyptian percussion instrument
F6:8 Or Perez-uzzah; 2Sm 5:20

---

him as he gathered his forces at **the stronghold**, Jerusalem, his new capital (vv. 7,9).

5:18 The **Valley of Rephaim** lay just southwest of Jerusalem.

5:19 David **inquired of the Lord** as he had on many other key occasions (1Sm 23:2,9-12; 30:7-8). The **Philistines** were a major threat to Saul and ultimately killed him; David, however, sought the Lord's guidance and received assurance of victory.

5:20 David was quick to give God the credit for his victory over the Philistines.

5:21 The Philistines **abandoned their idols**, and David and his men carried them off presumably to destroy them (cp. 1Ch 14:12 and note there).

5:23 God added a particular strategy to his encouragement of David to engage the Philistines again.

5:24 The **sound of marching** in the **balsam trees** was possibly produced by strong winds that typically would come up in the afternoon combined with an undisclosed act of God. When the Israelites heard this distinct sound, they would know God was marching before them, leading them to victory.

5:25 David cut off the Philistines' path of retreat and they had to flee northward down the Aijalon Valley instead of toward **Gezer**.

6:1 David wanted a large and representative delegation, so he assembled **choice men in Israel**.

6:2 Baale-judah was also known as Kiriath-jearim, located in Benjamin. The **ark of God** had been there since Samuel's days (1Sm 7:1). The **cherubim** adorned the mercy seat atop the ark, stretching their wings toward each other (Ex 25:20).

6:3 The people **set the ark . . . on a new cart** instead of carrying it on poles as the law prescribed (Ex 25:12-15). The people of God did no better than the pagan Philistines had done (1Sm 6:7). This decision would have disastrous consequences (2Sm 6:6-7).

6:4 On **Abinadab's house on the hill**, see note at 1Sm 7:1.

6:6-7 The site of **Nacon's threshing floor** is unknown. **Uzzah** meant well when he tried to steady the ark when the **oxen . . . stumbled**, but God **struck him dead** for his irreverence. Good intentions must be coupled with proper reverence when approaching God (cp. Heb 12:29).

6:8 David's anger was perhaps due to Uzzah's carelessness that led to God's anger being displayed. The king had not wanted such a joyous celebration to be marred by death. It is also possible that David's anger was directed at God, for humans often fail to comprehend God's justice.

6:9 David **feared the Lord that day** in a way he had never done before. His question was prompted by his own sense of sinfulness and uncleanness, and his realization of the holiness of God.

move the ark of the Lord to the city of David;[a] instead, he took it to the house of Obed-edom the Gittite. [11]The ark of the Lord remained in his house three months, and the Lord blessed Obed-edom[b] and his whole family.

[12]It was reported to King David: "The Lord has blessed Obed-edom's family and all that belongs to him because of the ark of God." So David went and had the ark of God brought up from Obed-edom's house to the city of David with rejoicing.[c] [13]When those carrying the ark of the Lord advanced six steps, he sacrificed an ox and a fattened calf.[d] [14]David was dancing[A] with all his might before the Lord wearing a linen •ephod.[e] [15]He and the whole house of Israel were bringing up the ark of the Lord with shouts and the sound of the ram's horn. [16]As the ark of the Lord was entering the city of David,[f] Saul's daughter Michal looked down from the window and saw King David leaping and dancing before the Lord, and she despised him in her heart.

[17]They brought the ark of the Lord and set it in its place inside the tent David had set up for it.[g] Then David offered •burnt offerings and •fellowship offerings in the Lord's presence. [18]When David had finished offering the burnt offering and the fellowship offerings, he blessed the people in the name of Yahweh of

cross-references:
a 6:10 Lk 2:4
b 6:11 1Ch 26:4-8
c 6:12 1Ch 15:25
d 6:13 1Kg 8:1-5
e 6:14 Ex 28:4-28; 1Sm 2:18
f 6:16 Lk 2:4
g 6:17 1Ch 15:1; 2Ch 1:4
h 6:12-19 1Ch 15:25–16:3
i 6:20 1Ch 16:43
j 6:21 1Sm 13:14; 15:28
k 7:1 2Sm 5:11
l 7:2 Ex 26:1; 1Ch 17:1

Hosts. [19]Then he distributed a loaf of bread, a date cake, and a raisin cake to each one in the entire Israelite community, both men and women.[h] Then all the people left, each to his own home.

[20]When David returned home to bless his household,[i] Saul's daughter Michal came out to meet him. "How the king of Israel honored himself today!" she said. "He exposed himself today in the sight of the slave girls of his subjects like a vulgar person would expose himself."

[21]David replied to Michal, "I was dancing[B] before the Lord who chose me over your father and his whole family to appoint me ruler over the Lord's people Israel.[j] I will celebrate before the Lord, [22]and I will humble myself even more and humiliate myself.[C,D] I will be honored by the slave girls you spoke about." [23]And Saul's daughter Michal had no child to the day of her death.

The Lord's Covenant with David

7 When the king had settled into his palace[k] and the Lord had given him rest on every side from all his enemies, [2]the king said to Nathan the prophet, "Look, I am living in a cedar house while the ark of God sits inside tent curtains."[l]

A 6:14 Or whirling   B 6:21 LXX; MT omits I was dancing   C 6:22 LXX reads more and I will be humble in your eyes   D 6:22 Lit more and I will be humble in my own eyes

6:10 The **ark of the Lord** ended up at the house of **Obed-edom** (1Ch 15:16-18). **Gittite** probably does not designate someone from Gath (21:19; 1Sm 17:4), but a person who lived near an olive press or wine press (Hb *gath*).

6:11 David delayed his plan for **three months**, perhaps to ensure the time of God's wrath had passed (v. 12), or perhaps out of reverent fear (v. 9).

6:13 David's sacrifice of **an ox and a fattened calf** after the ark had barely moved probably reveals he still had some concerns about the Lord's anger over the previous incident with Uzzah.

6:14 A **linen ephod** was a fine garment, typically worn by priests or Levites (Ex 28:6; 1Sm 2:18). Although David was **dancing** in worship **before the Lord**, the text does not indicate he actually assumed a priestly role. We should not understand verse 13 as meaning David actually performed the sacrifice, though he certainly was leading his people in worship.

6:16 The text states one reason why **Saul's daughter Michal . . . saw King David** and **despised him in her heart** is that his actions seemed vulgar to her (cp. v. 20 and note there). In addition to this, perhaps she was not sincere in her faith in the Lord (1Sm 19:13), or perhaps she was angry that David had taken her back from Paltiel (2Sm 3:13-16).

6:17 **Burnt offerings** marked general dedication to God, while **fellowship offerings** were sacrificial meals shared by priests and worshipers. Fellowship offerings were often of-

fered for special blessings, and bringing the ark to Jerusalem certainly would have qualified as a blessing.

6:20 **Michal** disapproved of David's dancing before **the slave girls of his subjects**, and she suggested his actions at least bordered on the **vulgar**. As a daughter of a king herself, she may have wanted King David to be more aloof from the common people.

6:21 David responded sharply. He had danced **before the Lord** to celebrate God's goodness on his life. God had chosen him to succeed Saul, Michal's **father**, as well as Saul's **whole family**. David mention of whole family was a subtle jab at Michal as well. Perhaps Michal was more a daughter of Saul than she was a wife of David.

6:22 Michal apparently did not think David should **humble** himself by celebrating as he did, but David insisted that he had acted appropriately and would continue to do so.

6:23 Some suggest Michal's childlessness was the result of God's direct judgment, but the text is not clear on this. Her childlessness may have resulted from her and David having no conjugal relations due to the obvious tension in their marriage.

7:1 David had secured his borders and subdued **all his enemies**, resulting in the nation's enjoyment of **rest on every side**. However, all of this came through God's blessing.

7:2 David's words further revealed his heart for the Lord. It made no sense to him that he had so much and **the ark of God** was housed only by **tent curtains**.

³ So Nathan told the king, "Go and do all that is on your heart, for the LORD is with you."

⁴ But that night the word of the LORD came to Nathan: ⁵ "Go to My servant David and say, 'This is what the LORD says: Are you to build a house for Me to live in?ᵃ ⁶ From the time I brought the Israelites out of Egypt until today I have not lived in a house; instead, I have been moving around with a tent as My dwelling.ᵇ ⁷ In all My journeys with all the Israelites, have I ever asked anyone among the tribes of Israel, whom I commanded to shepherd My people Israel: Why haven't you built Me a house of cedar?'

⁸ "Now this is what you are to say to My servant David: 'This is what the LORD of •Hosts says: I took you from the pasture and from following the sheep to be ruler over My people Israel.ᶜ ⁹ I have been with you wherever you have gone, and I have destroyed all your enemies before you. I will make a name for you like that of the greatest in the land.ᵈ ¹⁰ I will establish a place for My people Israel and plant them,ᵉ so that they may live there and not be disturbed again. Evildoers will not afflict them as they have done ¹¹ ever since the day I ordered judges to be over My people Israel.ᶠ I will give you rest from all your enemies.

"'The LORD declares to you: The LORD Himself will make a house for you. ¹² When your time comes and you rest with your fathers, I will raise up after you your descendant, who

will come from your body, and I will establish his kingdom.ᵍ ¹³ He will build a house for My name,ʰ and I will establish the throne of his kingdom forever.ⁱ ¹⁴ I will be a father to him, and he will be a son to Me.ʲ When he does wrong, I will discipline him with a human rod and with blows from others. ¹⁵ But My faithful love will never leave himᵏ as I removed it from Saul; I removed him from your way.ˡ ¹⁶ Your house and kingdom will endure before Meᴬ forever,ᵐ and your throne will be established forever.'"ⁿ

¹⁷ Nathan spoke all these words and this entire vision to David.

David's Prayer of Thanksgiving

¹⁸ Then King David went in,ᵒ sat in the LORD's presence, and said,

Who am I, Lord GOD, and what is my house that You have brought me this far? ¹⁹ What You have done so farᴮ was a little thing to You, Lord GOD, for You have also spoken about Your servant's house in the distant future. And this is a revelationᶜ for mankind, Lord GOD. ²⁰ What more can David say to You? You know Your servant,ᵖ Lord GOD. ²¹ Because of Your word and according to Your will, You have revealed all these great things to Your servant.

²² This is why You are great,ᑫ Lord GOD.

ᵃ7:5 1Kg 5:3; 8:19; 1Ch 22:8; 28:3
ᵇ7:6 Ex 25:8-9; 26:1
ᶜ7:8 1Sm 16:11-13
ᵈ7:9 1Sm 18:14; 2Sm 5:10; 8:6
ᵉ7:10 Ex 15:17
ᶠ7:11 Jdg 2:14-16; 1Sm 12:9-11
ᵍ7:12 Ac 13:23
ʰ7:13 1Kg 5:2-5; 6:12; 8:18-19; Ac 7:47
ⁱLk 1:32-33
ʲ7:14 Ps 2:7; Heb 1:5; Rv 21:7
ᵏ7:15 Ps 89:21,28,33
ˡ1Sm 15:24-28
ᵐ7:16 Lk 1:32-33
ⁿPs 89:3-4,26-37; Ezk 34:23-24; Rv 11:15
ᵒ7:18-29 1Ch 17:16-27
ᵖ7:20 Ps 139:1-4
ᑫ7:22 1Ch 16:25; 2Ch 2:5

ᴬ7:16 Some Hb mss, LXX, Syr; other Hb mss read *you*   ᴮ7:19 Lit *Yet this*   ᶜ7:19 Or *custom*, or *instruction*

7:3 **Nathan** is elsewhere called "Nathan the prophet" (1Kg 1:8,10,22-23). He apparently believed he did not need to consult **the LORD** about whether David should build God a temple, so he gave the king his blessing.

7:6 God had **brought the Israelites out of Egypt** over 400 years earlier and had led them to Sinai, where He gave them His statutes. During all that time, He had chosen to make His dwelling place among His people in **a tent**.

7:7 God's question **have I ever asked anyone** implied it was His prerogative to have a temple or not. He determined how His people should worship Him.

7:8 The Lord had taken David **from the pasture ... to be ruler**—from a very humble profession to the greatest position of leadership in the nation.

7:10 The Lord's promises of lasting security meant everything to people whose lives were subject to foreign invasions or raids by local tribes.

7:11 The Lord denied David's desire to build Him a house (temple), but He rewarded David's heart by building the king **a house** (dynasty)—composed of David's descendants.

7:12 God promised David the permanent dynasty Saul could have had (1Sm 13:13-14).

7:13 The phrase **I will establish the throne of his kingdom forever** did not imply that David's descendants would live forever but that his dynasty and kingdom would.

7:14 The concept of **discipline** implies reproof or correction, but generally with good intent (Is 2:4; Hab 2:1).

7:15 God promised David His **faithful love** (Hb *chesed*). This term is a rich word, encompassing all that would come to David's line because he belonged to God. On the other hand, the Lord had **removed** such love from **Saul** because of his misguided heart.

7:16 Ultimately God's promise to David was fulfilled in the king's most significant descendant, the Lord Jesus Christ, whose **throne** would be **established forever** (Lk 1:32-33).

7:18 David's questions, **Who am I ... what is my house**, reveal his amazement at God's grace toward him and his family. The king also pondered such issues about humanity in general when he wrote Psalm 8.

7:19 David affirmed that what the **Lord GOD** had **done so far** did not begin to challenge His power, and it was only the beginning of what He would do through David's line. The king's words **this is a revelation for mankind** can also be translated "This is instruction for mankind" or "This is the instruction of mankind," suggesting David thought God's work with him could be an example for all humanity. The Lord was willing to work through a surrendered heart.

7:20-21 David was aware of God's grace on his life, and he affirmed **all these great things** the Lord had promised would happen only in light of God's **word** and **will** (lit "heart").

There is no one like You, and there is no God besides You,[a] as all we have heard confirms. [23] And who is like Your people Israel? God came to one nation on earth in order to redeem a people for Himself, to make a name for Himself, and to perform for them[A] great and awesome acts, driving out nations and their gods before Your people You redeemed for Yourself from Egypt.[b] [24] You established Your people Israel to be Your own people forever, and You, Lord, have become their God.[c]

[25] Now, Lord God, fulfill the promise forever that You have made to Your servant and his house. Do as You have promised, [26] so that Your name will be exalted forever, when it is said, "The Lord of Hosts is God over Israel." The house of Your servant David[d] will be established before You [27] since You, Lord of Hosts, God of Israel, have revealed this to Your servant when You said, "I will build a house for you." Therefore, Your servant has found the courage to pray this prayer to You. [28] Lord God, You are God; Your words are true, and You have promised this grace to Your servant. [29] Now, please bless Your

servant's house so that it will continue before You forever. For You, Lord God, have spoken, and with Your blessing Your servant's house will be blessed forever.[e]

David's Victories

8 After this, David defeated the Philistines,[f] subdued them, and took Metheg-ammah[B] from Philistine control.[C,g] [2] He also defeated the Moabites, and after making them lie down on the ground, he measured them off with a cord. He measured every two cord lengths of those to be put to death and one length of those to be kept alive. So the Moabites became David's subjects and brought tribute.[h]

[3] David also defeated Hadadezer[i] son of Rehob, king of Zobah, who went to restore his control at the Euphrates River. [4] David captured 1,700 horsemen[D] and 20,000 foot soldiers from him, and he hamstrung all the horses[j] and kept 100 chariots.[E]

[5] When the Arameans of Damascus[k] came to assist King Hadadezer of Zobah, David struck down 22,000 Aramean men. [6] Then he placed garrisons in Aram of Damascus, and the Arameans became David's subjects and brought tribute. The Lord made David victorious wherever he went.[l]

---

a7:22 Mk 12:32
b7:23 Dt 4:32-38
c7:24 Ex 6:7; Dt 26:18
d7:26 Lk 1:69
e7:29 2Sm 22:51; Ps 89:28-29
f8:1-18 1Ch 18:1-17
g8:1 2Sm 3:18
h8:2 Nm 24:17
i8:3 2Sm 10:16-19
j8:4 Jos 11:6
k8:5 Gn 14:15; Ac 9:2-27
l8:6 2Sm 8:14

A7:23 Some Hb mss, Tg, Vg, Syr; other Hb mss read *you and David took tribute out of the hand of the Philistines*   B8:1 Or *took control of the mother city*; Hb obscure   C8:1 LXX reads *them,*   D8:4 LXX, DSS read *1,000 chariots and 7,000 horsemen*   E8:4 Or *chariot horses*

7:22 David's affirmation of the Lord's uniqueness contrasted sharply with the polytheistic views of the nations around him.

7:23 God established His covenant with Israel not only **to redeem a people for Himself,** but **to make a name for Himself** so other peoples could turn to Him (Is 45:22). His **great and awesome acts** included His miracles performed in Egypt and during the journey to the promised land. God's intent was to judge **nations and their gods** who lived in Canaan at the time Israel entered the land.

7:24 Israel's special covenant relationship with God (**You established Your people . . . forever**) did not preclude God using Israel to bless other nations (Gn 12:3). Nonetheless, Israel's covenant with God provided them a great blessing (Rm 3:1-2).

7:26 David wanted most of all that God's **name** would **be exalted forever** through all He did for David's house. Seeing **the Lord of Hosts** receive His proper glory had long been on David's heart (1Sm 17:26,36,45-47).

7:27 Like Daniel (Dn 9:2-5), David did not presume on God's promises but prayed for God to graciously fulfill them despite the unworthiness of humanity.

7:28 David knew God's **words** were **true** (the Hb word rendered "true" is related to the word "amen"). God's truth provided David a foundation for his life, just as it does for all believers (Jn 8:31-32).

7:29 Lasting **blessing** on David's **house** would naturally benefit the king and his descendants, but David seemed most

concerned with God's honor. He truly was a man loyal to God (1Sm 13:14).

8:1 The **Philistines** were never again a serious threat to Israel after David **subdued** them. **Metheg-ammah** (lit "bridle of the cubit") is an unknown site. Some suggest the expression is figurative, indicating David took the bridle (the reins of leadership) from his enemies.

8:2 The **Moabites** lived on Israel's southeast border beyond the Dead Sea. David allowed one-third of the defeated army to live; many kings of that time would not have been so merciful. Further, those who remained could then maintain the Moabite economy and thus bring **tribute** (regular tax that subject peoples were required to pay) to David.

8:3 **Zobah** was one of several Aramean (Syrian) city-states northeast of Israel. Through his conquest of **Hadadezer** and the other Aramean rulers, David gained control as far as the **Euphrates River**.

8:4 David **hamstrung all the horses** of the Arameans probably because chariot horses were not useful for most of Israel's rugged territory. David also affirmed that victory did not depend on horses but on God's will (Ps 20:7; Hos 1:7; cp. Dt 17:16).

8:5 Aramean city-states were known to band together against a common enemy.

8:6 Israelite garrisons in **Aram of Damascus** would ensure continued rule over the region. It also guaranteed Israel a profit from controlling major trade routes. God's power, however, was the determining factor in David's victories and blessing.

DAVID'S WARS OF CONQUEST

2Sm 8:1–12:21
1Ch 18:1-12

- • City
- ○ City (uncertain location)
- ▲ Mountain peak
- → David's routes of conquest
- → Edomite threat and retreat
- → Philistine threat
- → Aramean forces
- Saul's (now deceased) kingdom
- Territory of David's conquest

HAMATH

Tibhath

Byblos

Cun

10. David takes quantities of bronze from Tibhath, Cun, and Berothai to make the Bronze Sea in Solomon's temple

Berothai

3. David strikes Hadadezer, king of Zobah

ZOBAH

DAMASCUS

PHOENICIA

Sidon

Damascus

Abana River

BETH-REHOB

ARAM

Mt. Hermon

Pharpar River

Tyre

Litani River

Dan

MAACAH

Lake Huleh

Hazor

Acco

Sea of Galilee

GESHUR

Ashtaroth

6. Hadadezer assembles large Aramean army

Mt. Carmel

Mt. Tabor

Mt. Moreh

Helam

LAND OF TOB

Megiddo

Mt. Gilboa

Beth-shan

Ramoth-gilead

Yarmuk River

7. David pursues Hadadezer a second time, and inflicts serious defeat at Helam

MEDITERRANEAN SEA

Mt. Gerizim

Shechem

Jordan River

Mahanaim

Jabbok River

AMMON

Aphek

Yarkon River

9. David defeats the Ammonites (2Sm 8:3-12; 10:1-13; 12:26-31)

Bethel

Beth-horon

Gezer

Kiriath-jearim

Gibeon

Jericho

Rabbah (Amman)

Aijalon

Sorek River

Valley of Rephaim

Jerusalem

8. David sends Joab in retaliation of public humiliation

PHILISTIA

Gath

Baal-perazim

Medeba

Shephelah

1. David defeats Philistine advance, gains control of the Shephelah (2Sm 5:17-22)

Hebron

DEAD SEA

Gaza

N. Besor

Arnon River

Aroer

2. David defeats the Moabites (2Sm 8:2)

Arad

MOAB

Eastern Desert

Beer-sheba

Kir-hareseth

Negev

W. el-arish

Valley of Salt

Zered River

4. David defeats the Edomites (2Sm 8:13-14; 1Kg 11:14-18)

Arabah

EDOM

Bozrah

5. David's triumph in the Valley of Salt forces Edomite king to seek safety in Egypt

0 10 20 30 40 50 Miles
0 10 20 30 40 50 Kilometers

⁷David took the gold shields of Hadadezer's officers and brought them to Jerusalem.ᵃ ⁸King David also took huge quantities of bronze from BetahᴬLXX and Berothai, Hadadezer's cities.

⁹When King Toi of Hamathᵇ heard that David had defeated the entire army of Hadadezer, ¹⁰he sent his son Joram to King David to greet him and to congratulate him because David had fought against Hadadezer and defeated him, for Toi and Hadadezer had fought many wars. Joram had items of silver, gold, and bronze with him. ¹¹King David also dedicated these to the Lord, along with the silver and gold he had dedicated from all the nations he had subduedᶜ— ¹²from Edom,ᴮ Moab, the Ammonites, the Philistines, the Amalekites, and the spoil of Hadadezer son of Rehob, king of Zobah.

¹³David made a reputation for himself when he returned from striking down 18,000 Edomitesᶜ in the Valley of Salt.ᴰ,ᵈ ¹⁴He placed garrisons throughout Edom, and all the Edomites were subject to David.ᵉ The Lord made David victorious wherever he went.

¹⁵So David reigned over all Israel, administering justice and righteousness for all his people.

ᵃ 8:7 2Kg 11:10; 2Ch 23:9
ᵇ 8:9 Gn 10:15-18; Ezk 47:16-17
ᶜ 8:11 1Kg 7:51; 1Ch 26:26
ᵈ 8:13 2Kg 14:7
ᵉ 8:14 Gn 25:23; 27:29-40; Nm 24:18
ᶠ 8:18 2Sm 23:20-23
ᵍ 9:1 1Sm 18:3; 20:14-17,42
ʰ 9:3 2Sm 4:4

¹⁶   Joab son of Zeruiah was
        over the army;
      Jehoshaphat son of Ahilud was
        court historian;
¹⁷   Zadok son of Ahitub
        and Ahimelech son of Abiathar
        were priests;
      Seraiah was court secretary;
¹⁸   Benaiah son of Jehoiada was over
        the Cherethites and the Pelethites;ᶠ
      and David's sons were chief officials.ᴱ

David's Kindness to Mephibosheth

9 David asked, "Is there anyone remaining from Saul's family I can show kindness to because of Jonathan?"ᵍ ²There was a servant of Saul's family named Ziba. They summoned him to David, and the king said to him, "Are you Ziba?"

"I am your servant," he replied.

³So the king asked, "Is there anyone left of Saul's family that I can show the kindness of God to?"

Ziba said to the king, "There is still Jonathan's son who was injured in both feet."ʰ

⁴The king asked him, "Where is he?"

Ziba answered the king, "You'll find him in Lo-debar at the house of Machir son of

ᴬ8:8 Some LXX mss, Syr read Tebah   ᴮ8:12 Some Hb mss, LXX, Syr; other Hb mss read Aram; 1Ch 18:11   ᶜ8:13 Some Hb mss, LXX, Syr; other Hb mss read Arameans; 1Ch 18:12   ᴰ8:13 = the Dead Sea region   ᴱ8:18 LXX; MT reads were priests; 1Ch 18:17

8:7 **Gold shields** seem to have been a significant part of other kings' public displays as well (1Kg 14:26-27).

8:9 **King Toi of Hamath**, another Aramean region, sought a treaty with David since David had subdued **Hadadezer**, Toi's enemy (1Sm 27:2-7).

8:10 Lesser kings often sought a treaty with a superior king by sending large gifts (2Kg 16:7-9).

8:11 David **dedicated** these gifts **to the Lord**, because He had blessed him with victory over **all the nations he had subdued**.

8:12 David's victories are summarized here; his victory over the **Ammonites** is described later (10:1-14; 11:1; 12:26-31). Some manuscripts read "Aram" (Syria) instead of **Edom**, but Edom is more likely in light of verse 13.

8:13 Some early OT manuscripts read **Edomites** while others say "Arameans." The only difference between the two words in Hebrew is one slight variation in a letter. Since **the Valley of Salt** clearly designates a region by the Dead Sea, "Edomites" is more likely correct (see also v. 14).

8:15 The phrase **So David reigned over all Israel** indicates that David now controlled not only his own people's territory, but the land of all the surrounding peoples, and thus had secured his borders. David ruled with **justice and righteousness**, reflecting two aspects of God's character (Is 9:7; Jr 9:24).

8:16 **Joab**, David's nephew, is well known to the story (2:13-30; 3:22-30). **Jehoshaphat** should not be confused with a descendant of David by the same name (2Ch 17–20). This Jehoshaphat served as **court historian** (lit "the one causing to remember"), the person who supervised the preservation of important records and who perhaps coordinated the announcement of royal edicts.

8:17 **Zadok** would serve David throughout his reign (20:25) and also would serve David's son Solomon (1Kg 1:38-39; 2:35). He descended from faithful Eleazar's line (Nm 25:7-13); his followers were known as the Zadokites, a term that became "Sadducees" during Jesus' day (Mt 3:7; 16:1). **Abiathar** son of Ahimelech had escaped from Nob when Saul slaughtered all the **priests** (1Sm 22:20-21); he probably named his son **Ahimelech** in memory of his own father. **Seraiah** probably assisted Jehoshaphat in his administrative duties.

8:18 **Benaiah** served Solomon as well as David (1Kg 2:35). The meaning of **Cherethites** and **Pelethites** is uncertain, but many believe the terms designate special units of foreign-born royal bodyguards—perhaps from Crete and Philistia. **Chief officials** is literally "priests"; perhaps **David's sons** served as palace consultants to the priesthood (1Ch 18:17). However they served, it is clear that David desired a good relationship between his kingship and the priesthood.

9:1 David was determined to fulfill his promise regarding **Saul's family**, particularly because of **Jonathan** (1Sm 20:14-15; 23:17-18).

9:3 The phrase **Jonathan's son who was injured in both feet** refers to Mephibosheth, Jonathan's previously mentioned son (4:4); his name also appears as Merib-baal (1Ch 8:34).

9:4 **Lo-debar** lay east of the Jordan River in Gilead. **Machir son of Ammiel** was an influential man in that region who cared for Saul's son (17:27).

Ammiel." ⁵ So King David had him brought from the house of Machir son of Ammiel in Lo-debar.

⁶ Mephibosheth son of Jonathan son of Saul came to David, bowed down to the ground and paid homage. David said, "Mephibosheth!"

"I am your servant," he replied.

⁷ "Don't be afraid," David said to him, "since I intend to show you kindness because of your father Jonathan. I will restore to you all your grandfather Saul's fields, and you will always eat meals at my table."

⁸ Mephibosheth bowed down and said, "What is your servant that you take an interest in a dead dog like me?"

⁹ Then the king summoned Saul's attendant Ziba and said to him, "I have given to your master's grandson all that belonged to Saul and his family. ¹⁰ You, your sons, and your servants are to work the ground for him, and you are to bring in the crops so your master's grandson will have food to eat. But Mephibosheth, your master's grandson, is always to eat at my table." Now Ziba had 15 sons and 20 servants.

¹¹ Ziba said to the king, "Your servant will do all my lord the king commands."

So Mephibosheth ate at David'sᴬ table just like one of the king's sons. ¹² Mephibosheth had a young son whose name was Mica.ᵃ All those living in Ziba's house were Mephibosheth's servants. ¹³ However, Mephibosheth

ᵃ9:12 1Ch 8:34
ᵇ10:1-19 1Ch 19:1-19
ᶜ10:3 1Sm 11:1-10
ᵈ10:4 Is 7:20; 20:4

lived in Jerusalem because he always ate at the king's table. His feet had been injured.

War with the Ammonites

10 Some time later the king of the Ammonites died, and his son Hanun became king in his place.ᵇ ² Then David said, "I'll show kindness to Hanun son of Nahash, just as his father showed kindness to me."

So David sent his emissaries to console Hanun concerning his father. However, when they arrived in the land of the Ammonites, ³ the Ammonite leaders said to Hanun their lord, "Just because David has sent men with condolences for you, do you really believe he's showing respect for your father? Instead, hasn't David sent his emissaries in order to scout out the city, spy on it, and demolish it?"ᶜ ⁴ So Hanun took David's emissaries, shaved off half their beards, cut their clothes in half at the hips, and sent them away.ᵈ

⁵ When this was reported to David, he sent someone to meet them, since they were deeply humiliated. The king said, "Stay in Jericho until your beards grow back; then return."

⁶ When the Ammonites realized they had become repulsive to David, they hired 20,000 foot soldiers from the Arameans of Beth-rehob and Zobah, 1,000 men from the king of Maacah, and 12,000 men from Tob.

⁷ David heard about it and sent Joab and all the fighting men. ⁸ The Ammonites marched

---

ᴬ9:11 LXX; Syr reads *the king's*; Vg reads *your*; MT reads *my*

9:6 Mephibosheth **bowed** and **paid homage** despite the physical challenge of doing so.

9:7 David told Mephibosheth, **Don't be afraid**. Any descendant of Saul might expect the new king would kill him (1Sm 24:20-22). The restoration of **Saul's fields** near Gibeah would provide Mephibosheth income for future years, plus the king granted him the privilege of eating regularly with him in the palace.

9:8 Mephibosheth's question was a standard way of replying humbly; he was not considering turning down David's offer (cp. 7:18).

9:9-11 Ziba was given the task of caring for Mephibosheth's restored estate, and he submitted to David's command at first. However, he later attempted to secure the estate for himself and his **15 sons** (16:1-4; 19:17,24-30). The phrase **Mephibosheth ate at David's table just like one of the king's sons** is a touching comment in light of his father Jonathan's earlier prediction to David (1Sm 23:17)—a prediction that did not come true because Jonathan died in battle (1Sm 31:2). David thus took the son (Mephibosheth) of his brother by covenant (Jonathan) and treated him as a son.

9:12 Mica would later have four sons of his own (1Ch 8:35).

10:1 Ironically, the name **Hanun** means "gracious."

10:2 Nahash was the Ammonite ruler whom Saul defeated (1Sm 11:1-11). Nahash apparently honored Israel's terms of peace with the Ammonites on into David's reign.

10:3 The **Ammonite leaders** (lit "princes") suspected David had sent his **emissaries** on a spying mission. Their words suggest they feared a greater level of Israelite domination; probably their current arrangement gave them a certain amount of freedom.

10:4 Hanun **shaved off half their beards**, giving the men a ridiculous appearance but also making them appear to be in violation of the law of Moses (Lv 19:27) or in mourning (Is 15:2; Jr 41:5). He also **cut their clothes in half at the hips**, exposing their private parts.

10:5 David sent a delegation to the **deeply humiliated** men, advising them to **stay in Jericho** in the Jordan Valley about 15 miles below Jerusalem until their **beards** looked normal again. This would enable them to avoid further humiliation.

10:6 The **Ammonites** must have known their actions would make them **repulsive to David**, so Ammon had probably determined to try to free themselves of Israelite dominance. They also purchased (1Ch 19:6) the assistance of 33,000 additional **soldiers from the Arameans**. The Ammonites and Arameans thus banded together against David.

10:7 David realized his control to the north and east was in jeopardy, so he dispatched **Joab and all the fighting men** to counter his enemies.

10:8 The Ammonite-Aramean strategy was to force Israel to fight a war on two fronts—something Joab and his forces

out and lined up in battle formation at the entrance to the city gate while the Arameans of Zobah and Rehob and the men of Tob and Maacah were in the field by themselves. [9]When Joab saw that there was a battle line in front of him and another behind him, he chose some men out of all the elite troops of Israel and lined up in battle formation to engage the Arameans. [10]He placed the rest of the forces under the command of his brother Abishai who lined up in battle formation to engage the Ammonites.

[11]"If the Arameans are too strong for me," Joab said, "then you will be my help. However, if the Ammonites are too strong for you, I'll come to help you. [12]Be strong! We must prove ourselves strong for our people and for the cities of our God.[a] May the LORD's will be done."[A]

[13]Joab and his troops advanced to fight against the Arameans, and they fled before him. [14]When the Ammonites saw that the Arameans had fled, they too fled before Abishai and entered the city. So Joab withdrew from the attack against the Ammonites and went to Jerusalem.

[15]When the Arameans saw that they had been defeated by Israel, they regrouped. [16]Hadadezer sent messengers to bring the Arameans who were across the Euphrates River,

---

[a]10:12 Dt 31:6;
Jos 1:6
[b]11:1 2Sm
12:26-29; 1Ch
20:1
[c]11:3 2Sm
12:24; Ps 51
[d]Mt 1:6

---

and they came to Helam with Shobach, commander of Hadadezer's army, leading them.

[17]When this was reported to David, he gathered all Israel, crossed the Jordan, and went to Helam. Then the Arameans lined up in formation to engage David in battle and fought against him. [18]But the Arameans fled before Israel, and David killed 700 of their charioteers and 40,000 foot soldiers.[B] He also struck down Shobach commander of their army, who died there. [19]When all the kings who were Hadadezer's subjects saw that they had been defeated by Israel, they made peace with Israel and became their subjects. After this, the Arameans were afraid to ever help the Ammonites again.

David's Adultery with Bathsheba

11 In the spring when kings march out to war, David sent Joab with his officers and all Israel. They destroyed the Ammonites and besieged Rabbah, but David remained in Jerusalem.[b]

[2]One evening David got up from his bed and strolled around on the roof of the palace. From the roof he saw a woman bathing—a very beautiful woman. [3]So David sent someone to inquire about her, and he reported, "This is Bathsheba,[c] daughter of Eliam and wife of Uriah[d] the Hittite."[C]

[A]10:12 Lit *the LORD do what is good in His eyes*   [B]10:18 Some LXX mss; MT reads *horsemen*; 1Ch 19:18   [C]11:3 DSS add *Joab's armor-bearer*

---

did not realize they would have to do until they crossed the Jordan River.

10:9 Joab divided his troops into two groups. He determined the **Arameans** would prove the more challenging opponent, so he **chose some . . . elite troops** to fight them.

10:10 Joab's **brother Abishai**, another seasoned warrior (2:24; 1Sm 26:6-11), led the second group against the Ammonites. Nonetheless, such a strategy was risky.

10:12 Joab knew that if Israel lost this battle, Ammon and Aram might overrun Israel's territory and cities. He challenged Abishai to **be strong** and asked for **the LORD's will** to **be done** (lit "May the Lord do what is good in His eyes").

10:13 The Arameans **fled** before the Israelite army in defeat (1Sm 4:17; 31:1).

10:14 The **Ammonites** knew any hope of victory over Israel was gone when the **Arameans** fled. They **entered the city** of Rabbah (their capital) to defend it from siege. Joab withdrew, content for now to return to Jerusalem.

10:15 The **Arameans** probably feared an Israelite reprisal, so they **regrouped**.

10:16 **Hadadezer**, whom David had earlier subdued (8:3-4), gathered the **Arameans** even from the distant city-states across the **Euphrates River**. They gathered at **Helam** about 30 miles east of the Sea of Galilee.

10:17 David could not ignore this second threat, so he

crossed the Jordan River to face them. He wanted to keep the battle outside Israelite territory as much as possible.

10:18 Again **the Arameans fled before Israel** (see v. 13). The extent of the victory is indicated by the comment that David **struck down Shobach commander of their army**.

10:19 Israel's enemies realized the battle was lost, and they negotiated terms of **peace with Israel**—terms that probably included paying greater tribute to David than they had before.

11:1 Spring was an optimal time for **kings** to **march out to war**. The crops were growing and thus men were not needed as badly to work the fields, and the winter rains were letting up. David's forces under **Joab** had already put down the Ammonite threat (10:14), but David could not leave them unchecked. Israelite forces besieged **Rabbah**, the Ammonite capital. The words **David remained in Jerusalem** do not necessarily suggest David committed sin or folly by doing so. His men may have encouraged him to stay out of the battle (21:15-17), and David had not participated fully in some other battles as well (10:7).

11:2 The **roof of the palace** was probably on the highest ground, providing the king a commanding view of Jerusalem. He saw **a woman bathing** (lit "washing"); the text does not suggest she did so intentionally to lure David into an encounter.

11:3 David discovered the woman's identity—she was **Bathsheba, daughter of Eliam** (one of David's elite warriors; 23:34) and the **wife of Uriah the Hittite** (another of David's

⁴David sent messengers to get her, and when she came to him, he slept with her. Now she had just been purifying herself from her uncleanness.ᵃ Afterward, she returned home. ⁵The woman conceived and sent word to inform David: "I am pregnant."

⁶David sent orders to Joab: "Send me Uriah the Hittite." So Joab sent Uriah to David. ⁷When Uriah came to him, David asked how Joab and the troops were doing and how the war was going. ⁸Then he said to Uriah, "Go down to your house and wash your feet." So Uriah left the palace, and a gift from the king followed him. ⁹But Uriah slept at the door of the palace with all his master's servants; he did not go down to his house.

¹⁰When it was reported to David, "Uriah didn't go home," David questioned Uriah, "Haven't you just come from a journey? Why didn't you go home?"

¹¹Uriah answered David, "The ark, Israel, and Judah are dwelling in tents, and my master Joab and his soldiersᴬ are camping in the open field. How can I enter my house to eat and drink and sleep with my wife? As surely as you live and by your life, I will not do this!"ᵇ

¹²"Stay here today also," David said to Uriah, "and tomorrow I will send you back." So Uriah stayed in Jerusalem that day and the next. ¹³Then David invited Uriah to eat and drink with him, and David got him drunk. He went out in the evening to lie down on his cot

with his master's servants, but he did not go home.

Uriah's Death Arranged

¹⁴The next morning David wrote a letter to Joab and sent it with Uriah. ¹⁵In the letter he wrote:

> Put Uriahᶜ at the front of the fiercest fighting, then withdraw from him so that he is struck down and dies.

¹⁶When Joab was besieging the city, he put Uriah in the place where he knew the best enemy soldiers were. ¹⁷Then the men of the city came out and attacked Joab, and some of the men from David's soldiers fell in battle; Uriah the Hittite also died.

¹⁸Joab sent someone to report to David all the details of the battle. ¹⁹He commanded the messenger, "When you've finished telling the king all the details of the battle— ²⁰if the king's anger gets stirred up and he asks you, 'Why did you get so close to the city to fight? Didn't you realize they would shoot from the top of the wall? ²¹At Thebez, who struck Abimelech son of Jerubbesheth?ᴮ,ᶜ Didn't a woman drop an upper millstone on him from the top of the wall so that he died?ᵈ Why did you get so close to the wall?'—then say, 'Your servant Uriah the Hittite is dead also.'" ²²Then the messenger left.

When he arrived, he reported to David all

ᵃ11:4 Lv 15:18-30; 18:19
ᵇ11:11 1Sm 21:5
ᶜ11:15 Mt 1:6
ᵈ11:21 Jdg 9:50-54

ᴬ11:11 Lit *servants*   ᴮ11:21 LXX reads *Jerubbaal*   ᶜ11:21 = Gideon

---

elite soldiers; 23:39). She also may have been the granddaughter of Ahithophel, one of David's most trusted counselors (23:34). At any rate, her married status rendered her off-limits to the king.

11:4 David . . . slept with her—meaning he had intercourse with her. The narrative is silent about Bathsheba's feelings about coming to the palace and submitting to the king's wishes. Apparently the intent of the biblical writer was to place ultimate blame where it belonged—with Israel's king.

11:5 The news of Bathsheba's pregnancy presented special problems for the king because her husband Uriah had been away fighting the Ammonites and thus could not be the father of the child.

11:6 David sent orders to Joab without revealing the reason he was summoning **Uriah**.

11:7 Uriah must have wondered why the king had summoned him—one of David's valiant warriors—when a simple messenger could bring news about **the war** (v. 18).

11:8 The words of the king to Uriah, **wash your feet**, suggested a time of gentle relaxing at Uriah's **house**, where Bathsheba might arrange an intimate evening with her husband to make it appear that he was the baby's father. David even sent a **gift** along—probably some choice food and drink.

11:10 David questioned Uriah about his refusal to **go home**

as the king had invited him to do, while being careful not to appear overly eager to make sure Uriah went home.

11:11 Uriah answered David as a true soldier. With Israel's army engaging the enemy in battle, he would not leave the battlefield to enjoy the comforts of home. Ironically, Uriah swore by the king's own **life** to disobey David's command.

11:12 David delayed Uriah's return a few days while he contrived another plan.

11:13 David got Uriah **drunk** in an effort to get him to wander home to Bathsheba, but **he did not go home**. The king was becoming more desperate to cover his misdeed.

11:14 The **letter to Joab** ordering Uriah's death was delivered by Uriah's own hand.

11:15-16 Joab, a brilliant general, had to wonder what **Uriah** had done to deserve death, but he obeyed David's order.

11:18 Messengers (not elite soldiers as with Uriah; v. 6) routinely ran between **battle** lines and Jerusalem to provide updates on the war (18:19-23; 1Sm 4:12-17).

11:20 Joab knew that David, an experienced military man in his own right, might respond angrily if he heard a bad report that included what he considered foolish military tactics.

11:21 The account of **Abimelech** dying from an **upper millstone** that was thrown **from the top of the wall** was a vivid example from Israel's history (Jdg 9:50-54). The messenger

that Joab had sent him to tell. ²³The messenger reported to David, "The men gained the advantage over us and came out against us in the field, but we counterattacked right up to the entrance of the gate. ²⁴However, the archers shot down on your soldiers from the top of the wall, and some of the king's soldiers died. Your servant Uriah the Hittite is also dead."

²⁵David told the messenger, "Say this to Joab: 'Don't let this matter upset you because the sword devours all alike. Intensify your fight against the city and demolish it.' Encourage him."

²⁶When Uriah's ᵃ wife heard that her husband Uriah had died, she mourned for him.ᴬ ²⁷When the time of mourning ended, David had her brought to his house. She became his wife and bore him a son. However, the Lord considered what David had done to be evil.ᵇ

Nathan's Parable and David's Repentance

12 So the Lord sent Nathan to David.ᶜ When he arrived, he said to him:

There were two men in a certain city, one rich and the other poor. ²The rich man had a large number of sheep and cattle, ³but the poor man had nothing except

ᵃ11:26 Mt 1:6
ᵇ11:27 2Sm 12:9; 15:19
ᶜ12:1 Ps 51 title
ᵈ12:6 Ex 22:1; Lk 19:8
ᵉ12:7 1Sm 16:13
ᶠ12:9 Nm 15:30-31; 1Sm 15:19
ᵍMt 1:6

one small ewe lamb that he had bought. He raised it, and it grew up, living with him and his children. It shared his meager food and drank from his cup; it slept in his arms, and it was like a daughter to him. ⁴Now a traveler came to the rich man, but the rich man could not bring himself to take one of his own sheep or cattle to prepare for the traveler who had come to him. Instead, he took the poor man's lamb and prepared it for his guest.ᴮ

⁵David was infuriated with the man and said to Nathan: "As the Lord lives, the man who did this deserves to die! ⁶Because he has done this thing and shown no pity, he must pay four lambs for that lamb."ᵈ

⁷Nathan replied to David, "You are the man! This is what the Lord God of Israel says: 'I anointed you king over Israel,ᵉ and I delivered you from the hand of Saul. ⁸I gave your master's house to you and your master's wives into your arms,ᶜ and I gave you the house of Israel and Judah, and if that was not enough, I would have given you even more. ⁹Why then have you despised the command of the Lord by doing what I considerᴰ evil?ᶠ You struck down Uriahᵍ the Hittite with the sword and took his wife as your own wife—you murdered him

---

ᴬ11:26 Lit *her husband*   ᴮ12:4 Lit *for the man who had come to him*   ᶜ12:8 Lit *bosom*   ᴰ12:9 Alt Hb tradition reads *what He considers*

---

must have wondered, however, why Joab's suggestion to tell the king that **Uriah the Hittite** was **dead** might appease David's anger. Now two people, besides David and Bathsheba, knew a piece of David's secret.

11:24 The messenger did not wait for the king's reply to share the news of Uriah's death.

11:25 Again, when **David told the messenger** an encouraging word to relay to **Joab**, the messenger must have wondered why the king would have received the news without even challenging Joab's strategy as Joab had anticipated he might (vv. 20-21). As is almost always the case, sin proves hard to hide for David.

11:26 The text's description of Bathsheba only as **Uriah's wife** is probably intentional to accent David's sin. She **mourned** for Uriah, probably putting on mourner's clothes (Jr 6:26), throwing dirt or ashes on her head (2Sm 1:2), sitting in the dirt (Is 47:1), fasting (1Sm 31:13), and weeping.

11:27 The **time of mourning** is not given. Israel mourned Moses for 30 days (Dt 34:8), but Uriah's mourning probably was not that long. David then brought Bathsheba to **his house**, and soon she **bore him a son**. The king might have escaped detection from some who might have been in a position to report him—except that **the Lord** had seen the entire ugly ordeal.

12:1 The Lord sent Nathan to David to reveal His message to the king. Nathan had communicated to the king God's incredible promise about David's house (7:8-17). This time, the message would not be as pleasant.

12:3 Nathan's language emphasizes how the **one small ewe lamb** was more a member of the family than an asset comparable to the rich man's abundant sheep and cattle.

12:4 The **rich man** did the unthinkable in the name of hospitality.

12:5 David was **infuriated**, a fact that reveals he thought Nathan's words presented a real occurrence in his kingdom. **Deserves to die** is literally "is a son of death."

12:6 David judged that the rich man had responded in an unjust, calloused manner. **Four lambs** were the standard restitution for a stolen sheep (Ex 22:1).

12:7 With his powerful words, **You are the man**, the prophet drove home the application of the parable. The parable laid a foundation for what was to come; the words **this is what the Lord God of Israel says** then introduced God's indictment against the wayward king. The Lord then began to describe all He had done for David, beginning with giving him the kingship and delivering him **from the hand of Saul**.

12:8 The phrase **I would have given you even more** demonstrated the Lord's willingness to go even further with David's blessing if the king had only asked.

12:9 David had not merely neglected the **command** of the Lord; he had **despised** it with his grievous actions. Technically, the **Ammonite's sword** killed **Uriah**, but it was as if David had done it himself. And he had done this to cover his adultery with Uriah's wife.

with the Ammonite's sword.ᵃ ¹⁰Now therefore, the sword will never leave your houseᵇ
because you despised Me and took the wife of
Uriah the Hittite to be your own wife.'

¹¹"This is what the LORD says,ᶜ 'I am going to
bring disaster on you from your own family:
I will take your wives and give them to an-
otherᴬ before your very eyes, and he will sleep
with them publicly.ᴮ ¹²You acted in secret, but
I will do this before all Israel and in broad daylight.'"ᶜ

¹³David responded to Nathan, "I have sinned
against the LORD."ᵈ

Then Nathan replied to David, "The LORD has
taken away your sin; you will not die.ᵉ ¹⁴How-
ever, because you treatedᴰ the LORD with such
contempt in this matter, the son born to you
will die."ᶠ ¹⁵Then Nathan went home.

The Death of Bathsheba's Son

The LORD struck the baby that Uriah'sᵍ wife
had borne to David, and he became ill. ¹⁶Da-
vid pleaded with God for the boy. He fasted,
went home, and spent the night lying on the
ground.ʰ ¹⁷The elders of his house stood beside him to get him up from the ground, but
he was unwilling and would not eat anything
with them.

¹⁸On the seventh day the baby died. But David's servants were afraid to tell him the baby
was dead. They said, "Look, while the baby was
alive, we spoke to him, and he wouldn't listen
to us. So how can we tell him the baby is dead?
He may do something desperate."

¹⁹When David saw that his servants were
whispering to each other, he guessed that the
baby was dead. So he asked his servants, "Is
the baby dead?"

"He is dead," they replied.

²⁰Then David got up from the ground.
He washed, anointed himself, changed his
clothes, went to the LORD's house, and worshiped. Then he went home and requested
something to eat. So they served him food,
and he ate.

²¹His servants asked him, "What did you just
do? While the baby was alive, you fasted and
wept, but when he died, you got up and ate
food."

²²He answered, "While the baby was alive,
I fasted and wept because I thought, 'Who
knows? The LORD may be gracious to me and
let him live.' ²³But now that he is dead, why
should I fast? Can I bring him back again? I'll
go to him, but he will never return to me."ⁱ

The Birth of Solomon

²⁴Then David comfortedʲ his wife Bathsheba;
he went and slept with her. She gave birth to
a son and namedᴱ him Solomon.ᶠ,ᵏ The LORD
loved him, ²⁵and He sent a message through
Nathan the prophet, who namedᴳ him Jedidiah,ᴴ because of the LORD.

Capture of the City of Rabbah

²⁶Joab fought against Rabbah of the Ammon-
itesˡ and captured the royal fortress. ²⁷Then
Joab sent messengers to David to say, "I have

Cross references (center column)
ᵃ12:9 2Sm
11:14-17
ᵇ12:10 2Sm
12:18; 13:28-29;
18:14-18; 1Kg
2:22-25; 2Kg
11:1
ᶜ12:11-12 2Sm
16:21-22
ᵈ12:13 2Sm
24:10; Ps 32:5;
51:4
ᵉLv 20:10; 24:17;
Ps 32:1-5; Pr
28:13
ᶠ12:14 2Sm
12:18
ᵍ12:15 Mt 1:6
ʰ12:16 2Sm
13:31; Jb 1:20
ⁱ12:23 Jb 7:8-10
ʲ12:24 Gn
37:35; Ps 23:4;
119:76,82
ᵏ1Ch 22:9
ˡ12:26-31 1Ch
20:1-3

ᴬ12:11 Or *to your neighbor* ᴮ12:11 Lit *in the eyes of this sun* ᶜ12:12 Lit *and before the sun* ᴰ12:14 Ancient Jewish tradition, one
LXX ms; MT reads *treated the enemies of*; DSS read *treated the word of* ᴱ12:24 Alt Hb tradition reads *he named* ᶠ12:24 In Hb,
the name Solomon sounds like "peace." ᴳ12:25 Or *prophet to name* ᴴ12:25 = Beloved of the LORD

12:10 To despise God's command (v. 9) is to **despise** God;
conversely, believers show their love for God by loving and
keeping His commands (1Jn 5:3-4).

12:11 David's **own family** would be the instruments of God's
judgment. The words **I will take your wives and give them
to another** were fulfilled by David's son Absalom when Absalom tried to usurp the kingship (16:20-22).

12:13 David's response—**I have sinned**—contrasts sharply
with that of Saul when Samuel confronted him over his sin
(1Sm 15:15,20-21). Saul gave excuse after excuse, but David's heart (1Sm 13:14) would not let him do so. **Nathan** assured the king that his life would be spared.

12:14 The language of this verse is difficult and has been
rendered different ways. The words **you treated the LORD
with . . . contempt** emphasize David's careless treatment
of God's commands (v. 9). Other manuscripts read, "You
have caused the LORD's enemies to blaspheme," meaning
the enemies of God treated Him with disdain because they
had seen the hypocrisy of His chosen leader. In either case,
God's leader had committed a very public sin, a fact that
contributed to God's verdict: **the son born to you will die.**
God would not allow this child—a reminder of David's adultery and murder—to live.

12:16 David **pleaded** and **fasted**, spending the night **lying on
the ground** humbly before the Lord. He repented of his sin,
but he would struggle with sin's consequences.

12:21 David's behavior after his child died contradicted what
his servants thought might happen. Fasting normally followed the death of a loved one, but David **ate food**.

12:22 The king replied that he had been holding out hope
that **the LORD** might **let him live.** One never knows the full
extent of God's grace (Jl 2:14; Jnh 3:9).

12:23 The king's words **I'll go to him, but he will never
return to me** may be understood as meaning David would
one day join his infant child in heaven. Another possibility is that David was affirming that he would join him one
day in death, but the child would never join him in this life
again.

12:24 God's grace began anew in the lives of **David** and his
wife **Bathsheba**. Their next child was **Solomon**, who would
become Israel's next king. Another mark of God's grace was
that **the LORD loved** Solomon.

12:25 **Jedidiah**, another name for Solomon, means "Beloved of the Lord."

12:26 The account of Joab's battle with the **Ammonites**

fought against Rabbah and have also captured the water supply. ²⁸Now therefore, assemble the rest of the troops, lay siege to the city, and capture it. Otherwise I will be the one to capture the city, and it will be named after me." ²⁹So David assembled all the troops and went to Rabbah; he fought against it and captured it. ³⁰He took the crown from the head of their king,ᴬ and it was placed on David's head. The crown weighed 75 poundsᴮ of gold, and it had a precious stone in it. In addition, David took away a large quantity of plunder from the city. ³¹He removed the people who were in the city and put them to work with saws, iron picks, and iron axes, and to labor at brickmaking.ᵃ He did the same to all the Ammonite cities. Then he and all his troops returned to Jerusalem.

Amnon Rapes Tamar

13 Some time passed. David's son Absalomᵇ had a beautiful sister named Tamar,ᶜ and David's son Amnonᵈ was infatuated with her. ²Amnon was frustrated to the point of making himself sick over his sister Tamar because she was a virgin, but it seemed impossible to do anything to her. ³Amnon had a friend named Jonadab, a son of David's brother Shimeah.ᵉ Jonadab was a very shrewd man, ⁴and he asked Amnon, "Why are you, the king's son, so miserable every morning? Won't you tell me?"

Amnon replied, "I'm in love with Tamar, my brother Absalom's sister."

ᵃ12:31 Ex 1:13-14
ᵇ13:1 2Sm 3:3
ᶜ1Ch 3:9
ᵈ2Sm 3:2
ᵉ13:3 1Sm 16:9; 17:13; 1Ch 2:13
ᶠ13:12 Lv 18:9; 20:17

---

⁵Jonadab said to him, "Lie down on your bed and pretend you're sick. When your father comes to see you, say to him, 'Please let my sister Tamar come and give me something to eat. Let her prepare food in my presence so I can watch and eat from her hand.'"

⁶So Amnon lay down and pretended to be sick. When the king came to see him, Amnon said to him, "Please let my sister Tamar come and make a couple of cakes in my presence so I can eat from her hand."

⁷David sent word to Tamar at the palace: "Please go to your brother Amnon's house and prepare a meal for him."

⁸Then Tamar went to his house while Amnon was lying down. She took dough, kneaded it, made cakes in his presence, and baked them. ⁹She brought the pan and set it down in front of him, but he refused to eat. Amnon said, "Everyone leave me!" And everyone left him. ¹⁰"Bring the meal to the bedroom," Amnon told Tamar, "so I can eat from your hand." Tamar took the cakes she had made and went to her brother Amnon's bedroom. ¹¹When she brought them to him to eat, he grabbed her and said,ᶜ "Come sleep with me, my sister!"

¹²"Don't, my brother!" she cried. "Don't humiliate me, for such a thing should never be done in Israel.ᶠ Don't do this horrible thing! ¹³Where could I ever go with my disgrace? And you—you would be like one of the immoral men in Israel! Please, speak to the king, for he won't keep me from you." ¹⁴But he refused

---

ᴬ12:30 LXX reads *of Milcom*; some emend to *Molech*; 1Kg 11:5,33   ᴮ12:30 Lit *a talent*   ᶜ13:11 Lit *said to her*

---

that began in 11:1 now resumes. The **royal fortress** probably designates the part of the city where the palace stood.

12:27 Capturing a city's **water supply** ensured that its defeat was imminent. Cities that anticipated a siege would use extreme measures to guard their water (2Ch 32:3-4,30).

12:28 Joab wanted David to **lay siege to the city** and finish the job he had all but accomplished. The distance from Jerusalem to Rabbah was about 40 miles, but Joab was eager for the king to receive credit for the victory.

12:30 The placing of the former king's **crown . . . on David's head** symbolized the transfer of power from the Ammonite king to the king of Israel. David also dedicated the **plunder** to the Lord for the future temple's construction (1Ch 29:2-5).

12:31 David enslaved the captive Ammonite citizens and put them to work with **saws, iron picks, and iron axes, and to labor at brickmaking**. All these tasks were heavy labor. They suggest that David was fortifying key cities and areas throughout his territory.

13:1 David had several wives, and he fathered many children by them (3:2-5; 5:13-16). Both **Absalom** and **Tamar** had Maacah as their mother, whereas **Amnon**, David's firstborn son, had Ahinoam as his mother. The words **was infatuated with her** may also be translated as "loved her," but

the present translation is better because Amnon's actions toward Tamar show that he never really loved her.

13:2 Amnon was **frustrated** because he wanted **Tamar** for his wife, but he could not marry his half sister (Lv 18:11; 20:17).

13:3 **Jonadab** was Amnon's **friend** and cousin. **Shrewd** is literally "wise," but Jonadab's wisdom was clearly not used for godly means.

13:4 On **in love with**, see note at verse 1.

13:5 **Jonadab** devised a plan by which Amnon could get alone with and close to **Tamar**.

13:9 Amnon seems to have been in a larger room of the house. When **everyone left him**, he retreated to the bedroom to lie down.

13:10 The **bedroom** was normally the innermost room of the house and the least public.

13:11 **Sleep with me** is literally "lie with me"—have intercourse.

13:12 Three times Tamar urged her brother not to violate her. Doing **such a thing** was a serious offense in the law of Moses (Dt 22:25-29).

13:13 Tamar also insisted the crime would shame both her

to listen to her, and because he was stronger than she was, he raped her. [15] After this, Amnon hated Tamar with such intensity that the hatred he hated her with was greater than the love he had loved her with. "Get out of here!" he said.

[16] "No," she cried,[A] "sending me away is much worse than the great wrong you've already done to me!" But he refused to listen to her. [17] Instead, he called to the servant who waited on him: "Throw this woman out and bolt the door behind her!" [18] Amnon's servant threw her out and bolted the door behind her. Now Tamar was wearing a long-sleeved[B] garment, because this is what the king's virgin daughters wore. [19] Tamar put ashes on her head and tore the long-sleeved garment she was wearing. She put her hand on her head[a] and went away crying out.

[20] Her brother Absalom said to her: "Has your brother Amnon been with you? Be quiet for now, my sister. He is your brother. Don't take this thing to heart." So Tamar lived as a desolate woman[b] in the house of her brother Absalom.

Absalom Murders Amnon

[21] When King David heard about all these things, he was furious.[c] [22] Absalom didn't say anything to Amnon, either good or bad, because he hated Amnon since he disgraced his sister Tamar.

[23] Two years later, Absalom's sheepshearers were at Baal-hazor near Ephraim, and Absalom invited all the king's sons. [24] Then he went to the king and said, "Your servant has just hired sheepshearers. Will the king and his servants please come with your servant?"

[25] The king replied to Absalom, "No, my son, we should not all go, or we would be a burden to you." Although Absalom urged him, he wasn't willing to go, though he did bless him.

[26] "If not," Absalom said, "please let my brother Amnon go with us."

The king asked him, "Why should he go with you?" [27] But Absalom urged him, so he sent Amnon and all the king's sons.[D]

[28] Now Absalom commanded his young men, "Watch Amnon until he is in a good mood from the wine. When I order you to strike Amnon, then kill him. Don't be afraid. Am I not the one who has commanded you? Be strong and courageous!"[c] [29] So Absalom's young men did to Amnon just as Absalom had commanded. Then all the rest of the king's sons got up, and each fled on his mule.

[30] While they were on the way, a report

[a]13:19 Jr 2:37   [b]13:20 Is 54:1; 62:4   [c]13:28 Jos 1:9

[A]13:16 Lit she said to him   [B]13:18 Or an ornamented; Gn 37:3   [C]13:21 LXX, DSS add but he did not grieve the spirit of Amnon his son, for he loved him because he was his firstborn; 1Kg 1:6   [D]13:27 LXX adds And Absalom prepared a feast like a royal feast.

---

and her brother. Tamar then suggested that Amnon **speak to the king** about marrying her first. Her suggestion, however, may have been a means to escape the situation; it is unlikely David would have granted Amnon's request in violation of the Mosaic law (Lv 18:11; 20:17).

13:15 The words **Amnon hated Tamar** show that his feelings toward his half sister had been nothing more than lust (cp. vv. 1,4).

13:16 The Torah required a man who raped a virgin to pay her father a significant bride price, and he could never divorce her (Dt 22:28-29). The law protected women by warning men of the consequences of uncontrolled sexual urges. It was also probably assumed that the young woman's brothers would be sure the man who had dishonored their sister would be a good husband to her. Amnon's attempt to send Tamar **away** after he had assaulted her was **much worse than** the rape itself since it would ensure that her shame was permanent.

13:17 This woman was a disrespectful way to speak of Amnon's half sister whom he had hoped to marry.

13:19 Tamar's actions were typical signs of mourning.

13:20 Absalom found Tamar and discovered **Amnon** had raped her. **Be quiet for now** probably meant Absalom wanted Tamar to refrain from revealing what happened until he could think of a way to help her or to take vengeance on Amnon. As a **desolate woman**, Tamar would probably not marry; however, Absalom cared for her in his **house**.

13:21 David was **furious**, but he apparently did nothing. The law required that Amnon and Tamar should marry since

Amnon raped her (Dt 22:28-29), but it also prohibited sibling marriages (Lv 18:11). Thus this unusual case had no easy solution. David also may have feared challenging Amnon about Tamar because Amnon may have challenged him about his relationship with Bathsheba.

13:22 Absalom, Tamar's full brother, didn't say anything to Amnon, **either good or bad**, choosing instead to wait for an opportunity for revenge.

13:23 Two years later was a long time, but **Absalom** had not forgotten Amnon's sin. Sheep-shearing was a time of celebration (1Sm 25:7-8), so Absalom invited **all the king's sons** to Baal-hazor about 14 miles north of Jerusalem.

13:26 Absalom's request for **Amnon** to come may have been veiled as something David should do—send the crown prince if **the king** himself could not come. David challenged Absalom's request in light of the tension that probably was obvious between him and Absalom.

13:27 After much discussion, David sent **Amnon and all the king's sons**. Maybe David sent the others along in hopes of keeping things peaceful between Absalom and Amnon.

13:28 The narrative shifts suddenly to Baal-hazor. Absalom commanded his **young men** to strike **Amnon**. He reassured them because they probably feared reprisal from David. Amnon commissioned his hit men with words similar to those God spoke to Joshua (Jos 1:9).

13:29 The rest of the king's sons **fled**, perhaps fearing Absalom would kill them to eliminate rivals for the throne. A **mule** was the nobility's mount of choice (1Kg 1:33,38,44).

reached David: "Absalom struck down all the king's sons; not even one of them survived!" [31] In response the king stood up, tore his clothes, and lay down on the ground, and all his servants stood by with their clothes torn.[a]

[32] But Jonadab, son of David's brother Shimeah,[b] spoke up: "My lord must not think they have killed all the young men, the king's sons, because only Amnon is dead. In fact, Absalom has planned this[A] ever since the day Amnon disgraced his sister Tamar. [33] So now, my lord the king, don't take seriously the report that says all the king's sons are dead. Only Amnon is dead."

[34] Meanwhile, Absalom had fled. When the young man who was standing watch looked up, there were many people coming from the road west of him from the side of the mountain.[B] [35] Jonadab said to the king, "Look, the king's sons have come! It's exactly like your servant said." [36] Just as he finished speaking, the king's sons entered and wept loudly. Then the king and all his servants also wept bitterly.

[37] Now Absalom fled and went to Talmai son of Ammihud, king of Geshur.[c] And David mourned for his son[c] every day. [38] Absalom had fled and gone to Geshur where he stayed three years. [39] Then King David[D] longed to go to Absalom, for David had finished grieving over Amnon's death.

Absalom Restored to David

14 Joab son of Zeruiah observed that the king's mind was on Absalom. [2] So Joab sent someone to Tekoa[d] to bring a clever[e] woman from there. He told her, "Pretend to be in mourning: dress in mourning clothes and don't put on any oil.[f] Act like a woman who has been mourning for the dead for a long time. [3] Go to the king and speak these words to him." Then Joab told her exactly what to say.

[4] When the woman from Tekoa came[E] to the king, she fell with her face to the ground in homage and said, "Help me, my king!"

[5] "What's the matter?" the king asked her.

"To tell the truth, I am a widow; my husband died," she said.[g] [6] "Your servant had two sons. They were fighting in the field with no one to separate them, and one struck the other and killed him. [7] Now the whole clan has risen up against your servant and said, 'Hand over the one who killed his brother so we may put him to death for the life of the brother he murdered. We will destroy the heir!' They would extinguish my one remaining ember by not preserving my husband's name or posterity on earth."

[8] The king told the woman, "Go home. I will issue a command on your behalf."

[9] Then the woman of Tekoa said to the king, "My lord the king, may any blame be on me[h]

Cross-references:
[a]13:31 2Sm 1:11
[b]13:32 2Sm 13:3-5
[c]13:37 2Sm 3:3; 1Ch 3:2
[d]14:2 2Ch 20:20; Am 1:1
[e]2Sm 13:3; 14:20; 20:16; Jb 5:13
[f]Dn 10:2-3
[g]14:5 2Sm 12:1
[h]14:9 1Sm 25:24

A13:32 Lit *In fact, it was established on the mouth of Absalom*   **B**13:34 LXX adds *And the watchman came and reported to the king saying, "I see men on the Horonaim road on the side of the mountain."*   **C**13:37 Probably Amnon   **D**13:39 DSS, LXX, Tg read *David's spirit*   **E**14:4 Some Hb mss, LXX, Syr, Tg, Vg; other Hb mss read *spoke*

13:30 Perhaps he who reported to the king that Absalom had **struck down all the king's sons** was one of the first to flee Baal-hazor. Thus he was panicked and lacked full information. David must have regretted his decision to send all his sons to Baal-hazor (v. 27).

13:32 **Jonadab** clarified that only **Amnon** was dead, and he revealed that **Absalom** had planned Amnon's murder ever since Amnon had **disgraced his sister Tamar**. The text does not reveal how Jonadab knew Absalom's plans; perhaps it was only his theory, or perhaps he had overheard Absalom muttering threats.

13:34 **Coming from the road west of him** indicates David's sons had circled around rather than returning directly to Jerusalem.

13:37-38 **Talmai** was Absalom's maternal grandfather (3:3). He ruled **Geshur**, a small Aramean city-state along the eastern shore of the Sea of Galilee. Since Talmai was Absalom's grandfather and was on friendly terms with David, insisting on Absalom's return would have been politically difficult. Consequently, Absalom **stayed three years** in Geshur.

13:39 David missed **Absalom**, and he had **finished grieving over Amnon's death**. Yet he did not arrange for Absalom's homecoming. Whether from lack of fortitude or uncertainty about the right course of action, David's inaction would lead to further troubles.

14:1 Joab saw David's wounded heart, so he devised a plan to help heal the family and let David focus more on the matters of the kingdom.

14:2-3 **Tekoa** was approximately seven miles southwest of Jerusalem. Perhaps **Joab** thought Tekoa was far enough away that David would not recognize someone from there. Joab intended the **clever woman** to play a dramatic role that would influence **the king** to bring Absalom back to Jerusalem.

14:4 The clever woman (v. 2) **came to the king** and acted as if she were seeking David's judgment on a matter.

14:7 The woman's **clan** was attempting to execute justice and **put** her living son **to death**. However, if they killed the brother who killed his brother under extreme circumstances, they also would **destroy the heir** to the woman's estate, and her **husband's** family **name** would come to an end.

14:8 David assured the woman that he would **issue a command** protecting her living son, but the woman's words in verses 9-11 suggest the matter was not settled in her mind.

14:9 The woman's words suggested she had put David in a difficult position to let a murderer go free, and she asked that **any blame** rest on her and her family.

and my father's house, and may the king and his throne be innocent."

[10]"Whoever speaks to you," the king said, "bring him to me. He will not trouble you again!"

[11]She replied, "Please, may the king invoke the LORD your God, so that the avenger of blood will not increase the loss, and they will not eliminate my son!"[a]

"As the LORD lives," he vowed, "not a hair of your son will fall to the ground."[b]

[12]Then the woman said, "Please, may your servant speak a word to my lord the king?"

"Speak," he replied.

[13]The woman asked, "Why have you devised something similar against the people of God? When the king spoke as he did about this matter, he has pronounced his own •guilt. The king has not brought back his own banished one. [14]We will certainly die[c] and be like water poured out on the ground, which can't be recovered. But God would not take away a life; He would devise plans so that the one banished from Him does not remain banished.

[15]"Now therefore, I've come to present this matter to my lord the king because the people have made me afraid. Your servant thought: I must speak to the king. Perhaps the king will grant his servant's request. [16]The king will surely listen in order to rescue his servant from the hand of this man who would eliminate both me and my son from God's inheritance. [17]Your servant thought: May the word of my lord the king bring relief, for my lord the king is able to discern the good and the

bad like the Angel of God. May the LORD your God be with you."

[18]Then the king answered the woman, "I'm going to ask you something; don't conceal it from me!"

"Let my lord the king speak," the woman replied.

[19]The king asked, "Did Joab put you up to[A] all this?"

The woman answered. "As you live, my lord the king, no one can turn to the right or left from all my lord the king says. Yes, your servant Joab is the one who gave orders to me; he told your servant exactly what to say. [20]Joab your servant has done this to address the issue indirectly,[B] but my lord has wisdom like the wisdom of the Angel of God, knowing everything on earth."

[21]Then the king said to Joab, "I hereby grant this request. Go, bring back the young man Absalom."

[22]Joab fell with his face to the ground in homage and praised the king. "Today," Joab said, "your servant knows I have found favor with you, my lord the king, because the king has granted the request of your servant."

[23]So Joab got up, went to Geshur, and brought Absalom[d] to Jerusalem. [24]However, the king added, "He may return to his house, but he may not see my face." So Absalom returned to his house, but he did not see the king.[c]

[25]No man in all Israel was as handsome and highly praised as Absalom. From the sole of his foot to the top of his head, he did not have

[a]14:11 Nm 35:19-21; Dt 19:12   [b]Ac 27:34   [c]14:14 Jn 8:51   [d]14:23 2Sm 13:38

[A]14:19 Lit *Is the hand of Joab in*   [B]14:20 Lit *to go around the face of the matter*   [C]14:24 Lit *king's face*

14:10 David further assured her that no one would **trouble** her any more.

14:11 The woman persisted, asking David to **invoke** an oath before **the LORD** that her **son** would not die. David vowed that everything would be okay.

14:12 The woman had received her judgment, but she broke protocol and requested a chance to **speak** a further **word** to the king—a request David granted.

14:13 The woman gently but precisely drew a parallel between her situation and David's. Her words **the king . . . has pronounced his own guilt** implied David was unwilling to give himself the same judgment he gave the woman. He was unwilling to restore Absalom, who had murdered Amnon.

14:14 The woman also appealed to God's grace. The Lord takes sin seriously, but He also tries to restore **the one banished from Him**.

14:15-16 The woman acted as though she was returning to **the matter** of her **son** and her **inheritance**.

14:17 The woman's closing words were somewhat ambiguous in their application. Would **the word of . . . the king bring relief** for her or for David? Her blessing, **May the LORD**

your God be with you, may have hinted that just as the king could **discern the good and the bad** for others, perhaps with God's help he could discern for himself the wisest thing to do about Absalom.

14:18 David was indeed discerning, and he suspected the woman's collaboration with a member of the royal family.

14:20 The woman confessed that **Joab** had used her **to address the issue indirectly**, but David had seen through her presentation.

14:21 Despite David's recognition of Joab's ploy, he asked his nephew to bring **Absalom** from Geshur.

14:22 **Joab** appeared pleased to have played a part in beginning the reconciliation process between David and Absalom.

14:24 Ironically, David gave **Absalom** permission to **return to his house**, but he would not give Absalom an audience. David's "halfway" decision only inflamed the tension between himself and his son.

14:25 The description of Absalom's physical appearance makes him sound like a leader, and it prepares the reader for Absalom's coup attempt in chapter 15.

14:26 **Five pounds** is literally "200 shekels." Many manu-

a single flaw. [26] When he shaved his head—he shaved it every year because his hair got so heavy for him that he had to shave it off—he would weigh the hair from his head and it would be five pounds[A] according to the royal standard.

[27] Three sons were born to Absalom, and a daughter named Tamar, who was a beautiful woman. [28] Absalom resided in Jerusalem two years but never saw the king. [29] Then Absalom sent for Joab in order to send him to the king, but Joab was unwilling to come. So he sent again, a second time, but he still wouldn't come. [30] Then Absalom said to his servants, "See, Joab has a field right next to mine, and he has barley there. Go and set fire to it!" So Absalom's servants set the field on fire.[B]

[31] Then Joab came to Absalom's house and demanded, "Why did your servants set my field on fire?"

[32] "Look," Absalom explained to Joab, "I sent for you and said, 'Come here. I want to send you to the king to ask: Why have I come back from Geshur? I'd be better off if I were still there.' So now, let me see the king. If I am guilty, let him kill me."

[33] Joab went to the king and told him. So David summoned Absalom, who came to the king and bowed down with his face to the ground before him. Then the king kissed Absalom.

Absalom's Revolt

15 After this, Absalom got himself a chariot, horses, and 50 men to run before him.[a]

a15:1 1Sm 8:11; 1Kg 1:5
b15:2 Ru 4:1-11; 2Sm 19:8; Jb 29:7
c15:8 2Sm 13:37-38
d Gn 28:20-21; 1Sm 1:11
e15:9 1Sm 1:17
f15:10 1Kg 1:33-34; 2Kg 9:13

[2] He would get up early and stand beside the road leading to the city •gate.[b] Whenever anyone had a grievance to bring before the king for settlement, Absalom called out to him and asked, "What city are you from?" If he replied, "Your servant is from one of the tribes of Israel," [3] Absalom said to him, "Look, your claims are good and right, but the king does not have anyone to listen to you." [4] He added, "If only someone would appoint me judge in the land. Then anyone who had a grievance or dispute could come to me, and I would make sure he received justice." [5] When a person approached to bow down to him, Absalom reached out his hand, took hold of him, and kissed him. [6] Absalom did this to all the Israelites who came to the king for a settlement. So Absalom stole the hearts of the men of Israel.

[7] When four[c] years had passed, Absalom said to the king, "Please let me go to Hebron to fulfill a vow I made to the LORD. [8] For your servant made a vow when I lived in Geshur of Aram,[c] saying: If the LORD really brings me back to Jerusalem, I will worship the LORD in Hebron."[D,d]

[9] "Go in peace," the king said to him.[e] So he went to Hebron.

[10] Then Absalom sent messengers throughout the tribes of Israel with this message: "When you hear the sound of the ram's horn, you are to say, 'Absalom has become king in Hebron!'"[f]

[11] Two hundred men from Jerusalem went

A14:26 Lit 200 shekels   B14:30 DSS, LXX add So Joab's servants came to him with their clothes torn and said, "Absalom's servants have set the field on fire!"   C15:7 Some LXX mss, Syr, Vg; other LXX mss, MT read 40   D15:8 Some LXX mss; MT omits in Hebron

---

scripts say "100 shekels." Absalom's thick **hair** would have made him appear strong and powerful to many people.

14:27 Absalom had **a daughter named Tamar**. This was his way of honoring his sister.

14:28 Both David and **Absalom** lived in **Jerusalem**, but they did not speak to each other for **two years** as the tension between them mounted.

14:30 **Absalom** knew if he **set the field** of Joab **on fire**, Joab could no longer avoid talking to him as he had done up to that point.

14:32 Absalom asked **Joab** to get him an audience with David. He suggested it would have been preferable for him to remain in **Geshur**. Absalom wanted his father to decide once and for all how he would handle his murder of Amnon.

14:33 Absalom finally met with his father, David, but this one meeting would not heal a wound that had festered for five years (v. 28; 13:38).

15:1 By gathering **chariots, horses**, and **men**, Absalom took steps to enhance his position in the eyes of the people.

15:2 The **city gate** was the site of the city's important business transactions.

15:3 **Absalom** listened to the petitions that citizens planned to take to **the king**. He ostensibly sympathized with them over the fact that the king did **not have anyone** to help them with these concerns.

15:4 Absalom used the word **judge**, but he really intended for the people to think of him as "king." He insisted he would dispense **justice** better than his overburdened father.

15:5-6 Absalom prevented people from bowing to him, and he greeted them with a kiss (almost as equals). This **stole the hearts of the men of Israel**, many of whom began to believe that Absalom understood their problems better than David did.

15:7 Some manuscripts read "40 years" instead of **four years** while others read "40 days," but the HCSB reading seems most likely.

15:8 The law urged prompt fulfillment of a **vow** (Dt 23:21), so the passage of four years since Absalom's vow (2Sm 15:7) could have raised questions in David's mind. On the other hand, **Hebron**, located 19 miles south of Jerusalem, was Absalom's birthplace.

15:10 The sound of the **ram's horn** across the land, combined with Absalom's messengers shouting **Absalom has become king in Hebron**, would enable news of Absalom's assuming the throne to spread quickly. Absalom probably

with Absalom. They had been invited and were going innocently, for they knew nothing about the whole matter. [12]While he was offering the sacrifices, Absalom sent for David's adviser Ahithophel the Gilonite,[a] from his city of Giloh. So the conspiracy grew strong, and the people supporting Absalom continued to increase.

[13]Then an informer came to David and reported, "The hearts of the men of Israel are with Absalom."

[14]David said to all the servants with him in Jerusalem, "Get up. We have to flee, or we will not escape from Absalom![b] Leave quickly, or he will soon overtake us, heap disaster on us, and strike the city with the edge of the sword."

[15]The king's servants said to him, "Whatever my lord the king decides, we are your servants." [16]Then the king set out, and his entire household followed him. But he left behind 10 concubines to take care of the palace. [17]So the king set out, and all the people followed him. They stopped at the last house [18]while all his servants marched past him. Then all the Cherethites, the Pelethites, and the Gittites—600 men who came with him from Gath[c]—marched past the king.

[19]The king said to Ittai the Gittite,[d] "Why are you also going with us? Go back and stay with the new king since you're both a foreigner and an exile from your homeland. [20]Besides,

you only arrived yesterday; should I make you wander around with us today while I go wherever I can? Go back and take your brothers with you. May the Lord show you kindness and faithfulness."

[21]But in response, Ittai vowed to the king, "As the Lord lives and as my lord the king lives, wherever my lord the king is, whether it means life or death, your servant will be there!"

[22]"March on," David replied to Ittai. So Ittai the Gittite marched past with all his men and the children who were with him. [23]Everyone in the countryside was weeping loudly while all the people were marching past. As the king was crossing the Kidron Valley, all the people were marching past on the road that leads to the desert.

[24]Zadok was also there, and all the Levites with him were carrying the ark of the covenant of God. They set the ark of God down, and Abiathar offered sacrifices[A] until the people had finished marching past.[e] [25]Then the king instructed Zadok, "Return the ark of God to the city.[f] If I find favor in the Lord's eyes, He will bring me back and allow me to see both it and its dwelling place.[g] [26]However, if He should say, 'I do not delight in you,' then here I am—He can do with me whatever pleases Him."[B,h]

[27]The king also said to Zadok the priest,[i] "Look,[C] return to the city in peace and your

a 15:12 1Ch 27:33; Ps 41:9; 55:12-14
b 15:14 Ps 3 title
c 15:18 1Sm 27:2-7
d 15:19 2Sm 18:2
e 15:24 2Sm 8:17; 20:25
f 15:25 1Sm 4:3
g Ps 43:3
h 15:26 1Sm 3:18
i 15:27 2Sm 8:17; 20:25-26; 1Kg 1:7-8

A 15:24 Or Abiathar went up   B 15:26 Lit me what is good in His eyes   C 15:27 LXX; MT reads Are you a seer?

hoped he could get to Jerusalem and take power before David could prepare to defend himself.

15:12 David's adviser **Ahithophel** was one of the king's wisest men, making the **conspiracy** of Absalom even more **strong**.

15:14 David summoned his **servants with him in Jerusalem** and insisted they all needed to **flee** at once. He knew Absalom and his forces would head straight for the capital and attack it if necessary.

15:17 David and his officials **stopped at the last house** (perhaps the house at the edge of Jerusalem), probably to get organized for their flight eastward.

15:18 On **Cherethites** and **Pelethites**, see note at 8:18. David's influence among the Philistines had gained him the loyalty of **600 men . . . from Gath**.

15:19 **Ittai the Gittite** was **an exile** from Philistia who had cast his lot with David, perhaps during David's flight from Saul (1Sm 18-31).

15:21 David excused **Ittai** from accompanying him, but Ittai swore by the **Lord** and **the king** that he would stay with David whether it meant **life or death** for him. David's integrity still garnered respect.

15:23 The **Kidron Valley** skirted Jerusalem's eastern edge, separating the city from the Mount of Olives. Once David and his associates reached the top, they could travel **the road that leads to the desert** (lit "wilderness"), most likely

the ascent of Adummim that connected Jerusalem with Jericho in the Jordan Valley.

15:24 The **ark of the covenant of God** was probably brought to ensure God's presence and as a mark of David's legitimate right to reign. **Zadok** and **Abiathar** (see note at 8:17)

shalom

Hebrew Pronunciation	[shah LOAM]
HCSB Translation	peace
Uses in 2 Samuel	16
Uses in the OT	237
Focus Passage	2 Samuel 15:9,27

Shalom is in an important OT theological word family. The root occurs in all Semitic languages with meanings similar to Hebrew. *Shalom* usually means *peace* (Gn 15:15) and can function adverbially *(peaceably)* and adjectivally *(peaceful)*. Safety (Zch 8:10) is also a frequent connotation *(safe, safely)*. The noun indicates *welfare* (1Sm 17:18), *assurance* (1Sm 20:42), *prosperity* (Is 9:7), *success* (Is 45:7), or *strength* (Ps 38:3). *Shalom* can be a *favorable answer* (Gn 41:16) or *allies* (Ps 69:22). Other adverbial ideas are *well* (Gn 29:6), *quietly* (1Sm 29:7), *completely* (Jr 13:19), and *all right* (2Sm 18:29). Adjectivally, *shalom* can mean *satisfied* (Ex 18:23), *secure* (Jb 5:24), or *unscathed* (Jr 43:12). "Asking about *shalom*" is greeting (1Sm 30:21) or asking how someone is (1Sm 10:4). "Men of *shalom*" are people *trusted* (Jr 20:10) or *trusted friends* (Jr 38:22). "Speaking *shalom*" is speaking *in friendly ways* (Ps 28:3).

two sons with you: your son Ahimaaz and Abiathar's son Jonathan. [28]Remember, I'll wait at the fords of the wilderness until word comes from you to inform me." [29]So Zadok and Abiathar returned the ark of God to Jerusalem and stayed there.

[30]David was climbing the slope of the Mount of Olives, weeping as he ascended. His head was covered, and he was walking barefoot.[a] Each of the people with him covered their heads and went up, weeping as they ascended.

[31]Then someone reported to David: "Ahithophel is among the conspirators with Absalom."

"LORD," David pleaded, "please turn the counsel of Ahithophel into foolishness!"[b]

[32]When David came to the summit where he used to worship God, Hushai the Archite[c] was there to meet him with his robe torn and dust on his head. [33]David said to him, "If you go away with me, you'll be a burden to me, [34]but if you return to the city and tell Absalom, 'I will be your servant, my king! Previously, I was your father's servant, but now I will be your servant,' then you can counteract Ahithophel's counsel for me. [35]Won't Zadok and Abiathar the priests be there with you? Report everything you hear from the king's palace to Zadok and Abiathar the priests. [36]Take note: their two sons, Zadok's son Ahimaaz and Abi-

a15:30 Is 20:2-4; Mc 1:8
b15:31 2Sm 16:21; 17:14,23
c15:32 Jos 16:2
d15:37 1Ch 27:33
e16:1 2Sm 9:12
f16:4 2Sm 9:3-11

athar's son Jonathan, are there with them. Send me everything you hear through them." [37]So Hushai,[d] David's personal adviser, entered Jerusalem just as Absalom was entering the city.

Ziba Helps David

16 When David had gone a little beyond the summit,[A] Ziba, Mephibosheth's servant,[e] was right there to meet him. He had a pair of saddled donkeys loaded with 200 loaves of bread, 100 clusters of raisins, 100 bunches of summer fruit, and a skin of wine. [2]The king said to Ziba, "Why do you have these?"

Ziba answered, "The donkeys are for the king's household to ride, the bread and summer fruit are for the young men to eat, and the wine is for those to drink who become exhausted in the desert."

[3]"Where is your master's grandson?" the king asked.

"Why, he's staying in Jerusalem," Ziba replied to the king, "for he said, 'Today, the house of Israel will restore my grandfather's kingdom to me.'"

[4]The king said to Ziba, "All that belongs to Mephibosheth is now yours!"[f]

"I bow before you," Ziba said. "May you look favorably on me, my lord the king!"

Shimei Curses David

[5]When King David got to Bahurim, a man

A16:1 = Mount of Olives

---

stood by the king who had endorsed their respective ministries and the ministries of the **Levites** (6:12-18).

15:25-26 David determined that **the ark of God** properly belonged in Jerusalem, God's city. It would remain there, and it was up to God to either restore David to his throne in Jerusalem or not. The king was content to leave the matter in God's hands.

15:27 David created a spy network that included **Zadok**, Abiathar, and their respective sons **Ahimaaz** and **Jonathan**.

15:28 The **fords of the wilderness** were shallow places where the Jordan River could be crossed.

15:29 Absalom would probably assume David's supporters had fled. He may not have suspected **Zadok** and **Abiathar** of siding with his father.

15:30 Covering the **head** and **walking barefoot** were signs of deep personal anguish.

15:31 The news that **Ahithophel** had joined the **conspirators with Absalom** was a blow to David's cause. The king's prayer for God to **turn the counsel of Ahithophel into foolishness** was a prayer of great faith because Ahithophel's advice was taken to be like a word from the Lord (16:23).

15:32 **Hushai** would end up being the answer to David's prayer (v. 31).

15:34-35 Hushai's role was to **counteract Ahithophel's**

counsel (no small task in light of 16:23) and to **report everything** to **Zadok and Abiathar**.

15:36 **Ahimaaz** and **Jonathan** would then relay any information they received from their fathers directly to David.

15:37 **Hushai** and **Absalom** arrived in Jerusalem at the same time. The decisive moment when Absalom had to choose between Hushai's counsel or Ahithophel's counsel is delayed by 16:1-14 and resumes at 16:15.

16:1 A **little beyond the summit** on the eastern side of the Mount of Olives, David's delegation could not be seen by Absalom or anyone else in Jerusalem. **Ziba, Mephibosheth's servant**, had earlier arranged for Saul's estate to be restored to his master (9:1-10). Now he brought provisions for David's group, but with a different motive.

16:3 David expressed surprise that Mephibosheth had not come with him and others from his palace. Ziba informed David that Mephibosheth was **staying in Jerusalem** because he was hoping to take advantage of the situation to regain Saul's kingdom.

16:4 The truth of Ziba's assertion could not be substantiated, but David, in his turbulent emotional state, decided he believed **Ziba** and rewarded him with Mephibosheth's estate.

16:5 **Bahurim** was a nearby Benjaminite village. **Shimei son of Gera** is unknown except for his actions related to Absalom's revolt and David's flight (19:16-23) and his sentence during Solomon's reign (1Kg 2:8-9,36-46).

belonging to the family of the house of Saul was just coming out. His name was Shimei son of Gera,^{a} and he was yelling curses as he approached. ^{6}He threw stones at David and at all the royal^A servants, the people and the warriors on David's right and left. ^{7}Shimei said as he cursed: "Get out, get out, you worthless murderer! ^{8}The LORD has paid you back for all the blood of the house of Saul in whose place you rule, and the LORD has handed the kingdom over to your son Absalom. Look, you are in trouble because you're a murderer!"

^{9}Then Abishai son of Zeruiah said to the king, "Why should this dead dog^b curse my lord the king?^{c} Let me go over and cut his head off!"

^{10}The king replied, "Sons of Zeruiah, do we agree on anything?^{d} He curses^e me this way because the LORD^B told him, 'Curse David!' Therefore, who can say, 'Why did you do that?'" ^{11}Then David said to Abishai and all his servants, "Look, my own son, my own flesh and blood,^{c} intends to take my life^f—how much more now this Benjaminite! Leave him alone and let him curse me; the LORD has told him to. ^{12}Perhaps the LORD will see my affliction^D and restore goodness to me instead of Shimei's curses today." ^{13}So David and his men proceeded along the road as Shimei was going along the ridge of the hill opposite him.

As Shimei went, he cursed David, and threw stones and dirt at him. ^{14}Finally, the king and all the people with him arrived^E exhausted, so they rested there.

Absalom's Advisers

^{15}Now Absalom and all the Israelites came to Jerusalem. Ahithophel was also with him. ^{16}When David's friend Hushai the Archite came to Absalom, Hushai said to Absalom, "Long live the king! Long live the king!"^{g}

^{17}"Is this your loyalty to your friend?" Absalom asked Hushai. "Why didn't you go with your friend?"

^{18}"Not at all," Hushai answered Absalom. "I am on the side of the one that the LORD, the people, and all the men of Israel have chosen. I will stay with him. ^{19}Furthermore, whom will I serve if not his son? As I served in your father's presence, I will also serve in yours."^{h}

^{20}Then Absalom said to Ahithophel, "Give me your advice. What should we do?"

^{21}Ahithophel replied to Absalom, "Sleep with your father's concubines he left to take care of the palace.^{i} When all Israel hears that you have become repulsive to your father, everyone with you will be encouraged." ^{22}So they pitched a tent for Absalom on the roof, and he slept with his father's concubines in the sight of all Israel.^{j}

Cross references (center column)

^{a}16:5 1Kg 2:8-9,36-46
^{b}16:9 1Sm 24:14; 2Sm 9:8
^{c}Ex 22:28
^{d}16:10 2Sm 3:39; 19:22
^{e}1Sm 17:43; 2Sm 16:5; Ec 7:21-22
^{f}16:11 2Sm 12:10-11
^{g}16:16 1Sm 10:24; 1Kg 1:25; 2Kg 11:12
^{h}16:19 2Sm 15:34
^{i}16:21 2Sm 15:16; 20:3
^{j}16:22 2Sm 12:11-12

---

^{A}16:6 Lit all King David's ^{B}16:10 Alt Hb tradition reads If he curses, and if the LORD ^{C}16:11 Lit son who came from my belly ^{D}16:12 Some Hb mss, LXX, Syr, Vg; one Hb tradition reads iniquity; alt Hb tradition reads eyes; ancient Jewish tradition reads will look with His eye ^{E}16:14 LXX adds at the Jordan

---

16:8 The phrase **blood of the house of Saul** might have assumed that David participated in either Saul's death or Ishbosheth's death. Some interpreters believe David's giving of Saul's descendants to the Gibeonites for execution (21:5-9) had happened already, and that Shimei may have been alluding to that.

16:9 Abishai was disturbed that someone would **curse . . . the king** (cp. 19:21), and he offered to kill Shimei as he had offered to kill Saul several years before (1Sm 26:8).

16:10 Do we agree on anything? is literally "What to me and to you?" It may be rhetorically asking what interests David and Abishai have in common (cp. 19:22; Jdg 11:12; 1Kg 17:18; 2Kg 3:13; 2Ch 35:21; Jn 2:4). This expression reveals David's exasperation with the **sons of Zeruiah** his sister, here more specifically focused at Abishai. The sentence that begins with **He curses me this way** may also be translated as "if he curses me this way" and suggests that David was unsure of the source of Shimei's words (v. 11).

16:11 David highlighted his desperate situation. He was under threat of death from his **own son** Absalom, so perhaps Shimei's words were also part of God's instruction to the king.

16:12 David thought that perhaps if he bore **Shimei's curses** with patience, **the LORD** would **restore goodness** to him.

16:14 David and his officials were **exhausted** from the long journey and from the stress of Shimei's cursing as they traveled, so they took a much-needed rest.

16:15 Now is probably better translated as "meanwhile" to communicate the fact that even as David was fleeing, **Absalom** and his supporters arrived at **Jerusalem**. The conspirators took the city without a fight because David's forces had fled.

16:16 The account now picks up from 15:37. **Hushai** and **Absalom** entered Jerusalem about the same time, and Hushai's greeting, **Long live the king**, was the beginning of his attempt to convince Absalom he was on his side.

16:17 Absalom questioned Hushai's **loyalty** because he knew of Hushai's faithful service to his father, David.

16:18 Hushai's reply was more vague than Absalom realized. David—not Absalom—was the one whom **the LORD** had **chosen** (1Sm 16:12).

16:19 Hushai promised Absalom that just as he had served faithfully in David's **presence**, he now would continue to **serve** in the same way at Absalom's side.

16:21 Absalom's lying with his **father's concubines** would be a visible sign to everyone that Absalom was taking over the kingdom (including the harem) from David (12:8,11). Doing so would also sharpen the division between Absalom and his father and encourage others to forsake David and join Absalom.

16:22 In the sight of all Israel fulfilled God's words to David through the prophet Nathan (12:11).

16:23 The advice Ahithophel gave was normally **like some-**

²³Now the advice Ahithophel gave in those days was like someone asking about a word from God*—such was the regard that both David and Absalom had for Ahithophel's advice.

17 ¹Ahithophel said to Absalom, "Let me choose 12,000 men, and I will set out in pursuit of David tonight. ²I will attack him while he is weak and weary, throw him into a panic, and all the people with him will scatter. I will strike down only the king ³and bring all the people back to you. When everyone returns except the man you're seeking, all^A the people will be at peace." ⁴This proposal seemed good to Absalom and all the elders of Israel.

⁵Then Absalom said, "Summon Hushai the Archite also. Let's hear what he has to say as well."

⁶So Hushai came to Absalom, and Absalom told him: "Ahithophel offered this proposal. Should we carry out his proposal? If not, what do you say?"

⁷Hushai replied to Absalom, "The advice Ahithophel has given this time is not good." ⁸Hushai continued, "You know your father and his men. They are warriors and are desperate like a wild bear robbed of her cubs. Your father is an experienced soldier who won't spend the night with the people. ⁹He's probably already hiding in one of the caves^B or some other place. If some of our troops fall^C first, someone is sure to hear and say, 'There's been a slaughter among the people who follow Absalom.' ¹⁰Then, even a brave man with

the heart of a lion^b will melt because all Israel knows that your father and the valiant men with him are warriors. ¹¹Instead, I advise that all Israel from Dan to Beer-sheba—as numerous as the sand by the sea—be gathered to you and that you personally go into battle. ¹²Then we will attack David wherever we find him, and we will descend on him like dew on the ground. Not even one will be left of all the men with him. ¹³If he retreats to some city, all Israel will bring ropes to that city, and we will drag its stones into the valley until not even a pebble can be found there." ¹⁴Since the LORD had decreed^c that Ahithophel's good advice be undermined^d in order to bring about Absalom's ruin, Absalom and all the men of Israel said, "The advice of Hushai the Archite is better than Ahithophel's advice."

David Informed of Absalom's Plans

¹⁵Hushai then told the priests Zadok and Abiathar, "This is what^D Ahithophel advised Absalom and the elders of Israel, and this is what^E I advised. ¹⁶Now send someone quickly and tell David, 'Don't spend the night at the wilderness ford of the Jordan,^e but be sure to cross over, or the king and all the people with him will be destroyed.'"

¹⁷Jonathan and Ahimaaz were staying at En-rogel, where a servant girl would come and pass along information to them. They in turn would go and inform King David, because they dared not be seen entering the city. ¹⁸However,

*16:23 2Sm 15:12 *17:10 Am 3:8 *17:14 Pr 21:30; 1Co 1:19 *2Sm 15:31-34 *17:16 2Sm 15:28

^A17:3 LXX reads *to you as a bride returns to her husband. You seek the life of only one man, and all* ^B17:9 Or *pits, or ravines* ^C17:9 Lit *And it will be when a falling on them at* ^D17:15 Lit *Like this and like this* ^E17:15 Lit *and like this and like this*

one asking about a word from God. This time, however, his counsel was politically wise but immoral since David was still alive (Lv 20:11).

17:2 Ahithophel believed **panic** would envelop David and his followers if Absalom's forces came upon them while the king was **weak and weary**. Rather than turning the battle into a civil war, Ahithophel would then strike down **only the king**.

17:3 Ahithophel thought if David could be killed quickly, **all the people** would accept Absalom's kingship.

17:6 **Hushai** probably knew Ahithophel's **proposal** would succeed. He had to convince **Absalom** to delay in pressing the attack against David.

17:7 Hushai's negative evaluation was probably surprising to his hearers in view of Ahithophel's reputation (16:23).

17:8-10 Hushai cited David's military genius. The king would anticipate Absalom's quick strike and hence would not **spend the night with the people** but would hide in one of the many **caves** (or pits or ravines) on the northern edge of the Dead Sea. Further, any news of a setback among the people who followed Absalom could lead to popular support swinging back to David again.

17:11 From **Dan to Beer-sheba** was a distance of 110 miles.

The two cities basically served as the northern and southern points of Israel, so Hushai is calling for a nation-wide muster. Hushai's proposal was much more extensive and time-consuming, giving David and his forces time to regroup.

17:12 Hushai suggested that David and **all the men with him** should die—well beyond what Ahithophel had proposed. This strategy might appeal to Absalom's vengeful pride.

17:14 The Lord guided the fateful discussion to answer David's prayer (15:31).

17:15 Now that he knew Absalom's strategy, **Hushai** moved quickly to relay the information to **Zadok** and **Abiathar** (15:27-29).

17:16 Having received some escape time through Hushai's counsel to Absalom, David's forces needed to put distance between themselves and Absalom's forces as quickly as possible. Of course, if Absalom decided to follow Ahithophel's advice after all, Hushai's advice to David was all the more urgent.

17:17 **En-rogel** was a spring in the Kidron Valley about one-fourth of a mile from Jerusalem where the Kidron and Hinnom valleys met.

17:18 **Bahurim** was the village in Benjamin from which Shimei came (16:5).

a young man did see them and informed Absalom. So the two left quickly and came to the house of a man in Bahurim. He had a well in his courtyard, and they climbed down into it. ¹⁹Then his wife took the cover, placed it over the mouth of the well, and scattered grain on it so nobody would know anything.

²⁰Absalom's servants came to the woman at the house and asked, "Where are Ahimaaz and Jonathan?"

"They passed by toward the water,"ᴬ the woman replied to them. The men searched but did not find them, so they returned to Jerusalem.

²¹After they had gone, Ahimaaz and Jonathan climbed out of the well and went and informed King David. They told him, "Get up and immediately ford the river, for Ahithophel has given this advice against you." ²²So David and all the people with him got up and crossed the Jordan. By daybreak, there was no one who had not crossed the Jordan. ²³When Ahithophel realized that his advice had not been followed, he saddled his donkey and set out for his house in his hometown. He set his affairs in orderᴮ and hanged himself. So he died and was buried in his father's tomb.

²⁴David had arrived at Mahanaim by the time Absalom crossed the Jordan with all the men of Israel. ²⁵Now Absalom had appointed Amasaᵃ over the army in Joab's place. Amasa was the son of a man named Ithraᶜ the Israelite;ᴰ,ᵇ Ithra had married Abigail daughter of Nahash.ᴱ Abigail was a sister to Zeruiah, Joab's mother. ²⁶And Israel and Absalom camped in the land of Gilead. ²⁷When David

ᵃ17:25 2Sm 19:13; 20:9-12; 1Kg 2:5,32
ᵇ1Ch 2:13-17
ᶜ17:27 2Sm 10:1-2
ᵈ2Sm 12:26-29
ᵉ2Sm 9:4
ᶠ2Sm 19:31-32; 1Kg 2:7; Ezr 2:61
ᵍ18:3 2Sm 21:17

came to Mahanaim, Shobi son of Nahashᶜ from Rabbahᵈ of the Ammonites, Machir son of Ammiel from Lo-debar,ᵉ and Barzillai the Gileadite from Rogelimᶠ ²⁸brought beds, basins,ᶠ and pottery items. They also brought wheat, barley, flour, roasted grain, beans, lentils,ᴳ ²⁹honey, curds, sheep, and cheeseᴴ from the herd for David and the people with him to eat. They had reasoned, "The people must be hungry, exhausted, and thirsty in the desert."

Absalom's Defeat

18 David reviewed his troops and appointed commanders of hundreds and of thousands over them. ²He then sent out the troops, a third under Joab, a third under Joab's brother Abishai son of Zeruiah, and a third under Ittai the Gittite. The king said to the troops, "I will also march out with you."

³"You must not go!"ᵍ the people pleaded. "If we have to flee, they will not pay any attention to us. Even if half of us die, they will not pay any attention to us because you are worthⁱ 10,000 of us. Therefore, it is better if you support us from the city."

⁴"I will do whatever you think is best," the king replied to them. So he stood beside the gate while all the troops marched out by hundreds and thousands. ⁵The king commanded Joab, Abishai, and Ittai, "Treat the young man Absalom gently for my sake." All the people heard the king's orders to all the commanders about Absalom.

⁶Then David's forces marched into the field to engage Israel in battle, which took place in the forest of Ephraim. ⁷The people of Is-

ᴬ17:20 Or brook; Hb obscure   ᴮ17:23 Lit He commanded his house   ᶜ17:25 Or Jether   ᴰ17:25 Some LXX mss read Ishmaelite   ᴱ17:25 Some LXX mss read Jesse   ᶠ17:28 LXX reads brought 10 embroidered beds with double coverings, 10 vessels   ᴳ17:28 LXX, Syr; MT adds roasted grain   ᴴ 17:29 Hb obscure   ⁱ18:3 Some Hb mss, LXX, Vg; other Hb mss read because there would now be about

17:19 The woman **scattered grain** to make it look like the cover had not been recently disturbed.

17:20 **Absalom's servants** must have received word that **Ahimaaz and Jonathan** had gone to or toward Bahurim.

17:21 The advice of **Ahimaaz and Jonathan** further suggested that it was still uncertain what Absalom would do (v. 16).

17:23 Ahithophel knew that since **his advice had not been followed**, David would regain the throne. And when David was reestablished, Ahithophel would be considered a traitor. Thus he committed suicide.

17:24 **Mahanaim** was more than 30 miles from Jerusalem. So David and his men may have been about 20 miles from **Absalom** when he **crossed the Jordan**.

17:25 **Amasa** was another of David's nephews and a cousin of Joab and Abishai (19:13; 20:8-13).

17:27 **Machir** had cared for Mephibosheth before David brought Mephibosheth to his palace (9:4).

17:28-29 These men of influence knew about David's quick flight from Jerusalem, and they brought him food and supplies. These provisions restored the bodies and spirits of the king's group.

18:1 The phrase **commanders of hundreds and of thousands** shows that David had been able to rally considerable support for his cause.

18:2 Dividing his warriors into thirds would provide David more flexibility in battling Absalom's forces.

18:3 The people considered David's suggestion to march out with them too risky, so they prevailed on him to **support** them **from the city**—to stay away from direct confrontation with Absalom's forces.

18:5 The text makes it clear that David gave specific instructions about Absalom's treatment, and it emphasizes that **all the people heard the king's orders**.

18:6 The **forest of Ephraim** lay a few miles northwest of Mahanaim.

18:7-8 David divided his troops into three groups. This al-

rael were defeated by David's soldiers, and the slaughter there was vast that day—20,000 casualties. [8] The battle spread over the entire region, and that day the forest claimed more people than the sword.

Absalom's Death

[9] Absalom was riding on his mule when he happened to meet David's soldiers. When the mule went under the tangled branches of a large oak tree, Absalom's head was caught fast in the tree. The mule under him kept going, so he was suspended in midair.[A] [10] One of the men saw him and informed Joab. He said, "I just saw Absalom hanging in an oak tree!"

[11] "You just saw him!" Joab exclaimed.[B] "Why didn't you strike him to the ground right there? I would have given you 10 silver pieces[C] and a belt!"

[12] The man replied to Joab, "Even if I had the weight of 1,000 pieces of silver[D] in my hand, I would not raise my hand against the king's son. For we heard the king command you, Abishai, and Ittai, 'Protect the young man Absalom for me.'[E,a] [13] If I had jeopardized my own[F] life—and nothing is hidden from the king—you would have abandoned me."

[14] Joab said, "I'm not going to waste time with you!" He then took three spears in his hand and thrust them into Absalom's heart while he was still alive in the oak tree, [15] and 10 young men who were Joab's armor-bearers surrounded Absalom, struck him, and killed him.

[16] Afterward, Joab blew the ram's horn, and the troops broke off their pursuit of Israel because Joab restrained them. [17] They took Absalom, threw him into a large pit in the forest, and piled a huge mound of stones over him.[b] And all Israel fled, each to his tent.[c]

[18] When he was alive, Absalom had set up a pillar[d] for himself in the King's Valley,[e] for he had said, "I have no son[f] to preserve the memory of my name." So he gave the pillar his name. It is still called Absalom's Monument today.

[19] Ahimaaz son of Zadok[g] said, "Please let me run and tell the king the good news that the LORD has delivered him from his enemies."

[20] Joab replied to him, "You are not the man to take good news today. You may do it another day, but today you aren't taking good news, because the king's son is dead." [21] Joab then said to the •Cushite, "Go tell the king what you have seen." The Cushite bowed to Joab and took off running.

[22] However, Ahimaaz son of Zadok persisted and said to Joab, "No matter what, please let me also run behind the Cushite!"

Joab replied, "My son, why do you want to run since you won't get a reward?"

[23] "No matter what, I want to run!"

"Then run!" Joab said to him. So Ahimaaz ran by way of the plain and outran the Cushite.

[24] David was sitting between the two gates[h] when the watchman went up to the roof of the gate and over to the wall.[i] The watchman looked out and saw a man running alone. [25] He called out and told the king.

---

*a*18:12 2Sm 18:5 *b*18:17 Jos 7:24-26; 8:29 *c*1Sm 4:10; 2Sm 19:8; 20:1,22; 2Kg 8:21 *d*18:18 Gn 28:18; Dt 16:22; 1Sm 15:12; 2Kg 18:4 *e*Gn 14:17 *f*2Sm 14:27 *g*18:19 2Sm 15:36 *h*18:24 2Sm 19:8 *i*2Sm 13:34; 2Kg 9:17

A18:9 Lit was between heaven and earth **B**18:11 Lit Joab said to the man who told him **C**18:11 About 4 ounces of silver **D**18:12 About 25 pounds of silver **E**18:12 Some Hb mss, LXX, Tg, Vg; other Hb mss read Protect, whoever, the young man Absalom; Hb obscure **F**18:13 Alt Hb tradition reads jeopardized his

---

lowed him to spread Absalom's forces thinly **over the entire region**, preventing their united stand in the open country where their superior numbers would give them the advantage. A **forest** presented natural obstacles or threats such as wild animals, pits, low branches, and marshes.

18:11 Joab learned about Absalom's defenseless position. David's general had once again determined to take matters into his own hands for what he believed to be the king's own good.

18:12 This soldier was not ready to disobey a charge that David had given his generals. He also repeated David's charge; the writer is making it clear that Joab knew David's command.

18:13 The warriors did not trust Joab. If they killed Absalom, they thought Joab might let the blame fall on them.

18:14-15 Now at the place where Absalom was hanging **alive in the oak tree**, Joab and his men surrounded him, **struck him, and killed him** in violation of David's order.

18:16 Joab then **blew the ram's horn** to assemble the troops (2:28; 20:1,22). With Absalom dead, the battle was over.

18:17 All Absalom's supporters **fled**, uncertain what reprisal might come from David's victorious forces. Absalom's body was taken down and thrown into **a large pit in the forest** and covered with **a huge mound of stones**, thus denying him a place in his family's tombs and dishonoring him in his death (Jos 7:26).

18:18 Absalom had claimed that he had **no son**. Actually, he had three sons (14:27), so they must have preceded him in death.

18:19 Ahimaaz had been David's trusted messenger throughout the ordeal, and now he wished to carry the **good news** of David's victory. He also may have thought he could more gently break the news of Absalom's death to his father than another messenger could.

18:20 Certain runners brought **good news** and others brought bad news. That way, as soon as a runner was recognized, the people knew the basic outcome (v. 27). Sometimes a solitary runner indicated good news and two runners together indicated bad news (vv. 25-26).

18:23 Ahimaaz appears to have taken the longer but easier route and thus **outran the Cushite**.

The king said, "If he's alone, he bears good news."

As the first runner came closer, [26] the watchman saw another man running. He called out to the gatekeeper, "Look! Another man is running alone!"

"This one is also bringing good news," said the king.

[27] The watchman said, "The way the first man runs looks to me like the way Ahimaaz son of Zadok runs."[a]

"This is a good man; he comes with good news,"[b] the king commented.

[28] Ahimaaz called out to the king, "All is well," and then bowed down to the king with his face to the ground. He continued, "May the LORD your God be praised! He delivered up the men who rebelled against my lord the king."

[29] The king asked, "Is the young man Absalom all right?"

Ahimaaz replied, "When Joab sent the king's servant and your servant, I saw a big disturbance, but I don't know what it was."

[30] The king said, "Move aside and stand here." So he stood to one side.

[31] Just then the Cushite came and said, "May my lord the king hear the good news: today the LORD has delivered you from all those rising up against you!"

[32] The king asked the Cushite, "Is the young man Absalom all right?"

The Cushite replied, "May what has become of the young man happen to the enemies of my lord the king and to all who rise up against you with evil intent."[c]

[33A] The king was deeply moved and went up to the gate chamber and wept. As he walked, he cried, "My son Absalom! My son, my son Absalom! If only I had died instead of you, Absalom, my son, my son!"[d]

Cross-references
a18:27 2Kg 9:20
b1Kg 1:42
c18:32 1Sm 25:26
d18:33 2Sm 19:4
e19:4 2Sm 15:30
f19:7 Pr 14:28
g19:8 2Sm 18:4,24,33
h2Sm 18:17
i19:9 2Sm 8:1-14
j2Sm 5:20; 8:1
k2Sm 15:14

David's Kingdom Restored

19 It was reported to Joab, "The king is weeping. He's mourning over Absalom." [2] That day's victory was turned into mourning for all the troops because on that day the troops heard, "The king is grieving over his son." [3] So they returned to the city quietly that day like people come in when they are humiliated after fleeing in battle. [4] But the king hid his face[e] and cried out at the top of his voice, "My son Absalom! Absalom, my son, my son!"

[5] Then Joab went into the house to the king and said, "Today you have shamed all your soldiers—those who rescued your life and the lives of your sons and daughters, your wives, and your concubines. [6] You love your enemies and hate those who love you! Today you have made it clear that the commanders and soldiers mean nothing to you. In fact, today I know that if Absalom were alive and all of us were dead, it would be fine with you![B]

[7] "Now get up! Go out and encourage[c] your soldiers, for I swear by the LORD that if you don't go out, not a man will remain with you tonight.[f] This will be worse for you than all the trouble that has come to you from your youth until now!"

[8] So the king got up and sat in the •gate,[g] and all the people were told: "Look, the king is sitting in the gate." Then they all came into the king's presence.

Meanwhile, each Israelite had fled to his tent.[h] [9] All the people among all the tribes of Israel were arguing: "The king delivered us from the grasp of our enemies,[i] and he rescued us from the grasp of the Philistines,[j] but now he has fled from the land because of Absalom.[k] [10] But Absalom, the man we anointed over us, has died in battle. So why do you say nothing about restoring the king?"

A18:33 2Sm 19:1 in Hb   B19:6 Lit *be right in your eyes*   C19:7 Lit *speak to the heart of*

18:27 David's recognition of **Ahimaaz** brought the king hope that all was well.

18:28 Ahimaaz announced David's victory without specifically mentioning Absalom's death.

18:29 David's question revealed the focus of his concern. Ahimaaz, who knew the truth, suddenly found himself at a loss for words.

18:32 After the Cushite responded essentially as Ahimaaz had (vv. 28,31), David's further inquiry specifically about **Absalom** brought the reply **the king** did not want to hear. The kingdom was David's again, but he had lost another son.

18:33 The **gate chamber** over the gate provided isolation for David, though the sound of his wailing could be heard by others (19:1).

19:1 **Joab** returned to Mahanaim from the battle to hear about David's **mourning over Absalom**.

19:2 Victory was **turned to mourning** because victory had come through Absalom's death.

19:3 In this bittersweet moment, David's victorious troops **returned to the city** (lit "stole away"), acting as if they had lost the **battle**.

19:5-7 **Joab** recognized the serious public relations problem **the king** would face if he persisted in mourning the traitorous Absalom. David's soldiers, who had **rescued** David and all his family, would feel shame instead of a sense of victory because of the king's mourning. Joab told David to go out and **encourage** his **soldiers**, lest they abandon him. Joab's words in these verses are strong and blunt, but they may have saved David's kingship.

19:9-10 The **tribes of Israel** sensed that a public **restoring** of King David to his throne might help the nation heal from the wounds of its civil war.

¹¹King David sent word to the priests, Zadok and Abiathar:ᵃ "Say to the elders of Judah, 'Why should you be the last to restore the king to his palace? The talk of all Israel has reached the king at his house. ¹²You are my brothers, my flesh and blood.ᵇ So why should you be the last to restore the king?' ¹³And tell Amasa,ᶜ 'Aren't you my flesh and blood? May God punish me and do so severely if you don't become commander of the army from now on instead of Joab!'"

¹⁴So he won overᴬ all the men of Judah, and they sent word to the king: "Come back, you and all your servants." ¹⁵Then the king returned. When he arrived at the Jordan, Judah came to Gilgal to meet the king and escort him across the Jordan.

¹⁶Shimei son of Gera,ᵈ a Benjaminite from Bahurim, hurried down with the men of Judah to meet King David. ¹⁷There were 1,000 men from Benjamin with him. Ziba, an attendant from the house of Saul,ᵉ with his 15 sons and 20 servants also rushed down to the Jordan ahead of the king. ¹⁸They forded the Jordan to bring the king's household across and do whatever the king desired.ᴮ

When Shimei son of Gera crossed the Jordan, he fell down before the king ¹⁹and said to him, "My lord, don't hold me *guilty, and don't remember your servant's wrongdoing on the day my lord the king left Jerusalem.ᶠ May the king not take it to heart. ²⁰For your servant knows that I have sinned. But look! Today I am the first one of the entire house of Joseph to come down to meet my lord the king."

²¹Abishai son of Zeruiah asked, "Shouldn't Shimei be put to death for this, because he cursed the Lᴏʀᴅ's anointed?"ᵍ

²²David answered, "Sons of Zeruiah, do we agree on anything?ʰ Have you become my adversary today? Should any man be killed in Israel today? Am I not aware that today I'm king over Israel?" ²³So the king said to Shimei, "You will not die." Then the king gave him his oath.ⁱ

²⁴Mephibosheth,ʲ Saul's grandson, also went down to meet the king. He had not taken care of his feet, trimmed his mustache, or washed his clothes from the day the king left until the day he returned safely. ²⁵When he came from Jerusalem to meet the king, the king asked him, "Mephibosheth, why didn't you come with me?"

²⁶"My lord the king," he replied, "my servant Ziba betrayed me. Actually your servant said: 'I'll saddle the donkey for myselfᶜ so that I may ride it and go with the king'—for your servant is lame.ᵏ ²⁷Ziba slandered your servant to my lord the king.ˡ But my lord the king is like the Angel of God,ᵐ so do whatever you think best.ᴰ ²⁸For my grandfather's entire family deserves death from my lord the king, but you set your servant among those who eat at your table.ⁿ So what further right do I have to keep on making appeals to the king?"

²⁹The king said to him, "Why keep on

ᵃ19:11 2Sm 15:29	
ᵇ19:12 Gn 29:14; 2Sm 5:1	
ᶜ19:13 2Sm 17:25	
ᵈ19:16 2Sm 16:5; 1Kg 2:8	
ᵉ19:17 2Sm 16:1-4	
ᶠ19:19 2Sm 16:5-13	
ᵍ19:21 Ex 22:28	
ʰ19:22 2Sm 3:39; 16:10	
ⁱ19:23 1Kg 2:8-9,37,46	
ʲ19:24 2Sm 9:6	
ᵏ19:26 2Sm 4:4; 9:3	
ˡ19:27 2Sm 16:1-4	
ᵐ2Sm 14:17,20	
ⁿ19:28 2Sm 9:1-13	

ᴬ19:14 Lit he turned the heart of   ᴮ19:18 Lit do what is good in his eyes   ᶜ19:26 LXX, Syr, Vg read said to him, 'Saddle the donkey for me   ᴰ19:27 Lit do what is good in your eyes

---

19:11-12 Apparently because of a lack of response on the people's part, **King David** summoned **Zadok and Abiathar** to begin his restoration proceedings. He gave the **elders of Judah** first notice—an act of favoritism that would later cause consternation among the other tribes (vv. 41-43).

19:13 David's appointment of **Amasa**, who had headed Absalom's army (17:25), as **commander of the army** indicated that David planned to bear no animosity toward those who had sided with Absalom. Amasa was to replace **Joab**—a clear sign that David had heard about Joab's murder of Absalom, but the king felt it was politically unwise to put Joab to death for killing the person who had conspired for the throne.

19:16 Now that Absalom was dead, the "prophecy" of **Shimei** was clearly false. Moreover, he had cursed the king. He moved quickly to make amends.

19:17 Ziba, servant of Mephibosheth, also came to welcome David. He soon would be joined by Mephibosheth, creating an interesting dilemma for David (vv. 24-30).

19:20 Shimei confessed that he had **sinned**. He was trying to atone for his sin by being **the first one** of the **house of Joseph** (the northern tribes; Am 5:6) to welcome David back as king.

19:21 Abishai offered for the second time to kill **Shimei** for his harsh words against **the Lᴏʀᴅ's anointed** (16:9).

19:22 On **do we agree on anything**, see note at 16:10. Interestingly, **adversary** translates the Hebrew word satan. David was reluctant to add more bloodshed to the day when his kingdom was restored.

19:23 Shimei would later **die** when he violated Solomon's edict (1Kg 2:42-46).

19:24 Mephibosheth now met David, showing several signs of having been in mourning **from the day the king left**.

19:26 Mephibosheth contended that **Ziba** had **betrayed** (lit "deceived") him and had not provided him a **donkey** so Mephibosheth could **go with the king**.

19:27-28 Mephibosheth asserted his confidence in David's discernment and recognized that he deserved none of David's grace toward him. His final question, **what further right do I have to keep on making appeals to the king**, anticipated what he hoped would be a favorable ruling.

19:29 David had received Ziba's support as he fled, yet Mephibosheth's testimony seemed credible. David decided on a compromise under which the two of them would **divide the land**.

speaking about these matters of yours? I hereby declare: you and Ziba are to divide the land."[a]

[30] Mephibosheth said to the king, "Instead, since my lord the king has come to his palace safely, let Ziba take it all!"

[31] Barzillai the Gileadite[b] had come down from Rogelim and accompanied the king to the Jordan River to see him off at the Jordan. [32] Barzillai was a very old man—80 years old—and since he was a very wealthy man, he had provided for the needs of the king while he stayed in Mahanaim.[c]

[33] The king said to Barzillai, "Cross over with me, and I'll provide for you[A] at my side in Jerusalem."

[34] Barzillai replied to the king, "How many years of my life are left that I should go up to Jerusalem with the king? [35] I'm now 80 years old.[d] Can I discern what is pleasant and what is not? Can your servant taste what he eats or drinks? Can I still hear the voice of male and female singers? Why should your servant be an added burden to my lord the king?[e] [36] Since your servant is only going with the king a little way across the Jordan, why should the king repay me with such a reward? [37] Please let your servant return so that I may die in my own city near the tomb of my father and mother. But here is your servant Chimham:[f] let him cross over with my lord the king. Do for him what seems good to you."[B]

[38] The king replied, "Chimham will cross over with me, and I will do for him what seems good to you,[B] and whatever you desire from me I will do for you." [39] So all the people crossed the Jordan, and then the king crossed. The king kissed Barzillai and blessed him, and Barzillai returned to his home.

[40] The king went on to Gilgal, and Chimham went with him. All the troops of Judah and half of Israel's escorted the king. [41] Suddenly, all the men of Israel came to the king. They asked him, "Why did our brothers, the men of Judah, take you away secretly and transport the king and his household across the Jordan, along with all of David's men?"

[42] All the men of Judah responded to the men of Israel, "Because the king is our relative. Why does this make you angry? Have we ever eaten anything of the king's or been honored at all?"[c]

[43] The men of Israel answered the men of Judah: "We have 10 shares in the king,[g] so we have a greater claim to David than you. Why then do you despise us? Weren't we the first to speak of restoring our king?"[h] But the words of the men of Judah were harsher than those of the men of Israel.

Sheba's Revolt

20 Now a *wicked man, a Benjaminite named Sheba son of Bichri, happened

[a]19:29 2Sm 9:9; 16:4
[b]19:31 1Kg 2:7
[c]19:32 2Sm 17:27-29
[d]19:35 Ps 90:10
[e]2Sm 15:33
[f]19:37 1Kg 2:7; Jr 41:17
[g]19:43 1Kg 11:31
[h]2Sm 19:9-10

[A]19:33 LXX reads for your old age; Ru 4:15   [B]19:37,38 Lit what is good in your eyes   [C]19:42 LXX reads king's or has he given us a gift or granted us a portion

19:30 Mephibosheth's expression **let Ziba take it all** should be understood as a typical Middle Eastern overstatement to honor a ruler, just as his question in verse 28 was an understatement of his own value (cp. 9:8).

19:31-32 Although **Rogelim** was about 50 miles northeast of David's crossing point, **Barzillai**, who had **provided** food and other supplies for the **king** and his men while he stayed in **Mahanaim** (17:27-29), accompanied David to the Jordan River.

19:33 David wanted to reward **Barzillai** for his show of support during the king's desperate time of need.

19:37 Barzillai considered himself too old to enjoy royal privileges and preferred to remain in his **own city** near his family **tomb**, to finish his days in the surroundings he had known all his life, but he takes the opportunity to introduce **Chimham**, who was apparently a close relative, to benefit from David's offer.

19:39 Though **Barzillai returned to his home** after David **blessed him**, the king did not forget him, later instructing Solomon to continue to show kindness to Barzillai's household (1Kg 2:7). Jeremiah 41:17 mentions Geruth Chimham ("dwelling of Chimham") near Bethlehem—perhaps the fulfillment of David's words.

19:40 **Gilgal** was Israel's base camp during the days of Joshua's conquest (Jos 4:19).

19:41 Tensions between **Judah** and the other tribes that were evident earlier in Israel's history (2:10; 3:10; 12:8; 1Sm 11:8; 17:52; 18:16) now boiled to the surface again as the delegation from **Israel** challenged the king on the protocol for restoring him to Jerusalem. **Take you away secretly** is literally "stole you." The northern tribes also felt they were under-represented in comparison to the leaders from Judah (v. 40).

19:42 The **men of Judah** answered instead of allowing David to do so. They asserted that since David was their **relative** (a closer relative), they had taken the lead in restoring him as king. They insisted, however, that their tribe was not treated with favoritism.

19:43 The other tribes pointed out that David also ruled their **10 shares** (tribal territories) and they had been the **first to speak** of restoring David (vv. 9-10). The **men of Judah** responded even more harshly and ended the conversation, but the tension between the tribes grew stronger.

20:1 **Sheba son of Bichri** is not mentioned outside this account, but he was probably a leader among the **Benjaminite** delegation that escorted David back to Jerusalem. He **blew the ram's horn** and called the people of **Israel** to break off from David (cp. 18:16), citing the more distant relationship.

20:2 In the heat of the moment, following **Sheba** seemed to many people the right thing to do, so the men of **Israel deserted David**. Meanwhile, the men of **Judah** escorted David **all the way to Jerusalem** to guarantee his safety.

to be there. He blew the ram's horn and shouted:

> We have no portion in David,
> no inheritance in Jesse's son.
> Each man to his tent, Israel!

[2] So all the men of Israel deserted David and followed Sheba son of Bichri, but the men of Judah from the Jordan all the way to Jerusalem remained loyal to their king.[a]

[3] When David came to his palace in Jerusalem, he took the 10 concubines he had left to take care of the palace and placed them under guard.[b] He provided for them, but he was not intimate with them. They were confined until the day of their death, living as widows.

[4] The king said to Amasa, "Summon the men of Judah to me within three days and be here yourself." [5] Amasa went to summon Judah, but he took longer than the time allotted him. [6] So David said to Abishai, "Sheba son of Bichri will do more harm to us than Absalom. Take your lord's soldiers and pursue him, or he will find fortified cities and elude us."[A]

[7] So Joab's men, the Cherethites, the Pelethites, and all the warriors marched out under Abishai's command;[B] they left Jerusalem to pursue Sheba son of Bichri. [8] They were at the great stone in Gibeon when Amasa joined them. Joab was wearing his uniform and over it was a belt around his waist with a sword in its sheath. As he approached, the sword fell out. [9] Joab asked Amasa, "Are you well, my brother?" Then with his right hand Joab grabbed Amasa by the beard to kiss him.[c]

[10] Amasa was not on guard against the sword in Joab's hand, and Joab stabbed him in the stomach with it and spilled his intestines out on the ground. Joab did not stab him again for Amasa was dead.[d] Joab and his brother Abishai pursued Sheba son of Bichri.

[11] One of Joab's young men had stood over Amasa saying, "Whoever favors Joab and whoever is for David, follow Joab!" [12] Now Amasa was writhing in his blood in the middle of the highway, and the man had seen that all the people stopped. So he moved Amasa from the highway to the field and threw a garment over him because he realized that all those who encountered Amasa were stopping. [13] When he was removed from the highway, all the men passed by and followed Joab to pursue Sheba son of Bichri.

[14] Sheba passed through all the tribes of Israel to Abel of Beth-maacah. All the Berites[c] came together and followed him. [15] Joab's troops came and besieged Sheba in Abel of Beth-maacah. They built an assault ramp against the outer wall of the city. While all the troops with Joab were battering the wall to make it collapse, [16] a wise woman called out from the city, "Listen! Listen! Please tell Joab to come here and let me speak with him."

[17] When he had come near her, the woman asked, "Are you Joab?"

"I am," he replied.

"Listen to the words of your servant," she said to him.

He answered, "I'm listening."

[18] She said, "In the past they used to say, 'Seek

---

[a]20:1-2 1Kg 12:16-17
[b]20:3 2Sm 15:16; 16:21-22
[c]20:9 Mt 26:49; Mk 14:45; Lk 22:47
[d]20:10 1Kg 2:5

A 20:6 Lit *and snatch away our eyes*　　B 20:7 Lit *out following him*　　C 20:14 LXX, Vg read *Bichrites*

20:3 David compassionately provided for the welfare of the **10 concubines** with whom Absalom had had sex during his coup attempt (16:22). However, **he was not intimate with them** again, perhaps because of Torah considerations (Lv 18:15) but more likely to ensure no confusion arose within the royal line.

20:4-5 **Amasa**, the new head of David's army (19:13), was commanded to gather the **men of Judah** to crush Sheba's revolt. Time was of the essence, a fact that Amasa apparently did not grasp.

20:6 **Abishai** was David's next choice to lead the attack against **Sheba**.

20:7 On **Cherethites** and **Pelethites**, see note at 8:18.

20:8 **Gibeon**, about four miles northwest of Jerusalem, had been the site of Joab's encounter with Abner's forces (2:12-16). The site provided a panoramic view of the central Benjamin plateau and was large enough to gather a large fighting force. Amasa's late arrival may have received a mixed response from the army; after all, he had led Absalom's forces against David (17:25). **Joab** was present, though he was not in charge. His **sword** fell out of its **sheath**, probably a deceptive move by Joab so Amasa would not view him as drawing his weapon.

20:9 Joab grabbed Amasa **by the beard**—reached out and touched his face as he might do before greeting him with a **kiss**.

20:10 The **sword in Joab's hand** did not seem a threat to **Amasa** because it appeared that Joab was merely picking it up after dropping it (v. 8).

20:11 One of Joab's **young men** rallied everyone to **follow Joab** as their self-proclaimed, reappointed leader. Abishai apparently acquiesced to his brother's leadership.

20:14 **Sheba** retreated to the far north; **Abel of Beth-maacah** lay about 30 miles north of the Sea of Galilee.

20:15 Besieging a city generally involved surrounding it, cutting off its food and water supply, building an **assault ramp** to get over the wall, and constructing **battering** rams to break down the city's **wall**.

20:16 This woman is described as **wise** in retrospect because of what she did in the narrative.

20:17 **Joab** no doubt approached the woman cautiously (Jdg 9:50-55).

20:18-19 The city of **Abel**, a city of long standing within the nation, had a reputation as a place where wisdom often **settled disputes**.

counsel in Abel,' and that's how they settled disputes. ¹⁹I am a peaceful person, one of the faithful in Israel, but you're trying to destroy a city that is like a mother in Israel. Why would you devour the LORD's inheritance?"

²⁰Joab protested: "Never! I do not want to destroy! ²¹That is not my intention. There is a man named Sheba son of Bichri, from the hill country of Ephraim, who has rebelled against King David. Deliver this one man, and I will withdraw from the city."

The woman replied to Joab, "All right. His head will be thrown over the wall to you."
²²The woman went to all the people with her wise counsel,ᵃ and they cut off the head of Sheba son of Bichri and threw it to Joab. So he blew the ram's horn, and they dispersed from the city, each to his own tent. Joab returned to the king in Jerusalem.

²³Joab commanded the whole army of Israel;ᵇ Benaiah son of Jehoiada was over the Cherethites and Pelethites; ²⁴Adoramᴬ was in charge of forced labor; Jehoshaphat son of Ahilud was court historian; ²⁵Sheva was court secretary; Zadok and Abiathar were priests; ²⁶and in addition, Ira the Jairite was David's priest.

Justice for the Gibeonites

21 During David's reign there was a famine for three successive years, so David inquired of the LORD. The LORD answered, "It is because of the blood shed by Saul and his family when he killed the Gibeonites."

²The Gibeonites were not Israelites but rather a remnant of the Amorites. The Israelites had taken an oath concerning them,ᶜ but Saul had tried to kill them in his zeal for the Israelites and Judah. So David summoned the Gibeonites and spoke to them. ³He asked the Gibeonites, "What should I do for you? How can I make atonement so that you will bring a blessing onᴮ the LORD's inheritance?"

⁴The Gibeonites said to him, "We are not asking for money fromᶜ Saul or his family,ᵈ and we cannot put anyone to death in Israel."ᵉ

"Whatever you say, I will do for you," he said.

⁵They replied to the king, "As for the man who annihilated us and plotted to destroy us so we would not exist within the whole territory of Israel, ⁶let seven of his male descendants be handed over to us so we may hangᴰ them in the presence of the LORDᶠ at Gibeah of Saul,ᵍ the LORD's chosen."ʰ

The king answered, "I will hand them over."

⁷David spared Mephibosheth, the son of Saul's son Jonathan, because of the oath of the LORD that was between David and Jonathan, Saul's son.ⁱ ⁸But the king took Armoni and Mephibosheth, who were the two sons

ᵃ 20:22 Ec 9:14-15
ᵇ 20:23-26 2Sm 8:16-18; 1Kg 4:3-6
ᶜ 21:2 Jos 9:3-17
ᵈ 21:4 Nm 35:31-32
ᵉ Lv 24:21-22
ᶠ 21:6 Nm 25:4
ᵍ 1Sm 15:34
ʰ 1Sm 10:24
ⁱ 21:7 1Sm 18:3; 20:12-17; 23:18

ᴬ 20:24 Some Hb mss, LXX, Syr read *Adoniram*; 1Kg 4:6; 5:14   ᴮ 21:3 Lit *will bless*   ᶜ 21:4 Lit *"Not for us silver and gold with*   ᴰ 21:6 Or *impale,* or *expose*

20:21 Joab responded that his fight was not with the city's inhabitants, only with **Sheba**, whom they were harboring.

20:22 Once Sheba was dead, the revolt was ended. On blowing the **ram's horn**, see note at 2:28.

20:23 Joab had become commander of the **whole army of Israel** again, and David may have felt that he should leave well enough alone. After all, Joab had been a factor in reuniting Israel and restoring David's kingdom. Joab's sin, however, was not forgotten, and David later instructed his son Solomon to deal with it when he became king (1Kg 2:5-6). On **Benaiah** and the **Cherethites and Pelethites**, see note at 8:18.

20:24 Forced labor appears here for the first time; during Solomon's days, only non-Israelites made up this group (1Kg 9:20). Perhaps this was added late in David's reign. On **Jehoshaphat**, see note at 8:16.

20:25 Jehoshaphat was now assisted by **Sheva**, who had apparently replaced Seraiah (8:17) as **court secretary**. Zadok's influence would continue into Solomon's reign (1Kg 2:35), though **Abiathar** would side against Solomon during the transition of power from David to Solomon and suffer banishment from the priesthood (1Kg 1:7; 2:26-27).

20:26 Ira the Jairite, otherwise unknown, was **David's priest**, perhaps assisting him in matters of private worship, but certainly not functioning in place of Torah-prescribed patterns (unlike Micah in Jdg 17).

21:1 During David's reign is literally "in David's days." The last four chapters of 2 Samuel contain six accounts of matters pertaining to David's life, though not tied chronologically to the rest of the book. It appears the author had additional information he wished to include about David, and he decided this was the best place to put it. In the first account, God used continuing **famine** to prompt David to seek the reason behind this calamity. **The LORD** revealed the answer: **Saul and his family** had **killed the Gibeonites**.

21:2 The **Gibeonites** had remained in the land since the days of Joshua. The Israelites **had taken an oath** not to destroy them (Jos 9:3-17); Saul, however, had not honored that oath and had killed many of them.

21:3 When David asked **What should I do for you?** it showed his humble attitude and his concern for justice.

21:4 Israel probably did not allow their subject peoples to **put anyone to death** without Israelite sanction (cp. restrictions imposed on Israel by Roman authorities: Jn 18:31).

21:6 The Gibeonites asked for the death of **seven** of Saul's **male descendants**. Saul had probably killed many more Gibeonites than this; no doubt the number requested was a symbolic representation of the Gibeonite dead. **Gibeah** was Saul's hometown; since Saul had killed their people at Gibeon, the Gibeonites probably wanted to reciprocate by hanging his descendants in his hometown.

21:7 Even in complying with the Gibeonites request, **David**

whom Rizpah[a] daughter of Aiah had borne to Saul, and the five sons whom Merab[A,b] daughter of Saul had borne to Adriel son of Barzillai the Meholathite ⁹and handed them over to the Gibeonites. They hanged[B] them on the hill in the presence of the LORD; the seven of them died together. They were executed in the first days of the harvest at the beginning of the barley harvest.[c]

The Burial of Saul's Family

¹⁰Rizpah, Aiah's daughter, took •sackcloth and spread it out for herself on the rock from the beginning of the harvest[D] until the rain poured down from heaven on the bodies. She kept the birds of the sky from them by day and the wild animals by night.

¹¹When it was reported to David what Saul's concubine Rizpah, daughter of Aiah, had done, ¹²he went and got the bones of Saul and his son Jonathan from the leaders of Jabesh-gilead. They had stolen them from the public square of Beth-shan where the Philistines had hung the bodies the day the Philistines killed Saul at Gilboa.[c] ¹³David had the bones brought from there. They gathered up the bones of Saul's family who had been hung[B] ¹⁴and buried the bones of Saul and his son Jonathan at Zela in the land of Benjamin in the tomb of Saul's father Kish. They did everything the king commanded. After this, God answered prayer for the land.[d]

ᵃ21:8 2Sm 3:7
ᵇ1Sm 18:19
ᶜ21:12 1Sm 31:11-13
ᵈ21:14 2Sm 24:25
ᵉ21:17 2Sm 18:3; 1Kg 11:36; 15:4; 2Ch 21:7; Ps 132:17
ᶠ21:18-22 1Ch 20:4-8
ᵍ21:19 1Sm 17:7

The Philistine Giants

¹⁵The Philistines again waged war against Israel. David went down with his soldiers, and they fought the Philistines, but David became exhausted. ¹⁶Then Ishbi-benob, one of the descendants of the giant,[E] whose bronze spear weighed about eight pounds[F] and who wore new armor, intended to kill David. ¹⁷But Abishai son of Zeruiah came to his aid, struck the Philistine, and killed him. Then David's men swore to him: "You must never again go out with us to battle. You must not extinguish the lamp of Israel."[e]

¹⁸After this,[f] there was another battle with the Philistines at Gob. At that time Sibbecai the Hushathite killed Saph, who was one of the descendants of the giant.[E]

¹⁹Once again there was a battle with the Philistines at Gob, and Elhanan son of Jaare-oregim the Bethlehemite killed[G] Goliath the Gittite. The shaft of his spear was like a weaver's beam.[g]

²⁰At Gath there was still another battle. A huge man was there with six fingers on each hand and six toes on each foot—24 in all. He, too, was descended from the giant.[E] ²¹When he taunted Israel, Jonathan, son of David's brother Shimei, killed him.

²²These four were descended from the giant[E] in Gath and were killed by David and his soldiers.

ᴬ21:8 Some Hb mss, LXX, Syr, Tg; other Hb mss read *Michal*   ᴮ21:9,13 Or *impaled*, or *exposed*   ᶜ21:9 = March–April
ᴰ21:10 = April to October   ᴱ21:16,18,20,22 Or *Raphah*   ᶠ21:16 Lit *300* (shekels)   ᴳ21:19 1Ch 20:5 adds *the brother of*

---

spared Mephibosheth in accord with his earlier **oath** regarding **Jonathan** (9:1-10; 1Sm 18:3; 20:12-17; 23:18).

21:8 Rizpah was probably the same concubine with whom Abner had sexual relations (3:7).

21:9 The beginning of the **barley harvest** was normally during Nisan (March-April), the beginning of the religious year.

21:10 Rizpah performed a tragic act of love for her sons and Merab's sons, protecting their bodies from desecration by **birds** and **wild animals**. The **rain** mentioned normally fell in March and April between the barley and wheat harvest, so the exact length of Rizpah's vigil is unknown.

21:12-13 David heard about what Rizpah had done, and he took action to provide the dead an honored burial. The **bones of Saul and his son Jonathan** (and presumably those of Abinadab and Malchishua; 1Sm 31:2,12-13) were brought from **Jabesh-gilead** back to Benjamin. David also gathered up the bones of **Saul's family**.

21:14 The remains were placed in the family **tomb of Saul's father Kish** (see 1Sm 9:1). The exact location of **Zela** (other than in Benjamin) is unknown (Jos 18:28). **God answered prayer** means that the famine ceased (see v. 1).

21:16 Ishbi-benob is unknown outside this passage, but he may have been **one of the descendants of the giant** (Goliath; 1Sm 17:4), though some scholars understand the Hebrew word translated "giant" *(rapha)* as a proper name ("one of

the descendants of Rapha"). The man **intended to kill David** because killing him would deal Israel a serious blow.

21:17 David's nephew **Abishai** saved the king's life and **struck the Philistine**. As they pondered how close David had come to death, they told him not to participate with them in any more battles, an admonition the king seems to have taken to heart (11:1; 18:2; 20:4,6). Through his leadership David, as the figurative **lamp of Israel**, provided political, military, and spiritual light to the nation.

21:18 Gob ("cistern") may be either identified with or in the close vicinity of Gezer at the mouth of the Aijalon Valley near Philistine territory (1Ch 20:4). On **the giant**, see note at verse 16.

21:19 This verse raises the question of who killed **Goliath the Gittite**. First Samuel 17:50-51 credits David, but this verse credits **Elhanan**. One interpretation suggests two different Goliaths, though the identical description of Goliath's **spear** being **like a weaver's beam** (cp. 1Sm 17:7) makes this option doubtful. Another explanation is to understand Elhanan as David's original name and David as David's throne name, but this is not supported elsewhere in Scripture. By far the most likely explanation is that Elhanan killed not Goliath but Goliath's brother, as 1 Chronicles 20:5 states, and that an early scribe simply miscopied the present verse. Although this verse and 1Ch 20:5 read a bit differently in English,

David's Song of Thanksgiving

22 David spoke the words of this song to the LORD on the day the LORD rescued him from the hand of all his enemies and from the hand of Saul. 2 He said:[a]

The LORD is my rock, my fortress,[b]
and my deliverer,
3 my God, my mountain[A] where I seek
refuge.
My shield, the ·horn of my salvation,[c]
my stronghold,[d] my refuge,[e]
and my Savior, You save me
from violence.
4 I called to the LORD, who is worthy
of praise,[f]
and I was saved from my enemies.
5 For the waves of death engulfed me;[g]
the torrents of destruction terrified me.
6 The ropes of ·Sheol entangled me;
the snares of death confronted me.[h]
7 I called to the LORD in my distress;
I called to my God.[i]
From His temple He heard my voice,
and my cry for help reached His ears.
8 Then the earth shook and quaked;
the foundations of the heavens[B]
trembled;[j]
they shook because He burned
with anger.[k]
9 Smoke rose from His nostrils,
and consuming fire came
from His mouth;
coals were set ablaze by it.[C]
10 He parted the heavens and came down,[l]
a dark cloud beneath His feet.
11 He rode on a cherub and flew,
soaring[D] on the wings of the wind.
12 He made darkness a canopy
around Him,
a gathering[E] of water
and thick clouds.[m]
13 From the radiance of His presence,
flaming coals were ignited.
14 The LORD thundered from heaven;
the ·Most High projected His voice.[n]
15 He shot arrows and scattered them;[o]
He hurled lightning bolts
and routed them.[p]
16 The depths of the sea became visible,
the foundations of the world
were exposed
at the rebuke of the LORD,
at the blast of the breath[q]
of His nostrils.[r]
17 He reached down from heaven
and took hold of me;
He pulled me out of deep waters.[s]
18 He rescued me
from my powerful enemy
and from those who hated me,
for they were too strong for me.
19 They confronted me in the day
of my distress,
but the LORD was my support.
20 He brought me out to a spacious place;[t]
He rescued me because He delighted
in me.
21 The LORD rewarded me
according to my righteousness;[u]
He repaid me

[a]22:2-51 Ps 18:2-50 [b]22:2 Ps 31:3; 71:3 [c]22:3 Lk 1:69 [d]Ps 9:9; 59:9,16-17; 62:2,6 [e]Ps 14:6; 71:7; Jr 16:19 [f]22:4 1Ch 16:25; Ps 48:1; 96:4 [g]22:5 Ps 42:7; Jnh 2:3 [h]22:6 Ps 116:3 [i]22:7 Ps 116:4; 120:1; Jnh 2:2 [j]22:8 Jdg 5:4; Ps 77:18; 97:4 [k]Jb 26:11 [l]22:10 Ps 144:5; Is 64:1 [m]22:12 Ps 97:2 [n]22:14 Jb 37:4 [o]22:15 Dt 32:23; Ps 7:13; 77:17; Hab 3:11 [p]Ps 144:6 [q]22:16 Jb 4:9; Is 30:33 [r]Ex 15:8 [s]22:17 Ps 144:7 [t]22:20 Ps 31:8; 118:5 [u]22:21 1Sm 26:23; 1Kg 8:32; Ps 7:8

[A]22:3 LXX; MT reads *God of my mountain*; Ps 18:2 [B]22:8 Some Hb mss, Syr, Vg read *mountains*; Ps 18:7 [C]22:9 Or *ablaze from Him* [D]22:11 Some Hb mss; other Hb mss, Syr, Tg read *He was seen* [E]22:12 Or *sieve, or mass*; Hb obscure

in the Hebrew text only a minor alteration is required to change from one reading to another.

22:1 On the day is not a reference to a single day, but the general time at which David realized the Lord had given him the kingship and helped him subdue **all his enemies**. The **song** is very similar to Psalm 18, but has more emphasis on David's personal worship.

22:2 Rock denotes an immovable, jutting cliff, not a mere stone. This word commonly occurs in the Bible to describe God's support and defense of His people (1Sm 2:2; Ps 18:2; 95:1; Is 44:8).

22:3 Mary also used the expression **horn of my salvation** to describe God's work on her behalf (Lk 1:69). The Bible often uses the image of an animal horn to symbolize strength (1Sm 2:1). **Violence** (Hb *chamas*) denotes unjust violence (Gn 6:11; Ob 10).

22:5 Waves designates huge breakers coming in to shore. **Torrents** refers to canyons filled with rushing water during the rainy season.

22:6 The word **Sheol** often occurs in connection with **death** (Nm 16:33; Ps 16:10). David feared for his life as he fled from Saul.

22:7 Temple signifies the place of God's dwelling—either His heavenly temple (1Kg 8:27) or the tent where the ark of God rested (1Ch 16:1).

22:8-16 David described God's terrible fury. The imagery is intended to convey the awesomeness of His presence as He entered His world to intervene on behalf of His servant David.

22:18 David's enemies were **too strong** for him, but not too strong for the Lord.

22:19 The Lord was David's **support**, so David could lean on Him in times of trouble.

22:20 From **a spacious place** David could see enemy threats while they were still far away.

22:21 The Lord saw David's **righteousness** and blessed him for it. David's relationship with God made him want to please the Lord in the way he lived.

22:22 Kept can also be translated as "guarded."

according to the cleanness
of my hands.[a]
22 For I have kept the ways of the LORD[b]
and have not turned from my God
to wickedness.
23 Indeed, I have kept all His ordinances[c]
in mind[A]
and have not disregarded His statutes.
24 I was blameless before Him
and kept myself from sinning.
25 So the LORD repaid me
according to my righteousness,
according to my cleanness[B]
in His sight.

26 With the faithful
You prove Yourself faithful;
with the blameless man
You prove Yourself blameless;
27 with the pure
You prove Yourself pure,
but with the crooked
You prove Yourself shrewd.
28 You rescue an afflicted people,[d]
but Your eyes are set
against the proud—
You humble them.[e]
29 LORD, You are my lamp;
the LORD illuminates my darkness.[f]
30 With You I can attack a barrier,[C]
and with my God I can leap
over a wall.[g]
31 God—His way is perfect;[h]
the word of the LORD is pure.[i]
He is a shield to all who take refuge
in Him.

32 For who is God besides the LORD?
And who is a rock? Only our God.
33 God is my strong refuge;[D]
He makes my way perfect.[E]

[a]22:21 Ps 24:3-4
[b]22:22 Pr 8:32
[c]22:23 Ps 119:30,102
[d]22:28 Ps 72:12-13
[e]Is 2:11-12,17; Lk 1:51
[f]22:29 Jb 29:3; Ps 27:1
[g]22:30 2Sm 5:6-9
[h]22:31 Dt 32:4
[i]Ps 119:140
[j]22:35 Ps 144:1
[k]22:36 Eph 6:16-17
[l]22:40 Ps 44:5
[m]22:42 1Sm 28:6; Pr 1:28
[n]22:43 Is 10:6; Mc 7:10; Zch 10:5
[o]22:44 2Sm 2:8-10; 15:1-6; 20:1-2
[p]2Sm 8:1-14; Is 55:5
[q]22:46 Mc 7:17

34 He makes my feet like the feet of a deer
and sets me securely on the[F] heights.[G]
35 He trains my hands for war;[j]
my arms can bend a bow of bronze.
36 You have given me the shield
of Your salvation;[k]
Your help[H] exalts me.
37 You widen a place beneath me
for my steps,
and my ankles do not give way.
38 I pursue my enemies and destroy them;
I do not turn back until they are
wiped out.
39 I wipe them out and crush them,
and they do not rise;
they fall beneath my feet.
40 You have clothed me with strength
for battle;
You subdue my adversaries
beneath me.[l]
41 You have made my enemies retreat
before me;[I]
I annihilate those who hate me.
42 They look, but there is no one
to save them—
they look to the LORD, but He does not
answer them.[m]
43 I pulverize them like dust of the earth;
I crush them and trample them
like mud in the streets.[n]

44 You have freed me from the feuds
among my people;[o]
You have appointed me the head
of nations;
a people I had not known serve me.[p]
45 Foreigners submit to me grudgingly;
as soon as they hear, they obey me.
46 Foreigners lose heart
and come trembling
from their fortifications.[q]

[A]22:23 Lit *Indeed, all His ordinances have been in front of me* [B]22:25 LXX, Syr, Vg read *to the cleanness of my hands*; Ps 18:24 [C]22:30 Or *ridge* [D]22:33 DSS, some LXX mss, Syr, Vg read *God clothes me with strength*; Ps 18:32 [E]22:33 Some LXX mss, Syr; MT reads *He sets free the blameless His way*; Hb obscure [F]22:34 LXX; some Hb mss read *my*; other Hb mss read *His* [G]22:34 Or *on my high places* [H]22:36 LXX reads *humility*; Ps 18:35 [I]22:41 Lit *You gave me the neck of my enemies*

22:23 **Disregarded** is literally "turned aside."

22:24 **Blameless** does not mean sinless, but it reflects a deep moral character (Gn 6:9; Ps 119:1).

22:26 Qualities such as **faithful** and **blameless** are characteristic of both God and His children, who become more like Him as they grow in their relationship with Him (Rm 8:29).

22:28 **Humble** is literally "bring low."

22:29 Both **the LORD** and His Word function as a **lamp** for His people (Ps 119:105).

22:30 David was quick to credit the Lord as the source of his power (5:12,21; 1Sm 17:45-47).

22:32 David answered his two rhetorical questions; only Yahweh was God. **The LORD** is our **rock**.

22:34 The **deer** David described are very sure-footed. They are a powerful picture of the firm footing on which believers stand.

22:43 The words **pulverize . . . crush**, and **trample** describe the overwhelming victories David won with God's help (Rm 8:37).

22:44 David's sovereignty extended to the **nations** around him (5:17-25; 8:1-14; 10:1-19).

22:46 Reports of David's strength caused his enemies to **lose heart** before they ever battled him.

⁴⁷ The LORD lives—may my rock
    be praised!
God, the rock of my salvation,ᵃ
    is exalted.
⁴⁸ God—He gives me vengeance
    and casts down peoples under me.ᵇ
⁴⁹ He frees me from my enemies.
    You exalt me above my adversaries;
    You rescue me from violent men.ᶜ
⁵⁰ Therefore I will praise You, LORD,
    among the nations;
    I will sing about Your name.ᵈ
⁵¹ He is a tower of salvation forᴬ His king;
    He shows loyalty to His anointed,
    to David and his descendants forever.ᵉ

David's Last Words

23 These are the last words of David:

The declaration of David son of Jesse,ᶠ
the declaration of the man
    raised on high,ᴮ
the one anointed by the God of Jacob,ᵍ
the favorite singer of Israel:
² The Spirit of the LORD spoke
    through me,
His word was on my tongue.ʰ
³ The God of Israel spoke;
    the Rock of Israel said to me,
"The one who rules the people
    with justice,
who rules in the ˙fear of God,ⁱ
⁴ is like the morning light
    when the sun rises

ᵃ 22:47 Ps 89:26; 95:1
ᵇ 22:48 Ps 144:2
ᶜ 22:49 Ps 140:1
ᵈ 22:50 Rm 15:9
ᵉ 22:51 2Sm 7:12-16; Lk 1:55
ᶠ 23:1 Lk 3:32
ᵍ 1Sm 16:12-13; Ps 89:20
ʰ 23:2 Mt 22:43; 2Pt 1:21
ⁱ 23:3 Ps 72:1-3; Is 11:1-5
ʲ 23:5 Gn 9:16; 17:7,19; 1Ch 16:17; Ps 105:10
ᵏ 2Sm 7:12-16; Ps 89:29; Is 55:3
ˡ 23:8-39 1Ch 11:11-47

on a cloudless morning,
    the glisten of rain on sprouting grass."
⁵ Is it not true my house is with God?
For He has established
    an everlasting covenantʲ with me,
ordered and secured in every detail.ᵏ
Will He not bring about
    my whole salvation
    and my every desire?
⁶ But all the wicked are like thorns
    raked aside;
they can never be picked up by hand.
⁷ The man who touches them
    must be armed with iron and the shaft
    of a spear.
They will be completely burned up
    on the spot.

Exploits of David's Warriors

⁸These are the names of David's warriors:ˡ
Josheb-basshebeth the Tahchemonite was
chief of the officers.ᶜ He wielded his spearᴰ
against 800 men that he killed at one time.
⁹After him, Eleazar son of Dodo son of an
Ahohite was among the three warriors with David when they defied the Philistines. The men
of Israel retreated in the place they had gathered for battle, ¹⁰but Eleazar stood his ground
and attacked the Philistines until his hand was
tired and stuck to his sword. The LORD brought
about a great victory that day. Then the troops
came back to him, but only to plunder the
dead.
¹¹After him was Shammah son of Agee the

ᴬ22:51 DSS read *He gives great victory to*   ᴮ23:1 Or *raised up by the high God*   ᶜ23:8 Some Hb mss, LXX read *Three*   ᴰ23:8 Some
Hb mss; other Hb mss, LXX read *He was Adino the Eznite*

22:47 On **rock**, see note at verse 2.

22:51 Loyalty can also be translated as "faithfulness" or "covenant love." It denotes all that comes to God's children from Him. **Anointed** (Hb *mashiach*) designated God's
anointed king (1:14,16; 1Sm 24:6). **David and his descendants** would enjoy the blessings of God **forever** (7:16).

23:1 The heading for this chapter, **These are the last words
of David**, is not intended chronologically; other words of
David appear after this section and even in 1 Kings (1Kg
1:28-35; 2:1-9). Perhaps the section contains David's last recorded public statement or testimony to God's work through
his life. **Anointed** (Hb *mashiach*) emphasizes David's dedication to God's service. **God of Jacob** ties David to the history of
the patriarchs; God's work in David was the continuation of a
work that began with Abraham (Gn 12:1-3).

23:2 David's words should be understood not as boastful,
but as portraying a sense of wonder that God would use him
to convey His words.

23:3 On **Rock**, see note at 22:2. **Fear of God** denotes a
healthy reverence for His power and majesty; the book
of Proverbs associates such an attitude with wisdom and
knowledge (Pr 1:7; 9:10).

23:5 My house denotes David's family. God's **everlasting
covenant** with David's house was **ordered and secured in
every detail**. David was confident the Lord would bring its
every aspect to fruition.

23:6-7 David's experience had taught him that **the wicked**
had no future in God's plan. Since they were neither useful
nor usable, the day of their judgment would surely come.

23:8-39 These are the names and accounts of some of **David's warriors**—his most valiant soldiers. God blessed David
with exceptional military men. The list includes the three famous heroes who turned the tide of events in single combat
and the thirty warriors who served in a special detachment.
There were men from many different tribes of Israel and
even a few foreigners among the men who rallied to David.

23:9 Defied is the same word used of Goliath's words against
Israel (1Sm 17:10,26,36).

23:10 Eleazar displayed tenacity as he **attacked the Philistines**, yet the Lord brought the **victory**. The troops returned
later to **plunder the dead**, a means of securing "extra payment" for their military service.

23:11 Lentils were a common food source.

Hararite. The Philistines had assembled in formation where there was a field full of lentils. The troops fled from the Philistines, [12]but Shammah took his stand in the middle of the field, defended it, and struck down the Philistines. So the Lord brought about a great victory.

[13]Three of the 30 leading warriors went down at harvest time and came to David at the cave of Adullam,[a] while a company of Philistines was camping in the Valley of Rephaim. [14]At that time David was in the stronghold,[b] and a Philistine garrison was at Bethlehem. [15]David was extremely thirsty[A] and said, "If only someone would bring me water to drink from the well at the city gate of Bethlehem!" [16]So three of the warriors broke through the Philistine camp and drew water from the well at the gate of Bethlehem. They brought it back to David, but he refused to drink it. Instead, he poured it out to the Lord. [17]David said, "Lord, I would never do such a thing! Is this not the blood of men who risked their lives?" So he refused to drink it. Such were the exploits of the three warriors.

[18]Abishai, Joab's brother and son of Zeruiah,[c] was leader of the Three.[B] He raised his spear against 300 men and killed them, gaining a reputation among the Three. [19]Was he not more honored than the Three? He became their commander even though he did not become one of the Three.[d]

[20]Benaiah son of Jehoiada[e] was the son of a brave man from Kabzeel, a man of many exploits. Benaiah killed two sons[c] of Ariel[D] of Moab, and he went down into a pit on a snowy day and killed a lion. [21]He also killed an Egyptian, a huge man. Even though the Egyptian had a spear in his hand, Benaiah went down to him with a club, snatched the spear out of the Egyptian's hand, and then killed him with his own spear. [22]These were the exploits of Benaiah son of Jehoiada, who had a reputation among the three warriors. [23]He was the most honored of the Thirty, but he did not become one of the Three. David put him in charge of his bodyguard.

[24]Among the Thirty were:

Joab's brother Asahel,[f]
Elhanan son of Dodo of Bethlehem,
[25] Shammah the Harodite,
Elika the Harodite,
[26] Helez the Paltite,
Ira son of Ikkesh the Tekoite,
[27] Abiezer the Anathothite,
Mebunnai the Hushathite,
[28] Zalmon the Ahohite,
Maharai the Netophathite,
[29] Heleb son of Baanah the Netophahite,
Ittai son of Ribai from Gibeah
of the Benjaminites,
[30] Benaiah the Pirathonite,
Hiddai from the ˙wadis of Gaash,[E]
[31] Abi-albon the Arbathite,
Azmaveth the Barhumite,
[32] Eliahba the Shaalbonite,
the sons of Jashen,
Jonathan son of[F] [33] Shammah
the Hararite,
Ahiam son of Sharar the Hararite,
[34] Eliphelet son of Ahasbai
son of the Maacathite,

[a]23:13 1Sm 22:1   [b]23:14 1Sm 22:4-5   [c]23:18 1Sm 26:3-6   [d]23:19 1Ch 11:21   [e]23:20 2Sm 8:18; 20:23   [f]23:24 2Sm 2:18-23; 1Ch 27:7

[A]23:15 Lit And David craved   [B]23:18 Some Hb mss, Syr read the Thirty   [C]23:20 LXX; MT omits sons   [D]23:20 Or two warriors   [E]23:30 Or from Nahale-gaash   [F]23:32 Some LXX mss; MT omits son of; 1Ch 11:34

23:12 The **Philistines** and other enemies often came up Judah's valleys to raid food supplies.

23:13 The **cave of Adullam** was in the Valley of Elah (1Sm 17:2) below Bethlehem. The **Valley of Rephaim** lay southwest of Jerusalem.

23:14 The **stronghold** probably designates the cave in which David was stationed. A **Philistine garrison** occupied **Bethlehem**—perhaps a move designed to draw David out of hiding.

23:15 Probably David's vocalized wish came not only from his thirst, but from his desire that his hometown would once again know the peace that allowed people to **drink from the well at the city gate** freely.

23:16-17 Three of the warriors under David's command took their leader's wish as a challenge and made the 25-mile round-trip journey at the risk of their lives to secure **water from . . . Bethlehem**. David's response revealed the depth to which he was moved by his men's loyalty and bravery. The water from Bethlehem's well was a very precious gift because of the sacrifice the men made to get it. Consequently, it was a fitting sacrifice to David's God.

23:18 Abishai, Joab's brother, played a leading role in David's rise to power and kingship (v. 18; 10:10; 18:2-3).

23:20 Benaiah was a well-known warrior (8:18; 20:23). Despite his position in a **pit** and severe weather that hampered both his dexterity and his mobility, he **killed a lion**.

23:24 Asahel was a soldier who was killed by Abner during Israel's civil war following Saul's death (2:18-23).

23:25 Harodite may designate a person from the Harod Valley that leads from the Jezreel Valley down to Beth-shan (1Sm 31:10) in the Jordan Valley.

23:26 A **Tekoite** was a person from Tekoa, seven miles south of Jerusalem (Am 1:1).

23:27 Anathoth, located in Benjamin, was later the prophet Jeremiah's hometown (Jr 1:1).

23:29 Gibeah of the Benjaminites was Saul's hometown and capital, a fact that shows David had some following even there.

23:34 According to 11:3, **Eliam** was Bathsheba's father. If this is the same Eliam, then **Ahithophel**, counselor to David

Eliam son of Ahithophel the Gilonite,[a]

35 Hezro the Carmelite,

Paarai the Arbite,

36 Igal son of Nathan from Zobah,

Bani the Gadite,

37 Zelek the Ammonite,

Naharai the Beerothite, the armor-bearer for Joab son of Zeruiah,

38 Ira the Ithrite,

Gareb the Ithrite,

39 and Uriah[b] the Hittite.[c]

There were 37 in all.

David's Military Census

24 The LORD's anger burned against Israel again, and He stirred up David against them to say: "Go, count the people of Israel and Judah."[d]

2 So the king said to Joab, the commander of his army, "Go through all the tribes of Israel from Dan to Beer-sheba and register the troops so I can know their number."[e]

3 Joab replied to the king, "May the LORD your God multiply the troops 100 times more than they are[f]—while my lord the king looks on! But why does my lord the king want to do this?"

4 Yet the king's order prevailed over Joab and the commanders of the army. So Joab and the commanders of the army left the king's presence to register the troops of Israel.

5 They crossed the Jordan and camped in Aroer,[g] south of the town in the middle of the valley, and then proceeded toward Gad and Jazer. 6 They went to Gilead and to the land of the Hittites[A] and continued on to Dan-jaan and around to Sidon. 7 They went to the fortress of Tyre and all the cities of the Hivites and Canaanites. Afterward, they went to the •Negev of Judah at Beer-sheba.

8 When they had gone through the whole land, they returned to Jerusalem at the end of nine months and 20 days. 9 Joab gave the king the total of the registration of the troops. There were 800,000 fighting men from Israel and 500,000 men from Judah.[h]

10 David's conscience troubled him[i] after he had taken a census of the troops. He said to the LORD, "I have sinned greatly in what I've done. Now, LORD, because I've been very foolish,[j] please take away Your servant's •guilt."

David's Punishment

11 When David got up in the morning, a rev-

Cross references:
a 23:34 2Sm 15:12
b 23:39 Mt 1:6
c 2Sm 11:3-26
d 24:1-25 1Ch 21:1-28
e 24:2 Nm 1:2-3; 1Sm 13:15
f 24:3 Dt 1:11
g 24:5 Dt 2:36; Jos 13:19,16
h 24:9 Nm 1:45-46
i 24:10 1Sm 24:5
j Nm 12:9-12; 1Sm 13:13

A 24:6 LXX; MT reads of Tahtim-hodshi; Hb obscure

---

and Absalom (15:31; 16:20-23; 17:1-3,23), would be Bathsheba's grandfather.

23:36 **Zobah** may have been the Aramean city-state that David conquered (8:3-6). **Gadite** probably designates someone from Gad's territory east of the Jordan River.

23:37 David subdued Ammon on his eastern border; at some point **Zelek**, another foreigner, joined David's forces.

23:39 The text intentionally ends with the mention of **Uriah the Hittite**. Uriah was another foreigner among David's mighty men. He gave his life for David under the most evil of circumstances (11:14-17). The fact that **there were 37** members of the Thirty may be explained in one of two ways: either Thirty was a title rather than a specific figure, or the extra men were brought in to replace those who fell in battle.

24:1 The particular sin that brought about God's wrath is not given. First Chronicles 21:1 credits Satan with enticing David, but no contradiction exists. Both verses are correct; God is able to use even Satan to accomplish His purposes (Jb 1:12; 2:6). Here, God allowed Satan to entice David to **count the people**, an act that, while acceptable under certain circumstances (Ex 30:12), here probably revealed that David was putting trust in his military power rather than in the Lord's protection and guidance. Another possibility is that David failed to instruct his commanders to collect the half-shekel poll tax, bringing on the plague (Ex 30:12-13). In either case, God did not force David to make the wrong decision.

24:2 On **from Dan to Beer-sheba**, see note at 17:11.

24:3 **Joab** appears to have been concerned about his king's motives, though he veiled his concern with words of blessing.

24:4 **The king's order prevailed** is probably a reference to David telling **Joab** he wanted the census conducted—period.

24:5 **Aroer** was the southernmost part of Israel's territory east of the Jordan River. **Gad and Jazer** lay between the Jordan Valley and Ammon.

24:6 Some manuscripts read "Dan, Ijon" instead of **Dan-jaan**, referring to a second city near Dan at Israel's northern border. **Sidon**, a Phoenician city, nonetheless may have had an Israelite garrison there (5:11).

24:7 **Tyre** was also a Phoenician city. The expression **cities of the Hivites and Canaanites** probably designates areas that David had controlled. Joab may have counted the foreign population as well, or merely the Israelite soldiers maintaining order in those regions. The **Negev of Judah at Beer-sheba** completed their counterclockwise loop through the land, and Joab's delegation probably headed up the patriarchal highway through Hebron and back to Jerusalem with its census numbers.

24:9 On **men from Israel . . . men from Judah**, see note at 19:41. The numbers given in the parallel passage in 1Ch 21:5 differ significantly, but both authors appear to have rounded their numbers, and the Chronicler may have included Judah's number in Israel's number as well.

24:10 **David's conscience troubled him**, revealing again the work of God in his heart was not in vain. He confessed his sin and waited on the Lord's response.

24:11 The Lord's response came **in the morning**. The prophet Gad ministered during David's reign and committed certain events of David's life to writing (1Ch 29:29), though these writings have not been discovered.

elation from the Lord had come to the prophet Gad,[a] David's seer:[b] 12 "Go and say to David, 'This is what the Lord says: I am offering you three choices. Choose one of them, and I will do it to you.'"

13 So Gad went to David, told him the choices, and asked him, "Do you want three[A] years of famine to come on your land, to flee from your foes three months while they pursue you, or to have a plague in your land three days? Now, think it over and decide what answer I should take back to the One who sent me."

14 David answered Gad, "I have great anxiety. Please, let us fall into the Lord's hands because His mercies are great,[c] but don't let me fall into human hands."

15 So the Lord sent a plague on Israel from that morning until the appointed time, and from Dan to Beer-sheba 70,000 men died. 16 Then the angel extended his hand toward Jerusalem to destroy it,[d] but the Lord relented concerning the destruction[e] and said to the angel who was destroying[f] the people, "Enough, withdraw your hand now!" The angel of the Lord was then at the threshing floor of Araunah[B] the Jebusite.[g]

17 When David saw the angel striking the people, he said to the Lord, "Look, I am the one who has sinned; I am the one[c] who has done wrong. But these sheep, what have they done? Please, let Your hand be against me and my father's family."

a24:11 1Sm 22:5
b1Sm 9:9
c24:14 Ps 103:8-18; 119:156
d24:16 2Kg 19:35
eEx 32:14; Am 7:3-6
f1Co 10:10
g2Ch 3:1
h24:21 Nm 16:44-50
i24:22 1Sm 6:14; 1Kg 19:21
j24:25 2Sm 21:14

David's Altar

18 Gad came to David that day and said to him, "Go up and set up an altar to the Lord on the threshing floor of Araunah the Jebusite." 19 David went up in obedience to Gad's command, just as the Lord had commanded. 20 Araunah looked down and saw the king and his servants coming toward him, so he went out and bowed to the king with his face to the ground.

21 Araunah said, "Why has my lord the king come to his servant?"

David replied, "To buy the threshing floor from you in order to build an altar to the Lord, so the plague on the people may be halted."[h]

22 Araunah said to David, "My lord the king may take whatever he wants[D] and offer it. Here are the oxen for a •burnt offering and the threshing sledges and ox yokes for the wood.[i] 23 My king, Araunah gives everything here to the king." Then he said to the king, "May the Lord your God accept you."

24 The king answered Araunah, "No, I insist on buying it from you for a price, for I will not offer to the Lord my God burnt offerings that cost me nothing." David bought the threshing floor and the oxen for 20 ounces[E] of silver. 25 He built an altar to the Lord there and offered burnt offerings and •fellowship offerings. Then the Lord answered prayer on behalf of the land,[j] and the plague on Israel ended.

A24:13 LXX; MT reads *seven*; 1Ch 21:12   B 24:16 = Ornan in 1Ch 21:15-28; 2Ch 3:1   C24:17 LXX reads *shepherd*   D24:22 Lit *take what is good in his eyes*   E24:24 Lit *50 shekels*

24:13 David received three **choices** from the Lord through Gad—**famine**, military defeat, or **plague**. The seriousness of these punishments revealed the gravity of David's sin.

24:14 Again, David revealed his heart. He knew **mercies** might come from the Lord, but not from the **human hands** of his enemies. Who knew whether God's grace might avert disaster (see note at 12:22)?

24:16 When **the angel** whom God had sent to bring the plague extended his hand **toward Jerusalem to destroy it**, David's thinking proved correct. **The Lord relented** and spared the city. The Jebusites, part of the original Canaanite population during the days of Joshua (Jos 24:11), held Jerusalem until David conquered them (2Sm 5:6-8). **Araunah** apparently had continued to live in the area following David's conquest.

24:17 David asked the Lord, **these sheep, what have they done?** He pleaded with God to strike only him and his family, but sin often has consequences that affect others besides the person who has sinned.

24:18 This **altar to the Lord** would mark the point where the plague had stopped.

24:20 Araunah's threshing floor sat above Jerusalem to the north, in the area where Abraham offered Isaac as a sacrifice and where Solomon would later build the temple (2Ch 3:1). Since threshing utilized the wind, threshing floors probably were often in high parts of cities.

24:22 Araunah made David a generous offer: **My lord the king may take whatever he wants**. Probably his offer was sincere; besides, especially as a foreigner, he was not in a position to bargain with Israel's king. Or Araunah may have anticipated the king would respond with a price (Gn 23:7-16).

24:24 David, however, knew that all genuine sacrifice came at a **price**. To offer to the Lord **burnt offerings that cost . . . nothing** would have been to David a sign of the deepest ingratitude. In light of this, **20 ounces of silver** was probably more than a fair price.

24:25 **Burnt offerings** typically signified the general dedication of the worshiper (Lv 1). **Fellowship offerings** involved a meal shared by priest and worshiper, and they could be offered to express thankfulness—in this case thankfulness that **the plague on Israel**, while severe, had not destroyed Jerusalem.

1 Kings

Introduction

The titles of these books are certainly descriptive of their
contents: the history of the kings and the kingdoms
of Israel and Judah. First and Second Kings are part
of a larger body of the Old Testament known as the 12
Historical Books (Joshua–Esther). Originally, the books
were just one book, but were divided by the translators of
the Septuagint (the Gk translation of the Old Testament).

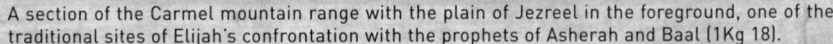

A section of the Carmel mountain range with the plain of Jezreel in the foreground, one of the
traditional sites of Elijah's confrontation with the prophets of Asherah and Baal (1Kg 18).

Circumstances of Writing

Author: Scholars cannot identify the authors of any portions of these books. Traditional guesses such as Samuel and Jeremiah lack evidence, although a prominent worshiper of Yahweh like Jeremiah would have been influential in the circles that produced these books. Since the books clearly incorporated many earlier documents, the complete authorship would be all writers who contributed to the source documents of this work. At some point, the Holy Spirit worked in the human authors to authenticate the inspired, inerrant books of 1 and 2 Kings. The final stage of composition or compilation had to come after the release of Jehoiachin from Babylonian imprisonment (ca 562 B.C.). That edition may have added only a postscript to a work completed years earlier, or it may have involved significant additions.

Background: The history recorded in 1 and 2 Kings covers approximately 410 years. First Kings begins around 970 B.C. with the death of King David, and 2 Kings ends around 560 B.C. with the release of King Jehoiachin from prison. During this time, the nation of Israel split into two kingdoms (930 B.C.), and both kingdoms went into exile (Israel in 722 B.C. and Judah in 587 B.C.).

Message and Purpose

The theological perspective of 1 and 2 Kings is expressed in a number of themes: (1) the sinfulness of the kings and the nation; (2) the conflict between the demands of practical politics and the demands of faith; (3) the glory that God gave to the obedient covenant kings; (4) God's harshness in judgment on some occasions and leniency on others; and (5) the conflict between the worship of the Lord and the worship of other gods.

The role of the king: The Davidic covenant established the king as the moral representative of the people for covenant purposes. Therefore, up through kings Azariah (also known as Uzziah) and Jotham, the moral state of the king was treated as equaling the moral state of the people. Covenant blessings were given or withheld on the basis of the king's behavior. Thus the behavior of the king was the important covenant and moral fact for any given reign.

1000 B.C.   **900 B.C.**

David 1010–970   **Solomon** 970–931   **Rehoboam** 931–913   **Jeroboam** 931–909

David becomes king of Judah. 1010

David becomes king over all Israel. 1003

David conquers Jerusalem. 1000?

Solomon becomes king. 970

Temple construction begins. 966

Temple of Solomon is dedicated. 959

Kingdom divides: Rehoboam, king of Southern Kingdom; Jeroboam I, king of Northern Kingdom 931

Pharaoh Shoshenq I (Shishak), founder of Egypt's 22nd Dynasty, invades Jerusalem and takes treasures from the temple and royal palaces. 926–917

First temple reform under Asa 897

Omri makes Samaria his capital. 880

Elijah's ministry 862–852

Ben-hadad attacks Samaria. 857

Elisha's ministry 850?–798?

Joel's ministry 836–796?

Second temple reform under Joash 812

The role of the prophet: This was the period of development of the office of the prophet. The nature of the prophetic office passed through several nonsequential stages from the ecstatic, miracle-working prophets represented by Saul (1Sm 19:24) and Elisha (2Kg 3:14-16); then through nonmiracle-working court prophets such as Gad and Micaiah; and finally to the great writing prophets attested in Scripture.

Revival: The last two revival kings of Judah (Hezekiah and Josiah) experienced individual revivals that had few effects on either the rest of the royal house or on the nation as a whole. The nation returned to apostasy on the death of each of these good kings. Therefore these two revivals did not bring a full restoration of international political power and wealth. Rather they simply delayed the inevitable judgment.

Contribution to the Bible

For the Bible writers, history could not have existed without God's purposes. This makes all history theological. The books of 1 and 2 Kings interpreted Hebrew history in light of OT covenant theology. The Babylonian exile created the need for this work of historical apologetics. The exiles needed to explain the failure of the religious program established by the sovereign God. In the Deuteronomic history—Joshua, Judges, 1 and 2 Samuel, and 1 and 2 Kings—this failure was consistently explained as the failures of the people to live up to their part of the covenant.

Structure

The organizing principle of 1 and 2 Kings is not story or narrative. Kings is unique because its basic structural units were the formulaic royal records. Formal openers (1Kg 15:9-10) and closers (1Kg 15:23-24) usually identify the boundaries of these records. Then the writer could insert other types of literature before, between, and after the openers and closers: narratives, prayers, descriptions, etc. But the most important element was the evaluation of the ruler's faithfulness to the covenant (1Kg 15:11-15). All of these materials made up a history of covenant obedience or disobedience.

---

800 B.C.   600 B.C.

Ahab 874–853   **Joash** 835–796

Events in Amos 783–746

First Olympiad celebrated in Greece 776

The first eclipse of the sun documented in
  Assyrian annals 763

Events in Hosea 750–722?

Events in Micah 750–686

Tiglath-pileser's invasions of Israel 745–732

Isaiah's ministry 742–700

Syro-Ephraimite War; Aram and Israel invade
  Judah. 735?

Hezekiah 715–686   **Josiah** 640–609

Samaria falls; Northern Kingdom taken
  into exile by Assyrians 722

Third temple reform under Hezekiah 715

Sennacherib's invasion of Judah 701

Jeremiah's ministry 627–586?

Fourth temple reform under Josiah 622

Josiah killed in battle by Pharaoh Neco 609

Nebuchadnezzar's three invasions of
  Judah 605, 597, 586

Temple of Solomon destroyed 586

Outline of 1 Kings

I. Final Days of King David (1:1–2:11)
  A. Adonijah tries to seize the throne (1:1-38)
  B. Solomon anointed as David's successor (1:39-53)
  C. David's charge to Solomon (2:1-11)

II. Solomon's Reign over the United Kingdom (2:12–11:43)
  A. Solomon deals with his opponents (2:12-46)
  B. Solomon's wisdom (3:1-28)
  C. Solomon's officials (4:1-19)
  D. Solomon's splendor (4:20-34)
  E. Solomon builds the temple (5:1–8:66)
  F. Solomon's fame and reputation (9:1–10:29)
  G. Solomon's sin and death (11:1-43)

III. The Divided Kingdoms of Judah and Israel (12:1–22:53)
  A. Judah's King Rehoboam (12:1-24)
  B. Israel's King Jeroboam (12:25–14:20)
  C. King Rehoboam of Judah (continued) (14:21-31)
  D. Judah's Abijam and Asa (15:1-24)
  E. Israel's Nadab and Baasha (15:25–16:7)
  F. Israel's Elah, Zimri, Tibni, and Omri (16:8-28)
  G. Israel's King Ahab and the prophet Elijah (16:29–22:40)
  H. Judah's King Jehoshaphat (22:41-50)
  I. Israel's King Ahaziah (22:51-53)

David's Last Days

1 Now King David was old and getting on in years.[a] Although they covered him with bedclothes, he could not get warm.[b] 2 So his servants said to him: "Let us[A] search for a young virgin for my lord the king.[c] She is to attend the king and be his caregiver. She is to lie by your side so that my lord the king will get warm." 3 They searched for a beautiful girl throughout the territory of Israel; they found Abishag[d] the Shunammite[B,e] and brought her to the king. 4 The girl was of unsurpassed beauty,[f] and she became the king's caregiver. She served him, but he was not intimate with[c] her.

Adonijah's Bid for Power

5 Adonijah son of Haggith[g] kept exalting himself, saying, "I will be king!" He prepared chariots, cavalry, and 50 men to run ahead of him.[D,h] 6 But his father had never once reprimanded[E,i] him by saying, "Why do you act this way?"[j] In addition, he was quite handsome[k] and was born after Absalom.[l] 7 He conspired[F] with Joab son of Zeruiah[m] and with Abiathar

Cross references (center column)

[a]1:1 2Sm 5:4; 1Kg 2:10-11; 1Ch 23:1
[b]Ec 4:11
[c]1:2 Est 2:2
[d]1:3 1Kg 1:15; 2:17
[e]Jos 19:18; 1Sm 28:4
[f]1:4 Est 2:7
[g]1:5 2Sm 3:4
[h]2Sm 15:1
[i]1:6 1Sm 3:13
[j]2Sm 13:21
[k]2Sm 14:25
[l]2Sm 3:3-4
[m]1:7 1Ch 11:6

[A]1:2 Lit *them*   [B]1:3 Shunem was a town in the hill country of Issachar at the foot of Mt. Moreh; Jos 19:17-18.   [C]1:4 Lit *he did not know*   [D]1:5 Heralds announcing his procession   [E]1:6 Or *grieved*   [F]1:7 Lit *His words were*

1:1-53 First Kings gives the reader a survey of sweeping social and religious forces that were vying to shape the future of Israel. The book begins with a power struggle between Adonijah and David over who would succeed David. At stake, many believed, was the identity of the nation. That Adonijah had no trouble garnering support in his quest for the throne indicates the deep divisions shaping up among the Hebrews.

At least six factors pressed for change in the kingdom. (1) The ideal of the violent, plundering warrior (Pr 1:10-19) was yielding in this new era to the ideal of the wise man (1Kg 4:32-34) and the successful businessman (Pr 22:29). (2) Central authority with a royal bureaucracy (1Kg 4:1-19) suppressed the power of the local elders and clan leaders. (3) The continued policy of converting and absorbing the many peoples of Canaan was creating a new nation united by Hebrew rulers and, nominally, by faith in Yahweh. (4) The new, national, chariot army (10:26; see note at 1:38) would replace the levies (military conscriptions) of the tribes and clans, thus changing the identity and capacities of Hebrew military forces. (5) The rise of international commerce and a new business class forced drastic changes in Hebrew society (Pr 7:19-21; 31:10-31). (6) The older moral values were giving way to new ones (e.g., Pr 7:16-21). Most of these trends were underway before Solomon, but under Solomon they created a new society.

The writer of 1 Kings spoke for the Davidic dynasty and faith in Yahweh, over against Adonijah and other representatives of an alternate future. Thus it is accurate to say that a major purpose of this opening chapter and many other portions of the OT is to support the politics of David and Solomon. Some would use the term *propaganda* to describe this purpose, but the only proper issue is whether or not the new trends were God's will for the nation. This is the author's focus.

1:1 The reign of **King David** had begun the first age of godly greatness, prosperity, and power in the history of the Hebrews. After David's death, could this greatness continue? In God's plan it was to continue with Solomon, but would God's purposes survive the crisis of David's death?

1:2 The strongest Hebrew word for **virgin** (*betulah*) is used here. The word for the nuptial sheets that provided proof of the bride's virginity (Dt 22:15) is derived from this word.

1:4 The ancients believed in the curative value of pairing a warm human body with an ill body, and so the phrase **was not intimate with her** speaks primarily to the fact that the sole purpose **the girl** served was to provide warmth and care. However, even among conservative scholars, some believe that given the context the above phrase may also indirectly indicate that aged David was no longer able to be intimate with a woman. In the eyes of his detractors, this would be taken as proof that David lacked the strength and fitness to continue as king. Once known, this may have encouraged Adonijah's attempt to seize the throne.

1:5-10 In the struggle for Israel's future, neither side (those aligned with David and his designated heir nor those against them) openly appealed to the tribal elders or other leaders for support (note tribal leaders in 12:1-7). Both sides believed that if they seized power in Jerusalem, the traditional leaders would accept the outcome. Adonijah gathered his supporters and tried to seize the throne. Some of David's loyal followers, such as Joab and Abiathar, joined with Adonijah. Perhaps they had given up on David, as he seems to have become rather detached and even irresponsible (e.g., 1:6).

Bathsheba and Nathan, supported by some of David's remaining brave warriors and David's loyal Cherethites and the Pelethites (see note at 1:38), reacted quickly and put an end to the attempted coup. Prudent human planning helped to gain David's active support. Nathan's warning to Bathsheba to act to save her and Solomon's lives (v. 12) showed the likelihood for violence of this struggle.

While there were moral positives and weaknesses to both sides, the decisive issue was which side God supported—despite its weaknesses. God's purposes and the future fortunes of the Hebrews were bound to the new ways, to the centralized government, and to the Davidic dynasty.

1:5 Kept exalting indicates that **Adonijah** had already been proclaiming his future kingship and establishing his entourage for seizing the throne. Coup attempts are not birthed overnight. David had already promised Bathsheba that her son Solomon would be king and had publicly announced to the assembled nation that Solomon was his heir (1Ch 28:5). Nevertheless, Adonijah seems to have made his moves with his father's silent acquiescence so that his will for the succession became unclear. In this context, the first to act might gain the throne.

Chariots and **cavalry** should probably be rendered "chariots" and "charioteers" since horse-mounted warriors (cavalry) are not documented for this early period. Early in the history of chariot warfare, the terms for chariot warriors were the same as the terms later used for cavalry warriors. By the time of Ahab (16:28ff), Assyrian records recognized the existence of mounted warriors in the region. During Solomon's rule the military would become a chariot army, probably made up of foreign mercenaries since developing a local chariot force was a long, expensive process.

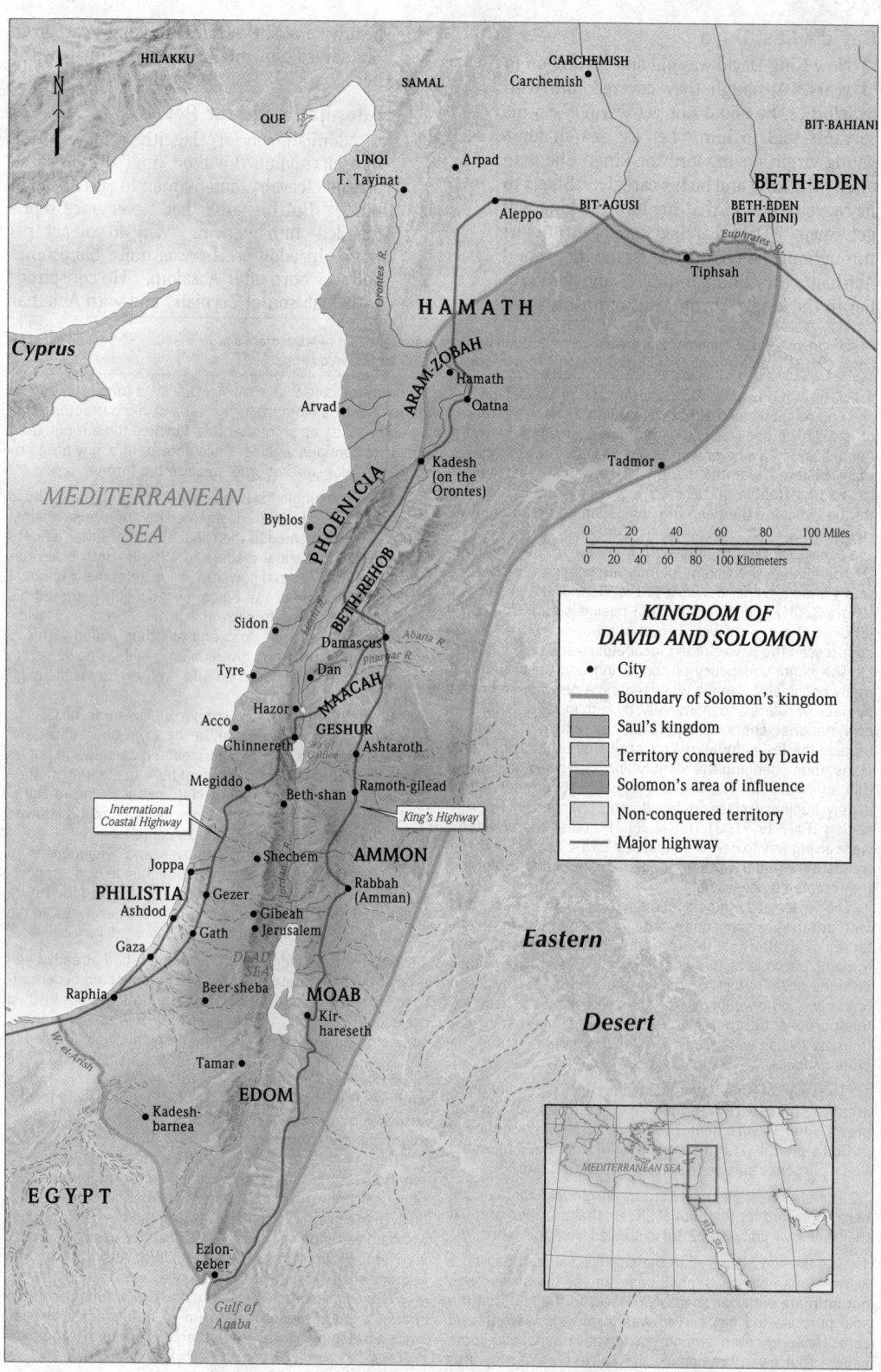

HILAKKU

N

QUE

SAMAL

CARCHEMISH
Carchemish

BIT-BAHIANI

UNQI
T. Tayinat

Arpad

BETH-EDEN

BIT-AGUSI

BETH-EDEN
(BIT ADINI)

Aleppo

Euphrates R.

Cyprus

Orontes R.

HAMATH

Tiphsah

ARAM-ZOBAH

Hamath

*MEDITERRANEAN
SEA*

Arvad

Qatna

Kadesh
(on the
Orontes)

Tadmor

Byblos

PHOENICIA

Sidon

BETH-REHOB

Tyre

Hazor

Damascus

Dan

Abana R.

Pharpar R.

Acco

MAACAH

Chinnereth

GESHUR

*Sea of
Galilee*

Ashtaroth

Megiddo

Beth-shan

Ramoth-gilead

International
Coastal Highway

King's Highway

Joppa

Shechem

AMMON

PHILISTIA

Gezer

Rabbah
(Amman)

Eastern

Ashdod

Gibeah

Gath

Jerusalem

Gaza

*DEAD
SEA*

Desert

Raphia

Beer-sheba

MOAB

W. el-'Arish

Tamar

Kir-
hareseth

EDOM

Kadesh-
barnea

EGYPT

Ezion-
geber

*Gulf of
Aqaba*

**KINGDOM OF
DAVID AND SOLOMON**

• City

Boundary of Solomon's kingdom

Saul's kingdom

Territory conquered by David

Solomon's area of influence

Non-conquered territory

Major highway

0   20   40   60   80   100 Miles

0 20 40 60 80 100 Kilometers

MEDITERRANEAN SEA

RED SEA

the priest.^a They supported^b Adonijah, ⁸ but Zadok the priest,^c Benaiah son of Jehoiada,^d Nathan the prophet,^e Shimei,^f Rei, and David's warriors^g did not side with Adonijah.

⁹ Adonijah sacrificed sheep, oxen, and fattened cattle near the stone of Zoheleth, which is next to En-rogel.^h He invited all his royal brothers and all the men of Judah, the servants of the king,ⁱ ¹⁰ but he did not invite Nathan the prophet, Benaiah, the warriors, or his brother Solomon.^j

Nathan's and Bathsheba's Appeals

¹¹ Then Nathan^k said to Bathsheba, Solomon's mother,^l "Have you not heard that Adonijah son of Haggith has become king^m and our lord David does not know it?ⁿ ¹² Now please come and let me advise^o you. Save your life and the life of your son Solomon.^p ¹³ Go, approach King David and say to him, 'My lord the king, did you not swear to your servant: Your son Solomon is to become king after me, and he is the one who is to sit on my throne?^q So why has Adonijah become king?' ¹⁴ At that moment, while you are still there speaking with the king, I'll come in after you and confirm your words."^r

¹⁵ So Bathsheba went to the king in his bedroom. Since the king was very old, Abishag the Shunammite was serving him.^s ¹⁶ Bathsheba bowed down and paid homage to the king, and he asked, "What do you want?"

¹⁷ She replied, "My lord, you swore to your servant by the Lord your God, 'Your son Solomon is to become king after me, and he is the one who is to sit on my throne.' ¹⁸ Now look, Adonijah has become king. And,^A my lord the king, you didn't know it. ¹⁹ He has lavishly sacrificed oxen, fattened cattle, and sheep. He

^a1:7 1Sm 22:20-23; 2Sm 20:25
^b1Kg 2:22
^c1:8 2Sm 20:25; 1Ch 16:39-40
^d2Sm 8:18
^e2Sm 7:2; 2:1-25
^f1Kg 4:18
^g2Sm 23:8-39
^h1:9 Jos 15:7; 18:16; 2Sm 17:17
ⁱ2Sm 15:11-12
^j1:10 1Kg 1:8,26
^k1:11 2Sm 12:1,25; 1Kg 1:8,10
^l2Sm 12:24
^m2Sm 15:10; 1Kg 1:25; 2:15
ⁿ2Sm 3:26; 1Kg 1:18; 2:32
^o1:12 Pr 15:22
^p1Kg 15:29; 2Kg 10:11
^q1:13 1Kg 1:17,30; 1Ch 22:9-13
^r1:14 1Kg 1:22-27
^s1:15 1Kg 1:1-4
^t1:21 Dt 31:16; 2Sm 7:12; 1Kg 2:10
^u1Kg 1:12
^v1:22 1Kg 1:14
^w1:29 2Sm 4:9

invited all the king's sons, Abiathar the priest, and Joab the commander of the army, but he did not invite your servant Solomon. ²⁰ Now, my lord the king, the eyes of all Israel are on you to tell them who will sit on the throne of my lord the king after him. ²¹ Otherwise, when my lord the king rests with his fathers,^t I and my son Solomon will be regarded as criminals."^u

²² At that moment, while she was still speaking with the king, Nathan the prophet arrived,^v ²³ and it was announced to the king, "Nathan the prophet is here." He came into the king's presence and bowed to him with his face to the ground.

²⁴ "My lord the king," Nathan said, "did you say, 'Adonijah is to become king after me, and he is the one who is to sit on my throne'? ²⁵ For today he went down and lavishly sacrificed oxen, fattened cattle, and sheep. He invited all the sons of the king, the commanders of the army, and Abiathar the priest. And look! They're eating and drinking in his presence, and they're saying, 'Long live King Adonijah!' ²⁶ But he did not invite me—me, your servant—or Zadok the priest or Benaiah son of Jehoiada or your servant Solomon. ²⁷ I'm certain my lord the king would not have let this happen without letting your servant^B know who will sit on my lord the king's throne after him."

Solomon Confirmed King

²⁸ King David responded by saying, "Call in Bathsheba for me." So she came into the king's presence and stood before him. ²⁹ The king swore an oath and said, "As the Lord lives, who has redeemed my life from every difficulty,^w ³⁰ just as I swore to you by the Lord

---

^A1:18 Some Hb mss, LXX, Vg, Syr; other Hb mss read *And now*   ^B1:27 Some Hb mss, LXX; alt Hb tradition reads *servants*

1:8 David's warriors (lit "great men") likely refers to (1) the remnants and/or successors of David's warriors (2Sm 23:8-39); or (2) David's loyal palace guard, the Cherethites and Pelethites (see note at 1Kg 1:38).

1:9 Adonijah's great feast amounted to an impromptu coronation, with many of the expected features: a revered setting, a military leader, a priest, pomp, and loyal followers.

1:11-12 With Adonijah's coup already in motion, someone with sufficient standing to be accepted by the people had to initiate a counter movement for Solomon or the throne would be lost. **Nathan**, the prophet, assumed this role. He warned **Bathsheba** that the penalty for inaction could be death for herself and **Solomon**, and probably others of David's loyalists as well. The losers in such power struggles were typically executed.

1:15-21 Bathsheba raised three issues to arouse David to action. First, by God's will David had promised the throne to **Solomon**. Second, Adonijah had proclaimed himself king without David's public support or knowledge. Third, she

pointed out that she and Solomon would be **regarded as criminals** if David did not act.

1:24-25 Nathan then came and reinforced the points Bathsheba had made to the king.

1:26-28 Nathan tactfully hinted at the danger to himself, Bathsheba, and David's loyal officials by revealing that David's inner circle had not been invited to the unofficial coronation. This cast them as outsiders, a dangerous place to be during a regime change.

Bathsheba had to be called in despite the fact that she was already in the king's bedroom with David when Nathan entered (v. 22). Readers may think the text is inconsistent here because it seems to forget that Bathsheba was already present. But we must remember that Hebrew narrative is often very spare, leaving out details that can be implied from context. In this case readers should conclude that sometime after verse 22 Bathsheba had temporarily left the king's room, appropriately giving Nathan private audience with his king.

God of Israel: Your son Solomon is to become king after me, and he is the one who is to sit on my throne in my place,[a] that is exactly what I will do this very day."[b]

[31]Bathsheba bowed with her face to the ground, paying homage to the king,[c] and said, "May my lord King David live forever!"[d]

[32]King David then said, "Call in Zadok the priest, Nathan the prophet, and Benaiah son of Jehoiada for me."[e] So they came into the king's presence. [33]The king said to them, "Take my servants[f] with you, have my son Solomon ride on my own mule,[g] and take him down to Gihon.[h] [34]There, Zadok the priest and Nathan the prophet are to anoint him as king over Israel.[i] You are to blow the ram's horn[j] and say, 'Long live King Solomon!'[k] [35]You are to come up after him, and he is to come in and sit on my throne. He is the one who is to become king in my place; he is the one I have commanded to be ruler[l] over Israel and Judah."[m]

[36]"Amen," Benaiah son of Jehoiada replied to the king. "May the LORD, the God of my lord the king, so affirm it.[n] [37]Just as the LORD was with my lord the king,[o] so may He[A] be with Solomon and make his throne greater than the throne of my lord King David."[p]

[38]Then Zadok the priest, Nathan the prophet, Benaiah son of Jehoiada, the Cherethites, and the Pelethites[q] went down, had Solomon ride on King David's mule, and took him to Gihon. [39]Zadok the priest took the horn of oil from the tabernacle and anointed Solomon.[r] Then they blew the ram's horn,[s] and all the people proclaimed, "Long live King Solomon!"[t] [40]All the people followed him, playing

flutes and rejoicing with such a great joy[u] that the earth split open from the sound.[B]

Adonijah Hears of Solomon's Coronation

[41]Adonijah and all the invited guests who were with him[v] heard the noise as they finished eating. Joab heard the sound of the ram's horn and said, "Why is the town in such an uproar?"[w] [42]He was still speaking when Jonathan son of Abiathar the priest,[x] suddenly arrived. Adonijah said, "Come in, for you are an excellent man, and you must be bringing good news."[y]

[43]"Unfortunately not," Jonathan answered him. "Our lord King David has made Solomon king. [44]And with Solomon, the king has sent Zadok the priest, Nathan the prophet, Benaiah son of Jehoiada, the Cherethites, and the Pelethites, and they have had him ride on the king's mule. [45]Zadok the priest and Nathan the prophet have anointed him king in Gihon.[z] They have gone from there rejoicing. The town has been in an uproar; that's the noise you heard. [46]Solomon has even taken his seat on the royal throne.[aa]

[47]"The king's servants have also gone to congratulate our lord King David, saying, 'May your God make the name of Solomon more well known than your name, and may He make his throne greater than your throne.'[ab] Then the king bowed in worship on his bed.[ac] [48]And the king went on to say this: 'May the LORD God of Israel be praised! Today He has provided one to sit on my throne,[ad] and I am a witness.'"[C]

Cross references (center column)

[a]1:30 1Kg 1:13
[b]1Kg 1:33-35
[c]1:31 1Kg 1:16
[d]Neh 2:3; Dn 2:4; 3:9
[e]1:32 1Kg 1:8,10,26
[f]1:33 2Sm 20:6
[g]2Sm 18:9; Est 6:8; Zch 9:9; Jn 12:14-15
[h]2Ch 32:30; 33:14
[i]1:34 1Sm 10:1; 16:3,13
[j]2Sm 15:10
[k]1Sm 10:24; 1Kg 1:25
[l]1:35 1Sm 13:14
[m]2Sm 2:4; 5:3
[n]1:36 Jr 28:6
[o]1:37 1Sm 20:13
[p]1Kg 1:47
[q]1:38 2Sm 8:18
[r]1:39 1Ch 29:22
[s]2Kg 11:14
[t]1Sm 10:24
[u]1:40 Ezr 6:16
[v]1:41 1Kg 1:5,7-10
[w]2Kg 11:12-13
[x]1:42 2Sm 15:27,36
[y]2Sm 18:26-27
[z]1:43-45 1Kg 1:33-35
[aa]1:46 1Ch 29:23
[ab]1:47 1Kg 1:37
[ac]Gn 47:31
[ad]1:48 2Sm 7:12; 1Kg 3:6

[A]1:37 Alt Hb tradition reads *so He will*   [B]1:40 LXX reads *the land resounded with their noise*   [C]1:48 Lit *and my eyes are seeing*

1:32 David responded with the orders that legitimized Solomon's succession. **Benaiah** seemed to be the leader of the Cherethites and the Pelethites. In the absence of any tribal levies, they were the dominant military force in the city.

1:33 The **mule** was the traditional mount of honor for that time. In an earlier age, the donkey had played that role, a custom still remembered as late as Zch 9:9. To ride the king's mule was to claim the throne. The **Gihon** spring was an ancient, revered, and necessary source of water for Jerusalem. Later it was the source of water for King Hezekiah's tunnel. Choosing it for the site of Solomon's coronation indicated that it carried special significance and authority for the people of Jerusalem just as Adonijah's selection of En-rogel recognized the significance of that site (v. 9).

1:34 The proper religious personnel were to anoint **Solomon**. This was done by the king's command and in the presence of the king's private army. These facts were sufficient for the people of Jerusalem to choose Solomon over Adonijah.

1:38 The **Cherethites** and the **Pelethites** were, formerly, Philistine mercenaries, personally loyal to David, and by this time, presumably converted to faith in Yahweh. They formed David's personal bodyguard and were effective infantry. The

probable reason why David's infantry could defeat Aramean chariots (2Sm 8:3-4), a rare skill for infantry, was the presence of these skilled Philistines.

1:40 The people who followed with **rejoicing** were probably the classes that benefited from several of the new ways that were emerging in the kingdom (see note at vv. 1-53). Both for good and for ill, Solomon's rule would enhance these new ways.

1:41 The conflicting coronations were occurring within 500 yards of each other, the distance between Gihon and En-rogel. Imagine the uneasiness when Adonijah's group **heard the noise** of Solomon's coronation.

1:44-46 All ceremonies for enthroning **Solomon** had been accomplished. Only major force could have reversed these actions. Adonijah's followers were not ready to battle for Jerusalem, especially since David had spoken and was still alive.

1:47-48 These two speeches were not merely friendly sentiments. First, they represented David's will. Then, repeated and recorded, they confirmed the new king in the same way that the public oath of office legitimizes an office holder in our time.

⁴⁹Then all of Adonijah's guests got up trembling and went their separate ways. ⁵⁰Adonijah was afraid of Solomon, so he got up and went to take hold of the horns of the altar.ᵃ

⁵¹It was reported to Solomon: "Look, Adonijah fears King Solomon, and he has taken hold of the horns of the altar, saying, 'Let King Solomon firstᴬ swear to me that he will not kill his servant with the sword.'"

⁵²Then Solomon said, "If he is a man of character, not a single hair of his will fall to the ground,ᵇ but if evil is found in him, he dies."ᶜ ⁵³So King Solomon sent for him, and they took him down from the altar. He came and paid homage to King Solomon, and Solomon said to him, "Go to your home."

David's Dying Instructions to Solomon

2 As the time approached for David to die,ᵈ he instructed his son Solomon, ²"As for me, I am going the way of all of the earth.ᵉ Be strong and be courageous like a man,ᶠ ³and keep your obligation to the LORD your God to walk in His ways and to keep His statutes, commands, ordinances, and decrees. This is written in the law of Moses, so that you will

have success in everything you doᵍ and wherever you turn, ⁴and so that the LORD will carry out His promise that He made to me: 'If your sons are careful to walk faithfully before Me with their whole mind and heart,ʰ you will never fail to have a man on the throne of Israel.'ⁱ

⁵"You also know what Joab son of Zeruiah did to meʲ and what he did to the two commanders of Israel's army, Abner son of Nerᵏ and Amasa son of Jether.ˡ He murdered them in a time of peace to avenge blood shed in war. He spilled that blood on his own waistband and on the sandals of his feet.ᴮ ⁶Act according to your wisdom, and do not let his gray head descend to ˚Sheol in peace.

⁷"Show loyalty to the sons of Barzillai the Gileadite and let them be among those who eat at your tableᵐ because they supported me when I fled from your brother Absalom.ⁿ

⁸"Keep an eye on Shimei son of Gera, the Benjaminite from Bahurim who is with you. He uttered malicious curses against me the day I went to Mahanaim.ᵒ But he came down to meet me at the Jordan River, and I swore to him by the LORD: 'I will never kill you with the sword.'ᵖ ⁹So don't let him go unpunished,

---

ᵃ1:50 Ex 21:12-14; 1Kg 2:28
ᵇ1:52 1Sm 14:45; 2Sm 14:11; Ac 27:34
ᶜ1Kg 2:23-25
ᵈ2:1 Gn 47:29; Nm 27:13
ᵉ2:2 Jos 23:14
ᶠJos 1:6-7,9
ᵍ2:3 Dt 29:9; 1Ch 22:12-13
ʰ2:4 Dt 6:5; Mt 22:37
ⁱ2Sm 7:12-13; 1Kg 8:25; 9:5
ʲ2:5 2Sm 18:5, 12,14
ᵏ2Sm 3:27
ˡ2Sm 20:10
ᵐ2:7 2Sm 9:7; 19:28
ⁿ2Sm 19:31-39
ᵒ2:8 2Sm 16:5-13
ᵖ2Sm 19:16-23

ᴬ1:51 Some Hb mss, LXX, Syr, Vg read *today*   ᴮ2:5 LXX, Old Lat read *on my waistband and . . . my feet*; v. 31

1:49 With the people of Jerusalem accepting Solomon's coronation, and Adonijah's followers having no stomach for fighting the Cherethites and the Pelethites, Adonijah's coup had failed.

1:50 Adonijah's failure was obvious when he took refuge at the **altar**, near the tabernacle. In popular attitudes of the day, such sanctuary may have involved magical protection rather than moral principle (see note at 2:30-33). The altar was the most sacred object outside the tabernacle proper, and over time, the **horns** became the most representative part of the altar.

2:2-3 David's instructions that Solomon be steadfast, firm, and obedient were the kind of covenant challenges presented to leaders and common Hebrews throughout the OT (cp. Jos 1:9). The result of obedience to the law was made explicit for Solomon: it would bring **success in everything** (Jos 1:6-8; Ps 1).

2:4 Obedience also assured the permanence of David's dynasty. Second Samuel 7:11-16 did not explicitly state this as the necessary condition for a permanent dynasty. This is another indication that the reader sometimes must examine several passages to get the whole picture. In terms of eternal salvation, this permanence depends on the eternal reign of the NT Messiah, the son of David. However, 1 and 2 Kings never overtly treated this permanence as anything more than the human, Davidic dynasty, though this concept is enriched and expanded in other parts of the OT.

2:5 David counseled Solomon about some real dangers to the state. David was accepted as a man after God's own heart in the old regime. Even so, as a man of blood David was not allowed to build God's temple (1Ch 22:7-9). Others, who were properly tolerated in the old days, were now

a threat to the new, more peaceful society. David was perhaps warning Solomon against tolerance for men whose character made them too dangerous for this new society. In this counsel David may have recognized a profound change from the ideal of the plundering warrior and conqueror king of yesterday to the mercantile emperor of the new day. Likewise there was a change from the violent, vengeful clan warrior to a professional soldier serving the interests of the centralized state.

Joab, the double murderer, was the first to be dealt with. His first murder, killing Abner, could have been construed as revenge, although **blood shed in war** was not normally avenged in **peace**. However, the murder of **Amasa** could not be justified. David seemed to be unable to act against powerful members of his own clan, although he did publicly distance himself from Joab's violence (2Sm 3:28-29). The **blood** on his **waistband** and **sandals** graphically indicated Joab's guilt. Finally, Joab's siding with Adonijah in what could have been a violent civil conflict outweighed any gratitude David owed to Joab for his past faithfulness.

2:7 David counseled **loyalty** to the house of **Barzillai**, who supported David in Absalom's rebellion. This word **loyalty** is the usual word for *covenant faithfulness*. For Barzillai, proper covenant faithfulness meant faithfulness to the king. For David, Barzillai's faithfulness deserved reciprocal faithfulness from the king and his house. David's counsel illustrated the mutual responsibility or loyalty in covenant relationships. These mutual covenant responsibilities were binding on both kings and God.

2:8 This counsel implied that **Shimei** still exercised some influence. At the time of David's return, tolerating Shimei may have been beneficial for stabilizing the country. By

for you are a wise man. You know how to deal with him to bring his gray head down to Sheol with blood."

[10] Then David rested with his fathers[a] and was buried in the city of David.[b] [11] The length of time David reigned over Israel was 40 years: he reigned seven years in Hebron and 33 years in Jerusalem.[c] [12] Solomon sat on the throne of his father David, and his kingship was firmly established.[d]

Adonijah's Foolish Request

[13] Now Adonijah son of Haggith[e] came to Bathsheba, Solomon's mother. She asked, "Do you come peacefully?"

"Peacefully," he replied,[f] [14] and then asked, "May I talk with you?"[A]

"Go ahead," she answered.

[15] "You know the kingship was mine," [g] he said. "All Israel expected me to be king, but then the kingship was turned over to my brother,[h] for the LORD gave it to him.[i] [16] So now I have just one request of you; don't turn me down."[B]

She said to him, "Go on."

[17] He replied, "Please speak to King Solomon since he won't turn you down. Let him give me Abishag the Shunammite[j] as a wife."

[18] "Very well," Bathsheba replied. "I will speak to the king for you."

[19] So Bathsheba went to King Solomon to speak to him about Adonijah. The king stood up to greet her, bowed to her, sat down on his throne, and had a throne placed for the king's mother.[k] So she sat down at his right hand.[l]

[20] Then she said, "I have just one small request of you. Don't turn me down."

"Go ahead and ask, mother," the king replied, "for I won't turn you down."

[21] So she said, "Let Abishag the Shunammite be given to your brother Adonijah as a wife."

[22] King Solomon answered his mother, "Why are you requesting Abishag the Shunammite for Adonijah? Since he is my elder brother,[m] you might as well ask the kingship for him,[n] for Abiathar the priest, and for Joab son of Zeruiah."[C,o] [23] Then Solomon took an oath by the LORD: "May God punish me and do so severely[p] if Adonijah has not made this request at the cost of his life. [24] And now, as the LORD lives, the One who established me, seated me on the throne of my father David, and made me a dynasty as He promised[q]—I swear Adonijah will be put to death today!" [25] Then King Solomon gave the order to Benaiah son of Jehoiada,[r] who struck down Adonijah, and he died.

Abiathar's Banishment

[26] The king said to Abiathar the priest,[s] "Go to your fields in Anathoth.[t] Even though you deserve to die, I will not put you to death today, since you carried the ark of the Lord GOD in the presence of my father David[u] and you suffered through all that my father suffered."[v] [27] So Solomon banished Abiathar from being the LORD's priest, and it fulfilled the LORD's prophecy He had spoken at Shiloh against Eli's family.[w]

Joab's Execution

[28] The news reached Joab. Since he had supported Adonijah[x] but not Absalom,[y] Joab fled to the LORD's tabernacle and took hold of the horns of the altar.[z]

Cross references (center column):
a2:10 Ac 2:29; 13:36
b2Sm 5:7
c2:11 2Sm 5:4-5; 1Ch 29:27
d2:12 1Kg 2:46; 1Ch 17:14
e2:13 1Kg 1:5, 51-53
f1Sm 16:4-5
g2:15 1Kg 1:11
h1Kg 1:38-46
i1Ch 23:9-10; 28:5,7; Dn 2:21; 4:17; Jn 19:11; Rm 13:1
j2:17 1Kg 1:3-4,15
k2:19 2Sm 15:16; 1Kg 15:13
lPs 110:1; Mt 20:21
m2:22 1Kg 1:6; 1Ch 3:2,5
n2Sm 16:20-22
o1Kg 1:7
p2:23 Ru 1:17; 1Sm 3:17
q2:24 2Sm 7:11-13
r2:25 1Kg 1:8, 26,38
s2:26 1Kg 1:7,19
tJos 21:18; Jr 1:1
u2Sm 15:24-25,29
v1Sm 22:20-23; 2Sm 19:11
w2:27 1Sm 2:31-35
x2:28 1Kg 1:7
y2Sm 18:1-5
zEx 21:12-14; 1Kg 1:50

A2:14 Lit then said, "I have a word for you."   B2:16 Lit don't make me turn my face   C2:22 LXX, Vg, Syr read kingship for him, and on his side are Abiathar the priest and Joab son of Zeruiah

---

contrast, Solomon's power was stable enough that Shimei, and any danger he represented, could be suppressed.

2:10-12 This formula statement, **David rested with his fathers**, provides a narrative transition from David's reign to Solomon's reign.

2:13 This incident is one of many clues (v. 19) that the queen mother was a position of great influence. The frequent listing of this position in the royal formulae of Judah also suggests its influence.

2:15 Adonijah's statement was true to someone who viewed only the human realities. However, it totally ignored the purposes of God.

2:17 One of the customs of the ancient world was for the new king to confirm his position by taking the wives of the former king (2Sm 16:22). Adonijah must have viewed Solomon as very weak to make this dangerous request.

2:18 It seems unbelievably naive for **Bathsheba** to intercede with Solomon in this request. Or did she see that encouraging Adonijah's foolishness was a good way to make clear to

Solomon the threat Adonijah represented? If so, her decision here moved Adonijah a step closer to his demise.

2:19 The protocol and ceremony of this scene again pointed to the influence of the queen mother.

2:22 Solomon's words grouped **Adonijah . . . Abiathar**, and **Joab** together as joint leaders of the failed coup. Adonijah's foolish attempt to extract some advantage from the failure gave Solomon the opportunity to deal with all the plotters.

2:26-27 Solomon's decisive action showed that both Solomon and the Bible writer believed that Solomon was removing major threats to his rule. **Abiathar** knew that his priestly participation in the abortive coronation was essential to Adonijah's plot; his participation was neither innocent nor casual. Mere banishment was a gentle penalty; death would have been justified. Banishment prevented him from playing an influential role either at the tabernacle or in the temple still to be built. Removal of Abiathar from office fulfilled the earlier judgment on **Eli's family** (1Sm 2:30-36).

2:28-29 As the commander of the army, **Joab's** support of **Adonijah** could have mobilized the old tribal and clan levies

²⁹It was reported to King Solomon: "Joab has fled to the LORD's tabernacle and is now beside the altar." Then Solomon sent[A] Benaiah son of Jehoiada[a] and told him, "Go and strike him down!"[b]

³⁰So Benaiah went to the tabernacle and said to Joab, "This is what the king says: 'Come out!'"[c]

But Joab said, "No, for I will die here."

So Benaiah took a message back to the king, "This is what Joab said, and this is how he answered me."

³¹The king said to him, "Do just as he says. Strike him down and bury him in order to remove from me and from my father's house the blood that Joab shed without just cause.[d] ³²The LORD will bring back his own blood on his head because he struck down two men more righteous and better than he, without my father David's knowledge. With his sword, Joab murdered Abner[e] son of Ner, commander of Israel's army, and Amasa[f] son of Jether, commander of Judah's army. ³³Their blood will come back on Joab's head and on the head of his descendants forever, but for David, his descendants, his dynasty, and his throne, there will be peace from the LORD forever."[g]

³⁴Benaiah son of Jehoiada[h] went up, struck down Joab, and put him to death. He was buried at his house in the wilderness.[i] ³⁵Then the king appointed Benaiah son of Jehoiada in Joab's place over the army,[j] and he appointed Zadok the priest in Abiathar's place.

Shimei's Banishment and Execution

³⁶Then the king summoned Shimei[k] and said to him, "Build a house for yourself in Jerusalem and live there, but don't leave there

and go anywhere else. ³⁷On the day you do leave and cross the Kidron Valley,[l] know for sure that you will certainly die. Your blood will be on your own head."[m]

³⁸Shimei said to the king, "The sentence is fair; your servant will do as my lord the king has spoken." And Shimei lived in Jerusalem for a long time.

³⁹But then, at the end of three years, two of Shimei's slaves ran away to Achish[n] son of Maacah, king of Gath.[o] Shimei was informed, "Look, your slaves are in Gath." ⁴⁰So Shimei saddled his donkey and set out to Achish at Gath to search for his slaves. He went and brought them back from Gath.

⁴¹It was reported to Solomon that Shimei had gone from Jerusalem to Gath and had returned. ⁴²So the king summoned Shimei and said to him, "Didn't I make you swear by the LORD and warn you, saying, 'On the day you leave and go anywhere else, know for sure that you will certainly die'? And you said to me, 'The sentence is fair; I will obey.' ⁴³So why have you not kept the LORD's oath and the command that I gave you?" ⁴⁴The king also said, "You yourself know all the evil that you did to my father David.[p] Therefore, the LORD has brought back your evil on your head, ⁴⁵but King Solomon will be blessed, and David's throne will remain established before the LORD forever."[q]

⁴⁶Then the king commanded Benaiah son of Jehoiada, and he went out and struck Shimei down, and he died. So the kingdom was established in Solomon's hand.[r]

The LORD Appears to Solomon

3 Solomon made an alliance[B] with Pharaoh king of Egypt by marrying Pharaoh's

A 2:29 LXX adds *Joab a message: "What is the matter with you, that you have fled to the altar?" And Joab replied, "Because I feared you, I have fled to the Lord." And Solomon the king sent*   B 3:1 Lit *Solomon made himself a son-in-law*

in support of Adonijah. Such a threat was virtually treasonous, and the treasonous potentialities remained as long as Joab lived. Furthermore, judging Joab for his murders was a necessary step in repudiating the old violent ways—a step that David never took.

2:30-33 Joab understood perfectly the consequences of his deeds and sought safety at the altar, where **Benaiah** executed the death sentence against him. In executing the commander in chief of the tribal levies, Solomon was either carrying out a risky deed to remove a popular enemy, or he was so secure in his power that he did not fear any repercussions. Executing Joab at the altar raised other questions. The devotion to Yahweh among the masses may not have risen far above the superstition that the horns of the altar provided magical protection. Assuming that Solomon's faith was real, his disbelief in the magical protection of the horns of the altar was a rejection of popular superstition and an assertion that real moral and social values transcended such superstitious magic (see note at 1:50). Joab might have hoped for sanctuary at the altar, but the right of

sanctuary only applied to those who committed accidental manslaughter (Ex 21:12-14).

2:35 Benaiah's appointment to **Joab's place over the army** indicated that Joab was the commander in chief up to his death. The later restructuring of government to minimize the traditional powers (chap. 4) could have indicated ongoing concerns about the loyalty of the traditional tribal authorities to Solomon.

2:36-46 Shimei's situation was the opposite of Abiathar's. Abiathar was a danger in the capital where he could meddle in centralized worship. Shimei was a danger away from **Jerusalem** where he could stir up trouble in distant locales. Therefore Shimei was placed under house arrest in Jerusalem. When Shimei violated his house arrest, possibly thinking Solomon's concern had diminished over the three-year period, he was executed. The **Kidron Valley**, just east of Jerusalem, served as one of the boundaries of Jerusalem.

3:1 Recalling Egypt's glorious past, some assume that **Solomon** was the junior member of this marriage alliance. Two

daughter.[a] Solomon brought her to live in the city of David[b] until he finished building his palace,[c] the LORD's temple,[d] and the wall surrounding Jerusalem.[e] [2]However, the people were sacrificing on the *high places,[f] because until that time a temple for the LORD's name[g] had not been built. [3]Solomon loved the LORD[h] by walking in the statutes of his father David,[i] but he also sacrificed and burned incense on the high places.

[4]The king went to Gibeon[j] to sacrifice there because it was the most famous high place. He offered 1,000 *burnt offerings on that altar.[k] [5]At Gibeon the LORD appeared to Solomon[l] in a dream at night.[m] God said, "Ask.[n] What should I give you?"

[6]And Solomon replied, "You have shown great and faithful love to Your servant, my father David, because he walked before You in faithfulness, righteousness, and[A] integrity. You have continued this great and faithful

love for him by giving him a son to sit on his throne,[o] as it is today.[p]

[7]"LORD my God, You have now made Your servant king in my father David's place.[q] Yet I am just a youth with no experience in leadership.[B,r] [8]Your servant is among Your people You have chosen,[s] a[c] people too numerous to be numbered or counted.[t] [9]So give Your servant an obedient heart to judge[u] Your people and to discern between good and evil. For who is able to judge this great people of Yours?"[v]

[10]Now it pleased the Lord that Solomon had requested this. [11]So God said to him, "Because you have requested this and did not ask for long life[D] or riches for yourself,[w] or the death[E] of your enemies, but you asked discernment for yourself to understand justice,[x] [12]I will therefore do what you have asked.[y] I will give you a wise and understanding heart, so that there has never been anyone like you before

[a]3:1 Dt 7:3; 1Kg 7:8; 9:24; Ezr 9:14
[b]2Sm 5:7; 7:8; 9:10
[c]2Sm 7:1-2
[d]2Sm 6:1,14; 1Kg 6:37; 7:51
[e]1Kg 9:15
[f]3:2 Dt 12:13-14 9Dt 14:23
[h]3:3 Dt 6:5
[i]1Kg 3:14
[j]3:4 Jos 9:3-27; 21:17
[k]2Ch 1:3,6
[l]3:5-15 2Ch 1:7-13
[m]3:5 Nm 12:6; 1Kg 9:2; 11:9
[n]Mt 7:7; Jn 15:7
[o]3:6 1Kg 1:48
[p]1Kg 2:4; 9:4; 2Ch 1:8
[q]3:7 2Ch 1:8
[r]1Ch 29:1; Jr 1:6-7
[s]3:8 Ex 19:5-6; Dt 7:6
[t]Gn 15:5; 22:17
[u]3:9 Dt 1:16-17
[v]2Ch 1:10
[w]3:11 Jms 4:3   [x]1Ch 22:12   [y]3:12 1Jn 5:14-15

[A]3:6 Lit and with You   [B]3:7 Lit am a little youth and do not know to go out or come in   [C]3:8 Lit chosen many   [D]3:11 Lit for many days
[E]3:11 Lit life

points counter that interpretation. (1) The Egyptians did not typically send princesses even to other great kingdoms. And it was probably quite unlikely for Egypt to send a princess to an inferior ally. (2) The fact that Pharaoh Siamun captured and burned Gezer, perhaps earlier during David's reign, but then gave it back to Solomon (see note at 9:16) speaks of Solomon's strength rather than his weakness. **Pharaoh** means "big house" and was a title, not a proper name, just as "the White House" serves as a popular title for the president of the United States. For such a prestigious wife, the cramped quarters of the original **city of David** were not suitable.

Some suggest that brides in political marriages, such as the one between Solomon and **Pharaoh's daughter**, conducted the business that in modern times is conducted by ambassadors. Therefore Solomon's granting his foreign wives and the representatives of their governments the right to worship their own gods while in Israel was, on the human level, a diplomatic courtesy. But the Lord regarded such courtesy toward false gods as apostasy. This was Solomon's first recorded example of conflict between prudent politics and faithfulness to Yahweh.

3:2-3a Archaeology shows that religious syncretism was always a part of popular Hebrew culture. The archaeological evidences for religious syncretism are as abundant for Judah as they are for Israel. The worship at the **high places**, or hilltop altars, might have been of three sorts: (1) the legal local worship of Yahweh before any formal recognition of a national shrine; (2) the illegal worship of Yahweh at such shrines after the recognition of a national shrine; and (3) the syncretistic worship of local Baals at local shrines. Not all scholars agree that the local worship of Yahweh was illegal *before* the temple was built. Further, it is not certain that God absolutely prohibited worship of Himself at the historic pagan holy sites. The two rules were (1) that the pagan equipment should be destroyed (Dt 7:5) and (2) that the site should be explicitly chosen or accepted by God (Dt 12:5; 1Kg 18:20-38), usually by an epiphany or an oracle.

Debate about the meaning of "high places" aside, the

normal locations for shrines for sky gods, such as Baal and Yahweh, were on the hilltops. These were closer to the sky, and were often situated over a cave that according to ancient lore could represent the underworld. The cave under the Mosque of Omar in Jerusalem today may have been the cave under the site of Solomon's temple. It is not certain that Solomon personally offered sacrifices.

3:3b-4 Even if a pious Solomon did sacrifice at the **high places** for Yahweh before the temple was built, it might have been proper worship because of Solomon's better attitude. Part of King Saul's offense (1Sm 13:9-13) was a disobedient attitude. After the temple was built, worshiping the Lord at the high places was sin. The numbers of the sacrifices may indicate that Solomon authorized the offering of abundant sacrifices by other, appropriate personnel.

3:5 Gibeon was the last of the pre-temple national shrines. It was located about six miles north of Jerusalem. How did it become a sacred city since it passed into Hebrew control by deception (Jos 9)? Holy places tended to remain holy through changes in time and local population. The Hebrews acknowledged its holy status when the tabernacle and the bronze altar were put there.

3:6 Faithful love (Hb *chesed*) almost always refers to covenant faithfulness. David was faithful in his obedience to God; God was, in turn, faithful in giving and keeping His covenant promises to David. Covenant faithfulness is a key concept in OT theology.

3:9-11 Solomon's prayer marked a major cultural shift in Hebrew life, a shift to peaceful values involving wisdom and skill rather than military craft. Solomon reflected these new values in asking for a heart that would be **obedient** (to the covenant) in judging the nation. Solomon's request was a request **to discern**. That a ruler of a great empire would desire an obedient, wise **heart** signaled a major change in values. These new values are also reflected in the royal psalm, Psalm 72. The old values are reflected in the title "man of war" (1Ch 28:3), assigned to David. In the old ways, prowess in war made a political leader mighty.

and never will be again.ᵃ ¹³In addition, I will give you what you did not ask for: both riches and honor,ᵇ so that no man in any kingdom will be your equal during your entire life.ᶜ ¹⁴If you walk in My ways and keep My statutes and commands just as your father David did, I will give you a long life."ᵈ

¹⁵Then Solomon woke upᵉ and realized it had been a dream.ᶠ He went to Jerusalem, stood before the ark of the Lord's covenant,ᵍ and offered burnt offerings and •fellowship offerings.ʰ Then he held a feastⁱ for all his servants.

Solomon's Wisdom

¹⁶Then two women who were prostitutes came to the king and stood before him.ʲ ¹⁷One woman said, "Please my lord, this woman and I live in the same house, and I had a baby while she was in the house. ¹⁸On the third day after I gave birth, she also had a baby and we were alone. No one elseᴬ was with us in the house; just the two of us were there. ¹⁹During the night this woman's son died because she lay on him. ²⁰She got up in the middle of the night and took my son from my side while your servant was asleep. She laid him at her breast, and she put her dead son in my arms. ²¹When I got up in the morning to nurse my son, I discovered he was dead. That morning, when I looked closely at him I realized that he was not the son I gave birth to."

²²"No," the other woman said. "My son is the living one; your son is the dead one."

The first woman said, "No, your son is the dead one; my son is the living one." So they argued before the king.

²³The king replied, "This woman says, 'This is my son who is alive, and your son is dead,' but that woman says, 'No, your son is dead, and my son is alive.'" ²⁴The king continued, "Bring me a sword." So they brought the sword to the king. ²⁵Solomon said, "Cut the living boy in two and give half to one and half to the other."

²⁶The woman whose son was alive spoke to the king because she felt great compassionᴮ·ᵏ for her son. "My lord, give her the living baby," she said, "but please don't have him killed!"

But the other one said, "He will not be mine or yours. Cut him in two!"

²⁷The king responded, "Give the living baby to the first woman, and don't kill him. She is his mother." ²⁸All Israel heard about the judgment the king had given, and they stood in awe of the king because they saw that God's wisdomˡ was in him to carry out justice.

Solomon's Officials

4 King Solomon ruled over Israel,ᵐ ²and these were his officials:ⁿ

Azariah son of Zadok, priest;
³Elihoreph and Ahijah the sons of Shisha, secretaries;
Jehoshaphat son of Ahilud, court historian;
⁴Benaiah son of Jehoiada, in charge of the army;
Zadok and Abiathar, priests;
⁵Azariah son of Nathan, in charge of the deputies;
Zabud son of Nathan, a priest and adviser to the king;

ᵃ 3:12 1Kg 4:29-31; 10:23-24
ᵇ 3:13 Mt 6:33; Lk 12:31
ᶜ 1Kg 10:23
ᵈ 3:14 1Kg 3:6; Pr 3:1-2
ᵉ 3:15 Gn 41:7
ᶠ Dn 2:3; 4:5
ᵍ 2Sm 6:12
ʰ 1Sm 11:15
ⁱ 1Kg 8:65
ʲ 3:16 Dt 16:18-19; 2Sm 15:2-4
ᵏ 3:26 Gn 43:30; Jr 31:20; Hs 11:8
ˡ 3:28 2Sm 14:20; 1Kg 3:9,11-12
ᵐ 4:1 2Sm 5:5; 8:15
ⁿ 4:2 1Kg 12:6

ᴬ3:18 Lit *No stranger*   ᴮ3:26 Lit *because her compassion grew hot*

3:12-13 Solomon thus got the best of both sets of values, the wisdom that marked the wise man or effective businessman, as well as the **riches . . . honor**, and power that marked success in the older values.

3:15 Solomon celebrated this oracle with a great sacrificial feast of **fellowship offerings** for his **servants**—perhaps for all the resident palace staff.

3:16 Though Solomon's reign involved a new, distant, imperial king, the people, at least those in Jerusalem, still had access to royal justice. The lack of such access during David's reign was used by Absalom to win the hearts of the people (2Sm 15:3-6).

3:16-27 Then marks the connection to the previous dream that Solomon had. He had asked for the ability to discern so he could judge God's people (v. 9). God answered his prayer (Jms 1:5) and gave more than he asked for. This passage is an example of the use of a God-given discerning mind. Ancient Mesopotamian kings kept records of exceptional legal decisions, which were presented to their gods to show that they had acted wisely (cp. D. J. Wiseman, *TOTC*, p. 87). Israel's historians evidently kept similar records.

4:1-34 This chapter gives an accurate description of Solomon's bureaucratic structure, but not for one particular time. Any person of renown, from any time in Solomon's reign, could be included since such people, by their stature and renown, showed Solomon's glory. Further, in showing Solomon's glory, they also glorified God, who gave such glory to Solomon. This structure totally bypassed the traditional tribal structures of the nation and replaced them with officials who were directly responsible to the king, with no loyalty to the ancient tribes and clans.

4:2 Azariah, the grandson of **Zadok**, was high priest at a later time in Solomon's rule though not at the very end of his rule (1Ch 6:8-10).

4:3 Though our knowledge of some terms is incomplete, **secretaries** could have been the heads of the royal scribes dealing with day-to-day matters. The **historian** might have been the keeper of the royal archives or chronicles.

4:4 The two competing high priests at the time of Solomon's coronation, **Zadok** and **Abiathar**, are both mentioned, though Abiathar was sent into exile almost immediately.

4:5 Deputies could have been the head officers of the

⁶ Ahishar, in charge of the palace; and Adoniram son of Abda, in charge of forced labor.

⁷ Solomon had 12 deputies for all Israel. They provided food for the king and his household; each one made provision for one month out of the year.ᵃᵇ These were their names:

Ben-hur, in the hill country of Ephraim;
⁹ Ben-deker, in Makaz, Shaalbim, Beth-shemesh, and Elon-beth-hanan;
¹⁰ Ben-hesed, in Arubboth (he had Socoh and the whole land of Hepher);
¹¹ Ben-abinadab, in all Naphath-dor (Taphath daughter of Solomon was his wife);
¹² Baana son of Ahilud, in Taanach, Megiddo, and all Beth-shean which is beside Zarethan below Jezreel, from Beth-shean to Abel-meholah, as far as the other side of Jokmeam;
¹³ Ben-geber, in Ramoth-gilead (he had the villages of Jair son of Manasseh, which are in Gilead, and he had the

region of Argob, which is in Bashan, 60 great cities with walls and bronze bars);
¹⁴ Ahinadab son of Iddo, in Mahanaim;
¹⁵ Ahimaaz, in Naphtali (he also had married a daughter of Solomon—Basemath);
¹⁶ Baana son of Hushai, in Asher and Bealoth;
¹⁷ Jehoshaphat son of Paruah, in Issachar;
¹⁸ Shimei son of Ela, in Benjamin;
¹⁹ Geber son of Uri, in the land of Gilead, the country of Sihon king of the Amorites and of Og king of Bashan.

There was one deputy in the land of Judah.ᴬ

Solomon's Provisions

²⁰ Judah and Israel were as numerous as the sand by the sea;ᵇ they were eating, drinking, and rejoicing. ²¹ᴮ Solomon ruled over all the kingdoms from the Euphrates River to the land of the Philistines and as far as the border of Egypt.ᶜ They offered tribute and served Solomon all the days of his life.ᵈ
²² Solomon's provisions for one day were 150

ᵃ4:7 1Kg 4:27 ᵇ4:20 Gn 22:17; 1Kg 3:8 ᶜ4:21 Gn 15:18; 2Ch 9:26 ᵈ2Sm 8:2,6

ᴬ4:19 LXX; MT omits *of Judah*   ᴮ4:21 1Kg 5:1 in Hb

---

military and bureaucratic forces garrisoned around the country and throughout the empire as well as the officers over forced labor levies (v. 6). Since the word **adviser** literally means "friend," this term probably referred to a close, intimate adviser to the king.

4:6 The official in charge of **the palace** (lit "the house") may have administered other properties of the king as well. On **forced labor**, see note at 5:13-18.

4:7 The following verses list the 12 appointed **deputies**, each of whom **provided food** for the royal **household** for one month of the year. There was no provision for the intercalary periods, which are days inserted into the calendar in order to compensate for the fact that the astronomical year is 12 lunar months plus a fraction of a month. These regions were not of equal size and wealth, and Judah is not included (see note at v. 19). Therefore this system probably created unfair burdens. Solomon certainly had other sources of revenue such as royally sponsored mercantile enterprises and tribute from subject nations or territories in his empire.

4:8 The **hill country of Ephraim** was roomy, but the settlement and economic development of Ephraim began in earnest only with the Hebrew conquest (cp. Jos 17:14-18). Therefore the large area assigned to Ben-hur might not have indicated a lighter burden since it might not have been fully productive.

4:9-10 One noted city, **Beth-shemesh**, plus three obscure names could indicate that **Ben-deker** administered a rather small region that likely found it a relatively heavy burden to provide "for the king and his household" (v. 7). The district controlled by **Ben-hesed** was about the same size, but it included some productive coastal plains and the fertile Shephelah region.

4:11 **Ben-abinadab** was one of two deputies married to

daughters of Solomon (cp. v. 15). His region included some coastal plains but was dominated by southern slopes of the Carmel range.

4:12 The district of **Baana** included several cities on trade routes that opened into the Plain of Esdraelon. For cities of such wealth, making a one-month provision for Solomon was a relatively light burden.

4:13-14 Ben-geber's district in the northern Transjordan, with its **60 great cities**, was large enough that the financial burden could have been relatively light. A second district around **Mahanaim** would have been relatively small and therefore more heavily burdened. A third in Transjordan (v. 19) is too vaguely defined for comment.

4:15-18 Each of these four districts consisted of the territory of one of Israel's smaller tribes; thus these were probably heavily burdened.

4:19 In the Hebrew text, **Judah** is not included in this burden. The HCSB follows the LXX in including a comment on Judah in this verse, although Judah was not one of the 12 districts. The Hebrew version of this comment could be construed as saying that each district had a single official. While some of the evaluations of burden given above are not proven, it is difficult to find a fair distribution of the financial burden in these districts.

4:20 This blissful picture of prosperity indicated that, since Solomon's rule brought prosperity to the entire nation, the responsibility of supporting Solomon's government and luxury was not as crippling a burden as it otherwise would have been.

4:21 The general extent of Solomon's empire included Hebrew tribal territories along with Moab and Edom, most or all of the old Philistine territories (but cp. 9:16), and most or all of the Aramean kingdoms west of the Euphrates River but not the Phoenician coastal cities. Not all of these re-

bushels[A] of fine flour and 300 bushels[B] of meal, [23] 10 fattened oxen, 20 range oxen, and 100 sheep, besides deer, gazelles, roebucks, and pen-fed poultry,[C,a] [24] for he had dominion over everything west of the Euphrates from Tiphsah to Gaza and over all the kings west of the Euphrates. He had peace on all his surrounding borders. [25] Throughout Solomon's reign, Judah and Israel lived in safety from Dan to Beer-sheba,[b] each man under his own vine and his own fig tree.[c] [26] Solomon had 40,000[D] stalls of horses for his chariots, and 12,000 horsemen.[d] [27] Each of those deputies for a month in turn provided food for King Solomon and for everyone who came to King Solomon's table. They neglected nothing. [28] Each man brought the barley and the straw for the chariot teams and the other horses[e] to the required place according to his assignment.[E]

Solomon's Wisdom and Literary Gifts

[29] God gave Solomon wisdom, very great insight, and understanding[f] as vast as the sand on the seashore. [30] Solomon's wisdom was greater than the wisdom of all the people of the East,[g] greater than all the wisdom of Egypt.[h] [31] He was wiser than anyone[i]—wiser than Ethan the Ezrahite,[j] and Heman, Calcol, and Darda, sons of Mahol.[k] His reputation extended to all the surrounding nations.[l]

[32] Solomon composed 3,000 proverbs,[m] and his songs numbered 1,005.[n] [33] He described trees, from the cedar in Lebanon to the hyssop growing out of the wall. He also taught about animals, birds, reptiles, and fish. [34] People came from everywhere, sent by every king on earth who had heard of his wisdom, to listen to Solomon's wisdom.[o]

Hiram's Building Materials

5 [F] Hiram king of Tyre[p] sent his servants to Solomon when he heard that he had been anointed king in his father's place,[q] for Hiram had always been friends with David.[r]

[2] Solomon sent this message to Hiram: [3] "You know my father David was not able to build a temple for the name of •Yahweh

Cross references
a4:22-23 1Kg 10:5; Neh 5:18
b4:25 Jdg 20:1; 1Sm 3:20
c Mc 4:3-4; Zch 3:10
d4:26 Dt 17:16; 1Kg 10:26; 2Ch 1:14
e4:28 Est 8:10,14
f4:29 1Kg 3:12
g4:30 Gn 29:1
hIs 19:11; Ac 7:22
i4:31 1Kg 3:12
iCh 15:19; Pss 88, 89 titles
k1Ch 2:6
l1Kg 10:1,6
m4:32 Pr 1:1; Ec 9:12
nSg 1:1
o4:34 1Kg 10:1,6
p5:1 2Ch 2:3
q1Kg 1:34,39
r2Sm 5:11; 1Ch 14:1

A4:22 Lit *30 cors*   B4:22 Lit *60 cors*   C4:23 Hb obscure   D4:26 2Ch 9:25 reads *4,000 stalls*   E4:28 Lit *judgment*   F5:1 1Kg 5:15 in Hb

gions were dominated to the same degree. Some authorities suggest that Philistia, except for Gezer, may actually have been under Egyptian control. This conflicts with the identification of Solomon's southern border as reaching to Gaza (4:24). But even that border indicated that Pharaoh Siamun may have moved the Egyptian boundary from the Wadi Arish north to the Wadi Besor, just south of Gaza.

4:22-23 Though our methods of analysis are proximate, the large quantities provided for Solomon's **provisions for one day** were far more than the expected needs of the palace in Jerusalem. Calculated at a pint of grain per day per person, the grain was sufficient for more than 20,000 persons. Likewise the meat supply easily fed 20,000 people, even when assuming that the livestock were relatively scrawny animals and each person ate an excessive figure of one pound of meat per day. In fact these quantities could be adequate not just for the needs of the palace, but also for the bureaucracy and the permanent resident military. Verses 27-28 hint that these provisions were possibly shared with the military establishment, though the link is unclear.

4:24-25 The north-south range of Solomon's **dominion** indicated here correlates with verse 21 on the north since **Tiphsah** was located on the **Euphrates** River, but in the south, **Gaza** was somewhat north of the Wadi Arish, the traditional border of Egypt (see note at v. 21). Solomon's control over this large region guaranteed the Israelites a degree of peace and security.

4:26 The writer then presents the major innovation of Solomon's military, a standing army of **chariots**. David did not use chariots. Two factors indicate that Solomon's chariot force was not a native Hebrew force. First, developing a home-grown chariot force was an expensive process involving years of training; hiring mercenaries was quicker. Second, Solomon's chariot armies disappeared in the conflict at Solomon's death, a likely clue that the charioteers returned to their native lands.

Ancient literature often used numbers symbolically, and so readers rightly ask in a given passage whether the numbers are meant to be literal. Taking the numbers as literal here and using the data from Chronicles, the following situation emerges. There were 1,400 chariots (10:26), an adequate number for a small empire with no competition from the great empires, **12,000** handlers for horses (probably including both the chariot warriors and the other support personnel for the horses), and facilities for housing and caring for **40,000** horses. The figure about the massive number of horses and the facilities for housing them is reasonable if the horses were scattered throughout the empire and in several different facilities, as would make strategic sense. No single facility in ancient times could house 40,000 horses. The Septuagint at 2Ch 9:25 gives a variant figure of 4,000, a reasonable figure for the facilities actually mobilized at any given time. First Kings 4:28 indicates that horse provisions, probably for the army at large, were also part of the levies, but not necessarily included in the listed provisions above (vv. 7-19).

4:31-34 Three of the four names listed here also appear in 1Ch 2:6, and a fourth is very close. In harmonizing these two lists, **Mahol** (lit "dance") may represent a professional or guild title while the Chronicles passage may present actual parentage. These may have been wise men of reputation from a different era. Solomon's reputation for **wisdom** transcended international and chronological boundaries.

5:1 David had traded with Tyre when collecting materials for the temple. Solomon also benefited from good relations with **Hiram king of Tyre** in purchasing materials. For Solomon, this cooperation was extended to joint international trade ventures. This was a wise policy since the Phoenicians were, at this time before Greek competition, continually tightening their grip on Mediterranean trade.

5:3-5 These verses state several major themes in biblical theology. (1) God had given **rest** to His people. Throughout the Bible this rest is given in various degrees and in various

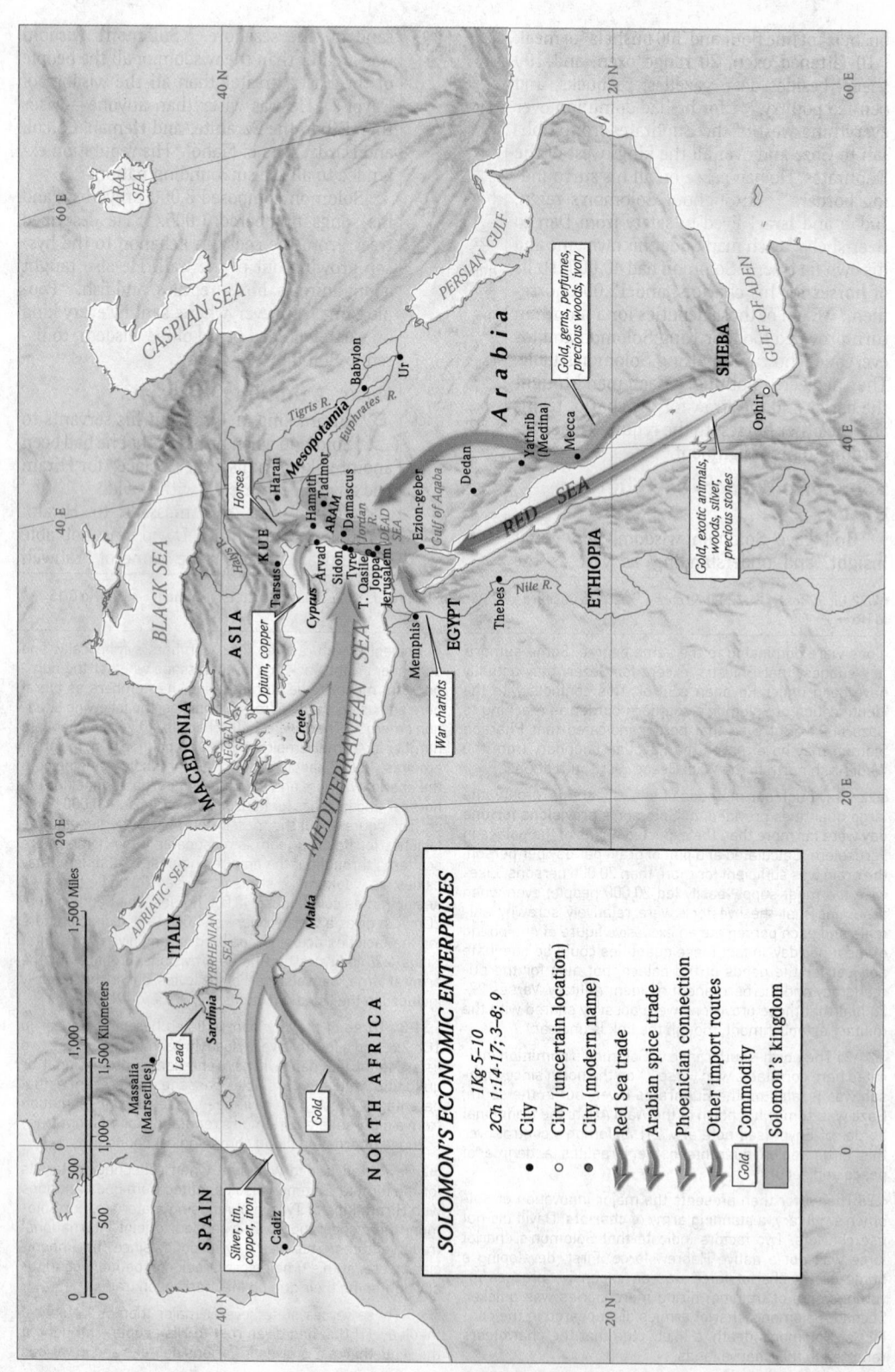

SOLOMON'S ECONOMIC ENTERPRISES

1Kg 5–10
2Ch 1:14-17; 3–8; 9

- ● City
- ○ City (uncertain location)
- ● City (modern name)
- Red Sea trade
- Arabian spice trade
- Phoenician connection
- Other import routes

Gold Commodity

Solomon's kingdom

Gold, gems, perfumes, precious woods, ivory

Gold, exotic animals, woods, silver, precious stones

Horses

Opium, copper

War chariots

Lead

Gold

Silver, tin, copper, iron

his God. This was because of the warfare all around him until the LORD put his enemies under his feet.[a] [4]"The LORD my God has now given me rest all around; there is no enemy or crisis.[b] [5]So I plan to build a temple for the name of Yahweh my God,[c] according to what the LORD promised my father David: 'I will put your son on your throne in your place, and he will build the temple for My name.'[d]

[6]"Therefore, command that cedars from Lebanon be cut down for me. My servants will be with your servants, and I will pay your servants' wages according to whatever you say, for you know that not a man among us knows how to cut timber like the Sidonians."[e]

[7]When Hiram heard Solomon's words, he greatly rejoiced and said, "May the LORD be praised today![f] He has given David a wise son to be over this great people!" [8]Then Hiram sent a reply to Solomon, saying, "I have heard your message; I will do everything you want regarding the cedar and cypress timber. [9]My servants will bring the logs down from Lebanon to the sea, and I will make them into rafts to go by sea to the place you indicate. I will break them apart there, and you can take them away. You then can meet my needs by providing my household with food."[g]

[10]So Hiram provided Solomon with all the cedar and cypress timber he wanted, [11]and Solomon provided Hiram with 100,000 bushels[A] of wheat as food for his household and 110,000 gallons[B] of oil from crushed olives.[h] Solomon did this for Hiram year after year.

[12]The LORD gave Solomon wisdom, as He had promised him.[i] There was peace between Hiram and Solomon, and the two of them made a treaty.[j]

Solomon's Work Force

[13]Then King Solomon drafted forced laborers from all Israel;[k] the labor force numbered 30,000 men. [14]He sent 10,000 to Lebanon each month in shifts; one month they were in Lebanon, two months they were at home. Adoniram was in charge of the forced labor. [15]Solomon had 70,000 porters and 80,000 stonecutters in the mountains,[l] [16]not including his 3,300[C] deputies[m] in charge of the work. They ruled over the people doing the work. [17]The king commanded them to quarry large, costly stones to lay the foundation of the temple with dressed stones.[n] [18]So Solomon's builders and Hiram's builders,[o] along with the Gebalites,[p] quarried the stone and prepared the timber and stone for the temple's construction.

Building the Temple

6 Solomon began to build the temple for the LORD in the four hundred eightieth year[q] after the Israelites came out of the land of Egypt, in the fourth year of his reign over Israel, in the second month, in the month of Ziv.[D,r] [2]The temple that King Solomon built for the LORD[s] was 90 feet[E] long, 30 feet[F] wide,

---

a 5:3 1Ch 28:2-3
b 5:4 1Kg 4:24-25
c 5:5 2Ch 2:4
d 2Sm 7:12-13
e 5:6 2Ch 2:8
f 5:7 1Kg 10:9
g 5:9 2Ch 2:16; Ezr 3:7
h 5:11 2Ch 2:10
i 5:12 1Kg 3:12
j 1Kg 15:19
k 5:13 1Kg 4:6; 9:15
l 5:15 2Ch 2:17-18
m 5:16 1Kg 9:23
n 5:17 1Kg 6:7; 1Ch 22:2
o 5:18 1Kg 5:6,9
p Jos 13:5
q 6:1 Ac 13:20
r 1Kg 6:37; 2Ch 3:1-2; Ezr 3:8
s 6:2 Ezr 5:11

A 5:11 Lit 20,000 cors B 5:11 LXX reads 20,000 baths; MT reads 20 cors C 5:16 Some LXX mss read 3,600; 2Ch 2:2,18
D 6:1 April–May E 6:2 Lit 60 cubits F 6:2 Lit 20 cubits

---

ways that finally culminated in the eternal rest described in Hebrews 4. (2) It gave a different perspective on David as a "man of war" (1Ch 28:3), since his wars were presented as defensive necessities. (3) Since no temple can contain God, this temple was to be the dwelling for **the name** of the Lord. And (4) this temple was built in response to the promise of a dynasty for David and his descendants.

5:6 The Israelites, as well as the Egyptians and Assyrians, used both the cedar and cypress lumber of **Lebanon** for their fine buildings. Phoenician artistic skills and manufactured products were also prized throughout the ancient world.

5:7 Hiram's praise for God probably did not represent real conviction or faith on his part. More likely the Bible writer was paraphrasing Hiram's diplomatic courtesies to express truth about God.

5:8-11 These were the terms of the business arrangements. Solomon bartered **food** for lumber and other products as well. Hiram's men would cut the lumber, bring it to the **sea**, and lash it into **rafts**. Then the rafts were floated south and beached, probably at Joppa, the port nearest Jerusalem. From there they were taken to Jerusalem by the road that passed near Gezer. The amount of grain mentioned here was somewhat more than half the amount of grain collected for Solomon's governmental structure (4:22-23). However, the book of 2 Chronicles adds an equal supply of barley to this amount (2Ch 2:10).

5:13-18 These projects were so big that Solomon sent Hebrew **forced laborers** to Phoenicia to help in the work. In this context *thousand* may be a general term with a meaning somewhat like "battalion." The **Gebalites** were the people of ancient Byblos. The few cedars of Lebanon that remain today are in the mountains inland from Byblos. This passage confirms that Byblos was then under Hiram's control.

6:1-38 There are three problems in understanding the technical language in this chapter and parts of the next. First, the original readers and hearers had background knowledge that we do not have; thus the author could presume a certain amount of knowledge on their part. Second, some issues touched on here are better covered in 2 Chronicles. And third, some issues raised here are better left to more detailed reference works devoted to architectural details of the temple.

6:1 Second Chronicles 3:2 dates this operation by the precise day in Solomon's reign. By contrast, 1 Kings dates it by its relationship to another great event in covenant history—the exodus from Egypt. The earlier event launched Hebrew life as a nation, and this event began Hebrew life with a

and 45 feet[A] high.[a 3] The portico in front of the temple sanctuary was 30 feet[B] long extending across the temple's width, and 15 feet deep[C] in front of the temple.[b 4] He also made windows with beveled frames[D] for the temple.[c]

[5] He then built a chambered structure[E] along the temple wall, encircling the walls of the temple, that is, the sanctuary and the inner sanctuary.[d] And he made side chambers[F] all around.[e] [6] The lowest chamber was 7¼ feet[G] wide, the middle was nine feet[H] wide, and the third was 10¼ feet[I] wide. He also provided offset ledges for the temple all around the outside so that nothing would be inserted into the temple walls. [7] The temple's construction used finished stones cut at the quarry so that no hammer, chisel, or any iron tool was heard in the temple while it was being built.[f]

[8] The door for the lowest[J] side chamber was on the right side of the temple. They[K] went up a stairway[D] to the middle chamber, and from the middle to the third. [9] When he finished building the temple,[g] he paneled it with boards and planks of cedar. [10] He built the chambers along the entire temple, joined to

the temple with cedar beams;[h] each story was 7¼ feet[G] high.

[11] The word of the LORD came to Solomon:[i] [12] "As for this temple you are building—if you walk in My statutes, observe My ordinances, and keep all My commands by walking in them,[j] I will fulfill My promise to you, which I made to your father David.[k 13] I will live among the Israelites and not abandon My people Israel."[l]

[14] When Solomon finished building the temple,[L,m 15] he paneled the interior temple walls with cedar boards; from the temple floor to the surface of the ceiling he overlaid the interior with wood. He also overlaid the floor with cypress boards.[n 16] Then he lined 30 feet[B] of the rear of the temple with cedar boards from the floor to the surface of the ceiling,[M] and he built the interior as an inner sanctuary, the most holy place.[o 17] The temple, that is, the sanctuary in front of the most holy place,[N] was 60 feet[O] long. [18] The cedar paneling inside the temple was carved with ornamental gourds[p] and flower blossoms. Everything was cedar;[q] not a stone could be seen.

---

[a]6:2 2Ch 3:3; Ezk 41:1
[b]6:3 2Ch 3:4; Ezk 40:49
[c]6:4 Ezk 41:16
[d]6:5 1Kg 6:16,19-21
[e]Jr 35:2; Ezk 41:5-6
[f]6:7 1Kg 5:17
[g]6:9 1Kg 6:1,14,38
[h]6:9-10 1Kg 5:6,8,10
[i]6:11 1Kg 3:5,11-15; 9:2
[j]6:12 1Kg 11:10
[k]2Sm 7:12-16; 1Kg 9:5
[l]6:13 Lv 26:11; Jos 1:5-6; Heb 13:5
[m]6:14 1Kg 6:1,38
[n]6:15 1Kg 5:8,10; 7:7; Ezk 41:16
[o]6:16 Ex 26:33-34; 1Kg 8:6; Heb 9:3
[p]6:18 1Kg 7:24
[q]1Kg 5:8,10

[A]6:2 Lit 30 cubits   [B]6:3,16 Lit 20 cubits   [C]6:3 Lit 10 cubits wide   [D]6:4,8 Hb obscure   [E]6:5 Lit built the house of chamber
[F]6:5 Lit made ribs or sides   [G]6:6,10 Lit five cubits   [H]6:6 Lit six cubits   [I]6:6 Lit seven cubits   [J]6:8 LXX, Tg; MT reads middle
[K]6:8 = people   [L]6:11-14 LXX omits these vv.   [M]6:16 LXX; MT omits of the ceiling; 1Kg 6:15   [N]6:17 Lit front of me; Hb obscure
[O]6:17 Lit 40 cubits

---

permanent dwelling for God. The figure of 480 years implies a fifteenth-century exodus (ca 1440 B.C.). Those who argue for a thirteenth-century exodus take this figure as representing 12 generations reflecting a generous life expectancy for that day (12 x 40 = 480). Allowing for overlapping generations, the actual length could then have been something like 12 x 25, or 300 years. Many of the other figures in 1 and 2 Kings are confirmed remarkably well by historical research. The month Ziv (Iyyar), the second month of the religious calendar, overlaps with our modern April and May.

6:3 The word **portico** (Hb 'ulam) has two different meanings, translated "hall [of pillars]" and "canopy with pillars" in 7:6. From those examples, this portico also might have been a covered hall or entrance with columns, 15 feet by 30 feet by 30 feet (2Ch 3:4). Most reconstructions of the temple show a covered entry without columns.

6:4 These **windows** pierced the walls above the height of the surrounding rooms (vv. 5-6).

6:5-6 These three levels of storage rooms surrounding the **temple** on the outside are omitted in Chronicles. The lower stories were narrower than the upper stories. The lowest ceiling beams pierced the outer **wall** of the storage room at the end away from the temple and rested on a ledge, one and one-half-feet wide, on the end toward the temple. This ledge was three feet from the temple wall. The second story beams pierced the same outer wall, but rested on another ledge, one and one-half-feet wide, that was one and one-half feet from the temple wall. The third story beams pierced the same outer wall but rested on a one and one-half-foot ledge that touched the temple wall itself but did not pierce it.

6:7 Cutting the **stones** to exact measure off-site and then putting them in place without further dressing with **iron** tools required great skill. This wording here permits a final polishing that smoothed the surfaces and equalized surfaces at the joints between the stones.

6:8 The Hebrew language of this verse is obscure. In the LXX it is said that the bottom story was accessed through a door on the **right**, or south (see note at 7:39), side of the structure. With only one door, access to other stories would have been by an interior doorway and **stairway**, of which we have no exact information. The Hebrew text suggests an external stair or ladder to the second story instead of the outer door mentioned above.

6:9 This verse addresses only the **planks of cedar** and cedar beams that covered the outer surfaces of the temple and surrounding chambers (for the interior surfaces, see vv. 15-22).

6:10 The stories of the outer rooms were 7¼ feet high, apparently including the thickness of the ceilings. Thus the total height of the three stories of outer rooms was 21¾ feet, about half the height of the temple itself.

6:11-13 God blessed the temple with the promise that He would **live among the Israelites** if they kept His commandments.

6:15 The interior walls were paneled with **cedar** while the flooring was **cypress** wood, probably Phoenician juniper or some other evergreen. The Chronicles account (2Ch 3:5) seems to use the word "cypress" as a general name for both cedar and cypress.

6:16-17 The **inner sanctuary** of the temple, **the most holy place**, was also paneled with cedar and separated from the

¹⁹He prepared the inner sanctuary*ᵃ* inside the temple to put the ark of the Lᴏʀᴅ's covenant*ᵇ* there. ²⁰The interior of the sanctuary was 30 feetᴬ long, 30 feetᴬ wide, and 30 feetᴬ high; he overlaid it with pure gold.*ᶜ* He also overlaid the cedar altar. ²¹Next, Solomon overlaid the interior of the temple with pure gold, and he hungᴮ gold chains*ᵈ* across the front of the inner sanctuary*ᵉ* and overlaid it with gold. ²²So he added the gold overlay to the entire temple until everything was completely finished, including the entire altar*ᶠ* that belongs to the inner sanctuary.

²³In the inner sanctuary he made two •cherubim*ᵍ* 15 feetᶜ high out of olive wood. ²⁴One wing of the first cherub was 7¹/₄ feet long,ᴰ and the other wing was 7¹/₄ feet long. The wingspan was 15 feetᶜ from tip to tip. ²⁵The second cherub also was 15 feet;ᶜ both cherubim had the same size and shape. ²⁶The first cherub's height was 15 feetᶜ and so was the second cherub's. ²⁷Then he put the cherubim inside the inner temple. Since their wings were spread out, the first one's wing touched one wall while the second cherub's wing touched the otherᴱ wall, and in the middle of the temple their wings were touching wing to wing.*ʰ* ²⁸He also overlaid the cherubim with gold.

²⁹He carved all the surrounding temple walls with carved engravings—cherubim,*ⁱ*

palm trees and flower blossoms—in both the inner and outer sanctuaries. ³⁰He overlaid the temple floor with gold in both the inner and outer sanctuaries.

³¹For the entrance of the inner sanctuary, he made olive wood doors.*ʲ* The pillars of the doorposts were five-sided.ᶠ ³²The two doors were made of olive wood. He carved cherubim, palm trees, and flower blossoms on them and overlaid them with gold, hammering gold over the cherubim and palm trees. ³³In the same way, he made four-sidedᶠ olive wood doorposts for the sanctuary entrance. ³⁴The two doors*ᵏ* were made of cypress wood; the first door had two folding sides, and the second door had two folding panels. ³⁵He carved cherubim, palm trees, and flower blossoms on them and overlaid them with gold applied evenly over the carving. ³⁶He built the inner courtyard*ˡ* with three rows of dressed stone*ᵐ* and a row of trimmed cedar beams.

³⁷The foundation of the Lᴏʀᴅ's temple was laid in Solomon's fourth year in the month of Ziv. ³⁸In his eleventh year in the eighth month, in the month of Bul,ᴳ the temple was completed in every detail and according to every specification.*ⁿ* So he built it in seven years.*ᵒ*

Solomon's Palace Complex

7 Solomon completed his entire palace complex after 13 years of construction.*ᵖ*

*ᵃ*6:19 Ezk 41:3-4
*ᵇ*Dt 10:16; Jos 3:11
*ᶜ*6:20 2Ch 3:8-9
*ᵈ*6:21 2Ch 3:14; Mt 27:51
*ᵉ*2Ch 3:16
*ᶠ*6:22 1Kg 7:48; Heb 9:3-4
*ᵍ*6:23-27 Ex 25:18-22; 2Ch 3:10-13
*ʰ*6:27 2Ch 5:8
*ⁱ*6:29 Ezk 41:18,25
*ʲ*6:31-32 Ezk 41:23
*ᵏ*6:34-35 Ezk 41:23-25
*ˡ*6:36 2Ch 4:9; Jr 36:10
*ᵐ*1Kg 7:12; Ezr 6:4
*ⁿ*6:38 1Kg 6:1,14
*ᵒ*1Kg 7:1
*ᵖ*7:1 1Kg 9:10; 2Ch 8:1

ᴬ6:20 Lit 20 cubits   ᴮ6:21 Lit he caused to pass across   ᶜ6:23,24,25,26 Lit 10 cubits   ᴰ6:24 Lit five cubits   ᴱ6:27 Lit the second
ᶠ6:31,33 Hb obscure   ᴳ6:38 = October–November

rest of the temple by a cedar wall. This produced the common three-part temple plan: (1) the court, (2) the sanctuary (the holy place), and (3) the inner sanctuary (the most holy place or the holy of holies).

6:18 The interior paneling was carved with **gourds** and **flower blossoms** as well as cherubim and palm trees (v. 29).

6:19-20 The height of the **inner sanctuary** was only **30 feet**, leaving about 15 feet between its top and the ceiling of the temple. The stone was completely covered (v. 18). However, the **pure gold** overlay in verse 21 and in 2Ch 3:7 does not necessarily demand that the entire surface was overlaid with gold. Like the ivory inlay in ivory beds (Am 6:4) or ivory palaces (Ps 45:8), this could refer to an esthetically selective usage of gold overlay. First Kings 6:35 ("applied evenly") may reveal the nature of this gold overlay. The best way to achieve such an even covering was to use gold that had been hammered into thin foil and then gently hammered onto selected surfaces until it adhered to those surfaces. Both the precious gold and the fine, expensive **cedar** wood showed God's glory.

6:22 Here, in agreement with the LXX, the altar of incense was the **altar that belongs to the inner sanctuary**. This indicated a new location of the altar of incense. In the tabernacle it was in the holy place just outside the veil. Here it was in the inner sanctuary itself (Heb 9:3-4). However, the

Hebrew language could be taken as ambiguous: "The altar that is to/for the . . .".

6:23-28 If the craftsmanship was typical for the time, the two larger **cherubim** were made of pieces of **olive wood** fastened together, probably glued, then carved, and then covered with **gold**, probably hammered gold foil (see note at vv. 19-20). Some suggest that the cherubim formed the throne of God. In the apocalyptic visions, similar beings seem to represent the glory of God. In pagan contexts, they were construed as supernatural protectors of kings and gods.

6:30 Even the **floor** was decorated or **overlaid . . . with gold**, but probably by a harder gold alloy.

6:34 This verse could describe each of the sanctuary **doors** as involving two hinged **panels**, perhaps like modern bifold doors.

6:36 The **courtyard** was enclosed by a wall that included **cedar beams**. This technique was often used to bind stone walls together for earthquake protection.

6:38 The **temple** was completed in the month of **Bul**, the eighth month of the Canaanite calendar (our modern October-November).

7:1 The word **palace complex** accurately translates the Hebrew word for "house." Solomon took **13 years** to build his palace complex in contrast with seven years for building the temple. This difference in time does not necessarily

²He built the House of the Forest of Lebanon.ᵃ It was 150 feetᴬ long, 75 feetᴮ wide, and 45 feetᶜ high on four rows of cedar pillars, with cedar beams on top of the pillars. ³It was paneled above with cedar at the top of the chambers that rested on 45 pillars, 15 per row. ⁴There were three rows of window frames, facing each otherᴰ in three tiers.ᴱ,ᵇ ⁵All the doors and doorposts had rectangular frames, the openings facing each otherᶠ in three tiers.ᴱ ⁶He made the hall of pillars 75 feetᴮ long and 45 feetᶜ wide. A portico was in front of the pillars, and a canopy with pillarsᴳ was in front of them. ⁷He made the Hall of the Throne where he would judgeᶜ—the Hall of Judgment. It was paneled with cedar from the floor to the rafters.ᴴ ⁸Solomon's own palace where he would live, in the other courtyard behind the hall, was of similar construction. And he made a house like this hall for Pharaoh's daughter, his wife.ᴵ,ᵈ

⁹All of these buildings were of costly stones, cut to size and sawed with saws on the inner and outer surfaces, from foundation to coping and from the outside to the great courtyard. ¹⁰The foundation was made of large, costly stones 12 and 15 feetᴶ long. ¹¹Above were also costly stones, cut to size, as well as cedar wood.

ᵃ7:2 1Kg 10:21; 2Ch 9:16 ᵇ7:3-4 1Kg 10:16-17 ᶜ7:7 1Kg 3:16-28 ᵈ7:8 1Kg 3:1; 9:24; 2Ch 8:11

ᴬ7:2 Lit *100 cubits* ᴮ7:2,6 Lit *50 cubits* ᶜ7:2,6 Lit *30 cubits* ᴰ7:4 Lit *frames, window to window* ᴱ7:4,5 Lit *three times; = at 3 different places* ᶠ7:5 Lit *frames, opposing window to window* ᴳ7:6 Hb obscure ᴴ7:7 Syr, Vg; MT reads *floor* ᴵ7:8 Lit *daughter he had taken* ᴶ7:10 Lit *ten cubits and eight cubits*

indicate that Solomon cared more for his house than for the Lord's temple. The shorter time spent on the temple could reflect a piously motivated rush and intensity in building. Conversely, the longer time spent on the palace complex may be explained by its greater complexity. It had to meet the many types of needs for administering an empire.

7:2-4 If verse 8 describes Solomon's personal dwelling, where he would "live" (or "sit"; v. 8), then these verses probably describe a large building dedicated to public business. The structure described for **the House of the Forest of Lebanon** is difficult for modern readers to visualize. Ancient Hebrew readers would likely understand it better given their familiarity with Hebrew idioms and terms, plus many early readers would have had a visual memory of the structure, which lessened the need for the author to describe it in a way that could easily be visualized. Our understanding is further complicated by the possibility that the Israelites used the same Hebrew word for more than one foreign architectural feature (see note at v. 6).

Understanding this description involves uniting the four rows of **pillars** that held up the central portion of the building (v. 2) with the three rows of pillars associated with three tiers of roof (vv. 3-4). If modeled after Egyptian architecture, these windows were placed in the roof where a change in ceiling height permitted the placing of windows between the columns and between the two different roof levels. The terminology for these windows is not well understood. The spaces between the two elevations and between the columns of the row left room for a row of windows. The whole row of columns left spaces for a tier of windows.

The three rows of pillars totaling **45 pillars, 15 per row**, would fit in well with the **three rows of window frames**, arranged in **three tiers**. Since the building would normally be symmetrical, with two sets of three tiers facing each other, we may be discussing six tiers of facing windows, three on each side of the high central portion of the palace. These windows then would be associated with six rows of columns, three on each side of the high central portion. Each tier of windows occupied the elevation between two roof levels of different height. The structures related above still leave several features that are not clearly defined. It is possible that the word **chambers** refers not to rooms above these pillars but to the beams on which the actual roof panels rested.

7:5 This verse seems to describe either three sets of ground level **doors** that faced each other across the width of the building or three matching sets across the front of the building. It is possible that the window **openings** in the doors were in **tiers**.

7:6 This verse uses the Hebrew word translated **portico** (Hb *'ulam*) with two different meanings. The first portico, translated **hall of pillars**, could be another covered court with columns (on portico, see note at 6:3). The second is sometimes translated as a *pilastered wall* with a roof or overhang. The HCSB communicates roughly the same idea by **canopy with pillars**. This context clearly indicates that the portico, whatever it was, was covered and may have had pillars.

7:7 The **Hall of the Throne** was another columned entrance or portico. The contextual association with the House of the Forest of Lebanon (see note at vv. 2-4) hints that this hall might have been the public entrance of the larger building, an appropriate place for the throne where people sought judgment.

7:8 The house in which Solomon **would live** also was another roofed structure with columns and walls paneled with cedar. Solomon's personal dwelling and the **house . . . for Pharaoh's daughter** were the same type of structure.

7:9-11 Since the inner, columnar supports for the roofs have been described, this verse describes the outer walls and perhaps some interior walls of these buildings. These walls

yaqar

Hebrew Pronunciation	[yah KAR]
HCSB Translation	precious
Uses in 1 Kings	7
Uses in the OT	36
Focus Passage	1 Kings 7:9-11

This root in other languages implies what is valuable, honored, or heavy. The word family occurs mostly in later Scripture. *Yaqar* describes *costly* building stones (1Kg 5:17) or *precious* gemstones (2Sm 12:30). Zion's people (Lm 4:2) and wisdom (Pr 3:15) are *precious*. God's love and the death of saints are *valuable* (Ps 36:7; 116:15). *Yaqar* indicates the *precious* life (Pr 6:26), or God's word as *rare* (1Sm 3:1). The adjective functions nominally as *glory* of pastures (Ps 37:20), *noble words* (Jr 15:19), or *honored women* (Ps 45:9). The moon moves *in splendor* (Jb 31:26). *Yaqar* indicates that folly *outweighs* wisdom (Ec 10:1). *Yeqar* (17x) means *honor* in Esther (Est 8:16), and elsewhere *valuables* (Jr 20:5), *treasure* (Jb 28:10), and *price* (Zch 11:13). The verb *yaqar* (11x) denotes *be well known* (1Sm 18:30), *precious* (2Kg 1:14), *scarce, rare* (Is 13:12), or *valued* (Zch 11:13).

¹²Around the great courtyard, as well as the inner courtyard of the Lᴏʀᴅ's temple and the portico of the temple, were three rows of dressed stone and a row of trimmed cedar beams.ᵃ

¹³King Solomon had HiramᴬᵇÞ brought from Tyre. ¹⁴He was a widow's son from the tribe of Naphtali, and his father was a man of Tyre, a bronze craftsman. Hiram had great skill,ᶜ understanding, and knowledge to do every kind of bronze work. So he came to King Solomon and carried out all his work.ᵈ

The Bronze Pillars

¹⁵He cast two hollow bronze pillars:ᵉ each 27 feetᴮ high and 18 feetᶜ in circumference.ᴰ,ᶠ ¹⁶He also made two capitalsᵍ of cast bronze to set on top of the pillars; 7¼ feetᴱ was the height of the first capital, and 7¼ feetᴱ was also the height of the second capital. ¹⁷The capitals on top of the pillars had gratings of latticework, wreathsᶠ made of chainwork—seven for the first capital and seven for the second.

¹⁸He made the pillars with two encircling rows of pomegranates on the one grating to cover the capital on top; he did the same for the second capital. ¹⁹And the capitals on top of the pillars in the portico were shaped like lilies, six feetᴳ high. ²⁰The capitals on the two pillars were also immediately above the rounded surface next to the grating, and 200 pomegranatesʰ were in rows encircling eachᴴ capital. ²¹He set up the pillars at the porticoⁱ

of the sanctuary: he set up the right pillar and named it Jachin;ⁱ then he set up the left pillar and named it Boaz.ʲ,ʲ ²²The tops of the pillars were shaped like lilies. Then the work of the pillars was completed.ᵏ

The Reservoir

²³He made the cast metal reservoir,ᴷ,ˡ 15 feetᴸ from brim to brim, perfectly round. It was 7¼ feetᴱ high and 45 feetᴹ in circumference. ²⁴Ornamental gourdsᵐ encircled it below the brim, 10 every half yard,ᴺ completely encircling the reservoir.ⁿ The gourds were cast in two rows when the reservoir was cast. ²⁵It stood on 12 oxen,ᵒ three facing north, three facing west, three facing south, and three facing east. The reservoir was on top of them and all their hindquarters were toward the center. ²⁶The reservoir was three inchesᵒ thick, and its rim was fashioned like the brim of a cup or of a lily blossom. It held 11,000 gallons.ᴾ

The Bronze Water Carts

²⁷Then he made 10 bronze water carts.ᵠ,ᵖ Each water cart was six feetᴳ long, six feetᴳ wide, and 4¼ feetᴿ high. ²⁸This was the design of the carts: They had frames; the frames were between the cross-pieces, ²⁹and on the frames between the cross-pieces were lions, oxen, and ˙cherubim.ᵠ On the cross-pieces there was a pedestal above, and below the lions and oxen were wreaths of hangingˢ work. ³⁰Each cartʳ

ᵃ7:12 1Kg 6:36
ᵇ7:13 1Kg 5:1-11; 2Ch 2:13-14
ᶜ7:14 Ex 31:2-5
ᵈ2Ch 4:11
ᵉ7:15 2Kg 25:16-17; 2Ch 3:15
ᶠ1Kg 7:41
ᵍ7:16 1Kg 7:42; 2Kg 25:17
ʰ7:20 2Ch 3:16; 4:13
ⁱ7:21 1Kg 6:3
ʲ2Ch 3:17
ᵏ7:22 2Kg 25:17
ˡ7:23 2Kg 25:13; 1Ch 18:8; 2Ch 4:6
ᵐ7:24 1Kg 6:18
ⁿ2Ch 4:3
ᵒ7:25 2Kg 16:17; 2Ch 4:4-5; Jr 52:20
ᵖ7:27 2Kg 25:13; 2Ch 4:14
ᵠ7:29 1Kg 6:29,32
ʳ7:30 2Kg 16:17

ᴬ7:13 = Huram in 2Ch 4:11   ᴮ7:15 Lit *18 cubits*   ᶜ7:15 Lit *12 cubits*   ᴰ7:15 LXX adds *and the thickness of the pillar was four fingers hollowed and similarly the second pillar*   ᴱ7:16,23 Lit *five cubits*   ᶠ7:17 Lit *tassels*   ᴳ7:19,27 Lit *four cubits*   ᴴ7:20 Lit *encircling the second*   ¹7:21 = He Will Establish   ʲ7:21 = In Him Is Strength   ᴷ7:23 Lit *sea*   ᴸ7:23 Lit *10 cubits*   ᴹ7:23 Lit *30 cubits*   ᴺ7:24 Lit *10 per cubit*   ᵒ7:26 Lit *a handbreadth*   ᴾ7:26 Lit *2,000 baths*   ᵠ7:27 Lit *bronze stands*   ᴿ7:27 Lit *three cubits*   ˢ7:29 Or *hammered-down*

---

were made of fine **stones** finished to measure—**sawed with saws**—on the exposed surfaces. This probably meant sawed to a close approximate shape and then finished smooth by some polishing technique (see note at 6:7). **Cedar wood** was also used on some upper parts of the walls.

7:12 On the construction of the temple **courtyard**, see note at 6:36.

7:13-14 For a devout follower of Yahweh, importing the Phoenician **craftsman** named **Hiram** (not to be confused with king Hiram) was more acceptable since his mother was Hebrew. Importing Phoenician artists was a regular practice in the ancient world.

7:15-21 The **pillars** were 27 feet high, with 7¼-foot-high capitals, for a total of over 34 feet. **Latticework** and ovoid art covered the structure of the capitals and their ornaments. The shape of the capitals, both for these pillars and for the pillars of the **portico**, was like an open lily blossom. Some have given these pillars a cosmic significance by translating their names as "He established/will establish/ establishes [from **Jachin**] in strength [from **Boaz**]." This could be more significant if one analyzes the temple itself as a cosmic symbol of the universe, as some have done (J. Walton, *Lost World of Genesis One*). On the other hand, the

"pillar" mentioned in 2Kg 11:14 and 23:3 could indicate that the Davidic dynasty, rather than the temple or universe, was established in strength.

7:23-26 A huge bronze vessel, containing about **11,000 gallons**, served as the main **reservoir** for water used for cleansing. Second Chronicles 4:6 indicates that this larger reservoir was allotted to priestly cleansing, which might imply that the bronze water carts (1Kg 7:27) were allotted to the Levites. We are not sure what shape the **ornamental gourds** represented since gourds come in many shapes. Since a cylindrical shape, in contrast to a conical shape, is needed for the stated capacity of the reservoir, the description, **fashioned like . . . a lily blossom**, could refer to only the rim of the reservoir.

7:27-28 The following is one possible understanding of the structure of the **bronze water carts**: They were essentially boxes on wheels for mobility. Each of the four sides had two square panels (**frames**) with carvings. There were carved **cross-pieces** both above and below the panels/frames. Above the top crosspieces were attached supports ("pedestal"; v. 29) presumably for the basin.

7:30 There were **axles** with two wheels under each end of **each cart**.

had four bronze wheels with bronze axles. Underneath the four corners of the basin were cast supports, each next to a wreath. [31] And the water cart's opening inside the crown on top was 18 inches[A] wide. The opening was round, made as a pedestal 27 inches[B] wide. On it were carvings, but their frames were square, not round. [32] There were four wheels under the frames, and the wheel axles were part of the water cart; each wheel was 27 inches[C] tall. [33] The wheels' design was similar to that of chariot wheels: their axles, rims, spokes, and hubs were all of cast metal. [34] Four supports were at the four corners of each water cart; each support was one piece with the water cart. [35] At the top of the cart was a band nine inches[D] high encircling it; also, at the top of the cart, its braces and its frames were one piece with it. [36] He engraved cherubim, lions, and palm trees[a] on the plates of its braces and on its frames, wherever each had space, with encircling wreaths. [37] In this way he made the 10 water carts using the same casting, dimensions, and shape for all of them.

Bronze Basins and Other Utensils

[38] Then he made 10 bronze basins[b]—each basin holding 220 gallons[E] and each was six feet[F] wide—one basin for each of the 10 water carts. [39] He set five water carts on the right side of the temple and five on the left side. He put the reservoir near the right side of the temple toward the southeast.[c] [40] Then Hiram made[d] the basins, the shovels, and the sprinkling basins.

Completion of the Bronze Works

So Hiram finished all the work that he was doing for King Solomon on the LORD's temple: [41] two pillars;[e] bowls for the capitals that were on top of the two pillars; the two gratings for covering both bowls of the capitals that were on top of the pillars;[f] [42] the 400 pomegranates for the two gratings (two rows of pomegranates for each grating covering both capitals' bowls on top of the pillars[g]); [43] the 10 water carts;[h] the 10 basins on the water carts;[i] [44] the reservoir;[j] the 12 oxen underneath the reservoir;[k] [45] and the pots, shovels, and sprinkling basins.[l] All the utensils that Hiram made for King Solomon at the LORD's temple were made of burnished bronze. [46] The king had them cast in clay molds in the Jordan Valley between Succoth[m] and Zarethan.[n] [47] Solomon left all the utensils unweighed because there were so many; the weight of the bronze was not determined.[o]

Completion of the Gold Furnishings

[48] Solomon also made all the equipment in the LORD's temple: the gold altar; the gold table that the ·bread of the Presence was placed on;[p] [49] the pure gold lampstands in front of the inner sanctuary, five on the right and five on the left;[q] the gold flowers, lamps, and tongs; [50] the pure gold ceremonial bowls, wick trimmers, sprinkling basins, ladles,[G] and firepans;[r] and the gold hinges for the doors of the inner temple (that is, the most holy place) and for the doors of the temple sanctuary.

[51] So all the work King Solomon did in the LORD's temple was completed.[s] Then Solomon brought in the consecrated things of his father David[t]—the silver, the gold, and the utensils—and put them in the treasuries of the LORD's temple.[u]

Solomon's Dedication of the Temple

8 At that time Solomon assembled the elders[v] of Israel,[w] all the tribal heads[x] and

[a]7:36 1Kg 6:29
[b]7:38 Ex 30:18; 2Ch 4:6
[c]7:39 2Ch 4:10
[d]7:40-51 2Ch 4:11-5:1
[e]7:41 1Kg 7:15
[f]1Kg 7:17
[g]7:42 1Kg 7:20
[h]7:43 1Kg 7:27
[i]1Kg 7:38
[j]7:44 1Kg 7:23
[k]1Kg 7:25
[l]7:45 Ex 27:3
[m]7:46 Gn 33:17
[n]Jos 3:16; 1Kg 4:12
[o]7:47 1Ch 22:3,14
[p]7:48 Ex 25:30; 30:1-3; 2Ch 29:18
[q]7:49 Ex 25:31-36
[r]7:50 2Kg 25:15
[s]7:51 1Kg 6:37-38
[t]2Sm 8:9-12; 2Ch 5:1
[u]2Ch 36:18
[v]8:1 Ex 3:16; Nm 11:16
[w]8:1-11 2Ch 5:2-14
[x]8:1 Nm 1:5-16; 7:2

7:31-37 The simplest understanding of verse 31 is that it describes an internal circular structure which, together with the pedestals and the four corner **supports**, supported a bronze basin (v. 38) and held it in place. Real **chariot wheels** were made of wood.

7:38 Then the **bronze basins** were set into the **water carts**. If their shape were more like a cylinder, a depth of slightly more than one foot would give a capacity of roughly 220 gallons. A more conical lily shape would demand a greater depth, possibly as much as three feet. Either could still fit into the cart with the water level about four and one-half feet above the ground.

7:39 The **right side** in descriptions of the temple is to the south, as if one is standing in the door of the temple looking out to the east.

7:40-45 These were generally the new items that had to be made anew for a new context.

7:47 Since **bronze** was a valuable commodity, it is an indication of Solomon's wealth that he did not have to keep track of the amount of bronze used.

7:48-51 When these implements were moved into the **temple**, the operation was finished.

8:1–9:9 This dedication was rooted in covenant history, and it was a reprise of many points of covenant theology. The specific offenses mentioned in Solomon's great prayer reflected the atmosphere, if not the very words, of Leviticus 26. On the other hand, much of the terminology also reflects particularly Deuteronomic sources. The prayer also focuses on more recent covenant history, especially the recently chosen dynasty, the dynasty's city, and the new permanent home for God's presence with His people.

8:1 Solomon here operated through traditional **tribal** and clan structures. Either his royal bureaucracy was not yet developed or he deferred to the traditional structures as

the ancestral leaders of the Israelites before him at Jerusalem in order to bring the ark of the LORD's covenant from the city of David,[a] that is •Zion.[b] 2So all the men of Israel were assembled in the presence of King Solomon in the seventh month, the month of Ethanim,[A] at the festival.[c]

3All the elders[d] of Israel came, and the priests[e] picked up the ark.[f] 4The priests and the Levites brought the ark of the LORD, the tent of meeting,[g] and the holy utensils that were in the tent.[h] 5King Solomon and the entire congregation of Israel, who had gathered around him and were with him in front of the ark, were sacrificing sheep and cattle that could not be counted or numbered, because there were so many.[i] 6The priests brought the ark of the LORD's covenant to its place, into the inner sanctuary of the temple, to the most holy place[j] beneath the wings of the •cherubim. 7For the cherubim were spreading their wings over[B] the place of the ark, so that the cherubim covered the ark and its poles from above.[k] 8The poles were so long that their ends were seen from the holy place in front of the inner sanctuary, but they were not seen from outside the sanctuary; they are there to this day.[l] 9Nothing was in the ark except the two stone tablets that Moses had put there at Horeb,[C,m] where the LORD made a covenant with the Israelites when they came out of the land of Egypt.[n]

10When the priests came out of the holy place, the cloud filled the LORD's temple,[o] 11and because of the cloud, the priests were not able to continue ministering, for the glory[p] of the LORD filled the temple.

12Then Solomon said:

> The LORD said that He would dwell
>   in thick darkness.[q]
> 13 I have indeed built an exalted temple[r]
>   for You,
> a place for Your dwelling forever.[s]

14The king turned around and blessed[t] the entire congregation of Israel while they were standing. 15He said:

> May the LORD God of Israel be praised!
> He spoke directly to my father David,
> and He has fulfilled the promise[u]
>   by His power.
> He said,
> 16 "Since the day I brought
>   My people Israel out of Egypt,[v]
> I have not chosen a city to build
>   a temple in
> among any of the tribes of Israel,
> so that My name[w] would be there.
> But I have chosen David to rule
>   My people Israel."[x]
> 17 It was in the desire of my father David
>   to build a temple for the name
>   of •Yahweh, the God of Israel.[y]

Cross references (center column):

a 8:1 2Sm 5:7
b 2Sm 6:12-15,17
c 8:2 Lv 23:34; Dt 16:13-15; 1Kg 8:65
d 8:3 Nm 11:16
e Dt 31:9; Jos 3:3,6
f 2Sm 6:12,17
g 8:4 2Ch 1:3
h 2Ch 5:4-5
i 8:5 2Ch 1:6; 30:24
j 8:6 1Kg 6:19
k 8:6-7 1Kg 6:23-28
l 8:8 Ex 25:13-15; 37:4-5
m 8:9 Ex 25:21; Dt 10:5
n Ex 24:7-8; Dt 4:13
o 8:10 Ex 40:34-35; 2Ch 7:1
p 8:11 2Ch 7:2; Ezk 10:4,18-19; 43:4-5
q 8:12 Ex 20:21; Lv 16:2; Dt 5:22
r 8:13 2Sm 7:13
s Ps 132:14
t 8:14 Ex 39:43; 2Sm 6:18; 1Kg 8:55
u 8:15 2Sm 7:15-16,25
v 8:16 2Sm 7:6; 1Ch 17:5
w Dt 12:5,11
x 1Sm 16:1; 2Sm 7:8
y 8:17 2Sm 7:2-3; 1Ch 22:7

A8:2 = September–October **B**8:7 LXX; MT reads *toward* **C**8:9 = Sinai

---

a courtesy. Moving the **ark** from David's private shrine on Mount Zion to the new national temple in **Jerusalem** restored the ark to its role as a national religious symbol.

8:2 All Israel was represented by these traditional leaders. Though the phrase **the men** here refers to people of both genders, to translate it in that way would be an acculturation rather than a translation. This assembly happened in **Ethanim** (aka Tishri, the seventh month, September-October), the month of the great Day of Atonement. The regular **festival** of this month was the Festival of Harvest (Ex 23:16)—Booths or Tabernacles—that was celebrated about a week after the Day of Atonement.

8:3-4 After the difficult lesson David learned concerning the proper movement of the ark (2Sm 6:7-8), all the transporting was implemented in the proper manner.

8:5 These extensive sacrifices were suitable for a pivotal point in covenant history.

8:6-7 The ark's place was under the wings of the great **cherubim** whose **wings** extended across the width of the inner sanctuary. Thus symbolically, the ark was restored to its rightful place under the symbols of God's glory and the agencies that protected that glory (see note at 6:23-28).

8:8-9 The **poles** had to remain since they could not be removed from the gold rings (Ex 25:15). Of the three original contents of the **ark**, the sample of manna and Aaron's rod had been lost so that only the **stone tablets** of the law

remained. These highlighted the covenant relationship between the Israelites and God.

8:10-11 God's impenetrable and unbearable **glory** filled the new sanctuary. We must go to 2Ch 7:1 to get any indication of a visible, supernatural descent of this glory (cp. Lv 9:24).

8:12-13 This brief introduction states several significant points of history and covenant theology. First, God showed Himself in overwhelming glory and **thick darkness**. Both prevented human eyes from seeing God. Then, the **temple** was to be God's **dwelling** despite the fact that neither earth nor heaven could contain God. Therefore, only the name (v. 18) of God dwelt in the temple. This tension recognizes that nothing can contain God, but God can, nevertheless, be present in some special way. Several schools of scholarship see God's name as reflective of God's reputation or fame. This suggests that one implication of a dwelling place for God's name was that the fame—the knowledge of God's great works—would go forth from that dwelling.

8:14 This scene acted out the role of the Davidic dynasty as the spiritual representative of the people. Solomon first stood before God speaking for the people. Then he turned from facing God to bless the **entire congregation**.

8:15 God practiced covenant faithfulness in keeping His promises to **David**.

8:16-17 Four major steps in advancing God's covenant agenda are described here. First, by implication, God had

18 But the LORD said to my father David,
"Since it was your desire to build
a temple for My name,
you have done well to have this desire.[a]
19 Yet you are not the one to build it;
instead, your son, your own offspring,
will build it for My name."[b]
20 The LORD has fulfilled
what He promised.
I have taken the place
of my father David,[c]
and I sit on the throne of Israel,
as the LORD promised.[d]
I have built the temple for the name
of Yahweh, the God of Israel.
21 I have provided a place there
for the ark,
where the LORD's covenant is
that He made with our ancestors
when He brought them out of the land
of Egypt.[e]

Solomon's Prayer

22 Then Solomon stood[f] before the altar of
the LORD in front of the entire congregation of
Israel and spread out his hands toward heav-
en.[g] 23 He said:

LORD God of Israel,
there is no God like You
in heaven above or on earth below,[h]
keeping the gracious covenant
with Your servants who walk before You
with their whole heart.[i]
24 You have kept what You promised
to Your servant, my father David.
You spoke directly to him
and You fulfilled Your promise
by Your power
as it is today.[j]
25 Therefore, LORD God of Israel,
keep what You promised
to Your servant, my father David:
You will never fail to have a man
to sit before Me on the throne
of Israel,[k]
if only your sons guard their walk
before Me
as you have walked before Me.[l]
26 Now LORD[A] God of Israel,
please confirm what You promised
to Your servant, my father David.[m]

27 But will God indeed live on earth?
Even heaven, the highest heaven,
cannot contain You,
much less this temple I have built.[n]
28 Listen[B] to Your servant's prayer
and his petition,[o]
LORD my God,
so that You may hear the cry
and the prayer
that Your servant prays
before You today,
29 so that Your eyes may watch over
this temple night and day,[p]
toward the place where You said:
My name will be there,[q]
and so that You may hear the prayer
that Your servant prays
toward this place.
30 Hear the petition of Your servant[r]
and Your people Israel,
which they pray toward this place.[s]
May You hear in Your dwelling place
in heaven.
May You hear and forgive.

31 When a man sins against his neighbor
and is forced to take an oath,[C,t]

a8:18 2Ch 6:8
b8:19 2Sm 7:12-13; 1Kg 5:5; Ac 7:47
c8:20 2Sm 7:12
d1Ch 28:5-6
e8:21 Dt 31:26; 1Kg 8:9
f8:22-53 2Ch 6:12-42
g8:22 1Kg 8:54; 2Ch 6:12
h8:23 1Sm 2:2; 2Sm 7:22
iDt 7:16; Neh 1:5; Dn 9:4
j8:24 2Sm 7:15-16
k8:25 1Kg 2:4; 9:5
l1Kg 9:4-9; 2Ch 7:17-22
m8:26 2Sm 7:25
n8:27 2Ch 2:6; Ac 7:47; 17:24
o8:28 Php 4:6
p8:29 2Ch 7:15; Neh 1:6
qDt 12:11
r8:30 Neh 1:6; Dn 9:4
sDn 6:10
t8:31 Ex 22:11; Jos 7:19; Jn 9:24

A8:26 Some Hb mss, LXX, Syr, Tg, Vg, 2Ch 6:16; other Hb mss omits *LORD* B8:28 Lit *Turn* C8:31 Lit *and he lifts a curse against him to curse him*

a dwelling place among His people. Second, this dwelling was the **temple** built by the Davidic dynasty. Third, it was in the **city chosen**, providentially, by David. And fourth, this was the dynasty chosen by God. These ideas added a sense of finality to choosing the Davidic dynasty and building the temple. Psalm 78 (esp. vv. 65-72) expresses the climactic significance of the Davidic dynasty in this program.

8:19-20 Solomon identified himself as the Davidic agent who had brought this program to completion. Here, the thematic spotlight was also on God's reliability and God's keeping **what He promised**.

8:22 Solomon then turned around again, this time to face God as the representative of the people. At some point (see v. 54), Solomon kneeled with his **hands** held upwards for this prayer.

8:23-24 Solomon stated more foundational points of covenant theology. The God of the Hebrews is unique. There is no God like Yahweh, **God of Israel**. God, uniquely, is a covenant-keeping God. That is, God observes (Hb *berith chesed*) covenant faithfulness, here translated as **gracious covenant**. Covenant faithfulness was a mutual responsibility for both parties.

8:25 God's covenant faithfulness guaranteed the permanency of the Davidic dynasty but only if Solomon's **sons guard their walk before** the Lord.

8:26 Keeping His covenant promises expressed God's (Hb) *chesed*. Solomon asked that this gracious faithfulness would continue.

8:27-30 After acknowledging that this house could not contain God, Solomon stated the major theme of this prayer: that God would confirm His covenant by being attentive to the **prayer** of His people, directed to this **temple** for the following concerns. This attentiveness would lead to forgiveness and restoration, recurrent themes in the remainder of

and he comes to take an oath
before Your altar in this temple,
32 may You hear in heaven and act.
May You judge Your servants,
condemning the wicked man
by bringing
what he has done on his own head
and providing justice for the righteous
by rewarding him according to
his righteousness.[a]

33 When Your people Israel are defeated
before an enemy,
because they have sinned against You,[b]
and they return to You and praise
Your name,
and they pray and plead with You
for mercy in this temple,
34 may You hear in heaven
and forgive the sin
of Your people Israel.
May You restore them to the land
You gave their ancestors.[c]

35 When the skies are shut and there is
no rain,
because they have sinned against You,[d]
and they pray toward this place
and praise Your name,
and they turn from their sins
because You are afflicting them,[e]
36 may You hear in heaven
and forgive the sin of Your servants
and Your people Israel,
so that You may teach them
the good way
they should walk in.[f]
May You send rain on Your land
that You gave Your people
for an inheritance.[g]

37 When there is famine on the earth,

when there is pestilence,
when there is blight, mildew, locust,
or grasshopper,[h]
when their enemy besieges them
in the region of their fortified cities,[A]
when there is any plague or illness,
38 whatever prayer or petition
anyone from Your people Israel
might have—
each man knowing his own afflictions[B,i]
and spreading out his hands
toward this temple[j]—
39 may You hear in heaven,
Your dwelling place,
and may You forgive, act, and repay
the man,
according to all his ways,
since You know his heart,
for You alone know
every human heart,[k]
40 so that they may •fear[l] You
all the days they live on the land[m]
You gave our ancestors.

41 Even for the foreigner who is not
of Your people Israel
but has come from a distant land[n]
because of Your name—
42 for they will hear of Your great name,
mighty hand,[o] and outstretched arm,
and will come[p] and pray
toward this temple—
43 may You hear in heaven,
Your dwelling place,
and do according to all the foreigner
asks You for.
Then all the people on earth will know[q]
Your name,
to fear You as Your people Israel do
and know that this temple I have built
is called by Your name.

[a]8:32 Dt 25:1 [b]8:33 Lv 26:17,25,39 [c]8:33-34 Lv 26:40-42 [d]8:35 Dt 28:23-24 [e]Dt 30:1-3; Am 4:7-8 [f]8:36 1Sm 12:23 [g]Dt 11:14; Jl 2:23 [h]8:37 Lv 26:16, 25-26 [i]8:38 2Ch 6:29 [j]Ex 9:29; 2Ch 6:29 [k]8:39 1Sm 16:7; 1Ch 28:9 [l]8:40 Dt 6:13 [m]Dt 12:1 [n]8:41 Lv 24:22; Dt 10:18-19 [o]8:42 Dt 3:24 [p]1Kg 10:1 [q]8:43 Jos 4:24; 1Sm 17:46

[A]8:37 Lit besieges him in the land of his gates [B]8:38 Lit knowing in his heart of a plague

this prayer. In effect, this prayer argued that God's covenant response to prayer, directed to this temple, guaranteed God's interest in all aspects of Israel's life.

8:31-32 When uncorroborated testimony must be supported by a solemn **oath**, the oath should be taken at this **temple**. In broad terms God would hear prayer to validate an honest oath and to maintain **justice** and integrity.

8:33-34 God would hear when the Israelites were **defeated** in war. In Solomon's hour of greatness, this prayer acknowledged that **sin** could produce defeat.

8:35-50 The following statements about sin, disaster, and restoration are not repetitious, stereotyped formulae. There is much freedom and creativity in composing the statements. Yet certain elements seem to recur. The whole process can involve: (1) sinning; (2) repentance; (3) acknowledgement of truth (either as "confessing" truth, as stating the truth in praise, or as stating the truth in thanks); (4)

prayer; (5) seeking favor; (6) God's hearing; (7) forgiveness; and (8) restoration.

8:37-40 Other natural disasters also were occasions for praying to God. The Lord would hear, forgive, and reward in accordance with **his** (the worshiper's) **ways**. This would result in the **fear** of God among His people. "Fear" is a rich word that includes a multitude of concepts, including formal worship of God, actual fear of God, and reverence for God.

8:41-43 Solomon states the theology of missions that is implicit in God's great works of witness. The **foreigner** should **hear** of God's works and then **pray toward** the **temple** to God. And God would hear that foreigner's prayer. The popular Christian misunderstanding that the OT was purely a Hebrew document, written by and for Hebrews alone, can easily miss this point. The intended result of OT revelation was the spread of the knowledge of God to **all the people on earth**.

44 When Your people go out to fight
    against their enemies,[A]
    wherever You send them,
    and they pray to Yahweh
    in the direction of the city
    You have chosen[a]
    and the temple I have built
    for Your name,
45 may You hear their prayer and petition
    in heaven
    and uphold their cause.[b]

46 When they sin against You—
    for there is no one who does not sin[c]—
    and You are angry with them
    and hand them over to the enemy,
    and their captors deport them
    to the enemy's country[d]—
    whether distant or nearby—
47 and when they come to their senses[B]
    in the land where they were deported
    and repent and petition You
    in their captors' land:
    "We have sinned and done wrong;
    we have been wicked,"[e]
48 and when they return to You
    with their whole mind and heart
    in the land of their enemies
    who took them captive,[f]
    and when they pray to You
    in the direction of their land
    that You gave their ancestors,
    the city You have chosen,[g]
    and the temple I have built
    for Your name,
49 may You hear in heaven,
    Your dwelling place,
    their prayer and petition and uphold
    their cause.
50 May You forgive Your people
    who sinned against You
    and all their rebellions[c]
    against You,
    and may You give them compassion
    in the eyes of their captors,

so that they may be compassionate
    to them.[h]
51 For they are Your people
    and Your inheritance;[i]
    You brought them out of Egypt,
    out of the middle of an iron furnace.[j]
52 May Your eyes be open
    to Your servant's petition
    and to the petition
    of Your people Israel,
    listening to them whenever they call
    to You.
53 For You, Lord GOD, have set them apart
    as Your inheritance
    from all the people on earth,
    as You spoke
    through Your servant Moses
    when You brought their ancestors
    out of Egypt.[k]

Solomon's Blessing

54 When Solomon finished praying this entire prayer and petition to the LORD, he got up from kneeling before the altar of the LORD, with his hands spread out toward heaven,[l] 55 and he stood and blessed the whole congregation of Israel[m] with a loud voice: 56 "May the LORD be praised! He has given rest[n] to His people Israel according to all He has said. Not one of all the good promises He made through His servant Moses has failed.[o] 57 May the LORD our God be with us as He was with our ancestors. May He not abandon us or leave us[p] 58 so that He causes us to be devoted[D] to Him,[q] to walk in all His ways, and to keep His commands, statutes, and ordinances, which He commanded our ancestors. 59 May my words I have made my petition with before the LORD be near the LORD our God day and night, so that He may uphold His servant's cause and the cause of His people Israel, as each day requires,[r] 60 and so that all the peoples of the earth may know that Yahweh is God. There is no other![s] 61 Let your heart be completely devoted to the LORD our God[t] to walk in His statutes and to keep His commands, as it is today."

Cross-references (center column):

a 8:44 Dt 12:11; 1Ch 5:20; 2Ch 14:11
b 8:45 Ps 9:4; 140:12
c 8:46 Rm 3:10,23
d Lv 26:33-34
e 8:47 Lv 26:40-42; Neh 1:6; Dn 9:5
f 8:48 Jr 29:10-14
g Dn 6:10
h 8:50 2Kg 25:28; 2Ch 30:9
i 8:51 Ex 32:11; Dt 9:26,29
j Dt 4:20
k 8:53 Ex 19:5-6; Dt 9:26-29
l 8:54 2Ch 6:12-13
m 8:55 Nm 6:23-26; 2Sm 6:18
n 8:56 Dt 12:10; 1Ch 22:18; Heb 3:18-19
o Jos 21:45; 23:15
p 8:57 Dt 31:6; Jos 1:5; Heb 13:5
q 8:58 Jos 24:23; Jr 31:33; Php 2:13
r 8:59 Pr 30:8; Mt 6:11
s 8:60 Dt 6:4; Jos 4:24; Mk 12:32
t 8:61 Dt 6:5; 1Kg 9:4; 11:4

[A] 8:44 Some Hb mss, some ancient versions, 2Ch 6:34; other Hb mss read *enemy*   [B] 8:47 Lit *they return to their heart*   [C] 8:50 Lit *rebellions that they have rebelled*   [D] 8:58 Lit *causes our hearts to be inclined*

8:46 Sin produces defeat in war and captivity. This truth could point to the occasional historical defeats and partial captivities of God's people, but it could also point to the two great national deportations of the people.

8:51-53 Solomon then looked to the historical basis for the covenant relationship between God and His people, particularly that He had delivered them from **Egypt**.

8:54-56 In his role as the spiritual representative of the people, Solomon had prayed in a posture of humble obeisance before God. This role as the spiritual intermediary between

the people and God continued when Solomon stood, turned to the people, and **blessed** them by announcing, **May the LORD be praised**.

8:57-59 Solomon prayed for God's presence with His people, for he knew that God's active participation (**causes us to be devoted**) was required to keep the people faithful to their covenant with God. The climactic location ("the altar of the LORD," v. 54) of this request tangibly represented God's ongoing presence among His people.

8:60-61 The result of this faithfulness brings us again to the

[62]The king and all Israel with him were offering sacrifices in the Lord's presence. [63]Solomon offered a sacrifice of *fellowship offerings to the Lord: 22,000 cattle and 120,000 sheep.[a] In this manner the king and all the Israelites dedicated[b] the Lord's temple.[c]

[64]On the same day, the king consecrated the middle of the courtyard that was in front of the Lord's temple because that was where he offered the *burnt offering, the *grain offering, and the fat of the fellowship offerings[d] since the bronze altar before the Lord was too small to accommodate the burnt offerings, the grain offerings, and the fat of the fellowship offerings.[e]

[65]Solomon and all Israel with him—a great assembly, from the entrance of Hamath[A,f] to the Brook of Egypt[g]—observed the festival at that time[h] in the presence of the Lord our God, seven days, and seven more days—14 days.[B,i] [66]On the fifteenth day[c] he sent the people away. So they blessed the king and went home to their tents rejoicing and with joyful hearts for all the goodness that the Lord had done for His servant David and for His people Israel.[j]

The Lord's Response

9 When Solomon finished building the temple of the Lord,[k] the royal palace, and all that Solomon desired to do,[l] [2]the Lord appeared to Solomon a second time just as He had appeared to him at Gibeon.[m] [3]The Lord said to him:

I have heard your prayer and petition you have made before Me. I have conse-

crated this temple you have built, to put My name there forever;[n] My eyes and My heart will be there at all times.[o]

[4]As for you, if you walk before Me as your father David walked, with a heart of integrity and in what is right, doing everything I have commanded you, and if you keep My statutes and ordinances,[p] [5]I will establish your royal throne over Israel forever, as I promised your father David: You will never fail to have a man on the throne of Israel.[q]

[6]If you or your sons turn away from following Me and do not keep My commands—My statutes that I have set before you—and if you go and serve other gods and worship them,[r] [7]I will cut off Israel from the land I gave them,[s] and I will reject[D] the temple I have sanctified for My name.[t] Israel will become an object of scorn and ridicule among all the peoples.[u] [8]Though this temple is now exalted,[E] everyone who passes by will be appalled and will mock.[F] They will say: Why did the Lord do this to this land and this temple?[v] [9]Then they will say: Because they abandoned the Lord their God who brought their ancestors out of the land of Egypt. They clung to other gods and worshiped and served them. Because of this, the Lord brought all this ruin on them.[w]

King Hiram's 20 Towns

[10]At the end of 20 years during which

Cross references (center column)

a 8:62-63 1Ch 29:21; 2Ch 7:4-5; Ezr 6:16-17
b 8:63 Dt 20:5; Ezr 6:16; Neh 12:27
c 2Ch 7:5
d 8:64 Lv 6-7
e 2Ch 7:7
f 8:65 Nm 13:21; 34:8
g Gn 15:18
h Lv 23:36; 1Kg 8:2
i 2Ch 7:9
j 8:66 2Ch 7:10
k 9:1-9 2Ch 7:11-22
l 9:1 1Kg 7:1-2; 2Ch 7:11
m 9:2 1Kg 3:5; 11:9
n 9:3 1Kg 8:29
o 2Ch 6:40
p 9:4 1Kg 3:6,14; 11:4,6; 1Ch 28:9
q 9:5 2Sm 7:12,15-16; 1Kg 2:4
r 9:6 Dt 28:15; 1Kg 11:10; 1Ch 28:9
s 9:7 Lv 26:33; Dt 28:63
t Dt 12:5; 1Kg 8:20
u Dt 28:37
v 9:8 Lv 26:32; Dt 29:24; Mt 23:38
w 9:9 Dt 29:25; 31:29

Footnotes

A 8:65 Or from Lebo-hamath   B 8:65 Temple dedication lasted seven days, and the Festival of Tabernacles lasted seven days.   C 8:66 Lit the eighth day   D 9:7 Lit send from My presence   E 9:8 Some ancient versions read temple will become a ruin   F 9:8 Lit hiss

Study notes

major theme of OT missions—that all the peoples of the earth may know that Yahweh is God. With these words, Solomon made a worldwide missions proclamation.

8:62-63 The large number of offerings, especially the fellowship offerings eaten by the worshipers, turned this into a huge, state-funded, national festival.

8:64 Everything that became a part of official worship had to be ritually consecrated.

8:65 This, and perhaps similar great national festivals, involved the entire empire (defined by its ideal bounds) from the entrance of Hamath on the north to the Brook of Egypt, on the south. Extrabiblical documents confirm that the Brook of Egypt was the Wadi Arish or was near this wadi.

9:1-3 At this point, about 946 B.C. in Solomon's twenty-fifth year, God again appeared to Solomon and reaffirmed the holy status of the temple. Though the human consecrations had occurred, the most important consecration was when God declared the temple fit for His residence. Three points were made. God's name would dwell there. God's eyes would be there, giving attention to the temple and in seeing out from it as well. And it would be the center of God's affections, or God's heart.

9:4-5 Turning to Solomon, God again promised him a permanent dynasty, conditioned upon his obedience.

9:6-9 If Solomon's royal descendants persistently worshiped false gods, the Lord would judge Israel. Since the kings were the spiritual representatives of the people, their disobedience was counted as the disobedience of the people. Then the greatest of the covenant punishments—loss of the land—could happen to the Israelites. Ironically, after this judgment the overthrow of Jerusalem and the ruins of the temple would cause Israel to become an object of scorn and ridicule among all the peoples, just the opposite of God's missionary purpose for Israel (see 8:60). In the OT there are two broad types of reaction to God's great works on behalf of His people, one positive and one negative. Positively, the great works of God often prompted recognition of God's holy character, which could cause a turning to Him (e.g., Rahab, Jos 2:9-10,12-13). Negatively, people could be filled with despair at the threat God posed (Jos 2:11), react with blasphemous obstinacy (e.g., Pharaoh hardening his heart; Ex 7:19-23), or be appalled or dismayed by seeing God's judgments against His own people.

9:10-25 The biblical writer then recorded, not in chronological

Solomon had built the two houses, the LORD's temple and the royal palace[a]— [11] Hiram king of Tyre[b] having supplied him with cedar and cypress logs and gold[c] for his every wish[d]—King Solomon gave Hiram 20 towns in the land of Galilee. [12] So Hiram went out from Tyre to look over the towns that Solomon had given him, but he was not pleased with them. [13] So he said, "What are these towns you've given me, my brother?" So he called them the Land of Cabul,[A] as they are still called today.[e] [14] Now Hiram had sent the king 9,000 pounds[B] of gold.[f]

Solomon's Forced Labor

[15] This is the account of the forced labor[g] that King Solomon had imposed to build the LORD's temple, his own palace, the supporting terraces,[h] the wall of Jerusalem,[i] and Hazor,[j] Megiddo,[k] and Gezer.[l] [16] Pharaoh king of Egypt had attacked and captured Gezer. He then burned it down, killed the Canaanites who lived in the city, and gave it as a dowry to his daughter, Solomon's wife.[m] [17] Then Solomon

rebuilt Gezer, Lower Beth-horon,[n] [18] Baalath,[o] Tamar[C,D] in the Wilderness of Judah, [19] all the storage cities that belonged to Solomon, the chariot cities,[p] the cavalry cities,[q] and whatever Solomon desired to build[r] in Jerusalem, Lebanon, or anywhere else in the land of his dominion.

[20] As for all the peoples who remained of the Amorites, Hittites, Perizzites, Hivites, and Jebusites, who were not Israelites— [21] their descendants who remained in the land after them, those whom the Israelites were unable to •completely destroy[s]—Solomon imposed forced labor on them; it is this way until today.[t] [22] But Solomon did not consign the Israelites to slavery;[u] they were soldiers, his servants, his commanders, his captains, and commanders of his chariots and his cavalry. [23] These were the deputies[v] who were over Solomon's work: 550 who ruled over the people doing the work.[w]

Solomon's Other Activities

[24] Pharaoh's daughter moved from the city

Cross references (center column)

a9:10 1Kg 6:38; 7:1; 2Ch 8:1
b9:11 1Kg 5:1
cDt 17:17
d1Kg 5:10
e9:11-13 2Ch 8:2
f9:14 Dt 17:17
g9:15 1Kg 5:13-16
h2Sm 5:9
i1Kg 3:1
jJos 11:1
kJos 17:11
lJdg 1:29
m9:16 1Kg 3:1; 7:8
n9:17 Jos 16:3; 2Ch 8:5
o9:18 Jos 19:44
p9:19 1Kg 10:26
q1Kg 4:26
r1Kg 9:1
s9:20-21 Jdg 1:21-36; 3:1; 2Ch 8:7-8
t9:21 Jdg 1:28, 35; Ezr 2:55,58
u9:22 Lv 25:39
v9:23 1Kg 5:16
w9:22-23 2Ch 8:9-10

A9:13 = Like Nothing   B9:14 Lit 120 talents   C9:18 Alt Hb traditions, LXX, Syr, Tg, Vg read Tamar; 2Ch 8:4   D9:18 Tamar was a city in southern Judah; Ezk 47:19; 48:28.

order, several general social and economic policies loosely related to Solomon's building operations. In terms of biblical theology, these describe Solomon's God-given glory. Some of the details of Solomon's administration involved a misuse, even grossly sinful misuse, of God's good gifts. However misused, they still revealed the glory that God gave to Solomon.

9:10-14 The scenario here is of two equal rulers haggling over an international business deal. Solomon may have driven a hard bargain with **Hiram**—large amounts of building materials plus **gold**—for some unproductive border villages. E. Merrill's analysis sees Hiram as paying Solomon despite Hiram's dissatisfaction with the deal. Hiram's words **my brother** probably indicated the treaty relationship between the two rulers. An international treaty could be called a treaty of brotherhood (Am 1:9).

9:15 Solomon's building operations were widespread and significant for politics, for forced labor economics, and for displaying glory and magnificence. First there were the building operations in Jerusalem: the **temple**, the royal **palace, the supporting terraces**, and **the wall of Jerusalem**. One thought about the supporting terraces, also called the *Millo*, is that they were needed to keep the walls from collapsing into the unsettled "fill" (Hb *millo*) of an earlier valley that had been filled or partially filled. The next three names—**Hazor, Megiddo, and Gezer**—referred to cities that guarded vulnerable routes of attack in the highland heart of Judah and that were fortified by Solomon, using **forced labor**. All of these operations demonstrated Solomon's power and glory and, on close examination, the potential abuses of that power and glory. Solomon and Amos gave principles to guide situations like this. Wealth, even luxury, gained by performing a service (Pr 10:4) is acceptable. But luxury that ruins a society (Am 6:6) is sinful.

9:16 This verse explains Solomon's control over **Gezer**. The

scholarly consensus is that David never completely subdued the Philistine cities, so Egypt felt free to invade Philistia even while David ruled. Then moving to an issue where scholarly consensus breaks down, possibly the **king of Egypt** realized that he had overreached in the invasion and he therefore ceded Gezer to Solomon. Gezer was strategic for Israel, permitting Solomon to control the coastal north-south trade route and one of the approaches from the coast to Jerusalem. In addition, **Pharaoh** was forced into an unusual, perhaps humiliating, marriage alliance in which he gave an Egyptian princess to a foreign king.

9:17-19 These verses describe more of Solomon's military building operations together with some of the more important names involved. These operations were more extensive and expensive than this brief description indicates. They involved garrison and provision cities for a world-class chariot army. This demanded huge initial expenses, road maintenance, and facilities for feeding and caring for the chariot horses as well as living quarters for the charioteers and support personnel. Since the charioteers represented a high degree of skill, which could not be quickly developed, it is likely that Solomon's charioteers were largely made up of international mercenary warriors. Later, as early as Zimri (16:9), Israel had homegrown chariot warriors. Since this text is ambiguous concerning Tamar (in southern Judah) and Tadmor (ancient Palmyra in Aramean territories), we are not positive which location is referred to here. Second Chronicles 8:4 clearly refers to Tadmor. Solomon's building in Tadmor probably referred to Solomon's imperial fortifications there.

9:20-21 There were two categories of Canaanite survivors among the Israelites. First, there were Canaanites, like the house of Rahab, the Gibeonite league, and apparently some of the sons of Hamor (Jdg 9:28) who had survived since the time of Jacob. These had more or less converted to faith in Yahweh and were assimilated into the Israelite population.

of David[a] to the house that Solomon had built for her;[b] he then built the terraces.[c]

[25] Three times a year Solomon offered ‑burnt offerings and ‑fellowship offerings on the altar he had built for the Lord, and he burned incense with them in the Lord's presence.[d] So he completed the temple.[e]

[26] King Solomon put together a fleet of ships at Ezion-geber,[f] which is near Eloth on the shore of the ‑Red Sea in the land of Edom. [27] With the fleet, Hiram sent his servants, experienced seamen, along with Solomon's servants. [28] They went to Ophir[g] and acquired gold there—16 tons[A]—and delivered it to Solomon.[h]

The Queen of Sheba

10 The queen of Sheba[i] heard about Solomon's fame[j] connected with the name of ‑Yahweh and came to test him with difficult questions.[k] [2] She came to Jerusalem with a very large entourage, with camels bearing[l] spices, gold in great abundance, and precious stones.[m] She came to Solomon and spoke to

him about everything that was on her mind. [3] So Solomon answered all her questions; nothing was too difficult for the king to explain to her. [4] When the queen of Sheba observed all of Solomon's wisdom, the palace he had built,[n] [5] the food at his table,[o] his servants' residence, his attendants' service and their attire, his cupbearers, and the ‑burnt offerings he offered at the Lord's temple, it took her breath away.

[6] She said to the king, "The report I heard in my own country about your words and about your wisdom is true. [7] But I didn't believe the reports until I came and saw with my own eyes. Indeed, I was not even told half. Your wisdom and prosperity far exceed the report I heard.[p] [8] How happy are your men.[B] How happy are these servants of yours, who always stand in your presence hearing your wisdom.[q] [9] May Yahweh your God be praised! He delighted in you and put you on the throne of Israel,[r] because of the Lord's eternal love

Cross references (center column)
a 9:24 2Sm 5:7
b 1Kg 7:8; 2Ch 8:11
c 1Kg 9:15; 11:27; 2Ch 32:5
d 9:25 Dt 16:16
e 2Ch 8:16
f 9:26 Nm 33:48; 1Kg 22:48
g 9:27-28 1Kg 10:11; 22:48-49
h 9:28 1Kg 9:11,14
i 10:1 2Ch 9:1; Mt 12:42
j 10:1-10 2Ch 9:1-12
k Jdg 14:12-14
l 10:2 Gn 24:10
m 1Kg 10:10
n 10:4 1Kg 7:1
o 10:5 1Kg 4:22-23
p 10:7 1Ch 29:25
q 10:8 Pr 8:34
r 10:9 2Sm 22:20; 1Kg 5:7

A 9:28 Lit *420 talents*　　B 10:8 LXX, Syr read *your wives*

The rights of these Canaanites were protected even when they were not completely assimilated (e.g., the Gibeonites, who could demand vengeance because Saul violated their rights; 2Sm 21:1-6). Second, there were the unconquered and still openly pagan Canaanites who were yet to be either killed or assimilated into Israelite society. Solomon's **forced labor** brigades were probably pressed into service from this second group.

9:24 Moving **Pharaoh's daughter** out of Jerusalem and so away from the temple can be interpreted in two ways: as an act of piety that removed pagan pollution from the vicinity of the temple, or as an act of respect for the most prestigious of Solomon's political marriages by giving her quarters worthy of her stature.

9:26-10:29 We must recognize Solomon's historical role in world trade as presented in these documents. North-south trade in luxury items was already producing wealth. Southern Arabia, Africa, and points further east were sources of expensive commodities such as gold, ivory, and jewels; esoteric luxury items such as apes and baboons; and spices. These goods could move from the region of southern Arabia north. Depending on the security of sea travel, they could come north by ships on the Red Sea, or they could come north by camel caravan on the Red Sea coast of the Arabian Peninsula. If they came by sea, they could move to the Mediterranean Sea either through Egypt, via the famed Wadi Hamamat, or they could move through the region of Palestine. In either case, once the goods reached the Mediterranean Sea, they went to points further west in Phoenician ships. At this time violent repercussions of Greek-speaking invaders still hampered sea trade to the north toward the Black Sea.

Solomon's joint sea ventures with Hiram were a way of controlling this trade and channeling it through Hebrew territory so that Solomon, instead of Pharaoh, shared in the wealth of such trade. Solomon, like Herod the Great and the Athenians, built a famed temple with the profits from international trade.

9:26-28 These verses indicate that Solomon implemented regular mercantile, seafaring expeditions from **Ezion-geber**. Some believe it is more accurate to speak in terms of caravan trade from the south rather than seafaring commerce. The decisive argument for seafaring trade is the fact that, according to Egyptian wall inscriptions, Shishak (14:25-26) destroyed the forts in the Arabah that protected the routes from **Eloth** north. This effort was frivolous if it was not aimed at diverting the sea trade via the Red Sea to Egyptian territory.

10:1-29 This chapter deals with Solomon's wealth, his international reputation, and his trade practices.

10:1 The author begins with the **the queen of Sheba** (Sabea in the southwestern corner of Arabia) investigating Solomon's rumored wisdom. Perhaps other political and economic interests motivated her visit as well.

10:2 Since the land routes were more convenient for traveling from southern Arabia, and perhaps because Solomon's fleets had cut her off from sea travel, the queen came with a camel caravan loaded with the luxury goods that made her land wealthy and famous. She and Hiram (9:10-14), in their dealings with Solomon, demonstrated one of the models for international commerce: that international trade could be conducted as gifts between heads of state. The gifts were delivered with all the generous appearances of real gifts, but the business managers probably were there to evaluate the real value of the exchanges. And, if an exchange was not fair, one of the partners could complain, as Hiram did (9:13).

10:4-5 These verses demonstrate the moral complexity and depth of the Bible writer's vision. As a manifestation of God's good gifts to Solomon, all this luxury was God-given. However, being abused in practice, this luxury also demonstrated the sinful excess that burdened the people and helped to bring down Solomon's empire.

10:6-9 There were two sides to the queen's glowing report of Solomon's greatness and the blissfulness of his servants. On the good side, it showed both God's glory and Solomon's

for Israel.[a] He has made you king to carry out justice and righteousness."[b]

[10] Then she gave the king four and a half tons[A] of gold,[c] a great quantity of spices, and precious stones. Never again did such a quantity of spices arrive as those the queen of Sheba gave to King Solomon.

[11] In addition, Hiram's fleet that carried gold from Ophir brought from Ophir a large quantity of almug[B] wood and precious stones.[d] [12] The king made the almug wood into steps for the LORD's temple and the king's palace and into lyres and harps for the singers. Never before had such almug wood come, and the like has not been seen again even to this very day.

[13] King Solomon gave the queen of Sheba her every desire—whatever she asked—besides what he had given her out of his royal bounty. Then she, along with her servants, returned to her own country.[e]

Solomon's Wealth

[14] The weight[f] of gold that came to Solomon annually was 25 tons,[c] [15] besides what came from merchants,[g] traders' merchandise, and all the Arabian kings and governors of the land.[h]

[16] King Solomon made 200 large shields of hammered gold; 15 pounds[D] of gold went into each shield. [17] He made 300 small shields of hammered gold; about four pounds[E] of gold went into each shield. The king put them in the House of the Forest of Lebanon.[i]

[18] The king also made a large ivory throne and overlaid it with fine gold. [19] The throne had six steps; there was a rounded top at the back of the throne, armrests on either side of the seat, and two lions standing beside the armrests. [20] Twelve lions were standing there on the six steps, one at each end. Nothing like it had ever been made in any other kingdom.

[21] All of King Solomon's drinking cups were gold, and all the utensils of the House of the Forest of Lebanon[j] were pure gold.[k] There was no silver, since it was considered as nothing in Solomon's time, [22] for the king had ships of Tarshish[l] at sea with Hiram's fleet, and once every three years the ships of Tarshish would arrive bearing gold, silver, ivory, apes, and peacocks.[F,m]

[23] King Solomon surpassed all the kings of the world in riches and in wisdom.[n] [24] The whole world wanted an audience with Solomon to hear the wisdom that God had put in his heart.[o] [25] Every man would bring his annual tribute: items[G] of silver and gold, clothing, weapons,[H] spices, and horses and mules.[p]

[26] Solomon accumulated 1,400 chariots and

---

[a]10:9 1Ch 17:22; 2Ch 2:11
[b]2Sm 8:15
[c]10:10 1Kg 9:28
[d]10:11 1Kg 9:27-28
[e]10:12-13 2Ch 9:11-12
[f]10:14-25 2Ch 9:13-24
[g]10:15 2Ch 1:16
[h]10:14-15 1Kg 9:28; 10:2
[i]10:17 1Kg 7:2-5
[j]10:21 1Kg 7:2-5
[k]1Kg 9:28
[l]10:22 Jnh 1:3
[m]1Kg 9:26-28; 22:48
[n]10:23 1Kg 3:13
[o]10:24 1Kg 3:28; 10:1
[p]10:23-25 2Ch 9:22-24

A10:10 Lit 120 talents   B10:11 = algum in 2Ch 2:8; 9:10-11   C10:14 Lit 666 talents   D10:16 Lit 600 (shekels)   E10:17 Lit three minas   F10:22 Or baboons   G10:25 Or vessels, or weapons   H10:25 Or fragrant balsam

---

glory and his capacity for producing wealth. But it also showed the short-sighted, luxurious misuse of those gifts.

10:10 **Sheba** was famous for spice production and probably also had its own maritime trade with points further east. The **gold** that the queen brought was probably in payment for goods that Solomon was shipping south.

10:11-12 In the absence of firm data about the technological status of the peoples and lands from which these items were imported, one can wonder if this trade was as exploitative as the early European trade with the primitive New World. From the biblical perspective this high-yield trade pictured Solomon's glory as well as God's glory.

10:13 Again, these gifts probably involved some businesslike bargaining.

10:14-15 These verses give a broader perspective on the wealth, trading partners, and tributary areas of Solomon's empire.

10:16-17 This **hammered gold** probably utilized a technology in which soft, nearly pure gold was hammered into thin sheets. Then this foil, because of its malleability, could be applied to almost any surface. This kind of fragile decoration was intended for purely ceremonial use. The **large shields** were modeled after the large rectangular shields more useful for heavy infantry lined up in formation in battle. The circular prototypes of the **small shields** were better suited for more mobile, light-armed infantry.

10:18 Like other luxurious trappings of glory already noted,

this **throne** was decorated with **ivory** inlay and hammered **gold** overlay.

10:19 Lions were a common motif associated with royalty in ancient times. For instance, the palaces of pagan kings often included carved lions representing supernatural beings who were thought to guard the king and his palaces. In Hebrew apocalyptic imagery, such creatures were more symbolic of God's glory. Thus they may here symbolize the king's glory, which ultimately derived from God's glory. **Two lions** here are described as **beside the armrests**. In some similar ancient thrones, the backs of the lions were the armrests while the legs of the lions formed the legs of the throne.

10:20 This description closes with the writer's boast about the uniqueness of Solomon's throne and dais—an expression more properly taken to indicate the king's unique glory rather than the purported uniqueness of structures related to his throne.

10:21 **Pure gold** is too malleable to use in table utensils; some variety of gold alloy is much more practical.

10:22 That the mercantile expeditions were undertaken **every three years** indicates that they were far-reaching, perhaps even bypassing the seafaring interests of possible allies such as Sheba. The expeditions also imply the existence of firm alliances with distant trading partners since the fleets had to have access to friendly harbors during the annual monsoon winds. **Tarshish** was likely in Spain. The Hebrew word translated **peacocks** is difficult to interpret. In light of the close diplomatic and cultural connections be-

12,000 horsemen[a] and stationed them in the chariot cities and with the king in Jerusalem.[b] 27The king made silver as common in Jerusalem as stones,[c] and he made cedar[d] as abundant as sycamore in the Judean foothills. 28Solomon's horses were imported from Egypt and Kue.[A] The king's traders bought them from Kue at the going price.[e] 29A chariot was imported from Egypt for 15 pounds[B] of silver, and a horse for about four pounds.[C] In the same way, they exported them to all the kings of the Hittites and to the kings of Aram through their agents.[f]

Solomon's Unfaithfulness to God

11 King Solomon loved many foreign women in addition to Pharaoh's daughter:[g] Moabite, Ammonite, Edomite, Sidonian, and Hittite women[h] 2from the nations that the LORD had told the Israelites about, "Do not intermarry with them, and they must not intermarry with you, because they will turn you away from Me to their gods."[i] Solomon was deeply attached to these women and loved them. 3He had 700 wives who were princesses and 300 concubines,[j] and they turned his heart away from the LORD.[k]

4When Solomon was old, his wives seduced him to follow other gods. He was not completely devoted to •Yahweh his God, as his father David had been.[l] 5Solomon followed •Ashtoreth,[m] the goddess of the Sidonians, and •Milcom,[n] the detestable idol of the Am-

monites.[o] 6Solomon did what was evil in the LORD's sight, and unlike his father David, he did not completely follow Yahweh.

7At that time, Solomon built a •high place[p] for Chemosh,[q] the detestable idol of Moab, and for Milcom,[D,r] the detestable idol of the Ammonites, on the hill across from Jerusalem.[s] 8He did the same for all his foreign wives, who were burning incense and offering sacrifices to their gods.

9The LORD was angry with Solomon, because his heart had turned away from Yahweh, the God of Israel, who had appeared to him twice.[t] 10He had commanded him about this, so that he would not follow other gods, but Solomon did not do what the LORD had commanded.[u]

11Then the LORD said to Solomon, "Since you have done this[E] and did not keep My covenant and My statutes, which I commanded you, I will tear the kingdom away from you and give it to your servant.[v] 12However, I will not do it during your lifetime because of your father David;[w] I will tear it out of your son's hand. 13Yet I will not tear the entire kingdom away from him. I will give one tribe to your son[x] because of my servant David and because of Jerusalem that I chose."

Solomon's Enemies

14So the LORD raised up[y] Hadad the Edomite as an enemy against Solomon. He was of the royal family in Edom. 15Earlier, when David was in Edom, Joab, the commander of

a10:26 1Kg 4:26
b1Kg 9:19
c10:27 Dt 17:17
d1Kg 5:10; 2Ch 1:15
e10:28 Dt 17:16; 2Ch 9:28
f10:29 2Ch 1:17
g11:1 1Kg 3:1; 7:8
hNeh 13:23-27
i11:2 Dt 7:3-4
j11:3 2Sm 5:13; Est 2:14-15; Sg 6:8
kDt 17:17
l11:4 1Kg 8:61; 9:4; 15:3,14; 1Ch 29:19
m11:5 Jdg 2:13; 10:6; 1Kg 11:33
nLv 18:21
oJdg 2:13; 1Sm 7:3-4
p11:7 Nm 33:52; 1Kg 3:2-3
qNm 21:29
r1Kg 11:33
s2Kg 23:13
t11:9 1Kg 3:5; 9:2
u11:10 1Kg 6:12; 9:6-7
v11:11 1Kg 11:29-31
w11:12 2Sm 7:12-16; 2Kg 19:34; 20:6
x11:12-13 1Kg 11:31-32
y11:14 1Kg 5:4; 1Ch 5:26

A10:28 = Cilicia   B10:29 Lit 600 shekels   C10:29 Lit 150 shekels   D11:7 Lit Molech   E11:11 Lit Since this was with you

tween Solomon and Egypt, the word may actually refer to a type of baboon native to Egypt.

10:26 In light of the data describing Solomon's imperial influence, this figure for a chariot army, **1,400**, seems appropriate or slightly on the low side. About a century later, Assyrian documents assert that Ahab of Israel could mobilize 2,000 chariots. The **12,000 horsemen** probably included the human handlers, trainers, other support personnel for the chariot horses, and the chariot warriors themselves.

10:28-29 An important part of Solomon's trade and commerce was his trade in chariots and chariot **horses**. The best chariots were made in Egypt. One of the major suppliers of horses was a place in northern Egypt known as Mitsri. This indicates that Solomon had established himself as the middleman for much of the north-south arms trade of his day.

11:1-43 This chapter describes Solomon's failures, which began in the early years of his rule.

11:1-2 David had also married **foreign** wives, but they did not change either his religious life or that of the nation. Solomon's wives, on the other hand, were known devotees of their national deities. Solomon's Hittite wives had historical ties with the old Hittite aristocracies of the preceding millennium. Ruth, the Moabitess, showed that there was no offense in marrying a foreigner who had converted (Ru 4:13).

11:3 Solomon's many political marriages demanded re-

spect for the resident princesses and the political groups they represented, especially when he was old and needed help in controlling the empire (vv. 14-40). **Princesses** probably designated his political wives in contrast to his 300 ordinary harem women, or **concubines**.

11:4-8 These religious compromises were likely seen as politically expedient acts of courtesy to Solomon's foreign **wives**, comparable to extraterritorial privileges that allow embassies in our time to conduct themselves according to the laws and customs of their native land, but these common-sense principles conflicted with faith in God and God's covenant with Israel. Both **Ashtoreth** (Astarte, Ishtar) and **Milcom** (Molech) were international deities worshiped under numerous names in different countries. **Chemosh**, by contrast, was a god of **Moab**, probably a god of war.

11:9-13 Two divine visions were not enough to keep Solomon faithful. His departure from the Lord produced a sentence of judgment, the execution of which was deferred and mitigated on account of his father David's faithfulness and on account of Jerusalem's reputation as Yahweh's city (v. 32).

11:14-40 God began to weaken Solomon so that his empire and most of his kingdom would be lost at his death. This was accomplished both by providential intervention in normal trends and, in the case of Jeroboam, by direct prophetic intervention (vv. 29-33).

11:14-17 Though God tolerated many character flaws,

the army, had gone to bury the dead and had struck down every male in Edom. [16]For Joab and all Israel had remained there six months, until he had killed every male in Edom.[a] [17]Hadad fled to Egypt, along with some Edomites from his father's servants. At the time Hadad was a small boy. [18]Hadad and his men set out from Midian and went to Paran.[b] They took men with them from Paran and went to Egypt, to Pharaoh king of Egypt,[c] who gave Hadad a house, ordered that he be given food, and gave him land. [19]Pharaoh liked Hadad so much that he gave him a wife, the sister of his own wife, Queen Tahpenes. [20]Tahpenes' sister gave birth to Hadad's son Genubath. Tahpenes herself weaned him in Pharaoh's palace, and Genubath lived there along with Pharaoh's sons.

[21]When Hadad heard in Egypt that David rested with his fathers and that Joab, the commander of the army, was dead, Hadad said to Pharaoh, "Let me leave, so I can go to my own country."

[22]But Pharaoh asked him, "What do you lack here with me for you to want to go back to your own country?"

"Nothing," he replied, "but please let me leave."

[23]God raised up Rezon son of Eliada as an enemy[d] against Solomon. Rezon had fled from his master Hadadezer king of Zobah[e] [24]and gathered men to himself. He became captain of a raiding party when David killed the Zobaites. He[A] went to Damascus,[f] lived there, and became king in Damascus. [25]Rezon was Israel's enemy throughout Solomon's reign, adding to the trouble Hadad had caused. He ruled over Aram,[B,g] but he loathed Israel.

[26]Now Solomon's servant,[h] Jeroboam son of Nebat, was an Ephraimite from Zeredah. His widowed mother's name was Zeruah. Jeroboam rebelled[i] against Solomon, [27]and this is the reason he rebelled against the king: Solomon had built the supporting terraces[j] and repaired the opening in the wall of the city of his father David. [28]Now the man Jeroboam was capable, and Solomon noticed the young man because he was getting things done. So he appointed him over the entire labor force of the house of Joseph.[k]

[29]During that time, the prophet Ahijah the Shilonite[l] met Jeroboam on the road as Jeroboam came out of Jerusalem. Now Ahijah had wrapped himself with a new cloak, and the two of them were alone in the open field. [30]Then Ahijah took hold of the new cloak he had on, tore it into 12 pieces,[m] [31]and said to Jeroboam, "Take 10 pieces for yourself, for this is what the LORD God of Israel says: 'I am about to tear the kingdom out of Solomon's hand. I will give you 10 tribes, [32]but one tribe will remain his because of my servant David[n] and because of Jerusalem, the city I chose out of all the tribes of Israel.[o] [33]For they have abandoned Me; they have bowed the knee to Ashtoreth, the goddess of the Sidonians, to Chemosh, the god of Moab, and to Milcom, the god of the Ammonites.[p] They have not walked in My ways to do what is right in My eyes and to carry out My statutes and My judgments as his father David did.[q]

[34]"'However, I will not take the whole kingdom from his hand but will let him be ruler all the days of his life because of My servant David, whom I chose and who kept My commands and My statutes. [35]I will take 10 tribes of the kingdom from his son's hand and give them to you. [36]I will give one tribe[r] to his son,[s] so that My servant David will always have a lamp before Me[t] in Jerusalem, the city I chose

*a*11:15-16 2Sm 8:13-14; 1Ch 18:12-13
*b*11:18 Nm 10:12; Dt 1:1
*c*1Kg 3:1
*d*11:23 1Kg 5:4
*e*2Sm 8:3
*f*11:24 2Sm 8:5
*g*11:25 Gn 10:22; 2Sm 10:19
*h*11:26 1Kg 11:11
*i*1Kg 11:40; 2Ch 13:6
*j*11:27 1Kg 9:15,24
*k*11:28 1Kg 5:13-16; 12:4
*l*11:29 1Kg 12:15; 14:2
*m*11:30 1Sm 15:27-28; 1Kg 11:11-13
*n*11:32 2Sm 7:15-16
*o*11:30-32 1Kg 11:11-13
*p*11:33 1Kg 11:5,7
*q*1Kg 3:14; 11:9-11
*r*11:36 1Kg 12:16-17
*s*11:34-36 1Kg 3:14; 11:12-13
*t*11:36 2Sm 21:17; 1Kg 15:4; 2Kg 8:19

A11:24 LXX; Hb reads *They*   B11:25 Some Hb mss, LXX, Syr read *Edom*

---

including excessive violence, in his chosen servants of Israel, this tolerance did not prevent their evil acts from yielding evil fruit. For instance, the resentment in Edom against **Joab** and **David** for their brutality (2Sm 8:13-14) helped to weaken Solomon years later. **All Israel** refers only to the group under discussion—the soldiers involved in the campaign against Edom.

11:18-22 God used Pharaoh's opportunism to weaken Solomon. **Pharaoh** exploited both **Hadad** and Jeroboam to undermine Solomon. The presence of foreign threats such as these could explain why Solomon willingly compromised his faith in order to appease his wives. He hoped better relations with his Egyptian wife might prompt Egypt to enact a more favorable foreign policy toward Israel. Even while Solomon lived, control over Edom was weak enough to permit Hadad to return home. An insecure Edom threatened the caravan routes from Eloth (9:26) northward.

11:23-25 Rezon, in moving from an outlaw warrior to a legitimate king, paralleled the career of King **David**. With Rezon's rule, **Damascus** became Israel's main enemy in **Aram**. Again, this situation developed while Solomon ruled.

11:26 Jeroboam is introduced as a rebel in an introductory summary of his career under Solomon.

11:29-32 God intervened in governmental affairs through the prophecy of **Ahijah**. The fact that **10 tribes** and **one tribe** does not account for all 12 tribes of Israel should not be taken as problematic. Levi may or may not be counted in such groupings, or Ahijah may have meant that one tribe would remain in addition to Judah (see note at 12:20).

11:33-34 God rejected Solomon because he encouraged false worship (vv. 5-8). He would be judged, but out of loyalty to **David** God would not completely reject Solomon's dynasty.

11:37-39 The only major idea of the Davidic covenant that was neither offered nor implied to Jeroboam was the rela-

for Myself to put My name there.[a] [37]I will appoint you,[b] and you will reign as king[c] over all you want,[d] and you will be king over Israel.

[38]"'After that, if you obey all I command you, walk in My ways, and do what is right in My sight in order to keep My statutes and My commands as My servant David did, I will be with you.[e] I will build you a lasting dynasty just as I built for David,[f] and I will give you Israel. [39]I will humble David's descendants, because of their unfaithfulness, but not forever.'"[A,g]

[40]Therefore, Solomon tried to kill Jeroboam,[h] but he fled to Egypt,[i] to Shishak king of Egypt,[j] where he remained until Solomon's death.

Solomon's Death

[41]The rest of the events of Solomon's reign, along with all his accomplishments and his wisdom, are written in the Book of Solomon's Events.[k] [42]The length of Solomon's reign in Jerusalem over all Israel totaled 40 years.[l] [43]Solomon rested with his fathers and was buried in the city of his father David. His son Rehoboam[m] became king in his place.[n]

The Kingdom Divided

12 Then Rehoboam[o] went to Shechem,[p] for all Israel[q] had gone to Shechem to make him king.[r] [2]When Jeroboam son of Nebat heard about it, for he was still in Egypt where he had fled from King Solomon's presence,[s] Jeroboam stayed in Egypt.[B] [3]They summoned him, and Jeroboam and the whole assembly of Israel came and spoke to Rehoboam: [4]"Your father made our yoke difficult.[t]

You, therefore, lighten your father's harsh service and the heavy yoke he put on us,[u] and we will serve you."

[5]Rehoboam replied, "Go home for three days and then return to me." So the people left. [6]Then King Rehoboam consulted with the elders[v] who had served his father Solomon when he was alive, asking, "How do you advise me to respond to these people?"

[7]They replied, "Today if you will be a servant to these people and serve them, and if you respond to them by speaking kind words to them, they will be your servants forever."[w]

[8]But he rejected the advice of the elders who had advised him[x] and consulted with the young men who had grown up with him and served him. [9]He asked them, "What message do you advise that we send back to these people who said to me, 'Lighten the yoke your father put on us'?"

[10]Then the young men who had grown up with him told him, "This is what you should say to these people who said to you, 'Your father made our yoke heavy, but you, make it lighter on us!' This is what you should tell them: 'My little finger is thicker than my father's loins! [11]Although my father burdened you with a heavy yoke, I will add to your yoke; my father disciplined you with whips, but I will discipline you with barbed whips.'"[C,y]

[12]So Jeroboam and all the people came to Rehoboam on the third day, as the king had ordered: "Return to me on the third day." [13]Then the king answered the people harshly. He rejected the advice the elders had given

Cross references (center column)

[a]11:36 1Kg 8:29; 11:13
[b]11:37 1Kg 11:11
[c]1Kg 14:7
[d]2Sm 3:21
[e]11:38 Jos 1:5; 1Kg 3:14; 11:11
[f]2Sm 7:11,27
[g]11:39 Ezk 37:15-28; Am 9:11-12
[h]11:40 1Kg 11:26-28
[i]1Kg 12:2
[j]1Kg 14:25-26; 2Ch 12:2-9
[k]11:41 1Kg 15:7,23; 2Ch 9:29
[l]11:42 2Sm 5:5
[m]11:43 1Kg 12:1
[n]11:42-43 2Ch 9:30-31
[o]12:1-19 2Ch 10:1-19
[p]12:1 Jos 12:1; 1Kg 12:25
[q]2Sm 20:1-2; 1Kg 12:16-17
[r]Jdg 9:6
[s]12:2 1Kg 11:40
[t]12:4 1Sm 8:11-18
[u]1Kg 4:20
[v]12:6 1Kg 4:2-19
[w]12:7 2Ch 10:7; Pr 15:1
[x]12:8 Lv 19:32
[y]12:10-11 Ex 1:13-14; 5:6-9; 2Ch 10:10-11

A11:38-39 LXX omits *and I will give . . . but not forever*   B12:2 LXX, Vg read *Jeroboam returned from Egypt*; 2Ch 10:2   C12:11 Lit *with scorpions*

---

tionship defined by the words, "I will be a father to him, and he will be a son to Me" (2Sm 7:14).

11:40 Solomon's attempt to **kill Jeroboam** reduced him to the same tyranny as Saul when Saul tried to kill David. By sheltering Jeroboam, **Shishak king of Egypt** again meddled in Solomon's affairs. The corrosion in Solomon's rule was clear.

11:41-43 The **Book of . . . Events** was probably the official, factual record of the king. This succession statement, like all future succession statements, ignored the traditional leaders of the tribes. This formal close to Solomon's rule was the writer's signal that he was finished with Solomon's era. Now the story moves to Solomon's successor.

12:1-33 There are two reasons for the great attention given here to the northern kings. First, because of the covenant offered to Jeroboam I (11:31,38), it was proper to record the evidence that the northern kings rejected God's covenant. Though God knew what the future would bring, Israel did not immediately disappear from the prophetic and historical picture. Being in the north, Israel was more exposed to the flow of events, both economic and political. Therefore, at its best, Israel's location guaranteed wealth and power.

At its worst, Israel's location exposed it to greater danger of foreign conquest.

12:1 Shechem was strategically located on the main road north of Jerusalem near the border of Ephraim and Manasseh. Therefore it was a good location for shadowing Jerusalem on the north and for gathering the traditional northern tribal leaders. The advantages of this location were confirmed when Jeroboam made Shechem his capital. David, earlier, had made a covenant with the elders for the kingship (2Sm 5:3), but these elders were ignored when Solomon came to power (1Kg 1). They were open to David's dynasty, but they wanted to negotiate. **Rehoboam** had to satisfy the traditional elders in order to become king. Clearly, if it had been God's choice for Rehoboam to rule the united empire, He could have accomplished it, but the Lord had rejected Solomon, so He permitted the forces of disunity to proceed.

12:2-4 Jeroboam was summoned from **Egypt** to speak for the elders. After Solomon's oppressive policies they demanded that the economic burdens be lightened.

12:8-16 Rehoboam's arrogance can be explained only by his presumption that he could demand and receive Solomon's absolute power. Rehoboam wanted to operate in terms

him [14]and spoke to them according to the young men's advice: "My father made your yoke heavy, but I will add to your yoke; my father disciplined you with whips, but I will discipline you with barbed whips."[A]

[15]The king did not listen to the people, because this turn of events came from the Lord[a] to carry out His word, which the Lord had spoken through Ahijah the Shilonite to Jeroboam son of Nebat.[b] [16]When all Israel saw that the king had not listened to them, the people answered him:

> What portion do we have in David?
> We have no inheritance in the son
>   of Jesse.[c]
> Israel, return to your tents;
> David, now look after your own house![d]

So Israel went to their tents, [17]but Rehoboam reigned over the Israelites living in the cities of Judah.[e]

[18]Then King Rehoboam sent Adoram,[B,f] who was in charge of forced labor, but all Israel stoned him to death. King Rehoboam man-

Cross references:
[a]12:15 Dt 2:30; 1Kg 12:24
[b]1Kg 11:29-39
[c]12:16 2Sm 5:3,5
[d]2Sm 20:1
[e]12:17 1Kg 11:13,36
[f]12:18 2Sm 20:24; 1Kg 4:6; 5:14

[A]12:14 Lit *with scorpions*   [B]12:18 LXX reads *Adoniram*; 1Kg 4:6; 5:14

---

comparable to the divine right of kings but with neither the military power nor the moral authority to enforce this approach. Rehoboam's younger (fortyish) companions, who had grown up in Solomon's absolutism, supported him with two proverbial similes and overrode the better counsel of the elders.

12:18 Rehoboam's naivete and foolishness were demonstrated by his sending **Adoram** (the same man as Adoniram; 5:14), director of the **forced labor** battalions, to enforce his rule. Adoram represented one of the heavier and more degrading of the burdens Solomon had placed on the people. The northerners killed him in a particularly insulting way, and Rehoboam barely escaped with his life.

Kings of the Divided Monarchy

JUDAH	(Bright)[1]	(Miller/Hays)[2]	ISRAEL	(Bright)[1]	(Miller/Hays)[2]
Rehoboam	922-915	924-907	Jeroboam I	922-901	924-903
Abijam	915-913	907-906	*Nadab	901-900	903-902
Asa	913-873	905-874			
			Baasha	900-877	902-886
			*Elah	877-876	886-885
			Zimri (suicide)	876	
			The Omrides	876-842	885-843
Jehoshaphat	873-849	874-850	Omri	876-869	885-873
			Ahab	869-850	873-851
			Ahaziah	850-849	851-849
Jehoram	849-843	850-843	*Jehoram	849-842	849-843
Ahaziah	843-842	843	Dynasty of Jehu	842-746	843-745
Athaliah (usurper)	842-837	843-837	Jehu	843/2-815	843-816
Joash	837-800	837-?	Jehoahaz	815-802	816-800
Amaziah	800-783	?-?	Jehoash (Joash)	802-786	800-785
Uzziah (Azariah)	783-742	?-?	Jeroboam II	786-746	785-745
Jotham	742-735	?-742	*Zechariah	746-745	745
			*Shallum	745	745
Ahaz	735-715	742-727	Menahem	745-737	745-736
			*Pekahiah	737-736	736-735
			*Pekah	736-732	735-732
			Hoshea	732-724	732-723
			Fall of Samaria	722	722
Hezekiah	715-687/6	727-698			
Manasseh	687/6-642	697-642			
Amon	642-640		Asterisk (*) indicates assassination		
Josiah	640-609	639-609			
Jehoaz	609	609	[1] Dates preferred by John Bright, *A History of Israel*, 3rd ed.		
Jehoiakim	609-598	608-598			
Jehoiachin	598/7	598/597	[2] Dates preferred by J. Maxwell Miller and John H. Hays, *A History of Ancient Israel and Judah*.		
Zedekiah	597-587	597-586			
Destruction of Jerusalem and the temple	586		▮ Indicates dynasty		

aged to get into the chariot and flee to Jerusalem. [19]Israel is in rebellion against the house of David until today.[a]

Rehoboam in Jerusalem

[20]When all Israel heard that Jeroboam had come back,[b] they summoned him to the assembly and made him king over all Israel.[c] No one followed the house of David except the tribe of Judah alone.[d] [21]When Rehoboam arrived in Jerusalem,[e] he mobilized 180,000 choice warriors from the entire house of Judah and the tribe of Benjamin[f] to fight against the house of Israel to restore the kingdom to Rehoboam son of Solomon. [22]But a revelation from God came to Shemaiah,[g] the man of God: [23]"Say to Rehoboam son of Solomon, king of Judah, to the whole house of Judah and Benjamin, and to the rest of the people, [24]'This is what the LORD says: You are not to march up and fight against your brothers, the Israelites. Each of you must return home, for I have done this.'"[h]

So they listened to what the LORD said and went back as He had told them.

Jeroboam's Idolatry

[25]Jeroboam built Shechem[i] in the hill country of Ephraim and lived there. From there he went out and built Penuel.[j] [26]Jeroboam said to himself, "The way things are going now, the kingdom might return to the house of David.[k] [27]If these people regularly go to offer sacrifices in the LORD's temple in Jerusalem,[l] the heart of these people will return to their lord, Rehoboam king of Judah. They will murder me and go back to the king of Judah." [28]So the king sought advice.

Then he made two golden calves, and he said to the people, "Going to Jerusalem is too difficult for you. Israel, here is your God[A] who brought you out of the land of Egypt."[m] [29]He set up one in Bethel,[n] and put the other in Dan.[o] [30]This led to sin;[p] the people walked in procession before one of the calves all the way to Dan.[B,q]

[31]Jeroboam also built shrines on the •high places[r] and set up priests from every class of people who were not Levites.[s] [32]Jeroboam made a festival in the eighth month on the fifteenth day of the month, like the festival in Judah.[t] He offered sacrifices on the altar; he made this offering in Bethel to sacrifice to the calves he had set up. He also stationed the priests in Bethel for the high places he had set up.[u] [33]He offered sacrifices on[c] the altar he had set up in Bethel on the fifteenth day of the eighth month. He chose this month on his own.[v] He made a festival for the Israelites,

a 12:19 2Kg 21:17
b 12:20 1Kg 12:3
c 1Kg 11:11
d 1Kg 11:13,36
e 12:21-24 2Ch 11:1-4
f 12:21 2Sm 19:17
g 12:22 2Ch 12:5,7
h 12:24 1Kg 12:15
i 12:25 Gn 12:6; Jdg 9:6; 1Kg 12:1
j 1Kg 8:8-9,17
k 12:26 1Kg 11:38
l 12:27 Dt 12:5-7,14
m 12:28 Ex 32:4,8
n 12:29 Gn 12:8; 28:19
o Jdg 18:29
p 12:30 1Kg 13:34; 2Kg 17:21
q Ex 20:4-6; Dt 5:8-10
r 12:31 1Kg 3:3; 11:7
s 2Kg 17:32
t 12:32 Lv 23:33-34; Nm 29:12
u 2Ch 11:15
v 12:33 Nm 15:39

A 12:28 Or here are your gods   B 12:30 Some LXX mss read calves to Bethel and the other to Dan   C 12:33 Or He went up to

12:20 In theory, the traditional authorities had exercised their right to elect the king. However, even in the north their elective rights would quickly give way to dynastic succession and military revolution. The statement that **the tribe of Judah alone** followed **David** is another true but rhetorical statement (cp. 11:35-36). It was true that only the tribe of Judah *completely* followed David, but portions of Benjamin, remnants of Simeon, many Levites, and even other northerners who wished to remain true to the covenant dynasty also followed the house of David (2Ch 11:13-17).

12:22-24 The divine oracle against fighting their **brothers** prevented hostilities for the moment, but this was just the beginning of recurrent, generally small-scale, border warfare.

12:25 The selection of **Shechem** as the capital should have pleased the northerners, for whom it was a natural site for conducting intertribal business. Then Jeroboam built or fortified **Penuel**, almost directly east across the Jordan rift from Shechem. This gave Jeroboam a fortified foothold on each side of the Jordan River.

12:26-27 Jeroboam's astute scheming showed his doubt of God's promises. The Lord promised Jeroboam 10 tribes, but Jeroboam speculated that God might prove untrue and the people of the north might **return to the house of David**.

12:28 The most sobering point in this verse is that **the king sought advice**, and rather than being turned from error, was encouraged to make **two golden calves**. This act was not simply rebellion against David; it was also the rejection of the proper worship of Yahweh by the leaders and counselors of Israel who advised Jeroboam. The king then set up

a new system of worship for the people to keep them from going to Jerusalem for worship. It was a shrewd innovation. Such golden images typically consisted of an image made of cheaper material, usually wood, covered with gold foil or gold plating. Possibly Jeroboam did not intend these images to represent the Lord Himself, but rather meant to imply that Yahweh was the invisible deity riding above the calves. Thus, the king may have intended to produce an alternate, nonidolatrous manner of worshiping the Lord. However, his was still a disobedient, human-made system that had its origins in unbelief and fear rather than faith and obedience.

12:29 Dan already had a history of illegal, idolatrous worship of Yahweh (Jdg 18). The calf shrine in **Bethel** was on the traditional border between Benjamin and Ephraim, barely 10 miles north of the national temple in Jerusalem. This was a deliberate insult to Jerusalem and the worship conducted there.

12:30-31 The Bible briefly depicts the pomp and circumstance of these consecrations: **the people walked in procession** before the calf installed at **Dan**. Jeroboam also set up other illegal shrines throughout the country which he staffed, illegally, with non-Levites. This dispossessing of the Levites from their assigned duties encouraged their emigration southward. Ironically, God may have used Jeroboam's idolatry to concentrate the Levites where their influence for good would be most effective.

12:32-33 Again, with political astuteness but religious disobedience, **Jeroboam** changed the calendar. He established a festival **like the festival in Judah**, on the fifteenth day of

offered sacrifices on the altar, and burned incense.[a]

Judgment on Jeroboam

13 A man of God[b] came from Judah to Bethel by a revelation from the LORD while Jeroboam was standing beside the altar to burn incense.[c] ²The man of God cried out against the altar by a revelation from the LORD: "Altar, altar, this is what the LORD says, 'A son will be born to the house of David, named Josiah, and he will sacrifice on you the priests of the •high places who are burning incense on you. Human bones will be burned on you.'"[d] ³He gave a sign[e] that day. He said, "This is the sign that the LORD has spoken: 'The altar will now be ripped apart, and the ashes that are on it will be poured out.'"[f]

⁴When the king heard the word that the man of God had cried out against the altar at Bethel, Jeroboam stretched out his hand from the altar and said, "Arrest him!" But the hand he stretched out against him withered, and he could not pull it back to himself. ⁵The altar was ripped apart, and the ashes poured from the altar, according to the sign that the man of God had given by the word of the LORD.

⁶Then the king responded to the man of God, "Plead for the favor of the LORD your God and pray for me[g] so that my hand may be restored to me." So the man of God pleaded for the favor of the LORD, and the king's hand was restored to him and became as it had been at first.

⁷Then the king declared to the man of God, "Come home with me, refresh yourself, and I'll give you a reward."[h]

⁸But the man of God replied, "If you were to give me half your house,[i] I still wouldn't go with you, and I wouldn't eat bread or drink water in this place, ⁹for this is what I was commanded by the word of the LORD:[j] 'You must not eat bread or drink water or go back the way you came.'" ¹⁰So he went another way; he did not go back by the way he had come to Bethel.

The Old Prophet and the Man of God

¹¹Now a certain old prophet was living in Bethel.[k] His son[A] came and told him all the deeds that the man of God had done that day in Bethel. His sons also told their father the words that he had spoken to the king.[l] ¹²Then their father said to them, "Which way did he go?" His sons had seen[B] the way taken by the man of God who had come from Judah. ¹³Then he said to his sons, "Saddle the donkey for me." So they saddled the donkey for him, and he got on it. ¹⁴He followed the man of God and found him sitting under an oak tree. He asked him, "Are you the man of God who came from Judah?"

"I am," he said.

¹⁵Then he said to him, "Come home with me and eat bread."

¹⁶But he answered, "I cannot go back with you, eat bread, or drink water with you in this place, ¹⁷for a message came to me by the word of the LORD: 'You must not eat bread or drink water there[m] or go back by the way you came.'"

¹⁸He said to him, "I am also a prophet[n] like you. An angel spoke to me by the word of the

Cross references

a 12:33 2Kg 23:15
b 13:1 1Kg 12:22; 2Kg 23:17
c 1Kg 12:32-33
d 13:2 2Kg 23:15-16
e 13:3 Is 7:14
f Jn 2:11,18
g 13:6 Jms 5:16
h 13:7 1Sm 9:7; 2Kg 5:15
i 13:8 Nm 22:18; Est 5:3; Mk 6:23
j 13:9 1Kg 13:1
k 13:11 1Kg 12:32; 13:1
l 1Kg 13:2-6
m 13:16-17 1Kg 13:8-9
n 13:18 1Jn 4:1

A 13:11 Some Hb mss, LXX, Syr, Vg read *sons*   B 13:12 LXX, Syr, Tg, Vg read *sons showed him*

---

the **eighth month**. This festival apparently replaced the observances in the seventh month, Tishri, which included both the Day of Atonement and the Festival of Ingathering (Ex 23:16; also known as the Festival of Booths). The text does not clarify whether Jeroboam's illegal act of **sacrifices** was a one-time event when he initiated the worship or a habitual act on his part.

13:1 The distinctive introductory statement of this account is literally, "And behold, a man of God came/was coming." This formula, announcing the arrival of **a man**, can occur at a dramatic new turn within the plot of an episode (Nm 25:6; Jdg 19:16), but it can also open a new story (1Sm 2:27; 2Kg 4:42). Therefore this chapter could be either a dramatic turn in the preceding story or an entirely different event on a later occasion when King Jeroboam officiated at a sacrifice.

13:2-3 The prophet's curse was especially insulting. Contact with human remains was one of the most powerful ways to pollute or desecrate any sacred object. This prophecy that **Josiah**, centuries later, would desecrate this altar with the corpses of its **priests** was a powerful statement of God's rejection of this disobedient worship. As related in the later story, these were corpses of already dead priests retrieved from a local cemetery (2Kg 23:16). The truth of the proph-

et's curse was attested by an immediate **sign**, the damaging of that altar with the spilling of **ashes** on the ground. Some suggest that irregular disposal of sacrificial ashes invalidated a sacrifice. If so, the spilling of the ashes here is symbolic of the unacceptability of sacrifices offered on this altar.

13:4-7 God also miraculously punished Jeroboam. The immediate healing of his **withered hand** as a result of the prophet's intercession should have been another witness to direct Jeroboam into faith and obedience. The king's spiritual shallowness was apparent when he trivialized the miraculous sign into an occasion to beg a personal **favor** from the prophet. Then Jeroboam offered the prophet a **reward** and thus treated God like a bargaining partner.

13:8-10 This prophet's steadfastness in obedience contrasts with Saul's willingness to give in to people (1Sm 28:23-25) and Gehazi's eagerness to benefit from Naaman's generosity (2Kg 5:20-27). To **eat bread** with Jeroboam might be perceived as withdrawing judgment and endorsing his kingdom (1Sm 15:24-31).

13:11-19 Jeroboam's shallow perception of God's holiness would be matched by **a certain old prophet** who lived in **Bethel**. This prophet lied to the prophet from **Judah**. Per-

LORD: 'Bring him back with you to your house so that he may eat bread and drink water.'" The old prophet deceived him,[a] [19]and the man of God went back with him, ate bread in his house, and drank water.

[20]While they were sitting at the table, the word of the LORD came to the prophet who had brought him back, [21]and the prophet cried out to the man of God who had come from Judah, "This is what the LORD says: 'Because you rebelled against the command of the LORD and did not keep the command that the LORD your God commanded you— [22]but you went back and ate bread and drank water in the place that He said to you, "Do not eat bread and do not drink water"—[b] your corpse will never reach the grave of your fathers.'"[c]

[23]So after he had eaten bread and after he had drunk, the old prophet saddled the donkey for the prophet he had brought back. [24]When he left,[A] a lion attacked[B] him along the way and killed him.[d] His corpse was thrown on the road, and the donkey was standing beside it; the lion was standing beside the corpse too.

[25]There were men passing by who saw the corpse thrown on the road and the lion standing beside it, and they went and spoke about it in the city where the old prophet lived. [26]When the prophet who had brought him back from his way heard about it, he said, "He is the man of God who disobeyed the command of the LORD. The LORD has given him to the lion, and it has mauled and killed him, according to the word of the LORD that He spoke to him."

[27]Then the old prophet instructed his sons, "Saddle the donkey for me." They saddled it,[e] [28]and he went and found the corpse of the man of God thrown on the road with the donkey and the lion standing beside the corpse. The lion had not eaten the corpse or mauled the donkey. [29]So the prophet lifted the corpse

of the man of God and laid it on the donkey and brought it back. The old prophet came into the city to mourn and bury him. [30]Then he laid the corpse in his own grave,[f] and they mourned over him: "Oh, my brother!"[g]

[31]After he had buried him, he said to his sons, "When I die, you must bury me in the grave where the man of God is buried; lay my bones beside his bones, [32]for the word that he cried out by a revelation from the LORD against the altar in Bethel[h] and against all the shrines of the high places[i] in the cities of Samaria[j] is certain to happen."[k]

[33]After all this[l] Jeroboam did not repent[m] of his evil way but again set up priests for the high places from every class of people.[n] He ordained whoever so desired it, and they became priests of the high places.[o] [34]This was the sin that caused the house of Jeroboam to be wiped out and annihilated from the face of the earth.[p]

Disaster on the House of Jeroboam

14 At that time Abijah son of Jeroboam became sick.[q] [2]Jeroboam said to his wife, "Go disguise yourself,[r] so they won't know that you're Jeroboam's wife, and go to Shiloh.[s] Ahijah the prophet is there; it was he who told about me becoming king over this people.[t] [3]Take with you 10 loaves of bread, some cakes, and a jar of honey,[u] and go to him. He will tell you what will happen to the boy."

[4]Jeroboam's wife did that: she went to Shiloh and arrived at Ahijah's house. Ahijah could not see; his gaze was fixed[C] due to his age.[v] [5]But the LORD had said to Ahijah, "Jeroboam's wife is coming soon to ask you about her son, for he is sick. You are to say such and such to her. When she arrives, she will be disguised."[w]

[6]When Ahijah heard the sound of her feet entering the door, he said, "Come in, wife of

a 13:18 Dt 13:1-3
b 13:21-22 1Kg 13:8-9
c 13:22 1Kg 13:30
d 13:24 1Kg 20:36
e 13:27 1Kg 13:13
f 13:30 1Kg 13:22,24
g Jr 22:18
h 13:32 1Kg 13:1-3
i 1Kg 12:31-32; 2Kg 17:29
j 1Kg 16:28-29,32
k 2Kg 23:16
l 13:33 1Kg 13:1-6,24
m 1Kg 12:28-33; 13:1; Ac 26:20
n 1Kg 12:31
o Jdg 17:5; 2Ch 13:9
p 13:34 1Kg 12:28-33; 2Kg 17:21-23
q 14:1 1Kg 14:12,17-18
r 14:2 1Sm 28:8; 2Sm 14:2-3
s Jos 18:1
t 1Kg 11:29-39
u 14:3 1Sm 9:7-8
v 14:4 1Sm 3:2; 4:15
w 14:5 2Sm 14:1-2

A 13:23-24 LXX reads *donkey, and he turned* [24] *and left, and*　B 13:24 Lit *met*　C 14:4 Lit *see, for his eyes stood*; 1Sm 4:15

---

haps the prophet of Bethel wanted the prophet of Judah to validate Bethel's ritual by sharing **bread** with him.

13:20-21 Then ironically, as they ate, God spoke His true judgment through the same **prophet** who had just moments earlier lied. God's judgment of the disobedient prophet from Judah is another example of His severe judgment in this book.

13:23-29 This account of the prophet's death is full of wonders. The **lion** did not devour the **corpse** or injure the **donkey**. The donkey stayed put instead of running away. And the lion did not threaten the old prophet when he came to retrieve the corpse—an act of nobility and bravery in contrast to his earlier deceit. To the ancient Israelites, loss of burial with one's own clan was a severe judgment.

13:30-32 The prophet from Judah was buried with honor

and respect, and the old prophet reaffirmed the truth of the message by sharing his burial place with the dead prophet.

13:33-34 Jeroboam trivialized and profaned sacred ritual by assuming the right to ordain **priests**, and in doing so, forfeited his covenant with God. This second statement of judgment on Jeroboam (see notes at vv. 2-3 and 14:10-11) focuses on this offense (cp. 2Kg 17:7-12).

14:1-3 Jeroboam continued his erratic, inconsistent behavior. The king was double-minded or indecisive (Jms 1:8), disobeying God and trying to seek favors from Him at the same time.

14:4-5 In dealing with the query of **Jeroboam's wife**, God again worked in supernatural ways. God was meeting the people at their own level.

14:6-9 Under all the OT covenants, God's people earned

Jeroboam! Why are you disguised?[a] I have bad news for you. [7]Go tell Jeroboam, 'This is what the Lord God of Israel says: I raised you up from among the people, appointed you ruler over My people Israel, [8]tore the kingdom away from the house of David, and gave it to you.[b] But you were not like My servant David, who kept My commands and followed Me with all of his heart, doing only what is right in My eyes. [9]You behaved more wickedly than all who were before you.[c] In order to provoke Me, you have proceeded to make for yourself other gods and cast images,[d] but you have flung Me behind your back.[e] [10]Because of all this, I am about to bring disaster on the house of Jeroboam:

> I will eliminate all of
>   Jeroboam's males,[A]
> both slave and free,[B] in Israel;
> I will sweep away the house
>   of Jeroboam
> as one sweeps away dung until it is
>   all gone![f]

[11]   Anyone who belongs to Jeroboam
>   and dies in the city,
> the dogs will eat,
> and anyone who dies in the field,
> the birds of the sky will eat,[g]
> for the Lord has said it!'

[12]"As for you, get up and go to your house. When your feet enter the city, the boy will die.[h] [13]All Israel will mourn for him and bury him. He alone out of Jeroboam's house will be put in the family tomb, because out of the house of Jeroboam the Lord God of Israel found something good only in him.[i] [14]The Lord will raise up for Himself a king over Israel, who will eliminate the house of Jeroboam.[j] This is the day, yes,[B] even today! [15]For the Lord will strike Israel and the people will shake as a reed shakes in water. He will uproot Israel from this good soil that He gave to their ancestors.[k] He will scatter them beyond the Euphrates[l] because they made their *Asherah poles, provoking the Lord.[m] [16]He will give up Israel because of Jeroboam's sins that he committed and caused Israel to commit."[n]

[17]Then Jeroboam's wife got up and left and went to Tirzah.[o] As she was crossing the threshold of the house, the boy died. [18]He was buried, and all Israel mourned for him, according to the word of the Lord He had spoken through His servant Ahijah the prophet.[p]

[19]As for the rest of the events of Jeroboam's reign, how he waged war[q] and how he reigned, note that they are written in the Historical Record of Israel's Kings. [20]The length of Jeroboam's reign was 22 years. He rested with his fathers, and his son Nadab became king in his place.[r]

Judah's King Rehoboam

[21]Now Rehoboam, Solomon's son, reigned in Judah.[s] Rehoboam was 41 years old when he became king; he reigned 17 years in Jerusalem, the city where *Yahweh had chosen from all the tribes of Israel to put His name.[t] Rehoboam's mother's name was Naamah the Ammonite.[u]

[22]Judah did what was evil in the Lord's eyes.[v] They provoked Him to jealous anger[w] more than all that their ancestors had done with the sins they committed. [23]They also built for themselves *high places,[x] sacred pillars,[y] and

[a]14:6 1Sm 28:12
[b]14:7-8 1Kg 11:28-31; 16:2
[c]14:9 1Kg 16:25,30
[d]1Kg 11:33; 12:28-33
[e]Neh 9:26; Ps 50:17
[f]14:10 1Kg 15:29; 21:21-22
[g]14:11 1Kg 16:4; 21:24
[h]14:12 1Kg 14:17
[i]14:13 2Ch 12:12; 19:3
[j]14:14 1Kg 15:27-29
[k]14:15 Dt 29:28
[l]2Kg 15:29; 17:6
[m]Ex 34:14-15; Dt 12:3-4
[n]14:16 1Kg 12:28-33; 13:34; 15:30
[o]14:17 1Kg 15:33; Sg 6:4
[p]14:18 1Kg 14:12-13
[q]14:19 1Kg 14:30; 2Ch 13:2-20
[r]14:20 1Kg 15:25-26
[s]14:21 1Kg 12:1-24
[t]Dt 12:5; 1Kg 9:3; 11:32,36
[u]2Ch 12:13
[v]14:22 2Kg 17:19; 2Ch 12:1,14
[w]Dt 32:21
[x]14:23 1Kg 3:2; 12:31
[y]Ex 23:24; Dt 16:21-22

---

earthly blessings from Him by obeying the stipulations of their covenants with the Lord. The king was to be the leader in obeying and enforcing obedience to the covenant. David was the model of a king who led the people in faithful commitment to loyal worship of the Lord. In their origins David and Jeroboam were similar—God had lifted both from obscurity to power (cp. 2Sm 7:8)—but Jeroboam, unlike David, failed to encourage proper worship. He led the people into false worship.

14:10-11 Therefore God pronounced a third statement of judgment on Jeroboam and his family (see notes at 13:2-3,33-34). This was a thorough judgment. It included such horrors as annihilation of the family and the disgrace of their corpses.

14:13 Since God had found **something good** in Jeroboam's sick son, a peaceful death and burial were his reward. The Bible does not reveal what the good thing was.

14:14-15 Jeroboam's sin resulted in God's raising up a new king who would destroy Jeroboam's dynasty. The ultimate seriousness of Jeroboam's sin and of this judgment was ex-

pressed by threatening the loss of the land (Lv 26:33). This is one of the earliest statements in 1 Kings that defined the place of exile as **beyond the Euphrates**. While the latter part of this prophesy would be almost 190 years in coming, God was preparing Baasha on that very **day** to wipe out Jeroboam's dynasty (15:29).

14:19-20 The record of Jeroboam ends with a conventional closing.

14:21-31 Rehoboam, Solomon's son, was the first of many kings for whom the Bible gives complete formal data. The typical pattern included: (1) a formal beginning; (2) an evaluation of his reign, perhaps including some relevant historical notes; and (3) a formal ending. Some of the formal elements of a king's record could be omitted or preempted by other elements.

14:21 Every element in this opening, except the description of Jerusalem as **the city . . . Yahweh had chosen**, is stereotypical formula. For the kings of Judah, it was common to list the **mother's name**.

14:22-24 This list of wicked deeds is even more degrad-

Asherah poles on every high hill and under every green tree; ²⁴there were even male cult prostitutes in the land.ᵃ They imitated all the detestable practices of the nations the LORD had dispossessed before the Israelites.ᵇ

²⁵In the fifth year of King Rehoboam, Shishak king of Egyptᶜ went to war against Jerusalem.ᵈ ²⁶He seized the treasuries of the LORD's temple and the treasuries of the royal palace. He took everything. He took all the gold shields that Solomon had made.ᵉ ²⁷King Rehoboam made bronze shields in their place and committed them into the care of the captains of the royal escortsᴬ,ᶠ who guarded the entrance to the king's palace. ²⁸Whenever the king entered the LORD's temple, the royal escorts would carry the shields, then they would take them back to the royal escorts' armory.ᵍ

²⁹The rest of the events of Rehoboam's reign,ʰ along with all his accomplishments, are written about in the Historical Record of Judah's Kings. ³⁰There was war between Rehoboam and Jeroboam throughout their reigns.ⁱ ³¹Rehoboam rested with his fathers and was buried with his fathers in the city of David. His mother's name was Naamah the Ammonite.ʲ His son Abijamᴮ,ᵏ became king in his place.

Judah's King Abijam

15 In the eighteenth year of Israel's King Jeroboam son of Nebat, Abijam became king over Judah ²and reigned three years in Jerusalem.ˡ His mother's name was Maacahᵐ daughterᶜ of Abishalom.

³Abijam walked in all the sins his father before him had committed,ⁿ and he was not completely devoted to the LORD his God as his ancestor David had been.ᵒ ⁴But because of David, the LORD his God gave him a lamp in Jerusalem to raise up his son after him and to establish Jerusalem.ᵖ ⁵For David did what was right in the LORD's eyes, and he did not turn aside from anything He had commanded him all the days of his life,�q except in the matter of Uriahʳ the Hittite.

⁶There had been war between Rehoboam and Jeroboam all the days of Rehoboam's life.ˢ ⁷The rest of the events of Abijam's reign, along with all his accomplishments, are written in the Historical Record of Judah's Kings.ᵗ There was also war between Abijam and Jeroboam.ᵘ ⁸Abijam rested with his fathers and was buried in the city of David.ᵛ His son Asa became king in his place.ʷ

ᵃ14:24 Dt 23:17
ᵇEx 23:24; Dt 18:9; 2Kg 16:3; 17:15; 21:2; 3Jn 11
ᶜ14:25 1Kg 11:40
ᵈ14:25-28 2Ch 12:2-11
ᵉ14:26 1Kg 10:16-17
ᶠ14:27 1Sm 22:17; 2Sm 15:1
ᵍ14:28 1Kg 10:17
ʰ14:29-31 2Ch 12:15-16
ⁱ14:30 1Kg 12:21-24; 15:6
ʲ14:31 1Kg 14:21
ᵏ1Kg 15:1-8; 2Ch 11:20; 13:1–14:1
ˡ15:1-2 2Ch 13:1-2
ᵐ15:2 1Kg 15:10,13; 2Ch 13:2
ⁿ15:3 1Kg 14:21-22
ᵒ1Kg 9:4; 11:4
ᵖ15:4 2Sm 21:17; 1Kg 11:36; 2Ch 21:7
q15:5 1Kg 9:4; 14:8
ʳ2Sm 11:3,15-17; 12:9-10
ˢ15:6 1Kg 14:30; 2Ch 12:15
ᵗ15:7 1Kg 14:29

ᵘ2Ch 13:4-20   ᵛ15:8 1Kg 14:31; 2Ch 14:1   ʷ1Kg 14:31; 2Ch 14-16

ᴬ14:27 Lit *the runners*   ᴮ14:31 = Abijah in 2Ch 13   ᶜ15:2 Possibly granddaughter; 2Ch 13:2

---

ing than the typical offenses of some northern kings. At this point, the north could claim to be worshiping Yahweh, though in a manner contrary to His instructions. **Judah** had sunk into degraded paganism. And the responsibility for this degradation is traceable directly to the throne. Judah's failure was Rehoboam's failure. The text notes that these were the vices of the people whom God had helped the Israelites to drive out of the promised land.

14:25 Including data from Egyptian records along with the Bible, we can see how weak the two Israelite kingdoms had become as a result of the invasion of **Shishak**. A briefly resurgent **Egypt** had a large army, and Pharaoh used this army for a devastating plundering raid into Palestine. These invaders, which Solomon's chariots at their height might have easily driven back, plundered both Judah and Israel—including the prosperous merchant cities that opened into the Plain of Esdraelon. Rehoboam's inexperienced levies, which had sounded so grand when mobilized to recapture Israel (12:21), were so helpless against Shishak's Libyan soldiers that they could not even protect **Jerusalem** from a siege. The Egyptian record of conquered places included a list of fortifications in the Arabah that were crucial for defending the trade route from the Red Sea. The reason for destroying these protective outposts was to divert the lucrative Red Sea maritime trade to Egypt.

14:26-28 Rehoboam's replacement of the plundered **gold shields** with less valuable **bronze shields** was a fitting symbol of the decline of the nation's glory and wealth. That they were kept ready in the **armory** when not in use, instead of on ceremonial display, speaks of the insecurity of the period.

14:29-31 Though not as clearly formal as the opener, the closing paragraph of Rehoboam's rule follows the typical format. It contains the formula statement that the remaining deeds of Rehoboam are recorded in Judah's **Historical Record**. It mentions the continual border warfare between the kingdoms. This was probably ineffective skirmishing since the military of both kingdoms seems to have been generally ineffective. The mention of Rehoboam's mother's **Ammonite** heritage may hint that her pagan influence (15:13) affected her son's character.

15:1-2 The only revealing detail in the formal opening for Abijam's ("Abijah" in Chronicles) record was that his mother **Maacah** was from the line of Absalom, or **Abishalom**. This relationship might indicate that Solomon's family had to make some accommodations with the family of Absalom, Solomon's half brother, to maintain rule over Judah (see 2Sm 15–18).

15:3-5 **Abijam** was bad, like **his father** (14:22-24), with the typical negative comparison with **David**, but then this record has one of several statements in 1 Kings to the effect that God spared Jerusalem and a wicked king because of the good king, David.

15:6 The reference to war between **Rehoboam and Jeroboam** departs from the normal pattern of dealing only with the current king. Other translations follow variant texts that read "Abijam" instead of "Rehoboam." Others consider this to be a scribal error. The HCSB translates this statement as a factual flashback reference to Rehoboam's rule.

15:7-8 The only distinctive point to note in this closer is the reference to continued **war between Abijam and Jeroboam**, a reference that is redundant if verse 6 also refers to Abijam. At this point these were still border skirmishes.

Judah's King Asa

[9] In the twentieth year of Israel's King Jeroboam,[a] Asa became king of Judah [10] and reigned 41 years in Jerusalem. His grandmother's[A] name was Maacah[b] daughter[B] of Abishalom.

[11] Asa did what was right in the Lord's eyes, as his ancestor David had done.[c] [12] He banished the male cult prostitutes[d] from the land and removed all of the idols that his fathers had made.[e] [13] He also[f] removed his grandmother[C] Maacah from being queen mother because she had made an obscene image of *Asherah. Asa chopped down her obscene image and burned it[g] in the Kidron Valley.[h] [14] The *high places were not taken away;[i] but Asa's heart was completely devoted to the Lord his entire life.[j] [15] He brought his father's consecrated gifts and his own consecrated gifts into the Lord's temple: silver, gold, and utensils.[k]

[16] There was war between Asa and Baasha king of Israel throughout their reigns.[l] [17] Israel's King Baasha went to war against Judah.[m] He built Ramah[n] in order to deny anyone access to Judah's King Asa. [18] So Asa withdrew all the silver and gold that remained in the treasuries of the Lord's temple[o] and the treasuries of the royal palace and put it into the hands

of his servants. Then King Asa sent them to Ben-hadad[p] son of Tabrimmon son of Hezion king of Aram who lived in Damascus,[q] saying, [19] "There is a treaty between me and you, between my father and your father.[r] Look, I have sent you a gift of silver and gold. Go and break your treaty with Baasha king of Israel[s] so that he will withdraw from me."

[20] Ben-hadad listened to King Asa and sent the commanders of his armies against the cities of Israel. He attacked Ijon,[t] Dan,[u] Abel-beth-maacah,[v] all Chinnereth,[w] and the whole land of Naphtali.[x] [21] When Baasha heard about it, he quit building Ramah and stayed in Tirzah.[y] [22] Then King Asa gave a command to everyone without exception in Judah, and they carried away the stones of Ramah and the timbers Baasha had built it with. Then King Asa built Geba[z] of Benjamin and Mizpah[aa] with them.

[23] The rest of all the events of Asa's reign,[ab] along with all his might, all his accomplishments, and the cities he built, are written in the Historical Record of Judah's Kings.[ac] But in his old age he developed a disease in his feet.[ad] [24] Then Asa rested with his fathers and was bur-

a 15:9 1Kg 15:1
b 15:10 1Kg 15:2
c 15:11 1Kg 9:4-5; 2Ch 14:2
d 15:12 Dt 23:17; 1Kg 14:24
e 15:11-12 1Kg 11:7; 14:23; 2Ch 14:3,5
f 15:13-15 2Ch 15:16-18
g 15:13 Ex 32:20
h 2Kg 23:6
i 15:14 1Kg 22:43
j 1Kg 8:61; 15:3
k 15:15 1Kg 7:51
l 15:16 1Kg 15:32
m 15:17-22 2Ch 16:1-6
n 15:17 Jos 18:25
o 15:18 1Kg 14:26
p 1Kg 20:1
q 1Kg 11:23-24
r 15:19 1Kg 5:12; 2Ch 16:7
s 1Kg 15:27-28
t 15:20 2Kg 15:29
u Jdg 18:29; 1Kg 12:29
v 2Sm 20:15; 2Kg 15:29
w Jos 11:2; 12:3
x Jos 19:32-39; 1Kg 20:34
y 15:21 1Kg 14:17; 15:33; 16:8,15-18
z 15:22 Jos 18:24; 21:17
aa Jos 11:3; 2Ch 16:6   ab 15:23-24 2Ch 16:11-14   ac 15:23 1Kg 14:29; 15:7   ad 2Ch 16:12

A 15:10 Lit *mother's*   B 15:10 Possibly granddaughter; 2Ch 13:2   C 15:13 Lit *mother*

15:9-24 With King Asa of Judah and Nadab of Israel, two parallel movements began. First, religious revival began under Asa so that God had a reason to restore blessings to the good kings of the south. This revival, led by two good kings, Asa and Jehoshaphat, lasted about 60 years. Then, early in the reign of Asa, the rule of Nadab began a bloody process of civil war and violence, which actually ended with the restoration of Hebrew economic and political power under Omri and Ahab. These two movements were inseparable because God used the renewed power of the wicked kings of the north to bring renewed blessing, power, and wealth to the good kings of the south. Chapters 15 and 16 trace the revival in the south and the resurgence of political power in the north. Asa's revival is recorded first.

15:9-10 The only unexpected point in Asa's opener is that he was a grandson of **Maacah**, from the line of Absalom, or **Abishalom**. Thus Absalom and Solomon were co-ancestors to the covenant royal line.

15:11-12 Asa, nevertheless, turned out to be a godly king. He was the first king since the division of the kingdom to do **what was right in the Lord's eyes**. What influenced him to choose obedience to God? From the data available, it seems that the presence of godly Levites in the south could have been a factor (2Ch 11:13-14).

15:13 As **queen mother**, Asa's **grandmother**, Maacah, was a stumbling block to faith in Yahweh. Part of cleansing the kingdom was removing her bad influence.

15:14 For all of the good kings, the **high places** that were **not taken away** were probably illegal shrines for worshiping the Lord away from the temple, not for worshiping pagan gods. Tolerating the pagan high places would have been out of

character for a good king and contrary to his general behavior as recorded.

15:15 The **gifts** to the temple, especially the **silver** and **gold**, marked the return of prosperity among the people.

15:16-17 With **Baasha**, whose formal record comes later (15:33-16:7), the border skirmishes became **war**. His offensives involved both Judah and the Philistine plain. These military advances were probably possible because of the newly reestablished chariot armies. Apparently, Baasha penetrated Benjamite territory and began building a fortress at **Ramah** about six miles north of Jerusalem. This could have cut off all trade on that road. There were two locations named Ramah just north of Jerusalem. The one in the middle of Benjamin would have posed the greater threat. This would have been a serious blow to whatever limited benefit Judah was gaining from north-south trade on the road through Jerusalem. Most of the significant trade bypassed Jerusalem by moving up the coastal plain and then inland through passes that opened into the Plain of Esdraelon. From there the trade moved to points west in Phoenician ships or by land to points northeast of Palestine.

15:18-22 This was such a serious threat that Asa purchased an alliance with the Arameans of **Damascus**. The Chronicler rebukes Asa for not trusting in the Lord instead (2Ch 16:7-10). This alliance must have been particularly humiliating since earlier years had been marked by alliances in which the Hebrews were dominant and collected tribute. Now the king of Judah had to pay the Arameans to deliver him from the threat of Israel. The Arameans' response was devastating to Israel. The northern regions were plundered, and **Baasha**, despite a small resurgence of Hebrew strength,

ied in the city of his ancestor David.[a] His son Jehoshaphat[b] became king in his place.

Israel's King Nadab

[25]Nadab son of Jeroboam[c] became king over Israel in the second year of Judah's King Asa;

he reigned over Israel two years. [26]Nadab did what was evil in the LORD's sight and followed the example of his father and the sin he had caused Israel to commit.[d]

[27]Then Baasha[e] son of Ahijah of the house of Issachar conspired against Nadab, and Baasha

[a] 15:24 1Kg 14:31; 15:8
[b] 1Kg 22:41-50
[c] 15:25 1Kg 14:20
[d] 15:26 1Kg 14:16; 15:30,34
[e] 15:27 1Kg 14:14; 15:16

had to take refuge in his capital, **Tirzah**. Asa then used the building materials at Ramah to build his own defenses north of Jerusalem at **Geba** and **Mizpah** in Benjamin. Depending on the location selected for Ramah, these fortifications would have formed a defense line just north of Ramah or two miles or so south of the other Ramah.

15:25–16:28 This section chronicles the reign of five kings of Israel: Nadab, Baasha, Elah, Zimri, and Omri. Israel had a favorable location for exacting some control over local transit trade. This trade financed a limited revival of Israel's military strength. Israel's military capacity had revived sufficiently for aggressive warfare against the Philistines as

early as Nadab, the son of Jeroboam. This new military was a local chariot force that included homegrown Hebrew warriors. Thus, eventually, a Hebrew chariot commander, Omri, could become king of Israel (16:16). Despite the civil wars and palace revolutions, this was a time of restoring the military power of Israel.

15:25-26 These two verses follow the typical formula. They tell of the beginning of the rule of **Nadab** over **Israel** and pass the usual negative moral judgment. Jeroboam's example was not only the measure of **evil** for Nadab, but for almost every other king of Israel.

15:27-29 This campaign against **Gibbethon**, just south of

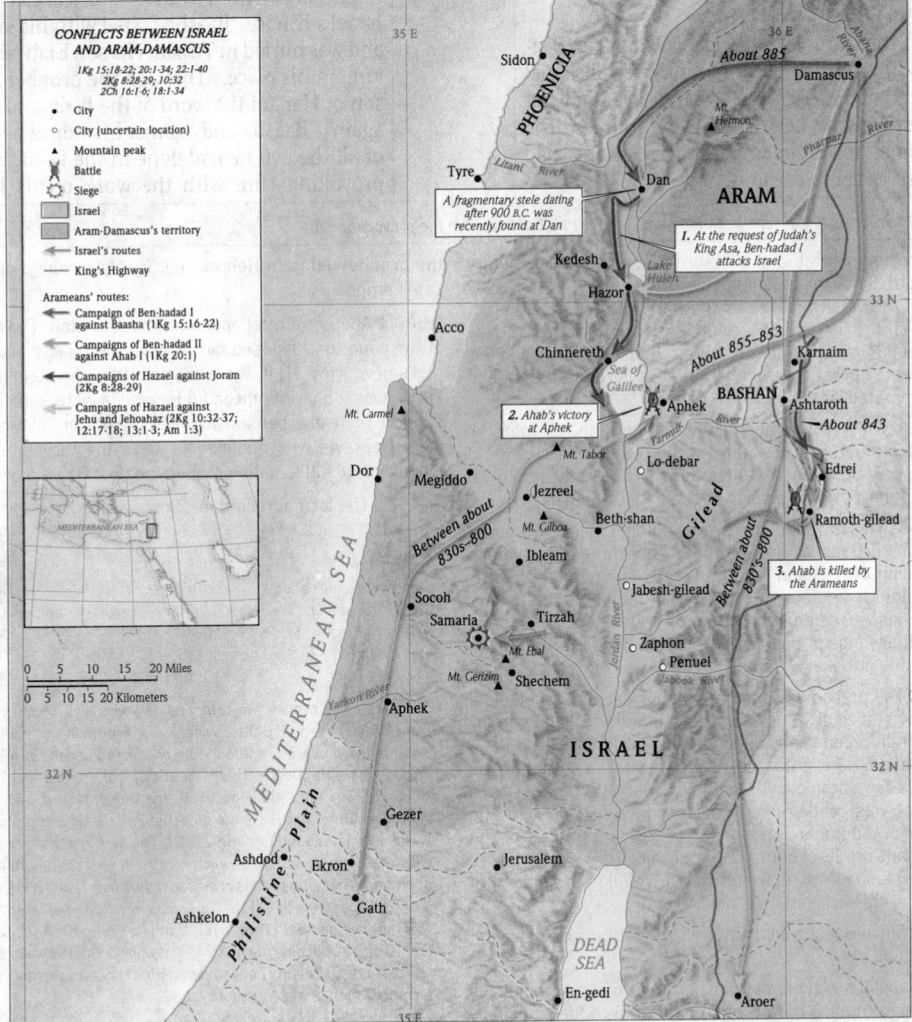

CONFLICTS BETWEEN ISRAEL AND ARAM-DAMASCUS

1Kg 15:18-22; 20:1-34; 22:1-40
2Kg 8:28-29; 10:32
2Ch 16:1-6; 18:1-34

- • City
- ○ City (uncertain location)
- ▲ Mountain peak
- ⚔ Battle
- ⚙ Siege
- Israel
- Aram-Damascus's territory
- ← Israel's routes
- — King's Highway

Arameans' routes:
- ← Campaign of Ben-hadad I against Baasha (1Kg 15:16-22)
- ← Campaigns of Ben-hadad II against Ahab (1Kg 20:1)
- ← Campaigns of Hazael against Joram (2Kg 8:28-29)
- ← Campaigns of Hazael against Jehu and Jehoahaz (2Kg 10:32-37; 12:17-18; 13:1-3; Am 1:3)

A fragmentary stele dating after 900 B.C. was recently found at Dan

1. At the request of Judah's King Asa, Ben-hadad I attacks Israel

2. Ahab's victory at Aphek

3. Ahab is killed by the Arameans

struck him down at Gibbethon[a] of the Philistines while Nadab and all Israel were besieging Gibbethon. [28]In the third year of Judah's King Asa,[b] Baasha killed Nadab[c] and reigned in his place.

[29]When Baasha became king, he struck down the entire house of Jeroboam.[d] He did not leave Jeroboam any survivors but[A] destroyed his family according to the word of the LORD He had spoken through His servant Ahijah the Shilonite.[e] [30]This was because Jeroboam had provoked[B] the LORD God of Israel by the sins he had committed and had caused Israel to commit.[f]

[31]The rest of the events of Nadab's reign, along with all his accomplishments, are written in the Historical Record of Israel's Kings.[g] [32]There was war between Asa and Baasha king of Israel throughout their reigns.[h]

Israel's King Baasha

[33]In the third year of Judah's King Asa, Baasha son of Ahijah became king over all Israel and reigned in Tirzah[i] 24 years. [34]He did what was evil in the LORD's sight and followed the example of Jeroboam and the sin he had caused Israel to commit.[j]

16 Now the word of the LORD came to Jehu[k] son of Hanani[l] against Baasha: [2]"Because I raised you up from the dust[m] and made you ruler over My people Israel,[n] but you have walked in the way of Jeroboam and have caused My people Israel to sin,[o] provoking Me with their sins, [3]take note: I will sweep away Baasha and his house, and I will make your house like the house of Jeroboam son of Nebat:[p]

[4] Anyone who belongs to Baasha and dies
    in the city,
  the dogs will eat,
and anyone who is his and dies
    in the field,
  the birds of the sky will eat."[q]

[5]The rest of the events of Baasha's reign, along with all his accomplishments and might, are written in the Historical Record of Israel's Kings.[r] [6]Baasha rested with his fathers and was buried in Tirzah. His son Elah became king in his place. [7]Through the prophet Jehu[s] son of Hanani the word of the LORD also came against Baasha and against his house because of all the evil he had done in the LORD's sight, provoking Him with the work of his hands

Cross references

a 15:27 Jos 19:44; 1Kg 16:15
b 15:28 1Kg 15:8-24; 2Ch 14-16
c 1Kg 16:8-10
d 15:29 1Kg 13:34
e 1Kg 14:10
f 15:30 1Kg 14:7-9
g 15:31 1Kg 14:19; 16:5
h 15:32 1Kg 15:16
i 15:33 1Kg 15:21
j 15:34 1Kg 14:16
k 16:1 1Kg 16:7; 2Ch 19:2
l 2Ch 16:7-10
m 16:2 1Sm 2:8
n 1Kg 14:7
o 1Kg 15:26,34
p 16:3 1Kg 14:10; 15:29
q 16:4 1Kg 14:11; 21:24
r 16:5 1Kg 14:19; 15:31
s 16:7 1Kg 16:1; 2Ch 19:2

A 15:29 Lit *Jeroboam anyone breathing until*   B 15:30 Lit *provoked in the provocation of*

Gezer, demonstrated the resurgence of Israel's military strength. Since the most effective arm of any offensive army in that era was typically the chariots (with the exception of David's), the text is likely referring to a chariot army. **Nadab** died in a battlefield revolution. Baasha, Nadab's killer, fulfilled the prophecy that the **house of Jeroboam** would be exterminated (14:10-11,14).

15:31-32 This closing again calls attention to the more or less continual war between the two kingdoms. The note about war between **Asa** and **Baasha** normally would be more at home in the closing section about Baasha.

15:33-34 This introduction reveals nothing distinctive about the rule of **Baasha**. He was the first of three kings whose beginning of rule and length of rule statements are combined into a single sentence. Translated literally, this formula was: "became king . . . for 24 years." Introductions to two other kings of this group, Elah (16:8) and Omri (16:23), show this unusual wording.

16:1-4 The preceding condemnation of Baasha's sin (15:34) did not sufficiently communicate his evil, so Jehu's judgment reinforced that condemnation. If Jehu's father was the **Hanani** who criticized Asa (2Ch 16:7) and Jehu was the Judean chronicler (2Ch 20:34), then another southern prophet was condemning a northern king (1Kg 13:1). The oracle of judgment was similar to the second half of the judgment on Jeroboam (14:11). Ironically, we learn more about Baasha from Asa's record (15:16-20) than we do from Baasha's record (see note at 22:41-44).

16:5-6 Since Baasha died naturally, he receives a full formal closer.

16:7 Baasha's wickedness was so great that even after his closing formula, a third condemnation was added, again by

the prophet Jehu. In Hebrew literary style, repetition indicates emphasis.

16:8-14 Another formal opener introduces **Elah**. The record of the coup that deposed him reveals three facts about Israel's new army: (1) It was a chariot army; the coup leader, **Zimri**, was a chariot officer. (2) Revenues were sufficient to support such an expensive army. (3) The officers of this force were Hebrews who qualified to seize the throne. Zimri's bloody purge fulfilled the prophecy against **Baasha** (vv. 3-4).

16:15-22 The formal record for **Zimri** begins here. His revo-

---

ka'as

Hebrew Pronunciation	[kah ASS]
HCSB Translation	be angry, provoke to anger
Uses in 1 Kings	10
Uses in the OT	54
Focus Passage	1 Kings 16:2,7,13,26,33

The verb *ka'as* occurs five times as *be angry* (Ezk 16:42) or *become furious* (Neh 4:1). Otherwise, *ka'as* is intensive or causative and means *provoke* (Ps 106:29) or *provoke to anger* (Dt 4:25). It implies *infuriate* (Dt 31:29), *enrage* (Dt 32:16), *trouble* (Ezk 32:9), or *taunt* (1Sm 1:6). God is generally the One *provoked*, and some verses assume that He is the object of *ka'as* without mentioning Him ("My" is supplied in 1Kg 21:22). The verb occurs five times with the noun *ka'as* (25x), which occurs in two slightly different spellings. The noun means *provocation [to anger]* (Dt 32:19), *insult* (Dt 32:27), *aggravation* (Pr 27:3), *displeasure* (Ec 7:9), or *resentment* (1Sm 1:16). It implies *grief* (Ps 6:7), *sorrow* (Ec 1:18), or *angry sorrow* (Ps 31:9). It appears adjectivally as *offensive* (Ezk 20:28) and *hot-tempered* (Pr 21:19). *Ka'as* may involve a combination of *anger*, *jealousy*, and *grief*.

and being like the house of Jeroboam, and because Baasha had struck down the house of Jeroboam.[a]

Israel's King Elah

[8] In the twenty-sixth year of Judah's King Asa, Elah son of Baasha became king over Israel and reigned in Tirzah[b] two years.

[9] His servant Zimri,[c] commander of half his chariots, conspired against him while Elah was in Tirzah getting drunk[d] in the house of Arza, who was in charge of the household[e] at Tirzah. [10] In the twenty-seventh year of Judah's King Asa, Zimri went in, struck Elah down, killing him. Then Zimri became king in his place.[f]

[11] When he became king, as soon as he was seated on his throne, Zimri struck down the entire house of Baasha. He did not leave a single male,[A,g] including his kinsmen and his friends. [12] So Zimri destroyed the entire house of Baasha, according to the word of the LORD He had spoken against Baasha through Jehu the prophet.[h] [13] This happened because of all the sins of Baasha and those of his son Elah, which they committed and caused Israel to commit, provoking the LORD God of Israel[i] with their worthless idols.[j]

[14] The rest of the events of Elah's reign, along with all his accomplishments, are written in the Historical Record of Israel's Kings.[k]

Israel's King Zimri

[15] In the twenty-seventh year of Judah's King Asa, Zimri became king for seven days in Tirzah.[l] Now the troops were encamped against Gibbethon of the Philistines.[m] [16] When these troops heard that Zimri had not only conspired but had also struck down the king, then all Israel made Omri, the army commander, king over Israel that very day in the camp. [17] Omri along with all Israel marched up from Gibbethon and besieged Tirzah.[n] [18] When Zimri saw that the city was captured, he entered the citadel of the royal palace and burned it down over himself. He died [19] because of the sin he committed by doing what was evil in the LORD's sight and by following the example of Jeroboam and the sin he caused Israel to commit.[o]

[20] The rest of the events of Zimri's reign, along with the conspiracy that he instigated, are written in the Historical Record of Israel's Kings. [21] At that time the people of Israel were divided: half the people followed Tibni son of Ginath, to make him king, and half followed Omri. [22] However, the people who followed Omri proved stronger than those who followed Tibni son of Ginath. So Tibni died and Omri became king.

Israel's King Omri

[23] In the thirty-first year of Judah's King Asa, Omri became king over Israel and reigned 12 years. He reigned six years in Tirzah,[p] [24] then he bought the hill of Samaria[q] from Shemer for 150 pounds[B] of silver, and he built up the hill. He named the city he built Samaria[C] based on the name Shemer, the owner of the hill.

[25] Omri did what was evil in the LORD's sight; he did more evil than all who were before him.[r] [26] He followed the example of Jeroboam son of Nebat and in his sins that he caused Israel to commit, provoking the LORD God of

Cross references (center column)

a16:7 1Kg 15:27,29
b16:8 1Kg 15:21
c16:9 2Kg 9:30-33
d1Sm 25:36; 1Kg 20:12,16; Pr 31:4-5; Eph 5:18
e1Kg 18:3
f16:10 1Kg 15:28
g16:11 1Sm 25:22; 1Kg 15:29
h16:12 1Kg 16:1-4
i16:13 1Kg 15:26,30
jDt 32:21; 1Kg 12:28-33
k16:14 1Kg 15:31
l16:15 1Kg 15:21
m1Kg 15:27
n16:17 1Kg 14:17
o16:19 1Kg 12:28-33
p16:23 1Kg 15:21
q16:24 1Kg 13:32
r16:25 1Kg 14:9; 16:30

A16:11 Lit leave him one who urinates against the wall　B16:24 Lit for two talents　C16:24 = Belonging to Shemer's Clan

---

lution was formally part of the record of Elah. **Omri**, a capable battlefield commander, led the troops to **Tirzah**, captured the city, and Zimri committed suicide after ruling only **seven days**. Omri then fought a five-year civil war with **Tibni son of Ginath**. When Tibni died, Omri became king.

16:23-28 Since Omri's power and wealth were partly based on an economic and marriage alliance with Ethbaal of Tyre, it is useful to review Phoenician mercantile power. At this time, the Phoenicians controlled Mediterranean trade. They had already established colonies as far away as North Africa and Spain, although the greatest Phoenician colony, Carthage, was yet to be founded. They produced manufactured goods for export throughout the Mediterranean. Omri's military skill and greatness made him a worthy ally for this maritime trade empire. The Phoenician merchants enhanced Hebrew prosperity by cooperating with Israel's trade just as they had cooperated with Solomon.

The greatest impact of Omri's dynasty was in religion. Omri's daughter-in-law was Jezebel. Jezebel's Baal was not a typical Palestinian Baal. Rather, he was Baal-melkart, the King of the City (Tyre), the patron deity for more than half of the contemporary trade wealth of the Mediterranean.

Ahab introduced this deity into Israel, creating a spiritual crisis. The next 50 years of Hebrew history and about 17 chapters of Kings (1Kg 16:23–2Kg 11:3) are devoted to this crisis; it was the occasion for the miraculous ministries of Elijah and Elisha.

16:23 The formal opener for **Omri** is unremarkable for such a great political figure.

16:24 The purchase of a new capital, **Samaria**, was Omri's outstanding achievement. Omri, like David, exercised personal ownership of his new capital.

16:25 Omri followed the pattern of Jeroboam's false cult, which led Israel into false worship. Omri's full, negative impact became clear only with the introduction of Baal-melkart (see note at vv. 23-28) into Israel. Despite his encouragement of idolatry, Omri established the power that restored wealth and empire to the two good kings of Judah.

16:26-28 These verses are Omri's closer, but again, they give an incomplete picture of Omri's spiritual importance. All the attention given to Ahab and the career of Elijah in the following chapters is an indirect reaction to Omri. Ahab and Jezebel were the rulers whom Elijah opposed, but the

Israel with their worthless idols.[a] [27]The rest of the events of Omri's reign, along with his accomplishments and the might he exercised, are written in the Historical Record of Israel's Kings. [28]Omri rested with his fathers and was buried in Samaria. His son Ahab became king in his place.

Israel's King Ahab

[29]Ahab son of Omri became king over Israel in the thirty-eighth year of Judah's King Asa; Ahab son of Omri reigned over Israel in Samaria 22 years. [30]But Ahab son of Omri did what was evil in the LORD's sight more than all who were before him.[b] [31]Then, as if following the sin of Jeroboam son of Nebat were a trivial matter, he married Jezebel,[c] the daughter of Ethbaal king of the Sidonians,[d] and then proceeded to serve •Baal and worship him.[e] [32]He set up an altar for Baal in the temple of Baal[f] that he had built in Samaria. [33]Ahab also made an •Asherah pole.[g] Ahab did more to provoke

the LORD God of Israel than all the kings of Israel who were before him.[h]

[34]During his reign, Hiel the Bethelite built Jericho. At the cost of Abiram his firstborn, he laid its foundation, and at the cost of Segub his youngest, he set up its gates, according to the word of the LORD He had spoken through Joshua son of Nun.[i]

Elijah Announces Famine

17 Now Elijah[j] the Tishbite, from the Gilead settlers,[A,k] said to Ahab, "As the LORD God of Israel lives,[l] I stand before Him, and there will be no dew or rain during these years except by my command!"[m]

[2]Then a revelation from the LORD came to him: [3]"Leave here, turn eastward, and hide[n] yourself at the •Wadi Cherith where it enters the Jordan. [4]You are to drink from the wadi. I have commanded the ravens[o] to provide for you there."

[5]So he did what the LORD commanded. Elijah left and lived by the Wadi Cherith where

---

Cross references (center column):

[a] 16:25-26 1Kg 16:13,19
[b] 16:30 1Kg 14:9; 16:25
[c] 16:31 Dt 7:3-4; 1Kg 18:4,13; Rv 2:20
[d] 1Kg 11:5
[e] Jdg 2:11
[f] 16:32 2Kg 10:21,26-27
[g] 16:33 2Kg 13:6
[h] 1Kg 16:30
[i] 16:34 Jos 6:26
[j] 17:1 1Kg 17-19; 2Kg 1-2; Mal 4:5; Mt 11:14
[k] Jdg 12:4
[l] 1Kg 18:10; 22:14
[m] Dt 11:16-17; Jms 5:17; Rv 11:6
[n] 17:3 1Kg 18:4
[o] 17:4 1Kg 17:9; Jb 38:41; Lk 12:24

A 17:1 LXX reads *from Tishbe of Gilead*

---

setting in which he opposed them and their Baalism was the product of Omri's policies. In God's economy, all of Omri's secular greatness amounted to nothing.

16:29-22:40 This section focuses on the reign of Ahab. Despite his succumbing to Jezebel's influence, Ahab was a capable warrior. His military career was marked by amazing highs and lows. At one time he was so firmly under the domination of Ben-hadad of Damascus (chap. 20) that only divine intervention delivered him from destruction, but then Assyrian records reveal that Ahab led the largest contingent of chariots against Assyria at the battle of Qarqar (853 B.C.), where the regional allies turned back a serious Assyrian invasion.

16:29-30 Ahab's opener makes two points: the date when he became king and how long he ruled. The evaluation reports that Ahab was the worst king Israel had up until that time. Jeroboam had set up an illegal cultic apparatus for serving the Lord, and this was enough to make him the archetypal representative of a bad king.

16:31-33 Ahab was even worse than Jeroboam. He not only followed Jeroboam's false worship; he, with Jezebel, went beyond Jeroboam in introducing into Israel the worship of Baal-melkart (see note at vv. 23-28). The **altar for Baal** and the **Asherah pole**, the symbol of his female consort, brought this powerful fertility cult to Israel.

16:34 Recording the rebuilding or refortifying of Jericho at this point identified it as a work of Ahab. This in turn illustrated the long reach of Ahab's foreign policy. A probable goal of this operation was to rebuild the fortifications, both of **Jericho** and of points further south in the Arabah, that protected the trade routes from Eloth. There is no evidence that either Omri or Ahab pushed these trade connections any further south. The deaths of the sons of **Hiel** could have been viewed as either the impact of an effective curse (Jos 6:26) or a human sacrifice to neutralize the curse.

17:1-19:21 This section describes the clash between the prophet Elijah and King Ahab of Israel. One of the greatest

missionary themes in OT theology was the witness of God's miraculous signs. The best literary pattern exemplifying this theology is Jethro's visit to Moses in the wilderness (Ex 18). Jethro heard of God's great deeds of deliverance (Ex 18:1) and visited God's people and learned even more about God's great works (Ex 18:8). He praised God (Ex 18:10-11) and then joined in a fellowship meal with God's people (Ex 18:12). These were the same signs that drew Rahab to the Lord (Jos 2:8-13) and threw other Canaanites into despair.

In biblical history, there are four extended periods of witness with great signs and wonders: (1) the exodus and conquest; (2) the age of Elijah and Elisha; (3) the first coming of Christ and the growth of the early church; and (4) the end of history with the miraculous wonders of the book of Revelation. In the age of Elijah and Elisha, faith in Yahweh clashed with one of the most dangerous false deities it ever faced, Baal-melkart of Tyre (see note at 16:23-28). The power encounter between these two rival religions was the setting for the miraculous works of these great prophets.

17:1 The HCSB suggests that **Elijah** was one of the **settlers** in Gilead. This raises the possibility that he was a non-Hebrew settler, since a Hebrew was typically described in terms of his tribe and family. Elijah's rustic appearance also set him apart as someone different. He was to announce to one of the most powerful kings in the region that God would send a devastating drought against the land.

17:2-3 The location of the **Wadi Cherith** is not clear. Some authorities identify it with the Wadi Qelt that passes just south of Jericho. Some translations place it east of the Jordan River, apparently taking the words **where it enters the Jordan** (lit "which is facing/before the Jordan") as being equal to "facing the Jordan from the east." If we permit Elijah's move eastward from delivering his oracle in Israel to include a great deal of southeasterly movement, the Wadi Qelt is possible.

17:4-7 In sign theology, miracles have meaning. God's miraculous provision of food for Elijah, at a time when God had cut off food for the nation, reminded any hearer/reader that

it enters the Jordan. [6]The ravens kept bringing him bread and meat in the morning and in the evening,[a] and he drank from the wadi. [7]After a while, the wadi dried up because there had been no rain in the land.

Elijah and the Widow

[8]Then the word of the Lord came to him: [9]"Get up, go to Zarephath[b] that belongs to Sidon and stay there. Look, I have commanded a woman who is a widow to provide for you there." [10]So Elijah got up and went to Zarephath. When he arrived at the city gate, there was a widow woman gathering wood. Elijah called to her and said, "Please bring me a little water in a cup and let me drink."[c] [11]As she went to get it, he called to her and said, "Please bring me a piece of bread in your hand."

[12]But she said, "As the Lord your God lives,[d] I don't have anything baked—only a handful of flour in the jar and a bit of oil[e] in the jug. Just now, I am gathering a couple of sticks in order to go prepare it for myself and my son so we can eat it and die."[f]

[13]Then Elijah said to her, "Don't be afraid; go and do as you have said. But first make me a small loaf from it and bring it out to me. Afterward, you may make some for yourself and your son, [14]for this is what the Lord God of Israel says, 'The flour jar will not become empty and the oil jug will not run dry until the day the Lord sends rain on the surface of the land.'"[g]

[15]So she proceeded to do according to the word of Elijah. Then the woman, Elijah, and her household ate for many days.[h] [16]The flour

[a] 17:6 Ex 16:8
[b] 17:9 Ob 20; Lk 4:26
[c] 17:10 Gn 24:17; Jn 4:7
[d] 17:12 1Kg 17:1
[e] 2Kg 4:2-7
[f] Gn 21:14,16
[g] 17:14 1Kg 17:1; Php 4:19
[h] 17:15 Mt 6:11
[i] 17:17 Ac 9:37
[j] 17:18 1Kg 12:22
[k] 2Sm 16:10; 2Kg 3:13
[l] Lk 5:8
[m] 17:19 Ac 9:37,39
[n] 17:20 2Kg 4:33
[o] 17:21 2Kg 4:34; Ac 20:10
[p] 17:22 Lk 7:14
[q] 17:23 Lk 7:15;
Heb 11:35
[r] 17:24 Jn 3:2
[s] 1Kg 22:16; Jn 17:17
[t] 18:1 1Kg 17:8
[u] 1Kg 17:1; Jms 5:17
[v] 1Kg 16:29-33

jar did not become empty, and the oil jug did not run dry, according to the word of the Lord He had spoken through[A] Elijah.

The Widow's Son Raised

[17]After this, the son of the woman who owned the house became ill. His illness became very severe until no breath remained in him.[i] [18]She said to Elijah, "Man of God,[j] what do we have in common?[k] Have you come to remind me of my *guilt[l] and to kill my son?"

[19]But Elijah said to her, "Give me your son." So he took him from her arms, brought him up to the upper room[m] where he was staying, and laid him on his own bed. [20]Then he cried out to the Lord[n] and said, "My Lord God, have You also brought tragedy on the widow I am staying with by killing her son?" [21]Then he stretched himself out over the boy three times.[o] He cried out to the Lord and said, "My Lord God, please let this boy's life return to him!"

[22]So the Lord listened to Elijah's voice, and the boy's life returned to him, and he lived.[p] [23]Then Elijah took the boy, brought him down from the upper room into the house, and gave him to his mother.[q] Elijah said, "Look, your son is alive."

[24]Then the woman said to Elijah, "Now I know you are a man of God[r] and the Lord's word from your mouth is true."[s]

Elijah's Message to Ahab

18 After a long time, the word of the Lord[t] came to Elijah in the third year:[u] "Go and present yourself to Ahab.[v] I will send rain

---

A 17:16 Lit *by the hand of*

God is the true provider of human needs. Unclean carrion birds (**ravens**) brought this food.

17:8-9 Then God sent Elijah to the Phoenician city of **Zarephath**, a Gentile city under Ethbaal's control, for provision and protection. Jesus Himself gave a theologically suitable interpretation of this passage (Lk 4:26-27)—that God sent His messenger with beneficial signs and wonders to a Gentile. God's witness through signs was not given to Israelites alone.

17:12 In referring to **the Lord your God**, the widow seemed to show she recognized that Elijah represented Yahweh, the God of the Hebrews, yet she did not turn him over to Ethbaal, the king of the Phoenicians. Ethbaal was the father-in-law of Ahab, from whom Elijah was hiding. Either that knowledge was insufficient to specifically identify Elijah to Ethbaal, or she deliberately chose not to betray Elijah.

17:15-16 This miraculous sign illustrated that God rewards faith and obedience, even that of a Gentile.

17:17-24 This miracle teaches three lessons: (1) not all illness is the result of sin; (2) God has power over sickness

and death; and (3) the purpose of the signs was to produce faith in **the Lord's word**.

18:1-46 This chapter describes one of history's great power encounters between God and evil; it is comparable to the encounter between the Lord and the gods of Egypt before the exodus. The prestige of Baal-melkart (see note at 16:23-28), with his association with Phoenician prosperity, was comparable to the historic prestige of the gods of Egypt. The power encounter with Egypt freed the Israelites from physical bondage. One might expect that God's confrontation with Baal-melkart freed Israel from spiritual bondage, but it is hard to find evidence for this. Neither Ahab nor Jezebel repented. The moral life of the northern kingdom was not noticeably influenced. But we cannot know how much worse things would have gone for faith in Yahweh without this encounter. Perhaps the 7,000 (19:18) who had not bowed to Baal were encouraged and strengthened, and thus kept the faith. Humanly speaking, without such manifestations of God's power as these, Hebrew faith might have perished long before the exile.

18:1 In **the third year** of the drought, God announced its end.

on the surface of the land." [2] So Elijah went to present himself to Ahab.

The famine was severe in Samaria.[a] [3] Ahab called for Obadiah, who was in charge of the palace.[b] Obadiah was a man who greatly *feared the LORD[c] [4] and took 100 prophets and hid them, 50 men to a cave, and provided them with food and water when Jezebel[d] slaughtered the LORD's prophets.[e] [5] Ahab said to Obadiah, "Go throughout the land to every spring of water and to every *wadi. Perhaps we'll find grass so we can keep the horses and mules alive and not have to destroy any cattle."[f] [6] They divided the land between them in order to cover it. Ahab went one way by himself, and Obadiah went the other way by himself.

[7] While Obadiah was walking along the road, Elijah suddenly met him.[g] When Obadiah recognized him, he fell with his face to the ground and said, "Is it you, my lord Elijah?"

[8] "It is I," he replied. "Go tell your lord, 'Elijah is here!'"

[9] But Obadiah said, "What sin have I committed,[h] that you are handing your servant over to Ahab to put me to death? [10] As the LORD your God lives, there is no nation or kingdom where my lord has not sent someone to search for you. When they said, 'He is not here,' he made that kingdom or nation swear they had not found you.

[11] "Now you say, 'Go tell your lord, "Elijah is here!"' [12] But when I leave you, the Spirit of the LORD may carry you off[i] to some place I don't know. Then when I go report to Ahab

and he doesn't find you, he will kill me. But I, your servant, have feared the LORD from my youth. [13] Wasn't it reported to my lord what I did when Jezebel slaughtered the LORD's prophets? I hid 100 of the prophets of the LORD, 50 men to a cave, and I provided them with food and water. [14] Now you say, 'Go tell your lord, "Elijah is here!"' He will kill me!"

[15] Then Elijah said, "As the LORD of *Hosts lives,[j] before whom I stand, today I will present myself to Ahab."

[16] Obadiah went to meet Ahab and told him. Then Ahab went to meet Elijah. [17] When Ahab saw Elijah, Ahab said to him, "Is that you, you destroyer of Israel?"[k]

[18] He replied, "I have not destroyed Israel, but you and your father's house have, because you have abandoned the LORD's commands[l] and followed the *Baals.[m] [19] Now summon all Israel to meet me at Mount Carmel,[n] along with the 450 prophets of Baal and the 400 prophets of *Asherah[o] who eat at Jezebel's table."

Elijah at Mount Carmel

[20] So Ahab summoned all the Israelites and gathered the prophets at Mount Carmel. [21] Then Elijah approached all the people and said, "How long will you hesitate between two opinions?[p] If *Yahweh is God, follow Him. But if Baal, follow him."[q] But the people didn't answer him a word.

[22] Then Elijah said to the people, "I am the only remaining prophet of the LORD,[r] but Baal's prophets are 450 men. [23] Let two bulls

Cross-references (center column)

a18:2 1Kg 16:24,29
b18:3 1Kg 16:9
cNeh 7:2; Pr 3:5-6
d18:4 1Kg 16:31; Rv 2:20
e1Kg 18:13
f18:5 Gn 47:4
g18:7 2Kg 1:6-8
h18:9 1Kg 17:18
i18:12 2Kg 2:16; Ac 8:39
j18:15 1Kg 17:1
k18:17 Jos 7:25; 1Kg 21:20
l18:18 1Kg 9:9; 16:25-26
m1Kg 16:31-32
n18:19 Jos 19:26; 2Kg 2:25
o1Kg 16:33; 22:6
p18:21 2Kg 17:41
qJos 24:15; Mt 6:24
r18:22 1Kg 19:10,14

This was an act of grace since neither Israel nor Israel's rulers had shown any repentance that warranted it.

18:3-5 Since these verses may have changed to a new story, verse 3 could predate the preceding verses. This would permit the translation, "Ahab *had* called." This scenario should be interpreted in terms of its historical conditions. It told of two high officials initiating a nationwide effort to find the resources to preserve the kingdom's chariot armies. The story's surface simplicity obscures a grave and historically realistic situation. How could they maintain the provisions for the chariot **horses** and baggage **mules** when forage and grazing were exhausted? This situation could have produced Israel's weakness in chariot forces in the first war of chapter 20.

18:6 Both **Ahab** and **Obadiah** were accompanied by soldiers and officials who purchased or confiscated the resources as needed.

18:7-8 The prophet **Elijah** made his approach through **Obadiah** as the latter **was walking along**, probably with his search party. Obadiah's deference to Elijah revealed Elijah's stature.

18:10 Obadiah's response made it clear that Elijah's time in Ethbaal's domains was "under cover" since Ahab had initiated a thorough search for the prophet.

18:13 This verse gives a remarkable view of the religious turmoil in Israel. With the government engaged in a bloody purge of those who worshiped the Lord, one of the king's chief political officials was protecting the minority religious party.

18:17 Despite Ahab's bravery and abilities in many areas, his accusation against Elijah showed that willful sin can blind a person to reality.

18:18-19 Elijah immediately took the conversation to the crucial issue—Ahab's disobedience of God. Then Elijah issued his challenge to set up a carefully planned and publicized power encounter pitting Elijah against the prophets of **Baal** and his consort, **Asherah**. Asherah is a generic name for any divine consort of any fertility god, but is also sometimes a title or name for a particular goddess.

18:20-21 From the course of events, we can see that some of the worshipers of Baal really believed in the power of their deity and that many who should have followed the Lord did not have much faith. Therefore, for many of the observers, this was a genuine open-ended power encounter to discover which deity was stronger.

18:22-25 Elijah then proposed the terms of the test: whichever god miraculously ignited and burned his sacrifice would prove to be the true deity who was worthy of the

be given to us. They are to choose one bull
for themselves, cut it in pieces, and place it
on the wood but not light the fire. I will prepare the other bull and place it on the wood
but not light the fire. 24 Then you call on the
name of your god, and I will call on the name
of Yahweh.[a] The God who answers with fire,
He is God."
All the people answered, "That sounds
good."
25 Then Elijah said to the prophets of Baal,
"Since you are so numerous, choose for yourselves one bull and prepare it first. Then call on
the name of your god but don't light the fire."
26 So they took the bull that he gave them,
prepared it, and called on the name of Baal
from morning until noon, saying, "Baal, answer us!" But there was no sound;[b] no one answered. Then they danced, hobbling around
the altar they had made.
27 At noon Elijah mocked them. He said,
"Shout loudly, for he's a god! Maybe he's thinking it over; maybe he has wandered away;[A] or
maybe he's on the road. Perhaps he's sleeping and will wake up!"[c] 28 They shouted loudly,
and cut themselves[d] with knives and spears,
according to their custom, until blood gushed
over them. 29 All afternoon they kept on raving
until the offering of the evening sacrifice,[e] but
there was no sound; no one answered, no one
paid attention.[f]
30 Then Elijah said to all the people, "Come
near me." So all the people approached him.
Then he repaired the LORD's altar that had been
torn down:[g] 31 Elijah took 12 stones—according to the number of the tribes of the sons
of Jacob, to whom the word of the LORD had
come, saying, "Israel will be your name"[h]—
32 and he built an altar[i] with the stones in
the name of Yahweh. Then he made a trench
around the altar large enough to hold about
four gallons.[B,C] 33 Next, he arranged the wood,
cut up the bull, and placed it on the wood. He
said, "Fill four water pots with water and pour
it on the offering to be burned and on the
wood." 34 Then he said, "A second time!" and
they did it a second time. And then he said, "A
third time!" and they did it a third time. 35 So
the water ran all around the altar; he even
filled the trench with water.
36 At the time for offering the evening sacrifice,[j] Elijah the prophet approached the altar
and said, "Yahweh, God of Abraham, Isaac,
and Israel,[k] today let it be known[l] that You
are God in Israel and I am Your servant, and
that at Your word I have done all these things.
37 Answer me, LORD! Answer me so that this
people will know that You, Yahweh, are God[m]
and that You have turned their hearts back."
38 Then Yahweh's fire fell and consumed the
•burnt offering, the wood, the stones, and the
dust, and it licked up the water that was in
the trench. 39 When all the people saw it, they
fell facedown[n] and said, "Yahweh, He is God!
Yahweh, He is God!"[o]
40 Then Elijah ordered them, "Seize the
prophets of Baal![p] Do not let even one of
them escape." So they seized them, and Elijah
brought them down to the Wadi Kishon[q] and
slaughtered them there.[r] 41 Elijah said to Ahab,
"Go up, eat and drink, for there is the sound
of a rainstorm."[s]

[a]18:24 Gn 4:26; Rm 10:13
[b]18:26 Jr 10:5; 1Co 8:4
[c]18:27 Hab 2:19
[d]18:28 Lv 19:28; Dt 14:1
[e]18:29 Ex 29:39,41
[f]2Kg 19:12; Is 16:12
[g]18:30 1Kg 19:10
[h]18:31 Gn 32:28; 35:10; 2Kg 17:34
[i]18:32 Gn 12:7,8; 22:9
[j]18:36 1Kg 18:29
[k]Ex 3:6; 4:5
[l]Nm 16:28
[m]18:37 Jos 4:24; Jn 11:42
[n]18:39 Lv 9:24; Mt 17:6
[o]1Kg 18:21,24
[p]18:40 1Kg 18:19,22
[q]18:40 Jdg 4:7; 5:21
[r]Dt 13:5; 2Kg 10:24-25
[s]18:41 1Kg 17:1; 18:1

[A]**18:27** Or *has turned aside*; possibly to relieve himself [B]**18:32** LXX reads *trench containing two measures of seed* [C]**18:32** Lit *altar corresponding to a house of two seahs of seed*

people's allegiance. Since Baal was the storm god, his followers believed he could answer with fire (lightning). But this encounter would show which deity really controlled the weather and provided what the people needed. At the same time, it would show who was a destroyer of Israel, rebellious Ahab or the Lord's prophet Elijah.

18:26 The priests of Baal entered into the contest with great zeal. The HCSB takes their dancing as imitating the steps of a lame person, since it uses the same Hebrew word as the one describing Mephibosheth (2Sm 4:4). Perhaps they danced this way as a result of their self-inflicted injuries (1Kg 18:28).

18:27 The Hebrew original possibly indicates that Elijah ridiculed Baal for relieving himself. Reducing deities to any level of human behavior is an insult. Therefore any suggestion that Baal was drawn away to perform a creaturely necessity was a poignant blow by Elijah.

18:28-29 The fanatical zeal of the priests of Baal led them to **cut** themselves. Some suggest that this self-inflicted pain may have been aimed at gaining the pity of the other gods so they would release Baal from his mythological death and thus bring rain. If this is true, these Baal worshipers were vicariously suffering pain for their god.

18:30-32 These verses draw on powerful symbols and names from the past—**12 stones** for the 12 **tribes**, and **Israel**, the name that Yahweh, the God of their covenant, had given them.

18:33-35 Elijah took steps to avoid any appearance of trickery or fraud. If his God could get a drenching wet sacrifice to burn, his God was God indeed.

18:36-39 Elijah's prayer was a powerful statement of the theology of God's great works. Just as the temple singers declared God's great works so the world could know God (Ps 66:3-4), Elijah prayed for a miraculous sign so **this people** would **know that You, Yahweh, are God**. The simplicity of Elijah's procedure is impressive. The prophet prayed, and the sacrifice was miraculously burned.

18:40 Elijah executed God's judgment on the false prophets that Moses commanded in Dt 13:5,13-18; 17:2-5. This was the law for the covenant community, God's holy nation.

18:41-46 Two final miraculous events on this day were

⁴²So Ahab went to eat and drink, but Elijah went up to the summit of Carmel.ᵃ He bowed down on the ground and put his face between his knees.ᵇ ⁴³Then he said to his servant, "Go up and look toward the sea."

So he went up, looked, and said, "There's nothing."

Seven times Elijah said, "Go back."

⁴⁴On the seventhᶜ time, he reported, "There's a cloud as small as a man's hand coming from the sea."

Then Elijah said, "Go and tell Ahab, 'Get your chariot ready and go down so the rain doesn't stop you.'"

⁴⁵In a little while, the sky grew dark with clouds and wind, and there was a downpour. So Ahab got in his chariot and went to Jezreel.ᵈ ⁴⁶The power of the Lordᵉ was on Elijah, and he tucked his mantle under his beltᶠ and ran ahead of Ahab to the entrance of Jezreel.

Elijah's Journey to Horeb

19 Ahab told Jezebelᵍ everything that Elijah had doneʰ and how he had killed all the prophets with the sword.ⁱ ²So Jezebel sent a messenger to Elijah, saying, "May the gods punish me and do so severelyʲ if I don't make your life like the life of one of them by this time tomorrow!"

³Then Elijah became afraid^A,ᵏ and immedi-

ately ran for his life.ˡ When he came to Beer-shebaᵐ that belonged to Judah, he left his servant there,ⁿ ⁴but he went on a day's journey into the wilderness. He sat down under a broom treeᵒ and prayed that he might die. He said, "I have had enough! Lord, take my life,ᵖ for I'm no better than my fathers." ⁵Then he lay down and slept under the broom tree.

Suddenly, an angel touched him.ᵍ The angel told him, "Get up and eat." ⁶Then he looked, and there at his head was a loaf of bread baked over hot stones, and a jug of water.ʳ So he ate and drank and lay down again. ⁷Then the angel of the Lordˢ returned for a second time and touched him. He said, "Get up and eat, or the journey will be too much for you." ⁸So he got up, ate, and drank. Then on the strength from that food, he walked 40 days and 40 nightsᵗ to Horeb, the mountain of God.ᵘ ⁹He entered a caveᵛ there and spent the night.

Elijah's Encounter with the Lord

Then the word of the Lord came to him, and He said to him, "What are you doing here, Elijah?"ʷ

¹⁰He replied, "I have been very zealousˣ for the Lord God of •Hosts, but the Israelites have abandoned Your covenant,ʸ torn down Your altars,ᶻ and killed Your prophetsᵃᵃ with the sword. I alone am left,ᵃᵇ and they are looking for me to take my life."ᵃᶜ

Cross references

ᵃ 18:42 1Kg 18:19
ᵇ 1Sm 12:17; Jms 5:18
ᶜ 18:44 Jos 6:15; Lk 12:54
ᵈ 18:45 Jos 17:16; Jdg 6:33
ᵉ 18:46 2Kg 3:15
ᶠ Ex 12:11; 2Kg 4:29; 9:1; Jr 1:17; 1Pt 1:13
ᵍ 19:1 1Kg 16:31; 18:4,14
ʰ 1Kg 18:30-38
ⁱ 1Kg 18:40
ʲ 19:2 1Sm 3:17; 1Kg 20:10; 2Kg 6:31
ᵏ 19:3 Pr 29:25
ˡ Gn 31:21
ᵐ Gn 21:31; Jdg 20:1
ⁿ Gn 22:5; Mt 14:23; 26:36
ᵒ 19:4 Jb 30:4
ᵖ Nm 11:15; Jnh 4:3,8
ᵍ 19:5 Gn 28:11-16
ʳ 19:6 1Kg 17:10-11
ˢ 19:7 Gn 16:7,9,11
ᵗ 19:8 Ex 24:18; Mt 4:2
ᵘ Ex 3:1; 4:27
ᵛ 19:9 Ex 33:22
ʷ Gn 3:9
ˣ 19:10 Nm 25:13; Ac 22:3
ʸ Dt 31:16
ᶻ 19:10 1Kg 18:30
ᵃᵃ 1Kg 18:4,13; Ac 7:52
ᵃᵇ 1Kg 18:22
ᵃᶜ 1Kg 19:2,14; Rm 11:3

---

^A 19:3 Some Hb mss, LXX, Syr, Vg; other Hb mss read *he saw*

---

(1) the coming of the **rain** as a result of Elijah's prayer and (2) Elijah's supernatural strength in leaving the scene and passing Ahab's **chariot** before the storm. Typically, the act of preceding the king's chariot could have been a friendly overture. It was an act of honor to the king and an honor to the runner to be permitted to run before the king. But if this was Elijah's intent, it was lost on Ahab and Jezebel.

19:1-21 This chapter presents facts that argue for the truth of both chapters 18 and 19. The preceding chapter was one of the best examples of a power encounter in the Bible, but chapter 19 demonstrates that God's miraculous works did not bring about repentance, at least not on a scale broad enough to be mentioned. Understandably, Elijah collapsed into an almost hysterical pessimism about what he took to be the failure of God's purposes. The clear lesson is that while power witness is both biblical and effective, sinful people can still reject the greatest of God's signs (Lk 16:31). So too, faithful disciples are wrong to suppose that they are all alone or that God's purposes have truly failed.

19:1-2 Jezebel's rejection of God's signs and the determined, defiant way in which she later faced death (2Kg 9:30-31) demonstrate her character as a person who did what she wanted, no matter the consequences. Sin breeds this self-destructive heedlessness.

19:3 Elijah's faith may have crumbled due to physical and emotional exhaustion. Although his future still included several tasks, it may be significant that his next task was to

choose his successor. **Beer-sheba**, about 100 miles south of Mount Carmel, served as a traditional southern boundary for Israelite territory (Jdg 20:1; 2Sm 24:2).

19:4 A **day's journey** would have taken Elijah out of Judean territory and into deeper desert. The **broom tree** under which the prophet sat provided shade, and its roots could be used for heat and food. Elijah was in deep depression.

19:5-8 God's miraculous provision was resumed, this time purely for the prophet. After Elijah **ate** and rested, he returned to the place where the covenant had been given, Mount **Horeb**, or Sinai. There, Elijah would have his personal faith renewed by God's presence.

19:9-10 Elijah explained his presence at Sinai by referring to his discouragement. Israel's immediate future, as hindsight shows, gave good reason for despair. Judah was to have one more period of God-given prosperity under the four good kings from Joash to Jotham, but during that time, Israel was to be deported to Assyria.

19:11-13 God first reveals His presence to Elijah in His greatness and power, but He did not speak from that position. The Lord instead spoke to Elijah in **a soft whisper**, showing Himself to be a God who communicates via a still, small voice as well as powerful displays.

19:15-16 God's commands first pointed to judgment. Elijah was to anoint **Hazael** as king over Aram, **Jehu** as king of Israel, and **Elisha** as his own successor. God was still controlling events.

[11]Then He said, "Go out and stand on the mountain in the LORD's presence."[a]

At that moment, the LORD passed by.[b] A great and mighty wind[c] was tearing at the mountains and was shattering cliffs before the LORD, but the LORD was not in the wind. After the wind there was an earthquake,[d] but the LORD was not in the earthquake. [12]After the earthquake there was a fire,[e] but the LORD was not in the fire. And after the fire there was a voice, a soft whisper.[f] [13]When Elijah heard it, he wrapped his face in his mantle[g] and went out and stood at the entrance of the cave.

Suddenly, a voice came to him and said, "What are you doing here, Elijah?"

[14]"I have been very zealous for the LORD God of Hosts," he replied, "but the Israelites have abandoned Your covenant, torn down Your altars, and killed Your prophets with the sword. I alone am left, and they're looking for me to take my life."[h]

[15]Then the LORD said to him, "Go and return by the way you came to the Wilderness of Damascus. When you arrive, you are to anoint Hazael[i] as king over Aram. [16]You are to anoint Jehu[j] son of Nimshi as king over Israel and Elisha[k] son of Shaphat from Abel-meholah as

[a]19:11 Ex 19:20
[b]Ex 33:21-22
[c]Ex 1:4; Ac 2:2
[d]Am 1:1; Rv 6:12; 16:18
[e]19:12 Ex 3:2
[f]Zch 4:6,10
[g]19:13 Ex 3:6
[h]19:14 1Kg 19:10; Rm 11:3
[i]19:15 2Kg 8:8-15
[j]19:16 2Kg 19:1-10
[k]1Kg 19:19

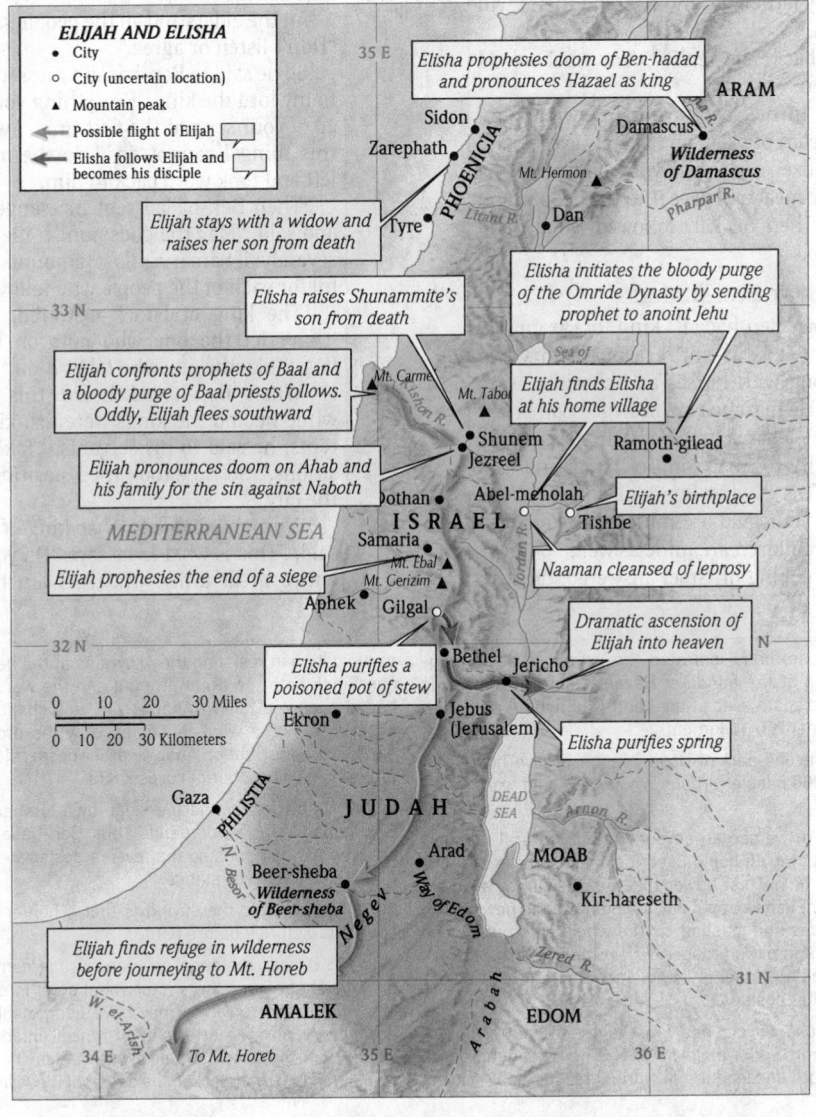

ELIJAH AND ELISHA
- • City
- ○ City (uncertain location)
- ▲ Mountain peak
- ← Possible flight of Elijah
- ← Elisha follows Elijah and becomes his disciple

Elisha prophesies doom of Ben-hadad and pronounces Hazael as king

Elijah stays with a widow and raises her son from death

Elisha raises Shunammite's son from death

Elisha initiates the bloody purge of the Omride Dynasty by sending prophet to anoint Jehu

Elijah confronts prophets of Baal and a bloody purge of Baal priests follows. Oddly, Elijah flees southward

Elijah finds Elisha at his home village

Elijah pronounces doom on Ahab and his family for the sin against Naboth

Elijah's birthplace

Elijah prophesies the end of a siege

Naaman cleansed of leprosy

Dramatic ascension of Elijah into heaven

Elisha purifies a poisoned pot of stew

Elisha purifies spring

Elijah finds refuge in wilderness before journeying to Mt. Horeb

ARAM
Sidon
Damascus
Zarephath
PHOENICIA
Wilderness of Damascus
Mt. Hermon
Pharpar R.
Tyre
Litani R.
Dan
Mt. Carmel
Mt. Tabor
Sea of
Shunem
Jezreel
Ramoth-gilead
Dothan
Abel-meholah
Tishbe
ISRAEL
Samaria
MEDITERRANEAN SEA
Mt. Ebal
Mt. Gerizim
Jordan R.
Aphek
Gilgal
Bethel
Jericho
Ekron
Jebus (Jerusalem)
Gaza
PHILISTIA
JUDAH
DEAD SEA
Arnon R.
Arad
MOAB
Beer-sheba
Wilderness of Beer-sheba
Kir-hareseth
Negev
Way of Edon
Zered R.
Arabah
AMALEK
EDOM
To Mt. Horeb
W. el-Arish
N. Besor
N.

0 10 20 30 Miles
0 10 20 30 Kilometers

35 E
33 N
32 N
31 N
34 E
35 E
36 E

prophet in your place. [17]Then Jehu will put to death whoever escapes the sword of Hazael,[a] and Elisha will put to death whoever escapes the sword of Jehu.[b] [18]But I will leave 7,000 in Israel[c]—every knee that has not bowed to •Baal[d] and every mouth that has not kissed him."[e]

Elisha's Appointment as Elijah's Successor

[19]Elijah left there and found Elisha[f] son of Shaphat as he was plowing. Twelve teams of oxen were in front of him, and he was with the twelfth team. Elijah walked by him and threw his mantle over him.[g] [20]Elisha left the oxen, ran to follow Elijah, and said, "Please let me kiss my father and mother, and then I will follow you."[h]

"Go on back," he replied, "for what have I done to you?"

[21]So he turned back from following him, took the team of oxen, and slaughtered them. With the oxen's wooden yoke and plow,[i] he cooked the meat and gave it to the people, and they ate. Then he left, followed Elijah, and served him.[j]

Victory over Ben-hadad

20 Now Ben-hadad[k] king of Aram assembled his entire army. Thirty-two kings,[l] along with horses and chariots, were with him. He marched up, besieged Samaria,[m] and fought against it. [2]He sent messengers into the city to Ahab king of Israel and said to him, "This is what Ben-hadad says: [3]'Your silver and your gold are mine! And your best wives and children are mine as well!'"[n]

[4]Then the king of Israel answered, "Just as

you say, my lord the king: I am yours, along with all that I have."

[5]The messengers then returned and said, "This is what Ben-hadad says: 'I have sent messengers to you, saying: You are to give me your silver, your gold, your wives, and your children. [6]But at this time tomorrow I will send my servants to you, and they will search your palace and your servants' houses. They will lay their hands on and take away whatever is precious to you.'"

[7]Then the king of Israel called for all the elders of the land and said, "Think it over and you will see that this one is only looking for trouble,[o] for he demanded my wives, my children, my silver, and my gold, and I didn't turn him down."

[8]All the elders and all the people said to him, "Don't listen or agree."

[9]So he said to Ben-hadad's messengers, "Say to my lord the king, 'Everything you demanded of your servant the first time, I will do, but this thing I cannot do.'" So the messengers left and took word back to him.

[10]Then Ben-hadad sent messengers to him and said, "May the gods punish me and do so severely[p] if Samaria's dust[q] amounts to a handful for each of the people who follow me."

[11]The king of Israel answered, "Say this: 'Don't let the one who puts on his armor boast[r] like the one who takes it off.'"

[12]When Ben-hadad heard this response, while he and the kings were drinking[s] in the tents, he said to his servants, "Take your positions." So they took their positions against the city.

[13]A prophet came to Ahab king of Israel and said, "This is what LORD says: 'Do you see this entire great army? Watch, I am handing it

a19:17 2Kg 9:14–10:25
b2Kg 2:24; 8:1
c19:18 Rm 11:4
d1Kg 16:31
eHs 13:2
f19:19 1Kg 19:16-17
g2Kg 2:8,13-14
h19:20 Mt 8:21-22
i19:21 1Sm 6:14; 2Sm 24:22
jLk 14:26,33
k20:1 1Kg 15:18,20
l1Kg 22:31
m1Kg 16:24,29
n20:3 2Kg 24:14-16; Dn 1:3-4
o20:7 2Kg 5:7
p20:10 1Kg 19:2; 2Kg 6:31
q2Sm 22:43
r20:11 Pr 27:1
s20:12 1Kg 16:9

19:17 This command indicated the extent of God's judgment—death at the hands of **Hazael**, death at the hands of **Jehu**, and death even at the hands of **Elisha** through His pronouncements of judgment.

19:18 The second part of God's response gave hope. God still had **7,000** people through whom He could work in the future.

19:19-21 Here we see an advance in agricultural technology—**teams of oxen** being used for deeper, more effective plowing (Pr 14:4). This showed that Elisha's family was quite prosperous. Elisha's capability to celebrate his new calling with sacrifices and feasting for the whole community also indicated his family's prosperity. The **mantle** or robe worn by Elijah was a symbol of his position and of Elisha's succession to that position.

20:1-3 This chapter clashes with the general pattern of Israelite strength under the dynasty of Omri. That general political strength and leadership culminated in Ahab's crucial

participation in resisting the Assyrians at the battle of Qarqar. Since both the great drought and the wars with Ben-hadad occurred late in Ahab's rule, this chapter probably describes a brief weakness caused by the drought (17:1) and also sheds light on Ahab's earlier desperate search for provisions for his chariot corps (18:5).

20:4-9 Ahab tried to end the siege by a total surrender to **Ben-hadad's** initial demands, but Ben-hadad then increased his demands so that even a desperate, weakened Ahab resorted to resistance.

20:11 The point of the saying is that a fighter should not count his victories before battle.

20:13-16 Divine revelation gave encouragement and guidance to **Ahab**. Since there is no mention of Israelite chariots, Ahab's chariot army may have been disabled by the drought. A surprise attack by provincial infantry brought victory for Ahab's army. God's intervention helped in the drunken panic that marked the defeat of the Aramean army.

over to you today so that you may know that I am •Yahweh.'"[a]

[14] Ahab asked, "By whom?"

And the prophet said, "This is what the LORD says: 'By the young men of the provincial leaders.'"

Then he asked, "Who is to start the battle?"[b]

He said, "You."

[15] So Ahab counted the young men of the provincial leaders, and there were 232. After them he counted all the Israelite troops: 7,000.[c] [16] They marched out at noon while Ben-hadad and the 32 kings[d] who were helping him were getting drunk in the tents. [17] The young men of the provincial leaders marched out first. Then Ben-hadad sent out scouts, and they reported to him, saying, "Men are marching out of Samaria."[e]

[18] So he said, "If they have marched out in peace,[f] take them alive, and if they have marched out for battle, take them alive."

[19] The young men of the provincial leaders and the army behind them marched out from the city, [20] and each one struck down his opponent.[g] So the Arameans fled and Israel pursued them,[h] but Ben-hadad king of Aram escaped on a horse with the cavalry. [21] Then the king of Israel marched out and attacked the cavalry and the chariots. He inflicted a great slaughter on Aram.

[22] The prophet approached the king of Israel and said to him, "Go and strengthen yourself, then consider what you should do, for in the spring[i] the king of Aram will march against you."

[23] Now the king of Aram's servants said to him, "Their gods are gods of the hill country.[j] That's why they were stronger than we were. Instead, we should fight with them on the plain; then we will certainly be stronger than they will be. [24] Also do this: remove each king from his position and appoint captains in their place. [25] Raise another army for yourself like the army you lost—horse for horse, chariot for chariot—and let's fight with them on the plain; and we will certainly be stronger than they will be." The king listened to them and did so.

[26] In the spring, Ben-hadad mobilized the Arameans and went up to Aphek[k] to battle Israel. [27] The Israelites mobilized, gathered supplies, and went to fight them. The Israelites camped in front of them like two little flocks of goats, while the Arameans filled the landscape.[l]

[28] Then the man of God[m] approached and said to the king of Israel, "This is what Yahweh says: 'Because the Arameans have said: Yahweh is a god of the mountains and not a god of the valleys,[n] I will hand over all this great army to you. Then you will know that I am the LORD.'"[o]

[29] They camped opposite each other for seven days. On the seventh day,[p] the battle took place, and the Israelites struck down the Arameans—100,000 foot soldiers in one day. [30] The ones who remained fled into the city of Aphek, and the wall fell on those 27,000 remaining men.

Ben-hadad also fled and went into an inner room[q] in the city. [31] His servants said to him, "Consider this: we have heard that the kings of the house of Israel are merciful kings. So let's put •sackcloth around our waists[r] and ropes

[a]20:13 1Kg 20:28
[b]20:14 Jdg 1:1; 20:18
[c]20:15 Jdg 7:2
[d]20:16 1Kg 20:1
[e]20:17 1Kg 16:24
[f]20:18 2Kg 14:8
[g]20:20 2Sm 2:15-16
[h]1Sm 14:13-14,22
[i]20:22 2Sm 11:1
[j]20:23 1Kg 14:23; Ps 139:7-12
[k]20:26 2Kg 13:17
[l]20:27 Jdg 6:5; 1Sm 13:5
[m]20:28 1Kg 17:18
[n]1Kg 20:23
[o]1Kg 20:13
[p]20:29 Jos 6:15
[q]20:30 1Kg 22:25
[r]20:31 Gn 37:34

The purpose of the divine intervention was that Ahab would recognize God's character. The lesson failed.

20:20 There are two views on the Aramean **cavalry**. One is that cavalry did not appear until later so that the ambiguous Hebrew word in this verse refers to charioteers. The other is that Assyrian records confirm the presence of cavalry in the region's armies at this time but the chariot was still the major strike force. So at this time Ben-hadad could have fled with the cavalry.

20:21 In this verse, **the cavalry and the chariots** are literally "horses and chariots," a combination that at this time would still more likely refer to chariotry. It is reasonable to conclude that much of the Israelite success came from God's blessing on the surprise infantry attack on the unprepared, unharnessed chariots of the Aramean army.

20:23-25 The Arameans then prepared for battle in the following year, most likely in the spring, the usual time for war (2Sm 11:1). They assumed that their mobile forces would be more effective in the plains instead of the mountains. But the reorganization of the Aramean chariots may have been disastrous. A feudal system in which kings provided the chariots was replaced by one in which central government officials maintained the chariots. In the long range, this was an advantage, but in the short range it may have replaced battle-tested nobility with less-experienced government officials. Their preparations included replacing the lost war machines, **chariot for chariot**.

20:26 The armies mobilized in the plains near **Aphek** in Bashan.

20:27 Ahab had rebuilt his chariot armies by the time of the battle of Qarqar (853 B.C.), probably two years after this battle with Ben-hadad. According to Assyrian records, Ahab led the largest opposing contingent of chariots, 2,000, at Qarqar. Thus it is fair to conclude that Ahab had partly rebuilt his chariot army by the time of this war with Ben-hadad. Both Ahab and Aram may have been fighting with rebuilt chariot armies, but the Aramean restructuring may have been more damaging. For a battle in the plains, the relative size of the armies was far less important than the quality of the chariot armies. Ahab's chariot force may have been superior.

20:30 The account given here is compatible with several

around our heads, and let's go out to the king of Israel. Perhaps he will spare your life."

³²So they dressed with sackcloth around their waists and ropes around their heads, went to the king of Israel, and said, "Your servant Ben-hadad says, 'Please spare my life.'"

So he said, "Is he still alive? He is my brother."

³³Now the men were looking for a sign of hope, so they quickly picked up on this^A and responded, "Yes, it is your brother Ben-hadad."

Then he said, "Go and bring him."

So Ben-hadad came out to him, and Ahab had him come up into the chariot. ³⁴Then Ben-hadad said to him, "I restore to you the cities that my father took from your father,^a and you may set up marketplaces for yourself in Damascus, like my father set up in Samaria."^b

Ahab responded, "On the basis of this treaty, I release you." So he made a treaty with him and released him.

Ahab Rebuked by the LORD

³⁵One of the sons of the prophets^c said to his fellow prophet by the word of the LORD, "Strike me!" But the man refused to strike him.

³⁶He told him, "Because you did not listen to the voice of the LORD, mark my words: When you leave me, a lion will kill you."^d When he left him, a lion attacked and killed him.

³⁷The prophet found another man and said to him, "Strike me!" So the man struck him, inflicting a wound. ³⁸Then the prophet went and waited for the king on the road. He disguised^e himself with a bandage over his eyes. ³⁹As the king was passing by, he cried out to the king and said, "Your servant marched out into the middle of the battle. Suddenly, a man turned aside and brought someone to me and said, 'Guard this man! If he is ever missing, it

will be your life in place of his life,^f or you will weigh out 75 pounds^B of silver.' ⁴⁰But while your servant was busy here and there, he disappeared."

The king of Israel said to him, "That will be your sentence; you yourself have decided it."^g

⁴¹He quickly removed the bandage from his eyes. The king of Israel recognized that he was one of the prophets. ⁴²The prophet said to him, "This is what the LORD says: 'Because you released from your hand the man I had set apart for destruction,^h it will be your life in place of his life and your people in place of his people.'" ⁴³The king of Israel left for home resentful and angry,^i and he entered Samaria.

Ahab and Naboth's Vineyard

21 Some time passed after these events. Naboth the Jezreelite had a vineyard; it was in Jezreel^j next to the palace of Ahab king of Samaria.^k ²So Ahab spoke to Naboth, saying, "Give me your vineyard^l so I can have it for a vegetable garden, since it is right next to my palace. I will give you a better vineyard in its place, or if you prefer, I will give you its value in silver."

³But Naboth said to Ahab, "I will never give my fathers' inheritance^m to you."

⁴So Ahab went to his palace resentful and angry^n because of what Naboth the Jezreelite had told him. He had said, "I will not give you my fathers' inheritance." He lay down on his bed, turned his face away,^o and didn't eat any food.^p

⁵Then his wife Jezebel came to him and said to him, "Why are you so upset that you refuse to eat?"

⁶"Because I spoke to Naboth the Jezreelite," he replied. "I told him: Give me your vineyard for silver, or if you wish, I will give you a vineyard in its place. But he said, 'I won't give you my vineyard!'"

Cross references (margin):
a 20:34 1Kg 15:20
b 2Sm 8:6
c 20:35 2Kg 2:3,5,7
d 20:36 1Kg 13:24
e 20:38 1Kg 14:2
f 20:39 Jos 2:14; 2Kg 10:24
g 20:40 2Sm 12:5
h 20:42 1Kg 19:16
i 20:43 1Kg 21:4
j 21:1 Jdg 6:33; 1Kg 18:45
k 1Kg 20:1
l 21:2 1Sm 8:14
m 21:3 Lv 25:23; Nm 36:7
n 21:4 1Kg 20:43
o 2Kg 20:2
p 1Sm 28:23

---

^A 20:33 Some Hb mss, alt Hb tradition, LXX; other Hb mss read *they hastened and caught hold; "Is this it?"*   ^B 20:39 Lit *a talent*

days of destruction against **Aphek** by Ahab's pursuing army as well as a house-to-house search for Ben-hadad.

20:34 This quick agreement, made in Ahab's chariot, raises puzzling questions. On the surface it seems unlikely that the Arameans had seized and held Israelite cities since the time of Omri, but there is much we do not know. It is clear that Ben-hadad relinquished claim to some Israelite cities and gave Ahab trading privileges in Aramean territory. From a human point of view, with the need to create an alliance with **Damascus** and anyone else who would join against the Assyrians, Ahab was politically wise and prudent in dealing gently with the defeated Arameans.

20:35-43 However prudent that policy may have been, the prophetic voices, speaking for God, condemned this act of prudent mercy. Once again, prudent politics conflicted

with following the Lord (see note at 3:1). As far as the prophets were concerned, Ben-hadad had been **devoted** to the ban, just like Jericho (Jos 6:18-19), and Ahab had violated that ban.

21:1-3 The law had legal provisions that protected the rights of Israelite land-holding families. The land could not be permanently alienated from the family, but it had to be returned either by redemption or by the free return in the Jubilee Year (Lv 25:10). There were no provisions for the selling or exchanging of land such as that which **Ahab** requested of **Naboth**. Therefore, Naboth refused to sell his **father's inheritance** to the king.

21:4 Ahab the mighty warrior pouted because Naboth the farmer had refused his offer.

21:7 If the descriptions of Phoenician royal tyranny given

[7] Then his wife Jezebel said to him, "Now, exercise your royal power over Israel. Get up, eat some food, and be happy. For I will give you the vineyard of Naboth the Jezreelite."[a] [8] So she wrote letters[b] in Ahab's name and sealed them with his seal.[c] She sent the letters to the elders[d] and nobles who lived with Naboth in his city. [9] In the letters, she wrote:

> Proclaim a fast[e] and seat Naboth at the head of the people. [10] Then seat two •wicked men[f] opposite him and have them testify against him, saying, "You have cursed God and the king!"[g] Then take him out and stone him to death.[h]

[11] The men of his city, the elders and nobles who lived in his city, did as Jezebel had commanded them, as was written in the letters she had sent them. [12] They proclaimed a fast and seated Naboth at the head of the people. [13] The two wicked men came in and sat opposite him. Then the wicked men testified against Naboth in the presence of the people, saying, "Naboth has cursed God and the king!" So they took him outside the city and stoned him to death with stones. [14] Then they sent word to Jezebel, "Naboth has been stoned to death."[i]

[15] When Jezebel heard that Naboth had been stoned to death, she said to Ahab, "Get up and take possession of the vineyard of Naboth the Jezreelite who refused to give it to you for silver,[j] since Naboth isn't alive, but dead." [16] When Ahab heard that Naboth was dead, he got up to go down to the vineyard of Naboth the Jezreelite to take possession of it.

The Lord's Judgment on Ahab

[17] Then the word of the Lord came to Elijah the Tishbite:[k] [18] "Get up and go to meet Ahab king of Israel,[l] who is in Samaria.[m] You'll find him in Naboth's vineyard, where he has gone to take possession of it. [19] Tell him, 'This is what the Lord says: Have you murdered[n] and also taken possession?'[o] Then tell him, 'This is what the Lord says: In the place where the dogs licked Naboth's blood, the dogs will also lick your blood!'"[p]

[20] Ahab said to Elijah, "So, you have caught me, my enemy."[q]

He replied, "I have caught you because you devoted[r] yourself to do what is evil in the Lord's sight. [21] This is what the Lord says:[A] 'I am about to bring disaster on you and will sweep away your descendants:

> I will eliminate all of Ahab's males,[B]
> 　both slave and free, in Israel;[s]

[22] I will make your house like the house of Jeroboam[t] son of Nebat and like the house of Baasha[u] son of Ahijah, because you have provoked My anger and caused Israel to sin.[v] [23] The Lord also speaks of Jezebel: The dogs will eat Jezebel in the plot of land[c] at Jezreel:[w]

[24] 　He who belongs to Ahab and dies
> 　　in the city, the dogs will eat,
> 　and he who dies in the field, the birds
> 　　of the sky will eat.'"[x]

[25] Still, there was no one like Ahab, who devoted himself to do what was evil in the Lord's sight, because his wife Jezebel incited him.[y] [26] He committed the most detestable acts by going after idols[z] as the Amorites[aa] had, whom the Lord had dispossessed before the Israelites.

[27] When Ahab heard these words, he tore his clothes, put •sackcloth over his body, and fasted. He lay down in sackcloth[ab] and walked

Cross references (margin)

[a] 21:7 1Sm 8:14
[b] 21:8 2Sm 11:14
[c] Est 3:12; 8:8,10
[d] 1Kg 20:7
[e] 21:9 1Sm 7:5-6; 2Ch 20:2-4
[f] 21:10 Dt 13:13
[g] Ex 20:16; 23:1; Dt 5:20; Ac 6:11
[h] Lv 24:15-16
[i] 21:14 Lv 24:16
[j] 21:15 1Kg 21:2-3
[k] 21:17 1Kg 17:2,8
[l] 21:18 1Kg 18:1
[m] 1Kg 16:29; 2Ch 22:9
[n] 21:19 Ex 20:13; Dt 5:17
[o] Lv 25:23
[p] 1Kg 22:38
[q] 21:20 1Kg 18:17
[r] 2Kg 17:17; Rm 7:14
[s] 21:21 2Kg 9:8
[t] 21:22 1Kg 14:10-11
[u] 1Kg 16:3-4
[v] 1Kg 12:30
[w] 21:23 2Kg 9:10,30-37
[x] 21:24 1Kg 14:11; 16:4
[y] 21:25 1Kg 16:30-33
[z] 21:26 2Kg 17:12
[aa] Gn 15:16; 2Kg 21:11
[ab] 21:27 Gn 37:34; 2Sm 3:31; 2Kg 6:30

A 21:21 LXX; MT omits *This is what the Lord says*　　B 21:21 Lit *eliminate Ahab's one who urinates against the wall*　　C 21:23 Some Hb mss, Syr, Tg, Vg, 2Kg 9:36; other Hb mss, LXX read *the rampart*

---

elsewhere are accurate, Jezebel brought an unbridled Phoenician tyranny to Israel.

21:8-10 Jezebel resolved Ahab's unhappiness with a scheme that involved perverting the law, perjury, and murder. First, she communicated a sense of seriousness by declaring a solemn **fast**. She then arranged for two **wicked men** to bring false accusations against Naboth. She knew Israelite law well enough to know that two witnesses were needed (Dt 17:6). Then she had Naboth accused of verbally abusing **God** and the **king**.

21:13-14 Jezebel's evil scheme had been executed. What is not related here, though it clearly happened, is that Naboth's male heirs were also killed (2Kg 9:25-26). This was necessary since as long as Naboth had surviving heirs, the land belonged to his family.

21:17-18 The prophet Elijah, who had faded into the background for a while, reenters the story.

21:19-24 The curse pronounced on Ahab came in two different statements. The first was expressed in God's words to Elijah and described the way **dogs** would **lick** Ahab's **blood** in the same place that they licked Naboth's blood and the blood of his sons (see note at vv. 13-14). Second, disaster would come on all the **males**, both slave and free (or as some translations suggest, both "weak and incapacitated"), of Ahab's **house**. Dogs and carrion **birds** would devour their corpses. The statement that dogs would lick Ahab's blood in the same place that they licked Naboth's blood did not happen exactly this way. Naboth was killed in Jezreel, and Ahab's chariot was washed out in Samaria (22:38). However, the Bible implies that this prophecy of Elijah was fulfilled when Joram, Ahab's son, was left for the dogs on Naboth's land in Jezreel (2Kg 9:24-26).

21:27-29 In a surprising acceptance of a very shallow repentance (note Ahab's continued rebellion in the next chapter), God pronounced that the prophesied destruction

around subdued. [28]Then the word of the Lord came to Elijah the Tishbite: [29]"Have you seen how Ahab has humbled himself before Me? I will not bring the disaster during his lifetime,[a] because he has humbled himself before Me. I will bring the disaster on his house during his son's lifetime."[b]

Jehoshaphat's Alliance with Ahab

22 There was[c] a lull of three years[d] without war between Aram and Israel. [2]However, in the third year, Jehoshaphat[e] king of Judah went to visit the king of Israel.[f] [3]The king of Israel had said to his servants, "Don't you know that Ramoth-gilead[g] is ours, but we have failed to take it from the hand of the king of Aram?" [4]So[h] he asked Jehoshaphat, "Will you go with me to fight Ramoth-gilead?"[i]

Jehoshaphat replied to the king of Israel, "I am as you are, my people as your people, my horses as your horses."[j] [5]But Jehoshaphat said to the king of Israel, "First, please ask what the Lord's will is."[k]

[6]So the king of Israel gathered the prophets, about 400 men,[l] and asked them, "Should I go against Ramoth-gilead for war or should I refrain?"

They replied, "March up, and the Lord will hand it over to the king."[m]

[7]But Jehoshaphat asked, "Isn't there a prophet of •Yahweh here anymore?[n] Let's ask him."

[8]The king of Israel said to Jehoshaphat, "There is still one man who can ask Yahweh, but I hate him[o] because he never prophesies

good about me,[p] but only disaster. He is Micaiah son of Imlah."

"The king shouldn't say that!" Jehoshaphat replied.

[9]So the king of Israel called an officer and said, "Hurry and get Micaiah son of Imlah!"

[10]Now the king of Israel and Jehoshaphat king of Judah,[q] clothed in royal attire, were each sitting on his own throne. They were on the threshing floor[r] at the entrance to Samaria's •gate, and all the prophets were prophesying in front of them. [11]Then Zedekiah[s] son of Chenaanah made iron horns[t] and said, "This is what the Lord says: 'You will gore the Arameans with these until they are finished off.'" [12]And all the prophets were prophesying the same: "March up to Ramoth-gilead[u] and succeed, for the Lord will hand it over to the king."

Micaiah's Message of Defeat

[13]The messenger[v] who went to call Micaiah instructed him, "Look, the words of the prophets are unanimously favorable for the king. So let your words be like theirs, and speak favorably."

[14]But Micaiah said, "As the Lord lives,[w] I will say whatever the Lord says to me."[x]

[15]So he went to the king, and the king asked him, "Micaiah, should we go to Ramoth-gilead for war, or should we refrain?"

Micaiah told him, "March up and succeed. Yahweh will hand it over to the king."

[16]But the king said to him, "How many times must I make you swear not to tell me

Cross-references (center column)

[a]21:29 2Kg 20:19; 2Ch 32:26
[b]2Kg 9:25-37; 10:6-11
[c]22:1-9 2Ch 18:1-8
[d]22:1 1Kg 20:1,26
[e]22:2 1Kg 15:24
[f]2Ch 18:2
[g]22:3 Dt 4:43; Jos 20:8; 1Kg 4:13
[h]22:4-6 2Kg 3:7-8
[i]22:4 2Kg 8:18,27
[j]2Kg 3:7
[k]22:5 1Sm 23:1-5; Jms 4:15
[l]22:6 1Kg 18:19
[m]1Kg 13:18
[n]22:7 2Kg 1:3; 3:11; 5:8
[o]22:8 1Kg 18:17; 21:20
[p]Am 5:10
[q]22:10-12 2Ch 18:9-11
[r]22:10 Jdg 6:37
[s]22:11 1Kg 22:24
[t]Dt 33:17; Zch 1:18-21
[u]22:12 1Kg 4:13
[v]22:13-28 2Ch 18:12-27
[w]22:14 1Kg 18:10,15
[x]Nm 22:28; 24:13

Study notes (bottom)

on Ahab's **house** would happen only after Ahab's death. We must accept God's sovereignty on those occasions when He seems harsh by our standards and also when He seems too merciful by our judgment.

22:1-3 For parts of **three years** there were no hostilities with Ben-hadad (ca 854–852 b.c.). During this time a successful defense against Assyria took place at the battle of Qarqar (853 b.c.). Then, within a year of that success, Ahab decided to retake Ramoth-gilead. This city should have already been returned under the terms of the informal treaty made in Ahab's chariot (see note at 20:34). The exact location of this city is disputed, but it had a history of serving as an important administrative center for Israelite holdings in Transjordan. The best explanation for the statement that Jehoshaphat **went to visit the king of Israel** was that he was reporting for duty as a loyal servant—as a vassal of Ahab.

22:4-5 Jehoshaphat's words in these two verses reflect the two different roles he was playing. In verse 4, his words show that he was a faithful vassal of Ahab, but in verse 5, Jehoshaphat, the pious king of Judah, wanted to consult a legitimate prophet of Yahweh.

22:6-7 Since these **prophets** came in response to Jehoshaphat's request, one might expect them to be followers of the Lord, but Jehoshaphat had to persist in asking for a real **prophet of Yahweh**.

22:8 Ahab's attitude toward prophets was pragmatic and agnostic, and it was determined by political expediency. He did not care what truth was. Prophets were tools for the king's political purposes.

22:11-12 Prophets could communicate their message through pantomime (see the pantomime involving Jeremiah and the false prophet Hananiah; Jr 28). Horns were symbols of power; **iron horns** represented an even more unbreakable and unyielding power, and they gave King Ahab exactly the message he wanted to hear. Ahab's superiority in chariot warfare supported this confidence in Israel's victory.

22:13-14 Expediency was the theme of the advice given to **Micaiah** by the **messenger** sent by the king, but Micaiah's response was a statement of faithfulness and truth.

22:15-18 Micaiah was so sarcastic that **the king** recognized his irony. He demanded that the prophet tell him **the truth**. Micaiah then gave Ahab a message from the Lord—a vision

anything but the truth in the name of Yahweh?"

[17] So Micaiah said:

> I saw all Israel scattered on the hills
> like sheep without a shepherd.[a]
> And the Lord said,
> "They have no master;
> let everyone return home in peace."[b]

[18] So the king of Israel said to Jehoshaphat, "Didn't I tell you he never prophesies good about me, but only disaster?"

[19] Then Micaiah said, "Therefore, hear the word of the Lord: I saw the Lord sitting on His throne,[c] and the whole heavenly •host[d] was standing by Him at His right hand and at His left hand. [20] And the Lord said, 'Who will entice Ahab to march up and fall at Ramoth-gilead?'[e] So one was saying this and another was saying that.

[21] "Then a spirit came forward, stood before the Lord, and said, 'I will entice him.'

[22] "The Lord asked him, 'How?'

"He said, 'I will go and become a lying spirit[f] in the mouth of all his prophets.'

"Then He said, 'You will certainly entice him and prevail.[g] Go and do that.'

[23] "You see, the Lord has put a lying spirit into the mouth of all these prophets of yours, and the Lord has pronounced disaster against you."

[24] Then Zedekiah[h] son of Chenaanah came up, hit Micaiah in the face, and demanded, "Did[A] the Spirit of the Lord leave me to speak to you?"[i]

[25] Micaiah replied, "You will soon see when

you go to hide yourself in an inner chamber on that day."[j]

[26] Then the king of Israel ordered, "Take Micaiah and return him to Amon, the governor of the city, and to Joash, the king's son,[k] [27] and say, 'This is what the king says: Put this guy in prison[l] and feed him only bread and water[B] until I come back safely.'"

[28] But Micaiah said, "If you ever return safely, the Lord has not spoken through me."[m] Then he said, "Listen, all you people!"[C,n]

Ahab's Death

[29] Then[o] the king of Israel and Judah's King Jehoshaphat went up to Ramoth-gilead.[p] [30] But the king of Israel said to Jehoshaphat, "I will disguise[q] myself and go into battle, but you wear your royal attire." So the king of Israel disguised himself and went into battle.[r]

[31] Now the king of Aram had ordered his 32 chariot commanders,[s] "Do not fight with anyone at all except the king of Israel."[t]

[32] When the chariot commanders saw Jehoshaphat, they shouted, "He must be the king of Israel!" So they turned to fight against him, but Jehoshaphat cried out. [33] When the chariot commanders saw that he was not the king of Israel, they turned back from pursuing him.

[34] But a man drew his bow[u] without taking special aim and struck the king of Israel through the joints of his armor. So he said to his charioteer, "Turn around and take me out of the battle,[D] for I am badly wounded!"[v]

[35] The battle raged throughout that day, and the king was propped up in his chariot facing the Arameans. He died that evening,[w] and

a22:17 Nm 27:16-17; Mt 9:36; Mk 6:34
b1Kg 22:35-36
c22:19 Is 6:1; Dn 7:9
dJb 1:6; Dn 7:10; Heb 1:7
e22:20 1Kg 22:4
f22:22 Jdg 9:23; 1Sm 16:14; Jr 20:7; Ezk 14:9
g2Th 2:11
h22:24 1Kg 22:11
i2Ch 18:23
j22:25 1Kg 20:30
k22:26 1Kg 22:40
l22:27 2Ch 16:10; Heb 11:36
m22:28 Dt 18:22
nMc 1:2
o22:29-33 2Ch 18:28-32
p22:29 1Kg 22:4
q22:30 1Sm 28:8
r2Ch 35:22
s22:31 1Kg 20:1,16
t2Ch 18:30
u22:34 2Kg 9:24
v2Ch 35:23
w22:34-35 1Kg 22:17,28; 2Ch 18:33-34

A22:24 Lit Which way did   B22:27 Lit him on bread of oppression and water of oppression   C22:28 LXX omits Then he said, "Listen, all you people!"   D22:34 LXX; MT reads camp

---

of **sheep without a shepherd**. This should have recalled the king's role as shepherd, but Ahab rejected this warning.

22:19-23 Some see a disconnect and an abrupt change in topic between verses 18 and 19, but the transition is consistent with the same man in the same context, engaging in rhetorical piling-on to make his point. How literally accurate is this presentation of God and His heavenly court (cp. Jb 1-2)? Probably as accurate as human language could ever be when describing eternal, heavenly realities that are beyond our customary experiences. A more difficult issue is God's usage of **a lying spirit** to accomplish His purposes. Similarly, God's anger "stirred up" David (2Sm 24:1) to sin by permitting Satan to incite David to sin (1Ch 21:1). Without pretending to answer all the questions about this issue, we can say that God, at the least, *permitted* a lying spirit to mislead Ahab for a time. Note too that the deceit was given to prophets who were already presenting false witness. In the end, the true prophet told Ahab the truth—he would die if he went to battle.

22:24-28 The remainder of this scene hardened the hostile

positions toward the prophet Micaiah that had already been taken by the king.

22:29-30 Some critics find a discrepancy and a second literary source in Ahab's instructions for Jehoshaphat to put on his **royal attire** when he already had it on in verse 10. However, it is reasonable to suggest that Jehoshaphat had changed out of these for the trip to battle at **Ramoth-gilead**. Both kings probably arrived at the site of battle in war armor rather than royal clothes. It might have seemed prudent to the vassal king to accept the strategy that ordered him to go into battle in royal robes, for this would typically draw heat away from Ahab, the superior king.

22:31-36 If, as the Assyrian report of the battle of Qarqar indicated, Ahab was stronger in chariotry than Ben-hadad, it was poor strategy to meet Ahab in a direct chariot battle. Perhaps concentrating his chariots on Ahab himself was a good alternate strategy for Ben-hadad. Ahab's counter strategy, having Jehoshaphat serve as the bait for such an attack, seemed to neutralize Ben-hadad's tactics. But God accomplished what human cunning could neither bring

blood from his wound flowed into the bottom of the chariot. ³⁶ Then the cry rang out in the army as the sun set, declaring:

> Each man to his own city,
> and each man to his own land!^a

³⁷ So the king died and was brought to Samaria. They buried the king in Samaria.^b ³⁸ Then someone washed the chariot at the pool of Samaria. The dogs licked up his blood, and the prostitutes bathed in it, according to the word of the Lord that He had spoken.^c ³⁹ The rest of the events of Ahab's reign, along with all his accomplishments, including the ivory palace^d he built, and all the cities he built, are written in the Historical Record of Israel's Kings.^e ⁴⁰ Ahab rested with his fathers,^f and his son Ahaziah^g became king in his place.

Judah's King Jehoshaphat

⁴¹ Jehoshaphat^h son of Asa became king over Judah in the fourth year of Israel's King Ahab. ⁴² Jehoshaphat was 35 years old when he became king; he reigned 25 years in Jerusalem. His mother's name was Azubah daughter of Shilhi. ⁴³ He walked in all the ways of his father Asa;ⁱ he did not turn away from them but did what was right in the Lord's sight. However, the •high places were not taken away;^A the people still sacrificed and burned incense

on the high places.^j ⁴⁴ Jehoshaphat also made peace with the king of Israel.^k

⁴⁵ The rest of the events of Jehoshaphat's reign, along with the might he exercised and how he waged war, are written in the Historical Record of Judah's Kings.^l ⁴⁶ He removed from the land the rest of the male cult prostitutes who were left from the days of his father Asa.^m ⁴⁷ There was no king in Edom;ⁿ a deputy served as king. ⁴⁸ Jehoshaphat made ships of Tarshish^o to go to Ophir^p for gold, but they did not go because the ships were wrecked at Ezi-on-geber.^q ⁴⁹ At that time, Ahaziah^r son of Ahab said to Jehoshaphat, "Let my servants go with your servants in the ships," but Jehoshaphat was not willing. ⁵⁰ Jehoshaphat rested with his fathers and was buried with them in the city of his ancestor David.^s His son Jehoram^t became king in his place.

Israel's King Ahaziah

⁵¹ Ahaziah^u son of Ahab became king over Israel in Samaria^v in the seventeenth year of Judah's King Jehoshaphat^w and reigned over Israel two years. ⁵² He did what was evil in the Lord's sight.^x He walked in the way of his father,^y in the way of his mother,^z and in the way of Jeroboam son of Nebat, who had caused Israel to sin.^{aa} ⁵³ He served •Baal and worshiped him.^{ab} He provoked the Lord God of Israel just as his father had done.^{ac}

---

^a22:36 2Sm 20:1; 1Kg 12:16; 22:17; 2Kg 14:12
^b22:37 1Kg 16:28
^c22:38 1Kg 21:19
^d22:39 Am 3:15
^e1Kg 16:27
^f22:40 1Kg 16:28
^g2Kg 1:2
^h22:41 2Ch 20:31
ⁱ22:43 1Kg 15:11 /1Kg 15:14
^k22:44 1Kg 22:2,4
^l22:45 1Kg 15:23; 2Ch 20:34
^m22:46 1Kg 15:12
ⁿ22:47 2Sm 8:14; 2Kg 3:9
^o22:48 1Kg 10:22
^p1Kg 9:28
^q1Kg 9:26
^r22:49 1Kg 22:40,51
^s22:50 1Kg 15:24; 2Ch 21:1
^t2Kg 1:17
^u22:51 1Kg 22:40
^v1Kg 16:24
^w1Kg 22:41-50
^x22:52 1Kg 15:26
^y1Kg 21:25-26
^z1Kg 16:31; 18:4; 21:25
^{aa}1Kg 12:28-33
^{ab}22:53 Jdg 2:11; 1Kg 16:32
^{ac}1Kg 16:33; 21:25

---

^A22:43 LXX, Syr, Vg read *he did not remove the high places*

---

about nor prevent by ordaining the flight of a randomly shot arrow.

22:37-38 The Bible writers, at this point, were able to live with partial fulfillment of Elijah's prophecy about Ahab's death. One part was fulfilled when the **dogs licked up his blood**, though Ahab did not die at the place the prophecy indicated (see note at 21:19-24). Later on dogs licked up the blood of one of Ahab's sons in Jezreel when Joram's body was dumped there (2Kg 9:24-26). Possibly this later event marks the complete fulfillment of the prophecy from 1Kg 21:19-24 since a fate pronounced over a father can be representatively fulfilled in his son and since, according to ancient understanding, the blood of a father courses through the veins of his son.

22:39 Ahab's **ivory palace** was probably a palace decorated with paneling containing ivory inlay.

22:40 Some interpreters argue that the statement that Ahab **rested with his fathers** is proof that the king died in peace and the text is a fictional recension. This conclusion is suggested by the fact that this statement is missing from the closers of other kings who died violently. However, to give this much weight to an irregularity in the formal closer opens the question of what to do with the fact that Ahab had no formulaic burial statement. Does

this then prove that Ahab was never buried (see v. 37)? Of course not.

22:41-44 More is said about King **Jehoshaphat** in the record of Ahab than is said about him in his own record. The formal statements are ordinary. The evaluative part tells us that Jehoshaphat was a good king, but the fact that he made **peace with the king of Israel** may contain a veiled criticism (2Ch 19:1), particularly since making peace with Israel meant accepting a vassal role to the king of Israel.

22:45-50 Despite Asa's good intentions, his reforms left some work undone. His son **Jehoshaphat** had to remove the remaining **male cult prostitutes**. Edom seems to have been controlled by Jehoshaphat through the agency of a deputy. But the most noteworthy event may have been the failed effort to revive the sea trade to Africa for **gold**. After one failed attempt, Jehoshaphat compromised his loyalty to the house of Ahab in refusing to cooperate with **Ahaziah** in another attempt at restoring that trade. Again, we cannot realize the importance of this refusal unless we know that Jehoshaphat was a vassal king to Israel.

22:51-53 The account of **Ahaziah** is contained at the end of 1 Kings and the beginning of 2 Kings. The assessment of his reign is simple: **He did what was evil in the Lord's sight** in that he supported the worship of **Baal** (Baal-melkart; see note at 16:23-28).

2 Kings

Introduction

See the Introduction to 1 Kings for the introductory material.

Outline of 2 Kings

I. The Divided Kingdom: From Israel's Ahaziah to the Fall of Israel (1:1–17:41)
  - A. Ahaziah and the prophet Elijah (1:1-18)
  - B. Elijah succeeded by Elisha (2:1-25)
  - C. Israel's King Joram (3:1-27)
  - D. Elisha's ministry of miracles (4:1–8:15)
  - E. Judah's King Joram (8:16-24)
  - F. Judah's King Ahaziah (8:25-29)
  - G. Israel's King Jehu and the prophet Elisha (9:1–10:36)
  - H. Queen Athaliah (11:1-16)
  - I. Three good kings: Joash, Amaziah, Azariah (11:17–15:7)
  - J. Five bad kings: Zechariah, Shallum, Menahem, Pekahiah, Pekah (15:8-31)
  - K. Jotham (15:32-38)
  - L. Ahaz (16:1-20)
  - M. Hoshea and God's indictment against Israel (17:1-41)

II. The Kingdom of Judah: From King Hezekiah to the Captivity (18:1–25:30)
  - A. Revival under Hezekiah and apostasy (18:1–21:26)
  - B. Revival under Josiah and apostasy (22:1–25:7)
  - C. Jerusalem falls to the Babylonians (25:8-30)

Ahaziah's Sickness and Death

1 After the death of Ahab, Moab[a] rebelled against Israel.[b] [2]Ahaziah[c] had fallen through the latticed window of his upper room in Samaria[d] and was injured. So he sent messengers instructing them: "Go inquire of Baal-zebub,[A,e] the god of Ekron,[f] if I will recover from this injury."[g]

[3]But the angel of the LORD said to Elijah the Tishbite,[h] "Go and meet the messengers of the king of Samaria[i] and ask them, 'Is it because there is no God in Israel that you are going to inquire of Baal-zebub, the god of Ekron?' [4]Therefore, this is what the LORD says: 'You will not get up from your sickbed—you will certainly die.'" Then Elijah left.

[5]The messengers returned to the king, who asked them, "Why have you come back?"

[6]They replied, "A man came to meet us and said, 'Go back to the king who sent you and declare to him: This is what the LORD says: Is it because there is no God in Israel that you're sending these men to inquire of Baal-zebub, the god of Ekron? Therefore, you will not get up from your sickbed—you will certainly die.'"

[7]The king asked them, "What sort of man came up to meet you and spoke those words to you?"

[8]They replied, "A hairy man with a leather belt around his waist."[j]

He said, "It's Elijah the Tishbite."[k]

[9]So King Ahaziah sent a captain of 50 with his 50 men[l] to Elijah. When the captain went up to him, he was sitting on top of the hill. He announced, "Man of God,[m] the king declares, 'Come down!'"

[10]Elijah responded to the captain of the 50, "If I am a man of God, may fire come down from heaven and consume you and your 50 men." Then fire came down from heaven and consumed him and his 50 men.[n]

[11]So the king sent another captain of 50 with his 50 men to Elijah. He took in the situation[B] and announced, "Man of God, this is what the king says: 'Come down immediately!'"

[12]Elijah responded, "If I am a man of God, may fire come down from heaven and consume you and your 50 men." So a divine fire[C] came down from heaven and consumed him and his 50 men.

[13]Then the king sent a third captain of 50 with his 50 men. The third captain of 50 went up and fell on his knees in front of Elijah and begged him, "Man of God,[o] please let my life and the lives of these 50 servants of yours be precious in your sight.[p] [14]Already fire has come down from heaven and consumed the first two captains of 50 with their fifties, but this time let my life be precious in your sight."

[15]The angel of the LORD[q] said to Elijah, "Go down with him. Don't be afraid of him."[r] So he got up and went down with him to the king.

[16]Then Elijah said to King Ahaziah, "This is what the LORD says: 'Because you have sent messengers to inquire of Baal-zebub, the god of Ekron—is it because there is no God in Israel for you to inquire of His will?—you will not get up from your sickbed; you will certainly die.'"

Cross references

[a]1:1 Gn 19:37; 2Sm 8:2
[b]2Kg 3:5
[c]1:2 1Kg 22:40,51-53
[d]1Kg 16:24; 22:51
[e]Jdg 10:6
[f]Jos 13:3; 2Kg 1:16
[g]2Kg 8:8-9
[h]1:3 1Kg 19:7
[i]1Sm 28:7-8
[j]1:8 Zch 13:4; Mt 3:4
[k]1Kg 17:1
[l]1:9 2Kg 6:13-14
[m]1Kg 13:1
[n]1:10 1Kg 18:36-38
[o]1:13 1Kg 13:1
[p]1Sm 26:21; Ps 72:14
[q]1:15 1Kg 19:7; 2Kg 1:3
[r]Jr 1:17; Ezk 2:6

[A]1:2 = Lord of the Flies   [B]1:11 Lit He answered   [C]1:12 Lit a fire of God

---

1:1 This brief statement about the Moabite rebellion and the later complete record of that war (3:4-27) brackets data that deals with Ahaziah, Elijah, and Joram. This bracketing indicates that all these materials should be related to the rebellion.

1:2 The first incident thus bracketed is Ahaziah's injury and subsequent query of **Baal-zebub**, "Lord of the Flies." Baal-zebub was the god of **Ekron**, one of the five cities of the Philistine pentapolis. Several scholars suggest that Baal-zebub is a mocking corruption of Baal-zebul ("Lord of Glory"). Turning to pagan deities was disloyalty to God and, by a slight extension of Ex 22:20, worthy of death. The bracketing hinted that one reason for losing the Moabite war was the idolatry of Israel described here.

1:3-4 The author tells us that **the angel** told Elijah what to say, **then Elijah left**, apparently after delivering the message. With an obedient prophet, compliance is implicitly simultaneous with command. Elijah condemned King Ahaziah for seeking counsel from a pagan deity. Ahaziah showed the same unbelieving pragmatism his father Ahab had when Ahab looked for a prophet who would give him the answer he wanted (1Kg 22:8). Elijah challenged King Ahaziah on this false worship. The question, **Is it because there**

is no God in Israel, rhetorically highlighted Ahaziah's lack of faith (v. 16). Then Elijah announced that Ahaziah would die.

1:9-10 Here is an encounter reminiscent of Elijah's conflict with the priests of Baal (1Kg 18) and of Moses' conflict with Pharaoh (Ex 7–11).

1:11-12 The king foolishly trusted in his power again and sent another company of **50 men** to be destroyed. Again we see the severity of God against the representatives of God's enemies.

1:13-15 The **third captain** had learned the lesson of God's power and appealed for mercy. At this point God, in contrast to the pattern of speaking directly through Elijah (vv. 10,12), sent an angel (cp. vv. 3-4) to instruct **Elijah** to go with the company.

1:16 Because of Ahaziah's rejection of God, Elijah again declared that he would not rise from his **sickbed**. Perhaps at this point Ahaziah recognized the power of God, but there is no evidence that it affected his attitudes and behavior.

1:17-18 **Ahaziah's** record ends with the statements of his death and the succession of his brother, **Joram**.

2:1-25 The departure of the prophet Elijah is described in this chapter. There was a literary reason for bracketing the departure of Elijah within the references to the Moab-

[17]Ahaziah died according to the word of the LORD that Elijah had spoken. Since he had no son, Joram[A,a] became king in his place. This happened in the second year of Judah's King Jehoram[b] son of Jehoshaphat.[B] [18]The rest of the events of Ahaziah's reign, along with his accomplishments, are written in the Historical Record of Israel's Kings.[C,c]

Elijah in the Whirlwind

2 The time had come for the LORD to take Elijah up to heaven[d] in a whirlwind.[e] Elijah and Elisha[f] were traveling from Gilgal,[g] [2]and Elijah said to Elisha,[h] "Stay here;[i] the LORD is sending me on to Bethel."[j]

But Elisha replied, "As the LORD lives and as you yourself live, I will not leave you."[k] So they went down to Bethel.

[3]Then the sons of the prophets[l] who were at Bethel came out to Elisha and said, "Do you know that the LORD will take your master away from you today?"[m]

He said, "Yes, I know. Be quiet."

[4]Elijah said to him, "Elisha, stay here; the LORD is sending me to Jericho."[n]

But Elisha said, "As the LORD lives and as you yourself live, I will not leave you." So they went to Jericho.

[5]Then the sons of the prophets who were in Jericho came up to Elisha and said, "Do you know that the LORD will take your master away from you today?"

He said, "Yes, I know. Be quiet."

[6]Elijah said to him, "Stay here; the LORD is sending me to the Jordan."[o]

But Elisha said, "As the LORD lives and as you yourself live, I will not leave you." So the two of them went on.

[7]Fifty men from the sons of the prophets came and stood facing them from a distance while the two of them stood by the Jordan. [8]Elijah took his mantle,[p] rolled it up, and struck the waters, which parted to the right and left. Then the two of them crossed over on dry ground.[q] [9]After they had crossed over, Elijah said to Elisha, "Tell me what I can do for you before I am taken from you."

So Elisha answered, "Please, let me inherit two shares[D] of your spirit."[r]

[10]Elijah replied, "You have asked for something difficult. If you see me being taken from you,[s] you will have it. If not, you won't."

[11]As they continued walking and talking, a chariot of fire with horses of fire[t] suddenly appeared and separated the two of them. Then Elijah went up into heaven in the whirlwind.[u] [12]As Elisha watched, he kept crying out, "My father, my father, the chariots and horsemen of Israel!"[v] Then he never saw Elijah again. He took hold of his own clothes and tore them into two pieces.[w]

Elisha Succeeds Elijah

[13]Elisha picked up the mantle[x] that had

Cross-reference column

[a]1:17 2Kg 3:1-3
[b]1Kg 22:50
[c]1:18 1Kg 22:39
[d]2:1 Gn 5:24; Heb 11:5
[e]2Kg 2:11
[f]1Kg 19:16-21
[g]Jos 4:19; 2Kg 4:38
[h]2:2 1Kg 19:16,19-21
[i]Ru 1:15
[j]1Kg 12:28-29
[k]1Sm 1:26; 2Kg 4:30
[l]2:3 1Sm 10:5; 1Kg 20:35; 2Kg 4:1,38
[m]Gn 5:24
[n]2:4 Jos 6:16; 1Kg 16:34
[o]2:6 Jos 3:8; Mt 3:5-6,13
[p]2:8 1Kg 19:13,19
[q]Ex 14:21-22; Jos 3:14-17
[r]2:9 Nm 11:16-25; Dt 21:15-17
[s]2:10 Ac 1:9-11
[t]2:11 2Kg 6:17
[u]2Kg 2:1
[v]2:12 2Kg 13:14
[w]Gn 37:29,34
[x]2:13 1Kg 19:19

A1:17 Lit *Jehoram*; 2Kg 8:16   B1:17 LXX omits *in the second year . . . Jehoshaphat*   C1:18 LXX adds 4 more vv. here similar to 2Kg 3:1-3.   D2:9 Two shares is the inheritance of blessing for the firstborn son; Dt 21:17. Here Elisha is asking for the leadership role among the prophets.

---

ite rebellion—it related Elijah's departure to the successful Moabite rebellion. This account, with its overtones of God's miraculous presence, would have reminded the reader that royal unfaithfulness, not any absence on God's part, caused this loss of empire.

2:1 The route of travel from northerly **Gilgal**, through Bethel, and then to Jericho, showed that this was not the well-known Gilgal near Jericho. The exact location of this Gilgal is unknown.

2:2 In this incident **Elijah** repeatedly urged **Elisha** to remain behind, perhaps to test his determination to be formally recognized as Elijah's successor. Persistence was a key trait of faithful prophets.

2:3 The presence of godly **sons of the prophets** indicated that prophets of Yahweh were still tolerated around **Bethel**, despite Bethel's illegal worship. The conversations show that Elijah's impending departure was common knowledge.

2:4-6 Again **Elisha** was urged to remain behind, again he insisted on following, and again the prophets—this time the **prophets** of **Jericho**—declared that Elijah's departure was near. The repetition underscores the importance of these events.

2:7-8 God's power was demonstrated again, in a very historic and traditional way, as **Elijah** miraculously made a path through the **Jordan** River, reminiscent of God opening the

Red Sea when His people left Egypt (Ex 14:21-31) and opening the Jordan as Israel prepared to take the promised land (Jos 3:14-17). An audience of **prophets** was there to report this miracle to the people.

2:9-10 In an age of God's miracles and power encounters, the identity of the next great miracle worker was important. The **two shares** was an indicator of the legitimate heir. Elisha's renewed request for that position highlighted the importance of the role and that Elisha was the person to assume the role. Since this role had already been assigned to Elisha, this request was not arrogant. However, despite the fact that **Elisha** had already been designated as Elijah's heir (1Kg 19:19-21), Elisha must still observe Elijah's departure for this promise to be implemented.

2:11 Adding marvelous deed upon marvelous deed was additional evidence of God's power for those who were willing to see (Is 6:9-10).

2:12 The words **chariots and horsemen of Israel** show that the value of the miracle-working men of God was more than just moral or didactic. They were channels for real power. These words would be repeated at Elisha's death (13:14). In the case of Elisha, there were specifically military grounds for the phrase as in the examples of miraculous military assistance rendered by Elisha in the wars with Aram (6:8–7:20).

2:13-15 Elijah's **mantle** showed that **Elisha** was the

fallen off Elijah and went back and stood on the bank of the Jordan. [14] Then he took the mantle Elijah had dropped and struck the waters. "Where is the LORD God of Elijah?" he asked. He struck the waters himself, and they parted to the right and the left, and Elisha crossed over.

[15] When the sons of the prophets from Jericho who were facing him saw him, they said, "The spirit of Elijah rests on Elisha." They came to meet him and bowed down to the ground in front of him.

[16] Then the sons of the prophets said to Elisha, "Since there are 50 strong men here with your servants, please let them go and search for your master. Maybe the Spirit of the LORD has carried him away and put him on one of the mountains or into one of the valleys."[a]

He answered, "Don't send them."

[17] However, they urged him to the point of embarrassment,[b] so he said, "Send them." They sent 50 men, who looked for three days but did not find him. [18] When they returned to him in Jericho[c] where he was staying, he said to them, "Didn't I tell you not to go?"

[19] Then the men of the city said to Elisha, "Even though our lord can see that the city's location is good, the water is bad and the land unfruitful."[d]

[20] He replied, "Bring me a new bowl and put salt in it."[e]

After they had brought him one, [21] Elisha went out to the spring of water, threw salt in it,[f] and said, "This is what the LORD says: 'I have healed this water. No longer will death or unfruitfulness result from it.'" [22] Therefore, the water remains healthy to this very day according to the word that Elisha spoke.

[23] From there Elisha went up to Bethel.[g] As he was walking up the path, some small boys came out of the city and harassed him,[h] chanting, "Go up, baldy! Go up, baldy!" [24] He turned around, looked at them, and cursed them in the name of the LORD.[i] Then two female bears came out of the woods and mauled 42 of the children. [25] From there Elisha went to Mount Carmel,[j] and then he returned to Samaria.[k]

Israel's King Joram

3 Joram son of Ahab became king over Israel in Samaria during the eighteenth year of Judah's King Jehoshaphat and reigned 12 years.[l] [2] He did what was evil in the LORD's sight, but not like his father and mother,[m] for he removed the sacred pillar of •Baal his father had made. [3] Nevertheless, Joram clung to the sins that Jeroboam son of Nebat had caused Israel to commit.[n] He did not turn away from them.

a2:16 1Kg 18:12; Ac 8:39
b2:17 Jdg 3:25; 2Kg 8:11
c2:18 2Kg 2:4
d2:19 Dt 28:15-18; Jos 6:26; 1Kg 16:34
e2:20 Lv 2:13; Nm 18:19
f2:21-22 Ex 15:25-26; 2Kg 4:41; 6:6
g2:23 2Kg 2:2-3
h2Ch 36:16; Ps 31:17-18
i2:24 Lv 26:21-22; Neh 13:25
j2:25 1Kg 18:19-20
k1Kg 16:24; 2Kg 1:2
l3:1 2Kg 1:17
m3:2 1Kg 21:25-26
n3:3 1Kg 16:31-32

Elisha's Spring at Jericho, which is the source for Elisha's well (2:19-22).

legitimate heir to **Elijah**. We should not attribute magic to the mantle any more than we attribute it to Moses' staff (Ex 14:16); the mantle was a concrete symbol of God's power to the watchers. The **sons of the prophets** recognized Elisha's new role with proper deference.

2:16-18 The unsuccessful search for Elijah's body confirmed that a miraculous work of God had occurred.

2:19-22 **Elisha** confirmed his role as a channel for God's works by performing a miracle—one that demonstrated the practical benefits of God's great acts.

2:23-24 In a context in which the destiny of the nation depended on its willingness to recognize God, and where the "man of God" (1:10) had replaced the apostate king as God's representative, it is understandable that severe penalty came to those who mocked God's chosen servant. God's severity had a purpose. The word translated as **boys** is often used for mature men (Boaz's "servant," Ru 2:5), but the behavior of the group suggests they were young. In all likelihood the **children** were preteens or younger teens. This passage is often overstated as if all the mockers were killed; **mauled** often connotes being wounded rather than killed.

2:25 Elisha lived at **Samaria** under the eye of the unfaithful kings of Israel.

3:1-3 These formal statements mark the beginning of Joram's record. **Joram** was bad, but not as bad as Ahab and Jezebel. He suppressed Baalism by removing Baal's **sacred pillar** (probably a short sacred stone rather than a column;

Moab's Rebellion against Israel

[4] King Mesha of Moab[a] was a sheep breeder. He used to pay[b] the king of Israel 100,000 lambs and the wool of 100,000 rams,[c] [5] but when Ahab died, the king of Moab rebelled against the king of Israel.[d] [6] So King Joram marched out from Samaria at that time and mobilized all Israel. [7] Then he sent a message to King Jehoshaphat[e] of Judah: "The king of Moab has rebelled against me.[f] Will you go with me to fight against Moab?"

Jehoshaphat said, "I will go. I am as you are, my people as your people, my horses as your horses."[g] [8] Then he asked, "Which route should we take?"

Joram replied, "The route of the Wilderness of Edom."

[9] So the king of Israel, the king of Judah, and the king of Edom[h] set out. After they had traveled their indirect route for seven days, they had no water for the army or their animals.

[10] Then the king of Israel said, "Oh no, the LORD has summoned three kings, only to hand them over to Moab."

[11] But Jehoshaphat said, "Isn't there a prophet of the LORD here? Let's inquire of *Yahweh through him."[i]

One of the servants of the king of Israel answered, "Elisha son of Shaphat,[j] who used to pour water on Elijah's hands, is here."

[12] Jehoshaphat affirmed, "The LORD's words are with him." So the king of Israel and Jehoshaphat and the king of Edom went to him.[k]

[13] However, Elisha said to King Joram of Israel, "We have nothing in common. Go to the prophets of your father and your mother!"[l]

But the king of Israel replied, "No, because it is the LORD who has summoned these three kings to hand them over to Moab."

[14] Elisha responded, "As the LORD of *Hosts lives,[m] I stand before Him. If I did not have respect for King Jehoshaphat of Judah,[n] I would not look at you; I wouldn't take notice of you. [15] Now, bring me a musician."[o]

While the musician played,[p] the LORD's hand[q] came on Elisha. [16] Then he said, "This is what the LORD says: 'Dig ditch after ditch in this *wadi.' [17] For the LORD says, 'You will not see wind or rain, but the wadi will be filled with water,[r] and you will drink—you and your cattle and your animals.' [18] This is easy in the LORD's sight.[s] He will also hand Moab over to you.[t] [19] Then you must attack every fortified city and every choice city. You must cut down every good tree and stop up every spring of water. You must ruin every good piece of land with stones."

a3:4 Gn 19:37; 2Kg 1:1
b2Sm 8:2
cIs 16:1-2
d3:5 2Kg 1:1
e3:7 1Kg 22:41-50
f2Kg 1:1
g1Kg 22:4
h3:9 1Kg 22:47; 2Kg 8:20
i3:11 1Kg 22:7
j1Kg 19:16,19-21; 2Kg 2:9
k3:12 2Kg 2:25
l3:13 1Kg 18:19,22; 22:6
m3:14 1Kg 17:1; 2Kg 5:16
n1Kg 22:41-50
o3:15 1Sm 10:5
p1Sm 16:23
qEzk 3:14
r3:17 Ps 107:35; Is 32:2
s3:18 Gn 18:14
t2Kg 3:7

---

but see 10:26), but there were still hundreds of priests of Baal when he died.

3:4-5 Finally, the text returns to the Moabite rebellion (1:1). **Moab**, Edom, and Judah were all subject to Israel. At this point Israel was a much smaller "empire" than what had been overseen by Solomon in the southern kingdom, although **Ahab** had regained some trade privileges in Damascus (1Kg 20:34). Mentioning this rebellion at 1:1 and 3:4-5 puts Ahaziah's unfaithfulness and Elijah's departure clearly in the context of this war. Chapter 2 showed that God's miraculous power was still available. When the story of this rebellion is brought into the picture, the message is clear that Moab's rebellion succeeded because of Israel's continued unfaithfulness and the people's rejection of God's great works.

3:6-7 King Joram **mobilized all Israel** and both of his remaining vassal kings, Jehoshaphat of Judah and the king of Edom (v. 9). Jehoshaphat used essentially the same statement of political self-subjection to Joram that he had earlier used with Ahab: **my people as your people, my horses as your horses** (1Kg 22:4).

3:8 The choice of the invasion **route** was particularly deliberate. Moab lay directly across the Dead Sea from Judah. Moab was most directly approached from the north, but the Moabite Stone indicates that Moab may have concentrated their military power in the north. The choice to attack Moab from the south through **Edom** thus evaded the Moabite strong points and helped to assure Edom's involvement in the campaign.

3:9-10 For all their intentionality in choosing the direction of attack, the **indirect route** of the invading army might be better described as "wandering around." The combined

three armies faced total disaster. The circumstances (**no water**) seem more compatible with wandering around in the dry wadis of Edom rather than the relatively open areas of the Arabah.

3:11-12 Once again, **Jehoshaphat** pointed a king of Israel toward seeking counsel from **the LORD** (cp. 1Kg 22:5). Two surprising facts then emerged. The first was that the man of God, **Elisha**, was there. God providentially worked to make the miracles of Elisha available for the armies. But the familiarity between Elisha and the king's household is even more surprising. This resembles the surprise one feels when learning that one of Jesus' disciples was on close terms with the household of a hostile high priest (Jn 8:15-16). God sometimes ordains surprising relationships in order to further His purposes.

3:13 The man of God boldly stated God's attitude toward the apostate **Joram**. This structurally highlighted the apostasy of Israel and God's mercy in delivering the nearly helpless kings. For a king with as little faith in God as Joram, it was hubris to say, **It is the LORD who has summoned these three kings**.

3:14-18 God responded only because of the godly **Jehoshaphat**. Elisha's **musician** provided the setting in which he could attend to God rather than being distracted. The result was that Elisha received and communicated God's word, giving instructions for receiving God's deliverance. Once again miraculous works revealed God's character and power, but Israel continued to reject His miraculous works.

3:19 God's command to devastate Moab contrasted with His command to care for the land of Palestine (Dt 20:19).

²⁰About the time for the •grain offering[a] the next morning, water suddenly came from the direction of Edom and filled the land.

²¹All Moab had heard that the kings[b] had come up to fight against them. So all who could bear arms, from the youngest to the oldest, were summoned and took their stand at the border. ²²When they got up early in the morning, the sun was shining on the water, and the Moabites saw that the water across from them was red like blood.[c] ²³"This is blood!" they exclaimed. "The kings[d] have clashed swords and killed each other. So, to the spoil, Moab!"

²⁴However, when the Moabites came to Israel's camp, the Israelites attacked them, and they fled from them. So Israel went into the land and struck down the Moabites. ²⁵They destroyed the cities, and each of them threw stones to cover every good piece of land. They stopped up every spring of water and cut down every good tree. In the end, only the buildings of Kir-hareseth[e] were left. Then men with slings surrounded the city and attacked it.

²⁶When the king of Moab saw that the battle was too fierce for him, he took 700 swordsmen with him to try to break through to the king of Edom,[f] but they could not do it. ²⁷So he took his firstborn son,[g] who was to become king in his place, and offered him as a •burnt offering on the city wall. Great wrath was on the Israelites, and they withdrew from him and returned to their land.

The Widow's Oil Multiplied

4 One of the wives of the sons of the prophets[h] cried out to Elisha, "Your servant, my husband, has died. You know that your servant •feared the LORD.[i] Now the creditor is coming to take my two children as his slaves."[j]

²Elisha asked her, "What can I do for you? Tell me, what do you have in the house?"

She said, "Your servant has nothing in the house except a jar of oil."[k]

³Then he said, "Go and borrow empty containers from everyone—from all your neighbors. Do not get just a few.[l] ⁴Then go in and shut the door behind you and your sons, and

a3:20 Ex 29:39-40
b3:21 2Kg 3:9
c3:22 Ex 7:17,20
d3:23 2Kg 3:9
e3:25 Jr 48:31,36
f3:26 2Kg 3:9
g3:27 Dt 12:31; 2Kg 16:3
h4:1 2Kg 2:3,15
iPr 1:7; 9:10
jLv 25:39-41
k4:2 1Kg 17:12
l4:3 2Kg 3:16

Once again, the reader is struck by the severity of God. We should not expect to easily understand or explain God's judgments.

3:21-24 Moab, fully mobilized, attacked and was defeated. The full details of how this worked are not clear, but it is no surprise that three invading armies were able to defeat Moab.

3:25 Then the combined armies devastated Moab except for the capital city, **Kir-hareseth**, modern Kerak. This devastation was also a blow to the north-south caravan route that passed through Transjordan and particularly through the Moabite capital.

3:26-27 Finally the devastation came to the point at which the **king of Moab** offered his own crown prince and heir as a human sacrifice. The lesson of these two chapters is clear: God's miraculous power could bring unfaithful Israel to the verge of victory, but God could also take that victory away. Whether from battle fatigue in foreign lands, shock at the desperate step the king of Moab took in sacrificing his son, superstitious fear of the magic power that such a sacrifice aimed to produce, or from seeing the **wrath** (whether of the Moabites or of God Almighty; the text is unclear), the coalition **withdrew** and Moab remained independent though thoroughly devastated.

4:1-7:20 These four chapters demonstrate two themes. First, they record more miraculous encounters between the followers of Yahweh and the paganism of the Israelites. Second, they report the work of the prophets, the new representatives of God, in correcting the pain brought on by the failure of the kings, who had forsaken their sacred responsibilities. These encounters began with Elijah.

Up to this point, the records of this conflict have been incorporated into the overall chronological structure of these books. In these four chapters the treatment of miracles changes. The writer here recorded miracles separated from the sequential structure of the book. Because of this

technique some of the events involve anonymous kings whose chronological place may be unclear. The sign ministry of Elisha covered a long period. Therefore some of these events could have taken place as late as the period of weakness between the reigns of Jehu and his grandson, Jehoash (798–782 B.C.). Unless chronological sequence is explicitly indicated, these events should not be taken as chronologically arranged. The normal chronological pattern of 1 and 2 Kings resumes with the record of Jehoram, son of Jehoshaphat (8:16).

Since these chapters develop the theme of power encounters, they are best understood in terms of the lessons they taught and their strengthening of faith in Yahweh in conflict with their unfaithfulness and paganism. The data indicate that the reputation of the miracle-working men of God extended beyond Hebrew territory. Because of this reputation the prophets could, on occasion, act in an international context. This wider influence, like the influence of the Jewish synagogue in the exile and early Christian era, indicates that God was affecting the larger Gentile world.

4:1 The social evil in this incident had two causes: societal evolution that broke down the old tribal and clan responsibilities, and the moral callousness that grew out of apostasy. When people find themselves in changed societal conditions where the traditional safety nets have disappeared, godlessness can lead to the creation of destructive new norms and practices. This incident (vv. 1-7) showed the power of God to relieve the hurts and pains that were inevitable in an increasingly godless society. When the covenant laws, which specified the responsibilities of the clan and tribe, were functioning properly, enslavement for debt would not have happened. Disallowing such abuses was one responsibility of a godly, responsible relative (Hb go'el; "redeemer") or even the king himself.

4:2-7 A miraculous provision by the man of God, **Elisha**, compensated for the injustice and the failure of the system

pour oil into all these containers. Set the full ones to one side." [5] So she left.

After she had shut the door behind her and her sons, they kept bringing her containers, and she kept pouring.[a] [6] When they were full, she said to her son, "Bring me another container."

But he replied, "There aren't any more." Then the oil stopped.

[7] She went and told the man of God,[b] and he said, "Go sell the oil and pay your debt; you and your sons can live on the rest."[c]

The Shunammite Woman's Hospitality

[8] One day Elisha went to Shunem.[d] A prominent woman who lived there persuaded him to eat some food. So whenever he passed by, he stopped there to eat.[e] [9] Then she said to her husband, "I know that the one who often passes by here is a holy man of God, [10] so let's make a small room upstairs and put a bed, a table, a chair, and a lamp there for him. Whenever he comes, he can stay there."[f]

The Shunammite Woman's Son

[11] One day he came there and stopped and went to the room upstairs to lie down. [12] He ordered his attendant Gehazi,[g] "Call this Shunammite woman." So he called her and she stood before him.

[13] Then he said to Gehazi, "Say to her, 'Look, you've gone to all this trouble for us. What can we do for you?[h] Can we speak on your behalf to the king or to the commander of the army?'"

She answered, "I am living among my own people."

[14] So he asked, "Then what should be done for her?"

Gehazi answered, "Well, she has no son, and her husband is old."

[a]4:5 Mt 14:17-21
[b]4:7 1Kg 12:22
[c]1Kg 17:16
[d]4:8 Jos 19:18
[e]Mt 10:40-42; 3Jn 5-8
[f]4:10 1Kg 17:19
[g]4:12 2Kg 4:29-31; 5:20-27
[h]4:13 2Kg 4:2
[i]4:16 Gn 18:9-14; Lk 1:7-13
[j]2Kg 4:28
[k]4:23 Nm 10:10; 28:11
[m]2Sm 18:28; 2Kg 4:26
[n]4:25 1Kg 18:19-20
[o]2Kg 4:12
[p]2Kg 4:8,12
[q]4:27 Mt 28:9

[15] "Call her," Elisha said. So Gehazi called her, and she stood in the doorway. [16] Elisha said, "At this time next year you will have a son in your arms."[i]

Then she said, "No, my lord. Man of God, do not deceive your servant."[j]

[17] The woman conceived and gave birth to a son at the same time the following year, as Elisha had promised her.

The Shunammite's Son Raised

[18] The child grew and one day went out to his father and the harvesters.[k] [19] Suddenly he complained to his father, "My head! My head!"

His father told his servant, "Carry him to his mother." [20] So he picked him up and took him to his mother. The child sat on her lap until noon and then died. [21] Then she went up and laid him on the bed of the man of God, shut him in, and left.

[22] She summoned her husband and said, "Please send me one of the servants and one of the donkeys, so I can hurry to the man of God and then come back."

[23] But he said, "Why go to him today? It's not a New Moon or a Sabbath."[l]

She replied, "Everything is all right."[m]

[24] Then she saddled the donkey and said to her servant, "Hurry, don't slow the pace for me unless I tell you." [25] So she set out and went to the man of God at Mount Carmel.[n]

When the man of God saw her at a distance, he said to his attendant Gehazi,[o] "Look, there's the Shunammite woman.[p] [26] Run out to meet her and ask, 'Are you all right? Is your husband all right? Is your son all right?'"

And she answered, "Everything's all right."

[27] When she came up to the man of God at the mountain, she clung to his feet.[q] Gehazi came to push her away, but the man of God

---

that God had established but that apostasy had corrupted. The provision for the woman and her children was a private act, but the canonical record of this deed was a public witness to God's provision, and the story may have been well known before it became canonical.

4:8-10 The **man of God** made such an impression that one **prominent** family wished to show special hospitality to him. In a society that had become largely pagan, a display of friendship to the man of God possibly indicated faith in God.

4:13 Apparently Elisha could have influence with an ungodly **king** or other authorities. This is an example for Christians living in a corrupted political system. The woman expressed contentment with her situation.

4:15-16 The woman was barren in a society in which both pagans and worshipers of the Lord thought of barrenness as one of the curses from the gods. At the same time, any

act of power could be a vindication of God's truth. Therefore this special help for the woman was a witness for God. More specifically, it was a statement that God could still give blessings to those who were faithful to Him.

4:18-26 When death entered the home of the **Shunammite** family, there was another opportunity to show that God could miraculously bless. The OT promise of earthly blessings for keeping the law was a general promise, not an absolute promise to every faithful person. There were many people who had faith but were not rewarded with freedom and prosperity, as in the case of Naaman's Jewish servant girl (5:2). Nevertheless, any blessing is an example of God's care for His faithful ones. To common perception, for the Shunammite woman to lose her son could send a negative message about God's dispensing of blessings.

4:27 Elisha modeled both sensitivity and a recognition of his own limitations. His words **the LORD has hidden it from**

said, "Leave her alone—she is in severe anguish,[a] and the LORD has hidden it from me. He hasn't told me."

[28] Then she said, "Did I ask my lord for a son? Didn't I say, 'Do not deceive me?'"[b]

[29] So Elisha said to Gehazi, "Tuck your mantle[c] under your belt, take my staff with you, and go. If you meet anyone, don't stop to greet him, and if a man greets you, don't answer him.[d] Then place my staff on the boy's face."

[30] The boy's mother said to Elisha, "As the LORD lives and as you yourself live, I will not leave you."[e] So he got up and followed her.

[31] Gehazi went ahead of them and placed the staff on the boy's face, but there was no sound or sign of life, so he went back to meet Elisha and told him, "The boy didn't wake up."[f]

[32] When Elisha got to the house, he discovered the boy lying dead on his bed.[g] [33] So he went in, closed the door behind the two of them, and prayed to the LORD.[h] [34] Then he went up and lay on the boy:[i] he put mouth to mouth, eye to eye, hand to hand. While he bent down over him, the boy's flesh became warm.[j] [35] Elisha got up, went into the house, and paced back and forth. Then he went up and bent down over him again. The boy sneezed seven times and opened his eyes.[k]

[36] Elisha called Gehazi and said, "Call the Shunammite woman." He called her and she came. Then Elisha said, "Pick up your son." [37] She came, fell at his feet, and bowed to the ground; she picked up her son and left.[l]

The Deadly Stew

[38] When Elisha returned to Gilgal,[m] there was a famine[n] in the land. The sons of the prophets[o] were sitting at his feet.[A,p] He said to his attendant, "Put on the large pot and make stew for the sons of the prophets."

[39] One went out to the field to gather herbs and found a wild vine from which he gathered as many wild gourds as his garment would hold. Then he came back and cut them up into the pot of stew, but they were unaware of what they were.

[40] They served some for the men to eat, but when they ate the stew they cried out, "There's death in the pot,[q] man of God!" And they were unable to eat it.

[41] Then Elisha said, "Get some meal." He threw it into the pot and said, "Serve it for the people to eat." And there was nothing bad in the pot.[r]

The Multiplied Bread

[42] A man from Baal-shalishah[s] came to the man of God with his sack full of 20 loaves of barley bread from the first bread of the harvest. Elisha said, "Give it to the people to eat."[t]

[43] But Elisha's attendant asked, "What? Am I to set 20 loaves before 100 men?"[u]

"Give it to the people to eat," Elisha said, "for this is what the LORD says: 'They will eat, and they will have some left over.'" [44] So he gave it to them, and as the LORD had promised, they ate and had some left over.[v]

Cross references:
a4:27 Ru 1:19-21; 1Sm 1:15; Zch 12:10
b4:28 2Kg 4:16
c4:29 1Kg 18:46; 2Kg 9:1
d Lk 10:4
e4:30 2Kg 2:2,4,6
f4:31 Jn 11:11
g4:32 2Kg 4:21
h4:33 Mt 6:6
i4:34 1Kg 17:21-23
j Ac 20:10
k4:35 2Kg 8:5
l4:37 Heb 11:35
m4:38 2Kg 2:1
n Lv 26:26; 2Kg 8:1
o2Kg 2:3,5,7
p Lk 10:39; Ac 22:3
q4:40 Ex 10:17
r4:41 Ex 15:25; 2Kg 2:21
s4:42 1Sm 9:4
t Mt 14:17
u4:43 Lk 9:13; Jn 6:9
v4:43-44 Mt 14:20

A 4:38 Lit *sitting before him*

---

me showed limitation to the knowledge and power God granted him.

4:28 Her ecstatic hopes are suddenly dashed, and her spirits are lower now than they had been before she was blessed with a son. Some grief is too painful to share with just anyone. Concealing her thoughts from her husband and from Gehazi, the woman wanted to deal with Elisha, the source of her blessing.

4:29-31 When sent to bring healing to the woman's son, **Gehazi** was to be focused on the task. Gehazi's failed attempt to bring healing also revealed the human limitations of the man of God. Elisha had seemed confident that sending Gehazi was sufficient to heal the woman's son.

4:32-35 When Elisha arrived, he carried out a more complicated procedure for healing the son. In that day and time, even some sincere worshipers of the Lord might have taken this healing act to be a result of magical power given by God. In this way some may have mistakenly taken Elisha to be a man gifted with rare powers. Such notions are contrary to biblical revelation. We must understand that in the era of epic power encounters between the men of God and representatives of darkness, men such as Elisha performed spectacular feats only because they served as channels for God's miraculous power. There was no magic to it; nor were the powers given to the men of God in such a way as to

make the powers their own. Here Elisha's success was dependent on his prayer **to the LORD**.

4:38 Since the text had earlier placed **Elisha** and the prophets in a northern **Gilgal** near Bethel (see note at 2:1), this is likely that same northern Gilgal. The prophets' way of life, at least on some occasions, demanded that they forage for their food. Apparently they partly supported themselves by such foraging and partly by gifts from pious Israelites.

4:39-40 While foraging, one of the prophets **gathered** some poisonous **gourds**. This may have happened on other occasions as well, but this time the occasion gave an opportunity for a miraculous provision.

4:41 Elisha neutralized the poison with another miraculous deed. The lesson was that God's power could protect His people from careless dangers even in a serious famine.

4:42 Another opportunity for a miraculous provision occurred when a supporter brought a gift of **bread** to the prophets. This gift could indicate that the giver had rejected the apostate priesthood of the north since he gave this gift to the faithful prophets of the Lord. The location of **Baal-shalishah** is uncertain.

4:43-44 This miracle sounds remarkably similar to the feeding of the 5,000 in the NT—similar enough that one could wonder if there are deeply rooted, long-lived reasons for

Naaman's Disease Healed

5 Naaman,[a] commander of the army for the king of Aram, was a great man in his master's sight[A] and highly regarded[b] because through him, the LORD had given victory to Aram. The man was a brave warrior, but he had a skin disease.[c]

[2] Aram had gone on raids[d] and brought back from the land of Israel a young girl who served Naaman's wife. [3] She said to her mistress, "If only my master would go to[B] the prophet who is in Samaria, he would cure him of his skin disease."

[4] So Naaman went and told his master what the girl from the land of Israel had said. [5] Therefore, the king of Aram said, "Go and I will send a letter with you to the king of Israel."

So he went and took with him 750 pounds[C] of silver, 150 pounds[D] of gold, and 10 changes of clothes.[e] [6] He brought the letter to the king of Israel, and it read:

When this letter comes to you, note that I have sent you my servant Naaman for you to cure him of his skin disease.

[7] When the king of Israel read the letter, he tore his clothes[f] and asked, "Am I God,[g] killing and giving life that this man expects me to cure a man of his skin disease? Think it over and you will see that he is only picking a fight with[E] me."[h]

[8] When Elisha the man of God heard that the king of Israel tore his clothes, he sent a message to the king, "Why have you torn your clothes? Have him come to me, and he will know there is a prophet in Israel."[i] [9] So Naaman came with his horses and chariots and stood at the door of Elisha's house.

[10] Then Elisha sent him a messenger,[j] who said, "Go wash[k] seven times[l] in the Jordan and your flesh will be restored and you will be •clean."

[11] But Naaman got angry and left, saying, "I was telling myself: He will surely come out, stand and call on the name of •Yahweh his God, and will wave his hand[m] over the spot and cure the skin disease. [12] Aren't Abana and Pharpar, the rivers of Damascus, better than all the waters of Israel?[n] Could I not wash in them and be clean?" So he turned and left in a rage.[o]

[13] But his servants approached and said to him, "My father,[p] if the prophet had told you to do some great thing, would you not have done it? How much more should you do it when he tells you, 'Wash and be clean'?" [14] So Naaman went down and dipped himself in the

---

Cross references (center column):
a5:1 Lk 4:27
bEx 11:3
c2Kg 7:3,8
d5:2 2Kg 6:23; 13:20
e5:5 Jdg 14:12; 2Kg 5:22
f5:7 Gn 37:29; 2Kg 11:14
g5:7 Gn 30:2
h1Kg 20:7
i5:8 1Kg 22:7
j5:10 Nm 5:1-4
kJn 9:7
lLv 14:7
m5:11 Ex 7:19
n5:12 Is 8:6
oPr 14:17; 19:11
p5:13 2Kg 2:12; 6:21; 13:14

A5:1 Lit *man before his master*   B5:3 Lit *master was before*   C5:5 Lit *10 talents*   D5:5 Lit *6,000 shekels*   E5:7 Lit *only seeking an occasion against*

---

the similarities (Mt 14:13-21). Perhaps Jesus consciously imitated this episode as yet another indication that He was the fulfillment of the OT (Mt 5:17). Here the instructive value of the miraculous work includes elements such as questioning the sufficiency of the gift, making an insufficient gift sufficient, distributing the food, and having more than was needed. The global lesson is God's ability to provide.

5:1-27 This chapter gives an example of God's miracle-working influence reaching out to the world and impacting a pagan nation, possibly at a time when that nation was a deadly enemy of Israel. This incident could have occurred during the time of Hebrew weakness and Aramean strength that occurred between Jehu's revolution and the resurgence of Hebrew power under Jehoash.

5:1 Though **Naaman** was regarded as a great military leader, we cannot identify the specific **victory** that earned him this respect. The Hebrew word for Naaman's illness (**skin disease**) is the word routinely translated "leprosy," but scholars have long felt that its meaning is broader than Hansen's Disease.

5:2-3 The kidnapping of a **young** Hebrew **girl** recalls God's description, given through Amos, of this border warfare: "They threshed Gilead with iron sledges" (Am 1:3). Yet the young Hebrew captive, in an attitude of faith and resigned to the brutality of the age, seemed to have accepted her situation with a positive attitude and to have retained her personal faith in God. She was able to love her enemy, and she wished that her **master** could experience God's miraculous healing.

5:4-6 The willingness to seek healing from a foreign god does not necessarily indicate a high international opinion of the deity, but considering God's hand on the internal political affairs of Damascus (8:7-12), a measure of international standing existed for Yahweh, the God of the Israelites.

5:7 The reaction of the **king of Israel**, particularly his fear that Damascus was seeking a pretext for war, showed that this was a time of weakness for Israel.

5:8-9 These verses give the most explicit statement of the story's intent—that people might **know there** was **a prophet in Israel**. This can easily be seen as an OT missionary statement.

5:10-12 The sequence of events recorded here fits best into a time when Elisha's residence was near the **Jordan** River. This story suggests that the author wished to present God and His work on God's terms, not the terms that humans would expect. **Naaman** represents the politicians and others who seemed to feel that God should approach them on man's terms. God's sovereignty transcended showing deference to pagan politicians, but God's grace was still available for those politicians and pagans who respected God. The lesson that God demanded obedience would also have been significant for the Hebrew audience. The **Abana** and **Pharpar** rivers, flowing from the slopes of Mount Hermon and coming to an end in the desert marshes east of **Damascus**, probably were more attractive and cleaner than the ever muddy Jordan.

5:13-14 Naaman's **servants** persuaded him to give up human pride, and then he was healed.

Jordan seven times, according to the command of the man of God. Then his skin was restored and became like the skin of a small boy, and he was clean.[a]

[15] Then Naaman and his whole company went back to the man of God, stood before him, and declared, "I know there's no God in the whole world except in Israel.[b] Therefore, please accept a gift[c] from your servant."

[16] But Elisha said, "As the Lord lives,[d] I stand before Him. I will not accept it."[e] Naaman urged him to accept it, but he refused.

[17] Naaman responded, "If not, please let your servant be given as much soil as a pair of mules can carry,[f] for your servant will no longer offer a *burnt offering or a sacrifice to any other god but Yahweh.[g] [18] However, in a particular matter may the Lord pardon your servant: When my master, the king of Aram, goes into the temple of Rimmon to worship and I, as his right-hand man,[A,h] bow in the temple of Rimmon—when I bow[B] in the temple of Rimmon, may the Lord pardon your servant in this matter."

[19] So he said to him, "Go in peace."[i]

Gehazi's Greed Punished

After Naaman had traveled a short distance from Elisha, [20] Gehazi,[j] the attendant of Elisha the man of God, thought: My master has let this Aramean Naaman off lightly by not accepting from him what he brought. As the Lord lives,[k] I will run after him and get something from him.

[21] So Gehazi pursued Naaman. When Naaman saw someone running after him, he got down from the chariot to meet him and asked, "Is everything all right?"

[22] Gehazi said, "It's all right.[l] My master has sent me to say, 'I have just now discovered that two young men from the sons of the prophets have come to me from the hill country of Ephraim. Please give them 75 pounds[c] of silver and two changes of clothes.'"[m]

[23] But Naaman insisted, "Please, accept 150 pounds."[D] He urged Gehazi and then packed 150 pounds[D] of silver in two bags with two changes of clothes. Naaman gave them to two of his young men who carried them ahead of Gehazi. [24] When Gehazi came to the hill,[E,n] he took the gifts from them and stored them in the house. Then he dismissed the men, and they left.

[25] Gehazi came and stood by his master. "Where did you go, Gehazi?" Elisha asked him.

"Your servant didn't go anywhere," he replied.

[26] But Elisha questioned him, "Wasn't my spirit[o] there[F] when the man got down from his chariot to meet you? Is it a time to accept money and clothes, olive orchards and vineyards, sheep and oxen, and male and female slaves? [27] Therefore, Naaman's skin disease will cling to you and your descendants forever." So Gehazi went out from his presence diseased—white as snow.[p]

The Floating Ax Head

6 The sons of the prophets[q] said to Elisha, "Please notice that the place where we live under your supervision[G] is too small for us.

[a]5:14 Lk 4:27
[b]5:15 Jos 2:11; 1Sm 17:46-47
[c]Gn 33:11
[d]5:16 1Kg 17:1; 2Kg 3:14
[e]Gn 14:22-23
[f]5:17 Ex 20:24
[g]Dt 6:4
[h]5:18 2Kg 7:2
[i]5:19 1Sm 1:17
[j]5:20 2Kg 4:12,31
[k]Ex 20:7
[l]5:21-22 2Kg 4:26
[m]5:22 2Kg 5:5
[n]5:24 2Kg 1:9
[o]5:26 2Kg 2:9,15
[p]5:27 Ex 4:6; Nm 12:10
[q]6:1 1Sm 10:5; 2Kg 2:3,5,7; 4:38

5:15 Naaman's next words to Elisha sounded like another paradigmatic statement of the expected consequences of God's great works—the response of faith on the part of those who experience or learn of God's great works (Ex 18:9-10; Jos 2:10-11; 1Kg 8:42-43; Ps 66:5-8).

5:16 Elisha was not in his ministry for the money. Then and now, ministry is a calling rather than a career.

5:17-19 Elisha's last words to Naaman implied two concessions to Naaman's new faith. First, as a man of new faith and incomplete understanding, Naaman believed there would be benefit in having **soil** from Israel at hand when he worshiped Israel's God. Elisha cooperated with Naaman's superstitious belief, much as the apostle Paul encourages mature believers to do with immature believers (Rm 14). A more significant concession was to allow Naaman to participate (seemingly in body only, not mind and heart) in his king's worship of the god **Rimmon**. "Rimmon" could have been a local name for the god Hadd/Hadad or a local manifestation of that god. Elisha's words, **go in peace**, imply acceptance of Naaman's requests.

5:20 Elisha's servant **Gehazi** decided to exploit his religious position for money, especially since it involved taking money from a foreigner. Contrast this with Elisha's attitude (v. 16).

5:21-23 When **Gehazi** asked for clothing and money based on his fabricated story, **Naaman** gave him twice the money he asked for and sent two men to help him take the treasures back and possibly to protect him on the trip.

5:25-26 **Gehazi** added lying to his other deceits, but this lie conflicted with knowledge that God had supernaturally imparted to **Elisha**. Elisha's answer listed some of the pleasures one could expect to gain with money.

5:27 As a leper, **Gehazi** was no longer fit to serve as Elisha's servant. As is commonly the case in other biblical narratives, we should not assume chronological order for the events narrated in this passage unless such order is explicitly indicated in the text. Therefore there is no necessary contradiction between the fact that Gehazi is here banished from Elisha and the fact that he is presented as Elisha's servant in 8:1-6. That incident, though recorded later in the book, could have occurred before Naaman's healing.

6:1-4 **Elisha** lived among and worked with the **prophets**. The communities of the prophets were fairly mobile and could

²Please let us go to the Jordan where we can each get a log and can build ourselves a place to live there."

"Go," he said.

³Then one said, "Please come with your servants."

"I'll come," he answered.

⁴So he went with them, and when they came to the Jordan, they cut down trees. ⁵As one of them was cutting down a tree, the iron ax head fell into the water, and he cried out, "Oh, my master, it was borrowed!"ᵃ

⁶Then the man of Godᵇ asked, "Where did it fall?"

When he showed him the place, the man of God cut a stick, threw it there, and made the iron float.ᶜ ⁷Then he said, "Pick it up." So he reached out and took it.

The Aramean War

⁸When the king of Aramᵈ was waging war against Israel, he conferred with his servants, "My camp will be at such and such a place."

⁹But the man of Godᵉ sent word to the king of Israel: "Be careful passing by this place, for the Arameans are going down there." ¹⁰Consequently, the king of Israel sent word to the place the man of God had told him about. The man of God repeatedlyᴬ warned the king, so the king would be on his guard.

¹¹The king of Aram was enraged because of this matter, and he called his servants and demanded of them, "Tell me, which one of us is for the king of Israel?"

ᵃ6:5 Ex 22:14
ᵇ6:6 2Kg 4:8-9
ᶜEx 15:25; 2Kg 2:21; 4:41
ᵈ6:8 2Kg 8:28-29
ᵉ6:9 2Kg 4:8-9
ᶠ6:13 Gn 37:17
ᵍ6:16 Ex 14:13
ʰ2Ch 32:7
ⁱ6:17 2Kg 2:11; Ps 34:7
ʲ6:18 Gn 19:11
ᵏ6:19 1Kg 16:24; 2Kg 3:6

¹²One of his servants said, "No one, my lord the king. Elisha, the prophet in Israel, tells the king of Israel even the words you speak in your bedroom."

¹³So the king said, "Go and see where he is, so I can send men to capture him."

When he was told, "Elisha is in Dothan,"ᶠ ¹⁴he sent horses, chariots, and a massive army there. They went by night and surrounded the city.

¹⁵When the servant of the man of God got up early and went out, he discovered an army with horses and chariots surrounding the city. So he asked Elisha, "Oh, my master, what are we to do?"

¹⁶Elisha said, "Don't be afraid,ᵍ for those who are with us outnumber those who are with them."ʰ

¹⁷Then Elisha prayed, "Lᴏʀᴅ, please open his eyes and let him see." So the Lᴏʀᴅ opened the servant's eyes. He looked and saw that the mountain was covered with horses and chariots of fireⁱ all around Elisha.

¹⁸When the Arameans came against him, Elisha prayed to the Lᴏʀᴅ, "Please strike this nation with blindness." So He struck them with blindness,ʲ according to Elisha's word. ¹⁹Then Elisha said to them, "This is not the way, and this is not the city. Follow me, and I will take you to the man you're looking for." And he led them to Samaria.ᵏ ²⁰When they entered Samaria, Elisha said, "Lᴏʀᴅ, open these men's eyes and let them see." So the Lᴏʀᴅ

ᴬ6:10 Lit *not once and not twice*

relocate whenever their homes or a neighborhood became crowded. To find room, they went to the lower **Jordan** River Valley to one of many places where the well-watered, lower flood plain abounded with thickets, **trees**, and other vegetation and also with pools and eddies of water. This well-watered strip near the river was the "pride [or 'rising,' or 'thickets'] of the Jordan" (Jr 12:5; Zch 11:3). The desert land beyond this fertile strip was generally barren.

6:5 It had been 200 years since the Israelites had relied on Philistines for **iron** tools (1Sm 13:19-22), but iron tools were still expensive.

6:6-7 The reaction of the **man of God** was almost perfunctory. He asked where the **ax** fell, threw a **stick** into the water, and miraculously recovered the ax head. The lesson was that God could do miraculous works of witness on behalf of His prophets in a time of national unfaithfulness to Yahweh.

6:8–8:15 This section, almost two chapters long, shows the man of God intervening in politics. Though His people had rejected Him, God did not abandon His people to their enemies or to their own rulers. A likely setting for these events was the political weakness under Jehu and his weak successor, Jehoahaz. In contrast with the severity shown to Elisha's greedy servant, God could still show mercy to Elisha's ungodly king. During this time, Elisha could live safely

in Samaria, though suffering occasional personal threats (6:32). The man of God helped Israel in two ways: by sharing supernatural knowledge of the enemy, and by serving as a rallying point and source of prophetic encouragement for Samaria.

6:8-9 Perhaps during an era of border harassment, the man of God regularly revealed the secret plans of the **Arameans** to the **king of Israel**. This was not as spectacular as destroying an enemy with hailstones (Jos 10:11), but it still showed that God was supernaturally working for His people.

6:12-13 The Arameans knew about Elisha's supernatural military intelligence.

6:14-15 The Arameans sent a major expedition to surround **Elisha** in **Dothan**, about 10 miles north of Samaria. The king of Damascus, with a pragmatic attitude similar to Ahab's, showed a typical reaction to God's miraculous works—defiant opposition.

6:16-17 A supernatural view of Dothan showed the servant that, contrary to what his unaided eyes told him, military leaders were not in control of coming events. A greater force was present, unseen but potent, ready to fight on behalf of the righteous.

6:18-20 God miraculously delivered the Aramean army into the hands of the Hebrews without bloodshed.

opened their eyes. They looked and discovered they were in Samaria.

²¹ When the king of Israel saw them, he said to Elisha, "My father,ᵃ should I kill them? I will kill them."

²² Elisha replied, "Don't kill them. Do you kill those you have captured with your sword or your bow? Set food and water in front of them so they can eat and drink and go to their master."ᵇ

²³ So he prepared a great feast for them. When they had eaten and drunk, he sent them away, and they went to their master. The Aramean raidersᶜ did not come into Israel's land again.

²⁴ Some time later, King Ben-hadadᵈ of Aram brought all his military units together and marched up to besiege Samaria. ²⁵ So there was a great famineᵉ in Samaria, and they continued the siege against it until a donkey's head sold for 80 silver •shekels,ᴬ and a cupᴮ of dove's dungᶜ sold for five silver shekels.ᴰ,ᶠ

²⁶ As the king of Israel was passing by on the wall, a woman cried out to him, "My lord the king, help!"

²⁷ He answered, "If the LORD doesn't help you, where can I get help for you? From the threshing floor or the winepress?"ᵍ ²⁸ Then the king asked her, "What's the matter?"ʰ

She said, "This woman said to me, 'Give up your son, and we will eat him today. Then we will eat my son tomorrow.' ²⁹ So we boiled my son and ate him, and I said to her the next day, 'Give up your son, and we will eat him,'ⁱ but she has hidden her son."

³⁰ When the king heard the woman's words, he tore his clothes.ʲ Then, as he was passing by on the wall, the people saw that there was •sacklothᵏ under his clothes next to his skin. ³¹ He announced, "May God punish me and do so severelyˡ if the head of Elisha son of Shaphat remains on his shoulders today."

³² Elisha was sitting in his house, and the eldersᵐ were sitting with him. The king sent a man ahead of him, but before the messenger got to him, Elisha said to the elders, "Do you see how this murdererⁿ has sent someone to cut off my head? Look, when the messenger comes, shut the door to keep him out. Isn't the sound of his master's feet behind him?"

³³ While Elisha was still speaking with them, the messengerᴱ came down to him. Then he said, "This disaster is from the LORD. Why should I wait for the LORD any longer?"ᵒ

Cross-references (center column):

ᵃ6:21 2Kg 2:12; 5:13
ᵇ6:22 2Ch 28:8-15; Rm 12:20
ᶜ6:23 2Kg 5:2; 24:2
ᵈ6:24 1Kg 20:1
ᵉ6:25 2Kg 4:38; 8:1
ᶠLv 26:26
ᵍ6:27 Hs 9:2
ʰ6:26-28 2Sm 14:4-5
ⁱ6:28-29 Lv 26:29; Dt 28:53,57
ʲ6:30 1Kg 21:27
ᵏGn 37:34
ˡ6:31 1Kg 19:2
ᵐ6:32 Ezk 8:1; 14:1
ⁿLk 12:31-32
ᵒ6:33 Jb 2:9; Is 8:21

ᴬ6:25 About 2 pounds of silver   ᴮ6:25 Lit *a fourth of a kab*   ᶜ6:25 Or *seedpods,* or *wild onions*   ᴰ6:25 About 2 ounces of silver   ᴱ6:33 Some emend to *king*

6:21-22 Several authorities argue that killing prisoners was not a common practice (but see 1Kg 11:16). Elisha's prohibition against killing the Arameans carried the implicit message that God had given this victory. There is no contradiction between this episode and the one just following (see next note). Since God's lessons fell on hardened hearts, it was inevitable that war would be resumed. The miraculous capture and release of the Aramean army did produce a brief period of peace between the weakened Israelites and the dominant Arameans. But in terms of God's larger purpose of witnessing through miraculous works, they were ineffective for both the Israelites and the Arameans. God's great works can be effective, but the impact of God's truth is determined more by the attitude of hearts than by the wonderment of miracles.

6:24–7:20 This account of the siege of Samaria demonstrated the failure of the king. In broad terms, he failed because of sin, but in this context he failed because of his rejection of the message of God's miraculous works. The account shows the king's interaction with the misery of the people and his personal failure. This failure came in a context in which God had provided past victories and lessons that could have led to peace and prosperity.

6:24-25 Since neither the Israelites nor the Arameans were changed by the demonstrations of God's power, war eventually returned. Ideally, the circumstances of God's people should never have reached such a sorry state; the biblical plan was that a righteous king would defeat the enemies and save his people from such misery (Ps 20:1-2,6-7). In this time of spiritual failure, war had come with a devastating siege of **Samaria** and starvation among the people. The siege was so pressing that ceremonially unclean and de-testable substances were being sold for exorbitant prices. This contrasted with the concept that the king was responsible to provide for his people's needs (Ps 72:12-13).

6:26-27 The people had the right to call to the **king** for help (Ps 72:12-13), but an unfaithful king could only make excuses and blame God.

6:28-29 The king's interview with one of the two women involved in cannibalism illustrated a depth of sin that had been prophesied much earlier (Lv 26:29).

6:30 The **king** was probably sincere in wearing **sackcloth** under his robes. He could honestly say that he felt the people's pain, and he skillfully displayed the evidences of his grief. He reacted to the woman's pain with great emotion.

6:31 The king was right to feel moral revulsion at this situation, but lack of moral wisdom led him to blame God and to pronounce an oath against God's prophet, **Elisha**. But this disaster was actually caused by the sin of the king and the people.

6:32 That the **elders** of the idolatrous city held Elisha in high respect is proven by the fact that they were **in his house . . . sitting with him.**

6:33 The strongest demonstration of the king's misdirected moral sensitivity came when the **messenger** asked why he should any longer trust a God who brought such disasters on His people. This recalled the scene when Ahab, the great destroyer of Israel, accused Elijah of being the destroyer (1Kg 18:17-18). The moral rebel often sees only what will justify his excuses. Furthermore, in blaming God, the king who should have represented the people to God instead became a blasphemer against God.

Aram Defeated

7 Elisha replied, "Hear the word of the Lᴏʀᴅ! This is what the Lᴏʀᴅ says: 'About this time tomorrow at the gate of Samaria, six quarts^A of fine meal will sell for a •shekel^B and 12 quarts^C of barley will sell for a shekel.'"^B,a

2 Then the captain, the king's right-hand man,^b responded to the man of God,^c "Look, even if the Lᴏʀᴅ were to make windows in heaven, could this really happen?"^d

Elisha announced, "You will in fact see it with your own eyes, but you won't eat any of it."^e

3 Four men with a skin disease^f were at the entrance to the gate. They said to each other, "Why just sit here until we die? 4 If we say, 'Let's go into the city,' we will die there because the famine is in the city, but if we sit here, we will also die. So now, come on. Let's go to the Arameans' camp.^g If they let us live, we will live; if they kill us, we will die."

5 So the diseased men got up at twilight to go to the Arameans' camp. When they came to the camp's edge, they discovered that there was not a single man there,^6 for the Lord^D had caused the Aramean camp to hear the sound of chariots, horses, and a great army.^h The Arameans had said to each other, "The king of Israel must have hired the kings of the Hittites^i and the kings of Egypt^j to attack us."^7 So they had gotten up and fled^k at twilight, abandoning their tents, horses, and donkeys. The camp was intact, and they had fled for their lives.

8 When these men came to the edge of the camp, they went into a tent to eat and drink. Then they picked up the silver, gold, and clothing and went off and hid them. They came back and entered another tent, picked

things up, and hid them.^l,9 Then they said to each other, "We're not doing what is right. Today is a day of good news.^m If we are silent and wait until morning light, our sin will catch up with us. Let's go tell the king's household."

10 The diseased men went and called to the city's gatekeepers and told them, "We went to the Aramean camp and no one was there—no human sounds. There was nothing but tethered horses and donkeys, and the tents were intact." 11 The gatekeepers called out, and the news was reported to the king's household.

12 So the king got up in the night and said to his servants, "Let me tell you what the Arameans have done to us. They know we are starving,^n so they have left the camp to hide in the open country, thinking, 'When they come out of the city, we will take them alive and go into the city.'"^o

13 But one of his servants responded, "Please, let messengers take five of the horses that are left in the city. Their fate is like the entire Israelite community who will die,^E so let's send them and see."

14 The messengers took two chariots with horses, and the king sent them after the Aramean army, saying, "Go and see." 15 So they followed them as far as the Jordan. They saw that the whole way was littered with clothes and equipment the Arameans had thrown off in their haste. The messengers returned and told the king. 16 Then the people went out and plundered the Aramean camp.^p

It was then that six quarts^A of fine meal sold for a shekel^B and 12 quarts^C of barley sold for a shekel,^B according to the word of the Lᴏʀᴅ.^q,17 The king had appointed the captain, his right-hand man,^r to be in charge of the gate, but the people trampled him in the

Cross references (center column)

a 7:1 2Kg 7:18
b 7:2 2Kg 5:18; 7:17
c 2Kg 4:8-9
d Mal 3:10
e 2Kg 7:17
f 7:3 Nm 5:2-4; 2Kg 5:1
g 7:4 2Kg 6:24
h 7:6 2Sm 5:24; 2Kg 5:16-17
i 1Kg 10:29
j 2Ch 12:2-3
k 7:7 Jdg 7:21
l 7:8 Jos 7:21
m 7:9 Pr 15:27; 21:17-18
n 7:12 2Kg 6:25
o Jos 8:4-12
p 7:16 2Kg 7:8
q 2Kg 7:1-2
r 7:17 2Kg 7:2

---

^A 7:1,16 Lit a seah ^B 7:1,16 About 1/2 ounce of silver ^C 7:1,16 Lit two seahs ^D 7:6 Some Hb mss read Lord ^E 7:13 Some Hb mss, LXX, Syr, Vg; other Hb mss read left in it. Indeed, they are like the whole multitude of Israel that are left in it; indeed, they are like the whole multitude of Israel who will die.

7:1 The story turns to the coming miraculous deliverance. **Elisha** announced that the next day at that same time, food would be available at bargain prices at the city **gate**. Despite the failure of the king, his lack of repentance, and no visible faith, God was still going to deliver—an act of undeserved grace.

7:2 In response to the blasphemous comment of the **captain**, Elisha prophesied that he would not share in the blessings.

7:3-4 Since the nation's leaders were such failures, the Lord brought knowledge of deliverance through four outcasts who were quarantined because of their **skin disease**. Despite their despair, they chose the least hopeless course of action and went to the Aramean camp.

7:5-7 God had already thrown the **Aramean** army into a supernatural panic that caused them to abandon their camp and foodstuffs to the besieged Hebrews. The **Hittites** referred to here were the neo-Hittites, remnants of

the older Hittite Empire from the second millennium B.C. In this context, **Egypt** was probably the northern Egypt from which Solomon imported **horses** (1Kg 10:28). The contrast between the miraculous power of God and the impotence of human agents is another great lesson of this story.

7:8-9 The outcasts, after gathering food and plunder for themselves, remembered their people. The outcasts brought news of the deliverance (or "victory," Ps 20:6) that a righteous king should have accomplished.

7:12-13 The **king**, still reacting to God's miracles with hopeless despair (Jos 2:11), was too paralyzed by fear to act, but his **servants** persuaded him to examine the situation.

7:14-15 A two-chariot scout group reconnoitered as far as the **Jordan** River and determined that the enemy really had been frightened away.

7:16-20 Now all of Elisha's prophecy was fulfilled. These

gateway. He died, just as the man of God had predicted when the king came to him. [18]When the man of God had said to the king, "About this time tomorrow 12 quarts[A] of barley will sell for a shekel[B] and six quarts[C] of fine meal will sell for a shekel[B] at the gate of Samaria," [19]this captain had answered the man of God, "Look, even if the LORD were to make windows in heaven, could this really happen?" Elisha had said, "You will in fact see it with your own eyes, but you won't eat any of it."[a] [20]This is what happened to him: the people trampled him in the gateway, and he died.

The Shunammite's Land Restored

8 Elisha said to the woman whose son he had restored to life,[b] "Get ready, you and your household, and go and live as a foreigner wherever you can. For the LORD has announced a seven-year famine,[c] and it has already come to the land."

[2]So the woman got ready and did what the man of God said. She and her household lived as foreigners in the land of the Philistines for seven years. [3]When the woman returned from the land of the Philistines at the end of seven years,[d] she went to appeal to the king for her house and field.[e]

[4]The king had been speaking to Gehazi,[f] the attendant of the man of God, saying, "Tell me all the great things Elisha has done."

[5]While he was telling the king how Elisha restored the dead son to life, the woman whose son he had restored to life came to appeal to the king for her house and field. So Gehazi said, "My lord the king, this is the

woman and this is the son Elisha restored to life."[g]

[6]When the king asked the woman, she told him the story. So the king appointed a court official for her, saying, "Restore all that was hers, along with all the income from the field from the day she left the country until now."

Aram's King Hazael

[7]Elisha came to Damascus[h] while Ben-hadad[i] king of Aram was sick, and the king was told, "The man of God[j] has come here." [8]So the king said to Hazael,[k] "Take a gift[l] with you and go meet the man of God. Inquire of the LORD through him, 'Will I recover from this sickness?'"[m]

[9]Hazael went to meet Elisha, taking with him a gift: 40 camel-loads of all kinds of goods from Damascus. When he came and stood before him, he said, "Your son,[n] Ben-hadad king of Aram, has sent me to ask you, 'Will I recover from this sickness?'"

[10]Elisha told him, "Go say to him, 'You are sure to[D] recover.' But the LORD has shown me that he is sure to die." [11]Then Elisha stared steadily at him until Hazael was ashamed.[o]

The man of God wept,[p] [12]and Hazael asked, "Why is my lord weeping?"

He replied, "Because I know the evil you will do to the people of Israel. You will set their fortresses on fire. You will kill their young men with the sword. You will dash their little ones to pieces. You will rip open their pregnant women."[q]

[13]Hazael said, "How could your servant, a mere dog,[r] do this monstrous thing?"

Cross references (center column)

a 7:18-19 2Kg 7:1-2
b 8:1 2Kg 4:8-37
c Gn 41:27,54
d 8:3 2Kg 7:1-2
e Dt 15:1-6
f 8:4 2Kg 4:12; 5:20-27
g 8:5 2Kg 4:35
h 8:7 1Kg 11:24
i 2Kg 6:24
j 2Kg 5:20
k 8:8 1Kg 19:15,17
l 1Kg 14:3
m 2Kg 1:2
n 8:9 2Kg 5:13
o 8:11 Jdg 3:25; 2Kg 2:17
p Lk 19:41
q 8:12 1Kg 19:17; 2Kg 10:32-33; 13:3
r 8:13 2Sm 9:8

A 7:18 Lit two seahs   B 7:18 About 1/2 ounce of silver   C 7:18 Lit a seah   D 8:10 Alt Hb tradition reads You will not

details, particularly those dealing with the death of the **captain**, were repeated in meticulous detail to highlight the fact that God is faithful. The unspoken lessons of God's reliable character were (1) that people, particularly the king and his officers, should obey and trust God, and (2) that God will care for His people when kings fail.

8:1-6 This incident almost certainly occurred at an earlier time and under an earlier king. Because **Gehazi** was serving Elisha and had an audience with the king, it is likely that this event took place before Gehazi became leprous (chap. 5). Though obviously related to the earlier incident of the healing of the Shunammite woman's son (4:32-37), this material may have been recorded here because it also dealt with issues of government and beneficial rule. Certainly beginning with 6:26, and perhaps earlier with 6:8, this section has dealt with the king's failure to perform his proper duties. This portion deals with justice for a **woman** who had abandoned her **land** in a time of distress and then had difficulty getting her land back. The prophet's influence helped her to get a just settlement of the issue. Though out of chronological order, this account is topically suited to this context.

8:7-15 Earlier (1Kg 19:15-16), God had instructed Elijah to

choose his successor and to anoint two kings. Up to this time, only one of those tasks—choosing his successor—had been accomplished. The other two anointings were to be done by Elisha "in the spirit and power of Elijah" (Lk 1:17). This would have had the same validity as the appearance of John the Baptist as Elijah (Mt 11:14). Apparently, Elisha's designation of these two kings was sufficient to fulfill the Lord's original command to Elijah.

8:7-8 Once again the prophet was presented as an international celebrity. God's mighty deeds gained influence even among foreigners, though such deeds did not always lead to faith.

8:10-11 Elisha gave a devious answer to Ben-hadad's request for an oracle. If one takes Elisha's message as meaning only that Ben-hadad's current illness was not terminal, it was true, but God also used Hazael's visit to Elisha to incite Hazael to commit murder and revolution.

8:12-13 Then Elisha shared his prophetic vision that **Hazael** would devastate Israel. From the perspective of covenant theology, Israel and Israel's king deserved such brutal judgment. This message ended with Elisha stating unambiguously that Hazael would become **king**. In giving that message, God and Elisha either instigated Hazael's treason

Elisha answered, "The LORD has shown me that you will be king over Aram."[a]

[14] Hazael left Elisha and went to his master, who asked him, "What did Elisha say to you?"

He responded, "He told me you are sure to recover." [15] The next day Hazael took a heavy cloth, dipped it in water, and spread it over the king's face. Ben-hadad died, and Hazael reigned instead of him.

Judah's King Jehoram

[16] In the fifth year[b] of Israel's King Joram[c] son of Ahab, Jehoram[A,d] son of Jehoshaphat became king of Judah, replacing his father.[B,e] [17] He was 32 years old when he became king and reigned eight years in Jerusalem.[f] [18] He walked in the way of the kings of Israel, as the house of Ahab had done, for Ahab's daughter was his wife. He did what was evil in the LORD's sight.[g] [19] The LORD was unwilling to destroy Judah because of His servant David, since He had promised to give a lamp[h] to David and his sons forever.[i]

[20] During Jehoram's reign, Edom rebelled against Judah's control and appointed their own king.[j] [21] So Jehoram crossed over to Zair with all his chariots. Then at night he set out to attack the Edomites who had surrounded him and the chariot commanders, but his troops fled to their tents.[k] [22] So Edom is still in rebellion against Judah's control today. Libnah[l] also rebelled at that time.

[23] The rest of the events of Jehoram's reign, along with all his accomplishments, are written in the Historical Record of Judah's Kings.[m] [24] Jehoram rested with his fathers and was buried with his fathers in the city of David, and his son Ahaziah became king in his place.[n]

Judah's King Ahaziah

[25] In the twelfth year of Israel's King Joram son of Ahab,[o] Ahaziah son of Jehoram became king of Judah.[p] [26] Ahaziah was 22 years old when he became king and reigned one year in Jerusalem. His mother's name was Athaliah, granddaughter of Israel's King Omri.[q] [27] He walked in the way of the house of Ahab and did what was evil in the LORD's sight like the house of Ahab,[r] for he was a son-in-law to Ahab's family.

[28] Ahaziah went with Joram son of Ahab to fight against Hazael[s] king of Aram in Ramoth-gilead,[t] and the Arameans wounded Joram. [29] So King Joram returned to Jezreel[u] to recover from the wounds that the Arameans had inflicted on him in Ramoth-gilead[c] when he fought against Aram's King Hazael.[v] Then Judah's King Ahaziah son of Jehoram went down to Jezreel to visit Joram son of Ahab since Joram was ill.

Cross references (center column):

[a] 8:13-15 1Kg 19:15
[b] 8:16-24 2Ch 21:5-20
[c] 8:16 2Kg 1:17; 3:1
[d] 2Ch 21:1
[e] 1Kg 22:50
[f] 8:17 2Ch 21:5
[g] 8:18 2Ch 21:6
[h] 8:19 1Kg 11:36; 15:4
[i] 2Ch 21:7
[j] 8:20 1Kg 22:47; 2Kg 3:9
[k] 8:21 2Sm 18:17; 19:8
[l] 8:22 Jos 21:13; 2Kg 19:8
[m] 8:23 1Kg 22:39; 2Kg 1:18
[n] 8:24 1Kg 22:40; 2Kg 1:17
[o] 8:25-29 2Ch 22:1-6
[p] 8:25 2Kg 9:29
[q] 8:26 1Kg 16:23; 2Ch 22:2
[r] 8:27 2Ch 22:3
[s] 8:28 1Kg 19:15
[t] 1Kg 22:3,29
[u] 8:29 1Kg 21:1
[v] 2Kg 9:15

A8:16 = The LORD is Exalted　　B8:16 Lit Judah; Jehoshaphat had been king of Judah　　C8:29 Lit Ramah

---

or encouraged the initiation of a treason that was already planned.

8:14-15 Hazael did, in fact, repeat the prophet's words to **Ben-hadad**, but then he proceeded to murder his king and take the throne.

8:16 With this record the data is again arranged chronologically.

8:18 After the formal opening, the evaluation reports that Joram was a bad king and observes that the corrupting influences of **Ahab** and Jezebel had reached into Judah. **The way of the kings of Israel** probably refers to the worship of Baal-melkart (see note at 1Kg 16:23-28). It was unlikely that the good king, Jehoshaphat, anticipated this outcome when he entered into a marriage alliance with Ahab.

8:19 Again, as in the case of the wicked king Abijam (1Kg 15:4-5), God tolerated and preserved a wicked king and his kingdom because of David's character. The example of Jeroboam I was an evil force that destroyed his successors. The faithful example of David preserved even wicked successors and a wicked kingdom from destruction.

8:20-21 During the reigns of Ahab and Jehoshaphat, both kingdoms could make claims of empire though Ahab was clearly the senior member of the alliance. These verses record the loss of Judah's last pretense to empire for this cycle as both kingdoms moved into a period of idol worship and weakness.

The brief description of the **night** attack against surrounding **Edomites** could be translated in two ways. The critical sentence could be either "at night he and his chariot officers attacked the surrounding Edomites" or "at night he attacked the surrounding Edomites and their chariot officers." The first option is more likely because, even in decline, Judah was more likely to have a small chariot division than Edom was. Then the next sentence, "The people (his troops) fled to their tents (homes)," is also ambiguous. "The people" could be the Edomites, who fled so that the rebellion was not crushed, or they could have been Jehoram's chariots, who went home without subduing the rebellion. This time the second option is more likely. By losing control of Edom, Judah lost control of the caravan routes to the south. Judah also lost Libnah on the border of the former Philistine territory.

8:22 Today refers to the date of the writing of an earlier document that was incorporated into the canonical version of 2 Kings. The final composer of 2 Kings incorporated parts of this earlier document into his finished work.

8:23-24 The closing statements for **Jehoram's** rule are completely formulaic.

8:25-27 The corrupting relationship with the house of Omri and Ahab is highlighted. The **way of . . . Ahab** probably alludes to bringing the worship of Baal-melkart into Judah (see note at 1Kg 16:23-28).

8:28-29 The notice about the continued conflict with **Hazael** of Damascus informs the reader that Israel, with Judah as an ally, could still contest control of Gilead with Hazael, the new, more aggressive ruler of Damascus. The big step in the decline of Israel's political power would come with Jehu's widespread massacres. There is no notice for the

Jehu Anointed as Israel's King

9 The prophet Elisha called one of the sons of the prophets[a] and said, "Tuck your mantle[b] under your belt, take this flask of oil[c] with you, and go to Ramoth-gilead.[d] 2 When you get there, look for Jehu[e] son of Jehoshaphat, son of Nimshi. Go in, get him away from his colleagues, and take him to an inner room. 3 Then, take the flask of oil, pour it on his head, and say, 'This is what the LORD says: "I anoint you king over Israel."'[f] Open the door and escape. Don't wait." 4 So the young prophet went to Ramoth-gilead.

5 When he arrived, the army commanders were sitting there, so he said, "I have a message for you, commander."

Jehu asked, "For which one of us?"

He answered, "For you, commander."

6 So Jehu got up and went into the house. The young prophet poured the oil on his head and said, "This is what the LORD God of Israel says: 'I anoint you king over the LORD's people, Israel. 7 You are to strike down the house of your master Ahab so that I may avenge the blood shed by the hand of Jezebel—the blood of My servants the prophets and of all the servants of the LORD.[g] 8 The whole house of Ahab will perish, and I will eliminate all of Ahab's males,[A] both slave and free, in Israel.[h] 9 I will make the house of Ahab like the house of Jeroboam son of Nebat and like the house of

Baasha son of Ahijah.[i] 10 The dogs will eat Jezebel in the plot of land at Jezreel—no one will bury her.'"[j] Then the young prophet opened the door and escaped.

11 When Jehu came out to his master's servants, they asked, "Is everything all right? Why did this crazy person[k] come to you?"

Then he said to them, "You know the sort and their ranting."

12 But they replied, "That's a lie! Tell us!"

So Jehu said, "He talked to me about this and that and said, 'This is what the LORD says: I anoint you king over Israel.'"

13 Each man quickly took his garment and put it under Jehu on the bare steps.[B,l] They blew the ram's horn[m] and proclaimed, "Jehu is king!"[n]

14 Then Jehu son of Jehoshaphat, son of Nimshi, conspired against Joram.[o] Joram and all Israel had been at Ramoth-gilead on guard against Hazael king of Aram. 15 But King Joram had returned to Jezreel to recover from the wounds that the Arameans had inflicted on him when he fought against Aram's King Hazael. Jehu said, "If you commanders wish to make me king, then don't let anyone escape from the city to go tell about it in Jezreel."

Jehu Kills Joram and Ahaziah

16 Jehu got into his chariot and went to Jezreel since Joram was laid up there and Aha-

a9:1 2Kg 2:3,5,7
b2Kg 4:29
c1Sm 10:1; 16:1;
1Kg 1:39
d1Kg 22:3,29;
2Kg 8:28-29
e9:2 1Kg 19:16-
17; 2Kg 9:14
f9:3 2Ch 22:7
g9:7 1Kg 18:4;
21:15
h9:8 1Kg 21:21;
2Kg 10:17
i9:9 1Kg 16:3-
5,11-12
j9:10 1Kg 21:23;
2Kg 9:30-37
k9:11 1Sm
10:11; Mk 3:21
l9:13 Mt 21:8
m2Sm 15:10
n1Kg 1:39
o9:14-16 2Kg
8:28-29; 2Ch
22:6

A9:8 Lit *eliminate Ahab's one who urinates against a wall*   **B9:13** Lit *on the bones of the steps*

---

end of Ahaziah's reign since his death is recorded later as part of Jehu's massacres.

9:1–15:12 The theological and moral reason for this coming period of weakness was the sin of the southern kings beginning with Jehoram, son of Jehoshaphat (8:18). But the immediate, political cause was the violence and destructiveness of Jehu's revolution against the dynasty of Omri. Decline began immediately with Jehu's massacres and continued into the rule of Jehu's son, Jehoahaz. This period of weakness was the most likely setting for several of the miracle events recorded in topical, non-chronological order in the general career of Elisha (see notes at chaps. 4–7).

Then, after Elisha's deathbed intervention in politics, Jehoash, grandson of Jehu, led the north in a new round of successful warfare. This culminated in the reign of Jeroboam II, during whose rule the wealth and power of the northern kingdom was greater than it had yet been. Both the Bible and archaeology bear witness to this. In God's providence, this restoration of power came just in time to bring material blessing to the successors of Joash of Judah.

9:1-4 The second anointing of a ruler commanded of Elijah by the Lord occurred when Elisha sent a young **prophet** to anoint **Jehu**, an experienced chariot commander, to be **king** of **Israel**. At that time Jehu was a commander of the chariots struggling with Aram for control of **Ramoth-gilead**. The delicacy of the situation is shown by the command to the young prophet to **escape** immediately.

9:6-10 In the account of Elisha commissioning the young

prophet, the message is summarized in six words (v. 3). Here in the account of delivering the message, the six words are expanded to more than a hundred words (in the HCSB translation) followed by an urgent departure. This expanded statement repeated the accusation against the **house of Ahab** and gave a detailed presentation of the penalty to be exacted.

9:11-13 The evaluation **Jehu** and **his master's servants** gave about the prophet seems confused. At first the prophet was described as **crazy** and **ranting**, but as soon as the group realized that they actually liked the message he had brought, they allowed the prophet's oracle and anointing of Jehu to instigate the revolution that destroyed the house of Ahab. Whatever Jehu's servants may have initially thought of the messenger, they recognized that his actions implied the divine approval of Jehu as king—a conclusion they apparently reached before Jehu himself did.

9:14 The formula used here to designate **Jehu** could be understood as: "Jehu, the son of Jehoshaphat, of the clan of Nimshi." **All Israel** should not be taken as referring literally to "all Israel" but to all Israel involved in conducting the war. This idiom is similar to the idiom involved in the sacrificial blood in which *all* (rightly translated "the rest" in the HCSB) of the blood was poured out on the base of the altar (Lv 4:34). From context, "all of the blood" referred to all of the remainder after the other functions had used much of the blood.

9:15 Jehu plotted with his fellow officers to prevent anyone

ziah king of Judah had gone down to visit Joram. [17] Now the watchman[a] was standing on the tower in Jezreel. He saw Jehu's troops approaching and shouted, "I see troops!"

Joram responded, "Choose a rider and send him to meet them and have him ask, 'Do you come in peace?'"[b]

[18] So a horseman went to meet Jehu and said, "This is what the king asks: 'Do you come in peace?'"

Jehu replied, "What do you have to do with peace?[A] Fall in behind me."

The watchman reported, "The messenger reached them but hasn't started back."

[19] So he sent out a second horseman, who went to them and said, "This is what the king asks: 'Do you come in peace?'"

Jehu answered, "What do you have to do with peace?[A] Fall in behind me."

[20] Again the watchman reported, "He reached them but hasn't started back. Also, the driving is like that of Jehu son of Nimshi[c]—he drives like a madman."

[21] "Harness!" Joram shouted, and they harnessed his chariot. Then Joram king of Israel and Ahaziah king of Judah set out, each in his own chariot, and met Jehu at the plot of land of Naboth the Jezreelite.[d] [22] When Joram saw Jehu he asked, "Do you come in peace, Jehu?"

He answered, "What peace can there be as long as there is so much prostitution and witchcraft from your mother Jezebel?"[e]

[23] Joram turned around and fled, shouting to Ahaziah, "It's treachery,[f] Ahaziah!"

[24] Then Jehu drew his bow and shot Joram between the shoulders. The arrow went through his heart, and he slumped down in his chariot.[g] [25] Jehu said to Bidkar his aide, "Pick him up and throw him on the plot of ground belonging to Naboth the Jezreelite.[h] For remember when you and I were riding side by side behind his father Ahab, and the LORD uttered this •oracle against him: [26] 'As surely as I saw the blood of Naboth and the blood of his sons yesterday'—this is the LORD's declaration—'so will I repay you on this plot of land'—this is the LORD's declaration. So now, according to the word of the LORD, pick him up and throw him on the plot of land."[i]

[27] When King Ahaziah of Judah saw what was happening, he fled up the road toward Bethhaggan. Jehu pursued him, shouting, "Shoot him too!" So they shot him in his chariot[B] at Gur Pass near Ibleam,[j] but he fled to Megiddo[k] and died there.[l] [28] Then his servants carried him to Jerusalem in a chariot and buried him in his fathers' tomb in the city of David.[m] [29] It was in the eleventh year of Joram son of Ahab that Ahaziah had become king over Judah.[n]

Jehu Kills Jezebel

[30] When Jehu came to Jezreel, Jezebel heard about it, so she painted her eyes,[o] adorned her head, and looked down from the window. [31] As

Cross references (center column):
- [a]9:17 1Sm 14:16
- [b]1Sm 16:4
- [c]9:20 1Kg 19:17; 2Kg 9:2
- [d]9:21 1Kg 21:1-7
- [e]9:22 1Kg 16:30-33; 2Ch 21:13
- [f]9:23 2Kg 11:14
- [g]9:24 1Kg 22:34-35
- [h]9:25 1Kg 21:1
- [i]9:25-26 1Kg 21:13,19,24
- [j]9:27 Jos 17:11; Jdg 1:27
- [k]2Kg 23:29
- [l]2Ch 22:7,9
- [m]9:27-28 2Kg 23:30; 2Ch 22:9
- [n]9:29 2Kg 8:25
- [o]9:30 Jr 4:30; Ezk 23:40

A9:18,19 Lit *What to you and to peace*   B9:27 LXX, Syr, Vg; MT omits *So they shot him*

---

from going to **Jezreel** to warn the king. Then he took a group of soldiers with him to seize the throne.

9:17 The term **troops** used to describe the approach of Jehu's group could refer to any rushing mass or torrent. No wonder **Joram** sent an officer to investigate. Although the term for **rider** could be used for either chariot drivers or horse riders, the chariot was more likely for this task (v. 21).

9:18 The quickness with which the messenger lined up behind **Jehu**, signaling a switch of allegiance, showed that personal loyalty to King Joram was as shallow in Jezreel as it had been in Ramoth-gilead and that Jehu was a persuasive leader.

9:19-20 After a **second** messenger defected to **Jehu**, the lookout thought he could identify the manner of chariot driving as distinctive of Jehu.

9:21 **Joram** behaved like a man of bravery and character in going to face the danger himself. King **Ahaziah** of **Judah** should also be given similar credit for going with him.

9:22 Taken in its literal meaning, the **prostitution** mentioned by **Jehu** probably referred to the temple prostitutes of Baalism associated with the local Baals of Palestine and Jezebel's imported Baalism from Phoenicia. However, it could easily be stretched to apply to the metaphorical religious adultery of worshiping any god other than the Lord. **Witchcraft** was also a routine part of pagan cults.

9:24-26 These events happened near the second royal palace, the summer palace, the place where **Naboth** and his sons were murdered. Jehu, remembering the time when he and **Bidkar**, his **aide**, were witnesses to those murders, enabled the fulfillment of the prophecy by dumping Joram's corpse on Naboth's land (see notes at 1Kg 21:13-14; 21:19-24; and 22:37-38). The Hebrew word for *aide*, meaning "third," indicates that Bidkar was a third person in addition to the chariot driver and Jehu.

9:27-28 Judah was a junior ally of the dynasty of Ahab and was also tied to Ahab by marriage and by the cult of Baal. Though he had not been commanded to do so, Jehu may have believed there was no reason to distinguish between purging the land of the house of Ahab and purging it of the related house of David in Jerusalem—so far had the house of David sunk. Jehu's men pursued and wounded King **Ahaziah** at the ascent into the **Gur Pass near Ibleam**, although some locate this pass close to the pass that led from Taanach south. The wounded Ahaziah was permitted to flee to **Megiddo** where he died. Neither Joram nor Ahaziah are given formal closers to their records since Jehu's massacres rendered such records superfluous.

9:30-37 This report, written by a follower of Yahweh who considered **Jezebel** the incarnation of evil, described the courage and resolve of this idolatress and murderess as she faced death. She tended to her appearance with black eye paint and then boldly faced her killer. Her fate again showed that the loyalty of the people to Ahab was quite shallow. Two

Jehu entered the gate, she said, "Do you come in peace, Zimri,^{A,a} killer of your master?"

³² He looked up toward the window and said, "Who is on my side? Who?" Two or three eunuchs^b looked down at him, ³³ and he said, "Throw her down!" So they threw her down, and some of her blood splattered on the wall and on the horses, and Jehu rode over her.^c

³⁴ Then he went in, ate and drank, and said, "Take care of this cursed^d woman and bury her, since she's a king's daughter."^e ³⁵ But when they went out to bury her, they did not find anything but her skull, her feet, and the palms of her hands. ³⁶ So they went back and told him, and he said, "This fulfills the LORD's word that He spoke through His servant Elijah the Tishbite: 'In the plot of land at Jezreel, the dogs will eat Jezebel's flesh.^f ³⁷ Jezebel's corpse will be like manure^g on the surface of the field in the plot of land at Jezreel so that no one will be able to say: This is Jezebel.'"

Jehu Kills the House of Ahab

10 Since Ahab had 70 sons in Samaria,^h Jehu wrote letters and sent them to Samaria to the rulers of Jezreel,ⁱ to the elders, and to the guardians of Ahab's sons,^B saying:

² When this letter^j arrives, since your master's sons are with you and you have chariots, horses, a fortified city, and weaponry, ³ select the most qualified^c of your master's sons, set him on his father's throne, and fight for your master's house.

⁴ However, they were terrified and reasoned, "Look, two kings^k couldn't stand against him; how can we?"

⁵ So the overseer of the palace, the overseer of the city, the elders, and the guardians sent a message to Jehu: "We are your servants, and we will do whatever you tell us. We will not

make anyone king. Do whatever you think is right."^{D,l}

⁶ Then Jehu wrote them a second letter, saying:

> If you are on my side, and if you will obey me, bring me the heads of your master's sons at this time tomorrow at Jezreel.

All 70 of the king's sons were being cared for by the city's prominent men. ⁷ When the letter came to them, they took the king's sons and slaughtered all 70, put their heads in baskets, and sent them to Jehu at Jezreel. ⁸ When the messenger came and told him, "They have brought the heads of the king's sons," the king said, "Pile them in two heaps at the entrance of the gate until morning."

⁹ The next morning when he went out and stood at the gate, he said to all the people, "You are innocent. It was I who conspired against my master and killed him.^m But who struck down all these? ¹⁰ Know, then, that not a word the LORD spoke against the house of Ahab will fail,ⁿ for the LORD has done what He promised through His servant Elijah."^o ¹¹ So Jehu killed all who remained of the house of Ahab in Jezreel—all his great men, close friends, and priests—leaving him no survivors.

¹² Then he set out and went on his way to Samaria. On the way, while he was at Beth-eked of the Shepherds, ¹³ Jehu met the relatives of Ahaziah king of Judah and asked, "Who are you?"

They answered, "We're Ahaziah's^p relatives. We've come down to greet the king's sons and the queen mother's^q sons."

¹⁴ Then Jehu ordered, "Take them alive." So they took them alive and then slaughtered them at the pit of Beth-eked—42 men. He didn't spare any of them.^r

¹⁵ When he left there, he found Jehonadab son of Rechab^s coming to meet him. He greet-

Cross references (center column)
^a9:31 1Kg 16:9-20
^b9:32 Est 1:10; 2:14
^c9:33 Ps 7:5
^d9:34 1Kg 21:21-24
^e1Kg 16:31
^f9:36 1Kg 21:23; 2Kg 9:10
^g9:37 Jr 8:1-2; Zph 1:17
^h10:1 1Kg 16:24,29
ⁱ1Kg 21:1; 2Kg 9:30
^j10:2 2Kg 5:6
^k10:4 2Kg 9:24,27
^l10:5 Jos 9:8,11; 1Kg 20:4,32; 2Kg 18:14
^m10:9 2Kg 9:14-24
^m10:10 2Kg 9:7-10
^o1Kg 21:19-29
^p10:13 2Kg 9:27-29
^q1Kg 2:19
^r10:14 2Ch 22:8
^s10:15 Jr 35:6-19

---

^A9:31 A sarcastic reference to Zimri who usurped the throne; 1Kg 16:8-20   ^B10:1 LXX; MT reads *of Ahab*   ^C10:3 Lit *the good and the upright*   ^D10:5 Lit *Do what is good in your eyes*

---

or three of Jezebel's eunuchized palace slaves, when challenged by Jehu, threw her to her death. Then, while Jehu **ate and drank**, the dogs destroyed the corpse of the Phoenician princess just as was prophesied (1Kg 21:23).

10:1-7 Having many wives and children was seen as one of the prerogatives of power, even for righteous men (Gideon in Jdg 8:30-31). Ahab's **sons** and grandsons were apparently distributed among the noble families to relieve the royal treasury and to provide loyal sets of eyes and ears in the homes where they lived. **Jehu** shrewdly offered the great families of **Samaria** a difficult choice—choose a king and fight for him or deliver evidence that they had killed Ahab's sons. By ordinary standards of the day, these male heirs of Ahab were legitimate targets. The surprise was

that their ruling brothers had permitted them to live that long.

10:8-10 Jehu used the cooperation of the leaders of Samaria to justify his revolution and to associate his slaughters—to that point, correctly—with God's will.

10:11 But Jehu went beyond killing the **house of Ahab** and killed Ahab's **great men** (perhaps the great men loyal to Ahab) and all of Ahab's **friends**. In these killings he clearly went beyond God's commands into excessive slaughter. By the standards of that day, the false **priests** were fair targets.

10:13-14 These verses report even more unnecessary slaughter of the southern royal family.

10:15-16 Jehu aligned himself with one of the major reli-

against Jerusalem. They besieged Ahaz but were not able to conquer him.[a] [6]At that time Rezin king of Aram recovered Elath for Aram and expelled the Judahites from Elath.[b] Then the Arameans came to Elath, and they live there until today.[c]

[7]So Ahaz sent messengers[d] to Tiglath-pileser[e] king of Assyria, saying, "I am your servant and your son. March up and save me from the power of the king of Aram and of the king of Israel, who are rising up against me." [8]Ahaz also took the silver and gold found in the LORD's temple and in the treasuries of the king's palace and sent them to the king of Assyria as a gift.[f] [9]So the king of Assyria listened to him[g] and marched up to Damascus and captured it.[h] He deported its people to Kir[i] but put Rezin to death.

Ahaz's Idolatry

[10]King Ahaz went to Damascus to meet Tiglath-pileser[j] king of Assyria. When he saw the altar that was in Damascus, King Ahaz sent a model of the altar and complete plans for its construction to Uriah the priest.[k] [11]Uriah built the altar according to all the instructions King Ahaz sent from Damascus. Therefore, by the time King Ahaz came back from Damascus, Uriah the priest had completed it. [12]When the king came back from Damascus, he saw the altar. Then he approached the altar[l] and ascended it. [13]He offered his •burnt offering[m] and his •grain offering, poured out his drink offering, and sprinkled the blood of his •fellowship offerings[n] on the altar. [14]He took the bronze altar[o] that was before the LORD in front of the temple between his altar and the LORD's temple, and put it on the north side of his altar.

[15]Then King Ahaz commanded Uriah the priest, "Offer on the great altar the morning burnt offering, the evening grain offering, and the king's burnt offering and his grain offering. Also offer the burnt offering of all the people of the land, their grain offering, and their drink offerings. Sprinkle on the altar all the blood of the burnt offering and all the blood of sacrifice. The bronze altar will be for me to seek guidance."[A] [16]Uriah the priest did everything King Ahaz commanded.

[17]Then King Ahaz cut off the frames of the water carts[B,p] and removed the bronze basin from each of them. He took the reservoir[C,q] from the bronze oxen that were under it and put it on a stone pavement. [18]To satisfy the king of Assyria, he removed from the LORD's temple the Sabbath canopy they had built in the palace, and he closed the outer entrance for the king.

[a] 16:5 2Kg 15:37; Is 7:1
[b] 16:6 1Kg 9:26
[c] 2Ch 26:2
[d] 16:7 2Ch 28:16
[e] 2Kg 15:29; 1Ch 5:26
[f] 16:8 1Kg 15:19; 2Kg 12:17-18; 18:15
[g] 16:9 2Ch 28:21
[h] Am 1:3-5
[i] Is 22:6; Am 9:7
[j] 16:10 2Kg 15:29
[k] Is 8:2
[l] 16:12 2Ch 26:16
[m] 16:13 Ex 29:40
[n] Lv 7:11-21
[o] 16:14 Ex 40:24
[p] 16:17 1Kg 7:27-28
[q] 1Kg 7:23-25

[A] **16:15** Hb obscure [B] **16:17** Lit *the stands* [C] **16:17** Lit *sea*

valuable territory, including the port of **Elath**, they could not conquer Ahaz.

16:7-9 **Ahaz** then voluntarily submitted to **Assyria**, who would rule Judah as a vassal for the next century. The text seems to indicate that the Assyrians intervened only because Judah hired them. However, history shows that Isaiah's prophesied deliverance (Is 7:7-9) might have come without Ahaz's meddling. Tiglath-pileser III had already planned to reconquer the region. The Assyrians would have been helped if Ahaz had just withheld support from the anti-Assyrian coalition. Shortly after Jerusalem was put under siege, Tiglath-pileser launched campaigns that conquered the Philistine coast, lifted the siege of Jerusalem, destroyed Damascus (732 B.C.), and reduced the size of Israel (15:29).

16:10-11 Ahaz's subjection to **Assyria** renewed the struggle between political prudence and loyalty to Yahweh. Though not always enforced, the general principle was that a vassal accepted the ruler's cultic symbols as signs of obedience to the ruling country and to its god. In this pagan worldview, Yahweh was treated as a local god, who, along with His country, also had submitted to Asshur—the chief Assyrian god—and was privileged to become a part of Asshur's divine council. Yahweh could even give oracles to the Assyrians, particularly when they suited Assyrian purposes (18:25). Unlike Amaziah's voluntary idolatry with the gods of Edom (2Ch 25:14), Ahaz's idolatry was forced on him by his submission to Assyria. Ahaz's imported **altar** was the cultic symbol of his submission to Assyria's main god. The priest **Uriah** represented the complicity of some priests and Levites in this religious corruption.

16:12-13 Ahaz entered into his religious responsibilities to Assyria's chief pagan god with diligence, though he also had time for other pagan deities as well (vv. 3-4). Ahaz, representing the Hebrew people, participated in the religious rituals at Asshur's altar. This contrasted with his failure to represent the people correctly before Yahweh, and it also contrasted with Solomon's representation of the people (see note at 1Kg 8:22).

16:14-15a Perhaps at the suggestion of some visiting Assyrian official (cp. v. 18), Ahaz moved the original **bronze altar** of Yahweh to a less central place in the temple to give prominence to the altar of the Assyrian god.

16:15b Ahaz, however, remained true to Yahweh in one activity. He designated the **bronze altar** of Yahweh as the king's private altar where he would seek guidance, presumably from the Lord. The traditional means of guidance was through the sacred lots, the Urim and Thummim, though some suggest that Ahaz used pagan divinations.

16:17 **Bronze** was a valuable commodity. So, as an accommodating subject, Ahaz stripped bronze off the sacred fittings of the temple and even sent the bronze from the 12 **oxen** of the bronze **reservoir** to Assyria as tribute. However, the valuable metal of Moses' bronze serpent was not sent to Assyria since it was still there years later (18:4).

16:18 The significance of removing the **Sabbath canopy** and closing the special **entrance for the king** is not clear. The only thing certain is that something in them offended the king of Assyria.

Ahaz's Death

[19] The rest[a] of the events of Ahaz's reign, along with his accomplishments, are written in the Historical Record of Judah's Kings.[b] [20] Ahaz rested with his fathers[c] and was buried with his fathers in the city of David, and his son Hezekiah became king in his place.

Israel's King Hoshea

17 In the twelfth year of Judah's King Ahaz, Hoshea[d] son of Elah became king over Israel in Samaria and reigned nine years. [2] He did what was evil in the Lord's sight, but not like the kings of Israel who preceded him.[e]

[3] Shalmaneser[f] king of Assyria attacked him,[g] and Hoshea became his vassal and paid him tribute money. [4] But the king of Assyria discovered Hoshea's conspiracy. He had sent envoys to So king of Egypt[h] and had not paid tribute money to the king of Assyria as in previous years.[A] Therefore the king of Assyria arrested him and put him in prison. [5] Then the king of Assyria invaded the whole land, marched up to Samaria, and besieged it for three years.[i]

The Fall of Samaria

[6] In the ninth year of Hoshea,[j] the king of Assyria captured Samaria. He deported[k] the Israelites to Assyria and settled them in Halah and by the Habor, Gozan's river, and in the cities of the Medes.[l]

Why Israel Fell

[7] This disaster happened because the people of Israel had sinned against the Lord their God who had brought them out of the land of Egypt from the power of Pharaoh king of Egypt[m] and because they had worshiped[B] other gods.[n] [8] They had lived according to the customs of the nations that the Lord had dispossessed before the Israelites[o] and the customs the kings of Israel had introduced.[p] [9] The Israelites secretly did what was not right[C] against the Lord their God. They built ·high places in all their towns from watchtower[q] to fortified city. [10] They set up for themselves sacred pillars[r] and ·Asherah poles[s] on every high hill and under every green tree.[t] [11] They burned incense on all the high places just like those nations that the Lord had driven out before them. They did evil things, provoking the Lord. [12] They served idols, although the Lord had told them, "You must not do this."[u] [13] Still, the Lord warned[v] Israel and Judah through every prophet and every seer, saying, "Turn from

Cross references (center column)
[a]16:19-20 2Ch 28:26-27
[b]16:19 2Kg 15:36
[c]16:20 Is 14:28
[d]17:1 2Kg 15:30
[e]17:2 2Kg 15:24,28
[f]17:3 Hs 10:14
[g]2Kg 18:9-12
[h]17:4 Is 31:1
[i]17:5 2Kg 18:9-10; Hs 13:16
[j]17:6 Hs 1:4; 13:16
[k]Dt 28:64; 29:27-28
[l]1Ch 5:26
[m]17:7 Jos 24:5-7
[n]Jdg 6:10
[o]17:8 Lv 18:3; Dt 18:9
[p]2Kg 16:3; 17:19
[q]17:9 2Kg 18:8
[r]17:10 Ex 23:24
[s]1Kg 14:15,23; 15:13; 2Kg 18:4
[t]Dt 12:2
[u]17:12 Ex 20:4-5
[v]17:13 Neh 9:29-30

[A]17:4 Lit as year by year [B]17:7 Lit feared [C]17:9 Or Israelites spoke untrue words

---

16:19-20 Ahaz's record closes with the typical formula statement.

17:1-2 The formulaic opener for **Hoshea** reveals that he was not as bad as his predecessors.

17:3-4 Hoshea was appointed king about 732 B.C. over an Israel greatly reduced by Tiglath-pileser III (15:29). At some point when **Assyria** was distracted elsewhere Hoshea declared his freedom. The identity of **So** among known Egyptian Pharaohs is uncertain. When Hoshea withheld tribute from Assyria, the end came. Tiglath-pileser died before he could return to **Samaria**, but his son, Shalmaneser V, invaded Israel (725 B.C.). After a three-year siege, he captured Samaria, imprisoned Hoshea, and **deported** the Hebrew population to Assyria (722 B.C.). Verse 4 seems to indicate that Shalmaneser arrested Hoshea before besieging Samaria. It is unlikely that the city would have resisted after Hoshea's arrest. It is easier to take verses 4 through 6 as topically structured. The topic of verse 4 is Hoshea, whom Shalmaneser **arrested** (confined by siege) and then **put . . . in prison** after the siege ended.

17:5-6a The temporal marker, **then**, is missing in the Hebrew. Rather, verses 5 and 6 probably consider the same time period with respect to the nation. Shalmaneser **besieged** the city for three years and then **deported** the population to points north and east of Israel. Sargon II, the next king of Assyria, may have expedited some of the deportations.

17:6b The Assyrians deported the Hebrews to several different areas. **Halah** was in the general area of Gozan. Some were settled along the **Habor** River, a tributary of the Euphrates that flowed south from the region of Haran and Gozan to the Euphrates. This region was only about 400 miles

northeast of Israel. However, other Israelites were settled in the territory of the **Medes** in mountain country east and northeast of the plains of Babylon and Assyria. These exiles were almost a thousand miles from home.

17:7-20 These verses contain one of the great theological statements of the OT—God's accusation against the Israelites for their covenant faithlessness and that of their kings. It also expresses the climactic moral statement of the Deuteronomic History. This condemnation covered both Judah and Israel although Judah's doom was still about 130 years in the future. The author gave a grief-filled statement of why this tragedy happened. The notes below recognize the major themes of this theological statement.

17:7 This verse repeats three fundamental truths of Israelite life that are repeated over and over again in OT theology. First, they **sinned against the Lord**. Second, this was the God who, by bringing them **out of . . . Egypt**, had made them His possession. Third, the people had **worshiped other gods**.

17:8 The Hebrews were so perverse in their idolatry that they, like King Amaziah (2Ch 25:14-15), adopted the gods who were incapable of defending their people against **the nations**.

17:9-10 The Israelites built numerous **high places**, at first **secretly** and then openly. The typical high place installation consisted of (1) a **sacred** stone or **pillar** for the male fertility deity, usually some Baal, and (2) a sacred pole or a **green tree** for the female consort of the Baal. The latter often represented the consort goddess or **Asherah**.

17:11-12 Then the message becomes a piling-on harangue that lists the discouraging catalogue of evils committed by the people. There are both general statements—**they did**

your evil ways and keep My commands and statutes according to all the law I commanded your ancestors and sent to you through My servants the prophets."[a]

[a]17:13 1Kg 9:6-9; 18:18-21
[b]17:14 Ex 32:9; 33:3; Nm 14:11
[c]17:15 Ex 24:6-8
[d]Jr 2:5; Rm 1:21-23
[e]Dt 12:30-31

jected His statutes and His covenant He had made with their ancestors[c] and the decrees He had given them. They pursued worthless idols and became worthless themselves,[d] following the surrounding nations the LORD had commanded them not to imitate.[e]

[14]But they would not listen. Instead they became obstinate like[A] their ancestors who did not believe the LORD their God.[b] [15]They re-

[16]They abandoned all the commands of the

[A]17:14 Lit they stiffened their neck like the neck of

evil things—as well as more specific general practices—they burned incense.

17:16-17 The author presents more accusations of idolatry and cruelties. The worship of the whole heavenly host, the gods of the heavenly bodies, had not been frequently men-

tioned so far, but they were mentioned by contemporaneous prophets (Am 5:26). The most extreme evil—offering infants to Baal by having them pass through the fire—is mentioned, as well as divination and omens. Divination focuses more on gaining knowledge by supernatural means while omens

The Exiles of Israel

Duane A. Garrett

Two related but distinct concepts that shaped the history of Israel are "exile" and "Diaspora." The "exile" is the forced removal of the bulk of the population, especially of the skilled and upper class people, from their homeland to another country. There were several Jewish exiles. The first was the exile of the Israelites of the northern kingdom (Samaria) carried out by the Assyrians. It occurred in two phases, first in 734 B.C. under Tiglath-pileser III (2Kg 15:29) and then, climactically, in 722 under Shalmaneser and his successor, Sargon II, when the city of Samaria was destroyed and the northern kingdom ceased to exist (2Kg 17:5–6). The next major exile involved the destruction of the southern kingdom (Judah) and the city of Jerusalem. It, too, took place in several phases, all under the Babylonian king Nebuchadnezzar II (Jr 52:28–30), the most terrible of which was in 586 B.C. (Jr 52:29). This was when Solomon's temple was destroyed and the dynasty of David came to an end.

The third major exile of the Jews took place under the Romans and also was in two phases. In A.D. 70 the Roman general (later emperor) Titus destroyed Jerusalem and Herod's temple. A second Jewish rebellion (called the Bar Kokhba revolt after the name of its Jewish leader) took place under Emperor Hadrian in the years A.D. 132–136. This was a bloody struggle, and at the end the victorious Romans decreed that no Jew would be allowed to live in Palestine. All of these events involved exile, the forcible deportation of Jews from the Holy Land by their conquerors.

The "Diaspora" is the scattering of Jews across the world. This process began around the time of the destruction of Samaria and it continued in the aftermath of the Babylonian exile. The story of Esther, for example, involves Jews dispersed across the Persian Empire; this dispersion persisted even though the Persians allowed the Jews to return to their traditional homeland. We know of some specific Jewish enclaves. For example, there was in the fifth century B.C. a Jewish community in Elephantine (in southern Egypt), and beginning in the third century B.C. there was another such community in Alexandria (in northern Egypt). The Jewish Diaspora has involved places as diverse as ancient Rome, medieval Spain, Yemen, Iraq, Russia, Germany, and the United States. It continues to this day even though there is now a Jewish homeland in Israel. Esther also accurately characterizes the experience of Jews in Diaspora. On the one hand, the Jews are a positive contribution to their host countries and are often highly successful, but on the other hand, they are relentlessly and often unjustly persecuted.

Exile and Diaspora are the punishments God imposed on Israel for idolatry and unbelief (Dt 28:64-68; Is 6:11-12; 39:1-7; Jr 6:1-8; 19:1-13; Ezk 5:5-12; Am 8:1-12). Perhaps the primary passage on the subject is Dt 29:24-28: "All the nations will ask, 'Why has the LORD done this to this land . . .' Then people will answer, 'It is because they abandoned the covenant of the LORD . . . They began to worship other gods . . . Therefore the LORD's anger burned . . . The LORD uprooted them from their land in His anger, fury, and great wrath, and threw them into another land where they are today.'"

But this is not the whole story. The prophets also claimed that God would restore David's fallen dynasty (Hs 3:5; Am 9:11) and give Israel a New Covenant to replace the one they had broken (Jr 31:31-34). And now, while Israel is in disobedience and Diaspora, the Gentiles are brought into the New Covenant (Rm 11:25-32). The true end of exile will be when Israel turns to their Messiah, Jesus, mourning over Him whom they have pierced (Zch 12:6-14).

LORD their God. They made cast images[a] for themselves, two calves, and an Asherah pole.[b] They worshiped the whole heavenly *host[c] and served *Baal.[d] [17]They made their sons and daughters pass through the fire[e] and practiced *divination and interpreted omens.[f] They devoted themselves to do what was evil in the LORD's sight and provoked Him.[g]

[18]Therefore, the LORD was very angry with Israel, and He removed them from His presence.[h] Only the tribe of Judah remained.[i] [19]Even Judah did not keep the commands of the LORD their God[j] but lived according to the customs Israel had introduced.[k] [20]So the LORD rejected all the descendants of Israel, afflicted them, and handed them over to plunderers until He had banished them from His presence.[l]

Summary of Israel's History

[21]When the LORD tore[m] Israel from the house of David, Israel made Jeroboam son of Nebat king.[n] Then Jeroboam led Israel away from following the LORD and caused them to commit great sin. [22]The Israelites persisted in all the sins that Jeroboam committed and did not turn away from them.[o] [23]Finally, the LORD removed Israel from His presence just as He had declared through all His servants the prophets. So Israel has been exiled to Assyria from their homeland until today.[p]

Foreign Refugees in Israel

[24]Then the king of Assyria brought people

from Babylon, Cuthah, Avva, Hamath, and Sepharvaim and settled them in place of the Israelites in the cities of Samaria. The settlers took possession of Samaria and lived in its cities.[q] [25]When they first lived there, they did not *fear *Yahweh. So the LORD sent lions among them, which killed some of them.[r] [26]The settlers spoke to the king of Assyria, saying, "The nations that you have deported and placed in the cities of Samaria do not know the requirements of the God of the land. Therefore He has sent lions among them that are killing them because the people don't know the requirements of the God of the land."

[27]Then the king of Assyria issued a command: "Send back one of the priests you deported.[s] Have him go and live there so he can teach them the requirements of the God of the land." [28]So one of the priests they had deported came and lived in Bethel,[t] and he began to teach them how they should fear Yahweh.

[29]But the people of each nation were still making their own gods in the cities where they lived and putting them in the shrines of the high places that the people of Samaria had made.[u] [30]The men of Babylon made Succoth-benoth, the men of Cuth made Nergal, the men of Hamath made Ashima, [31]the Avvites made Nibhaz and Tartak, and the Sepharvites burned their children in the fire[v] to Adrammelech and Anammelech, the gods of the Sepharvaim. [32]They feared the LORD, but they also appointed from their number priests to serve

a 17:16 1Kg 12:28
b 1Kg 14:15,23
c 2Kg 21:3
d 1Kg 16:31-33; Am 5:26; Zph 1:5
e 17:17 2Kg 16:3
f Lv 19:26; Dt 18:10-12; 2Kg 16:3
g 1Kg 21:20
h 17:18 2Kg 17:6
i 1Kg 11:13,32,36
j 17:19 1Kg 14:22-23
k 2Kg 16:3
l 17:20 2Kg 15:29; 17:6
m 17:21 1Kg 11,11,31
n 1Kg 12:20
o 17:21-22 1Kg 12:28-33
p 17:23 2Kg 17:6,13
q 17:24 Ezr 4:10
r 17:25 1Kg 13:24
s 17:27 2Kg 17:6
t 17:28 1Kg 12:29,32-33
u 17:29 1Kg 12:31; 13:32
v 17:31 2Kg 17:17

---

are the magical giving of knowledge and the exercise of magic power. Such dabbling with supernatural knowledge and power was part of King Saul's sin (1Sm 28:7-9) and was condemned by Moses (Lv 20:6; Dt 18:10-11).

17:18 After all these reports of idolatry and disobedience, **the LORD was very angry** seems like an understatement. The final penalty for repeated idolatry was the removal of the people from God's **presence** by taking them from the land He had given them.

17:19-20 The context of this judgment was primarily God's judgment of **Israel**, but the Lord proceeded to pronounce judgment on Judah as well. From this time, Judah's exile was also decreed.

17:21-23 Jeroboam (Jeroboam I) was the archetypical figure for the sin of **Israel** and the roots of Israel's destruction are traced back to him. Finally, Israel was **removed** from God's presence.

17:24 The origins of the Assyrian colonists were the following: (1) **Babylon** in lower Mesopotamia; (2) **Cuthah** in lower Mesopotamia just a few miles from Babylon; (3) **Avva**, also known as Ivva, of unknown location; (4) **Hamath**, north of Damascus on the Orontes River, near where the Battle of Qarqar was fought; and (5) **Sepharvaim**, somewhere in Aramean territory.

17:25 The word **fear** can carry a range of meanings, from

terror to reverential worship of God. It is not easy to know what level of terror or worship the word communicated in this context.

17:26-28 These verses give an accurate picture of religious attitudes in the ancient world. In general, ancient people believed that the gods were real and powerful enough that people had to manipulate them to gain benefits. This contrasted with Hebrew theology, which held that God cannot be manipulated. The Assyrians viewed foreign gods as lesser deities to be incorporated into their system of worship. Therefore, it seemed reasonable to them to send a priest of the territorial god back to the occupied region to teach the people there, many of whom were new arrivals, how to make peace with that god (or gods). Possibly this included providing a copy of the deity's sacred writings. This priest's work may have been the origin of the Samaritan Pentateuch.

17:29-34 The result of all these efforts was a group of people with mixed religious beliefs and practices. They **feared** the Lord while at the same time they still **worshiped their own gods**, and as a result eventually they did not fear the Lord. **Succoth-benoth** was similar to Sarpanitu, one of Marduk's goddess consorts. **Nergal**, the god of pestilence and one of many consorts of Erishkigal—queen of the underworld—had a shrine in **Cuth**. **Ashima** may have appeared also in the phrase "guilt (Hb *ashmath*) of Samaria" (Am 8:14). This deity was probably the same as Ashim Bethel

them in the shrines of the high places.ᵃ ³³They feared the LORD, but they also worshiped their own godsᵇ according to the custom of the nations where they had been deported from.

³⁴They are still practicing the former customs to this day. None of them fear the LORD or observe their statutes and ordinances, the law and commandments the LORD commanded the descendants of Jacob. He had renamed him Israel.ᶜ ³⁵The LORD made a covenant with them and commanded them, "Do not fear other gods; do not bow down to them;ᵈ do not serve them; do not sacrifice to them.ᵉ ³⁶Instead fear the LORD, who brought you from the land of Egypt with great powerᶠ and an outstretched arm.ᵍ You are to bow down to Him,

and you are to sacrifice to Him. ³⁷You are to be careful alwaysʰ to observe the statutes, the ordinances, the law, and the commandments He wrote for you; do not fear other gods. ³⁸Do not forget the covenant that I have made with you.ⁱ Do not fear other gods, ³⁹but fear the LORD your God, and He will deliver you from the hand of all your enemies."ʲ

⁴⁰However, they would not listen but continued practicing their former customs. ⁴¹These nations feared the LORD but also served their idols. Their children and grandchildren continue doing as their fathers did until today.ᵏ

Judah's King Hezekiah

18 In the third year of Israel's King Hosheaˡ son of Elah, Hezekiahᵐ son of

ᵃ 17:32 Jdg 17:5-13; 1Kg 12:31; 13:33
ᵇ 17:33 Zph 1:5
ᶜ 17:34 Gn 32:28; 35:10
ᵈ 17:35 Ex 20:5; Dt 5:9; Jdg 6:10
ᵉ Dt 5:9
ᶠ 17:36 Ex 14:15-30
ᵍ Ex 6:6; 9:15
ʰ 17:37 Dt 5:32
ⁱ 17:38 Dt 4:23; 6:12
ʲ 17:39 Ex 23:22; Dt 20:1-4; 23:14
ᵏ 17:41 1Kg 18:21; Ezr 4:2; Mt 6:24
ˡ 18:1 2Kg 17:1
ᵐ 2Ch 28:27

(or Eshem Bethel), who appeared as a fertility consort of Yahweh in the popular, syncretistic religion of the Jewish colony at Elephantine. Two unknown deities of the **Avvites** were **Nibhaz** and **Tartak**. **Adrammelech** and **Anammelech** of **Sepharvaim** cannot be clearly identified, though the fact that children were sacrificed to them tells something about their character. The general picture is one of typical ancient fertility religion, including major national deities and minor local deities.

17:35-39 These verses give a concluding summary of the historic mandate to the Israelites to obey the **covenant**.

17:40-41 If the Israelites, whom God had delivered from Egypt (vv. 34-39), would not obey God's covenant, how could the pagan idolaters that were relocated to Samaria do any better? In fact, we could argue that these pagans, eventually growing into some commitment to their own version of the Pentateuch, did deserve comparison with the Hebrews.

18:1–20:21 This section focuses on the reign of Hezekiah of

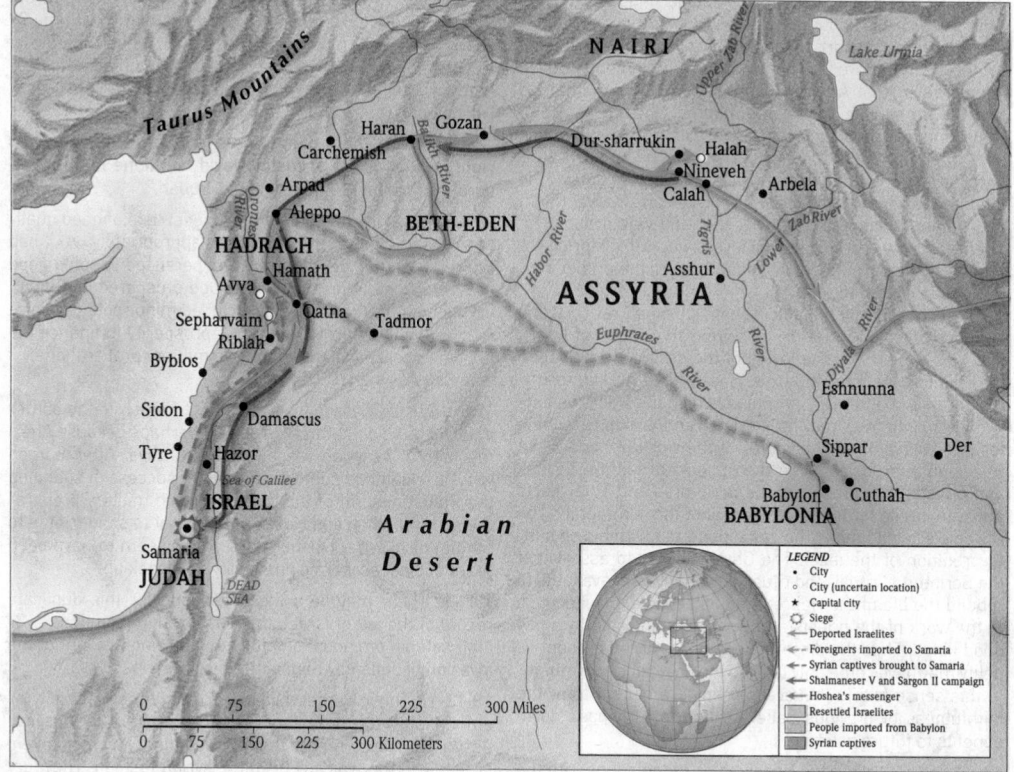

The Fall of Samaria and Deportation of the Israelites

Ahaz became king of Judah. [2]He was 25 years old when he became king and reigned 29 years in Jerusalem. His mother's name was Abi[A] daughter of Zechariah. [3]He did what was right in the LORD's sight just as his ancestor David had done.[a] [4]He removed the *high places, shattered the sacred pillars, and cut down the *Asherah poles.[b] He broke into pieces the bronze snake that Moses made,[c] for the Israelites burned incense to it up to that time. He called it Nehushtan.[B]

[5]Hezekiah trusted in the LORD God of Israel;[d] not one of the kings of Judah was like him, either before him or after him.[e] [6]He remained faithful to *Yahweh[f] and did not turn from following Him but kept the commands the LORD had commanded Moses.

[7]The LORD was with him, and wherever he went he prospered.[g] He rebelled against the king of Assyria and did not serve him.[h] [8]He defeated the Philistines as far as Gaza and its borders,[i] from watchtower[j] to fortified city.

Review of Israel's Fall

[9]In the fourth year of King Hezekiah, which was the seventh year of Israel's King

Hoshea son of Elah, Shalmaneser king of Assyria marched against Samaria and besieged it.[k] [10]The Assyrians captured it at the end of three years. In the sixth year of Hezekiah, which was the ninth year of Israel's King Hoshea, Samaria was captured. [11]The king of Assyria deported the Israelites to Assyria and put them in Halah and by the Habor, Gozan's river, and in the cities of the Medes,[l] [12]because they did not listen to the voice of the LORD their God but violated His covenant—all He had commanded Moses the servant of the LORD. They did not listen, and they did not obey.[m]

Sennacherib's Invasion

[13]In the fourteenth year of King Hezekiah, Sennacherib king of Assyria attacked all the fortified cities of Judah and captured them.[n] [14]So Hezekiah king of Judah sent word to the king of Assyria at Lachish,[o] saying, "I have done wrong;[p] withdraw from me. Whatever you demand from me, I will pay." The king of Assyria demanded 11 tons[C] of silver and one ton[D] of gold from King Hezekiah of Judah. [15]So Hezekiah gave him all the silver found in

Cross references (center column):
[a]18:2-3 2Ch 29:1-2
[b]18:4 2Kg 17:10; 18:22; 2Ch 31:1
[c]Nm 21:5-9
[d]18:5 2Kg 19:10
[e]1Kg 3:12; 2Kg 23:25
[f]18:6 Dt 10:20; Jos 23:8
[g]18:7 Gn 39:2-3; 1Sm 18:14
[h]2Kg 16:7
[i]18:8 2Ch 28:18; Is 14:29
[j]2Kg 17:9
[k]18:9 2Kg 17:3-7
[l]18:10-11 2Kg 17:6; 1Ch 5:26
[m]18:12 1Kg 9:6; 2Kg 17:7-18; Dn 9:6,10
[n]18:13 2Ch 32:1; Is 36:1
[o]18:14 2Kg 19:8
[p]Is 24:5; 33:8

[A]18:2 = Abijah in 2Ch 29:1   [B]18:4 = A bronze thing   [C]18:14 Lit 300 talents   [D]18:14 Lit 30 talents

---

Judah. He was a godly king, but he and his nation paid a terrible price for his godliness when Sennacherib invaded Judah. From man's short-range perspective, rebellion against the Assyrian Empire was a tragedy. The Bible and Assyrian annals agree that Assyrian reprisals devastated Judah so that the immediate gains were minimal. Even in terms of Deuteronomic theology, this revival just delayed the exile until after Hezekiah's death. Likewise for his great-grandson Josiah, judgment was just delayed. In this context, the long-range benefit and blessing of Hezekiah's revival might seem hard to discern. After all, the land was devastated. Then and now, persecuted believers pay a high price for little earthly gain. But earthly gain is never the proper motive of fidelity to God.

However, one identifiable benefit of these revivals and support for covenant teaching during the reigns of Hezekiah and Josiah was the laying of the essential foundation for religious life after the exile. Speaking in human terms, the Torah and other OT Scriptures, which the Hebrews took with them into exile, may have existed and/or been available for later teaching only because of the work of people like Hezekiah and Josiah. With the support of faithful Levites and priests, they preserved the Scriptures and other parts of covenant life for the future benefit of the community. The Chronicler could make the same point but with his own interpretation of the facts. The Chronicler could assert that the Scriptures, ritual, and ritual personnel were available to rebuild the life of the Hebrews after the exile only because of the work of the priests and Levites—supported by a few good kings. Thus the discernible benefits of the present fidelity may have come only later to the postexilic community. In this sense faithful believers in any era benefit from the faithfulness of previous believers and in turn pass down benefits to future believers.

18:1-2 The record of King **Hezekiah** of **Judah** opens with the usual formal statements. However, his dates, like Ahaz's

dates, present an unusual circumstance. Some point out that the length of Hezekiah's rule is compatible with the **29 years** of his sole regency (715–686 B.C.), while the date of the beginning of his rule refers to the beginning of his co-regency with his father, **Ahaz**. This began in the third year of Hoshea of Israel (729 B.C.).

18:3 The statement that King Hezekiah **did what was right . . . just as his ancestor David had done** is the standard formula for the good kings of Judah.

18:4-7a Hezekiah had one of the longest lists of good qualities of all the good kings. He acted appropriately (v. 4), had the right attitude of faith (v. 5), and persisted in doing good (v. 6). Because of his obedience, God prospered him in everything (v. 7). This prosperity included minor political victories (v. 8) and sufficient economic prosperity to finance building operations and expensive military preparations for war with Assyria (2Ch 32:1-5).

18:8 In 716 B.C. Sargon II advanced victoriously to the border of Egypt but did not threaten Judah, perhaps because Ahaz, the faithful Assyrian vassal, was still alive. After Sargon left, Hezekiah had some local military success in subduing the **Philistines**. All of this coincided with military preparations for rebellion and Hezekiah's refusal to send tribute to Sargon of Assyria. Furthermore, these seem to have been years of local economic prosperity for Hezekiah.

18:9-12 There may be a literary reason for this duplicate record of the fall of Israel, the northern kingdom (cp. 17:3-6). It sets an ominous tone for the following account of the invasion of Judah by Sennacherib of Assyria.

18:13-16 These verses fail to portray, either factually or emotionally, the devastation of the invasion by **Assyria**. Assyrian records report that 46 walled cities were taken, probably in the typically brutal Assyrian fashion. They further claim that 200,150 captives and much booty were also

Judah After the Fall of the Northern Kingdom

DATE [B.C.]	JUDAH	PROPHETS	EGYPT	ASSYRIA	MEDES	BABYLON
722	Ahaz (735–715); Vassal of Assyria	Isaiah Micah		Sargon II (722–705)		
715	Hezekiah (715–687) Hezekiah's rebellion against Assyria			Sennacherib (705–681) Campaign against Judah		Chaldean chieftan Merodach-baladan
700	Sennacherib's Campaign (701) Manasseh (687–642)		Tirhakah (690–664)	Sennacherib destroys Babylon Esar-haddon (681–669) attacks Egypt		
675	Corruption and pagan practices promoted by Manasseh's grip of Judah		Psammeticus (664–610)	Ashurbanipal II (669–627); sack of Thebes (663)		
650	Josiah (640–609)	Jeremiah (627–582) Nahum		Death of Ashurbanipal II (627)		Nabopolassar seized throne of Babylon (626)
625	Josianic reform "Book of the Law" (621)				Cyaxares (623–584)	
615	Death of Josiah (609)	Zephaniah Habakkuk	Neco II (610–594)	Sin-shar-ushkun (614) Assur sacked (614) Ashuruballit II; Nineveh destroyed (612) Haran falls (610)		
605	Jehoiakim (609–598) Rebellion against Babylon					Nebuchadnezzar (605–562) Battle of Carchemish
600						
598/97	1st siege of Jerusalem and deportation [Jehoiachin 598–597]	Ezekiel	Apries (Hophra) (589–570)			1st campaign against Judah
587/86	2nd siege of Jerusasalem; destruction of temple					2nd campaign against Judah; destruction of the temple

the LORD's temple and in the treasuries of the king's palace.

[16]At that time Hezekiah stripped the gold from the doors of the LORD's sanctuary and from the doorposts he had overlaid and gave it to the king of Assyria.[a]

[17]Then the king of Assyria sent the Tartan,[b] the Rab-saris, and the •Rabshakeh, along with a massive army, from Lachish to King Hezekiah at Jerusalem.[c] They advanced and came to Jerusalem, and[A] they took their position by the aqueduct of the upper pool, which is by the highway to the Fuller's Field.[d] [18]Then they called for the king, but Eliakim[e] son of Hilkiah, who was in charge of the palace, Shebnah[f] the court secretary, and Joah son of Asaph, the court historian, came out to them.[g]

The Rabshakeh's Speech

[19]Then[h] the Rabshakeh said to them, "Tell Hezekiah this is what the great king, the king of Assyria, says: 'What are you relying on?[B,i] [20]You think mere words are strategy and strength for war. What are you now relying on so that you have rebelled against me?[j] [21]Look, you are now trusting in Egypt, that splintered reed of a staff[k] that will enter and pierce the hand of anyone who leans on it.[l] This is how Pharaoh king of Egypt is to all who trust in him. [22]Suppose you say to me: We trust in the LORD our God. Isn't He the One whose high places and altars Hezekiah has removed,[m] say-

ing to Judah and to Jerusalem: You must worship at this altar in Jerusalem?'

[23]"So now make a bargain with my master the king of Assyria. I'll give you 2,000 horses if you're able to supply riders for them! [24]How then can you drive back a single officer[n] among the least of my master's servants and trust in Egypt for chariots and for horsemen? [25]Have I attacked this place to destroy it without the LORD's approval?[o] The LORD said to me, 'Attack this land and destroy it.'"

[26]Then Eliakim son of Hilkiah, Shebnah, and Joah said to the Rabshakeh, "Please speak to your servants in Aramaic,[p] since we understand it. Don't speak with us in Hebrew[c] within earshot of the people on the wall."

[27]But the Rabshakeh said to them, "Has my master sent me only to your master and to you to speak these words? Hasn't he also sent me to the men who sit on the wall, destined with you to eat their own excrement and drink their own urine?"[q]

[28]The Rabshakeh stood and called out loudly in Hebrew.[c] Then he spoke: "Hear the word of the great king, the king of Assyria. [29]This is what the king says: 'Don't let Hezekiah deceive[r] you; he can't deliver you from my hand.[s] [30]Don't let Hezekiah persuade you to trust in the LORD by saying: Certainly the LORD will deliver us! This city will not be handed over to the king of Assyria.'[t]

---

a 18:15-16 2Kg 12:18; 16:8; 2Ch 16:2
b 18:17 Is 20:1
c 2Ch 32:9
d 2Kg 20:20; Is 7:3
e 18:18 2Kg 19:2; Is 22:20
f Is 22:15
g 18:17-18 Is 36:2-3
h 18:19-37 Is 36:4-22
i 18:19 2Kg 18:5; 2Ch 32:10
j 18:20 2Kg 18:7
k 18:21 Is 30:2-3,7
l Ezk 29:6-7
m 18:22 2Kg 18:4; 2Ch 31:1; 32:11-12
n 18:24 Is 10:8
o 18:25 2Kg 19:6,22; 24:3; 2Ch 35:21
p 18:26 Ezr 4:7; Dn 2:4
q 18:26-27 Is 36:11-12
r 18:29 2Kg 19:10
s 2Ch 32:15
t 18:30 2Ch 32:18

A 18:17 LXX, Syr, Vg; MT reads *and came and*   B 18:19 Lit *What is this trust which you trust*   C 18:26,28 Lit *Judahite*

---

taken. Scholars have debated whether one or two Assyrian invasions of Judah are described in chapter 18. If there were two, these present verses may describe the first, and the second may be described in the following verses. If there was only one invasion, these verses could give a preliminary summary or preview of the overall campaign and then some of its details are further described below. Or perhaps there was only one campaign in which Hezekiah surrendered, made peace, and presented a huge tribute to Assyria, but the Assyrians then reneged on that agreement and tried to destroy Hezekiah and Jerusalem anyway. Some interpreters suggest the following scenario: Hezekiah promised this huge payment; Sennacherib had to leave without receiving it; Hezekiah sent the payment anyway.

18:17-18 Whatever had happened previously, the Assyrians were now threatening **Jerusalem**, the last outpost of orthodox worship of Yahweh. The **Tartan** was a high official, next to the king. If the Assyrians followed the Mesopotamian and Persian practice of using foreign eunuchs in high governmental positions, the meaning of the Hebrew word *saris* indicates that the **Rab-saris** was associated with those Assyrian officials. The title **Rabshakeh** is likely an honorific title that may have had little to do with the man's actual duties (cp. the chief cupbearer of Pharaoh; Gn 41:9). Here, he was the diplomatic spokesman for Sennacherib. Some have located the **Fuller's Field** near En-rogel on the southern approaches to Jerusalem. It may have been frequently visited by the royal family and dignitaries (1Kg 1:9). Though

this Assyrian deputation had asked for King Hezekiah, they received instead three high palace officials.

18:19-22 In human terms the Assyrian official spoke the truth: **Egypt** was weak; **Hezekiah** had torn down the shrines of Yahweh (though from the perspective of many who worshiped Yahweh, they were illegal) so that the Lord had no reason to protect the king. In fact, the Assyrian claimed that Yahweh was the deity who had sent the Assyrians to punish Hezekiah (v. 25).

18:23-24 The Rabshakeh mocked the military weakness of the Israelites.

18:25 The Rabshakeh claimed that the Lord had commissioned Assyria to attack and destroy Judah.

18:26 Aramaic was the normal language for international dealings, but the Assyrian diplomatic corps included **Hebrew** speakers.

18:28-30 Both the Assyrian propagandist and the author of 2 Kings continue to describe the depressing state of the Israelites and their faith in Yahweh. The **Rabshakeh** insisted on shouting, in **Hebrew** rather than Aramaic, his discouraging message to the soldiers on the wall.

18:31-32a The Rabshakeh offered temporary **peace** and then exile, which he described in rosy terms.

18:32b-35 The pessimistic appraisal continued with the accurate description of the helplessness of the **gods** of the other conquered **nations**. Even **Samaria** was mentioned.

³¹"Don't listen to Hezekiah, for this is what the king of Assyria says: 'Make peace^A with me and surrender to me. Then every one of you may eat from his own vine and his own fig tree,ᵃ and every one may drink water from his own cistern ³²until I come and take you away to a land like your own land—a land of grain and new wine, a land of bread and vineyards, a land of olive trees and honeyᵇ—so that you may liveᶜ and not die. But don't listen to Hezekiah when he misleads you, saying: The LORD will deliver us. ³³Has any of the gods of the nations ever deliveredᵈ his land from the power of the king of Assyria? ³⁴Where are the gods of Hamath and Arpad? Where are the gods of Sepharvaim, Hena, and Ivvah?^B Have they

ᵃ 18:31 1Kg 4:25
ᵇ 18:32 Dt 8:7-9; 11:12
ᶜ Dt 30:19
ᵈ 18:33 2Kg 19:12; Is 10:10-11
ᵉ 18:34 2Kg 17:24; 19:13
ᶠ 18:35 2Ch 32:14; Ps 2:1-4; Dn 3:15
ᵍ 18:37 2Kg 18:26; 19:2
ʰ 2Kg 6:30; Is 33:7

delivered Samaria from my hand?ᵉ ³⁵Who among all the gods of the lands has delivered his land from my power? So will the LORD deliver Jerusalem?'"ᶠ

³⁶But the people kept silent; they didn't say anything, for the king's command was, "Don't answer him." ³⁷Then Eliakim son of Hilkiah, who was in charge of the palace, Shebna the court secretary, and Joah son of Asaph, the court historian,ᵍ came to Hezekiah with their clothes tornʰ and reported to him the words of the Rabshakeh.

Hezekiah Seeks Isaiah's Counsel

19 When King Hezekiah heard their report, he tore his clothes, covered

---

^A 18:31 Lit *a blessing*   ^B 18:34 Some LXX mss, Old Lat read *Sepharvaim? Where are the gods of the land of Samaria?*

(On the nations mentioned here, see 19:12-13 and note at 19:10-13.)

18:36-37 The torn clothes were a formal declaration of grief.

19:1 Some have seen Hezekiah's inactivity at this point

as out of character. Two responses are proper. First, his seeking God and leading in repentance are very important actions. Second, this account was not structured to show Hezekiah's activities. It instead aims to show his faith as the world around him was collapsing. By his grief Hezekiah was demonstrating how bad things were.

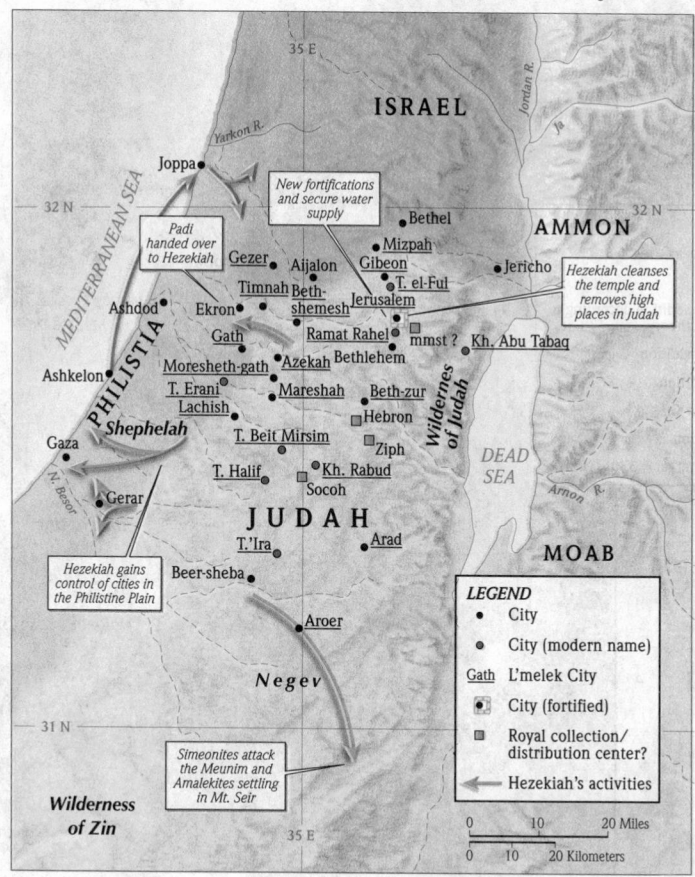

Hezekiah's Revolt

himself with *sackcloth,[a] and went into the LORD's temple.[b] [2] Then he sent Eliakim, who was in charge of the palace, Shebna the court secretary,[c] and the leading priests, who were wearing sackcloth,[d] to the prophet Isaiah[e] son of Amoz. [3] They said to him, "This is what Hezekiah says: 'Today is a day of distress, rebuke, and disgrace, for children have come to the point of birth,[f] but there is no strength to deliver them. [4] Perhaps *Yahweh your God[g] will hear[h] all the words of the *Rabshakeh, whom his master the king of Assyria sent to mock the living God, and will rebuke[i] him for

the words that Yahweh your God has heard. Therefore, offer a prayer for the surviving remnant.'"[j]

[5] So the servants of King Hezekiah went to Isaiah, [6] who said to them, "Tell your master this, 'The LORD says: Don't be afraid[k] because of the words you have heard, that the king of Assyria's attendants[l] have blasphemed[m] Me with. [7] I am about to put a spirit in him, and he will hear a rumor and return to his own land[n] where I will cause him to fall by the sword.'"[o]

[a]19:1 1Kg 21:27; 2Kg 18:37; Ps 69:11
[b]2Ch 32:20; Is 37:1
[c]19:2 2Kg 18:26,37
[d]2Sm 3:31
[e]Is 1:1; 2:1
[f]19:3 Hs 13:13
[g]19:4 1Sm 17:26; 2Kg 18:35
[h]Jos 14:12; 2Sm 16:12
[i]Ps 50:21
[j]2Kg 19:30; Is 37:4
[k]19:6 Is 37:6
[l]2Kg 18:17
[m]2Kg 18:22-25,30,35
[n]19:7 2Kg 7:6   [o]2Kg 19:35-37

19:2-3 Royal officers and the **leading priests** were a very prestigious delegation. The writer used Hezekiah's own words to **Isaiah** to reinforce how bad the situation was. The metaphor of failed childbirth powerfully demonstrated the Israelites' helplessness.

19:4 The Assyrians' insulting **words** about **Yahweh** might arouse God, the only resource remaining, to action.

19:5-7 After more than a chapter of bad news, these

verses describe the first of five steps of good news. The overall theme is that, no matter how bad circumstances appeared, God could and would deliver. Isaiah's response was that, despite the Assyrian's arrogance in insulting God, He would give the Assyrian king such a **spirit**—attitude or desire—that he would want to go **to his own land** where he would die.

19:8-9 Since Sennacherib left **Lachish** without returning, Lachish must have fallen about that time. Sennacherib was

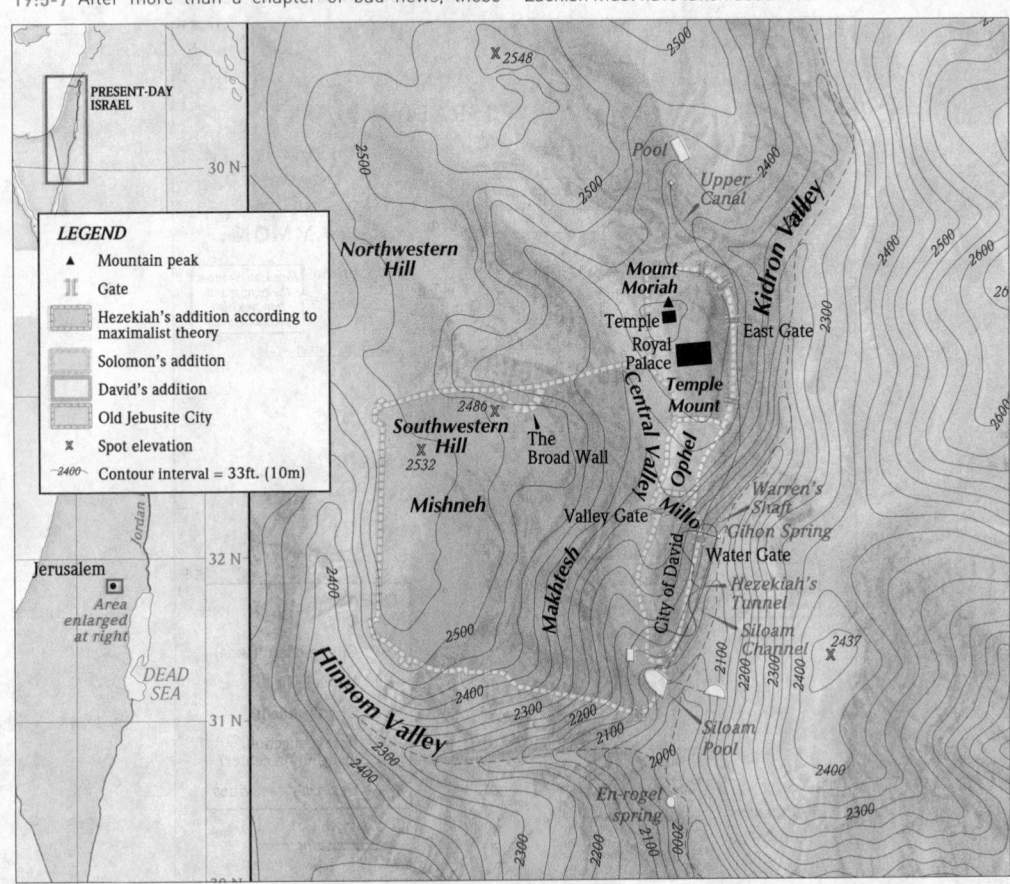

Hezekiah's Jerusalem

Sennacherib's Departing Threat

[8]When[a] the Rabshakeh heard that the king of Assyria had left Lachish,[b] he returned and found him fighting against Libnah.[c] [9]The king had heard this about Tirhakah king of *Cush: "Look, he has set out to fight against you." So he again sent messengers to Hezekiah, saying, [10]"Say this to Hezekiah king of Judah: 'Don't let your God, whom you trust,[d] deceive you by promising that Jerusalem will not be handed over to the king of Assyria.[e] [11]Look, you have heard what the kings of Assyria have done to all the countries: they *completely destroyed them. Will you be rescued? [12]Did the gods of the nations[f] that my predecessors destroyed rescue them—nations such as Gozan,[g] Haran,[h] Rezeph, and the Edenites[i] in Telassar? [13]Where is the king of Hamath, the king of Arpad, the king of the city of Sepharvaim, Hena, or Ivvah?'"[j]

Hezekiah's Prayer

[14]Hezekiah took[k] the letter[l] from the hand of the messengers, read it, then went up to the LORD's temple, and spread it out before the LORD.[m] [15]Then Hezekiah prayed before the LORD:

LORD God of Israel who is enthroned above the *cherubim,[n] You are God—You alone—of all the kingdoms of the earth. You made the heavens and the earth.[o] [16]Listen closely, LORD, and hear; open Your eyes, LORD, and see.[p] Hear the words that Sennacherib has sent to mock the living God.[q] [17]LORD, it is true that the kings of Assyria have devastated the nations and their lands.[r] [18]They have thrown their gods into the fire, for they were not gods but made by human hands—wood and stone.[s] So they have destroyed them. [19]Now, LORD our God, please save us from his hand so that all the kingdoms of the earth may know that You are the LORD God—You alone.[t]

God's Answer through Isaiah

[20]Then[u] Isaiah son of Amoz sent a message to Hezekiah: "The LORD, the God of Israel says: 'I have heard your prayer[v] to Me about Sennacherib king of Assyria.'[w] [21]This is the word the LORD has spoken against him:

Virgin Daughter *Zion[x]
despises you and scorns you:
Daughter Jerusalem
shakes her head behind your back.[A,y]
[22] Who is it you mocked
     and blasphemed?[z]
Against whom have you raised
     your voice
and lifted your eyes in pride?
Against the Holy One of Israel![aa]
[23] You have mocked the Lord[B] through[C]
     your messengers.[ab]
You have said:

With my many chariots[ac]
I have gone up to the heights
     of the mountains,
to the far recesses of Lebanon.
I cut down its tallest cedars,
its choice cypress trees.

Cross references (center column):
[a]19:8-13 Is 37:8-13
[b]19:8 2Kg 18:14
[c]Jos 10:29
[d]19:10 2Kg 18:5
[e]2Kg 18:29-30
[f]19:12 2Kg 18:33,35
[g]2Kg 17:6
[h]Gn 11:31
[i]Is 37:12
[j]19:13 2Kg 18:34
[k]19:14-19 Is 37:14-20
[l]19:14 2Kg 5:7
[m]Is 37:14
[n]19:15 Ex 35:22
[o]Gn 1:1; 2Kg 5:15; Is 44:6
[p]19:16 Dn 9:18
[q]2Kg 19:4; Ps 31:2; Is 37:17
[r]19:17 2Kg 18:34
[s]19:18 Is 44:9-20; Jr 10:3-5; Ac 17:29
[t]19:19 1Kg 8:42-43; Is 43:10-11
[u]19:20-34 Is 37:21-35
[v]19:20 2Kg 20:5
[w]Is 37:21
[x]19:21 Jr 14:17; Lm 2:13
[y]Ps 22:7-8; 109:25; Mt 27:39
[z]19:22 2Kg 19:4,6
[aa]Is 5:24; 30:11-15; Jr 51:5
[ab]19:23 2Kg 18:17; 19:4
[ac]Ps 20:7; Jr 50:37

[A]19:21 Lit *behind you*   [B]19:23 Many mss read LORD   [C]19:23 Lit *by the hand of*

---

dealing with **Libnah** when he heard that **Tirhakah** of Egypt was coming. Tirhakah was the last pharaoh of the Cushite dynasty of Egypt. His power consisted of a small group of ancient Egyptian royalty and nobility united with relatively effective Sudanese soldiers. Tirhakah's army was defeated, and Egypt ceased to be a threat.

19:10-13 Rabshakeh again warned **Hezekiah**, and again the message dealt with overwhelming Assyrian power. The warning was supported by a list of conquered peoples whose gods had not helped them: **Gozan**, on the Habor tributary of the Euphrates River near **Haran**; **Rezeph** northeast of Hamath on the trade route to the Euphrates; the **Edenites** (sometimes identified with the Aramean kingdom, Bit Adini, conquered by Assyria ca 855 B.C.), who like **Telassar** are unknown; **Hamath**, almost directly north of Damascus; **Arpad**, near the site of modern Aleppo; **Sepharvaim** and **Hena**, whose locations are unknown; and finally **Ivvah**, probably identical with Avva (17:31), whose gods are named but whose location is unknown. All of these sites were roughly on Assyria's approach route to Palestine.

19:15-16 Hezekiah's prayer depicted God as the sole Creator God. Although the Lord had not yet acted, this prayer implied that He would act when the time was right.

19:17-19 The second step (see note at vv. 5-7) in the good news was recognizing that the gods conquered by the Assyrians were **not gods**. The gods of those nations were idols made by men. Hezekiah, being so close to Isaiah, must have been influenced by Isaiah's teaching about idols (Is 40:18-20; 46:1-7). The intended impact of God's deliverance was to provide a testimony to **all the kingdoms of the earth**.

19:20-24 God presented the third stage of good news (see note at vv. 5-7) by describing the true power structure of the universe. This recalls the revelation to Elisha's servant (see note at 6:16-17).

19:21 First, the tables were turned to just the opposite of the Assyrians' attitudes. In truth, Jerusalem, or **Daughter Zion**, was in a position to mock the Assyrians.

19:22 In contrast to the idols destroyed by Assyria, the Assyrians were now facing the only true God, the **Holy One of Israel**, whose power surpassed anything the Assyrians had experienced.

19:23-24 Then came the most amazing principle of Isaiah's oracle. He admitted that the power of the Assyrian and his conquests were real. These verses use poetic figures of conquest, marching to the **mountains** of **Lebanon** and

I came to its farthest outpost,
its densest forest.
24 I dug wells,
and I drank foreign waters.
I dried up all the streams of Egypt[a]
with the soles of my feet.

25 Have you not heard?[b]
I designed it long ago;
I planned it in days gone by.
I have now brought it to pass,[c]
and you have crushed fortified cities
into piles of rubble.
26 Their inhabitants have
become powerless,
dismayed, and ashamed.
They are plants of the field,
tender grass,
grass on the rooftops,[d]
blasted by the east wind.[A]

27 But I know your sitting down,[B,e]
your going out and your coming in,
and your raging against Me.
28 Because your raging against Me
and your arrogance have reached
My ears,
I will put My hook in your nose[f]
and My bit in your mouth;
I will make you go back
the way you came.

29"This will be the sign[g] for you: This year
you will eat what grows on its own, and in the

second year what grows from that. But in the
third year sow and reap, plant vineyards and
eat their fruit. 30The surviving remnant[h] of the
house of Israel will again take root downward
and bear fruit upward. 31For a remnant will
go out from Jerusalem and survivors, from
Mount Zion.[i] The zeal of the LORD of •Hosts
will accomplish this.[j]

32   Therefore, this is what the LORD says
about the king of Assyria:
He will not enter this city
or shoot an arrow there
or come before it with a shield
or build up an assault ramp against it.[k]
33   He will go back
on the road that he came
and he will not enter this city.
This is the LORD's declaration.

34   I will defend this city and rescue it
for My sake and for the sake of My
servant David."[l]

Defeat and Death of Sennacherib

35That night the angel of the LORD went out
and struck down 185,000 in the camp of the
Assyrians. When the people got up the next
morning—there were all the dead bodies![m]
36So Sennacherib king of Assyria broke camp
and left. He returned home and lived in Nineveh.[n]
37One day, while he was worshiping in the
temple of his god Nisroch, his sons Adram-

a 19:24 Is 19:6
b 19:25 Is 40:21; 45:7
c Is 10:5
d 19:26 Ps 129:6
e 19:27 Ps 139:1-2
f 19:28 Ezk 19:9; 29:4; 38:4
g 19:29 Ex 3:14; 2Kg 20:8-9; Is 7:14
h 19:30 2Kg 19:4; 2Ch 32:22-23
i 19:31 Is 10:20
j Is 9:7
k 19:32 Is 8:7-10
l 19:34 1Kg 11:12-13; 2Kg 20:6; Is 31:5
m 19:35 2Ch 32:21; Is 37:36
n 19:36 Jnh 1:2

A 19:26 DSS; MT reads blasted before standing grain; Is 37:27   B 19:27 LXX, DSS read your rising up and your sitting down; Is 37:28

---

trampling the waters of many nations. No Assyrian court poet could have more effectively described the power and glory of Assyria in so few words.

19:25-26 Assyria had her way with surrounding nations for one reason: God ordained it.

19:27-28 The Assyrians were in God's hand. This brings us to the fourth point (see note at vv. 5-7) of good news: God would lead the Assyrians back to their land by His **hook** in their **nose** just as He would handle a stubborn draft animal.

19:29 The **year** of Jubilee was a second consecutive Sab-bath year, where fields were left fallow for two years (Lv 25:1-12). Many suspect that these commands were never consistently implemented. While possible, it is statistically unlikely that these two years under discussion would have coincided with the Jubilee. It is more likely that the author used these concepts and principles as metaphors to de-scribe the recovery of the land from devastation. Just as in the Jubilee, it would take two years of work and living on volunteer growth (plants arising from stray seeds not plant-ed by man) to restore the land. These words also suggest that the diminished population could survive on volunteer growth for two years. This message from Isaiah was both a sign, whose fulfillment proved God's reliability, and a prom-ise that volunteer growth would suffice for those two years.

19:30-31 This closing metaphor had three levels of mean-

ing. First, the remnants of the agricultural crops would take root and grow, and that growth would be an encouraging sign to God's people. Second, it promised that the **remnant** of the people would **take root** in the promised land, grow there, and survive this disaster. Third, this was a metaphor for the way in which God's people survive and recover from physical and spiritual enemies when they are fulfilling God's purposes.

19:32-33 Then God reiterated the fourth principle (vv. 27-28), adding that Jerusalem's deliverance would be so thorough that the Assyrians would not even **shoot an arrow** against Jerusalem.

19:35-36 The fifth and final step of good news (see note at vv. 5-7) was that God did send the **Assyrians** home. God miraculously damaged the Assyrian army so severely that they had to leave Judah. This apparently happened after the Assyrians had defeated the invading Egyptian army. All the events of this chapter probably took several weeks. Leaving Lachish, turning aside from Libnah, defeating the Egyptians, and then suffering a miraculous blow from God—perhaps a plague—would take some time.

19:37 Biblical Hebrew is often topically organized at the cost of chronological sequencing. The topic of these two chap-ters is God's triumph over Sennacherib. Though the end actually came some 10 or so years later, the Bible writer

melech[a] and Sharezer struck him down with the sword and escaped to the land of Ararat.[b] Then his son Esar-haddon[c] became king in his place.

Hezekiah's Illness and Recovery

20 In those days[d] Hezekiah became terminally ill.[e] The prophet Isaiah[f] son of Amoz came and said to him, "This is what the LORD says: 'Put your affairs in order,[A] for you are about to die; you will not recover.'"[g]

²Then Hezekiah turned his face to the wall[h] and prayed to the LORD, ³"Please LORD, remember[i] how I have walked before You faithfully and wholeheartedly and have done what pleases You."[B,j] And Hezekiah wept bitterly.[k]

⁴Isaiah had not yet gone out of the inner courtyard when the word of the LORD came to him: ⁵"Go back and tell Hezekiah, the leader[l] of My people, 'This is what the LORD God of your ancestor David says: I have heard your prayer;[m] I have seen your tears. Look, I will heal you. On the third day from now you will go up to the LORD's temple. ⁶I will add 15 years to your life. I will deliver you and this city from the hand of the king of Assyria. I will defend this city for My sake and for the sake of My servant David.'"[n]

⁷Then Isaiah said, "Bring a lump of pressed figs." So they brought it and applied it to his infected skin, and he recovered.[o]

⁸Hezekiah had asked Isaiah, "What is the sign[p] that the LORD will heal me and that I will go up to the LORD's temple on the third day?"

⁹Isaiah said, "This is the sign[q] to you from the LORD that He will do what He has promised: Should the shadow go ahead 10 steps or go back 10 steps?"

¹⁰Then Hezekiah answered, "It's easy for the shadow to lengthen 10 steps. No, let the shadow go back 10 steps." ¹¹So Isaiah the prophet called out to the LORD, and He brought the shadow[C] back the 10 steps it had descended on Ahaz's stairway.[D,r]

Hezekiah's Folly

¹²At that time[s] Merodach-baladan[E] son of Baladan, king of Babylon, sent letters and a gift to Hezekiah since he heard that he had been sick. ¹³Hezekiah gave them a hearing and showed them his whole treasure house—the silver, the gold, the spices, and the precious oil—and his armory, and everything that was found in his treasuries. There was nothing in his palace and in all his realm that Hezekiah did not show them.[t]

¹⁴Then the prophet Isaiah came to King Hezekiah and asked him, "Where did these men come from and what did they say to you?"

Hezekiah replied, "They came from a distant country, from Babylon."

a 19:37 2Kg 17:31
b Gn 8:4; Jr 51:27
c Gn 10:11; Ezr 4:2
d 20:1-11 Is 38:1-8
e 20:1 2Ch 32:24
f Is 1:1; 2:1
g 2Sm 17:23
h 20:2 1Kg 21:4
i 20:3 Neh 5:19; 13:14,22,31
j 2Kg 18:3-6
k 2Sm 12:21-22
l 20:5 1Sm 9:16; 10:1
m Ps 39:12
n 20:6 2Kg 19:34
o 20:7 Is 38:21
p 20:8 Jdg 6:17,37,39
q 20:9 Is 38:7
r 20:11 Jos 10:12-14; Is 38:8
s 20:12-19 Is 39:1-8
t 20:13 2Ch 32:27

A 20:1 Lit *Command your house*   B 20:3 Lit *what is good in Your eyes*   C 20:11 Lit *shadow on the steps*   D 20:11 Tg, Vg; DSS read *on the steps of Ahaz's roof chamber*; Is 38:8   E 20:12 Some Hb mss, LXX, Syr, Tg, some Vg mss, Is 39:1; other Hb mss read *Berodach-baladan*

recorded the end of that account—Sennacherib's death—before going on to begin another.

20:1-21 Most of this chapter (vv. 1-19) clearly occurred before Sennacherib's invasion. The major evidence is that Merodach-baladan's significant activities in Babylon occurred before this invasion. In the absence of explicit markers of chronological sequence, episodes in Hebrew narrative are not necessarily chronologically ordered. This chapter develops two points: (1) Hezekiah was so pious that God granted his prayer for extra years of life, and (2) Hezekiah, in pride, misused those extra years.

20:1-3 **In those days** may be interpreted as "in this same general time frame" (cp. 10:32; 15:37; Jdg 19:1). Told of his coming death, **Hezekiah** faced a difficult theological choice—either accept God's will or ask for special treatment. But the question can be stated in even more difficult terms. Should Hezekiah accept the will of the loving, omnipotent, sovereign Lord, or should he ask the immutable God to change His mind (Nm 23:19)? The Bible sometimes expects us to ask (Jms 4:2), and Hezekiah asked with sorrow, appealing to his righteous behavior.

20:4-6 God was neither surprised by nor unprepared for Hezekiah's **prayer**. He not only granted what was asked, but He also gave a promise of deliverance from the coming Assyrian invasion. Thus, this event was to strengthen Hezekiah's faith for that ordeal.

20:7 Some have suggested that what unfolded here was a divinely prescribed medical cure, meaning that God knew the treatment with figs would cure Hezekiah. More likely it was simply a miraculous healing. But in either case, God worked in response to prayer (v. 2).

20:8 An arrogant demand for a **sign** from **the LORD** is sin (Mt 16:1-4), but God might choose to honor a humble request for a sign (Jdg 6:36-40).

20:9-11 God let **Hezekiah** choose the final nature of the **sign**. Again, the purpose of this exercise was to strengthen Hezekiah's faith for the future.

20:12 This episode with **Babylon** also looked forward to Sennacherib's invasion. This invasion was a response to a worldwide conspiracy against Assyrian power. **Merodach-baladan** wanted to gain Hezekiah's support in such a rebellion.

20:13 Was Hezekiah's pride in the wealth he had accumulated? Wealth without empire may have been a relatively new thing in Judah. David and Solomon had great wealth, but their wealth grew from imperial power—control of international trade routes and foreign tribute. Or was Hezekiah's pride based on being sought as a player in the international politics of the day?

20:14-15 Hezekiah's brief answer indicated a reluctance to discuss the issue with **Isaiah**, but the prophet continued his

15Isaiah asked, "What have they seen in your
palace?"
Hezekiah answered, "They have seen everything in my palace. There isn't anything in my
treasuries that I didn't show them."
16Then Isaiah said to Hezekiah, "Hear the
word of the LORD: 17'The time will certainly
come when everything in your palace and all
that your fathers have stored up until this day
will be carried off to Babylon; nothing will be
left,'[a] says the LORD. 18'Some of your descendants who come from you will be taken away,[b]
and they will become eunuchs[A] in the palace
of the king of Babylon.'"[c]
19Then Hezekiah said to Isaiah, "The word
of the LORD that you have spoken is good,"[d]
for he thought: Why not, if there will be peace
and security during my lifetime?

Hezekiah's Death

20The rest of the events of Hezekiah's reign,
along with all his might and how he made the
pool[e] and the tunnel and brought water into
the city,[f] are written in the Historical Record
of Judah's Kings.[g] 21Hezekiah rested with his
fathers, and his son Manasseh became king in
his place.[h]

[a]20:17 2Kg 24:13; 2Ch 36:10
[b]20:18 2Kg 24:12; 2Ch 33:11
[c]Dn 1:3-7,11
[d]20:19 1Sm 3:18
[e]20:20 Neh 3:16; Is 7:3
[f]2Ch 32:30
[g]2Kg 16:19
[h]20:20-21 2Ch 32:32-33
[i]21:1-9 2Ch 33:1-9
[j]21:1 Is 62:4
[k]21:2 2Kg 20:16; Jr 15:4
[l]2Kg 16:3
[m]21:3 2Kg 18:4; 2Ch 31:1
[n]2Kg 23:26
[o]1Kg 16:32-33
[p]2Kg 17:16; 23:5
[q]21:4 2Kg 16:10-16
[r]Dt 12:11,14; 1Kg 11:13
[s]21:5 2Kg 23:4-5
[t]1Kg 7:12; 2Kg 23:12
[u]21:6 Lv 18:21; 2Kg 16:3; 2Ch 28:3
[v]Lv 19:26,31; Dt 18:10-12; 2Kg 23:24
[w]2Kg 23:26

Judah's King Manasseh

21 Manasseh[i] was 12 years old when he became king and reigned 55 years in Jerusalem. His mother's name was Hephzibah.[j]
2He did what was evil in the LORD's sight,[k]
imitating the detestable practices of the nations that the LORD had dispossessed before
the Israelites.[l] 3He rebuilt the •high places
that his father Hezekiah had destroyed[m] and
reestablished the altars for •Baal. He made an
•Asherah,[n] as King Ahab of Israel had done;[o]
he also worshiped the whole heavenly •host[p]
and served them. 4He built altars in the LORD's
temple,[q] where the LORD had said, "Jerusalem
is where I will put My name."[r] 5He built altars
to the whole heavenly host[s] in both courtyards of the LORD's temple.[t] 6He made his son
pass through the fire,[u] practiced witchcraft
and •divination, and consulted mediums and
spiritists.[v] He did a great amount of evil in the
LORD's sight, provoking Him.[w]
7Manasseh set up the carved image of Asherah, which he made, in the temple that the
LORD had spoken about to David and his son
Solomon, "I will establish My name forever
in this temple and in Jerusalem, which I have

[A]20:18 Or *court officials*

questioning until he received an answer from the king that merited comment.

20:16-18 Isaiah's prophecy concerning Hezekiah's wealth and descendants indicated the king had erred in showing all of Judah's wealth to the Babylonian embassy. The prideful sin may have included using God's blessings as bargaining points in an international political power play. This, then, could be another example of the recurrent conflict between playing a prudent role in international politics and failing to properly trust in the Lord.

20:19 Hezekiah's acceptance of God's punishment could have been either humble acceptance of God's will, or selfish rejoicing because he would experience **peace and security** in his day.

20:20-21 The story leaps over Sennacherib's invasion to the summary and conclusion of **Hezekiah's reign**. After the comment about the other records of Hezekiah's deeds, this conclusion turns the spotlight on one of Hezekiah's most important provisions for that war—the construction of a reservoir for water for a siege and of the **tunnel** that allowed water to come into the city of Jerusalem (see map on p. 634). The record of Hezekiah then closes with the statements of his death and the succession of his son **Manasseh** to the throne.

21:1-18 These verses cover the 55-year reign of Manasseh, including a co-regency with his father, which left him a sole regency of about 43 years. (Some reigns or periods can gain or lose a year both at the beginning and ending due to changing conventions in counting parts of a year.) If Manasseh was 12 when he began his co-regency, then he was 22 to 24 years old at the beginning of his sole rule. He would have been born before God's grant of 15 extra years of life to his father, Hezekiah.

21:2 We are told Manasseh **did what was evil**, but this statement hardly describes the depths of his apostasy. His wickedness was certainly associated with rejecting Hezekiah's anti-Assyrian policy. Manasseh is listed as a loyal vassal king who supplied troops for Ashurbanipal's expedition against Thebes in Egypt (ca 663 B.C.; see Nah 3:8). Assyrian vassals were expected to display religious loyalty to Asshur, the chief Assyrian god (see note at 16:10-11). Manasseh's acceptance of Assyrian deities evolved even further into a tolerant acceptance of any and all pagan deities.

21:3-6 Manasseh's restored **high places** may have included the illegal shrines of Yahweh, which Hezekiah had suppressed, and those altars devoted to other pagan deities.

banah

Hebrew Pronunciation	[bah NAH]
HCSB Translation	build
Uses in 2 Kings	12
Uses in the OT	377
Focus Passage	2 Kings 21:3-5

This root in Semitic languages means "build" but in some languages also signifies "create." *Banah* denotes *build* (2Sm 5:11). Sometimes *banah* is *make* (2Ch 8:12) or *construct* (Ezk 27:5). *Banah* is parallel to verbs like "prepare," "repair," and "set up." It implies *erect* (Ezk 39:15), *build up* (Is 60:10), or *rebuild* (Nm 21:27). *Banah* means *build a family* (Gn 30:3) or *have children* (Gn 16:2). God *builds* dynasties (2Sm 7:27) and *builds up* people (Jr 12:16). Those who are *built up* prosper (Mal 3:15) or *are renewed* (Jb 22:23). *Banah* involves *setting up* (Ex 24:4) or *establishing* (1Sm 2:35). It indicates *paneling* or *lining* (1Kg 6:15-16). It can suggest *complete* (1Kg 7:1).

chosen out of all the tribes of Israel.[a] [8]I will never again cause the feet of the Israelites to wander from the land I gave to their ancestors if only they will be careful to do all I have commanded them—the whole law that My servant Moses commanded them."[b] [9]But they did not listen; Manasseh caused them to stray so that they did greater evil than the nations the LORD had destroyed before the Israelites.[c]

[10]The LORD spoke through His servants the prophets, saying, [11]"Since Manasseh king of Judah has committed all these detestable things[d]—greater evil than the Amorites[e] who preceded him had done—and by means of his idols has also caused Judah to sin, [12]this is what the LORD God of Israel says: 'I am about to bring such disaster on Jerusalem and Judah that everyone who hears about it will shudder.[f] [13]I will stretch over Jerusalem the measuring line used on Samaria and the mason's level used on the house of Ahab,[g] and I will wipe[h] Jerusalem •clean as one wipes a bowl—wiping it and turning it upside down. [14]I will abandon the remnant[i] of My inheritance and hand them over to their enemies. They will become plunder and spoil to all their enemies, [15]because they have done what is evil in My sight and have provoked Me from the day their ancestors came out of Egypt until today.'"[j]

[16]Manasseh also shed so much innocent blood that he filled Jerusalem with it from one end to another.[k] This was in addition to his sin that he caused Judah to commit. Consequently, they did what was evil in the LORD's sight.

Manasseh's Death

[17]The rest[l] of the events of Manasseh's reign, along with all his accomplishments and the sin that he committed, are written in the Historical Record of Judah's Kings.[m] [18]Manasseh rested with his fathers and was buried in the garden of his own house, the garden of Uzza. His son Amon became king in his place.

Judah's King Amon

[19]Amon was 22 years old when he became king[n] and reigned two years in Jerusalem. His mother's name was Meshullemeth daughter of Haruz; she was from Jotbah. [20]He did what was evil in the LORD's sight as his father Manasseh had done.[o] [21]He walked in all the ways his father had walked; he served the idols his father had served, and he worshiped them.[p] [22]He abandoned the LORD God of his ancestors[q] and did not walk in the way of the LORD.[r]

[23]Amon's servants conspired against the king and killed him in his own house.[s] [24]Then the common people[A] executed[t] all those who had conspired against King Amon and made his son Josiah[u] king in his place.

[25]The rest of the events of Amon's reign, along with his accomplishments, are written in the Historical Record of Judah's Kings. [26]He was buried in his tomb in the garden of Uzza, and his son Josiah became king in his place.

Judah's King Josiah

22 Josiah[v] was eight years old when he became king and reigned 31 years in

[a]21:7 Dt 12:5; 1Kg 11:32
[b]21:8 2Sm 7:10; 1Kg 9:1-9
[c]21:9 1Kg 14:9
[d]21:11 2Kg 21:2; 24:3-4
[e]Gn 15:16; 1Kg 21:16
[f]21:12 1Sm 3:11; Jr 19:3
[g]21:13 Is 34:11; Am 7:7-8
[h]2Kg 23:27
[i]21:14 2Kg 19:4; Jr 6:9
[j]21:15 Ex 32:22; Jr 25:7
[k]21:16 2Kg 24:4
[l]21:17-18 2Ch 33:18-20
[m]21:17 2Kg 20:20
[n]21:19-24 2Ch 33:21-25
[o]21:20 2Kg 21:2-7,11,16
[p]21:21 2Kg 16:2
[q]21:22 1Kg 11:33
[r]2Kg 22:17
[s]21:23 2Kg 12:20; 14:19
[t]21:24 2Kg 14:5
[u]2Kg 22:1
[v]22:1-2 2Ch 34:1-2

[A]21:24 Lit *the people of the land*

They included the gods of the skies and heavens. Even worse, he desecrated the **temple** by worshiping these deities in the temple itself. Recent scholars have taken the word **mediums** as referring to a ritual pit for bringing up spirits serviced by the **spiritists** (1Sm 28:7).

21:7a **Asherah** was originally a tree or a wooden pole that represented any divine consort of the chief fertility god. Since the word here is not associated with any local Baal, it seems to refer to a particular female deity. In setting up this image, Manasseh came close to assigning Yahweh another female consort (see comments on Ashima in note at 17:29-34).

21:7b-9 The Lord had ceased His wanderings from tribe to tribe (2Sm 7:6) to dwell in the **temple** in **Jerusalem**. The covenant associated with it gave the Hebrews rest from wanderings. The corrupting of this temple would return the Israelites to wandering among the nations.

21:10-14 Just as Manasseh's list of sins is the longest of the kings of **Judah**, the judgment for those sins is one of the longest in the individual records.

21:13 The builder's **measuring** instruments symbolized God's judgment of a corrupt society.

21:15 The people's failure and rebellion dated **from the day their ancestors came out of Egypt**. This implied a more profound failure than the occasional transgressions of kings and people. There was a deeper, systemic problem that demanded a radically different solution, perhaps the new covenant written in their hearts (Jr 31:31-34).

21:16 The Bible gives no more specific data about Manasseh's filling Jerusalem with **innocent blood**, and 2 Kings mentions nothing about Manasseh's captivity, repentance, and building operations (2Ch 33:10-14).

21:20-22 Manasseh's son **Amon** learned nothing from God's judgment of his father.

21:23-24 **Amon** was assassinated by his own servants, probably a victim of the internal struggle between the pro-Assyrian and anti-Assyrian parties. The **common people** (lit "people of the land") emerged as the group that maintained loyalty to David's dynasty.

22:1–23:30 The reign of King Josiah of Judah is covered in these two chapters.

22:1-2 The formal statements are typical for a good king:

Jerusalem. His mother's name was Jedidah the daughter of Adaiah; she was from Bozkath.[a] 2 He did what was right in the LORD's sight and walked in all the ways of his ancestor David;[b] he did not turn to the right or the left.[c]

Josiah Repairs the Temple

3 In the eighteenth year of King Josiah, the king sent the court secretary Shaphan son of Azaliah, son of Meshullam, to the LORD's temple,[d] saying, 4 "Go up to Hilkiah the high priest so that he may total up the money brought into the LORD's temple—the money the doorkeepers have collected from the people.[e] 5 It is to be put into the hands of those doing the work—those who oversee the LORD's temple. They in turn are to give it to the workmen in the LORD's temple to repair the damage.[f] 6 They are to give it to the carpenters, builders, and masons to buy timber and quarried stone to repair the temple.[g] 7 But no accounting is to be required from them for the money put into their hands since they work with integrity."[h]

The Book of the Law Found

8 Hilkiah the high priest told Shaphan the court secretary, "I have found the book of the law[i] in the LORD's temple," and he gave the book to Shaphan, who read it.

9 Then Shaphan the court secretary went to the king and reported,[A] "Your servants have emptied out the money that was found in the temple and have put it into the hand of those doing the work—those who oversee the LORD's temple." 10 Then Shaphan the court secretary told the king, "Hilkiah the priest has given me a book," and Shaphan read it in the presence of the king.[j]

11 When the king heard the words of the book of the law, he tore his clothes.[k] 12 Then he commanded Hilkiah the priest, Ahikam[l] son of Shaphan, Achbor[m] son of Micaiah, Shaphan the court secretary, and the king's servant Asaiah: 13 "Go and inquire of the LORD for me, the people, and all Judah about the instruction in this book that has been found. For great is the LORD's wrath that is kindled against us because our ancestors have not obeyed the words of this book in order to do everything written about us."[n]

Huldah's Prophecy of Judgment

14 So[o] Hilkiah the priest, Ahikam, Achbor, Shaphan, and Asaiah went to the prophetess[p] Huldah, wife of Shallum son of Tikvah,[q] son of Harhas,[B] keeper of the wardrobe. She lived in Jerusalem in the Second District.[r] They spoke with her.

15 She said to them, "This is what the LORD God of Israel says, 'Say to the man who sent you to Me: 16 This is what the LORD says: I am about to bring disaster on this place and on its inhabitants, fulfilling all the words of the book that the king of Judah has read,[s] 17 because they have abandoned Me and burned incense to other gods in order to provoke Me with all the work of their hands. My wrath will be kindled against this place, and it will not be quenched.[t] 18 Say this to the king of Judah who sent you to inquire of the LORD: This is what the LORD God of Israel says: As for the words that you heard,[u] 19 because your heart was tender and you humbled yourself before the LORD[v] when you heard what I spoke against this place and against its inhabitants, that they would become a desolation and a curse,[w] and because you have torn your clothes and wept before Me, I Myself have heard you—this is the LORD's declaration— 20 therefore, I will indeed gather you to your fathers, and you will be gathered to your grave in peace.[x] Your eyes will not see all the disaster that I am bringing on this place.'"

Then they reported[C] to the king.

[a] 22:1 Jos 15:39
[b] 22:2 1Kg 14:8
[c] Dt 5:32; Jos 1:7
[d] 22:3 2Ch 34:8
[e] 22:4 2Kg 12:4,9-10
[f] 22:5 2Kg 12:5
[g] 22:6 2Kg 12:11-12
[h] 22:7 2Kg 12:15; 1Co 4:2
[i] 22:8 Dt 31:24-26; 2Ch 34:14-15
[j] 22:10 Dt 17:18-20
[k] 22:11 Gn 37:34; Jos 7:6
[l] 22:12 2Kg 25:22; Jr 26:24
[m] 2Ch 34:20
[n] 22:13 Dt 29:24-28; 31:17-18
[o] 22:14-20 2Ch 34:22-28
[p] 22:14 Ex 15:20
[q] 2Ch 34:22
[r] Zph 1:10
[s] 22:16 Dt 29:27; Dn 9:11-14
[t] 22:17 Dt 29:25-26; 1Kg 9:9
[u] 22:18 2Ch 34:26
[v] 22:19 1Sm 24:5; 1Kg 21:29
[w] Dt 28:15; Jr 26:6
[x] 22:20 2Kg 23:30

A **22:9** Lit *and returned a word to the king and said* B **22:14** = Hasrah in 2Ch 34:22 C **22:20** Lit *returned a word*

Josiah **walked in all the ways** of David, and he turned neither **to the right or the left**.

22:3-5 At 26 years old, Josiah pushed for the rebuilding of the **temple**. There was no argument over whose treasury was involved (see Joash; 12:4-8). The king either already had or then assumed the necessary authority for rebuilding the temple.

22:8 The Torah, or **book of the law**, had probably not been completely lost. Even the Samaritans had been preserving their Torah for almost a hundred years (17:28). Perhaps the copies available had been guarded from the previous idolatrous royal house.

22:11 Whatever had happened, **the king** had been ignorant of some provisions of the law.

22:12-13 Josiah's heart was tender toward God (v. 19). Just as he had searched for God when he was 16 years old (2Ch 34:3) and had pushed for rebuilding the temple, now he was equally willing to heed this message of sin, guilt, and judgment. He acknowledged that sin had aroused **the LORD's wrath**.

22:14 Despite the general false worship that was occurring throughout the land, a true **prophetess** was known and tolerated just as apostate Samaria had tolerated Elisha (6:32).

22:15-17 The message of the prophetess was that the sins of the nation must be judged.

22:18-20 Because of Josiah's grief over the sins of the nation, he was assured that destruction would not come until after his death.

Covenant Renewal

23 So the king sent messengers,[a] and they gathered all the elders[b] of Jerusalem and Judah to him. [2]Then the king went to the LORD's temple with all the men of Judah and all the inhabitants of Jerusalem, as well as the priests and the prophets—all the people from the youngest to the oldest. As they listened, he read all the words of the book of the covenant[c] that had been found in the LORD's temple.[d] [3]Next, the king stood by the pillar[A,e] and made a covenant[f] in the presence of the LORD to follow the LORD and to keep His commands, His decrees, and His statutes with all his mind and with all his heart,[g] and to carry out the words of this covenant that were written in this book; all the people agreed to[B] the covenant.[h]

Josiah's Reforms

[4]Then the king commanded Hilkiah[i] the high priest and the priests of the second rank[j] and the doorkeepers to bring out of the LORD's temple all the articles made for •Baal, •Asherah, and the whole heavenly •host.[k] He burned them outside Jerusalem in the fields of the Kidron and carried their ashes to Bethel.[l] [5]Then he did away with the idolatrous priests the kings of Judah had appointed to burn incense at the •high places[m] in the cities of Judah and in the areas surrounding Jerusalem. They had burned incense to Baal, and to the sun, moon, constellations, and the whole heavenly host.[n] [6]He brought out the Asherah pole[o] from the LORD's temple to the Kidron Valley outside Jerusalem. He burned it at the Kidron Valley,[p] beat it to dust,[q] and threw its dust on the graves of the common people.[C,r] [7]He also tore down the houses of the male cult prostitutes[s] that were in the LORD's temple, in which the women were weaving tapestries[D] for Asherah.[t]

[8]Then Josiah brought all the priests from the cities of Judah, and he defiled the high places[u] from Geba[v] to Beer-sheba,[w] where the priests had burned incense. He tore down the high places of the gates at the entrance of the •gate of Joshua the governor of the city (on the left at the city gate). [9]The priests of the high places, however, did not come up to the altar of the LORD in Jerusalem; instead, they ate unleavened bread with their fellow priests.[x]

[10]He defiled •Topheth,[y] which is in the Valley of Hinnom,[z] so that no one could make his son or daughter pass through the fire[aa] to •Molech.[ab] [11]He did away with the horses that the kings of Judah had dedicated to the sun. They had been at the entrance of the LORD's temple in the precincts by the chamber of Nathan-melech the court official, and he burned up the chariots of the sun.[ac]

[12]The king tore down the altars that were on the roof[ad]—Ahaz's upper chamber[ae] that the kings of Judah had made—and the altars that Manasseh had made[af] in the two courtyards of the LORD's temple. Then he smashed them[E] there and threw their dust into the Kidron Valley. [13]The king also defiled the high places that were across from Jerusalem, to the south of the Mount of Destruction, which King Solomon of Israel had built for •Ashtoreth, detestable idol of the Sidonians; for Chemosh, the detestable idol of Moab; and for •Milcom, the abomination of the Ammonites.[ag] [14]He broke the sacred pillars into pieces,[ah] cut down

Cross references (center column)

a 23:1 2Ch 34:29-32
b 2Kg 10:1
c 23:2 Dt 31:10-13
d 2Kg 22:8
e 23:3 1Kg 7:15; 2Kg 11:14
f 2Kg 11:17
g Dt 6:4-6; 13:4
h Ex 24:3-8; Jos 24:14-28
i 23:4 2Kg 22:8,14
j 2Kg 25:18; Jr 35:4; 52:24
k 2Kg 21:3,7; 2Ch 33:3
l 2Kg 23:15
m 23:5 2Kg 16:4
n 2Kg 21:3
o 23:6 1Kg 14:15,23; 2Kg 18:4; 21:7
p 1Kg 15:13
q 2Kg 23:15
r 2Ch 34:4; Jr 26:23
s 23:7 Dt 23:17; 1Kg 14:24; 15:12
t Ex 38:8; Ezk 16:16
u 23:8 2Kg 18:4
v Jos 21:17; 1Kg 15:22
w 1Sm 3:20
x 23:9 Ezk 44:10-14
y 23:10 Is 30:33; Jr 7:31-32
z Jos 15:8
aa Lv 18:21; 20:2-5
ab 1Kg 11:7; Jr 32:35
ac 23:11 Dt 4:19; Ezk 8:16
ad 23:12 Jr 19:13; Zph 1:4-5
ae 2Kg 20:11
af 2Kg 21:5; 2Ch 33:5
ag 23:13 1Kg 11:5-8
ah 23:14 Ex 23:24

A 23:3 2Ch 34:31 reads *platform*   B 23:3 Lit *people took a stand in*   C 23:6 Lit *the sons of the people*   D 23:7 Or *clothing*   E 23:12 Text emended; MT reads *he ran from*

23:1-2 All the purifying works of this chapter began quickly after the discovery of the law since, assuming chronological sequencing, these works culminated in the great Passover remembrance, still in Josiah's eighteenth year (1Kg 22:3; 23:23).

23:3 Perhaps this **pillar** was the same place used by Joash (see notes at 1Kg 7:15-21; 2Kg 11:14a) for a **covenant** renewal. The unclear parallel passage in Chronicles probably identifies this same location by a different object. King Josiah, then, committed himself to obedience to the covenant. **All the people** also committed themselves to the covenant.

23:4 Apparently Josiah's earlier piety had not moved him to a complete rejection of all false gods, but at this point his devotion to Yahweh became exclusive and the cleansing of Judah from false worship began in earnest.

23:5-7 In Judah the orders of **idolatrous priests**, founded and perhaps also funded by earlier kings, were deposed or disbanded rather than being slaughtered as in the north (v. 20). Allowing **male** religious **prostitutes** in the **temple** until this point indicated extreme degradation and a surprising tolerance for paganism.

23:8-9 Defiling the **high places** disqualified these altars for further use, at least until they were ritually purified. The **priests of the high places** seemed to have been incorporated into the ranks of the regular priests, although they were not permitted to come to **Jerusalem** to participate in worship. This leniency might indicate that these high places were illegal shrines for Yahweh worship rather than shrines for pagan deities.

23:10 To the bullet note information about **Topheth**, this verse adds that this altar honored the god **Molech**. Again, Josiah desecrated a sacred site in order to disable it.

23:11 Apparently these **horses** symbolically pulled the **chariots of the sun** across the heavens.

23:12-14 Josiah's program continued with the desecration of every illegal altar or place of worship he could find, even those founded by **Solomon**. These were also defiled by **human remains**.

the Asherah poles,[a] then filled their places with human bones.

[15] He even tore down the altar at Bethel[b] and the high place[c] that Jeroboam son of Nebat, who caused Israel to sin, had made. Then he burned the high place, crushed it to dust, and burned the Asherah.[d] [16] As Josiah turned, he saw the tombs there on the mountain. He sent someone to take the bones out of the tombs, and he burned them on the altar.[e] He defiled it according to the word of the LORD proclaimed by the man of God[A] who proclaimed these things.[f] [17] Then he said, "What is this monument I see?"

The men of the city told him, "It is the tomb of the man of God who came from Judah and proclaimed these things that you have done to the altar at Bethel."[g]

[18] So he said, "Let him rest. Don't let anyone disturb his bones." So they left his bones undisturbed with the bones of the prophet who came from Samaria.[h]

[19] Josiah also removed all the shrines of the high places that were in the cities of Samaria, which the kings of Israel had made to provoke the LORD.[i] Josiah did the same things to them that he had done at Bethel. [20] He slaughtered on the altars all the priests of the high places[j] who were there, and he burned human bones on the altars.[k] Then he returned to Jerusalem.

Passover Observed

[21] The king commanded all the people, "Keep the ·Passover of the LORD your God as written in the book of the covenant."[l] [22] No such Passover had ever been kept from the time of the judges who judged Israel through the entire time of the kings of Israel and Judah. [23] But in the eighteenth year of King Josiah, this Passover was observed to the LORD in Jerusalem.[m]

Further Zeal for the LORD

[24] In addition, Josiah removed the mediums, the spiritists,[n] household idols,[o] images, and all the detestable things[p] that were seen in the land of Judah and in Jerusalem. He did this in order to carry out the words of the law that were written in the book that Hilkiah the priest found in the LORD's temple.[q] [25] Before him there was no king like him who turned to the LORD with all his mind and with all his heart and with all his strength[r] according to all the law of Moses, and no one like him arose after him.[s]

[26] In spite of all that, the LORD did not turn from the fury of His great burning anger, which burned against Judah because of all that Manasseh had provoked Him with.[t] [27] For the LORD had said, "I will also remove Judah from My sight just as I have removed Israel.[u] I will reject this city Jerusalem, that I have chosen, and the temple about which I said, 'My name will be there.'"[v]

Cross-references (center column)

[a] 23:14 2Kg 18:4
[b] 23:15 1Kg 13:1-3
[c] 1Kg 12:28-33
[d] 2Kg 23:6
[e] 23:16 2Ch 34:5
[f] 1Kg 13:2
[g] 23:17 1Kg 13:1,31-32
[h] 23:18 1Kg 13:29-31
[i] 23:19 2Ch 34:6-7
[j] 23:20 1Kg 12:31; 13:2
[k] 2Kg 10:25; 11:18; 2Ch 34:5
[l] 23:21 Nm 9:1-14; Dt 16:1-8; 2Ch 35:1-6
[m] 23:22-23 2Ch 35:18-19
[n] 23:24 Lv 19:31; 2Kg 21:6
[o] Gn 31:19
[p] Dt 7:26; 2Kg 16:3
[q] 2Kg 22:8; 23:2-3
[r] 23:25 Dt 6:4-9; 2Kg 23:3
[s] 1Kg 3:12; 2Kg 18:5
[t] 23:26 2Kg 21:11-13; Jr 15:4
[u] 23:27 2Kg 18:11-12
[v] Dt 12:11; 1Kg 9:3; 2Kg 21:4

[A] 23:16 LXX adds *when Jeroboam stood by the altar of the feast. And he turned and raised his eyes to the tomb of the man of God*

23:15-20 It is almost certain that this cleansing of the north took place in the brief period between the fall of Assyrian imperial administration of Samaria and the time when the Egyptians seized control of Judah. It is difficult to tell whether this was political expansionism, religious cleansing, or both. If this cleansing all took place in Josiah's eighteenth year, it could not have been very thorough.

This expedition must have touched the developing Samaritan Jewish community with their alternate, Torah-based tradition. Seeing the general apostasy of Judah, the Samaritans could not have been much worse than the Judeans of that time. So we should not minimize the potential good influence of their loyalty to their Torah, whenever that loyalty developed. Josiah may have impacted this community in one of two ways. If his sense of orthodoxy made the Samaritan community enemies, he could have been a threat to their growth and development. On the other hand, his suppression of gross idolatry could have weakened forces hostile to their positive development. This expedition might have increased the number of pious northerners who shared in Josiah's Passover observance (2Ch 35:17).

23:15-16 Josiah had to travel only 10 miles north to cleanse **Bethel** by destroying its **high place** and desecrating the site with human remains.

23:17-18 Then Josiah became aware of the **tomb** of the Judean prophet who predicted the deeds Josiah had just done. The prophet's bones were left undisturbed, but Josiah had still desecrated other graves near Bethel. In this context **from Samaria** may indicate only that the prophet was native to Israel, often referred to collectively as "Samaria."

23:19-20 Josiah's reforms took a more brutal turn in the north with a systematic slaughter of the illegal **priests** of the north. Josiah desecrated the altars by killing the priests on their own **altars**.

23:21-23 The events detailed above must have occurred in Josiah's **eighteenth year** before the observance of the **Passover**. The high point of Josiah's reforms was this Passover celebration. The description here does not give adequate reason for this glowing evaluation, but in the Chronicles account (2Ch 35) its importance becomes clear. Chronicles comes close to presenting this Passover as the reestablishment of the guilds and personnel for the ritual life of the Israelites.

23:24 This verse contains a rare mention of the **household idols** in Judah (Jdg 17:5; 18:14-21; 1Sm 19:13). Archaeology documents the presence of this sin in the south as well as the north.

23:26-27 Once again, the writer returned to the theme of failure. The national repentance fell far short of what was needed to avoid God's judgment. History shows that the people had not been reached by this revival.

23:28 A formal closer concludes Josiah's reign, except for the following record of his death.

Josiah's Death

28The rest of the events of Josiah's reign,[a] along with all his accomplishments, are written in the Historical Record of Judah's Kings. 29During his reign, Pharaoh Neco king of Egypt[b] marched up to help the king of Assyria at the Euphrates River. King Josiah went to confront him, and at Megiddo[c] when Neco saw him he killed him. 30From Megiddo his servants carried his dead body in a chariot, brought him into Jerusalem, and buried him in his own tomb.[d] Then the common people[A] took Jehoahaz son of Josiah, anointed him, and made him king in place of his father.[e]

Judah's King Jehoahaz

31Jehoahaz[f] was[g] 23 years old when he became king and reigned three months in Jerusalem. His mother's name was Hamutal[h] daughter of Jeremiah, from Libnah. 32He did what was evil in the LORD's sight just as his ancestors had done.[i] 33Pharaoh Neco imprisoned him at Riblah[j] in the land of Hamath[k] to keep him from reigning in Jerusalem, and he imposed on the land a fine of 7,500 pounds[B] of silver and 75 pounds[C] of gold.

Judah's King Jehoiakim

34Then[l] Pharaoh Neco made Eliakim[m] son of Josiah king in place of his father Josiah and changed Eliakim's name to Jehoiakim.[n] But Neco took Jehoahaz and went to Egypt, and he died there.[o] 35So Jehoiakim gave the silver and the gold to Pharaoh, but at Pharaoh's command he taxed the land to give the money. He exacted the silver and the gold from the common people,[A] each man according to his assessment,[p] to give it to Pharaoh Neco.

36Jehoiakim was 25 years old when he became king and reigned 11 years in Jerusalem. His mother's name was Zebidah daughter of Pedaiah, from Rumah. 37He did what was evil[q] in the LORD's sight just as his ancestors had done.

Jehoiakim's Rebellion and Death

24 During[r] Jehoiakim's reign,[s] Nebuchadnezzar[t] king of Babylon[u] attacked.[v] Jehoiakim became his vassal for three years, and then he turned and rebelled against him. 2The LORD sent Chaldean, Aramean,[w] Moabite,[x] and Ammonite raiders against Jehoiakim. He sent them against Judah to destroy it, according to the word of the LORD He had spoken through His servants the prophets.[y] 3Indeed, this happened to Judah at the LORD's command to remove them from His sight.[z] It was because of the sins of Manasseh, according to all he had done,[aa] 4and also because of all the innocent blood he had shed. He had filled Jerusalem with innocent blood,[ab] and the LORD would not forgive.

5The rest of the events of Jehoiakim's reign, along with all his accomplishments, are written in the Historical Record of Judah's Kings.[ac] 6Jehoiakim rested with his fathers, and his son Jehoiachin became king in his place.[ad]

7Now the king of Egypt did not march out

Cross references (center column):

a 23:28-30 2Ch 35:20-27
b 23:29 Jr 46:2
c Jdg 5:19
d 23:30 2Kg 9:28
e 2Ch 36:1
f 23:31 1Ch 3:15; Jr 22:11
g 23:31-33 2Ch 36:2-3
h 23:31 2Kg 24:18
i 23:32 2Kg 21:2-7
j 23:33 2Kg 25:6
k 1Kg 8:65
l 23:34-37 2Ch 36:4-5
m 23:34 1Ch 3:15
n 2Kg 24:17; 2Ch 36:4
o Jr 22:11-12; Ezk 19:3-4
p 23:35 Ex 30:12-16; Lv 27:2-8
q 23:37 Jr 22:13-19; 36:1-26
r 24:1-6 2Ch 36:6-8
s 24:1 2Kg 23:26-27
t 2Kg 24:10-11; Dn 1:1
u 2Kg 20:14
v Jr 35:11
w 24:2 2Kg 6:23
x 2Kg 13:20
y 2Kg 23:27
z 24:3 2Kg 18:25
aa 2Kg 23:26
ab 24:4 2Kg 21:16
ac 24:5 2Kg 23:28
ad 24:5-6 Jr 22:18-19

A23:30,35 Lit *the people of the land*   B23:33 Lit *100 talents*   C23:33 Lit *one talent*

23:29-30 Assyria had earlier suffered major defeats. A coalition of Medes and Babylonians had destroyed Nineveh in 612 B.C. and captured Haran in 610 B.C. **Pharaoh Neco** of Egypt then went north toward the **Euphrates River** to help the Assyrians recapture Haran. Josiah intercepted the Egyptian army near **Megiddo**. He died from wounds he received in this battle. Josiah's accomplishments confirmed his greatness. Though his reforms did not halt God's judgment, his reestablishment of ritual and the religious guilds was essential for the renewal of Israel's religious life after the exile.

23:31-33 The people made Josiah's son, **Jehoahaz** (also referred to as Shallum; Jr 22:11-12), king. **Pharaoh Neco imprisoned** Jehoahaz and put Judah under tribute. Neco's victory over Josiah apparently eliminated the Judean army as a significant fighting force.

23:34-35 Jehoahaz's brother **Eliakim**, renamed **Jehoiakim** by Neco, was made king. Renaming a vassal symbolized the ruler's power over the subject king. Jehoiakim sent tribute to Pharaoh. Jehoahaz was a political prisoner in Egypt.

23:36-37 The formal opening statements for **Jehoiakim** identify him as another bad king. The prophet Jeremiah condemned him for social injustice in building a huge palace while ignoring the poor (Jr 22:13-17).

24:1 The background for this verse was the Babylonian capture of Carchemish (605 B.C.) that drove Egypt from Syria and Palestine. The object of the Babylonian attack was the Egyptian armies, and Jehoiakim yielded peaceably to **Nebuchadnezzar**, but then, after three years, Jehoiakim rebelled because Egypt temporarily drove the Babylonians northward again (601 B.C.).

24:2 The Babylonians, as God's instruments, compensated for this setback by encouraging the other local vassals mentioned here to harass **Judah**.

24:3-4 As in the condemnation of Judah at the time of Manasseh (21:15), the writer of 2 Kings took a longer, backward view in accounting for God's judgment on sin. He linked God's judgment and intent to remove the Hebrews **from His sight** to the sins of **Manasseh**. The sin of the times was the continuation of a sinful national character that had already been established and judged.

24:5-6 The Babylonians counterattacked and were soon approaching Jerusalem. **Jehoiakim** died either soon before or during the Babylonian siege. His rebellion was discredited. The absence of any formal statement about Jehoiakim's burial could confirm Jeremiah's prediction about the shameful circumstances of his death (Jr 22:18-19).

24:7 By this time Egypt had been driven out of Palestine,

of his land again,[a] for the king of Babylon took everything that belonged to the king of Egypt,[b] from the Brook of Egypt to the Euphrates River.[c]

Judah's King Jehoiachin

[8] Jehoiachin was 18 years old when he became king and reigned three months in Jerusalem. His mother's name was Nehushta daughter of Elnathan, from Jerusalem.[d] [9] He did what was evil in the LORD's sight as his father had done.

Deportations to Babylon

[10] At that time[e] the servants of Nebuchadnezzar[f] king of Babylon marched up to Jerusalem, and the city came under siege. [11] Then King Nebuchadnezzar of Babylon came to the city while his servants were besieging it. [12] Jehoiachin king of Judah, along with his mother, his servants, his commanders, and his officials, surrendered to the king of Babylon.[g]

So the king of Babylon took him captive in the eighth year of his reign. [13] He also carried off from there all the treasures of the LORD's temple and the treasures of the king's palace, and he cut into pieces all the gold articles that Solomon king of Israel had made[h] for the LORD's sanctuary, just as God had predicted.[i] [14] Then he deported all Jerusalem and all the commanders and all the fighting men,[j] 10,000 captives,[k] and all the craftsmen and metalsmiths.[l] Except for the poorest people of the land,[m] no one remained. [15] Nebuchadnezzar deported Jehoiachin to Babylon. Also, he took the king's mother, the king's wives, his officials, and the leading men of the land into exile from Jerusalem to Babylon.[n] [16] The king of Babylon also brought captive into Babylon all 7,000 fighting men and 1,000 craftsmen and metalsmiths—all strong and fit for war. [17] Then the king of Babylon made Mattaniah, Jehoiachin's[A] uncle,[B] king in his place and changed his name to Zedekiah.[o]

Judah's King Zedekiah

[18] Zedekiah[p] was 21 years old when he became king[q] and reigned 11 years in Jerusalem. His mother's name was Hamutal[r] daughter of Jeremiah, from Libnah. [19] Zedekiah did what was evil in the LORD's sight just as Jehoiakim had done.[s] [20] Because of the LORD's anger,[t] it came to the point in Jerusalem and Judah that He finally banished them from His presence.[u] Then, Zedekiah rebelled against the king of Babylon.[v]

Nebuchadnezzar's Siege of Jerusalem

25 In the ninth year[w] of Zedekiah's reign,[x] on the tenth day of the tenth month, King Nebuchadnezzar of Babylon advanced against Jerusalem with his entire army.[y] They laid siege to the city and built a siege wall against it all around.[z] [2] The city was under siege until King Zedekiah's eleventh year. [3] By the ninth day of the fourth month the famine was so severe in the city that the people of the land had no food.[aa] [4] Then the city was broken into,[ab] and all the warriors fled[ac] by night by way of the gate between the two walls near the king's garden,[ad] even though the Chaldeans surrounded the city. As the king made his way along the route to the •Arabah,[ae] [5] the Chaldean army pursued him and overtook him in the plains of Jericho. Zedekiah's entire army was scattered from him.[af] [6] The Chalde-

Cross references (center column)

a 24:7 Jr 37:5-7
b Jr 46:2
c Gn 15:18; 1Kg 4:21; Is 27:12
d 24:8-9 2Ch 36:9; Jr 22:24-30
e 24:10-17 2Ch 36:10
f 24:10 2Kg 24:1; Dn 1:1
g 24:12 2Kg 25:27; Jr 22:24-30
h 24:13 1Kg 7:48-50
i 2Kg 20:16-18; Is 39:5-7
j 24:14 Jr 24:1
k Jr 52:28
l Jr 24:1; 29:2
m 2Kg 25:12
n 24:15 2Ch 36:10; Jr 22:24-28
o 24:17 1Ch 3:15; 2Ch 36:11; Jr 1:3
p 24:18 Jr 27:1; 28:1
q 24:18-20 2Ch 36:11-12; Jr 52:1-3
r 24:18 2Kg 23:31
s 24:19 2Kg 23:37
t 24:20 Dt 4:26; 29:27; 2Kg 23:26
u 2Kg 13:23
v 2Ch 36:13; Ezk 17:15
w 25:1 Jr 32:1
x 25:1-7 Jr 39:1-7; 52:4-11
y 25:1 Jr 21:2; 34:1-2; Ezk 24:2
z Ezk 21:22
aa 25:3 2Kg 6:24-25; Lm 4:9-10
ab 25:4 Jr 39:2
ac Ezk 33:21
ad Neh 3:15
ae Dt 2:8
af 25:5 Lv 26:36; Ezk 12:14; 17:21

---

and all land north of the **Brook of Egypt** (the Wadi Arish) belonged to Babylon.

24:10-12 After a brief siege, Jehoiachin and all his high **officials** surrendered to **Nebuchadnezzar** of Babylon. Significantly, the expression **eighth year of his reign** must refer to Nebuchadnezzar's eighth year. This change to a pagan dating of events marked the impending end of Judah.

24:13 The plundering of the city of Jerusalem seemed to be very thorough. It is remarkable that there was still some **gold** from the time of **Solomon** left to be plundered after more than three centuries of foreign plundering.

24:14-16 Everyone except the **poorest** classes of the city were taken into captivity. The able-bodied **fighting men** might have been conscripted into the Babylonian army.

24:18-19 The formal opening statements and evaluation of **Zedekiah** are routine for a wicked, faithless king.

24:20 However, the grounds for Zedekiah's poor evaluation predated the wickedness of the current king. God was already angry, and judgment was inevitable (vv. 3-4; 21:15).

25:1 In 588 B.C. the pharaoh of Egypt led a general rebellion against Babylon that included the Phoenician coast and Transjordanian territories. Just as this rebellion was a coordinated joint rebellion of the region, the resulting Babylonian reprisal was a thorough destruction of the entire region—of non-Israelite territories in Transjordan as well. According to Jr 34:7, it seems that the Babylonians reduced all the other fortifications of Judah before turning to Jerusalem and that their approach at the end came from the southwest, from the Shephelah.

25:2-3 After a **siege** of 18 months, the **food** supply of Jerusalem failed.

25:4-5 When Jerusalem's wall was breached, the warriors and King Zedekiah fled, probably down the Kidron Valley to the road to **Jericho** and then to the **plains** near Jericho.

25:6-7 **Riblah** was the administrative center for Babylonian control in the region. There, **Zedekiah** was punished. His

ans seized the king[a] and brought him up to the king of Babylon[b] at Riblah,[c] and they passed sentence on him. [7]They slaughtered Zedekiah's sons before his eyes. Finally, the king of Babylon blinded Zedekiah, bound him in bronze chains, and took him to Babylon.[d]

Jerusalem Destroyed

[8]One[e] the seventh day of the fifth month, which was the nineteenth year of Nebuchadnezzar king of Babylon, Nebuzaradan, the commander of the guards, a servant of the king of Babylon, entered Jerusalem.[f] [9]He burned the LORD's temple,[g] the king's palace,[h] and all the houses of Jerusalem; he burned down[i] all the great houses. [10]The whole Chaldean army with the commander of the guards tore down the walls[j] surrounding Jerusa-

lem. [11]Nebuzaradan, the commander of the guards, deported the rest of the people who were left in the city, the deserters who had defected to the king of Babylon, and the rest of the population.[k] [12]But the commander of the guards left some of the poorest of the land to be vinedressers and farmers.[l]

[13]Now[m] the Chaldeans broke into pieces the bronze pillars[n] of the LORD's temple, the water carts, and the bronze reservoir,[o] which were in the LORD's temple, and carried the bronze to Babylon.[p] [14]They also took the pots, the shovels, the wick trimmers, the dishes, and all the bronze articles used in temple service.[q] [15]The commander of the guards took away the

a 25:6 Jr 34:21-22
b Jr 32:4
c Nm 34:11; 2Kg 23:33; Jr 52:9
d 25:7 Jr 39:6-7; Ezk 12:13
e 25:8-12 Jr 39:8-10; 52:12-16
f 25:8 2Kg 24:12; Jr 39:9; 52:12
g 25:9 1Kg 9:8; 2Ch 36:19
h Jr 39:8; Am 2:5
i Jr 17:27
j 25:10 2Kg 24:13; Neh 1:3; Jr 50:15
k 25:11 2Ch 36:20; Jr 5:19; 39:1-9
l 25:12 2Kg 24:14; Jr 39:10; 40:7
m 25:13-21 Jr 52:17-27
n 25:13 2Kg 20:17; 2Ch 36:18; Jr 52:17   o 1Kg 7:23; 2Ch 4:2-4
p Jr 27:19-22   q 25:14 Ex 27:3; 1Kg 7:47-50; 2Ch 4:16

sons were killed **before his eyes**, thus eliminating the threat of royal heirs to the throne. Zedekiah was **blinded** and taken to prison in **Babylon**. This fulfilled the prophecies that he would see Nebuchadnezzar (Jr 32:4) but would not see Babylon (Ezk 12:11-13).

25:8-10 The end of this historic phase of the Davidic covenant came with the total destruction of everything of significance in **Jerusalem**: literally, Yahweh's house, the king's house, all the houses of Jerusalem, all the great houses, and the wall of Jerusalem.

25:11-12 The **poorest of the land** were unlikely to have skills that could be of use in Babylon, and so they were left behind to be **farmers**.

25:13-17 The **temple** furnishings were plundered for their scrap-metal value. The list of plundered objects would have read to devout worshipers of Yahweh like an obituary list. All that was left for their faith in Yahweh was the documents that had already been taken and would be taken into captivity. The learned scholars of the time—according to current thinking, identified with the Levites—would continue to preserve and produce sacred writings.

Babylonian Invasion
586 B.C.

Babylon's King Nebuchadnezzar II took thousands of Judean residents as captives to Mesopotamia in three deportations: 605, 597, and 586 B.C. The third deportation took place when Jerusalem, its walls, and the temple were destroyed.

firepans and the sprinkling basins—whatever was gold or silver.[a]

[16] As for the two pillars, the one reservoir, and the water carts that Solomon had made for the LORD's temple, the weight of the bronze of all these articles was beyond measure.[b] [17] One pillar was 27 feet[A] tall and had a bronze capital on top of it. The capital, encircled by a grating and pomegranates of bronze, stood five feet[B] high. The second pillar was the same, with its own grating.[c]

[18] The commander of the guards[d] also took away Seraiah[e] the chief priest, Zephaniah[f] the priest of the second rank, and the three doorkeepers. [19] He took a court official who had been appointed over the warriors from the city; five trusted royal aides[C,g] found in the city; the secretary of the commander of the army, who enlisted the people of the land for military duty; and 60 men from the common people[D] who were found within the city. [20] Nebuzaradan, the commander of the guards, took them and brought them to the king of Babylon at Riblah.[h] [21] The king of Babylon put them to death at Riblah in the land of Hamath. So Judah went into exile from its land.[i]

Gedaliah Made Governor

[22] Nebuchadnezzar king of Babylon appointed Gedaliah[j] son of Ahikam, son of Shaphan, over the rest of the people he left in the land of Judah.[k] [23] When all the commanders of the armies—they and their men—heard that the king of Babylon had appointed Gedaliah, they came to Gedaliah at Mizpah.[l] The commanders included Ishmael son of Nethaniah, Johanan son of Kareah, Seraiah son of Tanhumeth the Netophathite, and Jaazaniah son of the Maacathite—they and their men.[m] [24] Gedaliah swore an oath to them and their men, assuring them, "Don't be afraid of the servants of the Chaldeans. Live in the land and serve the king of Babylon, and it will go well for you."[n]

[25] In the seventh month, however, Ishmael son of Nethaniah, son of Elishama, of the royal family, came with 10 men and struck down Gedaliah, and he died. Also, they killed the Judeans and the Chaldeans who were with him at Mizpah.[o] [26] Then all the people, from the youngest to the oldest, and the commanders of the army, left and went to Egypt, for they were afraid of the Chaldeans.[p]

Jehoiachin Pardoned

[27] On[q] the twenty-seventh day of the twelfth month of the thirty-seventh year of the exile of Judah's King Jehoiachin, in the year Evil-merodach became king of Babylon, he pardoned King Jehoiachin[r] of Judah and released him from prison.[s] [28] He spoke kindly[t] to him and set his throne over the thrones of the kings who were with him in Babylon.[u] [29] So Jehoiachin changed his prison clothes, and he dined regularly in the presence of the king of Babylon for the rest of his life.[v] [30] As for his allowance, a regular allowance[w] was given to him by the king, a portion for each day, for the rest of his life.

Cross references (center column):

[a] 25:15 2Kg 24:13; Jr 15:13; 20:5
[b] 25:16 1Kg 7:47
[c] 25:17 1Kg 7:15-22
[d] 25:18 Jr 39:9-13; 52:12-16,24
[e] 1Ch 6:14; Ezr 7:1
[f] Jr 21:1; 29:25,29
[g] 25:19 Jr 52:25
[h] 25:20 2Kg 23:33
[i] 25:21 Dt 28:63-64; 2Kg 23:27
[j] 25:22 Jr 39:14; 40:7-9
[k] Is 1:9; Jr 40:5
[l] 25:23 Jos 18:26
[m] Jr 40:7-8
[n] 25:24 Jr 40:9
[o] 25:25 Jr 41:1-2
[p] 25:26 Is 30:2; Jr 43:4-7
[q] 25:27-30 Jr 52:31-34
[r] 25:27 2Kg 24:12
[s] Gn 40:13,20
[t] 25:28 1Kg 8:50
[u] Ezr 5:5; 7:6,28
[v] 25:29 2Sm 9:7
[w] 25:30 Gn 43:34; Neh 12:47

[A]25:17 Lit *18 cubits*   [B]25:17 Lit *three cubits*   [C]25:19 Lit *five men who look on the king's face*   [D]25:19 Lit *the people of the land*

25:18-21 Representative leaders of Judah were selected for execution by the Babylonians after being taken to **Riblah**. Of the two, **Seraiah** is otherwise unknown. However, **Zephaniah**, a second tier leader of the priests, was known for being given the responsibility to root out supposedly false prophets, his major target being Jeremiah (Jr 29:26-29). The Babylonians were probably aware of his anti-Babylonian stance when they executed him. Also, **60 . . . common people**, probably randomly selected, were also executed.

25:22-25 A more detailed account of these events appears in Jr 40:6–41:9. Here it suffices to note that it was a story of alleged collaboration with the conquerors, wholesale murder by "freedom fighters," and the loss of any hope of civilized life for the Hebrews who remained in Palestine.

25:26 The feared repercussions after the assassination of Gedaliah resulted in a voluntary exodus from Palestine to Egypt. Though at the time there was little hope for the future, the Jewish colony at Elephantine would make their mark on history through documents (Elephantine papyri) that have survived to this day, and the Jewish community in Alexandria would become the intellectual rivals of rabbinic Judaism.

25:27-30 There was, however, one more optimistic development—Jehoiachin's release from prison and his place of honor among the captive kings. This favor probably resulted partly from his willing surrender to the Babylonians and may have been aimed at creating a better atmosphere for the exiles in Babylon. It may also have aroused hopes for restoration of the Davidic line in the person of Jehoiachin or one of his descendants. At the very least, it signaled a generally favorable Babylonian stance toward the Jewish captives—an optimistic development for God's people in Babylon.

1 Chronicles

The word *Chronicles* in Hebrew has the meaning of an ongoing account, almost like a journal or diary or minutes taken at a meeting. They are the first and second books of a four-book series that includes Ezra and Nehemiah. Together these four books provide a priestly history of Israel from the time of Adam to the rebuilding of the house of God and the walls of Jerusalem. At one time the book of Chronicles was probably one single scroll, which was divided later for convenience by those who translated the Old Testament into Greek (the Septuagint).

Eleven of Jerusalem's gates and the only one that is sealed. This gate existed during the time of Jesus but would have been destroyed in A.D. 70. The gate in the photo was built around A.D. 640. This is called the Golden Gate and is situated on the eastern side of Jerusalem just below the Temple Mount. A Jewish tradition says that the Messiah will enter Jerusalem through this gate. The Chronicler gives considerable attention to the temple and reminds his readers of God's presence in Israel's history as symbolized by the temple.

Circumstances of Writing

Author: An ancient tradition ascribes the authorship of Chronicles to Ezra. The author must have lived some time after the return of the Jews to Israel from the Babylonian exile. He also had a strong interest in the reimplementation of the law and the temple, and he must have had access to historical records. All of these criteria suit Ezra, and this identification is corroborated by the fact that the last verses of Chronicles are the first verses of the book of Ezra. However, since the book does not explicitly claim Ezra for its author, in these notes we will refer to him simply as the "Chronicler."

Background: The books of 1 and 2 Chronicles include extensive genealogies from the time of Adam and take the reader up to the period of the nation's exile and restoration. First Chronicles gives us the genealogies and focuses on the reign of King David. Second Chronicles focuses on all the kings who followed David up to the exile and restoration. It covers the same time period as 1 and 2 Kings, but 2 Chronicles focuses exclusively on the kings of Judah. The content of the books necessitates that they were written sometime after the return from the exile, perhaps the middle of the fifth century B.C.

Message and Purpose

Having resettled in Jerusalem after the exile, the people needed to reconnect with their identity as the people of God. Chronicles met this purpose by reminding them of their heritage and by directing them back to God's presence in their midst as symbolized by the temple. The important ideas that 1 and 2 Chronicles emphasize are: (1) a direct connection to God's people in the past; (2) the continuity of the line of David on the throne of Judah; (3) the centrality of the temple and its rituals in focusing on God; (4) the importance of music in worshiping God; (5) the invincibility of God's people when they obey Him; and (6) the inevitability of punishment when God's people disobey Him.

1000 B.C.

900 B.C.

David 1010–970

With the death of Saul, David becomes king of Judah. 1010

David becomes king over all Israel. 1003

David moves the ark of the covenant to Jerusalem. 1000

God's covenant with David 995

Solomon becomes Israel's third king. 970

Construction of the temple begins. 966

Solomon dedicates the temple. 959

Asa 911–870

Notched flute developed in Peru and Chile 900

First temple repair and reform under Asa 897

Jehoshaphat 872–848

Jehoram 853–841

Ahaziah 841

Etruscans settle in central Italy. 850–800

Athaliah 841–835

The books of 1 and 2 Chronicles convey several key themes. These include:

God's control of history: God desires to dwell among His people in a perfect relationship of holiness in which He is God and the redeemed live as His people. The tabernacle and the temple symbolize that desire, a desire that was ultimately fulfilled through Jesus Christ—the Son of David. Chronicles shows how God worked from the time of Adam but particularly in the time of David through Ezra and Nehemiah to accomplish His desire to dwell in holiness with His people.

The covenant with David: God chose David and His lineage to build His house. The final ruler in this lineage is the Son of David—the Messiah. Solomon built the temple in Jerusalem, but it is Jesus who is building and shall build to completion God's true house. Christ is the One who will reign forever. His people are those of Israel and indeed of all nations who will put their trust in Him.

The holy God is to be worshiped properly: The two books of Chronicles show us that the God who dwells in holiness must be approached according to the law that God gave to Moses. David, in seeking to unite his people around the presence of God, learned that God must be sought in the proper way. Worship by way of the altar of sacrifice as ministered by the Levitical priesthood was important, and the place of the altar of sacrifice was to be in Jerusalem at the threshing floor of Ornan (Araunah). There David erected the altar and Solomon built the temple according to God's directions.

The house of God: The books of Chronicles intended to encourage God's people to work together with God and with one another to build God's house. The people were challenged through these books to go up to Jerusalem to build God's house. Chronicles reminds the people of God's history of faithfulness to His people and to His house. God promised that He would bless their obedience to this challenge.

Contribution to the Bible

Chronicles brings together many dimensions of biblical revelation, such as historical events (as recounted

---

800 B.C.	700 B.C.	600 B.C.
Joash 835–796	**Hezekiah** 715–687	**Josiah** 641–609 **Zedekiah** 597–586
Second temple reform under Joash 812	Third temple reform under Hezekiah 715	Babylon under Nebuchadnezzar II becomes the largest city on earth. 600
Amaziah 796–767	Manasseh 697–643	Jehoiachin 598–597
Uzziah 792–740	Amon 643–641	The temple in Jerusalem destroyed under Zedekiah. 586
First Olympiad in Greece 776	Fourth temple reform under Josiah 622	Temple of Artemis in Ephesus, third of seven wonders of the ancient world 550
Traditional date for the founding of Rome 753	Jehoahaz 609	Statue of Zeus at Olympia, fourth of seven wonders of the ancient world 466–456
Jotham 750–732	Jehoiakim 609–598	
Ahaz 735–716		

in Genesis through Kings), temple ritual (as prescribed in Leviticus), sin and judgment (as preached by the prophets), and even some psalms. Because a recurring theme is that God will always accept people who return to Him no matter how wicked they may have been, it has been called, perhaps a little whimsically, "The Gospel According to Ezra." The books of 1 and 2 Chronicles give us the big picture of OT history, capturing the Davidic covenant in light of Israel's history back to Adam and pointing to the eternal continuation of that covenant through the reign of the Messiah.

Structure

The Hebrew Bible divides its books into three categories: the Law, the Prophets, and the Writings. In this arrangement, the books of Samuel and Kings are counted among the Prophets, whereas Chronicles belongs to the Writings. This classification may be partially due to the fact that Chronicles repeats information, such as the genealogies of Genesis and the histories of the kings of Judah from the books of Samuel and Kings. Still the Chronicler uses this repeated content to support his own point, and he also adds a lot of information that we find in Chronicles alone. He limits his discussion of the various kings almost entirely to those of Judah, the southern kingdom.

Outline of 1 Chronicles

I. The Genealogies (1:1–9:44)
  A. Genealogies of the human race (1:1-54)
  B. Genealogies of the twelve tribes (2:1–9:44)

II. The Reign of David (10:1–29:30)
  A. Fall of Saul's house and rise of David (10:1–14:17)
  B. Removal of the ark to Jerusalem (15:1–16:43)
  C. David's desire to build God a house (17:1-27)
  D. David's victories over Israel's enemies (18:1–21:30)
  E. David's preparations for building the temple (22:1-19)
  F. Arrangements for the service of the Levites (23:1–26:32)
  G. David's final days (27:1–29:30)

From Adam to Abraham

1 Adam,[a] Seth, Enosh,
2 Kenan, Mahalalel, Jared,
3 Enoch, Methuselah, Lamech,
4 Noah, Noah's sons:[A]
Shem, Ham, and Japheth.

5 Japheth's[b] sons: Gomer, Magog, Madai, Javan, Tubal, Meshech, and Tiras. 6 Gomer's sons: Ashkenaz, Riphath,[B] and Togarmah. 7 Javan's sons: Elishah, Tarshish, Kittim, and Rodanim.[C]

8 Ham's sons: Cush, Mizraim,[D] Put, and Canaan. 9 Cush's sons: Seba, Havilah, Sabta, Raama, and Sabteca. Raama's sons: Sheba and Dedan. 10 Cush fathered Nimrod, who was the first to become a great warrior on earth. 11 Mizraim[c] fathered Ludim, Anamim, Lehabim, Naphtuhim, 12 Pathrusim, Casluhim (the Philistines came from them), and Caphtorim.[d] 13 Canaan fathered Sidon as his firstborn, then Heth, 14 the Jebusites, Amorites, Girgashites, 15 Hivites, Arkites, Sinites, 16 Arvadites, Zemarites, and Hamathites.

17 Shem's[e] sons: Elam, Asshur, Arpachshad, Lud, Aram, Uz, Hul, Gether, and Meshech. 18 Arpachshad fathered Shelah, and

Shelah fathered Eber. 19 Two sons were born to Eber. One of them was named Peleg[E] because the earth was divided during his lifetime, and the name of his brother was Joktan. 20 Joktan fathered Almodad, Sheleph, Hazarmaveth, Jerah, 21 Hadoram, Uzal, Diklah, 22 Ebal, Abimael, Sheba, 23 Ophir, Havilah, and Jobab. All of these were Joktan's sons.

24 Shem,[f] Arpachshad, Shelah,
25 Eber, Peleg, Reu,
26 Serug, Nahor, Terah,
27 and Abram (that is, Abraham).

Abraham's Descendants

28 Abraham's sons: Isaac and Ishmael.

29 These[g] are their family records: Nebaioth, Ishmael's firstborn, Kedar, Adbeel, Mibsam, 30 Mishma, Dumah, Massa, Hadad, Tema, 31 Jetur, Naphish, and Kedemah. These were Ishmael's sons.

32 The sons[h] born to Keturah, Abraham's concubine: Zimran, Jokshan, Medan, Midian, Ishbak, and Shuah. Jokshan's sons: Sheba and Dedan. 33 Midian's sons: Ephah, Epher, Hanoch, Abida, and Eldaah. All of these were Keturah's sons.

34 Abraham[i] fathered Isaac. Isaac's sons: Esau and Israel.[j] 35 Esau's[k] sons: Eliphaz, Reuel, Jeush, Jalam, and Korah.

[a]1:1-4 Gn 4:25–5:32
[b]1:5-7 Gn 10:2-4
[c]1:11-16 Gn 10:13-18
[d]1:12 Dt 2:23; Am 9:7
[e]1:17-23 Gn 10:21-29
[f]1:24-27 Gn 11:10-26; Lk 3:34-36
[g]1:29-31 Gn 25:12-16
[h]1:32-33 Gn 25:1-4
[i]1:34 1Ch 1:28
[j]Gn 25:24-26; 32:28
[k]1:35-37 Gn 36:4-5,9-14

A1:4 LXX; MT omits *Noah's sons* B1:6 Some Hb mss, LXX, Vg; other Hb mss read *Diphath*; Gn 10:3 C1:7 Some Hb mss, Syr read *Dodanim*; Gn 10:4 D1:8 = Egypt E1:19 = Division

1:1 Even though the Chronicler was specifically writing for the Jews of his day, he began with this brief reminder that all people are creatures who are descended from the first man, **Adam**. **Seth** represented the ongoing hope after failure (Gn 4:25).

1:2-4 The line of ancient patriarchs moves quickly from **Adam** to **Noah**. Each of the men in this line had a son comparatively early in life, but he lived for many centuries afterwards. **Enoch** never actually died but was taken to heaven (Gn 5:24). **Methuselah** lived the longest with a total age of 969 years; he died after 1,650 years had elapsed since the birth of Adam. This is also the exact year in which Noah's flood occurred. Before going on with the main line of descent, the Chronicler frequently pursued a minor or alternative branch first, such as when he detailed the descendants of **Japheth** and **Ham** before returning to **Shem**.

1:5 **Japheth's** offspring moved to a more northern region than those of his brothers.

1:8-15 Many of **Ham's** sons lent their names to various nations, several of which became the chief opponents of Israel in the promised land.

1:17 The line of **Shem** was the most important one for the Chronicler because it includes Abraham.

1:18 Some scholars conjecture that Eber's name led to the name of the "Hebrews," but this inference is not certain.

1:19 The line of Shem divides with the brothers **Peleg** and **Joktan**. "Peleg" means "division." During his time the episode of the tower of Babel took place, and the entire human race was divided by the languages they spoke.

1:20 Again following a minor branch first, we read of the descendants of **Joktan**.

1:24-27 Here is a quick overview of the links between **Shem** and **Abraham**, based on the descendants of **Peleg**.

1:28 Although **Isaac** is mentioned in this verse, we are still a long way from the line that will eventually lead up to Judah. **Ishmael** and his **sons** come first.

1:32 Abraham spent an entire century waiting to have a single son with Sarah. Then, after Sarah's death, **Keturah** endowed him with many more sons.

1:34 Again **Isaac** is mentioned, along with Jacob, or **Israel**, but for the moment the Chronicler focuses on **Esau**, again an alternative branch.

1:35 We only have this list of names for **Esau's** sons and

³⁶Eliphaz's sons: Teman, Omar, Zephi, Gatam, and Kenaz; and by Timna, Amalek.ᴬ
³⁷Reuel's sons: Nahath, Zerah, Shammah, and Mizzah.

The Edomites

³⁸Seir'sᵃ sons: Lotan, Shobal, Zibeon, Anah, Dishon, Ezer, and Dishan.
³⁹Lotan's sons: Hori and Homam. Timna was Lotan's sister.
⁴⁰Shobal's sons: Alian, Manahath, Ebal, Shephi, and Onam.
Zibeon's sons: Aiah and Anah.
⁴¹Anah's son: Dishon.
Dishon's sons: Hamran, Eshban, Ithran, and Cheran.
⁴²Ezer's sons: Bilhan, Zaavan, and Jaakan.
Dishan's sons: Uz and Aran.

⁴³Theseᵇ were the kings who ruled in the land of Edom before any king ruled over the Israelites: Bela son of Beor. Bela's town was named Dinhabah. ⁴⁴When Bela died, Jobab son of Zerah from Bozrahᶜ ruled in his place. ⁴⁵When Jobab died, Husham from the land of the Temanitesᵈ ruled in his place. ⁴⁶When Husham died, Hadad son of Bedad, who defeated Midian in the country of Moab, ruled in his place. Hadad's town was named Avith. ⁴⁷When Hadad died, Samlah from Masrekah ruled in his place. ⁴⁸When Samlah died, Shaul from Rehoboth on the Euphrates River ruled in his place. ⁴⁹When Shaul died, Baal-hanan son of Achbor ruled in his place. ⁵⁰When Baal-hanan

ᵃ1:38-42 Gn 36:20-30
ᵇ1:43-50 Gn 36:31-39
ᶜ1:44 Is 34:6
ᵈ1:45 Jb 2:11
ᵉ1:51-54 Gn 36:40-43
ᶠ2:1-2 Gn 35:22-26; 46:8-25
ᵍ2:3-4 Gn 38:6-30
ʰ2:3 Gn 38:2-5; 46:12; Nm 26:19-22
ⁱ2:6 1Kg 4:31
ʲ2:7 Jos 7:1,16-26

died, Hadad ruled in his place. Hadad's city was named Pai, and his wife's name was Mehetabel daughter of Matred, daughter of Mezahab. ⁵¹Then Hadad died.

Edom'sᵉ chiefs: Timna, Alvah,ᴮ Jetheth, ⁵²Oholibamah, Elah, Pinon, ⁵³Kenaz, Teman, Mibzar, ⁵⁴Magdiel, and Iram. These were Edom's chiefs.

Israel's Sons

2 Theseᶠ were Israel's sons: Reuben, Simeon, Levi, Judah, Issachar, Zebulun, ²Dan, Joseph, Benjamin, Naphtali, Gad, and Asher.

Judah's Descendants

³Judah'sᵍ sons: Er, Onan, and Shelah.ʰ These three were born to him by Bathshua the Canaanite woman. Er, Judah's firstborn, was evil in the LORD's sight, so He put him to death. ⁴Judah's daughter-in-law Tamar bore Perez and Zerah to him. Judah had five sons in all.

⁵Perez's sons: Hezron and Hamul.
⁶Zerah's sons: Zimri, Ethan, Heman, Calcol, and Daraᶜ·ⁱ—five in all.
⁷Carmi's son: Achar,ᴰ·ʲ who brought trouble on Israel when he was unfaithful by taking the things •set apart for destruction.
⁸Ethan's son: Azariah.
⁹Hezron's sons, who were born to him: Jerahmeel, Ram, and Chelubai.ᴱ

ᴬ1:36 LXX; MT reads and Timna and Amalek; Gn 36:12   ᴮ1:51 Alt Hb tradition reads Aliah   ᶜ2:6 Some Hb mss, LXX, Syr, Tg, Vg read Darda; 1Kg 4:31   ᴰ2:7 = Trouble; Achan in Jos 7:1,16-26   ᴱ2:9 = Caleb

grandsons, but we know that this clan eventually led to the emergence of several large nations such as the Edomites.

1:38 Seir could be a proper name referring to an ancestor of the Edomites. It is also the name of a mountain in Edomite territory. The Edomites lived on the eastern side of the Jordan River in the vicinity of the Dead Sea. "Seirites" and "Meunites" are sometimes used as synonyms.

1:43-51a Little is known about these **kings . . . in the land of Edom**. They apparently lived around the time of the judges in Israel.

1:51b-54 The chapter concludes with a list of **Edom's chiefs**. The book of 1 Chronicles has now covered several minor lines in contrast to its major purpose of leading up to the kings of Judah. We have seen alternatives to Shem (Ham and Japheth), to Abraham (Ishmael and the sons of Keturah), and to Isaac (Esau and the Edomites), now we are ready for the main line of interest, the descendants of Jacob.

2:1 The Chronicler initially lists the sons of Jacob (Israel) in birth order. **Judah** became the most prominent, although

the oldest chronologically was **Reuben**, who forfeited the privilege of the firstborn (5:1-2).

2:2 As the first son of Jacob's favorite wife, **Joseph** could have carried the honors as the tribe of the firstborn, but his descendants are divided into the tribes of Ephraim and Manasseh.

2:3 We see God's grace in action as He selects the line that would lead to the kings and ultimately to the Messiah. All three of **Judah's** first sons had a **Canaanite** mother.

2:4 After **Judah's** first two sons were killed, he had two more sons by his daughter-in-law **Tamar**, another Canaanite woman, who had disguised herself as a prostitute (Gn 38). These were **Perez** and **Zerah**.

2:5 Perez continues the main line through **Hezron**. Hamul's line is the secondary alternative.

2:6 **Zerah's sons** constitute another alternative. This does not mean that they were unimportant—they may be the wise men of 1Kg 4:31 and the musicians in the titles of Psalms 88 and 89—only that they were not ancestors of the line of kings.

2:7 Carmi must be a person of a later generation. He is

a 2:21 Nm 26:29

¹⁰ Ram fathered Amminadab, and Amminadab fathered Nahshon, a leader of Judah's descendants. ¹¹ Nahshon fathered Salma, and Salma fathered Boaz. ¹² Boaz fathered Obed, and Obed fathered Jesse. ¹³ Jesse fathered Eliab, his firstborn; Abinadab was born second, Shimea third, ¹⁴ Nethanel fourth, Raddai fifth, ¹⁵ Ozem sixth, and David seventh. ¹⁶ Their sisters were Zeruiah and Abigail. Zeruiah's three sons: Abishai, Joab, and Asahel. ¹⁷ Amasa's mother was Abigail, and his father was Jether the Ishmaelite.

¹⁸ Caleb son of Hezron had children by his wife Azubah and by Jerioth. These were Azubah's sons: Jesher, Shobab, and Ardon. ¹⁹ When Azubah died, Caleb married Ephrath, and she bore Hur to him. ²⁰ Hur fathered Uri, and Uri fathered Bezalel. ²¹ After this, Hezron slept with the daughter of Machir the father of Gilead.ᵃ Hezron had married her when he was 60 years old, and she bore Segub to him. ²² Segub fathered Jair, who possessed 23 towns in the land of Gilead. ²³ But Geshur and Aram capturedᴬ Jair's Villagesᴮ along with Kenath and its villages—60 towns. All these were the sons of Machir father of Gilead. ²⁴ After Hezron's death in Caleb-ephrathah, his wife Abijah bore Ashhur to him. He was the father of Tekoa.

²⁵ The sons of Jerahmeel, Hezron's firstborn: Ram, his firstborn, Bunah, Oren, Ozem, and Ahijah. ²⁶ Jerahmeel

had another wife named Atarah, who was the mother of Onam. ²⁷ The sons of Ram, Jerahmeel's firstborn: Maaz, Jamin, and Eker. ²⁸ Onam's sons: Shammai and Jada. Shammai's sons: Nadab and Abishur. ²⁹ Abishur's wife was named Abihail, who bore Ahban and Molid to him. ³⁰ Nadab's sons: Seled and Appaim. Seled died without children. ³¹ Appaim's son: Ishi. Ishi's son: Sheshan. Sheshan's descendant: Ahlai. ³² The sons of Jada, brother of Shammai: Jether and Jonathan. Jether died without children. ³³ Jonathan's sons: Peleth and Zaza. These were the descendants of Jerahmeel. ³⁴ Sheshan had no sons, only daughters, but he did have an Egyptian servant whose name was Jarha. ³⁵ Sheshan gave his daughter in marriage to his servant Jarha, and she bore Attai to him.

³⁶ Attai fathered Nathan, and Nathan fathered Zabad. ³⁷ Zabad fathered Ephlal, and Ephlal fathered Obed. ³⁸ Obed fathered Jehu, and Jehu fathered Azariah. ³⁹ Azariah fathered Helez, and Helez fathered Elasah. ⁴⁰ Elasah fathered Sismai, and Sismai fathered Shallum. ⁴¹ Shallum fathered Jekamiah, and Jekamiah fathered Elishama.

⁴² The sons of Caleb brother of

ᴬ 2:23 Lit took from them   ᴮ 2:23 Or captured Havvoth-jair

mentioned only because he is the father of **Achar**, another bearer of scandal (aka Achan; Jos 7). Thus, the alternative branch goes: Zerah to Zabdi to Carmi to Achar.

2:9 Returning to the main line: Perez had **Hezron** (see note at v. 5). Now the line splits three ways based on Hezron's three sons: **Jerahmeel, Ram, and Chelubai**. Of these, Ram's line is the main one, and this time it gets mentioned first. Chelubai is another version of the name Caleb. There are many different men named Caleb in the list that follows.

2:10-12 Ram's line of descent connects through **Boaz** to **Jesse**, the father of David.

2:13-17 In this passage we are given the names of David's six older brothers and his two much older sisters **Zeruiah** and **Abigail**. These two were probably from an earlier marriage of David's father Jesse since according to 2Sm 17:25, their father was Nahash. So presumably Jesse married Nahash's widow. Zeruiah had three sons—**Abishai, Joab, and Asahel**—who were roughly David's age, and who would later become leaders in David's army. Abigail married an

Ishmaelite named **Jether** and gave birth to **Amasa**, who would become the leader of Absalom's army against David. These four were David's half nephews.

2:18-24 We go back to **Hezron**, son of Perez, who left a sizeable number of descendants—one of them even after his own death. His son **Caleb** (called Chelubai in v. 9) also had a number of sons.

2:25 The third line of descent coming from **Hezron**, joining those of Ram and Caleb, is that of **Jerahmeel**. His son **Ram** was the nephew of Hezron's brother, Ram.

2:34-35 **Sheshan** had been mentioned in verse 31, the sixth generation descendant of Jerahmeel. He did not have a male heir, but a daughter named Ahlai. **Jarha**, his Egyptian servant, provided him with a grandson named **Attai** to carry on the family name.

2:36-41 The list of Jerahmeel's descendants continues from **Attai** onward.

2:42-55 We have already had a list of the descendants of **Caleb** (Chelubai), the son of Perez. This time the descendants

Jerahmeel: Mesha, his firstborn, fathered Ziph, and Mareshah, his second son,^A fathered Hebron. ^43 Hebron's sons: Korah, Tappuah, Rekem, and Shema. ^44 Shema fathered Raham, who fathered Jorkeam, and Rekem fathered Shammai. ^45 Shammai's son was Maon, and Maon fathered Beth-zur. ^46 Caleb's concubine Ephah was the mother of Haran, Moza, and Gazez. Haran fathered Gazez. ^47 Jahdai's sons: Regem, Jotham, Geshan, Pelet, Ephah, and Shaaph. ^48 Caleb's concubine Maacah was the mother of Sheber and Tirhanah. ^49 She was also the mother of Shaaph, Madmannah's father, and of Sheva, the father of Machbenah and Gibea. Caleb's daughter was Achsah. ^50 These were Caleb's descendants.

The sons of Hur, Ephrathah's firstborn:
Shobal fathered Kiriath-jearim;
^51 Salma fathered Bethlehem,
and Hareph fathered Beth-gader.

^52 These were the descendants of Shobal the father of Kiriath-jearim: Haroeh, half of the Manahathites,^B ^53 and the families of Kiriath-jearim—the Ithrites, Puthites, Shumathites, and Mishraites. The Zorathites and Eshtaolites descended from these.

^54 Salma's sons: Bethlehem, the Netophathites, Atroth-beth-joab, and half of the Manahathites, the Zorites, ^55 and the families of scribes who lived in Jabez—the Tirathites, Shimeathites, and Sucathites. These are the Kenites who came from Hammath, the father of Rechab's family.

David's Descendants

3 These^a were David's sons who were born to him in Hebron:

Cross-references

^a 3:1-4a 2Sm 3:2-5
^b 3:4 2Sm 2:11; 5:4-5
^c 3:5-8 2Sm 5:14-16; 1Ch 14:4-7
^d 3:5 2Sm 12:24-25
^e 2Sm 11:3
^f 3:6 2Sm 5:15; 1Ch 14:5
^g 3:9 2Sm 13:1

Amnon was the firstborn, by Ahinoam of Jezreel;
Daniel was born second, by Abigail of Carmel;
^2 Absalom son of Maacah, daughter of King Talmai of Geshur, was third;
Adonijah son of Haggith was fourth;
^3 Shephatiah, by Abital, was fifth;
and Ithream, by David's wife Eglah, was sixth.
^4 Six sons were born to David in Hebron, where he ruled seven years and six months, and he ruled in Jerusalem 33 years.^b
^5 These^c sons were born to him in Jerusalem:
Shimea, Shobab, Nathan, and Solomon.^d These four were born to him by Bathshua^e daughter of Ammiel.
^6 David's other sons: Ibhar, Elishua,^C,f Eliphelet, ^7 Nogah, Nepheg, Japhia, ^8 Elishama, Eliada, and Eliphelet—nine sons.
^9 These were all David's sons, with their sister Tamar,^g in addition to the sons by his concubines.

Judah's Kings

^10 Solomon's son was Rehoboam;
his son was Abijah, his son Asa,
his son Jehoshaphat, ^11 his son Jehoram,^D,E
his son Ahaziah, his son Joash,
^12 his son Amaziah, his son Azariah,
his son Jotham, ^13 his son Ahaz,
his son Hezekiah, his son Manasseh,
^14 his son Amon, and his son Josiah.
^15 Josiah's sons:
Johanan was the firstborn, Jehoiakim second,
Zedekiah third, and Shallum fourth.
^16 Jehoiakim's sons:
his sons Jeconiah and Zedekiah.

David's Line After the Exile

^17 The sons of Jeconiah the captive:

---

^A 2:42 Lit *and the sons of Mareshah* ^B 2:52 Lit *Manuhoth* ^C 3:6 Lit *Elishama*; 2Sm 5:15; 1Ch 14:5 ^D 3:11 Lit *Joram* ^E 3:11 = The Lord is Exalted

---

mentioned are not individual people but the populations of towns that could trace themselves back to him in direct and indirect ways.

3:1 This chapter completes the line of Judah. We find the people who are most important for Chronicles: David and his descendants. **David's sons** are divided into two groups—those born in **Hebron** where David was king for seven years and those who were born in Jerusalem, David's capital for 33 years. This is a list of tragedy. **Amnon**, the firstborn, raped his sister Tamar and was eventually killed by Absalom (2Sm 13).

3:2 Absalom revolted against David and lost his life in the process (2Sm 15–18). **Adonijah** survived David's death, but then was killed in the struggle with Solomon over the throne (1Kg 1–2).

3:5 Bath-shua is more familiar to us as Bathsheba. **Solomon** carried the house of David forward.

3:10-16 These verses contain a quick overview of most of 2 Chronicles, the line of descendants of David who were kings of Judah. The significance is that David's descendants retained the throne.

his sons Shealtiel, [18] Malchiram, Pedaiah, Shenazzar, Jekamiah, Hoshama, and Nedabiah. [19] Pedaiah's sons: Zerubbabel and Shimei. Zerubbabel's sons: Meshullam and Hananiah, with their sister Shelomith; [20] and five others—Hashubah, Ohel, Berechiah, Hasadiah, and Jushab-hesed. [21] Hananiah's descendants: Pelatiah, Jeshaiah, and the sons of Rephaiah, Arnan, Obadiah, and Shecaniah.[A] [22] The son[B] of Shecaniah: Shemaiah. Shemaiah's sons: Hattush, Igal, Bariah, Neariah, and Shaphat—six. [23] Neariah's sons: Elioenai, Hizkiah, and Azrikam—three. [24] Elioenai's sons: Hodaviah, Eliashib, Pelaiah, Akkub, Johanan, Delaiah, and Anani—seven.

Judah's Descendants

4 Judah's sons:[a] Perez, Hezron, Carmi, Hur, and Shobal. [2] Reaiah son of Shobal fathered Jahath, and Jahath fathered Ahumai and Lahad. These were the families of the Zorathites. [3] These were Etam's sons:[C] Jezreel, Ishma, and Idbash, and their sister was named Hazzelelponi. [4] Penuel fathered Gedor, and Ezer fathered Hushah. These were the sons of Hur, Ephrathah's firstborn and the father of Bethlehem:

[5] Ashhur fathered Tekoa and had two wives, Helah and Naarah. [6] Naarah bore Ahuzzam, Hepher, Temeni, and Haahashtari to him. These were Naarah's sons. [7] Helah's sons: Zereth, Zohar,[D] and Ethnan. [8] Koz fathered Anub, Zobebah,[E] and the families of Aharhel son of Harum.

[9] Jabez[F] was more honorable than his brothers. His mother named him Jabez and said, "I gave birth to him in pain." [10] Jabez called out to the God of Israel: "If only You would bless me, extend my border, let Your hand be with me, and keep me from harm, so that I will not cause any pain."[G,H] And God granted his request.

[11] Chelub brother of Shuhah fathered Mehir, who was the father of Eshton. [12] Eshton fathered Beth-rapha, Paseah, and Tehinnah the father of Irnahash. These were the men of Recah. [13] Kenaz's sons: Othniel and Seraiah. Othniel's sons: Hathath and Meonothai.[I] [14] Meonothai fathered Ophrah, and Seraiah fathered Joab, the ancestor of those in the Valley of Craftsmen,[J] for they were craftsmen. [15] The sons of Caleb son of Jephunneh: Iru, Elah, and Naam. Elah's son: Kenaz. [16] Jehallelel's sons: Ziph, Ziphah, Tiria, and Asarel. [17] Ezrah's sons: Jether, Mered, Epher,

---

[A]3:21 LXX reads *Jeshaiah, his son Rephaiah, his son Arnan, his son Obadiah, and his son Shecaniah*   [B]3:22 LXX; MT reads *sons*   [C]4:3 LXX; MT reads *father*   [D]4:7 Alt Hb tradition reads *Izhar*   [E]4:8 Or *Hazzobebah*   [F]4:9 In Hb, the name Jabez sounds like "he causes pain."   [G]4:10 LXX reads *and act in knowledge which doesn't hurt me*   [H]4:10 Or *so that I will not experience pain*   [I]4:13 LXX, Vg; MT omits *and Meonothai*   [J]4:14 Or *the Ge-harashim*

3:17 The line continues after the Babylonian exile, even though there was not an official king of Judah from that point on.

3:19 Zerubbabel was the leader of the Jews when they returned from the exile. Under other circumstances, he would have been king. The list ends at a time that is perfectly matched for Ezra to have been the Chronicler.

4:1 In this verse the word **sons** refers loosely to "descendants," as happens frequently in biblical genealogies. Skipping several generations, the Chronicler emphasizes certain individuals in **Judah's** line. Adding to **Perez** and **Hezron**, he focuses on **Carmi, Hur, and Shobal**. Carmi may be the same person as the Carmi mentioned in 2:7.

4:4 Hur has already been mentioned in 2:20. As the father of Ephrathah (Bethlehem), he was an important ancestor.

4:5 Ashhur was mentioned earlier as the son who was born to Hezron posthumously.

4:9 We are not told in which way Jabez's brothers were

dishonorable. He obviously took his walk with God seriously. Jabez also labored under the stigma of a name with negative connotations because it means **pain**. People often thought that having a negative name would produce negative consequences for the person's life.

4:10 Jabez prayed a personal prayer, asking God for His blessing. He wanted more land, he wanted God's **hand** to be with him, and he wanted God to **keep** him **from harm**, which also included that he did not want to bring harm to others. Nothing in this passage indicates that we should pray these same words, let alone that we should pray them as if they represented a formula for blessing, but Jabez's prayer is an example for us in its honesty and fervency.

4:13 Othniel was the first judge (Jdg 2), and he must have been significantly younger than his uncle Caleb.

4:15 This **Caleb** is the spy of Numbers 13 who, along with Joshua, trusted God.

4:17-18 Once again a Gentile is part of the line, this time a daughter of a Pharaoh named **Bithiah**.

and Jalon. Mered's wife Bithiah gave birth to Miriam, Shammai, and Ishbah the father of Eshtemoa. ¹⁸ These were the sons of Pharaoh's daughter Bithiah; Mered had married her. His Judean wife gave birth to Jered the father of Gedor, Heber the father of Soco, and Jekuthiel the father of Zanoah. ¹⁹ The sons of Hodiah's wife, the sister of Naham: the father of Keilah the Garmite and the father of Eshtemoa the Maacathite. ²⁰ Shimon's sons: Amnon, Rinnah, Ben-hanan, and Tilon.

Ishi's sons: Zoheth and Ben-zoheth.

²¹ The sons of Shelah son of Judah: Er the father of Lecah, Laadah the father of Mareshah, the families of the guildᴬ of linen workers at Beth-ashbea, ²² Jokim, the men of Cozeba; and Joash and Saraph, who married Moabitesᴮ and returned to Lehem. These names are from ancient records. ²³ They were the potters and residents of Netaim and Gederah. They lived there in the service of the king.

Simeon's Descendants

²⁴ Simeon's sons:ᵃ Nemuel, Jamin, Jarib, Zerah, and Shaul;
²⁵ Shaul's sons: his son Shallum, his son Mibsam, and his son Mishma.
²⁶ Mishma's sons: his son Hammuel, his son Zaccur, and his son Shimei.

²⁷ Shimei had 16 sons and six daughters, but his brothers did not have many children, so their whole family did not become as numerous as the Judeans. ²⁸ They lived in Beer-sheba, Moladah, Hazar-shual, ²⁹ Bilhah, Ezem, Tolad, ³⁰ Bethuel, Hormah, Ziklag, ³¹ Beth-marcaboth, Hazar-susim, Beth-biri, and Shaaraim.

ᵃ4:24 Gn 46:10
ᵇ4:40 Jdg 18:7-10
ᶜ4:41 1Ch 4:33-38
ᵈNm 21:3; Dt 2:34; 7:2; 13:15; Jos 6:17-21
ᵉ4:42 Gn 36:8-9
ᶠ4:43 1Sm 15:7-8; 30:17
ᵍ5:1 Gn 29:32; 1Ch 2:1

These were their cities until David became king. ³² Their villages were Etam, Ain, Rimmon, Tochen, and Ashan—five cities, ³³ and all their surrounding villages as far as Baal. These were their settlements, and they kept a genealogical record for themselves.

³⁴ Meshobab, Jamlech, Joshah son of Amaziah,
³⁵ Joel, Jehu son of Joshibiah, son of Seraiah, son of Asiel,
³⁶ Elioenai, Jaakobah, Jeshohaiah, Asaiah, Adiel, Jesimiel, Benaiah, ³⁷ and Ziza son of Shiphi, son of Allon, son of Jedaiah, son of Shimri, son of Shemaiah—

³⁸ these mentioned by name were leaders in their families. Their ancestral houses increased greatly. ³⁹ They went to the entrance of Gedor, to the east side of the valley to seek pasture for their flocks. ⁴⁰ They found rich, good pasture, and the land was broad, peaceful, and quiet,ᵇ for some Hamites had lived there previously.

⁴¹ Theseᶜ who were recorded by name came in the days of King Hezekiah of Judah, attacked the Hamites' tents and the Meunites who were found there, and ˙set them apart for destruction,ᵈ as they are today. Then they settled in their place because there was pasture for their flocks. ⁴² Now 500 men from these sons of Simeon went with Pelatiah, Neariah, Rephaiah, and Uzziel, the sons of Ishi, as their leaders to Mount Seir.ᵉ ⁴³ They struck downᶠ the remnant of the Amalekites who had escaped, and they still live there today.

Reuben's Descendants

5 These were the sons of Reuben the firstborn of Israel. He was the firstborn,ᵍ but

---

ᴬ4:21 Lit house   ᴮ4:22 Or who ruled over Moab

4:21-23 Shelah was Judah's third son (2:3). His older brothers Er and Onan had been killed, and he should have become the husband of Tamar, but Judah prevented this (Gn 38:11-14). Shelah's descendants distinguished themselves as craftsmen.

4:24-37 Because Simeon was violent and cruel, his father Jacob predicted that his tribe would be dispersed in the land (Gn 49:7). At the time of the conquest, the tribe of Simeon received a territory that was adjacent to and intermingled with Judah. The parts that belonged to Simeon alone were mostly desert. As a consequence, Simeon became increasingly absorbed into Judah and Benjamin, and its identity faded. Despite numerous offspring, particularly from **Shimei**, the tribe as a whole remained undistinguished.

4:39-41 Some Simeonites retained their identity into the time of Hezekiah, when they took some fertile land from a group of **Hamites**. This accomplishment is particularly

noteworthy since they went on this military adventure to acquire further pasture land while the Assyrians were rampaging throughout the country.

4:42-43 Another group of Simeonites distinguished themselves by an excursion to **Mount Seir** (Edom), where they finally eliminated the **Amalekites** who were hiding out in that area. The Amalekites had frequently caused trouble for Israel (Ex 17; Nm 14:45; Jdg 3:13). They had been brought close to extinction by King Saul (1Sm 15:1-35) and defeated by David (1Sm 30:17), though a few escaped. These Simeonites finally finished the job.

5:1-5 The tribes that settled on the eastern side of the Jordan River (**Reuben**, Gad, and half of Manasseh) asked for this land when Moses and the Israelites first came to the promised land. They received this territory after their men had helped Joshua conquer the land on the river's western side. The tribes are discussed in this chapter, going south

his birthright was given to the sons of Joseph[a] son of Israel, because Reuben defiled his father's bed.[b] He is not listed in the genealogy according to birthright. [2]Although Judah became strong among his brothers[c] and a ruler came from him,[d] the birthright was given to Joseph.

[3] The sons of Reuben, Israel's firstborn:[e]
  Hanoch, Pallu, Hezron, and Carmi.
[4] Joel's sons: his son Shemaiah,
  his son Gog, his son Shimei,
[5] his son Micah, his son Reaiah,
  his son Baal, [6]and his son Beerah.

Beerah was a leader of the Reubenites, and Tiglath-pileser[A] king of Assyria took him into exile. [7]His relatives by their families as they are recorded in their genealogy:[f]

  Jeiel the chief, Zechariah,
  [8]and Bela son of Azaz,
  son of Shema, son of Joel.

They settled in Aroer[g] as far as Nebo and Baal-meon. [9]They also settled in the east as far as the edge of the desert that extends to the Euphrates River, because their herds had increased in the land of Gilead.[h] [10]During Saul's reign they waged war against the Hagrites,[i] who were defeated by their power. And they lived in their tents throughout the region east of Gilead.

Gad's Descendants

[11]The sons[j] of Gad lived next to them in the land of Bashan as far as Salecah:[k]
[12]Joel the chief, Shapham the second

in command, Janai, and Shaphat in Bashan.
[13]Their relatives according to their ancestral houses: Michael, Meshullam, Sheba, Jorai, Jacan, Zia, and Eber—seven.
[14]These were the sons of Abihail son of Huri,
  son of Jaroah, son of Gilead,
  son of Michael, son of Jeshishai,
  son of Jahdo, son of Buz.
[15]Ahi son of Abdiel, son of Guni, was head of their ancestral houses.
[16]They lived in Gilead, in Bashan and its towns, and throughout the pasturelands of Sharon.[l] [17]All of them were registered in the genealogies during the reigns of Judah's King Jotham[m] and Israel's King Jeroboam.[n]

[18]The sons of Reuben and Gad and half the tribe of Manasseh had 44,760 warriors who could serve[o] in the army—men who carried shield and sword, drew the bow, and were trained for war. [19]They waged war against the Hagrites,[p] Jetur,[q] Naphish, and Nodab. [20]They received help against these enemies because they cried out to God in battle, and the Hagrites and all their allies were handed over to them.[r] He granted their request because they trusted in Him.[s] [21]They captured the Hagrites' livestock—50,000 of their camels, 250,000 sheep, and 2,000 donkeys—as well as 100,000 people. [22]Many of the Hagrites were killed because it was God's battle.[t] And they lived there in the Hagrites' place[u] until the exile.[v]

Reference column:
a 5:1 Gn 48:15-22
b Gn 35:22; 49:4
c 5:2 Gn 49:8-10
d Mc 5:2; Mt 2:6
e 5:3 Gn 46:9; Nm 26:5-9
f 5:7 1Ch 5:17
g 5:8 Nm 32:34; Jos 12:2
h 5:9 Jos 22:8-9
i 5:10 1Ch 5:19-21; 11:38; 27:31
j 5:11-12 Gn 46:16; Nm 26:15-18
k 5:11 Dt 3:10
l 5:16 1Ch 27:29
m 5:17 2Kg 15:5,32
n 2Kg 14:16,28
o 5:18 Nm 1:3
p 5:19 1Ch 5:10
q 1Ch 1:31
r 5:20 2Ch 14:11-13
s Ps 9:10; 20:7-8
t 5:22 Jos 23:10; 2Ch 32:8
u 1Ch 4:41
v 2Kg 15:29; 17:6

A5:6 LXX; MT reads *Tilgath-pilneser*

to north. Reuben was located by the Dead Sea, a rough location that suited the status of Reuben. He lost his honor as the **firstborn** among the 12 sons of Jacob when he committed incest with Bilhah, one of Jacob's concubines and the mother of two of Reuben's brothers (Gn 35:25).

5:6 A quick and abbreviated genealogy of the tribe of Reuben leads us to **Beerah**, who had the bad fortune of being tribal leader when **Tiglath-pileser**, king of Assyria, carried the tribe into exile. The following Assyrian kings are important for the OT: Shalmaneser III (858–824 B.C.) is not mentioned in the Bible, but he fought against the northern kingdom of Israel and subjugated King Jehu. Tiglath-pileser III (744–727 B.C.) deported the tribes east of the Jordan River and conquered much of the northern kingdom. King Ahaz of Judah paid him tribute (2Ch 28:1-27). Shalmanezer V (726–722 B.C.) began the destruction of Israel's capital, Samaria (2Kg 17:6), which was completed by Sargon II (722–705 B.C.), who then deported the northern tribes. Sennacherib (704–681 B.C.) conquered Judah but was brought up short by God during the reign of Hezekiah when he attempted to vanquish Jerusalem (2Ch 32:1-23). Esar-haddon (681–669 B.C.) counted King Manasseh of Judah among his friends and supporters but then turned against him. Ashurbanipal

(668–627 B.C.) was the last major king of Assyria. Maintaining his alliance with Judah, he was successful in subduing Egypt, but toward the end of his reign the balance of power shifted from Assyria to Babylon.

5:9-10 Reuben's earlier successes had allowed this tribe to stretch all the way to the **Euphrates River** and to defeat the **Hagrites**. These were the Ishmaelites, the descendants of Hagar.

5:11-17 The tribe of **Gad** was located north of Reuben. The Chronicler's frequent reference to other written documents such as **genealogies** and historical records indicates that biblical writers had at their disposal written sources, and their use of such sources of information underscores the nature of the Bible as both human writing and the inspired Word of God. Cp. 29:29-30; Nm 21:14; Lk 1:1-4.

5:18-22 The eastern tribes combined forces in a number of military victories, and they accumulated a large amount of plunder. A constant theme in Chronicles is that when people attempt to fight in their own strength, God will not bless them, but, when He fights the **war**, His people see miraculous victories beyond human expectation. Thus, when **they cried out to God**, He rewarded them.

Half the Tribe of Manasseh

²³ The sons of half the tribe of Manasseh settled in the land from Bashan to Baal-hermon (that is, Senir[a] or Mount Hermon); they were numerous. ²⁴ These were the heads of their ancestral houses: Epher, Ishi, Eliel, Azriel, Jeremiah, Hodaviah, and Jahdiel. They were brave warriors, famous men, and heads of their ancestral houses. ²⁵ But they were unfaithful to the God of their ancestors. They prostituted themselves[b] with the gods of the nations[A] God had destroyed before them.[c] ²⁶ So the God of Israel put it into the mind of Pul[d] (that is, Tiglath-pileser[B]) king of Assyria to take the Reubenites, Gadites, and half the tribe of Manasseh into exile. He took them to Halah, Habor, Hara, and Gozan's river, where they are until today.

The Levites

⁶ ^c Levi's[e] sons: Gershom,[D] Kohath, and Merari.
² Kohath's sons: Amram, Izhar, Hebron, and Uzziel.
³ Amram's children: Aaron, Moses, and Miriam.
Aaron's sons: Nadab, Abihu, Eleazar, and Ithamar.
⁴ Eleazar fathered Phinehas;[f] Phinehas fathered Abishua;
⁵ Abishua fathered Bukki; Bukki fathered Uzzi;
⁶ Uzzi fathered Zerahiah; Zerahiah fathered Meraioth;
⁷ Meraioth fathered Amariah; Amariah fathered Ahitub;

⁸ Ahitub fathered Zadok; Zadok fathered Ahimaaz;
⁹ Ahimaaz fathered Azariah; Azariah fathered Johanan;
¹⁰ Johanan fathered Azariah, who served as priest in the temple that Solomon built in Jerusalem;
¹¹ Azariah fathered Amariah; Amariah fathered Ahitub;
¹² Ahitub fathered Zadok; Zadok fathered Shallum;
¹³ Shallum fathered Hilkiah; Hilkiah fathered Azariah;
¹⁴ Azariah fathered Seraiah; and Seraiah fathered Jehozadak.
¹⁵ Jehozadak went into exile when the LORD sent Judah and Jerusalem into exile at the hands of Nebuchadnezzar.[g]

^{16E} Levi's[h] sons: Gershom, Kohath, and Merari.
¹⁷ These are the names of Gershom's sons: Libni and Shimei.
¹⁸ Kohath's sons: Amram, Izhar, Hebron and Uzziel.
¹⁹ Merari's sons: Mahli and Mushi.
These are the Levites' families according to their fathers:
²⁰ Of Gershom: his son Libni, his son Jahath, his son Zimmah,
²¹ his son Joah, his son Iddo, his son Zerah, and his son Jeatherai.
²² Kohath's sons: his son Amminadab, his son Korah, his son Assir,
²³ his son Elkanah, his son Ebiasaph,

^a5:23 Dt 3:9 ^b5:25 Ex 34:15 ^c2Kg 17:7-8 ^d5:26 2Kg 15:19,29 ^e6:1-3 Gn 46:11; Ex 6:16,18,20,23; Nm 26:57-60 ^f6:4 Ex 6:25 ^g6:15 2Kg 24:1-2,10,14; 25:1,8,11,21; 1Ch 9:1 ^h6:16-19 Ex 6:16-19

---

^A5:25 Lit *the peoples of the land*   ^B5:26 LXX; MT reads *Tilgath-pilneser*   ^C6:1 1Ch 5:27 in Hb   ^D6:1 Levi's son's name is spelled Gershon in Ex.   ^E6:16 1Ch 6:1 in Hb

---

5:23 There was no tribe of Joseph. Instead, Joseph's sons became the ancestors of two separate tribes, Ephraim and **Manasseh**. The tribe of Manasseh occupied territory on both sides of the Jordan River.

5:25 This is the first reference to idolatry in Chronicles. Even though this part of the tribe of Manasseh contained some outstanding people, they deviated from God and adopted the idolatry of the **nations** around them.

5:26 **Tiglath-pileser** was a cruel and vicious king of **Assyria**, but God used him to punish His people for their idolatry. Long before the other tribes were captured by Assyria, the three eastern tribes fell into the hands of the Assyrians and were carried off into exile. The Chronicler leaves no doubt that this happened because of their idolatry.

6:1 We now switch to **Levi's** tribe, the tribe of priests. These are important for the Chronicler because after the exile, the time at which he was writing, reestablishing the proper priesthood was crucial. Anyone who wanted to serve as a priest in the rebuilt temple had to have a clear genealogy within the tribe of Levi. Levi had three sons, **Gershom, Kohath, and Merari**. Each of these three lines performed

distinctive duties in the worship of God (Nm 4:1-33). The most crucial line was the one that led to Aaron and, thus, to the priests. This is the line that stemmed from Levi's son Kohath. But not every descendant of Kohath got to be a priest—only those who could trace their lineage back to Aaron. Everyone else went into the larger pool of people who fulfilled general temple duties.

6:2 Most genealogies in Chronicles skip some links, and frequently the time that the Israelites spent in Egypt is either shortened or skipped altogether. This is the case here.

6:3-4 The descendants of **Aaron** who are mentioned here were priests. **Nadab** and **Abihu** lost their lives when they violated the sanctity of their duties (Lv 10:1-3), so **Eleazar** became Aaron's true successor, followed by **Phinehas**.

6:5-15 This list of priests is not complete. It does not mention Eli, the priest who raised Samuel (1Sm 1:3).

6:16-21 The second major list in this chapter includes Levites who were not of the priestly line.

6:22-30 We return to the descendants of **Kohath**. This list contains four men named **Elkanah**. The one mentioned in

his son Assir, [24] his son Tahath,
his son Uriel, his son Uzziah,
and his son Shaul.
[25] Elkanah's sons: Amasai and Ahimoth,
[26] his son Elkanah, his son Zophai,
his son Nahath, [27] his son Eliab,
his son Jeroham, and his son Elkanah.
[28] Samuel's sons: his firstborn Joel,[A,a]
and his second son Abijah.
[29] Merari's sons: Mahli, his son Libni,
his son Shimei, his son Uzzah,
[30] his son Shimea, his son Haggiah,
and his son Asaiah.

The Musicians

[31] These are the men David put in charge of the music in the LORD's temple[b] after the ark came to rest there.[c] [32] They ministered with song in front of the tabernacle, the tent of meeting, until Solomon built the LORD's temple in Jerusalem, and they performed their task according to the regulations given to them. [33] These are the men who served with their sons.

From the Kohathites:
Heman the singer,
son of Joel, son of Samuel,
[34] son of Elkanah, son of Jeroham,
son of Eliel, son of Toah,
[35] son of Zuph, son of Elkanah,
son of Mahath, son of Amasai,
[36] son of Elkanah, son of Joel,
son of Azariah, son of Zephaniah,
[37] son of Tahath, son of Assir,
son of Ebiasaph, son of Korah,
[38] son of Izhar, son of Kohath,
son of Levi, son of Israel.

[39] Heman's relative was •Asaph, who stood
at his right hand:
Asaph son of Berechiah, son of Shimea,

a6:28 1Sm 8:2
b6:31 1Ch 15:16-22; 16:4-6
c2Sm 6:17; 1Ch 15:25–16:1
d6:49 Ex 27:1-8
eEx 30:1-7
fEx 30:10-16
g6:50-53 1Ch 6:4-8
h6:54 Jos 21:4,10
i6:55-56 Jos 14:13; 15:13

[40] son of Michael, son of Baaseiah,
son of Malchijah, [41] son of Ethni,
son of Zerah, son of Adaiah,
[42] son of Ethan, son of Zimmah,
son of Shimei, [43] son of Jahath,
son of Gershom, son of Levi.

[44] On the left, their relatives were
Merari's sons:
Ethan son of Kishi, son of Abdi,
son of Malluch, [45] son of Hashabiah,
son of Amaziah, son of Hilkiah,
[46] son of Amzi, son of Bani,
son of Shemer, [47] son of Mahli,
son of Mushi, son of Merari,
son of Levi.

Aaron's Descendants

[48] Their relatives, the Levites, were assigned to all the service of the tabernacle, God's temple. [49] But Aaron and his sons did all the work of the most holy place. They presented the offerings on the altar of •burnt offerings[d] and on the altar of incense[e] to make atonement for Israel according to all that Moses the servant of God had commanded.[f]

[50] These[g] are Aaron's sons: his son
Eleazar,
his son Phinehas, his son Abishua,
[51] his son Bukki, his son Uzzi,
his son Zerahiah, [52] his son Meraioth,
his son Amariah, his son Ahitub,
[53] his son Zadok, and his son Ahimaaz.

The Settlements of the Levites

[54] These were the places assigned to Aaron's sons from the Kohathite family for their settlements in their territory, because the first lot was for them.[h] [55] They[i] were given Hebron in the land of Judah and its surrounding pasturelands, [56] but the fields and villages

---

A6:28 Some LXX mss, Syr, Arabic; other Hb mss omit Joel; 1Sm 8:2

---

verse 27 is the father of **Samuel** since Samuel is mentioned in the next verse. In 1Sm 1:1 Elkanah is referred to as being from Ephraim, whereas here we see him as belonging to the tribe of Levi. That verse refers to the location where he and his family had lived for many generations since Levi did not have its own territory. Chronicles gives us the actual bloodline, which places him in one of the privileged lines of Levi.

6:31 The Chronicler emphasizes the presence of **music** in the **temple**, as it was instituted by David and revived in later years.

6:33-47 There are three main musicians: **Heman** (Ps 88), **Asaph** (Pss 50; 73–83), and **Ethan** (also called Jeduthun at times; Ps 89). These three men represent the three branches of the sons of Levi, coming from Kohath, Gershom, and Merari, respectively. Heman was a descendant of Kohath, but not through Aaron, so he was not eligible for the priesthood.

6:48-53 Emphasizing the distinction between the descendants of **Aaron** and the other branches derived from Levi, the Chronicler once more lists those who were priests, but states that everyone else was also engaged in the service of the tabernacle.

6:54 The Levites worked in the tabernacle and later the temple, but they did not all live clustered around the sacred location. One reason for this is that before the building of the temple, there was no restriction on where sacrifices could be performed. Furthermore, once there was a temple and the restriction was in place, it would not have been economically feasible. At the time of the conquest, they were allocated territories and cities scattered throughout the tribes.

6:55-61 The Kohathites got a share of the important city of **Hebron**. The main inheritor of this location was **Caleb**, and

around the city were given to Caleb son of Jephunneh. ⁵⁷Aaron's sons were given:ᵃ

Hebron (a city of refuge), Libnah and its pasturelands, Jattir, Eshtemoa and its pasturelands, ⁵⁸HilenᴬÂ and its pasturelands, Debir and its pasturelands, ⁵⁹Ashan and its pasturelands, and Beth-shemesh and its pasturelands. ⁶⁰From the tribe of Benjamin they were given Geba and its pasturelands, Alemeth and its pasturelands, and Anathoth and its pasturelands. They had 13 towns in all among their families.

⁶¹To the rest of the Kohathites, 10 towns from half the tribe of Manasseh were assigned by lot.ᵇ

⁶²The Gershomites were assigned 13 towns from the tribes of Issachar, Asher, Naphtali, and Manasseh in Bashan according to their families.

⁶³The Merarites were assigned by lot 12 towns from the tribes of Reuben, Gad, and Zebulun according to their families.ᶜ ⁶⁴So the Israelites gave these towns and their pasturelands to the Levites.ᵈ ⁶⁵They assigned by lot the towns named aboveᵉ from the tribes of the Judahites, Simeonites, and Benjaminites.

⁶⁶Someᶠ of the families of the Kohathites were given towns from the tribe of Ephraim for their territory:

⁶⁷Shechem (a city of refuge) with its pasturelands in the hill country of Ephraim, Gezer and its pasturelands, ⁶⁸Jokmeam and its pasturelands, Beth-horon and its pasturelands, ⁶⁹Aijalon and its pasturelands, and Gath-rimmon and its pasturelands. ⁷⁰From half the tribe of Manasseh, Aner and its pasturelands, and Bileam and its pasturelands were given to the rest of the families of the Kohathites.

⁷¹The Gershomites received:

Golan in Bashan and its pasturelands, and Ashtaroth and its pasturelands from the families of half the tribe of Manasseh. ⁷²From the tribe of Issachar they received Kedesh and its pasturelands, Daberath

and its pasturelands, ⁷³Ramoth and its pasturelands, and Anem and its pasturelands. ⁷⁴From the tribe of Asher they received Mashal and its pasturelands, Abdon and its pasturelands, ⁷⁵Hukok and its pasturelands, and Rehob and its pasturelands. ⁷⁶From the tribe of Naphtali they received Kedesh in Galilee and its pasturelands, Hammon and its pasturelands, and Kiriathaim and its pasturelands.

⁷⁷The rest of the Merarites received:

From the tribe of Zebulun they received Rimmono and its pasturelands and Tabor and its pasturelands. ⁷⁸From the tribe of Reuben across the Jordan at Jericho, to the east of the Jordan, they received Bezer in the desert and its pasturelands, Jahzah and its pasturelands, ⁷⁹Kedemoth and its pasturelands, and Mephaath and its pasturelands. ⁸⁰From the tribe of Gad they received Ramoth in Gilead and its pasturelands, Mahanaim and its pasturelands, ⁸¹Heshbon and its pasturelands, and Jazer and its pasturelands.

Issachar's Descendants

7 Issachar's sons:ᵍ Tola, Puah, Jashub, and Shimron—four.
²Tola's sons: Uzzi, Rephaiah, Jeriel, Jahmai, Ibsam, and Shemuel, the heads of their ancestral houses. During David's reign, 22,600 descendants of Tola were recorded as warriors in their genealogies.ʰ
³Uzzi's son: Izrahiah.
Izrahiah's sons: Michael, Obadiah, Joel, Isshiah. All five of them were chiefs.
⁴Along with them, they had 36,000 troops for battle according to the genealogical records of their ancestral houses, for they had many wives and children. ⁵Their tribesmen who were warriors belonging to all the families of Issachar totaled 87,000 in their genealogies.

Benjamin's Descendants

⁶Threeⁱ of Benjamin's sons: Bela, Becher, and Jediael.

ᵃ 6:57 Jos 21:13,19
ᵇ 6:61 Jos 21:5; 1Ch 6:66-70
ᶜ 6:63 Jos 21:7; 1Ch 6:77-81
ᵈ 6:64 Jos 21:3,41-42
ᵉ 6:65 1Ch 6:57-60
ᶠ 6:66-81 Jos 21:20-40
ᵍ 7:1 Gn 46:13
ʰ 7:2 2Sm 24:1-9
ⁱ 7:6-12 Gn 46:21; Nm 26:38-41; 1Ch 8

Â6:58 Some Hb mss, LXX; other Hb mss read *Hilez*

it would also serve later for a time as capital city under David's monarchy.

6:62-81 A noticeable feature of this long list is that the Levites were given dwelling space among the eastern tribes of **Manasseh . . . Gad**, and **Reuben**, as well as in the main territory on the west. Even though eventually this arrangement would remove them far from the temple, it also allowed them to be distributed throughout the land so they could teach all the people.

7:1-5 The tribe of **Issachar** is mentioned primarily for the number of soldiers it supplied and its meticulous genealogies.

⁷Bela's sons: Ezbon, Uzzi, Uzziel, Jerimoth, and Iri—five. They were warriors and heads of their ancestral houses; 22,034 were listed in their genealogies. ⁸Becher's sons: Zemirah, Joash, Eliezer, Elioenai, Omri, Jeremoth, Abijah, Anathoth, and Alemeth; all these were Becher's sons. ⁹Their genealogies were recorded according to the heads of their ancestral houses—20,200 warriors. ¹⁰Jediael's son: Bilhan. Bilhan's sons: Jeush, Benjamin, Ehud, Chenaanah, Zethan, Tarshish, and Ahishahar. ¹¹All these sons of Jediael listed by heads of families were warriors; there were 17,200 who could serve in the army. ¹²Shuppim and Huppim were sons of Ir, and the Hushim were the sons of Aher.

Naphtali's Descendants

¹³Naphtali's sons:ᵃ Jahziel, Guni, Jezer, and Shallum—Bilhah's sons.

Manasseh's Descendants

¹⁴Manasseh'sᵇ sons through his Aramean concubine: Asriel and Machir the father of Gilead. ¹⁵Machir took wives from Huppim and Shuppim. The name of his sister was Maacah. Another descendant was named Zelophehad, but he had only daughters. ¹⁶Machir's wife Maacah gave birth to a son, and she named him Peresh. His brother was named Sheresh, and his sons were Ulam and Rekem.

ᵃ7:13 Gn 46:24-25
ᵇ7:14-19 Nm 26:29-34
ᶜ7:20-21a Nm 26:35-36
ᵈ7:24 Jos 16:3,5
ᵉ7:27 Ex 17:9-14; 24:13
ᶠ7:28 Jos 16:2

¹⁷Ulam's son: Bedan. These were the sons of Gilead son of Machir, son of Manasseh. ¹⁸His sister Hammolecheth gave birth to Ishhod, Abiezer, and Mahlah. ¹⁹Shemida's sons: Ahian, Shechem, Likhi, and Aniam.

Ephraim's Descendants

20 Ephraim'sᶜ sons: Shuthelah, and
　　his son Bered,
his son Tahath, his son Eleadah,
his son Tahath, ²¹his son Zabad,
his son Shuthelah, also Ezer,
　　and Elead.

The men of Gath, born in the land, killed them because they went down to raid their cattle. ²²Their father Ephraim mourned a long time, and his relativesᴬ came to comfort him. ²³He slept with his wife, and she conceived and gave birth to a son. So he named him Beriah, because there had been misfortune in his home.ᴮ ²⁴His daughter was Sheerah, who built Lower and Upper Beth-horonᵈ and Uzzen-sheerah,

25 his son Rephah,ᶜ his son Resheph,
　　his son Telah, his son Tahan,
26 his son Ladan, his son Ammihud,
　　his son Elishama, ²⁷his son Nun,
　　and his son Joshua.ᵉ

²⁸Their holdings and settlements were Bethelᶠ and its villages; Naaran to the east, Gezer and its villages to the west, and Shechem and its villages as far as

ᴬ7:22 Or his brothers　　ᴮ7:23 In Hb, the name Beriah sounds like "in misfortune."　　ᶜ7:25 Probably Ephraim's son

---

7:6-12 The first of several listings for **Benjamin** emphasizes the number of soldiers in this tribe. This was the tribe to which Saul, the first king of the Hebrews, belonged.

rosh

Hebrew Pronunciation	[ROESH]
HCSB Translation	head, top, leader
Uses in 1 Chronicles	73
Uses in the OT	600
Focus Passage	1 Chronicles 7:2-3,7,9,11,40

Rosh basically signifies a human (Gn 3:15) or animal (Lv 8:18) *head*. It denotes *leaders* (Ex 18:25), *masters* (2Kg 2:3), and household *heads* (Nm 1:4). It suggests *tops* of mountains (Gn 8:5) and *beginnings* of time periods (Ex 12:2). *Rosh* appears as *best* (Dt 33:15), *first* (Pr 8:26), *highest* (Jb 22:12), *chief* (Jr 52:24), and *leading* (2Sm 23:13). It signifies *sum* (Ps 139:17) or *entirety* (Ps 119:160), so implying *full* (Lv 6:5). "Lift the *head*" signifies *act arrogantly* (Ps 83:2), *pardon* (2Kg 25:27), or *take a census/count* (Ex 30:12; Nm 31:26). *Rosh* can mean *each* (Jdg 5:30) or connote a *life* (Dn 1:10). It is a scepter's *tip* (Est 5:2) or pole's *end* (1Kg 8:8). It describes street *corners* (Lm 4:1) and *forks* in roads (Ezk 21:19). *Heads* can suggest *source* (Gn 2:10) and be *divisions* (1Sm 11:11), *companies* (Jdg 7:16), or *units* (Jdg 9:44).

7:13 Naphtali is mentioned in only one short verse. Apparently his genealogy was not important in the Chronicler's day because after the exile there seems to be no large contingent from Naphtali among those who returned to Judah (9:3).

7:14 **Manasseh's** wife was **Aramean**, thus another Gentile was included in the lines of descent.

7:15 **Zelophehad** and his **daughters** made an important contribution to the culture of Israel. In Nm 27:1-6, Zelophehad's five daughters asked Moses to give them their inheritance in the land, and Moses granted their request. This event set a precedent that women could inherit property, something that most surrounding cultures did not allow.

7:20-29 **Ephraim** was one of the leading tribes, a consistent rival to Judah. When the kingdom split, Ephraim was foremost among the 10 northern tribes so that "Ephraim" is often synonymous with the entire northern kingdom. The deaths of **Ezer** and **Elead** must have happened while the Israelites were in Egypt, so that these men had ventured

Ayyah and its villages, [29] and along the borders of the sons of Manasseh, Beth-shean and its villages, Taanach and its villages, Megiddo and its villages, and Dor and its villages. The sons of Joseph son of Israel lived in these towns.

Asher's Descendants

[30] Asher's[a] sons: Imnah, Ishvah, Ishvi, and Beriah, with their sister Serah. [31] Beriah's sons: Heber, and Malchiel, who fathered Birzaith. [32] Heber fathered Japhlet, Shomer, and Hotham, with their sister Shua. [33] Japhlet's sons: Pasach, Bimhal, and Ashvath. These were Japhlet's sons. [34] Shemer's sons: Ahi, Rohgah, Hubbah, and Aram. [35] His brother Helem's sons: Zophah, Imna, Shelesh, and Amal. [36] Zophah's sons: Suah, Harnepher, Shual, Beri, Imrah, [37] Bezer, Hod, Shamma, Shilshah, Ithran, and Beera. [38] Jether's sons: Jephunneh, Pispa, and Ara. [39] Ulla's sons: Arah, Hanniel, and Rizia. [40] All these were Asher's sons. They were the heads of their ancestral houses, chosen men, warriors, and chiefs among the leaders. The number of men listed in their genealogies for military service was 26,000.

Benjamin's Descendants

8 Benjamin[b] fathered Bela, his firstborn; Ashbel was born second, Aharah third, [2] Nohah fourth, and Rapha fifth. [3] Bela's sons: Addar, Gera, Abihud, [4] Abishua, Naaman, Ahoah, [5] Gera, Shephuphan, and Huram. [6] These were Ehud's sons, who were the heads of the families living in Geba and who were deported to Manahath: [7] Naaman, Ahijah, and Gera. Gera

deported them and was the father of Uzza and Ahihud. [8] Shaharaim had sons in the country of Moab after he had divorced his wives Hushim and Baara. [9] His sons by his wife Hodesh: Jobab, Zibia, Mesha, Malcam, [10] Jeuz, Sachia, and Mirmah. These were his sons, heads of families. [11] He also had sons by Hushim: Abitub and Elpaal. [12] Elpaal's sons: Eber, Misham, and Shemed who built Ono and Lod and its villages, [13] Beriah and Shema, who were the heads of families of Aijalon's residents and who drove out the residents of Gath, [14] Ahio,[A] Shashak, and Jeremoth. [15] Zebadiah, Arad, Eder, [16] Michael, Ishpah, and Joha were Beriah's sons. [17] Zebadiah, Meshullam, Hizki, Heber, [18] Ishmerai, Izliah, and Jobab were Elpaal's sons. [19] Jakim, Zichri, Zabdi, [20] Elienai, Zillethai, Eliel, [21] Adaiah, Beraiah, and Shimrath were Shimei's sons. [22] Ishpan, Eber, Eliel, [23] Abdon, Zichri, Hanan, [24] Hananiah, Elam, Anthothijah, [25] Iphdeiah, and Penuel were Shashak's sons. [26] Shamsherai, Shehariah, Athaliah, [27] Jaareshiah, Elijah, and Zichri were Jeroham's sons. [28] These[c] were heads of families, chiefs according to their genealogies, and lived in Jerusalem.

[29] Jeiel[B,d] fathered Gibeon and lived in Gibeon. His wife's name was Maacah. [30] Abdon was his firstborn son, then Zur, Kish, Baal, Nadab, [31] Gedor, Ahio, Zecher, [32] and Mikloth who fathered Shimeah. These also lived opposite their relatives in Jerusalem, with their other relatives. [33] Ner fathered Kish, Kish fathered

a7:30-31 Gn 46:17; Nm 26:44-46 b8:1-5 Gn 46:21; Nm 26:38-41; 1Ch 7:6-12 c8:28-38 1Ch 9:34-44 d8:29 1Ch 9:35

A8:13-14 LXX reads Gath [14] and their brother   B8:29 LXX; MT omits Jeiel; 1Ch 9:35

north to Gaza. But the Chronicler often does not mention that geographical and historical setting, even though he was clearly aware of it (2Ch 9:28). Several of the towns inhabited by the Ephraimites, such as **Beth-shean** and **Megiddo**, were important because they were heavily fortified.

7:30-40 Asher's tribe, located in the north on the coast, was of secondary importance. However, a descendant of Asher—the prophetess Anna—praised God in the temple for the birth of Jesus.

8:1-2 A second listing for the tribe of **Benjamin** provides more detail than the first list (7:6-12). This chapter leads up to the tragic end of Saul's kingship (chap. 10). Saul was from Benjamin, but the throne had been promised to Judah

(Gn 49:10). Benjamin, the twelfth son of Jacob, had five sons who established their own large clans.

8:5 Gera was the father of Ehud, the left-handed judge who killed Eglon, king of the Amalekites (Jdg 3:15).

8:8-9 Shaharaim had at least three wives: **Hushim** and **Baara**—who presumably were Israelites—and **Hodesh**, who was a Moabite.

8:32 Not until David's reign as king did **Jerusalem** belong entirely to Israel. At the time referred to here, Benjaminites were living around Jerusalem, but the highest fortified part of the city was home to the Jebusites.

8:33 At this point the Chronicler casually mentions **Saul**, but without calling any special attention to him. **Esh-baal** (Ish-

Saul, and Saul fathered Jonathan, Malchishua, Abinadab, and Esh-baal.^A
³⁴ Jonathan's son was Merib-baal,^B and Merib-baal fathered Micah.
³⁵ Micah's sons: Pithon, Melech, Tarea, and Ahaz.
³⁶ Ahaz fathered Jehoaddah, Jehoaddah fathered Alemeth, Azmaveth, and Zimri, and Zimri fathered Moza.
³⁷ Moza fathered Binea. His son was Raphah, his son Elasah, and his son Azel.
³⁸ Azel had six sons, and these were their names: Azrikam, Bocheru, Ishmael, Sheariah, Obadiah, and Hanan. All these were Azel's sons.
³⁹ His brother Eshek's sons: Ulam was his firstborn, Jeush second, and Eliphelet third.
⁴⁰ Ulam's sons were warriors and archers.^C They had many sons and grandsons—150 of them.
All these were among Benjamin's sons.

After the Exile

9 All Israel was registered in the genealogies that are written in the Book of the Kings of Israel. But Judah was exiled^a to Babylon because of their unfaithfulness. ² The first^b to live in their towns on their own property again were Israelites, priests, Levites, and temple servants.^c

³ These people from the descendants of Judah, Benjamin, Ephraim, and Manasseh settled in Jerusalem:
⁴ Uthai son of Ammihud, son of Omri, son of Imri, son of Bani, a descendant^D of Perez son of Judah;
⁵ from the Shilonites:
Asaiah the firstborn and his sons;
⁶ and from the sons of Zerah:
Jeuel and 690 of their relatives.

⁷ The Benjaminites: Sallu son of Meshullam, son of Hodaviah, son of Hassenuah;
⁸ Ibneiah son of Jeroham;
Elah son of Uzzi, son of Michri;
Meshullam son of Shephatiah, son of Reuel, son of Ibnijah;
⁹ and 956^d of their relatives according to their genealogical records. All these men were heads of their ancestral houses.

¹⁰ The priests:^e Jedaiah; Jehoiarib; Jachin;
¹¹ Azariah son of Hilkiah, son of Meshullam, son of Zadok, son of Meraioth, son of Ahitub, the chief official^f of God's temple;
¹² Adaiah son of Jeroham, son of Pashhur, son of Malchijah;
Maasai son of Adiel, son of Jahzerah, son of Meshullam, son of Meshillemith, son of Immer;
¹³ and 1,760 of their relatives, the heads of households. They were capable men employed in the ministry of God's temple.

¹⁴ The Levites: Shemaiah son of Hasshub, son of Azrikam, son of Hashabiah of the Merarites;

^a9:1 1Ch 6:15
^b9:2-9 Neh 11:3-9
^c9:2 Ezr 2:43,58; 8:20
^d9:9 Neh 11:8
^e9:10-16 Neh 11:10-18
^f9:11 Jr 20:1

---

^A8:33 = Man of Baal   ^B8:34 = Baal Contends   ^C8:40 Lit *valiant ones who string the bow*   ^D9:4 Lit *Bani, from the sons*

---

bosheth) was Saul's son and a younger brother of Jonathan. In 2 Samuel 2–3 we find Esh-baal attempting to continue Saul's monarchy against David's claim. Joab eliminated virtually the entire clan.

8:34 Merib-baal (Mephibosheth), **Jonathan's** crippled son, was the only one who escaped the purge. Saul's line eventually did make a comeback. The tribe of Benjamin became strongly allied with David's and Solomon's unified kingdom and then with the kingdom of Judah. Jerusalem, the eventual capital, was located at the border of Judah and Benjamin.

9:1 Accurate **genealogies** were essential because so much was dependent on a person's tribal affiliation (Ezr 2:62). The northern kingdom of Israel was deported in 722 B.C. by the Assyrians. Judah went into exile in several stages, with the final deportation carried out by the Babylonians in 587 B.C. However, the exiles from Judah were allowed to return to their homeland approximately 40 years later.

9:2 The decree to return, issued by Cyrus of Persia, directed that they should rebuild the **temple** (2Ch 36:23). It was natural that most of these people would be directly

associated with the temple: **priests, Levites, and temple servants**.

9:3 Among those returning to Judah were also some people of the northern tribes, including **Ephraim** and **Manasseh**. Not everyone from the so-called 10 lost tribes was "lost." Still, the subsequent passage does not list anyone from the northern tribes by name.

9:4 The descendants of **Perez** listed here could be related to the royal line, but there was no more kingdom.

9:7 A large contingent of those returning to Judah were members of the tribe of Benjamin. This tribe had remained loyal to the southern kingdom of Judah, and they escaped the earlier deportation by Assyria and profited from the edict to return to their homeland.

9:10-13 The list of **priests** is significant. This listing indicates the accurate continuation of the genealogies and shows that the priests must have maintained their knowledge so they could take up their duties as soon as they returned to Judah.

9:14-16 The **Levites** were also ready to take up their duties again.

¹⁵Bakbakkar, Heresh, Galal, and Mattaniah, son of Mica, son of Zichri, son of ˙Asaph;
¹⁶Obadiah son of Shemaiah, son of Galal, son of Jeduthun;
and Berechiah son of Asa, son of Elkanah who lived in the villages of the Netophathites.

¹⁷The gatekeepers:ᵃ Shallum, Akkub, Talmon, Ahiman, and their relatives. Shallum was their chief; ¹⁸he was previously stationed at the King's Gate on the east side.ᵇ These were the gatekeepers from the camp of the Levites.
¹⁹Shallum son of Kore, son of Ebiasaph, son of Korah and his relatives from his ancestral household, the Korahites, were assigned to guard the thresholds of the tent.ᴬ Their ancestors had been assigned to the Lord's camp as guardians of the entrance.ᶜ ²⁰In earlier times Phinehas son of Eleazar had been their leader, and the Lord was with

him.ᵈ ²¹Zechariah son of Meshelemiah was the gatekeeper at the entrance to the tent of meeting.ᵉ

²²The total number of those chosen to be gatekeepers at the thresholds was 212. They were registered by genealogy in their villages. David and Samuel the seer had appointed themᶠ to their trusted positions. ²³So they and their sons were assigned to the gates of the Lord's temple, which had been the tent-temple. ²⁴The gatekeepers were on the four sides: east, west, north, and south. ²⁵Their relatives came from their villagesᵍ at fixed times to be with them seven days,ʰ ²⁶but the four chief gatekeepers, who were Levites, were entrusted with the rooms and the treasuries of God's temple.ⁱ ²⁷They spent the night in the vicinity of God's temple, because they had guard duty and were in charge of opening it every morning.ʲ
²⁸Some of them were in charge of the utensils used in worship. They would count them when they brought them in and when they took them out. ²⁹Others were put in charge of the furnishings and all the utensils of the

---

ᵃ9:17-22a 1Ch 26:1-19; Ezr 2:42; Neh 7:45; 11:19
ᵇ9:18 Ezk 46:1-2
ᶜ9:19 Nm 4:1-20; 26:11; 1Ch 6:22
ᵈ9:20 Nm 25:7-13
ᵉ9:21 1Ch 26:2,14
ᶠ9:22 1Ch 26:1
ᵍ9:25 1Ch 9:16
ʰ2Kg 11:5,7; 2Ch 23:8
ⁱ9:26 Neh 12:25
ʲ9:27 1Sm 3:3,15; 1Ch 23:30-32

ᴬ9:19 = the temple

9:17-18 **Shallum** was a veteran, having been in charge of a gate some 40 years earlier before the temple's destruction. Now he led the entire crew of **gatekeepers**.

9:19 Because of the makeshift nature of the rebuilt temple, its first appearance was not all that different from the tabernacle (cp. v. 23). Without the surrounding courtyards, guarding the entrance was similar to guarding the **thresholds of the tent**, a duty with a long and proud tradition.

9:22 We get a brief glimpse here of **Samuel** as administra-

tor of the tabernacle, setting a precedent that was resumed by **David**. The idea that guard duty was distributed among people from all over the country must have promoted a feeling of ownership among all Israelites.

9:28 The temple performed many functions, including many different types of sacrifices, all of which required **utensils**. Trustworthy people were needed to look after the utensils and other equipment.

9:30 A priest could not perform official religious duties un-

Mount Gilboa where Saul and his sons Jonathan, Abinadab, and Malchishua died at the hands of the Philistines.

sanctuary,^{a} as well as the fine flour,^{b} wine, oil, incense, and spices. ^{30}Some of the priests' sons mixed the spices.^{c} ^{31}A Levite called Mattithiah, the firstborn of Shallum the Korahite, was entrusted with baking the bread.^{A} ^{32}Some of the Kohathites' relatives were responsible for preparing the rows of the •bread of the Presence^d every Sabbath.

^{33}The singers,^{e} the heads of the Levite families, stayed in the temple chambers and were exempt from other tasks because they were on duty day and night.^{f} ^{34}These^g were the heads of the Levite families, chiefs according to their genealogies, and lived in Jerusalem.

Saul's Family

^{35}Jeiel fathered Gibeon and lived in Gibeon. His wife's name was Maacah. ^{36}Abdon was his firstborn son, then Zur, Kish, Baal, Ner, Nadab, ^{37}Gedor, Ahio, Zechariah, and Mikloth. ^{38}Mikloth fathered Shimeam. These also lived opposite their relatives in Jerusalem with their other relatives. ^{39}Ner fathered Kish, Kish fathered Saul, and Saul fathered Jonathan, Malchishua, Abinadab, and Esh-baal. ^{40}Jonathan's son was Merib-baal, and Merib-baal fathered Micah. ^{41}Micah's sons: Pithon, Melech, Tahrea, and Ahaz.^{B} ^{42}Ahaz fathered Jarah; Jarah fathered Alemeth, Azmaveth, and Zimri; Zimri fathered Moza. ^{43}Moza fathered Binea.

His son was Rephaiah, his son Elasah, and his son Azel. ^{44}Azel had six sons, and these were their names: Azrikam, Bocheru, Ishmael, Sheariah, Obadiah, and Hanan. These were Azel's sons.

The Deaths of Saul and His Sons

10 The Philistines^h fought against Israel, and Israel's men fled from them and were killed on Mount Gilboa. ^{2}The Philistines pursued Saul and his sons and killed Saul's sons Jonathan, Abinadab, and Malchishua. ^{3}When the battle intensified against Saul, the archers found him and severely wounded him. ^{4}Then Saul said to his armor-bearer, "Draw your sword and run me through with it, or these uncircumcised men will come and torture me!" But his armor-bearer wouldn't do it because he was terrified. Then Saul took his sword and fell on it. ^{5}When his armor-bearer saw that Saul was dead, he also fell on his own sword and died. ^{6}So Saul and his three sons died—his whole house died together.

^{7}When all the men of Israel in the valley saw that the army had fled and that Saul and his sons were dead, they abandoned their cities and fled. So the Philistines came and settled in them.

^{8}The next day when the Philistines came to strip the slain, they found Saul and his sons dead on Mount Gilboa. ^{9}They stripped Saul, cut off his head, took his armor, and sent messengers throughout the land of the Philistines to spread the good news to their idols and their people. ^{10}Then they put his armor in the

---

^{a}9:29 Nm 3:31
^{b}1Ch 23:29
^{c}9:30 Ex 30:23-25
^{d}9:32 Lv 24:5-9
^{e}9:33 1Ch 6:31-47; 25:1
^{f}Ps 134:1
^{g}9:34-44 1Ch 8:28-38
^{h}10:1-12 1Sm 31:1-13

---

^{A}9:31 Lit *with things prepared in pans* ^{B}9:41 LXX, Syr, Tg, Vg, Arabic; MT omits *and Ahaz*; 1Ch 8:35

---

til he turned 30 years old. The sons of many priests, while learning their profession, would also be involved in mixing the **spices** used in the sacrificial system.

9:31 This **Shallum** was the veteran gatekeeper (vv. 17-18).

9:33 The **singers** were expected to be ready at a moment's notice whenever a ceremony or sacrifice called for musical accompaniment.

9:35-44 The genealogy of Benjamin in these verses is the same as that in 8:29-38. In chapter 8 the emphasis was on their residence in Jerusalem (8:28,32); here the genealogy sets up the story of Saul in chapter 10.

10:1 Without going into any of the details leading up to this event, the Chronicler takes us right to the death of Saul and his sons. The **Philistines** had come upon Saul's army from the north, trapping Saul's men on **Mount Gilboa** and killing those who could not escape.

10:2 Jonathan and his two brothers were able warriors, but they could not hold out once the Israelite army had fled.

10:3 Because the **battle** was going so well for the Philistines, the **archers** were in the middle of the fight and were able to deal **Saul** a mortal blow.

10:4-5 Saul knew the Philistines would **torture** him, but this did not give him the right to take his own life, let alone to ask his **armor-bearer** to do it for him. Only when the boy refused did Saul kill himself, and then his armor-bearer also committed suicide.

10:6 Not every member of Saul's house **died** at that time, but the family unit, in the sense of Saul's dynasty (**his whole house**), came to a halt.

10:7 Having defeated Saul's army, the **Philistines** moved into the **abandoned** houses of the nearby villages, enjoying a false sense of security. They did not realize that David and his followers were already on their way.

10:9 The **Philistines** were more than willing to be a part of the celebration. They sent messengers out not only to inform the people but also to tell their **idols** about what had transpired. The irony of idolatry is that people entrust their lives to that which has no power. This is thoroughly satirized in Isaiah 44 and Jeremiah 10.

10:10 Saul's **armor**—perhaps the very armor that David once refused to wear in his confrontation with Goliath—became decoration pieces in the Philistines' temples.

temple of their gods and hung his skull in the temple of Dagon.[a]

[11]When all Jabesh-gilead heard of everything the Philistines had done to Saul, [12]all their brave men set out and retrieved the body of Saul and the bodies of his sons and brought them to Jabesh. They buried their bones under the oak[A] in Jabesh[b] and fasted seven days.

[13]Saul died for his unfaithfulness to the LORD because he did not keep the LORD's word.[c] He even consulted a medium for guidance,[d] [14]but he did not inquire of the LORD. So the LORD put

[a]10:10 1Sm
5:1-4; 17:54
[b]10:12 2Sm
21:12-14
[c]10:13 1Sm
13:13-14; 15:23
[d]1Sm 28:7
[e]10:14 1Sm
15:28; 1Ch 12:23
[f]11:1-3 2Sm
5:1-3

him to death and turned the kingdom over to David son of Jesse.[e]

David's Anointing as King

11 All Israel[f] came together to David at Hebron and said, "Here we are, your own flesh and blood.[B] [2]Even when Saul was king, you led us out to battle and brought us back. The LORD your God also said to you, 'You will shepherd My people Israel and be ruler over My people Israel.'"

[3]So all the elders of Israel came to the king at Hebron. David made a covenant with them

---

A10:12 Or *terebinth*, or *large tree*   B11:1 Lit *your bone and flesh*

A special place was reserved for Saul's **skull** in the temple of their main god, **Dagon**.

10:11-12 The inhabitants of **Jabesh-gilead** owed their lives to **Saul** (1Sm 11). Now they risked their lives to protect Saul's body from further desecration.

10:13 Saul was not as evil as many of the idolatrous kings

who came after him, but a king who outwardly followed God but inwardly went his own way was worse than a king who did not make any pretense of following God. Saul's apparent piety combined with his blatant disobedience (1Sm 13:7-14; 15:1-9) was unacceptable to God and served as a destructive example for onlookers.

10:14 Saul did make a show of inquiring of the Lord (1Sm

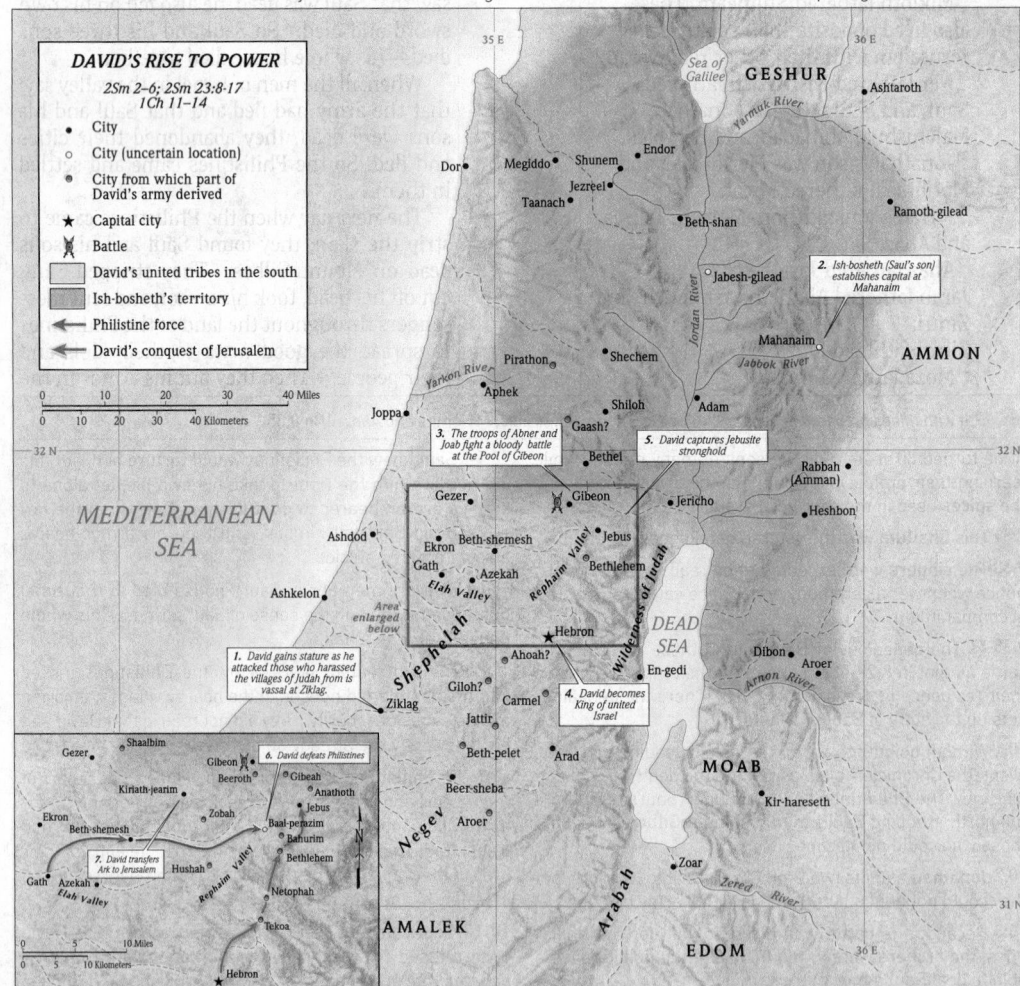

DAVID'S RISE TO POWER
2Sm 2–6; 2Sm 23:8-17
1Ch 11–14

- • City
- ○ City (uncertain location)
- ◉ City from which part of David's army derived
- ★ Capital city
- ⚔ Battle
- ▢ David's united tribes in the south
- ▨ Ish-bosheth's territory
- ← Philistine force
- ← David's conquest of Jerusalem

0 10 20 40 Miles
0 10 20 30 40 Kilometers

MEDITERRANEAN SEA

35 E
Sea of Galilee
GESHUR
Ashtaroth
Yarmuk River
Dor
Megiddo
Shunem
Endor
Jezreel
Taanach
Beth-shan
Ramoth-gilead
Jabesh-gilead

2. *Ish-bosheth (Saul's son) establishes capital at Mahanaim*

Jordan River
Mahanaim
Jabbok River
AMMON

Pirathon
Shechem
Adam
Yarkon River
Aphek
Shiloh
Gaash?
Joppa

3. *The troops of Abner and Joab fight a bloody battle at the Pool of Gibeon*

5. *David captures Jebusite stronghold*

Bethel
Rabbah (Amman)
Heshbon
32 N

Gezer
Gibeon
Jericho
Ashdod
Beth-shemesh
Ekron
Jebus
Gath
Azekah
Bethlehem
Ashkelon
Elah Valley
Rephaim Valley

Area enlarged below

Shephelah
Wilderness of Judah
Hebron
DEAD SEA
Ahoah?
En-gedi
Dibon
Aroer
Arnon River

1. *David gains stature as he attacked those who harassed the villages of Judah from is vassal at Ziklag.*

Ziklag
Giloh?
Carmel

4. *David becomes King of united Israel*

Jattir
Beth-pelet
Arad
MOAB
Kir-hareseth
Beer-sheba
Negev
Aroer

Zoar
Zered River
31 N

AMALEK
EDOM
36 E
Arabah

Gezer
Shaalbim
Gibeon
Beeroth
Gibeah
Anathoth
Kiriath-jearim
Jebus
Zobah
Ekron
Baal-perazim
Beth-shemesh
Bahurim
Bethlehem
Gath
Azekah
Hushah
Netophah
Elah Valley
Rephaim Valley
Tekoa
Hebron

6. *David defeats Philistines*

7. *David transfers Ark to Jerusalem*

0 5 10 Miles
0 5 10 Kilometers

at Hebron in the LORD's presence, and they anointed David king over Israel, in keeping with the LORD's word through Samuel.ᵃ

David's Capture of Jerusalem

⁴Davidᵇ and all Israel marched to Jerusalem (that is, Jebusᶜ); the Jebusites who inhabited the land were there. ⁵The inhabitants of Jebus said to David, "You will never get in here." Yet David did capture the stronghold of ˙Zion, that is, the city of David.

⁶David said, "Whoever is the first to kill a Jebusite will become chief commander." Joabᵈ son of Zeruiah went up first, so he became the chief.

⁷Then David took up residence in the stronghold; therefore, it was called the city of David. ⁸He built up the city all the way around, from the supporting terraces to the surrounding parts, and Joab restored the rest of the city. ⁹David steadily grew more powerful,ᵉ and the LORD of ˙Hosts was with him.

Exploits of David's Warriors

¹⁰The following were the chiefs of David's warriors who, together with all Israel, strongly supported him in his reign to make him king according to the LORD's word about Israel.ᶠ ¹¹Thisᵍ is the list of David's warriors:

Jashobeam son of Hachmoni was chiefʰ of the Thirty;ᴬ he wielded his spear against 300 and killed them at one time.

ᵃ11:3 1Sm 16:1-13
ᵇ11:4-9 2Sm 5:6-10
ᶜ11:4 Jos 15:8,63; Jdg 1:21
ᵈ11:6 2Sm 8:16; 1Ch 18:15
ᵉ11:9 2Sm 3:1
ᶠ11:10 1Ch 11:3
ᵍ11:11-25 2Sm 23:8-23
ʰ11:11 1Ch 12:18
ⁱ11:12 1Ch 27:4
ʲ11:13 2Sm 23:11-12
ᵏ11:15 1Sm 22:1
ˡ1Ch 14:9
ᵐ11:16 1Sm 22:4-5; 2Sm 5:9
ⁿ1Sm 10:5
ᵒ11:20 1Sm 26:6; 2Sm 18:2

¹²After him, Eleazar son of Dodoⁱ the Ahohite was one of the three warriors. ¹³He was with David at Pas-dammim when the Philistines had gathered there for battle. There was a portion of a field full of barley, where the troops had fled from the Philistines.ʲ ¹⁴But Eleazar and Davidᴮ took their stand in the middle of the field and defended it. They killed the Philistines, and the LORD gave them a great victory.

¹⁵Three of the 30 chief men went down to David, to the rock at the cave of Adullam,ᵏ while the Philistine army was encamped in the Valley of Rephaim.ˡ ¹⁶At that time David was in the stronghold,ᵐ and a Philistine garrisonⁿ was at Bethlehem. ¹⁷David was extremely thirstyᶜ and said, "If only someone would bring me water to drink from the well at the city gate of Bethlehem!" ¹⁸So the Three broke through the Philistine camp and drew water from the well at the gate of Bethlehem. They brought it back to David, but he refused to drink it. Instead, he poured it out to the LORD. ¹⁹David said, "I would never do such a thing in the presence of God! How can I drink the blood of these men who risked their lives?" For they brought it at the risk of their lives. So he would not drink it. Such were the exploits of the three warriors.

²⁰Abishai,ᵒ Joab's brother, was the leader of the Three.ᴰ He raised his spear against 300

ᴬ11:11 Alt Hb tradition reads *Three* ᴮ11:14 Lit *But they* ᶜ11:17 Lit *And David craved* ᴰ11:20 Syr reads *Thirty*

28:6), but this was purely fortune telling; he dashed off immediately to speak to the now-departed Samuel. Not even the king was allowed to treat God as though He were a daily horoscope. The Chronicler also reminds us that it was God who led things in this direction and that the goal was for David to be placed on the throne.

11:1-2 The Chronicler skips over a lengthy series of events and takes us directly to the time of David's coronation. David was not accepted immediately as king of Israel by everyone. He had opposition from Jonathan's surviving brother Esh-baal, and it took warfare and bloodshed before David emerged as the undisputed victor (2Sm 1–2). Thus, this peaceful assertion by **all Israel** of blood relationship with David and his entitlement to the throne was as pragmatic as it was firm. The people even quoted the Lord's approval of David, even though some of them had fought against him not too long ago.

11:3 David's initial coronation took place at **Hebron**, a city from which he ruled for seven years.

11:4-9 The last stronghold of the Canaanites in the promised land was the citadel of **Jebus** at the peak of **Jerusalem**. This was considered virtually impregnable. Despite the defiance declared by the **Jebusites**, David motivated his troops to capture this prize, and his half nephew **Joab** succeeded. He used the water shaft to gain entry into the compound (2Sm 5:8). Joab was rewarded by being designated **chief commander** of David's army, an office that he

had held *de facto* all along. David moved the capital from Hebron to Jerusalem.

11:10-47 The list of **David's** major **warriors** and heroes covers both individual exploits and victories of larger armies. It covers several decades, from the time that David was fleeing Saul until the end of David's 40-year reign. Not everyone on this list was around all that time. For example, **Asahel** was killed in the civil war against Esh-baal (2Sm 2:23), and **Uriah the Hittite** was sent to his death by David (2Sm 11:17). For this reason the list of **the Thirty** (v. 11) actually includes more than 30 people. It is best to think of "the Thirty" as an elite company of warriors, the number of which was not fixed at thirty. See note at verse 47.

11:11-14 Other English Bible versions set apart a special group of "Three" in addition to the **Thirty**, but the manuscripts in the original language do not support this distinction. Chronicles mentions only two men in the supposed group of "Three." A parallel list in 2 Samuel 23 adds a man named Shammah.

11:15-19 This anecdote illustrates the respect that **David** had for his heroes. When David complained of thirst, three of his men risked their lives to break through the **Philistine camp** and make off with some water from the city of Bethlehem for the king. But David **refused to drink it**. He poured it to the ground as an offering to God, stating that if he drank it, it would be as though he were drinking the **blood** of these three heroes.

11:20-21 It may seem a little confusing that **Abishai**, Joab's

men and killed them, gaining a reputation among the Three. [21]He was more honored than the Three and became their commander even though he did not become one of the Three.

[22]Benaiah son of Jehoiada[a] was the son of a brave man[A] from Kabzeel, a man of many exploits. Benaiah killed two sons of Ariel of Moab,[B] and he went down into a pit on a snowy day and killed a lion. [23]He also killed an Egyptian who was seven and a half feet tall.[C] Even though the Egyptian had a spear in his hand like a weaver's beam,[b] Benaiah went down to him with a club, snatched the spear out of the Egyptian's hand, and then killed him with his own spear. [24]These were the exploits of Benaiah son of Jehoiada, who had a reputation among the three warriors. [25]He was the most honored of the Thirty, but he did not become one of the Three. David put him in charge of his bodyguard.

[26]The fighting men[c] were:

Joab's brother Asahel,[d]
Elhanan son of Dodo of Bethlehem,
[27] Shammoth the Harorite,
Helez the Pelonite,
[28] Ira son of Ikkesh the Tekoite,
Abiezer the Anathothite,
[29] Sibbecai the Hushathite,
Ilai the Ahohite,
[30] Maharai the Netophathite,
Heled son of Baanah the Netophathite,
[31] Ithai son of Ribai from Gibeah
of the Benjaminites,
Benaiah the Pirathonite,
[32] Hurai from the *wadis of Gaash,
Abiel the Arbathite,
[33] Azmaveth the Baharumite,

Reference column (center):
[a]11:22 2Sm
8:18; 20:23;
23:20-23; 1Kg
1:8; 1Ch 18:17;
27:5-6,34
[b]11:23 1Sm
17:7; 1Ch 20:5
[c]11:26-47 2Sm
23:24-39
[d]11:26 2Sm
2:18-23
[e]11:34 2Sm
23:32
[f]12:1 1Sm
27:1-7

Eliahba the Shaalbonite,
[34] the sons of[D,e] Hashem the Gizonite,
Jonathan son of Shagee the Hararite,
[35] Ahiam son of Sachar the Hararite,
Eliphal son of Ur,
[36] Hepher the Mecherathite,
Ahijah the Pelonite,
[37] Hezro the Carmelite,
Naarai son of Ezbai,
[38] Joel the brother of Nathan,
Mibhar son of Hagri,
[39] Zelek the Ammonite,
Naharai the Beerothite,
the armor-bearer for Joab
son of Zeruiah,
[40] Ira the Ithrite,
Gareb the Ithrite,
[41] Uriah the Hittite,
Zabad son of Ahlai,
[42] Adina son of Shiza the Reubenite, chief
of the Reubenites, and 30 with him,
[43] Hanan son of Maacah,
Joshaphat the Mithnite,
[44] Uzzia the Ashterathite,
Shama and Jeiel the sons of Hotham
the Aroerite,
[45] Jediael son of Shimri and his brother
Joha the Tizite,
[46] Eliel the Mahavite,
Jeribai and Joshaviah, the sons
of Elnaam,
Ithmah the Moabite,
[47] Eliel, Obed, and Jaasiel the Mezobaite.

David's First Supporters

12 The following were the men who came to David at Ziklag while he was still banned from the presence of Saul son of Kish.[f] They were among the warriors who helped

---

[A]11:22 Or *was a valiant man*   [B]11:22 Or *He killed two Moabite warriors*   [C]11:23 Lit *who measured five cubits*   [D]11:34 LXX omits *the sons of*; 2Sm 23:32

brother, was the commander of **the Three** but was not actually one of them. Again, the manuscripts allow for greater flexibility in the translation. He may have been a commander of the "Thirty," but not a part of the most distinguished "Three." It also makes sense that the person in charge of an elite outfit would not necessarily be a participant in the mission of the group. Much the same occurs in modern militaries.

11:22-25 Another commander was **Benaiah**, whom David put in charge of his **bodyguard**. Benaiah's exploits included the killing of a giant. Victories over giants are mentioned several times in Chronicles (see 20:5 and note there), though the story of David and Goliath occurs only in 1 Samuel 17.

11:26 Asahel, brother of Joab and Abishai and half nephew of David, was also counted among the "Thirty." But he lost his life early on in the civil war against Esh-baal's supporters (2Sm 2:23).

11:34 Several sets of brothers are included in this list. We don't know how many **sons of Hashem** there were, but pairs of brothers are mentioned in verses 44, 45, and 46.

11:42 We see how flexible the designation of the "Thirty" was because **Adina** from Reuben was a part of this group, together with his own **30** supporters.

11:47 Assuming that there were only two sons of Hashem (and not counting Adina's 30 followers), the list adds up to 45 people, quite an expansive interpretation of the "Thirty." However, this is a problem only if one mistakenly takes approximations or figures of speech as exact numbers. A baseball team is called "nine," but the roster consists of 25 people, and that number would be higher still if it listed all who had been on the team over a 40-year period.

12:1 This chapter covers a long time span, encompassing the years from David's early days hiding from Saul in the desert to his coronation in Hebron. People were coming to him on their own, knowing that he would supersede the house of Saul. At the beginning of this chapter, **Saul** was

him in battle. ²They were archers who could use either the right or left hand, both to sling stones and shoot arrows from a bow.ᵃ They were Saul's relativesᵇ from Benjamin:

³Their chief was Ahiezer son of Shemaah the Gibeathite.
Then there was his brother Joash;
Jeziel and Pelet sons of Azmaveth;
Beracah, Jehu the Anathothite;
⁴Ishmaiah the Gibeonite, a warrior among the Thirty and a leader over the Thirty;
ᴬJeremiah, Jahaziel, Johanan, Jozabad the Gederathite;
⁵Eluzai, Jerimoth, Bealiah, Shemariah, Shephatiah the Haruphite;
⁶Elkanah, Isshiah, Azarel, Joezer, and Jashobeam, the Korahites;
⁷and Joelah and Zebadiah, the sons of Jeroham from Gedor.

⁸Some Gadites defected to David at his stronghold in the desert. They were fighting men, trained for battle, expert with shield and spear. Their faces were like the faces of lions, and they were as swift as gazelles on the mountains.ᶜ

⁹ Ezer was the chief, Obadiah second, Eliab third,
¹⁰ Mishmannah fourth, Jeremiah fifth,
¹¹ Attai sixth, Eliel seventh,
¹² Johanan eighth, Elzabad ninth,
¹³ Jeremiah tenth, and Machbannai eleventh.

¹⁴These Gadites were army commanders; the

ᵃ12:2 Jdg 3:15; 20:16
ᵇ1Ch 12:29
ᶜ12:8 2Sm 2:18
ᵈ12:14 Lv 26:8; Dt 32:30; Is 30:17
ᵉ12:15 Jos 3:15; 4:18
ᶠ12:16 1Sm 22:1-2
ᵍ12:18 Jdg 6:34; 2Ch 24:20
ʰ1Ch 2:17
ⁱ1Sm 25:5-6
ʲ12:19 1Sm 29:1-11
ᵏ12:21 1Sm 30:1-20

least of them was a match for a hundred, and the greatest of them for a thousand.ᵈ ¹⁵These are the men who crossed the Jordan in the first monthᴮ when it was overflowing all its banks,ᵉ and put to flight all those in the valleys to the east and to the west.

¹⁶Other Benjaminites and men from Judah also went to David at the stronghold.ᶠ ¹⁷David went out to meet them and said to them, "If you have come in peace to help me, my heart will be united with you, but if you have come to betray me to my enemies even though my hands have done no wrong, may the God of our ancestors look on it and judge."

¹⁸Then the Spirit took control ofᶜ,ᵍ Amasai,ʰ chief of the Thirty, and he said:

> We are yours, David,
> we are with you, son of Jesse!
> Peace, peace to you,
> and peace to him who helps you,ⁱ
> for your God helps you.

So David received them and made them leaders of his troops.

¹⁹Some Manassites defected to David when he went with the Philistines to fight against Saul. However, they did not help the Philistines because the Philistine rulers sent David away after a discussion. They said, "It will be our heads if he defects to his master Saul."ʲ ²⁰When David went to Ziklag, some men from Manasseh defected to him: Adnah, Jozabad, Jediael, Michael, Jozabad, Elihu, and Zillethai, chiefs of thousands in Manasseh. ²¹They helped David against the raiders,ᵏ for they were all brave warriors and commanders in

---

ᴬ12:4 1Ch 12:5 in Hb   ᴮ12:15 = Nisan (March–April)   ᶜ12:18 Lit Spirit clothed Himself with; Jdg 6:34; 2Ch 24:20

chayil

Hebrew Pronunciation	[KHAH yeel]
HCSB Translation	strength, wealth, army
Uses in 1 Chronicles	28
Uses in the OT	246
Focus Passage	1 Chronicles 12:8,21,25,28,30

The basic meaning of chayil is strength (Ec 10:10), with army (2Ch 26:11) and wealth (Pr 13:22) being two kinds of strength. When distinguished from gibbor ("strong"), chayil stresses bravery (1Sm 14:52). When chayil modifies gibbor, the phrase suggests fighting men (2Kg 24:14), wealthy men (2Kg 15:20), or brave warriors (1Ch 12:21). Chayil also modifies ben ("son") and 'iysh ("man") with similar meanings. "To do chayil" denotes being capable, triumphant, or powerful (Nm 24:18; Ru 4:11; Pr 31:29), and fighting bravely (1Sm 14:48) or gaining wealth (Dt 8:18). Chayil indicates entourage (2Ch 9:1), energy (Pr 31:3), or profits (Jb 20:18). It means influential (1Sm 9:1), able-bodied (Jdg 3:29), or excellent (1Kg 1:42). It describes those of noble character (Ru 3:11). Chayil can connote fearless (Is 5:22) or best (2Sm 11:16). Adverbially it signifies valiantly (Ps 108:13). God gives chayil (Ps 18:32).

still king. No one would have thought about Esh-baal's attempt to succeed his father because Jonathan was the obvious heir to the throne.

12:2-7 These ambidextrous **archers** and experts with the **sling** were some of Saul's own relatives from **Benjamin** who were already distancing themselves from him. David not only accumulated a sizeable number of supporters, but many of them were excellent warriors.

12:8-15 A group of hardened desert warriors from the tribe of Gad crossed the Jordan River to join David. They had the physical attributes and equipment necessary for being effective soldiers, and they were willing to endure hardship to join the effort.

12:16-18 David was not ready to trust all of these people, particularly those from the tribe of Benjamin. When he warned them of the dangers of betrayal, **Amasai**, the leader, confirmed his commitment under the inspiration of God. The Chronicler wants us to recognize divine guidance in David's cause.

12:19-22 Men from as far away as Manasseh signed up to support David. The **Philistines** balked at having David and

the army. [22]At that time, men came day after day to help David until there was a great army, like an army of God.[A,a]

David's Soldiers in Hebron

[23]The numbers of the armed troops who came to David at Hebron to turn Saul's kingdom over to him,[b] according to the Lord's word,[c] were as follows:

[24]   From the Judahites: 6,800 armed troops bearing shields and spears.

[25]   From the Simeonites: 7,100 brave warriors ready for war.

[26]   From the Levites: 4,600 [27]in addition to Jehoiada, leader of the house of Aaron, with 3,700 men; [28]and Zadok,[d] a young brave warrior, with 22 commanders from his own ancestral house.

[29]   From the Benjaminites, the relatives of Saul:[e] 3,000 (up to that time the majority of the Benjaminites maintained their allegiance to the house of Saul).

[30]   From the Ephraimites: 20,800 brave warriors who were famous men in their ancestral houses.

[31]   From half the tribe of Manasseh: 18,000 designated by name to come and make David king.

[32]   From the Issacharites, who understood the times[f] and knew what Israel should do: 200 chiefs with all their relatives under their command.

[33]   From Zebulun: 50,000 who could serve in the army, trained for battle with all kinds of weapons of war, with one purpose[g] to help David.[B]

[34]   From Naphtali: 1,000 commanders accompanied by 37,000 men with shield and spear.

[35]   From the Danites: 28,600 trained for battle.

[36]   From Asher: 40,000 who could serve in the army, trained for battle.

[37]   From across the Jordan—from the Reubenites, Gadites, and half the tribe of Manasseh: 120,000 men equipped with all the military weapons of war.

[38]All these warriors, lined up in battle formation, came to Hebron fully determined to make David king over all Israel. All the rest of Israel was also of one mind to make David king.[h] [39]They spent three days there eating and drinking with David, for their relatives had provided for them. [40]In addition, their neighbors from as far away as Issachar, Zebulun, and Naphtali came and brought food on donkeys, camels, mules, and oxen—abundant provisions of flour, fig cakes, raisins, wine and oil, oxen, and sheep.[i] Indeed, there was joy in Israel.

David and the Ark

13 David consulted with all his leaders, the commanders of hundreds and of thousands. [2]Then he said to the whole assembly of Israel, "If it seems good to you, and if this is from the Lord our God, let us spread out and send the message to the rest of our relatives in all the districts of Israel, including the priests and Levites in their cities with pasturelands,[j] that they should gather together with us. [3]Then let us bring back the ark of our God, for we did not inquire of Him[k] in Saul's days." [4]Since the proposal seemed right to all the people, the whole assembly agreed to do it.

[5]So David assembled all Israel,[l] from the Shihor of Egypt to the entrance of Hamath,[C,m]

a12:22 Gn 32:1-2; Jos 5:13-15
b12:23 1Sm 15:28; 1Ch 10:14
c1Ch 11:10
d12:28 2Sm 8:17; 1Ch 6:8,53; 9:11; 15:11; 16:39
e12:29 1Ch 12:2
f12:32 Est 1:13
g12:33 Ps 12:2
h12:38 2Sm 5:1-3
i12:40 1Sm 25:18
j13:2 Nm 35:1-8
k13:3 1Sm 7:1-2; 1Ch 10:14; 15:13
l13:5 2Sm 6:1; 1Ch 15:3
m1Kg 8:65

A12:22 Or like the ultimate army   B12:33 LXX; MT omits David   C13:5 Or to Lebo-hamath

---

his men fighting among them against Israel, fearing that David would suddenly turn on them and side with **Saul**.

12:23-38 Shifting now to the time of David's coronation at **Hebron**, an army totaling more than 300,000 gathered to follow David's command.

12:26-28 Not only did the **Levites** allow themselves to be conscripted, but even **Zadok**—soon to assume duty as high priest—let himself be counted.

12:29-30 The **Benjaminites** finally pledged their support to David. This was a great change of heart for them. Even though there had been some supporters from Benjamin early on (v. 16), at this point the entire tribe of Benjamin became loyal to David, though the number of their soldiers at **3,000** was still the smallest of the tribes.

12:32 The Chronicler specifically mentions the tribe of Issachar. He declares that they **understood the times**, showing their conviction that David should be made king over all Israel. A total of **200 chiefs** would have been in charge of a large number of soldiers.

12:37 The enrollment of tribes from the eastern side of the Jordan River—**Reubenites, Gadites, and half the tribe of Manasseh**—underscores the unity of this army.

12:38-40 These warriors were official representatives of their tribes. The times were not yet prosperous, so David could not feed all of them. They brought their own food, **provided** by **relatives**, and others sent caravans of provisions from as far away as the most northern tribes.

13:1 David consulted with all his leaders, but not the Levites, who could have kept him from the mistake he was about to make.

13:5-8 At this point the **ark** was at **Kiriath-jearim**, a town north of Jerusalem. It had rested there for several decades

to bring the ark of God from Kiriath-jearim.*
[6] David[b] and all Israel went to Baalah[c] (that is,
Kiriath-jearim that belongs to Judah) to take
the ark of God from there, which is called by
the name of the Lord who dwells between the
•cherubim.[d] [7] At Abinadab's house[e] they set
the ark of God on a new cart. Uzzah and Ahio[A]
were guiding the cart.

[8] David and all Israel were celebrating with
all their might before God with songs and with
lyres, harps, tambourines, cymbals, and trumpets.[f] [9] When they came to Chidon's threshing floor,[g] Uzzah reached out to hold the ark
because the oxen had stumbled. [10] Then the
Lord's anger burned against Uzzah, and He
struck him dead because he had reached out
to the ark.[h] So he died there in the presence
of God.[i]

[11] David was angry because of the Lord's outburst against Uzzah, so he named that place
Outburst Against Uzzah,[B] as it is still named
today. [12] David feared God that day and said,
"How can I ever bring the ark of God to me?"
[13] So David did not move the ark of God home[c]
to the city of David; instead, he took it to the
house of Obed-edom the Gittite.[j] [14] The ark of
God remained with Obed-edom's family in his
house for three months, and the Lord blessed
his family and all that he had.

*[a]13:51 Sm 6:21;
7:1
[b]13:6-14 2Sm
6:2-11
[c]13:6 Jos 15:9
[d]2Kg 19:15
[e]13:7 1Sm 7:1
[f]13:8 1Ch 15:16
[g]13:9 2Sm 6:6
[h]13:10 1Ch
15:13,15
[i]Lv 10:2
[j]13:13 1Ch 26:4-
5; 2Ch 25:23-24
[k]14:1-17 2Sm
5:11-25
[l]14:4-7 1Ch
3:5-8
[m]14:9 1Ch
11:15; 14:13

God's Blessing on David

14 King Hiram of Tyre sent envoys to
David,[k] along with cedar logs, stonemasons, and carpenters to build a palace for
him. [2] Then David knew that the Lord had established him as king over Israel and that his
kingdom had been exalted for the sake of His
people Israel.

[3] David took more wives in Jerusalem, and
he became the father of more sons and daughters. [4] These[l] are the names of the children
born to him in Jerusalem: Shammua, Shobab,
Nathan, Solomon, [5] Ibhar, Elishua, Elpelet,
[6] Nogah, Nepheg, Japhia, [7] Elishama, Beeliada,
and Eliphelet.

[8] When the Philistines heard that David had
been anointed king over all Israel, they all
went in search of David; when David heard
of this, he went out to face them. [9] Now the
Philistines had come and raided in the Valley of Rephaim,[m] [10] so David inquired of God,
"Should I go to war against the Philistines?
Will You hand them over to me?"

The Lord replied, "Go, and I will hand them
over to you."

[11] So the Israelites went up to Baal-perazim,
and David defeated the Philistines there. Then
David said, "Like a bursting flood, God has
used me to burst out against my enemies."

[A]13:7 Or *and his brothers*   [B]13:11 Or *Perez-uzzah*   [C]13:13 Lit *to himself*

after it had been returned by the Philistines. Seventy men
of the town of Beth-shemesh had been killed when they
looked inside it (1Sm 6:19). Since that time the ark had
been largely ignored. Abinadab, the owner of the property
on which the ark had settled, had prospered because of its
presence (1Sm 7:1). In their eagerness to move the ark to
Jerusalem, David's officials made sure that the procession
was as grandiose as possible. They got a **new cart**, the best
of oxen, and undoubtedly two of the most experienced oxen
drivers in the area. With much pomp and circumstance, accompanied by an impressive band, the procession set out
in high spirits.

13:9 Uzzah, fearing that the ark might slide off the cart,
reached out to hold it steady.

13:10 Good intentions aside, **Uzzah** was violating the sacredness of the **ark** by touching an object that the Lord had
declared untouchable. Lest there be any doubt about it, the
Chronicler insists that it was the Lord who struck Uzzah
dead.

13:11-12 David was **angry** that the Lord had interfered with
his plans for giving the **ark** such triumphal treatment. Then
his anger turned to fear. The display of the holiness and
power of God made David doubt whether he was able or
worthy to **bring the ark** to his city.

13:13-14 While David pondered what to do, **the ark of God**
was parked at the home of **Obed-edom**. Obed-edom's family—just as Abinadab's in Kiriath-jearim had done—enjoyed
special blessings from the Lord because they were hosting
the ark.

14:1 King Hiram of Tyre is a consistent presence throughout the reigns of David and Solomon. Even if he worshiped
the Phoenician gods outwardly, inwardly he worshiped
nothing as fervently as profit and material wealth. He initiated a possible sale of building materials to **David** for a
huge **palace**.

14:2 David saw this international recognition as confirmation from the Lord that **his kingdom** was approved by
God.

14:3-7 The Chronicler lists further **wives** whom David acquired after his capital was moved to **Jerusalem**. First
Chronicles does not recount his adulterous affair with Bathsheba, and Bathsheba is not invoked by name here, though
she had been mentioned earlier (3:5), and her children are
included in this list.

14:8 The **Philistines** had been held in check by **David**, but
they still lived in Israelite territory, trying to maintain their
power. When it became clear to them that David's kingdom was growing stronger, they joined forces to wage war
against Israel. David marched out with his army for a direct
confrontation.

14:9 The **Valley of Rephaim**, just south of Jerusalem, was
a natural path up to the capital city, but it was also an easy
place for an army to get locked in.

14:10-11 David must have learned his lesson from the disasters that beset Saul. He made sure that it was the Lord's
will to battle the **Philistines** in a direct attack. The Lord
gave him permission, and David caught the Philistines un-
awares.

Therefore, they named that place the Lord Bursts Out.ᴬ ¹²The Philistines abandoned their idols there, and David ordered that they be burned in the fire.

¹³Once again the Philistines raided in the valley. ¹⁴So David again inquired of God, and God answered him, "Do not pursue them directly. Circle around them and attack them opposite the balsam trees. ¹⁵When you hear the sound of marching in the tops of the balsam trees, then march out to battle, for God will have marched out ahead of you to attack the camp of the Philistines." ¹⁶So David did exactly as God commanded him, and they struck down the Philistine army from Gibeon to Gezer. ¹⁷Then David's fame spread throughout the lands, and the Lord caused all the nations to be terrified of him.ᵃ

The Ark Comes to Jerusalem

15 David built houses for himself in the city of David, and he prepared a place for the ark of God and pitched a tent for it.ᵇ ²Then David said, "No one but the Levites may carry the ark of God, because the Lord has chosen them to carry the ark of the Lord and to minister before Him forever."ᶜ

³David assembled all Israel at Jerusalemᵈ to bring the ark of the Lord to the place he had prepared for it.ᵉ ⁴Then he gathered together the descendants of Aaron and the Levites:

⁵From the Kohathites, Uriel the leader and 120 of his relatives; ⁶from the Merarites, Asaiah the leader and 220 of his relatives; ⁷from the Gershomites,ᴮ Joel the leader and 130 of

his relatives; ⁸from the Elizaphanites, Shemaiah the leader and 200 of his relatives; ⁹from the Hebronites, Eliel the leader and 80 of his relatives; ¹⁰from the Uzzielites, Amminadab the leader and 112 of his relatives.

¹¹David summoned the priests Zadokᶠ and Abiatharᵍ and the Levites Uriel, Asaiah, Joel, Shemaiah, Eliel, and Amminadab. ¹²He said to them, "You are the heads of the Levite families. You and your relatives must consecrate yourselvesʰ so that you may bring the ark of the Lord God of Israel to the place I have prepared for it.ⁱ ¹³For the Lord our God burst out in anger against us because you Levites were not with us the first time, for we didn't inquire of Him about the proper procedures."ʲ ¹⁴So the priests and the Levites consecrated themselves to bring up the ark of the Lord God of Israel. ¹⁵Then the Levites carried the ark of God the way Moses had commanded according to the word of the Lord: on their shoulders with the poles.ᵏ

¹⁶Then David told the leaders of the Levites to appoint their relatives as singers and to have them raise their voices with joy accompanied by musical instruments—harps, lyres, and cymbals.ˡ ¹⁷So the Levites appointed Heman son of Joel; from his relatives, Asaph son of Berechiah; and from their relatives the Merarites, Ethan son of Kushaiah. ¹⁸With them were their relatives second in rank: Zechariah, Jaaziel,ᶜ Shemiramoth, Jehiel, Unni, Eliab, Benaiah, Maaseiah, Mattithiah, Eliphelehu, Mikneiah, and the gatekeepers Obededom and Jeiel. ¹⁹The singers Heman, Asaph,

ᵃ14:17 Ex 15:14-16; Dt 2:25
ᵇ15:1 1Ch 16:1; 17:1-5
ᶜ15:2 Nm 4:15; Dt 10:8
ᵈ15:3 1Ch 13:5
ᵉ2Sm 6:12,17; 1Ch 15:12
ᶠ15:11 1Ch 12:28; 18:16; 24:3,6,31; 27:17; 29:22
ᵍ1Sm 22:20-23; 1Kg 1:7; 2:26-27,35; 1Ch 27:34
ʰ15:12 Ex 19:14; 2Ch 35:6
ⁱCh 15:1,3
ʲ15:13 2Sm 6:3; 1Ch 13:7
ᵏ15:15 Ex 25:12-15; Nm 4:6,15
ˡ15:16 1Ch 13:8; 25:1

ᴬ14:11 Or *Baal-perazim*   ᴮ15:7 = Gershonites   ᶜ15:18 Some Hb mss, LXX; other Hb mss read *Zechariah son and Jaaziel*

14:12 The **Philistines** were routed so thoroughly that they left their **idols** on the battlefield. Many ancient kings would have picked up these idols and either desecrated them or tried to gain some spiritual strength from them. David did not play any such spiritual games; he ordered that they be **burned**.

14:13-16 The **Philistines** must have thought that attacking through the same **valley** was the last thing anyone would expect, but if they were caught again they would be ready. This time the Lord commanded David to use a different strategy—to come from behind. God would give David a signal when it was time to **attack**. By following God's orders **exactly**, he eliminated the threat of the Philistines for a long time to come.

14:17 At this time Mesopotamia and Egypt were suffering from internal struggles. The Phoenicians were more interested in growth by trade than by military might. The Philistines had been put in their place; even though they were not eliminated, they were in no position to reestablish their military strength. David's kingdom was the strongest empire of the day. For the time being threats would not come from the traditional superpowers but from his neighbors who were trying to take advantage of the political vacuum.

15:1-3 Three months elapsed between the time of David's

first attempt to move the **ark** and this renewed effort. The king prepared **a tent** in **Jerusalem** as its official resting place. He followed the instructions given to him by the **Levites** on how the ark should be carried. Numbers 4:15 states that the ark should be carried only by Levites, and only by two long poles inserted through rings in the ark. These poles should rest on the shoulders of the transporting Levites (1Ch 14:15).

15:11 The last-minute council of the leaders among the **Levites** and **priests** included two priests, **Zadok and Abiathar**. The official tabernacle stood at Gibeon, with Zadok working as priest there, even though the ark had not been there for about a hundred years. Because David had no regular access to the tabernacle during Saul's reign, a Kohathite named Abiathar had become David's personal friend and priest (1Sm 22).

15:16-22 David also put the **Levites** in charge of the music, playing various **musical instruments**. The three main musicians—**Heman . . . Asaph**, and **Ethan**—took charge. Among the secondary musicians were **Obed-edom**, the last host of the ark, who would soon become one of the official gatekeepers.

15:23-24 The list flows on, from those who were a part of the procession to the organization that would be implemented

and Ethan were to sound the bronze cymbals; [20] Zechariah, Aziel, Shemiramoth, Jehiel, Unni, Eliab, Maaseiah, and Benaiah were to play harps according to *Alamoth*;[A] [21] and Mattithiah, Eliphelehu, Mikneiah, Obed-edom, Jeiel, and Azaziah were to lead the music with lyres according to the •Sheminith. [22] Chenaniah, the leader of the Levites in music, was to direct the music because he was skillful. [23] Berechiah and Elkanah were to be gatekeepers for the ark. [24] The priests, Shebaniah, Joshaphat, Nethanel, Amasai, Zechariah, Benaiah, and Eliezer, were to blow trumpets[a] before the ark of God. Obed-edom and Jehiah were also to be gatekeepers for the ark.

[25] David,[b] the elders of Israel, and the commanders of thousands went with rejoicing to bring the ark of the covenant of the Lord from the house of Obed-edom.[c] [26] While the Levites were carrying the ark of the covenant of the Lord, with God's help, they sacrificed seven bulls and seven rams.[d]

[27] Now David was dressed in a robe of fine linen, as were all the Levites who were carrying the ark, as well as the singers and Chenaniah, the music leader of the singers. David also wore a linen •ephod. [28] So all Israel brought up the ark of the covenant of the Lord with shouts, the sound of the ram's horn, trumpets, and cymbals, and the playing of harps and lyres. [29] As the ark of the covenant of the Lord was entering the city of David, Saul's daughter Michal looked down from the window and saw King David dancing[B] and celebrating, and she despised him in her heart.

16 They[e] brought the ark of God and placed it inside the tent David had pitched for

it.[f] Then they offered •burnt offerings and •fellowship offerings in God's presence. [2] When David had finished offering the burnt offerings and the fellowship offerings, he blessed the people in the name of •Yahweh. [3] Then he distributed to each and every Israelite, both men and women, a loaf of bread, a date cake, and a raisin cake.

[4] David appointed some of the Levites to be ministers before the ark of the Lord, to celebrate the Lord God of Israel, and to give thanks and praise to Him. [5] •Asaph was the chief and Zechariah was second to him. Jeiel, Shemiramoth, Jehiel, Mattithiah, Eliab, Benaiah, Obed-edom, and Jeiel played the harps and lyres, while Asaph sounded the cymbals [6] and the priests Benaiah and Jahaziel blew the trumpets regularly before the ark of the covenant of God.

David's Psalm of Thanksgiving

[7] On that day David decreed for the first time that thanks be given to the Lord by Asaph and his relatives:

[8] Give thanks[g] to Yahweh; call on
      His name;
   proclaim His deeds among
      the peoples.[h]
[9] Sing to Him; sing praise to Him;
   tell about all His wonderful works!
[10] Honor His holy name;
   let the hearts of those who seek Yahweh
      rejoice.
[11] Search for the Lord and for
      His strength;
   seek His face always.[i]

*a*15:24 1Ch 16:6
*b*15:25-29 2Sm 6:12-16
*c*15:25 1Ch 13:13
*d*15:26 Nm 23:1-4,29
*e*16:1-3 2Sm 6:17-19
*f*16:1 1Ch 15:1
*g*16:8-22 Ps 105:1-15
*h*16:8 1Kg 8:43; 2Kg 19:19
*i*16:11 Ps 24:6

A15:20 This may refer to a high pitch, perhaps a tune sung by soprano voices; the Hb word means "young women"; Ps 46 title
B15:29 Or *whirling*

after the **ark** arrived in Jerusalem. **Berechiah . . . Elkanah . . . Obed-edom**, and **Jehiah** would become gatekeepers, and permanent trumpet players would also be designated.

15:26 When the **ark** reached Jerusalem, the Levites performed a sacrifice consisting of **seven bulls and seven rams**. This number would be eclipsed by the huge sacrifices of Solomon a generation later, and it was echoed much later when King Hezekiah reopened the temple (2Ch 29:21).

15:27-29 When **Michal**, David's first wife, saw the king dancing before the ark in public (v. 25), she **despised him in her heart**. This moment finalized their estrangement. Of all David's wives, Michal never bore him any children.

16:1 This **tent** was a special place for the ark where priests could offer sacrifices. The company offered **burnt offerings**, signifying total commitment to the Lord, and **fellowship offerings**, indicating the covenant between God and His people.

16:2-3 David's coronation banquet had been a carry-in dinner, but now when David **blessed the people** and sent them home, each person received a small packet of food.

16:4-6 The site of the **ark** was not the main place for worship, which continued to be the tabernacle in Gibeon. As a symbol of the presence of God in their midst, the ark needed to be surrounded by people who praised the Lord. David appointed permanent musicians for this task. This group included **Asaph** on the cymbals, a string ensemble featuring **Obed-edom**, and the trumpeting priests **Benaiah** and **Jahaziel**.

16:7 Music had probably been a part of Israelite culture and worship for some time, but David made it an integral part of worship before the ark and at the tabernacle. In Jerusalem, he instructed **Asaph** to lead in thanksgiving songs, and he composed a psalm for the occasion. It had three parts that were later incorporated into the book of Psalms. Verses 8 through 22 constitute Ps 105:1-15; verses 23-33 are Ps 96:1-13; and verses 34-36 are Ps 106:1,47-48. The entire psalm as represented in 1 Chronicles comprises four segments exhorting the people to praise God, interspersed with three segments describing God's faithfulness, glory, and creatorship.

16:8-13 The first exhortation to **praise** is a call to remember

¹² Remember the wonderful works
    He has done,^a
His wonders, and the judgments
    He has pronounced,^{A,b}
¹³ you offspring of Israel His servant,
Jacob's descendants—His chosen ones.

¹⁴ He is the Lord our God;
His judgments govern the whole earth.^c
¹⁵ Remember His covenant forever—
the promise He ordained for a thousand
    generations,
¹⁶ the covenant He made with Abraham,
swore^B to Isaac,^d
¹⁷ and confirmed to Jacob as a decree,
and to Israel
    as an everlasting covenant:^e
¹⁸ "I will give the land of Canaan to you
as your inherited portion."^f

¹⁹ When they^C were few in number,
very few indeed,^g
    and temporary residents in Canaan
²⁰ wandering from nation to nation
and from one kingdom to another,
²¹ He allowed no one to oppress them;
He rebuked kings on their behalf:^h
²² "Do not touch My anointed ones
or harm My prophets."ⁱ

²³ Sing^j to the Lord, all the earth.
Proclaim His salvation from day to day.
²⁴ Declare His glory among the nations,
His wonderful works among all peoples.

²⁵ For the Lord is great
    and highly praised;^k
He is feared above all gods.^l
²⁶ For all the gods of the peoples
are idols,^m
but the Lord made the heavens.ⁿ
²⁷ Splendor and majesty are before Him;

strength and joy are in His place.
²⁸ Ascribe to the Lord, families
    of the peoples,
ascribe to the Lord glory and strength.
²⁹ Ascribe to Yahweh the glory
    of His name;
bring an offering and come before Him.
Worship the Lord
    in the splendor of His holiness;^o
³⁰ tremble^p before Him, all the earth.

The world is firmly established;
it cannot be shaken.
³¹ Let the heavens be glad and the earth
    rejoice,^q
and let them say among the nations,
    "The Lord is King!"
³² Let the sea and everything in it
    resound;
let the fields and all that is in them
    exult.^r
³³ Then the trees of the forest will shout
    for joy before the Lord,
for He is coming to judge the earth.

³⁴ Give thanks to the Lord, for He is good;
His faithful love endures forever.^s
³⁵ And say:^t "Save us,
    God of our salvation;
gather us and rescue us from
    the nations
so that we may give thanks to
    Your holy name
and rejoice in Your praise.
³⁶ May Yahweh, the God of Israel,
    be praised^u
from everlasting to everlasting."

Then all the people said, "'Amen" and "Praise
the Lord."
³⁷ So David left Asaph and his relatives there

Cross references (center column):

^a16:12 Ps 103:2
^bPs 78:43-68
^c16:14 Ps 48:10
^d16:16 Gn 17:2;
22:16-18; 26:3
^e16:17 Gn
35:11-12
^f16:18 Gn 13:15
^g16:19 Gn 34:30;
Dt 7:7
^h16:21 Gn 12:17;
20:3; Ex 7:15-18
ⁱ16:22 Gn 20:7
^j16:23-33 Ps 96
^k16:25 Ps
144:3-6
^lPs 89:7
^m16:26 Lv 19:4
ⁿPs 102:25
^o16:29 Ps 29:2
^p16:30-31 Ps
93:1
^q16:31 Is 44:23;
49:13
^r16:32 Ps 98:7
^s16:34 Ps 106:1;
136:1
^t16:35-36a Ps
106:47-48
^u16:36 1Kg
8:15,56; Ps
72:18

---

^A16:12 Lit *judgments of His mouth*   ^B16:16 Lit *and His oath*   ^C16:19 One Hb ms, LXX, Vg; other Hb mss read *you*

---

what God had done and to **proclaim His deeds**. In the Bible the praise of God often involves recalling and proclaiming what God has done in the past.

16:14-22 The first intermediate segment of David's psalm is a reminder of God's **covenant** with **Abraham** and how God had kept the covenant by bringing His people into the promised land.

16:23-24 These verses repeat Israel's obligation to praise God. They add the dimension that this praise should be done **among the nations**. The people who had not directly experienced God's guidance would learn about it from the Israelites.

16:25-27 This second segment describes the difference between God and **idols**. Because idols are man-made they do not have the power and **majesty** of **the Lord**.

16:28-30a To **ascribe** something to someone is to acknowledge they have that attribute. This exhortation to praise

connects praising God with worshiping Him with offerings. Just as praise of God is connected with His works, praise from the worshiper is connected with active service.

16:30b-33 In this segment of the psalm, the power of God is recognized by the firmness of the **world**, the witness of the **heavens**, the proclamation of the **sea**, and the shouts of joy of the **trees**. The created order gives testimony to Creator's glory.

16:34-36 The fourth and final exhortation to praise combines another reminder of God's glory with the need to rely on the Lord for **salvation**.

16:37-42 The Chronicler once more focuses on the service at the **ark** in Jerusalem and the service at the tabernacle in **Gibeon**. The ambiguity caused by having two sacred sites shows that a temple that unified worship was badly needed. **Zadok**, with the assistance of the musicians **Heman** and **Jeduthun** (Ethan), continued the sacrifices

before the ark of the LORD's covenant to minister regularly[a] before the ark according to the daily requirements.[b] [38]He assigned Obed-edom[c] and his[A] 68 relatives. Obed-edom son of Jeduthun and Hosah[d] were to be gatekeepers. [39]David left Zadok the priest and his fellow priests before the tabernacle of the LORD at the *high place in Gibeon[e] [40]to offer burnt offerings regularly, morning and evening, to the LORD on the altar of burnt offerings and to do everything that was written in the law of the LORD, which He had commanded Israel to keep.[f] [41]With them were Heman,[g] Jeduthun, and the rest who were chosen and designated by name[h] to give thanks to the LORD—for His faithful love endures forever.[i] [42]Heman and Jeduthun had with them trumpets and cymbals to play and musical instruments of God.[j] Jeduthun's sons were at the gate.

[43]Then all the people left for their homes, and David returned home to bless his household.[k]

The LORD's Covenant with David

17 When David[l] had settled into his palace, he said to Nathan the prophet, "Look! I am living in a cedar house while the ark of the LORD's covenant is under tent curtains."[m]

[2]So Nathan told David, "Do all that is on your heart, for God is with you."

[3]But that night[n] the word of God came to Nathan: [4]"Go to David My servant and say, 'This is what the LORD says: You are not the one to build Me a house to dwell in.[o] [5]From the time I brought Israel out of Egypt until today I have not lived in a house; instead, I have moved from tent to tent and from tabernacle to tabernacle.[p] [6]In all My travels throughout Israel, have I ever spoken a word to even one of the judges of Israel, whom I commanded to shepherd My people, asking: Why haven't you built Me a house of cedar?'[q]

[7]"Now this is what you will say to My servant David: 'This is what the LORD of *Hosts says: I took you from the pasture and from following the sheep to be ruler over My people Israel.'[r] [8]I have been with you wherever you have gone, and I have destroyed all your enemies before you. I will make a name for you like that of the greatest in the land. [9]I will establish a place for My people Israel and plant them,[s] so that they may live there and not be disturbed again. Evildoers will not continue to oppress them as they formerly have [10]ever since the day I ordered judges to be over My people Israel. I will also subdue all your enemies.

"'Furthermore, I declare to you that the LORD Himself will build a house for you. [11]When your time comes to be with your fathers, I will raise up after you your descendant, who is one of your own sons, and I will establish his kingdom. [12]He will build a house for Me,[t] and I will establish his throne forever. [13]I will be a father to him, and he will be a son to Me.[u] I will not take away My faithful love from him as I took it from the one who was before you.[v] [14]I will appoint him over My house and My kingdom forever, and his throne will be established forever.'"[w]

[15]Nathan reported all these words and this entire vision to David.

[a]16:37 1Ch 16:4-5
[b]2Ch 8:14; Ezr 3:4
[c]16:38 1Ch 13:13
[d]1Ch 26:10
[e]16:39 1Kg 3:4; 1Ch 21:29
[f]16:40 Ex 29:38-42; Nm 28:3-4
[g]16:41 1Ch 6:33
[h]1Ch 25:1-6
[i]2Ch 5:13
[j]16:42 1Ch 25:7; 2Ch 7:6; 29:27
[k]16:43 2Sm 6:19-20
[l]17:1-2 2Sm 7:1-3
[m]17:1 Hg 1:4
[n]17:3-15 2Sm 7:4-17
[o]17:4 1Ch 22:7-8; 28:2-3
[p]17:5 Ex 40:2-3; 2Sm 7:6
[q]17:6 2Sm 7:7
[r]17:7 1Sm 16:11-13
[s]17:9 Ex 15:17
[t]17:12 1Kg 5:2-5; 6:14,38; 8:17-20; 2Ch 6:2
[u]17:13 Heb 1:5
[v]1Sm 15:23-28; 1Ch 10:14
[w]17:14 Ps 89:29,36

that were commanded by the law at the tabernacle. Just as David had instituted a more consistent regimen surrounding the ark, he ordered similar provisions for the tabernacle.

17:1-2 Both David and **Nathan the prophet** were committed to the idea of building a temple. David felt that he was shortchanging the ark of the covenant by housing it in a tent. Nathan, who knew David's motives were pure, had no reason at this point to think that David should not proceed with his plans to build a temple.

17:3-14 God's message to **David** by way of **Nathan** about the temple was positive because that is how David took it. Eventually there would be a temple because God had promised Moses a central place of worship, which would become the exclusive place for sacrifices (Dt 12:5-7). David would not be allowed to build this **house** for God **to dwell in**, but God would give the king a far greater promise. The Lord declared that he would build David's **house**—a dynasty, a succession of kings that would last many generations (vv. 10-12). One of his sons would become the next king and would be the one to build the temple, and he would also continue the lineage of David for all eternity.

nagiyd

Hebrew Pronunciation	[nah GEED]
HCSB Translation	leader, ruler
Uses in 1 Chronicles	12
Uses in the OT	44
Focus Passage	1 Chronicles 17:7

Nagiyd relates to *neged* ("before, in front of") and *nagad* ("tell"); *nagad* may involve placing something before someone. *Nagiyd* indicates *nobleman* (Jb 29:10) and communicates specific leadership positions. It is a synonym for "king," designating the *ruler* of Tyre (Ezk 28:2) and the covenant *prince* Ptolemy Philometor of Egypt (Dn 11:22). Mostly it calls Israelite kings, including the Messiah (Dn 9:25), *rulers* (1Sm 10:1) or *leaders* (2Kg 20:5). *Nagiyd* describes national *leaders* (Ps 76:12). It designates the *chief official* of God's house (Neh 11:11) or of an Israelite tribe (1Ch 27:16). It denotes a palace *governor* (2Ch 28:7) and town or fortress *leaders* (2Ch 11:11). It is a *leader* of gatekeepers (1Ch 9:20) or an *officer* over community offerings (2Ch 31:12). *Nagiyd* specified *leaders* in Assyria's army who were one step below commanders (2Ch 32:21). Besides people, *nagiyd* can describe *noble things* (Pr 8:6).

David's Prayer of Thanksgiving

[16] Then[a] King David went in, sat in the Lord's presence, and said,

Who am I, Lord God, and what is my house that You have brought me this far? [17] This was a little thing to You,[A] God, for You have spoken about Your servant's house in the distant future. You regard me as a man of distinction,[B] Lord God. [18] What more can David say to You for honoring Your servant? You know Your servant. [19] Lord, You have done all this greatness, making known all these great promises because of Your servant and according to Your will.[b] [20] Lord, there is no one like You, and there is no God besides You, as all we have heard confirms. [21] And who is like Your people Israel? God, You came to one nation on earth to redeem a people for Yourself, to make a name for Yourself through great and awesome works by driving out nations before Your people You redeemed from Egypt.[c] [22] You made Your people Israel Your own people forever, and You, Lord, have become their God.[d]

[23] Now, Lord, let the word that You have spoken concerning Your servant and his house be confirmed forever, and do as You have promised. [24] Let Your name be confirmed and magnified forever in the saying, "'Yahweh of Hosts, the God of Israel, is God over Israel." May the house of Your servant David be established before You. [25] Since You, my God, have revealed to[C,e] Your servant that You will build him a house, Your servant has found courage to pray in Your presence. [26] Yahweh, You indeed are God, and You have promised this good thing to Your servant. [27] So now, You have been pleased to bless Your servant's house that it may continue before You forever. For You, Lord, have blessed it, and it is blessed forever.

David's Military Campaigns

18 After this,[f] David defeated the Philistines, subdued them, and took Gath and its villages from Philistine control. [2] He also defeated the Moabites, and they became David's subjects and brought tribute.

[3] David also defeated King Hadadezer of Zobah at Hamath when he went to establish his control at the Euphrates River. [4] David captured 1,000 chariots, 7,000 horsemen, and 20,000 foot soldiers from him, hamstrung all the horses, and kept 100 chariots.[D]

[5] When the Arameans of Damascus came to assist King Hadadezer of Zobah,[g] David struck down 22,000 Aramean men. [6] Then he placed garrisons[E,h] in Aram of Damascus, and the Arameans became David's subjects and brought

---

[a]17:16-27 2Sm 7:18-29   [b]17:19 Is 37:35   [c]17:21 Dt 4:32-38   [d]17:22 Ex 6:7; 19:5-6   [e]17:25 Ex 6:7; 19:5-6   [f]18:1-13 2Sm 8:1-14   [g]18:5 1Ch 18:9; 19:6   [h]18:6 2Sm 8:6

[A]17:17 Lit thing in Your eyes   [B]17:17 Hb obscure   [C]17:25 Lit have uncovered the ear of   [D]18:4 Or chariot horses   [E]18:6 Some Hb mss, LXX, Vg; other Hb mss omit garrisons; 2Sm 8:6

17:16 David understood the promise that his son would build the temple, even if he himself was not allowed to, as a positive affirmation from God.

17:21 In the fashion of biblical praise (16:8-36), David praised the Lord by referring to what He had done.

17:23-26 It may seem odd that David repeated what God had promised as though it were a petition directed to God, but there were three important points in this last half of David's prayer. First, he showed submission to what the Lord had planned for him. Second, he showed God that what he desired was whatever God wanted for him. Third, David tells us that it is never wrong to express our thoughts and desires to the Lord. Whether we are joyfully accepting what God has already said or struggling with trying to accept something He is making clear to us, God always knows what is on our hearts. We have the privilege of voicing our thoughts and feelings to Him.

17:27 The chapter ends with David's affirmation that God's blessing is irrevocable.

18:1 This chapter summarizes a number of military victories by David and the spoils that he collected. He defeated the **Philistines**, this time not by repelling their attack, but by taking control of one of the five principal cities and its outlying **villages**.

18:2 The same thing happened with the **Moabites**. Conquered by David, they contributed to his growing treasury.

18:3 The Arameans were a confederation of various kingdoms east of the Jordan River, ranging all the way from Damascus to the banks of the Euphrates River. **Hadadezer of Zobah** ruled over one of the most easterly regions. By taking over his territory at the Euphrates and by controlling Philistine territory to the south, David fulfilled the promise God had given to Abraham—that his descendants would eventually occupy the land all the way from the Euphrates River to the Brook of Egypt (Gn 15:8).

18:4 Today's readers may find the cutting of the tendons (**hamstrung**) of thousands of **horses** objectionable, but in David's time this was a standard method of crippling an enemy force. Without their horses, the soldiers were rendered immobile. The alternative to hamstringing the horses would have been to kill rather than immobilize the soldiers.

18:5-8 The **Arameans of Damascus** attempted to come to the rescue of **Hadadezer**, but this move led them into subjection by David. Now the rich trade city of Damascus belonged to the king. Even though he would never build the temple, David accumulated much of the materials for the building and for the utensils during his lifetime. The **bronze** objects mentioned here would be put to use by Solomon later on.

tribute. The LORD made David victorious wherever he went.

⁷David took the gold shields carried by Hadadezer's officers and brought them to Jerusalem. ⁸From Tibhath and Cun, Hadadezer's cities, David also took huge quantities of bronze, from which Solomon made the bronze reservoir, the pillars, and the bronze articles.ᵃ

⁹When King Tou of Hamath heard that David had defeated the entire army of King Hadadezer of Zobah, ¹⁰he sent his son Hadoram to King David to greet him and to congratulate him because David had fought against Hadadezer and defeated him, for Tou and Hadadezer had fought many wars. Hadoram brought all kinds of gold, silver, and bronze items. ¹¹King David also dedicated these to the LORD, along with the silver and gold he had carried off from all the nations—from Edom, Moab, the Ammonites, the Philistines, and the Amalekites.

¹²Abishai son of Zeruiah struck down 18,000 Edomites in the Valley of Salt. ¹³He put garrisons in Edom, and all the Edomites were subject to David. The LORD made David victorious wherever he went.

¹⁴So David reigned over all Israel,ᵇ administering justice and righteousness for all his people.

¹⁵   Joabᶜ son of Zeruiah was over the army;

Cross references:
ᵃ18:8 1Kg 7:15-47; 2Ch 3:15–4:18
ᵇ18:14-17 2Sm 8:15-18
ᶜ18:15 1Ch 11:6
ᵈ18:16 2Sm 8:17; 1Ch 24:6,31
ᵉ18:17 2Sm 23:20-23
ᶠ19:1-5 2Sm 10:1-5
ᵍ19:4 Is 7:20; 20:4

Jehoshaphat son of Ahilud was
    court historian;
¹⁶   Zadok son of Ahitub
    and Ahimelechᴬ,ᵈ son of Abiathar
    were priests;
Shavsha was court secretary;
¹⁷   Benaiah son of Jehoiadaᵉ was over
    the Cherethites and the Pelethites;
    and David's sons were the chief officials
    at the king's side.

War with the Ammonites

19 Some time later,ᶠ King Nahash of the Ammonites died, and his son became king in his place. ²Then David said, "I'll show kindness to Hanun son of Nahash, because his father showed kindness to me."

So David sent messengers to console him concerning his father. However, when David's emissaries arrived in the land of the Ammonites to console him, ³the Ammonite leaders said to Hanun, "Just because David has sent men with condolences for you, do you really believe he's showing respect for your father? Instead, hasn't David sent his emissaries in order to scout out, overthrow, and spy on the land?" ⁴So Hanun took David's emissaries, shaved them, cut their clothes in half at the hips, and sent them away.ᵍ

⁵It was reported to David about his men, so he sent messengers to meet them, since the

---

ᴬ18:16 Some Hb mss, LXX, Syr, Vg; other Hb mss read *Abimelech*; 2Sm 8:17

18:9-10 King Tou of Hamath decided that diplomacy was a better option than warfare. Because he had been at odds with **Hadadezer**, he considered the enemy of his enemy to be his ally, but he still needed to pay a tribute of numerous objects of precious metal.

18:11 David did not add all of these things to his personal wealth, but he placed them into a treasury that was **dedicated . . . to the LORD**. Later on, much of it would go into the building of the temple.

18:12-13 Abishai was Joab's brother and a general in his army. Abishai represented David in a campaign against the **Edomites**, and 18,000 enemy warriors were killed. Even though Abishai was the leader of the battle, David was the king, so this section reiterates David's unbroken record of victories.

18:14 A glorious time is depicted in this short verse. David looked after his people by making sure that **justice and righteousness** prevailed for everyone. No greater compliment can be paid to any ruler.

18:15-16 A quick overview of the most important people surrounding David starts with **Joab**, still his commander-in-chief. **Jehoshaphat**, the **court historian**, and **Shavsha**, the **court secretary**, kept records of what happened in the palace. There were still two high priests, **Zadok** and **Ahimelech** (who replaced his father Abiathar), because there were still two main places of worship.

18:17 The **Cherethites** and the **Pelethites**, who reported to **Benaiah**, apparently were Philistine groups who were loyal to David and who may have been his bodyguards (cp. 11:24-25). Why would David have Philistines as bodyguards? You don't need bodyguards against open, obvious enemies; you need bodyguards against people who work their way into the king's presence to carry out an assassination. Thus, bodyguards of a different ethnic origin were well-suited for this task.

19:1-2 King Nahash of the Ammonites was a consistent presence in the time of Saul and David. Unless this is a successor with the same name, it was he who had first given Saul the occasion to rise to the responsibilities of being king of Israel. He had besieged the town of Jabesh-gilead and agreed to a truce with the citizens of this village on the condition that he could gouge out each person's eye (1Sm 11:2). This threat had enabled Saul to rally the Israelites in a united war against the Ammonites, in which he roundly defeated them. The Bible does not disclose the details of the occasion when Nahash had treated David kindly, but when Nahash died, David sent a delegation to the new king **Hanun** to express his condolences.

19:3-4 Hanun's advisers persuaded him that David's ambassadors were spies looking for a way to conquer the Ammonites. Hanun gave the order that David's delegates should be humiliated and sent home. The Chronicler does not indicate why Hanun thought he could get away with this rash act.

19:5-7 The **humiliated** men did not return directly to David.

men were deeply humiliated. The king said, "Stay in Jericho until your beards grow back; then return."

⁶When the Ammonites realized[a] they had made themselves repulsive to David, Hanun and the Ammonites sent 38 tons[A] of silver to hire chariots and horsemen from Aram-naharaim, Aram-maacah, and Zobah.[b] ⁷They hired 32,000 chariots and the king of Maacah with his army, who came and camped near Medeba.[c] The Ammonites also came together from their cities for the battle.

⁸David heard about this and sent Joab and the entire army of warriors. ⁹The Ammonites marched out and lined up in battle formation at the entrance of the city while the kings who had come were in the field by themselves. ¹⁰When Joab saw that there was a battle line in front of him and another behind him, he chose some men out of all the elite troops[B,d] of Israel and lined up in battle formation to engage the Arameans. ¹¹He placed the rest of the forces under the command of his brother Abishai, and they lined up in battle formation to engage the Ammonites.

¹²"If the Arameans are too strong for me," Joab said, "then you'll be my help. However, if the Ammonites are too strong for you, I'll help you. ¹³Be strong! We must prove ourselves strong for our people and for the cities of our God.[e] May the LORD's will be done."[c]

¹⁴Joab and the people with him approached the Arameans for battle, and they fled before him. ¹⁵When the Ammonites saw that the Arameans had fled, they likewise fled before Joab's brother Abishai and entered the city. Then Joab went to Jerusalem.

¹⁶When the Arameans realized that they had been defeated by Israel, they sent messengers to summon the Arameans who were across the Euphrates. They were led by Shophach, the commander of Hadadezer's army.

¹⁷When this was reported to David, he gathered all Israel and crossed the Jordan. He came up to the Arameans and lined up in battle formation against them. When David lined up to engage them in battle, they fought against him. ¹⁸But the Arameans fled before Israel, and David killed 7,000 of their charioteers and 40,000 foot soldiers. He also killed Shophach, commander of the army. ¹⁹When Hadadezer's subjects saw that they had been defeated by Israel, they made peace with David and became his subjects. After this, the Arameans were never willing to help the Ammonites again.

Capture of the City of Rabbah

20 In the spring[D] when kings march out to war,[f] Joab led the army and destroyed the Ammonites' land. He came to Rabbah and besieged it, but David remained in Jerusalem.[g] Joab attacked Rabbah and demolished it. ²Then David took the crown from

Cross references

[a]19:6-19 2Sm 10:6-19
[b]19:6 1Ch 18:5,9
[c]19:7 Nm 21:30; Jos 13:9,16; Is 15:2
[d]19:10 2Sm 6:1
[e]19:13 Jos 1:6
[f]20:1-3 2Sm 12:26-31
[g]20:1 2Sm 11:1

[A]19:6 Lit *1,000 talents*   [B]19:10 Lit *the choice ones*; 2Sm 6:1   [C]19:13 Lit *the LORD do what is good in His eyes*   [D]20:1 Lit *At the time of the return of the year*

Instead they hid in shame in **Jericho**, where David told them to stay. It then dawned on the Ammonites that they had made a serious mistake. Still, rather than making amends, they gathered a large army to ward off David's inevitable retribution. Hanun mobilized various people who were friendly to him and acquired a huge mercenary force of Arameans, complete with many **chariots**. With this impressive force, the Ammonites thought they were ready to go against the Israelite army.

19:8-9 David delegated the responsibility for taking on the Ammonites to **Joab** as his commander in chief. By the time Joab arrived on the field and took stock of the situation, he found himself wedged between the **Ammonites**, who had their backs protected by the walls of the town of Medeba, and their Aramean allies on the other side. Israel's defeat seemed inevitable.

19:10-13 Joab decided to have his army fight on two fronts at the same time. He took command of one front against the **Arameans** and let his brother **Abishai** lead the other front against the **Ammonites**. They pledged that if either one ran into trouble, the other would come to his aid. If Joab had any anxiety, he did not show it as he encouraged his brother and expressed reliance on the Lord.

19:14-15 Apparently the **Arameans** had not expected this aggressive response from Joab and his brother. When they saw the Israelite army advancing, they turned and fled. This

was enough for the **Ammonites** to lose heart as well. When they saw the Arameans fleeing, they barricaded themselves behind the walls of Medeba.

19:16 Now it was the Arameans' turn to make an error in judgment. Even though they had already been defeated once by David, they decided to take advantage of the situation and turn back on David's forces. While Joab returned victoriously to Jerusalem (v. 15), the **Arameans** made another alliance, this time with their kinsman all the way on the eastern side of the **Euphrates** River, in order to take revenge against David.

19:17-18 This time David himself took charge of the Israelite army. With an even greater force than before, he defeated the combined Aramean army.

19:19 Being defeated by David was nothing new to Hadadezer (see 18:3 and note there). Twice now, this king's attempts to establish superiority among the **Arameans** had been thwarted by David. Regardless of their king's ambitions, his subjects had seen enough. They submitted to David—and blamed it all on the **Ammonites**.

20:1 The ideal time to **march out to war** in ancient times was **the spring** because the ground is not too wet or muddy, and the weather is not too cold or hot for soldiers to exert themselves. In addition, for food the army could plunder crops growing in the invaded territory. **Joab**, once again in command, crossed into the territory of Ammon to finish the

the head of their king,[A,B,a] and it was placed on David's head. He found that the crown weighed 75 pounds[c] of gold, and there was a precious stone in it. In addition, David took away a large quantity of plunder from the city. [3]He brought out the people who were in it and put them to work with saws,[D] iron picks, and axes.[E,b] David did the same to all the Ammonite cities. Then he and all his troops returned to Jerusalem.

The Philistine Giants

[4]After this,[c] a war broke out with the Philistines at Gezer. At that time Sibbecai the Hushathite killed Sippai, a descendant of the giants,[F] and the Philistines were subdued.

[5]Once again there was a battle with the Philistines, and Elhanan son of Jair killed Lahmi the brother of Goliath the Gittite. The shaft of his spear was like a weaver's beam.[d]

[6]There was still another battle at Gath where

there was a man of extraordinary stature with six fingers on each hand and six toes on each foot—24 in all. He, too, was descended from the giant.[G] [7]When he taunted Israel, Jonathan son of David's brother Shimei killed him.

[8]These were the descendants of the giant[G] in Gath killed by David and his soldiers.

David's Military Census

21 Satan[H,e] stood up against Israel and incited David[f] to count the people of Israel. [2]So David said to Joab and the commanders of the troops, "Go and count Israel from Beer-sheba to Dan and bring a report to me so I can know their number."[g]

[3]Joab replied, "May the LORD multiply the number of His people a hundred times over![h] My lord the king, aren't they all my lord's servants? Why does my lord want to do this? Why should he bring •guilt on Israel?"

[4]Yet the king's order prevailed over Joab. So

a 20:2 1Kg 11:5,7
b 20:3 2Sm 12:31
c 20:4-8 2Sm 21:18-22
d 20:5 1Sm 17:7; 1Ch 11:23
e 21:1 Jb 1:6; Zch 3:1-2
f 21:1-8 2Sm 24:1-10
g 21:2 1Ch 27:23-24
h 21:3 Dt 1:11

A 20:2 LXX, Vg read *of Milcom*   **B** 20:2 = Molech; 1Kg 11:5,7   **C** 20:2 Lit *a talent*   **D** 20:3 Text emended; MT reads *and sawed them with the saw*; 2Sm 12:31   **E** 20:3 Text emended; MT reads *saws*; 2Sm 12:31   **F** 20:4 Or *the Rephaites*   **G** 20:6,8 Or *Raphah*   **H** 21:1 Or *An adversary*; Jb 1:6; Zch 3:1-2

job started the previous year when the Ammonites had retreated. He traveled to the town of **Rabbah** and laid siege to this capital of the Ammonites. David did not accompany his troops, but he remained in Jerusalem. This is the time when David had his affair with Bathsheba, and this is the military campaign in which he sent her husband, Uriah, to his death (2Sm 11:2–12:25). The Chronicler omits this entire episode.

20:2-3 After Joab had destroyed the city, David was crowned with the Ammonites' **crown**. His men carried away anything of value. Then he may have commanded the inhabitants of the city to destroy their own buildings. To have them destroy their houses, which could be rebuilt, was an effective way to keep them under control without taking their lives or carrying them into slavery.

20:4 Further conflict with the **Philistines** was inevitable. The occasions mentioned here may have happened over a longer period of time; they are brought together here by the Chronicler to report on the various Philistine giants. The first giant mentioned was **Sippai**, referred to as a **descendant of the giants**. The Hebrew word is *rephaim*, which refers to a race of giants, of whom we know nothing more than that they were larger than normal men. Apparently the *rephaim* had left a genetic heritage, even though the last pure member of their race was Og, king of Bashan, whose bed was 13 feet long and six feet wide (Dt 3:11). Earlier in 1 Chronicles we learned of an Egyptian giant who was killed by Benaiah (11:23). In the case of Sippai, his killer was **Sibbecai the Hushathite**.

20:5 Goliath had a brother named **Lahmi**, who may have been as tall as Goliath (1Sm 17:4). He was killed by **Elhanan son of Jair**, who is not mentioned anywhere else in the Bible.

20:6-7 Another giant, whose name is not given, copied Goliath by taunting Israel. In addition to his extraordinary stature, he had an extra finger and toe on each **hand** and **foot**. This time the killing of a giant remained in David's family when his nephew **Jonathan** took care of the matter.

20:8 The elimination of giants is an important aspect of how David finally took possession of the entire promised land. Assuming the spies were giving an accurate report rather than an exaggerated report born of fear and faithlessness, giants were spotted in the promised land. This report initially deterred the Israelites from invading Canaan (Nm 13:33–14:9). Those giants would have been Anakites, descended from the Nephilim who were destroyed in Noah's flood (Gn 6:4) but whose genes must have been carried recessively by Noah's son Ham or his wife, among the eight survivors of the flood. About 40 years after the aborted invasion of the promised land Caleb had the opportunity to demonstrate his faith in God by eliminating the Anakites who lived around his new hometown of Hebron (Jdg 1:20). The defeat of these giants was a sign that the land had finally been completely conquered.

21:1 Satan is not mentioned often in the OT. When he does appear, he is the adversary of someone beloved by God (Jb 1:6; 2:7; Zch 3:1-2). The parallel passage in 2 Samuel makes it clear that Satan would not have been able to cause trouble for **David** if God had not let him (2Sm 24:1). The census itself was not an infraction of God's law (Nm 1:2; 26:2). David succumbed to the sin of pride. This could have included thinking that the men of Israel were his to enumerate, not God's, and that he could take refuge in military strength rather than God's sovereignty. He also violated rules that God had given for carrying out a legitimate census. The law stipulated that each man who was counted had to donate a half-shekel to the temple treasury (Ex 30:11-16). God had decreed that a census taken without these provisions would be punished by a plague.

21:2 David placed **Joab** in charge of this project, reinforcing the idea that the purpose of the census was to evaluate military capability. The expression **from Beer-sheba to Dan** signifies the entire country from south to north.

21:3 Joab knew that what David was proposing would bring harm to everyone, so he objected strongly.

Joab left and traveled throughout Israel and then returned to Jerusalem. [5] Joab gave the total troop registration to David. In all Israel there were 1,100,000 swordsmen and in Judah itself 470,000 swordsmen. [6] But he did not include Levi and Benjamin in the count because the king's command was detestable to him. [7] This command was also evil in God's sight, so He afflicted Israel.

[8] David said to God, "I have sinned greatly because I have done this thing. Now, please take away Your servant's guilt, for I've been very foolish."[a]

David's Punishment

[9] Then[b] the LORD instructed Gad,[c] David's seer,[d] [10] "Go and say to David, 'This is what the LORD says: I am offering you three choices. Choose one of them for yourself, and I will do it to you.'"

[11] So Gad went to David and said to him, "This is what the LORD says: 'Take your choice: [12] three years of famine, or three months of devastation by your foes with the sword of your enemy overtaking you, or three days of the sword of the LORD—a plague on the land, the angel of the LORD bringing destruction to the whole territory of Israel.' Now decide what answer I should take back to the One who sent me."

[13] David answered Gad, "I'm in anguish. Please, let me fall into the LORD's hands because His mercies are very great,[e] but don't let me fall into human hands."

[14] So the LORD sent a plague on Israel, and

a21:8 2Sm 12:13
b21:9-17 2Sm 24:11-17
c21:9 1Ch 29:29
d1Sm 9:9; 2Sm 24:11; 1Ch 25:5
e21:13 Ps 51:1; 130:4,7
f21:15 Ex 32:14; 1Sm 15:11; 2Sm 24:16; Am 7:3,6; Jnh 3:9-10
g21:16 1Kg 21:27
h21:18-27 2Sm 24:18-25
i21:18 2Ch 3:1

70,000 Israelite men died. [15] Then God sent an angel to Jerusalem to destroy it, but when the angel was about to destroy the city,[A] the LORD looked, relented concerning the destruction,[f] and said to the angel who was destroying the people, "Enough, withdraw your hand now!" The angel of the LORD was then standing at the threshing floor of Ornan[B] the Jebusite.

[16] When David looked up and saw the angel of the LORD standing between earth and heaven, with his drawn sword in his hand stretched out over Jerusalem, David and the elders, clothed in •sackcloth,[g] fell down with their faces to the ground. [17] David said to God, "Wasn't I the one who gave the order to count the people? I am the one who has sinned and acted very wickedly. But these sheep, what have they done? My LORD God, please let Your hand be against me and against my father's family, but don't let the plague be against Your people."

David's Altar

[18] So the angel of the LORD ordered Gad[h] to tell David to go and set up an altar to the LORD on the threshing floor of Ornan the Jebusite.[i] [19] David went up at Gad's command spoken in the name of the LORD.

[20] Ornan was threshing wheat when he turned and saw the angel. His four sons, who were with him, hid themselves. [21] David came to Ornan, and when Ornan looked and saw David, he left the threshing floor and bowed to David with his face to the ground.

[22] Then David said to Ornan, "Give me this threshing-floor plot so that I may build an

---

A21:15 Lit but as he was destroying   B21:15-28 = Araunah in 2Sm 24:16-24

21:5 The number that **Joab** came up with was astounding—over one million **swordsmen** from **Israel** and close to half a million swordsmen from Judah. This is one of the cases in which the numbers in Chronicles are different than those in 2 Samuel 24. The argument is frequently made that the Chronicler exaggerated the numbers found in the earlier books. These numbers should not be seen as mutually exclusive. In 2 Samuel "fighting men" are counted, while Chronicles reports on the number of "swordsmen." We do not know to what extent those two descriptions overlap. If they do overlap, it would account significantly for the large numbers. Given that we do not have fuller information, it would be presumptuous to claim that the Chronicler had contradicted earlier accounts or sought to supply misleading numbers.

21:6 Joab refused to include the tribes of **Levi** and **Benjamin**. Perhaps he did not want God's judgment to fall on the tribe of priests or the tribe in whose territory the tabernacle stood.

21:7 Exactly as God had foretold in Ex 30:12, He punished this illegitimate census with a plague.

21:8 Even before the effects of the punishment were apparent, **David** realized he had done wrong; he pleaded with God to forgive him.

21:9-13 Gad and Nathan were the two prophets associated with David. Both of them had the unpleasant duty of announcing divine punishment on the king they served (2Sm 12:7). Gad presented David with three options for punishment: (1) **three years of famine**, (2) **three months of devastation** by his enemies, or (3) **three days of . . . plague on the land**. David chose the plague, reasoning that it most directly involved the hand of God and therefore had the most potential for mercy.

21:14 David had wanted to know how many **men** he had at his disposal. By divine retribution he wound up with **70,000** fewer than he had before the census was taken.

21:15-17 The spread of the **plague** is attributed to an **angel** from God (2Ch 32:21). The angel was about to inflict the plague on Jerusalem. He was fully visible, hovering above the **threshing floor of Ornan**. David and the elders of Israel saw the angel floating in a menacing posture with his **sword . . . stretched out**. David pleaded with God to spare the innocent people and let him suffer God's punishment.

21:20-24 Ornan and his **four sons** received two shocks: they saw the hovering angel, and the king himself showed up on their property. David asked Ornan to sell him this location at its **full price**—without receiving a king's discount—because

altar to the LORD on it. Give it to me for the
full price, so the plague on the people may be
stopped."
23 Ornan said to David, "Take it! My lord the
king may do whatever he wants.[A] See, I give
the oxen for the •burnt offerings, the threshing sledges for the wood, and the wheat for
the •grain offering—I give it all."
24 King David answered Ornan, "No, I insist
on paying the full price, for I will not take for
the LORD what belongs to you or offer burnt
offerings that cost me nothing."
25 So David gave Ornan 15 pounds of gold[B]
for the plot. 26 He built an altar to the LORD
there and offered burnt offerings and •fellow-
ship offerings. He called on the LORD, and He
answered him with fire from heaven on the
altar of burnt offering.[a]
27 Then the LORD spoke to the angel, and he
put his sword back into its sheath. 28 At that
time, David offered sacrifices there when he
saw that the LORD answered him at the threshing floor of Ornan the Jebusite. 29 The tabernacle of the LORD, which Moses made in the
desert, and the altar of burnt offering were at
the •high place in Gibeon,[b] 30 but David could
not go before it to inquire of God, because he
was terrified of the sword of the LORD's angel.
22 1 Then David said, "This is the house of
the LORD God, and this is the altar of
•burnt offering for Israel."[c]

David's Preparations for the Temple

2 So David gave orders to gather the foreigners that were in the land of Israel,[d] and he appointed stonecutters to cut finished stones for
building God's house.[e] 3 David supplied a great
deal of iron to make the nails for the doors
of the gateways and for the fittings, together
with an immeasurable quantity of bronze,[f]
4 and innumerable cedar logs because the
Sidonians and Tyrians had brought a large
quantity of cedar logs to David.[g] 5 David said,
"My son Solomon is young and inexperienced,
and the house that is to be built for the LORD
must be exceedingly great and famous and
glorious in all the lands.[h] Therefore, I must
make provision for it." So David made lavish
preparations for it before his death.
6 Then he summoned his son Solomon and
instructed him to build a house for the LORD
God of Israel. 7 "My son," David said to Solomon, "It was in my heart to build a house for
the name of •Yahweh my God,[i] 8 but the word
of the LORD came to me: 'You have shed much
blood and waged great wars. You are not to
build a house for My name because you have
shed so much blood on the ground before Me.[j]
9 But a son will be born to you; he will be a
man of rest. I will give him rest from all his
surrounding enemies,[k] for his name will be
Solomon,[C,l] and I will give peace and quiet to
Israel during his reign.[m] 10 He is the one who
will build a house for My name. He will be My
son, and I will be his father. I will establish the
throne of his kingdom over Israel forever.'[n]
11 "Now, my son, may the LORD be with you,[o]
and may you succeed in building the house
of the LORD your God, as He said about you.
12 Above all, may the LORD give you insight and
understanding when He puts you in charge
of Israel so that you may keep the law of the
LORD your God.[p] 13 Then you will succeed if you
carefully follow the statutes and ordinances
the LORD commanded Moses for Israel.[q] Be

[a] 21:26 Lv 9:24; Jdg 6:21
[b] 21:29 1Kg 3:4; 1Ch 16:39
[c] 22:1 1Ch 21:18-28; 2Ch 3:1
[d] 22:2 1Kg 9:20-21; 2Ch 2:17
[e] 1Kg 5:17-18
[f] 22:3 1Ch 29:2,7
[g] 22:4 1Kg 5:6-10
[h] 22:5 1Ch 29:1
[i] 22:7 2Sm 7:2-3; 1Ch 17:1-2; 28:2
[j] 22:8 1Ch 28:3
[k] 22:9 1Kg 4:20,25
[l] 2Sm 12:24-25
[m] 1Ch 28:5
[n] 22:10 2Sm 7:13-14; 1Ch 17:12-13; 28:6-7
[o] 22:11 1Ch 22:16
[p] 22:12 1Kg 3:9-12; 2Ch 1:10-12
[q] 22:13 1Ch 28:7

A 21:23 Lit *do what is good in his eyes* B 21:25 Lit *600 shekels of gold by weight* C 22:9 In Hb, the name Solomon sounds like "peace."

he was afraid the Lord might not stop the plague if he did not pay the full amount.

21:25 The price for the plot of land mentioned here is **15 pounds of gold**, while in 2Sm 24:24 it is said to have been 50 ounces of silver. This difference can be explained if David purchased the properties in simultaneous but distinct transactions. Perhaps the silver was the price for the threshing floor while the gold purchased the surrounding property. Ornan may very naturally have priced these items apart from one another.

21:26-27 While the setting for the sacrifice was being prepared, the angel apparently continued to hover over the scene. God signaled His acceptance of the sacrifice by sending **fire from heaven**. The angel stopped threatening Jerusalem.

21:28-30 At the end of this episode, the basic arrangement of sacred locations changed. The ark was still in Jerusalem, and the **tabernacle** continued in **Gibeon**, but from here on, David no longer used the tabernacle. He performed his sacrifices on this **threshing floor**. Perhaps he was afraid the angel might come back if he left this site.

22:1 Since the threshing floor of Ornan had become the place where David worshiped the Lord, he declared that on this exact site the temple would be built. This temporary **altar** would mark the location of the permanent altar.

22:2-4 The temple would require **stones**, metal, and wood for its construction. David conscripted the **foreigners** living in the land to work as slaves to do the heavy labor of cutting stones for the temple and the foundation walls.

22:5 This is the first time we learn that **Solomon** would succeed David and build the temple.

22:6-10 In a private conversation, David gave instructions to **Solomon** about the building of the temple. David's personal history of warfare and **shed . . . blood** disqualified him from being the temple builder. On the other hand, Solomon would enjoy **peace** and **rest**. His name meant "man of peace." He would be allowed to build the temple.

strong and courageous. Don't be afraid or discouraged.[a]

[14]"Notice I have taken great pains to provide for the house of the Lord—3,775 tons of gold, 37,750 tons of silver,[A,b] and bronze and iron that can't be weighed because there is so much of it. I have also provided timber and stone, but you will need to add more to them. [15]You also have many workers: stonecutters, masons, carpenters, and people skilled in every kind of work [16]in gold, silver, bronze, and iron—beyond number. Now begin the work, and may the Lord be with you."[c]

[17]Then David ordered all the leaders of Israel to help his son Solomon: [18]"The Lord your God is with you, isn't He? And hasn't He given you rest on every side?[d] For He has handed the land's inhabitants over to me, and the land has been subdued before the Lord and His people. [19]Now determine in your mind and heart to seek the Lord your God.[e] Get started building the Lord God's sanctuary so that you may bring the ark of the Lord's covenant and the holy articles of God to the temple that is to be built[f] for the name of Yahweh."[g]

The Divisions of the Levites

23 When David was old and full of days,[h] he installed his son Solomon as king over Israel.[i] [2]Then he gathered all the leaders of Israel, the priests, and the Levites. [3]The Levites 30 years old or more were counted;[j]

the total number of men was 38,000 by headcount.[k] [4]"Of these," David said, "24,000 are to be in charge of the work on the Lord's temple,[l] 6,000 are to be officers and judges,[m] [5]4,000 are to be gatekeepers, and 4,000 are to praise the Lord with the instruments that I have made for worship."[n]

[6]Then David divided them into divisions according to Levi's sons:[o] Gershom,[B] Kohath, and Merari.

[7]The Gershonites: Ladan and Shimei.
[8]Ladan's sons: Jehiel was the first, then Zetham, and Joel—three.
[9]Shimei's sons: Shelomoth, Haziel, and Haran—three. Those were the heads of the families of Ladan.
[10]Shimei's sons: Jahath, Zizah,[c] Jeush, and Beriah. Those were Shimei's sons—four. [11]Jahath was the first and Zizah was the second; however, Jeush and Beriah did not have many sons, so they became an ancestral house and received a single assignment.
[12]Kohath's sons: Amram, Izhar, Hebron, and Uzziel—four.
[13]Amram's sons:[p] Aaron and Moses.

Aaron, along with his descendants,[q] was set apart forever to consecrate the most holy things, to burn incense in the presence of *Yahweh,[r] to minister to Him, and to pro-

Cross references (center column)
a 22:13 Jos 1:6-9
b 22:14 1Ch 29:4
c 22:16 1Ch 22:11
d 22:18 1Ch 22:9; 23:25
e 22:19 1Ch 28:9
f 1Kg 8:6,21; 2Ch 5:7
g 1Ch 22:7
h 23:1 1Ch 29:28
i 23:3 Nm 4:3-49
j 1Ch 23:24
k 23:4 Ezr 3:8-9
l 1Ch 26:29
m 23:5 1Ch 15:16
n 23:6 1Ch 6:1
o 23:13 Ex 6:20
p Ex 28:1
q Ex 30:6-10

A 22:14 Lit 100,000 talents of gold and 1,000,000 talents of silver　　B 23:6 Lit Gershon　　C 23:10 LXX, Vg; MT reads Zina

---

22:16 David encouraged Solomon not to delay in completing the project.

22:18-19 David emphasized that after all the wars he had fought, there would now be a period of **rest**. The time was right for the leaders to help Solomon build a permanent temple.

23:1 David intended for **Solomon** to be **king** after him. He had made this known to Solomon and to his advisers. Now he acted on this declaration and officially made Solomon co-regent alongside him. Despite David's public acclaim of Solomon, there would be vigorous dispute of this decision (1Kg 1–2). David reiterated his will on the matter several times (1Kg 1:38-39).

23:2-3 David called a meeting of the country's **leaders** and the **priests** and **Levites**. The first part of this chapter is directed to those Levites **30 years old** or older who would be ready to step into their roles as soon as the temple was built. Later on (v. 24) the minimum age is lowered to 20 years old. This lower number would include those who would have been in training and were not yet eligible for actual service, but who needed to be listed in their applicable categories. A total of **38,000** men were ready to get to work. With that many people, everyone would be able to lead a normal life at home for most of the year and be required to spend just a short time in Jerusalem pursuing temple duties.

23:4-5 The Levites were divided along several lines. The largest number (**24,000**) consisted of those who were actu-

ally doing temple work. Six thousand men were given the job of prescreening individuals and their potential sacrifices to make sure that neither the persons nor what they brought as offerings were unclean, and that everything proceeded in accordance with the law. The **4,000 . . . gatekeepers** were the guards. In keeping with David's vision for worship in the future, a large corps of musicians (**4,000**) would be available.

23:6 Having established the broad, professional divisions, the same large group also was allocated into the three lines of descent from Levi's sons: **Gershom, Kohath, and Merari**.

23:7 The Chronicler assumes his usual method with genealogies in following a specific line and then backtracking.

23:9 This Shimei must have been a fourth son of **Ladan**, named after his uncle, whose descendants are named according to his three sons. Ladan was also called "Libni" (6:17).

23:11 **Jeush** and **Beriah** were counted as one because they **did not have many sons**.

23:12 **Kohath's** clan included the priestly line of Aaron. Other members of this clan challenged Aaron's exclusive right to the priesthood, only to find themselves swallowed up by the earth as God's punishment (Nm 16).

23:13-14 For the Chronicler, the descendants of **Aaron** were far more important at this point than those of **Moses**.

23:21-22 The line of **Eleazar** continued by virtue of his

nounce blessings in His name forever. [14] As for Moses the man of God,[a] his sons were named among the tribe of Levi.

[15] Moses' sons: Gershom and Eliezer.
[16] Gershom's sons: Shebuel was first.
[17] Eliezer's sons were Rehabiah, first; Eliezer did not have any other sons, but Rehabiah's sons were very numerous.
[18] Izhar's sons: Shelomith was first.
[19] Hebron's sons: Jeriah was first, Amariah second, Jahaziel third, and Jekameam fourth.
[20] Uzziel's sons: Micah was first, and Isshiah second.
[21] Merari's sons: Mahli and Mushi. Mahli's sons: Eleazar and Kish.
[22] Eleazar died having no sons, only daughters. Their cousins, the sons of Kish, married them.
[23] Mushi's sons: Mahli, Eder, and Jeremoth—three.

[24] These were the sons of Levi by their ancestral houses—the heads of families, according to their registration by name in the headcount—20 years old or more, who worked in the service of the LORD's temple.[b] [25] For David said, "The LORD God of Israel has given rest to His people,[c] and He has come to stay in Jerusalem forever. [26] Also, the Levites no longer need to carry the tabernacle or any of the equipment for its service"[d]— [27] for according to the last words of David, the Levites 20 years old or more were to be counted— [28] "but their duty will be to assist the sons of Aaron

with the service of the LORD's temple, being responsible for the courts and the chambers, the purification of all the holy things, and the work of the service of God's temple— [29] as well as the rows of the *bread of the Presence,[e] the fine flour for the *grain offering,[f] the wafers of unleavened bread, the baking,[A,g] the mixing,[h] and all measurements of volume and length.[i] [30] They are also to stand every morning to give thanks and praise to the LORD, and likewise in the evening. [31] Whenever *burnt offerings are offered to the LORD on the Sabbaths, New Moons,[j] and appointed festivals, they are to do so regularly in the LORD's presence according to the number prescribed for them.[k] [32] They are to carry out their responsibilities for the tent of meeting, for the holy place,[l] and for their relatives, the sons of Aaron,[m] in the service of the LORD's temple."

The Divisions of the Priests

24 The divisions of the descendants of Aaron were as follows: Aaron's sons were Nadab, Abihu, Eleazar, and Ithamar.[n] [2] But Nadab and Abihu died before their father, and they had no sons, so Eleazar and Ithamar served as priests.[o] [3] Together with Zadok[p] from the sons of Eleazar and Ahimelech from the sons of Ithamar, David divided them according to the assigned duties of their service. [4] Since more leaders were found among Eleazar's descendants than Ithamar's, they were divided accordingly: 16 heads of ancestral houses were from Eleazar's descendants, and eight heads of ancestral houses were from Ithamar's. [5] They[q] were assigned by lot, for

Cross references
[a]23:14 Dt 33:1; Ps 90 title
[b]23:24 Nm 10:17,21
[c]23:25 1Ch 22:9,18
[d]23:26 Nm 4:5,15; 7:9
[e]23:29 Lv 24:5-9
[f]Lv 6:20
[g]1Ch 9:31
[h]Lv 6:14-15; 7:12
[i]Ex 29:40; 30:13; Lv 19:35-36
[j]23:31 Is 1:13-14
[k]Lv 23:2-4
[l]23:32 Nm 1:53; 1Ch 9:27
[m]Nm 3:6-9,38
[n]24:1 Ex 6:23
[o]24:2 Lv 10:1-2
[p]24:3 1Ch 15:11; 24:6,31
[q]24:5-6 1Ch 24:31

A23:29 Lit *the griddle*

---

daughters and the **sons of Kish** marrying one another. In 24:29 we learn that one of Kish's sons was Jerahmeel. The other supplementary information from 24:26-27 is that Merari had a third son, Jaaziah, who also had three sons.

23:24 The Chronicler was not obsessed with names for their own sake. Their significance lay in the fact that on the basis of this information, Levites during his own time would be reminded of where they fit in with the general program of service to **the LORD's temple**.

23:25 Anticipating what would not be reality until the time of Solomon, David declared that **rest** had come to **Israel** because there would now be a permanent place for the ark and for worship.

23:26-29 There was no longer any reason for the **tabernacle** to be carried. Those Levites who had this as their main duty would receive new assignments. The matter of moving the ark would not come up again until hundreds of years later (2Ch 35:2).

23:30-31 The Chronicler again emphasizes David's institution of regular temple music. The musicians must perform on a daily basis as well as at the major sacrifices and on special occasions.

24:1 Among all the **divisions** established at this time, the most important one was for the priests, who were divided into 24 segments. These 24 groupings were based on **Aaron's** two surviving sons, **Eleazar** and **Ithamar**.

24:2 The Chronicler does not mention that **Nadab** and **Abihu** died prematurely because they defiled the tabernacle (Lv 10:1-2). It was more important to him that since they died without children, they had no descendants to include in the priestly divisions.

24:3 Two men were serving as high priest during the time of David: **Zadok** who officiated at the tabernacle, and **Ahimelech** who was in charge of the ark in Jerusalem. Ahimelech was the son of Abiathar and grandson of the Ahimelech who was slaughtered at the tabernacle by King Saul's troops. Both men had a legitimate claim to the priesthood, representing the lines of Eleazar and Ithamar, respectively, so both of their descendants were included in this list.

24:4 Since **Eleazar's** descendants outnumbered those of **Ithamar** by a ratio of two to one, it made sense that of the 24 divisions, Eleazar should get **16** shifts, and Ithamar only **eight**.

there were officers of the sanctuary and officers of God among both Eleazar's and Ithamar's descendants.

⁶The secretary, Shemaiah son of Nethanel, a Levite, recorded them in the presence of the king and the officers, Zadok the priest, Ahimelech*ᵃ* son of Abiathar, and the heads of families of the priests and the Levites. One ancestral house was taken for Eleazar, and then one for Ithamar.

7 The first lot fell to Jehoiarib, the second to Jedaiah,

8 the third to Harim, the fourth to Seorim,

9 the fifth to Malchijah, the sixth to Mijamin,

10 the seventh to Hakkoz, the eighth to Abijah,ᵇ

11 the ninth to Jeshua, the tenth to Shecaniah,

12 the eleventh to Eliashib, the twelfth to Jakim,

13 the thirteenth to Huppah, the fourteenth to Jeshebeab,

14 the fifteenth to Bilgah, the sixteenth to Immer,

15 the seventeenth to Hezir, the eighteenth to Happizzez,

16 the nineteenth to Pethahiah, the twentieth to Jehezkel,

17 the twenty-first to Jachin, the twenty-second to Gamul,

18 the twenty-third to Delaiah, and the twenty-fourth to Maaziah.

¹⁹These had their assigned duties for service when they entered the LORD's temple, according to their regulations, which they received from their ancestor Aaron, as the LORD God of Israel had commanded him.

The Rest of the Levites

²⁰As for the rest of Levi's sons:

from Amram's sons: Shubael; from Shubael's sons: Jehdeiah.

²¹From Rehabiah: from Rehabiah's sons: Isshiah was the first.

²²From the Izharites: Shelomoth; from Shelomoth's sons: Jahath.

²³Hebron'sᴬ,ᶜ sons: Jeriah the first, Amariah the second, Jahaziel the third, and Jekameam the fourth.

²⁴From Uzziel's sons: Micah; from Micah's sons: Shamir.

²⁵Micah's brother: Isshiah; from Isshiah's sons: Zechariah.

²⁶Merari's sons: Mahli and Mushi, and from his sons, Jaaziah his son.ᴮ

²⁷Merari's sons, by his son Jaaziah:ᶜ Shoham, Zaccur, and Ibri.

²⁸From Mahli: Eleazar, who had no sons.

²⁹From Kish, from Kish's sons: Jerahmeel.

³⁰Mushi's sons: Mahli, Eder, and Jerimoth.

Those were the sons of the Levites according to their ancestral houses. ³¹They also cast lots the same way as their relatives the sons of Aaron did in the presence of King David, Zadok, Ahimelech, and the heads of the families of the priests and Levites—the family heads and their younger brothers alike.ᵈ

The Levitical Musicians

25 David and the officers of the army also set apart some of the sons of ˙Asaph, Heman,ᵉ and Jeduthun, who were to prophesyᶠ accompanied by lyres, harps, and cymbals.ᵍ This is the list of the men who performed their service:

²From Asaph's sons: Zaccur, Joseph, Nethaniah, and Asarelah, sons of Asaph, under Asaph's

ᵃ24:6 2Sm 8:17; 1Ch 18:16; 24:31
ᵇ24:10 Neh 12:4; Lk 1:5
ᶜ24:23 1Ch 23:19
ᵈ24:31 1Ch 24:5-6
ᵉ25:1 1Ch 6:33,39
ᶠ2Kg 3:15
ᵍ1Ch 15:16; 25:6

ᴬ24:23 Some Hb mss, some LXX mss; other Hb mss omit *Hebron's*; 1Ch 23:19   ᴮ24:26 Or *Mushi; Jaaziah's sons: Beno.*
ᶜ24:27 Or *sons, Jaaziah: Beno,*

24:6An official **secretary** kept a record, and there were overseers from both family lines as well as dignitaries who did not have a vested interest in how this matter was handled.

24:7-19 Since there were about 24 divisions within a pool numbering in the tens of thousands, the list of 24 divisions was not necessarily permanent, if even David envisioned it that way (Ezr 2:36-39; Neh 12:1-7). Still, some priestly divisions such as that of **Abijah** survived almost a thousand years (Lk 1:5).

24:20-31 The other Levites were also divided into 24 groups, though it is not easy to identify exactly 24 names in this list. The ancestral names of these 24 groups cover several generations, so their origin is uneven. It is clear that these

groupings were based to a large degree on the head count of the descendants of the more prominent ancestors. The ability to supply a sufficient number of workers within their groups was a more important consideration than maintaining exact genealogical parallels.

25:1 Music was certainly a part of the worship of God before David's time, but he made it a regular part of everyday worship in the tabernacle and at the site of the ark and later in the temple. David, a man of war, was also a man of music. He placed the **sons of Asaph, Heman, and Jeduthun** (also known as Ethan) in charge of the music for the future temple. The Chronicler equates the musical ministry with prophecy.

25:2-5 This time the numbers work out smoothly. **Asaph** had

authority, who prophesied under the authority of the king. ³From Jeduthun:ᵃ Jeduthun's sons: Gedaliah, Zeri, Jeshaiah, Shimei,ᴬ Hashabiah, and Mattithiah—six—under the authority of their father Jeduthun, prophesying to the accompaniment of lyres, giving thanks and praise to the LORD. ⁴From Heman: Heman's sons: Bukkiah, Mattaniah, Uzziel, Shebuel, Jerimoth, Hananiah, Hanani, Eliathah, Giddalti, Romamti-ezer, Joshbekashah, Mallothi, Hothir, and Mahazioth. ⁵All these sons of Heman, the king's seer,ᵇ were given by the promises of God to exalt him,ᴮ for God had given Heman fourteen sons and three daughters.

⁶All these men were under their own fathers' authority for the music in the LORD's temple, with cymbals, harps, and lyres for the service of God's temple. Asaph, Jeduthun, and Heman were under the king's authority. ⁷They numbered 288 together with their relatives who were all trained and skillful in music for the LORD. ⁸They cast lots for their duties, young and old alike, teacher as well as pupil.ᶜ

⁹ The first lot for Asaph fell to Joseph,
  his sons, and his brothers—   12
  to Gedaliah the second: him,
  his brothers, and his sons—   12
¹⁰ the third to Zaccur, his sons,
  and his brothers—   12
¹¹ the fourth to Izri,ᶜ his sons,
  and his brothers—   12
¹² the fifth to Nethaniah, his sons,
  and his brothers—   12
¹³ the sixth to Bukkiah, his sons,
  and his brothers—   12
¹⁴ the seventh to Jesarelah, his sons,
  and his brothers—   12
¹⁵ the eighth to Jeshaiah, his sons,
  and his brothers—   12
¹⁶ the ninth to Mattaniah, his sons,
  and his brothers—   12

ᵃ25:3 1Ch 16:41-42   ᵇ25:5 1Sm 9:9; 2Sm 24:11; 1Ch 21:9   ᶜ25:8 1Ch 26:13

¹⁷ the tenth to Shimei, his sons,
  and his brothers—   12
¹⁸ the eleventh to Azarel,ᴰ his sons,
  and his brothers—   12
¹⁹ the twelfth to Hashabiah, his sons,
  and his brothers—   12
²⁰ the thirteenth to Shubael,
  his sons, and his brothers—   12
²¹ the fourteenth to Mattithiah,
  his sons, and his brothers—   12
²² the fifteenth to Jeremoth, his sons,
  and his brothers—   12
²³ the sixteenth to Hananiah,
  his sons, and his brothers—   12
²⁴ the seventeenth to Joshbekashah,
  his sons, and his brothers—   12
²⁵ the eighteenth to Hanani, his sons,
  and his brothers—   12
²⁶ the nineteenth to Mallothi,
  his sons, and his brothers—   12
²⁷ the twentieth to Eliathah, his sons,
  and his brothers—   12
²⁸ the twenty-first to Hothir, his sons,
  and his brothers—   12
²⁹ the twenty-second to Giddalti,
  his sons, and his brothers—   12
³⁰ the twenty-third to Mahazioth,
  his sons, and his brothers—   12
³¹ and the twenty-fourth to Romamti-
  ezer, his sons, and his brothers— 12.

The Levitical Gatekeepers

26 The following were the divisions of the gatekeepers:

From the Korahites: Meshelemiah son of Kore, one of the sons of *Asaph. ²Meshelemiah had sons: Zechariah the firstborn, Jediael the second, Zebadiah the third, Jathniel the fourth, ³Elam the fifth, Jehohanan the sixth, and Eliehoenai the seventh. ⁴Obed-edom also had sons: Shemaiah the firstborn, Jehozabad the second,

ᴬ25:3 One Hb ms, LXX; other Hb mss omit *Shimei*   ᴮ25:5 Or *Him*; lit *by the words of God to lift a horn*   ᶜ25:11 Variant of Zeri
ᴰ25:18 Variant of Uzziel

four sons, **Jeduthun** had six, and **Heman** had 14. Thus there were 24 natural divisions, and it turned out that the larger number of their relatives came to 288, thus creating 24 divisions of exactly 12 each. Lots were drawn to draft these Levites into their groups.

25:6-31 These 288 musicians were the leaders, who had a total of 4,000 men to draw on (23:5). The men of the 24 divisions reported to the 12 sons of the three head musicians, and they in turn took their directions directly from the king. For most other temple functions, the high priest was the

final authority, but since the order of music was primarily David's innovation, he did not relinquish control over this part of the ministry.

26:1 The following list of **gatekeepers** is limited to the two Levitical clans of Kohath and Merari. Since Asaph the musician belonged to the clan of Gershom (6:39-43), the **Asaph** mentioned here is a different person. Possibly "Asaph" here should read "Ebiasaph" instead, as does the LXX. Compare also "Ebiasaph" at 9:19.

26:4-8 Obed-edom was a gatekeeper by profession, though

Joah the third, Sachar the fourth, Nethanel the fifth, ⁵Ammiel the sixth, Issachar the seventh, and Peullethai the eighth,

for God blessed him.

⁶Also, to his son Shemaiah were born sons who ruled over their ancestral houses because they were strong, capable men.

⁷Shemaiah's sons: Othni, Rephael, Obed, and Elzabad; his brothers Elihu and Semachiah were also capable men. ⁸All of these were among the sons of Obed-edom with their sons and brothers; they were capable men with strength for the work—62 from Obed-edom.

⁹Meshelemiah also had sons and brothers who were capable men—18.

¹⁰Hosah,ᵃ from the Merarites, also had sons: Shimri the first (although he was not the firstborn, his father had appointed him as the first), ¹¹Hilkiah the second, Tebaliah the third, and Zechariah the fourth. The sons and brothers of Hosah were 13 in all.

¹²These divisions of the gatekeepers, under their leading men, had duties for ministering in the LORD's temple, just as their brothers did. ¹³They cast lots for each gate according to their ancestral houses, young and old alike.ᵇ

¹⁴The lot for the east gate fell to Shelemiah.ᴬ They also cast lots for his son Zechariah, an insightful counselor, and his lot came out for the north gate. ¹⁵Obed-edom's was the south gate, and his sons' lot was for the storehouses; ¹⁶it was the west gate and the gate of Shalle-

ᵃ26:10 1Ch 16:38
ᵇ26:13 1Ch 24:5,31; 25:8
ᶜ26:20 1Ch 26:24,26; 28:12; Ezr 2:69
ᵈ26:26 2Sm 8:11; 1Ch 18:7-11

cheth on the ascending highway for Shuppim and Hosah.

There were guards stationed at every watch. ¹⁷There were six Levites each dayᴮ on the east, four each day on the north, four each day on the south, and two pair at the storehouses. ¹⁸As for the court on the west, there were four at the highway and two at the court. ¹⁹Those were the divisions of the gatekeepers from the sons of the Korahites and Merarites.

The Levitical Treasurers and Other Officials

²⁰From the Levites, Ahijah was in charge of the treasuries of God's temple and the treasuries of what had been dedicated.ᶜ ²¹From the sons of Ladan, who were the sons of the Gershonites through Ladan and were the heads of families belonging to Ladan the Gershonite: Jehieli. ²²The sons of Jehieli, Zetham and his brother Joel, were in charge of the treasuries of the LORD's temple.

²³From the Amramites, the Izharites, the Hebronites, and the Uzzielites: ²⁴Shebuel, a descendant of Moses' son Gershom, was the officer in charge of the treasuries. ²⁵His relative through Eliezer: his son Rehabiah, his son Jeshaiah, his son Joram, his son Zichri, and his son Shelomith.ᶜ ²⁶This Shelomithᶜ and his brothers were in charge of all the treasuries of what had been dedicated by King David,ᵈ by the heads of families who were the commanders of thousands and of hundreds, and by the army commanders. ²⁷They dedicated part of the plunder from their battles for the repair of the LORD's temple. ²⁸All that Samuel the seer, Saul son of Kish, Abner son of Ner, and Joab son of Zeruiah had dedicated, along with ev-

---

ᴬ26:14 Variant of Meshelemiah   ᴮ26:17 LXX; MT omits *each day*   ᶜ26:25,26 Or *Shelomoth*

---

he joined the musicians during the transport of the ark to Jerusalem (15:21). Now that plans were being set up for permanent duties, he figured prominently among the guards, coming uniquely equipped with a clan of **62** family members. **Shemaiah**, his son, is a different person than Shemaiah the secretary whose father was Nethanel (24:6).

26:12 The Chronicler emphasizes that the service these **gatekeepers** performed was just as significant as the duties of those who led in worship. Without dedicated gatekeepers, the ministry of the temple could not proceed.

26:13 Rather than dividing the gatekeepers into 24 shifts, their assignments were based on which gates they were assigned to guard.

26:14-15 The selection of leaders for each gate was made in the context of family membership, but capability must have been an overriding consideration. In those cases where sons and fathers seemed to be equally qualified, they were not held back because they belonged to the same family. Both son and father were placed in command of their own gates. This was true for **Shelemiah**

and his son **Zechariah**, as well as for Obed-edom and **his** sons.

26:16 The **Shallecheth** was the **gate** designated for disposal of refuse and materials left over from animal sacrifices.

26:17-18 Guard duty was not limited to the gates of the temple. Obviously the **storehouses** needed protection, and guards were also installed outside the temple grounds, specifically on the road leading to the temple. The external temple guards could deal with problems outside the temple compound, such as unacceptable sacrificial animals.

26:20-21 The gatekeepers came primarily from the clans of Merari and Kohath. The **Gershonites** were assigned to watch over the **treasuries** of the **temple**. This included guarding temple resources from theft or vandalism, as well as accounting for them and keeping them stored. **Ahijah** supervised this work. The treasuries included long-term deposits, as well as the funds needed for day-to-day operation of the temple.

26:26-27 When all of these arrangements were made, there still was no **temple**. David gave money for the cause, and

erything else that had been dedicated, were in the care of Shelomith[A] and his brothers.

[29] From the Izrahites: Chenaniah and his sons had the outside duties[a] as officers and judges[b] over Israel. [30] From the Hebronites: Hashabiah[c] and his relatives, 1,700 capable men, had assigned duties in Israel west of the Jordan for all the work of the Lord and for the service of the king. [31] From the Hebronites: Jerijah[d] was the head of the Hebronites, according to the genealogical records of his ancestors. A search was made in the fortieth year of David's reign and strong, capable men were found among them at Jazer[e] in Gilead. [32] There were among Jerijah's relatives, 2,700 capable men who were heads of families. King David appointed them over the Reubenites, the Gadites, and half the tribe of Manasseh as overseers in every matter relating to God and the king.[f]

David's Secular Officials

27 This is the list of the Israelites, the heads of families, the commanders of thousands and the commanders of hundreds, and their officers who served the king in every matter to do with the divisions that were on rotated military duty each month through-out[B] the year. There were 24,000 in each division:

[2] Jashobeam son of Zabdiel was in charge of the first division,[g] for the first month; 24,000 were in his division. [3] He

was a descendant of Perez and chief of all the army commanders for the first month.

[4] Dodai the Ahohite was in charge of the division for the second month, and Mikloth was the leader; 24,000 were in his division.

[5] The third army commander, as chief for the third month, was Benaiah son of Jehoiada the priest; 24,000 were in his division. [6] This Benaiah was a mighty man among the Thirty and over the Thirty, and his son Ammizabad was in charge[c] of his division.

[7] The fourth commander, for the fourth month, was Joab's brother Asahel, and his son Zebadiah was commander after him; 24,000 were in his division.

[8] The fifth, for the fifth month, was the commander Shamhuth the Izrahite; 24,000 were in his division.

[9] The sixth, for the sixth month, was Ira son of Ikkesh the Tekoite; 24,000 were in his division.

[10] The seventh, for the seventh month, was Helez the Pelonite from the sons of Ephraim; 24,000 were in his division.

[11] The eighth, for the eighth month, was Sibbecai the Hushathite, a Zerahite; 24,000 were in his division.

[12] The ninth, for the ninth month, was Abiezer the Anathothite, a Benjaminite; 24,000 were in his division.

[13] The tenth, for the tenth month, was

---

a 26:29 Neh 11:16
b 1Ch 23:4
c 26:30 1Ch 27:17
d 26:31 1Ch 23:19
e 1Ch 6:81
f 26:32 2Ch 19:11
g 27:2-15 2Sm 23:8-30; 1Ch 11:11-31

A 26:28 Or *Shelomith*   B 27:1 Lit *that came in and went out month by month for all months of*   C 27:6 LXX; MT omits *in charge*

---

many of his high-ranking officials and military officers also gave to the temple fund. A large share of these contributions was derived from the **plunder** of various military victories.

26:28 Even before there was any talk of building the temple, the leaders of Israel were dedicating treasures to the tabernacle. The accumulated items went all the way back to the prophet **Samuel**, King **Saul**, his commander in chief **Abner**, David's general **Joab**, and David himself.

26:29 One other group of Levites needed to be organized. These were the **officers and judges** who would enforce the divine law in Israel.

26:32 The tribes on the eastern side of the Jordan River—**Reubenites . . . Gadites**, and **half . . . of Manasseh**—were already becoming isolated from the rest of Israel. Only at the very end of his reign was David able to provide a suitable teacher for these more remote tribes.

27:1 The Chronicler spends a lot of time on the various participants in the temple service but relatively little time on the secular officials and the army. The most important category of classification here is that there were 12 **divisions** composed of **24,000** soldiers **each**. Each of those units was on duty for one **month** out of the year during times of peace. During times of war, obviously everyone would be

mobilized. Many of the names here appear in the list of the "Thirty" in chapter 11. Since David reigned for 40 years, this list is something of an abstraction, with different personnel probably in charge at various times. In many cases two names are mentioned (e.g., 27:4). In these cases the second person may have been the first one's adjutant early on, and then later his successor.

27:2-3 As a descendant of **Perez . . . Jashobeam** belonged to the expanded clan within Judah to which David was linked.

27:4 This is one of those instances with two names, where **Mikloth** may have reported to **Dodai** at first, and then may have replaced him later (see note at v. 1).

27:5-6 We have seen **Benaiah** several times already. He was the most honored of the Thirty (11:22), and he was in charge of the Philistine mercenaries (18:17). Here we see him commanding one of the 12 units of **24,000** as well. His own son **Ammizabad** was second in command to him.

27:7 The idealized nature of this list is brought out by the fact that **Asahel** was killed during the civil war between David and Esh-baal (2Sm 2:23). So for all practical purposes, the command of this unit belonged to **Zebadiah** the entire time.

27:11 Sibbecai is familiar because he had killed one of the Philistine giants (19:4).

Maharai the Netophathite, a Zerahite; 24,000 were in his division.

¹⁴The eleventh, for the eleventh month, was Benaiah the Pirathonite from the sons of Ephraim; 24,000 were in his division.

¹⁵The twelfth, for the twelfth month, was Heldai the Netophathite, of Othniel's family;ᴬ 24,000 were in his division.

¹⁶The following were in charge of the tribes of Israel:
For the Reubenites, Eliezer son of Zichri was the chief official;
for the Simeonites, Shephatiah son of Maacah;
¹⁷for the Levites, Hashabiah son of Kemuel; for Aaron, Zadok;
¹⁸for Judah, Elihu, one of David's brothers; for Issachar, Omri son of Michael;
¹⁹for Zebulun, Ishmaiah son of Obadiah;
for Naphtali, Jerimoth son of Azriel;
²⁰for the Ephraimites, Hoshea son of Azaziah;
for half the tribe of Manasseh, Joel son of Pedaiah;
²¹for half the tribe of Manasseh in Gilead, Iddo son of Zechariah;
for Benjamin, Jaasiel son of Abner;
²²for Dan, Azarel son of Jeroham.
Those were the leaders of the tribes of Israel.ᵃ

²³David didn't count the men aged 20 or under, for the LORD had said He would make Israel as numerous as the stars of heaven.ᵇ ²⁴Joab son of Zeruiah began to count them, but he didn't complete it. There was wrath against Israel because of this census,ᶜ and the number

ᵃ27:22 1Ch 28:1
ᵇ27:23 Gn 15:5
ᶜ27:24 2Sm 24:1-15; 1Ch 21:1-7
ᵈ27:28 1Kg 10:27; 2Ch 1:15
ᵉ27:29 1Ch 5:16
ᶠ27:31 1Ch 5:10,18-21; 11:38
ᵍ27:33 2Sm 15:12
ʰ2Sm 15:32,37

was not entered in the Historical Recordᴮ of King David.

²⁵Azmaveth son of Adiel was in charge of the king's storehouses.
Jonathan son of Uzziah was in charge of the storehouses in the country, in the cities, in the villages, and in the fortresses.
²⁶Ezri son of Chelub was in charge of those who worked in the fields tilling the soil.
²⁷Shimei the Ramathite was in charge of the vineyards.
Zabdi the Shiphmite was in charge of the produce of the vineyards for the wine cellars.
²⁸Baal-hanan the Gederite was in charge of the olive and sycamore treesᵈ in the Judean foothills.ᶜ
Joash was in charge of the stores of olive oil.
²⁹Shitrai the Sharonite was in charge of the herds that grazed in Sharon,ᵉ while Shaphat son of Adlai was in charge of the herds in the valleys.
³⁰Obil the Ishmaelite was in charge of the camels.
Jehdeiah the Meronothite was in charge of the donkeys.
³¹Jaziz the Hagriteᶠ was in charge of the flocks.
All these were officials in charge of King David's property.

³²David's uncle Jonathan was a counselor; he was a man of understanding and a scribe. Jehiel son of Hachmoni attendedᴰ the king's sons. ³³Ahithophelᵍ was the king's counselor. Hushaiʰ the Archite was the king's friend. ³⁴After Ahithophel came Jehoiada son of Bena-

---

ᴬ27:15 Lit belonging to Othniel   ᴮ27:24 LXX; MT reads Number   ᶜ27:28 Or the Shephelah   ᴰ27:32 Lit was with

27:16 This verse begins a list of those who were **in charge** of each tribe. We can think of them as governors of the **tribes**. Gad and Asher are left out, perhaps because they were governed by the leaders of another tribe. The number of men on the list comes to 12 because each of the two halves of Manasseh is represented separately (vv. 20-21) and Levi has two representatives (v. 17).

27:17 One person was in charge of the tribe of Levi at large, but the descendants of **Aaron**—the priests—were represented separately by **Zadok**.

27:18 Elihu was one of **David's brothers**. He is not listed among David's six brothers in 2:13-15. This could mean that this name is a variation on Eliab, David's older brother, or that this is a seventh brother who is not mentioned earlier by the Chronicler. This second interpretation makes sense because 1Sm 16:10 refers to seven brothers of David.

27:23-24 A potential army would have been much larger than the 288,000 mentioned here, but the Chronicler reminds us that no exact total is available because the census that David had ordered was contrary to God's directions and was punished by the Lord (see chap. 21).

27:25-33 These verses tell us about David's cabinet. **Azmaveth** was secretary of the treasury. Under him overseeing the various treasury locations around the nation was **Jonathan son of Uzziah**. There were also cabinet posts for the oversight of agriculture and herding.

27:32 This verse describes the inner circle of David's advisers, though again this is not a permanent group. **Jonathan**, despite these accolades, makes his only appearance in the record at this point. **Jehiel**, who tended David's sons, must have had great skill at diplomacy and conflict resolution.

27:33 Ahithophel was so wise that his advice was consid-

iah,[a] then Abiathar.[b] Joab was the commander of the king's army.[c]

David Commissions Solomon to Build the Temple

28 David assembled all the leaders of Israel in Jerusalem:[d] the leaders of the tribes, the leaders of the divisions in the king's service, the commanders of thousands and the commanders of hundreds, and the officials in charge of all the property and cattle of the king and his sons, along with the court officials, the fighting men,[e] and all the brave warriors. [2]Then King David rose to his feet and said, "Listen to me, my brothers and my people. It was in my heart to build a house as a resting place for the ark of the Lord's covenant[f] and as a footstool[g] for our God. I had made preparations to build, [3]but God said to me, 'You are not to build a house for My name because you are a man of war and have shed blood.'[h]

[4]"Yet the Lord God of Israel chose me out of all my father's household[i] to be king over Israel forever.[j] For He chose Judah as leader,[k] and from the house of Judah, my father's household, and from my father's sons,[l] He was pleased to make me king over all Israel. [5]And out of all my sons[m]—for the Lord has given me many sons—He has chosen my son Solomon to sit on the throne of the Lord's kingdom over Israel.[n] [6]He said to me,[o] 'Your son Solomon is the one who is to build My house and My courts, for I have chosen him to be My son, and I will be his father. [7]I will establish his kingdom forever if he perseveres in keeping My commands and My ordinances as he is today.'[p]

[8]"So now in the sight of all Israel, the assembly of the Lord, and in the hearing of our God, observe and follow all the commands of the Lord your God so that you may possess this good land and leave it as an inheritance to your descendants forever.

[9]"As for you, Solomon my son, know the God of your father, and serve Him with a whole heart and a willing mind,[q] for the Lord searches every heart and understands the intention of every thought.[r] If you seek Him, He will be found by you, but if you forsake Him, He will reject you forever.[s] [10]Realize now that the Lord has chosen you to build a house for the sanctuary. Be strong, and do it."[t]

[11]Then David gave his son Solomon the plans[u] for the portico[v] of the temple and

---

Cross references (center column):

[a] 27:34 2Sm 8:18; 1Kg 1:8; 1Ch 11:22-24; 18:17; 27:5-6
[b] 1Sm 22:20-23; 1Kg 1:7; 2:26-27,35; 1Ch 15:11; 18:16; 24:6
[c] 1Ch 11:6
[d] 28:1 1Ch 23:2; 27:1-31
[e] 1Ch 11:10-47
[f] 28:2 2Sm 7:1-3; 1Ch 17:1-2; 22:7
[g] Ps 132:7; Is 66:1
[h] 28:3 1Ch 22:8
[i] 28:4 1Sm 16:6-13
[j] 1Ch 17:23,27
[k] Gn 49:8-10; 1Ch 5:2
[l] 1Sm 16:1
[m] 28:5 1Ch 3:1-9; 14:3-7
[n] 1Ch 22:9
[o] 28:6-7 2Sm 7:13-14; 1Ch 22:10
[p] 28:7 1Ch 22:13
[q] 28:9 1Kg 8:61; 1Ch 29:17-19
[r] Gn 6:5; 1Sm 16:7; Ps 139
[s] 2Ch 15:2; Jr 29:13
[t] 28:10 1Ch 22:13
[u] 28:11 Ex 25:9,40; 1Ch 28:19
[v] 1Kg 6:3

---

ered almost like hearing from God himself (2Sm 16:23). Unfortunately, none of this wisdom prevented him from joining Absalom's rebellion and ending his life with suicide (2Sm 17:23). **Hushai** helped David by infiltrating Absalom's inner circle and frustrating Ahithophel's advice (2Sm 17:14).

27:34 Although this passage does not mention Ahithophel's death, it is implied by mentioning his successors. First came **Jehoiada son of Benaiah** (not to be confused with the hero Benaiah son of Jehoiada); then came **Abiathar**, who may have been either the priest who was David's friend during the king's time in the wilderness, or his grandson.

28:1 For the Chronicler, the questions of who would be the next king and who would build the temple are synonymous. David called another meeting of **all the leaders of Israel** (the first meeting occurred in chap. 22) in which he reiterated his answer to both questions.

28:2 This last speech by David calls to mind the time many decades earlier when representatives of the tribes came to David and declared, "Here we are, your own flesh and blood" (11:1). Now David addressed the people as **my brothers**. He reminded the people that he wanted to build the temple for God's **ark** (17:1) and as a **footstool for our God**.

28:3 David disclosed to the people what he had already told Solomon—the reason he could not build the temple (22:8; see note at 22:6-10).

28:4-6 David knew he was king only because God had willed it, and that by the same sovereign will God had now **chosen . . . Solomon** as his successor.

28:7 David repeated the covenant that God had made with him—that through Solomon the house of David would con-tinue on the throne (17:12). This was a blessing that Solomon should never take for granted. Having been called to be king by the Lord, Solomon must demonstrate his divine calling by **keeping** God's **commands** and **ordinances**.

28:8 For the first time since God had given the promise to Abraham (Gn 15:8), the people were living in the entire territory that God had set aside for them. With a faithful king on the throne and the people following him, this state of affairs could last **forever**. However, the people as well as the king must keep **all** of God's **commands**.

28:9 David turned to Solomon and exhorted him to single-minded devotion to the Lord. He reminded Solomon that nothing else would do because God knows our motivations and intentions (Ps 139:1-6). David directed Solomon's commitment not just to the law, but to the Lord. The covenant that God had made with David about the continuation of his house on the throne did not overrule Solomon's obligation to walk with the Lord.

28:10 David exhorted Solomon to **be strong**. Building the temple would bring about a revision of Israel's system of worship. For hundreds of years, sacrifices had been permitted anywhere in the country under the direction of many different priests. With the coming of the temple, sacrifices would be restricted to Jerusalem only and priests who had been specifically designated for this purpose (Dt 12:5-7). Only a strong, powerful leader would be able to sell that idea to all 12 tribes. In fact, as soon as the leadership in Jerusalem became weak and the kingdom split, the sacrificial system fell apart as well (2Ch 13:9).

28:11-18 David made a public display of handing Solomon the information that is recorded in the previous six chapters.

its buildings, treasuries, upper rooms, inner rooms, and a room for the •mercy seat.[a] [12] The plans contained everything he had in mind[A,b] for the courts of the LORD's house, all the surrounding chambers, the treasuries[c] of God's house, and the treasuries for what is dedicated. [13] Also included were plans for the divisions of the priests and the Levites; all the work of service in the LORD's house; all the articles of service of the LORD's house; [14] the weight of gold for all the articles for every kind of service; the weight of all the silver articles for every kind of service; [15] the weight of the gold lampstands[d] and their gold lamps, including the weight of each lampstand and its lamps; the weight of each silver lampstand and its lamps, according to the service of each lampstand; [16] the weight of gold for each table for the rows of the •bread of the Presence and the silver for the silver tables; [17] the pure gold for the forks, sprinkling basins, and pitchers; the weight of each gold dish; the weight of each silver bowl; [18] the weight of refined gold for the altar of incense;[e] and the plans for the chariot of[B,f] the gold •cherubim that spread out their wings and cover the ark of the LORD's covenant.[g]

[19] David concluded, "By the LORD's hand on me, He enabled me to understand everything in writing, all the details of the plan."[C]

[20] Then David said to his son Solomon, "Be strong and courageous,[h] and do the work. Don't be afraid or discouraged, for the LORD

God, my God, is with you. He won't leave you or forsake you[i] until all the work for the service of the LORD's house is finished. [21] Here are the divisions of the priests and the Levites for all the service of God's house.[j] Every willing man of any skill[k] will be at your disposal for the work, and the leaders and all the people are at your every command."

Contributions for Building the Temple

[29] Then King David said to all the assembly, "My son Solomon—God has chosen him alone—is young and inexperienced. The task is great[l] because the temple will not be for man but for the LORD God.[m] [2] So to the best of my ability I've made provision for the house of my God:[n] gold for the gold articles, silver for the silver, bronze for the bronze, iron for the iron, and wood for the wood, as well as onyx, stones for mounting,[D] antimony,[E,o] stones of various colors, all kinds of precious stones, and a great quantity of marble. [3] Moreover, because of my delight in the house of my God, I now give my personal treasures of gold and silver for the house of my God over and above all that I've provided for the holy house: [4] 100 tons[F,p] of gold (gold of Ophir[q]) and 250 tons[G] of refined silver for overlaying the walls of the buildings, [5] the gold for the gold work and the silver for the silver, for all the work to be done by the craftsmen. Now who will volunteer to consecrate himself to the LORD today?"

Cross-references (center column)

[a]28:11 Ex 25:17-22
[b]28:12 1Ch 28:19
[c]1Ch 26:20,22,24,26; Ezr 2:69
[d]28:15 Ex 25:31-39
[e]28:18 Ex 30:1-10
[f]Ps 18:10
[g]Ex 25:18-22; 1Kg 8:6-7; 2Ch 5:7-8
[h]28:20 Jos 1:6-7; 1Ch 22:13; 2Ch 32:7
[i]Dt 31:6; Jos 1:5,9; Heb 13:5
[j]28:21 1Ch 28:13
[k]Ex 35:25-35; 36:1-2
[l]29:1 1Ch 22:5
[m]1Ch 29:19
[n]29:2 1Ch 22:3-5
[o]Ex 28:18
[p]29:4 1Ch 22:14
[q]1Kg 9:28

[A]28:12 Or he received from the Spirit   [B]28:18 Or chariot, that is; Ps 18:10; Ezk 1:5,15   [C]28:19 Hb obscure   [D]29:2 Or mosaic   [E]29:2 In Hb, the word antimony is similar to "turquoise"; Ex 28:18.   [F]29:4 Lit 3,000 talents   [G]29:4 Lit 7,000 talents

---

28:20 The king pointed out that **the LORD** would be with Solomon for the entire building project and beyond. The Lord does not always guarantee success, even for those ministries to which He has called us, but He will always be present with us.

29:1 Turning again to the assembled people, David drew attention to Solomon's youth and lack of experience in the face of the immensity of the task. The temple must honor God, so it must reflect the greatness of God in its operation.

29:2 Since in verse 3 David refers to his giving his own wealth, the donations mentioned in this verse must be a part of the spoils of war that David had collected.

29:3-4 After serving as king for 40 years, David had accumulated quite a personal treasure, out of which he made a large contribution, including **100 tons of gold.**

29:5b David equated making an offering with consecrating oneself to the Lord. God is never as interested in the material substance we contribute as He is in our devotion to Him, of which our offering is an expression.

29:9 Obviously, not everyone had abundance to share, but everyone shared in the joy.

29:10 David's lengthy prayer began by focusing on God. He

did not minimize the gifts of the people, but he knew that their generosity was a product of God's mercy.

---

ratsah

Hebrew Pronunciation	[rah TSAH]
HCSB Translation	please, accept
Uses in 1 Chronicles	3
Uses in the OT	48
Focus Passage	1 Chronicles 29:3,17

Ratsah may involve two root words. One involves *being pleased with* (Mc 6:7) things or people. *Ratsah* in worship indicates offerings *accepted by* or *acceptable to* God (Lv 1:4; 22:23). God also *accepts* certain people (Gn 33:10) and *delights in* them (Is 42:1). *Ratsah* suggests *enjoy* (Jb 14:6), *approve* (Ps 49:13), or *value* (Ps 147:10). It signifies *being popular* (Est 10:3), *making friends* (Ps 50:18), or *becoming a friend* (Jb 34:9). *Ratsah* means *take delight* (Ps 102:14), *show favor* (Ps 77:7), and *please* (2Ch 10:7). It represents *taking pleasure* (Ps 149:4). To *regain favor* (1Sm 29:4) is to *make oneself acceptable*. The participle can denote *most favored* (Dt 33:24). *Ratsah* involves willingness, *being pleased to* do something (Ps 40:13).

Another root may imply *pay* (Lv 26:41) or *make up for* (Lv 26:34). The intensive verb means *beg from* (Jb 20:10), and the passive-reflexive means *be pardoned* (Is 40:2).

⁶Then the leaders of the households, the leaders of the tribes of Israel, the commanders of thousands and of hundreds,ᵃ and the officials in charge of the king's workᵇ gave willingly. ⁷For the service of God's house they gave 185 tonsᴬ of gold and 10,000 gold coins,ᴮ,ᶜ 375 tonsᶜ of silver, 675 tonsᴰ of bronze, and 4,000 tonsᴱ of iron. ⁸Whoever had precious stones gave them to the treasury of the Lord's house under the care of Jehielᵈ the Gershonite. ⁹Then the people rejoiced because of their leaders' willingness to give, for they had given to the Lord with a whole heart.ᵉ King David also rejoiced greatly.

David's Prayer

¹⁰Then David praised the Lord in the sight of all the assembly. David said,

May You be praised, Lord God of our father Israel, from eternity to eternity. ¹¹Yours, Lord, is the greatness and the power and the glory and the splendor and the majesty, for everything in the heavens and on earth belongs to You. Yours, Lord, is the kingdom, and You are exalted as head over all.ᶠ ¹²Riches and honor come from You, and You are the ruler of everything.ᵍ Power and might are in Your hand, and it is in Your hand to make great and to give strength to all.ʰ ¹³Now therefore, our God, we give You thanks and praise Your glorious name.

¹⁴But who am I, and who are my people, that we should be able to give as generously as this? For everything comes from You, and we have given You only what comes from Your own hand.ᶠ ¹⁵For we live before You as foreigners and temporary residents in Your presence as were all our ancestors.ⁱ Our days on earth are like a shadow, without hope.ʲ ¹⁶*Yahweh our God, all this wealth that we've provided for building You a house for Your

ᵃ29:6 1Ch 27:1; 28:1
ᵇ1Ch 27:25-31
ᶜ29:7 Ezr 2:69; Neh 7:70
ᵈ29:8 1Ch 23:8
ᵉ29:9 1Kg 8:61; 1Ch 28:9; 2Co 9:7
ᶠ29:11 Mt 6:13; Rv 5:13
ᵍ29:12 2Ch 1:12
ʰ2Ch 20:6
ⁱ29:15 Lv 25:23; Heb 11:13
ʲJb 14:2,10-12
ᵏ29:17 1Ch 28:9
ˡPs 15:2
ᵐ29:19 Ps 72:1
ⁿ1Ch 29:2
ᵒ29:20 Jos 22:33
ᵖEx 4:31
ᵍ29:21 1Kg 8:62-63
ʳ29:22 1Ch 23:1
ˢ1Kg 1:33-39
ᵗ29:23 1Kg 2:12
ᵘ29:25 2Ch 1:1
ᵛ1Kg 3:13; 2Ch 1:12

holy name comes from Your hand; everything belongs to You. ¹⁷I know, my God, that You test the heartᵏ and that You are pleased with what is right.ˡ I have willingly given all these things with an upright heart, and now I have seen Your people who are presentᴳ here giving joyfully andᴴ willingly to You. ¹⁸Lord God of Abraham, Isaac, and Israel, our ancestors, keep this desire forever in the thoughts of the hearts of Your people, and confirm their hearts toward You. ¹⁹Give my son Solomon a whole heart to keep and to carry out all Your commands, Your decrees, and Your statutes,ᵐ and to build the temple for which I have made provision.ⁿ

²⁰Then David said to the whole assembly, "Praise the Lord your God." So the whole assembly praised the Lord God of their ancestors.ᵒ They bowed down and paid homage to the Lord and the king.ᵖ

²¹The following day they offered sacrifices to the Lord and *burnt offerings to the Lord: 1,000 bulls, 1,000 rams, and 1,000 lambs, along with their *drink offerings, and sacrifices in abundance for all Israel.ᵍ ²²They ate and drank with great joy in the Lord's presence that day.

The Enthronement of Solomon

Then, for a second time,ʳ they made David's son Solomon king; they anointed himⁱ as the Lord's ruler,ˢ and Zadok as the priest. ²³Solomon sat on the Lord's throne as king in place of his father David. He prospered, and all Israel obeyed him.ᵗ ²⁴All the leaders and the mighty men, and all of King David's sons as well, pledged their allegiance to King Solomon. ²⁵The Lord highly exalted Solomon in the sight of all Israelᵘ and bestowed on him such royal majesty as had not been bestowed on any king over Israel before him.ᵛ

ᴬ29:7 Lit *5,000 talents*   ᴮ29:7 Or *drachmas, or darics*   ᶜ29:7 Lit *10,000 talents*   ᴰ29:7 Lit *18,000 talents*   ᴱ29:7 Lit *100,000 talents*
ᶠ29:14 Lit *and from Your hand we have given to You*   ᴳ29:17 Lit *found*   ᴴ29:17 Or *now with joy I've seen Your people who are present here giving*   ⁱ29:22 LXX, Tg, Vg; MT omits *him*

29:11-13 David praised the Lord by declaring who He is and what He had done.

29:14-17 As David continued to focus on God, he acknowledged some important truths. It is not possible to **give** anything to God because God owns everything. David also declared that it is not possible to deceive God. He knows exactly who is giving **willingly** out of true devotion to Him and who is giving just to be seen by others. The key is a **heart** that wants to please God.

29:22 After sacrifices and a feast, David **made . . . Solomon king** for **a second time**. Commentators are divided on the

reference to a first coronation and how to interpret 23:1, which states that David installed Solomon as king. Some interpreters see this verse as a general summary of the events that are amplified in this chapter, but this mention of a second coronation could be an understated reference to the turmoil we read about in 1 Kings 1. This turmoil resulted in David declaring Solomon to be king as an emergency measure in opposition to Adonijah's bid for the throne. In either case, the transfer of power from David to Solomon proceeded smoothly, and he was acclaimed by all Israel.

29:25 The statement that God **bestowed** on Solomon **such royal majesty as had not been bestowed on any king over**

A Summary of David's Life

[26] David son of Jesse was king over all Israel.[a] [27] The length of his reign over Israel was 40 years; he reigned in Hebron for seven years and in Jerusalem for 33.[b] [28] He died at a ripe old age,[c] full of days,[d] riches, and honor, and his son Solomon became king in his place. [29] As for the events of King David's reign, from beginning to end, note that they are written in the Events of Samuel the Seer,[e] the Events of Nathan the Prophet,[f] and the Events of Gad the Seer,[g] [30] along with all his reign, his might, and the incidents that affected him and Israel and all the kingdoms of the surrounding lands.

[a]29:26 1Ch 18:14
[b]29:27 2Sm 5:4-5; 1Kg 2:11
[c]29:28 Gn 15:15; Ac 13:36
[d]1Ch 23:1
[e]29:29 1Sm 9:9
[f]2Sm 7:2-4; 12:1-7
[g]1Sm 22:5

Israel before him may sound odd since Solomon was preceded on Israel's throne by only two men: Saul and David. See also 2Ch 1:12. But the point is that God established Solomon as the standard for grandeur which had never been attained before and which never would be reached again.

29:26-30 These verses summarize David's **reign** and give an assessment of his success. This formula was applied to every king after David in 2 Chronicles. In each case the Chronicler gives a bottom-line evaluation of each king. For David he has nothing but praise. **David** lived a long life, indicative of a blessing from God, and he enjoyed **riches** and **honor**. The Chronicler also mentions several additional sources of information about David. These ancient books are likely lost, but they could be reflected in our books of 1 and 2 Samuel, which record the ministry of **Samuel . . . Nathan**, and **Gad** during the reign of David (1Sm 16:13; 2Sm 12:1; 24:11).

2 Chronicles

Introduction

See the Introduction to 1 Chronicles for the introductory material.

Outline of 2 Chronicles

I. The Reign of Solomon (1:1–9:31)
  A. Solomon builds the temple (1:1–7:22)
  B. The glory of Solomon's kingdom (8:1–9:31)

II. The Reigns of Solomon's Successors (10:1–36:23)
  A. Rehoboam (10:1–12:16)
  B. Abijah (13:1-22)
  C. Asa (14:1–16:14)
  D. Jehoshaphat (17:1–20:37)
  E. Jehoram (21:1-20)
  F. Ahaziah and Athaliah (22:1-12)
  G. Joash (23:1–24:27)
  H. Amaziah (25:1-28)
  I. Uzziah (26:1-23)
  J. Jotham (27:1-9)
  K. Ahaz (28:1-27)
  L. Hezekiah (29:1–32:33)
  M. Manasseh (33:1-20)
  N. Amon (33:21-25)
  O. Josiah (34:1–35:27)
  P. Last kings of Judah (36:1-23)

Solomon's Request for Wisdom

1 Solomon son of David strengthened his hold on his kingdom.[a] The LORD his God was with him and highly exalted him.[b] [2] Then Solomon spoke to all Israel, to the commanders of thousands and of hundreds, to the judges, and to every leader in all Israel—the heads of the families.[c] [3] Solomon and the whole assembly with him went to the •high place that was in Gibeon[d] because God's tent of meeting, which the LORD's servant Moses had made[e] in the wilderness, was there. [4] Now David had brought the ark of God from Kiriath-jearim to the place[A] he had set up for it, because he had pitched a tent for it in Jerusalem,[f] [5] but he put[B] the bronze altar, which Bezalel son of Uri, son of Hur, had made,[g] in front of the LORD's tabernacle. Solomon and the assembly inquired of Him[C] there. [6] Solomon offered sacrifices there in the LORD's presence on the bronze altar at the tent of meeting; he offered 1,000 •burnt offerings on it.[h]

[7] That night[i] God appeared to Solomon and said to him: "Ask. What should I give you?"

[8] And Solomon said to God: "You have shown great and faithful love to my father David, and You have made me king in his place.[j] [9] LORD God, let Your promise to my father David now come true.[k] For You have made me king over a people as numerous as the dust of the earth.[l] [10] Now grant me wisdom and knowledge so that I may lead these people,[m] for who can judge this great people of Yours?"

[11] God said to Solomon, "Since this was in your heart, and you have not requested riches, wealth, or glory, or for the life of those who hate you, and you have not even requested long life, but you have requested for yourself wisdom and knowledge that you may judge My people over whom I have made you king, [12] wisdom and knowledge are given to you. I will also give you riches, wealth, and glory, unlike what was given to the kings who were before you, or will be given to those after you."[n] [13] So Solomon went to Jerusalem from[D] the high place that was in Gibeon in front of the tent of meeting, and he reigned over Israel.

Solomon's Horses and Wealth

[14] Solomon[o] accumulated 1,400 chariots and 12,000 horsemen,[p] which he stationed in the chariot cities[q] and with the king in Jerusalem. [15] The king made silver and gold as common in Jerusalem as stones, and he made cedar as abundant as sycamore in the Judean foothills. [16] Solomon's horses came from Egypt and Kue.[E] The king's traders would get

Cross references

[a] 1:1 1Kg 2:12,46
[b] 1Ch 29:25
[c] 1:2 1Ch 28:1
[d] 1:3 1Kg 3:4
[e] Ex 36:8-38
[f] 1:4 1Ch 13:1-14; 15:25–16:1
[g] 1:5 Ex 31:2-11; 38:1-7
[h] 1:6 1Kg 3:4
[i] 1:7-13 1Kg 3:5-15
[j] 1:8 1Ch 28:5
[k] 1:9 2Sm 7:12-16
[l] Gn 13:16; 22:17
[m] 1:10 1Sm 18:16; 2Sm 5:2
[n] 1:12 1Ch 29:25; 2Ch 9:22
[o] 1:14-17 1Kg 10:26-29; 2Ch 9:25-28
[p] 1:14 1Kg 4:26
[q] 1Kg 9:19

A 1:4 Vg; MT omits the place   B 1:5 Some Hb mss, Tg, Syr; other Hb mss, LXX, Vg read but there was   C 1:5 Or it   D 1:13 LXX, Vg; MT reads to   E 1:16 = Cilicia

1:1 At one point 1 and 2 Chronicles were bound together as one scroll, but here we come to a meaningful breaking point. The Chronicler starts afresh with his story, beginning by reviewing a number of details in the process. If we think of Chronicles as the "Gospel According to Ezra," then what follows in the reign of Solomon must be seen as an expression of God's grace because **the LORD . . . was with** Solomon and **highly exalted him**. This story is not just about a competent king, but the God who supported him. As a consequence, Solomon **strengthened his hold**. Solomon, though conscious of the need for military preparation, was not a military man. He united the people in other ways, primarily by fortifying the kingdom and generating a number of building projects, not the least of which was the temple.

1:2 We are not given the text of Solomon's inauguration address, but the fact that he gave one shows his acumen as a leader. As he set out to celebrate his new reign, he made sure that representatives from the entire kingdom were involved in the celebration.

1:3-5 The Chronicler reminds us of the ambivalent situation regarding the sacred sites in Israel. The tabernacle, the central place of worship, was still in **Gibeon**. This included the altar made by **Bezalel** in the time of Moses (Ex 38:1-3). The **bronze altar** was actually a wooden altar covered with a bronze plate.

1:6 Solomon presented **1,000** offerings, following a practice established by David (1Ch 29:21). All of Solomon's sacrifices were **burnt offerings**, meaning that all the animals were consumed by fire. In order to carry out all these sacrifices

within one day, dozens of animals must have been offered simultaneously.

1:10 In response to an open invitation from God (v. 7), Solomon asked for **wisdom**, demonstrating that he already had remarkable wisdom. Solomon was only about 20 years old. He had shown himself capable in asserting his leadership in eliminating Adonijah, his rival, and in uniting the priesthood in the person of Zadok (1Kg 1–2).

1:11-12 God was pleased with Solomon's request, and added a bonus—**riches, wealth, and glory**. To this day, the name of Solomon is synonymous with wisdom and wealth.

1:13 Solomon had honored the holy site that he was about to dismantle. The mention of the **tent of meeting** emphasizes the contrast to the new order he was about to initiate (2:1ff).

1:14 This is the first of two listings of Solomon's wealth (9:13-28). A total of **1,400 chariots and 12,000 horsemen** was an extremely large amount. Pharaoh, in pursuing the Israelites at the exodus, had 600 chariots (Ex 14:7) and Sisera of Hazor had 900 (Jdg 4:3). The size of Solomon's army is particularly noteworthy since he was not known as a man of war.

1:15 Solomon's own wealth devalued some of the most precious resources of the ancient world. This state of affairs did not outlive Solomon's reign; his wealth apparently did not benefit the common people in the long run.

1:16-17 Solomon invested heavily in **horses** and chariots as a basis for increasing his own wealth. He bought horses

them from Kue at the going price. [17]A chariot could be imported from Egypt for 15 pounds[A] of silver and a horse for about four pounds.[B] In the same way, they exported them to all the kings of the Hittites and to the kings of Aram through their agents.

Solomon's Letter to Hiram

2[c] Solomon decided to build a temple for the name of •Yahweh and a royal palace for himself,[a] [2D]so he assigned 70,000 men as porters, 80,000 men as stonecutters in the mountains, and 3,600 as supervisors over them.[b]

[3]Then Solomon sent word to King Hiram[E,c] of Tyre:[d]

Do for me what you did for my father David. You sent him cedars to build him a house to live in.[e] [4]Now I am building a temple for the name of Yahweh my God in order to dedicate it to Him for burning fragrant incense before Him,[f] for displaying the rows of the •bread of the Presence continuously,[g] and for sacrificing •burnt offerings for the morning and the evening,[h] the Sabbaths[i] and the New Moons, and the appointed festivals of the LORD our God. This is ordained for Israel

forever. [5]The temple that I am building will be great, for our God is greater than any of the gods.[j] [6]But who is able to build a temple for Him, since even heaven and the highest heaven cannot contain Him?[k] Who am I then that I should build a temple for Him except as a place to burn incense before Him? [7]Therefore, send me a craftsman who is skilled in engraving to work with gold, silver, bronze, and iron, and with purple, crimson, and blue yarn. He will work with the craftsmen who are with me in Judah and Jerusalem,[l] appointed by my father David.[m] [8]Also, send me cedar, cypress, and algum[F,n] logs from Lebanon, for I know that your servants know how to cut the trees of Lebanon. Note that my servants will be with your servants[o] [9]to prepare logs for me in abundance because the temple I am building will be great and wonderful. [10]I will give your servants, the woodcutters who cut the trees, 100,000 bushels[G] of wheat flour, 100,000 bushels[G] of barley, 110,000 gallons[H] of wine, and 110,000 gallons[H] of oil.

Hiram's Reply

[11]Then King Hiram of Tyre wrote a letter[I] and sent it to Solomon:

Cross references

[a]2:1 1Kg 5:5; 2Ch 2:12
[b]2:2 1Kg 5:15-16; 9:23; 2Ch 2:18; 8:10
[c]2:3 2Sm 5:11; 1Kg 5:1-2
[d]2:3-10 1Kg 5:2-6,10-11
[e]2:3 1Ch 14:1
[f]2:4 Ex 30:7
[g]Ex 25:30
[h]Ex 29:38-42
[i]Nm 28:9-10
[j]2:5 Ex 15:11; 1Ch 16:25
[k]2:6 1Kg 8:27; 2Ch 6:18
[l]2:7 Ex 31:3-5; 2Ch 2:13-14
[m]1Ch 22:14-16; 28:21
[n]2:8 1Kg 10:11-12
[o]2:8-9 2Ch 9:10-11

A1:17 Lit *600 shekels*   B1:17 Lit *150 shekels*   C2:1 2Ch 1:18 in Hb   D2:2 2Ch 2:1 in Hb   E2:3 Some Hb mss, LXX, Syr, Vg; other Hb mss read *Huram*; 2Sm 5:11; 1Kg 5:1-2   F2:8 = almug in 1Kg 10:11-12   G2:10 Lit *20,000 cors*   H2:10 Lit *20,000 baths*   I2:11 Lit *Tyre said in writing*

from **Egypt** and **Kue**, a region in Turkey, and then sold them to the **Hittites** and the Arameans. Although these items are mentioned here as representative of Solomon's material success, they were also a violation of God's ordinance. The law stated that a future king should not acquire horses from Egypt or accumulate large amounts of silver (Dt 17:16-17).

2:1 David assumed that Solomon would build the **temple**, and he made plans for this (1Ch 17:1). Solomon not only affirmed David's assumption in his own decisions, but he planned the temple and his own **palace** on a much more impressive scale than David's blueprints.

2:2 In verses 17-18, where the same list is repeated, we learn that the workers conscripted by Solomon were aliens living in Israel. At this time, Solomon did not force any Israelites to work on his building projects (10:4). The first part of the project was to construct the walls out of large blocks of stone. These stones were quarried **in the mountains**. By shaping this work off site, the laborers had more space to work on site, plus they reduced the weight of each block to its minimum, making transportation easier.

2:3 Despite all the materials that David had accumulated, Solomon needed more, particularly cedar wood. He also needed expert advice on how to work with these materials. So he consulted his father's old trading partner, **King Hiram of Tyre**.

2:4 Hiram was a shrewd trader. In proposing a business deal to Hiram, Solomon made sure he was informed about the importance of this project. He put Hiram on notice that

if he cut corners with the materials he supplied, he would be offending **Yahweh**. Solomon's letter briefly described the functions of the temple.

2:5 Solomon emphasized to Hiram that the greatness of this **temple** should exceed any other temple because **God** was **greater** than any other **gods**. If this statement was offensive to Hiram, who worshiped his own gods, his response did not show it (v. 12).

2:6 In contrast to pagan gods whose presence was limited to their temples, Yahweh was not confined to this temple. He filled all of **heaven** and earth.

2:7 Solomon asked Hiram for a craftsman who could work with precious metals as well as **bronze** and **iron**. In addition, he should be able to work with dyed textiles. The color **purple**, considered the color of royalty, was one of the chief exports of the Phoenicians. Solomon specified that this craftsman would be in charge of laborers who had been appointed by David. Solomon did not want Hiram to send a large labor force that might pose a military threat.

2:8-9 Not only did the Phoenicians have ready access to the wood that Solomon asked for, but they had more experience than the Israelites in working with it. Solomon sent Israelite **servants** to help with the labor and perhaps to assure the quality of the **logs**.

2:10 Tyre excelled in trade, but largely depended on other nations for food (Ac 12:20).

2:11-12 Hiram's response showed he understood that he was not just dealing with Solomon but with Solomon's God.

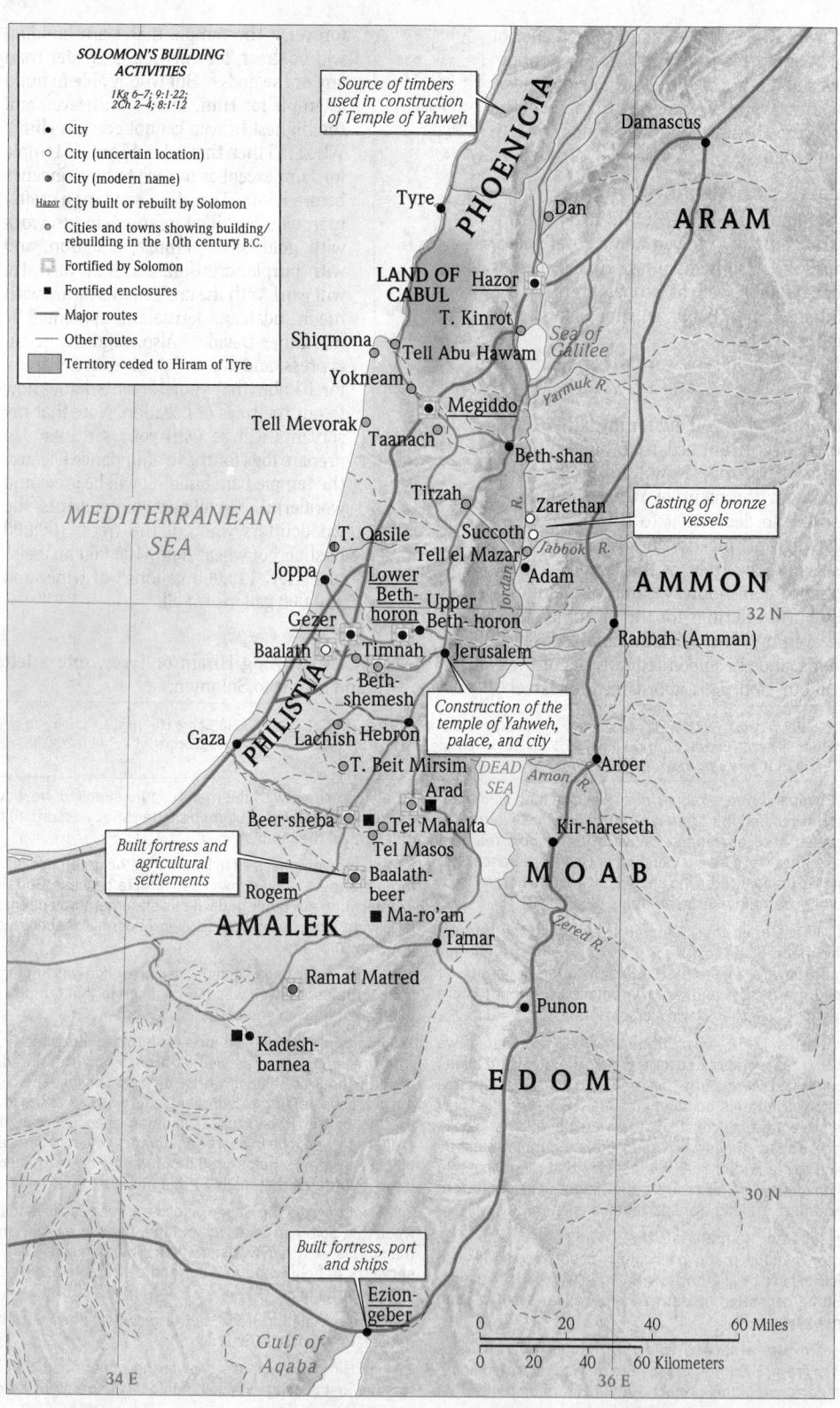

SOLOMON'S BUILDING ACTIVITIES

1Kg 6–7; 9:1-22;
2Ch 2–4; 8:1-12

- City
○ City (uncertain location)
● City (modern name)
Hazor City built or rebuilt by Solomon
○ Cities and towns showing building/
  rebuilding in the 10th century B.C.
☐ Fortified by Solomon
■ Fortified enclosures
— Major routes
— Other routes
░ Territory ceded to Hiram of Tyre

Source of timbers used in construction of Temple of Yahweh

PHOENICIA

Damascus

Tyre

Dan

ARAM

LAND OF CABUL
Hazor

T. Kinrot

Sea of Galilee

Shiqmona
Tell Abu Hawam
Yokneam

Yarmuk R.

Megiddo

Tell Mevorak
Taanach

Beth-shan

MEDITERRANEAN SEA

Tirzah

Zarethan

Casting of bronze vessels

Succoth

Jabbok R.

T. Qasile
Tell el Mazar
Adam

Joppa

AMMON

Lower Beth-horon
Upper Beth-horon

Gezer

Jerusalem

32 N

Rabbah (Amman)

Baalath
Timnah

PHILISTIA

Beth-shemesh

Construction of the temple of Yahweh, palace, and city

Gaza
Lachish Hebron

DEAD SEA

Aroer

Arnon R.

T. Beit Mirsim

Arad

Kir-hareseth

Beer-sheba
Tel Mahalta

Tel Masos

MOAB

Built fortress and agricultural settlements

Baalath-beer

Rogem

Ma-ro'am
Tamar

Zered R.

AMALEK

Ramat Matred

Punon

Kadesh-barnea

EDOM

30 N

Built fortress, port and ships

Ezion-geber

0   20   40   60 Miles

0   20   40   60 Kilometers

Gulf of Aqaba

34 E

36 E

Because the LORD loves His people, He set you over them as king.[a]

12Hiram also said:

May the LORD God of Israel, who made the heavens and the earth,[b] be praised! He gave King David a wise son with insight and understanding,[c] who will build a temple for the LORD and a royal palace for himself.[d] 13I have now sent Huram-abi,[A] a skillful man who has understanding.[e] 14He is the son of a woman from the daughters of Dan. His father is a man of Tyre. He knows how to work with gold, silver, bronze, iron, stone, and wood, with purple, blue, crimson yarn, and fine linen. He knows how to do all kinds of engraving and to execute any design that may be given him. I have sent him to be with your craftsmen and the craftsmen of my lord, your father David. 15Now, let my lord send the wheat, barley, oil, and wine to his servants as promised.[f] 16We will cut logs from Lebanon, as many as you need, and bring them to you as rafts by sea to Joppa. You can then take them up to Jerusalem.[g]

Solomon's Work Force

17Solomon took a census of all the foreign men in the land of Israel, after the census that his father David had conducted,[h] and the

a 2:11 1Kg 10:9; 2Ch 9:8
b 2:12 Ps 33:6; 102:25
c 1Kg 5:7
d 2Ch 2:1
e 2:13-14 1Kg 7:14
f 2:15 2Ch 2:10
g 2:16 1Kg 5:8-9
h 2:17 2Sm 24:1-9; 1Ch 21:1-5
i 2:18 1Kg 5:15-16; 2Ch 2:2
j 3:1-4 1Kg 6:1-3
k 3:1 Gn 22:2
l 3:7 1Kg 6:20-22
m 1Kg 6:29-35
n 3:8 1Kg 6:16

total was 153,600. 18Solomon made 70,000 of them porters, 80,000 stonecutters in the mountains, and 3,600 supervisors to make the people work.[i]

Building the Temple

3 Then Solomon began[j] to build the LORD's temple in Jerusalem on Mount Moriah[k] where the LORD[B] had appeared to his father David, at the site David had prepared on the threshing floor of Ornan[C] the Jebusite. 2He began to build on the second day of the second month in the fourth year of his reign. 3These are Solomon's foundations[D] for building God's temple: the length[E] was 90 feet,[F] and the width 30 feet.[G] 4The portico, which was across the front extending across the width of the temple, was 30 feet[G] wide; its height was 30 feet;[H,G] he overlaid its inner surface with pure gold. 5The larger room[I] he paneled with cypress wood, overlaid with fine gold, and decorated with palm trees and chains. 6He adorned the temple with precious stones for beauty, and the gold was the gold of Parvaim. 7He overlaid the temple—the beams, the thresholds, its walls and doors—with gold,[l] and he carved •cherubim on the walls.[m]

The Most Holy Place

8Then he made the most holy place; its length corresponded to the width of the temple, 30 feet,[G] and its width was 30 feet.[G,n] He

A 2:13 Lit Huram my father   B 3:1 LXX; Tg reads the Angel of the LORD; MT reads He   C 3:1 = Araunah in 2Sm 24:16-24   D 3:3 Tg reads The measurements which Solomon decreed   E 3:3 Lit length—cubits in the former measure—   F 3:3 Lit 60 cubits   G 3:3,4,8 Lit 20 cubits   H 3:4 LXX, Syr; MT reads 120 cubits   I 3:5 Lit The house

Hiram's praise of **the LORD** should not be taken to mean that he was a true follower of God. People of that time generally believed that each nation had its own god who was effective for his people, but who would have no jurisdiction over other geographic areas (2Kg 5:17). Hiram probably sincerely applauded the God of the Israelites, though Yahweh would have had no personal value to him as a non-Israelite.

2:13-14 Hiram proposed to send Solomon a man named **Huram-abi**. Son of an Israelite mother and a Tyrian father, Huram-abi was competent in all the skills specified by Solomon and presumably understood Israelite religion. Solomon was in ultimate control of the building project, and Huram-abi, the Phoenician, was next in charge. A number of Israelite supervisors oversaw the large force of non-Israelites and their foremen.

2:16 The Phoenicians were among the early pioneers of seafaring. They were willing to risk the dangerous but efficient method of shipping logs as **rafts** along the Mediterranean coast. Then they would be transported overland to **Jerusalem**.

2:17-18 On Solomon's forced laborers, see note at verse 2.

3:1 **Mount Moriah** was the place God had designated after David saw an angel and a plague was averted (1Ch 21).

3:2 Solomon began the actual building of the temple early in

the **fourth year of his reign**. This means he had not waited long after his coronation to start gathering building materials.

3:3-4 Even though the **temple** became complex in its details, the basic plan was straightforward. The outline of the temple was a rectangle, **30 feet by 90 feet**. Its entryway was a 30-foot tall portal that covered the entire width of the building. The most holy place, or holy of holies, was a 30-foot cube that constituted the far end, leaving a room 30 feet wide and 60 feet long as the holy place. This seems small, considering the crowds that would visit the temple, but sacrifices would be offered in the courtyard outside the temple. Only priests would enter the holy place, and then only twice a day—in the morning and in the evening—and only the high priest could enter the most holy place, only once a year.

3:5 The decorations of the holy place included **palm trees**. The use of botanical motifs went back to the tabernacle (Ex 37:20). God wants us to appreciate the beauty He has instilled in His creation. Embellishment of sacred places with natural objects is wrong only when they become objects of worship or detract from the true worship of God.

3:8-9 The **most holy place** was covered with **gold**. Gold is very heavy, but it is also soft. The easiest way to maintain the gold on the **ceiling** would have been to apply it to the ceiling beams before they were put in place. The golden **nails** must

overlaid it with 45,000 pounds[A] of fine gold. [9] The weight of the nails was 20 ounces[B] of gold, and he overlaid the ceiling with gold.

[10] He made[a] two cherubim of sculptured work, for the most holy place, and he overlaid them with gold. [11] The overall length of the wings of the cherubim was 30 feet:[C] the wing of one was 7¹/₂ feet,[D] touching the wall of the room; its other wing was 7¹/₂ feet,[D] touching the wing of the other cherub. [12] The wing of the other[E] cherub was 7¹/₂ feet,[D] touching the wall of the room; its other wing was 7¹/₂ feet,[D] reaching the wing of the other cherub. [13] The wingspan of these cherubim was 30 feet.[C] They stood on their feet and faced the larger room.[F]

[14] He made the veil of blue, purple, and

[a] 3:10-13 1Kg 6:23-28
[b] 3:14 Ex 26:31
[c] 3:15-17 1Kg 7:15-22; 2Kg 25:17; Jr 52:21-23
[d] 3:16 1Kg 6:21; 7:17
[e] 4:1 Ex 27:1-2; 2Kg 16:14

crimson yarn and fine linen, and he wove cherubim into it.[b]

The Bronze Pillars

[15] In front of the temple[c] he made two pillars, each 27 feet[G,H] high. The capital on top of each was 7¹/₂ feet[D] high. [16] He had made chainwork in the inner sanctuary and also put it on top of the pillars.[d] He made 100 pomegranates and fastened them into the chainwork. [17] Then he set up the pillars in front of the sanctuary, one on the right and one on the left. He named the one on the right Jachin[I] and the one on the left Boaz.[J]

The Altar, Reservoir, and Basins

4 He made a bronze altar[e] 30 feet[C] long, 30 feet[C] wide, and 15 feet[K] high.

[A] 3:8 Lit *600 talents*   [B] 3:9 Lit *50 shekels*   [C] 3:11,13;4:1 Lit *20 cubits*   [D] 3:11,12,15 Lit *five cubits*   [E] 3:12 Syr, Vg; MT reads *the one*   [F] 3:13 Lit *the house*   [G] 3:15 Hb uncertain   [H] 3:15 Lit *35 cubits*   [I] 3:17 = He Will Establish   [J] 3:17 = Strength Is in Him   [K] 4:1 Lit *10 cubits*

---

have had an iron core, or they could not have sustained hammer blows or held their place given the softness of gold.

3:10-13 On the back wall of the most holy place were **two cherubim**, each with two wings **7½ feet** long, adding up to **30 feet** in width, the exact width of the wall.

3:14 The curtain or **veil** became the highest expression of Phoenician art, with its fabric of many colors, including **blue, purple, and crimson**.

3:15-17 The design of the **temple** followed that of the tabernacle, though the temple was constructed from more permanent material. Solomon did add two new structures—**two pillars** that were taller than the portico. Each of

these pillars had a highly ornate capital, featuring a pomegranate motif. **Pomegranates** were a part of the decorative theme woven into the garments worn by priests (Ex 28:33), so the pomegranate decorations symbolized the priestly function connected to the temple. The names of the pillars, **Jachin** and **Boaz**, signified faith in God, meaning "He will establish" and "strength is in Him."

4:1 The various fixtures that Solomon installed in the temple complex were outside the building in the courtyard. The most dominant item was the **bronze altar**, which shared its dimensions with the most holy place, **30 feet** by **30 feet**. Because of its height (**15 feet**), it had a number of steps that priests had to climb to perform sacrifices.

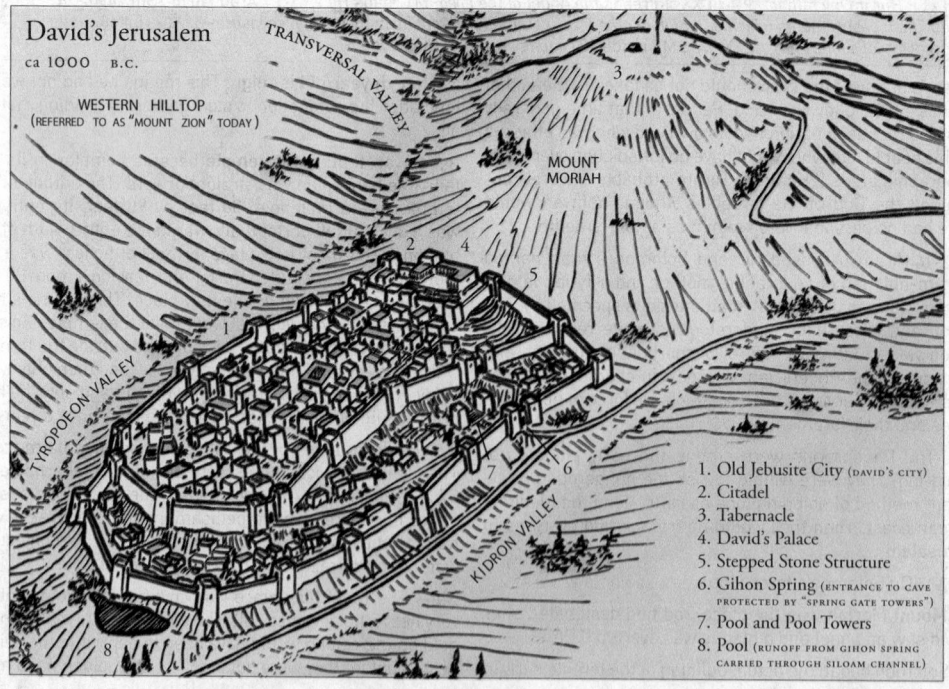

David's Jerusalem
ca 1000 B.C.

TRANSVERSAL VALLEY

WESTERN HILLTOP
(REFERRED TO AS "MOUNT ZION" TODAY)

MOUNT MORIAH

TYROPOEON VALLEY

KIDRON VALLEY

1. Old Jebusite City (DAVID'S CITY)
2. Citadel
3. Tabernacle
4. David's Palace
5. Stepped Stone Structure
6. Gihon Spring (ENTRANCE TO CAVE PROTECTED BY "SPRING GATE TOWERS")
7. Pool and Pool Towers
8. Pool (RUNOFF FROM GIHON SPRING CARRIED THROUGH SILOAM CHANNEL)

² Then he made the cast metal reservoir,ᵃ 15 feetᴬ from brim to brim, perfectly round. It was 7½ feetᴮ high and 45 feetᶜ in circumference. ³ The likeness of oxenᴰ was below it, completely encircling it, 10 every half yard,ᴱ completely surrounding the reservoir. The oxen were cast in two rows when the reservoir was cast. ⁴ It stood on 12 oxen, three facing north, three facing west, three facing south, and three facing east. The reservoir was on top of them and all their hindquarters were toward the center. ⁵ The reservoir was three inchesᶠ thick, and its rim was fashioned like the brim of a cup or a lily blossom. It could hold 11,000 gallons.ᴳ

⁶ He made 10 basins for washing and he put five on the right and five on the left.ᵇ The parts of the •burnt offering were rinsed in them,ᶜ but the reservoir was used by the priests for washing.

The Lampstands, Tables, and Courts

⁷ He made the 10 gold lampstands according to their specifications and put them in the sanctuary, five on the right and five on the left.ᵈ ⁸ He made 10 tables and placed them in the sanctuary, five on the right and five on the left.ᵉ He also made 100 gold bowls.

⁹ He made the courtyardᶠ of the priests and the large court, and doors for the court. He overlaid the doors with bronze. ¹⁰ He put the reservoir on the right side, toward the southeast.ᵍ ¹¹ Then Huramᴴ·ʰ madeⁱ the pots, the shovels, and the bowls.

Completion of the Bronze Furnishings

So Huram finished doing the work that he was doing for King Solomon in God's temple:

¹² two pillars; the bowls and the capitals on top of the two pillars; the two gratings for covering both bowls of the capitals that were on top of the pillars; ¹³ the 400 pomegranates for the two gratings (two rows of pomegranates for each grating covering both capitals' bowls on top of the pillarsʲ). ¹⁴ He also made the water cartsˡ·ᵏ and the basins on the water carts. ¹⁵ The one reservoir and the 12 oxen underneath it, ¹⁶ the pots, the shovels, the forks, and all their utensils—Huram-abiᴶ·ˡ made them for King Solomon for the LORD's temple. All these were made of polished bronze. ¹⁷ The king had them cast in clay molds in the Jordan Valley between Succoth and Zeredah. ¹⁸ Solomon made all these utensils in such great abundance that the weight of the bronze was not determined.

Completion of the Gold Furnishings

¹⁹ Solomon also made all the equipment in God's temple: the gold altar; the tables on which to put the •bread of the Presence;ᵐ ²⁰ the lampstands and their lamps of pure gold to burn in front of the inner sanctuary according to specifications;ⁿ ²¹ the flowers, lamps, and gold tongs—of purest gold; ²² the wick trimmers, sprinkling basins, ladles,ᴷ and firepans—of purest gold; and the entryway to the temple, its inner doors to the most holy place, and the doors of the temple sanctuary—of gold.

5 So all the work Solomon did for the LORD's temple was completed. Then Solomon brought the consecrated things of his father David—the silver, the gold, and all the utensils—and put them in the treasuries of God's temple.

ᵃ4:2-5 1Kg 7:23-26; Ezk 47:1-12; Rv 22:1 ᵇ4:6 1Kg 7:38-39 ᶜEzk 40:38 ᵈ4:7 Ex 37:17-24; 1Kg 7:49 ᵉ4:8 1Kg 7:48 ᶠ4:9 1Kg 6:36 ᵍ4:10 1Kg 7:39 ʰ4:11 1Kg 7:13,40,45 ⁱ4:11–5:1 1Kg 7:40-51 ʲ4:13 1Kg 7:20 ᵏ4:14 1Kg 7:27-37 ˡ4:16 1Kg 7:14; 2Ch 2:13 ᵐ4:19 Lv 24:5-9 ⁿ4:20 Ex 25:31-40; 2Ch 4:7

ᴬ4:2 Lit *10 cubits* ᴮ4:2 Lit *five cubits* ᶜ4:2 Lit *30 cubits* ᴰ4:3 = gourds in 1Kg 7:24 ᴱ4:3 Lit *10 per cubit* ᶠ4:5 Lit *a handbreadth* ᴳ4:5 Text emended; MT reads *3,000 baths* in 1Kg 7:26 ᴴ4:11 = Hiram in 1Kg 7:13,40,45 ᴵ4:14 Lit *the stands* ᴶ4:16 Lit *Huram my father* ᴷ4:22 Or *dishes*, or *spoons*; lit *palms*

4:2-4 The water **reservoir** was half the width of the altar in diameter. Here is where priests washed their hands and feet before performing their duties (Ex 30:18-21). Since the reservoir was **7½ feet high**, there must have been steps all around it to give the priests access to the water. Perhaps that was a function of the **12 oxen** decorations.

4:6 The large **reservoir** was reserved for the priests, but **10** smaller **basins** were provided in which to wash the sacrificial animals.

4:8 The **100 gold bowls** were probably intended to hold incense and coals.

4:9 A number of details that must have been a part of the **courtyard** are not specifically mentioned here. It probably featured amenities for the priests as well as storage areas.

4:11 Finally the name of **Huram**, chief craftsman on the project, comes up, even though he had been in charge of the artwork and decorations (2:13-14). He left his stamp particularly on the smaller items, the various **pots . . . shovels**, and **bowls** that would be used regularly at the altar.

With these accomplishments, Huram finished the work for which he had been hired.

4:12-16 This inventory of all the items that **Huram-abi** provided is a review of the things already mentioned, but this time with credit going to him.

4:17 The technique for making items out of bronze involved making clay **molds**, then filling them with hot molten metal, and removing the clay after the metal had cooled. This process required a lot of water. It was easier to create these items next to the **Jordan** River and transport them up to Jerusalem than to try to make them on site where water was not as abundant.

4:19-22 Most of the furnishings inside the temple were also made of gold. This **altar** was intended for the twice-daily burning of incense, not for animal sacrifice. Even though there was a curtain in front of the most holy place, there were also sets of golden doors in front of it and at the entrance to the actual temple building.

5:1 David might have been disappointed if he had known

Preparations for the Temple Dedication

[2] At that time[a] Solomon assembled at Jerusalem the elders of Israel—all the tribal heads, the ancestral chiefs of the Israelites—in order to bring the ark of the covenant of the Lord up from the city of David,[b] that is, *Zion. [3] So all the men of Israel were assembled in the king's presence at the festival; this was in the seventh month.[A]

[4] All the elders of Israel came, and the Levites picked up the ark. [5] They brought up the ark, the tent of meeting, and the holy utensils that were in the tent. The priests and the Levites brought them up. [6] King Solomon and the entire congregation of Israel who had gathered around him were in front of the ark sacrificing sheep and cattle that could not be counted or numbered because there were so many. [7] The priests brought the ark of the Lord's covenant to its place, into the inner sanctuary of the temple, to the most holy place, beneath the wings of the *cherubim.[c] [8] And the cherubim spread their wings over the place of the ark so that the cherubim formed a cover above the ark and its poles. [9] The poles were so long that their ends were seen from the holy place[B,d] in front of the inner sanctuary, but they were not seen from outside; they are there to this very day. [10] Nothing was in the ark except the two tablets that Moses had put in it at Horeb,[C,e] where the Lord had made a covenant with the Israelites when they came out of Egypt.

[11] Now all the priests who were present had consecrated themselves regardless of their divisions.[f] When the priests came out of the holy place, [12] the Levitical singers dressed in fine linen and carrying cymbals, harps, and lyres[g] were standing east of the altar, and with them were 120 priests blowing trumpets.[h] The Levitical singers were descendants of *Asaph, Heman, and Jeduthun and their sons[i] and relatives. [13] The trumpeters and singers joined together to praise and thank the Lord with one voice. They raised their voices, accompanied by trumpets, cymbals, and musical instruments,[j] in praise to the Lord:

> For He is good;
> His faithful love endures forever.[k]

The temple, the Lord's temple, was filled with a cloud.[l] [14] And because of the cloud, the priests were not able to continue ministering, for the glory of the Lord filled God's temple.[m]

Cross references (side column)
a 5:2-14 1Kg 8:1-11
b 5:2 2Ch 1:4
c 5:7 2Ch 3:10
d 5:9 1Kg 8:8
e 5:10 Dt 10:2-5; Heb 9:4
f 5:11 1Ch 24:1-5
g 5:12 1Ch 13:8; 15:16,24
h 2Ch 7:6
i 1Ch 25:1-4
j 5:13 1Ch 16:42
k 1Ch 16:34; 2Ch 7:3
l Ex 40:34-35; Lv 16:2; Nm 9:15-16
m 5:14 Ex 13:21-22; 40:34-38; Dt 4:11; 5:22; 31:14-15; 2Ch 7:1-3

Footnotes
A5:3 = Tishri (September–October)　B5:9 Some Hb mss, LXX; other Hb mss read *the ark*; 1Kg 8:8　C5:10 = Sinai

Study notes
that many of the valuable objects he commissioned for the **temple** (1Ch 28:12-18; 29:2-5) were relegated to the temple **treasuries** by Solomon.

5:2 The temple would serve as the only place of worship for all 12 tribes (Dt 12:14). Therefore, it was appropriate for Solomon to have representatives of all the tribes present for the dedication ceremony. The most important aspect of this celebration was moving the **ark of the covenant** from the tent where David had stored it into the temple.

5:3 Solomon arranged for the temple dedication to occur during the **festival** (probably the Festival of Booths). All Israelite men were supposed to be in Jerusalem for this celebration, now that a central sanctuary had been built (Ex 23:17; Lv 23:39-43). A large crowd of worshipers would thus take ownership of the temple right from the start.

5:4-6 This procession of the **ark** covered only a small distance, since it was moved from one part of Jerusalem to another. Simultaneously, a much longer procession carried the entire tabernacle (**tent of meeting**) from Gibeon up to Jerusalem, where it became integrated into the temple structure. The ark was carried by the proper people, the **Levites**, and in the proper manner, by threading two poles through grommets on the ark and then hoisting it on their shoulders.

5:7-9 More than a century earlier, the **ark** had been in the **most holy place** of the tabernacle. After that it had changed locations several times, but it had never been returned to its prescribed location in the tabernacle. Now finally the ark of the covenant resumed its proper place in the holy of holies. Once the ark was in its proper place, it was situated in such a way that the **cherubim** (3:10-13) created the impression of guarding the ark with their wings. The poles were too long to be confined to the holy of holies, so they jutted out into the temple. In the **very day** the Chronicler wrote these words, the ark was no longer in the temple but the poles were, presumably as a symbol of the missing ark.

5:10 By this time only the **two tablets** with the commandments were in the ark, but at one time it contained two other objects—a pot of manna and Aaron's rod that had sprouted miraculously (Heb 9:4).

5:11 Solomon followed David's plan for the division of the priests into different shifts, but all of the priests participated in the dedication service.

5:12-13 The descendants of the three chief musicians—**Asaph, Heman, and Jeduthun**—who had been divided between the tent of the ark in Jerusalem and the tabernacle in Gibeon were now reunited. Together with their clans, they started to make music. Everyone joined together in praising God because the temple was an expression of God's goodness and love for His people.

5:14 God approved of what the people had done, and He displayed His approval by revealing His **glory** through a cloud that **filled** the **temple**. There are three points of significance to the cloud and the momentary stoppage it forced on all activities. (1) It shows that God was pleased with the work the people had done. (2) It was a reminder that God's presence among His people is ultimately the focal point, not the many activities that the people carry out in worshiping God. (3) It brought the exodus to conclusion. Nearly 500 years earlier, the Israelites had followed God from point to point as they crisscrossed the desert for 40 years (1Kg 6:1). During that time, God had shown Himself as a cloud during the day and as a pillar of fire at night (Ex 13:21-22), always moving ahead of the people. Now, with the land possessed in its

Solomon's Dedication of the Temple

6 Then Solomon said:[a]

The LORD said He would dwell
in thick darkness,[b]
2 but I have built an exalted temple
for You,
a place for Your residence forever.

3 Then the king turned and blessed the entire congregation of Israel while they were standing. 4 He said:

May the LORD God of Israel be praised!
He spoke directly to my father David,
and He has fulfilled the promise
by His power.
He said,
5 "Since the day I brought
My people Israel
out of the land of Egypt,[c]
I have not chosen a city to build
a temple in
among any of the tribes of Israel,
so that My name would be there,
and I have not chosen a man
to be ruler over My people Israel.
6 But I have chosen Jerusalem
so that My name will be there,[d]
and I have chosen David
to be over My people Israel."[e]

7 Now it was in the heart
of my father David
to build a temple for the name
of •Yahweh, the God
of Israel.[f]

8 However, Yahweh said
to my father David,
"Since it was your desire to build
a temple for My name,
you have done well to have this desire.
9 Yet, you are not the one to build
the temple,
but your son, your own offspring,
will build the temple for My name."
10 So Yahweh has fulfilled
what He promised.
I have taken the place
of my father David
and I sit on the throne of Israel,
as Yahweh promised.
I have built the temple for the name
of Yahweh, the God of Israel.
11 I have put the ark there,
where Yahweh's covenant is
that He made with the Israelites.[g]

Solomon's Prayer

12 Then Solomon stood before the altar of the LORD in front of the entire congregation of Israel and spread out his hands. 13 For Solomon had made a bronze platform 7¹/₂ feet[A] long, 7¹/₂ feet[A] wide, and 4¹/₂ feet[B] high and put it in the court. He stood on it,[h] knelt down in front of the entire congregation of Israel, and spread out his hands toward heaven.[i] 14 He said:

LORD God of Israel,
there is no God like You
in heaven or on earth,[j]
keeping His gracious covenant
with Your servants who walk before You
with their whole heart.[k]

---

a 6:1-42 1Kg 8:12-53
b 6:1 Ex 20:21; Dt 4:11; 5:22
c 6:5-9 2Sm 7:1-13
d 6:6 2Ch 12:13
e 1Ch 28:4
f 6:7 1Kg 5:3
g 6:11 2Ch 5:7,10
h 6:13 Ex 9:29, 33; Ezr 9:5; Neh 8:4
i 1Kg 8:54
j 6:14 Ex 15:11; Dt 3:24
k Dt 7:9

A 6:13 Lit *five cubits*   B 6:13 Lit *three cubits*

---

entirety and a temple in place, the conquest had finally been finished, and the cloud came to rest inside the sanctuary.

6:1-2 Solomon responded to the cloud by observing that the temple was an **exalted** place where the people could be reminded of God's presence **forever**.

6:3-11 As the **entire congregation** rose to receive Solomon's blessings, he repeated the familiar story that led up to this point so everyone would understand the grace of God. The Lord had made a **promise** and now He had **fulfilled** it. It was He who had chosen **David**; and it was He who had designated Solomon as the temple builder.

6:12-13 Solomon had planned this moment by having a **platform** erected and assuming a public, reverent stance to pray. This way the people could focus on him as he represented the people before the Lord.

6:14-17 Solomon thanked God that the first half of what the Lord had **promised** had taken place: the temple had been built, and the son of David was on the throne. Then he petitioned God to keep the second part of the promise: the perpetual dynasty of David's descendants as long as they remain faithful.

---

shem

Hebrew Pronunciation	[SHAIM]
HCSB Translation	name
Uses in 2 Chronicles	45
Uses in the OT	864
Focus Passage	2 Chronicles 6:5-10,20,24,26,32-34

This root in various languages suggests a *distinguishing mark*. *Shem* was associated with *being*, *character*, and *public standing*. *Names* bore meanings (Ex 2:10,22), and changed *names* connoted changed characters (Gn 32:28). "Call the *name*" often appears as *name* (Gn 3:20) or *call* (Jr 20:3). One called by someone's *name* belonged to him (Is 4:1). God's *name* is synonymous with God (Ps 75:1); God's *name* dwells in His temple (Dt 16:2). Walking (Mc 4:5) or living (Ps 69:36) in His *name* is living as He instructs. "Calling on His *name*" is prayer (Ps 116:4) or *worship* (Gn 12:8). One acts in His *name* (Dt 18:5,22). *Shem* denotes *fame* (Is 63:12) or *reputation* (Jos 9:9). "*Name* of the day" signifies *today's date* (Ezk 24:2). One acts on someone's *behalf* (1Sm 25:9). *Shem* functions as *famous* (Zph 3:20), *prominent* (Nm 16:2), or *notorious* (Ezk 23:10). *Infamous* is "unclean of *name*" (Ezk 22:5).

15 You have kept what You promised
to Your servant, my father David.
You spoke directly to him,
and You fulfilled Your promise
by Your power,
as it is today.^a
16 Therefore, LORD God of Israel,
keep what You promised
to Your servant, my father David:
"You will never fail to have a man
to sit before Me on the throne
of Israel,^b
if only your sons guard their way
to walk in My Law
as you have walked before Me."
17 Now, LORD God of Israel, please confirm
what You promised
to Your servant David.

18 But will God indeed live on earth
with man?
Even heaven, the highest heaven,
cannot contain You,^c
much less this temple I have built.
19 Listen^A to Your servant's prayer
and his petition,
LORD my God,
so that You may hear the cry
and the prayer
that Your servant prays before You,
20 so that Your eyes watch over
this temple
day and night,
toward the place where You said
You would put Your name;^d
and so that You may hear the prayer
Your servant prays toward this place.
21 Hear the petitions of Your servant
and Your people Israel,
which they pray toward this place.
May You hear in Your dwelling place
in heaven.
May You hear and forgive.

<table>
<tr><td>a 6:15 1Ch 22:9-10</td></tr>
<tr><td>b 6:16 1Kg 2:4; 2Ch 7:18</td></tr>
<tr><td>c 6:18 2Ch 2:6</td></tr>
<tr><td>d 6:20 Dt 12:11</td></tr>
<tr><td>e 6:26 1Kg 8:35</td></tr>
</table>

22 If a man sins against his neighbor
and is forced to take an oath^B
and he comes to take an oath
before Your altar in this temple,
23 may You hear in heaven and act.
May You judge Your servants,
condemning the wicked man
by bringing
what he has done on his own head
and providing justice for the righteous
by rewarding him according to
his righteousness.

24 If Your people Israel are defeated
before an enemy,
because they have sinned against You,
and they return to You and praise
Your name,
and they pray and plead for mercy
before You in this temple,
25 may You hear in heaven
and forgive the sin of Your people Israel.
May You restore them to the land
You gave them and their ancestors.
26 When the skies are shut and there is
no rain
because they have sinned against You,
and they pray toward this place
and praise Your name,
and they turn from their sins
because You are afflicting^{C,e} them,
27 may You hear in heaven
and forgive the sin of Your servants
and Your people Israel,
so that You may teach them
the good way
they should walk in.
May You send rain on Your land
that You gave Your people
for an inheritance.
28 When there is famine on the earth,
when there is pestilence,

A 6:19 Lit *Turn* B 6:22 Lit *and he lifts a curse against him to curse him* C 6:26 LXX, Vg; MT reads *answering*; 1Kg 8:35

6:18-20 Solomon recognized that God was not confined to the **temple**. This was distinct from the common view in the ancient Near East that all deities were restricted to a particular location, such as a temple or a limited geographical region. In Israel's theology, the temple was a place where people could come to encounter the living God, but this living God was present everywhere.

6:21-39 There would be some needs for which the people would pray by directing themselves to the temple, and Solomon asked the Lord to listen and to respond.

6:22-23 The first scenario involved a man who had done some wrong and who needed to clear his name or to bring about the end of his punishment by taking **an oath** in the temple. Solomon did not ask that a guilty person would be set free, but that justice would be done.

6:24-25 The second scenario was one that is illustrated throughout the rest of 2 Chronicles. It involved the Israelites turning away from God and as a consequence being **defeated before an enemy**. Solomon asked that when the people came to their senses and prayed in the temple, God would **forgive** their sins and give them back the land they had lost.

6:26-27 The third scenario implied that a drought in the land had been caused by the Israelites' turning away from the Lord. Again, Solomon's prayer was that God would respond to sincere prayer in the temple by sending **rain**.

6:28-31 The fourth scenario included a number of disasters. Solomon petitioned God to listen to the prayers by people in the temple, but he stipulated that the prayers must be sincere because God knew **the human heart**. The temple was not an automatic forgiving machine.

when there is blight, mildew, locust,
   or grasshopper,
when their enemies besiege them
in the region of their fortified cities,^A,a
when there is any plague or illness,
29 whatever prayer or petition
anyone from your people Israel
   might have—
each man knowing his own affliction^B
   and suffering,
and spreading out his hands
   toward this temple—
30 may You hear in heaven,
   Your dwelling place,
and may You forgive and repay the man
according to all his ways,
   since You know his heart,
for You alone know the human heart,^b
31 so that they may •fear You
and walk in Your ways
all the days they live
   on the land
You gave our ancestors.

32 Even for the foreigner who is not of
   Your people Israel
but has come from a distant land
because of Your great name
and Your mighty hand
   and outstretched arm:^c
when he comes and prays
   toward this temple,
33 may You hear in heaven in Your
   dwelling place,
and do all the foreigner asks You.
Then all the peoples of the earth
   will know Your name,
to fear You as Your people Israel do
and know that this temple
   I have built
is called by Your name.^d

34 When Your people go out
   to fight against their enemies,
wherever You send them,
and they pray to You

^a6:28 Jos 2:7;
Jdg 16:2-3
^b6:30 1Sm 16:7;
1Ch 28:9
^c6:32 Is 56:6-8;
Zch 8:20-23;
14:16-21
^d6:33 2Ch 7:14
^e6:34 Dt 12:11
^f6:36 Jb 15:14-
16; Jms 3:2; 1Jn
1:8-10
^g6:40 2Ch 7:15;
Neh 1:6,11; Ps
17:1
^h6:41-42 Ps
132:8-10

in the direction of this city
   You have chosen^e
and the temple that I have built
   for Your name,
35 may You hear their prayer and petition
   in heaven
and uphold their cause.

36 When they sin against You—
for there is no one who does not sin^f—
and You are angry with them
and hand them over to the enemy,
and their captors deport them
to a distant or nearby country,
37 and when they come to their senses
in the land where they were deported
and repent and petition You
   in their captors' land,
saying: "We have sinned
   and done wrong;
we have been wicked,"
38 and when they return to You
   with their whole mind and heart
in the land of their captivity
   where they were taken captive,
and when they pray in the direction
   of their land
that You gave their ancestors,
and the city You have chosen,
and toward the temple I have built
   for Your name,
39 may You hear their prayer and petitions
   in heaven,
Your dwelling place,
and uphold their cause.^c
May You forgive Your people
who sinned against You.

40 Now, my God,
please let Your eyes be open
and Your ears attentive
to the prayer of this place.^g
41 Now therefore:^h

Arise, Lord God, come
   to Your resting place,

---

^A6:28 Lit if his (Israel's) enemies besiege him in the land of his gates; Jos 2:7; Jdg 16:2-3   ^B6:29 Lit plague   ^C6:39 Lit and do their judgment or justice

---

6:32-33 In the fifth scenario, Solomon made his request on behalf of every **foreigner** who might come to the **temple** to seek God. His prayer was that these foreigners would find their petitions answered, so God's name would be glorified among those who lived far away. Many ancient people believed their gods were restrained by their location. The god who responded to people from far away was a God who set Himself apart from the many false gods of the surrounding nations.

6:34-35 In the sixth scenario, Solomon asked God for strength in battle. Solomon was not asking God for a blanket support of military adventurism, but for Yahweh's help during those times when He would **send them** into war.

6:36-39 The seventh and last scenario would have been appropriate for the Chronicler and his contemporaries as they rebuilt the nation after the exile. The nation might be deported into a **distant . . . country**. This possibility had already been mentioned by Moses (Dt 28:33). Solomon asked that once the people repented and started to pray in the direction of the **temple** that the Lord would **forgive** them and bring them back to their own land.

6:41-42 Solomon concluded his prayer by asking God to take

You and Your powerful ark.
May Your priests, Lord God, be clothed
   with salvation,
and may Your godly people rejoice
   in goodness.
⁴² Lord God, do not reject
   Your anointed one;ᴬ
remember the loyalty
   of Your servant David.ᵃ

The Dedication Ceremonies

7 When Solomon finished praying,ᵇ fire
descended from heaven and consumed
the *burnt offering and the sacrifices,ᶜ and
the glory of the Lord filled the temple. ²The
priests were not able to enter the Lord's temple because the glory of the Lord filled the
temple of the Lord. ³All the Israelites were
watching when the fire descended and the
glory of the Lord came on the temple. They
bowed down on the pavement with their faces
to the ground. They worshiped and praised
the Lord:

For He is good,
   for His faithful love endures forever.ᵈ

⁴The king and all the people were offering
sacrifices in the Lord's presence.ᵉ ⁵King Solomon offered a sacrifice of 22,000 cattle and
120,000 sheep. In this manner the king and
all the people dedicated God's temple. ⁶The
priests and the Levites were standing at their
stations. The Levites had the musical instru-

ments of the Lord, which King David had made
to praise the Lord—"for His faithful love endures forever"—when he offered praise with
them.ᶠ Across from the Levites, the priests
were blowing trumpets, and all the people
were standing. ⁷Since the bronze altar that
Solomon had madeᵍ could not accommodate
the burnt offering, the *grain offering, and the
fat of the *fellowship offerings, Solomon first
consecrated the middle of the courtyardʰ that
was in front of the Lord's temple and then offered the burnt offerings and the fat of the fellowship offerings there.ⁱ

⁸So Solomon and all Israel with him—a
very great assembly, from the entrance to Ha-
mathᴮ to the Brook of Egypt—observed the
festival at that time for seven days. ⁹On the
eighth dayᶜ they held a sacred assembly,ʲ for
the dedication of the altar lasted seven days
and the festival seven days. ¹⁰On the twenty-
third day of the seventh month he sent the
people away to their tents, rejoicing and with
happy hearts for the goodness the Lord had
done for David, for Solomon, and for His people Israel.

¹¹So Solomon finished the Lord's temple and
the royal palace. Everything that had entered
Solomon's heart to do for the Lord's temple
and for his own palace succeeded.ᵏ

The Lord's Response

¹²Then the Lord appeared to Solomon at
night and said to him:

Cross references (center column):
ᵃ6:42 1Ch 16:8-22; Ps 105:1-15; Is 55:3
ᵇ7:1-10 1Kg 8:54
ᶜ7:1 Gn 15:7-17; Lv 9:24; Jdg 6:21-24; 1Kg 18:24,38
ᵈ7:3 1Ch 16:41; 2Ch 5:13; 20:21; Ezr 3:11; Ps 106:1; Jr 33:11
ᵉ7:4-5 1Kg 8:62-63
ᶠ7:6 1Ch 15:16-21; 16:42; 23:5; 2Ch 29:26-30; Neh 12:36
ᵍ7:7 2Ch 4:1
ʰ7:7-10 1Kg 8:64-66
ⁱ7:7 Lv 7:30-31
ʲ7:9 Lv 23:36
ᵏ7:11-22 1Kg 9:1-9

Aͧ6:42 Some Hb mss, LXX; other Hb mss read *ones*; Ps 132:10   Bͧ7:8 Or *from Lebo-hamath*   Cͧ7:9 = the day after the festival, or
the 15th day

---

over the temple so the **priests**, the **godly people**, and he—
the **anointed** king—might rejoice in the nearness of God.
He prayed that God would bless Israel for the sake of the
loyalty of **David**, which God did indeed do for Solomon and
many generations of Judah's kings (21:7; cp. 1Kg 11:11-13;
15:4; 2Kg 8:19; 19:34; 20:6).

7:1-2 **Fire** had **descended** from heaven once before on
an offering at precisely the same spot where the temple
stood—on David's sacrifice on the threshing floor of Ornan
(1Ch 21:25). This dramatic occurrence showed that God approved of what Solomon and the people had done. The **glory
of the Lord** was a cloud and a light so bright that no one
could stand in its presence (Ezk 1:28; 10:4).

7:3 This display of God's glory was publicly visible, reminding everyone of God's reality and His faithful character. The
praise of the worshipers focused on God.

7:4-6 The sacrifice of this many animals required rigor-
ous organization. The **priests** had specific tasks at their
designated area and the offerings were made virtually as-
sembly-line style, while the musicians took turns providing
background music, just as David had envisioned.

7:7 Sacrifices were supposed to be made on the altar of
the temple, but it was not large enough to accommodate
them all. Solomon **consecrated** the **courtyard** for this oc-

casion, and the animals were sacrificed right there on the
ground.

7:8-9 Since the dedication of the temple also coincided with
the **festival** (Festival of Booths), many people were in Jerusalem for the celebration of this feast. **Hamath** is in the
far north and the **Brook of Egypt** is the southern border of
Israel, so people were there from the whole country. It is not
often that a nation comes together in a celebration of joy,
but it surely was the case here.

7:10 Finally after three weeks, Solomon declared the festivities over and sent everyone home **to their tents**. This expression does not mean that most Israelites were still living in
tents rather than houses. This was a familiar figure of speech
(10:16). In addition, during the celebration of the Feast of
Booths, many people put up temporary shelters, or booths,
to signify Israel's period of wandering in the wilderness.

7:11 The Chronicler conflates the completion of the **temple**
and of Solomon's **royal palace** into one brief sentence. The
total time for building the temple, followed by the palace,
was 20 years (1Kg 6:38-7:1).

7:12 Ten years earlier, Solomon had begun his reign by visiting the tabernacle at Gibeon (1:7). Just as the Lord had done
at Gibeon, He **appeared to Solomon at night**. This time God
confirmed everything that Solomon had prayed for.

I have heard your prayer and have chosen this place for Myself as a temple of sacrifice.[a] [13]If I close the sky so there is no rain, or if I command the grasshopper to consume the land, or if I send pestilence on My people,[b] [14]and My people who are called by My name humble themselves, pray and seek My face, and turn from their evil ways, then I will hear from heaven, forgive their sin, and heal their land.[c] [15]My eyes will now be open and My ears attentive to prayer from this place.[d] [16]And I have now chosen and consecrated this temple so that My name may be there forever; My eyes and My heart will be there at all times.[e]

[17]As for you, if you walk before Me as your father David walked, doing everything I have commanded you, and if you keep My statutes and ordinances, [18]I will establish your royal throne, as I promised your father David: You will never fail to have a man ruling in Israel.[f]

[19]However, if you turn away and abandon My statutes and My commands that I have set before you and if you go and serve other gods and worship them,[g]

[20]then I will uproot Israel from the soil that I gave them, and this temple that I have sanctified for My name I will banish from My presence;[h] I will make it an object of scorn and ridicule among all the peoples.[i] [21]As for this temple, which was exalted, everyone who passes by will be appalled and will say:[j] Why did the Lord do this to this land and this temple? [22]Then they will say: Because they abandoned the Lord God of their ancestors who brought them out of the land of Egypt. They clung to other gods and worshiped and served them. Because of this, He brought all this ruin on them.

Solomon's Later Building Projects

8 At the end of 20 years[k] during which Solomon had built the Lord's temple and his own palace— [2]Solomon had rebuilt the cities Hiram[A] gave him and settled Israelites there— [3]Solomon went to Hamath-zobah and seized it. [4]He built Tadmor in the wilderness along with all the storage cities that he built in Hamath. [5]He built Upper Beth-horon and Lower Beth-horon[l]—fortified cities with walls, gates, and bars[m]— [6]Baalath, all the storage cities that belonged to Solomon, all

Cross-refs: a7:12 Dt 12:5,11 b7:13 2Ch 6:26-28 c7:14 2Ch 6:37-39 d7:15 2Ch 6:20,40 e7:16 2Ch 7:12 f7:18 2Ch 6:16 g7:19 Lv 26:14; Dt 28:15 h7:20 Lv 26:33; Dt 29:28; 1Kg 14:15 i Dt 28:37 j7:21-22 Dt 29:24-25 k8:1-10 1Kg 9:10-23 l8:5 1Ch 7:24 m2Ch 14:7

A8:2 = the king of Tyre

7:13-16 This promise presupposes a very specific context. It was given to God's **people who are called** by God's **name**, and it is a part of God's answer to Solomon's prayer. It refers to times when the Israelites have become faithless to God and are enduring the consequences, whether it was a famine, an invasion, or even the deportation to another country. To be **humble . . . pray . . . seek** God, and **turn** from sin are four aspects of one attitude: repentance. If Israel would repent, He would **forgive** them and **heal** their spiritual relationship with Him associated with the promised **land**. Furthermore, as was established earlier, the prayer mentioned is specifically intended to refer to prayer in the temple or, if that is not possible, prayer said facing in the direction of the temple. This promise is given specifically to God's covenant people, and by itself it should not be applied to other nations or to the church. However, these verses reflect God's gracious nature, and on that basis we may draw out a more fundamental principle—that any person, regardless of race or geography, can come to the Lord with a repentant heart and find forgiveness (see 6:32-33; Jl 2:32; Ac 2:21; Rm 10:13; 1Co 1:2).

7:17-22 The fact that Solomon had been allowed to build the **temple** showed that he was God's chosen king and the one whose offspring would continue the line of **David** on the **throne**. But if Solomon or his successors proved to be unworthy, a time might come when there was no longer a throne for David's offspring to occupy. Just as God was faithful in keeping His promise, He would also be faithful in carrying out His punishment for sin and rebellion. The Lord would not continue the kingdom if the kings refused to follow Him.

8:1 The building of the **temple** took seven years, and Sol-

omon's **palace** took another 13, making a total of **20 years** (see 1Kg 6:38–7:1).

8:2 A partial payment from Solomon to **Hiram** for the building materials he provided consisted of 20 **cities** (villages by modern standards) to add to Hiram's kingdom (1Kg 9:10-14). These locations would have been of use to Hiram only if they were affluent enough to pay taxes or could serve as military defenses. When Hiram went to visit his new acquisitions, he discovered they were worthless little hamlets, so he gave them back to the king of Judah. Solomon was willing to invest in these locations by having them **rebuilt** and resettled.

8:3 In contrast to his father David, Solomon undertook few military campaigns. One exception was his seizure of **Hamath-zobah**. In David's time Tou, king of Hamath, had surrendered to David and paid a tribute (1Ch 18:9-10). Apparently a new government of that city rebelled against Israel, so Solomon took it over and erected storage facilities there. This city was on the edge of Palestine, a natural destination for caravans crossing the desert between Mesopotamia and Lebanon.

8:4 Now all Solomon needed to do to take control of the trade across the Syrian Desert was to claim an oasis located halfway along the caravan route. **Tadmor** was such a location. By establishing it along with **Hamath**, Solomon dominated all the trade to and from Mesopotamia.

8:5-6 Solomon continued with his nationwide building program by fortifying the route leading up to Jerusalem. The cities of **Lower** and **Upper Beth-horon** were garrisons intended to keep invaders from reaching the capital city.

EXTERIOR

1. Altar
2. Sea
3. Boaz ("IN STRENGTH")
4. Joakin ("HE ESTABLISHES")
5. Portable Lavers
6. Solomon's Bronze
   Platform (NOT SHOWN ABOVE)

STOREROOMS

NORTH

THE HOLY
OF HOLIES

THE HOLY
PLACE

INTERIOR

7. Incense Altar
8. Lampstands
9. Tables
10. Veil and Doors

SOLOMON'S TEMPLE, Interior View (LOOKING WEST)

the chariot cities, the cavalry cities, and everything Solomon desired to build in Jerusalem, Lebanon, or anywhere else in the land of his dominion.

⁷As for all the peoples who remained of the Hittites, Amorites, Perizzites, Hivites, and Jebusites, who were not from Israel^a— ⁸their descendants who remained in the land after them, those the Israelites had not completely destroyed—Solomon imposed forced labor on them; it is this way today.^b ⁹But Solomon did not consign the Israelites to be slaves for his work; they were soldiers, commanders of his captains, and commanders of his chariots and his cavalry. ¹⁰These were King Solomon's deputies: 250 who ruled over the people.

¹¹Solomon brought the daughter of Pharaoh from the city of David to the house he had built for her,^c for he said, "My wife must not live in the house^A of David king of Israel because the places the ark of the Lord has come into are holy."

Public Worship Established at the Temple

¹²At that time^d Solomon offered •burnt offerings to the Lord on the Lord's altar he had made in front of the portico.^e ¹³He followed the daily requirement^f for offerings according to the commandment of Moses^g for Sabbaths, New Moons, and the three annual appointed festivals: the Festival of Unleavened Bread,

the Festival of Weeks, and the Festival of Booths.^h ¹⁴According to the ordinances of his father David, he appointed the divisions of the priests over their service,^i of the Levites over their responsibilities to offer praise and to minister before the priests following the daily requirement,^j and of the gatekeepers by their divisions with respect to each gate,^k for this had been the command of David, the man of God.^l ¹⁵They did not turn aside from the king's command regarding the priests and the Levites concerning any matter or concerning the treasuries.^m ¹⁶All of Solomon's work was carried out from the day the foundation was laid for the Lord's temple until it was finished. So the Lord's temple was completed.

Solomon's Fleet

¹⁷At that time^n Solomon went to Ezion-geber and to Eloth^o on the seashore in the land of Edom. ¹⁸So Hiram^B sent ships to him by his servants along with crews of experienced seamen. They went with Solomon's servants to Ophir, took from there 17 tons^c of gold, and delivered it to King Solomon.^p

The Queen of Sheba

9 The queen of Sheba heard of Solomon's fame,^q so she came to test Solomon with difficult questions at Jerusalem with a very large entourage, with camels bearing spices, gold in abundance, and precious stones. She

Cross references (center column)

^a8:7 Gn 15:18-21
^b8:8 1Kg 4:6; 9:21
^c8:11 1Kg 3:1; 7:8; 9:24
^d8:12-13 1Kg 9:25
^e8:12 2Ch 4:1
^f8:13 Ex 29:38-42
^g Nm 28:3
^h Ex 23:14-17
^i8:14 1Ch 24:1-3
^j1Ch 25:1
^k1Ch 26:1,13
^l Neh 12:24,36
^m8:15 1Ch 26:20-28
^n8:17-18 1Kg 9:26-28
^o8:17 2Kg 14:22
^p8:18 2Ch 9:10,13
^q9:1-12 1Kg 10:1-13; Mt 12:42; Lk 11:31

---

^A8:11 LXX reads *city*   ^B8:18 Lit *Huram*   ^C8:18 Lit *450 talents*

8:7-9 God's strict command to Joshua years before was that all Canaanites were to be eliminated (Jos 6:21), but the Israelites had not completely followed through on capturing all the territory until David conquered Jerusalem, the last bit of Canaanite-owned soil. There were still survivors, and these people now made up Solomon's slave force (**forced labor**) for his construction projects. **Israelites** were not supposed to become slaves. However, they did have to work for Solomon, and his requirements grew increasingly stringent.

8:11 In contrast to the record of 1 Kings, the Chronicler does not dwell on Solomon's shortcomings or his many marriages. He does mention Solomon's **wife** who was the **daughter of Pharaoh**, though only to emphasize that out of respect for the holiness of the **ark** and the facilities that David had erected, Solomon moved his Egyptian wife to quarters outside Jerusalem. Although the Chronicler does not condemn Solomon at this point, it is still impossible not to realize that Solomon, while observing every part of the ceremonial law by never missing a daily sacrifice, simultaneously undercut the law by importing idolatry right into his marriage bed. In 1Kg 11:6 we learn that Solomon even went so far as to participate in pagan sacrifices in order to please his wives.

8:12-16 Solomon fulfilled all the requirements associated with the temple to the letter, including the **daily . . . offerings** and all the various mandatory celebrations. He strictly maintained the division of labor and the shifts that had been ordered by his father, King David, before him.

8:17-18 The cities of **Ezion-geber** and **Eloth** were located at the southernmost end of Israel on the shore of the Red Sea. These locations made it possible for Solomon to carry on trade with the people on the Arabian Peninsula and possibly beyond. But Solomon had no ships and the Israelites knew nothing about sailing. On the other hand, King **Hiram** was the ruler of a seafaring people who were busy carrying on trade throughout the Mediterranean Sea, but if the Phoenicians wanted to establish trade relations with Arabia, they had to sail all the way through the Mediterranean down the west coast of Africa, around the Cape of Good Hope and back up north all the way along the east coast of Africa to Arabia. In short, Solomon had convenient harbors but no ships, while Hiram had ships but no convenient harbor. They were able to work together and haul in huge amounts of **gold**. The location of **Ophir** is unknown. Solomon considered the gold his personal property, so it was stored in his palace (9:15). The people eventually revolted against the king's practices when they declared, "What portion do we have in David? We have no inheritance in the son of Jesse" (10:16). The hard labor imposed by Solomon might have been more acceptable if it had resulted in nationwide economic benefits.

9:1 **Sheba** is identical with the ancient kingdom of Saba, located in what is today Yemen at the southern tip of the Arabian Peninsula. This was a thriving kingdom, strategically located between the more distant parts of Asia and the Middle East, thus able to profit from the trade between

came to Solomon and spoke with him about everything that was on her mind. ²So Solomon answered all her questions; nothing was too difficult for Solomon to explain to her. ³When the queen of Sheba observed Solomon's wisdom, the palace he had built, ⁴the food at his table, his servants' residence, his attendants' service and their attire, his cupbearers and their attire, and the ˙burnt offerings he offered at the LORD's temple, it took her breath away.

⁵She said to the king, "The report I heard in my own country about your words and about your wisdom is true. ⁶But I didn't believe their reports until I came and saw with my own eyes. Indeed, I was not even told half of your great wisdom! You far exceed the report I heard. ⁷How happy are your men.^A,^a How happy are these servants of yours, who always stand in your presence hearing your wisdom. ⁸May the LORD your God be praised! He delighted in you and put you on His throne as king for the LORD your God.^b Because Your God loved Israel enough to establish them forever, He has set you over them as king to carry out justice and righteousness."^c

⁹Then she gave the king four and a half tons^B of gold, a great quantity of spices, and precious stones. There never were such spices as those the queen of Sheba gave to King Solomon. ¹⁰In addition, Hiram's servants and Solomon's servants who brought gold from Ophir^d also brought algum wood and precious stones. ¹¹The king made the algum wood into

walkways for the LORD's temple and for the king's palace and into lyres and harps for the singers. Never before had anything like them been seen in the land of Judah.

¹²King Solomon gave the queen of Sheba her every desire, whatever she asked—far more than she had brought the king. Then she, along with her servants, returned to her own country.

Solomon's Wealth

¹³The weight of gold that came to Solomon^e annually was 25 tons,^C ¹⁴besides what was brought by the merchants and traders. All the Arabian kings and governors of the land also brought gold and silver to Solomon.

¹⁵King Solomon made 200 large shields of hammered gold; 15 pounds^D of hammered gold went into each shield. ¹⁶He made 300 small shields of hammered gold; about eight pounds^E of gold went into each shield. The king put them in the House of the Forest of Lebanon.^f

¹⁷The king also made a large ivory throne and overlaid it with pure gold. ¹⁸The throne had six steps; there was a footstool covered in gold for the throne, armrests on either side of the seat, and two lions standing beside the armrests. ¹⁹Twelve lions were standing there on the six steps, one at each end. Nothing like it had ever been made in any other kingdom.

²⁰All of King Solomon's drinking cups were gold, and all the utensils of the House of the Forest of Lebanon were pure gold. There was

---

Cross references:
^a 9:7 1Kg 10:8
^b 9:8 1Ch 28:5; 29:23
^c Dt 7:8; 2Ch 2:11
^d 9:10 2Ch 8:18
^e 9:13-24 1Kg 10:14-25
^f 9:16 1Kg 7:2-5

---

^A 9:7 LXX, Old Lat read wives; 1Kg 10:8   ^B 9:9 Lit 120 talents   ^C 9:13 Lit 666 talents   ^D 9:15 Lit 600 (shekels)   ^E 9:16 Lit 300 (shekels)

---

the two areas. When the combined fleet of Solomon and Hiram began to commute regularly between Arabia and Israel, Saba's economy may have been affected adversely because the two kings were able to eliminate Saba's role as a middleman. The **queen of Sheba** had heard many stories about this king who was noted for his wealth and wisdom. She made this long, arduous journey to meet Solomon face to face, to learn his secrets of statecraft, and presumably to be on the right side of any potential conflict. She attempted to impress this king who had more wealth than he could ever use by bringing him even more riches.

9:2-4 Solomon was able to answer **all her questions** and to **explain** many things to her. By the time the queen had seen everything of Solomon's material glory, as well as the extravagance of the **temple** and its rituals, **it took her breath away**. Solomon's intent to build a temple that demonstrated God's superiority to all other gods (1:5) had been accomplished.

9:5-9 The queen acknowledged that the reports she had heard about Solomon did not come close to the reality she saw. She was unaware of the unrest among Solomon's subjects that would reach a climax in the next chapter (and which is elaborated in 1Kg 11:26-40). She only saw the glo-

rious side of the kingdom and even gave the Lord credit for having arranged Solomon's reign. To show her appreciation for the king, she gave him **gold . . . spices, and precious stones**.

9:10-11 Algum, more commonly called almug, was one of several types of sandalwood known for its fragrance. It could be burned like incense. Solomon incorporated this wood into **walkways** for the **temple** and into musical instruments.

9:12 The presents of the **queen of Sheba** to Solomon turned out to be an investment because the king sent her home with **far more** wealth **than she had brought**.

9:13-16 Solomon, as we have seen (2:18; 8:7-8), used slave labor for his building projects and even instituted forced labor among the Israelites (10:4). He hoarded the accumulating amount of **gold** and devised an ingenious method of storing it by molding it into **shields** that covered the walls of his palace. People could admire it, but he had quick access to it if he needed it.

9:17-21 The Chronicler sees Solomon's wealth and his splendor as evidence of God's blessing (1:12). His acquisitions included ornate furniture and exotic animals, most

no silver, since it was considered as nothing in Solomon's time, [21] for the king's ships kept going to Tarshish[a] with Hiram's servants, and once every three years the ships of Tarshish would arrive bearing gold, silver, ivory, apes, and peacocks.[A]

[22] King Solomon surpassed all the kings of the world in riches and wisdom.[b] [23] All the kings of the world wanted an audience with Solomon to hear the wisdom God had put in his heart. [24] Each of them would bring his own gift—items[B] of silver and gold, clothing, weapons,[C,D] spices, and horses and mules—as an annual tribute.

[25] Solomon[c] had 4,000 stalls for horses and chariots, and 12,000 horsemen.[d] He stationed them in the chariot cities and with the king in Jerusalem. [26] He ruled over all the kings from the Euphrates River to the land of the Philistines and as far as the border of Egypt.[e] [27] The king made silver as common in Jerusalem as stones, and he made cedar as abundant as sycamore in the Judean foothills. [28] They were bringing horses for Solomon from Egypt and from all the countries.

Solomon's Death

[29] The remaining events[f] of Solomon's reign,

a 9:21 2Ch 20:36-37
b 9:22 1Kg 3:13;
2Ch 1:12
c 9:25-28 Dt 17:16; 1Kg 10:26-29; 2Ch 1:14-17
d 9:25 1Kg 4:26
e 9:26 Gn 15:18; 1Kg 4:21,24
f 9:29-31 1Kg 11:41-43
g 9:29 1Ch 29:29; 2Ch 12:15; 13:22
h 9:31 1Kg 2:10
i 10:1-19 1Kg 12:1-20
j 10:2 1Kg 11:40

from beginning to end, are written in the Events of Nathan the Prophet, the Prophecy of Ahijah the Shilonite, and the Visions of Iddo the Seer concerning Jeroboam son of Nebat.[g] [30] Solomon reigned in Jerusalem over all Israel for 40 years. [31] Solomon rested with his fathers and was buried in the city of his father David.[h] His son Rehoboam became king in his place.

The Kingdom Divided

10 Then Rehoboam went to Shechem,[i] for all Israel had gone to Shechem to make him king. [2] When Jeroboam son of Nebat heard about it—for he was in Egypt where he had fled from King Solomon's presence—Jeroboam returned from Egypt.[j] [3] So they summoned him. Then Jeroboam and all Israel came and spoke to Rehoboam: [4] "Your father made our yoke difficult. Therefore, lighten your father's harsh service and the heavy yoke he put on us, and we will serve you."

[5] Rehoboam replied, "Return to me in three days." So the people left.

[6] Then King Rehoboam consulted with the elders who had served his father Solomon when he was alive, asking, "How do you advise me to respond to these people?"

A 9:21 Or baboons   B 9:24 Or vessels, or weapons   C 9:24 LXX reads resin   D 9:24 Or fragrant balsam

coming to him as profit from his partnership with Hiram. Even the grandiose attitude that permeates this description was supposed to demonstrate to the Gentile world the reality of Yahweh's blessings of His king. But this does not mean that Solomon's policies, such as those that led to the devaluation of precious metals, were wise over the long haul. The overabundance of **silver** and **gold** in Jerusalem probably created a shortage in other lands, and it was only a short time before someone attempted to restore balance (12:9).

9:23-24 Even Solomon's legendary **wisdom** led to an increase in his wealth. Some of this wisdom has been preserved for us in the books of Proverbs and Ecclesiastes. Of particular note given Solomon's extraordinary wealth, at the end of his life that was so devoted to material acquisitions, he said: "Absolute futility. Everything is futile" (Ec 1:2).

9:25-28 On Solomon's accumulation of **horses and chariots**, see note at 1:16-17.

9:29-31 The Chronicler applies his standard summary of the life and rule of a king to **Solomon**, just as he had done for David (1Ch 29:26-30). If we compare Solomon's final notice with David's, we see that Solomon's obituary carries neither praise nor condemnation. Even though the Chronicler did not dwell on Solomon's shortcomings as the writer of 1 Kings did, he was certainly aware of them. He chose to focus on Solomon the temple builder rather than on Solomon the man. The temple that he built was of greater significance than the king himself.

10:1 Some of the kings throughout the rest of 2 Chronicles have similar names. Some of these kings appear under different names in 1 and 2 Kings. For this reason whenever a king is mentioned for the first time from this point on, we will give a quick summary of his identity.

Rehoboam: First king of Judah; son of Solomon; the king under whom the united kingdom split into the north (Israel) and the south (Judah). Initially there seemed to be little doubt in anyone's mind that Rehoboam should become the next king. He was the son of Solomon, and everyone knew that the descendants of David should occupy the throne. There seemed to be little question about Rehoboam's readiness for the kingship at 41 years old, so **all Israel** went to **Shechem** for his coronation.

10:2 Jeroboam: First king of Israel (where Israel refers only to the northern kingdom); leader in the revolt of the 10 northern tribes against Rehoboam; instituted official idol worship in the north. Jeroboam, from the tribe of Ephraim, at one time had been the leader of Solomon's labor force in Jerusalem (1Kg 11:26-40). One day when he was outside the city walls, the prophet Ahijah approached him and told him that he would be king over the 10 northern tribes (1Kg 11:29ff). Realizing that he had now been officially designated as a future traitor and that Solomon would execute him, Jeroboam fled to Egypt and remained there for the rest of Solomon's reign. As soon as Jeroboam heard about the impending coronation of Rehoboam, he made his way back from exile in Egypt to join the assembly.

10:3-4 Jeroboam's talent for leadership was known to the people, who immediately appointed him to be their spokesman and to convey to **Rehoboam** their desire for a reduction in forced labor.

10:5-7 King Solomon had been known for his wisdom and his ability to decide difficult questions (1Kg 3:28). His son, however, was unable to decide how to respond to this

⁷They replied, "If you will be kind to these people and please them by speaking kind words to them, they will be your servants forever."

⁸But he rejected the advice of the elders who had advised him, and he consulted with the young men who had grown up with him, the ones serving him. ⁹He asked them, "What message do you advise we send back to these people who said to me, 'Lighten the yoke your father put on us'?"

¹⁰Then the young men who had grown up with him told him, "This is what you should say to the people who said to you, 'Your father made our yoke heavy, but you, make it lighter on us!' This is what you should say to them: 'My little finger is thicker than my father's loins.ᴬ ¹¹Now therefore, my father burdened you with a heavy yoke, but I will add to your yoke; my father disciplined you with whips, but I, with barbed whips.'"ᴮ

¹²So Jeroboam and all the people came to Rehoboam on the third day, just as the king had ordered, saying, "Return to me on the third day." ¹³Then the king answered them harshly. King Rehoboam rejected the elders' advice ¹⁴and spoke to them according to the young men's advice, saying, "My father made your yoke heavy,ᶜ,ᵃ but I will add to it; my father disciplined you with whips, but I, with barbed whips."ᴮ

ᵃ10:14 1Kg 12:14
ᵇ10:15 2Ch 25:16-20
ᶜ1Kg 11:29-39
ᵈ10:16-17 2Sm 20:1-2
ᵉ10:16 1Kg 12:16
ᶠ10:18 1Kg 4:6; 5:14; 12:18
ᵍ11:1-4 1Kg 12:21-24
ʰ11:2 2Ch 12:5-7,15

¹⁵The king did not listen to the people because the turn of events came from God,ᵇ in order that the Lᴏʀᴅ might carry out His word that He had spoken through Ahijah the Shilonite to Jeroboam son of Nebat.ᶜ

¹⁶Whenᵈ all Israel sawᴰ,ᵉ that the king had not listened to them, the people answered the king:

What portion do we have in David?
We have no inheritance in the son
    of Jesse.
Israel, each man to your tent;
David, look after your own house now!

So all Israel went to their tents. ¹⁷But as for the Israelites living in the cities of Judah, Rehoboam reigned over them.

¹⁸Then King Rehoboam sent Hadoram,ᴱ,ᶠ who was in charge of the forced labor, but the Israelites stoned him to death. However, King Rehoboam managed to get into his chariot to flee to Jerusalem. ¹⁹Israel is in rebellion against the house of David until today.

Rehoboam in Jerusalem

11 When Rehoboam arrived in Jerusalem,ᵍ he mobilized the house of Judah and Benjamin—180,000 choice warriors—to fight against Israel to restore the reign to Rehoboam. ²But the word of the Lᴏʀᴅ came to Shemaiah,ʰ the man of God: ³"Say to Rehoboam

---

ᴬ10:10 Or waist   ᴮ10:11,14 Lit with scorpions   ᶜ10:14 Some Hb mss, LXX; other Hb mss read I will make your yoke heavy; 1Kg 12:14   ᴰ10:16 Some Hb mss, LXX; other Hb mss omit saw; 1Kg 12:16   ᴱ10:18 = Adoram in 1Kg 12:18

---

simple request. First he went to the older counselors, those who had served alongside Solomon, and asked them what he should do. They replied with the obvious answer: when you are confronted with an ultimatum from the populace and your entire kingdom is at stake, and you have it in your power to give in to the ultimatum with little difficulty, give the people what they ask for.

10:8-10 Rehoboam did not like the advice of the **elders**, so he consulted his peers, who are identified as **young men** (a comparative term, since they were roughly the same age as Rehoboam; see note at v. 1). They were in their forties, and they had been forced to wait for a long time to have any influence in the kingdom. These younger men saw the opportunity to assert themselves, and they suggested to Rehoboam that he speak sharply to the people. They coached their befuddled ruler into repeating an absurd saying that would have alienated even a person who had meant to support Rehoboam.

10:11 The HCSB correctly translates the word that is literally "scorpions" as **barbed whips**—a common instrument of discipline in the ancient Near East.

10:14 The king made the exact abusive speech that his younger advisers had programmed him to give (vv. 10-11).

10:15 The Chronicler makes it clear to his readers that in the final analysis Rehoboam was only carrying out what God had already prophesied through the prophet **Ahijah**—

that Rehoboam would lose almost all of his kingdom. Thus, even though Rehoboam was responsible for his actions, he was fulfilling what God had planned as punishment for Solomon's and Israel's unfaithfulness (1Kg 11:33).

10:16 When the people (**all Israel**) realized that Rehoboam was not willing to listen to their reasonable request, they turned their backs on him and went home (**to their tents**; see note at 8:17-18).

10:17 Rehoboam did not lose all his territory, but his kingdom was restricted to the tribe of **Judah**. Technically, this region also encompassed the area of Simeon, but this tribe had been assimilated into Judah over the centuries (though not entirely; see 1Ch 4:41). The tribe of Benjamin, once the fiercest opponent of the house of David, was now also fully integrated into Judah.

10:18-19 Still at Shechem, Rehoboam thought he could force the rebellious people to submit to him. He assigned **Hadoram**, his minister of labor, to call the Israelites back to their duty. The people of the northern tribes expressed their dissatisfaction with rocks and killed their would-be supervisor. Rehoboam managed to escape, but the kingdom was split for good.

11:2-4 Since God had brought about the split of the kingdom as a punishment, He informed **Rehoboam** through a prophet named **Shemaiah** that the king should give up any thought of invading and restoring the northern tribes.

son of Solomon, king of Judah, to all Israel in Judah and Benjamin, and to the rest of the people: ⁴'This is what the LORD says: You are not to march up and fight against your brothers.ᵃ Each of you must return home, for this incident has come from Me.'"ᵇ

So they listened to what the LORD said and turned back from going against Jeroboam.

Judah's King Rehoboam

⁵Rehoboam stayed in Jerusalem, and he fortified citiesᴬ,ᶜ in Judah. ⁶He built up Bethlehem, Etam, Tekoa, ⁷Beth-zur, Soco, Adullam, ⁸Gath, Mareshah, Ziph, ⁹Adoraim, Lachish, Azekah, ¹⁰Zorah, Aijalon, and Hebron, which are fortified cities in Judah and in Benjamin. ¹¹He strengthened their fortifications and put leaders in them with supplies of food, oil, and wine. ¹²He also put large shields and spears in each and every city to make them very strong. So Judah and Benjamin were his.

¹³The priests and Levites from all their regions throughout Israel took their stand with Rehoboam, ¹⁴for the Levites left their pasturelands and their possessionsᵈ and went to Judah and Jerusalem, because Jeroboam and his sons refused to let them serve as priests of •Yahweh.ᵉ ¹⁵Jeroboam appointed his own

priests for the •high places,ᶠ the goat-demons,ᵍ and the golden calves he had made.ʰ ¹⁶Those from every tribe of Israel who had determined in their hearts to seek Yahweh their God followed the Levites to Jerusalem to sacrifice to Yahweh, the God of their ancestors. ¹⁷So they strengthened the kingdom of Judah and supported Rehoboam son of Solomon for three years,ⁱ because they walked in the way of David and Solomon for three years.

¹⁸Rehoboam married Mahalath, daughter of David's son Jerimoth and of Abihail daughter of Jesse's son Eliab.ʲ ¹⁹She bore sons to him: Jeush, Shemariah, and Zaham. ²⁰After her, he married Maacah daughterᴮ,ᵏ of Absalom. She bore Abijah, Attai, Ziza, and Shelomith to him. ²¹Rehoboam loved Maacah daughterᴮ of Absalom more than all his wives and concubines. He acquired 18 wivesˡ and 60 concubines and was the father of 28 sons and 60 daughters.

²²Rehoboam appointed Abijah son of Maacah as chief, leader among his brothers, intending to make him king.ᵐ ²³Rehoboam also showed discernment by dispersing some of his sons to all the regions of Judah and Benjamin and to all the fortified cities. He gave them plenty of provisions and sought many wives for them.

ᵃ11:4 2Ch 28:8-11
ᵇ2Ch 10:15
ᶜ11:5 2Ch 8:2-6; 11:23
ᵈ11:14 Nm 35:2-5
ᵉ2Ch 13:9
ᶠ11:15 Ex 34:16-17
ᵍLv 17:7
ʰ1Kg 12:25-33; 13:33
ⁱ11:17 2Ch 12:1
ʲ11:18 1Sm 16:6
ᵏ11:20 2Ch 13:2
ˡ11:21 Dt 17:17
ᵐ11:22 Dt 21:15-17

ᴬ11:5 Lit he built cities for a fortress   ᴮ11:20,21 Possibly granddaughter; 2Ch 13:2

This was not time for a civil war; the people of **Judah and Benjamin** needed to go home and settle in under the new conditions. Thus, the army was disbanded and a war was avoided. The Chronicler mentions Jeroboam as head of the north, leaving it to the reader to infer that Jeroboam had indeed been crowned as king of the 10 northern tribes.

11:5-12 Instead of carrying out an invasion, **Rehoboam** assumed a defensive posture and **fortified cities** throughout the territory of **Judah and Benjamin**. Solomon had created large fortifications all over his kingdom, but many of those installations now belonged to the northern kingdom. Rehoboam needed to establish a smaller circle around Jerusalem. Cities that previously had not been that important, such as **Bethlehem**, now became crucial defensive posts. Not only did Rehoboam see to it that they were physically reinforced, but also that each of those places had a leader, a supply of **food, oil, and wine**, and **large shields and spears**. Having started off on the wrong foot, Rehoboam attempted to make up for his blunder by making sure that what remained of his kingdom was not vulnerable to attack.

11:13-16 Meanwhile, **Jeroboam** in the north was faced with a serious problem of his own. The mind-set of the people over whom he was supposed to rule made it almost impossible for him to be an effective king. He had broken away from Rehoboam and Jerusalem, but the temple was in **Jerusalem**, and the **priests** and **Levites** were still loyal to the temple. Prior to the building of the temple by Solomon, it was permissible for priests to perform sacrifices anywhere in the country, but the priests were not willing to return to that practice, and Jeroboam did not permit priests of the Jerusalem-bound religion to officiate in his new territory.

From all over the northern kingdom, they migrated to Jerusalem to participate in the true worship of the Lord. Thus, under Jeroboam's direction, the new kingdom of the north was rooted in idolatry right from the beginning. Jeroboam replaced the worship of God with the worship of **goat-demons** and two **golden calves**, one in the northern section of his kingdom at Dan, and the other in the south close to the border with Judah at Bethel. He also installed a new priesthood of those who were willing to serve these idols rather than the Lord. There were many laypersons within the northern tribes who were committed to serving the Lord, and they also relocated to Jerusalem so they could worship at the temple as the law required.

11:17 During the first **three years**, both kingdoms looked inward to strengthen themselves. The south rallied around the temple and the service of the Lord, while the north focused on the cult of idolatry instigated by Jeroboam.

11:18-21 **Rehoboam** had **18 wives**, many of them from within his wider circle of blood relations. **Mahalath** was his half cousin, **Abihail** was his great aunt, unless some intervening generations have not been mentioned. His favorite wife, **Maacah** (also called Micaiah), was probably Absalom's granddaughter by his son or son-in-law Uriel (13:2). She would become influential in leading the people into idolatry.

11:22-23 There was one matter in which **Rehoboam** proved to be a wiser ruler than either David or Solomon. Both of his predecessors had left their **sons** in Jerusalem, where they had been given important titles but not much responsibility. Having spent the first 41 years of his life in such a limbo, Rehoboam made sure that his sons had a meaningful purpose. He put them in charge of many of the newly **fortified cities** and provided them with numerous **wives**.

Shishak's Invasion

12 When Rehoboam had established his sovereignty and royal power,[a] he abandoned the law of the LORD—he and all Israel with him. [2]Because they were unfaithful to the LORD, in the fifth year of King Rehoboam, Shishak[b] king of Egypt went to war against Jerusalem[c] [3]with 1,200 chariots, 60,000 cavalrymen, and countless people who came with him from Egypt—Libyans,[d] Sukkiim, and Cushites. [4]He captured the fortified cities[e] of Judah and came as far as Jerusalem.

[5]Then Shemaiah[f] the prophet went to Rehoboam and the leaders of Judah who were gathered at Jerusalem because of Shishak. He said to them: "This is what the LORD says: 'You have abandoned Me; therefore, I have abandoned you into the hand of Shishak.'"[g]

[6]So the leaders of Israel and the king humbled themselves and said, "'Yahweh is righteous.'"[h]

[7]When the LORD saw that they had humbled themselves, the LORD's message came to Shemaiah: "They have humbled themselves; I will not destroy them but will grant them a little deliverance.[i] My wrath will not be poured out on Jerusalem through Shishak.[j] [8]However, they will become his servants so that they may recognize the difference between serving Me and serving the kingdoms of other lands."[k]

[9]So King Shishak of Egypt went to war[l] against Jerusalem.[m] He seized the treasuries of the LORD's temple and the treasuries of the royal palace. He took everything. He took the gold shields that Solomon had made.[n] [10]King Rehoboam made bronze shields in their place and committed them into the care of the captains of the royal escorts[A] who guarded the entrance to the king's palace. [11]Whenever the king entered the LORD's temple, the royal escorts would carry the shields and take them back to the royal escorts' armory. [12]When Rehoboam humbled himself, the LORD's anger turned away from him, and He did not destroy him completely.[o] Besides that, conditions were good in Judah.[p]

Rehoboam's Last Days

[13]King Rehoboam[q] established his royal power in Jerusalem. Rehoboam was 41 years old when he became king and reigned 17 years in Jerusalem, the city the LORD had chosen from all the tribes of Israel to put His name.[r] Rehoboam's mother's name was Naamah the Ammonite. [14]Rehoboam did what was evil, because he did not determine in his heart to seek the LORD.[s]

Cross references:
a12:1 2Ch 11:17; 12:13
b12:2 1Kg 11:40
c1Kg 14:25
d12:3 2Ch 16:8; Nah 3:9
e12:4 2Ch 11:5-12
f12:5 2Ch 11:2
g Dt 28:15,25; 2Ch 15:2
h12:6 Ex 9:27; Dn 9:14
i12:7 1Kg 21:29
j2Ch 34:25-27; Ps 78:38
k12:8 Dt 28:47-48
l12:9-11 1Kg 14:25-28
m12:9 2Ch 12:2
n2Ch 9:15-16
o12:12 2Ch 12:6-7
p2Ch 19:3
q12:13-14 1Kg 14:21-22
r12:13 Dt 12:5; 1Kg 9:3
s12:14 2Ch 19:3

A12:10 Lit the runners

12:1 All Israel in this context refers to residents of the kingdom of Judah, since the northern kingdom had already adopted Jeroboam's idolatry as the new state religion.

12:2-3 No sooner had Rehoboam fallen away into idolatry than **Shishak**, the new pharaoh of **Egypt**, mobilized his forces for an invasion of Judah (as well as Israel, as documented in his own records). Egypt had stayed in the background for a long time, having to deal with internal problems as well as several military setbacks over the last two centuries. In the thirteenth century, Ramesses II had set out on a disastrous attempt to subject the Hittites in the north to his rule, but he barely escaped with his army. This fact did not keep his subjects in Egypt from celebrating him as if he had achieved a major victory—for them it was a matter of national pride to put a positive spin on events. Egypt and the Hittites had seriously weakened each other, and Mesopotamia was gripped by a contest for power between Assyria and Babylonia. God had used these factors to enable David and Solomon to achieve great power. Furthermore, a while after Ramesses' misadventure, the Philistines had attempted to invade Egypt. Even though Egypt managed to hold them off, this episode left them weaker still. Solomon had married the daughter of a pharaoh whose entire dynasty ended with him. Now there was a new family of rulers, headed up by Shishak, known to history as Sheshonk I. Shishak was a Libyan. He was able to take control of the Egyptians as well as the adjoining people such as **Libyans, Sukkiim** (a nation related to the Libyans), **and Cushites**.

12:4 In spite of all the work that both Solomon and Rehoboam had put into fortifying the cities of Judah, these efforts did not keep away the pharaoh whom God had sent as punishment for the sins of the kingdom.

12:5-6 When the prophet **Shemaiah** (11:2) explained to King **Rehoboam** that his sin was the cause of this invasion, he and the people repented. Some subsequent kings, when confronted with their sin, did not listen to God, and thus received the full consequences of their sin.

12:9 Shishak's army arrived in **Jerusalem** and helped themselves to all the treasures that David and Solomon had collected. The **gold shields**, so conveniently stored on the walls of Solomon's palace, became easy objects for the Egyptian army to carry off (see note at 9:13-16). Yet just as Shemaiah had predicted, Shishak did not destroy Jerusalem. This unusual action fits with Shishak's own records of this military excursion. He listed in an inscription 41 cities that he captured and decimated, but Jerusalem was not among them.

12:10-11 Having lost the gold shields, Rehoboam replaced them with **bronze shields** and gave them more protection than he ever did to his father's legacy. He had been humiliated several times as he attempted to emulate his father. Now we see a little bit of self-assertion shining through this gesture.

12:12 Shishak's invasion was a lesson in humility. Shishak had apparently collected enough wealth to be satisfied. Despite the setback of the Egyptian invasion, on the whole life in **Judah** was **good**.

12:13-14 The customary death notice for Rehoboam is negative. On balance, despite his repentance and God's rescue, Rehoboam was considered an evil king who did not follow the law of the Lord.

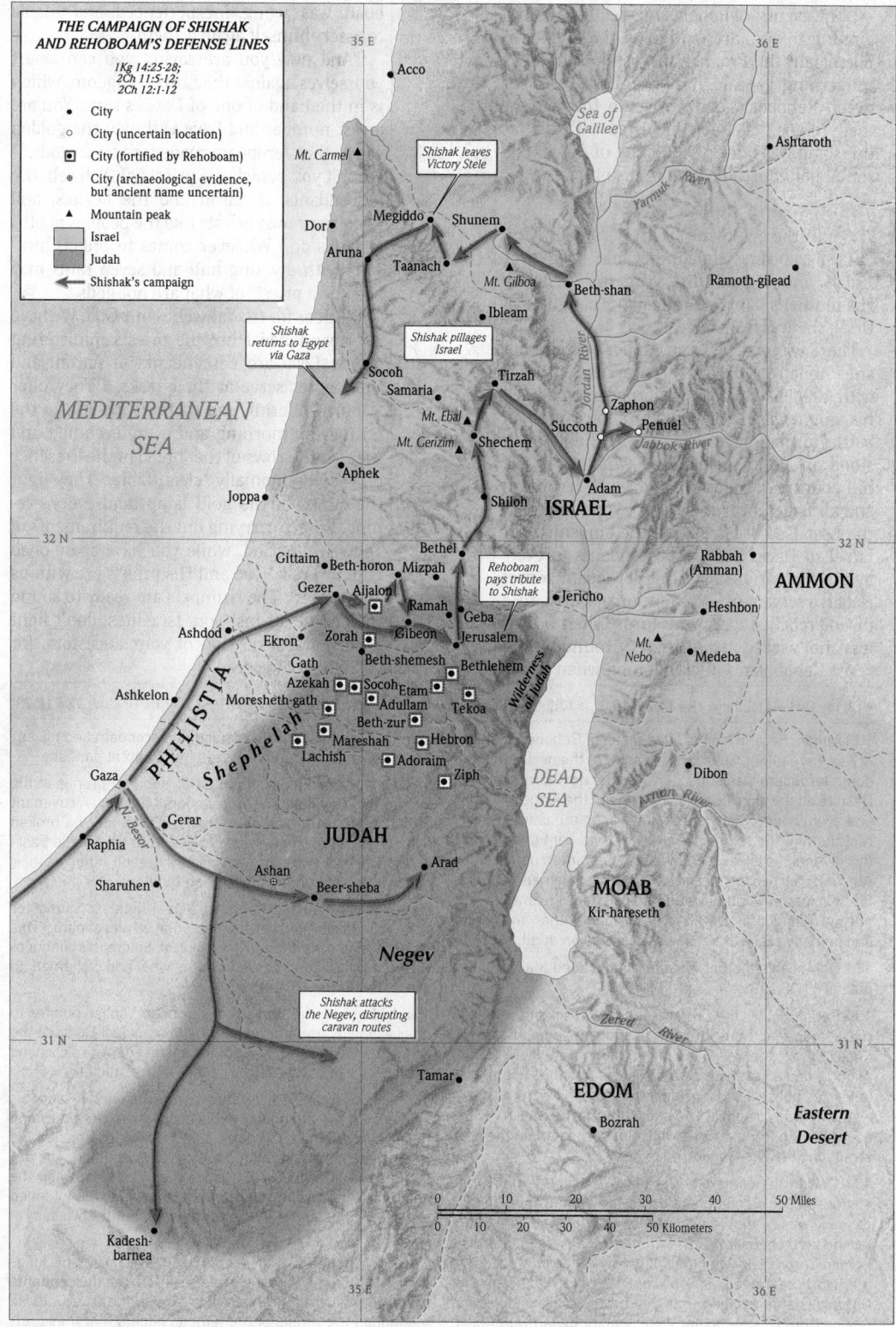

THE CAMPAIGN OF SHISHAK
AND REHOBOAM'S DEFENSE LINES

*1Kg 14:25-28;
2Ch 11:5-12;
2Ch 12:1-12*

- ● City
- ○ City (uncertain location)
- ▣ City (fortified by Rehoboam)
- ⊕ City (archaeological evidence, but ancient name uncertain)
- ▲ Mountain peak
- ▨ Israel
- ▨ Judah
- → Shishak's campaign

Acco

Sea of Galilee

Ashtaroth

Mt. Carmel ▲

Shishak leaves
Victory Stele

Dor

Megiddo Shunem

Yarmuk River

Aruna

Taanach

Mt. Gilboa ▲ Beth-shan

Ramoth-gilead

Ibleam

Shishak
returns to Egypt
via Gaza

Shishak pillages
Israel

Socoh

Tirzah

Samaria

Zaphon

Mt. Ebal ▲

Succoth

Penuel

Mt. Gerizim ▲ Shechem

Jabbok River

MEDITERRANEAN
SEA

Aphek

Shiloh

Adam

ISRAEL

Jordan River

Joppa

Bethel

Rabbah
(Amman)

AMMON

Gittaim Beth-horon Mizpah

Rehoboam
pays tribute
to Shishak

Jericho

Heshbon

Gezer Aijalon ▣

Ramah

Mt. Nebo ▲

Medeba

Ashdod

Ekron

Zorah ▣

Geba

Jerusalem

Gibeon

Gath

Beth-shemesh ▣

Ashkelon

Azekah ▣ Socoh ▣ Etam ▣

Bethlehem ▣

Moresheth-gath ▣ Adullam ▣

Tekoa ▣

Wilderness of Judah

Mareshah ▣ Beth-zur ▣

Lachish ▣ Hebron ▣

Dibon

Gaza

Adoraim ▣ Ziph ▣

N. Besor

Gerar

DEAD
SEA

Shephelah

PHILISTIA

Raphia

JUDAH

Ashan ⊕

Arad

MOAB

Sharuhen

Beer-sheba

Kir-hareseth

Arnon River

Negev

Shishak attacks
the Negev, disrupting
caravan routes

Zered River

Tamar

EDOM

*Eastern
Desert*

Bozrah

0   10   20   30   40   50 Miles

0   10   20   30   40   50 Kilometers

Kadesh-
barnea

¹⁵The events[a] of Rehoboam's reign, from beginning to end, are written in the Events of Shemaiah[b] the Prophet and of Iddo the Seer concerning genealogies.[c] There was war between Rehoboam and Jeroboam throughout their reigns. ¹⁶Rehoboam rested with his fathers and was buried in the city of David. His son Abijah[A,d] became king in his place.

Judah's King Abijah

13 In the eighteenth year[e] of Israel's King Jeroboam, Abijah[A] became king over Judah ²and reigned three years in Jerusalem. His mother's name was Micaiah[B,f] daughter of Uriel; she was from Gibeah.

There was war between Abijah and Jeroboam. ³Abijah set his army of warriors in order with 400,000 choice men. Jeroboam arranged his mighty army of 800,000 choice men in battle formation against him. ⁴Then Abijah stood on Mount Zemaraim,[g] which is in the hill country of Ephraim, and said, "Jeroboam and all Israel, hear me. ⁵Don't you know that the LORD God of Israel gave the kingship over Israel to David and his descendants forever[h] by a covenant of salt?[i] ⁶But Jeroboam son of Nebat, a servant of Solomon son of David, rose up and rebelled against his lord.[j] ⁷Then worthless and ˙wicked men gathered around him to resist Rehoboam son of Solomon when Rehoboam was young, inexperienced, and unable to assert himself against them.

⁸"And now you are saying you can assert yourselves against the LORD's kingdom, which is in the hand of one of David's sons. You are a vast number and have with you the golden calves that Jeroboam made for you as gods.[C,k] ⁹Didn't you banish the priests of ˙Yahweh, the descendants of Aaron and the Levites, and make your own priests like the peoples of other lands do?[l] Whoever comes to ordain himself[m] with a young bull and seven rams may become a priest[n] of what are not gods.[o]

¹⁰"But as for us, Yahweh is our God. We have not abandoned Him; the priests ministering to the LORD¯ are descendants of Aaron, and the Levites serve at their tasks. ¹¹They offer a ˙burnt offering and fragrant incense to the LORD every morning and every evening,[p] and they set the rows of the ˙bread of the Presence on the ceremonially ˙clean table.[q] They light the lamps of the gold lampstand every evening. We are carrying out the requirements of Yahweh our God, while you have abandoned Him.[r] ¹²Look, God and His priests are with us at our head. The trumpets are ready to sound the charge against you. Israelites, don't fight against the LORD God of your ancestors, for you will not succeed."[s]

Cross-references (center column)

a12:15-16 1Kg 14:29-31
b12:15 2Ch 12:5
c2Ch 9:29; 13:22
d12:16 1Kg 14:31–15:8
e13:1-2 1Kg 15:1-2,7
f13:2 1Kg 15:2; 2Ch 11:20,22
g13:4 Jos 18:22
h13:5 2Sm 7:12-16
iLv 2:13; Nm 18:19
j13:6 1Kg 11:26
k13:8 1Kg 12:28
l13:9 2Ch 11:14
mEx 29:29-33
n1Kg 13:33
oJr 2:11; 5:7
p13:11 Ex 29:38; 2Ch 2:4
qEx 25:30; Lv 24:5-9
rEx 25:31-40
s13:12 Nm 10:8-9

A12:16; 13:1 = Abijam in 1Kg 14:31–15:8   B13:2 LXX, Syr, Arabic read Maacah; 1Kg 15:2; 2Ch 11:22   C13:8 Or God; 1Kg 12:28

13:1 Abijah: Second king of Judah, son of Rehoboam, father of Asa, miraculous victor over an army of the northern kingdom. **Jeroboam** was still ruler over the northern kingdom. Despite all the shortcomings of many of the kings of Judah, and even though God would take drastic measures to correct them in the future, the line of David continued on the throne until the exile. There was one brief interruption when Athaliah usurped the throne (22:10), but even then the rightful heir was alive and eventually installed. In contrast, the northern kingdom saw no dynasty longer than five kings, and in many cases there was no succession at all.

13:2 On Abijah's mother **Micaiah** (also called Maacah), see note at 11:18-21.

13:3 Paradoxically, the Chronicler keeps track of the size of the army for each king, but only to make the point that in the final analysis, the size of the army did not matter. Jeroboam not only had an army twice as large as Abijah's, but he was able to establish his tactical **formation** so the army of Judah was practically trapped. The site of this **battle** was in the hill country of Ephraim, an area north of Jerusalem in the area straddling the two kingdoms.

13:4 Only in the context of the parallel account in 1 Kings 15 does Abijah's action take on its full significance. In that passage we see that Abijah was an idolater who cared little for the Lord or His laws. The moment that we see depicted here in Chronicles, when Abijah briefly relied on the Lord in a time of great need, is an exception, but it illustrates the Chronicler's affirmation that God protects the people who rely on Him. This particular case in point began with Abijah standing up and publicly repudiating **Jeroboam** and his entire army, an action that exposed him to great danger.

13:5 Abijah reminded everyone that God had promised the kingdom to **David** and his descendants **forever**. A **covenant of salt** refers to a binding promise that cannot be broken (Nm 18:19); the term may be derived from the Middle Eastern practice of two parties reassuring each other of their goodwill by consuming a bit of salt together.

13:6-7 Abijah depicted Rehoboam as a helpless youngster who was deceived by the manipulative **Jeroboam**. This made it sound as though the split of Solomon's kingdom was brought about by Jeroboam, who had schemed to grasp the throne.

13:8 Addressing the soldiers of Jeroboam, Abijah pointed to their action as another act of rebellion against God and the descendants of David. The **golden calves** they were carrying with them into battle were evidence of their idolatry.

13:9 Abijah combined Jeroboam, the instigator, and his soldiers a generation later in his accusation. Both they and their usurper king shared the guilt for having banished the true **priests** and substituting their own priesthood. The description of how one could become a priest by paying the going price of **a young bull and seven rams** was intended to raise doubts in the soldier's minds about the wisdom of this practice.

13:10-12 In contrast, Abijah pointed out that he and his kingdom had retained the true **priests** of God, the **descendants of Aaron**, and that they were worshiping the true God. He mentioned the rituals of the temple, hoping that these ref-

13Now Jeroboam had sent an ambush[a] around to advance from behind them. So they were in front of Judah, and the ambush was behind them. 14Judah turned and discovered that the battle was in front of them and behind them, so they cried out to the LORD.[b] Then the priests blew the trumpets, 15and the men of Judah raised the battle cry. When the men of Judah raised the battle cry, God routed Jeroboam and all Israel before Abijah and Judah.[c] 16So the Israelites fled before Judah, and God handed them over to them.[d] 17Then Abijah and his people struck them with a mighty blow, and 500,000 choice men of Israel were killed. 18The Israelites were subdued at that time. The Judahites succeeded because they depended on the LORD, the God of their ancestors.

19Abijah pursued Jeroboam and captured some cities from him: Bethel and its villages, Jeshanah and its villages, and Ephron[A] and its villages. 20Jeroboam no longer retained his power[B] during Abijah's reign; ultimately, the LORD struck him[e] and he died.[f]

21However, Abijah grew strong, acquired 14 wives, and fathered 22 sons and 16 daughters. 22The rest of the events of Abijah's reign, along with his ways and his sayings, are written in the Writing[g] of the Prophet Iddo.[h] 1CAbijah rested with his fathers and was bur-

ied in the city of David. His son Asa became king in his place.[i] During his reign the land experienced peace for 10 years.

Judah's King Asa

2DAsa did what was good and right[j] in the sight of the LORD his God. 3He removed the pagan altars and the *high places. He shattered their sacred pillars and chopped down their *Asherah poles.[k] 4He told the people of Judah to seek the LORD God of their ancestors and to carry out the instruction and the commands. 5He also removed the high places and the incense altars from all the cities of Judah,[l] and the kingdom experienced peace under him.

6Because the land experienced peace, Asa built fortified cities in Judah.[m] No one made war with him in those days because the LORD gave him rest.[n] 7So he said to the people of Judah, "Let's build these cities and surround them with walls and towers, with doors and bars.[o] The land is still ours because we sought the LORD our God. We sought Him and He gave us rest on every side." So they built and succeeded.

The Cushite Invasion

8Asa had an army of 300,000 from Judah bearing large shields and spears,[p] and 280,000 from Benjamin bearing regular shields and drawing the bow. All these were brave warriors.

a13:13 Jos 8:4-9
b13:14 2Ch 14:11
c13:15 2Ch 14:12
d13:16 2Ch 16:8
e13:20 1Sm 25:38
f1Kg 14:20
g13:22 2Ch 24:27
h1Kg 15:7; 2Ch 9:29; 12:15
i14:1 1Kg 15:8
j14:2-3 1Kg 15:11-12
k14:3 Ex 34:13; Dt 7:5
l14:5 2Ch 34:4,7
m14:6 2Ch 11:5
n2Ch 15:15
o14:7 2Ch 8:5
p14:8 2Ch 13:3

A13:19 Alt Hb tradition reads *Ephrain* B13:20 Lit *He did not restrain the power of Jeroboam* C14:1 2Ch 13:23 in Hb
D14:2 2Ch 14:1 in Hb

erences would induce the soldiers to understand that by having discarded their true legacy in favor of Jeroboam's contrivances, they were pursuing a lost cause.

13:13-18 While Abijah was attempting to persuade the northern army to abandon the fight, his enemies sent soldiers into the rear of his army to close the trap. The army of Judah **cried out**, fought with desperation, and God took it from there. They killed more than half of Jeroboam's army, but the Chronicler makes it clear that it was **the LORD** who was responsible for the victory.

13:19-20 Abijah and his army not only routed **Jeroboam**, but they also captured the town of **Bethel**—the southern sanctuary for Jeroboam's golden calves. For Jeroboam, this was the beginning of the end. God judged him severely, and after **he died**, his son Nadab was assassinated after only two years on the throne (1Kg 13–14; 15:25-28).

13:21 Abijah's reign was brief as well, but he remained powerful.

13:22 The **Writing of the Prophet Iddo** is not known to us.

14:1 In light of the single event of Abijah's life that the Chronicler highlights, Abijah received a neutral death notice. He was buried on Mount Zion in the vicinity of David's tomb. The line of succession passed on to his son Asa.

Asa: Third king of Judah; son of Abijah; devoted to God, but closed himself off from God at the end of his life. The years given for the kings' reigns make it clear that at times there was some overlap, when the father had already el-

evated his son as co-regent with him, just as David did with Solomon for a short while (1Ch 29:22). Thus, the **10 years** of **peace** could include the latter years of Abijah's reign and the first years of Asa's reign.

14:2-3 Asa receives high praise from the Chronicler. He **removed** all the objects of idol worship and exhorted the people to obey God. **High places** were places of worship to various gods. Many, but not all, were **pagan**. Frequently sites for idolatry are called "high places," as in this passage (11:15), but the expression is also used for places dedicated to Yahweh, the true God. **Asherah poles** were dedicated to the Canaanite goddess Asherah. The Canaanites believed that Asherah was the wife of the high god El and the mother of the main god Baal. She was a goddess of sexuality, and her worship was supposed to produce fertility for crops and animals by venerating sacred poles.

14:6-7 Encouraged by the time of **peace**, Asa set about redoing the fortifications throughout the land. He showed greater understanding than Rehoboam of the value of these fortifications. He told the people that they still owned the land because they had **sought the LORD**. Without the Lord's protection, the walls would be useless.

14:8-10 Asa's army was even larger than that of Abijah; the 400,000 warriors had grown to 580,000. Unfortunately, this huge number still put him at a disadvantage when **Zerah the Cushite** (an Ethiopian) came calling with an army of **one million men and 300 chariots**. Instead of concealing

⁹Then Zerah the •Cushite came against them with an army of one million men and 300ᴬ chariots. They came as far as Mareshah. ¹⁰So Asa marched out against him and lined up in battle formation in the Valley of Zephathah at Mareshah.ᵃ

¹¹Then Asa cried out to the LORD his God:ᵇ "LORD, there is no one besides You to help the mighty and those without strength. Help us, LORD our God, for we depend on You,ᶜ and in Your name we have come against this large army. •Yahweh, You are our God. Do not let a mere mortal hinder You."

¹²So the LORD routed the Cushites before Asa and before Judah,ᵈ and the Cushites fled. ¹³Then Asa and the people who were with him pursued them as far as Gerar.ᵉ The Cushites fell until they had no survivors, for they were crushed before Yahweh and His army. So the people of Judah carried off a great supply of loot. ¹⁴Then they attacked all the cities around Gerar because the terror of the LORD was on them.ᶠ They also plundered all the cities, since there was a great deal of plunder in them. ¹⁵They also attacked the tents of the herdsmen and captured many sheep and camels. Then they returned to Jerusalem.

Revival Under Asa

15 The Spirit of God came on Azariah son of Oded.ᵍ ²So he went out to meet Asa and said to him, "Asa and all Judah and Benjamin, hear me. The LORD is with youʰ when you are with Him. If you seek Him, He will be found by you,ⁱ but if you abandon Him, He will abandon you.ʲ ³For many years Israel has been without the true God,ᵏ without a teach-

ing priest, and without instruction,ˡ ⁴but when they turned to the LORD God of Israel in their distress and sought Him, He was found by them. ⁵In those times there was no peace for those who went about their daily activities because the residents of the lands had many conflicts. ⁶Nation was crushed by nation and city by city, for God troubled them with every possible distress. ⁷But as for you, be strong; don't be discouraged,ᴮ for your work has a reward."ᵐ

⁸When Asa heard these words and the prophecy of Azariah son of Oded the prophet, he took courage and removed the detestable idols from the whole land of Judah and Benjamin and from the cities he had captured in the hill country of Ephraim.ⁿ He renovated the altar of the LORD that was in front of the portico of the LORD's temple.ᵒ ⁹Then he gathered all Judah and Benjamin, as well as those from the tribes of Ephraim, Manasseh, and Simeon who had settled among them, for they had defected to him from Israel in great numbers when they saw that •Yahweh his God was with him.ᵖ

¹⁰They were gathered in Jerusalem in the third month of the fifteenth year of Asa's reign. ¹¹At that time they sacrificed to the LORD 700 cattle and 7,000 sheep from all the plunder they had brought.ᵍ ¹²Then they entered into a covenant to seek the LORD God of their ancestors with all their mind and all their heart.ʳ ¹³Whoever would not seek the LORD God of Israel would be put to death, young or old,ᶜ man or woman.ˢ ¹⁴They took an oath to the LORD in a loud voice, with shouting, with trumpets, and with rams' horns. ¹⁵All Judah rejoiced over the oath, for they had sworn it with all

Cross references (center column)

ᵃ14:10 2Ch 11:8
ᵇ14:11 2Ch 13:14
ᶜ2Ch 13:18
ᵈ14:12 2Ch 13:15
ᵉ14:13 Gn 10:19
ᶠ14:14 2Ch 17:10
ᵍ15:1 2Ch 20:14; 24:20
ʰ15:2 2Ch 20:17
ⁱDt 4:29; 2Ch 15:15; Jr 29:13-14
ʲ1Ch 28:9
ᵏ15:3 1Kg 12:28-33
ˡLv 10:8-11; 2Ch 17:9
ᵐ15:7 Jos 1:7,9
ⁿ15:8 2Ch 13:19
ᵒ2Ch 4:1; 8:12
ᵖ15:9 2Ch 11:16
ᵍ15:11 2Ch 14:13-15
ʳ15:12 2Ch 23:16
ˢ15:13 Ex 22:20; Dt 13:6-9; 17:2-7

ᴬ14:9 Syr, Arabic read *30,000*   ᴮ15:7 Lit *don't let your hands fail*   ᶜ15:13 Or *insignificant or great*

---

himself behind his newly built fortifications, Asa and his smaller army marched out to confront Zerah in the vicinity of **Mareshah**, a town in western Judah.

14:11 Asa knew the odds were against him, but he had evidently learned from his father's success against Jeroboam's army. He **cried out to the LORD** for help. The king believed the outcome of the battle would not be determined by **a mere mortal**.

14:12 Once again, it was **the LORD** who won the battle, with Asa and his army serving as His instruments.

14:13-15 Zerah and his huge army had advanced this far because they had received support from the people of **Gerar** and the cattle-raising nomads in the vicinity. The army of Judah plundered **all the cities** around Gerar.

15:1-2 Azariah son of Oded is one of many prophets who make brief appearances in the books of 1 and 2 Chronicles. He came with a message of encouragement for **Asa** to continue his devotion to the Lord.

15:3-7 Azariah reminded Asa of the cycles when the people had abandoned God, were punished (particularly by means of invasions of foreign armies), returned to God, enjoyed

God's blessings, and once again abandoned Him. The prophet's intent was to praise Asa and to motivate him to continue what he was doing.

15:8 It is not clear when this event occurred. It is possible that this passage is an elaboration of the introduction to Asa in 14:2, but we cannot rule out that Asa had not completely followed through on his earlier attempts at reform and that Azariah's message led him to become more aggressive in his purge of idolatry.

15:9-11 The people responded favorably to Asa's reforms, including further defections from the north (see note at 11:13-16). They held a major feast of sacrifice in the temple, which the king had renovated (15:8). The animals that were **sacrificed** came from the **plunder** of Asa's earlier victory (14:13-15).

15:12-15 Everyone took an oath of allegiance to the Lord, and they did so joyfully and voluntarily. This oath included an automatic death penalty for anyone who would **not seek the LORD**. The Lord rewarded their zeal and genuine repentance with **rest** (Dt 4:29; 1Sm 7:3); God reserves the right to

their mind. They had sought Him with all their heart, and He was found by them.[a] So the LORD gave them rest on every side.[b]

[16] King Asa[c] also removed Maacah, his grandmother,[A,d] from being queen mother because she had made an obscene image of *Asherah. Asa chopped down her obscene image, then crushed it and burned it in the Kidron Valley.[e] [17] The *high places were not taken away from Israel; nevertheless, Asa was wholehearted his entire life.[B] [18] He brought his father's consecrated gifts and his own consecrated gifts into God's temple: silver, gold, and utensils.

[19] There was no war until the thirty-fifth year of Asa's reign.

Asa's Treaty with Aram

16 In the thirty-sixth year of Asa,[f] Israel's King Baasha went to war against Judah. He built Ramah in order to deny access to anyone—going or coming—to Judah's King Asa. [2] So Asa brought out the silver and gold from the treasuries of the LORD's temple and the royal palace and sent it to Aram's King Ben-hadad, who lived in Damascus, saying, [3] "There's a treaty between me and you, between my father and your father. Look, I have sent you silver and gold. Go break your

treaty with Israel's King Baasha so that he will withdraw from me."

[4] Ben-hadad listened to King Asa and sent the commanders of his armies to the cities of Israel. They attacked Ijon, Dan, Abel-maim,[c] and all the storage cities[D] of Naphtali. [5] When Baasha heard about it, he quit building Ramah and stopped his work. [6] Then King Asa brought all Judah, and they carried away the stones of Ramah and the timbers Baasha had built it with. Then he built Geba and Mizpah with them.

Hanani's Rebuke of Asa

[7] At that time, Hanani[g] the seer came to King Asa of Judah and said to him, "Because you depended on the king of Aram and have not depended on the LORD your God,[h] the army of the king of Aram has escaped from your hand. [8] Were not the *Cushites and Libyans a vast army with many chariots and horsemen?[i] When you depended on *Yahweh, He handed them over to you.[j] [9] For the eyes of Yahweh roam throughout the earth[k] to show Himself strong for those whose hearts are completely His.[l] You have been foolish in this matter. Therefore, you will have wars from now on." [10] Asa was angry with the seer and put him in

Cross-references
[a]15:15 2Ch 15:2
[b]2Ch 14:6-7
[c]15:16-18 1Kg 15:13-15
[d]15:16 1Kg 15:2; 2Ch 11:22
[e]2Ch 14:2-5
[f]16:1-6 1Kg 15:17-22
[g]16:7 1Kg 16:1; 2Ch 19:2
[h]2Ch 14:11
[i]16:8 2Ch 12:3
[j]2Ch 14:9-13
[k]16:9 Gn 6:8; Ps 33:18; 34:15; Pr 15:3; Zch 4:10; 1Pt 3:12
[l]2Ch 15:17

[A]15:16 Lit mother; 1Kg 15:2; 2Ch 11:22　　[B]15:17 Lit wholehearted all his days　　[C]16:4 Abel-beth-maacah in 1Kg 15:20
[D]16:4 = all Chinnereth in 1Kg 15:20

---

ignore insincere repentance (Ps 66:18; Pr 1:28-31; 21:27; Jr 11:9-11).

15:16 One of the important acts of Asa was that he removed from power **Maacah**, his grandmother, because she was a supporter of idol worship.

15:17 This verse illustrates the difference between **high places** that were pagan sites and those that were used for worship of Yahweh (see note at 14:2-3). The high places that Asa did not remove were dedicated to the true God.

15:19 For a long time Asa did all the right things and avoided doing all the wrong things, and things went well for him and the kingdom.

16:1 Baasha: Third king of Israel; began his own dynasty; defeated by Asa of Judah. In the northern kingdom, Jeroboam's son Nadab had been replaced by Baasha, who decided to go to war against the southern kingdom. The first step in his strategy was to block access to Jerusalem by fortifying the town of **Ramah**. Baasha had also formed an alliance with Ben-hadad, king of Aram in Damascus. This meant that once Asa was cut off from the outside world, it would be an easy thing to capture Jerusalem.

16:2-6 Asa emptied the **treasuries** of the **temple** and bribed **Ben-hadad** of **Damascus** to break his treaty with Baasha of Israel. The king of Damascus not only complied willingly, but even sent his soldiers into Israel to compensate themselves for the booty they missed by not attacking Jerusalem. Asa was able to destroy Baasha's blockade and assert his dominance over his northern border area again.

16:7-9 Asa made a serious misjudgment in thinking that the Lord would be pleased if he did God's work for Him. Rather than reaping praise for his diplomatic achievement,

Asa was rebuked for his actions by **Hanani**. This prophet reminded the king that God wanted Asa to depend on Him and not on his own cleverness or on help from pagans. After Asa defeated the superior forces of the **Cushites and Libyans** he should have known that God rewards devotion with deliverance.

16:10 This was more than Asa could handle. His ego had

---

chazaq

Hebrew Pronunciation	[khah ZAHK]
HCSB Translation	be strong, strengthen, show oneself strong
Uses in 2 Chronicles	39
Uses in the OT	290
Key Passage	2 Chronicles 16:9

Chazaq means *be strong* (Dt 31:6), *harsh, fierce,* or *severe* (Gn 47:20). People *detain* or *pressure* (Ex 12:33). *Chazaq* implies *persevere* (1Ch 28:7), *devote energy, recover* (Is 39:1), *prevail,* and *defeat* (1Sm 17:50). Causative and intensive verbs signify *support* (Lv 25:35), *strengthen, encourage* (Dt 1:38), and *repair* (2Kg 12:5). Causatives signify *grab* (Gn 19:16), *seize, cling, hold fast, take hold, grasp, embrace, keep,* and *bring.* People *sustain, fortify, intensify, retain,* and *maintain* things. They *take charge* and *devote themselves* (Neh 5:16). Panic *grips.* Traps *catch.* People *join* (Neh 10:29), *triumph* (Dn 11:7), or *persuade* (2Kg 4:8). Intensives denote *give power* (Jdg 3:12), *brace,* and *harden* (Ex 4:21). People *fasten, tie, drive deep,* or *hold* things. Reflexive-passive forms indicate *be strengthened, establish oneself, assert oneself* (2Ch 13:7), *show/prove oneself strong* (2Ch 16:9), *summon courage/strength* (2Ch 23:1), *preserve* (Ezk 7:13), or *rally* (Jdg 20:22).

prison[A] because of his anger over this. And Asa mistreated some of the people at that time.

Asa's Death

[11] Note that the events[a] of Asa's reign, from beginning to end, are written in the Book of the Kings of Judah and Israel. [12] In the thirty-ninth year of his reign, Asa developed a disease in his feet, and his disease became increasingly severe. Yet even in his disease he didn't seek the Lord but only the physicians. [13] Asa died in the forty-first year of his reign and rested with his fathers. [14] He was buried in his own tomb that he had made for himself in the city of David. They laid him out in a coffin that was full of spices and various mixtures of prepared ointments;[b] then they made a great fire in his honor.[c]

Judah's King Jehoshaphat

17 His son Jehoshaphat became king in his place[d] and strengthened himself against Israel. [2] He stationed troops in every fortified city of Judah[e] and set garrisons in the land of Judah and in the cities of Ephraim that his father Asa had captured.[f] [3] Now the Lord was with Jehoshaphat because he walked in the former ways of his father David.[B] He did not seek the ·Baals [4] but sought the God of his father and walked by His commands, not according to the practices of Israel.[g] [5] So the Lord established the kingdom in his hand. Then all Judah brought him tribute, and he had riches and honor in abundance.[h] [6] His mind rejoiced in the Lord's

ways, and he again[i] removed the ·high places and ·Asherah poles from Judah.[j]

Jehoshaphat's Educational Plan

[7] In the third year of his reign, Jehoshaphat sent his officials—Ben-hail,[c] Obadiah, Zechariah, Nethanel, and Micaiah—to teach in the cities of Judah.[k] [8] The Levites with them were Shemaiah, Nethaniah, Zebadiah,[D] Asahel, Shemiramoth, Jehonathan, Adonijah, Tobijah, and Tob-adonijah; the priests, Elishama and Jehoram, were with these Levites. [9] They taught throughout Judah, having the book of the Lord's instruction with them.[l] They went throughout the towns of Judah and taught the people.

[10] The terror of the Lord was on all the kingdoms of the lands that surrounded Judah,[m] so they didn't fight against Jehoshaphat. [11] Some of the Philistines also brought gifts and silver as tribute to Jehoshaphat, and the Arabs brought him flocks: 7,700 rams and 7,700 male goats.[n]

Jehoshaphat's Military Might

[12] Jehoshaphat grew stronger and stronger. He built fortresses[o] and storage cities in Judah [13] and carried out great works in the towns of Judah. He had fighting men, brave warriors, in Jerusalem. [14] These are their numbers according to their ancestral families. For Judah, the commanders of thousands:

Adnah the commander and 300,000 brave warriors with him;

---

[a] 16:11-14 1Kg 15:23-24
[b] 16:14 Gn 50:2; Jn 12:7; 19:39-40
[c] 2Ch 21:19
[d] 17:1 1Kg 15:24
[e] 17:2 2Ch 11:5
[f] 2Ch 15:8
[g] 17:4 1Kg 12:28
[h] 17:5 2Ch 18:1
[i] 17:6 2Ch 14:2-3
[j] 2Ch 15:17
[k] 17:7 2Ch 15:3; 35:3
[l] 17:9 Dt 6:4-9; 17:18; 28:58,61; 29:21; 30:10; 31:24,26; Jos 1:8; 8:31,34; 23:6; 24:26
[m] 17:10 2Ch 14:14
[n] 17:11 2Ch 9:14; 26:8
[o] 17:12 2Ch 27:4

[A] 16:10 Lit the house of stocks   [B] 17:3 Some Hb mss, LXX omit David   [C] 17:7 = Son of Power   [D] 17:8 Some Hb mss, Syr, Tg, Arabic read Zechariah

---

been bruised, so he put the prophet Hanani **in prison** and abused other people. He had forgotten his earlier assertion that a mere mortal could not hinder God (14:11).

16:11-12 So the glorious reign of Asa, who had acted for God so effectively, came to a sour end. When he developed a serious **disease in his feet**, he avoided turning to the Lord and sought healing by **physicians** instead. His sin was not in turning to physicians, but in failing to ask God how he should proceed and to rely on God for the outcome (Jr 17:5).

16:14 Nevertheless, Asa received a glorious burial. The reference to **ointments** and **spices** may indicate that his death was due to diabetes, which could have brought on gangrene in his feet. The **great fire** was a tribute of honor from the people (cp. 21:19).

17:1 Jehoshaphat: Fourth king of Judah; son of Asa; thoroughly devoted to God, but made disastrous alliances with Ahab and Ahaziah of Israel.

17:2 Despite his dubious victory over Baasha, Asa had to endure further wars at the end of his reign (16:9). His son Jehoshaphat, who succeeded him on the throne, reworked all the fortifications and **stationed troops** in the older locations as well as in the newly captured **cities of Ephraim**.

17:3-6 Jehoshaphat was one of the outstanding kings of Judah. He stood for all the things that should characterize a king of Judah, and the Chronicler praises him almost as much as David, Solomon, and (later on) Hezekiah. Since his father Asa had lost his grip on the kingdom in his later years, Jehoshaphat had to purge the land of **high places and Asherah poles**.

17:7-9 An important part of David's original plan in assigning duties to the Levites was a contingent of teachers throughout the country (1Ch 26:29-32), but this proved impossible once the kingdom was divided. **Jehoshaphat** revived this idea and designated certain **Levites** as itinerant teachers. They carried copies of the law and instructed everyone in Judah how to live as God's people.

17:10-11 The Lord rewarded Jehoshaphat's single-minded commitment by causing the neighboring kingdoms to fear Judah; some even voluntarily brought **tribute**.

17:14-18 There was another increase in the size of the army of Judah. Rehoboam's army had numbered 180,000; Abijah had 400,000 soldiers; Asa's army numbered 580,000. The grand total for Jehoshaphat's army was 1,160,000 **fighting men**.

¹⁵ next to him, Jehohanan the commander and 280,000 with him; ¹⁶ next to him, Amasiah son of Zichri, the volunteer^a of the LORD, and 200,000 brave warriors with him; ¹⁷ from Benjamin, Eliada, a brave warrior, and 200,000 with him armed with bow and shield; ¹⁸ next to him, Jehozabad and 180,000 with him equipped for war.

¹⁹ These were the ones who served the king, besides those he stationed in the fortified cities throughout all Judah.^b

Jehoshaphat's Alliance with Ahab

18 Now Jehoshaphat^c had riches and honor in abundance,^d and he made an alliance with Ahab through marriage.^{A,e} ² Then after some years, he went down to visit Ahab in Samaria. Ahab sacrificed many sheep and cattle for him and for the people who were with him. Then he persuaded him to march up to Ramoth-gilead, ³ for Israel's King Ahab asked Judah's King Jehoshaphat, "Will you go with me to Ramoth-gilead?"

He replied to him, "I am as you are, my people as your people; we will be with you in the battle." ⁴ But Jehoshaphat said to the king of Israel, "First, please ask what the LORD's will is."

⁵ So the king of Israel gathered the prophets, 400 men, and asked them, "Should we go to Ramoth-gilead for war or should I refrain?"

They replied, "March up, and God will hand it over to the king."

⁶ But Jehoshaphat asked, "Isn't there a prophet of •Yahweh here anymore? Let's ask him."^f

^a17:16 Jdg 5:2,9; 1Ch 29:9 ^b17:19 2Ch 17:2 ^c18:1-34 1Kg 22:1-35 ^d18:1 2Ch 17:5 ^e1Kg 3:1; 2Kg 8:18; Ezr 9:14 ^f18:6 2Kg 3:11 ^g18:9 Ru 4:1 ^h18:13 Nm 22:35,38; 24:13

⁷ The king of Israel said to Jehoshaphat, "There is still one man who can ask Yahweh, but I hate him because he never prophesies good about me, but only disaster. He is Micaiah son of Imlah."

"The king shouldn't say that," Jehoshaphat replied.

⁸ So the king of Israel called an officer and said, "Hurry and get Micaiah son of Imlah!"

⁹ Now the king of Israel and King Jehoshaphat of Judah, clothed in royal attire, were each sitting on his own throne. They were sitting on the threshing floor at the entrance to Samaria's •gate,^g and all the prophets were prophesying in front of them. ¹⁰ Then Zedekiah son of Chenaanah made iron horns and said, "This is what the LORD says: 'You will gore the Arameans with these until they are finished off.'" ¹¹ And all the prophets were prophesying the same, saying, "March up to Ramoth-gilead and succeed, for the LORD will hand it over to the king."

Micaiah's Message of Defeat

¹² The messenger who went to call Micaiah instructed him, "Look, the words of the prophets are unanimously favorable for the king. So let your words be like theirs, and speak favorably."

¹³ But Micaiah said, "As the LORD lives, I will say whatever my God says."^{B,h}

¹⁴ So he went to the king, and the king asked him, "Micaiah, should we go to Ramoth-gilead for war, or should I^C refrain?"

Micaiah said, "March up and succeed, for they will be handed over to you."

¹⁵ But the king said to him, "How many times must I make you swear not to tell me

A18:1 Lit *made himself a son-in-law to Ahab*; 1Kg 3:1; Ezr 9:14   **B**18:13 LXX, Vg add *to me*; 1Kg 22:14   **C**18:14 LXX reads *we*; 1Kg 22:15

18:1 Ahab: Sixth king of Israel, son of Omri; made Baal worship the state religion of the northern kingdom (1Kg 16:31); formed an **alliance** with Jehoshaphat of Judah. **Jehoshaphat**, who needed no one's help to achieve greatness, acted as though he depended on other people for success. He contracted a **marriage** between his son Jehoram and Athaliah, daughter of Ahab and Jezebel.

18:2 Ahab's father, Omri, had built **Samaria** and made it the new capital of the northern kingdom. Jehoshaphat decided to pay **Ahab** a visit, and the king received him in grand style, even performing many sacrifices in Jehoshaphat's honor. Ahab's devotion to Baal was no secret, and thus Jehoshaphat was compromising his devotion to the Lord.

18:3-4 At Ahab's initiative, **Jehoshaphat** agreed to combine their armies to fight the Arameans. As an afterthought, Jehoshaphat asked that they consult the Lord on whether this was really **the LORD's will**.

18:5 Ahab had **400 prophets** on his payroll. These prophets, who were servants of Baal, were well-schooled in declaring whatever King Ahab wanted to hear, so they encouraged him to go ahead with his plans.

18:6 Conferring with false prophets was not what Jehoshaphat had in mind, so he asked if a prophet of **Yahweh** was available. This was an astounding request because prophets of Yahweh were not welcome at the court of Ahab and Jezebel.

18:10 Word had come to the prophets of Baal that what the king of Judah wanted to hear was the word of Yahweh. One of their leaders, **Zedekiah**, decided to add a visual touch to his prophecy. He decorated himself with a symbol of Baal, a set of **iron horns**, and began to act out the Lord's supposed prediction of Ahab's success in battle.

18:12-13 The court messenger wanted to avoid controversy and did not want to offend the king, so he encouraged Micaiah to go along with the crowd. As a true prophet, **Micaiah** knew he must speak the message God gave him (Nm 22:18; 2Co 2:17; Gl 1:10; 1Th 2:4).

18:14-15 There may have been a sarcastic tone in Micaiah's

anything but the truth in the name of Yahweh?"

¹⁶So Micaiah said:

I saw all Israel scattered on the hills
like sheep without a shepherd.ᵃ
And the Lord said,
"They have no master;
let each return home in peace."

¹⁷So the king of Israel said to Jehoshaphat, "Didn't I tell you he never prophesies good about me, but only disaster?"

¹⁸Then Micaiah said, "Therefore, hear the word of the Lord. I saw the Lord sitting on His throne, and the whole heavenly •host was standing at His right hand and at His left hand.ᵇ ¹⁹And the Lord said, 'Who will entice Ahab king of Israel to march up and fall at Ramoth-gilead?' So one was saying this and another was saying that.

²⁰"Thenᶜ a spirit came forward, stood before the Lord, and said, 'I will entice him.'

"The Lord asked him, 'How?'

²¹"So he said, 'I will go and become a lying spirit in the mouth of all his prophets.'

"Then He said, 'You will entice him and also prevail. Go and do that.'

²²"Now, you see, the Lord has put a lying spirit into the mouth ofᴬ these prophets of yours, and the Lord has pronounced disaster against you."

²³Then Zedekiah son of Chenaanah came up, hit Micaiah in the face, and demanded, "Which way did the spirit from the Lord leave me to speak to you?"

²⁴Micaiah replied, "You will soon see when you go to hide yourself in an inner chamber on that day."ᵈ

²⁵Then the king of Israel ordered, "Take Micaiah and return himᵉ to Amon, the governor of the city,ᶠ and to Joash, the king's son, ²⁶and say, 'This is what the king says: Put this guy in prisonᵍ and feed him only bread and waterᴮ until I come back safely.'"

²⁷But Micaiah said, "If you ever return safely, the Lord has not spoken through me." Then he said, "Listen, all you people!"ʰ

Ahab's Death

²⁸Then the king of Israel and Judah's King Jehoshaphat went up to Ramoth-gilead. ²⁹But the king of Israel said to Jehoshaphat, "I will disguise myself and go into battle, but you wear your royal attire." So the king of Israel disguised himself, and they went into battle.ⁱ

³⁰Now the king of Aram had ordered his chariot commanders, "Do not fight with anyone, small or great, except the king of Israel."

³¹When the chariot commanders saw Jehoshaphat, they shouted, "He must be the king of Israel!" So they turned to attack him, but Jehoshaphat cried outʲ and the Lord helped him. God drew them away from him. ³²When the chariot commanders saw that he was not the king of Israel, they turned back from pursuing him.

³³But a man drew his bow without taking special aim and struck the king of Israel through the joints of his armor. So he said to the charioteer, "Turn around and take me out of the battle,ᶜ for I am badly wounded!"ᵏ ³⁴The

Cross references
a 18:16 Nm 27:16-17; Ezk 34:5-8; Mt 9:36; Mk 6:34
b 18:18 Is 6:1-5; Dn 7:9-10
c 18:20-21 Dt 13:1-5; 1Sm 16:14; Jr 27:9-10; Ezk 14:9; 2Th 2:9-12
d 18:24 1Kg 20:30
e 18:25 2Ch 18:8
f 2Ch 34:8
g 18:26 2Ch 16:10
h 18:27 Mc 1:2
i 18:29 2Ch 35:22
j 18:31 2Ch 13:14-15
k 18:33 2Ch 35:23

A 18:22 Some Hb mss, LXX, Syr, Vg add *all*; 1Kg 22:23　　B 18:26 Lit *him on bread of oppression and water of oppression*
C 18:33 LXX, Vg; MT reads *camp*

---

first statement, because Ahab detected that it was not the truth.

18:16-17 Putting sarcasm aside, Micaiah stated that he saw **all Israel** scattered on the hills **like sheep without a shepherd**, implying that Ahab would be killed in the battle. Ahab said that this was precisely what he had come to expect from Micaiah.

18:18-24 Micaiah also stated that Ahab's court **prophets** were the instruments of a **spirit** sent by God with the specific intention of leading Ahab into destruction with a lie. While God does not lie, He does permit lying spirits to deceive those who will not believe the truth (2Th 2:9-12). In the end, God also sent Micaiah with the truth, so Ahab had a choice whom to believe. **Zedekiah** questioned Micaiah's divine authority by slapping him and accusing him of infringing on Zedekiah's right to speak for Yahweh. Micaiah replied that the matter would be settled on the day that Zedekiah, confronted by the defeat of Ahab's army, would try to protect himself by hiding in a toilet. The Chronicler did not record the precise confirmation of this prophecy.

18:27 Micaiah publicly announced he would submit to the test of a true prophet: whether his prediction came to pass (Dt 18:21-22).

18:29 Ahab, knowing that the Arameans wanted to kill him, made it look like Jehoshaphat was the only king on the battlefield. His superstition may have led him to think that a disguise could avert what was prophesied. It is hard to understand why Jehoshaphat would go along with this plan, unless he had already let Ahab have the upper hand in their relationship; see note at 1Kg 22:4-5.

18:30-32 The Arameans did, in fact, have orders to single out Ahab. Since **Jehoshaphat** was the only visible king, they focused on him and almost killed him. Jehoshaphat **cried out** to **the Lord**. God graciously caused the Arameans to back off by letting the Aramean **chariot commanders** recognize that Jehoshaphat was not Ahab, their intended target.

18:33-34 One lone Aramean archer shot a random arrow. The Hebrew could also be taken to mean that he "simply" shot or that he was merely doing what a good soldier should do. This arrow not only hit Ahab but penetrated **through the joints of his armor**, something even the best archer was unlikely to achieve on purpose. When Ahab **died at sunset**,

battle raged throughout that day, and the king of Israel propped himself up in his chariot facing the Arameans until evening. Then he died at sunset.

Jehu's Rebuke of Jehoshaphat

19 Jehoshaphat king of Judah returned to his home in Jerusalem in peace. ²Then Jehu*ª* son of Hanani the seer went out to confront him*ᴬ* and said to King Jehoshaphat, "Do you help the wicked and love those who hate the Lord?*ᵇ* Because of this, the Lord's wrath is on you.*ᶜ* ³However, some good is found in you, for you have removed the •Asherah poles from the land and have decided to seek God."*ᵈ*

Jehoshaphat's Reforms

⁴Jehoshaphat lived in Jerusalem, and once again he went out among the people from Beer-sheba to the hill country of Ephraim and brought them back to •Yahweh, the God of their ancestors.*ᵉ* ⁵He appointed judges in all the fortified cities of the land of Judah, city by city.*ᶠ* ⁶Then he said to the judges, "Consider what you are doing, for you do not judge for man, but for the Lord, who is with you in the matter of judgment.*ᵍ* ⁷And now, may the terror of the Lord be on you. Watch what you do, for there is no injustice or partiality or taking bribes with the Lord our God."*ʰ*

⁸Jehoshaphat also appointed in Jerusalem

some of the Levites and priests and some of the heads of the Israelite families for deciding the Lord's will and for settling disputes of the residents of*ᴮ* Jerusalem. ⁹He commanded them, saying, "In the •fear of the Lord, with integrity, and with a whole heart, you are to do the following: ¹⁰for every dispute that comes to you from your brothers who dwell in their cities—whether it regards differences of bloodguilt, law, commandment, statutes, or judgments*ⁱ*—you are to warn them, so they will not incur •guilt before the Lord and wrath will not come on you and your brothers.*ʲ* Do this, and you will not incur guilt.

¹¹"Note that Amariah, the chief priest, is over you in all matters related to the Lord, and Zebadiah son of Ishmael, the ruler of the house of Judah, in all matters related to the king, and the Levites are officers in your presence. Be strong; may the Lord be with those who do what is good."*ᵏ*

War against Eastern Enemies

20 After this, the Moabites and Ammonites, together with some of the Meunites,*ᶜ,ˡ* came to fight against Jehoshaphat. ²People came and told Jehoshaphat, "A vast number from beyond the Dead Sea and from Edom*ᴰ* has come to fight against you; they are already in Hazazon-tamar"*ᵐ* (that is, En-gedi). ³Jehoshaphat was afraid, and he resolved*ⁿ* to

Cross references (center column)

*ª*19:2 1Kg 16:1; 2Ch 20:34
*ᵇ*2Ch 18:1,3
*ᶜ*2Ch 24:18
*ᵈ*19:3 2Ch 12:14; 17:4,6
*ᵉ*19:4 2Ch 15:8-13
*ᶠ*19:5 Dt 16:18-20
*ᵍ*19:6 Lv 19:15; Dt 1:17
*ʰ*19:7 Gn 18:25; Dt 10:17-18; 32:4
*ⁱ*19:10 Dt 17:8
*ʲ*2Ch 19:2
*ᵏ*19:11 1Ch 28:20
*ˡ*20:1 2Ch 26:7
*ᵐ*20:2 Gn 14:7
*ⁿ*20:3 2Ch 19:3

---

*ᴬ*19:2 Lit *to his face* *ᴮ*19:8 LXX, Vg; MT reads *disputes and they returned to* *ᶜ*20:1 LXX; MT reads *Ammonites*; 2Ch 26:7
*ᴰ*20:2 Some Hb mss, Old Lat; other Hb mss read *Aram*

Micaiah, the prophet of Yahweh, had been vindicated, and Zedekiah, the prophet of Baal, had been repudiated.

19:1-3 Jehoshaphat was able to return safely to **Jerusalem** where he had to face God's evaluation of what he had just done. Just as Asa, his father, had been greeted by the prophet Hanani, now **Jehu son of Hanani** scolded Jehoshaphat, king of Judah. It was wrong for Jehoshaphat to team up with a king who was not a worshiper of God. But because Jehoshaphat was a good king who had gone further than any other in purging the land of idolatry, he would not have to face serious judgment as his father did.

19:4 Another difference between Asa and Jehoshaphat is that Jehoshaphat did not turn against the prophet who had declared God's anger to him but resumed his reforms.

19:5-7 In appointing regional **judges**, Jehoshaphat reminded them of two things: that God would be watching them, and that God was the model for impartiality. Jehoshaphat was not merely pragmatic in his governing but led the country in spiritual matters as well.

19:8-11 Jehoshaphat also carried out judicial reform in **Jerusalem**. Some of these judges were **Levites and priests** and thus were accountable only to the Lord. Their supervisor was not the king but **Amariah**, the high priest. They would serve as an appeals court for the regional judges. **Zebadiah . . . the ruler of the house of Judah**, along with the Levites, was to be the final authority in cases that involved the king himself.

20:1 With the northern kingdom of Israel occupied in war

against the Arameans, the countries east of the Jordan River and the Dead Sea decided to invade Judah. The **Meunites** were also referred to as the Edomites.

20:2 By the time the word of this invasion got to Jehoshaphat, the army had come as far as **En-gedi**, about 50 miles from Jerusalem on the west shore of the Dead Sea.

20:3-4 Jehoshaphat had learned to rely on **the Lord** and had

darash

Hebrew Pronunciation	[dah RASH]
HCSB Translation	seek, inquire, require
Uses in 2 Chronicles	30
Uses in the OT	165
Focus Passage	2 Chronicles 20:3

Seek is the basic meaning of *darash*, and God is what is most frequently sought (Is 55:6). The reward is finding (2Ch 15:2) or being answered (Ps 34:4); the opposite of seeking is *forsaking* (1Ch 28:9). *Darash* often occurs (14x) with *biqqesh* ("ask"). *Darash* implies *inquiring of* (Gn 25:22) or *consulting* (Ezk 20:1). It denotes *ask* (Dt 17:9) or *inquire about* (2Ch 32:31), and *investigate* (Dt 17:4) or *study* (Ps 111:2). It is *looking for* (Jr 30:14) or *searching for* (Ezk 34:8). More forcefully, it means *demand* (Ezk 34:10) or *require* (Gn 9:5). Then it indicates *demand an account* (2Ch 24:22), *call into account* (Ps 10:15), or *hold accountable* (Dt 18:19). It suggests *come looking for* (Dt 22:2) or *go after* (2Ch 25:20). Emotively, *darash* connotes *care for* (Is 62:12) or *about* (Jr 30:17). It can entail *selecting* (Pr 31:13) or *worshiping* (Ezr 4:2).

seek the LORD. Then he proclaimed a fast[a] for all Judah, [4]who gathered to seek the LORD. They even came from all the cities of Judah to seek Him.

Jehoshaphat's Prayer

[5]Then Jehoshaphat stood in the assembly of Judah and Jerusalem in the LORD's temple before the new courtyard. [6]He said:

[*]Yahweh, the God of our ancestors, are You not the God who is in heaven,[b] and do You not rule over all the kingdoms of the nations?[c] Power and might are in Your hand, and no one can stand against You. [7]Are You not our God who drove out the inhabitants of this land before Your people Israel[d] and who gave it forever to the descendants of Abraham[e] Your friend? [8]They have lived in the land and have built You a sanctuary in it for Your name and have said, [9]"If disaster comes on us—sword or judgment, pestilence or famine[f]—we will stand before this temple and before You, for Your name is in this temple.[g] We will cry out to You because of our distress, and You will hear and deliver."

[10]Now here are the Ammonites, Moabites, and the inhabitants of Mount Seir.[h] You did not let Israel invade them when Israel came out of the land of Egypt, but Israel turned away from them and did not destroy them.[i] [11]Look how they repay us by coming to drive us out of Your possession that You gave us as an inheritance. [12]Our God, will You not judge them?[j] For we are powerless before this vast number that comes to fight against us. We do not know what to do, but we look to You.[A,k]

God's Answer

[13]All Judah was standing before the LORD with their infants, their wives, and their children. [14]In the middle of the congregation, the Spirit of the LORD came on[l] Jahaziel (son of Zechariah, son of Benaiah, son of Jeiel, son of Mattaniah, a Levite from *Asaph's descendants), [15]and he said, "Listen carefully, all Judah and you inhabitants of Jerusalem, and King Jehoshaphat. This is what the LORD says: 'Do not be afraid or discouraged because of this vast number,[m] for the battle is not yours, but God's.[n] [16]Tomorrow, go down against them. You will see them coming up the Ascent of Ziz, and you will find them at the end of the valley facing the Wilderness of Jeruel. [17]You do not have to fight this battle. Position yourselves, stand still, and see the salvation of the LORD.[o] He is with you, Judah and Jerusalem. Do not be afraid or discouraged.[p] Tomorrow, go out to face them, for Yahweh is with you.'"[q]

[18]Then Jehoshaphat bowed with his face to the ground, and all Judah and the inhabitants of Jerusalem fell down before the LORD to worship Him.[r] [19]Then the Levites from the sons of the Kohathites and the Korahites[s] stood up to praise the LORD God of Israel shouting with a loud voice.

Victory and Plunder

[20]In the morning they got up early and went out to the wilderness of Tekoa. As they were about to go out, Jehoshaphat stood and said, "Hear me, Judah and you inhabitants of Jerusalem. Believe in Yahweh your God, and you will be established;[t] believe in His prophets, and you will succeed." [21]Then he consulted with the people and appointed some to sing for the LORD and some to praise the splendor

a20:3 1Sm 7:6; Ezr 8:21
b20:6 Dt 4:39
c1Ch 29:11
d20:7 Ps 135:10-12
eIs 41:8
f20:9 2Ch 6:28-30
g2Ch 6:20
h20:10 2Ch 20:1,22
iNm 20:14-21; Dt 2:4-9
j20:12 Jdg 11:27
kPs 25:15; 121:1-2
l20:14 2Ch 15:1; 24:20
m20:15 Ex 14:13; 2Ch 32:7-8
n1Sm 17:47; 2Ch 13:15; 14:12
o20:17 Ex 14:13-14
pJos 1:9
q2Ch 15:2
r20:18 2Ch 7:3
s20:19 Ex 6:18; 1Ch 9:19
t20:20 Is 7:9

A20:12 Lit *but on You our eyes*

taught his people the same. Earlier we saw that the total number of men in Jehoshaphat's army was 1,160,000. This was an enormous army, but Jehoshaphat was aware that neither the size of an army nor the depth of fortifications could protect him without the Lord's intervention.

20:5-9 In a public prayer in front of the **temple**, Jehoshaphat reaffirmed Solomon's prayer and God's response to it. This was precisely one of the scenarios that Solomon had envisioned (6:34): the kingdom was being invaded by a foreign power. On behalf of all the people, Jehoshaphat pleaded with the Lord for deliverance.

20:10-12 Jehoshaphat included in his prayer the events of long ago, when the Israelites had first come to the promised land. The **Ammonites** and **Moabites** had refused to allow the Israelites to pass through their territory (Nm 22:4). At the time the Israelites had not sought revenge against them; now Jehoshaphat appealed to God to judge them for their faithlessness.

20:14-17 God causes a priest to prophesy. **Jahaziel**, who came from a distinguished line of Levites reaching all the way back to Asaph—one of David's main musicians—conveyed God's approval to Jehoshaphat. He told the king to walk out to the place of confrontation with his army and to **stand** there and watch as God brings victory (Ex 14:13).

20:18-19 Jehoshaphat believed that Jahaziel had spoken God's message. There was nothing left to do but **worship** God, and a number of **Levites** took the lead in praising God. A meeting called to deal with a serious crisis turned into a **praise** and worship service.

20:21 The next day, as the army set out to march toward En-gedi, the only issue left to solve was what songs to sing and in which key. As they marched, one refrain kept coming up: **Give thanks to the LORD, for His faithful love endures forever**. This is the same chorus that was the theme song during the transport of the ark to Jerusalem (1Ch 16:34) and at the temple dedication (2Ch 5:13; 7:3,6).

of His holiness.[a] When they went out in front of the armed forces, they kept singing:[A]

> Give thanks to the LORD,
> for His faithful love endures forever.[b]

[22] The moment they began their shouts and praises, the LORD set an ambush[c] against the Ammonites, Moabites, and the inhabitants of Mount Seir who came to fight against Judah, and they were defeated. [23] The Ammonites and Moabites turned against the inhabitants of Mount Seir and ·completely annihilated them.[d] When they had finished with the inhabitants of Seir, they helped destroy each other.[e]

[24] When Judah came to a place overlooking the wilderness, they looked for the large army, but there were only corpses lying on the ground; nobody had escaped. [25] Then Jehoshaphat and his people went to gather the plunder. They found among them[B] an abundance of goods on the bodies[c] and valuable items. So they stripped them until nobody could carry any more. They were gathering the plunder for three days because there was so much. [26] They assembled in the Valley of Beracah[D] on the fourth day, for there they praised the LORD. Therefore, that place is still called the Valley of Beracah today.

[27] Then all the men of Judah and Jerusalem turned back with Jehoshaphat their leader, returning joyfully to Jerusalem, for the LORD enabled them to rejoice over their enemies. [28] So they came into Jerusalem to the LORD's temple with harps, lyres, and trumpets. [29] The terror of God[f] was on all the kingdoms

of the lands when they heard that Yahweh had fought against the enemies of Israel. [30] Then Jehoshaphat's kingdom was quiet, for his God gave him rest on every side.[g]

Summary of Jehoshaphat's Reign

[31] Jehoshaphat became king over Judah.[h] He was 35 years old when he became king and reigned 25 years in Jerusalem. His mother's name was Azubah daughter of Shilhi. [32] He walked in the way of Asa his father; he did not turn away from it but did what was right in the LORD's sight. [33] However, the ·high places were not taken away;[i] the people had not yet set their hearts on the God of their ancestors.[j]

[34] The rest of the events of Jehoshaphat's reign from beginning to end are written in the Events of Jehu[k] son of Hanani, which is recorded in the Book of Israel's Kings.[l]

Jehoshaphat's Fleet of Ships

[35] After this,[m] Judah's King Jehoshaphat made an alliance with Israel's King Ahaziah, who was ·guilty of wrongdoing. [36] Jehoshaphat formed an alliance with him to make ships to go to Tarshish,[n] and they made the ships in Ezion-geber. [37] Then Eliezer son of Dodavahu of Mareshah prophesied against Jehoshaphat, saying, "Because you formed an alliance with Ahaziah, the LORD has broken up what you have made." So the ships were wrecked and were not able to go to Tarshish.

Jehoram Becomes King Over Judah

21 Jehoshaphat rested with his fathers and was buried with his fathers in the city of David. His son Jehoram[E] became king in

[a]20:21 1Ch 16:29; Ps 29:2
[b]1Ch 16:34; 2Ch 5:13; 7:3; Ps 118:1,29; 136:1
[c]20:22 2Ch 13:13
[d]20:23 Ezk 38:21; Hg 2:22; Zch 14:13
[e]Jdg 7:22; 1Sm 14:20
[f]20:29 2Ch 14:14; 17:10
[g]20:30 2Ch 14:6-7; 15:15
[h]20:31-34 1Kg 22:41-45
[i]20:33 2Ch 17:6
[j]2Ch 19:3
[k]20:34 2Ch 19:2
[l]1Kg 16:1,7
[m]20:35-37 1Kg 22:48-49
[n]20:36 2Ch 9:21

[A]20:21 Lit *saying*   [B]20:25 LXX reads *found cattle*   [C]20:25 Some Hb mss, Old Lat, Vg read *goods, garments*   [D]20:26 = Blessing
[E]21:1 = Joram

20:22-23 There were three separate armies that did not know one another. They may have split up in order to arrive at their destination quickly. Suddenly, these armies heard what they took to be shouting—which was actually praising. In their God-ordained confusion they destroyed **each other**.

20:24-26 When Jehoshaphat's parade of musical soldiers arrived at the battlefield, there was nothing left to do but gaze at it in amazement, to **plunder** the enemy, and to praise God for this miraculous victory. Thus, this site was called the "Valley of Praise."

20:28 Music and praise continued to characterize the army under Jehoshaphat's spiritual leadership.

20:29-30 Word of the miraculous nature of this victory spread quickly. Due to Yahweh's reputation, no nation had any interest in picking a fight with Jehoshaphat or the kingdom of Judah. Thus, God's victory brought peace and prosperity.

20:32-33 The Chronicler gives Jehoshaphat high marks. No king since David had been as zealous in abolishing idolatry

and false worship. But despite his exemplary spiritual leadership, not all the people's hearts had been changed, so some **high places** still remained.

20:35-37 Jehoshaphat again tied himself to the northern kingdom by making a contract with **King Ahaziah** to build **ships**, which they would then send to **Tarshish** (possibly Spain). The best place to construct these ships appeared to be **Ezion-geber**, at the very tip of the Red Sea, not the Mediterranean coast. Once again, God did not allow Jehoshaphat to get away with such compromise. He sent a prophet named **Eliezer** to condemn Jehoshaphat's sin. As punishment, a storm came up and all the ships were destroyed.

21:1 Jehoram: Fifth king of Judah; son of Jehoshaphat; promoted Baal worship; brought calamity on Judah. In the next few chapters, we speed through several generations. Because the reigns end early, the kings get younger and younger, leading up to Athaliah usurping the throne of Judah when the next rightful heir was only one year old. Jehoshaphat was about 18 years old when Jehoram was born. Jehoshaphat ascended the throne at 35 and ruled for

his place.*a* 2He had brothers, sons of Jehoshaphat: Azariah, Jehiel, Zechariah, Azariah, Michael, and Shephatiah; all these were the sons of Jehoshaphat, king of Judah.A 3Their father had given them many gifts of silver, gold, and valuable things, along with fortified cities*b* in Judah, but he gave the kingdom to Jehoram because he was the firstborn. 4When Jehoram had established himself over his father's kingdom, he strengthened his position by killing with the sword all his brothers as well as some of the princes of Israel.

Judah's King Jehoram

5Jehoram*c* was 32 years old when he became king and reigned eight years in Jerusalem. 6He walked in the way of the kings of Israel, as the house of Ahab had done,*d* for Ahab's daughter was his wife.*e* He did what was evil in the Lord's sight, 7but because of the covenant the Lord had made with David, He was unwilling to destroy the house of David since the Lord had promised*f* to give a lamp*g* to David and to his sons forever.

8During Jehoram's reign, Edom rebelled against Judah's domination and appointed their own king. 9So Jehoram crossed into Edom with his commanders and all his chariots. Then at night he set out to attack the Edomites who had surrounded him and the chariot commanders. 10And now Edom is still

*a*21:1 1Kg 22:50
*b*21:3 2Ch 11:5
*c*21:5-10 2Kg 8:17-22
*d*21:6 1Kg 12:28-30
*e*2Ch 18:1
*f*21:7 2Sm 7:12-17; 1Kg 11:13
*g*1Kg 11:36; 15:4
*h*21:11 1Kg 11:7
*i*Lv 20:5
*j*21:12 2Ch 17:3-4
*k*2Ch 14:2-5
*l*21:13 2Ch 21:6
*m*1Kg 16:31-33
*n*2Ch 21:4
*o*21:15 2Ch 21:18-19

in rebellion against Judah's domination today. Libnah also rebelled at that time against his domination because he had abandoned ·Yahweh, the God of his ancestors. 11Jehoram also built ·high places*h* in the hills*B* of Judah, and he caused the inhabitants of Jerusalem to prostitute themselves,*i* and he led Judah astray.

Elijah's Letter to Jehoram

12Then a letter came to Jehoram from Elijah the prophet, saying:

This is what Yahweh, the God of your ancestor David says: "Because you have not walked in the ways of your father Jehoshaphat*j* or in the ways of Asa king of Judah*k* 13but have walked in the way of the kings of Israel,*l* have caused Judah and the inhabitants of Jerusalem to prostitute themselves like the house of Ahab*m* prostituted itself, and also have killed your brothers,*n* your father's family, who were better than you, 14Yahweh is now about to strike your people, your sons, your wives, and all your possessions with a horrible affliction. 15You yourself will be struck with many illnesses, including a disease of the intestines, until your intestines come out day after day because of the disease."*o*

A21:2 Some Hb mss, LXX, Syr, Vg, Arabic; other Hb mss read *Israel*   B21:11 Some Hb mss, LXX, Vg read *cities*

25 years. His son Jehoram ruled for eight years. Jehoram's son Ahaziah became king at age 22 but reigned for only one year. When Ahaziah died he left behind a one-year-old heir-apparent.

21:2-6 Jehoshaphat may have thought that by having his son **Jehoram** marry the daughter of Ahab and Jezebel (v. 6), Jehoram might eventually become ruler of a kingdom that was once again united, and thus perhaps return all Israel to the worship of God and obedience to the law. But rather than being a new David, Jehoram became the personification of Ahab in Judah. Together with Athaliah, his wife, Jehoram began to refashion the kingdom of Judah so it would look just like the northern kingdom, where Baal was supreme and assassination was the preferred method of changing government. As soon as Jehoram had full grasp of the southern kingdom, he proceeded to kill **all his brothers** and anyone else who might have some claim on the throne.

21:7 The only reason the Lord did not **destroy** Jehoram was that He graciously continued to fulfill His promise that a descendant of **David** would always be on the throne of Judah (see note at 6:41-42).

21:8-9 The **Edomites** had suffered defeat during the time of Jehoram's father, Jehoshaphat. When they realized that Jehoram was not worshiping the same powerful God as Jehoshaphat had done (see v. 10; cp. 20:29), they declared their independence from Judah and reestablished their own government. Jehoram set out to attack the insurgent Edomites, crossing into their territory with bulky **chariots**

and a large force, but God was not on his side. He quickly found himself **surrounded**.

21:10 The report that **Edom is still in rebellion . . . today** shows that Jehoram's mission was unsuccessful. Also, the town of **Libnah** in Judah rebelled against Jehoram. The citizens of this town refused to follow Jehoram because he had abandoned **Yahweh, the God of his ancestors**. Not everyone turned a blind eye to the disaster into which Jehoram was taking his country.

21:11 Jehoram kept busy installing places of idol worship throughout Judah. The statement that **he caused the inhabitants of Jerusalem to prostitute themselves** can be both literal and symbolic. In a symbolic sense, the people were committing spiritual adultery; in the literal sense, many of the pagan practices involved sexual lewdness. While it is the king's duty to provide spiritual leadership and he is held responsible when his people are led astray, ultimately the people are also responsible for their own actions. People can always refuse to follow a wicked king, as the people of Libnah proved (v. 10; cp. Ac 4:18-20).

21:12-15 Since Jehoram was Ahab's son-in-law, it is not surprising that the prophet **Elijah**—Ahab's long-standing opponent—chastised Jehoram for the same behavior for which he had rebuked Ahab. Elijah's **letter** mentioned the many sins that Jehoram had committed, including idolatry and fratricide, and promised a swift and harsh punishment. Just as Jehoram eliminated his brothers, now Jehoram's household would be eliminated.

Jehoram's Last Days

[16] The LORD put it into the mind of the Philistines and the Arabs[a] who live near the *Cushites to attack Jehoram.[b] [17] So they went to war against Judah and invaded it. They carried off all the possessions found in the king's palace and also his sons and wives; not a son was left to him except Jehoahaz,[A,c] his youngest son.

[18] After all these things, the LORD afflicted him in his intestines with an incurable disease. [19] This continued day after day until two full years passed. Then his intestines came out because of his disease, and he died from severe[B] illnesses. But his people did not hold a fire in his honor like the fire in honor of his fathers.[d]

[20] Jehoram[e] was 32 years old when he became king; he reigned eight years in Jerusalem. He died to no one's regret[C,f] and was buried in the city of David but not in the tombs of the kings.[g]

Judah's King Ahaziah

22 Then the inhabitants of Jerusalem made Ahaziah, his youngest son, king in his place, because the troops that had come with the Arabs[h] to the camp had killed all the older sons.[D] So Ahaziah son of Jehoram became king of Judah. [2] Ahaziah[i] was 22[E] years old when he became king and reigned one year in Jerusalem. His mother's name was Athaliah, granddaughter[F] of Omri.

[3] He walked in the ways of the house of Ahab, for his mother gave him evil advice. [4] So he did what was evil in the LORD's sight like the house of Ahab, for they were his advisers after the death of his father, to his destruction. [5] He also followed their advice and went with Joram[G] son of Israel's King Ahab to fight against Hazael, king of Aram, in Ramoth-gilead. The Arameans[H] wounded Joram, [6] so he returned to Jezreel to recover from the wounds they inflicted on him in Ramoth-gilead[I] when he fought against Aram's King Hazael. Then Judah's King Ahaziah[J] son of Jehoram went down to Jezreel to visit Joram son of Ahab since Joram was ill.

[7] Ahaziah's downfall came from God when he went to Joram.[j] When Ahaziah arrived, he went out with Joram to meet Jehu son of Nimshi,[k] whom the LORD had anointed to destroy the house of Ahab.[l] [8] So when Jehu executed judgment on the house of Ahab,[m] he found the rulers of Judah and the sons of Ahaziah's brothers who were serving Ahaziah, and he killed them. [9] Then Jehu looked for Ahaziah,[n] and Jehu's soldiers captured him (he was hiding in Samaria). So they brought Ahaziah to Jehu, and they killed him. The soldiers buried him, for they said, "He is the grandson of Jehoshaphat who sought the LORD with all his heart."[o] So no one from the house of Ahaziah had the strength to rule the kingdom.

Cross references (center column)

a21:16 2Ch 17:11; 22:1
b2Ch 33:11
c21:17 2Ch 25:23
d21:19 2Ch 16:14
e21:20 2Kg 8:17,24
fJr 22:18,28
g2Ch 24:25
h22:1 2Ch 21:16
i22:2-6 2Kg 8:24-29
j22:7 2Ch 10:15
k2Kg 9:21
l2Kg 9:6-7
m22:8 2Kg 10:11-14
n22:9 2Kg 9:27-28
o2Ch 17:4

Footnotes

A21:17 LXX, Syr, Tg read *Ahaziah*   B21:19 Lit *evil*   C21:20 Lit *He walked in no desirability*   D22:1 Lit *the former ones*
E22:2 Some LXX mss, Syr; MT reads *42*; 2Kg 8:26   F22:2 Lit *daughter*   G22:5 = Jehoram   H22:5 Lit *Rammites*
I22:6 Lit *in Ramah*   J22:6 Some Hb mss, LXX, Syr, Vg; other Hb mss read *Azariah*

21:16-17 It had not been long since the **Philistines** and their Arab neighbors had come calling on Jehoshaphat of Judah (17:11) to bring tribute. Now they came calling again, but this time they took back the tribute and everything else in **the king's palace**. They killed all of Jehoram's **sons** except **Jehoahaz** (who is subsequently called Ahaziah) and all his **wives** except Athaliah, the one who shared responsibility for this catastrophe.

21:18-20 Just as Elijah had predicted, Jehoram contracted a horrible disease **in his intestines** from which he eventually died. None of his subjects mourned his departure. He was not accorded a ceremonial **fire of honor**, and he was not buried alongside other kings of Judah.

22:1 Ahaziah: Sixth king of Judah; son of Jehoram and Athaliah; killed when Jehu annihilated the house of Ahab. Despite the people's dissatisfaction with Jehoram, when he died they acclaimed his son Ahaziah as the next king.

In order to make sense out of the events in this section, one must recognize the duplication of the names of the kings in the southern and northern kingdoms. In the northern kingdom of Israel, Ahab had two sons, Ahaziah and Jehoram. When Ahab died, his son Ahaziah succeeded him, and he in turn was succeeded by his brother, Jehoram. In the southern kingdom of Judah, Jehoshaphat was succeeded by his son Jehoram, and his successor was his son (and

Jehoshaphat's grandson), Ahaziah. Thus, the successions in the north were: Ahab, Ahaziah, Jehoram; in the south the successions were: Jehoshaphat, Jehoram, Ahaziah.

22:2-4 Ahaziah of Judah was just as evil as his father Jehoram. His mother **Athaliah** received a large share of the blame by misleading him. Because of the family connection to the house of Ahab, Ahaziah received **advice** from his relatives in the northern kingdom. Ahaziah followed the practices of the northern kingdom, including idolatry and violence.

22:5-6 Just as Jehoshaphat had gone with Ahab of Israel to fight against the Arameans, so **Ahaziah** of Judah went along with Joram of Israel to the same place for the same purpose. The result was almost identical. Joram was seriously wounded.

Ahaziah: Seventh king of Israel, son of Ahab and Jezebel; made a temporary naval alliance with Jehoshaphat of Judah. **Joram** (also called Jehoram): Eighth king of Israel, son of Ahab, brother of Ahaziah; killed by Jehu after he and Ahaziah of Judah fought against Hazael of Aram; last king of the house of Ahab in Israel.

22:7-9 Jehu: Ninth king of Israel; began a new dynasty when he eliminated the house of Ahab; killed Ahaziah of Judah as a part of his purge. God had decided to put an end to the dynasty of Ahab, and his chosen instrument for this task

Athaliah Usurps the Throne

[10] When[a] Athaliah, Ahaziah's mother, saw that her son was dead, she proceeded to annihilate all the royal heirs[A] of the house of Judah. [11] Jehoshabeath,[B] the king's daughter, rescued Joash son of Ahaziah from the king's sons who were being killed and put him and the one who nursed him in a bedroom. Now Jehoshabeath was the daughter of King Jehoram and the wife of Jehoiada the priest. Since she was Ahaziah's sister, she hid Joash from Athaliah so that she did not kill him. [12] While Athaliah ruled over the land, he was hiding with them in God's temple six years.

Athaliah Overthrown

23 Then, in the seventh year,[b] Jehoiada summoned his courage and took the commanders of hundreds into a covenant with him: Azariah son of Jeroham, Ishmael son of Jehohanan, Azariah son of Obed, Maaseiah son of Adaiah, and Elishaphat son of Zichri. [2] They made a circuit throughout Judah. They gathered the Levites from all the cities of Judah and the heads of the families of Israel, and they came to Jerusalem.

[3] Then the whole assembly made a covenant with the king in God's temple. Jehoiada said to them, "Here is the king's son! He must reign, just as the LORD promised[c] concerning David's sons. [4] This is what you are to do: a third of you, priests and Levites who are coming on duty on the Sabbath,[d] are to be gatekeepers.

[5] A third are to be at the king's palace, and a third are to be at the Foundation Gate, and all the troops will be in the courtyards of the LORD's temple. [6] No one is to enter the LORD's temple but the priests and those Levites who serve;[e] they may enter because they are holy, but all the people are to obey the requirement of the LORD. [7] You must completely surround the king with weapons in hand. Anyone who enters the temple is to be put to death. You must be with the king in all his daily tasks."[c]

[8] So the commanders of hundreds did everything Jehoiada the priest commanded. They each brought their men—those coming on duty on the Sabbath and those going off duty on the Sabbath—for Jehoiada the priest did not release the divisions.[f] [9] Jehoiada the priest gave to the commanders of hundreds King David's spears, shields, and quivers[D] that were in God's temple. [10] Then he stationed all the troops with their weapons in hand surrounding the king—from the right side of the temple to the left side, by the altar and by the temple.

[11] They brought out the king's son, put the crown on him, gave him the •testimony,[g] and made him king. Jehoiada and his sons anointed him and cried, "Long live the king!"[h]

[12] When Athaliah heard the noise from the troops, the guards, and those praising king, she went to the troops in the LORD's temple. [13] As she looked, there was the king standing by his pillar[E] at the entrance. The

[a]22:10-12 2Kg 11:1-3   [b]23:1-21 2Kg 11:4-20   [c]23:3 2Ch 21:7   [d]23:4 1Ch 9:25   [e]23:6 1Ch 23:28-32   [f]23:8 1Ch 24:1   [g]23:11 Ex 25:16,21; 31:18   [h]1Sm 10:24

[A]22:10 Lit seed   [B]22:11 = Jehosheba; 2Kg 11:2   [C]23:7 Lit king when he comes in and when he goes out   [D]23:9 Or spears and large and small shields   [E]23:13 LXX reads post

---

was Jehu **son of Nimshi** who led the revolution against the clan of Ahab and became king himself. Ahaziah of Judah was caught up in this revolution and was executed along with everyone else related to the **house of Ahab**.

22:10 Athaliah: Usurper of the throne of Judah; daughter of Jezebel and Ahab; wife of Jehoram; executed in Jehoiada's plot to reinstall Joash as king. Who would fill the vacant throne of Judah? There were some male heirs who were toddlers, but of course they were unable to rule the country. Athaliah, **Ahaziah's mother**, leaped at the chance and made herself queen of Judah. She had no legitimate claim to the throne because she was not descended from David. She followed her husband's earlier practice and killed anyone who had a claim to the throne, even her own grandchildren.

22:11-12 Still, there was one heir whom Athaliah was not able to eliminate. **Joash** was a baby, having been born about the time of Ahaziah's accession. Ahaziah's sister **Jehoshabeath** and her husband **Jehoiada** the high priest raised Joash in seclusion in the **temple** for **six years**.

23:1-2 Jehoiada waited patiently for six years before he carried out his plan to overthrow Athaliah. Jehoiada did not act rashly, but he made sure he had the military leaders on his side as well as the **Levites** and the prominent **families**. As

they gathered in Jerusalem, it was evident that Athaliah did not have much support from the people.

23:4-7 Jehoiada gathered a revolutionary force that was powerful, disciplined, and well prepared. He made it appear as though the **priests and Levites** were carrying on with their usual duties, with the normal one-third of the total work force serving in the temple. At the same time, the other Levites were in the immediate vicinity, half of them at the nearby **king's palace** and half at one of the major gates. The armed troops were in the **courtyards**, but Jehoiada insisted that the sanctity of the temple not be violated. The presence of the military would assure that nothing happened to Joash.

23:9 The **temple** contained an arsenal of weapons that had been stored there since the time of David. Thus, the soldiers were able to walk into the temple precinct unarmed, but they received weapons as soon as they entered.

23:11 Then they brought in Joash and began to acclaim the child as king. The **testimony** may have been a copy of the Torah, perhaps Deuteronomy, but it may also have been a copy of the agreement that Jehoiada had made with all the leaders acknowledging Joash as the rightful king.

23:13 The **pillar** was apparently where coronations traditionally took place (Jdg 9:6; 2Kg 11:14; 23:3). Athaliah probably

commanders and the trumpeters were by the king, and all the people of the land were rejoicing and blowing trumpets*a* while the singers with musical instruments were leading the praise. Athaliah tore her clothes and screamed, "Treason, treason!"

¹⁴ Then Jehoiada the priest sent out the commanders of hundreds, those in charge of the army, saying, "Take her out between the ranks, and put anyone who follows her to death by the sword," for the priest had said, "Don't put her to death in the LORD's temple." ¹⁵ So they arrested her, and she went by the entrance of the Horses' Gate*b* to the king's palace, where they put her to death.

Jehoiada's Reforms

¹⁶ Then Jehoiada made a covenant between himself, the king, and the people that they would be the LORD's people. ¹⁷ So all the people went to the temple of •Baal and tore it down. They broke its altars and images into pieces and killed Mattan, the priest of Baal, at the altars.*c*

¹⁸ Then Jehoiada put the oversight of the LORD's temple into the hands of the Levitical priests,*d* whom David had appointed*e* over the LORD's temple, to offer •burnt offerings to the LORD as it is written in the law of Moses,*f* with rejoicing and song ordained by^A David. ¹⁹ He stationed gatekeepers*g* at the gates of the LORD's temple so that nothing •unclean could enter for any reason. ²⁰ Then he took with him the commanders of hundreds, the nobles, the governors of the people, and all the people of

the land and brought the king down from the LORD's temple. They entered the king's palace through the Upper Gate and seated the king on the throne of the kingdom. ²¹ All the people of the land rejoiced, and the city was quiet, for they had put Athaliah to death by the sword.

Judah's King Joash

24 Joash*h* was seven years old when he became king and reigned 40 years in Jerusalem. His mother's name was Zibiah; she was from Beer-sheba. ² Throughout the time of Jehoiada the priest, Joash did what was right in the LORD's sight.*i* ³ Jehoiada acquired two wives for him, and he was the father of sons and daughters.

Repairing the Temple

⁴ Afterward,*j* Joash took it to heart to renovate*k* the LORD's temple. ⁵ So he gathered the priests and Levites and said, "Go out to the cities of Judah and collect money from all Israel to repair the temple of your God as needed year by year,*l* and do it quickly."

However, the Levites did not hurry. ⁶ So the king called Jehoiada the high priest and said, "Why haven't you required the Levites to bring from Judah and Jerusalem the tax imposed by the LORD's servant Moses and the assembly of Israel for the tent*m* of the testimony? ⁷ For the sons of that wicked Athaliah broke into the LORD's temple and even used the sacred things of the LORD's temple for the •Baals."

⁸ At the king's command a chest was made and placed outside the gate of the LORD's

*a*23:13 Nm 10:7-10
*b*23:15 Neh 3:28; Jr 31:40
*c*23:17 Dt 13:6-9; 1Kg 18:40
*d*23:18 2Ch 5:5
*e*1Ch 23:6,25-31
*f*2Kg 14:6; 2Ch 17:9; Ezr 7:6; Neh 8:1
*g*23:19 1Ch 9:22
*h*24:1-2 2Kg 11:21; 12:1-2
*i*24:2 2Ch 26:4-5
*j*24:4-12 2Kg 12:4-12
*k*24:4 2Ch 24:7
*l*24:5 Ex 30:12-16; 2Ch 34:9-10; Neh 10:32; Mt 17:24
*m*24:6 Nm 1:50

---

^A23:18 Lit *song on the hands of*

---

would not have recognized little Joash, so she concluded that someone was committing **treason**.

23:14 Jehoiada did not want to desecrate the temple by killing her there.

23:16-17 Jehoiada would speak for the child **king** while he was too young to make decisions. On behalf of the king, he and **the people** agreed to return to the Lord. They went to **the temple of Baal**, the main center of worship during the time of Jehoram, Ahaziah, and Athaliah. They destroyed the building, the **altars**, the idols, and the priest of Baal, **Mattan**.

23:18-19 Jehoiada restored order to the **temple**, following the plans outlined years before by **David**. He made sure that sacrifices would be conducted and that the joyful music David had made a part of the daily operation of the temple would be heard once again.

23:20-21 Jehoiada and his co-conspirators escorted young Joash to the royal **palace** and placed him on the **throne**. The word **quiet** is the same word used in Judges when the nation was at peace, with no threats (Jdg 3:11; cp. Jb 3:26; Is 32:17; Jr 30:10). **Athaliah** had been a source of conflict.

24:1-2 Joash: Seventh king of Judah; son of Ahaziah; installed while still a boy by Jehoiada when he dethroned Athaliah; obeyed God as long as Jehoiada was alive, but turned

to evil as soon as Jehoiada died. The **40 years** of Joash's reign matched the length of David's reign, but since Joash started at such an early age, it took him only into midlife.

24:4 Upon reaching adulthood, Joash decided it was time for **the LORD's temple** to be repaired and renovated. It had been largely ignored for many years.

24:5 Joash commissioned the **Levites** to travel throughout the kingdom of Judah and to **collect money** for this renovation. One wonders why Levites, whose jobs depended on the temple, had not made this a greater priority before Joash became king.

24:6-7 Jehoiada, as **high priest**, was supervisor of the **Levites**. Joash called him to account for the lack of speed by those who reported to him. As Joash issued this reprimand to Jehoiada, he appealed to those things that were closest to Jehoiada's heart—compliance with the law and the purity of the **temple**. The king stated that the collection of the **tax** for the temple had been instituted through **Moses** (Ex 30:14) and that many of the **sacred things**, or furnishings of the temple, had been stolen and used for the worship of **the Baals**.

24:8-10 Jehoiada did not send the Levites from town to town to collect the money. Instead, he sent them out to require

temple. ⁹Then a proclamation* was issued in Judah and Jerusalem that the tax God's servant Moses imposed on Israel in the wilderness be brought to the LORD. ¹⁰All the leaders and all the people rejoiced, brought the tax, and put it in the chest until it was full. ¹¹Whenever the chest was brought by the Levites to the king's overseers, and when they saw that there was a large amount of money, the king's secretary and the high priest's deputy came and emptied the chest, picked it up, and returned it to its place. They did this daily and gathered the money in abundance. ¹²Then the king and Jehoiada gave it to those in charge of the labor on the LORD's temple, who were hiring stonecutters and carpenters to renovate the LORD's temple, also blacksmiths and coppersmiths to repair the LORD's temple.ᵇ

¹³The workmen did their work, and through them the repairs progressed. They restored God's temple to its specifications and reinforced it. ¹⁴When they finished, they presented the rest of the money to the king and Jehoiada, who made articles for the LORD's temple with it—articles for ministry and for making *burnt offerings, and ladlesᴬ and articles of gold and silver. They regularly offered burnt offerings in the LORD's temple throughout Jehoiada's life.

Joash's Apostasy

¹⁵Jehoiada died when he was old and full of days; he was 130 years old at his death. ¹⁶He was buried in the city of David with the kingsᶜ because he had done what was good in Israel with respect to God and His temple.

¹⁷However, after Jehoiada died, the rul-

---

*24:9 2Ch 36:22
ᵇ24:12 2Kg 22:4-6
ᶜ24:16 2Ch 21:20; 24:25
ᵈ24:18 Ex 34:12-14
ᵉJos 22:20
ᶠ24:19 Jr 7:25
ᵍNeh 9:30; Ps 81:8-11; Jr 11:6-8
ʰ24:20 Jdg 6:34; 1Ch 12:18
ⁱNm 14:41
ʲ2Ch 15:2
ᵏ24:21 Mt 9:26; Mt 23:35; Lk 11:51
ˡ24:22 Gn 9:5
ᵐ24:23 2Kg 12:17
ⁿ24:24 2Ch 16:7-8
ᵒ2Ch 24:20
ᵖ24:25-27 2Kg 12:19-21

---

ers of Judah came and paid homage to the king. Then the king listened to them, ¹⁸and they abandoned the temple of *Yahweh, the God of their ancestors and served the *Asherah poles and the idols.ᵈ So there was wrathᵉ against Judah and Jerusalem for this *guilt of theirs. ¹⁹Nevertheless, He sent them prophetsᶠ to bring them back to the LORD; they admonished them, but the people would not listen.ᵍ

²⁰The Spirit of God took control ofᴮ,ʰ Zechariah son of Jehoiada the priest. He stood above the people and said to them, "This is what God says, 'Why are you transgressing the LORD's commands and you do not prosper?ⁱ Because you have abandoned the LORD, He has abandoned you.'"ʲ ²¹But they conspired against him and stoned him at the king's command in the courtyard of the LORD's temple.ᵏ ²²King Joash didn't remember the kindness that Zechariah's father Jehoiada had extended to him, but killed his son. While he was dying, he said, "May the LORD see and demandˡ an account."

Aramean Invasion of Judah

²³At the turn of the year, an Aramean army went to war against Joash.ᵐ They entered Judah and Jerusalem and destroyed all the leaders of the people among them and sent all the plunder to the king of Damascus. ²⁴Although the Aramean army came with only a few men, the LORD handed overⁿ a vast army to them because the people of Judah had abandonedᵒ Yahweh, the God of their ancestors. So they executed judgment on Joash.

Joash Assassinated

²⁵Whenᵖ the Arameans saw that Joash had many wounds, they left him. His servants con-

---

ᴬ24:14 Or *dishes*, or *spoons*; lit *palms*   ᴮ24:20 Lit *God clothed Himself with*; Jdg 6:34; 1Ch 12:18

---

the people to come to Jerusalem and deposit money in a **chest** that Joash had placed at the **gate of the . . . temple**. This plan worked.

24:12-13 The money collected went exactly where it was needed—to the **workmen** who were carrying out the renovation.

24:14 When all the construction work was done and the workers had been paid, there was enough money left over to replace the temple utensils so sacrificial rituals could be carried out efficiently and with dignity.

24:15-16 **Jehoiada** the high priest, Joash's adviser, died at the age of **130 years**. He was buried with honor normally accorded only to kings.

24:17-18 The people who won Joash's confidence had authority in various parts of Judah. They apparently preferred the old system, influenced by the kings of Israel. Like Rehoboam, Joash followed bad advice (10:8). They persuaded the king to abandon the Lord and to return to the idolatry that Joash along with **Jehoiada** had attempted to root out. The **wrath** of God cut into their prosperity (v. 20).

24:19 God did not give up on Joash but conveyed His will by way of **prophets**. Yet the king continued to support and encourage false worship.

24:20-22 Jehoiada's son **Zechariah** made a speech confronting the people with their idolatry. The king enlisted a number of functionaries who stoned Zechariah to death in the **courtyard** of the **temple**. Zechariah invoked God's vengeance on the faithless king. To this day, the tomb of Zechariah can be seen outside Jerusalem in the Kidron Valley. It was this Zechariah to whom Jesus referred when He accused the leaders of His day of hypocrisy (Lk 11:47-51).

24:23-24 Up to this point, Jehoshaphat and Ahaziah of Judah had participated in the northern kingdom's war against the Arameans. But there had been no direct conflict between Judah and Aram since the time Asa bought off Ben-hadad. Now this situation changed. With a weak and confused King **Joash** on the throne, and absent the Lord's protection, the Arameans were able to conquer Jerusalem with a small force and carry off valuables again.

24:25 The **Arameans** despised Joash so much that they left

spired against him, and killed him on his bed, because he had shed the blood of the sons of Jehoiada the priest. So he died, and they buried him in the city of David, but they did not bury him in the tombs of the kings.[a]

[26] Those who conspired against him were Zabad, son of the Ammonite woman Shimeath, and Jehozabad, son of the Moabite woman Shimrith.[A,b] [27] Concerning his sons, the many •oracles about him, and the restoration[c] of the LORD's temple, they are recorded in the Writing[d] of the Book of the Kings. His son Amaziah became king in his place.

Judah's King Amaziah

25 Amaziah[e] became king when he was 25 years old and reigned 29 years in Jerusalem. His mother's name was Jehoaddan; she was from Jerusalem. [2] He did what was right in the LORD's sight but not wholeheartedly.[f]

[3] As soon as the kingdom was firmly in his grasp,[B] he executed his servants who had murdered his father the king. [4] However, he did not put their children to death, because—as it is written in the Law, in the book of Moses,[g] where the LORD commanded—"Fathers must not die because of children, and children must not die because of fathers, but each one will die for his own sin."[h]

Amaziah's Campaign against Edom

[5] Then Amaziah gathered Judah and assembled them according to ancestral house,

[a]24:25 2Ch 24:16
[b]24:26 2Kg 12:21
[c]24:27 2Ch 24:12
[d]2Ch 13:22
[e]25:1-4 2Kg 14:2-6
[f]25:2 2Kg 25:14
[g]25:4 2Ch 17:9; 23:18
[h]Dt 24:16; Jr 31:30; Ezk 18:4,20
[i]25:5 Nm 1:3
[j]2Ch 26:13
[k]25:7 2Kg 4:9
[l]25:8 Ps 64:7-8
[m]2Ch 14:11; 20:6

according to commanders of thousands, and according to commanders of hundreds. He numbered those 20 years old or more[i] for all Judah and Benjamin. He found there to be 300,000 choice men who could serve in the army, bearing spear and shield.[j] [6] Then for 7,500 pounds[c] of silver he hired 100,000 brave warriors from Israel.

[7] However, a man of God[k] came to him and said, "King, do not let Israel's army go with you, for the LORD is not with Israel—all the Ephraimites. [8] But if you go with them, do it! Be strong for battle! But God will make you stumble before the enemy,[l] for God has the power to help[m] or to make one stumble."

[9] Then Amaziah said to the man of God, "What should I do about the 7,500 pounds[c] of silver I gave to Israel's division?"

The man of God replied, "The LORD is able to give you much more than this."

[10] So Amaziah released the division that came to him from Ephraim to go home. But they got very angry with Judah and returned home in a fierce rage.

[11] Amaziah strengthened his position and led his people to the Valley of Salt. He struck down 10,000 Seirites,[D] [12] and the Judahites captured 10,000 alive. They took them to the top of a cliff where they threw them off, and all of them were dashed to pieces.

[13] As for the men of the division that Amaziah sent back so they would not go with him

---

[A]24:26 = Shomer in 2Kg 12:21   [B]25:3 LXX, Syr; MT reads *was strong on him*; 1Kg 14:4   [C]25:6,9 Lit *100 talents*
[D]25:11 = Edomites

him to die after he was severely wounded. **His servants** took advantage of the situation and killed him as he was lying defenseless **on his bed**. Joash was buried unceremoniously outside the usual location for **the tombs of the kings**.

24:26 The two servants who assassinated Joash were Gentiles, sons of an **Ammonite woman** and a **Moabite woman**, respectively. Even these outsiders would not tolerate the king's evil actions.

25:1-4 Amaziah: Ninth king of Judah, son of Joash; turned from God to idol worship. Amaziah's reign was mediocre. Even though he had a basic commitment to the Lord and to God's law, he was not able to resist the lure of idolatry or the temptation to go to war unnecessarily. Amaziah **executed** the two men who had killed his father, but he did not follow the usual practice of executing an entire family (22:10; 2Kg 10:11), killing only the men and **not . . . their children** (Dt 24:16).

25:5-6 The nation of Edom had rebelled against Judah's control during the reign of Jehoram (21:8). Now **Amaziah** decided to bring the Edomites back in line, and he assembled an army for this purpose. This was the first serious military excursion by **Judah** since Jehoram's attempts to reconnect Edom. The army that Amaziah put together was also the smallest since the division of the kingdom. Even Abijah was able to muster 400,000 men, while Jehosha-

phat's army numbered over one million. Amaziah could only conscript **300,000** soldiers. He felt that this was not enough, so he hired **100,000** mercenaries from the northern kingdom of Israel. Once again a king of Judah allied himself with armed forces from **Israel**, though this time he did it in his own cause and at the hefty cost of **7,500 pounds of silver**, paid in advance.

25:7-10 A prophet appeared on the scene to issue a warning from God to the king. He told **Amaziah** that if he took the northern soldiers on his venture, he would ensure defeat. Amaziah was flabbergasted that the Lord expected him to waste all that silver, but when the prophet told him that this amount was tiny compared to what God could provide for him, he consented and released the soldiers, expecting them to go home since they had already been paid. The mercenaries, perhaps hoping for a large amount of plunder, did not see it that way. They grew **angry**. Before they returned **home** they attacked a number of cities of Judah. They helped themselves to plunder to compensate themselves for what they had missed by not participating in the war against Edom (v. 13).

25:11-12 As promised, Amaziah's expedition against Edom was a success. The army of Judah killed **10,000** Edomites in battle and then executed another **10,000** prisoners of war.

25:13 After being paid and released (see note at vv. 7-10),

into battle, they raided the cities of Judah from Samaria to Beth-horon, struck down 3,000 of their people, and took a great deal of plunder.

[14] After Amaziah came from the attack on the Edomites, he brought the gods of the Seirites[A] and set them up as his gods. He worshiped before them and burned incense to them.[a] [15] So the LORD's anger was against Amaziah, and He sent a prophet to him, who said, "Why have you sought a people's gods that could not deliver their own people from your hand?"[b]

[16] While he was still speaking to him, the king asked, "Have we made you the king's counselor? Stop, why should you lose your life?"

So the prophet stopped, but he said, "I know that God intends to destroy you, because you have done this and have not listened to my advice."

Amaziah's War With Israel's King Joash

[17] King Amaziah of Judah took counsel[c] and sent word to Jehoash[B] son of Jehoahaz, son of Jehu, king of Israel, saying, "Come, let us meet face to face."

[18] King Jehoash of Israel sent word to King Amaziah of Judah, saying, "The thistle that was in Lebanon sent a message to the cedar that was in Lebanon, saying, 'Give your daughter to my son as a wife.' Then a wild animal that was in Lebanon passed by and trampled the thistle.[d] [19] You have said, 'Look, I[c] have defeated Edom,' and you have become overconfident[e] that you will get glory. Now stay at home. Why stir up such trouble so that you fall and Judah with you?"

[20] But Amaziah would not listen, for this turn of events was from God in order to hand them over to their enemies because they went after the gods of Edom. [21] So King Jehoash of Israel advanced. He and King Amaziah of Judah faced off at Beth-shemesh in Judah. [22] Judah was routed before Israel, and each fled to his own tent. [23] King Jehoash of Israel captured Judah's King Amaziah son of Joash, son of Jehoahaz,[D,f] at Beth-shemesh. Then Jehoash took him to Jerusalem and broke down 200 yards[E] of Jerusalem's wall from the Ephraim Gate to the Corner Gate.[f,g] [24] He took all the gold, silver, all the utensils that were found with Obed-edom[h] in God's temple, the treasures of the king's palace, and the hostages. Then he returned to Samaria.

[a]25:14 2Ch 28:23 [b]25:15 2Ch 25:11-12 [c]25:17-24 2Kg 14:8-14 [d]25:18 Jdg 9:8-15 [e]25:19 2Ch 26:16; 32:25 [f]25:23 2Ch 21:17; 22:1 [g]2Kg 14:13 [h]25:24 1Ch 26:15

[A]25:14 = Edomites   [B]25:17 Lit Joash   [C]25:19 Some LXX mss, Old Lat, Tg, Vg; MT reads you   [D]25:23 = Ahazia in 2Kg 14:13   [E]25:23 Lit 400 cubits   [F]25:23 Some Hb mss; other Hb mss read to Happoneh

---

the irate mercenaries collected **plunder** within **Judah**. It is hard to understand how northern troops could plunder cities of Judah starting **from Samaria**. Perhaps Samaria is another name for Migron in Judah. Another possibility is that the troops were released immediately after mustering in Samaria, and they worked their way south from there into Judah. **Beth-horon** is northwest of Jerusalem.

25:14-15 Amaziah's next action is virtually unfathomable. A common mind-set in the ancient world was that the gods of a particular nation would help their people in battle. If they won, the gods were thought to be stronger than the gods of their enemies; but if they lost, then their gods were regarded as weak and unable to protect their own army. **Amaziah** had just won over the **Edomites**, and he did so after he had fulfilled God's ultimatum when the prophet assured him of victory on that basis. But incredibly, Amaziah took the **gods** of the people whom he had defeated and started to worship them. As a follower of Yahweh, he should have known that these idols were impotent and unreal because they had not protected the Edomites and therefore that it was a waste of time to worship them.

25:16 When God sent another **prophet** to rebuke the king, Amaziah reacted defensively and threatened to kill the prophet (cp. 32:25-26), but the prophet managed to get in the last word and told Amaziah his destruction was assured.

25:17 Jehoash: Twelfth king of Israel; **son of Jehoahaz**; defeated Amaziah of Judah in response to Amaziah's challenge. Once again, it is essential to keep track of the names of the kings because of the duplication of names in the northern and southern kingdoms. **Jehoahaz** of Israel was

the son of Jehu, who had killed Ahab and made himself king of Israel. **Jehoash** was Jehoahaz's son. Jehoash was the king of Israel contemporary with **Amaziah of Judah**. When Amaziah had returned home after his campaign against Edom and had learned of the damage done by the mercenaries from the north, he called for a show-down with Jehoash (though it would be difficult to prove that he was responsible for the way these men had behaved).

25:18-20 Amaziah had acquired an inflated sense of his military prowess, so when **Jehoash** tried to talk him out of going to war, Amaziah persisted with his plan to invade the northern kingdom. The Chronicler once again makes it clear that in the final analysis, this foolish action by the king was a part of God's plan to bring about his downfall (cp. 10:15; Jdg 14:4; 2Sm 17:14).

25:21-24 When **Jehoash** realized that **Amaziah** was not going to let up, he marched with his army into Judah, and Amaziah got the opportunity for a military confrontation that he had wanted. Jehoash decimated the army of Judah and captured Amaziah. The **Jehoahaz** referred to here (v. 23) is Amaziah's grandfather, usually called Ahaziah who, again, is not identical with the northern king of the same name. Jehoash used Amaziah as a hostage to allow him to head straight to Jerusalem, where he destroyed **200 yards** of the city **wall** and then plundered all the valuables from the **palace** and the **temple**, as well as taking **hostages**. **Obed-edom** stems from the name of the Levite on whose property the ark of the covenant was stored after David's first unsuccessful attempt to move it to Jerusalem (2Sm 6:10). Subsequently, he played in the musical ensemble when the ark was moved again, and he was made a guard of one of the

Amaziah's Death

25 Judah's King Amaziah[a] son of Joash lived 15 years after the death of Israel's King Jehoash son of Jehoahaz. 26 The rest of the events of Amaziah's reign, from beginning to end, are written in the Book of the Kings of Judah and Israel.

27 From the time Amaziah turned from following the LORD, a conspiracy was formed against him in Jerusalem, and he fled to Lachish. However, men were sent after him to Lachish, and they put him to death there. 28 They carried him back on horses and buried him with his fathers in the city of Judah.[A,b]

Judah's King Uzziah

26 All the people[c] of Judah took Uzziah,[B] who was 16 years old, and made him king in place of his father Amaziah. 2 He rebuilt Eloth[C,d] and restored it to Judah after Amaziah the king rested with his fathers.

3 Uzziah was 16 years old[e] when he became king and reigned 52 years in Jerusalem. His mother's name was Jecoliah from Jerusalem. 4 He did what was right in the LORD's sight as his father Amaziah had done. 5 He sought God[f] throughout the lifetime of Zechariah, the teacher of the ·fear[D,g] of God. During the

a25:25-28 2Kg 14:17-20
b25:28 2Kg 14:20
c26:1-2 2Kg 14:21-22
d26:2 1Kg 9:26; 2Kg 14:22; 16:6
e26:3-4 2Kg 15:2-3
f26:5 2Ch 24:2
gDn 1:17
h2Ch 15:2
i26:6 Is 14:29
j26:8 2Ch 17:11
k26:9 2Ch 25:23
lNeh 2:13,15; 3:13
m26:10 Gn 26:18-21

time that he sought the LORD, God gave him success.[h]

Uzziah's Exploits

6 Uzziah went out to wage war against the Philistines,[i] and he tore down the wall of Gath, the wall of Jabneh, and the wall of Ashdod. Then he built cities in the vicinity of Ashdod and among the Philistines. 7 God helped him against the Philistines, the Arabs that live in Gur-baal, and the Meunites. 8 The Ammonites[E] gave Uzziah tribute money,[j] and his fame spread as far as the entrance of Egypt, for God made him very powerful. 9 Uzziah built towers in Jerusalem at the Corner Gate,[k] the Valley Gate,[l] and the corner buttress, and he fortified them. 10 Since he had many cattle both in the Judean foothills[F] and the plain, he built towers in the desert and dug many wells.[m] And since he was a lover of the soil, he had farmers and vinedressers in the hills and in the fertile lands.[G]

11 Uzziah had an army equipped for combat that went out to war by division according to their assignments, as recorded by Jeiel the court secretary and Maaseiah the officer under the authority of Hananiah, one of the king's commanders. 12 The total number of heads of families was 2,600 brave warriors.

A25:28 Some Hb mss read *city of David*   B26:1 = Azariah in 2Kg 14:21   C26:2 LXX, Syr, Vg read *Elath*   D26:5 Some Hb mss, LXX, Syr, Tg, Arabic; other Hb mss, Vg read *visions*   E26:8 LXX reads *Meunites*   F26:10 Or *the Shephelah*   G26:10 Or *in Carmel*

---

gates of the temple while his sons were put in charge of the storehouse (1Ch 26:15). Apparently from that time on the storehouse was named "Obed-edom" in honor of this man, and thus it was by this name that the Chronicler referred to it as he described Jehoash's plundering.

25:25-28 Amaziah continued as king for many years, but just as his father **Joash** had done, he lost the confidence of his people. Eventually, because of an assassination plot against him, he had to flee Jerusalem and seek safety in the town of **Lachish**, but his pursuers caught up with him there and killed him. At least he was accorded a proper burial in the royal tombs in Jerusalem.

26:1 Uzziah: Tenth king of Judah; called Azariah in 2Kg 15; son of Amaziah; devoted to God, but was struck with a serious skin disease when he attempted to burn incense to God in the temple. When Uzziah became king of Judah at age **16**, it was probably as a co-regent during the time when his father **Amaziah** was held captive by King Jehoash of Israel, and then later when Amaziah was fleeing for his life from his assassins. Uzziah learned the lessons that his predecessor had refused to accept and became a godly and righteous king. His long reign of 52 years, though limited by being a co-regent for the first part and being in seclusion with a disease in the second part, was generally a time of peace and prosperity in the land.

26:2 One of the first things **Uzziah** did was to rebuild the seaport of **Eloth**, at the northern tip of the Red Sea. This meant that Judah was once again a player among the major powers and had access to the Mediterranean Sea and

the Red Sea. This move, perhaps not of grand consequence in itself, signaled that Judah was once again a force to be reckoned with.

26:5 This **Zechariah**, not the son of Jehoiada (24:20) or the prophet who has a book of the Bible named after him, fulfilled in some ways the same role for Uzziah as Jehoiada had done for Joash (24:2). When Zechariah died, Uzziah also weakened in his commitment to the Lord. Still, Uzziah's eventual waywardness occurred within the context of his worship of the Lord; he never strayed into idolatry.

26:6-10 For several hundred years, extending from the time of the judges through the time of Saul and David, the **Philistines** had been the main focus of Israel's military involvements. Then, after David had defeated them decisively, they remained in the background for a while. They appeared again during the time of Jehoshaphat when they presented tribute to the king in Jerusalem, and then again during the reign of Ahaziah when they invaded Jerusalem and carried off much treasure. Now Uzziah reasserted Judah's dominance over the Philistines by capturing their cities and destroying their walls. Uzziah was also able to bring back into line certain **Arabs**, the **Meunites** (Edomites), and the **Ammonites**. He not only fortified strategic corners in **Jerusalem**, but he also established settlements in the country, laying claim to the land not by military occupation but by agricultural development.

26:11-15 Uzziah had a different philosophy about the **army** than his predecessors. In the past, the idea had been to accumulate more and more men, so that the army of Judah

¹³ Under their authority was an army of 307,500 equipped for combat, a powerful force to help the king against the enemy.^a ¹⁴ Uzziah provided the entire army with shields, spears, helmets, armor, bows and slingstones. ¹⁵ He made skillfully designed devices in Jerusalem to shoot arrows and catapult large stones for use on the towers and on the corners. So his fame spread even to distant places, for he was marvelously helped until he became strong.

Uzziah's Disease

¹⁶ But when he became strong, he grew arrogant^b and it led to his own destruction. He acted unfaithfully against the LORD his God by going into the LORD's sanctuary to burn incense on the incense altar.^c ¹⁷ Azariah^d the priest, along with 80 brave priests of the LORD, went in after him. ¹⁸ They took their stand^e against King Uzziah and said, "Uzziah, you have no right to offer incense to the LORD^f—only the consecrated priests, the descendants of Aaron, have the right to offer incense.^g Leave the sanctuary, for you have acted unfaithfully! You will not receive honor from the LORD God."

¹⁹ Uzziah, with a firepan in his hand to offer incense, was enraged. But when he became

---

^a26:13 2Ch 25:5
^b26:16 Dt 32:15; 2Ch 25:19
^c1Kg 13:1-4
^d26:17 1Ch 6:10
^e26:18 2Ch 19:2
^fNm 16:39-40
^gEx 30:7-8
^h26:19 2Kg 5:25-27
ⁱ26:21-23 2Kg 15:5-7
^j26:21 Lv 13:46
^k26:22 Is 1:1
^l26:23 2Ch 21:20
^m27:1-3 2Kg 15:33-35
ⁿ27:1 2Ch 27:8

---

enraged with the priests, in the presence of the priests in the LORD's temple beside the altar of incense, a skin disease^h broke out on his forehead. ²⁰ Then Azariah the chief priest and all the priests turned to him and saw that he was diseased on his forehead. They rushed him out of there. He himself also hurried to get out because the LORD had afflicted him. ²¹ So King Uzziah was diseased to the time of his death.ⁱ He lived in quarantine^{A,j} with a serious skin disease and was excluded from access to the LORD's temple, while his son Jotham was over the king's household governing the people of the land.

²² Now the prophet Isaiah^k son of Amoz wrote about the rest of the events of Uzziah's reign, from beginning to end. ²³ Uzziah rested with his fathers, and he was buried with his fathers in the burial ground of the kings' cemetery,^l for they said, "He has a skin disease." His son Jotham became king in his place.

Judah's King Jotham

27 Jotham was 25 years old^m when he became king and reigned 16 years in Jerusalem.ⁿ His mother's name was Jerushah daughter of Zadok. ² He did what was right in the LORD's sight as his father Uzziah had done.

---

^A26:21 Lit *a house of freedom*

---

grew from 180,000 under Rehoboam to over one million at the time of Jehoshaphat. Instead of drastically increasing the size of his army, Uzziah had roughly the same number of men at his disposal as his father (**307,500**). But he organized them into more flexible divisions, and he made sure they had effective weapons. As a result, he became well-known and **strong**. The Chronicler emphasizes that

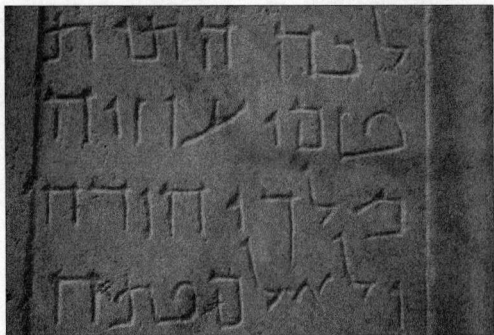

The reinterment funerary inscription of King Uzziah discovered in the nineteenth century. The translated Aramaic writing states: "Hither were brought the bones of Uzziah, King of Judah. Do not open." The inscription dates to the first century B.C. when Herod ordered all cemeteries to be moved outside the walls of Jerusalem, except for those of the Jewish kings. King Uzziah, who had been struck by God with a skin disease (26:16-21), was reinterred under Herod in the royal tombs, and this inscription was placed to mark the grave and act as a warning to looters.

this was because **he was marvelously helped**. The Lord undergirded all his efforts.

26:16 Although Uzziah did not commit idolatry, he still overstepped the authority that God had denied to any person who was not a descendant of Aaron of the tribe of Levi. He went into the holy place and burned **incense**, something that only a priest was allowed to do.

26:17-18 It was not an easy matter to call the king to account for his wrongdoing, but a priest, **Azariah**, and **80** of his colleagues did just that. They confronted the king and told him that what he was about to do was wrong. The priests declared to Uzziah that even if God did not punish him, He would not accept the king's worship, as expressed by the phrase, **You will not receive honor**.

26:19-21 Uzziah already had the incense **firepan** in his hand. Rather than listen to the priests, he became furious and continued. Immediately God punished him by having a **skin disease** break out **on his forehead**. The king dropped what he was doing and allowed himself to be led out of the **temple** into seclusion for the rest of his life. Though he was still officially the king, **his son Jotham** was placed in charge of the day-to-day duties of king.

26:23 Uzziah received a proper royal burial, though his tomb may have been separated from those of the previous kings because of the unclean condition caused by his skin disease.

27:1 **Jotham**: Eleventh king of Judah; son of Uzziah; devoted to God but not influential. Jotham's reign did not have a great impact on his kingdom. Much of his time on the throne overlapped with the time that his father, Uzzi-

In addition, he didn't enter the Lord's sanctuary,[a] but the people still behaved corruptly.

[3] Jotham built the Upper Gate of the Lord's temple, and he built extensively on the wall of Ophel.[b] [4] He also built cities in the hill country of Judah and fortresses and towers in the forests.[c] [5] He waged war against the king of the Ammonites. He overpowered the Ammonites, and that year they gave him 7,500 pounds[A] of silver, 50,000 bushels[B] of wheat, and 50,000 bushels[B] of barley. They paid him the same in the second and third years. [6] So Jotham strengthened himself because he did not waver in obeying[c] the Lord his God.[d]

[7] As for the rest of the events[e] of Jotham's reign, along with all his wars and his ways, note that they are written in the Book of the Kings of Israel and Judah. [8] He was 25 years old when he became king and reigned 16 years in Jerusalem. [9] Jotham rested with his fathers and was buried in the city of David. His son Ahaz became king in his place.

Judah's King Ahaz

28 Ahaz was 20 years old[f] when he became king and reigned 16 years in Jerusalem. He did not do what was right in the Lord's sight[g] like his ancestor David, [2] for he walked in the ways of the kings of Israel[h] and made cast images of the •Baals.[i] [3] He burned incense in the Valley of Hinnom[j] and burned his children in[D,k] the fire, imitating the detestable practices of the nations the Lord had dispossessed before the Israelites.[l] [4] He sacrificed and burned incense on the •high places,[m] on the hills, and under every green tree.

[5] So the Lord his God handed Ahaz over[n] to the king of Aram. He attacked him and took many captives to Damascus.

Ahaz was also handed over to the king of Israel, who struck him with great force: [6] Pekah son of Remaliah killed 120,000 in Judah in one day—all brave men—because they had abandoned the Lord God of their ancestors. [7] An Ephraimite warrior named Zichri killed the king's son Maaseiah, Azrikam governor of the palace, and Elkanah who was second to the king. [8] Then the Israelites took 200,000 captives from their brothers—women, sons, and daughters.[o] They also took a great deal of plunder from them and brought it to Samaria.

[9] A prophet of the Lord named Oded was there. He went out to meet the army that came to Samaria and said to them, "Look, the Lord God of your ancestors handed them over

[a]27:2 2Ch 26:16-18
[b]27:3 2Ch 33:14; Neh 3:26-27
[c]27:4 2Ch 11:5
[d]27:6 2Ch 26:5
[e]27:7-9 2Kg 15:36-38
[f]28:1-6 2Kg 16:2-4
[g]28:1 2Ch 27:2
[h]28:2 2Ch 22:3
[i]Ex 34:17
[j]28:3 Jos 15:8; 18:16; 2Kg 23:10; Jr 7:29-34; 19:2-6
[k]Lv 18:21; 2Kg 16:3; 2Ch 33:6
[l]2Ch 33:2
[m]28:4 2Ch 28:25
[n]28:5 2Ch 24:24
[o]28:8 2Ch 11:4

A27:5 Lit *100 talents*   B27:5 Lit *10,000 cors*   C27:6 Lit *he established his ways before*   D28:3 LXX, Syr, Tg read *and passed his children through*

---

ah, was king, though Uzziah was in isolation (see note at 26:19-21).

27:2 The Chronicler gives Jotham a good report card for his personal faith. He followed the example of his father, but he restrained himself from Uzziah's arrogance and did not violate the sanctity of the **sanctuary**. However, Jotham did not attempt to purify the land of idolatry or encourage the people to return to God.

27:3 Jotham took advantage of the peace that he inherited to reinforce the **wall** of Jerusalem and to carry out improvements on the **temple**.

27:5-6 Jotham continued his father's policy of controlling the **Ammonites** and carried out a successful military excursion against them. This garnered him a large amount of **silver** and grain for several years. As usual, these items are mentioned by the Chronicler not so much for their own sake but to show Jotham's obedience and God's reward for his faithfulness.

27:7-9 Jotham was a good king who came to the throne early, maintained the kingdom in good condition, was taken for granted by his people, and wound up not leaving much of a legacy. He received an appropriate royal burial, yet his reign served as a transition into a dark time for the kingdom of Judah.

28:1-4 Ahaz: Eleventh king of Judah; son of Jotham; confirmed idol worshiper; submitted voluntarily to Assyria. There was always some idolatry among the people, and there were always some people who remained true to the Lord, but in the earlier days, the decadent kings associated with the family of Ahab encountered some resistance among the people. By the time of Joash, the people were increasingly ignoring the religion of the king. By the time Ahaz took over the throne, the people and their king had become confirmed idol worshipers. Ahaz took the worship **of the Baals** to the point of burning his own **children** as an offering to Baal.

28:5-8 Pekah: Eighteenth and next-to-last king of Israel; scored a major victory over Judah, but released all of his prisoners in response to God's command. In the usual cause-and-effect sequence that characterizes the book of 2 Chronicles, Ahaz of Judah had forsaken the Lord so he was defeated by the **king** of **Damascus**, who carried away a number of hostages. Furthermore, Pekah, king of the northern kingdom of Israel, also defeated Ahaz of Judah. Again the Chronicler's assessment is that this happened because the people of Judah **abandoned the Lord**. Out of Judah's army, **120,000** were killed. This probably meant that Ahaz was left with less than half of his original army. Additionally, Ahaz lost his **son**, his chief of staff, and his prime minister. Pekah's army also took a huge number of people as hostages and transported them to the capital city of Samaria in Israel. The Chronicler reminds us that Israel and Judah were **brothers**, even though they were mortal enemies at this time.

28:9-11 Once again a prophet appeared, this time a man named **Oded**, who lived in **Samaria**. He confronted the returning victorious army with some basic facts about God's divine law. Their slaughter of their fellow Hebrews was not acceptable. Israelites were never to enslave other Israelites, but this is what Pekah was planning to do. Oded reminded

to you because of His wrath against Judah,[a] but you slaughtered them in a rage that has reached heaven.[b] [10] Now you plan to reduce the people of Judah and Jerusalem, male and female, to slavery. Are you not also *guilty before *Yahweh your God? [11] Listen to me and return the captives you took from your brothers,[c] for the LORD's burning anger is on you."

[12] So some men who were leaders of the Ephraimites—Azariah son of Jehohanan, Berechiah son of Meshillemoth, Jehizkiah son of Shallum, and Amasa son of Hadlai—stood in opposition to those coming from the war. [13] They said to them, "You must not bring the captives here, for you plan to bring guilt on us from the LORD to add to our sins and our guilt. For we have much guilt, and burning anger is on Israel."

[14] The army left the captives and the plunder in the presence of the officers and the congregation. [15] Then the men who were designated by name[d] took charge of the captives and provided clothes for their naked ones from the plunder. They clothed them, gave them sandals, food and drink,[e] dressed their wounds, and provided donkeys for all the feeble. The Israelites brought them to Jericho, the City of Palms,[f] among their brothers. Then they returned to Samaria.

[16] At that time King Ahaz asked the king of Assyria for help.[g] [17] The Edomites came again, attacked Judah, and took captives.[h] [18] The Phi-

listines also raided the cities of the Judean foothills[A] and the *Negev of Judah[i] and captured Beth-shemesh, Aijalon, Gederoth, Soco and its villages, Timnah and its villages, Gimzo and its villages, and they lived there. [19] For the LORD humbled Judah because of King Ahaz of Judah,[B] who threw off restraint in Judah and was unfaithful to the LORD. [20] Then Tiglath-pileser[C,j] king of Assyria came against Ahaz; he oppressed him and did not give him support.[k] [21] Although Ahaz plundered the LORD's temple and the palace of the king and of the rulers and gave the plunder to the king of Assyria, it did not help him.

[22] At the time of his distress, King Ahaz himself became more unfaithful to the LORD. [23] He sacrificed to the gods of Damascus which had defeated him; he said, "Since the gods of the kings of Aram are helping them, I will sacrifice to them so that they will help me."[l] But they were the downfall of him and of all Israel.

[24] Then Ahaz gathered up the utensils of God's temple, cut them into pieces,[m] shut the doors of the LORD's temple,[n] and made himself altars on every street corner in Jerusalem.[o] [25] He made high places in every city of Judah to offer incense to other gods, and he provoked the LORD, the God of his ancestors.

Ahaz's Death

[26] As for the rest of his deeds[p] and all his ways, from beginning to end, they are written in the

---

Cross references:
[a]28:9 Is 47:6
[b]Ezr 9:6; Rv 18:5
[c]28:11 2Ch 28:8
[d]28:15 2Ch 28:12
[e]2Kg 6:22; Pr 25:21-22
[f]Dt 34:3
[g]28:16 2Kg 16:7
[h]28:17 Ob 10-14
[i]28:18 Ezk 16:57
[j]28:20 1Ch 5:26
[k]2Ch 28:16
[l]28:23 Jr 44:17-18
[m]28:24 2Kg 16:17
[n]2Ch 29:7
[o]2Ch 30:14; 33:3-5
[p]28:26-27 2Kg 16:19-20

[A]28:18 Or the Shephelah　[B]28:19 Some Hb mss; other Hb mss read Israel　[C]28:20 Text emended; MT reads Tilgath-pilneser; 1Ch 5:6,26

---

the king of Israel that he too was **guilty** and could justly face similar punishment.

28:12-15 Some leaders of the northern kingdom realized the seriousness of the mistake they were about to make. The army of Israel abandoned the hostages, and some other people went in charge of making sure they returned to Judah. These captives were given **food** and **clothes**, and some even received **donkeys** on which they could ride back as far as Jericho (**the City of Palms**), where they were left.

28:16-21 Ahaz of Judah found himself under increasing pressure. The nation had already been defeated by Aram and the northern kingdom; now the **Edomites** and the **Philistines** returned to do damage. But rather than turning to the Lord for help, Ahaz tried to solve his problems by asking **Tiglath-pileser king of Assyria**, to protect him. He offered the Assyrian king all his possessions and everything that belonged to the **temple**. Tiglath-pileser did defeat Damascus (which he had planned to do anyway). Then he marched to Jerusalem and helped himself to more property.

28:22-23 Ahaz decided to pursue still another solution. Since the Arameans had defeated him earlier, the king concluded that the **gods of Damascus** must be strong, so he worshiped them (see note at 25:14-15). This was another futile move.

28:24-25 Ahaz seemed to become angry at God. His solution for dealing with these ineffective false gods was to empty

the **temple** of the true God, **shut** its **doors**, and continue to proliferate idolatrous worship sites. These were utterly irrational actions, but we can understand them a little bit more by calling on the description of some of the events recorded in Isaiah 7–8. Ahaz had placed himself in a state of war against God; regardless of the consequences, he was not about to let God win. The prophet Isaiah had specifically warned Ahaz against making this unreliable alliance with the Assyrians. When Ahaz rejected the admonition, Isaiah even gave him the opportunity to ask for a sign from God, to verify that God would protect him.

In a thoroughly hypocritical display of false piety, Ahaz responded to Isaiah by saying that he would never be so presumptuous as to ask for a sign from God. But Isaiah did not leave it alone. He said to Ahaz that if he were not going to ask for a sign, one would still be provided for him. He told him of the coming of a child (Is 7:14) who would grow up in a time of famine—referring to the consequences brought about soon by Ahaz's actions, but who would also represent God's presence with His people, thereby telescoping into the far future by predicting the coming Savior (Mt 1:23). This meant to Ahaz that God was going to actively oppose his efforts. So when the supposed alliance with Assyria did not work out, just as Isaiah had predicted, Ahaz blamed Isaiah's God.

28:26-27 The Chronicler's obituary of **Ahaz** is brief; the facts have spoken for themselves.

Book of the Kings of Judah and Israel. [27] Ahaz rested with his fathers and was buried in the city, in Jerusalem, but they did not bring him into the tombs of the kings of Israel. His son Hezekiah became king in his place.

Judah's King Hezekiah

29 Hezekiah was 25 years old[a] when he became king and reigned 29 years in Jerusalem. His mother's name was Abijah[A] daughter of Zechariah. [2] He did what was right in the Lord's sight[b] just as his ancestor David had done.

[3] In the first year of his reign, in the first month, he opened the doors of the Lord's temple and repaired them.[c] [4] Then he brought in the priests and Levites and gathered them in the eastern public square.[d] [5] He said to them, "Hear me, Levites. Consecrate yourselves[e] now and consecrate the temple of •Yahweh, the God of your ancestors. Remove everything impure from the holy place. [6] For our fathers were unfaithful and did what is evil in the sight of the Lord our God. They abandoned Him, turned their faces away from the Lord's tabernacle, and turned their backs on Him.[B,f] [7] They also closed the doors of the portico, extinguished the lamps, did not burn incense, and did not offer •burnt offerings in the holy place of the God of Israel. [8] Therefore, the wrath of the Lord was on Judah and Jerusalem, and He made them an object of terror, horror, and mockery,[C,g] as you see with your own eyes. [9] Our fathers fell by the sword, and our sons, our daughters, and our wives are in captivity because of this.[h] [10] It is in my heart now to make a covenant with Yahweh,

the God of Israel[i] so that His burning anger may turn away from us. [11] My sons, don't be negligent now, for the Lord has chosen you to stand in His presence, to serve Him, and to be His ministers and burners of incense."[i]

Cleansing the Temple

[12] Then the Levites stood up:

> Mahath[k] son of Amasai and Joel son of Azariah from the Kohathites;
> Kish son of Abdi and Azariah son of Jehallelel from the Merarites;[l]
> Joah son of Zimmah and Eden son of Joah from the Gershonites;
> [13] Shimri and Jeuel from the Elizaphanites;
> Zechariah and Mattaniah from the Asaphites;
> [14] Jehiel[D] and Shimei from the Hemanites;
> Shemaiah and Uzziel from the Jeduthunites.

[15] They gathered their brothers together, consecrated themselves,[m] and went according to the king's command by the words of the Lord[n] to cleanse the Lord's temple.[o]

[16] The priests went to the entrance of the Lord's temple to cleanse it. They took all the unclean things they found in the Lord's sanctuary to the courtyard of the Lord's temple. Then the Levites received them and took them outside to the Kidron Valley.[p] [17] They began the consecration on the first day of the first month, and on the eighth day of the month they came to the portico of the Lord's temple. They consecrated the Lord's temple

a29:1-2 2Kg 18:2-3
b29:2 2Ch 28:1; 34:2
c29:3 2Ch 28:24; 29:7
d29:4 Ezr 10:9; Neh 8:1
e29:5 2Ch 29:15,34; 35:6
f29:6 Ezk 8:16
g29:8 Dt 28:25; Jr 25:18
h29:9 2Ch 28:5-8,17
i29:10 2Ch 23:16
j29:11 Nm 3:6; 8:6
k29:12 2Ch 31:13
l Nm 3:19-20
m29:15 2Ch 29:5
n2Ch 30:12
o1Ch 23:28
p29:16 2Ch 15:16

A29:1 = Abi in 2Kg 18:2   B29:6 Lit and they gave the back of the neck   C29:8 Lit hissing   D29:14 Alt Hb tradition reads Jehuel

29:1-2 Hezekiah: Twelfth king of Judah; son of Ahaz; devoted to God; protected miraculously from Sennacherib of Assyria. Just as it looked as if things were so bad they could never be set right again, Hezekiah became king and led Judah in returning to God. With the highest compliment the Chronicler could pay a king, he compared Hezekiah to **David** because of his pursuit of righteousness.

29:3 Soon after becoming king, Hezekiah **opened the doors** of the **temple** again and undid the damage that Ahaz had caused.

29:4 Hezekiah knew that if he wanted to undertake a reformation, he would have some willing allies whom he could count on for support—the **priests and Levites**—who had gone unemployed during Ahaz's last years.

29:5 Hezekiah instructed them to clean the temple physically and to cleanse it spiritually.

29:8-9 Hezekiah saw that Judah's unfaithfulness had brought on the curse that had been predicted (Dt 28:15,25; 1Kg 9:6-9).

29:10 Hezekiah intended to restore the covenantal relationship that Judah was supposed to have with their God. **Yahweh** is His covenantal name (Ex 3:14-15).

29:11 He appealed to their professional pride as well as the need for the nation to return to God.

29:12 The Chronicler continues to draw a parallel between Hezekiah and David by mentioning the names of the leading Levites and the various divisions of the tribe they represented, as established by David (1Ch 23:6). The **Kohathites** included the division of Aaron, who made up the priesthood. The **Merarites** and **Gershonites**, descended from two other sons of Levi, were the guards, workers, musicians, and assistants to priests in the various duties associated with the temple.

29:13-14 The descendants of David's three main musicians—the **Asaphites . . . Hemanites**, and **Jeduthunites**—participated in this renewal (1Ch 25:1).

29:15-19 Before the **priests** could do anything in the **temple**, they first had to **cleanse** themselves so they would be in a state of spiritual and ritual purity. Otherwise, they would contaminate the temple as they were trying to purify it. Once they had taken care of this, they could remove all the things

for eight days, and on the sixteenth day of the first month they finished.

[18] Then they went inside to King Hezekiah and said, "We have cleansed the whole temple of the Lord, the altar of burnt offering and all its utensils, and the table for the rows of the *bread of the Presence and all its utensils. [19] We have set up and consecrated all the utensils that King Ahaz rejected during his reign[a] when he became unfaithful. They are in front of the altar of the Lord."

Renewal of Temple Worship

[20] King Hezekiah got up early, gathered the city officials, and went to the Lord's temple. [21] They brought seven bulls, seven rams, seven lambs, and seven male goats as a *sin offering for the kingdom, for the sanctuary, and for Judah. Then he told the descendants of Aaron, the priests, to offer them on the altar of the Lord. [22] So they slaughtered the bulls, and the priests received the blood and sprinkled it on the altar.[b] They slaughtered the rams and sprinkled the blood on the altar. They slaughtered the lambs and sprinkled the blood on the altar. [23] Then they brought the goats for the sin offering right into the presence of the king and the congregation, who laid their hands on them.[c] [24] The priests slaughtered the goats and put their blood on the altar for a sin offering, to make *atonement for all Israel,[d] for the king said that the burnt offering and sin offering were for all Israel.

[25] Hezekiah stationed the Levites in the Lord's temple with cymbals, harps, and lyres[e] according to the command of David,[f] Gad the king's seer,[g] and Nathan the prophet.[h] For the command was from the Lord through His prophets. [26] The Levites stood with the in-

[a]29:19 2Ch 28:24
[b]29:22 Lv 4:18
[c]29:23 Lv 4:15
[d]29:24 Lv 4:26
[e]29:25 1Ch 15:16; 25:6
[f]2Ch 8:14
[g]2Sm 24:11
[h]2Sm 7:2; 1Ch 29:29
[i]29:26 1Ch 23:5
[j]2Ch 5:12
[k]29:29 2Ch 20:18
[l]29:31 Ex 35:5,22; Ezr 1:4,6; 3:5
[m]29:34 2Ch 35:11
[n]Ps 32:11; 64:10
[o]2Ch 30:3
[p]29:35 Lv 3:16
[q]Nm 15:5-10

struments of David,[i] and the priests with the trumpets.[j]

[27] Then Hezekiah ordered that the burnt offering be offered on the altar. When the burnt offerings began, the song of the Lord and the trumpets began, accompanied by the instruments of David king of Israel. [28] The whole assembly was worshiping, singing the song, and blowing the trumpets—all of this continued until the burnt offering was completed. [29] When the burnt offerings were completed, the king and all those present with him bowed down and worshiped.[k] [30] Then King Hezekiah and the officials told the Levites to sing praise to the Lord in the words of David and of *Asaph the seer. So they sang praises with rejoicing and bowed down and worshiped.

[31] Hezekiah concluded, "Now you are consecrated[A] to the Lord. Come near and bring sacrifices and thank offerings to the Lord's temple." So the congregation brought sacrifices and thank offerings, and all those with willing hearts[l] brought burnt offerings. [32] The number of burnt offerings the congregation brought was 70 bulls, 100 rams, and 200 lambs; all these were for a burnt offering to the Lord. [33] Six hundred bulls and 3,000 sheep were consecrated.

[34] However, since there were not enough priests, they weren't able to skin all the burnt offerings, so their Levite brothers helped them[m] until the work was finished and until the priests consecrated themselves. For the Levites were more conscientious[B,n] to consecrate themselves than the priests were.[o] [35] Furthermore, the burnt offerings were abundant, along with the fat of the *fellowship offerings[p] and with the *drink offerings[q] for the burnt offering.

A29:31 Lit *Now you have filled your hands*　　B29:34 Lit *upright of heart*; Ps 32:11; 64:10

---

that did not belong there, particularly whatever was associated with idolatry. The **Kidron Valley** was used as a garbage dump where trash was burned (15:16; cp. 2Kg 23:4,6). They worked methodically by starting at the gate and moving toward the holy place and the holy of holies. When they were finished, they reported on their work to the king.

29:20-24 **Hezekiah** began the services in the temple with a **sin offering**, the type of sacrifice that was intended to atone for unwitting violations of the law (Lv 4:3-34). There were **seven** of each animal as a symbol of completeness. He and the priests followed the rules as given by God to Moses. Hezekiah did not usurp the privileges of the priests, but he did participate in the actual ceremony by laying his hands on the heads of the sacrificial animals, signifying that as the king he was looking to the Lord for forgiveness.

29:25-26 Hezekiah followed the precedents that had been established by **David**. He particularly saw to it that the music that had played such an important role for David was made a part of temple worship.

29:27 Next to be offered were **burnt offerings**, the sacrifice that expressed a person's total devotion to the Lord (Lv 1:1-17). As soon as the offering began, the musicians joined in.

29:30 These songs of **praise** by **David** and **Asaph** might have been the same as some of our psalms.

29:31-33 Now that the temple and the priests were ready, Hezekiah called for a sacrificial feast by the priests and the public. The different types of sacrifices were offered to God, including **thank offerings**. **Burnt offerings** signified devotion to God. Those who had **willing hearts** were able to offer these sacrifices, pledging their faithfulness to the Lord.

29:34-35 Killing and sacrificing these animals was hard work. **Not enough priests** were in a state of purity to be able to get it all done. **Levites**, who did not have priestly privileges, were called upon to do everything short of actually offering the sacrifices on the altar. They were able to assist by slaughtering and skinning animals.

So the service of the Lord's temple was established. [36] Then Hezekiah and all the people rejoiced over how God had prepared the people, for it had come about suddenly.

Celebration of the Passover

30 Then Hezekiah sent word throughout all Israel and Judah, and he also wrote letters to Ephraim and Manasseh to come to the Lord's temple in Jerusalem to observe the •Passover of •Yahweh, the God of Israel.[a] [2] For the king and his officials and the entire congregation in Jerusalem decided to observe the Passover of the Lord in the second month,[b] [3] because they were not able to observe it at the appropriate time. Not enough of the priests had consecrated themselves[c] and the people hadn't been gathered together in Jerusalem. [4] The proposal pleased the king and the congregation, [5] so they affirmed the proposal and spread the message throughout all Israel, from Beer-sheba to Dan,[d] to come to observe the Passover of Yahweh, the God of Israel in Jerusalem, for they hadn't observed it often,[A] as prescribed.[B]

[6] So the couriers[e] went throughout Israel and Judah with letters from the hand of the king and his officials, and according to the king's command, saying, "Israelites, return to Yahweh, the God of Abraham, Isaac, and Israel so that He may return to those of you who remain, who have escaped from the grasp of the kings of Assyria.[f] [7] Don't be like your fathers and your brothers who were unfaithful to Yahweh, the God of their ancestors[g] so that He made them an object of horror[h] as you yourselves see. [8] Don't become obstinate[C,i] now

like your fathers did. Give your allegiance[D] to Yahweh, and come to His sanctuary that He has consecrated forever. Serve the Lord your God so that He may turn His burning anger away from you,[j] [9] for when you return to Yahweh, your brothers and your sons will receive mercy in the presence of their captors and will return to this land.[k] For Yahweh your God is gracious and merciful;[l] He will not turn His face away from you if you return to Him."

[10] The couriers traveled from city to city in the land of Ephraim and Manasseh as far as Zebulun, but the inhabitants[E] laughed at them and mocked them.[m] [11] But some from Asher, Manasseh, and Zebulun humbled themselves and came to Jerusalem.[n] [12] Also, the power of God was at work in Judah to unite them[F] to carry out the command of the king and his officials by the word of the Lord.

[13] A very large assembly of people was gathered in Jerusalem to observe the Festival of Unleavened Bread in the second month. [14] They proceeded to take away the altars that were in Jerusalem,[o] and they took away the incense altars and threw them into the Kidron Valley.[p] [15] They slaughtered the Passover lamb[q] on the fourteenth day of the second month. The priests and Levites were ashamed, and they consecrated themselves and brought •burnt offerings to the Lord's temple. [16] They stood at their prescribed posts,[r] according to the law of Moses, the man of God. The priests sprinkled the blood received from the hand of the Levites, [17] for there were many in the assembly who had not consecrated themselves, and so the Levites were in charge of slaughtering the Passover lambs for every •unclean person to

---

a30:1 Ex 12:1-28; 13:1-10
b30:2 Nm 9:6-14; 2Ch 30:13,15
c30:3 2Ch 29:34
d30:5 Jdg 20:1
e30:6 Est 8:14; Jb 9:25; Jr 51:31
f2Ch 28:20
g30:7 Ezk 20:13
h2Ch 29:8
i30:8 Ex 32:9
j2Ch 29:10
k30:9 Dt 30:2-3
l Ex 34:6-7; Mc 7:18
m30:10 2Ch 36:16
n30:11 2Ch 30:18,21,25
o30:14 2Ch 28:24
p2Ch 29:16
q30:15 2Ch 30:2-3
r30:16 2Ch 35:10,15

A30:5 Or in great numbers   B30:5 Lit often, according to what is written   C30:8 Lit Don't stiffen your neck   D30:8 Lit hand
E30:10 Lit but they   F30:12 Lit to give them one heart

29:36 Hezekiah's revival started on the inside and then moved outward. He did not begin by smashing idols and then compelling the people to come to the temple, possibly against their will. He began with the restoration of the temple and a service of renewal and devotion. He made sure that right from the beginning there was music. After he had gone through the initial ceremony with the priests, he invited anyone who cared to do so to join in the joyful celebration, and the people complied. The revival became contagious. Hezekiah had not just reinstituted some ancient rules, but **God had prepared the people** so their hearts were changed. Just a short while before, everyone had been forced to share in the anger and misery of Ahaz. Now there was a brand new excitement, **for it had come about suddenly**.

30:1 The Assyrians had conquered Israel, so there was no longer any Israelite king to enforce separation from Judah. This enabled Hezekiah to invite everyone—citizens of **Judah** and **Israel** alike—to come to Jerusalem and participate in the **Passover** he was planning.

30:2-5 The **Passover** was **prescribed** to be observed the first

month every year, but that did not allow enough time for preparations, so the Passover observance was postponed until **the second month**. The law had a provision that it could be held a month later if necessary (Nm 9:9-11). **Beer-sheba to Dan** encompasses all of Judah and Israel.

30:6-11 The invitation to people from the northern kingdom to come to Jerusalem for the Passover expressed God's gracious willingness to extend **mercy** to those who repent and **return**. It met with mixed results (see note at v. 1). Some **mocked** the messengers and declined the invitation, but a few people decided to make the trip to **Jerusalem** for the Passover.

30:14 The **Kidron Valley** was where garbage was dumped and burned.

30:15-17 The **priests and Levites** who had been reluctant to participate became **ashamed** and **consecrated** themselves in order to return to their duties. Still, there was a shortage of purified priests, so the division of responsibilities by which Levites assisted the priests continued.

consecrate the lambs to the LORD.ª ¹⁸A large number of the people—many from Ephraim, Manasseh, Issachar, and Zebulun—were ritually unclean, yet they had eaten the Passoverᵇ contrary to what was written.ᶜ But Hezekiah had interceded for them, saying, "May the good LORD provide ˙atonement on behalf of ¹⁹whoever sets his whole heart on seeking God,ᵈ Yahweh, the God of his ancestors, even though not according to the purification rules of the sanctuary." ²⁰So the LORD heard Hezekiah and healed the people.ᵉ ²¹The Israelites who were present in Jerusalem observed the Festival of Unleavened Bread seven days with great joy,ᶠ and the Levites and the priests praised the LORD day after day with loud instruments. ²²Then Hezekiah encouragedᴬ'ᵍ all the Levites who performed skillfully before the LORD. They ate at the appointed festival for seven days, sacrificing ˙fellowship offerings and giving thanks to Yahweh, the God of their ancestors.ʰ

²³The whole congregation decided to observeⁱ seven more days, so they observed seven days with joy, ²⁴for Hezekiah king of Judah contributed 1,000 bulls and 7,000 sheep for the congregation. Also, the officials contributed 1,000 bulls and 10,000 sheep for the congregation,ʲ and many priests consecrated themselves.ᵏ ²⁵Then the whole assembly of Judah with the priests and Levites, the whole assembly that came from Israel, the foreigners who came from the land of Israel, and those who were living in Judah, rejoiced. ²⁶There was great rejoicing in Jerusalem, for nothing

like this was known since the days of Solomon son of David, the king of Israel.ˡ

²⁷Then the priests and the Levitesᵐ stood to bless the people,ⁿ and God heard their voice, and their prayer came into His holy dwelling placeᵒ in heaven.

Removal of Idolatry

31 When all this was completed, all Israel who had attended went out to the cities of Judah and broke up the sacred pillars, chopped down the ˙Asherah poles, and tore down the ˙high places and altarsᵖ throughout Judah and Benjamin, as well as in Ephraim and Manasseh, to the last one.ᴮ Then all the Israelites returned to their cities, each to his own possession.

Offerings for Levites

²Hezekiah reestablished the divisionsᑫ of the priests and Levites for the ˙burnt offerings and ˙fellowship offerings, for ministry, for giving thanks, and for praise in the gates of the camp of the LORD,ʳ each division corresponding to his service among the priests and Levites. ³The king contributedᶜ from his own possessionsˢ for the regular morning and evening burnt offerings, the burnt offerings of the Sabbaths, of the New Moons, and of the appointed feasts, as written in the law of the LORD.ᵗ ⁴He told the people who lived in Jerusalem to give a contributionᵘ for the priests and Levites so that they could devote their energy to the law of the LORD. ⁵When the word spread, the Israelites gave liberally of the best of the grain, new wine, oil, honey, and of all the

---

Cross references (center column):

ª30:17 2Ch 29:34
ᵇ30:18 Nm 9:10
ᶜEx 12:43-49
ᵈ30:19 2Ch 19:3
ᵉ30:20 Ps 41:4; Hs 14:4
ᶠ30:21 Ex 12:15; 13:6
ᵍ30:22 2Ch 32:6
ʰEzr 10:11
ⁱ30:23 1Kg 8:65
ʲ30:24 2Ch 35:7-8
ᵏ2Ch 29:34; 30:3
ˡ30:26 2Ch 7:8-10
ᵐ30:27 2Ch 23:18
ⁿNm 6:23-27
ᵒDt 26:15; Ps 68:5
ᵖ31:1 2Kg 18:4
ᑫ31:2 1Ch 23:6-23; 24:1-19
ʳ1Ch 23:28-31
ˢ31:3 2Ch 35:7
ᵗNm 28
ᵘ31:4 Nm 18:8

ᴬ30:22 Lit *spoke to the heart of*   ᴮ31:1 Lit *Manasseh, until finishing*   ᶜ31:3 Lit *The king's portion*

30:18-20 Many people from the north did not realize that before they were allowed to eat the **Passover** lamb or the unleavened bread, they had to go through personal **purification**. When King Hezekiah prayed for the people who had accidentally contaminated the feast, God did not hold it against them, and the occasion remained joyous.

30:21-22 Once again, the Chronicler emphasizes that joyful music was an important part of the celebration.

30:23-24 Hezekiah and a number of his officials **contributed** numerous animals to be offered as sacrifices. This eased the economic burden on some members of the **congregation**, and also contributed to the **joy** of the celebration, so by popular acclaim it was extended for another week.

30:25 Even **the foreigners**—some of the people who had just been resettled into the former northern kingdom by the Assyrian conquerors—came to Jerusalem and took part in the celebration. This added an evangelistic aspect to the festival.

30:26 The Chronicler states that Hezekiah's reign represented the revival of the kingdoms of **David** and **Solomon**. Hezekiah was a righteous man who was devoted to the Lord. He was the first king since Solomon to have positive influence over all of Israel since, with the conquest of the

northern kingdom by Assyria, there was no longer a divided kingdom.

30:27 When God **heard** them, it fulfilled the petition Solomon had made at the dedication of the temple (6:21).

31:1 After this lengthy Passover feast, the people demonstrated their renewed devotion by going throughout the area to destroy all the idols, pagan **altars**, and **Asherah poles**. They even went into the territory of the former northern kingdom—referred to as **Ephraim and Manasseh**—to carry out this purge.

31:2-3 When **Hezekiah** had finished establishing the priestly rotation, going back to the instructions laid down by David, a practical problem needed to be solved. Who would supply the animals for the sacrifices every morning and evening until this became a routine practice, with the people providing these sacrifices? The king himself contributed the sacrificial animals during this interim period.

31:4-6 Another problem was how to support the **priests and Levites** who had returned to **Jerusalem** to officiate in the temple on a regular basis. David's work schedule was based on the concept that most of these people would live in various parts of the kingdom, support themselves, and spend only one month a year in Jerusalem on temple duty. Hezeki-

produce of the field, and they brought in an abundance, a tenth[a] of everything. [6]As for the Israelites and Judahites who lived in the cities of Judah, they also brought a tenth of the cattle and sheep, and a tenth of the dedicated things that were consecrated to the LORD their God.[b] They gathered them into large piles. [7]In the third month they began building up the piles, and they finished in the seventh month. [8]When Hezekiah and his officials came and viewed the piles, they praised the LORD and His people Israel.

[9]Hezekiah asked the priests and Levites about the piles. [10]Azariah, the chief priest of the household of Zadok,[c] answered him, "Since they began bringing the offering to the LORD's temple, we eat and are satisfied and there is plenty left over because the LORD has blessed His people; this abundance is what is left over."[d]

[11]Hezekiah told them to prepare chambers[e] in the LORD's temple, and they prepared them. [12]The offering, the tenth, and the dedicated things were brought faithfully. Conaniah the Levite was the officer in charge of them, and his brother Shimei was second.[f] [13]Jehiel, Azaziah, Nahath, Asahel, Jerimoth, Jozabad, Eliel, Ismachiah, Mahath, and Benaiah were deputies under the authority of Conaniah and his brother Shimei by appointment of King Hezekiah and of Azariah the chief official of God's temple.

[14]Kore son of Imnah the Levite, the keeper of the East Gate, was over the freewill offerings to God to distribute the contribution to the LORD and the consecrated things.[g] [15]Eden,[h] Miniamin, Jeshua, Shemaiah, Amariah, and Shecaniah in the cities of the priests[i] were to faithfully distribute it under his authority to their brothers by divisions, whether large or small. [16]In addition, they distributed it to males registered by genealogy three[A,j] years old and above; to all who would enter the

LORD's temple for their daily duty,[k] for their service in their responsibilities according to their divisions. [17]They distributed also to those recorded by genealogy of the priests by their ancestral families and the Levites 20 years old and above,[l] by their responsibilities in their divisions; [18]to those registered by genealogy—with all their infants, wives, sons, and daughters—of the whole assembly (for they had faithfully consecrated themselves as holy); [19]and to the descendants of Aaron, the priests, in the common fields of their cities,[m] in each and every city. There were men who were registered by name[n] to distribute a portion to every male among the priests and to every Levite recorded by genealogy.

[20]Hezekiah did this throughout all Judah. He did what was good and upright and true before the LORD his God.[o] [21]He was diligent in every deed that he began in the service of God's temple, in the instruction and the commands, in order to seek his God, and he prospered.

Sennacherib's Invasion

32 After these faithful deeds, Sennacherib king of Assyria came and entered Judah. He laid siege to the fortified cities and intended[B] to break into them.[p] [2]Hezekiah saw that Sennacherib had come and that he planned[c] war on Jerusalem, [3]so he consulted with his officials and his warriors about stopping up the waters of the springs that were outside the city, and they helped him. [4]Many people gathered and stopped up all the springs[q] and the stream that flowed through the land;[r] they said, "Why should the kings of Assyria come and find plenty of water?" [5]Then Hezekiah strengthened his position by rebuilding the entire broken-down wall[s] and heightening the towers and the other outside wall.[t] He repaired the supporting terraces[u] of the city of David, and made an abundance of weapons and shields.

[a]31:5 Neh 13:12
[b]31:6 Lv 27:30; Dt 14:28
[c]31:10 1Ch 6:8-9
[d]Mal 3:10
[e]31:11 1Kg 6:5
[f]31:12 2Ch 35:9
[g]31:14 1Ch 26:26-28
[h]31:15 2Ch 29:12
[i]Jos 21:9-19
[j]31:16 1Ch 23:3
[k]Ezr 3:4
[l]31:17 1Ch 23:24
[m]31:19 Lv 25:34; Nm 35:2-5
[n]2Ch 31:12-15
[o]31:20 2Kg 20:3; 22:2
[p]32:1 2Kg 18:13; Is 36:1
[q]32:4 2Kg 20:20
[r]2Ch 32:30
[s]32:5 2Ch 25:23
[t]2Kg 25:4
[u]2Sm 5:9; 1Kg 9:15

A31:16 Or *30*; 1Ch 23:3   B32:1 Lit *said to himself*   C32:2 Lit *that his face was for*

---

ah implemented a regular **contribution** from all the people for the priests and Levites so they would be able to work in the temple without having to worry about supporting themselves. Upon Hezekiah's order, everyone contributed to this fund, providing a tithe of all their crops and livestock. This effort included people from both Israel and Judah.

31:16-19 Hezekiah charged various Levites to be responsible for distributing the abundant provisions to all the priests and Levites. In order to do this, it was necessary to pay close attention to the genealogies, so all who were entitled to participate received their share.

31:20-21 What **Hezekiah** accomplished was more than just a superficial redirection of the people to God and the tem-

ple. He managed to get grassroots support for his program. The people took a real interest in what was going on with the temple and the worship of the Lord. Because of his good work, Hezekiah was rewarded by God, and **he prospered**.

32:1 Hezekiah's faith in God was put to the test when **Sennacherib king of Assyria** invaded **Judah**. Before attacking Jerusalem, Sennacherib intended to demolish all the cities of Judah and make off with whatever plunder he could seize.

32:2-5 Sennacherib's strategy gave Hezekiah a chance to prepare for the impending siege of the capital city. In addition to rebuilding and strengthening the city **wall**, he made sure the Assyrians would not have access to the region's

⁶He set military commanders over the people and gathered the people in the square of the city gate. Then he encouraged them,^A,a saying, ⁷"Be strong and courageous!^b Don't be afraid or discouraged before the king of Assyria or before the large army that is with him, for there are more with us than with him.^c ⁸He has only human strength,^B but we have •Yahweh our God to help us and to fight our battles."^d So the people relied on the words of King Hezekiah of Judah.

Sennacherib's Servant's Speech

⁹After this,^e while Sennacherib king of Assyria with all his armed forces besieged^C Lachish, he sent his servants to Jerusalem against King Hezekiah of Judah and against all those of Judah who were in Jerusalem, saying, ¹⁰"This is what King Sennacherib of Assyria says: 'What are you relying on that you remain in Jerusalem under siege? ¹¹Isn't Hezekiah misleading you to give you over to death by famine and thirst when he says, "Yahweh our God will deliver us from the power of the king of Assyria"? ¹²Didn't Hezekiah himself remove His •high places and His altars^f and say to Judah and Jerusalem, "You must worship before one altar, and you must burn incense on it"?

¹³"Don't you know^g what I and my fathers have done to all the peoples of the lands? Have any of the national gods of the lands been able to deliver their land from my power? ¹⁴Who among all the gods of these nations that my predecessors •completely destroyed was able

^a32:6 2Ch 30:22
^b32:7 Dt 31:6; Jos 1:6-9; 10:25; 1Ch 22:13; Ps 31:24
^c2Kg 6:16; 1Jn 4:4
^d32:8 2Ch 20:17; Is 31:3; Jr 17:5
^e32:9-12 2Kg 18:17-22; Is 36:2-7
^f32:12 2Ch 31:1
^g32:13-14 2Kg 18:33-35; Is 36:18-20
^h32:14 Is 10:9-11
^i32:15-18 2Kg 18:28-30; Is 36:13-15
^j32:17 2Ch 32:14 19:15; Is 37:15-16
^k32:20 2Kg

to deliver his people from my power, that your God should be able to do the same for you?^h ¹⁵So now,^i don't let Hezekiah deceive you, and don't let him mislead you like this. Don't believe him, for no god of any nation or kingdom has been able to deliver his people from my power or the power of my fathers. How much less will your God deliver you from my power!'"

¹⁶His servants said more against the Lord God and against His servant Hezekiah. ¹⁷He also wrote letters to mock Yahweh, the God of Israel, saying against Him:

Just like the national gods of the lands that did not deliver their people from my power, so Hezekiah's God will not deliver His people from my power.^j

¹⁸Then they called out loudly in Hebrew^D to the people of Jerusalem, who were on the wall, to frighten and discourage them in order that he might capture the city. ¹⁹They spoke against the God of Jerusalem like they had spoken against the gods of the peoples of the earth, which were made by human hands.

Deliverance from Sennacherib

²⁰King Hezekiah and the prophet Isaiah son of Amoz prayed about this and cried out to heaven,^k ²¹and the Lord sent an angel who annihilated every brave warrior, leader, and commander in the camp of the king of Assyria. So the king of Assyria returned in disgrace to his land. He went to the temple of his god,

---

^A32:6 Lit *he spoke to their hearts*   ^B32:8 Lit *With him an arm of flesh*   ^C32:9 Lit *with his dominion was against*   ^D32:18 Lit *Judahite*

---

water supply. He closed off all external access to the **waters of the springs . . . outside the city** and built a tunnel that permitted his own people to get to the water (v. 30).

32:6-8 Hezekiah organized his army thoroughly. Then he called the people together and reminded them that Assyria was no match for the **strength** of **Yahweh**. The first sign of God's supernatural intervention was seen almost immediately in that the people **relied on the words of King Hezekiah**.

32:9-12 Sennacherib's propaganda minister came to **Jerusalem** and addressed the people from outside the city walls. This spokesman brought up a clever argument based on his own perceptions. Many people of the ancient Near East believed that each city and each nation had its own gods and that these gods had the responsibility to protect their own people. Any military confrontation was construed as a battle between gods, and the winner was thought to have the stronger gods. The Assyrian speaker knew that Hezekiah had destroyed sites outside the temple devoted to worship of Hezekiah's god. He taunted the people and asked how they could expect help from a God whose worship sites had just been eliminated by the king who was now asking them to trust in that god. It seemed to the Assyrian that Hezekiah had acted against his own deity and his own country. But of

course what Hezekiah had actually done was to remove the illegitimate worship sites and restore centralized worship at the temple in Jerusalem as God had ordained it.

32:13-15 The Assyrian spokesman continued his argument that the Assyrians were stronger than any of the **gods** of the lands they had so far encountered. It was statistically unlikely that Judah's **God** would deliver them.

32:16-19 Additional representatives of Assyria joined in to ridicule the notion that the people of Jerusalem could expect help from God. They spoke of God as **Hezekiah's God**, trying to drive a wedge between the people, the king, and the Lord. Some of the Assyrians were even able to speak directly **in Hebrew to the people**, conveying their propaganda about the superiority of the Assyrian gods.

32:20-22 The parallel passages of this event (2Kg 18; Is 36–37) provide a lengthier description of the verbal exchanges as well as more detailed information about the events surrounding this siege. For the Chronicler, the crucial thing was that Hezekiah, who received encouragement from the prophet **Isaiah**, trusted in God and received a miraculous reward. An Assyrian army of 185,000 gathered around Jerusalem, but the Lord went to work on behalf of his anointed. In one night the entire army was **annihilated**, and Sennach-

and there some of his own children struck him down with the sword.[a]

22 So the LORD saved Hezekiah and the inhabitants of Jerusalem from the power of King Sennacherib of Assyria and from the power of all others. He gave them rest[A,b] on every side.
23 Many were bringing an offering to the LORD to Jerusalem and valuable gifts to King Hezekiah of Judah, and he was exalted in the eyes of all the nations after that.[c]

Hezekiah's Illness and Pride

24 In those days Hezekiah became sick to the point of death, so he prayed to the LORD, and He spoke to him and gave him a miraculous sign.[d] 25 However, because his heart was proud,[e] Hezekiah didn't respond according to the benefit that had come to him. So there was wrath on him, Judah, and Jerusalem.[f]
26 Then Hezekiah humbled himself for the pride of his heart—he and the inhabitants of Jerusalem—so the LORD's wrath didn't come[g] on them during Hezekiah's lifetime.[h]

Hezekiah's Wealth and Works

27 Hezekiah had abundant riches and glory, and he made himself treasuries for silver, gold, precious stones, spices, shields, and every desirable item. 28 He made warehouses for the harvest of grain, new wine, and oil, and stalls for all kinds of cattle, and pens for flocks. 29 He made cities for himself, and he acquired herds of sheep and cattle in abundance, for God gave him abundant possessions.

30 This same Hezekiah blocked the outlet of the water of the Upper Gihon[i] and channeled it smoothly downward and westward to the city of David.[j] Hezekiah succeeded in everything he did. 31 When the ambassadors of Babylon's rulers[k] were sent[B] to him to inquire about the miraculous sign[l] that happened in the land, God left him to test him and discover what was in his heart.[m]

Hezekiah's Death

32 As for the rest of the events[n] of Hezekiah's reign and his deeds of faithful love, note that they are written in the Visions of the Prophet Isaiah son of Amoz,[o] and in the Book of the Kings of Judah and Israel.[p] 33 Hezekiah rested with his fathers and was buried on the ascent to the tombs of David's descendants. All Judah and the inhabitants of Jerusalem paid him honor at his death. His son Manasseh became king in his place.

Judah's King Manasseh

33 Manasseh was 12 years old[q] when he became king and reigned 55 years in Jerusalem. 2 He did what was evil in the LORD's sight, imitating the detestable practices of the nations that the LORD had dispossessed before the Israelites.[r] 3 He rebuilt the •high places that his father Hezekiah had torn down[s] and reestablished the altars for the •Baals. He made •Asherah poles, and he worshiped the whole heavenly •host and served them. 4 He built altars[t] in the LORD's temple, where •Yahweh had said, "Jerusalem is where My name will remain forever."[u] 5 He built altars to the whole heavenly host in both courtyards[v] of the LORD's temple. 6 He passed his sons through the fire

[a] 32:21 2Kg 19:35-37; Is 37:36-38
[b] 32:22 Ps 23:2
[c] 32:23 2Sm 8:10; 2Ch 9:23-24
[d] 32:24 2Kg 20:1-3,8-11; Is 38:1-3,7-8
[e] 32:25 2Ch 26:16; 32:31
[f] 2Ch 24:18
[g] 32:26 Jr 26:18-19
[h] 2Kg 20:18-19; Is 39:7-8
[i] 32:30 1Kg 1:33
[j] 2Kg 20:20
[k] 32:31 2Kg 20:12; Is 39:1
[l] 2Ch 32:24
[m] Dt 8:2; 13:3
[n] 32:32-33 2Kg 20:20-21
[o] 32:32 Is 36:1-39:8
[p] 2Kg 18:9–20:19
[q] 33:1-9 2Kg 21:1-9
[r] 33:2 2Ch 28:3
[s] 33:3 2Kg 18:4; 2Ch 31:1
[t] 33:4 2Ch 28:24
[u] 2Ch 7:16
[v] 33:5 2Ch 4:9

[A] 32:22 Lit *He led them*; Ps 23:2 [B] 32:31 LXX, Tg, Vg; MT reads *of Babylon sent*

erib was forced to withdraw and return to his homeland where he was eventually assassinated by his own sons.

32:23 Hezekiah's victory at the hand of **the LORD** did not go unnoticed. Many people came to the temple to bring offerings. Among them were people from other **nations** who also brought **valuable gifts** for the king. This brought international respect to Hezekiah, Jerusalem, Judah, and Yahweh.

32:24 Again, 2 Chronicles provides a shorter version of this event than the reports in 2 Kings and Isaiah. Hezekiah became **sick to the point of death**, but God heard his plea and gave him 15 more years of life. The Lord provided confirmation of this promise by the **miraculous sign** of having a shadow cast by the sun move in a counter clockwise direction (2Kg 20:1-11).

32:25-26 The **pride** for which Hezekiah was rebuked occurred when he received visitors from Babylon and showed them all his treasures (v. 31; 2Kg 20:12-19). The king did not react defensively when he was corrected on this point (cp. 2Ch 25:16), but **humbled himself** before God and became obedient.

32:27-31 As the Chronicler summarizes Hezekiah's reign, we are reminded of the time of Solomon. Hezekiah was able to acquire **abundant riches**, he carried out building projects (specifically the reworking of Jerusalem's water supply), he received **ambassadors** who had heard about his success, and the country flourished.

32:32-33 Hezekiah received a good evaluation by the Chronicler, and he was mourned by **all Judah**. He was buried with **honor** among the former kings of Judah.

33:1 Manasseh: Thirteenth king of Judah; son of Hezekiah; extreme idol worshiper; repented while in exile in Assyria; promoted worship of God upon return to Jerusalem.

33:1-6 Since **Manasseh** was only **12 years old** when he came to the throne, he would not have been alive at the time of the miraculous victory over the Assyrians. Furthermore, much of his early life was the time when Hezekiah's pride stood in the way of full devotion to the Lord, thus setting a negative example for Manasseh. Finally, when we consider that Manasseh reigned for **55 years**, we can get away from the idea that the complete reversal, which we associate with his reign, occurred almost all at once. Nevertheless, this king not only undid everything good that Hezekiah had done, but he brought the entire kingdom to a new low in idolatry and disobedience. He **rebuilt** all the sites for idol worship; he burned his **sons** as pagan sacrifices; he immersed himself

in the Valley of Hinnom.[a] He practiced witch-craft, *divination, and sorcery, and consulted mediums and spiritists.[b] He did a great deal of evil in the LORD's sight, provoking Him.

[7]Manasseh[c] set up a carved image of the idol he had made, in God's temple,[d] about which God had said to David and his son Solomon, "I will establish My name forever[A,e] in this temple and in Jerusalem, which I have cho-sen out of all the tribes of Israel.[f] [8]I will never again remove the feet of the Israelites from the land where I stationed your[B,g] ancestors,[h] if only they will be careful to do all that I have commanded them through Moses—all the law, statutes, and judgments." [9]So Manasseh caused Judah and the inhabitants of Jerusa-lem to stray so that they did worse evil than the nations the LORD had destroyed before the Israelites.

Manasseh's Repentance

[10]The LORD spoke to Manasseh and his peo-ple, but they didn't listen.[i] [11]So He brought against them the military commanders of the king of Assyria. They captured Manasseh with hooks, bound him with bronze shackles, and took him to Babylon.[j] [12]When he was in distress, he sought the favor of Yahweh his God and earnestly humbled himself[k] before the God of his ancestors. [13]He prayed to Him, so He heard his petition and granted his re-quest,[l] and brought him back to Jerusalem, to his kingdom. So Manasseh came to know that Yahweh is God.[m]

[14]After this, he built the outer wall of the city of David from west of Gihon[n] in the valley to the entrance of the Fish Gate;[o] he brought it around the Ophel,[p] and he heightened it considerably. He also placed military com-manders in all the fortified cities of Judah.

[15]He removed the foreign gods and the idol[q] from the LORD's temple, along with all the al-tars that he had built on the mountain of the LORD's temple and in Jerusalem, and he threw them outside the city. [16]He built[c] the altar of the LORD and offered *fellowship and thank of-ferings on it. Then he told Judah to serve Yah-weh, the God of Israel. [17]However, the people still sacrificed at the high places,[r] but only to Yahweh their God.

Manasseh's Death

[18]The rest of the events[s] of Manasseh's reign, along with his prayer[t] to his God and the words of the seers who spoke to him in the name of Yahweh, the God of Israel, are written in the Records of Israel's Kings. [19]His prayer and how God granted his request, and all his sin and unfaithfulness and the sites where he built high places and set up Asherah poles and carved images before he humbled him-self, they are written in the Records of Hozai. [20]Manasseh rested with his fathers, and he was buried in his own house. His son Amon be-came king in his place.

Judah's King Amon

[21]Amon was 22 years old when he became king and reigned two years in Jerusalem. [22]He did what was evil in the LORD's sight just as his father Manasseh had done.[u] Amon sacrificed to all the carved images that his father Ma-nasseh had made, and he served them. [23]But he did not humble himself before the LORD like his father Manasseh humbled himself;[v] instead, Amon increased his *guilt.

[24]So his servants conspired against him and put him to death[w] in his own house. [25]Then the common people[D] executed all those who

---

[a]33:6 2Kg 16:3; 2Ch 28:3
[b]Lv 19:31; 20:27; 2Kg 23:24
[c]33:7-8 1Kg 9:1-9
[d]33:7 Dt 16:21
[e]2Kg 21:7
[f]Dt 12:5; 1Kg 11:32
[g]33:8 2Kg 21:8
[h]2Sm 7:10
[i]33:10 2Kg 21:10-16
[j]33:11 2Ch 36:6
[k]33:12 2Ch 32:26
[l]33:13 Ezr 8:23
[m]Dn 4:32
[n]33:14 1Kg 1:33; 2Ch 32:30
[o]Neh 3:3
[p]2Ch 27:3
[q]33:15 2Ch 33:3-7
[r]33:17 2Ch 32:12
[s]33:18-25 2Kg 21:17-24
[t]33:18 2Ch 33:12-13
[u]33:22 2Ch 33:2
[v]33:23 2Ch 33:12,19
[w]33:24 2Ch 25:27

[A]33:7 LXX, Syr, Tg, Vg; 2Kg 21:7; MT reads *name for Elom*   [B]33:8 LXX, Syr, Vg read *land I gave to their*; 2Kg 21:8   [C]33:16 Some Hb mss, Syr, Tg, Arabic; other Hb mss, LXX, Vg read *restored*   [D]33:25 Lit *the people of the land*

---

in the occult; and ultimately he brought the entire nation down with him.

33:7-9 Manasseh even brought idols into the **temple**. The summary statement that **they did worse evil than the na-tions the LORD had destroyed before the Israelites** is a hor-rifying assessment. When God made a covenant with **David** and **Solomon**, He made a three-way connection between His dwelling in the **temple** in **Jerusalem**, the people dwell-ing in the promised **land**, and obedience to the **law**. If Ma-nasseh led the people in disobedience and displaced God from His temple, then they would be dispossessed from the promised land, just like the Canaanites before them.

33:11-13 The ultimate punishment that God had always held out as a possibility now came to pass. Manasseh was captured and carried off to **Babylon** by the **king of Assyria**. The parallel passage in 2 Kings 21 does not mention this exile and humiliation, nor does it say that he repented and

returned to the Lord. It was a sincere repentance that God honored, so Manasseh was able to return to **Jerusalem** and take up his duties as king once again.

31:14-17 Manasseh attempted to undo all the damage he had caused. He repaired the destruction that had been wrought by the Assyrian invasion; he purified the temple; he removed the idols; he reinstituted regular sacrifices; and he instructed the people to **serve Yahweh**. They did restrict their worship to Yahweh, but did not return to legitimate worship at the temple.

33:18-20 Manasseh's death notice includes references to the sources for the events that are related in 2 Kings as well as for this particular record of his repentance. He was not **buried** in the area reserved for kings but was laid to rest in **his own house**.

33:21-24 Amon: Fourteenth king of Judah; son of Manas-seh; idol worshiper; assassinated by his officials. Whatever

conspired against King Amon and made his son Josiah king in his place.

Judah's King Josiah

34 Josiah was eight years old[a] when he became king and reigned 31 years in Jerusalem. [2]He did what was right in the LORD's sight and walked in the ways of his ancestor David;[b] he did not turn aside to the right or the left.

Josiah's Reform

[3]In the eighth year of his reign, while he was still a youth, Josiah began to seek the God of his ancestor David,[c] and in the twelfth year he began to cleanse Judah and Jerusalem of the •high places, the •Asherah poles, the carved images,[d] and the cast images. [4]Then in his presence the altars of the •Baals were torn down, and he chopped down the incense altars that were above them. He shattered the Asherah poles, the carved images, and the cast images, crushed them to dust, and scattered[e] them over the graves of those who had sacrificed to them.[f] [5]He burned the bones of the priests on their altars.[g] So he cleansed Judah and Jerusalem. [6]He did the same in the cities[h] of Manasseh, Ephraim, and Simeon, and as far as Naphtali and on their surrounding mountain shrines.[A] [7]He tore down the altars, and he smashed the Asherah poles and the carved images to powder. He chopped down all the incense altars throughout the land of Israel and returned to Jerusalem.[i]

a 34:1-2 2Kg 22:1-2
b 34:2 2Ch 29:2
c 34:3 1Ch 28:9; 2Ch 11:16; 14:4; 15:12
d 2Ch 33:22
e 34:4 Ex 32:20
f 2Kg 23:6
g 34:5 2Kg 23:5,8,16,20
h 34:6 2Kg 23:15,19
i 34:7 2Ch 31:1
j 34:8-12 2Kg 22:3-7
k 34:8 2Ch 18:25
l 34:9 2Ch 34:14; 35:8
m 2Ch 30:10,18
n 34:12 1Ch 25:1

Josiah's Repair of the Temple

[8]In the eighteenth year of his reign,[j] in order to cleanse the land and the temple, Josiah sent Shaphan son of Azaliah, along with Maaseiah the governor[k] of the city and the court historian Joah son of Joahaz, to repair the temple of the LORD his God.

[9]So they went to Hilkiah[l] the high priest, and gave him the money brought into God's temple. The Levites and the doorkeepers had collected money from Manasseh, Ephraim,[m] and from the entire remnant of Israel, and from all Judah, Benjamin, and the inhabitants of Jerusalem. [10]They put it into the hands of those doing the work—those who oversaw the LORD's temple. They gave it to the workmen who were working in the LORD's temple, to repair and restore the temple; [11]they gave it to the carpenters and builders and also used it to buy quarried stone and timbers—for joining and making beams—for the buildings that Judah's kings had destroyed.

[12]The men were doing the work with integrity. Their overseers were Jahath and Obadiah, Levites from the Merarites, and Zechariah and Meshullam from the Kohathites as supervisors. The Levites were all skilled with musical instruments.[n] [13]They were also over the porters and were supervising all those doing the work task by task. Some of the Levites were secretaries, officers, and gatekeepers.

The Recovery of the Book of the Law

[14]When they brought out the money that

A 34:6 One Hb tradition reads *Naphtali with their swords*; alt Hb tradition, Syr, Vg read *Naphtali, the ruins all around*; Hb obscure

---

repentance or reform Manasseh attempted did not carry over to his son and successor, Amon. He picked up where his father had left off before his repentance, going back into idolatry. But with Amon there was no mid-life repentance. His servants assassinated him after he had reigned for **two years**. The people were probably outraged by the assassination, so they had Amon's killers **executed**.

34:1 Josiah: Fifteenth king of Judah; son of Amon; became king as a boy; carried out a thorough reform. Josiah came to the throne when he was only **eight years old**, but even at an early age he showed better judgment than many older kings.

34:2 Josiah received a good evaluation from the Chronicler. Like all the other good kings before him, he is compared to **David**.

34:3-5 Josiah did not come to faith in God immediately. In contrast to Joash, he did not have an older person to guide him in this direction. When he was 16 years old (**in the eighth year of his reign**), he decided to become a worshiper of God. Four years later he began to assert his will by removing the various idols from the land and abolishing all pagan places of worship. He desecrated the **graves** of past idolaters and defiled the pagan **altars**.

34:6-7 Josiah not only abolished the sites for idolatry in Judah, but he **tore down** those in the area of the northern tribes as well.

34:8 The Levites and priests had maintained their identity and had returned to work toward the end of Manasseh's reign. When Josiah issued orders for the **repair** of the **temple**, they were available and ready to make their contributions to Josiah's reform movement.

34:9-11 Josiah had sent emissaries to collect **money** for the repair of the temple. This money was allocated to **Hilkiah the high priest**. He distributed it among the contractors, who gave it to the **workmen**, who passed it on to those who were providing the raw materials. The Chronicler reminds the readers that the destruction of the temple, while often carried out by invaders, was ultimately the fault of **Judah's kings**.

34:12-13 Some **Levites** were placed in supervisory positions as overseers while others carried out clerical tasks for the construction project. The Chronicler also pointed out that some Levites apparently contributed to the effort by playing their **musical instruments**.

34:14 The **book of the law** that **Hilkiah** found was probably

had been deposited in the LORD's temple, Hilkiah the priest found the book of the law of the LORD written by the hand of Moses.[a] [15] Consequently,[b] Hilkiah told Shaphan the court secretary, "I have found the book of the law in the LORD's temple," and he gave the book to Shaphan.

[16] Shaphan took the book to the king, and also reported, "Your servants are doing all that was placed in their hands. [17] They have emptied out the money that was found in the LORD's temple and have put it into the hand of the overseers and the hand of those doing the work." [18] Then Shaphan the court secretary told the king, "Hilkiah the priest gave me a book," and Shaphan read from it in the presence of the king.[c]

[19] When the king heard the words of the law, he tore his clothes.[d] [20] Then he commanded Hilkiah, Ahikam son of Shaphan, Abdon son of Micah, Shaphan the court secretary, and the king's servant Asaiah, [21] "Go. Ask •Yahweh for me and for those remaining in Israel and Judah, concerning the words of the book that was found. For great is the LORD's wrath that is poured out on us[e] because our fathers have not kept the word of the LORD in order to do everything written in this book."

Huldah's Prophecy of Judgment

[22] So Hilkiah and those the king had designated[A] went to the prophetess Huldah, the wife of Shallum son of Tokhath, son of Hasrah, keeper of the wardrobe. She lived in Jerusalem in the Second District. They spoke with her about this.

[23] She said to them, "This is what Yahweh, the God of Israel says: Say to the man who sent you to Me, [24] 'This is what Yahweh says: I am about to bring disaster on this place and on its inhabitants,[f] fulfilling all the curses written in the book that they read in the pres-

ence of the king of Judah,[g] [25] because they have abandoned Me[h] and burned incense to other gods in order to provoke Me with all the works of their hands. My wrath will be poured out on this place, and it will not be quenched.' [26] Say this to the king of Judah who sent you to ask Yahweh, 'This is what Yahweh, the God of Israel says: As for the words that you heard, [27] because[i] your heart was tender and you humbled yourself before God when you heard His words against this place and against its inhabitants, and because you humbled yourself before Me, and you tore your clothes and wept before Me, I Myself have heard'—this is the LORD's declaration. [28] 'I will indeed gather you to your fathers, and you will be gathered to your grave in peace. Your eyes will not see all the disaster that I am bringing on this place and on its inhabitants.'"[j]

Then they reported to the king.

Affirmation of the Covenant by Josiah and the People

[29] So the king sent messengers and gathered all the elders of Judah and Jerusalem. [30] The king went up to the LORD's temple with all the men of Judah and the inhabitants of Jerusalem, as well as the priests and the Levites—all the people from great to small. He read in their hearing all the words of the book of the covenant that had been found in the LORD's temple.[k] [31] Then the king stood at his post[l] and made a covenant in the LORD's presence[m] to follow the LORD and to keep His commands, His decrees, and His statutes with all his heart and with all his soul[n] in order to carry out the words of the covenant written in this book.[o]

[32] He had all those present in Jerusalem and Benjamin agree[B] to it. So all the inhabitants of Jerusalem carried out the covenant of God, the God of their ancestors.

[33] So Josiah removed everything that was

Cross references (center column)
[a]34:14 Dt 31:24-26
[b]34:15-32 2Kg 22:8-23:3
[c]34:18 Dt 17:18-20
[d]34:19 Jos 7:6
[e]34:21 2Ch 29:8
[f]34:24 2Ch 36:15-21
[g]Dt 28:15-68
[h]34:25 2Ch 33:3
[i]34:27-28 1Kg 21:29; 2Ch 12:6-7; 32:26
[j]34:28 Is 57:1-2
[k]34:30 Neh 8:1-3
[l]34:31 2Kg 11:14; 2Ch 30:16
[m]2Ch 23:16; 29:10
[n]Dt 6:4-6
[o]Ex 24:3-8; Jos 24:14-28

---

one or more scrolls containing the entire Pentateuch—the books of Moses from Genesis through Deuteronomy.

34:18-21 When **Shaphan**, the king's secretary, started to read what was in the book, the king was overcome with dread because he knew that Judah had **not kept the word of the LORD** for a long time and severe punishment was likely. Josiah wanted specific guidance from **Yahweh** about what he should do.

34:22 Hilkiah and other royal officials consulted a **prophetess** named **Huldah** to determine God's perspective on the situation. As is normal in Chronicles, Huldah's genealogy is given. Other female prophets in the OT include Miriam (Ex 15:20) and Deborah (Jdg 4:4).

34:24-25 Huldah told them that God's punishment was in-

evitable, just as the book of the law predicted. There had been too many generations of wickedness in Judah.

34:27-28 But because of Josiah's attitude of repentance and his willingness to obey God, the calamity would not happen until after his death. The prophetess inserted **this is the LORD's declaration** into her prophecy to assure her hearers she was not speaking her own thoughts, but the very words of God.

34:29-32 King Josiah called a major convocation. Leaders and Levites as well as all the common people of Jerusalem came and heard the public reading of Scripture. The king publicly made a personal **covenant** with God that he would follow **the LORD**, and he compelled the crowd to follow him in this commitment.

34:33 Josiah continued to purge the land of idols. He also

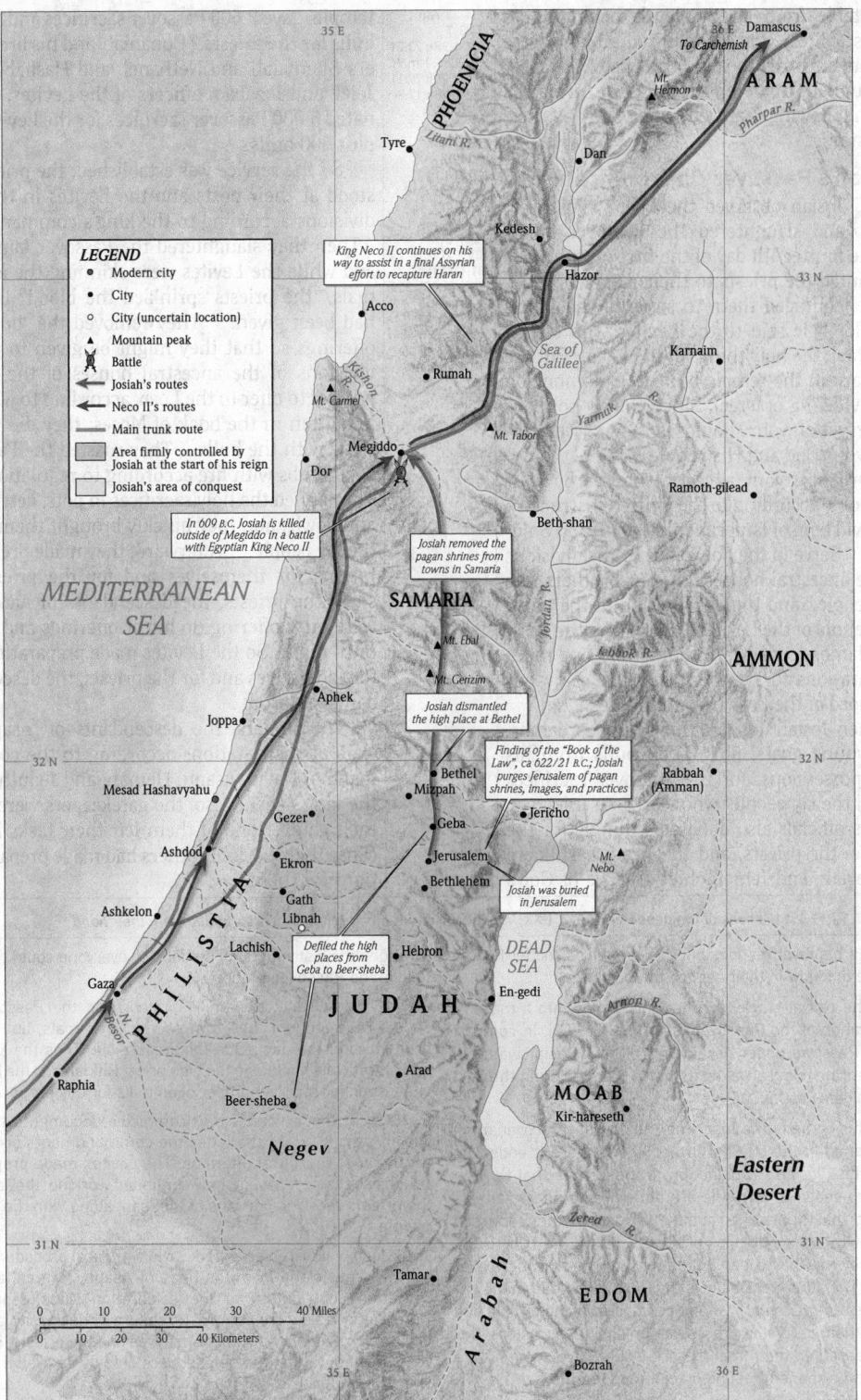

LEGEND

- ● Modern city
- ● City
- ○ City (uncertain location)
- ▲ Mountain peak
- ⚔ Battle
- ← Josiah's routes
- ← Neco II's routes
- — Main trunk route
- ▨ Area firmly controlled by Josiah at the start of his reign
- ▨ Josiah's area of conquest

King Neco II continues on his way to assist in a final Assyrian effort to recapture Haran

In 609 B.C. Josiah is killed outside of Megiddo in a battle with Egyptian King Neco II

Josiah removed the pagan shrines from towns in Samaria

Josiah dismantled the high place at Bethel

Finding of the "Book of the Law", ca 622/21 B.C.; Josiah purges Jerusalem of pagan shrines, images, and practices

Josiah was buried in Jerusalem

Defiled the high places from Geba to Beer-sheba

PHOENICIA

ARAM

To Carchemish

Damascus

Mt. Hermon

Tyre

Dan

Kedesh

Hazor

Acco

Karnaim

Rumah

Sea of Galilee

Mt. Carmel

Mt. Tabor

Megiddo

Dor

Beth-shan

Ramoth-gilead

MEDITERRANEAN SEA

SAMARIA

Mt. Ebal

Mt. Gerizim

AMMON

Aphek

Joppa

Mesad Hashavyahu

Bethel

Mizpah

Rabbah (Amman)

Gezer

Geba

Jericho

Ashdod

Ekron

Jerusalem

Ashkelon

Gath

Bethlehem

Mt. Nebo

Libnah

Lachish

Hebron

DEAD SEA

Gaza

En-gedi

JUDAH

Raphia

PHILISTIA

Arad

MOAB

Kir-hareseth

Beer-sheba

Negev

Eastern Desert

Tamar

EDOM

Bozrah

35 E

36 E

33 N

32 N

31 N

35 E

36 E

0   10   20   30   40 Miles

0   10   20   30   40 Kilometers

The Reign of Josiah

detestable from all the lands belonging to the Israelites,[a] and he required all who were present in Israel to serve the LORD their God. Throughout his reign they did not turn aside from following Yahweh, the God of their ancestors.

Josiah's Passover Observance

35 Josiah observed the LORD's •Passover[b] and slaughtered the Passover lambs on the fourteenth day of the first month.[c] 2 He appointed the priests to their responsibilities and encouraged them to serve in the LORD's temple.[d] 3 He said to the Levites who taught all Israel[e] the holy things of the LORD, "Put the holy ark in the temple built by Solomon son of David king of Israel. Since you do not have to carry it on your shoulders,[f] now serve •Yahweh your God and His people Israel.

4 "Organize your ancestral houses by your divisions[g] according to the written instruction of David king of Israel and that of his son Solomon.[h] 5 Serve in the holy place by the divisions of the ancestral houses for your brothers, the lay people,[A] and the distribution of the tribal household of the Levites.[i] 6 Slaughter the Passover lambs,[j] consecrate yourselves,[k] and make preparations for your brothers to carry out the word of the LORD through Moses."

7 Then Josiah donated 30,000 sheep, lambs, and young goats, plus 3,000 bulls from his own possessions, for the Passover sacrifices for all the lay people[A] who were present.

8 His officials also donated willingly for the people, the priests, and the Levites. Hilkiah, Zechariah, and Jehiel, chief officials of God's

temple, gave 2,600 Passover sacrifices and 300 bulls for the priests. 9 Conaniah[l] and his brothers Shemaiah and Nethanel, and Hashabiah, Jeiel, and Jozabad, officers of the Levites, donated 5,000 Passover sacrifices for the Levites, plus 500 bulls.

10 So the service was established; the priests stood at their posts and the Levites in their divisions according to the king's command.[m] 11 Then they slaughtered the Passover lambs, and while the Levites were skinning the animals,[n] the priests sprinkled the blood[B] they had been given.[C] 12 They removed the •burnt offerings so that they might be given to the divisions of the ancestral houses of the lay people[A] to offer to the LORD, according to what is written in the book of Moses; they did the same with the bulls. 13 They roasted the Passover lambs with fire according to regulation.[o] They boiled the holy sacrifices in pots, kettles, and bowls; and they quickly brought them to the lay people.[A] 14 Afterward, they made preparations for themselves and for the priests, since the priests, the descendants of Aaron, were busy offering up burnt offerings and fat until night. So the Levites made preparations for themselves and for the priests, the descendants of Aaron.

15 The singers, the descendants of •Asaph, were at their stations according to the command of David, Asaph, Heman, and Jeduthun the king's seer.[p] Also, the gatekeepers were at each gate.[q] None of them left their tasks because their Levite brothers had made preparations for them.

Cross references (margin)

a34:33 2Ch 34:3-7
b35:1 2Kg 23:21
cEx 12:6; Nm 9:3
d35:2 2Ch 29:11
e35:3 2Ch 17:8-9; Neh 8:7
f1Ch 23:26
g35:4 1Ch 9:10-13
h2Ch 8:14
i35:5 Ezr 6:18
j35:6 2Ch 35:1,11
k2Ch 29:5
l35:9 2Ch 31:12-13
m35:10 2Ch 35:5
n35:11 2Ch 29:34
o35:13 Ex 12:8-9
p35:15 1Ch 25:1
q1Ch 26:12-19

A35:5,7,12,13 Lit the sons of the people   B35:11 LXX, Vg, Tg; MT omits blood   C35:11 Lit sprinkled from their hand

---

fulfilled his royal responsibility to present a model for the people to follow in their service to God.

35:1 The revival started by the king turned into a massive celebration of the **Passover** (see note at 30:1). In contrast to the Passover under Hezekiah's reforms, Josiah was able to celebrate this festival on its normal day—during **the first month** (see note at 30:2-5).

35:3 This verse is the last time the **ark** of the covenant is mentioned in the OT. We do not know where it ended up after this. Josiah's explanation to the Levites that they no longer needed to carry the ark on their **shoulders** reflects the fact that they learned about this practice when they read the newly discovered book of the law (Ex 25:14; 1Ch 15:15), and they may have been holding it on their shoulders ever since. The other possibility is that Manasseh had made the Levites remove the ark when he desecrated the temple and made them carry it in procession on special occasions. Josiah reassured them that the ark would once again have a proper, permanent resting place in the **temple**.

35:4-6 Josiah implemented David's and Solomon's work schedule for the priests and Levites in the temple. He also

arranged the distribution of the food so everyone could partake of the **Passover** properly.

35:7-9 Theoretically all families celebrating the Passover should have brought their own sacrificial animals, but the economics of the day made this impossible. Thus the king and his **officials**, including the high priest **Hilkiah** and the **Levites**, supplied a large number of animals for this purpose.

35:10-14 In these verses the Chronicler documents that Josiah carried out to the letter the commandments of the Torah about sacrificial offerings. The Levites **made preparations** so that, even while they continued working, they and the **priests** received portions of the feast along with the **lay people**.

35:15 Josiah also implemented David's musical procedures, with the musicians from the lines of **Asaph, Heman, and Jeduthun** contributing to the celebration. **Gatekeepers** were stationed at the temple to ensure ritual purity and physical protection. As with themselves and the priests, Levites made sure that the gatekeepers on duty enjoyed their share of the feast.

35:18 The Chronicler declared this was the greatest Passover celebration since the kingship was first established in

[16] So all the service of the LORD was established that day for observing the Passover and for offering burnt offerings on the altar of the LORD, according to the command of King Josiah. [17] The Israelites who were present in Judah also observed the Passover at that time and the Festival of Unleavened Bread for seven days.[a] [18] No Passover had been observed[b] like it in Israel since the days of Samuel the prophet. None of the kings of Israel ever observed a Passover like the one that Josiah observed with the priests, the Levites, all Judah, the Israelites who were present in Judah, and the inhabitants of Jerusalem. [19] In the eighteenth year of Josiah's reign, this Passover was observed.

Josiah's Last Deeds and Death

[20] After all this[c] that Josiah had prepared for the temple, Neco king of Egypt[d] marched up to fight at Carchemish[e] by the Euphrates, and Josiah went out to confront him. [21] But Neco sent messengers to him, saying, "What is the issue between you and me, king of Judah?[f] I have not come against you today[A] but I am fighting another dynasty.[B] God told me to hurry. Stop opposing God who is with me; don't make Him destroy you!"

[22] But Josiah did not turn away from him; instead, in order to fight with him he disguised himself.[C,g] He did not listen to Neco's words from the mouth of God, but went to the Valley of Megiddo[h] to fight. [23] The archers shot King Josiah, and he said to his servants, "Take me away, for I am severely wounded!"[i] [24] So his servants took him out of the war chariot, carried him in his second chariot, and brought him to Jerusalem. Then he died, and they buried him in the tomb of his fathers. All Judah and Jerusalem mourned[j] for Josiah. [25] Jeremiah chanted a dirge[k] over Josiah, and all the singing men and singing women still speak of Josiah in their dirges to this very day. They established them as a statute for Israel, and indeed they are written in the Dirges.

[26] The rest of the events[l] of Josiah's reign, along with his deeds of faithful love according to what is written in the law of the LORD, [27] and his words, from beginning to end, are written in the Book of the Kings of Israel and Judah.

Judah's King Jehoahaz

36 Then[m] the common people[D] took Jehoahaz son of Josiah and made him king in Jerusalem in place of his father.

[2] Jehoahaz[E] was 23 years old when he became king and reigned three months in Jerusalem. [3] The king of Egypt deposed him in Jerusalem and fined the land 7,500 pounds[F] of silver and 75 pounds[G] of gold.

Judah's King Jehoiakim

[4] Then Neco king of Egypt made Jehoahaz's brother Eliakim king over Judah and Jerusalem and changed Eliakim's name to Jehoiakim. But Neco took his brother Jehoahaz[E] and brought him to Egypt.[n]

Cross-references (center column):
a35:17 2Ch 30:21
b35:18-19 2Kg 23:22-23
c35:20-25 2Kg 23:29-30a
d35:20 Jr 46:2
eIs 10:9
f35:21 Jdg 11:12; 2Ch 25:19
g35:22 2Ch 18:29
hJdg 5:19
i35:23 2Ch 18:33
j35:24 Zch 12:11
k35:25 Jr 22:10; Lm 4:20
l35:26-27 2Kg 23:28
m36:1-4 2Kg 23:30b-34
n36:4 Jr 22:10-12

A35:21 LXX, Syr, Tg, Vg; MT reads *Not against you, you today*   B35:21 Lit *house*   C35:22 LXX reads *he was determined*
D36:1 Lit *the people of the land*   E36:2,4 = Joahaz   F36:3 Lit *100 talents*   G36:3 Lit *one talent*

---

the days of Samuel. Perhaps the last good Passover celebration was when Israel first entered the promised land (Jos 5:10-11; cp. 2Kg 23:22). No king of Judah or Israel had celebrated so well. This evaluation may be a reference to the precise attention to the proper procedures, or to the joyful participation of the Levites, priests, gatekeepers, Israelites, and all the common people of Jerusalem. It was a true restoration of the ancient tradition, incorporating all the appropriate guilds and procedures.

35:20 The three superpowers of that time—Assyria, Babylonia, and Egypt—were about to fight for world supremacy. Egypt and Assyria had formed an alliance against the Babylonians. **Neco**, the pharaoh of Egypt, had assembled a large army and was heading to **Carchemish** in Mesopotamia to join the fight against Babylon.

35:21 Pharaoh **Neco** of Egypt was not an enemy of **Judah**. He had no intention of conquering Judah. Nevertheless, Josiah marched out to meet the Egyptian army in battle. Ominously, the Chronicler does not say that Josiah inquired of God whether he should fight.

35:22-24 Josiah confronted Neco on the large plain of **Megiddo**. To protect himself from any personal revenge by Neco, **he disguised himself**. But the king was mortally wounded by an arrow. He was transported to **Jerusalem** where he died. It is ironic that Josiah, one of the best kings of Judah, was killed in a manner remarkably similar to Ahab, perhaps the worst king of Israel (18:29-34).

35:25-27 Josiah's obituary contains many positive words, which makes his premature and unnecessary death all the more tragic.

36:1 Jehoahaz: Sixteenth king of Judah; son of Josiah; deposed and deported by Pharaoh Neco. The Chronicler states that the **common people** of Judah made Jehoahaz their next king. The point of this emphasis is the difference between the people's choice for a king and Neco's imposition of a king to his liking three months later.

36:2-3 The battle of Carchemish was won by Babylonia, reducing the power of both Assyria and Egypt. Thus, when Neco returned through Judah, he tried to make sure that the new king would not cause trouble as Josiah had done. He **deposed** Jehoahaz after he had reigned for only **three months**. According to 2Kg 23:32, Jehoahaz was about to perpetuate the same evil as some of the earlier kings. Although his deportation did not help the kingdom of Judah last much longer, it was no loss to the kingdom that Neco carried him off into exile and replaced him with his brother Eliakim (2Ch 36:4).

36:4 Jehoiakim: Seventeenth king of Judah; son of Josiah; installed by Pharaoh Neco of Egypt; pursued evil. After

⁵Jehoiakim was 25 years old when he became king and reigned 11 years in Jerusalem. He did what was evil in the sight of the Lord his God.[a] ⁶Now Nebuchadnezzar king of Babylon attacked him[b] and bound him in bronze[c] shackles to take him to Babylon.[d] ⁷Also Nebuchadnezzar took some of the utensils of the Lord's temple to Babylon and put them in his temple in Babylon.[e]

⁸The rest of the deeds of Jehoiakim,[f] the detestable things he did, and what was found against him, are written in the Book of Israel's Kings. His son Jehoiachin became king in his place.

Judah's King Jehoiachin

⁹Jehoiachin was 18[A] years old[g] when he became king and reigned three months and 10 days in Jerusalem. He did what was evil in the Lord's sight. ¹⁰In the spring[B][h] Nebuchadnezzar sent for him and brought him to Babylon along with the valuable utensils of the Lord's temple. Then he made Jehoiachin's brother Zedekiah king over Judah and Jerusalem.[i]

Judah's King Zedekiah

¹¹Zedekiah was 21 years old[j] when he became king and reigned 11 years in Jerusalem.

¹²He did what was evil in the sight of the Lord his God and did not humble himself[k] before Jeremiah the prophet at the Lord's command.[l] ¹³He also rebelled against[m] King Nebuchadnezzar who had made him swear allegiance by God. He became obstinate[C][n] and hardened his heart against returning to •Yahweh, the God of Israel. ¹⁴All the leaders of the priests and the people multiplied their unfaithful deeds, imitating all the detestable practices of the nations, and they defiled the Lord's temple that He had consecrated in Jerusalem.

The Destruction of Jerusalem

¹⁵But Yahweh, the God of their ancestors sent word against them by the hand of His messengers, sending them time and time again,[o] for He had compassion on His people and on His dwelling place. ¹⁶But they kept ridiculing God's messengers,[p] despising His words,[q] and scoffing at His prophets, until the Lord's wrath was so stirred up against His people that there was no remedy.[r] ¹⁷So He brought up against them the king of the Chaldeans,[s] who killed their choice young men with the sword in the house of their sanctuary. He had no pity on young men or young women, elderly or

a36:5 2Kg 23:36-37; Jr 22:13-18
b36:6 2Kg 24:1
c2Ch 33:11
dJr 22:18-19
e36:7 2Kg 24:1-4; Jr 22:13-19; 25:1-9; Dn 1:1; Hab 1:6
f36:8 2Kg 24:5-6
g36:9-10 2Kg 24:8-17
h36:10 2Sm 11:1
iJr 37:1
j36:11-13 2Kg 24:18-20; Jr 52:1-3
k36:12 2Ch 33:23
lJr 21:3-7
m36:13 Ezk 17:15
n2Ch 30:8
o36:15 Jr 7:13; 25:3,11-12
p36:16 2Ch 30:10; Jr 5:12-13
qPr 1:24-32
rEzr 5:12
s36:17 2Kg 25:1-7; Jr 52:4-11

A36:9 Some Hb mss, LXX; 2Kg 24:8; other Hb mss read *eight his neck*　　B36:10 Lit *At the return of the year*　　C36:13 Lit *He stiffened*

reimbursing himself for his trouble with a tribute of gold and silver (v. 2), Neco placed **Eliakim** on the throne. He changed his name to **Jehoiakim**, thereby associating his new vassal more closely with the God he supposedly served (with "Jh" being a reference to Yahweh), rather than using the more generic reference to God *(El)*. Either version means "God raises up," an ironic name for this godless king.

36:5-8 Jehoiakim was an **evil** king, committing idolatry and opposing the word from God that came to him by the prophet Jeremiah (Jr 36:10-26). He was eventually carried off by **Nebuchadnezzar** to **Babylon**, along with a number of

The Cyrus Cylinder, written in cuneiform, was discovered in 1879 in Nineveh, Iraq, by Hormuzd Rassam. It is now in the British Museum. The cylinder contains inscriptions in which Cyrus gives credit to the Babylonian god Marduk for choosing him and enabling him to conquer Babylon. The inscriptions express Cyrus's policy of allowing captive peoples, such as the Jews, to return to their homelands. The biblical writers saw God's hand in these world events (36:22-23; Ezr 1:2-4; Is 44:24-28; 45:1).

young men from leading families in Jerusalem. This was the first of three deportations, the one in which Daniel and his friends were relocated to Babylon (Dn 1:1-3).

36:9-10 Jehoiachin: Eighteenth and next-to-last king of Judah; son of Jehoiakim; deposed and deported by Nebuchadnezzar. Jehoiachin wound up having just 10 days longer (**three months and 10 days**) on the throne than Jehoahaz, but this was sufficient time for him to further aggravate **Nebuchadnezzar**. The king of Babylon returned to Jerusalem, collected more treasures, and carried a group back to Babylon into exile. This was the second deportation, which included the prophet Ezekiel (Ezk 1:1). The next king, Zedekiah, is called his **brother**; this should be interpreted as "kinsman" in this case. Zedekiah, Jehoahaz, and Eliakim/Jehoiakim were all sons of Josiah (v. 1; Jr 36:1; 37:1), and Jehoiachin was Jehoiakim's son, making Zedekiah Jehoiachin's uncle.

36:11-14 Zedekiah: Nineteenth and last king of Judah; son of Josiah; uncle of Jehoiachin; refused to submit to Nebuchadnezzar and witnessed the destruction of Jerusalem. Zedekiah thought he could get away with rebelling against **Nebuchadnezzar**, hoping that Egypt would come to his aid. But he was mistaken. He also brought Jerusalem and what little there was left of his kingdom to spiritual poverty, leading even the **priests** and Levites into false worship.

36:15-17 After God had graciously offered the people of Judah many opportunities to repent, He finally sent Nebuchadnezzar to eradicate Jerusalem and carry the people off to Babylon. When individual kings repented, God re-

aged; He handed them all over to him. [18] He took everything to Babylon—all the articles of God's temple, large and small, the treasures of the Lord's temple, and the treasures of the king and his officials. [19] Then the Chaldeans burned God's temple.[a] They tore down Jerusalem's wall, burned down all its palaces, and destroyed all its valuable articles.

[20] He deported those who escaped from the sword to Babylon, and they became servants to him and his sons until the rise of the Persian[A] kingdom.[b] [21] This fulfilled the word of the Lord through Jeremiah[c] and the land enjoyed its Sabbath rest all the days of the desolation[d] until 70 years were fulfilled.

The Decree of Cyrus

[22] In the first year of Cyrus king of Persia,[e] the word of the Lord spoken through[B] Jeremiah[f] was fulfilled. The Lord put it into the mind of King Cyrus[g] of Persia to issue a proclamation throughout his entire kingdom and also to put it in writing:

[23] This is what King Cyrus of Persia says: The Lord, the God of heaven, has given me all the kingdoms of the earth and has appointed me to build Him a temple at Jerusalem in Judah. Whoever among you of His people may go up, and may the Lord his God be with him.

a36:19-20 2Kg 25:9-11; Jr 52:13-15
b36:20 Jr 27:7
c36:21 Jr 25:11-12; 29:10
dLv 25:4; 26:33
e36:22-23 Ezr 1:1-3
f36:22 Jr 25:11-14; 27:22; 29:10-14; 33:7-10
gIs 44:28; 45:1

A36:20 LXX reads *Median*   B36:22 Lit *Lord by the mouth of*

---

peatedly provided a **remedy** (lit "healing"; 7:14; 30:20), but the accumulation of wrath against evil finally reached the tipping point. This passage is similar to the comment the Chronicler made about some of the northern tribes (1Ch 5:25-26).

36:21 The book of Jeremiah records his prophecy that, due to Judah's wickedness, the Babylonians would conquer Judah and deport its inhabitants.

36:22-23 But this story was not yet over. The Babylonians were eventually conquered by **Cyrus king of Persia**. Cyrus believed the gods of foreigners who were exiled in his territory could cause harm in the future. Thus, he decreed that all the foreign gods in Babylon and Persia should be transported back to their places of origin and that the people who worshiped them should return and build new temples for these deities. The Jews correctly saw Cyrus as God's instrument in issuing this command. A pagan king's orders allowed them to return to their homeland and rebuild the **temple** of the **Lord**.

Kings of Persia

PERSIAN KING	DATES (B.C.)	BIBLICAL CONNECTIONS	EVENTS AND ACCOMPLISHMENTS
Cyrus II (The Great)	559–530	Permitted return of the Jews from exile; facilitated rebuilding of the temple at Jerusalem (Ezr 1:1-4; 6:3-5); "His anointed" (Is 45:1)	King of Anshan, 559 B.C.; conquered kingdom of Media (550 B.C.) and Lydian kingdom (546 B.C.); conquered Babylon, 539 B.C.
Cambyses II	530–522	Not mentioned in the Bible	Son of Cyrus the Great; conquered Egypt, 525 B.C.; his death (suicide?) in 522 B.C. lead to two years of fighting between rival claimants to the throne
Darius I Hystaspes	522–486	Haggai and Zechariah preached during the second year of Darius I (520 B.C.); temple rebuilt and dedicated (515 B.C.; cp. Ezr 6:13-15)	Member of a collateral royal line; secured the throne ending the unrest following the death of Cambyses; reorganized the Persian Empire into satrapies; established royal postal system; began builiding Persepolis; invaded Greece and was defeated at Marathon, 490 B.C.; revolt in Egypt
Xerxes I	486–465	Possibly Ahasuerus of the book of Esther	Son of Darius I; continued building Persepolis; encountered numerous rebellions at the beginning of his reign (Egypt, Babylon); invaded Greece; sacked Athens (480 B.C.), but was defeated by the Greeks in a revolt engagement (Salamis, 480 B.C.), and on land (Plataea and Mycale, 479 B.C.); killed in a palace coup in 455 B.C.
Artaxerxes I Longimanus	465–425	Nehemiah, cupbearer to Artaxerxes; came to Judah (444 B.C.; cp. Neh 2:1; 13:6); traditional date of Ezra's mission in the seventh year of his reign (458 B.C.; cp. Ezr 7:7)	Faced revolt in Egypt; completed major buildings at Persepolis; made peace with the Greeks (Peace of Callas, 449 B.C.); died of natural causes
Xerxes II	423	Not mentioned in the Bible	Ruled less than two months
Darius II Nothus	423–404	Not mentioned in the Bible; Jews in Egypt appealed to Samaria and Jerusalem for help in rebuilding their temple about 407 B.C.	Peloponnesian War, 431–404 B.C.; Persia recovered several Greek cities in Asia Minor
Artaxerxes II Mnemon	404–359/8	Some scholars place Ezra's mission in the seventh year of Artaxerxes II, about 398 B.C.	Egypt regained freedom from Persia for a time; revolt of the Satraps, 366–360 B.C.
Artaxerxes II Ochus	359/8–338/7	Not mentioned in the Bible	Philip II of Macedon; rises to power about 359 B.C.; Alexander the Great born 356 B.C.; Persia reclaims Egypt, 342 B.C.
Arses	338/7–336	Not mentioned in the Bible	Son of Artaxerxes III; became king when his father and most of his family were murdered
Darius II Codomanus	336–330	Alexander subdues the Levant; Tyre and Gaza beseiged, 332 B.C.; conquest of Egypt by Alexander, 332 B.C.	Philip assassinated, 336 B.C.; Alexander the Great invades the Persian Empire, 334 B.C.; Darius III defeated by Alexander at Issus, 333 B.C. and Gaugamela, 331 B.C.; death of Darius, 330 B.C.

Ezra

The books of Ezra and Nehemiah bear the names of the key person in each of the books. Until the third century A.D., though, the books of Ezra and Nehemiah were regarded as a single book. Both books contain material found in the other, and they complete each other. The separation of the book in the Christian community took place through the influence of the Vulgate, the Latin translation prepared by Jerome who, following Origen before him, separated Ezra-Nehemiah into two distinct books. In the Jewish community, Ezra and Nehemiah were not separated into two distinct books until the fifteenth-century printing of the Hebrew Bible. In the Hebrew Bible, Ezra-Nehemiah is part of the third division of the canon, called the Writings (Hb *ketuvim*).

The Euphrates River at Dura Europas. The difficult journey from exile back to Judah was a thousand miles and likely proceeded along the trade route that ran parallel to the Euphrates River to Aleppo. Sheshbazzar led the first groups between 537 and 522 B.C. and Ezra the second group, 458 B.C.

Circumstances of Writing

Author: Ezra and Nehemiah are anonymous. Ancient Jewish sources usually credit Ezra as the author of Ezra-Nehemiah. More likely Ezra-Nehemiah was written by the "Chronicler," the person (or persons) responsible for 1 and 2 Chronicles. Not only is Ezra-Nehemiah linked to Chronicles at its introduction (Ezr 1:1-2 = 2Ch 36:22-23), it also shares many similarities in language, terminology, themes, and perspective.

Background: It is probably safe to assume that Ezra-Nehemiah was written soon after the conclusion of Nehemiah's ministry. Most likely the book was written no later than 400 B.C.

In Ezra-Nehemiah it is clear that Ezra came to Jerusalem first, probably in 458 B.C., and that Nehemiah followed him 13 years later, probably in 445 B.C. Nehemiah made no mention of Ezra, his ministry, or his reforms. Ezra and Nehemiah appear together in only two texts (Neh 8:9; 12:36). The two events in which Ezra and Nehemiah were together were significant. In Nehemiah 8, the context is the reading of the law to the people, while in Nehemiah 12 the two joyous processions walking around the city walls in the dedication ceremony include Ezra (Neh 12:36) and Nehemiah (Neh 12:38).

Message and Purpose

Ezra continues where 2 Chronicles left off. While it provides us with key historical insights, it is rich in messages for God's people.

The continuity of God's people: The events in Ezra-Nehemiah connect the Israelites with the preexilic community. The returning exiles experienced a new exodus and remained a part of God's redemptive plan. God even used pagan leaders like Cyrus and Artaxerxes to restore His people.

Holiness: For the people to continue the covenant relationship with God, it was important for them to separate and remain pure in matters of doctrine, ethics, and customs. Prior to the exile, the people experienced

600 B.C.	575 B.C.	550 B.C.
Neco II of Egypt commissions Phoenician sailors to be the first to sail around the continent of Africa. 615–595	Events in Ezekiel 593–571	Battle of Thymbra between Cyrus the Great and Croesus, commander of the Lydian army 546
Nebuchadnezzar's three invasions of Judah 605, 597, 586	Athens has two years with no *archon* (ruler), hence the term *anarchy*. 589	Cyrus's decree allows return of Jews from exile. 538
Events in Obadiah 605–586?	Cyrus the Elder, founder of the Persian Empire, is born. 581	Events in Ezra 538–457
Events in Daniel 605–530	Aesop, slave of Xanthus of Samos, is credited with collecting and creating fables. They were probably committed to writing at a later time. 570	Second temple construction under Zerubbabel's and Joshua's leadership 536–515
Temple of Solomon destroyed 586	Nebuchadnezzar II's successor, Evil-Merodach, releases Judah's King Jehoiachin, who has been a prisoner for 36 years. 560	

judgment because of their inability to remain faithful single-mindedly in their relationship to their covenant God. Ezra-Nehemiah shows us a renewed interest in remaining separated unto God.

Scripture: Ezra and Nehemiah reaffirm the centrality of the law to the life and practice of the Israelite community. They knew the authority of Scripture, but they were called back from their neglect of its teachings. Multiple times they showed that the people worked and behaved in accordance with what Moses had written (Ezr 3:2; 6:18; Neh 8:14-15; 13:1-3). Ezra and Nehemiah may give us the best example of the power of God at work through the written Word.

Worship: The returning exiles built an altar to sacrifice to God before they rebuilt the temple. Only after the place of worship was finished did they rebuild the walls. They got the projects in proper order, because worship and a proper relationship with God precede everything else.

Prayer: Alongside worship is an abundance of prayer in these books. Two extensive prayers are recorded (Ezr 9; Neh 9). Prayer and fasting are mentioned multiple times as they set out on tasks, and the whole rebuilding of the wall was bathed in prayer. Prayer is combined with action throughout Nehemiah, and both books underscore the need to approach God constantly in prayer.

Contribution to the Bible

The events which occurred in Ezra and Nehemiah, the rebuilt temple, the stabilizing of Jerusalem, and the Jewish community that developed, all played key roles in the life and ministry of Jesus recorded in the Gospels. The rebuilt temple may have paled in comparison to Solomon's temple, but it would serve the Jews for centuries until Christ removed the need for a physical temple.

Structure

Ezra-Nehemiah was written in two related but distinct languages—Hebrew and Aramaic. The Hebrew sections generally reflect the style of the postexilic era with some evidence of the impact of Aramaic on the language.

525 B.C.	500 B.C.	475 B.C.
Cambyses, son of Cyrus 530–522	Greeks develop instruments for surveying 500	Xerxes I, Ahasuerus, husband of Esther 486–465
Aeschylus, Greek tragedian (525–456) many of whose plays dealt with the Persian invasion of Greece, participated in the Greek victories at Marathon and Salamis.	Sugar cane cultivated in India 500	Esther's reign 479–465?
	Greeks, outnumbered almost five to one, defeat Persians in Battle of Marathon through superior military intelligence and strategy, forestalling Persian expansion into Europe. 490	Esther saves the Jews within the Persian Empire. 474?
Darius I or Darius the Great 521–486		Ezra goes to Jerusalem. 458
		Events in Nehemiah 445–430
Events in Haggai 520	Events in Esther 486–465	
Events in Zechariah 520–518	Greek victory over Persians in Battle of Salamis, 480, and Plain of Plataea, 479, thwarted Persian expansion into Europe.	
Second temple dedicated 515		

Aramaic, a Semitic language similar to Hebrew, occurs in two sections in the book of Ezra (Ezr 4:8–6:18; 7:12-26). During the Persian period (ca 540 to 330 B.C.), Aramaic was the official language of diplomacy and commerce.

Ezra-Nehemiah is similar to Samuel and Kings, and especially Chronicles, in that many sources were utilized in its composition. These include two major types of sources. Much of Ezra-Nehemiah consists of material from the Ezra Memoir and the Nehemiah Memoir. The Ezra Memoir, usually written in the first person, includes Ezra 7–10, along with Nehemiah 8 and probably chapter 9 as well, but embedded in this memoir are lists and records from other sources used by Ezra. The composition of the Nehemiah Memoir is regarded as including Nehemiah 1–7 as well as 11–13. But here also Nehemiah incorporated lists and records in his memoir. Ezra-Nehemiah also contains many lists, genealogies, inventories, letters, and census records throughout the book. For a community attempting to reestablish itself after the disaster of 586 B.C. and the subsequent exile to Babylon, this material was crucial in reordering their life as a community.

Outline of Ezra

I. **Return from Exile (1:1–6:22)**
   A. The decree of Cyrus (1:1-11)
   B. Exiles who returned (2:1-70)
   C. Restoration of worship (3:1-13)
   D. Opposition (4:1-24)
   E. Rebuilding the temple (5:1–6:22)

II. **Reform through Ezra (7:1–10:44)**
   A. Ezra's arrival (7:1-10)
   B. Artaxerxes' letter (7:11-28)
   C. Returnees with Ezra (8:1-14)
   D. Search for Levites (8:15-20)
   E. Preparing to return (8:21-30)
   F. Arrival in Jerusalem (8:31-36)
   G. Sin and confession (9:1–10:44)

The Decree of Cyrus

1 In[a] the first year of Cyrus king of Persia,[A] the word of the Lord spoken through Jeremiah was fulfilled.[b] The Lord put it into the mind[c] of King Cyrus to issue a proclamation throughout his entire kingdom and to put it in writing:

2 This is what King Cyrus of Persia says: "The Lord, the God of heaven, has given me all the kingdoms of the earth and has appointed me to build Him a house at Jerusalem in Judah.[d] 3 Whoever is among His people, may his God be with him, and may he go to Jerusalem in Judah and build the house of the Lord, the God of Israel,[e] the God who is in Jerusalem. 4 Let every survivor,[f] wherever he lives, be assisted by the men of that region with silver, gold, goods, and livestock, along with a freewill offering for the house of God in Jerusalem."

Return from Exile

5 So the family leaders of Judah and Benjamin, along with the priests and Levites—everyone God had motivated[B,g]—prepared to go up and rebuild the Lord's house in Jerusalem. 6 All their neighbors supported them[C,h] with silver articles, gold, goods, livestock, and valuables, in addition to all that was given as a freewill offering. 7 King Cyrus also brought out the articles of the Lord's house that Nebuchadnezzar had taken from Jerusalem and had placed in the house of his gods.[i] 8 King Cyrus of Persia had them brought out under the supervision of Mithredath the treasurer, who counted them out to Sheshbazzar the prince of Judah.[j] 9 This was the inventory:

30 gold basins, 1,000 silver basins,
29 silver knives, 10 30 gold bowls,
410 various[D] silver bowls,
and 1,000 other articles.

11 The gold and silver articles totaled 5,400. Sheshbazzar brought all of them when the exiles went up from Babylon to Jerusalem.

The Exiles Who Returned

2 These[k] now are the people of the province who came from those captive exiles King Nebuchadnezzar of Babylon[E] had deported to

Cross references

a 1:1 2Ch 36:22-23
b Jr 25:12; 29:10-14
c Ezr 7:27
d 1:2-3 Is 44:28; 45:1,13; Dn 9:17
e 1:3 Dn 6:26
f 1:4 Neh 1:2; Is 10:20-22
g 1:5 Ezr 1:1
h 1:6 Ezr 6:22
i 1:7 2Ch 36:7,10,18; Dn 1:2; 5:2-3
j 1:8 Ezr 5:14,16
k 2:1-70 Neh 7:6-73

A 1:1 Cyrus reigned 559–530 b.c.   B 1:5 Lit everyone whose spirit God had stirred   C 1:6 Lit supported their hands   D 1:10 Or similar
E 2:1 Nebuchadnezzar reigned 605–562 b.c.

1:1 The **first year of Cyrus** refers to the first year of his rule over Babylonia (538 b.c.) and not the first year of his reign in Persia that began in 559 b.c. and continued until 530 b.c. **Spoken through Jeremiah** may allude to Jeremiah's prophecy of the 70 years of captivity (Jr 29:10-14). More likely it is a reference to Jr 51:11, "The Lord has put it into the mind of the kings of the Medes." The same vocabulary occurs here in Ezr 1:1 where the **Lord put it into the mind** (lit "stirred up the spirit"; cp. Jr 51:1) **of King Cyrus**.

1:2-3 The "proclamation" (v. 1), often referred to as the "Edict of Cyrus," reflects Cyrus's policy to allow the exiles to return to their homeland. The edict, from the closing words of 2 Chronicles (2Ch 36:23), appears in two versions in the book of Ezra: here in Hebrew, reflecting a strong Jewish perspective, and in 6:3-5 written in Aramaic (the language of diplomacy in the Persian Empire), which appears to be an official court memorandum. Some scholars question whether a Persian king would refer to God as **The Lord, the God of heaven**. Possibly this reflects a paraphrase provided by the Jewish leaders in Babylon. One of Cyrus's tasks was to build **a house at Jerusalem in Judah**. House (Hb beth) often refers to the temple, the house of the Lord. The Babylonians had destroyed Solomon's temple in 586 b.c.

1:4 It is not clear if the **men of that region** refer to Jewish men or the entire population. If it refers to all the people, there may be a parallel here to the "spoiling of the Egyptians" (Ex 3; 11; 12). As the birth of the nation began with the spoils of the Gentiles, so the new beginning of God's people began with the **silver** and **gold** of their former oppressors.

1:5 The kingdom of Judah, conquered by the Babylonians in 586 b.c., consisted primarily of the region of **Judah and Benjamin**. Thus the exiles who returned represented three tribal groups: Judah, Benjamin, and Levi (**the priests and Levites**).

1:7 The **articles ... that Nebuchadnezzar had taken** when the Babylonians sacked the temple were not only extremely valuable but were of priceless spiritual worth to the returning exiles. Though plundered from Solomon's temple, they would again be used in worship in the second temple and would be an additional link to the worshiping community that existed before the great catastrophe of 586 b.c.

1:8 Both the name and title of **Mithredath** are Persian. This is the first mention of the enigmatic **Sheshbazzar** (vv. 8,11; 5:14,16). His name is Babylonian ("May Shamash [the sun god] protect the father"). His title, "prince of Judah," occurs nowhere else in the OT.

1:9-10 The variation in English translations of this passage reflects the difficulty in determining the exact identity of the items mentioned. Particularly uncertain is the reference to **29 silver knives** (Hb machalaphim). This rare term may instead refer to duplicate bowls (LXX) or possibly another type of bowl.

1:11 The figure of **5,400** is over twice the total of the figures given in verses 9-10. Possibly the items mentioned in the inventory (vv. 9-10) were only a portion of the material returned to Sheshbazzar. A textual corruption, more commonly occurring in lists of numbers, may also account for the disparity. The term **exiles** (Hb golah) can refer to either the exile to Babylon or the people of the exile. All but one of the 12 occurrences of the term in Ezra (6:21) refer to people of the exile.

2:1 The list of returnees probably reflects not the return from Babylon led by Sheshbazzar, but multiple waves of exiles over several decades. While it is possible that **the**

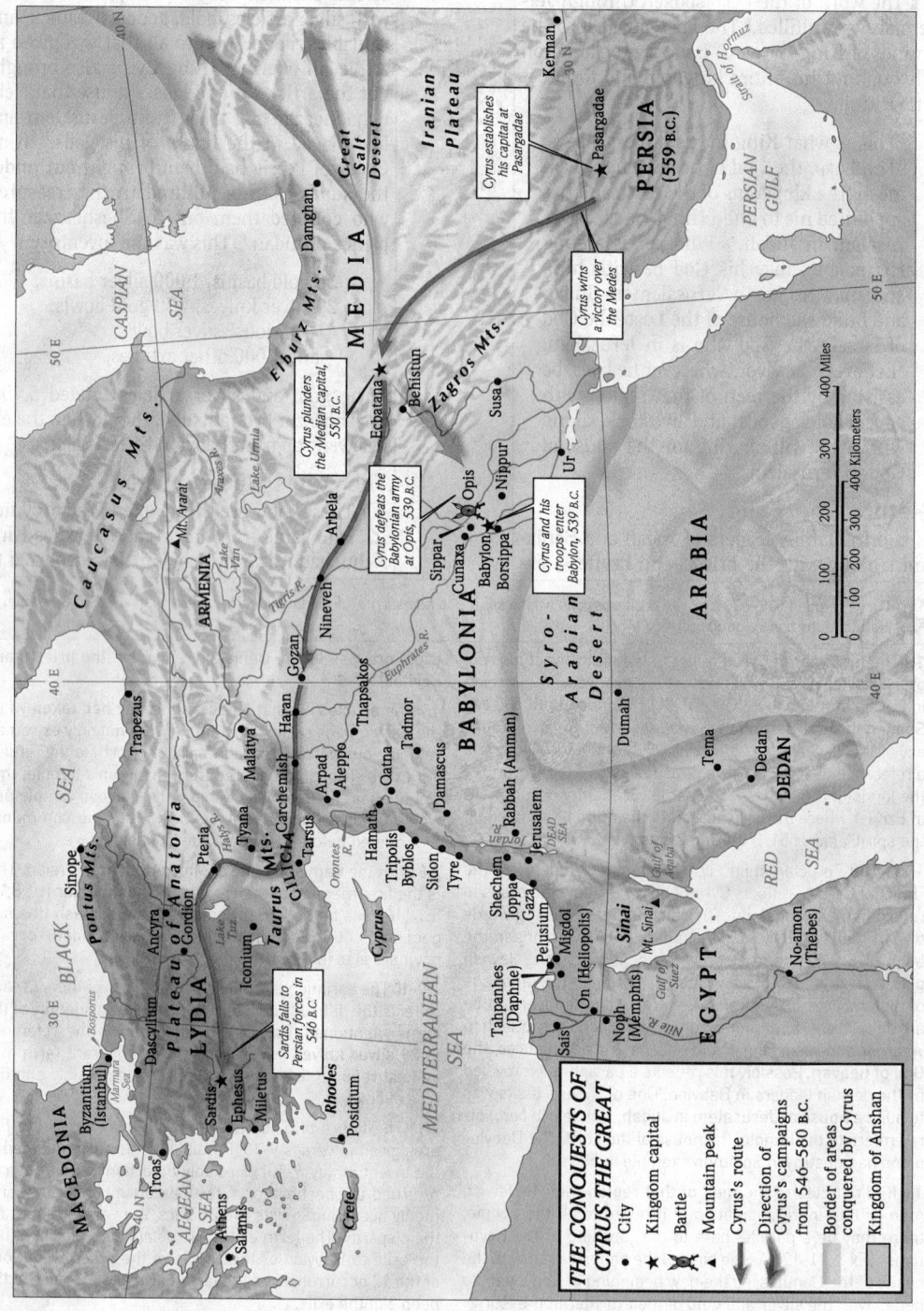

THE CONQUESTS OF
CYRUS THE GREAT

• City
★ Kingdom capital
⚔ Battle
▲ Mountain peak
↑ Cyrus's route
⬇ Direction of
  Cyrus's campaigns
  from 546–580 B.C.
  Border of areas
  conquered by Cyrus
  Kingdom of Anshan

Cyrus establishes
his capital at
Pasargadae

Cyrus wins
a victory over
the Medes

Cyrus plunders
the Median capital,
550 B.C.

Cyrus defeats the
Babylonian army
at Opis, 539 B.C.

Cyrus and his
troops enter
Babylon, 539 B.C.

Sardis falls to
Persian forces in
546 B.C.

PERSIA
(559 B.C.)

MEDIA

Iranian
Plateau

Kerman

Pasargadae

Great
Salt
Desert

Elburz Mts.

Damghan

CASPIAN
SEA

Zagros Mts.

Behistun

Ecbatana

Susa

Nippur

Ur

PERSIAN
GULF

Strait of Hormuz

Caucasus Mts.

Mt. Ararat

Araxes R.

Lake Urmia

Lake
Van

ARMENIA

Arbela

Nineveh

Gozan

Tigris R.

Euphrates R.

Sippar
Cunaxa
Opis
Babylon
Borsippa

BABYLONIA

Syro-
Arabian
Desert

ARABIA

Dumah

Tema

Dedan

DEDAN

Trapezus

Sinope

BLACK
SEA

Pontus Mts.

Ancyra
Gordion

Plateau of Anatolia

Lake
Tuz

Iconium

Pteria

Halys R.

Tyana

Malatya

Haran

Carchemish

Tarsus

Arpad
Aleppo

Thapsacus

Qatna

Tadmor

Hamath

Tripolis

Byblos

Sidon
Tyre

Damascus

Orontes R.

Shechem

Joppa

Gaza

Rabbah (Amman)

Jerusalem

Jordan R.

DEAD
SEA

Taurus Mts.

CILICIA

Cyprus

MEDITERRANEAN
SEA

Pelusium
Migdol
Tapanhes
(Daphne)

On (Heliopolis)

Noph
(Memphis)

Sais

EGYPT

Nile R.

Mt. Sinai

Sinai

Gulf of
Suez

Gulf of
Aqaba

RED
SEA

MACEDONIA

Byzantium
(Istanbul)

Bosporus

Dascylium

Marmara
Sea

Troas

Athens

Salamis

AEGEAN
SEA

Ephesus

Sardis

Miletus

Posidium

Rhodes

Crete

LYDIA

400 Miles

400 Kilometers

300

200

100

0

300

200

100

0

30 E

40 E

50 E

40 N

30 N

40 N

40 E

50 E

Babylon.[a] They returned to Jerusalem and Judah, each to his own town. [2]They came with Zerubbabel,[b] Jeshua,[c] Nehemiah, Seraiah,[d] Reelaiah, Mordecai, Bilshan, Mispar, Bigvai, Rehum, and Baanah.

The number of the Israelite men included:[A]

[3]	Parosh's descendants[e]	2,172
[4]	Shephatiah's descendants	372
[5]	Arah's descendants	775
[6]	Pahath-moab's descendants: Jeshua's and Joab's descendants	2,812
[7]	Elam's descendants	1,254
[8]	Zattu's descendants	945
[9]	Zaccai's descendants	760
[10]	Bani's descendants	642
[11]	Bebai's descendants	623
[12]	Azgad's descendants	1,222
[13]	Adonikam's descendants[f]	666
[14]	Bigvai's descendants	2,056
[15]	Adin's descendants	454
[16]	Ater's descendants: of Hezekiah	98
[17]	Bezai's descendants	323
[18]	Jorah's descendants	112
[19]	Hashum's descendants	223
[20]	Gibbar's descendants	95
[21]	Bethlehem's[g] people	123
[22]	Netophah's men	56
[23]	Anathoth's men	128
[24]	Azmaveth's people	42
[25]	Kiriatharim's, Chephirah's, and Beeroth's people	743
[26]	Ramah's[h] and Geba's people	621
[27]	Michmas's men	122
[28]	Bethel's and Ai's[i] men	223
[29]	Nebo's people	52
[30]	Magbish's people	156
[31]	the other Elam's people	1,254
[32]	Harim's people	320
[33]	Lod's, Hadid's, and Ono's people	725
[34]	Jericho's[j] people	345
[35]	Senaah's people	3,630

[36]The priests included:

	Jedaiah's descendants of the house of Jeshua	973
[37]	Immer's descendants	1,052
[38]	Pashhur's descendants	1,247
[39]	and Harim's descendants	1,017

[40]The Levites included:

| | Jeshua's and Kadmiel's descendants from Hodaviah's descendants | 74 |

[a] 2:1 2Ch 36:17-20
[b] 2:2 1Ch 3:19; Ezr 3:2; Hg 1:1; Zch 4:6
[c] Hg 1:1; Zch 3:1-10
[d] Neh 12:1
[e] 2:3 Ezr 8:3; 10:25; Neh 3:25
[f] 2:13 Ezr 8:13
[g] 2:21 Mc 5:2; Mt 2:1,6
[h] 2:26 Jr 31:15; Mt 2:18
[i] 2:28 Gn 12:8; Jos 7:2; 8:9
[j] 2:34 Jos 4:19; 5:13; 6:1-25

[A]2:2 Lit *the men of the people of Israel*

people of the province refers to the region in Babylon where the exiles had lived, it more likely refers to the province of Judah to which they returned. The province, called Yehud by the Persians, was probably much smaller than the hereditary territory of Judah (see note at 10:7-8). Nebuchadnezzar's series of deportations (597–582 B.C.) were now being reversed by God's power. Each returnee came back to **his own town**, emphasizing the continuity between the preexilic nation and the postexilic nation.

2:2 The names of the Jewish leaders who returned reflect the history of their nation. One name is Persian (**Bigvai**) while three others are Babylonian (**Zerubbabel . . . Mordecai**, and **Bilshan**). Zerubbabel probably served as the second governor of *Yehud* (Judah) after Sheshbazzar. As a grandson of king Jehoiachin, he was a crucial link with the Davidic dynasty. In the biblical books from the postexilic era, Zerubbabel is nearly always mentioned along with **Jeshua**, a grandson of Jozadak, Israel's last high priest before the destruction of the temple in 586 B.C. Thus Zerubbabel and Jeshua together link the reborn community in Yehud with the royal and priestly lines of preexilic Israel.

Nehemiah in this verse does not refer to the central figure in the book of Nehemiah, who arrived in Jerusalem almost 80 years later. Another person named Nehemiah is also mentioned in Neh 3:16, referring to a ruler over the region of Beth-Zur. Neither does the name Mordecai refer to the Mordecai in the book of Esther, who appeared a half-century after the Mordecai in Ezra 2.

2:3-60 These lists appear to be based on the nearly identical version in Neh 7:8-60. The divergences between the two are mostly inconsequential, consisting of alternative spellings of proper names and minor textual corruptions of the numbers. Because numbers were written in this era with small lines or marks, they were particularly prone to errors in copying. The

primary purpose of these lists was to ensure that those who returned to Judah were authentic Israelites. In both Ezra and Nehemiah, the purity of the people is emphasized.

2:3-35 The first list consists of Israelite laymen. In verses 3-20 they are listed by the names of their family patriarchs, and in verses 21-35 according to locality of origin. In verses 3-21 the returnees are referred to as the **descendants** of these family leaders (lit "sons"; Hb *beney*). In verses 22-35 they are more commonly called the **men** (Hb *anshey*) of the family leader. The variation is probably only stylistic.

2:20 The parallel list of **Gibbar's descendants** (Neh 7:25) reads "Gibeon," the town northwest of Jerusalem. It is difficult to decide which is original since the names that precede the verse are personal names while those that follow are place names.

2:21-35 All these places are in the immediate area surrounding Jerusalem. It reflects the greatly reduced size of Judah in the years before 586 B.C. Many of the towns were from the tribal area of Benjamin, north of Jerusalem. The only towns mentioned south of Jerusalem are Bethlehem and Netophah.

2:36-39 **Priests** make up about 10 percent of the returnees. Other priests returned later, because 8:2 mentions priestly families of Phinehas (Ex 6:23; Nm 25:1-11) and Ithamar, Aaron's fourth son (Ex 6:23).

2:40 Compared to the priests, the return of only 74 **Levites** seems very low. Possibly the nature of their work and their lowly status either kept them from being captured and deported in the first place, or it did not motivate many of them to return home. Many years later when Ezra was preparing to return (8:15), his recruitment efforts resulted in only 38 Levite volunteers.

[41]The singers included:

•Asaph's[a] descendants   128

[42]The gatekeepers'[b] descendants included:

Shallum's descendants,
Ater's descendants,
Talmon's descendants,
Akkub's descendants,
Hatita's descendants,
Shobai's descendants, in all   139

[43]The temple servants[c] included:

Ziha's descendants,
Hasupha's descendants,
Tabbaoth's descendants,
[44]Keros's descendants,
Siaha's descendants,
Padon's descendants,
[45]Lebanah's descendants,
Hagabah's descendants,
Akkub's descendants,
[46]Hagab's descendants,
Shalmai's[A] descendants,
Hanan's descendants,
[47]Giddel's descendants,
Gahar's descendants,
Reaiah's descendants,
[48]Rezin's descendants,
Nekoda's descendants,
Gazzam's descendants,
[49]Uzza's descendants,
Paseah's descendants,
Besai's descendants,
[50]Asnah's descendants,
Meunim's[B] descendants,
Nephusim's[C] descendants,
[51]Bakbuk's descendants,
Hakupha's descendants,
Harhur's descendants,

[a]2:41 1Ch 25:1; 2Ch 5:12; 35:15
[b]2:42 1Ch 9:17-32; Neh 12:25-26
[c]2:43 Ezr 8:20
[d]2:55 Neh 11:3

[52]Bazluth's descendants,
Mehida's descendants,
Harsha's descendants,
[53]Barkos's descendants,
Sisera's descendants,
Temah's descendants,
[54]Neziah's descendants,
and Hatipha's descendants.

[55]The descendants of Solomon's servants[d] included:

Sotai's descendants,
Hassophereth's descendants,
Peruda's descendants,
[56]Jaalah's descendants,
Darkon's descendants,
Giddel's descendants,
[57]Shephatiah's descendants,
Hattil's descendants,
Pochereth-hazzebaim's descendants,
and Ami's descendants.
[58]All the temple servants
and the descendants
of Solomon's servants   392.

[59]The following are those who came from Tel-melah, Tel-harsha, Cherub, Addan, and Immer but were unable to prove that their families and ancestry were Israelite:

[60]Delaiah's descendants,
Tobiah's descendants,
Nekoda's descendants   652

[61]and from the descendants of the priests: the descendants of Hobaiah, the descendants of Hakkoz, the descendants of Barzillai—who had taken a wife from the daughters of Barzillai the Gileadite and was called by their name. [62]These searched for their entries in the genealogical records, but they could not be found,

---

A2:46 Alt Hb tradition reads *Shamlai's*   B2:50 Alt Hb tradition reads *Meinim's*   C2:50 Alt Hb tradition reads *Nephisim's*

2:41 The presence of **singers** was important in establishing the continuity of worship as it existed before the exile. The term translated "singers" (Hb *meshorrim*) may be too narrow, as 1Ch 15:16-20 suggests that it included instrumentalists and worship leaders. Perhaps "musicians" better fits the context. Asaph was from the tribe of Levi.

2:42 Like the singers, the gatekeeper's position was established by King David (1Ch 9:18-27) and was regarded as part of the tribe of Levi (1Ch 6), although these gatekeepers are mentioned separately.

2:43-58 The **temple servants** were the fifth group of temple personnel (priests, Levites, singers, gatekeepers), and they had the lowest status. The Hebrew term for "temple servants" is *nethinim*, from the Hebrew verb *ntn*, "to give." They are the "given" ones, or "devoted" ones, designated to serve in the temple and its worship. **Solomon's servants** were part of this same group. A majority of the names are either foreign or are nicknames, reflecting their lowly status.

2:59-64 The final groups are of questionable status: three clans of laymen who could not verify their genealogy (vv. 59-60) and three clans of priestly families who could not prove their priestly lineage (vv. 61-64). The laymen, identified according their former residences in Babylon, presumably were allowed to remain in the Jewish community. The situation of the priests was more difficult. Because the purity of the priesthood and the temple was at stake, priests who could not prove their lineage were disqualified from their posts. This was not only a loss of status but of livelihood as well since priests were not allotted land and were dependent on the gifts given to the temple.

No mention of the use of the mysterious **Urim and Thummim** is found in the postexilic era. The term **governor** is an uncommon word for this position, appearing only five times in the OT, all in Ezra-Nehemiah. The word is *tirshat'a*, probably derived from the Old Persian language meaning "excellency." The term is later used to describe "Nehemiah the governor" (Neh 8:9; 10:1). Here it prob-

so they were disqualified from the priesthood. [63]The governor[a] ordered them not to eat the most holy things until there was a priest who could consult the •Urim and Thummim.[b]

[64]   The whole combined assembly
       numbered   42,360
[65]   not including their 7,337 male
       and female slaves,
       and their 200 male and female singers.[c]
[66]   They had 736 horses, 245 mules,
[67]   435 camels, and 6,720 donkeys.

Gifts for the Work

[68]After they arrived at the LORD's house in Jerusalem, some of the family leaders gave freewill offerings[d] for the house of God in order to have it rebuilt on its original site. [69]Based on what they could give, they gave 61,000 gold coins,[A] 6,250 pounds[B] of silver, and 100 priestly garments to the treasury[e] for the project. [70]The priests, Levites, singers, gatekeepers, temple servants, and some of the

people settled in their towns, and the rest of Israel settled in their towns.[f]

Sacrifice Restored

3 By the seventh month,[g] the Israelites had settled in their towns, and the people gathered together in Jerusalem.[h] [2]Jeshua son of Jozadak and his brothers the priests along with Zerubbabel son of Shealtiel[i] and his brothers began to build the altar of Israel's God in order to offer •burnt offerings on it, as it is written in the law of Moses, the man of God.[j] [3]They set up the altar on its foundation and offered burnt offerings for the morning and evening on it to the LORD even though they feared the surrounding peoples.[k] [4]They celebrated the Festival of Booths as prescribed, and offered burnt offerings each day, based on the number specified by ordinance for each festival day.[l] [5]After that, they offered the regular burnt offering and the offerings for the beginning of each month[C,m] and for all

Cross references (center column):
[a]2:63 Ezr 6:7; Neh 5:14; Hg 1:1
[b]Ex 28:30; Lv 8:8; Nm 27:21; Neh 7:65
[c]2:65 2Ch 35:25
[d]2:68 Nm 15:3; Ezr 1:4
[e]2:69 Ezr 8:33-34
[f]2:70 1Ch 9:2; Neh 11:3
[g]3:1 Lv 23:23-43; Nm 29:1-38
[h]Neh 7:73-8:1
[i]3:2 Ezr 3:8; 5:2; Hg 1:1; 2:21,23
[j]Ex 27:1-8
[k]3:3 Ezr 4:4
[l]3:4 Lv 23:33-43; Nm 29:12-38; Neh 8:13-18; Zch 14:16
[m]3:5 Nm 28:11-14; 1Sm 20:5

[A]2:69 Or *drachmas,* or *darics*   [B]2:69 Lit *5,000 minas*   [C]3:5 Lit *for the new moons*

---

ably refers to Zerubbabel, although some scholars prefer Sheshbazzar.

2:64-65 The **assembly** (Hb *qahal*) described the entire worshiping community, including both men and women. The sum of the returnees in the above list is only 29,818; probably the discrepancy reflects the number of women who also returned. While some commentators regard the presence of only 12,542 women as unlikely, it may suggest that most of those who returned were unattached, single men. The 42,360 returnees did not include the **slaves** who were regarded as property. The **singers** listed here are not those who participated in the temple worship but entertainers employed by wealthy families.

2:66-67 Since **horses** were more expensive than **donkeys**, it is not surprising that far more donkeys (6,720) than horses (736) were involved in the return to the land.

2:68-70 Just as Israelites gave gold and silver toward the construction of the tabernacle in Moses' time (Ex 35:21-29), so once again some of the people gave **freewill offerings** for the reconstruction of the temple. These **coins** (Hb *darkemonim*) probably refer to the Greek drachma. Verse 70 is awkward, as reflected in the Septuagint and in 1 Esdras, but its essential point is clear: both temple personnel and laymen had now returned to their cities and **towns** from which they or their forefathers had been exiled.

3:1-13 Neither Haggai nor Zechariah, who prophesied about the temple during this time, ever mentioned an early attempt to lay the foundation of the temple in the time of Cyrus as described in this chapter. They only recounted the laying of the foundation and the building of the temple during the time of Darius, with the completion of the temple in 515 B.C. The chronological indicators in the passage (vv. 6,8; 4:5,24; 5:1-2) attest to a short-lived attempt to rebuild in the time of Cyrus (3:1–4:3) followed by a second, ultimately successful attempt during the time of Darius (chaps. 5–6).

3:1-2 The seventh month was September–October 537 B.C. Taking the lead in reviving the proper sacrificial system was

Jeshua son of Jozadak (see note at 2:2). In Haggai he is always referred to as "Joshua," an alternative spelling, and nearly always called the "high priest," though never in Ezra-Nehemiah. Just as Joshua built an altar to the Lord when the people entered the promised land "according to what is written in the book of the law of Moses" (Jos 8:30-31), so those returning to the promised land built theirs the same way, with uncut stones that no iron tool had touched (Dt 27:5-6).

3:3 The morning and evening **burnt offerings**, called the (Hb) *Tamid,* were the basic daily sacrifices in which the entire lamb was burned up. The "burnt offerings" were part of the consecration of the new altar. Twice before in Israel's history the daily burnt offerings had ceased under godless kings and were reinstated, first by Joash (2Ch 24:14) and later by Hezekiah (2Ch 29:7,27-29). The term **surrounding peoples** (lit "the people of the lands") often has a pejorative sense. Here it probably refers to those with no desire to see a reconstituted Jewish population in the land.

3:4 The seventh month was also the time for the celebration of the **Festival of Booths** (also referred to as "Tabernacles," or by its Hebrew name *Succoth*), a harvest festival in which Israel remembered their sojourn in the wilderness and God's provision. The sacrifices during the seven-day festival were offered in accordance with the law of Moses as written in Nm 29:12-38, and would include 71 bulls, 15 rams, 105 lambs as well as seven goats—a major financial sacrifice for the small postexilic community.

3:5 The mention of **regular burnt offering** (Hb *'olat tamid*) is to show how the normal daily sacrificial schedule of offerings, as compared to the burnt offering at the dedication of the altar (v. 3), was reestablished. **Offerings for the beginning of each month** translates a single Hebrew word (*chodashim*) meaning "new moons." New moon celebrations were prescribed in the Mosaic law (Nm 28:11-15). They included the blowing of trumpets (Nm 10:10) along with the sacrifice of two bulls, a ram, and seven one-year-old male lambs, plus a male goat as a sin offering.

the LORD's appointed holy occasions, as well as the freewill offerings brought to[A] the LORD.

[6]On the first day of the seventh month they began to offer burnt offerings to the LORD,[a] even though the foundation of the LORD's temple had not yet been laid. [7]They gave money to the stonecutters and artisans, and gave food, drink, and oil to the people of Sidon and Tyre, so they could bring cedar wood from Lebanon to Joppa by sea,[b] according to the authorization given them by King Cyrus of Persia.[c]

Rebuilding the Temple

[8]In the second month of the second year after they arrived at God's house in Jerusalem, Zerubbabel son of Shealtiel, Jeshua son of Jozadak,[d] and the rest of their brothers, including the priests, the Levites, and all who had returned to Jerusalem from the captivity, began to build. They appointed the Levites who were 20 years old or more to supervise the work on the LORD's house.[e] [9]Jeshua with his sons and brothers, Kadmiel with his sons, and the sons of Judah[B] and of Henadad, with their sons and brothers, the Levites,[f] joined together to supervise those working on the house of God.

Temple Foundation Completed

[10]When the builders had laid the founda-

tion of the LORD's temple, the priests, dressed in their robes and holding trumpets, and the Levites descended from *Asaph,[g] holding cymbals, took their positions to praise the LORD, as King David of Israel had instructed.[h] [11]They sang with praise and thanksgiving to the LORD: "For He is good; His faithful love to Israel endures forever."[i] Then all the people gave a great shout of praise to the LORD because the foundation of the LORD's house had been laid.[j]

[12]But many of the older priests, Levites, and family leaders, who had seen the first temple, wept loudly when they saw the foundation of this house,[k] but many others shouted joyfully. [13]The people could not distinguish the sound of the joyful shouting from that of the[C] weeping,[l] because the people were shouting so loudly. And the sound was heard far away.

Opposition to Rebuilding the Temple

4 When the enemies of Judah and Benjamin[m] heard that the returned exiles[D,n] were building a temple for *Yahweh, the God of Israel, [2]they approached Zerubbabel and the leaders of the families and said to them, "Let us build with you, for we also worship your God and have been sacrificing to Him[E]

Cross-references column:
[a] 3:6 Lv 23:23-25; Nm 29:1-6
[b] 3:7 1Kg 5:1-11; 2Ch 2:3-16
[c] Ezr 1:2; 6:3-5
[d] 3:8 Ezr 4:3; 5:2; Hg 1:1
[e] 1Ch 23:4,24
[f] 3:9 Ezr 2:40
[g] 3:10 Ezr 2:41
[h] 1Ch 6:31; 25:1,6; 2Ch 29:25-26; Neh 12:24,45
[i] 3:11 1Ch 16:34; 2Ch 5:13; 7:3; Neh 12:31
[j] Hg 2:18; Zch 4:9
[k] 3:12 Hg 2:3
[l] 3:13 Ps 126:5-6
[m] 4:1 Neh 2:19-20
[n] Ezr 1:11; 2:1

[A]3:5 Lit well as those of everyone making a freewill offering to   [B]3:9 Or Hodaviah; Neh 7:43; 1 Esdras 5:58   [C]3:13 Lit the people
[D]4:1 Lit the sons of the exile   [E]4:2 Alt Hb tradition reads have not been sacrificing

---

3:6 The **first day of the seventh month** would most likely have been September 17, 538 B.C.

3:7 As soon as the sacrificial system was in place, the next order of business was the acquisition of building material. Payment was made to the **people of Sidon and Tyre** who cut down the famous cedars of Lebanon and floated the logs down the coast to Joppa, just south of present day Tel-Aviv, for transit overland to Jerusalem. While **stonecutters** were also hired, they were not as numerous as Solomon's 80,000 who worked on the first temple (2Ch 2:18) since some of the stones from the rubble of the first temple could be reused.

3:8 During the seven months preceding the **second month of the second year**, enough of the temple site had been cleared that work on the foundation could begin. **Zerubbabel** and **Jeshua** the priest led laymen as well as priests and Levites in the joint effort. In 5:16 Sheshbazzar is mentioned as laying the foundation of the temple. As the official governor, maybe he was credited with this event even though Zerubbabel carried on most of the work and would later succeed Sheshbazzar as governor.

3:10 The continuity of the people with their preexilic forefathers is again emphasized in the phrase **as King David of Israel had instructed**. When David brought the ark of the covenant into Jerusalem (1Ch 16:4-6), the Levites were to "give thanks and praise" while the priests blew the trumpets and Asaph "sounded the cymbals." Here the descendants of Asaph used the cymbals and the current priests blew their trumpets.

3:11 The Levites' antiphonal refrain, **For He is good; His**

faithful love to Israel endures forever, is found in slightly varying forms in the Psalms (Ps 100:4-5; 106:1; 107:1, 118:1; 136:1). The **shout** (Hb teru'ah) was commonly used in battle but also for other significant events, such as the shout of the people when the ark of the covenant was brought into Jerusalem by King David (1Ch 15:28).

3:12-13 The episode described here is not the same event as that described in Hg 2:1-5 which occurred almost 20 years later when the building of the temple finally resumed. Here the author prepares the way for chapter 4 with the opposition of enemies. Not only did the Lord's people hear the sound but so did their adversaries, who tried to thwart their plans.

4:1-2 The author's description of those who offered to help with the construction as **enemies** shows that their offer was not what it seemed. Their identity is clarified in that they had been **brought...here** by King Esar-haddon of Assyria. Second Kings 17 describes the policy of the Assyrian kings who deported many of the people in the northern kingdom of Israel and replaced them with people from Babylon and beyond. These events (2Kg 17) occurred half a century before Esar-haddon, and no report is given of deportations or resettlements during his reign (681-669 B.C.). But as the present verse indicates, he carried on the practice of resettlement.

The claim of these enemies that they also worshiped **your God** was probably true. The problem was that they worshiped the God of Israel along with the false gods of their homeland (2Kg 17:3-22). If **Zerubbabel** allowed these people to help in the construction, it would be impossible

since the time King Esar-haddon of Assyria[A] brought us here."[a]

[3] But Zerubbabel, Jeshua, and the other leaders of Israel's families answered them, "You may have no part with us in building a house for our God,[b] since we alone must build it for Yahweh, the God of Israel, as King Cyrus, the king of Persia has commanded us."[c] [4] Then the people who were already in the land[B] discouraged[C] the people of Judah and made them afraid[d] to build. [5] They also bribed officials to act against them to frustrate their plans[e] throughout the reign of King Cyrus of Persia and until the reign of King Darius of Persia.[D,f]

Opposition to Rebuilding the City

[6] At the beginning of the reign of Ahasuerus,[E,g] the people who were already in the land[B,h] wrote an accusation against the residents of Judah and Jerusalem. [7] During the time of King Artaxerxes of Persia,[F,i] Bishlam, Mithredath, Tabeel and the rest of his colleagues wrote to King Artaxerxes. The letter was written in Aramaic[j] and translated.[G,H]

[8] Rehum the chief deputy and Shimshai the

Cross references:
[a] 4:2 2Ki 17:24,27-32; 19:37; Is 37:38
[b] 4:3 Neh 2:20
[c] Ezr 1:1-4
[d] 4:4 Ezr 3:3
[e] 4:5 Neh 6:12-13; 13:2
[f] Ezr 5:5; 6:1
[g] 4:6 Est 1:1; Dn 9:1
[h] Ezr 3:3
[i] 4:7 Ezr 7:1; Neh 2:1
[j] Dn 1:4; 2:4

[A] 4:2 Esar-haddon reigned 681–669 B.C.   [B] 4:4,6 Lit *people of the land*   [C] 4:4 Lit *relaxed the hands of*   [D] 4:5 Darius reigned 521–486 B.C.   [E] 4:6 = Xerxes; he reigned 486–465 B.C.   [F] 4:7 Artaxerxes reigned 465–425 B.C.   [G] 4:7 Lit *translated. Aramaic:*   [H] 4:7 Ezr 4:8–6:18 is written in Aram.

---

to prevent them from worshiping there as well. Zerubbabel and the other returnees knew well the terrible price their nation had paid for their syncretistic practices and could never allow such a practice again.

4:3 In refusing their help, **Zerubbabel** did not cite their religious syncretism as the issue but focused on the legal decree of Cyrus that they were to build the temple (1:2-3). **You may have no part with us** is a variation on a Hebrew idiom that means "we have no common interests."

4:4-5 These verses highlight one aspect of the opposition from the **people who were already in the land** (lit "the peoples of the land," see note at 3:3): **they . . . bribed officials to act against them** (lit "they hired counselors against them"). In the vast Persian Empire, bribery of government officials was commonplace.

4:6-23 This unusual passage has confused and challenged interpreters. It is bracketed by statements (vv. 4-5,24) describing the cessation of building until the time of Darius. Chapter 5 continues with the renewed work in building the temple during the time of Darius. Yet in 4:6-23 the events described take place during the reigns of Ahasuerus (Xerxes) and Artaxerxes, successive kings in Darius's dynasty. Some critical scholars have charged that the author of Ezra-Nehemiah was chronologically confused. Such an assertion is unwarranted and unnecessary when one realizes that the author is not writing a chronological but a thematic account. Authors in the ancient world commonly ordered their material thematically rather than chronologically.

4:6 While earlier scholars identified **Ahasuerus** with various individuals, nearly all today identify him as Xerxes, the son of Darius. Ahasuerus (Xerxes) is mentioned nowhere else in the OT except for the book of Esther where he plays a central role.

4:7 Another letter was written to thwart the plans of the returned exiles, this time to **Artaxerxes** who took the throne following the death of his father Xerxes. His reign lasted over 40 years (465–425 B.C.). The ministry of Ezra and Nehemiah occurred during his reign, as well as the last writing prophet, Malachi. The Persian name **Mithredath** suggests he may have been a Persian official. The Hebrew name **Tabeel** ("God is good") finds its equivalent in the Aramaic name Tobiah, but it is unlikely the Tabeel mentioned in this verse is Tobiah, the Ammonite official who opposed Nehemiah (Neh 2:10,19).

4:8–6:18 With this verse begins the first of two sections written not in Hebrew but in Aramaic (4:8–6:18; 7:12-26). Aramaic, like Hebrew, is a Semitic language. It originated in Syria in the second millennium B.C. The Aramaic sections in the OT (here and in Dn 2:4–7:28) are written in "Official Aramaic" (or "Royal Aramaic"), a standardized language of government and diplomacy used throughout the Persian Empire. By the time of Jesus, Aramaic was the "mother tongue" of the Jewish people in Palestine. The Gospel of Mark records several quotes in Aramaic by Jesus. The first occurred as Jesus brought Jairus's daughter back to life (Mk 5:41) with the command *Talitha koum* ("Little girl, I say to you, get up"). Jesus later opened the ears of a deaf man (Mk 7:34) with the command *Ephphatha* ("Be opened"). Several Aramaic words and phrases are preserved in Paul's writings, such as "Abba" (Rm 8:15) and "Marana tha" (1Co 16:22).

4:8 The title **chief deputy** is literally "master of orders" (Aram *be'el-te'em*), a high-ranking official. Some scholars translate his title as "chancellor" or "high commissioner."

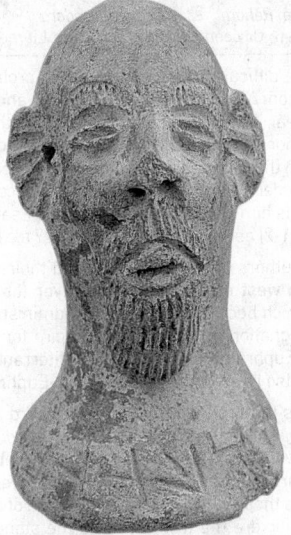

A pottery figure of a foreigner who came to Judea while the Jews were in captivity in Babylon. A Mediterranean background is suggested by the Aramaic writing on the base of the figure.

scribe[a] wrote a letter to King Artaxerxes concerning Jerusalem as follows:

[9] From Rehum[A] the chief deputy, Shimshai the scribe, and the rest of their colleagues—the judges and magistrates[B] from Tripolis, Persia, Erech, Babylon, Susa[b] (that is, the people of Elam),[C] [10] and the rest of the peoples whom the great and illustrious Ashurbanipal[D] deported and settled in the cities of Samaria[c] and the region west of the Euphrates River.[d]

[11] This is the text of the letter they sent to him:

To King Artaxerxes from your servants, the men from the region west of the Euphrates River:

[12] Let it be known to the king that the Jews who came from you have returned to us at Jerusalem. They are rebuilding that rebellious and evil city, finishing its walls, and repairing its foundations. [13] Let it now be known to the king that if that city is rebuilt and its walls are finished,[e] they will not pay tribute, duty, or land tax,[f] and the royal revenue[c] will suffer. [14] Since we have taken an oath of loyalty to the king,[E] and it is not right for us to witness his dishonor, we have sent to inform the king [15] that a search should be made in your fathers' record books.[g] In these

record books you will discover and verify that the city is a rebellious city, harmful to kings and provinces. There have been revolts in it since ancient times. That is why this city was destroyed. [16] We advise the king that if this city is rebuilt and its walls are finished, you will not have any possession west of the Euphrates.

Artaxerxes' Reply

[17] The king sent a reply to his chief deputy Rehum, Shimshai the scribe, and the rest of their colleagues living in Samaria and elsewhere in the region west of the Euphrates River:

Greetings.

[18] The letter you sent us has been translated and read[F,h] in my presence. [19] I issued a decree and a search was conducted. It was discovered that this city has had uprisings against kings since ancient times, and there have been rebellions and revolts in it. [20] Powerful kings have also ruled over Jerusalem and exercised authority over the whole region, and tribute, duty, and land tax were paid to them. [21] Therefore, issue an order for these men to stop, so that this city will not be rebuilt until a further decree has been pronounced by me.[i] [22] See that you not neglect this matter. Otherwise, the damage will increase and the royal interests[G] will suffer.

[a]4:8-9 Ezr 4:17,23-24
[b]4:9 Neh 1:1; Est 1:2; Dn 8:2
[c]4:10 2Kg 17:24
[d]4:10-11 Ezr 4:16-17,20
[e]4:13 Ezr 4:16,21; Neh 1:3
[f]Ezr 4:20; 7:24
[g]4:15 Ezr 5:17; 6:1
[h]4:18 Neh 8:8
[i]4:21 Neh 2:5,7-8

[A]4:9 Lit *Then Rehum*   [B]4:9 Or *ambassadors*   [C]4:9,13 Aram obscure   [D]4:10 Lit *Osnappar*   [E]4:14 Lit *have eaten the salt of the palace*   [F]4:18 Or *been read clearly*   [G]4:22 Lit *the kings*

4:9-10 The difficult Aramaic in verse 9b prohibits certainty in translation. After the mention of **judges and magistrates**, it is not clear if the next two terms refer to other officials or other locations. **Erech, Babylon**, and **Susa** are the homelands from which their forefathers had been deported by **Ashurbanipal** (a rendering borrowed from extra-biblical sources; the OT text calls him *Osnappar*), who followed Esar-haddon (see note at vv. 1-2) as king of Assyria (668-627 B.C.).

4:11 The authors of the letter specified their residences as **the region west of the Euphrates River** (lit "beyond [the] River"), which became the standard administrative and political designation in the Persian Empire for the vast area from the Euphrates River to the Mediterranean Sea. This region is also referred to as the "Trans-Euphrates."

4:12 This is the first occurrence of the word **Jews** in Ezra-Nehemiah. "Jew" (Aram *yehuday*; Hb *yehudi*) was derived from the word "Judah" (Hb *yehudah*). The Hebrew word *yehudi* appears in 2Kg 16:6 where it is translated "Judahites," referring to those who lived in the kingdom of Judah. During the postexilic era the term became the standard designation of the entire religious community of Israel, whether located in the land of Israel or elsewhere.

4:13 Xerxes' battles with the Greeks were a financial drain on the empire. Later, Artaxerxes' suppression of the revolt in Egypt was an additional financial burden. Rehum knew

that Artaxerxes could not afford the loss of **tribute, duty, or land tax**.

4:14-17 We have taken an oath of loyalty to the king translates an obscure Aramaic phrase (lit "We have salted the salt of the king"). On the suspicion that a scribal error has altered the original sentence, some scholars note that a minor change of the Aramaic verb would yield a more understandable rendering: "We have eaten the salt of the king." In the OT law, there are several references to the "salt of the covenant" (Lv 2:13; Nm 18:19), suggesting that salt, a valuable commodity in the ancient world, was used in the ritual of making a covenant. In a letter (Ezr 4:11-16) marked by exaggeration aimed at inciting suppression of the Jews, the concluding warning (v. 16) reached its crescendo: failure to stop the Jews from rebuilding would cause Artaxerxes to lose "Beyond the River"—the region **west of the Euphrates** River.

4:20 Powerful kings is likely a reference to foreign kings, such as Assyrian and Babylonian kings who once controlled the entire Jewish **region** and collected **tribute**. However, the context gives no indication of a change in subject. This most naturally suggests that Israelite kings were these "powerful kings." If this is correct, it is possibly another aspect of exaggerating the threat posed by the Jews and Jerusalem.

²³As soon as the text of King Artaxerxes' letter was read to Rehum, Shimshai the scribe, and their colleagues,ª they immediately went to the Jews in Jerusalem and forcibly stopped them.

Rebuilding of the Temple Resumed

²⁴Now the construction of God's house in Jerusalem had stopped and remained at a standstill until the second year of the reign of King Darius of Persia.ᵇ ¹But when the prophets Haggai and Zechariah son of Iddoᶜ prophesied to the Jews who were in Judah and Jerusalem, in the name of the God of Israel who was over them, ²Zerubbabel son of Shealtiel and Jeshua son of Jozadakᵈ began to rebuild God's house in Jerusalem. The prophets of Godᵉ were with them, helping them. ³At that time Tattenai the governor of the region west of the Euphrates River, Shethar-bozenai, and their colleaguesᶠ came to the Jews and asked, "Who gave you the order to rebuild this temple and finish this structure?"^A,g ⁴They also asked them, "What are the names of the workersᴮ who are constructing this building?" ⁵But God was watchingᶜ overʰ

Marginal references:
ª4:23 Ezr 4:8-10,17
ᵇ4:24 Ezr 4:1-5; Hg 1:1,14
ᶜ5:1 Ezr 6:14; Hg 1:1; Zch 1:1
ᵈ5:2 Ezr 3:2,8,10
ᵉEzr 6:14
ᶠ5:3 Ezr 6:6,13
ᵍEzr 1:1-4; 5:9,13; 6:3
ʰ5:5 Ezr 7:6,9,28; 8:18,22,31
ⁱ5:8 Ezr 6:3-4

the Jewish elders. These men wouldn't stop them until a report was sent to Darius, so that they could receive written instructions about this matter.

The Letter to Darius

⁶This is the text of the letter that Tattenai the governor of the region west of the Euphrates River, Shethar-bozenai, and their colleagues, the officials in the region, sent to King Darius. ⁷They sent him a report, written as follows:

To King Darius:

All greetings.

⁸Let it be known to the king that we went to the house of the great God in the province of Judah. It is being built with cutᴰ stones, and its beams are being set in the walls. This work is being done diligently and succeeding through the people's efforts.ⁱ ⁹So we questioned the elders and asked, "Who gave you the order to rebuild this temple and finish this structure?"^A ¹⁰We also asked them for their names, so

---

^A5:3,9 Or finish its furnishings   ᴮ5:4 One Aram ms, LXX, Syr; MT reads Then we told them exactly what the names of the men were   ᶜ5:5 Lit But the eye of their God was   ᴰ5:8 Or huge

---

4:23 Literally this text reads, "they made them cease by force and might." This must have been a painful and humiliating experience for the Jewish people.

4:24 The verse begins with an Aramaic preposition, be'dayin, that is usually translated "then," which suggests that verse 24 temporally follows verse 23. But as pointed out above, verses 6-23 form a parenthesis in which letters written to the Persian kings illustrate opposition to the Jews. Thus verse 5 and verse 24 serve as parallel bookends that bracket the lengthy parenthesis of verses 6-23.

5:1–6:22 After the thematic presentation of local opposition in chapter 4, the author returns to the situation in Darius's day when construction was resumed and completed (chaps. 5–6). The rebuilt temple and the fully restored sacrificial system not only demonstrated their continuity with the people of God before the exile but also served as a visible sign of God's restoration of what had been lost.

5:1 The impetus for a renewed attempt at construction began when **Haggai** and **Zechariah** brought their prophetic oracles to the Jews. In his first oracle, God asked the Jewish community, "Is it a time for you yourselves to live in your paneled houses, while this house lies in ruins?" (Hg 1:4). That same year Zechariah son of Iddo encouraged the people to respond to God's promise of future glory for Jerusalem. In this present verse Zechariah is said to be the "son of Iddo" while in Zch 1:1 he is the "son of Berechiah, son of Iddo." This is no contradiction. The term "son" (Aram bar) and its Hebrew equivalent (ben) can refer to a descendant such as "grandson." Thus Zch 1:1 and Ezr 5:1 are both correct.

5:2 Haggai and Zechariah also pointed to **Zerubbabel** and **Jeshua** the priest as those who led the people (2:2; 3:2,8; 4:3) in the renewed construction. **Helping them** did not im-

ply manual labor but encouragement and moral support for those doing the work.

5:3-5 **Tattenai** is called **governor** (Aram pechah) of "Beyond the River," the Trans-Euphrates region, even though he probably served as "sub-governor" under Ushtanu, a new governor appointed by Darius in 520 B.C., the year when construction on the temple resumed. Zerubbabel is also called "governor" (Hb pechah; Hg 1:14; 2:2,21), although he answered to Tattenai and was responsible solely for the region of Yehud (Judah).

Tattenai's question **who gave you the order to rebuild this temple** may have been a genuine concern for the legal authorization of the construction. The word **structure** translates an Aramaic term ('usharna) that could refer to wood used in the furnishings or, more probably, to the wood used in the construction of the walls (v. 8) and the roof. While Tattenai wanted to confirm the legality of the construction, he did not forbid it while waiting for **written instructions**.

5:5 The phrase **God was watching** is literally "the eye of their God was on" the elders. The idiom "the eye(s) of the Lord" occurs elsewhere in the OT (Jb 36:7; Ps 33:18; 34:15). In Ezra's Memoir (see "Structure" in the Introduction) a common idiom for God's providential care is "the hand of the Lord was with us" (Ezr 7:6,9; 8:18). This verse contains the first mention of the **Jewish elders** in the postexilic era. In the Persian period, real power was in the hands of the Persian-appointed authorities, while the elders more often were called together to witness important events and judicial decisions.

5:7 **All greetings** means literally "all peace."

5:8 Previously some scholars dismissed as implausible the use of the description **house of the great God** by a Persian official. However, the same term has been found in inscriptions at Persepolis, the great city of Darius and Xerxes.

that we could write down the names of their leaders for your information.

[11] This is the reply they gave us:

We are the servants of the God of heaven and earth and are rebuilding the temple that was built many years ago, which a great king of Israel built and finished.[a] [12] But since our fathers angered the God of heaven, He handed them over to King Nebuchadnezzar of Babylon, the Chaldean, who destroyed this temple and deported the people to Babylon.[b] [13] However, in the first year of Cyrus king of Babylon, he issued a decree to rebuild the house of God.[c] [14] He also took from the temple in Babylon the gold and silver articles of God's house that Nebuchadnezzar had taken from the temple in Jerusalem and carried them to the temple in Babylon.[d] He released them from the temple in Babylon to a man named Sheshbazzar, the governor by the appointment of King Cyrus.[e] [15] Cyrus told him, "Take these articles, put them in the temple in Jerusalem, and let the house of God be rebuilt on its original site."[f] [16] Then this same Sheshbazzar came and laid the foundation of God's house in Jerusalem.[g] It has been under construction from that time until now,[h] yet it has not been completed.

[17] So if it pleases the king, let a search of the royal archives[A] in Babylon be conducted to see if it is true that a decree was issued by King Cyrus to rebuild the house of God in Jerusalem.[i] Let the king's decision regarding this matter be sent to us.[j]

Darius's Search

6 King Darius gave the order, and they searched[k] in the library of Babylon in the archives.[B,l] [2] But it was in the fortress of Ecbatana in the province of Media[m] that a scroll was found with this record written on it:

[3] In the first year of King Cyrus, he issued a decree[n] concerning the house of God in Jerusalem:

Let the house be rebuilt as a place for offering sacrifices, and let its original foundations be retained.[C] Its height is to be 90 feet[D] and its width 90 feet,[D,E,o] [4] with three layers of cut[F] stones and one of timber.[p] The cost is to be paid from the royal treasury.[q] [5] The gold and silver articles of God's house that Nebuchadnezzar took from the temple in Jerusalem and carried to Babylon must also be returned. They are to be brought to the temple in Jerusalem where they belong[G] and put into the house of God.[r]

Cross references
a 5:11 1Kg 6:1,37-38
b 5:12 2Ch 36:19-20
c 5:13 2Ch 36:22-23; Ezr 1:1-4
d 5:14 2Ch 36:7,10,18; Ezr 1:7; Dn 5:2-3
e Ezr 1:8,11
f 5:15 Ezr 6:5
g 5:16 Ezr 3:10
h Ezr 5:1-5
i 5:17 2Ch 36:22-23; Ezr 1:1-4
j Ezr 6:1-12
k 6:1 Ezr 5:17
l Ezr 4:15
m 6:2 Dn 9:1; Ac 2:9
n 6:3 2Ch 36:22-23; Ezr 1:1-4
o 1Kg 6:2
p 6:4 1Kg 6:36; Ezr 5:8
q Ezr 3:7
r 6:5 Ezr 1:7

A 5:17 Lit treasure house   B 6:1 Lit Babylon where the treasures were stored   C 6:3 Lit be brought forth   D 6:3 Lit 60 cubits
E 6:3 A copyist seemingly overlooked the term for length and inadvertently read the 60 cubits for height and width. Like Solomon's temple, this temple was probably 90 feet long, 30 feet wide, and 45 feet high.   F 6:4 Or huge   G 6:5 Lit Jerusalem, to its place,

---

5:11 While the title "God of heaven" is used 12 times in Ezra-Nehemiah, this is the only use of the title **God of heaven and earth** in the Bible. The apostle Paul used a similar description in Athens, referring to God as "Lord of heaven and earth" (Ac 17:24). Solomon's name is not used here, only an oblique reference to **a great king of Israel**.

5:12 The phrase **our fathers angered the God of heaven** makes it clear that the cause of their nation's destruction and exile was their forefathers' failure to keep the covenant (2Ch 36:15-21; Neh 1:5-11; 9:5-37; Jr 4-6).

5:13 Although **Cyrus** was king of Persia, he also referred to himself as "King of Babylon" after he conquered Babylon in 539 B.C. Here the central claim of the Jewish leaders is put forth: Cyrus **issued a decree to rebuild the house of God**. This decree, if found, would verify their right to rebuild the temple.

5:15 The Neo-Babylonian kings who preceded Darius also showed great concern that fallen temples should be restored exactly on their original locations, strengthening the sense of continuity and legitimacy of the rebuilt temples.

5:16 The Jewish elders' claim that **Sheshbazzar . . . laid the foundation of God's house** has been the subject of debate (see note at 3:8). The claim that it had **been under construction from that time until now** is also difficult since both Haggai and Zechariah, as well as Ezra (4:5,23), say that construction had ceased for nearly 20 years. The claim

about ceaseless building appears to be a prevarication on the part of the Jewish elders, borne out of fear that any mention of a long halt of construction would weaken their case that their rebuilding efforts were sanctioned.

5:17 Tattenai suggested that a search be undertaken of **the royal archives** (lit "treasure house") **in Babylon** for Cyrus's decree allowing the Jewish exiles to return to their homeland. The record of the decree in fact was found in the Persian summer capital of Ecbatana (7:2). It appears that neither Sheshbazzar nor Zerubbabel had an official copy, since none was shown to their early opponents (4:1-5) or to Tattenai.

6:1-5 The first version of the Edict of Cyrus (1:2-4) was written in Hebrew and reflected a strong Jewish perspective. The second version given here, in Aramaic, explicitly decreed that funding for the temple would be **paid from the royal treasury**. Some scholars have dismissed this version as a literary fiction because they assume a Persian king would have no interest in paying to rebuild a **temple in Jerusalem**. Yet archaeological evidence shows that Persian kings, including Darius, were involved in state-supported reconstruction of temples outside Persia. Presumably, subjects are easier to govern when they are allowed to worship as they please.

6:3 The phrase **let its original foundations be retained** translates a difficult and uncertain Aramaic phrase. Other

Darius's Decree

[6]Therefore, you must stay away from that place, Tattenai governor of the region west of the Euphrates River, Shethar-bozenai, and your[A] colleagues, the officials in the region.[a] [7]Leave the construction of the house of God alone. Let the governor[b] and elders of the Jews rebuild this house of God on its original site.

[8]I hereby issue a decree concerning what you must do, so that the elders of the Jews can rebuild the house of God:

The cost is to be paid in full to these men out of the royal revenues[c] from the taxes of the region west of the Euphrates River, so that the work will not stop. [9]Whatever is needed—young bulls, rams, and lambs for *burnt offerings to the God of heaven, or wheat, salt, wine, and oil, as requested by the priests in Jerusalem—let it be given to them every day without fail,[d] [10]so that they can offer sacrifices of pleasing aroma to the God of heaven and pray for the life of the king and his sons.[e]

[11]I also issue a decree concerning any man who interferes with this directive:

Let a beam be torn from his house and raised up; he will be impaled on it, and his house will be made into a garbage dump

because of this offense.[f] [12]May the God who caused His name to dwell there[g] overthrow any king or people who dares[B] to harm or interfere with this house of God in Jerusalem. I, Darius, have issued the decree. Let it be carried out diligently.

[13]Then Tattenai governor of the region west of the Euphrates River, Shethar-bozenai, and their colleagues[h] diligently carried out what King Darius had decreed. [14]So the Jewish elders continued successfully with the building under the prophesying of Haggai the prophet and Zechariah son of Iddo.[i] They finished the building according to the command of the God of Israel and the decrees of Cyrus,[j] Darius, and King Artaxerxes[k] of Persia. [15]This house was completed on the third day of the month of Adar[C,l] in the sixth year of the reign of King Darius.

Temple Dedication and the Passover

[16]Then the Israelites, including the priests, the Levites, and the rest of the exiles, celebrated the dedication of the house of God with joy. [17]For the dedication of God's house they offered 100 bulls, 200 rams, and 400 lambs, as well as 12 male goats[m] as a *sin offering for all Israel—one for each Israelite tribe. [18]They also appointed the priests by their divisions and the Levites by their groups to the service of God in Jerusalem, according to what is written in the book of Moses.[n]

Cross references (center column)

a 6:6 Ezr 5:3,6; 6:13
b 6:7 Neh 5:14; Hg 1:1
c 6:8 Ezr 7:20
d 6:9 Ezr 7:17, 20-22
e 6:10 Ezr 7:23; 1Tm 2:1-2
f 6:11 Est 2:23; 9:14
g 6:12 Dt 12:5; 2Ch 6:2
h 6:13 Ezr 5:3,6; 6:6
i 6:14 Ezr 5:1; Hg 1:1; Zch 1:1
j Ezr 1:1-4; 6:3-5
k Ezr 7:12-26
l 6:15 Est 3:7
m 6:16-17 2Ch 7:4-5
n 6:18 Ex 29; Nm 18; 1Ch 24

A 6:6 Lit their   B 6:12 Lit who stretches out its hand   C 6:15 = February–March

---

translations assume the text is corrupted and change the term "foundations" (Aram 'ushohe) to "fire-offerings" (Aram 'eshohe), thus reading "and where the fire-offerings are brought."

The dimensions of the temple listed here are problematic. Only its width and height are mentioned, suggesting a cube that would be far larger than Solomon's glorious temple, which was "90 feet long, 30 feet wide, and 45 feet high" (1Kg 6:2). The text in Ezr 6:3 might reflect an ancient scribal error. It is most likely that the second temple would either be identical in size to Solomon's or smaller due to economic necessity.

6:4 The construction technique of **three layers of cut stones and one of timber** was based on the construction of Solomon's temple (1Kg 6:36). This translation reflects a slight change of the Aramaic text from "new (Aram chadath) timber" to "one (Aram chad) of timber." Unseasoned wood would not be used for such important construction.

6:6-7 Just as God was watching over His people (5:5) while they waited for Darius's decision, so His care for them was seen in Darius's decision that prohibited **Tattenai** and the other Persian officials from hindering the **construction** of the temple.

6:9-10 Darius's decree not only provided funds for reconstruction but for the daily sacrificial offerings as well. His motivation was not wholly altruistic, but that the people would **pray for . . . the king and his sons**. While Darius was

a devotee of Ahuramazda, he was willing to take spiritual support from any source.

6:11 The unusual terms in this Aramaic phrase (**raised up; he will be impaled on it**) have led some to translate it as "he will be set upon it (the beam) and struck," that is, flogged. However, "impaled" is probably correct. The Greek historian Herodotus claimed that Darius impaled 3,000 rebellious Babylonians when he recaptured the city.

6:13-15 **Tattenai** and his Persian colleagues knew how dangerous it was to disobey the king of Persia. The construction of the temple was done according to the decrees of **Cyrus, Darius, and King Artaxerxes of Persia**. The mention of Artaxerxes is odd since he became king a half-century after the temple was completed. Chapters 1-6 were probably the last chapters of Ezra-Nehemiah to be written. The author of this section, well aware both of Artaxerxes' opposition (4:6-22) and his support (7:11-26), included Artaxerxes in the list of those whose decrees involved the construction of the temple, even though his support came long after the events described in 6:13-15. Construction was most likely completed on March 12, 515 B.C.

6:16 In the OT law, the people were commanded to worship and celebrate their festivals with **joy** (Dt 12:7,12,18; 16:11,14). Just as the dedication of the first temple filled the people with joy (1Kg 8:66), and as the rededication of the temple and the restoration of Passover in Hezekiah's day

[19] The exiles[a] observed the •Passover[b] on the fourteenth day of the first month. [20] All of the priests and Levites were ceremonially •clean, because they had purified themselves. They killed the Passover lamb for themselves, their priestly brothers, and all the exiles.[c] [21] The Israelites who had returned from exile[d] ate it, together with all who had separated themselves from the uncleanness of the Gentiles of the land[A,e] in order to worship •Yahweh, the God of Israel. [22] They observed the Festival of •Unleavened Bread for seven days[f] with joy, because the LORD had made them joyful, having changed the Assyrian king's attitude toward them, so that he supported them[B] in the work on the house of the God of Israel.[g]

Ezra's Arrival

7 After these events, during the reign of King Artaxerxes[h] of Persia, Ezra—

Seraiah's[i] son, Azariah's son,
Hilkiah's[j] son, [2] Shallum's son,
Zadok's[k] son, Ahitub's son,
[3] Amariah's son, Azariah's son,
Meraioth's son, [4] Zerahiah's son,

Uzzi's son, Bukki's son,
[5] Abishua's son, Phinehas's son,
Eleazar's son, Aaron the chief priest's son[l]

[6] —came up from Babylon. He was a scribe skilled in the law of Moses,[m] which •Yahweh, the God of Israel, had given. The king had granted him everything he requested[n] because the hand of Yahweh his God was on him.[o] [7] Some of the Israelites, priests, Levites, singers, gatekeepers, and temple servants[p] accompanied him to Jerusalem in the seventh year of King Artaxerxes.

[8] Ezra[c] came to Jerusalem in the fifth month, during the seventh year of the king. [9] He began the journey from Babylon on the first day of the first month[q] and arrived in Jerusalem on the first day of the fifth month[r] since the gracious hand of his God was on him.[s] [10] Now Ezra had determined in his heart to study the law of the LORD, obey it, and teach[t] its statutes and ordinances in Israel.

Letter from Artaxerxes

[11] This is the text of the letter King Artaxer-

Cross-references (center column)

[a]6:19 Ezr 1:11; 2:1
[b]Ex 12:1-11; Nm 28:16
[c]6:20 2Ch 30:15-17
[d]6:21 Ezr 1:11; 2:1
[e]Ezr 9:11; Neh 10:28
[f]6:22 Ex 12:14-20; Dt 16:3-8
[g]Ezr 6:8-12
[h]7:1 Ezr 4:7; 6:14; Neh 2:1
[i]2Kg 25:18-21; Jr 52:24-27
[j]2Kg 22:4; 23:4
[k]7:2 1Sm 8:17; 1Kg 1:7-8; 2:35
[l]7:1-5 1Ch 6:3-15
[m]7:6 Ezr 7:11-12,21
[n]Neh 2:4-8
[o]Ezr 7:28; 8:22; Neh 2:8,18
[p]7:7 Ezr 2:1-58; Neh 7:6-60
[q]7:9 Ezr 8:15,21,31
[r]Ezr 8:32
[s]Ezr 7:28; 8:18,31; Neh 2:8,18
[t]7:10 Neh 8:1-8

A6:21 Lit land to them   B6:22 Lit their hands   C7:8 LXX, Syr, Vg read They

brought joy (2Ch 30:21), so now with the second temple the people responded with great joy.

6:19-20 The author had used Aramaic from 4:8–6:18 since he was working with official Persian correspondence written in Aramaic. With that correspondence completed, he returned to Hebrew. The new temple allowed the full implementation of the sacrificial system that existed before the disaster of 586 B.C. when the first temple was destroyed. This celebration of **Passover** (Hb *pesach*)—probably April 21, 515 B.C.—would have been a momentous occasion for God's people to remember their forefathers' deliverance from Egypt as well as their own deliverance from exile.

6:21 The OT law allowed even foreigners to celebrate Passover (Ex 12:48-49) as long as they were circumcised. Those **who had separated themselves** at least included proselytes. Likely it also included Israelites who had never been exiled but had remained in the land and continued to worship the God of Israel.

6:22 The **Festival of Unleavened Bread** began the day after Passover (Ex 12:14-20). The reference to King Darius of Persia as the **Assyrian** king seems unusual since the Assyrian Empire had collapsed more than a century earlier, but just as the Babylonians saw themselves as the successors of the Assyrians, so the Persian kings regarded themselves as the successors of the Assyrians and the Babylonians.

7:1–10:44 The second major part of Ezra consists primarily of the Ezra Memoir (see "Structure" in the Introduction) which tells of the ministry of Ezra the scribe in bringing spiritual renewal to the Jewish people. The final verses of chapter 6 take place in April 515 B.C. while the opening verses of chapter 7 begin with Ezra's journey to Jerusalem in 458 B.C., a gap of over 50 years. This section is written in Hebrew, except for the copy of Artaxerxes' letter (7:12-26) in Aramaic.

7:1 Ezra's name is a short form of the common Hebrew

name Azariah, meaning "Yahweh has helped," and is often followed by various titles, such as "Ezra the priest" (v. 12; 10:10,16; Neh 8:2), "Ezra the scribe" (Neh 8:4,13, 12:36), "Ezra the priest and scribe" (Ezr 7:11; Neh 8:1,4,9), and "Ezra the priest and expert in the law" (Ezr 7:21). The genealogy given for Ezra is representative and not complete, as a comparison with 1Ch 6:3-15 demonstrates.

7:6 Ezra was **a scribe** (Hb *sopher*), which in this context means more than reading, writing, and keeping records; it identifies a Torah expert who could read and interpret the law. Some scholars understand the term here and in verse 11 as designating Ezra as a Persian government official. However, it probably more accurately refers to his role in the Jewish community as a teacher and interpreter of the law.

7:7 Those returning to the land with Ezra are listed in the same order as in the return under Zerubbabel and Jeshua almost 80 years before (2:2-53).

7:8-9 Ezra's journey toward Jerusalem probably began on April 8, 458 B.C., but 8:15-31 tells of an immediate delay when it was discovered that no Levites were present. Taking the shortest route, this would be a journey of about 500 miles. However, such a route across the desert would be unlikely in summer, particularly during a time of political upheaval that made travel even more dangerous. The more common route covered about 900 miles. After a fourteen-week pilgrimage, they probably arrived in **Jerusalem** on August 4, 458 B.C.

7:10 Ezra's greatness is seen is his resolve to **study . . . obey**, and **teach** God's law to God's people.

7:11-28 Ezra came to Jerusalem bearing a letter from King Artaxerxes authorizing him and everyone who wanted to come with him to go to Jerusalem (v. 13). Some scholars in the past have dismissed this letter (vv. 12-26) as literary fiction. However, most now recognize its essential integrity.

xes gave to Ezra the priest and scribe, an expert in matters of the LORD's commands and statutes for Israel:^A

^a7:12 Ezk 26:7; Dn 2:37
^b7:13 Ezr 1:3
^c7:14 Est 1:14
^d7:15 Hg 2:8
^eDt 12:5-6; 2Ch 6:2
^f7:16 Ex 3:22; Ezr 1:6
^g7:17 Nm 15:1-14; Ezr 6:9
^h7:19 Ezr 8:33
^i7:20 Ezr 6:4,8; 7:22-23
^j7:21 Ezr 4:10; 7:25
^kEzr 6:8
^l7:23 Ezr 6:10
^m7:25 Ezr 7:10; Neh 8:1-3,8

¹²Artaxerxes, king of kings,^a to Ezra the priest, an expert in the law of the God of heaven:

Greetings.

¹³I issue a decree that any of the Israelites in my kingdom, including their priests and Levites, who want to go to Jerusalem, may go with you.^b ¹⁴You are sent by the king and his seven counselors^c to evaluate Judah and Jerusalem according to the law of your God, which is in your possession. ¹⁵You are also to bring the silver and gold the king and his counselors have willingly given to the God of Israel,^d whose dwelling is in Jerusalem,^e ¹⁶and all the silver and gold you receive throughout the province of Babylon, together with the freewill offerings given by the people and the priests to the house of their God in Jerusalem.^f ¹⁷Then you are to buy with this money as many bulls, rams, and lambs as needed, along with their *grain and *drink offerings, and offer them on the altar at the house of your God in Jerusalem.^g ¹⁸You may do whatever seems best to you and your brothers with the rest of the silver and gold, according to the will of your God. ¹⁹You must deliver to the God of Je-

rusalem all the articles given to you for the service of the house of your God.^h ²⁰You may use the royal treasury to pay for anything else needed for the house of your God.^i

²¹I, King Artaxerxes, issue a decree to all the treasurers in the region west of the Euphrates River:^j

Whatever Ezra the priest, an expert in the law of the God of heaven, asks of you must be provided promptly,^k ²²up to 7,500 pounds^B of silver, 500 bushels^C of wheat, 550 gallons^D of wine, 550 gallons^D of oil, and salt without limit.^E ²³Whatever is commanded by the God of heaven must be done diligently for the house of the God of heaven, so that wrath will not fall on the realm of the king and his sons.^l ²⁴Be advised that tribute, duty, and land tax must not be imposed on any priests, Levites, singers, doorkeepers, temple servants, or other servants of this house of God.

²⁵And you, Ezra, according to^F God's wisdom that you possess, appoint magistrates and judges to judge all the people in the region west of the Euphrates who know the laws of your God and to teach anyone who does not know them.^m ²⁶Anyone who does not keep the law of your God and the law of the king, let a fair judgment be executed against him,

---

^A7:11 Ezr 7:12-26 is written in Aram.   ^B7:22 Lit *100 talents*   ^C7:22 Lit *100 cors*   ^D7:22 Lit *100 baths*   ^E7:22 Lit *without instruction*
^F7:25 Lit *to your*

The letter was written in Aramaic (4:8) that was common to its era and in a format common throughout the Persian period. It is possible that Ezra himself composed the letter and submitted it to Artaxerxes for royal approval.

7:11 This verse, written in Hebrew, provides an introduction to Artaxerxes' **letter** that was written in Aramaic (vv. 12-26).

7:12 Artaxerxes used the common royal Persian title **king of kings**, used in the NT in reference to God (1Tm 6:15; Rv 19:16). The word **law** here is not the common Hebrew word *torah* but the word *dath*, a Persian loanword *(data)* found in both postexilic biblical Hebrew and Aramaic.

7:14 The Greek historian Herodotus described the practice of a Persian king having **seven** trusted advisers. Esther 1:13-14 names Xerxes' seven trusted counselors and states that they had personal access to the king.

7:15-17 Funds for Ezra's journey to **Jerusalem** and the purchase of sacrificial animals there came from the royal treasury and from gifts gathered from the Jewish exiles in Babylon.

7:19 It is not clear what the royal **articles** (Aram *ma'n*) were. In 5:14 the same term is used to describe the gold and silver articles looted from the temple by Nebuchadnezzar in 586 B.C. and returned by King Cyrus (1:7).

7:21-22 The provisions that Ezra was entitled to were used daily in the sacrifices at the temple. The quantities listed here would be sufficient for approximately two years. The **7,500 pounds** (lit "100 talents") **of silver** seems out of proportion to the other items. The entire annual tax for the "Beyond the River" region was 350 talents. A textual corruption, common when scribes were copying numbers, may explain the seemingly implausible amount of silver. A gift of even 10 talents of silver (750 pounds) would have been generous.

7:23 King Darius had asked the Jewish community to pray for the king and his sons (6:10). Now Artaxerxes commanded that the regular sacrifices and worship be properly maintained.

7:24 Persian texts and Greek writings about Persian practice confirm that exemption from taxes was granted to temples and the sacred personnel who served there.

7:25 The charge given to **Ezra** here is not clear. He was to **appoint magistrates and judges**, but it is not certain how their roles related to those of the regular Persian judges and officials. Probably these judges and magistrates dealt only with cases specific to the OT law.

7:26 Those who refused to keep **the law** were subject to

whether death, banishment, confiscation of property, or imprisonment.[a]

[27] Praise Yahweh the God of our fathers, who has put it into the king's mind[b] to glorify the house of the LORD in Jerusalem,[c] [28] and who has shown favor to me before the king,[d] his counselors, and all his powerful officers. So I took courage because I was strengthened by Yahweh my God,[A,e] and I gathered Israelite leaders to return with me.[f]

Those Returning with Ezra

8 These are the family leaders and the genealogical records of those who returned with me from Babylon during the reign of King Artaxerxes:[g]

[2] Gershom, from Phinehas's descendants;
Daniel, from Ithamar's descendants;
Hattush, from David's descendants,
[3] who was of Shecaniah's descendants;[h]
Zechariah, from Parosh's[i] descendants,
and 150 men[B] with him
who were registered by genealogy;
[4] Eliehoenai son of Zerahiah
from Pahath-moab's descendants,[j]
and 200 men with him;
[5] Shecaniah[C] son of Jahaziel
from Zattu's descendants,
and 300 men with him;
[6] Ebed son of Jonathan
from Adin's descendants,[k]

and 50 men with him;
[7] Jeshaiah son of Athaliah
from Elam's descendants,
and 70 men with him;
[8] Zebadiah son of Michael
from Shephatiah's descendants,
and 80 men with him;
[9] Obadiah son of Jehiel
from Joab's descendants,
and 218 men with him;
[10] Shelomith[D] son of Josiphiah
from Bani's descendants,
and 160 men with him;
[11] Zechariah son of Bebai
from Bebai's descendants,
and 28 men with him;
[12] Johanan son of Hakkatan
from Azgad's descendants,
and 110 men with him;
[13] these are the last ones,
from Adonikam's descendants,[l]
and their names are:
Eliphelet, Jeuel, and Shemaiah,
and 60 men with them;
[14] Uthai and Zaccur[E]
from Bigvai's descendants,
and 70 men with them.

[15] I gathered them at the river[F] that flows to Ahava,[m] and we camped there for three days. I searched among the people and priests, but found no Levites[n] there. [16] Then I summoned

Cross references column:
[a] 7:26 Ezr 6:11
[b] 7:27 Ezr 6:22
[c] Is 60:7,13
[d] 7:28 Ezr 9:9
[e] Ezr 7:6; 8:18
[f] Ezr 8:1-14,16
[g] 8:1 Ezr 7:7
[h] 8:3 1Ch 3:22
[i] Ezr 2:3; 10:25
[j] 8:4 Ezr 2:6
[k] 8:6 Ezr 2:15; Neh 7:20
[l] 8:13 Ezr 2:13
[m] 8:15 Ezr 8:21,31
[n] Ezr 2:40; 7:7

[A] 7:28 Lit because the hand of the LORD my God was on me   [B] 8:3 Or males; also in vv. 4-14   [C] 8:5 LXX, 1 Esdras 8:32; MT reads the descendants of Shecaniah   [D] 8:10 Some LXX mss, 1 Esdras 8:36; MT reads the descendants of Shelomith   [E] 8:14 Alt Hb tradition, some LXX mss read Zabud   [F] 8:15 Or canal

typical Persian punishments. **Imprisonment** was not stipulated in OT law, but it did occur in preexilic Israel, for example, in the case of Jeremiah the prophet (Jr 37–38).

7:27-28 With the completion of the official letter written in Aramaic (vv. 12-26), the author reverts to Hebrew. Here in verse 27 begins the first words of Ezra in the Ezra Memoir (see "Structure" in the Introduction).

8:1-14 Almost 80 years before Ezra came to Jerusalem, Zerubbabel and Jeshua led the first return of the Babylonian exiles to the land of their forefathers (chap. 2). The list of returnees at that time (2:2-61) numbered over 40,000 men (2:64) while the list here involves only about 1,500 men. In chapter 2 the list records the laity, the priests, and then the Levites. In chapter 8 the priests are mentioned first (v. 2a) followed by those of royal lineage (vv. 2b-3a) and then the listing of the laity (vv. 3b-14).

8:2a Gershom and **Daniel** represented the two branches of the Aaronic priesthood. Gershom traced his ancestry through Phinehas (Ex 6:25), the son of Eleazar, son of Aaron. Ezra himself was from this priestly lineage.

8:2b-3 Hattush's royal lineage from King David would certainly have been important to the postexilic community in Jerusalem. First Chronicles 3:19-22 gives his genealogy as: Zerubbabel/Hananiah/Shecaniah/Shemaiah/Hattush.

8:14 Mentioning two names (**Uthai and Zaccur**) for a family leader is unusual. The Hebrew text describes **70 men** literally "with him" (sg), suggesting some minor textual confu-

tsom

Hebrew Pronunciation	[TSOAM]
HCSB Translation	fast
Uses in Ezra	1
Uses in the OT	26
Focus Passage	Ezra 8:21

The noun tsom means fast, as does the verb tsum (21x; Ezr 8:23). Fasting was associated with grieving and often included wearing sackcloth and confessing sins (Neh 9:1-2). David fasted for defeated Israel (1Sm 31:13) partly because defeat signaled prior national sin (Dt 28:25). Fasting marked recognition of sin and attended the forsaking of idols (1Sm 7:2-6). People also fasted to plead with God for some request (Est 4:16), humbling themselves to pursue His mercy (1Kg 21:27-29), protection (Ezr 8:21), or healing (Ps 35:13). Yet self-humbling people anticipated divine responsiveness to petition, but fasting was needed to further His purposes (Is 58:4-6), being done for Him (Zch 7:5). God's refusal to respond signaled judgment (Jr 14:12). God (Jl 2:12) and kings (2Ch 20:3) called for fast days, and recurring official fast days followed the exile (Zch 8:19).

the leaders: Eliezer, Ariel, Shemaiah, Elnathan, Jarib, Elnathan, Nathan, Zechariah, and Meshullam,[a] as well as the teachers Joiarib and Elnathan. [17] I sent them to Iddo, the leader at Casiphia, with a message for[A] him and his brothers, the temple servants[b] at Casiphia, that they should bring us ministers for the house of our God. [18] Since the gracious hand of our God was on us,[c] they brought us Sherebiah[d]—a man of insight from the descendants of Mahli, a descendant of Levi son of Israel—along with his sons and brothers, 18 men, [19] plus Hashabiah,[e] along with Jeshaiah, from the descendants of Merari, and his brothers and their sons, 20 men. [20] There were also 220 of the temple servants,[f] who had

been appointed by David and the leaders for the work of the Levites. All were identified by name.

Preparing to Return

[21] I proclaimed a fast[g] by the Ahava River,[B] so that we might humble ourselves before our God and ask Him for a safe journey for us, our children, and all our possessions. [22] I did this because I was ashamed to ask the king for infantry and cavalry to protect us from enemies during the journey, since we had told him, "The hand of our God is gracious to all who seek Him, but His great anger is against all who abandon Him."[h] [23] So we fasted and pleaded with our God about this, and He granted our request.

a8:16 Ezr 10:15
b8:17 Ezr 2:43; Neh 7:46
c8:18 Ezr 7:6
d Ezr 8:24; Neh 8:7
e8:19 Neh 12:24
f8:20 Ezr 2:43; 7:7
g8:21 Is 58:3-8
h8:22 Dt 31:6,17

A8:17 Lit Casiphia, and I put in their mouth the words to speak to   B8:21 Or Canal

---

sion. Probably the original text read "Uthai son of Zaccur," a reading supported by the apocryphal 1 Esdras 8:40.

8:15 The term **river** (Hb *nahar*) can mean either "river" or "canal." It appears there were not enough priests to carry the gold and silver donated to the temple (vv. 24-30) and that the **Levites** were needed for this task. Ezra also wanted his group of returnees to be representative of the nation as a whole, where each major group took part in the return to the land of their ancestors.

8:16 The list of **leaders** and **teachers** is unusual in that it mentions three individuals named **Elnathan** who are not differentiated by a genealogical description, such as "son of

X." The term "teacher" (Hb *mevinim*) can be understood as a title ("teacher," "instructor") or as a descriptor ("who were wise," "men of understanding").

8:17 The distinguished entourage was sent to ask **Iddo** for Levites to join the exiles in their return to the land. Their request was significant, asking people to leave their homes and family on short notice for a difficult 900-mile journey.

8:21 The term **children** is not the normal Hebrew term but one (Hb *taph*) that indicates those unable to walk on the journey, such as the elderly, the infirm, and young children.

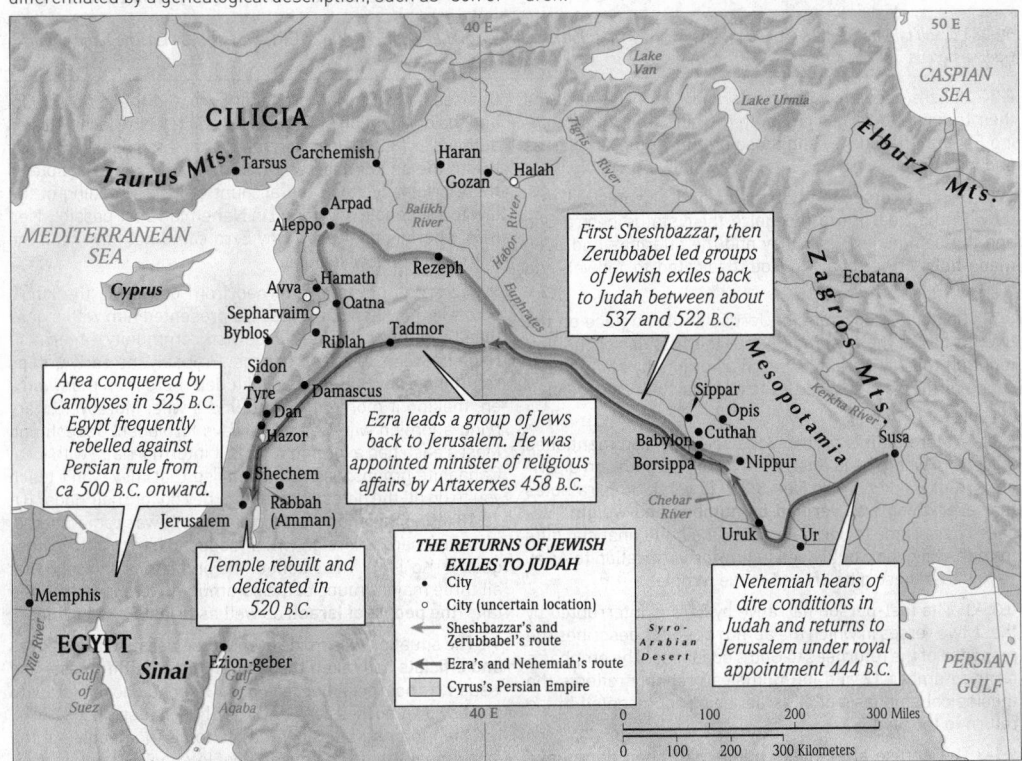

CILICIA

Taurus Mts.

MEDITERRANEAN SEA

Cyprus

EGYPT

Sinai

Memphis

Gulf of Suez

Nile River

Ezion-geber

Gulf of Aqaba

Tarsus   Carchemish   Haran   Halah
Gozan
Arpad
Aleppo   Balikh River   Habor River   Rezeph
Hamath   Tigris River
Avva   Oatna
Sepharvaim
Byblos   Riblah   Tadmor   Euphrates
Sidon
Tyre   Damascus
Dan
Hazor
Shechem
Rabbah (Amman)
Jerusalem

Lake Van
Lake Urmia

CASPIAN SEA

Elburz Mts.

Zagros Mts.

Ecbatana

Kertha River

Mesopotamia

Sippar   Opis
Babylon   Cuthah
Borsippa   Nippur

Chebar River

Uruk   Ur

Susa

Syro-Arabian Desert

PERSIAN GULF

First Sheshbazzar, then Zerubbabel led groups of Jewish exiles back to Judah between about 537 and 522 B.C.

Area conquered by Cambyses in 525 B.C. Egypt frequently rebelled against Persian rule from ca 500 B.C. onward.

Ezra leads a group of Jews back to Jerusalem. He was appointed minister of religious affairs by Artaxerxes 458 B.C.

Temple rebuilt and dedicated in 520 B.C.

Nehemiah hears of dire conditions in Judah and returns to Jerusalem under royal appointment 444 B.C.

THE RETURNS OF JEWISH EXILES TO JUDAH
• City
○ City (uncertain location)
→ Sheshbazzar's and Zerubbabel's route
← Ezra's and Nehemiah's route
    Cyrus's Persian Empire

40 E   50 E

0   100   200   300 Miles
0   100   200   300 Kilometers

²⁴I selected 12 of the leading priests, along with Sherebiah,ᵃ Hashabiah, and 10 of their brothers. ²⁵I weighed out to them the silver, the gold, and the articles—the contribution for the house of our God that the king, his counselors, his leaders, and all the Israelites who were present had offered. ²⁶I weighed out to them 24 tonsᴬ of silver, silver articles weighing 7,500 pounds,ᴮ 7,500 poundsᴮ of gold, ²⁷20 gold bowls worth 1,000 gold coins,ᶜ and two articles of fine gleaming bronze, as valuable as gold.ᵇ ²⁸Then I said to them, "You are holy to the Lᴏʀᴅ, and the articles are holy. The silver and gold are a freewill offeringᶜ to the Lᴏʀᴅ God of your fathers. ²⁹Guard them carefully until you weigh them out in the chambers of the Lᴏʀᴅ's house before the leading priests, Levites, and heads of the Israelite families in Jerusalem." ³⁰So the priests and Levites took charge of the silver, the gold, and the articles that had been weighed out, to bring them to the house of our God in Jerusalem.ᵈ

Arrival in Jerusalem

³¹We set out from the Ahava Riverᴰ on the twelfth day of the first month to go to Jerusalem. We were strengthened by our God,ᴱ,ᵉ and He protected us from the power of the enemy and from ambush along the way.ᶠ ³²So we arrived at Jerusalem and rested there for three days.ᵍ ³³On the fourth day the silver, the gold, and the articles were weighed out in the house of our God into the care of Meremoth the priest, son of Uriah. Eleazar son of Phinehas was with him. The Levites Jozabadʰ son of Jeshua and Noadiah son of Binnui were also with them. ³⁴Everything was verified by number and weight, and the total weight was recorded at that time.

³⁵The exiles who had returned from the captivityⁱ offered •burnt offerings to the God of Israel: 12 bulls for all Israel, 96 rams, and 77 lambs, along with 12 male goats as a •sin offering. All this was a burnt offering for the Lᴏʀᴅ.ʲ ³⁶They also delivered the king's edicts to the royal satraps and governors of the region west of the Euphrates,ᵏ so that they would support the people and the house of God.ˡ

Israel's Intermarriage with Pagans

9 After these things had been done, the leaders approached me and said: "The people of Israel, the priests, and the Levites have not separated themselvesᵐ from the surrounding peoples whose detestable practicesⁿ are like those of the Canaanites, Hittites, Perizzites, Jebusites, Ammonites, Moabites, Egyptians, and Amorites.ᵒ ²Indeed, the Israelite menᶠ have taken some of their daughters as wives for themselves and their sons, so that the holy

---

ᵃ 8:24 Neh 10:9,11
ᵇ 8:25-27 Ezr 7:15-20
ᶜ 8:28 Ezr 1:4; 2:68-69
ᵈ 8:29-30 Neh 13:4-5,9
ᵉ 8:31 Ezr 7:9; Neh 2:18
ᶠ Ezr 8:21-22
ᵍ 8:32 Neh 2:11
ʰ 8:33 Neh 11:16
ⁱ 8:35 Ezr 2:1; 6:16
ʲ Lv 1:3-15; 2Ch 29:24,27,31-35
ᵏ 8:36 Ezr 7:21,25
ˡ Ezr 7:21-24
ᵐ 9:1 Ezk 5:10-12
ⁿ Dt 12:29-31; Ezr 9:11
ᵒ Gn 15:18; Lv 18:24-30; Dt 7:1

ᴬ8:26 Lit *650 talents*   ᴮ8:26 Lit *100 talents*   ᶜ8:27 Or *1,000 drachmas, or 1,000 darics*   ᴰ8:31 Or *Canal*   ᴱ8:31 Lit *The hand of our God was on us*   ᶠ9:2 Lit *they*

8:24-25 Ezra appointed 12 **priests** and 12 Levites to bring their treasure to Jerusalem, both the gifts from those joining Ezra on the journey and those given by King Artaxerxes and his officials.

8:28-29 Ezra charged the 12 priests and 12 Levites entrusted with the treasure to recognize their status before God and the community. Both they and the offerings had been made **holy**, or set apart to God, dedicated to Yahweh and His worship.

8:31 The actual departure for Jerusalem took place **on the twelfth day of the first month**, not the first day of the first month (probably April 8, 538 B.C.) as originally planned because of the need to find Levites to join the returnees (vv. 15-20).

8:33-34 Meremoth is probably the same person mentioned in Neh 3:4 where he is referred to as "Meremoth son of Uriah, son of Hakkoz" (also Neh 3:21). In verse 34 Ezra notes that **everything was verified by number and weight**. Because Ezra came to Jerusalem bearing huge financial gifts from the king, he would need to provide verification to Artaxerxes that these gifts arrived at the temple.

8:35-36 The first-person narrative by Ezra is interrupted by these two verses in which the author or editor describes the response of the returnees to God's goodness. The emphasis on the number **12** and its multiples probably reflects the theological emphasis of all Israel being represented in the return to the land.

9:1-3 The phrase **after these things had been done** links this section with the worship of Ezra and the people (8:35) and the distribution of Artaxerxes' edicts to the local Persian authorities (8:36). However, many scholars suggest that between the end of chapter 8 and the beginning of chapter 9 there originally stood the account of Ezra's reading of the law to the people now found in Nehemiah 8 (or possibly Neh 8-9). There is no reason why Ezra could not have read the law on multiple occasions.

9:1 Ezra had not long returned from delivering the king's edicts (8:36) when some leaders presented him with a genuine threat to the postexilic Jewish community—intermarriage between Jews and pagans. Probably the early groups returning from Babylon had included more men than women, making it more difficult to find a wife. Moreover, marrying a foreign wife was not always forbidden. Joseph and Moses each had a foreign wife. But intermarriage with local Canaanite groups was forbidden "so that they won't teach you to do all the detestable things they do for their gods" (Dt 20:18). King Solomon's example certainly was remembered, as his numerous foreign wives "seduced him to follow other gods" (1Kg 11:4). The extent of the problem is shown in that all three major groups of the community were involved—the laity (**the people of Israel**) as well as **priests** and **Levites**.

9:2 The situation was made even worse because the **leaders and officials** had **taken the lead in this unfaithfulness**. The issue was not racial but religious. God had chosen Israel to be His "own possession" and His "holy nation" (Ex 19:5-6). His plan to bring blessing and life to all the peoples of the earth meant that His chosen people should maintain their

•seed*a* has become mixed with the surrounding peoples.*b* The leaders[A] and officials have taken the lead in this unfaithfulness!"*c* [3]When I heard this report, I tore my tunic and robe, pulled out some of the hair from my head and beard, and sat down devastated.*d*

Ezra's Confession

[4]Everyone who trembled at the words of the God of Israel*e* gathered around me, because of the unfaithfulness of the exiles,*f* while I sat devastated until the evening offering.*g* [5]At the evening offering, I got up from my humiliation, with my tunic and robe torn. Then I fell on my knees and spread out my hands to •Yahweh my God.*h* [6]And I said:*i*

My God, I am ashamed and embarrassed to lift my face toward You, my God, because our iniquities are higher than our heads and our •guilt is as high as the heavens.*j* [7]Our guilt has been terrible from the days of our fathers until the present. Because of our iniquities we have been handed over, along with our kings and priests, to the surrounding kings, and to the sword, captivity, plundering, and open shame,*k* as it is today. [8]But now, for a brief moment, grace has come from Yahweh our God to preserve a remnant*l* for us and give us a stake*m* in His holy place. Even in our slavery, God has given us new life and light to our eyes.*n* [9]Though we are slaves,*o* our God has not abandoned us in our slavery. He

has extended grace to us in the presence of the Persian kings,*p* giving us new life, so that we can rebuild the house of our God and repair its ruins,*q* to give us a wall in Judah and Jerusalem.

[10]Now, our God, what can we say in light of[B] this? For we have abandoned the commands [11]You gave through Your servants the prophets, saying: "The land you are entering to possess is an impure land. The surrounding peoples have filled it from end to end with their uncleanness by their impurity and detestable practices.*r* [12]So do not give your daughters to their sons in marriage or take their daughters for your sons.*s* Never seek their peace or prosperity,*t* so that you will be strong, eat the good things of the land, and leave it as an inheritance to your sons forever." [13]After all that has happened to us because of our evil deeds and terrible guilt—though You, our God, have punished us less than our sins deserve and have allowed us to survive[C,u]— [14]should we break Your commands again and intermarry with the peoples who commit these detestable practices?*v* Wouldn't You become so angry with us that You would destroy us, leaving no survivors?*w* [15]LORD God of Israel, You are righteous, for we survive as a remnant*x* today. Here we are before You with our guilt, though no one can stand in Your presence because of this.*y*

---

*a*9:2 Dt 14:2
*b*Dt 7:1-4; Ezr 9:12; Neh 13:1-3,23
*c*Neh 13:28
*d*9:3 2Kg 18:37–19:2; Neh 1:4; Dn 9:3
*e*9:4 Ezr 10:3; Is 66:2,5
*f*Ezr 2:1; 6:16
*g*Ex 29:38-39
*h*9:5 Ex 9:29; Dn 6:10
*i*9:6-15 Neh 1:5-11; Dn 9:4-19
*j*9:6 Jr 51:9; Rv 18:5
*k*9:7 Neh 9:30,36; Dn 9:7
*l*9:8 Is 10:20-22
*m*Is 10:23
*n*1Sm 14:29
*o*9:9 Neh 9:36
*p*2Kg 25:28; Ezr 6:22
*q*Ezr 1:4; 7:12-20
*r*9:10-11 Dt 12:29-31; Ezr 9:1
*s*9:12 Dt 7:1-4; Ezr 9:2; Neh 13:23-28
*t*Dt 7:3; 23:6
*u*9:13 Is 10:20-22
*v*9:14 Ezr 9:1-2; Neh 13:23-28
*w*Dt 29:26-28
*x*9:15 Neh 1:3
*y*Ps 130:3

[A]9:2 Lit *hand of the leaders*   [B]9:10 Lit *say after*   [C]9:13 Lit *and gave us a remnant like this*

---

identity. From them would come God's servant who would be "a light to the nations" (Is 42:6) and would bear the "iniquity of us all" (Is 53:6).

9:3 Ezra identified personally with the sins of his people, responding with actions associated with repentance and mourning.

9:4-5 Those who gathered around Ezra **trembled at the words of the God of Israel**—a phrase that occurs in three other OT passages (10:3; Is 66:2,5). It identified them as people fully committed to keeping God's law. Ezra got up from his **humiliation** (Hb *ta'anet*), a term that occurs only here in the Hebrew Bible but does occur in postbiblical Hebrew and in Aramaic. It probably implies a penitential act in this context.

9:6-15 Ezra's penitential prayer of confession, written in late biblical Hebrew, is similar to others from the postexilic era in content, style, and theological perspective (Neh 1:5-11; 9:6-38; Dn 9:4-19). It differs from them in that there is no petition or request to God. Its focus is confession.

9:6-7 Ezra began his prayer with his own shame and embarrassment but quickly shifted to a corporate confession of the nation's sins. In referring to **fathers**, he may have been looking back several generations to those who sinned be-

fore the destruction of the temple and the exile (5:12), but it is more likely that he used the term to go all the way back to Abraham, Isaac, and Jacob (Dt 6:10; 8:1; 2Ch 34:21). Thus Israel's entire history was a story of failure and guilt.

9:8-9 The term **stake** (Hb *yathed*) literally is "peg," a metaphor for the idea of permanence (Is 33:20) and stability (Is 22:23-25). That the postexilic community existed and had a temple was a sign of God's undeserved mercy. The reference to **slavery** may be misconstrued when read through the lens of American history. The postexilic people did not experience racially based servitude. Yet without question, they understood that they were not a free people. Except for a brief period during the time of the Maccabees (163–60 B.C.), they would remain under the control of foreign powers throughout the rest of biblical history.

9:10-12 Ezra's mention of the **prophets** reflects usage common in later OT texts that certainly includes Moses as well as others who spoke for God. The **commands** that the people had **abandoned** are spelled out in verses 11-12. The focus is the necessity of avoiding defilement of themselves and their nation through association with pagan people.

9:13-15 Ezra warned God's people that to intermarry with pagans once again could lead God to **destroy** them all. God had been merciful before when they sinned in this way

Sending Away Foreign Wives

10 While Ezra prayed and confessed, weeping and falling facedown[a] before the house of God, an extremely large assembly of Israelite men, women, and children gathered around him. The people also wept bitterly.[b] [2] Then Shecaniah son of Jehiel,[c] an Elamite, responded to Ezra: "We have been unfaithful to our God by marrying foreign women from the surrounding peoples,[d] but there is still hope for Israel in spite of this. [3] Let us therefore make a covenant before our God[e] to send away all the foreign wives and their children, according to the counsel of my lord and of those who tremble at the command of our God.[f] Let it be done according to the law. [4] Get up, for this matter is your responsibility,[g] and we support you. Be strong and take action!"[h]

[5] Then Ezra got up and made the leading priests, Levites, and all Israel take an oath to do what had been said; so they took the oath.[i] [6] Ezra then went from the house of God and walked to the chamber of Jehohanan son of Eliashib, where he spent the night.[A] He did not eat food or drink water, because he was mourning over the unfaithfulness of the exiles.[j]

[7] They circulated a proclamation throughout Judah and Jerusalem that all the exiles should gather at Jerusalem. [8] Whoever did not come within three days would forfeit all his possessions,[B] according to the decision of the leaders and elders, and would be excluded[k] from the assembly of the exiles.

[9] So all the men of Judah and Benjamin gathered in Jerusalem within the three days. On the twentieth day of the ninth month, all the people sat in the square at the house of God,[l] trembling because of this matter and because of the heavy rain. [10] Then Ezra the priest stood up and said to them, "You have been unfaithful by marrying foreign women, adding to Israel's *guilt.[m] [11] Therefore, make a confession to *Yahweh the God of your fathers and do His will. Separate yourselves from the surrounding peoples and your foreign wives."

[12] Then all the assembly responded with a loud voice: "Yes, we will do as you say! [13] But there are many people, and it is the rainy season. We don't have the stamina to stay out in the open. This isn't something that can be done in a day or two, for we have rebelled terribly in this matter. [14] Let our leaders represent the entire assembly. Then let all those in our towns who have married foreign women come at appointed times, together with the elders and judges of each town, in order to avert the fierce anger of our God[n] concerning[c] this matter." [15] Only Jonathan son of Asahel and Jahzeiah son of Tikvah opposed this, with Meshullam[o] and Shabbethai the Levite supporting them.

[16] The exiles did what had been proposed. Ezra the priest selected men[D] who were family leaders, all identified by name, to represent[E] their ancestral houses. They convened on the first day of the tenth month to investigate the matter, [17] and by the first day of the first month they had dealt with all the men who had married foreign women.

Those Married to Foreign Wives

[18] The following were found to have married foreign women from the descendants of the priests:

[a]10:1 Ezr 9:3,5; Neh 1:4; Dn 9:3-4,20
[b]Ezr 3:12-13
[c]10:2 Ezr 10:26
[d]Ezr 9:1-2; 10:18,44; Neh 13:23-28
[e]10:3 2Ch 34:31
[f]Ezr 9:4
[g]10:4 Ezr 7:25-26
[h]Jos 1:6-9
[i]10:5 Neh 10:29-30; 13:25
[j]10:6 Dt 9:18-19
[k]10:7-8 Ezr 7:26
[l]10:9 Neh 8:1
[m]10:10 Ezr 9:1-2; Neh 13:23-27
[n]10:14 2Ch 29:10; 30:8
[o]10:15 Ezr 8:16

[A]10:6 1 Esdras 9:2, Syr; MT, Vg read *he went*   [B]10:8 Lit *would *set apart all his possessions for destruction*   [C]10:14 Some Hb mss, LXX, Vg; other Hb mss read *until*   [D]10:16 1 Esdras 9:16, Syr; MT, Vg read *priest and men were selected*   [E]10:16 Lit *name, for*

---

because they survived as **a remnant today**, but they should not presume upon His grace. They needed to repent, specifically in the necessary but heart-breaking task of sending away their foreign wives and children (chap. 10).

10:1 The term **confessed** is from a Hebrew verb *(yadah)* that usually means "to praise, to give thanks." But in this verbal root (Hb *hithpael*), it has the connotation of "confessing" (Lv 5:5), as God is praised when His people acknowledge their sin and guilt before Him.

10:2-4 Shecaniah's radical solution of sending away **the foreign wives and their children** was not an expression of racial prejudice but an act to insure the survival of God's covenant people (9:14). The translation here follows most modern translations in reading "my lord" (Hb *adoni*) rather than the Masoretic Text "Lord" (Hb *adonay*). The context suggests that Shecaniah was referring to Ezra and not to God.

10:7-8 J. Blenkinsopp suggests the size of the Persian province of *Yehud* (Judah) was "no more than about thirty-five miles north to south and twenty-five miles east to west." Thus the three-day notice was sufficient time to notify the entire populace and for them to travel to **Jerusalem**. The term "forfeit" (Hb *charam*) is the word used in the OT to put something under the "ban," as were cities during the time of Joshua that were totally destroyed. It can also refer to things that were totally consecrated to divine use, as in the case of Achan (Jos 6–7), who stole items under the ban.

10:9 The threats for noncompliance with the proclamation had their desired effect. **All the men of Judah and Benjamin** met on the **twentieth day of the ninth month**—December 458 B.C.

10:12-15 It is significant that the people asked that individual cases of foreign marriage be handled by **leaders** (Hb *sar*) and not by priests who would seem to be the most likely ones to deal with these decisions. Since many priests were some of the worst offenders (vv. 18-22; 9:1), this disqualified them in the eyes of the people, who preferred to have respected family leaders (10:16) deal with this issue.

10:16-17 The **family leaders** selected by **Ezra** probably met from December 29, 458 to March 27, 457 B.C.

10:18-44 The list of offenders, which concludes the book of

from the descendants of Jeshua son of Jozadak and his brothers: Maaseiah, Eliezer, Jarib, and Gedaliah. [19] They pledged[A] to send their wives away, and being guilty, they offered a ram from the flock for their guilt;[a]

20 Hanani and Zebadiah from Immer's[b] descendants;

21 Maaseiah, Elijah, Shemaiah, Jehiel, and Uzziah from Harim's[c] descendants;

22 Elioenai, Maaseiah, Ishmael, Nethanel, Jozabad, and Elasah from Pashhur's[d] descendants.

23 The Levites:[e]

Jozabad, Shimei, Kelaiah (that is Kelita), Pethahiah, Judah, and Eliezer.

24 The singers:[f]

Eliashib.

The gatekeepers:[g]

Shallum, Telem, and Uri.

25 The Israelites:[h]

Parosh's descendants:[i] Ramiah, Izziah, Malchijah, Mijamin, Eleazar, Malchijah,[B] and Benaiah;

26 Elam's descendants:[j] Mattaniah, Zechariah, Jehiel, Abdi, Jeremoth, and Elijah;

27 Zattu's descendants:[k] Elioenai, Eliashib, Mattaniah, Jeremoth, Zabad, and Aziza;

28 Bebai's descendants:[l] Jehohanan, Hananiah, Zabbai, and Athlai;

29 Bani's descendants:[m] Meshullam, Malluch, Adaiah, Jashub, Sheal, and Jeremoth;

30 Pahath-moab's descendants:[n] Adna, Chelal, Benaiah, Maaseiah, Mattaniah, Bezalel, Binnui, and Manasseh;

31 Harim's descendants:[o] Eliezer, Isshijah, Malchijah, Shemaiah, Shimeon, [32] Benjamin, Malluch, and Shemariah;

33 Hashum's descendants:[p] Mattenai, Mattattah, Zabad, Eliphelet, Jeremai, Manasseh, and Shimei;

34 Bani's descendants:[q] Maadai, Amram, Uel, [35] Benaiah, Bedeiah, Cheluhi, [36] Vaniah, Meremoth, Eliashib, [37] Mattaniah, Mattenai, Jaasu, [38] Bani, Binnui, Shimei, [39] Shelemiah, Nathan, Adaiah, [40] Machnadebai, Shashai, Sharai, [41] Azarel, Shelemiah, Shemariah, [42] Shallum, Amariah, and Joseph;

43 Nebo's descendants:[r] Jeiel, Mattithiah, Zabad, Zebina, Jaddai, Joel, and Benaiah.

44 All of these[s] had married foreign women, and some of the wives had given birth to children.[t]

Cross references (center column):
[a]10:19 Lv 5:14–6:7
[b]10:20 1Ch 24:14
[c]10:21 1Ch 24:8
[d]10:22 1Ch 9:12
[e]10:23 Ezr 2:40
[f]10:24 Ezr 2:41
[g]Ezr 2:42
[h]10:25-43 Ezr 2:3-35; Neh 7:8-38
[i]10:25 Ezr 2:3
[j]10:26 Ezr 2:7; 10:2
[k]10:27 Ezr 2:8
[l]10:28 Ezr 2:11
[m]10:29 Ezr 2:10
[n]10:30 Ezr 2:6
[o]10:31 Ezr 2:32
[p]10:33 Ezr 2:19
[q]10:34 Ezr 2:10
[r]10:43 Ezr 2:29
[s]10:44 Ezr 10:18-43
[t]Neh 13:24

A10:19 Lit *gave their hand*   B10:25 Some LXX mss, 1 Esdras 9:26 read *Hashabiah*

Ezra, reflects a "top down" progression that begins with the high priest's own family (vv. 18-19). If the population of Judah at that time was over 30,000 people and only 113 people were identified as involved in the sin of intermarriage, this would be only one-third of one percent of the population. A number of suggestions have been offered for the surprising brevity of the list, among them: (1) only a partial list has been preserved; (2) only those found guilty of the charge of intermarriage are listed; and (3) only those who were found guilty and followed through by putting away their foreign wives and children are listed.

While there is no certainty on the exact nature of the list, it is clear that Ezra's ministry did not end the problem of intermarriage. Over 20 years later Nehemiah confronted it once again (Neh 13:23-29). The list in Ezra 10, like other OT lists, has variant names and variant spellings of some names.

10:18-19 The first four offenders were of the priestly family of Jedaiah (2:36). These priests vowed to put away their foreign wives and offered **a ram from the flock for their guilt**. While this action is recorded only here in reference to the priests, it is probable that this was the pattern for all who were found guilty.

10:20-22 Offenders from the three other priestly families (Immer, Pashhur, and Harim) represented in the return (2:37-39) are listed.

10:34 The second mention (v. 29) of the family name Bani is unusual since family names were usually unique and served as identifiers for their descendants. Some scholars suggest that the text originally read "Bigvai," a person mentioned in the return (2:14) and later in 8:14. The name **Uel** does not occur anywhere else in the OT. A variant of Uel is *Joel*.

10:40 The name **Machnadebai** is probably not a Hebrew name and is found nowhere else in the OT. Its position in the verse may suggest that it originally designated a family group, possibly "Zaccai's descendants" (2:9).

10:44 The abrupt ending of the book of Ezra, with no summations or conclusions, is attributable to the fact that Ezra was originally joined with Nehemiah. Thus this was not originally a closing to a book, but merely a closing to the section on Ezra's early ministry. The focus then shifted to Nehemiah, who, like Ezra, faithfully served God.

Nehemiah
Introduction

See the Introduction to Ezra for the introductory material.

Outline of Nehemiah

I.   Rebuilding the Walls (1:1–6:19)
    A. Jerusalem's plight and Nehemiah's prayer (1:1-11)
    B. Nehemiah's mission (2:1-10)
    C. Surveying the walls (2:11-20)
    D. Rebuilding begun (3:1-32)
    E. Opposition and oppression (4:1–6:19)

II. Restoration of the Community (7:1–13:31)
    A. Repopulating Jerusalem (7:1-73a)
    B. The covenant renewed (7:73b–10:39)
    C. Repopulating Jerusalem [continued] (11:1-21)
    D. Essential records (11:22-36)
    E. Temple personnel (12:1-26)
    F. Dedication of the wall (12:27-47)
    G. Nehemiah's further reforms (13:1-31)

1 The words of Nehemiah[a] son of Hacaliah:

News from Jerusalem

During the month of Chislev[A,b] in the twentieth year,[B,c] when I was in the fortress city of Susa,[d] [2] Hanani,[e] one of my brothers, arrived with men from Judah, and I questioned them about Jerusalem and the Jewish remnant[f] that had survived the exile.[g] [3] They said to me, "The remnant in the province,[h] who survived the exile, are in great trouble and disgrace. Jerusalem's wall has been broken down, and its gates have been burned down."[i]

Nehemiah's Prayer

[4] When I heard these words, I sat down and wept. I mourned for a number of days, fasting and praying[j] before the God of heaven.[k] [5] I said,[l]

•Yahweh, the God of heaven, the great and awe-inspiring God who keeps His gracious covenant with those who love Him[m] and keep His commands,[n] [6] let Your eyes be open and Your ears be attentive[o] to hear Your servant's prayer that I now pray to You day and night[p] for Your servants, the Israelites. I confess the sins[c] we have committed against You. Both I and my father's house have sinned.[q] [7] We have acted corruptly toward You and have not kept the commands, statutes, and ordinances You gave Your servant Moses.[r] [8] Please remember what You commanded Your servant Moses: "If you are unfaithful, I will scatter you among the peoples.[s] [9] But if you return to Me and carefully observe My commands, even though your exiles were banished to the ends of the earth,[D] I will gather them from there and bring them to the place where I chose to have My name dwell."[t] [10] They are Your servants and Your people. You redeemed them by Your great power and strong hand.[u] [11] Please, Lord, let Your ear be attentive[v] to the prayer of Your servant and to that of Your servants who delight to revere Your name. Give Your servant success today,[w] and have compassion on him in the presence of this man.[E,x]

At the time, I was the king's cupbearer.[y]

Cross references

a 1:1 Neh 10:1
b Zch 7:1
c Ezr 7:1,8; Neh 2:1
d Est 1:2; Dn 8:2
e 1:2 Neh 7:2
f Ezr 9:8,15; Is 10:20-22
g Ezr 1:11
h 1:3 Ezr 2:1; Neh 11:3
i Ezr 4:12-13,16; Neh 2:13
j 1:4 Ezr 9:3; 10:1; Ps 35:13; Dn 9:3; Lk 2:37; Ac 13:3
k Ezr 1:2; Neh 2:4
l 1:5-11 Dn 9:4-19
m 1:5 Dt 6:5; 7:9-11; Rm 8:28
n Dn 9:4
o 1:6 2Ch 6:40
p Ps 88:1-2; 2Tm 1:3
q Dn 9:5,8,20
r 1:7 2Ch 29:6; Dn 9:5-6,11
s 1:8 Dt 4:25-27; 28:64; Dn 9:7
t 1:9 Dt 30:1-5
u 1:10 Dt 9:29; Dn 9:15
v 1:11 2Ch 6:40
w Gn 24:12
x Neh 2:1
y Gn 40:20

A 1:1 = November–December   B 1:1 Artaxerxes reigned 465-425 B.C.   C 1:6 Lit sins of the Israelites   D 1:9 Lit skies   E 1:11 = the king

---

1:1 In both the Hebrew and the Greek OT, the books of Ezra and Nehemiah were originally a single book. Yet the connection between them is rather abrupt and without any real transition (see note at Ezr 10:44). Nehemiah, whose name means "Yahweh has comforted," is identified as **son of Hacaliah**, to distinguish him from other people named Nehemiah (3:16; 7:7; Ezr 2:2) in the same era. The prophet Nahum's name is a shorter form of Nehemiah's.

The text does not identify **the twentieth year**, but the context from Ezra 10 along with the statement of Neh 2:1 identifies it as the twentieth year of King Artaxerxes of Persia (445 B.C.). The mention of the month of **Chislev** is difficult because 2:1 describes a later event occurring in the month of Nisan, also in the twentieth year. Chislev was parallel to our late November to early December, while Nisan was in the spring. Since Nehemiah served in the royal Persian court, it is possible that he used the official regnal calendar in which the year began in the month a king came to power. In such a calendar Nisan could follow Chislev. **Susa**, in southwestern Iran, became the capital of Persia during the time of Darius. Later kings such as Xerxes and Artaxerxes used it as their winter palace.

1:2 Hanani is described by Nehemiah as **one of my brothers**. While this could be used loosely to refer to his Jewish companions, it probably means his literal brother due to the mention of Hanani in 7:2.

1:3 The people **in the province** of Judah (v. 2), which the Persians called (Hb) *Yehud*, were suffering because their city was in such terrible condition. Many scholars maintain that Nehemiah's response (v. 4) suggests this was a recent development, possibly referring to Rehum's opposition (Ezr 4:9-16). The HCSB translation of the verbs here, **has been broken down . . . have been burned**, reinforces this understanding of the passage.

1:4 Nehemiah's response was like that of his predecessor, Ezra (Ezr 9:3-5), who humbled himself before God.

1:5-11 Nehemiah's prayer, while shorter than Ezra's (see note at Ezr 9:6-15), is also written in late biblical Hebrew style found in other penitential prayers of that era (Neh 9:5-37; Dn 9:4-19). Like them it reflects the language of Deuteronomy, acknowledging that Israel's adversities had resulted from the nation's covenant unfaithfulness and that their present survival was due solely to God's abundant mercy.

1:5-6 Addressing God as **Yahweh, the God of heaven** is not common in the OT, but it does occur several other times (Gn 24:7; 2Ch 36:23; Jnh 1:9). This description of God is similar to the opening verse of Daniel's prayer: "the great and awe-inspiring God who keeps His gracious covenant with those who love Him and keep His commands" (Dn 9:4). Like Ezra (Ezr 9:6), Nehemiah also identified with the sin of his people, confessing that **both I and my father's house have sinned**.

1:8-9 Nehemiah alluded to Moses' warning (Dt 4:27; 28:64) that God would **scatter** Israel **among the peoples** if they were unfaithful to the covenant, and then he summarized God's promise through Moses (Dt 30:1-5) that repentance would bring restoration (Neh 1:9). Repentance is described as **return to Me**, using the primary OT term (Hb *shuv*) for repentance that depicts a turning from sin toward God.

1:10 Just as Moses had interceded for His sinful people, reminding God that Israel was His people whom He had brought out of Egypt (Ex 32:11), so too Nehemiah reminded God that they were His **servants** and His **people** whom He had **redeemed**.

1:11 The reference to **this man** has led some scholars to suggest impropriety on Nehemiah's part for referring to King Artaxerxes in such a way. But the context here is a private

Nehemiah Sent to Jerusalem

2 During the month of Nisan[A] in the twentieth year of King Artaxerxes,[a] when wine was set before him, I took the wine and gave it to the king. I had never been sad in his presence, [2] so the king said to me, "Why are you[B] sad, when you aren't sick? This is nothing but depression."[C,b]

I was overwhelmed with fear [3] and replied to the king, "May the king live forever! Why should I[D] not be sad when the city where my ancestors are buried lies in ruins and its gates have been destroyed by fire?"[c]

[4] Then the king asked me, "What is your request?"

So I prayed to the God of heaven[d] [5] and answered the king, "If it pleases the king, and if your servant has found favor with you, send me to Judah and to the city where my ancestors are buried,[E,e] so that I may rebuild it."[f]

[a]2:1 Ezr 7:1,8; Neh 1:1
[b]2:1-2 Pr 15:13
[c]2:3 Ezr 4:12,21; Neh 1:3
[d]2:4 Neh 1:4
[e]2:5 Neh 1:3
[f]Ezr 4:21; Dn 9:18

[A]2:1 = March–April; called Abib in the pre-exilic period; Ex 13:4; Dt 16:1   [B]2:2 Lit *Why is your face*   [C]2:2 Lit *sadness of heart*
[D]2:3 Lit *my face*   [E]2:5 Lit *city, the house of the graves of my fathers,*

---

prayer addressed to God who knew very well who "this man" was and that Nehemiah would need divine help in dealing with him. The Persian rulers were famous for the irrevocability of their laws, as Daniel discovered when the "law of the Medes and Persians" (Dn 6:8,12,15) was brought against him. Nehemiah faced the daunting task of asking Artaxerxes to reverse his previous proclamation (Ezr 4:23) stopping all construction in Jerusalem. Only at the end of the prayer does it become clear why a Jewish man like Nehemiah thought he would ever get to address the Persian king: **I was the king's cupbearer.** The cupbearer was not only responsible for choosing appropriate wines for the king, but he tasted them himself to assure they were not poisoned.

2:1-3 It is not clear why Nehemiah waited nearly four months to bring his request to King Artaxerxes (see note at 1:1 for the **month of Nisan**). It is possible that the king spent the winter in Babylon rather than in Susa. Ancient records attest to this happening occasionally. It is also possible that Nehemiah waited for the (Hb) *tukta,* a Persian feast in which the king would often grant the requests of his supplicants. Nehemiah's explanation for his sadness was carefully expressed. He did not mention Jerusalem by name, since it may have carried negative connotations from the past (Ezr 4:12), but he referred to it as **the city where my ancestors are buried.** The Persian rulers went to great expense building tombs for their ancestors. Nehemiah's concern for the condition of his ancestors' tombs would certainly strike a sympathetic chord with the Persian king.

2:5 Nehemiah's request to **rebuild** Jerusalem was bold in

The Return from Exile

PHASE	DATE	SCRIPTURE REFERENCE	JEWISH LEADER	PERSIAN RULER	EXTENT OF THE RETURN	EVENTS OF THE RETURN
First	538 B.C.	Ezra 1–6	Zerubbabel Jeshua	Cyrus	1) Anyone who wanted to return could go 2) The temple in Jerusalem was to be rebuilt 3) Royal treasury provided funding of the temple rebuilding 4) Gold and silver worship articles taken from temple by Nebuchadnezzar were returned	1) Burnt offerings were made 2) Festival of Booths was celebrated 3) The rebuilding of the temple was begun 4) Persian ruler ordered rebuilding to be ceased 5) Darius, King of Persia, ordered rebuilding to be resumed in 520 B.C. 6) Temple was completed and dedicated in 516 B.C.
Second	458 B.C.	Ezra 7–10	Ezra	Artaxerxes Longimas	1) Anyone who wanted to return could go 2) Royal treasury provided funding 3) Jewish civil magistrates and judges were allowed	Men of Israel intermarried with foreign women
Third	444 B.C.	Nehemiah 1–13	Nehemiah	Artaxerxes Longimas	Rebuilding of Jerusalem was allowed	1) Rebuilding of wall of Jerusalem was opposed by Sanballat the Horonite, Tobiah the Ammonite, and Gesham the Arab 2) Rebuilding of wall was completed in 52 days 3) Walls were dedicated 4) Ezra read the book of the law to the people 5) Nehemiah initiated reforms

⁶The king, with the queen seated beside him, asked me, "How long will your journey take, and when will you return?" So I gave him a definite time,ᵃ and it pleased the king to send me.

⁷I also said to the king: "If it pleases the king, let me have letters written to the governors of the region west of the Euphrates River,ᵇ so that they will grant me safe passage until I reach Judah.ᶜ ⁸And let me have a letter written to Asaph, keeper of the king's forest, so that he will give me timber to rebuild the gates of the temple's fortress,ᵈ the city wall, and the home where I will live."ᴬ,ᵉ The king granted my requests, for I was graciously strengthened by my God.ᴮ,ᶠ

⁹I went to the governors of the region west of the Euphrates and gave them the king's letters.ᵍ The king had also sent officers of the infantry and cavalry with me. ¹⁰When Sanballat the Horoniteʰ and Tobiah the Ammonite offi-

cial heard that someone had come to seek the well-being of the Israelites, they were greatly displeased.ⁱ

Preparing to Rebuild the Walls

¹¹After I arrived in Jerusalem and had been there three days,ʲ ¹²I got up at night and took a few men with me. I didn't tell anyone what my God had laid on my heart to do for Jerusalem. The only animal I tookᶜ was the one I was riding. ¹³I went out at night through the Valley Gate toward the Serpent'sᴰ Well and the Dung Gate,ᵏ and I inspected the walls of Jerusalem that had been broken down and its gates that had been destroyed by fire.ˡ ¹⁴I went on to the Fountain Gateᵐ and the King's Pool,ⁿ but farther down it became too narrow for my animal to go through. ¹⁵So I went up at night by way of the valley and inspected the wall. Then heading back, I entered through the Valley Gateᵒ and returned. ¹⁶The officials did not

ᵃ2:6 Neh 13:6
ᵇ2:7 Ezr 4:8-9; 8:36
ᶜEzr 8:22
ᵈ2:8 Neh 7:2
ᵉEzr 3:7
ᶠEzr 7:6; Neh 2:18
ᵍ2:9 Ezr 8:36
ʰ2:10 Jos 16:3,5; 18:13
ⁱNeh 4:7
ʲ2:11 Ezr 8:32
ᵏ2:13 Neh 3:13
ˡEzr 4:12; Neh 1:3
ᵐ2:14 Neh 3:15; 12:37
ⁿ2Kg 18:17; 20:20
ᵒ2:15 Neh 3:13

ᴬ2:8 Lit enter   ᴮ2:8 Lit for the gracious hand of my God was on me   ᶜ2:12 Lit animal with me   ᴰ2:13 Or Dragon's

---

light of the king's earlier decision (Ezr 4:12-16) to stop all construction on the project.

2:6 The word **queen** here is a rare term (Hb shagel) that occurs only here and in Ps 45:9. Both ancient and modern commentators suggest that this term identified this woman as a concubine or a sexual favorite of the king. This is suggested because the term derives from a verb (Hb shagal) that often indicates illicit sexual activity.

2:7-8 Nehemiah needed not only time away from Artaxerxes' court, but also official royal documents for the **governors . . . west of the Euphrates River** (lit "Beyond the River") who were opposed to any building in Jerusalem (v. 10). His request for timber for the **gates of the temple's fortress** probably refers to a military structure north of the temple that provided protection for the temple and its worshipers, and probably included the two towers mentioned in 3:1.

2:9 Some have criticized Nehemiah for accepting military protection, which Ezra refused (Ezr 8:22-23). Nehemiah's decision did not reflect a lack of faith on his part, but rather his trust that this was part of God's provision for him.

2:10 This verse introduces opposition as a recurring

theme throughout the book and mentions two of Nehemiah's three primary opponents. **Sanballat**, whose name is Babylonian (sin-uballat, "the god Sin has given life"), may have descended from a family displaced by the Assyrians and resettled in the region of Samaria (2Kg 17:24-33). He may have worshiped Yahweh, since his children Shelemiah and Delaiah both have names compounded with the divine name. Sanballat likely was serving already as governor of Samaria, the hill country region north of Judah (Hb Yehud). The description of Sanballat as **the Horonite** probably refers to his origin from either Upper or Lower Beth-horon northwest of Jerusalem (Jos 18:13). Some scholars contend that he was a high official working for Sanballat and that his description as **the Ammonite** reflects his ancestry. Others maintain that Tobiah was from a Jewish family living east of the Jordan River in the Ammonite region and that Tobiah was the governor of this province. Clearly both Sanballat and Tobiah were committed to thwarting Nehemiah's plans.

2:12 Nehemiah probably limited the number of men and animals during his night-time reconnaissance of Jerusalem to avoid detection by those who were sympathetic to Sanballat and Tobiah.

2:13-15 Nehemiah's description of his inspection of the city in this passage, along with the more detailed account of rebuilding in chapter 3, provide the best written information for reconstructing the dimensions of Jerusalem in the fifth century B.C. One school of thought argues that the walls rebuilt by Nehemiah included only the City of David and the temple area. Another maintains that the rebuilt walls followed the eighth-century walls, including the southwestern hill area that was within the walls of preexilic Jerusalem. Furthermore, some archaeologists maintain that Nehemiah abandoned the eastern wall because of the extensive rubble and built a new, more defensible wall on the crest of the hill. Others insist that he rebuilt the remains of the preexilic wall further down the slope. Nehemiah's inspection tour began on the western side of Jerusalem and proceeded counterclockwise around the city.

2:13 Nehemiah and his men headed south from the **Valley**

Golden drinking cup. Nehemiah was cupbearer for Artaxerxes I, king of Persia.

know where I had gone or what I was doing, for I had not yet told the Jews, priests, nobles, officials, or the rest of those who would be doing the work. ¹⁷So I said to them, "You see the trouble we are in. Jerusalem lies in ruins and its gates have been burned down.ᵃ Come, let's rebuild Jerusalem's wall,ᵇ so that we will no longer be a disgrace." ¹⁸I told them how the gracious hand of my God had been on me,ᶜ and what the king had said to me.

They said, "Let's start rebuilding," and they were encouragedᴬ to do this good work.

¹⁹When Sanballat the Horonite, Tobiah the Ammonite official,ᵈ and Geshem the Arabᵉ heard about this, they mocked and despised us, and said, "What is this you're doing? Are you rebelling against the king?"

²⁰I gave them this reply, "The God of heaven is the One who will grant us success. We, His servants, will start building, but you have no share, right, or historic claim in Jerusalem."ᶠ

Rebuilding the Walls

3 Eliashib the high priestᵍ and his fellow priests began rebuilding the Sheep Gate.ʰ

ᵃ2:17 Ezr 4:12;
Neh 1:3; 2:3
ᵇNeh 2:5
ᶜ2:18 Ezr 7:9;
Neh 2:8
ᵈ2:19 Neh 4:7
ᵉNeh 6:1,6
ᶠ2:19-20 Ezr
4:3-4
ᵍ3:1 Neh 12:10;
13:4,7,28
ʰNeh 3:32;
12:39; Jn 5:2
ⁱNeh 12:39; Zch
14:10
ʲ3:2 Ezr 2:34;
Neh 7:36
ᵏNeh 12:10
ˡ3:3 Neh 12:39;
Zph 1:10
ᵐNeh 6:1; 7:1
ⁿ3:4 Ezr 8:33
ᵒEzr 10:15; Neh
3:30; 6:17-18
ᵖ3:5 Neh 3:27;
Am 1:1
ᵠ3:6 Neh 12:39

They dedicated it and installed its doors. After building the wall to the Tower of the Hundred and the Tower of Hananel,ⁱ they dedicated it. ²The men of Jerichoʲ built next to Eliashib,ᵏ and next to them Zaccur son of Imri built.

Fish Gate

³The sons of Hassenaah built the Fish Gate.ˡ They built it with beams and installed its doors, bolts, and bars.ᵐ ⁴Next to them Meremothⁿ son of Uriah, son of Hakkoz, made repairs. Beside them Meshullamᵒ son of Berechiah, son of Meshezabel, made repairs. Next to them Zadok son of Baana made repairs. ⁵Beside them the Tekoitesᵖ made repairs, but their nobles did not lift a finger to helpᴮ their supervisors.

Old Gate, Broad Wall, and Tower of the Ovens

⁶Joiada son of Paseah and Meshullam son of Besodeiah repaired the Oldᶜ Gate.ᵠ They built it with beams and installed its doors, bolts, and bars. ⁷Next to them the repairs were done by Melatiah the Gibeonite, Jadon the Meronothite,

---

ᴬ2:18 Lit *they put their hands*   ᴮ3:5 Lit *not bring their neck to the work of*   ᶜ3:6 Or *Jeshanah*

Gate toward the **Serpent's Well** (Hb *en hattannin*), which could be translated as "Dragon's Well" or as "Serpent's/Dragon's Eye." Nehemiah continued south to the **Dung Gate** at the lower tip of the city. This gate led to the Valley of Hinnom where garbage was dumped and burned. The term "Gehenna" is derived from the Hebrew term *ge-hinnom* (Valley of Hinnom).

2:14 Nehemiah followed the ruins of the wall north to the **Fountain Gate and the King's Pool** (probably the same place as the "Pool of Shelah" mentioned in 3:15). With the ruined walls on his left and the steep Kidron Valley on his right, his way was blocked and he dismounted. Archaeological investigations have shown that preexilic Jerusalem extended down this slope (called the Millo) toward the Kidron Valley. This area of rubble, still visible today, is 15 feet thick in some places.

2:16 While some assume the **officials** here (Hb *segen*) were Persian officials, it probably refers to the various leaders mentioned among the **Jews, priests, nobles**, and officials.

2:17 The word **disgrace** (Hb *cherpah*), often translated "shame" or "reproach," is the same word used to describe the state of the people in Jerusalem when Nehemiah's brother and his friends gave their report (1:3). The present sad state of the city was a "disgrace" to the city, its people, and above all, its God.

2:19 Nehemiah's third primary opponent appears in this verse: **Geshem the Arab**. Arabs are mentioned in the Bible from the ninth century B.C. on, sometimes aiding the Israelites, as at the battle of Qarqar in 853, and sometimes attacking them, as in the time of King Jehoram of Judah (2Ch 21:16). During Nehemiah's time the Arabs were led by Geshem, whose vast domain stretched from the Negev south of Judah all the way to Lower Egypt. Together with Sanballat and Tobiah, he **mocked** Nehemiah and his follow-

ers, even accusing them of sedition against their Persian overlord.

2:20 Nehemiah did not try to refute his enemy's claims, but he stated his trust in the **God of heaven**. The meaning of the phrase **historic claim** is not certain in this context. The Hebrew term it is based on *(zikkaron)* normally means "remembrance." It is used to describe the Passover as a spiritual memorial for the people of Israel (Ex 12:14). This may mean that Nehemiah's enemies not only had no legal right to the land, but also no right to participate in the worship of the community.

3:1-32 With the conclusion of chapter 2, the first-person narrative of Nehemiah ends and does not resume until 4:1. Chapter 3, possibly written by someone other than Nehemiah, is a third-person account of the completion of the construction and the installation of the doors. Yet 6:1 and 7:1 explicitly state that the doors in the gates had not yet been hung. This chapter may have been an official archive that was kept in the temple and was incorporated into the book of Nehemiah, at a later date and out of sequence, because of its detailed description of the reconstruction.

3:1 Only here in this chapter is the dedication of the gate or the walls mentioned, a significant event because **Eliashib the high priest** led it. This marked the beginning of the endeavor and emphasized the priests' dependence on God for the successful completion of the project.

3:4-5 In verses 1-3 the workers are described as "building" the wall and gates (Hb *banah*) while in most of the chapter the builders **made repairs** (Hb *chazaq*; lit "to strengthen"). This may suggest that the wall in the northern section near the Sheep Gate was so devastated that they had to start from scratch.

3:6 The mention of **the Old** (Hb *hayeshanah*) **Gate** is problematic. The Hebrew text reads "the Jeshanah Gate," an unlikely name, since the gate leading to Jeshanah (2Ch

and the men of Gibeon[a] and Mizpah, who were under the authority[A,b] of the governor[c] of the region west of the Euphrates River.[d] [8] After him Uzziel son of Harhaiah, the goldsmith,[e] made repairs, and next to him Hananiah son of the perfumer made repairs. They restored Jerusalem as far as the Broad Wall.[f]

[9] Next to them Rephaiah son of Hur, ruler over half the district of Jerusalem, made repairs. [10] After them Jedaiah son of Harumaph made repairs across from his house.[g] Next to him Hattush the son of Hashabneiah made repairs. [11] Malchijah son of Harim and Hasshub son of Pahath-moab made repairs to another section, as well as to the Tower of the Ovens.[h] [12] Beside him Shallum son of Hallohesh, ruler over half the district of Jerusalem, made repairs—he and his daughters.

Valley Gate, Dung Gate, and Fountain Gate

[13] Hanun and the inhabitants of Zanoah repaired the Valley Gate. They rebuilt it and installed its doors, bolts, and bars, and repaired 500 yards[B] of the wall to the Dung Gate.[i] [14] Malchijah son of Rechab, ruler over the district of Beth-haccherem,[j] repaired the Dung Gate.[k] He rebuilt it and installed its doors, bolts, and bars.

[15] Shallun[C] son of Col-hozeh, ruler over the district of Mizpah, repaired the Fountain Gate.[l] He rebuilt it and roofed it. Then he installed its doors, bolts, and bars. He also made repairs to the wall of the Pool of Shelah[m] near the king's garden,[n] as far as the stairs that descend from the city of David.[o]

[16] After him Nehemiah son of Azbuk, ruler over half the district of Beth-zur,[p] made re-

pairs up to a point opposite the tombs of David,[q] as far as the artificial pool[r] and the House of the Warriors.[s] [17] Next to him the Levites[t] made repairs under Rehum son of Bani. Beside him Hashabiah, ruler over half the district of Keilah,[u] made repairs for his district. [18] After him their fellow Levites made repairs under Binnui[D] son of Henadad, ruler over half the district of Keilah. [19] Next to him Ezer son of Jeshua, ruler over Mizpah, made repairs to another section opposite the ascent to the armory at the Angle.[v]

The Angle, Water Gate, and Tower on the Ophel

[20] After him Baruch son of Zabbai[E] diligently repaired another section, from the Angle to the door of the house of Eliashib the high priest.[w] [21] Beside him Meremoth[x] son of Uriah, son of Hakkoz, made repairs to another section, from the door of Eliashib's[y] house to the end of his house. [22] And next to him the priests from the surrounding area made repairs.

[23] After them Benjamin and Hasshub made repairs opposite their house. Beside them Azariah son of Maaseiah, son of Ananiah, made repairs beside his house. [24] After him Binnui[z] son of Henadad made repairs to another section, from the house of Azariah to the Angle and the corner. [25] Palal son of Uzai made repairs opposite the Angle and tower that juts out from the upper palace[F] of the king,[aa] by the courtyard of the guard.[ab] Beside him Pedaiah son of Parosh, [26] and the temple servants[ac] living on Ophel[G,ad] made repairs opposite the Water Gate[ae] toward the east and the tower that juts out. [27] Next to him the Tekoites[af] made repairs to another section from a point

[a]3:7 Jos 9:3
[b]2Kg 25:23; Jr 40:5-12
[c]Neh 2:7-8; 5:14
[d]Neh 2:7,9
[e]3:8 Neh 3:31, 32
[f]2Ch 32:5; Neh 12:38
[g]3:10 Neh 3:23,28
[h]3:11 2Ch 26:9; Neh 12:38
[i]3:13 Neh 2:13
[j]3:14 Jr 6:1
[k]Neh 2:13
[l]3:15 Neh 2:14; 12:37
[m]Is 8:6; Jn 9:7
[n]2Kg 25:4
[o]Neh 12:37
[p]3:16 Jos 15:58; 1Ch 2:45
[q]1Kg 2:10; Ac 2:29
[r]2Kg 20:20; Is 22:9-11
[s]2Sm 23:8-39
[t]3:17 Ezr 2:40; Neh 7:43
[u]1Sm 23:1-5
[v]3:19 2Ch 26:9
[w]3:20 Neh 3:1; 12:10
[x]3:21 Ezr 8:33
[y]Neh 3:1
[z]3:24 Ezr 8:33
[aa]3:25 Neh 12:37
[ab]Jr 32:2
[ac]3:26 Ezr 2:43,55-58; 7:7
[ad]Ezr 8:20; Neh 11:21
[ae]Neh 8:1
[af]3:27 Neh 3:5; Am 1:1

[A]3:7 Or *Mizpah, the seat* [B]3:13 Lit *1,000 cubits* [C]3:15 Some Hb mss, Syr read *Shallum* [D]3:18 Some Hb mss, Syr, LXX; Neh 3:24; other Hb mss, Vg read *Bavvai* [E]3:20 Alt Hb tradition, Vg read *Zaccai*; Ezr 2:9 [F]3:25 Or *and the upper tower that juts out from the palace* [G]3:26 = a hill in Jerusalem

---

13:19) should be on the north wall. This translation, like most others, reads the word not as a proper name but as an adjective meaning "old," thus the "Old Gate." Another option is to understand it as the Mishnah Gate or the "Second Gate" that led to the second district of the city mentioned in 2Kg 22:14.

3:8 The word **restored** (Hb *'azav*) normally means "to abandon." Most translations assume this verse and 4:2 use a rare homonymic verb meaning "to restore." It is not clear why the author would depart from his normal term for "restore" (Hb *chazaq*) and use a verb found only twice in the Hebrew Bible. Thus, some scholars and translations read this phrase as "they *abandoned* Jerusalem," that is, they did not attempt to follow the eighth-century walls but left out the western hill section of the city (see note at 2:13-15).

3:12 The work crew of **Shallum son of Hallohesh** was unique. Possibly he had no sons, but his family still joined in the work through the labor of **his daughters**.

3:15 This verse details reconstruction of the southeast corner of the city. The **Pool of Shelah** is probably the same as the King's Pool (2:14).

3:16 The text continues to describe construction from south to north along the eastern side of the city. The fact that the descriptions are not of gates and prominent places along the wall but locations within the city may be indirect evidence that Nehemiah abandoned the eighth-century wall lower down the valley and established a new wall closer to the summit (2:14).

3:19 The **Angle** (Hb *miqtso'a*) may refer to a prominent place where the wall changed direction. However, the term appears again (vv. 24-25) in what would seem to be another location. Possibly the "Angle" was a natural feature such as a hillside or escarpment.

3:26-27 The term **Ophel** means "swelling" and is used here to describe a hill. It can refer to the entire southeastern hill

opposite the great tower that juts out, as far as the wall of Ophel.[a]

Horse Gate, Inspection Gate, and Sheep Gate

[28] Each of the priests made repairs above the Horse Gate,[b] each opposite his own house. [29] After them Zadok son of Immer made repairs opposite his house. And beside him Shemaiah son of Shecaniah, guard of the East Gate, made repairs. [30] Next to him Hananiah son of Shelemiah and Hanun the sixth son of Zalaph made repairs to another section.

After them Meshullam son of Berechiah made repairs opposite his room. [31] Next to him Malchijah, one of the goldsmiths,[c] made repairs to the house of the temple servants[d] and the merchants, opposite the Inspection[A] Gate,

and as far as the upper room of the corner. [32] The goldsmiths[e] and merchants made repairs between the upper room of the corner and the Sheep Gate.[f]

Progress in Spite of Opposition

4 [B] When Sanballat[g] heard that we were rebuilding the wall,[h] he became furious. He mocked the Jews[i] [2] before his colleagues and the powerful men[c] of Samaria,[j] and said, "What are these pathetic Jews doing? Can they restore it by themselves? Will they offer sacrifices? Will they ever finish it? Can they bring these burnt stones[k] back to life from the mounds of rubble?"[l] [3] Then Tobiah the Ammonite,[m] who was beside him, said, "Indeed, even if a fox[n] climbed up what they are building, he would break down their stone wall!"

A3:31 Or *Muster*   B4:1 Neh 3:33 in Hb   C4:2 Or *the army*

a3:27 Neh 11:21
b3:28 2Ch 23:15
c3:31 Neh 3:8
dNeh 7:46-56
e3:32 Neh 3:8,21
fNeh 3:1; Jn 5:2
g4:1 Neh 2:10,19; 4:7
hNeh 2:17,19
iNeh 2:19
j4:2 Ezr 4:9-10
k2Ch 26:19
l2Ch 26:19; Neh 1:3
m4:3 Neh 2:10,19; 6:1,14
nLm 5:18

of the ancient City of David or, as in this verse, to the area where the palace and the temple were situated. The **Water Gate** presumably provided access to the spring of Gihon. It was by the "Water Gate" that Nehemiah later gathered the people for a public reading of the Torah (8:1).

3:28 The prophet Jeremiah's reference to the **Horse Gate** (Jr 31:40) might suggest it was a gate on the eastern wall of the city, but the "Horses Gate" mentioned in 2Ch 23:15 was the gate at the entrance to the palace/temple complex within the city.

3:29 The **East Gate** was not in the outer city wall but led into the temple complex (Ezk 40:6). **Shemaiah** repaired the section of the wall near where he served.

3:31 The **Inspection Gate** (or the "Muster Gate" or the "Pa-

rade Gate") was probably on the northeast corner of the city wall. It may be identical to the Benjamin Gate where the prophet Jeremiah was arrested (Jr 37:13).

3:32 The **goldsmiths and merchants** "closed the loop" as they worked on repairing the walls up to where the work began at the **Sheep Gate** (v. 1) at the northeastern end of the city. D. J. Clines estimates the length of the wall around its perimeter to be about a mile and a half (p. 158). If Nehemiah's wall also included the western hill area of Jerusalem (v. 8), the distance was considerably greater.

4:1-6 These verses in the Hebrew Bible are a continuation of chapter 3 (3:33-38).

4:1-2 The Nehemiah Memoir (see "Structure" in the Introduction to Ezra) resumes again with the renewed op-

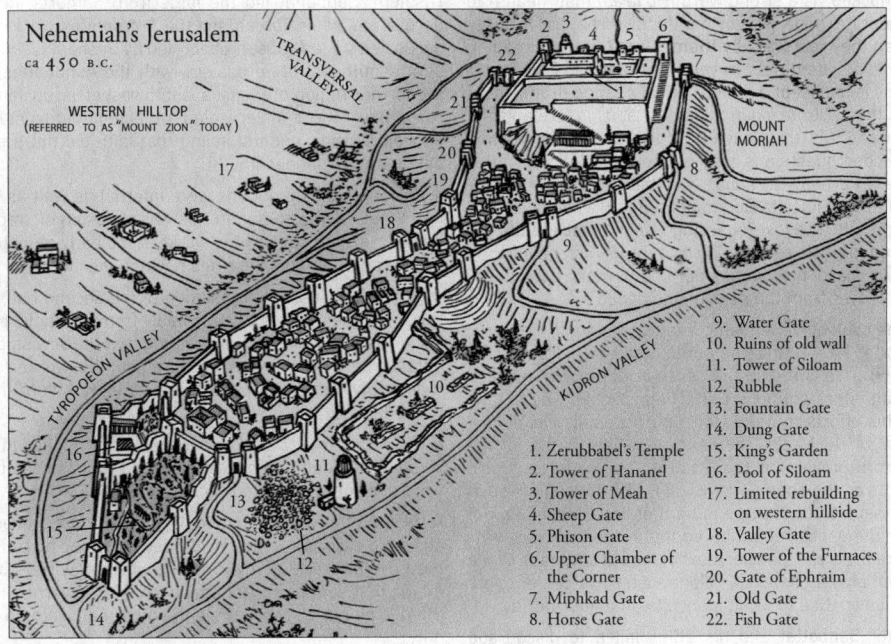

Nehemiah's Jerusalem
ca 450 B.C.

9. Water Gate
10. Ruins of old wall
11. Tower of Siloam
12. Rubble
13. Fountain Gate
14. Dung Gate
15. King's Garden
16. Pool of Siloam
17. Limited rebuilding on western hillside
18. Valley Gate
19. Tower of the Furnaces
20. Gate of Ephraim
21. Old Gate
22. Fish Gate

1. Zerubbabel's Temple
2. Tower of Hananel
3. Tower of Meah
4. Sheep Gate
5. Phison Gate
6. Upper Chamber of the Corner
7. Miphkad Gate
8. Horse Gate

⁴Listen, our God, for we are despised. Make their insults return on their own heads and let them be taken as plunder to a land of captivity. ⁵Do not cover their •guilt or let their sin be erased from Your sight, because they have provoked^A the builders.^a

⁶So we rebuilt the wall until the entire wall was joined together up to half its height, for the people had the will to keep working.^b

^{7B} When Sanballat, Tobiah, and the Arabs,^c Ammonites, and Ashdodites heard that the repair to the walls of Jerusalem was progressing and that the gaps were being closed,^d they became furious.^e ⁸They all plotted together to come and fight against Jerusalem and throw it into confusion. ⁹So we prayed to our God and stationed a guard because of them day and night.

¹⁰In Judah, it was said:^c

The strength of the laborer fails,
since there is so much rubble.
We will never be able
to rebuild the wall.

¹¹And our enemies said, "They won't know or see anything until we're among them and can kill them and stop the work." ¹²When the Jews who lived nearby arrived, they said to us time and again,^D "Everywhere you turn, they attack^E

us." ¹³So I stationed people behind the lowest sections of the wall, at the vulnerable areas. I stationed them by families with their swords, spears, and bows. ¹⁴After I made an inspection, I stood up and said to the nobles, the officials, and the rest of the people,^f "Don't be afraid of them.^g Remember the great and awe-inspiring Lord, and fight for your countrymen, your sons and daughters, your wives and homes."^h

Sword and Trowel

¹⁵When our enemies heard that we knew their scheme and that God had frustrated it, every one of us returned to his own work on the wall. ¹⁶From that day on, half of my men did the work while the other half held spears, shields, bows, and armor.ⁱ The officers supported all the people of Judah, ¹⁷who were rebuilding the wall. The laborers who carried the loads worked with one hand and held a weapon with the other. ¹⁸Each of the builders had his sword strapped around his waist while he was building, and the trumpeter was beside me. ¹⁹Then I said to the nobles, the officials, and the rest of the people:^j "The work is enormous and spread out, and we are separated far from one another along the wall.^k ²⁰Wherever you hear the trumpet sound, rally to us there. Our God will fight for us!"^l ²¹So we continued the work, while half of the men were holding

^a4:4-5 Neh 6:14; Jr 18:23
^b4:6 Neh 2:20; 6:1,15
^c4:7 Neh 2:19
^dNeh 4:2-3
^eNeh 2:10
^f4:14 Neh 2:16
^gDt 1:29; Ezr 3:3; 4:4
^h2Sm 10:12
ⁱ4:16 2Ch 18:33
^j4:19 Neh 2:16
^kNeh 3:1-32
^l4:20 Nm 10:1-9; Dt 1:30

^A4:5 Or *provoked You in front of*   ^B4:7 Neh 4:1 in Hb   ^C4:10 Lit *Judah said*   ^D4:12 Lit *us 10 times*   ^E4:12 Or *again from every place,* *"You must return to*

position of **Sanballat**. He **became furious** and **mocked the Jews**. "Mocked" is a strong word (Hb *la'ag*) that means "to jeer, to deride." The first of his derisive rhetorical questions, **Can they restore it by themselves?** involves reading a rare (and debated) Hebrew verb (see note at 3:8). Another possibility is to accept a minor textual change (from Hb *la-hem* "to them," to *le'lohim* "to God") and understand the question as, "Will they leave it all to God?" The meaning of the second question is also not certain: **Will they offer sacrifices?** Perhaps the sense was that the Jews would offer enough sacrifices to God to persuade Him to help them rebuild the city. The jest regarding bringing **back to life** the **burnt stones** was a recognition that the Jewish people had no time to quarry new stones but had to make do with the rubble left over from the destruction of 586 B.C.

4:4-5 The book of Nehemiah contains two lengthy prayers, one private (1:4-11) and one public (the prayer/confession of chap. 9). This is the first of seven brief prayers in which Nehemiah either petitions God's help or asks God to take note of his efforts to fulfill God's purposes for His people (5:19; 6:9,14; 13:14,22). The sentiment here is that of the imprecatory prayers of the Psalms that calls for God's judgments on the enemy (Pss 69; 83; 137; 139). While such a prayer seems out of place in light of Jesus' teaching (Mt 5:43-47), it must be remembered that Nehemiah was writing before the cross in the context of the old covenant. While we cannot pray a prayer like Nehemiah's, we can emulate his passion for God to bring justice to an unjust world.

4:7-9 After **Sanballat** and his allies failed to discourage

Nehemiah and the people, they virtually surrounded Jerusalem. Sanballat led the force from Samaria, north of Jerusalem, while **Tobiah** and the **Ammonites** were east of Jerusalem. The **Arabs**, probably led by Geshem (2:19), were south/southeast of Jerusalem, with the **Ashdodites**, from the former region of Philistia, southwest of Jerusalem. The response of those in Jerusalem reflected their trust in God as well as their understanding that faith did not preclude action but demanded it (v. 9).

4:10 Nehemiah's problems were internal as well as external. Whether the slogan in this verse was an oft-repeated jingle or a song sung by the workers, it clearly reflected the discouragement and pessimism within the city.

4:12 Another possible translation of the second half of the verse is, "they said to us repeatedly from all [their] places, 'You must return to us,'" suggesting that the Jewish people outside Jerusalem were encouraging the workers from their towns laboring in Jerusalem to leave before the city was attacked.

4:13-14 Nehemiah's skill as a leader is exemplified in these verses. Although enemies surrounded him and the people were discouraged, he took action.

4:15-17 As the work resumed, Nehemiah took precautions against a surprise attack. He divided the group he called **my men** (Hb *ne'aray*; lit "my youths"), which may have been a militia that supported Nehemiah's role as governor. Half of them joined in the work while the other half were on guard duty.

spears from daybreak until the stars came out. [22]At that time, I also said to the people, "Let everyone and his servant spend the night inside Jerusalem, so that they can stand guard by night and work by day." [23]And I, my brothers, my men, and the guards with me never took off our clothes. Each carried his weapon, even when washing.[A]

Social Injustice

5 There was a widespread outcry from the people and their wives against their Jewish countrymen. [2]Some were saying, "We, our sons, and our daughters are numerous. Let us get grain so that we can eat and live." [3]Others were saying, "We are mortgaging our fields, vineyards, and homes to get grain during the famine."[a] [4]Still others were saying, "We have borrowed money to pay the king's tax[b] on our fields and vineyards.[c] [5]We and our children are just like our countrymen and their children, yet we are subjecting our sons and daughters to slavery.[d] Some of our daughters are already enslaved,[e] but we are powerless[B] because our fields and vineyards belong to others."

[6]I became extremely angry[f] when I heard their outcry and these complaints. [7]After seriously considering the matter, I accused the nobles and officials, saying to them, "Each of you is charging his countrymen interest."[g] So I called a large assembly against them [8]and said, "We have done our best to buy back our Jewish countrymen who were sold to foreigners, but now you sell your own countrymen, and we have to buy them back."[h] They remained silent and could not say a word.[i] [9]Then I said, "What you are doing isn't right. Shouldn't you walk in the *fear of our God[j] and not invite the reproach of our foreign enemies?[k] [10]Even I, as well as my brothers and my servants, have been lending them money and grain. Please, let us stop charging this interest.[C] [11]Return their fields, vineyards, olive groves, and houses to them immediately,

*a*5:3 Hg 1:5-11
*b*5:4 Ezr 4:13; 7:24
*c*5:2-4 Dt 15:7-8
*d*5:5 Lv 25:39-43
*e*Ex 21:7-11
*f*5:6 Ex 11:8; Eph 4:26-27
*g*5:7 Ex 22:25; Dt 23:19-20
*h*5:8 Ex 21:8; Lv 25:39-42
*i*Jr 8:9
*j*5:9 Lv 25:36
*k*2Sm 12:14; Neh 4:4

A4:23 Lit *Each his weapon the water*   **B**5:5 Lit *but there is not the power in our hand*   **C**5:10 Or *us forgive these debts*

4:18-22 Because the defenders were spread so thinly around the city, Nehemiah had **the trumpeter** beside him, so they could concentrate their forces quickly in case of attack. Having everyone **spend the night inside Jerusalem** not only bolstered the defenses of the city but also kept the discouraged or the fearful from deserting during the night.

4:23 Nehemiah and his military entourage set the example for diligence in the face of danger: [we] **never took off our clothes**. Another possibility for understanding the final phrase of the verse is to read the last word of the Hebrew text (*hammayim*; "the water") as "the right hand" (Hb *hayyamin*), making the phrase, "each his weapon in his right hand." Nehemiah and his people in this chapter exemplify the Benedictine credo, (Lat) *ora et labora* ("pray and work"). They sought God's blessing and His protection while working with the strength He gave them to accomplish the task for which they prayed.

5:1-19 Nehemiah's effort in rebuilding the walls was a crucial step in securing the safety and prosperity of Jerusalem and Judah, but the need for workers inside Jerusalem made an already bad economic situation for the poor even worse. The postexilic prophets attest to the difficult economic conditions during this era, with crop failures and Persian taxes adding to their troubles (Hg 1:6-11; Mal 3:7-15). As in the eighth century B.C. (Am 2:6-8; 4:1-5), so once again the gap between rich and poor grew worse—the very situation the OT law discouraged by assuring property rights and the Year of Jubilee.

5:1 The first group of **people and their wives** complaining were the landless poor, who depended on their husband's work as day laborers for their daily food. Their absence from the home to work in Jerusalem was causing real distress.

5:3 The second group consisted of those who were forced to mortgage their property in order to survive. These loans would normally be paid back at harvest time in the fall, but with the men working in Jerusalem during August and early September, many were facing foreclosure.

5:4 The third group that brought their complaints had **bor-**rowed money to pay the king's tax. Documents from Babylonia and Egypt during this period attest to families unable to pay their taxes and thus forced to sell their children into servitude. Many finally lost their land and became part of the landless working poor. During this period the interest rate for borrowing money to pay taxes was often between 40 and 50 percent.

5:5 For all three groups (vv. 2-4) the result was the same: parents were selling their **children** into **slavery**. This was allowed under the OT law (Ex 21:2-11) but with some important qualifications (Lv 25:39-46). Often parents would sell their children before selling their property, because the sale of property precluded the possibility of earning the money to buy the children back. The situation was even more critical for **daughters** sold into servitude, because their master or his son could pressure them into marriage. Moreover, they were also more susceptible to sexual exploitation. Their daughters are described as **enslaved**, which is from a Hebrew term *(kavash)* that generally means "subdue," sometimes used in the OT with sexual connotations ("violate" in Est 7:8).

5:7 The translation of Nehemiah's accusation here assumes the issue was usury: **Each of you is charging his countrymen interest**. But the terms used in this context may suggest instead that the issue was acting as a creditor and seizing the properties of those in default—"pressing claims" or "seizing collateral." If this was the case, the actions of the "nobles and officials" were not illegal, but nevertheless unconscionable in light of the dire state of the people.

5:8 Most likely Nehemiah was not referring to buying back slaves while living in Babylonia, but recently having **to buy back** Israelites sold to neighboring nations. The nobles and officials were perpetuating the problem.

5:10 It is unlikely that Nehemiah was confessing sin about these issues. It was considered an act of kindness to lend to the poor (Ps 37:26; 112:5; Pr 19:17). What was wrong was taking advantage of the poor (Dt 15:7-11; 24:10-13) and demanding payment in light of the severe economic

along with the percentage[A] of the money, grain, new wine, and olive oil[a] that you have been assessing them."

[12] They responded: "We will return these things and require nothing more from them.[b] We will do as you say."

So I summoned the priests and made everyone take an oath[c] to do this. [13] I also shook the folds of my robe and said, "May God likewise shake from his house and property everyone who doesn't keep this promise. May he be shaken out[d] and have nothing!"

The whole assembly said, "•Amen," and they praised the LORD. Then the people did as they had promised.[e]

Good and Bad Governors

[14] Furthermore, from the day King Artaxerxes[f] appointed me to be their governor in the land of Judah—from the twentieth year until his thirty-second year, 12 years[g]—I and my associates never ate from the food allotted to the governor. [15] The governors[h] who preceded me had heavily burdened the people, taking food and wine from them, as well as a pound[B] of silver. Their subordinates also oppressed the people, but I didn't do this, because of the

fear of God.[i] [16] Instead, I devoted myself to the construction of the wall,[j] and all my subordinates were gathered there for the work. We didn't buy any land.[k]

[17] There were 150 Jews and officials, as well as guests from the surrounding nations at my table.[l] [18] Each[C] day, one ox, six choice sheep, and some fowl were prepared for me. An abundance of all kinds of wine was provided every 10 days.[m] But I didn't demand the food allotted to the governor, because the burden on the people was so heavy.

[19] Remember me favorably, my God, for all that I have done for this people.[n]

Attempts to Discourage the Builders

6 When Sanballat, Tobiah, Geshem the Arab, and the rest of our enemies[o] heard that I had rebuilt the wall and that no gap was left in it[p]—though at that time I had not installed the doors in the gates[q]— [2] Sanballat and Geshem[r] sent me a message: "Come, let's meet together in the villages of[D] the Ono Valley."[s] But they were planning to harm me.

[3] So I sent messengers to them, saying, "I am doing a great work and cannot come down. Why should the work cease while I leave it and

Cross references
[a]5:11 Neh 10:37
[b]5:12 Neh 10:31
[c]Ezr 10:5
[d]5:13 Ac 18:6
[e]Ezr 10:4-5; Neh 13:25
[f]5:14 Ezr 4:7; 7:1
[g]Neh 13:6
[h]5:15 Ezr 5:3,14; Hg 1:1
[i]Lv 25:36
[j]5:16 Neh 4:1; 6:1; 2Th 3:7-10
[k]Neh 5:3,7,11
[l]5:17 1Kg 4:27; 18:19
[m]5:18 1Kg 4:22-23
[n]5:19 Neh 13:14,22,31
[o]6:1 Neh 2:10,19
[p]Neh 4:6-7
[q]Neh 3:1
[r]6:2 Neh 2:10
[s]1Ch 8:12

[A]5:11 Lit hundredth   [B]5:15 Lit 40 shekels   [C]5:18 Lit And that which was prepared each   [D]6:2 Or together at Kephirim in

---

situation. As in Neh 5:7, there is a translation issue in this verse. Nehemiah's exhortation could be translated, "Let's stop pressing our claims on these loans."

5:12-13 The officials' agreement to Nehemiah's demands was followed by a solemn **oath**, the seriousness of which was reinforced by Nehemiah's ritual act of shaking the **folds** of his **robe** while reciting a curse on those who failed to **keep** it. The folds of the robe were used as pockets. Nehemiah was comparing his pockets to the rooms of a house and bidding God to evict the disobedient from their houses. The people had ample reason to say **Amen** (which means "so be it" or "surely"). This issue of social injustice could have splintered the community and brought about the same consequences their enemies had failed to achieve, but by God's grace Nehemiah produced a fair conclusion that allowed construction to continue.

5:14 This is the first mention of Nehemiah's appointment as **governor** (Hb pechah) of the province. Moreover, his duration as governor is given—probably from 445 to 432 b.c. Nehemiah distinguished his governance from his predecessors in that he declined to eat "the bread of the governor," or **the food allotted to the governor**. Such a refusal was at great personal cost to him, as verses 17-18 demonstrate.

5:15-16 The gap between Zerubbabel and Nehemiah was probably more than 60 years. Some scholars have argued that the governors whom Nehemiah criticized were the governors of Samaria, arguing that Judah (Hb Yehud) did not become a separate province until Nehemiah restored the city and its walls. Yet the historical evidence as well as the biblical record argues that Yehud had been a distinct political entity since the beginning of the Persian period. Ar-

chaeological finds have identified the names of some of the governors between Zerubbabel and Nehemiah on seals and coins, including Yeho'ezer, Ahzai, several named Elnatan, and Yehezqiyah.

Unlike his predecessors, Nehemiah wanted to fulfill his mission from God in restoring Jerusalem without adding to the burdens of the people who were already hard pressed. Nehemiah and his **subordinates** (lit "my youths"; 4:10) instead devoted themselves to their task of rebuilding. His assertion that they **didn't buy any land** is significant. Those at the center of power often use their power to get "sweetheart deals" to enrich themselves and their friends, but Nehemiah and his men did not take advantage of their power, especially when desperate people were willing to sell their properties for food.

5:17-18 On the **food allotted to the governor**, see note at verse 14.

5:19 Nehemiah's succinct prayer has often been criticized as selfish or as "works righteousness." But as J. G. McConville writes, "The invocation of God's favour is not so much a plea for a reward as an emphatic way of claiming that he has acted in good faith and from right motives. It is a statement of confidence that God is judge, and judges favourably those who sincerely seek to do his will" (McConville, Ezra, Nehemiah, and Esther; 102).

6:1-19 In chapter 6 the focus returns to construction of the wall and three attempts to thwart it by "intimidating" (vv. 9,14,19; Hb piel of yara'; "make afraid") Nehemiah and the workers.

6:1-4 News that the wall was completed (but not the gates) brought on a new attempt by **Sanballat, Tobiah**, and **Ge-**

go down to you?" ⁴Four times they sent me the same proposal, and I gave them the same reply.

⁵Sanballat*ᵃ* sent me this same message a fifth time by his aide, who had an open letter in his hand. ⁶In it was written:

It is reported among the nations—and Geshem*ᴬ,ᵇ* agrees—that you and the Jews plan to rebel. This is the reason you are building the wall. According to these reports, you are to become their king ⁷and have even set up the prophets in Jerusalem to proclaim on your behalf: "There is a king in Judah."*ᶜ* These rumors will be heard by the king. So come, let's confer together.

⁸Then I replied to him, "There is nothing to these rumors you are spreading; you are inventing them in your own mind."*ᵈ* ⁹For they were all trying to intimidate*ᵉ* us, saying, "They will become discouraged*ᴮ* in the work,*ᶠ* and it will never be finished."

But now, my God, strengthen me.*ᶜ,ᵍ*

Attempts to Intimidate Nehemiah

¹⁰I went to the house of Shemaiah son of Delaiah, son of Mehetabel, who was restricted to his house. He said:

Let us meet at the house of God inside the temple.

Let us shut the temple doors because they are coming to kill you. They are coming to kill you tonight!*ᴰ*

¹¹But I said, "Should a man like me run away? How can I enter the temple and live?*ʰ* I will not go." ¹²I realized that God had not sent him, because of the prophecy he spoke against me. Tobiah and Sanballat*ⁱ* had hired him. ¹³He was hired, so that I would be intimidated,*ʲ* do as he suggested, sin, and get a bad reputation, in order that they could discredit me.

¹⁴My God, remember*ᵏ* Tobiah and Sanballat for what they have done, and also Noadiah the prophetess*ˡ* and the other prophets who wanted to intimidate me.

The Wall Completed

¹⁵The wall was completed*ᵐ* in 52 days, on the twenty-fifth day of the month Elul.*ⁿ* ¹⁶When all our enemies*ᵒ* heard this, all the surrounding nations were intimidated*ᵖ* and lost their confidence,*ᴱ* for they realized that this task had been accomplished by our God.*ᵍ*

¹⁷During those days, the nobles of Judah sent many letters to Tobiah,*ʳ* and Tobiah's letters came to them. ¹⁸For many in Judah were bound by oath*ˢ* to him, since he was a son-in-law of Shecaniah son of Arah, and his son Jehohanan had married the daughter of Meshullam*ᵗ* son of Berechiah. ¹⁹These nobles kept mentioning Tobiah's good deeds to me,

ᵃ6:5 Neh 2:10
ᵇ6:6 Neh 2:19
ᶜ6:7 Zch 9:9
ᵈ6:8 Jb 13:4; Ps 52:2
ᵉ6:9 Ezr 3:3
ᶠEzr 4:4
ᵍNeh 5:19; 13:22; Ps 138:3
ʰ6:10-11 Nm 18:7
ⁱ6:12 Neh 2:10; 6:1
ʲ6:13 Ezr 3:3
ᵏ6:14 Neh 13:29
ˡRv 2:20
ᵐ6:15 Neh 4:1,7; 6:1
ⁿEzr 6:15
ᵒ6:16 Neh 2:10; 6:1
ᵖEx 14:25
ᵍ6:17 Neh 6:1; 13:4-5,7-8
ˢ6:18 Ezr 10:5
ᵗNeh 3:4,30

ᴬ6:6 Lit *Gashmu*   ᴮ6:9 Lit *saying, "Their hands will fail*   ᶜ6:9 Lit *my hands*   ᴰ6:10 Or *by night*   ᴱ6:16 Lit *and fell greatly in their eyes*

---

shem the Arab to stop construction, this time by focusing on Nehemiah himself. This translation follows the ancient versions in reading the Hebrew text as *kepharim* (**villages**) and not the Masoretic Text, which has *kephirim* (Kephirim). The versions leave us wondering which village was the proposed meeting place—perhaps it was different each of the **four times**. The MT specifies a location but it is not known to us. The Ono Valley, on the far northwest corner of Judah, may have been a neutral area between Judah and Samaria. Nehemiah recognized the offer to meet as a trap.

6:5-7 After four rejected invitations, **Sanballat** increased the pressure by trying to blackmail Nehemiah. The **open letter** in the hand of his aide made it clear that Sanballat's accusations against Nehemiah were for everyone to read. The letter charged Nehemiah with treason against King Artaxerxes, a charge that Sanballat knew had worked before to stop construction in Jerusalem (Ezr 4:7-16).

6:8-9 Nehemiah was not cowed by their slander. This translation of the end of verse 9, like most English translations, takes Nehemiah's words to be a brief prayer. However, the phrase "my God" (Hb *'elohay*) does not appear here as it does in the other brief prayers of Nehemiah (v. 14; 5:19; 13:14,22). Also, none of the early ancient versions (Gk, Lat, Syr) understood the closing phrase to be a prayer. With this in mind, a possible translation would be, "So now I increased my efforts."

6:10 **Shemaiah** ("Yahweh has heard") is a common OT name

shared by over 20 different people. Why Shemaiah was **restricted** or restrained is not clear. While he is not referred to as a prophet in this verse, his message to Nehemiah is called a prophecy in verse 12. Shemaiah tried a religious approach to trap Nehemiah, urging him to flee to the temple to save himself from assassination.

6:11-13 Nehemiah saw through this religious ruse intended to intimidate and **discredit** him. Moreover, had he entered the **temple** he could have been executed since by law only the priests could enter the temple (Nm 18:7).

6:14 Nehemiah knew that behind Shemaiah's "prophecy" were **Tobiah** and **Sanballat**, who evidently had persuaded others to do their bidding. **Noadiah** is mentioned only here in the OT.

6:15-16 In spite of myriad problems, the wall was **completed in 52 days**. The date of the **twenty-fifth day of the month** of **Elul** probably was October 2, 445 b.c. In less than six months, Nehemiah had traveled from Susa in Persia (modern-day Iran) to Jerusalem and had completed his mission of restoring the wall around the city. While Nehemiah's **enemies** had tried to intimidate him (vv. 9,14,19), they themselves **were intimidated**. They reluctantly understood that the completion of such a formidable task was due to God's help.

6:17-19 **During those days** suggests that this third attempt to intimidate Nehemiah may have been parallel to the other actions of intimidation. Verse 17 also explains

and they reported my words to him. And Tobiah sent letters to intimidate[a] me.

The Exiles Return

7 When the wall had been rebuilt and I had the doors installed,[b] the gatekeepers,[c] singers, and Levites were appointed. [2]Then I put my brother Hanani[d] in charge of Jerusalem,[e] along with Hananiah,[f] commander of the fortress,[g] because he was a faithful man who 'feared God[h] more than most. [3]I said to them, "Do not open the gates of Jerusalem until the sun is hot, and let the doors be shut and securely fastened while the guards are on duty. Station the citizens of Jerusalem as guards, some at their posts and some at their homes."[i]

[4]The city was large and spacious, but there were few people in it, and no houses had been built yet.[j] [5]Then my God put it into my mind[k] to assemble the nobles, the officials, and the people to be registered by genealogy. I found the genealogical record of those who came back first, and I found the following written in it:[l]

[6]These are the people of the province who went up among the captive exiles deported by King Nebuchadnezzar[m] of Babylon. Each of them returned to Jerusalem and Judah, to his own town.[n] [7]They came with Zerubbabel,[o] Jeshua,[p] Nehemiah, Azariah, Raamiah, Nahamani, Mordecai, Bilshan, Mispereth, Bigvai, Nehum, and Baanah.

The number of the Israelite men included:

[8]	Parosh's descendants[q]	2,172
[9]	Shephatiah's descendants	372
[10]	Arah's descendants	652
[11]	Pahath-moab's descendants:	
	Jeshua's and Joab's descendants	2,818
[12]	Elam's descendants	1,254
[13]	Zattu's descendants	845
[14]	Zaccai's descendants	760
[15]	Binnui's descendants	648
[16]	Bebai's descendants	628
[17]	Azgad's descendants	2,322
[18]	Adonikam's descendants[r]	667
[19]	Bigvai's descendants	2,067
[20]	Adin's descendants[s]	655
[21]	Ater's descendants: of Hezekiah	98
[22]	Hashum's descendants	328
[23]	Bezai's descendants	324
[24]	Hariph's descendants	112
[25]	Gibeon's[A] descendants	95
[26]	Bethlehem's[t] and Netophah's[u] men	188
[27]	Anathoth's[v] men	128
[28]	Beth-azmaveth's men	42
[29]	Kiriath-jearim's, Chephirah's, and Beeroth's men	743
[30]	Ramah's and Geba's men	621
[31]	Michmas's men	122
[32]	Bethel's and Ai's men[w]	123
[33]	the other Nebo's men	52
[34]	the other Elam's people	1,254
[35]	Harim's people	320
[36]	Jericho's people[x]	345
[37]	Lod's,[y] Hadid's, and Ono's people	721
[38]	Senaah's people	3,930

Cross references:
[a] 6:19 Neh 6:9,13
[b] 7:1 Neh 6:1
[c] Ezr 2:40-42; Neh 7:43-45
[d] 7:2 Neh 1:2
[e] Neh 3:9,12
[f] Neh 10:23
[g] Neh 2:8
[h] 1Kg 18:3; Neh 5:9,15
[i] 7:3 Neh 4:13,16,22-23
[j] 7:4 Neh 11:1
[k] 7:5 Pr 2:6
[l] 7:5-73 Ezr 2:1-70
[m] 7:6 2Ch 36:20
[n] Ezr 2:1
[o] 7:7 Hg 1:1
[p] Ezr 2:2; 5:2; Zch 3:3,8
[q] 7:8 Ezr 2:3; 8:3; 10:25; Neh 3:25
[r] 7:18 Ezr 2:13; 8:13
[s] 7:20 Ezr 2:15; 8:6
[t] 7:26 Ezr 2:21; Mc 5:2
[u] 2Sm 23:28; 2Kg 25:23; Ezr 2:22
[v] 7:27 Ezr 2:23; Neh 11:32; Jr 1:1
[w] 7:32 Gn 12:8; Jos 7:2; Ezr 2:28
[x] 7:36 Jos 6:1; Ezr 2:34; Neh 3:2
[y] 7:37 1Ch 8:12; Ezr 2:33; Ac 9:32

[A] 7:25 = Gibbar's in Ezr 2:20

why Nehemiah's enemies were so well informed of conditions within Jerusalem, because the **nobles of Judah sent many letters to Tobiah**. The term "letters" (Hb *iggereth*, from Akk *egirtu*) occurs only a dozen times in the OT, all in postexilic texts. These "nobles" were **bound by oath** (Hb *ba'alay-shevu'ah*; lit "masters of the oath") to Tobiah through marriage. Those aligned with Tobiah tried to convince Nehemiah of Tobiah's **good deeds**, yet his letters still were an attempt to **intimidate** Nehemiah.

7:1-3 Though the **wall had been rebuilt**, the danger was not over. Nehemiah's transfer of the **gatekeepers** from their positions in the temple to protection of the city is understandable. The walled city is in effect an extension of the temple courtyard. The mention of the **singers** and **Levites** suggests that Nehemiah needed these well-organized groups to take part in the city's defense. And with Tobiah's associates well entrenched in the city, he needed people he could trust such as **Hanani** and **Hananiah**.

No explanation is given on why the gates should remain closed **until the sun** was **hot**, a time when activity slowed. It may imply mid-morning rather than early morning, in order to give plenty of time for all the guards to come on duty. Another possibility is to understand the word "until" (Hb *'ad*) as "during," a less common meaning (Jdg 3:26; 2Kg 9:22; Jb 20:5; Jnh 4:2). This reading would suggest that the instruc-

tion was to *not* keep the gates open during the "siesta" period of the day, when the guards might become lethargic.

7:4-5 Most of the inhabitants of Jerusalem before the exile had been killed, deported, or scattered because of the catastrophe of 586 B.C. During the previous 80 years, thousands had returned from Babylonia, but the city's population still was small. Nehemiah was aware of the difficulty of trying to defend a sparsely populated city. The solution came when **God put it into** Nehemiah's **mind** (lit "heart") to gather the people to deal with the problem. Before Nehemiah could put his plan into action (11:1-2) he needed accurate census records of those who had returned from exile.

7:6-73a On the census of these returnees, see various notes at Ezra 2.

7:73b-10:39 The narrative about the repopulating of Jerusalem breaks off in 7:73a and does not resume until 11:1. Thus chapters 8-10 seem to be a parenthetical break that was actually part of the Ezra Memoir and originally stood chronologically between Ezra 8 and 9. Many scholars argue that this narrative was moved to its present position to link the ministries of Ezra and Nehemiah.

While it is likely that Ezra 8 (and probably Ezr 9) is part of the Ezra Memoir (see "Structure" in the Introduction to

³⁹The priests included:

Jedaiah's^a descendants of the house
   of Jeshua   973
⁴⁰ Immer's descendants   1,052
⁴¹ Pashhur's descendants   1,247
⁴² Harim's descendants   1,017.

⁴³The Levites^b included:

Jeshua's descendants: of Kadmiel
Hodevah's descendants   74.

⁴⁴The singers^c included:

•Asaph's descendants   148.

⁴⁵The gatekeepers^d included:

Shallum's descendants,
Ater's descendants,
Talmon's descendants,
Akkub's descendants,
Hatita's descendants,
Shobai's descendants   138.

⁴⁶The temple servants^e included:

Ziha's descendants,
Hasupha's descendants,
Tabbaoth's descendants,
⁴⁷Keros's descendants,
Sia's descendants, Padon's descendants,
⁴⁸Lebanah's descendants,
Hagabah's descendants,
Shalmai's descendants,
⁴⁹Hanan's descendants,
Giddel's descendants,
Gahar's descendants,
⁵⁰Reaiah's descendants,
Rezin's descendants,
Nekoda's descendants,
⁵¹Gazzam's descendants,
Uzza's descendants,
Paseah's descendants,
⁵²Besai's descendants,
Meunim's descendants,
Nephishesim's^A descendants,
⁵³Bakbuk's descendants,
Hakupha's descendants,
Harhur's descendants,
⁵⁴Bazlith's descendants,
Mehida's descendants,
Harsha's descendants,
⁵⁵Barkos's descendants,
Sisera's descendants,
Temah's descendants,
⁵⁶Neziah's descendants,
Hatipha's descendants.

a7:39 1Ch 24:7;
Ezr 2:36
b7:43 Ezr 2:40;
7:7; 8:15; Neh
13:30
c7:44 1Ch 15:16;
Ezr 2:41-43
d7:45 1Ch
9:17-27
e7:46 Neh 11:21
f7:57 1Kg 9:21;
Ezr 2:55
g7:60 Ezr 2:58
h7:61-62 Ezr
2:59-60
i7:65 Ezr 2:63;
5:14
jEx 28:30; Lv
8:8; Ezr 2:63
k7:69-72 Ezr
2:64-70

⁵⁷The descendants of Solomon's servants^f
included:

Sotai's descendants,
Sophereth's descendants,
Perida's descendants,
⁵⁸Jaala's descendants,
Darkon's descendants,
Giddel's descendants,
⁵⁹Shephatiah's descendants,
Hattil's descendants,
Pochereth-hazzebaim's descendants,
Amon's descendants.

⁶⁰ All the temple servants
and the descendants of
Solomon's servants^g   392.

⁶¹The following^h are those who came from
Tel-melah, Tel-harsha, Cherub, Addon, and
Immer, but were unable to prove that their
families and ancestors were Israelite:

⁶² Delaiah's descendants,
Tobiah's descendants,
and Nekoda's descendants   642

⁶³and from the priests: the descendants of Ho-
baiah, the descendants of Hakkoz, and the descendants of Barzillai—who had taken a wife
from the daughters of Barzillai the Gileadite
and was called by their name. ⁶⁴These
searched for their entries in the genealogical
records, but they could not be found, so they
were disqualified from the priesthood. ⁶⁵The
governorⁱ ordered them not to eat the most
holy things until there was a priest who could
consult the •Urim and Thummim.^j

⁶⁶ The whole combined assembly
    numbered   42,360
⁶⁷ not including their 7,337 male
    and female slaves,
    as well as their 245 male
    and female singers.
⁶⁸ They had 736 horses, 245 mules,^B
⁶⁹ 435 camels, and 6,720 donkeys.^k

⁷⁰Some of the family leaders gave to the
project. The governor gave 1,000 gold coins,^C
50 bowls, and 530 priestly garments to the
treasury. ⁷¹Some of the family leaders gave
20,000 gold coins and 2,200 silver minas^D
to the treasury for the project. ⁷²The rest of
the people gave 20,000 gold coins, 2,000 silver minas, and 67 priestly garments. ⁷³So the
priests, Levites, gatekeepers, temple singers,

A7:52 Alt Hb tradition reads *Nephushesim's* B7:68 Some Hb mss, LXX; Ezr 2:66; other Hb mss omit v. 68 C7:70 Or *drachmas,* or
darics; also in vv. 71-72 D7:71 A Babylonian coin worth 50 shekels

some of the people, temple servants, and all Israel settled in their towns.[A,a]

Public Reading of the Law

8 When the seventh month[b] came and the Israelites had settled in their towns, [1]all the people gathered together[c] at the square in front of the Water Gate.[d] They asked Ezra the scribe[e] to bring the book of the law of Moses[f] that the Lord had given Israel. [2]On the first day of the seventh month,[g] Ezra the priest[h] brought the law[i] before the assembly of men, women, and all who could listen with understanding. [3]While he was facing the square in front of the Water Gate,[j] he read out of it from daybreak until noon before the men, the women, and those who could understand. All the people listened attentively[B] to the book of the law.[k] [4]Ezra the scribe stood on a high wooden platform[l] made for this purpose.

Mattithiah, Shema, Anaiah, Uriah, Hilkiah, and Maaseiah stood beside him on his right; to his left were Pedaiah, Mishael, Malchijah, Hashum, Hash-baddanah, Zechariah, and Meshullam. [5]Ezra opened the book in full view of all the people, since he was elevated above everyone. As he opened it, all the people stood up. [6]Ezra praised the Lord, the great God, and with their hands uplifted[m] all the people said, "'Amen, Amen!'"[n] Then they bowed down and worshiped the Lord with their faces to the ground.[o]

[7]Jeshua, Bani, Sherebiah, Jamin, Akkub, Shabbethai, Hodiah, Maaseiah, Kelita, Azariah, Jozabad, Hanan, and Pelaiah,[p] who were Levites,[C,q] explained the law[r] to the people as they stood in their places. [8]They read out of the book of the law of God, translating and giving the meaning so that the people could understand what was read. [9]Nehemiah the

[a]7:73	1Ch 9:2; Ezr 2:70; Neh 7:6
[b]Lv 23:23-43; Ezr 3:1	
[c]8:1 Ezr 3:1	
[d]Neh 3:26; 8:16	
[e]Ezr 7:6,11,12; Neh 8:9,13	
[f]2Ch 34:14; Neh 8:7-9,13-14,18	
[g]8:2 Lv 23:23; Nm 29:1-6; Neh 6:15	
[h]Ezr 7:1-5	
[i]Neh 8:7,18	
[j]8:3 Neh 3:26	
[k]Dt 28:61; 2Ch 17:9; 25:4; 34:14-15	
[l]8:4 2Ch 6:13	
[m]8:6 1Tm 2:8	
[n]Neh 5:13	
[o]2Ch 20:18	
[p]8:7 Neh 9:4-5	
[q]Ezr 8:15,18-19; Neh 7:43	
[r]Lv 10:11; Mal 2:6,8	

[A]7:73 The second half of v. 73 is better understood when placed with 8:1.   [B]8:3 Lit The ears of all the people listened
[C]8:7 Vg, 1 Esdras 9:48; MT reads Pelaiah and the Levites

Ezra], this does not necessarily mean that the material has been displaced. While biblical writers sometimes present their material thematically and not chronologically (Ezr 4:6-24; Luke), there are no compelling reasons why Ezra could not be present for this reading of the law (Ezr 8) during the time of Nehemiah. It is not without biblical precedent (though it is odd) that Ezra and Nehemiah rarely mention each other even though their ministries overlapped. Thus it is suggested that the author of Ezra-Nehemiah turned from the Nehemiah Memoir he had used for Neh 1:1–7:73a and began drawing on the later section of the Ezra Memoir for Nehemiah 8 and possibly part of Nehemiah 9.

7:73b–8:2 Verse 73b is awkward. The final phrase (**the Israelites had settled in their towns**) is so similar to verse 73a (**all Israel settled in their towns**) that possibly a copyist mistakenly repeated the phrase. The **seventh month** (Tishri) was an important time in the Jewish calendar during which several events occurred. These events included the New Year, the Day of Atonement, and the Festival of Booths. Every seven years at the Festival of Booths the Law was to be read to the people (Dt 31:10-12). Those who are able to **listen with understanding** include children of a certain age (cp. 10:28; Ezr 10:1).

8:3 It is not stated why Ezra chose to have this assembly and reading of the Law at the **Water Gate** (see note at 3:26-27) rather than at the temple. Some speculate that tension between Nehemiah and the priests, some of whom were allied with Tobiah the Ammonite (6:17-19), may have encouraged Ezra and Nehemiah to have the meeting away from the temple complex. It is possible that the size of the crowd demanded a different location. Exactly what made up the **book of the law** has been the subject of intense discussion. Probably Ezra read the legal sections of a Pentateuch that was virtually identical to what we have today. It does not say that he read it in its entirety, but that **he read out of it**.

8:4 The term **platform** (Hb migdal) normally means "tower," but it is used to designate a platform here and in 2Ch 6:13. Little is known about the men who stood on **his right** and **his left**. Usually in Ezra-Nehemiah priests and Levites are distinguished from the "laity," so these people probably

were prominent lay leaders, such as representatives from the elders or heads of families.

8:5 The phrase **Ezra opened the book** is a little anachronistic since the book (codex) did not appear until the Christian era. Literally the phrase is, "Ezra unrolled the scroll." The apostle Paul specifically instructed that "Until I come, give your attention to public reading, exhortation, and teaching" (1Tm 4:13). Standing for the reading of the Word is as appropriate now as it was in Ezra's time.

8:6 Worship for the people was not just a mental exercise, but it involved the whole worshiper, who stood, spoke, and kneeled in humility before God.

8:7 Many of the 13 **Levites** who assisted Ezra were involved in the covenant renewal described in the following chapters. Eight of the 13 took part in the public confession (9:3-5), and nine are listed as signers of the covenant (10:9-13).

8:8 The term **translating** is one of several possibilities in understanding the Hebrew term (parash). This verb's basic meaning is to separate or to distinguish, reflected in the practice of the Jewish Masoretes, who divided the text of the Hebrew Bible into sections called parashoth. Thus Williamson translates verse 8a as, "They read from the book of the law paragraph by paragraph." Another possible rendering is to translate the verb as "to explain, make clear," a usage of the term that is uncommon in Hebrew (Nm 15:34) but common in related Semitic languages (Aramaic, Syriac, Mandean, Nabatean). The HCSB translation, which understands the Levites as "translating," is supported by the ancient Jewish tradition that the Levites were reading the Hebrew text but then providing the people with an Aramaic translation of the passage. The Jewish Talmud (b. Megillah 3a) cites this passage (Neh 8:8) as the source of the Targums, the Aramaic paraphrases of the Hebrew texts that became increasingly important as fewer Jewish people could read Hebrew. Targums were prepared for most of the OT books, but not for Ezra-Nehemiah or Daniel.

8:9 This verse is important because it links the ministries of **Nehemiah** and **Ezra**. Many critical scholars regard the mention of these great leaders together as an anachronis-

governor,[a] Ezra the priest and scribe,[b] and the Levites who were instructing the people said to all of them, "This day[c] is holy to the LORD your God. Do not mourn or weep."[d] For all the people were weeping as they heard the words of the law. [10] Then he said to them, "Go and eat what is rich, drink what is sweet, and send portions to those who have nothing prepared,[e] since today[f] is holy to our Lord. Do not grieve, because the joy of the LORD is your stronghold."[g] [11] And the Levites quieted all the people, saying, "Be still,[h] since today[i] is holy. Do not grieve." [12] Then all the people began to eat and drink, send portions, and have a great celebration,[j] because they had understood the words that were explained to them.

Festival of Booths Observed

[13] On the second day, the family leaders of all the people, along with the priests and Levites,[k] assembled before Ezra the scribe[l] to study the words of the law. [14] They found written in the law how the LORD had commanded through Moses that the Israelites should dwell in booths during the festival of the seventh month.[m] [15] So they proclaimed and spread this news throughout their towns and in Jerusalem, saying, "Go out to the hill country and bring back branches of olive, wild olive, myrtle, palm, and other leafy trees to make booths, just as it is written."[n] [16] The people went out, brought back branches, and made booths for themselves on each of their rooftops,[o] and courtyards, the court of the house of God, the square by the Water Gate,[p] and the square by the Gate of Ephraim.[q] [17] The whole community that had returned from exile[r] made booths and lived in them. They had not celebrated like this from the days of Joshua son of Nun until that day.[s] And there

a 8:9 Neh 5:14-15
b Ezr 7:1-6
c Nm 29:1-6
d Ezr 3:12-13; 10:1,6
e 8:10 2Sm 6:19; Est 9:22
f Nm 29:1-6
g Dt 16:11,14-15
h 8:11 Ps 46:10
i Nm 29:1-6
j 8:12 Est 9:22
k 8:13 Neh 10:28-29
l Ezr 7:6; Neh 8:1,9
m 8:14 Jn 7:2
n 8:14-15 Lv 23:4,34-42
o 8:16 Dt 22:8
p Neh 3:26; 8:1; 12:37
q 2Ch 25:23
r 8:17 Ezr 1:11; Neh 7:6
s 2Ch 7:9; Ezr 3:4

---

tic attempt to link together the ministries of two men who, according to these scholars, were not contemporaries. Yet there are no insurmountable problems, either textually or historically, that preclude the historicity of this event. Admittedly it seems odd that Nehemiah makes no mention of Ezra, a man of such prominence, until this point in the narrative. This does not necessarily mean that Ezra was not there. The prophets Haggai and Zechariah were contemporaries who both prophesied to the people of Jerusalem and Judah, yet neither mentions the other. Here the author clearly attests to a joint ministry of Ezra and Nehemiah, who participated together in the covenant renewal (chaps. 8–10) and took part together in the great procession and dedication of the walls of Jerusalem (12:27-43).

Nehemiah's command (or Ezra's?), **Do not mourn or weep**, seems baffling since the leaders would have been encouraged by the contrition and repentance of the people. However, this dedication of the wall occurred on the "first day of the seventh month" (v. 2) during the New Year celebration. The feast days were to be days of joy (Lv 23:24; Dt 12:12; 16:11), not mourning.

8:10 Rather than mourning, the people were commanded to **go and eat what is rich, drink what is sweet**. The term "rich" translates a Hebrew word *(mashmannim)* found in the OT only here in this verse but clearly related to the verb "to make fat, to be fat." It refers to choice foods appropriate for a celebration. The "sweet" drink (Hb *mamtaqqim*) mentioned here may have been wine mixed with honey, a popular drink long before the time of Christ. The people were to stop grieving because their strength came from **the joy of the LORD**. True security was found in Yahweh alone.

8:13 It is clear from the following context (v. 15) that most of the people returned to their homes after Ezra's reading of the law. It was harvest time, and there was much work to be done. However, many of the leaders remained in Jerusalem to **study the words of the law** and its implications.

8:14-15 The Festival of Booths is mentioned in four books of **the law** (Ex 23:16; Lv 23:39-43; Nm 29:12-38; Dt 16:13-15). Also called the Festival of Ingathering (Hb *chag-haqqatsir*), it was an eight-day agricultural festival that began on the fifteenth day of the seventh month, during the grain and grape

harvest (Dt 16:13). The legislation in Lv 23:39-43 is unique in two respects: (1) only in this passage are the Israelites commanded to dwell in a booth for the seven days of the feast, and (2) only in this passage is their dwelling in booths given a theological connection, "so that your generations may know that I made the Israelites live in booths when I brought them out of the land of Egypt" (Lv 23:43).

Since the celebration of the Festival of Booths required preparation, the leaders studying the law with Ezra **spread this news throughout their towns and in Jerusalem**. No passage in the OT expressly states the requirement to gather **branches** from **olive** and **myrtle** trees for the construction of **booths**. This seems to be an explanation and application of the command of Lv 23:40 to gather from "majestic trees—palm fronds, boughs of leafy trees, and willows of the brook."

8:16 Those living in Jerusalem erected their **booths** (Hb *sukkoth*) **on . . . their rooftops**, because most homes had flat roofs. Those who came from outside Jerusalem used whatever space was available, such as **the square by the Water Gate**, where they had read the law two weeks before, or in **the square by the Gate of Ephraim**. The Gate of Ephraim is not mentioned in the detailed description of the wall in chapter 3. However, its description in 2Kg 14:13 suggests it was on the north side of the wall. Thus, both locations provided easy access to the temple complex.

8:17 The celebration of the Festival of Booths was even more significant because the people **had not celebrated like this from the days of Joshua son of Nun until that day**. The phrase "had not celebrated like this" is literally "had not done (so)." The literal translation suggests that the festival had not been observed at all since Joshua's time, but this statement is incorrect and would have been understood as incorrect in Nehemiah's time because many people who were present for the festival had in fact celebrated the Festival of Booths soon after arriving in Jerusalem with Ezra (Ezr 3:4). Thus most commentators and some translations (including the HCSB) regard the statement as describing the *manner* in which the festival was celebrated. What made the present celebration different was likely the spiritual and theological emphasis that pervaded it. While earlier

was tremendous joy.[a] [18]Ezra[A] read out of the book of the law of God[b] every day, from the first day to the last. The Israelites celebrated the festival for seven days, and on the eighth day there was an assembly, according to the ordinance.[c]

National Confession of Sin

9 On the twenty-fourth day of this month[d] the Israelites assembled; they were fasting, wearing •sackcloth, and had put dust on their heads.[e] [2]Those of Israelite descent separated themselves from all foreigners,[f] and they stood[g] and confessed their sins and the •guilt of their fathers.[h] [3]While they stood in their places,[i] they read from the book of the law of the LORD their God for a fourth of the day and spent another fourth of the day[j] in confession[k] and worship of the LORD their God. [4]Jeshua, Bani, Kadmiel, Shebaniah, Bunni, Sherebiah, Bani, and Chenani stood on the raised platform built for the Levites[l] and cried out loudly to the LORD their God. [5]Then the Levites—Jeshua, Kadmiel, Bani, Hashabneiah, Sherebiah, Hodiah, Shebaniah, and Pethahiah[m]—said, "Stand up. Praise •Yahweh your God from everlasting to everlasting."[n]

Praise Your glorious name,[o]
and may it be exalted above all blessing
   and praise.
[6] You[B] alone are Yahweh.[p]
You created the heavens,
the highest heavens with all their host,
the earth and all that is on it,
the seas and all that are in them.
You give life to all of them,[q]
and the heavenly host worships You.[r]
[7] You are Yahweh,
the God who chose Abram
and brought him out of Ur
   of the Chaldeans,[s]
and changed his name to Abraham.[t]
[8] You found his heart faithful
   in Your sight,[u]
and made a covenant with him
to give the land of the Canaanites,
Hittites, Amorites, Perizzites,
Jebusites, and Girgashites—
to give it to his descendants.[v]
You have kept Your promise,
for You are righteous.
[9] You saw the oppression
   of our ancestors in Egypt[w]

Cross-references (center column)

[a]8:17 2Ch 30:21
[b]8:18 Neh 8:1,3
[c]Lv 23:34-36
[d]9:1 Neh 7:73; 8:2
[e]1Sm 4:12; Neh 1:4; Dn 9:3
[f]9:2 Ezr 6:21; 10:11; Neh 13:3
[g]Neh 8:5
[h]Neh 1:6; Dn 9:4,20
[i]9:3 Neh 8:5,7
[j]Neh 8:3
[k]Neh 1:6
[l]9:4 Neh 8:4
[m]9:4-5 Neh 8:7
[n]9:5 1Ch 16:36; Ps 41:13; 106:48
[o]1Ch 29:13
[p]9:6 Dt 6:4
[q]2Kg 19:15
[r]Ps 89:5-7; Lk 2:13
[s]9:7 Gn 11:28,31
[t]Gn 17:5
[u]9:8 Gn 15:6; 22:15-18
[v]Gn 15:18-21
[w]9:9 Ex 3:7; 14:10-14,31

A8:18 Some Hb mss, Syr read *They*   B9:6 LXX reads *And Ezra said: You*

---

celebrations may have focused on the harvest and thanksgiving aspects, this observance under Ezra returned to its theological underpinnings to recall God's provision and care during their forefathers' flight from Egypt, just as the people in Nehemiah's time rejoiced in God's care and provision for them in their flight from Babylon.

The author of Ezra-Nehemiah described well the experience of the people at the festival: **there was tremendous joy**. Critics have sometimes unfairly stigmatized Ezra-Nehemiah as banal, lifeless, or legalistic, but repeatedly this book emphasizes the joy that comes from living in covenant relationship with the God of Israel.

9:1-37 The penitential prayer of chapter 9 is a beautiful confession of God's faithfulness and mercy to His people as well as a confession by the people of their nation's persistent rebellion against God. Some argue that this chapter originally followed Ezra 10. They point out that while the people in Nehemiah 8 were commanded not to "mourn or weep" (8:9) during the Festival of Booths, the people in this chapter wept and confessed their sins. Yet it was not inappropriate to weep in contrition and repentance of sin; it was only inappropriate to do so during a festival where one was commanded to rejoice. With the completion of the Festival of Booths on the twenty-second day of the month, it was now permissible and appropriate to repent and confess on the twenty-fourth day of the month.

The prayer itself (vv. 9-37) is an example of the transformation of the lament, so commonly found in the Psalms, into a penitential prayer form common to the postexilic era. It shares many of the same characteristics and themes of the prayers of this era, such as Ezr 9:6-15; Neh 1:5-11; and Dn 9:4-19.

9:1 In the OT era there was a close connection between repentance and mourning. Just as mourners wore **sackcloth** (Gn 37:34) and **put dust** (Hb 'adamah) **on their heads** (2Sm 1:2) when someone died, so did those who mourned their sins and their spiritual condition.

9:2 Critical scholars who argue for the displacement of this chapter from its "original" location after Ezra 10 often point to the connection between the removal of foreign wives (Ezr 10) and this verse. However, in this verse the issue is not specifically foreign wives, but **foreigners** in general. God's chosen people, those **of Israelite descent** (lit "the seed of Israel"), were the ones who needed to confess, not the foreigners.

9:3 Presumably **they** who **stood in their places** were the Israelites who separated themselves from foreigners (v. 2), while **they** who **read from the book of the law** were those mentioned in the following verse (v. 4)—the Levites.

9:5 The prayer in verse 5 is probably a liturgical introduction distinct from the prayer itself that begins in verse 6. The call to **praise Yahweh your God from everlasting to everlasting** is close to King David's blessing in 1Ch 29:10 when he and the people generously gave for the building of the first temple.

9:6 The prayer begins with an acknowledgment of Yahweh's incomparability. Only Yahweh is the true God of creation who gives **life to all** and receives the worship of heavenly beings. While several biblical psalms allude to creation (Pss 8; 19; 95; 104), only in Psalm 136 does the theme of creation begin the psalm, as it does here.

9:7-8 Like **Abram**, many of those taking part in the penitential service had been brought **out of Ur of the Chaldeans** (Babylon). Abram, later renamed **Abraham**, received the

and heard their cry at the •Red Sea.

10 You performed signs and wonders
     against Pharaoh,
all his officials, and all the people
     of his land,ᵃ
for You knew how arrogantly
     they treated our ancestors.
You made a name for Yourself
that endures to this day.

11 You divided the sea before them,
and they crossed through it
     on dry ground.ᵇ
You hurled their pursuers
     into the depths
like a stone into churning waters.ᶜ

12 You led them with a pillar of cloud
     by day,
and with a pillar of fire by night,
to illuminate the way they should go.ᵈ

13 You came down on Mount Sinai,ᵉ
and spoke to them from heaven.
You gave them impartial ordinances,
     reliable instructions,
and good statutes and commands.

14 You revealed Your holy Sabbath
     to them,
and gave them commands, statutes,
     and instruction
through Your servant Moses.ᶠ

ᵃ9:10 Ex 3:20; 10:1
ᵇ9:11 Ex 14:21-22
ᶜEx 14:26-28
ᵈ9:12 Dt 1:32-33
ᵉ9:13 Ex 19:20
ᶠ9:13-14 Ex 20:1-17
ᵍ9:15 Ex 16:4
ʰEx 17:6
ⁱDt 1:8,21
ʲ9:16-17 Dt 1:26-33
ᵏ9:17 Nm 14:4
ˡEx 34:6; Ps 86:15; 103:8
ᵐ9:17-18 Ex 32:4

15 You provided bread from heavenᵍ
     for their hunger;
You brought them water from the rockʰ
     for their thirst.
You told them to go in and possess
     the land
You had swornᴬ to give them.ⁱ

16 But our ancestors acted arrogantly;
they became stiff-necked and did not
     listen to Your commands.

17 They refused to listen
and did not remember Your wonders
You performed among them.ʲ
They became stiff-necked
     and appointed a leader
to return to their slavery in Egypt.ᴮ,ᵏ
But You are a forgiving God,
gracious and compassionate,
slow to anger and rich in faithful love,ˡ
and You did not abandon them.

18 Even after they had cast an image
     of a calf
for themselves and said,
"This is your God who brought you
     out of Egypt,"ᵐ
and they had committed
     terrible blasphemies,

19 You did not abandon them
in the wilderness
because of Your great compassion.

ᴬ9:15 Lit *lifted Your hand*   ᴮ9:17 Some Hb mss, LXX; other Hb mss read *in their rebellion*

mercy of God, who **made a covenant** (Hb *berith*) **with him** (Gn 15; 17). Just as Abraham was **faithful**, so God also had been faithful—He had **kept** His **promise**.

9:9-11 The description of the exodus from Egypt is recounted with quotes and allusions from Exodus 3; 10; and 14. The

ziyd

Hebrew Pronunciation	[ZEED]
HCSB Translation	cook, act arrogantly
Uses in Nehemiah	3
Uses in the OT	10
Focus Passage	Nehemiah 9:10,16,29

The root indicates being *hot*. Jacob *cooks* stew (Gn 25:29). One lexicon, depending on Arabic, claims this idea represents a different root than other instances of *ziyd*, which describe *acting arrogantly* (Ex 18:11). Pharaoh and Egypt *treated* Israel *arrogantly* at the exodus (Neh 9:10). People *act willfully* by undertaking premeditated murder (Ex 21:14). They *act defiantly* (Dt 1:43) or *arrogantly* against God (Jr 50:29), *daring* to speak falsely for Him (Dt 18:20). The adjective (13x) describes *willful* or *deliberate* sins (Ps 19:13). The *proud* are accursed (Ps 119:21). *Arrogant* people will ultimately bring worldwide judgment (Is 13:11; Mal 4:1). With prepositions, the noun implies *arrogantly* ignoring God's messengers (Dt 17:12) or *presumptuously* proclaiming false prophecy (Dt 18:22). *Presumptuous* hearts are self-deceived, claiming invincibility against God (Jr 49:16).

term **arrogantly** translates a Hebrew verb (*ziyd*) meaning "to act presumptuously, to be arrogant." It is used to describe people or "nations who presume to have authority or rights that are not legitimately theirs" (NIDOTTE). The Egyptians regarded the Israelites as their slaves; in reality the Israelites were Yahweh's covenant people, and their redemption from Egypt was remembered as the central redemptive act of the OT. In this mighty act, God made **a name** for Himself as their Savior that endured to the time of Nehemiah and beyond.

9:12-15 The description of the wilderness period (vv. 12-21) begins with a recital of God's care and provisions for His people. Specific mention is made of the law about the **holy Sabbath**, which during the exilic and postexilic era became one of the primary markers of Jewish identity (13:15-22). God had provided for Israel's every need, and at Kadesh-barnea He commanded them **to go in and possess the land** He had promised the patriarchs (Nm 13–14).

9:16-17 In verse 10 it was the Egyptians who **arrogantly** mistreated Israel, but now the same verb (Hb *ziyd*) is used to describe the arrogance of Israel's **ancestors** (lit "fathers") against God and His commands, in spite of His care and provision. Their rebellion against God (v. 17) was both deliberate (**they refused to listen**) and nonsensical in their appointment of **a leader** to take them back to their **slavery in Egypt**.

9:18-21 God's mercy was put to the test in the making of the golden **calf** (see Ex 32). Yet even this serious offense was met with mercy. God's presence remained with them

During the day the pillar of cloud
never turned away from them,
guiding them on their journey.
And during the night the pillar of fire
illuminated the way they should go.[a]

20 You sent Your good Spirit[b]
to instruct them.
You did not withhold Your manna[c]
from their mouths,
and You gave them water
for their thirst.[d]

21 You provided for them
in the wilderness 40 years[e]
and they lacked nothing.
Their clothes did not wear out,
and their feet did not swell.[f]

22 You gave them kingdoms and peoples
and assigned them to be a boundary.
They took possession
of the land of Sihon[A] king of Heshbon
and of the land of Og king of Bashan.[g]

23 You multiplied their descendants
like the stars of heaven[h]
and brought them to the land
You told their ancestors to go in
and take possession of it.

24 So their descendants went in
and possessed the land:
You subdued the Canaanites
who inhabited the land before them
and handed their kings
and the surrounding peoples over to
them,[i]
to do as they pleased with them.

25 They captured fortified cities
and fertile land
and took possession of
well-supplied houses,
cisterns cut out of rock, vineyards,
olive groves, and fruit trees
in abundance.[j]
They ate, were filled,
became prosperous, and delighted
in Your great goodness.

[a]9:19 Ex 16:4; 17:6
[b]9:20 Nm 11:17; Neh 9:30
[c]Ex 16:14-15
[d]Ex 17:6
[e]9:21 Dt 2:7; 29:5
[f]Dt 8:4
[g]9:22 Nm 21:21-35
[h]9:23 Gn 15:5; 22:17
[i]9:24 Jos 11:23
[j]9:25 Dt 6:11; 11:11-12
[k]9:26 1Kg 14:9
[l]1Kg 18:4; 19:10
[m]9:26-28 Jdg 2:6-3:6
[n]9:29 Lv 18:5; Dt 30:16
[o]9:30 2Kg 17:13-18; Neh 9:20; Dn 9:6; 1Pt 1:10-12

26 But they were disobedient and rebelled
against You.
They flung Your law
behind their backs[k]
and killed Your prophets[l]
who warned them
in order to turn them back to You.
They committed terrible blasphemies.

27 So You handed them over
to their enemies,
who oppressed them.
In their time of distress, they cried out
to You,
and You heard from heaven.
In Your abundant compassion
You gave them deliverers,
who rescued them
from the power of their enemies.

28 But as soon as they had relief,
they again did what was evil
in Your sight.
So You abandoned them to the power
of their enemies,
who dominated them.
When they cried out to You again,
You heard from heaven
and rescued them
many times in Your compassion.[m]

29 You warned them to turn back
to Your law,
but they acted arrogantly
and would not obey Your commands.
They sinned against Your ordinances,
which a person will live by
if he does them.[n]
They stubbornly resisted,[B]
stiffened their necks,
and would not obey.

30 You were patient with them
for many years,
and Your Spirit warned them
through Your prophets,[o]
but they would not listen.

[A]9:22 One Hb ms, LXX; other Hb mss, Vg read *Sihon, even the land of the*   [B]9:29 Lit *They gave a stubborn shoulder*

---

in **the pillar of cloud** and **the pillar of fire**, and His provision continued during their entire **40 years** in **the wilderness**. God even sent His **good Spirit** (Hb *ruachka hatovah*) **to instruct** His people, probably a reference to the 70 elders chosen by Moses (Nm 11:16-17,23-30) who received some of the Spirit Moses had (Nm 11:25).

9:22-25 The final historical period, the giving of the land (vv. 22-31), is introduced with a synopsis primarily derived from Moses' review of the event in Deuteronomy. The defeat of **Sihon** and **Og** (see Nm 21; Dt 2-3) were crucial victories that secured Transjordan for Israel (Ps 135:11; 136:19-20). All that God had promised He faithfully brought about for His people, who **delighted** in His **great goodness**.

9:26-31 Just as God's faithfulness to His people in the wilderness (vv. 12-15) was rewarded with their rebellion (vv. 16-17), so God's faithfulness in the gift of the land was met with unbelief and unfaithfulness. In a poetic play on words not found elsewhere in the OT, the Israelites are described as those who **were disobedient and rebelled** (Hb *wayyameru wayyimredu*) against God (v. 26). Verses 27-30 recount the cycle of sin played out repeatedly in the book of Judges. Despite their persistent and repeated failure, God **did not destroy them or abandon them**.

Therefore, You handed them over
　to the surrounding peoples.[a]
31 However,
　in Your abundant compassion,
You did not destroy them
　or abandon them,[b]
for You are a gracious
　and compassionate God.[c]

32 So now, our God—the great,
　mighty,
and awe-inspiring God who keeps
　His gracious covenant[d]—
do not view lightly all the hardships
　that have afflicted us,
our kings and leaders,
our priests and prophets,
our ancestors and all Your people,
from the days of the Assyrian kings[e]
　until today.
33 You are righteous concerning all
　that has come on us,
because You have acted faithfully,
while we have acted wickedly.[f]
34 Our kings, leaders, priests,
　and ancestors
did not obey Your law
or listen to Your commands
and warnings You gave them.
35 When they were in their kingdom,

with Your abundant goodness that
　You gave them,
and in the spacious and fertile land
　You set before them,[g]
they would not serve You or turn
　from their wicked ways.

36 Here we are today,
slaves in the land You gave
　our ancestors
so that they could enjoy its fruit
　and its goodness.
Here we are—slaves in it![h]
37 Its abundant harvest goes to the kings
You have set over us,
because of our sins.
They rule over our bodies
and our livestock as they please.[i]
We are in great distress.

Israel's Vow of Faithfulness

38A In view of all this, we are making a binding agreement[j] in writing on a sealed document containing the names of our leaders, Levites, and priests.[k]

10 Those whose seals were on the document were:

Nehemiah the governor,[l]
　son of Hacaliah, and Zedekiah,
2 Seraiah,[m] Azariah, Jeremiah,

Cross-references (center column):
a 9:30 Jr 16:10-13
b 9:31 Jr 4:27
c Neh 9:17
d 9:32 Neh 1:5; Dn 9:4
e 2Kg 15:19; 17:3-6
f 9:33 Dn 9:7-8,14
g 9:35 Neh 9:25
h 9:35-36 Dt 28:47-48
i 9:37 Dt 28:33,51
j 9:38 2Ch 23:16
k Neh 10:1-39
l 10:1 Neh 5:14; 8:9; 12:26
m 10:2-8 Neh 12:1-7,11-21

A 9:38 Neh 10:1 in Hb

9:32-37 After the long review of Israel's broken promises and rebellion against God, the prayer finally turns from confession to a petition addressed to **our God**, the God who (unlike Israel) **keeps His gracious covenant**. The only request in this long prayer is that God would take note of their **hardships**. The term hardships (Hb *tela'ah*) occurs only rarely in the OT, but it is used to refer to times of great distress or trials, such as the exodus (Ex 18:8) or Jerusalem after its destruction at the hands of the Babylonians (Lm 3:5). While some have explained the mention of the **Assyrian kings** as a reference to the Persians (cp. Ezr 6:22), more likely it marks the beginning of foreign domination over Israel with the fall of the northern kingdom in the eighth century B.C., a condition that persisted in Nehemiah's time under the Persians.

Yet the prayer makes it clear (vv. 33-34) that the blame for all their hardships was their own and not God's. God was just. Both the Levites leading the prayer and all who joined in with them confessed their solidarity in sin, because they had **acted wickedly**. The tragic irony was that the land was God's great gift to them—if they would only keep the covenant. Instead they would lament, **Here we are—slaves in it!** While God's people hoped for God's intervention, they ended their prayer by acknowledging the sad reality: **We are in great distress**.

9:38-10:39 In the Hebrew Bible, 9:38 is the first verse of chapter 10, since its subject matter clearly relates to the covenant renewal ceremony that follows. The opening phrase of this section, **In view of all this**, links the covenant renewal with the penitential prayer of chapter 9. Many critical scholars maintain that chapter 10 is displaced from its

original position, yet there is no conclusive evidence that this is so. It is true that Ezra is not mentioned as a signatory of the covenant in chapter 10. It is also correct that some of the issues dealt with in 10:30-39 are issues that Nehemiah dealt with in chapter 13. Still, some of the issues dealt with in 10:30-39 are absent from chapter 13, while chapter 13 deals with issues not mentioned in 10:30-39. Moreover, one should not conclude that the pledges made in chapter 10 were fully kept from that time forward.

There are several possible explanations for why Ezra is not mentioned in the chapter. If he was the author of the covenant, there may have been no need for his signature. Also, since many of the names listed in the document (10:1-27), especially of the priests, are family names, it may be that Ezra was not mentioned since he was part of the Seraiah family of priests (Ezr 7:5). It is interesting that the high priest at this time, presumably still Eliashib (Neh 3:1), is not mentioned in the list of signatories. He too, like Ezra, was included under the Seraiah family signature. The discussion below will assume the events of chapter 10 follow logically and chronologically after the events of chapters 8-9.

9:38 After their corporate confession of sin, the leaders made **a binding agreement in writing**. The phrase "binding agreement" (Hb *korethim 'amanah*) is unique, combining the common Hebrew idiom for making (Hb *carath*; lit "cut") a covenant with the rare term "agreement" (Hb *'amanah*), derived from the Hebrew verb *('aman)* "to be faithful, to be trustworthy."

10:2-8 This list is similar to the listing of the priests who "went up with Zerubbabel" (12:1), although it contains some

3 Pashhur,[a] Amariah, Malchijah,
4 Hattush, Shebaniah, Malluch,
5 Harim, Meremoth, Obadiah,
6 Daniel, Ginnethon, Baruch,
7 Meshullam, Abijah, Mijamin,
8 Maaziah, Bilgai, and Shemaiah.
These were the priests.

9 The Levites[b] were:
Jeshua son of Azaniah,
Binnui of the sons of Henadad,
Kadmiel,
10 and their brothers
Shebaniah, Hodiah, Kelita, Pelaiah,
Hanan,
11 Mica, Rehob, Hashabiah,
12 Zaccur, Sherebiah, Shebaniah,
13 Hodiah, Bani, and Beninu.

14 The leaders of the people[c] were:
Parosh, Pahath-moab, Elam, Zattu,
Bani,
15 Bunni, Azgad, Bebai,
16 Adonijah, Bigvai, Adin,[d]
17 Ater, Hezekiah, Azzur,
18 Hodiah, Hashum, Bezai,
19 Hariph, Anathoth, Nebai,
20 Magpiash, Meshullam, Hezir,
21 Meshezabel, Zadok, Jaddua,
22 Pelatiah, Hanan, Anaiah,
23 Hoshea, Hananiah,[e] Hasshub,
24 Hallohesh, Pilha, Shobek,
25 Rehum, Hashabnah, Maaseiah,
26 Ahijah, Hanan, Anan,
27 Malluch, Harim, Baanah.

a10:3 1Ch 9:12
b10:9-13 Neh
8:7; 9:4-5;
12:8-9
c10:14-27 Ezr
2:1-61; Neh
7:6-63
d10:16 Ezr 8:6
e10:23 Neh 7:2
f10:28 Neh 8:2-3
g Neh 9:2; 13:3
h10:29 Ezr 10:5;
Neh 5:12
i Neh 8:1
j10:30 Ex 34:16;
Neh 13:23
k10:31 Neh
13:16
l Ex 23:10-11; Lv
25:1-7
m Dt 15:1-3
n10:32 Ex 30:11-
16; Mt 17:24
o10:33 Lv 24:5-9
p Nm 10:10

28 The rest of the people—the priests, Levites, gatekeepers, singers, and temple servants, along with their wives, sons, and daughters, everyone who is able to understand[f] and who has separated themselves from the surrounding peoples[g] to obey the law of God— 29 join with their noble brothers and commit themselves with a sworn oath[A,h] to follow the law of God given through God's servant Moses[i] and to carefully obey all the commands, ordinances, and statutes of •Yahweh our Lord.

Details of the Vow

30 We will not give our daughters in marriage to the surrounding peoples and will not take their daughters as wives for our sons.[j]

31 When the surrounding peoples bring merchandise or any kind of grain to sell on the Sabbath day, we will not buy from them on the Sabbath or a holy day.[k] We will also leave the land uncultivated in the seventh year[l] and will cancel every debt.[m]

32 We will impose the following commands on ourselves:

To give an eighth of an ounce of silver[B] yearly for the service of the house of our God:[n] 33 the bread displayed before the LORD,[C,o] the daily •grain offering, the regular •burnt offering, the Sabbath and New Moon offerings,[p] the appointed festivals, the holy things, the •sin offerings

---

A10:29 Lit and enter in a curse and in an oath   B10:32 Lit give one-third of a shekel   C10:33 Lit rows of bread

---

alternative spellings and minor textual corruption. None of the priests alive in Zerubbabel's time would have been present here, suggesting again that these are not the names of living people but the names of the founders of priestly divisions.

10:9-13 The names of **Levites** probably includes both family names (Jeshua, Binnui, and Kadmiel; 12:8; Ezr 3:9) and personal names (Neh 8:7; 9:4).

10:14-27 The list of the **leaders of the people** (Hb ra'she ha'am) likewise appears to list both family names and individual signers. The first half (vv. 14-19) generally matches the names of the returnees in the list of Ezra 2 and Nehemiah 7; the second half mentions people assigned to rebuild specific sections of the wall in Nehemiah 3.

10:28-29 Once the document was completed, **the rest of the people** had the opportunity to participate in the great event. This **sworn oath** first dealt broadly with obedience to God demonstrated in obedience to **the law of God given through God's servant Moses**. The particular areas of compliance to the law are then specified in verses 30-39.

10:30-39 These commands and prohibitions, prescribed in six crucial areas, are not just quotations from throughout the Pentateuch but an integration and application of the law to the present conditions. In some cases the OT laws are

given greater specification or are broadened and applied to Israel's new circumstances. What is clear is the presupposition of the absolute authority of law as God's revelation and the presupposition of its applicability to every generation.

10:30 In Ezra's earlier ministry (Ezr 9) the focus was on foreign wives. In this passage the issue is broadened to intermarriage with foreigners in general.

10:31a The law forbade any type of work on the **Sabbath**, but in Nehemiah's time, living in a multicultural situation, the question about buying from non-Israelites on the Sabbath came up. Here the prohibition is extended to the new cultural situation.

10:31b The pledge here is unique in that it brings together two ordinances not originally combined. The law commanding the **land** to remain fallow on the **seventh year** (Ex 23:10-11) is linked with the remission of all debts on the seventh year (Dt 15:1-6).

10:32 In Ex 30:11-16 Moses was commanded to collect a half shekel from every male 20 years old or over. The passage does not describe this as an annual taxation. However, in King Joash's time when the temple was being restored, the taxation of the people for the upkeep of the temple was assumed to be an annual occurrence (2Ch 24:4-6). It is not clear why in this passage the temple tax was only a third of

to *atone for Israel,[a] and for all the work of the house of our God.

[34] We have cast lots[b] among the priests, Levites, and people for the donation of wood by our ancestral houses at the appointed times each year. They are to bring the wood to our God's house to burn on the altar of the LORD our God,[c] as it is written in the law.

[35] We will bring the *firstfruits of our land and of every fruit tree to the LORD's house year by year.[d] [36] We will also bring the firstborn of our sons and our livestock, as prescribed by the law, and will bring the firstborn of our herds and flocks to the house of our God,[e] to the priests who serve in our God's house. [37] We will bring a loaf from our first batch of dough[f] to the priests at the storerooms of the house of our God. We will also bring the firstfruits of our grain offerings, of every fruit tree, and of the new wine and oil.[g] A tenth of our land's produce belongs to the Levites, for the Levites are to collect the one-tenth offering in all our agricultural towns.[h] [38] A priest of Aaronic descent must accompany the Levites when they collect the tenth,[i] and the Levites must take a tenth of this offering to the storerooms of the treasury in the house of our God.[j] [39] For the Israelites and the Levites are to bring the contributions of grain, new wine, and oil to the storerooms where the articles of the sanctuary are kept[k] and where the priests who minis-

ter are, along with the gatekeepers and singers. We will not neglect the house of our God.[l]

Resettling Jerusalem

11 Now the leaders of the people stayed in Jerusalem,[m] and the rest of the people cast lots[n] for one out of ten to come and live in Jerusalem, the holy city,[o] while the other nine-tenths remained in their towns.[p] [2] The people praised all the men who volunteered[q] to live in Jerusalem.

[3] These are the heads of the province who stayed in Jerusalem[r] (but in the villages of Judah each lived on his own property in their towns[s]—the Israelites, priests, Levites, temple servants, and descendants of Solomon's servants[t]— [4] while some of the descendants of Judah and Benjamin settled in Jerusalem):

Judah's[u] descendants:

Athaiah son of Uzziah, son of Zechariah, son of Amariah, son of Shephatiah, son of Mahalalel, of Perez's descendants; [5] and Maaseiah son of Baruch, son of Col-hozeh, son of Hazaiah, son of Adaiah, son of Joiarib, son of Zechariah, a descendant of the Shilonite. [6] The total number of Perez's descendants, who settled in Jerusalem, was 468 capable men.

[7] These were Benjamin's descendants:

Sallu son of Meshullam, son of Joed, son of Pedaiah, son of Kolaiah, son of Maaseiah, son of Ithiel, son of Jeshaiah, [8] and after him Gabbai and Sallai: 928. [9] Joel

---

[a]10:33 Nm 28:2–29:39
[b]10:34 Lv 16:8; Neh 11:1
[c]Lv 6:12-13; Neh 13:31
[d]10:35 Lv 26:1-10; Nm 18:12-13
[e]10:36 Ex 13:2,12-13
[f]10:37 Lv 23:17; Nm 15:20-21; Ezk 44:30
[g]Nm 18:12-13
[h]Lv 27:30
[i]10:38 Nm 18:26
[j]Neh 13:12-13
[k]10:39 Dt 12:6,11
[l]Neh 13:10-11
[m]11:1 Neh 7:4
[n]Neh 10:34
[o]Neh 11:18; Is 48:2; Rv 11:2; 21:2
[p]Ezr 2:70; Neh 7:73
[q]11:2 Jdg 5:9
[r]11:3 1Ch 9:2-34
[s]Neh 7:73; 11:20
[t]Neh 7:39-43,46-60
[u]11:4-19 1Ch 9:3-21

---

a shekel rather than the normal half shekel. Since there was not uniformity between monetary systems, it may be that the shekel in Nehemiah's time was more valuable than in earlier times.

10:34 The OT law commanded that "fire must be kept burning on the altar continually; it must not go out" (Lv 6:13). This required a lot of wood in a country not known for its forests. Thus the priests, Levites, and lay people shared the responsibility for providing wood.

10:35-39 The sixth and final obligation to which the Jews pledged themselves was to give the first and the best to God. This included the **firstfruits** of **every fruit tree**, a specification not found in OT law but a logical extension of the idea of giving the "firstfruits of the land" (Ex 23:19). Just as they brought the firstfruits (Hb *bikkurim*) of the land, so they brought the **firstborn** (Hb *bekoroth*) of their **sons** and **livestock**. Their sons (and the unclean livestock) would be redeemed (Ex 13:13; Lv 27:27) by a monetary payment (or the substitution of a clean animal for an unclean one), while the firstborn of a clean animal was offered **to the priests**. A tenth of the agricultural **produce** was given to the **Levites**, who in turn gave a tenth of the tenth to the temple. To en-

sure the proper allocation of these gifts and tenths, **a priest of Aaronic descent** was required to **accompany the Levites** when they accepted these donations (v. 38), a stipulation not found elsewhere in the OT.

11:1-2 Here the author returns to the Nehemiah Memoir (see "Structure" in the Introduction to Ezra) and the narrative about the repopulation of Jerusalem first introduced in 7:4-5. Jerusalem was underpopulated and consisted largely of the **leaders** (Hb *sarim*) **of the people**. There may be some degree of overstatement in the passage since the towns and villages would have needed local leadership as well. The solution to the problem was to have a tenth of the population come to **live in Jerusalem**, chosen by the casting of **lots**, a practice common in the OT and even into NT times (Ac 1:26). While this was a burden for those selected, this would not have been the selection of individuals but of families. It is not clear if the **men who volunteered** were in addition to those chosen by lot.

11:3-21 This list offers many textual challenges—a common phenomenon with names and numbers. The LXX reflects a much shorter version of verses 12-21 than does the Hebrew text. This list is also challenging in that it is clearly related

son of Zichri was the officer over them, and Judah son of Hassenuah was second in command over the city.

[10]The priests:

Jedaiah son of Joiarib, Jachin, and [11]Seraiah son of Hilkiah, son of Meshullam, son of Zadok, son of Meraioth, son of Ahitub, the chief official of God's temple, [12]and their relatives who did the work at the temple: 822. Adaiah son of Jeroham, son of Pelaliah, son of Amzi, son of Zechariah, son of Pashhur, son of Malchijah [13]and his relatives, the leaders of families: 242. Amashsai son of Azarel, son of Ahzai, son of Meshillemoth, son of Immer, [14]and their relatives, capable men: 128. Zabdiel son of Haggedolim, was their chief.

[15]The Levites:

Shemaiah son of Hasshub, son of Azrikam, son of Hashabiah, son of Bunni; [16]and Shabbethai and Jozabad, from the leaders of the Levites, who supervised the work outside the house of God; [17]Mattaniah son of Mica, son of Zabdi, son of ˙Asaph, the leader who began the thanksgiving in prayer;[a] Bakbukiah, second among his relatives; and Abda son of Shammua, son of Galal, son of Jeduthun.[b] [18]All the Levites in the holy city:[c] 284.

[19]The gatekeepers:

Akkub, Talmon, and their relatives, who guarded the gates: 172.

[20]The rest of Israel, the priests, and the Levites were in all the villages of Judah, each

on his own inherited property.[d] [21]The temple servants lived on Ophel;[A,e] Ziha and Gishpa supervised the temple servants.

The Levites and Priests

[22]The leader of the Levites in Jerusalem was Uzzi son of Bani, son of Hashabiah, son of Mattaniah, son of Mica, of the descendants of Asaph, who were singers for the service of God's house. [23]There was, in fact, a command of the king regarding them, and an ordinance regulating[B] the singers'[f] daily tasks. [24]Pethahiah son of Meshezabel, of the descendants of Zerah[g] son of Judah, was the king's[h] agent[C] in every matter concerning the people.

[25]As for the farming settlements with their fields:

Some of Judah's descendants lived
   in Kiriath-arba[i] and its villages,
Dibon[j] and its villages, and Jekabzeel
   and its villages;
[26]   in Jeshua, Moladah,[k] Beth-pelet,
[27]   Hazar-shual, and Beer-sheba[l]
   and its villages;
[28]   in Ziklag[m] and Meconah and its villages;
[29]   in En-rimmon, Zorah,[n] Jarmuth,[o] and
[30]   Zanoah[p] and Adullam
   with their villages;
in Lachish[q] with its fields and Azekah[r]
   and its villages.
So they settled from Beer-sheba[s]
   to the Valley of Hinnom.[t]

[31]   Benjamin's descendants:
   from Geba,[D,u] Michmash,[v] Aija,
   and Bethel[w]—and its villages,
[32]   Anathoth,[x] Nob,[y] Ananiah,
[33]   Hazor,[z] Ramah,[aa] Gittaim,[ab]
[34]   Hadid, Zeboim,[ac] Neballat,
[35]   Lod, and Ono,[ad] the Valley of Craftsmen.

Cross references (center column):

[a]11:17 1Ch 6:31,39; 2Ch 5:12
[b]1Ch 16:42
[c]11:18 Neh 11:1; Rv 21:2
[d]11:20 Nm 36:3; Neh 11:3
[e]11:21 Neh 3:26
[f]11:22-23 1Ch 15:16; Neh 7:44
[g]11:24 Gn 38:30; 1Ch 2:43
[h]Neh 2:1; 5:14
[i]11:25 Jos 14:15
[j]Jos 3:9,17
[k]11:26 Jos 15:26-28
[l]11:27 2Sm 17:11
[m]11:28 1Sm 27:6
[n]11:29 Jos 15:33
[o]Jos 10:5
[p]11:30 Jos 15:34-35
[q]Jos 10:3; 15:39
[r]Jos 10:10
[s]Jos 15:27
[t]2Kg 23:10
[u]11:31 Jos 21:17
[v]1Sm 13:2
[w]Jos 12:9
[x]11:32 Jos 21:18; Jr 1:1
[y]1Sm 21:1; 22:9
[z]11:33 Jos 11:1
[aa]Jos 18:25
[ab]2Sm 4:3
[ac]11:34 1Sm 13:18
[ad]11:35 1Ch 8:12; Ac 9:32

A11:21 = a hill in Jerusalem   B11:23 Lit for   C11:24 Lit was at the king's hand   D11:31 Or descendants from Geba lived in

to the list in 1Ch 9:1-17. Both lists (1Ch 9; Neh 11) originated in the postexilic era (1Ch 9:2) and recorded the names of those living in Jerusalem. Both have the same order of presentation: Israelites, priests, Levites, temple servants. Both list many of the same individuals, albeit with slightly different spelling of their names. Yet they differ greatly, with each including material not found in the other, and the 1 Chronicles 9 list is longer. A comparison of this list (Neh 11) with 1 Chronicles 9, along with the census lists of Ezra 2 and Nehemiah 7, suggests that this list must be selective and representative. Its purpose was to demonstrate that a representative cross section of the nation was now living in the holy city.

Descendants of the musicians **Asaph** and **Jeduthun** are mentioned, but not Heman (cp. 1Ch 25:1). This is probably a result of the few Levites who returned from Babylon (Ezr 2:40; 8:15-20).

11:22-24 It is likely that **Uzzi son of Bani** was a great-grandson of **Mattaniah**, who is listed first among the Levites (v.

17). The role of the Levites (v. 23) was regulated by the **command of the king**. While some regard this as a reference to the Persian king, this does not appear likely. The "command of the king" probably refers back to King David's ordering of temple worship (1Ch 23; 25), an identification supported by the reference to David and the Levites in Neh 12:45-46. **Pethahiah son of Meshezabel**, mentioned only here (v. 24) in the Bible, served as the **king's agent** (Hb leyad hammelek; lit "at the hand of the king"), probably in Judah.

11:25-36 An enigmatic chapter concludes with a puzzling description of the regions of Judah (vv. 25-30) and Benjamin (vv. 31-36). This list of towns and villages is unusual in what it contains as well as in what it omits. Towns that were far beyond the borders of Yehud (Hb for Judah) are mentioned, yet towns referred to in Ezra-Nehemiah are not mentioned, including Bethlehem, Mizpah, Gibeon, and Jericho. In general, the towns listed for Judah were south of Jerusalem, extending all the way into the Negev, while the towns listed

36 Some of the Judean divisions of Levites were in Benjamin.

12
These[a] are the priests and Levites[b] who went up with Zerubbabel[c] son of Shealtiel and with Jeshua:

Seraiah, Jeremiah, Ezra,
2 Amariah, Malluch, Hattush,
3 Shecaniah, Rehum, Meremoth,
4 Iddo,[d] Ginnethoi, Abijah,[e]
5 Mijamin, Maadiah, Bilgah,
6 Shemaiah, Joiarib, Jedaiah,[f]
7 Sallu, Amok, Hilkiah, Jedaiah.

These were the leaders of the priests and their relatives in the days of Jeshua.[g]

8 The Levites:

Jeshua, Binnui, Kadmiel,
Sherebiah, Judah, and Mattaniah[h]—
he and his relatives were in charge
of the praise songs.
9 Bakbukiah, Unni,[A] and their relatives
stood opposite them in the services.

10 Jeshua fathered Joiakim,
Joiakim fathered Eliashib,
Eliashib[i] fathered Joiada,
11 Joiada fathered Jonathan,
and Jonathan fathered Jaddua.[B]

a 12:1-7 Neh 12:12-21
b 12:1 Ezr 2:1-2; 7:7
c Ezr 3:2
d 12:4 Neh 12:16; Zch 1:1
e 1Ch 24:10
f 1Ch 24:7
g 12:7 Ezr 2:2; 3:2
h 12:8 Neh 11:17
i 12:10 Neh 3:20

12 In the days of Joiakim, the leaders of the priestly families were:

Meraiah   of Seraiah,
Hananiah   of Jeremiah,
13 Meshullam   of Ezra,
Jehohanan   of Amariah,
14 Jonathan   of Malluchi,
Joseph   of Shebaniah,
15 Adna   of Harim,
Helkai   of Meraioth,
16 Zechariah   of Iddo,
Meshullam   of Ginnethon,
17 Zichri   of Abijah,
Piltai   of Moadiah, of Miniamin,
18 Shammua   of Bilgah,
Jehonathan   of Shemaiah,
19 Mattenai   of Joiarib,
Uzzi   of Jedaiah,
20 Kallai   of Sallai,
Eber   of Amok,
21 Hashabiah   of Hilkiah,
and Nethanel of Jedaiah.

22 In the days of Eliashib, Joiada, Johanan, and Jaddua, the leaders of the families of the Levites and priests were recorded while Darius the Persian ruled. 23 Levi's descendants, the leaders of families, were recorded in the Book

A 12:9 Alt Hb tradition reads *Unno*   B 12:10-11 These men were high priests.

---

for Benjamin were northwest of Jerusalem extending into the Shephelah. While many proposed solutions have been offered for this passage, the most likely is that the list is of those towns that were not destroyed by the Babylonians in the sixth century B.C. and whose inhabitants remained in the land (Y. Aharoni, *The Land of the Bible*). This proposal accords well with the archaeological record that shows continuity of settlement in the region of Benjamin during this period.

12:1-26 This section of chapter 12 consists of temple personnel in supplementary lists appended to the repopulation list of chapter 11. These lists were representative of the situation a generation after Zerubbabel and Jeshua. Since they appear with little explanation or background, they bring about significant discussion in the scholarly community about their relationship to each other and in relation to the other lists of temple personnel mentioned in Ezra-Nehemiah (Ezr 2; Neh 7; 9; 10).

12:1-7 This list appears to enumerate individuals, while the second list (vv. 12-21) lists the leaders of the priests. However, it seems some of the names listed in verses 1-7 must be family names and not the name of individuals.

12:8-9 According to Ezr 2:40, there were only two Levitical families present in the return to the land under Zerubbabel (Jeshua and Kadmiel), numbering only 74 people. It is not clear why six families are listed here, especially since **Mattaniah** and **Bakbukiah** are mentioned as active in Nehemiah's time (v. 25; 11:17). The latter **stood opposite** the others either to offer support or to provide antiphonal music.

12:10-11 These verses list six high priests. The identity of the first and third are clear, with **Jeshua** serving with Zerubbabel in the return to the land (Ezr 2:2) and **Eliashib** serving

as high priest during Nehemiah's tenure (3:1,20). However, since there is nearly an 80-year gap between the first and the third postexilic high priests, it is possible that the list is only representative and not complete, or, as suggested by Blenkinsopp *(Ezra-Nehemiah)*, "there may have been times of political crisis . . . when the office was vacant."

The fourth priest, **Joiada** (also referred to by the longer form of his name, Jehoiada), is mentioned in 13:28 as the son of Eliashib the high priest, although Joiada himself did not yet bear that title. There is no other mention of **Jonathan** during this era. But verse 22 does identify an era by the listing of four priests: Eliashib, Joiada, Johanan, and Jaddua. The last named high priest, **Jaddua**, was mentioned by Josephus, who claimed that Alexander the Great met Jaddua (333 B.C.). However, since some of Josephus's work is considered legendary, it is probably unwise to date Jaddua that late. It is also possible that there were earlier and later high priests with the same name.

12:12-21 The second list of priestly names parallels the earlier one (vv. 1-7), although there is significant variation in the spelling of many names as well as an unexpected omission—Hattush (v. 2). Many of these names appear as signers of the pledge in chapter 10. The final six names are not on the earlier list (vv. 1-7) nor on the list of signatories in chapter 10. Of interest is the mention of **Zechariah of Iddo**, probably a reference to the prophet Zechariah (Ezr 5:1; 6:14; Zch 1:1).

12:22 The identification of **Darius the Persian** is not certain, and all three Persian kings named Darius have been suggested by scholars. Those who accept the veracity of Josephus's statement about Jaddua meeting Alexander the Great identify the Darius in this verse as Darius III Codomannus

of the Historical Records[a] during the days of Johanan son of Eliashib. [24] The leaders of the Levites—Hashabiah, Sherebiah, and Jeshua son of Kadmiel, along with their relatives opposite them—gave praise and thanks, division by division, as David the man of God had prescribed.[b] [25] This included Mattaniah,[c] Bakbukiah, and Obadiah. Meshullam, Talmon, and Akkub were gatekeepers who guarded the storerooms at the gates.[d] [26] These served in the days of Joiakim son of Jeshua, son of Jozadak, and in the days of Nehemiah the governor[e] and Ezra the priest and scribe.[f]

Dedication of the Wall

[27] At the dedication of the wall[g] of Jerusalem, they sent for the Levites wherever they lived and brought them to Jerusalem to celebrate the joyous dedication with thanksgiving and singing accompanied by cymbals, harps, and lyres.[h] [28] The singers gathered from the region around Jerusalem, from the villages of the Netophathites,[i] [29] from Beth-gilgal, and from the fields of Geba and Azmaveth, for they had built villages for themselves around Jerusalem. [30] After the priests and Levites had purified themselves, they purified the people, the gates, and the wall.[j]

[31] Then I brought the leaders of Judah up on top of the wall, and I appointed two large processions that gave thanks. One went to the right on the wall, toward the Dung Gate.[k] [32] Hoshaiah and half the leaders of Judah followed, [33] along with Azariah, Ezra, Meshullam, [34] Judah, Benjamin, Shemaiah, Jeremiah,

[35] and some of the priests' sons with trumpets, and Zechariah son of Jonathan, son of Shemaiah, son of Mattaniah, son of Micaiah, son of Zaccur, son of •Asaph followed [36] as well as his relatives—Shemaiah, Azarel, Milalai, Gilalai, Maai, Nethanel, Judah, and Hanani, with the musical instruments of David, the man of God.[l] Ezra the scribe[m] went in front of them. [37] At the Fountain Gate[n] they climbed the steps of the city of David[o] on the ascent of the wall and went above the house of David to the Water Gate[p] on the east.

[38] The second thanksgiving procession went to the left, and I followed it with half the people along the top of the wall, past the Tower of the Ovens[q] to the Broad Wall,[r] [39] above the Gate of Ephraim,[s] and by the Old Gate,[t] the Fish Gate,[u] the Tower of Hananel, and the Tower of the Hundred, to the Sheep Gate.[v] They stopped at the Gate of the Guard.[w] [40] The two thanksgiving processions stood in the house of God. So did I and half of the officials accompanying me, [41] as well as the priests:

> Eliakim, Maaseiah, Miniamin,
> Micaiah, Elioenai, Zechariah,
> and Hananiah, with trumpets;
> [42] and Maaseiah, Shemaiah, Eleazar,
> Uzzi, Jehohanan, Malchijah, Elam,
> and Ezer.

Then the singers sang, with Jezrahiah as the leader. [43] On that day they offered great sacrifices and rejoiced because God had given them great joy.[x] The women and children

Cross references (center column)

[a]12:23 1Ch 9:14-22
[b]12:24 1Ch 16:4; 23:30; 2Ch 29:25
[c]12:25 Neh 11:17
[d]1Ch 26:15,17; Ezr 2:42; Neh 11:19
[e]12:26 Neh 5:14; 10:1
[f]Neh 8:1-2,9
[g]12:27 Ezr 6:16
[h]1Ch 15:16
[i]12:28 1Ch 2:54; 9:16
[j]12:30 Neh 13:22,30
[k]12:31 Neh 2:13
[l]12:36 1Ch 15:16,19-21; 2Ch 8:14; Neh 12:24
[m]Neh 8:1,4
[n]12:37 Neh 2:14
[o]Neh 3:15
[p]Neh 3:26; 8:1
[q]12:38 Neh 3:11
[r]Neh 3:8
[s]12:39 2Kg 14:13; Neh 8:16
[t]Neh 3:6
[u]Neh 3:3
[v]Neh 3:1; Jn 5:2
[w]Neh 3:25
[x]12:43 Ezr 6:16-17,22

(336–331 B.C.). More likely Darius in this passage is a reference to Darius II Nothus (423–404 B.C.).

12:27-43 The grand finale of Nehemiah's ministry took place with the joyous dedication of the rebuilt wall around Jerusalem. While some scholars suggest that this dedication service took place immediately after the completion of the wall (6:15-16), it is more likely that the text is presenting an accurate chronology. Nehemiah's task, along with Ezra's, was to restore the people as well. Thus, the dedication celebrated the rebuilt wall as well as the revitalized people.

12:30 With the **Levites** and singers (vv. 28-29) present, the mandatory purification procedure could begin. For the priests and Levites (probably the "singers" as well, assuming they were included among the Levites at this point), this involved washing their clothes and abstaining from sexual intercourse (Ex 19:14-15), bringing special sacrifices (Nm 8:8-12), and being sprinkled with water (Nm 8:7).

12:31-37 The dedicatory procession began with Nehemiah (the text now resumes with the first-person account from the Nehemiah Memoir) bringing the **leaders** (Hb *sarim*) **up on top of the wall**, where they split into two groups. One group **went to the right on the wall**. The procession must have approached the city from the west, probably mounting the wall at the Valley Gate on the west side of the city. Here they "went

to the right"—or south—toward the **Dung Gate**. Archaeological evidence suggests that the top of the wall was about nine feet wide, allowing people to walk two or three abreast.

The leader of the procession was **Ezra the scribe**, a statement that many regard as impossible. Since many scholars do not believe there was any overlap between the ministries of Ezra and Nehemiah, they consider this statement a pious but flawed attempt to link the ministry of these two great men. However, as D. J. Clines writes, "It cannot be proved that Ezra's participation is unhistorical; it is not impossible that Ezra should have been brought from retirement or from Babylonia specifically to engage in this ceremony."

12:38-39 The second **procession** left the Valley Gate and **went to the left**, or north, in a clockwise direction, passing the **Fish Gate** (northwest corner of the city) and leaving the wall at the **Sheep Gate** at the north end of the city. From there they traveled to the **Gate of the Guard**, an uncertain location that may be identical with the courtyard of the guard (3:25) or the Inspection Gate (3:31). Presumably either location was near the temple.

12:40-43 The two **processions** met at **the house of God**, the temple. Nehemiah acknowledged the source of their **great joy** as **God**.

12:44-47 This section is linked to the dedication celebra-

also celebrated, and Jerusalem's rejoicing was heard far away.[a]

Support of the Levites' Ministry

[44] On that same day men were placed in charge of the rooms[b] that housed the supplies, contributions, •firstfruits, and tenths.[c] The legally required portions for the priests and Levites[d] were gathered from the village fields, because Judah was grateful to the priests and Levites who were serving.[e] [45] They performed the service of their God and the service of purification, along with the singers and gatekeepers,[f] as David and his son Solomon had prescribed.[g] [46] For long ago, in the days of David and Asaph,[h] there were leaders[A] of the singers and songs of praise and thanksgiving to God.[i] [47] So in the days of Zerubbabel[j] and Nehemiah,[k] all Israel contributed the daily portions[l] for the singers and gatekeepers.

They also set aside daily portions for the Levites, and the Levites set aside daily portions[m] for the descendants of Aaron.

Nehemiah's Further Reforms

13 At that time[n] the book of Moses[o] was read publicly to[B] the people.[p] The command was found written in it that no Ammonite or Moabite[q] should ever enter the assembly of God,[r] [2] because they did not meet the Israelites with food and water. Instead, they hired Balaam against them to curse them,[s] but our God turned the curse into a blessing.[t] [3] When they heard the law, they separated all those of mixed descent[u] from Israel.

[4] Now before this, Eliashib the priest[v] had been put in charge of the storerooms of the house of our God.[w] He was a relative[C] of Tobiah[x] [5] and had prepared a large room for him where they had previously stored the •grain offerings,

(reference column)

[a]12:43 Ezr 3:13
[b]12:44 Neh 13:4,13
[c]Neh 10:37-39
[d]Neh 7:39-43
[e]Dt 18:8
[f]12:45 Neh 7:44-45
[g]2Ch 8:14
[h]12:46 2Ch 29:30
[i]1Ch 9:33
[j]12:47 Neh 7:7; Hg 1:1
[k]Neh 1:1; 5:14
[l]Neh 11:23
[m]Nm 18:21
[n]13:1 Neh 12:27
[o]Dt 28:61; Neh 8:1-3
[p]Neh 9:3
[q]Neh 13:23
[r]Dt 23:3
[s]13:2 Nm 22:2-11; 23:7; 24:10; Dt 23:3-5
[t]Dt 23:4-5
[u]13:3 Dt 23:3,6
[v]13:4 Neh 12:10,22-23
[w]Neh 12:44
[x]Neh 2:10; 6:14

A12:46 Alt Hb tradition reads *there was a leader*   B13:1 Lit *read in the ears of*   C13:4 Or *an associate*

---

tion by the phrase **on that same day**, although the issues mentioned prepare the way for the following chapter. Many critical scholars regard the claim that the worship was exactly as **prescribed** by **David and his son Solomon** as a historical retrojection of postexilic worship back into the time of David and Solomon (1Ch 23–36). However, such a position probably reflects more on a scholar's presuppositions about the history of Israel than on exegesis of the biblical text.

13:1-3 At that time designates the era of reform under Nehemiah and not a specific date. During the now customary reading of the **book of Moses**, they read Dt 23:3-6 about the Ammonites and Moabites. The exclusion of the Moabites was because of their attempt to block the Israelites on their way to the promised land and their repeated attacks

(Jdg 3:13; 10:9-17). All those of **mixed descent** (Hb *'eyrev*) were **separated** from Israel, which probably did not mean deportation or breaking of marriages, but exclusion from the worshiping community.

13:4-5 While some identify **Eliashib** as the high priest (3:1,20-21), this is unlikely. The name Eliashib ("God repays" or "God leads back") was common in the postexilic era. Moreover, when Eliashib is identified he is called "the high priest" (3:1,20; 13:28) and never "the priest." Also, the Eliashib in verses 4-8 was the person responsible for the **storerooms** of the temple, which though a position of responsibility, was hardly a job for the high priest. That a **large room** in the temple complex was now empty of offerings and available for Tobiah's use points to the problem that Nehemiah dealt with later (vv. 10-13).

The tomb on the right is the tomb of Artaxerxes I. He died in 424 B.C. of natural causes. His wife is said to have died the same day.

the frankincense, the articles, and the tenths of grain, new wine, and oil[a] prescribed for the Levites, singers, and gatekeepers, along with the contributions for the priests.[b]

[6] While all this was happening, I was not in Jerusalem, because I had returned to King Artaxerxes[c] of Babylon[d] in the thirty-second year of his reign.[e] It was only later that I asked the king for a leave of absence[f] [7] so I could return to Jerusalem. Then I discovered the evil that Eliashib had done on behalf of Tobiah by providing him a room in the courts of God's house. [8] I was greatly displeased and threw all of Tobiah's household possessions out of the room. [9] I ordered that the rooms be purified,[g] and I had the articles of the house of God restored there, along with the grain offering and frankincense.[h] [10] I also found out that because the portions for the Levites had not been given,[i] each of the Levites and the singers performing the service had gone back to his own field.[j] [11] Therefore, I rebuked the officials, saying, "Why has the house of God been neglected?"[k] I gathered the Levites and singers together and

stationed them at their posts.[l] [12] Then all Judah brought a tenth of the grain, new wine, and oil into the storehouses.[m] [13] I appointed as treasurers over the storehouses Shelemiah the priest, Zadok the scribe, and Pedaiah of the Levites, with Hanan son of Zaccur, son of Mattaniah to assist them, because they were considered trustworthy.[n] They were responsible for the distribution to their colleagues.[o]

[14] Remember me for this, my God, and don't erase the deeds of faithful love I have done for the house of my God and for its services.[p]

[15] At that time I saw people in Judah treading wine presses on the Sabbath. They were also bringing in stores of grain and loading them on donkeys, along with wine, grapes, and figs. All kinds of goods were being brought to Jerusalem on the Sabbath day. So I warned them against selling food on that day.[q] [16] The Tyrians living there were importing fish and all kinds of merchandise and selling them on the Sabbath to the people of Judah in Jerusalem.[r]

[17] I rebuked the nobles of Judah and said to them: "What is this evil you are doing—pro-

[a]13:5 Neh 12:44
[b]Nm 13:21-32; Dt 14:28-29; 26:12-15
[c]13:6 Neh 2:1-8
[d]Ezr 5:13
[e]Neh 2:1; 5:14
[f]Neh 1:11; 2:6
[g]13:9 1Ch 23:28; 2Ch 29:5; Neh 13:30
[h]Neh 12:44
[i]13:10 Dt 12:19; Neh 12:44,47
[j]2Ch 29:5
[k]13:11 Neh 10:37-39; Mal 3:10
[l]Neh 12:44-45
[m]13:12 Neh 10:37-38
[n]13:13 Neh 7:2; Ac 6:1-5; 1Co 4:2
[o]Neh 12:47
[p]13:14 Neh 5:19; 13:31
[q]13:15 Ex 20:8-11; Dt 5:12-15
[r]13:16 Neh 10:31

13:6-7 With this verse (v. 6) it becomes clear how such a shameful situation could have occurred in the Lord's temple: Nehemiah was in Babylon. In 5:14, Nehemiah's time in Jerusalem was described as from Artaxerxes' "twentieth year until his thirty-second year—12 years," probably 445–432 B.C. Nehemiah stated that it was **only later** that he asked Artaxerxes for a **leave of absence** to return to Jerusalem and deal with the problems that had arisen. The description of his activity suggests that he returned as governor of the province and not just a private citizen. According to the Elephantine Papyri, a governor named Bagohi was active in Jerusalem in 407 B.C., thus giving a suggested end date for Nehemiah's second governorship.

13:8-13 Tobiah the Ammonite's profaning of the **rooms** provided by Eliashib meant they had to be **purified** before they were restored to their original function. These rooms were empty because during Nehemiah's absence the people had failed to provide a tenth of their produce. While the priests were provided for by their share of the sacrifices, the people had vowed to give a tenth of their produce (10:35-39) for the support of the Levites, singers, and gatekeepers. But in Nehemiah's absence, and with heavy Persian taxes, they had failed to keep their promises, and the Levites had been forced to return to farming. Nehemiah recalled the Levites and their associates back to the temple and insisted that the people give a tenth. To make sure such a situation would not happen again, Nehemiah appointed four **trustworthy** men who represented the various temple personnel to make an equitable **distribution** of the tenths.

13:14 The first of four brief prayers to God by Nehemiah in this chapter occurs in this verse (see note at 4:4-5). He asked the Lord not to **erase** his **deeds of faithful love** (Hb chesed). The thought is that in the records of heaven (Ps 69:28; Dn 7:10; 12:1; Mal 3:16) his acts of faithful love would remain and be acknowledged by the Lord. Nehemiah's "deeds" were those acts of faithfulness to the commission laid upon him by God. The phrase is not an example

of "works righteousness" but an expression of his faithfulness to his call by God to serve as governor.

13:15-16 In 10:31 the people had pledged that they would not buy any merchandise or any kind of grain on the **Sabbath**, but when Nehemiah returned for his second stint as governor, this is exactly what he found. Moreover, the people were working on the Sabbath as if it were just another day. The **Tyrians** were Phoenician traders whose homeland was the region of Tyre and Sidon.

13:17-18 The word **rebuked** is from a Hebrew term (riv) often used in a covenant lawsuit. Nehemiah contended with the nobles of Judah because of their violation of their covenant with God. Even if they were buying only from Gentile traders, their **evil** was clear; they were **profaning the Sabbath day**. During the postexilic era, Sabbath observance took on special significance and served as an important national mark-

'ud

Hebrew Pronunciation	[OOD]
HCSB Translation	be a witness, warn, call as witness
Uses in Nehemiah	6
Uses in the OT	40
Focus Passage	Nehemiah 13:15,21

Debate exists whether 'ud derives from 'ed (witness) or whether the reverse is true. 'Ud denotes be a witness (Mal 2:14), testify (Am 3:13), say on behalf of (Lm 2:13), or speak well of (Jb 29:11). It means warn (Gn 43:3), give a warning (Jr 6:10), charge (Zch 3:6), or admonish (Ps 81:8). It suggests call as witness (Dt 4:26), and occurs with 'ed as appoint or call in (Is 8:2; Jr 32:10). 'Ed (69x) indicates people or things as witnesses. It denotes testimony or evidence (Ex 20:16; 22:13). 'Edut (61x) refers to the two tablets of the Law as God's testimony (Ex 31:18), or to individual laws as testimonies (Jr 44:23). It means warning (Neh 9:34), decree (Ps 119:88), or ordinance (Ps 81:5).

faning the Sabbath day?[a] [18]Didn't your ancestors do the same, so that our God brought all this disaster on us and on this city?[b] And now you are rekindling His anger against Israel by profaning the Sabbath!"

[19]When shadows began to fall on the gates of Jerusalem just before the Sabbath, I gave orders that the gates be closed and not opened until after the Sabbath.[c] I posted some of my men at the gates, so that no goods could enter during the Sabbath day.[d] [20]Once or twice the merchants and those who sell all kinds of goods camped outside Jerusalem, [21]but I warned them, "Why are you camping in front of the wall? If you do it again, I'll use force[A] against you." After that they did not come again on the Sabbath. [22]Then I instructed the Levites to purify themselves[e] and guard the gates in order to keep the Sabbath day holy.[f]

Remember me for this also, my God,[g] and look on me with compassion in keeping with Your abundant, faithful love.[h]

[23]In those days I also saw Jews who had married women from Ashdod, Ammon, and Moab.[i] [24]Half of their children spoke the language of Ashdod or the language of one of the other peoples but could not speak Hebrew.[B][j] [25]I rebuked

them, cursed them, beat some of their men, and pulled out their hair.[k] I forced them to take an oath[l] before God and said: "You must not give your daughters in marriage to their sons or take their daughters as wives for your sons or yourselves![m] [26]Didn't King Solomon of Israel sin in matters like this? There was not a king like him among many nations. He was loved by his God and God made him king over all Israel, yet foreign women drew him into sin.[n] [27]Why then should we hear about you doing all this terrible evil and acting unfaithfully against our God by marrying foreign women?"[o]

[28]Even one of the sons of Jehoiada, son of Eliashib the high priest,[p] had become a son-in-law to Sanballat the Horonite.[q] So I drove him away from me.[r]

[29]Remember them, my God, for defiling the priesthood as well as the covenant of the priesthood and the Levites.[s]

[30]So I purified them from everything foreign[t] and assigned specific duties to each of the priests and Levites.[u] [31]I also arranged for the donation of wood at the appointed times and for the •firstfruits.[v]

Remember me, my God, with favor.[w]

A 13:21 Lit *again, I will send a hand*　**B** 13:24 Lit *Judahite*

Cross references (center column)

[a]13:17 Ex 20:8-11
[b]13:18 Ezr 9:10-11,13; Jr 17:21-23
[c]13:19 Lv 23:32
[d]Neh 7:1,3; Jr 17:21-22
[e]13:22 Neh 12:30; 13:30
[f]Ex 20:8
[g]Neh 5:19; 13:14,31
[h]Neh 1:5; 9:17,27,31
[i]13:23 Dt 23:3; Ezr 9:1-2; Neh 13:1-3; Mal 2:11
[j]13:24 Est 1:22; 8:9
[k]13:25 Ezr 9:3; Is 50:6
[l]Ezr 10:5
[m]Ezr 9:1-2; Neh 10:30
[n]13:26 1Kg 3:13; 11:1-10
[o]13:27 Ezr 9:1-2
[p]13:28 Neh 12:10,22-23
[q]Neh 2:10; 4:1; 6:1
[r]Lv 21:10,13-15
[s]13:29 Neh 6:14; Mal 2:4-8
[t]13:30 Neh 10:30
[u]Neh 12:44-47
[v]13:31 Neh 10:34-36
[w]Neh 5:19; 13:14,22

---

er that distinguished them from their Gentile neighbors. Nehemiah reminded the nobles of Judah of the terrible cost of their Sabbath violations in the past (Ezk 20:18-24) that had brought **this disaster on us and on this city**.

13:19-22 Nehemiah not only "rebuked" the leaders but took action. He closed the **gates** into Jerusalem during the **Sabbath**. Some merchants tried to get around his orders by setting up shop right outside the walls (v. 20), but he warned them that he would disperse them by **force** if it happened again. Posting his **men** to the city gates was only a temporary measure, so Nehemiah ordered the **Levites to purify themselves** and to **guard the gates . . . to keep the Sabbath day holy**. While this was an expansion of the Levites' duties, it was certainly in keeping with their overall purpose of maintaining the sanctity of the temple. The second of four brief prayers in this chapter (v. 22b) records Nehemiah's request that God honor his work in restoring the sanctity of the Sabbath and treat him in accordance with His **faithful love** (Hb *chesed*).

13:23-27 Ezra had dealt with the problem of intermarriage with Gentiles 30 years before (Ezr 10), but the people had reverted to their old ways—to the extent that half of their children spoke **the language of Ashdod** or one of the **other peoples** (lit "the tongue of a people and a people"). Some suggest this was a non-Semitic language related to the language of the Philistines. More likely it was either Aramaic or Phoenician, both of which were closely related to Hebrew and would be understandable to Hebrew speakers, but languages that were clearly distinct from Hebrew. Nehemiah's measures to secure the use of Hebrew appear to have had only temporary success. By the time of Jesus, Aramaic was the common language of the people. Nehemiah's response to this situation (v. 25) seems violent by modern standards, but even until recently the use of physical punishment was common and accepted in many Middle Eastern countries.

Nehemiah reacted strongly because he realized that the sin of intermarriage with Gentiles had been a major cause of the destruction of their nation and their temple.

13:28 To illustrate how serious this problem was, Nehemiah recounted the sad case of a grandson of the high priest **Eliashib** who had married the daughter of **Sanballat the Horonite** (see note at 2:10), the enemy of Nehemiah and God's people. Once again, Nehemiah's response was swift and decisive. Probably the man left Judah and moved to Samaria where his father-in-law was governor.

13:29 In Nehemiah's third prayer in this chapter, he asked God again to **remember**. However, he did not ask God to remember and bless, but to remember and judge. He asked God to remember **them**, probably referring to Sanballat and those within the priesthood who had defiled the **priesthood** by intermarriage with foreigners.

13:30-31 These final verses of the book of Nehemiah give a brief summary of some of Nehemiah's reforms. The fourth and final prayer of the chapter is also the shortest (just four words in Hebrew): **Remember me, my God, with favor** (Hb *tovah*). While the conclusion to Ezra-Nehemiah may seem anti-climactic, the ministries of Ezra and Nehemiah were crucial to the survival of the Jewish people. The small community of exiles struggled to preserve their people and their faith in a devastated land. They found in Ezra and Nehemiah two leaders who were used by the Lord to help them endure in a hostile environment, living as subjects of the Persian kings. That empire, with all its pomp and glory, would fall to Alexander the Great, while the Jewish community would survive not only Alexander and his descendants but the Romans as well. Ezra's and Nehemiah's faithfulness to God helped the Jewish people continue, so they could one day produce a son of Abraham, a son of David (Mt 1:1), who would redeem the world.

Esther

E sther is a unique book. It is the only book in the Bible that never mentions God, although His presence is implied due to Mordecai's allusion to divine providence (4:14). At times the book seems rather secular; historically this has contributed to questions regarding its place in the canon of the synagogue and the church. Esther is tightly connected with specific historical events, yet it is also a piece of literature, a narrative with all of the literary features necessary to make it a great story. It is a book in which its purposes are not always explicitly stated but are derived from the story as a whole.

Persepolis was one of four capitals of the Persian Empire; the others were Susa, Babylon, and Ecbatana. Darius the Great, father of Ahasuerus (Xerxes), began construction on the palace complex in Persepolis that took over a century to finish. Esther and her husband, Ahasuerus, lived during that construction.

Circumstances of Writing

Author: Like most OT books, the author of the book is unknown. In the Jewish Talmud it is suggested that the members of the Great Synagogue wrote the book. However, it is hard to imagine this prestigious group of religious scholars writing a book that mentions the Persian king 190 times but never mentions God. Many early writers, both Jewish as well as Christian, suggested Mordecai as the author.

Background: The story of Esther is rooted in the historical situation of King Xerxes (Ahasuerus), who ruled as king of Persia from 486–465 B.C.

Mid-twentieth century critical scholars tended to date the book late, even into the second century B.C. However, most now argue for an earlier date. The discovery of the Dead Sea Scrolls in 1947 showed that the Hebrew of Esther was very different from the Hebrew of the first century B.C. Also, there are no Greek words in the text of Esther, which would suggest that it was written before Alexander the Great's conquest (ca 333 B.C.) made Greek the language of the region. Most likely the book was written in the fourth century B.C.

The book gives every indication of being a historical narrative. For that reason the alleged historical anomalies in the text raise for many interpreters problems in accepting the historicity of the story. While it is regrettable not to have any extant extrabiblical confirmation of the main characters in the story (Esther, Haman, Mordecai), several points must be considered.

First, there are few extant Persian records for Xerxes' reign. Thus very few historical figures are known from this time. Moreover, the Greek writers, especially Herotodus, were writing their history particularly as it related to the Greeks—not as court historians for the Persians—thus, their material is selective and would leave unmentioned many significant figures. Second, the absence of extrabiblical evidence does not mean these people did not exist. Third, while there is no positive extrabiblical confirmation of these individuals, they appear in an account that even ardent critics acknowledge as being remarkably accurate in its description of the Persian era.

600 B.C.	575 B.C.	550 B.C.
Nineveh is sacked by the Babylonians and the Medes. The Assyrian Empire collapses. 612	Jeremiah's Ministry 627–586?	Cyrus the Great defeats King Astyages of Media at Pasargadae. 550
	Events in Obadiah 605–586?	
	Events in Ezekiel 593–571	Cyrus diverts the waters of the Euphrates and launches a surprise attack against the ancient city of Babylon, taking it without a struggle. 539
Nebuchadnezzar's three invasions of Judah 605, 597, 586	Events in Zechariah 593–571	
	Lamentations 586	
Events in Daniel 605–530		
	Cyrus 559–530	
Prince Nebuchadnezzar of Babylon defeats the Egyptians at the Battle of Carchemish. 605	Events in Haggai 520	Cyrus's decree allows return of Jews from exile. 538
Nebuchadnezzar II becomes king of Babylon. 604		Cyrus is killed in a campaign against the Massagatae of central Asia and his son Cambyses is crowned king of Persia. 530
Temple of Solomon is destroyed. 586		

Message and Purpose

The principle message of the book of Esther called all Jews to celebrate Purim. The purposes of Esther can be distinguished into two types: those purposes that pertain to the original audience of the book during the Persian period, and the broader, theological purposes that transcend the book's original readers.

Hope: For the Jewish people scattered around the Persian Empire, the book of Esther was a story that gave encouragement and hope. It provided a model of how Jewish people could not merely survive but also thrive in a Gentile environment. It showed how Jewish people could effectively serve in positions of high responsibility while maintaining their Jewish identity and their commitment to the God of Israel. It showed how Jewish leaders could be used to bring blessing to their Gentile rulers and neighbors. And for a people far from the land of their forefathers, it demonstrated that the God of Israel was still able to redeem His people in their oppression, whether they were in Egypt, Israel, or Persia.

Divine providence: It is unlikely the lack of any mention of God in the book is accidental. It leaves the reader to ponder the work of God, evident but unseen, in the unfolding story of deliverance and redemption. This is fitting since Jews in exile would be tempted to find lack of evidence for God's overt presence to be evidence for His actual absence. The book of Esther counters this notion, depicting God's providence as ruling even the events of foreign lands during exile.

God's unlikely instruments: Part of the mystery of God's providence in the book is how God can use such unlikely people to help accomplish His plans. Who would ever guess that a young Jewish woman named Hadassah (Esther), an orphan, would end up the queen of the greatest empire the world had ever known? Who but God could bring about such a powerful reversal through the "weakness" of a young woman?

475 B.C.	450 B.C.	400 B.C.
Events in Esther 486–465	Ezra goes to Jerusalem. 458	Greek historian Xenophon is born. 431
Aristotle, Plato's pupil, is born. 484	Events in Nehemiah 445–430	
Ahasuerus's 180-day feast; Vashti deposed 483	Jerusalem's walls are rebuilt under Nehemiah's leadership. 445	Greek playwright Sophochles writes *Oedipus the King.* 429
Esther becomes queen of Persia 479	Athens is defeated by Sparta, Peloponnesian War 431–404	Greek philosopher Plato, student of Socrates, is born. 427
Golden Age of Greek art 477–431		Events in Malachi 420?
At Haman's request, a royal decree is issued for the annihilation of the Jews in the Persian Empire. 474	Greek philosopher Empedocles speculates that the world is made up of four elements: earth, air, water, and fire. 430	The marble figure of *Nike* in the Temple of Athena 407
Esther intercedes with Ahasuerus for her people. 474		
First celebration of Purim 473		

Contribution to the Bible

Without ever mentioning God directly, the book of Esther underscores the providence of God. God's promise to give the Jews an eternal ruler remained in place, even in the face of threatened annihilation. Esther shows us that many Jews remained faithful to their God even in exile. They kept their identity as God's people through the synagogues that developed as the centers of the Jewish community wherever Jews settled. The synagogues would later play a significant role as the gospel spread throughout the Roman Empire, for these served as natural starting places for the deliverance of the gospel in the towns visited by the apostles (e.g., Ac 9:20; 17:1-2; 18:19; 19:8).

Structure

The Hebrew of the Masoretic Text used as the basis for the Holman Christian Standard Bible is a fairly straightforward text. It is written in a form of late biblical Hebrew common to the postexilic era and found in other biblical books of that time, such as Chronicles, Ezra-Nehemiah, and Daniel. Like Ezra-Nehemiah, Esther shows the growing influence of Aramaic in its grammar and vocabulary, as well as the presence of many Persian words.

Outline

I.   A Replacement Queen (1:1–2:20)
    A. Vashti angers the king (1:1-12)
    B. The king's decree (1:13-22)
    C. Search for a new queen (2:1-14)
    D. Esther becomes queen (2:15-20)

II. A Dangerous Threat (2:21–3:15)
    A. Mordecai saves the king (2:21-23)
    B. Haman's plan to kill the Jews (3:1-15)

III. Esther's Daring Decision (4:1–5:14)
    A. Mordecai's appeal to Esther (4:1-17)
    B. Esther approaches the king (5:1-14)

IV. The Great Reversal (6:1–10:3)
    A. Mordecai honored by the king (6:1-14)
    B. Haman is executed (7:1-10)
    C. Esther intervenes for the Jews (8:1-17)
    D. Victories of the Jews (9:1-32)
    E. Mordecai remembered (10:1-3)

Vashti Angers the King

1 These events took place during the days of Ahasuerus,[A,a] who ruled 127 provinces[b] from India[B] to ˙Cush. [2]In those days King Ahasuerus reigned from his royal throne[c] in the fortress at Susa.[d] [3]He held a feast[e] in the third year of his reign for all his officials and staff, the army of Persia and Media,[f] the nobles,[g] and the officials from the provinces. [4]He displayed the glorious wealth of his kingdom and the magnificent splendor of his greatness[h] for a total of 180 days.

[5]At the end of this time, the king held a week-long banquet[i] in the garden courtyard[j] of the royal palace[k] for all the people, from the greatest to the least,[l] who were present in the fortress of Susa.[m] [6]White and violet linen hangings were fastened with fine white and purple linen cords to silver rods on marble[c] columns.

*a*1:1 Ezr 4:6; Dn 9:1
*b*Est 8:9; 9:30
*c*1:2 1Kg 1:46
*d*Ezr 4:9; Neh 1:1; Dn 8:2
*e*1:3 Gn 40:20; 1Kg 3:15; Est 2:18
*f*Dn 5:28
*g*Est 6:9; Dn 1:3
*h*1:4 Dn 4:28-30
*i*1:5 Est 2:18
*j*2Kg 21:18; Est 7:7-8
*k*Est 2:8 *l*Est 1:20 *m*Ezr 4:9

[A]1:1 = Xerxes; he reigned 486-465 b.c. [B]1:1 = modern Pakistan [C]1:6 Or *alabaster*

1:1-2 Ahasuerus is the Hebrew name for King Xerxes, who ruled from 486–465 b.c., and who is mentioned only two other times in the rest of the OT (Ezr 4:6; Dn 9:1). Critical scholars regard the statement that Ahasuerus **ruled 127 provinces** as an error, yet this is not an impossible figure (cp. Dn 6:1). The Persian records speak of satrapies, which according to various accounts, would number between 20 and 31, but the term used in this verse is "provinces" (Hb *medinah*), which would be subdivisions of a satrapy. An example of this from Ezra-Nehemiah (see note at Ezr 4:11) would be the division of the satrapy of "Beyond the River" into many provinces, such as Samaria and *Yehud* (Hb for Judah). The easternmost border of the vast Persian Empire was the Indus River, now in Pakistan but once part of **India** during the time of the British *raj*. The westernmost extent of the empire was to **Cush**, the region south of Egypt called Upper Nubia, which today is part of northern Sudan.

Chapter 1 of Esther is set in the **fortress** (Hb *birah*) **at Susa**, one of the three capital cities of the Persian Empire along with Ecbatana and Persepolis (some would argue that Babylon was also a capital city). It is located in what is today southwestern Iran and was the capital of the ancient empire of Elam during the second millennium b.c. During

Xerxes' rule Susa was the usual location of his winter palace.

1:3-4 In the **third year** of Ahasuerus, probably 483 b.c., there occurred the first of 10 feasts recorded in Esther, which are important structural and thematic markers in the book. The word "feast" (Hb *mishteh*) is derived from the Hebrew verb *shathah*, meaning "to drink." The "feast" was more of a drinking bout than a meal. The ancient Greek writers mentioned that the Persians were famous (or infamous) for their prodigious drinking.

Many critical scholars assume the mention of **180 days** to be a legendary exaggeration. However, it is not clear whether verse 4 suggests that the party itself went on for 180 days, or instead that for a half year after the party there was a royal celebration in which Ahasuerus **displayed the glorious wealth of his kingdom**. It is more likely the latter, since it is hard to imagine how the government could function during a six-month drunken celebration. Also, it seems unlikely that a 180-day party would continue into the brutal summer heat, a time when the royal family normally relocated to their summer palace in Ecbatana.

1:5-8 Unlike the first feast, the second **banquet** (or "feast,"

Heart of the Persian Empire in the time of Esther

- ● City
- ○ Major Persian administrative center
- ⛫ Royal citadel of Persian kings
- ▲ Mountain peak
- ⚔ Battle
- PERSIS Satrapy or regional name
- — Royal road
- — Other road
- ☐ Persian Empire

Caucasus Mts.

Phasis

CASPIAN SEA

Trapezus

Cyrus River

ARMENIA   Mt. Ararat

Malatya   L. Van

Tigris River   Araxes River   L. Urmia

Carchemish   Nineveh   MEDIA   Elburz Mts.   HYRCANIA   Zadrakarta (Turang Tepe)   Tesmes (Meshed)

Haran   ATHURA   Arbela   Ecbatana   Rhagae   Damghan

Thapsakos   Asshur   Diyala River   Behistun   PARTHIA

Tadmor   Euphrates River   SAGARTIA

Eshnunna   SUSIANA   Gabae (Isfahan)   Iranian Plateau

Cunaxa   Sippar   Der

Babylon   Opis   Nippur   SUSA

Borsippa   BABYLONIA   ELAM

Xerxes sacks Babylon in 480 b.c.

Uruk   Ur   Winter capital of ancient Persia and setting of the Book of Esther

ARABIA   Dumah   Kerman

Pasargadae

PERSIS   Persepolis

Xerxes dies in a palace coup in 465 b.c.

Tema   Syro-Arabian Desert

Dedan   PERSIAN GULF

Gold and silver couches[a] were arranged on a mosaic pavement of red feldspar,[A] marble,[B] mother-of-pearl, and precious stones.

[7]Beverages were served in an array of gold goblets,[b] each with a different design. Royal wine flowed freely, according to the king's bounty[c] [8]and no restraint was placed on the drinking. The king had ordered every wine steward in his household to serve as much as each person wanted. [9]Queen Vashti also gave a feast for the women of King Ahasuerus's palace.

[10]On the seventh day, when the king was feeling good from the wine,[d] Ahasuerus commanded Mehuman, Biztha, Harbona,[e] Bigtha, Abagtha, Zethar, and Carkas, the seven eunuchs[f] who personally served him, [11]to bring Queen Vashti before him with her royal crown. He wanted to show off her beauty to the people and the officials, because she was very beautiful.[g] [12]But Queen Vashti refused to come at the king's command that was delivered by his eunuchs. The king became furious and his anger burned within him.[h]

[a]1:6 Est 7:8; Ezk 23:41; Am 6:4
[b]1:7 Dn 5:1-3
[c]Est 2:18
[d]1:10 2Sm 13:28
[e]Est 7:9
[f]2Kg 20:18; Est 2:21; 6:14; Mt 19:12
[g]1:11 Est 2:7
[h]1:12 Est 7:7; Pr 19:12
[i]1:13 Jr 10:7; Dn 2:2,12; Mt 2:1
[j]1Ch 12:32
[k]1:14 Ezr 7:14
[l]Dn 5:28
[m]2Kg 25:19
[n]Dn 2:48-49
[o]1:16 Est 1:1,3,5; 9:30

The King's Decree

[13]The king consulted the wise men[i] who understood the times,[C,j] for it was his normal procedure to confer with experts in law and justice. [14]The most trusted ones[D] were Carshena, Shethar, Admatha, Tarshish, Meres, Marsena, and Memucan. They were the seven officials[k] of Persia and Media[l] who had personal access to the king[m] and occupied the highest positions in the kingdom.[n] [15]The king asked, "According to the law, what should be done with Queen Vashti, since she refused to obey King Ahasuerus's command that was delivered by the eunuchs?"

[16]Memucan said in the presence of the king and his officials, "Queen Vashti has wronged not only the king, but all the officials and the peoples who are in every one of King Ahasuerus's provinces.[o] [17]For the queen's action will become public knowledge to all the women and cause them to despise their husbands and say, 'King Ahasuerus ordered Queen Vashti brought before him, but she did not come.' [18]Before this day is over, the noble women of

---

[A]1:6 Or of porphyry   [B]1:6 Or alabaster   [C]1:13 Or understood propitious times   [D]1:14 Lit Those near him

---

v. 3; Hb *mishteh*) was not for the nobility but for all the citizenry in the **fortress of Susa**. The event is described in great detail (v. 6) to highlight the opulence and wealth of the king. For the Persians, it must have been regarded as a fabulous party because the **royal wine flowed freely, according to the king's bounty** (lit "according to the hand of the king"). Moreover, by royal decree each guest could drink as much as he desired or was capable of drinking since **no restraint was placed on the drinking** (lit "as to the law [Hb *dath*] of the drinking, no restraint").

1:9 The third **feast** was given by **Queen Vashti**, who is first introduced in this verse, and it was only for **the women**. Both biblical and extrabiblical sources demonstrate that women were often present at the feasts, but their presence was not mentioned at the two earlier feasts (vv. 3,5). Neither Persian nor Greek records mention a queen named Vashti, but rather identify Amestris as queen during Xerxes' reign. Most critical scholars regard the reference to Vashti as a historical blunder on the part of the author of Esther. However, several prominent OT scholars suggest that Vashti may be not a proper name but a title, possibly related to the Avestan (ancient Indo-Iranian language) *Vahishta,* meaning "the best." Vashti disappears from the story when she is replaced by Esther (2:17).

1:10-12 Jewish readers who were well versed in the Scriptures would probably recognize the ominous mention of **feeling good from the wine**. King Belshazzar was also "under the influence of the wine" (Dn 5:2) when he literally saw the writing on the wall. Most of the references to **eunuchs** in the OT occur in the book of Esther. They held positions of power, such as serving as cupbearer, and could be trusted with the care of the royal wives and concubines. Three of the names listed for the eunuchs (**Mehuman, Biztha . . . Carkas**) have parallels with names found in the Elamite Persepolis texts (E. Yamauchi, *Persia and the Bible*). The king's call for **seven** eunuchs could suggest that

Queen Vashti was carried to the banquet on a royal litter.

No one was as shocked as King Ahasuerus when Queen Vashti **refused** his royal command. Both of the Jewish Targums of Esther (Aram paraphrases of the Hb text) state that the king commanded Vashti to appear before his drunken friends wearing *only* her **crown**, but this is an unlikely reading of the text. Ahasuerus's intense fury was predictable. His own wife had publicly disobeyed the most powerful man in the Persian Empire. The chronology of this event may give additional insight into the king's anger. If this occurred in "the third year" of Ahasuerus's rule (483 B.C.), it might coincide with the preparations for war with the Greeks. As Karen Jobes writes, "Ahasuerus needed his men to obey his commands as they went to war, but in his own palace he could not even get his own wife to obey."

1:13-14 Some suggest the phrase **who understood the times** refers to astrologers and translate the phrase as "who understood propitious times." However, the answer from these **wise men** does not mention the stars or the zodiac. More likely the reference to those who "understood the times" is like the usage in 1Ch 12:32 in which the men of Issachar "understood the times," that is, they were simply wise men. The names of the seven wise men, also called **officials** (Hb *sarim*), are not identifiable with known Persian individuals, but for three of the men (**Meres, Marsena, and Memucan**), Elamite parallels have been found for their names (Yamauchi).

1:16 Memucan's recommendation (vv. 19-20) was based on his assertion that Queen Vashti's action was not just a personal affront but also a universal affront against **all** (Hb *kol*) the **officials** and all (Hb *kol*) the **peoples** who lived in all (Hb *kol*) the **provinces**. Memucan's exaggeration served only to legitimize the poor advice he was about to give the king.

1:18 The syntax of the Hebrew text of verse 18 is difficult because there is no object for the verb "they will say" (Hb *to'marna*). One simple solution is to assume the loss of

Persia and Media who hear about the queen's act will say the same thing to all the king's officials, resulting in more contempt and fury.

[19] "If it meets the king's approval, he should personally issue a royal decree. Let it be recorded in the laws of Persia and Media, so that it cannot be revoked:[a] Vashti is not to enter King Ahasuerus's presence, and her royal position is to be given to another woman who is more worthy than she.[b] [20] The decree the king issues will be heard throughout his vast kingdom,[c] so all women will honor their husbands,[d] from the least to the greatest."[e]

[21] The king and his counselors approved the proposal, and he followed Memucan's advice. [22] He sent letters to all the royal provinces, to each province in its own script and to each ethnic group in its own language,[f] that every man should be master of his own house and speak in the language of his own people.

Search for a New Queen

2 Some time later,[g] when King Ahasuerus's rage[h] had cooled down, he remembered

Vashti, what she had done, and what was decided against her.[i] [2] The king's personal attendants[A] suggested, "Let a search be made for beautiful young women for the king.[j] [3] Let the king appoint commissioners[k] in each province of his kingdom, so that they may assemble all the beautiful young women to the harem at the fortress of Susa.[l] Put them under the care of Hegai, the king's eunuch,[m] who is in charge of the women,[n] and give them the required beauty treatments. [4] Then the young woman who pleases the king[o] will become queen instead of Vashti."[p] This suggestion pleased the king, and he did accordingly.

[5] In the fortress of Susa, there was a Jewish man named Mordecai[q] son of Jair, son of Shimei,[r] son of Kish,[s] a Benjaminite. [6] He had been taken into exile from Jerusalem with the other captives when King Nebuchadnezzar of Babylon took King Jeconiah[B] of Judah into exile.[t] [7] Mordecai was the legal guardian of his cousin[C] Hadassah (that is, Esther), because she didn't have a father or mother. The young woman had a beautiful figure and was

Cross references (center column)

[a] 1:19 Est 8:8; Dn 6:8,15
[b] Est 2:2,4,17
[c] 1:20 Est 1:1; 8:9
[d] Est 1:10-12; Eph 5:22,24,33; Col 3:18; 1Tm 2:12; 1Pt 3:1
[e] Est 1:5
[f] 1:22 Neh 13:24; Est 3:12; 8:9
[g] 2:1 Est 1:3,10
[h] Est 1:12; 7:10
[i] Est 1:10-12,16-21
[j] 2:2 1Kg 1:2
[k] 2:3 Gn 41:34
[l] Neh 1:1; Est 1:1; Dn 8:2
[m] Est 1:10
[n] Est 2:8-9,12-13
[o] 2:4 Est 2:17
[p] Est 1:19
[q] 2:5 Ezr 2:2; Est 2:15; 3:2
[r] 2Sm 6:5-13
[s] 1Sm 9:1
[t] 2:6 2Kg 24:10-15; 2Ch 36:10; Jr 24:1; 29:1-2

[A] 2:2 Lit *The young men of the king who served him*   [B] 2:6 = Jehoiachin in 2Kg 24; 25:27; 1Ch 3:16-17   [C] 2:7 Lit *uncle's daughter*

---

a definite article marker (Hb *'eth*) before the phrase **who hear**. This would give a translation such as "the noble women of Persia and Media will say *what* they have heard about the queen's act."

1:19 The irrevocability of the **laws of Persia and Media** is not documented either in Persian or Greek literature, although it is mentioned several times in the OT (8:8; Dn 6:8,12). Some scholars regard this as an historical inaccuracy on the part of the author; M. Fox writes, "It would be impossible to run a government by such a principle." But as D. J. Clines very plausibly notes, "The meaning here is that the decision should be incorporated among official decisions so that it will be strictly carried out." The consort was always called "Queen Vashti" until this verse; now she is simply "Vashti."

1:20 This passage is replete with irony and satire. King Ahasuerus, who could not control his own wife, now issues a universal **decree** that **all women** would **honor their husbands**.

1:22 The final phrase of the decree is unusual and has engendered much debate: **and speak in the language of his own people**. Some scholars suggest changing the text, while others follow the LXX and simply delete it (NRSV, NLT). Another possibility is to understand the phrase "speak in the language of the people" as referring to the decree and not to the husband. The issuance of the decree to the entire empire is ironic because it ensured that everyone in the empire would know about the king's marital struggles, and not just the "noble women" of Susa (v. 18).

2:1 The vague description **some time later** is of little help in determining the time frame in the story. It is clear from verse 16 that Esther did not meet King Ahasuerus until four years after the first events (479–478 B.C.). Some suggest that the search for a replacement queen only started when Ahasuerus returned from his fighting with the Greeks (479 B.C.).

2:2-3 The word translated **young women** (Hb *betulah*) does not necessarily mean "virgins," as the usage in verses 17-19 and Ezk 23:3-8 attests, but in this context it is clear that only young women without prior sexual experience would be acceptable to the king. Possible brides would be brought to the **harem** (lit "house of the women") at **Susa**.

2:5-7 In this important parenthetical flashback, two more main characters in the story are introduced—**Mordecai** and **Esther**. The name Mordecai was a common name, a Hebrew form of the Babylonian name Marduka, derived from Marduk, the principle god of Babylon.

Mordecai's genealogy is problematic if it is attempting to link him to **Kish** the father of King Saul (1Sm 9:1). This Kish could hardly have been Mordecai's great-grandfather, since

betulah

Hebrew Pronunciation	[beh too LAH]
HCSB Translation	young woman, virgin
Uses in Esther	4
Uses in the OT	50
Focus Passage	Esther 2:2-3,17,19

Betulah designated *young woman*, for *betulah* is paired with *bachur*, which implies *choice young man* (2Ch 36:17). A *betulah* was normally unmarried (Lv 21:14) and was expected to be a *virgin* because Israelite sexual law put a penalty on premarital sex (Dt 22:23-29). *Betulah* may not have had to entail virginity, for this fact is sometimes added after the word (Gn 24:16). Occasionally *betulah* must signify *virgin* (Est 2:2; Ezk 44:22). Tamar probably tore her dress, one worn by *virgins*, to mark her grief at losing this status (2Sm 13:18-19). *Betulah* can encompass an *engaged woman* (Jl 1:8). Harem *virgins* are still called *betulah* after spending a night with the king (Est 2:17), and a *betulah* can be ravished (Is 23:12). Whether *betulah* is *virgin* or *young woman* depends on what Scripture emphasizes. The stress can be on youth and stage in life (Ezk 9:6) or on virginity (Dt 22:19).

extremely good-looking. When her father and mother died, Mordecai had adopted her as his own daughter.[a]

[8] When the king's command and edict became public knowledge, many young women gathered at the fortress of Susa under Hegai's care. Esther was also taken to the palace and placed under the care of Hegai, who was in charge of the women. [9] The young woman pleased him and gained his favor[A] so that he accelerated the process of the beauty treatments and the special diet that she received. He assigned seven hand-picked female servants to her from the palace and transferred her and her servants to the harem's best quarters.

[10] Esther did not reveal her ethnic background or her birthplace, because Mordecai had ordered her not to. [11] Every day Mordecai took a walk in front of the harem's courtyard to learn how Esther was doing and to see what was happening to her.

[12] During the year before each young woman's turn to go to King Ahasuerus, the harem regulation required her to receive beauty treatments with oil of myrrh for six months and then with perfumes and cosmetics for another six months. [13] When the young woman

would go to the king, she was given whatever she requested to take with her from the harem to the palace. [14] She would go in the evening, and in the morning she would return to a second harem under the supervision of Shaashgaz, the king's eunuch in charge of the concubines.[b] She never went to the king again, unless he desired her and summoned her by name.[c]

Esther Becomes Queen

[15] Esther was the daughter of Abihail,[d] the uncle of Mordecai who had adopted her as his own daughter. When her turn came to go to the king, she did not ask for anything except what Hegai, the king's trusted official in charge of the harem, suggested. Esther won approval in the sight of everyone who saw her.[e]

[16] She was taken to King Ahasuerus in the royal palace in the tenth month, the month Tebeth, in the seventh year of his reign.[f] [17] The king loved Esther more than all the other women. She won more favor and approval from him than did any of the other young women. He placed the royal crown on her head and made her queen in place of Vashti.[g] [18] The king held a great banquet for all his of-

[a]2:7 Est 9:29
[b]2:14 1Kg 11:3; Dn 5:2
[c]Est 4:11
[d]2:15 Est 9:29
[e]Est 5:2,8
[f]2:16 Est 1:2
[g]2:17 Est 1:10-11; 2:4

[A]2:9 Lit and carried faithful love before him

---

the time gap between the two was over 500 years. Either a different Kish is in view, or it could be that the term "son of" means here "descendant of," a common usage in the OT that in this case would indicate that the author is choosing to identify only a handful of Mordecai's line of ancestors.

An additional difficulty is associated with verse 6—he **had been taken into exile from Jerusalem** during the time of Nebuchadnezzar. If "he" is Mordecai, this would make him almost 120 years old when Esther was chosen. It is possible to read verse 6 as identifying Kish as the "he" and not Mordecai, which would also lend credence to the theory that a different individual named Kish is intended here, not King Saul's father. Esther is introduced first with her Hebrew name, **Hadassah**, the name of the myrtle tree. Her "Gentile" name was Esther, derived from the name of the famous goddess Ishtar. Her physical beauty would give her an edge in replacing Vashti (1:9).

2:8-9 The statement that Esther **was also taken to the palace** does not necessarily suggest she was taken unwillingly, although one of the Jewish Targums of Esther suggests this. A later Midrash on the book of Esther states that Esther hid for four years before being captured and taken to the royal harem (Aggadath, *Esther* 2:8). Both the Targum and the Midrash can be commended for trying to protect Esther's virtue, but there is no biblical evidence that Esther resisted going to the harem, and clear evidence from this present passage shows she cooperated in the preparation for becoming the king's new queen. Esther's chances to become queen increased as she **pleased** Hegai, the eunuch in charge of the potential brides. He also gave her a **special diet** (Hb *minoth*). The Hebrew term used here usu-

ally means "portions," often in the sense of delicacies (Neh 8:10,12), which were probably not *kosher*.

2:10 It is not explicitly stated why Mordecai **ordered** Esther to hide her Jewish background. When Esther finally revealed her ethnicity to King Ahasuerus, he appeared untroubled by it (7:3). Yet clearly some people of that era, especially Haman (3:4-6), hated the Jews.

2:12-13 The mention of one-year **beauty treatments** for each **young woman** sounds excessive and indulgent. Probably it was intended to emphasize the grandeur and pomp of the king who deserved partners meticulously prepared for the privilege of being his consort. Each prospect could **take with her** whatever **she requested** when she went to the king, presumably perfumes, jewelry, and clothes.

2:16-18 Esther's turn to please the king came in what would have been the winter of 479–478 B.C. The story gives no hint of moral judgment about the actions of Esther, a young Jewish virgin who gave herself to a pagan, uncircumcised, Persian king. In the ethic of that era it was simply a given that kings had the right to collect a harem. More intriguing is the fact of God's working through another "divine coincidence." God's sovereignty was at work through the encounter of a pagan king and a Jewish virgin, for it would lead to the rescue of God's people.

The vacancy created by the deposing of Vashti was now filled by Esther, whose coronation was celebrated with **a great banquet**. This banquet contrasts with the fateful banquet where Queen Vashti refused to appear (1:12) and foreshadows the banquets yet to come, especially the crucial banquets with Haman (chaps. 5 and 7), and the banquets of rejoicing for the Jewish people in chapters 8 and 9.

ficials and staff.[a] It was Esther's banquet. He freed his provinces from tax payments and gave gifts worthy of the king's bounty.[b]

[19] When the young women[c] were assembled together for a second time, Mordecai was sitting at the King's Gate.[d] [20] Esther still had not revealed her birthplace or her ethnic background, as Mordecai had directed. She obeyed Mordecai's orders, as she always had while he raised her.

Mordecai Saves the King

[21] During those days while Mordecai was sitting at the King's Gate, Bigthan and Teresh, two eunuchs[e] who guarded the king's entrance, became infuriated and planned to assassinate[A] King Ahasuerus. [22] When Mordecai learned of the plot, he reported it to Queen Esther, and she told the king on Mordecai's behalf.[f] [23] When the report was investigated and verified, both men were hanged on the gallows.[g] This event was recorded in the Historical Record in the king's presence.

Haman's Plan to Kill the Jews

3 After all this took place, King Ahasuerus honored Haman, son of Hammedatha the Agagite.[h] He promoted him in rank and gave him a higher position than all the other officials.[i] [2] The entire royal staff at the King's Gate[j] bowed down and paid homage to Haman, because the king had commanded this to be done for him. But Mordecai would not bow down or pay homage.[k] [3] The members of the royal staff at the King's Gate asked Mordecai, "Why are you disobeying the king's command?" [4] When they had warned him day after day[l] and he still would not listen to them, they told Haman to see if Mordecai's actions would be tolerated, since he had told them he was a Jew.

[5] When Haman saw that Mordecai was not bowing down or paying him homage, he was filled with rage.[m] [6] And when he learned of Mordecai's ethnic identity, Haman decided not to do away with[B] Mordecai alone. He planned to destroy all of Mordecai's people, the Jews,[n] throughout Ahasuerus's kingdom.[o]

[7] In the first month, the month of Nisan,[C] in King Ahasuerus's twelfth year,[D,p] Pur (that is, the lot) was cast before Haman for each day in each month, and it fell on the twelfth month,[q] the month Adar.[E,r] [8] Then Haman informed King Ahasuerus, "There is one ethnic group, scattered throughout the peoples in every province of your kingdom,[s] yet living in isolation. Their laws are different from everyone else's and they do not obey the king's laws.[t] It is not in the king's best interest to tolerate them.[u] [9] If the king approves, let an order be

---

Cross references (center column):

[a] 2:18 Est 1:3
[b] Est 1:7
[c] 2:19 Est 2:12-14
[d] Est 5:13
[e] 2:21 Est 1:10,12; 2:3,14
[f] 2:22 Est 6:2-3
[g] 2:23 Gn 40:19,22; Est 5:14; 7:9-10
[h] 3:1 Ex 17:8-16; 1Sm 15:20
[i] Est 1:3,21; 2:18
[j] 3:2 Est 2:19,21
[k] Est 5:9
[l] 3:4 Gn 39:10
[m] 3:5 Est 1:12; 2:21; 7:7; Dn 3:19
[n] 3:6 Est 6:10
[o] Est 9:24; Ps 83:2-4
[p] 3:7 Est 1:2; 2:16
[q] Est 9:24-28
[r] Ezr 6:15
[s] 3:8 Est 1:1; 8:11,17; 9:2
[t] Jr 29:7; Ac 16:20-21
[u] Ezr 4:12-15

[A] 2:21 Lit *and they sought to stretch out a hand against*   [B] 3:6 Lit *to stretch out a hand against*   [C] 3:7 = March–April; called Abib in the pre-exilic period; Ex 13:4; Dt 16:1   [D] 3:7 474 B.C.   [E] 3:7 = February–March

---

The phrase **freed . . . from tax payments** translates a single Hebrew word *(hanachah)* that occurs only here in the OT. It has the connotation of "causing to rest," possibly indicating a rest from work in commemoration of the queen's coronation. This translation is supported by the mention of the giving of **gifts worthy of the king's bounty** and by the Latin translation as well.

2:19 It may be that the **young women** of the king's harem (vv. 12-14) were not allowed to be present at "Esther's Banquet" but got together at a different time to celebrate with their friend who was now queen. The mention of **Mordecai** at **the King's Gate** suggests that he was some kind of official in the Persian court. This would help explain why he was living in the fortress at Susa (1:2) and not in the city of Susa, and how he could be within earshot of conspirators who were plotting Ahasuerus's murder. The King's Gate in Susa was a massive monumental structure that measured 131 feet by 92 feet, with a column-like tower on each corner that was 40 feet high.

2:21-23 The story of Esther takes a new turn with Mordecai's discovery of a plot to **assassinate King Ahasuerus**. Mordecai informed the king through **Queen Esther**. Esther not only was Mordecai's best contact with the king, but her passing on of the news would have endeared her to the king. In terms of the narrative, this section of the story sets the stage for the delayed honoring of Mordecai at Haman's expense (chaps. 6–7). The seemingly mundane mention of the incident being **recorded in the Historical Record** serves as an important part of the plot, setting up Ahasuerus's later discovery of his failure to honor Mordecai (6:1-3).

3:1-6 This section is a critical part of the narrative that introduces the last protagonist in the story (Haman) and the conflict that now dominates the narrative (threat to the Jews). The initial incident that sparked the conflict was Mordecai's refusal to bow to Haman. A Jewish person was not forbidden by Scripture or cultural custom to bow down to a person in authority, but Mordecai, who presumably bowed down to the king and to other officials, repeatedly (vv. 2-4) refused to bow down to Haman. One of the most plausible explanations for Mordecai's refusal relates to Haman's name: **Haman . . . the Agagite**. While Mordecai was possibly from the line of King Saul (see 2:5-7 and note there), Haman was a descendant of Agag (1Sm 15:8-33), the leader of the Amalekites. King Saul's disobedience in sparing King Agag (1Sm 15:8-9) resulted in Samuel's announcement that the Lord had taken the kingdom away from him and by extension his descendants (1Sm 15:27). Possibly this ancient enmity explains Mordecai's refusal to bow to Haman the Agagite.

3:7 The **Pur** appears to derive from the Akkadian term *puru* meaning a "lot" or "fate." Presumably Haman wanted his astrologers or diviners to pick the most propitious date to launch his vengeance against Mordecai and his people. The month that was identified by lot was the month of **Adar** (normally March–April).

3:8-9 Haman cleverly began his presentation to Ahasuerus by starting with the truth (**There is one ethnic group, scattered throughout the peoples**) and ending with a lie (**they do not obey the king's laws**). His offer to give the crown

drawn up authorizing their destruction, and I will pay 375 tons of silver to[A] the accountants for deposit in the royal treasury."[a]

[10] The king removed his signet ring[b] from his finger and gave it to Haman son of Hammedatha the Agagite, the enemy of the Jewish people.[c] [11] Then the king told Haman, "The money and people are given to you to do with as you see fit."

[12] The royal scribes were summoned[d] on the thirteenth day of the first month, and the order was written exactly as Haman commanded. It was intended for the royal satraps,[e] the governors of each of the provinces, and the officials of each ethnic group and written for each province in its own script and to each ethnic group in its own language.[f] It was written in the name of King Ahasuerus[g] and sealed with the royal signet ring.[h] [13] Letters were sent by couriers[i] to each of the royal provinces telling the officials to destroy, kill, and annihilate all the Jewish people—young and old, women and children—and plunder their possessions on a single day,[j] the thirteenth day of Adar, the twelfth month.[B]

[14] A copy of the text, issued as law throughout every province, was distributed to all the peoples so that they might get ready for that day. [15] The couriers left, spurred on by royal command, and the law was issued in the for-

tress of Susa.[k] The king and Haman sat down to drink, while the city of Susa was in confusion.[l]

Mordecai Appeals to Esther

4 When Mordecai learned all that had occurred,[m] he tore his clothes,[n] put on *sackcloth and ashes,[o] went into the middle of the city, and cried loudly and bitterly.[p] [2] He only went as far as the King's Gate,[q] since the law prohibited anyone wearing sackcloth from entering the King's Gate. [3] There was great mourning among the Jewish people in every province where the king's command and edict[r] came. They fasted, wept, and lamented, and many lay on sackcloth and ashes.[s]

[4] Esther's female servants and her eunuchs came and reported the news to her, and the queen was overcome with fear.[t] She sent clothes for Mordecai to wear so he could take off his sackcloth, but he did not accept them. [5] Esther summoned Hathach, one of the king's eunuchs assigned to her, and dispatched him to Mordecai to learn what he was doing and why.[C] [6] So Hathach went out to Mordecai in the city square in front of the King's Gate. [7] Mordecai told him everything that had happened as well as the exact amount of money Haman had promised to pay the royal treasury for the slaughter of the Jews.[u]

[a] 3:9 Est 4:7
[b] 3:10 Gn 41:42; Est 8:2,8,10; Hg 2:23
[c] Est 7:6; 9:10
[d] 3:12 Est 8:9
[e] Ezr 8:36
[f] Est 1:22; 8:9
[g] 1Kg 21:8
[h] Est 8:10
[i] 3:13 2Ch 30:6; Est 8:14
[j] Est 8:11-13; 9:10
[k] 3:14-15 Est 8:13-14
[l] 3:15 Est 7:1; 8:15
[m] 4:1 Est 3:7-15
[n] 2Sm 1:11; 3:31; Ezr 9:3
[o] Is 58:5; Dn 9:3
[p] Ex 11:6
[q] 4:2 Est 2:19; 3:2
[r] 4:3 Est 3:12-15
[s] Est 8:17; Is 58:5; Dan 9:3; Jnh 3:5-6
[t] 4:4 Est 7:6
[u] 4:7 Est 3:9-15

[A] 3:9 Lit will weigh 10,000 silver talents on the hands of   [B] 3:13 LXX adds the text of Ahasuerus's letter here.   [C] 4:5 Lit what is this and why is this

375 tons of silver to pay for an empire-wide extermination may have encouraged Ahasuerus, whose coffers had been depleted by the war with the Greeks. The magnitude of the gift is apparent if one uses Herotodus's estimation of the income of the Persian king; such a gift from Haman would represent over half of the annual income of the Persian Empire. Yet it appears that the king may have refused the offer (v. 11), although both Mordecai and Esther assumed the king accepted it (4:7; 7:4).

3:10-11 Haman's request was granted by Ahasuerus, who gave him his **signet ring**, used by the king to put his official wax seal on a state document. With that ring, Haman now had the power to carry out his planned extermination. Ahasuerus's almost casual endorsement was chilling in its consequences. King Ahasuerus never even bothered to ask the identity of the ethnic group that Haman planned to destroy. **The money** is **given to you** may indicate that the king refused Haman's offer of "375 tons of silver" (v. 9).

3:12-15 The instructions were clear: all **young and old, women and children** were to be destroyed, killed, and annihilated (v. 13). The terrible decree was to be executed 11 months later, on the **thirteenth day of Adar**. Critics charge that such a decree that would be implemented almost a year later is ludicrous, since people would have had ample time to flee. But the Jews were dispossessed exiles whose lives depended on the king's good pleasure. Had they picked up to flee, undoubtedly the genocide would have been trig-

gered early, for their fleeing would have been seen as an attempt to evade the king's decree.

The picture of Haman and the king drinking and congratulating themselves on their solution to the problem of the Jews contrasts with the disposition of the city. The impression is that the people in Susa were not in favor of the decree nor did they share Haman's rabid anti-Semitism.

4:1-3 Mordecai's response to the king's edict was typical for his culture (see notes at Ezr 9:3; Neh 9:1). All who saw him recognized his grief, especially since he **cried loudly and bitterly** (lit "he cried out a great cry"). The term "to cry out" (Hb za'aq) is often used in the OT to describe a heartbroken howl over injustice (Gn 18:20), personal tragedy (2Sm 13:19), or national tragedy (Ezk 9:8). While Mordecai would not get the king's attention, he did get Esther's (Est 4:4), which was crucial. A law prohibiting a mourner to come into the palace is not attested in the ancient sources, but in a similar vein, Nehemiah stated that he had "never been sad" in King Artaxerxes' presence before, and when asked about it by Artaxerxes he "was overwhelmed by fear" (Neh 2:1-2). Mordecai was not alone in his grief. The **Jewish people in every province** wept and **lamented** and many lay on **sackcloth and ashes**. In many ways Mordecai epitomizes, or is representative of, the Jewish people.

4:4-7 The phrase **was overcome with fear** is from a Hebrew verb (chil) often translated as "writhe, tremble," occurring often in the context of childbirth. Here it is used to describe intense emotion, and it could be translated as "writhed in

⁸Mordecai also gave him a copy of the written decree issued in Susa ordering their destruction, so that Hathach might show it to Esther, explain it to her, and command her to approach the king, implore his favor, and plead with him personally for her people.ᵃ ⁹Hathach came and repeated Mordecai's response to Esther.

¹⁰Esther spoke to Hathach and commanded him to tell Mordecai, ¹¹"All the royal officials and the people of the royal provinces know that one law applies to every man or woman who approaches the king in the inner courtyardᵇ and who has not been summoned—the death penalty.ᶜ Only if the king extends the gold scepter will that person live.ᵈ I have not been summoned to appear before the kingᵉ for the lastᴬ 30 days." ¹²Esther's response was reported to Mordecai.

¹³Mordecai told the messenger to reply to Esther, "Don't think that you will escape the fate of all the Jews because you are in the king's palace. ¹⁴If you keep silent at this time, liberation and deliverance will come to the Jewish

people from another place,ᶠ but you and your father's house will be destroyed. Who knows, perhaps you have come to your royal position for such a time as this."ᵍ

¹⁵Esther sent this reply to Mordecai: ¹⁶"Go and assemble all the Jews who can be found in Susa and fast for me. Don't eat or drink for three days,ʰ day or night. I and my female servants will also fastⁱ in the same way. After that, I will go to the king even if it is against the law.ʲ If I perish, I perish."ᵏ ¹⁷So Mordecai went and did everything Esther had ordered him.

Esther Approaches the King

5 On the third day,ˡ Esther dressed up in her royal clothing and stood in the inner courtyardᵐ of the palace facing it. The king was sitting on his royal throne in the royal courtroom, facing its entrance. ²As soon as the king saw Queen Esther standing in the courtyard, she won his approval.ᴮ The king extended the gold scepter in his hand toward Esther, and she approached and touched the tip of the scepter.ⁿ

³"What is it, Queen Esther?" the king asked

Cross references:
ᵃ4:8 Est 7:3-4
ᵇ4:11 Est 5:1
ᶜDn 2:9,12-13
ᵈEst 5:2; 8:4
ᵉEst 2:14
ᶠ4:14 Gn 50:20
ᵍGn 45:5-7
ʰ4:16 Est 5:1; Jl 1:14
ⁱEst 9:31
ʲEst 5:1-2
ᵏGn 43:14
ˡ5:1 Est 4:16
ᵐEst 4:11
ⁿ5:2 Est 8:4

ᴬ4:11 Lit king these   ᴮ5:2 Lit she obtained favor in his eyes; Est 2:15,17

---

anguish" or "was agitated." The name **Hathach** possibly means "courier."

4:8-9 The courier was told to **explain** the decree. Either **Esther** was illiterate and the decree had to be read to her, or it was written in Persian and had to be translated into Aramaic. Mordecai was certainly aware of the danger he was putting Esther in by telling her to **plead . . . personally** with the king, but their situation was desperate. It is interesting how he emphasized that the Jews were "her people," the same people he had previously commanded her not to identify with (2:10).

4:10-11 Esther's response to Mordecai through Hathach was to remind him that to come to the king unbidden was certain **death**. Such a law was understandable in the Persian Empire with its long history of political assassinations (in fact Ahasuerus was murdered in his own bed less than ten years later). The one exception to this rule was if the king allowed an uninvited person to approach him, signified by his extending **the gold scepter**. Some assume that Esther's statement in verse 11 indicated that her absence from her husband was because she had fallen out of favor with him or that his passion for her had waned. Thus, the king might be less likely to respond to her unexpected presence and request. On the other hand, possibly her purpose was only to tell Mordecai that in the normal routine she did not see the king often, and this request would require her to make an unscheduled—and dangerous—visit.

4:13-14 Mordecai's reply to Esther was direct and to the point. Esther had no safe choices. Appearing unbidden before the king could mean death, but remaining silent, when so many servants and eunuchs knew of her connection to Mordecai the Jew, could likewise result in her death once the genocide was carried out.

Mordecai's statement that help would come **from another place** if Esther remained quiet is intriguing. The most

obvious interpretation is to understand the phrase "another place" (Hb *mimmaqom 'acher*) as a veiled reference to God, an interpretation supported by the Greek additions to Esther (Alpha Text 5:9), both Aramaic Targums, and Josephus. Others find it more likely that "another place" refers to a human source of deliverance, possibly Mordecai himself or another well-placed Jewish official similar to Nehemiah, who served Ahasuerus's son (Artaxerxes) as cupbearer. Mordecai and Esther would regard **liberation and deliverance**, whatever the source, as attributable ultimately to God's providential care for His people. This conclusion is supported by Mordecai's famous suggestion that Esther had **come to your royal position for such a time as this**. As T. Laniak notes, this meant God had a "destiny for Esther. Haven't all of the serendipitous events in the last four years put her in this position for this very moment?" (NIBC).

4:16 Often in times of crisis God's people would **fast** and pray, seeking God's help and deliverance (Jdg 20:26; 1Kg 21:9; Jr 36:9). Fasting took on an even more prominent role in the postexilic community (Ezr 8:21-23; Neh 1:4; 9:1-2). But this fast was unusually long, highlighting the severity of the threat to the Jewish people. Esther's last comment to Mordecai in this chapter (**If I perish, I perish**) is not just resigned fatalism. As M. Fox writes, this statement "does not suggest a person seeking an escape route, but one facing and coming to grips with a danger. The statement recognizes the possibility of failure, yet also expresses the hope—though not certainty—of success" (*Character*, p. 64).

5:1-2 On the **third day** of the three-day fast, Esther prepared herself for her surprise appearance before the king. She wore not her fasting and mourning clothes, but **her royal clothing**, possibly as a reminder to her husband that she was indeed the queen of Persia. When she **won his approval** (Hb *cheyn*), what could have precipitated her death had instead become her opportunity.

her. "Whatever you want, even to half the kingdom, will be given to you."[a]

[4] "If it pleases the king," Esther replied, "may the king and Haman come today to the banquet[b] I have prepared for them."

[5] The king commanded, "Hurry, and get Haman so we can do as Esther has requested." So the king and Haman went to the banquet Esther had prepared.

[6] While drinking the[A] wine,[c] the king asked Esther, "Whatever you ask will be given to you. Whatever you want, even to half the kingdom, will be done."

[7] Esther answered, "This is my petition and my request: [8] If the king approves of me[B] and if it pleases the king to grant my petition and perform my request,[d] may the king and Haman come to the banquet I will prepare for them.[e] Tomorrow I will do what the king has asked."

[9] That day Haman left full of joy and in good spirits.[C,f] But when Haman saw Mordecai at the King's Gate, and Mordecai didn't rise or tremble in fear at his presence, Haman was filled with rage toward Mordecai.[g] [10] Yet Haman controlled himself and went home. He sent for his friends and his wife Zeresh[h] to join him. [11] Then Haman described for them his glorious wealth and his many sons. He told them all how the king had honored him and promoted him in rank over the other officials and the royal staff.[i] [12] "What's more," Haman added, "Queen Esther invited no one but me to join the king at the banquet she had prepared. I am invited again tomorrow to join her with the king. [13] Still, none of this satisfies

[a]5:3 Est 7:2; Mk 6:23
[b]5:4 Est 1:3,5; 2:18
[c]5:6 Est 1:7-8,10; 7:1-2
[d]5:8 Est 7:3; 8:5
[e]Est 6:14
[f]5:9 1Kg 8:66; 2Ch 7:10; Pr 15:15
[g]Est 2:19; 3:2,5
[h]5:10 Est 6:13
[i]5:11 Est 3:1
[j]5:14 Est 6:4; 7:9-10
[k]Est 6:13
[l]6:1 Dn 6:18
[m]6:1-2 Est 2:21-23
[n]6:3 Est 10:2-3; Dn 2:48
[o]6:4 Est 5:14
[p]6:6 Est 3:8-9
[q]6:8-9 Gn 41:42-43

me since I see Mordecai the Jew sitting at the King's Gate all the time."

[14] His wife Zeresh and all his friends told him, "Have them build a gallows 75 feet[D] high.[j] Ask the king in the morning to hang Mordecai on it. Then go to the banquet with the king and enjoy yourself." The advice pleased Haman, so he had the gallows constructed.[k]

Mordecai Honored by the King

[6] That night sleep escaped[l] the king, so he ordered the book recording daily events to be brought and read to the king. [2] They found the written report of how Mordecai had informed on Bigthana and Teresh, two eunuchs who guarded the king's entrance, when they planned to assassinate King Ahasuerus.[m] [3] The king inquired, "What honor and special recognition have been given to Mordecai for this act?"[n]

The king's personal attendants replied, "Nothing has been done for him."

[4] The king asked, "Who is in the court?" Now Haman was just entering the outer court of the palace to ask the king to hang Mordecai on the gallows he had prepared for him.[o]

[5] The king's attendants answered him, "Haman is there, standing in the court."

"Have him enter," the king ordered.

[6] Haman entered, and the king asked him, "What should be done for the man the king wants to honor?"[p]

Haman thought to himself, "Who is it the king would want to honor more than me?" [7] Haman told the king, "For the man the king wants to honor: [8] Have them bring a royal garment that the king himself has worn[q] and a

---

[A]5:6 Lit During the banquet of   [B]5:8 Lit If I have found favor in the eyes of the king   [C]5:9 Lit left rejoicing and good of heart   [D]5:14 Lit 50 cubits

5:3-4 Ahasuerus's offer to Esther, **even to half the kingdom**, was not to be taken literally; it was an exaggeration meant to emphasize the generosity of the king (cp. Mk 6:23). Considering the breadth of the offer, the answer must have been surprising: an invitation for the **king** and **Haman** to come to a **banquet** (Hb *mishteh*) that Esther had prepared. Just as the first banquet in the story ended with the downfall of a queen (chap. 1), so this series of banquets would end with the downfall of the king's second in command (chap. 7).

5:4,8 Interpreters have speculated endlessly on Esther's motives in inviting Haman. A common suggestion is that Esther was trying to get Ahasuerus jealous and thus create a rift between her husband and Haman (7:7-8). Whatever the motivation, these scenes add to the story and make Haman's catastrophic fall all the more dramatic.

5:9 Haman's **rage** only got worse when he saw that Mordecai not only did not **rise** in his presence, but did not even **tremble** (Hb *zua'*, a verb used only five times in the OT) in **his presence**. Defying Haman did not even make Mordecai nervous.

5:14 Just as Jezebel once plotted with her husband to kill an innocent man (1Kg 21:7), so now **Zeresh**, along with Haman's **friends**, suggested a plan to publicly murder his enemy, Mordecai. Zeresh believed this plan would assuage her husband's murderous rage against his enemy. Haman was **pleased** with his wife's advice and he had the gallows constructed, believing the next day would be a triumphant moment in his life.

6:1-3 No reason is given for the king's insomnia. Some ancient Jewish writers suggested that Ahasuerus was worried about what Esther was going to ask for the next day at her second banquet. The LXX emphasizes the divine cause of his sleeplessness: "The Lord withdrew (Gk *aphistemi*) sleep (Gk *hupnos*) from the king." Apparently the king believed reading the tedious royal journal of **daily events** might lull him to sleep. Instead, it exposed a royal oversight as mention was made of Mordecai's unrewarded heroism.

6:8-9 Haman did not covet money or power, because he already had both. What he desired was the glory and splendor of royalty, including **royal** robes and a public **parade**.

horse the king himself has ridden,[a] which has a royal diadem on its head. [9]Put the garment and the horse under the charge of one of the king's most noble officials.[b] Have them clothe the man the king wants to honor, parade him on the horse through the city square, and proclaim before him, 'This is what is done for the man the king wants to honor.'"

[10]The king told Haman, "Hurry, and do just as you proposed. Take a garment and a horse for Mordecai the Jew,[c] who is sitting at the King's Gate. Do not leave out anything you have suggested." [11]So Haman took the garment and the horse. He clothed Mordecai and paraded him through the city square, crying out before him, "This is what is done for the man the king wants to honor."

[12]Then Mordecai returned to the King's Gate,[d] but Haman, overwhelmed,[A] hurried off for home with his head covered.[e] [13]Haman told his wife Zeresh and all his friends[f] everything that had happened. His advisers and his wife Zeresh said to him, "Since Mordecai

is Jewish, and you have begun to fall before him, you won't overcome him, because your downfall is certain."[g] [14]While they were still speaking with him, the eunuchs of the king[h] arrived and rushed Haman to the banquet Esther had prepared.[i]

Haman Is Executed

7 The king and Haman came to feast[B,j] with Esther the queen. [2]Once again, on the second day while drinking wine,[k] the king asked Esther, "Queen Esther, whatever you ask will be given to you. Whatever you seek, even to half the kingdom, will be done."[l]

[3]Queen Esther answered, "If I have obtained your approval,[c] my king, and if the king is pleased,[m] spare my life—this is my request; and spare my people—this is my desire.[n] [4]For my people and I have been sold out[o] to destruction, death, and extermination.[p] If we had merely been sold as male and female slaves,[q] I would have kept silent. Indeed, the trouble wouldn't be worth burdening the king."

Reference column (center):
[a] 6:8 1Kg 1:33
[b] 6:9 Est 5:11
[c] 6:10 Est 3:6
[d] 6:12 Est 5:9,13
[e] 2Sm 15:30
[f] 6:13 Est 5:10,14
[g] Dt 32:10; Zch 2:8
[h] 6:14 Est 1:10-11
[i] Est 5:7-8
[j] 7:1 Gn 40:20
[k] 7:2 Est 5:6
[l] Est 5:3,6
[m] 7:3 Est 2:17; 5:8
[n] Est 4:12-14
[o] 7:4 Est 3:9,13; 4:7
[p] Est 3:13; 8:11; 9:5-10
[q] Dt 28:48,68

[A]6:12 Lit mourning   [B]7:1 Lit drink   [C]7:3 Lit If I have found favor in your eyes

---

6:10-11 For Haman, events began to spin out of control. The greatest honor Haman could imagine receiving was bestowed on **Mordecai the Jew**, his enemy whom he had planned to hang that day.

6:12-13 To cover one's head was a sign of mourning (Jr 14:4). While no one had died, Haman was mourning his humiliation. The previous advice of Haman's **wife** and **friends** (5:14), who were presumably his **advisers** (lit "his wise ones," Hb chakamim), had been given as they offered a solution to Haman's problem with Mordecai. But now their counsel was ominous: once a person stumbles before a Jew, there is no hope. Why so? The text does not say. Some suggest that Haman's advisers were aware of Cyrus's decree (Ezr 1:1-11)

that had allowed the exiles to return home and reestablish themselves in Jerusalem. Or maybe the Jews had told their Persian friends about Balaam's oracle that prophesied blessings on the Jews in place of the curses sought by their enemies (Nm 24:1-10) or about how God had intervened for his people against genocidal Egyptian oppressors (Nm 24:8-9). This is how the Aramaic Targums understood it. On "Targums," see note at 1:10-12.

6:14 Haman had no time to react to their counsel because he was **rushed** to the **banquet Esther had prepared**. It is significant that this is the fourth mention of Haman "rushing" or "hurrying" in the last two chapters (vv. 10,12,14; 5:5). Previously he was in charge; now he was caught up in the rapid events of the moment.

7:1-10 Up to this point two intertwined conflicts have remained unresolved: the primary conflict, the threat of extinction of the Jews because of Haman's royal edict; and the secondary conflict, the personal struggle between Mordecai and Haman. The national threat is not resolved until chapter 9. This short chapter concludes the confrontation between Haman and Mordecai with poetic justice.

7:2 King Ahasuerus did not literally expect Esther to ask for half the kingdom, but her delayed answer must have convinced him that she had a well-thought-out, significant request.

7:3-4 Esther's request was direct and to the point: **spare** her **life** and spare her **people**. Esther continued with a carefully nuanced assertion: **For my people and I have been sold out**. She could hardly charge her husband directly ("You sold me out"), but she couched it in an indefinite passive voice ("have been sold out"; Hb nimkarnu). Esther had not told the king she was Jewish, and she did not identify "her people." But as she continued her plea, the king was given a clue: they had been sold out **to destruction, death, and extermination**, a direct quote from the edict crafted by Haman and authorized by her husband (3:13).

---

chaphets

Hebrew Pronunciation	[khah FAYTZ]
HCSB Translation	delight, desire, please
Uses in Esther	7
Uses in the OT	73
Focus Passage	Esther 6:6-7,9,11

Chaphets implies being delighted (Gn 34:19), pleased (Nm 14:8), satisfied (Dt 21:14), or impressed (Ps 147:10). People want (Dt 25:7), like (1Sm 19:1), desire (Hs 6:6), or favor (2Sm 20:11) others or things. They choose (Pr 21:1), prefer (Jb 13:3), or intend (Jdg 13:23). Chaphets can take another verb (Is 53:10). Someone finds/takes pleasure (Ezk 18:23) or delights in something (2Sm 22:20). Actions are appropriate (Sg 2:7). Chaphets (38x) indicates pleasure (Is 58:13b), will (Is 46:10), care (Jb 21:21), wish (Jb 31:16), want (1Kg 5:8), longing (Ps 107:30), desire (Pr 3:15), or delight (Ec 12:1). Stones are precious (Is 54:12). Chephets, like the root in Arabic, denotes activity or situation (Ec 3:1; 5:8). The name Hephzibah (2Kg 21:1) means "My Delight Is in Her" (Is 62:4). The adjective chaphets (13x), usually translated verbally, similarly involves desiring, wishing, wanting, willing, and delighting (Mc 7:18).

⁵King Ahasuerus spoke up and asked Queen Esther, "Who is this, and where is the one who would devise such a scheme?"[A,a]

⁶Esther answered, "The adversary and enemy[b] is this evil Haman."

Haman stood terrified[c] before the king and queen. ⁷Angered[d] by this, the king arose from where they were drinking wine and went to the palace garden.[e] Haman remained to beg Queen Esther for his life because he realized the king was planning something terrible for him.[f] ⁸Just as the king returned from the palace garden to the house of wine drinking, Haman was falling on the couch[g] where Esther was reclining. The king exclaimed, "Would he actually violate the queen while I am in the palace?" As soon as the statement left the king's mouth, Haman's face was covered.[h]

⁹Harbona, one of the royal eunuchs,[i] said: "There is a gallows 75 feet[B] tall at Haman's house that he made for Mordecai,[j] who gave the report that saved[C] the king."[k]

The king commanded, "Hang him on it."

¹⁰They hanged Haman on the gallows he had prepared for Mordecai.[l] Then the king's anger subsided.[m]

a 7:5 Est 3:5-6,8-9
b 7:6 Est 3:10
c Est 4:4
d 7:7 Est 1:12; Pr 20:2
e Est 1:5-6
f Est 6:13
g 7:8 Est 1:6
h Est 6:12; Jb 9:24
i 7:9 Est 1:12
j Est 5:14
k Est 2:21-23; 6:1-2
l 7:10 Est 5:14; Ps 7:16; 94:23; Pr 11:5,6; Dn 6:24
m Est 1:12; 2:1
n 8:1 Est 3:9; 5:11
o Est 3:10; 7:6
p Est 2:7,10
q 8:2 Est 3:10,12
r 8:3 Est 7:3-4,6
s Est 7:7
t Ex 17:8-16; Est 3:1
u 8:4 Est 3:5-6,8-15
v 8:4 Est 4:11; 5:2
w 8:5 Est 2:17; 5:8; 7:3
x Est 3:13-14
y 8:6 Est 4:13-14; 7:3-4
z Est 3:13

Esther Intervenes for the Jews

8 That same day King Ahasuerus awarded Queen Esther the estate[n] of Haman, the enemy of the Jews.[o] Mordecai entered the king's presence because Esther had revealed her relationship to Mordecai.[p] ²The king removed his signet ring he had recovered from Haman[q] and gave it to Mordecai, and Esther put him in charge of Haman's estate.

³Then Esther addressed the king again.[r] She fell at his feet, wept, and begged[s] him to revoke the evil of Haman the Agagite,[t] and his plot he had devised against the Jews.[u] ⁴The king extended the gold scepter[v] toward Esther, so she got up and stood before the king.

⁵She said, "If it pleases the king, and I have found approval before him, if the matter seems right to the king and I am pleasing in his sight,[w] let a royal edict be written. Let it revoke the documents the scheming Haman son of Hammedatha the Agagite, wrote to destroy the Jews who are in all the king's provinces.[x] ⁶For how could I bear to see the disaster that would come on my people?[y] How could I bear to see the destruction of my relatives?"[z]

⁷King Ahasuerus said to Esther the Queen

A 7:5 Lit who would fill his heart to do this   B 7:9 Lit 50 cubits   C 7:9 Lit who spoke good for

---

7:5-6 Both Ahasuerus's questions and Esther's reply reflect the intensity of their emotions. The term **terrified** (Hb niv'at) is the same word used to describe King David's terror when he was confronted by the angel of the Lord with a sword in his hand at Araunah's threshing floor (1Ch 21:30), and to portray Daniel's intense fear when the angel Gabriel approached him (Dn 8:17).

7:7 For the first time in the book of Esther the king had to make crucial decisions without his counselors. Suddenly he was forced to choose between his prime minister and his wife. But if he deposed Haman for threatening his wife and her people, would not Haman counter by revealing that the king himself had approved of the plan? While the king struggled with his decisions in the garden, Haman stayed back with Esther **to beg** (Hb lebaqqesh) **for his life**. Before, it was Esther (v. 3) who had sought ("desire," Hb baqqashah) to be spared, but now the tables were turned.

7:8 If the king was still undecided about Haman's fate as he returned from the garden, his decision was made certain as he caught Haman fawning over the queen. Court documents from the Assyrian period state that a man must not come closer than seven steps to one of the women in the palace (D. J. Clines). The Jewish Targums of Esther (Aram paraphrase of the Hb texts) state that Haman was **falling on the couch** because the angel Gabriel gave him a shove!

The author of the story skillfully used the concept of "falling" (Hb naphal). Haman was furious at Mordecai because he would not bow down to him (3:1-4). This resulted in the casting (Hb naphal) of the Pur to set the date for the extermination of the Jews (3:7). Then Haman's wife and friends warned him that "since Mordecai is Jewish, and you have begun to fall (Hb naphal) before him, you won't overcome him, because your downfall (Hb naphal) is certain" (6:13).

Only hours later Haman was falling (Hb naphal) on Esther's couch. With this final fall his fate was sealed.

7:10 The irony demonstrated in this verse is stated proverbially in Pr 26:27 and Mt 26:52.

8:1-2 All in the **same day** Haman was forced to honor Mordecai (6:4-11), went to the second banquet and was charged with trying to kill the queen and her people (7:1-8), and was hanged. The theme of reversal continues into chapter 8, as Esther, once threatened by Haman, was **awarded** his **estate**, which elevated her uncle Mordecai.

8:3-4 Many commentators have maintained that verse 3 introduces a new scene into the story, but the phrase **then Esther addressed the king again** need not be understood this way. While Esther was certainly pleased with the king's honoring of Mordecai, the larger issue of the death sentence upon her people had not been addressed. Rather than being annoyed at Esther's breach of royal protocol by falling at his feet, the king **extended the gold scepter toward Esther**, allowing her to state her request.

8:5-6 Esther prefaced her request with an extended version of the normal deferential statement one would make to a king. The first two phrases were standard (1:19; 5:4; 7:3), but she continued in order to make the king's decision seem like a referendum on his love for her. Esther did not point out the injustice of the decree (which the king had approved), but focused on how it would impact her.

8:7-8 The king's response is ambiguous in the Hebrew Bible. While some commentators think he was positive toward her request, others suggest a tone of exasperation or even irritation. Possibly the Greek (LXX) translation suggests this, as the king reminded her about all he had done for her and added, "What do you yet seek?" (Gk ti eti epizeyteis). Nevertheless, the king gave Esther and Mordecai the opportunity

and to Mordecai the Jew, "Look, I have given Haman's estate to Esther,[a] and he was hanged on the gallows because he attacked[A] the Jews.[b] [8]You may write in the king's name whatever pleases you[c] concerning the Jews, and seal it with the royal signet ring.[d] A document written in the king's name and sealed with the royal signet ring cannot be revoked."[e]

[9]On the twenty-third day of the third month[f] (that is, the month Sivan),[B] the royal scribes were summoned. Everything was written exactly as Mordecai[g] ordered for the Jews, to the satraps,[h] the governors, and the officials of the 127 provinces from India[C] to •Cush.[i] The edict was written for each province in its own script, for each ethnic group in its own language,[j] and to the Jews in their own script and language.

[10]Mordecai wrote in King Ahasuerus's name and sealed the edicts with the royal signet ring. He sent the documents by mounted couriers,[k] who rode fast horses[l] bred from the royal racing mares.

[11]The king's edict gave the Jews in each and every city the right to assemble and defend themselves, to destroy, kill, and annihilate every ethnic and provincial army hostile to them, including women and children, and to take their possessions as spoils of war.[m] [12]This would take place on a single day throughout all the provinces of King Ahasuerus, on the thirteenth day of the twelfth month, the month Adar.[D,n]

[13]A copy of the text, issued as law throughout every province, was distributed to all the peoples[o] so the Jews could be ready to avenge themselves against their enemies on that day. [14]The couriers rode out in haste on their royal

horses at the king's urgent command. The law was also issued in the fortress of Susa.[p]

[15]Mordecai went from the king's presence clothed in royal purple and white, with a great gold crown and a purple robe of fine linen.[q] The city of Susa shouted and rejoiced,[r] [16]and the Jews celebrated[E] with gladness, joy, and honor.[s] [17]In every province and every city, wherever the king's command and his law reached, joy and rejoicing took place among the Jews. There was a celebration and a holiday.[F,t] And many of the ethnic groups of the land professed themselves to be Jews because fear of the Jews[u] had overcome them.

Victories of the Jews

[9] The king's command and law[v] went into effect on the thirteenth day of the twelfth month,[w] the month Adar.[D] On the day when the Jews' enemies[x] had hoped to overpower them, just the opposite happened. The Jews overpowered those who hated them.[y] [2]In each of King Ahasuerus's provinces[z] the Jews assembled in their cities to attack those who intended to harm them.[G] Not a single person could withstand them; terror of them[aa] fell on every nationality.[ab]

[3]All the officials of the provinces, the satraps, the governors, and the royal civil administrators[H,ac] aided the Jews because they were afraid of Mordecai.[ad] [4]For Mordecai exercised great power in the palace,[ae] and his fame spread throughout the provinces as he became more and more powerful.[af]

[5]The Jews put all their enemies to the sword, killing and destroying them.[ag] They did what they pleased to those who hated them. [6]In the fortress of Susa[ah] the Jews killed and

Cross references (center column):

a 8:7 Est 3:9; 5:11; 8:1; Pr 13:22
b Est 7:9-10
c 8:8 Est 3:11
d Est 3:10,12; 8:2; Hg 2:23
e Est 1:19; Dn 6:8,12
f 8:9 Est 3:7,12
g Est 3:12
h Ezr 8:36
i Est 1:1; 3:13; 9:30
j Neh 13:24; Est 1:22; 3:12
k 8:10 Est 3:12-13
l 1Kg 4:26,28
m 8:11 Est 3:13; 9:10
n 8:12 Est 3:7
o 8:13 Est 3:14
p 8:14 Est 3:15
q 8:15 Gn 41:42; Est 5:11; Dn 5:29
r Est 3:15
s 8:16 Ezr 4:1-3; Ps 97:11
t 8:17 Est 4:3
u Dt 11:25; Est 9:3
v 9:1 Est 8:7-8,10
w Est 3:7; 8:12
x Est 3:10; 7:6; 8:1
y 2Sm 22:41; Est 3:5
z 9:2 Est 1:1; 8:9; 9:30
aa Est 8:17
ab Est 3:12,14; 8:13,17
ac 9:3 Est 3:12; 8:9
ad Est 8:17
ae 9:4 Est 10:2-3
af 2Sm 3:1; 1Ch 11:9
ag 9:5 Est 3:13
ah 9:6 Est 1:2; 3:15; 8:14

A8:7 Lit *stretched out his hand against*   **B**8:9 = May–June   **C**8:9 = modern Pakistan   **D**8:12; 9:1 = February–March   **E**8:16 Lit *had light*   **F**8:17 Lit *good day*   **G**9:2 Lit *cities to send out a hand against the seekers of their evil*   **H**9:3 Lit *and those who do the king's work*; Est 3:9

---

to write a new decree that would counter but not rescind his original order.

8:9 Since the Jewish people were speaking Aramaic, as were many in the Persian Empire, the counter-edict that was written **in their own script** must have been written in Hebrew.

8:10 The **edicts** were sealed with the **royal signet ring**, once worn by Haman in order to destroy the Jews, but now worn by Mordecai to save the Jews.

8:11-12 Just as Haman's edict decreed the destruction of the Jews on the thirteenth of Adar (3:12), the Jews now had the legal right to defend themselves that same day.

8:15-17 Mordecai had once torn his clothes and gone around in "sackcloth and ashes" (4:1); now he wore the **royal purple and white**. Once the city of Susa was "in confusion" (3:15); now the people **shouted and rejoiced**. The Jews had once "fasted, wept, and lamented, and . . . lay on sackcloth and ashes" (4:3); now they **celebrated with gladness, joy, and**

honor. While the Jews had once been in fear of the **ethnic groups** among whom they lived, now some of the ethnic groups were in **fear of the Jews**. The phrase **professed themselves to be Jews** is a single word in Hebrew (Hb *mityahadim*). Found only here in the OT, it is a reflexive verb derived from the proper noun "Jew" (Hb *yehudi*). Some understand the verb to mean "to become a Jew"—to convert to Judaism; this interpretation is supported by the Greek text (LXX). However, it is more likely that the term means that the people identified themselves with the Jewish people; this meaning may be supported by the Latin Vulgate.

9:1 The theme of reversal comes to its culmination on an empire-wide scale.

9:6-10 Haman's anti-Semitism, and the resentment of those who lost positions of influence when Mordecai replaced Haman, may explain why the Jews in the fortress of **Susa** had to kill **500 men**. Haman had taken pride in his **10 sons** (5:11); now they shared his fate.

destroyed 500 men, [7] including Parshandatha, Dalphon, Aspatha, [8] Poratha, Adalia, Aridatha, [9] Parmashta, Arisai, Aridai, and Vaizatha. [10] They killed these 10 sons[a] of Haman son of Hammedatha, the enemy of the Jews.[b] However, they did not seize[A] any plunder.[c]

[11] On that day the number of people killed in the fortress of Susa was reported to the king. [12] The king said to Queen Esther, "In the fortress of Susa the Jews have killed and destroyed 500 men, including Haman's 10 sons. What have they done in the rest of the royal provinces? Whatever you ask will be given to you. Whatever you seek will also be done."[d]

[13] Esther answered, "If it pleases the king, may the Jews who are in Susa also have tomorrow[e] to carry out today's law,[f] and may the bodies of Haman's 10 sons[g] be hung on the gallows."[h] [14] The king gave the orders for this to be done, so a law was announced in Susa, and they hung the bodies of Haman's 10 sons. [15] The Jews in Susa assembled again on the fourteenth day of the month of Adar[i] and killed 300 men in Susa, but they did not seize[A] any plunder.[j]

[16] The rest of the Jews in the royal provinces assembled, defended themselves, and got rid of[B] their enemies. They killed 75,000[c] of those who hated them,[k] but they did not seize[A] any plunder. [17] They fought on the thirteenth day of the month of Adar and rested on the four-

teenth, and it became a day of feasting and rejoicing.

[18] But the Jews in Susa had assembled on the thirteenth and the fourteenth days of the month. They rested on the fifteenth day of the month, and it became a day of feasting and rejoicing.[l] [19] This explains why the rural Jews who live in villages observe the fourteenth day of the month of Adar as a time of rejoicing and feasting. It is a holiday when they send gifts to one another.[m]

[20] Mordecai[n] recorded these events and sent letters to all the Jews in all of King Ahasuerus's provinces, both near and far. [21] He ordered[o] them to celebrate the fourteenth and fifteenth days of the month Adar every year [22] because during those days the Jews got rid of[D,p] their enemies. That was the month when their sorrow was turned into rejoicing and their mourning into a holiday.[q] They were to be days of feasting,[r] rejoicing, and of sending gifts to one another and the poor.

[23] So the Jews agreed to continue the practice they had begun, as Mordecai had written them to do. [24] For Haman son of Hammedatha the Agagite, the enemy of all the Jews,[s] had plotted against the Jews to destroy them. He cast the Pur (that is, the lot) to crush and destroy them.[t] [25] But when the matter was brought before the king,[u] he commanded by letter that the evil plan Haman had devised against the Jews return on his own head[v] and

[a]9:10 Est 5:11
[b]Est 3:10; 7:6; 8:1
[c]Est 3:13; 8:11
[d]9:12 Est 5:6; 7:2; 8:8
[e]9:13 Est 8:12; 9:1
[f]Est 8:11
[g]Est 5:11
[h]Est 7:9-10
[i]9:15 Est 9:1
[j]Est 8:11
[k]9:16 Lv 26:7-8; Est 9:5
[l]9:18 Est 8:16-17
[m]9:19 Neh 8:10,12; Est 9:22
[n]9:20 Est 8:15
[o]9:21 Est 8:15; 9:3-4
[p]9:22 Est 4:14
[q]Ps 30:11
[r]Est 8:17
[s]9:24 Est 3:1,10; 7:6
[t]Est 3:6-7
[u]9:25 Est 7:3-6
[v]Ps 7:16

A9:10,15,16 Lit not put their hands on   B9:16 Lit and gained relief from   C9:16 Some LXX mss read 10,107; other LXX mss read 15,000   D9:22 Lit Jews gained relief from

9:11-15 The **king** seemed unconcerned about the death of **500** of his subjects. After asking for a casualty report from the rest of the kingdom, he offered Esther any additional help she needed (v. 12). Apparently the struggle within the royal fortress was not finished because Esther requested

harag

Hebrew Pronunciation	[hah RAG]
HCSB Translation	kill, execute, murder
Uses in Esther	9
Uses in the OT	167
Focus Passage	Esther 9:6,10-12,15-16

Harag generally means kill (Gn 4:8) or slay (Is 14:30). God does it (Am 4:10), as do criminals (Ps 10:8). Qatal is a synonym (3x; Ps 139:19). Like tavach (11x; Ex 22:1), harag describes butchering cattle (Is 22:13). Harag portrays slaughtering people (1Kg 18:13). Harag denotes murder (Ex 21:14), although ratsach is the word in the Ten Commandments (Ex 20:13). Harag implies violent killing with nachah "strike down" (2Sm 12:9). Harag connotes put to death (2Sm 4:10) or execute (2Ch 25:3) as causative forms of muth ("die") regularly do. Harag conveys destroying a nation (Gn 20:4). The participle signifies murderer (Jr 4:31) or executioner (Hs 9:13). The passive participle indicates the slain (Is 10:4) and, somewhat figuratively, victims of adulteresses (Pr 7:26).

an additional day for the Jews to battle their enemies (v. 13). Her request to hang **the bodies of Haman's 10 sons** seems vindictive, but this was a common practice in the Persian period, especially for those who were convicted of insurrection (Herodotus 3:125). Moreover, the display of Haman's sons on the gallows would serve as a powerful deterrent to any who might contemplate further attacks against the Jewish people. Again, as in verses 10 and 16, the text emphasizes that the Jews were not out to pillage and enrich themselves, but only to defend their lives.

9:16-17 The phrase **got rid of** is based on the Hebrew verb nuach, meaning, "to rest." The death of **75,000 of those who hated them** seems unusually high, but the text itself is not certain. The Greek text (LXX) lists the number killed as 15,000, while the Alpha Text (Gk) has 10,107. Unlike the Jews in Susa, the **fourteenth** day of Adar was not a day of fighting for the Jews in the provinces. Instead they **rested** (Hb noach) and proclaimed a holiday.

9:19 A **holiday** is literally "a good day" (Hb yom tov).

9:21 Mordecai's letter appears to be commanding a two-day celebration for all Jews, an order that seems to conflict with verses 16-18,31, as well as later Jewish practice. However, he may have intended whatever day was appropriate for their location—the **fourteenth** in a walled city and the **fifteenth** in an open village—an interpretation probably supported by verse 27.

that he should be hanged with his sons on the gallows.[a] [26] For this reason these days are called Purim, from the word Pur.[b]

Because of all the instructions in this letter as well as what they had witnessed and what had happened to them, [27] the Jews bound themselves, their descendants, and all who joined[c] with them to a commitment that they would not fail to celebrate these two days each and every year according to the written instructions and according to the time appointed. [28] These days are remembered and celebrated by every generation, family, province, and city, so that these days of Purim will not lose their significance in Jewish life[A] and their memory will not fade from their descendants.[d]

[29] Queen Esther daughter of Abihail,[e] along with Mordecai the Jew,[f] wrote this second letter with full authority[g] to confirm the letter about Purim. [30] He sent letters with messages of peace and faithfulness to all the Jews who were in the 127 provinces of the kingdom of

[a]9:25 Est 5:14; 7:9-10; 9:13-14
[b]9:26 Est 3:7
[c]9:27 Est 8:17; Is 56:3,6; Zch 2:11
[d]9:28 Jos 4:6-7; 1Co 11:24-25
[e]9:29 Est 2:7,15
[f]Est 3:4-6; 5:13
[g]Est 8:8; Dn 6:8
[h]9:31 Est 4:16
[i]Est 4:1-3
[j]10:1 Est 1:1; 8:9
[k]Is 11:11; 24:15
[l]10:2 Est 1:4
[m]Est 8:15
[n]Est 2:23; 6:1-2
[o]10:3 Gn 41:40-43; 2Ch 28:7; Est 8:15; Dn 5:7
[p]Est 8:16-17
[q]Neh 2:10

Ahasuerus, [31] in order to confirm these days of Purim at their proper time just as Mordecai the Jew and Queen Esther had established them and just as they had committed themselves and their descendants to the practices of fasting[h] and lamentation.[i] [32] So Esther's command confirmed these customs of Purim, which were then written into the record.

Mordecai's Fame

10 King Ahasuerus imposed a tax throughout the land[j] even to the farthest shores.[B,k] [2] All of his powerful and magnificent accomplishments[l] and the detailed account of Mordecai's great rank to which the king had honored him,[m] have they not been written in the Historical Records of the Kings of Media and Persia?[n] [3] Mordecai the Jew was second only to King Ahasuerus,[o] famous among the Jews, and highly popular with many of his relatives.[p] He continued to seek good for his people and to speak for the welfare of all his descendants.[q]

[A]9:28 LXX reads will be celebrated into all times   [B]10:1 Or imposed forced labor on the land and the coasts of the sea

---

9:29-32 The meaning of verse 29 is uncertain. The sense is that both Esther and Mordecai confirmed the **authority** of the first letter (vv. 20-22), as well as placed their authority on the **second letter** (vv. 29-32), which, while odd, makes sense of the difficult syntax. Commentators come to differing conclusions about the practices of **fasting and lamentation**. Some maintain that this authorized certain fasts in the past (Zch 8:19) that were not commanded by the law but had become part of Jewish practice. But it is more likely that it stipulated a commemorative fast modeled on the time when the Jews mourned, fasted, and lamented (Est 4:3) after hearing of Haman's edict. That Esther's command was **written into the record** (Hb seypher) meant it became a permanent, official requirement for the Jewish people.

10:1-3 The mention of Ahasuerus imposing **a tax** (Hb mas) **throughout the land** seems out of place. Some interpreters suggest this may be another example of reversal, as the tax relief given to the empire when Ahasuerus married Esther (2:18) was now made up for with the new tax. More likely this is an echo of Joseph and his role as second in command in Egypt (Gn 41:40). Like Joseph before him, Mordecai the Jew helped a Gentile king bring prosperity to the crown.

The book of Esther ends with a picture of peace and tranquility, with Jewish people "living in harmony and mutual goodwill with the Gentile majority, under Jewish leaders who are respected and admired by the rulers, yet who are openly identified with the Jewish community and unashamed to advance its interests and to speak out in its defense" (J. Levenson, Esther, p. 234).

Job

The book of Job is named after the central character and speaker. The narrative deals with a man who lost everything and the subsequent discussions he had about the reason for his suffering. God alone had the final word and eventually restored all that Job had lost.

"See how He spreads His lightning around Him and covers the depths of the sea" (36:30).

Circumstances of Writing

Author: The author of Job is unknown. The author was a learned man whose knowledge embraced the heavens (22:12; 38:32-33) and earth (26:7-8; 28:9-11; 37:11,16). His knowledge touched on foreign lands (28:16,19), various products (6:19), and human professions (7:6; 9:26; 18:8-10; 28:1-11). He was familiar with plants (14:7-9) and animals (4:10-11; 38:39–39:30; 40:15–41:34). He was a wise man, familiar with traditional wisdom (6:5-6; 17:5; 28:12,28), but above all a man of spiritual sensitivity (1:1,5,8; 2:3; 14:14-15; 16:11-21; 19:23-27; 23:10; 34:26-28; 40:1-5; 42:1-6). He was doubtless an Israelite as confirmed by his frequent use of God's covenant name (Yahweh).

Background: The story of Job is set in the patriarchal period. In that era wealth consisted of the possession of cattle and servants. Like other OT patriarchal family heads, Job performed priestly duties, including offering sacrifices for his family. Like the patriarchs, Job lived to be more than 100 years old. Geographically, the action took place in the northern Arabian Peninsula, in the land of Uz (1:1), often associated with Edom. Job's three friends also had Edomite or southern associations, as did the young Elihu (see notes at 2:11; 32:2-3).

Although Job is set in the patriarchal period, its date of writing is unknown. Jewish tradition places the authorship of Job in the time of Moses.

Message and Purpose

The book of Job demonstrates that a sovereign, righteous God is sufficient and trustworthy for every situation in life, even in the most difficult of circumstances. Along with this truth, Job also carries several messages.

Character: A major portion of the book's discussion revolves around conduct that reflects correct ethical values. Job is introduced as a man of character (1:1), and God testified to his consistently blameless character (1:8; 2:3). In discussing Job's situation, Eliphaz initially suggested that Job's blameless character could prove to be to his benefit (4:7). Bildad, however, was not so sure (8:6,20). Both men later stated that no one can be

---

2200 B.C.

Eheduanna, the daughter of Sargon of Akkad, is the world's oldest known author whose works are written in cuneiform. **2285–2250**

The Dispute Between a Man and His Ba, Egyptian parallel to Job **2280–2050**

The Great Ziggurat at Ur **2200**

2100 B.C.

Abraham 2166–1991

Job 2100?–1900?

Isaac 2066–1886

Death in combat of Ur-nammu (king of Sumer, Ur, and Akkad) who standardized the weights and measures, and formulated a system of law that tried to establish justice for the underprivileged **2095**

2000 B.C.

Jacob 2006–1859

The Protests of the Eloquent Peasant, Egyptian parallel to Job **2000**

Man and His God, Sumerian parallel to Job **2000**

totally pure (15:14-15; 25:4-5). Job consistently maintained that his conduct was above reproach (27:5; see chap. 31), and he was willing to take his stand before God to prove it (23:7). As Job saw it, in God's dealings with man He does not appear always to reward a blameless and pure life (9:23; 10:14).

Righteousness: Job stated that his righteousness was the central issue in his situation (6:29), yet he wondered how he could convince God of this (9:2,15,20; 10:15). All three of Job's friends condemned Job's attitude as self-righteous (32:1). For Elihu, Job's fault was failing to see God's essential righteousness while maintaining his own (32:2; 34:5,17). In this Elihu anticipated God's own words to Job (40:8).

Justice: Job wanted to receive justice in his situation (19:7; 23:4). He renounced injustice (27:4) and modeled justice in his dealings with others (29:14; 31:13-15) but felt that God had not always dealt justly with him (14:3; 16:10-14; 23:10-16; 27:2-6; 34:5-6; 35:2). Job wanted to present his case before God (13:18), but he wondered whether he could get a hearing (9:32). Little is said about justice and injustice in the divine speeches, but the conclusion is evident. God's justice is seen in His administration of the physical universe and animal world as well as in human relationships. Only God has the wisdom and power to govern all of this with perfect harmony and justice. Rather than championing his own righteousness, Job should understand God's essential righteousness by which He justly administers the universe (40:7-14). When Job finally came to understand this (42:4-6), he experienced the justice he had sought and found his sufficiency in God.

Contribution to the Bible

The book of Job teaches that suffering comes to everyone, the righteous and unrighteous alike. God does not always keep the righteous from danger or suffering. Ultimately God controls all of life's situations, including limiting the power of Satan. God's comfort and strength are always available to the trusting soul.

Although the book of Job does take note of the problem of suffering, it focuses more on the nature of human conduct before a sovereign and holy God. In harmony with the rest of Scripture, the book teaches that even a consistent practice of religion is insufficient without a genuine heart relationship with God (Dt 6:4-6; Ps

1900 B.C.	1800–1100 B.C.
Joseph 1915–1805	**Moses** 1526–1406
	Joshua 1490?–1380?
Potter's wheel introduced to Crete 1900	
Egyptian town of El Lahun gives evidence of town planning with streets at right angles. 1900	*The Admonition of Ipu-wer*, Egyptian parallel of Job 1850–1600
Mesopotamian mathematicians discover what later came to be called the "Pythagorean theorem." 1900	*Ludlul Bel Nemeqi, Tabu-utul-Bel*, Babylonian parallel to Job 1700
Multiplication tables appear in Mesopotamia. 1900	Epic of Keret, Canaanite, extant copy 1360. Original date unknown
Khnumhotep II, an architect of Pharaoh Amenemhet II, develops encryption. 1900	*I Will Praise the Lord of Wisdom*, Mesopotamian 1290
	The Babylonian Theodicy, Mesopotamian 1100

86:11-12; Mt 22:37). The answer to life's problems and goals lies in a proper reverence for Him who is perfect in all His being and actions. Man needs not just to confess God but to surrender everything to Him. By letting Him truly be God in every area of life, a person will find Him sufficient.

Structure

The writer was a skilled storyteller, artistically characterizing the distinctions between the protagonist (Job), antagonist (Satan), and literary foils (the three friends and Elihu). The characterization demonstrates that God Himself is the ultimate protagonist (or "hero") of the story. Satan was as much challenging God as Job's piety. Although Job's three "comforters" applied traditional wisdom to Job's situation, each did it in a different way. Eliphaz, the rationalist, reasoned with Job (15:17-18); Bildad, the apologist, sought to defend God (25:1-6); and Zophar acted much like a prosecutor (11:1-6). The youthful Elihu served as a mediating influence in order to prepare for the divine speeches that follow (33:23-26). The writer constructed a well-developed plot built around dramatic dialogue. The fact that he related the account of Job's test in story form does not mean that Job was not a real person who underwent a real test.

Outline

I. Prologue: The Setting of the Test (1:1–2:13)
  A. Job's life before the test (1:1-5)
  B. Satan's first accusation and proposed test (1:6-12)
  C. Job's response to the first test (1:13-22)
  D. Satan's second accusation and proposed test (2:1-6)
  E. Job's response to the second test (2:7-10)
  F. The arrival of Job's comforters (2:11-13)

II. Development: Examining Job's Condition (3:1–27:23)
  A. Job's lament over his condition (3:1-26)
  B. Dialogues about Job's condition (4:1–27:23)

III. Dénouement: Explaining Job's Condition (28:1–37:24)
  A. Job's speeches about his condition (28:1–31:40)
  B. Elihu's speeches about Job's condition (32:1–37:24)

IV. Resolution: Job's Condition and God's Greatness (38:1–42:6)
  A. God's first speech: His sovereign power (38:1–40:2)
  B. Job's response: his self-renunciation (40:3-5)
  C. God's second speech: Job's impotence (40:6–41:34)
  D. Job's response: his repentance (42:1-6)

V. The Scene after the Test (42:7-17)
  A. Job and his three comforters (42:7-9)
  B. Job and his family (42:10-17)

Job and His Family

1 There was a man in the country of Uz[a] named Job.[b] He was a man of perfect integrity,[c] who *feared God and turned away from evil.[d] ²He had seven sons and three daughters. ³His estate included 7,000 sheep, 3,000 camels, 500 yoke of oxen, 500 female donkeys, and a very large number of servants. Job was the greatest man among all the people of the east.

⁴His sons used to take turns having banquets at their homes. They would send an invitation to their three sisters to eat and drink with them. ⁵Whenever a round of banqueting was over, Job would send for his children and purify them, rising early in the morning to offer burnt offerings for[A] all of them. For Job thought: Perhaps my children have sinned, having cursed God in their hearts. This was Job's regular practice.

Satan's First Test of Job

⁶One day the sons of God[e] came to present themselves before the LORD, and Satan[B] also came with them. ⁷The LORD asked Satan, "Where have you come from?"

"From roaming through the earth," Satan answered Him, "and walking around on it."

⁸Then the LORD said to Satan, "Have you considered My servant Job? No one else on earth is like him, a man of perfect integrity, who fears God and turns away from evil."

⁹Satan answered the LORD, "Does Job fear God for nothing? ¹⁰Haven't You placed a hedge around[g] him, his household, and everything he owns? You have blessed the work of his hands, and his possessions have increased in the land. ¹¹But stretch out Your hand and strike[h] everything he owns, and he will surely curse You to Your face."

¹²"Very well," the LORD told Satan, "everything he owns is in your power. However, you must not lay a hand on Job himself." So Satan left the LORD's presence.

¹³One day when Job's sons and daughters were eating and drinking wine in their oldest brother's house, ¹⁴a messenger came to Job and reported: "While the oxen were plowing and the donkeys grazing nearby, ¹⁵the Sabeans[i] swooped down and took them away. They struck down the servants with the sword, and I alone have escaped to tell you!"

¹⁶He was still speaking when another messenger came and reported: "A lightning storm[C] struck from heaven.[j] It burned up the sheep and the servants and devoured them, and I alone have escaped to tell you!"

¹⁷That messenger was still speaking when yet another came and reported: "The Chaldeans formed three bands, made a raid on the camels, and took them away. They struck down the servants with the sword, and I alone have escaped to tell you!"

a1:1 Jr 25:20; Lm 4:21
b Ezk 14:14,20; Jms 5:11
c Jb 2:3; 8:20; 9:20-22
d Jb 28:28; Pr 3:7
e 1:6 Gn 6:2,4; Jb 2:1; 38:7
f 1:7 1Pt 5:8
g 1:10 Ps 34:7
h 1:11 Jb 2:5; 4:5; 5:19
i 1:15 Gn 10:7; Jb 6:19; Is 45:14
j 1:16 Gn 19:24; 1Kg 18:38; 2Kg 1:10-14

A 1:5 Lit for the number of   B 1:6 Or the adversary   C 1:16 Lit The fire of God

---

1:1 The English rendering of Job's name comes from the Septuagint (LXX), the Greek translation of the OT. The Hebrew form reflects a name that is common in the ancient Near East, meaning "where is the (heavenly) father." The name carries a double significance for the story. Not only will Job wonder whether God has abandoned him, but it suggests the deeper questions: Is God really sufficient for every aspect of life? Will He be there when I need Him? **Uz** could name a place east of the Jordan River anywhere from Aram to Edom (Gn 10:22-23; Lm 4:21). Job's devotion to God was wholehearted. He had **perfect integrity** (lit he was "blameless and upright") and walked wisely before the Lord (28:28). This indicates that Job had a consistent spiritual walk, not that he was sinless.

1:2-3 The numbers seven (**seven sons** and **7,000 sheep**), three (**three daughters** and **3,000 camels**), and 1,000 (**500 yoke of oxen**, where a yoke represents a pair; and **500 female donkeys**) symbolized perfection and completeness. Job's impressive family, servants, livestock, and material wealth made him the **greatest man in the east**, where "east" could designate "virtually any place from Damascus to Arabia and as far east as Persia" (R. Alden, Job, 50).

1:5 To ensure his family's spiritual purity Job regularly acted as priest. The word **cursed** renders the Hebrew "blessed" (used as a euphemism in this case). Job's wife later used the same word in the same way (2:9).

1:6 The heavenly setting indicates that the **sons of God** are

angels (2:1; cp. Ps 29:1; 103:20). **Satan** (the Accuser; cp. Zch 3:1-2) also came to the heavenly council. He always opposes the work of the Lord (Mt 16:23; Rv 12:9) but is limited in his power (Jb 1:12; 2:6). **LORD** translates the Hebrew name of the covenant God of Israel (Yahweh).

1:7-8 The Lord's questions suggest that **Satan** came to the meeting uninvited but do not indicate that God was ignorant of Satan's activities. God's omniscience is attested throughout the Scriptures (Ps 139:7-12). Instances in which He asks questions are acts of accommodation that allow Him to relate to humans via dialogue.

1:9-11 Satan challenged Job's motives for fearing God. He suggested that Job's devotion to God depended on his life circumstances.

1:12 The limitation God imposed on Satan's testing demonstrated the Lord's desire that Job be a trophy of God's grace even in his suffering.

1:15 The **Sabeans** mentioned here were apparently nomads from northern Arabia, not the later wealthy kingdom of south Arabia whose fabled queen Sheba visited King Solomon (1Kg 10:1-13) and whose people Isaiah prophesied would submit to Israel (Is 45:14).

1:16 The **lightning storm** (lit "fire of God") is normally a divine weapon (2Kg 1:10-14). Ironically, Satan was given permission to use it against God's servants.

1:17 Like the Sabeans, the **Chaldeans** were nomadic

[18]He was still speaking when another messenger came and reported: "Your sons and daughters were eating and drinking wine in their oldest brother's house. [19]Suddenly a powerful wind swept in from the desert and struck the four corners of the house. It collapsed on the young people so that they died, and I alone have escaped to tell you!"

[20]Then Job stood up, tore[a] his robe, and shaved[b] his head.[A] He fell to the ground and worshiped, [21]saying:

> Naked I came
>   from my mother's womb,[c]
> and naked I will leave this life.[B,d]
> The LORD gives, and the LORD
>   takes away.
> Praise the name of •Yahweh.[e]

[22]Throughout all this Job did not sin or blame God for anything.[C,f]

Satan's Second Test of Job

2 One day the sons of God[g] came again to present themselves before the LORD, and Satan also came with them to present himself before the LORD. [2]The LORD asked Satan, "Where have you come from?"

"From roaming through the earth," Satan answered Him, "and walking around on it."

[3]Then the LORD said to Satan, "Have you considered My servant Job? No one else on earth is like him, a man of perfect integrity,[h] who •fears God and turns away from evil.[i] He still retains his integrity, even though you incited Me against him, to destroy him without just cause."

[4]"Skin for skin!" Satan answered the LORD. "A man will give up everything he owns in exchange for his life. [5]But stretch out Your hand and strike[j] his flesh and bones, and he will surely curse You to Your face."

[6]"Very well," the LORD told Satan, "he is in your power; only spare his life." [7]So Satan left the LORD's presence and infected Job with terrible boils from the sole of his foot to the top of his head.[k] [8]Then Job took a piece of broken pottery to scrape himself while he sat among the ashes.[A,l]

[9]His wife said to him, "Do you still retain your integrity? Curse God and die!"

[10]"You speak as a foolish woman speaks," he told her. "Should we accept only good from God and not adversity?" Throughout all this Job did not sin in what he said.[D]

Job's Three Friends

[11]Now when Job's three friends—Eliphaz the Temanite,[m] Bildad the Shuhite,[n] and Zophar the Naamathite—heard about all this adversity that had happened to him, each of them came from his home. They met together to go and sympathize with him and comfort[o] him. [12]When they looked from a distance, they could barely recognize him. They wept

Cross references (center column):
[a]1:20 Gn 37:29,34; Jos 7:6; Jb 2:12
[b]Jr 7:29; Ezk 7:18; Mc 1:16
[c]1:21 Jb 3:10-11; 10:17-18; Jr 20:17-18
[d]Ps 139:13,15
[e]Jb 38:1; Ps 113:2; 118:26
[f]1:22 Jb 2:10
[g]2:1 Gn 6:2,4; Jb 1:6; 38:7
[h]2:3 Jb 6:29
[i]Jb 1:1,8; 28:28; Pr 3:7
[j]2:5 Jb 1:11; 4:5; 19:21
[k]2:7 Dt 28:27,35
[l]2:8 2Sm 13:19; Jb 42:6
[m]2:11 Gn 36:34; 1Ch 1:45; Jb 42:9
[n]Gn 25:2; Jb 8:1; 18:1
[o]Jb 42:11; Ps 69:20; Jr 16:5

A1:20;2:8 This custom demonstrated mourning.   **B**1:21 Lit *will return there*; Ps 139:13,15   **C**1:22 Lit *or ascribe blame to God*   **D**2:10 Lit *sin with his lips*

---

raiders. King Nebuchadnezzar II of Babylon was a Chaldean (2Kg 24:1; Dn 1:1).

1:18-19 As after the Sabean raid (v. 15), a force of nature completed the attack against Job's family.

1:20 Tearing one's garments (Gn 37:34; 2Ch 34:19) and shaving one's **head** (Am 5:10) were symbolic acts of grief. Job's falling to the **ground** to worship God reflected a traditional method of showing reverence (Jos 5:14; Rv 1:17).

1:21-22 Job recognized that ultimately **the LORD** determines all things, so he submitted himself to God's sovereign will. The word **praise** occurs in verse 11 where it is translated "curse" (see note at v. 5). Rather than cursing God as Satan had predicted, Job blessed his **name** and did not **blame** God. The word "name" reflects the revealed character and reputation of God (Jl 2:26). The term *name* came to be a surrogate for God (Dn 9:18-19) and was later applied to Christ (Ac 5:41; 3Jn 7).

2:3 God denounced Satan's motives as pure hostility, first against God and then Job. Although Satan **incited** God to afflict Job, this does not mean that God can be manipulated against His will. Job was not a mere pawn in a superhuman struggle.

2:4-5 Satan's second test suggested that Job was callous and concerned only for himself. The proverbial saying **skin for skin** could indicate Job's willingness to give up all he had, including his family, in order to save his own life; or that if the Lord allowed Satan to afflict him bodily, Job would in turn deny the Lord.

2:6-7 Again (see note at 1:12) Satan's power to afflict Job was limited by the Lord. The severity of Job's condition would convince his friends that Job was being punished for sinning (Dt 28:35).

2:8 In scraping himself with **broken pottery**, Job may have been trying to get rid of the matter that oozed from his sores (so the LXX) and thus alleviate the itching. Job's sitting **among the ashes** symbolized his grief and despondency (2Sm 13:19; Est 4:3). Ash heaps were traditionally located at town dumps.

2:9 Job's wife avoided blasphemy by using a Hebrew euphemism, "bless," for her real intent: **curse**.

2:10 Job recognized that ultimately God is in control of every life, whether for **good** or for times of **adversity**.

2:11 Eliphaz came from Teman, a principle city in Edom (Ezk 25:13; Am 1:12-13). **Bildad** ("son of Hadad" the storm god) probably came from the tribe of Shuah, descended from Abraham through his second wife Keturah (Gn 25:1-2; 1Ch 1:32). **Zophar** may have been from northern Arabia.

2:12-13 Job's three friends responded to his gruesome appearance with actions symbolic of deep mourning: weeping (2Sm 18:33), tearing their robes (Jb 1:20), sitting on the

aloud,[a] and each man tore his robe and threw dust into the air and on his head.[b] [13]Then they sat on the ground with him seven days and nights,[c] but no one spoke a word to him because they saw that his suffering[d] was very intense.

Job's Opening Speech

3 After this, Job began to speak and cursed the day he was born. [2]He said:

[3] May the day I was born perish,
and the night when they said,
"A boy is conceived."[e]

[4] If only that day had turned
to darkness!
May God above not care about it,
or light shine on it.

[5] May darkness and gloom[f] reclaim it,
and a cloud settle over it.
May an eclipse of the sun[A] terrify it.

[6] If only darkness had taken
that night away!
May it not appear[B] among the days
of the year
or be listed in the calendar.[C]

[7] Yes, may that night be barren;
may no joyful shout[g] be heard in it.

[8] Let those who curse certain days
cast a spell[h] on it,
those who are skilled
in rousing •Leviathan.[i]

[9] May its morning stars grow dark.
May it wait for daylight but have none;
may it not see the breaking[D] of dawn.

[10] For that night did not shut
the doors of my mother's womb,
and hide sorrow from my eyes.

[11] Why was I not stillborn;
why didn't I die as I came
from the womb?[j]

[12] Why did the knees receive me,
and why were there breasts for me
to nurse?[k]

[13] Now I would certainly be lying down
in peace;
I would be asleep.[l]
Then I would be at rest[m]

[14] with the kings and counselors[n]
of the earth,
who rebuilt ruined cities
for themselves,

[15] or with princes who had gold,
who filled their houses[o] with silver.

[16] Or why was I not hidden
like a miscarried child,[p]
like infants who never see daylight?

[17] There the wicked[q] cease
to make trouble,
and there the weary find rest.

[18] The captives are completely
at ease;[r]
they do not hear the voice
of their oppressor.[s]

[19] Both small and great are there,
and the slave is set free
from his master.[t]

[20] Why is light given to one burdened
with grief,
and life to those whose existence
is bitter,[u]

[21] who wait for death,[v]
but it does not come,
and search for it more than
for hidden treasure,

[22] who are filled with much joy
and are glad when they reach
the grave?[w]

[a]2:12 Jdg 21:2; Ru 1:9,14; 2Sm 13:36	
[b]Jos 7:6; Lm 2:10; Ezk 27:30	
[c]2:13 Gn 50:10; Ezk 3:15; 45:21	
[d]Gn 34:5; Jb 16:6; Ps 39:2	
[e]3:3 Jb 5:7; Pr 23:25; Is 7:14	
[f]3:5 Jb 10:21-22; 12:22; 28:3	
[g]3:7 Jb 20:5; Ps 63:5	
[h]3:8 Nm 22:11,17; Jb 5:3; Pr 11:26	
[i]Jb 41; Ps 74:14; 104:26	
[j]3:10-11 Jb 1:21; 10:17-18; Jr 20:17-18	
[k]3:12 Sg 8:1; Is 66:12; Jl 2:16	
[l]3:13 Ps 13:3; Jr 51:39,57; Mt 8:24	
[m]Jb 17:16; Dn 12:13; Rv 14:13	
[n]3:14 Is 14:9; Jr 51:57; Ezk 32:29	
[o]3:15 Jb 17:13; 30:23; Ec 12:5	
[p]3:16 Nm 12:12; Ps 58:8; Ec 6:3	
[q]3:17 Jb 9:22; 11:20; 18:5	
[r]3:18 Pr 1:33; Jr 30:10; 46:27	
[s]Ex 3:7; 5:10,13-14; Jb 39:7	
[t]3:19 Jb 9:22; Ec 9:2-3; Is 14:9-10	
[u]3:20 Jb 23:2; Ps 71:20; Lm 1:4	
[v]3:21 1Kg 19:4; Jb 7:15; Jnh 4:3	
[w]3:22 Jb 5:26; 10:19; 17:1	

[A]3:5 Lit May a darkening of daylight　[B]3:6 LXX, Syr, Tg, Vg; MT reads rejoice　[C]3:6 Lit or enter the number of months　[D]3:9 Lit the eyelids

---

ground (Lm 2:10; Nah 1:4), and throwing **dust** on their heads (Jos 7:6; 2Sm 13:19). A seven-day period was observed in times of mourning for the dead (Gn 50:10; 1Sm 31:13). With due propriety Job's friends remained silent, waiting for Job to speak first. It is often best in sympathizing with those who are hurting just to be there and to be ready to listen.

3:3 The Hebrew word translated **boy** is usually used of an adult male (4:17), often with an indication of strength (Jr 41:16) or prominence (2Sm 23:1). Job's power and position mattered little to him now.

3:4-7 In language reminiscent of Gn 1:2-5, Job wished that his day of birth could become "uncreated."

3:8-9 As a great dragon gobbled up the sun in ancient Near Eastern mythology, so Job asked that the sun should never have brought light to his day of birth. **Leviathan** is known from ancient Ugaritic mythology as a sea monster, which the god Baal defeated. Leviathan appears in the OT sym-

bolically in connection with those forces that oppose God (26:12-14; Ps 74:12-14; 104:26; Is 27:1). The mythological allusions in Job (5:7; 7:12; 9:13; 18:13; 38:12) do not indicate scriptural endorsement of pagan theology or mythic zoology but serve as literary allusions. The **morning stars** were Venus and Mercury.

3:12 The **knees** probably refer to those of his mother either in childbirth (Gn 30:3) or in taking up her child for nursing.

3:13-19 Asleep is used frequently as a metaphor for death in the Bible, especially of the righteous (Jn 11:11-15; 1Co 15:20). Job's words should not be pressed to depict a common condition for all souls in the afterlife. Although the body may rest in the grave, the righteous have the sure hope of eternal life (Ps 16:9-17; 49:15; 73:25-26; Ac 2:25-28; 1Co 15:50-57; 2Co 5:1-8). The case of the wicked is far different (Ps 1:4-5; 49:14-15; Mt 8:12; 25:41,46).

23 Why is life given to a man whose path
  is hidden,[a]
  whom God has hedged in?
24 I sigh when food[b] is put before me,[A]
  and my groans pour out like water.[c]
25 For the thing I feared
  has overtaken me,
  and what I dreaded has happened
  to me.[d]
26 I cannot relax or be still;
  I have no rest,[e] for trouble comes.

FIRST SERIES OF SPEECHES

Eliphaz Speaks

4 Then Eliphaz the Temanite replied:

2 Should anyone try to speak with you
  when you are exhausted?
  Yet who can keep from speaking?
3 Indeed, you have instructed many
  and have strengthened[f] weak hands.
4 Your words have steadied the one
    who was stumbling
  and braced the knees
    that were buckling.[g]
5 But now that this has happened to you,
  you have become exhausted.
  It strikes[h] you, and you are dismayed.
6 Isn't your piety your confidence,
  and the integrity of your life[B]
    your hope?[i]
7 Consider: who has perished when he
    was innocent?
  Where have the honest
    been destroyed?[j]
8 In my experience,
    those who plow injustice
  and those who sow trouble[k] reap
    the same.[l]
9 They perish at a single blast[m] from God

and come to an end by the breath
  of His nostrils.[n]
10 The lion may roar and the fierce
    lion[o] growl,
  but the fangs of young lions
    are broken.[p]
11 The strong lion dies if it catches
    no prey,
  and the cubs of the lioness
    are scattered.[q]
12 A word was brought to me in secret;
  my ears caught a whisper of it.[r]
13 Among unsettling thoughts
    from visions in the night,[s]
  when deep sleep[t] descends on men,
14 fear and trembling came over me[u]
  and made all my bones shake.
15 A wind[C] passed by me,
  and I shuddered with fear.[D]
16 A figure stood there,
  but I could not recognize
    its appearance;
  a form loomed before my eyes.
  I heard a quiet voice:
17 "Can a person be more righteous
    than God,
  or a man more pure than his Maker?"[v]
18 If God puts no trust in His servants
  and He charges His angels
    with foolishness,[E,w]
19 how much more those who dwell
    in clay houses,[x]
  whose foundation is in the dust,
  who are crushed like a moth!
20 They are smashed to pieces from dawn
    to dusk;
  they perish forever
    while no one notices.[y]
21 Are their tent cords not pulled up?
  They die without wisdom.[z]

Cross references:
[a]3:23 Jb 19:8; Lm 3:9; Hs 2:6
[b]3:24 Jb 6:7; 33:20; Ps 102:4
[c]Ps 6:6; 22:1,14; 32:3
[d]3:25 Jb 9:28; 13:11; 30:15
[e]3:26 Jb 30:17; Pr 25:2; Ec 2:23
[f]4:3 Jb 26:2; Is 35:3; Heb 12:12
[g]4:4 Dt 3:28; Jb 16:15; Is 41:10
[h]4:5 Jb 5:19; 6:7; 19:21
[i]4:6 Jb 11:18; Ps 119:116; Jr 17:7
[j]4:7 Jb 8:20; Ps 37:25; Pr 12:21
[k]4:8 Jb 5:7; 15:35; Is 59:4
[l]Ps 7:15; Pr 22:8; Hs 8:7
[m]4:9 2Sm 22:26; Jb 37:10; Is 30:33
[n]Ex 15:8-10; Ps 18:15; 2Th 2:8
[o]4:10 Ps 10:9; 17:12; 22:13,21
[p]Jb 29:17; Ps 3:7; 58:6
[q]4:11 Ps 59:11; Pr 20:8,20; Is 33:3
[r]4:12 Jb 13:1; 33:16; 36:10,15
[s]4:13 Jb 7:14; 20:8; 33:15
[t]Gn 2:21; 15:12; Jb 33:15
[u]4:14 Jb 21:6; Ps 55:5; 119:120
[v]4:17 Jb 15:14; 25:4; Pr 20:9
[w]4:18 Jb 15:15; 21:22; 25:5
[x]4:19 Jb 10:9; 33:6; Is 64:8
[y]4:20 Jb 14:2; 20:7; Ps 90:5-6
[z]4:21 Jb 36:12; Pr 5:23; 10:21

[A]3:24 Or *My sighing serves as my food*   [B]4:6 Lit *ways*   [C]4:15 Or *A spirit*   [D]4:15 Or *and the hair on my body stood up*   [E]4:18 Or *error*; Hb obscure

---

3:23-25 The protective hedge that God had placed around Job (1:10) now hemmed him in to suffering.

4:1 Since Job had broken the silence (chap. 3), **Eliphaz** offered his concerned counsel, filled with various forms of traditional wisdom. Although Eliphaz's counsel contained truthful observations, they failed to address the reason for Job's condition.

4:4 Stumbling and **knees . . . buckling** relate as much to the psychological aspects of tragedy as to the physical (Ps 109:24; Ezk 21:7; Nah 2:10).

4:6-9 Eliphaz's advice was meant to be an encouragement and a gentle call for Job's self-reflection, yet it could have implied that Job's children deserved what they got.

4:10-11 This traditional wisdom from Eliphaz declared that individual strength could not deliver the wicked (Nah 2:11-

12). The **lion** is at times symbolic of the wicked (Ps 7:2) or those who rely on self rather than God (Ps 34:10).

4:12-16 Eliphaz seems to have been awakened out of **deep sleep** to receive a supernatural message. Whether this was a theophany (appearance of God) or an angelic visitation (Dn 2:5) is uncertain. Eliphaz thought his experience had provided him with wisdom to understand one of life's mysteries.

4:17 The basic question was not whether man is **more righteous than God**, but could he be truly righteous and pure before his **Maker** (25:4). No one can make special claim to God based on his supposed total moral integrity.

4:18-21 Eliphaz's point here was that because people are not sinless before God, they may expect difficulties in this life, even tragedy and death. People need to acquire godly **wisdom** in order to live properly before God.

5 Call out if you please. Will anyone
    answer you?
    Which of the holy ones[a] will you
        turn to?
2 For anger kills a fool,
    and jealousy slays the gullible.[b]
3 I have seen a fool taking root,
    but I immediately pronounced a curse
        on his home.
4 His children are far from safety.
    They are crushed at the city •gate,[c]
    with no one to rescue them.
5 The hungry consume his harvest,
    even taking it out of the thorns.[A]
    The thirsty[B] pant
        for his children's wealth.
6 For distress does not grow
        out of the soil,
    and trouble does not sprout
        from the ground.
7 But mankind is born for trouble[d]
    as surely as sparks fly upward.
8 However, if I were you, I would appeal
        to God
    and would present my case to Him.[e]
9 He does great[f]
        and unsearchable things,
    wonders without number.[g]
10 He gives rain to the earth
    and sends water to the fields.[h]
11 He sets the lowly on high,
    and mourners are lifted to safety.[i]

12 He frustrates the schemes of the crafty
    so that they[c] achieve no success.
13 He traps the wise in their craftiness
    so that the plans of the deceptive
    are quickly brought to an end.[j]
14 They encounter darkness by day,
    and they grope at noon
    as if it were night.[k]
15 He saves the needy
        from their sharp words[D,l]
    and from the clutches of the powerful.
16 So the poor have hope,
    and injustice shuts its mouth.[m]
17 See how happy the man is
        God corrects;
    so do not reject the discipline
        of the •Almighty.
18 For He crushes but also binds up;
    He strikes, but His hands also heal.[n]
19 He will rescue you from six calamities;
    no harm will touch you in seven.
20 In famine He will redeem you
        from death,
    and in battle, from the power
        of the sword.[o]
21 You will be safe from slander[E]
    and not fear destruction when it comes.[p]
22 You will laugh at destruction
        and hunger
    and not fear the animals of the earth.
23 For you will have a covenant
    with the stones of the field,

Cross-references:
a5:1 Jb 15:15; Ps 89:5-7; Dn 4:17
b5:2 Pr 12:16; 14:18; 19:19
c5:4 Jb 31:21; Pr 22:22; Is 29:21
d5:7 Jb 4:8; 15:35; Is 59:4
e5:8 Jb 13:18; 23:4; Lm 3:59
f5:9 Jb 9:10; 37:5; Ps 71:19
g5:9 Ps 40:5; 72:18
h5:10 Jb 36:27-28; 38:26-28; Jr 14:22
i5:11 1Sm 2:7; Ps 113:6-7; Mt 5:4
j5:13 Ps 9:15-16; Is 29:14; 1Co 3:19
k5:14 Dt 28:29; Jb 12:25; Is 59:10
l5:15 Ps 55:21; 59:7
m5:16 Ps 63:11; 107:42; Rm 3:19
n5:18 Dt 32:39; 1Sm 2:6; Hs 6:1
o5:20 Ps 33:19; 37:19; 144:10
p5:21 Ps 27:5; 31:20; 91:5

A5:5 Hb obscure   B5:5 Aq, Sym, Syr, Vg; MT reads *snares*   C5:12 Lit *their hands*   D5:15 Lit *from the sword of their mouth*; Ps 55:21; 59:7   E5:21 Lit *be hidden from the whip of the tongue*

5:1 The call-answer motif often expresses intimacy of fellowship between God and the believer (14:15; Is 65:24; Jr 33:3) and God's availability in times of distress (Jb 13:20-22; Ps 86:5-7; 102:1-2). Eliphaz told Job not to expect help from **the holy ones**. The need for a mediator is an important theme in Job (9:33; 16:19-20; 19:25).

5:2-7 Rather than being angry or resentful, Job should realize that **trouble** is part of the cycle of human life. The Hebrew word for **sparks** (lit "sons of flame" or "sons of Resheph") may contain an allusion to Resheph, the Canaanite god of pestilence and plague, reinforcing the inevitability of natural disasters.

5:9-16 This is a hymn of praise, possibly used in an ancient worship ceremony.

5:17 The rendering here of **the Almighty** (Hb *Shaddai*) represents a derivation from a verbal root known both in Hebrew and Akkadian indicating overpowering force. Other lexicographers suggest a literal meaning "Destroyer" or "(God of) the Mountain."

5:18 Eliphaz suggested that Job was in need of divine discipline, so he should bear his condition happily (Pr 1:2,7; 3:11-12; 23:12). Then God would bless him again with peace, prosperity, and a large family (Jb 5:18-26). For Eliphaz, as for Job, the evidence of personal piety was seen in God's external blessings.

5:19 The parallel use of **six** and **seven** is an example of a Semitic literary device in which a number and the next higher number are used to indicate indefiniteness. Where a definite number is intended, it is always the second one

---

ma'as

Hebrew Pronunciation	[mah AHS]
HCSB Translation	reject, despise
Uses in Job	11
Uses in the OT	74
Focus Passage	Job 5:17

Ma'as implies a *dismissive* evaluation and often involves *contempt*. It frequently occurs with near synonyms like "abhor" (*ga'al*; Lv 26:43), "despise" (*na'ats*; Is 5:24), or "spurn" (*zanach*; Ps 89:38). Antonyms include "choose" (*bachar*; Is 41:9) and "trust" (*batach*; Is 30:12). Israel tended to *reject* God (1Sm 8:7), His instruction (Jr 6:19), and His land (Nm 14:31). In return God *rejected* Israel (Ps 78:59). The pattern was *rejection* of God's word followed by God *rejecting* the offender (1Sm 15:26). When God *rejected*, He might abandon (Jr 7:29). *Ma'as* denotes *renounce, refuse,* and *dismiss* (Jb 9:21; 30:1; 31:13). *Despising* cities is comparable to disregarding human life (Is 33:8); *rejection* can be murderous (Jr 4:30). *Ma'as* can imply *giving up* on life (Jb 7:16), *taking back* words (Jb 42:6), or *despising* oneself (Pr 15:32). Occasionally it indicates good human behavior such as *refusing* what is bad or illegal (Is 7:16; 33:15).

and the wild animals will be at peace
   with you.^a
²⁴ You will know that your tent is secure,^b
   and nothing will be missing
     when you inspect your home.
²⁵ You will also know that your offspring
   will be many
   and your descendants like the grass
     of the earth.
²⁶ You will approach the grave^c
   in full vigor,^d
   as a stack of sheaves is gathered
     in its season.
²⁷ We have investigated this, and it is true!
   Hear it and understand it for yourself.

Job's Reply to Eliphaz

6 Then Job answered:

² If only my grief could be weighed
   and my devastation^e placed with it
     in the scales.^f
³ For then it would outweigh the sand
   of the seas!
   That is why my words are rash.
⁴ Surely the arrows of the *Almighty
   have pierced^A me;
   my spirit drinks their poison.
   God's terrors are arrayed against me.^g
⁵ Does a wild donkey bray
   over fresh grass
   or an ox low over its fodder?
⁶ Is bland food eaten without salt?
   Is there flavor in an egg white?^B
⁷ I refuse to touch them;
   they are like contaminated food.^h

⁸ If only my request would be granted
   and God would provide what I hope for:
⁹ that He would decide to crush me,

to unleash His power and cut me off!
¹⁰ It would still bring me comfort,
   and I would leap for joy
     in unrelenting pain
   that I have not denied^c the words
     of the Holy One.ⁱ
¹¹ What strength do I have that I should
   continue to hope?
   What is my future, that I should
     be patient?
¹² Is my strength that of stone,
   or my flesh made of bronze?
¹³ Since I cannot help myself,
   the hope for success has been banished
     from me.

¹⁴ A despairing man should receive loyalty
   from his friends,^{D,j}
   even if he abandons the *fear
     of the Almighty.
¹⁵ My brothers are as treacherous
   as a *wadi,
   as seasonal streams that overflow
¹⁶ and become darkened^E because of ice,
   and the snow melts into them.
¹⁷ The wadis evaporate
   in warm weather;
   they disappear from their channels
     in hot weather.
¹⁸ Caravans turn away from their routes,
   go up into the desert, and perish.
¹⁹ The caravans of Tema look
   for these streams.
   The traveling merchants of Sheba hope
     for them.
²⁰ They are ashamed because they
   had been confident of finding water.
   When they arrive there,
     they are frustrated.^k

Cross references: ^a5:23 Ps 91:12; Ezk 34:25; Hs 2:18 ^b5:24 Jb 8:6; 12:6; 21:9 ^c5:26 Jb 3:22; 10:19; 17:1 ^dGn 15:15; 25:8; Jb 21:23 ^e6:2 Jb 30:13; Ps 57:1; Pr 19:13 ^fJb 31:6; Dn 5:27; Mc 6:11 ^g6:4 Jb 30:15; Ps 38:2; 88:16 ^h6:7 Jb 3:24; 33:20; Ps 107:18 ⁱ6:10 Jb 22:22; 23:12; Ps 119:102 ^j6:14 Jb 19:21; Ps 38:11; Pr 17:17 ^k6:20 Jr 14:3; Jl 1:11; Am 4:8

---

^A6:4 Lit *Almighty are in*   ^B6:6 Hb obscure   ^C6:10 Lit *hidden*   ^D6:14 Lit *To the despairing his friend loyalty*   ^E6:16 Or *turbid*

and the details are spelled out (Pr 30:18-19,21-23,29-31; Am 1:3–2:8).

5:27 Eliphaz exhorted Job to apply the tested and **true** principles Eliphaz had just applied to Job's condition. In so doing Job would understand why God was disciplining him and be able to bear it profitably (v. 17).

6:3 The **sand of the seas** is often used as a metaphor for vastness (29:18; cp. Jos 11:4; 1Kg 4:20) or something beyond measure (Gn 22:17; Jdg 7:12; 1Kg 4:29; Hs 1:10).

6:4 God is often portrayed as the divine warrior whose **arrows** shatter the enemy (Dt 32:42; Ps 7:12-13; 18:14; Hab 3:11). God's mighty strength brings terror to the objects of His wrath (Ex 23:27; Is 2:10,19; Jr 49:5). Job felt he was the object of God's personal attack.

6:5 Animals, whether wild or compliant, do not complain when they are well tended. Job would not complain if he received just treatment in accordance with his righteousness.

6:6-7 The rhetorical question in verse 6 implied a negative answer. Rather than tasteful nourishment to Job's grieving soul, Eliphaz's words were like **contaminated food**.

6:8-10 Contrary to Eliphaz's advice, Job put his **hope** not in his piety (4:6-7) or God's disciplinary action (5:17), but in death (3:11-15; 10:21-22), God's final blow. God's granting of Job's wish to be crushed and **cut . . . off** would relieve his suffering and affirm his innocence.

6:14 Job complained about his treatment by his friends. As their suffering friend, he should receive **loyalty** (or lovingkindness) from them (Pr 14:21).

6:15 **Wadi** is an Arabian term for an intermittent desert stream—called an arroyo, gulch, gully, or wash in the American Southwest.

6:19 The oasis of **Tema** served as a trade center in northwestern Arabia.

21 So this is what you have now become
   to me.^A
   When you see something dreadful,
   you are afraid.
22 Have I ever said: "Give me something"
   or "Pay a bribe for me
   from your wealth"
23 or "Deliver me
   from the enemy's power"
   or "Redeem me from the grasp
   of the ruthless"?

24 Teach me, and I will be silent.
   Help me understand what I did wrong.
25 How painful honest words can be!
   But what does your rebuke prove?
26 Do you think that you can disprove
   my words
   or that a despairing man's words are
   mere wind?^a
27 No doubt you would cast lots
   for a fatherless child

a 6:26 Jb 8:2;
15:2; 16:3
b 6:27 Jl 3:3;
Nah 3:10; 2Pt
2:3
c 6:28 Jb 24:25;
27:4; 34:6
d 6:29 Jb 2:3
e 6:30 Jb 12:11;
27:4
f 7:1 Jb 14:14;
Is 40:2
g 7:3 Jb 30:17;
Ps 6:6; 42:3

   and negotiate a price to sell
   your friend.^b
28 But now, please look at me;
   would I lie to your face?^c
29 Reconsider; don't be unjust.
   Reconsider; my righteousness^d is still
   the issue.
30 Is there injustice on my tongue
   or can my palate not taste disaster?^e

7 Isn't mankind consigned
   to forced labor^f on earth?
   Are not his days like those
   of a hired hand?
2 Like a slave he longs for shade;
   like a hired man he waits for his pay.
3 So I have been made to inherit months
   of futility,
   and troubled nights have been assigned
   to me.^g
4 When I lie down I think:

---

^A 6:21 Alt Hb tradition reads *So you have now become nothing*

6:21 Seeing Job's **dreadful** condition, his friends were **afraid** to get close to him lest they also incur God's judgment.

6:22-23 Job had never asked his friends for special favors. Surely they could at least be loyal.

6:24-26 The Hebrew word behind **what I did wrong** *(shagah)* speaks of unintentional sin. If his friends thought Job had erred, they should tell him honestly but gently, not in a **painful** manner. Job's friends had not yet disproven his claim to innocence, they had only dismissed it.

6:27 Job compared his friends to merciless creditors who

would take an orphan or sell a friend into slavery in payment for a debt (Ex 22:22; 2Kg 4:1; Am 2:6; 8:6).

6:30 Job found Eliphaz's words tasteless (vv. 5-7), but his own words were not displeasing.

7:1-2 Job complained that God treated humans like a harsh master. The term **forced labor** could be used of military service, but here it involves the institution of service that was demanded of a man for a certain period (the corvée; cp. 1Kg 5:13-14). Hired hands usually worked for a day's **pay** (see Dt 24:14-15). To withhold a person's wages was a miscarriage of justice (Lv 19:13).

Job described his friends as being treacherous as a *wadi*, a rocky watercourse that is dry except during rainy seasons. These creek beds can become raging torrents when especially heavy rains fall. Seen here is Wadi Qilt, a deep valley that drains much of the northern Judean wilderness.

When will I get up?
But the evening drags on endlessly,
and I toss and turn until dawn.

5 My flesh is clothed with maggots
and encrusted with dirt.[A]
My skin forms scabs[B] and then oozes.[a]

6 My days pass more swiftly
than a weaver's shuttle;
they come to an end without hope.[b]

7 Remember that my life is but a breath.
My eye will never again see
anything good.[c]

8 The eye of anyone who looks on me
will no longer see me.
Your eyes will look for me, but I
will be gone.[d]

9 As a cloud fades away and vanishes,
so the one who goes down to ˙Sheol[e]
will never rise again.

10 He will never return to his house;
his hometown will no longer
remember[C] him.[f]

11 Therefore I will not restrain my mouth.
I will speak in the anguish of my spirit;
I will complain in the bitterness
of my soul.

12 Am I the sea[D,g] or a sea monster,[h]
that You keep me under guard?

13 When I say: My bed will comfort me,
and my couch will ease my complaint,

14 then You frighten me with dreams,
and terrify me with visions,[i]

15 so that I prefer strangling[E]—
death rather than life in this body.[F,j]

16 I give up! I will not live forever.
Leave me alone,[k] for my days are
a breath.[G]

17 What is man, that You think so highly
of him
and pay so much attention to him?[l]

18 You inspect him every morning,
and put him to the test
every moment.[m]

19 Will You ever look away from me,
or leave me alone long enough
to swallow?[H]

20 If I have sinned, what have I done
to You,
Watcher of mankind?
Why have You made me Your target,[n]
so that I have become a burden to You?[I]

21 Why not forgive my sin
and pardon my transgression?[o]
For soon I will lie down in the grave.[p]
You will eagerly seek me, but I
will be gone.[q]

Bildad Speaks

8 Then Bildad the Shuhite replied:

2 How long will you go on saying
these things?
Your words[r] are a blast of wind.[s]

3 Does God pervert justice?[t]
Does the ˙Almighty pervert
what is right?[u]

4 Since your children sinned
against Him,
He gave them over to their rebellion.

5 But if you earnestly seek[v] God
and ask the Almighty for mercy,[w]

6 if you are pure and upright,
then He will move even now
on your behalf

[a]7:5 Dt 28:35; Ps 38:5; Is 1:6
[b]7:6 Jb 14:19; 17:15; 19:10
[c]7:7 Jb 9:25; Ps 78:39; Jms 4:14
[d]7:8 Jb 7:21; 20:9; Ps 37:36
[e]7:9 Jb 11:8; 14:13; 17:13,16
[f]7:10 Jb 8:18; 20:9; Ps 103:16
[g]7:12 Jb 26:12; Ps 74:13
[h]Ps 148:7; Is 27:1; Ezk 32:2
[i]7:14 Jb 4:13; 20:8; 33:15
[j]7:15 1Kg 19:4; Jb 3:21; Jnh 4:3
[k]7:16 Jb 7:19; 10:20; Ps 39:13
[l]7:17 Ps 8:4; 144:3; Heb 2:6
[m]7:18 Ps 17:3; 73:14; 139:23
[n]7:20 Jb 16:12; Lm 3:12
[o]7:21 Jb 11:6; 13:23; 15:5
[p]Jb 17:16; 20:11; Is 26:19
[q]Jb 3:13; 7:8; Ps 37:36
[r]8:2 Jb 11:2; Pr 10:19; Ec 5:3
[s]Jb 6:26; 15:2; 16:3
[t]8:3 2Ch 19:6; Jb 34:12; Ps 9:16
[u]Gn 18:25; Jb 34:17; Rm 3:5
[v]8:5 Ps 63:1; 78:34; Is 26:9
[w]Jb 9:15; 33:24; Ps 30:8

[A]7:5 Or and dirty scabs   [B]7:5 Lit skin hardens   [C]7:10 Lit know   [D]7:12 Or the sea god   [E]7:15 Or suffocation   [F]7:15 Lit than my bones   [G]7:16 Or are futile   [H]7:19 Lit swallow my saliva?   [I]7:20 Ancient Jewish tradition, LXX; MT, Vg read myself

7:5 Job's boils (2:7) scabbed over only temporarily, then erupted, and the oozing pus became filled with **maggots**.

7:6 A play on words occurs here. The Hebrew word *tiqwah* can mean both "hope" and "thread." Like a weaver running out of thread, Job's life was moving **swiftly** toward its end, leaving him **without hope**.

7:9 In the OT **Sheol** is used both for the grave generally (1Kg 2:6; Ps 16:10; 49:15) and for the final state of the wicked specifically (Ps 49:13-14; Is 14:14-15). At times it reflects a commonly held ancient view of a dismal underworld into which all people passed after death.

7:12 In Canaanite mythology the **sea** god (Yam) and the **sea monster** (Tannin) were defeated by Baal. The allusion in verse 12 compares Job to some primordial adversary on which God is keeping watch. Such mythological allusions appear in the OT about God's victory over and control of the forces of nature in creation (9:13-14; 26:12-13), at the

Red Sea (Ps 74:14-15), and the forces of evil at the end of history (Is 27:1).

7:16 Breath (Hb *hevel*) can also designate something worthless or futile (Ec 1:2).

7:17-19 Unlike the viewpoint of the psalmist (Ps 8:3-8), Job answered his own rhetorical question in despairing fashion to indicate God's constant oppression of him.

7:20 If Job had sinned against God unintentionally (1:5), let the ever-watchful God tell him. Job used the title **Watcher** sarcastically.

8:2 Bildad acted like God's "defense attorney." He charged Job with speaking like an empty windbag.

8:3-4 Bildad's rhetorical question (v. 3) expected a negative answer. God is always righteous in His actions (Dt 32:4). Bildad believed Job's sinning **children** got what they deserved.

8:5-7 By implication Bildad suggested that Job had sinned, hence his condition. Because God had spared Job's life,

and restore the home where
  your righteousness dwells.[a]

7 Then, even if your beginnings
    were modest,
 your final days will be
   full of prosperity.[b]

8 For ask the previous generation,
 and pay attention to what
   their fathers discovered,[c]

9 since we were born only yesterday
    and know nothing.
 Our days on earth are but a shadow.[d]

10 Will they not teach you and tell you
 and speak from their understanding?

11 Does papyrus grow where there is
    no marsh?
 Do reeds flourish without water?

12 While still uncut shoots,
 they would dry up quicker than
   any other plant.

13 Such is the destiny[A] of all
    who forget God;
 the hope of the godless[e] will perish.

14 His source of confidence is fragile;[B]
 what he trusts in is a spider's web.[f]

15 He leans on his web, but it doesn't
    stand firm.
 He grabs it, but it does not hold up.

16 He is a well-watered plant
   in the sunshine;
 his shoots spread out over his garden.

17 His roots are intertwined around a pile
    of rocks.
 He looks for a home among the stones.

18 If he is uprooted[C] from his place,
 it will deny knowing him, saying,
   "I never saw you."[g]

19 Surely this is the joy of his way of life;

yet others will sprout from the dust.

20 Look, God does not reject a person
     of integrity,
 and He will not support evildoers.[h]

21 He will yet fill your mouth with laughter
 and your lips with a shout of joy.[i]

22 Your enemies will be clothed
     with shame;[j]
 the tent[k] of the wicked will exist
    no longer.

Job's Reply to Bildad

9 Then Job answered:

2 Yes, I know what you've said is true,
 but how can a person be justified
     before God?[l]

3 If one wanted to take[m] Him to court,
 he could not answer God[D] once
   in a thousand times.[n]

4 God is wise[o] and all-powerful.
 Who has opposed Him
   and come out unharmed?

5 He removes mountains
     without their knowledge,
 overturning them in His anger.[p]

6 He shakes the earth from its place
 so that its pillars tremble.

7 He commands the sun not to shine
 and seals off the stars.[q]

8 He alone stretches out the heavens[r]
 and treads on the waves of the sea.[E]

9 He makes the stars: the Bear,[F] Orion,
 the Pleiades,[s] and the constellations[G]
   of the southern sky.

10 He does great and unsearchable things,
 wonders without number.[t]

11 If He passes by me,
 I wouldn't see Him;[u]

Cross-reference column:

a 8:6 Jb 22:23; 42:10; Pr 3:33
b 8:7 Jb 36:11; 42:10,12; Jms 5:11
c 8:8 Dt 4:32; 32:7; Jb 15:18
d 8:9 Ps 102:11; 144:4; Ec 6:12
e 8:13 Jb 13:16; 15:34; 27:8
f 8:14-15 Jb 27:18; Is 59:5; Mt 7:26-27
g 8:18 Jb 7:10; 20:7; Ps 37:36
h 8:20 Gn 18:25; Jb 36:6; 2Pt 2:9
i 8:21 Jb 33:26; Ps 27:6; 47:5
j 8:22 Ps 35:26; 109:29; 132:18
k Jb 18:6,14; Ps 52:5; Pr 14:11
l 9:2 Jb 25:4; Ps 143:2; Rm 3:20
m 9:3 Jb 13:19; 33:13; 40:2
n Jb 9:14; 37:19; 40:2
o 9:4 Jb 11:6; 12:13; 36:5
p 9:5 Jdg 5:5; Ps 18:7; Mc 1:4
q 9:7 Is 13:10; Ezk 32:8; Jl 2:10,31
r 9:8 Ps 104:2-3; Is 40:22; 44:24
s 9:9 Jb 38:31-32; Is 40:26; Am 5:8
t 9:10 Jb 5:9; Ps 40:5; 72:18
u 9:11 Jb 23:8-9; 35:14

A 8:13 Lit *Such are the ways*   B 8:14 Or *cut off*; Hb obscure   C 8:18 Lit *swallowed*   D 9:3 Or *court, God would not answer him*   E 9:8 Or *and walks on the back of the sea god*   F 9:9 Or *Aldebaran*   G 9:9 Or *chambers*

---

there was yet hope for a change in Job's fortunes. **Home** more strictly denotes pasturage and by extension a dwelling place (5:3,24; cp. Jr 6:2; Zph 2:6).

8:8-9 Bildad appealed to traditional wisdom. Life is as short as a vanishing **shadow** (14:1-2; Ps 102:11; 109:23; 144:4; Ec 6:12).

8:11-13 As **papyrus** dies without water to nourish it, so the godless will perish. To succeed, man needs God, the "water of life."

8:16-19 The godless are like a vine that appears firmly established among the **rocks**. Yet it is easily **uprooted** leaving no trace.

8:20-22 Bildad summed up his case: If Job was truly righteous, God would sustain him.

9:2-4 A judicial image occurs throughout chapter 9. Job would like to present his case for innocence **before God** in **court** (vv. 3,16,19,32). As a finite plaintiff his arguments

were inadequate (vv. 3-4,14-15,20,32) before an omniscient and omnipotent judge (v. 15). Job needed a mediator to arbitrate his case (vv. 33-35; see note at 16:21).

9:5-10 Job called on a hymn extolling God's sovereignty as Creator. The imagery is metaphorical and is not to be taken as a cosmology.

9:5-6 **Mountains** are sometimes portrayed as **pillars** for the sky (26:11).

9:8 The heavens could be viewed as a great tent stretched out over the earth (Ps 104:2; Is 40:22). The image of God treading on **the waves of the sea** pictures God as controlling the forces of nature (Mc 1:3) much as a conqueror defeats his foes (Is 63:3; Hab 3:8,15).

9:9 Ancients often identified **stars** and **constellations** as gods and goddesses, used them as navigational guides, and noted their changing positions to mark the seasons.

9:11-12 God's mysterious and sovereign ways are often

if He goes right by,
I wouldn't recognize Him.

12 If He snatches something,
who can stop[A] Him?
Who can ask Him, "What are
You doing?"[a]

13 God does not hold back His anger;
•Rahab's[b] assistants cringe in fear
beneath Him!

14 How then can I answer Him
or choose my arguments against Him?

15 Even if I were in the right,
I could not answer.
I could only beg my Judge for mercy.[c]

16 If I summoned Him
and He answered me,
I do not believe He would
pay attention to what I said.

17 He batters me with a whirlwind[d]
and multiplies my wounds
without cause.

18 He doesn't let me catch my breath
but soaks me with bitter experiences.

19 If it is a matter of strength, look, He is
the Mighty One![e]
If it is a matter of justice, who can
summon[f] Him?[B]

20 Even if I were in the right,
my own mouth would condemn me;[g]
if I were blameless, my mouth would
declare me •guilty.

21 Though I am blameless,
I no longer care about myself;
I renounce my life.[h]

22 It is all the same. Therefore I say,
"He destroys both the blameless
and the wicked."[i]

23 When disaster brings sudden death,

He mocks the despair of the innocent.

24 The earth[c] is handed over
to the wicked;
He blindfolds[D] its judges.[j]
If it isn't He, then who is it?

25 My days fly by faster than a runner;[E,k]
they flee without seeing any good.[l]

26 They sweep by like boats made
of papyrus,
like an eagle swooping down
on its prey.[m]

27 If I said, "I will forget my complaint,
change my expression, and smile,"

28 I would still live in terror of all
my pains.[n]
I know You will not acquit me.[o]

29 Since I will be found guilty,[p]
why should I labor in vain?

30 If I wash myself with snow,
and cleanse my hands with lye,

31 then You dip me in a pit of mud,
and my own clothes despise me!

32 For He is not a man like me, that I can
answer Him,[q]
that we can take each other to court.

33 There is no one to judge between us,
to lay his hand on both of us.

34 Let Him take His rod away from me
so His terror will no longer
frighten me.[r]

35 Then I would speak and not fear Him.
But that is not the case; I am
on my own.

10 I am disgusted with my life.[s]
I will express my complaint
and speak in the bitterness of my soul.

2 I will say to God:

---

a9:12 Jb 11:10; Is 45:9; Rm 9:20
b9:13 Jb 26:12; Ps 89:10; Is 51:9
c9:15 Jb 8:5; 10:15
d9:17 Jb 30:22; Ps 83:15; Jnh 1:4
e9:19 Jb 9:4; Is 28:2; 40:26
f Jr 49:19; 50:44
g9:20 Jb 9:28; 40:8; Is 50:9
h9:21 Jb 7:16; 10:1
i9:22 Jb 3:19; Ec 9:2-3; Is 14:3-11
j9:24 Jb 12:6,17; Is 29:14; 44:25
k9:25 2Sm 18:19-33; 1Kg 1:5; Est 3:13,15
l Jb 7:7; Ps 78:39; Jms 4:14
m9:26 Jb 39:29; Is 18:2; Hab 1:8
n9:28 Jb 3:25; 13:11; 31:23
o Jb 10:14; Jl 3:21; Nah 1:3
p9:29 Jb 9:20; 40:8; Is 50:9
q9:32 Jb 41:13; Ps 143:2; Ec 6:10
r9:34 Jb 6:4; 13:21; Ps 39:10
s10:1 Jb 7:16; 9:21

A9:12 Or dissuade   B9:19 LXX; MT reads me   C9:24 Or land   D9:24 Lit covers the faces of   E9:25 = a royal messenger

---

unnoticed or incomprehensible to man. Mere humans cannot fault God for what He does.

9:13-14 Job felt that if the forces of nature could not withstand God, how could he hope to win his case before Him? Rahab suggests an ancient mythological sea monster. The image is that of God subduing and controlling the forces of nature (26:12-13; Ps 89:10; Is 51:9-10), a reminder that Yahweh alone is truly God and sovereign over all forces that seem to oppose Him.

9:15-16 Job suggested that if God should respond to his summons to court, he would have no chance of winning his case.

9:17-20 Job felt that God was mercilessly battering him. Since God is omnipotent, how could Job expect **justice**? His lack of eloquence would frustrate his defense.

9:21-24 Job displayed his hopelessness. He was certain of his innocence, but in his despair he imagined God to be capricious and an overbearing tyrant. Job felt Eliphaz (5:17-

26) and Bildad (8:20) were wrong: God did not distinguish between **the blameless and the wicked**. Since there is only one sovereign God, everything must ultimately trace back to Him.

9:25-26 Job's imagery heightened his lament for his life, which was fast ebbing away (7:6-8).

9:27-29 Job accused God of prejudging his case. Job felt that God was determined to hold him **guilty**.

9:30-31 Job suggested Bildad's views about repentance and self-purification were mistaken; Job feels these acts would be useless. Using **lye** rather than oil for cleansing indicates an extreme measure.

9:32-35 Job sensed the need for an arbitrator to adjudicate between himself and God (16:19-20; 19:25). Job had no angel or Mesopotamian personal god to aid him.

10:1-3 Since Job was convinced of his uprightness and innocence, he would like to know why God was oppressing him. For God had apparently rejected him, while looking

"Do not declare me •guilty!
Let me know why You prosecute me.
3   Is it good for You to oppress,
to reject the work of Your hands,
and favor[A] the plans of the wicked?
4   Do You have eyes of flesh,
or do You see as a human sees?
5   Are Your days like those of a human,
or Your years like those of a man,[a]
6   that You look for my wrongdoing[b]
and search for my sin,
7   even though You know that
I am not wicked
and that there is no one
who can deliver from Your hand?

8   "Your hands shaped me and formed me.
Will You now turn and destroy me?
9   Please remember that You formed me
like clay.
Will You now return me to dust?[c]
10 Did You not pour me out like milk
and curdle me like cheese?
11 You clothed me with skin and flesh,
and wove me together with bones
and tendons.
12 You gave me life and faithful love,
and Your care has guarded my life.

13 "Yet You concealed these thoughts
in Your heart;
I know that this was Your hidden plan:[B]
14 if I sin, You would notice,[C]
and would not acquit me
of my wrongdoing.[d]
15 If I am wicked, woe to me!
And even if I am righteous, I cannot
lift up my head.

I am filled with shame
and aware of my affliction.[e]
16 If I am proud,[D] You hunt me like a lion
and again display
Your miraculous power against me.[f]
17 You produce new witnesses[E] against me
and multiply Your anger toward me.
Hardships assault me, wave after wave.[F]

18 "Why did You bring me out of
the womb?[g]
I should have died and never been seen.
19 I wish[G] I had never existed
but had been carried from the womb
to the grave.[h]
20 Are my days not few? Stop it![H]
Leave me alone, so that I can smile
a little
21 before I go to a land of darkness
and gloom,[i]
never to return.
22 It is a land of blackness
like the deepest darkness,
gloomy and chaotic,
where even the light is
like[i] the darkness."

Zophar Speaks

11 Then Zophar the Naamathite replied:

2   Should this stream of words[i]
go unanswered
and such a talker[j] be acquitted?
3   Should your babbling put others
to silence,
so that you can keep on ridiculing
with no one to humiliate you?
4   You have said, "My teaching[k] is sound,

---

a10:5 Jb 36:26; Ps 90:4; 2Pt 3:8   b10:6 Jb 13:23,26; 14:17; 22:5   c10:9 Gn 2:7; Jb 4:19; 34:15   d10:14 Ex 34:7; Jb 7:21; Am 3:2   e10:15 Jb 9:15; Ps 25:18; Is 3:11   f10:16 Jb 5:9; Is 38:13; Lm 3:10   g10:18 Jb 1:21; 10:18-19; Jr 20:17-18   h10:19 Jb 3: 22; 5:26; 17:1   i10:21 Jb 3:5;12:22; 28:3   j11:2 Jb 8:2; Pr 10:19; Ec 5:3   k11:4 Dt 32:2; Pr 4:2; Is 29:24

A10:3 Lit *shine on*   B10:13 Lit *was with You*   C10:14 Lit *notice me*   D10:16 Lit *If he lifts up*   E10:17 Or *You bring fresh troops*
F10:17 Lit *Changes and a host are with me*   G10:19 Lit *As if*   H10:20 Alt Hb tradition reads *Will He not leave my few days alone?*
I10:22 Lit *chaotic, and shines as*   J11:2 Lit *a man of lips*

---

on approvingly at **the plans of the wicked**. Job's rhetorical question implied a negative response.

10:4-7 Job's rhetorical question amounted to a charge that God was acting from a human perspective in His investigation of Job. God knew that Job was **not wicked**. Nevertheless, Job viewed God as bringing charges against him just because He could.

10:8-12 The image of **dust** is reminiscent of man's creation in the cycle of life (Gn 2:7; 3:19; Ps 104:14). Like a divine **cheese** maker or weaver, God created Job and nurtured him. Why did He now seek to **destroy** him?

10:13-17 Job accused God of being a relentless prosecutor and unjust judge. His predetermined **plan** was to convict Job whether he was **wicked** or **righteous**. Job had lost all sense of self-worth and did not dare to **lift** his **head** (Lm 2:10).

10:18-19 Job reiterated his opening lament, wishing never to have been born or wishing to have died at birth (3:11-16; Jr 20:18).

10:20-22 Job pleaded with God to be compassionate and to **stop** His incessant persecution so he might enjoy his few remaining years (7:6-10,21). Job piled up the images in describing the afterlife as a place of **deepest darkness**. His despairing words reflect a common Mesopotamian understanding about the afterlife but not the biblical view (1Co 15:51-57).

11:2-3 Zophar began by attacking Job's answers much as a prosecuting attorney would press his case against a defendant. Zophar's rhetorical questions implied negative answers. He called Job a **talker** (lit a "man of lips"). The image of the lip is used in many ways in the OT. The lips of the fool lack knowledge (Pr 14:7), but those of the wise preserve it (Pr 5:2; 10:13; 20:15) and pass it on to others (Pr 15:7). Some lips speak arrogantly (Ps 12:4; Pr 12:7), rashly (Ps 106:33), or even mockingly (Ps 22:7).

11:4 Zophar misrepresented Job's position like an adversary at law who attacks the implications of another's position rather than its essence. Job had not claimed that his

and I am pure in Your sight."
5 But if only God would speak
and declare His case[A] against you,
6 He would show you the secrets
of wisdom,[a]
for true wisdom has two sides.
Know then that God has chosen
to overlook some of your sin.[b]

7 Can you fathom the depths of God
or discover the limits of the •Almighty?[c]
8 They are higher
than the heavens—what can you do?
They are deeper than •Sheol—what can
you know?[d]
9 Their measure is longer than the earth
and wider than the sea.

10 If He passes by and throws
someone in prison
or convenes a court, who can
stop Him?[e]
11 Surely He knows which people
are worthless.
If He sees iniquity, will He not
take note of it?[f]
12 But a stupid man
will gain understanding
as soon as a wild donkey is born a man!

13 As for you, if you redirect your heart
and lift up your hands to Him
in prayer—

[a]11:6 Jb 28:12; 38:36; Ec 7:23,25
[b]Ezr 9:13; Ps 103:10
[c]11:7 Ec 3:11; 8:17; Rm 11:33
[d]11:8 Dt 30:12-13; Ps 139:8-9; Am 9:2-3
[e]11:10 Jb 9:12; 23:13; Rv 3:7
[f]11:11 Jb 34:25; Ps 10:14
[g]11:15 Jb 22:26; Ps 119:6; 1Jn 3:21
[h]11:17 Jb 17:12; Ps 37:6; Is 58:8,10
[i]11:18 Jb 4:6; Ps 119:116; Jr 17:7 Jb 24:23; Ps 4:8; Pr 3:24
[k]11:19 Ps 45:12; Pr 19:6; 29:26
[l]11:20 Jb 3:17; 9:22; 18:5
[m]Jb 8:13; Pr 10:28; 11:7
[n]12:3 Jb 13:2; 15:9; 16:2

14 if there is iniquity in your hand,
remove it,
and don't allow injustice to dwell
in your tents—
15 then you will hold your head high,
free from fault.
You will be firmly established
and unafraid.[g]
16 For you will forget your suffering,
recalling it only as waters
that have flowed by.
17 Your life will be brighter than noonday;
its darkness[B] will be like the morning.[h]
18 You will be confident, because
there is hope.[i]
You will look carefully about
and lie down in safety.[j]
19 You will lie down without fear,
and many will seek your favor.[k]
20 But the sight of the wicked[l] will fail.
Their way of escape will be cut off,
and their only hope is their last breath.[m]

Job's Reply to Zophar

12 Then Job answered:

2 No doubt you are the people,
and wisdom will die with you!
3 But I also have a mind;
I am not inferior to you.
Who doesn't know the things you are
talking about?[C,n]

[A]11:5 Lit and open His lips   [B]11:17 Text emended; MT reads noonday; you are dark, you   [C]12:3 Lit With whom are not such things as these

---

teaching was flawless. Rather, he recognized that it lacked patience (6:11) and complete perspective (7:15,20). Job did not claim that he was sinless (i.e., **pure**), only blameless (9:21; 10:7) and upright (6:29).

11:5-6 Zophar pointed out that wisdom had **two sides**; this probably means the known and the unknown, the seen and the unseen. Only God understood the depths of true **wisdom** and could view things from all perspectives. If only Job could see both sides of his situation, he would realize that God's case against him was just. Zophar declared that God had only punished Job for part of his **sin**.

11:7-9 Zophar's rhetorical question indicated that Job was not in a position to understand fully all that was happening to him.

11:10-11 Because God was just and all-powerful, no one could **stop** or resist Him. Zophar implied that Job had sinned and God certainly knew the facts in Job's case.

11:13-14 Only if Job had a pure **heart** and clean **hands** (Ps 24:4) could he expect God's forgiveness and blessing (Is 1:15-17). The image is that of welcoming injustice as though it were a guest. To **dwell in your tents** is used metaphorically of sharing in someone's blessings (Gn 9:27) or occupying another's land (Ps 78:55). The tent is also used in the Bible to signify man's earthly body (2Co 5:1).

11:15-16 Zophar believed that confessed sin and a change of

lifestyle would restore Job's honor and his position before God and man. Although Job had gone through deep **waters** (see notes at Ps 69:1-2; Jnh 2:5), these would pass and be only a distant memory.

11:17-18 Zophar's encouraging words stood in stark contrast to Job's opening lament (3:4-7), to Eliphaz's observations about the fate of crafty schemers (5:12-14), and to Bildad's warning about evildoers (8:20).

11:19 Zophar assured Job that with restoration his fame and reputation would return. To be "sought out" functions at times idiomatically for the bringing of gifts (42:11; Ps 45:12).

11:20 Zophar concluded his speech with a dire warning. Unlike the blessings offered to a repentant sinner that he had just described, the unrepentant **wicked** could expect only suffering. Their prosperity would **fail** and their only **hope** of relief would be death itself.

12:2 Job lashed out sarcastically at all three friends, accusing them of being condescending. Although they claimed the wisdom of the ages, by their simplistic observations of his problem they had misapplied their learning. Acquired knowledge does not guarantee true wisdom.

12:3 Job reminded his friends that he had access to the same body of traditional wisdom that they described. By saying that he had a **mind**, Job implied that, unlike his

⁴ I am a laughingstock to my^A friends,
    by calling on God, who answers me.^B
    The righteous and upright man is
        a laughingstock.ᵃ
⁵ The one who is at easeᵇ holds calamity
        in contempt
    and thinks it is prepared for those
        whose feet are slipping.
⁶ The tents of robbers are safe,ᶜ
    and those who provoke God are secure;
    God's power provides this.^C,ᵈ

⁷ But ask the animals, and they will
        instruct you;
    ask the birds of the sky, and they will
        tell you.ᵉ
⁸ Or speak to the earth, and it will
        instruct you;
    let the fish of the sea inform you.
⁹ Which of all these does not know
    that the hand of the Lᴏʀᴅ
        has done this?ᶠ
¹⁰ The life of every living thing is
        in His hand,
    as well as the breath of all mankind.ᵍ
¹¹ Doesn't the ear test words
    as the palate tastes food?
¹² Wisdom is found with the elderly,
    and understanding comes
        with long life.ʰ

¹³ Wisdom and strength belong to God;
    counsel and understanding are His.ⁱ

¹⁴ Whatever He tears down cannot
        be rebuilt;
    whoever He imprisons cannot
        be released.ʲ
¹⁵ When He withholds the waters,
        everything dries up,
    and when He releases them,
        they destroy the land.ᵏ
¹⁶ True wisdom and power belong to Him.
    The deceived and the deceiver are His.
¹⁷ He leads counselors away barefoot
    and makes judges go mad.ˡ
¹⁸ He releases the bonds^D put on by kingsᵐ
    and fastens a belt around their waists.
¹⁹ He leads priests away barefoot
    and overthrows established leaders.ⁿ
²⁰ He deprives trusted advisers of speech
    and takes away the elders'
        good judgment.
²¹ He pours out contempt on nobles
    and disarms^E the strong.
²² He reveals mysteries from the darkness
    and brings the deepest darkness
        into the light.ᵒ
²³ He makes nations great,
        then destroys them;
    He enlarges nations,ᵖ
        then leads them away.
²⁴ He deprives the world's leaders
        of reason,
    and makes them wander
        in a trackless wasteland.q

ᵃ12:4 Jb 30:1,9; Jr 20:7; Lm 3:14
ᵇ12:5 Ps 123:4; Am 6:1
ᶜ12:6 Jb 5:24; 8:6; 21:9
ᵈPs 73:11; Jr 12:1; Mt 5:45
ᵉ12:7 Jb 35:11; Mt 6:26
ᶠ12:9 Ru 1:13; Jb 19:21; Is 41:20
ᵍ12:10 Gn 2:7; Jb 27:3; 33:4
ʰ12:12 Jb 12:20; 32:7,9; Ps 119:100
ⁱ12:13 Jb 9:4; 36:5; 38:36
ʲ12:14 Jb 11:10; Is 22:22; Rv 3:7
ᵏ12:15 Is 41:18; 42:15; 44:3,27
ˡ12:17 Jb 9:24; Is 29:14; 44:25
ᵐ12:18 Jb 12:21; Is 45:1
ⁿ12:19 Jb 40:23; Lk 1:52
ᵒ12:22 Ps 90:8; Dn 2:22; 1Co 4:5
ᵖ12:23 Ex 34:24; Is 9:3; 26:15
q12:24 Ps 107:40; Dn 4:33

---

^A12:4 Lit *his*   ^B12:4 Lit *him*   ^C12:6 Or *secure; to those who bring their god in their hands*   ^D12:18 Text emended; MT reads *discipline*   ^E12:21 Lit *and loosens the belt of*

---

friends, he weighed the evidence in order to make proper application.

12:5-6 Job could not reconcile his harsh condition with the **ease** the unrighteous seemed to enjoy. His words indicate that Zophar's closing remarks (11:13-19) simply did not fit the facts.

12:7-10 Job contended that all nature is tuned to understand that everything is in the **hand of the Lᴏʀᴅ** (see Is 64:8). The metaphor of God's hand usually conveys the image of strength or power (1Ch 29:12).

12:11-12 Job's rhetorical question suggested that mere knowledge was insufficient. A person needed to evaluate carefully what he heard. Job had expected to hear better advice from three supposedly wise men (v. 2).

12:13 In the ultimate sense, true **wisdom and strength** reside only in **God**. He alone is the omniscient and omnipotent One.

12:14-15 Job called attention to what he perceived to be negative features of God's actions. His destructive power was irreversible. His decisions could not be overturned. It seemed like it was either famine or flood.

12:16 Job's review of the scope of God's **wisdom and power** includes a stunning but true claim that even **the deceived and the deceiver**, both of whom are presumably bereft of true knowledge of God and do not willingly submit to Him, **are His**.

12:17-25 As Job cynically saw it, God arbitrarily directs social and political situations according to His inscrutable pleasure, with the result that **counselors . . . judges . . . kings . . . priests**, and all the **world's leaders** strive in vain to choose wise paths. In reality God's sovereignty is not arbitrary. He works all things "together for the good of those who love God" (Rm 8:28).

12:18 It is unclear what **bonds** and **a belt** are intended to convey with regard to **kings**. One possibility is that God easily strips kings of their robes and leads them away. Another is that God can release those whom kings have bound and bind the king instead. A third is that, if a king is defeated and bound, God can release him and gird him.

12:19 To be led away **barefoot** pictures defeat, captivity, and exile.

12:20 Under God's governance, **trusted advisers** can be deprived of the very things that made them advisers in the first place: their eloquence and **good judgment**.

12:22 Though Job is unable to make sense of his own sufferings, he recognizes God's power to reveal **mysteries**.

12:24-25 As Job viewed it, national leaders are caused by

25 They grope around in darkness
    without light;
    He makes them stagger
    like drunken men.[a]

13 Look, my eyes have seen all this;
    my ears[b] have heard
    and understood it.
2 Everything you know, I also know;
    I am not inferior to you.[c]
3 Yet I prefer to speak to the *Almighty
    and argue my case before God.[d]
4 But you coat the truth with lies;
    you are all worthless doctors.[e]
5 If only you would shut up
    and let that be your wisdom!

6 Hear now my argument,
    and listen to my defense.[A]
7 Would you testify unjustly
    on God's behalf
    or speak deceitfully for Him?
8 Would you show partiality[f] to Him
    or argue the case in His defense?
9 Would it go well if He examined you?
    Could you deceive Him
    as you would deceive a man?[g]
10 Surely He would rebuke you
    if you secretly showed partiality.

11 Would God's majesty not terrify you?[h]
    Would His dread not fall on you?
12 Your memorable sayings are proverbs
    of ash;[i]
    your defenses are made of clay.
13 Be quiet,[B] and I will speak.
    Let whatever comes happen to me.
14 Why do I put myself at risk[C]
    and take my life in my own hands?
15 Even if He kills me, I will hope
    in Him.[D]
    I will still defend[j] my ways before Him.
16 Yes, this will result in my deliverance,
    for no godless person[k] can appear
    before Him.
17 Pay close attention to my words;
    let my declaration ring in your ears.
18 Now then, I have prepared my case;[l]
    I know that I am right.
19 Can anyone indict me?
    If so, I will be silent and die.
20 Only grant these two things
    to me, God,
    so that I will not have to hide
    from Your presence:
21 remove Your hand from me,
    and do not let Your terror frighten me.[m]

[a]12:25 Dt 28:29; Jb 5:14; Is 59:10
[b]13:1 Jb 4:12; 33:16; 36:10,15
[c]13:2 Jb 12:3; 15:9; 16:2
[d]13:3 Jb 5:8; 23:4; 40:2
[e]13:4 Jb 16:2; Ps 69:20; Ec 4:1
[f]13:8 Dt 10:17; Jb 32:21; 34:19
[g]13:9 Ps 44:21; Pr 18:17; Jr 17:10
[h]13:11 Ex 15:16; Jb 31:23; Is 2:10
[i]13:12 1Sm 24:13; Pr 26:7,9; Is 44:20
[j]13:15 Jb 13:3; 15:3; 23:7
[k]13:16 Jb 8:13; 15:34; 27:8
[l]13:18 Jb 5:8; 23:4; Lm 3:59
[m]13:21 Jb 6:4; 9:34; Ps 39:10

A13:6 Lit to the claims of my lips   **B**13:13 Lit quiet before me   **C**13:14 Lit I take my flesh in my teeth   **D**13:15 Some Hb mss read I will be without hope

God to use poor judgment that leads to their disgrace (Ps 107:40).

13:1-2 Job made clear that Zophar's remarks about uninformed or stupid men (11:12) did not apply to him!

13:3 Job again (9:3,16,19,32) stated his desire to present his **case before God**. He'd had enough with making his case before finite, fallible men. He wanted a formal hearing before his divine adversary.

13:4-5 In Job's opinion, not only were his friends not as wise as they assumed themselves to be (12:1), but like unskilled physicians they had misdiagnosed his symptoms. Their best display of wisdom would be their silence (Pr 17:28).

13:6 **Hear** and **listen** are familiar calls to pay attention to what the teacher (Dt 6:4; Pr 4:1,10; 5:1; 7:24) or poet (Dt 32:1; Jdg 5:3) has to say.

13:7 Job's rhetorical questions implied that his friends, by taking God's side against Job, had twisted traditional wisdom and applied it **deceitfully**. Surely God could not be helped by false and unjust testimony.

13:8 The Hebrew idiom "lift up the face" is elsewhere used of showing respect for someone (Gn 32:21), but in the negative sense it means to **show partiality** (Ps 82:2; Pr 18:5), which was forbidden in Levitical legislation (Lv 19:15).

13:9-10 The way Job's friends applied their misguided traditional wisdom to Job's case was indefensible and would turn against them if God **examined** them instead.

13:11 If God called Job's friends to account for their treatment of him, they would learn something of the **majesty** of

God and it would **terrify** them. God's judgment against the wicked brings fear and **dread** (Ex 15:16; Jr 49:5; Rv 6:16).

13:12 A mixture of **ash** and water was sometimes used to write on a scroll, but the writing would soon disappear.

13:13 Job again asked for his friends' silence (vv. 5-6) so he might **speak** his mind regardless of the cost.

13:14 Job suggested that in speaking his mind plainly he was putting his **life . . . at risk** (lit "I take my flesh in my teeth"; i.e. "I expose myself to being consumed"). Yet he was so confident of his uprightness and integrity that he would take the chance and defend himself.

13:15 The Hebrew verb yachal can mean either "wait" (21:23) or "hope" (6:11). The HCSB has Job hoping in God (for vindication) even if God kills him. Alternatively, in the consonantal text (a Hb text that has no vowel points) the verb is preceded by a particle normally understood as a negative (see textual footnote), which would have Job observing that God might kill him, leaving him without hope (10:20-22). In either rendering, Job believed that his cause was just and that he must **defend** the uprightness of his **ways**. Job felt that he had nothing to lose by this risky move, because God seemed determined to find some charge against him in order to destroy him (9:20-21; 10:4-7).

13:16 If the Lord allowed Job to **appear before Him**, it would be proof of his uprightness.

13:20-21 Job contended that if he were not oppressed (hence the appeal, **remove Your hand from me**) or terrified (the typical reaction to being in God's presence; see Ex 20:18-19; Is 6:1ff), he might be able to state his case convincingly.

22 Then call, and I will answer,[a]
   or I will speak, and You can respond
     to me.
23 How many iniquities[b] and sins
     have I committed?[A]
   Reveal to me my transgression and sin.
24 Why do You hide Your face
   and consider me Your enemy?[c]
25 Will You frighten a wind-driven leaf?
   Will You chase after dry straw?
26 For You record bitter accusations
     against me
   and make me inherit the iniquities
     of my youth.
27 You put my feet in the stocks
   and stand watch over all my paths,
   setting a limit for the soles[B] of my feet.

28 Man wears out like something rotten,
   like a moth-eaten garment.[d]

14 Man born of woman
   is short of days and full of trouble.[e]
2 He blossoms like a flower,
     then withers;[f]
   he flees like a shadow and does not last.
3 Do You really take notice of one
     like this?

a13:22 Jb 9:16;
14:15; Jr 33:3
b13:23 Jb 7:21;
10:6,14; Is 43:25
c13:24 Jb 19:11;
33:10; Lm 2:5
d13:28 Ps
102:26; Is 50:9;
51:8
e14:1 Jb 5:7;
15:35; Is 59:4
f14:2 Ps 103:15-
16; Is 40:6-7;
Jms 1:10-11
g14:3 Jb 22:4;
Ps 143:2; 144:3
h14:5 Jb 21:21;
Ps 39:4; 90:12
i14:6 Jb 7:16;
10:20; Ps 39:13
j14:9 Jb 29:19;
Ps 1:3; Jr 17:8

   Will You bring me into judgment
     against You?[C,g]
4 Who can produce something pure
     from what is impure?
   No one!
5 Since man's days are determined
   and the number of his months depends
     on You,
   and since You have set[D] limits
     he cannot pass,[h]
6 look away from him and let him rest
   so that he can enjoy his day
     like a hired hand.[i]

7 There is hope for a tree:
   If it is cut down, it will sprout again,
   and its shoots will not die.
8 If its roots grow old in the ground
   and its stump starts to die
     in the soil,
9 the smell of water makes it thrive
   and produce twigs like a sapling.[j]
10 But a man dies and fades away;
   he breathes his last—where is he?
11 As water disappears from the sea
   and a river becomes parched and dry,
12 so man lies down never to rise again.

A13:23 Lit sins are to me   B13:27 Lit paths. You mark a line around the roots   C14:3 LXX, Syr, Vg read him   D14:5 Lit set his

13:22 Job applied the call-answer motif, expressing a desire for help or communion (Ps 102:1-2) in his situation (Jb 9:16; 12:4; 14:15). He longed for renewed fellowship with God either at God's invitation or Job's petition.

13:23 Job remained confident that he was suffering innocently (9:21; 10:7).

13:24 Idioms involving God's **face** can indicate the Lord's approval or blessing (Nm 6:24-26; 2Ch 30:9) or His disapproval and judgment (Ps 143:7; Jr 21:10).

13:25 In striking similes Job reminded God of his frailty as

---

balah

Hebrew Pronunciation	[bah LAH]
HCSB Translation	wear out
Uses in Job	2
Uses in the OT	16
Focus Passage	Job 13:28

This root in Akkadian means "die out, waste away." Balah indicates something is old and worn out, especially clothing (Dt 8:4). Sinners, the heavens, earth's foundations, and all mankind will wear out like a garment (Jb 13:28; Ps 102:26; Is 50:9; 51:6). People become shriveled up (Gn 18:12) and bones become brittle (Ps 32:3). Intensive forms take objects: God wears away flesh and skin (Lm 3:4). People spend their days (Jb 21:13) and fully enjoy, or wear out, the work of their hands (Is 65:22). Evildoers oppress others (1Ch 17:9). The related Aramaic bala' describes an end time king oppressing God's holy ones (Dn 7:25). Balah shows bodies wasting away in Sheol (Ps 49:14). Baleh (5x) describes worn-out, old, and threadbare items (Jos 9:4-5), and women worn out by adultery (Ezk 23:43).

a human being. **Dry straw** is often used metaphorically for that which is easily scattered (Ps 83:13; Is 40:23-24; Jr 13:24) or consumed in God's fiery judgment (Nah 1:10).

13:26 Job believed that he should not still be paying for the petty **iniquities** of his **youth**.

13:27 Job complained about God's constant scrutiny and mistreatment of him (7:19-20; 9:17-18; 10:4-5). Like an enemy prisoner, he was shackled and guarded, leaving him without freedom of movement.

13:28 Job again reminded God of the brevity of life (7:6; 9:25; 10:20). As rotting food, decaying wood, or a **moth-eaten garment** become useless and worthy only of being destroyed, so Job was wasting away toward his inevitable end. Although the similes are phrased with regard to **man** in general, Job clearly intended an application to his specific situation.

14:2 Job's similes emphasize that a person's life passes all too quickly, like a **flower** that is soon gone (Ps 103:15-16; Is 5:24; 40:6-8) or like a fleeting **shadow** (8:9; Ec 6:12).

14:3-4 Job wondered why God would spend so much time scrutinizing poor, powerless, short-lived mankind (7:17; 13:28–14:2). He could not understand why God seemed determined to bring him to judgment (7:19-20; 13:23-27). Actually, **no one** can be totally **pure** before God. Job never claimed to be sinless (7:21; 10:14-15); he merely insisted that he had done nothing to deserve his suffering (13:12-19).

14:5-6 Job reminded God that He had set the limits of human longevity. Job therefore urged the Lord to stop His constant surveillance (7:17-20) and fault-finding.

14:12 The **sleep** of death is as permanent as **the heavens**

They will not wake up until the heavens
   are no more;[a]
they will not stir from their sleep.

13 If only You would hide me in •Sheol[b]
   and conceal me
     until Your anger[c] passes.
   If only You would appoint a time for me
   and then remember me.
14 When a man dies, will he come back
   to life?
   If so, I would wait[d] all the days
     of my struggle[e]
   until my relief comes.
15 You would call, and I would
   answer You.
   You would long for the work
     of Your hands.[f]
16 For then You would count my steps[g]
   but would not take note[h] of my sin.
17 My rebellion would be sealed up
   in a bag,
   and You would cover over my iniquity.

18 But as a mountain collapses
   and crumbles
   and a rock is dislodged from its place,
19 as water wears away stones
   and torrents wash away the soil
     from the land,
   so You destroy a man's hope.[i]
20 You completely overpower him, and he
   passes on;
   You change his appearance
     and send him away.
21 If his sons receive honor, he does not
   know it;

Cross references (center column):
[a]14:12 Is 51:6; Rv 20:11; 21:1
[b]14:13 Jb 11:8; 17:16; Am 9:2
[c]Jb 16:9; 19:11; Ps 30:5
[d]14:14 Jb 6:8; 13:13; 35:14
[e]Jb 7:1; Is 40:2
[f]14:15 Jb 9:16; 10:3; 13:22
[g]14:16 Jb 10:6; 31:4; 34:21
[h]Jb 10:14; 33:11; Ps 130:3
[i]14:19 Jb 7:6; 17:15; 19:10
[j]14:21 Jb 21:21; Ec 9:5; Is 63:16
[k]15:2 Jb 2:10; 6:26; 27:12
[l]15:3 Jb 13:3,15; 23:7
[m]15:5 Jb 13:23,26; 14:17; 22:5
[n]15:6 2Sm 1:16; Jb 9:20; Lk 19:22
[o]15:7 Jb 38:21; Ps 90:2; Pr 8:25
[p]15:8 Jr 23:18; Rm 11:34; 1Co 2:11

   if they become insignificant,
   he is unaware of it.[j]
22 He feels only the pain of his own body
   and mourns only for himself.

SECOND SERIES OF SPEECHES

Eliphaz Speaks

15 Then Eliphaz the Temanite replied:

2 Does a wise man answer
   with empty[A] counsel[k]
   or fill himself[B] with the hot east wind?
3 Should he argue[l] with useless talk
   or with words that serve
     no good purpose?
4 But you even undermine the •fear
   of God
   and hinder meditation before Him.
5 Your iniquity[m] teaches you what to say,
   and you choose the language
     of the crafty.
6 Your own mouth condemns you, not I;
   your own lips testify against you.[n]

7 Were you the first person ever born,
   or were you brought forth
     before the hills?[o]
8 Do you listen in on the council of God,
   or have a monopoly on wisdom?[p]
9 What do you know that we don't?
   What do you understand that
     is not clear to us?
10 Both the gray-haired and the elderly
   are with us,
   men older than your father.

A 15:2 Lit *windy*; Jb 16:3   B 15:2 Lit *his belly*

(cp. Dt 11:20-21; Ps 89:28-29). In other contexts this speaks to the fact that earthly life is irrevocably lost upon death, but here Job seemingly expresses that he has no hope of afterlife.

14:13 In his despair Job continues to shift his stance. He now entertains the possibility that death might not end it all. Perhaps in time God's **anger** against him would pass, then He would **remember** Job favorably—that is, act on Job's behalf. This implies Job will have an ongoing existence beyond the grave. By **Sheol** Job referred to the grave (see notes at 7:9 and 26:5-6).

14:14-15 Job felt that if there was hope of life after death, he could endure his present struggle (7:1-5). The Hebrew word translated **relief** is used elsewhere to denote a change (Jdg 14:12-13). Job's hoped-for change would be to that of a new life of fellowship and communion with God. This is indicated by his use of the call-answer motif (Jb 13:22; Ps 102:1-2; Is 65:24).

14:16-17 Under these new and better conditions, Job would no longer experience God's scrutiny to determine his faults (7:17-19; 10:6; 13:27). His sins would be **sealed up**, never to be brought up again.

14:20-21 In his depression Job saw only God's oppressive might and the prospect of a painful future calamity followed by a dismal state of death.

15:2-3 Eliphaz's rhetorical questions suggested a negative answer. Unlike a truly wise man, Job's defense was self-serving and **empty**. Job displayed his passion like a **hot east wind** (Hb *khamsin*, or sirocco; cp. 1:19), which had entered the depths of his belly.

15:4 Eliphaz suggested that Job's intemperate attitude had affected his proper reverence for God. How then could Job claim to be wise? Wisdom begins with **the fear of God** (see Pr 1:7).

15:5-6 Eliphaz believed that Job's stance against his friends' counsel was dictated by an underlying **iniquity**. In defending himself Job used cunning terms to cover his guilt. Yet Job's words condemned him (9:20).

15:7-10 Eliphaz wanted Job to realize that he had no claim to superior wisdom (12:1-3; 13:1-2). In words bordering on sarcasm, Eliphaz stated that Job had neither priority of birth nor privileged access to the heavenly **council** (1:6; 2:1). Job should understand that time-tested **wisdom**, which had

11 Are God's consolations not enough
    for you,
  even the words that deal gently
    with you?
12 Why has your heart misled you,
  and why do your eyes flash
13 as you turn your anger^A against God
  and allow such words to leave
    your mouth?
14 What is man, that he should be pure,^a
  or one born of woman, that he
    should be righteous?
15 If God puts no trust in His holy ones^b
  and the heavens are not pure
    in His sight,^c
16 how much less one who is revolting
    and corrupt,^d
  who drinks injustice^e like water?

17 Listen to me and I will inform you.
  I will describe what I have seen,
18 what was declared by wise men
  and was not suppressed
    by their ancestors,^f
19 the land was given to them alone
  when no foreigner passed among them.
20 A wicked man writhes in pain
    all his days;
  only a few^B years are reserved
    for the ruthless.
21 Dreadful sounds fill his ears;
  when he is at peace, a robber
    attacks him.
22 He doesn't believe he will return
    from darkness;
  he is destined for the sword.^g

23 He wanders about for food, saying,
    "Where is it?"
  He knows the day of darkness is at hand.
24 Trouble^h and distress terrify him,
  overwhelming him like a king prepared
    for battle.
25 For he has stretched out his hand^i
    against God
  and has arrogantly opposed
    the •Almighty.
26 He rushes headlong at Him
  with his thick, studded shields.
27 Though his face is covered with fat^c
  and his waistline bulges with it,
28 he will dwell in ruined cities,
  in abandoned houses destined
    to become piles of rubble.^j
29 He will no longer be rich; his wealth
    will not endure.
  His possessions^D will not increase
    in the land.
30 He will not escape from
    the darkness;
  flames will wither his shoots,
  and by the breath of God's mouth,
    he will depart.^k
31 Let him not put trust
    in worthless things, being led astray,
  for what he gets in exchange
    will prove worthless.
32 It will be accomplished before his time,
  and his branch will not flourish.
33 He will be like a vine that drops
    its unripe grapes^l
  and like an olive tree that sheds
    its blossoms.

^a15:14 Jb 4:17; 25:4; Pr 20:9
^b15:15 Jb 5:1; Ps 89:5-7; Dn 4:17
^c15:15 Jb 4:18; 21:22; 25:5
^d15:16 Ps 14:3; 53:3
^e15:16 Jb 34:7; Ps 14:3
^f15:18 Dt 4:32; 32:7; Jb 8:8
^g15:22 Dt 32:41-42; Jb 19:29; Is 66:16
^h15:24 1Sm 22:2; Jb 36:19; Ps 107:6,13,19,28
^i15:25 Is 5:25; 9:16,20; Jr 21:5
^j15:28 Jb 3:14; Ps 109:10; Is 5:9
^k15:30 Jb 4:9; 22:20; 2Th 2:8
^l15:33 Is 18:5; Jr 31:29-30; Ezk 18:2

^A15:13 Or spirit   ^B15:20 Lit the number of   ^C15:27 Lit with his fat   ^D15:29 Text emended; MT reads their gain

been handed down long before Job's father, was on the side of his friends.

15:11-13 Eliphaz claimed that in his passion Job had thoughtlessly turned his **anger against God** with excessive language (7:1-2,11-20; 9:14-19; 10:3,17; 13:25-27).

15:14-16 If even angels were not trustworthy (4:18), **how much less** so mortal man. Man's basic nature is desperately **corrupt**.

15:17-19 Eliphaz appealed to his special grasp of traditional wisdom and wide experience (4:8-9,12-21; 5:3-7,27). His experience and understanding were in harmony with the wisdom that came from the early inhabitants of the land. That was a time of pure knowledge when **no foreigner** was present to bring corrupting influences to bear.

15:20 Job had maintained that God gave no special treatment to the blameless (9:22), but gave control of the earth to the **wicked** (9:24; 10:3). Eliphaz agreed with Zophar (11:20) that the wicked lived out their few years **in pain**. Neither of these polarized views corresponds with reality.

15:21 Dreadful sounds make the wicked person think someone is about to attack him. He is never truly **at peace**.

15:22 Unlike the righteous person (Ps 23:6; 27:13), the wicked person could look forward only to violent death and judgment (Ps 1:4-6).

15:23 The wicked person, asserts Eliphaz, fears he will become a vagrant.

15:26 The term **headlong** (lit "runs at Him with the neck") portrays of the wicked person as having reckless self-confidence.

15:27-29 Metaphorically, **fat** indicates a person possesses health and wealth (Gn 45:18). It can also carry a negative nuance associated with arrogance (Ps 73:3-7). Both ideas are expressed here.

15:30 As tender shoots **wither** before a scorching sun or a blasting desert wind, so the wicked will lose everything in God's judgment (4:8-9; Is 11:4). **God's mouth** can be used figuratively as the vehicle of His judgment. His **breath** represents the ease with which His mighty power accomplishes the deed and is a suitable figure for a desert wind.

15:32-33 Eliphaz used graphic descriptions of the sudden end of the wicked, whose potential will not be realized (22:15-16; Pr 10:27).

34 For the company of the godless[a]
   will have no children,
and fire will consume the tents of those
   who offer bribes.
35 They conceive trouble[b] and give birth
   to evil;
their womb[c] prepares deception.[d]

Job's Reply to Eliphaz

16 Then Job answered:

2 I have heard many things like these.
   You are all miserable comforters.[e]
3 Is there no end to your empty[A,f] words?
   What provokes you that you
     continue testifying?
4 If you were in my place I could
   also talk like you.
I could string words together
   against you
and shake my head at you.
5 Instead, I would encourage you
   with my mouth,
and the consolation from my lips
   would bring relief.[g]

6 Even if I speak, my suffering
   is not relieved,
and if I hold back, what have I lost?
7 Surely He[B] has now exhausted me.
   You have devastated my entire family.
8 You have shriveled me up[c]—
   it has become a witness;
My frailty rises up against me
   and testifies to my face.

9 His anger tears at me,
   and He harasses[h] me.
He gnashes His teeth at me.
   My enemy pierces me with His eyes.
10 They open their mouths against me
   and strike my cheeks with contempt;[i]
they join themselves together
   against me.
11 God hands me over to unjust men;[D]
   He throws me into the hands
     of the wicked.
12 I was at ease, but He shattered me;
   He seized me by the scruff of the neck
   and smashed me to pieces.
He set me up as His target;[j]
13 His archers[E] surround me.
He pierces my kidneys without mercy
   and pours my bile on the ground.
14 He breaks through my defenses again
   and again;[F]
He charges at me like a warrior.[k]
15 I have sewn •sackcloth over my skin;
   I have buried my strength[G] in the dust.[l]
16 My face has grown red with weeping,
   and darkness[m] covers my eyes,
17 although my hands are free
     from violence[n]
and my prayer is pure.

18 Earth, do not cover my blood;
   may my cry for help find
     no resting place.[o]
19 Even now my witness is in heaven,
   and my advocate is in the heights![p]

a15:34 Jb 8:13; 13:16; 27:8
b15:35 Jb 4:8; 5:7; Is 59:4
cJb 32:19; 37:1; Pr 20:27,30
dPs 7:14; Is 59:4; Hs 10:13
e16:2 Jb 13:4; Ps 69:20; Ec 4:1
f16:3 Jb 15:2
g16:5 Dt 3:28; Jb 4:4; Is 41:10
h16:9 Gn 49:23; Jb 30:21; Ps 55:3
i16:10 1Kg 22:24; Lm 3:30; Mc 5:1
j16:12 Jb 7:20; Lm 3:12
k16:14 Jb 30:14; Jl 2:7
l16:15 Jb 30:19; Ps 7:5; 75:10
m16:16 Ps 44:19; 107:10; Jr 13:16
n16:17 Is 53:9; 59:6; Jnh 3:8
o16:18 Gn 4:10; Is 26:21; Ezk 24:7-8
p16:19 Jb 22:12; Rm 1:9; 1Th 2:5

A16:3 Lit windy; Jb 15:2   B16:7 Or it   C16:8 Or have seized me; Hb obscure   D16:11 LXX, Vg; MT reads to a boy   E16:13 Or arrows   F16:14 Lit through me, breach on breach   G16:15 Lit horn

15:34 The unrighteous social practices of the **godless** wicked (Pr 17:8; Is 5:23; Mc 3:11; 7:3) will profit them nothing (Pr 15:27).

15:35 Rather than achieving their wicked goals, the godless metaphorically bear children named **trouble . . . evil**, and **deception**. What they did to others would cause their own downfall. **Womb** is the same word translated "himself" at the opening of Eliphaz's speech (see "his belly" in textual footnote at v. 2). Framing or bracketing a section of material in this way is a literary device called inclusio that is often not evident in the English translation.

16:4 Shaking the **head** was a gesture of mockery or contempt (2Kg 19:21; Ps 22:7).

16:6-17 Job observed that whether he spoke or said nothing, his suffering remained unaltered (v. 6). He would therefore speak, hoping that God would hear and be sympathetic (vv. 7-17).

16:7-8 Job switched the form of his verbs from third to second person; such changes are not uncommon in Hebrew poetry. Job addressed God as though He were present in the discussions among the four.

16:9 Gnashing of teeth conveys rage or hatred (Ps 37:12; Lm

2:16). Job called God his **enemy** who so scrutinized him that He seemed to look right through him (7:17-20).

16:10-11 Job's enemies showed their contempt by mocking him with **open . . . mouths** (Ps 22:13; Lm 2:16) as though to devour him. The enemies are **unjust** and **wicked** men; Job perceived that God had handed him over to them.

16:12-14 Job reminded his friends of his former state of **ease**. In graphic metaphors Job likened God to a **warrior** in command of a vast army. God had made him the object of His attack (7:20). Eventually an arrow struck Job's vital organ with tragic consequences (6:4). He compared himself to a besieged city whose defenses had been repeatedly assailed and finally penetrated by God's assaults.

16:15 In sorrow and mourning, Job had put on **sackcloth** (2Kg 19:1; Jl 1:13).

16:16-17 With reddened eyes that no longer saw clearly, Job viewed himself as good as dead. He felt he had done nothing to merit God's attack. He had maintained a **pure** attitude in **prayer** (1:22). Purity was an issue that had been brought up by his friends (4:17; 8:6; 11:4; 15:14-15).

16:18 Because Job must surely die soon, he pleaded that his spilled **blood** would not be covered (Gn 37:26). Like the

²⁰ My friends scoff at me
   as I weep before God.
²¹ I wish that someone might arbitrate
   between a man and God^a
   just as a *man pleads for his friend.
²² For only a few years will pass
   before I go the way of no return.

17

My spirit is broken.
   My days are extinguished.
   A graveyard^b awaits me.
² Surely mockers surround^A me
  and my eyes must gaze
   at their rebellion.^c

³ Make arrangements! Put up security
   for me.^{B,d}
  Who else will be my sponsor?^c
⁴ You have closed their minds
   to understanding,
  therefore You will not honor them.
⁵ If a man informs on his friends
   for a price,
  the eyes of his children will fail.

⁶ He has made me an object of scorn
   to the people;
  I have become a man people spit at.^{D,e}
⁷ My eyes have grown dim from grief,

Cross-reference column:

^a16:21 Jb 31:35; Ec 6:10; Is 45:9
^b17:1 Jb 3:22; 5:26; 10:19
^c17:2 Ps 22:7; 119:51; Jr 20:7
^d17:3 Gn 43:9; Ps 119:122; Pr 6:1
^e17:6 Nm 12:14; Is 50:6; Mt 27:30
^f17:8 Jb 18:20; 21:5; Dn 4:19
^g17:9 2Sm 22:21; Jb 22:30; Ps 24:4
^h17:12 Jb 11:17; Ps 37:6; Is 58:8,10
ⁱ17:14 Jb 3:15; 30:23; Ec 12:5
^j17:15 Jb 7:6; 14:19; 19:10
^k17:16 Jb 7:9; 11:8; 14:13

---

  and my whole body has become
   but a shadow.
⁸ The upright are appalled^f at this,
  and the innocent are roused
   against the godless.
⁹ Yet the righteous person will hold
   to his way,
  and the one whose hands are *clean^g
   will grow stronger.
¹⁰ But come back and try again,
   all of you.^E
  I will not find a wise man among you.

¹¹ My days have slipped by;
  my plans have been ruined,
   even the things dear to my heart.
¹² They turned night into day
  and made light seem near in the face
   of darkness.^h
¹³ If I await *Sheol as my home,
  spread out my bed in darkness,
¹⁴ and say to corruption: You are
   my father,
  and to the maggot: My mother
   or my sister,ⁱ
¹⁵ where then is my hope?^j
  Who can see any hope for me?
¹⁶ Will it go down to the gates of Sheol,^k
  or will we descend together to the dust?

---

^A17:2 Lit *are with*   ^B17:3 Lit *me with You*   ^C17:3 Lit *Who is there that will strike himself into my hand*   ^D17:6 Lit *become a spitting to the faces*   ^E17:10 Some Hb mss, LXX, Vg; other Hb mss read *them*

---

blood of innocent Abel, Job's blood would **cry** out from the ground for justice (Gn 4:10). He asked that his cry for vindication not be forgotten until his blood shed in innocence was avenged (Ezk 24:7-8).

16:19-20 Job wanted an audience with God to plead his case (9:34-35; 13:20-22). If his case came before God, a holy God would bear **witness** to his integrity. Job placed his hope for vindication in God alone, despite his verbal attacks against Him. He could expect no help from his **friends**; God remained his only **advocate**.

16:21 Job repeated his need of and desire for an arbitrator to represent him before God. Although he longed for an audience with God (13:3) where a fair hearing would vindicate him (13:15-16), he felt inadequate to represent himself (9:2-4,32-33). Jesus the Messiah became just such an intercessor for humanity (Is 2:4; 11:4; Rm 8:34; Heb 7:25; 1Jn 2:1).

16:22 Job lamented that his life expectancy was short at best (7:16,21; 9:25). With **few years** remaining, he faced only a death from which there was **no return** (10:20-21).

17:1 Job felt overwhelmed by what he believed was a hopeless situation (6:9; 9:21,25; 16:16,22).

17:3 Job again turned to God as his only hope. The image is that of a friend who was willing to be responsible for any debt should a default occur (Dt 24:6,10-13; Pr 6:1-5; 17:18; 22:26).

17:4 The HCSB translation here suggests that because those who might have helped Job were not capable of **un**derstanding the issues involved, God would not **honor** anything they might present on Job's behalf. Alternatively, Job might have reminded God that with his case not settled, God would not be honored.

17:5 In this verse Job appears to cite an ancient proverb that a person who was paid to inform on his **friends** endangered his **children**. If Job's friends were attempting to gain favor with God by taking His side against him, it could put their family in jeopardy.

17:7-8 Job's desperate condition should have stirred righteous people to compassion. If his friends were truly **upright**, they would have sought to defend him (7:14-21; 13:4; 16:2-5).

17:9 Job is nothing if not intent on staying the course.

17:10 Job challenged everyone, particularly his friends, to launch further arguments against him. They could only demonstrate that none of them was **wise** (see notes at 12:2; 13:4-5).

17:11-12 Because of Job's affliction, his **plans** had been thwarted and turned topsy-turvy.

17:13-16 By **Sheol** is meant the grave (see notes at 7:9; 14:13; 26:5-6). In a graphic metaphor, Job pictured the grave as his future home. Job used personification in calling the grave **my father** and the maggot that would feed on his body **my mother or my sister**. It was as though in the grave Job would enter into a new home housing a new family. "Gates" are often used metaphorically for entrance into the state of death (38:17; Ps 9:13; 107:18). The phraseology of Jb 17:13-16 bears similarities to ideas of the afterlife

Bildad Speaks

18 Then Bildad the Shuhite[a] replied:

2 How long until you stop talking?
  Show some sense, and then
    we can talk.
3 Why are we regarded as cattle,
  as stupid in your sight?
4 You who tear yourself in anger[A]—
  should the earth be abandoned
    on your account,
  or a rock be removed from its place?

5 Yes, the light[b] of the wicked[c]
    is extinguished;
  the flame of his fire does not glow.
6 The light in his tent grows dark,[d]
  and the lamp beside him is put out.
7 His powerful stride is shortened,
  and his own schemes trip him up.[e]
8 For his own feet lead him into a net,
  and he strays into its mesh.
9 A trap catches him by the heel;
  a noose seizes him.
10 A rope lies hidden for him
    on the ground,
  and a snare waits for him
    along the path.

11 Terrors frighten him on every side[f]
  and harass him at every step.
12 His strength is depleted;
  disaster lies ready for him to stumble.[B]
13 Parts of his skin are eaten away;
  death's firstborn consumes his limbs.
14 He is ripped from the security of his tent
  and marched away to the king of terrors.
15 Nothing he owned remains in his tent.
  Burning sulfur[g] is scattered
    over his home.
16 His roots below dry up,
  and his branches above wither away.[h]
17 All memory[i] of him perishes
    from the earth;
  he has no name anywhere.[C]
18 He is driven from light to darkness
  and chased from the inhabited world.
19 He has no children or descendants
    among his people,
  no survivor where he used to live.[j]
20 Those in the west are appalled[k]
    at his fate,
  while those in the east tremble in horror.
21 Indeed, such is the dwelling of the
    unjust man,
  and this is the place of the one
    who does not know God.[l]

---

*a*18:1 Jb 2:11; 8:1; 25:1
*b*18:5 Jb 21:17; Pr 13:9; 24:20
*c*Jb 3:17; 9:22; 11:20
*d*18:6 Jb 8:22; 18:14; Ps 52:5
*e*18:7 Jb 5:13; Pr 4:12
*f*18:11 Jb 20:25; 27:20; Jr 6:25
*g*18:15 Gn 19:24; Ps 11:6; Ezk 38:22
*h*18:16 Is 5:24; Hs 9:16; Am 2:9
*i*18:17 Ps 34:16; 109:13,15; Pr 10:7
*j*18:19 Gn 21:23; Is 14:22; Lm 2:22
*k*18:20 Jr 2:12; Ezk 27:35; 32:10
*l*18:21 Jb 21:28; Jr 9:3; 1Th 4:5

A 18:4 Lit *He who tears himself in his anger*   **B** 18:12 Or *disaster hungers for him*   **C** 18:17 Or *name in the streets*

---

in ancient Near Eastern mythology. It was believed that at death everyone entered into a dismal subterranean world with a city and gates ruled over by underworld deities. This is not the biblical view.

18:2 You in the original text is plural rather than singular. Because Bildad's speech was addressed to Job, the plural serves as a mark of politeness. The second line does not contain an imperative in the Hebrew text. Bildad was expressing a wish.

18:3 Bildad believed Job's rejection of their counsel was tantamount to calling them unthinking animals (12:7; Ps 73:22).

18:4 Bildad attempted to correct Job's perspective. It was not an angry God who was tearing at Job (12:14; 16:9) but his own **anger** at God. God was not obligated to empty the **earth** or move a **rock** just to satisfy Job's self-serving demands. As the physical order of the earth is established by divine law (Ps 104:5-7; Is 45:18), so are God's moral standards (Pr 11:20-21). For God to interrupt the laws of nature on Job's behalf would be as wrong as failing to hold him accountable for his sins.

18:5-6 As a **lamp** is **put out**, leaving a tent to grow **dark**, so misfortune would come to the **wicked** and his life would take a turn for the worse. **Light** represents a blessed life lived in accordance with the high standards of God, while darkness symbolizes the opposite (Pr 4:18-19). In other contexts light represents truth and knowledge, and darkness indicates error and ignorance (Dn 5:14; 2Pt 1:19).

18:7 The successful life is compared to walking without hindrance or stumbling (2Sm 22:33-37; Pr 4:10-12). The wicked person may appear to be walking well (with **pow-**erful stride**), but his **own schemes** will be his undoing (Pr 15:22; 26:27).

18:8-10 Six different words for "trap" are used to depict metaphorically the unanticipated dangers that could ensnare a wicked person.

18:11-13 The dangers that the wicked person encounters bring constant terror, including the prospect of death. In Job's plight, Bildad saw signs that the fate of the wicked lay before Job. **Death's firstborn** means either the plague or the most terrible manner of death.

18:14 Finally the wicked person will lose everything and will be claimed by death, the last enemy (1Co 15:26) and **the king of terrors**. The language is reminiscent of the Canaanite deity Mot (death), whose appetite was insatiable and whose mouth and throat were always open to receive his victims. Death is similarly portrayed in the OT (Is 5:14; Hab 2:5). Paul pointed out that man has victory over death through Christ (1Co 15:57; cp. Is 25:3-8).

18:15 The wicked person's **tent** (home) is destroyed by others. The scattering of **burning sulfur** over it ensured that it would never be rebuilt and occupied.

18:16 Like a dead tree whose roots **dry up** and branches **wither away**, the wicked will leave nothing behind (14:2-7; 15:30; 19:10).

18:17-20 The wicked person's family will also disappear, leaving no **memory** of him. It is as though he never existed. So total and devastating are the wicked person's demise and loss that people will **tremble** at his horrible end. Bildad built upon language used by Job in describing public reaction to his condition (17:7-8). **West** and **east** is a merismus

Job's Reply to Bildad

19 Then Job answered:

2 How long will you torment me
    and crush me with words?
3 You have humiliated me ten times now,
    and you mistreat[A] me without shame.[a]
4 Even if it is true that I have sinned,
    my mistake concerns only[B] me.
5 If you really want to appear superior[b]
        to me
    and would use my disgrace as evidence
        against me,
6 then understand that it is God
    who has wronged me
    and caught me in His net.[c]

7 I cry out: "Violence!"
    but get no response;[d]
    I call for help, but there is no justice.
8 He has blocked[e] my way so that
        I cannot pass through;
    He has veiled my paths with darkness.[f]
9 He has stripped me of my honor
    and removed the crown from my head.
10 He tears me down on every side so that
        I am ruined.[c]
    He uproots my hope like a tree.[g]
11 His anger[h] burns against me,

and He regards me as one of
    His enemies.[i]
12 His troops advance together;
    they construct a ramp[D] against me
    and camp[j] around my tent.

13 He has removed my brothers from me;
    my acquaintances have abandoned me.[k]
14 My relatives stop coming by,
    and my close friends
        have forgotten me.
15 My house guests[E] and female servants
        regard me as a stranger;
    I am a foreigner in their sight.[l]
16 I call for my servant, but he
        does not answer,
    even if I beg him with my own mouth.
17 My breath is offensive to my wife,
    and my own family[F] finds me repulsive.
18 Even young boys scorn me.
    When I stand up, they mock me.[m]
19 All of my best friends[G] despise me,[n]
    and those I love have turned
        against me.[o]
20 My skin and my flesh cling to my bones;
    I have escaped by the skin of my teeth.

21 Have mercy on me, my friends,[p]
    have mercy,

Cross references (center column):
a 19:3 Gn 31:7; Nm 14:22; Pr 25:8
b 19:5 Ps 35:26; 38:16; 55:12
c 19:6 Jb 27:2; Lm 3:5; Ezk 12:13
d 19:7 Jb 30:20; Lm 3:8; Hab 1:2
e 19:8 Jb 3:23; Lm 3:9; Hs 2:6
f Jb 29:3; 30:26; Is 59:9
g 19:10 Dt 28:63; Jb 24:20; Ps 52:5
h 19:11 Jb 16:9; 21:17; 40:11
i Jb 13:24; 33:10; Lm 2:5
j 19:12 Ps 27:3; Is 29:3; Jr 50:29
k 19:13 Ps 31:11; 38:11; 88:8,18
l 19:15 Gn 31:15; Ps 69:8; Mt 10:36
m 19:18 2Kg 2:23; Jb 29:8
n 19:19 Jb 30:10; Ps 89:38; Am 5:10
o Ps 41:9; 55:11-12; Jn 13:18
p 19:21 Jb 6:14; Ps 38:11; Pr 17:17

A 19:3 Hb obscure   B 19:4 Lit *mistake lives with*   C 19:10 Lit *gone*   D 19:12 Lit *they raise up their way*   E 19:15 Or *The resident aliens in my household*   F 19:17 Lit *and the sons of my belly*   G 19:19 Lit *of the men of my council*

(the use of two parts to represent the whole) to designate people everywhere.

19:2 Job began his speech by using Bildad's phraseology (18:2): **how long**? Because words can **crush**, they should be weighed and used appropriately (Pr 15:1,23; Eph 4:29).

19:3 Rather than being helpful, the words of Job's friends had added to his grief. The number **ten** represents the concept of totality.

19:4 Job admitted that he might have **sinned** unintentionally as all people do (6:24; 7:20). He felt, however, that he had done nothing worthy of such harsh treatment. His simple sins had harmed only himself, not his friends.

19:6 Bildad had suggested that a wicked man's lifestyle would lead him into being trapped (18:8-10) and that God does not pervert justice (8:3). On the contrary, Job declared that God had unjustly set out to trap him (7:19-20).

19:8 Job felt his course of life had been cut off. His prospects were dim, and he was haunted by the **darkness** that portended his death.

19:12 Job felt like a besieged city. An army had built a siege **ramp** against him to bring up their battering rams and penetrate his last defenses. He was just a weak human being who was more like a **tent** than a mighty city necessitating a strong attack. Contrary to Bildad's description of the lot of the wicked (18:14-15), Job's tent (lifestyle) had been battered undeservedly by God, who wanted to overpower him (14:20). The tent expresses the idea of impermanence (2Co 5:1), the brevity of life (Jb 7:16,21; 9:25-26; 10:20; 14:1-6).

19:15-16 Job's home life was in shambles. His situation had brought the disdain of his **guests . . . female servants**, and his personal male **servant**. It was as though these relationships had been turned upside down (Pr 30:21-23).

19:17 The phrase **my own family** renders the Hebrew phrase that literally reads, "children of my belly." The word "belly" is a euphemism referring to Job's loins; cp. Ps 132:11; Mc 6:7. But had Job not lost all his children (Jb 1:18-19)? These could be children by one of Job's concubines or slaves, or they could be grandchildren who escaped the earlier destruction and came to live in his house. Alternatively, some interpreters take "my belly" (Hb *bitni*) to refer to Job's mother, hence these "children" would be his blood brothers.

19:18 For children to **mock** an old man was a serious violation of Israelite social norms.

19:20 The Hebrew here suggests that in Job's weakness he felt as though his **bones** were clinging to his **skin** and **flesh** (33:21). He is emaciated. The idiom **skin of my teeth** heightens the effect. Job was so weak that he was barely alive.

19:21-22 Job's plea for his friends' understanding and compassion was based on his belief that he was innocent. God simply had attacked him. With their continued fault-finding, they joined God in His persecution of Job (7:17-20) as though they had become witnesses for the prosecution (10:17). The Hebrew idiom underlying Job's second question (19:22) is "to eat the flesh." It is used for slander or of levying accusations against someone (Ps 27:2; Dn 3:8; 6:24). Job lamented that by their unkind remarks his friends were consuming his last bastion of defense.

for God's hand[a] has struck me.[b]

22 Why do you persecute me as God does?
Will you never get enough of my flesh?

23 I wish that my words
were written down,
that they were recorded on a scroll
24 or were inscribed in stone forever
by an iron stylus and lead!
25 But I know my living Redeemer,[A,c]
and He will stand on the dust[B] at last.[C,d]
26 Even after my skin has been destroyed,[D]
yet I will see God in[E] my flesh.[e]
27 I will see Him myself;
my eyes will look at Him, and not
as a stranger.[F]
My heart longs[G] within me.[f]

28 If you say, "How will we pursue him,
since the root of the problem lies
with him?"[H]
29 then be afraid of the sword,
because wrath brings punishment
by the sword,[g]
so that you may know there is
a judgment.

Zophar Speaks

20 Then Zophar the Naamathite[h] replied:

2 This is why my unsettling thoughts
compel me to answer,
because I am upset![i]

3 I have heard a rebuke that insults me,
and my understanding[j]
makes me reply.[i]

4 Don't you know that
ever since antiquity,
from the time man was placed on earth,
5 the joy of the wicked has been brief
and the happiness of the godless
has lasted only a moment?[j]
6 Though his arrogance reaches heaven,
and his head touches the clouds,[k]
7 he will vanish forever
like his own dung.
Those who know[k] him will ask,
"Where is he?"[l]
8 He will fly away like a dream and never
be found;
he will be chased away like a vision
in the night.[m]
9 The eye that saw him will see him
no more,[n]
and his household will no longer
see him.[o]
10 His children will beg from[L] the poor,
for his own hands must give back
his wealth.
11 His bones may be full of youthful vigor,
but will lie down with him
in the grave.[p]
12 Though evil tastes sweet in his mouth
and he conceals it under his tongue,

Cross references (center column)

a19:21 Ru 1:13; Jb 12:9; Is 41:20
bJb 1:11; 2:5; 6:7
c19:25 Jb 16:19; Pr 23:11; Jr 50:34
dIs 44:6; 48:12; Rv 1:17-18
e19:26 Ps 17:15; Is 6:1; 1Co 13:12
f19:27 Ps 73:26; 84:2; 119:81
g19:29 Jb 15:22; Is 66:16; Ezk 32:10
h20:1 Jb 2:11; 11:1; 42:9
i20:3 Jb 19:3; 32:18; Ac 2:20
j20:5 Jb 8:12-13; Ps 37:35-36; 92:7
k20:6 Gn 11:4; Is 14:13-14; Ob 3-4
l20:7 Jb 4:20; Ps 90:5-6; Jms 4:14
m20:8 Ps 73:20; 90:5; Is 29:7
n20:9 Jb 7:8,21; Ps 37:36
oJb 7:10; 8:18; Ps 103:16
p20:11 Jb 7:21; 17:16; Ps 7:5

A19:25 Or know that my Redeemer is living   B19:25 Or earth   C19:25 Or dust at the last, or dust as the Last One   D19:26 Lit skin which they destroyed, or skin they destroyed in this way   E19:26 Or apart from   F19:27 Or not a stranger   G19:27 Lit My kidneys grow faint   H19:28 Some Hb mss, LXX, Vg; other Hb mss read me   I20:2 Lit because of my feeling within me   J20:3 Lit and a spirit from my understanding   K20:7 Lit have seen   L20:10 Or children must compensate

---

19:23-24 A **scroll** was made of papyrus or leather. Better yet, Job would like his words engraved in **lead** on a **stone** stele. Carved stelae are found throughout the ancient world. Although they often contain royal decrees, they could be used to record significant events in a person's life or boundary stones at the edge of one's property. Job's insistence on the carved letters being filled in with lead emphasized his desire for a permanent record of his innocence.

19:25 The Hebrew term **Redeemer** reflects an ancient custom whereby a person's nearest kinsman served as a guarantor of his rights and privileges (Lv 25:23-34,47-54; Dt 19:6-12; Jos 20:2-5; Ru 4:1-17). Although Job had repeatedly described God as his enemy and persecutor (Jb 7:17-21; 16:7-14; 19:7-12), he had also expressed his confidence in God (12:13-16; 13:15-18; 14:14-17; 16:18-20). He said that in the end God was his only hope (17:3). Job's underlying faith ultimately surfaced, breaking through his dark doubts about God. God was Job's Redeemer who alone could serve as a guarantor of his rights and vindicate his cause. If Job were to die, he was confident that the living God would stand on the dust of his grave and testify on his behalf.

19:26-27 Job built on his earlier mention of skin and flesh (v. 20). He pointed out the inevitability of that which he had come to expect (7:7-10; 10:18,21-22; 14:12; 17:13-16). Al-

though he would lie in the grave (19:25) with his body decayed, he would personally **see God**. No longer **as a stranger** (one outside of God's household, or an enemy), he would experience renewed fellowship. Job once again entertained the fond hope of personal life after death (14:14-15).

19:28-29 For Job's friends to **pursue him** with false accusations placed them in a dangerous position. They should become responsible counselors, or else they would face God's judicial **wrath**. The **sword** is a symbol of God's judgment (Dt 32:41; Rm 13:4).

20:3 Zophar still believed his **understanding** offered insight into Job's problems.

20:6-7 Although the wicked person may believe he is self-sufficient and the master of his own fate, eventually he will perish—like the arrogant king of Babylon (Is 14:12-15) and the proud, self-assured city of Nineveh (Zph 2:15).

20:11 The wicked person would die young, asserts Zophar. The word rendered **grave** here is literally "dust" (Hb aphar). Zophar was playing on Job's previous words (19:25). No longed-for Redeemer would appear over the dust of the wicked person's grave.

20:12-14 Much as a person savors honey under the tongue, the wicked person clings fondly to his ill-gotten gain. But

13 though he cherishes it and will not
      let it go
   but keeps it in his mouth,[a]
14 yet the food in his stomach turns
   into cobras' venom inside him.
15 He swallows wealth but must
      vomit it up;
   God will force it from his stomach.
16 He will suck the poison of cobras;
   a viper's fangs[A] will kill him.[b]
17 He will not enjoy the streams,
   the rivers flowing with honey
      and cream.[c]
18 He must return the fruit of his labor
      without consuming it;
   he doesn't enjoy the profits
      from his trading.
19 For he oppressed and abandoned
      the poor;
   he seized a house he did not build.[d]

20 Because his appetite is never satisfied,[B]
   he does not let anything
      he desires escape.
21 Nothing is left for him to consume;[e]
   therefore, his prosperity will not last.
22 At the height of his success[C]
      distress will come to him;[f]
   the full weight of misery[D]
      will crush him.
23 When he fills his stomach,

God will send His burning anger
   against him,
raining[g] it down on him
   while he is eating.[E]
24 If he flees from an iron weapon,
   an arrow from a bronze bow
      will pierce him.
25 He pulls it out of his back,
   the flashing tip out of his liver.[F]
   Terrors come over him.[h]
26 Total darkness is reserved
      for his treasures.
   A fire unfanned by human hands
      will consume[i] him;
   it will feed on what is left in his tent.
27 The heavens will expose his iniquity,[j]
   and the earth will rise up against him.[k]
28 The possessions in his house
      will be removed,
   flowing away on the day of God's anger.
29 This is the wicked man's lot[l] from God,
   the inheritance God ordained for him.

Job's Reply to Zophar

21 Then Job answered:

2 Pay close attention to my words;
   let this be the consolation you offer.
3 Bear with me while I speak;
   then after I have spoken, you may
      continue mocking.

Cross references:
a20:12-13 Ps 10:7; Pr 9:17; 20:17
b20:16 Dt 32:33; Pr 23:32; Is 59:5
c20:17 Dt 32:13; Jb 29:6; Ps 36:8
d20:19 Dt 28:30; Is 5:8; Mc 2:2
e20:20-21 Jb 15:29; Pr 17:1; Ec 5:13
f20:22 Jdg 2:15; Jb 21:17; Zph 1:17
g20:23 Gn 19:24; Ps 11:6; Ezk 38:22
h20:25 Jb 18:11; 27:20; Jr 6:25
i20:26 Jb 15:34; Ps 21:9; 50:3
j20:27 Jb 13:23,26; 15:5; 22:5
k Dt 4:26; Jb 16:18-19; Ps 50:4
l20:29 Jb 27:13; 31:2; Ps 17:14

A20:16 Lit *tongue*   B20:20 Lit *Because he does not know ease in his stomach*   C20:22 Lit *In the fullness of his excess*   D20:22 Some Hb mss, LXX, Vg; other Hb mss read *the hand of everyone in misery*   E20:23 Text emended; MT reads *him, against his flesh*   F20:25 Or *gallbladder*

---

that which tastes good in the **mouth** sometimes becomes harmful in the **stomach** (Pr 23:31-32).

20:15 As a physician may administer an emetic to force vomiting, so God would dislodge the **wealth** that the wicked person had coerced from others.

20:16 Obtaining wealth through illegitimate means was just as fatal as drinking **poison** or playing with a viper.

20:17 **Honey** was usually gathered from wild bees in ancient times (Jdg 14:8) rather than apiaries. "Honey" also designated thick date syrup. Together with refreshing **cream** (or fermented milk) honey symbolized an abundance of the best things in life (Ex 3:8; Jl 3:8).

20:19 The reason for the wicked man's fall is that he had gained his wealth by victimizing the less fortunate. In some cases he had **seized a house**, either in lieu of a debt or by some dishonest means (Mc 2:2).

20:21 The wicked person's ceaseless drive to get and use things would prove to be his undoing.

20:23 The image of **eating** expresses the idea of consuming life's pleasures and delicacies and enjoying them to the fullest.

20:24-25 Using the war implements of the day, Zophar described God's arsenal of weapons. It includes a sword made of **iron**, a powerful **bronze bow**, and arrows with metal tips (**flashing tip**). The force of the **arrow** is so great that it pierc-

es the wicked person's **liver** and goes through to his **back**. In attempting to remove the arrow, he pulls out his internal organs and only adds to his doom. Job had complained that God's arrows had been unleashed against him (16:13) and had pierced him (6:4). Zophar might have been hinting that, like this wicked person, Job was being justly judged.

20:26 So drastic will be the wicked person's end that even his valued belongings will suffer the **darkness** of death (15:22). He and anything that survives him will be destroyed in the **fire** of divine wrath (15:34; 22:20; Dt 32:22; Ps 21:8-9; 1Co 3:13).

20:27 The wicked man's guilt is so great that **the heavens** and **the earth** will testify against him. The imagery portrays a trial in which the wicked person is accused by everyone before the heavenly court. Job had maintained that his innocence and integrity were on record in heaven (16:18-19). Zophar hinted that it could be otherwise.

20:29 Zophar's final summation is not only a reiteration of his thesis with regard to retribution but a declaration that this is indeed God's decreed policy. Rather than leaving an **inheritance** for his heirs, the wicked person will inherit the just judgment that God has **ordained**.

21:3 Eliphaz had suggested that he and his friends were offering Job consolation (15:11), but Job contended that Zophar and the others were instead **mocking** him (16:20).

4 As for me, is my complaint[a]
     against a man?
  Then why shouldn't I be impatient?
5 Look at me and shudder;[b]
     put your hand over your mouth.[c]
6 When I think about it, I am terrified
     and my body trembles[d] in horror.
7 Why do the wicked continue to live,
     growing old and becoming powerful?
8 Their children are established
     while they are still alive,[A]
  and their descendants,
     before their eyes.
9 Their homes are secure
     and free of fear;[e]
  no rod from God strikes them.[f]
10 Their bulls breed without fail;
     their cows calve and do not miscarry.
11 They let their little ones run
     around like lambs;
  their children skip about,
12 singing to the tambourine and lyre
  and rejoicing at the sound of the flute.[g]
13 They spend[B] their days in prosperity[h]
  and go down to *Sheol in peace.
14 Yet they say to God: "Leave us alone!
  We don't want to know Your ways.[i]
15 Who is the *Almighty, that we
     should serve Him,

and what will we gain by pleading
  with Him?"[j]
16 But their prosperity is not
     of their own doing.
  The counsel of the wicked is far
     from me![k]
17 How often is the lamp[l] of the wicked
     put out?
  Does disaster[C] come on them?
  Does He apportion destruction
     in His anger?
18 Are they like straw before the wind,
  like chaff[m] a storm sweeps away?
19 God reserves a person's punishment
     for his children.[n]
  Let God repay the person himself,
     so that he may know it.
20 Let his own eyes see his demise;
  let him drink from
     the Almighty's wrath![o]
21 For what does he care about his family
     once he is dead,[p]
  when the number of his months
     has run out?[q]
22 Can anyone teach God knowledge,[r]
  since He judges the exalted ones?[D]
23 One person dies in excellent health,[E]
  completely secure[F] and at ease.

Cross references:
a 21:4 Jb 7:11; 10:1; 27:13
b 21:5 Jb 17:8; 18:20; Dn 4:19
c Jdg 18:19; Jb 29:9; 40:4
d 21:6 Jb 4:14; Ps 55:5; 119:120
e 21:9 Jb 5:24; 8:6; 12:6
f Jb 9:34; Ps 73:5
g 21:12 Jb 30:31; Ps 81:2; 150:4
h 21:13 Jb 36:11; Ps 37:7; 73:12
i 21:14 Jb 22:17; Ps 95:10; Pr 1:29
j 21:15 Ex 5:2; Jb 34:9; Mal 3:14
k 21:16 Jb 22:18; Ps 1:1; Pr 1:10
l 21:17 Jb 18:5; Pr 13:9; 24:20
m 21:18 Ps 1:4; 35:5; Is 17:13
n 21:19 Ex 20:5; Jr 31:29; Lm 5:7
o 21:20 Ps 75:8; Is 51:17; Jr 25:15
p 21:21 Jb 14:21; Ec 9:5; Is 63:16
q Jb 14:5; Ps 39:4; 90:12
r 21:22 Is 40:13-14; Rm 11:34; 1Co 2:16

A 21:8 Lit *established before them with them* angels B 21:13 Alt Hb tradition reads *fully enjoy* C 21:17 Lit *their disaster* D 21:22 Probably E 21:23 Lit *in bone of his perfection* F 21:23 Text emended; MT reads *health, all at ease*

Earlier Zophar had accused Job of mocking or ridiculing them (11:3).

21:4 Job's rhetorical question indicated that his **complaint** was against God (19:4,21-22), not **man**. He had grown **impatient** (lit "short of spirit") because he seemingly could not get through to God (7:11-21; 9:33-35; 16:21).

21:5-6 Job invited his friends to take another look at him (2:12; 17:7-8; 18:20). Rather than speaking so glibly, let them gaze at him in silent astonishment (29:9; 40:4; Mc 7:16). Even Job was **terrified** as he thought about his condition.

21:7 Job asserted that his friends' statements about the short-lived success of the wicked were wrong (15:20; 18:5-21; 20:5,15-18). The fact is that the wicked often live long, prosperous lives in positions of power (Ec 7:15).

21:8-13 Contrary to his friends' assertions (15:20-30; 18:5-19; 20:21-28), the wicked live out their lives and leave behind **children** who were also successful and prosperous.

21:14-15 As Job viewed it, the wicked succeed even while rejecting **the Almighty**. They neither serve Him nor recognize His lordship (Ps 73:9-12; 94:3).

21:16 In a parenthetical statement, Job acknowledged that **prosperity** comes from God and distanced himself from the defiant attitude the wicked express in the previous verses.

21:17 Job's rhetorical question implies that despite the **wicked** person's acts of evil and flagrant defiance of God, it does not appear that the Lord disciplines them. Thus Bil-

dad's statements did not hold up (18:5; cp. Ps 73:4-5,12).
Lamp is used metaphorically as a symbol of a happy life (Ps 18:28). An extinguished lamp refers to an untimely death (2Sm 21:17), often because of the judgment of God (Pr 13:9; 20:20; 24:20).

21:18 Wind-blown **straw** and **chaff** often symbolize judgment. As Job saw it, the wicked person escapes judgment while he lives. Job's remarks were born of pessimism because of his suffering, and they do not accurately reflect biblical teaching (Ps 1:4; Dn 2:35; Zph 2:1-2).

21:19-20 As Job saw it, God's punishment unfairly passes over the wicked person and lands on the next generation (Dt 24:16; Jr 31:29-30; Ezk 18:2-4). To **drink from the Almighty's wrath** reflects the figure of the cup of God's judgment (Ps 75:8; Is 51:17; Jr 25:15; Ezk 23:31-34). In other contexts the cup symbolizes God's blessing (Ps 23:5). The cup is also used to signify Jesus' willing surrender to become mankind's sin bearer (Jn 18:11) and the new covenant that He enacted (Mt 26:27-29; 1Co 11:25-26).

21:22 Job had asked previously whether anyone could rightly question God (9:12,19). Job's friends had declared that no one could be especially wise (11:7-9) or be absolutely pure in God's eyes—not even the angels (4:17-18). Yet his friends had acted as though they had special insight into God's ways and truth (4:12-21; 8:3-7; 11:5-6; 15:8-13; 20:4-5,20).

21:23-26 Job's observations on life pointed to facts that could not be accounted for in the worldview expressed by

24 His body is^A well fed,^B
and his bones are full of marrow.^C
25 Yet another person dies
with a bitter^a soul,
having never tasted prosperity.
26 But they both lie in the dust,
and worms cover them.^b

27 I know your thoughts very well,
the schemes you would wrong
me with.
28 For you say, "Where now is
the nobleman's house?"
and "Where are the tents^c the wicked
lived in?"
29 Have you never consulted
those who travel the roads?
Don't you accept their reports?^D
30 Indeed, the evil man is spared
from the day of disaster,
rescued from the day of wrath.
31 Who would denounce his behavior
to his face?
Who would repay^d him for what
he has done?
32 He is carried to the grave,
and someone keeps watch over
his tomb.
33 The dirt on his grave is^E sweet to him.
Everyone follows behind him,
and those who go before him are
without number.

Cross references (center column):
^a21:25 1Sm 1:10; Jb 7:11; 10:1
^b21:26 Jb 20:11; Ec 9:2-3; Is 14:11
^c21:28 Jb 8:22,18:21; Ps 55:15
^d21:31 Dt 7:10; Jb 34:11; Ps 62:12
^e22:2-3 Jb 35:7; Ps 16:2; Lk 17:10
^f22:4 Jb 14:3; Ps 143:2
^g22:6 Ex 22:26; Dt 24:6,17; Ezk:12,16
^h22:7 Jb 31:17; Is 58:7; Mt 25:42
^i22:9 Jb 24:3; Is 10:2; Ezk 22:7

34 So how can you offer me
such futile comfort?
Your answers are deceptive.

THIRD SERIES OF SPEECHES

Eliphaz Speaks

22 Then Eliphaz the Temanite replied:

2 Can a man be of any use to God?
Can even a wise man be of use to Him?
3 Does it delight the •Almighty if you
are righteous?
Does He profit if you perfect
your behavior?^e

4 Does He correct you and take you
to court
because of your piety?^f
5 Isn't your wickedness abundant
and aren't your iniquities endless?
6 For you took collateral^g
from your brothers without cause,
stripping off their clothes
and leaving them naked.
7 You gave no water to the thirsty
and withheld food from the famished,^h
8 while the land belonged
to a powerful man
and an influential man lived on it.
9 You sent widows away empty-handed,
and the strength of the fatherless^i
was^F crushed.

---

^A21:24 Or *His sides are;* Hb obscure   ^B21:24 Lit *is full of milk*   ^C21:24 Lit *and the marrow of his bones is watered*   ^D21:29 Lit *signs*
^E21:33 Lit *The clods of the wadi are*   ^F22:9 LXX, Syr, Vg, Tg read *you have*

---

his friends. As Job saw it, a person's goodness or wickedness had nothing to do with life's fortunes.

21:27 Job asserted that when his friends described the fate of the wicked, they were alluding to him (16:1-4), but they were wrong (19:1-6).

21:28 When Job's friends spoke of the loss of the **nobleman's house** and goods, he understood them to be applying that to his case (15:34; 18:14-21; 20:26-28). Their remarks were painful reminders to him of the loss of his children and all they had (1:13-19).

21:29-30 Job's questions imply that his friends' doctrine of swift retribution conflicts with facts that anyone who has traveled can observe. Rather than having their homes destroyed (18:14-15; 20:22), the wicked rich live securely in them.

21:31 Job's friends said that the wicked are on shaky ground and soon fall, but Job observes they are so powerful that no one can touch them.

21:32-33 Job's observation was that the wicked nobleman went to his **grave** with great honor and a large funeral procession (Ec 8:10), which was contrary to Bildad's remarks (Jb 18:17). The image of the **sweet . . . dirt** may indicate that as far as Job could tell, the wicked person's lot was pleasant even in death.

21:34 Job categorically denounced his friends' counsel as failing to provide **comfort** (v. 3; 16:2-3) and being **deceptive** (13:4).

22:2-3 Eliphaz began his speech with a series of rhetorical questions that expected a negative answer. Job's righteousness would not fill up a deficiency in God.

22:4-5 Previously Eliphaz had told Job that his **piety** would see him through his ordeal (4:6-7) after God's discipline had run its course (5:17-18). Now he accused Job of **wickedness** (see vv. 6-9). Later, Job defended himself against these charges (31:16-17).

22:6 Eliphaz charged Job with social crimes. He said Job had taken as **collateral** the outer garments or cloaks of those who were in debt to him. These should have been returned to the person each night as protection against the cool night air (Ex 22:26-27). Job later refuted Eliphaz's charge (see note at Jb 31:19-20).

22:7-8 Eliphaz accused Job of insensitivity. Although Job was a **powerful** and **influential man**, his actions showed he was not concerned about the needy. He supplied neither **water** nor **food** to them despite their circumstances (Is 58:7; Mt 10:41-42).

22:9 Eliphaz cited Job for failing to provide for **widows** and orphans. Care of the oppressed served as a standard of

¹⁰ Therefore snares surround you,
and sudden dread terrifies[a] you,
¹¹ or darkness, so you cannot see,
and a flood of water covers you.[b]
¹² Isn't God as high as the heavens?
And look at the highest stars—
how lofty they are!
¹³ Yet you say: "What does God know?
Can He judge through thick darkness?[c]
¹⁴ Clouds[d] veil Him so that He cannot see,
as He walks on the circle of the sky."
¹⁵ Will you continue on the ancient path
that wicked men have walked?
¹⁶ They were snatched away
before their time,
and their foundations[e]
were washed away by a river.
¹⁷ They were the ones who said to God,
"Leave us alone!"
and "What can the Almighty do
to us?"[A,f]
¹⁸ But it was He who filled their houses
with good things.
The counsel of the wicked is
far from me!
¹⁹ The righteous see this and rejoice;
the innocent mock them, saying,[g]

²⁰ "Surely our opponents are destroyed,
and fire has consumed
what they left behind."[h]
²¹ Come to terms with God and be
at peace;[i]
in this way[B] good will come to you.
²² Receive instruction from His mouth,[j]
and place His sayings[k] in your heart.
²³ If you return[l] to the Almighty, you will
be renewed.
If you banish injustice from your tent
²⁴ and consign your gold to the dust,
the gold of Ophir[m] to the stones
in the *wadis,
²⁵ the Almighty will be your gold
and your finest silver.
²⁶ Then you will delight[n] in the Almighty
and lift up your face to God.[o]
²⁷ You will pray to Him, and He will
hear you,[p]
and you will fulfill your vows.
²⁸ When you make a decision, it will be
carried out,[C]
and light will shine on your ways.[q]
²⁹ When others are humiliated
and you say, "Lift them up,"
God will save the humble.[D,r]

---

a 22:10 Jb 3:25; 23:15; 31:23
b 22:11 Jb 38:34; Ps 69:1-2; Lm 3:54
c 22:13 Ps 73:11; Is 29:15; Ezk 8:12
d 22:14 2Sm 22:12; Jb 26:8; 37:11
e 22:16 Jb 4:19; Lm 4:11; Ezk 30:4
f 22:17 Jb 21:14; Ps 95:10; 107:42
g 22:19 Ps 52:6; 58:10; Pr 1:26-27
h 22:20 Jb 1:16; 4:9; 15:30
i 22:21 Ps 119:165; Pr 3:2; Is 27:5
j 22:22 Dt 8:3; Pr 2:6; Mal 2:7
k Jb 6:10; 23:12; Ps 119:102
l 22:23 Is 31:6; 55:7; Mal 3:7
m 22:24 1Kg 9:28; Jb 28:16; Is 13:12
n 22:26 Jb 27:10; Ps 37:4; Is 55:2
o Jb 11:15; 27:10; Is 58:14
p 22:27 Jb 33:26; Ps 50:14; Is 58:9
q 22:28 Pr 4:18; Is 60:3; Dn 12:3
r 22:29 Ps 18:27; Mt 23:12; 1Pt 5:5

A 22:17 LXX, Syr; MT reads *him*   B 22:21 Lit *peace; by them*   C 22:28 Lit *out for you*   D 22:29 Lit *bowed of eyes*

---

common decency and social obligation in the ancient Near East (Dt 14:28-29; 24:17-22; Jms 1:27). The alleviation of their need was of concern to God (Dt 10:17-18; 27:19).

22:10-11 Eliphaz applied Bildad's remarks (18:8-11,18) metaphorically to Job's situation. Job's misdeeds had so ensnared him that he was overwhelmed like **water** that flooded the soul (27:20; Ps 69:15).

22:12-14 Eliphaz argues that if God controlled the vast universe (see note at 1Kg 8:27), He would know all about mankind. Eliphaz suggested that Job interpreted the same fact (God's control of the vast universe) in the opposite way: God was too distant to see man's actions. Eliphaz misrepresented Job's position, for Job had complained that God scrutinized his actions (Jb 7:12,17-20; 9:17-18; 10:4-8; 13:27). The **thick darkness** Job felt was his inability to get through to God (19:7-8).

22:15-16 Eliphaz implied that Job was treading the same route to destruction that had overtaken man since **ancient** times (Gn 7:20-24; 19:24-25). Contrary to Job's observation that the wicked defied God but were seldom punished (Jb 21:15-16), the witness of time confirms that in God's judgment they suffer the loss of everything.

22:17 The defiant ones Job said were permitted to prosper (21:14) were the very ones Eliphaz said died prematurely. Experience shows that neither man was entirely correct.

22:18 Eliphaz may here be agreeing with Job (21:16) that God **filled** the houses of the wicked **with good things**, but since they didn't acknowledge God their prosperity was short-lived. Their defiance of God (v. 17) is repulsive. Alternately, Eliphaz is saying that Job's statement that God had

blessed the wicked is the **counsel of the wicked** that is to be repudiated.

22:19-20 Eliphaz confirmed Zophar's counsel (20:26-29) that the wicked would lose everything in a fiery end. The **righteous** would **rejoice** at this justice (Ps 52:1-7).

22:21-22 Eliphaz argued it was in Job's best interest to learn from God's discipline (5:17-26). Job should take to **heart** God's wisdom that his friends had conveyed to him (Ps 78:2-4). Knowledge comes from God's **mouth** (Pr 2:6).

22:23-25 The verb **return** connotes turning from self to God with a deliberate choice to abandon sin and godlessness in order to live in submission to God and His standards (Jr 23:5; Ac 2:38). The verb translated **renewed** is literally "be built up." It implies a successful, godly lifestyle. The **gold of Ophir** was highly prized in the ancient Near East (1Kg 9:28), but Job should throw away his precious **gold** and let God be his treasure (Ps 16:5; Is 33:6; Mt 13:44; 19:21; Php 3:7-9; 1Tm 6:6).

22:26-27 Job had complained that he could get no answer from God when he prayed (13:20-24; 19:7-8). Eliphaz restated that when Job had submitted to God's discipline and had been renewed, he would enjoy restored fellowship with God (5:17-26).

22:28 Eliphaz suggested that when Job was restored his plans would no longer be frustrated. Rather than the darkness he now experienced (vv. 10-11; 19:8), the **light** of God's presence and guidance would **shine** on all he did (Ps 27:1; 56:13; 89:15; 1Jn 1:7).

22:29-30 With renewed fellowship with God, Job would become a blessing to others. God would hear Job's prayers, and Job would be a winsome example of godliness.

³⁰ He will even rescue the *guilty one,
who will be rescued by the purity
of your hands.ᵃ

Job's Reply to Eliphaz

23 Then Job answered:

² Today also my complaint is bitter.ᴬ,ᵇ
Hisᴮ hand is heavy
despite my groaning.
³ If only I knew how to find Him,
so that I could go to His throne.
⁴ I would plead my case before Himᶜ
and fill my mouth with arguments.
⁵ I would learn howᶜ He would
answer me;
and understand what He would say
to me.
⁶ Would He prosecuteᵈ me forcefully?
No, He will certainly pay attention
to me.
⁷ Then an upright man could reasonᵉ
with Him,
and I would escape
from my Judgeᶠ forever.

⁸ If I go east, He is not there,
and if I go west, I cannot
perceive Him.ᵍ
⁹ When He is at work to the north,
I cannot see Him;
when He turns south, I cannot
find Him.
¹⁰ Yet He knows the way I have taken;ᴰ
when He has tested me,ʰ I will emerge
as pure gold.

¹¹ My feet have followed in His tracks;
I have kept to His wayⁱ and not
turned aside.
¹² I have not departed
from the commands of His lips;
I have treasuredᴱ the wordsʲ
of His mouth
more than my daily food.

¹³ But He is unchangeable; who can
oppose Him?
He does what He desires.ᵏ
¹⁴ He will certainly accomplish
what He has decreed for me,
and He has many more things
like these in mind.ᶠ
¹⁵ Therefore I am terrifiedˡ
in His presence;
when I consider this, I am afraid
of Him.
¹⁶ God has made my heart faint;ᵐ
the *Almighty has terrified me.
¹⁷ Yet I am not destroyedᴳ
by the darkness,ⁿ
by the thick darkness that covers
my face.

24 Why does the *Almighty not reserve
times for judgment?ᵒ
Why do those who know Him never see
His days?
² The wicked displace boundary markers.
They steal a flock and provide pasture
for it.
³ They drive away the donkeys owned
by the fatherlessᵖ

ᵃ 22:30 2Sm
22:21; Jb 17:9;
Ps 24:4
ᵇ 23:2 Jb 7:11;
10:1; 21:4
ᶜ 23:4 Jb 5:8;
13:18; 35:14
ᵈ 23:6 Jb 13:19;
33:13; Is 45:9
ᵉ 23:7 Jb
13:3,15; 15:3
ᶠ Gn 18:25; Is
33:22; Jr 11:20
ᵍ 23:8 Jb 9:11;
35:14
ʰ 23:10 Ps 17:3;
66:10; 1Pt 1:7
ⁱ 23:11 Jb 17:9;
Ps 17:5; 44:18
ʲ 23:12 Jb 6:10;
22:22; Ps
119:102-3,111
ᵏ 23:13 Ps 115:3;
Is 14:27; Dn
4:35
ˡ 23:15 Jb 4:14;
22:10; 23:15
ᵐ 23:16 Dt 20:3;
Is 7:4; Jr 51:46
ⁿ 23:17 Jb 19:8;
29:3; 30:26
ᵒ 24:1 Ec 9:12; Is
2:12; Ac 1:7
ᵖ 24:3 Dt 27:19;
Jb 22:9; 31:21

ᴬ23:2 Syr, Tg, Vg; MT reads *rebellion* ᴮ23:2 LXX, Syr; MT reads *My* ᶜ23:5 Lit *the words* ᴰ23:10 Lit *way with me* ᴱ23:12 LXX, Vg read *treasured in my bosom* ᶠ23:14 Lit *these with Him* ᴳ23:17 Or *silenced*

23:2 Job answered Eliphaz with an attempt to justify his attitude. He felt that God was oppressing him (Ps 32:4).

23:3-4 Job lamented his inability to have an audience with God (9:32-35; 13:20-24) where he would expect to find justice (Ps 97:2).

23:5 Whatever God decided, Job would at least have the satisfaction of renewed contact with God.

23:6-7 Job had expressed fear about a hearing before God (9:34-35; 13:21-22). Now he felt his case for innocence would be established, and he would be acquitted of any wrongdoing (14:14-17).

23:8-9 Job experienced God as highly elusive. He sought God **east . . . west . . . north**, and **south** but could not **perceive Him**. At the same time, God was so close Job felt His relentless attacks.

23:10 As dross is removed from gold in the crucible, leaving a shining surface, so when God finished dealing with him, Job would appear as a shining example of righteousness (Pr 17:3).

23:11-12 The word translated **daily food** (Hb *choq*) means "portion" (Ex 29:28). A related word (Hb *chuqqah*) means

"statute" (Ex 29:9), suggesting that Job had prized God's precepts more than his own natural inclinations (Rm 7:23). The reading found in the Septuagint (LXX) and the Vulgate add the phrase "in my bosom" after **treasured**. This pictures that which was close to Job's heart (Ps 119:11).

23:13-14 Job acknowledged God's unchangeableness (lit "in/as one"; cp. Mal 3:6). God does what He **desires**, and His will is irresistible (Rm 9:19). God would yet finish what He had decided to do in testing Job.

23:15-17 Job was terrified (7:19; 9:34; 13:25) by God's omnipotence and **presence**. He lived in constant fear of the **darkness** of death that seemed near (16:16; 17:11-16).

24:1 Job's observations of society convinced him that God's justice was lacking. Those who kept His standards went unrewarded, and the wicked were not judged for their evil. God should establish times for administering justice.

24:2-3 The removal of **boundary markers** was a serious offense (Dt 19:14; Pr 23:10). Confiscation of animals in lieu of a debt was unforgivable, especially against the **fatherless** and **widows**. Care of the widow, orphans, and poor is a duty of righteousness (6:27; 22:9; Ps 82:3-4) and a priority to God (Dt 27:17; Ps 68:5).

and take the widow's ox as collateral.
4 They push the needy off the road;
the poor of the land are forced
into hiding.*a*
5 Like wild donkeys in the desert,
the poor go out to their task of foraging
for food;
the wilderness provides nourishment
for their children.
6 They gather their fodder in the field
and glean the vineyards
of the wicked.
7 Without clothing, they spend
the night naked,
having no covering against the cold.*b*
8 Drenched by mountain rains,
they huddle against*A* the rocks,
shelterless.
9 The fatherless infant is snatched
from the breast;
the nursing child of the poor is seized
as collateral.*B*
10 Without clothing,
they wander about naked.
They carry sheaves but go hungry.*c*
11 They crush olives in their presses;*C*
they tread the winepresses,
but go thirsty.
12 From the city, men*D* groan;
the mortally wounded cry for help,

*a*24:4 Jdg 5:6; Pr 28:28; Am 2:7
*b*24:7 Ex 22:26-27; Dt 24:12-13; Jb 22:6
*c*24:10 Dt 24:19; 2Tm 2:6; Jms 5:4
*d*24:12 Jb 1:22; Ps 69:26
*e*24:19 Jb 7:9; Ps 9:17; Pr 27:20
*f*24:20 Jb 18:17; Pr 10:7; Jr 11:19

yet God pays no attention
to this crime.*d*
13 The wicked are those who rebel
against the light.
They do not recognize its ways
or stay on its paths.
14 The murderer rises at dawn
to kill the poor and needy,
and by night he becomes a thief.
15 The adulterer's eye watches
for twilight,
thinking: No eye will see me;
he covers his face.
16 In the dark they break*E* into houses;
by day they lock themselves in,*F*
never experiencing the light.
17 For the morning is like darkness
to them.
Surely they are familiar
with the terrors of darkness!
18 They float*G* on the surface of the water.
Their section of the land is cursed,
so that they never go to their vineyards.
19 As dry ground and heat snatch away
the melted snow,
so •Sheol*e* steals those who have sinned.
20 The womb forgets them;
worms feed on them;
they are remembered*f* no more.

---

*A*24:8 Lit *they embrace*   *B*24:9 Text emended; MT reads *breast; they seize collateral against the poor*   *C*24:11 Lit *olives between their rows*   *D*24:12 One Hb ms, Syr read *the dying*   *E*24:16 Lit *dig*   *F*24:16 Lit *they seal for themselves*   *G*24:18 Lit *are insignificant*

24:4 The **needy** feared to travel the roads because the wicked might rob them.

24:6 The poor were left to the mercy of their **wicked** oppressors (Dt 24:14). They worked in the **field** and **vineyards** or gathered what remained behind the harvesters (Lv 19:9-10; Ru 2:2).

24:7-8 Lacking proper **clothing**, sometimes seized cruelly by the wicked (Dt 24:10-13,17), the poor were left to the mercy of the elements.

24:9 The poor, **fatherless**, and widows were often victims of the powerful (Is 10:2).

24:10-11 The poor toiled under oppressive conditions. Contrary to human decency (Mt 25:34-40), they were denied food and drink. They were not permitted portions of the produce they were hired to harvest (Dt 25:4; 1Tm 5:18). Grain, wine, and olive oil were basic staples (Jr 31:12).

24:12 Job complained that God did not rectify the prevailing injustice (9:23-24; 19:7). It was a familiar prophetic complaint (Jr 20:8; Hab 1:2-4), but the truth is God does act in His time (Is 29:15-21).

24:13-17 Evil persons use the cover of darkness to commit foul deeds, including murder, adultery, and theft. These are violations of the sixth, seventh, and eighth commandments. The verb **lock** (lit "seal") indicates that the wicked stay enclosed in their houses like a person who puts his seal on a document. The **dark** is a friend to evildoers, so **light** terrifies them (Jn 3:20; 1Co 4:5; Eph 5:8-11).

24:18-20 Job adapted his argument to his friends' teaching about the sudden demise of the wicked (18:14; 20:4-5; 22:16-18). As objects that **float on . . . water** move downstream, so the wicked pass on and their ill-gotten property becomes unusable. Their cycle of **injustice** is **broken**, and they are forgotten.

---

derek

Hebrew Pronunciation	[DEH rek]
HCSB Translation	way, road, path
Uses in Job	33
Uses in the OT	712
Focus Passage	Job 24:4,13,18,23

Derek, from verbal *darak (tread)*, indicates *way*, either as physical *path* (Nm 22:22) or metaphor for *behavior* (Ezk 16:27). It occurs alongside other words for *roadway*, and implies *highway* (Nm 20:17), *road* (1Sm 6:9), *route* (Dt 1:22), or *passageway* (Ezk 42:11). It suggests *journey* (Gn 24:21) or *trip* (Ex 3:18), especially when modified temporally. *Derek* can mean *distance* (Ex 8:27). With compass points it is untranslated, or suggests *direction* (1Kg 8:44) or *toward* (Ezk 42:7). Ethically, "walk in His *ways*" (Dt 10:12) implies *following* an *example* (1Kg 16:26), *instruction* (Dt 5:33), or *custom* (Gn 19:31). *Anything you do* is literally "your *ways*" (Dt 28:29). *Derek* signifies one's *course* (Jb 29:25), *works* (Jb 40:19), or *life* (Ps 119:26). In comparisons it can be *like* (Am 4:10). Scripture contrasts *ways* of life and death (Jr 21:8), the evil *way* (Pr 28:10), and the *way* of integrity (Ps 101:6).

So injustice is broken like a tree.

21 They prey on[A] the childless woman
     who is unable to conceive,
and do not deal kindly with the widow.

22 Yet God drags away[B] the mighty
     by His power;
when He rises up, they have
     no assurance of life.

23 He gives them a sense of security,
     so they can rely on it,[a]
but His eyes[b] watch over their ways.

24 They are exalted for a moment,
     then they are gone;
they are brought low and shrivel up
     like everything else.[c]
They wither like heads of grain.[c]

25 If this is not true, then who
     can prove me a liar[d]
and show that my speech is worthless?

[a]24:23 Jb 11:18;
Ps 4:8; Pr 3:24
[b]Ps 11:4; Pr
15:3; Jr 16:17
[c]24:24 Jb 14:21;
Ps 37:10; 106:43
[d]24:25 Jb 6:28;
27:4; 34:6
[e]25:2 2Ch 20:29;
Jb 13:11; Ps
36:1
[f]25:4 Jb 9:2; Ps
143:2; Rm 3:20
[g]Jb 4:17; 15:14;
Pr 20:9
[h]25:5 Jb 4:18;
15:15; 21:22
[i]25:6 Ps 8:4;
22:6; Is 41:14
[j]26:2 Jb 4:3; Is
35:3; Heb 12:12

Bildad Speaks

25 Then Bildad the Shuhite replied:

2 Dominion and dread[e] belong to Him,
     the One who establishes harmony
          in the heavens.[D]

3 Can His troops be numbered?
     Does His light not shine on everyone?

4 How can a person be justified
          before God?[f]
     How can one born of woman be pure?[g]

5 If even the moon does not shine
     and the stars are not pure in His sight,[h]

6 how much less man, who is a maggot,
     and the son of man, who is a worm![i]

Job's Reply to Bildad

26 Then Job answered:

2 How you have helped[j] the powerless

[A]24:21 LXX, Tg read *They harm*   [B]24:22 Or *God prolongs the life of*   [C]24:24 LXX reads *like a mallow plant in the heat*   [D]25:2 Lit *in His heights*

24:21-24 However much the wicked gain by preying on the helpless, it will not protect them against God's **power**. Although they feel secure, God is not unaware of their wickedness. They will experience short-lived success. Job acknowledged that God can and will judge. It just seems to be delayed.

24:25 Although the wicked might die prematurely, they do so without being brought to justice in this life (21:22-34). Job defied his friends to disprove his thesis (17:10).

25:2 Bildad summed up the friends' position against Job's claims. The might of God, who established **harmony** in the original creation (Gn 1:31; Ps 104:1-4) and maintained it (Ps 19:1-6; 103:19), should inspire **dread** in mankind (13:11).

25:3-6 Bildad asked a series of rhetorical questions implying negative answers. He restated the position of the three friends (4:17; 8:20; 11:14-16; 15:14-16; 22:4) as opposed to Job's claims of innocence and purity (13:18; 16:17; 23:4-7,10-12). If God's heavenly bodies were not **pure**, how could man claim to be (4:18-19; 15:15-16)? Job acknowledged that his life and man's destiny were tied to maggots and worms (7:5; 17:14; 21:26; 24:20), which speak of man's lowly existence (Ps 22:6) and terminal condition (Is 14:11).

26:2-4 Job replied sarcastically that Bildad had delivered **the path to success** (or "sound wisdom") to the **unwise** (Job). Yet Bildad had only parroted common knowledge (12:2-3) and his **words** originated with others (4:17-19; 25:4-6).

Reconstruction of an olive press (24:11) at Tel Ekron. Heavy weights were hung from each end of the large shaft. Olives were placed in cloth bags between stones under the fulcrum point. The oil ran out into the collection reservoir to the left of the press.

and delivered the arm that is weak!

3 How you have counseled the unwise[a]
   and thoroughly explained
      the path to success!

4 Who did you speak these words to?
   Whose breath came out of your mouth?

5 The departed spirits tremble
   beneath the waters and all that
      inhabit them.[b]

6 *Sheol[c] is naked before God,
   and *Abaddon[d] has no covering.[e]

7 He stretches the northern skies
      over empty space;
   He hangs the earth on nothing.

8 He wraps up the waters in His clouds,
   yet the clouds do not burst
      beneath their weight.[f]

9 He obscures the view of His throne,
   spreading His cloud over it.

10 He laid out the horizon on the surface
      of the waters[g]
   at the boundary between light
      and darkness.

11 The pillars that hold up
      the sky tremble,
   astounded at His rebuke.[h]

12 By His power He stirred[i] the sea,
   and by His understanding
      He crushed *Rahab.[j]

13 By His breath the heavens gained
      their beauty;
   His hand pierced the fleeing serpent.[A,k]

14 These are but the fringes of His ways;
   how faint is the word we hear of Him!
   Who can understand
      His mighty thunder?

---

a 26:3 Jb 11:6; Ps 73:24; Jms 1:5
b 26:5 Ps 88:10; Is 26:14,19; Rv 20:13
c 26:6 Pr 30:3,9; Pr 1:12; Is 5:14
d Jb 28:22; Pr 27:20; Rv 9:11
e Ps 139:8; Pr 15:11; Heb 4:13
f 26:8 Jb 37:11; 38:9; Pr 30:4
g 26:10 Ps 104:9; Pr 8:27,29; Jr 5:22
h 26:11 2Sm 22:16; Ps 18:15; 104:7
i 26:12 Is 51:15; Jr 31:35
j Jb 9:13; Ps 89:10; Is 51:9
k 26:13 Jb 41; Ps 33:6; Is 27:1
l 27:2 Jb 19:6; 34:5
m Ex 1:14; Ru 1:20; Jb 3:20
n 27:3 Gn 2:7; Jb 12:10; 33:4
o 27:5 Jb 2:3,9; 31:6; Pr 11:3
p 27:6 Ac 24:16; 1Co 4:4; Rv 9:11
q 27:8 Jb 17:8; 20:5; 36:13
r Jb 8:13; Mt 16:26; Lk 12:20
s 27:10 Jb 22:26; Ps 37:4; Is 55:2
t 27:12 Jb 2:10; 15:2
u 27:13 Jb 20:29; 31:2; Ps 17:14

---

27 Job continued his discourse, saying:

2 As God lives, who has deprived me
      of justice,[l]
   and the *Almighty who has
      made me bitter,[m]

3 as long as my breath is still in me
   and the breath from God remains
      in my nostrils,[n]

4 my lips will not speak unjustly,
   and my tongue will not utter deceit.

5 I will never affirm that you are right.
   I will maintain my integrity[B,o]
      until I die.

6 I will cling to my righteousness
      and never let it go.
   My conscience[p] will not accuse me
      as long as I live!

7 May my enemy be like the wicked
   and my opponent like the unjust.

8 For what hope does
      the godless man[q] have
      when he is cut off,
   when God takes away his life?[r]

9 Will God hear his cry
   when distress comes on him?

10 Will he delight[s] in the Almighty?
   Will he call on God at all times?

11 I will teach you about God's power.
   I will not conceal what the Almighty
      has planned.[C]

12 All of you have seen this for yourselves,
   why do you keep up this empty talk?[t]

13 This is a wicked man's lot[u] from God,
   the inheritance the ruthless receive
      from the Almighty.

A 26:13 = Leviathan   B 27:5 Lit will not remove my integrity from me   C 27:11 Lit what is with the Almighty

---

26:5-6 Job had previously delivered a discourse about God's dominion. Bildad had extolled God's heavenly rule (25:5). Job had added that **Sheol** was open to God's view (Pr 15:11). Sheol here refers to the place of the wicked **departed spirits**, quartered in **Abaddon** (the place of destruction; see note at 28:20-22). Elsewhere "Sheol" simply has the grave in view, with no specific reference to the fate of the wicked (see note at 7:9).

26:7-8 Northern refers to God's dwelling in the heavenly heights (Ps 48:1-2). God filled the **clouds** with water like celestial water skins that **do not burst** (see note at 38:36-38).

26:9-10 The clouds serve to keep people from beholding the glory of God in heaven (Ps 104:1-3; Am 9:6). The rising and setting of the sun appear most vividly at the far **horizon** of the sea's surface, where it separates **light and darkness**.

26:11 God's power is felt in His presence on the mountains, which stretch from deep below the sea (Jnh 2:6) into the sky like **pillars** (or standing columns; cp. 1Kg 7:15-21).

26:12-13 God's **power** and wisdom were evident in His control over the primal **sea** with its mighty creatures. **Stirred** may also be translated "stilled" (Jr 50:34). The reference to God destroying **Rahab** and the **fleeing serpent** counters ancient cosmologies in which mythical deities conquered chaos at creation. Job underscored the fact that Yahweh alone is God and the controller of everything (9:13-14; Ps 74:13; 89:10).

26:14 Mankind catches just a glimpse and a whisper of God's workings. Full knowledge is beyond human understanding (5:9; 11:8; 42:3).

27:4 The upright use their **lips** (Ps 141:3) and **tongue** wisely. Their organs of speech should praise God (Ps 51:14-15).

27:7-10 In their **godless** state, Job's detractors lived for self, not God. Therefore, God would not **hear** their cries for relief.

27:11-12 Job and his friends knew about **God's power** and providence. They lectured him about God's judgment of the wicked (11:5-6; 22:5) but misapplied it to Job's case.

27:13-23 Job displayed his understanding of the **wicked man's lot**, which his friends had described.

¹⁴ Even if his children increase,
　　they are destined for the sword;
his descendants will never
　　have enough food.
¹⁵ Those who survive him will be buried
　　by the plague,
yet their widows will not weep
　　for them.^a
¹⁶ Though he piles up silver like dust
　　and heaps up a wardrobe like clay—
¹⁷ he may heap it up, but the righteous
　　will wear it,
and the innocent will divide up
　　his silver.^b
¹⁸ The house he built is
　　like a moth's cocoon
or a booth set up by a watchman.^c
¹⁹ He lies down wealthy, but will do so
　　no more;
when he opens his eyes, it is gone.
²⁰ Terrors overtake him like a flood;^d
　　a storm^e wind sweeps him away
　　　at night.
²¹ An east wind picks him up,
　　and he is gone;
it carries him away from his place.
²² It blasts at him without mercy,
　　while he flees desperately
　　　from its grasp.
²³ It claps^f its hands at him
　　and scorns him from its place.

Job's Hymn to Wisdom

28 Surely there is a mine for silver
　　and a place where gold is refined.
² Iron is taken from the ground,
　　and copper is smelted from ore.
³ A miner puts an end to the darkness;
　　he probes^A the deepest recesses
　　for ore in the gloomy darkness.

⁴ He cuts a shaft far
　　from human habitation,
in places unknown to those who walk
　　above ground.^B
Suspended far away from people,
　　the miners swing back and forth.
⁵ Food may come from the earth,
　　but below the surface the earth
　　　is transformed as by fire.
⁶ Its rocks are a source of sapphire,^{C,g}
　　containing flecks of gold.
⁷ No bird of prey knows that path;
　　no falcon's eye has seen it.
⁸ Proud beasts have never walked on it;
　　no lion has ever prowled over it.
⁹ The miner strikes the flint
　　and transforms the mountains
　　　at their foundations.
¹⁰ He cuts out channels in the rocks,
　　and his eyes spot every treasure.
¹¹ He dams up the streams from flowing^D
　　so that he may bring to light
　　　what is hidden.

¹² But where can wisdom^h be found,
　　and where is understanding located?
¹³ No man can know its value,^E
　　since it cannot be found in the land
　　　of the living.
¹⁴ The ocean depths say, "It's not in me,"
　　while the sea declares, "I don't
　　　have it."ⁱ
¹⁵ Gold cannot be exchanged for it,
　　and silver cannot be weighed out
　　　for its price.
¹⁶ Wisdom cannot be valued in the gold
　　of Ophir,^j
in precious onyx or sapphire.^{C,k}
¹⁷ Gold and glass do not compare with it,

Cross references (center column)

^a27:15 Jb 18:19; Ps 78:64; Jr 22:10
^b27:17 Pr 13:22; 28:8; Ec 2:26
^c27:18 Jb 4:19; Is 1:8; Jnh 4:5
^d27:20 Jb 18:11; 20:25; Jr 6:25
^eJb 21:18; Ps 83:15; Is 29:6
^f27:23 Nm 24:10; Jb 34:37; Lm 2:15
^g28:6 Ex 24:10; Ezk 1:26; Rv 21:19
^h28:12 Jb 28:20; Pr 16:16; Ec 7:23,25
ⁱ28:14 Dt 30:11-13; Ps 92:5; Rm 11:33
^j28:16 1Kg 9:28; 10:11; Jb 22:24
^kPr 3:14-16; 8:10-11; 16:16

A 28:3 Lit *probes all*　**B** 28:4 Lit *far from with inhabitant, things forgotten by foot*　**C** 28:6,16 Or *lapis lazuli*　**D** 28:11 LXX, Vg read *He explores the sources of the streams*　**E** 28:13 LXX reads *way*

27:18 House portrays metaphorically the wicked person's life and possessions. A watchman's **booth** was a temporary structure built during harvest time as a shelter from which to guard the fields. After harvest it was allowed to fall into ruin.

27:19-23 The wicked person's prosperity can disappear overnight. Terrifying disasters haunt his soul constantly **like a flood** or tornadic wind (1:19; 38:24). Such could not designate Job. He might be discouraged, but he was confident of his integrity (27:5-6). The wicked must bear the scorn of those who rejoiced over his fall. Clapping the **hands**, hissing, and shaking the head were common gestures of contempt (Lm 2:15; Nah 3:19; Zph 2:15).

28:1-2 Mining and refining were widely known in the ancient world.

28:3-4 At times men were **suspended** in cages or baskets hung by ropes in order to pick out the minerals at the side of

the mineshaft. In some cases they cut horizontal tunnels. In dark places workers illuminated their way with torches.

28:5-6 Sometimes tunnel walls were heated with **fire** and then quickly drenched with water to crack hard stone. The rocks, which were then hauled to the surface, might contain **sapphire** (lapis lazuli, a dark blue stone), which typically contain **flecks** of gold-colored pyrite.

28:7-8 Neither the bird with keenest sight nor the proudest animal knew the way to the treasures that miners unearthed.

28:9-11 Miners developed and employed remarkable technology for their day.

28:12-13 Despite man's impressive technical expertise, he does not **know** the path to **wisdom** and **understanding**.

28:15-19 Glass was a valuable commodity in the ancient Near East. **Wisdom** is more valuable than precious metals

and articles of fine gold
  cannot be exchanged for it.*
18 Coral and quartz are not
    worth mentioning.
  The price of wisdom is beyond pearls.
19 Topaz from •Cush cannot compare
    with it,
  and it cannot be valued in pure gold.
20 Where then does wisdom come from,
  and where is understanding located?
21 It is hidden from the eyes
    of every living thing
  and concealed from the birds of the sky.
22 •Abaddon and Death* say,
  "We have heard news of it
    with our ears."
23 But God understands the way
    to wisdom,
  and He knows its location.
24 For He looks to the ends of the earth
  and sees everything under the heavens.
25 When God fixed the weight of the wind
  and limited the water by measure,*
26 when He established a limit*
    for the rain*
  and a path for the lightning,
27 He considered wisdom and evaluated it;
  He established it and examined it.
28 He said to mankind,
  "The •fear of the Lord is this: wisdom.
  And to turn from evil is understanding."*

Job's Final Claim of Innocence

29 Job continued his discourse, saying:

2 If only I could be as in months gone by,
  in the days when God watched over me,
3 when His lamp shone above my head,
  and I walked through darkness
    by His light!*

4 I would be as I was in the days
    of my youth
  when God's friendship* rested
    on my tent,
5 when the •Almighty was still with me
  and my children were around me,
6 when my feet were bathed in cream
  and the rock* poured out streams of oil
    for me!
7 When I went out to the city •gate
  and took my seat in the town square,
8 the young men saw me and withdrew,
  while older men stood to their feet.
9 City officials stopped talking
  and covered their mouths
    with their hands.*
10 The noblemen's voices were hushed,
  and their tongues stuck to the roof
    of their mouths.
11 When they heard me, they blessed me,
  and when they saw me, they spoke well
    of me.*
12 For I rescued the poor man
    who cried out for help,
  and the fatherless child who had no one
    to support him.*
13 The dying man blessed me,
  and I made the widow's heart rejoice.
14 I clothed myself in righteousness,*
  and it enveloped me;
  my just decisions were like a robe
    and a turban.
15 I was eyes to the blind
  and feet to the lame.*
16 I was a father to the needy,
  and I examined the case
    of the stranger.
17 I shattered the fangs of the unjust*
  and snatched the prey from his teeth.

*28:17 Ps 119:72; Pr 8:19; 20:15
*28:22 Jb 25:6; Ps 49:14; Pr 27:20
*28:25 Ps 135:7; Pr 30:4; Is 40:12
*28:26 Jb 5:10; 37:6; 38:25
*28:28 Dt 4:6; Pr 1:7; 9:10
*29:3 Jb 11:17; Ps 18:28; 119:105
*29:4 Ps 25:14; 55:14; Pr 3:32
*29:6 Dt 32:13; Jb 20:17; Ps 81:16
*29:9 Jdg 18:19; Jb 21:5; 40:4
*29:12 Ps 10:14; 72:12; Pr 21:13
*29:14 Ps 132:9; Is 59:17; Eph 6:14
*29:15 Is 35:6; 42:7,16; Mt 11:5
*29:17 Jb 4:10; Ps 3:7; 58:6

---

^A 28:26 Or decree   ^B 29:11 Lit When an ear heard, it called me blessed, and when an eye saw, it testified for me

---

and gem stones, including the famed **gold of Ophir** (see note at 22:23-25) or **topaz from Cush** (Ethiopia).

28:20-22 Wisdom (v. 12) is unseen by all creatures (see v. 7), living and dead (Lk 16:19-31). **Abaddon** and **Death** (here personified) have only **heard . . . of it**. Seeing and hearing are often paired in the Bible (42:6; cp. Is 64:4; 1Co 2:9).

28:23-27 The all-seeing God, the only true source of **wisdom**, established and balanced the laws and forces of nature.

28:28 God reveals to man what neither man nor creatures can find out on their own: **wisdom** resides with God, and man acts wisely when he follows God's standards and shuns **evil** (Dt 4:5-6; Ps 111:10; Pr 1:7; 9:10).

29:2-3 Job had complained about God's scrutiny (7:17-20; 13:27). Now he recalled previous days when God made him successful. The **lamp** symbolized God's blessings and direction. When it is extinguished, disaster follows (18:6; 21:17).

29:4-6 Job's prior life was filled with God's abundant blessings. **Cream** and **oil** symbolize life's finest pleasures (20:17; Ps 104:15). The **rock** was either the rocky soil where the olive trees grew or the stone press used to extract the oil.

29:7-10 The **town square** at the **city gate** served as a place for legal (Ru 4:1,11) and judicial decisions, a marketplace (2Kg 7:1), and general gathering place (Jr 17:19-20). Job's **seat** and the public reaction to his presence indicate prominence and respect.

29:11-13 Contrary to Eliphaz's charges (22:8-9), Job's beneficence toward the needs of the **poor**, orphan, **dying**, and widow earned the admiration of everyone.

29:14-17 In cases where Job served in an official capacity, he demonstrated **righteousness** as he defended the rights of the helpless and rendered their oppressors powerless.

29:18-20 Because of God's blessings and Job's righteousness, Job expected to live a long and healthy life (Dt 4:39-40;

18 So I thought: I will die in my own nest
and multiply my days as the sand.[A]

19 My roots will have access to water,[a]
and the dew will rest on my branches
all night.

20 My strength will be refreshed
within me,
and my bow will be renewed
in my hand.[b]

21 Men listened to me with expectation,
waiting silently for my advice.

22 After a word from me they did not
speak again;
my speech settled on them like dew.

23 They waited for me as for the rain
and opened their mouths as for
spring showers.

24 If I smiled at them, they couldn't
believe it;
they were thrilled at[B] the light
of my countenance.

25 I directed their course and presided
as chief.
I lived as a king among his troops,
like one who comforts those who mourn.

30 But now they mock[c] me,
men younger than I am,
whose fathers I would have refused
to put
with my sheep dogs.

2 What use to me was the strength
of their hands?
Their vigor had left them.

3 Emaciated from poverty and hunger,
they gnawed the dry land,
the desolate wasteland by night.

4 They plucked mallow[C,d]
among the shrubs,
and the roots of the broom tree were
their food.

5 They were expelled from human society;
people shouted at them
as if they were thieves.

6 They are living on the slopes
of the •wadis,
among the rocks and in holes
in the ground.

7 They bray among the shrubs;
they huddle beneath the thistles.

8 Foolish[e] men, without even a name.
They were forced to leave the land.

9 Now I am mocked by their songs;[f]
I have become an object of scorn
to them.

10 They despise me and keep
their distance from me;[g]
they do not hesitate to spit[h] in my face.

11 Because God has loosened
my[D] bowstring and oppressed me,
they have cast off restraint
in my presence.[i]

12 The rabble[E] rise up at my right;
they trap[F] my feet
and construct their siege ramp[G]
against me.[j]

13 They tear up my path;
they contribute to my destruction,[k]
without anyone to help them.

14 They advance as through
a gaping breach;
they keep rolling in through the ruins.[l]

15 Terrors[m] are turned loose against me;
they chase my dignity away
like the wind,
and my prosperity has passed by
like a cloud.

16 Now my life is poured out
before my eyes,
and days of suffering[n] have seized me.

17 Night pierces my bones,

Cross references (center column):

a 29:19 Jb 14:9; Ps 1:3; Ezk 31:7
b 29:20 Gn 49:24; Is 40:31; 41:1
c 30:1 Jb 12:4; Jr 20:7; Lm 3:14
d 30:4 Jb 12:4; Jr 20:7; Lm 3:14
e 30:8 Pr 26:7,12; Ec 7:5; Is 32:5-6
f 30:9 Jb 12:4; 30:1; Lm 3:14
g 30:10 Jb 19:19; Ps 89:38; Am 5:10
h Nm 12:14; Is 50:6; Mt 26:67
i 30:11 Jb 12:18; 29:20; Ps 32:9
j 30:12 Jb 16:10; 19:12; Ps 140:4-5
k 30:13 Jb 6:2; Ps 57:1; Pr 19:13
l 30:14 Jb 16:14; Jl 2:7
m 30:15 Jb 18:11; 27:20; Ps 73:19
n 30:16 Jb 10:15; 30:27; 36:21

A 29:18 Or *as the phoenix*   B 29:24 Lit *they did not cast down*   C 30:4 Or *saltwort*   D 30:11 Alt Hb tradition, LXX, Vg read *His*
E 30:12 Hb obscure   F 30:12 Lit *stretch out*   G 30:12 Lit *and raise up their destructive paths*

1Kg 3:14). **Sand** symbolizes things too numerous to count (6:3; Gn 22:17; 1Kg 4:29). A **nest** presents a secure image of home and family. The well-watered tree speaks of health and prosperity as well as Job's righteousness (Ps 1:1-3; 92:12). The **bow** symbolizes strength and virility (Gn 49:24).

29:21-23 Job's opinions and decisions were as valued as refreshing **rain** or **dew** in a dry region (Is 55:10-11).

29:24 Because he was considered both wise and powerful, everyone highly valued Job's approval.

30:1-4 Previously young and old, officials and nobles, had respected Job (29:7-11,21-23) and waited for his approval (29:24). Now he suffered humiliation at the hands of society's rabble (see note at 19:18). The mockers' fathers were worthless men whose indolent lifestyle sapped their vitality and forced them to scrounge for food. **Mallow** (or saltwort)

came from an edible plant that served as food for the poor. The **roots of the broom tree** were usually used to make charcoal rather than **food** (Ps 120:4).

30:7-8 These men cried from hunger like wild donkeys. To be referred to as having no **name** was an insult; it was the same as nonexistence.

30:9 Returning to the topic of verse 1, Job lamented the **songs** the young men created to mock him (Lm 3:14).

30:11-14 Job had hoped for renewed strength and vitality (29:20); now he lamented his weakness before his tormentors. He compared himself to a besieged city and his tormentors to invaders (16:13-14). Erecting siege ramps made from trees, stones, and earth to breach a wall was a common tactic in ancient warfare (Jr 6:6).

30:16-19 Job's life had disintegrated into **days** and nights of

but my gnawing pains never rest.[a]

18 My clothing is distorted
　　with great force;
He chokes me by the neck
　　of my garment.[A]
19 He throws me into the mud,
　　and I have become like dust and ashes.[b]
20 I cry out to You for help, but You
　　do not answer me;[c]
when I stand up, You merely look
　　at me.
21 You have turned against me
　　with cruelty;
You harass[d] me with Your strong hand.
22 You lift me up on the wind
　　and make me ride it;
You scatter me in the storm.[e]
23 Yes, I know that You will lead me
　　to death—
the place[f] appointed for all who live.

24 Yet no one would stretch out his hand
　　against a ruined man[B]
when he cries out to him for help
　　because of his distress.[g]
25 Have I not wept for those
　　who have fallen on hard times?
Has my soul not grieved for the needy?[h]
26 But when I hoped for good, evil came;
　　when I looked for light, darkness[i] came.
27 I am churning within[C] and cannot rest;
　　days of suffering confront me.
28 I walk about blackened, but not
　　by the sun.[D]
I stood in the assembly and cried out
　　for help.
29 I have become a brother to jackals

and a companion of ostriches.

30 My skin blackens and flakes off,[E]
　　and my bones burn with fever.[j]
31 My lyre is used for mourning
　　and my flute for the sound of weeping.[k]

31

I have made a covenant
　　with my eyes.[l]
How then could I look
　　at a young woman?[F,m]
2 For what portion[n] would I have
　　from God above,
or what inheritance from the •Almighty
　　on high?
3 Doesn't disaster come to the unjust
　　and misfortune to evildoers?
4 Does He not see my ways
　　and number all my steps?[o]

5 If I have walked in falsehood
　　or my foot has rushed to deceit,
6 let God weigh me in accurate scales,[p]
　　and He will recognize my integrity.[q]
7 If my step has turned from the way,
　　my heart has followed my eyes,
　　or impurity has stained my hands,[r]
8 let someone else eat what I have sown,
　　and let my crops be uprooted.[s]

9 If my heart has been seduced by
　　my neighbor's wife
or I have lurked at his door,
10 let my own wife grind grain
　　for another man,
　　and let other men sleep with[G] her.
11 For that would be a disgrace;

---

[a] 30:17 Jb 33:19; Ps 6:2; 38:3　[b] 30:19 Jb 16:15; Ps 7:5; 75:10　[c] 30:20 Jb 19:7; Ps 18:41; 88:13-14　[d] 30:21 Gn 49:23; Jb 16:9; Ps 55:3　[e] 30:22 Jb 9:17; Ps 83:15; Jnh 1:4　[f] 30:23 Jb 3:15; 17:13; Ec 12:5　[g] 30:24 Jb 12:5; 31:29; Pr 24:22　[h] 30:25 Jb 5:15; 24:4,14; 31:19　[i] 30:26 Jb 19:8; Is 59:9; Lm 3:2　[j] 30:30 Ps 102:3; Lm 4:8; 5:10　[k] 30:31 Is 24:8; Ezk 26:13; Mt 11:17　[l] 31:1 Pr 4:25; Is 33:15; 2Pt 2:14　[m] Ex 22:6; Pr 17:24; Mt 5:28　[n] 31:2 Jb 20:29; 27:13; Ps 17:14　[o] 31:4 Jb 14:16; 34:21; Pr 5:21　[p] 31:6 Jb 6:2; Dn 5:27; Mc 6:11　[q] Jb 2:3,9; 27:5; Pr 11:3　[r] 31:7 Nm 15:39; Jb 23:11; Ps 7:3　[s] 31:8 Lv 26:16; Dt 28:30; Jb 20:18

[A] 30:18 Hb obscure　[B] 30:24 Lit *a heap of ruins*　[C] 30:27 Lit *My bowels boil*　[D] 30:28 Or *walk in sunless gloom*　[E] 30:30 Lit *blackens away from me*　[F] 31:1 Or *a virgin*　[G] 31:10 Lit *men kneel down over*

---

unbearable suffering. It was as though God had bound him in a straitjacket and thrown him on the ground.

30:24 Job questioned the Lord's conduct. God's attack was like "kicking a man when he is down."

30:27-30 Job's suffering was total—physical, spiritual, and emotional. His **churning** insides and **fever** may have been a side-effect of the disease that **blackened** his **skin**. Abandoned by God and his fellow man, he compared his unheeded cries for help to the jackal's woeful howl and the mournful sound of the ostrich (Mc 1:8).

30:31 In bold figures Job portrayed his cries as the sounds of musical instruments. Rather than tunes of joy (21:12; Ps 33:2), praise (Ps 150:4), or comfort (1Sm 16:23), Job's **lyre** produced only dirge-like tones. His **flute** provided no happy melody (21:12; Mt 11:17), only a mourning **sound** (Mt 9:23).

31:1 Job began the final defense of his purity by declaring that he had never looked at a **young woman** lustfully. The **eyes** were considered the gateway to the inner person. The

wandering eye got Samson (Jdg 16:1) and David (2Sm 11:2-3) into serious trouble, and Jesus warned of its dangers (Mt 5:27-30). Job's **covenant** language underscored the seriousness of his purpose and his binding self-limitation.

31:2-4 Job posed three questions emphasizing God's dealing with him should he violate his covenant not to lust after a young woman. Job would have neither standing with God nor blessing, and God—who saw all that Job did (7:17-19)—would judge him as an evildoer (18:5-12; 27:13-23).

31:5-6 The metaphor of where one's **foot** walks expresses proper conduct (12:5; 23:11; Pr 4:26-27). The weighing of a man in the **scales** was a test of character (Dn 5:27).

31:7 The body parts mentioned here are often used figuratively to express ethical conduct: foot (Ps 17:5), **heart** or mind (Pr 23:19), **eyes** (Ps 101:3), and hands (Ps 24:4).

31:9-10 Adultery has dire consequences (Lv 20:10; 2Sm 12:7-10).

31:12 Illicit sex is likened to a **fire** that burns the person (Pr

it would be a crime
deserving punishment.[A][a]

12 For it is a fire that consumes down
to •Abaddon;
it would destroy my entire harvest.[b]

13 If I have dismissed the case of my male
or female servants
when they made a complaint
against me,

14 what could I do when God stands up
to judge?
How should I answer Him
when He calls me to account?

15 Did not the One who made me
in the womb also make them?
Did not the same God form us both
in the womb?[c]

16 If I have refused the wishes of the poor
or let the widow's[d] eyes go blind,

17 if I have eaten my few crumbs alone
without letting the fatherless
eat any of it—

18 for from my youth, I raised him
as his father,
and since the day I was born[B] I guided
the widow—

19 if I have seen anyone dying for lack
of clothing
or a needy person without a cloak,[e]

20 if he[c] did not bless me
while warming himself with the fleece
from my sheep,

21 if I ever cast my vote[D]
against a fatherless child

when I saw that I had support
in the city •gate,[f]

22 then let my shoulder blade fall
from my back,
and my arm be pulled from its socket.

23 For disaster from God terrifies me,
and because of His majesty
I could not do these things.[g]

24 If I placed my confidence in gold
or called fine gold my trust,[h]

25 if I have rejoiced because my wealth
is great
or because my own hand has acquired
so much,

26 if I have gazed at the sun
when it was shining
or at the moon moving in splendor,[i]

27 so that my heart was secretly enticed
and I threw them a kiss,[E]

28 this would also be a crime
deserving punishment,
for I would have denied God above.

29 Have I rejoiced over
my enemy's distress,
or become excited when trouble came
his way?

30 I have not allowed my mouth to sin
by asking for his life with a curse.

31 Haven't the members
of my household said,
"Who is there who has not had enough
to eat at Job's table?"

32 No stranger had to spend the night
on the street,

---

a 31:11 Gn 38:24; Lv 20:10; Dt 22:22,24
b 31:12 Jb 26:6; 28:22; Pr 6:27-29
c 31:15 Ps 119:73; 139:13; Jr 1:5
d 31:16 Jb 22:9; 24:3,21; 29:13
e 31:19 Ex 22:26; Jb 22:6
f 31:21 Jb 5:4; Pr 22:22; Is 29:21
g 31:23 Jb 13:11; 22:10; 23:15
h 31:24 Ps 52:7; Mt 6:19; Mk 10:24
i 31:26 Dt 4:19; 17:3; Ezk 8:16

[A]31:11 Lit *crime judges*   [B]31:18 Lit *and from my mother's womb*   [C]31:20 Lit *his loins*   [D]31:21 Lit *I raise my hand*   [E]31:27 Lit *and my hand kissed my mouth*

6:27-29) to the utmost—all the way to **Abaddon**, the realm of death and destruction (26:6; 28:22).

31:13-15 Any mishandling of his servants' complaints would make Job liable before his heavenly **judge** (Eph 6:9; 2Co 5:10). Just treatment of slaves and servants was expected of Israelites (Lv 25:42-43). Job had testified previously to God's care in creating him (Jb 10:8-12). Now he acknowledged that God is the Creator of all people, giving both servants and masters value in God's eyes.

31:16-22 Job offered a long list of if-then statements, calling down a curse on himself if he had failed to do the right thing in any of these cases.

31:16-18 Eliphaz had charged Job with dealing unjustly with the widow, **fatherless**, and **poor** (22:4-9). Job denied such wrongdoing. Even as a young man he had been concerned for the needs of the helpless.

31:19-20 Eliphaz had charged Job with taking the clothes of a debtor as collateral (22:6). Refuting this charge, Job stated that when any person lacked necessary clothing, he supplied it and they blessed him for it. The HCSB's **he** (lit "his loins") is a synecdoche where a part refers to the whole body.

31:21 Job denied that he had ever used his official position to take advantage of the weak, such as the **fatherless**, even though he had the backing of others.

31:22 See note at verses 16-22.

31:23 Job's obedience was motivated by the two aspects of the fear of the Lord: terror and awe.

31:24-28 Job offered another list of if-then statements (cp. vv. 16-22), denying that he had sinned in any of these ways (v. 28).

31:24-25 Job disavowed materialistic and greedy desires. Eliphaz's implied criticism was false (22:24-25).

31:26-27 Job had not secretly paid homage to false deities identified with the **sun** or **moon**, as some would do by throwing a **kiss** toward the heavens. Such false worship did affect the Israelites later (2Kg 21:3). Job understood that idolatry and paganism were an abomination to the Lord (Dt 4:19; 17:2-5).

31:29-30 Job had not gloated over an **enemy's** misfortune. This would violate accepted ethical standards (Pr 24:17-18; 25:21-22; Mt 5:43-47).

31:31-32 God's concern included the welfare of the **stranger**

for I opened my door
   to the traveler.
³³ Have I covered my transgressions^a
   as others do^A
by hiding my •guilt in my heart,^b
³⁴ because I greatly feared the crowds,
   and the contempt of the clans
     terrified me,
so I grew silent and would not
   go outside?

³⁵ If only I had someone to hear my case!^c
Here is my signature; let the Almighty
   answer me.
Let my Opponent compose
   His indictment.
³⁶ I would surely carry it on my shoulder
and wear it like a crown.^d
³⁷ I would give Him an account of all
   my steps;
I would approach Him like a prince.

³⁸ If my land cries out against me
and its furrows join in weeping,
³⁹ if I have consumed its produce
   without payment
or shown contempt for its tenants,^B
⁴⁰ then let thorns^e grow instead of wheat
and stinkweed^f instead of barley.

The words of Job are concluded.

Elihu's Angry Response

32 So these three men quit answering Job,
because he was righteous in his own

---

^a31:33 Jb 7:21; 22:5; 33:9
^bPs 32:3-5; Pr 28:13; 1Jn 1:8-10
^c31:35 Jb 16:21; Ec 6:10; Is 45:9
^d31:36 Pr 4:9; 12:4; 17:6
^e31:40 Gn 3:18; Is 34:13; Hs 9:6
^fPr 24:31; Is 5:2; Hs 10:4
^g32:1 Jb 10:7; 33:9; 34:5-6
^h32:2 Gn 22:21; Jr 25:23
ⁱJb 33:32; Jr 3:11; Ezk 16:51-52
^j32:6 Jb 15:17; 36:2
^k32:8 Gn 2:7; Jb 33:4; Is 42:5

---

eyes.^{g 2} Then Elihu son of Barachel the Buzite^h
from the family of Ram became angry. He was
angry at Job because he had justifiedⁱ himself
rather than God. ³ He was also angry at Job's
three friends because they had failed to refute
him and yet had condemned him.^c

⁴ Now Elihu had waited to speak to Job be-
cause they were all older than he. ⁵ But when
he saw that the three men could not answer
Job, he became angry.

⁶ So Elihu son of Barachel the Buzite re-
plied:

I am young in years,
   while you are old;
therefore I was timid and afraid
   to tell^j you what I know.
⁷ I thought that age should speak
and maturity should teach wisdom.
⁸ But it is a spirit in man^D
and the breath^k of the •Almighty
   that give him understanding.
⁹ It is not only the old who are wise
   or the elderly who understand
     how to judge.
¹⁰ Therefore I say, "Listen to me.
I too will declare what I know."

¹¹ Look, I waited for your conclusions;
I listened to your insights
   as you sought for words.
¹² I paid close attention to you.
Yet no one proved Job wrong;
   not one of you refuted his arguments.

---

^A31:33 Or *as Adam*   ^B31:39 Lit *or caused the breath of its tenants to breathe out*   ^C32:3 Ancient Jewish tradition reads *condemned God*   ^D32:8 Or *is the Spirit in a person*

(Lv 24:22; Dt 26:12; Ps 94:6-7). Hospitality is commended in both the OT and the NT (Gn 24:24-32; 1Tm 5:10).

31:33-34 Job had not covered up his sins by tucking them away in his **heart** (lit "bosom") like a thief concealing stolen goods. Job had not played the hypocrite by sinning in secret while pretending to be virtuous (2Kg 5:24-27). He had no need to shut himself up from public view (Gn 3:8-9). Jesus condemned spiritual hypocrisy (Mt 6:2-4; 23:25-28).

31:35-37 Job had repeatedly pleaded for a fair hearing before God (13:18-23; 23:2-7) even though he feared such a meeting (9:14-16) and felt the need for an arbitrator (9:32-35; 16:21). Job nonetheless felt so confident that his integrity would be vindicated that he signed his affidavit. His **signature** is literally his *tav*, the last letter in the Hebrew alphabet, in the form of an X in ancient Hebrew. The name of the letter means "mark" (Ezk 9:4). Documents were usually sealed with an engraved seal (1Kg 21:8), but when signed by hand even a literate person used the *tav*. When God presented His **indictment** (7:20), Job would place it proudly on his **shoulder** and approach the Lord as a **prince** wearing a victor's **crown**. Job was certain that he had proven his innocence and righteousness (23:3-7; 27:6).

31:38-40 Job finished with a final testimony toward his vindication in the form of two more conditional statements and a

curse (cp. vv. 16-22). He had demonstrated his integrity and righteousness toward his fellow man. He had neither overworked his **land** (cp. Lv 25:2-7) nor defrauded **its tenants** (24:10-11). He fortified his declaration with an imprecation involving the failure of his crops (Gn 3:18; Is 5:6).

32:2-3 The names **Elihu** ("He is my God") and **Barachel** ("God has blessed") testify to vital faith. The names Elihu and **Ram** appear in connection with the later family of David (Ru 4:19; 1Ch 27:18). Buz was the brother of Uz and Abraham's nephew (Gn 22:20-21). Job was from the land of Uz (Jb 1:1). Elihu was **angry** because he perceived that Job had argued for his own righteousness, implying that God was therefore unjust (cp. 40:8), and because Job's friends had **condemned** him without getting to the essential issue in his case.

32:6-10 Though he was **young**, Elihu maintained that wisdom was not the exclusive possession of the **old** but was available to everyone. God created man in His image (Gn 1:27), imparting His **breath** to him (Gn 2:7). Thus man is a rational creature (Jb 38:36; Pr 16:9), capable of acquiring vast knowledge (1Kg 4:29-34). Elihu implied that God had so enlightened his spirit that he must speak (Jb 32:17-20).

32:11-12 Elihu prefaced his remarks by noting that he had given due deference to his elders.

13 So do not claim,
    "We have found wisdom;
    let God deal with him, not man."
14 But Job has not directed his argument
    to me,
    and I will not respond to him
    with your arguments.

15 Job's friends are dismayed and can
    no longer answer;
    words have left them.
16 Should I continue to wait now that
    they are silent,
    now that they stand there
    and no longer answer?
17 I too will answer;[A]
    yes, I will tell what I know.
18 For I am full of words,
    and my spirit[B] compels me to speak.[a]
19 My heart[c] is like unvented wine;
    it is about to burst like new wineskins.[b]
20 I must speak so that I can find relief;
    I must open my lips and respond.
21 I will be partial to no one,[c]
    and I will not give anyone
    an undeserved title.
22 For I do not know how to give
    such titles;
    otherwise, my Maker would remove me
    in an instant.

Elihu Confronts Job

33 But now, Job, pay attention
    to my speech,
    and listen to all my words.

2 I am going to open my mouth;
    my tongue will form words
    on my palate.
3 My words come from
    my upright[d] heart,
    and my lips speak with sincerity
    what they know.
4 The Spirit of God has made me,
    and the breath of the •Almighty[e]
    gives me life.[f]
5 Refute me if you can.
    Prepare[g] your case against me;
    take your stand.[h]
6 I am just like you before God;
    I was also pinched off
    from a piece of clay.[i]
7 Fear[j] of me should not terrify you;
    the pressure I exert[D] against you
    will be light.

8 Surely you have spoken in my hearing,
    and I have heard these very[E] words:
9 "I am pure, without transgression;
    I am •clean and have no •guilt.[k]
10 But He finds reasons to oppose me;
    He regards me as His enemy.[l]
11 He puts my feet in the stocks;
    He stands watch[m] over all my paths."

12 But I tell you that you are wrong
    in this matter,
    since God is greater than man.[n]
13 Why do you take[o] Him to court
    for not answering anything
    a person asks?[F]

Cross references (center column):
- [a]32:18 Jb 19:3; 32:18; Ac 4:20
- [b]32:19 Jb 15:35; 37:1; Pr 20:27,30
- [c]32:21 Dt 10:17; Jb 13:8; 34:19
- [d]33:3 1Kg 9:4; Ps 25:21; 119:7
- [e]33:4 Jb 27:2; 32:8; 35:13
- [f]Gn 2:7; Jb 27:3; Is 30:33
- [g]33:5 Jb 23:4; 32:14; 37:19
- [h]1Sm 17:16; Ps 2:2; Jr 46:4,14
- [i]33:6 Jb 4:19; 10:9; 13:12
- [j]33:7 Jb 20:25; Ps 55:4; 88:15
- [k]33:9 Jb 9:21; 11:4; 34:6
- [l]33:10 Jb 13:24; 19:11; Lm 2:5
- [m]33:11 Jb 10:14; 14:16; Ps 130:3
- [n]33:12 Jb 4:17; 9:2; 15:14
- [o]33:13 Jb 9:3; 13:19; 40:2

[A]32:17 Lit answer my part   [B]32:18 Lit and the spirit of my belly   [C]32:19 Lit belly   [D]33:7 Lit you; my pressure   [E]33:8 Lit heard a sound of   [F]33:13 Lit court, for He does not answer all his words

---

32:13-14 Elihu agreed with Job (12:20; 13:12-19; 17:10; 21:34) that the friends had failed to demonstrate their claim to represent godly instruction (4:12-16) or traditional wisdom (15:17-19). Job would find Elihu a tougher opponent who would not follow the friends' line of argumentation.

32:15-17 Elihu noted the friends' dismay at exhausting their arguments against Job without refuting him successfully. Since they no longer had anything to say, Elihu would take up the controversy.

32:19 Elihu's **heart** (inner being; lit "belly") was so full that it was about to **burst**. New wine was normally put into **new wineskins**, which would expand with the fermentation process (Mt 9:17). If the wineskin was closed off without proper ventilation, it could burst.

32:21-22 Elihu was under divine obligation to speak his mind impartially. The word **partial** is literally "lift up the face." This idiom is used of showing respect (Gn 32:21) or partiality (Pr 18:5). The Bible condemns showing favoritism (Pr 28:21), especially in rendering judicial decisions (Lv 19:15) or by giving special treatment to prominent individuals (Jms 2:1-4). Elihu would not use flattering speech (Ps 12:1-3; Pr 28:23) by making reference to anyone's title.

33:3 Elihu spoke directly to Job from an **upright heart** (Ps 37:30; Pr 8:7-8). The heart was viewed as the source of thoughts (Ec 2:1,15), feelings (Ps 28:7), and will (Pr 23:12). Elihu's words would be carefully crafted from his heart (cp. Mt 15:18) and expressed **with sincerity** (Pr 16:23).

33:5 Elihu acted like an attorney in a legal proceeding. After he had stated his case, Job was free to try to **refute** him with counter arguments.

33:6-7 Although Elihu believed he was representing God in confronting Job, he claimed neither human superiority nor inferiority to Job. Therefore, Job need not **fear** a heavy-handed approach (13:21). The image of the **clay** portrays God as the heavenly potter and man as formed from clay (Gn 2:7; Is 64:8; Rm 9:21).

33:8-11 Elihu demonstrated that he had listened carefully to Job's claims of being pure and innocent (16:17; 23:7,10-12; 27:5-6), as well as being unjustly oppressed by God (10:6-7; 13:26-27; 19:11; 30:18-19).

33:12-13 Elihu reminded Job that as a finite man, he was not in a position to bring accusations against God (Is 55:8). Nor should God be called into **court** for Job's every wish (9:3,14-16; 13:2; 18:4).

14 For God speaks time and again,
　　but a person may not notice it.
15 In a dream, a vision[a] in the night,
　　when deep sleep falls on people[b]
　　as they slumber on their beds,
16 He uncovers their ears[c] at that time
　　and terrifies them[A] with warnings,
17 in order to turn a person
　　　from his actions
　　and suppress his pride.[B]
18 God spares his soul from the •Pit,[d]
　　his life from crossing the river
　　　of death.[C]
19 A person may be disciplined on his bed[e]
　　　with pain
　　and constant distress in his bones,[f]
20 so that he detests bread,
　　and his soul despises his favorite food.[g]
21 His flesh wastes away to nothing,[D]
　　and his unseen bones stick out.
22 He draws near to the Pit,
　　and his life to the executioners.
23 If there is an angel[h] on his side,
　　one mediator out of a thousand,
　　to tell a person what is right for him[E]
24 and to be gracious to him and say,
　　"Spare him from going down to the Pit;
　　I have found a ransom,"[i]
25 then his flesh will be healthier[F] than
　　　in his youth,
　　and he will return to the days
　　　of his youthful vigor.[j]
26 He will pray to God, and God
　　will delight in him.

That man will see His face[k] with a shout
　　of joy,
　　and God will restore his righteousness
　　　to him.[l]
27 He will look at men and say,
　　"I have sinned and perverted
　　　what was right;
　　yet I did not get what I deserved.[G]
28 He redeemed my soul from going down
　　　to the Pit,
　　and I will continue to see the light."
29 God certainly does all these things
　　two or three times to a man
30 in order to turn him back from the Pit,
　　so he may shine with the light of life.[m]
31 Pay attention, Job, and listen to me.
　　Be quiet, and I will speak.
32 But if you have something to say,[H]
　　　answer me;
　　speak, for I would like to justify you.
33 If not, then listen to me;
　　be quiet, and I will teach you wisdom.

34 Then Elihu continued,[I] saying:

2 Hear my words, you wise men,
　　and listen to me,
　　　you knowledgeable ones.
3 Doesn't the ear test words
　　as the palate tastes food?
4 Let us judge for ourselves what is right;
　　let us decide together what is good.
5 For Job has declared, "I am righteous,
　　yet God has deprived me of justice.[n]

Cross references (center column):
a 33:15 Jb 4:13; 7:14; 20:8
b Gn 2:21; 15:12; Jb 4:13
c 33:16 Jb 4:12; 13:1; 36:10,15
d 33:18 Jb 33:28,30; 36:16; Ps 30:9
e 33:19 Jb 7:13; Ps 41:3; Hs 7:14
f Jb 30:17; Ps 6:2; 38:3
g 33:20 Jb 3:24; 6:7; Ps 102:4
h 33:23 Ex 23:20,23; Ps 34:7; Is 63:9
i 33:24 Ex 30:12; Ps 49:7; Pr 21:18
j 33:25 Dt 34:7; 2Kg 5:14; Jb 20:11
k 33:26 Gn 33:10; Ps 11:7; 17:15
l Ps 23:3; 51:12; 1Jn 1:9
m 33:30 Ps 56:13; Jn 1:4,9
n 34:5 Jb 10:7; 27:2; 33:9

A 33:16 LXX; MT reads *and seals* ᴮ 33:17 Lit *and cover pride within a man* ᶜ 33:18 Or *from perishing by the sword* ᴰ 33:21 Lit *away from sight* ᴱ 33:23 Or *to vouch for a person's uprightness* ᶠ 33:25 Hb obscure ᴳ 33:27 Lit *and the same was not to me* ᴴ 33:32 Lit *If there are words* ᴵ 34:1 Lit *answered*

33:14-17 Job had complained that God might pass by him without his noting it (9:11) and that God had ignored his requests for Him to answer (13:24; 19:7; 30:20). Elihu implied that Job had failed to notice God's speaking to him. Elihu built upon Eliphaz's words about God instructing him in a nighttime visitation (4:12-19). To uncover the ear is to instruct, inform, or reveal (36:15; Ru 4:4; Is 22:14).

33:18 By the **Pit** is meant the grave or the state of death (16:10; 17:14). Just as Israel crossed the Jordan River to enter the promised land, so the image of the **river of death** portrays man's passing from this life into the next. "River" is the preferred rendering of a Hebrew word that also can be translated as "sword."

33:19-22 God may also communicate with a person through the discipline of **pain**. The **distress** may be so aggravating that **a person** loses all desire for food. In his severe pain, Job had expressed the fear that death was near (10:18-22; 16:16,22).

33:23-24 Elihu pointed out that the arbitrator Job had longed for between himself and God (9:33; 16:21) was available to bring a person to repentance. Angels often served in this capacity (Gn 48:15-16; Ps 34:6-7). God through His mediat-

ing angel supplies grace to ransom and deliver the repentant and surrendered person from death (Ex 14:19-20; Jb 17:3; Ps 49:7-9). In a deeper sense, such a work anticipates God's full revelation in Christ (2Co 5:18-19; Heb 9:12). Alternatively, the word translated **angel** may also be rendered as "messenger" (Jdg 11:13; 1Kg 20:2-10; Mal 2:7). Elihu may have sensed that he was serving as God's messenger to bring about Job's reconciliation with God (Jb 33:6-7).

33:29-30 God's offer to reclaim the sinner may be extended several times, but His grace should not be spurned continually (Jl 2:14; Heb 6:4-6).

33:31-33 Elihu asked for Job's further **attention** (vv. 1-5) while he developed his teaching. Job should interrupt only if he had something significant to add.

34:2 Elihu appears to be playing on Job's reference to his three friends as **wise men**. Since they had failed to refute Job (32:12-13), however, perhaps all involved could benefit from words of wisdom from Elihu.

34:3-4 Elihu referred to Job's earlier comments about the ear's ability to **test words** much as the **palate tastes food** (12:11). Elihu was confident that his words would stand up to scrutiny.

6 Would I lie about my case?[a]
My wound[A] is incurable,
though I am without transgression."
7 What man is like Job?
He drinks derision[b] like water.
8 He keeps company with evildoers
and walks with wicked men.
9 For he has said, "A man gains nothing
when he becomes God's friend."[c]

10 Therefore listen to me, you men
of understanding.
It is impossible for God to do wrong,
and for the ·Almighty to act unjustly.[d]
11 For He repays[e] a person according to
his deeds,
and He brings his ways on him.
12 Indeed, it is true that God does not
act wickedly
and the Almighty does not
pervert justice.[f]
13 Who gave Him authority
over the earth?
Who put Him in charge of
the entire world?[g]
14 If He put His mind to it
and withdrew the spirit[h] and breath
He gave,
15 every living thing
would perish together
and mankind would return to the dust.[i]

16 If you have understanding, hear this;
listen to what I have to say.
17 Could one who hates justice
govern the world?
Will you condemn the mighty
Righteous One,[j]
18 who says to a king, "Worthless man!"
and to nobles, "Wicked men!"?[k]
19 God is not partial[l] to princes
and does not favor the rich
over the poor,
for they are all the work of His hands.
20 They die suddenly in the middle
of the night;
people shudder, then pass away.
Even the mighty are removed
without effort.

21 For His eyes watch over a man's ways,
and He observes all his steps.[m]
22 There is no darkness, no deep darkness,
where evildoers can hide themselves.[n]
23 God does not need to examine
a person further,
that one should[B] approach Him
in court.
24 He shatters the mighty
without an investigation
and sets others in their place.[o]
25 Therefore, He recognizes their deeds[p]
and overthrows them by night,
and they are crushed.
26 In full view of the public,[C]
He strikes them for their wickedness,
27 because they turned aside
from following Him
and did not understand any of His ways
28 but caused the poor to cry out to Him,
and He heard the outcry of the afflicted.[q]

[a] 34:6 Jb 6:28; 24:25; 27:4
[b] 34:7 Jb 15:16; Pr 19:28
[c] 34:9 Ex 5:2; Jb 21:15; Mal 3:14
[d] 34:10 Dt 32:4; Ps 92:15; Rm 9:14
[e] 34:11 Dt 7:10; Jb 21:31; Is 59:18
[f] 34:12 2Ch 19:6; Jb 8:3; Ps 9:16
[g] 34:13 Jb 38:4; Ps 50:12; Is 40:12-14
[h] 34:14 Ps 104:29; Ec 3:19; 12:7
[i] 34:15 Gn 2:7; Jb 4:19; 10:9
[j] 34:17 Gn 18:25; 2Sm 23:3; Rm 3:5
[k] 34:18 Ex 22:28; Jb 12:21; Ps 107:40
[l] 34:19 Dt 10:17; Jb 13:8; 32:21
[m] 34:21 Jb 14:16; 31:4; Pr 5:21
[n] 34:22 Ps 139:12; Am 9:2-3; Heb 4:13
[o] 34:24 Jb 12:19; Ps 2:9; Dn 2:21
[p] 34:25 Jb 11:11; Ps 10:14
[q] 34:28 Ex 3:7; 22:23; Jms 5:4

[A] 34:6 Lit *arrow* [B] 34:23 Some emend to *God has not appointed a time for man to* [C] 34:26 Lit *In a place of spectators*

34:5-6 Elihu summarized Job's claims, which he was about to refute.

34:7-9 Elihu observed that Job was neither affected by the (justified) **derision** heaped upon him by others, nor was he above deriding others, especially God. In Elihu's opinion, this showed that Job had assumed the stance of an evildoer (cp. 21:7-15), especially when he complained that being righteous gained a person nothing before God (9:15,29-31).

34:10-12 In returning to his opening issue about God's justice (v. 5; cp. 32:2), Elihu denied Job's claim that God was treating him **unjustly** (27:2). All three friends had repeatedly applied in rigid fashion the doctrine of equal divine retribution: blessings for righteousness, judgment for unrighteousness, each in its proper degree (Jr 25:14; 30:11). Eliphaz had likewise championed that thesis but insisted that God's nature prohibited His wrongdoing (Dt 32:4; Ps 62:12; Jr 9:23-24). Elihu gave the implied answer to Bildad's earlier rhetorical question (Jb 8:2-3). God could not and did not act unrighteously or unjustly (Ps 92:15; Rm 3:5-6).

34:13-15 Elihu declared that as a sovereign and omnipotent God, the Lord is not accountable to anyone. Job had admitted as much (9:12), but he had questioned God's dealings with him (10:4-7). Elihu implied that for Job to question God was wrong and illogical. If God was sovereign, He had no reason to be unjust or show partiality. If mankind was dependent on God for sustenance, to question God's **authority** and justice puts a person in danger of judgment for rebellion.

34:17-18 As Elihu saw it, a being who is not truly righteous and all-powerful would not be able to **govern the world** properly. Without a just and omnipotent God, life on earth would be characterized by injustice and chaos.

34:21-23 Elihu built on Job's earlier remarks that God watches everything that men do on earth (7:20; 31:4). There is no place, however dark, where **evildoers** can escape God's view. Job had asked for a court appearance in order to present his case before God (9:32-35; 13:18; 21:3-7; 31:35-37). As the omniscient, all-seeing Judge, He does not need to come to court to **examine** a person's ways.

34:24-25 Elihu cited the example of wicked rulers. God did not need to launch **an investigation** of their deeds. He already knew everything.

34:26-28 God sees the godless **ways** of wicked rulers and hears the **outcry** of those whom they have oppressed. He judges wicked rulers and punishes them as a public example.

29 But when God is silent,
    who can declare Him *guilty?
When He hides His face, who can
    see Him?
Yet He watches over both individuals
    and nations,
30 so that godless men should not rule
    or ensnare the people.

31 Suppose someone says to God,
    "I have endured my punishment;
I will no longer act wickedly.
32 Teach me what I cannot see;
    if I have done wrong, I won't
        do it again."
33 Should God repay you on your terms
    when you have rejected His?
You must choose, not I!
    So declare what you know.
34 Reasonable men will say to me,
    along with the wise men who hear me,
35 "Job speaks without knowledge;ᵃ
    his words are without insight."
36 If only Job were tested to the limit,
    because his answers are like those
        of wicked men.
37 For he adds rebellion to his sin;
    he scornfully clapsᵇ in our presence,
    while multiplyingᶜ his words
        against God.

35

Then Elihu continued, saying:

2 Do you think it is just when you say,

"I am righteous before God"?
3 For you ask, "What does it profit You,ᴬ
and what benefit comes to me,
    if I do not sin?"ᵈ
4 I will answer you
    and your friends with you.
5 Look at the heavens and see;
    gaze at the clouds high above you.
6 If you sin, how does it affect God?
If you multiply your transgressions,
    what does it do to Him?
7 If you are righteous, what do you
        give Him,
or what does He receive
        from your hand?ᵉ
8 Your wickedness affects a person
    like yourself,
and your righteousness another
    human being.
9 People cry out because of
    severe oppression;
they shout for help because of the arm
    of the mighty.ᶠ
10 But no one asks, "Where is God
    my Maker,ᵍ
who provides us with songs
    in the night,ʰ
11 who gives us more understanding
    than the animals of the earth
and makes us wiser than the birds
    of the sky?"ⁱ
12 There they cry out,
    but He does not answer,

Cross references (center column):

ᵃ34:35 Jb 35:16; 38:2; 42:3
ᵇ34:37 Nm 24:10; Jb 27:23; Lm 2:15
ᶜJb 16:4; 35:16; Ezk 35:13
ᵈ35:3 Jb 9:29; 21:15; 34:9
ᵉ35:7 Jb 22:3; 41:11; Rm 11:35
ᶠ35:9 Ex 2:23; Jb 24:12; 34:28
ᵍ35:10 Dt 32:6; Is 51:13; Jr 2:8
ʰPs 42:8; 77:6; Ac 16:25
ⁱ35:11 Jb 12:7; Mt 6:26

ᴬ35:3 Some emend to *me*

34:29-30 Job felt that at times the unrighteous seem to have God's provision (12:6), but Elihu declared that such instances are illusions. Although God appears to ignore cases where wickedness prevails, He does see them. God's intervention may appear to be slow in coming, but He will rectify the situation in accordance with His wise and sovereign disposition of earthly affairs (2Pt 3:8-9).

34:31-33 Rather than repentance, Job had claimed his innocence and righteousness (27:2-6; 31:35-37). God's terms for the sinner's forgiveness and restoration to His favor are conditioned upon the sinner's repentance (22:21-27; 1Jn 1:8). Elihu challenged Job to consider his remarks and reply.

34:36-37 Elihu alluded to Zophar's initial declaration that God had not punished Job to the full **limit** for his sins (11:4-6). Because he had refused to acknowledge his sins, Job was rebelling against God. Elihu observed that Job had shown contempt for his friends (cp. Lm 2:15) while condemning God with his much speaking (Jb 16:12-17; 30:18-19). This put Job on dangerous ground (Ezk 25:6-7).

35:2-3 In a rhetorical question implying a negative answer, Elihu suggested that Job had established his righteousness apart from God, but Job had made no such assertion. Elihu based his argument on Job's remarks that keeping God's righteous standards appeared to gain mankind nothing (9:22,29-31; 10:1-3,17; 21:4-21; 27:1).

35:5-7 Since God is transcendent and superior to man, neither man's **sin** nor his righteousness can harm or benefit God (7:20; 22:2-3). God's character and glory are not conditioned by man's actions.

35:8 Far from enjoying an absolute moral autonomy without reference to others, our actions influence people for good or evil.

35:9-11 Elihu reminded Job that the oppressed often fail to consider the person and work of God. They are too concerned with their own situation rather than understanding that God may have a disciplinary purpose in their suffering (33:19-30). Elihu had shown that God will deal with oppressors in His own time and in His own way (34:11-22). The **songs** are the divine gift of music to alleviate painful nights of suffering (Ps 42:8; 77:6). These songs may be those of anticipated deliverance (Ps 30:4-5) or reminders of God's concern for His people in their need (Ps 118:1-7,14,28-29) or praise to God (Pss 96; 98). Job had pointed to the creatures of land, sea, and air as those who understand that God is the Creator and controller of all things (Jb 12:7-10). If creatures can appreciate the working of God, how much more should mankind, His special creation?

35:12-13 Elihu contended that when God is silent as the oppressed **cry out**, it is because their cry is born of **pride**, not contrition. God hears the penitent when they cry (Ps 4:3-4;

because of the pride of evil men.[a]

13 Indeed, God does not listen
      to empty cries,
   and the •Almighty does not take note
      of it—

14 how much less when[A] you complain[B]
   that you do not see Him,
   that your case[b] is before Him
   and you are waiting[c] for Him.

15 But now, because God's anger
      does not punish
   and He does not pay attention
      to transgression,[C]

16 Job opens his mouth in vain
   and multiplies words
      without knowledge.[d]

36 Then Elihu continued, saying:

2 Be patient with me a little longer,
   and I will inform you,
   for there is still more to be said
      on God's behalf.

3 I will get my knowledge from a
      distant place
   and ascribe justice to my Maker.

4 For my arguments are without flaw;[D]
   one who has perfect knowledge is
      with you.

5 Yes, God is mighty, but He despises
      no one;

He understands all things.[E,e]

6 He does not keep the wicked alive,[f]
   but He gives justice to the afflicted.

7 He does not remove His gaze
      from the righteous,
   but He seats them forever
      with enthroned kings,
   and they are exalted.

8 If people are bound with chains
   and trapped by the cords
      of affliction,

9 God tells them
      what they have done
   and how arrogantly
      they have transgressed.

10 He opens their ears[g] to correction
   and insists they repent from iniquity.

11 If they serve Him obediently,
   they will end their days in prosperity
   and their years in happiness.[h]

12 But if they do not obey,
   they will cross the river of death[F]
   and die without knowledge.[i]

13 Those who have a godless heart
      harbor anger;
   even when God binds them,
      they do not cry for help.

14 They die in their youth;
   their life ends among
      male cult prostitutes.[j]

Cross references:
[a]35:12 Pr 1:28; Is 1:15; Zch 7:13
[b]35:14 Jb 13:18; 23:4; 31:13
[c]Jb 6:8; 13:13; 14:14
[d]35:16 Jb 15:2; 21:22; 34:35
[e]36:5 Jb 9:4; 12:13; 38:36
[f]36:6 Gn 18:25; Jb 8:20; 2Pt 2:9
[g]36:10 Jb 4:12; 13:1; 33:16
[h]36:11 Jb 21:13; 22:2; Is 1:19
[i]36:12 Jb 4:21; 33:18; Hs 4:6
[j]36:14 Dt 23:17; 1Kg 14:24; 22:46

A35:14 Or *How then can*   B35:14 Lit *say*   C35:15 LXX, Vg; MT reads *folly*, or *arrogance*; Hb obscure   D36:4 Lit *my words are not false*   E36:5 Lit *He is mighty in strength of heart*   F36:12 Or *will perish by the sword*

22:23-24). If He does not answer, the fault lies with man, not God (2Ch 7:14; Jr 11:9-11).

35:14 Job had asked God why He did not answer his requests for the opportunity to state his case before Him (13:20-24; 23:2-7). Elihu suggested that God's silence (30:20) was not because He was unaware of Job's situation (33:21-23) but was due to Job's self-righteousness and pride in maintaining his innocence (27:2-6; 31:35-37) in the face of God's discipline (34:11-12). Job might be ignoring God's many attempts to communicate with him (33:8-17). He might be missing his opportunities to exercise his God-given wisdom (35:11) and to consider his Creator's provision for relief in his distress (v. 10).

35:15-16 Elihu ended this discourse on a similar note to his previous speech in which he recounted Job's rebellious tendencies (34:36-37). Because God had not given Job the full punishment that he deserved (11:6), he foolishly babbled on with meaningless prattle.

36:3-4 Elihu claimed to have access to the flawless mind of God. Here he professed **perfect knowledge** for himself; in 37:16 he attributed the same to God.

36:5 The phrase **He understands all things** is literally "He is mighty in strength of heart." The Hebrew word for "heart" can refer to the emotions or to the mind (Ps 77:6; see textual footnote at Jr 7:31). Elihu stated categorically that God's great power does not compromise His dealings with man-

kind. His strength of heart moves Him to deal with compassionate firmness of purpose.

36:6 Contrary to Job's insistence that he received no **justice** from God in his suffering (7:19; 9:27-35; 10:20-21; 16:18-22; 19:7; 30:16-23), Elihu declared that God's justice did extend to the **afflicted** (34:28).

36:7 Job had complained of God's constant scrutiny of him (7:17-20; 10:4-7), yet he had admitted that in times past when God watched over him, he experienced the good life (29:2-6). Elihu pointed out that the all-seeing God always looks to the good of the righteous.

36:8-9 Elihu pointed out that people's good includes their correction. God may allow the righteous to suffer like those **bound with chains** (i.e., like captives of war; cp. Nah 3:10) in order to keep them from going further along the path to destruction. Apparent injustice may be a disguised good in order that God may bring people's arrogance and sin to their attention.

36:10-12 The uncovered or opened ear symbolizes God's revelation and instruction to mankind (33:16; Is 50:4-5). The sinner's unopened ear indicates rebellion against God (Is 48:8). If a person's ears are opened to accept God's **correction**, he will obey God and serve Him faithfully. If the person's ear remains closed in disobedience, he will proceed in ignorance along the road to certain death (33:18).

36:13-14 Elihu pointed out that some people respond to

15 God rescues the afflicted by
  their affliction;
  He instructs them by their torment.
16 Indeed, He lured you from the jaws[A]
    of distress
  to a spacious and unconfined place.
  Your table was spread with choice food.
17 Yet now you are obsessed
    with the judgment due the wicked;
  judgment and justice have seized you.
18 Be careful that no one lures you
    with riches;[B]
  do not let a large ransom[C]
    lead you astray.[a]
19 Can your wealth[D] or all
    your physical exertion
  keep you from distress?[b]
20 Do not long for the night
  when nations will disappear
    from their places.
21 Be careful that you do not turn
    to iniquity,
  for that is why you have been tested
    by[E] affliction.

22 Look, God shows Himself exalted
    by His power.
  Who is a teacher like Him?
23 Who has appointed His way for Him,
    and who has declared, "You have
    done wrong"?[c]
24 Remember that you should praise
    His work,

which people have sung about.[d]
25 All mankind has seen it;
  people have looked at it
    from a distance.[e]
26 Yes, God is exalted
    beyond our knowledge;[f]
  the number of His years
    cannot be counted.[g]
27 For He makes waterdrops evaporate;[F]
  they distill the rain into its[G] mist,[h]
28 which the clouds pour out
  and shower abundantly on mankind.
29 Can anyone understand how the clouds
    spread out
  or how the thunder roars
    from God's pavilion?[i]
30 See how He spreads His lightning[j]
    around Him
  and covers the depths of the sea.
31 For He judges the nations with these;
  He gives food in abundance.[k]
32 He covers His hands with lightning
  and commands it to hit its mark.
33 The[H] thunder declares His presence;[I]
  the cattle also, the approaching storm.

37

1 My heart[I] pounds at this
  and leaps from my chest.[J]
2 Just listen to His thunderous voice
  and the rumbling that comes
    from His mouth.
3 He lets it loose beneath the entire sky;
  His lightning to the ends[m] of the earth.

Cross references (center column):
a 36:18 1Sm 12:3; Ps 26:10; Am 5:12
b 36:19 1Sm 22:2; Jb 15:24; Ps 107:6,13,19,28
c 36:23 Jb 34:10,13; Is 40:13-14; Rm 11:34
d 36:24 Ps 92:5; 104:33; Rv 15:3
e 36:25 Ps 19:3; Rm 1:19-20; Heb 11:13
f 36:26 Jb 9:10; 37:5,23; Ec 8:17
g Ps 90:2; 102:24,27; Heb 1:12
h 36:27 Gn 2:6; Jb 38:28; Ps 147:8
i 36:29 Jb 26:14; 37:16; Ps 105:39
j 36:30 2Sm 22:15; Jb 38:28; Ps 18:14
k 36:31 Jb 37:13; Ps 136:25; Ac 14:17
l 37:1 Jb 15:35; 32:19; Pr 20:27,30
m 37:3 Jb 38:13; Is 11:12; Ezk 7:2

A36:16 Lit *from a mouth of narrowness*   B36:18 Or *you into mockery*   C36:18 Or *bribe*   D36:19 Or *cry for help*   E36:21 Or *for you have preferred this to*   F36:27 Lit *He draws in waterdrops*   G36:27 Or *His*   H36:33 Lit *His*, or *Its*   I36:33 Lit *thunder announces concerning Him* or *it*   J37:1 Lit *from its place*

God's chastisement angrily. **Cult prostitutes** were involved in the worship of idols (Dt 23:17; 1Kg 14:22-24; Hs 4:14).

36:15 Rather than being a sign of God's unconcern as Job had reasoned (9:15-16), **affliction** is a mark of God's mercy, keeping one from the deadly path of ignorance (v. 12).

36:16 Elihu turned to Job's speech in which he had contrasted his former life and present situation (chaps. 29–30). Rather than complaining that he was suffering unjustly, Job should recognize that he was experiencing God's means of correction and restoration, as Eliphaz had also argued (5:17-26).

36:17-19 The prosperity of the wicked was distracting Job. Neither **wealth** nor personal effort could deliver Job from his **distress**. Only God's chastisement could work its intended result.

36:20-21 Job should neither wish for death (7:13-16; 10:19-22) nor resign himself to it (17:13-18; 30:20-23). Elihu warned Job that by seeking some alternative method of ending his **affliction**, he was committing **iniquity**. Rather, Job should learn the reasons for God's discipline in his life.

36:22-23 Elihu implied that Job should not accuse God of injustice in his case (10:6-7; 13:26-27; 19:11; 30:18-19; 33:8-11).

36:24-25 Rather than finding fault with God, Job should join **all mankind** in singing His **praise** (Ps 48:10; 100:1-2).

36:26–37:13 Elihu followed his own advice and launched into a long hymn-like praise of God. This prayer provides a setting for God's subsequent declarations to Job.

36:26 Elihu began his praise by pointing out that full **knowledge** of God is beyond human comprehension (42:3; Is 40:13-14). Mankind cannot fully appreciate His infinity (Ps 102:27). Job was in no position to criticize such a One, because His power and wisdom defied human understanding (Is 40:28).

36:27-30 The complexities of the hydrologic cycle are under God's control.

36:31-33 God's control of the forces of nature involves both the sustenance and the judgment of **the nations**. Like a mighty cosmic warrior shooting His arrows (Hab 3:8-13), God propels the **lightning** across the sky (37:3) as an instrument of judgment, unerringly hitting its **mark** (see Ps 18:14; 144:6). God's power and **presence** are felt by man and beast in the thunderstorm (Ps 77:18).

37:1-5 Elihu sensed God's power in the thunderstorm. The extent of its working is beyond human comprehension, but it is under the control of the Exalted One (36:26).

4 Then there comes a roaring sound;
   God thunders[a] with His majestic voice.
   He does not restrain the lightning
   when His rumbling voice is heard.
5 God thunders marvelously
   with His voice;
   He does great things that
   we cannot comprehend.
6 For He says to the snow,[b]
   "Fall to the earth,"
   and the torrential rains,
   His mighty torrential rains,
7 serve as His sign to all mankind,
   so that all men may know His work.
8 The wild animals enter their lairs
   and stay in their dens.[c]
9 The windstorm comes
   from its chamber,
   and the cold
   from the driving north winds.
10 Ice is formed by the breath of God,[d]
   and watery expanses are frozen.
11 He saturates clouds with moisture;[e]
   He scatters His lightning
   through them.
12 They swirl about,
   turning round and round
   at His direction,
   accomplishing everything
   He commands them
   over the surface of the inhabited world.
13 He causes this to happen
   for punishment,
   for His land, or for His faithful love.

14 Listen to this, Job.
   Stop and consider God's wonders.
15 Do you know how God directs
   His clouds
   or makes their lightning flash?
16 Do you understand
   how the clouds float,
   those wonderful works of Him who has
   perfect knowledge?
17 You whose clothes get hot
   when the south wind brings calm
   to the land,
18 can you help God spread out the skies
   as hard as a cast metal mirror?
19 Teach us what we should say to Him;[f]
   we cannot prepare our case because of
   our darkness.
20 Should He be told that I want to speak?
   Can a man speak when he is confused?
21 Now men cannot even look at the sun
   when it is in the skies,
   after a wind has swept through
   and cleared them away.
22 Yet out of the north He comes,
   shrouded in a golden glow;
   awesome[g] majesty surrounds Him.
23 The •Almighty—we cannot
   reach Him—
   He is exalted in power!
   He will not oppress justice and
   abundant righteousness,
24 Therefore, men •fear Him.
   He does not look favorably on any
   who are wise[h] in heart.

a 37:4 Jb 40:9; Ps 18:3; 29:3
b 37:6 Jb 6:16; 24:19; 38:22
c 37:8 Jb 38:40; Ps 104:22; Am 3:4
d 37:10 2Sm 22:21; Jb 4:9; Is 30:33
e 37:11 Jb 26:8; 36:29; 38:9
f 37:19 Jb 9:3,14; 40:2; Jms 1:5
g 37:22 Ex 15:11; Dt 7:21; Hab 3:2
h 37:24 Pr 3:7; 26:5,12,16; 28:11

37:6-8 Both the **snow** (38:22) and **torrential rains** (1Kg 18:45; Ezk 13:11) are under God's control. They testify to His handiwork. Under such conditions even beasts seek shelter from the elements. If winter is in view (as in Jb 37:9-10), Elihu may be noting the process of animal hibernation.

37:9-10 Elihu portrayed as the **breath of God** the chilling winds of winter, transforming the landscape by the power of the Lord and under His direction. Snow and ice are rare but not unheard of in Israel (2Sm 23:20).

37:11-13 God forms and controls all weather and sends it to accomplish His purposes. This may include **punishment** (lit "a rod") for disobedience or a special blessing and evidence of God's **faithful love** toward His people for covenant obedience (Dt 11:13-15). Elihu implied that Job should understand this so he may recognize God's dealing with him for correction and restoration (Ps 119:71).

37:17-18 Elihu now asked whether Job had any part in bringing the hot sirocco winds. The cloudless sky is like a vast **metal mirror** over the landscape.

37:19-20 Job had spoken previously of wanting to present his case before the Lord, confident that he was in the right (13:18; 23:4) and would be vindicated (31:35-37). Elihu maintained that no one has the wisdom to debate God, let alone win. If man cannot understand God's basic activities

in the natural world, how can he expect to speak boldly in His presence?

37:21-22 If the sun is too dazzling to behold, the splendor of the Lord is even more so (Ac 22:6-11; 26:13). Therefore, God softens His appearance (Ezk 1:4-28; Mt 17:2). The imagery may suggest the approach of a storm from the **north** (cp. Pr 25:23) as the sun's rays streamed through the gathering clouds with a **golden glow**. This would herald the Lord's presence (Ps 18:2). The north (Hb *tsaphon*) was linked with God's residence in some cultures of the ancient Near East (Jb 23:9; 26:7; cp. Ps 48:2; Is 14:13-14).

37:23 Elihu implied that Job's quest for a personal hearing before God (13:14-16; 31:35-37) was ill-founded. Elihu maintained that God was not singling out Job for persecution as he had complained (10:20; 16:12; 30:19,21). Such was impossible, because God's basic moral character functioned in accordance with His **justice** and **righteousness** (Dt 32:4; Jnh 4:2).

37:24 Elihu's final advice was to **fear** God (Ec 12:13). This is wise, as Job himself had admitted (Jb 28:28). But God does not **favorably** regard the person who is **wise in heart** (one who prides himself as having superior wisdom). True wisdom begins with reverential fear of God (Pr 1:7). Elihu was from the beginning angry with Job because he believed

The LORD Speaks

38 Then the LORD answered Job from the whirlwind.[a] He said:

2 Who is this who obscures My counsel
with ignorant words?[b]
3 Get ready to answer Me like a man;
when I question[c] you,
you will inform Me.
4 Where were you when I established[d]
the earth?
Tell Me, if you have[A] understanding.
5 Who fixed its dimensions?
Certainly you know!
Who stretched a measuring line
across it?
6 What supports its foundations?

Or who laid its cornerstone
7 while the morning stars sang together
and all the sons of God[e] shouted
for joy?
8 Who enclosed the sea behind doors
when it burst from the womb,
9 when I made the clouds its garment
and thick darkness its blanket,[B,f]
10 when I determined its boundaries[C]
and put its bars and doors in place,
11 when I declared: "You may come
this far, but no farther;
your proud waves stop here"?
12 Have you ever in your life commanded
the morning
or assigned the dawn its place,

*a*38:1 2Kg 2:11; Jb 40:6; Ezk 13:11,13 *b*38:2 Jb 34:35; 35:16; 42:3 *c*38:3 2Sm 11:7; Jb 40:7; 42:4 *d*38:4 Ps 89:11; 102:25; 104:5 *e*38:7 Gn 6:2,4; Jb 1:6; 2:1 *f*38:9 2Sm 22:10; Jb 22:13; 37:11

A38:4 Lit *know*   B38:9 Lit *swaddling clothes*   C38:10 Lit *I broke My statute on it*

---

that Job was self-righteous (Jb 32:2). Although Job feared God, he was playing God in his own life despite his constant acts of piety (1:5; cp. chap. 31). Job had been certain of his righteousness (27:6), but he had failed to recognize God's essential justice and righteousness (32:2; 37:23). Elihu's advice to Job was that he should truly fear (revere) God and turn from his self-centeredness. Then he would understand both God's power and His moral integrity (42:2-6). Thus Job would find God sufficient for his every trial.

38:1 God's speaking to Job from the **whirlwind** was not from a windstorm such as that which destroyed the house

"Then the LORD answered Job from the whirlwind. He said: Who is this who obscures My counsel with ignorant words?" (38:1-2)

of Job's children (1:18-19) or the winds of judgment (21:18). It was a theophany, a manifestation of God Himself (Ezk 1:4; cp. 2Kg 2:11). In the book of Job, the divine name LORD (Yahweh) had occurred previously only in the Prologue (it appears in Job's first response to Zophar in Jb 12:9, though some manuscripts read "God"). Although Job may have been upright and he was not suffering because of wrongdoing, his frequent complaints against God were tantamount to assuming the Lord's prerogatives—playing God in his life. Job needed to be reminded of who and what the LORD is in order to find Him sufficient for his situation.

38:3 The Lord addressed Job by challenging him to enter into a dialogue in full possession of his human strength and faculties. The Hebrew word translated **man** often reflects a man in his strength and virility (Jr 30:6). It is used at times of vigorous spiritual strength (Jb 16:21). **Get ready to answer** renders the Hebrew "gird up your loins." The idiom reflects the tucking of one's long garment between the legs and into the belt in preparation for an arduous task such as running (1Kg 18:46) or battle (Is 5:27). Job's difficult task consisted of fully understanding and answering God's questions.

38:4-6 God's first round of questions to Job challenged him to understand something of the Lord's creative power in both the inanimate (vv. 4-38) and animate (38:39–39:30) worlds. God alone brought the earth into being. The imagery here is that of a building carefully conceived, measured, and laid out. Its supporting pillars are securely fastened to its **foundations** (or sockets for the pillars). In an earlier image, the earth was conceived of as hanging in empty space (26:7).

38:7 The **stars** are personified as being able to sing. Music accompanied the dedication of Solomon's temple (2Ch 7:6). Music and singing also accompanied the laying of the second temple's foundation (Ezr 3:10-11). Alternatively, the **morning stars** may be a metaphor for the angels, who appear in the parallel line.

38:8-11 The origin of the **sea** is depicted in the imagery of childbirth. Although the delimitation of the oceans' **boundaries** has a significant place in the Genesis creation account (Gn 1:6-7; Ps 104:6-9), neither there nor here is there any hint of ancient Near Eastern mythology in which a primeval sea god is defeated.

13 so it may seize the edges of the earth
and shake the wicked out of it?
14 The earth is changed as clay is by a seal;
its hills stand out like the folds of
a garment.
15 Light^A is withheld from the wicked,
and the arm raised in violence
is broken.

16 Have you traveled to the sources
of the sea
or walked in the depths of the oceans?
17 Have the gates^a of death been revealed
to you?
Have you seen the gates
of deep darkness?
18 Have you comprehended the extent
of the earth?
Tell Me, if you know all this.

19 Where is the road to the home of light?
Do you know where darkness lives,
20 so you can lead it back to its border?
Are you familiar with the paths
to its home?
21 Don't you know? You were
already born;^b
you have lived so long!^B
22 Have you entered the place
where the snow is stored?
Or have you seen the storehouses
of hail,^c
23 which I hold in reserve for times
of trouble,

for the day of warfare and battle?^d
24 What road leads to the place
where light is dispersed?^C
Where is the source of the east wind
that spreads across the earth?
25 Who cuts a channel
for the flooding rain
or clears the way for lightning,
26 to bring rain on an uninhabited land,
on a desert with no human life,^D
27 to satisfy the parched wasteland
and cause the grass to sprout?^e
28 Does the rain have a father?
Who fathered the drops of dew?^f
29 Whose womb did the ice come from?
Who gave birth to the frost of heaven
30 when water becomes as hard as stone,^E
and the surface of the watery depths
is frozen?^g

31 Can you fasten the chains
of the Pleiades
or loosen the belt of Orion?
32 Can you bring out the constellations^F
in their season
and lead the Bear^G and her cubs?^h
33 Do you know the laws^i of heaven?
Can you impose its^H authority on earth?
34 Can you command^i the clouds
so that a flood of water covers you?^j
35 Can you send out lightning^k bolts,
and they go?
Do they report to you: "Here we are"?

Cross references (center column):

^a 38:17 Ps 9:13; 107:18; Is 38:10
^b 38:21 Jb 15:7; Ps 90:2; Pr 8:25
^c 38:22 Ex 9:18; Ps 105:32; Is 28:17
^d 38:23 Jos 10:11; Is 30:30; Rv 16:21
^e 38:27 Gn 1:11; 2Sm 23:4; Ps 107:35
^f 38:28 Jb 5:10; Ps 147:8; Jr 14:22
^g 38:29-30 Jb 37:10; Ps 147:16-17
^h 38:31-32 Jb 9:9; Is 40:26; Am 5:8
^i 38:33 Jr 31:35; 33:25
^j 38:34 Jb 22:11; Ps 69:1-2; Lm 3:54
^k 38:35 Ex 19:16; Ps 18:14; 97:4

^A 38:15 Lit *Their light*   ^B 38:21 Lit *born; the number of your days is great*   ^C 38:24 Or *where lightning is distributed*   ^D 38:26 Lit *life in it*   ^E 38:30 Lit *water hides itself as the stone*   ^F 38:32 Or *Mazzaroth*; Hb obscure   ^G 38:32 Or *lead Aldebaran*   ^H 38:33 Or *God's*   ^I 38:34 Lit *lift up your voice to*

38:12-15 Much as the appearance of clay is altered by a seal impression, so the landscape becomes dramatically changed by the rosy rays of dawn. The imagery is that of a garment whose folds—unseen in the darkness—become visible in the **light**. "Light" for the **wicked** is the darkness in which they accomplish their evil deeds. With the true light of day their "light" is extinguished. As an evildoer's arm is rendered impotent by being **broken**, so the plans of the wicked are thwarted by the light of day.

38:16-18 The extent of Job's experiential knowledge is questioned. His limited travels cannot have included going to the hidden springs that lie in the **depths of the oceans**. Job had not seen even the shadow of the **gates of death**, let alone passed through them. Earlier Job had described the realm of death as a gloomy place (10:21-22), yet he expressed a longing to find refuge there (14:13). An alternative proposal sees an allusion to ancient mythological concepts about the afterlife. Thus there is a movement from the depths of the sea to the underlying netherworld through whose gates one enters at death into a vast subterranean world ruled by underworld deities. If so, the force is apologetic, Yahweh being shown to be the true Lord. The point is that Job, with his limited perspective, should trust in Him who is infinite in wisdom, power, and knowledge.

38:19-21 **Light** and **darkness** are personified, each having a **home** from which they daily emerged and returned. The Lord satirically reminded Job that he was not born when God commanded the first light to penetrate the primeval darkness (15:7; Gn 1:2-5).

38:22-23 The imagery of these verses views God as keeping **snow** and **hail** in heavenly storehouses for His use at appropriate times. God could use them as weapons (Ex 9:18-26; Ps 68:14; 78:47-48; Is 28:2,19).

38:24 God reminded Job that his knowledge did not include the distribution of the lightning (see textual footnote; also 36:30,32; 37:3,11,15) or the place where the **east wind** originated. Such a mighty desert wind had swept away Job's family (1:19).

38:28-29 God reminded Job that only a master craftsman could account for the manifold forms that water can assume and the places where these may be found. The elemental forces of nature are under God's control (5:10; 28:25-26; 36:37; Ps 147:16-18).

38:31-33 God turned Job's attention to the constellations: **the Pleiades . . . Orion**, and **the Bear**. Job had mentioned them earlier in connection with God's creative activity (9:9). The meaning of the term **constellations** is uncertain and

³⁶ Who put wisdom*a* in the heart*A*
    or gave the mind understanding?
³⁷ Who has the wisdom to number
        the clouds?
    Or who can tilt the water jars of heaven
³⁸ when the dust hardens like cast metal
    and the clods of dirt stick together?

³⁹ Can you hunt prey for a lioness
    or satisfy the appetite of young lions*b*
⁴⁰ when they crouch in their dens
    and lie in wait within their lairs?
⁴¹ Who provides the raven's food*c*
    when its young cry out to God
    and wander about for lack of food?

39 Do you know when mountain goats
        give birth?
    Have you watched the deer in labor?
² Can you count the months
    they are pregnant*B*

a 38:36 Jb
28:12,18,20; Ps
51:6; Ec 2:26
b 38:39 Ps
104:21; 145:15-
16
c 38:41 1Kg
17:4,6; Ps 147:9;
Lk 12:24
d 39:6 Jb 24:5;
38:26; Jr 2:24
e Dt 29:23; Ps
107:34; Jr 17:6
f 39:7 Ex 3:7;
5:10,13-14; Jb
3:18

so you can know the time
        they give birth?
³ They crouch down to give birth
        to their young;
    they deliver their newborn.*c*
⁴ Their offspring are healthy and grow up
        in the open field.
    They leave and do not return.*D*
⁵ Who set the wild donkey free?
    Who released the swift donkey
        from its harness?
⁶ I made the wilderness*d* its home,
    and the salty*e* wasteland its dwelling.
⁷ It scoffs at the noise of the village
    and never hears the shouts
        of a driver.*f*
⁸ It roams the mountains
        for its pastureland,
    searching for anything green.

---

*A*38:36 Or *the inner self*; Ps 51:6   *B*39:2 Lit *months they fulfill*   *C*39:3 Or *they send away their labor pains*   *D*39:4 Lit *return to them*

may include the planets (2Kg 23:5). Although Job knew of their existence, he did not understand the **laws** of physics and astronomy and their effect on the earth. God alone exercises dominion over all of this.

38:36-38 God's questions implied that neither Job nor any human being had the **wisdom** to control the weather. In a metaphor the clouds are likened to giant **water jars** (or skins), which are tipped to spill their water on hard, dry soil (see Dt 28:23).

38:39-41 **Lions** are capable of securing their own prey, but it is God who established the complex relationship of predator and prey. God also cares for the needs of the **ravens**, scavengers that often feed on the remains of prey. His control of ravens included using them to care for one of His prophets (1Kg 17:4-6). The stately lion and lowly raven serve as a merism, the two extremes (stately and lowly) representing the whole animal world.

39:1-4 The female **mountain goats** (ibex) and **deer** are able to reproduce without human help. God controls the entire process.

A view of Orion Nebula, the constellation bearing the name of a giant Greek hunter who, according to the myth, was bound and placed in the heavens. Job 38:31 may allude to this myth. God is consistently portrayed as the creator of the Orion constellation (9:9; Am 5:8). The plural of the Hebrew term for Orion is rendered "constellations" in Isaiah 13:10.

⁹ Would the wild ox be willing
    to serve you?
Would it spend the night
    by your feeding trough?
¹⁰ Can you hold the wild ox*ᵃ* to a furrow
    by its harness?
Will it plow the valleys behind you?
¹¹ Can you depend on it because
    its strength is great?
Would you leave it to do
    your hard work?
¹² Can you trust the wild ox to harvest
    your grain
and bring it to your threshing floor?

¹³ The wings of the ostrich flap joyfully,
    but are her feathers and plumage
    like the stork's?ᴬ,ᵇ

ᵃ 39:10 Nm 23:22; 24:8; Dt 33:17
ᵇ 39:13 Ps 104:17; Jr 8:7; Zch 5:9
ᶜ 39:17 Jb 35:11; 38:36

¹⁴ She abandons her eggs on the ground
    and lets them be warmed in the sand.
¹⁵ She forgets that a foot may crush them
    or that some wild animal
    may trample them.
¹⁶ She treats her young harshly, as if
    they were not her own,
with no fear that her labor
    may have been in vain.
¹⁷ For God has deprived her of wisdom;
He has not endowed her
    with understanding.ᶜ
¹⁸ When she proudlyᴬ spreads her wings,
    she laughs at the horse and its rider.

¹⁹ Do you give strength to the horse?
    Do you adorn his neck with a mane?ᴬ
²⁰ Do you make him leap like a locust?

ᴬ **39:13,18,19** Hb obscure

39:5-8 God implied that He looks after the **wild donkey** in the **wilderness**, free from the work and constraints of its domesticated counterpart. There is a theme here: God has placed every animal in a suitable environment. The Hebrew word rendered **scoffs** can mean "laughs" or "plays"; it occurs six times in the divine speeches (vv. 7,18,22; 40:20; 41:5,29).

39:9-12 Only God can control the powerful **wild ox** (Hb *re'em*; probably the aurochs, *Bos primigenius*). Unlike the domesticated ox, the wild ox cannot be harnessed to **harvest** man's **grain**. The Assyrian King Sennacherib compared his indomitable courage and strength to that of the wild ox. Its long horns were symbolic of strength (Nm 23:22; 24:8; Dt 33:17).

39:13-18 The depiction of the **ostrich** conforms to popular conception rather than scientific observation. Because some females shared the same nesting area, one ostrich might look with disdain at another's eggs. Though they are unintelligent, they can outrun horses. Even this strange animal is designed and watched over by God.

39:19-25 The **horse** was particularly prized and possessed by royalty (1Kg 4:26; 10:26-28). The horse's great **strength** and swiftness made it an important part of ancient military forces, especially in pulling war chariots (Ex 15:1; Jdg 5:22; Jr 4:13; Nah 3:2). The leaping ability of locusts as well as their appearance and swift orderly advance when swarming made their comparison with horses a familiar one (Jl 2:4; Rv 9:7). The horse's fearlessness, eagerness, and confidence

The Pleiades, a brilliant grouping of six or seven visible stars located in the shoulder of the constellation Taurus (9:9; 38:31; Am 5:8).

His proud snorting fills one with terror.

21 He paws[A] in the valley and rejoices
in his strength;
He charges into battle.[B]

22 He laughs at fear, since he is afraid
of nothing;
he does not run from the sword.

23 A quiver rattles at his side,
along with a flashing spear
and a lance.[C]

24 He charges ahead[D] with trembling rage;
he cannot stand still
at the trumpet's sound.

25 When the trumpet blasts,
he snorts defiantly.[E]
He smells the battle from a distance;
he hears the officers' shouts
and the battle cry.

26 Does the hawk take flight
by your understanding
and spread its wings to the south?

27 Does the eagle soar at your command
and make its nest[a] on high?

28 It lives on a cliff where it spends
the night;
its stronghold is on a rocky crag.

29 From there it searches for prey;[b]
its eyes penetrate the distance.

30 Its brood gulps down blood,
and where the slain are, it is there.[c]

Cross references (center column):
[a]39:27 Jr 49:16; Ob 4; Hab 2:9
[b]39:29 Jb 9:26; Hab 1:8
[c]39:30 Ezk 39:17; Mt 24:28; Lk 17:37
[d]40:4 Ezr 9:6; Jb 29:9; 42:6
[e]40:5 Jb 9:3,15; 33:14; Ps 62:11
[f]40:6 Jb 38:1; Jr 30:23; Ezk 13:11,13
[g]40:7 2Sm 11:7; Jb 38:3; 42:4
[h]40:8 Jb 9:20,28; Ps 37:33; Is 50:9
[i]Jb 32:2; Ps 51:4; Rm 3:4
[j]40:10 Ps 93:1; 96:6; 104:1
[k]40:11 Jb 14:13; 19:11; 21:17

40

The LORD answered Job:

2 Will the one who contends
with the •Almighty correct Him?
Let him who argues with God
give an answer.[F]

3 Then Job answered the LORD:

4 I am so insignificant. How can I
answer You?[d]
I place my hand over my mouth.

5 I have spoken once, and I will not reply;
twice, but now I can add nothing.[e]

6 Then the LORD answered Job from the whirlwind:[f]

7 Get ready to answer Me like a man;
When I question[g] you, you will
inform Me.

8 Would you really challenge My justice?
Would you declare Me •guilty[h]
to justify yourself?[i]

9 Do you have an arm like God's?
Can you thunder with a voice like His?

10 Adorn yourself with majesty[j]
and splendor,
and clothe yourself with honor
and glory.

11 Unleash your raging anger;[k]

[A]39:21 LXX, Syr; MT reads *digs*   [B]39:21 Lit *He goes out to meet the weapon*   [C]39:23 Or *scimitar*   [D]39:24 Lit *He swallows the ground*   [E]39:25 Lit *he says, "Aha!"*   [F]40:2 Lit *God respond to it*

---

in the face of battle is personified as his saying "Aha!" (see textual footnote at Jb 39:25). The horse's amazing physical qualities can only be attributed to God's creative genius. He alone can strike terror into the otherwise fearless horse (Zch 12:4).

39:26-30 God closed this portion of His questioning of Job in the same way He began it. He challenged Job's understanding about the workings of nature (38:4). Job had not taught the **hawk** how to fly or when and where to migrate. The **eagle** did not build its lofty nest in an inaccessible **rocky crag** (Ob 4) at Job's direction. Job did not equip the eagle with keen eyesight. Eagles (and vultures) are at hand after military battles that leave dead bodies on the ground (Mt 24:28).

40:2 God questioned Job with a renewed challenge to either answer or make a rebuttal. Otherwise Job must admit that his criticism was groundless. Job had criticized the Lord often in the earlier dialogues (9:14-20; 16:11-12; 21:17-26) and had longed to present his case before God to see how He would answer him (23:2-5; 31:35-37). Job now had that opportunity.

40:3-5 Job's answer was a non-answer. The Hebrew phrase "I am insignificant" is literally "I am [too] light/little." Job did not disclaim his innocence. He had said all he could about his situation. Placing his **hand** over his **mouth** showed Job's reluctance to add anything further.

40:8 God now came to the heart of the matter. Was Job ready to condemn God who had demonstrated His loving care for

all creatures? Was Job so willing to defend his uprightness and innocence that he would declare God unjust? (cp. 27:2). Would Job **justify** himself (27:6) rather than see his suffering in the light of God's greater purposes? Job had an attitude problem that must be resolved if his fellowship with God was to be restored (14:15; 19:26-27; 29:2-6).

40:9 The **arm** is used figuratively for strength. God asked Job whether he had sufficient strength to enforce his decision if he were in charge of meting out justice. God's arm was stretched out against the Egyptians to redeem His people out of Egyptian slavery (Ex 6:6; Dt 4:34; 26:8). God brings justice to the world by His arm (Is 51:5; 63:5-6; Jr 21:3-5).

40:10 If Job was to be in charge, where were his royal garments and evidence of his authority? Such matters are characteristic of God's person (Ps 29:1-2; 112:9; 113:4; Rv 4:11).

40:11-14 Job had complained that God failed to bring the wicked to justice in this life (21:30-33; 24:1-17) while depriving God of justice (27:2). Should Job be able to demonstrate his ability to bring the wicked to justice, God would admit Job's sufficiency to care for his own situation. The **right hand** often symbolizes honor, authority, or power (Ps 110:1-2; 118:15-16). By it God lays hold of His enemies and the wicked and brings them to judgment (Ps 21:8-13). If Job was unable to deal similarly with the wicked, he must not accuse God of injustice.

40:15 Some have identified **Behemoth** as some kind of mythological beast, such as the bull of heaven in the Meso-

look on every proud person
and humiliate him.[a]
12 Look on every proud person
and humble him;[b]
trample the wicked where they stand.[A]
13 Hide them together in the dust;
imprison them in the grave.[B]
14 Then I will confess to you
that your own right hand[c]
can deliver you.[d]

15 Look at Behemoth,
which I made along with you.
He eats grass like an ox.
16 Look at the strength of his loins
and the power in the muscles
of his belly.
17 He stiffens his tail like a cedar tree;
the tendons of his thighs are woven
firmly together.
18 His bones are bronze tubes;
his limbs are like iron rods.
19 He is the foremost of God's works;[e]
only his Maker can draw the sword
against him.
20 The hills yield food for him,
while all sorts of wild animals
play there.
21 He lies under the lotus plants,
hiding in the protection[c]
of marshy reeds.
22 Lotus plants cover him
with their shade;

[a]40:11 Is 2:11; Ezk 21:26; Dn 4:37
[b]40:12 Ps 18:27; Is 13:11; 63:3
[c]40:14 Ps 17:7; 20:6; 108:6
[d]Ps 3:8; 49:7; 62:2
[e]40:19 Jb 26:14; Pr 8:22
[f]41:1 Jb 3:8; Ps 104:26; Is 27:1
[g]Is 19:8; Hab 1:15
[h]41:2 2Kg 19:28; Jb 40:24; Is 37:29
[i]41:4 Ex 21:6; Dt 15:17; 1Sm 27:12
[j]41:10 Jb 3:8; Jr 50:44

the willows by the brook surround him.
23 Though the river rages,
Behemoth is unafraid;
he remains confident, even if
the Jordan surges up to his mouth.
24 Can anyone capture him
while he looks on,[D]
or pierce his nose with snares?

41 [E] Can you pull in •Leviathan[f]
with a hook[g]
or tie his tongue down with a rope?
2 Can you put a cord[F] through his nose
or pierce his jaw with a hook?[h]
3 Will he beg you for mercy
or speak softly to you?
4 Will he make a covenant with you
so that you can take him
as a slave forever?[i]
5 Can you play with him like a bird
or put him on a leash[G] for your girls?
6 Will traders bargain for him
or divide him among the merchants?
7 Can you fill his hide with harpoons
or his head with fishing spears?
8 Lay a[H] hand on him.
You will remember the battle
and never repeat it!
9 [I] Any hope of capturing him proves false.
Does a person not collapse
at the very sight of him?
10 No one is ferocious enough
to rouse Leviathan;[j]

[A]40:12 Lit *wicked in their place*   [B]40:13 Lit *together; bind their faces in the hidden place*   [C]40:21 Lit *plants, in the hiding place*
[D]40:24 Lit *capture it in its eyes*   [E]41:1 Jb 40:25 in Hb   [F]41:2 Lit *reed*   [G]41:5 Lit *or bind him*   [H]41:8 Lit *your*   [I]41:9 Jb 41:1 in Hb

---

potamian *Epic of Gilgamesh* or the ferocious bullock, the Ugaritic goddess that Anat defeated. Allusions to mythological creatures had been made previously (3:8; 7:12; 9:13-14; 26:12-13), but the description here favors a living animal known to Job. The buffalo, a dinosaur, the rhinoceros, and (most often) the hippopotamus have been suggested. The term *behemoth* occurs elsewhere only in Ps 73:22 where the psalmist compared his formerly embittered soul to a brute beast.

40:17 The Hebrew verb *chaphats*, translated in verse 17 as **stiffens**, occurs only here with this meaning. The point of comparison between the short tail of the hippopotamus and the cedar tree may simply be the fact of their respective hardness. Elsewhere the same Hebrew word carries emphases such as "take pleasure in" or "delight." "Tail" could be a euphemism, hence speaking to Behemoth's virility. Readings found in manuscripts of ancient versions (LXX, Vg, Syr) support this possibility.

40:19 Only God would dare to face this creature alone (v. 24). Cattle (Hb *behemah*) were the first of God's created land animals. Behemoth (pl) would represent the **foremost** of all. Since Job could not face Behemoth, would he have the power to enforce justice against the wicked (vv. 10-14)? Job should entrust justice to the Lord, Behemoth's creator (v. 15).

40:20-22 Behemoth found **food** on the **hills** (cp. v. 15), but

it sought refuge in marshes where the **lotus plants** grew. Alternatively, this plant may refer to a thorny tree that grew in deep moist valleys.

40:24 Hunting parties attempted to **pierce** the **nose** of Behemoth to impair his breathing, making him vulnerable to **snares** or hooks. Such was no easy task while Behemoth was watching.

41:1 **Leviathan** has been identified by interpreters as a whale, shark, dinosaur, sea monster, and a crocodile. For its mythological associations, see notes at 3:8-9; 7:12. In ancient Egypt the crocodile could symbolize royal power, yet it was a hunted animal.

41:2-4 God's challenge indicates that Job would be unable to hunt and subdue Leviathan unaided. In the ancient Near East, stronger nations imposed treaty obligations on a weaker state. Fierce Leviathan would neither petition Job for such a **covenant** arrangement nor ask to be his perpetual slave (Ex 21:5-6; Dt 15:16-17).

41:6 Leviathan cannot be captured and sold.

41:7-9 It would be impossible for Job to face Leviathan alone with the usual hunting methods. Most likely Job would **collapse** in fear at seeing him.

41:10-11 If Job would not dare to face Leviathan single-handedly, how could he hope to confront God who owned

who then can stand against Me?

11 Who confronted Me, that I
    should repay him?
Everything under heaven belongs
    to Me.[a]

12 I cannot be silent about his limbs,
    his power, and his graceful proportions.

13 Who can strip off his outer covering?
Who can penetrate his double layer
    of armor?[A,b]

14 Who can open his jaws,[B]
    surrounded by those terrifying teeth?

15 His pride is in his rows of scales,
    closely sealed together.

16 One scale is so close to another[C]
    that no air can pass between them.

17 They are joined to one another,
    so closely connected[D] they cannot
    be separated.

18 His snorting[E] flashes with light,
    while his eyes are like the rays[F]
    of dawn.

19 Flaming torches shoot from his mouth;
    fiery sparks fly out!

20 Smoke billows from his nostrils[G]
    as from a boiling pot or burning reeds.

21 His breath sets coals ablaze,
    and flames pour out of his mouth.

22 Strength resides in his neck,
    and dismay dances before him.

23 The folds of his flesh
    are joined together,
    solid as metal[G] and immovable.

24 His heart is as hard as a rock,
    as hard as a lower millstone!

25 When Leviathan rises, the mighty[H]
    are terrified;

they withdraw because of his thrashing.

26 The sword that reaches him will have
    no effect,
nor will a spear, dart, or arrow.

27 He regards iron as straw,
    and bronze as rotten wood.

28 No arrow can make him flee;
    slingstones become like stubble to him.

29 A club is regarded as stubble,
    and he laughs[d] at the sound of a javelin.

30 His undersides are jagged potsherds,
    spreading the mud
    like a threshing sledge.[e]

31 He makes the depths seethe
    like a cauldron;
he makes the sea like an ointment jar.

32 He leaves a shining wake behind him;[i]
    one would think the deep had
    gray hair!

33 He has no equal on earth—
    a creature devoid of fear!

34 He surveys everything that is haughty;
    he is king over all the proud beasts.[J]

Job Replies to the LORD

42 Then Job replied to the LORD:

2 I[K] know that You can do anything
    and no plan of Yours can be thwarted.[f]

3 You asked, "Who is this who conceals
    My counsel with ignorance?"[g]
Surely I spoke about things I did not
    understand,
    things too wonderful for me to[L] know.[h]

4 You said, "Listen now, and I will speak.
When I question[i] you, you will
    inform Me."

---

[a] 41:11 Ps 24:1; Rm 11:35; 1Co 10:26   [b] 41:13 Jr 46:4; 51:3   [c] 41:20 2Sm 22:9; Jb 39:20; Ps 18:8   [d] 41:29 2Ch 30:10; Jb 39:7,18; Hab 1:10   [e] 41:30 Is 41:15; Am 1:3   [f] 42:2 Gn 18:14; Jr 23:20; Mt 19:26   [g] 42:3 Jb 34:35; 35:16; 38:2   [h] Ps 40:5; 131:1; 139:6   [i] 42:4 Jb 38:3; 40:7

[A] 41:13 LXX; MT reads *double bridle*   [B] 41:14 Lit *open the doors of his face*   [C] 41:16 Lit *One by one they approach*   [D] 41:17 Lit *another; they cling together and*   [E] 41:18 Or *sneezing*   [F] 41:18 Lit *eyelids*   [G] 41:23 Lit *together, hard on him*   [H] 41:25 Or *the divine beings*   [i] 41:32 Lit *a path*   [J] 41:34 Lit *the children of pride*   [K] 42:2 Alt Hb tradition reads *You*   [L] 42:3 Lit *me, and I did not*

---

everything (including Leviathan) in order to present and win an argument? (31:35-37).

41:12-17 God reminded Job of Leviathan's magnificent physical features that made him too formidable to face by any one person.

41:18-21 God's portrayal of Leviathan's foaming emergence from water is compared to that of a fire-breathing dragon. Similar creatures are described in Ugaritic mythology depicting Baal's defeat of Yam, the sea god.

41:22-25 Leviathan's **strength** and seemingly impregnable body were exceeded only by his inner courage and fearlessness. Leviathan's power and self-assurance made him a fitting symbol of Satan, the fearsome and fallen being whose raging is fully and finally quelled by God in the end times (Rv 20:10).

41:26-29 No human weapon had any **effect** on Leviathan. His fearlessness in the face of danger is compared to laughing.

41:30-31 A **threshing sledge** consisted of two boards whose

undersides were embedded with sharp stones for crushing grain, which would leave marks in the mud. When Leviathan dove into the water, he made it foam like ingredients boiled by the perfumer.

41:33-34 Fearless Leviathan was unequaled in power. If neither man nor beast dared to oppose God's foremost creature, certainly no one could challenge the Lord, its Creator (vv. 10-11).

42:1-2 Job confessed God's rightful sovereignty over all matters, including his situation. He had questioned God's actions previously (16:12-14). God's speeches about His ordering of the world caused Job's capitulation.

42:3 Job had questioned the equity and justice of God's dealings (7:20; 21:7-34). God's wise handling of the physical and natural worlds convinced him that, though he may have committed no overt sin, he had dabbled in questions beyond his understanding and experience.

42:4-5 Job now understood something of God's justice and

5 I had heard rumors about You,
  but now my eyes*a* have seen You.
6 Therefore I take back my words
  and repent in dust and ashes.^A

7After the LORD had finished speaking^B to Job, He said to Eliphaz the Temanite: "I am angry with you and your two friends, for you have not spoken the truth about Me, as My servant Job has. 8Now take seven bulls and seven rams, go to My servant Job, and offer a burnt offering for yourselves. Then My servant Job will pray for you.*b* I will surely accept his prayer and not deal with you as your folly deserves. For you have not spoken the truth about Me, as My servant Job has." 9Then Eliphaz the Temanite, Bildad the Shuhite, and Zophar the Naamathite went and did as the LORD had told them, and the LORD accepted Job's prayer.

God Restores Job

10After Job had prayed for his friends, the

a 42:5 Jb 19:27;
Ps 123:1-2;
141:8
b 42:8 Gn 20:17;
Nm 23:1; 1Jn
5:16
c 42:10 Ps 14:7;
Is 40:2; Mt 5:44
d 42:11 Jb 2:11;
19:13
e Gn 33:19; Jos
24:32
f Gn 24:22; 35:4;
Hs 2:13
g 42:14 Ps 45:8;
Sg 2:14; Jr 4:30
h 42:17 Gn 25:8;
35:29; 1Ch
29:28

LORD restored his prosperity and doubled his previous possessions.*c* 11All his brothers, sisters, and former acquaintances*d* came to his house and dined with him in his house. They sympathized with him and comforted him concerning all the adversity the LORD had brought on him. Each one gave him a *qesitah*^C,e and a gold earring.*f*

12So the LORD blessed the last part of Job's life more than the first. He owned 14,000 sheep, 6,000 camels, 1,000 yoke of oxen, and 1,000 female donkeys. 13He also had seven sons and three daughters. 14He named his first daughter Jemimah, his second Keziah, and his third Keren-happuch.*g* 15No women as beautiful as Job's daughters could be found in all the land, and their father granted them an inheritance with their brothers.

16Job lived 140 years after this and saw his children and their children to the fourth generation. 17Then Job died, old and full of days.*h*

---

^A 42:6 LXX reads *I despise myself and melt; I consider myself dust and ashes*   ^B 42:7 Lit *speaking these words*   ^C 42:11 The value of the currency is unknown.

---

wise dealings with the strongest of creatures. Although Job had previously considered himself to be upright, he confessed that he had been influenced by traditional but errant understandings (15:17-19; 16:2). By saying he now saw God, he meant that he had experienced God's presence and understood Him better.

42:6 Job was humbled that the Lord of the universe had spoken to him. This went beyond his fondest wish for reestablished fellowship (9:32-35; 19:26-27; 23:3-5; 29:2-6). With genuine contrition he abandoned self in full dependence on God.

42:7 God rebuked **Eliphaz** and his **friends** for their treatment of Job. While defending God they had attributed false reasons for Job's condition. They did not consider it possible that his suffering was not directly due to sin. They also misrepresented God as an insensitive enforcer of justice.

42:8-9 The friends had left Job. They must return to him and offer large sacrifices for their transgression so Job could intercede in prayer for them. Job's health apparently had been restored by now. Rather than bearing enmity against his friends, Job graciously prayed for them.

42:10 Job's restoration was complete. Because he was now pure in his attitude toward God and had demonstrated spiritual maturity toward his friends, the Lord accepted him into full fellowship. The **doubled** possessions (v. 12) reflect God's full acceptance of Job as His own (Dt 21:17; 2Kg 2:9). Not only had Job found God to be sufficient for his every need, but Satan had been proved wrong. He had remained blameless throughout his long ordeal (Jb 27:4-6; 28:28). Although

he had questioned God's dealings with him (10:18-21; 27:2) and had even accused the Lord of attacking him (13:20-27; 16:12-14; 23:2), he did not curse God as Satan had predicted he would (1:11; 2:5) or as his wife had urged him to do (2:9). In this at least, Job proved to be exemplary (Jms 5:11). By remembering Job's suffering and its outcome, believers can be encouraged to rejoice in times of their trial and testing (Jms 1:2-4; 1Pt 1:6-7). Rather than complaining or doubting God, they can humbly trust in God and His sufficiency so that Satan will not be given any advantage over them (1Pt 5:6-9).

42:11 Job's family and friends believed that **the LORD** controls and causes all events. They offered him the comfort they had formerly withheld (12:4; 16:20; 19:14). The (Hb) *qesitah* was a unit of silver used in the times covered in some of the earliest biblical accounts (Gn 33:19; Jos 24:32).

42:12-15 The fact that the number of Job's children was not doubled may indicate that at least the souls of his deceased children lived on after death. In a sense, then, his children now numbered twice what they were. Job's fairness toward everyone (29:12-17,21-25) is seen in his concern that his **daughters** would share the **inheritance** with their brothers.

42:16-17 Job's **140 years** may indicate that he was 70 at the time of his testing and may reflect the number of added years that he lived. His epitaph is the same accorded other godly men (Gn 25:8; 1Ch 29:28; 2Ch 24:15). The Septuagint (LXX) adds that Job "will rise again with the ones whom the Lord raises up."

Psalms

Introduction

The word for psalms in Hebrew is *Tehilîm*, which means "praise." The English title is derived from the Greek translation (LXX) *Psalmoi*, which means "songs of praise." Praise directed to Yahweh, the God of Israel, is certainly the primary emphasis in the psalms. Some have referred to the Psalms as Israel's hymnbook, which is partially true but overall is insufficient to account for all that is in the Psalms. More than one-third of the collection is made up of prayers to God. Therefore, it contains both hymns and prayers that were used in the context of Israel's worship.

Psalm 1, the gateway to this inspired collection, presents what has come to be called "the two ways." The process of winnowing chaff from grain is an apt image of the two ways and their consequences. The rest of the psalms elaborate on this theme in a variety of ways.

Circumstances of Writing

Author: Since the book is a collection of many different psalms written over a long time, there is not just one author for this collection. By far the most common designation in the titles is "Davidic," which may refer to David as the author of those psalms. David's role as a musician in Saul's court (1Sm 16:14-23) as well as his many experiences as a shepherd, a soldier, and a king make him a likely candidate for writing many of these psalms.

The problem is that the mention of his name in the titles consists of an ambiguous Hebrew construction. It is nothing more than a preposition attached to David's name. The preposition could be translated "written by," "belonging to," "for," or "about." This does nothing more than relate the psalms bearing that title to David in some way but not necessarily naming him as its author. The translation "Davidic" accurately conveys this same ambiguity.

Other titles include the designations of Solomon (Pss 72; 172), Asaph (Pss 50; 70–83), the sons of Korah (Pss 42; 44–49), Ethan (Ps 89), Heman son of Korah (Ps 88), and Moses (Ps 90). All of these use the same Hebrew preposition as appears with David's name and therefore have the same ambiguity about authorship. In the case of Asaph, although he was one of David's chief musicians (1Ch 6:39), the name itself became associated with a group of musicians bearing the same name (Ezr 2:40-41; see note at Ps 50 title). This might explain why an apparently postexilic psalm (Ps 74) includes the title "of Asaph."

Background: The book of Psalms consists of many different hymns and prayers composed by individuals but used by the community. If one were to take the names in the titles as authors, the date of composition ranges from the time of Moses (fifteenth century B.C.) to a time following the exile (sixth century B.C. or later). Some of the titles do contain historical information that might indicate the setting of the composition, although even this (like the authorship) is ambiguous. They might not refer to the date of composition but to the setting of its contents, being composed some time after the events had taken place. This is a more likely scenario since

---

3000 B.C.

1600 B.C.

1450 B.C.

Abraham 2166–1991

Isaac 2066–1886

Hymn to the Creator of the Heavens and the Earth, Ebla 3000–2000

Lament for Ur, Sumerian 2000–1500

Moses 1526–1406

Psalm 90, a prayer of Moses the man of God

Hymn to Ishtar, Sumero–Akkadian 1600

Hymns to Amun, Egypt 1550–1350

Book of the Dead, Egyptian texts appear on mummy wrappings. 1500

Rig Veda, a collection of over 1,000 hymns in Sanskrit, the oldest known major work in an Indo–European language 1500

The Phoenicians develop a 22–letter alphabet that consisted of consonants only. It was read from right to left and became an important step in the development of the modern Western alphabet. **1600**

Hymn of Amenhotep II, Egypt 1450–1425

Ba'al and Anat, Ugarit 1400

Events in Judges 1380?–1060?

"Hymn to the Sun," Akhenaten 1375–1358

some of these psalms describe life-threatening situations, where composing a psalm in the heat of the moment would not have been a top priority. In many cases, these psalms include thanksgiving sections as well, showing that they were written after God had answered the prayers.

Message and Purpose

There are myriad messages scattered through the 150 psalms, but overall, this record of the responses of God's people in worship and prayer serves the purpose of teaching us how to relate to God in various circumstances of life. The psalms also demonstrate God's sovereignty and goodness for His people in order to instill confidence in those who trust in Him.

Contribution to the Bible

The relationship between God's activities in the lives of His people and their responses to them is the most significant contribution of this book. God never spoke directly in any of the psalms, as He often did in the narratives and prophets. Therefore, they are written from the human perspective as authors work their way through various life situations. The struggle to understand how God's attributes, particularly His sovereignty and goodness, relate to life experiences is a major theme in the collection. These words are from people who had not lost their faith in God, although they might have been tempted to at times (Ps 73). They wrestled with how God was dealing with them personally and as a community.

Structure

The book of Psalms is, from first to last, a book of poetry. Hebrew poetry lacks rhyme and regular meter, but uses parallelism wherein two (or three) lines are balanced and complete a thought. Some parallelism is synonymous, where the second line echoes the first. Antithetic parallelism uses a contrast between the two segments, and in synthetic parallelism the second segment completes the idea in the first segment.

The psalms can be divided into classes. There are hymns (145–150) and songs of thanksgiving (30–32). Psalms

1000 B.C.	800 B.C.	600 B.C.
Saul is anointed king. 1050	Babylonian music makes use of five-tone and seven-tone scales. 800-700	Babylonians invade the Southern Kingdom on three occasions. Each time Judeans are taken to Babylon as exiles. 605, 597, 586
David becomes king over all Israel. 1003	Fall of Damascus to Tiglath-pileser of Assyria 732	Cyrus's decree allows return of Jews from exile. 538
73 Psalms of David, 14 of which are tied to events in David's life	Fall of Samaria to the Assyrians 722	Second temple is dedicated. 516
Solomon becomes king. 970	Assyrians invade Judah but fail to capture Jerusalem. 701	Jerusalem's walls are rebuilt. 445
Proverbs 970		
Song of Songs 970?	Greek poet Hesiod writes the *Theogony*, the oldest surviving account of the origin of the Greek gods. 700	Latest of the psalms are composed, including Psalm 137. These reflect Israel's exile and restoration. 400
Ecclesiastes 935?		
Israel divides into Northern and Southern Kingdoms. 931		

of lament (38–39) are prayers or cries to God on the occasion of distressful situations. Royal psalms (2; 110) are concerned with the earthly king of Israel. Enthronement psalms (96; 98) celebrate the kingship of Yahweh. Penitential psalms (32; 38; 51) express contrition and repentance, and wisdom or didactic psalms (19; 119) tend to be proverbial.

Outline

The book of Psalms is unlike most other biblical books since it contains many writings collected and compiled over a period of time and finally organized into its present form. For this reason, it is not possible to outline the book in the standard way. However, there is clearly a structure to the collection. The book is divided into five parts, also known as books. According to Jewish tradition, this fivefold division was based on the arrangement of the Torah (or Pentateuch), the first five books of the Bible. The book divisions are: Book 1 (Pss 1–41), Book 2 (Pss 42–72), Book 3 (Pss 73–89), Book 4 (Pss 90–106), and Book 5 (Pss 107–150).

Another part of the structure of the Psalms is that they are generally grouped together by their titles, such as the Asaph psalms and those of the sons of Korah. Following the close of each of the first of four books is a doxology or statement identifying the end of one book and the beginning of another. The psalms containing these statements are known as "seam" psalms because they show the "piecing together" of these psalms to form the collection as it now stands.

BOOK I
(Psalms 1–41)

Psalm 1
The Two Ways

1 How happy is the man
who does not follow[A] the advice
   of the wicked
or take[B] the path of sinners
or join a group[C] of mockers![a]
2 Instead, his delight is in the Lord's
   instruction,
and he meditates on it day and night.[b]
3 He is like a tree planted beside streams
   of water[D]
that bears its fruit in season[E,c]
and whose leaf does not wither.[d]
Whatever he does prospers.[e]

4 The wicked are not like this;
instead, they are like chaff
   that the wind blows away.[f]
5 Therefore the wicked will not survive[B]
   the judgment,[g]
and sinners will not be
   in the community of the righteous.

6 For the Lord watches over the way
   of the righteous,[h]
but the way of the wicked leads to ruin.[i]

Psalm 2
Coronation of the Son

1 Why[j] do the nations rebel[F,j]
and the peoples plot in vain?[k]
2 The kings of the earth take
   their stand,[l]
and the rulers conspire together

Cross references

*a*1:1 Ps 26:4-5;
Pr 4:14-15
*b*1:2 Jos 1:8; Ps
40:8; 119:14-16
*c*1:3 Rv 22:2
*d*Ps 92:12-14;
Jr 17:8
*e*Dt 5:33
*f*1:4 Jb 21:18; Ps
35:5; Hs 13:3
*g*1:5 Ps 5:5;
9:16; 76:7; Jr
25:31
*h*1:6 Jb 34:21;
Ps 37:18; Nah
1:7; Jn 10:14;
2Tm 2:19
*i*Pr 21:12; Jn
3:16
*j*2:1-2 Ac
4:25-26
*k*2:1 Is 17:12-13
*l*Ps 83:2-3
*m*2:2 Jr 49:19;
50:44

A1:1 Lit *not walk in*   **B**1:1,5 Lit *stand in*   **C**1:1 Or *or sit in the seat*   **D**1:3 Or *beside irrigation canals*   **E**1:3 Lit *in its season*
F2:1 Or *conspire*, or *rage*

1:1 **Happy** expresses the sense of joy and satisfaction in one's state or circumstances. It often is the result of blessing that comes from trust in and obedience to Yahweh (34:8; 40:4; 84:5; 89:15). Though related to God's blessing, it should be distinguished from the Hebrew word that is usually translated "blessed." The three descriptions that follow are expressed in the negative, showing what is *not* characteristic of this **man**. From the structure, it is better to understand these behaviors as parallel rather than progressing from lesser to greater sins.

1:2 The Hebrew word *torah* is sometimes translated as "law," but it is better understood as "teaching" or **instruction**. It is the revelation of God's will for His people rather than a body of legislative material or a collection of judicial decisions, both of which are notions often associated with the English word "law." Yahweh's instruction is not a burden (Dt 30:11; 1Jn 5:3) but a **delight** for those who trust in Him. "Meditating" (from Hb root *hgh*; Jos 1:8) has a literal meaning of mumbling to oneself, an activity closely related to concentrating on something in order to understand it.

1:3 The image of the righteous as flourishing trees is a common metaphor (92:12-14; Jr 17:8). It is also attested in other ancient Near Eastern material, most notably the Egyptian wisdom text, "The Instruction of Amen-em-ope" (*ANET*, 421f.). Bearing **fruit** is an extension of the metaphor and refers to the products of the spiritual life in the individual (Pr 12:12; Jn 15:5; Col 1:10).

1:4 The contrast here focuses on the destiny of the two ways rather than on their behavior, which is developed in verses 1-3. **Chaff**, the useless product of threshing, is a contrast to the fruit in the previous verse. **The wicked** are to be carried away by the **wind** (see note at 35:5; cp. Hs 13:3), being separated from what is useful and valuable.

1:5 **Survive the judgment** is literally "rise up in the judgment." In this context, rising up has the idea of being able to remain (or survive) during the time of judgment. Some have argued that this only refers to the final judgment of God because it is definite (the judgment). However, it seems better to understand this as God's judgment whether in this life or in the future. Since **sinners** are not among **the righteous**, they are judged and removed from the scene.

1:6 The final summary shows what is anticipated for those who follow the two ways: God's protection for **the righteous** and disaster (or **ruin**) for **the wicked**.

2:1 The question introduced by **why** is rhetorical and expresses surprise at the presumption of **the nations** in light of the reality of God's reign through His co-regent (vv. 6-9). Elsewhere, nations that **rebel** against God's authority are compared to the raging sea (Is 17:12-13). The word **plot** is the same Hebrew word as "meditates" in 1:2, only in this case it is used negatively to describe contemplation of plans to be free of God's dominion.

2:2 To **take** a **stand** is often used in military contexts to describe preparation for battle (1Sm 17:16; Jr 46:4). The **kings** and **rulers** are not just two specific groups but they represent all governing authorities and dignitaries on **the earth** (see Jdg 5:3; Hab 1:10). **Anointed** is translated into Greek

'ashrey

Hebrew Pronunciation	[ash RAY]
HCSB Translation	happy, blessed
Uses in Psalms	26
Uses in the OT	44
Focus Passage	Psalm 1:1

Ashrey, an interjection especially frequent in Psalms, means *happy* (Ps 1:1) and implies *blessed* twice (Ec 10:17; Dn 12:12). It is similar to *baruk* ("blessed") but probably more secular. *Ashrey* is never used of or by God. Though it announces a *happy* condition (2Ch 9:7), it often requires that people do things like waiting (Dn 12:12), obeying divine decrees (Ps 119:2), or showing kindness (Pr 14:21). *Ashrey* may have produced the verb *ashar* (10x), which would mean to "say *ashrey*" to someone. *Ashar* in intensive forms signifies *consider* or *declare fortunate* (Sg 6:9; Mal 3:12), and *call blessed* (Ps 72:17). It can be *bless* (Jb 29:11). The passive is *be blessed* (Ps 41:2; the passive participle indicates *happy* (Pr 3:18). Scholars disagree whether it is the same verb as the *ashar* meaning "proceed" (7x: Pr 4:14). The noun *osher* (Gn 30:13) and interjection *esher* (Pr 29:18) are translated as *happy*.

against the LORD
and His Anointed One:[A,a]
3 "Let us tear off their chains
and free ourselves
from their restraints."[B,b]

4 The One enthroned[C] in heaven laughs;
the Lord ridicules them.[c]
5 Then He speaks to them in His anger
and terrifies them in His wrath:[d]
6 "I have consecrated My King[D]
on *Zion, My holy mountain."[e]

7 I will declare the LORD's decree:
He said to Me, "You are My Son;[E]
today I have become Your[F] Father.[f]
8 Ask of Me,
and I will make the nations
Your[F] inheritance
and the ends of the earth
Your[F] possession.[g]
9 You will break[G] them with a rod of iron;
You[H] will shatter them like pottery."[i,h]

a2:2 1Sm 2:10;
12:3,5; 2Sm
22:51; Ps 18:50;
20:6; 28:8
b2:3 Is 58:6; Jr
5:5; Nah 1:13
c2:4 Ps 37:13;
59:8
d2:5 Ps 90:7
e2:6 Ps 48:2; Is
24:23
f2:7 Mt 3:17; Lk
3:22; Ac 13:33;
Heb 1:5; 5:5
g2:8 Jos 23:4;
Ps 111:6
h2:8-9 Ps 89:23;
Rv 2:26-27; 12:5;
19:15
i2:11 Heb 12:28
j2:12 Jn 3:18
k2Th 1:7-8
l2 Ps 5:11; 34:8,22
m3:title 2Sm
15:13-17
n3:1 2Sm 15:12;
Ps 69:4

10 So now, kings, be wise;
receive instruction, you judges
of the earth.
11 Serve the LORD with reverential awe
and rejoice with trembling.[i]
12 Pay homage to[J] the Son or He[K]
will be angry
and you will perish
in your rebellion,[L,j]
for His[M] anger may ignite
at any moment.[k]
All those who take refuge in Him[N]
are happy.[l]

Psalm 3
Confidence in Troubled Times

A psalm of David when he fled
from his son Absalom.[m]

1 LORD, how my foes increase!
There are many who attack me.[n]

---

as *christos*, and it refers to God's choice and establishment of His King. In this context, the anointed One is the Davidic king who is ultimately, in the progress of divine revelation, Jesus Christ (Eph 1:20-22).

2:3 The desire of these rulers for autonomy is pictured as tearing off **their chains** and freeing themselves from **restraints**. For those who rebel against God, His dominion is seen as nothing more than slavery. Ironically, these same terms are used to describe what God did for His people in freeing them from the oppression of the wicked (107:14; 129:4).

2:4 The **One enthroned in heaven** is parallel to **the Lord** (Hb *'adonai*, emphasizing God's sovereignty), indicating that God's place from which He reigns is heaven (11:4; 103:19). The combination of **laughs** and **ridicules** function together as one thought to show that God's response to the rebellion of the nations is to mock them, knowing that their attempts are futile and that their destiny is certain (37:13; 59:8).

2:5 Although God is laughing in derision in the previous verse, this attitude leads to action, which in this case is speaking to them in **anger**.

2:6 The opening phrase **I have consecrated** uses a separate first-person pronoun, which would otherwise be unnecessary. This adds emphasis to the subject, sometimes represented as "I Myself." The point is that God's **King** is established by God Himself, so there is no ambiguity about the legitimacy of His reign.

2:7 To validate the point of legitimacy further, there is a **decree** from Yahweh. This term is used to indicate royal protocol in order to validate the right to rule. This was a particular concern in the ancient world where there was often a conflict following newly established kings. The idea of the Davidic ruler being identified as God's **Son** was made clear in the covenant that God made with David (89:26-27; 2Sm 7:14).

2:8 The right of sonship includes the right to **inheritance**

and **possession** of what belongs to one's father. In this case, it is not limited but extends to **the ends of the earth**, an expression meaning the whole world and everything in it. This includes **the nations**, the same word used in verse 1 to identify those who were rebelling against God.

2:9 Some ancient manuscripts use "shepherd" instead of **break**, but the parallel **shatter** shows that "break" is better. Smashing nations **like pottery** represents the effortless way in which something is annihilated (Is 30:14; Jr 19:11). Such imagery appears in ancient Egyptian and Assyrian texts to indicate subjugation of one's enemies.

2:10-11 The word of warning for the rebellious nations is to **be wise** and **receive instruction**. This bears a remarkable resemblance to OT Wisdom literature (Pr 8:32-33). The nations are given an opportunity to change their ways and submit to God's King. Their submission should include **reverential awe** and **trembling**, showing the connection between fearing Yahweh and the acquisition of wisdom (Pr 9:10).

2:12 The word **Son** here is a different word than the one used in verse 7. It is an Aramaic word, causing some scholars to question its authenticity because (1) it seems out of place, and (2) Aramaic did not become the main language of the region until the Neo-Babylonian Empire under Nebuchadnezzar. Therefore, some have proposed that it should be changed to "His feet," adding a few Hebrew letters to the existing form. However, there is no good reason to reject this form as original since Aramaic, while not the main language of the region until later, had been in existence since Abraham's time and was a more commonly used Semitic language than Hebrew among other nations. To **pay homage** (see note at Hs 13:2) is to express obedience (Gn 27:26). The alternative is to **perish** as a result of God's **anger** that could **ignite at any moment**. This psalm ends where Psalm 1 began—with the word **happy**. The contrast is that those who follow Yahweh see His dominion as a place of **refuge** rather than slavery (v. 3).

2 Many say about me,
"There is no help for him in God."[a]
                              •Selah

3 But You, LORD, are a shield around me,[b]
  my glory,[c] and the One who lifts up
  my head.[d]

4 I cry aloud to the LORD,
  and He answers me
    from His holy mountain.[e]   Selah

5 I lie down and sleep;
  I wake again because the LORD
    sustains me.[f]

6 I am not afraid of the thousands
    of people
  who have taken their stand against me
    on every side.[g]

7 Rise up, LORD![h]
  Save me, my God!
  You strike all my enemies
    on the cheek;[i]

8 You break the teeth of the wicked.[j]

8 Salvation belongs to the LORD;[k]
  may Your blessing be on Your people.[l]
                              Selah

Psalm 4
A Night Prayer

For the choir director:
with stringed instruments.[m]
A Davidic psalm.

1 Answer me when I call,
  God, who vindicates me.[A,n]
  You freed me from affliction;[o]
  be gracious to me and hear my prayer.

2 How long, exalted men, will my honor
    be insulted?[p]
  How long will you love
    what is worthless[q]
  and pursue a lie?   •Selah

Marginal cross-references:

a3:2 Ps 22:7-8; 71:11
b3:3 Gn 15:1; Dt 33:29; Ps 5:12; 18:2; 28:7; 119:114
c Ps 62:7
d Ps 110:7
e3:4 Ps 2:6; 43:3; 48:1
f3:5 Lv 26:6; Ps 4:8; Pr 3:24
g3:6 Ps 23:4; 27:3; 118:10-13
h3:7 Ps 7:6
i Jb 16:10; Mc 5:1
j Ps 58:6
k3:8 Jnh 2:9; Rv 7:10; 19:1
l Dt 26:15
m4:title Ps 6 title; Is 38:20; Hab 3:19
n4:1 Ps 7:8; 26:1; 35:24
o Ps 25:17; 107:6,13
p4:2 Ps 69:7-10,19-20
q Ps 12:2

A4:1 Or God of my righteousness

Ps 3 title This is one of 14 psalms (3; 7; 18; 30; 34; 51; 52; 54; 56; 57; 59; 60; 63; 142) that are linked directly, by virtue of their titles, with specific events in the life of David. Though the titles reference specific events in David's life—in this case the time when **he fled from his son Absalom**—the actual content of these psalms is generalized. For this reason God's people who face the sort of life circumstances discussed in these psalms can identify with the author's words and be blessed. The episode of Absalom's rebellion and David's escape from him is recorded in 2 Samuel 15–18. David was grieved over the actions of his son (2Sm 18:33), but in this psalm he showed his dependence on Yahweh as his deliverer from those who attacked him.

3:1-2 In these verses the Hebrew root *rbb* shows up three times: **increase** (*rabbu*) in verse 1 and **many** (*rabbim*) appearing twice, once in each verse. This is the same root used in God's command to mankind to "multiply" on the earth (Gn 1:28) and in God's promise to Abraham that He would "multiply" his descendants (Gn 17:2). The problem in this psalm is that the situation is reversed, and it is the enemies of God and of His servant who are multiplying. These enemies are the aggressors by actively attacking the psalmist and declaring that God will not rescue him. In lament psalms, attacks on the psalmist and attacks against God are closely linked and are often used as an appeal for God to act because of His own reputation.

3:3 The image of God as a **shield** is common, especially in the Psalms (18:30; 115:9; 144:2). It represents protection during a time of attack. A more unusual description is identifying God as one's **glory**. The Hebrew word *kavod* (lit "heavy") is often used of a person's reputation or significance, sometimes being translated as "honor." Its use here seems to indicate that the psalmist found his own significance and honor linked to his relationship with Yahweh rather than in his own strength.

3:4 The word **answers** expresses the idea of completed action in the Hebrew (sometimes translated in the past tense: "answered"), but it seems to be used here in the sense of confidence that God always answers. The **holy mountain** is Zion, which is the place where God dwelt among His people (Jl 3:17).

3:5-6 To **lie down** and to **sleep** are poetic and tangible ways to describe a state of security. Only a person who feels secure will be able to sleep undisturbed by troubling thoughts. Psalm 4:8 uses the same combination of verbs and adds the phrase "in peace." The psalmist was confident that he would **wake again** because it is Yahweh Himself who sustained (i.e., supported or helped) him. The psalmist's security was unrelated to his circumstances even though he was surrounded by enemies. Confidence in God's protection does not depend on one's circumstances.

3:7-8 Although the fact that the psalmist was calling out to the Lord is stated in verse 4, it is verse 7 that identifies the content of his plea. The request is rather brief and made up of two imperatives: **rise up** and **save**. The first of these describes a change of state from rest to action. The action that brings salvation is expressed in vivid terms. Verse 8 contains a timeless theological truth—only Yahweh can be trusted to save His people.

Ps 4 title This is the first psalm in the collection to have musical instructions to the **choir director**. While there is no description of the specific setting of the psalm, its theme and content are similar to Psalm 3.

4:1 God, who vindicates me (lit "God of my righteousness/ justice") is an appeal to God's justice specifically as it relates to the psalmist's just cause. **Affliction** pictures the idea of being hemmed in or trapped by enemies. In response, God **freed me** (lit "made a broad place for me"). The verb expresses completed action and probably indicates the confidence of the psalmist that God would rescue him.

4:2 How long is an expression that shows concern about the duration of one's condition and is used in similar contexts in other psalms (79:5; 89:46). The enemies are called **exalted men**. In Hebrew this is literally "sons of a man" and refers to people of high social status or influence (62:9) and sometimes contrasted with the poor (49:2). The same expression is found in Egyptian and Babylonian texts to describe prominent and respected people who are to be distinguished from the poor.

3 Know that the Lord has set apart
the faithful for Himself;
the Lord will hear when I call to Him.
4 Be angry[A] and do not sin;[a]
on your bed, reflect in your heart
and be still.[b]   *Selah*
5 Offer sacrifices in righteousness[B,c]
and trust in the Lord.[d]

6 Many are saying, "Who can show us
anything good?"
Look on us with favor, Lord.[e]

7 You have put more joy in my heart
than they have when their grain
and new wine abound.[f]
8 I will both lie down and sleep in peace,[g]
for You alone, Lord, make me live
in safety.[h]

Psalm 5
The Refuge of the Righteous

For the choir director: with the flutes.
A Davidic psalm.

1 Listen to my words, Lord;
consider my sighing.[i]

2 Pay attention to the sound
of my cry,[j]
my King and my God,[k]
for I pray to You.

3 At daybreak,[l] Lord, You hear
my voice;
at daybreak I plead my case to You[m]
and watch expectantly.

4 For You are not a God who delights
in wickedness;
evil cannot dwell with You.[n]
5 The boastful cannot stand
in Your presence;[o]
You hate all evildoers.[p]
6 You destroy those who tell lies;[q]
the Lord abhors a man of bloodshed
and treachery.[r]

7 But I enter Your house
by the abundance
of Your faithful love;[s]
I bow down toward
Your holy temple
in reverential awe of You.[t]
8 Lord, lead me
in Your righteousness[u]

a4:4 Eph 4:26
bPs 77:6; 119:55
c4:5 Dt 33:19; Ps 51:19
dPs 37:3,5; 62:8
e4:6 Ps 80:3
f4:7 Is 9:3
g4:8 Ps 3:5
hLv 25:18; Dt 12:10; Jr 32:37; Ezk 34:25
i5:1 Ps 38:9
j5:2 Ps 28:2
kPs 84:3
l5:3 Ps 88:13
mJb 13:18; 23:4; Ps 50:21
n5:4 Ps 92:15
o5:5 Ps 1:5; 73:3; 75:4
pJb 8:20; Ps 11:5; 45:7
q5:6 Rv 21:8
rPs 55:23
s5:7 Ps 69:13; 86:5,15; 106:45; Is 63:7
tPs 138:2
u5:8 Ps 27:11

A4:4 Or *Tremble*   B4:5 Or *Offer right sacrifices*; lit *Sacrifice sacrifices of righteousness*

4:3 Set apart is not the normal expression for "make holy" (Hb *qadash*) but is a word that means "distinguish" or "separate" (Hb *palah*). The Lord makes a clear distinction between the **faithful** (those loyal to Him) and the "exalted men" in how He relates to each of them (cp. Ex 11:7). Therefore, the psalmist could have confidence that **the Lord** would **hear** when he called out to Him.

4:4 The Hebrew word translated **be angry** means to "shake" or "tremble" and is sometimes used literally for physical shaking (18:7; 77:18). When used of people it can mean trembling with fear (Ex 15:14; Dt 2:25), quarreling (Gn 45:24), or a fit of rage (2Kg 19:27-28). It can also refer to provoking God to anger (Jb 12:6). The basic sense of the term when it is not used literally seems to be agitation. The LXX translates it as "be angry" (from Gk *orgizo*), which is quoted by Paul in Eph 4:26. Though trembling with fear certainly works in the context of this psalm, the idea of anger also works if one assumes that this is a challenge to the angry enemies not to sin. In other words, their anger should not lead to attacks against God's people.

4:5 A further challenge to the enemies is to **offer sacrifices in righteousness**, which means those that are in keeping with God's righteousness that He has prescribed. The final challenge is for these enemies to turn from their ways by trusting in **the Lord**.

4:6 The quotation here seems to be coming from those who were restless and pessimistic about their own situation and fate. This is an example of those who were not trusting Yahweh within the community of God's people. The prayer for these people is that God would **look . . . with favor** on the entire community. The Hebrew here is "lift up on us the light of Your face" and is reminiscent of the Aaronic blessing in Nm 6:24-26.

4:7-8 The psalmist's own experience is in contrast to the pessimists' view in verse 6. He has both an abundance of **joy** and a sense of security because of his relationship with Yahweh. The same description of lying down and sleeping occurs in 3:5.

Ps 5 title Some interpreters have used this psalm and its designation as **a Davidic psalm** to argue that this phrase cannot mean "composed by David" since verse 7 seems to refer to the temple (see note at vv. 6-7).

5:1-2 The word **sighing** (Hb *hgg*) is perhaps related to the word meditate (Hb *hgh*; see note at 1:2). Some translate it as "consider my meditation," but since the basic meaning of the word is "to murmur," it seems better in this context to understand it as a low murmuring sound (similar to a sigh) made in a time of intense sorrow. **God** is also addressed as **King** (44:4; 68:24; 74:12; 84:3), indicating confidence in His dominion and His power to answer this prayer.

5:3 Daybreak is repeated and indicates the time of the prayer, which was early in the morning (88:13). **Plead my case** is literally "I prepare (or set in order)." While it could mean preparing a sacrifice, there is no other indication that a sacrifice was being offered. Instead, it was more likely preparing words (Jb 32:14) in a request for vindication.

5:4-5 The term **delights** is the same word as in 1:2, but here it is negated. Not only does God have no desire for **wickedness**, it cannot even exist in His presence. The arrogant, those who practice **evil**, liars, and the violent (v. 6) are all included in the explanation of those who **cannot stand** in God's **presence**. The word "stand" is the same term as in 2:2 describing those who "take their stand" against God. There is no contest between these wicked people and God; they cannot get anywhere near the Lord to attack Him.

5:6-7 The combination of **house** and **temple** has led many to assume that this psalm must have been written by some-

because of my adversaries;[A]
make Your way straight
     before me.[a]

9 For there is nothing reliable
      in what they say;[B,b]
   destruction is within them;
   their throat is an open grave;
   they flatter with their tongues.[c]
10 Punish them, God;
   let them fall
      by their own schemes.[d]
   Drive them out[e] because of
      their many crimes,
   for they rebel against You.[f]

11 But let all who take refuge
      in You rejoice;[g]
   let them shout
      for joy forever.
   May You shelter them,[h]
   and may those who love Your name
      boast about You.[i]
12 For You, LORD, bless
      the righteous one;
   You surround him with favor
      like a shield.[j]

a 5:8 Pr 4:11
b 5:9 Ps 52:2
c Ps 12:3; Pr 26:28; Rm 3:13
d 5:10 Ps 9:16; 35:8; 141:10
e Mt 13:41-42
f Pr 17:11
g 5:11 Ps 2:12; 64:10
h Ps 31:20; 61:4
i Ps 9:2
j 5:12 Gn 15:1; Dt 33:29; Ps 3:3; 18:2; 28:7; 119:114
k 6:title 1Ch 15:21; Ps 12 title
l 6:1 Ps 38:1; Jr 10:24
m 6:2 Ps 142:6
n Ps 41:4; Jr 17:14
o Jb 4:14
p 6:3 Jb 9:28; Jn 12:27
q Nm 14:27; Ps 13:1-2; 35:17; 79:5; 80:4
r 6:4 Ps 31:16; 109:26
s 6:4-5 Ps 30:9; 88:10-12; 115:17; Ec 9:10; Is 38:18
t 6:6 Ps 69:3; 119:28
u Ps 42:3; 102:9
v 6:7 Jb 17:7; Ps 31:9; 88:9

Psalm 6
A Prayer for Mercy

For the choir director:
with stringed instruments,
according to *Sheminith*.[k] A Davidic psalm.

1 LORD, do not rebuke me in Your anger;
   do not discipline me in Your wrath.[l]
2 Be gracious to me, LORD,
      for I am weak;[C,m]
   heal me,[n] LORD, for my bones
      are shaking;[o]
3 my whole being is shaken with terror.[p]
   And You, LORD—how long?[q]

4 Turn, LORD! Rescue me;
   save me because of Your faithful love.[r]
5 For there is no remembrance of You
      in death;
   who can thank You in *Sheol*?[s]

6 I am weary from my groaning;[t]
   with my tears I dampen my pillow[D]
   and drench my bed every night.[u]
7 My eyes are swollen from grief;[v]
   they[E] grow old because of all
      my enemies.

one other than David since Solomon's temple was built after David's time. However, the Hebrew word for "temple" is not only used for Solomon's temple, but also for the temporary temple at Shiloh (translated "tabernacle" in 1Sm 1:9; 3:3), which existed in David's time. God's house is the place where God dwelt among His people (Ps 26:8).

5:8 The connection between the plea for God's guidance and the **adversaries** is that the situation (i.e., attacks by enemies) calls for not only protection and rescue but also guidance in the midst of the crisis. It is also an affirmation of the intent to remain loyal to Yahweh even during the time of danger.

5:9-10 Throat and **tongues** are metaphors for speech. Since there is **nothing reliable in what they say**, all of the enemies' speech is deadly, pictured here as **an open grave**. A similar use of this word picture appears in Jr 5:16 where "their quiver is like an open grave," meaning their weapons bring death. Since the enemies here were intent on death and destruction, the psalmist asked that God let **their own schemes** bring about their destruction (64:8; 2Sm 15:31).

5:11-12 The emphasis in these verses is on God's protection of those who remain faithful to Him. The terms **take refuge in ... shelter ... surround**, and **shield** convey this thought. In this context, all these words evoke military ideas: Those who trust Yahweh often take refuge from their enemies in Him (17:7). The word for "shelter" can describe protective gear for battle (140:7). "Surround" is used to describe enemies preparing to attack (1Sm 23:26). And this word for "shield" describes a large piece of flattened metal that was placed in front of a soldier to protect his entire body; they were sometimes called "large shields" (1Kg 10:16).

Ps 6 title The word *Sheminith* is difficult to interpret. The

most commonly proposed root meaning is "eight," leading some to identify it with an eight-stringed instrument or an octave (an eight-note scale). In any case, it is part of the musical instructions for this psalm.

6:1 The combination of **rebuke ... discipline** and **anger ... wrath** indicates that the psalmist thought there was some sin behind his suffering, although the sin is not specified. The connection between sin and suffering is a common motif in lament psalms, and it shows how this relationship is part of the thinking of people who suffer even if there is no specific sin in mind; terms related to God's anger are a way of expressing this thought (38:1; 118:18). The opening to this psalm led the early church fathers to include it as one of the seven penitential psalms (along with 32; 38; 51; 102; 130; 143).

6:2-3 The parallelism between **my bones** and **my whole being** (or "my soul") demonstrates that the suffering was not only physical but also psychological and emotional. Suffering is never one-dimensional (only physical or psychological or spiritual); instead, it involves the whole person. The same Hebrew verb—meaning "shaken" when used literally but "terrified" in the figurative sense—is used for both subjects.

6:4-5 The plea has a twofold motivation. First, the appeal for Yahweh to act is **because of** His **faithful love** (Hb *chesed*). This is the covenant loyalty that God has for His people and the basis for the psalmist's trust (13:5; 26:3; 136). Second, the psalmist spoke of a loss of praise to Yahweh if he was allowed to go to **Sheol** (i.e., to die). This seems rather bold, but such appeals are common in lament psalms as a means of motivating God to act (30:9; 88:10; 115:17).

6:6-7 The extent of the psalmist's emotional distress is highlighted in these verses. His crying was so intense that

8 Depart from me, all evildoers,
    for the Lord has heard the sound
        of my weeping.[a]
9 The Lord has heard my plea
        for help;[b]
    the Lord accepts my prayer.[c]
10 All my enemies will be ashamed
        and shake with terror;
    they will turn back[d] and suddenly
        be disgraced.[e]

Psalm 7
Prayer for Justice

A *Shiggaion*[A] of David, which he sang to the Lord concerning the words of •Cush,[B] a Benjaminite.

1 •Yahweh my God, I seek refuge in You;[f]
    save me from all my pursuers
        and rescue me[g]
2 or they[C] will tear me like a lion,
    ripping me apart with no one
        to rescue me.[D,h]

3 Yahweh my God, if I have done this,
    if there is injustice on my hands,[i]

4 if I have done harm to one at peace
        with me[j]
    or have plundered[E] my adversary
        without cause,[k]
5 may an enemy pursue and overtake me;
    may he trample me to the ground[l]
        and leave my honor in the dust.[m]
                                    •Selah

6 Rise up, Lord, in Your anger;
    lift Yourself up against the fury
        of my adversaries;[n]
    awake for me;[F,o]
    You have ordained[G]
        a judgment.[p]
7 Let the assembly of peoples gather
        around You;[q]
    take Your seat[H] on high over it.[r]
8 The Lord judges the peoples;[s]
    vindicate me, Lord,
        according to my righteousness
        and my integrity.[I,t]

9 Let the evil of the wicked come
        to an end,[u]

Cross references
a6:8 Ps 18:6; 34:6; 40:1
b6:9 Ps 28:6
cPs 3:4; 66:19-20
d6:10 Ex 23:27
ePs 71:13
f7:1 Ps 11:1; 31:1; 71:1
gPs 31:15
h7:2 Ps 57:4; Is 5:29
i7:3 1Sm 24:11
j7:4 Ps 55:20
k1Sm 24:11; 26:18
l7:5 Am 2:7
m7:3-5 Jb 31:5-40
n7:6 Ps 3:7; 17:13
oPs 59:4
pJr 15:3
q7:7 Ps 22:27
rPs 68:18
s7:8 Ps 96:13; 98:9
tPs 26:1; 35:24; 43:1
u7:9 Ps 94:23

A7:title Perhaps a passionate song with rapid changes of rhythm, or a dirge   B7:title LXX, Aq, Sym, Theod, Jer read *of the Cushite*   C7:2 Lit *he*   D7:2 Lit *ripping, and without a rescuer*   E7:4 Or *me and have spared*   F7:6 LXX reads *awake, Lord my God*   G7:6 Or *me; ordain*   H7:7 MT reads *and return*   I7:8 Lit *integrity on me*

his **pillow** and bed were soaked with tears. The second image (**drench my bed**) is hyperbolic and literally reads "make my bed swim." The mention of **enemies** introduces another dimension to the suffering: helplessness before enemies because of the psalmist's condition of sickness.

6:8-10 The enemies of verse 7 are further described as **evildoers**. It is likely from the statement in verse 9 that the enemies were taunting the psalmist by saying that God would not deliver him (3:2; 22:7-8; 71:11). Instead of their perception of God's inactivity, these enemies would be shaken with **terror**. The word **shake** is the same Hebrew verb used twice in verses 2-3 to describe the condition of the psalmist in his suffering. In essence, the prayer ends with a statement of confidence that God will take away his suffering and inflict it upon his enemies.

Ps 7 title The word *Shiggaion* occurs only this one time in the psalm titles, and its meaning is unknown. Some have proposed that it comes from an Assyrian word *(shegu)* meaning "lament"; others have related it to a Hebrew root meaning "go astray" or "wander." The identity of **Cush, a Benjaminite** is also uncertain. Scholars have often related it to one of David's enemies from the tribe of Benjamin: Saul (1Sm 18–31), Shimei (2Sm 16:5-13), or Sheba (2Sm 20).

7:1-2 The use of the word **pursuers** to describe enemies indicates that the psalmist was a hunted man. He compared them collectively to a **lion, ripping . . . apart** its prey. This is a commonly used animal description of enemies in the psalms. Lions lurk in hiding places in order to attack their prey (10:9; 17:12); their mouths and teeth are fierce (58:6) as well as their roaring (22:13). In the NT, the same image of a roaring lion is used of Satan, the Christian's ultimate enemy (1Pt 5:8).

7:3-5 These verses contain a declaration of innocence in the form of an oath (cp. Jb 31:16-22). The **if** statements are rhetorical, assuming that the psalmist was innocent of those conditions ("if I have . . . and I have not"). The consequences are stated in a typical vow formula using the word **may**. This does not presuppose absolute innocence but is used to convey the notion of suffering without justifiable cause. There is no apparent sin or disobedience against God that would justify these results. It is another way of declaring that the psalmist had not knowingly acted unjustly toward anyone, intentionally harmed someone **at peace** with him, or stolen from anyone, including his enemy. Therefore, he should not be treated this way.

7:6-8 Calling down God's **judgment** on one's enemies is known as imprecation (see note at 109:1-31). The call for Yahweh to **rise up** was used as a battle cry for Israel when preparing to engage her enemies (Nm 10:35). The judgment that is called for is one that has already been **ordained** (lit "commanded") by God. Yahweh is the Judge of all the earth (Gn 18:25) and has promised to judge the whole world (1Sm 2:10; 1Ch 16:33), so this request is in keeping with God's character and promise. Some identify the **assembly of peoples** as the divine assembly of angels (82:1); however, "peoples" is most often used of nations and likely represents a gathering of the nations with Yahweh acting as the Judge. This section ends with a request for vindication based on the **righteousness** and **integrity** of the person praying (25:21; 26:1). As in the case of 7:3-5, this is not a statement of innocence from all sin but only from conscious sins that would justify this persecution.

7:9-11 Protection, pictured as a **shield**, is guaranteed by God's righteousness. The **thoughts and emotions** are literally "hearts and kidneys," imagery used to describe the inner parts of man that are not seen. In this case, it refers to inner thoughts and motives. Another text using a similar

but establish the righteous.[a]
The One who examines the thoughts
  and emotions[A]
is a righteous God.[b]
10 My shield is with[B] God,[c]
who saves the upright in heart.[d]
11 God is a righteous judge
and a God who shows His wrath
  every day.[e]
12 If anyone does not repent,
God[C] will sharpen His sword;[f]
He has strung[D] His bow
  and made it ready.[g]
13 He has prepared His deadly weapons;
He tips His arrows with fire.[h]

14 See, the wicked one is pregnant
  with evil,
conceives trouble, and gives birth
  to deceit.[i]
15 He dug a pit and hollowed it out
but fell into the hole he had made.[j]
16 His trouble comes back
  on his own head,
and his violence falls on the top
  of his head.[k]

17 I will thank the LORD
  for His righteousness;
I will sing about the name of Yahweh
  the *Most High.[l]

---

a 7:9 Is 9:7
b Heb 4:12
c 7:10 2Sm 22:3;
Ps 18:2; 144:2
d Ps 36:10
e 7:11 Ps 9:4;
Is 11:4
f 7:12 Nm 22:23;
Dt 32:41
g Ps 37:14
h 7:13 Ps 18:14;
45:5; 64:7; 144:6
i 7:14 Jb 15:35;
Is 59:4; Jms
1:15
j 7:15 Ps 9:15;
57:6; Pr 26:27;
28:10
k 7:16 1Sm
25:39; 1Kg 2:33;
Est 9:25
l 7:17 Ps 9:2;
71:15-16
m 8:title Ps
81,84 titles
n 8:1 Is 12:4
o Ps 113:4;
148:13
p 8:2 Mt 21:16
q 8:3 Ps 33:6;
136:9
r 8:4 Jb 7:17-18;
Ps 144:3
s 8:4-6 1Co
15:27; Eph 1:22;
Heb 2:5-8

Psalm 8
God's Glory, Man's Dignity

For the choir director: on the *Gittith.[m]
A Davidic psalm.

1 *Yahweh, our Lord,
how magnificent is Your name
  throughout the earth![n]

You have covered the heavens
  with Your majesty.[E,o]
2 Because of Your adversaries,
You have established a stronghold[F]
from the mouths of children
  and nursing infants[p]
to silence the enemy and the avenger.

3 When I observe Your heavens,
the work of Your fingers,
the moon and the stars,
which You set in place,[q]
4 what is man that You remember him,
the son of man that You look after him?[r]
5 You made him little less than God[G,H]
and crowned him with glory and honor.
6 You made him lord over the works
  of Your hands;
You put everything under his feet:[l,s]
7 all the sheep and oxen,
as well as the animals in the wild,
8 the birds of the sky,

A 7:9 Lit examines hearts and kidneys   B 7:10 Lit on   C 7:12 Lit He   D 7:12 Lit bent; that is, bent the bow to string it   E 8:1 Lit earth, which has set Your splendor upon the heavens   F 8:2 LXX reads established praise   G 8:5 LXX reads angels   H 8:5 Or gods, or a god, or heavenly beings; lit Elohim   I 8:6 Or authority

---

concept is Ps 139:13 where the idea is that God knows every part of a person; nothing is hidden from Him.

7:12-13 The imagery changes from God as a Judge to God as a Warrior. Such an image of God was part of Israel's history since He was the One who fought for His people (Dt 32:41-42). God was primed and ready to attack (i.e., judge) anyone who was unrepentant.

7:14-16 The terms **pregnant** and **birth** picture the wicked as creating, incubating, and unleashing their **evil** on the world as if it was their children (see Jb 15:35; Is 59:4, and Jms 1:15 for similar imagery). The plots of the wicked backfire (Ps 9:15; 35:8; 57:6; 141:10). This poetic justice is also described in Pr 26:27 and in the apocryphal book Sirach 27:25: "The one throwing a stone upward throws it on his own head."

7:17 Most High (Hb 'elyon) as a title for God first occurs in Gn 14:18-22, but it is also used throughout the OT to emphasize God's sovereignty over all mankind (Dt 32:8; Ps 47:2; Dn 4:17).

Ps 8 title Some propose that **Gittith** is some kind of musical instrument such as a lyre. The LXX translates it "for the winepress," relating it to a Hebrew root for grapes; in this sense, it could have been a song to be sung during the grape harvest.

8:1 This hymn of praise is more specifically identified as a creation hymn (along with 19:1-6; 33; and 104) in its focus

on **earth** and **the heavens**, terms describing the whole of creation (Gn 1:1; Ex 20:11; Neh 9:6). **Majesty**, a synonym for "honor" or "glory," and **name**, representing the person and not just the designation, are parallel. They demonstrate that God and His glory fill all of creation. This language distinguishes God from His creation (He is transcendent) but also shows that He is present (He is immanent) within it.

8:2 Even the feeblest of humanity, with their sometimes-inarticulate speech (**mouths**), function as firm testimonies (**a stronghold**) of God's glory and **silence the enemy and the avenger**. According to Jesus, children and their simple faith are the best representatives of God's kingdom (Mt 18:4). Paul also made a similar argument when he described God's use of weakness and foolishness to "shame the wise" of this world (1Co 1:26-29).

8:3-4 The vastness of creation is contrasted with the smallness and insignificance of **man**. This is in the form of a question: How is it that God would **remember** and **look after** (both words mean "pay attention to and care for") people? This is perplexing in light of the difference between the size and scope of the cosmos and the relative puniness of humanity. The terms *man* and **son of man** are parallel and are used to describe humankind as a collective whole (146:3; Nm 23:19; Is 51:12).

8:5-8 The answer to the perplexing question in verse 4 is found in these verses, which are essentially a commen-

and the fish of the sea
that pass through the currents
of the seas.[a]

9 Yahweh, our Lord,
how magnificent is Your name
throughout the earth!

Psalm 9

Celebration of God's Justice

For the choir director:
according to *Muth-labben*.[A]
A Davidic psalm.

1 I will thank •Yahweh
with all my heart;
I will declare all Your wonderful works.[b]
2 I will rejoice and boast about You;[c]
I will sing about Your name,
•Most High.[d]

3 When my enemies retreat,
they stumble and perish before You.[e]
4 For You have upheld my just cause;[B,f]
You are seated on Your throne
as a righteous judge.[g]
5 You have rebuked the nations:[h]

You have destroyed the wicked;[i]
You have erased their name forever
and ever.[j]
6 The enemy has come to eternal ruin;
You have uprooted the cities,
and the very memory of them
has perished.[k]

7 But the LORD sits enthroned forever;[l]
He has established His throne
for judgment.[m]
8 He judges the world
with righteousness;
He executes judgment on the nations
with fairness.[n]
9 The LORD is a refuge for the oppressed,
a refuge in times of trouble.[o]
10 Those who know Your name
trust in You
because You have not abandoned
those who seek You, Yahweh.[p]

11 Sing to the LORD, who dwells in •Zion;[q]
proclaim His deeds
among the nations.[r]
12 For the One who seeks an accounting
for bloodshed remembers them;[s]

a 8:7-8 Gn 1:26,28
b 9:1 1Ch 16:9,24; Ps 26:7; 96:3; 105:2
c 9:2 Ps 5:11
d Ps 7:17; 92:1
e 9:3 Lv 26:37; Ps 27:2; 92:9
f 9:4 1Kg 8:45,49,59; 2Ch 6:35,39
g Ps 7:11
h 9:5 Is 17:3
i Ps 68:2
j Zch 13:2
k 9:6 Ps 34:16
l 9:7 Ps 29:10; 102:12; Lm 5:19
m Ps 89:14
n 9:8 Ps 96:13; 98:9; Rv 19:11
o 9:9 Ps 14:6; Is 14:32
p 9:10 Ps 37:28; 94:14
q 9:11 Ps 76:2
r 1Ch 16:8; Ps 105:1
s 9:12 Gn 9:5

A 9:title Perhaps a musical term   B 9:4 Lit *my justice and my cause*

tary on Gn 1:26-28. While the perception is that humans are insignificant in the grand scheme of things, the reality is found in God's purpose for creating humanity. The word translated as **God** (Hb *'elohim*) is plural here and could be understood as indicating "gods" or "heavenly beings" instead of its usual sense of a plural of majesty emphasizing God's greatness. Therefore the LXX, which is quoted in Heb 2:7, translates it as "angels." The point is the same in both cases, even if the referent is different: Because of their divinely given purpose, humans are functionally closer to God and the angels than to the animals. We have been **made . . . lord over** creation, expressing humanity's function of dominion (Gn 1:26). The image of **everything under his feet** is developed in the rest of Scripture as a picture of the reign of God's King, Jesus Christ (the second Adam), over His kingdom (1Co 15:25,27; Eph 1:22; Heb 2:8).

8:9 The psalm ends as it began, forming an *inclusio* (essentially "bookends") for its content.

Ps 9 title The Hebrew word *Muth-labben* could be related to *alamoth*, which appears in the title of Psalm 46. It could be translated as "for the death of a son" in the sense of being used for that occasion. More likely it identifies a specific tune or style of music. Psalm 10 does not have a title and is joined to this psalm in the LXX and the Vulgate. Another reason for seeing Psalms 9 and 10 as one is that there is an alphabetic acrostic that begins in Psalm 9 and is continued in Psalm 10. However, there is a sufficient change that takes place, especially in terms of mood and form (Ps 9 focuses on thanksgiving whereas Ps 10 takes the form of a lament psalm). This seems to argue for them being two distinct psalms.

9:1 With all my heart means "sincerely" (86:12; 111:1; 119:10). **Wonderful works** is unspecified here, but elsewhere it refers to God's acts of creation (136:4), His works in

the natural order (Jb 5:9), or the redemptive acts performed on behalf of His people (Ex 3:20).

9:3 The **retreat** and stumbling of **enemies** describes either an event recently experienced or a frequent situation brought about by God (27:2; 56:4).

9:4-6 The verbs in these verses express completed action, indicating the confidence of the psalmist that the execution of God's justice was certain. In this context, the **throne** describes God's judgment (v. 7; 11:4) more than His rule, as it is sometimes used (45:6). Their **name** being erased and their **memory** perishing are related phrases; they refer to complete annihilation and the destruction of one's existence (21:10; 83:4; Dt 32:26).

9:7-8 Yahweh is **enthroned forever** (29:10; 93:2) and is portrayed as judging **the world** (see note at 7:6-8). Even though there will be a final judgment of the world in the future (96:13; 98:9), God is currently executing His justice on the world as well since He is and has always been the Judge of the earth (94:2).

9:9-10 The fact that Yahweh is on His throne is a comfort to **the oppressed** because He offers them protection (**a refuge**) from the wicked who afflict them. The phrases **know Your name** and **trust in You** and **seek You** have essentially the same meaning. They describe those who have personal, experiential knowledge of Yahweh ("know" is connected with love in 91:14), and who depend on Him and look to Him in times of need.

9:11 Sing and **proclaim** are parallel commands indicating the responsibility of those who know God and His works to tell others (30:4; 1Ch 16:8; Is 12:4).

9:12 Bloodshed is literally "bloods"; it is used in a phrase describing the avenging of murder (Gn 9:5; 42:22; Ezk 33:6).

He does not forget the cry
  of the afflicted.*a*

13 Be gracious to me, LORD;
  consider my affliction at the hands
    of those who hate me.*b*
  Lift me up from the gates of death,*c*
14 so that I may declare
    all Your praises.
  I will rejoice in Your salvation*d*
  within the gates of Daughter Zion.

15 The nations have fallen into the pit
    they made;
  their foot is caught in the net
    they have concealed.*e*
16 The LORD has revealed Himself;
  He has executed justice,*f*

striking down^A the wicked^B
  by the work of their hands.*g*
                         *Higgaion. *Selah

17 The wicked will return
    to *Sheol*^h—
  all the nations that forget God.*i*
18 For the oppressed will not always
    be forgotten;
  the hope of the afflicted^C will not perish
    forever.*j*

19 Rise up, LORD! Do not let man prevail;
  let the nations be judged
    in Your presence.*k*
20 Put terror in them, LORD;*l*
  let the nations know they are
    only men.*m*   Selah

a 9:12 Ps 12:5;
Pr 22:22-23
b 9:13 Ps 69:14
c Ps 30:3; 86:13
d 9:14 1Sm 2:1
e 9:15 Ps 7:15;
57:6; Pr 28:10
f 9:16 Is 56:1
g Ps 3:7; Is 11:4
h 9:17 Ps 31:17;
49:14; 55:15
i Jb 8:13; Ps
50:22
j 9:18 Ps 12:5;
72:4
k 9:19 Ps 82:8;
110:6
l 9:20 Ps 14:5
m Ps 62:9

^A 9:16 Or *justice, snaring*   ^B 9:16 LXX, Aq, Syr, Tg read *justice, the wicked is trapped*   ^C 9:18 Alt Hb tradition reads *humble*

9:13-14 The plea in verse 13 has a purpose, which is to **declare all Your praises**. This further expands the commands in verse 11 and shows how the psalmist's deliverance will be used to tell others about God's goodness. Rescue from **the gates of death** will allow him to once again enter **the gates of Daughter Zion**. This description of Jerusalem appears only here in the Psalms, but it is not uncommon in other books, especially Isaiah and Lamentations. It refers to more than the city itself, including its inhabitants as well.

9:15-16 The idea of enemies suffering the same fate that they had planned for someone else is found in other psalms (7:15-16; 35:8; 57:6). In this case, the enemies are **the nations** who are being judged by God for their rebellion against His authority (2:1). This is clear from the parallel designa-

tion **the wicked** in verse 16. *Higgaion* comes perhaps from a Hebrew root meaning "murmur." It might refer to the use of quieter instruments.

9:17-18 There is a play on the word "forget" in these verses. Those who **forget God** will go to **Sheol**, a place where they are forgotten (88:5), a concept similar to that of 9:5-6. In contrast, the future looks good for those who trust in Yahweh but are currently being persecuted by others; the God of justice will see to it that they are remembered.

9:19-20 **Rise up** is a martial call for the Lord to act (see note at 7:6-8). More specifically, He is asked to **put terror in them**. This is not the "fear of the Lord" that is characteristic of those who believe in Yahweh but the terror of people at the approach of an army (Dt 2:25; 11:25).

The Temple Mount and the old city of Jerusalem from the Mount of Olives (9:11,14)

Psalm 10

1 LORD,[A,B] why do You stand so far away?[a]
   Why do You hide in times of trouble?[b]
2 In arrogance the wicked
   relentlessly pursue the afflicted;
   let them be caught in the schemes
   they have devised.[c]

3 For the wicked one boasts about
   his own cravings;[d]
   the one who is greedy curses[C]
   and despises the LORD.[e]
4 In all his scheming,
   the wicked arrogantly thinks:[D]
   "There is no accountability,
   since God does not exist."[f]
5 His ways are always secure;[E]
   Your lofty judgments are beyond
   his sight;
   he scoffs at all his adversaries.[g]
6 He says to himself, "I will never
   be moved—
   from generation to generation
   without calamity."[h]
7 Cursing, deceit, and violence
   fill his mouth;
   trouble and malice are
   under his tongue.[i]
8 He waits in ambush near the villages;[j]
   he kills the innocent in secret places.
   His eyes are on the lookout
   for the helpless;[k]

9 he lurks in secret like a lion
   in a thicket.
   He lurks in order to seize the afflicted;
   he seizes the afflicted and drags him
   in his net.
10 So he is oppressed and beaten down;
   the helpless fall because of
   his strength.[l]
11 He says to himself, "God has forgotten;
   He hides His face and will never see."[m]

12 Rise up, LORD God! Lift up
   Your hand.[n]
   Do not forget the afflicted.[o]
13 Why has the wicked person
   despised God?
   He says to himself, "You will not
   demand an account."[p]
14 But You Yourself have seen trouble
   and grief,
   observing it in order to take the matter
   into Your hands.[q]
   The helpless entrusts himself to You;
   You are a helper of the fatherless.[r]
15 Break the arm of the wicked
   and evil person;[s]
   call his wickedness into account
   until nothing remains of it.[F,t]

16 The LORD is King forever and ever;[u]
   the nations will perish
   from His land.[v]
17 LORD, You have heard the desire
   of the humble;[G]

a10:1 Ps 22:1; 35:22; 38:21; 71:12
b Jb 13:24; Ps 44:24; 88:14
c10:2 Ps 7:15-16
d10:3 Ps 49:6
e 2Pt 2:3
f10:4 Ps 14:1; 53:1
g10:5 Ps 52:7
h10:6 Ps 49:11; Rv 18:7
i10:7 Ps 73:8; 140:3; Rm 3:13-14
j10:8 Ps 59:3
k Ps 64:4; 94:6
l10:8-10 Ps 17:11-12; Pr 28:15
m10:11 Jb 22:13; Ps 59:3
n10:12 Mc 5:9
o Ps 9:12
p10:13 Ps 73:11
q10:14 Ps 33:13-15
r Ps 68:5; 146:9
s10:15 Ps 37:17
t Ps 89:32
u10:16 Ex 15:18; Ps 29:10; Rv 11:15
v Dt 8:20

A10:1 Some Hb mss, LXX connect Pss 9–10.   B10:1 Together these 2 psalms form a partial 'acrostic.   C10:3 Or he blesses the greedy   D10:4 Lit wicked according to the height of his nose   E10:5 Or prosperous   F10:15 Lit account You do not find   G10:17 Some Hb mss, LXX, Syr read afflicted

10:1-2 The perceived absence of Yahweh in the psalmist's suffering is described as standing **far away** (35:22; 38:21) and hiding (13:1). This is another way of saying that God has not yet delivered the psalmist, although there is an implication of rejection as expressed more forcefully in other lament psalms (22:1). The specific affliction here is identified in 10:2 in the request for **the wicked** to be **caught** in their own **schemes** (see note at 7:14-16).

10:3-6 The arrogance of **the wicked one** climaxes in a statement denying God's existence. This is not metaphysical atheism, in which there is absolute unbelief in God's existence, but practical atheism, which denies that God pays any attention to what people are doing (14:1; 53:1). The enemy's security rests on his thinking, which is that he can get away with anything **his own cravings** allow. He **will never be moved** (15:5; 16:8; 21:7; 62:2; 112:6) in the sense that no higher being will divert him from doing what he desires.

10:7 Mouth and **tongue** are used for speech, describing the deadly arsenal of the enemy's words (5:9; 140:3). A similar image appears in 64:3 where a tongue is a sword and speech is an arrow.

10:8-10 The image of a wild animal, specifically a lion, is commonly used for the wicked (see note at 7:1-2). He preys

on **the innocent** (94:21; 106:38) and **the helpless**. This second term is used only in this psalm (vv. 10,14).

10:11 God's inactivity is evidence enough for the wicked that He has **forgotten** the righteous, reinforcing the practical atheism expressed in verse 4. This is coupled with the assumption that God was hiding Himself. For the afflicted, this apparent situation was a perplexing question (v. 1).

10:12-15 On **rise up**, see notes at 7:6-8 and 9:19-20. What is true in Psalm 9 is now in conflict with what appears to be happening in Psalm 10. God is asked **not** to **forget the afflicted**, but in 9:12,18 He does not forget them. Here the wicked think that God will **not demand an account**, but in 9:12 He clearly does. The tension is between appearance and reality, a common situation in the lament psalms. **Fatherless** is a better rendering than "orphan," since in Hebrew society it was the lack (or loss) of a father that made a person helpless by not having property or rights. Breaking the **arm of the wicked** would make them helpless as well (37:17), to be called into **account**.

10:16-18 Since Yahweh is sovereign **forever**, His justice will triumph. The statement that **nations will perish from His land** is reminiscent of the annihilation of the Canaanites from the promised land, a land that belonged to Yahweh

You will strengthen their hearts.
You will listen carefully,[a]
18 doing justice for the fatherless
and the oppressed
so that men of the earth
may terrify them no more.[b]

Psalm 11
Refuge in the LORD

For the choir director. Davidic.

1 I have taken refuge in the LORD.[c]
How can you say to me,
"Escape to the mountain like a bird!"[A,d]
2 For look, the wicked string the bow;
they put the[B] arrow on the bowstring
to shoot from the shadows
at the upright in heart.[e]
3 When the foundations are destroyed,
what can the righteous do?"[f]

4 The LORD is in His holy temple;[g]
the LORD's throne is in heaven.[h]
His eyes watch; He examines[C] •everyone.
5 The LORD examines the righteous
and the wicked.

He hates the lover of violence.[i]
6 He will rain burning coals[D] and sulfur
on the wicked;
a scorching wind will be their portion.[E,j]
7 For the LORD is righteous; He loves
righteous deeds.
The upright will see His face.[k]

Psalm 12
Oppression by the Wicked

For the choir director:
according to •Sheminith.[L] A Davidic psalm.

1 Help, LORD, for no faithful one remains;
the loyal have disappeared
from the •human race.[m]
2 They lie to one another;
they speak with flattering lips
and deceptive hearts.[n]
3 May the LORD cut off all flattering lips
and the tongue that speaks boastfully.[o]
4 They say, "Through our tongues
we have power;[F]
our lips are our own—who can be
our master?"[p]

Cross references

[a]10:17 2Ch 7:14; Ps 34:15
[b]10:18 Ex 22:22-24; Dt 10:18
[c]11:1 Ps 7:1; 31:1; 71:1
[d]Ps 121:1
[e]11:2 Ps 37:14; 64:4
[f]11:3 Ps 82:5
[g]11:4 Ps 27:4; Hab 2:20
[h]Ps 103:19; Is 66:1; Ac 7:49
[i]11:4-5 Ps 33:13-15
[j]11:6 Ezk 38:22
[k]11:7 Ps 17:15; Rv 22:4
[l]12:title 1Ch 15:21; Ps 6 title
[m]12:1 Ps 14:2-3; 53:2-3; Mc 7:2
[n]12:2 Ps 41:6; 144:8; Jr 9:8
[o]12:3 Ps 5:9
[p]12:4 Ps 73:8-9

Textual notes

A11:1 Lit to your mountain, bird   B11:2 Lit their   C11:4 Lit His eyelids examine   D11:6 Sym; MT reads rain snares, fire   E11:6 Lit be the portion of their cup   F12:4 Lit That say, "By our tongues we are strengthened

Notes

and was given to His people (Dt 7). The final result is that the wicked will no longer **terrify** others but will themselves be terrified (9:20).

11:1 A **bird** is a defenseless animal that can only fly away rather than stand its ground and fight (55:6; 124:7). The statement expresses the counsel of the psalmist's advisers or perhaps his own thoughts.

11:2 Comparing this verse to 7:12 where God is the One primed and ready to **shoot** at the wicked shows the irony of this situation.

11:3 The **foundations** are undefined here but could refer to moral foundations or the principles of justice within society. The activities of the wicked shake the foundations of justice and morality (82:5; Ezk 30:4).

11:4-5 The security of the psalmist rested in the fact that God had not left **His holy temple** (see Mc 1:2; Hab 2:20) and was still on His **throne** (103:19), both of which are in heaven. Though the wicked thought that God was not paying any attention to what was happening on earth (10:4; 14:1; 53:1), He was actually watching and examining **everyone** (33:13-14). This included both **the righteous and the wicked**.

11:6 The Hebrew text of this verse reads, "He will rain down traps on the wicked." This reading might have originated from a connection with verse 1, since the word "trap" most often describes something used to catch birds (Am 3:5). Another reading is "coals of fire," which only amounts to a slight variation of letters. This seems more likely in light of the parallel with **scorching wind**.

11:7 Seeing God's **face** is equivalent to experiencing God's favor or blessing (17:15; Jb 33:26). It is the opposite of God hiding His face (Ps 10:11). A related image is for God's face to "shine" on His people (Nm 6:25).

Ps 12 title On **Sheminith**, see note at Psalm 6 title.

12:1 These words were spoken from personal experience and conclude that there did not seem to be anyone left who was **faithful** or **loyal** to Yahweh (14:3; 53:3; Mc 7:2). This is similar to Elijah's experience when he believed he was the last person in the land who was faithful to the Lord (1Kg 19:10).

12:4 As in other descriptions of the wicked, their speech gave away their motives (5:9; 10:7; 59:12). In fact, they believed that their **power** resided in their speech, highlighting perhaps their ability to influence others by what they said.

chalaq

Hebrew Pronunciation	[khah LAHK]
HCSB Translation	smooth, flattering
Uses in Psalms	3
Uses in the OT	12
Focus Passage	Psalm 12:2-3

Chalaq refers to what is *smooth*, whether oil (Pr 5:3), skin (Gn 27:11), or stones (Is 57:6). "Mount *Halak*" (Jos 11:17) indicates "*Smooth* Mountain." *Chalaq* can imply *slippery places* (Ps 73:18) but usually suggests dangerous *flattery* (Dn 11:32) or *flattering* lips (Ps 12:3). *Flattering things* is complimentary once (Is 30:10), but in the context is false prophecy. *Chalaq* connotes deceit and ulterior motives (Hs 10:2). The verb *chalaq* (9x) means *be smooth* (Ps 55:21) or *devious* (Hs 10:2). Its derivation is probably different from that of *chalaq* meaning "divide." The causative describes *flattening* metal (Is 41:7) or *flattering* people (Ps 5:9). *Chalaqlaqqoth* (4x) means *slippery* (Ps 35:6) and *slippery paths* (Jr 23:12). It appears as *intrigue* and *insincerely* (Dn 11:21,34). *Cheleq* signifies seductive *flattery* (Pr 7:21). *Chelqah* denotes the *smooth part* of the neck (Gn 27:16) and a *flattering* tongue (Pr 6:24). *Challuq* portrays *smooth* stones (1Sm 17:40).

5 "Because of the oppression
     of the afflicted
and the groaning of the poor,
I will now rise up," says the LORD.
"I will put the one who longs for it
     in a safe place."[a]

6 The words of the LORD
     are pure words,
like silver refined
     in an earthen furnace,
purified seven times.[b]

7 You, LORD, will guard us;[A]
You will protect us[B]
     from this generation forever.[c]
8 The wicked wander[C] everywhere,
and what is worthless is exalted
     by the human race.[d]

Psalm 13
A Plea for Deliverance

For the choir director. A Davidic psalm.

1 LORD, how long will You forget me?
     Forever?
How long will You hide Your face
     from me?[e]
2 How long will I store up
     anxious concerns[D] within me,

(marginal references)
[a] 12:5 Ps 9:18; 72:4
[b] 12:6 Ps 18:30; 119:140; Pr 30:5
[c] 12:7 Ps 37:28; 97:10
[d] 12:8 Ps 4:2; 119:37
[e] 13:1 Jb 13:24; Ps 44:24; 89:46
[f] 13:2 Ps 6:3; 38:6; 42:9
[g] 13:3 Ezr 9:8; Ps 19:8; Pr 29:13
[h] 13:4 Ps 89:42
[i] 13:5 Ps 52:8
[j] Ps 9:14
[k] 13:6 Ps 119:17; 142:7
[l] 14:1 Ps 10:4; 53:1
[m] 14:2 Ps 33:13-15

agony in my mind every day?
How long will my enemy
     dominate me?[f]

3 Consider me and answer,
     LORD my God.
Restore brightness to my eyes;[g]
     otherwise, I will sleep in death.
4 My enemy will say, "I have triumphed
     over him,"
and my foes will rejoice
     because I am shaken.[h]

5 But I have trusted in Your faithful love;[i]
     my heart will rejoice in
     Your deliverance.[j]
6 I will sing to the LORD
     because He has treated me generously.[k]

Psalm 14
A Portrait of Sinners

For the choir director. Davidic.

1 The fool says in his heart,
     "God does not exist."[l]
They are corrupt; they do vile deeds.
There is no one who does good.
2 The LORD looks down from heaven
     on the •human race[m]
to see if there is one who is wise,
one who seeks God.

[A] 12:7 Some Hb mss, LXX, Jer; other Hb mss read *them*   [B] 12:7 Some Hb mss, LXX; other Hb mss read *him*   [C] 12:8 Lit *walk about*
[D] 13:2 Or *up counsels*

12:5 The familiar image of God rising up (7:6; 9:19) indicates that He is going to act. The picture of God acting as a result of hearing the cries of His people is similar to Ex 2:24.

12:6 In contrast to the unreliability of the words of the wicked (vv. 2-4; also 5:9), Yahweh's **words** are **pure** like **refined . . . silver**, meaning absolutely trustworthy (18:30; 19:7-10). **Seven times** refers to the fullest sense or the fact that a person cannot exceed this limit (Dn 3:19).

12:7-8 Yahweh **protects** His own (31:23), but **the wicked wander** about aimlessly. The Hebrew word translated "wander" is a common word for "walk," but in this form it expresses the idea of walking back and forth. When combined with **everywhere**, it means to walk around without any sense of purpose. The fact that **what is worthless is exalted** shows the extent of the influence of sin in society (Ec 8:11). God does not tolerate people who love what is worthless (Ps 4:2).

13:1-2 The phrase **how long** is not uncommon in the lament psalms (6:3; 35:17; 74:10; 79:5; 80:4; 94:3); however, it appears more times here (four times) than in any other single text. This highlights the fact that the psalmist had endured his suffering for a long time and was considering that Yahweh might have hidden His **face** from Him and forgotten Him. Both of these descriptions convey the idea of rejection (44:24).

13:3-4 Brightness in the **eyes** represents vitality and is the opposite of one's eyes growing dim during times of grief and suffering (6:7; 38:10; Jb 17:7). In this context it is contrasted

with **death**. The **enemy** was adding to the psalmist's suffering by proclaiming triumph over him. The statement **I am shaken** could refer to dying, but it could also be used to indicate defeat. In most contexts it is used with the negative as a statement of the assurance of security: "I will not be shaken" (16:8; 30:6; 62:6).

13:5-6 Even though the question about the time of God's intervention remained, the psalmist reaffirmed his trust in Yahweh's **faithful love**. This is the Hebrew word *chesed*, which is rooted in Yahweh's covenant with His people; sometimes it is even synonymous with the term *covenant* (see note at 89:28). The psalmist's trust was not in himself but in the God of the covenant who promised that He would show faithful love to those who love and obey Him (Dt 7:9; Neh 1:5; Dn 9:4).

14:1 The statement that **God does not exist** affirms practical rather than metaphysical atheism (see note at 10:3-6). The person making this claim is described as **the fool** (Hb *nabal*; 1Sm 25:25). This is not someone who was simple or gullible because it was outside his ability to be otherwise, but someone who was willfully ignorant, closing his mind off from God's wisdom and truth.

14:2 The LORD is depicted as one who, though He resides in **heaven**, is not ignorant of what happens on earth (11:4-5; 33:13-15). While in actuality God always knows the hearts of all mankind, here He is described in anthropomorphic terms as looking down to evaluate people. For similar terminology, see Gn 11:5; 18:21.

³ All have turned away;
    all alike have become corrupt.
    There is no one who does good,
    not even one.[A,a]

⁴ Will evildoers never understand?
    They consume My people
       as they consume bread;[b]
    they do not call on the LORD.[c]

⁵ Then[B] they will be filled with terror,
    for God is with those
       who are[c] righteous.[d]

⁶ You sinners frustrate the plans
       of the afflicted,[e]
    but the LORD is his refuge.[f]

⁷ Oh, that Israel's deliverance
       would come from *Zion!
    When the LORD restores the fortunes
       of His people,[D]
    Jacob will rejoice; Israel will be glad.[E,g]

Psalm 15
A Description of the Godly

A Davidic psalm.

¹ LORD, who can dwell
      in Your tent?[h]

Who can live on
    Your holy mountain?[i]

² The one who lives honestly,
      practices righteousness,
    and acknowledges the truth
      in his heart[j]—

³ who does not slander with his tongue,[k]
    who does not harm his friend
    or discredit his neighbor,[l]

⁴ who despises the one rejected
      by the LORD[F]
    but honors those who *fear the LORD,[m]
    who keeps his word whatever the cost,[n]

⁵ who does not lend his money
      at interest[o]
    or take a bribe against the innocent[p]—
    the one who does these things
      will never be moved.[q]

Psalm 16
Confidence in the LORD

A Davidic *Miktam.[r]

¹ Protect me, God, for I take refuge
      in You.[s]

² I[G] said to *Yahweh, "You are my Lord;
    I have nothing good besides You."[H,t]

Cross-references (center column):

a14:1-3 Ps 12:1; 53:1-3; Mc 7:2; Rm 3:10-12
b14:4 Ps 27:2; Mc 3:3
cIs 64:7
d14:5 Ps 53:5
e14:6 Ezr 4:5
fPs 9:9; 94:22
g14:7 Ps 53:6
h15:1 Ps 61:4
iPs 43:3
j15:1-2 Ps 24:3-5; Is 33:14-16
k15:3 Pr 10:18
lPr 3:29
m15:4 Gn 14:17-24; Ps 119:63
nLv 5:4; Dt 23:21-23
o15:5 Lv 25:35-38; Dt 33:19
pEx 23:18; Dt 16:19
qPss 16:8; 112:6
r16:title Ps 56–60 titles
s16:1 Ps 94:22
t16:2 Ps 73:25

[A]14:3 Some Hb mss, some LXX mss add the material found in Rm 3:13-18.   [B]14:5 Or *There*   [C]14:5 Lit *with the generation of the*   [D]14:7 Or *restores His captive people*   [E]14:7 Or *let Jacob rejoice; let Israel be glad.*   [F]15:4 Lit *in his eyes the rejected is despised*   [G]16:2 Some Hb mss, LXX, Syr, Jer; other Hb mss read *You*   [H]16:2 Or *"Lord, my good; there is none besides You."*

14:3 This verse expands the thought from the end of verse 1 by indicating that the psalmist felt isolated because he seemed to be the only one left who was faithful to Yahweh (12:1). Paul used this verse in a more absolute sense that no one among mankind is righteous since all are **corrupt**. Paul's usage is not contradictory to the original verse but extends its imagery to reflect the meaning that no person can claim righteousness apart from that which is given through faith in Jesus Christ.

14:4 The image of wicked people who devour or consume others is found elsewhere (27:2; Pr 30:14). It is perhaps related to the image of wild beasts such as lions that devour their prey (Ps 10:9; 17:12).

14:5-6 Terror is what the wicked bring to God's people (10:18), but the hope is that God will do the same to them (9:20). **The plans of the afflicted** will succeed when God frustrates the plans of the wicked (33:10).

14:7 The Hebrew for **restores . . . His people** is difficult. It is literally "turns with a turning His people." The Hebrew word for turn can also mean "return," and some understand this to mean the return of captives (perhaps from the exile). Such an event does not seem to fit this context. Here the idea is probably more general and describes God's blessings on His people.

15:1 The phrase **Your Tent** is parallel to **Your holy mountain** and refers to the sanctuary of Yahweh. This is the place of God's presence and protection (61:4). Certain people are not allowed in God's presence because of His holiness (5:4-5).

The desire of God's people is to be in His presence forever (65:4; 84:3-4).

15:2 Lives honestly is literally "walks blamelessly," and it refers to a life of integrity (18:23; 119:1). The **truth** of God is not just something proclaimed. It must reside in a person's **heart**, which is the mind or the inner person (Dt 6:6; Is 29:13).

15:3 God is intolerant of those who destroy others with their speech (101:5). Slandering and discrediting come from an attitude of hatred and a desire to **harm** others (10:12,18).

15:4 Despising the wicked and honoring the godly are attitudes that show we are made in God's image—we love what He loves and hate what He hates (139:21-22).

15:5 The command against lending at **interest** was only applicable to fellow Israelites and not to foreigners (Dt 23:20). However, someone who is close to the Lord will follow the spirit of the law and not just the letter. What is common between lending at interest and bribery is that both profit from someone else's misfortune or lack (Pr 15:27). Those who are able to enter God's sanctuary **will never be moved**. This is sometimes translated as "shaken," meaning that they will be secure (10:6; 13:4).

Ps 16 title *Miktam* occurs in the titles of six psalms (Pss 16; 56–60). Its meaning is difficult to determine. The Hebrew root from which the form is derived may mean "cover," "secret," or "inscribe." It is most likely a musical term, though its precise relationship with music is uncertain.

16:2 The phrase **nothing good besides You** is literally "my good (is) not above/beyond You" and is difficult in Hebrew.

3 As for the holy people who are
  in the land,[a]
they are the noble ones.
All my delight is in them.
4 The sorrows of those who take
  another god
for themselves will multiply;
I will not pour out
  their *drink offerings of blood,
and I will not speak their names
  with my lips.[b]

5 Lord, You are my portion[A]
and my cup of blessing;
You hold my future.[c]
6 The boundary lines have fallen for me
in pleasant places;
indeed, I have a beautiful inheritance.[d]

7 I will praise the Lord
  who counsels me[e]—
even at night my conscience
  instructs me.[f]
8 I keep the Lord in mind[B] always.
Because He is at my right hand,
I will not be shaken.[g]

9 Therefore my heart is glad
and my spirit rejoices;
my body also rests securely.[h]
10 For You will not abandon me
  to *Sheol;[i]
You will not allow Your Faithful One
  to see decay.[j]
11 You reveal the path of life to me;
in Your presence is abundant joy;[k]
in Your right hand are
  eternal pleasures.[l]

Psalm 17
A Prayer for Protection
A Davidic prayer.

1 Lord, hear a just cause;[m]
pay attention to my cry;
listen to my prayer—
from lips free of deceit.[n]
2 Let my vindication come from You,
for You see what is right.[o]
3 You have tested my heart;[p]
You have examined me at night.

a16:3 Dt 7:6; 14:2; 26:19
b16:4 Ex 23:13; Jos 23:7
c16:5 Nm 18:20; Ps 119:57; Lm 3:24
d16:6 Jr 3:19
e16:7 Ps 73:24
fPs 77:6
g16:8 Ps 15:5; 112:6
h16:9 Ps 4:7-8; 13:5
i16:10 Ps 49:10; 86:13
jJb 33:18,28; Ps 30:3; 103:4; Ac 13:35
k16:11 Ps 21:6
l16:8-11 Ac 2:25-28
m17:1 Ps 9:4
nJb 27:4; Ps 34:13; 1Pt 3:10
o17:2 Ps 26:1; 43:1
p17:3 Ps 66:10; Zch 13:9

A16:5 Or *allotted portion*   B16:8 Lit *front of me*

It is most likely related to a similar expression in 73:25 that carries the idea of finding nothing desirable on earth apart from the Lord.

16:3 Holy people (lit "holy ones") and **noble ones** are difficult to identify. Based on a common meaning of "holy ones" as heavenly beings, some have suggested angels or gods. Another suggestion is that these are leaders or rulers because of the designation "noble ones." The phrase **in the land** seems to argue for their identity as mortals. Most likely "holy" and "noble" are used to describe God's people in general. The more common word for God's people is the word meaning "faithful," as in "faithful ones" (50:5).

16:4 Multiplied **sorrows** is reminiscent of the curse in Gn 3:16 whereby God intensified "labor pains" for the woman. **Drink offerings of blood** could be a reference to human sacrifice (Is 57:5), although it is probably offerings made by those with impure motives who therefore remained guilty of sin (Is 1:15; 66:3).

16:5-6 My portion . . . cup of blessing and **boundary lines . . . inheritance** are terms usually used to describe the land promised to Israel. But the idea that God Himself is the true inheritance rather than the land was a promise specifically to Aaron and his sons (Nm 18:20; Dt 10:9). Here the concept is expressed more generally as true for anyone who is among God's people.

16:7 God guides His people with His counsel (33:11; 73:24). **Conscience** is literally "kidneys," which are often used in parallel with "heart" to signify the inner person (26:2; Jr 17:10).

16:8 In legal contexts the person who represented the defense of another was at the **right hand** (109:6). In military contexts the soldier protecting his comrade was at the right hand; also, it was the location for the sword, the primary weapon used in hand-to-hand combat. On **not be shaken**, see note at 13:3-4.

16:9-11 Along with verse 8, these verses are quoted (from the LXX) in the NT and explained as referring to Jesus' resurrection (Ac 2:25-31). Though in its original context it is possible to understand the terminology as meaning deliverance from death, it can also be used to describe resurrection from the dead. The language is sufficiently ambiguous to allow for both possibilities. The NT usage is within the range of meaning and is, according to Peter, the meaning that God ultimately intended in reference to Christ. Confidence is expressed in the fact that one can **rest securely**. As in the case of the imagery in verses 5-6, this language usually relates to the land (Dt 33:12,28; Jr 23:6; 33:16). The **path of life** usually means the way to life in OT Wisdom literature (Pr 5:6).

17:1-2 The concept of a **just cause** is also found in 9:4, although the Hebrew words are slightly different. In that context the psalmist praised God for hearing his case and answering his prayer. Here this forms part of the petition and is further identified as **vindication** and **what is right** in verse 2. In this context they are legal terms describing a case brought before Yahweh who is acting as judge in the case. **Lips free of deceit** refers to sincerity and truthfulness. God will not tolerate deceit (101:7).

17:3-5 God is the One who tests and tries people, particularly their motives (Pr 26:2; Jr 17:10). He is the only One who can declare a person righteous (Gn 15:6; Dt 6:25; Ps 37:6). Therefore, the truthfulness of this plea can be verified by God. As in the case of other declarations of innocence (see note at 7:3-5), this is not a statement of absolute righteousness, as found in the NT, but relative righteousness in terms of being habitually faithful to God and avoiding behavior that characterizes sin and rebellion against God (1:1; 26:4-5; Ezk 18:6-8).

You have tried me and found
nothing evil;[a]
I have determined that my mouth
will not sin.[A]

4 Concerning what people do:
by the word of Your lips[B]
I have avoided the ways of the violent.[b]

5 My steps are on Your paths;
my feet have not slipped.[c]

6 I call on You, God,
because You will answer me;[d]
listen closely to me; hear what I say.

7 Display the wonders
of Your faithful love,[e]
Savior of all who seek refuge[f]
from those who rebel
against Your right hand.[C]

8 Protect me as the pupil of Your eye;[g]
hide me in the shadow of Your wings[h]

9 from[D] the wicked
who treat me violently,[E]
my deadly enemies who surround me.[i]

10 They have become hardened;[F,j]
their mouths speak arrogantly.[k]

11 They advance against me;[G]
now they surround me.[l]
They are determined[H]
to throw me to the ground.[m]

12 They are[i] like a lion eager to tear,

like a young lion lurking
in ambush.[n]

13 Rise up, Lord!
Confront him; bring him down.[o]
With Your sword, save me
from the wicked.[p]

14 With Your hand, Lord, save me
from men,
from men of the world
whose portion is in this life:
You fill their bellies with what You have
in store;
their sons are satisfied,
and they leave their surplus
to their children.[q]

15 But I will see Your face in righteousness;[r]
when I awake, I will be satisfied
with Your presence.[J,s]

Psalm 18
Praise for Deliverance

For the choir director.
Of the servant of the Lord, David, who spoke
the words of this song to the Lord on the day
the Lord rescued him from the hand of all his
enemies and from the hand of Saul.[t] He said:

1 I love You, Lord, my strength.
2 The Lord is my rock,

Cross references (center column):

[a]17:3 Jb 23:10; Ps 26:2
[b]17:4 Pr 4:14-15
[c]17:5 Jb 23:11
[d]17:6 Ps 86:7
[e]17:7 Ps 85:7
[f]Ps 7:1
[g]17:8 Pr 7:2
[h]Ps 36:7; 57:1; 63:7; 91:1,4
[i]17:9 Ps 18:48
[j]17:10 Ps 119:70
[k]Ps 31:18
[l]17:11 Ps 88:17
[m]Ps 37:14; 62:4
[n]17:12 Ps 7:2; 10:9
[o]17:13 Ps 55:23
[p]Ps 7:12
[q]17:14 Ps 73:3-7
[r]17:15 Ps 11:7; Rv 22:4
[s]Ps 16:11; 21:6; 73:28
[t]18:title 2Sm 22

[A]17:3 Or evil; my mouth will not sin   [B]17:4 God's instruction   [C]17:7 Or love, You who save with Your right hand those seeking refuge from adversaries   [D]17:9 Lit from the presence of   [E]17:9 Or who plunder me   [F]17:10 Lit have closed up their fat   [G]17:11 Vg; one Hb ms, LXX read They cast me out; MT reads Our steps   [H]17:11 Lit They set their eyes   [i]17:12 Lit He is   [J]17:15 Lit form

---

17:7 Wonders is similar to "wonderful works" (see note at 9:1). Though this could be general enough to include works of creation, here it seems to be related to God's intervention in a time of need. The terms "wonders," **faithful love**, and **right hand** also occur together in Ex 15:11-13 where Moses in his song related the events of the exodus and God's wonderful acts that were part of Israel's redemption.

17:8 Both images in verse 8 convey the idea of protection. The **pupil of** the **eye** is that part of the body that is closely guarded (Dt 32:10; Pr 7:2). The image of being hidden **in the shadow of Your wings** portrays God as a mother bird protecting her young (36:7; 57:1).

17:10-12 The Hebrew in verse 10 is literally "they have closed up their fat." Fat represented prosperity, but such a state of abundance could and often did lead to callousness and rebellion (73:7; Dt 32:15; Jr 5:28). The idea here is that these enemies of God had become **hardened** toward Him and were surrounding the psalmist (both here and in v. 9) to attack a person who was faithful to God. The Hebrew text at the beginning of verse 11 is literally "our steps," which is difficult. Other texts read a verb such as **advance**, a reading that is more understandable and fits the context. On the **lion** imagery, see note at 7:1-2.

17:13-14 Rise up probably expresses the military idea of preparing for battle since it is linked with **Your sword** (see note at 7:6-8). The meaning of **world** here is similar to the use of the Greek *cosmos* in the NT to describe the world

system that is against God. These men belong to the world system, and their inheritance or **portion** was only in **this** earthly **life** (see Ec 9:9). God would **fill their bellies** with punishment, so much so that it would continue in the generations to come (Ex 20:5; Dt 5:9; Jb 21:19).

17:15 Seeing God's **face** is equivalent to receiving blessings from Him (see note at 4:6). There is a contrast between this faithful one being **satisfied** with God and the wicked being satisfied with God's punishment in verse 14. Its use in verse 14 is sarcastic in comparison to here.

Ps 18 title This title contains more information about its setting than any other psalm. It is linked with the Lord's deliverance of **David...from...all his enemies and from...Saul**. This rescue is not specified or described any further in the title. Neither does its parallel, 2 Samuel 22, give any detailed information about its precise setting in David's life. However, it is clearly set against the backdrop of a military victory where Yahweh fought for David and delivered him from his enemies. Such was the promise for those who obeyed Yahweh. He would fight for them and bring them victory (Dt 32:41-42). Elsewhere in the OT, only Moses and Joshua are called **the servant of the Lord** (cp. Ps 36 title).

18:1-2 In no other psalm is there such a large number of metaphors used to convey God's attributes. All of these relate to a military setting where God is seen as the real **strength** behind the person who fights. He also protects the

my fortress, and my deliverer,[a]
my God, my mountain
    where I seek refuge,
my shield[b] and the *horn
    of my salvation,[c]
my stronghold.
3 I called to the LORD, who is
    worthy of praise,[d]
and I was saved from my enemies.[e]

4 The ropes of death were wrapped
    around me;
the torrents of destruction terrified me.[f]
5 The ropes of *Sheol entangled me;
the snares of death confronted me.[g]
6 I called to the LORD in my distress,
and I cried to my God for help.
From His temple He heard my voice,[h]
and my cry to Him reached His ears.[i]

7 Then the earth shook and quaked;
the foundations of the mountains
    trembled;[j]
they shook because He burned
    with anger.
8 Smoke rose from His nostrils,
and consuming fire came
    from His mouth;
coals were set ablaze by it.[A,k]
9 He parted the heavens and came down,[l]

a dark cloud beneath His feet.
10 He rode on a cherub and flew,
soaring on the wings of the wind.[m]
11 He made darkness His hiding place,
dark storm clouds His canopy
    around Him.[n]
12 From the radiance of His presence,[o]
His clouds swept onward with hail
    and blazing coals.
13 The LORD thundered from[B] heaven;
the *Most High projected His voice.[C,p]
14 He shot His arrows
    and scattered them;
He hurled[D] lightning bolts
    and routed them.[q]
15 The depths of the sea became visible,
the foundations of the world
    were exposed,
at Your rebuke, LORD,
at the blast of the breath
    of Your nostrils.[r]

16 He reached down from heaven
and took hold of me;
He pulled me out of deep waters.[s]
17 He rescued me
    from my powerful enemy
and from those who hated me,
for they were too strong for me.[t]

Cross references (center column):

[a] 18:2 Ps 62:7; 94:22
[b] Gn 15:1; Dt 33:29; Ps 3:3; 5:12; 28:7; 119:114
[c] 1Sm 2:1,10; Lk 1:69
[d] 18:3 Ps 48:1; 96:4; 145:3
[e] Ps 138:7
[f] 18:4 Ps 124:4
[g] 18:5 Ps 116:3
[h] 18:6 Ps 3:4
[i] Ps 34:15
[j] 18:7 Is 13:13; Hg 2:6
[k] 18:8 Ps 21:9; 50:3
[l] 18:9 Ps 144:5; Is 64:1
[m] 18:10 Ps 104:3
[n] 18:11 Ps 97:2
[o] 18:12 Ps 50:2; Is 60:3
[p] 18:13 Ps 29:3; 104:7
[q] 18:14 Ps 144:6
[r] 18:15 Ex 15:8; Ps 106:9; Nah 1:4
[s] 18:16 Ps 144:7
[t] 18:17 Ps 35:10; 59:1; 142:6

[A] 18:8 Or *ablaze from Him*   [B] 18:13 Some Hb mss, LXX, Tg, Jer; other Hb mss read *in*   [C] 18:13 Some Hb mss read *voice, with hail and fiery coals*   [D] 18:14 Or *multiplied*

---

psalmist as a hiding place from the enemy (his **rock . . . fortress . . . mountain**, and **stronghold**). God also protects him by guarding him against the onslaught of weapons (He is his **shield**) and rescues him from his enemies (He is his **deliverer** and his **salvation**). In keeping with the military imagery in this psalm, the **horn** of **salvation** may refer to one of the horns of the altar, which represented a place of refuge (1Kg 1:50-51). However, it more likely refers to the horn of a wild animal that gored its enemies (Dt 33:17; Ps 92:10), signifying military strength.

18:3 Worthy of praise in some contexts is based on the attributes of God (48:1; 96:4; 145:3), but here it is clearly connected with specific events in the life of the psalmist.

18:4-5 The perception of the inevitability of death is pictured in a number of ways in the psalms (such as being near Sheol; 88:3). In this case it is pictured as being entangled in **ropes** and unable to escape (116:3; 119:61). **Torrents** is an image of being overwhelmed with water and in danger of drowning (Jnh 2:3,5). When pieced together such imagery describes being tangled in ropes while overtaken with a flood of water. There was absolutely no chance to swim away since the psalmist's limbs were bound and unable to move. Death itself **confronted** him in the same way enemies did (17:13) and would not allow him to escape.

18:6 Temple most likely refers to heaven in this context (see note at 11:4-5).

18:7-15 These verses describe a theophany where God reveals His power through natural phenomena such as an earthquake (v. 7) and a thunderstorm (vv. 13-14). **Mountains**

represent stability within the natural order, so their shaking and trembling describes God's power to bring upheaval to what seemed secure (Jdg 5:5; 1Sm 14:15). **Smoke** and **consuming fire** combined with God's voice that **thundered from heaven** is reminiscent of the Sinai experience (Ex 24:17; Dt 4:12,24; 9:3). The image of God acting as a warrior who fights for His people and uses the natural elements as His weapons is also connected with Israel's past experiences (Jos 10:11; Jdg 5:4,20). God's riding **on a cherub**—imagery found in creation hymns (19:1; 104:3)—blends the supernatural with the natural. Such a mixture is a common feature in many ancient Near Eastern myths, particularly those related to Baal, the Canaanite storm god. Some interpreters see this section of the psalm as a polemic against Baal, showing that Yahweh is the sovereign Lord of creation. Psalm 18:15 seems to be connected with the exodus event when **the depths of the sea became visible** because of God's breath (see Ex 14:21).

18:16-19 Reaching **down**, taking **hold**, and pulling **out** are anthropomorphic descriptions of God's condescension to rescue the psalmist in his time of need. These terms also allude to the image of a well as the place where one feels trapped during times of distress, connecting the concepts of "drawn up" and rescued (30:3; 40:2; Jr 38:10). The **deep waters** are related to the "torrents of destruction" in verse 4 and are identified more specifically as enemies. The **spacious place** is another illustration of being delivered from one's enemies (see note at 4:1). There is assurance that God delights in His people when He rescues them from harm and protects them from their enemies (41:11).

18 They confronted me in the day
    of my distress,
but the LORD was my support.ᵃ
19 He brought me out to a spacious place;ᵇ
He rescued me because He delighted
    in me.ᶜ

20 The LORD rewarded me
according to my righteousness;ᵈ
He repaid me
according to the cleanness of my hands.ᵉ
21 For I have kept the ways of the LORD
and have not turned from my God
    to wickedness.ᶠ
22 Indeed, I have kept all His ordinances
    in mindᴬ
and have not disregarded His statutes.ᵍ
23 I was blameless toward Himʰ
and kept myself from sinning.
24 So the LORD repaid me
according to my righteousness,ⁱ
according to the cleanness of my hands
    in His sight.ʲ

25 With the faithful
You prove Yourself faithful;
with the blameless man
You prove Yourself blameless;
26 with the pure
You prove Yourself pure,
but with the crooked
You prove Yourself shrewd.ᵏ
27 For You rescue an afflicted people,ˡ
but You humble those
    with haughty eyes.ᵐ
28 LORD, You light my lamp;
my God illuminates my darkness.ⁿ
29 With You I can attack a barrier,ᴮ
and with my God I can leap over a wall.ᵒ

30 God—His way is perfect;ᵖ
the word of the LORD is pure.ᑫ
He is a shield to all who take refuge
    in Him.ʳ
31 For who is God besides •Yahweh?ˢ
And who is a rock? Only our God.ᵗ
32 God—He clothes me with strengthᵘ
and makes my way perfect.
33 He makes my feet like the feet of a deerᵛ
and sets me securely on the heights.ᶜ,ʷ
34 He trains my hands for war;ˣ
my arms can bend a bow of bronze.ʸ
35 You have given me the shield
    of Your salvation;
Your right hand upholds me,ᶻ
and Your humility exalts me.
36 You widen a place beneath me
    for my steps,ᵃᵃ
and my ankles do not give way.ᵃᵇ

37 I pursue my enemies
    and overtake them;
I do not turn back until they are
    wiped out.ᵃᶜ
38 I crush them, and they cannot get up;
they fall beneath my feet.ᵃᵈ
39 You have clothed me with strength
    for battle;ᵃᵉ
You subdue my adversaries
    beneath me.ᵃᶠ
40 You have made my enemies retreat
    before me;ᴰ,ᵃᵍ
I annihilate those who hate me.ᵃʰ
41 They cry for help, but there is no one
    to save themᵃⁱ—
they cry to the LORD, but He does not
    answer them.ᵃʲ
42 I pulverize them like dust
before the wind;ᵃᵏ

Cross references (center column):

ᵃ18:18 Ps 55:22; 59:16
ᵇ18:19 Ps 31:8; 118:5
ᶜPs 41:11
ᵈ18:20 Ps 7:8
ᵉPs 24:4
ᶠ18:21 Jb 23:11; Ps 119:101
ᵍ18:22 Lv 18:4-5
ʰ18:23 Dt 18:13; Ps 37:18; 119:1
ⁱ18:24 2Ch 6:23
ʲPs 24:4
ᵏ18:25-26 Mt 16:27; Rv 22:12
ˡ18:27 Ps 72:12
ᵐPs 138:6
ⁿ18:28 Ps 112:4; Is 42:16
ᵒ18:29 Mt 19:26; Php 4:13
ᵖ18:30 Dt 32:4
ᑫPs 19:7
ʳPs 91:4; 144:2
ˢ18:31 Dt 32:39; 1Sm 2:2; Ps 86:8
ᵗPs 62:2
ᵘ18:32 Is 45:5
ᵛ18:33 Hab 3:19
ʷDt 32:13; Is 58:14
ˣ18:34 Ps 144:1
ʸJb 29:20
ᶻ18:35 Ps 89:21
ᵃᵃ18:36 Ps 31:8; 118:5
ᵃᵇPs 66:9; Pr 4:12
ᵃᶜ18:37 Ps 44:5
ᵃᵈ18:38 Ps 36:12
ᵃᵉ18:39 1Sm 2:4
ᵃᶠ1Ch 17:10; Ps 81:14
ᵃᵍ18:40 Ex 23:27
ᵃʰDt 7:10
ᵃⁱ18:41 Ps 50:22
ᵃʲMc 3:4
ᵃᵏ18:42 2Kg 13:7

ᴬ18:22 Lit *Indeed, all His ordinances have been in front of me*   ᴮ18:29 Or *ridge*   ᶜ18:33 Or *on my high places*   ᴰ18:40 Or *You gave me the necks of my enemies*

18:20-24 This declaration of innocence is set off by the same statements in verses 20 and 24. Unlike its use in prayers, these statements of innocence are part of thanksgiving for answered prayer, indicating why God delivered the psalmist from his calamity. Righteousness is further clarified as **cleanness of . . . hands**, meaning integrity in his obedience to God's commands (24:4; see note at 7:3-5). The psalmist was not absolutely perfect and free from sin, but he was **blameless** in terms of his faithfulness to God (15:2; Dt 18:13).

18:25-26 These verses make the connection between the statements of innocence in the previous section and Yahweh's covenant faithfulness. This is an outworking of the covenant stipulations in Deuteronomy 28 whereby God is **faithful** to those who are faithful to Him.

18:28-29 **Light** is sometimes connected with salvation (deliverance) and provides security and assurance that God protects His own (27:1). The security becomes confidence in 18:29 with the sense that the psalmist could **leap over a**

wall. In other words, he could accomplish the impossible with God on his side (Mt 19:26; Mk 9:23; Lk 18:27).

18:31 The uniqueness of Yahweh is significant in Israel's theology, and it forms the basis for the distinctiveness of Israel among the other nations (35:10; 89:8; Ex 15:11; Dt 4:32-40).

18:32-36 The descriptions in these verses are of traits that are important for warfare. **Strength** is the clothing (1Sm 2:4). **Feet of a deer** represent swiftness (2Sm 1:23; 2:18). God made the psalmist more skillful by training his **hands**. The **bow of bronze** is unusual since bows were not covered with metal. The point seems to be that it was strengthened and made more effective as a weapon (Jb 20:24). The **shield** is perhaps related to its earlier mention where it was identified with God Himself (vv. 2,30). On **widen a place**, compare verse 19 and see note at 4:1.

18:37-42 Rather than being pursued (7:1,5), those who are strengthened by God pursue their enemies (Ex 15:9). The

I trample them[A] like mud
　in the streets.[a]
43 You have freed me from the feuds
　among the people;
You have appointed me the head
　of nations;[b]
a people I had not known serve me.[c]
44 Foreigners submit to me grudgingly;
as soon as they hear,[B] they obey me.[d]
45 Foreigners lose heart
and come trembling
　from their fortifications.[e]

46 The LORD lives—may my rock
　be praised!
The God of my salvation is exalted.[f]
47 God—He gives me vengeance[g]
and subdues peoples under me.[h]
48 He frees me from my enemies.
You exalt me above my adversaries;
You rescue me from violent men.[i]
49 Therefore I will praise You, Yahweh,
　among the nations;
I will sing about Your name.[j]
50 He gives great victories to His king;[k]
He shows loyalty to His anointed,
to David and his descendants forever.[l]

[a] 18:42 Is 10:6; Mc 7:10
[b] 18:43 2Sm 8:1-14
[c] Is 55:5
[d] 18:44 Dt 33:29; Ps 66:3
[e] 18:45 Mc 7:17
[f] 18:46 Ps 62:2,6
[g] 18:47 2Sm 4:8; Ps 94:1
[h] Ps 47:3; 144:2
[i] 18:48 Ps 59:1; 140:1
[j] 18:49 Rm 15:9
[k] 18:50 Ps 144:10
[l] 2Sm 7:12-13; Ps 89:4,29
[m] 19:1 Ps 50:6; Rm 1:19-20
[n] 19:4 Rm 10:18
[o] Is 40:22
[p] 19:6 Ec 1:5

Psalm 19
The Witness of Creation and Scripture

For the choir director. A Davidic psalm.

1 The heavens declare the glory of God,
and the sky[C] proclaims the work
　of His hands.[m]
2 Day after day they pour out speech;
night after night
　they communicate knowledge.[D]
3 There is no speech; there are no words;
their voice is not heard.
4 Their message[E] has gone out to all
　the earth,
and their words to the ends
　of the world.[n]

In the heavens[F] He has pitched a tent
　for the sun.[o]
5 It is like a groom coming from
　the[G] bridal chamber;
it rejoices like an athlete
　running a course.
6 It rises from one end of the heavens
and circles[H] to their other end;[p]
nothing is hidden from its heat.

[A] 18:42 Some Hb mss, LXX, Syr, Tg; other Hb mss read *I poured them out*　[B] 18:44 Lit *At the hearing of the ear*　[C] 19:1 Or *expanse*
[D] 19:2 Or *Day to day pours out speech, and night to night communicates knowledge*　[E] 19:4 LXX, Sym, Syr, Vg; MT reads *line*　[F] 19:4 Lit
In them　[G] 19:5 Lit *his*　[H] 19:6 Lit *its circuit is*

shift between first-person and second-person forms in these verses indicates that God is the One who is at work through His warrior. Though God can work directly, He also uses people as His instruments to accomplish His purposes.

18:43-48 The designation **head of nations** along with the verb **subdues** refers to the dominion over the nations that was promised to the Davidic ruler of Israel (110:1-2; Jr 31:7). Some interpreters see this as recalling situations where David himself conquered other nations (2Sm 8:9-10; 10:19).

18:49 The **nations** are not just defeated and subdued by Israel's king; they become the audience for the **praise** of Yahweh among His people (57:9; 108:3) so that they too participate in singing praise to God (67:4).

18:50 The combination of **king . . . anointed . . . David and his descendants** makes the connection with the Davidic covenant even more explicit than the previous verses (110:1-2; 2Sm 7:8-14).

19:1 Although the **heavens** can refer to God's dwelling place, here it is clarified by **sky**, which is what can be seen from the perspective of those who live on the earth. The "sky" is the same Hebrew word as the expanse that separated water from water in Gn 1:6-8. Creation is sometimes personified as a witness to God's work among His people, particularly in the covenant relationship He has with them (Dt 4:26; 30:19; Is 1:2). In this context one specific part of creation is personified as declaring and proclaiming a message. The parallelism between **the glory of God** and **the work of His hands** indicates that the objects of creation are

demonstrations (or evidence) of God's glory (50:6; 89:5-8; 97:6; Rm 1:19-20).

19:2-3 Pour out is literally "gush" or "bubble up." This phrase is most often used for springs or fountains of water. The significance of the term here seems to be that **speech** never ceases. The concept is intensified by the doubling of the terms **day** and **night**. The message goes out all the time without ceasing. The paradox is that there is speech in verse 2, but there is **no speech** in verse 3. Although the same Hebrew term (*'omer*) appears in both verses, it is used differently. In the first instance it is equivalent to the message in verse 1; in the second instance it means **words**. Therefore, it is a message with clearly defined content, but it is not communicated with the words of human language.

19:4-6 While verse 2 says that the message comes at all times, this verse adds that it also comes to all places. The word for **world** (Hb *tevel*) is not the usual word for **earth** (as in the first line), but it denotes dry land that is capable of sustaining life (9:8; 24:1)—in other words, the inhabited world. No one can escape the message either in time or in space, and everyone is accountable for the message (Rm 1:20). The focus turns from the more general **heavens** to the most obvious and spectacular object in them: **the sun**. It is also personified and compared to **a groom** and **an athlete**. These images are used together to convey the idea of youthful strength, a concept that is elsewhere associated with the sun, especially when it rises (Jdg 5:31). The fact that **nothing is hidden** from the sun reinforces the idea that the message of God's glory is as obvious as the most visible and powerful object in God's creation.

7 The instruction of the LORD is perfect,
renewing one's life;[a]
the •testimony of the LORD
is trustworthy,
making the inexperienced wise.[b]

8 The precepts of the LORD are right,
making the heart glad;[c]
the command of the LORD is radiant,
making the eyes light up.[d]

9 The •fear of the LORD is pure,
enduring forever;[e]
the ordinances of the LORD are reliable
and altogether righteous.[f]

10 They are more desirable than gold—
than an abundance of pure gold;[g]
and sweeter than honey,
which comes from the honeycomb.[h]

11 In addition, Your servant is warned
by them;
there is great reward in keeping them.[i]

12 Who perceives his unintentional sins?
Cleanse me from my hidden faults.[j]

13 Moreover, keep Your servant
from willful sins;[k]
do not let them rule over me.[l]
Then I will be innocent
and cleansed from blatant rebellion.[m]

14 May the words of my mouth

Cross references:
[a] 19:7 Ps 111:7
[b] Ps 93:5; 119:130
[c] 19:8 Ps 119:14
[d] Ps 13:3
[e] 19:9 Ps 111:10
[f] Ps 119:30
[g] 19:10 Ps 119:72,127
[h] Ps 119:103
[i] 19:11 Pr 29:18
[j] 19:12 Ps 90:8
[k] 19:13 Nm 15:30
[l] Gn 4:7
[m] Ps 51:7; Ezk 36:25
[n] 19:14 Ps 104:34
[o] Ps 78:35
[p] 20:1 Ps 50:15; 77:2; 102:2
[q] Ps 46:7,11
[r] 20:2 Ps 3:4; 110:2; 128:5
[s] 20:3 Ps 119:108
[t] 20:4 Ps 21:2; 145:19
[u] Ps 138:8
[v] 20:5 Ps 21:1
[w] Is 13:2
[x] Ps 21:2; 1Pt 3:12

and the meditation of my heart
be acceptable to You,[n]
LORD, my rock and my Redeemer.[o]

Psalm 20
Deliverance in Battle
For the choir director. A Davidic psalm.

1 May •Yahweh answer you in a day
of trouble;[p]
may the name of Jacob's God
protect you.[q]

2 May He send you help
from the sanctuary
and sustain you from •Zion.[r]

3 May He remember
all your offerings
and accept your •burnt offering.[s]
          •*Selah*

4 May He give you what
your heart desires[t]
and fulfill your whole purpose.[u]

5 Let us shout for joy
at your victory[v]
and lift the banner in the name
of our God.[w]
May Yahweh fulfill
all your requests.[x]

19:7-9 The shift of subject between verses 1-6 and verses 7-14 seems abrupt. However, the common element in both cases is God's revelation of Himself and His purposes to mankind. In the first part of the psalm, it is God's creation (general revelation), whereas in the second part, it is the words that God specifically communicated to His people (special revelation). On the Hebrew word *torah* as **instruction**, see note at 1:2. **Perfect** is a term that is often used in relation to sacrifices that are acceptable to God because they are "unblemished" and "without defect" (Lv 1:3,10), but it can also refer to the perfect work of God (Dt 32:4). **Renewing one's life** means the restoration of strength or vitality (1Kg 17:22; Lm 1:11). **Making the eyes light up** seems like an unusual idiom, but it makes a connection between light and truth, or more specifically knowledge and understanding of the truth (119:105,130; Pr 6:23). The **fear of the LORD** is the only subject in this list that involves human response to God's instruction rather than a synonym for it. The concept involves obedience to God with an attitude of humility and reverence (see notes at 76:7 and 103:17-18). Its inclusion further demonstrates the relationship between fearing Yahweh and the knowledge and understanding of His truth (Pr 1:7; 9:10).

19:10-11 Gold and **honey** were valuable commodities in the ancient world, but God's words are even more valuable (119:103,127). The warning and **reward** are both positive benefits of knowing God's instruction because they keep God's servants from straying off the path of righteousness and provide them with blessings (119:35; Pr 4:18).

19:12-13 Unintentional or **hidden** sins can represent those that occur with or without proper instruction. The question is

rhetorical and assumes a negative answer. For this reason, continual cleansing is required for these sins. **Willful sins** are different in that they must be avoided or else they lead to being "cut off" from God and His people (Nm 15:30-31).

19:14 The final plea is that the psalmist's speech and thinking (**meditation**, from the Hb root *hgh*; see note at 1:2) reflect what is **acceptable** to God. The language of sacrifice is used to show that life should be lived as a sacrifice to God (Rm 12:1).

20:1 Day of trouble can refer to any distress (50:15; 77:2; 86:7), but in this case it is a crisis caused by enemies. This is validated by the main request of the psalm in 20:9 for the king's victory. **Name** appears three times in this psalm (vv. 1,5,7) and is used as a substitute for Yahweh Himself (68:4; 145:1-2). It can represent His protection (Pr 18:10). In the most general sense, it conveys God's self-revelation and represents His presence among His people (Dt 12:5,11; 1Kg 8:29). The use of **Jacob's** name as a reference to the nation of Israel also emphasizes the personal aspects of God's relationship with His people.

20:4 The heart's **desires** and **purpose** are related in the sense that God's purposes and His people's desires should be the same. The word "purpose" refers to counsel or plans, such as military advice (2Sm 16:20; 2Kg 18:20).

20:5 Banners were used in military campaigns to identify members of an army. These banners often included symbols or representations of the national gods who were fighting for the respective armies. Yahweh took on this role with Israel (Ex 15:3; Jos 23:10) and was identified as Israel's banner (Ex 17:15).

⁶ Now I know that the LORD gives victory
    to His anointed;ᵃ
He will answer him
    from His holy heaven
with mighty victories
    fromᴬ His right hand.ᵇ
⁷ Some take pride in chariots, and others
    in horses,
but we take pride in the name
    of Yahweh our God.ᶜ
⁸ They collapse and fall,
    but we rise and stand firm.ᵈ
⁹ LORD, give victory to the king!ᵉ
May Heᴮ answer us on the day
    that we call.

Psalm 21
The King's Victory

For the choir director. A Davidic psalm.

¹ LORD, the king finds joy
    in Your strength.
How greatly he rejoices
    in Your victory!ᶠ
² You have given him
    his heart's desireᵍ
and have not denied the request
    of his lips.ʰ   •Selah
³ For You meet him
    with rich blessings;
You place a crown of pure gold
    on his head.ⁱ
⁴ He asked You for life, and You gave it
    to him—

length of days forever and ever.ʲ
⁵ His glory is great through Your victory;
You confer majesty and splendor
    on him.ᵏ
⁶ You give him blessings forever;ˡ
You cheer him with joy
    in Your presence.ᵐ
⁷ For the king relies on the LORD;
through the faithful love
    of the •Most High
he is not shaken.ⁿ
⁸ Your hand will capture
    all your enemies;
your right hand will seize
    those who hate you.ᵒ
⁹ You will make them burn
    like a fiery furnace
    when you appear;
the LORD will engulf them
    in His wrath,
and fire will devour them.ᵖ
¹⁰ You will wipe their descendants
    from the earth
and their offspring
    from the •human race.�q
¹¹ Though they intend to harmᶜ you
    and devise a wicked plan,
    they will not prevail.ʳ
¹² Instead, you will put them to flight
when you aim your bowᴰ
    at their faces.ˢ
¹³ Be exalted, LORD, in Your strength;
    we will sing and praise Your might.ᵗ

ᵃ 20:6 Ps 18:50
ᵇ Ps 44:3; 98:1;
118:15
ᶜ 20:7 Ps 33:17;
Is 31:1
ᵈ 20:8 Is 2:11, 17;
Mc 7:8
ᵉ 20:9 Ps 18:50
ᶠ 21:1 Ps 28:7-8;
59:16-17
ᵍ 21:2 Ps 20:4;
145:19
ʰ Ps 20:5; 1Pt
3:12
ⁱ 21:3 2Sm 12:30;
1Ch 20:2
ʲ 21:4 Ps 61:6;
91:16
ᵏ 21:5 Ps 8:5;
96:6
ˡ 21:6 1Ch 17:27
ᵐ Ps 16:11
ⁿ 21:7 Ps 10:6;
16:8
ᵒ 21:8 Ex 15:6; Is
10:10
ᵖ 21:9 Ps 50:3;
97:3; Mal 4:1
q 21:10 1Kg
13:34; Ps 37:28;
Is 14:20
ʳ 21:11 Ps 2:1-3;
7:15-16; 10:2
ˢ 21:12 Ps 7:12
ᵗ 21:13 Ps 59:16;
81:1

ᴬ20:6 Some Hb mss, Aq, Sym, Jer, Syr read *with the victorious might of*   ᴮ20:9 Or *LORD, save. May the king*   ᶜ21:11 Lit *they stretch out evil against*   ᴰ21:12 Lit *aim with your bowstrings*

20:6 Anointed has the sense of being chosen, a title often related to Israel's king who was chosen by God to rule over His people (2:2; 45:7). In 20:2 help comes from Zion, but here help comes from **His holy heaven**. Although Yahweh dwelt among His people, His real domain from which He ruled was heaven (11:4; Is 66:1).

20:7-8 Human armaments were of no value if Yahweh was not fighting because He and His armies were more numerous and powerful than any human army (68:17). He had no concern or need for human weapons (147:10).

20:9 This verse specifies the purpose of the psalm—that the **king** would experience **victory**. Only Yahweh could grant this.

21:1-2 These verses tie this psalm to the previous one with the mention of **victory** (see note at 20:9) and **heart's desire** (see note at 20:4). This is a thanksgiving psalm that expressed thanks to Yahweh for giving victory to the king (21:1,7).

21:3 The **crown** is used as a sign of victory over a defeated power (2Sm 12:30).

21:4 Lengthening of **life** seems to be related to the king's victory over his enemies. To suffer defeat often meant to be killed, especially in the case of kings who led their own armies. Long life was apparently a common aim in prayer offered for kings (61:6; 72:17; 1Kg 3:11,14), and in a broader sense, this related not just to them but to their dynasties as well.

21:5 Majesty and splendor along with the crown of verse 3 recall the creation hymn in Psalm 8, where man himself is to function as God's co-regent. Together they are symbols of rule and dominion.

21:6-7 To be in the **presence** of God is the ultimate **joy** for a person who **relies** on Yahweh (16:11). On **Most High**, see note at 7:17.

21:8-10 The Hebrew word *yad* "hand" can mean power or strength, but when used of God it is often a symbol of His judgment (Ex 9:3; Dt 2:15; Jdg 2:15). **Fire** is associated with God's **wrath** (89:46), symbolizing the intensity and destructive power of God's judgment. Being wiped **from the earth** and having no **offspring** show the annihilation of a person or people (Dt 4:26; 2Sm 4:11; Am 9:8).

21:11-12 The **plan** of the wicked will not succeed because God will thwart them (2:1-2,9). In some contexts their evil plans come back to them (7:15-16; Pr 26:27), but here it is God Himself who will deal with them. **Put . . . to flight** is literally "turn a shoulder." It refers to the enemies turning

Psalm 22

From Suffering to Praise

For the choir director: according to "The Deer of the Dawn."[A] A Davidic psalm.

1 My God, my God, why have You
forsaken me?[a]
Why are You so far from my deliverance[b]
and from my words of groaning?[B,c]
2 My God, I cry by day, but You
do not answer,
by night, yet I have no rest.[d]
3 But You are holy,
enthroned on the praises of Israel.[e]
4 Our fathers trusted in You;
they trusted, and You rescued them.[f]
5 They cried to You and were set free;
they trusted in You
and were not disgraced.[g]

6 But I am a worm and not a man,[h]
scorned by men and despised by people.[i]
7 Everyone who sees me mocks me;
they sneer[C] and shake their heads:[j]
8 "He relies on[D] the LORD;
let Him rescue him;
let the LORD[E] deliver him,
since He takes pleasure in him."[k]

9 You took me from the womb,
making me secure
while at my mother's breast.[l]
10 I was given over to You at birth;[F]
You have been my God
from my mother's womb.[m]

11 Do not be far from me, because distress
is near
and there is no one to help.[n]

12 Many bulls surround me;
strong ones of Bashan encircle me.[o]
13 They open their mouths against me—
lions, mauling and roaring.[p]
14 I am poured out like water,[q]
and all my bones are disjointed;[r]
my heart is like wax,
melting within me.[s]
15 My strength is dried up like baked clay;[t]
my tongue sticks to the roof
of my mouth.[u]
You put me into the dust of death.[v]
16 For dogs have surrounded me;[w]
a gang of evildoers has closed in on me;
they pierced[G] my hands and my feet.[x]
17 I can count all my bones;
people[H] look and stare at me.[y]
18 They divided my garments
among themselves,
and they cast lots for my clothing.[z]

[a] 22:1 Mt 27:46; Mk 15:34 [b] Ps 10:1 [c] Ps 32:3; 38:8 [d] 22:2 Ps 42:3; 88:1 [e] 22:3 Ps 99:3 [f] 22:4 Ps 107:6 [g] 22:5 Ps 25:2; 31:1; 71:1; Is 49:23 [h] 22:6 Jb 25:6 [i] Ps 109:25; Is 53:3 [j] 22:7 Mt 27:39; Mk 15:29; Lk 23:35 [k] 22:8 Mt 27:43 [l] 22:9 Ps 71:6 [m] 22:10 Is 46:3; 49:1; Gl 1:15 [n] 22:11 2Kg 14:26; Ps 71:12; Is 63:5 [o] 22:12 Ps 68:30; Am 4:1 [p] 22:13 Ps 10:9; 17:12 [q] 22:14 Jb 30:16 [r] Jb 4:14; Ps 6:2; 32:3 [s] Nah 2:10 [t] 22:15 Ps 38:10 [u] Lm 4:4 [v] Ps 104:29 [w] 22:16 Ps 59:6,14 [x] Jn 20:25 [y] 22:17 Lk 23:35 [z] 22:18 Mt 27:35; Lk 23:34; Jn 19:24

[A] 22:title Perhaps a musical term [B] 22:1 Or *My words of groaning are so far from delivering me* [C] 22:7 Lit *separate with the lip* [D] 22:8 Or *Rely on* [E] 22:8 Lit *let Him* [F] 22:10 Lit *was cast on You from the womb* [G] 22:16 Some Hb mss, LXX, Syr; other Hb mss read *me; like a lion* [H] 22:17 Lit *they*

their back toward their attackers and running away (6:10; 9:3; Ex 23:27).

Ps 22 title "The Deer of the Dawn" was apparently a known tune of the time. The Hebrew word for "deer" (*'ayyeleth*) is similar to the rare word for "help" (*'eyaluth*) that is used in verse 19.

22:1 This psalm opens with a question about God's rejection, similar to other lament psalms (10:1; 13:1-2). This rejection is represented by the term **forsaken**. The same idea appears elsewhere in the psalm with God being "far away" (v. 19) and "hiding His face" (v. 24). In his suffering, the psalmist foreshadowed the Messiah; in His suffering, Jesus identified with the psalmist (Mt 27:46). When Jesus quoted this first line, He was probably calling attention to the whole psalm, including the theme of victory at the end.

22:3-5 These verses identify the psalmist with the nation of **Israel** and more specifically with Yahweh's covenant faithfulness to His people as shown by His deliverance of them time and time again (78:53; 107:6). **Enthroned on the praises** is unusual, picturing Yahweh's dwelling above the cherubim on the ark of the covenant (80:1; 99:1). However, in this instance it is the praise of God's people that is the focus because Yahweh is the praise of Israel (Dt 10:21).

22:6-8 Worm expresses humiliation (Jb 25:6; Is 41:14), an idea that is further developed with the scorn of the enemies. Shaking their **heads** was a physical gesture often associated with sneering and mocking (see textual footnote on 44:14; cp. 64:8). This disgrace was in direct contrast to the fact that Yahweh had kept Israel from disgrace (22:5). The thought that Yahweh would not rescue one of His own was a common assumption by Israel's enemies (3:2; 71:11).

22:9-10 The phrase **over to You** is in the emphatic position in the Hebrew text, emphasizing that Yahweh is the One in whom the psalmist has trusted since birth.

22:12-13 The connection between one's enemies and wild animals, especially **lions**, is found in other psalms (see note at 7:1-2). With **bulls** the point seems to be strength rather than fierceness.

22:14-15 The terminology in these verses conveys the notion of being drained of **strength**. A **heart** like melting **wax** is similar to the image of "melting hearts" in other contexts where the emotion of fear is so intense that all courage disappears (Dt 20:8; Jos 2:11; 7:5). **Dust of death** implies the nearness and inevitability of death (Jb 7:21; 10:9) and is sometimes linked with Sheol (Jb 17:16).

22:16 The Hebrew text is difficult, reading literally "like a lion my hands and my feet" for **pierced my hands and my feet**. Other manuscript traditions, including the LXX, read the Hebrew *ka'ari* ("like the lion") as a verb from the Hebrew root *krh*, meaning either "to bind" or "to dig." Digging could be synonymous with piercing. Christians have often adopted this reading and seen it as a prophetic allusion to Christ's crucifixion since NT authors quote so much of this psalm in relation to that event (e.g., Mt 27:46).

22:17-18 Counting **bones** seems to be related to imagery where a person was so emaciated from suffering or

19 But You, LORD, don't be far away.[a]
My strength, come quickly to help me.[b]
20 Deliver my life from the sword,[c]
my only life[A] from the power
of these dogs.
21 Save me from the mouth of the lion![d]
You have rescued[B] me
from the horns of the wild oxen.

22 I will proclaim Your name
to my brothers;
I will praise You in the congregation.[e]
23 You who *fear *Yahweh, praise Him![f]
All you descendants of Jacob,
honor Him!
All you descendants of Israel,
revere Him![g]
24 For He has not despised or detested
the torment of the afflicted.[h]
He did not hide His face from him[i]
but listened when he cried to Him
for help.[j]

25 I will give praise[C]
in the great congregation
because of You;[k]
I will fulfill my vows

26 before those who fear You.[D,l]
The humble[E] will eat
and be satisfied;[m]
those who seek the LORD
will praise Him.
May your hearts live forever![n]

27 All the ends of the earth
will remember
and turn to the LORD.
All the families of the nations
will bow down before You,[o]
28 for kingship belongs to the LORD;
He rules over the nations.[p]
29 All who prosper on earth will eat
and bow down;
all those who go down to the dust
will kneel before Him—
even the one who cannot preserve
his life.[q]
30 Their descendants will serve Him;
the next generation will be told
about the Lord.[r]
31 They will come and tell a people
yet to be born
about His righteousness—
what He has done.[s]

Cross references (center column):

a 22:19 Ps 10:1
b Ps 70:5
c 22:20 Jr 39:18
d 22:21 Ps 35:17; 2Tm 4:17
e 22:22 Ps 40:10; Heb 2:12
f 22:23 Rv 19:5
g Ps 135:20
h 22:24 Ps 69:33
i Ezk 39:29
j Ps 28:2
k 22:25 Ps 35:18; 40:9-10
l Ps 61:8
m 22:26 Ps 107:9
n Ps 40:16; 69:32
o 22:27 Ps 2:8; 86:9
p 22:28 1Ch 16:31; 2Ch 20:6; Mal 1:14; Rv 15:3
q 22:29 Is 45:23; Rm 14:11; Php 2:10
r 22:30 Ps 102:18,28
s 22:31 Ps 71:18; 78:6

[A]22:20 Lit *my only one*　[B]22:21 Lit *answered*　[C]22:25 Lit *my praise*　[D]22:25 Lit *Him*　[E]22:26 Or, *poor*, or *afflicted*

---

brutality that his bones were visible (102:5; Jb 19:20; 33:21). Dividing **garments** is an attested practice in Middle Assyrian laws where a criminal's clothes could be given to the prosecutor or to those carrying out the sentence. It was apparently practiced in other cultures, including Rome in the first century, as evident in the death of Jesus (Mt 27:35; Jn 19:23).

22:20-21 The psalmist uses imagery from animals to represent enemies. All are repeated with the exception of the **wild oxen** instead of bulls. Their **horns** that gored in an attack are the main focus in that image (see note at 18:1-2). **Dogs** might not seem like a negative image because of their role as pets in modern Western society, but in much of the ancient Near East they were never domesticated and were always wild and ravenous animals.

22:22-24 Verse 22 begins a new major section in this psalm, shifting the focus from petition to thanksgiving. The shift might indicate that the prayer of verses 1-21 had been answered or that such an answer was anticipated. Thanksgiving was to be offered **in the congregation** to evoke **praise** from the people of God. This was the responsibility of anyone whom Yahweh rescued, so that the entire community could rejoice in God's acts of deliverance (66:16). Whereas the psalmist praised God for being delivered from death, Jesus the Messiah brought glory to God through His death and resurrection.

22:25-26 The **vows** were those made during the time of prayer (50:14; 61:8; 66:13). Their fulfillment also took place **in the great congregation** as a further testimony of God's goodness to the psalmist. Any ceremonially clean person witnessing someone's praise offering was permitted to **eat** from it (Lv 7:11-21).

22:27-31 The psalm ends by broadening to the most univer-

sal purpose of God's kingdom over the earth. Israel's purpose was to be a testimony to other nations so they would **bow down** before Yahweh and serve Him (67:2; 72:11,17; 86:9). The growth of the kingdom throughout time is demonstrated in the phrase **a people yet to be born** (future generations). The inclusion of **those who go down to the dust** who would pay homage to Yahweh (v. 29) is unusual, since in other psalms it is clear that the dead cannot praise Him (6:5; 88:10-12). This is more likely a reference to the final stage of God's kingdom where even the dead are brought back to life to recognize Yahweh's authority over all things (Dn 12:2).

---

shevet

Hebrew Pronunciation	[SHAY vet]
HCSB Translation	scepter, rod, tribe
Uses in Judges	16
Uses in the OT	190
Focus Passage	Psalm 23:4

Shevet means *rod*. It indicates shepherds' *rods* (Ezk 20:37), used for counting (Lv 27:32) or protection (Ps 23:4). *Shevet* is also associated with applying discipline (Pr 13:24). Used symbolically as fury's power (Pr 22:8), *shevet* connotes *discipline* (Is 11:4) or *punishment* (Jb 37:13). Assyria was the *rod* of God's anger against Israel (Is 10:5). *Shevet* can be a military weapon, a *club* (2Sm 23:21) or *spear* (2Sm 18:14). *Shevet* as a symbol of power meant *scepter* (Gn 49:10) or *staff* (Jdg 5:14) of rule. It could represent one kingdom's destructive power over another (Is 14:29). A *scepter* of justice implies righteous rule (Ps 45:6). *Shevet* apparently became identified with those ruled in the most common denotation, *tribe*. The phrase "tribes of Israel" occurs 48x (Gn 49:28). Israel as a whole can be a *shevet* (Jr 10:16).

Psalm 23
The Good Shepherd

A Davidic psalm.

1 The Lord is my shepherd;[a]
there is nothing I lack.[b]
2 He lets me lie down in green pastures;[c]
He leads me beside quiet waters.[d]
3 He renews my life;
He leads me along the right paths[A]
for His name's sake.[e]
4 Even when I go
through the darkest valley,[B]
I fear no danger,

for You are with me;[f]
Your rod and Your staff[C]—
they comfort me.[g]

5 You prepare a table before me
in the presence of my enemies;
You anoint my head with oil;[h]
my cup overflows.[i]

6 Only goodness and faithful love
will pursue me
all the days of my life,[j]
and I will dwell in[D] the house
of the Lord
as long as I live.[E,k]

a 23:1 Ps 78:52; Jr 31:10; Ezk 34:11-13; Jn 10:11
b Ps 34:9-10; Php 4:19
c 23:2 Ps 65:11-13; Ezk 34:14
d Ps 36:8
e 23:3 Ps 5:8; Pr 4:11
f 23:4 Is 43:2
g Mc 7:14
h 23:5 Ps 92:10
i Ps 16:5
j 23:6 Ps 25:7; 109:21
k Ps 27:4-6

A 23:3 Or me in paths of righteousness   B 23:4 Or the valley of the shadow of death   C 23:4 A shepherd's equipment   D 23:6 LXX, Sym, Syr, Tg, Vg, Jer; MT reads will return to   E 23:6 Lit Lord for length of days; traditionally Lord forever

23:1 The Lord is often referred to as the **shepherd** of His people, Israel (74:1; 80:1; Is 40:11; Ezk 34:11-16). In the ancient Near East, kings were commonly known as the shepherds of their people. Since Yahweh is the true King, the title shepherd is most appropriate.

23:2-3 Lets me lie down is a Hebrew form implying causality, showing that God is the cause of the refreshment. On **renews my life**, see note at 19:7-9. **Right paths** might have a twofold idea. In keeping with the shepherd and sheep image, it can mean safe paths that are free from danger. In the larger context of Wisdom literature it refers to paths of righteousness, though usually that would contrast one path of life with another leading to death. The former idea is probably the primary meaning here.

23:4 Some argue that the Hebrew term *tsalmaweth* is related to an Akkadian word *(tselem)* that means "deep darkness." Others say it comes from two Hebrew words, *tsal* and *moth*, and means "shadow of death." It occurs approximately 20 times in the OT. It is clear that it implies intense darkness that represents extreme danger (Jb 10:21; 28:3; Jr 2:6). "Darkest" fits this specific context, since it is in the

darkest valley where the greatest danger (such as a predator) lurks for sheep.

23:5 The image shifts from shepherd to friend. The identification of Yahweh with a shepherd emphasizes His care and protection, but He is much more than that for a person who is in close fellowship with Him. While protection from **enemies** is still implied, it is intensified with the image of a banquet **(table)** that is served while the enemies look on. In Jewish society **oil** was a symbol for rejoicing (104:15) and was also used in the welcoming of guests (45:7; 92:10; Lk 7:46).

23:6 The verb **pursue** is commonly used for attackers, but here Yahweh's **goodness and faithful love** are personified as the ones who chased the psalmist throughout his life. **As long as I live** represents the Hebrew "for the length of days." This is equivalent to the parallel **all the days of my life**. Though some translate this as "forever," it is nowhere else used that way but always refers to one's earthly life (91:16; Pr 3:2,16). **Dwell** (Hb *yashav*) is similar to the word for "return" (Hb *shuv*). In this verbal form, it differs only in the vowels. It is possible that the request is to return to the sanctuary of Yahweh throughout one's life, although the preposition **in** argues for the idea of "dwell."

Shepherd leading his sheep

Psalm 24
The King of Glory

A Davidic psalm.

[1] The earth and everything in it,
the world and its inhabitants,
belong to the LORD;[a]

[2] for He laid its foundation on the seas
and established it on the rivers.[b]

[3] Who may ascend the mountain
of the LORD?
Who may stand in His holy place?[c]

[4] The one who has *clean hands
and a pure heart,[d]
who has not set his mind[A] on
what is false,[e]
and who has not sworn deceitfully.

[5] He will receive blessing from the LORD,[f]
and righteousness from the God
of his salvation.[g]

[6] Such is the generation of those
who seek Him,
who seek the face of the God
of Jacob.[B,h]   *Selah

[7] Lift up your heads, you gates!
Rise up, ancient doors!

[a] 24:1 Dt 10:14; Ps 89:11; 1Co 10:26
[b] 24:2 Ps 104:5; Pr 8:29
[c] 24:3 Ps 15:1
[d] 24:4 Jb 22:30; Ps 73:1; Mt 5:8
[e] Ps 31:6; 119:37
[f] 24:5 Ps 115:13
[g] Ps 65:5
[h] 24:6 Ps 27:8
[i] 24:7 Ps 118:19-20; Is 26:2
[j] 24:8 Ex 15:3; Ps 76:3-6
[k] 24:10 Is 24:23
[l] 25:1 Ps 38:15; 86:4
[m] 25:2 Ps 31:1; 71:1
[n] Ps 13:4; 41:11
[o] 25:3 Is 49:23
[p] Pr 2:22; Is 21:2
[q] 25:4 Ex 33:13; Ps 27:11; 86:11
[r] 25:5 Jn 16:13

Then the King of glory will come in.[i]
[8] Who is this King of glory?
The LORD, strong and mighty,
the LORD, mighty in battle.[j]

[9] Lift up your heads, you gates!
Rise up, ancient doors!
Then the King of glory will come in.

[10] Who is He, this King of glory?
The LORD of *Hosts,
He is the King of glory.[k]   Selah

Psalm 25
Dependence on the LORD

Davidic.

[1] LORD,[C] I turn to You.[D,l]

[2] My God, I trust in You.
Do not let me be disgraced;[m]
do not let my enemies gloat over me.[n]

[3] No one who waits for You
will be disgraced;[o]
those who act treacherously
without cause
will be disgraced.[p]

[4] Make Your ways known to me, LORD;
teach me Your paths.[q]

[5] Guide me in Your truth and teach me,[r]

[A] 24:4 Or not lifted up his soul [B] 24:6 LXX; some Hb mss, Syr read seek Your face, God of Jacob; other Hb mss read seek Your face, Jacob [C] 25:1 The lines of this poem form an *acrostic. [D] 25:1 Or To You, LORD, I lift up my soul

---

24:1-2 Everything on earth belongs **to the LORD** by right of creation (Dt 10:14). **World** (Hb tevel) refers to the inhabited world (see note at 19:4-6). According to the ancient Israelite conception, the earth rested on the waters (136:6; Ex 20:4); the **seas** and **rivers** are what was seen of this phenomenon. The **earth** was set on a firm **foundation**, so it was stable and secure (104:5; Is 51:13).

24:3-4 The use of rhetorical questions about those who are

kavod

Hebrew Pronunciation	[kah VOHD]
HCSB Translation	glory, honor, wealth
Uses in Psalms	51
Uses in the OT	200
Focus Passage	Psalm 24:7-10

Kavod relates to verbal kaved and adjectival kaved, which indicate heaviness. Kavod describes God's glory (Ex 16:7). The King of glory (Ps 24:10) is Israel's Glory (Jr 2:11), manifesting glory (Ex 24:17). The ark of the covenant represents Israel's glory (1Sm 4:22). People give glory to God (Jr 13:16). Earthly kings (Is 8:7) and thrones (Jr 17:12) have kavod. It is associated with natural (Is 60:13) or manufactured (Ex 28:2) beauty. Especially in Proverbs, kavod signifies honor (Pr 3:35). An antonym is disgrace (Hab 2:16). Kavod means wealth (Gn 31:1), riches (Is 61:6), abundance (Nah 2:9), splendor (Is 14:18), or reward (Nm 24:11). It implies burden (Is 22:24). A nation's kavod is its nobility (Mc 1:15) or dignitaries (Is 5:13). Kavod indicates the self, translated as I (Gn 49:6), soul (Ps 57:8), spirit (Ps 16:9), strength (Jb 29:20), or whole being (Ps 108:1). Adjectivally, kavod is glorious (Is 3:8) or honorable (Pr 20:3).

worthy to enter into Yahweh's presence is similar to Psalm 15. **Clean hands** and **a pure heart** represent innocence and integrity (73:13) in a similar sense as a person who "lives honestly" (see note at 15:2).

24:6 Seek means more than looking for something that is lost or hidden. It means turning to someone for advice and help; it is thus synonymous with trust (9:10). This is reinforced with the fact that seeking Yahweh results in life (Am 5:6).

24:7-10 Lift up your heads is a poetic way of saying "extend your height" in reference to the gates. Some think that **ancient doors** refers to the "gate of heaven" (Gn 28:17). These doors are represented in the earthly gates of the city of Jerusalem. There is certainly a connection between the heavenly throne at the temple of God and the temple existing on earth among His people, so this is a possibility. While "hosts" can refer to the objects in the sky (sun, moon, stars, etc.; Dt 4:19), it can also refer to armies (Ex 7:4) as it does here. The **LORD of Hosts** portrays Yahweh the Warrior and King returning from battle (1Sm 17:45).

25:2-3 Disgraced (Hb bosh) is used three times in these two verses and once more in verse 20. The belief of the psalmist was that Yahweh would not allow His people to be put to shame because of their faithfulness to Him and the fact that His reputation was at stake (69:6; 119:31).

25:4-5 Guide and **teach** are essentially synonymous in this context, and they refer to Yahweh's directing those who are faithful to Him. His **truth** is the guide for their lives (43:3). The **paths** are similar to "ways" in verse 10 and are connected not only to God's truth but also to His faithful love.

for You are the God of my salvation;[a]
I wait for You all day long.[b]

6 Remember, Lord, Your compassion
and Your faithful love,
for they have existed from antiquity.[A,c]

7 Do not remember the sins of my youth[d]
or my acts of rebellion;[e]
in keeping with Your faithful love,
remember me
because of Your goodness, Lord.[f]

8 The Lord is good and upright;[g]
therefore He shows sinners the way.[h]

9 He leads the humble in what is right[i]
and teaches them His way.[j]

10 All the Lord's ways show faithful love
and truth
to those who keep His covenant
and decrees.[k]

11 Because of Your name, •Yahweh,
forgive my sin, for it is great.[l]

12 Who is the man who •fears the Lord?[m]
He will show him the way
he should choose.[n]

13 He will live a good life,
and his descendants will inherit
the land.[B,o]

14 The secret counsel of the Lord
is for those who fear Him,
and He reveals His covenant to them.[p]

15 My eyes are always on the Lord,
for He will pull my feet out of the net.[q]

16 Turn to me and be gracious to me,
for I am alone and afflicted.[r]

17 The distresses of my heart increase;[C,s]
bring me out of my sufferings.[t]

18 Consider my affliction and trouble,[u]
and take away all my sins.[v]

19 Consider my enemies;
they are numerous,[w]
and they hate me violently.[x]

20 Guard me and deliver me;[y]
do not let me be put to shame,
for I take refuge in You.[z]

21 May integrity and what is right
watch over me,
for I wait for You.[aa]

22 God, redeem Israel, from all
its distresses.[ab]

Psalm 26
Prayer for Vindication

Davidic.

1 Vindicate me, Lord,
because I have lived with integrity
and have trusted in the Lord
without wavering.[ac]

2 Test me, Lord, and try me;
examine my heart and mind.[ad]

3 For Your faithful love
is before my eyes,
and I live by Your truth.[ae]

---

a 25:5 Ex 15:2
b Ps 40:1
c 25:6 Ps 98:3; 103:17
d 25:7 Jb 13:26
e Ps 51:1
f Neh 13:22
g 25:8 Ps 100:5; Nah 1:7
h Ps 32:8
i 25:9 Ps 23:3
j Ex 18:20; Ps 86:11
k 25:10 Ps 40:11; 103:17-18
l 25:11 Jb 7:21; Ps 103:3; Jr 31:34
m 25:12 Ps 31:19
n Ps 37:23
o 25:13 Ps 37:11; 69:36
p 25:14 Jn 7:17; 1Co 2:9
q 25:15 Ps 31:4; 124:7
r 25:16 Ps 70:5; 73:14
s 25:17 Lm 1:20
t Jr 10:19
u 25:18 Ps 31:7
v Rm 11:27; 1Jn 3:5
w 25:19 Ps 3:1
x Ps 9:13
y 25:20 Ps 17:8; 31:15
z Ps 86:2
aa 25:21 Ps 41:12
ab 25:22 Ps 34:22; 130:8
ac 26:1 2Kg 20:3; Ps 7:8
ad 26:2 Ps 7:9; 17:3; 139:23
ae 26:3 Ps 40:10; 86:11

A 25:6 Or everlasting   B 25:13 Or earth   C 25:17 Or Relieve the distresses of my heart

---

25:6-7 The juxtaposition of **remember . . . do not remember**, and **remember** in these verses is significant. The first demonstrates that Yahweh's consciousness of His own attributes is the motivation for Him to act beneficently toward His people. In contrast to this, the **sins** of the psalmist must not be remembered, that is, they must be forgiven (vv. 11,18). Only after this has taken place could Yahweh remember (act on behalf of) the psalmist (74:2; 106:4; 112:6).

25:8-10 **Way** and **ways** are probably not the way of life or conduct of God's people in this instance, as these terms are commonly used elsewhere (143:8; Dt 5:33; also note this use in Ps 25:12). They are more likely related to verses 4-5, and they represent Yahweh's instruction of His people in the **truth**. In this sense **the Lord's ways** are equivalent to **His covenant and decrees**.

25:11 As in the case of verse 6, it is Yahweh's reputation (His **name**) that is at stake in His forgiveness of the sins of the psalmist. God's reputation is closely connected with His actions toward His people (Ezk 36:22).

25:13 The promise of inheriting **the land** is closely tied with those who are faithful to God. The promise of the land was never a "blank check" for Israel, but it could be realized only when the people were faithful (Dt 4:1,28-30).

25:14 The Hebrew word *sod* expresses the idea of "confidential," referring either to the material that is **secret** or to a "circle of confidants." Given the parallel of **His covenant**,

it seems better to understand this as the content of God's secret **counsel**. God has the right to conceal what He wants (Pr 25:2), but He can also reveal His secret counsel to anyone He chooses. In this case it is revealed to **those who fear Him** (trust in Him and are faithful to Him).

25:15 **Eyes** are often used in the context of faith in the sense that a person "looks to" Yahweh as his source of help (123:2; 141:8).

25:17 The Hebrew text of this verse is difficult, reading literally "**the distresses of my heart**, they make wide." Although the form for "make wide" usually refers to relief from distress (4:2; 18:37), it can also express the meaning of "enlarge," which would be a figurative expression for **increase**. This idea is related to numerous enemies who surrounded the psalmist (v. 19).

25:20 **Put to shame** is similar to "disgrace" (see note at vv. 2-3).

25:21 **Integrity** and **what is right** are personified in a similar way as Yahweh's attributes were personified in 23:6. These characteristics will protect those who remain in God's will (37:37).

26:1-3 The request for vindication at the beginning sets the tone for this psalm that primarily involves a declaration of innocence. Although the terminology seems strong, it does not proclaim sinless perfection but moral and spiritual **integrity** (see note at 17:3-5). A sense of security comes

4 I do not sit with the worthless
or associate with hypocrites.
5 I hate a crowd of evildoers,
and I do not sit with the wicked.[a]
6 I wash my hands[A] in innocence[b]
and go around Your altar, LORD,[c]
7 raising my voice in thanksgiving[d]
and telling about
Your wonderful works.[e]

8 LORD, I love the house where You dwell,
the place where Your glory resides.[f]
9 Do not destroy me along with sinners,
or my life along with men of bloodshed[g]
10 in whose hands are evil schemes
and whose right hands are filled
with bribes.[h]

11 But I live with integrity;
redeem me and be gracious to me.[i]
12 My foot stands on level ground;[j]
I will praise the LORD in the assemblies.[k]

Psalm 27
My Stronghold

Davidic.

1 The LORD is my light and my salvation—
whom should I fear?[l]
The LORD is the stronghold of my life—
of whom should I be afraid?[m]
2 When evildoers came against me
to devour my flesh,[n]
my foes and my enemies stumbled
and fell.[o]

[a]26:4-5 Ps 1:1; Pr 4:14-15
[b]26:6 Ps 73:13
[c]Ps 43:4
[d]26:7 Jnh 2:9
[e]Ps 9:1
[f]26:8 Ps 27:4
[g]26:9 Ps 28:3
[h]26:10 Ex 23:8; Dt 16:19; Ps 15:5
[i]26:11 Jb 31:6; Ps 7:8
[j]26:12 Ps 27:11
[k]Ps 35:18; 40:9-10
[l]27:1 Is 60:20; Mc 7:8
[m]Ps 28:8; 118:6
[n]27:2 Ps 14:4
[o]Ps 9:3
[p]27:3 Ps 3:6
[q]27:4 Ps 23:6; 26:8
[r]Ps 93:5
[s]Mal 3:1
[t]27:5 Ps 31:20; 91:1; Is 25:4
[u]27:6 Ps 3:3
[v]Ps 54:6; 116:17
[w]Eph 5:19
[x]27:7 Ps 4:3; 30:10
[y]27:8 Ps 24:6; 105:4
[z]27:9 Ps 69:17; 102:2; 143:7
[aa]Ps 6:1
[ab]Ps 40:17

3 Though an army deploys against me,
my heart is not afraid;
though a war breaks out against me,
still I am confident.[p]

4 I have asked one thing
from the LORD;
it is what I desire:
to dwell in the house of the LORD
all the days of my life,[q]
gazing on the beauty of the LORD[r]
and seeking Him in His temple.[s]
5 For He will conceal me
in His shelter
in the day of adversity;
He will hide me under the cover
of His tent;
He will set me high on a rock.[t]
6 Then my head will be high
above my enemies around me;[u]
I will offer sacrifices in His tent
with shouts of joy.[v]
I will sing and make music
to the LORD.[w]

7 LORD, hear my voice when I call;
be gracious to me and answer me.[x]
8 My heart says this about You,
"You[B] are to seek My face."
LORD, I will seek Your face.[y]
9 Do not hide Your face from me;[z]
do not turn Your servant away
in anger.[aa]
You have been my helper;[ab]
do not leave me or abandon me,
God of my salvation.

[A]26:6 A ritual or ceremonial washing to express innocence [B]27:8 You is plural in Hb

from a life lived with integrity (Pr 10:9). This confidence is expressed in the psalmist's request that God **test** and **examine** him (Jr 12:3).

26:4-5 Evidence of a person's faithfulness toward Yahweh is not only in what is done but also in what is avoided, particularly in a person's associations with others. The repeated **do not sit with** in these verses recalls the language from 1:1.

26:6-7 Washing **hands** was part of an oath of purification symbolizing **innocence** (24:4; 73:13; Dt 21:6). Going **around** the **altar** is more difficult to interpret. Some suggest that the closest parallel is the activity of the priests of Baal on Mount Carmel (1Kg 18:26). However, their strange behavior, including self-mutilation, makes this an unlikely parallel. Instead, the present context suggests being around the altar and making sacrifices to Yahweh as part of a person's demonstration of purity and loyalty.

26:8 House is not necessarily Solomon's temple, but it may refer to the sanctuary in general (see note at 5:6-7). It was the place of Yahweh's **glory**, symbolizing God's presence among His people (Ex 40:34-35).

26:10 Some perverted the system of justice by the offering of bribes (15:5; Pr 17:23; 29:4).

26:12 Level ground is associated with the righteous way in which Yahweh leads His people (27:11; 143:10; Is 26:7).

27:1 Light is parallel to salvation, which in this context refers to rescue from danger. Darkness represents danger (23:4), but light dispels darkness, eliminating the immediate danger (18:28). With God's protection, there is no need to be **afraid** regardless of the danger (v. 3; Rm 8:31).

27:2 Devouring **flesh** is probably related to the imagery of wild animals as seen elsewhere in relation to enemies (see notes at 7:1-2 and 14:4).

27:4 To **dwell in the house of the LORD** may mean continually returning to the sanctuary for worship. It can also be more general in referring to living one's life in God's presence. In either case, the point is that there is constant fellowship with Yahweh throughout one's life (see note at 23:6).

27:5 The words **conceal** and **hide** mean protection when it is Yahweh hiding His people. Often the image is connected with a mother bird hiding her young under her wings (see note at 17:8).

27:6 Lifting one's **head . . . above** his **enemies** is another way of expressing triumph over those who are defeated (3:3).

27:8-9 Face is a key word in these verses, appearing three

10 Even if my father and mother
     abandon me,
the LORD cares for me.[a]

11 Because of my adversaries,
show me Your way, LORD,
and lead me on a level path.[b]

12 Do not give me over to the will
     of my foes,
for false witnesses rise up against me,
breathing violence.[c]

13 I am certain that I will see
     the LORD's goodness
in the land of the living.[d]

14 Wait for the LORD;
be strong[A] and courageous.[e]
Wait for the LORD.[f]

Psalm 28

My Strength

Davidic.

1 LORD, I call to You;
my rock, do not be deaf to me.[g]
If You remain silent to me,
I will be like those going down
     to the •Pit.[h]

2 Listen to the sound of my pleading
when I cry to You for help,
when I lift up my hands
toward Your holy sanctuary.[i]

3 Do not drag me away with the wicked,
with the evildoers,
who speak in friendly ways
     with their neighbors
while malice is in their hearts.[j]

4 Repay them according to what
     they have done—
according to the evil of their deeds.
Repay them according to the work
     of their hands;
give them back what they deserve.[k]

5 Because they do not consider
what the LORD has done
or the work of His hands,
He will tear them down and not
     rebuild them.[l]

6 May the LORD be praised,
for He has heard the sound
     of my pleading.[m]

7 The LORD is my strength and my shield;
my heart trusts in Him,
     and I am helped.[n]
Therefore my heart rejoices,
and I praise Him with my song.[o]

8 The LORD is the strength of His people;[B]
He is a stronghold of salvation
     for His anointed.[p]

9 Save Your people,
     bless Your possession,
shepherd them, and carry
     them forever.[q]

Cross references:
a 27:9-10 Ps 37:28; 94:14
b 27:11 Ps 25:4; 26:12
c 27:12 Ps 35:11; 41:2; Mt 26:59-60
d 27:13 Ex 33:19; Ps 116:9; 142:5
e 27:14 Jos 1:6
f Ps 37:34; 130:5
g 28:1 Ps 83:1
h Ps 88:4; 143:7
i 28:2 Ps 28:2; 134:2; 141:2; 1Tm 2:8
j 28:3 Ps 26:9-10
k 28:4 Jr 50:29; Rv 18:6; 22:12
l 28:5 Jb 34:26-28; Is 5:12
m 28:6 Ps 31:22
n 28:7 Gn 15:1; Dt 33:29; Ps 3:3; 5:12; 18:2; 119:114
o Ps 59:17; 69:30
p 28:8 Ps 20:6; 27:1
q 28:9 Ps 33:12; Is 40:11

A 27:14 Lit LORD; *let your heart be strong*   **B** 28:8 Some Hb mss, LXX, Syr; other Hb mss read *strength for them*

---

times. To **seek** God's face is to petition Yahweh, most often in the context of worship (2Ch 11:16). It involves complete devotion to God in the same sense as turning toward Him (Dt 4:29; Ps 24:6).

27:11 On the significance of **level**, see note at 26:12.

27:13 The **land of the living** is in contrast to Sheol, the realm of the dead (Ezk 32:27). Being cut off from the land of the living is another way to express being killed (Jr 11:19). The psalmist anticipated receiving Yahweh's blessings (**goodness**) while he was still alive.

27:14 Waiting **for the LORD** is an abbreviated way to express waiting for an answer to prayer. Rather than taking matters into their own hands, the people of God should **wait** patiently for Yahweh's response (37:7; 40:1; Pr 20:22).

28:1 Deaf and **silent** are often connected with being "far from" (35:22) and "silent" (83:1). These concepts describe God's lack of intervention in a time of need. "Pit" is sometimes parallel with Sheol, the realm of the dead (30:3; Jb 33:18; Pr 1:12; Is 14:15), so **those going down to the Pit** refers to those who are going to die.

28:2 Lifting up **hands** was a common gesture for prayer, perhaps related to the image of showing that one's hands were clean and therefore his motives were pure before the Lord (134:2; 1Kg 8:35,38,42). **Sanctuary** is a specific word (Hb *devir*) referring to the innermost part of the sanctuary—the most holy place. This was the place where the ark of the

covenant resided, but more importantly it was the location of the mercy seat—the place from which Yahweh dispensed mercy on His people (Ex 26:34).

28:3-5 The psalmist's plea that he not be punished (i.e., dragged away) **with the wicked** is because he was not connected with them, either in association or in activities (26:9-10). **Repay them** appears twice as a call for retribution on one's enemies; it is also known as an imprecation (see note at 109:1-31). The reason for this request for judgment on these **evildoers** is that they did not **consider what the LORD** had **done**. Some think that this refers to God's judgment on the wicked; however, the phrase **work of His hands** is more commonly used for God's work of creation (19:1; 102:25) or for His work in delivering His people (143:5; Is 60:21). The second of these options seems more likely in this context where there is praise for Yahweh's help.

28:6 The shift from petition to thanksgiving is common in lament psalms (see note at 22:22-24).

28:8-9 The relationship between the individual and the community is evident in identifying Yahweh as the psalmist's strength in verse 7 and **the strength of His people** in verse 8. Though **His anointed** can refer to the Davidic king of Israel (18:50; 20:6; 45:7), in this case it is parallel to "His people" and represents the nation as a whole (105:15; Hab 3:13). Israel was also known as Yahweh's **possession** (see 135:4; Ex 19:5 and notes there). On the designation **shepherd**, see note at 23:1.

Psalm 29

The Voice of the LORD

A Davidic psalm.

1 Ascribe to ˙Yahweh,
   you heavenly beings,[A]
ascribe to the LORD glory and strength.
2 Ascribe to Yahweh the glory due
   His name;
worship Yahweh
   in the splendor of His holiness.[B,a]

3 The voice of the LORD is
   above the waters.
The God of glory thunders—
   the LORD, above vast waters,[b]
4 the voice of the LORD in power,
   the voice of the LORD in splendor.[c]
5 The voice of the LORD breaks the cedars;
   the LORD shatters the cedars
   of Lebanon.[d]
6 He makes Lebanon skip like a calf,[e]
   and Sirion,[C] like a young wild ox.[f]
7 The voice of the LORD flashes
   flames of fire.[g]

8 The voice of the LORD shakes
   the wilderness;
the LORD shakes the wilderness
   of Kadesh.[h]
9 The voice of the LORD makes the deer
   give birth[D,i]
and strips the woodlands bare.[j]

In His temple all cry, "Glory!"

10 The LORD sat enthroned at the flood;
   the LORD sits enthroned, King forever.[k]
11 The LORD gives His people strength;[l]
   the LORD blesses His people with peace.[m]

Psalm 30

Joy in the Morning

A psalm; a dedication song
for the house. Davidic.

1 I will exalt You, LORD,
   because You have lifted me up[n]
and have not allowed my enemies
   to triumph over me.[o]
2 LORD my God,

Cross references:
a 29:1-2 1Ch 16:28-29; Ps 96:7-9
b 29:3 Jb 37:4-5; Ps 18:13; 104:7
c 29:4 Ps 68:33
d 29:5 Ps 104:16
e 29:6 Ps 114:4,6
f Dt 3:8-9
g 29:7 Dt 4:12,33
h 29:8 Nm 13:26
i 29:9 Jb 39:1-3
j Is 24:1,3
k 29:10 Ps 9:7; 10:17
l 29:11 Ps 28:8; 68:35
m Php 4:7
n 30:1 Ps 3:3
o Ps 25:2; 35:19

A 29:1 Or *you angels,* or *you sons of the mighty;* lit LORD *sons of the gods*   B 29:2 Or *in holy attire,* or *in holy appearance*
C 29:6 = Mount Hermon   D 29:9 Or *the oaks shake*

29:1 To **ascribe** something to someone is to acknowledge they have that attribute. **Heavenly beings** is literally "sons of gods." The word for "gods" (Hb *'elim*), although similar to the word for "God" (Hb *elohim*), is never used of Him. The term has a background in ancient Near Eastern mythologies as referring to the divine assembly of the gods (see note at 82:1). In fact, it sometimes refers to pagan gods (Ex 15:11; Dn 11:36), though not as an affirmation that they existed but only as a recognition that other nations believed in them. It can also refer to people, with the meaning of "mighty ones" (Jb 41:25). In this context it is best to understand the term as angelic beings (Ps 89:6). The angels are witnesses of God's creation (Jb 38:7) and are allowed access to God in heaven (Jb 1:6; 2:1). They surround His throne to praise and worship Him (Is 6; Ezk 1). It is most appropriate to address them as those who worship Yahweh.

29:2 The word for **splendor** can mean "adornment," such as the ornate clothing worn by rulers or dignitaries. In the case of Yahweh, He is clothed in His own attributes (93:1), which in this case is His **holiness** (96:9; 2Ch 20:21).

29:3-4 Voice here and through verse 9 is used as Yahweh's audible expression of His **power**, comparable to **thunder**. The imagery of a thunderstorm for God's power is used in military contexts picturing Yahweh as a warrior (see note at 18:7-15); however, this context does not have any explicit military references and more likely compares Yahweh to the formidable physical phenomenon itself. In the ancient Near East, "waters" represented the primeval chaos that could not be tamed. The description of God's voice **above the waters** shows His dominion over them (93:3-4; Jr 10:13; 51:16).

29:5-6 Lebanon was known for its **cedars**, the strongest and most majestic trees in Israel (104:16; Sg 5:15; Is 2:13). **Sirion** refers to Mount Hermon, the tallest mountain in that

area (Dt 3:9). Together these represent the greatest spectacles of creation in and around Israel.

29:7 Lightning, which accompanies thunder in storms, is called **flames of fire** that flash and come from Yahweh's **voice** (18:12,14).

29:8-9 The verb for **shakes** is commonly used to mean "tremble with fear" (96:9; 114:7), so that the picture is of creation itself trembling before Yahweh's power. In this psalm **His temple** is heaven (11:4; Mc 1:2) where **all** is the "heavenly beings" in verse 1.

29:10-11 The flood continues the image in verse 3, relating it to "waters," but here the unleashing of the destructive powers of chaos in a flood makes this even more significant than the earlier reference. Some interpreters relate it directly to the flood of Noah's time (Gn 6-7), while others see it as the waters at creation (Gn 1:7; Ps 148:4). The point in either case is that Yahweh rules over (**sat enthroned**) the most powerful forces in the natural world. Because of this great power, **His people** find **strength** in Him.

Ps 30 title If **Davidic** means "authored by David," then the inclusion of **a dedication song for the house** might have been added later to indicate how this psalm was used by the nation of Israel. This is a good possibility since psalms composed by individuals within a specific historical setting were later used by the community during worship or for special occasions.

30:1-2 Lifted . . . up is from a Hebrew word (*dlh*) that is most often used to describe drawing water from a well (Ex 2:16,19; Pr 20:5). Though **enemies** are not always the immediate cause of the psalmist's affliction, they aggravate the suffering, adding insult to injury (41:5,11). This seems to be the case here since the problem was more likely sickness, as indicated by the word **healed** in verse 2.

I cried to You for help,
and You healed me.[a]

3 LORD, You brought me up from *Sheol;[b]
You spared me from among those
going down[A] to the *Pit.[c]

4 Sing to *Yahweh, you His faithful ones,
and praise His holy name.[d]

5 For His anger lasts only a moment,
but His favor, a lifetime.
Weeping may spend the night,
but there is joy in the morning.[e]

6 When I was secure, I said,
"I will never be shaken."[f]

7 LORD, when You showed Your favor,
You made me stand
like a strong mountain;[g]
when You hid Your face, I was terrified.[h]

8 LORD, I called to You;
I sought favor from my Lord:[i]

9 "What gain is there in my death,
if I go down to the Pit?
Will the dust praise You?
Will it proclaim Your truth?[j]

10 LORD, listen and be gracious to me;
LORD, be my helper."[k]

11 You turned my lament into dancing;
You removed my *sackcloth
and clothed me with gladness,[l]

[a]30:2 Ps 88:13
[b]30:3 Ps 86:13
[c]Ps 28:1; 88:4;
143:7
[d]30:4 Ps 50:5;
149:1
[e]30:5 Ps 103:9;
Is 54:7-8; 2Co
4:17
[f]30:6 Ps 10:6;
62:2,6
[g]30:7 Ps 20:8
[h]Ps 104:29
[i]30:8 Ps 119:58
[j]30:9 Ps 6:5;
88:10-12
[k]30:10 Ps 4:1;
27:7
[l]30:11 Ec 3:4; Is
61:10; Jr 31:13
[m]30:12 Ps 44:8;
108:1
[n]31:1 Ps 25:2
[o]31:2 Ps 71:1-2
[p]31:3 Ps 18:2;
71:3
[q]Ps 23:3; 25:11
[r]31:4 Ps 25:15;
46:1
[s]31:5 Lk 23:46
[t]Ps 25:5
[u]31:6 Ps 26:5;
Jnh 2:8

12 so that I can sing to You and not
be silent.
LORD my God, I will praise You forever.[m]

Psalm 31
A Plea for Protection

For the choir director. A Davidic psalm.

1 LORD, I seek refuge in You;
let me never be disgraced.[n]
Save me by Your righteousness.

2 Listen closely to me;
rescue me quickly.
Be a rock of refuge for me,
a mountain fortress to save me.[o]

3 For You are my rock and my fortress;[p]
You lead and guide me
because of Your name.[q]

4 You will free me from the net
that is secretly set for me,
for You are my refuge.[r]

5 Into Your hand I entrust my spirit;[s]
You redeem[B] me, LORD, God of truth.[t]

6 I[c] hate those who are devoted
to worthless idols,
but I trust in the LORD.[u]

7 I will rejoice and be glad
in Your faithful love
because You have seen my affliction.

[A]30:3 Some Hb mss, LXX, Theod, Orig, Syr; other Hb mss, Aq, Sym, Tg, Jer read *from going down*   [B]31:5 Or *You have redeemed*, or *You will redeem*, or *spirit. Redeem*   [C]31:6 One Hb ms, LXX, Syr, Vg, Jer read *You*

30:3 Sheol in many instances is a synonym for death. To be near Sheol is to be close to death (88:3), so being **brought . . . up** from Sheol or **spared** from the Pit is equivalent to being rescued from death (28:1; 88:4).

30:4-5 The personal experience of the individual becomes a lesson to be learned by the community. It is the individual's responsibility to communicate to the community what Yahweh has done (see note at 22:22-24). The lesson is that times of suffering pale in comparison to Yahweh's deliverance (30:5). On the connection between God's **anger** and human suffering, see note at 6:1.

30:6-7 These verses recall the time before the affliction in order to point out a likely reason for the suffering, which is the need for humility. Before God allowed the psalmist to suffer, he was so **secure** that he felt he could **never be shaken**. The security apparently became a source of overconfidence even though it was Yahweh who **showed** His **favor** and made him **like a strong mountain** (5:12). In other words, the blessing of God gave him a false sense of security. The suffering began when Yahweh **hid** His **face** (see note at 13:1-2).

30:9 The psalmist seeks to motivate God to act on behalf of His people by emphasizing the loss of praise and testimony for Yahweh if the sufferer were to die (6:5; 88:10-12). This may seem bold, but it demonstrates a key element in Israel's purpose—to be a testimony for Yahweh to the nations by proclaiming His **truth** (Dt 4:6-8; see note at Ps 18:49).

30:11-12 Lament is parallel with **sackcloth**, the clothing used to represent a time of mourning (Gn 37:34; Est 4:3; Ezk 27:31). **Dancing** and being **clothed . . . with gladness** are also related ideas showing the dramatic change after Yahweh delivered the psalmist from death. The purpose of the deliverance is praise and testimony. This demonstrates the change in perspective from the false sense of security to a renewed sense of purpose in keeping with the reason why God had called out His people from among the nations (30:9).

31:1-4 A number of different Hebrew words are used in these verses for **refuge . . . rock**, and **fortress**, all conveying the sense of Yahweh as a source of security and protection (18:1-2). Fortresses were places of protection from an enemy (27:1). Rocks also symbolize stability, something in which a person can place his trust (Is 26:4). A **net** was metaphorically a malicious plot (35:7; 140:5).

31:5 Spirit could represent the person as a whole or the life-giving force that God gives to each person (Gn 7:22; Is 38:16). **Hand** means possession or control (Jos 7:7). Although here the expression of trust in Yahweh is in the context of being protected from harm (or, more specifically, death), Jesus used these words as He was dying on the cross to describe the release of His own spirit to His Father (Lk 23:46).

31:6 Those who are faithful to Yahweh and remain close to Him should **hate** what He hates (101:3; 119:113; 139:12; see note at 15:4).

You have known the troubles of my life[a]

8 and have not handed me over
    to the enemy.[b]
You have set my feet
    in a spacious place.[c]

9 Be gracious to me, LORD,
    because I am in distress;[d]
my eyes are worn out
    from angry sorrow—
    my whole being[A] as well.[e]

10 Indeed, my life is consumed with grief
    and my years with groaning;[f]
my strength has failed
    because of my sinfulness,[B]
    and my bones waste away.[g]

11 I am ridiculed by all my adversaries
    and even by my neighbors.
I am dreaded by my acquaintances;
    those who see me in the street
    run from me.[h]

12 I am forgotten: gone from memory
    like a dead person—
    like broken pottery.[i]

13 I have heard the gossip of many;
    terror is on every side.[j]
When they conspired against me,
    they plotted to take my life.[k]

14 But I trust in You, LORD;
    I say, "You are my God."[l]

15 The course of my life is in Your power;[m]
    deliver me from the power
    of my enemies
    and from my persecutors.[n]

16 Show Your favor to Your servant;

save me by Your faithful love.[o]

17 LORD, do not let me be disgraced
    when I call on You.[p]
Let the wicked be disgraced;
    let them be silent[C,D] in •Sheol.[q]

18 Let lying lips be quieted;[r]
    they speak arrogantly
        against the righteous
    with pride and contempt.[s]

19 How great is Your goodness
    that You have stored up for those
        who •fear You
    and accomplished in the sight
        of •everyone
    for those who take refuge in You.[t]

20 You hide them in the protection
        of Your presence;
    You conceal them in a shelter[E]
    from the schemes of men,
    from quarrelsome tongues.[u]

21 May the LORD be praised,
    for He has wonderfully shown
        His faithful love to me
    in a city under siege.[F,v]

22 In my alarm I had said,
    "I am cut off from Your sight."[w]
But You heard the sound
        of my pleading
    when I cried to You for help.[x]

23 Love the LORD, all His faithful ones.[y]
The LORD protects the loyal,
    but fully repays the arrogant.[z]

24 Be strong[G] and courageous,
    all you who put your hope in the LORD.[aa]

a31:7 Ps 10:14
b31:8 Dt 32:30
c Jb 36:16
d31:9 Ps 69:17
e Ps 6:7; 63:1
f31:10 Ps 102:3
g Ps 32:3; 38:3
h31:11 Jb
19:13; Ps 38:11;
88:8,18
i31:12 Ps 88:5;
Ec 9:5
j31:13 Jr 20:10
k Ps 41:7; Mt
27:1
l31:14 Ps 140:6
m31:15 Jb 14:5;
24:1
n Ps 59:1
o31:16 Ps 6:4;
119:135
p31:17 Ps 25:2-
3,20
q Ps 94:17;
115:17
r31:18 Ps 120:2
s1Sm 2:3; Ps
94:4
t31:19 Ps 5:11;
23:5
u31:20 Ps 27:5;
32:7
v31:21 Ps 28:6
w31:22 Ps 88:5;
Is 38:11-12
x Ps 66:19;
145:19
y31:23 Ps 30:4
z Ps 94:2
aa31:24 Ps
27:14

A31:9 Lit *my soul and my belly*   B31:10 LXX, Syr, Sym read *affliction*   C31:17 LXX reads *brought down*   D31:17 Or *them perish*, or
them wail   E31:20 Lit *canopy*   F31:21 Or *a fortified city*   G31:24 Lit *Let your heart be strong*

31:8 Spacious place conveys the notion of being delivered from surrounding enemies who have someone enclosed without an exit (see note at 4:1).

31:9-10 Physical suffering often accompanies emotional distress. **Worn out . . . eyes**, most likely from crying (6:7; 88:9; Jb 17:7), and **bones** that were wasting away (see 6:2; 22:14; 102:5) are figurative expressions describing **sorrow** and **grief**. The additional idea of **my sinfulness** as the cause shows the common perception that suffering is the result of sin. While this is true universally and generally, it is not always the case individually and specifically. The same issue is involved in the identification of suffering with God's anger (see note at 6:1).

31:11 Suffering often results not only in ridicule from enemies but also in abandonment (being **dreaded**) by friends (38:11; 88:18; Jb 16:20; 19:1). In a very real sense, enemies and friends are not easily distinguished during such times.

31:13 The phrase **terror . . . on every side** occurs frequently in Jeremiah (Jr 6:25; 20:10; 46:5) and is a vivid way to describe being surrounded by enemies. Enemies also **plotted** to take Jeremiah's **life** (Jr 11:19; 18:23). It is characteristic of the wicked to plot against the righteous (Ps 21:11; 37:12).

31:15 The request to be in God's **power** instead of the power of one's **enemies** is the central plea in this psalm (v. 5; cp. 2Sm 24:14).

31:17-18 The disgrace of one of God's faithful ones reflects negatively on Yahweh's reputation (see notes at 22:6-8 and 25:2-3). **Sheol** is equivalent to "the land of silence" (94:17; 115:17) where the dead are no longer able to communicate with the living. Death is the only thing that will quiet the deception (**lying lips**) of these enemies.

31:19 God is often said to **store up** the sins and punishment of people (Jb 21:19; Hs 13:12), but here it is God's **goodness** that is stored up for those who **fear** Him (1Co 2:9).

31:20 On **hide** and **conceal**, see note at 17:8.

31:22 To be **cut off** means to be separated, as in the case of being cut off from the Israelite community (Ex 12:15; Nm 19:13). The most extreme form of separation is death (Ex 9:15; 31:14; Jr 9:21). Being cut off from God's **sight** refers to His rejection that results in separation from Him. It is similar to other terms for rejection such as God being "far away" or "hiding" from the psalmist (see note at 10:1-2).

31:24 The phrase **strong and courageous** recalls the words

Psalm 32
The Joy of Forgiveness

Davidic. A *Maskil.

1 How joyful is the one
whose transgression is forgiven,
whose sin is covered![a]
2 How joyful is the man
the LORD does not charge with sin[b]
and in whose spirit is no deceit![c]

3 When I kept silent, my bones
became brittle
from my groaning all day long.[d]
4 For day and night Your hand was heavy
on me;[e]
my strength was drained[A]
as in the summer's heat.[f]   •Selah
5 Then I acknowledged my sin to You
and did not conceal my iniquity.
I said,
"I will confess my transgressions
to the LORD,"
and You took away the •guilt of my sin.[g]
Selah

6 Therefore let everyone who is faithful
pray to You
at a time that You may be found.[B,h]
When great floodwaters come,
they will not reach him.[i]
7 You are my hiding place;[j]
You protect me from trouble.[k]
You surround me with joyful shouts
of deliverance.   Selah

8 I will instruct you and show you
the way to go;[l]
with My eye on you,
I will give counsel.[m]
9 Do not be like a horse
or mule,
without understanding,
that must be controlled with bit
and bridle
or else it will not come near you.[n]

10 Many pains come to the wicked,[o]
but the one who trusts in the LORD
will have faithful love
surrounding him.[p]

a32:1 Ps 85:2
b32:1-2 Rm
4:7-8
c32:2 Jn 1:47
d32:3 Ps 31:10;
38:8
e32:4 Jb 23:2;
Ps 38:2
f Ps 22:15; 39:10
g32:5 Lv 26:40;
Ps 38:18; Pr
28:13; 1Jn 1:9
h32:6 Is 55:6
i Ps 124:4-5; Is
43:2
j32:7 Ps 31:20;
91:1
k Ps 121:7
l32:8 Ps 25:8,12
m Ps 33:18;
73:24
n32:9 Pr 26:3;
Jms 3:3
o32:10 Pr 13:21;
Rm 2:9
p Ps 5:12

A32:4 Hb obscure   B32:6 Lit *time of finding*

---

of God to Joshua and Israel to prepare them for the conquest of the promised land (Dt 31:6-7,23; Jos 1:6-7,9,18).

Ps 32 title *Maskil* may be derived from a root word meaning "insight." For this reason, some have suggested that psalms with this title deal with wisdom or instruction. The problem is that many of the psalms bearing this title do not have teaching elements (even though this psalm does have them in vv. 8-9). It is also possible to connect the word with the idea of "skill," which is closely tied to the OT concept of "wisdom." In this sense, the title refers to a "skillful" or an "artistic" psalm.

32:1-2 On **joyful**, see note at 1:1. Four different Hebrew terms are used for **sin** in these verses, highlighting different aspects of sin: (1) *pesha'* (translated **transgression**) has the basic idea of rebellion, (2) *hata'ah* (translated **sin**) is a more general term referring to a deliberate offense, (3) *'awon* (also translated **sin**) has the idea of going astray, and (4) *remiyyah* (translated **deceit**) emphasizes falsehood or even hypocrisy. There are also three different Hebrew verbs asso-

ciated with the first three of these terms for sin, also showing different aspects of forgiveness: (1) the root *ns'* (translated **forgiven**) is literally "lifted up" and emphasizes the burden of sin being lifted from the person, (2) the root *kasah* (translated **covered**) means to hide or cover something that is offensive, and (3) the root *chashav* (translated **charge**) can mean "reckon" or "regard," but in legal contexts it means to reckon as liable for punishment (impute with guilt).

32:3-4 The silence here is quite specific—not confessing sin (v. 5). The references to **bones . . . brittle . . . groaning**, and **strength . . . drained** represent physical manifestations of a person who is suffering (see note at 31:9-10). The **heavy hand** of God represents God's wrath and punishment (38:2; 39:10), but here it is specifically due to the conviction of sin.

32:5 In contrast to the suffering in verses 3-4, the confession of **sin** brings relief because God **took away the guilt** of sin, which is another way of describing forgiveness. Guilt is not a subjective feeling but liability for punishment in a legal sense. Mere removal of the feelings over sin is clearly not intended, since God brings the conviction. What is needed is forgiveness (vv. 1-2).

32:6-7 **Floodwaters** represent the overwhelming **trouble** or disaster that the psalmist was facing as a result of his sin (18:16; Is 28:2,17; 30:28). The **hiding place** is not used in the same sense as in other psalms where it means protection from enemies. Here it is **deliverance** from the overwhelming guilt that was brought about by God's reaction to the psalmist's own sin.

32:8-9 This is a wisdom section in the psalm as evidenced by the terms **instruct** and **counsel**. This might be related to its designation as a *Maskil* (see note at Ps 32 title). **A horse** and **mule** need to be **controlled** in order to be useful to people. Otherwise, they are too obstinate and will not obey their masters. In the human world, they are best compared to fools (Pr 26:3).

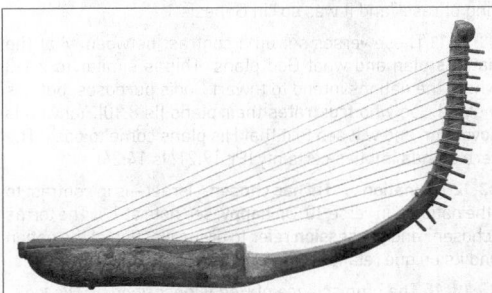

This wooden harp (33:2), dating from 1379-1320 B.C., is similar to the instrument David would have played as a young man.

11 Be glad in the LORD and rejoice,
you righteous ones;
shout for joy,
all you upright in heart.[a]

Psalm 33

Praise to the Creator

1 Rejoice in the LORD, you righteous ones;
praise from the upright is beautiful.[b]
2 Praise the LORD with the lyre;
make music to Him
with a ten-stringed harp.[c]
3 Sing a new song to Him;[d]
play skillfully on the strings,
with a joyful shout.[e]

4 For the word of the LORD is right,
and all His work is trustworthy.[f]
5 He loves righteousness and justice;[g]
the earth is full of the LORD's
unfailing love.[h]

6 The heavens were made by the word
of the LORD,[i]
and all the stars, by the breath
of His mouth.[j]
7 He gathers the waters of the sea
into a heap;[A]
He puts the depths into storehouses.[k]
8 Let the whole earth tremble
before the LORD;
let all the inhabitants of the world
stand in awe of Him.[l]
9 For He spoke, and it came into being;
He commanded, and it came
into existence.[m]

10 The LORD frustrates the counsel
of the nations;
He thwarts the plans of the peoples.[n]
11 The counsel of the LORD stands forever,
the plans of His heart from generation
to generation.[o]
12 Happy is the nation whose God
is •Yahweh—
the people He has chosen to be
His own possession![p]

13 The LORD looks down from heaven;
He observes everyone.[q]
14 He gazes on all the inhabitants
of the earth
from His dwelling place.[r]
15 He alone shapes their hearts;
He considers all their works.[s]

16 A king is not saved by a large army;
a warrior will not be delivered
by great strength.[t]

[a]32:11 Ps 64:10; 68:3; 97:12 [b]33:1 Ps 32:11; 147:1; Php 4:4 [c]33:2 Ps 92:3; 144:9 [d]33:3 Ps 40:3; 96:1; Is 42:10 [e]Ps 150:4 [f]33:4 Ps 19:8 [g]33:5 Ps 11:7; 37:28 [h]Ps 119:64 [i]33:6 Heb 11:3; 2Pt 3:5 [j]Jb 26:13; Ps 104:30 [k]33:7 Ex 15:8; Jos 3:13; Ps 78:13 [l]33:8 Ps 67:7; 96:9 [m]33:9 Gn 1:3; Ps 147:15,18; 148:5 [n]33:10 Ps 2:1-3; Is 8:10; 19:3 [o]33:11 Ps 139:17; Pr 19:21; Is 55:8 [p]33:12 Ex 19:5; Dt 7:6; Ps 144:15 [q]33:13 Jb 28:24; Ps 11:4; 14:2; 53:2 [r]33:14 Ps 102:19 [s]33:15 Jb 34:21 [t]33:16 Ps 44:6; 60:11

A33:7 LXX, Tg, Syr, Vg, Jer read *sea as in a bottle*

32:11 After the psalmist confessed and experienced forgiveness, he became a conduit for God's praise and called on others to do the same (see note at 30:11-12).

33:1-3 This is a typical beginning for a descriptive praise psalm, which has the two main elements: a call to praise (vv. 1-3) and a cause for praise (vv. 4-22). The relationship between the beginning of this psalm and the end of Psalm 32 is evident in the use of **righteous ones** and **upright**. Since there is no title to this psalm, the connection is even more pronounced. Even though only the **lyre** and **harp** are mentioned, they probably represent all the musical instruments used for worship. A **new song** might be one newly composed for a special occasion or it might mean a new experience of God's acts through the singing of this psalm. Worship in Israel often involved "entering into history" in order to experience events as if they were happening at that moment.

33:4 God's **word** (or revelation) is worthy of exaltation and praise because it is **trustworthy** (see note at 19:7-9).

33:5 Loving **righteousness and justice** means doing acts of righteousness and justice (99:4; Jr 9:24). They are not just abstract attributes but they involve actions, whether directed toward God or His people.

33:6 This verse and what follows specify this psalm as a creation hymn (along with Pss 8 and 104). Even though they refer to different things, **the word of the LORD** here and in verse 4 are related in that they both originate with God. The Lord of creation is the God of revelation. This is distinctive from other ancient world religions that had myths of creation involving a "creative word" but did not tie that act to any subsequent history. In the biblical text, the God of history who interacts with His people is the same God who spoke the world into existence (see note at v. 9). This brings together the general revelation of creation and the special revelation that God gave to His people (see note at 19:7-9).

33:7 **The depths** uses the same word (Hb *tehom*) as "watery depths" (Gn 1:2), only here it is plural. The gathering of **the waters** in that context is the initial act of God's forming and filling the earth with the separation of waters above and below the expanse. Though some interpreters argue that this could describe the exodus event, the immediate context argues for creation.

33:8 By right of creation, Yahweh is the God of all mankind; therefore, everyone should fear Him. This is in fact the ultimate goal of the kingdom of God (see notes at 8:5-8 and 22:27-31).

33:9 The phrase **it came into being** is similar to the recurring phrase "and it was so" in Genesis 1.

33:10-11 These verses set up a contrast between what **the nations** plan and what God plans. This is similar to 2:1-3 where the nations intend to thwart God's purposes, but it is instead God who **frustrates** their plans (Is 8:10). Yahweh is sovereign and will see to it that His plans come to pass. The verb **stands** implies certainty (Pr 19:21; Is 14:24).

33:12 The **nation . . . He has chosen**—Israel—is in contrast to "the nations" in verse 10. On **happy**, see note at 1:1. The terms "chosen" and **possession** refer to divine election of the nation and its unique relationship to Yahweh (Ex 19:5; Dt 7:6).

33:13-15 The omniscience of God is described as His looking down, observing, and gazing on the **inhabitants of the earth**. Even though His **dwelling place** is **heaven**, this does not mean that He is unconcerned with what is happening

17 The horse is a false hope for safety;
   it provides no escape by its great power.[a]

18 Now the eye of the LORD is on those
      who ·fear Him—
   those who depend on His faithful love[b]

19 to deliver them from death
   and to keep them alive in famine.[c]

20 We wait for Yahweh;[d]
   He is our help and shield.[e]

21 For our hearts rejoice in Him[f]
   because we trust in His holy name.[g]

22 May Your faithful love rest on us,
      Yahweh,
   for we put our hope in You.[h]

Psalm 34

The LORD Delivers the Righteous

Concerning David, when he pretended to
be insane in the presence of Abimelech,[A,i]
who drove him out, and he departed.

1 I[B] will praise the LORD at all times;
   His praise will always be on my lips.[j]

2 I will boast in the LORD;[k]

the humble will hear and be glad.[l]

3 Proclaim ·Yahweh's greatness with me;[m]
   let us exalt His name together.[n]

4 I sought the LORD, and He answered me
   and delivered me from all my fears.[o]

5 Those who look to Him are[c] radiant
      with joy;[p]
   their faces will never be ashamed.[q]

6 This poor man cried, and the LORD
      heard him
   and saved him from all his troubles.[r]

7 The Angel of the LORD encamps
      around those who ·fear Him,
      and rescues them.[s]

8 Taste and see that the LORD is good.[t]
   How happy is the man who takes refuge
      in Him![u]

9 You who are His holy ones,
      fear Yahweh,
   for those who fear Him lack nothing.[v]

10 Young lions[D] lack food and go hungry,[w]
   but those who seek the LORD
   will not lack any good thing.[x]

Cross references:
[a]33:17 Ps 20:7; 147:10; Hs 1:7
[b]33:18 Jb 36:7; Ps 34:15; 1Pt 3:12
[c]33:19 Jb 5:20; Ps 37:19; 56:13
[d]33:20 Ps 130:6; Is 8:17
[e]Gn 15:1; Dt 33:29; Ps 3:3; 5:12; 18:2; 28:7; 115:9-11
[f]33:21 Ps 13:5; 28:7; Jn 16:22
[g]Zph 3:12
[h]33:22 Ps 130:7; 147:11
[i]34:title 1Sm 21:10-15
[j]34:1 Ps 71:6; Eph 5:20
[k]34:2 Ps 44:8; Jr 9:24; 1Co 1:31
[l]Ps 69:32
[m]34:3 Lk 1:46
[n]Ps 69:30
[o]34:4 Ps 34:6,17,19
[p]34:5 Is 60:5
[q]Ps 25:3
[r]34:6 Ps 34:4
[s]34:7 Ps 91:11; Heb 1:14
[t]34:8 1Pt 2:3
[u]Ps 2:12
[v]34:9 Ps 23:1
[w]34:10 Jb 4:10-11
[x]Ps 84:11

[A]34:title Probably Achish, king of Gath   [B]34:1 The lines of this poem form an ·acrostic.   [C]34:5 Some Hb mss, LXX, Aq, Syr, Jer read *Look to Him and be*   [D]34:10 LXX, Syr, Vg read *The rich*

on earth, even if the nations and the enemies of Israel think this is the case (see note at 10:3-6). Moreover, He not only knows what is happening but He is actively involved in it. The word **shapes** (Hb *yzr*) is the same word used in the creation account of God's shaping man from the dust of the earth (Gn 2:7-8). This also connects the creative acts of God with His involvement in history.

33:16-17 Human weaponry is of no use if God does not support it (see note at 20:7-8).

33:18-19 Eye is in an emphatic position in verse 18. Literally it is "behold the eye," emphasizing God's close watch on His people. This is even more intense than the descriptions in verses 13-15 since Yahweh has a concern for His own people that is unique in comparison to the other nations. Here, as in the previous verses, it is not only His knowledge but also His activity that is in view to **deliver** His people and to **keep them alive** (protect them).

33:20 Shield represents protection and is often identified with Yahweh Himself (3:3; 18:30; 115:9; 144:2)

Ps 34 title The incident mentioned here is found in 1Sm 21:10-15. It relates David's deliverance from King Achish of Gath (see textual footnote). Although an unusual account of deliverance, this psalm praises Yahweh for rescuing the psalmist. The content of the psalm is not tied to the specific event, so it could be used in a general way by God's people.

34:2 Boast in the LORD is best defined in Jr 9:23-24 where it means to "understand and know" Yahweh, which is further explained as knowing that Yahweh shows "faithful love, justice, and righteousness on the earth." In other words, it is knowing who God is and what He does, having a personal knowledge and experience of Him through trusting in Him.

34:5 Look to is another way of expressing trust in time of need (145:15) and is equivalent to "seek" in some contexts (Is 31:1).

34:6 A person who is in need and prays to Yahweh often identifies himself with the **poor**. The term can also designate someone who is humble or, in the more negative sense, humiliated. The word for "afflicted" (Hb *'ani*) is closely related and is often in parallel with the poor. There is not a strong distinction between these since it is assumed that the poor were the weakest and most helpless in society and were often the objects of oppression by stronger and more influential persons. Therefore, the term "poor" in the psalms should not be limited to economic hardship alone.

34:7 The **Angel of the LORD** can also be translated as "messenger of Yahweh." In most contexts there is a distinction between God and this angel. For example, in the story of Gideon, the angel of the Lord vanished (Jdg 6:21), but Gideon continued to speak to Yahweh (Jdg 6:22-24). This seems to indicate that they were different. However, in other contexts the angel of the Lord spoke as if he were God Himself (Gn 22:11-12; Ex 3:2). In this sense the angel could be a theophany (an appearance of Yahweh). Christian tradition has often identified such angels with the preincarnate appearances of Jesus Christ, but as noted above, this does not work in every instance. It is best to treat each context on its own merit and not impose the same meaning in every text. The connection between the "Angel of the Lord" and military imagery (note the word **encamps**) appears elsewhere to show that Yahweh fights for His people (2Kg 19:35). The "commander of the Lord's army" in Jos 5:13-15 may also be related to this angel.

34:8 Taste can mean "judge" in the sense of determine for oneself (Pr 31:18). **See** most likely carries the same sense in order to reinforce the concept.

34:9-10 God cares for His people more than the rest of His creation (8:5-8). Other texts use the argument that if God cares for His creation, He will care for mankind (104:14-15) and especially for His own people (Mt 6:28-30). **Lack**

11 Come, children, listen to me;
   I will teach you the fear of the LORD.[a]
12 Who is the man who delights in life,
   loving a long life to enjoy
      what is good?[b]
13 Keep your tongue from evil
   and your lips from deceitful speech.[c]
14 Turn away from evil and do
      what is good;[d]
   seek peace and pursue it.[e]

15 The eyes of the LORD are
      on the righteous,
   and His ears are open to their cry
      for help.[f]
16 The face of the LORD is set
   against those who do what is evil,[g]
   to erase[A] all memory of them
      from the earth.[h]
17 The righteous[B] cry out,
   and the LORD hears,
   and delivers them from all
      their troubles.[i]
18 The LORD is near the brokenhearted;
   He saves those crushed in spirit.[j]

19 Many adversities come to the one
      who is righteous,
   but the LORD delivers him
      from them all.[k]
20 He protects all his bones;
   not one of them is broken.[l]
21 Evil brings death to the wicked,
   and those who hate the righteous
      will be punished.[m]
22 The LORD redeems the life
   of His servants,

[a] 34:11 Ps 66:16; 111:10
[b] 34:12 Ec 3:13; 6:6
[c] 34:13 Ps 39:1; 141:3; Pr 13:3; Jms 1:26
[d] 34:14 Ps 37:27; Is 1:16-17
[e] Rm 14:19; Heb 12:14
[f] 34:15 Jb 36:7; Ps 33:18; 1Pt 3:12
[g] 34:12-16 1Pt 3:10-12
[h] 34:16 Am 9:4
[i] 34:17 Ps 145:19
[j] 34:18 Ps 51:17; 147:3; Is 61:1
[k] 34:19 Ps 71:20; 2Tm 3:11-12
[l] 34:20 Jn 19:33,36
[m] 34:21 Ps 94:23; 140:11; Pr 24:16
[n] 34:22 Ps 37:40; Rm 8:33-34
[o] 35:1 Ex 14:25; Is 49:25
[p] 35:2 Ps 5:12; 91:4
[q] 35:3 Ps 13:5; 40:17
[r] 35:4 Ps 40:14; 70:2; 129:5
[s] 35:5 Jb 21:18; Ps 83:13; Is 29:5
[t] 35:6 Ps 73:18; Jr 23:12
[u] 35:7 Ps 140:5
[v] 35:8 Jb 18:8; Ps 7:15
[w] 35:9 Ps 9:14; 13:5
[x] 35:10 Ex 15:11; Ps 86:8; Mc 7:18

and all who take refuge in Him will not
   be punished.[n]

Psalm 35
Prayer for Victory
Davidic.

1 Oppose my opponents, LORD;
   fight those who fight me.[o]
2 Take Your shields—large and small—
   and come to my aid.[p]
3 Draw the spear and javelin
      against my pursuers,
   and assure me: "I am your deliverance."[q]

4 Let those who seek to kill me
   be disgraced and humiliated;
   let those who plan to harm me
   be turned back and ashamed.[r]
5 Let them be like chaff in the wind,
   with the angel of the LORD
      driving them away.[s]
6 Let their way be dark and slippery,
   with the angel of the LORD
      pursuing them.[t]
7 They hid their net for me without cause;
   they dug a pit for me without cause.[u]
8 Let ruin come on him unexpectedly,
   and let the net that he hid ensnare him;
   let him fall into it—to his ruin.[v]

9 Then I will rejoice in the LORD;
   I will delight in His deliverance.[w]
10 My very bones will say,
   "LORD, who is like You,[x]
rescuing the poor from one too strong
   for him,

[A] 34:16 Or cut off   [B] 34:17 Lit They

---

nothing also appears in the context of Yahweh's role as a shepherd in 23:1.

34:11 The identification of the psalmist's listeners as children recalls a common wisdom motif of parents instructing their children (Ex 12:26; Dt 6:6-9) and shows that Ps 34:11-14 form a wisdom section in this psalm (similar to 32:8-9). To be taught the fear of the LORD is preferable to learning it through experience. Fearing the Lord is where wisdom begins (Pr 9:10).

34:15 The reference to eyes in relation to Yahweh's watchful care of His people is similar to the singular form in 33:18. His open ears describe His attentiveness to their prayers (18:6; 130:2).

34:16 To erase the memory of someone from the earth is another way to describe annihilation (see note at 9:4-6).

34:18 Brokenhearted and crushed in spirit further develop the image of oppression, although the emphasis in these terms is on internal suffering. Yahweh is near those who are broken and humble (51:17) as opposed to those who have "hearts of stone" (Ezk 11:19; 36:26).

34:20 Broken bones are often symbols of physical affliction

(51:8; Is 38:13) or oppression (Mc 3:3). God protects His own from these dangers.

34:21 Evil (Hb ra'ah) can mean disaster and calamity as well as the abstract concept of evil. In this case it is personified as the one who kills the wicked. Note how this contrasts with goodness and faithful love pursuing the person who trusts in Yahweh (23:6).

35:1 The description of Yahweh as a warrior who fights for His people is a common image in the OT (see note at 7:12-13).

35:2 On large shields, see note at 5:11-12.

35:5 Chaff was the waste from threshing (see note at 1:4). The angel of the LORD is sometimes used in military contexts as the one who fought for Israel (see note at 34:7).

35:6-8 It is a common request that one's enemies fall into their own traps (9:15; 31:4; 57:6; 141:10; see note at 7:14-16).

35:10 Bones often represent suffering. In this case they are used for the whole person, but they emphasize that Yahweh protects His people from suffering. Needy (Hb 'evyon) is of-

the poor or the needy from one
  who robs him?"[a]

11 Malicious witnesses come forward;
    they question me about things
    I do not know.[b]
12 They repay me evil for good,
    making me desolate.[c]
13 Yet when they were sick,
    my clothing was *sackcloth;
    I humbled myself with fasting,
    and my prayer was genuine.[A,d]
14 I went about grieving as if for my friend
      or brother;
    I was bowed down with grief,
    like one mourning a mother.[e]
15 But when I stumbled, they gathered
      in glee;
    they gathered against me.
    Assailants I did not know
    tore at me and did not stop.[f]
16 With godless mockery[B]
    they gnashed their teeth at me.[g]

17 Lord, how long will You look on?[h]
    Rescue my life from their ravages,
    my only one from the young lions.[i]
18 I will praise You
      in the great congregation;
    I will exalt You among many people.[j]
19 Do not let my deceitful enemies rejoice
      over me;
    do not let those who hate me
      without cause[k]

look at me maliciously.[l]
20 For they do not speak in friendly ways,
    but contrive deceitful schemes[c]
    against those who live peacefully
      in the land.[m]
21 They open their mouths wide
      against me and say,
    "Aha, aha! We saw it!"[D,n]

22 You saw it, LORD; do not be silent.
    Lord, do not be far from me.[o]
23 Wake up and rise to my defense,
    to my cause, my God and my LORD![p]
24 Vindicate me, LORD my God,
    in keeping with Your righteousness,
    and do not let them rejoice over me.[q]
25 Do not let them say in their hearts,
    "Aha! Just what we wanted."
    Do not let them say,
    "We have swallowed him up!"[r]
26 Let those who rejoice at my misfortune
    be disgraced and humiliated;
    let those who exalt themselves over me
    be clothed with shame and reproach.[s]

27 Let those who want my vindication
    shout for joy and be glad;
    let them continually say,
    "The LORD be exalted.
    He takes pleasure in
      His servant's well-being."[t]
28 And my tongue will proclaim
      Your righteousness,
    Your praise all day long.[u]

[a] 35:10 Ps 72:12; 82:4	
[b] 35:11 Ps 27:12; Pr 19:5,9	
[c] 35:12 Ps 38:20; 109:5; Jr 18:20	
[d] 35:13 Ps 69:10-11	
[e] 35:14 Ps 38:6	
[f] 35:15 Jb 30:1,8,12; Ob 12	
[g] 35:16 Jb 16:9; Ps 37:12; Lm 2:16	
[h] 35:17 Ps 13:1; Hab 1:13	
[i] Ps 22:20-21	
[j] 35:18 Ps 22:22,25; 40:9-10; Heb 2:12	
[k] 35:19 Ps 38:19; Jn 15:25	
[l] Ps 13:4; 30:1; 38:16	
[m] 35:20 Ps 55:21; Jr 9:8; Mc 6:12	
[n] 35:21 Jb 16:10; Ps 22:13; 40:15; 70:3	
[o] 35:22 Ps 10:1; 22:11; 28:1	
[p] 35:23 Ps 7:6; 44:23; 59:4	
[q] 35:24 Ps 26:1; 43:1	
[r] 35:25 Ps 124:3; Lm 2:16	
[s] 35:26 Jb 8:22; Ps 40:14; 109:29	
[t] 35:27 Ps 40:16; 70:4	
[u] 35:28 Ps 71:8,15,24	

[A] 35:13 Lit *prayer returned to my chest*   [B] 35:16 Hb obscure   [C] 35:20 Lit *but devise deceitful words*   [D] 35:21 Lit *Our eyes saw!*

ten parallel to **poor** and is used to make the connection between poverty and oppression (see note at 34:6).

35:11-14 **Witnesses** who were caught lying in their accusations were to receive the punishment they intended for the accused (Dt 19:18-19). It is clear from this context that their accusations were unfounded ("without cause," Ps 35:19). They were most likely fellow Israelites since the psalmist identified with their suffering as a **friend** and **brother**. In this way friends were no different from enemies (41:9; 55:12-14).

35:15 The **glee** of these people toward the psalmist's troubles also put them in the same category as enemies who triumphed over the afflictions of God's people (see note at 30:1-2).

35:16 Gnashing the **teeth** was a sign of anger (37:12; 112:10; Jb 16:9; Lm 2:16), so this **mockery** was more than playful ridicule; it included a "malicious" intent (vv. 11,19).

35:17 **How long** is used to show how there is a perceived delay in God's acting on behalf of His suffering servant (see notes at 4:2 and 13:1-2). Enemies are often represented as vicious wild animals, especially **lions** (see note at 7:1-2).

35:20 **Live peacefully** (lit "quietly") **in the land** is a phrase that occurs only here in the OT, but it describes those who are faithful to Yahweh since God promised to give His

people peace in the land when they obeyed Him (Lv 26:6). The usual word for peace (Hb *shalom*) is actually in the first line and is translated as **friendly ways**. The irony is that those who are not peaceful are plotting against those who are at peace.

35:21 **Aha** is used in contexts involving ridicule. It attempts to shame further those who have suffered some calamity (40:16; 70:4; Ezk 25:3; 26:2; 36:2).

35:22 **You saw it** is in contrast to "we saw it" in the previous verse. In that case it was the enemies who ridiculed the psalmist because they saw his affliction; here it is Yahweh who saw his suffering and was called upon to act on it.

35:23 **Wake up** is parallel to **rise** and probably has the same idea as other contexts calling for Yahweh to "rise up" for His people (see note at 7:6-8).

35:26 Clothing is a figure of speech often used with attributes such as majesty in the case of Yahweh (93:1; 104:1) or salvation in the case of priests (132:16). In this instance **shame and reproach** are negative attributes that are to be worn (as clothing) by the enemies.

35:27-28 God's **righteousness** is connected with the psalmist's **vindication**. The term for righteousness (Hb *tsedaqah*) can also mean "justice," so the call for vindication is actually a request for the execution of God's justice in the psalmist's situation.

Psalm 36
Human Wickedness and God's Love

For the choir director. A psalm of David, the LORD's servant.

1 An *oracle within my heart
concerning the transgression of the
wicked person:
There is no dread of God before his eyes,[a]

2 for in his own eyes he flatters himself
too much
to discover and hate his sin.[b]

3 The words of his mouth are malicious
and deceptive;[c]
he has stopped acting wisely
and doing good.[d]

4 Even on his bed he makes
malicious plans.[e]
He sets himself on a path that is not good
and does not reject evil.[f]

5 LORD, Your faithful love reaches
to heaven,
Your faithfulness to the clouds.[g]

6 Your righteousness is
like the highest mountains;
Your judgments, like the deepest sea.[h]
LORD, You preserve man and beast.[i]

7 God, Your faithful love is so valuable
that *people take refuge in the shadow
of Your wings.[j]

8 They are filled from the abundance
of Your house;
You let them drink
from Your refreshing stream,[k]

9 for with You is life's fountain.[l]
In Your light we will see light.[m]

10 Spread Your faithful love over those
who know You,
and Your righteousness
over the upright in heart.[n]

11 Do not let the foot of the arrogant man
come near me
or the hand of the wicked one
drive me away.[o]

12 There the evildoers fall;
they have been thrown down
and cannot rise.[p]

Psalm 37
Instruction in Wisdom

Davidic.

1 Do[A] not be agitated by evildoers;
do not envy those who do wrong.[q]

---

[a] 36:1 Rm 3:18
[b] 36:2 Dt 29:19; Ps 10:3; 49:18
[c] 36:3 Ps 10:7
[d] Jr 4:22
[e] 36:4 Pr 4:16
[f] Ps 10:7; Is 65:2
[g] 36:5 Ps 57:10; 103:11; 108:4
[h] 36:6 Ps 71:19
[i] Ps 104:14-15
[j] 36:7 Ru 2:12; Ps 17:8; 57:1; 91:4
[k] 36:8 Ps 46:4; 65:4; Jr 31:12-14
[l] 36:9 Jn 4:10,14
[m] Jn 1:9; Ac 26:18
[n] 36:10 Pr 11:6; Jr 22:16
[o] 36:11 Ps 38:16; 119:122
[p] 36:12 Ps 1:5; 140:10; Is 26:14
[q] 37:1 Ps 73:3; Pr 3:31; 23:17; 24:19

[A]37:1 The lines of this poem form an *acrostic.

36:1 The Hebrew word *ne'um*, translated here as **oracle**, is used by the prophets in a more formal sense to signify God's official declarations through the prophets to His people (note especially its use in Jeremiah; e.g., Jr 1:8,15,19). Its use here could also refer to an official prophetic oracle against **the wicked**. The difference between this and the prophets is that the message originated within the psalmist's **heart** and not from God's spoken word to him.

36:2 The Hebrew text is difficult here and literally reads,

'awen

Hebrew Pronunciation	[AH vehn]
HCSB Translation	evil, malicious, disaster, sorrow
Uses in Psalms	29
Uses in the OT	85
Focus Passage	Psalm 36:3-4,12

'Awen, a root occurring only in Hebrew and appearing largely in poetic and prophetic texts, signifies *evil* (Is 31:2), *wickedness* (1Sm 15:23), *sin* (Ps 56:7), and *iniquity* (Is 1:13). Specifically, it connotes *crime* (Ps 55:10), *malice* (Jr 4:15), *injustice* (Hab 1:3), or *evil intent* (Is 29:20). *'Awen* denotes evil's consequences of *disaster* (Nm 23:1), *distress* (Jb 5:6), and *sorrow* (Ps 90:10). It specifies evil's emptiness as *falsehood* (Zch 10:2), *delusion* (Is 41:29), *nothing* (Am 5:5), and *idol* (Is 66:3). *'Awen* appears alongside *'amal* ("trouble") 11 times (Jb 4:8). Adjectivally, *'awen* is *malicious, wicked, sinful,* and *crooked* (Is 10:1). The phrase *po'aley* ("doers of") *'awen* (22x) is normally translated *evildoers* (Ps 36:12). *'Awen* names a valley Aven (Am 1:5) and once seems a shortened form of Beth-aven (Hs 10:8; cp. v. 5). *'Awen* is part of the place name Beth-*aven* (7x). Beth-*aven* might derogatorily substitute for Bethel (Hs 4:15; cp. Am 5:5).

"for it is smooth to him in his eyes to find his sin to hate." The word for "smooth" (Hb *chalaq*) is sometimes used in the context of speech and associated with flattery (12:3; Dn 11:32). This concept makes sense here even though it is not directly related to speech. **In his own eyes** means in his own estimation; in other words, it is perception and not reality that prevents this wicked person from hating **his sin**.

36:4 The **malicious plans** are made in **bed** so they can be carried out during the daytime (Mc 2:1).

36:5-6 **Heaven** and **clouds** illustrate the extent of Yahweh's covenant faithfulness as do the extremes of **highest mountain** and **deepest sea**. There is no limit to God's love for His people (Rm 8:35-39) nor any place that is beyond His reach (Ps 139:7-12).

36:8 **Abundance** is literally "oil" and represents blessing (Is 55:2). The imagery of oil and **refreshing stream** bring together the same images as those in Psalm 23 (see notes at 23:2-3 and 23:5).

36:9 **Life's fountain** is used elsewhere to describe Yahweh as the source of life (Jr 2:13; 17:13). **Light** can refer to truth (43:3) or salvation (27:1). The combination of life and light is particularly significant in John's Gospel and is applied to Jesus Christ (Jn 1:4; 8:12).

36:10 **Spread Your faithful love** may relate to the image of a mother bird's "wings" in verse 7.

36:11 Victory in the ancient world was often represented by the victor's **foot** on the neck of the vanquished (110:1).

37:1 To **envy** the wicked is a temptation when one sees them prospering. Such an attitude is in essence doubting God's

2 For they wither quickly like grass
and wilt like tender green plants.*a*

3 Trust in the LORD and do
what is good;*b*
dwell in the land and live securely.^A,c

4 Take delight in the LORD,
and He will give you
your heart's desires.*d*

5 Commit your way to the LORD;
trust in Him, and He will act,*e*

6 making your righteousness shine
like the dawn,
your justice like the noonday.*f*

7 Be silent before the LORD and wait
expectantly for Him;*g*
do not be agitated by one who prospers
in his way,
by the man who carries out evil plans.*h*

8 Refrain from anger and give up
your rage;
do not be agitated—it can only
bring harm.*i*

9 For evildoers will be destroyed,
but those who put their hope
in the LORD
will inherit the land.^B,j

10 A little while, and the wicked person
will be no more;

though you look for him, he will not
be there.*k*

11 But the humble will inherit the land^B,l
and will enjoy abundant prosperity.*m*

12 The wicked person schemes
against the righteous
and gnashes his teeth at him.*n*

13 The Lord laughs at him*o*
because He sees that his day
is coming.*p*

14 The wicked have drawn the sword
and strung the^c bow
to bring down the afflicted and needy
and to slaughter those whose way
is upright.*q*

15 Their swords will enter
their own hearts,
and their bows will be broken.*r*

16 The little that the righteous man has
is better
than the abundance
of many wicked people.*s*

17 For the arms^D of the wicked
will be broken,*t*
but the LORD supports the righteous.*u*

18 The LORD watches over the blameless
all their days,
and their inheritance will last forever.*v*

*a*37:2 Ps 92:7; 129:6; Jms 1:11
*b*37:3 Ps 62:8
*c*Pr 2:21
*d*37:4 Ps 21:2; 145:19; Is 58:14
*e*37:5 Ps 55:22; Pr 16:3; 1Pt 5:7
*f*37:6 Ps 97:11; Is 58:8,10
*g*37:7 Ps 40:1; Lm 3:26
*h*Jr 12:1
*i*37:8 Eph 4:31; Col 3:8
*j*37:9 Pr 2:21; Is 57:13; 60:21
*k*37:10 Jb 7:10; 24:24; Ps 37:35-36
*l*37:11 Mt 5:5
*m*Ps 72:7
*n*37:12 Ps 31:13,20; 35:16
*o*37:13 Ps 2:4; 59:8; Hab 1:10
*p*1Sm 26:10
*q*37:14 Ps 11:2; Lm 2:4
*r*37:15 1Sm 2:4; Ps 46:9
*s*37:16 Pr 15:16; 16:8
*t*37:17 Ps 10:15
*u*Ps 145:14
*v*37:18 Ps 1:6

^A37:3 Or *and cultivate faithfulness* ^B37:9,11 Or *earth* ^C37:14 Lit *their* ^D37:17 Or *power*

justice (73:3) and is prohibited here as well as in other texts (Pr 23:17; 24:1,19).

37:2 To refrain from envying the wicked is easier if we stop to consider their destiny (cp. 73:3,17-20). **Grass** and **tender green plants** are temporary and do not last (103:15; Jb 14:2; Is 40:6; Mt 6:30).

37:3 God's covenant promise to His people was that they would **dwell in the land . . . securely** if they obeyed His commands (see notes at 25:13 and 35:20). "The land" is significant in this psalm as the "inheritance" of those who were loyal to Yahweh (37:9,11,22,29,34).

37:4 When there is close fellowship with Yahweh, a person's **heart's desires** will match God's will and purposes (see note at 20:4; cp. Mt 6:33 and Lk 12:31).

37:6 The images of **shine like the dawn** and **like the noon-day** could mean either that the psalmist's vindication (the demonstration of God's **justice** in his life) will be seen by all or that God's justice is as certain as the rising of the sun. In either case, there is comfort in the fact that God will answer His people's prayers for justice.

37:7 **Be silent** is a command similar to being "quiet" before the Lord (62:1,5). Sometimes it is the result of discipline (Lm 3:28), but here it means to **wait** on the Lord instead of acting on one's own (see note at 27:14).

37:8-9 The psalmist's **anger** was apparently caused by the observation that the wicked were prospering and God had not judged them (v. 1). The prohibition on anger and agita-

tion is repeated, as is the reason—the promise of the destruction of **evildoers**.

37:10 Although from the human perspective God was delaying the execution of His justice, from His perspective it was only **a little while** (Jb 24:24; 2Pt 3:8-9).

37:11 The **humble** are similar to the "poor," "needy," and "afflicted" in other psalms. They are those who are "brokenhearted" before Yahweh (see note at 34:18).

37:12-13 On gnashing **teeth**, see note at 35:16. The combination of the **schemes** of **the wicked** and God's laughing at them in ridicule is reminiscent of 2:1-4.

37:14 The **wicked** are pictured as those who are poised with their weapons ready and aimed at the righteous (see note at 7:12-13).

37:16 **Little** is the same word used in verse 10 to describe the time before God dispenses His justice. Here it refers to the quantity of the possessions of **the righteous** in comparison to the **abundance** (wealth and prosperity) of **many wicked people**. This is perhaps a play on the word in order to emphasize that what was now the case would change shortly.

37:17 **Arms** often refer to power (89:10), so breaking one's arm means to render someone powerless (10:15; Jb 38:15; Jr 48:25; Ezk 30:21).

37:18 The promise of the **inheritance** of the land was **forever**, in the sense that it would go to their descendants (Jos 14:9; Ezr 9:12).

¹⁹ They will not be disgraced in times
  of adversity;
  they will be satisfied in days
  of hunger.^a

²⁰ But the wicked will perish;
  the LORD's enemies, like the glory
  of the pastures,
  will fade away—
  they will fade away like smoke.^b

²¹ The wicked man borrows
  and does not repay,
  but the righteous one is gracious
  and giving.^c

²² Those who are blessed by Him
  will inherit the land,^A
  but those cursed by Him
  will be destroyed.^d

²³ A man's steps are established
  by the LORD,
  and He takes pleasure in his way.^e

²⁴ Though he falls, he will not
  be overwhelmed,
  because the LORD holds his hand.^{B,f}

²⁵ I have been young and now I am old,
  yet I have not seen
  the righteous abandoned
  or his children begging for bread.^g

²⁶ He is always generous, always lending,
  and his children are a blessing.^h

²⁷ Turn away from evil and do
  what is good,
  and dwell there^C forever.ⁱ

²⁸ For the LORD loves justice
  and will not abandon His faithful ones.^j

They are kept safe forever,
  but the children of the wicked
  will be destroyed.^k

²⁹ The righteous will inherit the land^A
  and dwell in it permanently.^l

³⁰ The mouth of the righteous
  utters wisdom;
  his tongue speaks what is just.^m

³¹ The instruction of his God is
  in his heart;
  his steps do not falter.ⁿ

³² The wicked one lies in wait
  for the righteous
  and seeks to kill him;^o

³³ the LORD will not leave him
  in the power of the wicked one
  or allow him to be condemned
  when he is judged.^p

³⁴ Wait for the LORD and keep His way,
  and He will exalt you to inherit
  the land.
  You will watch when the wicked
  are destroyed.^q

³⁵ I have seen a wicked, violent man
  well-rooted^D like
  a flourishing native tree.^r

³⁶ Then I passed by and^E noticed
  he was gone;
  I searched for him, but he could not
  be found.^s

³⁷ Watch the blameless and observe
  the upright,
  for the man of peace will have
  a future.^{F,t}

Cross-references

^a37:19 Jb 5:20; Ps 33:19
^b37:20 Ps 68:2; Hs 13:3
^c37:21 Ps 112:5,9
^d37:22 Pr 3:33
^e37:23 1Sm 2:9; Ps 66:9
^f37:24 Ps 145:14; Pr 24:16; Mc 7:8
^g37:25 Is 41:17
^h37:26 Dt 15:8; Ps 112:5,9; Mt 5:42
ⁱ37:27 Ps 34:14; 102:28
^j37:28 Dt 31:6; Heb 13:5
^kPs 21:10; Pr 2:22
^l37:29 Pr 2:21; Is 60:21
^m37:30 Ps 49:3; 119:13; Pr 10:13
ⁿ37:31 Dt 6:6; Ps 40:8; 119:11
^o37:32 Ps 10:8; 17:11
^p37:33 Ps 34:22; 109:31; 2Pt 2:9
^q37:34 Ps 27:14; 52:5-6; 91:8
^r37:35 Jb 5:3; Jr 12:2
^s37:36 Jb 20:5
^t37:37 Is 57:1-2

Textual notes

^A37:22,29 Or earth   ^B37:24 Or LORD supports with His hand   ^C37:27 = dwell in the land   ^D37:35 Hb obscure   ^E37:36 DSS, LXX, Syr, Vg, Jer; MT reads Then he passed away, and I   ^F37:37 Or posterity

37:20 Pastures recalls the same image as "grass" in verse 2. The word **smoke** conveys the same notion of transience (68:2; 102:3; Is 51:6).

37:21 The generosity of the righteous comes from Yahweh's **gracious** acts toward them. God will provide for their needs to such an extent that they will be able to help others (Dt 15:6; 28:12,44). This idea is further developed in Ps 37:25-26 (cp. Ps 112).

37:23-24 Figuratively, **established** refers to security and stability, and **steps** are related to one's way of life, often represented as a path or road. Therefore, the Lord is the One who brings about a person's stability in life.

37:25-26 The principle of verse 21 is part of the psalmist's life experience and not just empty words.

37:28 Safety is sometimes related to the image of Yahweh as a strong fortress or tower (Pr 18:10).

37:31 Instruction is the Hebrew word torah (see note at 1:2). The idea of Yahweh's instruction being in the **heart** has theological significance in its relation to the new covenant (Jr 31:33; Ezk 36:27). Even before the benefits of that covenant occur, the people of God are known as those "in whose heart is My instruction" (Is 51:7). True devotion of God's people is evident in the heart and not just in outward actions.

37:32 On the **wicked** and the **righteous**, see note at verse 14.

37:35 I have seen is a common expression in Wisdom literature to indicate that what follows is from personal experience (Jb 5:3; Pr 7:6; 24:30; Ec 2:1). A **flourishing . . . tree** is an image generally referring to the righteous (see note at 1:3), but here the situation is different in that it seems the **wicked** have the stability (**well-rooted**) in life that only the righteous are supposed to have.

37:36 The appearance of stability in verse 35 was an illusion (v. 10).

37:37-38 Future is equivalent to "destiny," "end," or "fate" (73:17; Nm 23:10; Dt 32:29). This reinforces the idea that perception is not reality since **the upright** and **transgressors** have different fates.

³⁸ But transgressors will all
   be eliminated;
the future^A of the wicked
   will be destroyed.^a

³⁹ The salvation of the righteous is
   from the Lᴏʀᴅ,
their refuge in a time of distress.^b

⁴⁰ The Lᴏʀᴅ helps and delivers them;
He will deliver them from the wicked
   and will save them
because they take refuge in Him.^c

Psalm 38
Prayer of a Suffering Sinner

A Davidic psalm for remembrance.^d

¹ Lᴏʀᴅ, do not punish me in Your anger
   or discipline me in Your wrath.^e

² For Your arrows have sunk into me,
   and Your hand has pressed down on me.^f

³ There is no health in my body
because of Your indignation;
there is no strength^B in my bones
because of my sin.^g

⁴ For my sins have flooded over my head;
they are a burden too heavy for me
   to bear.^h

⁵ My wounds are foul and festering
because of my foolishness.ⁱ

⁶ I am bent over and brought low;

---

all day long I go around in mourning.^j

⁷ For my loins are full of burning pain,
and there is no health in my body.^k

⁸ I am faint and severely crushed;
I groan because of the anguish
   of my heart.^l

⁹ Lord, my every desire is known to^C You;
my sighing is not hidden from You.^m

¹⁰ My heart races, my strength leaves me,
and even the light of my eyes has faded.^{D,n}

¹¹ My loved ones and friends stand back
   from my affliction,
and my relatives stand at a distance.^o

¹² Those who seek my life set traps,
and those who want to harm me
   threaten to destroy me;
they plot treachery all day long.^p

¹³ I am like a deaf person;
   I do not hear.
I am like a speechless person
who does not open his mouth.^q

¹⁴ I am like a man who does not hear
and has no arguments in his mouth.^r

¹⁵ I put my hope in You, Lᴏʀᴅ;
You will answer, Lord my God.^s

¹⁶ For I said, "Don't let them rejoice
   over me—
those who are arrogant toward me
   when I stumble."^t

¹⁷ For I am about to fall,
and my pain is constantly with me.^u

Cross references (center column):

^a37:38 Ps 1:4-6; Pr 2:22
^b37:39 Ps 3:8; 9:9; 62:1
^c37:40 Ps 22:4; 34:22; 54:4
^d38:title Ps 70 title
^e38:1 Ps 6:1
^f38:2 Jb 6:4; Ps 32:4
^g38:3 Jb 33:19; Ps 31:10; 102:10
^h38:4 Ezr 9:6; Ps 40:12
ⁱ38:5 Is 1:6
^j38:6 Ps 35:14
^k38:7 Ps 38:3; Lm 1:13
^l38:8 Jb 3:24; Ps 6:6; 32:3; Lm 2:11
^m38:9 Ps 10:17
ⁿ38:10 Ps 6:7; 69:3; 88:9
^o38:11 Jb 19:13-20; Ps 31:11; 88:18
^p38:12 Ps 35:4,20; 54:3; 140:5
^q38:13 Ps 39:2,9
^r38:14 Jb 23:4
^s38:15 Ps 17:6; 39:7
^t38:16 Ps 13:4; 35:26
^u38:17 Ps 13:2; 35:15

---

^A37:38 Or *posterity*   ^B38:3 Hb *shalom*   ^C38:9 Lit *is in front of*   ^D38:10 Or *and the light of my eyes—even that is not with me*

37:39-40 The psalm ends with a statement of confidence and certainty, in contrast to the agitation and envy in verse 1.

Ps 38 title The word **remembrance** may refer to a memorial offering that was a part of the grain offering in Israel (Lv 2:2,9,16; 5:12). This title also appears in Psalm 70. The request for Yahweh to remember is another way of asking Him to act in a situation (see note at 25:6-7). Both this psalm and Psalm 70 are prayers and fit this concept.

38:1-2 God's **anger** and **discipline** are often mentioned in lament psalms, indicating the belief that sin is the reason for suffering. Although in some cases it may only be an assumption (see note at 6:1), in this psalm the language is much more certain and indicates that sin is the primary issue. The **arrows** recall weapon imagery used of enemies (11:2) and of Yahweh when He fights for His people (7:13; 18:14). However, this instance pictures Yahweh as an enemy of the psalmist because of his sin.

38:3-8 The relationship between psychological suffering and physical pain is common in lament psalms (see note at 6:2-3). **Bones** seem to be used most frequently in relation to the image of physical pain (see note at 22:17-18). While the language need not be literal, it conveys the idea of intense pain and suffering that is clearly connected to Yahweh's discipline. It is significant how many times the phrase **because of** is used in this context. Its objects are **Your indignation . . . my sins . . . my foolishness**, and **the anguish of my heart**. These make it clear why the psalmist was suffering.

38:9 The phrase **known to You** is literally "in front of You" (in Your presence). Sin cannot dwell in God's presence (see note at 5:4-5), but when there is a change in a person's attitude toward sin, represented here by **my every desire** (or "longing"), God accepts and acts on it (55:16).

38:10 Light in one's **eyes** is similar to "brightness" and represents vitality (see note at 13:3-4).

38:11-12 It is a common experience of a person who is suffering intensely that even **friends** reject him (88:8,18; Jb 19:14-15). Many scholars believe that the juxtaposition of friends in Ps 38:11 with enemies in verse 12 makes it possible that the friends had become like enemies (109:3-4; Lm 1:2; see note at Ps 31:11).

38:13-14 The psalmist was **speechless** and had **no arguments** (defense) because he knew that God was the One who was punishing him for his sins. This is much different from the suffering of the innocent where there is a plea for God to act based on His promises to the faithful (Pss 17; 26). In this instance the only thing Yahweh will hear is a confession of sin, which is also the only chance for relief from the suffering (32:3-5).

38:16 On the rejoicing of enemies over the psalmist's misfortune, see note at 30:1-2.

38:17 Fall in this case is not a moral fall—since the psalmist was already in sin—but defeat and perhaps death. It is a term often applied to the downfall of one's enemies (5:10; 35:8).

18 So I confess my •guilt;
I am anxious because of my sin.[a]
19 But my enemies are vigorous
and powerful;[A]
many hate me for no reason.[b]
20 Those who repay evil for good
attack me for pursuing good.[c]

21 LORD, do not abandon me;
my God, do not be far from me.[d]
22 Hurry to help me,
Lord, my Savior.[e]

Psalm 39
The Fleeting Nature of Life

For the choir director, for Jeduthun.
A Davidic psalm.

1 I said, "I will guard my ways
so that I may not sin with my tongue;
I will guard my mouth with a muzzle
as long as the wicked are
in my presence."[f]
2 I was speechless and quiet;
I kept silent, even from speaking good,
and my pain intensified.[g]
3 My heart grew hot within me;
as I mused, a fire burned.[h]
I spoke with my tongue:
4 "LORD, reveal to me the end of my life
and the number of my days.

Let me know how short-lived I am.[i]
5 You, indeed, have made my days short
in length,
and my life span as nothing
in Your sight.
Yes, every mortal man is only a vapor.[j]
•Selah

6 "Certainly, man walks about
like a mere shadow.
Indeed, they frantically rush around
in vain,
gathering possessions
without knowing who will get them.[k]
7 Now, Lord, what do I wait for?
My hope is in You.[l]
8 Deliver me from all my transgressions;
do not make me the taunt of fools.[m]
9 I am speechless; I do not open my mouth
because of what You have done.[n]
10 Remove Your torment from me;
I fade away because of the force
of Your hand.[o]
11 You discipline a man with punishment
for sin,
consuming like a moth
what is precious to him;[p]
every man is only a vapor.[q]   Selah

12 "Hear my prayer, LORD,
and listen to my cry for help;
do not be silent at my tears.[r]

---

a 38:18 Ps 32:5; 2Co 7:9-10
b 38:19 Ps 18:17; 35:19
c 38:20 Ps 35:12; 109:5; 3Jn 11
d 38:21 Ps 22:19; 35:22
e 38:22 Ps 40:13,17
f 39:1 Ps 34:13; Jms 3:5-12
g 39:2 Jb 40:4; Ps 38:13
h 39:3 Ps 32:4; Jr 20:9; Lk 24:32
i 39:4 Ps 78:39; 90:12; 103:14
j 39:5 Ps 62:9; 89:47; 144:4
k 39:6 Ps 49:10; Ec 2:18-19; Lk 12:20; 1Co 7:31
l 39:7 Ps 38:15
m 39:8 Ps 44:13; 79:4; 119:22
n 39:9 Ps 39:2
o 39:10 Jb 9:34; 13:21; Ps 32:4
p 39:11 Is 50:9
q Ps 39:5
r 39:12 Ps 35:22

[A] 38:19 Or *numerous*

38:18 Guilt is parallel to **sin** and means a liability for punishment rather than a subjective feeling (see note at 32:5). Sin is why the psalmist was deserving of punishment.

38:19-22 Once the confession took place, the problem of the enemies still existed. In fact, it probably was more intense since the psalmist was now **pursuing good**, and his enemies were repaying **evil for good**. The big difference is that God would no longer be against him as well. Instead, the psalmist could legitimately ask for Yahweh not to **abandon** him; he could ask for His **help** and be confident that God would respond.

Ps 39 title Jeduthun (probably another name for Ethan) also appears in the titles of Psalms 62 and 77. According to 1Ch 16:41, he was one of David's chief musicians. If this is not a reference to Jeduthun himself, it may refer to his descendants or a group of musicians using his name (perhaps derived from his own musical style or school).

39:1-2 The reason for the psalmist's silence was to keep from sinning by voicing his protest to God. The same idea occurs in 73:15, but in that text the protest is specifically identified as the belief that God is ignoring the prosperity of the wicked. In this psalm it could be a condition of suffering that caused these feelings to emerge.

39:3 A **heart** growing **hot** is an expression for exasperation (Dt 19:6; Jr 20:9). **Fire** can mean anger, but here it seems to refer to pent-up emotions waiting to escape.

39:4-6 This request for God to **reveal** to the psalmist that his **days** were **short-lived** shows that he knew his inner feelings must be held in check. He already knew this, but he wished for Yahweh to instruct him. **Vapor** (Hb *hevel*) is sometimes translated as "breath" (Jb 7:7). It denotes in its literal sense a small puff of air. Figuratively, it refers to a meaningless existence or futile activities (Ps 94:11; Ec 1:2). When used together with **shadow**, the word emphasizes the fleeting nature of life (see note at Ps 144:4). The lesson to be learned involves seeing everything as God sees it—from His perspective, rather than from the human perspective. Human accomplishments, however great they seem, fade away with the steady march of history. For those who trust in God, life has a meaning and significance that is not tied to earthly achievements.

39:8 Suffering for God's people often includes being taunted by enemies (see note at 22:6-8), who are here described as **fools**, which implies they are godless (14:1).

39:9 The psalmist was **speechless** because there was no point in complaining about what God was doing in his life.

39:10-11 The most severe suffering from the psalmist's perspective was God's **torment**, which was being used as a corrective measure to bring him to his senses and to help him learn the lesson in verses 4-6. One way that God uses suffering in the lives of His people is to **discipline** them as His children in a loving and corrective way (Heb 12:5-11).

39:12 Foreigner and **temporary resident** are terms for those who were not native inhabitants in the promised land. The

For I am a foreigner residing with You,
a temporary resident like all
my fathers.[a]

13 Turn Your angry gaze from me
so that I may be cheered up
before I die and am gone."[b]

Psalm 40
Thanksgiving and a Cry for Help

For the choir director. A Davidic psalm.

1 I waited patiently for the LORD,
and He turned to me and heard my cry
for help.[c]

2 He brought me up from a desolate[A] pit,
out of the muddy clay,[d]
and set my feet on a rock,
making my steps secure.[e]

3 He put a new song in my mouth,
a hymn of praise to our God.[f]
Many will see and fear
and put their trust in the LORD.[g]

4 How happy is the man
who has put his trust in the LORD
and has not turned to the proud
or to those who run after lies![h]

5 LORD my God, You have done
many things—
Your wonderful works and Your plans
for us;
none can compare with You.

If I were to report and speak of them,
they are more than can be told.[i]

6 You do not delight in sacrifice
and offering;
You open my ears to listen.[B]
You do not ask for
a whole •burnt offering
or a •sin offering.[j]

7 Then I said, "See, I have come;
it is written about me in the volume
of the scroll.[k]

8 I delight to do Your will, my God;[l]
Your instruction lives within me."[C,m]

9 I proclaim righteousness
in the great assembly;
see, I do not keep my mouth closed[D]—
as You know, LORD.[n]

10 I did not hide Your righteousness
in my heart;
I spoke about Your faithfulness
and salvation;
I did not conceal Your constant love
and truth
from the great assembly.[o]

11 LORD, do not withhold Your compassion
from me;
Your constant love and truth
will always guard me.[p]

12 For troubles without number
have surrounded me;

[a]39:121Ch 29:15; Heb 11:13; 1Pt 2:11
[b]39:13 Jb 7:19; 10:20-21; Ps 102:24
[c]40:1 Ps 27:14; 34:15; 37:7
[d]40:2 Ps 69:2,14
[e]Ps 27:5; 37:23
[f]40:3 Ps 33:3
[g]Dt 13:11
[h]40:4 Jb 23:11; Ps 84:12
[i]40:5 Jb 5:9; Ps 71:15; 139:17-18
[j]40:6 1Sm 15:22; Ps 51:16; Am 5:22
[k]40:7 Lk 24:44
[l]40:8 Ps 119:16,24; Jn 4:34
[m]40:6-8 Ps 119:11; Heb 10:5-9
[n]40:9 Ps 22:22,25
[o]40:10 Ac 20:20
[p]40:11 Ps 36:5; 57:3; 61:7

[A]40:2 Or watery   [B]40:6 Lit You hollow out ears for me   [C]40:8 Lit instruction within my inner being   [D]40:9 Lit not restrain my lips

---

Israelites were to consider themselves as foreigners and "temporary residents" in Yahweh's land (119:19; Lv 25:23; 1Ch 29:15). The use of the words here seems to indicate that the lesson of Ps 39:4-6 about the insignificance and fleeting nature of this earthly life had been learned.

40:1 Waited patiently shows faithfulness to Yahweh in refraining from taking things into one's own hands (see note at 27:14) or going to another source for help. Yahweh is the only source of help for those who trust in Him (40:17; 70:5).

40:2 Pit can refer to a deep well. Someone trapped in a well would probably sink down in the **muddy clay** and die if someone did not pull him out (Jr 38:6,10). Figuratively the term is related to Sheol, representing death (see note at Ps 28:1). To be **brought . . . up** means to be rescued from death (30:4).

40:3 The **new song** likely refers to the newness of life after being delivered from death (see note at 30:3).

40:4 On **happy**, see note at 1:1.

40:5 The shift from personal experience to identification with the community of Israel is significant in linking the psalmist to God's covenant promises to the nation (see note at 28:8-9). God's **wonderful works** are His saving acts on behalf of His people (see note at 9:1). The experience of the psalmist's personal deliverance is intricately connected with God's salvation of His people.

40:6-8 Some interpreters think this verse repudiates the act of

sacrifice, even though God Himself had commanded it. However, the most important issue is **delight** in God's **will**. In other words, acts of sacrifice must be accompanied by cheerful obedience. This was precisely the problem with Israel when God said He was tired of their sacrifices because they were not offered with pure motives of love and faithfulness to Him (Is 1:11). The phrase **open my ears to listen** (lit "dig/hollow out ears for me") is a symbol of being attentive to Yahweh in order to obey Him (the opposite of closed or "uncircumcised" ears; see Jr 6:10). This emphasizes the importance of obedience over sacrifice (1Sm 15:22). **See, I have come** is similar to Isaiah's expression, "Here I am" (Is 6:8), showing submission to God's will. Jesus' sacrifice on the cross was the ultimate expression of submission (Heb 10:5-10). The meaning of **the volume of the scroll** is unclear. Some suggest it was the book where the deeds of people were recorded (51:1; 56:8; 87:6; 139:16), but in this context it may refer to God's will (His instruction) in general (note "will" in 40:8).

40:9-10 Personal experiences, especially those involving rescue by Yahweh, were to be related to those in the congregation of Israel in order to instruct the community (see note at 22:22-24).

40:12 Overtaken is used mostly with enemies as the subject (7:6; Jr 39:5; Lm 1:3), but here it is the psalmist's **sins** that have overtaken him. His **troubles** (apparently the result of his sins) surrounded him in the same way as enemies who were ready to attack.

my sins have overtaken me;
I am unable to see.
They are more than the hairs
of my head,
and my courage leaves me.[a]

13 Lord, be pleased to deliver me;
hurry to help me, Lord.[b]

14 Let those who seek to take my life
be disgraced and confounded.
Let those who wish me harm
be driven back and humiliated.[c]

15 Let those who say to me, "Aha, aha!"
be horrified because of
their shame.[d]

16 Let all who seek You rejoice
and be glad in You;
let those who love Your salvation
continually say,
"The Lord is great!"[e]

17 I am afflicted and needy;
the Lord thinks of me.
You are my helper and my deliverer;
my God, do not delay.[f]

Psalm 41
Victory in Spite of Betrayal

For the choir director. A Davidic psalm.

1 Happy is one who cares for the poor;
the Lord will save him in a day
of adversity.[g]

Cross-references (center column):
[a] 40:12 Ps 38:4; 65:3
[b] 40:13 Ps 70:1
[c] 40:14 Ps 35:4,26; 63:9; 70:2
[d] 40:15 Ps 35:21,25; 70:3
[e] 40:16 Ps 35:27; 70:4
[f] 40:17 Ps 86:1; 109:22
[g] 41:1 Ps 82:3-4; Pr 14:21
[h] 41:2 Ps 37:22,28
[i] Ps 27:12
[j] 41:3 Jr 17:14
[k] 41:4 Ps 6:2; 51:4
[l] 41:5 Ps 38:12
[m] 41:6 Ps 12:2; 62:4; Pr 26:24-26
[n] 41:7 Ps 56:5
[o] 41:8 Ps 71:10-11
[p] 41:9 Jb 19:19; Ps 55:12-13; Jn 13:18
[q] 41:10 Ps 9:13

---

2 The Lord will keep him
and preserve him;
he will be blessed in the land.[h]
You will not give him over to the desire
of his enemies.[i]

3 The Lord will sustain him
on his sickbed;
You will heal him on the bed
where he lies.[j]

4 I said, "Lord, be gracious to me;
heal me, for I have sinned against You."[k]

5 My enemies speak maliciously
about me:
"When will he die and be forgotten?"[l]

6 When one of them comes to visit,
he speaks deceitfully;
he stores up evil in his heart;
he goes out and talks.[m]

7 All who hate me whisper together
about me;
they plan to harm me.[n]

8 "Lethal poison has been poured
into him,
and he won't rise again from where
he lies!"[o]

9 Even my friend[A] in whom I trusted,
one who ate my bread,
has raised his heel against me.[p]

10 But You, Lord, be gracious to me
and raise me up;
then I will repay them.[q]

[A]41:9 Lit *Even a man of my peace*

40:14-15 It is a common request for the disgrace intended by enemies against the psalmist to be turned back on them (7:14-16; 35:4,26; 70:3). **Aha** is an expression often associated with ridicule (see note at 35:21).

40:16-17 All who seek You is equivalent to those who are faithful to Yahweh (see note at 9:9-10). The phrase **afflicted and needy** refers to those who are humble and dependent on Yahweh as their only help (see notes at 34:6 and 35:10).

41:1 On **happy**, see note at 1:1. **Poor** (Hb *dal*) has the basic idea of "low" in the sense that they are humbled or brought low by their own circumstances or by others. It could be used to mean those faithful to Yahweh, as do the terms "humble," "afflicted," or "needy" (72:13; see note at 34:18). However, the verb **cares for** might indicate that the idea is economic hardship. Those who are close to Yahweh will be generous to those in need (see note at 37:21).

41:2 To be **blessed in the land** was the hope of all those in Israel who were loyal to Yahweh and to His covenant with them (see note at 37:3).

41:3 Sustain is not quite identical to **heal**. It refers to God's support (v. 12) of someone during a time of adversity, whether it is an illness or some danger (18:38; 20:2; 94:18). Even when there is a delay in God's intervention, there is still His sustaining power that strengthens the person who is suffering. This is in fact when God's strength is most evident in those who trust Him (2Co 12:10).

41:4 Sin is mentioned but not specified or developed (in contrast to Pss 38 and 51). In some cases sin may be assumed, but it is not the main cause of the suffering (see note at 6:1). Evidence of this is that the psalmist considered himself as having "integrity" (41:12), indicating either that the sin was already confessed or that there was no specific sin involved. The primary issue seems to be physical illness, since there are references to "heal" (v. 3), "sickbed" (v. 3), and "poison" (v. 8), which is how his enemies described his condition (as if he were poisoned).

41:5-8 The **enemies** are vividly described, with their activities against the psalmist as the focal point. Their intentions were malicious, as demonstrated by their speech and their desire for his demise. To **be forgotten** is equivalent to dying (see 31:12). **Stores up evil** expresses the idea of harvesting it like one does grain. Some think this might be a reference to gossip, which in this case involved **evil** things said about someone. This idea is reinforced by their whispering about the psalmist (v. 7). Their intention was for him to **die**, so they spoke about his death as if it were a certainty (v. 8).

41:9 Some think the mention of **friend** here is synonymous with the enemies of verses 5-8. In instances of extreme suffering, friends can take on the role of enemies (see notes at 31:11; 35:11-14; and 38:11-12). Indeed there is the adversarial phrase **raised his heel against me**, so there appears to be more than just abandonment in this context.

11 By this I know that You delight in me:[a]
   my enemy does not shout in triumph
   over me.[b]
12 You supported me because of
   my integrity[c]
   and set me in Your presence forever.[d]
13 May •Yahweh, the God of Israel,
   be praised
   from everlasting to everlasting.
   •Amen and amen.[e]

BOOK II
(Psalms 42–72)

Psalm 42
Longing for God

For the choir director. A •Maskil
of the sons of Korah.

1 As a deer longs for streams of water,
   so I long for You, God.[f]
2 I thirst for God, the living God.

When can I come and appear
   before God?[g]
3 My tears have been my food
   day and night,
   while all day long people say
   to me,
   "Where is your God?"[h]
4 I remember this as I pour out
   my heart:[i]
   how I walked with many,
   leading the festive procession
   to the house of God,
   with joyful and thankful shouts.[j]

5 Why am I so depressed?
   Why this turmoil within me?
   Put your hope in God, for I will
   still praise Him,
   my Savior and my God.[k]
6 I[A] am deeply depressed;
   therefore I remember You
   from the land of Jordan
   and the peaks of Hermon,
   from Mount Mizar.[l]

[a]41:11 Ps 37:23
[b]Ps 25:2
[c]41:12 Ps 37:17
[d]Ps 21:6
[e]41:13 Ps 72:18-19; 89:52
[f]42:1 Ps 84:2; 119:131
[g]42:2 Ps 63:1
[h]42:3 Ps 79:10; 115:2
[i]42:4 Ps 62:8
[j]Ps 55:14; 100:4
[k]42:5 Ps 38:6; 43:5; Mt 26:38
[l]42:6 Ps 61:2; Jnh 2:7

[A]42:5-6 Some Hb mss, LXX, Syr; other Hb mss read Him, the salvation of His presence. [6] My God, I

41:11 Yahweh's **delight** in someone is not a mere emotion but involves actions and is equivalent to blessing or showing favor to someone (18:19; 22:8; 35:27).

41:12 To be in God's **presence** is the ultimate reward for the person who is faithful to Him (see note at 15:1).

41:13 This verse marks the close of Book 1 of the Psalms (1–41). It is a doxology including a call to praise followed by a congregational response (**amen and amen**). There are four psalms (41; 72; 89; 106) that end a book before the beginning of a new one; each has similar material. Such statements were most likely added at the time the Psalms were joined together in their canonical form. Some refer to these as "seam" psalms because of the way they pieced the books together to form the complete book of Psalms.

Ps 42 title On **Maskil**, see note at Psalm 32 title. The phrase **sons of Korah** appears in the titles of 11 psalms (42; 44–49; 84–85; 87–88). According to 1Ch 9:17-24 and 26:1-19, the Korahites were the gatekeepers in the temple. In 2Ch 20:19 they stood up in the congregation of Israel and praised Yahweh. Most scholars believe they became associated with musicians (perhaps a group of singers) who were involved in the worship of Yahweh. Many have argued that although Psalms 42 and 43 are separated in the Hebrew text, they might actually have been composed as one psalm. One reason is that there is no title for the latter. While this is not unusual in comparison to all the psalms, in the second book only Psalms 43 and 71 lack titles. The strongest evidence for connecting the two psalms is the occurrence of the same questions and response in 42:5,11 and 43:5. These verses seem to end each of the sections of the psalm consisting of three strophes or poetic divisions. Psalm 43 would be the third strophe if they were joined as one psalm.

42:1-2 Longing and thirsting pictures a prolonged drought where even the animals are dying (Jr 14:1-6; Jl 1:20). **Streams of water** recalls the blessings of God for the righteous who are often represented by flourishing trees (see note at 1:3). Also, in the shepherd image of 23:2 Yahweh leads His people to refreshing water. What the psalmist desired was to **appear before God** (lit "see the face of God"), which probably refers to receiving God's blessing and favor in His presence (84:7).

42:3 The profusion of **tears** from crying is pictured as drenching furniture in 6:6. In this context they were the psalmist's only **food**. This hyperbolic expression shows the depths of his grief (80:5).

42:4 The **house of God** means the sanctuary of God where Yahweh dwelt among His people (see note at 5:6-7). The house of God represents His presence, which for some reason was distant from the psalmist, and he longed to be back among God's people in the context of worship.

42:5 The questions and the response of verse 5 also appear in verse 11 and in 43:5 (perhaps because Ps 43 is part of this psalm; see note at Ps 42 title). The psalmist was speaking to himself (lit "my soul") in an attempt to bring comfort and security. In answer to the questions focusing on his depression, he literally commands himself to **hope in God**. This means waiting on God during a time of crisis, trusting that He will answer prayer (see note at 27:14). The point the psalmist seems to be making is that there was no reason for his depression if God was his **Savior**. The fact that he repeated this several times shows the difficulty of internalizing this truth.

42:6 The geographical descriptions could refer to the place where the psalmist was praying since he was distant from the sanctuary, according to verse 3. The **land of Jordan** could refer to the entire Jordan River Valley, but in connection with Mount **Hermon**, which was in the extreme north of Israel, it probably refers to the sources for the river in the mountains of northern Israel. **Mount Mizar** is not as easy to identify, but it was probably part of the same mountain range as Mount Hermon in the north.

7 Deep calls to deep in the roar
  of Your waterfalls;
  all Your breakers and Your billows
  have swept over me.ᵃ
8 The LORD will send His faithful love
  by day;ᵇ
  His song will be with me in the night—
  a prayer to the God of my life.

9 I will say to God, my rock,ᶜ
  "Why have You forgotten me?
  Why must I go about in sorrow
  because of the enemy's oppression?"ᵈ
10 My adversaries taunt me,
  as if crushing my bones,
  while all day long they say to me,
  "Where is your God?"ᵉ
11 Why am I so depressed?
  Why this turmoil within me?
  Put your hope in God, for I will
  still praise Him,
  my Savior and my God.ᶠ

Psalm 43ᴬ

1 Vindicate me, God, and defend
  my cause
  against an ungodly nation;
  rescue me from the deceitful
  and unjust man.ᵍ

2 For You are the God of my refuge.
  Why have You rejected me?
  Why must I go about in sorrow
  because of the enemy's oppression?ʰ

3 Send Your light and Your truth;
  let them lead me.ⁱ
  Let them bring me
  to Your holy mountain,
  to Your dwelling place.ʲ
4 Then I will come to the altar of God,
  to God, my greatest joy.ᵏ
  I will praise You with the lyre,
  God, my God.ˡ

5 Why am I so depressed?
  Why this turmoil within me?
  Put your hope in God, for I will
  still praise Him,
  my Savior and my God.ᵐ

Psalm 44
Israel's Complaint

For the choir director. A *Maskil
of the sons of Korah.

1 God, we have heard with our ears—
  our ancestors have told us—
  the work You accomplished
  in their days,

Cross references (center column):
ᵃ42:7 Ps 69:1-2; Jnh 2:3
ᵇ42:8 Jb 35:10; Ps 77:6
ᶜ42:9 Ps 18:2; 31:3
ᵈPs 43:2
ᵉ42:10 Jl 2:17
ᶠ42:11 Ps 43:5; Mt 26:38
ᵍ43:1 Ps 5:6; 26:1; 35:24
ʰ43:2 Ps 42:9; 88:14
ⁱ43:3 Ps 36:9
ʲPs 2:6; 46:4; 84:1
ᵏ43:4 Ps 26:6
ˡPs 33:2; 57:8
ᵐ43:5 Ps 42:5,11

ᴬPs 43 Many Hb mss connect Pss 42–43

42:7 This verse is perhaps related to the Jordan River in verse 6. Even if this is the case, the imagery goes beyond the physical and describes the depths of the psalmist's depression symbolized by **deep** waters churning around and sweeping over him. For similar imagery, see 18:4-5; 29:10-11; 32:6-7.

42:8 Song is parallel to **prayer** and might refer to a joyful **song . . . in the night**, as in Is 30:29.

'emeth

Hebrew Pronunciation	[eh MET]
HCSB Translation	truth, faithfulness
Uses in Psalms	37
Uses in the OT	127
Focus Passage	Psalm 43:3

Emeth, from *'aman* (be faithful), chiefly denotes *truth* (Ex 34:6) but indicates *faithfulness* in personal relations (Ps 54:5). It connotes *integrity* (Ps 51:6) and *fairness* (Pr 29:14). Once it implies *promise* (Ps 132:11). Adjectivally, it suggests *true, truthful* (Pr 12:19), *faithful, reliable* (Ps 19:9), *sure* (Jos 2:12), and *trustworthy* (Ex 18:21). It describes *right* paths (Gn 24:48). With the preposition *b* ("in"), it implies *really* or *faithfully* (Jos 9:15,16). *'Emunah* (49x), also from *'aman*, mainly means *faithfulness* (Is 11:5). It connotes *faith* (Hab 2:4), *loyalty* (1Sm 26:23), *security* (Is 33:6), and *integrity* (2Kg 12:15). It suggests *faithful, steady* (Ps 37:24), *trustworthy* (Ps 33:4), and *true* (Ps 119:86). It appears as *fairly* (Ps 119:75) and *securely* (Ps 37:3). With *b* it implies *honestly* (Is 59:4), to *trusted positions* (1Ch 9:22,26), and *entrusted* (1Ch 9:22,26). *'Emeth* (33x) and *'emunah* (11x) frequently appear with *chesed* ("love, faithful love, kindness").

42:10 The **taunt** is the same as in verse 3. This reflects a common belief by the enemies of the psalmist that Yahweh was not concerned about the plight of his servant and would not act (3:2; 22:7-8; 71:11).

42:11 See note at verse 5.

43:1 Vindication is a common request in psalms that assume the innocence and integrity of the psalmist (Pss 17 and 26). **Ungodly nation** is parallel to **deceitful and unjust man**. It is difficult to determine whether these enemies were Gentiles who were not a part of Yahweh's covenant or Israelites who were disloyal to the covenant.

43:2 Rejection by God is a common assumption when one's prayers seem to go unanswered (see notes at 13:1-2 and 22:1).

43:3-4 Light and **truth** are placed together when they refer to Yahweh's instruction (or His will) for His people (Pr 6:23). The psalmist was requesting guidance in order once again to be in Yahweh's presence, represented here by the three descriptions: **Your holy mountain . . . Your dwelling place**, and **the altar of God**. If this is a continuation of Psalm 42, then the request in 42:2 is further specified.

43:5 See note at 42:5.

Ps 44 title On *Maskil*, see note at Psalm 32 title. On **sons of Korah**, see note at Psalm 42 title.

44:1-3 The psalm begins with a rehearsal of what Yahweh has done for Israel. This is similar to the "wonderful works," or God's saving acts on behalf of His people (9:1; Ex 3:20; 15:11). It is clear from the mention of **ancestors** and

in days long ago:[a]

2 to plant them,
You drove out the nations
    with Your hand;
to settle them,
You crushed the peoples.[b]

3 For they did not take the land
    by their sword—
their arm did not bring them victory—
but by Your right hand, Your arm,
and the light of Your face,
for You were pleased with them.[c]

4 You are my King, my God,
who ordains[A] victories for Jacob.[d]

5 Through You we drive back our foes;
through Your name we trample
    our enemies.[e]

6 For I do not trust in my bow,
and my sword does not
    bring me victory.[f]

7 But You give us victory over our foes
and let those who hate us
    be disgraced.[g]

8 We boast in God all day long;
we will praise Your name forever.[h]
                                          •Selah

9 But You have rejected
    and humiliated us;
You do not march out with our armies.[i]

10 You make us retreat from the foe,

and those who hate us
have taken plunder for themselves.[j]

11 You hand us over to be eaten like sheep
and scatter us among the nations.[k]

12 You sell Your people for nothing;
You make no profit from selling them.[l]

13 You make us an object of reproach
    to our neighbors,
a source of mockery and ridicule
    to those around us.[m]

14 You make us a joke among the nations,
a laughingstock[B] among the peoples.[n]

15 My disgrace is before me all day long,
and shame has covered my face,[o]

16 because of the voice of the scorner
    and reviler,
because of the enemy and avenger.[p]

17 All this has happened to us,
but we have not forgotten You
or betrayed Your covenant.[q]

18 Our hearts have not turned back;
our steps have not strayed
    from Your path.[r]

19 But You have crushed us in a haunt
    of jackals
and have covered us
    with deepest darkness.[s]

20 If we had forgotten the name of our God
and spread out our hands
    to a foreign god,[t]

21 wouldn't God have found this out,

---

a44:1 Dt 32:7; Ps 78:3
b44:2 2Sm 7:10; Ps 78:55; 80:8
c44:3 Dt 7:7-8; Ps 77:15; Hs 1:7
d44:4 Ps 42:8; 74:12
e44:5 Ps 60:12; 108:13; Zch 10:5
f44:6 1Sm 17:47; Ps 33:16
g44:7 Ps 35:4; 53:5
h44:8 Ps 30:12; 34:2
i44:9 Ps 60:1,10; 74:1; 108:11
j44:10 Lv 26:17; Dt 28:25; Jos 7:8,12
k44:11 Lv 26:33; Dt 4:27; 28:64; Ps 106:27
l44:12 Dt 32:30; Jdg 2:14; 3:8; Is 52:3-4
m44:13 Dt 28:37; Ps 79:4
n44:14 Jb 17:6; Ps 109:25; Jr 24:9
o44:15 2Ch 32:21; Ps 69:7
p44:16 Ps 8:2; 74:10
q44:17 Ps 119:61,153
r44:18 Jb 23:11; Ps 37:31; 119:51,157
s44:19 Jb 30:29; Jr 9:11
t44:20 Dt 6:14; Jb 11:13

A44:4 LXX, Syr, Aq; MT reads *King, God; ordain*   B44:14 Lit *shaking of the head*

---

days long ago that this refers to an early time, specifically the time of conquest and settlement of the promised land. Being "planted" (80:8; 2Sm 7:10; Jr 11:17; 12:2) is the opposite of being "uprooted" (Dt 29:28) and serves to picture Yahweh's **work** as a farmer planting something like a tree on his land. The emphasis especially in verse 3 is that it was Yahweh's **hand** and **arm** that **accomplished** this rather than Israel's weaponry. The combination of hand and arm is used in contexts referring to God's power displayed in the deliverance of Israel from Egypt (Dt 4:34; 5:15; 7:19; 11:2; 26:8).

44:4 The terms **King** and **Jacob** recall the unique covenant relationship that Yahweh had with Israel (Dt 33:1-5).

44:5 When the people of Israel were faithful to Yahweh, He fought for them (v. 7; see note at 18:7-15). His **name** represents Yahweh Himself and is closely aligned with His reputation (see note at 20:1).

44:6 Human weaponry is of no use if God is not behind it (see note at 20:7-8).

44:8 Boasting **in God** is in contrast to boasting in one's own power or skill (see note at 34:2).

44:9 This perception is in stark contrast to Yahweh's past acts when He fought for His people (v. 5; cp. 60:10; 108:11).

44:11 The imagery of **sheep** that were handed over **to be eaten** is similar to verse 22 where they were "slaughtered." God was the shepherd of Israel (see note at 23:1), but to the

psalmist it seemed He was not protecting His sheep but giving them to other **nations** to be killed.

44:12 Selling was a common way of describing God giving His people over to the power of their enemies (Dt 32:30; Jdg 2:14; 3:8; 4:2,9; 10:7). It occurs most often in the context of God's response to Israel's rebellion against Him.

44:13-16 Almost every Hebrew word for **ridicule** is used in these verses. The word for **joke** (Hb *mashal*) expresses the idea of a byword or proverbial saying. The **shame** of Israel was so extensive and had lasted so long that **the nations** were using them as the butt of jokes and sayings.

44:17-18 This is a declaration of innocence similar to those of individual lament psalms (Pss 17; 26), but here it expresses the innocence of the nation. The psalmist protested that they had done nothing to deserve this treatment. **Turned back** is similar to the idea of "turning aside" in reference to the proper **path** of God. It expresses the idea of rejecting God's commands (78:57; 119:51; Dt 5:32). The protest that people had not **strayed** from God's path is reminiscent of Job's protest (Jb 23:11) and also of the psalmist in Ps 17:5.

44:20 Spreading out **hands** was a gesture used in the context of prayer and worship (88:9; 141:2; 143:6; Ex 9:29,33; Ezr 9:5; Is 1:15).

44:21 The **secrets of the heart** are attitudes and motives. A person's integrity could be tested by God to determine if he was innocent of false motives (26:2; Jr 12:3).

since He knows the secrets
   of the heart?[a]
22 Because of You we are slain
   all day long;
   we are counted as sheep
   to be slaughtered.[b]

23 Wake up, LORD! Why are You sleeping?
   Get up! Don't reject us forever![c]
24 Why do You hide Yourself
   and forget our affliction
   and oppression?[d]
25 For we have sunk down to the dust;
   our bodies cling to the ground.[e]
26 Rise up! Help us!
   Redeem us because of
   Your faithful love.[f]

Psalm 45
A Royal Wedding Song

For the choir director: according to
"The Lilies."[A] A *Maskil* of the sons
of Korah. A love song.

1 My heart is moved by a noble theme
   as I recite my verses to the king;
   my tongue is the pen
   of a skillful writer.[g]

Cross-references column:
[a] 44:21 Ps 139:1-2; Jr 17:10; Heb 4:13
[b] 44:22 Is 53:7; Jr 12:3; Rm 8:36
[c] 44:23 Ps 7:6; 35:23; 78:65
[d] 44:24 Jb 13:24; Ps 88:14
[e] 44:25 Ps 119:25
[f] 44:26 Ps 25:22
[g] 45:1 Ezr 7:6
[h] 45:2 Lk 4:22
[i] Ps 21:6
[j] 45:3 Is 49:2; Rv 1:16; 19:15
[k] 45:4 Ps 65:5; 98:1
[l] 45:5 Dt 23:14; Ps 18:14
[m] 45:6-7 Heb 1:8-9
[n] 45:6 Ps 93:2
[o] 45:7 Ps 33:5
[p] 45:8 Sg 4:14; Jn 19:39
[q] 45:9 Sg 6:8

2 You are the most handsome of •men;
   grace flows from your lips.[h]
   Therefore God has blessed you forever.[i]

3 Mighty warrior, strap your sword
   at your side.
   In your majesty and splendor[j]—
4 in your splendor ride triumphantly
   in the cause of truth, humility,
   and justice.
   May your right hand show
   your awe-inspiring acts.[k]
5 Your arrows pierce the hearts
   of the king's enemies;
   the peoples fall under you.[l]

6 Your throne,[m] God, is[B] forever and ever;
   the scepter of Your[C] kingdom is
   a scepter of justice.[n]
7 You love righteousness
   and hate wickedness;[o]
   therefore God, your God,
   has anointed you with the oil of joy
   more than your companions.
8 Myrrh, aloes, and cassia perfume
   all your garments;
   from ivory palaces harps bring you joy.[p]
9 Kings' daughters are
   among your honored women;[q]

[A] 45:title Possibly a tune; Pss 60; 69; 80   [B] 45:6 Or *Your divine throne is*, or *Your throne is God's*   [C] 45:6 Or *your*

44:23-26 **Wake up** calls God to act. **Rise up** is similar, but with military connotations (see note at 7:6-8). **The dust** is often used to represent humiliation in defeat at the hands of an enemy (7:5; 72:9; Is 49:23). It could also refer to humility before Yahweh either in worship or in prayer (Dt 9:18; 2Ch 20:18).

Ps 45 title **The Lilies** was apparently a known tune at the time of composition, similar to "The Deer of the Dawn" in Psalm 22. On *Maskil*, see note at Psalm 32 title. On **sons of Korah**, see note at Psalm 42 title. The psalm is further identified as **a love song**, a description that fits the context of this royal wedding psalm.

45:1-2 It was a common practice in the ancient Near East to compose songs in honor of kings to perpetuate their memory for later generations. Such hyperbolic designations as **most handsome** and **grace flows from your lips** are usually a part of these songs.

45:4 While **truth** and **justice** were common traits that were admired by kings and people in the ancient world, **humility** was something more specific to Israel. Kings of the ancient world were rarely humble, seeing humility as a sign of weakness. For a servant of Yahweh, this was a characteristic that signified a close relationship with Him (Pr 15:33; 18:12; Zph 2:3).

45:6 A **scepter** symbolized royal dominion. Its size and shape varied in different times and cultures, but it was often associated with military power. In some cases it was actually a military weapon. God's **throne** is linked with this king because Israel's king was to function as God's co-regent over His kingdom (2:6-9; 2Sm 7:14; 19:21; 1Ch 28:6).

45:7 The king of Israel was often referred to as God's **anointed** (see note at 20:6). **Oil** was a symbol of both **joy** and God's blessing (see notes at 23:5 and 36:8).

45:8 The phrase **ivory palaces** does not refer to palaces made completely of ivory but having their interior and perhaps furniture covered with ivory (1Kg 22:39; Am 3:15; 6:4).

selah

Hebrew Pronunciation	[see LAH]
HCSB Translation	Selah
Uses in Psalms	71
Uses in the OT	74
Focus Passage	Psalm 46:3,7,11

Selah, an expression found in Psalms and Hab 3:3,9,13, remains obscure. Always occurring with "choir director" or *mizmor* ("psalm"), *selah* may specify musical or recitation style. It could be a later addition, for the Septuagint translation *diapsalma*, possibly a new word representing *selah* and indicating musical pause, appears 81 times. *Selah* might derive from *salal* ("lift up, exalt") and call worshipers to lift their eyes to heaven and repeat the psalm, or raise their voices and repeat a refrain. Alternatively, musicians might lift their instruments to perform a musical interlude. An ancient theory suggests that *selah*, read and pronounced *netsah* ("forever"), called worshipers to respond with a praise refrain. If from the root *sl* ("bow, pray"), *selah* could ask worshipers to bow in prayer. *Selah* could indicate the sound of the strings if related to a Persian word for song. *Selah* could abbreviate a phrase signaling a change in voice.

the queen, adorned with gold
from Ophir,
stands at your right hand.[a]

10 Listen, daughter, pay attention
and consider:
forget your people
and your father's house,[b]

11 and the king will desire your beauty.
Bow down to him, for he is your lord.[c]

12 The daughter of Tyre,
the wealthy people,
will seek your favor with gifts.[d]

13 In her chamber, the royal daughter
is all glorious,
her clothing embroidered
with gold.[e]

14 In colorful garments she is led
to the king;
after her, the virgins, her companions,
are brought to you.[f]

15 They are led in with gladness
and rejoicing;
they enter the king's palace.[g]

16 Your sons will succeed
your ancestors;
you will make them princes
throughout the land.[h]

17 I will cause your name
to be remembered
for all generations;
therefore the peoples will praise you
forever and ever.[i]

---

[a]45:9 1Kg 9:28; 10:11
[b]45:10 Ru 1:16-17
[c]45:11 Eph 5:33
[d]45:12 Ps 68:29; 72:10-11; Is 49:23
[e]45:13 Ex 39:2-3; Rv 19:7-8
[f]45:14 Ezk 16:18; 26:16
[g]45:15 Jr 22:4
[h]45:16 1Pt 2:9; Rv 1:6; 5:10
[i]45:17 Mal 1:11
[j]46:title 1Ch 15:20
[k]46:1 Ps 9:9; 62:7-8
[l]46:2 Ps 18:7; 82:5
[m]46:3 Ps 93:3-4; Jr 5:22
[n]46:4 Ps 43:3; Rv 22:1-2
[o]46:5 Is 12:6; Zch 2:10-11
[p]46:6 Ps 2:1; Jr 25:30
[q]46:7 Ps 9:9; Jl 3:16
[r]46:8 Ps 66:5

Psalm 46
God Our Refuge

For the choir director.
A song of the sons of Korah.
According to *Alamoth*.[A,j]

1 God is our refuge and strength,
a helper who is always found
in times of trouble.[k]

2 Therefore we will not be afraid,
though the earth trembles
and the mountains topple
into the depths of the seas,[l]

3 though its waters roar and foam
and the mountains quake
with its turmoil.[m]   •Selah

4 There is a river—
its streams delight the city of God,
the holy dwelling place
of the •Most High.[n]

5 God is within her;
she will not be toppled.
God will help her
when the morning dawns.[o]

6 Nations rage, kingdoms topple;
the earth melts when He lifts
His voice.[p]

7 The LORD of •Hosts is with us;
the God of Jacob is our stronghold.[q]
Selah

8 Come, see the works of the LORD,
who brings devastation on the earth.[r]

[A]46:title This may refer to a high pitch, perhaps a tune sung by soprano voices; the Hb word means "young women."

45:9 **Gold from Ophir** is synonymous with the finest gold (Jb 28:16; Is 13:12). The exact location of Ophir is uncertain.

45:10-11 "Forgetting" then "bowing down" represent a change in loyalty from the bride's own people and country to the king whom she was marrying.

45:12 **Tyre**, a major trading center on the Mediterranean Sea, was known for its extravagance and wealth.

45:14 **Virgins** and **companions** were essentially maids who accompanied the bride (Est 2:9).

45:16-17 The final wish is for a permanent dynasty for this king that would exalt his **name** (his reputation and fame) beyond that of his **ancestors**.

Ps 46 title On **sons of Korah**, see note at Psalm 42 title. *Alamoth* also occurs in 1Ch 15:20 and is used in the same way to designate a song. It is similar to at least part of the title in Psalm 9 that reads *al-Muth-labben*. Except for the *labben* the rest is essentially the same. However, what is the same would read something like "concerning death," which certainly does not fit the content of this psalm. Suggested renderings include "maidens" (Aquila and Jerome) and "hidden things" (LXX).

46:2-3 Trembling **earth** and quaking **mountains** represent unsettling motion in parts of nature that are supposed to be stable (see note at 18:7-15). The **waters**, which God restrained at creation, here threaten to become chaotic again (see notes at 29:3-4 and 29:10-11).

46:4 The **river** here is difficult to identify precisely. It does not appear to be a literal river in Jerusalem, unless it refers to something like Hezekiah's tunnel. Instead, it seems more likely to refer to God's presence and blessings that fill Jerusalem and flow to other nations (Zch 14:8).

46:5 The strength of Jerusalem was not in its fortified walls but in Yahweh who was its "stronghold" (vv. 7,11; Jl 3:17; Zph 3:15).

46:6 **Nations rage** is reminiscent of the rebellion of the nations against Yahweh and His anointed (2:1). However, the parallel of **kingdoms topple** indicates that it probably refers to the common experience of wars between nations and kingdoms rising and falling. But the final command in verse 10 may indicate that these wars were still an affront to God. **The earth melts** probably symbolizes fear at the voice of God (Ex 15:15; Is 14:31).

46:7 On **LORD of Hosts**, see note at 24:7-10.

46:8-10 Yahweh is in absolute control of all warfare as well as peace among nations. The final command, **stop your fighting**, is probably addressed to the nations to stop their hostilities, which were ultimately directed against God (2:10).

9 He makes wars cease
    throughout the earth.
He shatters bows and cuts spears
    to pieces;
He burns up the chariots.[A][a]

10 "Stop your fighting—and know that
    I am God,
exalted among the nations,
    exalted on the earth."[b]

11 •Yahweh of Hosts is with us;
    the God of Jacob is our stronghold.[c]
              Selah

Psalm 47
God Our King

For the choir director. A psalm
of the sons of Korah.

1 Clap your hands, all you peoples;[d]
    shout to God with a jubilant cry.[e]
2 For •Yahweh, the •Most High,
    is awe-inspiring,
a great King over all the earth.[f]
3 He subdues peoples under us
    and nations under our feet.[g]
4 He chooses for us our inheritance—
    the pride of Jacob, whom He loves.[h]
              •*Selah*

5 God ascends among shouts of joy,
    the LORD, among the sound
    of trumpets.[i]
6 Sing praise to God, sing praise;
    sing praise to our King, sing praise![j]
7 Sing a song of wisdom,[B]
    for God is King of all the earth.[k]

8 God reigns over the nations;

God is seated on His holy throne.[l]
9 The nobles of the peoples
    have assembled
with the people of the God of Abraham.[m]
For the leaders[c] of the earth
    belong to God;
He is greatly exalted.[n]

Psalm 48
Zion Exalted

A song. A psalm of the sons of Korah.

1 The LORD is great and highly praised
    in the city of our God.[o]
His holy mountain, 2 rising splendidly,
    is the joy of the whole earth.
Mount •Zion on the slopes of the north
    is the city of the great King.[p]
3 God is known as a stronghold
    in its citadels.[q]

4 Look! The kings assembled;
    they advanced together.[r]
5 They looked and froze with fear;
    they fled in terror.[s]
6 Trembling seized them there,
    agony like that of a woman in labor,[t]
7 as You wrecked the ships of Tarshish
    with the east wind.[u]

8 Just as we heard, so we have seen
    in the city of •Yahweh of •Hosts,
in the city of our God;
    God will establish it forever.[v]   •*Selah*

9 God, within Your temple,
    we contemplate Your faithful love.[w]
10 Your name, God, like Your praise,

Cross references (center column)

a46:9 Ps 76:3; Is 2:4; Mc 4:3
b46:10 Ps 100:3; Is 2:11,17
c46:11 Ps 9:9; Jl 3:16
d47:1 Is 55:12
ePs 95:1
f47:2 Dt 7:21; Neh 1:5; Mal 1:14
g47:3 Ps 2:8; 18:47
h47:4 Am 8:7; Nah 2:2
i47:5 2Sm 6:15; Ps 68:18; 98:6
j47:6 Ps 68:4; 89:18
k47:7 Zch 14:9; 1Co 14:15
l47:8 1Ch 16:31; Ps 22:28; 97:2
m47:9 Ps 102:22
nPs 72:11; Is 49:7,23
o48:1 Ps 2:6; Mc 4:1; Zch 8:3
p48:2 Mt 5:35
q48:3 Ps 46:7; 50:2
r48:4 2Sm 10:6-19
s48:5 Ex 15:15
t48:6 Is 13:8; Hs 13:13
u48:7 1Kg 22:48; Jr 18:17; Ezk 27:26
v48:8 Ps 87:5; Is 2:2; Mc 4:1
w48:9 Ps 26:3; 40:10

A46:9 Lit *chariots with fire*   B47:7 Hb a *Maskil*   C47:9 Lit *shields*

Ps 47 title On **sons of Korah**, see note at Psalm 42 title.

47:1 The clapping of **hands** is an expression of joy that is used elsewhere to praise a new king (98:8; 2Kg 11:12).

47:2-3 **Most High** is a title for God expressing His sovereignty over the earth (see note at 7:17; cp. 24:1; 95:4; 97:5). **Subdues** (Hb *yadber*) occurs only in this verbal form here and in 18:47 where it refers to Israel's military campaigns in which nations were subjugated. **Under** the **feet** is a place of submission; it is a concept further developed in Scripture as a picture of the dominion of God's kingdom (see note at 8:5-8).

47:4 **Pride of Jacob** is parallel to **inheritance** and refers to the promised land (Is 58:14; Am 8:7).

47:5 **Ascends** could refer to God going up into heaven (Gn 17:22; 35:13; Jdg 13:20) or to the ark of the covenant (representing Yahweh's presence) being carried up to the temple (2Sm 6:5,16-17). In this psalm it probably expresses the more general idea of Yahweh ascending His earthly throne.

47:7 **Song of wisdom** uses the word *Maskil* (see note at Ps 32 title).

47:9 **Leaders** is literally "shields" and is used to represent those who lead nations, usually kings (84:9; 89:18).

Ps 48 title On **sons of Korah**, see note at Psalm 42 title.

48:2 **North** can also be translated as Zaphon, a place name. According to Ugaritic myths, Zaphon was the place where the gods assembled. There might be a play on the word to say that Jerusalem is the place where the true God actually lives. However, there is also the reality that Israel was the kingdom in the north compared to some nations around them, such as Cush, Egypt, Edom, and Moab.

48:4-5 These verses recall the conquest of Canaan when Yahweh caused the people in the land to be terrified of the Israelites (Jos 2:9).

48:6 The image of **a woman in labor** is often used to represent fear (Is 13:8; 21:3; Jr 4:31). Perhaps it referred to the fear of death during the process of giving birth, something common in that time.

48:7 The destruction of **the ships of Tarshish** may refer to an actual event (1Kg 22:48), or this verse could use Tarshish as a representative of the enemies of God (Ps 72:10).

reaches to the ends of the earth;[a]
Your right hand is filled with justice.[b]

11 Mount Zion is glad.
The towns[A] of Judah rejoice
because of Your judgments.[c]

12 Go around Zion, encircle it;
count its towers,

13 note its ramparts; tour its citadels
so that you can tell
a future generation:[d]

14 "This God, our God forever and ever—
He will always lead us."[B,e]

Psalm 49
Misplaced Trust in Wealth

For the choir director. A psalm
of the sons of Korah.

1 Hear this, all you peoples;
listen, all who inhabit the world,[f]

2 both low and high,[C]
rich and poor together.[g]

3 My mouth speaks wisdom;
my heart's meditation
brings understanding.[h]

4 I turn my ear to a proverb;
I explain my riddle with a lyre.[i]

5 Why should I fear in times of trouble?
The iniquity of my foes surrounds me.[j]

6 They trust in their wealth
and boast of their abundant riches.[k]

7 Yet these cannot redeem a person[D]

or pay his ransom to God[l]—

8 since the price of redeeming him is
too costly,
one should forever stop trying[E,m]—

9 so that he may live forever
and not see the •Pit.[n]

10 For one can see that wise men die;
foolish and stupid men also
pass away.[o]
Then they leave their wealth to others.[p]

11 Their graves are their eternal homes,[F]
their homes from generation
to generation,
though they have named estates
after themselves.[q]

12 But despite his assets,[G]
man will not last;
he is like the animals that perish.[r]

13 This is the way of those
who are arrogant,
and of their followers,
who approve of their words.[H,s]   •Selah

14 Like sheep they are headed for •Sheol;
Death will shepherd them.
The upright will rule over them
in the morning,[t]
and their form will waste away
in Sheol,[I]
far from their lofty abode.[u]

15 But God will redeem my life
from the power of Sheol,
for He will take me.[v]   Selah

Cross-references (center column):

[a]48:10 Ps 113:3; Mal 1:11
[b]Ps 45:4
[c]48:11 Ps 97:8
[d]48:12-13 Ps 78:5-7; 122:7
[e]48:14 Ps 23:3-4; Is 58:11
[f]49:1 Ps 78:1; Mc 1:2
[g]49:2 Ps 62:9
[h]49:3 Ps 37:30
[i]49:4 Nm 12:8; Mt 13:35
[j]49:5 Ps 23:4; 27:1
[k]49:6 Jb 31:24; Ps 52:7; Pr 11:28
[l]49:7 Jb 36:18-19; Mt 25:8-9
[m]49:8 Mt 16:26
[n]49:9 Jb 33:28; Ps 16:10
[o]49:10 Ec 2:16
[p]Ps 39:6; Ec 2:18-19; Lk 12:20
[q]49:11 Ps 5:9; 10:6
[r]49:12 Ec 3:19
[s]49:13 Ps 31:23; Pr 16:18; 21:24
[t]49:14 Rv 2:26
[u]Jb 24:19; Ps 9:17
[v]49:15 Ps 16:10; 56:13; Hs 13:14

Footnotes:

[A]48:11 Lit *daughters*   [B]48:14 Some Hb mss, LXX; other Hb mss read *over death*   [C]49:2 Lit *both sons of Adam and sons of man*   [D]49:7 Or *Certainly he cannot redeem himself*, or *Yet he cannot redeem a brother*   [E]49:8 Or *costly, it will cease forever*   [F]49:11 LXX, Syr, Tg; MT reads *Their inner thought is that their houses are eternal*   [G]49:12 Or *honor*   [H]49:13 Lit *and after them with their mouth they were pleased*   [I]49:14 Hb obscure

---

48:10 On **name**, see note at 20:1. The **right hand** often represented power and was especially significant in military contexts (see note at 16:8).

48:12-13 "Encircling" the city sounds like some sort of inspection, but in the context of a psalm and worship, it probably refers to a thanksgiving procession around the city (Neh 12:27-30).

Ps 49 title On **sons of Korah**, see note at Psalm 42 title.

49:1-4 The terms in these verses identify this psalm as a wisdom psalm, providing instruction for those who pay attention.

49:5 Usually the psalmist referred to enemies who surrounded him, but here the emphasis is on their **iniquity**.

49:6 Trusting in **wealth** is apparently the main issue in this psalm since this idea is developed in verses 10-12 and 16-20. As taught elsewhere in Wisdom literature, wealth is unstable (Pr 23:5).

49:7-9 **Redeem** and **ransom** fit the theme of money and what it can buy. To **see the Pit** is to experience death (7:15; 16:10; see note at 28:1). The point of 49:8 is that a person

cannot buy life, so it is pointless to try. In Jesus' words, it is possible for someone to "gain the whole world" but still "lose his soul" (Mt 16:26; Lk 9:25). "Ransom" is an especially significant word in light of how it is used in the NT to describe Jesus' payment through His sacrifice (Mt 20:28).

49:10-12 This section as well as verses 16-20 are similar to the arguments in other Wisdom texts, especially Ecclesiastes, about the futility of wealth: it is left **to others** (39:6; Ec 2:18), **graves** are the **eternal homes** of the wealthy (Ec 12:5), they are **like . . . animals that perish** (Ec 3:19), they will take nothing with them (Jb 27:19; Ps 49:17), and they praise themselves (v. 18; Dt 29:18; Lk 12:19).

49:14 The **sheep** and **shepherd** imagery is used in positive contexts where God shepherds His people (see note at 23:1); it is used negatively when describing evil leaders who misdirect God's people and lead them into sin (Ezk 34:2-10). Here it is clearly a negative image personifying **Death** as the shepherd of those who trust in their wealth. It leads them into **Sheol**, Death's realm.

49:15 **Redeem** is used again as in verses 7-8, but here God does have the power to redeem His own.

16 Do not be afraid when a man gets rich,
   when the wealth[A]
     of his house increases.[a]
17 For when he dies, he will take
   nothing at all;
   his wealth[A] will not follow him down.[b]
18 Though he praises himself
   during his lifetime—
   and people praise you when you do well
   for yourself[c]—
19 he will go to the generation
   of his fathers;
   they will never see the light.[d]
20 A man with valuable possessions[B]
   but without understanding
   is like the animals that perish.[e]

Psalm 50

God as Judge

A psalm of •Asaph.[f]

1 •Yahweh, the God of gods[c] speaks;
   He summons the earth from east
     to west.[D,g]
2 From •Zion, the perfection of beauty,
   God appears in radiance.[E,h]
3 Our God is coming; He will not
     be silent!
   Devouring fire precedes Him,
   and a storm rages around Him.[i]
4 On high, He summons heaven and earth
   in order to judge His people.[j]
5 "Gather My faithful ones to Me,
   those who made a covenant with Me
   by sacrifice."[k]

6 The heavens proclaim His righteousness,[l]
   for God is the Judge.[m]   •Selah
7 "Listen, My people, and I will speak;
   I will testify against you, Israel.
   I am God, your God.[n]
8 I do not rebuke you for your sacrifices
   or for your •burnt offerings,
   which are continually before Me.[o]
9 I will not accept a bull
     from your household
   or male goats from your pens,[p]
10 for every animal of the forest is Mine,
   the cattle on a thousand hills.
11 I know every bird of the mountains,[F]
   and the creatures of the field are Mine.[q]
12 If I were hungry, I would not tell you,
   for the world and everything in it
     is Mine.[r]
13 Do I eat the flesh of bulls
   or drink the blood of goats?[s]
14 Sacrifice a thank offering to God,[t]
   and pay your vows to the •Most High.[u]
15 Call on Me in a day of trouble;
   I will rescue you,
     and you will honor Me."[v]

16 But God says to the wicked:
   "What right do you have to recite
     My statutes
   and to take My covenant on your lips?[w]
17 You hate instruction
   and turn your back on My words.[G,x]
18 When you see a thief,
   you make friends with him,
   and you associate with adulterers.[y]

Cross references

a49:16 Ps 37:7
b49:17 Jb 27:19;
Ps 17:14; 1Tm
6:7
c49:18 Dt 29:19;
Ps 10:3,6
d49:19 Gn 15:15;
Jb 33:30; Ps
56:13
e49:20 Ec 3:19
f50:title 1Ch
16:5,7
g50:1 Jos 22:22;
Ps 113:3
h50:2 Dt 33:2;
Ps 48:2; Lm
2:15
i50:3 Ps 18:12-
13; 97:3
j50:4 Dt 4:26;
31:28; 32:1;
Is 1:2
k50:5 Ex 24:4-8;
2Ch 6:11
l50:6 Ps 89:5;
97:6
mPs 75:7; 96:13
n50:7 Dt 31:21;
Ps 81:8
o50:8 1Sm
15:22; Ps 40:6;
51:16
P50:9 Ps 69:31
q50:10-11 Ex
19:5; Ps 104:24
r50:12 Dt 10:14;
Ps 24:1; 1Co
10:26
s50:13 Is 1:11
t50:14 Lv 7:12;
Ps 107:22;
116:17
u Dt 23:21; Ps
76:11
v50:15 Ps 20:1;
59:16; 77:2
w50:16 Is 29:13
x50:17 Pr 5:12;
12:1
y50:18 Rm 1:32;
1Tm 5:22

A49:16,17 Or glory   B49:20 Or with honor   C50:1 Or The Mighty One, God, the Lord, or The God of gods, the Lord   D50:1 Lit from the rising of the sun to its setting   E50:2 Or God shines forth   F50:11 LXX, Syr, Tg read heavens   G50:17 Or and cast My words behind you

---

49:16-20 On the wealthy and their destiny, see note at verses 10-12.

Ps 50 title Asaph was one of David's chief musicians (1Ch 6:39; 15:17,19; 16:5,7; 2Ch 5:12). He was also the ancestor of a group of temple musicians (Ezr 2:40-41). As in the case of Jeduthun (Ps 39), the name might have come to represent his descendants or the musicians who followed him rather than Asaph himself.

50:1 From east to west means all the people of the whole earth.

50:2 Perfection of beauty is associated with the glorification of Jerusalem as the city of God (48:2; Lm 2:15).

50:3 Fire and **storm** are both common in theophanies (visible manifestations of God; 18:12-13; 97:3).

50:4 Heaven and earth represent all of creation (69:34; 115:15; 121:2). They were witnesses to Yahweh's covenant with Israel (Dt 4:26; 30:19) and were personified as witnesses in a legal setting where Yahweh judged His people for their violations of the covenant (Is 1:2).

50:5 Sacrifice could refer to God's initial covenant with Abram (Gn 15:9-18) or Israel's acceptance of the Ten Commandments (Ex 24:3-8).

50:8-13 The practice of sacrifice was not Israel's main problem; it was that they did not serve Yahweh with the proper motives (see note at 40:6-8). The reason offered here is that God owned **every** kind of **animal**, so He did not need them. The issue in worship is not giving God something He needs but offering oneself fully and completely, which is what He desires (Dt 6:5; 10:16).

50:14-15 In contrast to the sacrifices in verses 8-13, something much more personal and "from the heart" should be offered. This included calling on Yahweh in a time of need followed by a **thank offering**, which was usually made with **vows** during the petition (see note at 22:25-26).

50:16 The **wicked** in this context were those within Israel who only pay lip service to God's commands.

50:17-20 Verse 17 is a summary accusation followed by a list of violations that prove the accusation. This is a common formula, particularly in prophetic material. The violations include participation in theft (v. 18; Ex 20:15), adultery (Ps 50:18; Ex 20:14), and false accusations against fellow Israelites (Ps 50:19-20; Ex 20:16).

¹⁹ You unleash your mouth for evil
and harness your tongue for deceit.^a
²⁰ You sit, maligning your brother,
slandering your mother's son.^b
²¹ You have done these things,
and I kept silent;
you thought I was just like you.^c
But I will rebuke you
and lay out the case before you.^{A,d}

²² "Understand this, you who forget God,
or I will tear you apart,
and there will be no one to rescue you.^e
²³ Whoever sacrifices a thank offering
honors Me,
and whoever orders his conduct,
I will show him the salvation of God."^f

Psalm 51

A Prayer for Restoration

For the choir director. A Davidic psalm,
when Nathan the prophet came to him
after he had gone to Bathsheba.^g

¹ Be gracious to me, God,
according to Your faithful love;

according to Your abundant
compassion,
blot out my rebellion.^h
² Wash away my *guilt
and cleanse me from my sin.ⁱ
³ For I am conscious of my rebellion,
and my sin is always before me.^j
⁴ Against You—You alone—
I have sinned
and done this evil in Your sight.^k
So You are right
when You pass sentence;
You are blameless when You judge.^l
⁵ Indeed, I was guilty when I was born;
I was sinful when my mother
conceived me.^m
⁶ Surely You desire integrity
in the inner self,
and You teach me wisdom deep within.ⁿ
⁷ Purify me with hyssop,
and I will be *clean;
wash me, and I will be
whiter than snow.^o
⁸ Let me hear joy and gladness;
let the bones You have crushed rejoice.^p

Cross references (center column)

^a50:19 Ps 10:7; 36:3; 52:2
^b50:20 Jb 19:18; Mt 10:21
^c50:21 Is 42:14; 57:11
^dPs 90:8
^e50:22 Jb 8:13; Ps 9:17
^f50:23 Ps 85:13; 91:16; Gl 6:16
^g51:title 2Sm 12:1
^h51:1 Is 43:25; Ac 3:19
ⁱ51:2 Is 1:16; Jr 33:8; 1Jn 1:7,9
^j51:3 Ps 32:5; Pr 28:13; Is 59:12
^k51:4 Ps 41:4
^lRm 3:4
^m51:5 Jb 15:14; Ps 58:3; Rm 5:12-13
ⁿ51:6 Jb 38:36; Pr 2:6; Ec 2:26
^o51:7 Lv 14:4,49; Nm 19:18; Is 1:18
^p51:8 Ps 35:10; Is 38:13

^A50:21 Lit *out before your eyes*

50:21 God's silence (or delay in executing justice) is sometimes assumed to mean that He will not act. The wicked are especially characterized by this assumption (see notes at 10:3-6 and 10:11).

50:22 Tear you apart uses imagery of a wild animal and its prey. This is often used for enemies (see note at 7:1-2), but here God takes on the role of an enemy against those who violate His covenant (see note at 38:1-2).

50:23 Orders his conduct refers to obedience, which is preferable to sacrifice (1Sm 15:22; see note at Ps 40:6-8).

Ps 51 title This psalm has a clearly defined historical setting, which was David's confession of his sins after being confronted by **Nathan the prophet** (2Sm 12:1; the entire background of the sins is in 2Sm 11–12). As in other psalms with a specific setting (such as Ps 18), the language of the psalm is general enough to be applied in other contexts. This fits the purpose of the psalms and their various applications.

51:1-2 Blot out . . . wash away, and **cleanse** are terms for forgiveness, which is David's main plea (see note at 32:1-2 for similar terms). He relied completely on God's mercy, which is evident in the terms **gracious . . . faithful love**, and **abundant compassion**. In David's case, his sins were severe enough that sacrifice was not acceptable (v. 16). According to God's laws, deliberate and premeditated sins such as adultery and murder were referred to as sins of "the high hand" ("defiantly" in Nm 15:30-31). Their punishment was being "cut off" from the community, which in many cases meant death (see note at Ps 31:22).

51:3 Verses 3-5 include the recognition of sin without specifying the sins, allowing this psalm to be used in a variety of contexts (see note at title). **My rebellion** is in the emphatic position in the Hebrew text, showing that this is the main focus of attention in this confession.

51:4 The statement **against You . . . alone** does not mean that others were not involved in the effects of the sin, but that even in sinning against others the ultimate affront was against God Himself. This was clearly David's emphasis when he was confronted with this sin (2Sm 12:13).

51:5 This verse has prompted a variety of interpretations. Some have interpreted it to mean that marriage and childbearing are a curse; this is untenable in light of the rest of Scripture (127:3; Heb 13:4). Another interpretation is that this refers to a specific sin, perhaps adultery, committed by David's mother, but there is no evidence of this in the biblical texts. Others connect this verse with ceremonial uncleanness in childbirth (Lv 12:2,5; 15:18), but this is not the same as sin. Some say David is using rhetorical overstatement to describe his sinfulness. One of the most common interpretations in Christian history is that this verse teaches the doctrine of original sin. While not aiming to strictly identify the origin of human sinfulness with events at biological conception, David recognizes that sin pervades humankind as a universal condition from the very outset of our existence. Sin is everywhere and in everyone, and David confessed that it had been with him since birth. Far from forming the basis of an excuse (i.e., "Why should I be blamed for my sins when I was born this way?"), David's confession contrasts the "blameless" (Ps 51:4) ways of God with the innately evil ways of men.

51:6 God desires obedience to His commands from within (with **integrity**). Yahweh is the source of wisdom (Pr 2:6), but it must be communicated to a person's heart. This is similar to the idea of God's commands residing in the heart (see note at Ps 37:31).

51:8 Bones are often mentioned in the context of suffering (see note at 34:20).

9 Turn Your face away[A] from my sins
and blot out all my guilt.[a]

10 God, create a clean heart for me
and renew a steadfast[B] spirit
within me.[b]

11 Do not banish me from Your presence
or take Your Holy Spirit
from me.[c]

12 Restore the joy of Your salvation to me,
and give me a willing spirit.[C,d]

13 Then I will teach the rebellious
Your ways,
and sinners will return to You.[e]

14 Save me from the guilt of bloodshed,
God,[f]
the God of my salvation,
and my tongue will sing
of Your righteousness.[g]

15 Lord, open my lips,
and my mouth will declare
Your praise.[h]

16 You do not want a sacrifice,
or I would give it;

You are not pleased
with a *burnt offering.[i]

17 The sacrifice pleasing to God is[D]
a broken spirit.
God, You will not despise a broken
and humbled heart.[j]

18 In Your good pleasure, cause *Zion
to prosper;
build[E] the walls of Jerusalem.[k]

19 Then You will delight
in righteous sacrifices,
whole burnt offerings;
then bulls will be offered on Your altar.[l]

Psalm 52
God Judges the Proud

For the choir director. A Davidic *Maskil.
When Doeg the Edomite went and
reported to Saul, telling him, "David
went to Ahimelech's house."[m]

1 Why brag about evil, you hero![n]
God's faithful love is constant.[o]

Cross references:
[a]51:9 Jr 16:17
[b]51:10 Ps 24:4; Mt 5:8; Jms 4:8
[c]51:11 2Kg 13:23; Is 63:10-11; Jr 7:15
[d]51:12 Ps 13:5
[e]51:13 Ex 33:13; Ps 25:4; Jr 2:33
[f]51:14 Ps 26:9
[g]Ps 35:28; 71:15
[h]51:15 Ex 4:15; Ps 9:14
[i]51:16 1Sm 15:22; Ps 40:6
[j]51:17 Ps 34:18
[k]51:18 Ps 69:35; 102:16; 147:2
[l]51:19 Ps 4:5; 66:13,15; Mal 3:3
[m]52:title 1Sm 22:9
[n]52:1 Ps 94:4
[o]Ps 40:10-11; 138:2

Footnotes:
[A]51:9 Lit *Hide Your face* [B]51:10 Or *right* [C]51:12 Or *and sustain me with a noble spirit* [D]51:17 Lit *The sacrifices of God are*
[E]51:18 Or *rebuild*

51:9 Turning away the **face** implies forgiving and forgetting (vv. 1-2).

51:10 The renewal of one's **heart** and **spirit** are common images representing not only forgiveness (vv. 1-2,7-9) but also a change that enables a person to live in obedience to Yahweh's commands (1Sm 10:6,9; Jr 32:39; Ezk 36:26). Note also the use of "willing spirit" in Ps 51:12.

51:11 **Holy Spirit** is taken by some to mean Yahweh's **presence**. However, in the larger context of the biblical text, it seems to refer to God Himself (Is 63:10-14) in the same way that "heart" and "spirit" can refer to people. The division among the persons of the Godhead (the Trinity) is not a concept developed in the OT, although texts such as this allow for the establishment of the doctrine as God's revelation progresses through the NT (e.g., Mt 3:16-17, where Father, Son, and Spirit are all present yet distinct at Jesus' baptism).

51:13-15 Publicly praising God and teaching others about Him was part of the response of God's deliverance in a person's life (see note at 22:22-24).

51:16-17 God desires a **broken spirit** (or heart) rather than acts of sacrifice (see notes at 34:18 and 40:6-8).

51:18 Some think **build the walls** refers to Nehemiah's time, but this is not necessary if it is used figuratively. It simply refers to strengthening **Zion**, which is where Yahweh dwelt among His people (65:1).

51:19 **Righteous sacrifices** must be connected with verses 16-17, meaning those offered with the proper motives (see notes at 40:6-8 and 50:8-13).

Ps 52 title On *Maskil*, see note at Psalm 32 title. The historical setting specified in this psalm is when **Doeg the Edomite**, one of Saul's chief herdsmen, informed Saul that David had gone to **Ahimelech's house** (1Sm 22:9). He had also informed Saul of the help David received from the priests

of Nob (1Sm 21:7), so he was the one responsible for the slaughter of 85 priests accused of treason against King Saul (1Sm 22:11-23). As in other psalms with a specific setting (such as Ps 18), the language of the psalm is general enough to be applied in other contexts.

52:1 To **brag about evil** is a much stronger denunciation than most passages dealing with boasting. People apart from God commonly boast about their abilities (Jr 9:23) or their wealth (Ps 49:6), but this person was boasting about his sins (10:3). Those who are faithful to Yahweh boast only in the fact that they know Him (see note at 34:2).

52:2 **Razor** symbolizes sharpness that could be used as a weapon of **destruction**. In other contexts, a sharpened **tongue** is a common image for destructive speech (57:4;

qawah

Hebrew Pronunciation	[kah WAH]
HCSB Translation	hope, wait, put hope in
Uses in Psalms	17
Uses in the OT	47
Focus Passage	Psalm 52:9

Qawah describes *waiting for* pay (Jb 7:2), *expecting* good grapes (Is 5:2), or *hoping* for peace (Jr 8:15). Showers *wait* for nobody (Mc 5:7). *Qawah* stands parallel with "seeking" (Lm 3:25) and "looking for" (Jb 6:19); it connotes *looking* for (Is 5:7). God is often the object (22x). *Waiting for* (Is 26:8) or *putting hope in* (Ps 69:6) Him involves *trusting* (Is 40:31). God is good to those who *wait for* Him (Lm 3:25); they will inherit the land, not evildoers (Ps 37:9). *Qawah* need not imply godly *hoping*; the wicked *hope* to destroy the righteous (Ps 119:95). One motif concerns *hoping* for something that does not come (Jr 8:15). *Qawah* has a homonym meaning "gather" (Gn 1:9) that occurs twice. The noun *tiqwah* (32x) indicates *hope* except twice when translated *expectation* because of another word for "hope" (Pr 10:28; 11:7). *Miqweh* (5x; Jr 17:13) signifies *hope*.

2 Like a sharpened razor,
your tongue devises destruction,
working treachery.[a]

3 You love evil instead of good,
lying instead of speaking truthfully.[b]
•Selah

4 You love any words that destroy,
you treacherous tongue![c]

5 This is why God will bring
you down forever.
He will take you, ripping you out of
your tent;
He will uproot you from the land
of the living.[d]   Selah

6 The righteous will look on with awe
and will ridicule him:[e]

7 "Here is the man
who would not make God his refuge,
but trusted in the abundance
of his riches,
taking refuge
in his destructive behavior."[A,f]

8 But I am like a flourishing olive tree
in the house of God;[g]
I trust in God's faithful love
forever and ever.[h]

9 I will praise You forever for what
You have done.
In the presence of Your faithful people,
I will put my hope in Your name,
for it is good.[i]

Psalm 53
A Portrait of Sinners

For the choir director: on Mahalath.[B,j]
A Davidic •Maskil.

1 The fool says in his heart,
"God does not exist."

They are corrupt, and they do
vile deeds.
There is no one who does good.[k]

2 God looks down from heaven
on the •human race
to see if there is one who is wise,
one who seeks God.[l]

3 All have turned away;
all alike have become corrupt.
There is no one who does good,
not even one.[m]

4 Will evildoers never understand?
They consume My people
as they consume bread;[n]
they do not call on God.[o]

5 Then they will be filled with terror—
terror like no other[p]—
because God will scatter
the bones of those who besiege you.[q]
You will put them to shame,
for God has rejected them.[r]

6 Oh, that Israel's deliverance
would come from •Zion!
When God restores the fortunes
of His people,[C]
Jacob will rejoice; Israel will be glad.[s]

Psalm 54
Prayer for Deliverance

For the choir director:
with stringed instruments. A Davidic •Maskil.
When the Ziphites went and said to Saul,
"Is David not hiding among us?"[t]

1 God, save me by Your name,
and vindicate me by Your might![u]

2 God, hear my prayer;
listen to the words of my mouth.[v]

3 For strangers rise up against me,

Cross references (center column)

[a]52:2 Ps 5:9; 50:19; 59:7
[b]52:3 Ps 58:3; Jr 9:4-5
[c]52:4 Ps 10:7; Pr 17:4
[d]52:5 Ps 27:13; Pr 2:22
[e]52:6 Jb 22:19-20; Ps 37:34
[f]52:7 Ps 10:6; 49:6; Pr 11:28
[g]52:8 Ps 1:3; 128:3; Jr 11:16
[h]Ps 143:8
[i]52:9 Ps 30:12; 54:6
[j]53:title Ps 88 title
[k]53:1 Ps 10:4; 14:1
[l]53:2 Ps 33:13-15
[m]53:2-3 Rm 3:10-12
[n]53:4 Ps 27:2; Mc 3:3
[o]Is 64:7
[p]53:5 Lv 26:36
[q]Jr 8:1-2
[r]Ps 44:7
[s]53:6 Ps 14:7; Is 52:7-9; Jr 30:18-19
[t]53:title 1Sm 23:19; 26:1
[u]54:1 Ps 6:1; 7:8; 35:24; 43:1
[v]54:2 Ps 5:1; 17:6; 55:1

[A]52:7 Or riches, and grew strong in his evil desire; lit his destruction   [B]53:title Perhaps a tune, a musical instrument, or a dance; this may be related to Hb word for "sickness."   [C]53:6 Or restores His captive people

---

64:3; 140:3). Human speech, symbolized by the tongue, has the power of death (Pr 18:21).

52:4 The word for **destroy** is literally "swallow" (Hb bl'), picturing destructive speech as devouring others (see note at 14:4).

52:5 Bring . . . down is commonly used for judgment on the wicked (147:6; 2Sm 22:48). **Uproot** is the most common description of a wicked person being removed from Yahweh's land (Dt 29:28; 2Ch 7:20; Pr 2:22).

52:6 This verse does not refer to the same malicious mocking since that is forbidden (Pr 24:17); it is part of a request for divine retribution (Dt 32:35; see note at Ps 28:3-5).

52:7 On dependence on **riches**, see note at 49:10-12.

52:8 The righteous are often pictured as **a flourishing . . . tree** (see note at 1:3).

Ps 53 title Mahalath may be related to a Hebrew word mean-

ing "sickness." It is unclear whether it refers to a song tune or a musical form. On **Maskil**, see note at Psalm 32 title.

53:1-4 These verses are essentially the same as 14:1-4 (see notes at 14:1, 2, 3, and 4).

53:5 This verse includes a more extended image of God's judgment on the wicked than 14:5-6. Scattering **bones** often pictures the dead on the battlefield (141:7; Jr 8:1-2; Ezk 6:5; 37:1-6).

53:6 On **Israel's deliverance**, see note at 14:7.

Ps 54 title The historical setting for this psalm relates to the **Ziphites**, who lived southeast of Hebron and informed **Saul** of David's hiding place (1Sm 23:19; 26:1). On **Maskil**, see note at Psalm 32 title.

54:1 For **vindicate** see notes at 17:1-2 and 35:27-28.

54:3 The word **strangers** (Hb zarim) denotes outsiders with

and violent men seek my life.
They have no regard for God.[A,a]

            •Selah

4 God is my helper;
    the Lord is the sustainer of my life.[B,b]
5 He will repay my adversaries
        for their evil.
    Because of Your faithfulness,
        annihilate them.[c]

6 I will sacrifice a freewill offering
        to You.[d]
    I will praise Your name, •Yahweh,
    because it is good.[e]
7 For He has delivered me
        from every trouble,
    and my eye has looked down on
        my enemies.[f]

Psalm 55
Betrayal by a Friend

For the choir director:
with stringed instruments.
A Davidic •Maskil.

1 God, listen to my prayer
    and do not ignore[C] my plea for help.[g]
2 Pay attention to me and answer me.[h]
    I am restless and in turmoil
        with my complaint,[i]
3 because of the enemy's voice,
    because of the pressure[D] of the wicked.
    For they bring down disaster on me[E]
    and harass me in anger.[j]

4 My heart shudders within me;[k]
    terrors of death sweep over me.

5 Fear and trembling grip me;
    horror has overwhelmed me.[l]
6 I said, "If only I had[F] wings like a dove!
    I would fly away and find rest.[m]
7 How far away I would flee;
    I would stay in the wilderness.[n]

            •Selah

8 I would hurry to my shelter
    from the raging wind and the storm."[o]
9 Lord, confuse[G] and confound
        their speech,[H,p]
    for I see violence and strife in the city;
10 day and night they make the rounds
        on its walls.
    Crime and trouble are within it;[q]
11 destruction is inside it;
    oppression and deceit never leave
        its marketplace.[r]

12 Now it is not an enemy
        who insults me—
    otherwise I could bear it;
    it is not a foe who rises up
        against me—
    otherwise I could hide from him.
13 But it is you, a man who is my peer,
    my companion and good friend![s]
14 We used to have close fellowship;
    we walked with the crowd
        into the house of God.[t]

15 Let death take them by surprise;[u]
    let them go down to •Sheol alive,
    because evil is in their homes
        and within them.[v]
16 But I call to God,
    and the Lord will save me.[w]

Cross references (center column)
a 54:3 Ps 86:14; 143:3; Is 25:5
b 54:4 Ps 118:7; Is 41:10
c 54:5 Ps 94:23; 143:12
d 54:6 Nm 15:3; Ps 116:17
e Ps 52:9
f 54:7 Ps 59:10; 92:11
g 55:1 Lm 3:56
h 55:1-2 Ps 4:1; 5:1-2; 54:2
i 55:2 Ps 64:1; 142:2
j 55:3 2Sm 16:7-8; Ps 71:11
k 55:4 Ps 38:8
l 55:4-5 Ps 18:4-5; 116:3
m 55:6 Jb 3:13
n 55:7 Jr 9:2
o 55:8 Is 4:6; 25:4
p 55:9 Gn 10:25; 11:7
q 55:9-10 Jr 6:7; Hab 1:3
r 55:11 Ps 5:9; 10:7
s 55:12-13 Jb 19:13,19; Ps 41:9; 88:18
t 55:14 Ps 42:4
u 55:15 Pr 6:15; Is 47:11; 1Th 5:3
v Nm 16:30,33
w 55:16 Ps 119:46

A 54:3 Lit They do not set God before them   B 54:4 Or is with those who sustain my life   C 55:1 Lit hide Yourself from   D 55:3 Or threat, or oppression   E 55:3 LXX, Syr, Sym; MT reads they cause me to totter   F 55:6 Lit "Who will give to me . . . dove?   G 55:9 Or destroy   H 55:9 Lit and divide their tongue

regard to Yahweh's covenant and people (Is 1:7; 14:1; Eph 2:12). **No regard for God** is similar to descriptions of the wicked who think God will not execute His justice (see notes at 10:3-6 and 14:1).

54:5 Repay is a term used in contexts describing divine retribution (Dt 32:35).

54:6 Freewill offering is used instead of thank offering because there was no vow made in the request as in other cases (see note at 22:25-26). Instead, this is a voluntary and spontaneous offering that was not done out of obligation.

54:7 Looked down expresses the idea of triumph over one's **enemies** (58:10; 59:10; 92:11).

Ps 55 title On *Maskil*, see note at Psalm 32 title.

55:3 Harass is a rare word (Hb *stm*) that expresses the idea of animosity or hatred, often connected with hostility (Gn 49:23; Jb 30:21). This emphasizes malicious intent rather than playful mocking.

55:4-5 Sweep over and **overwhelmed** portray being overtaken by troubles as if by a flood (see note at 32:6-7).

55:6-8 The hope of escape is pictured as a bird flying away to safety. This is the reaction of an animal that has no hope of defending itself any other way (see note at 11:1).

55:9-11 These verses recall when God judged those who were building the tower of Babylon by confounding their **speech** (Gn 11:1-9). The terms **city** and **walls** and the description of the wickedness associated with them are further connections to Babylon. Since the main issue in this psalm is the "voice" of the enemy (v. 3), this is a most appropriate request.

55:12-14 The shift here is significant in demonstrating that the culprit was not some distant **enemy** but a close **friend**, a worship companion. This "friend" did not merely abandon the psalmist (see notes at 31:11 and 35:11-14), but actually participated in the malicious **insults**.

55:15 Going **down to Sheol alive** is reminiscent of the fate

¹⁷ I complain and groan morning, noon,
     and night,^a
and He hears my voice.^b
¹⁸ Though many are against me,
He will redeem me
     from my battle unharmed.^c
¹⁹ God, the One enthroned
     from long ago,^d
will hear and
     will humiliate them   *Selah*
because they do not change
and do not *fear God.^e

²⁰ My friend^f acts violently
against those at peace
     with him;^g
he violates his covenant.^h
²¹ His buttery words are smooth,^A
but war is in his heart.
His words are softer than oil,
but they are drawn swords.ⁱ

²² Cast your burden on the LORD,
and He will sustain you;^j
He will never allow the righteous
     to be shaken.^k

²³ God, You will bring them down
to the *Pit of destruction;^l
men of bloodshed and treachery
will not live out half their days.^m
But I will trust in You.ⁿ

Psalm 56
A Call for God's Protection

For the choir director: according to
"A Silent Dove Far Away."^B A Davidic *Miktam.
When the Philistines seized him in Gath.^o

¹ Be gracious to me, God,
     for man tramples me;
he fights and oppresses me
     all day long.
² My adversaries trample me all day,
for many arrogantly fight
     against me.^{C,p}

³ When I am afraid,
I will trust in You.^q
⁴ In God, whose word I praise,
in God I trust; I will not fear.
What can man do to me?^r

⁵ They twist my words all day long;
all their thoughts against me are evil.^s
⁶ They stir up strife,^D they lurk;
they watch my steps
while they wait to take my life.^t
⁷ Will they escape in spite of such sin?
God, bring down the nations in wrath.^u

⁸ You Yourself have recorded
     my wanderings.^E
Put my tears in Your bottle.
Are they not in Your records?^v

Cross-references

^a55:17 Ps 92:2
^bPs 64:1; 142:2
^c55:18 Ps 56:2; 103:4
^d55:19 Ps 93:2
^eDt 33:27
^f55:20 Ps 55:13
^gPs 7:4
^hPs 89:34
ⁱ55:21 Ps 12:2; 28:3
^j55:22 1Pt 5:7
^kPs 37:24; 112:6
^l55:23 Is 38:17; Ezk 28:8
^mPs 5:6
ⁿPs 56:3
^o56:title 1Sm 21:10-11; 22:1
^p56:1-2 Ps 35:1; 57:3
^q56:3 Ps 112:7; Pr 29:25; Is 12:2
^r56:4 Ps 27:1; 118:6; Heb 13:6
^s56:5 Ps 41:7; 2Pt 3:16
^t56:6 Ps 10:8-10; 59:3
^u56:7 Ezk 17:15; Rm 2:3
^v56:8 2Kg 20:5; Ps 139:3; Mal 3:16

---

^A55:21 Some Hb mss, Sym, Syr, Tg, Jer read *His speech is smoother than butter*   ^B56:title Possibly a tune   ^C56:2 Or *many fight against me, O exalted One*, or *many fight against me from the heights*   ^D56:6 Or *They attack*   ^E56:8 Or *misery*

---

of those who followed Korah in his rebellion against God (Nm 16:31-33).

55:17 The phrase **morning, noon, and night** most likely implies constant prayer rather than specific times of prayer (22:2; 88:1; 119:164; 1Th 5:7).

55:19 Enthroned from long ago describes God's eternal rule beginning at creation (29:10; 45:6; Lm 5:19).

55:20 His covenant (Hb *berith*) in this context is not a reference to God's covenant with His people but is used in the more "secular" sense of a promise or oath made between people. Here it refers to one who does not fear God (v. 19) violating a friendship (vv. 12-14).

55:21 War . . . in his heart relates to the earlier term "harass" (v. 3), which refers to open hostility. The point here is that hostile speech comes from hostile intentions (Mt 12:34; Lk 6:45).

55:22 This verse is quoted in 1Pt 5:7. Similar constructions are used to describe committing one's way (Ps 37:5) and works (Pr 16:3) to Yahweh.

55:23 Pit is equivalent to "Sheol" (v. 15) and refers to death (see note at 28:1).

Ps 56 title A Silent Dove Far Away was probably a known song tune (see note at Ps 22 title). On *Miktam*, see note at Psalm 16 title. The historical setting for this psalm is the same as Psalm 34 (1Sm 21:10-11; see note at Ps 34 title).

56:1-2 Tramples (Hb *sh'p*) appears twice in these verses. There are two meanings for this Hebrew word: (1) "pant" or "long for" (Is 42:14; Jr 2:24) and (2) "crush" or "trample" (Ps 57:4; Am 8:4). Since the first of these is more common, some translations take that as the meaning here. However, the parallel terms **fights** and **oppresses** argue for the second meaning.

56:4 Man is literally "flesh" (Hb *basar*), which represents man's weakness and mortality (Is 2:22; 31:3; 40:6). This word is often used to contrast man's weakness with God's power (2Ch 32:8). The same words in verses 3-4 are repeated in verses 10-11.

56:5 Twist (Hb *'atsav*) expresses the idea of "shape" or "fashion" (Jb 10:8). It portrays these enemies as shaping the psalmist's words into whatever they wanted for their own **evil** purposes.

56:6 Lurk describes the psalmist's enemies as predatory animals waiting to attack their prey (10:9; 17:12).

56:8 Tears probably refers to prayers or, more specifically, laments that involve crying. The **bottle** refers to God's storing of these prayers so He can act on them later. This is similar to the image of incense in Revelation to represent the prayers of the saints (Rv 5:8; 8:3-4). The **records** is similar to the "books of remembrance" referred to in Dn 7:10 and Mal 3:16.

9 Then my enemies will retreat
on the day when I call.[a]
This I know: God is for me.[b]
10 In God, whose word I praise,
in the LORD, whose word I praise,
11 in God I trust; I will not fear.
What can man do to me?[c]

12 I am obligated by vows[A] to You, God;
I will make my thank offerings to You.[d]
13 For You delivered me from death,
even my feet from stumbling,
to walk before God in the light of life.[e]

Psalm 57
Praise for God's Protection

For the choir director: "Do Not Destroy."[B]
A Davidic •*Miktam*. When he fled
before Saul into the cave.[f]

1 Be gracious to me, God, be gracious
to me,
for I take refuge in You.
I will seek refuge in the shadow
of Your wings
until danger passes.[g]
2 I call to God •Most High,
to God who fulfills His purpose
for me.[C,h]
3 He reaches down from heaven
and saves me,
challenging the one who tramples me.[i]
•Selah
God sends His faithful love and truth.[j]
4 I am surrounded by lions;
I lie down with those
who devour •men.
Their teeth are spears and arrows;
their tongues are sharp swords.[k]
5 God, be exalted above the heavens;
let Your glory be over the whole earth.[l]
6 They prepared a net for my steps;
I was despondent.
They dug a pit ahead of me,
but they fell into it![m] *Selah*

7 My heart is confident, God, my heart
is confident.
I will sing; I will sing praises.[n]
8 Wake up, my soul![D]
Wake up, harp and lyre!
I will wake up the dawn.[o]
9 I will praise You, Lord,
among the peoples;
I will sing praises to You
among the nations.[p]
10 For Your faithful love is as high as
the heavens;
Your faithfulness reaches the clouds.[q]
11 God, be exalted above the heavens;[r]
let Your glory be over the whole earth.[s]

Psalm 58
A Cry against Injustice

For the choir director: "Do Not Destroy."[B]
A Davidic •*Miktam*.

1 Do you really speak righteously,
you mighty ones?[E]
Do you judge •people fairly?[t]

[a]56:9 Ps 9:3
[b]Ps 118:6; Rm 8:31
[c]56:10-11 Ps 112:7; Pr 29:25; Is 12:2
[d]56:12 Ps 50:14
[e]56:13 Jb 33:30; Ps 116:8-9
[f]57:title 1Sm 22:1; 24:1-3
[g]57:1 Ru 2:12; Ps 17:8; 91:1,4
[h]57:2 Ps 138:8
[i]57:3 Ps 56:1-2
[j]Ps 25:10; 40:11
[k]57:4 Ps 58:6; 64:3; Pr 30:14
[l]57:5 Ps 108:5; 113:4
[m]57:6 Ps 9:15; 35:8; Pr 28:10
[n]57:7 Ps 59:17; 112:7
[o]57:8 Jdg 5:12; Ps 33:2; 81:2
[p]57:9 2Sm 22:50; Ps 9:11; 18:49
[q]57:10 Ps 36:5; 103:11; Lm 3:22-23
[r]57:11 Ps 113:4
[s]57:7-11 Ps 108:1-5
[t]58:1 Ps 82:2

[A]56:12 Lit *On me the vows* [B]57: title; 58:title Possibly a tune [C]57:2 Or *who avenges me* [D]57:8 Lit *glory* [E]58:1 Or *Can you really speak righteousness in silence?*

56:12 Vows were commonly made during petition and fulfilled through **thank offerings** (see note at 22:25-26).

56:13 Light is used as a synonym for **life** (Jb 3:20) but also may represent joy (Is 9:2) and salvation (Is 58:8). See notes at Ps 27:1 and 36:9.

Ps 57 title Do Not Destroy was probably a known song tune of the time (see note at Ps 22 title). On ***Miktam***, see note at Psalm 16 title. There are two possibilities for the historical setting of this psalm, both of which involved David fleeing from **Saul** and going into a **cave** (1Sm 22:1; 24:1-3; cp. Ps 142).

57:1 On **shadow of Your wings**, see notes at 17:8 and 27:5.

57:2 Most High emphasizes God's sovereignty over the whole earth (see note at 7:17).

57:3 On **tramples**, see note at 56:1-2.

57:4 Enemies are often portrayed as **lions** that **devour** people (see notes at 7:1-2 and 14:4). **Tongues** probably refers to their speech, which is often destructive (see note at 52:2).

57:5 Glory (Hb *kavod*) carries the idea of "heavy" or "weighty" in the sense of important (see word study at 24:7-10). God's glory can either be a physical manifestation, such as that which came down on the ark of the covenant (Ex 40:34-35), or used to represent His significance, perhaps connected with His reputation or "name" (Ps 29:2; 66:2). In this verse His significance is **over the whole earth**, meaning beyond anything on earth. Verse 11 repeats the same words as verse 5.

57:6 The desire for enemies to fall into their own traps is a common request in these types of prayers (see note at 7:14-16).

57:8 My soul here is literally "my glory" from the same Hebrew word *(kavod)* as verse 5. Here it represents the person but creates an interesting wordplay within the psalm.

57:9 The **praise . . . among the peoples** and **nations** demonstrates that Yahweh's authority is over all the nations of the earth (see notes at 18:49 and 22:27-31).

Ps 58 title On **Do Not Destroy**, see note at Psalm 57 title. On ***Miktam***, see note at Psalm 16 title.

58:1 The Hebrew word for **mighty ones** is *'elim*. Sometimes it refers to angelic beings or the gods of the nations (see note at 29:1), but here it refers to people (note esp. the reference to birth in 58:3). The combination of **righteously**

2 No, you practice injustice
in your hearts;
with your hands you weigh out violence
in the land.[a]
3 The wicked go astray from the womb;
liars err from birth.[b]
4 They have venom like the venom
of a snake,
like the deaf cobra
that stops up its ears,[c]
5 that does not listen to the sound
of the charmers
who skillfully weave spells.[d]
6 God, knock the teeth
out of their mouths;
LORD, tear out the young lions' fangs.[e]
7 They will vanish like water that flows by;
they will aim their useless arrows.[A,B,f]
8 Like a slug that moves along in slime,
like a woman's miscarried child,
they will not see the sun.[g]
9 Before your pots can feel the heat of
the thorns—
whether green or burning—
He will sweep them away.[C,h]
10 The righteous one will rejoice
when he sees the retribution;[i]
he will wash his feet in the blood
of the wicked.[j]
11 Then people will say,
"Yes, there is a reward
for the righteous!
There is a God who judges
on earth!"[k]

Psalm 59

God Our Stronghold

For the choir director: "Do Not Destroy."[D]
A Davidic *Miktam*. When Saul sent agents
to watch the house and kill him.[l]

1 Deliver me from my enemies,
my God;[m]
protect me from those who rise up
against me.[n]
2 Deliver me from those
who practice sin,
and save me from men of bloodshed.[o]
3 LORD, look! They set an ambush
for me.[p]
Powerful men attack me,
but not because of any sin or rebellion
of mine.[q]
4 For no fault of mine,
they run and take up a position.
Awake to help me, and take notice.[r]

[a] 58:2 Ps 94:20; Is 10:1; Mal 3:15
[b] 58:3 Ps 51:5; Is 48:8
[c] 58:4 Dt 32:33; Ps 140:3
[d] 58:5 Ec 10:11; Jr 8:17
[e] 58:6 Jb 4:10; 29:17; Ps 3:7
[f] 58:7 Jos 7:5; Ps 112:10; Ezk 21:7
[g] 58:8 Jb 3:16; Ec 6:3
[h] 58:9 Jb 27:21; Pr 10:25; Ec 7:6
[i] 58:10 Jb 22:19
[j] Ps 68:23; Jr 11:20; 20:12
[k] 58:11 Ps 9:8; 67:4; 75:7
[l] 59:title 1Sm 19:11
[m] 59:1 Ps 143:9
[n] 2Sm 22:18; Ps 18:17; 91:14
[o] 59:2 Ps 5:6; 17:7
[p] 59:3 Pr 1:11,18
[q] 1Sm 20:1; 24:11
[r] 59:4 Ps 7:3-4; 69:4

A 58:7 Or *their arrows as if they were circumcised*; Hb obscure B 58:7 Or *they wither like trampled grass* C 58:9 Or *thorns, He will sweep it away, whether raw or cooking, or thorns, He will sweep him away alive in fury* D 59:title Possibly a tune

(referring to justice) and **judge** shows that they were most likely rulers or judges who were responsible for rendering justice. The designation "mighty ones" is sarcastic since this is how they viewed themselves.

58:2 Injustice in your hearts contrasts with the fact that they were responsible for judging fairly (v. 1). The "heart" was often used to depict the place of one's motives (see notes at 17:3-5 and 44:21) as well as the human will where decisions were made (1Sm 7:3; 1Kg 8:47-48).

58:3 This verse has been used to argue for the doctrine of original sin, but the subject is restrictive, having in view **the wicked** and **liars** rather than humanity in general. We know from elsewhere (e.g., Rm 3:23) that it is not just the wicked and liars who **go astray** and **err**. Speaking of the wicked and liars specifically, the psalmist traces their errant ways to **the womb** and **birth** not in a bid to argue that they are constituted differently from the general population, but rather to express the deep-rootedness of their sinfulness. See note at 51:5.

58:4-5 The comparison of these wicked rulers to a **snake** emphasizes their deadliness (their **venom**). The other main point of comparison is stopping up their **ears** and not listening to **charmers**. In the context of judging, it probably refers to not listening to someone's case and therefore not rendering justice fairly.

58:6 The imagery of **lions** is common for enemies (see note at 7:1-2). Since the power of predatory animals was in their **teeth**, the psalmist requested that they be knocked out.

58:7 The vanishing **water** here may be a reference to a wadi, a seasonal stream that flowed only during the rainy season. The rest of the time it was nothing more than a dry river bed (or valley).

58:8 The image of the **slug** and its **slime** seems to reflect a common perception in the ancient world that the slug was melting away as it moved along.

58:9 Thorns were often used as fuel to heat food in **pots**. Therefore, this implies the swiftness of God's judgment (see notes at 37:10 and 37:36).

58:10 Seeing **retribution** and washing one's **feet in . . . blood** (spilled blood or death) are parallel concepts. Though the second image is more vivid, the point is the same—**the righteous** will witness God's judgment on these wicked rulers.

58:11 God's judgment on the wicked will be a lesson for all **people**. The lessons are that Yahweh is a God of justice, and He is not distant and removed but is involved in matters **on earth** (82:8; 94:2; Gn 18:25).

Ps 59 title On **Do Not Destroy**, see note at Psalm 57 title. On ***Miktam***, see note at Psalm 16 title. The "him" in the phrase **kill him** refers to David. The background for this setting is found in 1Sm 19:11.

59:2 Men of bloodshed is literally "men of blood." It refers to those who were known for their violence (5:6; 26:9; 55:23), in this case those who desired the death of the psalmist.

59:4 No fault of mine is a statement of innocence, meaning that the psalmist had done nothing to provoke the attacks of his enemies (see note at 7:3-5).

5 LORD God of *Hosts, You are the
   God of Israel,
 rise up to punish all the nations;
 do not show grace
   to any wicked traitors.[a]   *Selah

6 They return at evening,
   snarling like dogs
 and prowling around the city.[b]

7 Look, they spew from their mouths—
 sharp words from[A] their lips.[c]
 "For who," they say, "will hear?"[d]

8 But You laugh at them, LORD;
 You ridicule all the nations.[e]

9 I will keep watch for You, my[B] strength,
 because God is my stronghold.[f]

10 My faithful God[C] will come
   to meet me;
 God will let me look down on
   my adversaries.[g]

11 Do not kill them; otherwise, my people
   will forget.
 By Your power, make them
   homeless wanderers[h]
 and bring them down,
 Lord, our shield.[i]

12 For the sin of their mouths and the
   words of their lips,
 let them be caught in their pride.
 They utter curses and lies.[j]

13 Consume them in rage;
 consume them until they are gone.[k]

Then people will know
   throughout[D] the earth
 that God rules over Jacob.[l]   Selah

14 And they return at evening,
   snarling like dogs
 and prowling around the city.[m]

15 They scavenge for food;
 they growl if they are not satisfied.[n]

16 But I will sing of Your strength
 and will joyfully proclaim
 Your faithful love in the morning.[o]
 For You have been a stronghold for me,
 a refuge in my day of trouble.[p]

17 To You, my strength, I sing praises,
 because God is my stronghold—
 my faithful God.[q]

Psalm 60
Prayer in Difficult Times

For the choir director: according to
"The Lily of Testimony."[E] A Davidic *Miktam
for teaching. When he fought with
Aram-naharaim and Aram-zobah,
and Joab returned and struck Edom
in the Valley of Salt, killing 12,000.[r]

1 God, You have rejected us;
 You have broken out[F] against us;
 You have been angry. Restore us![G,s]
2 You have shaken the land
 and split it open.
 Heal its fissures, for it shudders.[t]

Cross references:
[a]59:5 Jr 18:23
[b]59:6 Ps 22:16
[c]59:7 Ps 52:2; 57:4; 64:3
[d]Ps 73:11
[e]59:8 Ps 2:4; 37:13
[f]59:9 Ps 28:8; Jr 16:19
[g]59:10 Ps 54:7
[h]59:11 Hs 9:17
[i]Gn 15:1; Dt 33:29; 2Sm 22:3,31; Ps 3:3; 5:12; 18:2; 28:7; 119:114
[j]59:12 Ps 10:7; Pr 12:13
[k]59:13 Ps 104:35
[l]Ps 83:18
[m]59:14 Ps 22:16
[n]59:15 Jb 15:23; Ps 109:10
[o]59:16 Ps 5:3; 88:13; 92:2
[p]Is 25:4; Nah 1:7
[q]59:17 Ps 28:8; Jr 16:19
[r]60:title 1Ch 18:3,12
[s]60:1 Ps 44:9,23; 79:5
[t]60:2 Ps 18:7

[A]59:7 Lit *swords are on*   [B]59:9 Some Hb mss, LXX, Vg, Tg; other Hb mss read *his*   [C]59:10 Alt Hb tradition reads *My God in His faithful love*   [D]59:13 Lit *know to the ends of*   [E]60:title Possibly a tune; Pss 45; 69; 80   [F]60:1 Lit *have burst through*   [G]60:1 Or *Turn back to us*

59:5 LORD God of Hosts is a military image that describes Yahweh as a warrior who fights for His people (see note at 24:7-10).

59:6-7 Dogs were not domesticated and had a negative connotation in the ancient Near East. They were viewed no differently than other wild and dangerous animals (see note at 22:20-21). **Prowling** is also characteristic of wild dogs foraging for food. Note the same image in verses 14-15. Spewing **from their mouths** perhaps pictures dogs slobbering or foaming at the mouth. **Sharp words** is a common description of vicious speech (see note at 52:2).

59:8 God's response to these wicked people was to **laugh at them** and **ridicule** them (see notes at 2:4 and 37:12-13).

59:9 Keep watch pictures the psalmist as a watchman, a common role for Israel's prophets (Is 21:11-12; Ezk 3:17; 33:2-9). The watchman warned people of foes, but also watched for the approach of friends (2Sm 18:27; Is 52:8).

59:11 Unlike other psalms that call for annihilation of the wicked, this psalm asks that Yahweh spare their lives so His **people** will not **forget**. This reinforces the image of the watchman in verse 9 since God's power and His punishment of them could no longer be used to warn people (Ex 9:16; 1Sm 17:46).

59:12 The request that the wicked **be caught in their pride** is reminiscent of enemies being caught in their own traps (see note at 7:14-16). The idea of pride (Gk *hubris*) as that which leads to one's demise became a common element in Greek tragedies of later centuries.

59:13 The wicked are often pictured as those who **consume** others (see note at 14:4). In a turn of poetic justice, Yahweh consumes them.

59:16 Praising Yahweh **in the morning** is common in the psalms (5:3; 30:5).

Ps 60 title The Lily of Testimony was perhaps a known song tune of the time (see note at Ps 22 title). On *Miktam*, see note at Psalm 16 title. The additional term **teaching** indicates that this psalm had the purpose of instruction, although it is not specifically a wisdom psalm according to its form. The historical setting is quite specific about an incident in David's life. This is found in 1Ch 18:3,12. As in other psalms with a specific setting (such as Ps 18), the language of the psalm is general enough to be applied in other contexts.

60:1 Rejected us indicates that this is a communal lament similar to Psalm 44.

60:2 The shaking of the **land** could refer to an actual earthquake, though it can also represent Yahweh's power. In this

³ You have made Your people
　　suffer hardship;
You have given us wine to drink
　　that made us stagger.ᵃ
⁴ You have given a signal flag to those
　　who •fear You,
so that they can flee
　　before the archers.ᴬ·ᵇ　　　　•Selah
⁵ Save with Your right hand,
　　and answer me,
so that those You love
　　may be rescued.ᶜ

⁶ God has spoken in His sanctuary:ᴮ
"I will triumph!
　　I will divide up Shechem.ᵈ
I will apportion the Valley of Succoth.ᵉ
⁷ Gilead is Mine, Manasseh is Mine,
and Ephraim is My helmet;ᶠ
Judah is My scepter.ᵍ
⁸ Moab is My washbasin.ʰ
I throw My sandal on Edom;ⁱ
I shout in triumph over Philistia."ʲ

⁹ Who will bring me to the fortified city?
Who will lead me to Edom?ᵏ
¹⁰ God, haven't You rejected us?
God, You do not march out
　　with our armies.ˡ
¹¹ Give us aid against the foe,
for human help is worthless.ᵐ
¹² With God we will perform valiantly;ⁿ
He will trample our foes.ᵒ

ᵃ60:3 Is 51:17-
23; Jr 25:15-17
ᵇ60:4 Is 5:26;
11:12; 13:2
ᶜ60:5 Ps 17:7;
20:6; 138:7
ᵈ60:6 Gn 12:6;
33:18
ᵉGn 33:17
ᶠ60:7 Dt 33:17;
Jos 13:31
ᵍGn 49:10
ʰ60:8 2Sm 8:2
ⁱ2Sm 8:14
ʲ2Sm 8:1
ᵏ60:9 Jr 1:18
ˡ60:10 Ps 44:9
ᵐ60:11 Ps 146:3
ⁿ60:12 Nm
24:18; Ps 44:5;
118:15-16
ᵒ60:5-12 Ps
108:6-13
ᵖ61:1 Ps 17:1;
88:2; 142:6
ᑫ61:2 Ps 88:4
ʳPs 27:5
ˢ61:3 Pr 18:10
ᵗ61:4 Ru 2:12;
Ps 17:8; 91:4
ᵘ61:5 Jb 22:27;
Ps 56:12
ᵛMal 4:2
ʷ61:6 Ps 21:4
ˣ61:7 Ps 41:12
ʸPs 40:11
ᶻ61:8 Ps 7:17;
9:2; 18:49
ᵃᵃPs 65:1;
116:14,18

Psalm 61
Security in God

For the choir director:
　on stringed instruments. Davidic.

¹ God, hear my cry;
　pay attention to my prayer.ᵖ
² I call to You from the ends
　　of the earth
when my heart is without strength.ᑫ
Lead me to a rock that is
　　high above me,ʳ
³ for You have been a refuge for me,
a strong towerˢ in the face
　　of the enemy.
⁴ I will live in Your tent forever
and take refuge under the shelter
　　of Your wings.ᵗ　　　　•Selah

⁵ God, You have heard my vows;ᵘ
You have given a heritage
　　to those who •fear Your name.ᵛ
⁶ Add days to the king's life;
may his years span
　　many generations.ʷ
⁷ May he sit enthroned
　　before God forever;ˣ
appoint faithful love and truth
　　to guard him.ʸ
⁸ Then I will continually sing
　　of Your name,ᶻ
fulfilling my vows day by day.ᵃᵃ

ᴬ60:4 Or *can rally before the archers*, or *can rally because of the truth*　　ᴮ60:6 Or *has promised by His holy nature*

case it is in the context of judgment on His people (see note
at 18:7-15).

60:3 Drinking **wine** that makes one **stagger** is an image related to God's judgment, usually represented by His "cup"
(Is 51:17,22).

60:4 A **signal flag** is probably the same as a "banner,"
which was used primarily in military campaigns (see note
at 20:5).

60:5 Yahweh's **right hand** refers to His power that was demonstrated in His actions against His enemies and on behalf
of His people (see note at 16:8).

60:6-8 The place names in these verses are probably used to
represent the whole territory of Canaan, which was owned
by Yahweh and given to His people (see note at 10:16-18).
Shechem was in the north (40 miles north of Jerusalem).
Succoth was east of the Jordan River near the Jabbok River. **Gilead** and **Manasseh** were both on the eastern side of
the Jordan, together extending from the south (the Arnon
River) to the extreme north (the hill country of **Ephraim**)...**Moab**...**Edom**, and **Philistia** were never a permanent part of Israel but represented the outer extremes
of Israel's territory to the east, south, and west, respectively. The **helmet** probably represents Ephraim's military
strength (Dt 33:17). **Judah** received God's **scepter**, which
was the right to rule over His kingdom (Gn 49:10).

60:10 Yahweh no longer seemed to fight for His people (see
note at 44:9; cp. 108:11).

60:11-12 Only **with God** did Israel have any hope to conquer
her enemies because **human** weaponry and armies without
God were **worthless** (see note at 20:7-8).

61:2-3 The verb translated **without strength** (Hb *'tp*) is used
with other subjects such as "spirit" to describe exhaustion
(77:3; 142:3; 143:4; Jnh 2:7). On **rock** and **refuge**, see notes
at 18:1-2 and 31:1-4.

61:4 Your tent seems to be used in a way similar to "house"
or "temple" as a figurative reference to Yahweh's presence.
Being in Yahweh's presence is the hope of all the faithful
(see note at 15:1). On **shelter of Your wings**, see notes at
17:8 and 27:5.

61:5 The **vows** here are most likely those made during a time
of petition. They were to be fulfilled by a thank offering (see
notes at 22:25-26 and 50:14-15). Note the same idea in 61:8.

61:6-7 The request of a long **life** for the king was sometimes used in the context of protection from harm, but in its
broader sense it meant the longevity of a dynasty (see note
at 21:4). The promise of being **enthroned...forever** and
having God's **faithful love** is closely related to the language
of the Davidic covenant (2Sm 7:13,15-16).

Psalm 62
Trust in God Alone

For the choir director:
according to Jeduthun.[a] A Davidic psalm.

1 I am at rest in God alone;
my salvation comes from Him.[b]
2 He alone is my rock and my salvation,[c]
my stronghold; I will never be shaken.[d]

3 How long will you threaten a man?
Will all of you attack[A]
as if he were a leaning wall
or a tottering stone fence?[e]
4 They only plan to bring him down
from his high position.
They take pleasure in lying;
they bless with their mouths,
but they curse inwardly.[f] *Selah*

5 Rest in God alone, my soul,
for my hope comes from Him.[g]
6 He alone is my rock and my salvation,[h]
my stronghold; I will not be shaken.[i]
7 My salvation and glory depend on God,
my strong rock.
My refuge is in God.[j]
8 Trust in Him at all times, you people;
pour out your hearts before Him.
God is our refuge.[k] *Selah*

9 *Men are only a vapor;
exalted men, an illusion.
Weighed in the scales, they go up;
together they are less than a vapor.[l]

10 Place no trust in oppression,
or false hope in robbery.
If wealth increases,
pay no attention to it.[B,m]
11 God has spoken once;
I have heard this twice:
strength belongs to God,[n]
12 and faithful love belongs to You, Lord.
For You repay each according to
his works.[o]

Psalm 63
Praise God Who Satisfies

A Davidic psalm. When he was
in the Wilderness of Judah.[p]

1 God, You are my God;
I eagerly seek You.
I thirst for You;
my body faints for You
in a land that is dry, desolate,
and without water.[q]
2 So I gaze on You in the sanctuary
to see Your strength and Your glory.[r]
3 My lips will glorify You
because Your faithful love is better
than life.[s]
4 So I will praise You as long as I live;
at Your name, I will lift up my hands.[t]
5 You satisfy me as with rich food;[C,u]
my mouth will praise You
with joyful lips.[v]

Cross references:
[a] 62:title Ps 39 title
[b] 62:1 Ps 33:20; 37:39
[c] 62:1-2 Dt 32:15; 2Sm 22:47
[d] 62:2 Ps 37:24; 55:22
[e] 62:3 Is 30:13
[f] 62:4 Ps 4:2; 55:21
[g] 62:5 Ps 71:5
[h] 62:6 Ps 89:26; 95:1
[i] Ps 16:8; 21:7
[j] 62:7 Ps 18:2
[k] 62:8 Ps 91:2; 118:8-9
[l] 62:9 Ps 39:5-6,11; Is 40:17
[m] 62:10 Jb 31:24-25; Mk 4:19; 1Tm 6:10,17-19
[n] 62:11 Jb 40:5
[o] 62:12 Mt 16:27; Rm 2:6; Rv 22:12
[p] 63:title 2Sm 16:14; 17:2,29
[q] 63:1 Ps 42:2; Is 26:9
[r] 63:2 Jb 19:26-27; Ps 17:15; 27:4
[s] 63:3 Ps 69:16
[t] 63:4 Ps 28:2; 143:6; Lm 3:41
[u] 63:5 Ps 36:8
[v] Ps 71:23

A62:3 Some Hb mss read *you be struck down*   B62:10 Lit *increases, do not set heart*   C63:5 Lit *with fat and fatness*

Ps 62 title On **Jeduthun**, see note at Psalm 39 title.

62:1 **Rest** (Hb *dumiyah*) expresses the idea of silence. In 22:2 it is used with a negative ("not silent") to describe the restlessness of actively praying for something. Here it most likely refers to rest in the sense of waiting on Yahweh and feeling secure that He will answer prayer and protect the psalmist. It appears as a command in 62:5.

62:2 On **rock** and other terms here and in verses 6-8, see notes at 18:1-2 and 31:1-4.

62:3 The enemies described here have the common characteristic of oppressing those who were weak or vulnerable, like a **leaning wall** and **tottering . . . fence.**

62:4 **High position** indicates that the person being attacked by these enemies was a person of some importance, perhaps a leader. It could refer to the king himself.

62:8 **Pour out your hearts** is an idiom for opening up to God with all one's requests (42:4; 102:1; 142:2). It is joined with the idea of **trust** to indicate that through prayer a person can rely on God to meet his needs.

62:9-10 **Vapor** (Hb *hevel*) represents lack of significance or the fleeting nature of life (see note at 39:4-6). It is parallel with **exalted men**, showing the contrast between human perception and reality. Since vapor literally refers to a small

puff of air, the idea of weighing it on **scales** is absurd. All who think of themselves as prominent weigh **less than a vapor.** Trusting in anything other than God is futile. The mention of **wealth** in this way is developed elsewhere (see notes at 49:6 and 49:10-12).

62:11 **Once . . . twice** is used for emphasis to show that something has been repeated and is therefore significant (Jb 33:14; 40:5). In this case it is a lesson to be learned.

62:12 **Repay** refers to retribution (see note at 28:3-5).

Ps 63 title The historical setting for this psalm has less detail than other psalms and could refer to David's flight from Saul or from Absalom (1Sm 23:14; 24:2; 2Sm 16:14; 17:2,29).

63:1 On the connection between drought conditions and longing for Yahweh, see note at 42:1-2.

63:2 **Gaze on You in the sanctuary** is probably not a theophany but is similar to the idiom "looking to God" for help in the sense of trusting Him (see note at 34:5).

63:4 Lifting up **hands** is a gesture for praying (see note at 28:2).

63:5 **Rich food** is a combination of two Hebrew words for "fat," implying being satisfied beyond one's need. Fat represents prosperity in the OT (73:7; Dt 32:15; Jr 5:28).

⁶ When I think of You as I lie on my bed,
I meditate on You
   during the night watches^a
⁷ because You are my helper;^b
I will rejoice in the shadow
   of Your wings.^c
⁸ I follow close to You;
Your right hand holds on to me.^d

⁹ But those who seek to destroy my life
will go into the depths of the earth.^e
¹⁰ They will be given over to the power
   of the sword;^f
they will become the jackals' prey.
¹¹ But the king will rejoice in God;^g
all who swear by Him^A will boast,
for the mouths of liars will be shut.^h

Psalm 64
Protection from Evildoers

For the choir director. A Davidic psalm.

¹ God, hear my voice when I complain.ⁱ
Protect my life from the terror
   of the enemy.^j
² Hide me from the scheming
   of wicked people,^k
from the mob of evildoers,^l
³ who sharpen their tongues like swords
and aim bitter words like arrows,^m
⁴ shooting from concealed places
   at the innocent.
They shoot at him suddenly
and are not afraid.ⁿ

⁵ They encourage each other
   in an evil plan;^{B,C}
they talk about hiding traps and say,
"Who will see them?"^{D,o}
⁶ They devise crimes and say,
"We have perfected a secret plan."^p
The inner man and the heart
   are mysterious.

⁷ But God will shoot them with arrows;
suddenly, they will be wounded.^q
⁸ They will be made to stumble;
their own tongues work against them.
All who see them will shake
   their heads.^r
⁹ Then everyone will fear
and will tell about God's work,
for they will understand
   what He has done.^s

¹⁰ The righteous one rejoices in the Lord
and takes refuge in Him;
all those who are upright in heart
will offer praise.^t

Psalm 65
God's Care for the Earth

For the choir director. A Davidic psalm. A song.

¹ Praise is rightfully Yours,^E
God, in •Zion;
vows to You will be fulfilled.^u
² All humanity will come to You,
the One who hears prayer.^v

Cross-references:

^a63:6 Ps 77:6; 119:148
^b63:7 Ps 27:9; 40:17
^cPs 17:8; 36:7; 57:1
^d63:8 Ps 18:35
^e63:9 Ps 55:15; Ezk 26:20; 31:14-18
^f63:10 Jr 18:21; Ezk 35:5
^g63:11 Ps 21:1
^hPs 107:42; Rm 3:19
ⁱ64:1 Ps 55:2
^jPs 140:1
^k64:2 Ps 35:20; 37:12
^lPs 22:16; 26:5
^m64:3 Ps 52:2; 57:4; Pr 25:18
ⁿ64:4 Ps 10:8; 11:2
^o64:5 Ps 35:7; 140:5; 141:9
^p64:6 Ps 21:11; 83:3
^q64:7 Ps 7:13; 45:5; 144:6
^r64:8 Jr 18:16; 48:27; Lm 2:15
^s64:9 Ps 40:3
^t64:10 Ps 32:11; 68:3; 97:11-12
^u65:1 Ps 50:14; 116:18
^v65:2 Ps 86:9; Is 2:2-4; 66:23

---

^A63:11 Or *him*   ^B64:5 Or *thing*; lit *word*   ^C64:5 Or *They hold fast to an evil purpose,* or *They establish for themselves an evil purpose*
^D64:5 Or *us,* or *it*   ^E65:1 Or *Praise is silence to You,* or *Praise awaits You*

63:6 On **meditate** (Hb *hgh*), see note at 1:2.

63:7 On **shadow of Your wings**, see notes at 17:8 and 27:5.

63:8 The **right hand** represented strength and the place from which Yahweh protected and helped His people (see note at 16:8).

63:9 The **depths of the earth** is another way of describing Sheol or death (86:13; Is 44:23; Ezk 26:20).

63:10 The first line is literally "they will be poured out on the hands of the sword," where "hands" refers to power. This is a more intensive way of expressing the idea of the psalmist's enemies receiving what was coming to them (Jr 18:21; Ezk 35:5).

63:11 **Swear by Him** is a way of saying that Yahweh is the only source of security. It is essentially another way of describing a person's trust in God. Yahweh's people are to boast only because they know Him (see notes at 34:2 and 52:1).

64:3 **Sharpen** is often used with **tongues** to describe destructive speech (55:21; 57:4; see note at 52:2).

64:4 **Shooting from concealed places** pictures the enemies hiding in ambush and waiting to strike without notice (10:8; 11:2). This was not open conflict but guerrilla warfare. **Not**

afraid is perhaps an abbreviated way to say "no dread of God" (36:1).

64:5 The enemies did not believe God was paying attention (see notes at 10:3-6 and 14:1).

64:6 The **heart** is **mysterious** in the sense that it is full of concealed wickedness, as revealed in actions (Pr 12:20; Jr 17:9).

64:7 God takes on the role of warrior (7:12), with the picture of Him shooting **arrows** at the psalmist's enemies, even while they were hiding and waiting to **shoot** the innocent (v. 4).

64:8 The phrase **tongues work against them** may be a reference to the enemies' provoking God through their destructive speech. Shaking the head was a gesture often associated with mocking (see note at 22:6-8).

64:9 One of the purposes in God's punishment of the wicked is to teach others (see note at 59:11).

65:1 **Vows** were often used in the context of prayer and were fulfilled with thank offerings (see notes at 22:25-26 and 50:14-15).

65:2 **All humanity** is literally "all flesh" and refers to the eschatological hope of mankind as a whole trusting in Yahweh

3 Iniquities overwhelm me;
only You can •atone for[A]
our rebellions.[a]

4 How happy is the one You choose
and bring near to live
in Your courts!
We will be satisfied with the goodness
of Your house,
the holiness of Your temple.[B,b]

5 You answer us in righteousness,
with awe-inspiring works,
God of our salvation,
the hope of all the ends of the earth
and of the distant seas.[c]

6 You establish the mountains
by Your[C] power,
robed with strength.[d]

7 You silence the roar of the seas,
the roar of their waves,
and the tumult of the nations.[e]

8 Those who live far away are awed
by Your signs;
You make east and west
shout for joy.[f]

9 You visit the earth
and water it abundantly,
enriching it greatly.
God's stream is filled with water,
for You prepare the earth[D]
in this way,
providing people with grain.[g]

10 You soften it with showers and bless
its growth,
soaking its furrows and leveling
its ridges.[h]

---

a 65:3 Ps 38:14; 40:12; 79:9
b 65:4 Ps 27:4; 84:4
c 65:5 Dt 10:21; 2Sm 7:23; Ps 46:8
d 65:6 Ps 93:1; Am 4:13
e 65:7 Ps 107:29; Is 17:13; Mt 8:26
f 65:8 Ps 2:8; 139:9; Is 24:16
g 65:9 Ps 104:13; 147:8; Is 45:8
h 65:10 Dt 3:22; Ps 72:6; 147:8
i 65:11 Ps 104:28; 147:14
j 65:12 Jb 38:26-27; Is 55:12; Jl 2:22
k 65:13 Ps 72:16; 144:13; Is 30:23
l Is 44:23
m 66:1 Ps 98:4; 100:1
n 66:1-2 1Ch 16:29; Ps 48:10
o 66:3 Ps 18:44; 47:2; 145:6
p 66:4 Ps 72:11; Is 66:23; Zph 2:11
q 66:5 Ps 46:8
r 66:6 Ex 14:21; Ps 106:9
s Ex 15:1-21
t 66:7 Ps 14:2; 33:13-14; Pr 15:3
u Ps 140:8

---

11 You crown the year
with Your goodness;
Your ways overflow with plenty.[E,i]

12 The wilderness pastures overflow,
and the hills are robed with joy.[j]

13 The pastures are clothed with flocks
and the valleys covered with grain.[k]
They shout in triumph; indeed,
they sing.[l]

Psalm 66
Praise for God's Mighty Acts

For the choir director. A song. A psalm.

1 Shout joyfully to God, all the earth![m]

2 Sing about the glory of His name;
make His praise glorious.[n]

3 Say to God, "How awe-inspiring
are Your works!
Your enemies will cringe before You
because of Your great strength.[o]

4 All the earth will worship You
and sing praise to You.
They will sing praise to Your name."[p]
•*Selah*

5 Come and see the wonders of God;[q]
His acts for •humanity
are awe-inspiring.

6 He turned the sea into dry land,
and they crossed the river on foot.[r]
There we rejoiced in Him.[s]

7 He rules forever by His might;
He keeps His eye on the nations.[t]
The rebellious should not
exalt themselves.[u]   *Selah*

[A]65:3 Or *can forgive,* or *can wipe out*   [B]65:4 Or *house, Your holy temple*   [C]65:6 Some LXX mss, Vg; MT reads *His*   [D]65:9 Lit *prepare it*   [E]65:11 Lit *ways drip with fat*

---

and coming to Him in **prayer** and worship (86:9; Is 2:2-4; see note at Ps 22:27-31).

65:3 The Hebrew word for **atone** (*kpr*) is difficult to define since its origin is uncertain. The two most likely options are "cover" and "cleanse." When sin is its object (as it is here), it is probably another way of describing forgiveness. On other expressions for forgiveness, see note at 32:1-2.

65:4 On **happy,** see note at 1:1. **In Your courts** is equivalent to **house** and **temple,** all of which represent being in Yahweh's presence. The **goodness** probably refers to spiritual refreshment that a person experiences in God's presence. This is often pictured as a feast (23:5; 36:8) and may refer to a sacrificial meal.

65:5-8 The language here is reminiscent of other texts where Yahweh demonstrates His power over **all . . . the earth** because all of it is His by right of creation (see note at 24:1-2). The connection between **roar of the seas** and **tumult of the nations** is significant since the nations are often represented by the restless and chaotic sea (see note at 2:1).

65:9-10 Visit (Hb *pqd*) describes God's grace and provision, especially in times of need ("paid attention" in Ru 1:6). Since

water is the sustainer of life, God's provision of water identifies Him as the source and sustainer of life.

65:11-13 Crown the year with Your goodness refers to a year "adorned" with blessings. The repetition of **overflow** symbolizes abundance of blessing. This also relates to the image of water flowing all over the land, not as a disastrous flood but as that which brings nourishment to everything.

66:1-4 All the earth signifies all mankind. Israel's praise of Yahweh has the purpose of leading everyone to praise Him (see note at 22:27-31).

66:5-6 One example of God's "works" (v. 3) is given here: Israel's crossing of the Red Sea when God delivered them from Egypt. These **acts** benefited **humanity;** Israel would be the conduit through which God would redeem the world.

66:7 Although God **rules** over the earth by right of creation, His saving acts toward Israel represented His intervention in history and demonstrated His sovereignty over the world. **His eye on the nations** means that He pays close attention to what is happening and that He can act at any time (see note at 33:13-15).

8 Praise our God, you peoples;
let the sound of His praise be heard.[a]
9 He keeps us alive[A]
and does not allow our feet to slip.[b]

10 For You, God, tested us;
You refined us as silver is refined.[c]
11 You lured us into a trap;
You placed burdens on our backs.[d]
12 You let men ride over our heads;
we went through fire and water,
but You brought us out to abundance.[B,e]

13 I will enter Your house
with •burnt offerings;
I will pay You my vows[f]
14 that my lips promised
and my mouth spoke
during my distress.[g]
15 I will offer You fattened sheep
as burnt offerings,
with the fragrant smoke of rams;
I will sacrifice oxen with goats.[h] *Selah*

16 Come and listen, all who •fear God,
and I will tell what He has done
for me.[i]
17 I cried out to Him with my mouth,

and praise was on my tongue.[j]
18 If I had been aware of malice
in my heart,
the Lord would not have listened.[k]
19 However, God has listened;
He has paid attention to the sound
of my prayer.[l]
20 May God be praised!
He has not turned away my prayer
or turned His faithful love from me.[m]

Psalm 67
All Will Praise God

For the choir director:
with stringed instruments. A psalm. A song.

1 May God be gracious to us and bless us;
look on us with favor[n] •*Selah*
2 so that Your way may be known
on earth,
Your salvation among all nations.[o]

3 Let the peoples praise You, God;
let all the peoples praise You.[p]
4 Let the nations rejoice and shout for joy,
for You judge the peoples with fairness
and lead the nations on earth.[q] *Selah*

Cross references:
[a] 66:8 Ps 98:4
[b] 66:9 Ps 94:18; 121:3
[c] 66:10 Jb 23:10; Ps 17:3; Is 48:10
[d] 66:11 Lm 1:13; Ezk 12:13; 17:20
[e] 66:12 Ps 18:19; Is 43:2
[f] 66:13 Ps 22:25; 116:14; Ec 5:4
[g] 66:14 Ps 18:6
[h] 66:15 Nm 6:14; Ps 51:19
[i] 66:16 Ps 9:1; 34:11; 71:15,24
[j] 66:17 Ps 35:28
[k] 66:18 Jb 36:21; Jn 9:31
[l] 66:19 Ps 116:1-2
[m] 66:20 Ps 22:24; 68:35
[n] 67:1 Nm 6:25; Ps 4:6; 80:3,7,19
[o] 67:2 Ps 98:2; Is 52:10; Ti 2:11
[p] 67:3 Ps 45:17; 66:4; 117:1
[q] 67:4 Ps 96:10,13; 100:1-2; Is 11:4

[A] 66:9 Lit He sets our soul in life [B] 66:12 Or a place of satisfaction

66:9 The image of **feet** not slipping off the path of righteousness is connected with remaining physically and spiritually **alive** (19:10-11; Dt 30:20; Pr 10:30).

66:10 Refining was a process for testing and purification. It can describe the testing of motives and integrity (26:2; Pr 17:3; 27:21). It often depicts a time of severe trials meant to purify God's people (Is 1:25; 48:10; Jr 9:7; Zch 13:9; Mal 3:2-3).

66:11 Lured us into a trap indicates that the people were unaware of what God was doing. If this is related to the time of Egyptian bondage, there is a possible link to Joseph's situation of being caught in a trap and sold into slavery. This event led Israel into Egypt, and later **burdens** were placed on their **backs**.

66:12 Men riding over the **heads** is a description of oppression. There is also perhaps an allusion to the chariots of Egypt. **Fire** and **water** are used elsewhere in the context of trials (Is 43:2), but they may also allude to God's pillar of fire and the water of the Red Sea. Since they are transitional from the burdens (Ps 66:11-12) to the blessings (v. 12), it is possible that there is a double meaning here.

66:13-15 These **offerings** represent the fulfillment of **vows** made during a time of prayer (see notes at 22:25-26 and 50:14-15). Considering the quantity being offered, it is possible that this represents others who were joining in as a result of God's answer to prayer. This reinforces the connection between God's work in the life of a person and His work in the community.

66:16 Public testimony and praise is a responsibility of those who have experienced answered prayer (see note at 22:22-24).

66:18-19 Awareness of **malice** means that a person is conscious of wrong motives. Hypocrisy is a barrier in one's relationship with God and is reflected in God's refusal to listen to prayer (Is 59:2-4). The fact that God did answer proves there was no hypocrisy.

67:1-2 God's acts on behalf of His people have the greater purpose of bringing others into fellowship with Him (see note at 30:9).

67:3-5 The **praise** of the nations accomplishes the goal of bringing the whole world into the recognition of Yahwe sovereignty (cp. "fear" in v. 7; see note at 22:27-31).

bachan

Hebrew Pronunciation	[bah KHAN]
HCSB Translation	test
Uses in Psalms	9
Uses in the OT	29
Focus Passage	Psalm 66:10

Bachan means *test* (Jr 9:7) or *put to the test* (Jb 7:18). One *assays* (Jr 6:27), *examines* (Ps 11:4), or *tries* (Ps 95:9). The intensive passive suggests something *is a trial* (Ezk 21:13). *Bachan* indicates spiritual *testing* twice with *nasah* ("test"; Ps 95:9) and five times with *tsaraph* ("refine, try"; Ps 17:3). *Tsaraph* usually retains its primary association with refining metals, *nasah* never describes testing metals, and *bachan* may be in between. *Bachan* has about seven clear associations with metal refining, and related *bachon* signifies an *assayer* of metals (Jr 6:27). *Bachan* connotes experiential *testing* (Jb 12:11), sometimes aimed at producing desired results (Jb 23:10). God is usually the subject of *bachan*, with the object often human hearts (1Ch 29:17) or minds (Jr 11:20). Several ancient translations render *bochan* as tested (Is 28:16), but some Dead Sea Scrolls saw a homonym meaning "fortress," indicating a large stone used in fortresses.

⁵ Let the peoples praise You, God,
  let all the peoples praise You.*ᵃ*

⁶ The earth has produced its harvest;
  God, our God, blesses us.*ᵇ*

⁷ God will bless us,
  and all the ends of the earth
    will •fear Him.*ᶜ*

Psalm 68

God's Majestic Power

For the choir director. A Davidic psalm. A song.

¹ God arises. His enemies scatter,
  and those who hate Him flee
    from His presence.*ᵈ*

² As smoke is blown away,
  so You blow them away.
  As wax melts before the fire,
  so the wicked are destroyed
    before God.*ᵉ*

³ But the righteous are glad;
  they rejoice before God and celebrate
    with joy.*ᶠ*

⁴ Sing to God! Sing praises to His name.
  Exalt Him who rides on the clouds*ᴬ* —
  His name is •Yahweh*ᴮ*—and rejoice
    before Him.*ᵍ*

⁵ God in His holy dwelling is
  a father of the fatherless
  and a champion of widows.*ʰ*

⁶ God provides homes for those
    who are deserted.
  He leads out the prisoners to prosperity,*ᶜ*
  but the rebellious live
    in a scorched land.*ⁱ*

ᵃ67:5 Ps 45:17; 66:8; 117:1
ᵇ67:6 Lv 26:4; Ps 85:12; Ezk 34:27; Hs 2:22
ᶜ67:7 1Kg 8:43; 2Ch 6:33; Ps 33:8
ᵈ68:1 Nm 10:35; Ps 7:6; Ezk 30:26
ᵉ68:2 Ps 37:20; Hs 13:3
ᶠ68:3 Ps 32:11; 40:16; 64:10
ᵍ68:4 Dt 33:26; Ps 7:17; 66:4; Is 19:1
ʰ68:5 Dt 24:17,19; Ps 146:9
ⁱ68:6 Ps 107:14; 113:9; 146:7
ʲ68:7-8 Ex 19:16-18; Jdg 5:4-5
ᵏ68:9 Lv 26:4; Ezk 34:26
ˡ68:10 Ps 74:19; 78:20; 107:9
ᵐ68:11 1Sm 18:6-7
ⁿ68:12 Jos 10:16; Jdg 5:30
ᵒ68:13 Gn 49:14; Jdg 5:16
ᵖ68:14 Jos 10:10; Jdg 9:48
ᵍ68:15 Ps 36:6
ʳ68:16 Ps 48:1-2; 132:13-14; Is 2:2-4

⁷ God, when You went out
    before Your people,
  when You marched through the desert,
                              •Selah

⁸ the earth trembled and the skies
    poured down rain
  before God, the God of Sinai,*ᴰ*
  before God, the God of Israel.*ʲ*

⁹ You, God, showered abundant rain;
  You revived Your inheritance
    when it languished.*ᵏ*

¹⁰ Your people settled in it;
  God, You provided for the poor
    by Your goodness.*ˡ*

¹¹ The Lord gave the command;
  a great company of women brought
    the good news:*ᵐ*

¹² "The kings of the armies flee—
    they flee!"
  She who stays at home divides the spoil.*ⁿ*

¹³ While*ᴱ* you lie among the sheepfolds,*ᶠ*
  the wings of a dove are covered
    with silver,
  and its feathers with glistening gold.*ᵒ*

¹⁴ When the •Almighty scattered kings
    in the land,
  it snowed on Zalmon.*ᴳ,ᵖ*

¹⁵ Mount Bashan is
    God's towering mountain;
  Mount Bashan is a mountain
    of many peaks.*ᵍ*

¹⁶ Why gaze with envy,
    you mountain peaks,
  at the mountain*ᴴ* God desired
    for His dwelling?
  The Lᴏʀᴅ will live there forever!*ʳ*

ᴬ68:4 Or *rides through the desert*   ᴮ68:4 Lit *Yah*   ᶜ68:6 Or *prisoners with joyous music*; Hb uncertain   ᴰ68:8 Lit *God, this Sinai*
ᴱ68:13 Or *If*   ᶠ68:13 Or *campfires, or saddlebags*; Hb obscure   ᴳ68:14 Or *Black Mountain*   ᴴ68:16 = Mount Zion

---

67:6 Harvest indicates the exact blessing that is the main point of this psalm. The blessing of one's crops was an outworking of God's covenant with His people as long as they were obedient to Him (Dt 28:4).

68:1-2 The image of Yahweh as a warrior who **scatters** the enemies of Israel is similar to Psalm 18. **Smoke** represents something insignificant that can easily be **blown away** (see note at 37:20). Melting **wax** recalls the image of Israel's enemies in the conquest of Canaan (Dt 20:8; Jos 2:11; 7:5).

68:4 Rides on the clouds overturns the common mythic imageries of Baal, the storm god of the Canaanites (19:1; 104:3; see note at 18:7-15).

68:5 Fatherless (see note at 10:12-15) and **widows** represented the weakest and most vulnerable members of society who were often the most oppressed (94:6). Yahweh Himself took on the role of their defender (Dt 10:18).

68:7-8 Went out before Your people perhaps alludes to the pillars of cloud and fire that led them in the desert (Ex 13:21) or to the ark of the covenant (Nm 10:35; Jos 3:14).

68:9 Rain is especially significant as that which allows crops to grow and feeds the people (see note at 65:9-10).

68:11-12 The **women** praise Yahweh for the spoils of war brought back by their husbands.

68:13 The image of a **dove** covered with **silver** and **gold** is especially difficult to interpret. Suggestions include prosperity, the glory of the Lord, plunder taken from enemies, and the women of verses 11-12 dressed in fine garments that were part of the plunder. Perhaps this last suggestion fits the context best, although it is uncertain.

68:14 Zalmon as a mountain is only mentioned one other place in the Bible (Jdg 9:48), but it is uncertain how snow relates to it here. It might be a reference to the **scattered kings** being tormented by bad weather from God.

68:15-16 Mount Bashan probably refers to the highest mountain in the region (Mount Hermon?). God's choice of the much smaller Zion made the higher mountains envious.

68:17 The repetition of **thousands** indicates that the armies under God's control cannot be counted (see note at 20:7-8).

¹⁷ God's chariots are tens of thousands,
  thousands and thousands;^a
 the Lord is among them
  in the sanctuary^A
 as He was at Sinai.^b
¹⁸ You ascended to the heights,
  taking away captives;
 You received gifts from^B people,
 even from the rebellious,
 so that the Lord God
  might live there.^{C,c}
¹⁹ May the Lord be praised!
 Day after day He bears our burdens;
 God is our salvation.^d   *Selah*
²⁰ Our God is a God of salvation,
 and escape from death belongs
  to the Lord God.^e
²¹ Surely God crushes the heads
  of His enemies,
 the hairy head of one who goes on
  in his •guilty acts.^f
²² The Lord said, "I will bring them back
  from Bashan;
 I will bring them back from the depths
  of the sea^g
²³ so that your foot may wade^D in blood
 and your dogs' tongues may have
  their share
 from the enemies."^h
²⁴ People have seen Your procession, God,
 the procession of my God,
 my King, in the sanctuary.^{A,i}
²⁵ Singers^E lead the way,
 with musicians following;

among them are young women
  playing tambourines.^j
²⁶ Praise God in the assemblies;
 praise the Lord from the fountain
  of Israel.^k
²⁷ There is Benjamin, the youngest,
  leading them,
 the rulers of Judah in their assembly,^F
 the rulers of Zebulun, the rulers
  of Naphtali.^l
²⁸ Your God has decreed your strength.
 Show Your strength, God,
 You who have acted on our behalf.^m
²⁹ Because of Your temple at Jerusalem,
 kings will bring tribute to You.ⁿ
³⁰ Rebuke the beast^G in the reeds,
 the herd of bulls with the calves
  of the peoples.^o
 Trample underfoot those with bars
  of silver.^H
 Scatter the peoples who take pleasure
  in war.^p
³¹ Ambassadors will come^I from Egypt;
 •Cush will stretch out its hands^J to God.^q
³² Sing to God, you kingdoms
  of the earth;
 sing praise to the Lord,^r   *Selah*
³³ to Him who rides in the ancient,
  highest heavens.^s
 Look, He thunders
  with His powerful voice!^t
³⁴ Ascribe power to God.
 His majesty is over Israel,
 His power among the clouds.^u

Cross references (center column):

^a68:17 Hab 3:8
^bDt 33:2
^c68:18 Dt 21:10; Ps 7:7; Eph 4:8
^d68:19 Ps 55:22; Is 46:3-4
^e68:20 Dt 32:39; Ps 49:15; 56:13
^f68:21 Ps 110:6; Hab 3:13
^g68:22 Nm 21:33; Am 9:1-4
^h68:23 1Kg 21:19; 22:38; Jr 15:3
ⁱ68:24 Ps 42:4; Is 60:11
^j68:25 Ex 15:20; Jdg 11:34; 1Sm 18:6
^k68:26 Ps 22:25; 26:12
^l68:27 Jdg 5:14,18; 1Sm 9:21
^m68:28 Ps 44:4; Is 26:12
ⁿ68:29 Ps 72:10; Is 18:7; Hg 2:7
^o68:30 Ps 22:12
^pPs 18:42; 89:10
^q68:31 Is 45:14; Zph 3:10
^r68:32 Ps 67:4; 102:22
^s68:33 Dt 33:26
^tPs 29:3-5; 46:6; Is 30:30
^u68:34 Ps 29:1; 150:1

---

^A68:17,24 Or *in holiness*   ^B68:18 Lit *among*   ^C68:18 Or *even those rebelling against the Lord God's living there*, or *even rebels are living with the Lord God*; Hb obscure   ^D68:23 LXX, Syr read *dip*   ^E68:25 Some Hb mss, LXX, Syr read *Officials*   ^F68:27 Hb obscure   ^G68:30 Probably Egypt   ^H68:30 Or *peoples, trampling on those who take pleasure in silver*, or *peoples, trampling on the bars of silver*, or *peoples, who trample each other for bars of silver*   ^I68:31 Or *They bring red cloth*, or *They bring bronze*   ^J68:31 Probably with tribute or in submission

---

68:21 Hairy head may refer to the ancient practice of wearing one's hair long as a symbol of power over others during a time of military campaigns. The biblical connections are the Nazirite vow (Nm 6:1-5) and the story of Samson (Jdg 13–16).

68:22-23 Bring them back is probably a reference to returning with enemies rather than the restoration of Israel, as some suggest. The enemies are brought to be executed (see note at 58:10).

68:24-26 This **procession** pictures the grand array of a king returning from battle. In this case it is Yahweh, the great King of Israel.

68:27 Benjamin, the **youngest** of Jacob's sons, is leading the procession. One interpretation is that this refers to Benjamin's dominion over the other tribes during Saul's reign, though it is difficult to say whether this psalm was written during that time. Another option is that Benjamin represents Jerusalem since it was technically in that tribe's territory. The southern kingdom was often called "Judah and Benjamin" (2Ch 11:1), and Zebulun and Naphtali might represent the north (1Ch 12:40). Perhaps the best option is that this procession mimics an earlier military campaign when Israel went to war against Sisera (Jdg 5:14).

68:29 Dominion over other peoples was often connected with the bringing of **tribute** to the dominant power. The dominion of God and His people over the other nations is part of the eschatological hope (see note at 22:27-31). Note also 68:31.

68:30 The beast in the reeds is perhaps a reference to Egypt (v. 31; Ezk 32:2), one of the greatest world powers of that time.

68:31 Stretching out **hands** is similar to spreading out one's hands in the context of worship (see note at 44:20), but in this case it probably pertains more to paying homage than to worshiping.

68:33-34 Rides in the . . . heavens along with the reference to **clouds** recalls the imagery of verse 4.

35 God, You are awe-inspiring
   in Your sanctuaries.
The God of Israel gives power
   and strength to His people.
May God be praised!ᵃ

Psalm 69

A Plea for Rescue

For the choir director: according to
"The Lilies."ᴬ Davidic.

1 Save me, God,
   for the water has risen to my neck.ᵇ
2 I have sunk in deep mud, and there is
      no footing;
   I have come into deep waters,
   and a flood sweeps over me.ᶜ
3 I am weary from my crying;
   my throat is parched.
   My eyes fail, looking for my God.ᵈ
4 Those who hate me without cause
   are more numerous than the hairs
      of my head;
   my deceitful enemies, who would
      destroy me,
   are powerful.ᵉ
   Though I did not steal, I must repay.ᶠ

5 God, You know my foolishness,
   and my •guilty acts are not hidden
      from You.ᵍ
6 Do not let those who put their hope
      in You
   be disgraced because of me,
   Lord Goᴅ of •Hosts;
   do not let those who seek You
   be humiliated because of me,
   God of Israel.ʰ

7 For I have endured insults
      because of You,
   and shame has covered my face.ⁱ
8 I have become a stranger
      to my brothers
   and a foreigner to my mother's sonsʲ
9 because zeal for Your house
      has consumed me,ᵏ
   and the insults of those who insult You
   have fallen on me.ˡ
10 I mourned and fasted,
   but it brought me insults.ᵐ
11 I wore •sackcloth as my clothing,
   and I was a joke to them.
12 Those who sit at the city •gate
      talk about me,
   and drunkards make up songs
      about me.ⁿ

13 But as for me, Lᴏʀᴅ,
   my prayer to You is for a time of favor.
   In Your abundant, faithful love, God,
   answer me with Your sure salvation.ᵒ
14 Rescue me from the miry mud;
      don't let me sink.
   Let me be rescued from those
      who hate me
   and from the deep waters.ᵖ
15 Don't let the floodwaters sweep over me
   or the deep swallow me up;
   don't let the •Pit close its mouth
      over me.ᵠ
16 Answer me, Lᴏʀᴅ,
   for Your faithful love is good;
   in keeping with
      Your great compassion,
   turn to me.ʳ

ᵃ68:35 Dt 10:21; Ps 29:11; Is 40:29 ᵇ69:1 Jb 22:11; Ps 32:6; Jnh 2:5 ᶜ69:2 Ps 40:2; 124:4; Jnh 2:3 ᵈ69:3 Ps 6:6; 38:10; 119:82,123 ᵉ69:4 Ps 38:19 ᶠLv 6:2-5; Ps 35:19; Jn 15:25 ᵍ69:5 Ps 38:5; 44:21 ʰ69:6 Ps 25:2-3 ⁱ69:7 Ps 44:15; Is 50:6; Jr 51:51 ʲ69:8 Jb 19:13-14; Ps 31:11; 38:11 ᵏ69:9 Jn 2:17 ˡPs 89:50; Rm 15:3 ᵐ69:10 Ps 35:13; 109:24-25 ⁿ69:11-12 Jb 17:6; 30:9; Ps 44:14; Jr 24:9 ᵒ69:13 Ps 109:4; Is 49:8; 2Co 6:2 ᵖ69:14 Ps 144:7 ᵠ69:15 Nm 16:33; Ps 55:23 ʳ69:16 Ps 25:16; 109:21

ᴬ69:title Possibly a tune; Pss 45; 60; 80

Ps 69 title On The Lilies, see note at Psalm 45 title.

69:1-2 The imagery of being trapped in a well and sinking in **mud** was a common way to describe life-threatening danger (see note at 40:2). A **flood** is also used to represent disaster (see notes at 18:4-5 and 32:6-7).

69:3 Physical exhaustion and suffering are often the result of psychological pain (see note at 6:2-3).

69:4 The righteous being outnumbered by the wicked seems to run counter to the plan of God (see note at 3:1-2).

69:5 This amounts to a confession of sin so that there is no hypocrisy (nothing **hidden**) that becomes a barrier in the psalmist's relationship with God (17:1; 26:1; see note at 66:18-19).

69:6-7 **Disgraced** and **humiliated because of me** refers not to the psalmist's sins, which were "not hidden" (v. 5), but to his **shame**. The point is that others might lose their faith in Yahweh if the suffering of this psalmist is not relieved. This is the converse of the principle that a person's rescue by the Lord leads to the faith of others being strengthened (see notes at 22:22-24 and 30:4-5).

69:8 **Stranger** refers to an outsider (see note at 54:3). Alienation by friends and family members was a common experience of those who were suffering (see note at 31:11).

69:9 It is unclear how the psalmist's **zeal** for God's **house** (the sanctuary or temple) was expressed. Some suggest it refers to the rebuilding of the temple in the postexilic period, but this is not clear. It probably refers to his intense desire to be in Yahweh's presence, especially in the context of worship (27:4; 63:1-2; see notes at 42:1-2 and 42:4). The **insults** that were intended for Yahweh had fallen on the psalmist because of his close connection to God. He was identified with Yahweh, and therefore those who were against Yahweh were also against him. This is similar to the fact that God's enemies and those of His people are the same (139:21). In the NT, both halves of this verse are applied to Jesus and His humiliation (Jn 2:17; Rm 15:3).

69:10-12 On **insults** and **joke** (Hb *mashal*), see note at 44:13-16. On **songs** see Jb 30:9 and Lm 3:13-14.

69:14-15 On the imagery in these verses, see note at verses 1-2. **The deep** and **the Pit** are parallel and represent death,

17 Don't hide Your face
from Your servant,
for I am in distress.
Answer me quickly![a]
18 Draw near to me and redeem me;
ransom me because of my enemies.[b]

19 You know the insults I endure—
my shame and disgrace.
You are aware of all my adversaries.[c]
20 Insults have broken my heart,
and I am in despair.
I waited for sympathy,
but there was none;
for comforters, but found no one.[d]
21 Instead, they gave me gall[A]
for my food,
and for my thirst
they gave me vinegar to drink.[e]

22 Let their table set before them be
a snare,
and let it be a trap for their allies.[f]
23 Let their eyes grow too dim to see,
and let their loins continually shake.[g]
24 Pour out Your rage on them,
and let Your burning anger
overtake them.[h]
25 Make their fortification desolate;
may no one live in their tents.[i]
26 For they persecute the one You struck
and talk about the pain of those
You wounded.[j]
27 Add guilt to their guilt;
do not let them share
in Your righteousness.[k]

28 Let them be erased from the book
of life
and not be recorded with the righteous.[l]

29 But as for me—poor and in pain—
let Your salvation protect me, God.[m]
30 I will praise God's name with song
and exalt Him with thanksgiving.[n]
31 That will please ·Yahweh more than
an ox,
more than a bull with horns
and hooves.[o]
32 The humble will see it and rejoice.
You who seek God, take heart![p]
33 For the LORD listens to the needy
and does not despise
His own who are prisoners.[q]

34 Let heaven and earth praise Him,
the seas and everything that moves
in them,[r]
35 for God will save ·Zion
and build up[B] the cities of Judah.
They will live there and possess it.[s]
36 The descendants of His servants
will inherit it,
and those who love His name will live
in it.[t]

Psalm 70
A Call for Deliverance

For the choir director. Davidic.
To bring remembrance.[u]

1 God, deliver me.
Hurry to help me, LORD![v]

[a] 69:17 Ps 27:9; 102:2 [b] 69:18 Ps 119:134 [c] 69:19 Jr 15:15 [d] 69:20 Ps 142:4; Is 63:5 [e] 69:21 Mt 27:34,48; Jn 19:29 [f] 69:22 Ps 35:4-8; Rm 11:9-10; 1Th 5:3 [g] 69:23 Is 6:10; Ezk 29:7; Dn 5:6 [h] 69:24 Ps 79:6; Ezk 21:31; Zph 3:8 [i] 69:25 Mt 23:38; Lk 13:35; Ac 1:20 [j] 69:26 2Ch 28:9; Is 53:4; Zch 1:15 [k] 69:27 Neh 4:5; Ps 109:14 [l] 69:28 Ex 32:32; Dn 12:1; Rv 3:5 [m] 69:29 Ps 20:1; 70:5 [n] 69:30 Ps 100:4; 107:22 [o] 69:31 Ps 50:13-14; 51:16 [p] 69:32 Ps 22:26; 34:2 [q] 69:33 Ps 12:5; 68:6; 146:7 [r] 69:34 Ps 96:11; Is 44:23; 49:13 [s] 69:35 Ps 147:2; Is 44:26 [t] 69:36 Ps 102:28; Is 65:9 [u] 70:title Ps 38 title [v] 70:1 Ps 38:22

[A] 69:21 A bitter substance [B] 69:35 Or *and rebuild*

which is personified as something that swallows its victims (see note at 28:1).

69:17 For God to **hide** His **face** implies rejection (see notes at 10:1-2 and 13:1-2).

69:20 The mention of **comforters** here is similar to Job's situation where his friends were unsympathetic (Jb 16:2).

69:21 **Gall** (essentially poison) and **vinegar** were by no means suitable for quenching **thirst**. These terms are used figuratively here, but in Jesus' suffering they were literal (Mt 27:34,48; Jn 19:28-29).

69:22 The **set . . . table** may refer to sacrificial meals rather than ordinary feasts. If that is the case, eating in Yahweh's presence with such "guilt" (v. 27) would be an affront to Him and a practice worthy of His wrath (vv. 23-25).

69:23-25 These requests are imprecations, calling down God's judgment on one's enemies (see note at 109:1-31). The request that their **tents** be made empty is a request that the enemies be annihilated.

69:26 The wicked were not willing to let Yahweh's discipline of the psalmist stand as correct and complete, but had added further insult and injury to it.

69:27 **Guilt** means liability for punishment (see note at 32:5). The psalmist's enemies were deserving of God's punishment.

69:28 The **book of life** should be distinguished from the book of remembrance with the prayers of those who suffer (see note at 56:8) and the book with a list of everyone's deeds (see note at 40:6-8). It is probably the book where the names of the righteous are listed (Ex 32:32; Dn 12:1; Rv 3:5; 13:8; 17:8; 20:12,15; 21:27).

69:30 This was most likely a vow made during petition that was fulfilled by a thank offering (see notes at 22:25-26 and 50:14-15).

69:31 God is more pleased with loving obedience than with sacrifice (see notes at 40:6-8 and 50:8-13). The **horns** indicate a **bull** in its prime, and the cloven **hooves** (Hb *prs*) designate a ceremonially acceptable animal.

69:32-33 On **humble** and **needy**, see notes at 34:6 and 35:10.

69:34-35 Creation is personified as a witness of God's workings with His people (see notes at 19:1 and 50:4). Here it voices its **praise** of God's saving work among His people.

Ps 70 title On **remembrance**, see note at Psalm 38 title.

70:1-5 See notes at 40:14-15 and 40:16-17; these verses are the same.

2 Let those who seek my life
be disgraced and confounded;
let those who wish me harm
be driven back and humiliated.
3 Let those who say, "Aha, aha!"
retreat because of their shame.[a]
4 Let all who seek You rejoice and be glad
in You;
let those who love Your salvation
continually say, "God is great!"[b]
5 I am afflicted and needy;
hurry to me, God.
You are my help and my deliverer;
LORD, do not delay.[c]

Psalm 71

God's Help in Old Age

1 LORD, I seek refuge in You;
let me never be disgraced.[d]
2 In Your justice, rescue and deliver me;
listen closely to me and save me.[e]
3 Be a rock of refuge for me,
where I can always go.
Give the command to save me,
for You are my rock and fortress.[f]
4 Deliver me, my God, from the power
of the wicked,
from the grasp of the unjust
and oppressive.[g]
5 For You are my hope, Lord GOD,
my confidence from my youth.[h]
6 I have leaned on You from birth;
You took me from my mother's womb.[i]
My praise is always about You.[j]
7 I have become an ominous sign
to many,
but You are my strong refuge.[k]
8 My mouth is full of praise
and honor to You all day long.[l]
9 Don't discard me in my old age;
as my strength fails,
do not abandon me.[m]
10 For my enemies talk about me,
and those who spy on me
plot together,[n]
11 saying, "God has abandoned him;
chase him and catch him,
for there is no one to rescue him."[o]
12 God, do not be far from me;
my God, hurry to help me.[p]
13 May my adversaries be disgraced
and destroyed;
may those who seek my harm
be covered with disgrace
and humiliation.[q]
14 But I will hope continually
and will praise You more and more.[r]
15 My mouth will tell
about Your righteousness
and Your salvation all day long,
though I cannot sum them up.[s]
16 I come because of the mighty acts
of the Lord GOD;
I will proclaim Your righteousness,
Yours alone.[t]

17 God, You have taught me
from my youth,
and I still proclaim
Your wonderful works.[u]
18 Even when I am old and gray,
God, do not abandon me.[v]
Then I will[A] proclaim Your power
to another generation,
Your strength to all who are to come.[w]
19 Your righteousness
reaches heaven, God,
You who have done great things;
God, who is like You?[x]
20 You caused me to experience

[a]70:2-3 Ps 35:25; 40:14-15
[b]70:4 Ps 35:27; 77:13
[c]70:5 Ps 40:17; 141:1
[d]71:1 Ps 25:20
[e]71:2 Ps 17:6
[f]71:1-3 Ps 31:1-3
[g]71:4 Ps 140:1,4
[h]71:5 Ps 39:7; Jr 17:13
[i]71:6 Ps 22:9-10
[j]Ps 34:1
[k]71:7 Ps 61:3; 62:7; 91:2,9
[l]71:8 Ps 35:28; 63:5
[m]71:9 Ps 27:9; 71:18; Is 46:3-4
[n]71:10 Ps 31:13; 56:6; 83:3
[o]71:11 Ps 3:2
[p]71:12 Ps 22:19; 38:21-22; 40:13
[q]71:13 Ps 71:24
[r]71:14 Ps 84:4; 130:7; 147:11
[s]71:15 Ps 35:28; 40:5; 96:2
[t]71:16 Ps 51:14; 106:2
[u]71:17 Dt 4:5; 6:7
[v]71:18 Is 46:4
[w]Ps 22:30-31; 78:4,6
[x]71:19 Ex 15:11; Dt 3:24; Ps 86:8

[A]71:18 Lit *me until I*

71:3 Rock . . . refuge, and **fortress** convey the idea of Yahweh's protection (see notes at 18:1-2 and 31:1-4).

71:5-6 The combination of **youth . . . birth**, and **mother's womb** shows that the psalmist had been loyal to Yahweh throughout his life. For **always**, note also verses 8 and 14.

71:7 Ominous sign (Hb *mopheth*) can refer to an extraordinary display of divine power to terrify enemies (Ex 7:3; 11:9; Dt 6:22) or an extraordinary sign that points to a future event (1Kg 13:3,5; Is 20:3). Here, the psalmist apparently displays evidence of suffering that **many** observers consider some kind of warning. It is similar to "I am dreaded" in 31:11.

71:9 Discard (Hb *shlk*) is a common word for "throw" or "cast." In this context it refers to God abandoning the psalmist (51:11), perhaps because of his loss of **strength**. Note also verse 12.

71:10-11 The psalmist's **enemies** assumed that God was no longer paying attention to him (Jb 19:13-21). **No one to rescue him** recalls similar texts that use the image of wild animals devouring their prey (7:2; 50:22).

71:13 On prayer for the disgrace of enemies, see notes at 35:26 and 40:14-15.

71:15-16 Righteousness and **salvation** are often paired in testimonies of God's **mighty acts** toward His people (40:10; 51:14). Public praise is the responsibility of a person who experiences deliverance by Yahweh (see note at 22:22-24).

71:17-18 The instruction of Yahweh in the psalmist's life is passed on to other generations. This was part of his vow to the Lord for delivering him from suffering.

71:19 Reaches heaven means "beyond comprehension" (36:5; 57:10)

71:20 On **depths of the earth**, see note at 63:9. The psalmist was brought up from the very edge of death.

many troubles and misfortunes,[a]
but You will revive me again.[b]
You will bring me up again,
even from the depths of the earth.[c]

21 You will increase my honor
and comfort me once again.[d]

22 Therefore, I will praise You
with a harp
for Your faithfulness, my God;
I will sing to You with a lyre,
Holy One of Israel.[e]

23 My lips will shout for joy
when I sing praise to You
because You have redeemed me.[f]

24 Therefore, my tongue will proclaim
Your righteousness all day long,
for those who seek my harm
will be disgraced and confounded.[g]

Psalm 72

A Prayer for the King

Solomonic.[h]

1 God, give Your justice to the king
and Your righteousness
to the king's son.[i]

2 He will judge Your people
with righteousness
and Your afflicted ones with justice.[j]

3 May the mountains bring prosperity[A]
to the people
and the hills, righteousness.[k]

4 May he vindicate the afflicted
among the people,
help the poor,
and crush the oppressor.[l]

5 May he continue[B] while the
sun endures

and as long as the moon,
throughout all generations.[m]

6 May he be like rain that falls
on the cut grass,
like spring showers that water the earth.[n]

7 May the righteous[C] flourish in his days
and prosperity[A] abound
until the moon is no more.[o]

8 May he rule from sea to sea
and from the Euphrates
to the ends of the earth.[p]

9 May desert tribes kneel before him
and his enemies lick the dust.[q]

10 May the kings of Tarshish
and the coasts and islands
bring tribute,
the kings of Sheba and Seba offer gifts.[r]

11 Let all kings bow down to him,
all nations serve him.[s]

12 For he will rescue the poor who cry out
and the afflicted who have no helper.[t]

13 He will have pity on the poor
and helpless
and save the lives of the poor.[u]

14 He will redeem them from oppression
and violence,
for their lives are[D] precious[E]
in his sight.[v]

15 May he live long!
May gold from Sheba be given to him.
May prayer be offered
for him continually,
and may he be blessed all day long.[w]

16 May there be plenty of grain in the land;
may it wave on the tops
of the mountains.
May its crops be like Lebanon.

Cross-references (center column):

[a] 71:20 Ps 60:3
[b] Ps 85:6
[c] Hs 6:1-2
[d] 71:21 Ps 86:17; Is 12:1; 49:13
[e] 71:22 Ps 33:2; 81:2; 92:1-3
[f] 71:23 Ps 34:22; 55:18
[g] 71:24 Ps 35:28; 71:13
[h] 72:title Ps 127 title
[i] 72:1 1Kg 3:9; 1Ch 22:12-13; Ps 24:5
[j] 72:2 Is 9:7; 11:2-5; 32:1
[k] 72:3 Is 11:9; 52:7; 55:12
[l] 72:4 Ps 109:31; Is 11:4
[m] 72:5 Ps 89:36-37
[n] 72:6 Dt 32:2; 2Sm 23:3-4; Hs 6:3
[o] 72:7 Ps 37:11; Is 2:4; 60:21
[p] 72:8 Gn 15:18; Ex 23:31; Zch 9:10
[q] 72:9 Ps 22:29; Is 49:23; Mc 7:17
[r] 72:10 1Kg 10:22; 2Ch 9:21; Is 60:6
[s] 72:11 Ps 86:9; 138:4; Is 49:23
[t] 72:12 Jb 29:12-17
[u] 72:13 Pr 19:17; 28:8
[v] 72:14 Ps 69:18; 116:15
[w] 72:15 Is 60:6

A 72:3,7 Or *peace*   B 72:5 LXX; MT reads *May they fear you*   C 72:7 Some Hb mss, LXX, Syr, Jer read *May righteousness*   D 72:14 Lit *their blood is*   E 72:14 Or *valuable*

71:22 Holy One of Israel is a favorite title for Yahweh in the book of Isaiah. Here it links the psalmist who is suffering with the nation of Israel and with Yahweh's covenant promises.

Ps 72 title Solomonic probably functions similarly to "Davidic" (Ps 127; see note at Ps 5 title). It could mean "authored by," "written for," or "in the style of."

72:1-4 Justice and **righteousness** are the dominant terms in these verses. They refer to the king's role of dispensing God's justice. The king of Israel was to function as Yahweh's royal representative and co-regent over His kingdom (see note at 45:6). When the king and the people were obedient, Yahweh would bring **prosperity** to the land (v. 16).

72:5 Continue may refer to a long reign or to a long dynasty, similar to the request that the king have a long life (see note at 21:4).

72:6-7 Rain symbolizes blessing (68:9; see note at 65:9-10)

and is used here to request that the king's reign be blessed with **prosperity**.

72:8-11 This is a list of far distant places. **Tarshish** represents Phoenicia and **Sheba** represents Arabia. **Seba** could be somewhere in Africa; Josephus identified it with Ethiopia. The summary statement in verse 11 makes the point that these places represent **all kings** and **all nations**. On the dominion of Israel over all nations, see notes at 22:27-31 and 68:29.

72:12-14 The **poor . . . helpless**, and **afflicted** are the downtrodden in society. If a king rendered justice to the poor, his reign would be particularly blessed (Pr 29:14).

72:15 On the prayer for the king to **live long**, see note at 21:4.

72:16 These blessings recall those promised to Israel in God's covenant (Dt 28:2-14).

May people flourish in the cities
like the grass of the field.[a]
17 May his name endure forever;
as long as the sun shines,
may his fame increase.
May all nations be blessed by him
and call him blessed.[b]

18 May the LORD God, the God of Israel,
who alone does wonders, be praised.[c]
19 May His glorious name
be praised forever;
the whole earth is filled with His glory.[d]
•Amen and amen.
20 The prayers of David son of Jesse
are concluded.[e]

BOOK III
(Psalms 73–89)

Psalm 73
God's Ways Vindicated

A psalm of •Asaph.[f]

1 God is indeed good to Israel,
to the pure in heart.[g]
2 But as for me, my feet almost slipped;
my steps nearly went astray.[h]
3 For I envied the arrogant;
I saw the prosperity of the wicked.[i]
4 They have an easy time until they die,[A]
and their bodies are well fed.[B,j]
5 They are not in trouble like others;
they are not afflicted like most people.[k]
6 Therefore, pride is their necklace,
and violence covers them
like a garment.[l]
7 Their eyes bulge out from fatness;
the imaginations of their hearts
run wild.[m]
8 They mock,
and they speak maliciously;
they arrogantly threaten oppression.[n]
9 They set their mouths against heaven,
and their tongues strut
across the earth.[o]
10 Therefore His people turn to them[C]
and drink in their
overflowing words.[D,p]
11 The wicked say, "How can God know?
Does the •Most High know everything?"[q]
12 Look at them—the wicked!
They are always at ease,
and they increase their wealth.[r]

13 Did I purify my heart
and wash my hands in innocence
for nothing?[s]
14 For I am afflicted all day long
and punished every morning.[t]

[a]72:16 Jb 5:25; Ps 104:16 [b]72:17 Gn 12:2-3; 22:18; Ps 89:36 [c]72:18 Jb 9:10; Ps 86:10; 136:4 [d]72:19 Nm 14:21; Is 6:3 [e]72:20 2Sm 23:1 [f]73:title 1Ch 16:5,7 [g]73:1 Ps 24:4; 51:10; Mt 5:8 [h]73:2 Ps 17:5; 66:9; 94:18 [i]73:3 Ps 37:1; Pr 23:17; 24:1 [j]73:4 Jb 21:23-24 [k]73:5 Jb 21:4 [l]73:6 Ps 37:35; Pr 16:29; 21:24 [m]73:7 Jb 15:27; Jr 5:28 [n]73:8 Ps 17:10; 2Pt 2:18; Jd 16 [o]73:9 Rv 13:6 [p]73:10 Jb 15:16 [q]73:11 Jb 22:13; Ps 10:4,11; Is 29:15 [r]73:12 Ps 49:6; 52:7; Jr 49:31 [s]73:13 Ps 26:6; Mt 27:24 [t]73:14 Jb 33:19; Ps 38:6; 118:18

[A]73:4 Lit *For there are no pangs to their death* [B]73:4 Lit *fat* [C]73:10 Lit *turn here* [D]73:10 Lit *and waters of fullness are drained by them*

72:17-19 Name represents reputation and fame (see note at 20:1). It is significant that the name of the king and the name of Yahweh are intertwined in praise. **Amen and amen** probably form the end of a doxology used to close Book 2 of the Psalms (see note at 41:13).

72:20 These comments were probably added as part of the close of Book 2. This is similar in form to Jb 31:40 where "The words of Job are concluded." As in the case of Job, this does not mean that everything preceding the comment was from David. It seems to separate the previous psalms from the grouping of Asaph's psalms beginning with Psalm 73.

Ps 73 title On **Asaph**, see note at Psalm 50 title.

73:1 Indeed represents a certainty that the statement is true.

73:2 Feet almost slipped refers to slipping off the path of following Yahweh. This is the same as the path of life or righteousness (66:9; see note at 19:10-11). In this case "almost slipping" means almost losing faith in God.

73:3 Being envious of the **prosperity** of the wicked occurs elsewhere in the psalms. This is a common temptation when God's justice on the wicked is delayed (see note at 37:1).

73:4 Easy time and **well fed** refer to prosperity (v. 3). "Well fed" is literally "fat bellies," evidence of having more than a person needs (see notes at 17:10-12 and 63:5).

73:5 Like most people is an assessment from observation. From the psalmist's own experience, the degree of wickedness and prosperity seem to go together.

73:6 A **necklace** signified status and prominence (Dn 5:29); the wicked wore their **pride** as a status symbol. They also did not bother to hide their malicious **violence**.

73:7 Eyes and **imaginations** are parallel, representing the desires of the wicked in what they saw and thought. "Imagination" (Hb *maskiyyoth*) is also used of idols (Nm 33:52; Ezk 8:12). It has the connotation of "idols of the heart."

73:9 Heaven is a substitute for God Himself, so the mocking of the wicked is against God. The image of tongues strutting **across the earth** further emphasizes their brash arrogance.

73:10 His people could refer to those who were connected with these wicked people, but the shift from plural to singular is awkward. If "heaven" in verse 9 represents God, then it is the nearest singular antecedent. In this case the speech of the wicked even leads God's people astray, something this psalmist would not do with his words (v. 15).

73:11 It was a common belief among the wicked that God did not pay attention to them and would not punish them (Is 29:15; see notes at Ps 10:11 and 14:1). In fact, God does know everything (44:21; 139:1-12; Dn 2:2; Hs 7:2; Heb 4:13; 1Jn 3:20).

73:12 Always at ease means that the wicked did not seem to experience problems (v. 4).

73:13 Washing **hands** was part of an oath of **innocence** (see note at 26:6-7).

73:14 The psalmist's affliction was in stark contrast to the wicked's being "at ease" (v. 12).

¹⁵ If I had decided to say
    these things aloud,
I would have betrayed Your people.^{A,a}
¹⁶ When I tried to understand all this,
    it seemed hopeless^{B,b}
¹⁷ until I entered God's sanctuary.
    Then I understood their destiny.^c
¹⁸ Indeed, You put them in slippery places;
    You make them fall into ruin.^d
¹⁹ How suddenly they become
    a desolation!
    They come to an end, swept away
    by terrors.^e
²⁰ Like one waking from a dream,
    Lord, when arising, You will despise
    their image.^f
²¹ When I became embittered
    and my innermost being^C was wounded,^g
²² I was stupid and didn't understand;
    I was an unthinking animal
    toward You.^h
²³ Yet I am always with You;
    You hold my right hand.ⁱ
²⁴ You guide me with Your counsel,
    and afterward You will take me up
    in glory.^{D,j}
²⁵ Who do I have in heaven but You?

And I desire nothing on earth but You.^k
²⁶ My flesh and my heart may fail,
    but God is the strength^E of my heart,
    my portion forever.^l
²⁷ Those far from You will certainly perish;
    You destroy all who are
    unfaithful to You.^m
²⁸ But as for me, God's presence is
    my good.
    I have made the Lord God my refuge,
    so I can tell about all You do.ⁿ

Psalm 74

Prayer for Israel

A *Maskil* of *Asaph.*^o

¹ Why have You rejected us forever, God?
    Why does Your anger burn
    against the sheep of Your pasture?^p
² Remember Your congregation,
    which You purchased long ago
    and redeemed as the tribe
    for Your own possession.^q
    Remember Mount *Zion
    where You dwell.^r
³ Make Your way^F
    to the everlasting ruins,

Cross references:
^a73:15 Ps 44:17; 89:33
^b73:16 Ec 8:17
^c73:17 Jb 8:13; Ps 37:38
^d73:18 Ps 35:6,8
^e73:19 Nm 16:21; Jb 18:11; Is 47:11
^f73:20 Ps 35:23; 59:5; 78:65
^g73:21 Ps 109:22
^h73:22 Jb 11:12; Ps 92:6
ⁱ73:23 Ps 63:8
^j73:24 Ps 49:15; Is 58:11
^k73:25 Ps 16:2; Php 3:8
^l73:26 Ps 16:5; 38:10; 84:2
^m73:27 1Ch 5:25; Ps 37:20
ⁿ73:28 Ps 40:5; 118:17
^o74:title 1Ch 16:5,7
^p74:1 Ex 32:11; Ps 60:1,10; 108:11
^q74:2 Is 63:17; Jr 10:16; 51:19
^rIs 8:18

---

^A73:15 Lit *betrayed the generation of Your sons*   ^B73:16 Lit *it was trouble in my eyes*   ^C73:21 Lit *my kidneys*   ^D73:24 Or *will receive me with honor*   ^E73:26 Lit *rock*   ^F74:3 Lit *Lift up Your steps*

73:15 In addition to the normal word for **say** (Hb *'mr*), there is another word (Hb *spr*) meaning "recount" in the sense of something more developed. This is not just stating a fact but developing a story, which was obviously the psalmist's temptation. His "betrayal" would have been to undermine the faith of others.

73:16 Hopeless (Hb *'ml*) is the same word as that in verse 5 translated "trouble." The wicked did not have trouble, but the psalmist's attempts to **understand** this phenomenon gave him nothing but trouble.

73:17 The phrase **until I entered . . . then I understood** has caused much speculation by scholars. Exactly what happened in the **sanctuary**? Suggestions include: the psalmist received an oracle from God, witnessed a theophany, or engaged in ritual acts. It is perhaps best to leave it unanswered and realize the main issue is that Yahweh's presence in the sanctuary enlightened the psalmist. This is what became the psalmist's hope later in verse 28 and seems to be reflective of the principle that nearness to Yahweh (close fellowship with Him) provides a change of perspective.

73:18 There is a contrast with the psalmist's feet "almost slipping" in verse 2 and the **slippery places** of the wicked.

73:19 Suddenly shows that, despite appearances, God's judgment on the wicked is sure and swift (see notes at 37:10 and 37:36).

73:20 The phrase **waking from a dream** could refer to the psalmist's own state before his change of perspective, but it probably refers to God's waking (**arising**, meaning "to act"; see notes at 7:6 and 35:23). The dream is equivalent to **image** and emphasizes as in verse 19 that the swift destruc-

tion of the wicked will make their former prosperity seem like a dream.

73:21-22 The psalmist's bitterness apparently blinded him and made him **stupid** like an **animal** (92:6).

73:23 Holding someone's **right hand** is used in some contexts to refer to honor (Is 45:1). Here it refers to protection (Ps 63:8; Is 41:10,13; 42:6; Jr 31:32).

73:24 Some argue that **take me up in glory** refers to being honored (similar to the image of the "right hand" in v. 23). However, there is no good reason to doubt that this could refer to life after death. The OT does not develop a thorough or consistent concept of life after death, but the afterlife could have been a belief in Israel, as it was among the other nations (Gn 5:24).

73:26 Flesh and **heart** probably refers to earthly existence, and they reinforce the idea of life after death from verse 24. A **portion** is another way of describing a person's inheritance (see note at 16:5-6).

73:28 The **presence** of Yahweh is the ultimate hope of those who trust Him (15:1; 21:6-7).

Ps 74 title On **Asaph**, see note at Psalm 50 title.

74:1 Sheep of Your pasture depicts Yahweh as the shepherd of Israel (100:3; see note at 23:1).

74:2 On **remember**, see note at 25:6-7. **Purchased** and **possession** denote Yahweh's ownership of Israel (see note at 28:8-9).

74:3 Everlasting ruins is used elsewhere to describe the annihilation of an enemy (9:6).

to all that the enemy has destroyed
in the sanctuary.[a]
4 Your adversaries roared
in the meeting place
where You met with us.[A]
They set up their emblems as signs.[b]
5 It was like men in a thicket of trees,
wielding axes,[c]
6 then smashing all the carvings
with hatchets and picks.[d]
7 They set Your sanctuary on fire;
they utterly[B] desecrated
the dwelling place of Your name.[e]
8 They said in their hearts,
"Let us oppress them relentlessly."
They burned down every place
throughout the land
where God met with us.[C,f]
9 There are no signs for us to see.
There is no longer a prophet.
And none of us knows how long
this will last.[g]
10 God, how long will the enemy mock?
Will the foe insult Your name forever?[h]
11 Why do You hold back Your hand?
Stretch out[D] Your right hand
and destroy them![i]
12 God my King is from ancient times,
performing saving acts on the earth.[j]
13 You divided the sea with Your strength;
You smashed the heads
of the sea monsters
in the waters;[k]
14 You crushed the heads of •Leviathan;
You fed him to the creatures
of the desert.[l]
15 You opened up springs and streams;[m]
You dried up ever-flowing rivers.[n]
16 The day is Yours, also the night;
You established the moon and the sun.[o]
17 You set all the boundaries of the earth;
You made summer and winter.[p]
18 Remember this: the enemy
has mocked •Yahweh,
and a foolish people has insulted
Your name.[q]
19 Do not give the life of Your dove
to beasts;[E]
do not forget the lives
of Your poor people forever.[r]
20 Consider the covenant,[s]
for the dark places of the land
are full of violence.[t]

[a]74:3 Ps 79:1; Is 61:4 [b]74:4 Nm 2:2; Lm 2:6-7 [c]74:5 Jr 46:22 [d]74:6 Lm 2:2 [e]74:7 2Kg 25:9; Ps 79:1 [f]74:8 Ps 83:4 [g]74:9 1Sm 3:1; Lm 2:9; Ezk 7:26 [h]74:10 Ps 79:12; 89:51 [i]74:11 Ps 59:13; Lm 2:3 [j]74:12 Ps 47:6-8; 95:3; Jr 10:10 [k]74:13 Ex 14:21; Is 51:9; Ezk 32:2 [l]74:14 Jb 41:1; Ps 104:26; Is 27:1 [m]74:15 Ps 104:10-11 [n]Is 42:15; 44:27 [o]74:16 Gn 1:14-18; Ps 104:19 [p]74:17 Gn 8:22; Jb 38:10-11; Pr 8:29; Jr 5:22 [q]74:18 Ps 14:1; 53:1; 89:51 [r]74:19 Ps 9:18; 68:10 [s]74:20 Dt 4:31; Ps 106:45 [t]Ezk 7:23

[A]74:4 Lit *in Your meeting place* [B]74:7 Lit *they to the ground* [C]74:8 Lit *every meeting place of God in the land* [D]74:11 Lit *From Your bosom* [E]74:19 One Hb ms, LXX, Syr read *Do not hand over to beasts a soul that praises You*

74:4 **Roared** depicts enemies as wild animals who have entered the sanctuary (22:13). **Emblems** are likely related to banners that were used in military campaigns to identify the armies (see note at 20:5).

74:5-6 The **men** with **axes** portrays highly energized destructive activity without thought or concern.

74:7 The **dwelling place of Your name** refers to the promise that Yahweh made to Israel about His presence among them (Dt 12:11). "Name" is sometimes used for Yahweh and often represents His presence among His people (see note at 20:1).

74:8 The allusion to multiple meeting places in **the land** probably does not refer to high places, which had been abolished by Josiah. Rather it probably includes the various locations in history where the sanctuary had been located—such as Shiloh (Jos 18:1; 1Sm 1:3), Mizpah (Jdg 20:1), Bethel (Gn 12:8; 1Sm 7:16), Gilgal (1Sm 10:8), and now Jerusalem.

74:9 **Signs** is parallel with **prophet**. It indicates that Yahweh was no longer speaking to His people—an indication of abandonment. The signs the people were apparently looking for were those that would answer their "why" (vv. 1,11) and "how long" (v. 10) questions.

74:10 **How long** emphasizes God's delay in intervening (see note at 13:1-2). Enemies are often depicted as mocking and insulting those whom they oppress, who in this case was the nation of Israel (44:13-14).

74:11 The **right hand** was the place of Yahweh's power (see note at 16:8).

74:12 God's authority was demonstrated by His **saving acts** toward His people (see note at 66:7).

74:13 **Sea monsters** (Hb *tanninim*) is used elsewhere for serpents (91:13; Ex 7:10,12; Dt 32:33). It is parallel to "sea" in Jb 7:12 and to "Rahab" in Is 51:9. It probably refers to the great creatures of the sea that were untamable, but there could also be some connection to Canaanite beliefs. Baal was supposed to have defeated the seas, represented by seven-headed sea monsters, but in response to that mythology, Yahweh is depicted as the One who defeats these creatures by His power.

74:14 **Leviathan** also appears in other biblical texts (104:26; Jb 3:8; 41; Is 27:1). He represents the most fierce and powerful sea creature. Whether this creature can be linked to a specific animal in the known world is uncertain, although suggestions range from a crocodile to a dinosaur. There certainly is a connection in Canaanite mythology that links this creature with chaos. Therefore, God defeated chaos and **fed him to the creatures of the desert**, which could mean wild beasts.

74:15 Drying up **ever-flowing rivers** could be a reference to God's saving acts at the Red Sea (Ex 14:21-22) or the Jordan River (Jos 3:15-17), the latter of which makes more sense for a river. Some have also suggested mythological imagery here, since Baal was supposed to have defeated the rivers by drying them up.

74:17 The **boundaries of the earth** could refer to the boundary between land and sea established at creation (Gn 1:9-10), but it is more likely the regularity of the seasons (Gn 1:14) since it is parallel to **summer and winter**.

74:19 **Dove** was a term of affection (Sg 6:9). It is used as a designation for Israel here.

74:20 **Dark places of the land** may be metaphorical for evil,

21 Do not let the oppressed turn away
      in shame;
   let the poor and needy
      praise Your name.[a]
22 Rise up, God, defend Your cause![b]
   Remember the insults
   that fools bring against You
      all day long.[c]
23 Do not forget the clamor
      of Your adversaries,
   the tumult of Your opponents
      that goes up constantly.[d]

Psalm 75
God Judges the Wicked

For the choir director: "Do Not Destroy."[A]
A psalm of •Asaph.[e] A song.

1 We give thanks to You, God;
   we give thanks to You, for Your name
      is near.
   People tell about
      Your wonderful works.[f]

2 "When I choose a time,
   I will judge fairly.[g]
3 When the earth and all
      its inhabitants shake,
   I am the One who steadies its pillars.[h]
                              •Selah
4 I say to the boastful, 'Do not boast,'
   and to the wicked, 'Do not lift up
      your •horn.[i]

---

a 74:21 Ps 9:9;
103:6; Is 41:7
b 74:22 Ps 9:19;
82:8
c Ps 79:12
d 74:23 Ps 65:7
e 75:title 1Ch
16:5,7
f 75:1 Dt 4:7; Ps
26:7; 145:18
g 75:2 Ps 9:8;
96:10
h 75:3 1Sm 2:8;
Ps 46:6; Is 24:19
i 75:4 Pr 27:1;
Jr 9:23
j 75:5 1Sm 2:3;
Ps 94:4
k 75:6-7 1Sm
2:7-8; Ps 50:6;
Lk 1:52-53
l 75:8 Is
51:17,22; Jr
25:15-17
m 75:9 Ps 9:2;
18:49; 81:1
n 75:10 Jr 48:25
o Ps 89:17;
92:10; 148:14
p 76:title 1Ch
16:5,7
q 76:1 Jr 10:6;
Mal 1:11
r 76:2 Gn 14:18;
Ps 9:11

---

5 Do not lift up your horn
      against heaven
   or speak arrogantly.'"[j]

6 Exaltation does not come
   from the east, the west, or the desert,
7 for God is the Judge:
   He brings down one
      and exalts another.[k]
8 For there is a cup in the LORD's hand,
   full of wine blended with spices,
      and He pours from it.
   All the wicked of the earth will drink,
   draining it to the dregs.[l]

9 As for me, I will tell about Him forever;
   I will sing praise to the God of Jacob.[m]
10 "I will cut off all the horns
      of the wicked,[n]
   but the horns of the righteous will be
      lifted up."[o]

Psalm 76
God, the Powerful Judge

For the choir director:
with stringed instruments.
A psalm of •Asaph.[p] A song.

1 God is known in Judah;
   His name is great in Israel.[q]
2 His tent is in Salem,[B]
   His dwelling place in •Zion.[r]

A 75:title Possibly a tune   B 76:2 = Jerusalem

---

or it could refer to places where enemies hid to attack the
unsuspecting.

74:21 The words **poor** and **needy** often represent those who
are faithful to Yahweh (see notes at 34:6 and 35:10).

74:22 Rise up is used to call God to act (see note at 7:6-8).
Yahweh's **cause** is the same as Israel's, and He should act
on behalf of His reputation.

Ps 75 title On **Do Not Destroy**, see note at Psalm 57 title. On
Asaph, see note at Psalm 50 title.

75:1 Name represents Yahweh's presence among His people (see note at 20:1). **Wonderful works** can refer either to
God's creative acts or to His saving acts on behalf of His
people (see note at 9:1-2).

75:2 Choose a time refers to a "set" or "appointed" time,
which in this case is God's time for judging. He is orderly
in His actions and has appointed times for the seasons (Gn
1:14), the festivals of Israel (Lv 23:2), and a final time when
He will bring His justice to the world (Dn 12:7).

75:3 "Shaking" probably refers to earthquakes that were
regular occurrences in and around Israel. **Pillars** of the
earth (1Sm 2:8; Jb 9:6) are equivalent to "foundations of the
earth" (Jb 38:4; Ps 104:5; Pr 8:29; Is 51:13; Mc 6:2).

75:4 Horn was a symbol of power, often used in military contexts (see notes at 18:1-2 and 22:20-21). Lifting up a horn is

parallel to boasting, probably about one's might. The only
boasting appropriate for God's people is that they know Him
(Jr 6:23-24; see note at Ps 34:2). Note also 75:10.

75:5 Against heaven means that this arrogance was directed against God Himself (see note at 73:9).

75:6 Exaltation is from the same Hebrew root (rum) as "lifting up" in verses 4-5, linking the two concepts together.

75:7 God is the Judge is a statement of His sovereignty and
His right to bring down or exalt anyone He wants (147:6;
1Sm 2:6-7; Lk 1:52-53). This extends to the whole earth (Gn
18:25; see note at Ps 7:6-8).

75:8 Cup depicts God's judgment (60:3; Is 51:17; Jr 25:15,28;
49:12; 51:7). Since **all the wicked of the earth** are referred
to, God's judgment will fall on all humanity.

75:9 On **God of Jacob**, see note at 20:1.

Ps 76 title On **Asaph**, see note at Psalm 50 title.

76:1 The ancient Near Eastern concept of the **name** reflects
identity, reputation, and character. The combination of **Judah** and **Israel** in subsequent lines indicates all 12 tribes
witnessed to God's name.

76:2 Salem is a shortened form of Jerusalem. **Zion** also
refers to Jerusalem. The place where the name dwells is
commonly associated with the divine presence of God. **His**

3 There He shatters the bow's
    flaming arrows,
the shield, the sword, and the weapons
    of war.*a*   •*Selah*

4 You are resplendent and majestic
coming down from the mountains
    of prey.*b*
5 The brave-hearted
    have been plundered;
they have slipped into their final sleep.
None of the warriors was able to lift
    a hand.*c*
6 At Your rebuke, God of Jacob,
both chariot and horse lay still.*d*

7 And You—You are to be •feared.*A*
When You are angry,
who can stand before You?*e*
8 From heaven
    You pronounced judgment.
The earth feared and grew quiet*f*
9 when God rose up to judge
and to save all the lowly of the earth.*g*
            Selah

10 Even human wrath will praise You;
You will clothe Yourself
    with their remaining wrath.*B,h*

11 Make and keep your vows
to the LORD your God;*i*

*a*76:3 Ps 46:9; Is 2:4; Jr 49:35
*b*76:4 Is 14:25; Nah 2:13
*c*76:5 Jr 51:39
*d*76:6 Ex 13:1,21
*e*76:7 Ps 1:5; 130:3; Nah 1:6
*f*76:8 2Ch 20:29-30; Ps 33:8; Hab 2:20
*g*76:9 Ps 9:7-8; Is 3:13-15
*h*76:10 Ex 9:16; Rm 9:17
*i*76:11 Ps 50:14
*j*Ps 68:29; Is 18:7
*k*76:12 Dn 4:37
*l*77:title 1Ch 16:5,7
*m*77:1 Ps 3:4; 142:1
*n*77:2 Gn 37:35; Jb 11:13; Jr 31:15
*o*77:3 Ps 42:5,11; 43:5; 55:17; 143:4
*p*77:4 Ps 39:9
*q*77:5 Dt 32:7; Ps 143:5
*r*77:6 Ps 4:4; 42:8

let all who are around Him
    bring tribute
to the awe-inspiring One.*C,j*
12 He humbles the spirit of leaders;
He is feared by the kings of the earth.*k*

Psalm 77
Confidence in a Time of Crisis

For the choir director: according to
    Jeduthun. Of •Asaph.*l* A psalm.

1 I cry aloud to God,
aloud to God, and He will hear me.*m*
2 I sought the Lord in my day of trouble.
My hands were continually lifted up
    all night long;
I refused to be comforted.*n*
3 I think of God; I groan;
I meditate; my spirit becomes weak.*o*
            •*Selah*

4 You have kept me from closing
    my eyes;
I am troubled and cannot speak.*p*
5 I consider days of old,
    years long past.*q*
6 At night I remember
    my music;
I meditate in my heart,
    and my spirit ponders.*r*

---

*A*76:7 Or *are awe-inspiring*   *B*76:10 Hb obscure   *C*76:11 Or *tribute with awe*

---

tent should perhaps be rendered "booth" in this context. The Hebrew term *sukkah* refers to a hut built from intertwined tree branches. "Booth" nicely parallels **dwelling place**, a shelter protected by thick vegetation. "Booth" and "dwelling place" figuratively describe Yahweh's presence in the temple.

76:3 Flaming arrows, a metaphor for strength, can also mean "lightning bolts." The psalmist used imagery depicting Yahweh as a divine warrior who defeated the enemy (29:7; 78:48; Dt 32:24; Hab 3:5).

76:4 The psalmist addressed God directly, using the second person **You**. By calling God **resplendent**, he equated God's presence to "light," corresponding to verses 1-2. The Hebrew word *min* could indicate that God's majesty and strength exceed that of the mountains. The idea corresponds to the statement of victory in verse 3.

76:5 God's enemies do not show courage by challenging Him; instead, their actions demonstrate their stubborn nature (Is 46:12). **They have slipped** suggests that exhaustion eventually ended in permanent sleep, or death. **Hand** metaphorically refers to strength; the warriors could no longer find strength to fight.

76:6 Jacob refers to the 12 tribes descended from the patriarch. God's spoken word brings about miraculous events, causing waters to stand or divide (18:15; 104:7; Is 50:2) and people to perish (Ps 80:16). The **rebuke** of God, coupled with the mention of **chariot and horse**, alludes to the exodus event, a recurrent theme in the psalms of Asaph (Ex 15:1,4).

The chariot and horse **lay still**, a term describing a comatose state or deep sleep. The metaphor for death (Ex 15:16) fits well with the imagery in Ps 76:5.

76:7 The repetition of **You** emphasizes the Lord. Fear of God is a combination of humility, obedience, awe, and respect. No creature that opposes God's righteous anger can endure in His presence (147:17; Nah 1:6).

76:8-9 The Hebrew term *shaqat* never denotes a silence or quietness derived from terror. So this is a reverent fear that stems from a sense of security and comfort as a result of God's correction of injustice and oppression. The Lord's righteousness produces hope, trust, and peace (Is 30:15; 32:17).

76:10 God uses all things to fulfill His divine will and purpose. Even human **wrath** serves to exalt God, perhaps because it is powerless to defy God or overthrow His justice.

76:11 A vow is a solemn promise or oath. God's people, encouraged to praise Him for deliverance from their enemies, bring sacrifices and offerings in gratitude. The faithful surround God to willingly bring worship, an ironic contrast to verse 10, where human wrath encompassed God but, despite contrary intentions, only managed to glorify Him.

Ps 77 title On **Jeduthun**, see note at Psalm 39 title. On **Asaph**, see note at Psalm 50 title.

77:1-3 This psalm begins with a lament, an intense longing to hear from God (see note at 22:1).

77:4-6 Pondering a time when the worship experience was better caused grief and sleeplessness.

7 "Will the Lord reject forever
   and never again show favor?ᵃ

8 Has His faithful love ceased forever?
   Is His promise at an end
     for all generations?ᵇ

9 Has God forgotten to be gracious?
   Has He in anger
     withheld His compassion?"ᶜ   *Selah*

10 So I say, "I am grievedᴬ
   that the right hand of the •Most High
     has changed."ᵈ

11 I will remember the Lᴏʀᴅ's works;
   yes, I will remember
     Your ancient wonders.ᵉ

12 I will reflect on all You have done
   and meditate on Your actions.ᶠ

13 God, Your way is holy.
   What god is great like God?ᵍ

14 You are the God
   who works wonders;

You revealed Your strength
   among the peoples.ʰ

15 With power You redeemed Your people,
   the descendants of Jacob and Joseph.ⁱ
                   Selah

16 The waters saw You, God.
   The waters saw You; they trembled.
   Even the depths shook.ʲ

17 The clouds poured down water.
   The storm clouds thundered;
   Your arrows flashed back and forth.ᵏ

18 The sound of Your thunder was
     in the whirlwind;
   lightning lit up the world.ˡ
   The earth shook and quaked.ᵐ

19 Your way went through the sea
   and Your path through
     the great waters,
   but Your footprints were unseen.ⁿ

20 You led Your people like a flockᵒ
   by the hand of Moses and Aaron.ᵖ

Cross-references:
ᵃ77:7 Ps 44:9,23; 74:1; Lm 2:7; 3:31
ᵇ77:8 Ps 33:11; 85:5; 89:49
ᶜ77:9 Ps 25:6; 40:11; Is 49:15
ᵈ77:10 Ps 31:22; 73:14
ᵉ77:11 Ps 105:5; 143:5
ᶠ77:12 Ps 9:11; 90:16; 145:5
ᵍ77:13 Ex 15:11; Ps 71:19; 86:8
ʰ77:14 Ps 72:18; 106:8
ⁱ77:15 Ex 6:6; Dt 9:29; Ps 74:2
ʲ77:16 Ps 114:3; Hab 3:8,10
ᵏ77:17 Ps 18:14; Hab 3:11; Zch 9:14
ˡ77:16-18 Ps 29:3,9; 97:4
ᵐ77:18 2Sm 22:8; Ps 18:7; Is 13:13
ⁿ77:19 Is 43:16
ᵒ77:20 Ps 78:52; 80:1
ᵖPs 105:26; Is 63:11-13

ᴬ77:10 Lit "My piercing

77:7 Typical of Asaph psalms (74:1-2; 80:3-4; 83:1; 88:14), the psalmist characterized God's slow response as rejection and asked how long before the restoration of the Lord's **favor**.

77:8 Faithful love (Hb *chesed*) could be rendered as "covenant love" or "covenant loyalty" in this context (see word study at 136:1-26). The psalmist hoped an appeal to Yahweh's faithful love would persuade God to respond to the crisis. He used language normally associated with the exodus from Egypt and the appearance of God at Sinai.

77:9 Gracious and compassionate often occur together in poetic contexts. While grace parallels the idea of showing favor in verse 7, **compassion** derives from the Hebrew root meaning "womb," suggesting a filial relationship that parallels faithful love in verse 8. A literal rendering of the Hebrew text reads, "has He [God] closed up His womb in anger," a figurative expression denoting the absence of parental love and concern for His offspring.

77:10 God's **right hand** represents the power by which He works (60:5). God's immutability guarantees His unchangeable character. The psalmist was not claiming that God's nature had changed; instead, he was disappointed because God had responded differently than expected.

77:13 A hymn (vv. 13-20) immediately follows the end of the lament. God's **way** (Hb *derek*), the determination and exercise of His divine will, reflects His **holy** character. The rhetorical question **What god is great like God** often introduces incomparability statements in hymns emphasizing the Lord's sovereignty (18:31; Ex 15:11; 2Sm 22:32; Is 40:18), omnipotence (Ex 15:11; Dt 3:24; Ps 71:19; 89:8), omniscience (Is 44:7), stature (Ps 113:5; Is 40:25), and capacity for forgiveness (Mc 7:18).

77:14 God's **strength**, revealed through Israel's redemption from bondage, alludes to the exodus, which provided the paradigm against which Israel anticipated the Lord's deliverance from future enemies. The reference to "descendants of Jacob and Joseph" in verse 15 reinforces the exodus allusion.

77:15 With power is literally "by arm." By His powerful arm, God redeems, saves, and executes judgment (44:3; 89:13; 98:1; 118:15; Is 50:2; 51:5; 52:10; 59:1).

77:16-18 Using divine warrior imagery, the psalmist declared that cosmic upheaval accompanies God's presence (18:7-15; 114:3-5; Ex 19:16-19), and creation exults in worship before Him. The Lord's **arrows** (v. 17) refer to lightning bolts (29:7; 76:3). The storm language depicts His control over all of nature's forces.

77:19 Referring to Israel's procession through the parted **waters** of the Red **Sea**, the psalmist recalled the mysterious work of the Lord, who was **unseen** yet present.

77:20 The psalms of Asaph often use shepherd and **flock** imagery to emphasize the Lord's compassion and care.

---

zakar

Hebrew Pronunciation	[zah KAHR]
HCSB Translation	remember, think of, mention
Uses in Psalms	54
Uses in the OT	235
Focus Passage	Psalm 77:3,6,11

Zakar chiefly means *remember* (Gn 8:1) but also *mention, refer to,* or *think about* (Jr 20:9; 23:36; 31:20). It implies *consider* (Ec 5:20), *think* (Ps 109:16), *recall* (Jb 11:16), *think of* (Ps 63:6), *give orders to* (Nah 2:5), *invoke* (2Sm 14:11), or *hold against* (Ps 79:8). "Not remember" connotes *forget, abandon* (Lm 2:1), or *break* (Am 1:9). Passive-reflexive verbs signify *be worth mentioning* (Jb 28:18) or *be thought of again* (Is 23:16). Causative verbs mean *remind* (1Kg 17:18), *preserve the memory* (2Sm 18:18), or *bring remembrance.* They suggest *take to court* (Is 43:26) or *warn* (Jr 4:16). They convey *draw attention to* (Ezk 21:23), *make known* (Is 63:7), *proclaim* (Ps 71:16), *declare, praise* (Sg 1:4), *celebrate,* or *take pride in* (Ps 20:7). Someone *offers* incense memorially (Is 66:3). *"Mentioning a name"* implies *naming* (Is 49:1). Participles represent *court historian* (2Sm 8:16), *historian, record keeper,* or *recorder.*

Psalm 78
Lessons from Israel's Past

A *Maskil* of *Asaph.[a]*

1 My people, hear my instruction;
listen to what I say.[b]

2 I will declare wise sayings;
I will speak mysteries from the past[c]—

3 things we have heard and known
and that our fathers have passed down
to us.[d]

4 We must not hide them
from their children,
but must tell a future generation
the praises of the LORD,
His might, and the wonderful works
He has performed.[e]

5 He established a *testimony in Jacob
and set up a law in Israel,
which He commanded our fathers
to teach to their children[f]

6 so that a future generation—
children yet to be born—might know.
They were to rise and tell
their children[g]

7 so that they might put their confidence
in God
and not forget God's works,
but keep His commands.[h]

8 Then they would not be
like their fathers,
a stubborn and rebellious generation,
a generation whose heart was not loyal
and whose spirit was not faithful
to God.[i]

9 The Ephraimite archers turned back
on the day of battle.[j]

10 They did not keep God's covenant
and refused to live by His law.[k]

11 They forgot what He had done,
the wonderful works
He had shown them.[l]

12 He worked wonders in the sight of
their fathers
in the land of Egypt, the region
of Zoan.[m]

13 He split the sea
and brought them across;
the water stood firm like a wall.[n]

14 He led them with a cloud by day
and with a fiery light
throughout the night.[o]

15 He split rocks in the wilderness
and gave them drink as abundant
as the depths.[p]

16 He brought streams out of the stone
and made water flow down like rivers.[q]

17 But they continued to sin against Him,
rebelling in the desert
against the *Most High.[r]

18 They deliberately[A] tested God,
demanding the food they craved.[s]

19 They spoke against God, saying,
"Is God able to provide food
in the wilderness?

20 Look! He struck the rock and water
gushed out;
torrents overflowed.[t]
But can He also provide bread
or furnish meat for His people?"[u]

---

a 78:title 1Ch 16:5,7
b 78:1 Pr 5:7; 7:24; Is 55:3
c 78:2 Ps 49:4; Pr 1:6; Mt 13:35
d 78:3 Ps 44:1
e 78:4 Dt 6:7; 11:19; Ps 145:4
f 78:5 Ps 19:7; 81:5; 147:19
g 78:6 Dt 11:19; Ps 22:31; 102:18
h 78:7 Dt 6:12; Ps 103:2; Pr 3:1
i 78:8 Dt 31:27; 2Kg 17:14; 2Ch 30:7
j 78:9 Ps 44:10
k 78:10 1Kg 11:11; 2Kg 17:15; Jr 32:23
l 78:11 Ps 106:13
m 78:12 Ex 7–12; Ps 78:43
n 78:13 Ex 14:21; 15:8; Ps 136:13
o 78:14 Ex 13:21; Nm 14:14; Ps 105:39
p 78:15 Ex 17:6; Nm 20:8-13; Is 48:21
q 78:16 Ps 105:41; 114:8
r 78:17 Dt 9:22; Is 63:10; Heb 3:16
s 78:18 Ex 17:2,7; Ps 106:14; 1Co 10:5-10
t 78:20 Nm 20:11
u 78:19-20 Ex 16:3; Nm 11:4; 21:5

A 78:18 Lit *in their heart*

Ps 78 title On *Maskil*, see note at Psalm 32 title. On **Asaph**, see note at Psalm 50 title.

78:1 The people are exhorted to listen to the Lord's **instruction**. Translating Hebrew *torah* as "law" obscures the essence of Torah as God's instructions for sustaining a relationship with Him (see note at 1:2).

78:2 The psalmist couched the epic psalm in terms of a riddle or paradox, describing Israel's inability to trust God despite God's repeated acts of faithfulness. The Hebrew word *chiydoth* means **mysteries** or "parables" (Nm 12:8; Jdg 14:12-19; Pr 1:6; cp. Mt 13:35).

78:5 A **testimony** or decree relates what is required of the Lord's people.

78:6-7 Reciting Israel's early history to future generations assures the perpetuation of the account. This would connect generations far removed from the original event to the promises and instructions governing Israel's relationship to God.

78:8 The goal was to educate the children so they did not become another **stubborn and rebellious generation** (66:7; Ex 17:1-7; Is 1:23; 30:1; 65:2). Israel continued to be disloyal to the Lord throughout the ages, despite His covenant loyalty and mercy.

78:9-10 The sons of Ephraim were well known for their military role as **archers** (Zch 9:13). They broke the **covenant** during the mutiny of the northern tribes.

78:12 God revealed Himself to Israel through His words and His ways. **Zoan** was a major Egyptian city that later became its capital (Is 19:11,13; 30:4; Ezk 30:14).

78:13 This verse describes the crossing of the Red Sea (Ex 14:21-22). The waters **stood firm like a wall** (lit "like a heap" 33:7; Ex 15:8; Jos 3:13,16).

78:14 **Cloud** and **light** refer to the pillars of cloud and fire representing the Lord's presence (Ex 14:19-20; 40:36-38).

78:15-16 **Split rocks** and **stone** describe water from the rock at Horeb and Meribah (Ex 17:1-7; Nm 20:7-11).

78:17 Compare verses 17-20 with verses 56-58. The Israelites continued to be rebellious (lit "bitter, strive") against Moses and the Lord. Compare the reversal of drought in Isaiah as a metaphor for the restoration of fertility in Israel following the exile (107:35; Is 53:2; Jr 2:6; 50:12; 51:43).

78:18-20 The Israelites **tested** God (see note at 95:8-9; cp. 1Co 10:8), presuming that He could not **provide food** (lit "prepare a table"; see note at 23:5).

²¹ Therefore, the L<small>ORD</small> heard
   and became furious;
then fire broke out against Jacob,
and anger flared up against Israel^a
²² because they did not believe God
   or rely on His salvation.^b
²³ He gave a command to the clouds above
   and opened the doors of heaven.^c
²⁴ He rained manna for them to eat;
He gave them grain from heaven.^d
²⁵ People^A ate the bread of angels.^B
He sent them an abundant supply
   of food.^e
²⁶ He made the east wind blow in the skies
   and drove the south wind
   by His might.^f
²⁷ He rained meat on them like dust,
   and winged birds like the sand
   of the seas.
²⁸ He made them fall in His camp,
all around His tent.^{C,D,g}
²⁹ They ate and were completely satisfied,
for He gave them what they craved.^h
³⁰ Before they had satisfied their desire,
while the food was still in their mouths,
³¹ God's anger flared up against them,
and He killed some of their best men.
He struck down Israel's choice
   young men.ⁱ
³² Despite all this, they kept sinning
and did not believe
   His wonderful works.^j
³³ He made their days end in futility,
their years in sudden disaster.^k
³⁴ When He killed some of them,
the rest began to seek Him;
they repented and searched for God.^l
³⁵ They remembered that God was
   their rock,
the Most High God, their Redeemer.^m

³⁶ But they deceived Him
   with their mouths,
they lied to Him with their tongues,ⁿ
³⁷ their hearts were insincere toward Him,
and they were unfaithful
   to His covenant.^o
³⁸ Yet He was compassionate;
He •atoned for^E their •guilt
and did not destroy them.
He often turned His anger aside
and did not unleash^F all His wrath.^p
³⁹ He remembered that they were
   only flesh,
a wind that passes and does not return.^q
⁴⁰ How often they rebelled against Him
in the wilderness
and grieved Him in the desert.
⁴¹ They constantly tested God^r
and provoked the Holy One of Israel.^s
⁴² They did not remember
   His power shown
on the day He redeemed them
   from the foe,^t
⁴³ when He performed
   His miraculous signs in Egypt
and His wonders in the region of Zoan.^u
⁴⁴ He turned their rivers into blood,
and they could not drink
   from their streams.^v
⁴⁵ He sent among them swarms of flies,^w
which fed on them,
and frogs, which devastated them.^x
⁴⁶ He gave their crops to the caterpillar
and the fruit of their labor
   to the locust.^y
⁴⁷ He killed their vines with hail
and their sycamore fig trees
   with a flood.
⁴⁸ He handed over their livestock to hail
and their cattle to lightning bolts.^z

^a78:21 Nm 11:1
^b78:22 Dt 1:23;
9:23; Heb 3:18
^c78:23 Gn 7:11;
Mal 3:10
^d78:24 Ex
16:4,31; Jn 6:31
^e78:25 Ex 16:3
^f78:26 Nm 11:31
^g78:27-28 Ex
16:13; Ps 105:40
^h78:29 Nm
11:4,34
ⁱ78:30-31 Nm
11:33-34; Jb
20:23
^j78:32 Nm
14:16-17
^k78:33 Nm
14:29,35
^l78:34 Nm 21:7;
Ps 63:1; Hs 5:15
^m78:35 Is 44:6,8
ⁿ78:36 Is 29:13;
57:11; Ezk 33:31
^o78:37 Ps 51:10;
78:8; Ac 8:21
^p78:38 Nm
14:18-20; Dt
4:31; Is 12:1
^q78:39 Dt 31:27;
Ps 107:11
^r78:41 Ps 95:8-9
^sDt 9:7-8,22;
Ps 106:29; Zch
8:14
^t78:42 Jdg 8:34;
Ps 44:3; 106:10
^u78:43 Ex 4:21;
7:3; Ps 105:27
^v78:44 Ex 7:14-
25; Ps 105:29
^w78:45 Ex 8:17;
Ps 105:31
^xEx 8:3-6; Ps
105:30
^y78:46 Ex 10:14-
15; Ps 105:34
^z78:47-48 Ex
9:23-24; Ps
105:32

---

^A78:25 Lit *Man*   ^B78:25 Lit *mighty ones*   ^C78:28 LXX, Syr read *in their camp, all around their tents*   ^D78:28 Or *in its camp, all around its tents*   ^E78:38 Or *He wiped out*, or *He forgave*   ^F78:38 Or *stir up*

78:21-22 The Lord sent **fire** in punishment (Nm 11:1-3) as the consequences of the Israelites' disbelief (Dt 9:23; Jnh 3:4-5).

78:23-25 Manna was the basic food that sustained Israel during the wilderness wanderings (Ex 16:4-5). This is the only place in the OT where the Hebrew word *'abbirim* (lit "strong, powerful ones," "valiant ones") refers to angels (Jb 24:22; 34:20).

78:26-31 When Israel murmured against God and desired **meat**, the Lord sent quail (**winged birds**; Nm 11:18-20,31-35). Then God became angry that they had complained about their "hardship" (Nm 11:1) and punished them with a plague.

78:33 Israel's history was filled with conflict and oppression, and she spent her years in contention with foreign nations

(2:5; 48:6; 83:16; 104:29; Ex 15:15; Is 13:8). The people's lives were short and marked by fear.

78:34-35 Following divine discipline, Israel sought God (Is 26:9; Hs 5:15). **Rock** and **Redeemer** refer to the power and salvation of the Lord (18:31; 19:14; Gn 49:24; Dt 32:4,15).

78:36-39 Israel's worship of the Lord was insincere and hypocritical. Their actions did not reflect their words (Ac 8:21). God consistently forgave Israel's sin and restrained His anger because of humanity's weakness and transitory nature (Ps 78:35,39,41).

78:42 Although the Lord remembered Israel by redeeming them from the enemy, they did not **remember** God (vv. 35,39,41).

78:44-51 The plagues described in these verses do not follow the sequence in Exodus (Ex 7-11). Egypt suffered **rivers**

49 He sent His burning anger
    against them:
  fury, indignation, and calamity—
  a band of deadly messengers.[A,a]
50 He cleared a path for His anger.
  He did not spare them from death
  but delivered their lives to the plague.[b]
51 He struck all the firstborn[c] in Egypt,
  the first progeny of the tents of Ham.[B,d]
52 He led His people out like sheep
  and guided them like a flock
    in the wilderness.[e]
53 He led them safely,
    and they were not afraid;
  but the sea covered their enemies.[f]
54 He brought them to His holy land,
  to the mountain
    His right hand acquired.[g]
55 He drove out nations before them.[h]
  He apportioned their inheritance by lot
  and settled the tribes of Israel
    in their tents.[i]

56 But they rebelliously tested
    the Most High God,
  for they did not keep His decrees.[j]
57 They treacherously turned away
    like their fathers;
  they became warped like a faulty bow.[k]
58 They enraged Him
    with their ·high places
  and provoked His jealousy
    with their carved images.[l]
59 God heard and became furious;
  He completely rejected Israel.[m]

60 He abandoned the tabernacle at Shiloh,
  the tent where He resided
    among men.[C,n]
61 He gave up His strength[D] to captivity
  and His splendor to the hand of a foe.[o]
62 He surrendered His people to the sword
  because He was enraged
    with His heritage.[p]
63 Fire consumed His chosen young men,
  and His young women
    had no wedding songs.[E,q]
64 His priests fell by the sword,
  but the[F] widows could not lament.[G,r]

65 Then the Lord awoke as if from sleep,
  like a warrior from the effects of wine.[s]
66 He beat back His foes;
  He gave them lasting shame.[t]
67 He rejected the tent of Joseph
  and did not choose the tribe
    of Ephraim.
68 He chose instead the tribe of Judah,
  Mount ·Zion, which He loved.[u]
69 He built His sanctuary
    like the heights,[H]
  like the earth that
    He established forever.[v]
70 He chose David His servant
  and took him from the sheepfolds;[w]
71 He brought him from tending ewes
  to be shepherd over His people Jacob—
  over Israel, His inheritance.[x]
72 He shepherded them with a pure heart
  and guided them
    with his skillful hands.[y]

Cross references:
[a] 78:49 Ex 12:13,23; 2Sm 24:16
[b] 78:50 Ex 12:29-30
[c] 78:51 Ex 13:15; Ps 105:36
[d] Ps 105:23,27
[e] 78:52 Ex 15:22; Ps 77:20
[f] 78:53 Ex 14; 15:19; Jos 24:7; Ps 106:11
[g] 78:54 Ex 15:17; Ps 74:2
[h] 78:55 Jos 11:16-23; Ps 44:2
[i] Jos 13:7; 23:4; Ps 135:12
[j] 78:56 Jdg 2:11-13
[k] 78:57 Ezk 20:27-28; Hs 7:16
[l] 78:58 Jdg 2:12; 1Kg 3:2; Ezk 20:28
[m] 78:59 Dt 32:19; Ps 106:40; Am 6:8
[n] 78:60 Jr 7:12,14; 26:6
[o] 78:61 1Sm 4:17
[p] 78:62 Jdg 20:21; 1Sm 4:10
[q] 78:63 Jr 7:34; 16:9; Lm 2:21
[r] 78:64 Jb 27:15; Ezk 24:23
[s] 78:65 Ps 73:20; 121:4; Is 42:13
[t] 78:66 1Sm 5:6; Ps 40:14
[u] 78:67-68 Ps 87:2
[v] 78:69 1Kg 6
[w] 78:70 1Sm 16:11-13
[x] 78:71 Ps 28:9; Is 40:11
[y] 78:72 1Kg 9:4; Ps 101:2

[A] 78:49 Or angels   [B] 78:51 Ham's descendants who settled in Egypt   [C] 78:60 Hb adam   [D] 78:61 = the ark of the covenant
[E] 78:63 Lit virgins were not praised   [F] 78:64 Lit His   [G] 78:64 War probably prevented customary funerals.   [H] 78:69 Either the heights of heaven or the mountain heights

---

of **blood** (Ex 7:14-24), **flies** (Ex 8:20-32), **locust** (Ex 10:1-15), **hail** (Ex 9:13-26), and the death of the **firstborn** (Ex 11:1-11). The **tents of Ham** is a name for Egypt (105:23,27; Gn 10:6).

78:52-53 On leading Israel as a **flock** through the **sea**, see note at 77:20.

78:54 To His holy land is literally "the border of His holiness." This **mountain** cannot be Zion since the events at the sanctuary at Shiloh preceded Zion chronologically (v. 60).

78:55 The conquest and settlement of Canaan is recorded in Joshua 6–22.

78:58 The **high places** were separate sanctuaries and altars constructed for the worship of pagan gods.

78:60 The total rejection of Israel manifested itself by the departure of the Lord's presence from the sanctuary at **Shiloh**, an early shrine in Canaan where Joshua housed the ark in the tent of meeting.

78:61 His strength to captivity is a reference to the capture of the ark by the Philistines (1Sm 4–6). The ark symbolized

the power and presence of the Lord among His people, and it often preceded Israel in battle (Jos 6:6-14).

78:62-64 These verses refer to the judgment suffered by Israel following the loss of the ark.

78:65 A figurative expression describing the Lord's delay, the waking of the Lord indicates His resumption of deliverance and the conclusion of His punishment (35:23; 44:24; 59:5-6). The imagery pictures rousing the divine **warrior** from **sleep** to do battle (1Kg 18:27; Is 42:13-16; 51:9-11).

78:67-68 The elevation of **Judah** over **Ephraim** as the location of the Lord's temple and the center of the Davidic monarchy resulted in part from Ephraim's failure to protect the ark when it was in Shiloh. The text reinforces the Lord's choice of **Zion** as His dwelling place.

78:70-71 David was selected from among the common shepherds of Israel to rule over **Jacob**. The Lord often uses those who are least important to serve in important leadership roles.

78:72 David served his kingly role with integrity and care, shepherding God's people and guiding them with wisdom (77:20).

Psalm 79

Faith amid Confusion

A psalm of *Asaph.*[a]

1 God, the nations have invaded
    Your inheritance,
  desecrated Your holy temple,
  and turned Jerusalem into ruins.[b]
2 They gave the corpses of Your servants
    to the birds of the sky for food,
  the flesh of Your godly ones
    to the beasts of the earth.[c]
3 They poured out their blood
    like water all around Jerusalem,
  and there was no one to bury them.[d]
4 We have become an object of reproach
    to our neighbors,
  a source of mockery and ridicule
    to those around us.[e]

5 How long, *Yahweh? Will You
    be angry forever?
  Will Your jealousy keep burning
    like fire?[f]
6 Pour out Your wrath on the nations
    that don't acknowledge You,

on the kingdoms that don't call on
    Your name,[g]
7 for they have devoured Jacob
    and devastated his homeland.[h]
8 Do not hold past sins[A] against us;
  let Your compassion come
    to us quickly,
  for we have become weak.[i]

9 God of our salvation, help us[j]—
    for the glory of Your name.
  Deliver us and *atone for[B] our sins,
    because of Your name.[k]
10 Why should the nations ask,
    "Where is their God?"[l]
  Before our eyes,
  let vengeance for the shed blood
    of Your servants
  be known among the nations.[m]
11 Let the groans of the prisoners
    reach You;
  according to Your great power,
  preserve those condemned to die.[n]

12 Pay back sevenfold to our neighbors[o]
  the reproach they have hurled at You,
    Lord.[p]

Cross references

a 79:title 1Ch 16:5,7
b 79:1 Jr 26:18; Lm 1:10; Mc 3:12
c 79:2 Dt 28:26; Jr 7:33; 16:4
d 79:3 Jr 14:16; 16:4; 22:19
e 79:4 Ps 44:13-14; 80:6; Dn 9:16
f 79:5 Ps 74:10; 78:58; 80:4
g 79:6 Ps 14:4; Jr 10:25
h 79:7 Ps 53:4
i 79:8 Ps 142:6; Is 64:9
j 79:9 1Ch 16:35; Ps 85:4
k Ps 25:11; 106:8; Jr 14:7
l 79:10 Ps 42:3,10; 115:2
m Dt 32:43; Ps 94:1-2; Jr 46:10
n 79:11 Ps 102:20
o 79:12 Lv 26:21,28
p Ps 74:10,18,22

A 79:8 Or *hold the sins of past generations*   B 79:9 Or *and wipe out*, or *and forgive*

Ps 79 title On **Asaph**, see note at Psalm 50 title.

79:1 The nations **invaded** Jerusalem in 586 B.C. and **desecrated** the temple. The cultic term "desecrated" or "defiled" means "to make ceremonially unclean." Verses 1-3 detail the extensive nature of the devastation since the enemies destroyed Israel's place of worship and harmed the Lord's people.

79:2 Normal burial practices in Israel included wrapping the deceased carefully to preserve them and burying the bodies in family plots (cp. Dt 28:26). Consequently, leaving the bodies exposed to the elements where they were consumed by animals signifies humiliation and insult.

79:3 The life is in the **blood** (Gn 9:4-6), so blood was sacred for ritual but unfit for consumption. The violation of God's people consisted of illegal bloodshed and the outpouring (Hb *shaphak*) of blood for consumption by animals.

79:4 Jerusalem's inhabitants had become an **object of reproach** (lit "a taunt"), mocked, and "ridiculed" (lit "cursed" or "shamed"; see note at v. 12).

79:5 **How long** reflects the frustration of the psalmist, who connected the absence or abandonment of God with His failure to respond immediately to the plight of Jerusalem's citizens (see note at 13:1-2). By focusing on the duration of the Lord's anger, the psalmist presumed an end to judgment and eventual restoration.

79:6 The psalmist asked God to redirect His anger to **the nations**. Since Babylon poured out the blood of God's people, He should pour out His anger on the enemy. The ironic request in this verse is one of a number of wordplays in this psalm that appeal to God to invoke a reversal of vengeance (see notes at 7:14-16 and 79:12). **Kingdoms that don't call on Your name** is a common idiom distinguishing between the Lord's people and those who opposed Him.

79:7 As the birds and beasts consumed the corpses as food (Hb *ma'akal*; v. 2) and the nations made ruins of Jerusalem (v. 1), so the enemy has **devoured** (Hb *'akal*) Jerusalem and **devastated** Judah's territory.

79:8 The cultic term translated **hold** is idiomatic and literally means "to remember." When the Lord ceased to remember sin, the transgression no longer existed.

79:9 The psalmist's appeal to the glory of God's **name** evokes all the Lord's previous saving activity on behalf of His people. Moses served as a mediator following the golden calf incident (Ex 32) and prayed for forgiveness for the people so the Lord's name and reputation among the nations would be glorified. The divine name, characterized by mercy and compassion coupled with holiness and judgment, provides the basis to **atone** ("wipe off, cleanse, cover"; see note at 65:3) Judah's iniquities (78:38).

79:10 The rhetorical question asked by the nations, **Where is their God**, echoes the response of Israel's enemies to her destruction (42:3; Jl 2:17; Mc 7:10). Calamity and oppression often represent the absence of God's protection. **Vengeance** refers to divine retribution, a privilege belonging to God alone. **Be known among the nations** could be translated "be poured out upon the nations," preserving the wordplay on the Hebrew root *shophek*, "pour out" in verses 3,6.

79:11 In a wordplay, the **groans** of the prisoners evoke God's "avenging of blood" (v. 10). **Those condemned to die** literally reads "sons of death."

79:12 **Pay back sevenfold** emphasizes the enduring nature of the vengeance God will inflict upon the nations (Gn 4:15,24; Lv 26:18,21,24). Just as Jacob became a taunt to her neighbors (see note at Ps 79:4), so the psalmist asked the Lord to return the **reproach** (lit "taunts") that they had **hurled** (lit "taunted") at the Lord.

13 Then we, Your people, the sheep
    of Your pasture,[a]
will thank You forever;
we will declare Your praise
    to generation after generation.[b]

Psalm 80
A Prayer for Restoration

For the choir director: according to
"The Lilies."[A] A testimony of *Asaph.[C] A psalm.

1 Listen, Shepherd of Israel,
    who leads Joseph like a flock;[d]
You who sit enthroned
    on the *cherubim,[e]
    rise up[f]
2 before Ephraim,
    Benjamin, and Manasseh.[B,g]
Rally Your power and come
    to save us.[h]
3 Restore us, God;
    look on us with favor,
    and we will be saved.[i]

4 LORD God of *Hosts,
    how long will You be angry

with Your people's prayers?[j]
5 You fed them the bread of tears
    and gave them a full measure[C]
    of tears to drink.[k]
6 You make us quarrel with our neighbors;
    our enemies make fun of us.[l]
7 Restore us, God of Hosts;
    look on us with favor, and we will be
    saved.[m]

8 You uprooted a vine from Egypt;
    You drove out the nations
    and planted it.[n]
9 You cleared a place for it;
    it took root and filled the land.[o]
10 The mountains were covered
    by its shade,
and the mighty cedars[D]
    with its branches.[p]
11 It sent out sprouts toward the Sea[E]
    and shoots toward the River.[F,q]

12 Why have You broken down its walls
    so that all who pass by pick its fruit?[r]
13 The boar from the forest tears it
    and creatures of the field feed on it.[s]
14 Return, God of Hosts.[t]

Cross references:
a 79:13 Ps 74:1; 100:3
b Ps 89:1; Is 43:21
c 80:title 1Ch 16:5,7
d 80:1 Ezk 34:11,16,31
e Ps 99:1
f Ps 44:26
g 80:2 Nm 2:17-24
h Ps 35:23; 106:47; 118:25
i 80:3 Ps 60:1; 85:4; Lm 5:21
j 80:4 Ps 74:10; 79:5; 85:5
k 80:5 Ps 102:9; Is 30:20; Hs 9:4
l 80:6 Ps 44:13; 79:4
m 80:7 Ps 60:1; Lm 5:21
n 80:8 Jr 2:21; 32:41
o 80:9 Am 9:15
p 80:10 Ezk 17:22-24
q 80:11 Ex 23:31; Dt 11:24; Ps 72:8
r 80:12 Ps 89:40; Is 5:5
s 80:13 Jr 5:6
t 80:14 Ps 6:4; 90:13

A 80:title Possibly a tune; Pss 45; 60; 69   B 80:2 This is the marching order for the camp of Israel.   C 80:5 Lit *a one-third measure*
D 80:10 Lit *the cedars of God*   E 80:11 = the Mediterranean   F 80:11 = the Euphrates

---

Ps 80 title On **The Lilies**, see note at Psalm 45 title. On **Asaph**, see note at Psalm 50 title.

80:1 The imperative form for **listen** is a polite request, as from an inferior to his superior. **Shepherd of Israel** is a metaphor indicating God's intimate relationship with His people as protector and provider (23:1; 121:4). This metaphor connects this psalm with the concluding verse of Psalm 79. **Joseph** was a name for Israel normally associated with the northern tribes. **Enthroned on the cherubim** refers to the ark of the covenant upon which the presence of the Lord resided, emphasizing His kingship (18:10; 97:2; 99:1). The ark, sometimes referred to as the "footstool of the Lord," preceded Israel in holy battle. **Rise up** is meant in the sense that a star rises; it could mean "shine forth," reflecting the coming of the Lord in His glory (94:1; Dt 33:2).

80:2 Ephraim, Benjamin, and Manasseh represent the tribes of Israel, settled in central Palestine. "Benjamin" means "son of the right hand," an allusion to verses 15,17. **Rally** is an allusion to Is 63:15,17 in language referring to God's inactivity.

80:3 The psalmist called on God to **restore us**, returning the people to their previous state of blessing. **Look on us with favor** is literally "let your face shine," a reference to the priestly blessing in Nm 6:25.

80:4 The psalmist appealed to the LORD **God of Hosts**. This evokes divine warrior language, typical imagery in ancient Near Eastern cultures. Since Israel's current circumstances were a direct result of God's judgment, the writer asked **how long** (cp. 79:5; 83:1; 88:14), focusing on the duration of God's wrath.

80:5 Grief (**the bread of tears**) was the only sustenance for

the psalmist in the midst of persecution. Tears as a source of food or drink denotes the lack of God's intervention (42:3).

80:7 Repetition of the refrain from verse 3 (**restore us**) forms a natural break in the transition to the second part of the psalm.

80:8 Vine from Egypt alludes to the exodus (Ex 15:17). However, the metaphor extends as far back as Joseph (Gn 49:22), who is characterized as a fruitful vine. Early imagery of Israel as a sprout or branch planted by the Lord in Canaan reached full development in the prophets, particularly Jeremiah, who used the planting metaphor throughout his book (Jr 1:10; 12:10; Ezk 17:1-10; 19:10-14).

80:9-11 The expansion of the vine denotes the spread of territorial and political influence. The Davidic empire eventually occupied territory in Canaan extending from the Mediterranean **Sea** to the Euphrates **River**.

80:12-13 Linguistic and contextual similarities between verses 12-13 and imagery in Is 5:1-7 suggest an intentional allusion to the prophet. The vineyard **walls** protected the crop from wild animals. In Isaiah, the Lord planted a vineyard and tended it carefully, yet the plants produced bad fruit (Is 5:1-4). Consequently, the Lord removed the protective hedges surrounding the vineyard and compromised the walls (Is 5:5), rendering the land barren and useless (Is 5:6). The vineyard, representing Israel, belonged to the Lord of Hosts, and the plants corresponded to the people. Similarly, God permitted the break in the wall protecting the vineyard (Israel), giving boars (foreigners) access to the **fruit** (Israel).

80:14 In a sequential list of actions (**return . . . look down . . . see; take care**), the people's perceived absence of God relates to suffering, captivity, and oppression. The turning

Look down from heaven and see;
take care of this vine,

15 the root[A] Your right hand has planted,
the shoot[B] that You made strong
for Yourself.[a]

16 It was cut down and burned up;[C]
they[D] perish at the rebuke
of Your countenance.[b]

17 Let Your hand be with the man
at Your right hand,
with the son of man
You have made strong for Yourself.[c]

18 Then we will not turn away from You;
revive us, and we will call on Your name.[d]

19 Restore us, *Yahweh, the God of Hosts;[e]
look on us with favor, and we will
be saved.[f]

Psalm 81

A Call to Obedience

For the choir director:
on the *Gittith. Of *Asaph.[g]

1 Sing for joy to God our strength;
shout in triumph to the God of Jacob.[h]

2 Lift up a song—play the tambourine,
the melodious lyre, and the harp.[i]

3 Blow the horn on the day of our feasts[E,F]
during the new moon[j]
and during the full moon.

4 For this is a statute for Israel,
a judgment of the God of Jacob.[k]

5 He set it up as an ordinance for Joseph
when He went throughout[G] the land
of Egypt.[l]

I heard an unfamiliar language:

6 "I relieved his shoulder from the burden;
his hands were freed from carrying
the basket.[m]

7 You called out in distress,
and I rescued you;
I answered you from the thundercloud.[n]
I tested you at the waters of Meribah.[o]
*Selah

8 Listen, My people, and I will
admonish you.
Israel, if you would only listen to Me![p]

9 There must not be a strange god
among you;
you must not bow down to a foreign god.[q]

a 80:14-15 Is 63:15
b 80:16 Ps 39:11; 76:6; Is 33:12
c 80:17 Ps 89:21
d 80:18 Ps 71:20; 85:6
e 80:19 Ps 60:1; 85:4; Lm 5:21
f Mal 1:9
g 81:title 1Ch 16:5,7; Ps 8,84 titles
h 81:1 Ps 59:16; 95:1-2; 98:4
i 81:2 Ps 33:2; 71:22; 92:3
j 81:3 Lv 23:24; Nm 10:10; 29:1
k 81:4 1Ch 16:17; Ps 105:10
l 81:5 Ps 78:5; 122:4
m 81:6 Is 9:4; 10:27
n 81:7 Ex 14:24; 20:18-20
o Ex 17:1-7; Nm 20:2-13
p 81:8 Ps 50:7
q 81:9 Ex 20:3-5; 22:20; 34:14

A 80:15 Hb obscure   B 80:15 Or son   C 80:16 Lit burned with fire   D 80:16 Or may they   E 81:3 Lit feast   F 81:3 Either Passover or Tabernacles   G 81:5 LXX, Syr, Jer read out of

away of God's face (v. 3) indicates God's refusal to respond. The psalmist implored Yahweh to "turn" His attention back toward the nation and restore it (Is 63:15-18).

80:15 The **right hand** signifies a privileged position or serves as the instrument that executes divine action. **Root** (lit "stem or shoot") occurs only here. **Shoot** is never used literally in an agricultural sense and always denotes a living being, in this case alluding to the "son of man" in verse 17.

80:16 The Lord Himself planted the root (Israel) and nurtured it, only to permit its destruction in judgment. **At the rebuke of Your countenance** signifies that sinful people could not survive in the presence of God.

80:17 Let your hand be denotes a request from a subordinate to a superior. The transfer of divine power flows through God's hand and into his agent. The **man at Your right hand** is usually a king (110:1; cp. Is 45:1) who received divine appointment and approval. In the NT, Christ is seated at the right hand of God, identical with God in authority, power, and holiness (Heb 1:3).

Ps 81 title On **Gittith** see note at Psalm 8 title. On **Asaph**, see note at Psalm 50 title.

81:1 Jacob is a designation for the 12 tribes of Israel, who all serve one God.

81:3 The assembly blew the **horn** (Hb shophar) to herald the beginning of a cultic celebration or before entering into battle. A **new moon** marked the beginning of festivities, which concluded with the full moon. According to the Hebrew calendar, this time paralleled a series of cultic activities celebrated during two weeks of autumn.

81:4 A feast stipulated by the Torah indicates that the song accompanied one of three great cultic celebrations. **Judgment** means "ordinance" in this context.

81:5-6 Psalms of Asaph frequently mention **Joseph** as a designation for Israel (50; 73; 83). The song does not refer to the historical person Joseph, but to Israel as Joseph's descendants. The formal establishment of the law occurred long after Joseph's death and only after Israel departed from Egypt. The **unfamiliar language** (lit "a tongue I did not know") does not refer to a divine oracle or prophetic utterance, but to direct communication between God and His people during the exodus. Israel **heard** and understood God. Although the psalmist was not present, the exodus events of the past were clearly understood by the present community. The Lord freed Israel from the burden of Egyptian bondage. During Israel's slavery under Pharaoh, the workers used a **basket** to carry bricks and construction materials.

81:7 Along with verse 6, this verse recollects the exodus and the Lord's faithful response to the suffering of His people. Yahweh spoke to Israel **from the thundercloud** (lit "from hidden thunder") in the desert. The thundercloud evokes the appearance of God in Exodus 19. During the sojourn in the wilderness, Rephidim, renamed **Meribah** (see note at Ex 17:1-7), was the place where the Israelites tested Yahweh's faithfulness and ability to provide water. However, the psalmist depicted the event as one in which the Lord **tested** Israel's faithfulness and dependence on Him.

81:8 The Hebrew concept of hearing—shema—is the central theme of the psalm. Hearing involves obedience to instruction. Thus, a person does not truly hear God without a response of obedience. **Admonish** conveys the meaning of "warn" or "testify." If Israel had listened to the Lord, she would have experienced victory and prosperity (vv. 14-15).

81:9 The phrase **there must not be a strange god** recalls the first of the Ten Commandments (Ex 20:3-4; Dt 5:7-8). The current plight of the Lord's people resulted from idolatrous

¹⁰ I am •Yahweh your God,
who brought you up from the land
of Egypt.^a
Open your mouth wide, and I will fill it.^b

¹¹ "But My people did not listen to Me;
Israel did not obey Me.^c

¹² So I gave them over
to their stubborn hearts
to follow their own plans.^d

¹³ If only My people would listen to Me
and Israel would follow My ways,^e

¹⁴ I would quickly subdue their enemies
and turn My hand against their foes."^f

¹⁵ Those who hate the LORD
would pretend submission to Him;^g
their doom would last forever.^h

¹⁶ But He would feed Israel^A
with the best wheat.
"I would satisfy you with honey
from the rock."ⁱ

Psalm 82
A Plea for Righteous Judgment

A psalm of •Asaph.^j

¹ God has taken His place
in the divine assembly;
He judges among the gods:^{B,k}

---

² "How long will you judge unjustly
and show partiality to the wicked?^l

•Selah

³ Provide justice for the needy
and the fatherless;
uphold the rights of the oppressed
and the destitute.^m

⁴ Rescue the poor and needy;
save them from the power of
the wicked."ⁿ

⁵ They do not know or understand;
they wander in darkness.^o
All the foundations of the earth
are shaken.^p

⁶ I said, "You are gods;^q
you are all sons of the •Most High.^r

⁷ However, you will die like men
and fall like any other ruler."^s

⁸ Rise up, God, judge the earth,
for all the nations belong to You.^t

Psalm 83
Prayer against Enemies

A song. A psalm of •Asaph.^u

¹ God, do not keep silent.
Do not be deaf, God; do not be idle.^v

---

^a81:10 Ex 20:2; Dt 5:6
^bPs 78:25; 107:9
^c81:11 Jr 7:24; 13:10
^d81:12 Jb 8:4; Jr 11:8
^e81:13 Dt 5:29; Is 48:18
^f81:14 Ps 18:47; 47:3; Am 1:8
^g81:15 Ps 18:44; 66:3
^hDt 32:35
ⁱ81:16 Nm 18:12; Dt 32:13-14; Ps 147:14
^j82:title 1Ch 16:5,7
^k82:1 Jb 21:22; Ps 7:8; 58:11
^l82:2 Dt 1:17; Pr 18:5; Mal 2:9
^m82:3 Dt 24:17; Is 11:4; Jr 22:16
ⁿ82:4 Jb 29:12; Pr 24:11
^o82:5 Pr 2:13; Is 44:18
^pPs 11:3
^q82:6 Jn 10:34
^rPs 82:1; Lk 6:35
^s82:7 Ps 49:12
^t82:8 Ps 58:11; 96:13
^u83:title 1Ch 16:5,7
^v83:1 Ps 28:1; 39:12; Is 62:1

---

^A81:16 Lit him   ^B82:1 Or the heavenly beings, or the earthly rulers; lit elohim

---

practices. God's resolution of Israel's situation presupposed their obedience.

81:10 A formulaic expression **I am Yahweh your God** (Ex 6:6-8; Dt 20:1; Jdg 6:13) recollects the revelation of God to Moses (Ex 3:14). **Open your mouth wide, and I will fill it** describes Yahweh's faithful provision.

81:11-12 Israel refused to listen to the Lord, as shown by her failure to respond. **Did not obey** expresses an unwillingness to yield to the leadership of Yahweh. Therefore, as a result of their covenant disobedience, Yahweh relinquished His people to **their stubborn hearts** (Dt 29:18; Jr 3:17; 7:24; 23:17). Israel demonstrated her arrogance by taking pride in her own reasoning faculties and ignoring the counsel of God.

81:15 Those who hate the LORD include any individual or nation who refused to hear Him and to follow His covenant stipulations.

81:16 Two phrases, the **best wheat** and **honey from the rock,** allude to Dt 32:13-14. In Deuteronomy 32, Moses recounted the history of Yahweh's relationship with Israel, noting Israel's frequent rebellion against Him. When Yahweh first established His people in Canaan, the nation enjoyed prosperity and peace. The people eventually became too comfortable in God's providence and failed to keep God's law. The passage from Deuteronomy provides the interpretive model for this psalm.

Ps 82 title On **Asaph,** see note at Psalm 50 title.

82:1 The phrase **God has taken His place** indicates sentencing or judgment in progress (74:22; 94:2; Is 3:13; 33:10)

since judges normally sat (Ex 18:14; Jdg 4:5; Is 28:6). The **divine assembly** has its equivalents in Ugaritic, Mesopotamian, and Egyptian mythology, where it refers to "lesser gods" in a pantheon. In the OT, the designation either refers to heavenly servant beings (103:19) or judges and governors appointed by God as political leaders (Ex 21:6; 22:8; 2Ch 19:5-6). The Scriptures place God in the presence of a divine council consisting of good and evil spirits (1Kg 22:19-22), sometimes designated as "sons of God" (Jb 1:6-12; Ps 82:6). The emphasis on judgment (vv. 1-3,8) reinforces the failure of God's servants.

82:2 God formally indicted the appointed officials for social injustice since their decisions favored those who were **wicked.**

82:5 The psalmist characterized the officials as those who did **not know or understand,** using language reminiscent of the impotent idols often depicted by the prophet Isaiah as blind, deaf, mute, and powerless (Is 44:9,18; 46:1-2,6-7; Jr 10:3-5). The distorted administration of justice disrupted the cosmic order as originally intended by God, threatening the **foundations** on which God had established the world.

82:6-7 Kings who failed to perform responsibly and ethically deserved death. The concept finds support in the book of Ezekiel (Ezk 28:1-19), where the Lord banished His divine servant, the king of Tyre, from His presence to die like a common man.

82:8 The Lord as Creator and King restores cosmic balance through the exercise of divine judgment on **the nations**.

Ps 83 title On **Asaph,** see note at Psalm 50 title.

2 See how Your enemies make an uproar;
   those who hate You
     have acted arrogantly.[A,a]
3 They devise clever schemes
   against Your people;
  they conspire against
     Your treasured ones.[b]
4 They say, "Come, let us wipe them out
   as a nation
  so that Israel's name will no longer
     be remembered."[c]
5 For they have conspired with one mind;
   they form an alliance[B] against You[d]—
6 the tents of Edom and the Ishmaelites,[e]
   Moab and the Hagrites,[f]
7 Gebal, Ammon, and Amalek,[g]
   Philistia with the inhabitants of Tyre.[h]
8 Even Assyria has joined them;
   they lend support[C] to the sons of Lot.[D,i]
          •Selah

9 Deal with them as You did with Midian,[j]
   as You did with Sisera
  and Jabin at the Kishon River.[k]
10 They were destroyed at En-dor;
   they became manure for the ground.[l]
11 Make their nobles like Oreb and Zeeb,[m]
   and all their tribal leaders like Zebah
     and Zalmunna,[n]
12 who said, "Let us seize God's pastures
   for ourselves."[o]

13 Make them like tumbleweed, my God,

like straw before the wind.[p]
14 As fire burns a forest,
   as a flame blazes
     through mountains,[q]
15 so pursue them with Your tempest
   and terrify them with Your storm.[r]
16 Cover their faces with shame
   so that they will seek
     Your name •Yahweh.[s]
17 Let them be put to shame
   and terrified forever;
  let them perish in disgrace.[t]
18 May they know that You alone—
   whose name is Yahweh—
  are the •Most High over all the earth.[u]

Psalm 84
Longing for God's House

For the choir director: on the •Gittith.[v]
A psalm of the sons of Korah.

1 How lovely is Your dwelling place,
   Lord of •Hosts.[w]
2 I long and yearn
   for the courts of the Lord;
  my heart and flesh cry out
     for[E] the living God.[x]

3 Even a sparrow finds a home,
   and a swallow, a nest for herself
  where she places her young—
     near Your altars, Lord of Hosts,

Cross references:
a 83:2 Ps 2:1; Is 17:12
b 83:3 Jb 5:12-13; Ps 37:12; 64:2
c 83:4 Ps 41:5; Jr 11:19
d 83:5 Ps 2:2
e 83:6 Gn 25:12-16; Ps 137:7
f 1Ch 5:10; 2Ch 20:10
g 83:7 Jos 13:5; 1Sm 15:2
h 1Sm 4:1; Ezk 27:3
i 83:8 2Kg 15:19
j 83:9 Nm 31:7; Jdg 7:1-24
k Jdg 4:7; 5:21
l 83:10 Jr 9:22; 16:4; 25:33
m 83:11 Jdg 7:25; 8:3
n Jdg 8:5-21
o 83:12 2Ch 20:11
p 83:13 Jb 21:18; Ps 1:4; Is 17:13
q 83:14 Is 9:18; 10:16-19
r 83:15 Jb 9:17; Ps 58:9
s 83:16 Ps 35:26; 109:29; 132:18
t 83:17 Ps 35:4; 70:2
u 83:18 Ps 97:9
v 84:title Ps 8,81 titles
w 84:1 Ps 43:3; 132:5
x 84:2 Ps 42:1-2; 63:1

A 83:2 Lit *have lifted their head*   B 83:5 Lit *they cut a covenant*   C 83:8 Lit *they are an arm*   D 83:8 = Moab and Edom   E 84:2 Or *flesh shout for joy to*

83:1 A communal lament, this final psalm of Asaph makes three urgent requests of Yahweh. Using terms generally attributed to lifeless, false gods (81:9), the community seeks God's response to the current crisis.

83:2 In contrast to the Lord's silence and apparent inactivity (v. 1), the adversaries made **an uproar**, lifting their heads in a defiant gesture of independence.

83:3 The imagery in verses 3-5 echo 2:1-3, without the messianic emphasis. Nations "rebel" and "plot" (2:1), gathering together to challenge the Lord and His anointed (2:2-3). Similarly the enemies "make an uproar" (83:2), **devise clever schemes**, and **conspire against** God's **treasured ones** (lit "sheltered, protected ones"; Is 7:5-6; 17:12-13).

83:4 The rare Hebrew term for **wipe . . . out** denotes complete annihilation, making it as if it had never existed (9:4-6; Ex 23:23; 1Kg 13:34).

83:6-7 While the context implies that all 10 enemy nations originated from Lot (v. 9), only **Moab** and **Ammon** descended from him (Gn 19:36-38). The nations listed here divide into two separate groups. The **Ishmaelites** and the **Hagrites** are synonymous with Moab and **Edom**. The remaining nations make up a familiar list of all Israel's fiercest enemies, with the exception of **Gebal**, about which little is known.

83:8 Assyria, as the enemy par excellence, lent **support** (lit

"arm"), a term figuratively denoting military resources and strength.

83:9-12 In an extended imprecation (see note at 109:1-31), the lament evokes memories of Yahweh's intervention in two major victories. **Sisera** and **Jabin** were defeated by Deborah and Barak (Jdg 4-5), and the nation of **Midian**—including **Oreb . . . Zeeb . . . Zebah**, and **Zalmunna**—was defeated by Gideon (Jdg 6:1–8:21).

83:13 The opposition will be like **straw**, separated from the grain and blown away by the evening **wind**, implying that the enemy's power lacked substance.

83:15 **Storm** imagery is associated with the execution of God's wrath (18:7-15; 50:3; 107:24-30; Jnh 1:4).

83:16-18 Three Hebrew terms for "shame" in these verses reinforce the extent of the Lord's judgment and His complete humiliation of the oppressors, culminating in the annihilation of hostile peoples. The fate the adversaries sought to inflict on God's people (v. 4) will be exacted on them (see note at 7:14-16). Only then would the nations recognize the Lord as sovereign King.

Ps 84 title On **Gittith** see note at Psalm 8 title. On **Sons of Korah**, see note at Psalm 42 title.

84:2 The courts refers to the outer precincts of the temple where worshipers gathered.

my King and my God.[a]

4 How happy are those who reside
    in Your house,
who praise You continually.[b]   *Selah*

5 Happy are the people whose strength
    is in You,
whose hearts are set on pilgrimage.[c]

6 As they pass through the Valley
    of Baca,[A]
they make it a source of springwater;
even the autumn rain will cover it
    with blessings.[B,d]

7 They go from strength to strength;
each appears before God in *Zion.[e]

8 LORD God of Hosts, hear my prayer;
listen, God of Jacob.[f]   *Selah*

9 Consider our shield,[C] God;[g]
look on the face
    of Your anointed one.[h]

10 Better a day in Your courts
than a thousand anywhere else.
I would rather be at the door
    of the house of my God
than to live in the tents
    of wicked people.[i]

11 For the LORD God is a sun and shield.[j]
The LORD gives grace and glory;
He does not withhold the good
from those who live with integrity.[k]

---

[a] 84:3 Ps 5:2; 43:4
[b] 84:4 Ps 65:4
[c] 84:5 Ps 119:2; 122:1
[d] 84:6 Ezk 34:26; Jl 2:23
[e] 84:7 Pr 4:18; Is 40:31
[f] 84:8 Ps 39:12; 54:2; 86:6
[g] 84:9 Ps 3:3; 115:9-11
[h] 1Sm 2:10; 2Ch 6:42; Ps 132:17
[i] 84:10 Ps 27:4
[j] 84:11 Ps 3:3; 5:12; 18:2; 28:7; 119:114; Is 60:19-20; Rv 21:23
[k] Pr 2:7
[l] 84:12 Ps 40:4
[m] 85:1 Ps 106:4
[n] Dt 30:3; Ps 14:7; Jr 29:14
[o] 85:2 1Kg 8:34; Ps 32:1,5
[p] 85:3 Ps 78:38; 106:23; Jnh 3:9
[q] 85:4 Ps 27:9; 79:9; 80:3,7
[r] 85:5 Ps 74:1; 79:5; 80:4
[s] 85:6 Ps 71:20; 80:18; 149:2
[t] 85:7 Ps 69:13; 119:41
[u] 85:8 Hg 2:9; Zch 9:10

---

12 Happy is the person who trusts in You,
    LORD of Hosts![l]

Psalm 85
Restoration of Favor

For the choir director. A psalm
of the sons of Korah.

1 LORD, You showed favor to Your land;[m]
You restored Jacob's prosperity.[D,n]

2 You took away Your people's *guilt;
You covered all their sin.[o]   *Selah*

3 You withdrew all Your fury;
You turned from Your burning anger.[p]

4 Return to us, God of our salvation,
and abandon Your displeasure
    with us.[q]

5 Will You be angry with us forever?
Will You prolong Your anger for all
    generations?[r]

6 Will You not revive us again
so that Your people may rejoice
    in You?[s]

7 Show us Your faithful love, LORD,
and give us Your salvation.[t]

8 I will listen to what God will say;
surely the LORD will declare peace
to His people, His godly ones,
and not let them go back
    to foolish ways.[u]

[A] 84:6 Or *Valley of Tears*   [B] 84:6 Or *pools*   [C] 84:9 = the king   [D] 85:1 Or *restored Jacob from captivity*

84:4-5 On **happy**, see note at 1:1. These verses mirror the structure of the Beatitudes (Mt 5:3-12), setting forth some of the conditions of happiness. **Whose hearts are set on pilgrimage** is literally "the highways are on their hearts." This describes the minds of the godly, their thoughts focused on the ascent to Zion.

84:6 The **Valley of Baca** derives from the Hebrew term *baka'*, "to weep." The joyful tears of the pilgrims transformed the source of sadness and grief into a spring of blessing, just as the early rains of autumn restored water to the valley.

84:9 God as a **shield** is a metaphorical reference to the protection provided by the king for his people.

84:10 The psalmist would rather stand outside at the entrance to the temple without shelter than to **live** in comfort among the **wicked**.

Ps 85 title On **sons of Korah**, see note at Psalm 42 title.

85:1 The perfect form of the Hebrew verbs, denoting completed action, supports a postexilic date for this psalm that celebrates Jacob's return from Babylonian captivity. The idiomatic expression "restore the fortunes" includes the concept of a release from imprisonment or debt combined with the return of the Lord's people to their homeland (14:7; 53:6; 126:4; Dt 30:3; Jr 29:14; 30:3,18; Am 9:14; Zph 2:7). As a key word of the psalm, the root *shuv* ("turn," "return," "restore") occurs five times (Ps 85:1,3,4,6,8).

85:2 The Hebrew term for **covered**, when combined with the word for sin, means "forgave," especially in context with "took away" in the previous line (32:1).

85:3 The Hebrew root *'avar* ("anger, fury") functions as a wordplay with a second related Hebrew root *'avar*, meaning "pass over, forgive" ("pardon" in Jb 7:21). The Lord has forgiven Israel's sins and **turned** (Hb *shuv*) His anger away from them.

85:4 If God had already forgiven, restored, and showed favor to the exiles, why did the psalmist call on Him to do so again? His request acknowledged that God's renewal of His wrath against the people remained a tangible reality.

85:5 On **will You be angry with us forever**, compare 79:5; 80:4; 88:14. To **prolong . . . anger for all generations** recalls Ex 34:7, where the Lord promised to punish descendants for the sins of their fathers. The nation of Israel experienced suffering as a consequence of previous sin, suggesting that all God's people shared responsibility for the welfare and moral condition of the nation.

85:6-7 **Faithful love** (Hb *chesed*; "covenant loyalty") is a cultic term indicating a unique relationship between the Lord and His people, a relationship built on loyalty by those not obligated to demonstrate that loyalty. **Revive us again** (lit "restore our lives") uses the Hebrew word *shuv*. Yahweh restores Israel's fortunes by turning His anger from them, thereby restoring Jacob's vitality. The **salvation** of the Lord results from a demonstration of His covenant loyalty.

85:8 **Go back** is the Hebrew word *shuv* (cp. vv. 1,3,6).

9 His salvation is very near
those who ·fear Him,
so that glory may dwell in our land.[a]
10 Faithful love and truth
will join together;
righteousness and peace will embrace.[b]
11 Truth will spring up from the earth,
and righteousness will look
down from heaven.[c]
12 Also, the LORD will provide
what is good,
and our land will yield its crops.[d]
13 Righteousness will go before Him
to prepare the way for His steps.[e]

Psalm 86
Lament and Petition

A Davidic prayer.

1 Listen, LORD, and answer me,
for I am poor and needy.[f]
2 Protect my life, for I am faithful.[g]
You are my God; save Your servant
who trusts in You.[h]
3 Be gracious to me, Lord,
for I call to You all day long.[i]
4 Bring joy to Your servant's life,
because I turn to You, Lord.[j]
5 For You, Lord, are kind and ready
to forgive,[k]
rich in faithful love to all who call
on You.[l]
6 LORD, hear my prayer;
listen to my plea for mercy.[m]
7 I call on You in the day of my distress,
for You will answer me.[n]
8 Lord, there is no one like You
among the gods,
and there are no works like Yours.[o]
9 All the nations You have made
will come and bow down
before You, Lord,
and will honor Your name.[p]
10 For You are great
and perform wonders;
You alone are God.[q]

11 Teach me Your way, ·Yahweh,
and I will live by Your truth.
Give me an undivided mind to ·fear
Your name.[r]
12 I will praise You with all my heart,
Lord my God,
and will honor Your name forever.[s]
13 For Your faithful love for me is great,
and You deliver my life from the depths
of ·Sheol.[t]

14 God, arrogant people have attacked me;
a gang of ruthless men seeks my life.
They have no regard for You.[u]
15 But You, Lord, are a compassionate
and gracious God,
slow to anger and rich in faithful love
and truth.[v]
16 Turn to me and be gracious to me.
Give Your strength to Your servant;
save the son of Your female servant.[w]
17 Show me a sign of Your goodness;
my enemies will see and be put
to shame
because You, LORD, have helped
and comforted me.[x]

[a] 85:9 Is 46:13; Zch 2:5; Jn 1:14
[b] 85:10 Ps 72:3; 89:14
[c] 85:11 Is 45:8
[d] 85:12 Ps 65:12-13; 67:6; Ezk 34:27
[e] 85:13 Ps 89:14; Is 40:3,10; 58:8
[f] 86:1 Ps 17:6; 31:2; 70:5
[g] 86:2 1Sm 2:9; Ps 37:28
[h] Ps 109:26
[i] 86:3 Ps 25:5; 88:9
[j] 86:4 Ps 25:1; 43:5
[k] 86:5 Ps 130:4
[l] Ps 103:8; 145:8
[m] 86:6 Ps 55:1-2
[n] 86:7 Gn 35:3; Ps 17:6; 20:1
[o] 86:8 Ex 15:11; Dt 3:24; Ps 89:6
[p] 86:9 Ps 22:7; Is 66:24; Rv 15:4
[q] 86:10 2Kg 19:15; Ps 72:18; 83:18; Jr 10:6
[r] 86:11 Ps 25:4-5; 26:3
[s] 86:12 Ps 111:1
[t] 86:13 Ps 30:3; Ezk 26:20
[u] 86:14 Ps 54:3
[v] 86:15 Ex 34:6; Nm 14:18; Neh 9:17
[w] 86:16 Ps 25:16; 68:35
[x] 86:17 Ps 112:10; 132:18

85:9-10 Reconciliation is characterized by renewal and the return of peace and prosperity to the **land** (119:151; 145:18; Is 50:8; 55:6; 62:2).

85:11-12 Personification of God's attributes as pastoral imagery reinforce the connection between material prosperity and the perfect state of fairness and righteousness operative under the Lord's kingship. Fertility and abundant rainfall affirm God's faithfulness (Is 30:23-25; 32:15-18; 45:8; 55:10; 61:11; Am 9:13).

85:13 Righteousness accompanies the Lord in His procession back to Jerusalem (43:3; 89:14; 96:6; Is 40:10; 58:8; 62:11), representing a reversal from when the land was overrun by injustice.

86:3 In many individual laments, the psalmist's unceasing prayers (**all day long**) continued until God delivered him.

86:4-5 An appeal to the Lord's kindness, forgiveness, and covenant loyalty (**faithful love**) is a variation of the formula that occurs again in verse 15. Psalm 103:8 associates forgiveness of sin with the Lord's covenant loyalty.

86:6 Hear requests a respondent who is fully alert. **Plea for mercy** is a supplication, the seeking of divine favor (28:2; 31:23; 130:2; 140:7).

86:7 God will **answer** (Hb *'anan*) the prayer of the humble ("poor"; Hb *'ani*); see verse 1 (see note at 34:6).

86:8-9 A statement about the incomparability of God often precedes a call for the universal recognition of His sovereignty (Ex 15:11; 2Sam 7:22; 1Kg 8:23; Mc 7:18).

86:13 Sheol refers to the underworld (Is 14:9; Ezk 31:16) or a place of separation from God (Ps 6:5; Is 38:18) from which there is no praise. Figuratively, mention of Sheol may depict imminent death or the removal of a person from the divine presence (Jnh 2:3).

86:14 Arrogant people do not recognize or regard the Lord (19:13; 54:3).

86:15 The psalmist emphasized the positive attributes of the Lord as **compassionate**, merciful, **slow to anger**, and great in covenant loyalty and **truth**. Note the absence of the second half of the formula, which describes God's wrathful response to sin (Ex 34:6-7; see note at Ps 86:4-5).

86:16 Your female servant is figurative for Israel.

Psalm 87
Zion, the City of God

A psalm of the sons of Korah. A song.

¹ His foundation is
on the holy mountains.ᵃ

² The Lord loves the gates of •Zion
more than all the dwellings of Jacob.ᵇ

³ Glorious things are said about you,
city of God.ᶜ   •Selah

⁴ "I will mention those who know Me:
•Rahab, Babylon, Philistia, Tyre,
and •Cush—
each one was born there."ᵈ

⁵ And it will be said of Zion,
"This one and that one were born
in her."
The •Most High Himself
will establish her.ᵉ

⁶ When He registers the peoples,
the Lord will record,
"This one was born there."ᶠ   Selah

⁷ Singers and dancers alike will say,
"My whole source of joy isᴬ in you."ᵍ

Psalm 88
A Cry of Desperation

A song. A psalm of the sons of Korah.
For the choir director: according to Mahalath
Leannoth. A •Maskil of Heman the Ezrahite.ʰ

¹ Lord, God of my salvation,
I cry out before You day and night.ⁱ

² May my prayer reach Your presence;
listen to my cry.ʲ

³ For I have had enough troubles,
and my life is near •Sheol.ᵏ

⁴ I am counted among those going down
to the •Pit.ˡ
I am like a man without strength,ᵐ

⁵ abandonedᴮ among the dead.
I am like the slain lying
in the grave,ⁿ
whom You no longer remember,
and who are cut off from Your care.ᶜ,ᵒ

⁶ You have put me in the lowest part
of the Pit,
in the darkest places, in the depths.ᵖ

⁷ Your wrath weighs heavily on me;ᵟ
You have overwhelmed me with all
Your waves.ʳ   •Selah

⁸ You have distanced my friends
from me;
You have made me repulsive
to them.ˢ
I am shut in and cannot go out.

⁹ My eyes are worn out from crying.ᵗ
Lord, I cry out to You all day long;ᵘ
I spread out my hands to You.ᵛ

¹⁰ Do You work wonders for the dead?
Do departed spirits rise up
to praise You?ʷ   Selah

¹¹ Will Your faithful love be declared
in the grave,
Your faithfulness in •Abaddon?ˣ

Cross references (center column)
ᵃ87:1 Ps 78:69; Is 28:16
ᵇ87:2 Ps 78:67-68
ᶜ87:3 Ps 48:8
ᵈ87:4 Is 19:23-25; 56:6-7; Zch 2:10-12
ᵉ87:5 Ps 48:8; Is 2:2
ᶠ87:6 Is 4:3; Ezk 13:9
ᵍ87:7 Ps 46:4; 68:25
ʰ88:title 1Kg 4:31; 1Ch 2:6
ⁱ88:1 Ps 22:2; 86:3; Lk 18:7
ʲ88:2 Ps 18:6; 31:2; 86:1
ᵏ88:3 Ps 16:10; 116:3
ˡ88:4 Ps 28:1; 143:7
ᵐPs 61:2
ⁿ88:5 Ps 31:12
ᵒPs 31:22; Is 53:8
ᵖ88:6 Ps 69:15; 86:13; Ezk 26:20
ᵟ88:7 Ps 32:4; 39:10
ʳPs 42:7
ˢ88:8 Jb 19:13-22; Ps 31:11
ᵗ88:9 Ps 6:7; 31:9
ᵘPs 86:3
ᵛPs 143:6
ʷ88:10 Ps 6:5; 30:9
ˣ88:11 Jb 26:6; Pr 15:11; 27:20

ᴬ87:7 Lit "All my springs, are   ᴮ88:5 Or set free   ᶜ88:5 Or hand

Ps 87 title On **sons of Korah**, see note at Psalm 42 title.

87:1 His foundation or "established city" (Jerusalem) renders the mountain **holy**.

87:2 Court proceedings, social interaction, and commercial transactions normally took place in the **gates** of a city (Ru 4:1-2; Jb 29:7-10; Pr 24:7). The Lord reinforced Jerusalem as the preferred location for His sanctuary.

87:3 City of God means belonging to God, as a possession.

87:4 The universal outlook of the psalm is evident as the psalmist recounted major powers of Mesopotamia, all once historical enemies of Israel. **Rahab**, the mythical dragon-like chaos monster, represented Egypt (Is 30:7). **Babylon** was known for its oppression while **Philistia** had a reputation for aggression. These, along with the wealthy of **Tyre**, and the Cushites, from the Nubian kingdom south of Egypt, would attain the status of naturalized citizens with full privileges though they were born in another country. From an eschatological perspective, these nations would be qualified to participate in Israel's feasts and Torah instruction since all national distinctions would be eliminated under the Lord's kingship (Is 2:2-4; 49:18-23; 56:3,6-7; Zch 14:16-18).

87:5-7 Despite the inclusion of Gentile nations, the Lord would appoint Israel to a special position of leadership in the eschatological kingdom because of her birthright (Is 60; 62:1-5).

Ps 88 title On **sons of Korah**, see note at Psalm 42 title. **Heman the Ezrahite**, a famous wise man during Solomon's reign, served as the king's seer. **According to Mahalath Leannoth** may designate this as a psalm of penitence associated with purification from illness (see note at Ps 53 title).

88:3 I have had enough troubles means literally "my soul is sated with turmoil." The psalmist described his condition as grave, as his **life** drew near **Sheol** (see note at 86:13; cp. Jb 7:11-21; 13:18-28; 30:20-23).

88:4 The **Pit** is another name for Sheol. The psalmist compared himself to a weakened man, about to die.

88:5 The psalmist passed from memory since the dead were **cut off** from interaction with God and others (Is 53:8).

88:6 The **lowest part of the Pit** (cp. 86:13) is often portrayed as the roots of the mountains in the deep sea (Jnh 2:6; Mc 7:19).

88:8 The Hebrew word for "repulsive" (to'evah) often describes unethical practices such as child sacrifice or idolatry ("detestable" in Dt 12:31; 27:15). Those who committed such heinous acts were ceremonially unclean and were ostracized from the community.

88:9 The **hands** being **spread out** implies submission and helplessness.

12 Will Your wonders be known in
   the darkness
   or Your righteousness in the land
   of oblivion?ᵃ

13 But I call to You for help, LORD;
   in the morning my prayer meets You.ᵇ

14 LORD, why do You reject me?ᶜ
   Why do You hide Your face from me?ᵈ

15 From my youth,
   I have been afflicted and near death.
   I suffer Your horrors; I am desperate.ᵉ

16 Your wrath sweeps over me;
   Your terrors destroy me.ᶠ

17 They surround me like water
   all day long;
   they close in on me from every side.ᵍ

18 You have distanced loved one
   and neighbor from me;
   darkness is my only friend.ᴬ,ʰ

Psalm 89

Perplexity about God's Promises

A *Maskil* of Ethan the Ezrahite.ⁱ

1 I will sing about the LORD's
   faithful love forever;ʲ
   I will proclaim Your faithfulness to all
   generations
   with my mouth.ᵏ

2 For I will declare,
   "Faithful love is built up forever;
   You establish Your faithfulness
   in the heavens."ˡ

3 The LORD said,
   "I have made a covenant
   with My chosen one;
   I have sworn an oath to David
   My servant:

4 'I will establish your offspring forever
   and build up your throne
   for all generations.'"ᵐ   •Selah

5 LORD, the heavens praise
   Your wondersⁿ—
   Your faithfulness also—
   in the assembly of the holy ones.ᵒ

6 For who in the skies can compare
   with the LORD?
   Who among the heavenly beingsᴮ is
   like the LORD?ᵖ

7 God is greatly •feared in the council
   of the holy ones,
   more awe-inspiring thanᶜ
   all who surround Him.ᵠ

8 LORD God of •Hosts,
   who is strong like You, LORD?ʳ
   Your faithfulness surrounds You.

9 You rule the raging sea;
   when its waves surge, You still them.ˢ

10 You crushed •Rahab like one
   who is slain;ᵗ
   You scattered Your enemies
   with Your powerful arm.ᵘ

11 The heavens are Yours; the earth also
   is Yours.
   The world and everything in it—
   You founded them.ᵛ

Cross-references (center column):
ᵃ88:12 Ec 9:5
ᵇ88:13 Ps 5:3; 119:147
ᶜ88:14 Ps 43:2
ᵈJb 13:24; Ps 10:1; 13:1
ᵉ88:15 Jb 31:23
ᶠ88:16 Jb 6:4; 9:34
ᵍ88:17 Ps 22:12,16; 118:10-12
ʰ88:18 Jb 19:13; Ps 31:11; 38:11
ⁱ89:title 1Kg 4:31; 1Ch 2:6
ʲ89:1 Ps 101:1
ᵏPs 92:2; 119:90
ˡ89:2 Ps 36:5
ᵐ89:3-4 2Sm 7:8-16; 1Ch 17:7-14; Jr 33:17-21
ⁿ89:5 Ps 19:1; 97:6
ᵒPs 149:1
ᵖ89:6 Ps 86:8; 113:5
ᵠ89:7 Ps 89:5; 96:4
ʳ89:8 Ex 15:11; 2Sm 7:22
ˢ89:9 Jb 38:11; Ps 104:9; Mt 8:23-27
ᵗ89:10 Is 30:7; 51:9-10
ᵘPs 68:1; 92:9
ᵛ89:11 1Ch 29:11; Ps 24:1

ᴬ88:18 Or *from me, my friends. Oh darkness!*   ᴮ89:6 Or *the angels*, or *the sons of the mighty*   ᶜ89:7 Or *ones, revered by*

88:10-12 A series of four rhetorical questions expect negative answers, typical of disputation speeches. The psalmist asked if God performed miracles on behalf of the dead in order to receive praise in the grave. On the contrary, God blesses the living to receive glory on earth and in heaven. **Departed spirits** could be translated as "shades," a figurative expression for "spirits of the dead" (Jb 26:5; Is 14:9; 26:14,19). **Abaddon**, a place of destruction, is synonymous with Sheol or the Pit (Jb 26:6; 28:22; Pr 15:11).

88:13-14 Prayers were often answered in the **morning** (5:3; 90:14; 143:8), so the psalmist, feeling his prayer had been ignored, accused God of rejecting him as one who was unclean.

88:16 Terrors acted as the Lord's agents of destruction (Jb 6:4) against the psalmist. Typically, God exercised His "terror" against enemies (Dt 32:25; Jb 13:21).

Ps 89 title Ethan the Ezrahite was a Levitical musician (1Ch 15:17,19). The connections of this psalm with 2 Samuel 7 and 1 Chronicles 17 are unmistakable.

89:1 On **faithful love**, see note at 77:8.

89:2 The covenant significance of the verb **built up** is seen in 2Sm 7:5,13,27; 1Ch 17:4,10,12.

89:3 I have made a covenant implies obligation and binding responsibility. The Lord assumes responsibility while imposing obligations on Israel as part of the covenant. **My chosen one** may refer to David, or collectively, to his descendants.

89:4 As the Lord's covenant loyalty is "built up" (v. 2), so the Lord will **establish** David's throne. The longevity of David's dynasty is compared to the Lord's faithfulness; both have been established **forever**.

89:5 Heavens could be a metonymy for "heavenly beings" (see note at 82:1).

89:6 Skies refers metaphorically to the heavenly realm (Jb 37:18). The expression **heavenly beings** is part of a formulaic expression typical of statements describing the incomparability of the Lord (18:31; 82:1; Ex 15:11; Is 40:18; 44:7).

89:7 On **council of the holy ones**, see verse 5 and note at 82:1.

89:8 Hosts (Hb *tseva'oth*; "armies") is military language describing the Lord as warrior.

89:9-10 Rahab, the name for an ancient Near Eastern mythological chaos monster, was associated with the chaotic sea (Jb 26:12; Is 51:9). In contrast with that myth, God created the ocean and continues to demonstrate His sovereignty over it (Ps 74:13-17).

¹² North and south—You created them.^a
   Tabor and Hermon shout for joy
      at Your name.^b
¹³ You have a mighty arm;
   Your hand is powerful;
   Your right hand is lifted high.^c
¹⁴ Righteousness and justice are
      the foundation
   of Your throne;^d
   faithful love and truth go before You.^e
¹⁵ Happy are the people who know
      the joyful shout;^f
   •Yahweh, they walk in the light
      of Your presence.^g
¹⁶ They rejoice in Your name all day long,
   and they are exalted
      by Your righteousness.^h
¹⁷ For You are their magnificent strength;ⁱ
   by Your favor our •horn is exalted.^j
¹⁸ Surely our shield^A belongs to the Lord,
   our king to the Holy One of Israel.^k

¹⁹ You once spoke in a vision
      to Your loyal ones
   and said: "I have granted help
      to a warrior;
   I have exalted one chosen^B
      from the people.^l
²⁰ I have found David My servant;
   I have anointed him
      with My sacred oil.^m
²¹ My hand will always be with him,
   and My arm will strengthen him.ⁿ
²² The enemy will not afflict^C him;
   no wicked man will oppress him.^o
²³ I will crush his foes before him
   and strike those who hate him.^p
²⁴ My faithfulness and love will be
      with him,
   and through My name
      his horn will be exalted.^q
²⁵ I will extend his power to the sea
   and his right hand to the rivers.^r

Cross references:
^a 89:12 Jb 26:7
^b Ps 133:3; Jr 46:18
^c 89:13 Ps 98:1; 118:16
^d 89:14 Ps 97:2
^e Ps 85:13
^f 89:15 Ps 98:6
^g Ps 56:13; 1Jn 1:7
^h 89:16 Ps 20:5; 105:3
ⁱ 89:17 Ps 28:8
^j Ps 148:14
^k 89:18 Ps 84:9
^l 89:19 2Sm 17:10; 1Kg 11:34; Ps 78:70
^m 89:20 1Sm 16:13; Ps 47:9; Ac 13:22
ⁿ 89:21 Ps 18:35; 80:17
^o 89:22 2Sm 7:10
^p 89:23 2Sm 7:9; Ps 2:9
^q 89:24 Ps 21:7; 132:17
^r 89:25 Ps 72:8

^A89:18 = the king   ^B89:19 Or *exalted a young man*   ^C89:22 Or *not exact tribute from*

89:12 North and south is a merism, the two extremes referring to everything between them. The Hebrew word for "create" *(bara')* is always used of God. **Tabor** and **Hermon** were noteworthy mountains in the north.

89:13 The Lord's right hand is **lifted high** (lit "exalted"), ready to exact judgment.

89:14 Righteousness and **justice** serve as the platform or pedestal on which the Lord builds His majesty. Ancient Near Eastern myths used figures of "righteousness" and "justice" as divine powers that function as throne supports. Combined with **faithful love** and **truth**, the four characteristics summarize the essential attributes of the Lord. The Lord's **throne** denotes the worldwide realm of His kingship (97:2).

89:15-17 God's **people** recognize the call to praise, and they are **happy** in His **presence** (see notes at 1:1 and 15:1).

yamiyn

Hebrew Pronunciation	[yah MEEN]
HCSB Translation	right hand, right, south
Uses in Psalms	42
Uses in the OT	141
Focus Passage	Psalm 89:12-13,25,42

Yamiyn signifies *right hand* (Is 41:10) and *right* as opposed to left (Gn 13:9). People oriented themselves by looking toward the sunrise, so *yamiyn* signifies *south*, the *right* side when facing eastward (Ezk 16:46). "To the *right* or to the *left*" connotes *elsewhere* (Gn 24:49). It suggests deviation from paths of moral integrity (Pr 4:27) or covenant obedience (Jos 1:7). The ancients viewed the *right hand* as the hand of action and power, whether for God or the wicked (Ps 21:8; 26:10). One phrase for *left-handed* means "restricted in one's *right* hand" (Jdg 3:15). The place of honor was at someone's *right hand* (Ps 45:9; 110:1). One giving assistance is pictured at the *right hand* of the one helped (Ps 109:31; 110:5). Courtroom accusers stood at the defendant's *right hand* (Zch 3:1). Distinguishing *right* and left shows maturity (Jnh 4:11). *Right* symbolizes uprightness in contrast with the left (Ec 10:2).

When the Lord's right hand is exalted (89:13), His people are **exalted**. Israel receives esteem, honor, and recognition through God's gracious **favor**. **Horn**, a figurative term for power or strength (75:4), reappears in 89:24, where the Lord raises David's horn through the divine name.

89:18 The **shield** of Israel was their **king**, who with God's help protected and defended the people. The king was given by God and was the servant of God (vv. 19-20), and therefore belonged to Him.

89:19 The **vision** refers to verses 3 and 4 and the larger context of the oracle of Nathan to David in 2Sm 7:1-17. The **warrior** selected from the people refers to David as the Lord's anointed and divinely empowered warrior. The Lord's right hand was exalted (v. 13). As a result, God's people were exalted (v. 16) and their horn of victory was exalted (v. 17); now the Lord has **exalted** the king.

89:20-38 This passage is similar to 2Sm 7:14-17 and 1Ch 17:3-15, suggesting a conceptual and literary relationship between them.

89:20 Kings and priests were **anointed** with **oil** in a formal inauguration ceremony, figuratively denoting divine approval, a close association with the Lord, and endowment with the Holy Spirit (Lv 4:3-4,16; Jdg 9:8; 1Kg 19:16; Is 61:1).

89:21 The **hand** of God establishes His faithfulness (v. 2), the Davidic dynasty (v. 4), and divine power (v. 21). As the Lord's **arm** is empowered with strength, so His divinely appointed agents will be empowered.

89:23 The promise in 2Sm 7:10 is here applied to David alone.

89:24 On **horn**, see note at verse 17; on **exalted**, see notes at verses 13, 15-17, and 19.

89:25 David will act with divine authority, which will extend from the Mediterranean **sea** in the west to the Tigris and Euphrates **rivers** in the east. The **right hand** always denotes the actions of God and His representative with authority and dominion (see word study at vv. 12-13,25,42, and note at v. 13).

26 He will call to Me, 'You are my Father,[a]
my God, the rock of my salvation.'[b]

27 I will also make him My firstborn,
greatest of the kings of the earth.[c]

28 I will always preserve My faithful love
for him,
and My covenant with him
will endure.[d]

29 I will establish his line forever,
his throne as long as heaven lasts.[A,e]

30 If his sons forsake My instruction
and do not live by My ordinances,[f]

31 if they dishonor My statutes
and do not keep My commands,[g]

32 then I will call their rebellion
to account with the rod,
their sin with blows.[h]

33 But I will not withdraw
My faithful love from him
or betray My faithfulness.[i]

34 I will not violate My covenant
or change what My lips have said.[j]

35 Once and for all
I have sworn an oath by My holiness;
I will not lie to David.[k]

36 His offspring will continue forever,
his throne like the sun before Me,[l]

37 like the moon, established forever,
a faithful witness in the sky."[m]   Selah

38 But You have spurned and rejected him;
You have become enraged
with Your anointed.[n]

39 You have repudiated the covenant
with Your servant;
You have completely dishonored
his crown.[B,o]

40 You have broken down all his walls;
You have reduced his fortified cities
to ruins.[p]

41 All who pass by plunder him;[q]
he has become an object of ridicule
to his neighbors.[r]

42 You have lifted high the right hand
of his foes;
You have made all his enemies rejoice.[s]

43 You have also turned back
his sharp sword
and have not let him stand in battle.[t]

44 You have made his splendor[C] cease
and have overturned his throne.[u]

45 You have shortened the days of his youth;
You have covered him with shame.[v]
                                              Selah

Cross references (center column):

[a]89:26 2Sm 7:14; 1Ch 22:10
[b]2Sm 22:47; Ps 18:2
[c]89:27 Ex 4:22; Jr 31:9; Col 1:15
[d]89:28 2Ch 13:5; Ps 105:8
[e]89:29 Is 9:7; Jr 33:17
[f]89:30 2Sm 7:14; 1Kg 2:4
[g]89:31 1Sm 12:15
[h]89:32 Jb 9:34
[i]89:33 2Sm 7:15
[j]89:34 Lv 26:44; Jdg 2:1
[k]89:35 Am 4:2
[l]89:36 Ps 72:5,17
[m]89:37 Jb 16:19; Lk 1:33
[n]89:38 1Ch 28:9; Ps 44:9
[o]89:39 Ps 74:7; Lm 2:7; 5:16
[p]89:40 Ps 80:12; Lm 2:2,5
[q]89:41 Jr 30:16
[r]Ps 44:13; 79:4
[s]89:42 Ps 13:4; 80:6
[t]89:43 Ps 44:10
[u]89:44 Ezk 28:7
[v]89:45 Is 54:4; Ezk 7:18; Ob 10

A89:29 Lit *as days of heaven*   B89:39 Lit *have dishonored his crown to the ground*   C89:44 Hb obscure

89:26 Father exemplifies the language of adoption. Near Eastern and Egyptian mythology appropriated this concept, in which the pharaoh or the divinely appointed king was considered a divine "son" of God. This psalm reached ideal fulfillment in Christ as a descendant of David and as the actual Son of God.

89:27 The father-son relationship in 2Sm 7:14 refers to David's son Solomon, while the idea in this psalm centers on David alone. The **firstborn** son usually received a special blessing from the father and a double inheritance. **Greatest** is the same Hebrew word that describes God as the "Most High" (87:5; 91:1). While these words fit David, they were fulfilled in Christ.

89:28 The **covenant** promises of God to His people will be realized through the line of David.

89:29 The longevity of David's seed is guaranteed by the Lord, and the eternal rule of David's dynasty will continue **as long as heaven lasts**. Psalm 72:5,17 compares the king's enduring reign with the life of the sun. The concept reflects an expression common in ancient Near Eastern thought.

89:30-32 If David's descendants should fail to exemplify righteous living and the fear of God, the Lord would not hesitate to discipline them. He would punish the dynasty with a staff or **rod**, a symbol of His royalty and kingship, and by natural means, such as disease or plague.

89:33-34 Despite disobedience, corruption, and divine correction, the Lord's promises will not be invalidated (Lv 26:44; Jr 14:21; Zch 11:10). God's nature is unchangeable (Mal 3:6; Heb 13:8), so His promises are immutable (Ps 102:27-28; Is 51:6,8; 55:10-11).

89:35 Only the Lord can swear **an oath** by His holy nature. Because He is holy, He cannot **lie** (78:36; Is 57:11; Heb 6:18).

89:36-37 The stability of the Davidic throne is as reliable as the course of the **sun** and the **moon** (72:5,17), established forever. The language of the psalm resembles that of ancient royal grant covenants, unilateral in nature as a gift to those who show themselves faithful. The **faithful witness in the sky** could be the moon, God's **throne**, or the Lord Himself.

89:38-39 A tone of accusation in a series of charges toward Yahweh (vv. 38-45) suggests the psalmist saw his current circumstances as a breach of God's **covenant** agreement. **Repudiated** implies the removal of the Lord's covenant loyalty from His servant.

89:40-41 Jerusalem became vulnerable to enemies through a breach in her defenses and the destruction of her strongholds. On **object of ridicule** see note at 44:13-16.

89:42 In an ironic twist, the Lord had **lifted high** (lit "exalted") the **hand** of David's enemies. In verse 13 the Lord's hand was "lifted high" against Israel's enemies; Israel's horn was "exalted" through God's favor (vv. 16-17); God's anointed was "exalted" from among the people (v. 19); and the Anointed One's horn would be "exalted" (v. 24).

89:43 Not only did the Lord empower David's enemies, but He also removed David's military power.

89:44 Splendor is literally "purity." This cessation of purity connects the political downfall to a state of cultic defilement, eliminating access to God. As the king's crown had been defiled by dust, so the king's **throne** had been overturned, reinforcing his humiliation.

89:45 On the shortening of one's **days**, see note at 102:23-24.

46 How long, LORD? Will You hide
   Yourself forever?
   Will Your anger keep burning like fire?[a]
47 Remember how short my life is.
   Have You created •everyone
     for nothing?[b]
48 What man can live and
   never see death?
   Who can save himself from the power
     of •Sheol?[c]   *Selah*
49 Lord, where are the former acts
   of Your faithful love
   that You swore to David
   in Your faithfulness?[d]
50 Remember, Lord, the ridicule
   against Your servants—
   in my heart I carry abuse from all
   the peoples—
51 how Your enemies have ridiculed, LORD,
   how they have ridiculed every step
   of Your anointed.[e]

52 May the LORD be praised forever.
   •Amen and amen.[f]

BOOK IV
(Psalms 90–106)

Psalm 90
Eternal God and Mortal Man

A prayer of Moses, the man of God.

1 Lord, You have been our refuge[A]
   in every generation.[g]

Cross references (center column):
[a] 89:46 Ps 6:3; 13:1; 35:17; 79:5
[b] 89:47 Ps 39:6-7; 90:5-6,9-10
[c] 89:48 Ps 16:10; 22:29
[d] 89:49 2Sm 7:15; Jr 30:9; Ezk 34:23
[e] 89:50-51 Ps 69:9; 74:10,18,22
[f] 89:52 Ps 41:13; 72:19-20; 106:48
[g] 90:1 Ps 71:3
[h] 90:2 Jb 36:26; Ps 102:27; Pr 8:25
[i] 90:3 Gn 3:19; Ec 12:7
[j] 90:4 2Pt 3:8
[k] 90:5 Jb 14:12
[l] 90:5-6 Jb 14:1-2; Ps 37:2; 103:15-16
[m] 90:7 Ps 39:11
[n] 90:8 Ps 19:12; Ec 12:14
[o] 90:9 Ps 78:33
[p] 90:10 Jb 20:8; Ps 78:39

2 Before the mountains were born,
   before You gave birth to the earth
     and the world,
   from eternity to eternity,
     You are God.[h]
3 You return mankind to the dust,
   saying, "Return,
     descendants of Adam."[i]
4 For in Your sight a thousand years
   are like yesterday that passes by,
   like a few hours of the night.[j]
5 You end their lives;[B] they sleep.[k]
   They are like grass that grows
     in the morning—
6 in the morning it sprouts and grows;
   by evening it withers and dries up.[l]
7 For we are consumed by Your anger;
   we are terrified by Your wrath.[m]
8 You have set our unjust ways
     before You,
   our secret sins in the light
     of Your presence.[n]
9 For all our days ebb away
     under Your wrath;
   we end our years like a sigh.[o]
10 Our lives last[C] seventy years
   or, if we are strong, eighty years.
   Even the best of them are[D] struggle
     and sorrow;
   indeed, they pass quickly and we
     fly away.[p]
11 Who understands the power
   of Your anger?

[A] 90:1 Some Hb mss, LXX; other Hb mss read *dwelling place*   [B] 90:5 Or *You overwhelm them*; Hb obscure   [C] 90:10 Lit *The days of our years in them*   [D] 90:10 LXX, Tg, Syr, Vg read *Even their span is*; Hb obscure

---

89:46 On **how long**, see notes at 13:1-2 and 79:5.

89:47 The psalmist questioned God's motives in creating mankind and establishing a covenant with David that He later appeared to break. The inquiry underscores the psalmist's frustration and his inability to understand the Lord's actions.

89:49 Appealing to God's promise to David, the psalmist called on the Lord to act faithfully, remembering that the continuation of the dynasty depended on God's protection and providence.

89:50-51 The repetition of **ridicule** reinforces the continual torment experienced by the Lord's Anointed (80:12-15). By repeating **Your** (servants, enemies, anointed), the psalmist calls on God to defend His people who represent His name.

89:52 See note at 41:13.

Ps 90 title No other psalm is labeled a **prayer of Moses**. The Hebrew preposition may identify Moses as the author, or it may just suggest the poem reflects a Mosaic perspective.

90:1-2 Throughout Israel's history, the Lord provided physical aid and spiritual sanctuary for His people. The psalmist emphasized God's immutability as the basis for His faithfulness. The nuance of **gave birth** when referring to God always emphasizes His role as Creator and Almighty Father (Col 1:15-17).

90:3 The sovereignty of God over creation includes His authority over life and death. **Descendants of Adam** could also be translated "sons of man" (8:5). The psalm contrasts humanity's limitations and God's eternality.

90:4 The nature of God makes Him unconstrained by time. The expression **a thousand years** implies infinity.

90:5-6 **You end their lives** is literally "You interrupted them." **Grass** is a favorite OT metaphor for mankind's frailty and the brevity of human life (103:15-16; Is 40:6-8; Jms 1:9-11).

90:8 **Secret sins** are transgressions committed discreetly or unrecognized by the individual (19:13). But God is always aware of mankind's **unjust ways** because He is omniscient.

90:10 **Seventy** or **eighty** years may represent the average lifespan of God's people, since dietary restrictions and attention to purity promote longevity. **Even the best of them** alludes to the difficulties of daily life in temporal bodies, but see note at verses 14-15.

90:11 **Who understands** is literally "who knows" (2Sm 12:22; Pr 24:22; Ec 3:21; 6:12; Jnh 3:9). God's inscrutability troubled the psalmist since God's ways are unknowable.

Your wrath matches the fear that
   is due You.[a]
12 Teach us to number our days carefully
   so that we may develop wisdom
   in our hearts.[A,b]

13 LORD—how long?
   Turn and have compassion
      on Your servants.[c]
14 Satisfy us in the morning
   with Your faithful love
   so that we may shout with joy
   and be glad all our days.[d]
15 Make us rejoice for as many days
   as You have humbled us,
   for as many years as
   we have seen adversity.[e]
16 Let Your work be seen by Your servants,
   and Your splendor by their children.[f]
17 Let the favor of the Lord our God be
   on us;
   establish for us the work
      of our hands—
   establish the work of our hands![g]

Psalm 91
The Protection of the Most High

1 The one who lives under the protection
   of the •Most High
   dwells in the shadow
   of the •Almighty.[h]

2 I will say[B] to the LORD, "My refuge
      and my fortress,
   my God, in whom I trust."[i]

3 He Himself will deliver you
      from the hunter's net,[j]
   from the destructive plague.
4 He will cover you with His feathers;
   you will take refuge
      under His wings.[k]
   His faithfulness will be
      a protective shield.[l]
5 You will not fear the terror
      of the night,
   the arrow that flies by day,[m]
6 the plague that stalks in darkness,
   or the pestilence that ravages
      at noon.[n]
7 Though a thousand fall
      at your side
   and ten thousand at your right hand,
   the pestilence will not reach you.[o]
8 You will only see it with your eyes
   and witness the punishment
      of the wicked.[p]

9 Because you have made the LORD—
      my refuge,[q]
   the Most High—
      your dwelling place,[r]
10 no harm will come to you;
   no plague will come near your tent.[s]

Reference column:
[a] 90:11 Ps 76:7
[b] 90:12 Dt 32:29; Ps 39:4
[c] 90:13 Dt 32:36; Ps 135:14
[d] 90:14 Ps 36:8; 65:4; 103:5
[e] 90:15 Ps 86:4; 92:4
[f] 90:16 Ps 96:6; Is 35:2
[g] 90:17 Ps 27:4; Is 26:12
[h] 91:1 Ps 27:5; 32:7; 121:5
[i] 91:2 Ps 18:2; 61:4; 62:7-8
[j] 91:3 Ps 124:7; 141:9; Ec 9:12
[k] 91:4 Ps 57:1; 63:7
[l] Ps 5:12
[m] 91:5 Ps 58:7; 76:3
[n] 91:5-6 Jb 5:19-23
[o] 91:7 2Ch 20:9
[p] 91:8 Ps 37:34; 58:10
[q] 91:9 Ps 18:2; 62:7-8
[r] Ps 121:5
[s] 91:10 Pr 12:21

A90:12 Or *develop a heart of wisdom*   B91:1-2 LXX, Syr, Jer read 2 *Almighty, saying,* or 2 *Almighty, he will say*

90:12 The psalmist asked the Lord to **teach us** to take advantage of our short lives on earth in order to nurture a heart directed by wisdom (1Kg 3:12; Pr 16:23; Ec 8:5; 10:2).

90:13 The Lord "returns" (Hb *shuv*) all living things to dust (v. 3), but the psalmist implored God to **turn** to His people. On **how long**, see note at 13:1-2. The psalmist identified no specific enemy but perceived God as the agent of distress.

90:14-15 God's provision and answer to prayer traditionally occurred in the **morning** (88:13). The psalmist did not expect to live a life without **adversity**. Rather, he asked the Lord for an equal balance of blessing and adversity. A life without trials would lead to an attitude of self-sufficiency and independence from God.

90:16-17 The blessings of God's people are visual witnesses to His faithfulness. **Establish . . . the work of our hands** implies that Israel does have a role in provision, and also makes a direct connection between success and God's providence.

91:1 Under the protection (lit "hiding place") refers to the protection of the sanctuary (27:5; 31:20; 61:4; Jb 40:21). **Shadow** denotes protection or security (121:5; Is 30:2,3; 49:2; 51:16). **The Almighty** is a name for God describing His dual roles as nurturer and protector.

91:2 The psalmist's safety is guaranteed by the Lord's presence. On **my refuge**, see note at verse 4.

91:3 Destructive plague shows the psalmist's fear of physical illness (vv. 5-8).

91:4 The imagery of **wings** alludes to the cherubim surrounding the ark of the covenant. The Lord covers the psalmist, shutting him off from danger. "Wings," a figurative term for "cloak," denotes protection (17:8; 36:8; 57:2; 61:5; 63:8; Ru 2:12). Compare Is 40:28 for eagle imagery. Those who seek God's protection will be shielded by His faithfulness.

91:5 On **terror of the night**, compare 121:6.

91:6 The plague includes flood, famine, hail, fire, or anything that threatens livestock and human beings. **Pestilence** is often personified as a demon. The connection in ancient Near Eastern thought between an evil spirit and disease is well attested. The psalmist sought safe haven from thieves, wild animals, persecutors, and sickness, all threats that existed in the **darkness**.

91:7 If the petitioner were surrounded by illness to which his neighbors succumbed, he would experience preservation at the Lord's hand.

91:8 Though the psalmist would be spared, he witnessed the Lord's **punishment** (lit "repayment, retribution") of the wicked. God executes judgment in proportion to the measure of evil.

91:9 On **refuge**, see notes at verses 1 and 4. The Hebrew word for **dwelling place** implies a remote, protected place (71:3; 90:1).

91:10 The word **plague** (infection, hit, infestation) reinfor the concept of serious physical threat (Lv 13:2; 14:3,32

11 For He will give His angels orders
　　concerning you,
　　to protect you in all your ways.[a]
12 They will support you with their hands
　　so that you will not strike your foot
　　against a stone.[b]
13 You will tread on the lion
　　and the cobra;
　　you will trample the young lion
　　and the serpent.[c]

14 Because he is lovingly devoted to Me,
　　I will deliver him;
　　I will protect him because he knows
　　My name.[d]
15 When he calls out to Me,
　　I will answer him;
　　I will be with him in trouble.
　　I will rescue him and give him honor.[e]
16 I will satisfy him with a long life[f]
　　and show him My salvation.[g]

Psalm 92
God's Love and Faithfulness

A psalm. A song for the Sabbath day.

1 It is good to praise *Yahweh,
　　to sing praise to Your name,
　　*Most High,[h]
2 to declare Your faithful love
　　in the morning

and Your faithfulness at night,[i]
3 　　with a ten-stringed harp
　　and the music of a lyre.[j]

4 For You have made me rejoice, Lord,
　　by what You have done;
　　I will shout for joy
　　because of the works of Your hands.[k]
5 How magnificent are Your works, Lord,
　　how profound Your thoughts![l]
6 A stupid person does not know,
　　a fool does not understand this:[m]
7 though the wicked sprout like grass
　　and all evildoers flourish,
　　they will be eternally destroyed.[n]
8 But You, Lord, are exalted forever.[o]
9 For indeed, Lord, Your enemies—
　　indeed, Your enemies will perish;
　　all evildoers will be scattered.[p]
10 You have lifted up my *horn[q]
　　like that of a wild ox;
　　I have been anointed[A] with oil.[r]
11 My eyes look down on my enemies;
　　my ears hear evildoers when they
　　　　attack me.[s]

12 The righteous thrive like a palm tree
　　and grow like a cedar tree in Lebanon.[t]
13 Planted in the house of the Lord,
　　they thrive in the courts of our God.[u]
14 They will still bear fruit in old age,
　　healthy and green,[v]

Cross references:
[a] 91:11 Ps 34:7
[b] 91:11-12 Mt 4:6; Lk 4:10-11
[c] 91:13 Lk 10:19
[d] 91:14 Ps 9:10; 37:40; 107:41
[e] 91:15 2Sm 22:20; Ps 18:19; 50:15
[f] 91:16 Dt 4:40; Ps 21:4
[g] Ps 50:23
[h] 92:1 Ps 135:3; 147:1
[i] 92:2 Ps 59:16; 89:1; Lm 3:22-23
[j] 92:3 Ps 33:2
[k] 92:4 Ps 40:5; 143:5
[l] 92:5 Ps 139:17; Is 55:8-9
[m] 92:6 Ps 73:22
[n] 92:7 Ps 90:5-6
[o] 92:8 Ps 93:4
[p] 92:9 Ps 37:20; 68:1
[q] 92:10 Ps 89:17,24; 112:9
[r] Ps 45:7
[s] 92:11 Ps 37:34; 54:7
[t] 92:12 Ps 1:3; Is 61:3; Jr 17:8
[u] 92:13 Is 60:21
[v] 92:14 Is 37:31; 46:4

A 92:10 Syr reads *You have anointed me*

91:11-12 The Lord's **angels** serve as His messengers and agents of His power outside the sanctuary (103:20; Gn 24:7; Heb 1:14). These divine beings have superior power, involving the ability to protect the Lord's people from harm (Gn 19:10-11; 24:40; Is 63:90; Dn 3:28). On **strike . . . a stone**, see 121:3,7-8.

91:13 The metaphors of the predatory **lion** and the poisonous **cobra** suggest creatures that stalked their prey or hid in wait. In the ancient Near East, gods were often depicted as creatures.

91:14-16 Those who know God's **name** are in covenant relationship with Him. The Lord delivers, protects, answers, honors, satisfies, and reveals His **salvation** through the preservation and blessing of Israel (95:7-11).

92:1 On **Most High**, see note at 47:2-3 (cp. 83:18; 91:9; 97:9).

92:2 Deuteronomy 6 teaches God's people to speak His word day and **night**, reflecting on His covenant **love** and **faithfulness** in the presence of the family and the community. The wise person finds delight in meditating on the Torah regularly (1:2). Creation testifies to God's constant care (19:1).

92:4 The chiastic structure of the Hebrew, which is not reflected in the English, emphasizes the Lord's works. **I will shout for joy** is the last element of the verse in Hebrew.

92:5 The term **profound** underscores the unfathomable and mysterious nature of God's thoughts (40:5; 139:17; Is 55:9-10).

92:6 Using wisdom terminology, the psalmist admonished

the **stupid** ("uneducated, brutish") **person** and the **fool**. Both fail to sustain a close relationship to God, and they reject the wisdom necessary for right living. The prophet Isaiah depicted Israel as more stupid and foolish than brutish beasts (Is 1:3).

92:7 The vulnerability and temporal nature of the wicked compares to vegetation that sprouts temporarily, then withers and disappears, leaving no evidence of its existence (see note at 37:2). The psalmist took comfort in knowing that **evildoers** would experience eternal destruction.

92:8 The sovereignty and immutability of God contrast with the weakness and finitude of man.

92:10 **Lifted up my horn** is a figurative expression denoting restored vitality and power (89:17; 148:4; 1Sm 2:1). Being **anointed with oil** can mean consecration for service (Lv 8:10-12), but here probably refers to an act of hospitality that symbolizes favor (Ps 23:5).

92:12 The **righteous** blossom and grow strong like trees, whereas the wicked blossom then wither away like grass (v. 7). **Lebanon** was known for its abundant supply of **cedar** trees used in construction. Trees often refer figuratively to the characteristics of national leaders.

92:13-14 The **house of the Lord** refers to the temple. This is a pattern for paradise, representing the order of creation and a place of rest in the presence of the Lord. The righteous **thrive** as the result of God's providence (1:3; Jr 17:8). **Old age** will not take away their vitality.

15 to declare: "The LORD is just;
   He is my rock,
   and there is no unrighteousness
      in Him."[a]

Psalm 93
God's Eternal Reign

1 The LORD reigns! He is robed
      in majesty;
   The LORD is robed,
      enveloped in strength.
   The world is firmly established;
      it cannot be shaken.[b]
2 Your throne has been established
      from the beginning;[A]
   You are from eternity.[c]
3 The floods have lifted up, LORD,
   the floods have lifted up their voice;
   the floods lift up their pounding waves.[d]
4 Greater than the roar
      of many waters—
   the mighty breakers of the sea—
   the LORD on high is majestic.[e]

5 LORD, Your testimonies
      are completely reliable;[f]
   holiness is the beauty of [B] Your house
   for all the days to come.[g]

Psalm 94
The Just Judge

1 LORD, God of vengeance—
   God of vengeance, appear.[h]
2 Rise up, Judge of the earth;
   repay the proud what they deserve.[i]

3 LORD, how long will the wicked—
      how long will the wicked gloat?[j]
4 They pour out arrogant words;
      all the evildoers boast.[k]
5 LORD, they crush Your people;
      they afflict Your heritage.[l]
6 They kill the widow and the foreigner
      and murder the fatherless.[m]
7 They say, "The LORD doesn't see it.
   The God of Jacob
      doesn't pay attention."[n]

8 Pay attention, you stupid people!
   Fools, when will you be wise?[o]
9 Can the One who shaped the ear
      not hear,
   the One who formed the eye not see?[p]
10 The One who instructs nations,
   the One who teaches
      man knowledge—
   does He not discipline?[q]
11 The LORD knows man's thoughts;
   they are meaningless.[r]

12 LORD, happy is the man You discipline
   and teach from Your law[s]
13 to give him relief from troubled times
   until a pit is dug for the wicked.[t]
14 The LORD will not forsake His people
   or abandon His heritage,[u]
15 for justice will again be righteous,
   and all the upright in heart
      will follow[C] it.[v]

16 Who stands up for me
      against the wicked?
   Who takes a stand for me
      against evildoers?[w]

---

[a]92:15 Dt 32:4; Ps 18:2; 94:22
[b]93:1 1Ch 16:30-31; Ps 96:10; 97:1
[c]93:2 Ps 9:7; 90:2; 103:19
[d]93:3 Ps 96:11; 98:7-8
[e]93:4 Ps 65:7; 89:9; Ezk 43:2
[f]93:5 Ps 19:7
[g]94:1 2Sm 22:48; Ps 18:47-48; Jr 46:10
[h]94:1 2Sm 22:48; Ps 18:47-48; Jr 46:10
[i]94:2 Ps 7:6; 28:4; 98:9
[j]94:3 Ps 74:10; Rv 6:10
[k]94:4 1Sm 2:3; Ps 31:18
[l]94:5 Is 3:15
[m]94:6 Dt 27:19; Is 10:2
[n]94:7 Jb 22:13; Ps 10:11
[o]94:8 Ps 92:6
[p]94:9 Ex 4:11; Pr 20:12
[q]94:10 Jb 35:11; Is 28:26
[r]94:11 Ps 139:2; Is 66:18; 1Co 3:20
[s]94:12 Ps 25:5,9; 71:17; Is 48:17
[t]94:13 Ps 7:15; 9:15; Pr 26:27
[u]94:14 1Sm 12:22; Rm 11:2
[v]94:15 Ps 36:10; 64:10; 97:11
[w]94:16 Ps 59:2

A93:2 Lit *from then*   B93:5 Or *holiness characterizes*   C94:15 Or *heart will support*; lit *heart after*

92:15 The strength of the righteous demonstrates Yahweh's reliability and impartiality. The enemy prospers but is destroyed after attempting to present himself as genuine. Those who are truly the Lord's have no hypocrisy or deceit; their prosperity endures.

93:1-2 The Hebrew word for **reigns** is a verb form implying completed action or an established condition. Reference to **the beginning** and **eternity** means Yahweh's kingship is timeless. On **robed in majesty**, see note at 104:1 (cp. Is 51:9; 59:17). The Lord **established** ("measured, regulated") the world, and the order of the cosmos is not subject to disruptions. To **be shaken** often occurs in texts that describe the impotence of false gods (Is 54:10). The term reinforces the reliability of the Lord's character and His commitment to creation (Ps 96:10; 99:1; 104:5).

93:3-4 The psalmist personified primeval forces that threatened creation and then demonstrated the Lord's sovereignty over them. On **on high**, compare 7:7; 68:16; 144:7.

93:5 God's **testimonies** or decrees are as stable as His throne and the earth (19:8; 25:10; 99:7; 132:12; Dt 4:45; 6:17,20). **Beauty** refers to a suitable adornment (Sg 1:10).

94:1 **Vengeance** ("retribution, vindication") generally describes God's judgment on the nations; rarely does the term apply to Israel. The expression parallels Jr 51:56, in which the Lord executed final judgment on destructive peoples and powers (Is 35:4; 66:6). The psalmist requested an epiphany, the Lord's return to rescue His people.

94:2 Yahweh is **Judge of the earth**, especially the nations (7:8; 58:11; 76:8; 82:8; 96:10; 98:9).

94:3 On **how long**, see note at 13:1-2.

94:4 To **pour out** speech is figurative for the empty, incessant babbling of the arrogant and deceitful.

94:5-6 The enemy seeks to obliterate God's people (143:3). The evildoers target the most vulnerable groups in society, whom the Lord will defend (see note at 68:5; cp. 146:8; Ex 22:21-22).

94:12 God will **discipline** those He loves, correcting and instructing them to bring them back into relationship with Him (Heb 12:3-13). God recognizes humanity's inherent weaknesses.

94:14 Compare this verse with verse 5.

17 If the LORD had not been my helper,
   I would soon rest in the silence
     of death.[a]
18 If I say, "My foot is slipping,"
   Your faithful love will support me, LORD.[b]
19 When I am filled with cares,
   Your comfort brings me joy.[c]
20 Can a corrupt throne—
   one that creates trouble by law—
   become Your ally?[d]
21 They band together against the life
   of the righteous
   and condemn the innocent to death.[e]
22 But the LORD is my refuge;
   my God is the rock of my protection.[f]
23 He will pay them back for their sins
   and destroy them for their evil.
   The LORD our God will destroy them.[g]

Psalm 95
Worship and Warning

1 Come, let us shout joyfully to the LORD,
   shout triumphantly to the rock
     of our salvation![h]
2 Let us enter His presence
   with thanksgiving;
   let us shout triumphantly to Him
   in song.[i]
3 For the LORD is a great God,
   a great King above all gods.[j]
4 The depths of the earth are in His hand,

and the mountain peaks are His.[k]
5 The sea is His; He made it.
   His hands formed the dry land.[l]
6 Come, let us worship and bow down;
   let us kneel before the LORD our Maker.[m]
7 For He is our God,
   and we are the people of His pasture,
   the sheep under His care.[A,n]

Today, if you hear His voice:[o]
8 Do not harden your hearts as at Meribah,
   as on that day at Massah
     in the wilderness[p]
9 where your fathers tested Me;
   they tried Me, though they had seen
     what I did.[q]
10 For 40 years I was disgusted
   with that generation;
   I said, "They are a people whose hearts
     go astray;
   they do not know My ways."[r]
11 So I swore in My anger,
   "They will not enter My rest."[s]

Psalm 96[t]
King of the Earth

1 Sing a new song to the LORD;
   sing to the LORD, all the earth.[u]
2 Sing to *Yahweh, praise His name;
   proclaim His salvation from day to day.[v]
3 Declare His glory among the nations,
   His wonderful works among all peoples.[w]

---

a94:17 Ps 124:1-2
b94:18 Ps 18:35; 66:9; 121:3
c94:19 Is 57:18; 66:13
d94:20 Ps 50:16; 58:2
e94:21 2Kg 21:16; Ps 106:38; Jr 26:15
f94:22 2Sm 22:3; Ps 46:1,7; 62:2,6
g94:23 Ps 73:27; 94:23; 101:5,8
h95:1 Jb 38:7; Ps 81:1; 98:4,6
i95:2 Ps 100:4; Jnh 2:9
j95:3 Dt 10:17; Ps 47:2; 96:4
k95:4 Ps 135:6
l95:5 Gn 1:9-10; Ps 146:6; Jnh 1:9
m95:6 Ps 96:9; 100:3; Is 17:7
n95:7 Ps 79:13
o Heb 3:7-11,15; 4:7
p95:8 Ex 17:7; Dt 6:16
q95:9 Nm 14:22; Ps 78:18
r95:10 Dt 9:7; Ac 13:18; Heb 3:10,17
s95:11 Nm 14:23,28-30; Dt 12:9
t Ps 96† Ch 16:23-33
u96:1 1Ch 16:23; Ps 98:1; Is 42:10
v96:2 Is 25:9; 52:7
w96:3 1Ch 16:9,24; Ps 145:12

A95:7 Lit *sheep of His hand*

94:20 Corrupt rulers enact legislation that persecutes the righteous and enables wickedness, which is clearly contrary to God's will.

95:1 The **rock of our salvation** is a metaphorical expression denoting security and safety. The Hebrew word for "rock" describes the steadfast character of God (18:1-2,31; 73:26; 92:15; 144:1; Dt 32:15; 2Sm 22:47; Is 44:8).

95:3 The LORD **is a great God** is an expression prevalent in the psalms that celebrate the Lord's kingship (47:3,7-8; 48:2-3; 96:4; 97:9; 136:2; 149:2). On **above all gods**, see notes at 29:1 and 82:1.

95:4 God understands incomprehensible things such as the foundations of the **earth** (Jr 31:37), the depths of the ocean (Jb 38:16), or the depth of God Himself (Jb 11:7). The power of God extends from the bottom of the sea to the **mountain peaks**.

95:5 The **sea** and the **dry land** belong to God because He created them. In Jnh 1:9 the same phrase is part of the prophet's confessional statement about His identity.

95:6 The same God who created the world created humanity as well. Both the cosmos and humanity **kneel** before their Creator.

95:7 The Lord, who created the world, also created Israel. On **people of His pasture**, compare 79:13. He serves

a dual role as Creator and Shepherd in Is 43:1,15. Those who truly belong to the Lord will **hear His voice** and respond to Him.

95:8-11 These verses recall Ex 17:1-7 and Nm 20:2-13. The psalm relies heavily on the covenantal associations and language of the two texts.

95:8-9 **Do not harden** warns against the self-reliance of God's people, who followed their own counsel and complained in the wilderness. The names **Meribah** (lit "contention, controversy") and **Massah** ("test") were given by Moses to the location where God provided water from a rock after the people **tested** God (Ex 17:7; Nm 20:13; Dt 6:16). The Lord tested Israel's faithfulness in the wilderness (Dt 8:2; 33:8). The Hebrew word for "tested" describes the refining of precious metals by smelting (Zch 13:9).

95:10 Although the original group that departed Egypt would not enter Canaan because of their sinfulness, Caleb and Joshua would lead the next generation into the promised land (Nm 14:30).

95:11 On **enter My rest**, compare Dt 12:9. A person may rest at home or rest through relief from enemies. God rested on the Sabbath (Gn 2:2) and rests among His people (2Ch 6:41-42). The concept of rest reaches its full development in Heb 4:3-11.

96:1-3 This **new song** was cosmic praise for Yahweh's

⁴ For the LORD is great and is
   highly praised;
   He is feared above all gods.ᵃ
⁵ For all the gods of the peoples
   are idols,
   but the LORD made the heavens.ᵇ
⁶ Splendor and majesty are before Him;
   strength and beauty are
      in His sanctuary.ᶜ

⁷ Ascribe to the LORD, you families
   of the peoples,
   ascribe to the LORD glory and strength.ᵈ
⁸ Ascribe to Yahweh the glory
   of His name;ᵉ
   bring an offering and
      enter His courts.ᶠ

⁹ Worship the LORD in the splendor
   of His holiness;ᵍ
   tremble before Him, all the earth.ʰ

¹⁰ Say among the nations:
   "The LORD reigns.ⁱ
   The world is firmly established;
      it cannot be shaken.ʲ
   He judges the peoples fairly."ᵏ
¹¹ Let the heavens be glad
   and the earth rejoice;
   let the sea and all that fills it resound.ˡ
¹² Let the fields and everything
      in them exult.
   Then all the trees of the forest
      will shout for joyᵐ
¹³ before the LORD, for He is coming—

ᵃ96:4 1Ch 16:25; Ps 47:2; 95:3
ᵇ96:5 1Ch 16:27; Jr 10:11
ᶜ96:6 Ps 104:1
ᵈ96:7 1Ch 16:28-29; Ps 29:1
ᵉ96:8 Ps 79:9
ᶠPs 100:4
ᵍ96:8-9 Ps 29:2
ʰ96:9 Ps 33:8; 114:7
ⁱ96:10 Ps 93:1; 97:1
ʲ1Ch 16:30
ᵏPs 9:8; 67:4; 98:9
ˡ96:11 1Ch 16:31-32; Ps 69:34; 98:7
ᵐ96:12 Is 35:1; 55:12-13

reign over a universal kingdom comprising all peoples (98:1; 144:9; 149:1; Is 42:10; see note at Ps 33:1-3). Mention of the sanctuary (96:6) implies a preexilic origin for this psalm. A threefold repetition of "sing" followed by three imperatives—**praise . . . proclaim**, and **declare**—underscore the purpose of the song: to glorify the Lord's **works** of **salvation**.

96:4 On **He is feared above all gods**, see notes at 29:1 and 82:1.

96:5 The psalmist contrasted the impotence of **idols** with the creative power of the Lord, challenging all association between false gods and the natural forces of the cosmos. The **gods of the peoples** are worthless or powerless (97:7; Is 42:5,8,17).

96:6 Four descriptive nouns—**splendor . . . majesty . . .**

strength, and **beauty**—are personified as divine escorts preceding the Lord's processional entrance into the temple.

96:7-9 These verses represent an expansion of 29:1-2, substituting **families** (lit "tribes, clans") **of the people** for "sons of God" (29:1), while adding **bring an offering and enter His courts**, and **tremble before Him, all the earth**. The modifications redirect the praise of the Lord from the heavenly realm to the earthly sphere, functioning as a polemic against other deities. To **ascribe** something to someone is to acknowledge they have that attribute.

96:10 With the phrase **the LORD reigns**, the psalmist reinforced the Lord's dual roles as King and Creator.

96:11-12 The personification of **heaven . . . earth . . . the sea . . . fields**, and **trees** in cosmic praise for the Lord recalls imagery from the prophet Isaiah (Is 44:23; 49:13).

The Huleh Basin in northern Israel is known for its farming and grazing fields (96:12).

for He is coming to judge the earth.
He will judge the world
with righteousness
and the peoples with His faithfulness.[a]

Psalm 97
The Majestic King

1 The LORD reigns! Let the earth rejoice;
let the many coasts and islands
be glad.[b]
2 Clouds and thick darkness
surround Him;
righteousness and justice are
the foundation of His throne.[c]
3 Fire goes before Him
and burns up His foes on every side.[d]
4 His lightning lights up the world;
the earth sees and trembles.[e]
5 The mountains melt like wax
at the presence of the LORD—
at the presence of the Lord of all
the earth.[f]
6 The heavens proclaim
His righteousness;[g]
all the peoples see His glory.[h]
7 All who serve carved images,
those who boast in idols, will be
put to shame.[i]
All the gods[A] must worship Him.[j]
8 ˙Zion hears and is glad,
and the towns[B] of Judah rejoice
because of Your judgments, LORD.[k]
9 For You, LORD,
are the ˙Most High over all the earth;
You are exalted above all the gods.[l]
10 You who love the LORD, hate evil![m]
He protects the lives
of His godly ones;[n]
He rescues them from the power of
the wicked.[o]
11 Light dawns[C,D] for the righteous,
gladness for the upright in heart.[p]
12 Be glad in ˙Yahweh,
you righteous ones,
and praise His holy name.[E,q]

Psalm 98
Praise the King

A psalm.

1 Sing a new song to the LORD,[r]
for He has performed wonders;
His right hand and holy arm
have won Him victory.[s]
2 The LORD has made
His victory known;
He has revealed
His righteousness
in the sight of the nations.[t]
3 He has remembered His love
and faithfulness to the house
of Israel;
all the ends of the earth
have seen our God's victory.[u]
4 Shout to the LORD, all the earth;
be jubilant, shout for joy, and sing.[v]

[a] 96:13 Ps 98:9; Rv 19:11 [b] 97:1 Ps 93:1; 96:10 [c] 97:2 Dt 4:11; 5:20; Ps 18:11 [d] 97:3 Ps 18:8; 50:3 [e] 97:4 Ex 19:16; Ps 77:18 [f] 97:5 Neh 1:5; Mc 1:4 [g] 97:6 Ps 50:6 [h] Is 40:5; 66:18 [i] 97:7 Is 44:9,11; Jr 10:14; 50:2 [j] Heb 1:6 [k] 97:8 Ps 48:11; Zph 3:14 [l] 97:9 1Ch 16:25; Ps 95:3; 96:4 [m] 97:10 Am 5:15 [n] Ps 145:20 [o] Ps 37:40 [p] 97:11 Ps 112:4; Pr 4:18 [q] 97:12 Ps 30:4; 32:11 [r] 98:1 Ps 33:3 [s] Ex 15:6; Is 52:10 [t] 98:2 Is 56:1; 62:2 [u] 98:3 Ps 22:27; Is 52:10 [v] 98:4 Ps 66:1; 100:1; Is 44:23

[A] 97:7 LXX, Syr read *All His angels*; Heb 1:6 [B] 97:8 Lit *daughters* [C] 97:11 One Hb ms, LXX, some ancient versions read *rises to shine*; Ps 112:4 [D] 97:11 Lit *Light is sown* [E] 97:12 Or *memory, of His holiness*; lit *praise the mention*

97:1 The **coasts and islands** represent the farthest known habitable places, conveying the scope of the Lord's dominion and praise (Is 20:5,6; 41:1; 42:4,10,12,15).

97:2 **Clouds and thick darkness** recollect the storm imagery on Mount Sinai, where the thick clouds hid God, and from which He spoke. In prophetic texts these Hebrew words usually describe a state of judgment (Is 60:2; Jl 2:2). On **righteousness . . . His throne**, see note at 89:14.

97:3-5 **Fire** combined with **lightning**, earthquakes, and volcanic activity typify the cosmic upheaval experienced at the approach of God (77:16-18; Ex 19:16; Mc 1:3-4). Even the created order responds to the Creator.

97:6 Cosmic disturbances and defeat of the Lord's enemies demonstrate the Lord's **righteousness** and **glory** to all the earth's inhabitants (19:1). The saving power of God demonstrated by divine acts of victory magnify His sovereignty so that the whole world recognizes His glory.

97:7 The Hebrew word for "worthless gods" always refers to the impotence of **carved images** and pagan **gods**. **All the gods must worship Him** could be translated "all the gods humble themselves before Him," conveying the irony of the psalm.

97:9 While idol worshipers are ashamed and pagan deities are subjugated before God (v. 7), Yahweh is the **Most High**, raised to a superior rank and appropriating the authority of these impotent gods.

97:10 Those who **love** God should share His hatred of **evil** (15:4; 139:21; Pr 8:13; Am 5:15; Zch 8:17; Rm 12:9).

97:11 The psalmist equated **light** with joy and righteousness, a connection developed further in Isaiah (Is 10:17; 30:29; 42:6; 49:6; 58:10; 60:1-3,19-20), who described the Lord's return to Jerusalem. Zion as the Lord's dwelling place shines forth, Yahweh's glory is described as light, and the restored nation of Israel reflects the light of God's presence. All nations will be drawn from the darkness to the light of Jerusalem (Is 60:2-3).

98:1 The Lord's **right hand** and His **holy arm** refer to His immeasurable power (see note at 16:8). In this psalm, **victory** implies judgment on the nations and salvation for Israel.

98:3 A reference to God's covenantal **faithfulness** combined with the **house of Israel** places this psalm in the preexilic period.

98:4 **Be jubilant** or "break forth" always occurs in combina-

5 Sing to the LORD with the lyre,
with the lyre and melodious song.[a]
6 With trumpets and the blast
of the ram's horn
shout triumphantly
in the presence of the LORD,
our King.[b]
7 Let the sea and all that fills it,
the world and those who live in it,
resound.[c]
8 Let the rivers clap their hands;
let the mountains shout together
for joy[d]
9 before the LORD,
for He is coming to judge the earth.
He will judge the world righteously
and the peoples fairly.[e]

Psalm 99

The King Is Holy

1 The LORD reigns! Let
the peoples tremble.
He is enthroned
above the •cherubim.[f]
Let the earth quake.[g]
2 •Yahweh is great in •Zion;
He is exalted above all the peoples.[h]
3 Let them praise Your great
and awe-inspiring name.[i]
He is holy.[j]
4 The mighty King loves justice.
You have established fairness;
You have administered justice
and righteousness in Jacob.[k]
5 Exalt the LORD our God;
bow in worship at His footstool.[l]
He is holy.[m]
6 Moses and Aaron were
among His priests;[n]
Samuel also was among
those calling on His name.
They called to Yahweh
and He answered them.[o]
7 He spoke to them in a pillar
of cloud;[p]
they kept His decrees and the statutes
He gave them.
8 LORD our God, You answered them.
You were a forgiving God to them,[q]
an avenger of their sinful actions.[r]
9 Exalt the LORD our God;
bow in worship
at His holy mountain,
for the LORD our God is holy.[s]

Psalm 100

Be Thankful

A psalm of thanksgiving.

1 Shout triumphantly to the LORD,
all the earth.[t]
2 Serve the LORD with gladness;
come before Him
with joyful songs.[u]

[a]98:5 Ps 51:3; Is 51:3
[b]98:6 Nm 10:10; 2Ch 15:14
[c]98:7 1Ch 16:31-32; Ps 93:1; 97:1
[d]98:8 Ps 89:12; Is 55:12
[e]98:9 Ps 9:8; 67:4; 96:13
[f]99:1 Ex 25:22; 1Sm 4:4; Ezk 11:22
[g]Ps 33:8
[h]99:2 Ps 48:1; 113:4
[i]99:3 Ps 111:9
[j]Is 6:3
[k]99:4 Ps 33:5; 103:6; Jr 23:5
[l]99:5 Ps 132:7
[m]Is 6:3
[n]99:6 Ex 24:6-8; Lv 8:1-30
[o]1Sm 12:18
[p]99:7 Nm 12:5; 14:14; Dt 31:15-18
[q]99:8 Ps 78:38
[r]Jr 46:28
[s]99:9 Ps 2:6; 48:1; Ezk 20:40
[t]100:1 Ps 66:1; 98:4
[u]100:1-2 Ps 95:1-2; 98:4-6

tion with **shout for joy** or "ring out" (Is 14:7; 44:23; 49:13; 52:9; 54:1; 55:12).

98:6 The second part of this verse is literally "shout before King Yahweh." The LXX rendering, "Shout before the king, O Lord," assumes the poem was performed before a human king, but a reference to an earthly ruler seems out of place in a text that lauds the attributes of the Lord.

98:7 Compare this verse with 96:11.

98:8 The only other place **mountains shout** is in Isaiah's prophecies (Is 44:23; 49:13).

98:9 Compare this verse with 96:13.

99:1 On **He is enthroned above the cherubim**, see note at 80:1. The ark of the covenant was regarded as the throne of the invisible God, or His footstool (132:7-8; Jr 3:16-17). Because the ark of the covenant was the central symbol of God's presence with His people Israel, its mysteries remained appropriately veiled within the inner sanctuary of the living God. **Let the earth quake**, as though knocked off balance (Is 6:1-4).

99:3 Awe-inspiring (lit "to be feared") denotes both respect and worship. The psalmist declared God's holiness three times (vv. 3,5,9) as in Is 6:3.

99:4 Righteousness characterizes God's people (85:10-12; Is 62:1-3) as an extension of the Lord Himself (Ps 96:13; Is 42:1-4).

99:5 At His footstool associates the Lord's presence with the ark of the covenant (1Ch 28:2) or a central place of worship (Ps 132:7). In the days preceding Solomon's temple, King David instructed the priests to bring the ark, symbolizing the Lord's presence (2Sm 6:12). Isaiah equated the ark with the sanctuary (Is 60:13), later describing heaven as the Lord's throne and the earth as His footstool (Is 66:1). Enemies become Christ's footstool, showing subjugation (Heb 1:13; 9:5).

99:6 Moses . . . Aaron, and **Samuel** served intercessory roles as priests, administering God's justice. They communicated closely with God, obeying His commands.

99:7 The Lord showed His presence to the Israelites in the form of a **pillar of cloud** and fire, from which He communicated His divine will to Israel's leaders during the wilderness experience (Ex 14:19; 16:10; 33:9; 40:36).

99:8 Even after God forgave sins, actions had consequences. The Lord punished Moses and Aaron for their **sinful actions** (Nm 20:12).

100:1-2 Praising the Lord and serving Him joyfully were two conditions for entering the sanctuary or presence of God (40:8; 42:2; 43:4; 66:13; 86:9; 118:19-20).

3 Acknowledge that •Yahweh is God.
  He made us, and we are His[A,a] —
  His people, the sheep of His pasture.[b]
4 Enter His gates with thanksgiving[c]
  and His courts with praise.
  Give thanks to Him and praise
    His name.[d]
5 For Yahweh is good, and His love
    is eternal;
  His faithfulness endures
    through all generations.

Psalm 101
A Vow of Integrity

A Davidic psalm.

1 I will sing of faithful love and justice;
  I will sing praise to You, LORD.[e]
2 I will pay attention to the way
    of integrity.
  When will You come to me?
  I will live with a heart of integrity
    in my house.[f]
3 I will not set anything worthless
    before my eyes.
  I hate the practice of transgression;
    it will not cling to me.[g]
4 A devious heart will be far from me;
  I will not be involved with[B] evil.[h]

5 I will destroy anyone
  who secretly slanders
    his neighbor;[i]
  I cannot tolerate anyone
  with haughty eyes
    or an arrogant heart.[j]

6 My eyes favor the faithful
    of the land
  so that they may sit down with me.
  The one who follows the way
    of integrity
  may serve me.[k]
7 No one who acts deceitfully
  will live in my palace;
  no one who tells lies
  will remain in my presence.[C,l]
8 Every morning I will destroy
  all the wicked of the land,
  eliminating all evildoers
    from the LORD's city.[m]

Psalm 102
Affliction in Light of Eternity

A prayer of an afflicted person who is weak
and pours out his lament before the LORD.[n]

1 LORD, hear my prayer;
  let my cry for help come before You.[o]
2 Do not hide Your face from me
    in my day of trouble.
  Listen closely to me;
  answer me quickly when I call.[p]

3 For my days vanish like smoke,
  and my bones burn like a furnace.[q]
4 My heart is afflicted,
    withered like grass;[r]
  I even forget to eat my food.[s]
5 Because of the sound of my groaning,
  my flesh sticks to my bones.[t]
6 I am like a desert owl,[D]
  like an owl among the ruins.[u]

Cross references:
a 100:3 Dt 32:6; Ps 95:6
b Ps 79:13; 95:7
c 100:4-5 Ps 119:90; 136:1; Lm 3:22-23
d 100:4 Ps 75:1; 116:17
e 101:1 Ps 89:1; 145:7
f 101:2 1Kg 9:4; Ps 119:1
g 101:3 Dt 15:9; Ps 40:4
h 101:4 Pr 3:32; 14:2
i 101:5 Ps 50:20
j Ps 18:27; Is 5:15
k 101:6 Ps 119:1; Pr 11:20
l 101:7 Ps 31:18; 52:3; 63:11
m 101:8 Ps 119:119; Jr 21:12
n 102:title Ps 142:2
o 102:1 Ps 18:6; 39:12; 61:1
p 102:2 Ps 27:9; 31:2; 69:17
q 102:3 Jb 30:30; Ps 31:10; Lm 1:13
r 102:4 Ps 37:2
s Ezr 10:6; Jb 33:20
t 102:5 Jb 19:20; Lm 4:8
u 102:6 Is 34:11; Zph 2:14

A 100:3 Alt Hb tradition, some Hb mss, LXX, Syr, Vg read *and not we ourselves*   B 101:4 Lit *not know*   C 101:7 Lit *in front of my eyes*   D 102:6 Or *a pelican of the desert*

100:3 The combined roles of the Lord as Creator and Shepherd occur in 95:7 (see note at that verse).

101:1 The king's responsibilities toward his people consisted of **faithful love** (Hb *chesed*; "covenant loyalty") and **justice**, prompting his promise to live with integrity and to eradicate God's enemies.

101:2 **Integrity** is a cultic term denoting the lack of imperfections or blemishes. It refers to purity of thought or behavior (78:72). Integrity governs private life as well as public life (Dt 5:32-33; 6:5-7). The wisdom overtones of this verse establish a connection between wisdom and the royal court.

101:3 The **eyes** of the king is a metaphor for his jurisdiction. **Transgression** is a covenantal term denoting anyone or anything opposed to God and His law. **It will not cling** means the king will not permit evil to remain in his kingdom for any amount of time.

101:4 Saying that a **heart** is **devious** acknowledges humanity's tendency to sin.

101:5-8 These verses focus on the king's promotion of righteousness in the community. The wise ruler rejects slanderers and the **arrogant** but surrounds himself with those

who are blameless (see note at v. 2) and **faithful** (Dt 10:8; 17:12; 21:5). The moral standards of the king should be reflected by those who **serve** him; therefore, the ruler will remove from his palace anyone who deceives and **tells lies**. The **evildoers** would be exiled from the precincts of Jerusalem (48:2,9; 87:3; Is 60:14).

102:2 **Do not hide Your face** is a figurative expression used by the psalmist, who thought God had forsaken him (10:11; 13:1-2; 69:17; Is 28:21; 33:10). God's face represents the blessing of His presence (see note at Ps 4:6).

102:3 **My days vanish like smoke**, which immediately dissipates into the air (37:20; 68:2; Hs 13:3). Life passed quickly as the psalmist suffered physical pain (Ps 69:18; Is 33:14). The **furnace** could be a hearth or brazier (Jr 36:23).

102:4-5 The **heart**, or seat of morale, has been **afflicted** as if by disease. **Withered like grass** shows the discouragement of the psalmist. He longed for death as the ultimate deliverance from a life of persecution and oppression (Pss 39; 90).

102:6 **An owl among the ruins** denotes the psalmist's loneliness resulting from ostracism.

102:7-8 The psalmist suffered abuse, ridicule, and false ac-

⁷ I stay awake;^a
  I am like a solitary bird on a roof.
⁸ My enemies taunt me all day long;
  they ridicule and curse me.^b
⁹ I eat ashes like bread
  and mingle my drinks with tears^c
¹⁰ because of Your indignation and wrath;
  for You have picked me up
    and thrown me aside.^d
¹¹ My days are like a lengthening shadow,
  and I wither away like grass.^e

¹² But You, Lord, are enthroned forever;^f
  Your fame endures to all generations.^g
¹³ You will rise up and have compassion
    on 'Zion,
  for it is time to show favor to her—
  the appointed time has come.^h
¹⁴ For Your servants take delight
    in its stones
  and favor its dust.ⁱ

¹⁵ Then the nations will fear the name
    of 'Yahweh,
  and all the kings of the earth Your glory,^j
¹⁶ for the Lord will rebuild Zion;
  He will appear in His glory.^k
¹⁷ He will pay attention to the prayer
    of the destitute
  and will not despise their prayer.^l

¹⁸ This will be written
    for a later generation,
  and a newly created people will praise
    the Lord:^m
¹⁹ He looked down from
    His holy heights—
  the Lord gazed out from heaven
    to earthⁿ—
²⁰ to hear a prisoner's groaning,
  to set free those condemned
    to die,^{A,o}
²¹ so that they might declare
  the name of Yahweh in Zion
  and His praise in Jerusalem,^p
²² when peoples and kingdoms
    are assembled
  to serve the Lord.^q

²³ He has broken my^B strength
    in midcourse;
  He has shortened my days.^r
²⁴ I say: "My God, do not take me
  in the middle of my life!^C
  Your years continue
    through all generations.^s
²⁵ Long ago You established
    the earth,
  and the heavens are the work
    of Your hands.^t

---

^a102:7 Ps 77:4
^b102:8 Ps 31:11; 69:19
^c102:9 Ps 42:3; 80:5
^d102:10 Jb 30:22
^e102:11 Jb 8:9; Ps 109:23
^f102:12 Ps 9:7; Lm 5:19
^gPs 135:13
^h102:13 Is 60:10; Zch 1:12
ⁱ102:14 Neh 4:2; Lm 4:1
^j102:15 Ps 138:4; Is 60:3
^k102:16 Ps 147:2; Is 60:1-2
^l102:17 Ps 22:24
^m102:18 Dt 31:19; Ps 22:30-31; 78:6
ⁿ102:19 Ps 14:2; 33:13; 53:2
^o102:20 Ps 79:11
^p102:21 Ps 22:22
^q102:22 Ps 22:27; 86:9; Zch 8:20-23
^r102:23 Ps 39:5; 89:45
^s102:24 Jb 36:26; Ps 90:2
^t102:25 Neh 9:6; Ps 96:5; Heb 1:10-12

---

^A102:20 Lit *free sons of death*   ^B102:23 Some Hb mss, LXX read *His*   ^C102:24 Lit *my days*

cusations day and night. **Taunt** is a common term describing unrelenting torment (see notes at 79:4 and 79:12).

102:9-10 On **mingle my drinks with tears**, compare Is 30:20, and "bread of tears" in note at Ps 80:5. The psalmist perceived his circumstances as a direct result of God's casting him out of His presence (Jb 27:21; 30:19,22; Is 64:5).

102:11 A metaphorical expression for imminent death, the phrase **like a lengthening shadow** associates the setting sun with the end of life. On **wither away like grass**, see note at verses 4-5.

102:12 The psalmist began a new section of the psalm by contrasting the frailty and vulnerability of humanity with the eternal and immutable nature of the Lord. While God's name **endures** throughout the generations, man is remembered no more after he dies (9:6; 103:16).

102:13 The rising of the Lord signifies judgment (see notes at 7:6-8 and 80:1). The psalmist anticipated the imminent restoration of Zion and the return of the Lord's presence to the Holy City. The Lord's attributes of righteousness, mercy, and compassion are revealed through His mighty acts of deliverance from the enemy.

102:14 Your servants, the members of a unified community (79:2,10; 89:5; 90:13), took **delight in** Jerusalem even after it was reduced to **stones** and **dust** (see note at Mc 1:6). The value of Zion to her people did not diminish in spite of the Babylonian invasion (Ezk 26:12).

102:15 The return of the Lord has cosmological implications. All the **nations** and their leaders will recognize and worship the God of Israel (Is 2:1-5; 49:7-23; 60–62; Zch 14).

102:16-17 The glory and omnipotence of the Lord will be

revealed through the rebuilding of Jerusalem and His abiding presence among His people (51:18; 147:2; Is 52:10; 60:1,10; Mc 7:11).

102:18 The **later generation** consists of **a newly created people** not yet in existence. The psalmist anticipated the Lord's immediate future response.

102:19 When the Lord **looked down** and **gazed** at the earth below, He heard the cries of the exiles, acknowledged the plight of His people, and brought deliverance (Dt 26:15; Is 63:15). Hundreds of years earlier, God had also heard the Israelites in Egypt and looked upon them with great concern (Ex 2:24).

102:20 The prisoner's **groaning** may also be rendered "groans" (79:11; Mal 2:13). **Those condemned to die** (lit "sons of death") describes the hopelessness of the captives (Ps 79:11; 146:7; Is 49:9).

102:21 God's faithful deliverance of His remnant from Babylon testifies to His holy **name**. In the ancient Near East, a person's name reflected his nature and character. The emphasis on **Zion** and **Jerusalem** reinforces the association of the divine name with the capital city.

102:22 The assembly of nations for universal worship occurs at the Lord's return to Zion (Is 2:1-5; 66:23-24; Zch 14:16-21).

102:23-24 The psalmist acknowledged God as the Creator and sustainer of life, and he pleaded for God not to take his **life** prematurely. The eternality of God contrasts with the temporal nature of humanity.

102:25 By right of creation, Yahweh earned the authority to rule and reign over the cosmos (24:1-2,7-10; 89:6-15; Jb 38:4; Is 40:21-23; 48:13; 51:13-16).

26 They will perish, but You will endure;
all of them will wear out like clothing.
You will change them like a garment,
and they will pass away.[a]
27 But You are the same,
and Your years will never end.[b]
28 Your servants' children
will dwell securely,
and their offspring will be established
before You."[c]

Psalm 103
The Forgiving God

Davidic.

1 My soul, praise •Yahweh,
and all that is within me, praise
His holy name.[d]
2 My soul, praise the LORD,
and do not forget all His benefits.[e]
3 He forgives all your sin;[f]
He heals all your diseases.[g]
4 He redeems your life from the •Pit;[h]
He crowns you with faithful love
and compassion.[i]
5 He satisfies you[A] with goodness;[j]
your youth is renewed
like the eagle.[k]
6 The LORD executes acts of righteousness
and justice for all the oppressed.[l]
7 He revealed His ways to Moses,[m]
His deeds to the people of Israel.[n]
8 The LORD is compassionate and gracious,
slow to anger and rich in faithful love.[o]
9 He will not always accuse us
or be angry forever.[p]
10 He has not dealt with us as
our sins deserve
or repaid us according to our offenses.[q]
11 For as high as the heavens are above
the earth,
so great is His faithful love
toward those who •fear Him.[r]
12 As far as the east is from the west,
so far has He removed
our transgressions from us.[s]
13 As a father has compassion
on his children,
so the LORD has compassion on those
who fear Him.[t]
14 For He knows what we are made of,
remembering that we are dust.[u]

[a]102:26 Is 34:4; 51:6; Mt 24:35
[b]102:27 Mal 3:6; Jms 1:17
[c]102:28 Ps 69:36; 89:4; 112:2
[d]103:1 Ps 30:4; 97:12; 104:1
[e]103:2 Dt 6:12; 8:11
[f]103:3 Is 43:25
[g]Jr 30:17
[h]103:4 Ps 49:15
[i]Ps 5:12
[j]103:5 Ps 107:9
[k]Is 40:31
[l]103:6 Ps 147:7
[m]103:7 Ex 33:13
[n]Ps 78:11; 99:7
[o]103:8 Ex 34:6; Nm 14:18; Neh 9:17
[p]103:9 Is 57:16; Jr 3:12; Mc 7:19
[q]103:10 Ezr 9:13; Lm 3:22
[r]103:11 Ps 36:5; 57:10
[s]103:12 Is 43:25; Mc 7:19
[t]103:13 Mal 3:17
[u]103:14 Gn 3:19; Ps 78:39

[A]103:5 Lit *satisfies your ornament*; Hb obscure

102:26-27 The unchanging nature of God extends beyond the course of history. Although the heavens and earth will **wear out like clothing** (Is 50:9; 51:6,8; cp. Heb 1:10-12), they will undergo transformation at the return of Christ (Rv 21:1).

102:28 The psalmist trusted that God would protect his descendants for many generations.

103:1-2 The threefold repetition of **praise** represents the highest form of worship (Is 6:3). The Hebrew word translated **benefits** *(gemul,* from *gamal)* means paying back what is deserved (28:4; 94:2; 116:12; 142:7). It most often describes God's divine wrath and retribution toward the enemy (Is 59:18), but here it describes the Lord's blessings enumerated in verses 3-5.

103:3 **Forgives** (Hb *soleach*), a cultic expression common in Leviticus and Numbers, finds fuller development in Is 33:24; 43:25, although only Is 55:7 includes the expressed condition of repentance. God **heals** Israel physically and spiritually, yet we should not associate all physical distress with sin. The Lord heals both body and spirit through forgiveness, providing a sense of wholeness (147:3; Is 53:5).

103:4-5 The word **redeems** denotes the payment of a ransom price. The Israelite redeemed his firstborn (Ex 13:1-16). The family redeemer exacted revenge for wrongful death of a near relative, and he adopted the responsibility of raising a son to carry on a dead brother's lineage (Dt 19:1-13; 25:5-10; Ru 3:8-9). **Pit** refers to Sheol, the place of the dead. The people of God are adorned with covenant loyalty and mercy, like a wreath of honor or esteem presented to a dignitary or king. These verses convey a sense of divine providence and peace, so that youthful strength is **renewed** (lit "renews itself") like an **eagle** (Is 40:31; 57:10).

103:6-7 **Righteousness** and **justice** toward the poor and needy in society reflect the ethical integrity of the king as God's representative. The Lord's revealing **His ways to Moses** refers to the divine formula describing God's character (Ex 34:6-7). God demonstrated His compassion through His mighty works of victory and the sustenance of His people in the wilderness.

103:8-9 In this allusion to Ex 34:6-7, the psalmist used the divine formula as the basis on which Israel experienced the Lord's forgiveness (cp. Is 57:16 for parallel expressions and terms).

103:10 While God's holiness demands payment for sin, God's mercy and compassion restrain His discipline. The Hebrew word *gamal,* rendered **repaid**, forms a wordplay with verse 2. The Lord's people enjoy His "benefits" *(gemul)* because He does not pay them back *(gamal)* for their sins.

103:11-12 The extent of the Lord's covenant loyalty is incomprehensible, and His capacity for removing transgression is immeasurable. Once the Lord forgives sin it no longer exists (Is 43:25), and the sinner is delivered from the Pit (Is 38:17). The language alludes to Is 55:6-9.

103:13 A godly **father** disciplines his child not out of malice, but because he loves him (Heb 12:3-13). The Lord demonstrates mercy and compassion toward His children through forgiveness of sin and blessing, in spite of their weaknesses.

103:14 The Hebrew word *yetser* (**what we are made of**; "our formation") comes from the verb *yatsar,* which denotes the shaping of clay by a craftsman into an acceptable vessel. God's intimate knowledge of His created beings affirms their origin and frailty.

103:15-16 The temporary nature of life is compared to the brief blossoming of **grass** and a **flower**, easily wilted by the

¹⁵ As for man, his days are like grass—
he blooms like a flower of the field;^a
¹⁶ when the wind passes over it,
it vanishes,
and its place is no longer known.^{A,b}
¹⁷ But from eternity to eternity
the LORD's faithful love is toward
those who fear Him,
and His righteousness
toward the grandchildren^c
¹⁸ of those who keep His covenant,
who remember to observe His precepts.^d
¹⁹ The LORD has established His throne
in heaven,
and His kingdom rules over all.^e

²⁰ Praise the LORD,
all His angels of great strength,
who do His word,
obedient to His command.^f
²¹ Praise the LORD, all His armies,
His servants who do His will.^g
²² Praise the LORD, all His works
in all the places where He rules.^h
My soul, praise Yahweh!

Psalm 104
God the Creator

¹ My soul, praise •Yahweh!
LORD my God, You are very great;

You are clothed with majesty
and splendor.ⁱ
² He wraps Himself in light as if it were
a robe,
spreading out the sky like a canopy,^j
³ laying the beams of His palace
on the waters above,^k
making the clouds His chariot,^l
walking on the wings of the wind,^m
⁴ and making the winds
His messengers,^B
flames of fire His servants.ⁿ

⁵ He established the earth
on its foundations;
it will never be shaken.^o
⁶ You covered it with the deep
as if it were a garment;
the waters stood
above the mountains.^p
⁷ At Your rebuke the waters fled;
at the sound of Your thunder
they hurried away^q—
⁸ mountains rose and valleys sank^c—
to the place You established
for them.^r
⁹ You set a boundary
they cannot cross;
they will never cover
the earth again.^s

^a103:15 Jb 14:2; 1Pt 1:24
^b103:15-16 Is 40:6-7
^c103:17 Ex 20:6; Dt 5:10; Ps 25:6
^d103:18 Dt 7:9; Ps 25:10
^e103:19 Ps 11:4; 47:2
^f103:20 Ps 29:1; 148:2
^g103:21 1Kg 22:19; Neh 9:6
^h103:22 Ps 145:10
ⁱ104:1 Ps 93:1; 103:22
^j104:2 Jb 9:8; Is 40:22
^k104:3 Am 9:6
^lIs 19:1
^mPs 18:10
ⁿ104:4 Ps 148:8; Heb 1:7
^o104:5 Jb 38:4; Ps 24:2; 93:1; 96:10
^p104:6 Gn 7:19
^q104:7 Ps 18:15; 106:9
^r104:8 Ps 65:6; Am 4:13
^s104:9 Jb 26:10; 38:10-11; Jr 5:22

^A103:16 Lit *place no longer knows it*   ^B104:4 Or *angels*   ^C104:7-8 Or *away. They flowed over the mountains and went down valleys*

elements. The same metaphor in Isaiah contrasts the power of God's word and the impotence of humanity (Is 40:6-8).

103:17-18 Although God's people struggle with unfaithfulness, the Lord's covenant loyalty endures for those who **fear Him** (v. 11). The Hebrew word *yara'* ("fear") combines obedience and respect with humility before a sovereign God.

103:20 Angels of great strength, or "His angels, warriors of strength," act on God's behalf and minister to His people (91:11; 104:4; 148:2).

103:21 God's **armies** (or "hosts") refer to divine beings who dwell with God and serve Him.

103:22 The saving works of the Lord toward His people testify to His majesty and power (98:3; Is 40:5).

104:1-35 This psalm is a companion hymn to Psalm 103. It begins with the same words that end that psalm. This psalm alludes to the Noahic covenant and the six days of creation. It resembles ancient Near Eastern texts in form and content. The psalm is an argument against sun worship.

104:1 To be **clothed with majesty and splendor** represents royal language typically associated with kingship (96:6; 111:3; 145:5-12; Jb 40:10; Is 2:10,19-20; 35:2).

104:2 God is identified with **light** (Gn 15:17; 1Jn 1:5), and light signifies the Lord's presence in Jerusalem (Ps 89:15; Is 60:1; Ezk 43:1-2). Light, the first created element, dispels darkness and reveals evil (Jn 3:20; 8:12; 2Co 4:5-6; 1Jn 2:8). On **spreading out the sky**, compare Is 40:22; Zch 12:1.

104:3 The **palace** (or "chamber") refers to God's dwelling

place, which contains rain (v. 13; Am 9:6). The Lord rides the clouds (Ps 68:4,17). To walk **on the wings of the wind** refers to God's dominion (18:10).

104:4 The **winds** and rain, controlled by God, are agents of judgment and blessing. **Flames of fire** refers to lightning (29:7; 148:8; cp. Heb 1:7). In the ancient Near East, the heavenly bodies and natural elements were worshiped as deities, but in this psalm all of these "deities" fall under the Lord's authority as Creator.

104:5 While verses 1-4 describe the Lord's sovereignty over natural forces, the emphasis in this verse shifts to the Lord as King over the earth. By divine command, God **established** the earth on its axis. **It will never be shaken** could be rendered as "it will never totter," based on the nuance of the Hebrew verb *mut* ("to tip over, fall off balance"; 82:5; 93:1; 96:10; Is 24:19; 40:20; 41:7).

104:6-8 God **covered** the earth **with the deep** and the waters **stood above the mountains**. The imagery is consistent with the cosmic flood in Genesis (Gn 7:18-20). At God's **rebuke**, the waters **fled** like warriors fleeing from battle (114:3-6) and **hurried away** (i.e., in alarm) at the sound of God's voice. The floodwaters receded, uncovering the mountains and redefining the valleys, restoring the earth to its natural state. Just as the Lord established the earth (v. 5), so the mountains and valleys remained in the places God established for them.

104:9 As sovereign Creator, God appointed a boundary that the waters could not transcend, so that **they will never cover the earth again** (Jb 37:8-11). This expression recalls

¹⁰ He causes the springs to gush
  into the valleys;
they flow between the mountains.^a
¹¹ They supply water for every wild beast;
the wild donkeys quench their thirst.^b
¹² The birds of the sky live
  beside the springs;
they sing among the foliage.^c
¹³ He waters the mountains
  from His palace;
the earth is satisfied by the fruit
  of Your labor.^d
¹⁴ He causes grass to grow
  for the livestock
and provides crops for man to cultivate,
producing food from the earth,^e
¹⁵ wine that makes man's heart glad—
making his face shine with oil—
and bread that sustains man's heart.^f
¹⁶ The trees of the Lord flourish,^A
the cedars of Lebanon that He planted.^g
¹⁷ There the birds make their nests;
the stork makes its home
  in the pine trees.^h
¹⁸ The high mountains are
  for the wild goats;
the cliffs are a refuge for hyraxes.ⁱ
¹⁹ He made the moon to mark
  the^B festivals;^C
the sun knows when to set.^j
²⁰ You bring darkness,
  and it becomes night,
when all the forest animals stir.^k
²¹ The young lions roar for their prey

and seek their food from God.^l
²² The sun rises; they go back
and lie down in their dens.^m
²³ Man goes out to his work
and to his labor until evening.ⁿ
²⁴ How countless are Your works, Lord!
In wisdom You have made them all;
the earth is full of Your creatures.^{D,o}
²⁵ Here is the sea, vast and wide,
teeming with creatures
  beyond number—
living things both large and small.^p
²⁶ There the ships move about,
and •Leviathan, which You formed
  to play there.^q
²⁷ All of them wait for You
to give them their food at the right time.^r
²⁸ When You give it to them,
they gather it;
when You open Your hand,
they are satisfied with good things.^s
²⁹ When You hide Your face,
they are terrified;
when You take away their breath,
they die and return to the dust.^t
³⁰ When You send Your breath,^E
they are created,
and You renew the face of the earth.^u
³¹ May the glory of the Lord
  endure forever;
may the Lord rejoice in His works.^v
³² He looks at the earth, and it trembles;
He touches the mountains,
and they pour out smoke.^w

---

^a104:10 Ps 107:35; Is 41:18 ^b104:11 Jb 39:5 ^c104:12 Mt 8:20 ^d104:13 Jb 5:10; Ps 65:9 ^e104:14 Jb 28:5; Ps 147:8 ^f104:15 Gn 18:5; Ps 141:5 ^g104:16 Nm 24:6 ^h104:17 Lv 11:19 ⁱ104:18 Lv 11:5; Pr 30:26 ^j104:19 Gn 1:14; Ps 19:6; 74:16 ^k104:20 Is 45:17 ^l104:21 Jb 38:39 ^m104:22 Jb 37:8 ⁿ104:23 Gn 3:19 ^o104:24 Pr 3:19; Jr 10:12; 51:15 ^p104:25 Gn 1:21; Ps 69:34 ^q104:26 Jb 41:1; Ps 74:14; Is 27:1 ^r104:27 Ps 136:25; 145:15; 147:9 ^s104:28 Ps 145:16 ^t104:29 Jb 10:9; Ps 90:3 ^u104:30 Jb 33:4 ^v104:31 Ps 72:17 ^w104:32 Ex 19:18; Ps 144:5

---

^A104:16 Lit are satisfied   ^B104:19 Lit moon for   ^C104:19 Or the appointed times   ^D104:24 Lit possessions   ^E104:30 Or Spirit

the Lord's covenant with Noah, when He promised never to destroy the earth by flood again (Gn 9:11).

104:10-11 The psalmist transformed the destructive role of water into a constructive role—the provision of water for sustaining the life of His creatures.

104:13 On **palace** see note at verse 3.

104:14 Vegetation provides food for cattle and mankind alike. Humanity stands at the center of the psalm, representative of God's finest creature and the crowning achievement of His creation (Ps 8).

104:15 To make a man's **face shine with oil** figuratively describes the abundance of God's provision and the satisfaction of rich foods. **Bread** denotes any type of food.

104:16 **Flourish** is literally "are satisfied."

104:19-20 The solar and lunar cycles regulate the seasons, reflecting God's dependability and sovereignty over creation. God controls the **darkness** and the light and the life cycles of **night** and day creatures.

104:25 **Vast and wide** is literally "great and broad its hands."

104:26 **Leviathan** (Jb 3:8; Is 27:1) refers to a large sea creature that would **play** in the water (Zch 8:5).

104:27 God's faithfulness to His creation allows His creatures to anticipate His future provision (145:5; 146:5; Is 38:18).

104:28 The Hebrew word for **satisfied** (sb') is a key term in the psalm. The earth is "satisfied" (v. 13), the trees are satisfied ("flourish" v. 16), and all of the earth's inhabitants are "satisfied" (v. 28).

104:29-30 The hiding of God's **face** refers to abandonment. The term **terrified** denotes a state of chaos, and it may also be translated "confused." Only God has power over life and death (Gn 2:7; 6:17). When man dies, he returns to dust (Gn 3:19), and when God sends forth His **breath** (Hb ruach; "spirit"), He creates life.

104:32 The focused attention of God causes the **earth** to tremble (2:11; 55:5; Jb 4:14; Is 33:14). The presence of the omnipotent God causes **mountains** to smoke (18:8; 144:5; 2Sm 22:9; Is 4:5; 6:4), often as part of an appearance of the Lord (Ex 19:18; 20:18).

104:35 In the LXX, **Hallelujah** begins Psalm 105; thus Psalms

33 I will sing to the LORD all my life;
　　I will sing praise to my God
　　　while I live.*a*

34 May my meditation be pleasing to Him;
　　I will rejoice in the LORD.*b*

35 May sinners vanish from the earth
　　and wicked people be no more.*c*
　　My soul, praise Yahweh!
　　·Hallelujah!

Psalm 105
God's Faithfulness to His People

1 Give thanks to ·Yahweh, call on
　　His name;
　　proclaim His deeds among the peoples.*d*
2 Sing to Him, sing praise to Him;
　　tell about all His wonderful works!*e*
3 Honor His holy name;
　　let the hearts of those who seek
　　　Yahweh rejoice.*f*
4 Search for the LORD and for His strength;
　　seek His face always.*g*
5 Remember the wonderful works
　　He has done,
　　His wonders, and the judgments
　　He has pronounced,*A,h*
6 you offspring of Abraham His servant,
　　Jacob's descendants—His chosen ones.*i*

7 He is the LORD our God;
　　His judgments govern the whole earth.*j*

8 He remembers His covenant forever,
　　the promise He ordained
　　for a thousand generations*k*—
9 the covenant He made with Abraham,
　　swore*B* to Isaac,*l*
10 and confirmed to Jacob as a decree
　　and to Israel as an everlasting covenant:*m*
11 "I will give the land of Canaan to you
　　as your inherited portion."*n*

12 When they were few in number,
　　very few indeed,
　　and temporary residents in Canaan,*o*
13 wandering from nation to nation
　　and from one kingdom to another,*p*
14 He allowed no one to oppress them;
　　He rebuked kings on their behalf:*q*
15 "Do not touch My anointed ones,*r*
　　or harm My prophets."*s*

16 He called down famine
　　against the land
　　and destroyed the entire food supply.*t*
17 He had sent a man ahead of them—
　　Joseph, who was sold as a slave.*u*
18 They hurt his feet with shackles;
　　his neck was put in an iron collar.*v*
19 Until the time his prediction came true,
　　the word of the LORD tested him.*w*
20 The king sent for him
　　and released him;
　　the ruler of peoples set him free.*x*

Cross-references:

*a*104:33 Ps 63:4; 146:2
*b*104:34 Ps 19:14
*c*104:35 Ps 37:10; 59:13
*d*105:1 Ps 9:11; Is 12:4
*e*105:2 Ps 96:3
*f*105:3 Ps 33:21
*g*105:4 Ps 27:8; 63:2
*h*105:5 Ps 77:11; 119:13
*i*105:6 Ps 135:4
*j*105:7 Is 26:9
*k*105:8 Dt 7:9; Ps 106:45; Lk 1:42
*l*105:9 Gn 12:7; 22:16-18
*m*105:10 Gn 28:13-15
*n*105:11 Gn 13:15; 15:18; Ps 78:55
*o*105:12 Gn 34:30; Dt 7:7
*p*105:13 Dt 26:5
*q*105:14 Gn 12:17; 20:3,7
*r*105:15 Gn 20:6-7; 26:11
*s*105:1-15 1Ch 16:8-22
*t*105:16 Gn 41:54; Lv 26:26; Ezk 4:16
*u*105:17 Gn 37:28-36; 45:5; Ac 7:9
*v*105:18 Gn 39:20
*w*105:19 Gn 40:20-21
*x*105:20 Gn 41:14

A105:5 Lit *judgments of His mouth*　　**B**105:9 Lit *and His oath*

103–106 each end with the same phrase they begin with—"My soul, praise Yahweh!" in 103 and 104, and "Hallelujah!" in 105 and 106. "Hallelujah" is literally "praise Yah." *Yah* is a shortened form of Yahweh. The psalmist was inviting his audience to join him in praising Yahweh.

105:1-45 This psalm, an epic poem, resembles Psalms 78 and 106 in form and content. Verses 1-15 recur in 1Ch 16:8-22, a song associated with the Davidic procession ushering the ark of the covenant into Jerusalem.

105:3 Honor denotes continuous praise.

105:4 Strength is figurative for the ark (78:61) that symbolized the Lord's presence and preceded Israel in battle (Jos 6:6-7; 1Sm 4:3).

105:5 As long as Israel remembered God's miraculous **works**, the Lord remembered His covenant promises (v. 8). God's **judgments** are His ordinances (119:13; Ex 24:3).

105:6 The threefold covenant promise made to the patriarchs (seed, land, blessing) was realized by Israel as God's **chosen ones**. The descendants of **Abraham** and Isaac were God's "elect" people (v. 43), who enjoyed the blessings of prosperity in the land designated by the Lord.

105:7-11 As sovereign God, the Lord affirmed the **covenant** with Israel (Gn 35:10-15), focusing specifically on the land as their inheritance.

105:12-13 The psalmist outlined the birth and growth of the nation of Israel, beginning with the time of the patriarchs, a nomadic people (Gn 12:1; 13:1; 20:1) traveling throughout **Canaan**.

105:14 The word **allowed** derives from the Hebrew *noach* ("leave untouched, settle securely, repose"). The verb serves a dual role, since God's refusal to permit oppression allowed the patriarchs to dwell safely. **He rebuked kings** refers to the divine protection of Sarah from Pharaoh (Gn 12:17) and Sarah and Rebekah from Abimelech (Gn 20:13; 26:11).

105:15 God's **anointed ones** would include kings, priests, and **prophets**, all of whom received anointing in a dedication ceremony.

105:16 The **famine** in the land of Canaan (Gn 41:53-57) eventually brought Jacob and his sons to Egypt. **The entire food supply** is literally "every staff of bread." The staff could refer to a rod on which bread, shaped in rings, was hung up to protect it from rodents, or it could be speaking figuratively of bread as the staff of life.

105:17 Jacob's son **Joseph**, sold by his brothers to nomads, entered the land of Egypt and was providentially raised to a high office in Pharaoh's court (Gn 37:12-26; 45:5).

105:18 Joseph was unjustly imprisoned in Egypt following accusations by Potiphar's wife (Gn 39:20).

105:19-22 Tested describes the smelting process that removed dross from fine metal. Joseph's imprisonment

21 He made him master
  of his household,
  ruler over all his possessions[a]—
22 binding[A] his officials at will
  and instructing his elders.[b]
23 Then Israel went to Egypt;
  Jacob lived as a foreigner in the land
  of Ham.[B,c]
24 The Lord[C] made His people
  very fruitful;
  He made them more numerous
  than their foes,[d]
25 whose hearts He turned to hate
  His people
  and to deal deceptively with His servants.[e]
26 He sent Moses His servant,
  and Aaron, whom He had chosen.[f]
27 They performed His miraculous signs
  among them,
  and wonders in the land of Ham.[B,g]
28 He sent darkness, and it became dark—
  for did they not defy[D]
  His commands?[h]
29 He turned their water into blood
  and caused their fish to die.[i]
30 Their land was overrun with frogs,
  even in their royal chambers.[j]
31 He spoke, and insects came[k]—
  gnats throughout their country.[l]
32 He gave them hail for rain,
  and lightning throughout their land.[m]
33 He struck their vines and fig trees
  and shattered the trees
  of their territory.[n]
34 He spoke, and locusts came—
  young locusts without number.

35 They devoured all the vegetation
  in their land
  and consumed the produce
  of their land.[o]
36 He struck all the firstborn
  in their land,
  all their first progeny.[p]
37 Then He brought Israel out with silver
  and gold,
  and no one among
  His tribes stumbled.[q]
38 Egypt was glad when they left,
  for the dread of Israel[E] had fallen
  on them.[r]
39 He spread a cloud as a covering
  and gave a fire to light up the night.[s]
40 They asked, and He brought quail
  and satisfied them with bread
  from heaven.[t]
41 He opened a rock, and water
  gushed out;
  it flowed like a stream in the desert.[u]
42 For He remembered
  His holy promise
  to Abraham His servant.[v]
43 He brought His people out
  with rejoicing,
  His chosen ones with shouts of joy.[w]
44 He gave them the lands
  of the nations,
  and they inherited
  what other peoples had worked for.[x]
45 All this happened
  so that they might keep His statutes
  and obey His instructions.[y]
  •Hallelujah!

---

[a]105:21 Gn 41:40-43 [b]105:22 Gn 41:44 [c]105:23 Gn 46:6; Ac 7:15; 13:17 [d]105:24 Ex 1:7,9; Dt 26:5 [e]105:25 Ex 1:8-14; Ac 7:19 [f]105:26 Ex 3:10; 4:12,14 [g]105:27 Ex 7:3; 11:9-10; Ps 78:43-51 [h]105:28 Ex 10:21-23; Ps 99:7 [i]105:29 Ex 7:20-21 [j]105:30 Ex 8:3,6 [k]105:31 Ex 8:21 [l]Ex 8:16-17 [m]105:32-33 Ex 9:23-25 [n]105:33 Ps 78:47 [o]105:34-35 Ex 10:12-15 [p]105:36 Ex 12:29; 13:15; Ps 78:51 [q]105:37 Ex 12:35-36 [r]105:38 Ex 12:33; 15:16 [s]105:39 Ex 13:21; Neh 9:12; Ps 78:14 [t]105:40 Ex 16:15; Ps 78:24 [u]105:41 Ex 17:6; Nm 20:11; Ps 78:15 [v]105:42 Ex 2:24 [w]105:43 Ex 15:1; Ps 106:12 [x]105:44 Jos 24:13; Ps 78:55 [y]105:45 Dt 4:1,40; Ps 78:7

[A]105:22 LXX, Syr, Vg read *teaching* [B]105:23,27 = Egypt [C]105:24 Lit *He* [D]105:28 LXX, Syr read *for they did defy*
[E]105:38 Lit *them*

---

increased his trust in the Lord. Pharaoh eventually **released him** because of his prophetic dreams and interpretations and he installed Joseph over his house, all his possessions, and all other officials (Gn 41:39-42).

105:23 The designation **Israel** refers to **Jacob** and his sons (Gn 46). **The land of Ham** is another name for Egypt (78:51; 106:22; Gn 10:6).

105:24 The Hebrew word translated as **more numerous** implies "stronger," with the nuance of physical power.

105:25 This psalm emphasizes God's sovereign control of all people and events in Israel's history, including those that seemed bad at the time (cp. v. 16).

105:28 The psalmist listed the plague of **darkness** out of order because it was the first sign that resulted in Egypt's acknowledgment of the Lord's power (Ex 10:21ff).

105:29-36 The psalmist recounted some of the plagues in Egypt that enabled the Lord's people to escape. The plagues were **water into blood** (Ex 7:14-24), **frogs** (Ex 8:5-15), **gnats** (Ex 8:16-19), **hail** (Ex 9:13-35), **locusts** that consumed all

the vegetation (Ex 10:1-20), culminating in the death of **the firstborn** of Egypt (Ex 11:1-10). The firstborn represented the virility and strength of the family. In Egyptian culture, Pharaoh and his firstborn son claimed to have the status of deity.

105:39 The **cloud** and **fire** refer to the pillar of cloud and fire (Ex 13:20-22; 14:19-20; 40:36-37) that guided the Israelites throughout their journey in the wilderness.

105:40-42 The Lord provided **quail** when the Israelites complained about the manna **from heaven** (78:25; Ex 16:4; Nm 11:4-35), and He also gave them **water** from a **rock** (Ex 17:1-7; Nm 20:9-11). God's provision for His people reflects His faithfulness to the covenant first initiated with **Abraham**.

105:44-45 The **lands of the nations** refers to Canaan, which contained wicked peoples deserving judgment. Israel conquered the peoples and inhabited their cities, consumed their harvests, and possessed their flocks. The purpose of the Lord's protection and provision was to motivate Israel to maintain a relationship with Him through their obedience.

Psalm 106

Israel's Unfaithfulness to God

1 •Hallelujah!
Give thanks to the LORD,
for He is good;
His faithful love endures forever.[a]
2 Who can declare the LORD's mighty acts
or proclaim all the praise due Him?[b]
3 How happy are those
who uphold justice,
who practice righteousness
at all times.[c]

4 Remember me, LORD,
when You show favor to Your people.[d]
Come to me with Your salvation
5 so that I may enjoy the prosperity
of Your chosen ones,
rejoice in the joy of Your nation,
and boast about Your heritage.[e]

6 Both we and our fathers have sinned;
we have done wrong
and have acted wickedly.[f]
7 Our fathers in Egypt did not grasp
the significance of
Your wonderful works
or remember Your many acts
of faithful love;
instead, they rebelled by the sea—
the •Red Sea.[g]
8 Yet He saved them
because of His name,
to make His power known.[h]
9 He rebuked the Red Sea,
and it dried up;
He led them through the depths
as through a desert.[i]
10 He saved them from the hand
of the adversary;
He redeemed them from the hand
of the enemy.[j]
11 Water covered their foes;
not one of them remained.[k]
12 Then they believed His promises
and sang His praise.[l]

13 They soon forgot His works
and would not wait for His counsel.[m]
14 They were seized with craving
in the wilderness
and tested God in the desert.[n]
15 He gave them what they asked for,
but sent a wasting disease
among them.[o]

16 In the camp they were envious of Moses
and of Aaron, the LORD's holy one.[p]
17 The earth opened up
and swallowed Dathan;
it covered the assembly of Abiram.[q]
18 Fire blazed throughout their assembly;
flames consumed the wicked.[r]

[a] 106:1 1Ch 16:34,41; Ps 100:5
[b] 106:2 Ps 145:4,12; 150:2
[c] 106:3 Ps 15:2
[d] 106:4 Ps 119:132
[e] 106:5 Dt 32:9; Ps 105:6,43
[f] 106:6 Lv 26:40; Jr 3:25; 14:20
[g] 106:7 Ex 14:10-12; Ps 78:17
[h] 106:8 Ex 9:16; Ezk 20:9
[i] 106:9 Ps 18:15; 104:7; Is 63:11-13
[j] 106:10 Ex 14:30; Ps 107:2
[k] 106:11 Ex 14:27-28; 15:5; Ps 78:53
[l] 106:12 Ex 14:31; 15:1-21; Ps 105:43
[m] 106:13 Ex 15:24; Ps 78:11; 107:11
[n] 106:14 Nm 11:4; Ps 78:18
[o] 106:15 Nm 11:31; Ps 78:29
[p] 106:16 Nm 16:1-3
[q] 106:17 Nm 16:31-32; Dt 11:6
[r] 106:18 Nm 16:35

106:1-48 While Psalm 105 focuses on trust, Psalm 106 emphasizes repentance. The absence of conflict between the northern and southern kingdoms suggests a setting for this psalm during the monarchy. It consists of a historical chronology of the exodus and conquest.

yasha'

Hebrew Pronunciation	[yah SHAH]
HCSB Translation	save, deliver, rescue
Uses in Psalms	57
Uses in the OT	205
Focus Passage	Psalm 106:8,10,21,47

Yasha' in causative verbs denotes *save* (Ex 14:30), *deliver* (Jdg 3:31), and *rescue* (Dt 22:27). Passive-reflexive verbs give passive ideas: *be saved* (Ps 80:3). *Yasha'* signifies *give* (Dt 20:4), *win* (Ps 98:1), *bring* (Ps 44:3), or *accomplish* (Is 63:5) *victory*. It is *help* (Lm 4:17), *preserve* (Ps 36:6), and *spare* (Jos 22:22). It can be *avenge* (1Sm 25:26). God *makes victorious* (1Ch 18:6). The passive-reflexive connotes *be safe* (Ps 119:117). Causative participles mean *savior* (Ps 17:7) or *deliverer* (Jdg 3:15); passive-reflexive ones imply *saved* and *victorious* (Zch 9:9). *Yasha'* appears several times with related *yeshu'ah* (78x) and *teshu'ah* (34x). *Yeshu'ah* means *salvation* (Gn 49:18), *deliverance* (1Sm 14:45), *help* (Ps 3:2), and *victory* (Is 26:18); *teshu'ah* does too (Jdg 15:18; Ps 60:11; Pr 11:14; Is 45:17). *Yeshu'ah* also suggests *saving act* (Ps 74:12) and *prosperity* (Jb 30:15), while *teshu'ah* connotes *safety* (Ps 33:17).

106:2 God's incomparable works reveal His glory (19:1-2).

106:3 The consequences of the Lord's relationship with Israel include community peace and the integrity of its individual members who practiced **righteousness**.

106:7 Israel stubbornly refused to recognize God's miraculous **works** (Ex 4:1,8; 6:9; 14:11) and **rebelled** instead.

106:9 The parting of the **Red Sea** occurred during Israel's departure from Egypt (104:7; 114:3; Ex 14:21-22; Is 63:13).

106:10 The **adversary** is literally "the one who hated."

106:11-12 Compare these verses with Ex 14:28–15:1.

106:13 In verse 4 the psalmist asked God to "remember" him, yet Israel continually **forgot** God (Dt 4:9,23,31; 6:12; 9:7; 25:19; 32:18). Although the Lord supplied all their needs, they grew impatient in the wilderness.

106:14 Israel became greedy in the wilderness (Nm 11:31-34). On **tested God**, see note at 95:8-9 (cp. Ex 17; Dt 6:16).

106:15 God granted Israel's request, only to send a plague (possibly consumption) as a response to their rebellious attitude.

106:16-18 The Israelites grew **envious** (Hb *qana'*) of Moses and Aaron (Nm 16:1-14,31-39). The Hebrew word often refers to God's righteous jealousy on behalf of His name (Ex 20:5; 34:14; Ezk 39:25). As **the LORD's holy one**, Aaron served a unique role as the first anointed high priest.

106:19-20 Israel replaced God's **glory** with a manmade

19 At Horeb they made a calf
  and worshiped the cast metal image.[a]
20 They exchanged their glory[A,B]
  for the image of a grass-eating ox.[b]
21 They forgot God their Savior,
  who did great things in Egypt,[c]
22 wonderful works in the land of Ham,[C]
  awe-inspiring acts at the Red Sea.[d]
23 So He said
  He would have destroyed them—
  if Moses His chosen one
  had not stood before Him in the breach
  to turn His wrath away
  from destroying them.[e]

24 They despised the pleasant land
  and did not believe His promise.[f]
25 They grumbled in their tents
  and did not listen to the Lord's voice.[g]
26 So He raised His hand against them
  with an oath
  that He would make them fall
  in the desert[h]
27 and would disperse their descendants[D]
  among the nations,
  scattering them throughout the lands.[i]

28 They aligned themselves with •Baal
  of Peor
  and ate sacrifices offered
  to lifeless gods.[E,j]
29 They provoked the Lord with their deeds,
  and a plague broke out against them.[k]
30 But Phinehas stood up and intervened,
  and the plague was stopped.[l]
31 It was credited to him
  as righteousness

throughout all generations
  to come.[m]

32 They angered the Lord at the waters
  of Meribah,
  and Moses suffered[F] because of them;[n]
33 for they embittered his spirit,[G]
  and he spoke rashly with his lips.[o]

34 They did not destroy the peoples
  as the Lord had commanded them[p]
35 but mingled with the nations
  and adopted their ways.[q]
36 They served their idols,
  which became a snare to them.[r]
37 They sacrificed their sons
  and daughters to demons.[s]
38 They shed innocent blood—
  the blood of their sons and daughters
  whom they sacrificed to the idols
  of Canaan;
  so the land became polluted with blood.[t]
39 They defiled themselves by their actions
  and prostituted themselves
  by their deeds.[u]

40 Therefore the Lord's anger burned
  against His people,
  and He abhorred His own inheritance.[v]
41 He handed them over to the nations;
  those who hated them ruled them.[w]
42 Their enemies oppressed them,
  and they were subdued
  under their power.[x]
43 He rescued them many times,
  but they continued to rebel deliberately
  and were beaten down by their sin.[y]

Cross-references:

a 106:19 Ex 32:4; Dt 9:8; Ac 7:41
b 106:20 Jr 2:11; Rm 1:23
c 106:21 Dt 10:21; Ps 78:11
d 106:22 Ps 105:27
e 106:23 Ex 32:10; Dt 9:14; Ezk 20:8
f 106:24 Nm 14:31; Dt 9:23; Heb 3:19
g 106:25 Nm 14:2; Dt 1:27
h 106:26 Nm 14:28-35; Ezk 20:15; Heb 3:11
i 106:27 Lv 26:33; Dt 4:27; Ps 44:11
j 106:28 Nm 25:3; Dt 4:3; Hs 9:10
k 106:29 Nm 25:4
l 106:30 Nm 25:7-8
m 106:31 Gn 15:6; Nm 25:10-13
n 106:32 Nm 20:2-13; Ps 81:7
o 106:33 Ps 78:40; Is 63:10
p 106:34 Dt 7:2,16; Jdg 1:21,27-36
q 106:35 Jdg 3:5-6
r 106:36 Dt 7:16; Jdg 2:12
s 106:37 Lv 17:7; Dt 32:17
t 106:38 Nm 35:33; Is 24:5
u 106:39 Ezk 20:18,30-31; Lv 18:24
v 106:40 Dt 32:19; Ps 78:59
w 106:41 Jdg 2:14; Neh 9:27
x 106:42 Jdg 4:3; 10:12
y 106:43 Jdg 2:16-18; Ps 81:12

---

image (Ex 32; Dt 9:12). The unique relationship that God had shared with the Israelites had served as a testimony to the other nations. Israel eliminated the one thing that distinguished them from all other peoples. The sin of idolatry is cited in this psalm as the single most significant breach of covenant fidelity.

106:23 Moses **stood before** God **in the breach**, mediating on behalf of the wayward people in the wilderness and offering his life to prevent their destruction (105:26; Ex 32:10-11,31). Compare Ps 106:19-23 with Dt 9:8-21.

106:24-27 Following the reports of Joshua and Caleb about the inhabitants of the land of Canaan, Israel showed a lack of trust and rejected the promised **land** (78:59,67; Nm 11:20; 14:11). Consequently, Israel's **descendants** experienced exile and dispersion (Lv 26:33; Dt 4:26-27; 28:64-65; Ezk 20:23). Compare Ps 106:24-27 with Nm 13:25–14:45; Dt 1:21-33.

106:28-31 Israel participated in a fertility cult at Peor in Moab, further endangering their relationship with the Lord. Over 24,000 died from the **plague** that resulted (Nm 25:1-9). In later Scripture, **Baal of Peor** symbolizes apostasy (Hs

9:10). **Phinehas** demonstrated faith by his zeal for God, and God counted it as **righteousness** to him and all who follow his example (cp. Gn 15:6).

106:32-33 The rebellion at **Meribah** (81:7; 95:8; Ex 17:1-7; Nm 20:2-13) provided the catalyst for Moses' sin of presumption (Nm 8–13). As a result, he did not enter Canaan.

106:34-38 The Israelites were instructed to annihilate all the inhabitants of the cities they conquered (Ex 34:11; Dt 7:1; 20:16; Jdg 1:21; 2:3), but they failed to do so. Consequently they intermarried with foreigners and adopted many of their idolatrous practices, including infant sacrifice (cp. Lv 18:21; 2Kg 16:3; 21:6; 23:10). God's faithfulness to His divine promise and covenant was met with infidelity by Israel (Ex 23:32).

106:39-40 Israel's abominations rendered the people and the land of Canaan ritually and ethically unclean, thus unacceptable to the Lord.

106:41-44 The Lord allowed the oppression of Israel by other **nations** as divine judgment. The goal was discipline and restoration to divine favor (Jdg 2:14; 3:1). The book of

44 When He heard their cry,
He took note of their distress,[a]
45 remembered His covenant with them,
and relented according to the riches
of His faithful love.[b]
46 He caused them to be pitied
before all their captors.[c]

47 Save us, *Yahweh our God,
and gather us from the nations,
so that we may give thanks
to Your holy name
and rejoice in Your praise.[d]

48 May Yahweh, the God of Israel,
be praised
from everlasting to everlasting.[e]
Let all the people say, "*Amen!"
Hallelujah![f]

BOOK V
(Psalms 107–150)

Psalm 107
Thanksgiving for God's Deliverance

1 Give thanks to the LORD, for He is good;
His faithful love endures forever.[g]
2 Let the redeemed of the LORD proclaim
that He has redeemed them
from the hand of the foe[h]
3 and has gathered them
from the lands—
from the east and the west,
from the north and the south.[i]

4 Some[A] wandered
in the desolate wilderness,
finding no way to a city
where they could live.[j]
5 They were hungry and thirsty;
their spirits failed[B] within them.[k]
6 Then they cried out to the LORD
in their trouble;
He rescued them
from their distress.[l]
7 He led them by the right path
to go to a city where they could live.[m]
8 Let them give thanks to the LORD
for His faithful love
and His wonderful works for
all *humanity.[n]
9 For He has satisfied the thirsty
and filled the hungry
with good things.[o]

10 Others[A] sat in darkness and gloom[C]—
prisoners in cruel chains[p]—
11 because they rebelled
against God's commands
and despised the counsel
of the *Most High.[q]
12 He broke their spirits[D] with hard labor;
they stumbled, and there was no one
to help.[r]
13 Then they cried out to the LORD
in their trouble;
He saved them from their distress.[s]
14 He brought them out of darkness
and gloom[C]
and broke their chains apart.[t]

[a]106:44 Jdg 3:3; 6:7; 10:10 [b]106:45 Lv 26:42; Ps 105:8 [c]106:46 1Kg 8:50; 2Ch 30:9; Ezr 9:9 [d]106:47 Ps 107:3; 147:2 [e]106:48 Ps 41:13; 72:18; 89:52 [f]106:47-48 1Ch 16:35-36 [g]107:1 1Ch 16:34; Ps 100:5; 106:1 [h]107:2 Ps 78:42; 106:10 [i]107:3 Is 11:12; 43:5; Ezk 20:34 [j]107:4 Nm 14:33; 32:13 [k]107:5 Ps 77:3 [l]107:6 Ps 106:44 [m]107:7 Jr 31:9 [n]107:8 Ps 75:1 [o]107:9 Ps 22:26; 34:10; Lk 1:53 [p]107:10 Ps 102:20; Is 42:7; Lk 1:79 [q]107:11 2Ch 36:16; Ps 78:40; 106:7 [r]107:12 Ex 6:9; Dt 26:6; Is 14:3 [s]107:13 Ex 2:23-25 [t]107:14 Jr 2:20

A107:4,10 Lit *They* B107:5 Lit *their soul fainted* C107:10,14 Or *the shadow of death* D107:12 Lit *hearts*

Judges recounts the repeated cycle of disobedience, oppression, entreaty, and restoration.

106:45-46 The Lord **remembered** (v. 4; see note at 25:6-7) the Abrahamic **covenant** and exercised compassion on the basis of His covenant **love** and mercy (105:8,42; Jdg 2:18; Jl 2:13; Jnh 4:2). In His sovereignty, He caused the captors to show compassion toward His people (2Kg 25:27-30).

106:47-48 The psalmist appealed to God's saving acts toward Israel as the grounds for imploring the Lord to **gather** and restore the nation once again (cp. 1Ch 16:35-36; Is 61:7-14). Every book of the Psalms ends with praise (see note at 41:13).

107:1 Faithful love (Hb *chesed*; "covenant loyalty") is a key word in this psalm, reinforcing the Lord's unconditional love, the basis on which He intervened on behalf of His people.

107:2 The concept of redemption (Hb *go'el*; "redeem") relates to blood vengeance exercised by the Lord upon the enemy. The idea is rooted in Levitical law (Nm 35:12,19-27; Dt 19:6-12).

107:3 This verse refers to the return of Israel from exile (Is 42:10-13; 43:5-7).

107:4 While the **wilderness** normally implies the wanderings following the exodus, the context suggests the exiles journeyed through the Syrian-Arabic desert. The exiles were unable to assimilate into the culture and lifestyle of their captors, anticipating the Lord's rescue at any time.

107:5 Hungry and thirsty is a dual reference to physical hunger and thirst as well as the absence of organized worship and cultic practice (Am 8:11).

107:6 This sentence is repeated in verses 13,19,28. God's people continually sought the Lord's intervention from adversity and danger (Is 51:13-16).

107:7 The psalmist envisioned a homeward procession led by the Lord (Is 35:8-10; 40:9-11; 42:10-12; 49:5,9-12,22-24; 52:7-12; 59:9-12).

107:8 This sentence is repeated in verses 15,21,31. Salvation should result in testimony and praise (see note at 22:22-24). God's **wonderful works** on behalf of Israel ultimately benefitted **all humanity** in Christ (Gn 12:3).

107:9 This verse expresses God's response to the hunger and thirst of the exiles (v. 5).

107:10-14 Those who dwelt **in darkness and gloom—prisoners in cruel chains** recounts the terrible fate of those who were removed from social interaction with the community.

15 Let them give thanks to the LORD
for His faithful love
and His wonderful works for
all humanity.[a]

16 For He has broken down
the bronze gates
and cut through the iron bars.[b]

17 Fools suffered affliction
because of their rebellious ways
and their sins.[c]

18 They loathed all food
and came near the gates of death.[d]

19 Then they cried out to the LORD
in their trouble;
He saved them from their distress.[e]

20 He sent His word and healed them;
He rescued them from the •Pit.[f]

21 Let them give thanks to the LORD
for His faithful love
and His wonderful works for
all humanity.[g]

22 Let them offer sacrifices of thanksgiving
and announce His works with shouts
of joy.[h]

23 Others[A] went to sea in ships,
conducting trade on the vast waters.[i]

24 They saw the LORD's works,
His wonderful works in the deep.[j]

25 He spoke and raised a tempest
that stirred up the waves of the sea.[B,k]

26 Rising up to the sky, sinking down
to the depths,
their courage[C] melting away
in anguish,[l]

27 they reeled and staggered
like drunken men,
and all their skill was useless.[m]

28 Then they cried out to the LORD
in their trouble,
and He brought them
out of their distress.[n]

29 He stilled the storm to a murmur,
and the waves of the sea[D] were hushed.[o]

30 They rejoiced when the waves[E]
grew quiet.
Then He guided them to the harbor
they longed for.[p]

31 Let them give thanks to the LORD
for His faithful love
and His wonderful works for
all humanity.[q]

32 Let them exalt Him in the assembly
of the people
and praise Him in the council
of the elders.[r]

33 He turns rivers into desert,
springs of water into thirsty ground,[s]

34 and fruitful land into salty wasteland,
because of the wickedness
of its inhabitants.[t]

35 He turns a desert into a pool of water,
dry land into springs of water.[u]

36 He causes the hungry to settle there,
and they establish a city
where they can live.[v]

37 They sow fields and plant vineyards
that yield a fruitful harvest.[w]

38 He blesses them,
and they multiply greatly;[x]
He does not let
their livestock decrease.[y]

39 When they are diminished
and are humbled
by cruel oppression and sorrow,[z]

Cross-references (center column):

a 107:15 Ps 75:1
b 107:16 Is 45:1-2
c 107:17 Jr 30:14-15
d 107:18 Jb 33:20
e 107:19 Nm 21:7-9
f 107:20 Jb 33:28,30; Ps 30:3
g 107:21 Ps 75:1
h 107:22 Ps 9:11; 105:43; 116:17
i 107:23 Is 42:10
j 107:24 Is 33:21
k 107:25 Ps 93:3-4; Ezk 26:19
l 107:26 Ps 22:14; 119:28
m 107:27 Jb 12:25; Is 29:9
n 107:28 Jnh 1:14; Mk 4:39
o 107:29 Ps 89:9; Mt 8:26; Lk 8:24
p 107:30 Ex 15:13; Ps 78:72
q 107:31 Ps 75:1
r 107:32 Ps 22:22,25
s 107:33 Is 42:15; 50:2
t 107:34 Gn 19:24-28; Dt 29:23
u 107:35 Is 35:6-7; 41:18
v 107:36 Ps 60:9; 146:7
w 107:37 Is 65:21; Am 9:14
x 107:38 Gn 12:2; Ex 1:7
y Dt 7:14
z 107:39 Ps 44:25

A 107:23 Lit *They*   B 107:25 Lit *of it*   C 107:26 Lit *souls*   D 107:29 Lit *of them*   E 107:30 Lit *when they*

When they repented, He **saved them** (cp. Is 42:7; 58:6; Jr 30:8).

107:16 The Lord rescued those who were restrained with chains and irons (v. 10). See Is 45:1-22, especially verse 2 for a literary connection.

107:17-18 These verses summarize the fate of those who suffered debilitating illness as a result of their disobedience and guilt.

107:20 The Lord's word healed the diseased and saved those who were close to death (Is 25:7-8; 35:5-6; 54:1; 57:18; 65:19-20).

107:23-32 The OT does not elaborate on the maritime activity of Israel, and commercial seafaring is rarely mentioned (Gn 49:13; 2Ch 9:21; 20:36).

107:23-26 The terminology and rhythm of this section mimic the up-and-down movement of the waves. The Lord exercises sovereign control over the fierce sea (Jb 38:8-11; Jnh 1:4-16; Mt 8:26-27). God's powerful word brings all things to pass (Jb 37:6-13; Ps 147:15-20; Is 40:6-8; 55:8-11).

107:27 The sailors' actions are compared to those of drunken men (Pr 23:29-35). The Hebrew term *hagag* (**reeled**) normally describes celebration and dancing. **Their skill was useless** could be translated "their wisdom was confounded."

107:29-30 The psalmist recounted the Lord's deliverance of the sailors described in verses 23-28.

107:33-35 Many of those exiled in Babylon became comfortable and were not anxious to return to Judah, so the psalmist, in an effort to encourage native Judeans to return to Jerusalem, reminded them that God could bring about a reversal in natural resources. The **rivers** of Babylon could fail, while the **desert** areas of Judah could flourish (Is 41:17-18).

107:36-38 The destruction of hunger and homelessness reflects a reversal of verses 4-5,7. The hungry will become agriculturally independent, producing crops and cattle.

107:39-41 In an ironic twist, those who suffered **oppression**, grief, and misfortune will enjoy prosperity, while those who inflicted misery will be frustrated (7:14-16; Jb 12:21,24).

40 He pours contempt on nobles[a]
and makes them wander
in a trackless wasteland.[b]

41 But He lifts the needy out of
their suffering[c]
and makes their families multiply
like flocks.[d]

42 The upright see it and rejoice,[e]
and all injustice shuts its mouth.[f]

43 Let whoever is wise pay attention
to these things
and consider[A] the LORD's acts
of faithful love.[g]

Psalm 108
A Plea for Victory

A song. A Davidic psalm.

1 My heart is confident, God;[B]
I will sing; I will sing praises
with the whole of my being.[C,h]

2 Wake up, harp and lyre!
I will wake up the dawn.[i]

3 I will praise You, LORD,
among the peoples;
I will sing praises to You
among the nations.[j]

4 For Your faithful love is higher
than the heavens,
and Your faithfulness reaches to
the clouds.[k]

5 God, be exalted above the heavens,[l]
and let Your glory be over
the whole earth.[m]

6 Save with Your right hand
and answer me
so that those You love may be rescued.[n]

7 God has spoken in His sanctuary:[D]
"I will triumph!
I will divide up Shechem.[o]
I will apportion the Valley of Succoth.[p]

8 Gilead is Mine, Manasseh is Mine,
and Ephraim is My helmet;[q]
Judah is My scepter.[r]

9 Moab is My washbasin;[s]
I throw My sandal on Edom.[t]
I shout in triumph over Philistia."[u]

10 Who will bring me
to the fortified city?
Who will lead me to Edom?[v]

11 God, haven't You rejected us?
God, You do not march out
with our armies.[w]

12 Give us aid against the foe,
for human help is worthless.[x]

13 With God we will perform valiantly;[y]
He will trample our foes.[z]

Psalm 109
Prayer against an Enemy

For the choir director. A Davidic psalm.

1 God of my praise, do not be silent.[aa]

2 For wicked and deceitful mouths open
against me;
they speak against me
with lying tongues.[ab]

3 They surround me with hateful words
and attack me without cause.[ac]

4 In return for my love
they accuse me,
but I continue to pray.[E,ad]

5 They repay me evil for good,
and hatred for my love.[ae]

---

[a]107:40 Jb 12:21
[b]Jb 12:24
[c]107:41 1Sm 2:8; Ps 113:7-8
[d]Jb 21:11
[e]107:42 Jb 22:19; Ps 64:10
[f]Jb 5:16
[g]107:43 Ps 64:9; Hs 14:9
[h]108:1 Ps 59:17; 112:7
[i]108:2 Jdg 5:12; Ps 33:2; 81:2
[j]108:3 2Sm 22:50; Ps 9:11; 18:49
[k]108:4 Ps 36:5; 103:11; Lm 3:22-23
[l]108:5 Ps 113:4
[m]108:1-5 Ps 57:7-11
[n]108:6 Ps 17:7; 20:6; 138:7
[o]108:7 Gn 12:6; 33:18
[p]Gn 33:17
[q]108:8 Dt 33:17; Jos 13:31
[r]Gn 49:10
[s]108:9 2Sm 8:2
[t]2Sm 8:14
[u]2Sm 8:1
[v]108:10 Jr 1:18
[w]108:11 Ps 44:9
[x]108:12 Ps 146:3
[y]108:13 Nm 24:18; Ps 44:5; 118:15-16
[z]108:6-13 Ps 60:5-12
[aa]109:1 Ps 28:1; 83:1
[ab]109:2 Ps 10:7; 52:4; 120:2
[ac]109:3 Ps 35:7; 69:4; Jn 15:25
[ad]109:4 Ps 69:13
[ae]109:5 Ps 35:12; 38:20

A107:43 Lit and let them consider   B108:1 Some Hb mss, LXX, Syr add my heart is confident   C108:1 Lit praises, even my glory
D108:7 Or has promised by His holy nature   E109:4 Lit but I, prayer

---

107:43 The psalm concludes with a wisdom saying centering on God's covenant loyalty.

108:1-13 This psalm is a combination of 57:7-11 (vv. 1-5) and 60:5-12 (vv. 6-13).

108:1 **The whole of my being** is literally "my glory."

108:2 The Hebrew word shachar (**dawn**) refers to the first light of morning. The psalmist began the day with praise (Jb 38:12).

108:7 God's promises are certain, sworn on His immutable character. In His sovereignty He allotted the tribes of Jacob portions of land.

108:8 Judah was the location of the king, symbolized by the **scepter.**

108:9 **Moab . . . Edom,** and **Philistia** were three long-standing enemies of Israel. They are symbolically assigned denigrating roles.

108:11-13 The psalmist sought reassurance of the Lord's

presence (cp. 44:9; 60:10). The community needed divine help; it could not attain victory without God's intervention (44:6; Is 41:25; 63:6; Zch 10:5).

109:1-31 This is called an imprecatory psalm, in which the psalmist pronounced curses in relation to the covenant (Dt 27:15-26; 28:15-46). This plays a significant role in certain psalms (note esp. 7:6-10; 35:8-11; 69:6-7,22-29; 83:9-18). These curses do not convey petty personal anger; they reflect curses against those who had mistreated God's people. They also express a firm belief in the righteousness of God and a hatred for sin.

109:1-2 God's silence is contrasted with the **deceitful** speech of the persecutors (see notes at 28:1; 50:21; 83:2). **Lying tongues** reflects legal terminology—false testimony (10:4,6-7; 12:3-5; 59:7,12; cp. Ex 20:16).

109:3-4 The psalmist had been maligned **without cause** by those he was close to (vv. 9-10,13-14,17-18). Friends had

6 Set a wicked person over him;
    let an accuser[A] stand at his right hand.[a]
7 When he is judged, let him
    be found *guilty,
    and let his prayer be counted as sin.[b]
8 Let his days be few;
    let another take over his position.[c]
9 Let his children be fatherless
    and his wife a widow.[d]
10 Let his children wander as beggars,
    searching for food far[B]
    from their demolished homes.[e]
11 Let a creditor seize all he has;
    let strangers plunder what he has
    worked for.[f]
12 Let no one show him kindness,
    and let no one be gracious
    to his fatherless children.[g]
13 Let the line of his descendants
    be cut off;
    let their name be blotted out
    in the next generation.[h]
14 Let his ancestors' guilt
    be remembered before the Lord,[i]
    and do not let his mother's sin
    be blotted out.[j]
15 Let their sins[c] always remain
    before the Lord,
    and let Him erase[D] all memory of them
    from the earth.[k]
16 For he did not think
    to show kindness,

but pursued the afflicted, poor, and
    brokenhearted
    in order to put them to death.[l]
17 He loved cursing—let it fall on him;
    he took no delight in blessing—
    let it be far from him.[m]
18 He wore cursing like his coat—
    let it enter his body like water
    and go into his bones like oil.[n]
19 Let it be like a robe he wraps
    around himself,
    like a belt he always wears.[o]
20 Let this be the Lord's payment
    to my accusers,
    to those who speak evil against me.[p]

21 But You, *Yahweh my Lord,
    deal kindly with me
    because of Your name;[q]
    deliver me because of the goodness
    of Your faithful love.[r]
22 For I am afflicted and needy;[s]
    my heart is wounded within me.[t]
23 I fade away like a lengthening shadow;[u]
    I am shaken off like a locust.
24 My knees are weak from fasting,
    and my body is emaciated.[E,v]
25 I have become an object of ridicule
    to my accusers;[F]
    when they see me, they shake
    their heads in scorn.[w]
26 Help me, Lord my God;
    save me according to Your faithful love[x]

Cross references:
a109:6 Zch 3:1
b109:7 Ps 1:5; Pr 28:9
c109:8 Ps 55:23; Ac 1:20
d109:9 Ex 22:24
e109:10 Jb 30:5-8; Ps 59:15
f109:11 Dt 28:43-44; Lm 5:2
g109:12 Jb 5:4
h109:13 Jb 18:17,19; Ps 9:5; Pr 10:7
i109:14 Ex 20:5; Nm 14:18
j Neh 4:5; Jr 18:23
k109:15 Ps 34:16; 90:8; Jr 16:17
l109:16 Ps 34:18; 94:6
m109:17 Pr 14:14; Ezk 35:6; Mt 7:2
n109:18 Nm 5:22
o109:19 Ps 73:26
p109:20 Ps 54:5; 94:23; Is 3:11
q109:21 Ps 79:9; 106:8
r Ps 69:16
s109:22 Ps 40:17; 86:1
t Ps 143:4
u109:23 Ps 102:11
v109:24 Jb 16:8; Ps 35:13
w109:25 Ps 22:6-7; 69:19
x109:26 Ps 119:86

A109:6 Or *adversary* B109:10 LXX reads *beggars, driven far* C109:15 Lit *Let them* D109:15 Or *cut off* E109:24 Lit *denied from fat* F109:25 Lit *to them*

become adversaries (see note at 38:11-12). Despite their accusations, the psalmist continued to **pray**.

109:6 The psalmist asked God to **set** (or "appoint") a **wicked person** against his adversary. In some situations the defense attorney stood at the **right hand** of the defendant (v. 31; cp. 16:8). Those who testified for the prosecution also stood in that place (Zch 3:1). In either case, the psalmist wanted an **accuser** (Hb *satan*) there.

109:8-11 After the adversary was tried and convicted, the psalmist called on the Lord to shorten his life. He deserved death because he had inflicted death on others (vv. 16,31). The loss of property and posterity was the worst punishment Israel could imagine, so the psalmist wished poverty and homelessness on the adversary's family.

109:12 Just as the oppressors did not show **kindness** toward the afflicted, so they deserved no demonstration of covenant loyalty or compassion.

109:13 See note at verses 8-11.

109:14-15 Children often suffer for the sins of their fathers and mothers (Ex 34:7). While the Lord blotted out the sins of His people (Ps 51:2,9; Is 43:25; 44:22), the psalmist prayed that the sins of the adversaries would **remain before the Lord**, and that their names would be erased as if they had never existed.

109:16 The psalmist was poor and needy and his heart

was pierced (v. 22), much like those whom the adversaries **pursued**.

109:17 The law of (Lat) *lex talionis* required that all injustices be remedied by an equal punishment of the perpetrator (Ex 21:23-25). The psalmist prayed that the oppressor would be cursed, just as he had cursed others.

109:18-19 While God clothed Himself in glory and light (104:1-2), the adversaries would clothe themselves with **cursing**. Using metaphorical language, the psalmist asked that the adversary would fall under the power and influence of their own curses.

109:20 Through the adversary's punishment, the people of God and the psalmist in particular would receive vindication and justice (vv. 4,6,29; see Is 65:7).

109:21 The Lord's faithfulness to rescue and deliver His wronged people reflects positively on His reputation (**name**) among the nations.

109:22 See note at verse 16.

109:23 The weakness of the psalmist is compared to the **lengthening** of his **shadow**, a figurative expression denoting nearness of death (102:11). He also experienced alienation as a result of his sufferings (102:10).

109:24-25 The psalmist was concerned that his prolonged

27 so they may know that this is
   Your hand
   and that You, Lord, have done it.*a*
28 Though they curse, You will bless.
   When they rise up, they will be
      put to shame,
   but Your servant will rejoice.*b*
29 My accusers will be clothed
      with disgrace;
   they will wear their shame
      like a cloak.*c*
30 I will fervently thank the Lord
      with my mouth;
   I will praise Him in the presence
      of many.*d*
31 For He stands at the right hand of
      the needy
   to save him from those who would
      condemn him.*e*

Psalm 110
The Priestly King

A Davidic psalm.

1 This is the declaration of the Lord
   to my Lord:
   "Sit at My right hand
   until I make Your enemies
      Your footstool."*f*
2 The Lord will extend
   Your mighty scepter from •Zion.

---

*a*109:27 Jb 37:7
*b*109:28 2Sm
16:11-12; Is
65:14
*c*109:29 Jb
8:22; Ps 35:26;
132:18
*d*109:30 Ps
22:22,25; 35:18;
111:1
*e*109:31 Ps 16:8;
110:5; 121:5
*f*110:1 Mt 22:44;
Mk 12:36; Lk
20:42-43; Ac
2:34-35; 1Co
15:25; Heb 1:13
*g*110:2 Ps 45:6;
Ezk 19:14
*h*110:3 Jdg 5:2
*i*1Ch 16:29; Ps
96:9
*j*110:4 Gn 14:18;
Heb 5:6,10;
7:17,21
*k*110:5 Ps 16:8;
68:14
*l*110:6 Is 66:24;
Rv 19:17-18
*m*Ps 68:21
*n*110:7 Jdg 7:5-6
*o*Ps 27:6
*p*111:1 Ps 35:18;
149:1
*q*111:2 Ps 92:5;
143:5

   Rule*A* over Your surrounding*B* enemies.*g*
3 Your people will volunteer
   on Your day of battle.*C,h*
   In holy splendor, from the womb
      of the dawn,
   the dew of Your youth belongs to You.*D,i*
4 The Lord has sworn an oath
   and will not take it back:
   "Forever, You are a priest
   like Melchizedek."*j*
5 The Lord is at Your right hand;
   He will crush kings on the day
      of His anger.*k*
6 He will judge the nations,
      heaping up corpses;*l*
   He will crush leaders
      over the entire world.*m*
7 He will drink from the brook
      by the road;*n*
   therefore, He will lift up His head.*o*

Psalm 111
Praise for the Lord's Works

1 •Hallelujah!*E*
   I will praise the Lord with all my heart
   in the assembly of the upright
      and in the congregation.*p*
2 The Lord's works are great,
   studied by all who delight in them.*q*

---

*A*110:2 One Hb ms, LXX, Tg read *You will rule*   *B*110:2 Lit *Rule in the midst of Your*   *C*110:3 Lit *power*   *D*110:3 Hb obscure
*E*111:1 The lines of this poem form an •acrostic.

---

fasting and prayer had gone unnoticed, while his **accusers** mocked him with impunity.

109:26-28 The Lord's intervention and salvation would demonstrate the sovereign power and righteousness of God.

109:29 Not only would the false witnesses be clothed with curses (v. 18), but they would suffer dishonor and **shame** similar to that experienced by the accused. The sin of the **accusers** would be evident to the entire community.

109:30 It is appropriate for deliverance to be followed by public praise (see note at 22:22-24).

109:31 The Lord stands at the **right hand** of those who rely on Him to defend them (cp. v. 6). He oversees the fair execution of justice for those who are weak and vulnerable (see note at 68:5).

110:1-7 This is a royal psalm with messianic implications that culminate in the person of Jesus Christ. As a psalm of messianic promise, the poem is the most frequently cited psalm in the NT (Ac 2:34-35; 1Co 15:25; Eph 1:20; Col 3:1; Heb 1:3; 7:17,21; 1Pt 3:22). Although the psalm seems to address the Davidic dynasty, the ideal is never realized except in the Messiah.

110:1 The Lord addresses the Davidic king as His divinely appointed representative. The **right hand** denotes a place of strength, honor, and privilege (45:9). The king as God's co-regent derives his authority from God (see note at 80:17; cp. Heb 1:3). The expression **make Your enemies Your foot-**

stool conveys the idea of being victorious and forcing submission (Jos 10:24).

110:2 To **extend** the **scepter** meant to establish a person's authority and power over the land (45:6). Genesis 49:10 describes Judah as the Lord's scepter, a metaphorical reference to divinely ordained regal authority.

110:3 This verse is often characterized as the most obscure in the entire book of Psalms. The first line is literally, "Your people (will be) freewill offerings in the day of Your strength." Some interpreters emend **in holy splendor** (Hb *behaderey-qodesh*) to "on the holy mountains" (*beharerey-qodesh*), referring to Zion. **From the womb of the dawn** denotes the young men's eagerness to do battle for the Lord. The young men are descendants of the king, and thereby, of the Lord.

110:4 The reference to **Melchizedek** derives from Gn 14:17-24. The concept of a priestly kingship seems unusual, yet kings served as priests on special occasions or in exceptional circumstances. God promised an eternal dynasty to David (2Sm 7:14-17; see Ps 89:29). Jesus Christ, as a descendant of David and as the Son of God, fulfills the dual roles of king and priest **forever** (Heb 7:17,21).

110:5-6 The **right hand** denotes protection. The Lord will **judge** (Is 42:1-7) among **the nations** and destroy their wicked **leaders** (Ezk 32:5; 35:8).

110:7 Drinking from **the brook by the road** possibly relates to the rite of drinking from the Gihon Spring as part of an enthronement ceremony (1Kg 1:38), or to pausing to

3 All that He does is splendid
and majestic;[a]
His righteousness endures forever.[b]
4 He has caused His wonderful works
to be remembered.[c]
The LORD is gracious and compassionate.[d]
5 He has provided food for those
who fear Him;[e]
He remembers His covenant forever.[f]
6 He has shown His people the power
of His works
by giving them the inheritance
of the nations.[g]
7 The works of His hands are truth
and justice;
all His instructions are trustworthy.[h]
8 They are established forever and ever,
enacted in truth and in what is right.[i]
9 He has sent redemption to His people.[j]
He has ordained His covenant forever.
His name is holy and awe-inspiring.[k]

10 The *fear of the LORD is the beginning
of wisdom;[l]
all who follow His instructions[A] have
good insight.[m]
His praise endures forever.[n]

Psalm 112
The Traits of the Righteous

1 *Hallelujah![B]
Happy is the man who *fears the LORD,
taking great delight in His commands.[o]

2 His descendants will be powerful
in the land;
the generation of the upright
will be blessed.[p]
3 Wealth and riches are in his house,[q]
and his righteousness
endures forever.[r]
4 Light shines in the darkness
for the upright.[s]
He is gracious, compassionate,
and righteous.[t]
5 Good will come to a man
who lends generously
and conducts his business fairly.[u]
6 He will never be shaken.[v]
The righteous man will be
remembered forever.[w]
7 He will not fear bad news;
his heart is confident,
trusting in the LORD.[x]
8 His heart is assured;
he will not fear.[y]
In the end he will look in triumph
on his foes.[z]
9 He distributes freely to the poor;
his righteousness endures forever.[aa]
His *horn will be exalted in honor.[ab]

10 The wicked man will see it
and be angry;
he will gnash his teeth in despair.[ac]
The desire of the wicked man will come
to nothing.[ad]

[a]111:3 Ps 145:5
[b]Ps 112:3,9; 119:142
[c]111:4 Ps 78:4
[d]Ps 103:8; 145:8
[e]111:5 Mt 6:31-33
[f]Ps 105:8
[g]111:6 Dt 4:38; 32:8; Ps 78:55
[h]111:7 Ps 19:7; 93:5
[i]111:8 Ps 119:160; Is 40:8; Mt 5:18
[j]111:9 Lk 1:68
[k]Ps 99:3; Lk 1:49
[l]111:10 Pr 1:7; 9:10
[m]Ps 119:98
[n]Ps 44:8; 145:2
[o]112:1 Ps 1:2; 119:16; 128:1
[p]112:2 Ps 102:28
[q]112:3 Pr 3:16; 8:18
[r]Ps 111:3
[s]112:4 Ps 97:11
[t]Ex 34:6; Neh 9:17; Ps 116:5
[u]112:5 Ps 15:5; 37:26
[v]112:6 Ps 55:22
[w]Pr 10:7
[x]112:7 Ps 56:4; 57:7; Pr 1:33
[y]112:8 Ps 27:1; 56:11
[z]Ps 54:7; 59:10
[aa]112:9 2Co 9:9
[ab]Ps 75:10; 89:17
[ac]112:10 Jb 16:9; Ps 35:16
[ad]Pr 10:28; 11:7

[A]111:10 Lit *follow them*   [B]112:1 The lines of this poem form an *acrostic.

---

refresh oneself before continuing the pursuit of the vanquished foe (Jdg 8:4).

111:1-10 This psalm is an acrostic, the first letter of each half verse following the order of the Hebrew alphabet (vv. 9 and 10 are three lines each). This psalm provides the theological basis for Psalm 112.

111:1 On **Hallelujah** see note at 104:35. The psalmist praised the Lord both privately and publicly.

111:5 Food is from the Hebrew word for "prey" *(tereph)*, possibly implying provision in the wilderness (Ex 16; Nm 11:31-32; Jb 24:5). On **those who fear Him**, see note at 112:8.

111:6 The two lines of verse 6 form the center of the psalm, with 10 lines on either side. To give **the inheritance of the nations** reinforces the Lord's gift of land to Israel during the conquest of Canaan. The Lord handed over the heritage inhabited by other nations to His chosen people.

111:9 Redemption (Hb *padah*) denotes the exchange of a payment price for liberation (Dt 7:8; Is 35:10; 50:2; 51:11) and it occurs in this noun form only three other times (Ex 8:23 "distinction"; Ps 130:7; Is 50:2). The phrase **His name is . . . awe-inspiring** (lit "to be feared") implies a covenantal relationship (68:35; 89:7; 99:3; Ex 34:10; Dt 7:21; 28:58).

111:10 The beginning of wisdom is a wisdom expression (112:1; Jb 28:28; Pr 1:7; 15:33).

112:1-10 This psalm contains wisdom features and vocabulary, and it shares language and acrostic form with Psalm 111. It applies the theology expressed in Psalm 111.

112:2 Descendants (lit "seed") will serve as a conduit of the Lord's strength—not **powerful** in themselves, but through God's blessing.

112:4 On **light**, see notes at 18:28 and 27:1.

112:5 The upright mirror the character of the Lord. **Conducts** (Hb *kul*) expresses the idea of consistent behavior. The upright do not commit usury or charge interest (Lv 25:35-36; Dt 15:7-11).

112:6 Just as the foundations of the world will not be **shaken** (82:5; 96:10; 99:1; 104:5), so nothing will ever make the **righteous** person slip or fall.

112:8 Trust in the Lord prevents **fear** (vv. 1,7). The **assured . . . heart** conveys the idea of support (111:8).

112:9 The **righteousness** of the generous person **endures**, just as God's instructions (111:8) and praise (111:10) last **forever**. The **horn** is symbolic of power (see notes at 18:1-2; 89:15-17).

112:10 Those who are evil will witness the elevation of the righteous. The term **angry** can be rendered "confused" or "troubled" (Hb *qaʿas*). Those who **desire** anything other than God will ultimately be frustrated.

Psalm 113
Praise to the Merciful God

1 •Hallelujah!
Give praise, servants of •Yahweh;
praise the name of Yahweh.[a]
2 Let the name of Yahweh be praised
both now and forever.[b]
3 From the rising of the sun
to its setting,
let the name of Yahweh
be praised.[c]

4 Yahweh is exalted above
all the nations,[d]
His glory above the heavens.[e]
5 Who is like Yahweh our God—
the One enthroned on high,[f]
6 who stoops down to look
on the heavens and the earth?[g]
7 He raises the poor from the dust
and lifts the needy
from the garbage pile[h]
8 in order to seat them with nobles—
with the nobles of His people.[i]
9 He gives the childless woman
a household,
making her the joyful mother
of children.[j]
Hallelujah!

[a]113:1 Ps 34:22; 69:36; 135:1
[b]113:2 Ps 115:18; 145:21
[c]113:3 Mal 1:11
[d]113:4 Ps 99:2
[e]Ps 57:5,11; 148:13
[f]113:5 Ex 15:11; Ps 89:6
[g]113:6 Ps 11:4; 138:6
[h]113:7 1Sm 2:8; Ps 107:41
[i]113:8 Jb 36:7
[j]113:9 1Sm 2:5; Ps 68:6
[k]114:1 Ex 13:3; Ps 81:5
[l]114:2 Ex 15:17; Ps 78:68-69
[m]114:3 Ex 14:21; Ps 77:16
[n]Jos 3:13-16
[o]114:4 Ex 19:18; Ps 29:6
[p]114:5 Hab 3:8
[q]114:6 Hab 3:10
[r]114:7 Ps 96:9
[s]114:8 Ex 17:6; Nm 20:11; Dt 8:15

Psalm 114
God's Deliverance of Israel

1 When Israel came out of Egypt—
the house of Jacob from a people
who spoke a foreign language[k]—
2 Judah became His sanctuary,
Israel, His dominion.[l]

3 The sea looked and fled;[m]
the Jordan turned back.[n]
4 The mountains skipped like rams,
the hills, like lambs.[o]
5 Why was it, sea, that you fled?
Jordan, that you turned back?[p]
6 Mountains, that you skipped
like rams?
Hills, like lambs?[q]

7 Tremble, earth, at the presence
of the Lord,
at the presence of the God of Jacob,[r]
8 who turned the rock
into a pool of water,
the flint into a spring of water.[s]

Psalm 115
Glory to God Alone

1 Not to us, •Yahweh, not to us,
but to Your name give glory

113:1 This psalm is one of a set of songs recited during Passover. The phrase **servants of Yahweh** refers to the priests (134:1; 135:1). Yahweh's **name** in the ancient Near East represented the revelation of His powerful presence and impeccable character (Ex 34:5-7; see note at Ps 20:1).

113:2 The praising of God's **name** means the recognition of His position of power and authority.

113:3 This verse forms a chiasm with verse 2, centering on God's eternality. The travel of the **sun** across the sky is described in 19:4-6 as indicating God's omniscience, and in 72:5,17 it is associated with the longevity of the kingly reign.

113:4 On the concept of God's glory in heaven, see 99:2; 138:5; Is 57:15; Eph 3:10.

113:5 The statement **who is like Yahweh** (cp. Ex 15:11) introduces a hymn praising the Lord. His enthronement **on high** denotes superiority and sovereignty (103:11; Is 7:11; 55:9).

113:6 The word for **stoops down** generally means to "humble or abase" (2:4; 18:16; 104:3). God lowers Himself from above the cosmos to consider His creation (33:13).

113:7 Just as the Lord lowers Himself to gaze at His creation, so He **lifts** (lit "raises") the **poor** and **needy** from the **dust** of the street and the **garbage pile**, or ash heap—an unsanitary place where rubbish and filth were dumped (Jb 2:8; Lm 4:5).

113:8 In a role reversal, the Lord confers royal status to the humble, affirming the equal value of all human beings.

113:9 Barrenness often resulted in shame since the status of a woman was determined by her ability to bear **children**.

114:1 This psalm resembles Psalm 29, which celebrates God's revelation. **Israel** here refers to the 12 tribes, not just the northern kingdom.

114:2 The reference to **Judah** as a **sanctuary** seems anachronistic since the central sanctuary was not established until the Davidic kingship, but this could simply mean that Judah was God's metaphorical "holy place." The reference to **Israel** as the Lord's political domain indicates the psalmist had Israel's election as the Lord's people in view.

114:3 **The sea looked and fled** draws on mythological imagery to describe the parting of the Red Sea (Ex 14:21-22; 15:4-12). The course reversal of the **Jordan** River occurred when Joshua and the people entered Canaan (Jos 3–5). See Ps 66:6 for a similar combination of the Red Sea and Jordan events.

114:4 The **mountains skipped** refers to the shaking of Mount Sinai (Ex 19:16). The cosmos responds to God's presence (Ps 29:2,8; Is 40:4; 64:1; Hab 3:6-7; Zch 14:4).

114:5-8 Introducing a rhetorical question, the psalmist reflected on the might and majesty of the Lord who caused such phenomena.

115:1-18 This psalm contains a number of lines that are identical to those in Psalm 135.

because of Your faithful love, because of
 Your truth.*a*
2 Why should the nations say,
 "Where is their God?"*b*
3 Our God is in heaven
 and does whatever He pleases.*c*

4 Their idols are silver and gold,
 made by human hands.*d*
5 They have mouths but cannot speak,
 eyes, but cannot see.
6 They have ears but cannot hear,
 noses, but cannot smell.*e*
7 They have hands but cannot feel,
 feet, but cannot walk.*f*
 They cannot make a sound
  with their throats.*g*
8 Those who make them are^A just
  like them,
 as are all who trust in them.*h*

9 Israel,^B trust in the LORD!*i*
 He is their help and shield.*j*
10 House of Aaron, trust in the LORD!*k*
 He is their help and shield.*l*
11 You who •fear the LORD,
  trust in the LORD!*m*
 He is their help and shield.
12 The LORD remembers us
 and will bless us.
 He will bless the house of Israel;
 He will bless the house of Aaron;*n*
13 He will bless those who fear the LORD—
 small and great alike.*o*

14 May the LORD add to your numbers,
 both yours and your children's.*p*
15 May you be blessed by the LORD,
 the Maker of heaven and earth.*q*
16 The heavens are the LORD's,^C
 but the earth He has given
  to the •human race.*r*
17 It is not the dead who praise
  the LORD,
 nor any of those descending
  into the silence of death.*s*
18 But we will praise the LORD,
 both now and forever.*t*
 •Hallelujah!

Psalm 116

Thanks to God for Deliverance

1 I love the LORD because He has heard
 my appeal for mercy.*u*
2 Because He has turned His ear to me,
 I will call out to Him as long as I live.*v*

3 The ropes of death were wrapped
  around me,
 and the torments of •Sheol
  overcame me;
 I encountered trouble and sorrow.*w*
4 Then I called on the name of •Yahweh:
 "Yahweh, save me!"*x*

5 The LORD is gracious and righteous;
 our God is compassionate.*y*
6 The LORD guards the inexperienced;

Cross-reference column:

a115:1 Ezk 36:22; Dn 9:18-19
b115:2 Ps 42:3,10; 79:10
c115:3 Ps 135:6; Dn 4:35
d115:4 2Kg 19:18; Is 37:19
e115:5-6 Is 46:7
f115:7 Jr 10:5
g Hab 2:18
h115:4-8 Ps 135:15-18
i115:9 Ps 118:2
j Gn 15:1; Dt 33:29; Ps 3:3; 5:12; 18:2; 28:7; 33:20; 119:114
k115:10 Ps 118:3; 135:19
l115:10-11 Ps 33:20
m115:11 Ps 22:23; 118:4
n115:12 Ps 98:3
o115:13 Rv 11:18; 19:5
p115:14 Dt 1:11
q115:15 Ps 121:2; 124:8; 134:3
r115:16 Ps 89:11
s115:17 Ps 6:5; 31:17; 88:10-12
t115:18 Ps 113:2; Dn 2:20
u116:1 Ps 18:1; 66:19
v116:2 Ps 17:6; 40:1
w116:3 Ps 18:4-5
x116:4 Ps 18:6; 118:5
y116:5 Ex 34:6; Neh 9:17; Ps 112:4

A115:8 Or *May those who make them become* B115:9 Some Hb mss, LXX, Syr read *House of Israel* C115:16 Lit *LORD's heavens*

115:2 The **nations** questioned the presence of Israel's God in light of her dire circumstances. The setting may be exilic, prompting the question, or the question may be a general remark on the absence of any visible manifestation of Israel's God.

115:3 This phrase expresses God's sovereignty (135:6; Pr 21:1; cp. Ec 8:3).

115:4-8 Compare these verses with 135:15-18. **Idols**, created by humans, are lifeless. The nations' gods are impotent. The prophet Isaiah also declared the weakness of idols (Is 6:10; 40:19-20; 41:7; 46:1-7). While the molten images appear to have human characteristics, they are unable to act under their own power. Those who create idols and place their trust in them will be **just like them**—powerless and ineffective.

115:9-13 Verses 12-13 list the consequences of verses 9-11; Israel trusts God, and God blesses Israel.

115:14 Increased descendants is a sign of the Lord's favor and blessing.

115:15 The Lord created all things; He is not created by human hands (v. 4). This expression occurs frequently in poetical texts that herald the Lord's superiority.

115:17-18 Those who have descended into **silence** is a figure for those who are dead—lifeless idols and their makers.

Conversely, those who trust in God are alive, and they bless His name **forever**.

116:1-19 This psalm shares a number of words and ideas with Jnh 2:2-9, pointing to a literary relationship between these two inspired writings.

116:1 "Love" (Hb *'ahav*) here implies love associated with a covenantal relationship. The concept is used in ancient Near Eastern covenants between the victorious and the vanquished. Compare 119:47-48,97,113; Dt 6:5; 11:1; 13:3, all of which restrict the use of "love" to a disciple's love for God's word and will.

116:2 When the Lord turns **His ear**, the petitioner is granted his request. The Lord's faithfulness led the psalmist to continue to **call** upon Him.

116:3 The psalmist compared the threat of immanent death to lethal **ropes** that would pull him down to **Sheol** (18:4-5; Jnh 2:2,5-6).

116:5 On **gracious** and **compassionate**, compare 103:8; Ex 34:6-7.

116:6 The Lord **guards the inexperienced**, or "simple ones" (see note at Pr 1:4). God dispenses mercy without prejudice and apart from social status. The Hebrew word for **helpless** *(dll)* means "lowly" or "weak."

I was helpless, and He saved me.[a]
7 Return to your rest, my soul,
for the LORD has been good to you.[b]
8 For You, LORD, rescued me from death,
my eyes from tears,
my feet from stumbling.[c]
9 I will walk before the LORD
in the land of the living.[d]
10 I believed, even when I said,
"I am severely afflicted."[e]
11 In my alarm I said,
"Everyone is a liar."[f]

12 How can I repay the LORD
for all the good He has done for me?[g]
13 I will take the cup of salvation
and call on the name of Yahweh.[h]
14 I will fulfill my vows to the LORD
in the presence of all His people.[i]
15 The death of His faithful ones
is valuable in the LORD's sight.[j]
16 LORD, I am indeed Your servant;
I am Your servant, the son
of Your female servant.
You have loosened my bonds.[k]
17 I will offer You a sacrifice
of thanksgiving
and call on the name of Yahweh.[l]
18 I will fulfill my vows to the LORD
in the presence of all His people,[m]
19 in the courts of the LORD's house—
within you, Jerusalem.[n]
•Hallelujah!

a116:6 Ps 19:7; 79:8; 142:6
b116:7 Ps 13:6; Jr 6:16
c116:8 Ps 49:15; 56:13
d116:9 Ps 27:13
e116:10 2Co 4:13
f116:11 Ps 31:22; 62:9; Rm 3:4
g116:12 2Ch 32:25; 1Th 3:9
h116:13 Ps 16:5; 105:1
i116:14 Ps 22:25; 50:14
j116:15 Ps 72:14
k116:16 Jb 12:18; Ps 86:16; 107:14
l116:17 Lv 7:12; Ps 50:14
m116:18 Ps 22:25; 50:14
n116:19 Ps 96:8; 102:21
o117:1 Rm 15:11
p117:2 Ps 100:5; 103:11; 146:6
q118:1 2Ch 5:13; Ezr 3:11; Ps 100:5
r118:2 Ps 115:9
s118:3 Ps 115:10; 135:19
t118:4 Ps 22:23; 115:11
u118:5 Ps 18:6; 120:1
vPs 18:19
w118:6 Ps 56:4,11; Heb 13:6
x118:7 Ps 54:4,7; 59:10

Psalm 117

Universal Call to Praise

1 Praise the LORD, all nations!
Glorify Him, all peoples![o]
2 For His faithful love to us is great;
the LORD's faithfulness endures forever.[p]
•Hallelujah!

Psalm 118

Thanksgiving for Victory

1 Give thanks to the LORD, for He is good;
His faithful love endures forever.[q]
2 Let Israel say,
"His faithful love endures forever."[r]
3 Let the house of Aaron say,
"His faithful love endures forever."[s]
4 Let those who fear the LORD say,
"His faithful love endures forever."[t]

5 I called to the LORD in distress;[u]
the LORD answered me
and put me in a spacious place.[A,v]
6 The LORD is for me; I will not be afraid.
What can man do to me?[w]
7 The LORD is my helper,
Therefore, I will look in triumph
on those who hate me.[x]

A118:5 Or *answered me with freedom*

116:8-11 Deliverance from **death** brought a resolve and transformation in the life of the psalmist, who promised to **walk . . . in the land of the living** (cp. 27:3; Jnh 2:6-7). Faith enabled him to prevail through adversity and his perception that everyone was out to deceive him.

116:12 The Hebrew word translated **good** comes from a root *(gml)* that means "payback," here in the good sense of "reward" or "benefit" (see note at 103:1-2; cp. Pr 12:14; 19:17).

116:13 Giving someone a "cup" normally denoted forcing something negative on someone, such as "fury" and "staggering" (Is 51:17,22). Here the psalmist received **salvation** from God. Alternatively, it could refer to a libation or drink offering from the psalmist (Ex 29:40-41; Nm 15:5,7; cp. Mt 26:26-29; 1Co 10:16).

116:15 Those in service to the Lord who are threatened with **death** are **valuable** to God, and are thus saved (72:14; Is 43:4). Though they may not escape physical death, they will experience eternal life (Mt 10:29-31; Lk 21:16-18; Jn 10:28-29).

116:17-18 Compare these verses to Jnh 2:9.

116:19 The psalmist intended to fulfill his vow publicly in the temple precincts (see note at 22:22-24). In the LXX, **Hallelujah** begins Psalm 117 (see note at 104:35).

117:1 The worship of the Lord by **all nations** and **all peoples** conveys a universal outlook consistent with the return of Christ (22:27; 63:4; 113:1; 135:1; 145:4; 147:12; Rv 19–21). **Glorify** (Hb *shibbach*) occurs only seven other times in the Old Testament.

117:2 Faithful love denotes the enduring qualities of the Lord's *chesed* (Hb for "covenant loyalty"; 25:10; 57:4; 85:10; 89:15; see word study at 136:1-26). **Hallelujah** is literally "Praise Yah" (104:35; 105:45; 106:1).

118:1-29 This psalm describes the triumphal entry of the king in terms of humiliation and glory.

118:1 His faithful love endures forever, a standard liturgical formula, recurs in verses 2, 3, and 4 (cp. 100:5; 105:1; 106:1; 136).

118:2 Compare this verse with 115:9-11; 135:19.

118:3 House of Aaron refers to priests—descendants of the first high priest (Nm 26:59-60).

118:4 The obligation of all believers is to **fear the LORD** (cp. 22:23,25; 34:7; 112:1; 145:19).

118:5 Distress (Hb *metsar*) is a rare term (116:3; Lm 1:3) from a related word that suggests confinement or restriction. The Lord's remedy is a **spacious place**.

118:6 On **what can man do to me**, compare 23:4; 56:4,11.

118:7 The term **helper** applies to Eve in Gn 2:18 and frequently describes God and His actions on behalf of people (Ex 18:4; Dt 33:7,29; 1Sm 7:12; Ps 20:2; 115:9-11; 121:2; 124:8; Is 41:10-13). To **look in triumph** is to overcome, as if in war.

8 It is better to take refuge in the LORD
than to trust in man.[a]

9 It is better to take refuge in the LORD
than to trust in nobles.[b]

10 All the nations surrounded me;
in the name of •Yahweh
I destroyed them.[c]

11 They surrounded me, yes,
they surrounded me;
in the name of Yahweh
I destroyed them.[d]

12 They surrounded me like bees;[e]
they were extinguished like a fire
among thorns;
in the name of Yahweh
I destroyed them.[f]

13 You[A] pushed me[B] hard to make me fall,
but the LORD helped me.[g]

14 The LORD is my strength and my song;
He has become my salvation.[h]

15 There are shouts of joy and victory
in the tents of the righteous:
"The LORD's right hand
performs valiantly![i]

16 The LORD's right hand is raised.
The LORD's right hand
performs valiantly!"[j]

17 I will not die, but I will live
and proclaim what the LORD has done.[k]

18 The LORD disciplined me severely
but did not give me over to death.[l]

19 Open the gates of righteousness for me;
I will enter through them

and give thanks to the LORD.[m]

20 This is the gate of the LORD;
the righteous will enter through it.[n]

21 I will give thanks to You
because You have answered me
and have become my salvation.[o]

22 The stone that the builders rejected
has become the cornerstone.[p]

23 This came from the LORD;
it is wonderful in our eyes.[q]

24 This is the day the LORD has made;
let us rejoice and be glad in it.[r]

25 LORD, save us!
LORD, please grant us success![s]

26 He who comes in the name
of the LORD is blessed.[t]
From the house of the LORD
we bless you.[u]

27 The LORD is God and has given us light.
Bind the festival sacrifice with cords
to the horns of the altar.[v]

28 You are my God, and I will give
You thanks.
You are my God; I will exalt You.[w]

29 Give thanks to the LORD, for He is good;
His faithful love endures forever.[x]

Psalm 119
Delight in God's Word

א Alef

1 How[c] happy are those whose way
is blameless,[y]

Cross references:

[a]118:8 Ps 40:4; 108:12; Jr 17:5
[b]118:9 Ps 146:3
[c]118:10 Ps 3:6; 88:17
[d]118:11 Ps 18:40
[e]118:12 Dt 1:44
[f]Ps 58:9; Nah 1:10
[g]118:13 Ps 140:4
[h]118:14 Ex 15:2; Ps 27:1; Is 12:2
[i]118:15 Ex 15:6; Lk 1:51
[j]118:16 Ps 89:13
[k]118:17 Ps 73:28; Hab 1:12
[l]118:18 Ps 86:13; Jr 30:11; 2Co 6:9
[m]118:19 Is 26:2
[n]118:20 Ps 24:3-6; Rv 22:14
[o]118:21 Ps 116:1
[p]118:22 Lk 20:17; Ac 4:11; 1Pt 2:4,7
[q]118:23 Mt 21:42; Mk 12:11
[r]118:24 Ps 31:7
[s]118:25 Neh 2:20; Ps 122:6-7
[t]118:25-26 Mt 21:9; Mk 11:9-10; Lk 13:35; Jn 12:13
[u]118:26 Ps 129:8
[v]118:27 Ex 27:2; Ps 18:28; 1Pt 2:9
[w]118:28 Is 25:1
[x]118:29 2Ch 5:13; Ezr 3:11; Ps 100:5
[y]119:1 Ps 101:6; Pr 11:20

A118:13 Perhaps the enemy   B118:13 LXX, Syr, Jer read *I was pushed*   C119:1 The stanzas of this poem form an •acrostic.

118:8-9 The proverbial expressions in these verses are introduced by **better to**. This formulaic wisdom saying occurs several times in Proverbs (Pr 15:16-17; 16:32; 19:1,22), while the concept of taking **refuge in the LORD** also enjoys wider usage (61:4; 64:10; 71:1; 141:8; 143:9; 144:2; Dt 32:37; 2Sm 22:3,31; Is 14:32; 57:13). **Nobles** were those who distributed wealth willingly (see note at 146:3). People should prefer God over common men as well as over those in authority and power.

118:10-12 To act **in the name of Yahweh** could mean the king served as His regent and acted on His behalf, or that the king fought **the nations** relying on the strength of the Lord (v. 14).

118:13 Here the psalmist probably addressed the nations, who had **pushed** him when he was surrounded (vv. 10-12).

118:14 On **my strength** and **my salvation**, compare Ex 15:2; Is 12:2.

118:15-16 The Lord's **right hand** executes judgment, renders justice, and accomplishes salvation (see note at 16:8). **Performs valiantly** has a military tone. The raising of the Lord's right hand depicts judgment (89:13; 102:13).

118:18 The king acknowledged the discipline of Yahweh. The

king's current circumstances reflected the Lord's rebuke, but his life would be spared (v. 17).

118:19 The plural form of **gates** refers to the Eastern Gate of the temple, a gate with two sections (24:7-10). On **enter . . . and give thanks**, compare 96:8.

118:22 The **cornerstone** bears the weight of a building and serves as the standard for leveling the rest of the structure. The rejected king has been restored to a place of prominence. The imagery of a cornerstone representing the character of the Lord (Zch 4:7) is further developed in the NT (Mt 21:42; Ac 4:11; Eph 2:20-21; 1Pt 2:4-8).

118:25-29 The last section of the psalm consists of a series of praises to the Lord motivated by the desire of the psalmist for rescue. The Hebrew word *na'*, a particle of entreaty, occurs twice in this verse, emphasizing the desperate pleas of the psalmist. This was part of the expression "Hosanna" (please save) in the triumphal entry (Mt 21:9), where the crowd alluded to verses 25-26 of this psalm. The phrase **Bind the festival sacrifice with cords to the horns of the altar** is unusual since there is no evidence that a sacrifice was ever tied to the altar. However, this concept was fulfilled when Christ was nailed to the cross.

119:1-176 Psalm 119 is an acrostic *par excellence*. The

who live according to the LORD's
   instruction!*a*
2 Happy are those who keep His decrees*b*
   and seek Him with all their heart.*c*
3 They do nothing wrong;*d*
   they follow His ways.
4 You have commanded
   that Your precepts*e*
   be diligently kept.
5 If only my ways were committed
   to keeping Your statutes!*f*
6 Then I would not be ashamed*g*
   when I think about all Your commands.
7 I will praise You with a sincere heart*h*
   when I learn Your righteous judgments.
8 I will keep Your statutes;
   never abandon me.*i*

‎ב *Bet*

9 How can a young man keep his way
   pure?
   By keeping Your^A word.*j*
10 I have sought You with all my heart;*k*
   don't let me wander
   from Your commands.*l*
11 I have treasured Your word
   in my heart*m*
   so that I may not sin against You.
12 LORD, may You be praised;
   teach me Your statutes.*n*
13 With my lips I proclaim
   all the judgments from Your mouth.*o*
14 I rejoice in the way revealed by
   Your decrees*p*
   as much as in all riches.

15 I will meditate on Your precepts*q*
   and think about Your ways.*r*
16 I will delight in Your statutes;*s*
   I will not forget Your word.

‎ג *Gimel*

17 Deal generously with Your servant*t*
   so that I might live;
   then I will keep Your word.
18 Open my eyes so that
   I may contemplate
   wonderful things from Your instruction.
19 I am a stranger on earth;*u*
   do not hide Your commands from me.
20 I am continually overcome
   with longing for Your judgments.*v*
21 You rebuke the proud,
   the ones under a curse,*w*
   who wander from Your commands.*x*
22 Take insult and contempt away
   from me,*y*
   for I have kept Your decrees.
23 Though princes sit together speaking
   against me,*z*
   Your servant will think
   about Your statutes;*aa*
24 Your decrees are my delight
   and my counselors.*ab*

‎ד *Dalet*

25 My life is down in the dust;*ac*

*a*119:2 Ps 128:1; Mc 4:2
*b*Ps 25:10; 119:10,22,168
*c*Dt 4:29; 10:12; 11:13; 13:3; 30:2
*d*119:3 1Jn 3:9; 5:18
*e*119:4 Dt 4:13; Neh 9:13; Ps 19:8
*f*119:5 Dt 12:1; 2Ch 7:17; Pr 4:26
*g*119:6 Jb 22:26; Ps 119:80
*h*119:7 Ps 119:62,106
*i*119:8 Ps 38:21; 71:9,18
*j*119:9 2Sm 22:31; Ps 12:6; 19:9-10; 119:140; Pr 20:11; 30:5; Php 4:8
*k*119:10 Ps 119:2
*l*Ps 119:21,118
*m*119:11 Ps 37:31; 40:8; Lk 2:19,51
*n*119:12 Ps 119:26,64,108, 124,135,171
*o*119:13 Ps 40:9; 119:72
*p*119:14 Ps 119:111,162; Pr 3:13-15; 8:10,11,18,19
*q*119:15 Ps 1:2; 119:23,48, 78,97,148
*r*Ps 25:4; 27:11; Is 58:2
*s*119:16 Ps 1:2; 119:24,47,70, 77,92,143,174
*t*119:17 Ps 13:6; 119:144
*u*119:19 1Ch 29:15; Ps 39:12; 119:54; Heb 11:13
*v*119:20 Ps 42:1,2; 63:1; 84:2; 119:40,131
*w*119:21 Dt 27:26
*x*Ps 119:10,118
*y*119:22 Ps 39:8; 119:39
*z*119:23 Ps 119:161
*aa*Ps 119:15, 27-28
*ab*119:24 Ps 119:16; Rm 7:22
*ac*119:25 Ps 44:25

---

^A119:9 Or *keeping it according to Your*

---

eight-verse sections are arranged according to the order of the Hebrew alphabet. Nearly every verse contains one of eight words for God's revelation: "instruction," "decree," "precept," "statute," "command," "judgment," "promise," and "word."

119:1-8 To be **blameless** derives from the Hebrew word for "perfect, unblemished." The psalmist prayed for total commitment to obedience. His conscience reminded him of his weaknesses (vv. 5-6). The Hebrew word for **sincere** (*yshr*; v. 7) means "upright," or "straight."

119:9-16 A **young man** is one who lacks experience and wisdom. He is easily tempted by worldly desires (Pr 1:8-19; 2:1-22) and enticed away from God. The loyalty of the righteous is maintained by the value they place on God's **word**. To **meditate** is not to empty one's mind, but to fill it with the Torah in order to internalize it.

119:17-24 Deal generously translates the Hebrew word for "recompense" or "benefit" (see note at 103:1-2). **Contemplate** means "consider carefully" ("think about" in v. 15). The psalmist characterized himself as a **stranger**, a resident alien living on God's **earth** and dependent on Him. The purpose of **rebuke** is to correct and bring God's people back into relationship with Him (Mt 18:15).

119:25-32 The Lord is the source of all life. Only He can

torah

Hebrew Pronunciation	[toe RAH]
HCSB Translation	law, instruction, teaching
Uses in Psalms	36
Uses in the OT	223
Focus Passage	Psalm 119:1,18,29,34,44

Singular (Lv 14:32) or plural (Pr 7:2), *torah* indicates particular *laws* or *instructions*. *Torah* as a collective denotes *instruction* for particular individuals (Dt 17:11) or nations (Dt 33:4). *Torah* describes civil (Ex 18:16) and religious (Lv 6:9) *laws*, the book of Deuteronomy (Dt 1:5), all of Moses' writings (Jos 8:31), the Prophets (Dn 9:10), or the whole Word of God (Ps 19:7). The focus of *torah* is not a specific literary form but divine authority; any communication from God constitutes *torah*. *Torah* also pictures a parent's *teaching* (Pr 6:20). It appears as *ritual* (Nm 5:30), *revelation* (2Sm 7:19), *ruling* (Hg 2:11), *legal* (Nm 19:2), and *legally required* (Neh 12:44). *Torah* derives from *yarah* (47x), which means *teach* (Ex 4:12), *instruct* (Dt 17:10), or *show* (Ex 15:25). Once *yarah* is *determine* (Lv 14:57), *prepare* (Gn 46:28), and *gesture* (Pr 6:13). *Yarah* and *torah* appear together seven times (Dt 17:11).

give me life[a] through Your word.

26 I told You about my life,
and You listened to me;
teach me Your statutes.[b]
27 Help me understand
the meaning of Your precepts
so that I can meditate on Your wonders.[c]
28 I am weary[A] from grief;
strengthen me through Your word.[d]
29 Keep me from the way of deceit
and graciously give me
Your instruction.
30 I have chosen the way of truth;
I have set Your ordinances
before me.[e]
31 I cling to Your decrees;
LORD, do not put me to shame.[f]
32 I pursue the way of Your commands,
for You broaden my understanding.[B,g]

ח **He**

33 Teach me, LORD, the meaning[C]
of Your statutes,
and I will always keep them.[D,h]
34 Help me understand Your instruction,[i]
and I will obey it
and follow it with all my heart.[j]
35 Help me stay on the path
of Your commands,[k]
for I take pleasure in it.[l]
36 Turn my heart to Your decrees[m]
and not to material gain.[n]
37 Turn my eyes
from looking at what is worthless;[o]
give me life in Your ways.[E,p]
38 Confirm what You said
to Your servant,[q]
for it produces reverence for You.
39 Turn away the disgrace I dread;[r]
indeed, Your judgments are good.
40 How I long for Your precepts![s]
Give me life through
Your righteousness.

ו **Vav**

41 Let Your faithful love come to me, LORD,[t]
Your salvation, as You promised.[u]
42 Then I can answer the one
who taunts me,[v]
for I trust in Your word.
43 Never take the word of truth
from my mouth,
for I hope in Your judgments.[w]
44 I will always obey Your instruction,
forever and ever.[x]
45 I will walk freely in an open place[y]
because I seek Your precepts.[z]
46 I will speak of Your decrees before kings
and not be ashamed.[aa]
47 I delight in Your commands,
which I love.[ab]
48 I will lift up my hands[ac]
to Your commands,
which I love,
and will meditate on Your statutes.[ad]

ז **Zayin**

49 Remember Your word to Your servant;
You have given me hope through it.
50 This is my comfort in my affliction:[ae]
Your promise has given me life.
51 The arrogant constantly ridicule me,
but I do not turn away
from Your instruction.[af]
52 LORD, I remember Your judgments
from long ago
and find comfort.
53 Rage seizes me[ag] because of the wicked
who reject Your instruction.[ah]
54 Your statutes are the theme of my song
during my earthly life.[F]
55 Yahweh, I remember Your name[ai]
in the night,[aj]
and I obey Your instruction.

---

[a]119:25 Ps 119:37,40,88, 93,107,149,154, 156,159
[b]119:26 Ps 25:4; 86:11; 119:12, 64,68,124, 135,171
[c]119:27 Ps 105:2; 119:15,73,125; 145:5
[d]119:28 1Pt 5:10
[e]119:30 Ps 16:8
[f]119:31 Ps 119:116
[g]119:32 1Kg 4:29; 2Co 6:11,13
[h]119:33 Ps 119:112; Mt 10:22; Heb 3:6; Rv 2:26
[i]119:34 Ps 119:125,144,169
[j]1Ch 22:12; Ps 119:2,69
[k]119:35 Ps 25:4; Is 40:14
[l]Ps 119:16
[m]119:36 1Kg 8:58
[n]Ezk 33:31; Mk 7:21,22; Lk 12:15; Heb 13:5
[o]119:37 Is 33:15
[p]Ps 119:25
[q]119:38 2Sm 7:25
[r]119:39 Ps 119:22
[s]119:40 Ps 119:20
[t]119:41 Ps 119:77
[u]Ps 119:58,76, 116,170
[v]119:42 Ps 102:8; Pr 27:11
[w]119:43 Ps 119:49,74,81, 114,147
[x]119:44 Ps 119:33
[y]119:45 Pr 4:12
[z]Ps 119:94,155
[aa]119:46 Mt 10:18; Ac 26:1,2
[ab]119:47 Ps 119:16,97, 127,159
[ac]119:48 Ps 63:4
[ad]Ps 119:15
[ae]119:50 Rm 15:4
[af]119:51 Jb 23:11; Ps 44:18
[ag]119:53 Ezr 9:3; Neh 13:25; Ps 119:158
[ah]Ps 89:30
[ai]119:55 Ps 63:6
[aj]Ps 42:8; 92:2; Is 26:9; Ac 16:25

A 119:28 Or I weep   B 119:32 Lit You enlarge my heart   C 119:33 Lit way   D 119:33 Or will keep it as my reward   E 119:37 Some Hb mss, Tg read word   F 119:54 Lit song in the house of my sojourning

---

rejuvenate those who are bowed down. The psalmist sought clarity, relying on God to help him understand and apply the Torah to his life. The righteous person rejects the way of deceivers (1:6; 16:11; 32:8), and depends on the Lord to keep him on the path of righteousness.

119:33-40 This section focuses on God's reward for obedience. The pursuit of **material gain** leads to sin, but life is found in the ways of the Lord. On **with all my heart**, compare Dt 6:5.

119:41-48 The psalmist longed for expressions of God's chesed (Hb for "covenant loyalty, faithful love"; see word study at 136:1-26) in light of the persecution and hostility against him. He sought God's **salvation** from oppression.

The freedom offered the person who walks according to God's word enables him to remain strong through adversity and to maintain his focus on God's decrees. The righteous person is courageous enough to **speak of** the Lord, and he will **not be ashamed** (vv. 6,31,42).

119:49-56 The righteous person is comforted by the Lord's **judgments**, certain that He will execute justice with integrity (v. 52). As the Lord rescued Israel in the past through His miraculous intervention, so the expectations of the psalmist were based on the testimony of God's works. The psalmist expressed righteous indignation against the **arrogant** and the **wicked** who neglected the instructions of God (see notes at 15:4 and 109:1-31).

56 This is my practice:
I obey Your precepts.[a]

ח Khet

57 The LORD is my portion;[A,b]
I have promised to keep Your words.
58 I have sought Your favor[c] with all
my heart;
be gracious to me[d] according to
Your promise.
59 I thought about my ways[e]
and turned my steps back
to Your decrees.
60 I hurried, not hesitating
to keep Your commands.
61 Though the ropes of the wicked[f]
were wrapped around me,
I did not forget Your instruction.[g]
62 I rise at midnight to thank You[h]
for Your righteous judgments.[i]
63 I am a friend to all who ·fear You,[j]
to those who keep Your precepts.
64 LORD, the earth is filled with
Your faithful love;[k]
teach me Your statutes.[l]

ט Tet

65 LORD, You have treated
Your servant well,
just as You promised.
66 Teach me good judgment
and discernment,[m]
for I rely on Your commands.
67 Before I was afflicted I went astray,[n]
but now I keep Your word.
68 You are good,[o] and You do
what is good;[p]
teach me Your statutes.
69 The arrogant have smeared me
with lies,[q]
but I obey Your precepts with all
my heart.[r]
70 Their hearts are hard
and insensitive,[s]
but I delight in Your instruction.[t]
71 It was good for me to be afflicted[u]
so that I could learn Your statutes.

72 Instruction from Your lips[v] is better
for me
than thousands of gold and silver pieces.

י Yod

73 Your hands made me and formed me;[w]
give me understanding
so that I can learn Your commands.[x]
74 Those who fear You will see me
and rejoice,[y]
for I put my hope in Your word.[z]
75 I know, LORD, that Your judgments
are just
and that You have afflicted me fairly.[aa]
76 May Your faithful love comfort me
as You promised Your servant.
77 May Your compassion come to me[ab]
so that I may live,
for Your instruction is my delight.[ac]
78 Let the arrogant be put to shame[ad]
for slandering me with lies;
I will meditate on Your precepts.
79 Let those who fear You,
those who know Your decrees,
turn to me.
80 May my heart be blameless
regarding Your statutes[ae]
so that I will not be put to shame.

כ Kaf

81 I long for Your salvation;[af]
I put my hope in Your word.[ag]
82 My eyes grow weary
looking for what You have promised;[ah]
I ask, "When will You comfort me?"
83 Though I have become like a wineskin
dried by smoke,
I do not forget Your statutes.
84 How many days must
Your servant wait?
When will You execute judgment
on my persecutors?[ai]
85 The arrogant have dug pits for me;[aj]
they violate Your instruction.
86 All Your commands are true;
people persecute me with lies—
help me![ak]

Cross references (center column)

a 119:56 Ps 119:22,69,100
b 119:57 Ps 16:5; Lm 3:24
c 119:58 1Kg 13:6
d Ps 41:4; 56:1; 57:1
e 119:59 Lk 15:17
f 119:61 Jb 36:8; Ps 140:5
g Ps 119:83,141,153,176
h 119:62 Ps 119:55
i Ps 119:7
j 119:63 Ps 101:6
k 119:64 Ps 33:5
l Ps 119:12
m 119:66 Php 1:9,10
n 119:67 Ps 119:71,75; Jr 31:18,19; Heb 12:5-11
o 119:68 Ps 100:5; 106:1; 107:1
p Ps 125:4
q 119:69 Jb 13:4; Ps 109:2
r Ps 119:56
s 119:70 Ps 17:10
t Ps 119:16
u 119:71 Ps 119:67,75
v 119:72 Ps 19:10; 119:127; Pr 8:10,11,19
w 119:73 Jb 10:8; 31:15; Ps 100:3; 139:15-16
x Ps 119:34
y 119:74 Ps 34:2; 107:42
z Ps 119:43
aa 119:75 Ps 119:138; Heb 12:10
ab 119:77 Ps 119:41
ac Ps 119:16
ad 119:78 Jr 50:32
ae 119:80 Ps 119:1
af 119:81 Ps 84:2
ag Ps 119:43
ah 119:82 Ps 69:3; 119:123; Is 38:14
ai 119:84 Rv 6:10
aj 119:85 Ps 35:7; 57:6; Jr 18:22
ak 119:86 Ps 35:19; 109:26; 119:78

A 119:57 Lit You are my portion, LORD

119:57-64 Just as the Levites received no allotment of land during the settlement of Canaan and thus relied on God, so the psalmist depended on God alone for his livelihood. The threat of the **wicked** endangered the psalmist's life, but he remained focused on God's **righteous judgments**.

119:65-72 The psalmist's past affliction was the direct result of the Lord's discipline. In retrospect, he acknowledged his moral weaknesses (v. 67), and realized God's rebuke served him well (v. 71). The rebellious ones **smeared** him **with lies**.

The court language suggests false accusations. The value of God's instructions is beyond measure (19:7-10).

119:73-80 The psalmist did not want to be ashamed, but he prayed that the arrogant would **be put to shame** and reiterated his request to be **blameless**.

119:81-88 This section consists of a lament, in which the psalmist asked **when** the Lord would bring relief. Although near death, he remained loyal to God's precepts, putting his hope in God for life itself (vv. 87-88).

87 They almost ended my life on earth,
but I did not abandon Your precepts.
88 Give me life in accordance with
Your faithful love,
and I will obey the decree
You have spoken.

ל Lamed

89 Lord, Your word is forever;[a]
it is firmly fixed in heaven.
90 Your faithfulness is for all generations;[b]
You established the earth,
and it stands firm.[c]
91 They stand today in accordance with
Your judgments,[d]
for all things are Your servants.[e]
92 If Your instruction had not been
my delight,
I would have died in my affliction.[f]
93 I will never forget Your precepts,
for You have given me life
through them.[g]
94 I am Yours; save me,[h]
for I have sought Your precepts.[i]
95 The wicked hope to destroy me,[j]
but I contemplate Your decrees.
96 I have seen a limit to all perfection,
but Your command is without limit.

מ Mem

97 How I love Your instruction![k]
It is my meditation all day long.[l]
98 Your commands make me wiser
than my enemies,[m]
for they are always with me.
99 I have more insight than
all my teachers
because Your decrees are
my meditation.[n]
100 I understand more than the elders[o]
because I obey Your precepts.[p]
101 I have kept my feet from every evil path[q]
to follow Your word.
102 I have not turned from
Your judgments,[r]
for You Yourself have instructed me.

103 How sweet Your word is[s] to my taste—
sweeter than honey in my mouth.
104 I gain understanding
from Your precepts;[t]
therefore I hate every false way.[u]

נ Nun

105 Your word is a lamp for my feet[v]
and a light on my path.
106 I have solemnly sworn[w]
to keep Your righteous judgments.
107 I am severely afflicted;
Lord, give me life through Your word.[x]
108 Lord, please accept my willing offerings
of praise,[y]
and teach me Your judgments.[z]
109 My life is constantly in danger,[A]
yet I do not forget Your instruction.[aa]
110 The wicked have set a trap for me,[ab]
but I have not wandered
from Your precepts.[ac]
111 I have Your decrees as a heritage forever;
indeed, they are the joy of my heart.[ad]
112 I am resolved to obey Your statutes
to the very end.[B,ae]

ס Samek

113 I hate those who are double-minded,[af]
but I love Your instruction.[ag]
114 You are my shelter and my shield;[ah]
I put my hope in Your word.[ai]
115 Depart from me,[aj] you evil ones,
so that I may obey my God's commands.[ak]
116 Sustain me as You promised,[al]
and I will live;
do not let me be ashamed of my hope.[am]
117 Sustain me so that I can be safe[an]
and always be concerned about
Your statutes.[ao]
118 You reject all who stray
from Your statutes,[ap]
for their deceit is a lie.
119 You remove all the wicked on earth
as if they were[C] dross;[aq]

---

a 119:89 Ps 89:2; 119:160; Is 40:8; Mt 24:35; 1Pt 1:25   b 119:90 Ps 89:1,2   c Ps 148:6; Ec 1:4   d 119:91 Jr 31:35   e Ps 104:2-4   f 119:92 Ps 119:16,50   g 119:93 Ps 119:16,25   h 119:94 Ps 119:146   i Ps 119:45   j 119:95 Ps 40:14   k 119:97 Ps 119:47,127,163,165   l Ps 1:2; 119:15   m 119:98 Dt 4:6; Ps 119:130   n 119:99 Ps 119:15   o 119:100 Jb 32:7-9   p Ps 119:56   q 119:101 Pr 1:15   r 119:102 Dt 17:20; Jos 23:6; 1Kg 15:5   s 119:103 Ps 19:10; Pr 8:11; 24:13,14   t 119:104 Ps 119:130   u Ps 119:128   v 119:105 Pr 6:23   w 119:106 Neh 10:29   x 119:107 Ps 119:25,50   y 119:108 Hs 14:2; Heb 13:15   z Ps 119:12   aa 119:109 Ps 119:16   ab 119:110 Ps 140:5; 141:9   ac Ps 119:10   ad 119:111 Ps 119:14,162   ae 119:112 Ps 119:33,36   af 119:113 1Kg 18:21; Jms 1:8; 4:8   ag Ps 119:47   ah 119:114 Gn 15:1; Dt 33:29; Ps 3:3; 28:7; 115:9-11; 144:2; Pr 2:7   ai Ps 119:74   aj 119:115 Ps 6:8; 139:19; Mt 4:10   ak Ps 119:22   al 119:116 Ps 54:4   am Ps 25:20; 31:1; Rm 9:33; Php 1:20   an 119:117 Pr 29:25   ao Ps 119:15   ap 119:118 Ps 119:10,21   aq 119:119 Is 1:25; Ezk 22:18,19

A 119:109 Lit in my hand   B 119:112 Or statutes; the reward is eternal   C 119:119 Some Hb mss, DSS, LXX, Aq, Sym, Jer read All the wicked of the earth You count as

---

119:89-96 The **word** of God is the central theme of these verses. The Lord's judgments that maintain order in the cosmos provide order for human life as well. Verse 96 could be a summary of the book of Ecclesiastes (Ec 12:8-14).

119:97-104 An intimate acquaintance with God's **word** results in wise and discerning behavior (Dt 4:5-6; Jr 15:16; Ezk 3:3). Just as those with God's word are **wiser** than those without (vv. 98-100), so also the gospel is understood by "infants" but hidden from the worldly wise (Lk 10:21; 1Co 1:18-21; 2:8).

119:105-112 The lighted **path** is not whatever we want it to be, but **righteous judgments** and God's **precepts**; on such a path there is no **danger** or **trap** but a **heritage** and **joy**. Thus the guidance of the Lord's instruction enabled the psalmist to negotiate right and wrong (19:11-13; Pr 6:23; Jn 8:16).

119:113-120 The upright life surrenders to God's divine instruction for maintaining a relationship with Him. The presence of the wicked and deceitful remains pervasive in this section, suggesting the severe hostility that threatened the psalmist.

therefore, I love Your decrees.[a]

120 I tremble[A] in awe of You;[b]
I fear Your judgments.

ע Ayin

121 I have done what is just and right;[c]
do not leave me to my oppressors.
122 Guarantee Your servant's well-being;[d]
do not let the arrogant oppress me.
123 My eyes grow weary[e] looking for
Your salvation
and for Your righteous promise.
124 Deal with Your servant based on
Your faithful love;[f]
teach me Your statutes.
125 I am Your servant;[g]
give me understanding[h]
so that I may know Your decrees.
126 It is time for the LORD to act,[i]
for they have violated
Your instruction.
127 Since I love Your commands[j]
more than gold, even the purest gold,
128 I carefully follow[B] all Your precepts[k]
and hate every false way.[l]

פ Pe

129 Your decrees are wonderful;[m]
therefore I obey them.[n]
130 The revelation of Your words[o]
brings light
and gives understanding
to the inexperienced.[p]
131 I open my mouth and pant[q]
because I long for Your commands.
132 Turn to me and be gracious to me,[r]
as is Your practice toward those
who love Your name.
133 Make my steps steady
through Your promise;[s]
don't let any sin dominate me.[t]
134 Redeem me from human oppression,[u]
and I will keep Your precepts.
135 Show favor to Your servant,[v]
and teach me Your statutes.[w]
136 My eyes pour out streams of tears[x]

because people do not follow
Your instruction.

צ Tsade

137 You are righteous, LORD,[y]
and Your judgments are just.
138 The decrees You issue are righteous
and altogether trustworthy.[z]
139 My anger overwhelms me
because my foes forget Your words.[aa]
140 Your word is completely pure,[ab]
and Your servant loves it.[ac]
141 I am insignificant and despised,[ad]
but I do not forget Your precepts.[ae]
142 Your righteousness is
an everlasting righteousness,
and Your instruction is true.[af]
143 Trouble and distress have overtaken me,
but Your commands are my delight.[ag]
144 Your decrees are righteous forever.[ah]
Give me understanding,
and I will live.

ק Qof

145 I call with all my heart; answer me, LORD.
I will obey Your statutes.[ai]
146 I call to You; save me,
and I will keep Your decrees.[aj]
147 I rise before dawn and cry out for help;[ak]
I put my hope in Your word.
148 I am awake through each watch
of the night
to meditate on Your promise.[al]
149 In keeping with Your faithful love,
hear my voice.
LORD, give me life in keeping with
Your justice.[am]
150 Those who pursue evil plans[C,an]
come near;
they are far from Your instruction.
151 You are near, LORD,[ao]
and all Your commands are true.[ap]
152 Long ago I learned from Your decrees
that You have established
them forever.[aq]

[a]119:119 Ps 119:47　[b]119:120 Jb 4:14; Hab 3:16　[c]119:121 Jb 29:14　[d]119:122 Ps 119:134　[e]119:123 Ps 119:82　[f]119:124 Ps 51:1; 109:26; 119:88,149,159　[g]119:125 Ps 116:16　[h]Ps 119:27　[i]119:126 Jr 18:23　[j]119:127 Ps 19:10; 119:47　[k]119:128 Ps 19:8　[l]Ps 119:104　[m]119:129 Ps 119:18　[n]Ps 119:22　[o]119:130 Pr 6:23　[p]Ps 19:7　[q]119:131 Ps 42:1　[r]119:132 Ps 25:16　[s]119:133 Ps 17:5　[t]Ps 19:13; Rm 6:12　[u]119:134 Ps 142:6; Lk 1:74　[v]119:135 Ps 31:16; 80:3,7,19　[w]Ps 119:12　[x]119:136 Jr 9:1; 14:17; Lm 3:48　[y]119:137 Neh 9:33; Ps 129:4; 145:17; Lm 1:18　[z]119:138 Ps 19:7-9; 119:86, 90,144,172　[aa]119:139 Ps 69:9; Jn 2:17　[ab]119:140 Ps 12:6; 19:9　[ac]Ps 119:47　[ad]119:141 Ps 22:6　[ae]Ps 119:61　[af]119:142 Ps 119:151,160　[ag]119:143 Ps 119:24　[ah]119:144 Ps 19:9　[ai]119:145 Ps 119:10,55　[aj]119:146 Ps 3:7　[ak]119:147 Ps 5:3　[al]119:148 Ps 119:15　[am]119:149 Ps 119:25, 124　[an]119:150 Pr 6:17,18; 12:20; 14:22; 24:8　[ao]119:151 Ps 34:18; 145:18; Is 50:8　[ap]Ps 119:142　[aq]119:152 Ps 119:89; Lk 21:33

[A]119:120 Lit My flesh shudders　[B]119:128 Lit I therefore follow carefully　[C]119:150 Some Hb mss, LXX, Sym, Jer read who maliciously persecute me

119:121-128 The upright are loyal, showing righteous anger toward God's enemies (v. 126; cp. v. 53). The frustration of the psalmist is apparent, as he called on the Lord to intervene.

119:129-136 The **revelation** is literally the "door" or "opening" (v. 130). Like a hungry and thirsty animal, the psalmist longed for God's instruction (v. 131). Though sometimes the psalmist expressed righteous indignation at those who did not obey God (vv. 53,126,139,158), here he

expressed sorrow (v. 136; cp. Mt 23:37; Lk 19:41; Ac 20:31; Rm 9:2-3; Php 3:18).

119:137-144 On verse 138, compare 19:7; on verse 140, compare 19:9. The psalmist reinforced God's role as Judge.

119:145-152 The psalmist called on the Lord, seeking His help in overcoming those who devised evil plans against him. He expressed trust and assurance in the Lord's faithfulness. While his enemies were physically **near**, they were

ר Resh

153 Consider my affliction and rescue me,[a]
for I have not forgotten
Your instruction.[b]

154 Defend my cause and redeem me;[c]
give me life as You promised.

155 Salvation is far from the wicked
because they do not seek Your statutes.[d]

156 Your compassions are many, LORD;[e]
give me life according to Your judgments.

157 My persecutors and foes are many.[f]
I have not turned from Your decrees.[g]

158 I have seen the disloyal[h] and feel disgust[i]
because they do not keep Your word.

159 Consider how I love Your precepts;
LORD, give me life according to
Your faithful love.[j]

160 The entirety of Your word is truth,
and all Your righteous judgments
endure forever.[k]

ש Sin / ש Shin

161 Princes have persecuted me
without cause,
but my heart fears only Your word.[l]

162 I rejoice over Your promise[m]
like one who finds vast treasure.

163 I hate and abhor falsehood,[n]
but I love Your instruction.[o]

164 I praise You seven times a day
for Your righteous judgments.[p]

165 Abundant peace belongs to those[q]
who love Your instruction;
nothing makes them stumble.[r]

166 LORD, I hope for Your salvation[s]
and carry out Your commands.

167 I obey Your decrees
and love them greatly.[t]

168 I obey Your precepts and decrees,
for all my ways are before You.[u]

ת Tav

169 Let my cry reach You, LORD;[v]
give me understanding according to
Your word.[w]

170 Let my plea reach You;[x]
rescue me according to Your promise.[y]

171 My lips pour out praise,[z]
for You teach me Your statutes.[aa]

172 My tongue sings about Your promise,[ab]
for all Your commands are righteous.[ac]

173 May Your hand be ready to help me,[ad]
for I have chosen Your precepts.[ae]

174 I long for Your salvation, LORD,
and Your instruction is my delight.[af]

175 Let me live, and I will praise You;[ag]
may Your judgments help me.

176 I wander like a lost sheep;[ah]
seek Your servant,[ai]
for I do not forget Your commands.[aj]

Psalm 120

A Cry for Truth and Peace

A *song of ascents.

1 In my distress I called to the LORD,
and He answered me.[ak]

2 "LORD, deliver me from lying lips
and a deceitful tongue."[al]

3 What will He give you,
and what will He do to you,
you deceitful tongue?[am]

4 A warrior's sharp arrows
with burning charcoal![A,an]

5 What misery that I have stayed
in Meshech,[B,ao]
that I have lived among the tents
of Kedar![C,ap]

Cross references:
[a]119:153 Ps 119:50; Lm 5:1
[b]Ps 119:16; Hs 4:6
[c]119:154 1Sm 24:15; Ps 35:1; Mc 7:9
[d]119:155 Ps 119:45,94
[e]119:156 2Sm 24:14
[f]119:157 Ps 7:1
[g]Ps 119:51
[h]119:158 Pr 14:14
[i]Ps 139:21
[j]119:159 Ps 119:25,47
[k]119:160 Ps 119:89,142,152
[l]119:161 Ps 119:23,120
[m]119:162 Ps 119:14,111
[n]119:163 Ps 119:104,128; Pr 13:5
[o]Ps 119:47
[p]119:164 Ps 119:7,160
[q]119:165 Pr 3:1,2; Is 26:3; 32:17
[r]Pr 3:23; Is 63:13
[s]119:166 Gn 49:18; Ps 119:81,174
[t]119:167 Ps 119:47,129
[u]119:168 Ps 139:3; Pr 5:21
[v]119:169 Ps 18:6; 102:1; 140:6
[w]Ps 119:144
[x]119:170 Ps 28:2; 130:2; 143:1
[y]Ps 22:20; 59:1
[z]119:171 Ps 51:15; 63:3
[aa]Ps 119:12
[ab]119:172 Ps 51:14
[ac]Ps 119:138
[ad]119:173 Ps 37:24; 73:23
[ae]Jos 24:22
[af]119:174 Ps 119:16, 24,166
[ag]119:175 Ps
119:25 [ah]119:176 Is 53:6; Jr 50:6 [ai]Mt 18:12; Lk 15:4 [aj]Ps
119:16 [ak]120:1 Ps 18:6; Jnh 2:2 [al]120:2 Pr 12:22 [am]120:3 Zph
3:13 [an]120:4 Pr 25:18,22 [ao]120:5 Ezk 27:13 [ap]Sg 1:5; Ezk 27:21

A120:4 Lit *with coals of the broom bush*   **B**120:5 = a people far to the north of Palestine   **C**120:5 = a nomadic people of the desert to the southeast

---

spiritually **far** from the **commands** that protected the psalmist because the Lord was **near** (vv. 150-151).

119:153-160 Realizing his utter dependence on God, the psalmist prayed that God would give him **life** (vv. 154,156, 159). The psalmist despised the way of the wicked (vv. 155, 158; cp. v. 53).

119:161-168 Peace fills the lives of those who trust in God's **instruction**. The goal is not to **obey** God's **precepts** for the sake of obedience, but in order to enjoy abundant life in God's presence (v. 168).

119:169-176 The psalmist concluded the psalm with words of praise, an affirmation of his faithfulness to the Torah, and a final, heartfelt plea for intervention.

120 title This is the first of 15 psalms of **ascents** (Pss 120-

134). These psalms were designed for pilgrimage processions to celebrate seasonal feasts in Jerusalem. The hymns contain numerous references to Jerusalem or Zion, the temple, Israel, peace, and adversity. The 15 songs, adapted from ancient hymns heralding the blessings and salvation of Zion, may have been sung on the 15 steps leading up to the temple.

120:2 Metaphorically, **lying lips** and a **deceitful tongue** denote the spread of gossip and baseless rumors (109:2).

120:3-4 Those who spoke lies—possibly while swearing by God that they were not lying—would face severe judgment. **Burning charcoal** is literally "coals of broom," that is, charcoal derived from a hard-stemmed plant called a broom tree (1Kg 19:4-5; Jb 30:4).

120:5 Meshech was located southeast of the Black Sea.

⁶ I have lived too long
  with those who hate peace.^a
⁷ I am for peace; but when I speak,
  they are for war.^b

Psalm 121
The Lord Our Protector

A *song of ascents.

¹ I lift my eyes toward the mountains.
  Where will my help come from?^c
² My help comes from the Lord,
  the Maker of heaven and earth.^d

³ He will not allow your foot to slip;
  your Protector will not slumber.^e
⁴ Indeed, the Protector of Israel
  does not slumber or sleep.^f

⁵ The Lord protects you;
  the Lord is a shelter right by your side.^{A,g}
⁶ The sun will not strike you by day
  or the moon by night.^h

⁷ The Lord will protect you from all harm;
  He will protect your life.ⁱ
⁸ The Lord will protect your coming
  and going
  both now and forever.^j

Psalm 122
A Prayer for Jerusalem

A Davidic *song of ascents.

¹ I rejoiced with those who said to me,

"Let us go to the house of the Lord."^k
² Our feet are standing
  within your gates, Jerusalem^l—

³ Jerusalem, built as a city should be,
  solidly joined together,^m
⁴ where the tribes, *Yahweh's tribes,
    go up
  to give thanks to the name of Yahweh.ⁿ
  (This is an ordinance for Israel.^o)
⁵ There, thrones for judgment are placed,
  thrones of the house of David.^p

⁶ Pray for the peace of Jerusalem:
  "May those who love you prosper;^q
⁷ may there be peace within your walls,
  prosperity within your fortresses."^r
⁸ Because of my brothers and friends,
  I will say, "Peace be with you."^s
⁹ Because of the house of the Lord
    our God,
  I will seek your good.^t

Psalm 123
Looking for God's Favor

A *song of ascents.

¹ I lift my eyes to You,
  the One enthroned in heaven.^u
² Like a servant's eyes
    on his master's hand,
  like a servant girl's eyes
    on her mistress's hand,
  so our eyes are on the Lord our God
  until He shows us favor.^v

---

^a120:6 Ps 35:20
^b120:7 Ps 109:4
^c121:1 Ps 87:1; 123:1
^d121:2 Ps 115:15; 124:8
^e121:3 Ps 41:2; 66:9; 127:1
^f121:4 Dt 33:29
^g121:5 Ps 16:8; 91:1,4
^h121:6 Is 49:10; Rv 7:16
ⁱ121:7 Ps 41:2; 91:10-12
^j121:8 Dt 28:6
^k122:1 Is 2:3; Mc 4:2; Zch 8:21
^l122:2 Ps 9:14; Jr 7:2
^m123:3 Neh 4:6; Ps 147:2
ⁿ122:4 Is 2:3; Mc 4:2
^o1Ch 22:13
^p122:5 Dt 17:8; 2Ch 19:8
^q122:6 Ps 51:18; Jr 29:7
^r122:7 Ps 48:3
^s122:8 1Sm 25:6; Ps 85:8
^t122:9 Neh 2:10; Est 10:3
^u123:1 Ps 2:4; 121:1; 141:8
^v123:2 Ps 25:15

---

^A121:5 Lit *is your shelter at your right hand*

Kedar was an eastern plain located at the northern fringe of the Syrian-Arabian desert. It was normally inhabited by Arab tribes. Together they represent places far and near where Israelites lived as aliens.

121 title On **ascents**, see note at Psalm 120 title.

121:1-8 In this psalm the writer exploited the broad semantic range of the Hebrew verb *shamar* ("guard, keep, protect, observe") using the term six times (vv. 3,4,5,7[2x],8). The HCSB consistently translates it as "protect" or "Protector" in this psalm.

121:1 The **mountains** may have seemed like a potential place to hide (11:1), a symbol of God's stability and deliverance (31:2; 125:2; Nah 1:15), or a looming menace (Jnh 2:6). Any of these could prompt the question concerning the source of **help**.

121:2 The Creator is the faithful source of help and blessing (124:8; 134:3; 146:6).

121:5-8 God **protects** His people from the perils of the road **by day** or **by night**.

122 title On **ascents**, see note at Psalm 120 title.

122:1-9 Sharing terminology and imagery with Is 2:2-4, this psalm may be an adaptation of that prophetic passage. The focus of the psalm is on the features of the city: house (vv.

1,5,9), gates (v. 2), thrones (v. 5), walls (v. 7), and fortresses (v. 7).

122:1 On **go to the house of the Lord**, compare Is 2:3; Jr 31:6.

122:2 **Standing within** the **gates** means entering the Lord's presence.

122:4 The **tribes** are the 12 tribes of Israel. **Yahweh's tribes** occurs only here in the Bible. Attendance at the three yearly festivals was mandatory. These were Passover, the Day of Atonement (Yom Kippur), and the Festival of Booths (Ex 23:14-17; Lv 23; Dt 16).

122:5 The phrase **thrones for judgment** refers to the judicial function of the central sanctuary (Dt 17:8-13; 2Sm 8:15; 15:2-6), while the **thrones of the house of David** refers to kings of Davidic descent. Solomon's temple contained a "hall of thrones" (1Kg 7:7).

122:6-7 **Peace** permits the pursuit of **prosperity** (1Kg 4:20-25; 1Tm 2:1-2).

122:8-9 The pilgrimage to the temple prompted the psalmist to **seek . . . good** for everyone in the community.

123 title On **ascents**, see note at Psalm 120 title.

123:2 A **servant** might watch **his master's hand** intently for a gesture that would signify approval.

³ Show us favor, Lord, show us favor,
for we've had more than enough
contempt.ᵃ
⁴ We've had more than enough
scorn from the arrogant
and contempt from the proud.ᵇ

Psalm 124
The Lord Is on Our Side

A Davidic •song of ascents.

¹ If the Lord had not been
on our side—
let Israel say—
² If the Lord had not been
on our sideᶜ
when men attacked us,ᵈ
³ then they would have
swallowed us alive
in their burning anger against us.ᵉ
⁴ Then the waters would have
engulfed us;
the torrent would have swept
over us;
⁵ the raging waters would have swept
over us.ᶠ

⁶ Praise the Lord,
who has not let us be ripped apart
by their teeth.ᵍ
⁷ We have escaped like a bird
from the hunter's net;
the net is torn, and we have escaped.ʰ
⁸ Our help is in the name of •Yahweh,
the Maker of heaven and earth.ⁱ

ᵃ123:3 Neh 4:4;
Ps 4:1; 119:22
ᵇ123:4 Is
32:9,11; Am 6:1
ᶜ124:1-2 Ps
94:17
ᵈ124:2 Ps 129:1
ᵉ124:3 Ps 35:25;
56:1; Pr 1:12
ᶠ124:4-5 Jb
22:11; Ps 32:6;
69:2
ᵍ124:6 Ps 27:2;
Pr 30:14
ʰ124:7 Ps 91:3
ⁱ124:8 Ps
115:15; 121:2
ʲ125:1 Ps 46:5
ᵏ125:2 Zch 2:5
ˡ125:3 Ps 89:22;
Is 14:5
ᵐ125:4 Ps 7:10;
119:68
ⁿ125:5 Ps
92:7,9; 94:4
ᵒ125:4-5 Ps
128:5-6
ᵖ126:1 Ps 85:1;
Jr 29:14

Psalm 125
Israel's Stability

A •song of ascents.

¹ Those who trust in the Lord are
like Mount •Zion.
It cannot be shaken;
it remains forever.ʲ
² Jerusalem—the mountains
surround her.
And the Lord surrounds
His people,
both now and forever.ᵏ

³ The scepter of the wicked
will not remain
over the land allotted
to the righteous,
so that the righteous will not apply
their hands to injustice.ˡ
⁴ Do what is good, Lord, to the good,
to those whose hearts are upright.ᵐ
⁵ But as for those who turn aside
to crooked ways,
the Lord will banish them
with the evildoers.ⁿ

Peace be with Israel.ᵒ

Psalm 126
Zion's Restoration

A •song of ascents.

¹ When the Lord restored the fortunes
of •Zion,ᴬ
we were like those who dream.ᵖ

ᴬ126:1 Or Lord returned those of Zion who had been captives

123:3 The Hebrew term for **contempt** [buz] is related to the verb "despise" (31:18; 107:40; Is 37:22).

124 title On **ascents**, see note at Psalm 120 title.

124:2 The **men attacked us** is literally "men stood up against us" (3:1; 86:14; 92:11).

124:4-5 Fast-moving **waters** and floods would have washed away all evidence of Israel's existence (69:2,15; Is 30:28; 66:12). The Hebrew term translated **raging** is related to a word that means "arrogant" (Dt 17:13; Neh 9:10,29), characterizing the destructive **waters** and the oppressive enemy.

124:6 Hostile people are depicted as devouring, unrestrained monsters (79:7; Is 9:12; Jr 51:34).

124:7 The mouth of a bird trap (Pr 7:23; Am 3:5) has been **torn** and the captured bird has **escaped**, as if from prison. The setting of a fowler's trap suggests premeditation by the opposition, who lay in wait to capture God's people.

125 title On **ascents**, see note at Psalm 120 title.

125:1 For Israel, **Zion** represented the center of the earth and the place where the Lord dwelt. The Hebrew word mut (**shaken**) functions as a wordplay with Hebrew hammattiym; "turn aside" (v. 5). Those who trust Yahweh will remain

stable, while those who depend on evil ways will be turned aside.

125:2 The psalm emphasizes the protection of Zion and her inhabitants as the Lord's chosen nation.

125:3 An unusual expression, **the scepter of the wicked** refers to the authority of evildoers (Ezk 19:11-14), which would not continue to dominate the **land of the righteous**. On Judah as the "scepter of righteousness," see Gn 49:10. Those who lived in the land of their inheritance would conduct themselves as God's people, avoiding evil and injustice (Ps 82:2; 107:42).

125:4 The actions and motives of the righteous coincide.

125:5 On **those who turn aside**, see note at verse 1. The Lord will **banish** evildoers (lit "lead them away"; cp. Jb 12:17,19).

126 title On **ascents**, see note at Psalm 120 title.

126:1 Restored the fortunes refers to the return of the Babylonian exiles to Jerusalem as an event that had already taken place (84:6; 85:1). The appeal in 126:4 to "restore our fortunes" is difficult since the verb assumes that the action has not yet occurred. While verse 1 refers to the return of

a126:2 Jb 8:21
bPs 51:14
cPs 71:19
d126:3 Is 25:9
e126:4 Is 35:6;
43:19
f126:5 Jr 31:9
g126:6 Is 35:10;
51:11
h127:1 Ps 78:69
iPs 121:4
j127:2 Ps 3:5;
4:8; Pr 3:24
k127:3 Dt 7:13;
Ps 113:9
l127:4 Ps 120:4
m127:5 Ps
128:2-3
nJl 2:26-27
o128:1 Ps 112:1;
119:1,3
p128:2 Is 3:10
qEc 8:12
r128:3 Ps 52:8;
Ezk 19:10
s128:4 Ps 115:13
t128:5 Ps 20:2;
134:3; 135:21
u128:6 Ps 125:5;
Pr 17:6

2 Our mouths were filled
   with laughter then,*a*
and our tongues with shouts of joy.*b*
Then they said among the nations,
"The Lord has done great things
   for them."*c*
3 The Lord had done great things for us;
we were joyful.*d*

4 Restore our fortunes,^A^ Lord,
like watercourses in the •Negev.*e*
5 Those who sow in tears
will reap with shouts of joy.*f*
6 Though one goes along weeping,
carrying the bag of seed,
he will surely come back with shouts
   of joy,
carrying his sheaves.*g*

Psalm 127
The Blessing of the Lord

A Solomonic •song of ascents.

1 Unless the Lord builds a house,
its builders labor over it in vain;*h*
unless the Lord watches over a city,
the watchman stays alert in vain.*i*
2 In vain you get up early and stay up late,
working hard to have enough food—
yes, He gives sleep to the one
   He loves.^B,*j*^

3 Sons are indeed a heritage
   from the Lord,
children, a reward.*k*

4 Like arrows in the hand of a warrior
are the sons born in one's youth.*l*
5 Happy is the man who has filled
   his quiver with them.*m*
Such men will never be put
   to shame
when they speak with their enemies
   at the city •gate.*n*

Psalm 128
Blessings for Those Who Fear God

A •song of ascents.

1 How happy is everyone who •fears
   the Lord,
who walks in His ways!*o*
2 You will surely eat
what your hands have worked for.*p*
You will be happy,
and it will go well for you.*q*
3 Your wife will be like a fruitful vine
within your house,
your sons, like young olive trees
around your table.*r*
4 In this very way
the man who fears the Lord
will be blessed.*s*

5 May the Lord bless you from •Zion,
so that you will see the prosperity
   of Jerusalem
all the days of your life*t*
6 and will see your children's children!*u*

Peace be with Israel.*u*

---

^A^126:4 Or *Return our captives*   ^B^127:2 Or *yes, He gives such things to His loved ones while they sleep*

Israel, verse 4 may refer to the restoration of prosperity and peace in the land (122:6-7). **Like those who dream** refers to those who eagerly anticipate the future.

126:2 God's intervention on Israel's behalf testifies to His omnipotence and superiority (96:3; 113:4; Is 61:9; 66:19; Jr 31:10; Ezk 36:23).

126:4-6 In verse 1 Yahweh restores Zion as the political and religious center, but verses 4-6 focus on the productivity of the land. The **watercourses in the Negev** refer to seasonal streams or wadis, which occasionally blessed the land with a sudden overabundance of water. Along with sudden bounty like a wadi, God also made use of methodical processes and hard labor like agriculture. The person who remains humble before God will **surely** enjoy God's blessings in the land.

127 title On **ascents**, see note at Psalm 120 title.

127:1 No task succeeds apart from God's will. While building a dwelling is the literal meaning here, a **house** could also refer to a household or family, connecting this verse to verses 3-5.

127:2 Humanity struggles to provide for its needs, **working hard to have enough food** (lit "eating the bread of toil"; 80:5;

102:9; Gn 3:17; Is 30:20). The Lord provides rest by blessing the work of the godly.

127:3 While food generally came from hard work, amid the uncertainties of the ancient Near Eastern life, **children** came from God (Gn 30:2; Dt 7:14). The psalmist focused specifically on **sons**, who could continue the family lineage.

127:4-5 A full **quiver** of arrows represented prestige and protection. Like **arrows** for a **warrior**, children were useful in the agricultural society. The man who had many children also enjoyed respect in Near Eastern society (on **gate**, see note at 87:2).

128 title On **ascents**, see note at Psalm 120 title.

128:1-6 This is a companion psalm to Psalm 127. The psalmist affirmed the significance of descendants, revisiting the original promise God made to Abraham in Gn 12:1-3.

128:3 Just as Joseph was described as a **fruitful vine** (Gn 49:22), so a **wife** who is blessed with children expands the family. **Olive trees** were known for vitality, strength, productivity, and longevity.

128:5-6 In the ancient Near East, the ultimate earthly blessing would be **prosperity** for one's nation, long life, healthy offspring, and **peace**.

Psalm 129
Protection of the Oppressed

A •song of ascents.

1 Since my youth they have often
    attacked me—
let Israel say—
2 Since my youth they have often
    attacked me,
but they have not prevailed
    against me.[a]
3 Plowmen plowed over my back;
they made their furrows long.[b]
4 The LORD is righteous;
He has cut the ropes of the wicked.[c]

5 Let all who hate •Zion
be driven back in disgrace.[d]
6 Let them be like grass
    on the rooftops,
which withers before it grows up[A,e]
7 and can't even fill the hands
    of the reaper
or the arms of the one
    who binds sheaves.[f]
8 Then none who pass by will say,
"May the LORD's blessing be on you."

We bless you in the name of •Yahweh.[g]

Psalm 130
Awaiting Redemption

A •song of ascents.

1 Out of the depths I call
    to You, •Yahweh![h]
2 Lord, listen to my voice;

let Your ears be attentive
    to my cry for help.[i]
3 Yahweh, if You considered sins,
Lord, who could stand?[j]
4 But with You there is forgiveness,
so that You may be revered.[k]

5 I wait for Yahweh; I wait
and put my hope in His word.[l]
6 I wait for the Lord
more than watchmen
    for the morning—
more than watchmen for the morning.[m]

7 Israel, put your hope in the LORD.[n]
For there is faithful love with the LORD,
and with Him is redemption
    in abundance.[o]
8 And He will redeem Israel
from all its sins.[p]

Psalm 131
A Childlike Spirit

A Davidic •song of ascents.

1 LORD, my heart is not proud;
my eyes are not haughty.[q]
I do not get involved with things
too great or too difficult for me.[r]
2 Instead, I have calmed
    and quieted myself
like a little weaned child
    with its mother;
I am like a little child.[s]

3 Israel, put your hope in the LORD,
both now and forever.[t]

[a]129:1-2 Jr 1:19; 20:11
[b]129:3 Mc 3:12
[c]129:4 Ps 2:3
[d]129:5 Ps 35:4; 70:3; 71:13
[e]129:6 2Kg 19:26; Is 37:27
[f]129:7 Ps 79:12
[g]129:8 Ru 2:4; Ps 118:26
[h]130:1 Ps 69:2; Lm 3:55
[i]130:2 2Ch 6:40; Ps 28:6; 140:6
[j]130:3 Ps 76:7; Mal 3:2; Rv 6:17
[k]130:4 1Kg 8:39-40; Ps 86:5; Jr 33:8-9
[l]130:5 Ps 33:20; 119:74,81
[m]130:6 Ps 63:6; 119:147
[n]130:7 Ps 131:3
[o]Ps 111:9
[p]130:8 Lk 1:68; Ti 2:14
[q]131:1 Ps 101:5; Rm 12:16
[r]Jb 42:3; Ps 139:6
[s]131:2 Mt 18:3; 1Co 14:20
[t]131:3 Ps 130:7

[A]129:6 Or *it can be pulled out*

129 title On **ascents**, see note at Psalm 120 title.

129:1 Israel **often** suffered affliction from enemies in her early days (106:41-43). On **let Israel say**, compare 118:2-4; 124:1.

129:3 Slaves were often beaten by overseers and owners, creating stripes on their backs (Ex 5:14; Is 50:6; 53:4-6).

129:4 The Lord will prevent the **wicked** from harming His people by eliminating the weapons used to force submission (46:9; Jb 39:10).

129:5-7 The psalmist prayed an imprecation or curse upon those who hated the Lord and His people (see note at 109:1-31). Those who oppose the Lord will be like **grass** that sprouts briefly only to become scorched and withered, not living long enough to bear fruit. This is the opposite of 126:6, where the righteous person rejoiced in his harvest.

129:8 Those who hate Zion (v. 5) will suffer God's curse on their harvest. No one who sees them will offer a cheerful greeting (cp. Ru 2:4).

130 title On **ascents**, see note at Psalm 120 title.

130:3-4 To consider **sins** is literally to "watch over" or "guard" them (Hb *shamar*). All would be lost if God made no provision to let sins go. The penitent person relies on the mercy and compassion of the Lord to forgive (103:3); otherwise, the Lord would not acknowledge his worship (Ezr 9:15). **Revered** brings out the dual connotation of "fear" and "worship," depicting God's mercy in forgiveness and His judgment of unrighteousness.

130:5 **Hope** in adversity anticipates God's response on the basis of **His word** (119:42,49,74,81).

130:7 While Israel's **hope** of forgiveness is generated by the Lord's **faithful love** (Hb *chesed*), her **redemption** (Hb *paha'*; "deliverance from an obligation through a payment") depicts the visible result of that forgiveness (Neh 1:10; Is 50:2).

131 title On **ascents**, see note at Psalm 120 title.

131:1 Humility characterizes the faithful, who depend on the Lord and exalt Him.

131:2-3 Israel should adopt the attitude of an infant, depending on **the LORD** for protection and nurture (Mt 18:3).

Psalm 132
David and Zion Chosen

A •song of ascents.

1 LORD, remember David
and all the hardships he endured,[a]
2 and how he swore an oath to the LORD,
making a vow to the Mighty One
of Jacob:[b]
3 "I will not enter my house[A]
or get into my bed,[B]
4 I will not allow my eyes to sleep
or my eyelids to slumber[c]
5 until I find a place for the LORD,
a dwelling for the Mighty One
of Jacob."[d]

6 We heard of the ark
in Ephrathah;[C,e]
we found it in the fields of Jaar.[D,f]
7 Let us go to His dwelling place;
let us worship at His footstool.[g]
8 Rise up, LORD, come to
Your resting place,
You and Your powerful ark.[h]
9 May Your priests be clothed
with righteousness,

and may Your godly people shout
for joy.[i]
10 Because of Your servant David,
do not reject Your anointed one.[E,j]

11 The LORD swore an oath to David,
a promise He will not abandon:
"I will set one of your descendants[F]
on your throne.[k]
12 If your sons keep My covenant
and My decrees that I will teach them,
their sons will also sit on
your throne forever."[l]

13 For the LORD has chosen •Zion;
He has desired it for His home:[m]
14 "This is My resting place forever;
I will make My home here
because I have desired it.[n]
15 I will abundantly bless its food;
I will satisfy its needy with bread.[o]
16 I will clothe its priests with salvation,
and its godly people will shout
for joy.[p]
17 There I will make a •horn grow
for David;[q]
I have prepared a lamp for
My anointed one.[r]

a 132:1 2Sm 16:12
b 132:2 Gn 49:24; Is 49:26; 60:16
c 132:3-4 Pr 6:4
d 132:5 1Ch 22:7; Ac 7:46
e 132:6 Gn 35:19; Ru 4:11; 1Sm 17:12; Mc 5:2
f 1Sm 7:1
g 132:7 1Ch 28:2; Ps 99:5
h 132:8 2Ch 6:41; Ps 68:1; 78:61
i 132:9 Jb 29:14; Ps 149:5
j 132:10 2Ch 6:42
k 132:11 2Sm 7:12-16; Ps 89:3; Ac 2:30
l 132:12 1Kg 8:25; Lk 1:32
m 132:13 Ps 68:16; 78:68
n 132:14 Mt 23:21
o 132:15 Ps 107:9; 147:14
p 132:16 2Ch 6:41
q 132:17 2Sm 23:5; Lk 1:69
r 1Kg 11:36

A 132:3 Lit *enter the tent of my house*   B 132:3 Lit *into the couch of my bed*   C 132:6 = Bethlehem   D 132:6 = Kiriath-jearim
E 132:10 = the king   F 132:11 Lit *set the fruit of your womb*

132 title On **ascents**, see note at Psalm 120 title. This royal psalm must have been written after David's time, since it looks back at King David's plan to build a temple for the ark (vv. 5-8). Also, another anointed king appeals to God's grace in David's name (v. 10).

132:1 The **hardships** David **endured** probably refer to his longing to bring the ark to Jerusalem and his anguish over the incident with Uzzah (2Sm 6:6-8).

132:2 **Mighty One of Jacob** alludes to Israel's heritage in God (Gn 49:24).

132:3-4 David's promise is revisited in verses 3-5, while verses 6-8 recall its fulfillment. The Hebrew grammar in these verses shows determination or will, reinforcing David's commitment to bring the ark of the covenant to Jerusalem and install it in a permanent structure.

132:6 The psalmist summarized the history of the installation of the ark in a tabernacle in Jerusalem (1Sm 5-6; 2Sm 6-7). **Ephrathah** was an area near Bethlehem where David received news about the ark, otherwise known as Kiriath-jearim (1Sm 6:21-7:2), was where the ark was recovered from the Philistines.

132:7 Remembering the ceremonial procession that accompanied the ark to Jerusalem, the psalmist appealed to the congregation to enter the temple (1Ch 15-16). **His footstool** is a term referring to the ark (see note at 99:5; cp. 1Ch 16; Is 66; Heb 1:13).

132:8 Verses 8-10 recur in 2Ch 6:41. The ark denotes the Lord's **resting place** (Nm 10:33-35), serving as a visible representation of God's presence (1Sm 4:4; Is 6:1) and playing a pivotal role in holy war (Jos 6:6-7; 1Sm 4:3-8).

132:9 The priests were **clothed with righteousness**, bound to obedience and ethical behavior (v. 16; cp. Is 11:5; 61:10). **Your godly people** derives from the Hebrew term for "covenant love."

132:10 **Reject** is literally "turn one's face from" (cp. Ezk 14:6). The **anointed one** is the king.

132:11 Just as David swore an oath to the Lord (v. 2), so **the LORD swore an oath** of fidelity to David (89:35; 110:4). The Lord promised to sustain the Davidic monarchy by keeping one of his **descendants** on the throne (89:3-4,28-29; 2Sm 7).

132:12 Conditionality was always implicit in this promise (89:38-39; 2Sm 7:14). God's divinely ordained leader was expected to obey His law, serving as a role model to the community.

132:13 The designation of **Zion** as the Lord's eternal **resting place** (68:16; 78:68; 87:2) brought a false sense of security to Israel; they believed the Lord would never allow Jerusalem to be captured or destroyed (Jr 7:3-12; Mc 3:11).

132:16 Just as the priests were expected to exhibit integrity in behavior (v. 9), so they were entrusted with **salvation**. This expressed their responsibility as divine mediators for the spiritual welfare of the people (Ezk 3:18).

132:17 The **horn** represents victory and salvation. The Hebrew word for **grow** (89:17; 148:14) is sometimes associated with a future Messiah, often figuratively referred to as a "branch" or "sprout" (Jr 23:5; 33:15; Ezk 29:21; Zch 3:8; 6:12). To prepare **a lamp** describes metaphorically the permanence of the dynasty and God's visible presence on the throne (18:28; 2Sm 21:17; 22:29; 1Kg 11:36; Jb 18:6).

18 I will clothe his enemies
   with shame,[a]
but the crown he wears[A]
   will be glorious."[b]

Psalm 133
Living in Harmony

A Davidic *song of ascents.

1 How good and pleasant it is
   when brothers live together
   in harmony![c]
2 It is like fine oil on the head,
   running down on the beard,
   running down Aaron's beard
   onto his robes.[d]
3 It is like the dew of Hermon[B]
   falling on the mountains
   of *Zion.[e]
For there the Lord has appointed
   the blessing—
life forevermore.[f]

[a]132:18 Jb 8:22
[b]Ps 21:3
[c]133:1 Gn 13:8;
Heb 13:1
[d]133:2 Ex
30:25,30; Lv 8:12
[e]133:3 Ps 48:1-
2; Mc 5:7
[f]Ps 21:4
[g]134:1 1Ch 9:23-
27; Ps 135:1-2
[h]134:2 Ps 28:2;
63:2; 1Tm 2:8
[i]134:3 Ps
115:15; 128:5
[j]135:1 Ps 113:1;
134:1
[k]135:2 Ps 92:13;
116:19

Psalm 134
Call to Evening Worship

A *song of ascents.

1 Now praise the Lord,
   all you servants of the Lord
   who stand in the Lord's house
      at night![g]
2 Lift up your hands in the holy place
   and praise the Lord![h]

3 May the Lord,
   Maker of heaven and earth,
   bless you from *Zion.[i]

Psalm 135
Yahweh Is Great

1 *Hallelujah!
   Praise the name of *Yahweh.
   Give praise, you servants of Yahweh[j]
2 who stand in the house of Yahweh,
   in the courts of the house of our God.[k]

[A]132:18 Lit *but on him his crown*   [B]133:3 The tallest mountain in the region, noted for its abundant precipitation

A view of the snow-capped peaks of Mount Hermon, mentioned in several psalms (42:6; 89:12; 133:3)

132:18 God's priests will display righteousness and salvation (vv. 9,16), but the unrighteous will reflect **shame**. The divinely ordained king will stand out among the nations as the Lord's anointed.

133 title On **ascents**, see note at Psalm 120 title.

133:1 Brothers can denote any fellow Israelite. The psalmist holds up unity as an ideal.

133:2-3 Unity in a society is compared to extravagant blessing of consecrating oil (see notes at 23:5; 36:8; 89:20; and 92:10) or dewfall on dry ground (Gn 27:28; Pr 19:12). **Zion** was the epitome of blessing because **there** God commanded (**appointed**) eternal **life**—possibly alluding to what Christ accomplished in Jerusalem.

134 title This is the last of the 15 Psalms of Ascents (see note at Ps 120 title).

134:1 Praise and "bless" are the same word in Hebrew *(brk)*. To bless a person is to speak well of him. When people speak well of God, it is praise. When God speaks well of a person, that person is blessed (Gn 24:35; Jb 42:12). After the exile, **servants** designated the faithful community that exemplified an attitude of service (19:11,13; 79:2,10; 86:4,16; 90:13). Congregational singing at the temple often occurred in the evening.

134:2 On **praise**, see note at verse 1.

134:3 The "blessing" of the Lord represents divine attention (see note at v. 1; cp. 128:5; Nm 6:24; Dt 14:29). **Maker of heaven and earth** differentiates God the Creator from all false gods.

135:1-21 Nearly every verse of this psalm quotes or is quoted by other Scripture, such as Psalm 115.

135:1 On **Hallelujah** see note at 104:35.

135:2 People stood in the temple to worship (134:1; Neh 9:3), pray (2Ch 20:9), and serve (Dt 10:8; Ezk 44:15).

135:3 The Lord's **name** is His character or reputation (see v. 13; see note at 20:1).

3 Praise Yahweh, for Yahweh is good;
sing praise to His name,
for it is delightful.[a]
4 For Yahweh has chosen Jacob
for Himself,
Israel as His treasured possession.[b]

5 For I know that Yahweh is great;
our Lord is greater than all gods.[c]
6 Yahweh does whatever He pleases
in heaven and on earth,
in the seas and all the depths.[d]
7 He causes the clouds to rise
from the ends of the earth.
He makes lightning for the rain
and brings the wind
from His storehouses.[e]

8 He struck down the firstborn of Egypt,
both man and beast.[f]
9 He sent signs and wonders
against you, Egypt,
against Pharaoh and all his officials.[g]
10 He struck down many nations
and slaughtered mighty kings:[h]
11 Sihon king of the Amorites,
Og king of Bashan,
and all the kings of Canaan.[i]
12 He gave their land as an inheritance,
an inheritance to His people Israel.[j]

13 Yahweh, Your name endures forever,
Your reputation, Yahweh,
through all generations.[k]
14 For Yahweh will vindicate His people
and have compassion on His servants.[l]

15 The idols of the nations are of silver
and gold,
made by human hands.[m]
16 They have mouths but cannot speak,[n]
eyes, but cannot see.
17 They have ears but cannot hear;
indeed, there is no breath
in their mouths.[o]
18 Those who make them are just like them,
as are all who trust in them.[p]

19 House of Israel, praise Yahweh![q]
House of Aaron, praise Yahweh![r]
20 House of Levi, praise Yahweh!
You who revere the LORD,
praise the LORD![s]
21 May the LORD be praised from ˚Zion;[t]
He dwells in Jerusalem.[u]
Hallelujah!

Psalm 136
God's Love Is Eternal

1 Give thanks to the LORD,
for He is good.[v]
His love is eternal.

[a] 135:3 Ps 100:5; 147:1
[b] 135:4 Ex 19:5; Dt 7:6-7; 10:15
[c] 135:5 Ps 95:3; 97:9
[d] 135:6 Ps 115:3; Is 45:7; Lm 3:37-38; Dn 4:35
[e] 135:7 Jb 28:25-26; Jr 10:13; 51:16
[f] 135:8 Ex 12:12; Ps 78:51; 105:36
[g] 135:9 Dt 6:22; Ps 78:43
[h] 135:10 Ps 44:2; 136:17-22
[i] 135:11 Nm 21:21-35
[j] 135:12 Dt 29:8; Ps 78:55
[k] 135:13 Ex 3:15; Ps 102:12
[l] 135:14 Dt 32:36; Ps 90:13; 106:46
[m] 135:15 2Kg 19:18; Is 37:19
[n] 135:16 Hab 2:18
[o] 135:16-17 Is 46:7
[p] 135:15-18 Ps 115:4-11
[q] 135:19 Ps 115:9; 118:2
[r] Ps 115:10; 118:3
[s] 135:20 Ps 22:23; 115:11; 118:4
[t] 135:21 Ps 128:5
[u] Ps 132:13-14
[v] 136:1 Ps 106:1; 107:1; 118:1

135:4 God's **treasured possession** (Hb *segullah*) always referred to Israel (Ex 19:5; Dt 7:6; 14:2; 26:18; Mal 3:17).

135:5 On **greater than all gods**, see notes at 29:1 and 82:1.

135:6 Compare this verse with 115:3. The Lord's decree accomplishes His purposes (Is 55:11). The **depths** (24:2; Ex 20:4) and the **seas** (Is 24:15-16; 42:10) illustrate the Lord's authority over all creation.

135:7 An identical verse occurs in Jr 10:13; 51:16 (cp. Jb 38:22). God controls the weather. The Hebrew word *'otser* (**storehouses**) is also used for a temple treasury or royal storeroom.

135:8-9 Verses 8-12 are similar to Psalm 136. The God-ordained death of the **firstborn** in **Egypt** was virtually equivalent to killing their gods, since Pharaoh and his offspring were considered divine. The plagues were Yahweh's polemic against false Egyptian gods. The direct address **against you, Egypt** could be translated "in the midst of Egypt."

135:11-12 **Sihon** and **Og** were kings who denied Israel passage through their lands (Nm 21:33-35; cp. Ps 136:19-20). During the conquest of Canaan, the Lord gave Israel the land that had belonged to these kings.

135:15-18 See note at 115:4-8.

135:19-20 Each sector is called upon to bless and acknowledge Yahweh as their God, beginning with the nation (**Israel**), the high priest (**Aaron**), the priesthood (**Levi**), and concluding with the community (cp. 115:9-11).

136:1-26 This psalm recollects events from creation to Israel's conquest of Canaan. Each verse concludes with the refrain, **His love is eternal** (cp. 118:1-4), which may have been sung by the congregation in response to the priests. On **love** see word study on *chesed*.

136:1-2 Compare these verses with 135:3.

chesed

Hebrew Pronunciation	[KHEH sed]
HCSB Translation	faithful love, kindness, loyalty
Uses in Psalms	129
Uses in the OT	249
Focus Passage	Psalm 136:1-26

The etymology of *chesed* is unknown. Half the word's occurrences are in Psalms, where it is closely associated with God. *Chesed* is *faithful love* (Ex 34:6), *love* (Is 54:8), or *constant love* (Ps 40:10). It is a quality that binds people together: *kindness* (Gn 19:19), *loyalty* (Jb 6:14), *goodness* (Is 40:6), or *faithfulness* (Mc 6:8). *Chesed* implies *favor* (Est 2:9) and *grace* (Ezr 9:9). Adjectivally, it appears as *gracious* (Dn 9:4), *kind* (Pr 11:17), *faithful* (Is 57:1), and *loving* (Pr 31:26). It occurs with *'asah* ("do") as *deal faithfully* (1Sm 20:8), *show kindness or loyalty* (2Sm 9:1; 22:51), and *treat well* (Jdg 1:24). The plural implies *acts/deeds of faithful love* (Ps 107:43) or *good deeds* (Neh 13:14). *Chasiyd* (34x) denotes *faithful* (Ps 86:2), *godly* (Mc 7:2), *loyal* (Ps 89:19), or *gracious* (Ps 145:17) and functions nominally. *Chasad* (2x) means *prove oneself faithful* (Ps 18:25).

2 Give thanks to the God of gods.
   His love is eternal.
3 Give thanks to the Lord of lords.*a*
   His love is eternal.
4 He alone does great wonders.*b*
   His love is eternal.
5 He made the heavens skillfully.*c*
   His love is eternal.
6 He spread the land on the waters.*d*
   His love is eternal.
7 He made the great lights:*e*
   His love is eternal.
8 the sun to rule by day,
   His love is eternal.
9 the moon and stars to rule by night.*f*
   His love is eternal.
10 He struck the firstborn of the Egyptians*g*
   His love is eternal.
11 and brought Israel out from among
   them
   His love is eternal.
12 with a strong hand
   and outstretched arm.*h*
   His love is eternal.
13 He divided the •Red Sea*i*
   His love is eternal.
14 and led Israel through,*j*
   His love is eternal.
15 but hurled Pharaoh and his army
   into the Red Sea.*k*
   His love is eternal.
16 He led His people in the wilderness.*l*
   His love is eternal.
17 He struck down great kings
   His love is eternal.
18 and slaughtered famous kings—
   His love is eternal.
19 Sihon king of the Amorites
   His love is eternal.

20 and Og king of Bashan—
   His love is eternal.
21 and gave their land as an inheritance,
   His love is eternal.
22 an inheritance to Israel His servant.*m*
   His love is eternal.
23 He remembered us in our humiliation*n*
   His love is eternal.
24 and rescued us from our foes.*o*
   His love is eternal.
25 He gives food to every creature.*p*
   His love is eternal.
26 Give thanks to the God of heaven!*q*
   His love is eternal.

Psalm 137
Lament of the Exiles

1 By the rivers of Babylon—
   there we sat down and wept
   when we remembered •Zion.*r*
2 There we hung up our lyres
   on the poplar trees,*s*
3 for our captors there asked us
      for songs,
   and our tormentors, for rejoicing:
   "Sing us one of the songs of Zion."*t*
4 How can we sing the LORD's song
   on foreign soil?*u*
5 If I forget you, Jerusalem,
   may my right hand forget its skill.*v*
6 May my tongue stick to the roof
      of my mouth
   if I do not remember you,
   if I do not exalt Jerusalem
      as my greatest joy!*w*

7 Remember, LORD,
   what the Edomites said

*a*136:2-3 Dt 10:17
*b*136:4 Jb 9:10; Ps 72:18
*c*136:5 Pr 3:19; Jr 10:12; 51:15
*d*136:6 Ps 24:2
*e*136:7 Ps 74:16
*f*136:8-9 Gn 1:16
*g*136:10 Ex 12:29; Ps 78:51; 135:8
*h*136:12 Ex 6:1; Dt 4:34
*i*136:13 Ex 14:21; Ps 66:6; 78:13
*j*136:14 Ex 14:21-22; Ps 106:9
*k*136:15 Ex 14:27; Ps 78:53; 106:11
*l*136:16 Dt 8:15; Ps 78:52
*m*136:17-22 Nm 21:21-35; Ps 135:10-12
*n*136:23 Ps 106:45
*o*136:24 Ps 107:2
*p*136:25 Ps 104:27; 145:15
*q*136:26 Neh 1:5
*r*137:1 Ezk 1:1,3
*s*137:2 Jb 30:31; Ezk 26:13
*t*137:3 Ps 80:6
*u*137:4 Neh 12:46
*v*137:5 Is 65:11
*w*137:6 Jb 29:10; Ps 22:15; Ezk 3:26

136:4 On **wonders**, see 72:18; 75:1; 78:4; 96:3; 98:1; 105:5; 106:7,22; 107:8.

136:5 Skillfully is literally "through understanding" (78:72; Jb 26:12; Is 44:19; Jr 10:12; 51:15).

136:6-9 The psalmist summarized creation in terms of the separation of **land** and **waters** and the appointment of the **sun . . . moon**, and **stars** to regulate seasons and times (Gn 1:3-8,14-19). Noticeably absent are references to living creatures.

136:10 On **firstborn of the Egyptians**, see note at 135:8-9.

136:11-15 Strong hand and outstretched arm always refers to God's power and the deliverance of Israel (Dt 4:34; 5:15; 26:8; Jr 32:21), but especially to Israel's crossing of the Red Sea (Ex 14:2).

136:16 The **wilderness** refers to the 40 years of wandering by the Israelites (Dt 8:2; 29:4-5).

136:17-22 Compare this with 135:10-11. These **kings** were

famous for their military power. On **Sihon** and **Og**, see note at 135:11-12.

136:23-25 The Lord encouraged the Israelites in the land of Canaan, providing abundant resources for their livelihood (104:14-15,27-28; 145:15-16; 146:7; 147:9).

137:1 The rivers of Babylon were a series of canals running through the southern plain (Ezk 1:1; Dn 8:2). During the exile, the assembled community grieved there.

137:2 The **trees** of Babylon were not the familiar olive and cedar trees of the promised land.

137:3 By asking the community to sing **songs of Zion**, Israel's **captors** were tormenting and mocking them (42:3,10; 79:10).

137:4 The Israelites could not engage in worship since the land of Babylon was unclean and Israel had no temple.

137:5 The psalmist took an oath to stay loyal to **Jerusalem**, which represented the city, the land, and the temple, symbols of God's promise to Israel.

137:7 Remember reflects the theme of the psalm. Israel "re-

that day[A] at Jerusalem:
"Destroy it! Destroy it
down to its foundations!"[a]

8 Daughter Babylon,
doomed to destruction,
happy is the one who pays you back
what you have done to us.[b]

9 Happy is he who takes your little ones
and dashes them against the rocks.[c]

Psalm 138
A Thankful Heart

Davidic.

1 I will give You thanks
with all my heart;[d]
I will sing Your praise
before the heavenly beings.[B,e]

2 I will bow down
toward Your holy temple
and give thanks to Your name
for Your constant love and truth.
You have exalted Your name
and Your promise above
everything else.[f]

3 On the day I called, You answered me;
You increased strength within me.[C,g]

4 All the kings on earth
will give You thanks, Lord,
when they hear
what You have promised.[D,h]

5 They will sing of the Lord's ways,
for the Lord's glory is great.[i]

References (center column):

a137:7 Is 34:5-6; Ezk 35:2; Ob 10-14
b137:8 Jr 50:1-46; 51:1-64
c137:9 2Kg 8:12; Is 13:16; Nah 3:10
d138:1 Ps 111:1
e Ps 82:1,6-7; 95:3; 96:5
f138:2 1Kg 8:29; Ps 5:7; 28:2
g138:3 Ps 28:7; 46:1
h138:4 Ps 72:11; 102:15
i138:5 Ps 21:5; 145:7
j138:6 Ps 113:4-7; Pr 3:34; Jms 4:6
k138:7 Ps 23:4
l Ps 20:6; 60:5
m138:8 Ps 57:2; Php 1:6
n Jb 10:3; Ps 100:3
o139:1 Ps 17:3; 44:21; Jr 12:3
p139:2 2Kg 19:27; Is 66:18; Mt 9:4
q139:3 Jb 14:16; 31:4
r139:4 Heb 4:13
s139:5 Jb 9:33; Ps 125:2
t139:6 Jb 42:3; Rm 11:33

---

6 Though the Lord is exalted,
He takes note of the humble;
but He knows the haughty
from a distance.[j]

7 If I walk into the thick of danger,
You will preserve my life
from the anger of my enemies.[k]
You will extend Your hand;
Your right hand will save me.[l]

8 The Lord will fulfill His purpose
for me.[m]
Lord, Your love is eternal;
do not abandon the work of Your hands.[n]

Psalm 139
The All-Knowing, Ever-Present God

For the choir director. A Davidic psalm.

1 Lord, You have searched me
and known me.[o]

2 You know when I sit down and when
I stand up;
You understand my thoughts
from far away.[p]

3 You observe my travels and my rest;
You are aware of all my ways.[q]

4 Before a word is on my tongue,
You know all about it, Lord.[r]

5 You have encircled me;
You have placed Your hand on me.[s]

6 This extraordinary knowledge is
beyond me.
It is lofty; I am unable to reach it.[t]

A137:7 The day Jerusalem fell to the Babylonians in 586 B.C.   B138:1 Or *before the gods*, or *before judges*, or *before kings*; Hb *elohim*   C138:3 Hb obscure   D138:4 Lit *hear the words of Your mouth*

---

membered" Zion (v. 1), made a pledge to remember Jerusalem (vv. 5–6), and asked the Lord to "remember" Jerusalem's devastation by the Edomites (v. 7). The Edomites descended from Esau, the twin brother of Jacob, and served as Babylon's allies in the destruction of Jerusalem (Ezk 25:12; 36:5). **Destroy it** is literally "strip it down," that is, "raze it."

137:8 Who pays you back what you have done to us reinforces the concept of (Lat) *lex talionis*, or receiving a punishment equal to the crime (Ex 21:23-25; Mt 5:38-42). God pays back those who reject Him (Dt 7:10; 32:35; Is 65:6), and He specifically promised to repay Babylon for their crimes against His people (Jr 51:56).

137:9 This imprecation (see note at 109:1-31) is startling. Out of the psalmist's intense emotional state, seething with righteous anger, he called for the execution of just vengeance against the wicked who had perhaps done the described acts (**takes . . . and dashes**) to Israel's **little ones** (see note at Is 13:16).

138:1 On **before the heavenly beings**, or "before the gods," see note at 82:1.

138:2 Constant love translates the Hebrew word *chesed* (see word study at 136:1-26). The fulfillment of God's promises surpasses all previous revelation.

138:4-5 The universal outlook of the psalmist reflects a fairly new understanding for David—that **all the kings on earth** would someday worship the Lord (22:27-28). Solomon came to know it (72:11; 2Ch 6:33), and it was spoken through the prophets (Is 2:1-4; Rv 21:24).

138:6 From heaven (14:2; 33:13; 34:15; 102:19; 113:5; Is 57:15), God stoops to act on behalf of the downtrodden (**humble**; see note at 113:6), but He withholds assistance from those who are **haughty** or arrogant.

139:1-24 This psalm celebrates the attributes of God.

139:1-4 The Hebrew verbs can be interpreted as timeless truth: "You search me and You know me." God's attributes are not restricted to time. The words **know . . . understand . . . observe**, and **are aware** speak of God's omniscience. The word "observe" comes from the Hebrew root *zarah*, which means "measure." The Hebrew word for **ways** does not necessarily denote literal walking but daily behavior.

139:5 God's omnipresence guarantees protection. The first line is literally, "Back and front, You enclosed me." **Your hand on me** denotes absolute control over the psalmist, who was subject to the Lord's loving care and discipline.

139:6 God's attributes of omniscience and omnipresence are beyond human comprehension.

7 Where can I go to escape Your Spirit?
Where can I flee from Your presence?*[a]*
8 If I go up to heaven, You are there;*[b]*
if I make my bed in •Sheol,
You are there.*[c]*
9 If I live at the eastern horizon
or settle at the western limits,[A]
10 even there Your hand will lead me;
Your right hand will hold on to me.*[d]*
11 If I say, "Surely the darkness
will hide me,
and the light around me
will be night"—*[e]*
12 even the darkness is not dark to You.
The night shines like the day;
darkness and light are alike to You.*[f]*
13 For it was You who created
my inward parts;[B]
You knit me together
in my mother's womb.*[g]*
14 I will praise You
because I have been remarkably
and wonderfully made.[C,D]
Your works are wonderful,
and I know this very well.*[h]*
15 My bones were not hidden from You
when I was made in secret,
when I was formed in the depths
of the earth.*[i]*

16 Your eyes saw me when
I was formless;
all my days were written in Your book
and planned
before a single one of them began.*[j]*
17 God, how difficult[E] Your thoughts are
for me to comprehend;
how vast their sum is!
18 If I counted them,
they would outnumber the grains
of sand;*[k]*
when I wake up,[F] I am still with You.*[l]*
19 God, if only You would kill
the wicked—
you bloodthirsty men, stay away
from me*[m]*—
20 who invoke You deceitfully.
Your enemies swear by You falsely.*[n]*
21 Lord, don't I hate those who hate You,
and detest those who rebel
against You?
22 I hate them with extreme hatred;
I consider them my enemies.*[o]*
23 Search me, God, and know my heart;
test me and know my concerns.*[p]*
24 See if there is any
offensive[G] way in me;
lead me in the everlasting way.*[q]*

---

[a] 139:7 Jr 23:24
[b] 139:8 Am 9:2-4
[c] Jb 26:6; Is 14:11
[d] 139:9-10 Ps 23:2-3
[e] 139:11 Jb 22:13-14
[f] 139:12 Jb 34:22; Dn 2:22
[g] 139:13 Jb 10:11; Ps 119:73
[h] 139:14 Ps 40:5
[i] 139:15 Jb 10:8-10; Ps 63:9; Ec 11:5
[j] 139:16 Jb 14:5
[k] 139:17-18 Ps 40:5; 92:5
[l] 139:18 Ps 3:5
[m] 139:19 Ps 5:6; 6:8; Is 11:4
[n] 139:20 Ex 20:7; Jd 15
[o] 139:21-22 Ps 26:5; 31:16
[p] 139:23 Jb 31:6; Ps 26:2
[q] 139:24 Ps 16:11

A 139:9 Lit *I take up the wings of the dawn; I dwell at the end of the sea*   B 139:13 Lit *my kidneys*   C 139:14 DSS, some LXX mss, Syr, Jer read *because You are remarkable and wonderful*   D 139:14 Hb obscure   E 139:17 Or *precious*   F 139:18 Some Hb mss read *I come to an end*   G 139:24 Or *idolatrous*

139:7 The psalmist could not remove himself from the realm of God's transcendence, nor could he run from God's immanent and personal engagement with him (Jr 23:24; Am 9:2-4; Heb 4:13). The concept is both frightening and comforting.

139:8 The notion of escaping to heaven and hell finds its roots in ancient Near Eastern mythology. The OT acknowledges God's ability to access **Sheol** because He is sovereign (Jb 26:6; Am 9:2), but banishment to the underworld removes a person from God's blessing (Ps 6:5; Ec 9:10).

139:9 Live at the eastern horizon is literally "take up the wings of the dawn" (see textual footnote). The LXX renders the phrase, "if I lift my wings to the dawn," reinforcing the concept of flying a long distance to avoid God's presence.

139:10 The Lord's authority extends beyond the cosmos, and His sovereignty recognizes no limits. Every human being is under the power, protection, and authority of God.

139:11 Evildoers cannot conceal their deeds from God (Jb 22:11-14; 34:22).

139:12 Light and **darkness** are artificial distinctions for the Lord, who transcends creation.

139:13 Humankind is the Lord's possession and His creation (Gn 14:19,22; Dt 32:6). **Inward parts** (lit "kidneys") often denote the seat of emotion or affection (16:7; 73:21; Jb 19:27).

139:14 The expression **wonderfully made** is a forceful ren-

dering of the text. God's creation testifies to His power and majesty (Rm 1:20).

139:15 The phrase **depths of the earth** is normally associated with death (63:9; Ezk 26:20), but here it is figurative for the concealment of the womb.

139:16 The concept of the Lord's book that records the existence of all human beings reinforces God's sovereignty over life and death (69:28; Ex 32:32-33).

139:17 How vast their sum denotes the superiority of God's knowledge in quality and quantity.

139:18 The sum of everything God knows is immeasurable (Is 55:8). **When I wake up** could refer to having pondered God's knowledge all night, or to the resurrection.

139:19-22 On hate for enemies, see notes at 15:4 and 109:1-31. The psalmist wished to escape the influence of wicked liars. His zeal for God and righteousness gave him a single-minded determination. Such zeal is commendable (Jn 2:17; 2Co 7:11), but in calmer times it is directed toward love and mercy (Gl 1:14-16; Php 3:6-7).

139:23-24 Concluding with an appeal for God to **search me** (cp. v. 1), the psalmist submitted his thoughts and motives (**concerns**) to the Lord's scrutiny. He asked God to reveal any **offensive way** (lit "way of hardship") in him. The Scriptures speak of two opposite ways: that of the upright and that of the wicked (Ps 1; Pr 12:28; Mt 7:13-14).

Psalm 140
Prayer for Rescue

For the choir director. A Davidic psalm.

1 Rescue me, LORD, from evil men.
Keep me safe from violent men[a]
2 who plan evil in their hearts.
They stir up wars all day long.[b]
3 They make their tongues
as sharp as a snake's bite;
viper's venom is under their lips.[c]
•Selah

4 Protect me, LORD,
from the clutches of the wicked.[d]
Keep me safe from violent men
who plan to make me stumble.[A,e]
5 The proud hide a trap with ropes for me;
they spread a net along the path
and set snares for me.[f]　Selah

6 I say to the LORD, "You are my God."
Listen, LORD, to my cry for help.[g]
7 Lord GOD, my strong Savior,
You shield my head on the day of battle.[h]
8 LORD, do not grant the desires
of the wicked;
do not let them achieve their goals.
Otherwise, they will become proud.[i]
Selah

9 When those who surround me rise up,[B]
may the trouble their lips cause
overwhelm them.[j]
10 Let hot coals fall on them.
Let them be thrown into the fire,
into the abyss, never again to rise.[k]

11 Do not let a slanderer stay in the land.
Let evil relentlessly[c] hunt down
a violent man.[l]
12 I[D] know that the LORD upholds
the just cause of the poor,
justice for the needy.[m]
13 Surely the righteous will praise
Your name;
the upright will live in Your presence.[n]

Psalm 141
Protection from Sin and Sinners

A Davidic psalm.

1 LORD, I call on You; hurry to help me.
Listen to my voice when I call on You.[o]
2 May my prayer be set before You
as incense,[p]
the raising of my hands
as the evening offering.[q]

3 LORD, set up a guard for my mouth;
keep watch at the door of my lips.[r]
4 Do not let my heart turn
to any evil thing
or perform wicked acts
with men who commit sin.
Do not let me feast on their delicacies.[s]
5 Let the righteous one strike me—
it is an act of faithful love;
let him rebuke me—
it is oil for my head;
let me[E] not refuse it.[t]
Even now my prayer is against
the evil acts of the wicked.[F,u]

---

[a]140:1 Ps 18:48; 71:4
[b]140:2 Ps 36:4; 56:6; Pr 6:14
[c]140:3 Ps 58:4; Rm 3:13; Jms 3:8
[d]140:4 Ps 71:4
[e]Ps 36:11
[f]140:5 Ps 35:7; 141:9; 142:3
[g]140:6 Ps 31:14; 130:2
[h]140:7 Ps 28:8; 118:14
[i]140:8 Ps 10:2-3
[j]140:9 Ps 7:16; Pr 18:7
[k]140:10 Ps 11:6; 36:12
[l]140:11 Ps 34:21
[m]140:12 1Kg 8:45,49; Ps 9:4; 82:3
[n]140:13 Ps 11:7; 64:10
[o]141:1 Ps 22:19; 38:22; 70:5
[p]141:2 Ex 30:8
[q]Lk 1:10; Rv 5:8; 8:3-4
[r]141:3 Ps 34:13; 39:1; Pr 13:3; Mc 7:5
[s]141:4 Ps 119:36; Pr 23:6; Is 32:6
[t]141:5 Ec 7:5; Gl 6:1
[u]Ps 109:4

A140:4 Lit *to trip up my steps*　B140:9 Lit *Head of those who surround me*　C140:11 Hb obscure　D140:12 Alt Hb tradition reads *You*　E141:5 Lit *my head*　F141:5 Lit *of them*

140:1 On **violent men**, compare verses 4 and 11.

140:2-3 The metaphor of battle terminology refers to verbal attacks on the psalmist by his enemies. The reference to their **tongues** further supports verbal contention or litigation (58:5; 64:4; 120:4). Those who oppose God are often characterized as poisonous vipers or snakes (10:7; 55:21; 57:4; cp. Rm 3:13).

140:4 Clutches is a figurative expression denoting influence or control. **Violent men** were making false accusations and trying to trap the psalmist (v. 1).

140:5 Those who were **proud** believed their plans were beyond discovery. The psalms often describe the deceitful actions of wicked men in terms of traps and **snares** (9:15-16; 10:8-9; 31:4; 57:6; 119:110; 124:7; 141:9).

140:6 The psalmist sought the Lord's favorable response to the persecution he faced (28:2; 31:22; 86:6; 130:2).

140:9 The psalmist asked God to bring the lies of his attackers back down on their **heads** (7:15-16; 40:14-15; Pr 26:27).

140:10 Based on Aramaic and Ugaritic usage, the Hebrew word for **abyss** probably means "watery pits."

140:12 The Lord defends the most vulnerable people in society (10:18; 68:5; 146:7-9; Dt 10:18).

140:13 To **live in Your presence** is literally "dwell before You." To stand, walk, or live in God's presence implies a good relationship with God (16:11; 41:12; 56:13; Gn 17:1; 1Kg 2:4; 3:6; 8:23).

141:2 Offerings of **incense** were prescribed for both morning and **evening** (Ex 30:7-8; 2Kg 16:15). These represented prayers rising to God in heaven (Neh 13:5,9; Is 1:13; Jr 41:5). The lifting of **hands** was a common practice in worship (28:2; 63:4; 134:2).

141:3 The phrase **door of my lips**, figurative for exercising prudent speech, occurs only here.

141:4 The **delicacies** probably refer metaphorically to illicit sacrificial offerings and pleasurable acts of sin.

141:5 Pouring oil on the head was considered refreshing in that culture (23:5; 45:7; 133:2; Is 61:3; Jms 5:14). Constructive criticism from a **righteous one** is desirable; it would be foolish to **refuse it** (Pr 8:33-36; 15:32). The psalmist remains resolute in his opposition to evil.

6 When their rulers[A] will be thrown off
   the sides of a cliff,
   the people[B] will listen to my words,
   for they are pleasing.[a]

7 As when one plows and breaks up
      the soil,
   turning up rocks,
   so our[C] bones have been scattered
   at the mouth of *Sheol.[b]

8 But my eyes look to You, Lord GOD.
   I seek refuge in You; do not
      let me die.[D,c]

9 Protect me from[E] the trap they have set
      for me,
   and from the snares of evildoers.[d]

10 Let the wicked fall into their own nets,
   while I pass by safely.[e]

Psalm 142
A Cry of Distress

A Davidic *Maskil*. When he was
in the cave.[f] A prayer.

1 I cry aloud to the LORD;[g]
   I plead aloud to the LORD for mercy.[h]

2 I pour out my complaint before Him;
   I reveal my trouble to Him.[i]

3 Although my spirit is weak within me,
   You know my way.[j]

   Along this path I travel
   they have hidden a trap for me.[k]

4 Look to the right and see:[F]
   no one stands up for me;

---

a141:6 2Ch 25:12
b141:7 Ps 53:5; 88:3-5
c141:8 Ps 7:1; 57:1; 144:2
d141:9 Ps 38:12; 140:5
e141:10 Ps 7:15; 35:8; 57:6
f142:title 1Sm 22:1; 24:3
g142:1 Ps 3:4; 77:1
h30:8
i142:2 Ps 77:2; 102 title
j142:3 Ps 77:3; 143:4
k Ps 140:5
l142:4 Ps 69:20; Jr 25:35
m142:5 Ps 16:5; 27:13
n142:6 Ps 79:8; 116:6
o Ps 18:17
p142:7 Ps 13:6; 143:11
q143:1 Ps 71:2; 140:6
r143:2 Jb 14:3
s Jb 15:14; Ps 130:3; Rm 3:23
t143:3 Ps 88:3-6; Lm 3:6
u143:4 Ps 77:3; 142:3

---

   there is no refuge for me;
   no one cares about me.[l]

5 I cry to You, LORD;
   I say, "You are my shelter,
   my portion in the land of the living."[m]

6 Listen to my cry,
   for I am very weak.[n]
   Rescue me from those who pursue me,
   for they are too strong for me.[o]

7 Free me from prison
   so that I can praise Your name.
   The righteous will gather around me
   because You deal generously with me.[p]

Psalm 143
A Cry for Help

A Davidic psalm.

1 LORD, hear my prayer.
   In Your faithfulness listen to my plea,
   and in Your righteousness answer me.[q]

2 Do not bring Your servant
      into judgment,[r]
   for no one alive is righteous
      in Your sight.[s]

3 For the enemy has pursued me,
   crushing me to the ground,
   making me live in darkness
   like those long dead.[t]

4 My spirit is weak within me;
   my heart is overcome with dismay.[u]

5 I remember the days of old;
   I meditate on all You have done;

A141:6 Or *judges*   B141:6 Lit *cliff, and they*   C141:7 DSS reads *my*; some LXX mss, Syr read *their*   D141:8 Or *not pour out my life*
E141:9 Lit *from the hands of*   F142:4 DSS, LXX, Syr, Vg, Tg read *I look to the right and I see*

141:6 The psalmist will be vindicated. When the wicked rulers are deposed, their followers will come to see that the psalmist has been right.

141:7 The psalmist feels as though his people had been slaughtered and then not provided a proper burial (79:2-4).

141:8 The psalmist affirms his trust in God (2:12; 5:12; 57:1; 64:10; 71:1; 118:8; Is 14:32; 57:13).

141:9-10 While the **evildoers** sought to trap the psalmist, he asked God to cause the **wicked** to **fall** into their own snares (7:16; 9:16; 35:8; 69:22; 106:36; 140:9-11; Pr 26:27).

Ps 142 title The **cave** referred to here could be Adullam (1Sm 22:1) or En-gedi (1Sm 24:3-4; cp. Ps 57).

142:1-3 Turning to God when in distress showed that David trusted Him. David referred to his spirit as **weak**, denoting spiritual or physical collapse (77:3; 102 title; 143:4).

142:4 An advocate or defender normally stood on a person's **right** (16:8; 109:6; 110:5; 121:5). **No one stands up for me** is literally "no one recognizes me." **No one cares about me** is literally "no one seeks my soul." The psalmist lacked support.

142:5 A **portion** is another way of describing a person's inheritance (see note at 16:5-6).

142:6 In asking God to **listen**, David also wants God to act (55:2).

142:7 Being hunted and having to hide was like being in **prison**. It is appropriate for deliverance to be followed by public **praise** (see note at 22:22-24). **You deal generously with me** is literally "You pay back (Hb *gamal*) on my behalf," which could have double meaning: God would reward David and punish his false accusers (see note at 103:1-2).

143:1-12 In this psalm, David asked God, in His faithful love, to do what He had promised in His covenant.

143:2 Bring Your servant into judgment uses legal courtroom terminology typical of a covenant lawsuit (Jb 9:32; 14:3; Ec 11:9). As the psalmist began praying, he became self-conscious of his sinfulness. He acknowledged humanity's weaknesses (**no one . . . is righteous**) as a basis for a positive response from the Lord. The covenant relationship depended on the Lord's willingness to forgive (130:3-4; Jb 4:17; 9:2; 25:4; Rm 3:20; Gl 2:16).

143:4 As a result of being pursued, the psalmist was physically and spiritually exhausted (142:3).

143:5-6 The **work** of God's **hands** probably refers to all of His acts of creation and sustenance (8:6; 19:1; 28:5; 102:26; Is

I reflect on the work of Your hands.*a*

6 I spread out my hands to You;
I am like parched land before You.*b*
                        •*Selah*

7 Answer me quickly, LORD;
my spirit fails.*c*
Don't hide Your face from me,
or I will be like those
going down to the •Pit.*d*

8 Let me experience
Your faithful love in the morning,
for I trust in You.*e*
Reveal to me the way I should go
because I long for You.*f*

9 Rescue me from my enemies, LORD;
I come to You for protection.*A,g*

10 Teach me to do Your will,
for You are my God.*h*
May Your gracious Spirit
lead me on level ground.*i*

11 Because of Your name, •Yahweh,
let me live.
In Your righteousness deliver me
from trouble,*j*

12 and in Your faithful love
destroy my enemies.
Wipe out all those who attack me,
for I am Your servant.*k*

Psalm 144
A King's Prayer

Davidic.

1 May the LORD, my rock, be praised,*l*
who trains my hands for battle

and my fingers for warfare.*m*

2 He is my faithful love and my fortress,
my stronghold and my deliverer.
He is my shield,*n* and I take refuge
in Him;*o*
He subdues my people*B* under me.*p*

3 LORD, what is man,
that You care for him,
the son of man, that You think of him?*q*

4 Man is like a breath;
his days are like a passing shadow.*r*

5 LORD, part Your heavens
and come down.*s*
Touch the mountains,
and they will smoke.*t*

6 Flash Your lightning and scatter
the foe;*C*
shoot Your arrows and rout them.*u*

7 Reach down*D* from heaven;*v*
rescue me from deep water,
and set me free
from the grasp of foreigners*w*

8 whose mouths speak lies,
whose right hands are deceptive.*x*

9 God, I will sing a new song to You;
I will play on a ten-stringed harp
for You*y*—

10 the One who gives victory to kings,
who frees His servant David
from the deadly sword.*z*

11 Set me free and rescue me
from the grasp of foreigners*aa*
whose mouths speak lies,
whose right hands are deceptive.*ab*

Cross references (center column)

*a*143:5 Ps 77:5,10-12
*b*143:6 Jb 11:13; Ps 42:2; 63:1
*c*143:7 Ps 69:17; 102:2
*d*Ps 28:1; 88:4
*e*143:8 Ps 90:14
*f*Ps 25:1,4
*g*143:9 Ps 31:15; 59:1; 142:6
*h*143:10 Ps 25:4-5; 31:14; 63:1; 86:2; 119:12
*i*Ps 23:3
*j*143:11 Ps 25:11; 71:20
*k*143:12 Ps 54:5; 116:16
*l*144:1 1Sm 2:2; Ps 18:2; 19:14; 92:15; 95:1; Is 26:4
*m*Ps 18:34
*n*144:2 Dt 33:29; Ps 3:3; 28:7; 115:9-11; Pr 2:7
*o*2Sm 22:3; Ps 18:2; 71:1-3; 91:4; 144:2; Pr 30:5
*p*Ps 18:39,47
*q*144:3 Jb 7:17; Ps 8:4; Heb 2:6
*r*144:4 Ps 102:11; 109:23
*s*144:5 2Sm 22:10; Ps 18:9-10
*t*Ps 104:32
*u*144:6 Ps 18:14; Hab 3:11; Zch 9:14
*v*144:7 Ps 18:16
*w*Ps 69:14
*x*144:8 Ps 12:2; 41:6; 106:26
*y*144:9 Ps 33:2-3; 40:3
*z*144:10 Ps 18:50
*aa*144:11 Ps 69:14
*ab*Ps 12:2; 41:6; 106:26

A143:9 One Hb ms, LXX; some Hb mss read *I cover myself to You*   **B**144:2 Some Hb mss, DSS, Aq, Syr, Tg, Jer read *subdues peoples*; 2Sm 22:48; Ps 18:47   **C**144:6 Lit *scatter them*   **D**144:7 Lit *down Your hands*

5:12). When David looked back on what God had done in the past, he deeply desired God.

143:7 The **Pit**, like Sheol, meant death or the grave (30:3; 88:3-4; Is 14:11).

143:8 Based on the **faithful love** of the Lord, the psalmist asked for God's guidance in avoiding the traps set by the enemy (142:3).

143:10 In his weakness (v. 2), David recognized he needed God to **teach** him and **lead** him (cp. "Rescue" and "deliver" in vv. 9,11). **Level ground** refers to a path with nothing that would cause one to slip or stumble.

143:12 David appealed to God's **faithful love** when asking Him to **destroy** his **enemies**.

144:1-15 This psalm has a number of similarities with portions of Psalms 8 and 18. Isaiah developed some of these same themes.

144:1 Compare this verse with 18:34. On the Lord as a **rock**, see note at 18:1-2.

144:2 Compare this verse with 18:2,46-50.

144:3 On **son of man**, see note at 8:3-4. The emphasis of this verse is on God's concentrated attention on and His intimate knowledge of humanity.

144:4 The life of **man** is compared to a mere **breath**, reinforcing the fleeting nature of human existence (103:14-15; Is 40:6-8). On **like a passing shadow**, see note at 102:11.

144:5 Compare this verse with 18:9. The metaphorical imagery is consistent with the language of Psalm 18 and descriptions of the divine warrior (Am 9:5). **Mountains** tremble, **smoke** appears, and lightning accompanies the presence of the Lord.

144:6 The Lord scatters **lightning** bolts over the earth, directing them like arrows (18:14; Ezk 5:16; Zch 9:14).

144:7-8 Foreigners probably refer to those who worship false gods (18:44). **Lies** is literally "emptiness" (Is 59:4). **Whose right hands are deceptive** refers to those who swore falsely with a raised right hand (Dt 32:40) or while shaking hands (Pr 6:1).

144:9 On **new song**, see note at 33:1-3.

144:11 See note at verses 7-8.

12 Then our sons will be like plants
nurtured in their youth,
our daughters, like corner pillars
that are carved in the palace style.[a]
13 Our storehouses will be full,
supplying all kinds of produce;[b]
our flocks will increase by thousands
and tens of thousands in
our open fields.[c]
14 Our cattle will be well fed.[A]
There will be no breach in the walls,
no going into captivity,[B]
and no cry of lament in
our public squares.[d]
15 Happy are the people with
such blessings.
Happy are the people whose God
is •Yahweh.[e]

Psalm 145

Praising God's Greatness

A Davidic hymn.

1 I[C] exalt You, my God the King,
and praise Your name forever and ever.[f]
2 I will praise You every day;
I will honor Your name
forever and ever.[g]
3 •Yahweh is great and is highly praised;[h]
His greatness is unsearchable.[i]
4 One generation will declare Your works
to the next
and will proclaim Your mighty acts.[j]
5 I[D] will speak of Your splendor and
glorious majesty
and[E] Your wonderful works.[k]
6 They will proclaim the power
of Your awe-inspiring acts,
and I will declare Your greatness.[F,l]
7 They will give a testimony
of Your great goodness
and will joyfully sing
of Your righteousness.[m]
8 The LORD is gracious
and compassionate,
slow to anger and great in faithful love.[n]
9 The LORD is good to everyone;[o]
His compassion rests
on all He has made.[p]
10 All You have made will thank You, LORD;
the[G] godly will praise You.[q]
11 They will speak of the glory
of Your kingdom
and will declare Your might,[r]
12 informing all •people
of Your mighty acts

[a] 144:12 Ps 92:12-14; 128:3 [b] 144:13 Ps 107:37-38 [c] Pr 3:9-10 [d] 144:14 Is 24:11; Jr 14:2 [e] 144:15 Ps 33:12 [f] 145:1 Ps 30:1; 34:1; 99:5,9 [g] 145:2 Ps 146:2 [h] 145:3 Ps 48:1; 147:5 [i] Jb 5:9; 9:10; Is 40:28 [j] 145:4 Ps 22:30-31 [k] 145:5 Ps 119:27 [l] 145:6 Dt 10:21; Ps 106:2 [m] 145:7 Is 63:7 [n] 145:8 Ex 34:6; Ps 86:5,15; 103:8 [o] 145:9 Ac 14:17 [p] Ps 100:5 [q] 145:10 Ps 19:1; 103:22 [r] 145:11 Jr 14:21

[A] 144:14 Or *will bear heavy loads*, or *will be pregnant* [B] 144:14 Or *be no plague, no miscarriage* [C] 145:1 The lines of this poem form an •acrostic. [D] 145:5 LXX, Syr read *They* [E] 145:5 LXX, Syr read *and they will tell of* [F] 145:6 Alt Hb tradition, Jer read *great deeds* [G] 145:10 Lit *Your*

144:12 On **sons . . . like plants**, see notes at 80:8 and 80:9-11. The OT often refers to God's people in agrarian terms (44:2; Ex 15:17; Is 5:7; Hs 10:1).

144:14 Some interpreters believe the phrases **breach in the walls** and **going into captivity** look back on Jerusalem's destruction and Judah's exile, proving that this psalm was written after the exile. Others say it is a prophetic warning similar to that in Deuteronomy (Dt 28:52,63-64).

144:15 On **happy**, see note at 1:1.

145:1-21 This is an acrostic psalm. Each verse begins with a different letter of the Hebrew alphabet, and it has marked similarities with Psalm 111. The MT has no line beginning with the Hebrew letter *nun*.

145:1 The introduction places this psalm with other poems that herald the Lord as **King** (Pss 47; 93; 96–99).

145:3 Compare this verse with 96:4. God's superiority goes beyond comprehension (cp. 139:6; Is 40:28).

145:4 **One generation . . . to the next** is literally "generation to generation." The construction resembles "day after day" and "night after night" in 19:2. Both passages emphasize continuous praise of the Lord.

145:5 The Hebrew word *siyach* (**speak**) could be translated "meditate" (77:3,6,12).

145:7 **They will give a testimony** is literally "they will pour out a memory" (cp. 19:2).

145:8 The language of this verse exemplifies God's covenant love toward His people (103:4; 111:4; Ex 34:6-7).

145:9 God's benevolence extends to all His creatures (Mt 5:45). Often called "common grace," the concept is contrasted with God's particular grace, extended only to His chosen people, believers (Ps 145:18-20; Mt 24:31; Rm 11:5; 2Th 2:13).

145:10-12 **All people** will recognize God's sovereignty and dominion.

hadar

Hebrew Pronunciation	[hah DAHR]
HCSB Translation	splendor, honor
Uses in Psalms	13
Uses in the OT	30
Focus Passage	Psalm 145:5,12

The root in Aramaic denotes "honor" or "ornament." Arabic may add the idea of "swelling." *Hadar* particularly describes God's *splendor* (17x; Ps 104:1), which can be terrifying (Is 2:10). *Hadar* also indicates the *splendor* of animals (Dt 33:17), landscape (Is 35:2), people (Is 53:2), and cities (Lm 1:6). Trees are *majestic* (Lv 23:40). *Hadar* means *honor* (Ps 8:5). It is a collective signifying *dignitaries* (Is 5:14). *Hadar* is God's *blessing* in the sense of what is *splendid* (Mc 2:9). The verb *hadar* (7x) means *honor* (Lv 19:32) or *show respect* (Lm 5:12), but also *show favoritism* (Ex 23:3) and *give preference* (Lv 19:15). The passive participle means *splendid* (Is 63:1); it describes *uneven places* that are leveled (Is 45:2). The reflexive verb means *brag* (Pr 25:6). *Hadarah* (5x) refers to the *splendor* of God's holiness (Ps 96:9) except for one reference to a king's *splendor* (Pr 14:28).

and of the glorious splendor
of Your^A kingdom.^a

13 Your kingdom is
an everlasting kingdom;
Your rule is for all generations.^b
The Lord is faithful in all His words
and gracious in all His actions.^B,c

14 The Lord helps all who fall;
He raises up all who are oppressed.^C,d

15 All eyes look to You,
and You give them their food at the
proper time.^e

16 You open Your hand
and satisfy the desire
of every living thing.^f

17 The Lord is righteous in all His ways
and gracious in all His acts.^g

18 The Lord is near all who call out to Him,
all who call out to Him with integrity.^h

19 He fulfills the desires of those
who ˙fear Him;
He hears their cry for help
and saves them.^i

20 The Lord guards all those who love Him,
but He destroys all the wicked.^j

21 My mouth will declare Yahweh's praise;
let every living thing
praise His holy name forever and ever.^k

Psalm 146
The God of Compassion

1 ˙Hallelujah!
My soul, praise the Lord.^l

2 I will praise the Lord all my life;
I will sing to my God as long as I live.^m

---

a 145:12 Ps
105:1; 145:5
b 145:13 Ps
10:16; 2Pt 1:11
c Ps 103:8
d 145:14 Ps
37:24; 146:8
e 145:15 Ps
104:27; 136:25
f 145:16 Ps
104:28
g 145:17 Ps
116:5
h 145:18 Dt 4:7;
Ps 34:18; Jn
4:23-24
i 145:19 Ps
10:17; 21:2; 37:4
j 145:20 Ps
31:23; 97:10
k 145:21 Ps 65:2;
150:6
l 146:1 Ps 103:1
m 146:2 Ps 63:4;
104:33
n 146:3 Ps 60:11;
108:12; 118:8-9
o 146:4 Gn 2:7;
3:19
p 146:5 Ps
144:15; Jr 17:7
q 146:6 Ps
115:15; Ac 14:15
r Ps 117:2
s 146:7 Ps 103:6;
107:9
t Is 61:1
u 146:8 Mt 9:27-
30; Jn 9:7
v Ps 145:15
w Ps 11:7
x 146:9 Ex 22:22-
23; Dt 10:18
y Ps 147:6
z 146:10 Ex
15:18; Ps 10:16
aa 147:1 Ps 33:1;
135:3
ab 147:2 Ps
51:18; 102:16
ac Dt 30:3; Ezk
39:28

---

3 Do not trust in nobles,
in man, who cannot save.^n

4 When his breath^D leaves him,
he returns to the ground;
on that day his plans die.^o

5 Happy is the one whose help is the God
of Jacob,
whose hope is in the Lord his God,^p

6 the Maker of heaven and earth,
the sea and everything in them.^q
He remains faithful forever,^r

7 executing justice for the exploited
and giving food to the hungry.^s
The Lord frees prisoners.^t

8 The Lord opens the eyes of the blind.^u
The Lord raises up those
who are oppressed.^C,v
The Lord loves the righteous.^w

9 The Lord protects foreigners
and helps the fatherless
and the widow,^x
but He frustrates the ways
of the wicked.^y

10 The Lord reigns forever;
˙Zion, your God reigns
for all generations.^z
Hallelujah!

Psalm 147
God Restores Jerusalem

1 ˙Hallelujah!
How good it is to sing to our God,
for praise is pleasant and lovely.^aa

2 The Lord rebuilds Jerusalem;^ab
He gathers Israel's exiled people.^ac

A 145:12 LXX, Syr, Jer; MT reads *His*   B 145:13 One Hb ms, DSS, LXX, Syr; some Hb mss omit *The Lord is faithful in all His words and gracious in all His actions.*   C 145:14; 146:8 Lit *bowed down*   D 146:4 Or *spirit*

145:14 The Hebrew term *samak* (**help**) suggests sustenance and support (146:8).

145:16 Compare this verse with 104:28.

145:18-19 For those who trust Him, God is **near** like a friend and ready to help (cp. 138:6; Is 55:6; Jn 14:14).

145:21 Yahweh's **name** represents the revelation of His powerful presence and impeccable character (see note at 20:1).

146:1 The last five psalms each begin and end with **Hallelujah!** (see note at 104:35).

146:3 **Nobles** were the best of men—generous, giving freely (the "willing" in Ex 35:5,22). Such a person could help immensely in this life but could not bestow eternal life (Ps 118:9; cp. "ruler" in Pr 19:6).

146:4 The fleeting nature of life affects everyone, and every man (Hb *'adam* in v. 3) eventually returns to the **ground** (Hb *'adamah*), reversing creation (Gn 2:7; 3:19). Kings and leaders suffer the same fate (Ps 39:5-6; 90:3-6; 102:11).

146:5 The phrase **God of Jacob** recalls Israel's early history before it became an established nation (20:1; 46:7,11; 84:8; cp. Ex 3:15).

146:6 The formula **Maker of heaven and earth . . . and everything in them** often occurs as a polemic, underscoring the omnipotence of the Lord and contrasting His power with impotent gods and leaders (96:5; Neh 9:6; Is 37:16; 44:24; 45:18). The Lord's integrity is guaranteed by His holy nature.

146:7-9 The psalmist emphasized God's faithful provision and His role as deliverer (68:6; 82:3-4; Is 42:7). He defends the cause of Israel's most vulnerable citizens (see note at Ps 68:5). This practice is based in cultic law that was established early in Israel's history (Ex 22:21-22; Dt 24:17).

146:10 The Lord, as Israel's King, will reign **forever**, rendering the help earthly kings cannot provide (cp. vv. 3-4).

147:1 On **Hallelujah!** see note at 146:1.

147:2-3 The restoration and return of Israel to the land is expressed as spiritual and physical healing. Isaiah 61:1 uses

3 He heals the brokenhearted
   and binds up their wounds.*a*
4 He counts the number of the stars;
   He gives names to all of them.*b*
5 Our Lord is great, vast in power;
   His understanding is infinite.*A,c*
6 The LORD helps the afflicted
   but brings the wicked to the ground.*d*

7 Sing to the LORD with thanksgiving;
   play the lyre to our God,*e*
8 who covers the sky with clouds,
   prepares rain for the earth,
   and causes grass to grow on the hills.*f*
9 He provides the animals with their food,
   and the young ravens, what they cry for.*g*

10 He is not impressed by the strength
   of a horse;
   He does not value the power*B* of a man.*h*
11 The LORD values those who fear Him,
   those who put their hope
   in His faithful love.*i*

12 Exalt the LORD, Jerusalem;
   praise your God, *Zion!*j*
13 For He strengthens the bars
   of your gates
   and blesses your children within you.*k*
14 He endows your territory
   with prosperity;*C,l*
   He satisfies you with the finest wheat.*m*

15 He sends His command
   throughout the earth;
   His word runs swiftly.*n*
16 He spreads snow like wool;
   He scatters frost like ashes;*o*
17 He throws His hailstones
   like crumbs.
   Who can withstand His cold?*p*
18 He sends His word and melts them;
   He unleashes His winds,*D*
   and the waters flow.*q*

19 He declares His word to Jacob,
   His statutes and judgments to Israel.*r*
20 He has not done this for any nation;
   they do not know*E* His judgments.*s*
   Hallelujah!

Psalm 148
Creation's Praise of the LORD

1 *Hallelujah!*
   Praise the LORD from the heavens;
   praise Him in the heights.*t*
2 Praise Him, all His angels;
   praise Him, all His *hosts.*u*
3 Praise Him, sun and moon;
   praise Him, all you shining stars.*v*
4 Praise Him, highest heavens,
   and you waters above the heavens.*w*
5 Let them praise the name of *Yahweh,

Cross references
a147:3 Ps 34:18; Is 61:1
b147:4 Gn 15:5; Is 40:26
c147:5 Ps 48:1; Is 40:28
d147:6 Ps 146:8-9
e147:7 Ps 33:2; 95:1-2
f147:8 Jb 5:10; 38:27; Ps 104:14
g147:9 Jb 38:41; Ps 104:27-28
h147:10 Ps 33:17
i147:11 Ps 33:18; 149:4
j147:12 Ps 99:5,9
k147:13 Neh 7:3
l147:14 Is 54:13
m Dt 32:14; Ps 81:16
n147:15 Ps 104:4
o147:16 Jb 37:6; 38:29
p147:17 Jb 37:9-10
q147:18 Ps 33:9; 107:20
r147:19 Dt 33:2-4; Mal 4:4
s147:20 Dt 4:7,32-34
t148:1 Ps 69:34; Mt 21:9
u148:2 Ps 103:20-21
v148:3 1Co 15:41
w148:4 Gn 1:7; Dt 10:14; 1Kg 8:27

A147:5 Lit *understanding has no number*   B147:10 Lit *legs*   C147:14 Or *peace*   D147:18 Or *breath*   E147:20 DSS, LXX, Syr, Tg read *He has not made known to them*

---

some of the same words—to **bind up** the **brokenhearted**—which Jesus the Messiah fulfilled (Lk 4:18-21).

147:4-5 While the Lord **counts** (Hb *mispar*) the **stars** (Is 40:26), humanity is unable to measure (Hb *mispar*) the Lord's **understanding**.

147:6 God rights wrongs and reverses fortunes (7:14-16; 18:27; 113:8; 1Pt 5:5).

147:7 On **sing to the LORD** and **lyre**, see note at 33:1-3.

147:8 Three lines trace the progression from **clouds**, to **rain**, to vegetation. The Lord attends to every aspect of the cosmos, and nothing escapes His attention (72:6; 85:11; 104:14; Is 45:8; 61:11).

147:9 Compare the imagery of this verse with Jb 38:41.

147:10-11 God determines the outcome of any situation, and when He evaluates the participants, **strength** and **power** do not impress Him (33:16-17). Rather, He seeks to intervene on behalf of those who **fear** and trust Him (2Ch 16:9).

147:13 In a clever wordplay, the psalmist described the Lord as strengthening the **bars** (Hb *beriychey*) of Jerusalem's **gates** and blessing (Hb *barak*) her **children** (Hb *beniyk*; "sons") in her midst (Hb *beqirbek*). The Lord will restore Judah's protection and offspring.

147:14 The sovereign Lord controls the productivity of the land. His blessing is described in terms of the abundance that Israel will enjoy.

147:15 In a progressive development of the **word** of God, the Lord **sends** (Hb *shalach*) forth **His command**. His spoken **word** accomplishes all that He declares (v. 18; Is 55:10-11).

147:16-17 Compare these verses with Job 37–38 for God's sovereignty over the weather. Nothing is unaffected by the Lord's **cold**, which permeates creation.

147:18 The psalmist reinforced the association between the Lord's creative word and His spoken **word**. The Hebrew word for **winds** (*ruach*) could also be translated "breath."

147:19-20 Describing the Lord's **word** as revelatory, the psalmist alluded to Dt 4:7-8, a text characterizing Israel as unique, with divinely ordained standards to regulate her relationship with God.

148:1 On **Hallelujah!** see note at 146:1. Compare this verse with 19:1; 29:1.

148:2-3 A military term denoting armies, **hosts** often refers to the stars and other heavenly bodies (1Kg 22:19; 2Kg 23:5; Jr 31:35; cp. 1Sm 17:45).

148:4 **Waters above the heavens** is figurative for celestial waters, the reservoirs from which God is said to have brought rain (104:3; Gn 1:6-7; 7:11).

148:5 The powerful word of the Lord (33:9) spoke the world into existence (Gn 1). The Hebrew word *bara'* ("create") is only used in reference to God.

for He commanded,
and they were created.[a]

6 He set them in position forever and ever;
He gave an order that will never
pass away.[b]

7 Praise the LORD from the earth,
all sea monsters and ocean depths,[c]

8 lightning[A] and hail, snow and cloud,
powerful wind that executes
His command,[d]

9 mountains and all hills,
fruit trees and all cedars,[e]

10 wild animals and all cattle,
creatures that crawl and flying birds,[f]

11 kings of the earth and all peoples,
princes and all judges of the earth,[g]

12 young men as well as young women,
old and young together.[h]

13 Let them praise the name of Yahweh,
for His name alone is exalted.
His majesty covers heaven and earth.[i]

14 He has raised up a •horn for His people,
resulting in praise to all His godly ones,
to the Israelites, the people
close to Him.[j]
Hallelujah!

Psalm 149
Praise for God's Triumph

1 •Hallelujah!
Sing to the LORD a new song,[k]
His praise in the assembly of the godly.[l]

2 Let Israel celebrate its Maker;

let the children of •Zion rejoice
in their King.[m]

3 Let them praise His name
with dancing
and make music to Him
with tambourine and lyre.[n]

4 For •Yahweh takes pleasure
in His people;[o]
He adorns the humble
with salvation.[p]

5 Let the godly celebrate
in triumphal glory;
let them shout for joy on their beds.[q]

6 Let the exaltation of God be
in their mouths[B]
and a double-edged sword
in their hands,[r]

7 inflicting vengeance on the nations
and punishment on the peoples,[s]

8 binding their kings with chains
and their dignitaries with iron shackles,[t]

9 carrying out the judgment
decreed against them.
This honor is for all His godly people.[u]
Hallelujah!

Psalm 150
Praise the LORD

1 •Hallelujah!
Praise God in His sanctuary.
Praise Him in His mighty heavens.[v]

2 Praise Him for His powerful acts;[w]
praise Him for His abundant greatness.[x]

[a]148:5 Ps 33:6,9
[b]148:6 Jr 31:35-36; 33:20,25
[c]148:7 Gn 1:2,21; Ps 74:13
[d]148:8 Ps 18:12; 103:20; 147:16
[e]148:9 Is 44:23; 49:13; 55:12
[f]148:10 Is 43:20; Hs 2:18
[g]148:11 Ps 102:15
[h]148:11-12 Rv 7:9
[i]148:13 Ps 8:1; 113:4; Is 12:4
[j]148:14 Dt 10:21; Jr 17:14; Eph 2:17
[k]149:1 Ps 33:3
[l]Ps 35:18; 89:5
[m]149:2 Ps 95:6; Zch 9:9
[n]149:3 Ps 30:11; 81:2
[o]149:4 Ps 147:11; Rm 8:8; 1Co 1:21
[p]Ps 35:27; Is 61:3
[q]149:5 Jb 35:10; Ps 132:16
[r]149:6 Ps 66:17; Heb 4:12
[s]149:7 Ezk 25:16-17; Mc 5:15
[t]149:8 Jb 36:8
[u]149:9 Ps 148:14; Ezk 28:26
[v]150:1 Ps 11:4; 19:1
[w]150:2 Ps 145:12
[x]Dt 3:24

A 148:8 Or *fire*   B 149:6 Lit *throat*

148:6 God established creation and set boundaries, exercising sovereign control over the cosmos (104:9; Gn 1:6-10; 9:11; Jb 28:26; 38:8-10).

148:7 The psalmist contrasted the three levels of heaven (vv. 5-6) with three levels of the earth. Even **sea monsters** (Hb *tannin*) are called on to praise God (69:34).

148:8 The elements of nature perform at God's command (103:20; 104:4).

148:9-10 The psalmist hinted at the creation account in these verses, using peculiar expressions typical of Genesis 1.

148:11-12 The list of people represents descending social status. All people are united in worship (Rm 10:12; Gl 3:28; Col 3:11). Prophets, priests, and other temple personnel were not mentioned, perhaps because they were the ones who were calling all others to praise God.

148:14 To raise **a horn** signifies strength (see notes at 18:1-2; 75:4; 89:15-17).

149:1 On **Hallelujah!** see note at 146:1. This introduction **sing . . . a new song** usually denotes dynamic intervention not previously experienced by the writer (33:1-3; 96:1; 98:1;

Is 42:10; 61:1). **The godly** (see note at 132:9) is a designation for Israel.

149:2 The Hebrew for **its Maker** (be'osayw) is a plural of majesty (Jb 35:10; Is 54:5). Israel is doubly obligated to honor God since He is both their Creator and their **King**.

149:3 **Dancing** and **music** were typical modes of worship in the temple (30:11; 87:7; 150:4).

149:4-5 Just as Israel glorified God, so the Lord adorned Israel by saving them and giving them **glory** (Is 60:9; 61:1-3).

149:6 The Hebrew word for **double-edged** consists of a variation on the word *peh* ("mouth"), an archaic form of the plural *(piphiyyoth)* meaning "multi-mouthed." Isaiah 41:15 has the same word, translated "many teeth." In Pr 5:4 "double-edged" is the plural "mouths" and in Jdg 3:16 it is literally "two mouths."

149:7-9 God will put the sword (v. 6) in Israel's hand to execute retaliation for wrongdoing (18:47; 58:11; 79:10; 94:1; cp. Est 9:5; Is 13:3; Rm 13:4). Just as God's people were captured and imprisoned, so the Lord will bind **kings** with **chains** and **shackles** (Is 45:14). Submission of world powers to God's **people** will bring **honor** to Israel.

150:1 On **Hallelujah!** see note at 146:1.

3 Praise Him with trumpet blast;[a]
   praise Him with harp
      and lyre.[b]
4 Praise Him with tambourine
      and dance;[c]
   praise Him with flute
      and strings.[d]

[a]150:3 Ps 98:6
[b]Ps 33:2
[c]150:4 Ps 149:3
[d]Jb 21:12; Ps 45:8
[e]150:5 2Sm 6:5; 1Ch 13:8
[f]150:6 Ps 145:21

5 Praise Him
      with resounding cymbals;
   praise Him with clashing cymbals.[e]
6 Let everything that breathes
      praise the LORD.[f]
   Hallelujah!

150:3-5 The sophistication of ancient sacred music is clear from the wide range of instruments used in temple worship. All three classifications—wind instruments, strings, and percussion—are represented.

150:6 It is only logical that everything that has been given the breath of life from the Creator ought to praise Him (149:2).

Proverbs

What is a proverb? A secular proverb seeks to state a general (not absolute) truth, such as "a fool and his money are soon parted." It is typically pithy, that is, it is brief but rich in meaning: "No pain, no gain." A proverb is practical; it gives advice that is useful in the real world: "A stitch in time saves nine." It should be applied; the reader should consider what changes he should make in his own life in light of the proverb: "Charity begins at home." A proverb is derived from astute observations about how life usually works; the creator of a proverb shows himself very knowledgeable and perceptive, able to see what is generally true and to draw conclusions from it: "The pen is mightier than the sword."

"Wisdom calls out in the street; she raises her voice in the public squares. She cries out above the commotion; she speaks at the entrance of the city gates: 'How long, foolish ones, will you love ignorance?'" (1:20-22a).

In addition to all this, the proverbs in the book of Proverbs are also divinely inspired. Since they come from God, we know they are true and we can be certain they are beneficial: "The one who understands a matter finds success, and the one who trusts in the LORD will be happy" (16:20). Biblical proverbs not only offer practical advice for this life but also guide the reader to eternal life: "For the discerning the path of life leads upward, so that he may avoid going down to Sheol" (15:24).

Circumstances of Writing

Author: Solomon is credited with the proverbs in chapters 1–29 of the book of Proverbs (1:1; 10:1). There is biblical evidence that Solomon was wise and a collector of wise sayings (1Kg 3:5-14; 4:29-34; 5:7,12; 10:2-3,23-24; 11:41). Chapters 1–24 may have been written down during his reign, 970–931 B.C. The proverbs in chapters 25–29 were Solomon's proverbs collected by King Hezekiah, who reigned 716–687 B.C. (25:1). The last two chapters are credited to Agur and Lemuel (30:1; 31:1), about whom nothing else is known. An editor was inspired to collect the proverbs of Solomon, Agur, and Lemuel into the book that we now have.

Background: The reign of Solomon represented the peak of prosperity for the nation of Israel. The period saw the greatest extent of the territory, and there was peace and international trade (1Kg 4:20-25; 10:21-29). It is likely that Solomon knew about the ancient tradition of wisdom in Egypt (1Kg 3:1), but through inspiration and God's gift he composed even better sayings (1Kg 3:12; 10:6-7,23). Solomon addressed his teaching to his son or sons, but these inspired wise sayings are applicable to all people. The book of Proverbs, like the rest of the Bible, contains stories, teaching, and examples. People should make appropriate application of these truths to their own situation (1Co 10:11).

Message and Purpose

Because these proverbs are in the Bible, they do not just entertain; they exhort, encourage, and offer hope. Solomon called readers, especially youth, to pursue wisdom rather than foolishness. He encouraged the inexperienced to become wise rather than mockers, to be teachable rather than incorrigible, to live rather than to

5000 B.C.

1800 B.C.

Abraham 2166–1991

The Instruction of Prince Hardjedef, Egyptian Old Kingdom 2686–2160

The Royal Instruction of Khety to Merikare, Egyptian 2160

The Instructions Addressed to Kagemni, Egyptian 2600

The Instruction of a Man for His Son, Egyptian Middle Kingdom 2040–1640

The Instruction of Ptah-Hotep, Egypt's Old Kingdom 2575–2134

The Instruction of King Amenemhet I for His Son Sesostris I, Egyptian 1925

Collections of proverbs found among the royal archives at Ebla 2450–2250

Instructions of Shuruppak, Sumerian Proverb Collection 1900–1700

die. He predicted that people who pursued wisdom would generally find success and happiness in this life, but he promised that they would absolutely find joy and blessing in eternity.

There is a close connection between wisdom and God. For example, both prescribe obedience and morality and both promise success and eternal life. They are connected because wisdom presupposes the fear of God; because God is the source of this inspired, godly advice; and because God is the One who guarantees the blessings that wisdom promises. The benefits of wisdom and of God are the same. What wisdom promises is what God grants (4:4-8).

Structure

The book of Proverbs is in the wisdom genre. Wisdom books consist of the intelligent author's observations on the world and the people in it. However, without an inspired godly perspective, the world would be depressing and hopeless, as parts of Job and Ecclesiastes show. Ultimately, biblical wisdom is informed by and founded on faith in God.

The process of observation, contemplation, and inspiration can be seen in Pr 24:30-34. After observing the deteriorated condition of "the field of a slacker" and "the vineyard of a man lacking sense," Solomon contemplated what he was seeing and was inspired: "I saw, and took it to heart; I looked, and received instruction" (v. 32). He either composed a new proverb or applied a familiar proverb to the situation: "a little sleep, a little slumber, a little folding of the arms to rest, and your poverty will come like a robber, your need, like a bandit" (vv. 33-34).

Proverbs is written as Hebrew poetry. Hebrew poetry is terse and concise, it uses a lot of imagery, and generally the second line complements or contrasts the thought of the first. Contemplating how the second line relates to the first is a profitable way to meditate on a proverb.

In chapters 1–9 Solomon used imagery and sustained arguments to teach about the value of wisdom and the

---

1600 B.C.

1200–800 B.C.

Moses 1526–1406

The Phoenicians develop a 22-letter alphabet that consisted of consonants only. It was read from right to left and became an important step in the development of the modern Western alphabet. This was the world's first purely phonetic alphabet. It was based on sounds and not symbolic representations of objects. 1600

The Counsels of Wisdom, Akkadian 1500–1200

Events in Judges 1380?–1060?

Samuel 1105?–1025?

The Instruction of Amenemope, Egypt 1186–1069

Saul anointed king 1050

David becomes king over all Israel. 1003

Solomon becomes king. 970

Proverbs 970

seduction of evil. In 22:17–24:34 there are "sayings" made up of several verses each, and in chapters 30–31 there are more sayings, including numerical sayings and an alphabetic acrostic in praise of a capable wife. In the rest of the book, each proverb is generally one verse. Some scholars argue that these individual proverbs are carefully arranged in groups and each should be interpreted in the context of its group. Other scholars view the collection as unsystematic and argue that the immediate context seldom has any bearing on interpretation.

In either case, it is important to interpret any single proverb in the context of the book of Proverbs and the Bible as a whole. For example, while 21:14 may seem to encourage bribery, the rest of the book of Proverbs is clearly against it (15:27), as is the rest of Scripture (Ex 23:8; Ec 7:7).

Outline

I. Solomon's Exhortations and Warnings (1:1–9:18)
  A. Contrast between wisdom and riches (1:1–3:20)
  B. Praise of wisdom, love, and worthy conduct (3:21–4:27)
  C. Warnings against lust, idleness, and deceit (5:1–7:27)
  D. A portrayal of wisdom (8:1–9:18)

II. Solomon's Proverbs (10:1–29:27)
  A. Collected proverbs (10:1–22:16)
  B. Thirty sayings of the wise (22:17–24:22)
  C. More sayings of the wise (24:23-34)
  D. Hezekiah's collection (25:1–29:27)

III. Other Proverbs (30:1–31:31)
  A. Words of Agur (30:1-33)
  B. Words of Lemuel (31:1-9)
  C. Praise of a capable wife (31:10-31)

PROVERBS TOPICAL CHART

HUMAN BEINGS

EMOTIONS

ANGER	indignation, vexation	12:16a; 17:25; 21:19; 27:3
	anger, indignation	14:17a; 14:29; 15:1; 16:32; 19:11a; 21:14; 22:24-25; 24:17-18; 27:4; 29:8b; 29:22; 30:33
	wrath, rage	11:4; 11:23b; 14:35; 20:2; 22:8
	rage, anger, troubled, sullen	19:12; 22:14
	burning anger, wrath, rage	6:34; 15:1; 15:18; 16:14; 19:19; 21:14; 22:24-25; 27:4; 29:22
ANXIETY	12:25a	
BITTERNESS	14:10a; 17:25	
DESIRE, JEALOUSY	lust, passion	10:24; 11:23; 13:12; 13:19a; 18:1; 19:22; 21:25-26; 23:6; 24:1
	desire, lust	3:15
	desire, lust, mischief	10:3; 17:4
	envy, jealousy	3:31; 6:34; 14:30; 23:17; 24:1a; 24:19b; 20:20b; 27:4
	desire, delight	21:20
GRIEF, SADNESS	10:1; 14:13; 17:21a	
HAPPY, BLESSED	8:32-36; 14:21b; 16:20b; 20:7; 31:28	
HEALING	3:7-8; 4:20-22; 12:18b; 13:17b; 14:30a; 15:4a; 16:24; 17:22a; 29:1	
HOPE	10:28a; 11:7a; 11:23; 13:12a; 19:18a; 23:18; 24:14; 26:12; 29:20	
JOY	10:28; 12:20b; 13:9a; 14:10b; 14:13b; 15:13a; 15:21a; 15:23a; 15:30; 17:21b; 21:15a; 23:15; 24:17; 27:9a; 27:11; 29:2a; 29:3a; 29:6b	
DELIGHT, REJOICING	8:30-31	
LOVE AND HATE	8:35-36; 9:8a; 10:12; 13:24; 14:20	
	love	1:22; 4:6b; 5:19a; 7:18; 8:17; 8:20-21; 9:8b; 15:9b; 16:13; 17:9a; 17:19a; 18:21; 19:8; 21:17; 27:5-6
	hate	1:29; 5:12; 6:16; 8:13; 10:18; 11:15; 12:1b; 13:5a; 14:17a; 14:20; 15:10b; 15:17; 15:27; 19:7a; 25:17; 25:21-22; 26:24-26; 26:28; 27:6; 28:16; 29:10a; 29:24; 30:21-23
PANIC, DREAD	1:33; 3:25-26; 28:14	
SEPARATION	17:11; 18:1	
SHAME	shame, ignominy, and disgrace	3:35; 6:32-33; 9:7a; 11:2a; 12:16; 13:18; 18:3; 25:8-10a
	causing shame	10:5b; 14:34-35; 17:2a; 19:26; 29:15b
SPIRIT	1:23; 11:29; 14:29; 15:4b; 15:13a; 16:2; 16:18-19; 16:32; 17:22b; 17:27b; 18:14; 25:28; 29:23	
FAMILY	11:29a; 15:27a; 17:13; 27:8	
	wife	5:18b-19; 12:4; 18:22; 19:13b-14b; 21:9; 21:19; 25:24; 27:15-16; 31:10-31
	both parents	1:8-9; 6:20-24; 10:1; 20:20; 23:22; 23:24-25; 28:24; 30:11-14; 30:17
	father	3:12; 4:1-9; 13:1; 15:5; 17:6; 19:13; 22:28; 28:7; 29:3
	mother	7:7; 10:1; 10:5; 13:1; 13:24; 14:26a; 15:20a; 17:2; 17:6; 17:25; 19:13a; 19:18; 19:26; 19:27; 20:7; 27:11; 28:7; 29:15; 29:17; 31:28a
	children	31:28a
	youth, boys	7:7; 20:11; 20:20; 22:6; 22:15; 23:13-14; 29:15
	grandchildren	13:22a; 17:6
	brother	6:19b; 17:17b; 18:19a; 18:24; 19:7; 27:10b
	widows	15:25b
	orphans	22:28; 23:10-11; 31:8
	ancestors	22:28; 23:10a

HUMAN BEINGS

FRIENDS, NEIGHBORS, STRANGERS, ENEMIES	friends, intimate companions, chief	16:28b; 17:9b
	neighbor, companion, friend	3:28-29; 6:1-5; 6:29; 11:9; 11:12; 12:26; 14:20-21; 16:29; 17:17a; 17:18; 18:17; 18:24a; 19:4; 19:6b-7; 21:10; 22:11; 24:28-29; 25:8-10; 25:17-18; 26:18-19; 27:9-10; 27:14; 29:5
	companions: good and bad	2:20; 3:31-32a; 13:20; 14:7; 19:6; 19:7; 20:19; 22:24-25; 23:20-21; 24:1-2; 24:21-22; 27:17; 29:5; 29:6
	nobles, philanthropists	17:7; 17:26; 18:16; 19:6
	stranger	5:10; 6:1-2; 11:15; 14:10; 20:16; 27:2; 27:13
	foreigner, stranger	5:10; 5:20; 6:23-24; 7:4-5; 20:16; 27:2; 27:13
	enemy	16:7; 24:17-18; 25:21-22; 27:6
	adulterer	6:26-35; 30:20
	other women	9:13; 14:1; 31:2-3
	strange woman, alien, foreign woman	2:16-19; 5:3-14; 5:20; 6:23-24; 7:4-5; 27:13
	whore	6:23-26; 7:4-27; 23:28
	virgin	30:18-19; 30:21-23
DYNAMICS OF RELATING	gossip and secrets	11:12-13; 16:28; 25:9b-10; 26:20
	the witness	6:19a; 12:17; 14:5; 14:25; 19:5; 19:9; 19:28; 21:28; 24:28-29; 25:9-10; 25:18; 26:18-19
	betrayal (treachery)	11:6; 13:2; 13:15; 21:18b; 25:19; 26:18-19; 26:28; 29:12
	braggart	27:1-2
	meddling	26:17
	disputes — quarreling	22:10
	disputes — strife, contention	3:30; 15:18; 17:1; 17:14; 17:19a; 18:6a; 20:3; 26:17; 26:21
	disputes — strife	13:10; 17:19

OUR TONGUES AND BODIES

LONGEVITY	3:1-2; 3:16-18; 4:10; 8:35-36; 9:11; 10:11; 12:28; 13:3a; 13:12b; 13:14; 14:12; 14:27; 14:32b; 15:27b; 16:22; 18:21; 19:16; 19:23a; 23:17-18
STRENGTH — strength, mighty, fierce	10:29a; 21:22; 24:5; 30:25; 31:17a; 31:25
STRENGTH — strength, vigor, power	14:4; 14:26; 18:10; 18:19; 20:29; 21:22; 24:5; 24:10
STRENGTH — strength, valor, might	8:14; 21:22
STRENGTH — strength, power, valor, army	12:4; 31:3
OUR BODY	3:6-8; 5:3-6; 6:10-11; 6:12-14a; 6:16-19; 6:20-26; 7:1-3; 12:13-15a; 14:30; 15:30; 20:27; 25:19; 31:12-13
BONES	12:4; 14:30; 15:30; 17:22b; 25:15
HEAD	1:8-9; 25:22
GRAY HAIR	16:31; 20:27
FACE	7:13; 10:26; 15:13; 20:12-13; 21:29a; 23:9; 24:23; 27:19-20; 30:11-14
EYE	4:25; 6:4; 15:3; 16:30a; 17:24; 20:8; 21:4; 22:12; 23:5; 23:26; 28:27; 29:13
EAR	2:2; 4:20; 5:1; 15:31; 21:13; 22:17; 23:12; 25:12; 28:9
MOUTH, TONGUE, LIPS	4:24; 6:1-3; 7:21; 8:6-9; 8:13b; 10:6; 10:11; 10:13-14; 10:18-21a; 10:31-32; 11:9a; 11:12-13; 12:13a; 12:14; 12:17-19; 12:22; 12:25b; 13:2a; 13:3; 14:3; 14:7; 14:23; 15:1-2; 15:4; 15:7; 15:14b; 15:23; 15:26b; 15:28; 16:1; 16:10; 16:13; 16:21b; 16:23-24; 16:27b; 16:28b; 17:4; 17:7; 17:20b; 17:27a; 17:28; 18:4; 18:6-8; 18:13; 18:17; 18:20-21; 19:1; 19:9; 19:28; 20:15; 20:17; 20:19; 20:25; 21:6; 21:23; 21:28; 22:11-12; 22:14; 22:18; 23:9; 23:16; 24:2; 24:7; 24:26; 24:28-29; 25:9b-10; 25:11-15; 25:18; 25:23; 26:7; 26:9; 26:20-28; 27:2; 29:20; 30:10; 30:32; 31:8-9; 31:26
NECK	1:8-9; 3:3-4; 3:21-22; 6:20-21
HAND	12:14; 14:1; 21:25; 31:13b; 31:16b; 31:19-20; 31:31a
HEART	3:5; 4:23; 6:20-21; 13:12a; 14:10; 14:13; 15:11; 15:13a; 15:15b; 15:21a; 15:28a; 15:32b; 16:9a; 17:3b; 17:22a; 18:12; 18:15; 19:3; 19:8a; 19:21; 20:5a; 20:9; 20:30; 23:15; 24:12
FOOT	1:15-16; 3:6; 3:23-26; 4:11; 4:14-19; 4:26-27; 5:5; 5:21; 6:28-29b; 7:11; 16:9; 20:24; 26:6; 29:5

GODLY TRAITS

BLESSED	blessed, benediction	3:33; 5:18a; 10:6a; 10:7a; 10:22; 11:11; 11:24; 11:26; 20:21; 22:9; 24:25; 27:14; 28:20; 30:11
	blessed, happy	See Human Beings/Emotions/Happy, Blessed
COVER, CONCEAL		10:6b; 10:11b; 10:12; 10:18; 11:13; 12:16b; 12:23; 17:9; 24:31; 25:2; 26:26

Proverbs Topical Chart

HUMAN BEINGS

GODLY TRAITS (CONTINUED)

DISCERNING, JUDICIOUS, ASTUTE	17:10; 17:24a; 28:2; 28:7; 28:11	
DISCRETION	discretion, devising, plotting	2:11; 3:21; 5:2; 8:12; 11:19; 12:2; 12:12a; 14:17; 14:19; 24:8c
	discretion, taste, flavor	11:22
FEAR	fear, to be afraid, to revere	1:29; 2:2,5; 3:7; 8:13; 9:10; 10:24; 10:27; 14:2; 14:16; 14:26-27; 15:16a; 15:33a; 16:6b; 19:23; 22:4; 23:17; 24:21; 28:14; 29:25; 31:30b
	fear	1:26-27; 1:33; 3:25
GLORY	4:8-9	
	glory, ornament, beauty, finery	16:31; 17:6; 20:29
	honor, respect, reverence	3:9; 3:16; 3:35; 8:18; 11:16a; 15:33b; 18:12b; 20:3; 21:21; 22:4; 25:27; 26:1; 26:8; 29:23
	ornament, splendor, honor	14:28
EVEN, STRAIGHT, LEVEL	1:3; 2:9-10	
HUMBLE, LOWLY, MEEK	3:34; 15:33b; 18:12; 22:4	
INTEGRITY, BLAMELESS, WHOLENESS	2:7; 2:21; 10:9a; 11:3; 11:5a; 11:20b; 13:6a; 19:1; 20:7; 28:6; 28:18; 29:10	
LEARNING, INSTRUCTION	1:5a; 4:2a; 9:9; 16:21; 16:23	
PRACTICAL WISDOM	8:14; 18:1	
PRUDENCE	astute, cunning, crafty	8:5a; 8:12; 12:16b; 12:23; 13:16a; 14:8a; 14:15b; 14:18b; 15:5; 17:2; 19:25a; 22:3; 27:12
	wise, skillful	10:19b; 15:24; 16:20a; 17:2; 19:14b
	good sense, insight	12:8a; 13:15a; 16:22a; 19:11a; 21:16
PURE	pure, clean	16:2a; 20:9; 20:11; 21:8b
	purity, clean	15:26; 20:9; 22:11; 30:12
RIGHTEOUS	2:9-10; 2:20; 3:33; 4:18; 8:8; 8:15-16; 8:18; 8:20-21; 10:2b-10:3a; 10:6a; 10:7a; 10:11a; 10:16a; 10:20a; 10:21a; 10:24-25; 10:28-32; 11:4b-11; 11:18b-19a; 11:21; 11:23a; 11:28b; 11:30a; 11:31; 12:3b; 12:5a; 12:7b; 12:10; 12:12b; 12:13b; 12:17; 12:21a; 12:26a; 12:28a; 13:5a; 13:6a; 13:9a; 13:21b; 13:22a; 13:25a; 14:19b; 14:32b; 14:34a; 15:6a; 15:28a; 15:29b; 16:8; 16:12; 16:13; 16:31; 17:15; 17:26a; 18:5b; 18:10; 18:17; 20:7; 21:3; 21:12; 21:15; 21:18a; 21:21; 21:26; 23:24-25; 24:15-16; 25:5; 25:26; 28:1; 28:12; 28:28; 29:2; 29:6b-7a; 29:16; 29:27; 31:9	
SATISFIED, TO BE FULL	12:11a; 12:14a; 14:14; 18:20; 19:23; 20:13; 27:20; 30:15b	
UNDERSTANDING	understanding reason, intelligence	2:1-8; 2:10-15; 3:13-20; 5:1-2; 8:1; 10:23b; 11:12; 14:29a; 15:21b; 17:27b; 18:2; 19:8; 20:5; 21:30; 24:3-7; 28:16
	understanding, discernment, perception	4:1-9; 7:4; 8:5; 8:14; 9:6; 9:10; 10:13a; 14:6b; 16:16b; 17:28; 19:25b; 23:23; 28:11; 30:2-3
UPRIGHT, INTEGRITY	2:21; 3:32; 4:11; 8:6; 8:9; 9:15; 11:3a; 11:6a; 11:11; 12:6b; 12:15; 14:2a; 14:9a; 14:11b; 14:12; 15:8b; 15:19b; 15:21b; 16:13; 16:17; 16:25; 17:26b; 20:11; 21:2; 21:8b; 21:18b; 21:29; 23:16; 28:10; 29:10; 29:27	

UNGODLY TRAITS

ABOMINATION, HORRIBLE DEED	3:32; 6:16-19; 8:7; 11:1; 11:20; 12:22; 13:19b; 15:8a; 15:9a; 15:26a; 16:5; 16:12; 17:15; 20:10; 20:23; 21:27; 24:9b; 26:24-25; 28:9; 29:27	
BACKSLIDER	14:14a	
BOORISH, BRUTISH, STUPID	12:1b; 30:2	
CRUEL	5:9; 11:17b; 12:10b; 17:11; 27:4	
DECEIT	deceit, fraud	11:1; 12:5; 12:17; 12:20a; 14:8; 14:25; 20:23b; 26:24
	deceit, treacherous	13:2; 13:15b; 22:12; 25:19
	lie, falsehood, deceit	10:18; 11:18; 12:19; 12:22a; 13:5; 14:5; 17:4; 17:7; 20:17; 21:6; 25:14; 25:18; 26:28; 29:12; 31:30a

HUMAN BEINGS

UNGODLY TRAITS (CONTINUED)

DECEIVE, ENTICE		24:28b
EVIL	evil, distress, adversity	2:12-15; 3:7b; 3:29-30; 4:14-17; 4:26-27; 6:6-19; 6:12-15; 8:13; 11:14a; 11:21a; 11:27b; 12:13a; 12:20a; 12:21b; 13:20b-21a; 14:16a; 14:22a; 14:32a; 15:3; 15:10a; 15:15a; 15:26a; 15:28; 16:6b; 16:17a; 16:27a; 16:30b; 17:4; 17:11; 17:13; 17:20b; 19:23; 20:8; 20:22; 20:30; 21:10; 21:12; 22:3; 23:6-8; 24:1-2; 24:8; 24:15-20; 25:20; 26:23; 27:12a; 28:5; 28:10; 28:14b; 28:22; 29:6a; 31:12
	evil, trouble, sorrow, wickedness	6:12-15; 6:16-19; 10:29; 12:21a; 17:4; 19:28b; 21:15; 22:8a; 30:20
FOOLS	folly, foolishness	5:23; 12:23b; 13:16b; 14:1b; 14:8b; 14:17a; 14:18a; 14:24b; 14:29b; 15:2b; 15:14b; 16:22b; 17:12; 18:13; 19:3; 22:15; 24:9a; 26:4-5; 26:11; 27:22
	foolish, stupid	7:22; 10:8; 10:10; 10:14b; 10:21b; 11:29b; 12:15a; 12:16a; 14:3a; 14:9; 15:5a; 16:22b; 17:28; 20:3; 24:7; 27:3; 27:22; 29:9
	fool, dullard	1:22; 1:32; 3:35; 8:5; 9:13; 10:1b; 10:18b; 10:23; 12:23b; 13:16b; 13:19b; 13:20b; 14:8b; 14:16; 14:24b; 15:2b; 15:7; 15:14b; 15:20b; 17:10; 17:12; 17:16; 17:21b; 17:24; 17:25; 18:2; 18:6-7; 19:1; 19:10; 19:29; 21:20; 23:9; 26:1-12; 28:26a; 29:11; 29:20
	foolish, ignoble, senseless	17:7; 17:21b; 30:21-23; 30:32
GLUTTONY, DRINKING		13:25; 15:17; 19:24; 20:1; 20:17; 21:17; 23:1-3; 23:20-21; 23:29-35; 24:13; 25:16; 25:25; 25:27; 26:9; 26:15; 27:8; 30:20; 31:4-7
PERVERSE	bent, twisted	2:15; 3:32; 4:24; 14:2b
	crooked	4:24; 6:12; 8:8; 10:9b; 11:20; 17:20; 19:1; 22:5; 28:6; 28:18
	fickle, froward	2:12,14b; 8:13b; 10:31b; 10:32b; 16:28; 16:30; 21:8; 23:33
	perverted, twisted, crooked	11:3; 15:4; 19:3
	perverse	12:8
PRIDE	comely, adorning, beautifying	14:3; 15:25a; 16:18-19; 29:23
	arrogant	21:24
	insolent, presumptuous	11:2; 13:10; 21:24
	proud, haughty	21:4
	vain	21:6
	haughty	16:5; 16:18; 18:12; 25:27
REPROACH	to dig, to be put to shame	13:5b; 19:26;
	reprove, taunt, defy	6:33; 14:31; 18:3a; 27:11
SCOFFERS, SCORNER		1:22; 3:34; 9:7a; 9:8a; 9:12; 13:1; 14:6b; 15:12; 19:25a; 19:28a; 19:29; 20:1a; 21:11a; 21:24; 22:10; 24:9b; 29:8a
SHAME	shame, bashfulness, shy	10:5; 14:35; 19:26; 27:2; 29:15
	shame, ignominy, disgrace, dishonor	3:35; 6:33; 9:7a; 11:2, 13:18a; 18:3b; 22:10
	shame, insult, reproach, humiliation	18:13; 25:8-10
SIMPLE-MINDED, FOOL		1:22; 1:32; 7:7; 8:5; 9:4; 9:6; 9:13; 14:15a; 14:18a; 19:25a; 21:11a; 22:3; 27:12
SIN	sin, guilt	1:10-19; 5:22; 10:16b; 13:21a; 13:22a; 14:21a; 14:34; 20:9; 21:4; 24:9
	sin, perversion, wrong	5:22; 16:6a
	sin, transgression	10:19; 12:13; 17:9a; 17:19; 28:2; 28:13; 28:21; 28:24; 29:6a; 29:16; 29:22
	guilt	14:9a
TRAITOR, TREACHEROUS		2:22; 11:3b; 11:6b; 13:2; 13:15; 21:18; 22:12; 23:28
VANITY	emptiness, vanity, nothingness	28:19
	vanity, nothingness, worthlessness	30:7-9
	vapor, hot air, vanity	13:11; 21:6
VENGEANCE		6:34; 20:22; 24:29
WICKED, VICIOUSNESS, OFFENSE		2:22; 3:25; 3:33; 4:14-19; 5:22; 8:7; 9:7; 10:2a; 10:3b; 10:6b; 10:7b; 10:11b; 10:16b; 10:20b; 10:24-25; 10:27b-32; 11:4b-11; 11:18a; 11:23b; 11:31; 12:2; 12:3a; 12:5b-6a; 12:7a; 12:10a; 12:12a; 12:21b; 13:5b; 13:6b; 13:9b; 13:17; 13:25; 14:11a; 14:19b; 14:32a; 15:6b; 15:8a; 15:9a; 15:28; 15:29a; 16:4; 16:12; 17:15; 17:23; 18:3a; 18:5a; 19:28b; 20:26; 21:4; 21:7; 21:10; 21:12; 21:18a; 21:27; 21:29a; 24:15-16; 24:19-20; 24:24-25; 25:5; 25:26; 28:1; 28:4; 28:12; 28:15; 28:28; 29:2; 29:7b; 29:12; 29:16; 29:27

OUR WORLD

ECONOMIC MATTERS

ECONOMIC JUSTICE, INJUSTICE	to judge, to administer justice	31:9
	judgment, right	13:23
	oppression	14:31a; 22:16; 28:3;
	violence	4:17; 10:6b; 10:11b; 22:2-23; 23:10-11
	slaves, servants	11:29; 12:9; 14:35; 17:2; 19:10; 22:7; 29:19; 29:21; 30:10; 30:21-23
POVERTY, WEALTH	10:4; 10:15; 11:24; 13:7-8; 14:20; 18:23; 19:4; 21:17; 22:2; 22:7a; 22:16; 28:6; 28:11; 28:22; 30:7-9	
	poverty	6:11; 13:18a; 13:23; 17:5; 19:1; 19:7; 19:22; 20:13; 24:33-34; 28:3; 28:6; 28:19; 28:27; 29:13; 30:7-9; 31:6-7
	low, weak, humble	10:15b; 14:31; 19:17; 21:13; 22:9; 22:16; 22:22-23; 26:7; 28:3; 28:8; 28:15; 29:6b-7a; 29:14
	humble, afflicted	14:21b; 15:15; 16:19; 22:22-23; 30:11-14; 31:4-5; 31:9
	need, deficiency	6:11; 11:24; 14:23; 21:5; 21:17; 22:16; 24:33-34; 28:27
	destitute, needy, poor	14:31; 31:9; 31:20
	riches, wealth	3:16; 8:18-19; 10:4; 10:22; 11:16b; 11:28a; 14:24a; 22:1; 22:4; 23:4-5; 28:20
	treasure	8:21; 10:2a; 15:16; 21:6
	wealth, riches, capital	1:13; 3:9; 8:18; 10:15; 11:4; 12:27; 13:7; 13:11; 13:22; 18:11; 19:14; 24:4; 27:24; 28:8; 28:22; 29:3b
WORK, WORK HABITS	10:4; 14:23; 20:11; 21:5; 21:8; 24:12	
	lazy, sluggard	6:6-11; 10:26; 13:4; 15:19a; 19:24; 20:4; 21:25; 22:13; 24:30-34; 26:13-16
	slothfully, deceitfully	10:4-5; 12:24; 12:27; 19:15
OCCUPATION, BUSINESS	18:9; 22:29; 24:27; 20:13	
	wages, hire, rent	11:18
BUSINESS PRACTICES	property	5:15-17
	honesty	11:1; 15:27; 16:11; 20:10; 20:23
BORROWING, LENDING	6:1-2; 11:14-15; 17:18; 20:16; 22:7b; 22:26-27; 27:13	
	buying and selling	11:26; 20:14
INHERITANCE, POSSESSION, PROPERTY	13:22a; 14:26a; 17:2; 19:14; 20:21	
LOTTERY	1:14; 16:33; 18:18	
FARMING	5:15-18a; 13:23; 14:4; 20:4; 24:27; 27:23-28; 28:19; 30:33	

POLITICAL MATTERS

POLITICAL JUSTICE, INJUSTICE	to judge, to administer justice	8:16
	justice, judgment	13:23; 28:5; 29:4; 29:26
	oppression	28:15-16
	violence	10:6b; 10:11b; 13:2; 16:29; 24:11; 28:15
	violence, havoc, destruction	21:7; 24:1-2
	violent, terrible ruthless	11:16b
WAR	20:18; 21:22; 21:31; 24:5-6	
THOSE IN AUTHORITY	king	8:15-16; 14:28; 14:34-35; 16:10; 16:12-15; 19:12; 20:2; 20:8; 20:26; 20:28; 21:1; 22:11; 22:29; 24:21-22; 25:1-6; 29:4; 29:14; 30:21-23; 30:27-28; 30:29-31; 31:4
	prince	6:7; 19:10; 28:2; 31:4
	ruler	6:6-7; 12:24a; 16:32; 17:2; 19:10; 23:1-3; 28:15; 29:2; 29:12; 29:26
	dictator, ruler	6:6-7; 25:15a
	messenger	13:17; 16:14a; 17:11
	ambassador	13:17; 25:13

NATURE

CREATION	3:19-20; 8:21-31; 25:3; 30:4
WATER	5:15-16; 9:17; 17:14a; 18:4; 20:5; 21:1; 25:21; 25:26; 27:17-19; 30:16b

OUR WORLD

NATURE (CONTINUED)

BIRDS AND ANIMALS	insects	6:6-8; 30:15; 30:25; 30:27
	birds	23:5; 26:2; 30:17; 30:19; 30:31
	land animals	17:2; 19:12; 20:2; 26:3; 28:1; 30:28; 30:30; 30:31
WEATHER, STORMS	1:26b-27; 11:29; 16:15b; 25:13-14; 25:23; 26:1-3; 27:16; 30:4	
SILVER, GOLD, JEWELS	2:4-5; 3:13-15; 8:10-11; 8:18; 10:20; 16:16; 17:3; 20:15; 22:1b; 25:4; 25:11-12; 27:21	

CITIES

CITY, TOWN	16:32b; 21:22; 25:28
TOWN, CITY	8:3; 9:3; 9:14; 11:10a; 11:11; 18:11; 18:19a; 29:8a

PRINCIPLES

PRINCIPLES	1:2-6	
COMMANDMENTS	2:1-5; 3:1-2; 4:4; 6:20-24; 7:1-3; 13:13b; 19:16	
COUNSEL	1:25; 1:29-31; 8:14; 11:14; 12:15; 13:10b; 15:22; 16:30; 19:20-21; 20:5a; 20:18; 21:30; 27:9	
GUIDANCE, COUNSEL, WISDOM	11:14; 20:18; 24:6	
SECRET COUNSEL	3:32; 11:13; 15:22; 20:19a	
DISCIPLINE	discipline, reproof, chastisement	3:11-12; 4:1a; 4:20-22; 5:1-2; 5:11-14; 5:23; 6:20-24; 7:22; 8:33; 10:17; 12:1; 13:1; 13:18; 13:24; 15:5; 15:10; 15:31-33a; 19:18; 19:20; 19:27; 22:15; 23:12-13; 23:23; 24:32; 29:17; 29:19
	correction, chastisement, reproof	1:23; 1:25; 1:29-31; 3:11-12; 5:11-14; 6:23; 9:8; 10:17; 12:1; 13:18; 15:5; 15:10; 15:12a; 15:31-32b; 19:25b; 29:15
GOOD	2:20a; 3:27; 4:2; 8:11; 8:19; 11:23; 11:27; 12:2a; 12:9; 14:14a; 12:25b; 13:2; 13:15a; 13:21b; 13:22a; 14:14b; 14:19a; 14:22b; 15:2a; 15:3; 15:13a; 15:23; 15:30b; 16:16; 16:19-20; 16:29; 16:32; 17:1; 17:13; 17:20a; 17:26a; 18:5; 19:1-2; 19:8; 20:23b; 21:9; 21:19; 22:1; 22:9; 24:13; 24:23b; 25:25; 25:27; 27:5; 27:10; 28:10; 28:21; 31:18	
GRACE	grace, favor	1:9; 3:4; 3:22; 3:34; 4:9; 5:19; 11:16a; 13:15a; 14:31b; 22:1b; 22:11; 28:23
	grace, favor, acceptance	8:35; 11:20; 11:27; 12:2a; 14:9; 14:35; 15:8; 16:13; 16:15; 18:22
JUSTICE AND INJUSTICE	to judge, to administer justice	19:29; 29:9
	judgment, justice	2:7b-9; 8:20-21; 12:5a; 13:23; 16:8; 16:10; 16:11; 17:23; 18:5b; 19:28a; 21:3; 21:7; 21:15; 24:23; 28:5; 28:17; 28:21; 29:4; 29:26
	injustice	22:8
KNOWLEDGE	1:7; 1:22b; 1:29-31; 2:5-6; 2:10; 3:20; 5:2; 8:8a; 8:9b; 8:10b; 9:10; 10:14a; 11:9; 12:1a; 12:23a; 13:16a; 14:6b; 14:7; 14:18b; 15:2a; 15:7; 15:14a; 17:27; 18:15; 19:2a; 19:25b; 19:27; 20:15; 21:11; 22:12; 22:17-21; 23:12; 24:3-7; 24:14; 28:2; 29:7b; 30:2-3	
LAW	1:8-9; 3:1-2; 4:2; 6:20-24; 7:2; 13:14; 28:4; 28:7; 28:9; 29:18; 31:26	
MERCY	3:3-4; 11:17a; 14:22b; 14:34; 16:6a; 18:10a; 19:22; 20:6; 20:28; 21:21; 31:26	
NAME, REPUTATION	18:10a; 22:1; 30:7-9	
PEACE	3:1-2; 3:17; 12:20; 16:7	
REBUKE, SCOLD	13:1; 17:10	
TRUTH AND LIES	12:17-19; 12:22; 14:5; 14:25	
	truth	3:3-4; 8:7a; 12:19; 14:22b; 16:6a; 20:6; 20:28; 22:20-21; 23:23
	falsehood and lying	6:16-19; 10:18; 11:18; 12:17; 12:19; 13:5a; 14:5; 17:4; 17:7; 19:5; 19:9; 20:17; 21:6; 25:14; 25:18; 26:28; 29:12
	lying	19:22b; 21:28; 23:3; 24:28; 26:24
WISDOM	1:7; 1:20-33; 2:1-15; 3:7-8; 3:13-26; 3:35; 4:1-9; 4:10-11; 5:1-2; 8:1; 9:12; 10:8a; 10:11a; 10:14a; 10:23b; 10:31a; 11:2b; 11:29b; 12:15b; 12:18b; 13:1; 13:10b; 13:14; 13:20; 14:1a; 14:3b; 14:8a; 14:16a; 14-24a; 14:33; 14:35a; 15:2a; 15:12b; 15:20a; 15:31; 16:14; 16:16a; 16:21a; 16:23a; 17:16; 17:24a; 17:28; 18:15b; 19:20; 20:1b; 20:26; 21:11; 21:20; 21:22; 21:30; 23:15; 23:19; 23:23; 23:24-25; 24:3-7; 24:13-14; 28:11; 28:26; 29:3; 29:11; 30:2-3; 30:24-28; 31:26	
WORD	1:6; 1:23; 2:12; 4:4; 8:6; 10:19; 12:25; 13:5a; 14:23; 15:1; 16:13; 17:9; 18:4a; 18:8; 18:13; 21:28; 22:12; 23:8; 24:2; 24:26; 25:11; 27:11; 29:12; 29:20; 30:1a; 30:5-6; 31:1a	

The Purpose of Proverbs

1 The proverbs of Solomon[a] son of David,
king of Israel:

2 For learning what wisdom
and discipline are;
for understanding insightful sayings;

3 for receiving wise instruction
in righteousness, justice,
and integrity;[b]

4 for teaching shrewdness
to the inexperienced,[A,c]
knowledge and discretion[d]
to a young man—

5 a wise man will listen and increase
his learning,[e]
and a discerning man
will obtain guidance—

6 for understanding a proverb
or a parable,[B]

the words of the wise,
and their riddles.[f]

7 The ·fear of the LORD
is the beginning of knowledge;[g]
fools despise wisdom
and discipline.[h]

Avoid the Path of the Violent

8 Listen, my son,
to your father's instruction,
and don't reject
your mother's teaching,[i]

9 for they will be a garland[j] of grace
on your head
and a gold chain
around your neck.[k]

10 My son, if sinners entice you,[l]
don't be persuaded.[m]

11 If they say—"Come with us!

Cross references:
[a]1:1 1Kg 4:32; Pr 10:1; 25:1; Ec 12:9
[b]1:3 Pr 2:9
[c]1:4 Pr 8:5
[d]Pr 2:11; 3:21
[e]1:5 Pr 9:9; 16:21,23
[f]1:6 Nm 12:8; Jdg 14:12; Ps 49:4; Hab 2:6
[g]1:7 Jb 28:28; Ps 111:10; Pr 9:10; 15:33
[h]Eph 5:17
[i]1:8 Pr 6:20; 31:1
[j]1:9 Pr 4:9
[k]Gn 41:42; Pr 6:21; Dn 5:29
[l]1:10 Pr 16:29
[m]Ps 141:4

[A]1:4 Or *simple*, or *gullible*   [B]1:6 Or *an enigma*

1:1 A proverb is a pithy allusion or parable that is rich in truth and meaning. **King of Israel** here refers to Solomon, who was the last king of united Israel (1Kg 1–11).

1:2 Wisdom is having mastery of a subject of knowledge; it encompasses discipline, knowledge, prudence, and other virtues. It is the ability to apply knowledge to overcome any problem in life. Biblical "wisdom," which is a gift from God (2:6), includes morality and the knowledge of God. **Discipline** has to do with warnings about the consequences of errant behavior, or loving correction to those who have failed to heed such warnings. It can involve physical punishment. The Hebrew word is often translated "instruction" (v. 3) because the goal is always edification and education, not just punishment. **Understanding** means internalizing knowledge so that it directs action. **Insightful sayings** are those that reveal truth.

1:3 Wise instruction is literally "the discipline (see note at v. 2) of prudence." Prudence is skill or cleverness; a talent for insight, observation, or scrutiny; practical wisdom that leads to success. The word is translated "wise/wiser/wisdom" (v. 3; 14:35; 16:23; 17:2; 21:11,16), "prudent" (10:5), "discerning" (15:24), "understands" (16:20), "succeeds" (17:8), "sensible" (19:14), and "considers" (21:12). This cleverness is morally guided by **righteousness** (agreement with God's directives), **justice** (restoration of what is right), and **integrity** (what is straight, right, and fair).

1:4 The **inexperienced** are naive people, usually young (7:7), who are still uncommitted. They generally lack shrewdness (8:5) or common sense (9:4,16; 22:3; 27:12). They have neither chosen wisdom nor become entrenched in folly like the mocker (1:22), but they are willing to believe anything (14:15,18). Those who try to remain uncommitted are condemned because they have not set out on the way of righteousness (1:32; 9:6). They should take warning from those who have chosen the wrong way (19:25; 21:11). The Hebrew word for **shrewdness** always has a positive connotation in the book of Proverbs (the adjective is translated "shrewd" in 12:23 and "sensible" in 12:16; 13:16; 14:8,15,18; 15:5; 22:3; 27:12). Such a person foresees and deals with difficulties (22:3). However, in other books it usually means "cunning" or "craftiness" that is in direct defiance of God's will (Gn 3:1; Jb 5:12). **Knowledge** is collected, memorized information

(Hb *da'ath*; see word study at 8:9). Knowledge is the tool; wisdom is the workman. Without wisdom to apply it, knowledge is ineffective. **Discretion** is the ability to ponder and plan, to think independently. The negative side is scheming (12:2; 14:17; 24:8). In Proverbs a **young man** is one who is on the verge of maturity; he is making decisions about the course of his life (22:6).

1:5 A **discerning man** has the capacity to understand what he hears and sees and to internalize knowledge so that it directs his actions.

1:6 The words **proverb** and **parable** are synonyms (v. 1). The **words of the wise** may refer to sayings that are more than two lines long; two sections are introduced as such (22:17; 24:23; cp. 30:1; 31:1; Ec 9:17; 12:11). A riddle is a proverb that is tricky or difficult to understand (Jdg 14:12; 1Kg 10:1).

1:7 The **fear of the LORD** involves awe, reverence, love, and trust in God. It accompanies knowledge, humility, obedience, and blessing (8:13; 10:27; 14:26-27; 16:6; 19:23; 22:4). The **beginning** is what must come first, the prerequisite; it is also the chief or supreme principle (4:7). All three kinds of "fool" are obstinately immoral (1:22; 17:7). This fool (Hb *'ewiyl*; see word study at 10:8) is self-sufficient and detests **wisdom** or any advice or correction.

1:8 On **instruction**, see "discipline" in note at verse 2. **Teaching** implies a person of authority passing on moral guidelines; in other contexts the same word means "law" (28:4,7,9; cp. Dt 4:44). The reader should not make too much of the pairing of instruction with the father and teaching with the mother. Splitting them is merely an aspect of Hebrew poetry (Pr 4:3; 6:20; 19:26; 23:22; 30:11,17). Both parents participated in this homeschooling.

1:9 The **garland** and **chain** were symbols of honor, guidance, and protection.

1:10 The Hebrew word for **entice** is related to the word for "inexperienced" (see note at v. 4).

1:11 Just for fun is literally "for nothing" ("foolish" in v. 17; "without cause" in 3:30 and 24:28; "for no reason" in 23:29; "undeserved" in 26:2). **Attack** is literally "hide away," a synonym for "ambush."

Let's set an ambush[a] and kill someone.[A]
Let's attack some innocent person[b]
just for fun![B]
12 Let's swallow them alive,[c] like •Sheol,
still healthy as they go down
to the •Pit.[d]
13 We'll find all kinds
of valuable property
and fill our houses with plunder.[e]
14 Throw in your lot with us,
and we'll all share our money"[C]—
15 my son, don't travel that road
with them[f]
or set foot on their path,[g]
16 because their feet run toward trouble
and they hurry to commit murder.[D,h]
17 It is foolish to spread a net
where any bird can see it,
18 but they set an ambush
to kill themselves;[E]
they attack their own lives.
19 Such are the paths of all who make
profit dishonestly;[i]
it takes the lives of those
who receive it.[F]

Wisdom's Plea
20 Wisdom calls out in the street;

she raises her voice
in the public squares.[j]
21 She cries out above[G] the commotion;
she speaks at the entrance
of the city •gates:
22 "How long, foolish ones, will you
love ignorance?
How long will you mockers[k]
enjoy mocking
and you fools hate knowledge?[l]
23 If you respond to my warning,[H,m]
then I will pour out my spirit on you[n]
and teach you my words.
24 Since I called out and you refused,[o]
extended my hand and no one
paid attention,[p]
25 since you neglected all my counsel[q]
and did not accept my correction,
26 I, in turn, will laugh at your calamity.[r]
I will mock when terror strikes you,
27 when terror strikes you like a storm
and your calamity comes
like a whirlwind,
when trouble and stress overcome you.
28 Then they will call me,
but I won't answer;
they will search for me, but won't
find me.[s]

Cross references:
[a] 1:11 Pr 12:6; Jr 5:26
[b] Ps 10:8
[c] 1:12 Ps 124:3
[d] Ps 28:1
[e] 1:13 Pr 24:4
[f] 1:15 Ps 1:1; Pr 4:14
[g] Ps 119:101; Pr 16:19
[h] 1:16 Pr 6:17-18; Is 59:7; Rm 3:15
[i] 1:19 Pr 15:27; Ezk 22:27; Hab 2:6-12
[j] 1:20 Pr 8:1-3; 9:3
[k] 1:22 Ps 1:1 (Jb 21:14; Pr 1:29; 5:12
[m] 1:23 Pr 3:11; 15:5,31-32
[n] Jl 2:28
[o] 1:24 Is 65:12; 66:4; Jr 7:13; Zch 7:11
[p] Is 65:2; Rm 10:21
[q] 1:25 Ps 107:11; Lk 7:30
[r] 1:26 Ps 2:4
[s] 1:28 1Sm 8:18

Translation footnotes:
[A] 1:11 Lit Let's ambush for blood   [B] 1:11 Lit person for no reason   [C] 1:14 Lit us; one bag will be for all of us   [D] 1:16 Lit to shed blood   [E] 1:18 Lit they ambush for their blood   [F] 1:19 Lit takes the life of its masters   [G] 1:21 Lit at the head of   [H] 1:23 Lit back to my reprimand

1:12 **Sheol** is the grave, and the **Pit** pictures the opening to a grave; both are symbols of death. Sheol is the destiny of the wicked, but the righteous will be rescued from it (15:11). The victim was **alive** and **still healthy**, not expecting death.

1:14 One's **lot** can mean one's destiny (Is 17:14). There may be a pun here: "Choose our way as your 'destiny' and join us in casting 'lots' to divide up the plunder."

1:15 The book of Proverbs frequently warns the reader to avoid the **road . . . path**, or way of wickedness and instead choose the way of righteousness (4:13-15). The lifestyle a person chooses leads to a certain destiny. A person should not try the wicked lifestyle even for a moment.

1:16 **Trouble** comes from the common Hebrew word for "evil" (ra'a'; see word study at 24:8,18-19). "Evil" is the concept (2:12), the intention is "harm" (3:29), the consequence is "trouble" or "misery" (12:21; 15:15), and the ultimate result is "ruin" or "disaster" (5:14; 21:12)—the same Hebrew word. In 20:14 the buyer uses the word to claim that something is "worthless" or contemptible.

1:17-18 An animal that sees a **net** has the sense to avoid it, but the wicked who know their lifestyle is self-destructive don't have the sense to turn away.

1:19 The gang described in verses 10-19 is summarized as those who **make profit dishonestly** (15:27; 28:16; Jr 6:13; 8:10; Ezk 22:27; Hab 2:9). The practice is self-destructive (Pr 1:18,31-32; 2:19; 8:36; 29:6,24).

1:20-33 **Wisdom** is personified as a woman who **calls out** a warning in **public**. Those who reject her guidance will suffer disaster. What she offers is success in practical matters in this life but eternal life as well (3:22).

1:20-21 The **public** square was the marketplace, and the **city** gate was where civic debate and official business were carried out (see note at 24:7).

1:22 On **foolish** and **ignorance**, see "inexperienced" in note at verse 4. A mocker is obnoxiously obstinate in his folly and not willing to change. He treats righteousness with ridicule and contempt (17:5). He is proud (21:24), a source of conflict (22:10), and unpopular (24:9). Because he is not open to correction (9:7-8; 13:1; 15:12), he is unable to learn (14:6) and is thus condemned (3:34; 9:12; 19:29). He is suitable only as a negative example for the inexperienced (19:25; 21:11). This kind of fool (Hb kesiyl; see word study at 17:10) is a close synonym to ewiyl (1:7; cp. 17:7). Along with being obstinately immoral, he perhaps adds a smug overconfidence that increases his pigheadedness. Because he delights in evil conduct, he is dangerous to be around.

1:23 To warn is to call someone to account; it includes an implicit threat of physical punishment.

1:24 Extending the **hand** could be a threatening (Ex 7:5) or a friendly (Is 65:2) gesture.

1:26-27 A **calamity** is the sudden onset of severe destruction (Dt 32:35; Jr 48:16). **Terror** is intense fear that causes uncontrollable trembling. Wisdom rejoices that through calamity the world is set right—the wicked are punished and the righteous are rewarded. The **storm** and **whirlwind** leave only devastation (10:25; Hs 8:7). The basic idea behind the Hebrew words for **trouble** and **stress** is confinement or being squeezed (24:10).

29 Because they hated knowledge,
   didn't choose to fear the LORD,[a]
30 were not interested in my counsel,
   and rejected all my correction,[b]
31 they will eat the fruit of their way[c]
   and be glutted with
     their own schemes.[d]
32 For the turning away
   of the inexperienced will kill them,[e]
   and the complacency of fools
     will destroy them.
33 But whoever listens to me
   will live securely
   and be free from the fear of danger."[f]

Wisdom's Worth

2 My son, if you accept my words[g]
   and store up my commands within you,
2 listening closely[A] to wisdom
   and directing your heart
     to understanding;
3 furthermore, if you call out to insight
   and lift your voice to understanding,
4 if you seek it like silver

and search for it like hidden treasure,[h]
5 then you will understand the *fear
     of the LORD
   and discover the knowledge of God.
6 For the LORD gives wisdom;
   from His mouth come knowledge
     and understanding.[i]
7 He stores up success[B] for the upright;
   He is a shield for those who live
     with integrity[j]
8 so that He may guard the paths
     of justice
   and protect the way
     of His loyal followers.[k]
9 Then you will understand
     righteousness, justice,
   and integrity—every good path.
10 For wisdom will enter your mind,
   and knowledge will delight your heart.
11 Discretion will watch over you,
   and understanding will guard you,[l]
12 rescuing you from the way of evil—
   from the one who says perverse things,

Cross references
a 1:29 Pr 1:7
b 1:30 Pr 5:12; 15:5
c 1:31 Jr 6:19
d Pr 14:14; 28:19
e 1:32 Jr 2:19
f 1:33 Ps 112:7-8; Pr 3:24-26
g 2:1 Pr 4:10
h 2:4 Jb 3:21; Mt 13:44
i 2:6 Jb 32:8
j 2:7 Ps 84:11; Pr 10:9; 20:7; 28:18; 30:5
k 2:8 1Sm 2:9; Ps 66:9
l 2:11 Pr 4:6; 6:22

A 2:2 Lit you, stretching out your ear   B 2:7 Or resourcefulness

1:28 This Hebrew word for **search** implies eager seeking under stress (Ps 63:1; 78:34; Hs 5:15). God patiently permits Himself to be found (Pr 8:17; cp. Dt 4:29; 2Ch 7:14; Jr 29:13), but He doesn't respond to insincere seekers (Is 1:15; 59:2-3), and eventually it becomes too late (Jr 11:11; 14:12; Ezk 8:17-19; Hs 5:6; 2Pt 3:9-10).

1:31 On **glutted**, see "satisfied" in note at 18:20; compare 28:19.

1:32 The Hebrew word for **turning away** from God (Hs 11:7) can also be translated "unfaithfulness, apostasy, or rebellion." **Complacency** is a false sense of security in which some people trust (Ps 30:6; Jr 22:21; Ezk 16:49).

tevunah

Hebrew Pronunciation	[tuh vew NAH]
HCSB Translation	understanding
Uses in Proverbs	19
Uses in the OT	42
Key Passage	Proverbs 2:2,3,6,11

Tevunah (understanding, competence, sound judgment) refers to competency at a particular skill or task relevant to living successfully within society. It does not connote a deep intellectual understanding of this world or thought, an idea prominently associated with the synonymous *binah (understanding)*. Rather, *tevunah* refers to the skillful *know-how* of a craftsman (Ex 31:3; 35:31; 36:1; 1Kg 7:14), the business *savvy* of a king (Ezk 28:4), the *skill* of the idol-maker (Hs 13:2), and *skill* at speech (Jb 32:11). It may refer to *skill* at discerning the plans and purposes of God (Dt 32:28), sociopolitical realities (Ob 7-8), or spiritual realities (Is 44:19). Both David (Ps 78:72) and Solomon (1Kg 4:29) were endowed with *understanding* to rule skillfully (cp. Pr 28:16). *Understanding* leading to skillful living is the gift of God (Ex 31:3; 1Kg 4:29) and may be gained through long life (Jb 12:12). The person who acquires *understanding* is happy (3:13), quiet (11:12), patient (14:29; 17:27), humble (18:2), and successful (19:8).

1:33 This Hebrew word translated **securely** generally involves false security if the object of trust is not God (11:28; 28:26). Lady Wisdom promises true security because there is a close connection between wisdom and God (2:6).

2:1-22 The first four verses of this chapter are a condition (**if**), followed by two results (**then**) in verses 5-8 and 9-11. Verses 12-15 and 16-19 describe the benefits of the results—being rescued from the way of evil and from the forbidden woman. Verses 20-22 are the conclusion.

2:1-5 Rather than just learning about **wisdom**, the student is first told to **accept** (rather than despise or reject; 1:7,30) and internalize wisdom, then to **call out to** and passionately **seek** it. The result is a reverent (that is, with appropriate **fear**) relationship (**knowledge**) with God, which is a prerequisite of true wisdom (1:7).

2:7 As we store up God's commands (v. 1), **He stores up success** as our reward. Success is competence (3:21; 8:14) or sound judgment (18:10). **Upright** means "corresponding to God's ethical instruction" (Hb *yashar*; see word study at 21:2). The Hebrew word for **integrity** implies genuineness and reliability; it is also translated "honorable" (10:29) and "honest" (29:10).

2:8 On **protect**, see "keep" in note at 4:4,6.

2:9-10 Understanding is a further result (**then**; cp. v. 5) of seeking wisdom. A person can live ethically when he has **wisdom** in his **mind** (lit "heart"; see note at 4:23) and **heart** (Hb *nephesh*; see note at 13:2-4). God's wisdom entering a person and making him **delight** in godly knowledge is regeneration (Jr 31:31-33; Ezk 36:27; 1Co 1:18). On **path**, see note at 1:15.

2:11 Having **discretion** (see note at 1:4) and **understanding** (see note at 1:2) will prevent self-destructive behavior (1:19).

2:12 On **evil**, see note at 1:16. **Perverse** is literally "turned over" (Jdg 7:13; 2Kg 21:13), making something into something else (Dt 23:5; Is 29:16; Jr 2:21; Am 5:7)—in this case, turning truth into a lie (Jr 23:36).

13 from those who abandon
    the right paths
to walk in ways of darkness,[a]
14 from those who enjoy doing evil[b]
    and celebrate perversion,
15 whose paths are crooked,[c]
    and whose ways are devious.[d]
16 It will rescue you
    from a forbidden woman,[e]
    from a stranger[A]
    with her flattering talk,[f]
17 who abandons the companion
    of her youth[g]
    and forgets the covenant of her God;
18 for her house sinks down to death
    and her ways to the land
    of the departed spirits.[h]
19 None return who go to her;
    none reach the paths of life.[i]
20 So follow the way of good people,[j]
    and keep to the paths of the righteous.
21 For the upright will inhabit the land,
    and those of integrity will remain in it;[k]
22 but the wicked will be cut off
    from the land,[l]
    and the treacherous uprooted from it.[m]

Trust the Lord

3 My son, don't forget my teaching,
    but let your heart keep
    my commands;[n]

2 for they will bring you
    many days, a full life,[B,o] and well-being.[p]
3 Never let loyalty and faithfulness
    leave you.
Tie them around your neck;
    write them on the tablet of your heart.[q]
4 Then you will find favor
    and high regard
    in the sight of God and man.[r]
5 Trust in the Lord with all your heart,[s]
    and do not rely on
    your own understanding;[t]
6 think about Him in all your ways,
    and He will guide you
    on the right paths.[C,u]
7 Don't consider yourself to be wise;[v]
    *fear the Lord and turn away from evil.[w]
8 This will be healing for your body[D,x]
    and strengthening for your bones.[y]
9 Honor the Lord with your possessions
    and with the first produce
    of your entire harvest;[z]
10 then your barns will be
    completely filled,
    and your vats will overflow
    with new wine.[aa]
11 Do not despise the Lord's instruction,
    my son,

---

[a]2:11-13 Ps 82:5; Pr 15:19; 16:17; Jn 3:19,20
[b]2:14 Pr 10:23
[c]2:15 Ps 125:5; Pr 21:8
[d]Pr 3:32; 14:2
[e]2:16 Pr 9:13-18
[f]Pr 5:3,20; 6:24; 7:5,21; 23:27
[g]2:17 Mal 2:14-15
[h]2:18 Pr 7:27; 9:18; 21:16
[i]2:16-19 Ps 16:11; Pr 5:6; 7:5,21-27; 23:27-28; Ec 7:26
[j]2:20 Heb 6:12
[k]2:21 Pr 10:30; Mt 5:5-6
[l]2:22 Ps 37:38
[m]Dt 28:63; Ps 52:5
[n]3:1 Dt 30:16
[o]3:2 Ps 91:16; Pr 3:16; 4:10; 9:11; 10:27
[p]3:1-2 Pr 4:1-4; 6:20-23; 7:1-3
[q]3:3 Pr 1:9; 6:21; 7:3; 2Co 3:3
[r]3:4 Dt 4:6; 1Sm 2:26; Lk 2:52; Rm 14:18
[s]3:5 Ps 37:3,5
[t]Jr 9:23
[u]3:6 Pr 11:5
[v]3:7 Pr 26:5,12; 28:11,26; Rm 12:16
[w]Jb 1:1; 28:28; Ps 37:27; Pr 16:6
[x]3:8 Pr 4:22 [y]Jb 21:24 [z]3:9 Ex 23:19; Lv 23:9-14; Dt 26:2
[aa]3:10 Dt 28:8; Mal 3:10

[A]2:16 Or foreign woman   [B]3:2 Lit days, years of life   [C]3:6 Lit will make your paths straight   [D]3:8 Lit navel

---

2:14 To do **evil** is to undermine society and applaud its overthrow.

2:15 Crooked is the opposite of "upright" (v. 7); it means "twisted" (11:20) or "distorted" (28:6). On **paths** and **ways**, see note at 1:15.

2:16 The **forbidden woman** has turned away from her husband (v. 17) and wants to destroy society (5:3,20; 7:5; 22:14). The **stranger** has allegiance to a different community and has no interest in preserving the community of the faithful (5:20; 6:24; 7:5; 23:27). **Flattering** (lit "smooth") speech always has an agenda that includes the destruction of others (5:3; 7:5,21; 26:28; 28:23; 29:5; Ps 55:21). This warning applies to any person who appeals to base instincts with ulterior motives.

2:18-19 Joining the forbidden woman/stranger is self-destructive (1:19). The Hebrew word for **departed spirits** is the same as the Rephaim, a Canaanite people (Dt 2:20-21), but in Hebrew poetry it refers to the residents of the grave (Pr 9:18; 21:16; cp. Is 14:9).

2:20-22 These **good people** have moral excellence. Figuratively, to **inhabit the land** means to enjoy God's blessing through a relationship with Him (Ps 37:3; Jr 7:5-7). While the warning of Pr 2:16-19 is specifically against illicit sexual relations, this suggests a broader application. Those who choose the good will enjoy God's blessings eternally (Ps 37:29; Is 60:21; Mt 5:5), but **the wicked** (impious, evil, selfish, violently antisocial) will be eternally **cut off** from God's blessing. **Treacherous** people are unfaithful in relationships; here they have abandoned commitment to God.

3:1-12 In this section the odd-numbered verses give a command and the even-numbered verses a promised result (in vv. 5-6 the command spills over).

3:2 To have **well-being** is to be healthy, free from threat or need, and thus fulfilled, content, prosperous, and at peace in a way that only God can grant (Ps 4:8; 119:165).

3:3 Loyalty (Hb chesed; see note at 19:22) and **faithfulness** summarize godliness in contrast to the selfish malice and infidelity of the wicked (14:22; 16:6; 20:28; cp. Mt 22:37-40). The son should make them his permanent characteristics, externally and internally.

3:5 To **trust** anything or anyone other than **the Lord** results in disaster (11:28; 28:26; cp. Ps 52:7; 62:10; Is 30:12-13; Ezk 16:15). To **rely on** something—a synonym for "trust"—is to lean on it as if it were a crutch (2Sm 1:6; Jb 8:14-15; Is 50:10). **Understanding** is good (16:16), but only if it is from the Lord (9:10).

3:6 To **think about** God **in all your ways** is to invite His presence into all daily activities and decisions. **Guide . . . on the right paths** is literally "make straight" or "smooth." God will make righteousness attainable.

3:7 Turning away from **evil** and worshiping **the Lord** is the gist of repentance (Ac 8:22; 26:20), which requires humility (Jr 31:19).

3:8 Body (lit "navel"; Sg 7:2) and **bones** stand for the entire person.

3:9-10 Possessions is the word for abundant "wealth" (8:18; 10:15; 11:4; 12:27; 13:7,11; 18:11; 19:4,14; 28:8,22; 29:3) or

and do not loathe His discipline;[a]

12 for the LORD disciplines the one
He loves,
just as a father, the son he delights in.[b]

Wisdom Brings Happiness

13 Happy is a man who finds wisdom[c]
and who acquires understanding,

14 for she is more profitable than silver,
and her revenue is better than gold.[d]

15 She is more precious than jewels;[e]
nothing you desire compares with her.[f]

16 Long life[A] is in her right hand;
in her left, riches and honor.[g]

17 Her ways are pleasant,[h]
and all her paths, peaceful.

18 She is a tree of life[i] to those
who embrace her,
and those who hold on to her
are happy.

19 The LORD founded the earth
by wisdom[j]
and established the heavens
by understanding.

20 By His knowledge the watery depths
broke open,[k]
and the clouds dripped with dew.[l]

21 Maintain your competence
and discretion.

My son, don't lose sight of them.[m]

22 They will be life for you[B,C,n]
and adornment[D] for your neck.

23 Then you will go safely on your way;
your foot will not stumble.[o]

24 When you lie[E] down, you will not
be afraid;[p]
you will lie down, and your sleep
will be pleasant.

25 Don't fear sudden danger
or the ruin of the wicked
when it comes,[q]

26 for the LORD will be your confidence[F]
and will keep your foot from a snare.[r]

Treat Others Fairly

27 When it is in your power,[G]
don't withhold good[s] from the one
it belongs to.

28 Don't say to your neighbor, "Go away!
Come back later.
I'll give it tomorrow"—when it is there
with you.[t]

29 Don't plan any harm
against your neighbor,[u]
for he trusts you and lives near you.

30 Don't accuse anyone without cause,[v]
when he has done you no harm.

31 Don't envy a violent man[w]
or choose any of his ways;

Cross references

a3:11 Pr 5:11-13; 15:5,31-33
b3:12 Dt 8:5; Jb 5:17-18; Pr 13:24; Heb 12:5-7
c3:13 Pr 8:32,34
d3:14 Jb 28:15-19; Pr 8:10,19; 16:16; 22:1
e3:15 Jb 28:18
f Pr 8:11; 20:15
g3:16 Pr 8:18; 21:21; 22:4
h3:17 Mt 11:19
i3:18 Gn 2:9; Pr 11:30; 13:12; 15:4; Rv 2:7
j3:19 Ps 104:24; Pr 8:27
k3:20 Gn 7:11
l Dt 33:28; Jb 36:28
m3:21 Pr 4:21
n3:22 Pr 4:22
o3:23 Ps 91:12; Pr 4:12
p3:24 Jb 11:19; Ps 3:5; Pr 6:22
q3:25 Jb 5:21; Ps 91:5; 1Pt 3:14
r3:26 1Sm 2:9
s3:27 Gl 6:10
t3:28 Lv 19:13; Dt 24:15
u3:29 Pr 6:14; 14:22
v3:30 Pr 24:28; Rm 12:18
w3:31 Ps 37:1; Pr 23:17; 24:1,19

A3:16 Lit *Length of days*　B3:22 Or *be your throat*　C3:22 In Hb, *nephesh* can mean throat, soul, or life.　D3:22 Or *grace*　E3:24 LXX reads *sit*　F3:26 Or *be at your side*　G3:27 Lit *in the power of your hands*

---

sufficiency (see "enough" in 30:15-16), the stored resources that are ready for use. The **first produce** was the earliest and best of the crop (Dt 18:4). Those who **honor** God with their wealth will receive more with which to honor Him (Mal 3:10; Lk 19:17,26).

3:11-12 To ask God to refrain from giving us **discipline** would be to ask Him to love us less (Jb 7:17-19; 10:10).

3:13-18 This poem praising **wisdom** begins and ends with the word **happy**. To be happy is to discover the good life that the Creator intended (8:32,34; 14:21; 16:20; 20:7; 28:14; Ps 1:1; 32:1; 144:15; Is 30:18). This Hebrew word is associated with the Greek word in Mt 5:3-12 that describes the present and future blessings enjoyed by the godly person. Godly wisdom is better than **silver . . . gold**, and **jewels** because **she** (where "she" is a personification of wisdom) gives enduring **riches** along with honor, inner peace, and eternal life.

3:14 This could be the profit gained in trading up to wisdom (4:7) or the subsequent profit made by applying wisdom (8:18-21; 21:20; 24:4).

3:16 The Hebrew word for **honor** is literally "weightiness" ("heavy" in 27:3; "burden" in Is 22:24); it implies ascribing value or esteem to something or taking it seriously (Ps 50:15; Pr 3:9; Mal 1:6). It is also translated "glory," especially when describing God (Ex 40:34; Ps 96:7; Pr 25:2).

3:18 A **tree of life** is a source provided by God for healing and eternal life (11:30; 13:12; 15:4; cp. Gn 2:9; 3:22; Rv 2:7; 22:2). Thus godly wisdom functions symbolically to replace

what was lost in the garden of Eden. Jesus Christ fulfilled wisdom's promise.

3:19 God **established** and sustains creation through **wisdom**. Solomon offered this same wisdom to his son to firmly establish and sustain his life (4:26; 12:3; 16:3; 24:3).

3:20 In Palestine **dew** was an important source of moisture.

3:21 Maintain is literally "guard." On **discretion**, see note at 1:4.

3:22 Wisdom is the key to **life**—a full life now and eternal life in the future—because it is anchored in the fear of the Lord and it includes practical advice (vv. 2,18; 1:33; 4:13,22-23; 6:23; 8:35; 10:16-17; 11:19; 12:28; 14:27; 16:22; 19:23; 21:21; 22:4; cp. Mk 10:30; 1Tm 4:8).

3:23-26 On **safely**, see "securely" in note at 1:33. Though the **wicked** will suddenly come to **ruin** at their ending (Ps 35:8; Is 10:3; 47:11; 1Th 5:3), those who maintain wisdom (Pr 3:21) will never be in such danger—whether up and about or sleeping—because **the LORD** will protect them.

3:29-30 Harm is literally "evil" (see note at 1:16). The mention of one who **lives near you** emphasizes the trust inherent in community. It does not mean that treachery is permissible against distant strangers; it is always wrong (Jdg 18:7,27; 2Sm 3:27; 20:9-10; Ps 55:12-14; Mt 26:14). **Without cause** (see note at 1:11; cp. 24:28; 1Kg 2:31; Ps 35:7; 119:161) is literally "for nothing" (Gn 29:15; 2Sm 24:24) or "for no reason" (1Sm 19:5; Lm 3:52). Bringing accusations without just cause is malicious betrayal of community trust.

3:31 A **violent man** is one who, out of greed and hate,

³² for the devious are detestable
    to the LORD,
but He is a friend^A to the upright.^a
³³ The LORD's curse is on the household
    of the wicked,^b
but He blesses the home
    of the righteous;
³⁴ He mocks those who mock,
but gives grace to the humble.^c
³⁵ The wise will inherit honor,
but He holds up fools to dishonor.^B

A Father's Example

4 Listen, my sons,
    to a father's discipline,^d
and pay attention so that
    you may gain understanding,
² for I am giving you good instruction.^e
Don't abandon my teaching.
³ When I was a son with my father,
tender and precious to my mother,
⁴ he taught me and said:
"Your heart must hold on to my words.
Keep my commands and live.^f
⁵ Get wisdom, get understanding;^g
don't forget or turn away
    from the words of my mouth.
⁶ Don't abandon wisdom, and she will
    watch over you;
love her,^h and she will guard you.
⁷ Wisdom is supreme—so get wisdom.
And whatever else you get,
    get understanding.ⁱ

⁸ Cherish her, and she will exalt you;
if you embrace her, she will honor you.^j
⁹ She will place a garland of grace
    on your head;
she will give you a crown of beauty."^k

Two Ways of Life

¹⁰ Listen, my son. Accept my words,^l
and you will live many years.^m
¹¹ I am teaching you the way of wisdom;
I am guiding you on straight paths.ⁿ
¹² When you walk, your steps will not
    be hindered;^o
when you run, you will not stumble.^p
¹³ Hold on to instruction; don't let go.^q
Guard it, for it is your life.
¹⁴ Don't set foot on the path
    of the wicked;^r
don't proceed in the way of evil ones.
¹⁵ Avoid it; don't travel on it.
Turn away from it, and pass it by.
¹⁶ For they can't sleep
unless they have done what is evil;
they are robbed of sleep
unless they make someone stumble.^s
¹⁷ They eat the bread of wickedness
and drink the wine of violence.
¹⁸ The path of the righteous is
    like the light of dawn,^t
shining brighter and brighter
    until midday.
¹⁹ But the way of the wicked is
    like the darkest gloom;^u

Cross references:

^a 3:32 Ps 25:14; Pr 11:20; 12:22; 15:8-9
^b 3:33 Zch 5:3-4; Mal 2:2
^c 3:34 Jms 4:6; 1Pt 5:5
^d 4:1 Ps 34:11; Pr 1:8
^e 4:2 Jb 11:4
^f 4:4 Pr 3:1-2; 6:20-23; 7:1-2
^g 4:5 Pr 16:16
^h 4:6 2Th 2:10
ⁱ 4:7 Pr 16:16
^j 4:8 1Sm 2:30
^k 4:9 Pr 1:9; 16:31
^l 4:10 Pr 2:1
^m Pr 3:2
ⁿ 4:11 1Sm 12:23
^o 4:12 Jb 18:7; Ps 18:36
^p Pr 3:23
^q 4:13 Pr 3:18
^r 4:14 Ps 1:1; Pr 1:15
^s 4:16 Ps 36:4; Mc 2:1
^t 4:18 2Sm 23:4
^u 4:19 Is 59:9-10; Jr 23:12; Jn 12:35

---

^A3:32 Or *confidential counsel*   ^B3:35 Or *but haughty fools dishonor*, or *but fools exalt dishonor*

---

commits crimes against society such as oppression and exploitation (10:6,11; 13:2; 16:29).

3:32 The devious, those who turn aside from what is right, are **detestable** to God, offensive, abhorrent, an abomination; they virtually turn His stomach. He will not pay them any attention except to punish them (15:8; 16:5; 21:27; 28:9). But with **the upright** God is **a friend**, an intimate counselor (15:22; Jb 29:4; Ps 25:14; 55:14).

3:33 God's **curse** is the removal of His sustaining presence. A **household** includes all a person's family, possessions, and property. Individual members of the family can be redeemed from the curse (Ezk 18:17,20).

3:34 God will treat with contempt those who ridicule Him (see note at 1:22). The **humble** (16:19) are those who are poor (14:21; 31:20) not from laziness but because they are exploited or oppressed (15:15; 22:22; 30:14; 31:5,9).

3:35 An inheritance is a permanent possession. On **honor**, see note at 3:16. Fools (Hb *kesiyl*; see note at 1:22) are "exalted" to a state of **dishonor**—a sarcastic statement.

4:3 Being a true **son** implies obedience, not merely being a male child. A **tender** child is delicate as well as teachable. **Precious** means to be treated as if an only child (Jr 6:26; Am 8:10; Zch 12:10).

4:4,6 To **keep . . . commands** is to listen attentively, retain,

and obey; it could also be translated "guard." Those who keep their way in godly wisdom (v. 21; 2:20; 5:2; 7:1-2; 8:32; 10:17; 16:17; 19:16; 22:5) will in turn be watched over and guarded by **wisdom** or the Lord (2:8,11; 3:26; 6:22,24; 7:5; 14:3).

4:5-8 Get translates a common Hebrew word for "purchase." There is a great emphasis here that **wisdom** and **understanding** are the most important acquisitions (16:16; 18:15; 23:23; cp. 17:16)—literally "in all your purchasing, purchase understanding" (4:7), that is, spend all your assets on understanding. **Supreme** could also mean the beginning (1:7), the first thing to get. As with salvation, the cost of godly wisdom is not silver and gold. Rather, a person must stop desiring anything else and **love . . . cherish**, and **embrace** only the one thing—that's part of what it means to give up one's life for something. Paradoxically, the cost is both nothing and everything (Is 55:1; Mt 13:44-46; 16:24; 19:21,27; Lk 5:11,28; Php 3:8).

4:9 The **garland** and **crown** are symbolic of God's grace and favor being visible in one's life.

4:10-19 The **wicked** are addicted to doing **evil**—it is their refreshment and their nourishment (vv. 16-17). The son is exhorted to **hold on** to the good and warned not even to try the bad (vv. 13-15; cp. 1:15). Quantity and quality of life are the incentives (vv. 10,13,22; 8:35 see note at 3:22). The righteous increase in **light** while the wicked **stumble** in **gloom**

they don't know what makes
  them stumble.[a]

The Straight Path

20 My son, pay attention to my words;
    listen closely to my sayings.[b]
21 Don't lose sight of them;[c]
    keep them within your heart.
22 For they are life to those
      who find them,
    and health to one's whole body.
23 Guard your heart above all else,[A]
    for it is the source of life.[d]
24 Don't let your mouth
      speak dishonestly,[e]
    and don't let your lips talk deviously.
25 Let your eyes look forward;
    fix your gaze[B] straight ahead.[f]
26 Carefully consider the path[c]
      for your feet,[g]
    and all your ways will be established.
27 Don't turn to the right or to the left;[h]
    keep your feet away from evil.

Avoid Seduction

5 My son, pay attention to my wisdom;
   listen closely[D] to my understanding[i]
2 so that you may maintain discretion
   and your lips safeguard knowledge.[j]
3 Though the lips
     of the forbidden woman drip honey

and her words are[E] smoother than oil,
4 in the end she's as bitter
     as •wormwood[k]
   and as sharp as a double-edged sword.[l]
5 Her feet go down to death;
   her steps head straight for •Sheol.[m]
6 She doesn't consider the path of life;
   she doesn't know that her ways
     are unstable.

7 So now, my sons, listen to me,
   and don't turn away from the words
     of my mouth.[n]
8 Keep your way far from her.
   Don't go near the door of her house.[o]
9 Otherwise, you will give up your vitality
     to others
   and your years to someone cruel;
10 strangers will drain your resources,
   and your earnings will end up
     in a foreigner's house.
11 At the end of your life, you will lament
   when your physical body
     has been consumed,
12 and you will say,
     "How I hated discipline,
   and how my heart
     despised correction.[p]
13 I didn't obey my teachers
   or listen closely[F] to my mentors.

---

[a] 4:19 Pr 24:16; Jn 11:10
[b] 4:20 Pr 5:1
[c] 4:21 Pr 3:21
[d] 4:23 Mt 15:19; Mk 7:18-23
[e] 4:24 Pr 6:12
[f] 4:25 Heb 12:2
[g] 4:26 Pr 5:6,21; Heb 12:13
[h] 4:27 Dt 5:32-33; 28:13-14; Jos 1:7; 23:6; 1Kg 15:5
[i] 5:1 Pr 4:20; 22:17
[j] 5:2 Mal 2:7
[k] 5:4 Pr 5:8-11; 6:32-33; Ec 7:26
[l] Ps 55:21; 57:4
[m] 5:5 Pr 7:27; 9:18
[n] 5:7 Pr 7:24
[o] 5:8 Pr 2:18; 7:8; 9:14
[p] 5:12 Ps 107:11; Pr 1:7,28-31; 12:1; 13:18

A 4:23 Or heart with all diligence   B 4:25 Lit eyelids   C 4:26 Or Clear a path   D 5:1 Lit wisdom; stretch out your ear   E 5:3 Lit her palate is   F 5:13 Lit or turn my ear

---

(vv.18-19; cp. Jb 29:2-3; 1Pt 2:9; Rv 21:23-24). The foolish wicked **don't know** that there is a connection between sin and punishment (5:6; 7:23; 9:18; 28:22).

4:22 On **life**, see note at 3:22.

4:23 Above all else is literally "more than all guarding." To **guard** something is to make sure that it doesn't get away and that it is safe from attack. In Hebrew the **heart** is the location of knowledge and also the preconscious source of decisions (27:19; Mt 15:18). Your heart is who you are, the "true you" that directs all your thoughts and emotions. You can educate your heart (Pr 24:32)—consciously form and modify a worldview—after which decisions and actions flow from it (16:9,23; Lk 6:45; Rm 10:10; 2Co 9:7). This education can be worldly, carried out by yourself, or godly, carried out by the Holy Spirit (Pr 2:6; Jr 24:7; Ezk 36:26-27; Ac 16:14; Rm 2:29). The inclination of your heart directs your mortal **life** and determines whether you enter eternal life (3:22).

4:25-27 Undivided attention to the right **path** (cp. 17:24; 27:20) and a determination not to even sample **evil** (cp. vv. 13-15; 1:15) assure that **your ways will be established**. The passive voice implies that it is God who does it. "Established" is fixed and firm, secure, not subject to change or to destruction (12:3; "achieved" in 16:3; 24:3; 25:5). **Right or . . . left** expresses the whole range of evil paths. That is not to say that a middle road, a compromise, is the good way, but that it is important not to leave the only good way.

5:2 To **maintain** and **safeguard** wisdom includes the responsibility to pass it along (Mal 2:7).

5:3-6 The **forbidden woman** with her smooth **words** (see note at 2:16) seems attractive, but she is in fact deadly. On **in the end**, see note at verse 11. **Wormwood** was a shrub that produced a bitter flavor (Lm 3:15,19). In Hebrew **double-edged** is literally "with mouths," a pun on the way she devours people (Is 1:20). She is headed for eternal **death** (see note at 1:12), along with anyone she can entice to join her, because she does not focus her eyes on **the path of life** (4:25). She is **unstable**—wandering (Gn 4:12; Nm 32:13; 2Sm 15:20; Ps 59:11; 109:10; Lm 4:15), staggering (Ps 107:27; Is 24:20; Am 4:8)—and she doesn't even know it (see note at Pr 4:10-19).

5:9-10 The unwise son gives up his **vitality**; he is not overpowered and robbed (1:11). The **others** to whom he gives his **resources** may be the family of the adulteress (6:29-35). Vitality could also be translated "authority" (Nm 27:20) or "splendor" (Hs 14:6); it describes a man in his prime. A **cruel** person shows no mercy (Jr 6:23).

5:11 At the end describes the outcome of a course of action—what happens later, the ultimate result (v. 4; 14:12; 19:20; 20:21; 23:32; 29:21).

5:12-14 How introduces an expression of grief (Gn 44:34). To hate **discipline**, despise **correction**, and not **obey** or **listen** are characteristics of a fool (see notes at 1:7 and 1:22), which the son was **on the verge** of becoming, despite his father's warnings (1:30-31; 3:11; cp. 12:1; 15:10). These are

14 I am on the verge of complete ruin
    before the entire community."

Enjoy Marriage

15 Drink water from your own cistern,
    water flowing from your own well.ᵃ
16 Should your springs flow in the streets,
    streams of water in the public squares?ᵇ
17 They should be for you alone
    and not for you to share with strangers.
18 Let your fountain be blessed,
    and take pleasure in the wife
      of your youth.ᶜ
19 A loving doe, a graceful fawn—
    let her breasts always satisfy you;ᵈ
    be lost in her love forever.
20 Why, my son, would you be infatuated
    with a forbidden woman
    or embrace the breast of a stranger?ᵉ
21 For a man's ways are
    before the Lᴏʀᴅ's eyes,ᶠ
    and He considers all his paths.ᵍ
22 A wicked man's iniquities entrap him;ʰ
    he is entangled in the ropes
      of his own sin.ⁱ

23 He will die because there is
    no discipline,ʲ
    and be lost because of
    his great stupidity.

Financial Entanglements

6 My son, if you have put up security
    for your neighborᴬ
    or entered into an agreement
    withᴮ a stranger,ᶜ,ᵏ
2 you have been trapped by the words
    of your lipsᴰ—
    ensnared by the words of your mouth.
3 Do this, then, my son, and free yourself,
    for you have put yourself
    in your neighbor's power:
    Go, humble yourself, and plead
    with your neighbor.
4 Don't give sleep to your eyes
    or slumber to your eyelids.ˡ
5 Escape like a gazelle from a hunter,ᴱ
    like a bird from a fowler's trap.ᴱ,ᵐ

Laziness

6 Go to the ant,ⁿ you slacker!ᵒ

Cross references

ᵃ5:15 Sg 4:12,15
ᵇ5:16 Pr 7:12
ᶜ5:18 Ec 9:9; Mal 2:14
ᵈ5:19 Sg 4:5
ᵉ5:20 Pr 2:16
ᶠ5:21 Jb 14:16; Ps 119:168; Hs 7:2; Heb 4:13
ᵍPr 4:25-26
ʰ5:22 Nm 32:23; Ps 7:15-16
ⁱPr 11:6
ʲ5:23 Jb 4:21
ᵏ6:1 Pr 11:15; 17:18; 20:16; 22:26; 27:13
ˡ6:4 Ps 132:4
ᵐ6:5 Ps 91:3; 124:7
ⁿ6:6 Pr 30:24-25
ᵒPr 10:26; 13:4; 20:4; 26:16

ᴬ6:1 Or *friend*   ᴮ6:1 Lit *or shaken hands for* or *with*   ᶜ6:1 The Hb word for *stranger* can refer to a foreigner, an Israelite outside one's family, or simply to another person.   ᴰ6:2 Lit *mouth*   ᴱ6:5 Lit *hand*

---

not school **teachers** but parents (1:8) or sages (1:6; 30:1; 31:1; Ec 12:9). The destiny of a fool is **ruin** (see "trouble" in note at 1:16) **before the . . . community**, convened as if for a trial (26:26; cp. Jr 26:7-11).

5:15-19 The many figurative references to **water**—cistern, flowing, well, springs, streams, fountain—are interpreted as one's wife. The allusion is to quenching one's sexual thirst (9:17; Sg 5:1). Many houses had their own private cisterns to store rain water. Wells, springs, and streams supplied sweet, refreshing water. The father prayed that God would bless his son's wife, with the result that the son would always **take pleasure** in her since something that is blessed is by definition able to **satisfy** (3:33; 22:9). The **wife of your youth** is the first wife (2:17; Is 54:6; Mal 2:14-15); a man should not seek another wife or a different woman. **Loving** implies sexual love (7:18; Hs 8:9). "Satisfy" (Jr 31:25) also means "drench" or "watered" (Is 16:9; 58:11; cp. Pr 7:18). In this context, to **be lost** is to drift unconsciously in pleasure. In other contexts it is used of intoxication (20:1; Sg 5:1) or straying from righteousness (Pr 19:27; cp. 5:23).

5:20 Why suggests the action is inexcusable. To be **infatuated** is literally to "stray" (19:27; Ps 119:118; Ezk 34:6) or to "err, sin" (Lv 4:13; Jb 19:4); it is translated "be lost" in Pr 5:19,23. On **forbidden woman** and **stranger**, see note at 2:16. The **breast** is the part of the body involved in an em-**brace**, also translated "in one's arms" (6:27; cp. 2Sm 12:8; Mc 7:5).

5:23 The wicked man (v. 22) will **be lost** (vv. 19-20) to eternal death because he didn't let **discipline** replace his **stupidity** with wisdom (6:23; 15:10). "Stupidity" comes from Hb *ewiyl* (see note at 1:7; cp. 12:23; 13:16; 14:8).

6:1 To **put up security** is "to pledge oneself as a guarantee for another's debts"; if the debtor defaulted, the son would have to pay or be liable to seizure. **Entered into an agree-**ment is literally "struck your palm," probably referring to a gesture that made it official (Ru 4:7-8), an ancient equivalent of shaking hands or signing a contract. To risk one's assets and reputation for a **neighbor** or friend is inadvisable (17:18), much less for a **stranger** (11:15; 20:16; 27:13; cp. 22:26).

6:3 The **son** is in his **neighbor's power** (lit "palm"; see v. 2) because if the neighbor defaults, the son must pay. He should **plead** (lit "assault" his neighbor) incessantly to be released from the security agreement. The word translated **humble yourself** could also be translated "weary yourself."

6:4 Sleep and **slumber** when a person should be working leads to ruin (vv. 9-11).

6:5 A "fowler" is one who hunts birds (Ps 91:3; Jr 5:26; Hs 9:8).

6:6 A **slacker** is a lazy person (26:14) who hopes to sustain

The Rhorr gazelle (6:5) is one species of antelope found in Israel.

Observe its ways and become wise.
7 Without leader, administrator, or ruler,
8 it prepares its provisions in summer;
it gathers its food during harvest.[a]
9 How long will you stay in bed,
you slacker?
When will you get up from your sleep?
10 A little sleep, a little slumber,
a little folding of the arms to rest,[b]
11 and your poverty will come like
a robber,
your need, like a bandit.[c]

The Malicious Man

12 A worthless person,[d] a wicked man
goes around speaking dishonestly,[e]
13 winking[f] his eyes, signaling
with his feet,
and gesturing with his fingers.
14 He always plots evil[g] with perversity
in his heart—
he stirs up trouble.[h]
15 Therefore calamity
will strike him suddenly;
he will be shattered instantly—
beyond recovery.[i]

What the Lord Hates

16 The Lord hates six things;
in fact, seven are detestable to Him:
17 arrogant eyes,[j] a lying tongue,[k]
hands that shed innocent blood,[l]
18 a heart that plots wicked schemes,[m]
feet eager to run to evil,[n]
19 a lying witness who gives
false testimony,[o]
and one who stirs up trouble
among brothers.[p]

Warning against Adultery

20 My son, keep your father's command,
and don't reject
your mother's teaching.[q]
21 Always bind them to your heart;
tie them around your neck.[r]
22 When you walk here and there,
they will guide you;
when you lie down, they will
watch over you;
when you wake up, they will
talk to you.
23 For a command is a lamp,
teaching is a light,[s]
and corrective discipline is the way
to life.[t]
24 They will protect you
from an evil woman,[A]
from the flattering[B] tongue
of a stranger.[u]
25 Don't lust in your heart for her beauty[v]
or let her captivate you
with her eyelashes.[w]
26 For a prostitute's fee is only a loaf
of bread,[C]

[a]6:8 Pr 10:5; 30:25 [b]6:10 Pr 26:14; Ec 4:5 [c]6:10-11 Pr 20:13; 24:33-34; Ec 4:5 [d]6:12 1Sm 25:25; Pr 16:27; 19:28 [e]Pr 4:24 [f]6:13 Ps 35:19; Pr 10:10; 16:30 [g]6:14 Pr 3:29; Mc 2:1 [h]Pr 6:19; 16:27-28; 28:25 [i]6:15 2Ch 36:16; Pr 24:22; 29:1; Is 30:13-14; Jr 19:11 [j]6:17 Ps 18:27; Pr 21:4; 30:13 [k]Ps 31:18; 120:2; Pr 12:22; 17:7 [l]Dt 19:10; Pr 1:16; Is 1:15; 59:7 [m]6:18 Gn 6:5 [n]Pr 1:16 [o]6:19 Ex 20:16; Ps 27:12; Pr 12:17; 14:5,25 [p]Pr 6:14; 16:27-28; 28:25 [q]6:20 Pr 1:8; 31:1 [r]6:21 Pr 1:9; 3:3; 7:3 [s]6:23 Ps 119:105 [t]Pr 3:1-2; 4:4; 7:2; 19:16 [u]6:24 Pr 7:5 [v]6:25 Mt 5:28 [w]Sg 4:9

[A]6:24 LXX reads *from a married woman* [B]6:24 Lit *smooth* [C]6:26 Or *On account of a prostitute, one is left with only a loaf of bread*

his life without actually working (20:4; 21:25)—he literally refuses to lift a hand (19:24). He makes excuses not to work (22:13). Unlike the oppressed (31:9), the slacker has brought his poverty on himself and is not an object of pity. His opposite is a diligent person (13:4). As the son listens to his father admonishing the slacker, he himself is warned against laziness (19:25). A wise person learns from observation (24:32; 30:24-28; see "prudence" in note at 1:3).

6:8 This verse describes harvester ants that store grain in their nests.

6:9 Asking **how long** generally implies that something bad has been going on for too long (1:22; cp. Ex 10:3; Ps 74:10).

6:10 On **sleep** and **slumber**, see note at verse 4.

6:11 **Poverty** in this context is destitution brought on oneself (13:18; 28:19). It is not the same as oppressed people who are poor because of circumstances beyond their control, and who deserve pity (19:17). The **robber** is literally a "traveler," perhaps a vagabond or drifter. The **bandit** is literally a "man with a shield," an armed man. His attack is sudden and unexpected.

6:12 The Hebrew word *beliyya'al* (**worthless**) identifies a troublemaker who rebels against all good and godly authority (16:27; 19:28; 2Ch 13:7; Jb 34:18). It is translated "perverted" in Judges (Jdg 19:22; 20:13) and "wicked" in many places (Dt 13:13; 1Sm 2:12; 2Sm 20:1). He is described in Pr 6:12-14. "Belial" became a synonym for Satan (2Co 6:15).

6:13 This body language was apparently conspiratorial or deceptive (16:30; Is 58:9). He literally "compresses" his **eyes**, "shuffles" his **feet**, and "throws in" his **fingers**.

6:14 On **perversity**, see note at 2:12. To stir up **trouble** is to spread dissension and strife (6:19; 16:28; Jr 15:10).

6:15 **Suddenly** implies surprise (24:22; Jos 10:9; Ec 9:12; Is 47:11). **Instantly** further emphasizes the speed of the destruction (Is 29:5-6; 30:13; cp. Jr 4:20). The last words are literally "there is no healing."

6:16 On **detestable**, see note at 3:32.

6:17 **Arrogant** is literally "raised high." It describes proud people who deny God's authority (21:4; 30:13; cp. 2Kg 19:22; Ps 18:27; 131:1; Is 10:12; 37:23).

6:19 To be a **lying witness** and to give **false testimony** are the same; the two expressions are used for clarity (14:5; 19:5). On **trouble**, see note at verse 14.

6:20-24 Instruction that has been internalized sustains the person who faces moral challenges (Ps 119:11). While verse 21 refers to **them**, verse 22 literally says "she" **will guide you**, perhaps referring to the **command** or the **teaching** in verse 20 or to Lady Wisdom, a common personification of wisdom. The word for "guide" is the same as "leads" in Ps 23:3. Walking, lying down, and waking up covers all aspects of daily life (Dt 6:7; Ps 139:2). On **life**, see note at 3:22; on **stranger** and **flattering**, see note at 2:16.

6:26 This is not to excuse prostitution (1Co 6:15-20) but to

but an adulteress[A] goes after
a precious life.[a]

27 Can a man embrace fire[B]
and his clothes not be burned?

28 Can a man walk on burning coals
without scorching his feet?

29 So it is with the one who sleeps with
another man's wife;
no one who touches her
will go unpunished.[b]

30 People don't despise the thief
if he steals
to satisfy himself when he is hungry.[c]

31 Still, if caught, he must pay
seven times as much;[d]
he must give up all the wealth
in his house.

32 The one who commits adultery[C]
lacks sense;
whoever does so destroys himself.[e]

33 He will get a beating[D] and dishonor,
and his disgrace will never be removed.

34 For jealousy enrages a husband,[f]
and he will show no mercy
when he takes revenge.

35 He will not be appeased by anything
or be persuaded by lavish gifts.

7 My son, obey my words,
and treasure my commands.[g]

2 Keep my commands and live;[h]
protect my teachings
as the pupil of your eye.[i]

3 Tie them to your fingers;
write them on the tablet of your heart.[j]

4 Say to wisdom, "You are my sister,"[k]
and call understanding your relative.

5 She will keep you
from a forbidden woman,
a stranger with her flattering talk.[l]

A Story of Seduction

6 At the window of my house
I looked through my lattice.[m]

7 I saw among the inexperienced,[E]
I noticed among the youths,
a young man lacking sense.

8 Crossing the street near her corner,
he strolled down the road to her house

9 at twilight, in the evening,
in the dark of the night.[n]

10 A woman came to meet him
dressed like a prostitute,[o]
having a hidden agenda.[F]

11 She is loud and defiant;[p]
her feet do not stay at home.[q]

12 Now in the street, now in the squares,[r]
she lurks at every corner.[s]

13 She grabs him and kisses him;
she brazenly says[G] to him,

Cross references (center column):

a 6:26 Pr 2:18-19; 7:21-23,27; 23:27-28; Ezk 13:18
b 6:29 Pr 16:5
c 6:30 Jr 49:9; Ob 5
d 6:31 Ex 22:1-4; Ps 79:12
e 6:32 Pr 7:22-23
f 6:34 Pr 27:4; Sg 8:6
g 7:1 Pr 2:1
h 7:2 Pr 3:1-2; 4:4; 6:23; 19:16
i Dt 32:10; Ps 17:8; Zch 2:8
j 7:3 Dt 11:18; Pr 3:3; 6:21
k 7:4 Sg 4:9
l 7:5 Pr 5:3,20; 6:24; 7:21
m 7:6 Jdg 5:28; Sg 2:9
n 7:9 Jb 24:15
o 7:10 Gn 38:14-15
p 7:11 Pr 9:13
q 1Tm 5:13
r 7:12 Pr 5:16; 9:14
s Pr 23:28

A 6:26 Lit *but a wife of a man*   B 6:27 Lit *man take fire to his bosom*   C 6:32 Lit *commits adultery with a woman*   D 6:33 Or *plague*
E 7:7 Or *simple*, or *gullible*, or *naive*   F 7:10 Or *prostitute with a guarded heart*   G 7:13 Lit *she makes her face strong and says*

---

illustrate the terrible penalty of adultery by way of comparison; the adulteress will destroy someone's **life**.

6:27-29 These verses illustrate the inevitability of punishment. To **go unpunished** is a legal term meaning to be acquitted, declared innocent, pardoned, or released; to be set free from guilt, liability, or punishment (Ex 21:19; Nm 5:31). The basic meaning of the word is to be pure, clean, or free. To say that someone will not go unpunished is more emphatic than simply saying he will be punished (Pr 11:21; 16:5; 17:5; 19:5,9; 28:20; cp. Ex 34:7; 1Kg 2:9; Jr 25:29; 49:12).

6:30-33 A **thief** is guilty of a crime and must pay a severe penalty, but if there are mitigating circumstances he does not totally lose the respect of the community. **Seven times** is not literal here but is an expression that implies he must pay the full penalty, from twice to five times what he stole (Ex 22:1,7,9; cp. Lk 19:8); a repeat offender could go broke. An adulterer, on the other hand, suffers punishment plus complete, permanent **disgrace**. The person who brings this on himself **lacks sense** (lit "has no heart"; see note at 4:23; cp. 8:5)—he is brainless.

6:34-35 While a court can be satisfied when a fine is paid (v. 31), a jealous **husband** can never be satisfied (27:4; cp. Sg 8:6). On **appeased**, see "show partiality" in note at 18:5. Verse 35a can be translated, "He will not look favorably on any kind of ransom." The **gifts** are literally a "bribe" to subvert justice (17:8,23; 21:14).

7:1-5 This section may connect with 6:20-24 to conclude the speech begun there, or it may introduce 7:6-27. The origin of the Hebrew word translated **pupil** is "little man," the tiny reflection one sees in another person's eye. Because the eye is sensitive yet indispensable, it is closely guarded (Dt 32:10; Zch 2:8). To **write** something on the **heart** is to internalize it so that it directs one's actions (2:1-4; 6:20-24; Jr 17:1; 31:31-34). On **forbidden woman . . . stranger**, and **flattering talk**, see note at 2:16.

7:6 In ancient times a **window** had a **lattice** that let in light and air (Jdg 5:28; 2Kg 1:2; Sg 2:9).

7:7 The **young man** whom Solomon observed had not yet acquired protection by committing himself to wisdom and discretion (1:4; 2:11; 4:6). **Youths** is literally "sons." On **inexperienced**, see note at 1:4; on **lacking sense**, see note at 6:30-33.

7:11 The word translated **loud** implies restless movement as well as noise—commotion (1:21); uproar (1Kg 1:41).

7:12 Lurks is literally "ambush" (1:11; 23:28; 24:15; Dt 19:11).

7:13 To speak **brazenly** is to lie with arrogance (21:29).

7:14-15 She includes religion in her lie. Her flattery includes the lie that she searched specifically for him. In reality she was on the hunt for any vulnerable young man.

7:16-17 She seduces him by describing her **bed** (cp. 31:22) with its luxurious and suggestive perfumes (cp. Sg 4:14).

14 "I've made •fellowship offerings;^A
today I've fulfilled my vows.^a
15 So I came out to meet you,
to search for you, and I've found you.
16 I've spread coverings on my bed^b—
richly colored linen from Egypt.^c
17 I've perfumed my bed
with myrrh, aloes, and cinnamon.^d
18 Come, let's drink deeply of lovemaking
until morning.^e
Let's feast on each other's love!
19 My husband isn't home;
he went on a long journey.
20 He took a bag of money with him
and will come home at the time
of the full moon."
21 She seduces him
with her persistent pleading;
she lures with her flattering^B talk.
22 He follows her impulsively
like an ox going to the slaughter,
like a deer bounding toward a trap^C
23 until an arrow pierces its^D liver,^f
like a bird darting into a snare^g—
he doesn't know it will cost him
his life.
24 Now, my sons, listen to me,
and pay attention to the words
of my mouth.
25 Don't let your heart turn aside
to her ways;
don't stray onto her paths.^h

Cross references (center column):
^a 7:14 Lv 7:11-18; Dt 23:18; Ps 56:12
^b 7:16 Pr 31:22
^c Ezk 27:7
^d 7:17 Ex 30:23; Ps 45:8
^e 7:18 Sg 5:1
^f 7:21-23 Pr 2:16-19; 5:3-6; 23:27-28
^g 7:23 Ec 9:12
^h 7:25 Pr 5:8
^i 7:27 Pr 2:18; 5:5; 9:18; 1Co 6:9; Rv 22:15
^j 8:1-3 Pr 1:20-21; 9:3,13-15
^k 8:3 Jb 29:7
^l 8:7 Ps 37:30
^m 8:8 Dt 32:5; Pr 2:15; Php 2:15
^n 8:9 Pr 14:6

26 For she has brought many
down to death;
her victims are countless.^E
27 Her house is the road to •Sheol,
descending to the chambers of death.^i

Wisdom's Appeal

8 Doesn't Wisdom^j call out?
Doesn't Understanding make her voice
heard?
2 At the heights overlooking the road,
at the crossroads, she takes her stand.
3 Beside the gates^k at the entry
to^F the city,
at the main entrance, she cries out:
4 "People, I call out to you;
my cry is to mankind.
5 Learn to be shrewd,
you who are inexperienced;
develop common sense,
you who are foolish.
6 Listen, for I speak of noble things,
and what my lips say is right.
7 For my mouth tells the truth,^l
and wickedness is detestable to my lips.
8 All the words of my mouth
are righteous;
none of them are deceptive
or perverse.^m
9 All of them are clear to the perceptive,^n
and right to those
who discover knowledge.
10 Accept my instruction instead of silver,

---

^A 7:14 Meat from a fellowship offering had to be eaten on the day it was offered; therefore she is inviting him to a feast at her house.　^B 7:21 Lit *smooth*　^C 7:22 Text emended; MT reads *like a shackle to the discipline of a fool*; Hb obscure　^D 7:23 Or *his*　^E 7:26 Or *and powerful men are all her victims*　^F 8:3 Lit *the mouth of*

7:18 Drink deeply is the same Hebrew word as "satisfy" in 5:19; she claims to offer what only a wife should give (Sg 5:1). This is not true **love** but lust (2Sm 13:1; Hs 8:9; cp. Sg 8:6-7).

7:19-20 She promises they won't get caught, ignoring the eternal consequences of their sin (v. 23). The length of the husband's business trip is indicated by the amount of **money** he took with him.

7:22 Impulsively is literally "suddenly" (see note at 6:15).

7:23 The **liver** was considered the reservoir of life-blood. A **snare** seems attractive but is deadly (22:5; Jos 23:13; Am 3:5; cp. Pr 1:17-18). On **he doesn't know**, see note at 4:10-19.

7:26 Brought many down to death and **victims** are military terms.

7:27 On **Sheol**, see note at 1:12. She lures youths to eternal **death** (2:18; 5:5,23).

8:1-3 Like the forbidden woman (7:5), **Wisdom**—again personified as a lady (1:20-21)—extends an invitation to the inexperienced (8:5; cp. 7:7). Unlike the forbidden woman, Wisdom's invitation is very public in broad daylight, her appeal is spiritual not sexual, and her promise is life not

death. Wisdom and **Understanding** are two names for the same "lady."

8:4 Her appeal to **people** and **mankind** (lit "sons of Adam") may emphasize her broad appeal (Ps 49:1-2) or the mortality of her audience (2Ch 14:11; Ps 39:5; 90:3; Is 51:12).

8:5 On **shrewd** and **inexperienced**, see note at 1:4. **Common sense** is literally an "understanding heart"—a mind that functions as it should (4:23; cp. 6:32). On **foolish**, see "fool" in note at 1:22.

8:6 The word translated **noble** might also mean "morally straight" (v. 9).

8:7 On **detestable**, see note at 3:32.

8:8 On **perverse**, see "crooked" in note at 2:15.

8:9 Both **clear** and **right** relate to what is straight in front of a person, not twisted, crooked, or off to the side. A **perceptive** person is insightful, intelligent, and discerning (1:5). Those who seek **knowledge** diligently will **discover** it (2:1-5).

8:10 One must choose to pursue either godly wisdom or riches; there is no third way (4:27; Mt 6:24). Yet there is often monetary reward with wisdom (Pr 8:18-21; cp. 1Kg 3:11-13).

and knowledge rather than pure gold.[a]

11 For wisdom is better than jewels,[b]
and nothing desirable can compare
with it.[c]

12 I, Wisdom, share a home
with shrewdness
and have knowledge and discretion.[d]

13 To °fear the LORD is to hate evil.[e]
I hate arrogant pride, evil conduct,
and perverse speech.

14 I possess good advice and competence;[A]
I have understanding and strength.[f]

15 It is by me that kings reign[g]
and rulers enact just law;

16 by me, princes lead,
as do nobles and all righteous judges.[B]

17 I love those who love me,[h]
and those who search for me find me.[i]

18 With me are riches and honor,[j]
lasting wealth and righteousness.[k]

19 My fruit is better than solid gold,
and my harvest than pure silver.[l]

20 I walk in the way of righteousness,
along the paths of justice,

21 giving wealth as an inheritance
to those who love me,
and filling their treasuries.

22 "The LORD made[C] me
at the beginning of His creation,[D]
before His works of long ago.[m]

23 I was formed before ancient times,
from the beginning,
before the earth began.[n]

24 I was born
when there were no watery depths[o]
and no springs filled with water.

25 I was delivered
before the mountains and hills
were established,[p]

26 before He made the land, the fields,
or the first soil on earth.

27 I was there when He established
the heavens,[q]
when He laid out the horizon
on the surface of the ocean,[r]

28 when He placed the skies above,
when the fountains of the ocean
gushed out,

29 when He set a limit for the sea
so that the waters would not violate
His command,[s]
when He laid out the foundations
of the earth.[t]

30 I was a skilled craftsman[E] beside Him.[u]

---

a 8:10 Pr 3:14-15; 8:19; 16:16
b 8:11 Jb 28:12-19
c Pr 3:15; 20:15
d 8:12 Pr 1:4
e 8:13 Pr 16:6
f 8:14 Ec 7:19
g 8:15 2Ch 1:10; Dn 2:21; Rm 13:1
h 8:17 1Sm 2:30; Jn 14:21
i Pr 1:28; 2:4-5; Jms 1:5
j 8:18 Pr 3:16
k Ps 112:3; Mt 6:33
l 8:19 Jb 28:15; Pr 3:14; 8:10; 16:16
m 8:22 Gn 1:1; Jb 28:26-28; Ps 104:24
n 8:23 Jn 1:1-3; 17:5
o 8:24 Gn 1:2; Pr 3:20
p 8:25 Ps 90:2
q 8:27 Pr 3:19
r Jb 26:10
s 8:29 Jb 38:8-11; Ps 104:9
t Jb 38:4-5; Ps 104:5
u 8:30 Jb 28:20-27; 38-39; Pr 3:19-20; Jr 10:12; 51:15; Zch 13:7; Jn 1:2-3

A 8:14 Or resourcefulness   B 8:16 Some Hb mss, LXX read nobles who judge the earth   C 8:22 Or possessed, or begot   D 8:22 Lit way
E 8:30 Or a confidant, or a child, or was constantly

8:11 Lady Wisdom is speaking (vv. 1,4,12), commending **wisdom**.

8:12-14 The point of **Wisdom** sharing **a home** with or possessing the other virtues is that if you find one you find the others. Those who **fear the LORD** have the mind of Christ and therefore view **evil** the same way that God does (1Co 2:15-16). **Arrogant pride** translates two Hebrew words for pride; the first is found in 15:25 and 16:19, the second in

16:18. Pride and arrogance are characteristics of those who refuse to acknowledge God's rule. **Good advice and competence** implies counsel that brings success (19:20; 20:18; Is 28:29). These kinds of qualities belong to God (Jb 12:13). The Spirit (Is 11:2) and the Son (1Co 1:30) mediate wisdom's qualities to godly people.

8:16 A "noble" was a powerful and respected royal courtier (17:7,26; 19:6; 25:7), the opposite of the boorish fool (Is 32:5,8); the same Hebrew word describes those who have a generous and willing spirit (Ex 35:5,22; 2Ch 29:31; Ps 51:12).

8:17 To **love** and to **search** imply emotional passion and diligence.

8:18 Riches and **honor** involve wealth granted by Lady Wisdom without social stigma (3:16; 11:22; 22:4; Jms 2:6; 5:1). Ironically, those who pursue riches get dishonor (Jr 17:11; 1Tm 6:10). **Lasting wealth** is wealth in this life that does not evaporate (11:7; 13:11; 27:23-24; 28:22), and it includes treasures in heaven as well (Mt 6:20; 1Tm 6:17-18).

8:19 Pure is literally "choice," meaning "desired, precious" (Ps 132:13).

8:20-21 Where Wisdom "walks" is where she can be found and where she will lead her followers so they will be rewarded. The reward of her **way** contrasts with the disastrous way of the wicked and fools (2:15; 4:14; 5:8-10; 22:5; see note at 1:15). On **inheritance**, see note at 3:35.

8:22-29 Wisdom was **made** by God **before the earth began**. Wisdom witnessed all the rest of God's creative activity, and Wisdom was a craftsman in creation. Therefore, Wisdom is in a unique position to explain creation to mortals (Jb 38:2-4). Since wisdom is a skill dependent on knowledge, it is not

---

da'ath

Hebrew Pronunciation	[DAH aht]
HCSB Translation	knowledge
Uses in Proverbs	39
Uses in the OT	88
Key Passage	Proverbs 8:9,10,12

Fundamentally, da'ath (knowledge) refers to a relational awareness of people or objects gained through the senses. Knowledge is gained through practical involvement with the object of knowledge, and da'ath only infrequently expresses the concept of abstract intellectual knowledge apart from relationship. In Proverbs, there are two understandings of knowledge. In chapters 1-9, knowledge focuses more on insight gained through theological reflection (1:7,29; 2:5,6,10; 3:20; 9:10), while in chapters 10-29, knowledge focuses primarily upon the ability to handle interpersonal relationships (10:14; 11:9; 12:1; 14:6; 17:27; 19:25; 21:11; 23:12). In theological contexts, God possesses knowledge (Jb 10:7; Pr 3:20), and He disseminates it to men (Jb 21:22; Ps 94:10; 119:66; Is 40:14). The fear of the Lord is the beginning of knowledge (da'ath; Pr 1:7; 2:5), and the perception of God's plans and purposes through relationship with Him is referred to as knowledge (Is 5:13; 11:2; 58:2; Jr 10:14; 51:17).

I was His[A] delight every day,
always rejoicing before Him.
31 I was rejoicing in His inhabited world,[a]
delighting in the •human race.[b]

32 "And now, my sons, listen to me;
those who keep my ways are happy.[c]
33 Listen to instruction and be wise;[d]
don't ignore it.
34 Anyone who listens to me is happy,[e]
watching at my doors every day,
waiting by the posts of my doorway.
35 For the one who finds me finds life[f]
and obtains favor from the LORD,[g]
36 but the one who misses me[B]
harms himself;[h]
all who hate me love death."[i]

Wisdom versus Foolishness

9 Wisdom has built her house;[j]
she has carved out her seven pillars.
2 She has prepared her meat;[k]
she has mixed her wine;[l]
she has also set her table.[m]
3 She has sent out her female servants;[n]
she calls out from the highest points
of the city:[o]

4 "Whoever is inexperienced,
enter here!"
To the one who lacks sense,[p] she says,
5 "Come, eat my bread,[q]
and drink the wine I have mixed.
6 Leave inexperience behind,
and you will live;
pursue the way of understanding.
7 The one who corrects a mocker
will bring dishonor on himself;
the one who rebukes a wicked man
will get hurt.[C]
8 Don't rebuke a mocker, or he will
hate you;[r]
rebuke a wise man, and he will
love you.[s]
9 Instruct a wise man, and he will be
wiser still;
teach a righteous man, and he will
learn more.[t]

10 "The •fear of the LORD is the beginning
of wisdom,[u]
and the knowledge of the Holy One[v]
is understanding.
11 For by Wisdom your days will be many,

Cross-references
a8:31 Jb 38:4-7
bHeb 2:6-8
c8:32 Ps 119:1-2; 128:1; Lk 11:28
d8:33 Pr 4:1
e8:34 Pr 3:13
f8:35 Pr 4:4,22; 7:2; 9:11; 12:28; Jn 17:3
gPr 3:4; 12:2; 13:13; 18:22
h8:36 Pr 15:32
iPr 11:19; 21:6
j9:1 Pr 14:1; Eph 2:20-22; 1Pt 2:5
k9:2 Mt 22:4
lSg 8:2
mLk 14:17
n9:3 Ps 68:11; Mt 22:3
o Pr 8:2-3; 9:14-15; Mt 10:27
p9:4 Pr 6:32
q9:5 Is 55:1; Jn 6:27,51
r9:8 Pr 15:12; Mt 7:6
sPs 141:5
t9:9 Pr 1:5; 16:21,23
u9:10 Jb 28:28; Ps 111:10; Pr 1:7; 15:33
vPr 30:3; Hs 11:12; Rv 16:5

A8:30 LXX; MT omits *His*   B8:36 Or *who sins against me*   C9:7 Lit *man his blemish*

really an entity that can be created. So this is a figurative way to say that God is its source. Thus true wisdom can only come from Him. The concept that God created wisdom also conveys that all God created and all He does are the products of His infinite wisdom. Because Wisdom existed before creation and was involved in creation (Pr 3:19-20; 8:22,30) and because the same is said of Christ (Jn 1:3; 1Co 8:6; Col 1:15-16), Wisdom has been identified with Christ. However, the NT never cites Proverbs or the Hebrew word for "wisdom" (*sophia*) with regard to the preexistence of Christ. Also, Pr 8:22-25 declare that Wisdom was made, **formed**, and **born**, but Christ is coeternal with the Father. Wisdom was a spectator during creation, but Christ is the Creator (Jn 1:3; Col 1:16). Christ displays God's wisdom in atonement (1Co 1:20-25,30), in which Wisdom had no role. Christ is similar to Wisdom in some ways but far superior (Mt 12:42); He is Wisdom's source and consummate expression.

8:30-31 Wisdom was **beside** God, but only God was the Creator. Wisdom was **rejoicing** in God's creation; it would be sinful to celebrate creation without acknowledging God. Within creation, Wisdom's ultimate object of rejoicing and **delighting** is humankind.

8:32-34 And now draws a logical conclusion from what was just said. Because Wisdom is ancient and was with God in creation and delights in humanity, she can teach people how to be truly **happy** (see note at 3:13-18). The key is to listen to her, not ignore instruction (1:25; 13:18; 15:32), and desire her so much as to hang around her **doors** in order not to miss her invitation (9:4).

8:35-36 On **life**, see note at 3:22. To obtain **favor** is to become someone in whom **the LORD** delights (11:20; 12:2,22; 15:8; 18:22) and whom He blesses. This word for sin is literally "miss the mark" or "fall short" (Is 65:20), an apt contrast to

finds. Harm refers to violence (Lm 2:6; Ezk 22:26; Zph 3:4) or brutality (Jr 22:3). Rejecting Wisdom is self-destructive (Pr 1:18-19,31-32; 2:18-19; 26:6; 29:6,24).

9:1-2 Lady **Wisdom** is preparing a banquet to dedicate her **house** (cp. 1Kg 8:62-66). The **seven pillars**, the number of perfection, suggest that it was a large, durable house. **Mixed . . . wine** contained honey or spices (Ps 75:8; Sg 8:2). Symbolically, she is ready to share her enjoyable and beneficial instruction.

9:3 Through **her . . . servants**, she **calls out**; the messengers speak in the name of the sender (Nm 22:5). Her servants are sages, teachers, pastors, and parents. Her invitation is very public (Pr 1:21; 8:1-4).

9:4-6 Enter is literally "turn"; it implies leaving one path in favor of another (3:7; 4:27; 5:7; 11:22; 13:14,19; 14:16,27; 16:6; 22:6). She invites the **inexperienced** (see note at 1:4), **who lacks sense** (see note at 6:30-33), to **leave** his path and **pursue** her **way** (see note at 1:15) that leads to life (Jn 6:27,51-58). There is no middle road (see note at Pr 4:25-27); if he does not choose Wisdom, he will end up a mocker (1:22).

9:7-9 The teacher is warned to avoid the unteachable (Mt 7:6). **Dishonor** could also be translated "insults" (12:16). Indirectly, this encourages the inexperienced not to become the obstinate, malevolent **mocker** (1:22) or the hostile **wicked** person (2:22), but instead the benevolent **wise** and **righteous** person who continues to **learn more**. The wise never reach the point where they can't become **wiser still** (1:5; 4:18; 12:1; 13:1; 19:25; 21:11; Mt 13:12).

9:10 The wise are teachable (10:9) because they are humble and they **fear . . . the LORD** (see note at 1:7).

9:11 These phrases imply both a long **life** and eternal life (see note at 3:22).

and years will be added to your life.

12 If you are wise, you are wise
for your own benefit;[a]
if you mock, you alone will bear
the consequences."

13 The woman Folly is rowdy;[b]
she is gullible and knows nothing.[c]

14 She sits by the doorway of her house,
on a seat at the highest point
of the city,

15 calling to those who pass by,
who go straight ahead on their paths:[d]

16 "Whoever is inexperienced, enter here!"
To the one who lacks sense, she says,

17 "Stolen water is sweet,
and bread eaten secretly is tasty!"[e]

18 But he doesn't know
that the departed spirits are there,[f]
that her guests are in the depths
of *Sheol.[g]

A Collection of Solomon's Proverbs

10 Solomon's proverbs:[h]

A wise son brings joy to his father,
but a foolish son, heartache
to his mother.[i]

2 Ill-gotten gains do not profit anyone,
but righteousness rescues from death.[j]

3 The LORD will not let the righteous
go hungry,[k]
but He denies the wicked
what they crave.[l]

4 Idle hands make one poor,
but diligent hands bring riches.[m]

5 The son who gathers during summer
is prudent;
the son who sleeps during harvest
is disgraceful.[n]

6 Blessings are on the head
of the righteous,
but the mouth of the wicked
conceals violence.[o]

7 The remembrance of the righteous is
a blessing,
but the name of the wicked will rot.[p]

8 A wise heart accepts commands,[q]
but foolish lips will be destroyed.

9 The one who lives with integrity
lives securely,[r]

a9:12 Jb 22:2
b9:13 Pr 7:11
cPr 5:6
d9:14-15 Pr 7:11-12; 9:3-4
e9:17 Pr 20:17
f9:18 Pr 2:18; 21:16
gPr 5:5; 7:27
h10:1 Pr 1:1
iPr 15:20; 17:25; 23:24-25; 29:3,15
j10:2 Pr 11:4,18; 12:28; 21:6; Ezk 7:19; Lk 12:19-20
k10:3 Ps 37:25; Mt 6:33
lPs 112:10
m10:4 Pr 12:24,27; 13:4,11; 19:15; 21:5
n10:5 Pr 6:6-11; 30:25
o10:6 Pr 10:11
p10:7 Ps 9:5-6; 112:6
q10:8 Mt 7:24
r10:9 Ps 23:4; Pr 2:7; 3:23; 19:1; 20:7; 28:6,18; Is 33:15-16

9:12 This verse emphasizes the individual nature of rewards and **consequences** (see Ezk 18), but a person's family (Pr 20:7; 23:25) and a leader's followers (11:10; 29:2,4) are also affected.

9:13 On **Folly**, see "fool" in note at 1:22; on **rowdy**, see "loud" in note at 7:11. Lady Folly is **gullible** (the same Hebrew word as "inexperienced"—see note at 1:4—but in her case she has chosen a path) and ignorant of morality and the consequences of choosing against it (v. 18; 4:19; 5:6; 23:35; 28:22).

9:14 While Wisdom is industrious (vv. 1-3), Folly **sits**. Chairs were rare in ancient times. Only kings and honored teachers sat (2Sm 19:8; 1Kg 2:12,19; Est 5:1; Ps 29:10; Mt 5:1; 23:2; Lk 4:20)—so her **seat** (lit "throne") was her pretentious claim of authority to rule or teach.

9:15-16 The **inexperienced** person (see note at 1:4) was going **straight ahead**, but he lacked the resolve and ability to resist the temptation to turn aside (v. 4; 4:10-19,25-27; 1Jn 2:19). Folly tempts vulnerable people (Pr 1:11; Mt 23:14-15).

9:17 Lady Wisdom offers a feast (vv. 2,5), Folly only **water** and **bread**, but her appeal is the attraction that sin has for fallen man (Ps 52:3; Jr 14:10; Mc 3:2; Jn 3:19; 1Pt 4:3).

9:18 Neither Folly (v. 13) nor fallen man knows that death is the outcome of this path (4:19; 5:3-5; 8:36; 14:12). On **departed spirits**, see note at 2:18-19; on **Sheol**, see note at 1:12.

10:1 Chapters 1–9 contain discourses on wisdom. From here to the end of the book the sayings are proverbs proper.

10:2 **Ill-gotten gains** are literally "treasures of wickedness," wealth obtained by harming another person.

10:3 This proverb should not be taken as a universal promise that **the righteous** will never go **hungry** in this life, but it is certainly true that the life of wisdom and righteousness tends to promote a healthy and secure lifestyle. This lifetime is destined to have its struggles. God's care for His children has its ultimate application in eternity. On the characteristics of proverbs, see the Introduction.

10:4-5 Hard work and prudence (see note at 1:3) are rewarded.

10:7 It was considered a curse to have no one remember

'ewiyl

Hebrew Pronunciation	[eh VEEL]
HCSB Translation	fool
Uses in Proverbs	19
Uses in the OT	26
Key Passage	Proverbs 10:8,10,14,21

In Proverbs, 'ewiyl (fool) refers to one who is morally deficient from the standpoint of being able to make reasoned moral judgments. He willfully refuses to make moral choices, choosing neither good nor rejecting evil. He arrogantly refuses to receive moral instruction and to learn from his mistakes (1:7; 12:15; 15:5). The fool is characterized by foolishness ('iwweleth), an internal moral corruption that renders the fool impotent to make reasonable moral judgments in life (15:21; 16:22). While he is young, there is hope that a youth can be separated from his foolishness (22:15), but later in life the fool is irrevocably marked by his folly (27:22). His moral deficiency manifests itself in matters of speech, morality, discipline, religion, and daily life. He speaks either the wrong thing or at the wrong time (10:8,10,14,21; 14:3), and he is quick to show his anger (12:16; 20:3) and to refuse resolution (29:9).

but whoever perverts his ways will be found out.[a]

10 A sly wink of the eye[b] causes grief,
and foolish lips will be destroyed.

11 The mouth of the righteous is
a fountain of life,[c]
but the mouth of the wicked
conceals violence.[d]

12 Hatred stirs up conflicts,
but love covers all offenses.[e]

13 Wisdom is found on the lips
of the discerning,
but a rod is for the back of the one
who lacks sense.[f]

14 The wise store up knowledge,
but the mouth of the fool
hastens destruction.[g]

15 A rich man's wealth is his fortified city;[h]
the poverty of the poor is
their destruction.

16 The labor of the righteous leads to life;
the activity of the wicked leads to sin.[i]

17 The one who follows instruction is
on the path to life,
but the one who rejects correction
goes astray.[j]

18 The one who conceals hatred has
lying lips,
and whoever spreads slander is a fool.[k]

19 When there are many words,
sin is unavoidable,
but the one who controls his lips
is wise.[l]

20 The tongue of the righteous is
pure silver;
the heart of the wicked is
of little value.[m]

21 The lips of the righteous feed many,
but fools die for lack of sense.[n]

22 The LORD's blessing enriches,[o]
and struggle adds nothing to it.[A,p]

23 As shameful conduct is pleasure
for a fool,[q]
so wisdom is for a man
of understanding.

24 What the wicked dreads will come
to him,[r]
but what the righteous desire
will be given to them.[s]

25 When the whirlwind passes,
the wicked are no more,[t]
but the righteous
are secure forever.[u]

26 Like vinegar to the teeth and smoke
to the eyes,[v]
so the slacker is to the one
who sends him on an errand.

27 The *fear of the LORD prolongs life,[B,w]
but the years of the wicked
are cut short.[x]

28 The hope of the righteous is joy,[y]
but the expectation of the wicked
comes to nothing.[z]

29 The way of the LORD is a stronghold
for the honorable,
but destruction awaits the malicious.[aa]

---

[a]10:9 Pr 26:26; Mt 10:26; 1Tm 5:25
[b]10:10 Ps 35:19; Pr 6:13; 16:30
[c]10:11 Ps 37:30; Pr 13:14; 14:27; 16:22
[d]Pr 10:6
[e]10:12 Pr 17:9; Jms 5:20; 1Pt 4:8
[f]10:13 Pr 19:29; 26:3
[g]10:14 Pr 10:8; 12:13; 13:3; 18:7
[h]10:15 Ps 52:7; Pr 18:11
[i]10:16 Pr 11:19
[j]10:17 Pr 5:12-13,22-23; 6:23; 13:13-14
[k]10:18 Pr 11:13
[l]10:19 Pr 17:27-28; Jms 1:19; 3:2
[m]10:20 Pr 8:19; 10:32
[n]10:21 Hs 4:6
[o]10:22 Gn 24:35; 26:12; Dt 8:18; Jms 1:17
[p]Mt 6:31-32
[q]10:23 Pr 2:14; 15:21
[r]10:24 Pr 1:26-27; Is 66:4; Heb 10:27
[s]Ps 37:4; 145:19; Pr 11:23; Mt 5:6; 1Jn 5:14-15
[t]10:25 Jb 21:18; Is 29:5-7
[u]Ps 15:5; Pr 10:30; 12:3,7; Mt 7:24-27
[v]10:26 Pr 26:6
[w]10:27 Pr 3:2
[x]Jb 15:32-33; Pr 14:26-27; 15:16; 19:23
[y]10:28 Pr 11:23; 23:18; Jr 29:11
[z]Jb 8:13; 14:9; Pr 11:7; Ezk 37:11
[aa]10:29 Pr 13:6; 21:15

A10:22 Or *and He adds no trouble to it*   **B**10:27 Lit LORD *adds to days*

you (Ex 17:14) or to fail to pass down your **name** to the next generation (Ps 109:13; cp. Ps 45:17).

10:9 On **integrity**, see notes at 2:7 and 11:20.

10:10 A **wink** was apparently some kind of signal used by dishonest people (6:13).

10:11 The things that **righteous** people say tend to promote eternal **life** (see note at 3:22).

10:12 Loving people, unlike hateful ones, are willing to put up with insults or slander and to forgive those who wrong them.

10:13-14 This is a case where two verses clarify each other, though each could stand on its own. The **one who lacks sense** is likely to spout off and hasten **destruction**, while **wise** and **discerning** people **store up knowledge** and speak wisely, avoiding public condemnation in this life and eternal destruction as well.

10:15 This is an observation about the way things look from an earthly perspective. Other proverbs, including the next

verse, teach long-term and eternal principles about wealth and poverty (11:28; 18:10-11).

10:18 This verse does not mean a person should display hatred. Rather, the person who has **hatred** concealed within himself inevitably tells lies.

10:21 The **righteous** produce life-giving nourishment (v. 11), while **fools** cannot even keep themselves alive.

10:22 If wealth is gained apart from acknowledgment of God's **blessing**, often all kinds of **struggle** accompany it—greedy "friends," legal trouble, fear of loss (Mt 6:19), and the temptation of pride (Dt 8:17-18).

10:24 This observation on the **wicked** is often valid in this life and always true in eternity.

10:26 Vinegar, or soured wine, had an astringent quality that irritated the **teeth**.

10:27 On **life**, see note at 3:22.

10:29 The **honorable** do not dread the imposition of truth (Rm 13:3), but when God's kingdom comes (Mt 6:10) and

30 The righteous will never be shaken,
but the wicked will not remain
on the earth.[a]

31 The mouth of the righteous
produces wisdom,[b]
but a perverse tongue
will be cut out.[c]

32 The lips of the righteous know
what is appropriate,[d]
but the mouth of the wicked,
only what is perverse.[e]

11 Dishonest scales are detestable
to the LORD,[f]
but an accurate weight is His delight.[g]

2 When pride comes, disgrace follows,
but with humility comes wisdom.[h]

3 The integrity of the upright
guides them,[i]
but the perversity of the treacherous
destroys them.[j]

4 Wealth is not profitable on a day
of wrath,
but righteousness rescues
from death.[k]

5 The righteousness of the blameless
clears his path,
but the wicked person will fall
because of his wickedness.

6 The righteousness of the upright
rescues them,
but the treacherous are trapped
by their own desires.[l]

7 When the wicked man dies,
his expectation comes to nothing,
and hope placed in wealth[A,B]
vanishes.[m]

8 The righteous one is rescued
from trouble;
in his place, the wicked one goes in.[n]

9 With his mouth the ungodly
destroys his neighbor,
but through knowledge the righteous
are rescued.

10 When the righteous thrive,
a city rejoices,[o]
and when the wicked die, there is
joyful shouting.

11 A city is built up by the blessing
of the upright,[p]
but it is torn down by the mouth
of the wicked.[q]

12 Whoever shows contempt
for his neighbor lacks sense,
but a man with understanding
keeps silent.[r]

13 A gossip goes around revealing a secret,
but a trustworthy person keeps
a confidence.[s]

14 Without guidance, people fall,
but with many counselors
there is deliverance.[t]

15 If someone puts up security
for a stranger,
he will suffer for it,[u]
but the one who hates such agreements
is protected.

[a]**10:30** Ps 21:7; 37:29; 125:1; Pr 2:21-22; 12:3 [b]**10:31** Ps 37:30 [c]Ps 37:38; 120:2-4 [d]**10:32** Ec 10:12 [e]Pr 2:12; 10:20; 15:28 [f]**11:1** Dt 25:13-16; Pr 20:10,23; Mc 6:10-11 [g]Lv 19:36; Pr 16:11; Ezk 45:10 [h]**11:2** Pr 15:33; 18:12; 22:4; 29:23 [i]**11:3** Pr 13:6 [j]Pr 11:17-19; 19:3 [k]**11:4** Gn 7:1; Pr 10:2; 11:28; 12:28; Zph 1:18 [l]**11:6** Ps 7:15-16; Pr 5:22; Ec 10:8 [m]**11:7** Jb 8:13; Pr 10:28; 24:14 [n]**11:8** Pr 21:18 [o]**11:10** Pr 28:12 [p]**11:11** Pr 14:34 [q]Pr 14:1; 29:4 [r]**11:12** Pr 14:21 [s]**11:13** Lv 19:16; Pr 10:18; 20:19; 1Tm 5:13 [t]**11:14** Pr 15:22; 20:18; 24:6 [u]**11:15** Pr 6:1-2; 17:18; 22:26

[A]11:7 LXX reads *hope of the ungodly* [B]11:7 Or *strength*

every knee bows to Christ (Php 2:10), **the way of the LORD** will be **destruction**, in the ultimate sense, for **the malicious** (Am 5:18-20; 7:7-9).

10:30 This proverb uses promised-land terminology (cp. 2:22). Just as disobedient Israel was sent into exile, so **the wicked will not remain** in God's grace.

10:31 The person who speaks what is **perverse** (see note at 2:12) will be excluded from the community and ultimately from God's presence (Lv 18:29).

10:32 The Hebrew word translated **what is appropriate** also means "favor, delight" (8:35).

11:1 On **dishonest scales**, see Dt 25:13-16.

11:2 **Pride** makes a person an obstinate fool or mocker (see note at 1:22) who will be disgraced (13:18). **Wisdom** comes from the fear of the Lord (9:10), which comes from faith and presupposes **humility**—giving up pride and self-sufficiency.

11:3 **Integrity** implies genuineness and reliability. **Perversity** implies subversion and deceit, treachery (see note at 2:20-22) and destructiveness.

11:5 To clear a **path** is literally to make it straight, to improve it so it is easy to walk on. A **blameless** person will not grow weary or **fall** on such a path and so will reach his destination.

11:7 This verse implies that when a righteous person **dies**, his **hope** does not vanish. The book of Proverbs supports this implication of eternal rewards, including verses 6 and 8 here (see note at 3:22).

11:9 Though the **ungodly** spread slander, the **righteous** are **rescued** through their own **knowledge** and that of their acquaintances. Those who know them realize the slander is untrue.

11:12 On **lacks sense**, see note at 6:30-33.

11:13 A **gossip** spreads slander (Lv 19:16; Jr 6:28; 9:4; Ezk 22:9).

11:16 This proverb teaches that there is something more important than **riches** (cp. v. 28; 22:1). It is also significant

16 A gracious woman gains honor,
but violent^A men gain only riches.

17 A kind man benefits himself,^a
but a cruel man brings disaster
on himself.^b

18 The wicked man earns an empty wage,
but the one who sows righteousness,
a true reward.^c

19 Genuine righteousness leads to life,^d
but pursuing evil leads to death.^e

20 Those with twisted minds
are detestable to the Lord,
but those with blameless conduct are
His delight.^f

21 Be assured^B that the wicked
will not go unpunished,^g
but the offspring of the righteous
will escape.

22 A beautiful woman who rejects
good sense
is like a gold ring in a pig's snout.^h

23 The desire of the righteous
turns out well,^i
but the hope of the wicked
leads to wrath.^j

24 One person gives freely,

yet gains more;^k
another withholds what is right,
only to become poor.^l

25 A generous person will be enriched,^m
and the one who gives a drink of water
will receive water.^n

26 People will curse^o anyone
who hoards grain,
but a blessing will come to the one
who sells it.^p

27 The one who searches for what is good^q
finds favor,
but if someone looks for trouble,
it will come to him.^r

28 Anyone trusting in his riches will fall,^s
but the righteous will flourish
like foliage.^t

29 The one who brings ruin
on his household^u
will inherit the wind,^v
and a fool will be a slave
to someone whose heart is wise.

30 The fruit of the righteous is a tree
of life,^w
but violence^C takes lives.

31 If the righteous will be repaid on earth,
how much more the wicked and sinful.^x

Cross references (center column):

^a 11:17 Mt 5:7; 25:34-36
^b Pr 11:3
^c 11:18 Pr 10:2-3; Hs 10:12; Gl 6:8-9; Jms 3:18
^d 11:19 Pr 10:16-17; 19:23
^e Rm 6:23; Jms 1:15
^f 11:20 1Ch 29:17; Ps 119:1; Pr 3:32; 12:22; 13:6; 15:8-9,26
^g 11:21 Pr 16:5
^h 11:22 Gn 24:47
^i 11:23 Ps 37:4-5; Pr 10:24; Jr 29:11
^j Pr 10:28; 11:7; Rm 2:8-9
^k 11:24 Ps 112:9; Pr 11:25; 21:26
^l Pr 13:7; 22:16; 28:27
^m 11:25 Pr 3:9-10; 2Co 9:6-11
^n Mt 5:7; 10:42
^o 11:26 Pr 24:24
^p Gn 42:6
^q 11:27 Php 4:8
^r Est 7:10; Ps 7:15-16
^s 11:28 Ps 49:6
^t Ps 1:3; 92:12; Pr 11:4; 14:11; Jr 17:8
^u 11:29 Pr 15:27
^v Ec 5:16
^w 11:30 Pr 3:18
^x 11:31 Dt 32:25; Pr 13:21; 1Pt 4:18

---

^A 11:16 Or *ruthless*   ^B 11:21 Lit *Hand to hand*   ^C 11:30 LXX, Syr; MT reads *but a wise one*

---

that one **gracious woman** might obtain a greater reward than many **violent men**.

11:17 The **kind man** is one who acts with faithful love (Hb *chesed*; see note at 19:22). He looks out for others. Conversely, the **cruel man** is merciless and unfaithful, having no concern for others.

11:18 The **empty wage** is insubstantial, deceptive—its appearance differs from reality. The **true reward** is dependable. There is a Hebrew pun in this verse. The word for "empty" is *sheqer* and the word for "reward" is *seker*.

11:19 On **life**, see note at 3:22.

11:20 This proverb has connections to 10:9; 19:1; and 28:6. The word **blameless** here is related to the word "integrity" in those three verses above (see note at 2:7); **twisted** here is related to "perverts" in 10:9, "deceitful" in 19:1, and "distorted" in 28:6 (see "crooked" in note at 2:15); and **conduct** is related to "his ways" in 10:9 and "right and wrong" in 28:6. So a poor man with integrity (19:1; 28:6), and whose conduct is blameless, is well off because the Lord delights in him. Conversely, the person with a twisted mind or deceitful lips (19:1), who perverts his ways (10:9) and distorts right and wrong (28:6), is at a great disadvantage, even if he is rich, because he will be found out (10:9) and is **detestable to the Lord**. If he persists, he's a fool (Hb *kesiyl*; 19:1).

11:21 Be assured is literally "hand to hand." It may mean that it is as sure as a contract solemnized by a handshake (6:1). On **not go unpunished**, see note at 6:27-29. Righ-

teousness is so powerful that even the next generation of **the righteous** is likely to **escape** eternal death due to the influence a parent's righteousness has on their offspring (Ex 20:6; cp. Ezk 18).

11:22 The pig was an unclean animal; no amount of adornment could make up for this fundamental defect.

11:23 The **righteous . . . desire** to do good to others, and this **turns out well** for them. The **wicked** intend **wrath** for others, but their only **hope** for the future is wrath upon themselves.

11:24 To give **freely** is literally to "scatter"—to be generous without worrying about where the blessings fall.

11:26 The king of Moab refused to sell grain to the traveling Israelites and came under God's **curse** (Dt 2:26-31), while Joseph sold grain during a famine and was blessed (Gn 41:56; 47:13-20).

11:29 To **inherit the wind** is to end up with nothing.

11:30 The second part of this verse is difficult. The Hebrew reads literally "the one taking lives is wise." Elsewhere in the Bible the phrase "to take a life" is always negative (1:19; 1Sm 24:11; 1Kg 19:10,14; Ps 31:13; Ezk 33:6); it never means "to win a soul." But it doesn't fit with the rest of Scripture to say that the person who kills people is wise, so there must be another explanation. The LXX implies that the original Hebrew might have read "violence" (*chamas*) instead of "wise" (*chakam*). That is how the HCSB has translated it.

11:31 How much more argues from the lesser to the greater

12 Whoever loves discipline
loves knowledge,
but one who hates correction is stupid.[a]

2 The good person obtains favor
from the LORD,[b]
but He condemns a man who schemes.[c]

3 Man cannot be made secure
by wickedness,
but the root of the righteous
is immovable.[d]

4 A capable wife[A] is her husband's crown,[e]
but a wife who causes shame
is like rottenness in his bones.[f]

5 The thoughts of the righteous are just,
but guidance from the wicked
leads to deceit.

6 The words of the wicked are
a deadly ambush,[g]
but the speech of the upright
rescues them.[h]

7 The wicked are overthrown and perish,[i]
but the house of the righteous
will stand.[j]

8 A man is praised for his insight,
but a twisted mind is despised.

9 Better to be dishonored, yet have
a servant,
than to act important but have
no food.[k]

10 A righteous man cares about
his animal's health,[l]
but even the merciful acts
of the wicked are cruel.

11 The one who works his land will have
plenty of food,[m]
but whoever chases fantasies
lacks sense.[n]

12 The wicked desire
what evil men have,[B]
but the root of the righteous
produces fruit.

13 An evil man is trapped
by his rebellious speech,[o]
but a righteous one escapes
from trouble.[p]

14 A man will be satisfied with good
by the words of his mouth,[q]
and the work of a man's hands
will reward him.[r]

15 A fool's way is right in his own eyes,[s]
but whoever listens to counsel is wise.

16 A fool's displeasure is known at once,
but whoever ignores an insult
is sensible.[t]

17 Whoever speaks the truth declares
what is right,
but a false witness, deceit.[u]

18 There is one who speaks rashly,
like a piercing sword;[v]
but the tongue of the wise
brings healing.[w]

19 Truthful lips endure forever,
but a lying tongue, only a moment.[x]

20 Deceit is in the hearts of those
who plot evil,
but those who promote peace
have joy.[y]

Cross references (center column):

a12:1 Pr 3:11; 5:11-13; 15:5,31-32
b12:2 Pr 8:35
cPr 14:17; 24:8
d12:3 Ps 16:8; 21:7; Pr 10:30
e12:4 Pr 18:22; 19:14; 31:10
fPr 14:30
g12:6 Pr 1:11
hPr 14:2
i12:7 Jb 34:25
jPs 103:17-18; Pr 10:25; Mt 7:24-27
k12:9 Pr 11:24; 13:7; Rm 12:3
l12:10 Dt 25:4; Pr 27:23; Jnh 4:11
m12:11 Pr 24:27
nPr 28:19
o12:13 Pr 10:14; 13:3; 18:7
pPr 21:23; 29:6
q12:14 Pr 13:2; 18:20
rPr 1:31; 28:19; Is 3:10
s12:15 Pr 16:2; 21:2
t12:16 Pr 11:13; 12:23; 17:9; 29:11
u12:17 Pr 6:19; 14:5,25
v12:18 Ps 57:4
wPr 4:22; 15:4
x12:19 Ps 52:4-5; Pr 19:9
y12:20 Pr 14:22

A12:4 Or *A wife of quality,* or *A wife of good character*   B12:12 Or *desire a stronghold of evil*

(15:11; 17:7; 19:7,10; 21:27). This is not to say that the punishment of the **wicked** is more certain than the blessing of the **righteous**. But if God's impartial judgment begins with the righteous, then the **sinful** will not escape (1Pt 4:18).

12:1 Obviously the **stupid** person is one without average human intelligence (30:2). But something more is in view here. The "stupid" person is more like a brutish, irrational animal (Ps 73:22). That he **hates correction** reveals a heart problem more than a head problem.

12:2 On **schemes**, see "discretion" in note at 1:4.

12:4 This is the same Hebrew phrase as that in the portrayal of the **capable wife** in 31:10 and the description of Ruth as "a woman of noble character" (Ru 3:11). **Rottenness** in the **bones** implies loss of joy and strength.

12:8 The Hebrew word for **insight** is related to prudence (see "wise instruction" in note at 1:3).

12:9 On **better . . . than** proverbs, see note at 15:16-17. To have one **servant** signified a modest standard of living in ancient times.

12:10 What the **wicked** person thinks is **merciful** is still **cruel**.

12:11 The opposite of productive **works** is the pursuit of **fantasies** or delusions, such as get-rich-quick schemes, gambling, or idly "waiting for my ship to come in."

12:14 After a person accomplishes **good** things through his **words**, good in turn will provide a reward for him (8:10; 13:2,21; 18:20).

12:17 This is courtroom terminology. The person who **speaks the truth** is the opposite of the **false witness** who has first-hand knowledge but utters lies (6:19; 14:5,25; 19:5,9). To declare **what is right** is to provide the necessary information for a correct verdict, which could literally save the life of an innocent person (14:25).

12:18 Speaking **rashly**, without thinking, could involve either

21 No disaster overcomes the righteous,[a]
but the wicked are full of misery.

22 Lying lips are detestable to the Lord,[b]
but faithful people are His delight.[c]

23 A shrewd person conceals knowledge,
but a foolish heart publicizes stupidity.[d]

24 The diligent hand will rule,
but laziness will lead to forced labor.[e]

25 Anxiety in a man's heart
weighs it down,
but a good word cheers it up.[f]

26 A righteous man is careful in dealing
with his neighbor,[A]
but the ways of the wicked
lead them astray.[g]

27 A lazy man doesn't roast his game,[h]
but to a diligent man, his wealth
is precious.[i]

28 There is life in the path
of righteousness,
but another path leads to death.[B,j]

13 A wise son responds to his
father's discipline,
but a mocker doesn't listen to rebuke.

2 From the words of his mouth,
a man will enjoy good things,[k]

but treacherous people have an appetite
for violence.[l]

3 The one who guards his mouth
protects his life;[m]
the one who opens his lips invites
his own ruin.[n]

4 The slacker craves, yet has nothing,
but the diligent is fully satisfied.[o]

5 The righteous hate lying,
but the wicked act disgustingly
and disgracefully.

6 Righteousness guards people
of integrity,[C]
but wickedness undermines
the sinner.[p]

7 One man pretends to be rich
but has nothing;[q]
another pretends to be poor but has
great wealth.[r]

8 Riches are a ransom for a man's life,[s]
but a poor man hears no threat.

9 The light of the righteous
shines brightly,[t]
but the lamp of the wicked is put out.[u]

10 Arrogance leads to nothing but strife,[v]
but wisdom is gained by those
who take advice.

Cross references (center column):

[a]12:21 Ps 91:10; 1Pt 3:13
[b]12:22 Rv 22:15
[c]Pr 3:32; 11:20; 15:8–9,26
[d]12:23 Pr 11:13; 12:16; 13:16; 15:2
[e]12:24 Pr 10:4; 13:4; 19:15
[f]12:25 Ps 94:19; Pr 15:13; 16:24; Mt 6:25-34
[g]12:26 Pr 14:22
[h]12:27 Pr 19:15,24; 26:15
[i]Pr 10:4; 13:4
[j]12:28 Pr 10:2; 13:14; 14:27
[k]13:2 Pr 12:14
[l]Pr 1:10–12,31; 18:20–21; Is 32:6-8
[m]13:3 Pr 18:21; 21:23; Jms 3:2
[n]Pr 10:14; 12:13; 18:7
[o]13:4 Pr 10:4; 12:24,27; 19:15
[p]13:6 Pr 10:29; 11:3
[q]13:7 Pr 11:24; Lk 12:20-21; 1Tm 6:17-19; Rv 3:17-18
[r]Lk 12:33; 2Co 6:10; Jms 2:5
[s]13:8 Jb 2:4; Pr 10:15
[t]13:9 Pr 4:18
[u]Jb 18:5-6; Pr 20:20; 24:20
[v]13:10 Pr 17:19

[A]12:26 Or *man guides his neighbor*   [B]12:28 Or *righteousness, and in its path there is no death*   [C]13:6 Lit *guards integrity of way*

saying something inconsiderate (Nm 20:10; Ps 106:33) or making reckless vows (Lv 5:4).

12:20 Peace is the opposite of **evil** in the sense that success or welfare is the opposite of disaster (Is 45:7; Jr 29:11).

12:22 On **detestable**, see note at 3:32.

12:23 On **shrewd**, see note at 1:4. The shrewd person holds his tongue unless the situation is right. What he has is **knowledge**. The **foolish** (Hb *kesiyl*) person does not restrain himself. What's worse, his speech is pure **stupidity** (see note at 5:23).

12:24 For examples of **forced labor**, see Ex 1:11; Jdg 1:28; 1Kg 5:13-14; 12:18; Lm 1:1.

12:26 The **righteous man** literally "spies out" (Nm 13:2) or "investigates" (Ec 7:25) **his neighbor** to make sure he will not mislead him.

12:27 The **lazy man** (v. 24; 10:4; 19:15; cp. "slacker" in note at 6:6) has failed to put in the time it takes to obtain any **game**, but the **diligent man** has obtained **precious . . . wealth**. This proverb may also imply that the lazy man does not finish what he started and **roast** what he has brought home, so it goes to waste, but the diligent man takes care of what God has given him.

12:28 On **life**, see note at 3:22.

13:2-4 These three verses have the Hebrew multipurpose word *nephesh* ("soul, self, appetite, throat, or mouth"; see note at v. 19). **Treacherous people** (see note at 2:20-22) will

not receive **good things** and in fact have no **appetite** (*nephesh*) for them. Instead, their treachery will backfire as violence (4:17), that is, fierceness, ruthlessness, or malice. In 13:3 the wise man **guards his mouth** (*nephesh*). In verse 4 *nephesh* is implied. **The slacker . . . has nothing** for his mouth (Hb *nephesh*), but the mouth (*nephesh*) of the **diligent is fully satisfied**.

13:5 Act disgustingly is literally "stink" (Gn 34:30; Ex 5:21).

13:6 Undermines is literally "overturns," but it implies being frustrated or subverted (Ex 23:8; Dt 16:19; Jb 12:19) and brought to ruin (Pr 19:3; 21:12; 22:12).

13:7 One person **pretends** to have the blessings that are reserved for the wise and righteous and demands social status that he does not deserve. The other covers up his blessings—perhaps so he doesn't have to share with the needy—and does not give God the glory.

13:8 No one should trust in **riches** (11:28), and you cannot buy eternal life (Ps 49:5-9). However, it is an accurate observation that a rich man can pay a **ransom** to save his earthly **life**. The **poor man** doesn't have to worry because no gangster would typically bother with him. Another possible meaning is that the rich man is able to respond to the rebuke (another meaning of **threat**) of those whom he has wronged and is willing to give all his money to make his life right. However, if a poor person is rebuked for his guilt, he is forced to ignore the rebuke and endure the guilt.

13:9 On **lamp**, see note at 20:20.

11 Wealth obtained by fraud will dwindle,[a]
but whoever earns it through labor[A]
will multiply it.[b]

12 Delayed hope makes the heart sick,
but fulfilled desire is a tree of life.[c]

13 The one who has contempt
for instruction will pay the penalty,[d]
but the one who respects a command
will be rewarded.[e]

14 A wise man's instruction is a fountain
of life,[f]
turning people away from the snares
of death.[g]

15 Good sense wins favor,[h]
but the way of the treacherous
never changes.[B]

16 Every sensible person
acts knowledgeably,
but a fool displays his stupidity.[i]

17 A wicked messenger falls into trouble,
but a trustworthy courier
brings healing.[j]

18 Poverty and disgrace come to those
who ignore discipline,

but the one who accepts correction
will be honored.[k]

19 Desire fulfilled is sweet to the taste,
but to turn from evil[l]
is an abomination to fools.

20 The one who walks with the wise
will become wise,
but a companion of fools
will suffer harm.

21 Disaster pursues sinners,
but good rewards the righteous.[m]

22 A good man leaves an inheritance
to his[c] grandchildren,
but the sinner's wealth is stored up
for the righteous.[n]

23 The uncultivated field of the poor yields
abundant food,
but without justice, it is swept away.

24 The one who will not use the rod hates
his son,[o]
but the one who loves him disciplines
him diligently.[p]

25 A righteous man eats
until he is satisfied,

a13:11 Pr 10:2; 20:21; 23:5
b Pr 10:4; 21:5-6
c 13:12 Pr 11:30; 15:4
d 13:13 Nm 15:31; 2Ch 36:16
e Pr 3:1-2; 4:4; 6:23
f 13:14 Pr 10:11; 14:27
g Ps 18:5; 116:3
h 13:15 Pr 3:4
i 13:16 Pr 12:23; 15:2; Ec 10:3
j 13:17 Pr 25:13
k 13:18 Pr 5:12-14; 12:1; 15:31-33
l 13:19 Pr 16:22; 29:27
m 13:21 Ps 32:10; Pr 11:31; 13:13
n 13:22 Jb 27:13-17; Pr 28:8; Ec 2:26
o 13:24 Pr 19:18; 22:15; 23:13-14; 29:15,17
p Dt 8:5; Pr 3:12; Heb 12:5-7

A 13:11 Lit whoever gathers upon his hand   B 13:15 LXX, Syr, Tg read treacherous will perish   C 13:22 Or inheritance: his

13:11 The Hebrew word for **fraud** here is *hevel*, the word translated "futility" in Ecclesiastes. It is literally "breath" or "vapor," something with no substance. Here it means "ill-gotten" or "rashly" (10:2; 12:11). The same word is used to say that wealth is a "vanishing mist" (21:6) and beauty is "fleeting" (31:30).

13:13 To have **contempt for instruction** is to despise the Lord's word. Such a person is always condemned (Nm 15:31; 2Sm 12:9; 2Ch 36:16; cp. 1Sm 2:17). **Pay the penalty** is literally "pledge collateral to it," in other words, be in debt to it.

13:15 Good sense is literally "insight of good" (see "insight" in note at 1:3). Sensible people can advance by winning the **favor** of God and men, while **the treacherous** cannot improve **the way** they go.

13:17 Accurate news and effective diplomacy benefited the officials and communities served by a good **courier**.

13:19 The Hebrew word for **taste** is *nephesh* (see note at vv. 2-4). The desires of the righteous will be **fulfilled** (v. 25; 10:24; 11:23) because they fear God and turn from evil (3:7; 14:16). **Fools** (Hb *kesiyl*) refuse to **turn from evil** because good disgusts them (29:27); therefore, their desires will not be fulfilled.

13:22 The Hebrew word for **wealth** can stand for "strength" as well. **The sinner's** possessions along with all his capabilities and resources are granted to **the righteous**.

13:23 The **field** that went uncultivated could refer to the marginal lands that the poor were forced to live on, or to the fields that were supposed to be left fallow on the Sabbatical Year for the sake of the poor (Ex 23:10-11; Lv 25:1-7). In the latter case, the lack of **justice** was the failure to observe the command (Lv 26:34-35,43; 2Ch 36:21).

Replica of an open courtyard of a typical Old Testament dwelling (14:1). Shown are mortar and pestle, storage pot, ladder to a sleeping loft, and an oven with a cooking pot.

but the stomach of the wicked
is empty.[a]

14 Every wise woman builds her house,[b]
but a foolish one tears it down
with her own hands.[c]

2 Whoever lives with integrity
°fears the Lord,[d]
but the one who is devious in his ways
despises Him.[e]

3 The proud speech of a fool brings a rod
of discipline,[A]
but the lips of the wise protect them.[f]

4 Where there are no oxen, the
feeding trough is empty,[B]
but an abundant harvest comes
through the strength of an ox.

5 An honest witness does not deceive,
but a dishonest witness utters lies.[g]

6 A mocker seeks wisdom
and doesn't find it,
but knowledge comes easily
to the perceptive.

7 Stay away from a foolish man;
you will gain no knowledge
from his speech.[h]

8 The sensible man's wisdom is
to consider his way,
but the stupidity of fools deceives them.

9 Fools mock at making restitution,[C]
but there is goodwill
among the upright.

10 The heart knows its own bitterness,
and no outsider shares in its joy.

11 The house of the wicked
will be destroyed,
but the tent of the upright will stand.[D,i]

12 There is a way that seems right
to a man,[j]
but its end is the way to death.[k]

13 Even in laughter a heart may be sad,
and joy may end in grief.[l]

14 The disloyal one will get
what his conduct deserves,

---

[a]13:25 Pr 10:3
[b]14:1 Ru 4:11; Pr 9:1; 24:3; 31:10-27
[c]Pr 11:11; 29:4
[d]14:2 Pr 19:1; 28:6
[e]Pr 2:15
[f]14:3 Pr 12:6
[g]14:5 Ex 20:16; 23:1; Pr 6:19; 12:17; 14:25
[h]14:7 Pr 20:15
[i]14:11 Pr 10:25; 11:28; 12:7; Mt 7:24-27
[j]14:12 Pr 12:15; 16:25
[k]Pr 5:4; Rm 6:21
[l]14:13 Ec 2:1-2; Lk 6:25

[A]14:3 Some emend to *In the mouth of a fool is a rod for his back*   [B]14:4 Or *clean*   [C]14:9 Or *at guilt offerings*   [D]14:11 Lit *flourish*

13:24 Parents who love their children seek **diligently** to apply the best and most appropriate method of discipline (Heb 12:5-11). In some cases that is the **rod** (22:15; 23:13-14; 29:15), which is appropriate punishment for the fool (10:3; 26:3). Only a parent who **hates** his child would withhold discipline and permit him to remain a fool, knowing that foolishness leads to misery, shame, and ultimately death.

14:1 This **wise woman** is not wisdom personified, as in chapters 8-9, but a flesh-and-blood woman. Solomon is urging his son (1:8) to look for a wise woman (31:10) to build up a **house** (the word can also mean "household"; see note at 3:33). Women in turn are encouraged to be the kind who build rather than tear down.

14:4 Empty could also be translated "clean" in the sense of "pure." You don't have to worry about having feed on hand and cleaning up after **oxen** if you don't have any, but you also won't have an **abundant harvest**. Sometimes the benefits of an investment outweigh the costs and inconveniences involved.

14:5 A person can tell the quality of testimony by considering the character of the **witness** (cp. 6:19; 27:21).

14:6 Because of the pride of a **mocker** (21:24; see note at 1:22), God does not respond to his seeking (3:34); humility must precede **wisdom** (15:33). Mockers are skeptical and therefore do not take in knowledge. The **perceptive** person, while not naive, is still open to learning (vv. 15,18; 8:9).

14:8 This verse says literally **the stupidity** (Hb *ewiyl*; see notes at 1:7 and 5:23) **of fools** (Hb *kesiyl*; see note at 1:22) is deceit. This could mean that they deceive themselves through their own stupidity, or that their stupidity is evident in the deceit they practice on others.

14:9 It is safe to conclude that **the upright** respect the need for **restitution**, and **fools** enjoy no **goodwill**.

14:10 No one can completely know what another person's

heart is feeling. While it is good to try to empathize (Rm 12:15), God alone knows our hearts fully (1Kg 8:39; Ps 44:21; Pr 15:11; Lk 9:47; 16:15; Ac 1:24; 15:8), and He sympathizes with our trials (Heb 4:15).

14:11 Stand is literally "sprout"—it grows with new life.

14:12 On **end**, see note at 5:11.

14:14 Although things don't always look fair in this life, in eternity everyone will **get** (lit "be satiated with") what they deserve. A **disloyal** person is literally "one whose heart turned back." He set out on the good way but then turned back (Heb 6:4-6).

---

chakam

Hebrew Pronunciation	[kha KAHM]
HCSB Translation	wise
Uses in Proverbs	47
Uses in the OT	138
Key Passage	Proverbs 14:1,3,16,24

Chakam (wise) describes one with a high degree of knowledge and skill in a particular area. *Chakam* may describe a skilled craftsman in a task such as sewing (Ex 28:3; 35:25) or construction (Ex 31:6; 36:1,2,4,8). Second, *chakam* may refer to skillfulness in exercising good judgment in managing interpersonal relations. The *wise* can manage people and affairs of state (Gn 41:33,39; 1Kg 5:7; Pr 20:26) and adjudicate impartially (Dt 1:13,15; 16:19; 1Kg 2:9; Pr 24:23). Third, *chakam* may refer to skillfulness in devising a scheme or plan (shrewd, clever, cunning; 2Sm 13:3; 14:2; 20:16). In Proverbs and Ecclesiastes, *chakam* carries both intellectual and moral connotations and describes the skill of right living. In contrast to the fool, the *wise* have ethical, religious, and pragmatic wisdom. They foresee the ramifications of their actions and consequently change them. The *wise* obey the Lord (Ps 107:43; Hs 14:9), exercise discernment (Pr 16:21; Ec 2:14) and turn from evil (Pr 14:16).

and a good man,
what his deeds deserve.*a*

15 The inexperienced one believes
anything,*b*
but the sensible one watches^A his steps.

16 A wise man is cautious and turns
from evil,*c*
but a fool is easily angered
and is careless.^B

17 A quick-tempered man acts foolishly,
and a man who schemes is hated.*d*

18 The inexperienced inherit foolishness,
but the sensible are crowned
with knowledge.

19 The evil bow before those
who are good,
the wicked, at the gates
of the righteous.

20 A poor man is hated even
by his neighbor,*e*
but there are many who love the rich.*f*

21 The one who despises
his neighbor sins,*g*
but whoever shows kindness
to the poor will be happy.*h*

22 Don't those who plan evil go astray?*i*

*a*14:14 Pr 1:31;
12:14; 18:20;
28:19
*b*14:15 Eph 4:14;
Jms 1:5-8
*c*14:16 Jb 28:28;
Ps 34:14; Pr 3:7;
22:3
*d*14:17 Pr 12:2;
24:8
*e*14:20 Pr 19:7
*f*Pr 19:4
*g*14:21 Pr 11:12
*h*Ps 41:1
*i*14:22 Pr 6:14-
15; 12:26
*j*Pr 12:20
*k*14:23 Pr 21:5
*l*14:25 Pr 6:19;
12:17; 14:5
*m*14:26 Pr 29:25
*n*14:27 Pr 13:14;
16:22; 19:23
*o*14:29 Pr 16:32;
19:11; Ec 7:9;
Jms 1:19
*p*14:30 Pr 3:8;
4:22; 16:24
*q*Pr 12:4; 27:4;
Jms 3:16

But those who plan good find loyalty
and faithfulness.*j*

23 There is profit in all hard work,
but endless talk^C leads only to poverty.*k*

24 The crown of the wise is their wealth,
but the foolishness of fools
produces foolishness.

25 A truthful witness rescues lives,
but one who utters lies is deceitful.*l*

26 In the fear of the LORD one has
strong confidence
and his children have a refuge.*m*

27 The fear of the LORD is a fountain
of life,
turning people away from the snares
of death.*n*

28 A large population is a king's splendor,
but a shortage of people is
a ruler's devastation.

29 A patient person shows great
understanding,*o*
but a quick-tempered one
promotes foolishness.

30 A tranquil heart is life to the body,*p*
but jealousy is rottenness
to the bones.*q*

---

^A14:15 Lit *the prudent understand*   ^B14:16 Or *and falls*   ^C14:23 Lit *but word of lips*

14:15 While the mocker rejects everything (see note at v. 6), the **inexperienced** person accepts **anything**. He will inevitably be led astray. The **sensible** person is guided by godly wisdom to "watch" (lit "understand") his own **steps**—to practice discretion.

14:16 The Hebrew word translated **is cautious** is literally "fears." This could imply that **a wise man** fears the Lord and **turns from evil** (3:7; 16:6). In contrast, the fool's (Hb *kesiyl*) hot temper gets him into trouble. He is **careless** or self-confident because he thinks he is secure (see note at 1:33), but he is wrong.

14:17 A **quick-tempered man** does bad things impetuously because he doesn't think first. A schemer (see "discretion" in note at 1:4) does bad things purposely because he is malicious (24:8). Neither thrives. The former squanders his life in foolishness (14:29), and the latter is **hated** and condemned (12:2).

14:18 Inexperienced people (see note at 1:4) who refuse to seek wisdom remain naive and gullible and thus **inherit** (see note at 3:35) **foolishness**.

14:19 It is implied that **the wicked** will bow down to **the righteous**. The **gates** of cities were where judgment took place, suggesting that the righteous person will have a prominent place in the city (31:23) and stand in judgment of the wicked. This does not always prove to be true in this life, but it will certainly be true in eternity.

14:20 This is not a promise or endorsement (see the next verse); it is an astute observation of human nature.

14:21 On **happy**, see note at 3:13-18.

14:22 On **loyalty and faithfulness**, see note at 3:3.

14:23 **Endless talk** is literally "words of the lips"; it could also be translated "mere words" (2Kg 18:20). **Hard work** is labor that is physically or emotionally draining. Outside of the Lord's blessing, it is vain (10:22; Ps 127:1-2). But diligent work (Pr 6:6-11) is better than recklessness (21:5), idleness (10:4), fraud (13:11), or get-rich-quick schemes (28:20).

14:24 On **crown**, see note at 4:9. **Fools** (Hb *kesiyl*) end up where they started.

14:25 On **truthful** and **utters lies**, see note at 12:17.

14:26 On **strong confidence**, see note at 21:22.

14:27 This proverb is the same as 13:14 except that **the fear of the LORD** is in place of "a wise man's instruction." The two ideas are nearly interchangeable because wisdom presupposes the fear of the Lord (9:10; 15:33).

14:28 When a **ruler's** followers desert him, he can be devastated or terrified (1Sm 13:11-12; 30:6; 1Kg 12:1-20).

14:29 **Patient** is literally "slow at becoming angry." Outside of Proverbs, the phrase is always used of God in the OT (Ex 34:6; Nm 14:18; Neh 9:17; Ps 86:15; 103:8; 145:8; Is 48:9; Jr 15:15; Jl 2:13; Jnh 4:2; Nah 1:3).

14:30 It is not wrong to be passionate or zealous for a proper cause (Nm 25:11; 1Kg 19:10; Ps 69:9), but a person should not be envious or jealous of sinners (Pr 3:31; 23:17; 24:1,19)

31 The one who oppresses the poor person
insults his Maker,[a]
but one who is kind to the needy
honors Him.[b]

32 The wicked one is thrown down
by his own sin,[c]
but the righteous one has a refuge
in his death.[d]

33 Wisdom resides in the heart
of the discerning;[e]
she is known[A] even among fools.

34 Righteousness exalts a nation,
but sin is a disgrace to any people.[f]

35 A king favors a wise servant,[g]
but his anger falls on a disgraceful one.

15 A gentle answer turns away anger,[h]
but a harsh word stirs up wrath.[i]

2 The tongue of the wise
makes knowledge attractive,
but the mouth of fools
blurts out foolishness.[j]

3 The eyes of the LORD are everywhere,
observing the wicked and the good.[k]

4 The tongue that heals is a tree of life,[l]
but a devious tongue[B] breaks the spirit.

5 A fool despises his father's discipline,

but a person who accepts correction
is sensible.[m]

6 The house of the righteous
has great wealth,
but trouble accompanies the income
of the wicked.

7 The lips of the wise
broadcast knowledge,
but not so the heart of fools.

8 The sacrifice of the wicked is detestable
to the LORD,[n]
but the prayer of the upright is
His delight.[o]

9 The LORD detests the way
of the wicked,
but He loves the one
who pursues righteousness.[p]

10 Discipline is harsh for the one
who leaves the path;
the one who hates correction
will die.

11 •Sheol and •Abaddon lie open
before the LORD[q]—
how much more, human hearts.[r]

12 A mocker doesn't love one
who corrects him;[s]
he will not consult the wise.

a14:31 Pr 17:5; 21:13; Mt 25:40; 1Jn 3:17
bPr 3:9; 14:21; 19:17; 22:2
c14:32 Ps 17:15; 73:24; Pr 24:16; 2Co 1:9; 5:8; 2Tm 4:18
dPr 10:25
e14:33 Pr 15:14; 18:15; Ec 7:9
f14:34 Pr 11:11
g14:35 Pr 22:29; Mt 24:45-47; 25:21
h15:1 Jdg 8:1-3; Pr 25:15; Ec 10:4
i1Sm 25:10-13; 1Kg 12:13-16
j15:2 Pr 12:23; 13:16; 15:28
k15:3 2Ch 16:9; Jb 31:4; Zch 4:10; Heb 4:13
l15:4 Pr 11:30; 13:12
m15:5 Pr 3:11; 12:1; 15:31-33
n15:8 Pr 21:27; 28:9; Ec 5:1; Is 1:11; Jr 6:20; Mc 6:7
oPr 15:29
p15:9 Pr 3:32; 11:20; 12:22; 1Tm 6:11
q15:11 Jb 26:6; Ps 139:8
r1Sm 16:7; 2Ch 6:30; Ps 44:21; Ac 1:24
s15:12 Pr 9:8; Am 5:10

A14:33 LXX reads unknown B15:4 Lit but crookedness in it

or of the assignment God has given to others (Ps 106:16; Ec 4:4; Jms 3:16).

14:32 Even while he is dying or after his death (the Hebrew is ambiguous), the **righteous** person looks for and finds refuge in the Lord.

14:33 **Wisdom** among **fools** (Hb kesiyl) is merely **known**; among the **discerning**, she literally "comes to rest."

14:34 While many proverbs promote personal ethics, this proverb takes ethics to a national level.

14:35 **Servant** of a **king** probably refers to a royal official, not a household slave.

15:1 The Hebrew word used to describe a **gentle answer** is related to that used to describe Josiah's "tender heart" in 2Kg 22:19. He demonstrated humility, not obstinacy. The word also describes how a wound is "soothed" or softened with oil (Is 1:6). A soothing answer is not ineffective (Pr 25:15). **Harsh word** is literally "word of pain."

15:3 The Hebrew word for **observing** or being vigilant implies that proper action will be taken with regard to what is observed. It is used of the capable wife who watches over her household (31:27), of the watchman in Ezekiel who is obligated to sound the alarm (Ezk 33:6), and of God Himself who watches and judges the nations (Ps 66:7).

15:4 **Heals** could also be translated "is tranquil." The author may have intended both meanings. A tranquil tongue heals, and a healing tongue must surely be tranquil (v. 1). Both concepts are also the opposite of fracturing **the spirit**.

15:6 This Hebrew word for **wealth** includes produce, possessions, and treasures. The **trouble** could refer to the destruction that a **wicked** person causes others in order to gain **income**, but in Proverbs it usually refers to the ruin he brings on himself (v. 27; 11:17,29).

15:8 God hates the **sacrifice** of those who do not honor Him because they take an occasion for confession and reduce it to magic—the attempt to manipulate a god through ritual (1Sm 15:22; Is 1:10-17; Jr 7:22-23; Hs 6:6; Am 5:21-24; Mt 23:23). The **prayer of the upright** is offered in faith and worship (Heb 11:6).

15:10 This verse refers to the **path** of life (v. 24; 5:6; 10:17), the path of the righteous (4:18; 8:20; 12:28), or the right path (3:6). The person who **leaves** the path is the same as **the one who hates correction**; such people are condemned to eternal death (2:11-19).

15:11 **Sheol** is the grave (see note at 1:12), and **Abaddon** (Jb 26:6; 28:22; 31:12; Ps 88:11) is the "place of destruction." Sheol is the realm of both the righteous and the unrighteous dead. It is generally observed that one cannot see God from Sheol (Ps 6:5) and can never hope to get out (Jb 7:9; Ps 89:48; cp. Lk 16:26), but God can see into Sheol and He can bring His elect out (Ps 16:10; 30:3; 49:15; 86:13; Hs 13:14). If God can see into the obscure depths of the grave, **how much more** (see note at 11:31) can He see the recesses of **human hearts**.

15:12 On **mocker**, see note at 1:22.

13 A joyful heart makes a face cheerful,
   but a sad heart produces
      a broken spirit.[a]

14 A discerning mind seeks knowledge,[b]
   but the mouth of fools feeds
      on foolishness.[c]

15 All the days of the oppressed
      are miserable,
   but a cheerful heart has
      a continual feast.

16 Better a little
      with the •fear of the LORD
   than great treasure with turmoil.[d]

17 Better a meal of vegetables
      where there is love
   than a fattened ox[e] with hatred.[f]

18 A hot-tempered man stirs up conflict,[g]
   but a man slow to anger[h] calms strife.

19 A slacker's way is like a thorny hedge,
   but the path of the upright is
      a highway.[i]

20 A wise son brings joy to his father,
   but a foolish man despises his mother.[j]

21 Foolishness brings joy to one
      without sense,
   but a man with understanding walks
      a straight path.[k]

22 Plans fail when there is no counsel,
   but with many advisers they succeed.[l]

23 A man takes joy in giving an answer;[A]
   and a timely word—how good
      that is![m]

24 For the discerning the path of life
      leads upward,
   so that he may avoid going down
      to Sheol.

25 The LORD destroys the house
      of the proud,
   but He protects the widow's territory.[n]

26 The LORD detests the plans
      of an evil man,
   but pleasant words are pure.[o]

[a]15:13 Pr 12:25; 14:30; 15:30; 17:22; 18:14
[b]15:14 Pr 14:33; 18:15
[c]Mt 12:34
[d]15:16 Ps 37:16; Pr 16:8; Ec 4:6; 1Tm 6:6
[e]15:17 Mt 22:4; Lk 15:23
[f]Pr 16:19; 17:1
[g]15:18 Pr 16:28; 26:21; 29:22
[h]Pr 14:29
[i]15:19 Pr 16:17,31; 22:5-6
[j]15:20 Pr 10:1; 23:24-25; 29:3,15
[k]15:21 Pr 4:11,25; 10:23; Eph 5:15
[l]15:22 Pr 8:14-16; 11:14; 24:6
[m]15:23 Pr 25:11; Is 50:4
[n]15:25 Ps 68:5; 146:9
[o]15:26 Pr 11:20; 15:8-9; 16:24

[A]15:23 Lit in an answer of his mouth

15:13 In this proverb sadness seems to affect a person more deeply than joy since the **heart** is more profound than the **face**. Perhaps Solomon wanted to scare his readers away from a lifestyle that might lead to such despair.

15:14 On **discerning**, see note at 1:5.

15:15 The parallelism in this verse suggests that even if a person is **oppressed** and **miserable**, if he has a **cheerful heart** he can experience a virtual **continual feast**.

15:16-17 These are typical examples of **better . . . than** proverbs (12:9; 16:8,19; 17:1; 19:1; 27:5,10; 28:6; cp. 3:14; 8:11,19). In each proverb of this type, two categories are considered. Having little or none of one and a lot of the other is compared with the other way around. In 15:16 one category is wealth and the other is a good relationship with God. A little wealth and a very good relationship with God (characterized by **fear**) are better than a lot of wealth and little relationship with God (which brings **turmoil**). In verse 17 one category is lavish food and the other is family **love**. Having no lavish food and a lot of love is better than having the best food and no love. That a person who fears the Lord may have **little** speaks to the fact that righteousness is not always immediately rewarded in this life.

A **meal** is a daily allowance, like that given a traveler (Jr 40:5). **Vegetables** were the normal, everyday food. A **fattened ox** was a great luxury (Lk 15:23). While normally an ox would be worked during its life then slaughtered when it was old and tough, a fattened ox was kept in a stall and carefully fed, then slaughtered in its prime. The result was moist and tender meat, but the profit from the labor of the animal was forfeited.

15:18 The Hebrew word translated **strife** here is also used for a lawsuit or court case (18:17; 22:23; 23:11; 25:9; see Ex 23:2; Hs 4:1), but it often has a nonlegal sense of a dispute or quarrel (Pr 17:1,14; 18:6; 20:3; 26:17,21; 30:33). On **hot-tempered**, see note at 14:17; on **conflict**, see "trouble" in note at 6:14; on **slow to anger**, see note at 14:29.

15:19 A **hedge** made from thorns was a painful obstacle (Is 5:5; cp. Mc 7:4). A **highway** was an efficient road built up and cleared of obstacles.

15:20 The fool (Hb *kesiyl*) **despises his mother** because she offers wisdom (1:8; 31:1) and requires obedience (30:17)—both of which the fool hates (1:7).

15:21 Foolishness implies moral waywardness. The person who lacks **sense** (see note at 6:30-33) actually finds pleasure in sinning (10:23; Heb 11:25). The **man with understanding** knows that even if he does not receive a reward in this life, there is a great reward in heaven (Lk 16:25; Heb 12:2).

15:22 On **plans**, see "schemes" in note at 16:9. **Counsel** is private, personal advice from intimate friends. In 3:32 God is a "friend" (same Hb word) "to the upright." Independent, selfish fools don't seek out advice (13:10; 18:1) and **fail**. **Advisers** (see "counselors" in 11:14) are generally advantageous, but those who speak contrary to the Lord's will bring failure (19:21; cp. Dt 13:1-3; 1Kg 12:13-15; 22:1-37).

15:23 This Hebrew word for **answer** means the most appropriate and effective thing to say in the given circumstance (v. 1; 16:1). The failure of Job's friends to answer his speeches angered Elihu (Jb 32:3,5).

15:24 On **discerning**, see "wise/prudent" in note at 1:3. Solomon understood God's revelation about eternal life. The discerning person is on the **path of life** because he trusts in the Lord (3:22; 16:20) and thereby avoids going to **Sheol**.

15:25 The widow represents those who were vulnerable to wicked, greedy people. God Himself **protects the widow's territory** (lit her "boundary") from those who might move the boundary markers (22:28; 23:10).

27 The one who profits dishonestly[a]
    troubles his household,
    but the one who hates bribes will live.[b]

28 The mind of the righteous person
    thinks before answering,[c]
    but the mouth of the wicked blurts out
    evil things.[d]

29 The LORD is far from the wicked,[e]
    but He hears the prayer
    of the righteous.[f]

30 Bright eyes cheer the heart;
    good news strengthens[A] the bones.[g]

31 One who[B] listens to life-giving rebukes[h]
    will be at home among the wise.

32 Anyone who ignores discipline
    despises himself,[i]
    but whoever listens to correction
    acquires good sense.[C,j]

33 The fear of the LORD is what
    wisdom teaches,
    and humility comes before honor.[k]

16 The reflections of the heart
    belong to man,
    but the answer of the tongue is
    from the LORD.[l]

2 All a man's ways seem right to him,
    but the LORD evaluates the motives.[D,m]

3 Commit your activities to the LORD,
    and your plans will be achieved.[n]

4 The LORD has prepared everything
    for His purpose—
    even the wicked for the day of disaster.[o]

5 Everyone with a proud heart is
    detestable to the LORD;[p]
    be assured,[E] he will not
    go unpunished.[q]

6 Wickedness is *atoned for by loyalty
    and faithfulness,[r]
    and one turns from evil by the *fear
    of the LORD.[s]

7 When a man's ways please the LORD,
    He[F] makes even his enemies to be
    at peace with him.[t]

[a]15:27 Pr 1:19; Jr 17:11
[b]Ex 23:8; Dt 16:19; Ps 15:5; Pr 17:23; 28:16
[c]15:28 Pr 18:13; 1Pt 3:15
[d]Pr 15:2
[e]15:29 Ps 18:41; Pr 28:9
[f]Ps 145:18-19; Pr 15:8
[g]15:30 Pr 14:30; 15:13; 17:22
[h]15:31 Pr 3:11
[i]15:32 Pr 12:1
[j]Pr 3:11; 5:12-14
[k]15:33 Pr 18:12; 22:4; 29:23
[l]16:1 Pr 16:9; 19:21
[m]16:2 1Sm 16:7; Pr 17:3; 19:21; 21:2
[n]16:3 Ps 37:4-5
[o]16:4 Ex 9:16; Rm 9:21-22
[p]16:5 2Ch 32:25; Pr 6:16-17; 8:13
[q]Ps 101:5; Pr 11:21; 16:18
[r]16:6 Dn 4:27; Lk 11:41
[s]Jb 28:28; Pr 3:7; 14:16
[t]16:7 2Ch 17:10

[A]15:30 Lit makes fat   [B]15:31 Lit An ear that   [C]15:32 Lit acquires a heart   [D]16:2 Lit weighs spirits   [E]16:5 Lit hand to hand   [F]16:7 Or he

---

15:26 On **detests** (v. 8; 21:27; 28:9), see note at 3:32. **Pure** is "ceremonially clean," acceptable to offer to God.

15:27 On **profits dishonestly**, see note at 1:19. There are two Hebrew words for a **bribe** (21:14 has both words). This one, *mattan/mattanah*, often is simply a "gift" (18:16; 19:6), but in the context of dishonest profit it clearly represents a bribe. The other word, *shochad* (17:8,23), is never a gift without strings attached. God hates bribes because they subvert justice (17:23; cp. 18:5; Dt 16:19; Ps 15:5; Ec 7:7; Is 5:23). Therefore, the person who **hates** bribes agrees with God, and the one who totally agrees with God—that is, who has the mind of Christ—**will live** (Rm 7:16; 1Co 2:16; 1Tm 6:3).

15:29 To say that the Lord is **far from** somebody is not a limit on His omnipresence, but refers to losing out on His communion, favor, and help (Gn 3:8,23; Ps 22:12,19; 35:22; 38:21; 71:12). Sometimes God moved away from Israel (Ezk 8:6), but sometimes Israel moved away from God (Jr 2:5). In both cases the cause was sin. It is impossible for God and sin to dwell together (Ps 5:4).

15:30 The phrase **bright eyes** implies spiritual vitality (29:13; cp. Ezr 9:8; Ps 13:3; 19:8; 38:10). **Bones** represent the inner core, the seat of health (3:8; cp. Jb 20:11; 21:24). To strengthen the bones is literally to "make them fat," to satiate them. Thus **good news** refreshes and strengthens a person (25:25).

15:31-32 To be **at home** is literally "to spend the night." To ignore or neglect the Lord's counsel and **discipline** is not just harmful (13:18), it is ultimately fatal (1:25,32). To do so is to despise or reject one's very self. To acquire **good sense** is literally to "buy a heart" (19:8; cp. "lacks sense" at 6:32).

15:33 The phrase **what wisdom teaches** probably means "the instruction that results in wisdom." **Humility** and **the**

fear of the LORD are prerequisites for gaining wisdom and **honor** (see notes at 1:7; 3:16; 14:6; 18:12; cp. 9:10).

16:1 The Hebrew word translated **reflections** has to do with arranging things in an orderly manner. On **answer**, see note at 15:23.

16:2 To evaluate something is to compare it with a standard. If **a man's ways** are not compared to God's standards, it will all **seem right** or pure (20:11; cp. Jb 11:4; 33:9). But **the LORD** evaluates the inner **motives** (lit the "spirit") of a man (cp. "hearts" in 24:12 and "actions" in 1Sm 2:3).

16:3 On **achieved**, see "established" in note at 4:25-27.

16:4 **Prepared** could also be translated "created"; either way God is sovereign. A **day of disaster** is literally an "evil day."

16:5 **Proud** is literally "high" (cp. 18:12). The same word describes "haughty" eyes (Ps 101:5) or a "proud" spirit (Ec 7:8). All of these imply arrogance, thinking oneself better than anyone, including God. On **detestable**, see note at 3:32; on **be assured**, see note at 11:21; on **not go unpunished**, see note at 6:27-29.

16:6 The **fear of the LORD** (see note at 1:7) represents faith, and **loyalty and faithfulness** (see note at 3:3) represent good works that demonstrate faith (Jms 2:14-26). Such works of faith atone (see Lv 23:27; Is 6:7) for **wickedness** in the past and turn a person away from following an **evil** path in the future.

16:7 The Hebrew is ambiguous whether it is a man or God that transforms **his enemies**. Often those who have a right relationship with God are respected (Gn 26:28; 33:4; 1Sm 2:26; 2Ch 17:10; Lk 2:52; Ac 2:46-47; Rm 12:18). However, there are also cases where the righteous are persecuted (2Tm 3:12).

8   Better a little with righteousness
    than great income with injustice.*

9   A man's heart plans his way,
    but the LORD determines his steps.*

10 God's verdict is on the lips of a king;^A,c
    his mouth should not give
        an unfair judgment.*

11 Honest balances and scales are
        the LORD's;
    all the weights in the bag^B are
        His concern.*

12 Wicked behavior^c is detestable
        to kings,*
    since a throne is established
        through righteousness.*

13 Righteous lips are a king's delight,
    and he loves one who speaks honestly.

14 A king's fury is a messenger of death,
    but a wise man appeases it.*

15 When a king's face lights up,
        there is life;
    his favor is like a cloud
        with spring rain.

16 Get wisdom—

how much better it is than gold!
And get understanding—
    it is preferable to silver.*

17 The highway of the upright^j avoids evil;
    the one who guards his way protects
        his life.*

18 Pride comes before destruction,
    and an arrogant spirit before a fall.*

19 Better to be lowly of spirit
        with the humble^D,m
    than to divide plunder with the proud.*

20 The one who understands a matter
        finds success,*
    and the one who trusts in the LORD
        will be happy.*

21 Anyone with a wise heart
        is called discerning,
    and pleasant speech^E
        increases learning.*

22 Insight is a fountain of life^r
        for its possessor,
    but the discipline of fools is folly.

23 A wise heart instructs its mouth
    and increases learning
        with its speech.^F,s

Cross references (center column):

*16:8 Ps 37:16; Pr 15:16-17; 16:19; 28:6
*16:9 Ps 37:23; Pr 16:1; 19:21; 20:24; Jr 10:23
*16:10 2Sm 14:17,20; 1Kg 3:28
*2Sm 23:2-3; Pr 18:14-15
*16:11 Lv 19:36; Pr 11:1; Ezk 45:10; Mc 6:11
*16:12 Pr 31:3-5
*Ps 101; Pr 25:5
*16:14 Ec 10:4
*16:16 Pr 3:14; 8:10,19; 22:1
*16:17 Is 35:8
*Pr 2:11-13; 15:19
*16:18 Pr 11:2; 16:5; 18:12; 29:23; Dn 4:37; Ob 3-4
*16:19 Pr 29:23; Is 57:15
*Ex 15:9; Ps 37:16; Pr 1:13-14; 15:16-17; 16:8
*16:20 Pr 19:8
*Ps 2:12; 34:8; 40:4; 84:12; 146:5; Jr 17:7
*16:21 Pr 1:5; 9:9; 16:23
*16:22 Pr 10:11; 13:14; 14:27
*16:23 Ps 37:30; Pr 1:5; 9:9; Mt 12:34

---

^A16:10 Or *A divination is on the lips of a king*   ^B16:11 Merchants kept the stones for their scales in a bag.   ^C16:12 Either the king's or someone else's behavior   ^D16:19 Alt Hb tradition reads *afflicted*   ^E16:21 Lit *and sweetness of lips*   ^F16:23 Lit *learning upon his lips*

16:8 Choosing **righteousness** or **injustice** in this life determines where a person spends eternity. On **better . . . than** proverbs, see note at 15:16-17.

16:9 This word for **plans** in Proverbs usually involves wicked schemes (v. 30; 24:8; cp. Ps 140:2; Nah 1:9), but it can also refer to good strategies and tactics (Pr 12:5; 16:3; 21:5) or thinking deeply about something (Ps 73:16; 119:59). Even good plans can only be established by the sovereign Lord (Pr 16:3; 19:21). On **determines**, see "established" in note at 4:25-27.

16:10 God's verdict is literally "divination," which is usually condemned, but the Hebrew word can refer to seeking God legitimately (Ps 27:4). In this context it refers to a **king** seeking God's mind when passing **judgment**. Because God expects a king to be just (v. 12; cp. 1Kg 10:9; Is 16:5; Jr 22:15; 23:5), and because his subjects look at a king's verdict as if it came from God Himself (1Sm 29:9; 2Sm 14:17,20; 19:27), the king has a great responsibility to judge fairly. Ultimately, God causes the king to fulfill His will (Pr 21:1).

16:12 A wise king will find **wicked behavior . . . detestable** because he knows that nothing is **established** apart from God's will (vv. 3,9; 4:26), and only those kings who rule with **righteousness** will gain God's favor (20:28; 25:5; 29:4,14; Dt 17:18-20).

16:13 A wise king knows that dishonest counselors can be disastrous (1Kg 12; 22).

16:14-15 A king of ancient times held the power of **life** and **death**. Thus unlike a jealous but powerless husband's rage (6:35), a **king's fury** could be appeased (the same Hb word

as "atoned" in v. 6). **Spring rain** symbolized life because it gave a boost to the grain and fruit crops before harvest.

16:16 On **get**, see note at 4:5-8; cp. 23:23.

16:19 It is **better** to avoid the **proud** who are destined for destruction (v. 18) and those pursuing **plunder** who are self-destructive (1:13,18). Furthermore, the **humble** will receive grace from God (3:34) and gain honor (29:23). On "better . . . than" proverbs, see note at 15:16-17.

16:20 The person who **understands a matter** could also be translated "the one who attends to business" or "the one who pays attention to the way" (Ps 101:2). The Hebrew for "understands" implies prudence (see note at Pr 1:3). On **happy**, see note at 3:13-18.

16:21 On **discerning**, see note at 1:5. **Pleasant speech** is literally "sweetness of lips." "Sweetness" is used literally for honey (24:13; Jdg 14:18; Ps 19:10; Ezk 3:3) and metaphorically for something that is revitalizing or encouraging (Pr 16:24).

16:22 The internal **fountain of life** that **insight** (see note at 12:8) provides to its **possessor** is comparable to what Christ is for Christians (Jn 4:14). It is possible that the **discipline** (see note at 1:2) **of fools** is referring to the teaching that fools try to do, which results in mere **folly**, but more likely it means that through their own folly, fools are disciplined. They reap the punishment of their errant lifestyle (6:33; 14:14,24; 19:3).

16:24 One expects anything medicinal to be bitter and anything sweet to be harmful, but **pleasant words**—morally uplifting speech—are both **sweet** and health-giving.

²⁴ Pleasant words are a honeycomb:^a
sweet to the taste^A and health
to the body.^{B,b}

²⁵ There is a way that seems right
to a man,
but its end is the way to death.^c

²⁶ A worker's appetite works for him
because his hunger^C urges him on.

²⁷ A worthless man digs up evil,
and his speech is like
a scorching fire.^d

²⁸ A contrary man spreads conflict,
and a gossip separates close friends.^e

²⁹ A violent man lures his neighbor,^f
leading him in a way that is
not good.^g

³⁰ The one who narrows his eyes
is planning deceptions;
the one who compresses his lips
brings about evil.^h

³¹ Gray hair is a glorious crown;ⁱ
it is found in the way
of righteousness.^j

³² Patience is better than power,

---

^a16:24 Ps 19:10; Pr 15:26
^bPr 4:22; 15:30; 25:13
^c16:25 Pr 14:12; 24:20
^d16:27 Pr 6:12; 19:28; 26:23; Jms 3:6
^e16:28 Pr 6:14,19; 17:9; 26:20-21; 28:25
^f16:29 Pr 1:10
^g1Sm 12:23; Ps 36:4; Pr 28:10
^h16:30 Ps 35:19; Pr 6:12-14; 10:10
ⁱ16:31 Lv 19:32; Pr 4:9; 20:29
^jPr 3:1-2
^k16:32 Pr 25:15,28; 29:11
^l16:33 Pr 16:1; 19:21; 21:31
^m17:1 Pr 15:17; 21:9,19; 25:24
ⁿ17:3 Pr 27:21
^o1Ch 29:17; Ps 26:2; Pr 16:2; 21:2; Is 48:10; Jr 17:10; Mal 3:3
^p17:5 Pr 14:31; 21:13
^qJb 31:29; Pr 24:17; Lm 1:21-22; Ezk 25:6-7; 35:15; Ob 12

---

and controlling one's temper,^D
than capturing a city.^k

³³ The lot is cast into the lap,
but its every decision is
from the LORD.^l

17 Better a dry crust with peace
than a house full of feasting
with strife.^m

² A wise servant will rule over
a disgraceful son
and share an inheritance
among brothers.

³ A crucible for silver, and a smelter
for gold,ⁿ
and the LORD is the tester of hearts.^o

⁴ A wicked person listens to
malicious talk;^E
a liar pays attention to
a destructive tongue.

⁵ The one who mocks the poor insults
his Maker,^p
and one who rejoices over calamity
will not go unpunished.^q

⁶ Grandchildren are the crown
of the elderly,

---

^A16:24 Lit throat   ^B16:24 Lit bones   ^C16:26 Lit mouth   ^D16:32 Lit and ruling over one's spirit   ^E17:4 Lit to lips of iniquity

---

16:26 This worker is one who struggles in miserable labor (Ec 2:18,22). On **appetite**, see note at 13:2-4. The slacker is not similarly motivated (21:25).

16:27 The Hebrew word translated **digs up** could also be translated "purchases" or "cooks up." However he gets it, the **worthless man** (see note at 6:12) is intent on using **evil** destructively.

16:28 A **contrary man** is one who distorts speech, who turns things upside down, who "says perverse things" (see notes at 2:12 and 10:31). It may be that he speaks his own lies or that he subverts others' speech by the way he spins it. A **gossip** is someone who grumbles (Dt 1:27; Ps 106:25; Is 29:24) or finds fault but avoids open discussion or confrontation.

16:29 On **violent**, see note at 3:31. Sinners often want to lure others to join them in sin (see "entice" in notes at 1:4 and 1:10) to excuse their own sinfulness. Misbehavior, like misery, loves company.

16:30 Narrowing one's **eyes** and compressing one's **lips** might refer to subtle nonverbal cues that the wise person should be aware of, or they could refer to gestures made by those **planning deceptions** to signal their accomplices (6:12-14; 10:10).

16:31 The person who stays on the **way of righteousness** is likely to live to a ripe old age (12:28; 13:6) and attain the respect that elders deserve (Lv 19:32).

16:32 On **patience**, see note at 14:29. A person who does not let his passions control him is **better than** a powerful military hero who lacks such control.

16:33 The **lot** was a stone the ancient Israelites used to make decisions the same way we might roll dice or flip a coin. The **lap** was a fold or pocket in one's garment. Perhaps the lot was dropped into the pocket for storage, or it was shaken in the pocket, or else the pocket area was where the lot was revealed for its decision.

17:1 On **better . . . than** proverbs, see note at 15:16-17. Bread that is **dry** means either that it is old (Jos 9:5) or that there is no oil or sauce to dip it in (Ru 2:14). **Peace** implies security; **strife** is human conflict. The **feasting** was a communion sacrifice, which was supposed to make peace between God and the people in the **house**.

17:2 This is probably metaphor or hyperbole. There was no provision in the law for a **servant** to displace a **disgraceful son**, though a "rebellious" son could be stoned (Dt 21:18-21).

17:3 The **crucible** and **smelter** were small clay vessels in which metals were melted at very high temperatures to refine them. To be tested is to be evaluated to see if something is genuine. The process of testing can bring about purification (Jb 23:10). God cannot be deceived when He evaluates **hearts** (1Ch 29:17; Ps 7:9; 26:2; Jr 11:20; 12:3).

17:4 A **wicked . . . liar** makes his situation worse by listening to more of the same.

17:5 To mock someone is to treat him with ridicule and contempt (1:22). Since God made the **poor** (14:31), to mock them is an insult to God. God protects the disadvantaged (14:21; 15:25; 22:16,22-23). On **calamity**, see note at 1:26-27; on **not go unpunished**, see note at 6:27-29.

17:6 The **crown** is the celebrated symbol of status. The eldery's reward is the **pride** their **sons** and **grandchildren**

and the pride of sons is
their fathers.

7 Eloquent words are not appropriate
on a fool's lips;
how much worse are lies
for a ruler.

8 A bribe*a* seems like a magic stone
to its owner;
wherever he turns, he succeeds.*b*

9 Whoever conceals an offense
promotes love,*c*
but whoever gossips about it
separates friends.*d*

10 A rebuke cuts into
a perceptive person
more than a hundred lashes
into a fool.

11 An evil man seeks only rebellion;
a cruel messenger*A,e* will be sent
against him.

12 Better for a man to meet a bear robbed
of her cubs*f*
than a fool in his foolishness.

13 If anyone returns evil for good,*g*
evil will never depart from his house.*h*

14 To start a conflict is to release a flood;
stop the dispute before it breaks out.*i*

15 Acquitting the •guilty and condemning
the just*j*—
both are detestable to the Lord.

16 Why does a fool have money
in his hand
with no intention of buying wisdom?*k*

17 A friend loves at all times,*l*
and a brother is born for
a difficult time.

18 One without sense enters
an agreement*B*
and puts up security for his friend.*m*

*a*17:8 Ex 23:8; Is 1:23; Am 5:12
*b*Pr 18:16; 19:6; 21:14
*c*17:9 Pr 10:12; Jms 5:20; 1Pt 4:8
*d*Lv 19:16; Pr 11:13; 16:28
*e*17:11 Ps 78:49
*f*17:12 2Sm 17:8; Hs 13:8
*g*17:13 Ps 35:12; 109:5
*h*2Sm 12:10
*i*17:14 Pr 20:3; 25:8
*j*17:15 Ex 23:7; Pr 17:26; 18:5; 24:23-24; Is 5:23
*k*17:16 Pr 4:5,7; 18:15; 23:23
*l*17:17 Ru 1:16; Pr 18:24; 27:10
*m*17:18 Pr 6:1-5; 11:15; 22:26

A17:11 Or *a merciless angel*   **B**17:18 Lit *sense shakes hands*

take in them. To obtain such blessing a person needs to pursue wisdom.

17:7 *Nabal*, the Hebrew word used here for fool (see Nabal in 1Sm 25:25), connotes the most irreligious of fools. It is one who curses God (Jb 2:9-10) and denies His existence (Ps 14:1; cp. Is 32:6). On the other kinds of "fool," see notes at Pr 1:7 and 1:22. If it is bad for this kind of fool to chatter, even though his words will be ignored, **how much** more important (see note at 11:31) it is for a **ruler** (see "noble" in note at 8:16) to watch what he says since his words carry weight.

17:8 The **magic stone** is literally "a stone of favor"—a charm that makes people treat others favorably. **Seems like . . . to its owner** is literally "in the eyes of its master." The owner is the one who gives a **bribe** (see note at 15:27). He only apparently **succeeds** in this life; ultimately God, who hates bribes, will condemn him.

17:9 The person who **conceals** another person's **offense** is the one who literally "seeks" **love**. To overlook being offended (19:11), and to leave any vengeance to God, is to promote good relationships in the future.

17:10 Unlike the **perceptive person**, who is sensitive to a mere spoken **rebuke**, the **fool** (Hb *kesiyl*) is so obstinate that he does not respond to extreme discipline. **A hundred lashes** is hyperbole; only 40 were allowed by law (Dt 25:3).

17:11 Rebellion implies turning away from God defiantly (Dt 31:27). The word for **messenger** can also be translated "angel." The "cruel messenger" is God's angel of death (16:14; 1Ch 21:15; Ps 78:49).

17:12 The female Syrian brown **bear** had a reputation for fierceness (2Kg 2:24; Lm 3:10) that was intensified if she was **robbed of her cubs** (2Sm 17:8; Hs 13:8).

17:14 To **stop** a **dispute** is to "leave it alone" or drop it (26:20). On **conflict**, see "trouble" in note at 6:14.

17:15 Corrupt judges in Israel were **acquitting the guilty**

and denying the innocent their day in court (Is 5:23). On **detestable**, see note at 3:32.

17:16 On **buying wisdom**, see note at 4:5-8. There is no better use for **money** than buying wisdom, but the **fool** (Hb *kesiyl*) is ignorant of that fact or obstinately against it (**with no intention** is lit "but there is no heart").

17:17 The purpose of a **brother** is to uphold a family member in **a difficult time**. The Hebrew word can be used generally of relatives (Gn 13:8; 29:15; Jdg 14:3). An unlikely but possible interpretation is that a **friend** is better because he **loves at all times**, not just in difficult times.

17:18 On **enters an agreement** and **puts up security**, see note at 6:1; on **without sense**, see note at 6:30-33.

kesiyl

Hebrew Pronunciation	[keh SEEL]
HCSB Translation	fool
Uses in Proverbs	49
Uses in the OT	70
Focus Passage	Proverbs 17:10,12,16,21,24-25

Kesiyl indicates someone *foolish* because of laziness and complacency. The *kesiyl* has a stupidity stemming from apathy toward moral issues, not willful disregard of them. This apathy distinguishes him from the *ewiyl*, a *fool* who is intentionally immoral. The *kesiyl* harbors anger, is easily provoked (Ec 7:9), and in consequence becomes careless (Pr 14:16). He is amused by purposeless activity (Ec 7:4-6) and speaks without thinking (Pr 15:2). Being self-indulgent (Pr 19:10), he squanders resources (Pr 21:20). Like the *ewiyl*, he displays his *foolishness* (Pr 13:16), loves ignorance (Pr 1:22), and repeats *foolish* behavior (Pr 26:11). He brings harm to companions (Pr 13:20), is self-deceived (Pr 14:8), and self-destructive (Ec 4:5). *Kesel* (6x) is *confidence* (Pr 3:26) but also *stupidity* (Ec 7:25) or *arrogance* (Ps 49:13). *Kislah* denotes *foolish ways* (Ps 85:8) or *confidence* (Jb 4:6), and *kesiylut* signifies *folly* (Pr 9:13). *Kasal* means *be foolish* (Jr 10:8).

19 One who loves to offend loves strife;[a]
one who builds a high threshold
   invites injury.

20 One with a twisted mind
      will not succeed,
and one with deceitful speech will fall
   into ruin.[b]

21 A man fathers a fool to his own sorrow;
the father of a fool has no joy.[c]

22 A joyful heart is good medicine,
but a broken spirit dries up the bones.[d]

23 A wicked man secretly takes a bribe[e]
to subvert the course of justice.[f]

24 Wisdom is the focus of the perceptive,
but a fool's eyes[g] roam to the ends
   of the earth.

25 A foolish son is grief to his father
and bitterness to the one
   who bore him.[h]

26 It is certainly not good to fine
      an innocent person
or to beat a noble for his honesty.[A,i]

27 The intelligent person restrains
      his words,[j]

[a]17:19 Pr 29:22
[b]17:20 Jr 23:36
[c]17:21 Pr 10:1;
17:25; 19:13;
23:24-25
[d]17:22 Ps 22:15;
Pr 14:30; 15:13;
18:14
[e]17:23 Pr 17:8
[f]Dt 16:19; Ps
15:5; Pr 18:5; Mc
3:11; 7:3
[g]17:24 Ec 2:14
[h]17:25 Pr 10:1;
17:21; 19:13
[i]17:26 Pr 17:15;
18:5; 24:23-24
[j]17:27 Pr 10:19;
Jms 1:19; 3:2
[k]17:28 Jb 13:5;
Pr 10:19
[l]18:2 Pr 12:23;
13:16; Ec 10:3
[m]18:4 Pr 20:5
[n]18:5 Lv 19:15;
Dt 1:17; 24:17;
Ps 15:5; 82:2; Pr
24:23-24; 28:21
[o]Pr 17:15
[p]18:6 Pr 19:29

and one who keeps a cool head[B]
is a man of understanding.

28 Even a fool is considered wise
      when he keeps silent,
discerning when he seals his lips.[k]

18 One who isolates himself pursues
      selfish desires;
he rebels against all sound judgment.

2 A fool does not delight
      in understanding,
but only wants to show off
      his opinions.[C,l]

3 When a wicked man comes,
      contempt also does,
and along with dishonor, disgrace.

4 The words of a man's mouth
      are deep waters,[m]
a flowing river, a fountain of wisdom.[D]

5 It is not good to show partiality
      to the •guilty[n]
by perverting the justice
      due the innocent.[o]

6 A fool's lips lead to strife,
and his mouth provokes a beating.[p]

A 17:26 Or *noble unfairly*   **B** 17:27 Lit *spirit*   **C** 18:2 Lit *to uncover his heart*   **D** 18:4 Or *waters; a fountain of wisdom is a flowing river.*

17:19 It is necessary to step over the **threshold** to enter a house. A **high** threshold would be hard to step over, possibly causing **injury** to guests. Or a high threshold could indicate someone who arrogantly built his house on a mound or hill above his neighbors. Such a proud person **invites** the Lord's destruction on himself (16:5).

17:20 Twisted and **deceitful** are both literally "turned" around, like those who call evil good (28:6,18).

17:21 The first kind of **fool** (Hb *kesiyl*) is immoral, obstinate, and dangerous (see note at 1:22). The second kind (*Hb nabal*) is sacrilegious (see note at 17:7).

17:22 In 15:13 a **joyful heart** causes a good face; here it is a **good** cure. A sad heart produces a **broken spirit** (see note at 15:13). Dried-up **bones** represent people who have lost their vitality (Ezk 37:11). The opposite would be bones saturated with marrow or oil (Jb 21:24; Ps 109:18).

17:23 The word **secretly** is literally "from the bosom" (cp. "covert" in 21:14), which elsewhere means from inside the folds of one's cloak (Ex 4:7) or from being wrapped in one's arms (1Kg 17:19). On **bribe**, see note at 15:27.

17:24 Wisdom is literally "with the face of" the **perceptive**, that is, he is facing it. The **ends of the earth** is a place far from the chosen people of Israel, out where ungodly people are (Dt 13:7; 28:49). The "**fool**" (Hb *kesiyl*) looks for easy income, illegal profit, or ways to avoid hard work.

17:25 Bitterness is misery, not malice (Jr 6:26).

17:26 The **innocent person** is literally "righteous." On **noble**, see note at 8:16; on **honesty**, see "upright" in note at 2:7.

17:27-28 In Egyptian wisdom, which shared some concepts of Israelite wisdom, to be cool or dispassionate was the ideal personality type. Jesus was the ultimate example of restraint (Is 53:7; Mk 14:61). There is an implied *a fortiori* argument here: if **even a fool** (Hb *ewiyl*) **is considered wise when . . . silent,** how much more will an intelligent person be respected for restraint. On **discerning**, see note at 1:5.

18:1 Desires are cravings (21:25-26; cp. Nm 11:4; Ps 10:3). **Sound judgment** is competence (3:21; 8:14) that leads to success (see note at 2:7).

18:3 This is probably not teaching that a **wicked man** brings contempt, **dishonor**, and **disgrace** to others. Instead, society dishonors him.

18:4 This could be saying that good speech can be really **deep** and meaningful—a source of **wisdom**. Or it could mean that typical human speech is often useless (20:5), but wisdom's **fountain** is a useful, flowing **river**.

18:5 To **show partiality** is literally to "lift the face." It may refer to a superior lifting his own face and looking on an inferior with a smile and a favorable judgment (Nm 6:26; cp. Ps 4:6), or to the inferior who had been bowed and groveling on the ground having his face or head lifted by the superior in vindication (Gn 40:13; Jb 11:15). Besides partiality, it means that the inferior "appeases" the superior (Pr 6:35) and that the superior "accepts" (Jb 42:9) or "grants the request of" the inferior (Gn 19:21; 1Sm 25:35). To pervert **justice** is literally "to turn aside from judgment" (Is 29:21; Am 5:12; Mal 3:5).

18:6-7 Lips and **mouth** refer to what the fool (Hb *kesiyl*) says, which causes trouble, escalating from **strife** and a **beating** to **devastation** (or terror) and ultimately to death.

7 A fool's mouth is his devastation,
and his lips are a trap for his life.[a]

8 A gossip's words are like choice food
that goes down
to one's innermost being.[A,b]

9 The one who is truly lazy in his work
is brother to a vandal.[B,c]

10 The name of •Yahweh is
a strong tower;[d]
the righteous run to it
and are protected.[C,e]

11 A rich man's wealth is his fortified city;
in his imagination it is like a high wall.[f]

12 Before his downfall a man's heart
is proud,[g]
but humility comes before honor.[h]

13 The one who gives an answer
before he listens—
this is foolishness and disgrace
for him.[i]

14 A man's spirit can endure sickness,
but who can survive a broken spirit?[j]

15 The mind of the discerning
acquires knowledge,
and the ear of the wise seeks it.[k]

16 A gift opens doors[D] for a man
and brings him before the great.[l]

17 The first to state his case seems right
until another comes and cross-
examines him.[m]

18 Casting the lot[n] ends quarrels
and separates powerful opponents.

19 An offended brother is harder to reach[E]
than a fortified city,
and quarrels are like the bars
of a fortress.

20 From the fruit of his mouth
a man's stomach is satisfied;
he is filled with the product
of his lips.[o]

21 Life and death are in the power
of the tongue,
and those who love it will eat its fruit.[p]

22 A man who finds a wife finds
a good thing[q]
and obtains favor from the LORD.[r]

23 The poor man pleads,[s]
but the rich one answers roughly.[t]

24 A man with many friends
may be harmed,[F]

Cross references:

[a] 18:7 Ps 64:8; 140:9; Pr 10:14; 12:13; 13:3; Ec 10:12
[b] 18:8 Pr 26:22
[c] 18:9 Pr 28:24
[d] 18:10 Ps 18:2; 61:3; 91:2; 144:2
[e] Pr 29:25
[f] 18:11 Pr 10:15
[g] 18:12 Pr 16:18
[h] Pr 11:2; 15:33; 29:23
[i] 18:13 Pr 15:28
[j] 18:14 Pr 15:13; 17:22
[k] 18:15 Pr 14:33; 15:14
[l] 18:16 Gn 32:20; 1Sm 25:27; Pr 17:8; 19:6; 21:14
[m] 18:17 1Kg 3:16-28
[n] 18:18 Pr 16:33
[o] 18:20 Pr 1:31; 12:14; 14:14
[p] 18:21 Pr 13:2; Mt 12:37; 15:11,18-20; Jms 3:8
[q] 18:22 Pr 12:4; 19:14; 31:10-31
[r] Pr 8:35
[s] 18:23 Pr 19:7
[t] Jms 2:6

A 18:8 Lit *to the chambers of the belly*   B 18:9 Lit *master of destruction*   C 18:10 Lit *raised high*   D 18:16 Lit *gift makes room*
E 18:19 LXX, Syr, Tg, Vg read *is stronger*   F 18:24 Some LXX mss, Syr, Tg, Vg read *friends must be friendly*

18:8 On gossip, see note at 16:28. **Choice food** is readily and greedily swallowed. The **words** go **down** to the hearer's **innermost being** (lit "chamber of the belly") where they infect his thinking and poison his heart.

18:9 To be **truly lazy** is to sink down, relax, and let go to the point of being slack, feeble, or ineffective. **Brother** implies solidarity—that he has the same characteristics (Jb 30:29) and supports the same causes (cp. "companion" in Pr 28:24). **Vandal** is literally "master (Hb *ba'al*) of destruction" (cp. "skilled at destruction" in Ezk 21:31).

18:10-11 These two proverbs illustrate a genuine and an imaginary refuge, respectively. A **strong tower** was a central place in a region or city to which people could **run** when threatened (Jdg 9:51). Yahweh's **name** implies His character as the eternal, powerful, faithful, covenant-keeping God (Ex 3:15; 6:6-7; Dt 7:9). The **righteous** people, who call on, rely upon, and have faith in the character of God, will be **protected** (lit "exalted" or lifted up so the enemy cannot reach them). A rich man relies on his **wealth** when he is threatened. To him it seems like a **high** (lit "exalted") **wall** around a **fortified city** (cp. 10:15), but that is only **in his imagination.** In reality, wealth cannot save (11:28; cp. Jb 31:24-28; 36:18-19; Ps 49; 52:5-7; Mt 16:26; Mk 10:24-25).

18:12 This proverb goes beyond 16:5,18 to teach that **humility** brings **honor** (see note at 3:16; cp. 15:33; 22:4; 29:23; see also "wisdom" in note at 11:2). This Hebrew word for "humility" implies being bowed down by affliction and then, when affliction shows that we are not self-sufficient, having a trusting relationship with God.

18:15 Unlike the fool who hates knowledge (1:22), refuses to listen (18:13), and does not intend to buy wisdom (17:16), the **wise** seek to hear **knowledge** (see note at 1:4), and the **discerning** (see note at 1:5) mind **acquires** (see note at 4:5-8) knowledge.

18:16 This **gift** is a bribe (see note at 15:27). It "makes room" or provides relief and **brings . . . a man** safely (the word is used of shepherds leading their sheep) into the presence of important people, such as kings and judges. This is an astute observation: bribery appears to work (17:8; 19:6; 21:14). However, only those who hate bribes will ultimately prosper (15:27).

18:17 To cross-examine is literally to "search," to diligently test or scrutinize to find what is hidden (25:2; 28:11).

18:18 On the **lot**, see note at 16:33. Flipping a coin can put an end to even the harshest argument. This is the only place in Proverbs where **separates** has a good sense (cp. v. 1; 16:28; 17:9; 19:4).

18:19 The **brother** is **offended**, having suffered a perceived loss or crime. Metal **bars** were used to reinforce the doors of a **fortress.** It was nearly impossible to get through in order to reconcile the situation.

18:20 **Fruit** is the harvest that results over time from what was initiated, as wheat comes from a sown field. **Satisfied** and **filled** are the same word in Hebrew. In a bad sense it can mean "glutted" (25:16-17). The approach a person takes in his speech will return to him. If his speech is wicked, he will get his fill of depravity (1:31); if his speech is honorable,

but there is a friend who stays closer
than a brother.[a]

19 Better a poor man who lives
with integrity[b]
than someone who has deceitful lips
and is a fool.

2 Even zeal is not good
without knowledge,[c]
and the one who acts hastily[A] sins.[d]

3 A man's own foolishness leads
him astray,
yet his heart rages against the Lord.[e]

4 Wealth attracts many friends,[f]
but a poor man is separated
from his friend.

5 A false witness will not go unpunished,[g]
and one who utters lies
will not escape.[h]

6 Many seek a ruler's favor,[i]
and everyone is a friend of one
who gives gifts.[j]

7 All the brothers of a poor man
hate him;[k]

how much more do his friends
keep their distance from him!
He may pursue them with words,[l]
but they are not there.[B]

8 The one who acquires good sense[c]
loves himself;
one who safeguards understanding
finds success.[m]

9 A false witness will not go unpunished,
and one who utters lies perishes.[n]

10 Luxury is not appropriate
for a fool[o]—
how much less for a slave to rule
over princes![p]

11 A person's insight gives him patience,[q]
and his virtue is to overlook
an offense.[r]

12 A king's rage is like the roaring
of a lion,[s]
but his favor is like dew on the grass.[t]

13 A foolish son is his father's ruin,[u]
and a wife's nagging is
an endless dripping.[v]

Cross references:
[a] 18:24 Pr 17:17; 27:10; Jn 15:13
[b] 19:1 Ps 26:11; 37:16; Pr 10:9; 14:2; 20:7; 28:6
[c] 19:2 Rm 10:2
[d] Pr 21:5; 28:20; 29:20
[e] 19:3 Is 8:21
[f] 19:4 Pr 14:20; 19:6
[g] 19:5 Dt 19:16-19; Pr 19:9; 21:28
[h] Pr 6:19
[i] 19:6 Pr 29:26
[j] Pr 14:20; 17:8; 19:4
[k] 19:7 Ps 38:11
[l] Pr 18:23
[m] 19:8 Pr 16:20
[n] 19:9 Pr 19:5; 21:28
[o] 19:10 Pr 17:7; 26:1
[p] Pr 30:22; Ec 10:6-7
[q] 19:11 Pr 14:29
[r] Pr 11:13; 17:9
[s] 19:12 Pr 16:14
[t] Ps 133:3; Pr 20:2; 28:15; Hs 14:5; Mc 5:7
[u] 19:13 Pr 10:1; 17:25; 28:7
[v] Pr 21:9,19; 27:15

A 19:2 Lit *who is hasty with feet*   B 19:7 Hb uncertain   C 19:8 Lit *acquires a heart*

---

he will get all the good things he needs (12:14; cp. 14:14; 28:19).

18:21 The **tongue** is powerful (Jms 3:1-12). Those who **love** the tongue and **eat its fruit** are those who choose to live or die under its **power**, like those who live by the sword (Gn 27:40; Mt 26:52), by the law (Neh 9:29; Ezk 20:11; Rm 10:5; Gl 3:12), or by faith (Hab 2:4; Rm 1:17; Gl 3:11). Prudent speech brings **life** (v. 20; 12:14; 13:2; 21:23), and wicked or excessive speech brings **death** (13:3; Mt 15:18-19).

18:22 The **good thing** is literally abstract "good"; in other contexts it is translated "success" (16:20; 17:20; 19:8). On **favor**, see note at 19:6.

18:24 The first **friends** are neighbors or companions, who may be attracted by money (19:4). The second kind of **friend** is literally "one who loves." Jesus is such a friend to His followers (Jn 15:13-14).

19:1 On **poor** and **integrity**, see note at 11:20; on **better . . . than** proverbs, see note at 15:16-17.

19:2 **Zeal** is literally "appetite, desire" (Hb *nephesh*; see note at 13:2-4). Romans 10:2 reinforces this proverb.

19:3 It is the fool's (Hb *ewiyl*) own fault when **foolishness** literally "undermines his way" (see note at 13:6), but because he is obstinate (see note at 1:7), he gets angry at God.

19:4 In both cases these are false **friends** (see note at 18:24; cp. 16:28; 17:9). On **wealth**, see "possessions" in note at 3:9-10.

19:5 On **not go unpunished**, see note at 6:27-29. God sees to it that liars **will not escape** judgment (v. 9; 11:21).

19:6 On "ruler," see "noble" in note at 8:16. To **seek . . . favor** is literally "to make the face pleasant" (18:5). It is used

when an inferior is petitioning a superior, trying to get him to "smile" at him (Ex 32:11; 1Sm 13:12; Jb 11:19; see note at Pr 18:5). This is sometimes done through **gifts** or offerings (Ps 45:12), which may degenerate into bribery (Pr 15:27). It is better to wait on the Lord (29:26).

19:7 On **how much more**, see note at 11:31. These **friends** are like royal advisers (Gn 26:26) or a groom's attendants (Jdg 14:11,20; 15:2,6).

19:8 On **acquires**, see note at 4:5-8; on **good sense**, see notes at 6:30-33 and 8:5. Putting this proverb together with 15:32, if a person **loves himself** (1Sm 20:17; Mt 22:39; Eph 5:29) he should be open to discipline and should listen to correction so he can acquire good sense and ultimately find **success** (lit "good"; cp. 16:20). The alternative is to harm oneself and love death (8:36).

19:10 On **how much less**, see note at 11:31. **Appropriate** means "patently wrong"—not suitable or fitting, threatening to the social order (17:7; 26:1; 30:21). However, a wise **slave** may rightly supplant a wicked prince (see note at 17:2).

19:11 **Virtue** is literally a "beautiful adornment," translated "glory" in 20:29. When through **insight** (see notes at 1:3 and 12:8) a person gains **patience** (see note at 14:29), he gains the admirable capacity to **overlook** it when someone sins against him (10:12; 17:9; Mt 6:14-15).

19:12 A king in ancient times had great power over his subjects; he could order someone executed (2Sm 1:15; cp. Pr 16:14) or set him up for life (2Sm 9:7).

19:13 Both of these things irritate and frustrate a person. There is an Arabic word related to the Hebrew word for **dripping** that means "a leaky roof." **Nagging** is bitter conflict and discord, strife and dissension, contention and quarreling (21:9,19; 25:24; 27:15; cp. 5:18-19).

14 A house and wealth are inherited
from fathers,[a]
but a sensible wife is from the LORD.

15 Laziness induces deep sleep,
and a lazy person will go hungry.[b]

16 The one who keeps commands
preserves himself;[c]
one who disregards[A] his ways will die.[d]

17 Kindness to the poor is a loan
to the LORD,[e]
and He will give a reward
to the lender.[B,f]

18 Discipline your son while there is hope;
don't be intent on killing him.[C,g]

19 A person with great anger bears
the penalty;
if you rescue him, you'll have to do
it again.[h]

20 Listen to counsel
and receive instruction
so that you may be wise later in life.[D,i]

21 Many plans are in a man's heart,
but the LORD's decree will prevail.[j]

22 What is desirable in a man is
his fidelity;
better to be a poor man than a liar.[k]

23 The •fear of the LORD leads to life;
one will sleep at night[E]
without danger.[l]

24 The slacker buries his hand in the bowl;
he doesn't even bring it back
to his mouth.[m]

25 Strike a mocker, and the inexperienced
learn a lesson;[n]
rebuke the discerning,
and he gains knowledge.[o]

26 The one who assaults his father
and evicts his mother
is a disgraceful and shameful son.

27 If you stop listening to correction,
my son,
you will stray from the words
of knowledge.

28 A worthless witness mocks justice,
and a wicked mouth swallows iniquity.[p]

29 Judgments are prepared for mockers,
and beatings for the backs of fools.[q]

[a]19:14 2Co 12:14 [b]19:15 Pr 6:9-11; 10:4; 13:4; 21:25 [c]19:16 Lk 10:28 [d]Pr 3:1-2; 4:4; 13:13 [e]19:17 Dt 15:7-10; Pr 14:31; 28:27; Ec 11:1-2; Mt 10:42; 25:40; 2Co 9:6-8; Heb 6:10 [f]Lk 6:38 [g]19:18 Pr 13:24; 23:13-14; 29:17 [h]19:19 Pr 22:24-25; 29:22 [i]19:20 Pr 12:1; 15:5,31-32 [j]19:21 Ps 33:10-11; Pr 16:1,9,33; 21:31; Is 14:26-27 [k]19:22 Pr 19:1; 28:6 [l]19:23 Pr 14:26-27 [m]19:24 Pr 12:27; 20:4; 26:14-15 [n]19:25 Pr 21:11 [o]Pr 9:8 [p]19:28 Jb 15:16; 34:7 [q]19:29 Pr 10:13; 18:6; 26:3

[A]19:16 Or *despises*, or *treats lightly* [B]19:17 Lit *to him* [C]19:18 Lit *don't lift up your soul to his death* [D]19:20 Lit *in your end*
[E]19:23 Lit *will spend the night satisfied*

19:14 Many things are seen as arising from human activity, but a **sensible wife** (unlike a nagging wife, v. 13) is truly a gift from God (18:22; 31:10).

19:15 On the connection between **laziness . . . sleep**, and poverty, see notes at 6:4; 6:6; 6:11 and 24:30-34. In a **deep** sleep, a person is unaware of what is happening around him (Gn 2:21; 1Sm 26:12).

19:16 **Keeps** and **preserves** both come from the Hebrew word *shamar*. The **commands** are not just God's commandments, but instruction from any good source. Also, the mention of **his ways** probably does not refer directly to God's ways because God is not mentioned in context. Disregarding one's own ways has to do with not wanting to watch carefully what one is doing, not taking responsibility—the opposite of making sure that one's ways are God's ways (8:32).

19:17 God takes care of those who care for the **poor** (14:21,31; 22:9; 28:27). The **reward** (lit "repayment," related to *shalom*, "wholeness"; 13:13; 25:22) from God is not necessarily money and will not necessarily come in this life.

19:18 The **son** who is not disciplined will remain a slacker or a fool and will perish—physically and spiritually. The parent should strive not to let this happen (3:12; 5:23; 13:24; 22:15; 23:13-14; 29:15; Heb 12:5-11). As long as a son is alive, **there is hope**.

19:19 A person with a hot temper (see note at 14:17) should be left to pay the consequences—it is the only way he will learn.

19:20 On **later in life**, see "at the end" in note at 5:11.

19:21 **Prevail** is literally "stand" (cp. "succeed" in 15:22).

19:22 The Hebrew word *chesed*, translated "faithful love," can also mean **fidelity** (3:3; 20:6,28) or "kindness" (11:17). It is used of the faithful covenant love that God has for His people (Ex 20:6; Dt 7:9; 2Sm 7:15; Ps 23:6; Is 16:5; 54:8; Jr 31:3). There is a homonym *chesed* that means "shame." If every word in the first line is given a negative spin, it reads, "The craving of a human is his shame." It is **better** to be a faithful **poor man** than someone who craves what he does not have and lies to get it.

19:24 On **bowl** and **slacker**, see note at 26:15.

19:25 On **inexperienced**, see note at 1:4. The **mocker** (see note at 1:22) does not learn (13:1; 14:6; 15:12), but the **discerning** (see note at 1:5) is willing to learn from **rebuke** (9:8; 28:23).

19:27 The Hebrew does not have **if**; instead, it is sarcastic: "**stop listening** . . . in order to stray." To **stray** is to be lost, stagger, or be misled (5:23; 20:1; 28:10; cp. "disregard his ways" in 19:16). On **correction**, see "discipline" in note at 1:2.

19:28 The meaning of **swallows iniquity** is uncertain. Perhaps the **wicked** person considers sin a tasty morsel. Or perhaps the **worthless** (see note at 6:12) **witness** (see note at 12:17) will be forced to "swallow" the consequences of his lies (19:29).

19:29 Judgment is always God's final punishment; it is never meant for correction. **Beatings** are potentially corrective, but **fools** (Hb *kesiyl*; see note at 1:22) are obstinate and do not change.

20 Wine is a mocker,ᵃ beer is a brawler,
and whoever staggers
because of them is not wise.

² A king's terrible wrath is
like the roaring of a lion;
anyone who provokes him
endangers himself.ᵇ

³ It is honorable for a man to resolve
a dispute,ᶜ
but any fool can get himself
into a quarrel.ᵈ

⁴ The slacker does not plow
during planting season;ᴬ
at harvest time he looks,ᴮ and there is
nothing.ᵉ

⁵ Counsel in a man's heart is deep water;ᶠ
but a man of understanding
draws it out.

⁶ Many a man proclaims
his own loyalty,
but who can find
a trustworthy man?ᵍ

⁷ The one who lives with integrity
is righteous;ʰ
his childrenᶜ who come after him
will be happy.ⁱ

⁸ A king sitting on a throne to judge
sifts out all evil with his eyes.ʲ

⁹ Who can say, "I have kept
my heart pure;
I am cleansed from my sin"?ᵏ

¹⁰ Differing weights
and varying measuresᴰ—
both are detestable to the LORD.ˡ

¹¹ Even a young man is known
by his actions—
if his behavior is pure and upright.ᵐ

¹² The hearing ear and the seeing eye—
the LORD made them both.ⁿ

¹³ Don't love sleep, or you will
become poor;
open your eyes, and you'll have
enough to eat.ᵒ

¹⁴ "It's worthless, it's worthless!"
the buyer says,
but after he is on his way, he gloats.

¹⁵ There is gold and a multitude
of jewels,
but knowledgeable lips are
a rare treasure.ᵖ

¹⁶ Take his garment,ᴱ
for he has put up security
for a stranger;
get collateral if it is for foreigners.۩

¹⁷ Food gained by fraud is sweet
to a man,ʳ

ᵃ 20:1 Gn 9:21; Pr 23:29-30; Is 28:7; Hs 4:11
ᵇ 20:2 Nm 16:38; Est 4:11; Pr 8:36; 19:12; Hab 2:10
ᶜ 20:3 Pr 17:14
ᵈ Pr 15:18; 18:6; 22:10
ᵉ 20:4 Pr 24:27,30-34
ᶠ 20:5 Pr 18:4
ᵍ 20:6 Ps 53:2-3; Pr 28:20; Ec 7:28; Lk 18:8
ʰ 20:7 Pr 2:7,20-21; 10:9; 13:6
ⁱ Ps 37:26; 112:2
ʲ 20:8 Pr 20:26; 25:5; Mt 25:32
ᵏ 20:9 1Kg 8:46; Jb 15:15-16; Ps 14:2-3; Ec 7:20; Rm 3:9-12; 1Jn 1:8
ˡ 20:10 Dt 25:14-15; Pr 11:1; 20:23; Mc 6:10-11
ᵐ 20:11 Pr 21:8; Mt 7:16
ⁿ 20:12 Ex 4:11; Ps 94:9; Pr 22:2; 29:13
ᵒ 20:13 Pr 6:10-11; 19:15; 24:33-34
ᵖ 20:15 Pr 3:15; 8:11
۩ 20:16 Dt 24:12-13; Pr 6:1-5; 11:15; 27:13
ʳ 20:17 Pr 9:17

ᴬ 20:4 Lit *plow in winter*   ᴮ 20:4 Lit *inquires*   ᶜ 20:7 Lit *sons*   ᴰ 20:10 Lit *Stone and stone, measure and measure*   ᴱ 20:16 A debtor's outer garment was held as collateral.

20:1 On **mocker**, see note at 1:22. A **brawler** is loud and rowdy (7:11; 9:13). To "stagger" is literally to "wander" into something (19:27) and "get lost" in it (5:19-20,23).

20:2 On **king's . . . wrath**, see note at 19:12. The last phrase could be literally translated either "he misses (fails to hit) his life" or "he sins against himself"; the essential meaning is the same.

20:4 The ground has to be plowed to prepare it for **planting**, but the **slacker** avoids work and does not think ahead (6:6-11). "During planting season" is literally "from winter," that is, starting in about November. **He looks** is literally "he asks," that is, he comes to the fields to inquire about his harvest.

20:5 **Water** in a **deep** well is useful but hard to draw up.

20:6 On **loyalty**, see "faithful love" in note at 19:22. It is easy for someone to proclaim it, but truly **trustworthy** (cp. 13:17) people, who will act in time of need, are rare. **Who can find** is a rhetorical question that assumes the answer, "no one."

20:7 On **integrity**, see note at 2:7; on **happy**, see note at 3:13-18. The promise of happiness for children must be balanced by Ezekiel 18.

20:8 **Sifts out** is to throw grain up in the wind with a winnowing shovel so that the chaff scatters (Ru 3:2; Ps 106:27; Is 30:24; 41:16; Ezk 5:10; cp. Pr 20:26).

20:9 The word for **cleansed** is used for being ritually clean and suitable for temple worship (Nm 8:6). This rhetorical question makes the point that no human being is perfect, and no human effort can remove sin (Jb 15:14; 25:4; Rm 3:23; 1Jn 1:8). Only God can forgive sin and cleanse a person (Is 55:7; Mk 2:5-11; 1Jn 1:7).

20:11 The Hebrew word for **is known** probably means to present oneself to be recognized. A **young man** is measured against purity and uprightness.

20:12 God can open the **ear** and **eye** to wisdom.

20:13 To **become poor** is literally to "be dispossessed" (Jos 3:10), or to be deprived of possessions (Gn 45:11; Zch 9:4; cp. Pr 23:21; 30:9).

20:14 This is a humorous look at bartering, but it also shows that many people are self-idolizing liars. **He gloats** is literally "he praises himself." On **worthless**, see "trouble" in note at 1:16.

20:15 These **jewels** were probably coral (Lm 4:7) or pearls (Jb 28:18).

20:16 Someone has been foolish enough to **put up security for a stranger** (see note at 6:1). A person might as well take the pledge and **collateral** from him now because it is as good as lost.

20:17 On **gravel**, compare Lm 3:16.

but afterward his mouth is full
of gravel.

18 Finalize plans with counsel,[a]
and wage war with sound guidance.[b]

19 The one who reveals secrets is
a constant gossip;[c]
avoid someone with a big mouth.[d]

20 Whoever curses his father or mother[e]—
his lamp will go out in deep darkness.[f]

21 An inheritance gained prematurely
will not be blessed ultimately.[g]

22 Don't say, "I will avenge this evil!"[h]
Wait on the Lord,[i] and He will
rescue you.[j]

23 Differing weights[A] are detestable
to the Lord,[k]
and dishonest scales[l] are unfair.

24 A man's steps are determined
by the Lord,[m]
so how can anyone understand
his own way?

25 It is a trap for anyone to dedicate
something rashly
and later to reconsider his vows.[n]

26 A wise king separates out the wicked[o]
and drives the threshing wheel[p]
over them.

27 The Lord's lamp sheds light on
a person's life,[B]
searching the innermost parts.[C,q]

28 Loyalty and faithfulness deliver a king;
through loyalty he maintains
his throne.

29 The glory of young men is
their strength,
and the splendor of old men is
gray hair.[r]

30 Lashes and wounds purge away evil,[s]
and beatings cleanse
the innermost parts.[D]

21 A king's heart is like streams of water
in the Lord's hand:
He directs it wherever He chooses.[t]

2 All a man's ways seem right to him,
but the Lord evaluates the motives.[E,u]

3 Doing what is righteous and just
is more acceptable to the Lord
than sacrifice.[v]

[a]20:18 Pr 11:14; 15:22
[b]Pr 24:6; Lk 14:31
[c]20:19 Lv 19:16; Pr 11:13
[d]Pr 13:3
[e]20:20 Ex 21:17; Pr 24:20; 30:11
[f]Jb 18:5
[g]20:21 Pr 21:5; 23:5; 28:22; Lk 15:11-13
[h]20:22 Pr 24:29; Mt 5:39; Rm 12:17,19; 1Th 5:15; 1Pt 3:9
[i]Ps 27:14
[j]Ps 37:7-9
[k]20:23 Pr 20:10; Mc 6:11
[l]Pr 11:1
[m]20:24 Pr 16:9,33; 19:21
[n]20:25 Nm 30:2; Dt 23:21; Ec 5:4-6
[o]20:26 Pr 20:8
[p]Is 28:27
[q]20:27 Ps 139:23; Pr 20:30; 1Co 2:11
[r]20:29 Lv 19:32; Pr 16:31
[s]20:30 Is 53:5
[t]21:1 Ezr 6:22
[u]21:2 Pr 12:15; 16:2; 17:3; 24:12; Lk 16:15
[v]21:3 1Sm 15:22; Pr 15:8; Hs 6:6; Mc 6:7-8; Mt 9:13

[A]20:23 Lit *A stone and a stone*   [B]20:27 Lit *breath*   [C]20:27 Lit *the chambers of the belly*   [D]20:30 Lit *beatings the chambers of the belly*   [E]21:2 Lit *Lord weighs the hearts*

20:18 To **finalize plans** is to "establish" or "achieve" them, which ultimately only God can do (4:26; 16:3,9). Often God works through the **counsel** and **guidance** of wise, godly advisers.

20:19 On **gossip**, see note at 11:13.

20:20 To "curse" is literally to "declare inconsequential" or to treat with contempt (Gn 12:3; 2Sm 16:7; cp. "defiling" in 1Sm 3:13). One's **lamp** going **out** is metaphorical for untimely death (13:9; 24:20; 2Sm 21:17; cp. Ex 20:12; Eph 6:2-3).

20:21 This proverb is proved true in the parable of the lost son (Lk 15:11-13).

20:22 To **avenge** is to exact payment; God is in charge of payments and rewards (11:31; 19:17; 24:29; Dt 32:35). To **wait** implies hope (Ps 25:3; 27:14; 37:9,34; 39:7; 40:1; 130:5).

20:24 This word for "man" implies strength and virility (see "warrior" in 24:5). If God determines the conduct of even the strongest man, no one can claim absolute control over **his own** life.

20:25 A fool's mouth can be a **trap** (cp. 18:7; Jdg 11:29-40). To **reconsider** is to inquire into something carefully. The fool only **later** checks to see if he can fulfill **his vows.**

20:26 The process of **threshing** actually begins with the **wheel**, which removes the chaff from the grain. Then the chaff is separated by throwing it up in the wind (v. 8).

20:27-28 To be delivered is to be guarded or kept. On **loyalty and faithfulness**, see notes at 3:3 and 19:22.

20:29 These are "choice" or "select" **young men** (Jos 8:3). **Gray hair** represents the achievement of honorable old age; few wicked people reach it (10:27; 16:31).

20:30 Corporal punishment, when appropriate, is effective (13:24; 22:15; 23:14). To **cleanse** is to remove tarnish through rubbing or scouring (Lv 6:28; Jr 46:4). On **innermost**, see verse 27 and note at 18:8.

21:1 God is sovereign even over a king—and not just Israel's kings (1Kg 11:23; Ezr 6:22; Is 44:28; Jr 25:9; Ac 4:27-28).

21:3 **Sacrifice** stands for the outward actions of religious observance, equivalent to "doing church."

21:4 This Hebrew word for **lamp that guides** could also be

Oil lamp (20:20) from the late Iron Age II or the Persian period. Such an item would have been very common in an ancient Israelite home.

⁴ The lamp^A that guides the wicked—
   haughty eyes
   and an arrogant heart^a—is sin.

⁵ The plans of the diligent certainly lead
      to profit,
   but anyone who is reckless
      certainly becomes poor.^b

⁶ Making a fortune
      through a lying tongue
   is a vanishing mist,^B a pursuit
      of death.^C,D,c

⁷ The violence of the wicked
      sweeps them away
   because they refuse to act justly.

⁸ A •guilty man's conduct is crooked,^d
   but the behavior of the innocent
      is upright.^e

⁹ Better to live on the corner
      of a roof
   than to share a house
      with a nagging wife.^f

¹⁰ A wicked person desires evil;
   he has no consideration^E
      for his neighbor.^g

¹¹ When a mocker is punished,
   the inexperienced become wiser;
   when one teaches a wise man,
   he acquires knowledge.^h

¹² The Righteous One considers the house
      of the wicked;
   He brings the wicked to ruin.

¹³ The one who shuts his ears to the cry
      of the poor
   will himself also call out
      and not be answered.^i

¹⁴ A secret gift soothes anger,
   and a covert bribe,^F fierce rage.^j

¹⁵ Justice executed is a joy
      to the righteous
   but a terror to those
      who practice iniquity.^k

¹⁶ The man who strays from the way
      of wisdom
   will come to rest
   in the assembly
      of the departed spirits.^l

¹⁷ The one who loves pleasure
      will become a poor man;
   whoever loves wine and oil will not
      get rich.^m

¹⁸ The wicked are a ransom
      for the righteous,
   and the treacherous, for^G the upright.^n

¹⁹ Better to live in a wilderness
   than with a nagging
      and hot-tempered wife.^o

Cross-references:
^a 21:4 Ps 101:5; Pr 6:16-17; 30:13
^b 21:5 Pr 10:4; 14:23; 21:20; 28:22
^c 21:6 Pr 8:36; 13:11; 20:21
^d 21:8 Pr 2:15
^e Pr 20:11
^f 21:9 Pr 15:16-17; 17:1; 21:19; 25:24
^g 21:10 Pr 14:21
^h 21:11 Pr 19:25
^i 21:13 Pr 14:31; 17:5; Mt 18:30-34; Jms 2:13; 1Jn 3:17
^j 21:14 Pr 17:8; 18:16; 19:6
^k 21:15 Pr 10:29; Rm 13:13
^l 21:16 Ps 49:14; Pr 2:18; 9:18
^m 21:17 Ec 2:1-3,10-11
^n 21:18 Pr 11:8; Is 43:3
^o 21:19 Pr 21:9

---

^A21:4 Some Hb mss, ancient versions read *tillage*   ^B21:6 Or *a breath blown away*   ^C21:6 Some Hb mss, LXX, Vg read *a snare of death*   ^D21:6 Lit *is vanity, ones seeking death*   ^E21:10 Or *favor*   ^F21:14 Lit *a bribe in the bosom*   ^G21:18 Or *in place of*

---

translated "unplowed field of." Just as an unplowed field produces weeds, **haughty eyes** (see "arrogant eyes" and note at 6:17) and an **arrogant heart** (immodesty and lack of restraint) produce **sin**. In contrast, a commandment and teaching guide the righteous (6:23).

21:5 The **reckless** person is literally "hasty" (19:2; cp. 29:20) or "in a hurry" (28:20); he lacks forethought and diligence.

21:6 On **mist**, see note at 13:11. It is literally "blown away" like smoke (cp. Ps 68:2). This **fortune** cannot save from eternal **death** (10:2; 20:21).

21:8 To be **crooked** is to be perverse or deceptive.

21:9 On **better . . . than** proverbs, see note at 15:16-17; on **nagging**, see note at 19:13. Houses in ancient Israel had flat roofs, and it was possible to build a shelter on them (2Kg 4:10) or to sleep there in the summer (1Sm 9:25-26). Normally, however, the inside of the house was "better."

21:10 The Hebrew words for **evil** *(ra')* and **neighbor** *(rea')* look and sound similar.

21:11 A mocker's only contribution is as a negative example (see note at 1:22). **He** in the second part of this verse could refer to **the inexperienced** (see note at 1:4), who first becomes **wiser**, then **acquires knowledge**.

21:12 On **brings . . . to ruin**, see "undermines" in note at 13:6.

21:13 God does not answer cries for help if they are insincere (1:28; Is 1:15; Jr 11:9-12; Ezk 8:16-18; Mc 3:4; Zch 7:13; 1Pt 3:7).

21:14 While it cannot be denied that a **bribe** is effective (see note at 15:27; cp. 17:8), God hates bribery. On **covert**, see "secretly" in note at 17:23.

21:15 Amos warned that **justice** on the day of the Lord would be **terror** to the wicked in Israel (Am 5:18), and Paul taught that rulers are only a terror to the wicked (Rm 13:3).

21:16 On **strays**, compare 7:25-27; on **departed spirits**, see note at 2:18-19.

21:17 **Wine** and **oil** were blessings from God (Dt 7:13; Ps 104:14-15), as was **pleasure** (lit "joy"; Ps 21:6), but when God's blessings are pursued without God, they become vices.

21:18 One should not conclude from this proverb that sinners somehow pay the debt of the godly; in fact Christ, the sinless One, paid for the sins of all (Ps 49:7-9,15; Gl 3:13; 1Tm 2:6). While this doesn't explain the means of salvation, it does express the outcome: **the righteous** go free and **the treacherous** will be punished.

21:19 On **nagging . . . wife**, see note at 19:13. A **hot-tempered** person vexes others, causes grief and aggravation, and expresses displeasure (12:16; 17:25; 27:3).

²⁰ Precious treasure and oil are
in the dwelling of a wise person,
but a foolish man consumes them.^(A,a)

²¹ The one who pursues righteousness
and faithful love
will find life, righteousness, and honor.^b

²² A wise person went up against a city
of warriors
and brought down its secure fortress.^c

²³ The one who guards his mouth
and tongue
keeps himself out of trouble.^d

²⁴ The proud and arrogant person,
named "Mocker,"
acts with excessive pride.^e

²⁵ A slacker's craving will kill him
because his hands refuse to work.^f

²⁶ He is filled with craving^B all day long,
but the righteous give and don't
hold back.^g

²⁷ The sacrifice of a wicked person
is detestable—
how much more so

when he brings it
with ulterior motives!^h

²⁸ A lying witness will perish,^i
but the one who listens
will speak successfully.

²⁹ A wicked man puts on a bold face,^j
but the upright man considers
his way.

³⁰ No wisdom, no understanding,
and no counsel
will prevail against the LORD.^k

³¹ A horse is prepared for the day
of battle,^l
but victory comes from the LORD.^m

22 A good name is to be chosen
over great wealth;
favor is better than silver and gold.^n

² The rich and the poor have this
in common:^C
the LORD made them both.^(D,o)

³ A sensible person sees danger
and takes cover,

Cross references (center column):
^a 21:20 Jb 20:15,18; Ps 112:3; Pr 10:4; 28:20; Mt 25:1-13
^b 21:21 Pr 3:16; 8:18; 15:9; Mt 5:6; 6:33
^c 21:22 2Sm 5:6-9; Pr 14:26; 24:5; Ec 7:19; 9:14-18
^d 21:23 Pr 12:13; 13:3; Jms 3:2
^e 21:24 Ps 1:1; Pr 1:22; 21:11
^f 21:25 Pr 10:4; 12:24; 13:4; 19:15,24
^g 21:26 Ps 37:26; Pr 11:24-25
^h 21:27 Pr 15:8; 28:9; Is 66:3
^i 21:28 Pr 19:5,9
^j 21:29 Pr 7:13
^k 21:30 Is 8:9-10; 1Co 3:19-20
^l 21:31 Ps 20:7; 33:17; 108:10-13; Is 31:1
^m Jr 3:23; 1Co 15:57
^n 22:1 Pr 10:7; 8:10; Ec 7:1
^o 22:2 Jb 31:13,15; Pr 29:13

---

^A 21:20 Lit *it*   ^B 21:26 Lit *He craves a craving*   ^C 22:2 Lit *poor meet*   ^D 22:2 Lit *all*

21:20 To "consume" is literally to "gulp down" (1:12; 19:28). The **wise** person accumulates valuable savings but the **foolish man** (Hb *kesiyl*) spends his income as fast as it is produced.

21:21 On **faithful love**, see note at 19:22. Those who pursue godliness also **find** God's blessing (1Kg 3:10-14; Mt 6:33).

21:22 Secure fortress in this verse uses the same two Hebrew words as "strong confidence" in 14:26. However, those who trust in this mighty fortress have unfounded con-

fidence. A **wise** person can overcome the most formidable obstacles.

21:24 On **Mocker**, see note at 1:22. **Pride** is the key to the mocker's character.

21:25-26 The slacker (see note at 6:6) has selfish **craving** that is unfilled because he is too lazy; he will experience physical and spiritual death. **Righteous** people are generous yet contented (19:24).

21:27 God hates hypocrisy (15:8), but even **more so** (see note at 11:31) when there is a plan to harm others (2Sm 15:7-13; Mt 23:14).

21:28 The person who **listens** could be one who paid attention to the report of a crime so that he could give accurate second-hand testimony, or it could be the accused person who listened to a **lying witness** against him and then gave a good rebuttal.

21:29 To put on a **bold face** is to act brazenly (7:13) or arrogantly (Dn 11:12).

21:30-31 God is sovereign (19:21; Ps 33:10-11). **A horse** is an example of human **understanding**—military technology—that cannot succeed apart from God's will (Ps 20:7; 33:17; Is 31:1; Jr 3:23).

22:1 A person's **name** is his character in life (21:24) and the way he is remembered after death (10:7). **Favor** is respect from people and grace from God, a benefit of wisdom (3:1-4).

22:2 To **have this in common** is literally "meet" or "intersect" (cp. 29:13). There is no class structure in God's eyes (Jb 34:19; Rm 10:12; Gl 3:28; Col 3:11).

22:3 On **sensible**, see "shrewd" in note at 1:4. The punishment here is literally a "fine" or "penalty" (17:26; 19:19), which implies financial consequences for remaining **inexperienced** (see note at 1:4; cp. 8:5; 9:6).

---

yashar

Hebrew Pronunciation	[yah SHAHR]
HCSB Translation	straight, right, upright
Uses in Proverbs	25
Uses in the OT	119
Focus Passage	Proverbs 21:2,8,18,29

Adjectival *yashar*, from the verb *yashar* (go *straight*), means *straight* (Is 26:7) or *smooth* (Jr 31:9). People are *upright* (Nm 23:10), *true* (Dt 32:4), *just* (Ps 92:15), *honest* (Jb 4:7), or *honorable* (1Sm 29:6). Actions are *right* (Ex 15:26), *laws impartial* (Neh 9:13), journeys *safe* (Ezr 8:21), and hearts *one* (2Kg 10:15). "*Yashar of heart*" implies *conscientious* (2Ch 29:34). "*Yashar in his eyes*" suggests *fine to him* (2Sm 19:6), *whatever he wants* (Jdg 17:6), and *what pleases him* (Jr 34:15) or *seems right* (Jr 40:4). *Book of Jasher* is literally "Book of the *Upright*" (Jos 10:13). Related *yosher* (15x) and *meshar* (19x) mean *integrity, uprightness, rightness,* and *agreement* (Dn 11:6,17). Additionally, *yosher* connotes *sincerity* (Ps 119:7), *honesty* (Pr 17:26), *accuracy* (Ec 12:10), and *straightness* (Pr 4:11). *Meshar* connotes *fairness* (Ps 9:8), *levelness* (Is 26:7), and *smoothness* (Pr 23:31). *Yishrah* means *integrity* (1Kg 3:6).

but the inexperienced keep going
   and are punished.[a]

4   The result of humility is *fear
       of the LORD,
    along with wealth, honor, and life.[b]

5   There are thorns and snares
       on the path of the crooked;[c]
    the one who guards himself stays
       far from them.

6   Teach a youth about the way
       he should go;[d]
    even when he is old he will not depart
       from it.

7   The rich rule over the poor,[e]
    and the borrower is a slave
       to the lender.[f]

8   The one who sows injustice
       will reap disaster,[g]
    and the rod of his fury
       will be destroyed.

9   A generous person[A] will be blessed,[h]
    for he shares his food
       with the poor.[i]

10 Drive out a mocker,[j] and conflict
       goes too;
    then quarreling and dishonor
       will cease.[k]

11 The one who loves a pure heart
    and gracious lips—the king is
       his friend.[l]

Cross references column

[a]22:3 Pr 14:16;
27:12; Is 26:20
[b]22:4 Pr 15:33;
21:21; 29:23
[c]22:5 Pr 7:23;
15:19
[d]22:6 Eph 6:4
[e]22:7 Pr 18:23;
Jms 2:6
[f]Dt 28:12-13
[g]22:8 Jb 4:8; Hs
10:13-14
[h]22:9 Pr 19:17;
2Co 9:6
[i]Lk 14:13-14
[j]22:10 Gn
21:9-10
[k]Pr 26:20
[l]22:11 Pr 16:13
[m]22:13 Pr 26:13
[n]22:14 Pr 2:16-
19; 7:5,21,27;
23:27-28; Ec
7:26
[o]22:15 Pr 13:24;
23:13-14; 29:15
[p]22:16 Pr 11:24;
22:7; 28:27
[q]22:17 Pr 5:1

12 The LORD's eyes keep watch
       over knowledge,
    but He overthrows the words
       of the treacherous.

13 The slacker says,
       "There's a lion outside!
    I'll be killed in the public square!"[m]

14 The mouth of the forbidden woman is
       a deep pit;
    a man cursed by the LORD will fall
       into it.[n]

15 Foolishness is tangled up in the heart
       of a youth;
    the rod of discipline will drive it away
       from him.[o]

16 Oppressing the poor to enrich oneself,
    and giving to the rich—both lead
       only to poverty.[p]

Words of the Wise

17 Listen closely,[B] pay attention
       to the words of the wise,[q]
    and apply your mind to my knowledge.

18 For it is pleasing if you keep them
       within you
    and if[C] they are constantly on your lips.

19 I have instructed you today—
       even you—
    so that your confidence may be
       in the LORD.

20 Haven't I written for you thirty sayings[D]
    about counsel and knowledge,

[A]22:9 Lit Good of eye   [B]22:17 Lit Stretch out your ear   [C]22:18 Or you; let them be, or you, so that   [D]22:20 Text emended; one Hb tradition reads you previously; alt Hb tradition reads you excellent things; LXX, Syr, Vg read you three times

22:5 These are large **thorns**—big enough to drag prisoners with (Am 4:2; cp. Jb 5:5). On **snares**, see note at 7:23.

22:6 Teach is literally to "dedicate" something, such as a building—to have a celebration commemorating the first time it is put to its intended use (Dt 20:5; 1Kg 8:63). Here, the **youth** is consecrated to a life of godly wisdom (4:11). "Youth" typically refers to pre-teen to late-teen years. The Hebrew words translated **about the way he should go** speak of orienting the initiation to fit the challenges of young people. Youth are known for foolishness and lack of discretion or sense (v. 15; 1:4; 7:7); left to themselves, they fall into disgrace (29:15,21). Thus, if a youth is initiated in a manner that is appropriate to his age (1:4; 23:13), it is likely to stick with him. However, this is not a promise, and it does not make the teacher responsible for the student (Ezk 18:20).

22:8 God will avenge the arrogant use of power.

22:9 A **generous person** is literally "the good of eye"; the opposite is the "evil eye" of the "stingy" or "greedy" person (23:6; 28:22).

22:10 On **mocker**, see note at 1:22.

22:11 A good **king** is a **friend** of those who value genuine, godly purity (Ps 51:10) and elegant speech.

22:12 God **overthrows** (see "undermines" in note at 13:6) those who teach treachery (see note at 2:20-22).

22:13 This is a preposterous excuse.

22:14 The **forbidden woman** lures men with her words (see note at 2:16; cp. 7:21; 23:27-28; Jr 18:22). To be **cursed** by God is to experience His indignation (Ezk 22:31). The wicked will realize they are cursed when they **fall** (Ps 81:11-12; Rm 1:24-28).

22:15 Tangled up means both "tied to" and voluntarily "wrapped up" (Gn 44:30). **Foolishness** (from Hb ewiyl) is an innate quality that youth cling to (Gn 8:21; Ps 51:5). On **rod**, see note at 13:24.

22:16 The person who gives to **the rich** likely has ulterior motives (Lk 14:12).

22:17-21 This passage introduces a collection of proverbs that runs through 24:22. This is also the first of the **thirty sayings**. On **words of the wise**, see note at 1:6. These sayings were also probably Solomon's (10:1). There are three motivations given for gaining wisdom, two practical and one theological: to be **pleasing**, to have **confidence . . . in the** LORD, and to be dependable when commissioned (v. 21; cp. 10:26; 25:13). **True** words promote justice. **Dependable report** translates the same Hebrew words as **reliable words**.

21 in order to teach you true
 and reliable words,
so that you may give
 a dependable report[A,a]
to those who sent you?[b]

22 Don't rob a poor man
 because he is poor,
and don't crush the oppressed[c]
 at the •gate,[d]
23 for the Lord will take up their case[e]
and will plunder those
 who plunder them.

24 Don't make friends
 with an angry man,[B]
and don't be a companion
 of a hot-tempered man,[f]
25 or you will learn his ways[g]
and entangle yourself in a snare.

26 Don't be one of those
 who enter agreements,[C]
who put up security for loans.[h]
27 If you have no money to pay,
even your bed will be taken
 from under you.[i]

28 Don't move
 an ancient boundary marker,
that your fathers set up.[j]

29 Do you see a man skilled in his work?
He will stand in the presence of kings.
He will not stand in the presence
 of unknown men.[k]

23 When you sit down to dine
 with a ruler,
consider carefully what[D] is before you,
2 and put a knife to your throat
if you have a big[E] appetite;
3 don't desire his choice food,[l]
for that food is deceptive.

4 Don't wear yourself out to get rich;[m]
stop giving your attention to it.
5 As soon as your eyes fly to it,
 it disappears,[n]
for it makes wings for itself
and flies like an eagle to the sky.

6 Don't eat a stingy person's bread,[F,o]
and don't desire his choice food,[p]
7 for it's like someone calculating
 inwardly.[G,q]
"Eat and drink," he says to you,
but his heart is not with you.[r]
8 You will vomit the little
 you've eaten
and waste your pleasant words.

9 Don't speak to[H] a fool,
for he will despise the insight
 of your words.[s]

10 Don't move
 an ancient boundary marker,[t]
and don't encroach on the fields
 of the fatherless,
11 for their Redeemer is strong,[u]
and He will take up their case
 against you.[v]

a22:21 Lk 1:3-4
b Pr 10:26; 25:13
c 22:22 Ex 23:6; Jb 31:16; Zch 7:10; Mal 3:5
d Ru 4:11; Pr 24:7; Zch 8:16
e 22:23 1Sm 25:39; Ps 12:5; 35:10; 68:5; 140:12; Pr 23:10-11; Is 3:13-15
f 22:24 Pr 15:18; 19:19
g 22:25 1Co 15:33
h 22:26 Pr 6:1-5; 11:15; 17:18
i 22:27 Ex 22:26; Pr 20:16
j 22:28 Dt 19:14; 27:17; Jb 24:2; Pr 23:10; Hs 5:10
k 22:29 Gn 41:46; 1Kg 10:8; Pr 14:35
l 23:3 Gn 27:4; Pr 23:6; Dn 1:8
m 23:4 Pr 15:27; 28:20; Mt 6:19; 1Tm 6:9-10; Heb 13:5
n 23:5 Pr 27:24
o 23:6 Dt 15:9; Pr 28:22; Mt 6:23
p Pr 23:3
q 23:7 Mt 6:21; Lk 12:34
r Pr 26:24-25
s 23:9 Mt 7:6
t 23:10 Pr 22:28
u 23:11 Jr 50:34
v Pr 22:22-23

A22:21 Lit *give dependable words*   B22:24 Lit *with a master of anger*   C22:26 Lit *who shakes hands*   D23:1 Or *who*   E23:2 Lit *you are the master of an*   F23:6 Lit *eat bread of an evil eye*   G23:7 LXX reads *it is like someone swallowing a hair in the throat*   H23:9 Lit *in the ears of*

22:22-23 The city **gate** was where legal proceedings took place (24:7). God is like the ultimate defense attorney (23:11; Ps 43:1; 119:154; Jr 50:34; Mc 7:9; 1Jn 2:1). Since God is also Judge, the accuser cannot prevail (Rv 12:10).

22:24-25 A **hot-tempered man** is constantly in trouble (15:18; 19:19; 29:22); his **companion** could get trapped (12:13; 18:7; 29:6).

22:26-27 On **security for loans**, see note at 6:1.

22:28 On **boundary marker**, see note at 23:10-11.

22:29 The wise learn from what they **see** (24:32). To be **skilled** is to be experienced, learned, efficient, and accurate in one's vocation (Ezr 7:6; Ps 45:1; "quick" in Is 16:5). To **stand** in a ruler's **presence** is to offer oneself to be recognized or commissioned (Ex 8:20; Dt 31:14; Jb 1:6; Zch 6:5).

23:1-3 A **ruler** could have ulterior motives to test or obligate his guest (cp. vv. 6-8). A **big appetite**, or lack of discipline, might annoy the ruler, which could be fatal (16:14). The admonition to **put a knife to your throat** is hyperbole (Mt 18:9); it calls for total abstinence if restraint is not possible. **Choice food** is the same as the "delicious food" that caused trouble between Jacob, Isaac, and Esau (Gn 27).

23:4-5 Diligence along with godliness and wisdom brings riches (8:18; 10:4; 22:4), but only if God blesses (10:22). It is futile to try to get **rich** easily, illegally, or quickly (13:11; 20:21; 28:20,22).

23:6-8 It is futile to try to please an unwilling host. **Stingy** person is literally "evil eye" (28:22; Dt 15:9; 28:54,56; contrast Pr 22:9). On **choice food**, see note at verses 1-3. Eventually the inner character of a person will show. A host in ancient times was obligated to offer food and **drink** to any person who visited, but it could be done insincerely. The guest of an insincere host gains nothing: the food is lost and compliments go to **waste**.

23:9 On the obstinacy of a **fool**, see note at 1:22; on **insight**, see note at 12:8.

23:10-11 Joshua established the boundaries of the tribes when Israel entered Canaan (22:28; Dt 19:14; Jos 14-19). Private property was marked off by pillars or cairns and was intended to be kept within a family forever (Lv 25:23-28; Nm 36:7; 1Kg 21:3). Moving a marker amounted to stealing land. God defends the oppressed (Dt 10:18; Pr 22:22-23). On **Redeemer**, see Lv 25:23-28,47-55; Nm 35:19 ("avenger of blood"); Ru 3:9-4:14; Ps 103:4; Is 59:20; Hs 13:14.

¹² Apply yourself to discipline
and listen to words of knowledge.

¹³ Don't withhold discipline from a youth;
if you beat him with a rod,
he will not die.^a

¹⁴ Strike him with a rod,
and you will rescue his life
from •Sheol.^b

¹⁵ My son, if your heart is wise,
my heart will indeed rejoice.^c

¹⁶ My innermost being will cheer
when your lips say what is right.^d

¹⁷ Don't let your heart envy sinners;^e
instead, always •fear the LORD.^f

¹⁸ For then you will have a future,
and your hope will never fade.^g

¹⁹ Listen, my son, and be wise;
keep your mind on the right course.

²⁰ Don't associate with those who drink
too much wine^h
or with those who gorge themselves
on meat.ⁱ

²¹ For the drunkard and the glutton
will become poor,
and grogginess will clothe them
in rags.^j

²² Listen to your father who gave you life,
and don't despise your mother
when^A she is old.^k

²³ Buy—and do not sell—truth,
wisdom, instruction,
and understanding.^l

²⁴ The father of a righteous son
will rejoice greatly,

and one who fathers a wise son
will delight in him.^m

²⁵ Let your father and mother have joy,ⁿ
and let her who gave birth to you
rejoice.

²⁶ My son, give me your heart,
and let your eyes observe my ways.

²⁷ For a prostitute is a deep pit,^o
and a stranger is a narrow well;

²⁸ indeed, she sets an ambush
like a robber^p
and increases those among men
who are unfaithful.

²⁹ Who has woe? Who has sorrow?
Who has conflicts?
Who has complaints?
Who has wounds for no reason?^q
Who has red eyes?

³⁰ Those who linger over wine,
those who go looking for mixed wine.^r

³¹ Don't gaze at wine because it is red,^s
when it gleams in the cup
and goes down smoothly.^t

³² In the end it bites like a snake
and stings like a viper.

³³ Your eyes will see strange things,
and you will say absurd things.^{B,u}

³⁴ You'll be like someone sleeping
out at sea
or lying down on the top
of a ship's mast.

³⁵ "They struck me, but^C I feel no pain!
They beat me, but I didn't know it!^v
When will I wake up?
I'll look for another drink."^w

---

^a23:13 Pr 13:24; 19:18; 22:15	
^b23:14 1Co 5:5	
^c23:15 Pr 10:1; 15:20; 23:24-25; 29:3	
^d23:16 Pr 8:6	
^e23:17 Ps 37:1; Pr 24:1,19	
^fPr 28:14	
^g23:18 Ps 9:18; Pr 10:28; 24:14; Jr 29:11	
^h23:20 Pr 20:1; 23:29-30; Is 5:22; Mt 24:49; Lk 21:34; Rm 13:13; Eph 5:18	
ⁱPr 28:7	
^j23:21 Pr 6:10-11	
^k23:22 Pr 1:8; 15:20; Eph 6:1	
^l23:23 Pr 4:5,7; 16:16; 18:15; Mt 13:44	
^m23:24 Pr 10:1; 23:15; 29:3	
ⁿ23:25 Pr 27:11	
^o23:27 Pr 22:14	
^p23:28 Pr 6:26; 7:12,22-23; Ec 7:26	
^q23:29 Pr 23:35	
^r23:30 Is 5:11,22	
^s23:31 Eph 5:18	
^tSg 7:9	
^u23:33 Is 28:7	
^v23:35 Pr 23:29; Jr 5:3	
^wIs 56:12	

---

^A23:22 Or *because*   ^B23:33 Or *will speak perversities* or *inverted things*   ^C23:35 LXX, Syr, Tg, Vg read *me," you will say, "But*

23:12 On **discipline**, see note at 1:2.

23:13-14 Corporal punishment, properly applied, will actually save a youth from death. He will as a rule escape physical death by avoiding dangerous situations and escape spiritual death (symbolized by **Sheol**) by learning to fear God (19:18). But corporal punishment must be administered out of love, not dominance (Hs 11:4; Col 3:21; Heb 12:9).

23:15-16 Innermost being is literally "kidneys" (18:8). It was seen as the seat of the strongest emotions (Ps 73:21).

23:17-18 A future is literally "what comes after" (see note at 5:11; cp. 14:12; 24:14,20). Those who treasure **the LORD** rather than **sinners** have **hope** for eternity (3:31-32; 24:19-20; Mt 6:19-21).

23:19-21 To **listen** is a prerequisite; to **be wise** and have a disciplined **mind** follow. To **associate** with **the drunkard** **and the glutton** runs the risk of becoming like them and sharing their fate (24:21; Jos 23:7; Ps 1:1; 26:4) or of implying approval (1Co 5:11). **Grogginess** is lack of vigilance (Ps 121:3-4; Is 5:27; 56:10).

23:22-25 To say something both positively and negatively—

buy and do not sell—is a Hebrew method of emphasis (Gn 40:23). On **despise**, see note at 1:7; on "buy," see note at 4:5-8.

23:26-28 Heart and **eyes** are the key to sexual temptation; both should be given to the instructor in godly wisdom rather than the **prostitute** (5:1-23; 6:20–7:27; 9:13-18; 22:14; 1Co 6:15-18). **Pit** and **ambush** describe the prostitute's predatory nature (7:21-23; 30:20).

23:29-35 Woe and **sorrow** are exclamations of hopelessness and despair (Is 6:5). The Hebrew behind **red eyes** is unclear; it may mean "bloodshot" or "bleary" (cp. Gn 49:12). **Wine** could be **mixed** with spices (9:2; Sg 8:2; cp. mixed beer in Is 5:22). To **go looking** is to "investigate" wine by "sampling." We are called to flee tempting things (1Co 6:18; 10:14; 1Tm 6:11; 2Tm 2:22), not **gaze at** them. **Gleams** is literally "gives its eye," that is, to show luster. **In the end** (see note at 5:11), like the forbidden woman, wine destroys people (23:26-28). **Absurd** is literally "perverse" (2:12; 8:13; 10:31-32). These are the ramblings of an alcoholic who is physically and mentally out of touch.

24 Don't envy evil men[a]
or desire to be with them,[b]
2 for their hearts plan violence,
and their words stir up trouble.[c]

3 A house is built by wisdom,[d]
and it is established by understanding;
4 by knowledge the rooms are filled
with every precious
and beautiful treasure.

5 A wise warrior is better
than a strong one,[A]
and a man of knowledge than one
of strength;[B,e]
6 for you should wage war
with sound guidance—
victory comes with many counselors.[f]

7 Wisdom is inaccessible to[c] a fool;[g]
he does not open his mouth
at the •gate.[h]

8 The one who plots evil[i]
will be called a schemer.
9 A foolish scheme is sin,
and a mocker is detestable to people.

10 If you do nothing in a difficult time,
your strength is limited.
11 Rescue those being taken off to death,
and save those stumbling
toward slaughter.[j]
12 If you say, "But we didn't know
about this,"
won't He who weighs hearts[k]
consider it?
Won't He who protects your life[l] know?
Won't He repay a person according to
his work?[m]

13 Eat honey,[n] my son, for it is good,
and the honeycomb is sweet
to your palate;[o]
14 realize that wisdom is the same
for you.[p]
If you find it, you will have a future,
and your hope will never fade.[q]

15 Wicked man, don't set an ambush,
at the camp of the righteous man;[r]
don't destroy his dwelling.
16 Though a righteous man falls
seven times,
he will get up,[s]
but the wicked will stumble into ruin.[t]

[a]24:1 Ps 37:1; Pr 23:17; 24:19
[b]Ps 1:1; Pr 1:15
[c]24:2 Ps 10:7
[d]24:3 Pr 14:1
[e]24:5 Pr 21:22
[f]24:6 Pr 11:14; 15:22; 20:18
[g]24:7 Pr 14:6; 17:16,24
[h]Jb 5:4; Ps 127:5
[i]24:8 Rm 1:30
[j]24:11 Ps 82:4; Is 58:6-7
[k]24:12 1Sm 16:7; Ps 44:21; Pr 21:2
[l]Ps 121:3-8
[m]Jb 34:11; Ps 62:12
[n]24:13 Pr 25:16
[o]Sg 5:1
[p]24:14 Ps 19:10; 119:103
[q]Pr 10:28; 23:18; Jr 29:11
[r]24:15 Pr 10:9-10
[s]24:16 Jb 5:19; Ps 37:24
[t]Pr 14:32; 29:16

[A]24:5 LXX, Syr; MT reads one is in strength   [B]24:5 LXX, Syr, Tg; MT reads knowledge exerts strength   [C]24:7 Lit is too high for

---

24:1-2 This warning is similar to that in 23:17-18. Involvement in **violence** and **trouble** will lead to a person's downfall.

24:3-4 Just as God established the world through **wisdom . . . understanding**, and **knowledge** (3:19-20), so a **house** is **established** by the same. **Treasure** represents both material and spiritual blessings. Sinners also hope to fill their houses, but their methods are self-destructive (1:13,18).

24:5-6 Verse 5 is difficult to translate; the second line might

ra'a'

Hebrew Pronunciation	[rah AH]
HCSB Translation	be evil, do evil
Uses in Proverbs	7
Uses in the OT	97
Focus Passage	Proverbs 24:8,18-19

Ra'a' means be evil, difficult, or a mistake (Gn 21:11; 38:10; 48:17). Someone is displeased (Jnh 4:1) or sad and suffers (Ps 106:32). "Your heart is evil" implies you are troubled (1Sm 1:8). "Your eye is evil" means you are stingy (Dt 15:9), look grudgingly, or begrudge. "Be evil in one's eyes" connotes resenting (1Sm 18:8) or being upset; something seems wrong (Jr 40:4), or one considers something evil. The passive-reflexive means suffer harm (Pr 13:20). Causative verbs denote do evil or harm (Gn 19:7,9) and act wickedly. With "do" it conveys behave wickedly or wrongly. One treats badly, mistreats (Nm 16:15), afflicts, injures, or destroys. Causatives also suggest bring/cause tragedy (harm, trouble, disaster) (Jr 25:29). Participles denote evildoer (Is 1:4) or wicked person. Another ra'a' (8x) signifies crush (Ps 44:3), smash, break, or shatter. Teeth are rotten. The reflexive-passive implies be devastated (Is 24:19) or harmed.

read, "a man of knowledge increases strength." In any case, wisdom and sound guidance are the keys to success in any situation.

24:7 Important and knowledgeable people oversaw legal and commercial business at the city **gate** (1:21; 22:22; 31:23; Dt 21:19; Jos 20:4; Ru 4:1; 2Sm 15:2).

24:8-9 What a person is **called** is his reputation (16:21; 21:24), which is difficult to overcome. On **schemer**, see "discretion" in note at 1:4. A **scheme** is a shameful, depraved act (Lv 18:17). On **mocker**, see note at 1:22; on **detestable**, see note at 3:32.

24:10-12 To **do nothing** is literally to go slack (see "truly lazy" in note at 18:9). A **difficult time** is literally a "time of restriction" (Hb tsarah). To be **limited** is literally to be "restricted" (Hb tsar). So to avoid losing **strength**, act. **Death** could be physical or spiritual death or any other misfortune, whether they are **being taken off** by others or they are **stumbling** toward disaster on their own (Ps 82:4; Is 58:6-7). Those who are not on the way of wisdom are on a path to disaster and need to be saved (Pr 10:17; 12:28; 14:12; 15:24). To deny knowledge is futile because God **weighs hearts** (21:12; Ps 44:21). Inactivity is complicity (Ezk 3:17-18). God can withdraw His protection to **repay a person** for his sin.

24:13-14 **Wisdom**, like **honey**, is beneficial as well as pleasant (16:24; but see 25:16,27). On **future**, see note at 23:17-18.

24:15-16 The malicious actions of a **wicked man** are futile. **Seven** is the number of completion (6:31; 9:1; 26:16,25; Mt 18:21). If the **righteous** falls until he is utterly down, maybe even dead, he will still **get up . . . Into ruin** could also be translated "by means of evil." The righteous and the wicked get their just rewards—sometimes in this life but certainly in eternity.

17 Don't gloat when your enemy falls,
and don't let your heart rejoice
when he stumbles,*a*

18 or the LORD will see, be displeased,
and turn His wrath away
from him.

19 Don't be agitated by evildoers,
and don't envy the wicked.*b*

20 For the evil have no future;*c*
the lamp of the wicked
will be put out.*d*

21 My son, •fear the LORD, as well as
the king,*e*
and don't associate with rebels,*A*

22 for destruction from them
will come suddenly;
who knows what distress these two
can bring?

23 These sayings also
belong to the wise:*f*

It is not good to show partiality
in judgment.*g*

24 Whoever says to the •guilty,
"You are innocent"*h*—
people will curse him,*i* and tribes
will denounce him;

25 but it will go well with those
who convict the guilty,
and a generous blessing will come
to them.

26 He who gives an honest answer
gives a kiss on the lips.

27 Complete your outdoor work,
and prepare your field;*j*
afterward, build your house.

28 Don't testify against your neighbor
without cause.*k*
Don't deceive with your lips.

29 Don't say, "I'll do to him what he did
to me;
I'll repay the man for what
he has done."*l*

30 I went by the field of a slacker
and by the vineyard of a man
lacking sense.

31 Thistles had come up everywhere,
weeds covered the ground,*m*
and the stone wall was ruined.

32 I saw, and took it to heart;
I looked, and received instruction:

33 a little sleep, a little slumber,
a little folding of the arms to rest,

34 and your poverty will come
like a robber,
your need, like a bandit.*n*

Hezekiah's Collection

25 These too are proverbs of Solomon,*o*
which the men of Hezekiah,*p*
king of Judah, copied.

2 It is the glory of God to conceal
a matter*q*
and the glory of kings to investigate
a matter.

3 As the heaven is high and the earth
is deep,

*a*24:17 Ps 35:15,19; Pr 17:5; Ob 12; Mc 7:8
*b*24:19 Ps 37:1; Pr 23:17; 24:1
*c*24:20 Ps 37:38; Pr 14:11; 16:25
*d*Jb 18:5; 21:17; Pr 13:9; 20:20
*e*24:21 Mt 22:21; Rm 13:1-7; 1Pt 2:13-14,17
*f*24:23 Pr 1:6; 22:17
*g*Dt 1:17; 16:19; Pr 18:5; 28:21
*h*24:24 Pr 17:15
*i*Pr 11:26
*j*24:27 Pr 20:4
*k*24:28 Ex 20:16; Pr 25:18
*l*24:29 Dt 32:35; Pr 20:22; Mt 5:39; Rm 12:17,19
*m*24:31 Gn 3:18; Pr 20:4
*n*24:34 Pr 6:10-11; 20:13
*o*25:1 Pr 1:1
*p*2Kg 18-20
*q*25:2 Dt 29:29; Rm 11:33

^A24:21 Or *those given to change*

24:17-18 It is literally "evil in the eyes" of God when someone gloats over another person's misfortune (Jb 31:29; Ps 35:11-14; Lk 6:27,35; Rm 12:20-21).

24:19-20 To worry is to be **agitated** with anger (Ps 37:1,7-8). While it is right to be angry because **evildoers** are sinning, it is wrong to be angry because they are prospering. They don't have a **future**, but the righteous do (23:17-18). On **lamp**, see note at 20:20.

24:21-22 The **king** is God's agent for social justice (Rm 13:1-4; 1Pt 2:13-14). God and the king are the **two** who **bring** so much **distress** on evildoers that no one **knows** (cp. Ec 3:21; 6:12; 8:1) its potential magnitude. On **suddenly**, see note at 6:15.

24:23-34 These are miscellaneous **sayings** collected by Solomon (10:1) beyond the "thirty" (22:20).

24:23-25 To **show partiality** is literally "to take notice of a face" (28:21; Dt 16:19)—to treat people differently based on their status or position. A judge should treat "small and great alike" (Dt 1:17). **People** hate an unjust judge (17:15). That the phrase **blessing will come** is in the passive voice implies that the blessing comes from God.

24:26 A **kiss** symbolizes loyal love and solidarity in a family

(Gn 33:4; 45:15) or among very close friends (1Sm 20:41). "Honesty" also demonstrates love.

24:27 A young man should first establish his means of income. Besides the structure, to **build** a **house** could include marrying, having children, and hiring servants (v. 3; 14:1).

24:28-29 To **testify . . . without cause** (see note at 3:29-30) might be to volunteer to give testimony without being called and without being an eyewitness. A person should not seek vengeance (20:22).

24:30-34 Whatever a **slacker** (see note at 6:6) who lacks **sense** (see note at 6:30-33) builds or inherits comes to ruin. Elsewhere **thistles** (Is 34:13; Hs 9:6) and **weeds** (Zph 2:9) are symbolic of God's judgment. A wise person learns from observation. Verses 33-34 echo Pr 6:10-11; it fits both situations.

25:1 The **proverbs** in chapters 25–29 were collected by **the men of Hezekiah** (cp. 1:1; 10:1; 22:17; 24:23), who was a godly king until late in his life (2Kg 18-20).

25:2-3 Both **God** and **kings** are unfathomable; their respective subjects cannot entirely comprehend their knowledge and motives. **A matter** may include science and creation (1Kg 4:33), philosophy (Ec 1:13), and personal motives and

so the hearts of kings cannot
  be investigated.

4 Remove impurities from silver,[a]
and a vessel will be produced[A]
  for a silversmith.[b]
5 Remove the wicked
  from the king's presence,[c]
and his throne will be established
  in righteousness.[d]

6 Don't brag about yourself
  before the king,
and don't stand in the place
  of the great;
7 for it is better for him to say to you,
  "Come up here!"
than to demote you in plain view
  of a noble.[B,e]

8 Don't take a matter to court hastily.[f]
Otherwise, what will
  you do afterward
if your opponent[C] humiliates you?
9 Make your case with your opponent[C]
without revealing another's secret;[g]
10 otherwise, the one who hears
  will disgrace you,
and you'll never live it down.[D]

11 A word spoken at the right time
is like gold apples on a silver tray.[E,h]
12 A wise correction to a receptive ear[i]
is like a gold ring or an ornament
  of gold.

13 To those who send him,
  a trustworthy messenger
is like the coolness of snow
  on a harvest day;
he refreshes the life of his masters.[j]

14 The man who boasts about a gift
  that does not exist
is like clouds and wind without rain.[k]
15 A ruler can be persuaded
  through patience,
and a gentle tongue can break a bone.[l]
16 If you find honey,[m] eat only
  what you need;
otherwise, you'll get sick from it
  and vomit.[n]
17 Seldom set foot
  in your neighbor's house;
otherwise, he'll get sick of you
  and hate you.

18 A man giving false testimony
  against his neighbor[o]
is like a club, a sword,
  or a sharp arrow.[p]
19 Trusting an unreliable person in a
  difficult time
is like a rotten tooth or a faltering foot.[q]
20 Singing songs to a troubled heart
is like taking off clothing on a cold day
or like pouring vinegar on soda.[F,r]
21 If your enemy is hungry, give him food
  to eat,

---

a25:4 Ezk 22:18; Mal 3:2-3
b25:5 2Tm 2:21
c25:5 Pr 20:8,26
d Pr 16:12
e25:7 Lk 14:7-11
f25:8 Pr 17:14; Mt 5:25; 1Co 6:7
g25:9 Pr 17:9; Mt 18:15
h25:11 Pr 8:10; 15:23; 16:16
i25:12 Pr 15:31
j25:13 Pr 13:17; 16:24; 25:25
k25:14 Jd 12
l25:15 Pr 15:1; 16:14,32; Ec 10:4
m25:16 Jdg 14:8; 1Sm 14:25
n Pr 25:27
o25:18 Ex 20:16; Pr 24:28
p Ps 57:4; Pr 12:18
q25:19 2Kg 18:21
r25:20 Rm 12:15

A25:4 Lit will come out; Ex 32:24   B25:7 Lit you before a noble whom your eyes see   C25:8,9 Or neighbor   D25:10 Lit and your evil report will not turn back   E25:11 Or like apples of gold in settings of silver   F25:20 Lit natron, or sodium carbonate

---

legal testimony (Pr 18:17; 25:8; 28:11). God is glorious because His creation is so intricate (Jb 38–41). Kings gain **glory** by delving into things that improve their ability to rule.

25:5 The people in **the king's presence** are his servants, officials, and advisers. For a **throne to be established** suggests at least uncontested rule, and possibly a dynasty (see note at 16:12; cp. 2Sm 5:9-12; 1Kg 2:46; 9:5).

25:6-7 Prideful self-promotion is not wise (11:2; 29:23; Rm 12:3). There may have been a specified order in which the officials were supposed to stand **before the king**; to **stand** in someone else's **place** would be pretentious. On **noble**, see note at 8:16. It is possible that the last few words (translated **in plain view**) go with the next verse, which means: "That which your eyes have seen, don't be hasty to take to court."

25:8-10 Frivolous litigation and divulging confidences will ruin one's reputation. **You'll never live it down** is literally "a bad report will not return"—that is, the person who disgraces you will not have to eat his words. On **afterward**, see "at the end" in note at 5:11.

25:11-12 These decorative **apples** (or apricots; Sg 2:3,5; 7:8; 8:5) are not just golden in color, but are apparently made of **gold**. They could be spheres set on the **tray** or images inlaid into it. When a person is receptive to a **wise** rebuke, he is improved (9:8; 19:25).

25:13 Harvest time could be dangerously hot (2Kg 4:18-20). For **snow** to fall at harvest time could be disastrous, but the wealthy sometimes had it carried down from the mountains for refreshment.

25:14 This is literally a "lying" **gift** (cp. 6:17). Most **rain** in Palestine comes during windy thunderstorms.

25:15 A **bone** is the hardest part of a person; here it represents strong resistance to persuasion.

25:16-17 Too much of a good thing (v. 27; 16:24; 24:13) is bad, so even a good guest should exercise moderation. **Seldom set foot** is literally "make your foot precious (on account of its rarity)" (3:15; 20:15). To **get sick** is literally to be satisfied (12:14; 13:25; 18:20) or glutted (1:31).

25:19 Unreliable is literally "treacherous" (2:22; cp. 20:6). On **difficult time**, see note at 24:10-12 (cp. 17:17).

25:20 Here are some actions that make things worse. Cheery **songs** can make a **troubled** person worse (Ec 3:4; Rm 12:15; but see 1Sm 16:14-16). **Pouring vinegar on soda** makes the vinegar foam; it also neutralizes both and makes them worthless. The word translated "soda" could also be "a deep wound"; pouring vinegar on it would bring suffering with no benefit.

25:21-22 To **heap . . . coals on his head** does not imply ven-

and if he is thirsty, give him water
to drink;[a]

²² for you will heap burning coals
on his head,
and the LORD will reward you.[b]

²³ The north wind produces rain,
and a backbiting tongue, angry looks.

²⁴ Better to live on the corner of a roof
than to share a house
with a nagging wife.[c]

²⁵ Good news from a distant land
is like cold water
to a parched throat.[A,d]

²⁶ A righteous person who yields
to the wicked[e]
is like a muddied spring
or a polluted well.[f]

²⁷ It is not good to eat too much honey[g]
or to seek glory after glory.[B,h]

²⁸ A man who does not control
his temper[i]
is like a city whose wall
is broken down.[j]

26

Like snow in summer and rain
at harvest,[k]
honor is inappropriate for a fool.[l]

² Like a flitting sparrow
or a fluttering swallow,[m]

an undeserved curse goes nowhere.[n]

³ A whip for the horse, a bridle
for the donkey,[o]
and a rod for the backs of fools.[p]

⁴ Don't answer a fool according to
his foolishness[q]
or you'll be like him yourself.

⁵ Answer a fool according to
his foolishness[r]
or he'll become wise in his own eyes.[s]

⁶ The one who sends a message
by a fool's hand[t]
cuts off his own feet
and drinks violence.[u]

⁷ A proverb in the mouth of a fool
is like lame legs that hang limp.

⁸ Giving honor to a fool
is like binding a stone in a sling.[C]

⁹ A proverb in the mouth of a fool
is like a stick with thorns,
brandished by[D] the hand of a drunkard.

¹⁰ The one who hires a fool or who hires
those passing by
is like an archer
who wounds everyone.

¹¹ As a dog returns to its vomit,
so a fool repeats his foolishness.[v]

¹² Do you see a man who is wise
in his own eyes?[w]

Cross references

a 25:21 Ex 23:4-5; 2Kg 6:22; 2Ch 28:15; Mt 5:44; Rm 12:20
b 25:22 Mt 6:4
c 25:24 Pr 15:17; 17:1; 21:9,19
d 25:25 Pr 15:30
e 25:26 Dt 13:6-8; Gl 2:4-5
f Ezk 32:2; 34:18-19
g 25:27 Pr 25:16
h Pr 27:2
i 25:28 Pr 16:32; 29:11
j Neh 1:3
k 26:1 1Sm 12:17
l Pr 17:7; 19:10
m 26:2 Pr 27:8
n Nm 23:8; Dt 23:5; 2Sm 16:12
o 26:3 Ps 32:9
p Pr 10:13; 19:29
q 26:4 Pr 23:9; 29:9; Mt 7:6; Lk 23:9
r 26:5 Mt 16:1-4; 21:24-27
s Pr 26:12; 28:11; Rm 12:16
t 26:6 Pr 10:26; 25:13
u Pr 13:2
v 26:11 2Pt 2:22
w 26:12 Pr 3:7; 26:5; Rm 12:16

A 25:25 Or *a weary person*   B 25:27 Lit *seek their glory, glory*   C 26:8 A stone bound in a sling would not release and could harm the person using the sling. A modern equivalent is jamming a cork in a gun barrel.   D 26:9 Lit *thorn that goes up into*

---

geance because God does not **reward** vengeance (20:22; Lv 19:18; Rm 12:17-20). Rather, it may refer to the shame an enemy feels when his assaults are met with good deeds.

25:23 In Palestine rain actually comes from the west (1Kg 18:44; Lk 12:54). **North** may suggest the cold wind that accompanies **rain**. Also, "north" comes from a word that means "hidden," which is a pun on **backbiting** (lit "secret"). The second half is ambiguous in Hebrew and could be reversed: "and angry looks, a backbiting tongue."

25:24 On **nagging wife**, see note at 19:13.

25:25 On **throat**, see note at 13:2-4. It could take many months to receive **news** from a **distant land**.

25:26 Finding a **well** to be **polluted** could be disastrous to a traveler in Palestine. When a **righteous person**, a supposed "fountain of life" (10:11), betrays those who trust him, it can be disastrous (25:19).

25:27 The second line is difficult. It could mean, "and to investigate matters that are too weighty is not honorable" (cp. vv. 2-3; Ps 131).

26:1-12 The word **fool** (Hb *kesiyl*; see note at 1:22) occurs in every verse in this section except verse 2.

26:1 Snow in summer and rain at harvest would not only be unusual; they could be catastrophic, destroying the crops and endangering society.

26:2 On **undeserved**, see "just for fun" in note at 1:11. Ultimately, God determines whether a blessing or **curse** will be fulfilled (Nm 23:8; Dt 23:5; Ps 109:28).

26:3 Like an animal, **fools** must be prodded and directed.

26:4-5 A person should not **answer a fool** by resorting to foolish methods. Yet, someone needs to expose his **foolishness**, even if he won't listen (23:9).

26:6 To trust a fool as a messenger is as self-destructive as self-mutilation or taking poison (1:19).

26:7 A **lame** person has **legs** but can't use them.

26:8 A **sling** was a leather strap with a pouch in the middle. A **stone** would be placed in the pouch, then the slinger held both ends of the strap and swung it over his head two or three times. When he let go of one strap, the stone would be released. It would be ridiculous to tie the stone in the pouch. The weapon would be useless, and it could hurt the slinger.

26:9 A **fool** would give a **proverb** a wrong application, causing chaos and destruction, like a belligerent **drunkard** swinging a thorny **stick**.

26:10 The Hebrew here was hard to understand before scholars discovered that *rav* could mean **archer** (Jb 16:13; Jr 50:29) as well as "great." Hiring a **fool** or someone at random is as harmful to society as a berserk shooter (v. 18; cp. the English idiom "loose cannon").

26:11 Because a **fool** doesn't accept correction (1:22; 23:9), he never advances, but returns to what everyone else can see is repulsive.

26:12 A **fool** might respond to corporal punishment or even arguments (23:3,5), but the self-deluded will not.

There is more hope for a fool
than for him.[a]

13 The slacker says, "There's a lion
in the road—
a lion in the public square!"[b]

14 A door turns on its hinges,
and a slacker, on his bed.[c]

15 The slacker buries his hand
in the bowl;
he is too weary to bring it
to his mouth.[d]

16 In his own eyes, a slacker is wiser[e]
than seven men
who can answer sensibly.

17 A person who is passing by and meddles
in a quarrel that's not his
is like one who grabs a dog
by the ears.

18 Like a madman who throws
flaming darts and deadly arrows,[f]

19 so is the man who deceives
his neighbor
and says, "I was only joking!"

20 Without wood, fire goes out;
without a gossip, conflict dies down.[g]

21 As charcoal for embers and wood
for fire,
so is a quarrelsome man
for kindling strife.[h]

22 A gossip's words are like choice food
that goes down to
one's innermost being.[A,i]

23 Smooth[B] lips with an evil heart
are like glaze on an earthen vessel.[j]

24 A hateful person disguises himself
with his speech
and harbors deceit within.

25 When he speaks graciously,
don't believe him,
for there are seven abominations
in his heart.[k]

26 Though his hatred is concealed
by deception,
his evil will be revealed in the assembly.

27 The one who digs a pit will fall into it,
and whoever rolls a stone—
it will come back on him.[l]

28 A lying tongue hates those it crushes,
and a flattering mouth causes ruin.

27 Don't boast about tomorrow,
for you don't know what a day
might bring.[m]

2 Let another praise you, and not
your own mouth—
a stranger, and not your own lips.[n]

3 A stone is heavy and sand, a burden,
but aggravation from a fool
outweighs them both.

4 Fury is cruel, and anger a flood,
but who can withstand jealousy?[o]

5 Better an open reprimand
than concealed love.[p]

6 The wounds of a friend
are trustworthy,[q]
but the kisses of an enemy
are excessive.[r]

7 A person who is full tramples
on a honeycomb,[s]
but to a hungry person, any bitter thing
is sweet.

8 A man wandering from his home
is like a bird wandering from its nest.[t]

Cross references (center column):

[a] 26:12 Pr 29:20
[b] 26:13 Pr 22:13
[c] 26:14 Pr 6:9-10; 19:15
[d] 26:15 Pr 12:27; 19:24
[e] 26:16 Pr 26:5,12; 28:11
[f] 26:18 Is 50:11
[g] 26:20 Pr 16:28; 22:10
[h] 26:21 Pr 15:18
[i] 26:22 Pr 18:8
[j] 26:23 Mt 23:27; Lk 11:39
[k] 26:25 Ps 28:3
[l] 26:27 Est 7:10; Jb 4:8; Pr 28:10; Dn 6:24; Mt 26:52
[m] 27:1 Lk 12:19-20; Jms 4:13-14
[n] 27:2 Pr 25:27; 2Co 10:12,18; 12:11
[o] 27:4 Pr 6:34
[p] 27:5 Pr 28:23
[q] 27:6 Ps 141:5
[r] Lk 22:48
[s] 27:7 Pr 25:16
[t] 27:8 Pr 26:2

A 26:22 Lit *to the chambers of the belly*   B 26:23 LXX; MT reads *Burning*

26:13 On a **slacker** and his excuses, see note at 22:13.

26:14 This is a sarcastic image of the only "work" a **slacker** does. An ancient hinge was a hole in the threshold on which the door pivoted.

26:15 In ancient times, food was eaten by hand from a communal dish. The **slacker** does not have the gumption to **bring** food **to his mouth**, which has physical consequences (6:9-11; 20:4; 21:25; cp. 19:15).

26:16 A sensible **answer** implies discernment. **Seven** suggests this is a complete group of counselors (Ezr 7:14).

26:17 **Meddles in** could be translated as "is provided by" (20:2). Alternatively, it could be the **dog** that **is passing by**, i.e., a stray. Therefore, this could be translated, "One who gets riled up by a quarrel that's not his is like one who grabs a stray dog by the ears." The point is the same.

26:18-19 A liar who calls himself a jester if he gets caught is as dangerous to society as a berserk warrior (v. 10).

26:20 On **gossip**, see note at 16:28.

26:22 On **choice food**, see note at 18:8.

26:23-28 Though verses 23, 27, and 28 could each stand as independent proverbs, with 24-26 they develop a single theme. The Hebrew *keseph siygiym* ("silver dross"; cp. 25:4) has been emended to *kesaphsagiym* (**glaze**). Silver dross—lead monoxide—was also used as a glaze on pottery, so the point is the same. A flatterer (see note at 2:16) with evil intentions appears nice, but it's an artificial veneer, a pretense. Though a **hateful person disguises himself**, the wise person perceives that his **heart** is detestable. His driving force is **hatred**, the wicked person's passion to destroy anything good and godly. The person who hates will eventually be **revealed** publicly (5:14), and he will suffer the fate he wished on others (Ps 7:15-16; 9:15-16). The last line is ambiguous—the liar seeks the **ruin** of the godly, but he causes his own ruin.

27:4 On **jealousy**, see notes at 6:34-35 and 14:30.

⁹ Oil*a* and incense bring joy to the heart,
and the sweetness of a friend is better
than self-counsel.ᴬ

¹⁰ Don't abandon your friend
or your father's friend,*b*
and don't go to your brother's house
in your time of calamity;
better a neighbor nearby than a brother
far away.*c*

¹¹ Be wise, my son, and bring
my heart joy,*d*
so that I can answer anyone
who taunts me.*e*

¹² A sensible person sees danger
and takes cover;
the inexperienced keep going
and are punished.*f*

¹³ Take his garment,ᴮ
for he has put up security
for a stranger;
get collateral if it is for foreigners.ᶜ,*g*

¹⁴ If one blesses his neighbor
with a loud voice early in the morning,
it will be counted as a curse to him.

¹⁵ An endless dripping on a rainy day

and a nagging wife are alike.*h*

¹⁶ The one who controls her controls
the wind
and grasps oil with his right hand.

¹⁷ Iron sharpens iron,
and one man sharpens another.ᴰ

¹⁸ Whoever tends a fig tree*i* will eat
its fruit,*j*
and whoever looks after his master
will be honored.

¹⁹ As water reflects the face,
so the heart reflects the person.

²⁰ •Sheol and •Abaddon*k* are
never satisfied,*l*
and people's eyes are never satisfied.*m*

²¹ A crucible for silver, and a smelter
for gold,
and a man for the words of his praise.ᴱ,*n*

²² Though you grind a fool
in a mortar with a pestle
along with grain,
you will not separate his foolishness
from him.*o*

²³ Know well the condition of your flock,*p*

Cross references (center column):

*a*27:9 Ps 23:5
*b*27:10 2Sm 10:2
*c*Pr 17:17
*d*27:11 Pr 10:1;
23:24-25; 29:3
*e*Ps 119:42;
127:5
*f*27:12 Pr 22:3
*g*27:13 Pr 6:1-5;
11:15; 20:16
*h*27:15 Pr 19:13
*i*27:18 Am 7:14
*j*Sg 8:12; 1Co
3:8; 9:7; 2Tm 2:6
*k*27:20 Jb 26:6;
Pr 15:11
*l*Pr 30:15-16;
Hab 2:5
*m*Ec 1:8; 4:8
*n*27:21 Pr 16:2;
17:3
*o*27:22 Pr 23:35;
26:11; Jr 5:3
*p*27:23 Ezk
34:12; Jn
10:3,14; Ac 20:28

ᴬ27:9 LXX reads *heart, but the soul is torn up by affliction*   ᴮ27:13 A debtor's outer garment held as collateral; Dt 24:12-13,17;
Jb 22:6; Am 2:8   ᶜ27:13 Lit *a foreign woman*   ᴰ27:17 Lit *and a man sharpens his friend's face*   ᴱ27:21 Or *gold, but a man is tested
by his praise*

27:6 A friend imparts constructive criticism out of love, but an enemy gives **kisses** (24:26) with deceit in mind.

27:7 On **honeycomb**, see note at 24:13-14.

27:8 The word translated **wandering** (cp. Jb 15:23; Hs 9:17) could also be translated "fleeing" (Ps 55:7; Is 16:2; Jr 4:25; 9:10).

27:9 Being anointed with **oil** and enjoying **incense** were ancient pleasures. The second line could be saying that the **sweetness** (see "pleasant" in note at 16:21) **of a friend** comes from sincere counsel.

27:10 On **better . . . than** proverbs, see note at 15:16-17. Long-term friendships are at times more dependable than blood relations (17:17; 18:24).

27:11 A parent might be publicly criticized if he cannot control his own children (1Tm 3:4-5).

27:12 On **punished**, see note at 22:3.

27:13 On **security for a stranger**, see note at 6:1.

27:14 There are two possible interpretations: For someone who is "not a morning person," a **loud** greeting **early in the morning** will be annoying. Or, a person who rushes over to shout a blessing is probably insincere, and God will **curse** a hypocrite.

27:15-16 On **dripping**, see note at 19:13. Controlling a **nagging wife** seems as impossible as stopping the **wind** or grabbing **oil** in one's fist.

27:17 As a file **sharpens** an ax or a sharpening steel a carving knife, good friends encourage one another to grow in

wisdom and godliness, even if it requires painful criticism (v. 6).

27:18 If a person patiently serves his employer with integrity (Eph 6:5; Col 3:22; 1Tm 6:1-2; Ti 2:9-10; 1Pt 2:18), God will see to it that he is properly rewarded—if not in this life, then in eternity.

27:20 Sheol (see note at 1:12) and **Abaddon** (see note at 15:11) represent death, which can always take more victims (30:16). **People's eyes** represent their insatiable capacity for lust, envy, and greed (30:15).

27:21 Praise here could mean the praise a person receives or the praise he gives. This proverb has several possible meanings. As **a crucible** proves **silver . . . a man** should evaluate the praise he receives before he accepts it, dismissing flattery and insincerity. If you wonder about the praise a person receives or gives, look to the person; his character will show whether it is genuine. Over time, a person can refine the praise he receives or gives. The Hebrew could also be translated, "and a man according to his praise." That is, a man is tested (17:3) and proven by what kind of praise he receives and how graciously he receives it.

27:22 A **mortar** was a bowl made of fired clay or carved from stone. A **pestle** was a stone or fired-clay rod with a rounded tip. The worker would put a small amount of **grain** (hulled barley, in this case) into the mortar and pound and **grind** it until it became meal or flour. **Foolishness** taints every molecule of a **fool** (Hb *ewiyl*).

27:23-27 Just as a farmer cares for his livestock, Solomon here instructed his son the prince to **pay attention** to his

and pay attention to your herds,
24 for wealth is not forever;[a]
not even a crown lasts
for all time.
25 When hay is removed
and new growth appears
and the grain from the hills
is gathered in,
26 lambs will provide your clothing,
and goats, the price of a field;
27 there will be enough goat's milk
for your food—
food for your household
and nourishment for your
female servants.[b]

28 The wicked flee when no one
is pursuing them,[c]
but the righteous are as bold
as a lion.[d]

2 When a land is in rebellion, it has
many rulers,[e]
but with a discerning
and knowledgeable person,
it endures.

3 A destitute leader[A] who oppresses
the poor
is like a driving rain that leaves
no food.[f]

4 Those who reject the law
praise the wicked,[g]
but those who keep the law battle
against them.[h]

5 Evil men do not
understand justice,[i]

but those who seek the LORD
understand everything.[j]

6 Better a poor man who lives
with integrity[k]
than a rich man who distorts right
and wrong.[B,l]

7 A discerning son keeps the law,
but a companion of gluttons humiliates
his father.[m]

8 Whoever increases his wealth
through excessive interest[n]
collects it for one who is kind
to the poor.[o]

9 Anyone who turns his ear
away from hearing the law—
even his prayer is detestable.[p]

10 The one who leads the upright
into an evil way
will fall into his own pit,[q]
but the blameless will inherit
what is good.[r]

11 A rich man is wise in his own eyes,
but a poor man who has discernment
sees through him.

12 When the righteous triumph,
there is great rejoicing,[C]
but when the wicked come to power,
people hide themselves.[s]

13 The one who conceals his sins
will not prosper,[t]
but whoever confesses
and renounces them
will find mercy.[u]

---

a 27:24 Lk 16:9
b 27:27 Pr 31:15
c 28:1 Lv 26:17; Ps 53:5
d Eph 6:19-20
e 28:2 1Kg 16:8-28; 2Kg 15:8-15
f 28:3 Ex 9:25
g 28:4 Rm 1:32
h 1Kg 18:18; Neh 13:11,15; Mt 3:7; 14:4; Eph 5:11
i 28:5 Ps 92:6
j Ps 119:100; Jn 7:17; 1Co 2:15; Jms 1:5; 1Jn 2:20,27
k 28:6 Pr 19:1; 20:7
l Pr 16:8,19; 19:22; Is 5:20
m 28:7 Dt 21:20; Pr 17:25; 23:20; 29:3
n 28:8 Ex 22:25; Lv 25:36
o Jb 27:17; Pr 13:22; Ec 2:26; Ezk 18:13,17
p 28:9 Ps 109:7; Pr 15:8,29; 21:27
q 28:10 Ps 7:15; Pr 16:29; 26:27; Mt 18:6
r Mt 5:6
s 28:12 Pr 11:10; 28:28; 29:2; Ec 10:5-6
t 28:13 Jb 31:33; Ps 32:3
u Ps 32:5; Jms 5:16; 1Jn 1:9

A 28:3 LXX reads A wicked man   B 28:6 Lit who twists two ways   C 28:12 Lit glory

---

people. While **wealth** is fickle (23:4-5) and a dynasty can end, flocks and crops (people and land) are a steady source of sustenance if they are well maintained (24:27). After **hay** was harvested **new** grass appeared for grazing. Later, **grain** was harvested, which along with the hay provided feed for livestock. **Lambs** provided wool. Females were kept for breeding and **milk**, while some male **goats** were sold for income that could be reinvested. All people in positions of leadership should be good stewards of their human and material resources.

28:1 God gives irrational terror to **the wicked** and courage to **the righteous** (Lv 26:17; Dt 28:25; Jos 1:5-6; Ac 9:31; Rm 15:5).

28:2 People usually do not rebel against a wise king. The last phrase could also be translated, "right **endures**."

28:3 A hard **rain** at the wrong time could sweep away (Jr 46:15) a crop.

28:5 To **seek the LORD** can mean to consult Him for wisdom and knowledge (Ex 33:7; 2Sm 21:1) or to pursue a relationship with Him (Dt 4:29; Ps 27:4; Zph 2:3).

28:6 On **poor man . . . with integrity**, see note at 11:20; on **better . . . than** proverbs, see note at 15:16-17.

28:7 On **discerning**, see note at 1:5.

28:8 In this life or in eternity, God will punish those who exploit **the poor** and reward those who help them.

28:9 To reject God's **law** implies lack of trust, which precludes prayer (1:23-31; Heb 11:6).

28:10 On **inherit**, see note at 3:35.

28:11 On **rich**, see notes at 10:15 and 18:10-11; on **wise in his own eyes**, see note at 26:12.

28:12 To see the end of the matter, read this verse along with verse 28 and 29:2,16. Under **righteous** leadership there is a public celebration of "glory" or "beauty" (4:9; 15:31; 17:6; 20:29). Under **wicked** leaders, literally "a man is sought."

28:13 It is a good thing to conceal others' **sins** (17:9), but not one's own. To confess and renounce sins is the definition of repentance. The person who finds **mercy** will prosper in the ultimate sense in eternity.

¹⁴ Happy is the one who is always
    reverent,^a
but one who hardens his heart falls
    into trouble.^b

¹⁵ A wicked ruler over a helpless people^c
is like a roaring lion
    or a charging bear.^d

¹⁶ A leader who lacks understanding
is very oppressive,
but one who hates dishonest profit
prolongs his life.^e

¹⁷ A man burdened by bloodguilt^A
will be a fugitive until death.^f
Let no one help him.^g

¹⁸ The one who lives with integrity
    will be helped,
but one who distorts right and wrong^B
will suddenly fall.^h

¹⁹ The one who works his land
will have plenty of food,ⁱ
but whoever chases fantasies
will have his fill of poverty.^j

²⁰ A faithful man will have
    many blessings,^k
but one in a hurry to get rich^l
will not go unpunished.

²¹ It is not good to show partiality^m—
yet a man may sin for a piece
    of bread.ⁿ

²² A greedy man^C is in a hurry for wealth;

he doesn't know that poverty will come
    to him.^o

²³ One who rebukes a person
    will later find more favor^p
than one who flatters^D with his tongue.^q

²⁴ The one who robs his father or mother^r
and says, "That's no sin,"^s
is a companion to a man who destroys.^t

²⁵ A greedy person provokes conflict,^u
but whoever trusts in the LORD
    will prosper.^v

²⁶ The one who trusts in himself^E is a fool,
but one who walks in wisdom
    will be safe.^w

²⁷ The one who gives to the poor
will not be in need,
but one who turns his eyes away^F
will receive many curses.^x

²⁸ When the wicked come to power,
people hide,
but when they are destroyed,
the righteous flourish.^y

29 One who becomes stiff-necked,
    after many reprimands
will be shattered instantly—
beyond recovery.^z

² When the righteous flourish,
    the people rejoice,
but when the wicked rule,
    people groan.^{aa}

Cross references (center column):

^a 28:14 2Ch 19:7; Pr 23:17
^b Ps 95:8
^c 28:15 Ex 1:14; Pr 29:2; Mt 2:16
^d Pr 19:12; 1Pt 5:8
^e 28:16 1Kg 12:1-19; Ps 15:5; Pr 15:27
^f 28:17 Gn 4:14; 9:6; Ex 21:14
^g Nm 35:31
^h 28:18 Pr 2:7; 10:9; 20:7
ⁱ 28:19 Pr 24:27
^j Pr 1:31; 12:11,14; 14:14
^k 28:20 Pr 10:6; Mt 25:21
^l Pr 20:21; 28:22; 1Tm 6:9
^m 28:21 Pr 18:5; 24:23
ⁿ Ezk 13:19
^o 28:22 Pr 13:11; 20:21; 21:5; 22:16
^p 28:23 Pr 27:5-6
^q Pr 26:28; 29:5
^r 28:24 Pr 19:6
^s Pr 30:20; Mk 7:11
^t Pr 18:9
^u 28:25 Pr 15:18
^v Ps 37:3-5; Pr 3:5-6; Jr 17:7-8
^w 28:26 Pr 3:5-7
^x 28:27 Pr 11:24; 19:17; 22:16
^y 28:28 Pr 28:12; 29:2
^z 29:1 Pr 1:24-31; 6:14-15
^{aa} 29:2 Ex 2:23; Est 8:15; Pr 11:10; 28:12,28

---

^A 28:17 Lit *the blood of a person*   ^B 28:18 Lit *who is twisted regarding two ways*   ^C 28:22 Lit *A man with an evil eye*   ^D 28:23 Lit *is smooth*   ^E 28:26 Lit *his heart*   ^F 28:27 Lit *who shuts his eyes*

28:14 On **happy**, see note at 3:13-18. The Hebrew word for **reverent** usually refers to terror (1:26-27), but in this context it is synonymous with the fear of the Lord. To have a hard **heart** is to refuse to turn and obey God (Ex 7:3; Ezk 3:7).

28:15 A **wicked ruler** is destructive out of anger (19:12; 20:2).

28:16 Very oppressive is literally "much extortion" (Is 33:15). On **dishonest profit**, see note at 1:19.

28:17 Until death is literally "to the Pit" (1:12). The innocent should be rescued from death (24:11), but not those guilty of shedding innocent blood (Dt 19:11-13).

28:18 On **integrity**, see note at 11:20.

28:19 On "work," see note at 12:11. **Have plenty** and **have his fill** translate the same Hebrew word (18:20).

28:20 It is implied that the person **in a hurry to get rich** is willing to use illegal or immoral means. On **not go unpunished**, see note at 6:27-29.

28:21 An unjust judge may eventually give in to small bribes (24:23; Dt 16:19).

28:22 On **in a hurry for wealth**, see notes at verse 19 and verse 20.

28:23 One exception to this is rebuking a mocker (9:7).

28:24 Refusing to call a **sin** a sin **destroys** society. It is sinful to justify stealing money from one's parents (Mt 15:5-6; cp. Pr 20:21; Lk 15:12). A person is known by what kind of companions he has (Ps 1:1; 119:63; Pr 4:14; Jr 15:17).

28:25 **Greedy** is literally "enlarged throat" (Is 5:14) or appetite (Hab 2:5); see (Hb) *nephesh* in note at Pr 13:2-4. To **prosper** is literally to "be fat" (15:30). On the benefit of trusting, cp. 16:20; 29:25.

28:26 **Be safe** is literally "escape (judgment)" (19:5, cp. 19:9). This implies the **fool** will perish (1:32) because the object of his trust cannot save him (11:28).

28:28 On **the wicked** in **power**, see note at verse 12. To **flourish** is to increase in number and power (29:16).

29:1 At the end of God's patient call to obedience comes sudden judgment against the obstinate (2Kg 17:13-14,18; 2Ch 36:16; Neh 9:29-30; Jr 7:2-29; Ac 7:51; 2Pt 3:9-10).

29:2 On **righteous flourish**, see note at 28:12. **People groan** when oppressed (Ex 2:23) or devastated (Lm 1:4,8,11,21).

3 A man who loves wisdom brings joy
    to his father,[a]
but one who consorts with prostitutes
    destroys his wealth.[b]

4 By justice a king brings stability
    to a land,[c]
but a man who demands
    "contributions"[A]
    demolishes it.[d]

5 A man who flatters[B] his neighbor
    spreads a net for his feet.[e]

6 An evil man is caught by sin,[f]
but the righteous one sings
    and rejoices.[g]

7 The righteous person knows the rights[c]
    of the poor,[h]
but the wicked one does not
    understand these concerns.

8 Mockers inflame a city,[i]
but the wise turn away anger.

9 If a wise man goes to court with a fool,
there will be ranting and raving
    but no resolution.[D,j]

10 Bloodthirsty men hate
    an honest person,[k]
but the upright care about him.[E]

11 A fool gives full vent to his anger,[F,l]
but a wise man holds it in check.[m]

12 If a ruler listens to lies,[n]
all his officials will be wicked.

13 The poor and the oppressor have this
    in common:[G]
the LORD gives light to the eyes of both.[o]

14 A king who judges the poor
    with fairness—
his throne will be
    established forever.[p]

15 A rod of correction imparts wisdom,[q]
but a youth left to himself[H]
    is a disgrace to his mother.[r]

16 When the wicked increase,
    rebellion increases,
but the righteous will see
    their downfall.[s]

17 Discipline your son, and it will bring
    you peace of mind[t]
and give you delight.

18 Without revelation[I,u] people run wild,[v]
but one who listens to instruction
    will be happy.[w]

19 A slave cannot be disciplined by words;
though he understands,
    he doesn't respond.[x]

20 Do you see a man who speaks
    too soon?[y]
There is more hope for a fool
    than for him.[z]

21 A slave pampered from his youth
will become arrogant[J] later on.

22 An angry man stirs up conflict,

Cross references (center column):

[a] 29:3 Pr 10:1; 15:20; 23:24-25; 27:11; 28:7
[b] Pr 5:9-10; 6:26; Lk 15:13,30
[c] 29:4 2Ch 9:8; Pr 29:14
[d] Pr 17:23
[e] 29:5 Pr 26:28; 27:6; 28:23
[f] 29:6 Pr 12:13; 18:7; Ec 9:12
[g] Ex 15:1
[h] 29:7 Jb 29:16; Ps 41:1
[i] 29:8 Pr 11:11; 26:21; 29:22
[j] 29:9 Pr 26:4
[k] 29:10 Gn 4:5-8; 1Jn 3:12
[l] 29:11 Pr 12:16
[m] Pr 16:32; 25:28
[n] 29:12 1Kg 22:8,21-23
[o] 29:13 Pr 22:2
[p] 29:14 Ps 72:4; Pr 16:12; 25:5; Is 11:4
[q] 29:15 Pr 13:24; 22:15
[r] Pr 10:1; 17:25
[s] 29:16 Ps 37:34,36; 58:10; 91:8; 92:11
[t] 29:17 Pr 13:24
[u] 29:18 1Sm 3:1; Ps 74:9; Am 8:11-12
[v] Ex 32:25
[w] Ps 119:2; Pr 8:32; Jn 13:17; Jms 1:25
[x] 29:19 Mt 18:17
[y] 29:20 Lv 5:4; Jdg 11:30-31,34; Pr 10:19; 17:27; 19:2; 20:25
[z] Pr 26:12

[A]29:4 The Hb word for "contributions" usually refers to offerings in worship.   [B]29:5 Lit *is smooth on*   [C]29:7 Lit *justice*
[D]29:9 Lit *rest*   [E]29:10 Or *person, and seek the life of the upright*   [F]29:11 Lit *spirit*   [G]29:13 Lit *oppressor meet*   [H]29:15 Lit *youth sent away*   [I]29:18 Lit *vision*   [J]29:21 Hb obscure

---

29:3 This could refer to the father's or the man's **wealth**. Since a father is responsible for a son's debts, and a son hopes for an inheritance, the outcome is the same.

29:4 On **justice** and **king**, see note at 16:12. The Hebrew in the second line could refer to one who **demands** or who gives bribes, either of which subverts justice.

29:5 On **flatters**, see note at 2:16. His **feet** could be the neighbor's or the speaker's own feet (see v. 6; cp. 26:28).

29:6 The first line is literally "In the rebellion of a man of evil [is] a snare." Sin contains the seeds of self-destruction (1:19), but the **righteous** person **rejoices** in security.

29:7 The **rights** refers to a legal decision (Ezr 7:26; Dn 7:22).

29:9 **Ranting and raving** is literally "shakes (in rage; Jb 39:24) and laughs" (Pr 26:19).

29:10 The second line is difficult to translate (cp. 11:30). It is literally "and the upright ones, they seek his life." Do **bloodthirsty men** seek to kill **the upright**? The phrase "seek his life" almost always means "try to kill," but "upright" is plural and "his life" is singular. Or do the upright seek to take **care** of the **honest person**? That fits best with the rest of

Proverbs, and "seek" can mean to "demand justice" ("require" in 2Sm 4:11).

29:12 A **ruler** who likes to hear **lies** will end up accumulating **wicked** attendants.

29:13 On **this in common**, see note at 22:2. **Light to the eyes** means life. **The LORD** determines the outcome of both lives.

29:14 On **king** and **fairness**, see note at 16:12.

29:15 On this verse, see note at 23:13-14 (cp. 10:5,13; 17:2).

29:16 On leadership of the **wicked** and the **righteous**, see note at 28:12.

29:17 **Peace of mind** means being free from emotional and physical threats (Jb 3:26; Ps 116:7; Is 14:3,7). A wise **son** provides necessities as well as **delight** (Gn 49:20; Lm 4:5).

29:18 **Revelation**, like instruction, probably refers to the inspired wisdom in Proverbs. True happiness (see note at 3:13-18) is found within God's plan.

29:19 A foolish **slave** only responds to corporal punishment (see note at 13:24).

29:21 A **slave**, like any other person, needs to be prepared

and a hot-tempered man[A]
　increases rebellion.[a]

23　A person's pride will humble him,[b]
　but a humble spirit will gain honor.[c]

24　To be a thief's partner is to hate oneself;
　he hears the curse but
　　will not testify.[B,d]

25　The fear of man is a snare,[e]
　but the one who trusts in the LORD
　　is protected.[C,f]

26　Many seek a ruler's favor,[g]
　but a man receives justice
　　from the LORD.[h]

27　An unjust man is detestable
　　to the righteous,
　and one whose way is upright
　　is detestable to the wicked.[i]

The Words of Agur

30　The words of Agur son of Jakeh.
　　The oracle.[D,j]

The man's oration to Ithiel, to Ithiel
　and Ucal:[E]

2　I am more stupid than
　　any other man,[F]
　and I lack man's ability
　　to understand.[k]

3　I have not gained wisdom,
　and I have no knowledge
　　of the Holy One.[l]

4　Who has gone up to heaven
　　and come down?[m]
　Who has gathered the wind
　　in His hands?
　Who has bound up the waters
　　in a cloak?[n]
　Who has established all the ends
　　of the earth?[o]
　What is His name,
　and what is the name of His Son—
　　if you know?[p]

5　Every word of God is pure;[G,q]
　He is a shield to those who take refuge
　　in Him.[r]

6　Don't add to His words,[s]

Cross-references

[a] 29:22 Pr 15:18; 26:21; 28:25
[b] 29:23 2Sm 22:28; Mt 23:12; Jms 4:6
[c] Pr 11:2; 15:33; 18:12; 22:4
[d] 29:24 Lv 5:1
[e] 29:25 Gn 12:12; 20:2; 1Sm 13:11; Lk 12:4; Jn 12:42-43
[f] Pr 14:27; 18:10
[g] 29:26 Pr 16:15; 19:6
[h] Is 49:4; 1Co 4:4-5
[i] 29:27 Pr 29:10; Mt 10:22; Jn 15:18; 1Jn 3:13
[j] 30:1 Nm 24:3; Pr 31:1; Nah 1:1; Hab 1:1; Zch 9:1; Mal 1:1
[k] 30:2 1Kg 3:7
[l] 30:3 Pr 9:10
[m] 30:4 Jn 3:13; Eph 4:9-10
[n] Jb 26:8; 38:9
[o] Jb 38:4-5; Ps 93:1; 119:90; Is 45:18
[p] Mt 11:27; Rv 19:12-13
[q] 30:5 Ps 12:6; 18:30
[r] Ps 3:3
[s] 30:6 Dt 4:2; 12:32; Rv 22:18

[A] 29:22 Lit *a master of rage*　[B] 29:24 When a call for witnesses was made public, anyone with information who did not submit his testimony was under a curse.　[C] 29:25 Lit *raised high*　[D] 30:1 Or *son of Jakeh from Massa*; Pr 31:1　[E] 30:1 Hb uncertain. Sometimes read with different word division as *oration: I am weary, God, I am weary, God, and I am exhausted*, or *oration: I am not God, I am not God, that I should prevail.* LXX reads *My son, fear my words and when you have received them repent. The man says these things to the believers in God, and I pause.*　[F] 30:2 Lit *I am more stupid than a man*　[G] 30:5 Lit *refined*

---

during **his youth** to fulfill his life's responsibilities (22:6). On **later on**, see "at the end" in note at 5:11.

29:24 Associating with the wicked is self-destructive (1:19; 24:21-22). In an unsolved case, the legal system would announce a **curse** on the perpetrator and any accomplices (Lv 5:1). If witnesses came forward or the thief turned himself in, they could be exonerated (Jdg 17:2). But God's curse would be on this **partner** if he refused to testify against the thief (Zch 5:3-4; cp. Nm 5:21).

29:25 A **snare** can be fatal (13:14; 14:27; 18:7). **Fear** is literally "sheer terror" (1Sm 14:15; Is 21:4; Dn 10:7). A wise person does not fear mortal **man**. The One to fear is the LORD, who is able to protect or destroy (18:10; Lk 12:4-5).

29:27 To detest an **unjust man** is to agree with God (3:32; 11:1; 12:22; 15:8-9,26; 16:5,12; 17:15; 20:10,23; 21:27; 28:9; Ps 139:21-22; 2Co 6:14-16), but hating the **upright** is wrong (v. 10; Ps 69:4; Mt 10:22; 24:9; Jn 15:18; 17:14; 1Jn 3:13).

30:1 On **Jakeh** and **the oracle**, see the textual footnote at verse 1. **Agur**, the author of this chapter (cp. 1:1; 31:1), and **Ithiel and Ucal**, the recipients, are otherwise unknown. These proverbs, though written for specific individuals, have application for all people. An oracle is a message from God (2Kg 9:25; Ezk 12:10; Mal 1:1; cp. Jr 23:33-40). **Oration** (Hb *ne'um*), which usually announces a declaration of the Lord (Gn 22:16; 1Sm 2:30; Hg 2:4), is used twice for the "oracle" or "proclamation" of men (Nm 24:3,15; 2Sm 23:1).

30:2-3 Some men claim to have a grasp on God. What Job eventually came to realize (Jb 40:4), Agur reverently states at the beginning: **I have no knowledge of the Holy One**.

30:4 Gathering **wind** and binding **waters** refer to God's control of thunderstorms, which are important for the agricultural cycle. Asking about God's **name** is asking whether the hearer knows His character. **His Son** could refer to Israel (Hs 11:1) or to anyone whom God teaches (Dt 8:5; Heb 12:6), but Jesus fulfilled the role perfectly (Mt 2:15; Lk 9:35).

A copper ink pot found at Qumran along with the Dead Sea Scrolls which contained portions of Proverbs.

or He will rebuke you, and you will be
proved a liar.[a]

7 Two things I ask of You;
don't deny them to me before I die:
8 Keep falsehood and deceitful words
far from me.
Give me neither poverty nor wealth;
feed me with the food I need.[b]
9 Otherwise, I might have too much[c]
and deny You,[d] saying,
"Who is the LORD?"[e]
or I might have nothing and steal,[f]
profaning[A] the name of my God.[g]

10 Don't slander a servant to his master
or he will curse you,[h] and you will
become •guilty.

11 There is a generation that curses
its father
and does not bless its mother.[i]
12 There is a generation that is pure
in its own eyes,[j]
yet is not washed from its filth.
13 There is a generation—how haughty
its eyes
and pretentious its looks.[B]
14 There is a generation whose teeth
are swords,[k]
whose fangs are knives,[l]
devouring the oppressed from the land[m]
and the needy from among mankind.

15 The leech has two daughters:
"Give, Give!"

16 Three things[n] are never satisfied;
four never say, "Enough!":
•Sheol;[o] a childless womb;[p]
earth, which is never satisfied
with water;
and fire, which never says, "Enough!"

17 As for the eye that ridicules a father[q]
and despises obedience to a mother,
may ravens of the valley pluck it out
and young vultures eat it.[r]

18 Three things are beyond me;
four I can't understand:
19 the way of an eagle in the sky,
the way of a snake on a rock,
the way of a ship at sea,
and the way of a man
with a young woman.

20 This is the way of an adulteress:
she eats and wipes her mouth
and says, "I've done nothing wrong."[s]

21 The earth trembles
under three things;
it cannot bear up under four:
22 a servant when he becomes king,[t]
a fool when he is stuffed with food,
23 an unloved woman when she marries,[u]
and a servant girl when she ousts
her queen.

24 Four things on earth are small,
yet they are extremely wise:
25 the ants are not a strong people,

Cross references (center column):
a 30:6 Dt 18:22
b 30:8 Jb 23:12; Mt 6:11; Php 4:11-12
c 30:9 Dt 6:10-12; 8:11-14
d Jos 24:27; Jb 31:28
e Ex 5:2
f Ex 20:5; Eph 4:28
g Lv 19:11-12
h 30:10 Ec 7:21
i 30:11 Ex 21:17; Pr 20:20
j 30:12 Pr 16:2; Lk 18:11
k 30:14 Ps 57:4 Jb 29:17
m Ps 14:4
n 30:15 Pr 6:16; 30:18,21,29
o 30:16 Pr 27:20; Hab 2:5
p Gn 30:1
q 30:17 Gn 9:22
r Dt 28:26
s 30:20 Pr 28:24; 1Jn 1:8
t 30:22 Pr 19:10; Ec 10:7
u 30:23 Gn 29:30-31; Dt 21:15

A 30:9 Lit grabbing B 30:13 Lit and its eyelids lifted up

30:7-9 This prayer is comparable to Jesus' model prayer (Mt 6:9-13). Both ask God's protection from temptation; both ask for basic needs (1Tm 6:8; cp. Php 4:12); both are concerned with upholding God's honor. The indulgent person may become a liar and a mocker (Ex 5:2); the destitute person may become a thief (Pr 6:30). The thief profanes God by implying that God can't provide.

30:11-15 A **generation** is a group of people of a certain time with certain characteristics in common. Jesus condemned an evil "generation" of His day (Mt 11:16; 12:39-45; 17:17).

30:11 On **curses**, see note at 20:20.

30:12 **Filth** is literally "excrement" (Dt 23:13; 2Kg 18:27; Ezk 4:12). It refers figuratively to obvious, detestable sin.

30:13-14 Arrogance leads to exploitation.

30:15-16 The blood-sucking **leech** takes without contributing. Until God restores paradise (Rm 8:19-22; Rv 21:1), **Sheol** and **fire** will always try to destroy, and the **womb** and the soil will always strive to produce (Gn 3:16-17).

30:17 The **eye that ridicules** indicates a haughty person (v. 13).

30:18-20 A **man** is a strong, virile man (20:24), and the **young woman** is of marriageable age, presumably a virgin (Gn 24:43; Is 7:14). If Pr 30:18-19 stand alone, the point might

be that the progress of love is as marvelous and mysterious as the motion of the other three items. If verse 20 is connected to the saying, the interpretation is far different. The first three things leave no tracks. The man, like the **adulteress** who **wipes her mouth**, thinks fornication with the young woman leaves no trace. (The adulteress thinks sex is as casual and amoral as a meal.) However, in the end there are consequences (5:4; 14:12). These things are **beyond** Agur (Jb 42:3; Ps 131:1), but God knows (Jr 32:17).

30:21-23 This could be a humorous observation or a serious commentary on the collapse of social order. The **servant** could be an official who seized the kingdom. On **fool**, see note at 17:7. **Unloved** is literally "hated"; it may refer to a wicked woman who was rightly rejected. All these become destructive when they move into a position they should not be in.

30:24-28 A perceptive person can learn from observing God's creation (6:6-8; cp. 24:32). Each of these **small** animals overcomes potentially fatal limitations. **Ants** and **hyraxes** are metaphorically called **people** as if they were a nationality. Ants show forethought. A hyrax (Procavia syriacus) is a herbivore the size of a rabbit that lives in herds in cavities among the rocks. Wise men also rely on the Lord as their rock of protection. **Locusts** have unity of purpose, maintaining **ranks** without infighting. The **lizard** (or spider) is vulnerable, yet it can be found in unexpected places.

yet they store up their food
   in the summer;[a]
26 hyraxes are not a mighty people,
   yet they make their homes
     in the cliffs;[b]
27 locusts have no king,
   yet all of them march in ranks;[c]
28 a lizard[A] can be caught in your hands,
   yet it lives in kings' palaces.

29 Three things are stately in their stride,
   even four are stately in their walk:
30 a lion, which is mightiest among beasts
   and doesn't retreat before anything,
31 a strutting rooster,[B] a goat,
   and a king at the head of his army.[C]

32 If you have been foolish
   by exalting yourself
   or if you've been scheming,
   put your hand over your mouth.[d]
33 For the churning of milk
   produces butter,
   and twisting a nose draws blood,
   and stirring up anger produces strife.[e]

The Words of Lemuel

31 The words of King Lemuel,
  an oracle[D,f] that his mother
   taught him:

2 What should I say, my son?
  What, son of my womb?[g]

What, son of my vows?
3 Don't spend your energy[h] on women
  or your efforts on those
   who destroy kings.[i]
4 It is not for kings, Lemuel,
  it is not for kings[j] to drink wine[k]
  or for rulers to desire beer.
5 Otherwise, they[E] will drink,
  forget what is decreed,[l]
  and pervert justice for all
   the oppressed.[F,m]
6 Give beer to one who is dying
  and wine to one whose life is bitter.[n]
7 Let him drink so that he can forget
  his poverty
  and remember his trouble no more.[o]
8 Speak up[G] for those who have
  no voice,[H,p]
  for the justice of all
   who are dispossessed.[I]
9 Speak up,[G] judge righteously,[q]
  and defend the cause of[J] the oppressed
  and needy.[r]

In Praise of a Capable Wife

10 Who can find a capable wife?[K,s]
  She is far more precious than jewels.[L]
11 The heart of her husband trusts in her,
  and he will not lack anything good.
12 She rewards him with good, not evil,
  all the days of her life.

a 30:25Pr 6:6-8
b 30:26Lv 11:5; Ps 104:18
c 30:27Jl 2:7-8
d 30:32Jb 21:5; Mc 7:16
e 30:33Pr 10:12; 29:22
f 31:1Pr 30:1
g 31:2Is 49:15
h 31:3Pr 5:9
i Dt 17:17; 1Kg 11:1; Neh 13:26
j 31:4 1Kg 16:9; 20:16; Ec 10:17
k Pr 20:1
l 31:5Hs 4:11
m Ps 72:1-2; Is 28:7
n 31:6Jb 3:20
o 31:7Ps 104:15
p 31:8Jb 29:12-17
q 31:9Lv 19:15; Dt 1:16
r Is 1:17; Jr 22:16
s 31:10Ru 3:11; Pr 12:4; 18:22; 19:14

A 30:28 Or *spider* B 30:31 Or *a greyhound* C 30:31 LXX reads *king addressing his people* D 31:1 Or *of Lemuel, king of Massa, or of King Lemuel, a burden* E 31:5 Lit *he* F 31:5 Lit *sons of affliction* G 31:8,9 Lit *Open your mouth* H 31:8 Lit *who are mute* I 31:8 Lit *all the sons of passing away* J 31:9 Lit *and justice for* K 31:10 Or *a wife of quality,* or *a wife of noble character* L 31:10 Vv. 10-31 form an *acrostic.

30:29-31 Stately is literally "good"; that is, they excel in the quality of their **stride**. The **lion** is literally a "hero" (1Sm 17:51). Each of these is supreme in its realm. The phrase that modifies the **king** is obscure.

30:32-33 On **foolish**, see note at 17:7. Putting one's **hand** over one's **mouth** means to immediately stop speaking out of fear (Jdg 18:19; Jb 21:5; 40:4; Mc 7:16). **Churning . . . twisting**, and **stirring up** are all the same word in Hebrew, which has to do with force or pressure and twisting or wringing. The scheming social climber is cautioned that his maneuverings will inevitably bring violence against him.

31:1 This chapter was written by **Lemuel** (cp. 1:1; 30:1). He was not a **king** in Israel, so he was probably a foreign king who converted to the worship of Israel's God (cp. Dn 4:34).

31:2 The Hebrew word for **what** is probably an implicit call to listen (1:8; 4:1) or a rhetorical question, "What should you do?" Lemuel's mother probably made a vow before his conception (1Sm 1:11).

31:3 Women . . . who destroy kings are either adulteresses (6:26,32; 30:20) or multiple wives (Dt 17:17; 1Kg 11:1-4). David diverted his **energy** to an affair, and it distorted his judgment and ruined his family (2Sm 11–12).

31:4-5 People in positions of authority should avoid **wine** and **beer**, which could affect their judgment (Is 5:22-23; Am 6:6; Eph 5:18; Ti 1:7). Since all persons wear a hat of authority at

some point—whether as a parent or a voter in a representative organization—this warning applies to all persons. The king has a special responsibility to protect **the oppressed** (vv. 8-9; cp. 3:34; 29:4,14).

31:6-7 This is a sarcastic command (cp. 19:27) intended to emphasize that alcohol is not appropriate for kings.

31:8-9 Having **no voice** means being unable to be effective in court and get a fair hearing. The **dispossessed** are literally "vanishing." Each person needs to help the **needy** (Ps 82:3; Is 1:17).

31:10-31 This poem is an alphabetic acrostic. While Proverbs 1–9 describe the virtues of the symbolic Lady Wisdom, this passage celebrates the ideal flesh-and-blood wife. Just as most of the exhortations to the "son" in the rest of Proverbs can be applied to all people of both genders, everyone can learn from the example of this capable wife.

31:10 Capable implies practical competence (v. 29; cp. Gn 47:6), physical strength ("energy" in Pr 31:3; cp. Jdg 3:29), and financial wealth (Pr 13:22; cp. Ps 49:6), as well as "noble character" (Ru 2:1; 3:11).

31:11 This is the only case where the Bible commends trusting in anything but God; her husband can trust her because she is godly. **Anything good** is literally "spoil"; it refers to her abundant profits (v. 18).

13 She selects wool and flax
   and works with willing hands.
14 She is like the merchant ships,
   bringing her food from far away.*a*
15 She rises while it is still night*b*
   and provides food for her household
   and portions*A* for her female servants.*c*
16 She evaluates a field and buys it;
   she plants a vineyard
      with her earnings.*B,d*
17 She draws on her strength*C*
   and reveals that her arms are strong.*e*
18 She sees that her profits are good,
   and her lamp never goes out at night.*f*
19 She extends her hands
      to the spinning staff,
   and her hands hold the spindle.*g*
20 Her hands reach*D* out to the poor,
   and she extends her hands
      to the needy.*h*
21 She is not afraid for her household
      when it snows,
   for all in her household
      are doubly clothed.*E*
22 She makes her own bed coverings;*i*
   her clothing is fine linen*j* and purple.*k*

23 Her husband is known
      at the city •gates,
   where he sits among the elders
      of the land.*l*
24 She makes and sells linen garments;
   she delivers belts*F* to the merchants.
25 Strength*m* and honor are her clothing,*n*
   and she can laugh at the time
      to come.*o*
26 She opens her mouth with wisdom
   and loving instruction*G* is
      on her tongue.
27 She watches over the activities
      of her household*p*
   and is never idle.*H*
28 Her sons rise up and call her blessed.
   Her husband also praises her:
29 "Many women*I* are capable,
   but you surpass them all!"*q*
30 Charm is deceptive and beauty
      is fleeting,*r*
   but a woman who •fears the LORD
      will be praised.
31 Give her the reward of her labor,*J*
   and let her works praise her
      at the city gates.

*a*31:14 1Kg 10:22
*b*31:15 Pr 20:13
*c*Pr 27:27; Lk 12:42
*d*31:16 Mt 21:33
*e*31:17 Pr 31:25
*f*31:18 Mt 25:8
*g*31:19 Pr 31:13
*h*31:20 Dt 15:11; Pr 22:9; 31:9; Rm 12:13; Eph 4:28
*i*31:22 Pr 7:16
*j*Gn 41:42; Rv 19:8,14
*k*Jdg 8:26; Lk 16:19
*l*31:23 Ru 4:1-2; Pr 24:7; 31:31
*m*31:25 Pr 31:17
*n*1Tm 2:9-10
*o*Pr 31:21
*p*31:27 Pr 31:15
*q*31:29 Pr 12:4; 31:10; Sg 6:8-9
*r*31:30 1Pt 3:3-4

*A*31:15 Or *tasks*   *B*31:16 Or *vineyard by her own labors*   *C*31:17 Lit *She wraps strength around her like a belt*   *D*31:20 Lit *Her hand reaches*   *E*31:21 LXX, Vg; MT reads *are dressed in scarlet*   *F*31:24 Or *sashes*   *G*31:26 Or *and the teaching of kindness*   *H*31:27 Lit *and does not eat the bread of idleness*   *I*31:29 Lit *daughters*   *J*31:31 Lit *the fruit of her hands*

31:13 Flax fibers were used to make linen (Dt 22:11; Ezk 44:18).

31:14 She could afford imported **food.**

31:15 Food is literally "prey" (Ps 111:5; Mal 3:10), implying diligence, strength, and cunning (Jb 24:5; 38:39).

31:16-17 It requires tremendous **strength** to earn the extra money to buy a **vineyard**, then to clear it of stones, plant the vines, dig a winepress, and build a tower to protect it (Is 5:2).

31:18 The burning **lamp** symbolizes long life and prosperity (20:20).

31:19 The **spinning staff** and **spindle** were used to make thread and to twist it into yarn.

31:22 These **bed coverings** were probably for comfort and decoration (7:16). **Fine linen** may have been imported from Egypt, and **purple** dye came from Phoenicia (Ezk 27:7).

31:23 On **gates**, see note at 24:7. She enabled her husband to sit **among the elders**, a respected local authority.

31:24 She **sells** everything, from the inner **linen garments** that are put on first, to the outer belt or sash.

31:25 She has **strength** like the young and **honor** like the old (20:29).

31:26 Her **instruction** arises out of **wisdom** and love (Hb *chesed*; see note at 19:22).

31:28-31 Here the wife is recognized and rewarded for her character and **works**. Even if all the rare **capable** women were gathered, her **husband** says she would **surpass** them. **Charm** is grace or favor (11:16; 22:1), and **beauty** is outward appearance (6:25; Ezk 16:14); both are temporary (see "fraud" in note at Pr 13:11). The end **reward** of wisdom depends on its beginning: the fear of the Lord (see 1:7; 9:10; 15:33 and notes there).

Ecclesiastes

Introduction

The Bible is never shy about confronting painful truths or hard questions. The book of Ecclesiastes faces the issue of how we can find meaning in life in light of the seemingly futile nature of everything. It will not allow the reader to retreat into superficial answers. It does not answer this problem by comforting us with hollow slogans. To the contrary, its motto is "Everything Is Futile." But by forcing us to face the futility of human existence, it guides us to a life free of empty purpose and deceitful vindication.

"All the streams flow to the sea, yet the sea is never full. The streams are flowing to the place, and they flow there again" (1:7).

Circumstances of Writing

Author: According to 1:1 and 1:12, the author was David's son and a king over Israel from Jerusalem. Also, 12:9 speaks of the author as a writer of proverbs, so Solomon appears to be the author. Many scholars believe that Ecclesiastes was written too late in Israel's history for this to be true, and they want to date the book at least 500 years after Solomon's time (later than 450 B.C.). However, strong evidence attests that the book does come from the age of Solomon. For instance, it displays a great knowledge of literature from early Mesopotamia and Egypt.

One example is that the book shows an awareness of the "Harper Songs," poetry from Egypt that is much older than the age of Solomon. Ecclesiastes 9:7-9 is similar to that poetry, and it also resembles a portion of the famous *Epic of Gilgamesh* from Mesopotamia. It makes sense that Solomon, who had close contacts with Egypt and whose empire stretched up to the Euphrates River, would know and reflect on such texts. It is very doubtful that an anonymous Jew writing 500 or more years later, when Egyptian and Mesopotamian glory was finished and when Judah was a backwater nation, would have had access to these texts or could have understood them. By contrast, Ecclesiastes shows no similarities to the Greek philosophy that flourished in the fifth century B.C. and later. All of these conditions point to the traditional view that Solomon authored this book.

Background: Ecclesiastes is Wisdom literature, meaning that it is in the part of the Bible that is especially concerned with helping readers cope with the practical and philosophical issues of life. It has roots in the wisdom literature of Egypt and Babylon. Books like Proverbs and Ecclesiastes are the biblical answer to the search for truth. Proverbs is basic wisdom, giving the reader fundamental principles to live by. Ecclesiastes, by contrast, is for a more mature reader. It engages the question of whether death nullifies all purpose and meaning in life.

Message and Purpose

Ecclesiastes shows us that since we and our works are futile—that is, destined to perish—we must not waste

---

5000–2000 B.C.

2000–1800 B.C.

Abraham 2166–1991

Moses 1526–1406

Light wooden plows, Mesopotamia **4000**

Copper smelting, Mesopotamia **4000**

Irrigation developed, Mesopotamia **3500**

Epic of Gilgamesh developed **2700–1400**

The Instruction of Ptah-Hotep, Egypt's Old Kingdom **2575–2134**

Chinese Literature, First of Seven Periods **2000–600**

The Man Who Was Tired of Life, Egyptian **1990–1800**

The Complaints of Khakheperre-Sonb, Egyptian **1900**

Egyptians develop an alphabet of 24 signs.

Egyptians use the flooding of the Nile to their agricultural advantage by building systems of irrigation.

our lives trying to justify our existence with pursuits that ultimately mean nothing. Put simply, Ecclesiastes examines major endeavors of life in light of the reality of death. The book warns us about the pursuit of several different purposes in life.

1. *Intellectual accomplishments.* Ecclesiastes affirms that wisdom helps us cope with life, but it denies that acquiring knowledge as such is meaningful. Ultimately, the wise person and his works, like the fool and his deeds, perish.

2. *Wealth and luxury.* Wealth does not give life purpose. More than that, those who pursue riches waste their lives in bitterness, anxiety, and toil. Money does matter, and Ecclesiastes affirms that we need a strategy for maintaining a basic level of prosperity. But wealth of itself is a fraudulent substitute for true contentment.

3. *Politics.* Political power is inherently corrupting, and the worst evils in the world are committed by cruel or incompetent people with power. At the same time, government is necessary, and Ecclesiastes counsels the reader on how to survive in a world of political competition, and thus how to have a stable, peaceful life.

4. *Religion.* Zeal for religion also comes in for criticism in Ecclesiastes. Its two warnings are that we should not try to impress God and we should not wear ourselves out with irrational excess.

Positively, Ecclesiastes recommends that we do two things in light of the brevity of our days.

1. *Enjoy life.* This is not a philosophy of hedonism, nor does it involve neglect of other duties because there is a time for everything under the sun. But a life without enjoyment is no life at all.

2. *Fear God.* This is an honest humility before God arising from an awareness of our weakness and sin. It includes awareness of our dependence on Him and a remembrance of the fact that He is our judge.

1800–1500 B.C.	1500–1200 B.C.	1200–800 B.C.
The Admonitions of Ipuwer, Egypt 1600–1400	Heavy import and export trade, Egypt 1500–1000	The Harper's Song for Inherkhway, Egyptian 1160
The Satirical Letter of Hori, Egypt 1570–1070	Words of Ahiqar, Egypt 1500–500	The Babylonian Theodicy, Mesopotamian 1100
Declarations of Innocence from the Egyptian Book of the Dead 1530–1500	Events in Joshua 1406–1380?	David becomes king over all Israel. 1003
	Events in Judges 1380?–1060?	Solomon becomes king. 970
	Epic of Gilgamesh is recorded. 1200	Proverbs 970
		Song of Songs 970?
		Ecclesiastes 935?

Contribution to the Bible

Ecclesiastes must be read with care because some of its verses, if read in isolation, seem to contradict other biblical teachings. It seems to deny the afterlife (3:18-22), to warn us against being too righteous (7:16), and to recommend a life of pleasure (10:19). But the real purpose of Ecclesiastes is to force us to take our mortality seriously and thus to consider carefully how we should live. Ecclesiastes knocks away all the façades by which we disguise the fact that life is short and we deny that all our accomplishments will pass away. In this sense, Ecclesiastes anticipates the NT teaching that only God's grace, and not excessive zeal, saves us.

Structure

Ecclesiastes does not have the kind of structure we usually look for in a book of the Bible. At first glance it seems to move to and fro among various topics in a way that seems almost incoherent. It has no simple hierarchical outline, and it often jumps rapidly from one topic to the next. But a closer look reveals a structure that alternates between two perspectives: that of human existence apart from God and that of existence lived before God. If Ecclesiastes were music, it would be seen as antiphonal. The resolution of the tensions that permeate Ecclesiastes is found in the affirmation that the most important thing in life is to "fear God and keep His commands" (12:13).

Outline

I.   God and the Futility of Life (1:1–2:26)
   A. The humdrum of life (1:1-11)
   B. The Teacher's quest (1:12-18)
   C. The emptiness of pleasure (2:1-3)
   D. The emptiness of possessions (2:4-11)
   E. The limits of wisdom (2:12-17)
   F. The emptiness of work (2:18-23)
   G. Pleasure, possessions, wisdom, and work in God's perspective (2:24-26)

II. Time and Eternity (3:1-22)
   A. The rhythm of time (3:1-8)
   B. Eternity in time (3:9-15)
   C. Eternity and death (3:16-22)

III. Society (4:1-16)
   A. A place of injustice (4:1-6)
   B. A place of comfort (4:7-12)
   C. The more things change (4:13-16)

IV. Religion (5:1–6:12)
   A. Authentic religion (5:1-7)
   B. Wealth: God's perspective (5:8–6:12)

V.   Wise Sayings (7:1-29)
   A. Proverbs (7:1-14)
   B. The value of moderation (7:15-22)
   C. Wisdom's limitations (7:23-29)

Everything is Futile

1 The words of the Teacher,[A,a] son of David, king in Jerusalem.[b]

2 "Absolute futility," says the Teacher.
"Absolute futility. Everything is futile."[c]

3 What does a man gain for all his efforts
that he labors at under the sun?[d]

4 A generation goes and a generation
comes,
but the earth remains forever.[e]

5 The sun rises and the sun sets;
panting, it returns to its place[f]
where it rises.

6 Gusting to the south,
turning to the north,
turning, turning, goes the wind,[g]
and the wind returns in its cycles.

7 All the streams flow to the sea,
yet the sea is never full.
The streams are flowing to the place,
and they flow there again.

8 All things[B] are wearisome;

man is unable to speak.
The eye is not satisfied by seeing[h]
or the ear filled with hearing.

9 What has been is what will be,
and what has been done is
what will be done;
there is nothing new under the sun.

10 Can one say about anything,
"Look, this is new"?
It has already existed in the ages
before us.

11 There is no remembrance of those
who[c] came before;[i]
and of those who[c] will come after
there will also be no remembrance
by those who follow them.

The Limitations of Wisdom

12 I, the Teacher,[j] have been[D] king over Israel in Jerusalem. 13 I applied my mind to seek[k] and explore through wisdom all that is done under heaven.[l] God has given •people this miserable task to keep them occupied.[m] 14 I have seen all the things that are done under the sun and

Cross references:
a 1:1 Ec 1:12; 7:27; 12:8-10
b 1 Kg 2:12; Pr 1:1
c 1:2 Ps 39:5-6; 62:9; 144:4; Ec 12:8; Rm 8:20
d 1:3 Ec 2:11,22; 3:9; 5:16
e 1:4 Ps 104:5; 119:90; 1 Jn 2:17
f 1:5 Ps 19:6
g 1:6 Ec 11:5; Jn 3:8
h 1:8 Pr 27:20; Ec 4:8
i 1:11 Dt 9:14; Ec 2:16; 9:5
j 1:12 Ec 1:1; 7:27; 12:8-10
k 1:13 Ec 1:17
l Kg 4:29-34; Ec 3:10-11; 7:25; 8:17
m Gn 3:19; Ec 2:23,26; 3:10; 4:8

A 1:1 Or of Qoheleth, or of the Leader of the Assembly　　B 1:8 Or words　　C 1:11 Or of the things that　　D 1:12 Or Teacher, was

---

1:1 The Hebrew word qoheleth, here translated as **Teacher**, probably means "assembly leader." It is not the ordinary word for "teacher." It is a rare Hebrew word (found seven times in Ecclesiastes and nowhere else in the Bible), and it could mean "public speaker." It is the author's self-designation throughout the book. For this reason the book of Ecclesiastes is often called "Qoheleth." The words **son of David, king in Jerusalem** could refer to any Davidic king of Judah, but only Solomon was king over all Israel from Jerusalem (v. 12).

1:2 Hevel, the Hebrew word for **futile**, basically means "vapor" or "breath," but it comes to mean "vain," "transitory," or "futile." It does not necessarily mean that something is altogether worthless, but it implies that something is at best only of fleeting value. In the context of Ecclesiastes,

it means that things done "under the sun" are only of temporary significance and therefore, set against eternity, they have no real value.

1:3-7 The phrase **under the sun** means here on earth; it speaks of the temporal and temporary nature of humanity. The **sun . . . wind**, and waters (**streams**) are in constant motion, but they never accomplish anything. It is simply a constant cycle of coming and going. In the same way, each **generation** comes and goes but does not change the world in any fundamental way. Worse yet, each generation of people (unlike the sun, wind, and waters) passes away.

1:8 The phrase **all things are wearisome** could be translated "all words are weary." It refers to our inability to find either meaning or satisfaction in creation. No one can **speak** in the face of all the ceaseless motion of the sun, wind, and waters. That is, the world cannot be adequately explained or in any way affected by the human word. We stand dumb before it. Similarly, we neither see nor hear anything that fully satisfies.

1:9-10 When Ecclesiastes says that **there is nothing new under the sun**, it means that there is nothing that changes the fundamental facts of the human condition. This does not deny that there are technological innovations or new works of art, literature, and architecture, but these things are all variations on what had already existed, and they do not deliver humanity from its bondage to death. The "new thing" that really changes life can only come from God (Jr 31:31-34; Lk 22:20; Heb 9:15).

1:11 This verse does not claim that no human is ever remembered in history. The point is that people move on and that fame and glory have no lasting significance.

1:12-18 These verses describe the futility of the quest for knowledge. The claim is not that intellectual pursuits are evil; they are vain and frustrating because no person by learning finds the answers to his fundamental questions.

1:12 A king does not stop serving as king until he dies. The

hevel

Hebrew Pronunciation	[HEH vel]
HCSB Translation	breath, futility
Uses in Ecclesiastes	38
Uses in the OT	73
Focus Passage	Ecclesiastes 1:2,14

Hevel may originate in the sound of *breath* (Is 57:13). It may have produced a verb (*haval*) that occurs five times, once used as *keep up empty talk* (Jb 27:12). Haval denotes *become worthless* (Jr 2:5) or *place false hope* (Ps 62:10). The causative means *make worthless* (Jr 23:16). *Breath* as transient and apparently insignificant underlies all metaphorical uses of *hevel*. It can indicate *vapor* (Ps 39:5) or *mist* (Pr 21:6), but the idea of little worth is always present. *Hevel* connotes *fraud* (Pr 13:11). It signifies *empty* (Jb 27:12), *worthless* (Jr 10:3), *meaningless* (Ps 94:11), *futile* (Jb 21:34), *fleeting* (Pr 31:30), or *in vain* (Zch 10:2). It describes man (Ps 62:9). This key word in Ecclesiastes suggests *futility* except at Ec 9:9. *Absolute futility* is literally "futility of futilities" (Ec 1:2). The plural often denotes *worthless idols* (Dt 32:21) since context clarifies what the *hevel* is.

have found everything to be futile, a pursuit of the wind.[A,a]

15 What is crooked cannot
      be straightened;[b]
   what is lacking cannot be counted.

[16]I said to myself,[B] "Look, I have amassed wisdom far beyond all those who were over Jerusalem before me,[c] and my mind has thoroughly grasped[C] wisdom and knowledge." [17]I applied my mind to know wisdom and knowledge,[d] madness and folly;[e] I learned that this too is a pursuit of the wind.[A,f]

18 For with much wisdom is
      much sorrow;[g]
   as knowledge increases, grief increases.

The Emptiness of Pleasure

2 I said to myself, "Go ahead, I will test you with pleasure;[h] enjoy what is good." But it turned out to be futile. [2]I said about laughter,[i] "It is madness," and about pleasure, "What does this accomplish?" [3]I explored with my mind how to let my body enjoy life[D] with wine[j]

and how to grasp folly[k]—my mind still guiding me with wisdom—until I could see what is good for •people to do under heaven[E] during the few days of their lives.[l]

The Emptiness of Possessions

[4]I increased my achievements. I built houses[m] and planted vineyards[n] for myself. [5]I made gardens[o] and parks for myself and planted every kind of fruit tree in them. [6]I constructed reservoirs of water for myself from which to irrigate a grove of flourishing trees.[p] [7]I acquired male and female servants and had slaves who were born in my house.[q] I also owned many herds of cattle and flocks, more than all who were before me in Jerusalem.[r] [8]I also amassed silver and gold for myself, and the treasure of kings and provinces.[s] I gathered male and female singers for myself,[t] and many concubines, the delights of men.[F,G] [9]So I became great and surpassed all who were before me in Jerusalem;[u] my wisdom also remained with me. [10]All that my eyes desired, I did not deny them.[v] I did not refuse myself any pleasure, for I took pleasure

Cross references (center column)
[a]1:14 Pr 27:16; Ec 2:11,17; 4:4; 6:9
[b]1:15 Ec 7:13
[c]1:16 1Kg 3:12; 4:30; 10:23; Ec 2:9
[d]1:17 Ec 1:13
[e]Ec 2:12; 7:25
[f]Ec 2:11,17; 4:4,6,16; 6:9
[g]1:18 Ec 2:23; 12:12
[h]2:1 Ec 7:4; 8:15; Lk 12:19
[i]2:2 Pr 14:13; Ec 7:3,6
[j]2:3 Ps 104:15; Ec 10:19
[k]Ec 7:25
[l]Ec 2:24; 3:12,13; 5:18; 8:15
[m]2:4 1Kg 7:1-12
[n]Sg 8:11
[o]2:5 Sg 4:16
[p]2:6 Neh 2:14; 3:15-16
[q]2:7 Gn 14:14; 15:3
[r]1Kg 4:23
[s]2:8 1Kg 9:28; 10:10,14,21
[t]2Sm 19:35
[u]2:9 1Ch 29:25; Ec 1:16
[v]2:10 Ec 6:2

[A]1:14,17 Or a feeding on wind, or an affliction of spirit [B]1:16 Lit said with my heart [C]1:16 Or discerned [D]2:3 Lit to pull my body [E]2:3 Two Hb mss, LXX, Syr read the sun [F]2:8 LXX, Theod, Syr read and male cupbearers and female cupbearers; Aq, Tg, Vg read a cup and cups; Hb obscure [G]2:8 Or many treasures that people delight in

---

phrase **have been king** does not mean that the Teacher had stopped being king. Rather, the point is that he had, in his lifetime, been in a position to have the wealth and freedom to carry out the investigations described in this book.

1:13 The quest for wisdom is usually thought of as noble and fulfilling, but it is here called **this miserable task**, meaning that it is just a hard job.

1:15 This verse is a proverb. **What is crooked cannot be straightened** refers to a problem that cannot be solved. **What is lacking cannot be counted** refers to working with insufficient information. The problem of understanding life is beyond mere humans.

1:18 Instead of answering all our questions and bringing happiness, great learning or **wisdom** only leads to less certainty and more pain.

2:1-2 These verses summarize in advance the whole of verses 1-11. Solomon looked into finding meaning through riches, and he found it **futile**.

2:3 The word **wine** is literal wine, but it also stands for all the pleasure-giving luxuries of life. **Folly** refers to parties, frivolity, and self-indulgence. When the Teacher said **my mind still guiding me with wisdom**, he meant that he did not give himself over to total dissipation. Anyone can see that a person who has cast off all self-restraint, such as the alcoholic, will not be happy. Solomon never lost self-control or became an addict. Still, even pleasures pursued in moderation will not bring happiness.

2:4-8 The Teacher was rich in every way, including palatial homes, the natural beauty of **vineyards** and **gardens**, abundant and varied food from his herds and estates, riches in the form of livestock and precious metals, and feats of engineering in the form of **reservoirs** and aqueducts. He was free of hard labor and was served by an army of **slaves**.

He was entertained by **singers**, and his sexual desires were fulfilled by **concubines**.

2:9 Solomon's assertion that **my wisdom also remained with me** is important. If he had lost all self-control and had become an addict, then the fact that his wealth and luxury had not made him happy would be self-evident. But he did handle the prosperity well and did not fall into debauchery. It is not only excess and dissipation that leads to ruin, but even indulgence with moderation does not satisfy.

2:10 The Teacher's quest for happiness through wealth

simchah

Hebrew Pronunciation	[sim KHAH]
HCSB Translation	joy, gladness
Uses in Ecclesiastes	8
Uses in the OT	94
Focus Passage	Ecclesiastes 2:1-2,10,26

Simchah, derived from samach (rejoice, be glad), reflects several of the verb's meanings, occurring 10x with it. Simchah signifies joy (Gn 31:27), rejoicing (Neh 12:43), or shout of joy (1Sm 18:6). It connotes happiness (Jb 20:5), pleasure (Pr 21:17), enjoyment (Ec 8:15), celebration (Neh 8:12), and gratitude (Neh 12:44). Simchah appears 13x with sason ("joy, delight"), usually as gladness (Ps 51:8), and several times each with giyl ("rejoicing"; Is 16:10) and rinnah ("shout of joy, singing"; Zph 3:17). Simchah accompanied feasting (Est 9:17-19), harvest (Is 9:3), and especially music (21 vv.). It could arise from folly or wisdom (Pr 15:21,23). The adjective sameach (21x) describes people rejoicing (1Kg 1:40). It appears as joy (Dt 16:15) and joyful (Ps 113:9). It implies enjoying (oneself) (Est 5:14; Pr 2:14), taking pleasure (Ec 2:10), and being full of joy (Est 5:9). Carouser translates "sameach of heart" (Is 24:7).

in all my struggles. This was my reward for all my struggles.[a] [11] When I considered all that I had accomplished[A] and what I had labored to achieve, I found everything to be futile and a pursuit of the wind.[b] There was nothing to be gained under the sun.[c]

The Relative Value of Wisdom

[12] Then I turned to consider wisdom,[d] madness, and folly, for what will the man be like who comes after the king? He[B] will do what has already been done.[e] [13] And I realized that there is an advantage to wisdom over folly, like the advantage of light over darkness.[f]

[14]   The wise man has eyes in his head,
        but the fool walks in darkness.[g]

Yet I also knew that one fate comes to them both.[h] [15] So I said to myself, "What happens to the fool will also happen to me. Why then have I been overly wise?"[i] And I said to myself that this is also futile. [16] For, just like the fool, there is no lasting remembrance of the wise man,[j] since in the days to come both will be forgotten. How is it that the wise man dies just like the fool? [17] Therefore, I hated life because the work that was done under the sun was distressing to me. For everything is futile and a pursuit of the wind.

The Emptiness of Work

[18] I hated all my work that I labored at under the sun[k] because I must leave it to the man who comes after me.[l] [19] And who knows whether he will be a wise man or a fool?[m] Yet he will take over all my work that I labored at skillfully under the sun. This too is futile. [20] So I began to give myself over[C] to despair concerning all my work that I had labored at under the sun. [21] When there is a man whose work was done with wisdom, knowledge, and skill,[n] and he must give his portion to a man who has not worked for it, this too is futile and a great wrong. [22] For what does a man get with all his work and all his efforts[o] that he labors at under the sun? [23] For all his days are filled with grief, and his occupation is sorrowful;[p] even at night, his mind does not rest.[q] This too is futile.

[24] There is nothing better for man than to eat, drink, and enjoy[D,E] his work.[r] I have seen that even this is from God's hand,[s] [25] because who can eat and who can enjoy life[F] apart from Him?[G] [26] For to the man who is pleasing in His sight, He gives wisdom, knowledge, and joy,[t] but to the sinner He gives the task of gathering and accumulating in order to give to the one who is pleasing in God's sight.[u] This too is futile and a pursuit of the wind.[v]

Cross references

[a] 2:10 Ec 3:22; 5:18; 9:9
[b] 2:11 Ec 1:14; 2:22-23
[c] Ec 1:3; 3:9; 5:16
[d] 2:12 Ec 1:17
[e] Ec 1:9-10; 3:15
[f] 2:13 Ec 7:11-12,19; 9:18; 10:10
[g] 2:14 Pr 2:10-13; 1Jn 2:11
[h] Ps 49:10; Ec 3:19; 6:6; 7:2; 9:2-3
[i] 2:15 Ec 6:8,11; 7:16
[j] 2:16 Dt 32:26; 2Sm 18:18; Ec 1:11; 9:5
[k] 2:18 Ec 1:3; 2:11
[l] Ps 39:6; 49:10; Pr 13:22
[m] 2:19 Ezk 18:9-10
[n] 2:21 Ec 4:4
[o] 2:22 Ec 1:3; 2:11
[p] 2:23 Jb 5:7; 14:1
[q] Ps 127:2
[r] 2:24 Ec 2:3; 3:12-13,22; 5:18; 6:12; 8:15; 9:7; Is 56:12; Lk 12:19; 1Co 15:32; 1Tm 6:17
[s] Ec 3:13
[t] 2:26 Jb 32:8; Pr 2:6
[u] Jb 27:16-17; Pr 13:22; 28:8
[v] Ec 1:14

Footnotes

[A] 2:11 Lit all my works that my hands had done   [B] 2:12 Some Hb mss read They   [C] 2:20 Lit And I turned to cause my heart
[D] 2:24 Syr, Tg; MT reads There is no good in man who eats and drinks and enjoys   [E] 2:24 Lit and his soul sees good   [F] 2:25 LXX, Theod, Syr read can drink   [G] 2:25 Some Hb mss, LXX, Syr read me

Commentary

failed, but not for lack of trying. He **did not deny** himself any pleasure.

2:11 Not only did Solomon realize his treasures and accomplishments failed to give him satisfaction, he also understood that none would endure. Consider that virtually nothing remains of all of Solomon's architectural achievements—they were all doomed to disappear.

2:12-17 The quest for knowledge is a source of frustration and pain because it is futile; no human mind can solve the mysteries of life. Wisdom has some practical value, but it is subject to great limitations. The advantages it offers are temporary.

2:12 Solomon compared **wisdom, madness, and folly** to see if there was any real value in one way of living over another. The last part of this verse has some extraordinarily difficult Hebrew. Literally it says, "For what is the man who will come after the king whom they already made?" Most interpreters take the **king** to be Solomon himself and so read the text more or less as the HCSB has done. It is possible, however, that "whom they already made" refers to the creation of man in Gn 1:26, where God is referred to in the plural ("Let Us make man"). If so, then "the king" is not Solomon but Adam, and the point is that any **man** (in Hb the word is 'adam) **who comes after** Adam must learn to make moral choices involving wisdom and folly. Adam started this when he ate from the tree of the knowledge of good and evil. How can a man who comes after Adam not wrestle with these things?

2:13-15 The Teacher did not deny that wisdom is a good

thing. The **fool** will fall into all kinds of troubles because of the poor decisions he makes. This refers to the kind of practical wisdom and folly that Proverbs describes. The fool may be lazy, quarrelsome, not handle money well, or fall into promiscuity. All these things bring about ruin. On the other hand, wisdom can do nothing to save a person from death, the greatest calamity of all. One person may be prudent and another foolish, but **one fate comes to them both**.

2:16 The **wise man** cannot even count on having a legacy that outlasts that of the **fool**.

2:18-23 In this section Ecclesiastes returns to the subject of wealth and pleasure. But unlike verses 1-11, which focus on the impossibility of finding satisfaction in riches, this text focuses on the absurdity of devoting one's life to acquiring wealth only to leave it all behind to someone else. A person may toil ceaselessly for wealth, so that **his days are filled with grief**, but he must lose it all to someone who had none of his skill and who did not work for it.

2:24-26 The words **There is nothing better for man than to eat, drink, and enjoy his work** must be understood in context. Ecclesiastes is preoccupied with how death nullifies all of man's accomplishments. It emphasizes that our days under the sun are limited, and thus that it is a tragedy to waste those days with excessive labor and grief. There are obviously many more things to a good life than just eating, drinking, and enjoying one's work, and Ecclesiastes does not suggest that we abandon ourselves to pleasure-seeking or our careers, but we ought to recognize that life is short and not miss out on its basic pleasures. These, too, are a gift of God.

The Mystery of Time

3 There is an occasion for everything,
and a time for every activity
under heaven:[a]

2 a time to give birth and a time to die;[b]
a time to plant and a time to uproot;[A]

3 a time to kill and a time to heal;
a time to tear down and a time to build;

4 a time to weep and a time to laugh;[c]
a time to mourn and a time to dance;[d]

5 a time to throw stones and a time
to gather stones;[e]
a time to embrace and a time
to avoid embracing;[f]

6 a time to search and a time to count
as lost;
a time to keep and a time
to throw away;

7 a time to tear and a time to sew;
a time to be silent and a time to speak;[g]

8 a time to love and a time to hate;
a time for war and a time for peace.[h]

Cross-references:
[a]3:1 Ec 3:17; 8:6
[b]3:2 Jb 14:5; Heb 9:27
[c]3:4 Rm 12:15
[d]Ex 15:20
[e]3:5 2Kg 3:19,25; Is 5:2
[f]1Co 7:5
[g]3:7 Am 5:13; 1Co 14:26-32
[h]3:8 Mt 5:9; 10:34
[i]3:9 Ec 1:3
[j]3:10 Ec 1:13; 2:26
[k]3:11 Gn 1:31
[l]Jb 5:9; Ec 7:23; 8:17; Rm 11:33
[m]3:13 Ec 2:24; 5:19
[n]3:14 Rv 22:18-19
[o]Ex 7:5; Ezk 36:23
[p]3:15 Ec 1:9; 6:10
[q]3:16 Ec 4:1; 5:8; 8:9
[r]3:17 Ec 11:9; Mt 16:27; Rm 2:6-10; 2Th 1:6-9

9 What does the worker gain from his struggles?[i] 10 I have seen the task that God has given •people to keep them occupied.[j] 11 He has made everything appropriate[B] in its time.[k] He has also put eternity in their hearts,[C] but man cannot discover the work God has done from beginning to end.[l] 12 I know that there is nothing better for them than to rejoice and enjoy the[D] good life. 13 It is also the gift of God whenever anyone eats, drinks, and enjoys all his efforts.[m] 14 I know that all God does will last forever; there is no adding to it or taking from it.[n] God works so that people will be in awe of Him.[o] 15 Whatever is, has already been,[p] and whatever will be, already is. God repeats what has passed.[E]

The Mystery of Injustice and Death

16 I also observed under the sun: there is wickedness at the place of judgment and there is wickedness at the place of righteousness.[q] 17 I said to myself, "God will judge the righteous and the wicked,[r] since there is a time

---

[A]3:2 Lit uproot what is planted   [B]3:11 Or beautiful   [C]3:11 Or has put a sense of past and future into their minds, or has placed ignorance in their hearts   [D]3:12 Lit his   [E]3:15 Or God calls the past to account, or God seeks what is past, or God seeks the persecuted; lit God seeks the pursued

---

3:1-11 These verses, the most famous text in Ecclesiastes, must be read from the context of the fundamental claim of the book: that we are mortals, doomed to perish, and that our work will perish with us. No human work is eternal, and our activities, whether building or tearing down, must change as the situation dictates. We naturally prefer to stay on the positive side of the list—to laugh rather than to weep, to love rather than to hate, and to have peace rather than war—but as long as we live in a world of change, conflict, and death, we must accept the fact that we cannot have unchanging bliss. Even so, as verse 11 says, everything is "appropriate in its time." Mourning and separation are painful, but there is a time when it is right and even beautiful to mourn. We must accept the fundamental fact of mortality: we are creatures who live in time. We must respond appropriately to the seasons of life as they come.

3:5 The meaning of throwing or gathering **stones** is uncertain. It may refer to clearing a field for planting versus building a wall, or spoiling a field (2Kg 3:25) versus clearing it (Is 5:2). A rabbinical tradition takes it to be a euphemism for participating in or refraining from sexual relations.

3:11 The fact that God **has also put eternity in their hearts** tells us that although we are creatures of time, we are not like the animals, who are fully and exclusively creatures of time. God made us as hybrids, so to speak, in that we are temporal but we have an inner longing for eternity. We can never be fully at peace in this life because, although we are mortal, we yearn for immortality.

3:12-14 The fact that we are creatures of time is another reason to enjoy the days we have. Giving ourselves to excessive mourning and toil is as wrong as indulging in excessive laughter and dancing.

3:15 The phrase **God repeats what has passed** is literally, "God seeks the pursued" or "God seeks the persecuted." Such a translation suggests that God cares about and seeks

out those who are harassed and oppressed. This anticipates the text on injustice that follows (vv. 16-17).

3:16-17 An absurdity of life is that where there ought to be

"A time to dance" (3:4). Jewish men dancing during a private ceremony in the Court of the Men at the Wailing Wall in Jerusalem.

for every activity and every work."[a] [18]I said to myself, "This happens concerning people, so that God may test them and they may see for themselves that they are like animals."[b] [19]For the fate of people and the fate of animals is the same.[c] As one dies, so dies the other; they all have the same breath. People have no advantage over animals since everything is futile. [20]All are going to the same place; all come from dust, and all return to dust.[d] [21]Who knows if the spirit of people rises upward and the spirit of animals goes downward to the earth? [22]I have seen that there is nothing better than for a person to enjoy his activities[e] because that is his reward. For who can enable him to see what will happen after he dies?[A,f]

4 Again, I observed all the acts of oppression being done under the sun.[g] Look at the tears of those who are oppressed; they have no one to comfort them. Power is with those who oppress them; they have no one to comfort them. [2]So I admired the dead,[h] who have already died, more than the living, who are still alive. [3]But better than either of them is the one who has not yet existed,[i] who has not seen the evil activity that is done under the sun.

The Loneliness of Wealth

[4]I saw that all labor and all skillful work is

a 3:17 Ec 3:1
b 3:18 Ps 49:12,20; 73:22
c 3:19 Ec 9:12
d 3:20 Gn 3:19; Ec 12:7
e 3:22 Ec 2:24
f Ec 2:18; 6:12; 8:7; 10:14
g 4:1 Jb 35:9; Ec 3:16; 5:8
h 4:2 Jb 3:11-26
i 4:3 Ec 6:3; Lk 23:29
j 4:4 1Sm 18:9; Ec 2:21; Ac 13:45; 2Co 12:20
k Ec 1:14
l 4:5 Pr 6:10; 24:33
m Is 9:20
n 4:6 Pr 15:16-17
o 4:8 Pr 27:20; Ec 1:8; 5:10
p 4:11 1Kg 1:1-4
q 4:13 Ec 9:15
r 4:14 Gn 41:14,41-43

due to a man's jealousy of his friend.[j] This too is futile and a pursuit of the wind.[k]

5 The fool folds his arms[l]
   and consumes his own flesh.[m]
6 Better one handful with rest
   than two handfuls with effort and a
   pursuit of the wind.[n]

[7]Again, I saw futility under the sun: [8]There is a person without a companion,[B] without even a son or brother, and though there is no end to all his struggles, his eyes are still not content with riches.[o] "So who am I struggling for," he asks, "and depriving myself from good?" This too is futile and a miserable task. [9]Two are better than one because they have a good reward for their efforts. [10]For if either falls, his companion can lift him up; but pity the one who falls without another to lift him up. [11]Also, if two lie down together, they can keep warm; but how can one person alone keep warm?[p] [12]And if someone overpowers one person, two can resist him. A cord of three strands is not easily broken.

[13]Better is a poor but wise youth than an old but foolish king who no longer pays attention to warnings.[q] [14]For he came from prison to be king,[r] even though he was born poor in his kingdom. [15]I saw all the living, who move

---

A 3:22 Lit after him   B 4:8 Lit person, but there is not a second,

---

justice in the law courts, there is often corruption, oppression, and a perversion of justice. Even so, we may take comfort in the fact that God has appointed a final day for judging the world.

3:18-22 These verses are disturbing to Christian readers because they appear to deny the hope of eternal life. What they actually deny is that people *within themselves* have the power to transcend death. By contrast, Egyptian religion was so certain that people were immortal that the ancient Egyptians were obsessed with preparing their tombs for the afterlife. According to the Bible, death is an enemy (1Co 15:26); it is not merely a doorway to a new level of existence. God's people will experience eternal life only because they are known by God and will be raised by His power. Our hope is based entirely on the resurrection of Christ. The Teacher of Ecclesiastes wanted people to take death seriously so they would use well the time they had under the sun. It does not deny that God can raise us from the dead.

4:1-3 Returning to the topic of **oppression** (see note at 3:16-17), Ecclesiastes asserts that political corruption is terrible precisely because it does not allow common people to do the thing the book recommends—to enjoy their days **under the sun**. Oppression is innately wrong, and it also deprives its victims of the freedom to partake of the ordinary pleasures of life.

4:3 This verse is "hyperbole," the use of exaggeration for rhetorical effect. Someone who says, "I wish I had never been born," rarely means it literally. When Ecclesiastes declares that **one who has not yet existed** is the most for-

tunate of all, it is merely saying in an emphatic way that the corruption practiced **under the sun** is a cause for great sorrow.

4:4-8 Ecclesiastes returns to the theme of wealth, describing how foolish it is to spend one's life in the pursuit of riches. First, Solomon declares that people **work** hard not out of love for the task but out of a desire to do better than their peers. The work and the wealth it brings give no satisfaction; there is only the pathetic pleasure of beating others in a race for success. Second, a conventional proverb declares that laziness brings on poverty. Against this, verse 6 gives a counter lesson—that it is better to have little with peace than to have much with a constant hunger for more. A strong work ethic is not wrong, but it needs to be balanced with an appreciation for the joys of life. In verse 8, the example of the person who works ceaselessly to acquire but who has no one with whom to share it shows how sad is the life that is governed by a desire for more.

4:9-12 Friendship is the theme of this section. The advantages of friends are that they help one another get work done, that one friend sustains another when disaster strikes, that they give comfort to one another against the bitterness of life, and that they protect one another from enemies. Interestingly, friendship is one area of life that Ecclesiastes never calls "futile."

4:11-12 These verses do not refer to lying together sexually. It is an image of travelers sleeping outdoors in the desert who must huddle together to **keep warm**. The fact that

about under the sun, follow[A] a second youth who succeeds him. [16]There is no limit to all the •people who were before them, yet those who come later will not rejoice in him. This too is futile and a pursuit of the wind.[a]

Caution in God's Presence

5 [B]Guard your steps when you go to the house of God. Better to draw near in obedience than to offer the sacrifice as fools do,[b] for they ignorantly do wrong. [2C]Do not be hasty to speak, and do not be impulsive to make a speech before God. God is in heaven and you are on earth, so let your words be few.[c] [3]For dreams result from much work and a fool's voice from many words.[d] [4]When you make a vow to God,[e] don't delay fulfilling it, because He does not delight in fools. Fulfill what you vow. [5]Better that you do not vow than that you vow and not fulfill it.[f] [6]Do not let your mouth bring •guilt on you,[g] and do not say in the presence of the messenger that it was a mistake.[h] Why should God be angry with your words and destroy the work of your hands? [7]For many dreams bring futility, so do many words.[i] Therefore, •fear God.

The Realities of Wealth

[8]If you see oppression of the poor[j] and perversion of justice and righteousness in the province, don't be astonished at the situation,[k] because one official protects another of-

Cross references
a 4:16 Ec 1:14
b 5:1 1Sm 15:22; Mt 5:23-24
c 5:2 Pr 10:19; Mt 6:7
d 5:3 Jb 11:2
e 5:4 Nm 30:2; Dt 6:13; 23:21-22; Pr 20:25
f 5:5 Pr 20:25; Mt 5:33-37; Ac 5:4; Jms 5:12
g 5:6 Jdg 11:30-31,34
h Nm 15:25
i 5:7 Ec 6:11
j 5:8 Ec 4:1
k 1Pt 4:12
l 5:9 Pr 27:23-27
m 5:13 Ec 6:1-2
n 5:15 Jb 1:21
o 5:16 Ec 1:3
p Pr 11:29
q 5:17 Ps 127:2
r 5:18 Ec 2:24
s Ec 2:10
t 5:19 2Ch 1:12

ficial, and higher officials protect them. [9]The profit from the land is taken by all; the king is served by the field.[D,l]

[10]The one who loves money is never satisfied with money, and whoever loves wealth is never satisfied with income. This too is futile. [11]When good things increase, the ones who consume them multiply; what, then, is the profit to the owner, except to gaze at them with his eyes? [12]The sleep of the worker is sweet, whether he eats little or much, but the abundance of the rich permits him no sleep.

[13]There is a sickening tragedy I have seen under the sun: wealth kept by its owner to his harm.[m] [14]That wealth was lost in a bad venture, so when he fathered a son, he was empty-handed. [15]As he came from his mother's womb, so he will go again, naked as he came;[n] he will take nothing for his efforts that he can carry in his hands. [16]This too is a sickening tragedy: exactly as he comes, so he will go. What does the one gain[o] who struggles for the wind?[p] [17]What is more, he eats in darkness all his days,[q] with much sorrow, sickness, and anger.

[18]Here is what I have seen to be good:[r] it is appropriate to eat, drink, and experience good in all the labor one does under the sun during the few days of his life God has given him, because that is his reward.[s] [19]God has also given riches and wealth to every man,[t] and He has

---

[A]4:15 Lit with   [B]5:1 Ec 4:17 in Hb   [C]5:2 Ec 5:1 in Hb   [D]5:9 Or *An advantage for the land in every respect is a king for a cultivated field*; Hb obscure

---

verse 12 asserts that **three** are better than **two** makes it clear that these are friends, not lovers.

4:13-16 This section illustrates how fleeting political power is. There are two people here. The first person is an old **king**, who in his youth was **poor** but he rose to power through skill and perseverance. This king is now **old but foolish**. He has been in power for so long that he has lost touch with changing political circumstances. The second person is a **youth** who, possessing the political skills the old king once had but lost, is now ready and able to usurp him (this is the youth of v. 13, who is called the **second youth** in v. 15). But even though the second youth is successful for a time and pleases the crowd, he will also eventually get old, lose touch, and be abandoned. He is just the latest in a long line of kings who come and go. Political power and popularity are by nature fleeting.

5:1-7 This passage deals with religious behavior, and it warns that we should not try to impress God. It is in two parallel parts. First, positively, come to the **house of God** in humble **obedience**; negatively, don't try to impress God with big sacrifices and big vows; and then there is a proverb that big **dreams** and **many words** come from an overworked fool. Second, positively, fulfill your **vow**; negatively, don't make a vow you cannot keep; and then a proverb, **many dreams** and **many words** are futile, so it is better to **fear God**. The foundation of these teachings is our mortality: **God is in heaven and you are on earth**. Because we are

weak, small, and prone to fail, we should give up on trying to impress God with vows, gifts, and promises. We cannot impress Him; our place is to be humble and obedient. This text calls on us to depend on the grace of God and not on our religious deeds.

5:8-9 Once again, the Teacher looks at political matters. In these verses he tells us not to be surprised at corruption. Layers of governmental bureaucracy are supposed to insure that every official is accountable to others and is behaving properly, but all these layers of government can make for more layers of corruption. If that is the case, should we abandon the idea of government and embrace anarchy? No. Government, although never free from corruption, is not something we can do without. Verse 9 could be translated, "And among everything a land's advantage is this: a king for a cultivated field." That is, the **king** is a benefit to agriculture (which represents the economy). For example, the king protected his people from enemies, maintained irrigation canals, and settled property disputes. Government is necessary, but corruption is inescapable.

5:10–6:6 This is a lengthy passage on wealth. It makes the point that a life spent pursuing wealth is futile. Ecclesiastes 5:10-20 gives us a series of seven reasons not to devote ourselves to getting rich. First, seeking wealth is an endless quest, because those who want to get rich never feel that they have enough (v. 10). Second, if you get rich, you attract people who care nothing for you but just want your

allowed him to enjoy them, take his reward, and rejoice in his labor.[a] This is a gift of God,[b] [20] for he does not often consider the days of his life because God keeps him occupied with the joy of his heart.

6 Here is a tragedy I have observed under the sun,[c] and it weighs heavily on humanity:[A] [2] God gives a man riches, wealth, and honor[d] so that he lacks nothing of all he desires for himself,[e] but God does not allow him to enjoy them. Instead, a stranger will enjoy them. This is futile and a sickening tragedy. [3] A man may father a hundred children and live many years. No matter how long he lives,[B] if he is not satisfied by good things and does not even have a proper burial,[f] I say that a stillborn child is better off than he.[g] [4] For he comes in futility and he goes in darkness, and his name is shrouded in darkness. [5] Though a stillborn child does not see the sun and is not conscious, it has more rest than he. [6] And if he lives a thousand years twice, but does not experience happiness, do not both go to the same place?

7   All man's labor is for his stomach,[C,h] yet the appetite is never satisfied.

[8] What advantage then does the wise man have over the fool?[i] What advantage is there for the poor person who knows how to conduct himself before others? [9] Better what the eyes see than wandering desire.[j] This too is futile and a pursuit of the wind.[k]

[10] Whatever exists was given its name long ago,[D,l] and it is known what man is. But he is not able to contend with the One stronger than he.[m] [11] For when there are many words, they increase futility.[n] What is the advantage for man? [12] For who knows what is good for man in life, in the few days of his futile life that he spends like a shadow?[o] Who can tell man what will happen after him under the sun?

Wise Sayings

7   A good name is better than
       fine perfume,[p]
       and the day of one's death than the day
       of one's birth.[q]
2   It is better to go to a house
       of mourning
       than to go to a house of feasting,
       since that is the end of all mankind,
       and the living should take it to heart.[r]

Cross references:
a 5:19 Ec 6:2
b Ec 3:13
c 6:1 Ec 5:13
d 6:2 1Kg 3:13
e Ps 17:14; 73:7
f 6:3 Is 14:20; Jr 8:2; 22:19
g Jb 3:16; Ec 4:3
h 6:7 Pr 16:26
i 6:8 Ec 2:15
j 6:9 Ec 11:9
k Ec 1:14
l 6:10 Gn 2:19; Ec 1:9–10; 3:15
m Jb 9:32; Is 45:9
n 6:11 Pr 10:19; Mt 6:7
o 6:12 Ec 3:22
p 7:1 Pr 22:1; Ezk 36:21
q Ec 4:2
r 7:2 Ps 90:12

A 6:1 Or it is common among men   B 6:3 Lit how many years   C 6:7 Lit mouth   D 6:10 Lit name already

money (v. 11a). Third, once you acquire much money, you can't do anything with it but look at it (v. 11b). Fourth, working people are not full of anxieties and they **sleep** well; the rich are awake at night worrying about their investments (v. 12). Fifth, wealthy people live in a world of high-stakes financial deals. They can lose their money in bad business deals just when they need the money for their families. In the world of finance, men put their families at risk (vv. 13–14). Sixth, at death you lose it all. You can't take it with you (vv. 15–16). Seventh, the quest for riches is hard and bitter, and days are spent in tedious and vexing work. It is far better to get by with fewer things and less money and be able to enjoy life (vv. 17–20).

6:1-6 A person who has money but who derives no real joy from his privileges is a pitiful wretch. His money serves no purpose but to be passed on to others. Ecclesiastes again wants us to see that because life is short, it should be enjoyed. A life spent huddled over work or eaten away by anxieties is wasted.

6:2-3 These verses describe typical measures of prosperity: **wealth**, honors, **children**, and long life (in ancient societies, having many children was a measure of success). But none of these is any good if a person is not able to **enjoy** them.

6:3-6 These verses use a **stillborn child** for rhetorical purposes, to make the point that a life without joy, no matter how rich a person may be, is wasted. This text should not be used for attempting to discern what happens to the souls of stillborn children.

6:7-9 This passage contains three proverbs, and it makes the transition from a major discussion of wealth (5:10–6:6) to a major discussion of wisdom and death (6:10–7:4). The proverbs teach that **appetite** is the thing that drives us, but it **is never satisfied**, that wisdom cannot save us from our appetite or from poverty, and that it is important to be satisfied with what we have. These proverbs can relate equally well to the desire for riches or for knowledge. Both are important in their places, but neither is the key to life.

6:10-7:4 The main point of this passage is given in 6:10: the fundamental truths of life are well **known** and that there is nothing to be added. This means that the quest for great knowledge is folly, since no one will find out something that

tovah

Hebrew Pronunciation	[toh VAH]
HCSB Translation	goodness, well-being, happiness
Uses in Ecclesiastes	7
Uses in the OT	67
Focus Passage	Ecclesiastes 6:3,6

Feminine *tovah* connotes *goodness* (Ps 65:11) more often than masculine *tov* and frequently contrasts with *ra'ah* ("evil"). It means *good*, *good things*, and *good work* or *deed*. *Tovah* indicates *friendship*, *grace*, *prosperity*, *happiness*, *well-being*, or *favor*. It suggests *well* (Jdg 9:16), *kindly*, or *favorably*. The verb *tov* (44x) means *be better* (Sg 4:10), *beautiful*, *favorable*, or *well off*. It connotes *prosper* (Dt 5:33) or *be better*. Infinitives signify *good* or *better*; causative verbs mean *do well* (1Kg 8:18). *Be good* "in the eyes" or "before" indicates *please* (Nm 24:1), *meet/find approval*, *seem right* or *good*, *be agreed on*, or *prefer*. With "heart" as subject, one *feels good* (Est 1:10) or *is in a good mood*. *Tuv* (32x), the most common word for *goodness* (Ex 33:19), signifies *goods*, *the best*, *best products*, *bounty*, and *prosperity*. It implies *good*, *glad*, *cheerful* (Dt 28:47), *thriving*, *lovely*, and *fine*.

3 Grief is better than laughter,
  for when a face is sad, a heart
    may be glad.[a]
4 The heart of the wise is in a house
    of mourning,
  but the heart of fools is in a house
    of pleasure.
5 It is better to listen to rebuke
    from a wise person
  than to listen to the song of fools,[b]
6 for like the crackling of burning thorns
    under the pot,[c]
  so is the laughter of the fool.
  This too is futile.
7 Surely, the practice of extortion turns
    a wise person into a fool,[d]
  and a bribe destroys the mind.[e]
8 The end of a matter is better
    than its beginning;
  a patient spirit is better
    than a proud spirit.[f]
9 Don't let your spirit rush to be angry,
  for anger abides in the heart of fools.[g]
10 Don't say, "Why were the former days
    better than these?"[h]
  since it is not wise of you to ask this.
11 Wisdom is as good as an inheritance
  and an advantage to those who see
    the sun,

Cross references:
a 7:3 Pr 14:13
b 7:5 Pr 13:1
c 7:6 Ps 58:9; 118:12
d 7:7 Ec 4:1
e Dt 16:19; Pr 17:8
f 7:8 Pr 14:29
g 7:9 Pr 14:17; Jms 1:19
h 7:10 Jdg 6:13
i 7:12 Pr 3:18
j 7:13 Ec 3:11
k Ec 1:15
l 7:14 Ec 3:22
m Lm 3:38
n 7:15 Ec 6:12; 9:9
o Ec 8:14
p Ec 8:12-13
q 7:16 Ec 2:15; Rm 12:3
r 7:17 Jb 22:16; Ps 55:23; Pr 10:27
s 7:19 Ec 9:13-18

12 because wisdom is protection as money
    is protection,
  and the advantage of knowledge
  is that wisdom preserves the life
    of its owner.[i]
13 Consider the work of God,[j]
  for who can straighten out
  what He has made crooked?[k]

14 In the day of prosperity be joyful,[l] but in the day of adversity, consider: God has made the one as well as the other,[m] so that man cannot discover anything that will come after him.

Avoiding Extremes

15 In my futile life[A] I have seen everything:[n] there is a righteous man who perishes in spite of his righteousness,[o] and there is a wicked man who lives long in spite of his evil.[p] 16 Don't be excessively righteous, and don't be overly wise.[q] Why should you destroy yourself? 17 Don't be excessively wicked, and don't be foolish. Why should you die before your time?[r] 18 It is good that you grasp the one and do not let the other slip from your hand. For the one who •fears God will end up with both of them.

19 Wisdom makes the wise man stronger
    than ten rulers of a city.[s]

A 7:15 Lit days

---

changes the basic truths of life. Thus, a person should not prattle on about supposedly new insights (6:11). Our understanding is limited, as is shown by our inability to predict the future (6:12). Therefore, the truly **wise** give attention to the fact of **death** (7:1-4). Funerals should sober us to the reality of death and encourage us to live well and happily.

7:5-6 Fools can neither give nor take good advice. The **song of fools** stands for a life of carefree merrymaking. The pain of a **rebuke** is better than the encouragement to party that fools offer. Also, fools receive wisdom with smirking **laughter**. The image of **thorns under the pot** indicates that fools are prickly to those who try to deal with them but ultimately are useless, just as thorns are good for nothing but burning.

7:7-9 In these three maxims, the main focus is on how the **wise person** confronts political reality. First, corruption is pervasive and can bring anyone down; one should beware of it. Second, one should not judge by first appearances; those who are winning now may someday come to ruin. One should be **patient** and understand that virtue is proved right in **the end**, and so flee temptations to bribery. Third, abiding **anger** over a current situation in life shows you are a fool.

7:10 People see the evil in their own times and wrongly presume that earlier times were better.

7:11-14 Ecclesiastes acknowledges that people do need money. In discouraging the pursuit of riches, it does not say that **money** is unnecessary or evil. At the same time, we should accept with patience whatever God allots to us.

7:15-18 These verses seem to say that a little sinning is

acceptable. That is not the point; the passage is about an extreme zeal for religious duties that makes life unbearably harsh (an example would be constant fasting). In this context, **excessively righteous** refers to being unreasonably demanding on yourself about moral or religious duties.

7:19 Wisdom is a good thing, but a person can be overly zealous about attaining it and end up disappointed (v. 23).

---

matsa'

Hebrew Pronunciation	[mah TSAH]
HCSB Translation	find, discover
Uses in Ecclesiastes	17
Uses in the OT	457
Focus Passage	Ecclesiastes 7:14,24,26-29

Matsa' denotes find (Gn 8:9), discover, expose, and find or figure out. Trials happen or come to (Dt 31:21), confront, afflict, overtake, or overwhelm. Matsa' means encounter (Ps 116:3), meet, see, reach, catch up with, or spread to. People obtain (Lv 25:26), acquire, get, reap, receive, take, or feel (Jr 10:18). They catch (Jr 2:34), seize, or reach out to seize. "Finding favor" involves pleasing (Nm 11:15), allowing, granting, approving, liking, or indulging. "Find hands" implies ability to act (Ps 76:5). "Hand finds" signifies have sufficient means (Lv 12:8) or afford. Passive verbs indicate be, be present (Est 1:5), live (Jr 5:26), or be enough. They suggest be verified (Est 2:23) or traced to. "Be found with" connotes belong to (Dt 21:17), possess, or have. The participle entails surviving (2Kg 19:4) or remaining. Causative verbs denote bring (Lv 9:12), hand or turn over, and cause to happen.

20 There is certainly no righteous man
on the earth
who does good and never sins.[a]

21 Don't pay attention[A] to everything •people
say, or you may hear your servant cursing
you,[b] 22 for you know that many times you
yourself have cursed others.

What the Teacher Found

23 I have tested all this by wisdom. I resolved,
"I will be wise," but it was beyond me. 24 What
exists is beyond reach and very deep.[c] Who can
discover it? 25 I turned my thoughts to know,
explore, and seek wisdom[d] and an explanation
for things, and to know that wickedness is stupidity and folly is madness. 26 And I find more
bitter than death[e] the woman who is a trap,[f]
her heart a net, and her hands chains. The
one who pleases God will escape her, but the
sinner will be captured by her. 27 "Look," says
the Teacher, "I have discovered this by adding
one thing to another to find out the explanation, 28 which my soul continually searches for
but does not find: among a thousand people I
have found one true man, but among all these
I have not found a true woman.[g] 29 Only see
this: I have discovered that God made people
upright,[h] but they pursued many schemes."

Wisdom, Authorities, and Inequities

8 Who is like the wise person, and who
knows the interpretation of a matter?
A man's wisdom brightens his face, and the
sternness of his face is changed.[i]

2 Keep[B] the king's command because of your
oath made before God.[j] 3 Do not be in a hurry;
leave his presence,[k] and don't persist in a bad
cause, since he will do whatever he wants.
4 For the king's word is authoritative, and who
can say to him, "What are you doing?"[l] 5 The
one who keeps a command will not experience
anything harmful,[m] and a wise heart knows
the right time and procedure. 6 For every activity there is a right time and procedure,[n] even
though man's troubles are heavy on him. 7 Yet
no one knows what will happen[o] because who
can tell him what will happen? 8 No one has
authority over the wind[C] to restrain it,[p] and
there is no authority over the day of death;[q]
there is no furlough in battle, and wickedness
will not allow those who practice it to escape.
9 All this I have seen, applying my mind to all
the work that is done under the sun, at a time
when one man has authority over another to
his harm.

10 In such circumstances, I saw the wicked
buried. They came and went from the holy
place,[r] and they were praised[D] in the city
where they did so. This too is futile. 11 Because
the sentence against a criminal act is not carried out quickly,[s] the heart of •people is filled
with the desire to commit crime. 12 Although
a sinner commits crime a hundred times and
prolongs his life,[t] yet I also know that it will
go well with God-fearing people,[u] for they are
reverent before Him. 13 However, it will not
go well with the wicked,[v] and they will not
lengthen their days like a shadow,[w] for they
are not reverent before God.

14 There is a futility that is done on the earth:
there are righteous people who get what the
actions of the wicked deserve,[x] and there are
wicked people who get what the actions of the
righteous deserve.[y] I say that this too is futile.
15 So I commended enjoyment because there
is nothing better for man under the sun than
to eat, drink, and enjoy himself,[z] for this will
accompany him in his labor during the days of
his life that God gives him under the sun.

16 When I applied my mind to know wisdom[aa]

[a] **7:20** 1Kg 8:46; Rm 3:23
[b] **7:21** Pr 30:10
[c] **7:24** Rm 11:33
[d] **7:25** Ec 1:15,17
[e] **7:26** Pr 5:4
[f] Pr 6:25
[g] **7:28** 1Kg 11:3
[h] **7:29** Gn 1:27
[i] **8:1** Dt 28:50
[j] **8:2** Ex 22:11; 2Sm 21:7; Ezk 17:18
[k] **8:3** Ec 10:4
[l] **8:4** Jb 9:12; Dn 4:35
[m] **8:5** Rm 13:3
[n] **8:6** Ec 3:1,17
[o] **8:7** Ec 3:22; 6:12; 9:12; 10:14
[p] **8:8** Ps 148:8; Pr 30:4; Mk 4:39
[q] Jn 10:18; 2Tm 1:10
[r] **8:10** Ec 9:5
[s] **8:11** Rm 2:4; 2Pt 3:9
[t] **8:12** Ec 7:15
[u] Dt 12:25; Ps 37:11; Pr 1:33; Is 3:10
[v] **8:13** Is 3:11
[w] Jb 14:2; Ec 6:12
[x] **8:14** Ec 7:15
[y] Jb 21:7; Ps 73:3; Jr 12:1
[z] **8:15** Ec 2:24
[aa] **8:16** Ec 1:13-14

[A] **7:21** Lit *Don't give your heart* [B] **8:2** Some Hb mss, LXX, Vg, Tg, Syr; other Hb mss read *I, keep* [C] **8:8** Or *life-breath* [D] **8:10** Some Hb mss, LXX, Aq, Theod, Sym; other Hb mss read *forgotten*

7:20-24 Awareness that everyone has sinned should lead to forbearance and patience with others.

7:25-29 This passage seems to say that women are more evil than men. However, it needs to be understood in its context; this was a male sage giving advice to other male sages and to men generally. Because Ecclesiastes was originally intended for men (few women were literate), it predominantly reflects the man's point of view. Furthermore, this text is a reflection on the fall into sin, alluded to in verse 29. The point is that because of sin, the fundamental relationship between male and female, especially husband and wife, is broken (as implied in Gn 3:16). This is why men often have better friendships with other men (in the sense that they encourage and accept one another) than they have with their own wives. The phrase **I have not found a true woman** does not mean that women are intrinsically evil, but that Solomon, as a man, could not find a woman with whom his relationship was without guile, tension, or conflict. He in fact also found that such honest friendships with men were extremely rare (**I have found one true man**). If Ecclesiastes were written more for women, it would reflect their point of view, stating that many women have more caring relationships with other women than they have with their husbands. As it stands, both genders benefit from the God-given wisdom found in this book.

8:1-6 A **wise person** respects authority and knows how to approach an authority figure tactfully and at the right moment. No matter how bad things seem (**even though man's troubles are heavy on him**), approach a person in authority in the right way and at the right time.

8:7-8 We mortals are by nature frail, limited in our understanding, and incapable of predicting the future. Ultimately, everything is in God's hands.

and to observe the activity that is done on the earth (even though one's eyes do not close in sleep day or night), [17]I observed all the work of God and concluded that man is unable to discover the work that is done under the sun. Even though a man labors hard to explore it, he cannot find it;[a] even if the wise man claims to know it, he is unable to discover it.

Enjoy Life Despite Death

9 Indeed, I took all this to heart and explained it all: the righteous, the wise, and their works are in God's hands.[b] *People don't know whether to expect love or hate. Everything lies ahead of them. [2]Everything is the same for everyone:[c] there is one fate for the righteous and the wicked,[d] for the good and the bad,[A] for the *clean and the *unclean, for the one who sacrifices and the one who does not sacrifice. As it is for the good, so it is for the sinner; as for the one who takes an oath, so for the one who fears an oath. [3]This is an evil in all that is done under the sun: there is one fate for everyone. In addition, the hearts of people are full of evil, and madness is in their hearts while they live[e]—after that they go to the dead. [4]But there is hope for whoever is joined[B] with all the living, since a live dog is better than a dead lion. [5]For the living know that they will die, but the dead don't know anything. There is no longer a reward for them because the memory of them is forgotten.[f] [6]Their love, their hate, and their

envy have already disappeared, and there is no longer a portion for them in all that is done under the sun.

[7]Go, eat your bread with pleasure, and drink your wine with a cheerful heart, for God has already accepted your works.[g] [8]Let your clothes be white all the time, and never let oil be lacking on your head.[h] [9]Enjoy life with the wife you love all the days of your fleeting[c] life,[i] which has been given to you under the sun, all your fleeting days. For that is your portion in life and in your struggle[j] under the sun. [10]Whatever your hands find to do, do with all your strength,[k] because there is no work, planning, knowledge, or wisdom[l] in *Sheol where you are going.

The Limitations of Wisdom

[11]Again I saw under the sun that the race is not to the swift,[m] or the battle to the strong,[n] or bread to the wise, or riches to the discerning, or favor to the skillful; rather, time and chance happen to all of them. [12]For man certainly does not know his time:[o] like fish caught in a cruel net or like birds caught in a trap,[p] so people are trapped in an evil time[q] as it suddenly falls on them.[r]

[13]I have observed that this also is wisdom under the sun, and it is significant to me: [14]There was a small city with few men in it. A great king came against it, surrounded it, and built large siege works against it. [15]Now a poor wise man was found in the city,[s] and

[a]8:17 Ec 3:11; 7:25-29; 11:5
[b]9:1 Dt 33:3
[c]9:2 Jb 9:22
[d]Ec 2:14
[e]9:3 Ec 1:17
[f]9:5 Ec 2:16
[g]9:7 Ec 2:24; 3:13; 5:18; 8:15
[h]9:8 Ps 23:5
[i]9:9 Ec 6:12; 7:15
[j]Ec 2:10
[k]9:10 Rm 12:11; Col 3:23
[l]Ec 9:5
[m]9:11 Am 2:14-15
[n]2Ch 20:15
[o]9:12 Ec 8:7
[p]Pr 7:23
[q]Pr 29:6
[r]Lk 21:34-35
[s]9:15 Ec 4:13

A9:2 LXX, Aq, Syr, Vg; MT omits *and the bad*　B9:4 Alt Hb tradition reads *chosen*　C9:9 Or *futile*

8:9–9:1 This passage focuses on God's governance of the world; it struggles with the question of why evil sometimes seems to triumph. Examples of this include: cruel people rising to power (8:9), wicked people being honored in public (8:10), wicked people avoiding punishment (8:11), and good people suffering while the wicked do well (8:14). Against this, Ecclesiastes affirms that God does set things right (8:12-13) and asserts that a person should enjoy life and not always brood over evil (8:15). More than that, we must acknowledge that God alone knows what He is doing and why He does it, and we must be content to let Him rule the world (8:16–9:1).

9:2-6 When Ecclesiastes says **there is one fate for the righteous and the wicked**, it means physical death, not heaven or hell. We cannot control or avoid death by our works. But people draw the wrong conclusion from this; they assume that since there is nothing they can do to change the fact that death awaits all, they might as well cast away all restraint and live for themselves. They become **full of evil, and madness**. They cling to life, and use proverbs such as **a live dog is better than a dead lion**. Indeed, Ecclesiastes wants us to take death seriously. If we do, we will realize how fleeting are the passions that fuel our lives. But despair and self-abandonment are not the answer.

9:7-10 The proper response to death is to treat life as precious. The simple matters of eating and drinking should be

done **with a cheerful heart**. Wearing clothes that are **white** and having **oil** on the **head** refers to dressing up, as for a party. The message is that we should treat most days as times of celebration and not of mourning. To **enjoy life with** one's **wife** is to find sexual pleasure in the proper way.

9:10 Sheol refers to the grave. The point of saying that **no work, planning, knowledge, or wisdom** occurs there is not to deny the possibility of the afterlife, but to assert that we have only one opportunity to enjoy this world.

9:11-12 Another aspect of our mortality is that we are governed by time and circumstances. Ecclesiastes does not deny the sovereignty of God over human affairs. The Teacher asserts that no matter how capable we are, many things are beyond our control. Above all, the moment of death is not ours to choose.

9:13-10:17 The teachings and proverbs in this section focus on making one's way in the world, and they are especially focused on political life. The people described here are likely to have direct contact with the king (10:4). This suggests that the original audience was not the peasant or merchant class, but the aristocracy. In the modern world, many of these teachings apply to what we might describe as "office politics."

9:13-16 In this anecdote, a **poor** but **wise man** conceived of a strategy that saved his city from destruction. This proves that wisdom is better than power, but the man's lack of

he delivered the city by his wisdom.[a] Yet no one remembered that poor man. [16]And I said, "Wisdom is better than strength,[b] but the wisdom of the poor man is despised, and his words are not heeded."

[17] The calm words of the wise are heeded
more than the shouts of a ruler
over fools.
[18] Wisdom is better than weapons of war,
but one sinner can destroy
much good.[c]

The Burden of Folly

10 Dead flies make a perfumer's oil
ferment and stink;[d]
so a little folly outweighs wisdom
and honor.
[2] A wise man's heart goes to the[A] right,
but a fool's heart to the[A] left.
[3] Even when the fool walks
along the road, his heart lacks sense,
and he shows everyone he is a fool.[e]
[4] If the ruler's anger rises against you,
don't leave your place,[f]
for calmness puts great offenses
to rest.[g]

[a]9:15 2Sm 20:22
[b]9:16 Ec 7:19
[c]9:18 Jos 7:1
[d]10:1 Ex 30:25
[e]10:3 Pr 13:16; 18:2
[f]10:4 Ec 8:3
[g]1Sm 25:24-33; Pr 25:15
[h]10:6 Est 3:1; Pr 28:12; 29:2
[i]10:7 Pr 19:10
[j]Est 6:8-10
[k]10:8 Ps 7:15
[l]Am 5:19
[m]10:11 Jr 8:17
[n]10:12 Pr 10:32; 22:11; Lk 4:22

[5]There is an evil I have seen under the sun, an error proceeding from the presence of the ruler:

[6] The fool is appointed to great heights,[h]
but the rich remain in lowly positions.
[7] I have seen slaves on horses,[i]
but princes walking on the ground
like slaves.[j]

[8] The one who digs a pit may fall into it,[k]
and the one who breaks through a wall
may be bitten by a snake.[l]
[9] The one who quarries stones
may be hurt by them;
the one who splits trees
may be endangered by them.
[10] If the ax is dull, and one does not
sharpen its edge,
then one must exert more strength;
however, the advantage of wisdom is
that it brings success.
[11] If the snake bites before it is charmed,[m]
then there is no advantage
for the charmer.[B]
[12] The words from the mouth
of a wise man are gracious,[n]

[A]10:2 Lit *his*   [B]10:11 Lit *master of the tongue*

---

power meant that he was not properly rewarded for his work. A person needs wisdom to deal with the world's problems, but this does not ensure that he will achieve wealth or glory.

9:17-10:1 In this section two contrasting ideas are set against each other. On the one hand, **wisdom** is more effective for governing people than is the brutal exercise of force and violence, described as **shouts** and **weapons of war** (9:17-18a). On the other hand, a single mistake can do a lot of damage and nullify the work of much wisdom (9:18b-10:1). The point of 10:1 is that **dead flies** in a fine

sakal

Hebrew Pronunciation	[sah KAHL]
HCSB Translation	fool
Uses in Ecclesiastes	5
Uses in the OT	7
Focus Passage	Ecclesiastes 10:3,14

Like *kesiyl* and *'ewiyl*, *sakal* denotes *fool*. A related Akkadian adjective describes a *simpleminded*, *clumsy*, or *foolish* person so intellectually weak that he cannot evaluate his actions. An Arabic cognate means "doubtful." The *sakal* doesn't recognize when something is absurd (Jr 5:21), lacks understanding, and knows to do evil but not good (Jr 4:22). Contrasted with a wise man, he displays *folly*, multiplies words, and dies prematurely (Ec 2:19; 7:17; 10:3,14). The verb *sakal* (8x) is *be foolish* in the passive-reflexive (2Sm 24:10), *act foolishly* (Gn 31:28) or *be a fool* (1Sm 26:21) in the causative, and *turn into foolishness* in the intensive (2Sm 15:31). *Sikluth*, or *folly* (7x), appears only in Ecclesiastes. It includes drunken behavior (Ec 2:3) and is contrasted with wisdom as a kind of madness leading to evil madness (Ec 2:13; 10:1,13). *Sekel* means *folly*, specifically, a *fool* (Ec 10:6)

ointment make that ointment disgusting. In the same way, one fool can ruin an administration and one mistake can ruin a career.

10:2-3 Folly is usually self-evident. The word **right** in the ancient world meant skillful and the word **left** connoted ineptness and clumsiness. Ancient society made no special provision for left-handers; all soldiers, for example, held their shields in their left hand and their swords in their right hands.

10:4 A person must maintain tact and self-control, showing wisdom, when dealing with the **anger** of a superior.

10:5-7 Even though folly is usually self-evident (v. 3), sometimes kings and other rulers appoint inept people to high offices but let the competent languish **in lowly positions**. In this context, **slaves** refers to people whose skill and wisdom are so limited they ought to be restricted to doing simple manual labor.

10:8-9 These verses contain two pairs of proverbs that are juxtaposed against each other. Verse 8 describes criminal activity: digging a **pit** refers to setting a trap in order to rob or murder someone, and breaking through a **wall** refers to breaking into a house to plunder it. Traditional wisdom teaches that people who engage in such criminal action inevitably destroy themselves (Ps 7:15; 9:15; Pr 26:27). On the other hand, Ec 10:9 teaches that even honest labor, such as quarrying **stones** or cutting **trees**, can result in severe injury. That is, criminal activity can destroy you, but so can honest work. The Teacher did not intend to discourage honesty but to say we have no guarantee of safety in this life. Even wise behavior can end in disaster. Ultimately, we must trust not in wisdom or in ethical behavior but in God for our security.

10:10-11 Wisdom can make **success** easier to accomplish,

but the lips of a fool consume him.[a]

13 The beginning of the words
   of his mouth is folly,
   but the end of his speaking
   is evil madness.

14 Yet the fool multiplies words.
   No one knows what will happen,
   and who can tell anyone
   what will happen after him?[b]

15 The struggles of fools weary them,
   for they don't know how to go
   to the city.

16 Woe to you, land, when your king is
   a youth[c]
   and your princes feast in the morning.

17 Blessed are you, land, when your king
   is a son of nobles
   and your princes feast
   at the proper time—
   for strength and not for drunkenness.[d]

18 Because of laziness the roof caves in,
   and because of negligent hands
   the house leaks.

19 A feast is prepared for laughter,
   and wine makes life happy,[e]
   and money is the answer
   for everything.[f]

20 Do not curse the king
   even in your thoughts,[g]

and do not curse a rich person
   even in your bedroom,[h]
for a bird of the sky may carry
   the message,
and a winged creature may report
   the matter.

Invest in Life

11 Send your bread on the surface
   of the waters,[i]
   for after many days you may find it.
2 Give a portion to seven or even
   to eight,[j]
   for you don't know what disaster
   may happen on earth.
3 If the clouds are full, they will pour out
   rain on the earth;
   whether a tree falls to the south
   or the north,
   the place where the tree falls,
   there it will lie.
4 One who watches the wind
   will not sow,
   and the one who looks at the clouds
   will not reap.
5 Just as you don't know the path
   of the wind,
   or how bones develop in[A] the womb
   of a pregnant woman,

[a]10:12 Pr 18:7
[b]10:14 Ec 8:7,17
[c]10:16 Pr 30:21-22; Is 3:4,12
[d]10:17 Pr 31:4; Is 5:11
[e]10:19 Ps 104:15
[f]Ec 7:12
[g]10:20 Ex 22:28
[h]2Kg 6:12; Lk 12:3
[i]11:1 Dt 15:10; Pr 19:17; Mt 10:42; Gl 6:9-10; Heb 6:10
[j]11:2 Ps 112:9; Mt 5:42; Lk 6:30; 1Tm 6:18-19

A11:5 Or *know how the life-breath comes to the bones in*

but **wisdom** must be applied in a timely manner or it will do no good.

10:12-15 The primary service of a counselor was giving advice to a king, and the quality of his advice marked the counselor as either a sage or a fool. The mark of a foolish counselor is that he says far more than he knows. Since **no one knows what will happen**, the wise counselor limits the amount of advice he gives. It is impossible to speak of the future with any certainty. By contrast, the foolish counselor tries to cover for his lack of knowledge by speaking on and on. This is well illustrated by the verbose but confusing directions fools give to someone who does not know the way to a location (v. 15 could be translated, "The effort of fools wearies him who does not know the way to the city").

10:16-17 Ultimately, the success or failure of a political entity (or of a business) depends on the quality of its leaders. These verses conclude the general discussion of 9:13–10:17 on wisdom in the political world with the remark that few things matter so much in this area as leadership.

10:18-20 These verses contain a series of three proverbs on what makes a safe, pleasant life. First, we must do the work needed to insure that we have the basic comforts that all people desire. Second, we must have some money and pleasure in order to enjoy a good life. In isolation from the rest of the book, this seems to recommend pure hedonism and greed, but this misreads the verse. There are things, such as a good meal, that almost all people enjoy. Money helps us to deal with all kinds of problems (**money** does not literally solve **everything**, but in fact many of our ordinary problems are financial in nature). Third, we should

be careful in dealing with authorities in order to stay out of trouble.

11:1-6 This section focuses on making sound investments. It may seem odd that the Bible has such teachings, but much of Proverbs is concerned with advice on how to avoid poverty by prudent action. Most of us need a certain degree of prosperity in order to have a good life, and the advice here is valuable for both ancient and modern readers.

11:1-2 These verses deal with financial investment, not charity. The phrase **bread on the surface of the waters** refers to investing in overseas trading ventures (1Kg 9:26-27). The phrase **after many days you may find it** refers to an eventual return on the investment, and the phrase **to seven or even to eight** refers to diversifying one's investments.

11:3-5 These verses expand on the reason that a person must diversify his investments. No one knows what will happen, so it is best to be ready for anything. Verse 3 essentially states that there are some signs that indicate what will happen in the future. Dark **clouds** do not guarantee—but they suggest—that a storm is coming. Certain trends are likely to remain the same. A fallen tree almost certainly will stay where it is. On the other hand, a person can be too concerned with looking for indications of what will happen. Verse 4 says that people who will not commit until they are absolutely certain of success never do anything. Verse 5 tells us that we know very little about the processes that govern the world. Understanding all about the weather or the formation of a fetus is beyond us. Thus, we should not demand infallible information about the future before making any investments.

so you don't know the work of God
   who makes everything.[a]
6 In the morning sow your seed,
   and at evening do not let
     your hand rest,
because you don't know
   which will succeed,
whether one or the other,
or if both of them will be equally good.
7 Light is sweet,
   and it is pleasing for the eyes to see
     the sun.[b]
8 Indeed, if a man lives many years,
   let him rejoice in them all,
   and let him remember the days
     of darkness,[c] since they will be many.
All that comes is futile.
9 Rejoice, young man,
     while you are young,
and let your heart be glad in the days
     of your youth.
And walk in the ways of your heart
and in the sight of your eyes;[d]
but know that for all of these things
     God will bring you to judgment.

10 Remove sorrow from your heart,
   and put away pain from your flesh,[e]
because youth and the prime of life
   are fleeting.

The Twilight of Life

12 So remember your Creator in the days
    of your youth:

Before the days of adversity come,
   and the years approach
     when you will say,[f]
   "I have no delight in them";
2 before the sun and the light
   are darkened,[g]
and the moon and the stars,
and the clouds return after[A] the rain;
3 on the day when the guardians
   of the house tremble,
and the strong men stoop,
the women who grind cease because
   they are few,
and the ones who watch
   through the windows see dimly,[h]
4 the doors at the street are shut
while the sound of the mill fades;[i]

Cross references:
[a]11:5 Jb 10:10-11; Ps 139:14-16; Is 55:9; Jn 3:6-8; Rm 11:33
[b]11:7 Ec 6:5; 7:11
[c]11:8 Ec 12:1
[d]11:9 Ec 2:24; 3:12-13,22; 5:18; 8:15; 9:7-9
[e]11:10 2Co 7:1; 2Tm 2:22
[f]12:1 Ec 11:8
[g]12:2 Is 5:30; Ezk 32:7-8
[h]12:3 Gn 27:1; 48:10; 1Sm 3:2
[i]12:4 Jr 25:10; Rv 18:22

A 12:2 Or with

11:6 A final word of advice on achieving prosperity: work hard in the hopes that at least one of your ventures will **succeed**.

11:7–12:7 Ecclesiastes is primarily concerned with making us understand that we are mortal, that our days are few, that all our works will fade away, and that we should govern our lives accordingly. In this, the last major passage of Ecclesiastes, the book reviews its essential conclusions about how we should spend the time we have. Essentially, the conclusion is twofold: enjoy your days under the sun and fear God.

11:7-8 In the Bible, light is often associated with life and darkness is associated with death. Light is beautiful, but the main point of **light is sweet** is that it is good to be alive. The assertion that **the days of darkness . . . will be many** does not deny the concept of an afterlife, nor does it specifically allude to an interim period between death and bodily resurrection. It is simply a way of saying that life is short but death is long. Enjoy these days because they are few and they pass quickly.

11:9-10 In these verses two pieces of advice are in tension with each other. The first is that we should enjoy life and the second is that we should fear God. The danger is that some people will try to enjoy life by doing things that are offensive to God. Whoever does such things destroys himself and loses both happiness and God. On the other hand, those who have the wrong kind of fear of God believe that anything that makes people happy must be bad and thus they deprive themselves of legitimate joys. A **young man** is specifically addressed because men (not women) were the original audience for Ecclesiastes and because the elderly, as described in 12:1-7, are already in the grip of death; the capacity to enjoy life has to a degree already passed them by.

12:1-7 Approaches to this passage differ, but it most likely is an extended series of metaphors describing the troubles of old age, culminating in death. The fact that old age is in view is suggested by the details of the metaphors and also by the exhortation in 11:10 to enjoy life while youthful vigor still exists. This text tells the young man, "This is what you have in your future, so enjoy your youth while it lasts."

12:1 God is called the **Creator** here for two reasons. First, as maker of heaven and earth He is our judge; we must **remember** Him in the sense that we live in fear of Him and never forget that we are accountable to Him for our actions. Second, God as Creator calls us to enjoy life; He made the light, the earth and sky, food and drink, man and woman, and all the other things that in Genesis 1 He calls "good." **The days of adversity**, as described in the verses that follow, are the days when a person is feeble and failing.

12:2 The phrase **the sun and the light are darkened** allude to the great works of creation in Gn 1:3-8—the creation of light, sun, moon, and sky. In apocalyptic texts, such as Jr 4:23-28 and Jl 2:10-11, the Day of the Lord is described as an unmaking of creation itself, including the darkening of the sun and moon. For every human being, death is a personal apocalypse; it is the end of the world for us. This, rather than failing eyesight, is probably the main point of this verse (failing eyesight is described in the next verse).

12:3 The phrase **when the guardians of the house tremble** probably refers to the hands. They are what a person uses to protect himself, and the hands of the elderly are sometimes subject to trembling. The **strong men** who **stoop** refer to the legs and back; these are the largest muscle groups in the body and they become flaccid in old age, leading to bent posture. The **women who grind** are the teeth, because they grind food. In the ancient world, where dental care was nonexistent, even the pharaohs of Egypt lost their teeth if they lived into old age. The teeth are referred to as "women" because typically women in a household did the work of grinding meal for bread. The **ones who watch through the windows** refer to the eyes. Here, however, the language is

when one rises at the sound of a bird,
and all the daughters of song grow faint.
⁵ Also, they are afraid of heights
and dangers on the road;
the almond tree blossoms,
the grasshopper loses its spring,ᴬ
and the caper berry has no effect;
for man is headed to his eternal home,ᵃ
and mourners will walk around
in the street;ᵇ
⁶ before the silver cord is snapped,ᴮ
and the gold bowl is broken,ᶜ
and the jar is shattered at the spring,
and the wheel is broken into the well;
⁷ and the dust returns to the earth
as it once was,
and the spirit returns to God
who gave it.ᵈ

⁸"Absolute futility," says the Teacher. "Everything is futile."ᵉ

The Teacher's Objectives and Conclusion

⁹In addition to the Teacher being a wise man, he constantly taught the •people knowledge; he weighed, explored, and arranged many proverbs.ᶠ ¹⁰The Teacher sought to find delightful sayings and write words of truth accurately. ¹¹The sayings of the wise are like goads,ᵍ and those from masters of collections are like firmly embedded nails.ʰ The sayings are given by one Shepherd.ᶜ

¹²But beyond these, my son, be warned: there is no end to the making of many books,ⁱ and much study wearies the body.ʲ ¹³When all has been heard, the conclusion of the matter is: •fear Godᵏ and keep His commands, because this is for all humanity.ˡ ¹⁴For God will bring every act to judgment,ᵐ including every hidden thing, whether good or evil.

ᵃ12:5 Jb 17:13; 30:23
ᵇJr 9:17
ᶜ12:6 Zch 4:2-3
ᵈ12:7 Gn 2:7; 3:19; Ec 3:21
ᵉ12:8 Ec 1:2
ᶠ12:9 1Kg 4:32; Pr 1:1
ᵍ12:11 Pr 1:6; 22:17
ʰEzr 9:8; Is 22:23
ⁱ12:12 1Kg 4:32-33; Jn 21:25
ʲEc 1:18
ᵏ12:13 Pr 1:7; Ec 3:14; 5:7; 7:18; 8:12-13
ˡPs 97:5; Ac 4:12; Rm 10:12
ᵐ12:14 Ec 3:17; 11:9; Rv 20:12

ᴬ12:5 Or grasshopper is weighed down, or grasshopper drags itself along   ᴮ12:6 Alt Hb tradition reads removed   ᶜ12:11 Or by a shepherd

---

a metaphor for poor eyesight; there is no apocalyptic language, as there is in verse 2.

12:4 This verse describes two aspects of the effects of old age on hearing. On the one hand, people no longer hear well, and sounds are muffled and **faint** as if **doors** have been shut. On the other hand, many old people do not sleep well, and even a faint sound awakens them.

12:5 Solomon abandons metaphorical language with the phrase **they are afraid of heights and dangers on the road**. Old people fear falling down and are easy prey for criminals. **Almond tree blossoms** almost certainly refers to white hair. **The grasshopper loses its spring** and **the caper berry has no effect** may refer to impotence; it appears that the caper was regarded as an aphrodisiac. A **man** going to his **eternal home** with **mourners** walking **in the street** obviously alludes to a funeral.

12:6 The **cord**, the **bowl**, the **jar . . . shattered at the spring**, and the **wheel . . . broken** at **the well** all refer to drawing up water from a well, a spring, or a cistern. Water in the Bible is frequently associated with life (this is understandable, considering the near-desert climate of ancient Israel). Thus, if these things are broken, death has occurred. Describing these objects as **silver** and **gold** implies that life is precious.

12:7 This verse alludes to Gn 2:7; 3:19.

12:8 This verse repeats the theme of the book stated in 1:2. These two verses—1:2 and 12:8—bracket the whole of the book, and it properly ends at this point. What follows, verses 9-14, is an epilogue.

12:9-14 These verses reveal a few more details about the author's life and give the reader some parting exhortations.

12:9 This verse is consistent with the view that Solomon was the author of Ecclesiastes (1Kg 4:30-32).

12:10 This verse indicates that the Teacher not only sought

to give sound teaching, but to present it in a way that was appealing and appropriate. This suggests that there is more care in the wording and arrangement of books such as Proverbs and Ecclesiastes than first meets the eye.

12:11 The essential teaching of this verse—that God has given us wisdom in order to guide us through life—is clear. A pastoral metaphor governs at least part of the verse. God (the **one Shepherd**) prods us along just as shepherds prod animals with **goads**—sticks with sharp points (Ac 26:14). It is not certain whether **embedded nails** refers to nails inserted at the ends of goads (1Sm 13:21), or whether this is a different metaphor, describing proverbs as fixed and dependable, like nails driven in a wall. If the latter, it implies that we can hang our lives on these fixed truths.

12:12 Proverbs are important, but the Teacher warns against study done for its own sake. Too much **study** deprives a person of the joys that Ecclesiastes recommends. This verse does not oppose scholarship, but it does demand that scholars approach their work with humility and with balance in their lives.

12:13-14 The meaning of the phrase **because this is for all humanity** is much debated. The Hebrew literally says, "for this [is] the whole of man." The phrase could mean, as the HCSB renders it, that the rule to fear God applies to every person. Alternatively, it could mean obedience to God is the proper role for man in the universe. In other words, to live in the fear of God is to be truly human. To do otherwise is to lose the essence of our humanity. The conclusion of Ecclesiastes, to **fear God**, is in keeping with the message of the book—that we are mortal and weak but He is almighty. Although the book recommends, among other things, that we should enjoy our brief time under the sun, the advice to fear God trumps everything. The whole of the book has been focused on the brevity of earthly life and on how we should live in light of this reality. But at the end, the book looks beyond this life to the final judgment.

Song of Songs

Introduction

The Song of Songs celebrates the love of Solomon and his bride, who is called Shulamith or the Shulammite (6:13). The excitement of courtship, the beauty of the wedding night, the sexuality of the first night and subsequent nights, as well as tender friendship—all of these elements make this book a celebration of romance and marital sensuality as God intended them to be.

"Listen! My love is approaching. Look! Here he comes, leaping over the mountains, bounding over the hills. My love is like a gazelle or a young stag" (2:8-9).

Circumstances of Writing

Author: The Song claims authorship by Solomon in its title, "The Song of Songs which is Solomon's." The church has long accepted this at face value, but modern critics raise objections to Solomon as author.

First, critics claim that the title did not originate with the Song but was added later by someone who wanted to attribute the work to the famous Solomon. However, no evidence supports this claim. Moreover, the structure of the book suggests that the title is integral to the book's composition and is thus original. Like other biblical writers, the writer often structured content with attention to certain numbers—three, seven, and ten being some of the most common. Within the Song, for example, the author designed seven sections (see below), a sevenfold praise (4:1-5), twice a tenfold praise (5:10-16; 7:1-5), and a tenfold occurrence of the abstract word for love (2:4-5,7; 3:5; 5:8; 7:6; 8:4,6-7). Apart from the title (1:1), he wove Solomon's name into six other places (1:5; 3:7,9,11; 8:11-12): two in the last section, three in the central, and one in the first. With the inclusion of "Solomon" in the title, the name appears a perfect seven times and is symmetrically balanced within the Song: twice in the first section balanced by twice in the last one, with three in the central. The title is thus as cleverly integrated with the lyrics as possible. It not only conforms to their melodic alliteration and meter, but it completes the sevenfold occurrence of "Solomon" and in a manner that artistically balances it throughout the Song. In fact, the tenfold occurrence of "love" joins the sevenfold appearance of "Solomon" to show the Song's subject and author. Hardly a later addition, the title seems to have been original, constituting its first verse.

Another common objection to Solomon's authorship is the king's well-known possession of 700 wives and 300 concubines (1Kg 11:3). How could a man who lived like that write a song about devotion to one woman? It appears he could do so only because grace touched his heart. In this respect he foreshadowed other biblical writers who, except for God's grace and calling, were the least qualified to write Scripture. For example, Paul, the great apostle, wrote most eloquently of grace and his unworthiness (e.g., 1Tm 1:12-16). Solomon was a man immersed in power and pleasure, but God opened his eyes to true love. Solomon also authored the book

---

3000–2000 B.C.

2000–1800 B.C.

Abraham 2166–1991

Stonehenge construction, phase I 2900

Stonehenge construction, phase II 2900–2400

Epic of Gilgamesh oral tradition developed from 2700 to 1400

First libraries in Egypt 2500–2000

Stonehenge construction, phase III 2400–1600

The Love Poem of a Persistent Woman, Old Babylonian 2017–1794

Dumuzi-Inanna Love Songs, Sumerian 2000

An Old Akkadian Love Charm 2000

Love Lyrics of Rim-Sin, Akkadian 1822–1763

of Proverbs. Just as he did not always follow the precepts he recorded there, so too he evidently composed a great love song despite his failure to live in accordance with its ideals.

Background: A compelling historical reason to date the Song as coming from the time of Solomon is its nearest literary parallel—the Egyptian love songs. No one doubts their origin prior to or contemporaneous with the time of Solomon, and the Egyptian love songs are indisputably the Song's closest literary parallels.

Message and Purpose

The central theme of the Song of Songs is a celebration of the goodness and beauty of romantic love. The Song's romantic ideals are as captivating as its imagery: emotional intimacy, sensitive communication, delightful sexuality, profound companionship, common perspective, willing forgiveness, respect, integrity, security, love's devotion through bleak seasons of winter, and love's renewal in new seasons of spring.

Since the Song portrays a perfect love, it is natural for the songwriter to compare it to the love of God for Israel. Solomon's love is like God's love for His people, and Shulamith's love is like a response from those people to God. If the NT will later *tell* us that a man's love for his wife should emulate Christ's love for his bride (Eph 5:22-33), Solomon's song *shows* such a marriage patterned after divine love.

Since the Song captures ideal love in its reflection of God's love for Israel, its romance also reflects the ideal love that God intended for a husband and wife. We see a return to paradise in a courtship that blossomed in the uncluttered beauty of nature (1:15–2:3; 2:8-14), in a wedding night consummated with allusions to the garden of paradise (4:12–5:1), and in a marriage that delights in innocent lovemaking (4:1–5:1; 7:1–8:3).

The Song's last praise of love captures all of this (8:5-7). The flames of love are like the fire of the Lord. In Genesis, God ruled over the waters of chaos to make the heavens and earth, creating in His image Adam and Eve to reflect His love in their union. In Exodus, God ruled over the deathly waters of the Red Sea to establish a new nation for His people. Since God's love is like fire (Dt 4:24; 32:21-22), and since the love of Solomon and

1600–1200 B.C.	1200–800 B.C.
Moses 1526–1406	
Message of Lundingirra to His Mother, Old Babylonian 1800–1600	*Love Lyrics of Nabu and Tasmetu,* Neo–Assyrian 1180–609
Love Lyrics of Nanay and Muati, Old Babylonian 1711–1684	*The Harper's Song for Inherkhway,* Egyptian 1160
Heavy import and export trade, Egypt 1500–1000	David becomes king over all Israel 1003
Events in Joshua 1406–1380?	Solomon becomes king 970
Events in Judges 1380?–1060?	Proverbs 970
Egyptian Love Poetry 1305–1150	Song of Songs 970?
	Ecclesiastes 935?

Shulamith recovers the innocence of Adam and Eve and reflects God's love for Israel, the Song compares the power of romantic love to the eternal fire of God that no waters or rivers can quench.

Contribution to the Bible

A beautiful love song inspires us like grace, creating within us a desire for its beauty. Like such an enchanting love song, Solomon's Song inspires a pursuit of the love it portrays. This romantic delight is not a modern fairy tale or fantasy from the past, but reflects God's desire to form within us a pure and devoted love. We discover that there is a bliss in married love that is reflective of the greater love believers experience as the bride of Christ. As this book's imagery informs us of romantic love, it also helps us anticipate the full consummation of our relationship with Christ when He returns for His bride.

Structure

The Song of Songs is a poem whose components form a chiastic structure. A chiasm takes the form:

    A
       B
          C
      B'
    A'

where A and A' mirror each other and where the central element, C, conveys the main point of the poem. The outline below shows the structure of the Song of Songs. The author intended to emphasize the central elements of the structure, the day and night of the wedding (section IV). When God inspired Solomon to write this song, He gave divine approval to romantic love.

The Hebrew text makes a distinction between the various speakers through a change in gender and number. The HCSB text has added subheadings to clarify when the speakers change.

Structure and Outline

I. Section A: Their Story Begins (1:2–2:7)
   A. Shulamith, Solomon, and the daughters of Jerusalem (1:2-4)
   B. Her brothers, their vineyards, and her appearance (1:5-6)
   C. Her character and beauty (1:7-11)
   D. Love's expression (1:12–2:5)
   E. Refrains conclude Section A and begin Section B (2:6-7)

II. Section B: Invitation to Enjoy a Spring Day (2:6-17)
   A. Refrains of longing and patience (2:6-7)
   B. Her beloved's invitation to come from her house to enjoy spring (2:8-14)
   C. Refrains (after caution) of unity and invitation to her breasts (2:15-17)

III. Section C: Night of Separation Preceding Wedding (3:1-5)
   A. She is awakened, alone, and longing for him (3:1)
   B. Leaves home to find him (3:2)
   C. Is found by guards (3:3a)
   D. Asks for help (3:3b)

C'. Finds Solomon (3:4a)

B'. Returns home with him (3:4b)

A'. Is reunited with him through the night (3:4b); transition (3:5)

IV. Section D: Wedding Day and Night (3:6–5:1)

    A. Songwriter's own words (3:6-11)

    B. Celebration of the wedding's beginning (3:6-11)

          C. Wedding night (4:1–5:1)

    B'. Celebration of the wedding's consummation (5:1a)

    A'. Songwriter's own words (5:1b)

V. Section C': Night of separation following wedding night (5:2–7:9)

    A. She is awakened, alone, and reluctant (5:2-8)

    B. Awakened to give tenfold praise (5:9-16)

    C. Aware of his presence in the garden (6:1-3)

    D. Receives his praise in the garden (6:4-10)

    C'. Recounts her journey to the garden (6:11-13)

    B'. Receives tenfold praise (7:1-5)

    A'. Delightfully makes love, together drift off to sleep (7:6-9)

VI. Section B': Invitation to Enjoy a Spring Day (7:10–8:4)

    C'. Enjoyment of breasts and refrain of unity (7:7-8,10)

    B'. Her invitation to come enjoy spring then return to her house (7:11–8:2)

    A'. Refrains of longing and patience (8:3-4)

VII. Section A': Their Story Complete (8:3-14)

    E'. Refrains conclude Section B' and begin Section A' (8:3-4)

    D'. Love's devotion (8:5-7)

    C'. Shulamith's character and beauty (8:8-9)

    B'. Her brothers, their vineyards, and her appearance (8:10-12)

    A'. Shulamith, Solomon, and Shulamith's companions (8:13-14)

The design of the Song underscores its central theme: a celebration of the goodness and beauty of romantic love (Glickman, *Solomon's Song of Love*, p. 241).

1

Solomon's Finest Song.[A,a]

W[B]

2 Oh, that he would kiss me
   with the kisses of his mouth!
   For your[c] love is[D] more delightful
      than wine.[b]
3 The fragrance of your perfume
      is intoxicating;[c]
   your name is perfume poured out.[d]
   No wonder young women[E] adore you.
4 Take me with you[e]—let us hurry.
   Oh, that the king would bring[F] me
      to his chambers.

Y   We will rejoice and be glad for you;
         we will praise your love
            more than wine.

W   It is only right that they adore you.

5 Daughters of Jerusalem,[f]
   I am dark like the tents of Kedar,[g]

[a]1:1 1Kg 4:32
[b]1:2 Sg 4:10
[c]1:3 Jn 12:3
[d]Ec 7:1
[e]1:4 Hs 11:4
[f]1:5 Sg 2:7; 3:5,10; 5:8,16; 8:4
[g]Ps 120:5; Is 60:7
[h]Sg 2:14; 4:3; 6:4
[i]1:6 Ps 69:8
[j]Sg 8:11
[k]1:7 Sg 3:1-4
[l]Sg 2:16; 6:3
[m]Is 13:20; Jr 33:12
[n]Sg 8:13
[o]1:8 Sg 5:9; 6:1

   yet lovely[h] like the curtains
      of Solomon.
6 Do not stare at me because I am dark,
   for the sun has gazed on me.
   My mother's sons were angry with me;[i]
   they made me a keeper
      of the vineyards.[j]
   I have not kept my own vineyard.[G]

7 Tell me, you, the one I love:[k]
   Where do you pasture your sheep?[l]
   Where do you let them rest at noon?[m]
   Why should I be like one who veils
      herself[H,i]
   beside the flocks of your companions?[n]

M[J]

8 If you do not know,
   most beautiful of women,[o]
   follow[K] the tracks of the flock,
   and pasture your young goats
      near the shepherds' tents.

[A]1:1 Or *The Song of Songs, which is Solomon's* [B]1:2 The W, M, Y, N, and B indicate the editors' opinions of the changes of speakers: W = Woman, M = Man, Y = Young women of Jerusalem, N = Narrator, B = Brothers. If a letter is in parenthesis (W), there is a question about the identity of the speaker. [C]1:2 Unexpected change of grammatical persons, here from *he* and *his* to *your*, is a Hb poetic device. [D]1:2 Or *your caresses are*, or *your lovemaking is* [E]1:3 Or *wonder virgins* [F]1:4 Or *The king has brought* [G]1:6 Lit *my vineyard, which is mine* [H]1:7 Or *who wanders* [I]1:7 To express shame or grief, or to conceal identity as a prostitute would; Gn 38:14-15 [J]1:8 Some understand the young women to be the speakers in this verse. [K]1:8 Lit *go out for yourself into*

1:1 Solomon's Finest Song (lit "The Song of Songs which is Solomon's"), like many of the lyrics, is alliterative and melodic. The form of the phrase "which is Solomon's" normally indicates authorship (cp. Pss 72 and 127).

1:2 Oh, that he would kiss me with the kisses of his mouth begins the Song like love often begins: with sudden intensity and excitement. The abrupt beginning artistically weds style to content, signaling to the reader that the Song will move at a quick and entrancing pace. The speaker is unidentified at this point. Later we learn that she is "the Shulammite" (6:13). For reasons explained in the note at 6:11-13, we will refer to her by the name "Shulamith."

1:3 Name (Hb *shem*) and **perfume** (Hb *shemen*) are similar in Hebrew, so the Song presents here the first of its frequent wordplays. Since names were thought to capture

essence, the praise also begins an important theme—that desire arises out of delight.

1:4 Solomon's attractive qualities are apparent to others, and are not mere fantasies of infatuation.

1:5-6 Shulamith explained her darkened appearance as the consequence of her brothers' (**my mother's sons**) assignment to work outside in **vineyards**. We later discover they had leased this vineyard from Solomon (8:10-12).

1:7 As a shepherd finds shade for his flock during the heat of the day, Solomon could provide protection from the gaze of the women (vv. 5-6) and the anger of the brothers (v. 6) that burned like the sun. So Shulamith could ask **Where do you let them** (the flock) **rest at noon**, implicitly requesting relief in Solomon's protection from the "sun's" heat. This extended metaphor resumes in Shulamith's comparison of Solomon to a tree in the forest in whose "shade" she delighted (2:3) and concludes in her being compared to the morning star (or dawn light in 6:10). "Dawn" (or morning star, Hb *shakar*) is a play on "dark" (Hb *shekorah*; 1:6), the effect of the sun on the skin. Love transformed the young woman darkened by the sun into the light of dawn.

In a wordplay, **why** appears in this form only here in the OT. The archaic relative pronoun (*she*) is attached to the interrogative with the *lamed* prefix (Hb *lamah*) to form *shallamah*. Since the consonants are exactly the same as the name "Solomon," the original readers might first have thought it should be translated "Solomon," making the sentence read, "Solomon, I will be like a veiled woman by the flocks." This is perhaps just the sort of playful thing young lovers would say.

One who veils herself is likely an allusion to Tamar, who disguised herself as a prostitute by donning a veil and then enticed Judah to fulfill his duty to provide for her (Gn 38:14-

---

dod

Hebrew Pronunciation	[DOHD]
HCSB Translation	love, uncle
Uses in Song of Songs	39
Uses in the OT	61
Focus Passage	Song of Songs 1:2,4,13-14,16

Dod has two distinct meanings that likely developed from a single verb *yadad* (love). In Song of Songs, *dod* refers to Solomon and always has a pronominal modifier identifying Solomon as the woman's romantic *love* (Sg 1:13). Elsewhere, this sense of *dod* appears only when Isaiah refers to Yahweh as his *loved one* (Is 5:1). The concept of romantic relationship occurs in the abstract plural use of *dod* to indicate sexual *love* (Sg 5:1) or *lovemaking* (Pr 7:18). *Dod* also denotes the important *uncle* on the father's side (Lv 10:4).

⁹ I compare you, my darling,ᵃ
　　to aᴬ mare among Pharaoh's chariots.ᴮ,ᵇ
¹⁰ Your cheeks are beautiful
　　with jewelry,ᶜ
　　your neck with its necklace.
¹¹ We will make gold jewelry for you,
　　accented with silver.

W

¹² While the king is on his couch,ᶜ
　　my perfumeᴰ releases its fragrance.ᵈ
¹³ My love is a sachet of myrrh to me,ᵉ
　　spending the night between my breasts.

ᵃ1:9 Sg 1:15
ᵇ2Ch 1:16-17
ᶜ1:10 Sg 5:13
ᵈ1:12 Sg 4:14;
Mk 14:3; Jn 12:3
ᵉ1:13 Ps 45:8;
Jn 19:39
ᶠ1:14 Sg 4:13
ᵍ1Sm 23:29
ʰ1:15 Sg 4:1
ⁱ1:16 Sg 2:3

M

¹⁴ My love is a cluster of henna blossoms
　　to me,ᶠ
　　in the vineyards of En-gedi.ᴱ,ᵍ

¹⁵ How beautiful you are, my darling.
　　How very beautiful!
　　Your eyes are doves.ʰ

W

¹⁶ How handsome you are, my love.ⁱ
　　How delightful!
　　Our bed is lush with foliage;

ᴬ1:9 Lit *my*　ᴮ1:9 Pharaoh's chariot horses were stallions.　ᶜ1:12 Or *is at his table*　ᴰ1:12 Lit *nard*　ᴱ1:14 = Wellspring of the Young Goat

---

15). Like Tamar, Shulamith was not what she appeared to be: She was no more a common laborer than Tamar was a prostitute. But unlike Tamar, she did not have to use manipulation since Solomon was willing. So why indeed should Shulamith veil herself to conceal her motives? Later Shulamith is likened to a "palm tree," which is *tamar* in Hebrew (Sg 7:7-8).

1:8 Most beautiful of women is a term of address used twice elsewhere by the young women of Jerusalem for Shulamith (5:9; 6:1). Perhaps these other occurrences are evidence that the women of Jerusalem also speak here. If so, the reader can imagine that in 1:7 Shulamith addressed Solomon in soliloquy, similar to verses 2b-4a. **Young goats** is literally "female kids" (used only here in the OT), and it invites a figurative explanation for such an unusual flock. It likely anticipates the praise of Shulamith's long, flowing hair being like a flock of goats descending a mountain (4:1).

1:9 A **mare among Pharaoh's chariots** would stir the chariots' stallions, just as Shulamith would attract the attention of men. "Shepherds" (Hb *ra'ah*; v. 8), which evidently refers to "companions" (v. 7), is a wordplay with **my darling** (Hb *ra'yah*), Solomon's first term of endearment for Shulamith. The name thus underscores their companionate friendship (5:16), in the imagery of shepherd and shepherdess.

1:10 Archaeological drawings show jewels decorating bridles of horses, so the imagery of jewels on the **cheeks** and in necklaces likely extends the metaphor of the mare.

1:12-2:5 This section is in chiastic balance with 8:5-7 in the design of the Song (see outline in the Introduction): (a) he was a **sachet of myrrh . . . between my breasts** (1:13) and she requested to be a seal over his heart (8:6); (b) they enjoyed the "house" of nature and the "house of wine" (lit for **banquet hall**) (1:17; 2:4) but "all the wealth of his house" (lit) could not buy love (8:7); (c) she delighted in him, likened him to an **apricot** (or apple) **tree** (2:3), and she awakened his love under the apricot (or apple) tree (8:5); (d) she was "faint from love" (lit in 2:5) and she emerged from the wilderness "leaning on the one she loved" (8:5).

1:12 One may also translate **on his couch** as "in his realm," similar to its meaning in 1Kg 6:29 and 2Kg 23:5 ("surrounding"), the only other times this phrase appears in the OT.

1:13-14 Spending the night personifies the **sachet of myrrh**, suggesting it was like a pillow a young woman would hold pretending it was her lover. While Solomon was away and about his realm, Shulamith's thoughts about him were as evocative as myrrh. **En-gedi** was an oasis in the desert, per-

haps continuing the metaphor of Solomon's protection from the sun (vv. 6-7).

1:15-2:3 Mutual praise escalates, each building upon the imagery introduced by the other: his praise of her beauty and **eyes** like **doves** (1:15) elicited like praise (1:16a) to which she added additional imagery (1:16b-17); her comparison of herself to a flower (2:1) then elicited like praise (2:2a) from him to which he added additional imagery (2:2b), which she reciprocated (**like an apricot tree**), but also climactically embellished (she delighted **to sit in his shade**, 2:3). Doves were repeatedly shown in the drawings of the day as literal "messengers of love." The look of love in lovers' eyes is unmistakable. **Our bed is lush with foliage** (1:16) may also be translated "our resting place is in the branches' foliage," which is perhaps more consistent with the context and other OT usage.

One of the few natural waterfalls in Israel is located at En-gedi on the west side of the Dead Sea.

17 the beams of our house are cedars,
   and our rafters are cypresses.[A]

2 I am a rose[B,C] of Sharon,
   a lily[D] of the valleys.[a]

M

2 Like a lily among thorns,
   so is my darling
      among the young women.

W

3 Like an apricot[E] tree among the trees
      of the forest,
   so is my love among the young men.
   I delight to sit in his shade,
   and his fruit is sweet to my taste.

4 He brought me
      to the banquet hall,[F,b]
   and he looked on me with love.[G,c]

5 Sustain me with raisins;
   refresh me with apricots,[H]
   for I am lovesick.[d]

6 His left hand is under my head,

[a] 2:1	Sg 5:13; 7:2; Hs 14:5
[b] 2:4	Sg 1:4
[c]	Ps 20:5
[d] 2:5	Sg 5:8
[e] 2:6	Sg 8:3
[f] 2:7	Sg 3:5; 5:8; 8:4
[g] 2:8	Is 52:7
[h] 2:9	Sg 2:17; 8:14
[i] 2:10	Sg 2:13

   and his right arm embraces me.[I,e]

7 Young women of Jerusalem,
   I charge you
by the gazelles and the wild does
   of the field:
do not stir up or awaken love
   until the appropriate time.[J,f]

8 Listen! My love is approaching.
   Look! Here he comes,
   leaping over the mountains,[g]
   bounding over the hills.

9 My love is like a gazelle
   or a young stag.[h]
   Look, he is standing behind our wall,
   gazing through the windows,
   peering through the lattice.

10 My love calls to me:

M   Arise,[i] my darling.
   Come away, my beautiful one.

11 For now the winter is past;
   the rain has ended and gone away.

[A] 1:17 Or firs, or pines   [B] 2:1 Or meadow saffron   [C] 2:1 Not the modern flower but a common wildflower in northern Israel
[D] 2:1 Or lotus   [E] 2:3 Or apple   [F] 2:4 Lit the house of wine   [G] 2:4 Or and his banner over me is love   [H] 2:5 Or apples   [I] 2:6 Or Let his
left hand be under . . . and his right arm embrace me   [J] 2:7 Lit until it pleases

---

2:1 The Hebrew *shushan* was probably not the **lily** (*Lilium spp.*) but the water lily or lotus flower (*Nymphaea lotus L.*), which the ancient world associated with almost magical, life-giving powers. This association is consistent with references in the Song: the life-giving princess (v. 1); the source of life that bonds Solomon to her (v. 16); the erotic setting of her breasts (4:5); his lips flowing with liquid myrrh (5:13); flowers enjoyed before a reconciliation (6:3); and the flowers that surround her abdomen and navel. There is also a wordplay: Solomon praised Shulamith as a mare (Hb *susa*; 1:9) that drew the attention of others; she responded that she was also a life-giving flower (Hb *shushan*). She not only received attention; she gave attention as well.

2:2-3 The significance of the lotus flower's place **among thorns** is similar to the tree's **shade** and **fruit** in a dangerous forest: both are places of safety surrounded by danger. The implication is that their love was likewise a place of safety in a hostile world. "Fruit" is often a metaphor for speech (Pr 12:14; 13:2; 18:20) that can be described as sweet not only in Proverbs (Pr 16:24), but also in the Song (Sg 5:13,16).

2:4-5 Banquet hall is literally "house of wine," inviting a contrast with the house of nature in 1:17 and the house of wealth in 8:6-7; the latter is the corresponding section in the chiastic structure. **He looked on me with love** assumes that the root meaning behind the military banner was the concept of looking. The alternate reading, "His banner over me is love," is supported by the fact that drawings in the ancient Near East show groups carrying banners with symbols identifying the group. Solomon's love for Shulamith is clear and public. **I am lovesick** affirms the intensity of romantic love.

2:6-17 Between the two refrains of verses 6-7 and the two of verses 16-17 is Solomon's invitation to Shulamith during courtship to come from her house and enjoy a spring day that reflects the new life love has given (vv. 8-15). This section is in chiastic contrast with Shulamith's invitation to

Solomon during marriage to enjoy a spring day and go to her house (7:10-8:4). This latter section is also framed by similar refrains (see outline in the Introduction). The wives of kings commonly had separate quarters from the king.

2:6-7 These refrains conclude the first section and begin the second, just as they appear in chiastic balance in 8:3-4 to conclude the sixth section and begin the last (see outline in the Introduction).

2:6 One may also render **His left hand is** as a wish: "Let his left hand be . . ." Wishes appear in the Song's opening request, "Oh, that he would kiss me" (1:1), and even on the wedding night, "Let my love come to his garden" (4:16). Here a wish appears even more likely. It is a public context (2:4-5,7), and afterwards comes an admonition advocating restraint until the appropriate time. The wedding night at that time, as evidenced in its fulfillment of a wish for intimacy (cp. 2:17 with 4:5-6) and the praise of Shulamith's virgin purity (4:12).

2:7 Shulamith asked the women to promise **by the gazelles and the wild does of the field**. Gazelles (Hb *tseva'oth*) is precisely like "hosts" (Hb *tseva'oth*) in "Lord of Hosts," and wild does of the field (Hb *'ayloth hasadeh*) is similar to El Shaddai—two wordplays that might go unnoticed except that Shulamith's request is in the form of the traditional oath formula normally requesting a promise "by the Lord" (Gn 24:3). The play on the names of God is instructive. Shulamith asked for a promise of patience in love. So she asked for the promise not by the Lord of Hosts nor by the Almighty God but by the creatures whose manner modeled romantic ways. Love, as she expresses it here, awakens not in response to the coercive power of an army or the might of God, but to love expressed with the gentle sensitivity of the gazelles or does of the meadow. **Until the appropriate time** (lit "until it pleases") personifies love as their guide.

2:8-14 Listen! My love is approaching is literally "The voice

¹² The blossoms appear
   in the countryside.
The time of singing^A has come,
and the turtledove's cooing is heard
   in our land.^a
¹³ The fig tree ripens its figs;^b
the blossoming vines give off
   their fragrance.^c
Arise, my darling.
Come away, my beautiful one.

¹⁴ My dove,^d in the clefts of the rock,^e
in the crevices of the cliff,
let me see your face,^B
let me hear your voice;^f
for your voice is sweet,
and your face is lovely.^g

(W)
¹⁵ Catch the foxes for us^h—
the little foxes that ruin
   the vineyards—
for our vineyards are in bloom.ⁱ

W
¹⁶ My love is mine and I am his;^j

Cross references column:
^a2:12 Jr 8:7
^b2:13 Mt 24:32
^cSg 7:12
^d2:14 Sg 5:2; 6:9
^eJr 48:28
^fSg 8:13
^gSg 1:5
^h2:15 Ezk 13:4
ⁱSg 2:13
^j2:16 Sg 6:3; 7:10; 8:6
^k2:17 Sg 2:9
^lSg 4:5-6; 8:14
^m3:1 Sg 1:7
ⁿSg 5:6
^o3:2 Jr 5:1
^p3:3 Sg 5:7
^q3:4 Sg 8:2

he feeds among the lilies.
¹⁷ Before the day breaks^C
and the shadows flee,
turn to me, my love, and be
   like a gazelle
or a young stag^k
   on the divided mountains.^{D,l}

3 In my bed at night^E
I sought the one I love;^m
I sought him, but did not find him.^{F,n}
² I will arise now and go about the city,
through the streets and the plazas.^o
I will seek the one I love.
I sought him, but did not find him.
³ The guards who go about the city
   found me.^p
I asked them, "Have you seen the one
   I love?"
⁴ I had just passed them
when I found the one I love.
I held on to him and would not
   let him go
until I brought him
to my mother's house^q—

^A2:12 Or *pruning*   ^B2:14 Or *form*   ^C2:17 Lit *breathes*   ^D2:17 Or *the Bether mountains, or the mountains of spices*; Hb obscure
^E3:1 Or *bed night after night*   ^F3:1 LXX adds *I called him, but he did not answer me*

of my beloved!" Voice can also mean "sound," which may be the sense of it here, but the same word appears in verse 12 to refer to the **cooing** (lit "voice") of the dove and in verse 14 to refer to the voice of Shulamith. The "voice" is thus at the beginning, middle, and end of this section and a theme of these lyrics develops around it: the desire of each to hear the voice of the other, to communicate in the uncluttered freedom of nature—a theme begun in 1:4 that does not conclude until the last lyrics of the Song (8:13) but is distinctively developed in 2:8-14.

2:8 Bounding (Hb *qaphats*; v. 8) plays on the word "pleases" (Hb *chaphets*) in "until the appropriate time" (v. 7). Solomon approached in response to the leading of love.

2:10-14 Solomon's address to Shulamith comprises two lyrical sets: the first (vv. 10-13) describes the beauty of spring with the singing voice of the turtledove as its centerpiece; the second (v. 14) describes the hidden Shulamith as the real dove whose appearance and voice he wished to hear.

2:12 The word for **singing** may also mean "pruning," but the parallelism with the **turtledove's cooing** confirms the translation here.

2:15-17 These verses conclude section B with refrains resumed in part at the transition (7:7-8,10) beginning the corresponding section B' (7:10–8:4; see Introduction).

2:15 The term **vineyards** refers to Shulamith (1:6; 8:12). **In bloom** anticipates the vineyard's beauty before the harvest, and thus describes the beauty of the two lovers anticipating marriage; **foxes** extend the metaphor to anything harmful to the romance. Perhaps the primary warning is against a "premature harvest" of the fruit Shulamith offered Solomon on the wedding night (4:16). The speaker of **Catch . . . for us** could be Solomon, Shulamith, or both, and the ambiguity is likely intentional, suggesting mutual resolve.

2:16 My love is mine and I am his later transforms to "I am

my love's and my love is mine" (6:3) and finally to "I belong to my love and his desire is for me" (7:10)—all similar but differing in ways that show a progression in Shulamith's security. First her possession of him was primary, then secondary, then finally omitted completely, as she found security not in her possession of him, but in his devoted love of her (see note at 7:10). On **lilies**, see note at verse 1. The flower becomes increasingly erotic and evidently associated with tenderness—her breasts, his lips, her abdomen.

2:17 The request in this verse is answered in similar language on the wedding night (4:6). **Gazelle or a young stag** is identical to the phrase in verse 9 that describes Solomon's behavior in courtship. Shulamith longed for the same delight on the wedding night. **Divided mountains** (lit "mountains of separation") is a poetic reference to her breasts (see note at 4:1-7). In Solomon's answer to this request, he embellished the metaphor as the "mountain of myrrh and hill of frankincense" (4:6; cp. 8:14), adding fragrance to the image. The enjoyment of Shulamith's breasts is again poetically expressed in a later night of lovemaking (7:7-8). So Solomon displayed in the Song what he encouraged in Proverbs, "Rejoice in the wife of your youth . . . Let her be your loving deer, your graceful doe. And drink your fill from her breasts of wine so you are always drunk with her love" (Pr 5:18-19, trans. by Glickman, *Solomon's Song of Love*, p. 230). Until Solomon answered Shulamith's request, the night remained and with it the anxiety of anticipation (3:1-4).

3:1-4 Shulamith and Solomon began the night apart but ended it together, aided by the watchmen of the walls. This is set in chiastic balance with section C' where again they began the night apart but fell asleep together (5:2-7:9; see Introduction), though hindered by the watchmen—one of many contrasts in the chiasm (see note at 5:2-8). The shorter length of this section as compared to the one corresponding to it is not uncommon in Hebrew chiasm.

to the chamber of the one
who conceived me.
5 Young women of Jerusalem,
I charge you
by the gazelles and the wild does
of the field:
do not stir up or awaken love
until the appropriate time.[A,a]

N

6 What is this[b] coming up
from the wilderness
like columns of smoke,
scented with myrrh and frankincense[c]
from every fragrant powder
of the merchant?
7 It is Solomon's royal litter[B]
surrounded by 60 warriors
from the mighty of Israel.
8 All of them are skilled with swords
and trained in warfare.
Each has his sword at his side[d]
to guard against the terror
of the night.[e]

9 King Solomon made a sedan chair[C]
for himself

*a*3:5 Sg 2:7;
5:8; 8:4
*b*3:6 Sg 6:10; 8:5
*c*Sg 4:6,14
*d*3:8 Ps 45:3
*e*Ps 91:5
*f*3:10 Sg 1:5
*g*3:11 Is 3:16-17;
4:4
*h*Is 62:5
*i*4:1 Sg 1:15;
5:12
*j*Sg 6:5
*k*4:2 Sg 6:6
*l*4:3 Jos 2:18

with wood from Lebanon.
10 He made its posts of silver,
its back[D] of gold,
and its seat of purple.
Its interior is inlaid with love[E]
by the young women
of Jerusalem.[f]
11 Come out, young women of •Zion,[g]
and gaze at King Solomon,
wearing the crown his mother placed
on him
the day of his wedding[h]—
the day of his heart's rejoicing.

M

4 How beautiful you are, my darling.
How very beautiful!
Behind your veil,
your eyes are doves.[i]
Your hair is like a flock of goats
streaming down Mount Gilead.[j]
2 Your teeth are like a flock
of newly shorn sheep
coming up from washing,
each one having a twin,
and not one missing.[F,k]
3 Your lips are like a scarlet cord,[l]

A3:5 Lit *until it pleases*   **B**3:7 A conveyance carried on the shoulders of servants   **C**3:9 In Hb, the term sedan chair is possibly a synonym for "litter"; it is also called a palanquin.   **D**3:10 Or *base*, or *canopy*   **E**3:10 Or *leather*   **F**4:2 Lit *and no one bereaved among them*

3:5 Young women of Jerusalem begins a repetition of the refrain of 2:7 (see note at 2:7) and is a transition to the central section of the wedding day and night (3:6–5:1; see outline in the Introduction).

3:6–5:1 These verses feature the songwriter's own words at beginning and end, first celebrating the pageant of the wedding day and then the beauty of the wedding night. Solomon is more central in the wedding day, his name appearing three times and the pageantry proclaiming his lavish wedding (3:6-11). Shulamith is more central in the wedding night, in praise of her beauty and character (4:1–5:1).

3:6 The word **this** is feminine in Hebrew, perhaps indicating Shulamith was in the procession coming to Solomon. **Coming up from the wilderness** (see 8:5) suggests two complimentary allusions: (1) Israel's emergence from the wilderness they had entered after deliverance from Egypt and (2) Adam and Eve's emergence from the wilderness they had entered after disobedience. The imagery of Shulamith as a garden paradise on the wedding night is evidence of the latter. The implicit comparisons of Shulamith to Israel are evidence of the former (see Introduction). Both allusions underscore the ideals of romantic love. Like Israel's new land, their love was the foundation of a new life together; like a new paradise, their love recovered what romantic love was meant to be.

3:7-11 This section describes the powerful and magnificent retinue of King Solomon.

4:1–5:1 The wedding night begins with praise of seven aspects of Shulamith (4:1-7), then proceeds to invitation (4:8), lovemaking (4:9-11), and poetic consummation (4:12–5:1).

4:1-7 The praise begins and ends with compliment of the whole person. Within these comprehensive statements Solomon admired Shulamith's eyes, hair, teeth, lips, mouth (see notes at v. 2 and v. 5), neck, and breasts. Between the compliment of her breasts and the concluding summary compliment is Solomon's answer to Shulamith's request of 2:17. The placement of the answer just after the imagery of her breasts but within the overall praise is significant in

yapheh

Hebrew Pronunciation	[yah FEH]
HCSB Translation	beautiful
Uses in Song of Songs	13
Uses in the OT	42
Focus Passage	Song of Songs 4:1,7

The adjective *yapheh* generally describes someone physically *beautiful* (Gn 12:11). It is part of a word family applying regularly to feminine beauty but also to men and other things. Frequently the words "form" *(to'ar)* or "appearance" *(mar'eh)* modify *yapheh*. These phrases indicate *shapely* and *beautiful* women (Gn 29:17) or *well-built* and *handsome* men (Gn 39:6). The second phrase covers *healthy-looking* cows (Gn 41:2). *Yapheh* alone depicts *beautiful* eyes (1Sm 16:12), voice (Ezk 33:32), or tree branches (Ezk 31:3). Describing a city's elevation, *yapheh* implies *splendidly* (Ps 48:2). Twice it connotes *appropriate* (Ec 3:11; 5:18). The noun *yophiy* (19x) is usually *beauty* (Ps 45:11), but characterizes wisdom as *magnificent* (Ezk 28:7). The verb *yaphah* (8x) means *be beautiful* (Ezk 16:13) or *handsome* (Ps 45:2). Love *is delightful* (Sg 4:10). The reflexive denotes *beautify oneself* (Jr 4:30), the intensive *decorate* (Jr 10:4). The reduplicated adjective *yepheh-piyyah* signifies *very beautiful* (Jr 46:20).

and your mouth[A] is lovely.
Behind your veil,
　your brow[B] is like a slice
　　of pomegranate.[a]
4　Your neck is like the tower of David,[b]
　constructed in layers.
　A thousand bucklers
　　are hung on it—
　all of them shields of warriors.[c]
5　Your breasts are like two fawns,
　twins of a gazelle,[c] that feed
　　among the lilies.
6　Before the day breaks[D]
　and the shadows flee,[d]
　I will make my way to the mountain
　　of myrrh
　and the hill of frankincense.[e]
7　You are absolutely beautiful,[f]
　　my darling,
　with no imperfection in you.

Cross references:
[a]4:3 Sg 6:7
[b]4:4 Sg 7:4
[c]4:5 Sg 7:3
[d]4:6 Sg 2:17
[e]Sg 3:6; 4:14
[f]4:7 Sg 1:15; Eph 5:27
[g]4:8 1Kg 4:33
[h]Is 62:5
[i]Dt 3:9; 1Ch 5:23
[j]4:9 Sg 6:5; 7:5
[k]Sg 5:1-2
[l]4:10 Sg 1:2,4
[m]4:11 Pr 5:3

8　Come with me from Lebanon,[E,g]
　　my bride[h]—
　with me from Lebanon!
　Descend from the peak of Amana,
　from the summit of Senir
　　and Hermon,[i]
　from the dens of the lions,
　from the mountains of the leopards.
9　You have captured my heart,[j]
　　my sister,[F,k] my bride.
　You have captured my heart
　　with one glance of your eyes,
　with one jewel of your necklace.
10　How delightful your love is, my sister,
　　my bride.
　Your love is much better than wine,[l]
　and the fragrance of your perfume
　　than any balsam.
11　Your lips drip sweetness like
　　the honeycomb, my bride.[m]

[A]4:3 Or *speech*　[B]4:3 Or *temple*, or *cheek*, or *lips*　[C]4:4 Perhaps describing the woman's necklace　[D]4:6 Lit *breathes*　[E]4:8 In Hb, the word for Lebanon is similar to "frankincense" in Sg 4:6,14,15.　[F]4:9 A term of endearment

---

that it supports the interpretation that "divided mountains" of 2:17 and "mountain of myrrh and the hill of frankincense" in 4:6 are metaphors for her breasts.

4:1 Doves were associated with love in the ancient world, appearing as literal messengers of love in Egyptian art. Shulamith's eyes were messengers of love to Solomon (see note at 1:15). **A flock of goats streaming down Mount Gilead** describes her long, flowing hair. "Streaming" derives from a verb meaning "bubbling" or "boiling," suggesting movement within the whole, as if individual animals were leaping within the group, though merged within it. The metaphor suggests lively curls and healthy, flowing hair.

4:2 Shulamith's **teeth** were gleaming and white. A festive sheep-shearing may be suggested, too, by **coming up from washing**, occurring after they were shorn, so perhaps Solomon praised her smile as well.

4:3 The prostitute Rahab hung a scarlet cord from her window as a sign to the invading Israelites to protect her home (Jos 2:18). Shulamith's speech, which expressed her character, was her protection. This indicated she belonged to God, just as Rahab's scarlet ribbon indicated she belonged to God and His people (Glickman, p. 207). **Your brow** could be translated "your lips" (Hb *raqqah*). In addition, the word translated **slice** is more precisely rendered "sliced opening," which is consistent with the drawings from this era that show the pomegranate sliced open but not cut into slices (O. Keel, *The Song of Songs*, p. 144). These compliments are a dazzling array of movement and color. The colors proceed from white doves to black goats to white sheep to red lips and mouth. They also alternate movement: doves flying out, a flock scampering down, shorn sheep scurrying up, lips beckoning up.

4:4 The **neck** expresses the body language of character. If Shulamith's neck was like a military fortress, she had a character that demanded respect: Solomon admired her completely. The tower **shields** probably correspond metaphorically to her necklace (v. 9).

4:5 The **lilies**, or lotus flowers (see note at 2:1), suggest the life-giving effect of her breasts. The comparison to **fawns**

perhaps suggests Solomon responded as if to playful, baby animals he wanted to hold and caress.

4:6 Before can be rendered "until" (see note at 2:17), which suggests the promise of love through the night. This **mountain** imagery occurs at the end of the first two sections (2:17), at the end of the last two sections (8:14), and here in the center of the central section.

4:7 No imperfection refers to both inner and outer perfection, so it is an apt summary of Solomon's praise of Shulamith's beauty and character.

4:8 The Hebrew for the end of verse 6 and beginning of verse 7 is *hallevonah kulak* and is translated as ". . . frankincense. You are absolutely," where "absolutely" is literally "completely." This phrase sounds like the phrase here translated as: **from Lebanon, my bride** (Hb *millevanon kallah*). This wordplay draws attention to a connotation of "bride" as the "completed one," and furnishes an alliterative transition between the closely related sections. The use of the simpler "bride" here rather than "my sister, my bride" (vv. 9,10,12 and 5:1) allows for the wordplay. **From the peak . . . from the dens of the lions, from the mountains of the leopards** perhaps are metaphors of the fearful places within Shulamith that she must leave in order to open her heart fully to Solomon.

4:9 "Sister" and "brother" were terms of endearment in Egyptian love songs as well as Sumerian love poetry. It is perhaps implied in Adam's expression of unity with Eve: "This one, at last, is bone of my bone, and flesh of my flesh" (Gn 2:23)—a level of unity particularly fitting for siblings, and a metaphor, therefore, of the closest possible relationship. The "brother" metaphor for Solomon in 8:1 justifies a gentle kiss from Shulamith even in public. **My sister, my bride**—a phrase implying a bond as close as that of Adam and Eve—introduces each stage of increasing sexual intimacy: arousal from her presence; delight in her love and fragrance (v. 10); beginning of consummation (v. 12); and the celebration of their union (5:1). **Captured my heart** may also be rendered "made my heart beat faster."

4:11 The phrase **Your lips drip sweetness like the**

Honey and milk[a] are
   under your tongue.
The fragrance of your garments is like
   the fragrance of Lebanon.

12 My sister, my bride, you are
   a locked garden—
   a locked garden[A] and a sealed spring.[b]
13 Your branches are a paradise[B]
   of pomegranates
   with choicest fruits,[c]
   henna with nard—
14 nard and saffron, calamus
   and cinnamon,[d]
   with all the trees of frankincense,[e]
   myrrh and aloes,[f]
   with all the best spices.
15 You are a garden spring,
   a well of flowing water[g]
   streaming from Lebanon.

W
16 Awaken,[h] north wind—

Cross references (center column):
a 4:11 Ex 3:8,17; Nm 14:8; 16:13-14
b 4:12 1Kg 21:8; Est 8:10; Jb 9:7
c 4:13 Sg 7:13
d 4:14 Ex 30:23
e Sg 4:6
f Sg 3:6; Jn 19:39
g 4:15 Gn 26:19; Lv 14:5; Jr 2:13
h 4:16 Sg 2:7; 3:5; 8:4
i Sg 7:13
j 5:1 Pr 5:19
k 5:2 Sg 2:8

   come, south wind.
Blow on my garden,
   and spread the fragrance of its spices.
Let my love come to his garden
   and eat its choicest fruits.[i]

M
5 I have come to my garden—my sister,
   my bride.
I gather[c] my myrrh with my spices.
I eat my honeycomb with my honey.
I drink my wine with my milk.

N Eat, friends!
Drink, be intoxicated with love![D,j]

W
2 I sleep, but my heart is awake.
A sound! My love is knocking![k]

M Open to me, my sister, my darling,
   my dove, my perfect one.
For my head is drenched with dew,
   my hair with droplets of the night.

A 4:12 Some Hb mss read *locked fountain*   B 4:13 Or *park*, or *orchard*   C 5:1 Lit *pluck*   D 5:1 Or *Drink your fill, lovers*

---

honeycomb is alliterative in Hebrew, suggesting the sound of dripping honey. **Honey and milk** not only describes passionate kisses but likely alludes to the richness of the land that God gave Israel (Ex 3:8,17; Nm 14:8; 16:13-14). Solomon found the same richness in Shulamith and implied she was also a gift from God.

4:12-5:1 These lyrics include three principal metaphors in the consummation sequence: a garden, a fountain, and a banquet. Solomon compared Shulamith to a **garden** and spring, or fountain (4:12), expanding first upon the garden (4:13-14) and then the **spring** (4:15). Shulamith continued the metaphor in her invitation to the wind to blow upon the garden, causing its spices to "flow like a stream" (lit for "spread" in "spread the fragrance of its spices," 4:16). Solomon then celebrated in the metaphor of a festive banquet (5:1) that drew together the imagery of the garden (4:12,16) with its **myrrh** and **spices** (4:14) and the honey and milk of Shulamith's kisses (4:11). The banquet imagery continues in the songwriter's encouragement to celebrate (5:1) (Glickman, pp. 30-35).

4:12 The phrases **locked garden** and **sealed spring** praise virgin purity in the imagery of a garden paradise and pristine mountain streams (cp. v. 15).

4:13-14 The word **paradise** may mean simply "park" or "orchard," but it may also allude to the perfection of Eden. The Hebrew rendered **branches** is difficult to translate but not difficult to understand. It refers to all the "extensions" from the garden soil: all the fruits, trees, and spices. It is not the word for "garden," but for all that the garden contains, so it anticipates the entire description in verses 13-14. **Pomegranates** were symbols of lovemaking and fertility; **henna** had small red and white blossoms; **nard** was famous for its aroma; **saffron** was linked with nard, possibly because the spices were in the saffron's stigmata, which when gathered together resembled a handful of yarn, perhaps providing a delicate metaphor of Shulamith's sexuality. **Calamus** (Hb *qaneh*) **and cinnamon** (Hb *qinnamon*) are alliterative and, like nard and saffron, combine plant (the long, green-ribboned leaves of the calamus that grew in marshes) with fragrance. The **trees of frankincense** continue the movement to the larger, more overwhelming beauty of the garden, perhaps a metaphor for the increasing intensity of the experience.

4:15 Garden spring joins the metaphors of "garden" and "spring." Water **from Lebanon** completes the embellishment of spring water with the image of pure, mountain streams. An allusion to Shulamith's sexual response in the metaphor of the waters is consistent with the metaphor of a well in Pr 5:15-18.

4:16 If the previous imagery suggests the peak of excitement, then Shulamith's invitation to Solomon is perfectly placed. She continued the previous metaphors in her poetic request for the winds to **blow** upon her **garden** (lit "let its spices flow like a stream"; the verb rendered "streams flowing" in v. 15 is the same verb rendered "flow like a stream" here). So Shulamith resumed both the garden and the spring metaphors. She asked the winds to entice Solomon into the garden with its intoxicating fragrances. **Awaken** is the same word used in the refrain advocating patient restraint (2:7; 3:5). The songwriter thus reminds the reader that such restraint is no longer needed.

5:1 Solomon celebrated the consummation (see note at 4:12-5:1). The songwriter's words began this section and now conclude it (see outline in the Introduction). Since **friends** in the singular was Solomon's customary name for Shulamith (rendered "darling" in 1:9,15; 2:2,10,13; 4:1,7; 6:4) and **love** in the singular was Shulamith's customary name for Solomon (rendered "my love" in 1:13,14,16; 2:3,8,9,16,17; 4:16; 5:2,4,5,6,8,9,10,16; 6:1,2,3; 7:9,11; 8:14), an alternative translation is "Eat, O darling companions (Hb *reyim*); drink and drink deeply, O beloveds (Hb *dodim*)." In other words, it appears the songwriter addresses the couple by the names they most commonly called each other.

This blessing is at the center of the song's lyrics and is the conclusion of its central section (see outline in the Introduction). As if Shakespeare stepped onto the stage of *Romeo and Juliet*, the songwriter dramatically appears.

W 3 I have taken off my clothing.ᵃ
How can I put it back on?
I have washed my feet.
How can I get them dirty?
4 My love thrust his hand
   through the opening,
and my feelings were stirred for him.
5 I rose to open for my love.
My hands dripped with myrrh,ᵇ
my fingers with flowing myrrh
on the handles of the bolt.
6 I opened to my love,
but my love had turned
   and gone away.
I was crushedᴬ that he had left.ᴮ
I sought him, but did not find him.ᶜ
I called him, but he did not answer.
7 The guards who go about the city
   found me.ᵈ
They beat and wounded me;

they took my cloakᶜ from me—
the guardians of the walls.ᵉ
8 Young women of Jerusalem,
   I charge you:ᶠ
if you find my love,
tell him that I am lovesick.ᵍ

Y 9 What makes the one you love better
   than another,
most beautiful of women?ʰ
What makes him better than another,
that you would give us this charge?

W
10 My love is fit and strong,ᴰ,ⁱ
notable among ten thousand.ʲ
11 His head is purest gold.
His hair is wavyᴱ,ᵏ
and black as a raven.
12 His eyes are like dovesˡ
beside streams of water,

ᵃ5:3 Lk 11:7
ᵇ5:5 Sg 5:13
ᶜ5:6 Sg 3:1-2
ᵈ5:7 Sg 3:3
ᵉSg 8:9-10
ᶠ5:8 Sg 2:7;
3:5; 8:4
ᵍSg 2:5
ʰ5:9 Sg 1:8; 6:1
ⁱ5:10 1Sm 16:12
ʲPs 45:2
ᵏ5:11 Sg 5:2
ˡ5:12 Sg 1:15;
4:1

ᴬ**5:6** Lit *My soul went out*   ᴮ**5:6** Or *spoken*   ᶜ**5:7** Or *veil, or shawl*   ᴰ**5:10** Or *is radiant and ruddy*   ᴱ**5:11** Or *is like palm leaves;*
Hb obscure

After encouraging the wedding guests at the end of the wedding day (3:11), he blesses the wedding couple at the end of the wedding night (5:1). His authorial perspective is all-knowing and all-present, hinting that he speaks for God. Readers have often thought it curious that the mothers appear five times (3:4,11; 6:9; 8:2,5) but fathers not at all, even where expected (8:8-9). Perhaps it is because the voice of the songwriter speaks for the ultimate Father who orchestrates the romance. As the wedding's preeminent guest, the Great Songwriter gives blessing to love and the lovers.

5:2-7:9 This is the lengthiest section of the Song. This night of relative apathy (5:2a) following the wedding night is structurally opposite the night of anxiety preceding the wedding day (see outline in the Introduction). As such this later section provides some obvious contrasts, but it also more broadly captures common romantic sequences within marriage that compare and contrast with the wedding night and all that precedes it. This section is also distinguished by the most developed internal chiasm in the Song. Despite its length, its beginning with Shulamith sleeping alone (5:2a) and conclusion with her sleeping romantically with Solomon (7:9) artistically maintains its chiastic balance with the corresponding section, 3:1-5. The outline of events is evident in the outline of the book (see Introduction). In addition, the two questions posed by the women of Jerusalem (5:9; 6:1) are poetic guides to the movement of the lyrics. After the problem created by Shulamith's reluctance (5:2), the first question (5:9) introduces her tenfold praise of Solomon (5:10-16) and the second question (6:1) introduces the reconciliation (6:1-13) that leads to Solomon's tenfold praise of her (7:1-5).

5:2-8 The contrast with the night before the wedding is apparent. On that earlier night (see note at 3:1-4), Shulamith couldn't sleep because of her anxiety over Solomon's absence; here, sleep comes easily, and she wants continued slumber out of apathy from his presence, as evidenced by Solomon's pleading to **open to me**. In 3:1-4 the watchmen of the walls assisted Shulamith to find him; here, they hinder her, mistaking her for a criminal. In 3:1-4 Shulamith's

night ended united with Solomon; here, lengthy anxiety and reconciliation precedes the night of reunion.

5:2 Solomon's fourfold terms of endearment, the most of any place in the Song, underscore the contrast of his fervor with her apathetic response.

5:4-5 Many of the terms in these verses have euphemistic possibilities, suggesting a double entendre. She may have been dreaming. **My feelings were stirred** is literally "my insides were agitated."

5:8 Shulamith is no longer apathetic but **lovesick** (lit "faint from love am I"), just as she was in the peak of courtship (2:5).

5:9 This is the first of two questions (v. 9; 6:1; see note at 5:2-7:9) that guide the movement of this section.

5:10-16 This section contains tenfold praise that moves downward from head to feet, enclosed by comprehensive summary praise in verse 10 and verse 16b. The praise of Solomon's mouth in verse 16 is not likely an interruption of the movement since it is apparently a praise of his speech and not his literal lips that are praised in verse 13 (see note at 2:2-3). This section is in chiastic balance with the tenfold praise of Shulamith that moves upward from feet to head (7:1-5, see outline in the Introduction).

5:10 Fit and strong is literally "radiant and red," implying fitness and strength. **Among ten thousand** is clearly a ratio emphasizing uniqueness.

5:11 Gold is consistent with the lustrous radiance, and its color and value are paramount in the metaphor. The Hebrew word translated **wavy** may be associated with "palm leaves," a precursor to the palm tree simile of Shulamith in 7:7.

5:12 Eyes ... like doves is the only identical praise of each by the other (1:15; 4:1). Each had eyes expressing love. Whereas other aspects of Shulamith's praise are expanded at most by one phrase, this simile is expanded by three: **beside streams of water, washed in milk and set like jewels** (lit "perched over a pool"). The phrases contribute to imagery of happy, loving eyes. They also

washed in milk
and set like jewels.^{A}
13 His cheeks^a are like beds of spice,
towers of^B perfume.
His lips are lilies,
dripping with flowing myrrh.^{b}
14 His arms^c are rods of gold
set^D with topaz.^{E,c}
His body^F is an ivory panel
covered with sapphires.^{d}
15 His legs are alabaster pillars
set on pedestals of pure gold.
His presence is like Lebanon,^{e}
as majestic as the cedars.^{f}
16 His mouth is sweetness.
He is absolutely desirable.^{g}
This is my love, and this is my friend,
young women of Jerusalem.

Y

6 Where has your love gone,
most beautiful of women?
Which way has he^G turned?
We will seek him with you.

W

2 My love has gone down to his garden,^{h}
to beds of spice,^{i}
to feed in the gardens^j
and gather lilies.^{k}
3 I am my love's and my love is mine;^{l}
he feeds among the lilies.

---

^{a}5:13 Sg 1:10
^{b}Sg 5:5
^{c}5:14 Ex 28:20;
39:13; Ezk 1:16
^{d}Ex 24:10
^{e}5:15 Sg 7:4-5
^{f}1Kg 4:33
^{g}5:16 Sg 4:7
^{h}6:2 Sg 4:16; 5:1
^{i}Sg 5:13
^{j}Sg 1:7
^{k}Sg 2:1
^{l}6:3 Sg 2:16;
7:10; 8:6
^{m}6:4 Nm 2:2-3;
Sg 6:10
^{n}6:5 Sg 4:9
^{o}Sg 4:1
^{p}6:6 Sg 4:2
^{q}6:7 Sg 4:3
^{r}6:8 1Kg 11:3
^{s}6:9 Sg 2:14; 5:2
^{t}Pr 31:29
^{u}Gn 30:13
^{v}6:10 Sg 3:6; 8:5

M 4 You are as beautiful as Tirzah,^{H}
my darling,
lovely as Jerusalem,
awe-inspiring as an army
with banners.^{m}
5 Turn your eyes away from me,
for they captivate me.^{n}
Your hair is like a flock of goats
streaming down from Gilead.^{o}
6 Your teeth are like a flock
of ewes
coming up from washing,
each one having a twin,
and not one missing.^{I,p}
7 Behind your veil,^{q}
your brow^J is like a slice
of pomegranate.
8 There are 60 queens
and 80 concubines^r
and young women^K without number.
9 But my dove,^{s} my virtuous one,
is unique;^{t}
she is the favorite of her mother,
perfect to the one who gave her birth.
Women see her and declare
her fortunate;^{u}
queens and concubines also,
and they sing her praises:

Y^L

10 Who is this^{M,v} who shines
like the dawn—

---

^{A}5:12 Lit *milk sitting in fullness*　　^{B}5:13 LXX, Vg read *spice, yielding*　　^{C}5:14 Lit *hands*　　^{D}5:14 Lit *filled*; Sg 5:2,12　　^{E}5:14 Probably
yellow topaz　　^{F}5:14 Lit *abdomen*　　^{G}6:1 Lit *your love*　　^{H}6:4 = a mountain city in Manasseh　　^{I}6:6 Lit *and no one bereaved among
them*　　^{J}6:7 Or *temple, or cheek, or lips*　　^{K}6:8 Or *and virgins*; Sg 1:3　　^{L}6:10 Some see v. 10 as spoken by **M.**　　^{M}6:10 In Hb, the
word for "this" is feminine.

---

possibly allude to the power of love that triumphs over waters of chaos (8:6-7). Doves looking at rushing streams become doves perched over still water, with reflections of doves looking back to their source (Glickman, pp. 101, 151, 212).

5:13 The visual metaphors of verses 11-12 give way to more sensual, aromatic ones in this verse: fragrant spices and perfume describe Solomon's cheeks; liquid **myrrh** drips from his lips. **Lilies** are literally life-giving "lotus flowers" (see note at 2:1). Shulamith praised Solomon's fragrant, intoxicating kisses.

5:14 **His arms** are literally "his hands," and the **rods of gold** are likely his fingers, a metaphor in praise of Solomon's valued touch. **His body** (lit "his abdomen") is hard and polished like **ivory**, but rippled, as if **covered with sapphires**.

5:15 **Alabaster** was a valuable mineral normally used for small objects, so its use to create massive **pillars** emphasizes value, like gold, ivory, or sapphires. "Pillars" imply **legs** of grandeur and strength. The **pedestals of pure gold** of Solomon's feet show gold from head to toe, a visual metaphor for his complete desirability (v. 16).

5:16 **Mouth** is likely a reference to speech (see note at 2:2-3). The affirmation of **love** and friendship intertwined continues the theme begun in 1:9 (see note at 1:9).

6:1 This is the second of two questions (5:9; see note at 5:2-7:9) that guide the movement of this section.

6:2-13 This section first answers the question, showing Shulamith's awareness of Solomon's location, then recounts his affirming praise and the account of their reconciliation.

6:2-3 **Lilies** are "lotus flowers" (see note at 2:1). **I am my love's** continues the transformation of this refrain (see note at 2:16). **Feeds among the lilies** anticipates Solomon's life-giving praise that brings reconciliation (see note at 2:16).

6:4-10 This section consists of praise designed to reconcile. Although on the wedding night one glance of Shulamith's eyes aroused Solomon (4:9), here Solomon asked that she turn her eyes from him because they captivated (lit "aroused") him. He did not want to express his love physically until they reunited emotionally, which the praise was designed to achieve. He avoided the most erotic of lovemaking praise. He emphasized instead that Shulamith was God's gift for whom his love was unchanged from the wedding night. His comparison of her to the beauty of Israel (6:4,10) implies she was as wonderful a gift to him as the land was to God's people (see note at 4:11).

Solomon's comparison of Shulamith to **Tirzah** and **Jerusalem** (v. 4), Israel's most prominent cities in the south and the north, appears to be in chiastic balance with the

as beautiful as the moon,
bright as the sun,
awe-inspiring as an army
  with banners?[a]

W

11 I came down to the walnut grove
to see the blossoms of the valley,
to see if the vines were budding[b]
and the pomegranates blooming.
12 Before I knew it,
my desire put me
among the chariots of
my noble people.[A]

Y

13B Come back, come back,
Shulammite![C,D]
Come back, come back, that
we may look at you!

a6:10 Sg 6:4
b6:11 Sg 7:12
c6:13 Jdg 21:21
d Gn 32:2; 2Sm 17:24
e7:1 Ps 45:13
f7:3 Sg 4:5
g7:4 Sg 4:4

M Why are you looking
at the Shulammite,
as you look at the dance[c]
of the two camps?[E,d]

7 How beautiful are your sandaled feet,
  princess![F,e]
The curves of your thighs
are like jewelry,
the handiwork of a master.
2 Your navel is a rounded bowl;
it never lacks mixed wine.
Your waist[G] is a mound of wheat
surrounded by lilies.
3 Your breasts are like two fawns,
twins of a gazelle.[f]
4 Your neck is like a tower of ivory,[g]
your eyes like pools in Heshbon
by the gate of Bath-rabbim.
Your nose is like the tower of Lebanon
looking toward Damascus.

A6:12 Or *of Amminadib*, or *of my people of a prince*; Hb obscure   B6:13 Sg 7:1 in Hb   C6:13 Or *the peaceable one*   D6:13 Perhaps an inhabitant of the town of Shunem, or a feminine form of Solomon's name   E6:13 Or *dance of Mahanaim*   F7:1 Lit *daughter of a nobleman or prince*   G7:2 Or *belly*

---

description of her as **beautiful as the moon, bright as the sun**, since both lyrics end with the phrase: **awe-inspiring as an army with banners**. "An army with banners" may also be translated "bannered hosts" (i.e., "of heaven," which would be "stars," or "of armies," depending on the context). So Solomon compared Shulamith to the cities and military of Israel, which were like the moon, the sun, and the stars—perhaps recalling the imagery of Israel as the sun, moon, and stars in Joseph's dream (Gn 37:9).

6:11-13 In these verses Shulamith recounted the reconciliation. **If the vines were budding and the pomegranates blooming** is a metaphor expressing their desire to begin a new season of life together (2:17; 7:12). No easy explanation exists for the phrase **among the chariots of my noble people**, but the implication is that Shulamith had resumed a position of royal prominence. She is here identified as **the Shulammite** for the first time in the Song (or, as we have rendered it throughout the study notes, the word can also be rendered "Shulamith," the feminine form of Solomon's name). As the feminine form of Solomon, the name shows she and Solomon were "soulmates" who through their hardship and reconciliation had entered into a deeper relationship (8:10). Alternately, rather than a personal or pet name the word might mean she was from the town of Shulam, which is otherwise unknown, or from Shunem (Jos 19:18; 1Sm 28:4; 2Kg 4:8).

The **two camps** is Mahanaim in Hebrew. This was the place where Jacob and Esau's reconciliation took place (Gn 32-33)—an appropriate parallel for the resolution of conflict between husband and wife. Solomon was using the illustration of God's love for Israel to illustrate his love for Shulamith. The people were gazing (as if in a vision) at an illustration of the reconciliation God always wants to achieve with His people.

7:1-5 Solomon's tenfold praise of Shulamith from head to toe in this section is in chiastic balance with her tenfold praise of Solomon from toe to head in 5:10-16 (see outline in the Introduction). This praise also offers interesting comparisons with the lovemaking praise of the wedding night (4:1-7). It is more intimate and lavish—more lavish,

in the royal imagery of a **princess** with hair not like a flock descending a mountain but like fine **purple** threads holding **captive** a king; more intimate, in praising not only her **breasts** again (more sensually), but her **thighs** (lit "hips"), **navel**, and **waist** (lit "abdomen") for the first time. The praise poetically portrays the greater depth of intimacy that reconciliation and time have achieved.

7:1 Princess is literally "daughter of a prince" (Hb *bath nadiv*). If this is not a wordplay, it is certainly a link to "my noble people" (6:12; Hb *'ammi nadiv*). These are the only occurrences of "prince" (Hb *nadiv*) in the Song, and its repetition links the reconciliation section with the lovemaking praise. **Thighs** refer to their upper part, inclusive of the hips, which bear the **curves** that Solomon praised. The **handiwork of a master** (or "of a master craftsman") is another creative way of describing Shulamith as a gift.

7:2 Although some lexical evidence from Arabic suggests the possibility that **navel** is "vulva," the other two occurrences of this word in the OT refer to the body in general (Pr 3:8) and to the umbilical cord (Ezk 16:4). In addition, "navel" is more probable here since it is more like the image of a **rounded bowl** (or "wine chalice") to which it is compared. On the other hand, the image of wine and wheat, coupled with the reference to the pomegranate in 8:2 with its wordplay on "drink" and "kiss" (see note at 8:1-2), and the prior wordplays on "love" and "mandrakes," and then on "doors" and "openings" (see note at 7:12-13), suggests that "navel" may be a euphemism for Shulamith's more intimate sexuality. On **surrounded by lilies**, see note at 2:1. Solomon envisioned lotus flowers surrounding the wine and wheat of Shulamith's navel and abdomen that brought delight to him.

7:3 The phrase **breasts are like two fawns** repeats a praise from the wedding night (4:5) but significantly omits "that feed among the lilies." This emphasizes the "feeding" (lit "grazing") among the lotus flowers just implied by their surrounding the wine and wheat of Shulamith's abdomen. Solomon used the metaphor of a palm tree and its fruit to describe his delight in Shulamith's breasts (7:7-8).

7:4 A **tower of ivory** is smooth to the touch but it has a demeanor that inspires respect (see note at 4:4). **Eyes like**

5 Your head crowns you[A]
   like Mount Carmel,
   the hair of your head
   like purple cloth—
   a king could be held captive[a]
   in your tresses.
6 How beautiful you are
   and how pleasant,[b]
   my love, with such delights!
7 Your stature is like a palm tree;
   your breasts are clusters of fruit.
8 I said, "I will climb the palm tree
   and take hold of its fruit."[c]
   May your breasts be like clusters
   of grapes,
   and the fragrance of your breath
   like apricots.[d]

9 Your mouth[B] is
   like fine wine[e]—

W   flowing smoothly for my love,
    gliding past my lips and teeth![C]
10 I belong to my love,
    and his desire[f] is for me.[g]
11 Come, my love,
    let's go to the field;
    let's spend the night
    among the henna blossoms.[D]
12 Let's go early to the vineyards;
    let's see if the vine has budded,
    if the blossom has opened,
    if the pomegranates are in bloom.[h]
    There I will give you my love.
13 The mandrakes[i] give off a fragrance,

a 7:5 Sg 4:9
b 7:6 Sg 1:15-16
c 7:8 Pr 5:19
d Sg 2:3
e 7:9 Sg 5:16
f 7:10 Gn 3:16; 4:7
g Sg 2:16; 6:3; 8:6
h 7:12 Sg 6:11
i 7:13 Gn 30:14-16

A 7:5 Lit *head upon you is*   **B** 7:9 Lit *palate*   **C** 7:9 LXX, Syr, Vg; MT reads *past lips of sleepers*   **D** 7:11 Or *the villages*

---

pools in Heshbon perhaps continues the theme of Solomon's eyes like doves "perched over a pool" (see note at 5:12), implying that the pool his dovelike eyes perched over were Shulamith's eyes. They were tranquil waters (perhaps "of understanding," Heshbon arising from the root for "explanation") so that they gave rest by the city gates (**Bath-rabbim**, lit "daughter of many," indicating a busy thoroughfare into the city). The peace and wholeness each found in the other contrasts with the chaos of city crowds. **Nose . . . like the tower of Lebanon looking toward Damascus** describes a capacity for appropriate anger. "Nose" is from the word for anger, arising from its evidence in the flaring of the nostrils; "tower" connotes strength with a military image; Damascus was the capital of potential enemies that might violate Israel's borders. Shulamith's anger would flare at anyone who violated her boundaries as well.

7:5 Mount Carmel has majesty like Shulamith's, giving the capability to bind even the **king** with the power of her **hair** like **purple cloth** (lit "threads"—that can bind). The royal imagery of princess and king continues, albeit in irony. The king who stooped to admire the sandaled feet of the princess (v. 1) was bound by her silken hair (v. 5).

7:6-9 The fervor of this section is in chiastic balance with the apathy of 5:2-8 (see outline in the Introduction). This lovemaking following praise also invites comparison with the lovemaking following the praise of 4:1-7. If the focus of the wedding night is its beautiful consummation (4:12–5:1), the focus of this later night is the peaceful nurture their love brings. They fell asleep tasting kisses like wine (see note at 7:9). Sexual intimacy consummates marriage and nurtures it as well.

7:6 The Hebrew underlying **my love, with such delights** is difficult to translate. Linguistic data favors "love" (Hb *'ahavah*) not as a term of address but as an abstract word for "love," as it is in its other nine references in the Song (v. 6; 2:4-5,7; 3:5; 5:8; 8:4,6-7), one of which is in chiastic parallelism with this verse (5:8). So love is likely the subject, just as a new subject follows the only other place in the Song where the two Hebrew words rendered **beautiful** and **pleasant** appear (1:16). To paraphrase, Solomon says, "Love flows through your tender affection." This is a beautiful lyric about the heartfelt source of Shulamith's love.

7:7-8 The **fruit** of the **palm tree** transforms from "stalks of dates" (lit "fruit" in v. 8) to **clusters of grapes**, demonstrating first a view from a distance and then the object of Solomon's caresses. "At a distance her breasts seem like

clusters of dates on the palm tree. But held close, they are like supple, juicy clusters of grapes" (Glickman, p. 127).

7:9 The last phrase in this verse could be translated "past the lips of sleepers" (Hb *yeshenim*). This section begins with Shulamith sleeping alone (Hb *yeshenah*, 5:2) and ends with the couple sleeping together (see outline in the Introduction) just as the section in chiastic balance with this does as well (3:1-4). So their kisses—hers as fragrant as apricots and both of theirs as intoxicating as **wine**—lingered on as they drifted peacefully off to sleep.

7:10 This verse repeats the similar refrain where Shulamith affirmed their exclusive bond (see note at 2:16). "Desire" in **his desire is for me** is used only twice elsewhere in the OT: at Gn 3:16, in God's words to Eve describing the consequences of disobedience ("Your desire will be for your husband, yet he will rule over you") and in God's words to Cain describing sin personified as a lion crouching at the door ("Its desire is for you, but you must rule over it," Gn 4:7). So "desire" may connote the desire to rule. This verse has been interpreted in at least three ways: (1) Now Solomon has a desire (to love or to rule) equal to the desire of Shulamith; (2) now Solomon has a desire to love, but not to dominate;

duda'iym

Hebrew Pronunciation	[doo dah EEM]
HCSB Translation	mandrakes
Uses in Song of Songs	1
Uses in the OT	6
Focus Passage	Song of Songs 7:13

Mandrakes (duda'iym) are in the nightshade family and grow natively in the Mediterranean region. The best-known species, *Mandragora officinarum*, has a short stem; large leaves of pungent odor; whitish, purple flowers; and a thick, pulpy root that often forks. The fruit is golden, juicy, about the size of an apple, and not poisonous. From ancient times, the *mandrake* was considered an aphrodisiac and used to promote conception by removing sterility. The plant appears frequently in Egyptian drawings from the New Kingdom era (1540–1075 B.C.), where its odor is used to arouse sexual desire. Rachel sold Leah the right to an evening with their husband Jacob in exchange for *mandrakes* (Gn 30:14-16). As a sign of her readiness for love, Solomon's lover mentions mandrakes giving off their fragrance (Sg 7:12-13). *Duda'iym* may derive from the root behind the noun *love (dod)* that stands before and after it, so wordplay may occur.

and at our doors is every delicacy—
new as well as old.
I have treasured them up for you,
my love.

8 If only I could treat you like my brother,[A]
one who nursed at my mother's breasts,
I would find you in public and kiss you,
and no one would scorn me.
2 I would lead you, I would take you,

to the house of my mother[a]
who taught me.[B]
I would give you spiced wine
to drink
from my pomegranate juice.
3 His left hand is under my head,
and his right arm embraces me.[b]
4 Young women of Jerusalem,
I charge you:

a8:2 Sg 3:4
b8:3 Sg 2:6

A8:1 Lit *Would that you were like a brother to me*   B8:2 LXX adds *and into the chamber of the one who bore me*

---

and (3) now Solomon, and not Shulamith, has a desire to "rule" in a benevolent sense, perhaps as the sun and moon "rule" (or "govern") the day and night, providing guiding light (Gn 1:18) or as God's "rule" provides loving care for His people (Ps 22:28; 59:13; 66:7; 89:9). In any case, after a wonderful reconciliation and time of intimacy, Shulamith affirmed her complete security in Solomon's love.

7:11–8:4 This section is in chiastic balance with 2:6-17 (see note there).

7:11-13 This section contains Shulamith's invitation to enjoy spring. It balances Solomon's earlier invitation to do the same (2:8-14). His invitation concluded with a request to hear her voice (2:14); hers concluded with a request to make love (7:12-13). The Song will conclude on precisely these themes: Solomon's request to hear her voice (8:13) and her request to make love (8:14)—artistically portraying unending seasons of spring in their love.

7:11 The phrase **let's spend the night among the henna blossoms** uses language from 1:13-14 where Shulamith compared Solomon to henna blossoms in En-gedi after comparing him to a pouch of myrrh which spent the night between her breasts. During courtship her thoughts were of him who was like henna blossoms who would "spend the night" with her; now she asked to spend the night with him "among the henna blossoms."

7:12-13 These verses contemplate a new season of spring in their experience. **Love** (Hb *doday*) is a wordplay on **mandrakes** (Hb *duda'iym*), an appropriate name for these plants associated with love and fertility. **Delicacy** is the same word twice rendered "choicest fruits" referring to erotic delicacies of the wedding night (4:13,16). **New** and **old** refer literally to fresh fruit from the harvest and dried fruits from the past. This refers figuratively to lovemaking "delicacies" that were in part fresh and new and in part familiar and constant. "Old" (Hb *yeshanim*) plays on "of the ones sleeping" (Hb *yeshenim*; v. 9). Since this is the peaceful sleep after lovemaking (see note at v. 9), the poet associates the familiar lovemaking with security and comfort.

The location of delicacies at **our doors** (Hb *pethachenu*) is a play on **has opened** (Hb *pittach*; "of blossoms," v. 12), both words derived from the same root. The poet's intention to create the wordplay is underscored by his rejection of a different word for door that he could have used (Hb *chomah*, used in 8:9) without creating the wordplay. "Our doors" is thus a very erotic play on "our openings." Her "openings" and openness are like the opening of flower blossoms.

8:1-2 In these verses the couple moves inside. On the earlier spring day Solomon's description prepared for his request to see and hear Shulamith. Similarly, now she first wished for a kiss outside with all the innocence of a kiss from a brother, and that prepares for her wish for more intimate kissing in innocence—"without scorn"—as well. **I would . . . kiss you** (Hb *'eshaqka*; v. 1) is a play on **I would give you . . . to drink** (Hb *'ashqeka*). They would have been

identical in the original Hebrew, which did not write the vowels. "I would give you . . . to drink from" could be taken as "I would let you kiss from."

Spiced wine . . . from my pomegranate juice is a smooth translation, but the literal is more dramatic: "from the wine—the spiced wine—from the sweet wine of my pomegranate." The repetition of "from" reinforces the image of drinking from a container and probably resumes these images: (1) the image of the navel as the chalice of wine (see note at 7:2), (2) the image of drinking her kisses like wine (7:9), and (3) the image of drinking from a mother's breast (8:1). The "spiced wine" (Hb *reqach*) is likely a play on "mouth" or "opened lips" (as opposed to "brow," Hb *raqqah*; see note at 4:3). The moisture of Shulamith's mouth was like the sliced opening of a pomegranate on the wedding night; now the moisture of "my pomegranate" is like "spiced wine."

8:3-14 This section concludes the themes introduced in 1:1–2:7 (see outline in the Introduction). Refrains similar to the ones that concluded the first section now begin the last one in chiastic balance. And once again the Song appropriately reintroduces Shulamith's brothers and explains the circumstances introduced in the first section and how the lovers first met.

8:3 This refrain again functions to close the prior section and to introduce the next. It appropriately requests consummation from Solomon (see note at 2:6) and leads to a variation on the refrain that previously urged patience.

8:4 Caution in love is important, but when **the time** is **appropriate**, don't let its joy pass you by.

The blossoms and fruit of a pomegranate tree (3:4; 6:7; 8:2). The pomegranate is a frequent image in Jewish art and was found atop the columns on the façade to the temple.

do not stir up or awaken love
until the appropriate time.*ᵃ*

Y
⁵ Who is this*ᵇ* coming up
  from the wilderness,
leaning on the one she loves?

W
I awakened you under the apricot tree.*ᶜ*
There your mother conceived you;
there she conceived and gave
  you birth.
⁶ Set me as a seal on your heart,
as a seal on your arm.*ᵈ*
For love is as strong as death;*ᵉ*
ardent love is as unrelenting
  as •Sheol.
Love's flames are fiery flames*ᶠ*—
the fiercest of all.*ᴬ*
⁷ Mighty waters cannot extinguish love;
rivers cannot sweep it away.

*ᵃ*8:4 Sg 2:7; 3:5
*ᵇ*8:5 Sg 3:6; 6:10
*ᶜ*Sg 2:3
*ᵈ*8:6 Sg 2:16; 6:3; 7:10
*ᵉ*Rm 8:38-39; 1Co 13:8
*ᶠ*Dt 32:21-22; Pr 6:34; 27:4
*ᵍ*8:7 Pr 6:35
*ʰ*8:8 Ezk 16:7
*ⁱ*8:9 1Kg 6:15
*ʲ*8:11 Ec 2:4
*ᵏ*Mt 21:33

If a man were to give all his wealth*ᴮ*
  for love,*ᵍ*
it would be utterly scorned.

B ⁸ Our sister is young;
  she has no breasts.*ʰ*
What will we do for our sister
  on the day she is spoken for?
⁹ If she is a wall,
  we will build a silver parapet on it.
If she is a door,
  we will enclose it with cedar planks.*ᶜ,ⁱ*

W
¹⁰ I am*ᴰ* a wall
and my breasts like towers.
So in his eyes I have become
like one who finds peace.*ᴱ*

¹¹ Solomon owned a vineyard
  in Baal-hamon.*ʲ*
He leased the vineyard to tenants.*ᵏ*

---

*ᴬ*8:6 Or *the blaze of the* LORD   *ᴮ*8:7 Lit *all the wealth of his house*   *ᶜ*8:8-9 Vv. 8-9 may record what the girl's brothers used to say.
*ᴰ*8:10 Or *was*   *ᴱ*8:10 In Hb, the word for peace sounds similar to Solomon and Shulammite.

8:5-7 All earlier praise, though differing at times in purpose (see note at 6:4-10) was in praise of the lovers. The lyrics of this section, however, praise love itself. The love that pleased to awaken Solomon and Shulamith has a fiery origin in the love of Yahweh.

8:5 Who is this coming up from the wilderness begins a new section introduced with words identical to those that begin the wedding procession and with the same complimentary allusions (see note at 3:6). Solomon and Shulamith have left the wilderness created by Adam and Eve to experience a paradise, and their love is like God's for His people, particularly when after the hardships of the wilderness they emerged trusting and "leaning" on Him.

8:6-7 The **seal** is the valuable possession by which all of a person's possessions are identified. **Strong as death** is a stark metaphor, showing that just as death conquers, so does love. But perhaps it implies love has the last word.

'ur

Hebrew Pronunciation	[OOR]
HCSB Translation	awaken, stir up
Uses in Song of Songs	9
Uses in the OT	80
Focus Passage	Song of Songs 8:4-5

'Ur functions as the imperative *wake up* (Is 52:1), *awake* (Jdg 5:12), or *come alive* (Hab 2:19). All verb conjugations describe *rousing* someone (Jb 41:10). The intensive verb also means *stir up* (Is 14:9) or *rally* (Ps 80:2). One *brandishes* whips (Is 10:26) and *raises* (2Sm 23:18) or *wields* (1Ch 11:11) spears. People *raise* cries (Is 15:5). The causative verb also means *awaken* (Is 50:4), *raise up* (Is 45:13), or *unleash* (Ps 78:38). One *puts into the mind* or *motivates* (Ezr 1:1,5). God *moves* on someone's behalf (Jb 8:6). People *stir* fires (Hs 7:4). The infinitive indicates *arising* (Ps 73:20). The reflexive-passive verb signifies *be excited* (Jb 31:29) or *wake oneself* (Is 51:17). The passive-reflexive shows people *stirring* from sleep (Jb 14:12). It suggests *taking* sheaths from bows (Hab 3:9). God *is coming* from heaven (Zch 2:13). The noun *'ir* denotes *agitation* (Jr 15:8) or *rage* (Hs 11:9).

If death conquers mortality, then love may as well. **Unrelenting as Sheol** extends this image, showing that as the grave pursues all mortals, so love pursues the beloved. The **ardent love** is often attributed to God, who expresses it in fiery concern for those whom He loves (Dt 4:24; 32:21-22). Since its **fiery flames** are the blaze of the Lord (see textual footnote), it cannot be extinguished. Any improper attempts to attain love are **scorned**.

8:8-12 This section explains how Shulamith found love properly—by preparing herself for it and by a fortuitous meeting with Solomon in the vineyard. These sections are in chiastic balance with the introductory sections of the Song (see outline in the Introduction) and are a flashback to the life with her brothers assumed in 1:6.

8:8-9 Shulamith's brothers took responsibility for her care when **she** was **young** and had **no breasts**, promising restrictions if she was promiscuous (**if she is a door**) but rewards if she was responsible (**if she is a wall**) as they prepared for **the day** she was **spoken for**.

8:10 Shulamith affirmed the development of her character (**I am a wall**) and her body (**my breasts like towers**) continuing the imagery of verses 8-9. There may be an allusion to Ruth, who found favor in the eyes of Boaz (Ru 2:2,10,13) under circumstances similar to Shulamith's. The poet artfully changes the traditional expression that dates back to the story of Noah, who "found favor in the eyes of the LORD" (Gn 6:8): Shulamith found **peace** in the **eyes** of Solomon. It is an appropriate change and wordplay, since Shulamith and "Shelomoh" (Hb for "Solomon") are feminine and masculine forms of names derived from *shalom* "peace." Shulamith found *shalom* with Shelomoh. Boaz saw Ruth working in the field after the death of her husband left her destitute, but then Boaz's marriage to her raised her to a position of prominence. Solomon's observation of Shulamith working in the vineyard after the mistreatment by her brothers led to the same.

8:11-12 These verses describe what happened after Shulamith's brothers leased vineyards from Solomon and placed Shulamith there to work (1:6). Their agreement re-

Each was to bring for his fruit
1,000 pieces of silver.[a]
12 I have my own vineyard.[A,b]
The 1,000 are for you, Solomon,
but 200 for those who guard
its fruits.

M
13 You[B] who dwell in the gardens—

[a]8:11 Is 7:23
[b]8:12 Sg 1:6
[c]8:13 Sg 1:7
[d]Sg 2:14
[e]8:14 Sg 2:17

companions[c] are listening
for your voice—
let me hear you![d]

W
14 Hurry to me, my love,
and be like a gazelle
or a young stag
on the mountains of spices.[e]

[A]8:12 Lit *My vineyard, which is mine, is before me*; Sg 1:6　　[B]8:13 In Hb, the word for You is feminine.

---

quired them to pay **1,000 pieces of silver** to the owner, Solomon, and allowed them, the caretakers, to keep **200** for themselves. Just as Solomon could do what he wanted with his own literal vineyard, Shulamith was free to do what she pleased with the figurative vineyard of herself (**my . . . vineyard**). Love cannot be purchased, but it can be given. **Those who guard its fruits** are the brothers who temporarily cared for the figurative vineyard that was Shulamith (vv. 8-9), just as they cared for Solomon's literal vineyard. In light of the hardships placed upon her at times by her brothers (1:6), Shulamith in effect forgave them, perhaps in recognition that their harshness resulted in her meeting Solomon.

8:13-14 These verses echo the themes of the days in spring (see note at 7:12-13). In the tarnished mirror of the world

after Eden, the romantic love God designed to reflect His own love seldom does adequately. An almost universal distortion of this love is the stereotype that in companionship women seek only communication and security while men seek only sexual gratification. The recovery of ideal love displayed in the Song restores the right balance. Both enjoyed loving communication and both enjoyed sexual expression. However, quite remarkably, the themes of spring echoed at the end of the Song show it was Solomon who initiated and longed for communication while it was Shulamith who responded in desire to make love. Not only does this shatter the stereotype and recover the ideal of romantic love, it also reflects the love of God toward us: "We love because He first loved us" (1Jn 4:19).

The Hebrew Prophets in History
(9th–5th century B.C.)

PROPHET	APPROX. DATES (B.C.)	LOCATION/ HOME	BASIC BIBLE PASSAGE	CENTRAL TEACHING	KEY VERSE
Elijah	875–850	Tishbe	1Kg 17:1–2Kg 2:18	Yahweh, not Baal, is God	1Kg 18:21
Micaiah	856	Samaria	1Kg 22; 2Ch 18	Judgment on Ahab; proof of prophecy	1Kg 22:28
Elisha	855–800	Abel Meholah	1Kg 19:15-21; 2Kg 2–9; 13	God's miraculous power	2Kg 5:15
Jonah	786–746	Gath Hepher	2Kg 14:25; Jonah	God's universal concern	Jnh 4:11
Hosea	786–746	Israel	Hosea	God's unquenchable love	Hs 11:8-9
Amos	760–750	Tekoa	Amos	God's call for justice and righteousness	Am 5:24
Isaiah	740–698	Jerusalem	2Kg 19–20; Isaiah	Hope through repentance and suffering	Is 1:18; 53:4-6
Micah	735–710	Moresheth Gath/ Jerusalem	Jr 26:18; Micah	Call for humble mercy and justice	Mc 6:8
Oded	733	Samaria	2Ch 28:9-11	Do not go beyond God's command	2Ch 28:9
Nahum	686–612	Elkosh	Nahum	God's jealousy protects His people	Nah 1:2-3
Zephaniah	640–621	?	Zephaniah	Hope for the humble and righteous	Zph 2:3
Jeremiah	626–584	Anathoth/ Jerusalem	2Ch 36:12; Jeremiah	Faithful prophet points to new covenant	Jr 31:33-34
Huldah (the prophetess)	621	Jerusalem	2Kg 22; 2Ch 34	God's book is accurate	2Kg 22:16
Habakkuk	608–598	?	Habakkuk	God calls for faithfulness	Hab 2:4
Ezekiel	593–571	Babylon	Ezekiel	Future hope for new community of worship	Ezk 37:12-13
Obadiah	580	Jerusalem	Obadiah	Doom on Edom to bring God's kingdom	Ob 21
Joel	539–531	Jerusalem	Joel	Call to repent and experience God's Spirit	Jl 2:28-29
Haggai	520	Jerusalem	Ezr 5:1; 6:14; Haggai	The priority of God's house	Hg 2:8-9
Zechariah	520–514	Jerusalem	Ezr 5:1; 6:14; Zechariah	Faithfulness will lead to God's universal rule	Zch 14:9
Malachi	500–450	Jerusalem	Malachi	Honor God and wait for His righteousness	Mal 4:2

Isaiah

Isaiah was an eighth-century B.C. prophet. His book is the first of the prophets in the English canon and the first of the Latter Prophets in the Hebrew canon. Isaiah is powerful in its poetic imagination, intriguing in its prophetic vision, and complex in its structure. One can never read or study the book without having new insights into the nature of God and our relationship with Him. The authors of the New Testament read the book of Isaiah in light of the coming of Christ and realized that this prophet anticipated Messiah's coming with remarkable clarity. For this reason they quoted Isaiah more than any other Old Testament book.

"You will indeed go out with joy and be peacefully guided; the mountains and the hills will break into singing before you, and all the trees of the field will clap their hands. Instead of the thornbush, a cypress will come up, and instead of the brier, a myrtle will come up; it will make a name for Yahweh as an everlasting sign that will not be destroyed" (55:12-13).

Circumstances of Writing

Author: The book presents itself as the writing of one man, Isaiah son of Amoz. The superscription to the book dates his prophetic activity as spanning the reigns of four kings of Judah: Uzziah (783–742 B.C.; Isaiah's call is dated to this king's last year, 6:1), Jotham (742–735 B.C.), Ahaz (735–716 B.C.), and Hezekiah (716–686 B.C.). Not much is known about Isaiah apart from his prophecy.

Isaiah's authorship of the whole book has been vehemently contested in the modern period. Many scholars have argued that the historical Isaiah could not have written chapters 40–66. For those who believe that God knows the future and can reveal it to His servants, it is not problematic that God through Isaiah predicted the rise of Babylon, its victory against Judah, the exile, and the return.

Background: Isaiah 6:1 records that Isaiah received his prophetic call in the last year of Uzziah's reign over Judah (ca 742 B.C.). Uzziah's reign was a particularly prosperous time in the history of Judah, but storm clouds were on the horizon. Assyria was on the rise again in the person of Tiglath-pileser III (745–727 B.C.). The Assyrian king threatened to engulf Syria and the northern kingdom of Israel. After the death of Tiglath-pileser, his successors, Shalmaneser and Sargon, defeated the northern kingdom in 722 B.C. and deported its citizens. This event brought Judah even more under the shadow of that great empire. Isaiah 37:38 suggests that the prophet lived until the death of Sennacherib in 681 B.C.

Isaiah's vision extended beyond the eighth century, through the rest of the OT period and beyond. The NT authors cited Isaiah as finding fulfillment in the great events surrounding Jesus Christ, the Messiah and Suffering Servant.

Message and Purpose

Isaiah's message is relatively simple. First, Isaiah accused God's people of sin, rebelling against the One who made them and redeemed them. Second, Isaiah instructed these sinners to reform their ways and act obedi-

---

750 B.C.

Death of King Uzziah of Judah 740

Isaiah's call to be a prophet 740

Tiglath-pileser III's invasions of Israel 734–732

Pekah of Israel and Rezin of Damascus form a mutual defense alliance against Assyria and invite Ahaz of Judah to join them. 734

Ahaz refuses Isaiah's counsel and seeks protection from Assyria by paying tribute to them, creating a heavy financial burden on Judah for years to come. 734

Alliance between Syria and Israel collapses with the fall of Damascus (732) and the fall of Samaria. 722

725 B.C.

Hezekiah of Judah initiates reforms and shows resistance to Assyria. 715–701

Hezekiah prepares for war against Assyria, strengthens Jerusalem's defenses, and receives Merodach-baladan's envoys from Babylon. 705–701

Sennacherib of Assyria defeats the Phoenicians, Philistines, and Egyptians; destroys most cities in Judah; and besieges Jerusalem. 701

God delivers Jerusalem from the Assyrian forces. 701

ently. Third, Isaiah announced God's judgment on the people because of their sin. Finally, God revealed His future restoration of the people, or at least of the faithful remnant that survived the judgment. As part of the restoration of God's people, Isaiah foresaw both judgment on the nations (chaps. 13–23) and a future turning of the nations to God (2:1-4). The first part of the book (chaps. 1–39) emphasizes sin, the call to repentance, and judgment; the second part (chaps. 40–66) emphasizes the hope of restoration. Other topics should be noted:

God, the Holy One of Israel: From the beginning to the end of the book, God is called the Holy One of Israel. At the time of Isaiah's call, the seraphim cried out, "Holy, holy, holy is the LORD of Hosts" (6:3). God is set apart, completely removed from sin, the very epitome of moral perfection. God's people were to reflect the character of their holy God according to the requirements of the Torah (Lv 11:44-45; 19:2; 20:7), but they had fallen far short. Isaiah was commissioned to remind them of this high standard.

Trust and confidence: Isaiah called God's people to trust God, and when they did not, he condemned them for it. They were to fear God, not other human beings. Most often the Israelites betrayed God by trusting a powerful foreign nation or false gods.

God versus the idols: Because of the tendency of God's people to trust false gods, Isaiah's prophetic word often contrasted the true God with the false gods of the nations. God acted in history; idols did not. God could reveal the future; idols could not. God is eternal; idols were man-made and amounted to nothing.

Messiah and Servant: Perhaps more than any other part of Isaiah, the passages describing a future anointed king (Messiah; 9:1-7; 11:1-9) and those describing the Servant (42:1-9; 49:1-6; 50:4-6; 52:13–53:12) have attracted the interest of Christian readers of the book. From the time of the NT, Christian readers have understood Jesus Christ as the ultimate fulfillment of the expectation of a future king and Suffering Servant.

700 B.C.	500 B.C.
According to extra-biblical tradition Isaiah was martyred early in the reign of Manasseh. 699?	Babylonians attack Jerusalem and lead citizens of Judah into exile. 605, 597, 586
Manasseh succeeds his father Hezekiah as king of Judah. 687	Cyrus captures Babylon without resistance. 539
Ashurbanipal (668–631) rules over a declining Assyrian Empire that experiences revolts in 642, contributed to the assassination of Amon of Judah (641) and the rise of his son Josiah (641–609).	Cyrus issues a decree allowing the Jews to return to Judah. 538
Josiah killed by the Egyptians at Megiddo 609	Work begins on rebuilding the temple in Jerusalem. 536–537
Babylonians defeat Pharaoh Neco of Egypt at Carchemish. 605	Renewed work on the temple 520–518
	New temple dedicated 515

Structure

The book of Isaiah is a combination of both prose and poetry. The prose is found primarily in chapters 36–39, a section that forms a bridge between the two sections of the book (see Message and Purpose). Isaiah's poetry is rich and varied. He wrote hymns, wisdom poetry, and even poetry that resembles a love song (5:1-7). The richness is seen in Isaiah's vocabulary. He used over 2,200 different Hebrews words, far more variety than found in any other OT book.

Outline

I. Rebuke and Promise from the Lord (1:1–6:13)
    A. Rebellion met with judgment and grace (1:1-31)
    B. Chastisement will bring future glory (2:1–4:6)
    C. Judgment and exile for the nation (5:1-30)
    D. Isaiah cleansed and commissioned (6:1-13)

II. The Promise of Immanuel (7:1–12:6)
    A. Immanuel rejected by worldly wisdom (7:1-25)
    B. God's deliverance and the coming Deliverer (8:1–9:7)
    C. Exile is coming for proud Samaria (9:8–10:4)
    D. Promise of a future glorious empire (10:5–12:6)

III. Coming Judgment upon the Nations (13:1–23:18)
    A. Babylon (13:1–14:23)
    B. Assyria (14:24-27)
    C. Philistia (14:28-32)
    D. Moab (15:1–16:14)
    E. Damascus and Syria (17:1-3)
    F. Israel (17:4-14)
    G. Cush (18:1-7)
    H. Egypt (19:1–20:6)
    I. Babylon, additional judgment (21:1-10)
    J. Dumah (21:11-12)
    K. Arabia (21:13-17)
    L. Jerusalem (22:1-25)
    M. Tyre (23:1-18)

IV. First Cycle of General Judgment and Promise (24:1–27:13)
    A. Universal judgment for universal sin (24:1-23)
    B. Praise to the Lord as Deliverer (25:1-12)
    C. A song of comfort for Judah (26:1-21)
    D. Promise of preservation for God's people (27:1-13)

V. Woes upon the Unbelievers of Israel (28:1–33:24)
    A. God's dealings with drunkards and scoffers (28:1-29)
    B. Judgment for those who try to deceive God (29:1-24)
    C. Confidence in man vs. confidence in God (30:1-33)
    D. Deliverance through God's intervention (31:1–32:20)
    E. Punishment of deceivers and triumph of Christ (33:1-24)

1 The vision[a] concerning Judah and Jerusalem that Isaiah[b] son of Amoz saw during the reigns[A,B] of Uzziah,[c] Jotham,[d] Ahaz,[e] and Hezekiah,[f] kings of Judah.[g]

Judah on Trial

2 Listen, heavens,
　　and pay attention, earth,[h]
　for the LORD has spoken:
　"I have raised children[C]
　　and brought them up,
　but they have rebelled against Me.[i]

3 The ox knows its owner,
　and the donkey its master's
　　feeding trough,
　but Israel does not know;
　My people do not understand."[j]

4 Oh sinful nation,
　people weighed down with iniquity,[k]
　brood of evildoers,[l]
　depraved children![C]
　They have abandoned[m] the LORD;
　they have despised[n] the Holy One
　　of Israel;[o]
　they have turned their backs on Him.

5 Why do you want more beatings?
　Why do you keep on rebelling?
　The whole head is hurt,
　and the whole heart is sick.

6 From the sole of the foot
　　even to the head,[p]
　no spot is uninjured[q]—
　wounds, welts, and festering sores
　not cleansed, bandaged,
　or soothed with oil.

7 Your land is desolate,
　your cities burned with fire;[r]
　foreigners devour your fields
　before your very eyes—
　a desolation demolished by foreigners.

8 Daughter •Zion[s] is abandoned
　like a shelter in a vineyard,
　like a shack in a cucumber field,
　like a besieged city.

9 If the LORD of •Hosts[t]
　had not left us a few survivors,[u]
　we would be like Sodom,
　we would resemble Gomorrah.[v]

10 Hear the word of the LORD,[w]
　you rulers of Sodom!
　Listen to the instruction of our God,
　you people of Gomorrah![x]

11 "What are all your sacrifices to Me?"
　asks the LORD.
　"I have had enough of •burnt offerings
　　and rams
　and the fat of well-fed cattle;
　I have no desire for the blood of bulls,

Cross references (center column)

[a]1:1 Pr 29:18; Dn 8:1; Ob 1; Nah 1:1; Hab 2:2-3
[b]Is 2:1; 13:1
[c]2Ch 26:3-5
[d]2Kg 15:32-38
[e]2Kg 16:1-4
[f]2Kg 18:1-8
[g]Hs 1:1; Mc 1:1
[h]1:2 Dt 4:26; 32:1; Is 30:1; Mc 1:2
[i]Is 30:1
[j]1:3 Jr 8:7
[k]1:4 Is 13:11
[l]Is 14:20; Mt 3:7
[m]Dt 4:31
[n]Nm 14:11; Dt 31:20; Pr 5:12; Is 5:24
[o]Is 5:19,24; 10:20; 12:6; 29:19; 30:11-15
[p]1:6 Jb 2:7
[q]Ps 38:3
[r]1:7 Lv 26:33; Dt 28:51-52; Is 6:11-12; Jr 44:6
[s]1:8 Is 10:32; 37:22; Zch 2:10; 9:9
[t]1:9 1Sm 17:45
[u]Is 10:21-22
[v]Gn 19:24-25; Is 3:9; 13:19; Rm 9:29
[w]1:10 Is 28:14
[x]Is 3:9; Ezk 16:46-49,55; Rv 11:8

A1:1 Lit saw in the days　B1:1 ca 792–686 B.C.　C1:2,4 Or sons

1:1 On the historical setting for Isaiah's ministry, see Introduction.

1:2 The opening oracle of the book puts Judah on trial. The call goes out to the **heavens** and the **earth** to hear the charges against God's people. In Deuteronomy the heavens and earth are invoked as witnesses to the covenant (Dt 4:26; 30:19). Isaiah called on the witnesses to listen to the charges filed in the following verses and to render judgment. God Himself describes the rebellion of His people, referring to them as His **children**, underlining the scandal of the betrayal.

1:3 God stood amazed at the stupidity of His people. They were dumber than an **ox**; even dumber than a **donkey**. The former was smart enough to recognize its owner; the latter might not recognize its **owner**, but it knew where it got its food. Israel did not even have that level of intelligence as it denied God, its master and sustainer.

1:4 The opening **Oh** marks the beginning of what is commonly called a "woe oracle." This literary form derives from funeral processions and often signifies the sense that the object of the Oh—in this case the **sinful nation** (Judah)—is as good as dead. As in verse 2, the heart of Judah's transgression is identified as a betrayal of God. Isaiah frequently refers to God as **the Holy One of Israel**. This title emphasizes God's separation from and profound aversion toward sin. When Isaiah encountered God in the temple, he experienced this absolute purity as he heard the seraphim cry out, "Holy, holy, holy, is the LORD of Hosts" (6:3).

1:5-6 Judah's rebellion had already reaped consequences.

They were like a sick man whose injuries stemmed from a beating, perhaps a poetic allusion to Assyrian military threats in 722 B.C. when the northern kingdom of Israel fell, or perhaps to a later incursion in 701 B.C. (see Introduction).

1:7-8 Judah's sin resulted in a foreign military intrusion in the land (see notes at 2:5 and 2:6). **Daughter Zion** is a personification of Zion, the most holy place in Judah, the mountain where the temple was built. It reminds the reader of the intimate relationship God enjoyed with the people He must judge. A **shelter in a vineyard** or a **shack in a cucumber field** were both fragile. Without upkeep they would crumble, providing an illuminating analogy for the desolation of Jerusalem.

1:9 God had been gracious. He did not completely destroy His people and make them like **Sodom** and **Gomorrah** (Gn 19). Rather, some would survive the judgment; restoration would follow the cleansing of judgment.

1:10-15 In these verses God expressed His revulsion at the religious practices of His people.

1:10 Though God will not punish the people with total annihilation as He did the cities of **Sodom** and **Gomorrah** (cp. v. 9), it is not as if they did not deserve that fate. Their rulers were like the inhabitants of those depraved cities who denied hospitality to strangers and engaged in perverse sexual acts.

1:11 God commanded His people to offer sacrifices (Lv 1–7; **burnt offerings** are specifically described in Lv 1), but the sacrifices of His people were reprehensible to Him. They

lambs, or male goats.[a]

12 When you come to appear before Me,
who requires this from you—
this trampling of My courts?

13 Stop bringing useless offerings.[b]
Your incense is detestable to Me.
New Moons and Sabbaths,[c]
and the calling of solemn assemblies[d]—
I cannot stand iniquity[e] with a festival.

14 I hate your New Moons
and prescribed festivals.
They have become a burden to Me;
I am tired of putting up with them.

15 When you lift up your hands in prayer,[f]
I will refuse to look at you;
even if you offer countless prayers,
I will not listen.[g]
Your hands are covered with blood.[h]

Purification of Jerusalem

16 "Wash yourselves. Cleanse yourselves.[i]
Remove your evil deeds
from My sight.
Stop doing evil.[j]

17 Learn to do what is good.
Seek justice.[k]
Correct the oppressor.[A]
Defend the rights of the fatherless.
Plead the widow's cause.

18 "Come, let us discuss this,"[l]
says the LORD.
"Though your sins are like scarlet,
they will be as white as snow;[m]
though they are as red as crimson,
they will be like wool.

19 If you are willing and obedient,

you will eat the good things
of the land.[n]

20 But if you refuse and rebel,
you will be devoured by the sword."[o]
For the mouth of the LORD has spoken.[p]

21 The faithful city—
what an adulteress[B] she has become!
She was once full of justice.
Righteousness once dwelt in her—
but now, murderers!

22 Your silver has become dross,[C]
your beer[D] is diluted with water.

23 Your rulers are rebels,
friends of thieves.[q]
They all love graft
and chase after bribes.[r]
They do not defend the rights
of the fatherless,
and the widow's case never comes
before them.[s]

24 Therefore the Lord GOD of Hosts,
the Mighty One of Israel, declares:
"Ah, I will gain satisfaction
from My foes;
I will take revenge against My enemies.[t]

25 I will turn My hand against you[u]
and will burn away
your dross[c] completely;[E]
I will remove all your impurities.[v]

26 I will restore your judges[w] to what
they once were,[F]
and your advisers to their former state.[G]
Afterward you will be called
the Righteous City,[x]
a Faithful City."

Cross references (center column)

[a]1:11 1Sm 15:22; Jr 6:20; Hs 6:6; Am 5:21-24; Mt 23:23; Mk 12:33
[b]1:13 Mal 1:10
[c]Nm 28:11; 1Ch 23:31
[d]Ex 12:16; Lv 23:36
[e]Is 13:11
[f]1:15 1Kg 8:22
[g]Is 59:2; Jr 7:16; Ezk 8:18; Am 5:23; Hab 1:2; Zch 7:13
[h]Pr 1:28; Is 59:1-3; Mc 3:4
[i]1:16 Ps 26:6; Is 4:4; 52:11
[j]Jr 25:5
[k]1:17 Dt 16:20; 1Kg 3:11; Ps 89:14; Is 10:2; 11:4; Am 5:15; Zch 7:9
[l]1:18 Is 41:1,21; 43:26; Mc 6:2
[m]Ps 51:7; Is 43:25; 44:22; Rv 7:14
[n]1:19-20 Dt 30:15-20
[o]1:20 Jr 12:12
[p]Is 24:3; 40:5; 58:14; Mc 4:4
[q]1:23 Hs 5:10
[r]Ex 23:8; Mc 7:2-6
[s]Ex 22:22; Dt 24:17; Is 10:2; Jr 5:28; Ezk 22:7; Zch 7:10
[t]1:24 Is 35:4; 59:18; Jr 46:10
[u]1:25 Ps 81:14; Is 5:25; Am 1:8
[v]Ezk 22:20; Mal 3:3
[w]1:26 Is 60:17; Mt 19:28
[x]Is 33:5; 60:14; 62:1-2; Zch 8:3

Footnotes

[A]1:17 Or Aid the oppressed   [B]1:21 Or prostitute   [C]1:22,25 Or burnished lead   [D]1:22 Or wine   [E]1:25 Lit dross as with lye   [F]1:26 Lit judges as at the first   [G]1:26 Lit advisers as at the beginning

Study notes

were not offered with pure motives of sincere repentance. Rather, they were offered with hands covered with blood (Is 1:15).

1:13-14 God also commanded that Israel consecrate holy times on a weekly (**Sabbaths**) and yearly (**New Moons . . . solemn assemblies . . . festivals**) cycle, but they were loathsome to God because of the hypocrisy of His people.

1:15 This oracle has delayed the problem with the people's ritual practice until the very last line. Their sacrifices, times of worship, and even prayers were not acceptable because their hands were **covered with blood**. That is, they sinned and did not repent but still participated in worship. God did not tolerate such hypocritical behavior.

1:16-17 The oracle gives a prescription for change—repent. The metaphor for transformation here is a good washing. Transformation involves a cessation of evil activities as well as the requirement of good deeds. The good deeds are defined as social justice, particularly resisting oppressors and promoting the interests of the vulnerable (the **fatherless** and the widow).

1:18-20 The Lord presented two options to the people. One was to repent and obey. A remarkable transformation would result. Now they were blood red as a result of their sin, but repentance would turn them a glorious **white**. They could be cleansed (v. 16) with the result that life would be good. The second option was continued rebellion, a course of action that would end with their destruction.

1:21-22 God's people were not always corrupt. A formerly **faithful city**—Jerusalem—had gone bad. The worship of false gods, idolatry, is often described as a form of adultery. **Dross** and watered-down **beer** are symbols of impurity.

1:23 The **rulers** of Judah were corrupt. They sought their own financial advantage and neglected the rights and needs of the socially vulnerable (the widow and the **fatherless**).

1:24 Therefore marks the transition from indictment (vv. 21-23) to judgment. God will not let the guilty escape their punishment.

1:25-26 The judgment is not just punitive; it purifies. The people started a faithful city (v. 21) and after their cleansing, they will again be a **Faithful City**.

27 Zion will be redeemed by justice,
    her repentant ones by righteousness.[a]

28 But both rebels and sinners
    will be destroyed,
    and those who abandon the LORD
    will perish.

29 Indeed, they[A] will be ashamed
    of the sacred trees
    you desired,[b]
    and you will be embarrassed because of
    the gardens
    you have chosen.[c]

30 For you will become like an oak
    whose leaves are withered,
    and like a garden without water.[d]

31 The strong one will become tinder,
    and his work a spark;
    both will burn together,[e]
    with no one to quench the flames.[f]

The City of Peace

2 The vision that Isaiah[g] son of Amoz saw concerning Judah and Jerusalem:

2 In[h] the last days[i]
    the mountain of the LORD's house[j]
    will be established
    at the top of the mountains
    and will be raised above the hills.
    All nations will stream to it,[k]

3 and many peoples will come and say,
    "Come, let us go up to the mountain
    of the LORD,

to the house of the God of Jacob.[l]
    He will teach us about His ways
    so that we may walk in His paths."
    For instruction will go out of •Zion
    and the word of the LORD
    from Jerusalem.

4 He will settle disputes among the nations
    and provide arbitration
    for many peoples.
    They will turn their swords into plows
    and their spears into pruning knives.[m]
    Nations will not take up the sword
    against other nations,
    and they will never again train for war.[n]

The Day of the LORD

5 House of Jacob,
    come and let us walk in the LORD's light.[o]

6 For You have abandoned[p] Your people,
    the house of Jacob,
    because they are full of •divination
    from the East
    and of fortune-tellers[q]
    like the Philistines.[r]
    They are in league[B] with foreigners.

7 Their[C,D] land is full of silver and gold,
    and there is no limit to their treasures;
    their land is full of horses,
    and there is no limit to their chariots.[s]

8 Their land is full of idols;[t]
    they bow down to the work
    of their hands,

Cross references

a 1:27 Rm 3:26
b 1:29 Is 2:8; 57:5; Hs 4:13
c Is 65:3; 66:17
d 1:30 Ps 1:3; Is 64:6
e 1:31 Is 5:24; 9:19; 26:11; 33:11-14
f Is 66:24; Mt 3:12; Mk 9:43
g 2:1 2Kg 19:2; 20:1; 2Ch 26:22; 32:20; Is 1:1; 13:1
h 2:2-4 Mc 4:1-4; Rm 2:20
i 2:2 Nm 24:14; Dt 4:30; Ezk 38:16; Hs 3:5
j 2Ch 33:15; Is 27:13; 66:20
k Ps 22:27; Is 56:7; Zch 14:10
l 2:3 Is 29:23; 45:23; 60:13; 66:18
m 2:4 Is 11:6-9; 32:17-18; Jl 3:10
n Ps 72:3,7; Is 9:7; Hs 2:18; Zch 9:10
o 2:5 Ps 27:1; 43:3
p 2:6 Dt 31:17; Ps 94:14; Is 1:4
q Lv 19:26; Dt 18:10-14; 2Kg 21:6; 2Ch 33:6; Jr 27:9; Mc 5:12
r Jdg 14:3; 1Sm 6:2; 2Kg 1:2-6
s 2:7 Dt 17:17
t 2:8 Is 10:10-11; 19:1-3; 31:7; Jr 2:28

Footnotes

A 1:29 Some Hb mss; other Hb mss, Tg read *you*   B 2:6 Or *They teem*, or *They partner*; Hb obscure   C 2:7 Lit *Its*   D 2:7 = the house of Jacob

---

1:29 The people of God sinned by their idolatry that often took the form of worshiping false gods with foreign rituals. One common form of this false worship involved **sacred trees** that were probably connected with worship of a Canaanite fertility goddess called Asherah, the mother of Baal.

1:30-31 The oracle charged that Judah (**you**) would become like an **oak**. Here the tree image stands for the pride and resistance of God's people. But such apparent strength is undermined by the fact that the tree was not watered and therefore would quickly **burn** when set on fire.

2:2-4 This oracle is virtually identical to that found in Isaiah's near contemporary, the prophet Micah (Mc 4:1-3).

2:2 The phrase **last days** refers to the future, a time beyond the judgment on the sin of God's people. The **mountain of the LORD's house** is a reference to Zion, where the temple was built. Zion was where God made His presence known in a special way among His people. In actuality, Zion was not a physically imposing mountain—indeed, the nearby Mount of Olives was considerably taller—but in terms of spiritual importance, Zion stood above all the other mountains of the world.

2:3 The vision anticipates a day when not only Israel but all the nations will stream toward this **mountain** that represents the presence of God on earth. God had promised Abraham that He would bless the nations through his descendants (Gn 12:1-3). Today the church is composed of people from many different nations who have aligned themselves with God, thus fulfilling this vision in at least a preliminary way.

2:4 The **nations** seeking the Lord will experience a great transformation. They will not exert their energies and resources to destruction (**swords . . . spears**), but rather to productive activities (**plows . . . pruning knives**).

2:5 Some scholars believe this call to obey God's way concludes the previous oracle. If so, it invites Israel to follow God as the least they can do in anticipation of the fact that the nations will turn to God in the future. However, verse 6 begins with "For," marking the verses that follow as motivation for the repentance of Israel called for in this verse.

2:6 God had removed His presence from His **people** because they had imbibed of the superstitions of their neighbors to the **East** (Edom and Mesopotamia, for instance) and the west (Philistia). In particular, they practiced **divination**. Divination tries to access the divine realm via rituals, with the aim of foretelling the future and warding off evil. The Torah forbade such practices (Lv 19:26; Dt 18:9-14).

2:7 Deuteronomy 17:14-20 prohibited kings from accumulating precious metals and military assets (**horses** and **chariots**).

2:8 The root of the evil of idolatry is expressed here when the oracle states that idols are man-made (**the work of their hands**). Paul reflected this understanding when he referred

to what their fingers have made.[a]

9 So humanity is brought low,
and man is humbled.
Do not forgive them![b]

10 Go into the rocks[c]
and hide in the dust
from the terror of the Lord[d]
and from His majesty splendor.[e]

11 Human pride[A] will be humbled,[f]
and the loftiness of men
will be brought low;
the Lord alone will be exalted
on that day.

12 For a day belonging to the Lord
of •Hosts is coming
against all that is proud and lofty,[g]
against all that is lifted up—it will
be humbled—

13 against all the cedars of Lebanon,[h]
lofty and lifted up,
against all the oaks of Bashan,[i]

14 against all the high mountains,[j]
against all the lofty hills,

15 against every high tower,[k]
against every fortified wall,

16 against every ship of Tarshish,[l]
and against every splendid sea vessel.

17 So human pride will be brought low,
and the loftiness of men will be humbled;
the Lord alone will be exalted
on that day.[m]

18 The idols will vanish completely.

a 2:8 Is 41:21-29; 44:9-17
b 2:9 Ex 34:7
c 2:10 Rv 6:15
d 1Sm 11:7; 2Ch 14:14; 17:10; 19:7; Is 2:19,21
e 2Th 1:9
f 2:11 Ps 18:27; Is 2:17; Mc 2:3; 2Co 10:5
g 2:12 Mal 4:1
h 2:13 Ps 29:5; Is 14:8; Hs 14:5
i Ezk 27:6; Zch 11:2
j 2:14 Is 40:4
k 2:15 Is 25:12; Zph 1:16
l 2:16 1Kg 10:22; Is 23:1,14; 60:9
m 2:17 Mt 25:13
n 2:19 Is 2:10
o Ps 18:7; Is 13:13; 24:1,19-20; Hg 2:6-7; Heb 12:26
p 2:20 Is 30:22; 31:7
q 2:21 Is 2:10
r 2:22 Ps 39:11; 144:4; 146:3; Jr 17:5; Jms 4:14
s 3:2 2Kg 24:14; Ezk 17:13-14

19 People will go into caves in the rocks[n]
and holes in the ground,
away from the terror of the Lord
and from His majestic splendor,
when He rises to terrify the earth.[o]

20 On that day people will throw
their silver and gold idols,[p]
which they made to worship,
to the moles and the bats.

21 They will go into the caves
of the rocks
and the crevices in the cliffs,
away from the terror of the Lord
and from His majestic splendor,[q]
when He rises to terrify the earth.

22 Put no more trust in man,
who has only the breath
in his nostrils.[r]
What is he really worth?

Judah's Leaders Judged

3 Observe this: The Lord God of •Hosts
is about to remove from Jerusalem
and from Judah
every kind of security:
the entire supply of bread and water,

2 the hero and warrior,[s]
the judge and prophet,
the fortune-teller and elder,

3 the commander of 50
and the dignitary,
the counselor, cunning magician,[B]
and necromancer.[C]

A 2:11 Lit Mankind's proud eyes   B 3:3 Or skilled craftsman   C 3:3 Or medium

---

to the folly of exchanging "the glory of the immortal God for images resembling mortal man, birds, four-footed animals, and reptiles" (Rm 1:23).

2:11 With the words **human pride will be humbled**, Isaiah

shaphel

Hebrew Pronunciation	[shah FAIL]
HCSB Translation	be low, humbled
Uses in Isaiah	15
Uses in the OT	30
Focus Passage	Isaiah 2:9,11,17

Isaiah has half the uses of shaphel, which means be lowly (Pr 16:19) or sink (Is 32:19). People are humbled (Is 2:9) or brought down (Is 29:4). Trees are felled (Is 10:33) and mountains leveled (Is 40:4). Causative verbs mean humiliate (Jb 40:11), humble (Pr 29:23), demote (Pr 25:7), bring down or low (Is 25:11-12), stoop down (Ps 113:6), and send down (Is 57:9). Shephelah (20x) is the name for the Judean foothills (Jos 9:1). The adjective shaphal (17x) denotes low (Ezk 17:6), lowly (Is 57:15), humble (Ezk 17:14), or humiliated (Mal 2:9). Once it is lowliest (Ezk 29:15). The phrase "lower than" is translated beneath (Lv 13:20). The noun shephel means humiliation (Ps 136:23) or lowly position (Ec 10:6). Shiplah, meaning depths, occurs with the verb shaphel (Is 32:19). "Lowness (shiphluth) of hands" suggests negligent hands hanging down (Ec 10:18). The adjective shaphel implies humbled (Is 2:12).

expressed one of the major themes of his book. Through judgment, God cuts down the sinful pretensions of His people.

2:12-17 The prophets often spoke of a coming **day belonging to the Lord** (Jl 1:15; Am 2:1,11,31; 5:18,20; Zph 1:7,14; Zch 14:1). This day is one of judgment of sinners, which means the redemption of God's people. However, God's people in this verse were the object of His anger since they were rebelling against Him. While the "Day of the Lord" ultimately points to the final judgment, God's temporal punishments of His people are often understood to be anticipatory fulfillments of the final judgment. **Lebanon** and **Bashan** were well known for their fertile lands and, in particular, their impressive trees. Thus, they are representative of arrogance built on abundance. God's judgment is against all kinds of **pride**.

2:19-20 People will flee in **terror** from the coming judgment of God. Out of fear, they will throw away their precious **idols**.

2:22 The last verse of the oracle states an important and pervasive theme in Isaiah connected to the prophet's concern that God's people act with humility. They were not to **trust in man**, but to put their confidence in God.

3:1-3 Since God's people trust in man (2:22) rather than in God, He will remove from them **every kind of security**. While various political, military, and religious leaders are on the list, it begins with the staples of **bread and water**.

4 "I will make youths their leaders,[a]
and the unstable[A] will govern them."
5 The people will oppress one another,[b]
man against man, neighbor
against neighbor;
the youth will act arrogantly
toward the elder,
and the worthless
toward the honorable.
6 A man will even seize his brother
in his father's house, saying:
"You have a cloak—you be our leader!
This heap of rubble will be
under your control."
7 On that day he will cry out, saying:
"I'm not a healer.
I don't even have food or clothing
in my house.
Don't make me the leader
of the people!"
8 For Jerusalem has stumbled
and Judah has fallen
because they have spoken and acted
against the LORD,[c]
defying His glorious presence.[d]
9 The look on their faces testifies
against them,
and like Sodom,[e] they flaunt their sin.
They do not conceal it.
Woe to them,
for they have brought evil
on themselves.[f]
10 Tell the righteous that it will go well
for them,
for they will eat the fruit of their labor.
11 Woe to the wicked—it will go badly
for them,
for what they have done will be done
to them.
12 Youths oppress My people,[g]

a3:4 Ec 10:16
b3:5 Mc 7:3-6
c3:8 Ps 73:9-11
d Nm 14:22-23;
Is 43:7; 48:11;
59:19
e3:9 Is 1:9-10;
13:19
f Rm 6:23
g3:12 Is 3:4
h Is 28:14-22
i3:13 Ps 7:6;
Hs 4:1
j3:14 Mc 3:1-3
k Ezk 18:10-18;
33:15
l3:16 Is 32:9-15;
1Pt 3:3-4
m3:18 Is 27:12
n Jdg 8:21,26
o3:20 Ezk 24:17
p3:21 Gn 24:47;
Ezk 16:12

and women rule over them.
My people, your leaders mislead you;
they confuse the direction
of your paths.[h]
13 The LORD rises to argue the case
and stands to judge the people.[i]
14 The LORD brings this charge
against the elders and leaders
of His people:[j]
"You have devastated the vineyard.
The plunder from the poor is
in your houses.[k]
15 Why do you crush My people
and grind the faces of the poor?"
This is the declaration
of the Lord GOD of Hosts.

Jerusalem's Women Judged

16 The LORD also says:

Because the daughters of •Zion
are haughty,[l]
walking with heads held high
and seductive eyes,
going along with prancing steps,
jingling their ankle bracelets,
17 the Lord will put scabs on the heads
of the daughters of Zion,
and the LORD will shave
their foreheads bare.

18 On that day[m] the Lord will strip their finery: ankle bracelets, headbands, crescents,[n] 19 pendants, bracelets, veils, 20 headdresses, ankle jewelry, sashes, perfume bottles, amulets,[o] 21 signet rings, nose rings,[p] 22 festive robes, capes, cloaks, purses, 23 garments, linen clothes, turbans, and veils.

24 Instead of perfume there will be
a stench;

A3:4 Or mischief-makers

3:4-5 With the removal of the leaders in whom the people trust comes the installation of **youths** to replace them. The result will be social chaos and oppression.

3:6-7 In such a disorderly society, it did not take much to be a leader among men. In the vignette described in these verses, the people are so unwilling and unfit to lead that a **man** will be pressed into a leadership role just because he has a **cloak**. But what would be left for him to lead? Only a **heap of rubble**.

3:9 Again, God's oracle compares Judah to **Sodom**, the preeminent early example of open, flagrant sin as well as God's determined judgment (Gn 19; see note at Is 1:9).

3:10-11 But not all people will experience the severe judgment of God. The **righteous** will find reward in a good life, and the **wicked** will suffer. In both cases, they will get what they deserve (see note at Ps 103:1-2).

3:13-15 Isaiah returned to the legal language with which the

book began (1:2). The leaders were guilty of destroying the **vineyard**, the land of Judah (5:1-7), through their exploitation of the poor.

3:16 The proud **daughters of Zion** stand for the city and the inhabitants of Jerusalem (1:8), not just its female inhabitants. Though clearly the inhabitants included its share of rich, snooty women, the fact that the city is clearly described by such a female personification in 3:25-26 confirms the view that the daughters should not be restricted to the female population. For another oracle against women, see 32:9-20.

3:17-24 God will humiliate these proud women who represent the city and inhabitants of Jerusalem. Their physical appearance will be spoiled and their **finery** will be removed. They will end up wearing **sackcloth**, ugly and uncomfortable. While this language should be understood figuratively of the city of Jerusalem, it also has a literal significance.

instead of a belt, a rope;
instead of
    beautifully styled hair,[a] baldness;[b]
instead of fine clothes, *sackcloth;[c]
instead of beauty, branding.[A]

25 Your men will fall by the sword,
    your warriors in battle.
26 Then her gates[d] will lament
        and mourn;
    deserted, she will sit on the ground.[e]

4 On that day seven women
    will seize one man,[f] saying,
"We will eat our own bread
and provide our own clothing.
Just let us be called by your name.
Take away our disgrace."[g]

Zion's Future Glory

[2] On that day the Branch of[B] the LORD will be beautiful and glorious,[h] and the fruit of the land[i] will be the pride and glory[j] of Israel's survivors.[k] [3] Whoever remains in *Zion and whoever is left in Jerusalem[l] will be called holy[m]—all in Jerusalem who are destined to live[n]— [4] when the Lord has washed away the filth[o] of the daughters of Zion and cleansed the bloodguilt[p] from the heart of Jerusalem by a spirit of judgment[q] and a spirit of burning.[r]

[5] Then the LORD will create[s] a cloud of smoke by day[t] and a glowing flame of fire by night over the entire site of Mount Zion and over its assemblies. For there will be a canopy over all the glory,[C] [6] and there will be a booth for shade from heat by day, and a refuge and shelter from storm and rain.[u]

Song of the Vineyard

5 I will sing about the one I love,
    a song about my loved one's vineyard:[v]
The one I love had a vineyard
on a very fertile hill.
2 He broke up the soil, cleared it
        of stones,
and planted it with the finest vines.[w]
He built a tower in the middle of it
and even dug out a winepress there.
He expected[x] it to yield good grapes,
but it yielded worthless grapes.[y]

3 So now, residents of Jerusalem
    and men of Judah,
    please judge between Me
    and My vineyard.

[a]3:24 1Pt 3:3
[b]Is 15:2; 22:12;
Ezk 27:31; Am
8:10; Mc 1:16
[c]Gn 37:34; Is
15:3; Jr 48:36-
38; Lm 2:10
[d]3:26 Jr 14:2;
Lm 1:4
[e]Jb 2:13; Is 47:1;
Lm 2:10
[f]4:1 Is 3:25
[g]Gn 19:31-32;
30:23; Neh 1:3;
Is 54:4; Lk 1:25
[h]4:2 2Sm 23:4-
5; Ps 132:17; Jr
23:5; 33:15; Zch
3:8; 6:12
[i]Ps 72:16; Is
27:6
[j]Is 3:18
[k]Gn 45:7; Jdg
21:17; 2Kg
19:30-31; Is
10:20; 37:31-32;
Jl 2:32; Ob 17
[l]4:3 Is 28:5; Rm
11:4-5
[m]Is 52:1; 62:12
[n]Ex 32:32; Ps
69:28; 139:16; Is
49:16; Ezk 13:9;
Lk 10:20; Ac
13:48
[o]4:4 2Ch 4:6;
Ezk 40:38; Zch
13:1
[p]Is 1:15; 3:13-15
[q]Is 28:6
[r]Is 1:31; 9:19;
33:14; Mal 3:2;

Mt 3:11; Lk 3:17   [s]4:5 Gn 1:1; Is 40:26,28; 41:20; 43:1,7,15;
45:7-8; 65:17-18   [t]Ex 13:21-22; 14:20; 40:34; Nm 9:15-23
[u]4:6 Ps 27:5; Is 25:4; 32:1-2   [v]5:1 Ps 80:8; Jr12:10; Mt 21:33;
Lk 20:9   [w]5:2 Jr 2:21   [x]Is 40:31   [y]Mt 21:19; Mk 11:13; Lk 13:6

[A]3:24 DSS read shame   [B]4:2 Or plant   [C]4:5 Or For glory will be a canopy over all

---

Wealthy, beautiful, well-dressed women would be reduced to such a state in the midst of the coming military siege.

3:25–4:1 War will severely reduce the male population of Jerusalem. There will not be enough **men** to go around for all the women. Women without husbands were socially vulnerable. Thus, **seven women** will beg a single man to make them their wives. He will not even need to provide their food (**bread**) and **clothing** (something mandated even for unloved secondary wives in Ex 21:10-11).

4:2-6 This oracle marks a sudden shift from judgment described in the oracles of 2:5–4:1 to future salvation. A similar dynamic has been observed in the abrupt transition of judgment speeches in 1:2-31 to the powerful picture of salvation in 2:1-4.

4:2 That day is a future day, a time that comes after the judgment described in 2:5–4:1. Indeed, the new restored state of Zion is a product of passing through the crucible of judgment. The remnant is here described as **Israel's survivors**. The reference to the **Branch of the LORD** is provocative. After all, the branch has a messianic connotation in Jr 23:5; 33:18; Zch 3:8; 6:12. Many scholars have pointed out that the branch in this verse is parallel with **the fruit of the land** and may indicate the rich abundance that Zion will enjoy in the future. But the two readings may not be mutually exclusive since in Hebrew parallelism the second idea is often not strictly synonymous, but expands the thought of the first idea.

4:3 The remnant will be **holy**. Holiness means set apart or consecrated for service to the Lord. Such a relationship implies an obedient lifestyle.

4:4 This verse explicitly states that Zion's blessed future

condition will be accomplished through **judgment**. It is an act of the grace of God. God's people must wash themselves (1:16), but it is God who makes them clean.

4:5 After the exodus from Egypt, God guided Israel through the desert by **a cloud** and **flame** (cp. Ex 40:38), which represented God's mysterious and powerful presence with His people. Isaiah used this language to teach that the future remnant will again enjoy an intimate and assuring relationship with God after the judgment.

5:1-7 This poem has been identified as a parable, an allegory, and a love poem. Whatever its precise genre, its message is clear and compelling. It uses imagery to make the point that the people of God deserve the punishment coming their way. While previous oracles have hinted at hope beyond the judgment, this poem does not.

5:1 The loved one in the song turns out to be none other than God Himself, and His **vineyard** stands for His people (v. 7). The image of the vineyard is appropriate for Israel because grapes were one of its main crops.

5:2 The singer continues by describing the labor that went into preparing the vineyard. To create a vineyard was no easy matter. There was a period of a few years that passed from clearing the area of **stones** (pervasive through the hill country of Israel), planting expensive vines, and building a **tower** and a **winepress**. Similarly, God expended great effort in creating the right conditions for Israel to flourish as a godly nation. But in spite of all the work, the vineyard produced **worthless grapes**. This signified that the people of God did not live up to their promise of being an obedient and blessed people who would also bless the nations around them.

5:3-6 In these verses the first-person speaker is God, the

4 What more could I have done
   for My vineyard
   than I did?*a*
   Why, when I expected a yield
   of good grapes,
   did it yield worthless grapes?
5 Now I will tell you
   what I am about to do
   to My vineyard:
   I will remove its hedge,*b*
   and it will be consumed;
   I will tear down its wall,*c*
   and it will be trampled.
6 I will make it a wasteland.*d*
   It will not be pruned or weeded;
   thorns and briers will grow up.*e*
   I will also give orders to the clouds
   that rain should not fall on it.
7 For the vineyard of the LORD
   of Hosts
   is the house of Israel,*f*
   and the men*A* of Judah,
   the plant He delighted in.
   He looked for justice
   but saw injustice,
   for righteousness,
   but heard cries of wretchedness.

Judah's Sins Denounced

8 Woe to those who add house
   to house*g*
   and join field to field
   until there is no more room
   and you alone are left in the land.

9 I heard the LORD of Hosts say:

   Indeed, many houses*h*
   will become desolate,
   grand and lovely ones
   without inhabitants.
10 For a ten-acre*B* vineyard will yield
   only six gallons,*C*
   and 10 bushels*D* of seed will yield
   only one bushel.*E*

11 Woe to those who rise early
   in the morning
   in pursuit of beer,*i*
   who linger into the evening,
   inflamed by wine.
12 At their feasts they have lyre, harp,
   tambourine, flute, and wine.
   They do not perceive
   the LORD's actions,*j*
   and they do not see the work
   of His hands.*k*

13 Therefore My people will go
   into exile
   because they lack knowledge;*l*
   her*F* dignitaries are starving,
   and her*F* masses are parched
   with thirst.
14 Therefore *Sheol enlarges its throat
   and opens wide its enormous jaws,*m*
   and down go *Zion's dignitaries,
   her masses,
   her crowds, and those who carouse
   in her!
15 Humanity is brought low,
   man is humbled,
   and haughty eyes are humbled.*n*
16 But the LORD of Hosts is exalted
   by His justice,*o*
   and the holy God*p* is distinguished
   by righteousness.*q*
17 Lambs will graze

Cross references (center column)

a 5:4 Mc 6:3-4; Mt 23:37
b 5:5 Ps 89:40; Jr 5:10
c Ps 80:12
d 5:6 2Ch 36:19-21; Is 7:19-25; 24:1,3; 27:2-6; Jr 25:11
e Gn 3:18; Is 7:23-25; 9:18; 10:17; 27:4; 32:13
f 5:7 Ps 80:8-11
g 5:8 Jr 22:13-17; Mc 2:2; Hab 2:9-12
h 5:9 Am 3:10,15
i 5:11 Lv 10:9; Nm 6:3; Dt 29:6; Jdg 13:4; Is 5:22; 24:9; 28:7; 56:12
j 5:12 Dt 32:4; Jb 34:27; 36:24; Ps 28:5; 44:1; 64:9-10
k Ex 32:16; 34:10; Ps 8:3,6; 19:1; 92:4-5; Is 10:12; 29:23
l 5:13 Is 1:3; 27:11; Hs 4:6; Lk 11:52; 19:42; 1Tm 1:13
m 5:14 Pr 30:16; Hab 2:5
n 5:15 Is 2:9,11,17; 10:33
o 5:16 Is 33:5,10
p Is 6:3
q Is 8:13; 29:23; 1Pt 3:15

A 5:7 Lit man   *B* 5:10 Lit ten-yoke   *C* 5:10 Lit one bath   *D* 5:10 Lit one homer   *E* 5:10 Lit one ephah   *F* 5:13 Lit its

---

owner of the vineyard, demanding an accounting of His grapes, the people of Israel.

5:3-4 When God called on the **residents of Jerusalem** to **judge** between Him and His **vineyard**, He in essence was calling on them to judge themselves. In this way, this poem functions similarly to the parable of Nathan as he confronted David about his sin with Bathsheba (2Sm 12:1-15).

5:5-6 The owner was incensed that the results of His hard labor had produced useless grapes, so He took His anger out on the vineyard.

5:7 The last verse of the poem makes explicit the identification of the **vineyard** as the people of God. It also gives the explanation for their punishment by means of a wordplay. In the land there was **injustice** (Hb *mispach*) and not **justice** (Hb *mishpat*), **cries of wretchedness** (Hb *tse'aqah*) and not **righteousness** (Hb *tsedaqah*).

5:8-30 The previous passage described Israel as a vineyard that produced worthless grapes. The six woes (on "woe," see

note at 1:4) that follow illustrate why Israel was so worthless. Judgment oracles follow the description of the woes.

5:8 The first **woe** is directed toward those who expanded their real estate holdings. Since God graciously provided the land so all of His people had some, buying up land was always done at the cost of another person. Ahab's seizure of Naboth's vineyard is a concrete illustration of this exploitation (1Kg 21).

5:9-10 While the wealthy intended to grab land to get richer, the result will be the opposite—empty **houses** and poor harvests.

5:11-12 The second **woe** is directed toward those who indulged in excessive drinking of alcoholic beverages (**beer** and **wine**). They drank and ate and sang, forgetting what was really important—the **work** of God.

5:14 As God's people indulged themselves with drink and food, so **Sheol** will open its large mouth and swallow them. Sheol refers to the grave and in some contexts signifies the underworld. The idea of Sheol swallowing its victims did

as if in[A] their own pastures,[a]
and strangers[B] will eat
among the ruins of the rich.

18 Woe to those who drag wickedness
with cords of deceit[b]
and pull sin along with cart ropes,
19 to those who say:
"Let Him hurry up and do
His work quickly
so that we can see it!
Let the plan[c] of the Holy One of Israel[d]
take place
so that we can know it!"
20 Woe to those who call evil good
and good evil,[e]
who substitute darkness for light
and light for darkness,
who substitute bitter for sweet
and sweet for bitter.
21 Woe to those who are wise
in their own opinion
and clever in their own sight.[C,f]
22 Woe to those who are heroes
at drinking wine,
who are fearless at mixing beer,[g]
23 who acquit the •guilty for a bribe[h]
and deprive the innocent of justice.

24 Therefore, as a tongue of fire
consumes straw
and as dry grass shrivels
in the flame,
so their roots will become
like something rotten
and their blossoms will blow away
like dust,
for they have rejected[i]
the instruction of the LORD of Hosts,
and they have despised
the word of the Holy One
of Israel.[j]

25 Therefore the LORD's anger burns[k]
against His people.
He raised His hand against them
and struck them;
the mountains quaked,[l]
and their corpses were like garbage
in the streets.
In all this, His anger is
not removed,
and His hand is still raised
to strike.[m]

26 He raises a signal flag
for the distant nations[n]
and whistles[o] for them from the ends
of the earth.
Look—how quickly and swiftly
they come!
27 None of them grows weary
or stumbles;[p]
no one slumbers or sleeps.
No belt is loose
and no sandal strap broken.
28 Their arrows are sharpened,
and all their bows strung.
Their horses' hooves are
like flint;
their chariot wheels are
like a whirlwind.
29 Their roaring is like a lion's;[q]
they roar like young lions;[r]
they growl and seize their prey
and carry it off,
and no one can rescue it.
30 On that day they will roar over it,
like the roaring of the sea.
When one looks at the land,
there will be darkness
and distress;
light will be obscured
by clouds.[D]

[a] 5:17 Mc 2:12
[b] 5:18 Pr 5:22; Is 59:4-8; Jr 23:10-14
[c] 5:19 Jb 38:2; 42:3; Ps 33:11; 106:13; 107:11; Pr 19:21; Is 14:26; 19:17; 46:10-11
[d] Is 1:4
[e] 5:20 Pr 17:15; Am 5:7; Mal 2:17
[f] 5:21 Pr 3:7; Rm 12:16; 1Co 3:18
[g] 5:22 Is 5:11
[h] 5:23 Ex 23:8; Pr 17:15; Is 1:23; 33:15
[i] 5:24 Is 8:6; 30:9,12; Am 2:4; Ac 13:41
[j] Is 5:19; Jr 51:5
[k] 5:25 Nm 11:10,33; 32:10-13; Dt 6:15; Jos 7:1; 23:16; 2Kg 13:3; Ps 106:40
[l] Am 1:1; Zch 14:5
[m] Is 9:12,17,21; 10:4; 14:27
[n] 5:26 Is 10:5; 11:10,12; 13:2; 18:3
[o] Is 7:18; Zch 10:8
[p] 5:27 1Jn 2:10
[q] 5:29 Jdg 14:5; Hs 13:8; Jl 1:6; Nah 2:12-13
[r] Rv 9:17

[A] 5:17 Syr reads *graze in* [B] 5:17 LXX reads *sheep* [C] 5:21 Lit *clever before their face* [D] 5:30 Lit *its clouds*

not originate with the Hebrews, but may stem from the Canaanite story that describes the god of death *(Mot)* swallowing his victims.

5:18-19 The third **woe** begins by picturing people whose sins were so heavy that they ended up pulling it along in a **cart** behind them. Their sin was one of cynicism. With a tone of disbelief, they challenged God to act. In particular they might be thinking of God's work of judgment. They sinned and did not yet see God's punishment.

5:20 The fourth **woe** is against those who confused ethical categories. They classified actions as **evil** that God would call **good** and vice versa. While the principle is broader than judicial, such moral confusion was particularly reprehensible in the courtroom (v. 23).

5:21 As with the previous verse, the issue of the fifth **woe** is human autonomy. On being wise in one's own eyes, see Pr 3:7; 26:12; 28:11,26.

5:22-23 The sixth and final **woe** returns to the earlier issue of excessive drinking (**heroes at drinking wine**) and also twisting justice for money.

5:24-25 Two judgment speeches follow (**therefore** introduces vv. 24 and 25) the woes.

5:26 God will call for foreign armies to descend on His people. Though these armies are not mentioned by name, we know from later history that these nations were Assyria and Babylon. Notice that God would signal them with a whistle, and they would immediately respond. This illustrates God's sovereign rule over the nations.

5:29 Assyrian royal inscriptions often compare their kings to **lions**.

Isaiah's Call and Mission

6 In the year that King Uzziah[a] died, I saw the Lord[b] seated on a high and lofty[c] throne,[d] and His robe[A] filled the temple. [2]Seraphim[B] were standing above Him; each one had six wings:[e] with two he covered his face, with two he covered his feet, and with two he flew.[f] [3]And one called to another:

Holy, holy, holy is the Lord of °Hosts;
His glory[g] fills the whole earth.[h]

[4]The foundations of the doorways shook[i] at the sound of their voices, and the temple was filled with smoke. [5]Then I said:

Woe is me[j] for I am ruined[C]
because I am a man
    of °unclean lips
and live among a people
    of unclean lips,[k]
and because my eyes have seen
    the King,
the Lord of Hosts.

[6]Then one of the seraphim flew to me, and in his hand was a glowing coal that he had taken from the altar[l] with tongs. [7]He touched my mouth[m] with it and said:

Now that this has touched your lips,
your wickedness is removed
and your sin is atoned for.[n]

[8]Then I heard the voice of the Lord saying:

Who should I send?
Who will go for Us?

I said:

Here I am. Send me.

[9]And He replied:

Go! Say to these people:
Keep listening,
    but do not understand;[o]
keep looking, but do not perceive.
[10] Dull the minds[D] of these people;
deafen their ears and blind
    their eyes;
otherwise they might see
    with their eyes
and hear with their ears,
understand with their minds,
turn back, and be healed.[p]

[11]Then I said, "Until when, Lord?"[q] And He replied:

Until cities lie in ruins
    without inhabitants,[r]
houses are without people,
the land is ruined and desolate,
[12] and the Lord drives the people far away,
leaving great emptiness in the land.
[13] Though a tenth will remain in the land,
it will be burned again.
Like the terebinth or the oak
that leaves a stump when felled,
the holy °seed[s] is the stump.[t]

Cross references:
a 6:1 2Kg 15:1-7; Is 1:1; 14:28
b Gn 32:30; Ex 3:1-6; 24:9-10; Jos 5:13-15; 1Kg 22:19; Is 31:3; Jn 1:18; 4:24; 12:41
c Is 52:13; 57:15
d Ps 9:7; 11:4; 45:6; Is 66:1; Jr 3:17; Ezk 1:26; 10:1; 43:7
e 6:2 Rv 4:8
f Ezk 1:14
g 6:3 Ex 16:10; 24:16-17; 40:34-35; 1Kg 8:11; Is 35:2; 40:5; 60:1; Ezk 1:28; Lk 9:32
h Nm 14:21; Ps 72:19
i 6:4 Ex 19:8; Hab 3:3-10; Rv 15:8
j 6:5 Ex 33:20; Jdg 13:22; Is 59:3; Jr 9:3-8; Lk 5:8
k Ex 6:12,30
l 6:6 Lv 6:12-13; 17:11
m 6:7 Jr 1:9; Dn 10:16
n Ex 21:30; 30:12-16
o 6:9-10 Mt 13:14-15; Mk 4:12; Lk 8:10; Jn 12:40; Ac 28:26-27
p 6:10 Zch 7:11-12; 1Th 2:16
q 6:11 Ps 79:5; 89:46
r Is 1:7; 27:10
s 6:13 Is 41:8; 43:5; 45:25; 53:10; 59:21; 65:9,23; 66:22
t Is 11:1

A 6:1 Lit *seam*   B 6:2 = heavenly beings   C 6:5 Or *I must be silent*   D 6:10 Lit *heart*

6:1-13 Most prophets record a time when God called them to their ministry. Moses received God's call at the burning bush (Ex 3). Jeremiah heard God tell him that he had been chosen from the womb to deliver a message of judgment and salvation to the nations (Jr 1:4-10). Ezekiel experienced an incredible vision while he was in exile in Babylon (Ezk 1:4–3:27). Isaiah received his commissioning vision in the temple, but in his vision the temple was transformed into the throne room of heaven itself.

6:1 King Uzziah (called "Azariah" in 2Kg 15:3) died about 740 B.C. He had been a relatively good king, and did "what was right in the Lord's sight" (2Kg 15:3), though he did not remove the high places. God also blessed Uzziah's reign with prosperity and military success. His death, coupled with the rise of Assyria, created great uncertainty in Judah. Note that God is so great that **His robe** (the Hb suggests just the seam of His robe) filled the temple.

6:2 The **seraphim** were angelic creatures of great power and importance. Their name means "burning ones," and the implication of fire evokes thoughts of danger and mystery. Covering their eyes shielded them from the brilliance of the divine glory. Covering their feet (possibly used here as a euphemism) may have been a posture of submission.

6:3 The word **holy** spoken three times is emphatic or super-

lative and points to God's otherness. He is completely separated from anything profane or sinful. His sovereignty is underlined by the fact that His glory filled **the whole earth**.

6:5 In the presence of such holiness, Isaiah felt the weight of his own sinfulness. He feared for himself because he knew that God did not tolerate uncleanness in His presence.

6:6-7 God prepared Isaiah by cleansing his **lips**, the instrument by which he would execute his prophetic task. He did this symbolically by having one of His seraphim touch the prophet's lips with a burning coal. Fire can purify (Nm 31:22-23), and this burning coal was taken from the altar where sacrifices were offered to atone for **sin** (1Ch 6:49).

6:8 Isaiah's readiness to serve contrasts with the reluctance of Moses and Jeremiah (Ex 4:1-17; Jr 1:6).

6:9-10 Isaiah was a prophet with a message of judgment. God's commission recognized that, because of its sin, Israel's healing could only come about through their punishment. Isaiah's message from God would serve only to distance them even more from God.

6:11-13 From the start Isaiah knew that his message would not lead God's people to repentance. They would experience destruction. Even so, a remnant would survive. This remnant is pictured as a **stump** that is left after a mighty tree falls.

The Message to Ahaz

7 This took place during the reign of Ahaz, son of Jotham, son of Uzziah king of Judah:*a* Rezin king of Aram, along with Pekah, son of Remaliah, king of Israel, waged war against Jerusalem,*b* but he could not succeed. ²When it became known to the house of David*c* that Aram had occupied Ephraim,*d* the heart of Ahaz*A* and the hearts of his people trembled like trees of a forest shaking in the wind. ³Then the Lord said to Isaiah, "Go out with your son Shear-jashub*e* to meet Ahaz at the end of the conduit of the upper pool,*f* by the road to the Fuller's Field. ⁴Say to him: Calm down and be quiet. Don't be afraid or cowardly*g* because of these two smoldering stubs of firebrands, the fierce anger of Rezin and Aram, and the son of Remaliah. ⁵For Aram, along with Ephraim and the son of Remaliah, has plotted harm against you. They say, ⁶'Let us go up against Judah, terrorize it, and conquer it for ourselves. Then we can install Tabeel's son as king in it.'"

⁷This is what the Lord God says:

It will not happen; it will not occur.*h*
⁸ The*B* head of Aram is Damascus,
the head of Damascus is Rezin
(within 65 years
Ephraim will be too shattered to be
a people),
⁹ the head of Ephraim is Samaria,
and the head of Samaria is the son
of Remaliah.
If you do not stand firm in your faith,
then you will not stand at all.

The Immanuel Prophecy

¹⁰Then the Lord spoke again to Ahaz: ¹¹"Ask for a sign*i* from the Lord your God—from the depths of •Sheol to the heights of heaven." ¹²But Ahaz replied, "I will not ask. I will not test the Lord." ¹³Isaiah*j* said, "Listen, house of David! Is it not enough for you to try the patience of men? Will you also try the patience of my God?*k* ¹⁴Therefore, the Lord Himself will give you*c*

*a*7:1 Is 1:1
*b*2Kg 15:25,37; 16:5
*c*7:2 Is 7:13; 9:7; 16:5; 22:9,22; 29:1; 37:35; 38:5; 55:3
*d*Is 8:12; 9:9
*e*7:3 Is 8:3,18
*f*2Kg 18:17; Is 36:2
*g*7:4 Gn 15:1; Ex 14:13; 20:20; Nm 14:9; Dt 20:3; 31:6; Jos 10:8,25; Is 10:24; 35:4; 41:14
*h*7:7 Is 8:10
*i*7:11 2Kg 19:29; Is 37:30; 38:7-8; 55:13
*j*7:13 Mt 3:3; 12:17
*k*Is 1:14; 43:24; Jr 15:6; 20:9; Mal 2:17

A7:2 Lit *Aram has rested upon Ephraim, his heart*   **B7:8** Lit *For the*   **C7:14** In Hb, the word *you* is pl

7:1-2 The political situation was tense in Jerusalem. In the early 730s B.C. the aggressive Assyrian king Tiglath-pileser III was busy on his northern frontier. During this time, **Rezin**, the king of **Aram** with its capital in Damascus, and **Pekah**, the king of **Israel** (also known as **Ephraim**), joined forces to withstand the almost certain Assyrian attack that would follow Tiglath-pileser's victory in the north. Rezin and Pekah wanted Judah to support them, but **Ahaz** wanted nothing to do with the alliance. By this time he might already have paid (or at least was contemplating paying) the Assyrians to rescue him from these kings (2Kg 16:6-9). He probably feared Tiglath-pileser, but he apparently realized the Syro-Ephraimite coalition was a more immediate threat. Isaiah confronted the king with a question: What was the source of his trust: Yahweh or the Assyrians?

7:3 The name of Isaiah's son, **Shear-jashub**, means "a remnant will return," a theme that has already played a significant role in the first six chapters of the book (1:9,26; 4:2-6; 6:13).

7:6 Though no other certain references to Tabeel exist in the Bible or outside of it, the political intentions of Rezin and Pekah were clear. They wanted to remove Ahaz from the throne because of his unwillingness to join their coalition and they intended to install a puppet **king** who would be more easily manipulated.

7:8 The reference to **65 years** is puzzling. If this oracle is dated to 735 B.C. or thereabouts, then it would point to approximately 670 B.C., but the northern kingdom was soundly defeated by Assyria in 722 B.C. Of course, that is "within 65 years," but perhaps the reference is to some unknown event among the survivors of the northern kingdom around 670 B.C. It is also possible that the deportations of Israelites and the importation of foreigners into their former region happened around that time.

7:9 The challenge that the oracle presented to Ahaz was

that he should trust God and not Assyria as he faced the threat from Rezin and Pekah.

7:11 The purpose of **a sign** was to give Ahaz even more reason to have confidence in God rather than Assyria to rescue him from Rezin and Pekah. **Sheol** refers to the underworld.

7:12 From Isaiah's reaction, the reader can discern that Ahaz's reply, which on the surface seems pious, was actually impious. The king seemed to cite scriptural precedent (Dt 6:16), but the law prohibited the type of rebellious testing that took place at Massah (Ex 17:1-7), not a test offered by a true prophet of the Lord. It may be that Ahaz had already decided to call on Assyria for help.

7:14 The context indicates that the preliminary fulfillment

'aman

Hebrew Pronunciation	[ah MAHN]
HCSB Translation	be faithful, believe
Uses in Isaiah	15
Uses in the OT	105
Focus Passage	Isaiah 7:9

'*Aman*, related to '*emeth (truth)* and '*emunah (faithfulness)*, might reflect one or two roots. Participles denote *nurses* (2Sm 4:4), *guardians* (2Kg 10:1), and *foster fathers* (Is 49:23) who *take care of people* (Ru 4:16). The passive participle is *reared* (Lm 4:5). The passive-reflexive indicates *being carried* (Is 60:4). Perhaps as another root, passive-reflexives mean *endure* (2Sm 7:16) and *be faithful* (Nm 12:7), *reliable* (Ps 93:5), or *confirmed* (Gn 42:20). Promises *come true* (2Ch 1:9). Participles imply *faithful, trustworthy* (Is 8:2), *trusted, assured* (Is 33:16), *certain* (Hs 5:9), *confirmed* (1Sm 3:20), or *firm* (Is 22:25). They connote *chronic, lasting* (Dt 28:59), and *enduring* (Ps 89:28). Causative verbs signify *believe* (Gn 15:6), *trust* (Nm 14:11), *rely* (Mc 7:5), *have confidence* (Jr 12:6) or *assurance* (Jb 24:22), and *be certain* (Ps 27:13).

Significance of the Dead Sea Scrolls

Peter W. Flint

The Dead Sea Scrolls are ancient manuscripts that were found at several sites near the western shore of the Dead Sea. The most important site was near Qumran, where eleven caves containing scrolls or artifacts were discovered from 1946 to 1956. Also notable are discoveries at Murabba'at (1951), Nahal Hever (1951 or 1952), Wadi Seiyal (1951 or 1952), and Masada (1963–65). Professor W. F. Albright, America's foremost archaeologist, described the scrolls as "the greatest archaeological find of modern times."

At least 941 scrolls were discovered in the Qumran caves (715 in Cave 4 alone). They are dated on paleographic and radiocarbon grounds to between ca 250 B.C. and A.D. 68, when the site was destroyed by the Romans. The Qumran library is divided into two basic categories: 240 biblical scrolls and 701 nonbiblical scrolls. The nonbiblical scrolls are further divided into: Apocryphal scrolls (such as Tobit), Sectarian scrolls (such as the *Rule of the Community*), and Pseudepigraphic scrolls (such as the *Prayer of Nabonidus*).

Most scholars agree that the Sectarian scrolls were produced by a group of Essenes who had a settlement at Qumran. Proposals to the contrary may be discounted due to lack of firm evidence.

Five Reasons Why the Dead Sea Scrolls Are Significant

The scrolls were discovered and copied in Palestine (Israel). In fact, they are virtually the only manuscripts that survive from the Second Temple period (which ended in A.D. 70). It is even possible—though not likely—that Jesus or some of His followers handled some of these manuscripts before they were brought to Qumran.

The scrolls were written in the three languages of Scripture. Of the 240 biblical scrolls from Qumran, 235 are written in Hebrew and 5 in Greek, and of the 701 nonbiblical scrolls, 548 are written in Hebrew, 137 in Aramaic, and 5 in Greek. This means that at least some Jews could speak Greek in late Second Temple Palestine, and reinforces the idea that Jesus and His followers knew Greek.

The biblical scrolls both affirm and enhance the Hebrew Bible used by scholars. Prior to their discovery, the oldest complete Hebrew Bible was the *Leningrad Codex* (A.D. 1008), on which most scholarly editions are based. Even older medieval manuscripts are the *Aleppo Codex* (early tenth century), part of which is missing, and some fragments from the Cairo Genizeh (ninth century onwards). In contrast, the oldest Bible scroll found at Qumran (4QExod-Lev^f) is dated from about 250 B.C., and the latest ones to A.D. 68. This puts scholars much closer to the time of the texts' origins. Two of the most prominent and best-preserved Bible scrolls are the Great Isaiah Scroll (1QIsa^a, about 125 B.C.) and the Great Psalms Scroll (11QPs^a, A.D. 30–50).

Scrolls with sufficient writing for an assessment to be made fall into four textual groups: Proto-Masoretic (i.e., the consonantal text behind the Masoretic Text, represented by about 40% of the scrolls), Proto-Samaritan (about 15%), Pre-Septuagint (about 5%), and mixed or nonaligned (about 40%). The Proto-Masoretic scrolls in particular affirm the accuracy and great age of the Hebrew text found in modern Bible editions.

On the other hand, many scrolls (in all four groups) preserve original or preferable readings that are convincing enough to have been adopted by modern English OT translations. One example is at Isaiah 19:18, where the Masoretic Text reads "City of Destruction," but two scrolls (1QIsa^a, 4QIsa^b) and even a few Masoretic manuscripts read "City of the Sun," which makes better sense. The reading found in the scrolls has also been adopted by many modern Bibles, including the HCSB, RSV, and NRSV. A second example is the missing verse in the acrostic Psalm 145. This verse is present in 11QPs^a and the LXX, and hence it is now included as verse 13b in the HCSB, RSV, NRSV, NIV, and so forth. At least 100 such examples have gotten modern Bible translators closer to the original text, and the majority of these discoveries have been adopted by the Holman Christian Standard Bible.

Most of the nonbiblical scrolls throw light on Judaism in the late Second Temple period. Certain scrolls illuminate our understanding of Jewish sects, namely the Pharisees, Sadducees, and Essenes. Sectarian documents such as the *Community Rule* and the *Damascus Document* reveal the doctrines and teachings of the Essenes: for example, their expectation of two separate Messiahs (of Aaron and of David) and their ascetic lifestyle. One fascinating text named *Some of the Works of the Law* (4QMMT) is a manifesto which details how the Essene interpretation of some 25 laws from the Pentateuch differed from those of the Pharisees.

Some scrolls illuminate our understanding of Jesus and the early Christians. None of the Qumran scrolls was written by or for Christians, but several are relevant for understanding the historical context of Christian origins. The three books most commonly found at Qumran are Psalms (36 scrolls), Deuteronomy (30), and Isaiah (21). These are also the books quoted most often in the New Testament (Psalms 79x, Isaiah

a sign: The virgin will conceive,[A] have a son, and name him Immanuel.[B,a] [15] By the time he learns to reject what is bad and choose what is good,[b] he will be eating butter[C] and honey.[c] [16] For before the boy knows to reject what is bad and choose what is good, the land of the two kings you dread will be abandoned. [17] The LORD will bring on you, your people, and the house of your father, such a time as has never been since Ephraim separated from Judah[d]—the king of Assyria[e] is coming."

[18] On that day[f]
the LORD will whistle[g] to the fly
that is at the farthest streams of the Nile
and to the bee that is in the land
of Assyria.
[19] All of them will come and settle
in the steep ravines, in the clefts
of the rocks,[h]
in all the thornbushes, and in all the
water holes.

[20] On that day the Lord will use a razor[i] hired from beyond the Euphrates River—the king of Assyria[j]—to shave the head, the hair on the legs, and to remove the beard as well.

[21] On that day
a man will raise a young cow
and two sheep,
[22] and from the abundant milk they give
he will eat butter,
for every survivor in the land
will eat butter and honey.[k]

[23] And on that day
every place where there were 1,000 vines,
worth 1,000 pieces of silver,
will become thorns and briers.[l]
[24] A man will go there with bow
and arrows
because the whole land will be thorns
and briers.
[25] You will not go to all the hills
that were once tilled with a hoe,

Cross references:
a 7:14 Is 8:8,10; Mt 1:23; Lk 1:31
b 7:15 Dt 1:39
c Ex 3:8; 2Sm 17:29; Is 7:22; 8:15
d 7:17 1Kg 12:16
e 2Ch 28:20; Is 8:7-8; 10:5-6
f 7:18 Is 27:12
g Is 5:25
h 7:19 Is 2:19; Jr 16:16
i 7:20 2Kg 18:13-16; Is 24:1; Ezk 5:1-4
j Is 8:7; 11:15; Jr 2:18
k 7:22 Is 8:15
l 7:23 Is 5:6

A 7:14 Or *virgin is pregnant, will*   B 7:14 = God With Us   C 7:15 Or *sour milk*

of this sign must have taken place within a few years of its utterance—the time between a child's conception and his knowing right from wrong (vv. 15-16), traditionally at age 12. The Hebrew word translated **virgin** means "young woman of marriageable age" and often has the implication of virginity. Thus many scholars feel that the referent is a woman whom Isaiah would marry and, if so, then the birth is mentioned in 8:1-4. This may be the immediate fulfillment of this sign. But its ultimate and more exalted fulfillment is noted in Mt 1:23 as it cites the more specific Greek word found in the Septuagint, *parthenos*, which means "virgin." **Immanuel** means "God is with us."

7:15 The first phrase could also be translated, "In order to learn," meaning that hardship will motivate the child to turn to God. The significance of eating **butter and honey** is that the devastation of the land's agriculture (vv. 23-24) will be such that other foods will not be available.

7:16 The Aramean kingdom of Rezin was destroyed in 732 B.C. Tiglath-pileser reduced the size of the northern kingdom of Pekah in 733 B.C., and the king was assassinated and replaced by Hoshea. Even so, the northern kingdom was totally defeated in 722 B.C., about 13 years after the Immanuel prophecy.

7:17 But it was not just Syria and the northern kingdom that would experience Assyrian devastation. Judah would also experience God's punishment. As later events showed, paying Tiglath-pileser to take care of Ahaz's northern problem was not the smartest strategy. From that point on Ahaz paid a heavy tribute as Assyria's vassal (2Kg 16:10-18).

7:18-19 The **fly** (Egypt) and the **bee** (Assyria) will infest (occupy) the land.

7:20 The **razor** is Tiglath-pileser, who will ravage the land of Judah.

66x, and Deuteronomy 54x). This is hardly a coincidence, but speaks to similar messianic expectations and covenantal themes among the Qumranites and the early Christians.

Key nonbiblical scrolls are just as pertinent. For example, the *Messianic Apocaplyse* (4Q521) describes the works and wonders that will accompany the Messiah's coming in language that is very close to Jesus' words in Luke 4:18-19 (will bring good news to the poor, set the captives free, open the eyes of the blind, and lift up the oppressed) and in Matthew 11:4-5 and Luke 7:21-22 (will open the eyes of the blind, make the dead live, and bring good news to the poor). This scroll helps Bible readers see that Jesus is claiming to be a prophetic Messiah in the Gospel passages just mentioned. Another striking example is *Some of the Works of the Law* (4QMMT), since the term "works of the Law" occurs nowhere else except in Romans (e.g., 3:20, 28) and Galatians (e.g., 3:2,5,10). In this light we now know that Paul is using a term identified with the Essenes, and so is criticizing Essene Jews or Christians who have been influenced by Essene doctrines concerning works of the Law. A final example is the sectarian New Jerusalem Text, which is found in several scrolls (1Q32, 2Q24, 4Q544-55, 5Q15, 11Q18), and describes the coming New Jerusalem with language that would be developed further in the Book of Revelation (21:9-27).

In conclusion, the Dead Sea Scrolls help scholars get closer to the original OT texts where variants have entered the tradition, plus they help set the historical and cultural context for the Intertestamental and New Testament eras.

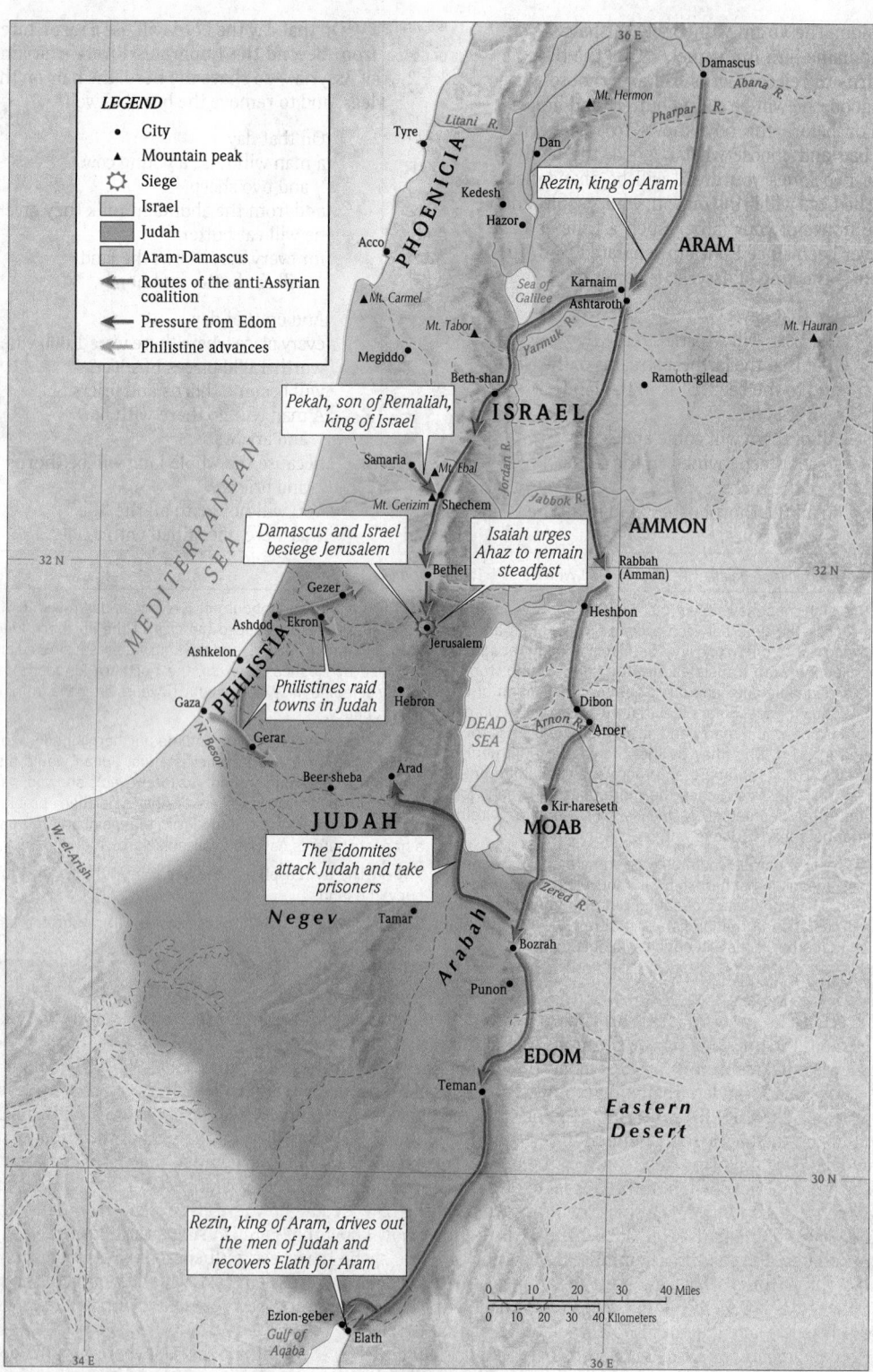

Damascus

Mt. Hermon

Rezin, king of Aram

Tyre

Dan

Kedesh

Hazor

ARAM

Acco

PHOENICIA

Litani R.

Abana R.

Pharpar R.

36 E

Mt. Carmel

Sea of
Galilee

Karnaim

Ashtaroth

Mt. Hauran

Megiddo

Mt. Tabor

Yarmuk R.

Ramoth-gilead

Beth-shan

*Pekah, son of Remaliah,
king of Israel*

ISRAEL

Samaria

Mt. Ebal

Mt. Gerizim

Shechem

Jordan R.

Jabbok R.

AMMON

*Damascus and Israel
besiege Jerusalem*

*Isaiah urges
Ahaz to remain
steadfast*

Rabbah
(Amman)

32 N

32 N

Bethel

Jerusalem

Heshbon

Gezer

MEDITERRANEAN SEA

Ashdod

Ekron

Ashkelon

PHILISTIA

*Philistines raid
towns in Judah*

Hebron

Dibon

Aroer

Arnon R.

DEAD
SEA

Gaza

Gerar

N. Besor

Beer-sheba

Arad

JUDAH

Kir-hareseth

MOAB

*The Edomites
attack Judah and take
prisoners*

W. et-Arish

Negev

Tamar

Arabah

Zered R.

Bozrah

Punon

EDOM

Teman

Eastern
Desert

30 N

*Rezin, king of Aram, drives out
the men of Judah and
recovers Elath for Aram*

Ezion-geber

Gulf of
Aqaba

Elath

34 E

36 E

0   10   20   30   40 Miles

0 10 20 30 40 Kilometers

The Syro-Ephraimite War

for fear of the thorns and briers.
Those hills will be places for oxen
　　to graze
and for sheep to trample.

The Coming Assyrian Invasion

8 Then the LORD said to me, "Take a large piece of parchment[A] and write on it with an ordinary pen:[B,a] Maher-shalal-hash-baz.[C] 2 I have appointed[D] trustworthy witnesses—Uriah the priest and Zechariah son of Jeberechiah."[b]

3 I was then intimate with the prophetess, and she conceived and gave birth to a son. The LORD said to me, "Name him Maher-shal-al-hash-baz, 4 for before the boy knows how to call out father or mother,[c] the wealth of Damascus and the spoils of Samaria will be carried off to the king of Assyria."[d]

5 The LORD spoke to me again:

6　Because these people rejected
　the slowly flowing waters of Shiloah
　and rejoiced with[E] Rezin
　and the son of Remaliah,[e]
7　the Lord will certainly bring
　　against them
　the mighty rushing waters
　　of the Euphrates River—
　the king of Assyria and all his glory.

It will overflow its channels
and spill over all its banks.
8　It will pour into Judah,
flood over it, and sweep through,
reaching up to the neck;[f]
and its spreading streams[F]
will fill your entire land, Immanuel![g]

9　Band together, peoples, and be broken;
pay attention, all you distant lands;
prepare for war, and be broken;
prepare for war, and be broken.
10　Devise a plan; it will fail.[h]
Make a prediction; it will not happen.
For God is with us.[G,i]

The LORD of Hosts, the Only Refuge

11 For this is what the LORD said to me with great power, to keep[H] me from going the way of this people:[j]

12　Do not call everything an alliance
these people say is an alliance.[k]
Do not fear what they fear;[l]
do not be terrified.
13　You are to regard only the LORD
of •Hosts as holy.[m]
Only He should be •feared;[n]
only He should be held in awe.

Cross-references
a 8:1 Is 30:8; Hab 2:2
b 8:2 2Kg 16:10-11,15-16
c 8:4 Is 7:16
d Is 7:8-9
e 8:6 Is 7:1
f 8:8 Is 30:28
g Is 7:14; 8:10
h 8:10 Is 14:27
i Is 8:8
j 8:11 Ezk 2:8
k 8:12 Is 7:2; 30:1
l Pt 3:14
m 8:13 Nm 20:12
n 1Pt 3:15

A 8:1 Hb obscure　B 8:1 Lit with the pen of a man　C 8:1 = Speeding to the Plunder, Hurrying to the Spoil　D 8:2 Vg; MT, one DSS ms read I will appoint; one DSS ms, LXX, Syr, Tg read Appoint　E 8:6 Or and rejoiced over　F 8:8 Or wings　G 8:10 Or For Immanuel H 8:11 DSS; MT reads instruct

8:1 There is nothing unusual about the use of **parchment** and **pen** in this verse. Nor would there be anything unusual if, as some scholars suggest, the Hebrew here indicates a clay tablet and a stylus. The significance of the **large** size of the parchment may simply be that the writing was prominent and clear. The name **Maher-shalal-hash-baz** means "Speeding to the Plunder, Hurrying to the Spoil," and it signifies the rapid future advance of Assyria.

8:2 The presence of **witnesses** indicates that the writing of this prophecy had the force of a legal document. If the prophecy did not come true, then these two witnesses could attest to its falsity. If it did come true, they could proclaim that it was written before, and not after, the fact. It is possible that **Uriah** is mentioned in 2Kg 16:10-18. He was the high priest during Ahaz's reign who, at the king's request, modified the altar to conform to the one in Damascus.

8:3 On **intimate with the prophetess**, see note at 7:14. The first fulfillment of the Immanuel prophecy may well be connected with the birth of Maher-shalal-hash-baz recorded here. Isaiah's wife was a prophetess (cp. Miriam, Ex 15:20; Deborah, Jdg 4:4; Huldah, 2Kg 22:14; Anna, Lk 2:36).

8:4 The point of the prophecy is that within just a few years the Assyrian army would advance to crush **Damascus**, the capital of Rezin's Syria, and **Samaria**, the capital of Pekah's northern kingdom of Israel.

8:5-8 It was good news to Judah that Assyria would defeat Syria and Israel, the two nations that were allied against it. In this light **rejoiced with Rezin**, the translation and meaning of which is debated, likely refers to Judah's rejoicing in

Rezin's coming defeat. The oracle states that such rejoicing might be premature since the Assyrian threat would come to its doorstep as well.

8:6 The **waters of Shiloah** refer to the small water channel that carried water from pools outside Jerusalem into the city. Here it stands for God Himself contrasting with the raging river mentioned in the next verse. Thus, Judah's rejection of Shiloah signifies their rejection of God.

8:7 The **mighty rushing waters** of the **Euphrates** represent the Assyrian king and thus Assyrian might. By calling on Tiglath-pileser to help him against the Syro-Ephraimite alliance, Ahaz was choosing a foreign nation rather than God.

8:8 The waters that represent Assyria will come up to Judah's **neck**. They will not be drowned, but they will find themselves paying annual tribute. On occasion the Assyrian army will threaten their independent existence.

8:9-10 However, Assyria will not completely subjugate Judah. After all, God was still with them.

8:11 God spoke to Isaiah (**me**) so he would not conform to the people's beliefs.

8:12 The **alliance** (alternatively "conspiracy," NRSV) may refer to the alliance between Syria and the northern kingdom of Israel against Judah or perhaps an inner-Judean alliance against the pro-Assyrian party of Ahaz. Whatever the exact alliance in view, the point was that Isaiah must not be afraid like the people were.

8:13 The fear of God overshadows all other fears (Lk 12:5). The reason Isaiah and others must not fear threatening

¹⁴ He will be a sanctuary;[a]
but for the two houses of Israel,
He will be a stone[b] to stumble over
and a rock to trip over,[c]
and a trap and a snare
to the inhabitants of Jerusalem.
¹⁵ Many will stumble over these;[d]
they will fall and be broken;
they will be snared and captured.

¹⁶ Bind up the •testimony.[e]
Seal up the instruction[f]
among my disciples.
¹⁷ I will wait for the LORD,[g]
who is hiding His face from the house
of Jacob.[h]
I will wait for Him.

¹⁸ Here I am with the children the LORD has given me[i] to be signs and wonders in Israel from the LORD of Hosts who dwells on Mount •Zion. ¹⁹ When they say to you, "Consult the spirits of the dead and the spiritists who chirp and mutter,"[j] shouldn't a people consult their God?[A] Should they consult the dead on behalf of the living?[k] ²⁰ To the law and to the testimony![l] If they do not speak according to this word, there will be no dawn for them.

²¹ They will wander through the land, dejected and hungry. When they are famished, they will become enraged, and, looking upward, will curse their king and their God. ²² They will look toward the earth[m] and see only distress,

[a]8:14 Is 4:6;
25:4; Ezk 11:16
[b]Ps 91:12; Is
26:4
[c]Lk 2:34; Rm
9:33; 1Pt 2:8
[d]8:15 Is 28:13;
59:10; Lk 20:18;
Rm 9:32
[e]8:16 Is 8:1-2;
29:11-12
[f]Dn 12:4
[g]8:17 Ps 27:14;
33:20; 37:34;
130:5-6; Is 25:9;
30:18; Lm 3:26;
Hab 2:3; 1Co
1:7; Php 3:20
[h]Dt 31:17; Is
1:15; 45:15; 54:8
[i]8:18 Heb 2:13
[j]8:19 Lv 20:6;
2Kg 21:6; 23:24;
Is 19:3; 29:4;
47:12-13
[k]1Sm 28:8-11
[l]8:20 Is 1:10; Lk
16:29
[m]8:22 Is 5:30;
59:9; Jr 13:16;
Am 5:18,20; Zph
1:14-15
[n]9:1 Mt 4:15
[o]9:2 Mt 4:16;
Eph 5:8
[p]Lk 1:79
[q]9:3 Is 26:15
[r]1Sm 30:16
[s]9:4 Is 10:27;
14:25
[t]Jdg 7:25; Is
10:26
[u]9:6 Is 7:14;
11:1-2; 53:2; Lk
2:11; Jn 3:16
[v]Is 22:22; Mt
28:18; 1Co
15:25

darkness, and the gloom of affliction, and they will be driven into thick darkness.

Birth of the Prince of Peace

9[B] Nevertheless, the gloom of the distressed land will not be like that of the former times when He humbled the land of Zebulun and the land of Naphtali.[n] But in the future He will bring honor to the Way of the Sea, to the land east of the Jordan, and to Galilee of the nations.

²[C] The people walking in darkness
have seen a great light;[o]
a light has dawned
on those living in the land of darkness.[p]
³ You have enlarged the nation
and increased its joy.[D,q]
The people have rejoiced before You
as they rejoice at harvest time
and as they rejoice
when dividing spoils.[r]
⁴ For You have shattered
their oppressive yoke[s]
and the rod on their shoulders,
the staff of their oppressor,
just as You did on the day of Midian.[t]
⁵ For the trampling boot of battle
and the bloodied garments of war
will be burned as fuel for the fire.
⁶ For a child will be born for us,
a son will be given to us,[u]
and the government will be
on His shoulders.[v]

[A]8:19 Or gods   [B]9:1 Is 8:23 in Hb   [C]9:2 Is 9:1 in Hb   [D]9:3 Alt Hb tradition reads have not increased joy

alliances is because God is the only One who should be feared. There is a difference in the quality of the two fears described in these verses. The fear of human beings may be described as terror (v. 12), while the fear of God is described as **awe.**

8:14 The **sanctuary** image highlights God's holiness and suggests that He protects His people, but because they have rejected Him, the Judeans will experience Him as a stumbling **stone.**

8:16 The **testimony,** also called the **instruction,** refers to the words of God that have come to Isaiah. These are to be kept safely (**bind up . . . seal up**) by Isaiah's **disciples.** They will keep the oracles of God secure until the events prove them true.

8:17 Because of their sin, God will withdraw His saving presence (**hiding His face**) from His people (**the house of Jacob**). The faithful, represented by Isaiah, **will wait** for His certain return.

8:18 The **children** who are **signs and wonders** are Shear-jashub (7:3) and Maher-shalal-hash-baz (8:1).

8:19-20 The people wanted Isaiah to engage in necromancy along the lines of the witch of En-dor (1Sm 28). Such divination was strictly prohibited in the OT (Dt 18:9-14). They should put their trust in God and seek only His guidance through His **word.**

9:1 **Zebulun** and **Naphtali** were two northern tribes hit hard by the Assyrian invasion led by Tiglath-pileser in 733 B.C. At that time, the Assyrians reduced the land holdings of the northern empire and integrated three new provinces into their empire. These three provinces were called Magiddo (**Galilee**), Du'ru (**the Way of the Sea**), and Gal'aza (**the land east of the Jordan**).

9:2 The Assyrian invasion brought great devastation (**darkness**), but the people still had great reason to hope (**light has dawned**). The verbs in this section are in what is often called the "prophetic perfect." Though the events were in the future, they are described as if they had already happened.

9:4 The type of deliverance the oracle pictures seemed impossible. After all, Assyria was a world power and God's people were weak and crushed. Thus, the oracle alludes to the **day of Midian.** This refers to the events of Jdg 6 and 7 when Gideon with just a handful of troops—but with the power of God—defeated the oppressive Midianites and expelled them from the land.

9:6-7 Twice earlier in this section of Isaiah, the birth of children has been described as having prophetic significance (7:14; 8:1-4). For a third time, the reader learns of a future birth. Some commentators believe the text means that this

He will be named
Wonderful Counselor,[a] Mighty God,[b]
Eternal Father,[c] Prince of Peace.[d]
7 The dominion will be vast,
and its prosperity will never end.[e]
He will reign on the throne of David
and over his kingdom,
to establish and sustain it
with justice and righteousness
from now on and forever.
The zeal of the LORD of •Hosts
will accomplish this.[f]

The Hand Raised against Israel

8 The Lord sent a message
against Jacob;
it came against Israel.
9 All the people—
Ephraim and the inhabitants
of Samaria[g]—will know it.
They will say with pride and arrogance:
10 "The bricks have fallen,
but we will rebuild with cut stones;
the sycamores have been cut down,
but we will replace them with cedars."
11 The LORD has raised up
Rezin's adversaries against him
and stirred up his enemies.
12 Aram from the east and Philistia
from the west
have consumed Israel
with open mouths.
In all this, His anger is not removed,
and His hand is still raised to strike.[h]

a9:6 Is 28:29
bDt 10:17; Neh
9:32; Is 10:21
cIs 63:16; 64:8
dIs 26:3,12;
54:10; 66:12
e9:7 Ps 89:4; Dn
2:44; Lk 1:32-33
fIs 37:32; 59:17
g9:9 Ac 1:8
h9:12 Is 5:25
i9:14 Is 19:15
j9:15 Is 3:2-3
kIs 28:15; 59:3-
4; Jr 23:14,32;
Mt 24:24
l9:17 Is 1:4;
10:6; 14:20;
31:2; 32:6
m9:18 Ps 83:14;
Is 1:7; Nah 1:10;
Mal 4:1
n9:19 Is 1:31;
24:6
oMc 7:2,6
p9:20 Is 8:21-22

13 The people did not turn to Him
who struck them;
they did not seek the LORD of Hosts.
14 So the LORD cut off Israel's head
and tail,[i]
palm branch and reed in a single day.
15 The head is the elder, the honored one;[j]
the tail is the prophet,
the lying teacher.[k]
16 The leaders of the people mislead them,
and those they mislead
are swallowed up.[A]
17 Therefore the Lord does not rejoice
over[B] Israel's young men
and has no compassion
on its fatherless and widows,
for everyone is a godless evildoer,[l]
and every mouth speaks folly.
In all this, His anger is not removed,
and His hand is still raised to strike.
18 For wickedness burns like a fire[m]
that consumes thorns and briers
and kindles the forest thickets
so that they go up in a column
of smoke.
19 The land is scorched
by the wrath of the LORD of Hosts,
and the people are like fuel for the fire.[n]
No one has compassion on his brother.[o]
20 They carve meat on the right,
but they are still hungry;[p]
they have eaten on the left,
but they are still not satisfied.

A9:16 Or are confused   B9:17 DSS read not spare

---

future royal child will be a purely human descendant of David who will be proclaimed king and lead God's people to a new level of freedom and prosperity. Both Hezekiah and Josiah have been identified as this child. However, the titles given to this child and the description of His kingdom far surpass anything that was applicable to Hezekiah or Josiah. The only feasible interpretation of this passage is messianic. This child will be given names that signify His character. He will be a sage characterized by extraordinary wisdom (**Wonderful Counselor**). He will have life that is never ending (**Eternal Father**). He will bring peace (**Prince of Peace**). But the most extraordinary thing of all that confirms He is simply not to be identified with a Hezekiah or a Josiah is His title, **Mighty God** (cp. 8:21). In the NT, Jesus is identified as the Davidic descendant who fulfilled this great promise (Mt 1:1,22-23).

9:9-10 The preeminent sin of God's people, **pride and arrogance**, is again pointed out. They believed they did not need God to survive and prosper. They continued in their pride even after experiencing devastation at the hands of Tiglathpileser. They foolishly claimed they not only could rebuild, they could even improve themselves by their own resources and strength (**cut stones** replace **bricks . . . cedars** replace **sycamores**).

9:11 Rezin was the king of Syria (Aram) whose **adversaries** were Assyria and its vassals.

9:12 Israel was beset by enemies to the northeast (**Aram**, who under their king, Rezin, allied and exploited them for its purposes) and **Philistia** to its immediate west. Note that the last two parts of this verse are repeated in verses 17 and 21, as well as 10:4.

9:13 God's punishment of His people was intended to convince them to return to His ways, but they were so dull of mind and spirit that they did not respond.

9:14 After the first Assyrian incursion into the north (733 B.C.), Israel continued in its sinful ways. God soon brought a more devastating judgment in 722 B.C., ending their independent existence. The expression **head and tail, palm branch and reed** points to a totality (19:15).

9:15-16 It was particularly the leaders (including the **elder** and the **prophet**) who were responsible for the people going in the wrong direction.

9:18-19 Devastation is seen as the natural consequence of wickedness itself (**wickedness burns like a fire**) as well as the result of divine anger (**the land is scorched by the wrath of the LORD of Hosts**). Sin breaks up human relationships, even brotherly love.

9:20 The greediness of the people led them to consume everyone and everything in their path. Eventually their hunger turned them on themselves.

Each one eats the flesh
   of his own arm.[a]
21 Manasseh is with Ephraim,
   and Ephraim with Manasseh;
together, both are against Judah.[b]
In all this, His anger is not removed,
and His hand is still raised to strike.[c]

10

Woe to those enacting
   crooked statutes
and writing oppressive laws
2 to keep the poor from getting
   a fair trial
and to deprive the afflicted
   among my people of justice,
so that widows can be their spoil
and they can plunder the fatherless.
3 What will you do on the day
   of punishment
when devastation comes
   from far away?
Who will you run to for help?
Where will you leave your wealth?
4 There will be nothing to do
except crouch among the prisoners
or fall among the slain.
In all this, His anger is not removed,
and His hand is still raised to strike.

Assyria, the Instrument of Wrath

5 Woe to Assyria, the rod of My anger—
   the staff in their hands is My wrath.

a 9:20 Dt 28:53-
57; Is 49:26
b 9:21 2Ch
28:6,8; Is 11:13
c Is 5:25
d 10:6 2Sm
22:43; Ps 18:42;
Ezk 26:11; Mc
7:10
e 10:9 Ac 1:8

6 I will send him against
   a godless nation;
I will command him to go
   against a people destined
   for My rage,
to take spoils, to plunder,
and to trample them down like clay[d]
   in the streets.
7 But this is not what he intends;
   this is not what he plans.
It is his intent to destroy
and to cut off many nations.
8 For he says,
"Aren't all my commanders kings?
9 Isn't Calno like Carchemish?
Isn't Hamath like Arpad?
Isn't Samaria[e] like Damascus?[A]
10 As my hand seized
   the idolatrous kingdoms,
whose idols exceeded
   those of Jerusalem
   and Samaria,
11 and as I did to Samaria
   and its idols
will I not also do to Jerusalem
   and its idols?"

Judgment on Assyria

12 But when the Lord finishes all His work against Mount ·Zion and Jerusalem, He will say, "I[B] will punish the king of Assyria for his

---

A 10:9 Cities conquered by Assyria   B 10:12 LXX reads *Jerusalem, He*

9:21 Manasseh and **Ephraim** were two large northern tribes whose founding fathers were brothers, the sons of Joseph (Gn 41:50-52; 48:5). They turned against each other, illustrating lack of compassion toward a brother (Is 9:19). Then together they turned against **Judah**.

10:1-2 On **woe**, see note at 1:4. God's law protected the socially vulnerable: the **poor** (see Ex 23:6,11; Dt 15:4-11), **widows** (see Ex 22:22), and the **fatherless** (see Dt 10:18). Isaiah condemned man-made laws that corrupted justice.

10:4 With the fourth repetition of the refrain concerning God's **anger** (cp. 9:12,17,21), the section comes to a close. The refrain identifies the main theme of the passage (9:8–10:4). Though punishment has come, God's people still have not repented. More judgment will follow.

10:5 The oracle opens with a **woe** against Assyria. On "woe" see note at 1:4 (see also 5:8-30). This woe is directed toward the enemy rather than toward God's people (10:1). Assyria is the tool He will use to bring punishment against Israel and Judah. The reference to a rod brings to mind the extensive teaching in Proverbs about using a rod to drive the folly out of a child (Pr 10:13; 22:15) and how a rod is applied to one's son to encourage him to travel the right path (Pr 13:24; 23:13-14).

10:6 The **godless nation** is ironically not Assyria but Israel. They will become the object of God's anger. The phrase **to take spoils, to plunder** is reminiscent of the name Maher-

shalal-hash-baz, "Speeding to the Plunder, Hurrying to the Spoil" (8:1).

10:7 There was a difference between the divine intention and the intention of Assyria. This difference was no obstacle to God's use of Assyria for His purposes, but it did bode poorly for the tool of God's anger. While God's intention was to promote His own glory by punishing His sinful people, Assyria was interested only in imperialistic expansion.

10:9 These three pairs of cities each begin with the southernmost of the two. Thus, **Calno** (also known as Calneh) was south of Carchemish, **Hamath** was south of Arpad, and **Samaria** was south of Damascus. These cities were paired and listed for geographical and not chronological reasons since **Carchemish** was conquered by the Assyrians in 717 B.C., Calno in 738, Hamath in 738 and 720, and **Arpad** in 740. The claim of the Assyrian king was an imperialistic one, again demonstrating that his intention was different from God's.

10:11 The comparisons of southern cities to northern ones culminate in a final comparison between **Samaria** in the north and **Jerusalem** in the south: both were practicing idolatry as the Syrian cities did (v. 9).

10:12 God will overrule Assyria's imperialistic intentions. Indeed, He will use their godless motivation to accomplish His own goal of punishing His idolatrous people. Nonetheless, the **king of Assyria** and his nation will not get off the hook.

10:13-14 The boastful quotation from the Assyrian king reflects the type of bombastic language used in contemporary

arrogant acts and the proud look in his eyes."
¹³For he said:

ᵃ10:20 Is 1:4
ᵇ10:22 Rm
9:27-28
ᶜ10:26 Jdg 7:25

> I have done this by my own strength
> and wisdom, for I am clever.
> I abolished the borders of nations
> and plundered their treasures;
> like a mighty warrior, I subjugated
>   the inhabitants.ᴬ
> ¹⁴ My hand has reached out, as if
>   into a nest,
> to seize the wealth of the nations.
> Like one gathering abandoned eggs,
> I gathered the whole earth.
> No wing fluttered;
> no beak opened or chirped.

> ¹⁵ Does an ax exalt itself
> above the one who chops with it?
> Does a saw magnify itself
> above the one who saws with it?
> It would be like a staff waving the one
>   who liftsᴮ it!
> It would be like a rod lifting a man
>   who isn't wood!
> ¹⁶ Therefore the Lord Gᴏᴅ of •Hosts
> will inflict an emaciating disease
> on the well-fed of Assyria,
> and He will kindle a burning fire
> under its glory.
> ¹⁷ Israel's Light will become a fire,
> and its Holy One, a flame.
> In one day it will burn up
>   Assyria's thorns and thistles.
> ¹⁸ He will completely destroy
> the glory of its forests and orchards
> as a sickness consumes a person.
> ¹⁹ The remaining trees of its forest

will be so few in number
that a child could count them.

The Remnant Will Return

²⁰On that day the remnant of Israel and the survivors of the house of Jacob will no longer depend on the one who struck them, but they will faithfully depend on the Lᴏʀᴅ, the Holy One of Israel.ᵃ

> ²¹ The remnant will return, the remnant
>   of Jacob,
> to the Mighty God.
> ²² Israel, even if your people were
>   as numerous
> as the sand of the sea,
> only a remnant of them will return.ᵇ
> Destruction has been decreed;
> justice overflows.
> ²³ For throughout the land
> the Lord Gᴏᴅ of Hosts
> is carrying out a destruction
>   that was decreed.

²⁴Therefore, the Lord Gᴏᴅ of Hosts says this: "My people who dwell in Zion, do not fear Assyria, though he strikes you with a rod and raises his staff over you as the Egyptians did. ²⁵In just a little while My wrath will be spent and My anger will turn to their destruction." ²⁶And the Lᴏʀᴅ of Hosts will brandish a whip against him as He did when He struck Midian at the rock of Oreb;ᶜ and He will raise His staff over the sea as He did in Egypt.

God Will Judge Assyria

> ²⁷ On that day
> his burden will fall
>   from your shoulders,

ᴬ10:13 Or I brought down their kings   ᴮ10:15 Some Hb mss, Syr, Vg read wave he who lifts

---

Assyrian royal inscriptions. The image of the Assyrian king stealing **eggs** from an abandoned **nest** emphasizes his cruelty in taking advantage of weaker nations. Indeed, no one can put up a substantial challenge to his growing power.

10:15 The Assyrian king's boasts are ill-founded. From his perspective, he was a mighty warrior and a great leader of armies. From a heavenly perspective, he was a mere tool used by God to accomplish His purposes. The use of rhetorical questions directed to the king has the function of scolding and embarrassing him in his pretension. Each question has the implied answer, "Of course not."

10:16-19 The conjunction **therefore** serves as a transition from indictment to judgment. The description of the punishment by **disease** and **fire** could be taken literally or metaphorically, or both. The point is clear: glorious and prosperous **Assyria** will soon be weakened by the judgment of God.

10:17 The image of God as **Light** is typically used for positive purposes (Ps 27:1), but like the light of the sun, God both illuminates so people can see clearly and also scorches and kills in judgment.

10:20 The **remnant** will turn their trust to God rather than a foreign power.

10:22 God had promised Abraham that his descendants would be **as numerous as the sand of the sea** (see Gn 22:17; 32:12; 41:49), but because of their punishment, only a **remnant** would survive and even that would be an act of God's grace.

10:24 The present Assyrian threat is compared to the bondage in Egypt. This comparison evokes memories of God's deliverance of His people at the Red Sea (Ex 14–15).

10:26 Oreb was a Midianite leader who oppressed the Israelites during the period of the judges. He was defeated by the forces of Gideon and executed at a rock that was given his name, the **rock of Oreb** (Jdg 7:24-25). The reference to God's staff in Egypt recalls the crossing of the Red Sea. Moses raised his **staff**, representing God's presence. God caused the sea to divide, allowing the Israelites to escape the Egyptian army (Ex 14:21-31).

10:27 The **yoke** is an image of political domination frequently

and his yoke from your neck.
The yoke will be broken
  because of fatness.^A
²⁸ Assyria has come to Aiath
and has gone through Migron,
storing his equipment
  at Michmash.
²⁹ They crossed over at the ford, saying,
"We will spend the night
  at Geba."
The people of Ramah are trembling;
those at Gibeah of Saul have fled.
³⁰ Cry aloud, daughter of Gallim!
Listen, Laishah!
Anathoth is miserable.
³¹ Madmenah has fled.
The inhabitants of Gebim
  have sought refuge.
³² Today he will stand at Nob,
shaking his fist at the mountain
  of Daughter Zion,
the hill of Jerusalem.
³³ Look, the Lord GOD of Hosts
will chop off the branches
  with terrifying power,

^a11:1 Is 9:7;
11:10; Ac 13:23
^bIs 14:19; 60:21;
Jr 23:5; 33:15;
Dn 11:7; Zch
3:8; 6:12
^c11:2 Is 42:1;
48:16; 61:1; Mt
3:16; Jn 1:32
^d11:3 Jn 2:25;
7:24

and the tall trees will be cut down,
the high trees felled.
³⁴ He is clearing the thickets of the forest
with an ax,
and Lebanon with its majesty
  will fall.

Reign of the Davidic King

11 Then a shoot will grow
  from the stump of Jesse,^a
and a branch^b from his roots
  will bear fruit.
² The Spirit of the LORD will rest
on Him^c—
a Spirit of wisdom
  and understanding,
a Spirit of counsel and strength,
a Spirit of knowledge and of the •fear
of the LORD.
³ His delight will be in the fear
of the LORD.
He will not judge
by what He sees with His eyes,^d
He will not execute justice
by what He hears with His ears,

---

^A10:27 Hb obscure

---

used by the prophets (14:25; 47:6; 58:6; Jr 27:11; 30:8; Ezk 30:18).

10:28-32 The oracle in these verses describes the march of the Assyrian army from the north to the very doorstep of Jerusalem. While some have suggested that this describes an actual attack on Jerusalem, it cannot be equated with the Assyrian advance that took place in 701 B.C. under Sennacherib because the army took a different route. This leads certain scholars to propose a second, later Assyrian campaign on Judah, but this is doubtful. The route described in these verses is unlikely to be one taken by an actual army since the terrain would be difficult to cross. The best understanding of these verses is as a visionary image of an attack, not a description of an actual attack. The route described is the most direct route "as the crow flies," indicating that not even natural obstacles could slow down the army's advance.

10:28 Aiath is likely identified with Ai (Jos 8), which was about 30 miles north of Jerusalem. But the Hebrew term *Ai* means "ruin" and Aiath is plural, "ruins," so the name could be given to a number of different sites. **Migron** refers to the Wadi Swenit, a dry riverbed between **Michmash** and Geba.

10:29 Ramah and **Gibeah** were on the major central hill route north of Jerusalem.

10:30 Gallim . . . Laishah, and **Anathoth** (known as the hometown of the prophet Jeremiah; Jr 1:1) were small towns just north of Jerusalem.

10:31 Madmenah and **Gebim** are still not identified, but they were probably villages just north of Jerusalem.

10:32 Nob is typically associated with modern Mount Scopus, just northeast of Jerusalem. As a person stands on Nob, he has a commanding view of the city of Jerusalem. Nob was where David received sustenance and the sword of Goliath as he began his flight from Saul. King Saul repaid the priests at Nob by slaughtering them (1Sm 21:1-9;

22:11-23). Nob is also mentioned in Neh 11:32 as near Anathoth.

10:33-34 The oracle ends with a sudden reversal. Assyria marched on Jerusalem, but the army met with destruction. They will become **trees** (a cedar from **Lebanon** is implied by the final line) that will be felled by none other than God Himself. The Assyrians had been the ax in God's hand against His people (v. 15), but God will wield an ax against them.

11:1 Judgment in Isaiah is often described as a cutting down of trees (6:13; 10:33-34). The **stump of Jesse** indicates that the Davidic line has also been cut down, but the tree is yet living. The **shoot** that springs up shows that David's line will have new life. It will be restored and will once again bear fruit. The association of the stump with Jesse rather than David indicates that there is a new beginning here, a going back to origins, and a distancing from the later corrupt kings of Judah. The continuation of the Davidic line is an indication of the grace of God based on the covenant of kingship with David: "Your house and kingdom will endure before Me forever, and your throne will be established forever" (2Sm 7:16). As redemptive history progressed, the new Davidic dynasty was not realized in later Davidic descendants like Zerubbabel (Ezr 3; Zch 4), but in Jesus Christ.

11:2 The shoot is different in character than other descendants of David, most of whom were self-seeking, fearful, and cruel. The **Spirit of the LORD** will characterize this descendant. The Spirit will fill this leader with **wisdom**: the ability to rule, and **strength**: the power to rule. Scripture makes it clear that the Spirit brings wisdom (Ex 31:3; Dt 34:9) and that wisdom leads to productive and just rule (1Kg 4:29; Pr 8:15-16).

11:3 The **fear of the LORD** is the basic characteristic of a wise, godly person (Pr 1:7). The fear described here is not terror but awe. This wise, Spirit-filled person will not judge

4   but He will judge the poor righteously[a]
     and execute justice for the oppressed
        of the land.
     He will strike the land
        with discipline[A] from His mouth,[b]
     and He will kill the wicked[c]
        with a command[B] from His lips.[d]
5   Righteousness will be a belt
        around His loins;[e]
     faithfulness will be a belt
        around His waist.[f]
6   The wolf will live with the lamb,[g]
     and the leopard will lie down
        with the goat.
     The calf, the young lion, and the fatling
        will be together,
     and a child will lead them.
7   The cow and the bear will graze,
     their young ones will lie down together,
     and the lion will eat straw like the ox.
8   An infant will play
        beside the cobra's pit,
     and a toddler will put his hand
        into a snake's den.
9   None will harm or destroy another
     on My entire holy mountain,
     for the land will be as full
     of the knowledge of the LORD
     as the sea is filled with water.[h]

Israel Regathered

10   On that day the root of Jesse[i]
     will stand as a banner for the peoples.[j]
     The nations will seek Him,[k]
     and His resting place will be glorious.[l]

11   On that day[m] the Lord will extend His
     hand a second time to recover—from Assyria,
     Egypt, Pathros, *Cush, Elam, *Shinar, Hamath,
     and the coasts and islands of the west—the
     remnant of His people who survive.[n]

12   He will lift up a banner for the nations
     and gather the dispersed of Israel;[o]
     He will collect the scattered of Judah
     from the four corners of the earth.[p]
13   Ephraim's envy will cease;[q]
     Judah's harassment will end.
     Ephraim will no longer be envious
        of Judah,
     and Judah will not harass Ephraim.
14   But they will swoop down
     on the Philistine flank to the west.
     Together they will plunder the people
        of the east.[r]
     They will extend their power
        over Edom and Moab,
     and the Ammonites will be
        their subjects.[s]
15   The LORD will divide[C,D] the Gulf of Suez.[E]
     He will wave His hand
        over the Euphrates
     with His mighty wind[t]
     and will split it into seven streams,
     letting people walk through on foot.
16   There will be a highway
        for the remnant of His people
     who will survive from Assyria,[u]
     as there was for Israel
     when they came up from the land
        of Egypt.[v]

[a]11:4 Ps 72:2,13-14; Is 3:14
[b]Ps 2:9; Is 49:2; Mal 4:6
[c]Gn 18:25; Ps 139:19; Ezk 3:18-19; 18:20-24; 33:8-15
[d]Jb 4:9; Is 30:28,33; 2Th 2:8
[e]11:5 Eph 6:14
[f]Eph 6:14
[g]11:6 Is 65:25; Jr 5:6; Hs 2:18; 13:6-9
[h]11:9 Ps 98:2-3; Is 45:6; 52:10; 66:18-23; Hab 2:14
[i]11:10 Is 11:1
[j]Is 49:22; 62:10; Jn 3:14-15; 12:32
[k]Rm 15:12; Rv 5:5
[l]Is 14:3; 28:12; 32:17-18
[m]11:11 Is 27:12
[n]Is 10:20-22; 37:4,31-32; 46:3
[o]11:12 Is 56:8; Zph 3:10; Zch 10:6
[p]Rv 7:1; 20:8
[q]11:13 Is 9:21; Jr 3:18; Ezk 37:16-17,22; Hs 1:11
[r]11:14 Jr 49:28
[s]Ps 60:8; 83:6
[t]11:15 Is 7:20; 8:7; Rv 16:12
[u]11:16 Is 19:23; 35:8; 40:3; 62:10
[v]Ex 14:26-29

A 11:4 Lit *the rod*   B 11:4 Lit *with the breath*   C 11:15 Text emended; MT reads *destroy*   D 11:15 Or *dry up*   E 11:15 Lit *the Sea of Egypt*

according to external appearances, but he will cut to the heart of the truth.

11:4 The wicked kings of Israel and the Near East exploited and took advantage of the weak (**the poor** and **the oppressed**; see notes at 3:13-15 and 10:1-2), but this king will rule with justice and protect their rights.

11:5 The term translated **belt** (Hb 'ezor) refers to an intimate piece of apparel. The idea is that these two fundamental characteristics of covenant fidelity will be an integral part of the future Davidic king's character.

11:6-9 The future rule is described in Edenic terms where there is no animosity among God's creatures. The **knowledge of the LORD** will permeate this future ideal world ushered in by the shoot of the stump of Jesse.

11:10 The **root of Jesse** is a variant reference to what is called the "stump of Jesse" (see note at v. 1). Of course, the stump would include the root of the tree, but perhaps this way of referring to the image is a way of emphasizing the hidden life that remains. The root of Jesse is here a **banner**, which refers to a standard around which an army rallied. This same Hebrew word is used in 5:26 (translated "signal flag"). In 5:26 the signal flag was a rallying point

for the nations as they assembled to attack God's people. Here the banner is a rallying point for the regathering of the remnant.

11:11 The list of nations in this verse probably should not be taken as a literal reference as if God's people would return from all of these nations, but from all directions. **Assyria . . . Elam**, and **Shinar** (Mesopotamia) were to the east; **Egypt, Pathros**, and **Cush** were to the south; **Hamath** was to the north; and **the coasts and islands** were to the west.

11:12 On **banner**, see note at verse 10.

11:13 At least from the time of Rehoboam, Solomon's son, enmity and political division had existed between **Judah** and **Ephraim** (the northern kingdom of Israel also known as Samaria). The future will bring an end to hostilities and a reunion of God's people.

11:14 A reunited Israel will expand its borders to encompass the small nations to the east: **Edom . . . Moab**, and Ammon. These nations harassed Israel whenever they could.

11:15-16 Exodus imagery is used to describe the return of the **remnant** from **Assyria**. God will split the **Euphrates** River like He did the Red Sea, but in this case He won't split it into two parts but **seven**.

A Song of Praise

12 On that day you will say:
"I will praise You, LORD,
although You were angry with me.
Your anger has turned away,
and You have had compassion[a] on me.

2 Indeed, God is my salvation;
I will trust Him and not be afraid,
for •Yah, the LORD,
is my strength and my song.
He has become my salvation."[b]

3 You will joyfully draw water[c]
from the springs of salvation,

4 and on that day you will say:
"Give thanks to Yahweh;
proclaim His name!
Celebrate His works
among the peoples.[d]
Declare that His name is exalted.

5 Sing to Yahweh, for He has done
glorious things.[e]
Let this be known
throughout the earth.

6 Cry out and sing, citizen of •Zion,
for the Holy One of Israel[f] is among you
in His greatness."

An Oracle against Babylon

13 An •oracle[g] against Babylon[h] that Isaiah son of Amoz saw:

2 Lift up a banner on a barren mountain.[i]
Call out to them.
Wave your hand, and they will go
through the gates of the nobles.

3 I have commanded My chosen ones;
I have also called My warriors,
who exult in My triumph,
to execute My wrath.[j]

4 Listen, a tumult on the mountains,
like that of a mighty people!
Listen, an uproar among the kingdoms,
like nations being gathered together!
The LORD of •Hosts is mobilizing
an army for war.

5 They are coming from a far land,
from the distant horizon—
the LORD and the weapons
of His wrath—
to destroy the whole country.[A]

6 Wail! For the day of the LORD is near.[k]
It will come like destruction
from the •Almighty.[l]

---

a 12:1 Is 40:1
b 12:2 Ex 15:2; Ps 118:14
c 12:3 Jn 4:10; 7:37-38
d 12:4 1Ch 16:8; Ps 105:1; 145:4
e 12:5 Ex 15:1; Ps 98:1; Is 24:14; 42:10-11; 44:23
f 12:6 Is 1:4
g 13:1 Is 14:28; 15:1; 17:1; 19:1; 21:1,11,13; 22:1; 23:1; 30:6
h Is 13:19; 14:4; 47:1-15; Jr 24:1; 50:1-51:64; Mt 1:11; Rv 14:8
i 13:2 Is 5:26; Jr 50:2
j 13:3 Ps 78:21,50; Ezk 5:15; 20:8
k 13:6 Is 2:12; 10:3; 13:9; 34:2,8; 61:2; Ezk 30:3; Am 5:18; Zph 1:7
l Is 10:25; 14:23; Jl 1:15

A 13:5 Or *earth*

12:1 On that day points to a future date. That date is unspecified, but it is a day that will certainly come. Up to this point in the text, the phrase has been used in reference to the coming judgment (2:20; 3:18; 4:1; 7:18,20-21,23), but now it points to the time after the storm, the time of salvation.

12:2 Yah is a shortened form of the divine name Yahweh, God's personal covenant name that He revealed to Moses at the burning bush (Ex 3:14-15).

12:3 In a relatively dry land like Israel, **water** and the refreshment it brings was an apt image for **salvation**. The picture of water bubbling up in a spring evokes freshness and abundance.

12:4 The praise of God serves as a testimony not just within God's people, but also to the nations. They were also recipients of God's blessing through Abraham's descendants (Gn 12:1-13).

13:1 Oracle (Hb *massa'*; lit "burden") is often used in the context of judgment pronouncements against the nations. This is a "war oracle," a declaration of war. **Babylon** is the object, which is surprising since Babylon was not the major player on the world scene in Isaiah's time. But Babylon will play a major role in the judgment of God's people in Judah. Babylon represented cultural arrogance and human self-reliance.

13:2 The call to lift a **banner** is a call to rally troops before a battle (5:26; 11:10,12). The identity of the army and the object of their attack are unspecified. Even though an actual gate of **the nobles** is unknown, the name evokes ideas of elitism, power, and pride.

13:3 My warriors might be angelic, but the reference is more likely to human warriors whom God will use for His purposes. Since they may not be conscious of such a divine purpose (10:5-11), they are not necessarily an army of the faithful.

13:4 The LORD of Hosts is God's name that signifies His activity in warfare. The **tumult on the mountains** emanates from God's army that gathers there. While it is possible that the mountains are the Zagros east of Babylon, it is not certain.

13:5 The **far land** is not specified, but it may be a reference to the Medes (v. 17) whom God will use (as part of the Persian Empire) to defeat Babylon (**the whole country**).

za'am

Hebrew Pronunciation	[ZA am]
HCSB Translation	indignation, wrath
Uses in Isaiah	5
Uses in the OT	22
Focus Passage	Isaiah 13:5

Za'am indicates God's *wrath* (Is 10:5) seven times. It refers to God in all but two instances: God fills Jeremiah with *indignation* (Jr 15:17), and the tongues of ungodly leaders produce *cursing* (Hs 7:16). Za'am appears 10 times as *indignation*, sometimes with other words for God's "wrath": *qetseph*, which stresses *rage* (Ps 102:10); *chemah*, which emphasizes heat (Nah 1:6); and *'aph*, which implies *anger* (Hab 3:12). Further words for "wrath" include *charon* (Ps 2:5), which connotes *burning* (Ex 15:7), and *'ebrah*, which involves *outbursts* (Jb 21:30). Za'am suggests *fury* (Is 30:27), *rage* (Jr 10:10), and *fierceness* (Lm 2:6). The verb za'am (12x) means *show wrath* (Is 66:14), *be angry* (Zch 1:12), and *rage* (Dn 11:30). It can involve *executing justice* (Ps 7:11). When the angry expression is verbal, za'am denotes *denounce* (Nm 23:7) and *curse* (Mal 1:4). Passive forms describe *angry* looks (Pr 25:23) and an *accursed* short measure (Mc 6:10).

7 Therefore everyone's hands
   will become weak,
and every man's heart will melt.
8 They will be horrified;
pain and agony will seize them;
they will be in anguish like a woman
   in labor.[a]
They will look at each other,
   their faces flushed with fear.
9 Look, the day[b] of the LORD is coming—
cruel, with rage and burning anger—
to make the earth a desolation
and to destroy the sinners on it.[c]
10 Indeed, the stars of the sky
   and its constellations[A]
will not give their light.
The sun will be dark when it rises,
and the moon will not shine.[d]
11 I will bring disaster on the world,
and their own iniquity,[e] on the wicked.
I will put an end to the pride
   of the arrogant[f]
and humiliate the insolence of tyrants.
12 I will make man scarcer than gold,
and mankind more rare than the gold
   of Ophir.[g]
13 Therefore I will make
   the heavens tremble,
and the earth will shake
   from its foundations[h]
at the wrath of the LORD of Hosts,
on the day of His burning anger.

14 Like wandering gazelles
   and like sheep without a shepherd,[i]
each one will turn to his own people,
each one will flee to his own land.
15 Whoever is found will be stabbed,
and whoever is caught will die
   by the sword.
16 Their children will be smashed to death
   before their eyes;[j]
their houses will be looted,
and their wives raped.
17 Look! I am stirring up the Medes
   against them,[k]
who cannot be bought off with[B] silver
and who have no desire for gold.
18 Their bows will cut young men
   to pieces.
They will have no compassion
   on little ones;
they will not look with pity on children.

19 And Babylon, the jewel of the kingdoms,
the glory of the pride of the Chaldeans,
will be like Sodom and Gomorrah
when God overthrew them.[l]
20 It will never be inhabited
or lived in from generation
   to generation;[m]
a nomad will not pitch his tent there,
and shepherds will not let their flocks
   rest there.
21 But desert creatures will lie down there,
and owls will fill the houses.

---

[a]13:8 Is 26:17; Jr 4:31; Jn 16:21
[b]13:9 Mt 25:13
[c]Dt 32:43
[d]13:10 Is 34:4; Mt 24:29; Mk 13:24-25; Lk 21:26; Rv 8:12
[e]13:11 Jr 23:2; 36:31; 44:29
[f]Is 2:11; 23:9; Dn 5:22-23
[g]13:12 1Kg 9:28; Jb 28:16; Ps 45:9
[h]13:13 Ps 18:7; Is 2:19; 24:1,19-20; Hg 2:6
[i]13:14 1Kg 22:17; Mt 9:36; Mk 6:34; 1Pt 2:25
[j]13:16 Ps 137:8-9; Is 13:18; 14:21; Hs 10:14; Nah 3:10
[k]13:17 Jr 51:11; Dn 5:28
[l]13:19 Gn 19:24; Jr 14:18; 50:40; Am 4:11
[m]13:20 Is 14:23; 34:10-15; Jr 51:37-43

[A]13:10 Or Orions   [B]13:17 Lit who have no regard for

13:6 The **day of the LORD** is a future time when God will wage war against those who oppose Him.

13:7 Weak **hands** and a melted **heart** refer to physical and psychological reactions to fear.

13:8 Isaiah used the theme of **a woman in labor**, one that appears often in prophetic literature (21:3; Jr 4:31; 6:24; 22:23; 30:6; Mc 4:9). It is a graphic image of the pain and distress that will result from God's warring activity.

13:10 The incursion of God as warrior causes nature to go into convulsions. On the day of God's judgment, the **sun . . . moon**, and **stars**, which God created to provide the world with light (Gn 1:14-19), will go out, plunging the world into darkness (Ezk 32:7; Jl 2:2; 3:1,15; Am 5:18; Mc 3:6; Mt 24:29; Lk 21:25; Rv 8:12).

13:11 The object of God's wrath is **pride** that leads people to trust in themselves rather than in Him.

13:12 God's warring judgment will reduce the population of the earth dramatically.

13:13 When the divine warrior appears, not only will the heavenly bodies convulse (v. 10); so will the **earth**.

13:14-15 The destroyed city had residents from many different lands. Once destroyed, the people will be leaderless and will quickly run (**like wandering gazelles**) back to their homeland. However, they may not make it back. The road will be lined with dangers, including robbers and perhaps even an enemy army.

13:16 In ancient times defeated cities endured the horrible atrocities described in this verse. The worst was that their **children** would be killed.

13:17 At last, the attacking army is described as the implacable **Medes**, a people known as early as the ninth century B.C. They came from the Zagros Mountains east of the Mesopotamian plain. These warlike people are known in history as Babylon's allies when they defeated Assyria. However, in the sixth century B.C. they were engulfed by Persia. The combined armies of the Medes and Persians defeated Babylon in 539 B.C.

13:19 For the first time **Babylon** is named as the object of God's warring activity. They are described as the **jewel of the kingdoms** in anticipation of the position they will assume after their defeat of Assyria at the end of the seventh century B.C. The **Chaldeans** were the leading tribe that produced the leaders (Nabopolassar and Nebuchadnezzar) who led the Babylonian resurgence. The destruction of **Sodom and Gomorrah** is described in Gn 19. This account in Isaiah implies a horrible end. It associates Babylon with the perverse sin that led to the destruction of those cities.

13:21-22 These verses describe animals that lived in ruins and desolate places. **Ostriches** and **owls** were considered unclean (Lv 11:15-16).

Ostriches will dwell there,
and wild goats will leap about.[a]

22 Hyenas will howl in the fortresses,
and jackals, in the luxurious palaces.
Babylon's time is almost up;
her days are almost over.

Israel's Return

14 For the LORD will have compassion[b] on Jacob and will choose Israel again.[c] He will settle them on their own land.[d] The foreigner will join them and be united with the house of Jacob.[e] 2 The nations will escort Israel and bring it to its homeland. Then the house of Israel will possess them as male and female slaves in the LORD's land.[f] They will make captives of their captors and will rule over their oppressors.

Downfall of the King of Babylon

3 When the LORD gives you rest from your pain,[g] torment, and the hard labor[h] you were forced to do, 4 you will sing this song of contempt about the king of Babylon[i] and say:

How the oppressor has quieted down,
and how the raging[A] has become quiet!

5 The LORD has broken the staff
of the wicked,
the scepter of the rulers.

6 It struck the peoples in anger
with unceasing blows.

It subdued the nations in rage
with relentless persecution.

7 All the earth is calm and at rest;
people shout with a ringing cry.

8 Even the cypresses and the cedars
of Lebanon
rejoice over you:[j]
"Since you have been laid low,
no woodcutter has come against us."

9 •Sheol below is eager to greet
your coming.
He stirs up the spirits of the departed
for you—
all the rulers[B] of the earth.
He makes all the kings of the nations
rise from their thrones.

10 They all respond to you, saying:
"You too have become as weak
as we are;
you have become like us!

11 Your splendor has been brought down
to Sheol,
along with the music of your harps.
Maggots are spread out under you,
and worms cover you."

12 Shining morning star,[C,k]
how you have fallen from the heavens![l]
You destroyer of nations,
you have been cut down to the ground.

13 You said to yourself:

a13:21 Is 34:11-15; Zph 2:14; Rv 18:2
b14:1 1Kg 3:26
cDt 7:7; Ps 102:13; Zch 1:17
dDt 12:10; 2Sm 7:1
eDt 14:21,29; Zch 8:22, 23; Eph 2:12-14
f14:2 Is 9:7; 45:14-25; 49:22-26; 60:9; 61:5; 66:19-24
g14:3 Gn 3:16; Is 14:3; Jr 44:19
hEx 1:14
i14:4 Mc 2:4; Hab 2:6
j14:8 Ps 104:16; Is 55:12; Ezk 31:16
k14:12 2Pt 1:19; Rv 2:28; 22:16
lIs 34:4; Lk 10:18; Rv 8:10; 9:1

A14:4 DSS; Hb uncertain   B14:9 Lit rams   C14:12 Or Day Star, son of the dawn

14:1-2 An oracle anticipating the restoration of God's people appears in the midst of the oracle against Babylon. While this seems awkward, Babylon's fall correlates with the rise of a restored Judah. Indeed, this restoration provides the context for the taunt song against Babylon's king in verses 4-21.

14:1 Just as God chose **Israel** in Egypt and freed them from bondage, He will do so again in Mesopotamia. As foreigners traveled with God's people from Egypt, they will do so again.

14:2 The **nations** had escorted God's people out of the promised land when they were exiled, so in the future they will escort them back. Power relations will be reversed. Israel had been the slave of the nations; now the nations will serve God's people.

14:3-4 The following song (vv. 4b-21) has its setting after Israel's return to the land. The song is a **song of contempt** or a taunt song (Hb *mashal*). It was directed toward the **king of Babylon**. The song speaks as if the king is a definite individual, but the lack of a specific name may mean that the king is depicted as the apex of the imperialistic machine that oppressed the people of God.

14:5 The **staff** and the **scepter** were held by the king, and they represented his power. The staff may be a shepherd's staff, and it could refer to the king's responsibility to shepherd the people. The scepter was an ornamented mace used as a weapon, representing the king's fearsome power. The fact that God has broken them indicates His superior power.

14:8 It is not just the inhabitants of the earth, and in particular the people of God, who rejoice over Babylon's downfall, but even the trees, which had been cut down to produce siege works.

14:9 Sheol refers to the grave and in some contexts signifies the underworld. In this verse Sheol is personified and pictured as warmly greeting its new citizen, the Babylonian king. Indeed, Sheol will rouse all the **spirits of the departed** kings to greet the Babylonian king when he arrives in the realm of the dead. Some believe this reference to the activities of the dead is just a poetic device, but it is better understood as evidence that the Israelites at the time of Isaiah had an awareness of the afterlife.

14:10 Though conscious, the spirits of the departed kings will confess that they are **weak** in the afterlife. This weakness contrasts with the oppressive power they had exercised in life.

14:11 Maggots and **worms** will crawl over the corpse in the grave. This plays on the idea that Sheol was considered both the grave and the underworld.

14:12-15 Commentators have often connected this passage to Lk 10:18 and Rv 12:8-9, but the context seems clear that the one fallen from **the heavens** is not Satan (even though the KJV translated **shining morning star** as "Lucifer") but is instead the Babylonian king. If there is a double application the Bible never indicates as much. The poetic theme of this passage may be modeled on the Canaanite account of

"I will ascend to the heavens;[a]
I will set up my throne
above the stars of God.[b]
I will sit on the mount
of the gods' assembly,
in the remotest parts of the North.[A,c]

14 I will ascend above the highest clouds;
I will make myself like the •Most High."

15 But you will be brought down to Sheol
into the deepest regions of the •Pit.[d]

16 Those who see you will stare at you;
they will look closely at you:
"Is this the man who caused the earth
to tremble,
who shook the kingdoms,

17 who turned the world
into a wilderness,[e]
who destroyed its cities
and would not release the prisoners
to return home?"

18 All the kings of the nations
lie in splendor, each in his own tomb.

19 But you are thrown out
without a grave,
like a worthless branch,
covered by those slain with the sword
and dumped into a rocky pit
like a trampled corpse.

20 You will not join them in burial,
because you destroyed your land
and slaughtered your own people.
The offspring of evildoers
will never be remembered.[f]

21 Prepare a place of slaughter
for his sons,
because of the iniquity[g]
of their fathers.
They will never rise up to possess
a land
or fill the surface of the earth
with cities.

22 "I will rise up against them"—this is the declaration of the LORD of •Hosts—"and I will cut off from Babylon her reputation, remnant, offspring, and posterity"—this is the LORD's declaration. 23 "I will make her a swampland and a region for screech owls,[B] and I will sweep her away with a broom of destruction."
This is the declaration
of the LORD of Hosts.

Assyria Will Be Destroyed

24 The LORD of Hosts has sworn:

As I have purposed, so it will be;
as I have planned it, so it will happen.[h]

25 I will break Assyria[i] in My land;
I will tread him down on My mountain.
Then his yoke will be taken from them,
and his burden will be removed
from their shoulders.

26 This is the plan[j] prepared
for the whole earth,
and this is the hand stretched out
against all the nations.

27 The LORD of Hosts Himself
has planned it;
therefore, who can stand in its way?

a14:13 Jr 51:53; Ezk 28:2; Am 9:2
bDn 5:22-23; 8:10; 2Th 2:4
cPs 48:2
d14:15 Ps 28:1; Is 38:18; Ezk 28:8; Mt 11:23; Lk 10:15
e14:17 Jl 1:19-20; 2:3,22; 4:19
f14:20 Jb 18:16,19; Ps 21:10; 37:28; Is 1:4; 31:2
g14:21 Is 13:11
h14:24 Pr 16:4; Is 46:11; Jr 23:20; 30:24; 51:29; Zch 1:6; Eph 1:11; Rv 17:17
i14:25 Is 8:7; 10:5-15,27
j14:26 Is 5:19

A14:13 Or of Zaphon   B14:23 Or hedgehogs

a lesser god that tried to usurp the position of the high God. Such pride resulted in a quick and horrible fall.

14:12 The **shining morning star** may figuratively refer to a Canaanite deity whose story provides the pattern for this taunting lament for the Babylonian king. But in any case, Venus is the morning "star" that falls so quickly through the sky.

14:13 The attempt of a human, no matter how powerful, to take the place of God is the ultimate expression of arrogance. In Canaanite mythology, which is exploited here to make a point about human pride, the mountain of Baal, the chief god, was in the **remotest parts of the North**. Indeed, his mountain was named Mount North (Hb *Zaphon*).

14:15 Pride tries to lift a human being up to the level of God, but it always causes a rapid fall to a position below humanity (the **Pit**).

14:16-17 In death the powerful, oppressive king will look weak and helpless. The nameless people who will see him are quoted as expressing amazement at how powerless he looks.

14:18-20 There is even a contrast with other kings, who were buried in fine tombs. This king will not even be given a decent burial but will lie dead on the battlefield, surrounded

and even covered by other dead bodies. Again, the idea is that a person who was powerful in life will be reduced to a humiliating circumstance in death.

14:21 It was an expectation of a powerful king that, when he died, his son would become the next king and would continue his imperialistic pretensions, but because of the depredations of the fathers, the **sons** would meet an untimely death.

14:22-23 God will bring this judgment. Babylon, particularly its most southern part, was a **swampland**. God would reduce the entire nation to this in the anger of His judgment.

14:24-27 The oracle shifts focus to the northern center of Mesopotamian power, **Assyria**. Assyria was the nation that under Tiglath-pileser III reduced the size of the northern kingdom of Israel in the 730s B.C. and then in 722, under Shalmaneser, deported its citizens. But God will bring even this strong kingdom to an end.

14:24 On a human level Assyria seemed invincible, but God assured His people of His determination to judge the Assyrian people.

14:25 The **yoke** was a common metaphor for political servitude (10:27; 47:6; 58:6; Jr 27:11; 30:8; Ezk 30:18).

It is His hand that is outstretched,
so who can turn it back?

An Oracle against Philistia

²⁸In the year that King Ahaz died,^a this •oracle came:^b

²⁹ Don't rejoice, all of you in Philistia,
because the rod of the one
who struck you^c is broken.
For a viper will come from the root^A
of a snake,
and from its egg comes
a flying serpent.^d
³⁰ Then the firstborn^e of the poor will be
well fed,
and the impoverished will lie down
in safety,
but I will kill your root with hunger,
and your remnant will be slain.^B
³¹ Wail, you gates!^f Cry out, city!
Tremble with fear,^g all Philistia!
For a cloud of dust is coming
from the north,^h
and there is no one missing from
the invader's ranks.
³² What answer will be given
to the messengers from that nation?
The Lord has founded •Zion,ⁱ
and His afflicted people find refuge
in her.

An Oracle against Moab

15 An •oracle against Moab:^j

Ar in Moab is devastated,^k
destroyed in a night.
Kir in Moab is devastated,
destroyed in a night.
² Dibon went up to its temple
to weep at its •high places.
Moab wails on Nebo and at^C Medeba.
Every head is shaved;
every beard is cut off.
³ In its streets they wear •sackcloth;
on its rooftops and in its public squares
everyone wails,
falling down and weeping.
⁴ Heshbon and Elealeh cry out;
their voices are heard as far away
as Jahaz.^l
Therefore the soldiers of Moab cry out,
and they tremble.^D
⁵ My heart cries out over Moab,
whose fugitives flee as far as Zoar,^m
to Eglath-shelishiyah;
they go up the slope of Luhith weeping;
they raise a cry of destruction
on the road to Horonaim.
⁶ The waters of Nimrimⁿ are desolate;
the grass is withered, the foliage is gone,
and the vegetation has vanished.

^a14:28 2Kg 16:20; 2Ch 28:27; Is 6:1 ^bIs 13:1 ^c14:29 1Sm 17:50; 18:25-30; 19:8; 23:1-5; 2Sm 5:17-25; 8:1 ^dEx 4:2-3; 7:10-12; Is 30:6 ^e14:30 Ex 4:22 ^f14:31 Is 3:26; 24:12; 45:2 ^gJos 2:9,24 ^hIs 41:25; Jr 1:13-14; 4:6; 6:1; 47:2; 50:3,9,41 ⁱ14:32 Ps 87:1,5; 102:16; Is 28:16; 44:28; 54:11 ^j15:1-7 Gn 19:31-37; Is 11:14; 25:10; Jr 48:1-38; Ezk 25:8-11; Am 2:1-3; Zph 2:8-9 ^k15:1 Nm 21:28 ^l15:4 Nm 21:28; 32:3; Jr 48:34 ^m15:5 Gn 19:21-22 ⁿ15:6 Nm 32:3,36; Jos 13:27

---

^A14:29 Or *stock*   ^B14:30 DSS, Syr, Tg; MT reads *and he will kill within himself*   ^C15:2 Or *wails over Nebo and over*   ^D15:4 Lit *out, he trembles*

14:28-32 The oracle against **Philistia** is the first in a series of oracles against nations that were immediate neighbors of Israel. Indeed, Philistia occupied part of the promised land in a region west of Jerusalem and on the coast of the Mediterranean Sea. The book of Genesis records interaction between the patriarchs and the Philistines (Gn 10:14; 21:32,34), but it was not until the period of the united monarchy that we hear of a sizeable presence of Philistines in the region. Both Saul and David waged war against them. A remnant of Philistines lasted until the sixth century (Jr 47).

14:28 The year that King Ahaz died is debated. It may have been as early as the 720s, but it certainly was not later than 715 b.c.

14:29 Debate surrounds the exact reference to the figurative language of this verse, but the broken **rod** may be a reference not to a particular king but to weakness in Assyria, perhaps in the period after Sargon II took the throne. However, the warning is that, though apparently weak, Assyria is not done. From its slumber will come **a flying serpent** against Philistia. Under Sennacherib, Esar-haddon, and Ashurbanipal, Assyria did experience a major resurgence.

14:30 Because of Philistia's oppression of Judah, the poor had grown poorer, but with its destruction, there will be a reversal of their fortunes.

14:31 The **cloud of dust** coming from the north will be none other than the Assyrian army that will destroy Philistia.

14:32 This verse envisions Philistine envoys trying to convince Judah to join them in resisting the Assyrian army. But Judah's trust should be in **Zion**, or God, not foreign alliances.

15:1–16:14 The oracle against **Moab** is the second in a series of oracles against nations that were immediate neighbors of Israel. Moab was located in Transjordan opposite Jericho and on the east bank of the Dead Sea. The Bible and other sources (the Moabite Stone, for example) record a long history of conflict between Israel and Moab whose origins go back to the incestuous union between Lot and his daughter (Gn 19:30-38). See Jr 48 for a similar oracle against Moab.

15:1 Ar was a city on the wadi Arnon in the middle part of Moab, and **Kir** (the same place as Kir-hareseth; 16:7) was further south.

15:2 Nebo and **Medeba** were two northern Moabite sites east of the northern tip of the Dead Sea. Nebo was further known as the mountain that Moses ascended to catch sight of the promised land before he died (Dt 34:1). **Dibon** was further south about midway down the coast of the Dead Sea and some 20 miles inland. Its **temple** was dedicated to Chemosh, the main god of the Moabites. Shaving hair from the **head** and **beard** was an ancient mourning rite.

15:3 Sackcloth was a very rough material, irritating to the skin, worn as part of mourning rites.

15:4 Heshbon and Elealeh were northeastern cities in Moab. **Jahaz** was further south parallel to Dibon.

15:5-9 The oracle in these verses describes the attempt-

7 So they carry their wealth
   and belongings
over the *Wadi of the Willows.*[a]
8 For their cry echoes
throughout the territory of Moab.
Their wailing reaches Eglaim;
   their wailing reaches Beer-elim.
9 The waters of Dibon[A] are full of blood,[b]
but I will bring on Dibon[A] even more
   than this—
a lion for those who escape from Moab,
and for the survivors in the land.[c]

16 Send lambs to the ruler of the land,[d]
from Sela in the desert[e]
to the mountain of Daughter *Zion.
2 Like a bird fleeing,
   forced from the nest,
the daughters of Moab
will be at the fords of the Arnon.

3 Give us counsel and make a decision.
Shelter us at noonday
with shade that is as dark as night.
Hide the refugees;[f]
   do not betray the one who flees.
4 Let my refugees stay with you;
be a refuge for Moab[B]
   from the aggressor.

When the oppressor has gone,
   destruction has ended,

and marauders have vanished
   from the land.
5 Then in the tent of David
a throne will be established
   by faithful love.[g]
A judge who seeks what is right
and is quick to execute justice
will sit on the throne forever.

6 We have heard of Moab's pride[h]—
how very proud he is—
his haughtiness, his pride, his arrogance,
and his empty boasting.
7 Therefore let Moab wail;
let every one of them wail for Moab.
Mourn, you who are
   completely devastated,
for the raisin cakes[i] of Kir-hareseth.[j]
8 For Heshbon's terraced vineyards
and the grapevines of Sibmah
   have withered.
The rulers of the nations
have trampled its choice vines
that reached as far as Jazer[k]
and spread to the desert.
Their shoots spread out
and reached the Dead Sea.[l]
9 So I join with Jazer
to weep for the vines of Sibmah;
I drench Heshbon and Elealeh
   with my tears.

[a]15:7 Is 30:6; Jr 48:36
[b]15:9 2Kg 3:22-23
[c]2Sm 23:20; 1Ch 11:22
[d]16:1 2Kg 3:4
[e]2Kg 14:7; Is 42:11
[f]16:3 1Kg 18:4
[g]16:5 Is 9:6-7; 32:1; 55:4; Dn 7:14; Mc 4:7; Lk 1:33
[h]16:6 Jr 48:29; Am 2:1; Ob 3-4; Zph 2:8,10
[i]16:7 2Sm 6:19; 1Ch 16:3; Sg 2:5; Hs 3:1
[j]2Kg 3:25; Jr 48:31
[k]16:8 Nm 21:32; Jos 13:25
[l]Jr 48:32

A15:9 DSS, some LXX mss, Vg; MT reads *Dimon*   B16:4 Or *you; Moab—be a refuge for him*

---

ed escape route of those who survived the devastation of northern **Moab**.

15:5 While the location of some of these sites (**Zoar**, for instance) is debated, the fact that others (**Eglath-shelishiyah** and **Horonaim**) were in the south suggests that all the sites mentioned here were in the south. This implies that the destruction was in the northern part of Moab and the refugees fled south.

15:6 The **waters of Nimrim** may be associated with the wadi Numeira, continuing the naming of southern Moabite sites.

15:7 The **Wadi of the Willows** may be a reference to the Zered River, the Wadi el-Hesa, which separated Moab from Edom on the south.

15:8 The locations of **Eglaim** and **Beer-elim** are uncertain.

15:9 The Hebrew text says the "waters of Dimon," but good textual evidence (as listed in the textual footnote in the HCSB) leads to the change of Dimon to **Dibon**. The oracle reverts from the south to the midpoint of Moab, but this may be due to the fact that Dibon was the most important city. The point is that those who escaped the devastation of the attack would be eaten by lions.

16:1-5 The Moabites will turn to Judah (**Zion**) to request refuge.

16:1 Sela (commonly identified as the cliff fortress of Petra) was in Edom, so the Moabite refugees apparently will go that far. Then they will send gifts (**lambs**) to Jerusalem (**Zion**).

16:2 The previous verses place the refugees in Edom, so it is odd that they will now say they are at the **fords of the Arnon** which is in the center of Moab. The metaphor of the bird pushed from the **nest** presupposes that they were out of their home in Moab. Oswalt suggests that it may be a "stereotyped phrase which has been pressed into service here to express the agitated flight of the Moabites" (*Isaiah 1–39*, p. 342).

16:3 The request for **shelter** as well as **shade** is a request for protection, and it implies that Moab will be willing to become a vassal state of Judah.

16:5 The oracle evokes the picture of a just descendant of **David** ruling **on the throne forever**. The language is a reminder of the Davidic covenant in 2Sm 7:12-16 (cp. Is 9:7; 11:1-9), and it hints at the expectation of the Messiah.

16:6-12 In response to Moab's request for shelter, the prophet can only lament its destruction. This part of the oracle is similar in wording and imagery to Jr 48:29-39.

16:6 In keeping with a major theme throughout the book of Isaiah, the heart of Moab's sin is described as **pride**.

16:7 **Raisin cakes** were a delicacy mentioned in Sg 2:5 along with apples as providing sustenance for lovemaking, though it may not have been an aphrodisiac. Hosea 3:1 suggests that raisin cakes were associated with pagan rituals.

16:8-9 Moab was known for its wine production. **Jazer** was in the north on the border with Ammon, and **Sibmah** is of uncertain location. Jazer will weep for itself as God wept for Sibmah.

Triumphant shouts have fallen silent[A]
over your summer fruit
and your harvest.
10 Joy and rejoicing[a] have been removed
from the orchard;
no one is singing or shouting for joy
in the vineyards.[b]
No one tramples grapes[B]
in the winepresses.
I have put an end to the shouting.
11 Therefore I moan like the sound of
a lyre for Moab,[c]
as does my innermost being for
Kir-heres.
12 When Moab appears on the *high place,
when he tires[c] himself out[d]
and comes to his sanctuary to pray,
it will do him no good.[e]

13 This is the message that the LORD previously announced about Moab. 14 And now the LORD says, "In three years, as a hired worker counts years,[f] Moab's splendor will become an object of contempt, in spite of a very large population. And those who are left will be few and weak."

An Oracle against Damascus

17 An *oracle[g] against Damascus:[h]

Look, Damascus is no longer a city.
It has become a ruined heap.
2 The cities of Aroer are forsaken;
they will be places for flocks.

They will lie down without fear.
3 The fortress disappears from Ephraim,[i]
and a kingdom from Damascus.
The remnant of Aram will be
like the splendor of the Israelites.
This is the declaration
of the LORD of *Hosts.

Judgment against Israel

4 On that day
the splendor of Jacob will fade,
and his healthy body[D]
will become emaciated.[j]
5 It will be as if a reaper had gathered
standing grain—
his arm harvesting the heads of grain—
and as if one had gleaned heads of grain
in the Valley of Rephaim.[k]
6 Only gleanings will be left in Israel,[l]
as if an olive tree had been beaten—
two or three berries at the very top
of the tree,
four or five on its fruitful branches.
This is the declaration of the LORD,
the God of Israel.

7 On that day people will look to their Maker and will turn their eyes to the Holy One of Israel.[m] 8 They will not look to the altars[n] they made with their hands or to the *Asherahs and incense altars[o] they made with their fingers.

9 On that day their strong cities will be
like the abandoned woods
and mountaintops[E]

a16:10 Is 24:8; Jr 48:33
b Jdg 9:27; Is 24:7; Am 5:11,17
c16:11 Is 15:5; 63:15; Jr 48:36; Hs 11:8; Php 2:1
d16:12 1Kg 18:29
e Is 15:2
f16:14 Jb 7:1; 14:6; Is 21:16
g17:1 Is 13:1
h Gn 14:15; 15:2; 2Kg 16:9; Jr 49:23; Am 1:3-5; Zch 9:1; Ac 9:2
i17:3 Is 7,8,16; 8:4
j17:4 Is 10:16
k17:5 2Sm 5:18,22
l17:6 Dt 4:27; Is 24:13; 27:12; Ob 5; Rm 11:19
m17:7 Is 1:4
n17:8 2Ch 34:7; Is 27:9
o Ex 34:13; Dt 7:5; Mc 5:14

A16:9 Or Battle cries have fallen   B16:10 Lit wine   C16:12 DSS read place, he will tire   D17:4 Lit and the fat of his flesh
E17:9 Some Hb mss read like the Horesh and the Amir; LXX reads like the Amorites and the Hivites

16:10 Because of the devastation, **joy . . . singing**, and wine will vanish from the land of Moab.

16:12 Moabite worship is ineffective. **His sanctuary** refers to the temple of Chemosh, who was no god and therefore could not respond to prayer.

16:13-14 The concluding comment about the Moabite oracle declares that it actually had been delivered at an earlier time, but from this moment Moab had only three more years. Presumably a **hired worker** would count the time until his work was over with great attention and precision. Most scholars associate this Moabite devastation with the Assyrian king Sargon's campaign against the people of northwest Arabia in approximately 718 B.C.

17:1-3 The next **oracle** is directed **against Damascus**, an ancient city and the capital of Syria. From the time of Solomon (1Kg 11:23-25) to the mid-eighth century, there was fighting between Israel and Syria. Isaiah 7 describes how Isaiah encouraged Ahaz of Judah to resist the threat of a Syrian-Ephraimite alliance. Assyria under Tiglath-pileser III absorbed Damascus into its growing empire.

17:2 The best known **cities of Aroer** were in Moab, but it seems odd that they are mentioned in the middle of an oracle against Damascus. Perhaps these are a different set of cities or perhaps, as some have suggested, the text should

be emended to say "its cities are deserted forever" (Childs, *Isaiah*, p. 137).

17:3 As the next passage demonstrates, it is not good for Aram that its **splendor** will be like that of Israel (v. 4). Both of these nations will be destroyed.

17:4 **On that day** (vv. 7,9) points to a future but unspecified period. The first image of the destruction of Israel is a diseased **body**.

17:5 A second image of destruction is a **reaper** picking grain. The **Valley of Rephaim** was southwest of Jerusalem. The meaning of its name is ominous: "Valley of the Departed."

17:6 The third image of destruction concerns the harvesting of an **olive tree**. It was shaken and the fallen olives were eaten. But this image also shows that, though the devastation will be extensive, it will not be total. A remnant, represented by **berries** that stayed attached to the tree, will survive.

17:7-8 **On that day** (v. 4) points to a time beyond the judgment. Indeed, the judgment of God will cause the remnant to turn from false worship to the worship of the true God who created them. Asherah was a Canaanite goddess of love and war. The plural form (**Asherahs**) signifies that the reference is to wooden poles or trees associated with her worship.

that were abandoned because of
  the Israelites;
there will be desolation.
¹⁰ For you have forgotten the God
    of your salvation,
  and you have failed to remember
    the rock of your strength;ᵃ
  therefore you will plant beautiful plants
  and set out cuttings from exotic vines.
¹¹ On the day that you plant,
    you will help them to grow,
  and in the morning
  you will help your seed to sprout,
  but the harvest will vanish
  on the day of disease and incurable pain.

Judgment against the Nations

¹² Ah! The roar of many peoples—
    they roar like the roaring of the seas.
  The raging of the nations—
    they rage like the raging
      of mighty waters.ᵇ
¹³ The nations rage like the raging
      of many waters.ᶜ
  He rebukes them, and they flee far away,ᵈ
  driven before the wind like chaff
    on the hillsᵉ
  and like tumbleweeds before a gale.
¹⁴ In the evening—sudden terror!
  Before morning—it is gone!
  This is the fate of those who plunder us
  and the lot of those who ravage us.

ᵃ17:10 Is 8:14;
26:4
ᵇ17:12 Ps 93:1-
5; Is 8:9-10; Lk
21:25
ᶜ17:13 Is 33:3
ᵈPs 9:5; Is 41:11
ᵉJb 21:18; Ps
1:4; 83:13; Is
29:5; 41:15-16
ᶠ18:1 2Kg 19:9;
Is 20:3-5; Ezk
30:4-5,9; Zph
2:12; 3:10

The Lord's Message to Cush

18 Ah! The land of buzzing insect wingsᴬ
  beyond the rivers of •Cushᶠ
²   sends couriers by sea,
  in reed vessels on the waters.

Go, swift messengers,
  to a nation tall and smooth-skinned,
  to a people feared far and near,
  a powerful nation
    with a strange language,ᴮ
  whose land is divided by rivers.
³ All you inhabitants of the world
  and you who live on the earth,
  when a banner is raised
    on the mountains, look!
  When a trumpet sounds, listen!

⁴ For, the Lord said to me:

I will quietly look out from My place,
  like shimmering heat in sunshine,
  like a rain cloud in harvest heat.
⁵ For before the harvest,
    when the blossoming is over
  and the blossom becomes
    a ripening grape,
  He will cut off the shoots
    with a pruning knife,
  and tear away and remove
    the branches.
⁶ They will all be left for the birds of prey
  on the hills

ᴬ18:1 Or *of sailing ships*   ᴮ18:2 Hb obscure

17:9 On that day signals the future time of judgment again
(see v. 4). The destruction will turn cities into **abandoned
woods and mountaintops**. The reason for their abandonment is the Israelites, who, as verse 10 explains, have
sinned by forgetting God.

17:10-11 To **remember** God involves more than a mental
activity; it implies obeying and worshiping Him. To forget
Him points to Israel's disobedience. Isaiah spoke of Israel's
bad end by using a plant analogy. Israel worked hard to grow
beautiful plants. They exerted their energy but ended up with
nothing. Israel's self-sufficient efforts will also end up empty.

17:12 The opening exclamation **Ah** is the same word earlier
translated as "Oh" (see 1:4). It begins an oracle that has
the form of a funeral dirge. The nations were agitated; they
roared and raged (Ps 2:1-4). Their agitation is compared to
the pounding of waves. **Mighty waters** is often an image of
social and religious chaos (Ps 18:16; 29:3; 32:6).

17:13 Though the **nations rage**, God's rebuke will quiet them
by driving them away (Pss 2; 48). **Chaff** was light and wind
blew it away, so God's rebuke will blow away the tumultuous nations.

17:14 God's judgment comes quickly, in a single day (**in
the evening . . . before morning**). The victim of the nations
(God's people) speaks here in the first person (**us**).

18:1-7 The statement about **Cush** is not called an oracle as

the previous chapters have specified, but the opening word
Ah signals a type of judgment speech (see notes at 1:4 and
17:12). The land of Cush was south of Egypt, on the upper
(southern) portion of the Nile River, roughly identical to
modern Ethiopia.

18:1 The best explanation for the reputation of the region
beyond the rivers of Cush as being a **land of buzzing insect
wings** is that it was renowned for its bugs.

18:2 Cush sent envoys on **reed vessels**, typical of Egypt and
Cush, down the Nile River toward Judah. Then follows a
command to go to a nation described as having **tall and
smooth-skinned** inhabitants who spoke a **strange language** and were feared. The best understanding of this is
that the command is addressed to Judean envoys to go to
Cush since the description describes that nation, rather
than as a command to the Ethiopian messengers to return
home. The verse describes hectic diplomatic activity.

18:3 In spite of human diplomatic efforts, a decisive moment will occur in the future when an army gathers for
battle. The **banner** marks the rallying point (5:26; 11:10,12;
13:2), and the **trumpet** signals the start of war.

18:4 In contrast to the frenetic efforts of diplomacy, God
was calmly in control.

18:5-6 God's judgment is compared to pruning a grapevine

and for the wild animals of the land.
The birds will spend the summer
    on them,
and all the animals, the winter on them.

⁷ At that time a gift will be brought to •Yah-
weh of •Hosts from^A a people tall and smooth-
skinned,^a a people feared far and near, a powerful
nation with a strange language, whose land is
divided by rivers—to Mount •Zion, the place of
the name of Yahweh of Hosts.

An Oracle against Egypt

19 An •oracle^b against Egypt:^c

Look, the LORD rides on a swift cloud^d
and is coming to Egypt.
Egypt's idols will tremble before Him,^e
and Egypt's heart will melt within it.^f
² I will provoke Egypt against Egypt;
each will fight against his brother^g
and each against his friend,
city against city,
    kingdom against kingdom.^h
³ Egypt's spirit will be disturbed within it,
and I will frustrate its plans.
Then they will seek idols, ghosts,
spirits of the dead, and spiritists.^i
⁴ I will deliver Egypt into the hands
    of harsh masters,^j
and a strong king will rule it.
            This is the declaration
            of the Lord GOD of •Hosts.

⁵ The waters of the sea will dry up,
and the river will be parched and dry.
⁶ The channels will stink;
they will dwindle, and Egypt's canals
    will be parched.
Reed and rush will die.^B
⁷ The reeds by the Nile, by the mouth
    of the river,
and all the cultivated areas of the Nile
will wither, blow away, and vanish.
⁸ Then the fishermen will mourn.
All those who cast hooks into the Nile
    will lament,
and those who spread nets on the water
    will shrivel up.
⁹ Those who work with flax
    will be dismayed;^k
the combers and weavers
    will turn pale.^C
¹⁰ Egypt's weavers^D will be dejected;
all her wage earners
    will be demoralized.

¹¹ The princes of Zoan are complete fools;^l
Pharaoh's wisest advisers
    give stupid advice!
How can you say to Pharaoh,
"I am one^E of the wise,
a student of eastern^F kings"?
¹² Where then are your wise men?
Let them tell you and reveal

^a18:7 Ps 68:31; Is 45:14; Zph 3:10; Ac 8:27-38 ^b19:1 Is 13:1 ^cJr 46:13-26; Ezk 29:1-31:2; 31:18-32:32; Jl 3:19 ^dPs 18:9-10; 104:3; Mt 26:64; Rv 1:7 ^eEx 12:12; Jr 43:12; 44:8 ^fJos 2:11; Is 13:7 ^g19:2 Mk 13:12 ^hJdg 7:22; 1Sm 14:20; 2Ch 20:23; Mt 10:21,36; Mk 13:8; Lk 21:10 ^i19:3 1Ch 10:13; Is 8:19; Dn 2:2 ^j19:4 Is 20:4; Jr 46:26; Ezk 29:19 ^k19:9 Pr 7:16; Ezk 27:7 ^l19:11 Nm 13:22; Ps 78:12,43; Is 30:4

---

^A18:7 DSS, LXX, Vg; MT omits *from*   ^B19:6 Or *wilt*, or *become black*   ^C19:9 DSS, Tg; MT reads *weavers of white cloth*   ^D19:10 Or *foundations*   ^E19:11 Lit *a son*   ^F19:11 Lit *a son of ancient*

---

before the grapes got ripe. Those fallen in battle would be left to the **wild animals**.

18:7 The Ethiopians (Cushites), described as a **tall and smooth-skinned** people (v. 2), are pictured as bringing tribute. This is a sign of their submission to God's temple on **Zion** after the judgment.

19:1 The **swift cloud**, a storm cloud, is God's war chariot. The image is found elsewhere in Scripture (Ps 18:10; 68:33; 104:3; Nah 1:3) and even has an older ancient Near Eastern background (the god Baal is often described as a "cloud rider"). Fear strikes the hearts of **Egypt's idols** again, just as the plagues were described as a victory over Egypt's gods at the time of the exodus (Ex 12:12).

19:2 God will use Egyptian civil war to judge that nation. During much of the eighth century Egypt was at war with itself. There were conflicts between power centers at Tanis, Thebes, and in the delta. There were also conflicts between Cushite rulers and the rulers at Sais. Not until 712 B.C. was Egypt united under one pharaoh, the Cushite king Shabaka. Even though conditions through much of the eighth century are described by this verse, the picture is so general that it could apply to a different, future time as well.

19:3 Egyptian religion was filled with many gods and mysterious rites, but this verse describes a darker religious turn born out of frustration.

19:4 Egypt's punishment is to be delivered into the control of **harsh masters**, a **strong king**. The lack of specificity does not allow the identification of a concrete historical figure. The description reminds the reader that Egypt at an earlier point had been a harsh master for Israel in bondage.

19:5-7 The waters of the **Nile** River were the lifeblood of Egypt. Its fresh waters running northward from the south to the delta and out into the Mediterranean Sea were the only source of drinkable water in the country. Egypt's prosperity was enhanced by the early development of an irrigation system. God's judgment of Egypt is pictured as a drying up of the **waters**. As a result farmland will vanish.

19:8 The disappearance of the Nile waters will not only affect farmers but also those who make their living by fishing.

19:9-10 Another major industry associated with Egypt was the production of **flax**, a fiber from which clothes were made. The loss of this industry would lead to economic depression.

19:11 **Zoan** was an important city (also known as Tanis), formerly a capital of Egypt. It is mentioned in this verse because it was the residence of Pharaoh's wisest advisers. Egypt was known as a center of wisdom in the ancient Near East. This oracle mocks their wisdom.

19:12 The ignorance of the **wise men** of Egypt is revealed by their ignorance of God's plans for their country.

what the LORD of Hosts has planned against Egypt.
13 The princes of Zoan have been fools; the princes of Memphis are deceived.[a] Her tribal chieftains have led Egypt astray.
14 The LORD has mixed within her a spirit of confusion.
The leaders have made Egypt stagger in all she does,
as a drunkard staggers in his vomit.
15 No head or tail, palm or reed,[b] will be able to do anything for Egypt.

Egypt Will Know the LORD

16 On that day Egypt will be like women. She will tremble with fear because of the threatening hand of the LORD of Hosts when He raises it against her. 17 The land of Judah will terrify Egypt; whenever Judah is mentioned, Egypt will tremble because of what the LORD of Hosts has planned[c] against it.

18 On that day five cities in the land of Egypt will speak the language of Canaan and swear loyalty to the LORD of Hosts. One of the cities will be called the City of the Sun.[A,B]

19 On that day there will be an altar to the LORD in the center of the land of Egypt and a pillar to the LORD near her border.[d] 20 It will be a sign and witness to the LORD of Hosts in the land of Egypt. When they cry out to the LORD because of their oppressors, He will send them a savior and leader, and he will rescue them.[e] 21 The LORD will make Himself known to Egypt, and Egypt will know the LORD on that day. They will offer sacrifices and offerings;[f] they will make vows to the LORD and fulfill them. 22 The LORD will strike Egypt, striking and healing. Then they will return to the LORD and He will hear their prayers and heal them.

23 On that day there will be a highway[g] from Egypt to Assyria. Assyria will go to Egypt, Egypt to Assyria, and Egypt will worship with Assyria.

24 On that day Israel will form a triple alliance with Egypt and Assyria—a blessing within the land. 25 The LORD of Hosts will bless them, saying, "Egypt My people, Assyria My handiwork,[h] and Israel My inheritance are blessed."[i]

No Help from Cush or Egypt

20 In the year that the chief commander,[j] sent by Sargon king of Assyria, came to Ashdod[k] and attacked and captured

Cross references (center column):
a19:13 Jr 2:16; 46:14,19; Ezk 30:13
b19:15 Is 9:14-16
c19:17 Is 5:19
d19:19 Gn 28:18; Ex 24:4; Jos 22:10,26-27
e19:20 Jdg 3:9,15; 6:7; 10:10
f19:21 Is 56:7; 60:7; Zch 14:16-18
g19:23 Is 11:16; 35:8; 49:11; 62:10
h19:25 Ps 100:3; Is 29:23; 45:11; 60:21; 64:8; Eph 2:10
iDt 9:26,29; 32:9; Ps 28:9; Is 47:6; 63:17
j20:1 2Kg 18:17
k1Sm 5:1

A19:18 Some Hb mss, DSS, Sym, Tg, Vg, Arabic; other Hb mss read *of Destruction*; LXX reads *of Righteousness*   B19:18 = the ancient Egyptian city Heliopolis

19:14 Egyptian **leaders** and wise men are pictured as drunk, in a state of heightened confusion. The image of a **drunkard** staggering and passing out, representing the demise of God's enemies, occurs frequently in the Prophets. It is often connected with the theme of the cup of God's wrath (Jr 25:15-38), but sometimes not explicitly (Jr 48:26-28; Nah 3:11). See also Ps 75:8; Lm 4:21; Ezk 23:32-33; Hab 2:16; Zch 12:2; Mt 26:42; Rv 14:10; 16:19; 17:4; 18:6. The image recurs in Is 51:17-23 and is alluded to in 63:6.

19:15 The expression **head or tail, palm or reed** points to a totality (9:14). Nothing can protect Egypt against God's devastating judgment.

19:16 **On that day** points to a future but unspecified time (vv. 18-19,23). It was an insult to say that Egypt's troops will be **like women** (Jr 50:37; 51:30).

19:17 Egypt was always militarily superior to **Judah**, so Judah was tempted to depend on Egypt for military support, but this verse envisions Egypt fearing Judah, a shameful reversal for this proud nation.

19:18 **On that day**, see note at verse 16. While Hebrew settlements were known from the postexilic period on, it is more likely that this verse refers to a conversion of at least some Egyptians to Yahweh. The **five cities** cannot be identified and may be a symbolic number for "a few." But the **City of the Sun** is well known. It was Heliopolis, closely associated with the worship of the sun god. That the worship of Yahweh would be taken up in this city is a sign of a radical transformation.

19:19 **On that day**, see note at verse 16. As a sign of an Egyptian conversion to the worship of the true God, there will be an **altar** set up in the center of the land and a memorial **pillar** at the border. The land will be dedicated to the worship of the true God.

19:20 The language of this verse is reminiscent of that of the book of Judges. Here, however, sending someone to rescue a repentant nation from an oppressor describes the situation in future Egypt.

19:22 Egypt's conversion will be after that country experiences God's judgment; **healing** will follow **striking**.

19:23 **On that day**, see note at verse 16. **Highway** is a "favorite metaphor in Isaiah for the removal of alienation and separation (11:16; 33:8; 35:8; 40:3; 49:11; 62:10)" (Oswalt, *Isaiah 1-39*, p. 380). **Assyria** and **Egypt** had been enemies for many years, but this amazing passage envisions a time when travel will be free and easy between them and they will be united in the worship of God.

19:24 Israel was a land bridge between **Egypt and Assyria**. Both of these nations had tried to control Israel to get a foothold against the other. Here **Israel** is added to Assyria and Egypt in an intimate relationship of love and worship of the Lord.

19:25 The description of God blessing Israel and the two most powerful Gentile nations of the time anticipates the fulfillment of the Abrahamic promise that God would **bless** not only Abraham's descendants but other nations as well (Gn 12:1-3).

20:1 The events narrated in this verse took place between 713 and 711 B.C. Sargon II attacked the Philistine city of **Ashdod** after its king, Azuri, revolted. Azuri probably thought that Egypt under Shabaka would provide aid. The Assyrians deposed Azuri and placed his brother Ahimeti on the throne. But Ahimeti was deposed by a person named

it— ² during that time the LORD had spoken through Isaiah[a] son of Amoz, saying, "Go, take off your •sackcloth[A] and remove the sandals from your feet," and he did so, going naked and barefoot[b]— ³ the LORD said, "As My servant Isaiah has gone naked and barefoot three years as a sign and omen against Egypt and •Cush,[c] ⁴ so the king of Assyria will lead the captives of Egypt[d] and the exiles of Cush, young and old alike, naked and barefoot, with bared buttocks—to Egypt's shame. ⁵ Those who made Cush their hope and Egypt their boast will be dismayed and ashamed.[e] ⁶ And the inhabitants of this coastland will say on that day, 'Look, this is what has happened to those we relied on and fled to for help to rescue us from the king of Assyria! Now, how will we escape?'"

A Judgment on Babylon

21 An •oracle[f] against the desert by the sea:[g]

Like storms that pass over the •Negev,
   it comes from the desert, from the land
   of terror.

² A troubling vision is declared to me:
   "The treacherous one
     acts treacherously,[h]
   and the destroyer destroys.
   Advance, Elam! Lay siege, you Medes!
   I will put an end to all her groaning."

³ Therefore I am[B] filled with anguish.
   Pain grips me, like the pain of a woman
     in labor.[i]
   I am too perplexed to hear,
   too dismayed to see.

⁴ My heart staggers;
   horror terrifies me.
   He has turned my last glimmer
     of hope[c]
   into sheer terror.[j]

⁵ Prepare a table,[k] and spread out
   a carpet!

Cross references

ᵃ20:2 Mt 3:3; 12:17
ᵇ1Sm 19:24; Mc 1:8
ᶜ20:3 Is 8:18
ᵈ20:4 Is 19:4
ᵉ20:5 2Kg 18:21; Is 30:3-5; 31:1; Ezk 29:6-7
ᶠ21:1 Is 13:1
ᵍIs 13:20-22; 14:23; 21:9; Jr 51:41-44
ʰ21:2 Is 24:16; 33:1
ⁱ21:3 Ps 48:6; Is 13:8; 16:11; 26:17-18; Jr 4:31; 6:24; 22:23; 30:6; 50:43; Mc 4:9-10; 1Th 5:3
ʲ21:4 Dt 28:67
ᵏ21:5 Jr 51:39,57; Dn 5:1-4

A20:2 Lit off the sackcloth from your loins   B21:3 Lit Therefore my loins are   C21:4 Lit my twilight

---

Yamani, so Sargon had to come back. Yamani fled to Egypt, but under the Assyrian threat, Egypt handed the rebel over. This should have served as a warning to others who believed Egypt could provide help against their enemies.

20:2 God commanded Isaiah to perform a symbolic action that would support his spoken oracle. Isaiah had been wearing **sackcloth**, a symbol of mourning, but he was told to go about **naked**. This would represent the coming humiliation and destitution of Egypt.

20:5 Those who trusted **Egypt** and **Cush** for help against their enemies would be sorely disappointed. God was the only proper object of the people's trust.

20:6 The oracle envisioned other nations coming to recognize that Egypt was an unreliable ally. The implicit message is that Judah should come to the same realization.

bagad

Hebrew Pronunciation	[bah GAD]
HCSB Translation	act treacherously, betray
Uses in Isaiah	12
Uses in the OT	49
Focus Passage	Isaiah 21:2

This root in south Arabic means "deceive." *Bagad* means *be treacherous* (Is 48:8) or *act treacherously* (Ex 21:8). It denotes *be unfaithful* (1Sm 14:33), *treat deceitfully* (Jdg 9:23), or *betray* (Is 33:1). Wine *betrays* (Hab 2:5). *Deal treacherously* (Is 24:16) is *bagad* with *beged* (2x), *treachery*. The participle (23x) denotes *the treacherous* (Pr 2:22). It is *those who are unfaithful* (Pr 23:28), the *disloyal* (Ps 119:158), an *unreliable person* (Pr 25:19), or a *traitor* (Is 33:1). Family members (Jr 12:6) and friends (Jb 6:14-15) may *be treacherous*. *Bagad*, associated with *rebellion* (Is 48:8) and *covenant violation* (Hs 6:7), describes *political treachery* (Is 21:2). *Bagad* indicates *adultery* (Jr 9:2), *marital disloyalty*, and *infidelity to God* (Mal 2:11,14). Israel *betrayed* God as women *betray lovers* (Jr 3:20). The opposite of treachery is uprightness (Pr 11:3,6). *Bagod* means *treacherous* (Jr 3:7,10), and the noun *bogedoth* appears as *treacherous* (Zph 3:4).

21:1-10 The oracle in these verses was against the **desert by the sea**. This designation is ambiguous when first stated, but the end of the passage (v. 9) makes it clear that Babylon was meant. The description of the fall of Babylon is mysterious. Debate surrounds whether it anticipates an Assyrian defeat of Babylon in the late eighth or early seventh century B.C. (three times: 710, 700, 689) or the ultimate defeat of Babylon by Persia in 539 B.C. A good argument can be made that both the earlier and the later defeats are alluded to in this prophecy. The intention of this prophecy at the time of Isaiah was to show that Babylon would not be an effective ally against Assyria as even King Hezekiah of Judah at one point had hoped (chap. 39).

21:1 The **desert** (lit "wilderness") **by the sea** in connection with Babylon could be taken as a reference to the area in the extreme south of Mesopotamia, the swampland next to what today is called the Persian Gulf. This area was the center of Babylonian revolts against Assyria at the end of the eighth century (Merodach-baladan) as well as in the late part of the seventh century (Nabopolassar). The **Negev** was to the extreme south of Jerusalem and was itself a wilderness area. The storms that pass through that area even today are particularly violent.

21:2 **Elam** and Media (**Medes**) were countries on the Iranian plateau east of Babylon. In this verse they are called to advance, but against whom? In the late eighth century B.C., they were allies with Babylon and would have fought against Assyria. In 539 B.C. they were both parts of the Persian Empire that defeated Babylon. Perhaps the ambiguity intends the reader at a later time to recognize allusions to both events.

21:3 Isaiah used the theme of a **woman in labor**, one widely used in prophetic literature (13:8; Jr 4:31; 6:24; 22:23; 30:6; Mc 4:9). This was a graphic image of the pain and distress that would fall on the object of God's warring activity.

21:5 Attack would come in the midst of celebrative feasting, reminiscent of Daniel 5 when Belshazzar ate and drank on the eve of Babylon's destruction. It is unclear whether such

Eat and drink!
Rise up, you princes, and oil the shields!

6 For the Lord has said to me,
"Go, post a lookout;
let him report what he sees.
7 When he sees riders—
pairs of horsemen,
riders on donkeys,
riders on camels—
he must pay close attention."
8 Then the lookout[A] reported,
"Lord, I stand on the watchtower
all day,[a]
and I stay at my post all night.
9 Look, riders come—
horsemen in pairs."
And he answered, saying,
"Babylon has fallen,[b] has fallen.
All the images of her gods
have been shattered on the ground."[c]

10 My people who have been crushed
on the threshing floor,[d]
I have declared to you
what I have heard from the LORD
of *Hosts,
the God of Israel.

An Oracle against Dumah

11 An oracle[e] against Dumah:[B,f]

One calls to me from Seir,[g]
"Watchman, what is left of the night?
Watchman, what is left of the night?"

---

[a]21:8 Hab 2:1
[b]21:9 2Sm 1:19; Is 3:8; 14:12; Jr 51:8; Ezk 32:22; Rv 14:8; 18:2
[c]Is 46:1; Jr 50:2; 51:44
[d]21:10 Jr 51:33; Mc 4:13
[e]21:11 Is 21:1
[f]Gn 25:14
[g]Dt 2:8; Ezk 35:2
[h]21:13 Jr 25:23-24; 49:28
[i]Gn 10:7; Jr 25:23; 49:8; Ezk 27:15
[j]21:14 Gn 25:15; Jb 6:19
[k]21:16 Is 16:14
[l]Ps 120:5; Sg 1:5; Is 42:11; 60:7; Jr 2:10; Ezk 27:21
[m]22:1 Is 13:1
[n]Ps 125:2; Jr 21:13; Jl 3:12,14
[o]Is 15:3
[p]22:2 Is 23:7; 32:13

---

12 The watchman said,
"Morning has come, and also night.
If you want to ask, ask!
Come back again."

An Oracle against Arabia

13 An oracle against Arabia:[h]

In the desert[C] brush
you will camp for the night,
you caravans of Dedanites.[i]
14 Bring water for the thirsty.
The inhabitants of the land of Tema[j]
meet[D] the refugees with food.
15 For they have fled from swords,
from the drawn sword,
from the bow that is strung,
and from the stress of battle.

16 For the Lord said this to me: "Within one year,[k] as a hired worker counts years, all the glory of Kedar[l] will be gone. 17 The remaining Kedarite archers will be few in number." For the LORD, the God of Israel, has spoken.

An Oracle against Jerusalem

22 An *oracle[m] against the Valley of Vision:[n]

What's the matter with you?
Why have all of you gone up
to the rooftops?[o]
2 The noisy city, the jubilant town,[p]
is filled with revelry.
Your dead did not die by the sword;

[A]21:8 DSS, Syr; MT reads *Then a lion*　　[B]21:11 Some Hb mss, LXX read *Edom*　　[C]21:13 LXX, Syr, Tg, Vg read *desert at evening*
[D]21:14 LXX, Syr, Tg, Vg read *meet* as a command

---

banqueting indicated a lack of preparedness for battle or whether it was a pre-battle rally (Est 1). The reference to the oiling of **shields** may indicate the latter since this was done before battle.

21:6 The **lookout** was posted at some point distant from the battle, perhaps at the city of the attackers. He looked for signs of victory or defeat.

21:9 The attacking army returned intact with the announcement that **Babylon has fallen**. The focus is on the defeat of Babylon's gods.

21:10 The **crushed** people were the people of Israel. The prophet confirmed to them that the destruction of Babylon had been announced by none other than God Himself.

21:11-12 Dumah was an oasis in Arabia that controlled trade routes. In the eighth century it was an object of Assyrian invasion under Sennacherib and was an ally of Babylon. In the sixth century when the last Babylonian king, Nabonidus, moved to Tema in Arabia, he tried to control all the trade routes in that region. Besides designating an oasis in north central Arabia, the Hebrew word *Dumah* means "silence," like the silence of death (Ps 94:17). Thus, the name sets the mood for the oracle. The Greek translation of the OT understood Dumah as a reference to Edom. **Seir** is a reference to an important part of Edom, but here Edom spoke to Dumah.

The theme of the **watchman** continues from the preceding oracle. The question the watchman was asked is enigmatic, but it may be a way of asking how much longer the suffering (**night**) would last.

21:13-17 Dedan, Tema, and Kedar are references to geographical and/or political entities in northern **Arabia**. They were likely allies of Babylon during the eighth century B.C. Childs (*Isaiah*, p. 154) has pointed out that these tribes were defeated by Assyria between 691–689 B.C.

21:16 Presumably a **hired worker** counted the time until his work was over with great attention and precision (see note at 16:13-14).

22:1 From later in the oracle, it is clear that the **Valley of Vision** is a reference to Jerusalem, even though this name is not used elsewhere of the city. It could be satirical, that is, the Valley of Vision was blind to the divine purpose. Or perhaps it could be a reference to Hinnom, where divinatory practices took place (Walton, *IVP BBC*, p. 613). The significance of the **rooftops** is also difficult, but it probably refers to their getting a better perspective on the withdrawal of a besieging army. Most think the historical reference is to the withdrawal of the Assyrian army from Jerusalem in 701 B.C. (chaps. 36–37).

22:2 The inhabitants were **jubilant** because the attacking army had withdrawn from its siege. The reference to those

they were not killed in battle.
3 All your rulers have fled together,
captured without a bow.
All your fugitives
were captured together;
they had fled far away.
4 Therefore I said,
"Look away from me!
Let me weep bitterly!ᵃ
Do not try to comfort me
about the destruction
of my dearᴬ people."
5 For the Lord Gᴏᴅ of •Hosts
had a day of tumult, trampling,
and confusionᵇ
in the Valley of Vision—
people shoutingᴮ and crying
to the mountains;
6 Elam took up a quiver
with chariots and horsemen,ᶜ
and Kirᶜ uncovered the shield.
7 Your best valleys were full of chariots,
and horsemen were positioned
at the gates.
8 He removed the defenses of Judah.

On that day you looked to the weapons in the House of the Forest.ᵈ 9 You saw that there were many breaches in the walls of the city of David.ᵉ You collected water from the lower pool.ᶠ 10 You counted the houses of Jerusalem so that you could tear them down to fortify

ᵃ22:4 Is 15:3; 33:7; Jr 9:1; Zch 12:10
ᵇ22:5 Is 10:6; 37:3; 63:3
ᶜ22:6 2Kg 16:9; Am 1:5; 9:7
ᵈ22:8 1Kg 7:2; 10:17
ᵉ22:9 Lk 2:4
ᶠ2Kg 20:20; Neh 3:16
ᵍ22:11 2Kg 25:4; Jr 39:4
ʰ2Kg 20:20; 2Ch 32:3-4
ⁱ22:12 Is 32:11; Jl 1:13; 2:17
ʲ22:13 Is 56:12; 1Co 15:32
ᵏ22:14 Is 5:9
ˡ1Sm 3:14; Ezk 24:13
ᵐ22:15 2Kg 18:18,26,37; Is 36:3,11,22; 37:2
ⁿ22:16 2Sm 18:18; 2Ch 16:14; Mt 27:60

the wall. 11 You made a reservoir between the wallsᵍ for the waters of the ancient pool,ʰ but you did not look to the One who made it, or consider the One who created it long ago.

12 On that day the Lord Gᴏᴅ of Hosts
called for weeping,ⁱ for wailing,
for shaven heads,
and for the wearing of •sackcloth.
13 But look: joy and gladness,
butchering of cattle,
slaughtering of sheep,
eating of meat, and drinking of wine—
"Let us eat and drink, for tomorrow
we die!"ʲ
14 The Lᴏʀᴅ of Hosts has directly revealed
to me:ᵏ
"This sin of yours will neverᴰ be
wiped out."ˡ
The Lord Gᴏᴅ of Hosts has spoken.

An Oracle against Shebna

15 The Lord Gᴏᴅ of Hosts said: "Go to Shebna,ᵐ that steward who is in charge of the palace, and say to him: 16 What are you doing here? Who authorized you to carve out a tomb for yourself here, carving your tomb on the height and cutting a crypt for yourself out of rock?ⁿ 17 Look, you strong man! The Lᴏʀᴅ is about to shake you violently. He will take hold of you, 18 wind you up into a ball, and sling you into a wide land.ᴱ There you will die, and there

ᴬ22:4 Lit of the daughter of my   ᴮ22:5 Or Vision—a tearing down of a wall, or Vision—Kir raged; Hb obscure   ᶜ22:6 Lit chariots of man   ᴰ22:14 Lit will not until you die   ᴱ22:17-18 Hb obscure

who died apart from battle may be a reference to those who starved or contracted disease during the siege.

22:3 The description of fleeing **rulers** does not accord with what we know about the siege of 701 B.C., but some connect it with an Assyrian account of the battle that mentions the capture of some of Hezekiah's paid troops.

22:4 The prophet Isaiah (the first-person speaker) did not share the joy of the city. After all, although the siege was lifted, people died.

22:6 Elam (located on the Iranian plateau east of Babylon) and **Kir** (of uncertain location) appear to have fought along with the Assyrians.

22:8 The **House of the Forest** is likely the same as the storehouse in the palace complex known as the House of the Forest of Lebanon (1Kg 7:1-12). **Weapons** were stored there. The people should have been looking to God for help, but they put their trust in their weapons instead.

22:10-11 Refortifying the wall with construction materials taken from demolished homes and building an emergency reservoir within the city are taken again by the prophet as a sign of human self-reliance. They should have been looking to God for help. After all, he was **the One who created it long ago**. The reference to collecting water from the lower **pool** may connect to the fact that Hezekiah built a tunnel to bring water inside the city walls (2Kg 20:20).

22:12 Shaving one's head and wearing **sackcloth** were rituals of mourning in ancient Israel.

22:13-14 God called for mourning (v. 12), but the people celebrated the lifting of the siege on the city. The people lived for the moment. The fact that the **sin** of the people would never be removed boded poorly for the future of the city.

22:15-25 The oracle against Jerusalem in these verses concludes with an evaluation of two stewards. Shebna abused his office and would be replaced by Eliakim. Eliakim was competent, and Isaiah praised him, but even Eliakim eventually failed. The message is that politicians cannot be relied on to solve problems that only God can solve.

22:15 The office of **steward** was an important role, analogous to the chief of staff of a president. **Shebna** is known elsewhere as a high-ranking officer in the court of Hezekiah (36:3,11,22; 37:2; 2Kg 18:18; 19:2), though in these passages he is called a "secretary" which may indicate that he had been demoted.

22:16 Shebna was concerned more about himself and his own glory than with the well-being of the city. Rock-hewn tombs from antiquity may be seen today all around Jerusalem, but particularly east of the city. Archaeologists discovered a tomb near Jerusalem that contained an inscription with the title of a person who was "in charge of the palace" (v. 15). However, there was no name on the tomb. Since he was demoted, it was probably not Shebna's.

your glorious chariots will be—a disgrace to the house of your lord. ¹⁹ I will remove you from your office; you will be ousted from your position.

²⁰ "On that day I will call for my servant, Eliakim son of Hilkiah.ᵃ ²¹ I will clothe him with your robe and tie your sash around him. I will put your authority into his hand, and he will be like a father to the inhabitants of Jerusalem and to the House of Judah.ᵇ ²² I will place the keyᶜ of the House of David on his shoulder; what he opens, no one can close; what he closes, no one can open.ᵈ ²³ I will drive him, like a peg, into a firm place. He will be a throne of honor for his father's house. ²⁴ They will hang on him the whole burden of his father's house: the descendants and the offshoots—all the small vessels, from bowls to every kind of jar. ²⁵ On that day"—the declaration of the LORD of Hosts—"the peg that was driven into a firm place will give way, be cut off, and fall, and the load on it will be destroyed." Indeed, the LORD has spoken.

An Oracle against Tyre

23 An •oracleᵉ against Tyre:ᶠ

Wail, ships of Tarshish,ᵍ
for your haven has been destroyed.

Word has reached them from the land
of Cyprus.ᴬ·ʰ
² Mourn, inhabitants
of the coastland,
you merchants of Sidon;ⁱ
your agents have crossed the seaᴮ
³ on many waters.
Tyre's revenue was the grain
from Shihor—
the harvest of the Nile.
She was the merchant
among the nations.ʲ
⁴ Be ashamed Sidon, the stronghold
of the sea,
for the sea has spoken:
"I have not been in labor
or given birth.
I have not raised young men
or brought up young women."
⁵ When the news reaches Egypt,
they will be in anguish over the news
about Tyre.ᵏ
⁶ Cross over to Tarshish;
wail, inhabitants of the coastland!
⁷ Is this your jubilant city,
whose origin was in ancient times,
whose feet have taken her
to settle far away?

ᵃ22:20 2Kg 18:18; Is 36:3,22; 37:2
ᵇ22:21 Gn 45:8; Jb 29:16
ᶜ22:22 Mt 16:19; Rv 3:7
ᵈJb 12:14
ᵉ23:1 Is 13:1
ᶠJos 19:29; 1Kg 5:1; Jr 25:22; 47:4; Ezk 26:1–27:36; Jl 3:4-8; Am 1:9; Zch 9:2-4
ᵍGn 10:4; 1Kg 10:22
ʰJr 2:10; Ezk 27:6; Ac 11:19
ⁱ23:2 Gn 10:15; Jos 19:28; Jr 25:22; 27:3; Ezk 27:8; 32:30; Jl 3:4; Zch 9:2
ʲ23:3 Ezk 27:3-23
ᵏ23:5 Ac 21:7

ᴬ23:1 Hb *Kittim*   ᴮ23:2 DSS; MT reads *Sidon, whom the seafarers have filled*

22:18 Shebna not only exalted himself by the type of tomb he was building, but also by driving **glorious chariots**.

22:19 Because of his vanity and self-promotion, God will replace him in his **position** as steward.

22:20 Shebna's replacement will be **Eliakim son of Hilkiah**, also known as a high official in King Hezekiah's court (36:3,11,22; 37:22; 2Kg 18:18,26,37). He will be God's **servant**, a title used elsewhere for Isaiah (20:3).

22:21 The **robe** and **sash** were symbols of the office of steward. As opposed to self-serving Shebna, Eliakim will function **like a father**, looking after the needs of his people.

22:22 The **key**, whether literal or metaphorical, indicates the control the steward had over the distribution of resources.

22:23 Eliakim will not be shaken like Shebna but will be a firmly implanted **peg**. The metaphor probably refers to a peg driven into a plastered wall to hold up shelves.

22:24-25 Eliakim is compared to a shelf on which his family put a tremendous burden. The weight ultimately sheared off the **peg**, causing the shelf (Eliakim) to crash and its contents (his family's burdens) to break. The message of the oracle seems to be that the people could not trust even a competent, well-intentioned person to resolve Jerusalem's problems.

23:1 Tyre was the southernmost major city of Phoenicia. It was a wealthy city, due to its development and control of sea trade. As an island city (with overflow population living on the mainland) its major port was easily protected. Tyre had established a trading colony on **Tarshish**, thought to be in what is modern Spain (Tartessus). The ships of Tarshish were particularly impressive, since they traveled so far between Tyre

and Iberia. The destruction of Tyre prophetically described in this oracle is difficult to pin down from the description made here. In the latter part of the eighth century and the early seventh century B.C., the Assyrians tried to take Tyre a number of times. However, the oracle may also look forward to Nebuchadnezzar's attack on Tyre (including a thirteen-year siege) in the sixth century and perhaps even to the final destruction of Tyre by Alexander the Great in 332 B.C. **Cyprus** was a large island about 75 miles west of Tyre and would have been the last port of call before reaching Tyre.

23:2 Sidon was another important Phoenician trade port north of Tyre. Its mention indicates that, though the oracle was specifically directed toward Tyre (the city closest to Jerusalem), the whole of Phoenicia was under judgment.

23:3 Shihor is a name for the Nile valley. Phoenicia carried on trade with Egypt during much of its history. Egypt was well known for its production and export of **grain**.

23:4 The **sea** here is personified, perhaps evoking the idea that the sea (Hb *yam*) was an important god and rival of the Canaanite god Baal (though the following description fits a female much better). In any case, the sea will lament for its barrenness, perhaps a reference to the loss of Sidon.

23:5 Egypt will be upset because it had lost an important trading partner.

23:6 Because of the destruction of the Phoenician **coastland**, its inhabitants will have to disperse, some perhaps going as far as the trading colony **Tarshish** (see note at v. 1).

23:7 The **jubilant city** is Tyre, the ancient city that established Tarshish as a colony. After it is destroyed, its inhabitants will flee to Tarshish.

8 Who planned this against Tyre,
   the bestower of crowns,
   whose traders are princes,
   whose merchants are the honored ones
      of the earth?
9 The LORD of ˙Hosts planned it,
   to desecrate all its glorious beauty,
   to disgrace all the honored ones
      of the earth.
10 Overflow^A your land like the Nile,
      daughter of Tarshish;
   there is no longer anything
      to restrain you.^B
11 He stretched out His hand
      over the sea;^a
   He made kingdoms tremble.
   The LORD has commanded
   that the Canaanite fortresses
      be destroyed.
12 He said,
   "You will not rejoice anymore,
   ravished young woman,
      daughter of Sidon.
   Get up and cross over to Cyprus^b—
   even there you will have no rest!"
13 Look at the land of the Chaldeans—
   a people who no longer exist.
   Assyria destined it for desert creatures.
   They set up their siege towers
   and stripped its palaces.
   They made it a ruin.
14 Wail, ships of Tarshish,
   because your fortress is destroyed!

^a 23:11 Ex 14:21;
Is 14:26
^b 23:12 Is 23:1;
Jr 2:10; Ezk
27:6; Ac 4:36;
11:19-20; 13:4,
15:39; 21:3,16;
27:4
^c 23:17 Jr
25:11,22
^d Ac 21:7

15 On that day Tyre will be forgotten for 70 years—the life span of one king. At the end of 70 years, what the song says about the prostitute will happen to Tyre:

16 Pick up your lyre,
   stroll through the city,
   prostitute forgotten by men.
   Play skillfully,
   sing many a song,
   and you will be thought
      of again.

17 And at the end of the 70 years,^c the LORD will restore Tyre^d and she will go back into business, prostituting herself with all the kingdoms of the world on the face of the earth. 18 But her profits and wages will be dedicated to the LORD. They will not be stored or saved, for her profit will go to those who live in the LORD's presence, to provide them with ample food and sacred clothing.

The Earth Judged

24 Look, the LORD is stripping
      the earth bare
   and making it desolate.
   He will twist its surface and scatter
      its inhabitants:
2 people and priest alike,
   servant and master,
   female servant and mistress,
   buyer and seller,
   lender and borrower,
   creditor and debtor.

---

^A 23:10 DSS, LXX read *Work*   ^B 23:10 Or *longer any harbor*

23:8 Tyre's wealth had brought her great power and prestige.

23:9 In answer to the question of verse 8, the oracle proclaims that the One who planned the fall of the magnificent city of Tyre was none other than the **LORD of Hosts**. Thus, this oracle continues the teaching that God is sovereign over all nations.

23:10 The Nile's waters **overflow** annually, leaving a rich, fertile soil. As a result, the Nile also overflowed with human population. Now **Tarshish** will overflow with all the refugees from the destroyed cities of the Phoenician coastland.

23:11 God determines the fate of even the most powerful human cities and strikes terror in the hearts of the nations (Ps 2). Phoenicia was considered a part of Canaan, and its fortresses may be referred to as **Canaanite fortresses**.

23:12 Sidon is compared to a rape victim, who must leave to seek refuge in **Cyprus**.

23:13 An analogy is drawn between the fall of the **Chaldeans** (the Aramaic-speaking tribe that produced the two rebels against Assyria—Merodach-baladan at the end of the eighth century and Nabopolassar at the end of the seventh century B.C.) and the fall of Tyre. Since the verse goes on to imply the fall of Babylon at the hands of the Assyrians, it

probably refers to the first of these, not the second in which Babylon was victorious.

23:15-18 The oracle against Tyre ends with a note about its restoration. It also suggests that the city will turn to the Lord.

23:15 Interestingly, **70 years** is cited as the length of the exile and punishment of the people of God (Jr 25:12; Dn 9:2; Zch 1:12). There have been some attempts to identify such a time period (from the death of Sennacherib to the time of Nebuchadnezzar), but this cannot be done with certainty.

23:16 This song may have been popular in ancient Israel. It speaks of an old **prostitute forgotten by men** who tried to attract attention by singing songs. The revived Tyre is like this prostitute. The image of the prostitute suggests Tyre itself, since it was a trading city.

23:18 Surprisingly, though, Tyre's restored trade will go to the work of the Lord, specifically to the priests.

24:1 While chapters 13–23 focused on the judgment of particular nations, chapters 24–27 speak of the whole **earth** (a word repeated 23x) as the object of God's punishment.

24:2 This long list of pairs of opposites is a striking way of saying that all human inhabitants of the earth will be judged without regard for social standing.

24:5 The cause of this horrific judgment is human sin. The

3 The earth will be stripped
   completely bare
and will be totally plundered,
for the Lord has spoken
   this message.[a]

4 The earth mourns and withers;
the world wastes away and withers;
the exalted people of the earth
   waste away.

5 The earth is polluted
   by its inhabitants,[b]
for they have transgressed teachings,
overstepped decrees,
and broken the everlasting covenant.[c]

6 Therefore a curse has consumed
   the earth,[d]
and its inhabitants have become •guilty;
the earth's inhabitants
   have been burned,
and only a few survive.

7 The new wine mourns;[e]
the vine withers.
All the carousers now groan.

8 The joyful tambourines[f] have ceased.
The noise of the jubilant has stopped.
The joyful lyre has ceased.

9 They no longer sing and drink wine;
beer is bitter to those who drink it.

10 The city of chaos is shattered;[g]
every house is closed to entry.[h]

11 In the streets they cry[A] for wine.
All joy grows dark;
earth's rejoicing goes into exile.

12 Only desolation remains in the city;
its gate has collapsed in ruins.

13 For this is how it will be on earth
among the nations:
like a harvested olive tree,
like a gleaning after a grape harvest.[i]

14 They raise their voices, they sing out;
they proclaim in the west
the majesty of the Lord.

15 Therefore, in the east honor the Lord!
In the islands of the west
honor the name of •Yahweh,
the God of Israel.

16 From the ends of the earth
   we hear songs:
The Splendor of the Righteous One.[j]

But I said, "I waste away! I waste away![B]
Woe is me."
The treacherous act treacherously;
the treacherous deal
   very treacherously.[k]

17 Panic, pit, and trap await you[l]
who dwell on the earth.[m]

18 Whoever flees at the sound of panic
will fall into a pit,
and whoever escapes from the pit
will be caught in a trap.
For the windows are opened
   from heaven,[n]
and the foundations of the earth
   are shaken.[o]

19 The earth is completely devastated;
the earth is split open;
the earth is violently shaken.

20 The earth staggers like a drunkard[p]
and sways like a hut.

---

[a]24:3 Is 1:20; 6:11
[b]24:5 Gn 3:17; 6:5,11-12; Nm 35:33; Is 9:17; 10:6
[c]Gn 9:16; 17:7; Ex 31:16; Lv 24:8; 2Sm 23:5; Ps 105:10; Is 55:3; 61:8; Jr 32:40; Ezk 16:60
[d]24:6 Jos 23:15; Is 34:5; 43:28; Zch 5:3-4
[e]24:7 Is 16:10; Jl 1:10,12
[f]24:8 Ex 15:20; Jdg 11:34; 1Sm 18:6; Is 30:32; Jr 31:4
[g]24:10 Is 34:11
[h]Is 23:1
[i]24:13 Is 17:6
[j]24:16 Ex 9:27; Pr 21:12; Ac 3:14; 7:52; 22:14
[k]Is 21:2; 33:1; Jr 3:20; 5:11
[l]24:17 Am 5:19
[m]24:17-18 Jr 48:43-44
[n]24:18 Gn 7:11
[o]Ps 18:7; 46:2; Is 2:19,21; 13:13
[p]24:20 Is 19:14

[A]24:11 Lit *streets she cries*   [B]24:16 Hb obscure

---

people have broken the covenant between God and Israel (Ex 19–24). The reference to **everlasting covenant** reminds the reader of the Noahic covenant between God and all the inhabitants of the earth (Gn 9:16).

24:6 The covenant form called for **a curse** if the law was broken (see Dt 27–28 in relationship to Dt 5–26). The remnant theme is seen here in the fact that a **few** will **survive**.

24:7-9 God's judgment brings joyful singing and drinking alcoholic beverages to an end. Both of these involved celebration. **Wine** and **beer** were the two main types of alcoholic drinks in the ancient Near East.

24:10 The **city of chaos** is not a specific city. It represents evil men and women who are subject to God's judgment.

24:11 Wine production will decline, so the people will **cry** for wine but go unsatisfied. Wine is associated with joy and celebration; the judgment of God will bring such festivities to an end. Wine also blunts pain. This may be another reason the people will cry out for wine—because of the suffering that God's judgment will produce.

24:12 The **gate** in a walled city represented its defenses.

24:13 A harvested **olive tree** or a **grape** vine after **harvest**

had only a few olives or grapes. So the cities of the nations will have just a few people left when God's judgment falls.

24:14-16a Those who **sing out** are not specifically identified. They could be Israel or the remnant from all the nations. The fact that they are in the **west**, the **east**, the **islands of the west**, and the **ends of the earth**, suggests that if it does refer to Israel, then it imagines a time when they will be scattered among the nations. In any case, these verses indicate that there were some people who celebrated the downfall of the wicked described in the previous verses.

24:16b Isaiah (the first-person speaker) does not join the chorus of celebration of verses 14-16a. Perhaps he was horrified by the destruction or, more likely, by the depth of the transgression of the nations.

24:17-18 The words **panic, pit, and trap** (*pachad, wapachat, wapach*) play on the similarity of sound of these three words in Hebrew. They stand for the judgment that God has prepared for the sinful inhabitants of the earth. The open **windows** of the sky imply rain and suggest devastating flood. The shaking **foundations** would be experienced as earthquakes.

24:20 A **drunkard** cannot think or stand straight. A lightweight **hut** sways in the wind. Both ultimately will fall down.

Earth's rebellion weighs it down,
and it falls, never to rise again.

21 On that day[a] the LORD will punish
the host of heaven above
and kings of the earth below.
22 They will be gathered together
like prisoners in a pit.[b]
They will be confined to a dungeon;[c]
after many days they will be punished.
23 The moon will be put to shame
and the sun disgraced,
because the LORD of •Hosts will reign
as king
on Mount •Zion in Jerusalem,
and He will display His glory
in the presence of His elders.[d]

Salvation and Judgment on That Day

25 •Yahweh, You are my God;[e]
I will exalt You. I will praise
Your name,
for You have accomplished wonders,
plans formed long ago,
with perfect faithfulness.
2 For You have turned the city into a pile
of rocks,[f]
a fortified city, into ruins;
the fortress of barbarians[g] is no longer
a city;

it will never be rebuilt.
3 Therefore, a strong people
will honor You.
The cities of violent nations
will •fear You.
4 For You have been a stronghold
for the poor,
a stronghold for the needy[h] person
in his distress,
a refuge from the rain, a shade
from the heat.[i]
When the breath of the violent
is like rain against a wall,
5 like heat in a dry land,
You subdue the uproar of barbarians.
As[A] the shade of a cloud cools the heat
of the day,
so He silences the song of the violent.
6 The LORD of •Hosts will prepare a feast[j]
for all the peoples
on this mountain[B,k]—
a feast of aged wine, choice meat,[c]
finely aged wine.
7 On this mountain
He will destroy the burial shroud,
the shroud over all the peoples,
the sheet covering all the nations;[l]
8 He will destroy death forever.[m]
The Lord GOD will wipe away the tears

a24:21 Is 27:12	
b24:22 Rv 20:1-3	
cRv 20:2	
d24:23 Is 2:2-4;	
1Co 15:54	
e25:1 Ex 15:2;	
Ps 118:28; Is	
7:13; 44:17	
f25:2 Is 17:1;	
26:5	
gCol 3:11	
h25:4 Mt 11:29	
iIs 4:6; 32:2	
j25:6 Is 24:23;	
Rv 19:9	
kIs 2:2-4	
l25:7 2Co 3:15-	
16; Eph 4:18	
m25:8 Hs 13:14;	
1Co 15:54; Rv	
21:4	

A25:5 Lit *In*   B25:6 = Mount Zion   C25:6 Lit *wine, fat full of marrow*

This judgment is connected to **rebellion** against God by virtually all people on earth.

24:21 The phrase **on that day** points to a future but unspecified time. God's judgment is extensive. It not only covers the earth but also the **host of heaven**, a phrase that either indicates the stars (perhaps also suggesting pagan deities) or fallen angels.

kaved

Hebrew Pronunciation	[kah VAID]
HCSB Translation	be heavy, honor
Uses in Isaiah	20
Uses in the OT	114
Focus Passage	Isaiah 25:3

Kaved, related to *kavod (glory)* and adjectival *kaved (heavy)*, means *be heavy* (Neh 5:18), *weigh, weigh down,* or *be heavily loaded.* One *receives honor* (Jb 14:21). Fighting *is fierce* or *intensifies.* Sin *is serious.* Ears *are deaf,* and eyesight *is poor.* The "hand *being heavy* on" (Ps 32:4) implies *getting the upper hand* or *severely oppressing.* Passive-reflexive verbs denote *be honored* or *glorified.* Something *is a burden.* Springs *are filled.* God reveals or *displays glory;* people *honor themselves* and *receive* or *enjoy glory.* Participles indicate *dignitaries* and signify *honored, important, high in rank, glorious,* or *highly respected.* The intensive verb means *honor* (Ex 20:12), *glorify, show respect for,* or *reward.* It is also *harden.* The causative verb involves *loading, heavily burdening, weighing down,* or *making heavy.* One *deafens* or *closes* ears and *hardens* hearts. God *brings honor,* and people *get glory.* The reflexive-passive verb signifies *act important* or *multiply oneself.*

24:23 Even the **moon** and **sun** will pale in comparison with the brilliant light emanating from God as He exercises His sovereign rule from the temple.

25:1 The prophet Isaiah is the first-person speaker (**I**) who praises God for His plan that includes judgment. His judgment is an example of **perfect faithfulness** because His covenant promised that punishment would follow rebellion.

25:2 The **city** described in this and the following verses is the same as the "city of chaos" of 24:10. It is not a specific place but a city that represents human evil.

25:3 Because of God's judgment of sin, even **people** who are **violent** will fear Him.

25:4-5 The **poor** and the **needy** are the antithesis of the powerful and proud inhabitants of the city that God has judged. God is their protection, not city walls or weapons. God's protection of the humble poor is illustrated by the image of **a refuge from the rain** and **a shade from the heat**. Violent people are the rain and the heat from which God provides protection for the vulnerable.

25:6 Feasting follows victory, and the Lord prepares a fine **feast** for His people. The **mountain** refers to the mountain of God's presence—Zion.

25:7-8 God not only conquers the evil nations, but **death** and sorrow (**tears**) and **disgrace**. The verb translated **destroy** is better rendered as "swallow." Here there is likely an allusion to the Baal myth of Ugarit where death swallowed the god Baal. Here Yahweh swallows death.

from every face[a]
and remove His people's disgrace[b]
from the whole earth,
for the Lord has spoken.

⁹ On that day it will be said,
"Look, this is our God;
we have waited for Him, and He has
saved us.
This is the Lord; we have waited
for Him.
Let us rejoice and be glad
in His salvation."[c]

¹⁰ For the Lord's power will rest
on this mountain.

But Moab[d] will be trampled
in his place[A]
as straw is trampled in a dung pile.

¹¹ He will spread out his arms
in the middle of it,
as a swimmer spreads out his arms
to swim.
His pride will be brought low,
along with the trickery of his hands.[e]

¹² The high-walled fortress
will be brought down,
thrown to the ground, to the dust.[f]

The Song of Judah

26 On that day this song will be sung in
the land of Judah:

We have a strong city.
Salvation is established as walls
and ramparts.[g]

² Open the gates
so a righteous nation can come in—

one that remains faithful.

³ You will keep the mind that is
dependent on You
in perfect peace,[h]
for it is trusting in You.

⁴ Trust in the Lord forever,
because in •Yah, the Lord, is
an everlasting rock![i]

⁵ For He has humbled those who live
in lofty places—
an inaccessible city.[j]
He brings it down; He brings it down
to the ground;
He throws it to the dust.

⁶ Feet trample it,
the feet of the humble,
the steps of the poor.

God's People Vindicated

⁷ The path of the righteous is level;[k]
You clear a straight path
for the righteous.

⁸ Yes, Yahweh, we wait for You
in the path of Your judgments.
Our desire is for Your name
and renown.[l]

⁹ I long for You in the night;[m]
yes, my spirit within me
diligently seeks You,
for when Your judgments are
in the land,
the inhabitants of the world
will learn righteousness.

¹⁰ But if the wicked man is
shown favor,
he does not learn righteousness.

Cross references

[a]25:8 Is 30:19; 35:10; 51:11; 65:19; Rv 7:17; 21:4
[b]Ps 89:50-51; Is 51:7; 54:4; Mt 5:11; 1Pt 4:14
[c]25:9 Is 35:1-2,10; 66:10
[d]25:10 Nm 24:17; Is 15:1
[e]25:11 Is 2:10-12,15-17; 16:6,14
[f]25:10-12 Is 26:5-6
[g]26:1 Is 60:18
[h]26:3 Is 26:12; 27:5; 57:19; 66:12
[i]26:4 Ps 73:26; Is 17:10; 30:29; 44:8
[j]26:5-6 Is 25:10-12
[k]26:7 Ps 27:11
[l]26:8 Ex 3:15
[m]26:9 Ps 77:2; 84:2; 119:20,81

[A]25:10 Or trampled under Him

25:9 On that day, see note at 24:21. **Salvation** indicates rescue from powerful, evil enemies.

25:10 The **mountain** is where God will make His presence known—Zion. Up to this point the nations have been referred to generically. Now **Moab**, a small nation east of the Dead Sea, becomes the subject of the oracle. Moab is a prime example of the sinful pride of the nations.

25:11 Continuing the image from the previous verse, Isaiah described Moab as swimming in dung.

26:1 The **strong city** contrasts with the "city of chaos" (see note at 24:10). That city represents human evil and has walls that crumble, but this city's strength (its **walls and ramparts**) is defined by **salvation**. Oswalt states that this city is "a state of mind more than a geographical place" (*Isaiah 1-39*, p. 297).

26:2 The **righteous nation** includes faithful Israelites but might also suggest other peoples as well, since the defining characteristic of the nation is that it **remains faithful** to God and His law.

26:3-4 Trust is the defining trait of those who depend on God (on **Yah**, see note at 12:2), not on other nations. The image

of the **everlasting rock** points to God's persistent protection of His people. The rock is one in which the faithful can find shelter (Ex 33:22).

26:5 The **inaccessible city**, like the "city of chaos" (see note at 24:10), represents the proud who do not humble themselves before God. Though it is called "inaccessible," God is able to defeat this city in spite of its pretensions.

26:6 Thanks to God's intervention, the **humble . . . poor** will trample on the arrogant.

26:7 The image of the **path** is drawn from wisdom literature (Pr 1-9) and stands for the course of a person's life. A level or straight path is a life with few problems (Heb 12:13).

26:8 In this verse Isaiah spoke on behalf of himself and the righteous as he expressed longing for God and specifically for God's coming judgment on the wicked. But even in the context of passionate desire for God, they did not demand His actions but expressed confidence (**we wait**).

26:9-10 People learn about **righteousness** when wickedness is punished. Otherwise, evil behavior is encouraged (Ec 8:11).

In a righteous land
    he acts unjustly
and does not see the majesty
    of the Lord.

11 Lord, Your hand is lifted up
    to take action,
but they do not see it.
They will see Your zeal for Your people,
    and they will be put to shame.
The fire for Your adversaries
    will consume them!
12 Lord, You will establish peace for us,
for You have also done all our work
    for us.
13 Yahweh our God, lords other than You
    have ruled over us,
but we remember Your name alone.ᵃ

14 The dead do not live;
departed spirits do not rise up.
Indeed, You have visited
    and destroyed them;
You have wiped out all memory
    of them.ᵇ
15 You have added to the nation, Lord.ᶜ
You have added to the nation;
    You are honored.
You have expanded all the borders
    of the land.ᵈ
16 Lord, they went to You
    in their distress;ᵉ
they poured out whispered prayers
because Your discipline fell on them.ᴬ
17 As a pregnant woman
    about to give birth
writhes and cries out in her pains,ᶠ
so we were before You, Lord.

18 We became pregnant, we writhed
    in pain;
we gave birth to wind.
We have won no victories on earth,
and the earth's inhabitants
    have not fallen.

19 Your dead will live; their bodiesᴮ
    will rise.ᵍ
Awake and sing, you who dwell
    in the dust!
For you will be covered
    with the morning dew,ᶜ
and the earth will bring out
    the departed spirits.

20 Go, my people, enter your rooms
    and close your doors behind you.
Hide for a little while until the wrath
    has passed.ʰ
21 For look, the Lord is coming
    from His placeⁱ
to punish the inhabitants of the earth
    for their iniquity.ʲ
The earth will reveal the blood shed
    on it
and will no longer conceal her slain.

Leviathan Slain

27 On that day the Lord with His harsh, great, and strong sword, will bring judgment on *Leviathan,ᵏ the fleeing serpent—Leviathan, the twisting serpent. He will slay the monster that is in the sea.ˡ

The Lord's Vineyard

2 On that day
    sing about a desirable vineyard:ᵐ

Cross references (center column):
ᵃ26:13 Jn 10:25
ᵇ26:14 Jb 18:17; Ps 9:6
ᶜ26:15 Is 9:3
ᵈIs 33:17; 54:2-3
ᵉ26:16 Is 37:3; Hs 5:15
ᶠ26:17 Is 13:8
ᵍ26:19 Is 25:8; Ezk 37:1-14; Dn 12:2; Hs 13:14; Mt 11:5; Lk 7:22; Jn 8:51
ʰ26:20 Is 10:5,25; 13:5; 34:2; 66:14
ⁱ26:21 Mc 1:3
ʲIs 13:11
ᵏ27:1 Jb 3:8; 41:1,34; Ps 74:14; 104:26
ˡIs 51:9
ᵐ27:2 Ps 80:8; Is 5:7; Jr 2:21

ᴬ26:16 Hb obscure   ᴮ26:19 Lit *live; my body they*   ᶜ26:19 Lit *For your dew is a dew of lights*

26:11 God's upraised **hand** is an image of the imminent judgment against the wicked.

26:12 Contrary to the fate of the wicked, God's righteous people will experience **peace**, not destruction. While it is hard to pinpoint the exact nature of the prophet's reference to God's **work**, it certainly includes the punishment of the wicked.

26:13 The faithful acknowledge that other **lords** have **ruled** over them. These would include the Assyrians and eventually the Babylonians and others. But for the faithful there is only one true ruler—God Himself.

26:14 A contrast exists between this statement and verse 19. In this verse, the wicked **dead** stay dead. God's judgment will not be reversed. A fuller understanding of the afterlife awaits the NT period (though it is anticipated in passages like Dn 12:2).

26:15 In contrast to the wicked whom He punishes, God blesses the righteous. In this verse His blessing takes the form of an expanded **land**, evoking the memory that God promised Abraham his descendants would become a "great nation" (Gn 12:2).

26:17-18 Turning from the future back to the present, God's people experienced suffering similar to the excruciating pain of a woman in labor. A pregnant woman goes through that pain with a positive result at the end—a baby. However, God's people went through the pain and simply passed gas (**gave birth to wind**). There was no deliverance, no victory over enemies.

26:19 In contrast to the wicked who die and stay dead (v. 14), God's people will **live** again. The **morning dew** is an image of freshness and renewal.

26:20-21 The call to **hide** during the judgment is reminiscent of the first Passover when God's people stayed in their homes while God took the lives of the Egyptian firstborn (Ex 12).

27:1 **On that day** refers to a future but unspecified time. **Leviathan** was well-known from ancient Canaanite mythology. Leviathan was a sea monster, representing chaos and evil in this verse. Childs says that Isaiah used this image to proclaim that God "will destroy not only historical forms of evil, but strike against its cosmic source once and for all" (*Isaiah*, p. 196).

3   I, *Yahweh, watch over it;
    I water it regularly.
    I guard it night and day
    so that no one disturbs it.
4   I am not angry,
    but if it produces thorns and briers[a]
        for Me,
    I will fight against it, trample it,
    and burn it to the ground.
5   Or let it take hold of My strength;
    let it make peace with Me—
    make peace with Me.
6   In days to come, Jacob will take root.[b]
    Israel will blossom and bloom[c]
    and fill the whole world with fruit.

7   Did the Lord strike Israel
    as He struck the one
        who struck Israel?[d]
    Was he killed like those killed
        by Him?
8   You disputed with her
    by banishing and driving her away.[A]
    He removed her
        with His severe storm
    on the day of the east wind.
9   Therefore Jacob's iniquity[e]
        will be purged in this way,
    and the result of the removal of his sin
        will be this:[f]
    when he makes all the altar stones
    like crushed bits of chalk,
    no *Asherah poles or incense altars
        will remain standing.
10 For the fortified city will be deserted,

pastures abandoned and forsaken
    like a wilderness.
Calves will graze there,
and there they will spread out and strip
    its branches.
11 When its branches dry out, they will be
    broken off.
Women will come and make fires
    with them,
for they are not a people
    with understanding.[g]
Therefore their Maker[h] will not
    have compassion on them,
and their Creator will not be gracious
    to them.

12 On that day[i]
    the Lord will thresh grain
        from the Euphrates River
    as far as the *Wadi of Egypt,[j]
    and you Israelites will be gathered
        one by one.
13 On that day
    a great trumpet[k] will be blown,
    and those lost in the land of Assyria
        will come,
    as well as those dispersed in the land
        of Egypt;
    and they will worship the Lord
    at Jerusalem on the holy mountain.

Woe to Samaria

28 Woe to the majestic crown
    of Ephraim's drunkards,[l]
    and to the fading flower
        of its beautiful splendor,

Cross references:
a 27:4 2Sm 23:6; Is 10:17
b 27:6 Is 37:31
c Is 35:1-2; Hs 14:5-6
d 27:7 Is 10:12,17; 30:31-33; 31:8-9; 37:36-38
e 27:9 Is 13:11
f Rm 11:27
g 27:11 Ps 32:9; 49:20; Jr 4:22
h Jb 4:17; Ps 95:6; Pr 14:31; Is 17:7; 29:16; 44:2; 45:9,11; 51:13; 54:5; Hs 8:14
i 27:12 Is 3:18; 7:18,20; 11:11; 24:21; Zch 12:8
j Gn 15:18
k 27:13 Lv 25:9; 1Ch 15:24; Mt 24:31; 1Th 4:16; Rv 11:15
l 28:1 Is 28:7; Hs 7:5

A 27:8 Hb obscure

27:2-6 The **desirable vineyard** is a metaphor for God's people. The poem has many contrasts with the vineyard song of 5:1-7. There the vineyard image is used to emphasize God's judgment on sin; here the vineyard image describes the restoration of His people after judgment.

27:4-5 In these verses the **thorns and briers** seem to represent rebellion against God—the type of behavior that led to judgment in the first place. The thorns and briers have two possible courses of action: they can experience the devastating punishment of God or they can **make peace** with Him.

27:6 The phrase **in days to come**, like "on that day" (see note at v. 1), refers to a future but unspecified time. The prophet Isaiah saw a prosperous future for God's people, one that would bring prosperity to the **whole world** (Gn 12:1-3).

27:7 God indeed will judge His people, but He will not annihilate them as He will do with those whom He uses to punish them (Assyria in the eighth century B.C. and Babylon in the sixth).

27:8 Rather than annihilating His people, God will scatter them. The image of a windy storm (the **east wind** was a particularly hot, dangerous wind coming off the desert) evokes the picture of chaff being blown away.

27:9 God's punishment of His people will be a cleansing (**will be purged**), a renewing, not a complete destruction. In particular, their idolatrous practices will be removed. On **Asherah poles** see note at 17:7-8.

27:10-11 The **fortified city**, like the "city of chaos" (see note at 24:10) and the "inaccessible city" (see note at 26:5), represents arrogant human evil. In the aftermath of God's judgment, this city will become grazing land.

27:12 On that day, see note at 24:21. The **Euphrates River** and the **Wadi of Egypt** were the far northern and southern boundaries of the promised land. The image of threshing **grain** is an image of refining judgment since the process separated the wheat from the chaff. But the aftermath of the punishment will bring a regathering of God's dispersed people.

27:13 On that day, see note at 24:21. The Israelites will come back for the purpose of worship. The **holy mountain** refers to Zion, the location of the temple.

28:1 Woe marks the beginning of an oracle connected to a funeral procession (see note at 1:4). This is the first woe in chapters 28-33 (29:1,15; 30:1; 31:1; 33:1). The effect of the oracle is to announce that the object of the oracle, in this case the northern kingdom of Israel (called by the name of

which is on the summit above
  the rich valley.
Woe to those overcome with wine.
2 Look, the Lord has a strong
  and mighty one[a]—
like a devastating hail storm,
like a storm with strong flooding waters.
He will bring it across the land
  with His hand.
3 The majestic crown
  of Ephraim's drunkards
will be trampled underfoot.
4 The fading flower
  of his beautiful splendor,
which is on the summit
  above the rich valley,
will be like a ripe fig
  before the summer harvest.[b]
Whoever sees it will swallow it
while it is still in his hand.
5 On that day
the LORD of 'Hosts will become a crown
  of beauty
and a diadem of splendor[c]
to the remnant of His people,
6 a spirit of justice
to the one who sits in judgment,[d]
and strength

to those who turn back the battle
  at the gate.
7 These also stagger because of wine
and stumble under the influence
  of beer:
priest and prophet stagger
  because of beer,
they are confused by wine.[e]
They stumble because of beer,
they are muddled in their visions,
they stumble in their judgments.
8 Indeed, all their tables are covered
  with vomit;
there is no place without a stench.
9 Who is he[A] trying to teach?
Who is he[A] trying to instruct?
Infants[B] just weaned from milk?
Babies[B] removed from the breast?
10 For he says: "Law after law, law after law,
line after line, line after line,
a little here, a little there."[C,D]
11 So He will speak to this people
with stammering speech
and in a foreign language.[f]
12 He had said to them:
"This is the place of rest,
let the weary rest;[g]

a28:2 Is 8:7; 40:10
b28:4 Hs 9:10; Mc 7:1; Nah 3:12
c28:5 Is 62:3
d28:6 1Kg 3:28; Is 11:2; 32:1,15-16; Jn 5:30
e28:7 Is 5:11,22; 9:15; 22:13; 56:12; Hs 4:11
f28:11-12 Is 5:26-29; 33:19; 1Co 14:21
g28:12 Is 11:10; 30:15; 32:17-18; Jr 6:16; Mt 11:28-29

A28:9 Or He   B28:9 Lit Those   C28:10 Hb obscure   D28:10 Perhaps the mockers of v. 9 are mimicking the prophet's words as baby talk.

its major tribe Ephraim), is as good as dead. The **majestic crown** of Ephraim may be a reference to its capital city Samaria, which sat atop a large hill overlooking the area. The reference to heavy drinking in the northern kingdom may be because of an abuse of alcohol in the region, particularly among its leaders, but this also fits with the prophetic theme of the cup of wrath (Jr 12). God will make the object of His anger drink from this cup so they will become disoriented and eventually pass out (see note at Is 19:14).

28:2 God's judgment is compared to the devastating effects

navel

Hebrew Pronunciation	[nah VALE]
HCSB Translation	wither, lose heart
Uses in Isaiah	11
Uses in the OT	20
Focus Passage	Isaiah 28:1,4

The fundamental idea of *navel* is *wither* (Is 1:30), but its earliest use was metaphorical. Moses will *wear out* if he tries to judge the people alone (Ex 18:18). Soldiers *lose heart* and surrender (2Sm 22:46). Mountains *crumble* (Jb 14:18), and the world itself *withers* and wastes away (Is 24:4). Eleven times *navel* refers to plants *withering* or flowers *fading* (Is 28:1), but usually in comparison with people or objects. Sinners *wither* (Is 64:6); the word of God does not (Is 40:8). The concept of decay is associated with *withering*, and the related noun *nevelah* (48x) signifies the *carcass* of an animal (Lv 5:2) or *corpse* of a person (Dt 21:23). It refers to dead *bodies* (Is 26:19). Sometimes *nevelah* signifies an *animal that dies naturally* (Lv 7:24). Once it conveys the *lifelessness* of idols (Jr 16:18).

of a **hail storm** and a flood. Joshua 10 recounts the time when God defeated a coalition of southern Canaanite city-states by pelting them with hailstones. The great flood (Gn 6–9) and the crossing of the Red Sea (Ex 14–15) illustrate how God used floodwaters to defeat His enemies.

28:3-4 Appealing again to the images of **crown** and **flower** from verse 1, the prophet describes the devastating punishment coming on Ephraim. He adds the picture of the **ripe fig** ready to be plucked and devoured.

28:5-6 On that day, see note at 24:21. While the majestic crown of Ephraim will be "trampled underfoot" (28:3), God Himself will become a **crown of beauty** for the remnant—for the righteous who survive the punishments to come and form the nucleus for a new people of God. Inspired by God, judges will again be just and soldiers will again have the strength to defend their city.

28:7-13 While verses 1–6 criticize the nobility for their drunken behavior, this section focuses on the priests and prophets.

28:7-8 The priests and prophets were crucial to the spiritual leadership of the nation, but here they had clouded their thought with drink. They had drunk so much alcohol that they were covered with **vomit**, an unflattering and undignified portrait of people who had such an important task.

28:9-10 These decadent leaders were acting as if they were teaching **babies** and not adults. The content of their teaching was mocked. What they said was repetitive and meaningless.

28:11-12 Since God's people had been so irresponsible, and

this is the place of repose."
But they would not listen.

13 Then the word of the LORD came
to them:
"Law after law, law after law,
line after line, line after line,
a little here, a little there,"^A,B
so they go stumbling backward,
to be broken, trapped, and captured.^a

A Deal with Death

14 Therefore hear the word of the LORD,^b
you mockers^c
who rule this people in Jerusalem.
15 For you said, "We have cut a deal
with Death,
and we have made an agreement
with •Sheol;
when the overwhelming scourge
passes through,^d
it will not touch us,
because we have made falsehood
our refuge
and have hidden behind treachery."
16 Therefore the Lord GOD said:
"Look, I have laid a stone^e in •Zion,
a tested stone,
a precious cornerstone,
a sure foundation;^f
the one who believes
will be unshakable.^C,g
17 And I will make justice
the measuring line
and righteousness the mason's level."^h

Hail will sweep away the false refuge,
and water will flood your hiding place.
18 Your deal with Death will be dissolved,
and your agreement with Sheol
will not last.
When the overwhelming scourge
passes through,
you will be trampled.
19 Every time it passes through,
it will carry you away;
it will pass through every morning—
every day and every night.
Only terror^i will cause you
to understand the message.^D
20 Indeed, the bed is too short
to stretch out on,
and its cover too small to wrap up in.
21 For the LORD will rise up as He did
at Mount Perazim.^j
He will rise in wrath, as at the Valley
of Gibeon,^k
to do His work, His strange work,
and to perform His task,
His disturbing task.
22 So now, do not mock,
or your shackles will become stronger.
Indeed, I have heard from the Lord GOD
of Hosts
a decree of destruction
for the whole land.^l

God's Wonderful Advice

23 Listen and hear my voice.
Pay attention and hear what I say.

Cross references: ^a 28:13 Is 8:15; Mt 21:44 ^b 28:14 Is 1:10; 39:5,8; 66:5 ^c Is 29:20 ^d 28:15 Is 8:7-8 ^e 28:16 Is 8:14; 26:4 ^f Mt 21:42; Mk 12:10; Lk 20:17; Ac 4:11; 1Co 3:11; Eph 2:20 ^g Rm 9:33; 1Pt 2:6 ^h 28:17 2Kg 21:13; Is 5:16; 30:18; 61:8; Am 7:7-9 ^i 28:19 2Ch 29:8; Jr 15:4; 24:9; 29:18 ^j 28:21 2Sm 5:20; 1Ch 14:11 ^k Jos 10:10,12; 2Sm 5:25; 1Ch 14:16 ^l 28:22 Is 10:22-23; Rm 9:27-28

^A 28:13 Hb obscure ^B 28:13 The LORD quotes the mockers' words in v. 10 to represent the unintelligible language of the Assyrian invaders. ^C 28:16 Lit will not hurry ^D 28:19 Or The understanding of the message will cause sheer terror

had refused to **rest** contentedly in God, He will speak to His people with **stammering speech** and in a **foreign language**—Akkadian, the language of the Assyrians.

28:14-22 The oracle now shifts its focus from the northern kingdom to the southern.

28:14 Mockers were those who did not fear God and who made fun of those who did (Pr 1:22; 9:7-8,12; 13:1).

28:15 The rulers of Judah had entered a dangerous agreement. The agreement is said to be with **Death** and **Sheol.** Sheol refers to the grave and in some contexts signifies the underworld. Isaiah probably referred to treaties with foreign nations to try to keep Assyria (**the overwhelming scourge**) from defeating them.

28:16 But it was not foreign alliances that made Judah strong. It was their relationship with God. He was the One who had built it, **cornerstone** and **foundation.** A precise identification of the **tested stone** is elusive. Goldingay (*Isaiah*, p. 156) remarks that the stone "has been identified with the law, the temple, the monarchy, the city, the saving work of Yahweh, the people's relationship with Yahweh, the true believing community, Zion itself, the Messiah, faith, the remnant, or the actual promise about the one who trusts." The allusion may be to all of the above.

28:17 God's standards are **justice** and **righteousness**—fair treatment of fellow citizens and trusting obedience. Both were lacking in Judah.

28:18 The dark pact with **Death** (see note at v. 15) is doomed to failure.

28:20 The arrangements that Judah had made to protect itself against Assyria were inadequate, like a **bed** that was **too short**.

28:21 At **Perazim** (described in 2Sm 5:20 as a "bursting flood") God gave David a great victory over the Philistines. At the **Valley of Gibeon,** God used hailstones to allow Joshua to defeat the southern coalition of Canaanite city-states (Jos 10:11). Though this oracle and many of Isaiah's oracles describe God's violent judgment against the nations, here it is called **strange** and **disturbing.** It was not the typical, normal, hoped-for mode of relationship, particularly with His covenant people.

28:22 Though God's judgment against the mocking leaders of Judah is certain, their future behavior will determine whether it becomes even worse (**your shackles will become stronger**).

28:23-29 In this section Isaiah drew an analogy between a farmer's task and God's treatment of Judah. Good results

24 Does the plowman plow every day
  to plant seed?
  Does he continuously break up
  and cultivate the soil?
25 When he has leveled its surface,
  does he not then scatter black cumin
  and sow cumin?
  He plants wheat in rows and barley
  in plots,
  with spelt as their border.
26 His God teaches him order;
  He instructs him.
27 Certainly black cumin is not threshed
  with a threshing board,
  and a cart wheel is not rolled
  over the cumin.
  But black cumin is beaten out
  with a stick,
  and cumin with a rod.
28 Bread grain is crushed,
  but is not threshed endlessly.
  Though the wheel
  of the farmer's cart rumbles,
  his horses do not crush it.
29 This also comes from the LORD
  of Hosts.
  He gives wonderful advice;
  He gives great wisdom.ᵃ

Woe to Jerusalem

29 Woe to Ariel,ᴬ Ariel,
  the city where David camped!ᵇ
  Continue year after year;
  let the festivals recur.
2 I will oppress Ariel,
  and there will be mourning and crying,
  and she will be to Me like an Ariel.ᴬ
3 I will camp in a circle around you;

---

*ᵃ*28:29 Is 9:6; Jr 32:19
*ᵇ*29:1 2Sm 5:9
*ᶜ*29:4 Is 8:19
*ᵈ*29:5 Is 17:13; 41:15-16
*ᵉ*Is 17:14; 30:13; 47:11; 1Th 5:3
*ᶠ*29:6 Ex 9:23; 19:16,19; 20:18; 1Sm 2:10; 12:18; Jb 40:9; Ps 77:18; Zch 14:5; Rv 4:5; 11:13
*ᵍ*29:7 Mc 4:11-12; Zch 12:9
*ʰ*Jb 20:8; Ps 73:20; Is 17:14

  I will besiege you with earth ramps,
  and I will set up my siege towers
  against you.
4 You will be brought down;
  you will speak from the ground,
  and your words will come from low
  in the dust.
  Your voice will be like that of a spirit
  from the ground;ᶜ
  your speech will whisper
  from the dust.
5 Your many foesᴮ will be like fine dust,ᵈ
  and many of the ruthless,
  like blowing chaff.
  Then suddenly, in an instant,ᵉ
6 you will be visited by the LORD
  of •Hosts
  with thunder, earthquake,
  and loud noise,
  storm, tempest, and a flame
  of consuming fire.ᶠ
7 All the many nationsᵍ
  going out to battle against Ariel—
  all the attackers, the siege works
  against her,
  and those who oppress her—
  will then be like a dream, a vision
  in the night.ʰ
8 It will be like a hungry one who dreams
  he is eating,
  then wakes and is still hungry;
  and like a thirsty one who dreams
  he is drinking,
  then wakes and is still thirsty,
  longing for water.
  So it will be for all the many nations
  who go to battle against Mount •Zion.

ᴬ29:1,2 Or *Altar Hearth*, or *Lion of God*; Hb obscure   ᴮ29:5 Lit *foreigners*

---

come from different actions and different methods applied at different times. The passage has the feel of a parable.

28:24-26 The farmer (**plowman**) does not just keep plowing, he also sows seed. He places the various seeds in their separate places. This **order** comes from God Himself.

28:27 Each plant has its proper treatment. The analogy may point to the fact that God exercises His judgment against sinners in a way that is appropriate to their specific situation.

28:28-29 But the crushing and threshing, images of judgment, are not endless activities. It comes to an end. Threshing and the cessation of threshing produce good bread, so judgment and its aftermath produce good results as well. The order of the farmer's task as well as God's "strange work" (v. 21) are a result of God's **great wisdom**.

29:1 **Ariel** stands for Jerusalem. What the word means is difficult to discern. It could mean "lion of God," but more likely it refers to "altar hearth," its meaning in Ezk 43:15 in reference to the hearth of the sanctuary. This chapter is a **woe** oracle (see note at 1:4) against Jerusalem. This is the

second woe presented in chapters 28–33 (28:1; 29:15; 30:1; 31:1; 33:1).

29:2 God will turn Jerusalem into an **Ariel**—an altar hearth. The meaning seems to be that He will destroy it by fire.

29:3 Though on a literal level it will be Assyria that will set up a siege around Jerusalem, the prophet knew that it would do so only as an agent of the Lord.

29:4 God speaks to Jerusalem in the second person (**you . . . your**) and thus personifies the city. He will kill Jerusalem, and it will be like a buried body (**speak from the ground**).

29:5-8 Suddenly the oracle shifts from judgment against Jerusalem to the restoration of the city. It imagines a situation like Sennacherib's campaign against Judah. His initial successes fizzled out at the siege of Jerusalem (chap. 37).

29:6 When God comes as warrior, He often takes the form of **storm . . . earthquake**, and **fire**.

29:8 Those armies that move against Jerusalem will ultimately be unsuccessful. Their early successes will give way to failure, so that their first actions will seem like a dream.

⁹ Stop and be astonished;
   blind yourselves and be blind!
  They are drunk,^A but not with wine;
   they stagger,^B but not with beer.^a
¹⁰ For the LORD has poured out on you
   an overwhelming urge to^c sleep;^b
  He has shut your eyes—the prophets,
   and covered your heads—the seers.^c

¹¹ For you the entire vision will be like the words of a sealed document.^d If it is given to one who can read and he is asked to read it,^D he will say, "I can't read it, because it is sealed." ¹²And if the document is given to one who cannot read and he is asked to read it,^E he will say, "I can't read."

¹³ The Lord said:

Because these people approach Me
   with their mouths^e
to honor Me with lip-service^F—
yet their hearts are far from Me,
and their worship consists of
   man-made rules
learned by rote—
¹⁴ therefore I will again confound
   these people
with wonder after wonder.^f
The wisdom of their wise men
   will vanish,^g
and the understanding of the perceptive
   will be hidden.

¹⁵ Woe to those who go to great lengths
   to hide their plans from the LORD.^h
  They do their works in darkness,

and say, "Who sees us?
   Who knows us?"^i
¹⁶ You have turned things around,
   as if the potter were the same
     as the clay.
  How can what is made say
   about its maker,
  "He didn't make me"?^j
  How can what is formed
  say about the one who formed it,
  "He doesn't understand
   what he's doing"?
¹⁷ Isn't it true that in just
     a little while
  Lebanon will become an orchard,
  and the orchard will seem
     like a forest?^k
¹⁸ On that day the deaf will hear^l
  the words of a document,
  and out of a deep darkness
  the eyes of the blind will see.
¹⁹ The humble will have joy
  after joy in the LORD,
  and the poor people will rejoice^m
  in the Holy One of Israel.^n
²⁰ For the ruthless one will vanish,
  the scorner will disappear,^o
  and all those who lie in wait
     with evil intent
  will be killed—
²¹ those who, with their speech,
  accuse a person of wrongdoing,
  who set a trap at the •gate
     for the mediator,

Cross references (center column):
^a 29:9 Lk 1:15
^b 29:10 Ps 69:23; Is 6:9-10; Mc 3:6
^c Rm 11:8
^d 29:11 Is 8:16; Dn 12:4,9; Mt 13:11; Rv 5:1
^e 29:13 Ezk 33:31; Mt 15:8-9; Mk 7:6-7
^f 29:14 Is 6:9-10; 28:21; 65:7; Hab 1:5
^g Is 44:25; Jr 8:9; 49:7; 1Co 1:19
^h 29:15 Ps 10:11,13; Is 28:15; 30:1
^i Jb 22:13; Is 57:12; Ezk 8:12
^j 29:16 Rm 9:20
^k 29:17 Ps 84:6; 107:33,35; Is 32:15
^l 29:18 Is 35:5; 42:18-19; 43:8; Mt 11:5; Mk 7:37
^m 29:19 Ps 69:32; Is 49:13
^n Is 1:4
^o 29:20 Is 28:14

---

^A 29:9 LXX, Tg, Vg read *Be drunk*   ^B 29:9 Tg, Vg read *wine; stagger*   ^C 29:10 Lit *you a spirit of*   ^D 29:11 Lit *If one gives it to one who knows the document, saying, "Read this, please"*   ^E 29:12 Lit *who does not know the document, saying, "Read this, please"*   ^F 29:13 Lit *their mouth and honor Me with its lips*

29:9-10 The oracle shifts again to the spiritual hardness and punishment of the people of God. They will **blind** themselves, but God will **shut** their **eyes**. They will get **drunk**, but God will give them an **overwhelming urge to sleep**. The oracle recognizes the people's sinful actions and God's sovereign control.

29:11-12 God has laid it all out for the people (**the entire vision**), but they were spiritually dull and could not make sense of it. They will not heed God's warnings and will suffer the consequences. In ancient Israel documents were written on papyrus or vellum scrolls. After being rolled into a tube, they were **sealed** with wax or clay, then stamped with an impression that identified the sender.

29:13 The **worship** of the people was empty and meaningless. They were just going through the motions.

29:15 A new **woe** oracle (see note at 1:4) begins with this verse and extends to the end of the chapter. This is the third woe presented in chapters 28–33 (v. 1; 28:1; 30:1; 31:1; 33:1). Those who did evil thought they could **hide** their actions from God. It may be that these plans included a decision to seek help against Assyria from Egypt. Such presumption would not go unpunished.

29:16 The metaphor of God as a **potter** is used in a few key places in prophetic literature (45:9; 64:8; Jr 18:1-12; see also Rm 9:21). It evokes the description of the creation of Adam from the dust of the ground (Gn 2:7). The prophets pointed out how crazy it was for God's creature, the pot made from clay, to challenge or question their Maker, the Potter.

29:17-24 As with the previous woe oracle, there is a shift in this oracle from judgment to hope (see note at vv. 5-8).

29:17 Lebanon was known for its cedar forests, but it will be transformed into an **orchard**—a place for fruit-bearing trees. The cedar is often used in the Bible as a symbol of power and arrogance, so perhaps the transformation has to do with a change from pride to humble service.

29:18 The coming transformation is also pictured as the **deaf** hearing and the **blind** seeing. The **document** probably is an allusion to verses 11-12. In those verses the document could not be understood, but here it could.

29:21 The **gate** of a walled city was where public hearings and judicial proceedings were held. The **mediator** was the person who heard a case. His removal would lead to injustice.

and without cause deprive
  the righteous of justice.ᵃ

²²Therefore, the LORD who redeemed Abraham*ᵇ* says this about the house of Jacob:

Jacob will no longer be ashamed
  and his face will no longer be pale.
²³ For when he sees his children,
  the work of My hands within his nation,
  they will honor My name,
  they will honor the Holy One of Jacobᶜ
  and stand in awe of the God of Israel.ᵈ
²⁴ Those who are confused
    will gain understanding,
  and those who grumble
    will accept instruction.

Condemnation of the Egyptian Alliance

30 Woe to the rebellious children!ᵉ
    This is the LORD's declaration.
They carry out a plan,ᶠ but not Mine;
they make an alliance,
but against My will,
piling sin on top of sin.
² They set out to go down to Egyptᵍ
  without asking My advice,
  in order to seek shelter
    under Pharaoh's protection
  and take refuge in Egypt's shadow.ʰ
³ But Pharaoh's protection will become
    your shame,
  and refuge in Egypt's shadow
    your disgrace.ⁱ

⁴ For though hisᴬ princes are at Zoanʲ
  and his messengers reach
    as far as Hanes,
⁵ everyone will be ashamed
  because of a people who can't help.
  They are of no benefit, they are no help;
  they are good for nothing but shame
    and reproach.ᵏ

⁶An •oracleˡ about the animals of the •Negev:ᴮ

Through a land of trouble and distress,
  of lioness and lion,
  of viper and flying serpent,ᵐ
they carry their wealth on the backs
    of donkeys
and their treasures on the humps
    of camels,
to a people who will not help them.
⁷ Egypt's help is completely worthless;
  therefore, I call her:
  •Rahab Who Just Sits.ⁿ

⁸ Go now, write it on a tablet
    in their presence
  and inscribe it on a scroll;
  it will be for the future,
  forever and ever.
⁹ They are a rebellious people,
  deceptive children,ᵒ
  children who do not want to obey
    the LORD's instruction.
¹⁰ They say to the seers, "Do not see,"
  and to the prophets,

ᵃ 29:21 Is 32:7; Am 5:10,12
ᵇ 29:22 Is 41:8; 51:2; 63:16
ᶜ 29:23 2Sm 23:1; Ps 24:6; 76:6; 114:7; Is 2:3
ᵈ Is 5:16; 8:13
ᵉ 30:1 Dt 21:18-21; Is 1:2,23; 30:9; 65:2
ᶠ Is 29:15
ᵍ 30:2 Is 31:1; Jr 43:7
ʰ Is 36:9
ⁱ 30:3 Is 20:5-6; 36:6; Jr 42:18,22
ʲ 30:4 Is 19:11
ᵏ 30:5 Jr 2:36
ˡ 30:6 Is 13:1
ᵐ Dt 8:15
ⁿ 30:7 Ps 87:4; 89:10; Is 51:9; Ezk 29:3,7
ᵒ 30:9 Is 30:1

ᴬ30:4 Or *Judah's*   ᴮ30:6 Or *Southland*

29:22 The oracle invokes the election of **Abraham** (Gn 12:1-3), the father of God's people. **Jacob** is another name for the nation of Israel.

29:23-24 God will fulfill His promise to Abraham and Jacob by transforming His people.

30:1 On **woe**, see note at 1:4. This is the fourth woe in chapters 28–33 (28:1; 29:1,15; 31:1; 33:1). The **rebellious children** were God's people who sought help from a foreign nation rather than from God Himself.

30:2 The plan was to form an alliance with **Egypt** to counter the Assyrian threat. **Shelter . . . protection**, and **shadow** imply the relationship with Egypt would not be as equal partners; God's people would be the junior partner. This arrangement involved the payment of annual tribute as well as the forfeiture of an independent foreign policy. The description of Egypt in this oracle fits with the time of King Hezekiah of Judah and may indicate the threat of an invasion by Sennacherib in 701 B.C.

30:3 The purpose of the foreign alliance was to protect Israel against an Assyrian invasion, but rather than preserving Israel's glory, it would lead to **shame** because Egypt was an unreliable ally.

30:4 Zoan was an important city (also known as Tanis), formerly a capital of Egypt, mentioned in this verse because it

was the residence of Pharaoh's wisest advisers (see note at 19:11). This is the only mention of **Hanes** in the Bible. According to extrabiblical sources, it "was an important regional capital" identified with Heracleopolis Magna (Walton, p. 621).

30:6 The **Negev** was the wilderness region south of the southern Israelite city of Beersheba. It was on the way to Egypt. Nomadic peoples and various animals such as those listed in the first part of this verse populated this area. The people who carried their **wealth on the backs of donkeys** describe those who took tribute to Egypt to buy protection against the Assyrian threat. Isaiah saw this as a waste of money.

30:7 In the book of Job, **Rahab** is a monster representing chaos, which is parallel to Leviathan (Jb 26:12-13), but the name is used here and elsewhere to refer to Egypt (Ps 87:4).

30:8 A record of the prophecy of destruction would demonstrate to future generations that it had been predicted.

30:9 On **rebellious people**, see note at verse 1. They did not obey God's **instruction**, which refers to His law and perhaps to His prohibition against entering into alliances with other nations.

30:10-11 People want to hear pleasant things, not the hard

"Do not prophesy the truth to us.
Tell us flattering things.[a]
Prophesy illusions.
11 Get out of the way!
Leave the pathway.
Rid us of the Holy One of Israel."[b]
12 Therefore the Holy One of Israel says:
"Because you have rejected this message
and have trusted in oppression
and deceit,
and have depended on them,
13 this iniquity[c] of yours will be
like a spreading breach,
a bulge in a high wall
whose collapse will come
in an instant—suddenly!
14 Its collapse will be like the shattering
of a potter's jar,[d] crushed to pieces,
so that not even a fragment of pottery
will be found among
its shattered remains—
no fragment large enough to take fire
from a hearth
or scoop water from a cistern."
15 For the Lord God, the Holy One
of Israel, has said:
"You will be delivered by returning
and resting;
your strength will lie in quiet confidence.
But you are not willing."
16 You say, "No!
We will escape on horses"—
therefore you will escape!—
and, "We will ride on fast horses"—

but those who pursue you will be faster.[e]
17 One thousand will flee at the threat
of one,[f]
at the threat of five you will flee,
until you alone remain
like a solitary pole on a mountaintop
or a banner on a hill.

The Lord's Mercy to Israel
18 Therefore the Lord is waiting
to show you mercy,
and is rising up
to show you compassion,[g]
for the Lord is a just God.
All who wait patiently for Him are happy.

19 For you people will live on *Zion in Jerusalem and will never cry again. He will show favor to you at the sound of your cry; when He hears, He will answer you. 20 The Lord will give you meager bread and water during oppression,[h] but your Teacher[A] will not hide Himself[B] any longer. Your eyes will see your Teacher,[A] 21 and whenever you turn to the right or to the left, your ears will hear this command behind you: "This is the way. Walk in it."[i] 22 Then you will defile your silver-plated idols and your gold-plated images. You will throw them away like menstrual cloths, and call them filth.

23 Then He will send rain for your seed that you have sown in the ground, and the food, the produce of the ground, will be rich and plentiful. On that day your cattle will graze in open pastures.[j] 24 The oxen and donkeys that work the ground will eat salted fodder

---

a 30:10 1Kg 22:8,13; Jr 6:14; 23:17,26; Ezk 13:8-16; Rm 16:18; 2Tm 4:3-4
b 30:11 Is 1:4; 41:14-20; 43:14; 45:11; 48:17; 49:7; 54:5; 55:5; 60:9,14
c 30:13 Is 13:11
d 30:14 Ps 2:9; Jr 19:10-11
e 30:16 Is 31:1,3
f 30:17 Lv 26:36; Dt 28:25; 32:30; Jos 23:10; Pr 28:1
g 30:18 2Pt 3:9
h 30:20 1Kg 22:27; Ps 80:5
i 30:21 Is 35:8-9
j 30:23 Ps 144:13; Is 32:20; Hs 4:16

---

things that prophets like Isaiah told them. True prophets warned them of coming judgment and urged them to restore their relationship with God, but they responded by declaring they wanted nothing to do with this God. The **Holy One of Israel** is one of Isaiah's favorite titles for God, appearing more than 25 times in his book. It emphasizes God's distaste for sin (see note at 1:4).

30:12-14 The people **rejected** the prophet's admonition to trust in God alone, and instead **trusted in oppression and deceit** by seeking the protection of Egypt. As a result, God will cause them to collapse. They thought that Egypt would be a **high wall** of protection against the Assyrians, but the wall had a huge crack. It would eventually be obliterated.

30:15-17 The healthy alternative was to relax and trust in God, but such an easy course was too hard for God's people to accept. The result of their refusal to listen to God is that they would flee from the threat of just a few of the enemy (Dt 32:30).

30:18-26 After the judgment described in this oracle, God would restore His people to His favor.

30:18 God was **waiting** for the people to repent before turning His judgment into **compassion** and restoration.

30:19 The **cry** of the people refers to their repentance, an

acknowledgment of their sin, and a turn to God for help. As a result, He would respond with His **favor**. They will live on **Zion in Jerusalem** near the presence of God. The beginning of the fulfillment of this promise occurred after the Jews began returning from Babylonian exile in 539 B.C.

30:20 The word **oppression** refers to the future exile and political oppression by foreign nations (Assyria, followed by Babylon, followed by Persia) that happened because of their sin. The **Teacher** of the people of God is a reference to God Himself who would show them the right way to behave.

30:21 Walking in the **way** is reminiscent of the language of Psalm 1 and Proverbs. There are two ways—a crooked path that represents an evil life heading toward death and the straight path of godliness that leads to life.

30:22 The spiritual transformation of the people of God involves moving toward the true God and away from false gods. **Menstrual cloths** were especially impure because a woman was considered unclean during her menstrual period (Lv 15:19-24).

30:23-24 Based on the lists of covenant blessings found in places like Deuteronomy 28, God will grant agricultural prosperity to His restored people. While they had nothing but bread and water (Is 30:20) during their oppression, they

scattered with winnowing shovel[a] and fork. [25] Streams flowing with water will be on every high mountain and every raised hill on the day of great slaughter when the towers fall. [26] The moonlight will be as bright as the sunlight, and the sunlight will be seven times brighter[b]—like the light of seven days—on the day[c] that the LORD bandages His people's injuries and heals the wounds He inflicted.[d]

Annihilation of the Assyrians

[27] Look, •Yahweh[A] comes from far away,
His anger burning and heavy
  with smoke.[B]
His lips are full of fury,
and His tongue is like a consuming fire.
[28] His breath is like an overflowing torrent[e]
that rises to the neck.[f]
He comes to sift the nations in a sieve
  of destruction
and to put a bridle on the jaws
  of the peoples
to lead them astray.[g]
[29] Your singing will be like that
on the night of a holy festival,
and your heart will rejoice
like one who walks to the music
  of a flute,
going up to the mountain of the LORD,
to the Rock of Israel.[h]
[30] And the LORD will make the splendor
  of His voice heard

and reveal His arm[i] striking in
  angry wrath
and a flame of consuming fire,
in driving rain, a torrent, and hailstones.
[31] Assyria will be shattered by the voice
  of the LORD.
He will strike with a rod.
[32] And every stroke of the appointed[c] staff
that the LORD brings down on him
will be to the sound of tambourines
  and lyres;
He will fight against him
  with brandished weapons.
[33] Indeed! •Topheth has been ready[j]
for the king for a long time now.
Its funeral pyre is deep and wide,
with plenty of fire and wood.
The breath of the LORD,[k] like a torrent
  of brimstone,
kindles it.

The LORD, the Only Help

31 Woe to those who go down
  to Egypt for help[l]
and who depend on horses!
They trust in the abundance of chariots
and in the large number of horsemen.[m]
They do not look[n] to the Holy One
  of Israel
and they do not seek the LORD's help.
[2] But He also is wise and brings disaster.[o]
He does not go back on what He says;[p]

Cross references (center column)
a 30:24 Mt 3:12
b 30:26 Is 24:23; 60:19-20; Rv 21:23; 22:5
c Mt 25:13
d Is 33:24; Jr 33:6; Hs 6:1-2
e 30:28 Is 11:4; 30:33; 2Th 2:8
f Is 8:8
g 2Kg 19:28; Is 37:29
h 30:29 Is 8:14; 26:4
i 30:30 Ex 6:6; Dt 4:34; Jb 40:9; Is 53:1; Jr 32:17; Ezk 20:33
j 30:33 2Kg 23:10; Jr 7:31; 19:6
k Is 40:7
l 31:1 Is 30:2,7; 36:6
m Dt 17:16; Ps 20:7; 33:17; Is 2:7; 30:16; 36:9
n Is 9:13; 17:7-8; Dn 9:13; Am 5:4-8
o 31:2 Is 45:7
p Nm 23:19; Is 22:14; Jr 44:29

A 30:27 Lit *the name Yahweh*   B 30:27 Hb obscure   C 30:32 Some Hb mss read *punishing*

---

would have large quantities of food in the future. Even the **oxen and donkeys** would have plenty of good food.

30:25 Israel's prosperity was normally tenuous because of limited water supplies. Here the picture is of overflowing waters. The reference to the **great slaughter** and the fall of **towers** is probably a reference to the downfall of their oppressors.

30:26 Not only will there be abundant food and water, but **light** as well. Light represents what is good and godly.

30:27-33 The oracle in these verses describes God's appearance as a judging warrior. The object of His wrath is not revealed until verse 31 where Assyria, the oppressor of God's people, is named.

30:27-28 God's anger is described in human terms as if He had **lips . . . tongue . . . breath**, and **neck**. He is hot with anger. He will take the wayward nations and **bridle** them as if they were a donkey or horse. Then He will guide them in the way He wants them to go.

30:29 The scene shifts to the people of God who will celebrate this act of God. The judgment of their enemies is a cause for rejoicing. They will praise God as if it were a **holy festival** like Passover or the Festival of Booths. The **mountain of the LORD** refers to Zion where God (their **Rock**, a title that signifies shelter and protection) will make His presence known.

30:30 God often uses weather as His weapons against the objects of His anger (see 28:21).

30:31 The **voice of the LORD** is powerful (Ps 29). **Assyria**, the region's superpower, will be punished.

30:32 The blows of weapons are compared to the beating of **tambourines**. Babylon was the **appointed staff** of God to bring down Assyria in the late seventh century B.C.

30:33 Topheth was located in the Valley of Ben Hinnom (Jr 7:30-34). This valley was immediately south and west of Jerusalem. At times, it functioned as a garbage heap for the city. In Greek, this valley was known as *Gehenna*, which became associated with hell. We do not know for certain what the word "Topheth" means or where it came from, but we do know that King Josiah had desecrated this place earlier during his religious reforms (2Kg 23:10-11). It had been a place where the foreign god Molech was worshiped. Jeremiah said it epitomized the sin and guilt of the people (Jr 7:30-32; 19:6-13). God explicitly had forbidden human sacrifice as well as the worship of Molech (Lv 18:21; Dt 12:31; 18:10; see also Is 57:5,9; Jr 19:5; 32:35; Ezk 16:20-21; 20:25-26,31; 23:37,39). Here though it is being used for a good purpose—the burning of the body of the king of Assyria after his defeat.

31:1 On **woe**, see note at 1:4. This is the fifth woe in chapters 28-33 (28:1; 29:1,15; 30:1; 33:1). The issue again is that God's people were trusting foreign nations (in this case Egypt) rather than God for help against their enemies (30:1-17). The "holy war" theme of the OT makes it clear that Israel's safety depended on God, not on the size of their army.

He will rise up against the house
  of wicked men
and against the allies of evildoers.
3 Egyptians are men, not God;
  their horses are flesh, not spirit.
When the LORD raises His hand
  to strike,
the helper will stumble
and the one who is helped will fall;
both will perish together.

4 For this is what the LORD said to me:

As a lion or young lion growls
  over its prey[a]
when a band of shepherds is called out
  against it,
and is not terrified by their shouting
or subdued by their noise,
so the LORD of •Hosts will come down
  to fight on Mount •Zion
and on its hill.[b]

5 Like hovering birds,
  so the LORD of Hosts
  will protect Jerusalem[c]—
by protecting it, He will rescue it,
by sparing it, He will deliver it.

6 Return to the One the Israelites have greatly rebelled against.[d] 7 For on that day, every
one of you will reject the silver and gold idols
that your own hands have sinfully made.[e]

8 Then Assyria will fall,
  but not by human sword;

a sword will devour him,
  but not one made by man.[f]
He will flee from the sword;
  his young men will be put
    to forced labor.[g]
9 His rock[A] will pass away
    because of fear,[h]
  and his officers will be afraid because of
    the signal flag.[i]

This is the LORD's declaration—whose fire is
in Zion and whose furnace is in Jerusalem.[j]

The Righteous Kingdom Announced

32 Indeed, a king will reign righteously,
     and rulers will rule justly.[k]
2 Each will be like a shelter
    from the wind,
  a refuge from the rain,[l]
  like streams of water[m] in a dry land
  and the shade of a massive rock
    in an arid land.
3 Then the eyes of those who see will not
    be closed,
  and the ears of those who hear
    will listen.[n]
4 The reckless mind will gain knowledge,
  and the stammering tongue[o]
    will speak clearly and fluently.
5 A fool will no longer be called a noble,[p]
  nor a scoundrel said to be important.
6 For a fool speaks foolishness
  and his mind plots iniquity.
He lives in a godless way

Cross references (center column)
a31:4 Nm 24:9; Hs 11:10; Am 3:8
b Is 42:13; Zch 12:8
c31:5 Dt 32:11; Ps 91:4
d31:6 Is 1:5; 59:13
e31:7 Is 2:20; 30:22
f31:8 Is 37:7,36-38
g Gn 49:15; Is 14:2
h31:9 Dt 32:31,37
i Is 5:26; 13:2; Jr 4:6,21; 51:12,27
j Lv 10:2; Is 10:17; 30:33
k32:1 Ps 72:1-4; Is 9:6-7; 11:4-5; Jr 23:5; Zch 9:9; 14:9
l32:2 Is 4:6; 25:4
m Is 30:25
n32:3 Is 29:18
o32:4 Is 33:19
p32:5 Ps 107:40; 118:9; 146:3

A31:9 Perhaps the Assyrian king

Examples include the battle of Jericho (Jos 7), Gideon's victory over the Midianites (Jdg 7–8) and countless other accounts (Ps 20:7).

31:2-3 Israel's attempt to get help from Egypt will backfire because God will cause both **helper** (Egypt) and **helped** (God's people) to be destroyed.

31:4-5 God is the only One who can protect His people. In these verses, Isaiah uses two images to describe God's protection. He is a fearless **lion** on behalf of Israel against the foreign armies (represented by the **shepherds** who try to fend Him off). He is also **hovering** over His people like **birds** hover over their prey. The point is that God will see to the deliverance of His people.

31:6-7 The restoration of God's people has two sides: returning to Him, which implies repentance, and rejecting false gods in the form of **silver and gold idols**.

31:8 God is the real reason **Assyria will fall**. He will use Babylon for this task, but God is the One who will give Babylon the victory.

31:9 Though the reference is unusual, the **rock** is probably a reference to the Assyrian king. A rock is something that provides shelter and protection, but in this case the rock will fail to provide defense. The **signal flag** is a reference to a battle standard used to rally troops. Zion's **fire** and Jerusalem's

furnace may be a reference to the altar fire (see the explanation of Ariel in note at 29:1), but in the context of judgment it may point to the fire that will come out of Jerusalem to destroy the attacking enemy.

32:1 Scholars are divided over whether the **king** who will **reign righteously** is a direct reference to the Messiah or whether it describes a historical king like Hezekiah or Josiah. Of course, the Messiah is the ideal king, and Hezekiah and Josiah were pale anticipations of the Messiah. The point is that the future will bring just leadership.

32:2 The benefits the people will experience because of their righteous leaders are described metaphorically. They are protection and provision in difficult circumstances.

32:3 Righteous rule will result in greater discernment among the subjects of the just king.

32:4-5 The Teacher in Ecclesiastes (Ec 10:16-17) pointed out how dangerous it is when a fool becomes a ruler; the world turns upside down. Here there may be a wordplay on **fool** (Hb nabal) and **noble** (Hb nadiv).

32:6 The book of Proverbs makes it clear that a **fool** is someone who rejects God and has a detrimental effect on the community. Here Isaiah claims that folly among the leadership leads to hunger and thirst.

and speaks falsely about the LORD.
He leaves the hungry empty
and deprives the thirsty of drink.[a]
7 The scoundrel's weapons
  are destructive;
he hatches plots to destroy the needy
  with lies,
even when the poor says what is right.
8 But a noble person plans noble things;
he stands up for noble causes.

9 Stand up, you complacent women;[b]
listen to me.
Pay attention to what I say,
you overconfident daughters.
10 In a little more than a year
you overconfident ones will shudder,
for the vintage will fail
and the harvest will not come.
11 Shudder, you complacent ones;
tremble, you overconfident ones!
Strip yourselves bare[c]
and put •sackcloth around your waists.
12 Beat your breasts in mourning[d]
for the delightful fields
  and the fruitful vines,[e]
13 for the ground of my people
growing thorns and briers,[f]
indeed, for every joyous house
  in the joyful city.
14 For the palace will be forsaken,
the busy city abandoned.
The hill and the watchtower
  will become
barren places forever,
the joy of wild donkeys,
and a pasture for flocks,
15 until the Spirit from heaven
is poured out on us.[g]

Then the desert will become
  an orchard,
and the orchard will seem
  like a forest.[h]
16 Then justice will inhabit
  the wilderness,
and righteousness will dwell
  in the orchard.
17 The result of righteousness
  will be peace;[i]
the effect of righteousness
will be quiet confidence forever.
18 Then my people will dwell
  in a peaceful place,
in safe and secure dwellings.
19 But hail will level the forest,[A,j]
and the city will sink into the depths.[k]
20 Those who sow seed are happy
beside abundant waters;[l]
they let ox and donkey range freely.[m]

The LORD Rises Up

33 Woe, you destroyer
  never destroyed,
you traitor never betrayed!
When you have finished destroying,
you will be destroyed.
When you have finished betraying,
they will betray you.[n]

2 LORD, be gracious to us! We wait
  for You.[o]
Be our strength every morning
and our salvation in time of trouble.[p]
3 The peoples flee
  at the thunderous noise;[q]
the nations scatter when You rise
  in Your majesty.
4 Your spoil will be gathered as locusts
  are gathered;

Cross references (center column)

a 32:6 Is 3:15; 10:2
b 32:9 Is 47:8; Am 6:1; Zph 2:15
c 32:11 Is 47:2-3
d 32:12 Nah 2:7
e Mk 14:25
f 32:13 Is 5:6; 7:23-25; 9:18; 27:4
g 32:15 Is 11:2; 44:3; 59:21; Ezk 39:29; Jl 2:28
h Is 29:17; 35:1-2
i 32:17 Ps 72:2-3; 85:8; 119:165; Is 2:4; Rm 14:17; Jms 3:18
j 32:19 Is 28:2,17; 30:30
k Is 24:10,12; 26:5; 27:10; 29:4
l 32:20 Nm 24:7; Ec 11:1; Is 30:23-24
m Is 30:24
n 33:1 2Kg 18:14-36; Is 17:14; 21:2
o 33:2 Is 25:9; 26:8
p Ex 15:2; Ps 28:8; Is 12:2; 17:10; 51:5
q 33:3 Is 17:13; 21:15

A 32:19 Hb obscure

32:9 The prophetic oracle now addresses the **women** in the community of the people of God. They also show pride in human resources rather than in the Lord. They are **complacent** and **overconfident**. For an earlier oracle against women, see note at 3:16–4:1.

32:10 It appears that the security of these women is in the abundant produce of the land, but Isaiah pointed out that this prosperity is temporary. In the next year wine (**vintage**) and crop production (**harvest**) will fail.

32:11-12 Tearing and removing one's clothes (**strip yourselves bare**) and replacing them with **sackcloth** along with beating one's breast were mourning customs. The oracle suggests the people should move directly into ritual mourning in anticipation of future judgment.

32:13 The land will produce **thorns and briers**, useless plants, instead of grains and vines. The idea is similar to the curse against Adam in Gn 3:18.

32:14 Not only will the fields be desolate and unproductive,

but so will the city of Jerusalem. It will be turned into the haunt of wild animals.

32:15 However, because of God (**the Spirit from heaven**) a miraculous transformation will take place in the future. What has been unproductive will produce fruit-bearing trees.

33:1 This is the sixth and final **woe** in chapters 28–33 (28:1; 29:1,15; 30:1; 31:1). The woe pronounces the destruction of a betrayer. Many interpreters believe the reference is to Sennacherib, whom King Hezekiah of Judah paid to back off from the siege of Jerusalem (chaps. 36–37). But others believe it is a general reference to the deception of the nations. They will receive their due.

33:2 Since the nations have let them down, God's people have no recourse but to **wait** for God to save them.

33:3-4 God will be victorious over Israel's enemies. **Locusts** are often symbols of a large destroying army (Jl 1; Nah 3:15-16).

people will swarm over it
    like an infestation of locusts.

5 The Lord is exalted, for He dwells
    on high;
He has filled •Zion with justice
    and righteousness.

6 There will be times of security
    for you—
a storehouse of salvation, wisdom,
    and knowledge.
The •fear of the Lord is Zion's treasure.ᵃ

7 Listen! Their warriors cry loudly
    in the streets;
the messengers of peace weep bitterly.ᵇ

8 The highways are deserted;
    travel has ceased.
An agreement has been broken,ᶜ
cities^A despised,
and human life disregarded.

9 The land mourns and withers;ᵈ
Lebanon is ashamed and decayed.
Sharon is like a desert;
Bashan and Carmel shake off
    their leaves.

10 "Now I will rise up,"ᵉ says the Lord.
"Now I will lift Myself up.
Now I will be exalted.

11 You will conceive chaff;ᶠ
you will give birth to stubble.
Your breath is fire that will
    consume you.

12 The peoples will be burned to ashes,

like thorns cut down and burned
    in a fire.

13 You who are far off, hear what
    I have done;
you who are near,ᵍ know My strength."

14 The sinners in Zion are afraid;
trembling seizes the ungodly:
"Who among us can dwell
    with a consuming fire?ʰ
Who among us can dwell with
    ever-burning flames?"

15 The one who lives righteously
and speaks rightly,ⁱ
who refuses gain from extortion,
whose hand never takes a bribe,
who stops his ears from listening
    to murderous plots^B
and shuts his eyes to avoid
    endorsing evil^C,ʲ—

16 he will dwell on the heights;
his refuge will be the rocky fortresses,
his food provided, his water assured.

17 Your eyes will see the King
    in His beauty;ᵏ
you will see a vast land.ˡ

18 Your mind will meditate
    on the past terror:
"Where is the accountant?^D
Where is the tribute collector?^E
Where is the one who spied out
    our defenses?"^F

ᵃ33:6 Is 11:2-3; Ac 9:31
ᵇ33:7 2Kg 18:18,37; Is 36:3,22
ᶜ33:8 2Kg 18:14-17; Is 24:5
ᵈ33:9 Is 3:26; 24:4; 29:2
ᵉ33:10 Ps 12:5; Is 2:19,21
ᶠ33:11 Ps 7:14; Is 26:18; 59:4; Jms 1:15
ᵍ33:13 Is 18:2; Eph 2:17
ʰ33:14 Is 30:27,30; 66:15; Heb 12:29
ⁱ33:15 Ps 15:2; 24:4; Is 58:6-11
ʲPs 119:37
ᵏ33:17 Is 6:5; 24:23; 33:21-22; Zch 9:9
ˡIs 54:2-3

---

^A33:8 DSS read *witnesses*   ^B33:15 Lit *to bloods*   ^C33:15 Lit *eyes from seeing evil*   ^D33:18 Lit *counter*   ^E33:18 Lit *weigher*
^F33:18 Lit *who counts towers*

33:6 Zion's **treasure** is not gold, silver, or weapons. Its treasure is the **fear of the Lord**. A relationship of dependence and trust leads to action by a warring God on behalf of His people (Pr 1:7).

33:7-13 This passage describes a future attack (perhaps Sennacherib's attack on Jerusalem in 701 B.C.; v. 1) as if it were happening in the present.

33:7 Diplomacy has broken down. The diplomats weep as **warriors** control the streets.

33:8 The **broken . . . agreement** may be a direct reference to the agreement that Sennacherib made to withdraw from Jerusalem after being paid tribute—a promise he did not honor. Since the army is on the brink of attack, all **travel has ceased**.

33:9 **Lebanon** was north of Israel. **Sharon**, the western foothills famous for its wild flowers, as well as **Bashan and Carmel** were known as lush regions. But because of conflict these areas are described as bare wilderness.

33:10 At this moment of tension, a time when Israel's abilities are insufficient, God will rise up. This shows He is about to make an appearance as a warrior. A number of psalms call on God to "rise up" to fight on behalf of the psalmist and his people (Pss 7; 17).

33:11-12 In spite of the efforts of the enemy army to win a

victory, they will achieve nothing productive. They **conceive** and **give birth**, not to life but to death, here represented by dead vegetation that is good for nothing (**chaff** and **stubble**).

33:13 God's warring activity will be a testimony to the whole world, both **near** and **far off**, of His **strength**.

33:14 The anticipation of such a powerful, judging God frightens sinners and causes everyone to ask, **Who . . . can dwell** with such a God? The question and the answer in the following verses are similar to Psalms 15 and 24, thought to be liturgies used by those entering the sacred space of the sanctuary.

33:15 Righteousness is described in this verse in relational terms. God will dwell with those who refrain from acts that exploit other people. The righteous person will avoid **extortion**, bribery, and murder.

33:16 The righteous will be protected and sustained by God.

33:17 The King is none other than God Himself (cp. v. 22; "the Lord is our King"). The picture of the **King in His beauty** looks to the future after the judgment and the destruction of the enemy when God's people will be restored.

33:18 In this glorious future, no longer will there be emissaries from the oppressive enemy to take the resources of the people of God (**accountant** and **tribute collector**) or

19 You will no longer see the barbarians,
a people whose speech is difficult
to comprehend—
who stammer in a language that is
not understood.[a]

20 Look at Zion, the city
of our festival times.
Your eyes will see Jerusalem,
a peaceful pasture,[b] a tent
that does not wander;
its tent pegs will not be pulled up
nor will any of its cords be loosened.[c]

21 For the majestic One, our LORD,
will be there,[d]
a place of rivers and broad streams
where ships that are rowed will not go,
and majestic vessels will not pass.[e]

22 For the LORD is our Judge,
the LORD is our lawgiver,[f]
the LORD is our King.
He will save us.[g]

23 Your ropes are slack;
they cannot hold the base of the mast
or spread out the flag.
Then abundant spoil will be divided,
the lame will plunder it,

24 and none there will say, "I am sick."
The people who dwell there
will be forgiven[h] their iniquity.[i]

The Judgment of the Nations

34 You nations, come here
and listen;
you peoples, pay attention![j]

Let the earth hear, and all that fills it,
the world and all that comes from it.[k]

2 The LORD is angry with all
the nations—
furious with all their armies.[l]
He will set them apart
for destruction,[m]
giving them over to slaughter.

3 Their slain will be thrown out,
and the stench of their corpses
will rise;[n]
the mountains will flow[A]
with their blood.[o]

4 All[B] the heavenly bodies[p] will dissolve.
The skies will roll up like a scroll,[q]
and their stars will all wither
as leaves wither on the vine,
and foliage on the fig tree.[r]

The Judgment of Edom

5 When My sword has drunk its fill[C,s]
in the heavens,
it will then come down on Edom[t]
and on the people I have ·set apart
for destruction.

6 The LORD's sword is covered with blood.
It drips with fat,
with the blood of lambs and goats,
with the fat of the kidneys of rams.[u]
For the LORD has a sacrifice in Bozrah,[v]
a great slaughter in the land of Edom.

a 33:19 Dt 28:49-50; Is 28:11; Jr 5:15
b 33:20 Ps 46:5; 125:1-2; Is 32:18
c Is 54:2
d 33:21 Rm 8:31
e Is 41:18; 43:19-20; 48:18; 66:12
f 33:22 Is 1:10; 51:4,7; Jms 4:12
g 2Sm 22:3; 23:5; 2Kg 19:19,34; Is 25:9; 35:4; 38:20
h 33:24 Is 40:2; 44:22; Jr 50:20; Mc 7:18-19; 1Jn 1:7-9
i Is 13:11
j 34:1 Ps 49:1; Is 1:2; 41:1; 43:9; 45:20
k Ps 24:1; Is 6:3; 42:5
l 34:2 Is 13:5; Jr 10:10; 50:13
m Jos 6:21; 1Sm 15:3; Is 11:5; 24:1,6; 43:28
n 34:3 Is 14:21; 18:6; Ezk 39:17; Jl 2:10; Am 4:10; Rv 19:17-19
o Ps 46:2-3
p 34:4 2Kg 17:16; 21:3,5; 23:4-5
q Rv 6:12-14
r Ps 102:25-27; Is 13:10; 51:6; Ezk 32:7-8; Jl 3:15; Mt 24:29; Mk 13:24-25; 2Pt 3:10,12
s 34:5 Dt 32:41-43; Jr 46:10; Ezk 21:3-5
t Nm 20:14-21; Is 63:1; Jr 49:7-8,20; Ezk 25:12-14;
35:1-15; Jl 3:19; Am 1:11-12; Ob 1-14; Mal 1:4
30:32; Jr 46:10; 51:40; Ezk 39:17; Zph 1:7-9
u 34:6 Is 25:6;
v Gn 36:33; Is 63:1; Jr 49:13,22

A 34:3 Or melt, or dissolve   B 34:4 DSS read And the valleys will be split, and all   C 34:5 DSS read sword will appear

---

those who try to prepare for battle against them (**the one who spied out our defenses**).

33:19 The **barbarians** at the end of the eighth century were the Assyrians, who spoke a **language** (Akkadian) that the people of God could not understand. They destroyed the northern kingdom and subjected the south to vassalage and threatened their existence.

33:20-21 Describing Jerusalem as a **tent** may be a way of emphasizing the fragility of the city. A tent is easy to pull down or destroy. However, since God will be for them, this tent will not move. To describe **Zion** as a place of **rivers and broad streams** is to paint a picture of future blessing since Jerusalem had nothing of the kind. The prevention of shipping in these rivers may refer to war vessels.

33:22 God is **Judge . . . lawgiver**, and **King**, offices that provide internal and external stability and security.

33:23 It appears that the oracle changes the addressee. **Your** must refer to the enemy who tries to capture the people of God. The ship imagery (**ropes . . . base of the mast**) may point to those ships (v. 21) that try to assail Zion. But rather than taking plunder away, even the lame among the people of God will receive a portion.

33:24 The change from judgment to salvation for the people

of God takes place for one reason: they will be **forgiven their iniquity**.

34:1 God is not just the God of Israel. He is the God of the whole **world**, so He calls on all the **nations** to **hear** Him when He speaks.

34:2-3 God's anger is directed toward the armies of the **nations**. While He used some of them for His own purposes, they were only thinking of their desires for empire. Not only will they be defeated and killed, but they will suffer indignities such as lack of burial.

34:4 God's warring activity has cosmic implications. The nations thought of the **stars** as representing their gods. This language points to the fact that their gods, who are not gods at all, will suffer defeat at the hands of the true God.

34:5 Victory over heavenly forces (v. 4) is followed by a description of one representative nation, **Edom**. This nation was south of Moab in the region southeast of the Dead Sea. **Set apart for destruction** translates a single Hebrew verb (cherem) that is used frequently in Joshua to indicate that every man, woman, and child would be killed. It also describes the death of the enemy as a type of sacrifice to God.

34:6-7 The language of **sacrifice** is explicit in these verses. **Bozrah** was the capital of ancient Edom.

7 The wild oxen will be struck[A] down
       with them,
   and young bulls with the mighty bulls.
   Their land will be soaked with[B] blood,
   and their soil will be saturated with fat.

8 For the Lord has a day of vengeance,[a]
   a time of paying back Edom
   for its hostility against •Zion.
9 Edom's streams will be turned
       into pitch,
   her soil into sulfur;[b]
   her land will become burning pitch.
10 It will never go out—day or night.
   Its smoke will go up forever.[c]
   It will be desolate, from generation
       to generation;
   no one will pass through it forever
       and ever.[d]
11 The desert owl[C] and the screech owl[D]
       will possess it,
   and the great owl and the raven
       will dwell there.[e]
   The Lord will stretch out
       a measuring line
   and a plumb line over her
   for her destruction and chaos.[f]
12 No nobles will be left to proclaim
       a king,
   and all her princes will come
       to nothing.
13 Her palaces will be overgrown
       with thorns;
   her fortified cities, with thistles
       and briers.[g]

Reference column:
[a]34:8 Is 13:6; 35:4; 47:3; 61:2; 63:4
[b]34:9 Gn 19:24; Dt 29:23; Ps 11:6; Is 30:33; Ezk 38:22
[c]34:10 Is 1:31; 66:24; Rv 14:11; 19:3
[d]Is 13:20-22; Ezk 29:11; Mal 1:3-4
[e]34:11 Is 13:21-22; 14:23; Zph 2:14
[f]2Kg 21:13; Is 24:10; Lm 2:8
[g]34:13 Is 32:13
[h]Ps 44:19; Is 13:22; Jr 9:11; 10:22; Mal 1:3
[i]34:15 Dt 14:13
[j]34:16 Ps 40:7; 139:16; Is 8:16; 30:8; Dn 7:10; Mal 3:16; Rv 20:12
[k]34:17 Nm 24:18
[l]35:1 Ps 65:12; Is 6:11; 7:21-25; 27:10; 32:15; 41:18-19; 51:3; 55:12-13

   She will become a dwelling for jackals,
   an abode[E] for ostriches.[h]
14 The desert creatures will meet hyenas,
   and one wild goat will call to another.
   Indeed, the screech owl will stay there
   and will find a resting place for herself.
15 The sand partridge[F] will make
       her nest there;
   she will lay and hatch her eggs
   and will gather her brood
       under her shadow.
   Indeed, the birds of prey
       will gather there,
   each with its mate.[i]
16 Search and read the scroll of the Lord:[j]
   Not one of them will be missing,
   none will be lacking its mate,
   because He has ordered it
       by my[G] mouth,
   and He will gather them by His Spirit.
17 He has ordained a lot for them;
   His hand allotted their portion
       with a measuring line.
   They will possess it forever;[k]
   they will dwell in it from generation
       to generation.

The Ransomed Return to Zion

35 The wilderness and the dry land
       will be glad;
   the desert will rejoice and blossom
       like a rose.[H,l]
2 It will blossom abundantly
   and will also rejoice with joy
       and singing.

[A]34:7 Or will go [B]34:7 Or will drink its fill of [C]34:11 Or The pelican [D]34:11 Or the hedgehog [E]34:13 DSS, LXX, Syr, Tg; MT reads jackals, grass [F]34:15 Or The arrow snake, or The owl [G]34:16 Some Hb mss; other Hb mss, DSS, Syr, Tg read His [H]35:1 Or meadow saffron [l]35:1 Not the modern flower but a common wildflower in northern Israel

34:8 Edom had a reputation for taking advantage of Israel whenever Israel was weak (Ps 137:7; Lm 4:22; Ezk 35:15; Ob 10-14).

34:9-10 God would punish Edom with the same type of punishment (**pitch . . . sulfur . . . burning pitch**) that He had brought against Sodom and Gomorrah (Gn 19:24-28), though those cities are not explicitly mentioned. Earlier Isaiah had described the punishment on God's people as devastating but not as bad as that on Sodom (Is 1:9). In the oracle against Babylon, though, its punishment is said to be equivalent (13:19). Interestingly, Jeremiah used similar language in his oracle against Edom (Jr 49:7-22), linking its destruction to those infamous cities (Jr 49:18).

34:11 This verse describes animals that lived in ruins and desolate places. The **owl** was considered unclean (Lv 11:15-16). For similar use of the word in contexts of judgment, see Is 34:13; Jr 50:38; Mc 1:8. God's judgment will be premeditated and extensive. While the **measuring line** and **plumb line** were normally used in construction, God will use them to plan for the destruction of Edom.

34:12 Edom's kingship was ancient, preceding that of Israel

(Gn 36:31-43), but God will bring that institution to an end since He is bringing the nation itself to a close.

34:13-15 The theme of this verse is that of a city becoming a wilderness. Not only will the public buildings of the nation be **overgrown** out of neglect, but wild animals—a number of which were considered unclean (Lv 15)—will make their homes among the ruins.

34:16-17 The meaning of the **scroll of the Lord** is unknown. It may be a reference to a heavenly scroll, but if so, it is hard to know how the hearer could refer to this document. The appeal to the scroll could be a rhetorical device to emphasize the certainty of Edom's destruction and its transformation into a haunt for wild animals.

35:1-10 This chapter is a mirror image of chapter 34 where God announced that He would turn the nations into a wilderness. In chapter 35, He proclaimed that He would transform the people of God from a wilderness into a garden. The principle of both chapters is that God's people should trust Him, not the nations.

35:2 Lebanon . . . Carmel, and **Sharon** were regions especially lush in vegetation (33:9).

The glory of Lebanon will be given to it,
the splendor of Carmel and Sharon.[a]
They will see the glory of the LORD,[b]
the splendor of our God.[c]
3 Strengthen the weak hands,
steady the shaking knees![d]
4 Say to the cowardly:
"Be strong; do not fear!
Here is your God; vengeance is coming.[e]
God's retribution is coming; He will
save you."[f]
5 Then the eyes of the blind
will be opened,
and the ears of the deaf unstopped.[g]
6 Then the lame will leap like a deer,[h]
and the tongue of the mute will sing
for joy,[i]
for water will gush in the wilderness,
and streams in the desert;[j]
7 the parched ground will become a pool
of water,
and the thirsty land springs of water.[k]
In the haunt of jackals,[l] in their lairs,
there will be grass, reeds, and papyrus.
8 A road will be there and a way;[m]
it will be called the Holy Way.[n]
The •unclean will not travel on it,[o]
but it will be for the one who walks
the path.[p]
Even the fool will not go astray.
9 There will be no lion there,
and no vicious beast will go up on it;
they will not be found there.
But the redeemed will walk on it,
10 and the redeemed of the LORD
will return[q]
and come to •Zion with singing,
crowned with unending joy.
Joy and gladness will overtake them,
and sorrow and sighing will flee.[r]

Sennacherib's Invasion

36 In the fourteenth year of King Hezekiah,[s] Sennacherib king of Assyria
attacked all the fortified cities of Judah and
captured them. 2 Then the king of Assyria sent
the •Rabshakeh, along with a massive army,
from Lachish[t] to King Hezekiah at Jerusalem.
The Assyrian stood near the conduit of the
upper pool, by the road to the Fuller's Field.[u]
3 Eliakim son of Hilkiah, who was in charge of
the palace, Shebna the court secretary,[v] and
Joah son of Asaph, the court historian, came
out to him.
4 The Rabshakeh said to them, "Tell Hezekiah:

The great king, the king of Assyria, says
this: What are you relying on?[A] 5 I[B] say
that your strategy and military preparedness are mere words. What are you now
relying on that you have rebelled against
me?[w] 6 Look, you are trusting in Egypt,
that splintered reed of a staff[x] that will

[a] 35:2 Sg 2:1; 5:15; 7:5; Is 33:9 [b] Ex 16:7,10; Lv 9:6,23; Nm 29:6; Is 40:5; Ezk 1:28; 3:23 [c] Ps 45:3-4; 96:6; 104:1; 145:5,12; Is 2:10,19,21; 53:2; 63:1; Ezk 16:14 [d] 35:3 Heb 12:12 [e] 35:4 Is 1:24; 34:8; 47:3; 59:17; 61:2; 63:4 [f] Is 33:22 [g] 35:5 Is 29:18; 32:3-4; 42:7,16,18; 50:4; Mt 11:5; Lk 7:22; Jn 9:6-7 [h] 35:6 Zph 3:19; Mt 11:5; 15:30-31; 21:14; Ac 3:1-8; 8:7; 14:8-10 [i] Ex 4:11; Mk 7:32; 9:25 [j] Is 41:18; 43:19; Jn 7:38-39 [k] 35:7 Is 49:10 [l] Is 13:22; 34:13 [m] 35:8 Is 40:3; 42:16; 43:16,19; 49:11; 51:10; 57:14; 62:10 [n] Is 4:3; 52:1; Mt 7:13-14; 1Pt 1:15-16 [o] Is 52:1; Rv 21:27 [p] Ps 139:24; Is 2:3; 8:11; 30:21; 42:24; 48:17; 58:13 [q] 35:10 Is 51:11 [r] Is 65:19; Rm 9:2; Rv 21:4 [s] 36:1-22 2Kg 18:13,17-37; 2Ch 32:1-16,18

[t] 36:2 Jos 15:20,39 [u] Is 7:3 [v] 36:3 Is 22:15,20-21 [w] 36:5 2Kg 18:7 [x] 36:6 Ezk 29:6-7

[A] 36:4 Lit *What is this trust that you trust* [B] 36:5 DSS read *You*

35:3-4 God will save His people from the godless nations that oppress them. **God's retribution** refers to the punishment due the wicked and the reward due the righteous. For this reason, the latter can be **strong** and not fearful.

35:5-7 God's work transforms those who are **blind . . . deaf . . . lame**, and **mute**. Elsewhere in Isaiah these physical disabilities are metaphors for spiritual shortcomings (29:18; 42:18-19; 43:8). They have been physically dead to godliness, but in the future they will come alive. Not only will the lame walk, but they will **leap like a deer**. Not only will the mute speak, but they will **sing for joy**. A similar transformation is described with the language of nature. The **parched ground** will flow with water. Land that was only suitable for wilderness animals like **jackals** will be verdant.

35:8 Israel, with its deep wadis and mountainous terrain, was a hard land to cross, but Isaiah foresaw a **road**. This road will be the **Holy Way**, a name indicating that it would provide access to God. While the **unclean** would not travel on it since it led to the presence of a holy God, even the **fool** would not get lost if he seeks to walk this **path**.

35:9-10 The road described in verse 8 will be a safe road, and it will lead to **Zion**, where God makes His presence known to His people.

36:1 The year was 701 B.C. The Assyrians had defeated the northern kingdom of Israel in 722 B.C. and put Judah in a position where they had to pay annual tribute to keep the Assyrians from attacking them. In 703 B.C. **Sennacherib** succeeded his father Sargon on the throne of Assyria. Many nations, including Judah, seized upon this succession in leadership as an opportunity to rebel against Assyria. After taking care of rebellions in other parts of his empire, Sennacherib turned his attention to Judah in 701 B.C. He easily took many of the smaller **fortified cities** on the way to Jerusalem. For accounts of this confrontation, see 2Kg 18–19 and 2Ch 32.

36:2 **Lachish** was an important garrison city about 30 miles west of Jerusalem. Along with other cities, it guarded the road that led to Jerusalem. The king of Assyria, along with his armies, was still at Lachish when he sent one of his chief officials, the **Rabshakeh** (perhaps a Hebrew representation of an Akkadian title "chief cupbearer"), to present an ultimatum to Jerusalem. The Rabshakeh stood at the same place where Isaiah had confronted Ahaz at an earlier time (7:3). This reminds the reader that the earlier Judean king was told not to trust the Assyrians, but Ahaz did not heed this advice, and this led to the present situation.

36:3 **Eliakim . . . Shebna**, and **Joah** were high-ranking Judean officials who negotiated on behalf of King Hezekiah. On Shebna and Eliakim, see note at 22:15-25.

36:4-5 The purpose of the Rabshakeh's speech was to try to get **Hezekiah** to surrender. He questioned the basis of Hezekiah's refusal by trying to undermine the foundations of his confidence. He first questioned whether the people of Judah were militarily prepared to counter the Assyrian threat.

36:6 The Rabshakeh then undermined any confidence the

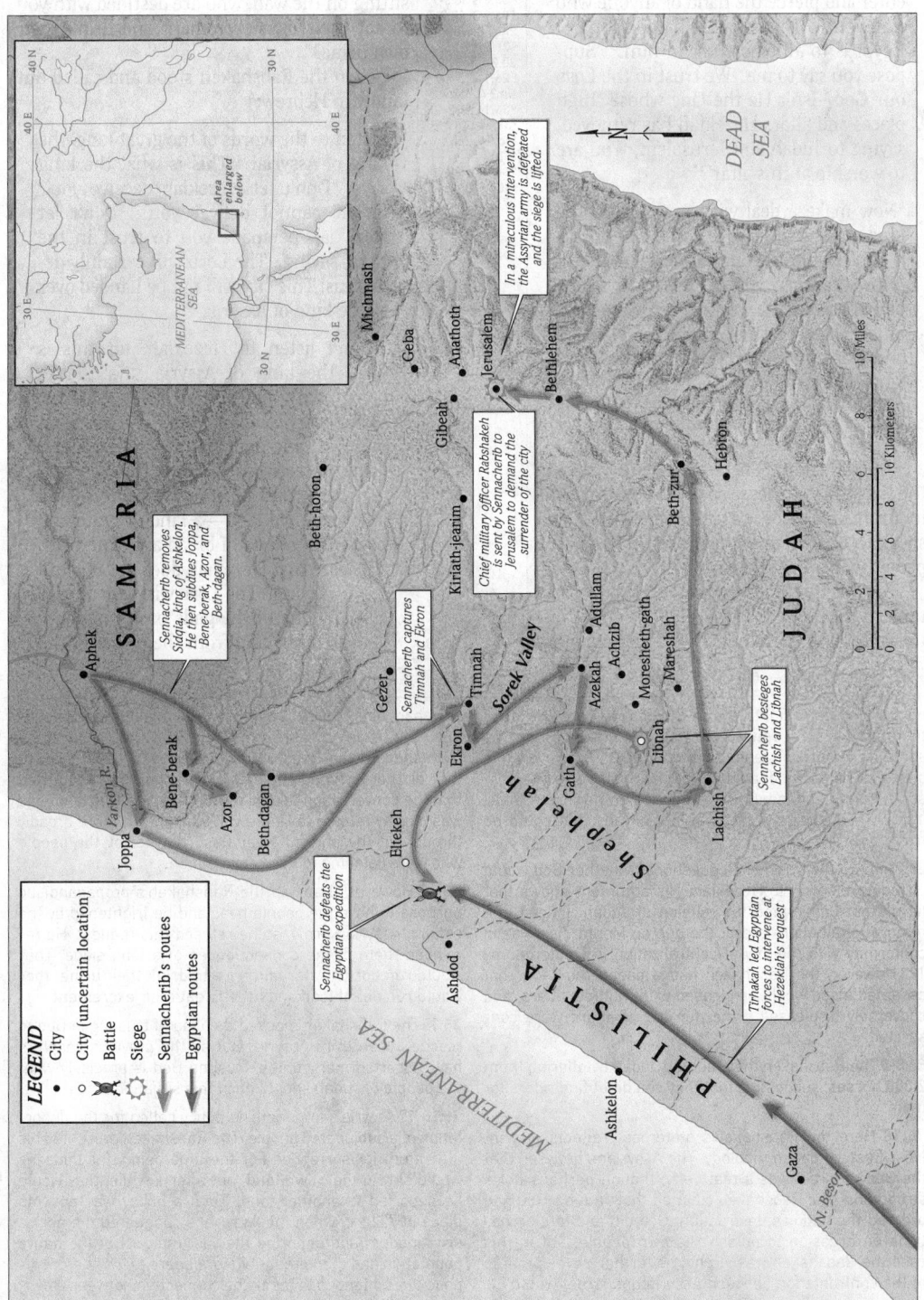

Sennacherib's Campaign Against Judah

LEGEND
- City
- City (uncertain location)
- Battle
- Siege
- Sennacherib's routes
- Egyptian routes

MEDITERRANEAN SEA

PHILISTIA

SAMARIA

JUDAH

Shephelah

Sorek Valley

DEAD SEA

N

Gaza

Ashkelon

Ashdod

Joppa

Azor

Bene-berak

Beth-dagan

Aphek

Yarkon R.

N. Besor

Eltekeh

Gezer

Ekron

Timnah

Gath

Libnah

Lachish

Azekah

Adullam

Achzib

Moresheth-gath

Mareshah

Kiriath-jearim

Gibeah

Geba

Michmash

Anathoth

Jerusalem

Bethlehem

Beth-zur

Hebron

Beth-horon

Sennacherib removes Sidqia, king of Ashkelon. He then subdues Joppa, Bene-berak, Azor, and Beth-dagan.

Sennacherib captures Timnah and Ekron

Chief military officer Rabshakeh is sent by Sennacherib to Jerusalem to demand the surrender of the city

In a miraculous intervention, the Assyrian army is defeated and the siege is lifted.

Sennacherib besieges Lachish and Libnah

Sennacherib defeats the Egyptian expedition

Tirhakah led Egyptian forces to intervene at Hezekiah's request

MEDITERRANEAN SEA

Area enlarged below

40 N

30 N

40 E

30 E

10 Miles

10 Kilometers

enter and pierce the hand of anyone who leans on it. This is how Pharaoh king of Egypt is to all who trust in him.[a] ⁷Suppose you say to me, 'We trust in the LORD our God.' Isn't He the One whose •high places and altars Hezekiah has removed, saying to Judah and Jerusalem, 'You are to worship at this altar'?[b]

⁸Now make a deal with my master, the king of Assyria. I'll give you 2,000 horses if you're able to supply riders for them! ⁹How then can you drive back a single officer among the weakest of my master's officers and trust in Egypt for chariots and horsemen?[c] ¹⁰Have I attacked this land to destroy it without the LORD's approval? The LORD said to me, 'Attack this land and destroy it.'"

¹¹Then Eliakim, Shebna, and Joah said to the Rabshakeh, "Please speak to your servants in Aramaic,[d] since we understand it. Don't speak to us in Hebrew[A] within earshot of the people who are on the wall."

¹²But the Rabshakeh replied, "Has my master sent me to speak these words to your master and to you, and not to the men who are

ᵃ36:6 Is 30:3-7
ᵇ36:7 Dt 12:2-5;
2Kg 18:4-5
ᶜ36:9 Is 20:5;
30:2-5,7; 31:3
ᵈ36:11 Ezr 4:7;
Dn 2:4
ᵉ36:14 Is 37:10
ᶠ36:16 1Kg 4:25;
Mc 4:4; Zch
3:10
ᵍ36:18 Is 37:10
ʰ1Ch 5:25; Is
37:12

sitting on the wall, who are destined with you to eat their own excrement and drink their own urine?"

¹³Then the Rabshakeh stood and called out loudly in Hebrew:[A]

Listen to the words of the great king, the king of Assyria! ¹⁴This is what the king says: "Don't let Hezekiah deceive you,[e] for he cannot deliver you. ¹⁵Don't let Hezekiah persuade you to trust in the LORD, saying, 'The LORD will certainly deliver us! This city will not be handed over to the king of Assyria.'"

¹⁶Don't listen to Hezekiah, for this is what the king of Assyria says: "Make peace[B] with me and surrender to me. Then every one of you may eat from his own vine and his own fig tree[f] and drink water from his own cistern ¹⁷until I come and take you away to a land like your own land—a land of grain and new wine, a land of bread and vineyards. ¹⁸Beware that Hezekiah does not mislead you by saying, 'The LORD will deliver us.'[g] Has any one of the gods of the nations[h] delivered his land from the power of the

---

A36:11,13 Lit *Judahite*   B36:16 Lit *a blessing*

---

nation of Judah might have in **Egypt** as an ally. He used the metaphor of a **splintered reed of a staff**. A staff was something a person leaned on for support. However, this staff was made out of a reed that could not support a person's weight. Indeed, God through Isaiah had been making the same point. Egypt was not an ally that could be trusted.

36:7 Finally, the Rabshakeh questioned whether God would provide protection to **Hezekiah**. His argument shows that he did not understand the religion of Judah. Indeed, the removal of all altars except the one on Mount Zion was in conformity with the law of centralization in Deuteronomy 12. However, the Rabshakeh had a pagan mind-set that assumed a god would be pleased with multiple altars, and conversely displeased if the number of altars were constricted.

36:8-9 The Rabshakeh then taunted Judah by offering them **2,000 horses**, suggesting that they could not find riders for them.

36:10 Here the Rabshakeh's statement reflects ancient Near Eastern pagan theology. The Assyrians believed that the God of Israel was a real deity, though perhaps not a strong one. The Rabshakeh claimed that Judah's God had ordered the nation's destruction. God did use foreign nations on occasion to punish His own people, but in this case the Rabshakeh was wrong, as further developments of the confrontation between Assyria and Israel would indicate.

36:11 The Assyrians spoke a dialect of Akkadian, and the Judeans spoke **Hebrew** at this time. The Rabshakeh prob-

ably had been speaking Hebrew to the Judean delegation. The leaders of Judah did not want the people to be frightened by the Rabshakeh's speech. Perhaps because they did not know how to speak Akkadian, they requested that the conversation take place in **Aramaic**. This language was closely related to Hebrew. It was known more broadly throughout the ancient Near East, but not by the people who were listening to this conversation.

36:12 However, it served the Rabshakeh's propagandistic purpose to have the people hear and be frightened by the coming Assyrian army, so he refused this request. He reminded them of the consequences of a long siege. They would run out of water and have to **drink** their **urine**; they would run out of food and have to **eat** their **excrement**.

36:15 The Rabshakeh mocked the idea of trusting in God to rescue Judah from Assyria. But as the previous chapters have asserted many times, trusting God is precisely what the people of Judah should do in this situation.

36:16-17 Assyria's imperialistic policy called for the deportation of a subjugated people. The Rabshakeh presented his ultimatum for surrender. For the time being, the Judeans would stay in their own **land**, but after a while, they would be deported to another land. Such a policy was put into place in 722 B.C. when the Assyrians conquered the northern kingdom and deported the vast majority of the native population and then brought in foreigners to live there. This policy was intended to break the connection between a people and the god of their land.

36:18-20 The Rabshakeh argued that the God of Judah, Yahweh, could not save Judah any more than the **gods** of other

king of Assyria? [19]Where are the gods of Hamath and Arpad?[a] Where are the gods of Sepharvaim? Have they delivered Samaria from my power?[b] [20]Who among all the gods of these lands ever delivered his land from my power? So will the LORD deliver Jerusalem."

[21]But they kept silent; they didn't say anything, for the king's command was, "Don't answer him."[c] [22]Then Eliakim son of Hilkiah, who was in charge of the palace, Shebna the court secretary, and Joah son of Asaph, the court historian, came to Hezekiah with their clothes torn and reported to him the words of the Rabshakeh.

[a]36:19 Is 10:9-11; 37:11-13; Jr 49:23
[b]2Kg 17:6
[c]36:21 Pr 26:4
[d]37:1-35 2Kg 19:1-34
[e]37:1 Gn 37:34; 2Sm 3:31; 1Kg 21:27; Is 3:24
[f]37:3 Is 22:5; 26:16; 33:2; Nah 1:7; Hab 3:16
[g]Is 26:17-18; 66:9; Hs 13:13
[h]37:4 Dt 5:26; 1Sm 17:26,36; Jr 10:10

Hezekiah Seeks Isaiah's Counsel

37 When King Hezekiah heard their report,[d] he tore his clothes, put on •sackcloth,[e] and went to the LORD's temple. [2]Then he sent Eliakim, who was in charge of the palace, Shebna the court secretary, and the leading priests, who were wearing sackcloth, to the prophet Isaiah son of Amoz. [3]They said to him, "This is what Hezekiah says: 'Today is a day of distress, rebuke, and disgrace,[f] for children have come to the point of birth, and there is no strength to deliver them.[g] [4]Perhaps •Yahweh your God will hear all the words of the •Rabshakeh, whom his master the king of Assyria sent to mock the living God,[h] and will

---

nations and cities that had been defeated by Assyria. He specifically mentioned the defeat of three cities whose gods were unable to rescue their inhabitants. **Arpad** and **Hamath** were cities in northern Syria known to have been defeated by Assyria at an earlier time. The exact identification of **Sepharvaim** is unknown.

36:21-22 Hezekiah did not give his officials authority to negotiate with Assyria. They simply **reported** the proceedings to the king. Their **clothes** that were **torn** were a customary sign of mourning, showing their deep distress.

37:1 The report from Hezekiah's officials (36:22) led the king to assume a posture of mourning, indicated by the customary tearing of his **clothes** and putting on **sackcloth**, a rough and uncomfortable material. He then went to the temple, demonstrating the proper response to such a crisis. He did not turn to a foreign nation like Egypt for help, but he turned to God.

37:2-4 Hezekiah then sent two of his officials, **Eliakim** and **Shebna**, along with senior priests, to elicit prayers on behalf of the nation from the **prophet Isaiah**. One of the main roles

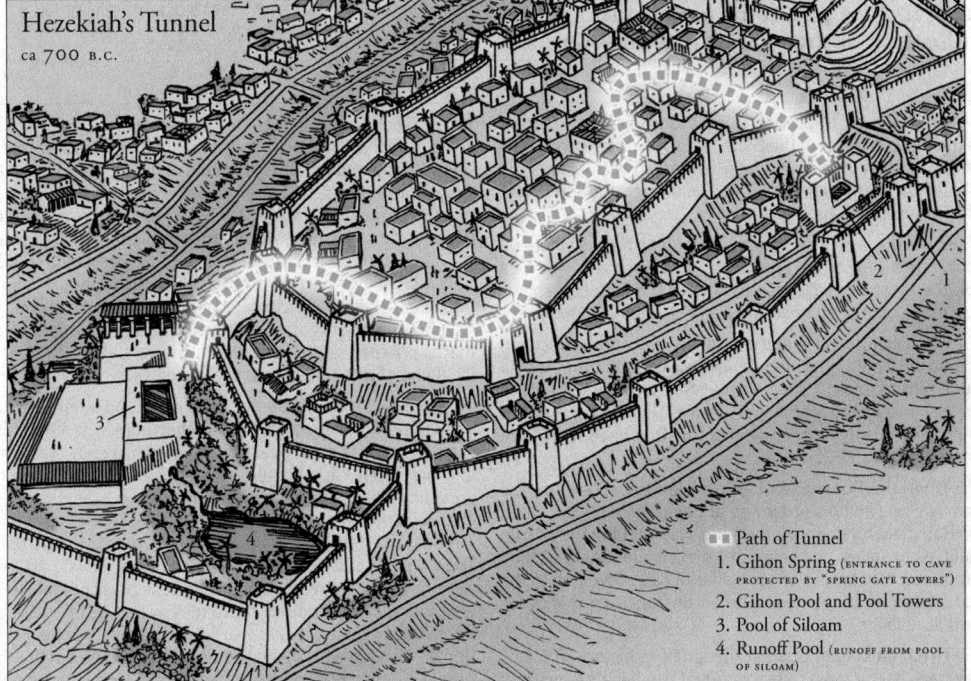

Hezekiah's Tunnel
ca 700 B.C.

Path of Tunnel
1. Gihon Spring (ENTRANCE TO CAVE PROTECTED BY "SPRING GATE TOWERS")
2. Gihon Pool and Pool Towers
3. Pool of Siloam
4. Runoff Pool (RUNOFF FROM POOL OF SILOAM)

In 711 B.C. Sargon II of Assyria captured Ashdod. Hezekiah foresaw a time when the Assyrian army might besiege Jerusalem. He fortified Jerusalem and organized an army. Knowing that a source of water was crucial within the city walls, Hezekiah constructed a 1,750-foot tunnel through solid rock from the spring of Gihon to the Siloam pool. On the east wall of the tunnel conduit, about 20 feet from the Pool of Siloam, an inscription was found that represents one of the oldest Hebrew inscriptions of significant length. Although the inscription was broken in an attempt to steal it, the fragments are now in the Istanbul Archaeology Museum.

rebuke him for the words that Yahweh your God has heard. Therefore offer a prayer for the surviving remnant.'"[a]

[5] So the servants of King Hezekiah went to Isaiah, [6] who said to them, "Tell your master this, 'The LORD says: Don't be afraid[b] because of the words you have heard, which the king of Assyria's attendants have blasphemed Me with.[c] [7] I am about to put a spirit[d] in him and he will hear a rumor and return to his own land, where I will cause him to fall by the sword.'"[e]

Sennacherib's Letter

[8] When the Rabshakeh heard that the king of Assyria had left Lachish,[f] he returned and found him fighting against Libnah.[g] [9] The king had heard this about Tirhakah king of •Cush:[h] "He has set out to fight against you." So when he heard this, he sent messengers to Hezekiah, saying, [10] "Say this to Hezekiah king of Judah: 'Don't let your God, whom you trust, deceive you[i] by promising that Jerusalem won't be handed over to the king of Assyria. [11] Look, you have heard what the kings of Assyria have done to all the countries: they •completely destroyed them. Will you be rescued? [12] Did the gods of the nations[j] that my predecessors destroyed rescue them—Go-

zan,[k] Haran,[l] Rezeph, and the Edenites in Telassar? [13] Where is the king of Hamath, the king of Arpad, the king of the city of Sepharvaim, Hena, or Ivvah?'"

Hezekiah's Prayer

[14] Hezekiah took the letter from the messengers, read it, then went up to the LORD's temple and spread it out before the LORD.[m] [15] Then Hezekiah prayed[n] to the LORD:

[16] LORD of •Hosts, God of Israel, who is enthroned above the •cherubim,[o] You are God[p]—You alone[q]—of all the kingdoms of the earth.[r] You made the heavens and the earth.[s] [17] Listen closely, LORD, and hear;[t] open Your eyes, LORD, and see.[u] Hear all the words that Sennacherib has sent to mock the living God.[v] [18] LORD, it is true that the kings of Assyria have devastated all these countries and their lands. [19] They have thrown their gods into the fire, for they were not gods[w] but made by human hands[x]—wood and stone.[y] So they have destroyed them. [20] Now, LORD our God, save us from his power so that

[a] 37:4 Is 1:9; 46:3
[b] 37:6 Is 7:4; 35:4
[c] Ps 44:7,13-16; Is 52:5; Rm 2:24
[d] 37:7 Nm 5:14; Is 19:14; Hs 4:12; Zch 13:2; 2Tm 1:7
[e] Is 37:36-38
[f] 37:8 Jos 10:31-32
[g] Nm 33:20; Jos 10:29
[h] 37:9 Is 18:1; 20:5
[i] 37:10 Is 36:14-15
[j] 37:12 Is 36:18
[k] 2Kg 17:6; 18:11
[l] Gn 11:31; 12:1-4; Ac 7:2
[m] 37:14 Dt 22:17; 1Kg 8:22; Ezk 2:10
[n] 37:15 2Ch 32:20
[o] 37:16 Ex 25:22; Nm 7:89; 1Sm 4:4; 2Sm 6:2; Ps 80:1; 99:1
[p] Dt 10:17; 2Sm 7:28; Ps 86:10; 90:2; 136:2-3
[q] 1Kg 8:39; Neh 9:6; Ps 4:8; 83:18; 86:10; Rv 15:4
[r] 2Ch 36:20; Ps 68:32; Rv 11:15
[s] Ex 20:11; Neh 9:6; Ps 146:6; Ac 4:24
[t] 37:17 2Ch 6:40; Ps 17:6; Dn 9:18
[u] Is 42:5; 45:12; Jr 10:12
[v] Is 37:4
[w] 37:19 Dt 32:17; 2Ch 13:9; Jr 2:11; 5:7; 16:20; Hs 8:6; Ac 19:26; Gl 4:8
[x] Is 2:8,20; 17:8; 31:7; 41:24,29; 44:9-20; 46:6
[y] Dt 4:28; 28:36,64; 29:17; Ezk 20:32

of a prophet was to provide intercessory prayer. The first mention of a prophet in the Bible links the office with prayer (Gn 20:7). Most of the prophets, beginning with Moses (Ex 33) and Samuel (1Sm 12:23), demonstrated the important role of prayer in their work.

37:5-6 Isaiah assured King Hezekiah through his men that God would remedy the threat presented by the Assyrian army. God took the Assyrian challenge personally. The king had shown trust in the Lord by approaching Isaiah, His servant, to pray.

37:7 God would send a **spirit** of deception to the Assyrian king so he would hear and believe a falsehood that would cause him to retreat. The fact that God would send such a spirit evokes memory of the "evil spirit" God sent to torment Saul (1Sm 16:14) and the "lying spirit" God used to deceive King Ahab (1Kg 22:22).

37:8 When the **Rabshakeh** had traveled to Jerusalem, the Assyrian king and his army was at **Lachish** (36:2), but when the Rabshakeh returned, the king was at **Libnah**, a town about eight miles northeast of Lachish. Sennacherib had completed the capture of Lachish and had moved on to the next city on what seemed to be an unstoppable march toward Jerusalem.

37:9 Tirhakah king of Cush at this point in history (701 B.C.) may have been crown prince of Egypt. He became pharaoh of all Egypt in 690 B.C. and ruled until 664 B.C.

37:10 The rumor of Tirhakah's advance on his rear flank caused Sennacherib to retreat from his advance on **Jerusalem**, but before he left he sent a message in the form of a "letter" (v. 14) to warn Hezekiah that his departure was only temporary.

37:11-13 Sennacherib again told Hezekiah (see the Rabshakeh's speech in 36:18-20) that he should not trust Yahweh. After all, the **gods** of other **nations** and cities conquered by Assyria in the past had been unable to help them. Most of the sites listed here were in what is today eastern Turkey (**Haran**, the city where Abraham and his family stayed for a while before descending into the promised land; see Gn 11:31-32) or northern Syria (**Gozan . . . Rezeph** and Eden). One site, **Telassar**, has been associated with a location (Til-Ashshuri) in what is today Iraq near the Diyala River. On **Hamath . . . Arpad**, and **Sepharvaim**, see note at 36:18-20. The locations of **Hena** and **Ivvah** are unknown.

37:16 Hezekiah addressed his prayer to God whom he described as **enthroned above the cherubim**. The cherubim were among the most powerful of God's heavenly creatures and are often represented at places close to the divine presence. In particular, this refers to the statues of two cherubim whose wings covered the ark of the covenant as it rested in the holy of holies in the tabernacle and temple. Their wings touched and their heads were bowed so they were not overwhelmed by God's glorious presence since He was said to be enthroned above their wings with the ark as His footstool (Ex 25:18-22; 1Kg 8:6-7). Hezekiah appealed to God as the One who **made the heavens and the earth**—the One who is sovereign over all kingdoms, not just Judah—since Sennacherib had mocked God as a mere local deity.

37:18-20 Sennacherib had dared to compare the true God to mere idols and suggested that he would defeat Yahweh's people as easily as he had defeated the **gods** of the other **countries**. Hezekiah appealed to God based on His glory. If Judah should be defeated, then the nations, and in par-

all the kingdoms of the earth may know
that You are the LORD^a—You alone.^b

God's Answer through Hezekiah

²¹ Then Isaiah son of Amoz sent a message to
Hezekiah: "The LORD, the God of Israel, says:
'Because you prayed to Me about Sennacherib
king of Assyria, ²² this is the word the LORD has
spoken against him:

> Virgin Daughter *Zion^c
> despises you and scorns you:
> Daughter Jerusalem shakes her head^d
> behind your back.^A
> ²³ Who is it you have mocked^e
> and blasphemed?
> Who have you raised your voice against
> and lifted your eyes in pride?^f
> Against the Holy One of Israel!^g
> ²⁴ You have mocked the LORD
> through^B your servants.
> You have said, "With my many chariots^h
> I have gone up to the heights
> of the mountains,
> to the far recesses of Lebanon.
> I cut down its tallest cedars,
> its choice cypress trees.
> I came to its distant heights,
> its densest forest.
> ²⁵ I dug wells^c and drank water.
> I dried up all the streams of Egypt
> with the soles of my feet."ⁱ
> ²⁶ Have you not heard?^j

> I designed it long ago;
> I planned it in days gone by.^k
> I have now brought it to pass,
> and you have crushed fortified cities^l
> into piles of rubble.
> ²⁷ Their inhabitants have
> become powerless,
> dismayed, and ashamed.
> They are plants of the field,
> tender grass,
> grass on the rooftops,
> blasted by the east wind.^D

> ²⁸ But I know^E your sitting down,
> your going out and your coming in,^m
> and your raging against Me.
> ²⁹ Because your raging against Me
> and your arrogance have reached
> My ears,ⁿ
> I will put My hook in your nose^o
> and My bit in your mouth;^p
> I will make you go back
> the way you came.

³⁰ "'This will be the sign for you:^q This year
you will eat what grows on its own, and in the
second year what grows from that. But in the
third year sow and reap, plant vineyards and
eat their fruit. ³¹ The surviving remnant of the
house of Judah will again take root^r downward
and bear fruit upward. ³² For a remnant^s will
go out from Jerusalem and survivors, from
Mount Zion. The zeal of the LORD of Hosts will
accomplish this.'^t

^a37:20 Jos 4:24; 1Kg 8:60; 20:13; Is 45:3,6
^bIs 37:16
^c37:22 Is 1:8; 3:16–17; 4:4; 52:2; 62:11; Lm 2:13
^dPs 22:7; 109:25; Jb 16:4; Jr 18:16; Lm 2:15
^e37:23 Ps 74:10,18; Is 37:4; Gl 6:7
^fIs 2:11; 5:15,21
^gGn 12:3; Ex 23:22
^h37:24 Ex 14:26–28; 15:4,19; Dt 20:1; Jos 11:4–9; 2Ch 16:8; Ps 68:17
ⁱ37:25 Dt 11:10; 1Kg 20:10
^j37:26 Is 40:21,28
^kIs 5:19; 10:5–6; 14:24–26; 22:11; 46:11; Jr 18:11; Ac 2:23; 4:27–28; 1Pt 2:8
^lIs 34:13
^m37:28 Ps 139:1
ⁿ37:29 Is 10:12
^oEzk 19:9; 29:4; 38:4
^pIs 30:28
^q37:30 Ex 3:12; 1Sm 2:34; 1Kg 13:3; Is 7:14; 38:7; Jr 44:29; Lk 2:12
^r37:31 Is 27:6
^s37:32 Ezr 9:14; Is 10:20–22
^t2Kg 19:31; Is 9:7; 59:17; Jl 2:18; Zch 1:14

^A37:22 Lit behind you   ^B37:24 Lit by the hand of   ^C37:25 DSS add in foreign lands   ^D37:27 DSS; MT reads rooftops, field before standing grain   ^E37:28 DSS read know your rising up and

ticular Assyria, would believe that Yahweh was just like the false gods of all the other nations.

37:21 God responded to **Hezekiah** through His divinely chosen spokesman, the prophet **Isaiah**. As Isaiah spoke, he spoke in the name of **God**.

37:22 **Daughter Zion** is a personification of Zion, the most holy location in Judah. This reminds the reader of the intimate relationship God enjoyed with His people. The response was addressed to none other than Sennacherib, so the use of this title for God's people shows from the start how important they were to Yahweh.

37:23 God was enraged by Sennacherib's mocking condescension toward Him, treating Him as a local and powerless deity. He was the **Holy One of Israel**, one of Isaiah's favorite titles for God, emphasizing His separateness, moral perfection, and uniqueness.

37:24 Lebanon's cedar forests were well known throughout the ancient Near East, and glory was attached to anyone who could go there and take its precious wood.

37:25 It was always the dream of Mesopotamian kings to defeat Egypt. Sennacherib had boasted that he was able to travel to Egypt.

37:26–27 Now God revealed to Sennacherib the true nature

of things. Sennacherib had boasted of his achievements, but God announced that he had done nothing without divine design. His victories had come about only because God had willed it.

37:28 In language reminiscent of Psalm 139, God asserted His extensive knowledge of the Assyrian king. Yahweh was in control.

37:29 It was Assyrian practice, as illustrated in the bas-reliefs that adorned their palaces, to put a **hook** in the nose or the mouth of captives as they carried them into exile. God told Sennacherib that he would be subjected to this brutal and degrading treatment.

37:30–32 God directed these words to Hezekiah, king of Judah, to show him that the future would see a turn for the better for God's people.

37:30 Because of the siege by Assyria, the Judeans were penned up behind the walls of Jerusalem and had not been able to plant their crops. Thus, they would eat what grew **on its own**, an unreliable volunteer crop. After Assyria lifted the siege, they would be able to plant, but not until the third year would agriculture get back to normal.

37:31–32 Now the oracle speaks of a metaphorical harvest—of the **surviving remnant** of the people of God. The future will see the remnant become productive.

³³"Therefore, this is what the LORD says about the king of Assyria:

> He will not enter this city
> or shoot an arrow there
> or come before it with a shield
> or build up an assault ramp
> against it.
> ³⁴ He will go back
> the way he came,
> and he will not enter this city.
> This is the LORD's declaration.

> ³⁵ I will defend this city and rescue it
> because of Me^a
> and because of My servant David."^b

Defeat and Death of Sennacherib

³⁶Then^c the angel of the LORD^d went out and struck down 185,000 in the camp of the Assyrians. When the people got up the next morning—there were all the dead bodies! ³⁷So Sennacherib king of Assyria broke camp and left. He returned home and lived in Nineveh.^e

³⁸One day, while he was worshiping in the temple of his god Nisroch, his sons Adrammelech and Sharezer struck him down with the sword and escaped to the land of Ararat.^f Then his son Esar-haddon^g became king in his place.

^a37:35 Is 43:25; 48:9,11
^b1Kg 11:13,32-38; 2Kg 20:6; Ezk 34:23
^c37:36-38 2Kg 19:35-37; 2Ch 32:21
^d37:36 Gn 16:7-11; Ex 3:2; Nm 22:22-35; Jdg 6:11-12; 2Sm 24:16; Ps 34:7
^e37:37 Gn 10:11; Jnh 1:2; 3:3; 4:11; Zph 2:13
^f37:38 Gn 8:4; Jr 51:27
^gEzr 4:2
^h38:1-8 2Kg 20:1-6,9-11; 2Ch 32:24
ⁱ38:1 2Sm 17:23
^j38:3 Gn 17:1; 1Kg 3:6; 8:23; 2Kg 18:5-6; Ps 26:3
^kDt 6:18
^l38:5 2Kg 18:2,13
^m38:6 Is 31:5; 37:35
ⁿ38:7 Is 37:30
^o38:8 Jos 10:12-14
^p38:10 Ps 102:24
^qPs 107:18

Hezekiah's Illness and Recovery

38 In those days Hezekiah became terminally ill.^h The prophet Isaiah son of Amoz came and said to him, "This is what the LORD says: 'Put your affairs in order,^{A,i} for you are about to die; you will not recover.'"^B ²Then Hezekiah turned his face to the wall and prayed to the LORD. ³He said, "Please, LORD, remember how I have walked before You faithfully and wholeheartedly,^j and have done what pleases You."^{C,k} And Hezekiah wept bitterly.

⁴Then the word of the LORD came to Isaiah: ⁵"Go and tell Hezekiah that this is what the LORD God of your ancestor David says: I have heard your prayer; I have seen your tears. Look, I am going to add 15 years to your life.^{D,l} ⁶And I will deliver you and this city from the power of the king of Assyria; I will defend this city.^m ⁷This is the sign to youⁿ from the LORD that He will do what^E He has promised:^F ⁸I am going to make the sun's shadow that goes down on Ahaz's stairway go back by 10 steps."^o So the sun's shadow^G went back the 10 steps it had descended.

⁹A poem by Hezekiah king of Judah after he had been sick and had recovered from his illness:

> ¹⁰ I said: In the prime^H of my life^{D,p}
> I must go to the gates of ‧Sheol;^q

^A38:1 Lit *Command your house*   ^B38:1 Lit *live*   ^C38:3 Lit *what is good in Your eyes*   ^D38:5,10 Lit *days*   ^E38:7 Lit *this thing*
^F38:7 Lit *said*   ^G38:8 Lit *And the sun*   ^H38:10 Lit *quiet*

37:33-35 God directed His attention back to the **king of Assyria**. He announced that Sennacherib would fail at his attempt to take the city. He would not even begin the assault but would return to Assyria. God would do this for His own glory and because of the promise He had made to **David**. God promised David that "your house and kingdom will endure before Me forever, and your throne will be established forever" (2Sm 7:16).

37:36-37 God sent His **angel** to kill the **Assyrians** without a battle. No proximate cause is given for the death of the enemy soldiers, though it is likely that God used disease to accomplish His goal.

37:38 Nisroch was an unknown Assyrian god or, more likely, the name given by the Hebrews to a god known by another name. **Ararat** was a region located around Lake Van north of Assyria. It was known in antiquity as Urartu and was a long-standing foe of Assyria, thus a likely place for the murderous sons of Sennacherib to escape. While **Adrammelech and Sharezer** are not known by name, **Esar-haddon** is known to have succeeded his father Sennacherib after the king's death in 683 B.C. Since these events happened in 683 B.C., it appears that almost 20 years passed from the time Sennacherib withdrew from Jerusalem in 701 B.C. to the time when he died at the hands of his sons.

38:5 God **heard** the **prayer** of Hezekiah and increased his lifespan by **15 years**. Interestingly, God is described as **the LORD God of your ancestor David**. Hezekiah was the descendant of David, who had been promised a son on the throne in

Jerusalem forever. Hezekiah may not have had an heir at this time (his heir, Manasseh, was 12 years old when Hezekiah died; 2Kg 21:1). This meant that if he died prior to the fifteen-year extension, the Davidic dynasty would come to an end.

38:6 The reference to the deliverance of the city from the **king of Assyria** may indicate that this episode took place during the Assyrian threat described in chapters 36-37.

38:7 Hezekiah's **sign** brings to mind the sign offered to his father Ahaz in chapter 7. While Ahaz was not interested in receiving a sign, probably because he had other plans in mind, Hezekiah did not try to refuse the sign. Their contrasting responses reveal the difference between Ahaz, who trusted in other nations, and Hezekiah, who trusted in God.

38:8 The return of the **sun's shadow** on the stairway indicated a lengthening of the day that would be comparable to God's lengthening of the life of Hezekiah. The parallel account in 2Kg 20:9-11 indicates that Hezekiah was allowed to choose whether the shadow would go ahead or go back **10 steps**. Hezekiah chose the latter since he considered that the more difficult feat.

38:9 The introduction to Hezekiah's poem states that it was written **after he had been sick and had recovered**. In this respect, the poem is like the thanksgiving songs in Psalms. In the first part of this poem, Hezekiah spoke as if he were going to die, but from the second half of the poem it is clear that it was written after he was healed.

38:10 Sheol refers to the grave and in some contexts signifies the ancient concept of an underworld.

I am deprived of the rest of my years.

¹¹ I said: I will never see the LORD,
the LORD in the land of the living;^a
I will not look on humanity any longer
with the inhabitants of what is
  passing away.^A

¹² My dwelling is plucked up and removed
  from me
like a shepherd's tent.^b
I have rolled up my life like a weaver;^c
He cuts me off from the loom.^{B,d}
You make an end of me from day
  until night.^e

¹³ I thought until the morning:
He will break all my bones like a lion;
You make an end of me day and night.

¹⁴ I chirp like a swallow or a crane;
I moan like a dove.^f
My eyes grow weak looking upward.
Lord, I am oppressed; support me.^g

¹⁵ What can I say?
He has spoken to me,
and He Himself has done it.
I walk along slowly all my years^h
because of the bitterness of my soul,ⁱ

¹⁶ Lord, because of these promises
  people live,^j
and in all of them is the life of my spirit
  as well;
You have restored me to health^k
and let me live.^l

¹⁷ Indeed, it was for my own welfare
that I had such great bitterness;^m
but Your love has delivered me
from the *Pit of destruction,ⁿ
for You have thrown all my sins
  behind Your back.^o

¹⁸ For Sheol cannot thank You;

Death cannot praise You.^p
Those who go down to the Pit
cannot hope for Your faithfulness.

¹⁹ The living, only the living
  can thank You,
as I do today;
a father will make Your faithfulness
  known to children.^q

²⁰ The LORD will^c save me;
we will play stringed instruments
all the days of our lives
at the house of the LORD.^r

²¹Now Isaiah^s had said, "Let them take a lump of pressed figs and apply it to his infected skin, so that he may recover." ²²And Hezekiah had asked, "What is the sign that I will go up to the LORD's temple?"

Hezekiah's Folly

39 At that time^t Merodach-baladan son of Baladan, king of Babylon, sent letters and a gift to Hezekiah since he heard that he had been sick and had recovered. ²Hezekiah was pleased with them, and showed them his treasure house—the silver, the gold, the spices, and the precious oil—and all his armory, and everything that was found in his treasuries.^u There was nothing in his palace and in all his realm that Hezekiah did not show them.^v

³Then the prophet Isaiah came to King Hezekiah and asked him, "Where did these men come from and what did they say to you?"

Hezekiah replied, "They came to me from a distant country, from Babylon."

⁴Isaiah asked, "What have they seen in your palace?"

Hezekiah answered, "They have seen everything in my palace. There isn't anything in my treasuries that I didn't show them."

Cross-reference column:

^a38:11 Ps 27:13; 116:9
^b38:12 2Co 5:1,4; 2Pt 1:13-14
^cJb 7:6; Heb 1:12
^dJb 6:9
^eJb 4:20; Ps 73:14
^f38:14 Is 59:11; Ezk 7:16; Nah 2:7
^gJb 17:3; Ps 119:122
^h38:15 1Kg 21:27
ⁱSm 1:10; Ezk 27:31; Jb 3:20; 7:11; 10:1
^j38:16 Ps 119:71,75
^kPs 39:13
^lPs 119:25
^m38:17 Heb 12:11
ⁿJb 33:18,30; Ps 103:4; 106:23; Ezk 20:17; Jnh 2:6
^oIs 43:25; Jr 31:34; Mc 7:19
^p38:18 Ps 6:5; 30:9; 88:10-12; 115:17
^q38:19 Dt 6:7; 11:19; Ps 78:5-7
^r38:20 Ps 23:6; 116:17-19
^s38:21-22 2Kg 20:7-8
^t39:1-8 2Kg 20:12-19; 2Ch 32:31
^u39:2 2Kg 18:15-16
^v2Ch 32:25

---

^A38:11 Some Hb mss, Tg read *of the world*   ^B38:12 Lit *thrum*   ^C38:20 Lit *to*

38:11 The **land of the living** refers to this world and leaves open the question about Hezekiah's belief in the afterlife.

38:12 Hezekiah used multiple metaphors to describe the fragility and brevity of life.

38:13 On God as a **lion**, see Lm 3:10; Hs 5:14; Am 3:8.

38:14 The groans of Hezekiah's lamentation sound like the chirping of a bird.

38:15-16 God had **spoken**, and King Hezekiah had been delivered from a premature death.

38:17 Hezekiah's **bitterness** (see also v. 15) refers to his mournful reaction to news of his impending death. This bitterness is what led him to seek God in prayer and ultimately to God's relenting from His death sentence. The king referred to the grave (and the afterworld) as a **Pit of destruction**. After all, in the grave the body rots and turns to dust.

38:18 **Sheol** (see note at v. 10) and **Death** are personified.

The implication, as made clear by the phrase **those who go down to the Pit**, is that the dead can no longer praise God.

38:19 God benefits from keeping His saints alive. The living can praise God and they can share that praise with the following generations.

38:21-22 These verses are an appendix that fills in some facts from earlier in the story.

39:1 **Merodach-baladan** was king of Babylon, at this time a province of the Assyrian Empire, during two different times—721-710 B.C. and 705-703 B.C. In 703 B.C. Sennacherib, to whom Merodach-baladan had been a constant irritant looking for opportunities to revolt, removed him. Even after his removal from Babylon, Merodach-baladan went to Elam and continued to plot against Assyria until his death. The **letters and a gift** that he sent to Hezekiah were part of a strategy to get Hezekiah to join with him in a rebellious alliance.

39:2 Hezekiah responded positively to Merodach-baladan,

5 Then Isaiah said to Hezekiah, "Hear the
word of the LORD of •Hosts:[a] 6 'The time will
certainly come when everything in your palace and all that your fathers have stored up
until this day will be carried off to Babylon;
nothing will be left,' says the LORD.[b] 7 'Some of
your descendants who come from you will be
taken away, and they will become eunuchs in
the palace of the king of Babylon.'"

8 Then Hezekiah said to Isaiah, "The word of
the LORD that you have spoken is good," for
he thought: There will be peace and security
during my lifetime.[c]

God's People Comforted

40 "Comfort, comfort My people,"[d]
says your God.
2 "Speak tenderly to[A] Jerusalem,
and announce to her
that her time of forced labor is over,
her iniquity[e] has been pardoned,[f]
and she has received
from the LORD's hand
double for all her sins."[g]

3 A voice of one crying out:

Prepare the way of the LORD
in the wilderness;[h]
make a straight highway for our God
in the desert.[i]
4 Every valley will be lifted up,
and every mountain and hill
will be leveled;
the uneven ground will become smooth
and the rough places, a plain.[j]
5 And the glory of the LORD will appear,[k]
and all humanity[B] together will see it,[l]
for the mouth of the LORD has spoken.[m]

6 A voice was saying, "Cry out!"
Another[C] said, "What should I cry out?"
"All humanity is grass,[n]
and all its goodness is like the flower
of the field.[o]
7 The grass withers, the flowers fade
when the breath[D] of the LORD blows
on them;[E]
indeed, the people are grass.
8 The grass withers, the flowers fade,[p]
but the word of our God
remains forever."[q]

9 •Zion, herald of good news,
go up on a high mountain.[r]
Jerusalem, herald of good news,[s]
raise your voice loudly.
Raise it, do not be afraid!
Say to the cities of Judah,
"Here is your God!"[t]
10 See, the Lord GOD comes with strength,
and His power establishes His rule.[u]
His reward is with Him,[v]
and His gifts accompany Him.
11 He protects His flock like a shepherd;[w]

[a] 39:5 Is 28:14; Zch 7:4; 8:1,18
[b] 39:6 2Kg 24:13; 25:13-15; Jr 20:5
[c] 39:8 2Ch 32:26
[d] 40:1 Is 12:1; 49:13; 51:3,12; 52:9; 61:2; 66:13; Jr 31:10-14; Zph 3:14-17; 2Co 1:4
[e] 40:2 Is 13:11
[f] Lv 26:41,43; Is 27:9
[g] Ex 22:7-8; Jr 16:18; Zch 9:12; Rv 18:6
[h] 40:3 Mal 3:1; 4:5-6
[i] Mt 3:3; Mk 1:3; Lk 3:4; Jn 1:23
[j] 40:4-5 Lk 3:5-6
[k] 40:5 Is 35:2
[l] Is 52:10; Jl 2:28
[m] Is 1:20; 34:16; 58:14
[n] 40:6-8 1Pt 1:24-25
[o] 40:6 Jb 14:2; Ps 102:11; 103:15
[p] 40:8 Jms 1:11
[q] Is 55:11; 59:21; Mk 13:31; Lk 21:33
[r] 40:9 Is 52:7
[s] Is 61:1
[t] Is 25:9; 35:2
[u] 40:10 Is 59:16-18
[v] Is 62:11; Rv 22:12
[w] 40:11 Jr 31:10; Ezk 34:12-14,23,31; Mc 5:4; Jn 10:11,14-16

[A] 40:2 Lit *Speak to the heart of* [B] 40:5 Lit *flesh* [C] 40:6 DSS, LXX, Vg read *I* [D] 40:7 Or *wind*, or *Spirit* [E] 40:7 Lit *it*

showing him the wealth of his kingdom as well as the strength of his armaments.

39:5-7 God through the prophet **Isaiah** expressed his great displeasure with **Hezekiah**. The king's actions demonstrated that he was trusting foreign nations like **Babylon** for his protection rather than God. The Lord's punishment would take away the wealth that Hezekiah had been showing off to Merodach-baladan. Another part of the punishment was that some of the king's **descendants** would be taken away and would become **eunuchs** in Babylon. Babylonian records indicate that a number of the Babylonian king's advisers were eunuchs. Some have speculated that Daniel and his three friends (described as "from the royal family and from the nobility") were also made eunuchs since Ashpenaz's title is literally rendered "chief of the eunuchs" (Dn 1:3).

39:8 The implication of the announced punishment was that it would happen in a future generation. Hezekiah's selfish relief does not speak well for him. The reference is likely to the turbulent end of the Davidic dynasty in Judah and specifically to the events surrounding the exile and removal of the last king, Zedekiah.

40:1 Though the hearer of God's words are not here specified, it is best to see these words as being directed to the prophet Isaiah, who was commanded to bring words of **comfort** rather than judgment to God's people. The words address the prophet as if he were living in the time of the future exile of Judah to Babylon. God anticipated the questions that His people would have as they experienced His judgment.

40:2 The **time of forced labor** refers to the future Babylonian exile (586–539 B.C.). That the people had received **double** punishment is a way of saying that their sentence was fully satisfied before God.

40:3-4 A herald rallied his hearers to prepare a road that would make quick and easy access for God to return to the promised land in order to restore His people. The wilderness was difficult to cross because it had deep wadis and high mountains, but in preparation for the return this rough terrain would become like **a plain**, easy to travel. The fulfillment most immediately in view is the return of Jewish people after the end of the exile, but the ultimate fulfillment of these verses is in the work of Jesus Christ as signaled by the quotation of verse 3 along with Mal 3:1 in Mk 1:2-3 and the identification of the voice as that of John the Baptist.

40:5 Sin had broken the fellowship between God and His people, but Isaiah looked beyond their punishment to the return of **the glory of the LORD**.

40:6-8 Another herald compared humanity to **grass** and the **flower of the field**, both of which have short-lived and fragile beauty. The contrast is with the word of God that endures. Perhaps the contrast implies that the Babylonians, though seemingly powerful, would fade, but God's word that had promised His people restoration would not fail.

He gathers the lambs in His arms
and carries them in the fold
    of His garment.
He gently leads those that are nursing.

12 Who has measured the waters
    in the hollow of his hand
or marked off the heavens
    with the span of his hand?[a]
Who has gathered the dust of the earth
    in a measure
or weighed the mountains in a balance
and the hills in the scales?
13 Who has directed[A] the Spirit
    of the LORD,
or who gave Him His counsel?[b]
14 Who did He consult with?
Who gave Him understanding[c]
and taught Him the paths of justice?
Who taught Him knowledge
and showed Him the way
    of understanding?
15 Look, the nations are like a drop
    in a bucket;
they are considered as a speck of dust
    in the scales;
He lifts up the islands like fine dust.
16 Lebanon is not enough for fuel,
    or its animals enough
    for a •burnt offering.[d]
17 All the nations are as nothing
    before Him;
they are considered by Him
    as nothingness and emptiness.[e]
18 Who will you compare God with?
What likeness will you compare Him to?[f]

19 To an idol?—something that
    a smelter casts,
and a metalworker plates with gold
and makes silver welds for it?[g]
20 To one who shapes a pedestal,
    choosing wood that does not rot?[B]
He looks for a skilled craftsman
to set up an idol that will not fall over.[h]
21 Do you not know?[i]
Have you not heard?
Has it not been declared to you
    from the beginning?
Have you not considered
    the foundations of the earth?[j]
22 God is enthroned above the circle
    of the earth;
its inhabitants are like grasshoppers.[k]
He stretches out the heavens
    like thin cloth[l]
and spreads them out like a tent
    to live in.[m]
23 He reduces princes to nothing[n]
and makes judges of the earth
    irrational.
24 They are barely planted, barely sown,
    their stem hardly takes root
    in the ground
when He blows on them
    and they wither,
and a whirlwind carries them away
    like stubble.[o]
25 "Who will you compare Me to,[p]
    or who is My equal?"
    asks the Holy One.
26 Look up[c] and see:

A 40:13 Or measured, or comprehended   B 40:20 Or who is too poor for such an offering, or who chooses mulberry wood as a votive gift; Hb obscure   C 40:26 Lit Lift up your eyes on high

40:11 In the Bible and throughout the ancient Near East, the shepherd was a familiar image for a ruler. Judah had been subject to weak and evil shepherds or kings (Ezk 34), but the nation would once again have a strong and compassionate shepherd—God Himself (Ps 23).

40:12-26 The series of rhetorical questions that appear in these verses have one intention—to demonstrate the uniqueness of the one true God. This assured God's people that God not only wanted to deliver them, but He was able to do so.

40:12 God is in control and knows everything about His creation, both heavens and earth. Unlike the gods of the surrounding nations that were identified with aspects of nature (Baal was the god of storm, thunder, and lightning), Judah's God created the world and measured it.

40:13-14 God does not need a teacher. He is inherently wise and gives advice to others (Jb 38:1–42:5).

40:15-17 Babylon must have seemed invulnerable once Judah suffered defeat by the Babylonians and her leaders were carted off into exile, but no human power, not even

Babylon, could compare with God. They were like a drop in a bucket. Lebanon was famous for its massive forests and its abundant wildlife, but they were not sufficient to produce a burnt offering before God. The message is that God could and would deliver Judah from Babylonian captivity. On islands, see note at 41:1.

40:18-20 God is nothing like the gods of the nations. Many thought otherwise, believing that Babylon was able to defeat Judah because the Babylonian gods were stronger than Yahweh, but the Babylonian gods were nothing but wood and metal—the creation of human craftsmen (41:6-7; 42:17; 44:9-20; 46:5-7; 48:5).

40:21-24 God is not only superior to the gods of the nations; He is far above the rulers of the nations as well (princes . . . judges). He is the ultimate ruler. His throne is not on earth, but above the circle of the earth. Like grass (vv. 6-8), they are fragile and short-lived and as easily disposed of as stubble carried away by a whirlwind. They are no match for God.

40:25-26 Nothing compares to God—not even the starry host. The religions of the ancient Near East believed the

who created[a] these?
He brings out the starry host
　by number;
He calls all of them by name.[b]
Because of His great power
　and strength,
not one of them is missing.

27 Jacob, why do you say,
and Israel, why do you assert:
"My way is hidden from the Lord,
and my claim is ignored by my God"?[c]
28 Do you not know?
Have you not heard?
•Yahweh is the everlasting God,[d]
the Creator of the whole earth.
He never grows faint or weary;
there is no limit to His understanding.[e]
29 He gives strength to the weary
and strengthens the powerless.
30 Youths may faint and grow weary,
and young men stumble and fall,
31 but those who trust in the Lord
will renew their strength;[f]
they will soar on wings like eagles;[g]
they will run and not grow weary;
they will walk and not faint.

The Lord versus the Nations' Gods

41 "Be silent before Me, islands![h]
　　And let peoples renew
　　　their strength.
Let them approach,
　then let them testify;
let us come together for the trial.
2 Who has stirred him up from the east?[i]
He calls righteousness to his feet.[A,j]

---

a40:26 Is 42:5;
48:12-13
bPs 147:4-5
c40:27 Is 7:13;
49:4,14
d40:28 Gn 21:33;
Ps 90:2
ePs 147:5; Rm
11:33
f40:31 Jb 17:9;
Ps 103:5; 2Co
4:8-10,16; 12:9
gEx 19:4; Dt
32:11; Lk 18:1;
2Co 4:1,16; Gl
6:9; Heb 12:3
h41:1 Is 11:11;
Hab 2:20; Zch
2:13
i41:2 Is 41:25;
45:1-3; 46:11; Rv
16:12
jIs 42:6
k2Ch 36:23;
Ezr 1:2
l41:4 Is 43:10;
44:6; Rv 1:8,17;
22:13
mIs 43:13; 46:4;
48:12
n41:5 Ps 67:7
o41:7 Is 40:19
pIs 40:20; 46:7
q41:8 Is 42:19;
43:10; 44:1-2,21;
45:4; 48:20;
49:3; 54:17; Ezk
28:25; 37:25;
Lk 1:54
rIs 42:1;
43:10,20; 44:1-2;
45:4; 49:7;
65:9,15,22
s2Ch 20:7; Jms
2:23
t41:9 Is 43:5-7

The Lord hands nations over to him,[k]
and he subdues kings.
He makes them like dust
　with his sword,
like wind-driven stubble with his bow.
3 He pursues them, going on safely,
hardly touching the path with his feet.
4 Who has performed and done this,
calling the generations
　from the beginning?
I, •Yahweh, am the first,
and with the last[l]—I am He."[m]

5 The islands see and are afraid,
the whole earth trembles.[n]
They approach and arrive.
6 Each one helps the other,
and says to another, "Take courage!"
7 The craftsman encourages
　the metalworker;[o]
the one who flattens
　with the hammer
supports the one who strikes the anvil,
saying of the soldering, "It is good."
He fastens it with nails so that
　it will not fall over.[p]

8 But you, Israel, My servant,[q]
Jacob, whom I have chosen,[r]
descendant of Abraham, My friend[s]—
9 I brought[B] you from the ends
　of the earth
and called you
　from its farthest corners.
I said to you: You are My servant;
I have chosen you and not
　rejected you.[t]

A41:2 Hb obscure　B41:9 Or seized

---

stars were gods. Judah's religion asserted that God created the stars. The fact that He knew them by name indicates that they were His creation and they were protected (**not one of them is missing**) by His power.

40:27 When Judah experienced God's punishment, Isaiah anticipated that the people would ask why God had abandoned them. The following verses summarize the answer given in the first part of the chapter. God wanted to deliver His people, and He was fully able to do so.

40:28 God had the power and wisdom to bring about Judah's deliverance.

40:29-31 God not only had strength, but He distributed that strength to His people. The criterion for receiving God's strength was not youth but **trust**. Those who trusted God would have an unlimited source of strength.

41:1 The **islands** refer to far-off lands and thus represent all the nations of the world. The prophets often used the language of the courtroom. Here God will try the nations and their idols. The nations were to be quiet as God presented evidence in support of His case.

41:2 The one **from the east** who subdues kings is a refer-

ence to Cyrus, king of Persia (45:1), whom God used to defeat Babylon in 539 b.c. This brought the exile of Judah to an end.

41:3 The conquests of Cyrus were quick, and he remained safe until he had extended Babylon's boundaries.

41:4 Though Cyrus was the human agent behind these predicted events, God took credit because Cyrus succeeded under His sovereign control.

41:5-7 On **islands**, see note at verse 1. The **craftsman** and the **metalworker** were those who created the idols in whom the nations trusted.

41:8 While the nations felt the wrath of God at the hands of His agent Cyrus, God again would make Israel His **friend**. By calling Israel the **descendant of Abraham**, God called to mind the promise to the patriarch that his descendants would be a "great nation" (Gn 12:2). On the basis of this ancient covenantal promise, God acted to restore His people Israel.

41:9 God's punishment of Judah led to exile in 586 b.c. when many of its leading citizens were taken to Babylon and from

¹⁰ Do not fear, for I am with you;^a
do not be afraid, for I am your God.^b
I will strengthen you; I will help you;
I will hold on to you with My righteous
    right hand.^c

¹¹ Be sure that all who are enraged
    against you
will be ashamed and disgraced;^d
those who contend with you
will become as nothing and will perish.

¹² You will look for those who contend
    with you,
but you will not find them.
Those who war against you
will become absolutely nothing.

¹³ For I, Yahweh your God,^e
hold your right hand
and say to you: Do not fear,
I will help you.

¹⁴ Do not fear, you worm Jacob,^f
you men^A of Israel:
I will help you—
           this is the Lord's declaration.
Your Redeemer^g is the Holy One
    of Israel.^h

¹⁵ See, I will make you
    into a sharp threshing board,
new, with many teeth.
You will thresh mountains
    and pulverize them
and make hills into chaff.ⁱ

¹⁶ You will winnow them^j
and a wind will carry them away,
a gale will scatter them.
But you will rejoice in the Lord;
you will boast in the Holy One of Israel.

¹⁷ The poor and the needy seek water,
    but there is none;
their tongues are parched with thirst.

I, Yahweh, will answer them;^k
I, the God of Israel, will not
    forsake them.

¹⁸ I will open rivers
    on the barren heights,^l
and springs in the middle
    of the plains.
I will turn the desert into a pool
    of water
and dry land into springs of water.^m

¹⁹ I will plant cedars in the desert,
acacias, myrtles, and olive trees.ⁿ
I will put juniper trees in the desert,
elms and cypress trees together,

²⁰ so that all may see and know,
consider and understand,
that the hand of the Lord
    has done this,^o
the Holy One of Israel has created^p it.

²¹ "Submit your case," says the Lord.
"Present your arguments,"
    says Jacob's King.

²² "Let them come and tell us
what will happen.^q
Tell us the past events,
so that we may reflect on them
and know the outcome,
or tell us the future.

²³ Tell us the coming events,^r
then we will know that you are gods.
Indeed, do something good or bad,
then we will be in awe^B and perceive.

²⁴ Look, you are nothing^s
and your work is worthless.
Anyone who chooses you is detestable.

²⁵ "I have raised up one from the north,^t
    and he has come,
one from the east^u who invokes
    My^c name.^v

---

^a41:10 Gn 26:24; 28:15; Is 43:5; Jr 1:19; 15:20; 42:11
^bEzk 34:31
^cEx 15:6,12; Ps 18:35; 48:10; 63:8; 138:7; 139:10
^d41:11 Is 45:24
^e41:13 Is 43:3
^f41:14 Jb 25:6; Ps 22:6
^gIs 43:14; 44:6,24; 47:4; 48:17; 49:7,26; 54:5,8; 59:20; 60:16; 63:16
^hIs 1:4
ⁱ41:15 Mc 4:13; Hab 3:12
^j41:16 Jr 51:2
^k41:17 Is 43:20; 44:3; 49:10; 55:1
^l41:18 Is 30:25
^mPs 107:35; Is 35:6-7; 48:21
ⁿ41:19 Is 35:1; 55:13; 60:13
^o41:20 Jb 12:9; Is 66:14
^pIs 4:5
^q41:22 Is 44:7-8; 45:21; 46:10
^r41:23 Is 42:9; 45:3; Jn 13:19
^s41:24 Ps 115:8; Is 44:9; 1Co 8:4
^t41:25 Jr 50:3
^uIs 41:2; 46:11
^vEzr 1:2-4

---

^A41:14 LXX reads *small number*; DSS read *dead ones*   ^B41:23 DSS read *we may hear*   ^C41:25 DSS read *his*

---

there scattered throughout the empire. Restoration involved bringing them back **from the ends of the earth**.

41:10 God's statement **I am with you** is a concise way of describing the covenant relationship between Him and His people. God's **right hand** is often associated with His military might, thus His ability to protect His people.

41:11-12 God assured His people that their enemies would not have the ability or the power to harm them.

41:13-14 The inability of the nations to contend with Israel was because of divine protection and intimacy (**I ... hold your right hand**). Israel did not have the strength or ability to protect itself, but God would sustain them.

41:15 The **threshing board** was a heavy wooden sledge with many stone or iron teeth on its underside. It was dragged across sheaves to separate the grain from the chaff in the winnowing process. The metaphor emphasizes how thoroughly and violently Israel would defeat the nations.

41:16 Winnowing involved throwing grain in the air so the wind caught the chaff, or waste matter, and blew it away.

41:17-18 The phrase **the poor and the needy** here refers to God's own down-and-out people whom He has punished. But God will restore them, turning their dry land into a watery paradise.

41:19-20 The **desert** has become an orchard, an act that only God could perform—the word translated **created** (Hb *bara'*) is the same as in Gn 1:1.

41:21 Again (see note at v. 1) God used legal language as He challenged the nations and their idols. **Jacob's King** is none other than God Himself.

41:22-24 The idols were ignorant of the future, demonstrating that they were not gods. Indeed, they were **nothing**.

41:25 King Cyrus of Persia is in mind here. He is said to be from the **east** (see note at v. 2) because his homeland was

He will march over rulers as if
   they were mud,
like a potter who treads the clay.
26 Who told about this
   from the beginning,
so that we might know,
and from times past,
so that we might say: He is right?
No one announced it,
no one told it,
no one heard your words.
27 I was the first to say to •Zion:[A]
Look! Here they are!
And I gave a herald of good news
   to Jerusalem.[a]
28 When I look, there is no one;
there is no counselor among them;
when I ask them, they have
   nothing to say.[b]
29 Look, all of them are a delusion;[B]
their works are nonexistent;
their images are wind and emptiness.

The Servant's Mission

42 "This[c] is My Servant;[d]
   I strengthen Him,
this is My Chosen One;[e] I delight
   in Him.[f]

I have put My Spirit on Him;[g]
He will bring justice[c] to the nations.[h]
2 He will not cry out or shout
or make His voice heard in the streets.
3 He will not break a bruised reed,
and He will not put out
   a smoldering wick;
He will faithfully bring justice.
4 He will not grow weak
   or be discouraged
until He has established justice
   on earth.
The islands will wait
   for His instruction."[i]

5 This is what God, •Yahweh, says—
who created the heavens and stretched
   them out,[j]
who spread out the earth
   and what comes from it,[k]
who gives breath to the people
   on it
and life[D] to those who walk on it[l]—
6 "I, Yahweh, have called You
for a righteous purpose,[E,m]
and I will hold You by Your hand.[n]
I will keep You and appoint You
to be a covenant for the people[o]

Cross-references:
a 41:27 Is 40:9; 44:28; 52:7; Nah 1:15
b 41:28 Is 46:7
c 42:1-4 Mt 12:18-21
d 42:1 Is 49:3-7; 50:10
e Is 41:8-9; Lk 9:35; 23:35; 1Pt 2:4,6
f Mt 3:17; 17:5; Mk 1:11; Lk 3:22; 2Pt 1:17
g Nm 11:16-17; 1Sm 16:13; Ps 33:6; 139:7; Is 11:2; 40:7; 59:21; Lk 4:18-21
h Is 2:4; 51:4-5
i 42:4 Is 11:11; 24:15; 42:10,12; 49:1; 51:5; 60:9; 66:19
j 42:5 Ps 104:2; Is 40:22
k Ps 136:6; Is 34:1
l Jb 12:10; 33:4; Is 57:16; Dn 5:23; Ac 17:25
m 42:6 Is 5:7,16; 9:7; 11:4-5; 32:1; 41:2; 45:8,13; 51:5-8; 56:1; 60:21; Jr 23:5-6
n Is 41:10,13
o Is 49:8

A 41:27 Lit *First to Zion* B 41:29 DSS, Syr read *are nothing* C 42:1 DSS read *His justice* D 42:5 Lit *spirit* E 42:6 Or *you by My righteousness*; lit *you in righteousness*

---

geographically east of Israel. On the other hand, he could at the same time be from the **north** because that was the direction from which he attacked Babylon.

41:26-27 While the idols were ignorant because they did not really exist, God knew the future. Indeed He knew about this **from the beginning**. The coming of Cyrus was **good news to Jerusalem** because his defeat of Babylon would mean that the exiles could come home.

41:28-29 The false gods of the nations were **nonexistent**, thus they could not give advice.

42:1-9 A number of songs in the latter half of Isaiah focus on the Servant of the Lord (49:1-6; 50:4-6; 52:13–53:12). The identity of the Servant is much debated, and most modern commentaries give full lists of options. The context of these verses points in the first instance to Israel or Judah filling the role of the Servant. After all, 41:8-9 addresses the nation as the Servant. In answer to the objection that this song's description of the Servant is much too positive to refer to the nation as a whole, it can be conceded that Isaiah spoke of the remnant that would emerge from the purifying fires of judgment. However, even the postexilic survivors did not live up to the hope expressed in these verses. Accordingly, Christian readers recognize that the NT writers (Mt 12:15-21) applied the description of the Servant, both here and in the three other songs, to Jesus Christ (so the HCSB appropriately capitalizes *Servant*).

42:1 God will choose and anoint His Servant with the **Spirit**. Such anointing in the OT granted the recipient the ability to perform a divinely given task, in this case to bring justice to the nations. God commissioned Israel with this task begin-

ning with the promises to Abraham that included their being a blessing to the **nations** (cp. Gn 12:1-3), but it is Jesus who will perform His Father's will perfectly in this regard. Jesus' work of justice included bringing judgment on sinners (Mt 12:15-21; Rv 19:11).

42:2 The Servant will not be loud or obnoxious in carrying out His task. He will not cry out in pain. This assumes suffering as part of the Servant's future (chap. 53). At Gethsemane Jesus went quietly when arrested (Mt 26:47ff). Later He quietly bore the crossbeam of His cross a portion of the way as He walked the streets toward His execution site: Golgotha (Jn 19:17).

42:3 The Servant's work of bringing justice to the world is also characterized by compassion. Like God who would not destroy Sodom and Gomorrah if just 10 righteous people could be found there, so the Servant will not crush anyone, provided there is even a glimmer of hope in them (a bruised reed . . . a smoldering wick).

42:4 The word **islands** refers to the distant nations, so it is a way of referring to all the nations. The whole earth will heed God's **instruction**, bringing justice to the world. In 2:2-4 the same idea is presented in the form of a picture of the nations streaming to Zion to receive the law.

42:5 God is not a part of creation, He is its Creator. He is also not a human being, but the One who created human beings. He gave them **breath**, starting with Adam (Gn 2:7).

42:6 God had entered into a **covenant** with Abraham on behalf not only of future Israel, but also of the **nations** (Gn 12:1-3). But history shows Israel's miserable failure. Again, God's purposes were fulfilled in the good news of Jesus

and a light to the nations,[a]

7 in order to open blind eyes,[b]
to bring out prisoners
from the dungeon,[c]
and those sitting in darkness
from the prison house.

8 I am Yahweh, that is My name;
I will not give My glory
to another[d]
or My praise to idols.

9 The past events
have indeed happened.
Now I declare new events;[e]
I announce them to you
before they occur."

A Song of Praise

10 Sing a new song to the LORD;[f]
sing His praise from the ends
of the earth,
you who go down to the sea with all
that fills it,[g]
you islands with your[A] inhabitants.

11 Let the desert and its cities shout,
the settlements where Kedar dwells
cry aloud.[h]
Let the inhabitants of Sela
sing for joy;[i]
let them cry out
from the mountaintops.

12 Let them give glory to the LORD
and declare His praise in the islands.

13 The LORD advances like a warrior;
He stirs up His zeal like a soldier.[j]

He shouts, He roars aloud,
He prevails over His enemies.

14 "I have kept silent from ages past;
I have been quiet
and restrained Myself.[k]
But now, I will groan like a woman
in labor,[l]
gasping breathlessly.

15 I will lay waste mountains and hills
and dry up all their vegetation.
I will turn rivers into islands
and dry up marshes.[m]

16 I will lead the blind by a way
they did not know;[n]
I will guide them on paths
they have not known.
I will turn darkness to light in front
of them[o]
and rough places into level ground.[p]
This is what I will do for them,
and I will not forsake them.[q]

17 They will be turned back
and utterly ashamed—
those who trust in idols
and say to metal-plated images:
You are our gods![r]

Israel's Blindness and Deafness

18 "Listen, you deaf!
Look, you blind, so that you may see.[s]

19 Who is blind but My servant,[t]
or deaf like My messenger
I am sending?

Cross references

a 42:6 Is 49:6
b 42:7 Ac 26:17-18
c Is 35:5; 49:9; 61:1; Heb 2:14-15
d 42:8 Ex 20:3-5; Is 48:11
e 42:9 Is 43:19; 48:3,6; Rv 21:4
f 42:10 Ps 33:3; 96:1; 98:1; 144:9
g Ps 96:11; 98:7
h 42:11 Is 21:16; 60:7
i Is 16:1
j 42:13 Is 9:7; 26:11; 37:32; 59:17
k 42:14 Ps 50:21; Is 57:11; 62:1; 64:12; 65:6
l Is 13:8
m 42:15 Is 44:27; 50:2; Nah 1:4-6
n 42:16 Is 29:18; 30:21; 32:3; Jr 31:8-9; Lk 1:78-79
o Eph 5:8
p Is 40:4; Lk 3:5
q Jos 1:5; Ps 94:14; Is 41:17; Heb 13:5
r 42:17 Ps 97:7; Is 1:29; 44:9,11; 45:16
s 42:18 Is 35:5
t 42:19 Is 41:8-9; 43:10; 44:1-2,21; 45:4; 48:20; 49:3; 54:17; Ezk 28:25; 37:25; Lk 1:54

A 42:10 Lit *their*

Christ whose death and resurrection brought hope (**light**) to the Gentiles. He was the One who established the new covenant anticipated by Jeremiah (Jr 31:31-34; Lk 22:20).

42:7 The Servant brought those who were in spiritual and physical **darkness** into the light of God's grace.

42:8-9 God is superior to the **idols** that are really nothing at all. After all, they can neither interpret the significance of **past events** nor announce what will happen in the future (cp. 41:22).

42:10-17 This song celebrating God's making all things new through His judgment follows the first Servant Song.

42:10 The expression **new song** occurs only in Isaiah, Psalms (Ps 33:3; 40:3; 98:1; 149:1), and Revelation (Rv 5:9; 14:3). With only minor exceptions, "new song" is associated, as here, with the image of God as a warrior. It is the warrior who causes all things to become new through His refining warfare (see note at Ps 149:1). All the nations are urged to join in the praise. On **islands**, see note at 41:1.

42:11 The litany of the far-flung participants in the song of praise of God continues. **Kedar** refers to a desert-dwelling Arabic tribe, while **Sela** was a major city in Edom, a mountainous region. The two sites thus represent isolated desert and mountain regions.

42:12 On **islands**, see note at 41:1.

42:13 The first explicit mention of God as **a warrior** comes at the time of the crossing of the Red Sea (Ex 15:4) when He rescued His helpless people and destroyed Egypt's elite chariot troops. Earlier anticipations extend back to the stationing of cherubim at the entrance to the garden of Eden (Gn 3:24). When God appears as a warrior, there is no uncertainty about the outcome.

42:14 God has been **silent**. He has not made an appearance as a warrior for a long time, but that is about to change. He is about to give birth to His righteous anger toward the enemy of His people.

42:15 God's appearance as a warrior is often described as having catastrophic results for the physical creation. Fertility stops for a time, and water sources go dry (24:4-13; Nah 1:4-6).

42:16-17 God will rescue His people (**the blind**) and will make their way smooth. **Those who trust in idols** will not be helped but will experience shame.

42:18-25 The chapter ends with an oracle that explains why God's people will experience judgment before they receive the deliverance described in the previous hymn (vv. 10-17).

42:18-20 God describes His **servant** Israel as **blind** and **deaf**. These physical disabilities represent spiritual disabilities; they don't perceive God's guidance.

Who is blind like My dedicated one,[A]
or blind like the servant of the LORD?
20 Though seeing many things,[B]
you do not obey.
Though his ears are open,
he does not listen."[a]

21 The LORD was pleased, because of
His righteousness,
to magnify His instruction
and make it glorious.
22 But this is a people plundered
and looted,
all of them trapped in holes
or imprisoned in dungeons.
They have become plunder[b]
with no one to rescue them
and loot, with no one saying,
"Give it back!"
23 Who among you will pay attention
to this?
Let him listen and obey in the future.
24 Who gave Jacob to the robber,[c]
and Israel to the plunderers?
Was it not the LORD?
Have we not sinned against Him?
They were not willing to walk
in His ways,

[cross references column]
[a]42:20 Rm 2:21-23
[b]42:22 Dt 1:39; Jr 2:14; Ezk 34:8; 36:4
[c]42:25 Is 29:13; 47:7; 57:1; Jr 12:11; Hs 7:9
[d]43:1 Is 43:7,15,21; 44:2,21,24
[e]Is 44:22-23; 48:20
[f]Gn 32:28; Is 45:3-4
[g]43:2 Dt 31:6,8,23; Jos 1:5; 3:7; Jr 1:8; 30:11; 46:28
[h]Ps 66:12; Is 8:7-8
[i]Is 29:6; 30:27-29; Dn 3:25,27
[j]43:3 Ex 20:2; Is 41:13
[k]Is 19:20; 43:11; 45:15,21; 49:26; 60:16; 63:8

and they would not listen
to His instruction.
25 So He poured out on Jacob
His furious anger
and the power of war.
It surrounded him with fire,
but he did not know it;
it burned him, but he paid
no attention.[D,c]

Restoration of Israel

43 Now this is what the LORD says—
the One who created you, Jacob,
and the One who formed you, Israel[d]—
"Do not fear, for I have redeemed you;[e]
I have called you by your name;
you are Mine.[f]
2 I will be with you[g]
when you pass through the waters,[h]
and when you pass
through the rivers,
they will not overwhelm you.
You will not be scorched
when you walk through the fire,[i]
and the flame will not burn you.
3 For I ·Yahweh your God,[j]
the Holy One of Israel,
and your Savior,[k]

[A]42:19 Hb obscure   [B]42:20 Alt Hb tradition reads *You see many things;*   [C]42:24 Lit *to loot*   [D]42:25 Lit *he did not put on heart*

42:21 The people's inability to see and hear God's instruction was not a failure on God's part. He magnified His **instruction** and made it **glorious**. Only the most spiritually insensitive could miss it. God had even sent the prophets—men like Isaiah and later Jeremiah and Ezekiel—to make His instruction clearer, but still they did not obey.

42:22 God's people have become **plunder**, a reference to the judgment He will bring on them, specifically the exile. No one will help them. The reference to **holes** is to makeshift prisons, similar to the cistern in which Jeremiah was held (Jr 38).

42:24-25 God is the One who has allowed Israel to be the plunder of the nations as punishment for not following His law.

43:1 Calling a person by his **name** indicates a high level of familiarity. The phrase might even hint at the fact that God gave them their names, an act to indicate superiority and perhaps even ownership. God gave Israel its name when He changed the name of the patriarch Jacob to Israel (Gn 32:28). The intention of this oracle is expressed clearly at the start (**Do not fear**; see also Is 43:5). God informed His people about their coming deliverance to keep them from caving in to fear.

43:2 The **waters** can be naturally dangerous just like the **fire** mentioned in the second half of the verse. However, the waters in particular can stand for the forces of chaos and evil (Dn 7:1-9) or some kind of personal duress (Ps 69:1-3). The background for this symbolic use of water comes from ancient Near Eastern creation stories where there was a conflict between the creator god and the god or goddess of water. The promise that God will be with His people is a cov-

enant formula that indicates the close relationship between God and His people.

43:3-4 God's people are so **precious** that He is willing to save them at the price (**ransom**) of **Egypt . . . Cush**, and **Seba**. The land of Cush was south of Egypt, on the upper (southern) portion of the Nile River, roughly identical to modern Ethiopia. Seba's location is unknown. Some scholars take this as a reference to the fact that while King Cyrus of Persia decreed the restoration of Judah, his successors

yatsar

Hebrew Pronunciation	[yah TSAR]
HCSB Translation	form
Uses in Isaiah	27
Uses in the OT	63
Focus Passage	Isaiah 43:1,7,10,21

This common Semitic verb means *form* (Gn 2:7), especially regarding pottery. The participle denotes *potter* (Is 29:16) or *craftsman* (Hab 2:18); *pottery* is sometimes literally "article of a *potter*" (Ps 2:9). *Yatsar* signifies *make* (Is 44:9), *craft* (Ps 33:15), *plan* (Is 46:11), or *shape* (Ps 33:15). Men *create* trouble (Ps 94:20). The participle describes God as *Creator* or *Maker* (Is 27:11; 45:9). So comparing God to a *potter* is natural (Jr 18:2-6). God *forms* mountains (Am 4:13), locust swarms (Am 7:1), and man's spirit (Zch 12:1). *Yatsar* occurs alongside *bara'* ("create"; 5x; Is 45:18) and *'asah* ("make"; 21x; Jr 33:2). Twice *yatsar* accompanies related *yetser* (9x), where the noun means *shape* (Hab 2:18) or *what is formed* (Is 29:16). *Yetser* also indicates *intention* (1Ch 28:9), *scheme* (Gn 6:5), *inclination* (Gn 8:21), *mind* (Is 26:3), *desire* (1Ch 29:18), and *what someone is made of* (Ps 103:14).

give Egypt as a ransom for you,
˙Cush and Seba in your place.
4 Because you are precious in My sight[a]
and honored, and I love you,[b]
I will give people in exchange for you
and nations instead of your life.
5 Do not fear, for I am with you;
I will bring your descendants
from the east,[c]
and gather you from the west.[d]
6 I will say to the north: Give them up!
and to the south:
    Do not hold them back!
Bring My sons from far away,[e]
and My daughters from the ends
of the earth[f]—
7 everyone called by My name
and created for My glory.
I have formed him;
    indeed, I have made him."

8 Bring out a people who are blind,
yet have eyes,[g]
and are deaf, yet have ears.
9 All the nations are gathered together,
and the peoples are assembled.[h]
Who among them can declare this,[i]
and tell us the former things?
Let them present their witnesses
to vindicate themselves,
so that people may hear and say,
    "It is true."
10 "You are My witnesses"[j]—
       this is the LORD's declaration—
"and My servant
    whom I have chosen,[k]

so that you may know and believe Me
and understand that I am He.[l]
No god was formed before Me,
and there will be none after Me.[m]
11 I, I am Yahweh,
and there is no other Savior but Me.[n]
12 I alone declared, saved,
    and proclaimed—
and not some foreign god[A] among you.
So you are My witnesses"—
       this is the LORD's declaration—
"and[B] I am God.[o]
13 Also, from today on I am He alone,
and none can deliver from My hand.[p]
I act, and who can reverse it?"[q]

God's Deliverance of Rebellious Israel

14 This is what the LORD, your Redeemer,[r] the Holy One of Israel[s] says:

Because of you, I will send to Babylon
and bring all of them as fugitives,[c]
even the Chaldeans[t] in the ships
in which they rejoice.[D]
15 I am Yahweh, your Holy One,
the Creator of Israel, your King.

16 This is what the LORD says—
who makes a way in the sea,
and a path through surging waters,[u]
17 who brings out the chariot and horse,[v]
the army and the mighty one together
(they lie down, they do not rise again;
they are extinguished,
    quenched like a wick[w])—
18 "Do not remember the past events,

a 43:4 2Kg 1:13-14; Ps 36:7; 72:14; Pr 3:15; Is 28:16
b Is 63:9
c 43:5 Is 41:8; 61:9
d Is 49:12
e 43:6 2Co 6:18
f Is 45:22
g 43:8 Is 6:9; 42:19; Ezk 12:2
h 43:9 Is 34:1; 41:1
i Is 41:22-23,26 Ac 1:8
j 43:10 Is 44:8; Ac 1:8
k Is 41:8
l Is 41:4
m Is 44:6,8; 45:5-6
n 43:11 Is 43:3; 45:21; Hs 13:4
o 43:12 Ps 46:10; 50:7; Is 45:22; 46:9
p 43:13 Dt 32:39; Jn 10:28-29
q Jb 9:12; Is 14:27
r 43:14 Jb 19:25; Ps 19:14; 78:35; Pr 23:11; Is 41:14; Jr 50:34
s Is 1:4
t Is 23:13
u 43:16 Ex 14:21-22; Ps 77:19; Is 11:15; 44:27; 50:2; 51:10; 63:11-12
v 43:17 Ex 15:19
w Ps 118:12; Is 1:31

A 43:12 Lit *not a foreigner*   B 43:12 Or *that*   C 43:14 Or *will break down all their bars*   D 43:14 Hb obscure

went on to attack Egypt and Cush. Indeed, God is willing to give much more than these three countries in place of His people.

43:5-6 God will **gather** His people from all over the world, **east** and **west . . . north** and **south**. The reference is to the restoration from the exile. The returns under Sheshbazzar and Zerubbabel as well as the later returns under Ezra and Nehemiah show that the Lord kept His promise.

43:7 The exile will not result in the eradication of God's special people. After all, He **created** them. They will preserve their distinct identity and not be merged into foreign populations.

43:8 Israel, God's servant, is a people who were **blind** and **deaf** (see note at 42:18-20). Since they had functioning **eyes** and **ears**, the reference is to spiritual insensitivity.

43:9 The challenge to find someone among the **nations** who could tell the significance of past events is another sarcastic comment on the mute, powerless idols of the nations (41:22; 42:9).

43:10-12 God called to the assembled nations (v. 9) to be a witness. He also called on His people, whom He identified

as His **servant**, to be His **witnesses**. The calling of witnesses associates this passage with the courtroom. Not only is God better than the foreign gods, those gods do not exist at all. The nations were silent when asked to witness to their gods' work in their lives. God's people functioned as God's witness to the fact that He had saved them in the past.

43:14 God will turn the Babylonians into **fugitives**, suggesting that their cities will be defeated and they will wander from place to place. **Chaldeans** were an Aramaic-speaking tribe of Babylon that rose up in the seventh century B.C. to lead the charge against Assyria, thus establishing the Neo-Babylonian Empire. The Chaldean tribe's home base was at the point where the Tigris and Euphrates rivers emptied into what is today called the Persian Gulf. Thus shipping was very important to them.

43:16-17 God called on His people to remember their great deliverance from the Egyptians at the Red Sea (Ex 14).

43:18-19 The exodus poetically described in verses 16-17 is described as **past events**, the **things of old**. But God turns the hearers' attention to **something new**, a new exodus. This time God will create not "a way in the sea" (v. 16), but

pay no attention to things of old.[a]

19 Look, I am about to do
    something new;[b]
even now it is coming.
    Do you not see it?
Indeed, I will make a way
    in the wilderness,[c]
rivers[A] in the desert.

20 The animals of the field
    will honor Me,
jackals and ostriches,
because I provide water
    in the wilderness,
and rivers in the desert,[d]
    to give drink to My chosen people.

21 The people I formed for Myself
    will declare My praise.[e]

22 "But Jacob, you have not called on Me,
because, Israel, you have become weary
    of Me.[f]

23 You have not brought Me your sheep
    for *burnt offerings
or honored Me with your sacrifices.[g]
I have not burdened you with offerings
    or wearied you with incense.[B]

24 You have not bought Me aromatic cane
    with silver,
or satisfied Me with the fat
    of your sacrifices.
But you have burdened Me
    with your sins;
you have wearied Me[h]
    with your iniquities.[i]

25 "It is I who sweep away
    your transgressions[j]
    for My own sake[k]

and remember your sins no more.[l]

26 Take Me to court; let us argue
    our case together.[m]
State your case, so that you may
    be vindicated.

27 Your first father sinned,[n]
and your mediators have rebelled
    against Me.[o]

28 So I defiled the officers
    of the sanctuary,
and *set Jacob apart
    for destruction[p]
and Israel for abuse.

Spiritual Blessing

44 "And now listen, Jacob My servant,
    Israel whom I have chosen.[q]

2 This is the word of the LORD
    your Maker who formed you
        from the womb;
He[C] will help you:
Do not fear; Jacob is My servant;
    I have chosen Jeshurun.[D,r]

3 For I will pour water on
        the thirsty land
and streams on the dry ground;
I will pour out My Spirit[s]
        on your descendants
and My blessing on your offspring.

4 They will sprout among[E] the grass
    like poplars by flowing streams.

5 This one will say, 'I am the LORD's';
another will call himself by the name
    of Jacob;
still another will write on his hand,
    'The LORD's,'

---

[a]43:18 Is 65:17; Jr 23:7
[b]43:19 Is 42:9; 48:6; 2Co 5:17
[c]Ex 17:6; Nm 20:11; Dt 8:15; Ps 78:16; Is 35:1,6; 41:18-19; 49:10; 51:3
[d]43:20 Is 41:17-18; 48:21
[e]43:21 Ps 102:18; Is 42:12; Lk 1:74-75; 1Pt 2:9
[f]43:22 Mc 6:3; Mal 1:13; 3:14
[g]43:23 Zch 7:5-6; Mal 1:6-8
[h]43:24 Ps 95:10; Is 1:14; 7:13; Ezk 6:9; Mal 2:17
[i]Is 13:11
[j]43:25 Is 44:22; 55:7; Jr 50:20; Heb 2:17
[k]Is 37:35; 48:9,11; Ezk 36:22
[l]Is 38:17; Jr 31:34; Mk 2:7
[m]43:26 Is 1:18; 41:1; 50:8
[n]43:27 Is 51:2; Ezk 16:3
[o]Is 9:15; 28:7; 29:10; Jr 5:31
[p]43:28 Is 24:6; 34:5; Jr 24:9; Dn 9:11; Zch 8:13
[q]44:1 Is 41:8-9; 42:1; 43:10,20; 45:4; 49:7; 65:9,15,22
[r]44:2 Dt 32:15; 33:5,26
[s]44:3 Is 32:15; Jl 2:28

A43:19 DSS read *paths* B43:23 With demands for offerings and incense C44:2 Lit *from the womb, and He* D44:2 = Upright One, referring to Israel E44:4 Some Hb mss, DSS, LXX read *as among*

---

a way in the wilderness. This future deliverance is pictured as a reversal of nature, with **rivers in the desert**.

43:20-21 Because of the new provision of water in the wilderness, the animals that live there will be pleased. In the same way, God's people who have been oppressed by the Babylonians will find new freedom.

43:22-24 Whether Israel literally stopped offering **sacrifices** or whether they simply offered them hypocritically is not important; proper sacrifices were not being offered. The passage revolves around the word "weary." The people were **weary** of God so they did not offer requisite sacrifice. But it was not God's fault—the purpose of the sacrificial laws was not to weary them but to free them from their sins. Since the people refused to see this, God was instead **wearied** by the **sins** of His people.

43:25 The people sinned, but God forgave. The idea of removal of sin is communicated by the action of sweeping as well as the mental act of forgetting. To remember something is to act on it, and to forget is to hold back from acting.

43:26-28 Once again a court setting is introduced. God challenged His people to **argue** their **case** against Him. The reference to Israel's **first father** is likely Jacob, whose name was changed to Israel. Jacob was well known for his foolish and sinful ways (Hs 12:1-6).

44:1 Again, **Jacob** or **Israel** is explicitly identified as God's **servant** (v. 21; 41:8-9; 42:19; 43:1). God had **chosen** Israel from among the nations to be His special people (Dt 7:7-11). In this way, He created Israel.

44:2-3 The phrase **formed you from the womb** evokes the metaphor of God as the mother who gave birth to Israel. **Jeshurun** is used as a name for Israel (Dt 32:15; 33:5,26) in contexts that indicate it is a term of endearment. It is obscure in meaning but may be related to the Hebrew word *yashar*, which means "virtuous." The theme of turning dry land into fertile land is an image of physical and/or spiritual transformation. The results are growth, in this case among the **descendants** of the people of God.

44:5 Writing on one's **hand** signified intimacy, though some (Walton, pp. 628–29) believe it refers to a slave mark show-

and name himself by the name
  of Israel."

No God Other Than Yahweh

⁶This is what the Lord, the King of Israel
and its Redeemer,ᵃ the Lord of *Hosts, says:

I am the first and I am the last.ᵇ
There is no God but Me.ᶜ
⁷ Who, like Me, can announce
    the future?
Let him say so and make a case
    before Me,ᵈ
since I have established
    an ancient people.
Let these gods declareᴬ
    the coming things,
and what will take place.
⁸ Do not be startled or afraid.
Have I not told you and declared it
    long ago?
You are my witnesses!ᵉ
Is there any God but Me?ᶠ
There is no other Rock;ᵍ
    I do not know any.

⁹ All who make idols are nothing,
and what they treasure does not profit.
Their witnesses do not see
    or know anything,
so they will be put to shame.ʰ
¹⁰ Who makes a god or casts
    a metal image
for no profit?ⁱ
¹¹ Look, all its worshipers will be
    put to shame,
and the craftsmen are humans.
They all will assemble and stand;
they all will be startled
    and put to shame.

¹² The ironworker labors over the coals,
shapes the idol with hammers,

and works it with his strong arm.
Also he grows hungry
    and his strength fails;
he doesn't drink water and is faint.
¹³ The woodworker stretches out
    a measuring line,
he outlines it with a stylus;
he shapes it with chisels
and outlines it with a compass.
He makes it according to
    a human likeness,ʲ
like a beautiful person,
to dwell in a temple.
¹⁴ He cuts downᴮ cedars for his use,
or he takes a cypress or an oak.
He lets it grow strong among the trees
    of the forest.
He plants a laurel, and the rain
    makes it grow.
¹⁵ It serves as fuel for man.
He takes some of it
    and warms himself;
also he kindles a fire
    and bakes bread;
he even makes it into a god
    and worships it;
he makes an idol from it
    and bows down to it.
¹⁶ He burns half of it in a fire,
and he roasts meat on that half.
He eats the roast and is satisfied.
He warms himself and says, "Ah!
I am warm, I see the blaze."
¹⁷ He makes a god or his idol with the rest
    of it.
He bows down to it and worships;
He prays to it,ᵏ "Save me, for you are
    my god."
¹⁸ Such peopleᶜ do not comprehend
and cannot understand,

ᵃ44:6 Is 41:14;
43:14
ᵇIs 41:4; 43:10;
48:12; Rv 1:8,17;
22:13
ᶜIs 43:11; 44:8;
45:5-6
ᵈ44:7 Is 41:22,26
ᵉ44:8 Is 43:10
ᶠDt 4:35,39; 1Sm
2:2; Is 45:5; Jl
2:27
ᵍIs 17:10; 26:4;
30:29
ʰ44:9 Ps 97:7;
Is 42:17; 44:11;
45:16
ⁱ44:10 Is 41:29;
Jr 10:5; Hab
2:18; Ac 19:26
ʲ44:13 Ps
115:5-7
ᵏ44:17 1Kg
18:26,28; Is
45:20

ᴬ44:7 Lit *declare them*—   ᴮ44:14 Lit *To cut down for himself*   ᶜ44:18 Lit *They*

---

ing ownership. In either case, the idea is that people will want to identify and align themselves with the Lord.

44:6 A long argument against idols begins with an assertion of the uniqueness of God.

44:7 Only God can reveal the **future**, something that He does through His prophets (cp. 41:22; 42:9).

44:8 The invocation of **witnesses** places this passage in a courtroom setting. These witnesses will bear testimony to the fact that only Yahweh is a **Rock**—a place of protection and stability—not the false gods of the nations.

44:12-20 These verses describe the construction and worship of an idol. Ancient texts describing the making and care of idols confirm such a process. Pagan Near Eastern religious leaders probably did not believe that an idol was the actual god, but they did believe that the god made its power and presence known in the physical object. Thus the

idol was seen as a potent representation of the deity. Laypeople, on the other hand, likely made a stronger association between idols and the deities, taking the graven wood or metal to be true deity. In any case, Isaiah's argument was one that reduced all idolatry to its absurd foundation.

44:12-13 Some ancient idols were made from metal and others from wood. The description of their manufacture emphasizes that these were human creations.

44:14 Isaiah went back in this verse to the beginning of the process of constructing an idol—the planting and cultivation of a tree.

44:15-19 These verses express the ultimate absurdity of idolatry. The same wood used to construct an idol was also used to kindle a **fire** to keep warm and to cook food. Isaiah was aware that ancient Near Eastern people utilized rituals that intended to turn the wooden idol into an object

for He has shut their eyes[A]
    so they cannot see,
and their minds
    so they cannot understand.
[19] No one reflects,
no one has the perception or insight
    to say,
"I burned half of it in the fire,
I also baked bread on its coals,
I roasted meat and ate.
I will make something detestable[a]
    with the rest of it,
and I will bow down to a block
    of wood."
[20] He feeds on[B] ashes.
His deceived mind has led him astray,
and he cannot deliver himself,
or say, "Isn't there a lie
    in my right hand?"[b]

[21] Remember these things, Jacob,
and Israel, for you are My servant;
I formed you, you are My servant;
Israel, you will never be forgotten
    by Me.[C,c]
[22] I have swept away your transgressions
    like a cloud,[d]
and your sins like a mist.
Return to Me,[e]
for I have redeemed you.[f]
[23] Rejoice, heavens,[g] for the LORD
    has acted;
shout, depths of the earth.
Break out into singing, mountains,
forest, and every tree in it.

For the LORD has redeemed Jacob,
and glorifies Himself through Israel.[h]

Restoration of Israel through Cyrus

[24] This is what the LORD, your Redeemer[i] who formed you from the womb,[j] says:

I am •Yahweh, who made everything;
who stretched out the heavens
    by Myself;[k]
who alone spread out
    the earth;
[25] who destroys the omens
    of the false prophets
and makes fools of diviners;
who confounds the wise
and makes
    their knowledge foolishness;[l]
[26] who confirms the message
    of His servant
and fulfills the counsel
    of His messengers;
who says to Jerusalem, "She will
    be inhabited,"
and to the cities of Judah, "They will
    be rebuilt,"
and I will restore her ruins;
[27] who says to the depths of the sea,
    "Be dry,"
and I will dry up your rivers;
[28] who says to Cyrus,[m] "My shepherd,
he will fulfill all My pleasure"[n]
and says to Jerusalem, "She will
    be rebuilt,"[o]
and of the temple, "Its foundation
    will be laid."

---

[a]44:19 Dt 27:15; 1Kg 11:5,7; 2Kg 23:13-14
[b]44:20 Is 57:11; 59:3-4,13; Rm 1:25
[c]44:21 Is 49:15
[d]44:22 Ps 51:1,9; Is 43:25; Ac 3:19
[e]Is 31:6; 55:7
[f]Is 43:1; 48:20; 1Co 6:20; 1Pt 1:18-19
[g]44:23 Ps 69:34; 96:11-12; Is 42:10; 49:13
[h]Is 49:3; 61:3
[i]44:24 Is 41:14; 43:14
[j]Is 44:2
[k]Is 40:22; 42:5; 45:12,18; 51:13
[l]44:25 2Sm 15:31; Jb 5:12-14; Ps 33:10; Is 29:14; Jr 51:57; 1Co 1:20,27
[m]44:28 Is 45:1
[n]Eph 1:9
[o]2Ch 36:22-23; Ezr 1:1; Is 14:32; 45:13; 54:11

[A]44:18 Or *for their eyes are shut*   [B]44:20 Or *He shepherds*   [C]44:21 DSS, LXX, Tg read *Israel, do not forget Me*

---

of worship. In Mesopotamia these were called "opening of the mouth" rituals. Via this ritual, the presence of the god was thought to enter the piece of wood. Jeremiah 10:1-5 expresses a similar idea.

44:20 The **lie** in a person's **right hand** is a reference to an idol that represented a false god and was really nothing at all.

44:21 Israel will benefit from remembering the lesson about the absurdity of idolatry since that will keep God's people from practicing false worship. God **formed** His people; they did not form their god like the idolaters did. Israel was the **servant** of God (v. 1; 41:8-9; 42:19; 43:1).

44:23 In idolatry, a bit of nature, a piece of wood, was worshiped. Here God's creation—especially the **forest, and every tree in it**—worships God.

44:24-28 In these verses God's sovereignty over His creation and the future is asserted. God affirmed His prophets over against those prophets who deceived.

44:24 On the image of God stretching out the **heavens** and spreading the **earth**, see note at 42:5. This description demonstrates God's control over the cosmos. He puts it up like a Bedouin erects a tent.

44:25 The sovereign God confuses and destroys those who claim to reveal the future. Such people are condemned and contrasted with true prophets in Dt 18:9-22. The type of "prophets" this verse has in mind were diviners, not those who received revelation from God. Diviners manipulated or observed such things as sheep livers, cloud formations, and the stars to determine the future.

44:26 In contrast to the false prophets are God's messengers with the message that Jerusalem will be rebuilt and reinhabited.

44:27 God's ability to restore Jerusalem is affirmed by reference to His control of nature, specifically that He can make bodies of water go **dry**. Since water is often a symbol of the forces of chaos, perhaps the meaning of this verse is that God will subdue those chaotic forces that held Judah captive.

44:28 God announced the agent of His rescue of exiled Judah—**Cyrus** the Great. Thus Isaiah, whose ministry spanned four kings whose reigns stretched from 742 to 686 B.C., named a ruler who was not yet born. The prophetic reference is to Persia's defeat of Babylon under the leadership of Cyrus in 539 B.C., an event that led to permission for the Jews to return to their homeland and rebuild Jerusalem. Cyrus is called a **shepherd**, a common metaphor for a royal figure.

45 The LORD says this to Cyrus,
  His anointed,[a]
  whose right hand I have grasped[b]
  to subdue nations before him,
  to disarm[A] kings,[c]
  to open the doors before him
  and the gates will not be shut:
2 "I will go before you
  and level the uneven places;[B,d]
  I will shatter the bronze doors
  and cut the iron bars in two.[e]
3 I will give you the treasures of darkness
  and riches from secret places,[f]
  so that you may know that I,
  ·Yahweh,
  the God of Israel call you
  by your name.[g]
4 I call you by your name,
  because of Jacob My servant[h]
  and Israel My chosen one.
  I give a name to you,
  though you do not know Me.
5 I am Yahweh, and there is no other;[i]

there is no God but Me.[j]
  I will strengthen[c] you,
  though you do not know Me,
6 so that all may know from the rising
    of the sun to its setting
  that there is no one but Me.[k]
  I am Yahweh, and there is no other.
7 I form light and create darkness,[l]
  I make success and create disaster;[m]
  I, Yahweh, do all these things.

8 "Heavens, sprinkle from above,
  and let the skies shower righteousness.[n]
  Let the earth open up
  so that salvation will sprout
  and righteousness will spring up
    with it.[o]
  I, Yahweh, have created it.

9 "Woe to the one who argues
    with his Maker—
  one clay pot among many.[D]
  Does clay say to the one forming it,
  'What are you making?'[p]

Cross references (center column):

a45:1 Is 44:28
bPs 73:23; Is 41:13; 42:6
cJb 12:21; Is 45:5
d45:2 Is 40:4
ePs 107:16
f45:3 Jr 41:8; 50:37
gEx 33:12,17; Is 43:1; 49:1
h45:4 Is 41:8; 42:19
i45:5 Is 45:6,14,18,21; 46:9
jIs 44:6,8
k45:6 Ps 102:15; Is 37:20; Mal 1:11
l45:7 Ps 104:20; 105:28
mGn 50:20; 1Sm 16:14; 1Kg 21:21; 22:8; 2Kg 6:33; Ps 78:49; Jb 2:10; Is 13:11; 31:2; 47:11; Jr 1:14; Lm 3:38; Am 3:6
n45:8 Hs 10:12
oPs 85:11; Is 61:11
p45:9 Is 29:16; 64:8; Jr 18:6; Rm 9:20-21

A45:1 Lit *unloosen the loins*   B45:2 DSS, LXX read *the mountains*   C45:5 Lit *gird*   D45:9 Lit *a clay pot with clay pots of the ground*

The rebuilding of Jerusalem is associated with the rebuilding of the **temple**, a hope that became reality in 515 B.C.

45:1-8 In this section, written at least 140 years before it was fulfilled, God speaks to Cyrus and announces how He intends to use Him as His agent. The passage divinely commissions Cyrus. There is no reason to believe that Cyrus was conscious of His role as God's agent of redemption any more than Assyria or Babylon were conscious that they were used as the tool of God's anger. Indeed, the final lines of verses 4 and 5 state as much.

45:1 God called Cyrus His **anointed**. The Hebrew word can be rendered "Messiah" in English. Here the use is metaphorical of God's invisible commissioning of this earthly king to function as a royal deliverer of His people. In the ancient Near East, when a god **grasped** the **right hand** of someone, it indicated special favor, commissioning, guidance, and divine endowment with skill.

45:2 God will cause the strong defenses of enemy cities to fall before Cyrus. He will level the **uneven places** (cp. 40:3-6) to speed his attack.

45:3 As Cyrus defeated nations (including Medes, Lydians, and Babylonians), their wealth would come into his possession. These **treasures** were hidden away from the world and thus are associated with **darkness** and considered **secret**.

45:4 God's actions toward Cyrus have nothing to do with God's love for Cyrus or the Persians. He will use them on behalf of His people whom He calls His **servant** (see note at 44:1). The fact that God named Cyrus and called him shows that the Persian king was under His control. The fact that God could forename Cyrus through Isaiah also shows God's ability to read the future.

45:5-7 No one should ascribe these great acts of redemption to any other god than Yahweh, the only true God. His lordship is not just over Israel but the entire world (**from the rising of the sun to its setting**). He is in control not only of the good things but also of the difficult things that occur in history.

45:8 This verse describes more than literal fruitfulness; it talks about how, on God's command, the future will see the earth morally replenished.

45:9-13 The woe oracle in these verses responds to those who would argue with God for using a pagan king like Cyrus to accomplish His purposes.

45:9 On **woe** oracles, see notes at 1:4 and 5:8-30. Human beings are the **pot** and God is the potter. This image reminds humans of their proper place in relationship to God. There may be an allusion here to Gn 2:7 where God took the dust of the ground and formed Adam. The ancient Near Eastern myths of Atrahasis and Enuma Elish describe human beings as the product of clay. Where the biblical and

bara'

Hebrew Pronunciation	[bah RAH]
HCSB Translation	create
Uses in Isaiah	21
Uses in the OT	48
Focus Passage	Isaiah 45:7-8,12,18

Bara', occurring in the active and passive, is theological in that it has no clear subject other than God. *Bara'* always connotes *create*, though occasionally it is better translated *be done* (Ex 34:10) or *bring about* (Nm 16:30). It suggests *creating* something new (Jr 31:22). The participle refers to God as *Creator* (Is 40:28). He not only *created* the whole universe (Gn 1:1) but such particulars as sea creatures (Gn 1:21), heavenly bodies (Is 40:26), and wind (Am 4:13). *Bara'* most frequently describes the creation of human beings (Is 45:12), both peoples and individuals (Ezk 21:30; 28:15). *Bara'* applies to providential acts such as new generations (Ps 102:18). God *creates* disaster as well as words of praise (Is 45:7; 57:19). Spiritually, He *creates* clean hearts (Ps 51:10) and will *create* Jerusalem to be a joy (Is 65:18). The related noun *beriyah*, translated *something unprecedented*, indicates circumstances that God would create (Nm 16:30).

Or does your work say,
'He has no hands'?[A]

10 How absurd is the one who says
    to his father,
'What are you fathering?'
or to his mother,
'What are you giving birth to?'"

11 This is what the LORD,
    the Holy One of Israel[a]
    and its Maker, says:
"Ask Me what is to happen to[B] My sons,[b]
and instruct Me about the work
    of My hands.[c]

12 I made the earth,
and created man on it.
It was My hands that stretched out
    the heavens,[d]
and I commanded all their host.

13 I have raised him up
    in righteousness,[e]
and will level all roads for him.
He will rebuild My city,[f]
and set My exiles free,[g]
not for a price or a bribe,"
says the LORD of •Hosts.

God Alone is the Savior

14 This is what the LORD says:

The products of Egypt
    and the merchandise of •Cush
and the Sabeans, men of stature,[h]
will come over to you[i]
and will be yours;
they will follow you,
they will come over in chains
and bow down to you.
They will confess[C] to you:
God is indeed with you,[j] and there is
    no other;
there is no other God.

15 Yes, You are a God who hides Himself,[k]
    God of Israel, Savior.[l]

16 All of them are put to shame,
    even humiliated;[m]
the makers of idols
    go in humiliation together.

17 Israel will be saved by the LORD
with an everlasting salvation;
you will not be put to shame
    or humiliated
for all eternity.[n]

18 For this is what Yahweh says—
God is the Creator of the heavens.
He formed the earth and made it.
He established it;
He did not create it to be empty,
but formed it to be inhabited[o]—
"I am Yahweh,
and there is no other.

19 I have not spoken in secret,[p]
somewhere in a land of darkness.
I did not say to the descendants
    of Jacob:
Seek Me in a wasteland.[q]
I, Yahweh, speak truthfully;[r]
I say what is right.

20 "Come, gather together,
and draw near, you fugitives
    of the nations.
Those who carry their wooden idols,
and pray to a god who cannot save,[s]
have no knowledge.[t]

21 Speak up and present your case[D,u]—
yes, let them take counsel together.
Who predicted this long ago?
Who announced it from ancient times?
Was it not I, Yahweh?
There is no other God but Me,
a righteous God and Savior;[v]

---

[a] 45:11 Is 1:4
[b] Jr 31:9
[c] Is 19:25; 29:23; 60:21; 64:8
[d] 45:12 Ps 104:2; Is 42:5; 44:24
[e] 45:13 Is 41:2
[f] 2Ch 36:22-23; Is 44:28
[g] Is 52:3
[h] 45:14 Is 18:1; 43:3
[i] Is 14:1-2; 49:23; 54:3
[j] 1Co 14:25
[k] 45:15 Ps 44:24; Is 1:15; 8:17; 57:17
[l] Is 43:3
[m] 45:16 Is 42:17; 44:9
[n] 45:17 Is 49:23; 50:7; 54:4
[o] 45:18 Gn 1:26; Ps 115:16
[p] 45:19 Is 48:16
[q] 2Ch 15:2; Ps 78:34; Jr 29:13-14
[r] Ps 19:8; Is 45:23; 63:1
[s] 45:20 Is 44:17; 46:1,7; Jr 10:5
[t] Is 44:18-19; 48:5-7
[u] 45:21 Is 41:21-23; 43:9
[v] Is 43:3,11

[A] 45:9 Or making? Your work has no hands.   [B] 45:11 Or Me the coming things about   [C] 45:14 Lit pray   [D] 45:21 Lit and approach

---

ancient Near Eastern accounts differ profoundly is in the second element that forms humans. In the Bible God used his own breath, indicating a high view of humanity. In Mesopotamian accounts the second element was the blood of a demon god, expressing a lower view of human life.

45:10 The second metaphor of God as parent (father and mother) and His human creation as the child also expresses an unbalanced power relationship. A baby does not question his birth any more than a pot questions its creation. So why should Israel question God's plan?

45:11 On Holy One of Israel, see note at 1:4.

45:12 On stretched out the heavens, see note at 42:5.

45:14 Egypt and Cush (Ethiopia; see note at 18:1-7) were nations associated with the Nile Valley. The Sabeans were an Arabian tribe. This verse anticipates a time when these foreign nations will recognize that the God of the Israelites is the one true God.

45:15 On God hiding Himself, see note at verse 19.

45:16 Shame comes on those who trust in idols because their confidence is misplaced.

45:18 The claim that God did not create the world to be uninhabited (empty) may be a polemic against an ancient Near Eastern myth, according to which human beings were created only after the minor gods went on strike from digging irrigation canals and thus needed a workforce.

45:19 While God hid Himself in the sense that He is far above creation (v. 15), He pursues relationship and makes Himself known to His creatures.

45:20 The description of the nations as fugitives may imply a previous judgment against them.

45:21 The challenge to speak up and present your case indicates that this passage has a legal background. The issue involves the gods' ability to reveal the future.

there is no one except Me.[a]

22 Turn to Me and be saved,
all the ends of the earth.
For I am God,
and there is no other.
23 By Myself I have sworn;[b]
Truth has gone from My mouth,[c]
a word that will not be revoked:
Every knee will bow[d] to Me,
every tongue will swear allegiance.
24 It will be said to Me: Righteousness
and strength
is only in the LORD."
All who are enraged against Him
will come to Him and be put to shame.[e]
25 All the descendants of Israel
will be justified and find glory
through the LORD.

There is No One Like God

46 Bel crouches; Nebo cowers.[f]
Their idols are consigned to beasts
and cattle.
The images you carry are loaded,
as a burden for the weary animal.
2 The gods cower; they crouch together;
they are not able to rescue the burden,
but they themselves go into captivity.[g]

3 "Listen to Me, house of Jacob,
all the remnant of the house of Israel,
who have been sustained
from the womb,
carried along since birth.
4 I will be the same until your old age,[h]
and I will bear you up when you
turn gray.
I have made you,
and I will carry you;
I will bear and save you.

5 "Who will you compare Me or make Me
equal to?
Who will you measure Me with,
so that we should be like each other?[i]
6 Those who pour out their bags of gold
and weigh out silver on scales—
they hire a goldsmith and he makes it
into a god.
Then they kneel and bow down
to it.[j]
7 They lift it to their shoulder
and bear it along;[k]
they set it in its place, and there
it stands;
it does not budge from its place.[l]
They cry out to it but it doesn't answer;
it saves no one from his trouble.

8 "Remember this and be brave;[A]
take it to heart, you transgressors!
9 Remember what happened long ago,[m]
for I am God, and there is no other;
I am God, and no one is like Me.
10 I declare the end from the beginning,
and from long ago what is not yet done,
saying: My plan will take place,
and I will do all My will.[n]
11 I call a bird of prey[B] from the east,[o]
a man for My purpose
from a far country.
Yes, I have spoken; so I will also
bring it about.[p]
I have planned it; I will also do it.
12 Listen to me, you hardhearted,
far removed from justice:
13 I am bringing My justice near;[q]
it is not far away,
and My salvation will not delay.
I will put salvation in •Zion,
My splendor in Israel.

---

[a]45:21 Dt 4:35;
6:4; Mk 12:32
[b]45:23 Gn 22:16;
Is 62:8; Heb
6:13
[c]Is 55:11
[d]Rm 14:11; Php
2:10
[e]45:24 Is 41:11
[f]46:1 Jr 50:2-4;
51:44
[g]46:2 Jdg 18:17-
18,24; 2Sm 5:21;
Jr 43:12-13;
48:7; Hs 10:5-6
[h]46:4 Ps 71:18
[i]46:5 Is 40:18,25
[j]46:6 Is 40:19;
41:7; 44:12-17;
Jr 10:4
[k]46:7 Is 45:20;
46:1; Jr 10:5
[l]Is 40:20; 41:7
[m]46:9 Dt 32:7; Is
42:9; 65:17
[n]46:10 Ps 33:11;
Pr 19:21; Is
5:19; 14:24;
25:1; 40:8; Ac
5:39
[o]46:11 Is
44:28-45:1
[p]Nm 23:19; Is
14:24; 37:26
[q]46:13 Is 51:5;
61:11; Rm 3:21

A46:8 Hb obscure   B46:11 = Cyrus

46:1-4 A contrast is drawn in these verses between the idols that had to be carried and God who carried the burdens of His people.

46:1 Bel means "lord" and is likely a reference to Marduk, the chief god of Babylon. **Nebo** is the Hebrew name for Nabu, Marduk's son and an important deity in his own right. Nabu was the god of wisdom, the god of the scribes. These gods, or more precisely the idols that represented them (see note at 44:12-20), had to be carried on carts to move from one place to another. They were a heavy burden for the draft animals that carried them.

46:2 When one ancient Near Eastern power defeated another, they would carry off the idols of the vanquished nation. The Gilgamesh epic contains a description of the gods cowering in the presence of the powerful force of the flood.

46:3-4 The **remnant** were those Israelites who would survive the coming judgment. God had carried (**sustained**) His people from their birth.

46:5-7 The gods of the surrounding nations were divinized portions of the creation. Thus Enlil was the god of war, Inanna the goddess of love, Ea the god of wisdom, etc. But God was not exactly like anything on earth. It is true that the great metaphors of the Bible taught about God's nature and actions through comparing Him to a king, a warrior, a rock, light, a storm, and so forth, but these metaphors throw light on who God is without identifying Him with these objects or elements of creation. The idols, on the other hand, were associated with and even identified with the creation. There was nothing transcendent about them. They were human-made objects, a point that Isaiah had already made (see note at 44:12-13).

46:8-9 To **remember** means to draw strength by contemplating God's past acts of power.

46:11 Cyrus—the king of Persia (45:1), a country **east** of Israel—was the **bird of prey**.

The Fall of Babylon

47 "Go down and sit in the dust,[a]
Virgin Daughter Babylon.[b]
Sit on the ground without a throne,
Daughter Chaldea!
For you will no longer be called
pampered and spoiled.
2 Take millstones and grind meal;[c]
remove your veil,
strip off your skirt, bare your thigh,
wade through the streams.
3 Your nakedness will be uncovered,
and your shame will be exposed.[d]
I will take vengeance;
I will spare no one.[A]
4 The Holy One of Israel is
our Redeemer;[e]
•Yahweh of •Hosts is His name.

5 "Daughter Chaldea,
sit in silence[f] and go into darkness.
For you will no longer be called
mistress of kingdoms.
6 I was angry with My people;
I profaned My possession,
and I placed them under your control.
You showed them no mercy;
you made your yoke very heavy
on the elderly.
7 You said, 'I will be
the mistress forever.'
You did not take these things to heart
or think about their outcome.

8 "So now hear this, lover of luxury,
who sits securely,[g]
who says to herself,
'I exist, and there is no one else.
I will never be a widow
or know the loss of children.'[h]
9 These two things will happen to you
suddenly, in one day:
loss of children and widowhood.
They will happen to you
in their entirety,
in spite of your many sorceries[i]
and the potency of your spells.
10 You were secure in your wickedness;
you said, 'No one sees me.'[j]
Your wisdom and knowledge
led you astray.
You said to yourself,
'I exist, and there is no one else.'
11 But disaster will happen to you;
you will not know how to avert it.
And it will fall on you,
but you will be unable to ward it off.[B]
Devastation will happen
to you suddenly
and unexpectedly.[k]
12 So take your stand with your spells
and your many sorceries,
which you have wearied yourself with
from your youth.
Perhaps you will be able to succeed;
perhaps you will inspire terror!

[a]47:1 Is 3:26; Jr 48:18
[b]Ps 137:8; Jr 50:42; 51:33; Zch 2:7
[c]47:2 Ex 11:5; Jb 31:10; Mt 24:41
[d]47:3 Jr 13:26; Lm 1:8; Ezk 16:37; Nah 3:5
[e]47:4 Is 41:14; 43:14
[f]47:5 Is 23:2; Jr 8:14; Lm 2:10; 3:2,28
[g]47:8 Zph 2:15
[h]Rv 18:7
[i]47:9 Is 47:13; Nah 3:4; Rv 18:23
[j]47:10 Ps 139:3,11
[k]47:11 Is 13:6; Jr 51:8,43; Lk 17:27; 1Th 5:3

A47:3 Hb obscure   B47:11 Or to atone for it

47:1 To **sit in the dust**, just like sitting on the **ground**, was a sign of subservience and humiliation. Babylon, the mighty nation that achieved special status among the other nations of the world (**pampered and spoiled**), will be put in a position of shame. Up to this point in the book, only God's people have been called **daughter** by the Lord (1:8; 3:16; 37:22). In this passage not only is Babylon given this title of intimacy, but it is qualified with **virgin**, indicating purity as well as dependence on the father, or God. However, here "virgin" is sarcastic. **Chaldea** refers to the Aramaic-speaking tribe of the southern marsh region of Babylon that came to dominate the entire nation during the Neo-Babylonian period (626–586 b.c.).

47:2-3 Babylon, personified as a young woman, will do her lowly chores—in contrast to her former exalted status—and then will **strip** to cross a stream. As she does so, her **shame** (her promiscuity that contradicted her apparent virginity) will be exposed.

47:4 On **Holy One of Israel**, see notes at 1:4 and 30:10-11.

47:5 On **Daughter Chaldea**, see note at verse 1. Under leaders like Nabopolassar (626–605 b.c.) and his better-known son Nebuchadnezzar (605–562 b.c.), Babylon had achieved dominance among the nations of the world, but its former glory will be turned to oblivion.

47:6-7 God has used Babylon as the tool of His anger against Judah. Babylon's **yoke** is an image of their political domina-tion over Judah (see note at 10:27). But Babylon overplayed its hand and sought its own glory, not realizing that its pride would lead to retribution.

47:8-9 Babylon is personified as a woman consistently in this chapter. Before she was the Virgin Daughter, but in these verses she is a woman who is blessed with marriage and **children**. The future judgment of Babylon is compared to a woman who will lose husband and children in **one day**. A woman without husband and children had no meaning and no protection in ancient times. This disaster will befall Babylon even though she was a sorceress (see Nah 3:4 for a similar description of Assyria).

47:10-11 **Wisdom** includes the ability to navigate life in a way that avoids pitfalls and also includes the skill to get out of jams if hardship should fall. However, in this case wisdom is useless and unable to ward off **disaster**. In other words, Babylonian wisdom is actually foolishness. This affirmation is not far from the NT idea that the wisdom of the world is folly (1Co 1–2). Babylon will fall because it was "wise in its own eyes" rather than trustful in the one true God (Pr 3:5-8).

47:12-13 Babylonian culture was known for its infatuation with **sorceries** and **spells**, which represented a way to ma-nipulate the gods. In particular, Babylon was known for attempts to determine the future by consulting the stars. Indeed, even after Babylon disappeared as an empire, the term "Chaldean" was used to designate **astrologers**.

¹³ You are worn out
     with your many consultations.
So let them stand and save you—
     the astrologers,^A who observe
     the stars,^a
who predict monthly
     what will happen to you.
¹⁴ Look, they are like stubble;^b
fire burns them up.^c
They cannot deliver themselves
     from the power^B of the flame.
This is not a coal
     for warming themselves,
or a fire to sit beside!
¹⁵ This is what they are to you—
     those who have wearied you
and have traded with you
     from your youth—
each wanders on his own way;
no one can save you.

Israel Must Leave Babylon

48 "Listen to this, house of Jacob—
     those who are called
     by the name Israel
and have descended from^c Judah,^d
who swear by the name of •Yahweh^e
and declare the God of Israel,
but not in truth or righteousness.
² For they are named
     after the Holy City,
and lean on the God of Israel;^f
His name is Yahweh of •Hosts.
³ I declared the past events long ago;
they came out of My mouth;
     I proclaimed them.
Suddenly I acted, and they occurred.
⁴ Because I know that you are stubborn,
and your neck is iron^D
and your forehead bronze,^g
⁵ therefore I declared to you long ago.

I announced it to you
     before it occurred,
so you could not claim, 'My idol
     caused them;
my carved image and cast idol
     control them.'^h
⁶ You have heard it. Observe it all.
Will you not acknowledge it?
From now on I will announce
     new things to you,
hidden things that
     you have not known.ⁱ
⁷ They have been created now, and not
     long ago;
you have not heard of them
     before today,
so you could not claim, 'I already
     knew them!'
⁸ You have never heard; you have
     never known;
For a long time your ears have not
     been open.
For I knew that you
     were very treacherous,
and were known as a rebel from birth.^j
⁹ I will delay My anger for the honor
     of My name,
and I will restrain Myself
     for your benefit and for My praise,
so that you will not be destroyed.
¹⁰ Look, I have refined you,^k but not
     as silver;
I have tested^E you in the furnace
     of affliction.
¹¹ I will act for My own sake,
     indeed, My own,^l
for how can I^F be defiled?
I will not give My glory to another.^m

¹² "Listen to Me, Jacob,
     and Israel, the one called by Me:

^a47:13 Is 8:19; 44:25; 47:9; Dn 2:2,10 ^b47:14 Is 5:24; Nah 1:10; Mal 4:1 ^cIs 10:17; Jr 51:30-32,58 ^d48:1 Nm 24:7; Dt 33:28; Ps 68:26 ^eDt 6:13; Is 45:23; 65:16 ^f48:2 Is 10:20; Jr 7:4; 21:2; Mc 3:11; Rm 2:17 ^g48:4 Ex 32:9; Dt 31:27; Ezk 2:4; 3:7-9 ^h48:5 Jr 44:15-18 ⁱ48:6 Is 42:9; 43:19 ^j48:8 Dt 9:7,24; Ps 58:3; Is 46:8 ^k48:10 Dt 4:20; 1Kg 8:51; Jr 11:4; Ezk 22:18-22; 1Pt 1:7 ^l48:11 Is 43:25; Ezk 20:9 ^mIs 42:8

---

^A47:13 Lit *dividers of the heavens*   ^B47:14 Lit *hand*   ^C48:1 Lit *have come from the waters of*   ^D48:4 Lit *is an iron sinew*   ^E48:10 Or *chosen*   ^F48:11 DSS, Syr; MT reads *it*

48:1 Isaiah addressed those connected to God by their genealogical descent from the patriarchs. Though part of **Israel**, they did not have a true relationship because of their disobedience (vv. 4,8).

48:3 The **past events** refers to the judgment of God on His people. He announced what would happen to sinful Judah through Isaiah, Jeremiah, Ezekiel, and other prophets. He proclaimed what He would do and then **acted** on His words.

48:4 Nothing can get through a **bronze** forehead. An **iron . . . neck** is stiff and cannot turn around. This imagery shows the refusal of God's people to hear Him or to repent.

48:6 Up to this point God has been announcing judgment, but now He will announce **new things**—a message of grace after the judgment. Why had God kept the news of eventual restoration **hidden**? According to Childs, "God chose

to keep the entrance of the new hidden until the very last moment because he knew that Israel would abuse its foreknowledge" (*Isaiah*, p. 375). The new things include God's use of Cyrus to deliver His people (vv. 14-15).

48:8 God's people had closed their ears to God's commands for **a long time**, thus the call for them to listen in this chapter (vv. 1,12,14,16). To hear means more than just listening; it implies acting on what is heard.

48:9 God will not completely destroy His people. A remnant will survive the judgment.

48:10 Pure **silver** is made by subjecting it to high temperatures and removing the impurities. The image of refining is often used in the Bible to refer to removing sin from a person or a community (1:22), in this case, through **affliction**.

I am He; I am the first,
I am also the last.[a]

13 My own hand founded the earth,
and My right hand spread out
the heavens;[b]
when I summoned them,
they stood up together.

14 All of you, assemble and listen!
Who among the idols[A] has declared
these things?
The LORD loves him;[B]
he will accomplish His will
against Babylon,[c]
and His arm will be against
the Chaldeans.

15 I—I have spoken;
yes, I have called him;[d]
I have brought him,
and he will succeed in his mission.[e]

16 Approach Me and listen to this.
From the beginning I have not spoken
in secret;[f]
from the time anything existed,
I was there."
And now the Lord GOD
has sent me and His Spirit.[g]

17 This is what the LORD, your Redeemer,[h] the
Holy One of Israel[i] says:

I am Yahweh your God,
who teaches you for your benefit,
who leads you in the way
you should go.

18 If only you had paid attention
to My commands.
Then your peace would have been
like a river,[j]

and your righteousness like the waves
of the sea.[k]

19 Your descendants would have been
as countless as the sand,[l]
and the offspring of your body
like its grains;
their name would not be cut off
or eliminated from My presence.

20 Leave Babylon,
flee from the Chaldeans!
Declare with a shout of joy,
proclaim this,
let it go out to the end of the earth;
announce,
"The LORD has redeemed
His servant[m] Jacob!"

21 They did not thirst
when He led them
through the deserts;
He made water flow for them
from the rock;[n]
He split the rock, and water
gushed out.

22 "There is no peace for the wicked,"
says the LORD.[o]

The Servant Brings Salvation

49 Coastlands,[C] listen to me;
distant peoples, pay attention.
The LORD called[p] me
before I was born.
He named me while I was
in my mother's womb.[q]

2 He made my words
like a sharp sword;[r]
He hid me in the shadow
of His hand.[s]

---

[a]48:12 Is 41:4; 43:10-13; 46:4; Rv 1:17
[b]48:13 Ps 102:25; Is 42:5; 45:12,18; Heb 1:10-12
[c]48:14 Is 13:4-5,17-19; 46:10-11
[d]48:15 Is 41:2; 45:1-2
[e]Is 53:10
[f]48:16 Is 45:19
[g]Nm 27:18; Ps 51:11; Is 61:1; 63:7,10; Zch 2:9,11
[h]48:17 Is 41:14; 43:14
[i]Is 1:4
[j]48:18 Is 32:16-18; 66:12
[k]Dt 5:29; 32:29; Ps 81:13-16; Am 5:24
[l]48:19 Gn 22:17; Is 10:22; 44:3-4; 54:3; Hs 1:10
[m]48:20 Is 41:8-9; 42:19; 43:10; 44:1-2,21; 45:4; 49:3; 54:17; Lk 1:54
[n]48:21 Ex 17:6; Ps 78:15-16
[o]48:22 Is 57:21
[p]49:1 Is 44:2,24; 46:3; Jr 1:5
[q]Lk 1:15
[r]49:2 Is 11:4; Heb 4:12; Rv 1:16; 2:12,16
[s]Is 51:16

A48:14 Lit among them   B48:14 = Cyrus   C49:1 Or Islands

48:13 On the image of God spreading and stretching out the **heavens** and the **earth**, see note at 42:5. Since God is the Creator, His people should pay attention to Him.

48:14-15 The one whom the Lord **loves** is Cyrus (44:24–45:8)—the pagan king of Persia whom the Lord will use to deliver his people from the Babylonians. On **Chaldeans**, see note at 13:19.

48:16 Isaiah concluded this section by affirming that God was the One who had brought him to the people.

48:17-18 On **Holy One of Israel**, see note at 1:4. Israel's past judgment was the result of their refusal to follow God.

48:19 Isaiah had earlier announced that Israel's population would be reduced to a remnant (see note at 10:22). The allusion to **sand** goes back to the patriarchal promise that Abraham would have numerous descendants (Gn 22:17; 32:12; 41:49). It was Israel's sin that led to a reduction of the population.

48:20-22 The chapter ends with a divine directive to **leave Babylon**, the nation that was the source of Judah's oppres-

sion. The assumption is that the people should do this after the work of God's messiah, Cyrus (see note at 45:1).

48:20 On **Chaldeans**, see note at 13:19.

48:21 The prophet alluded to the wilderness wandering when God brought His people out of Egypt and into the promised land. Isaiah had earlier used what might be called the "second exodus" theme (4:5; 11:15-16; 40:3-5; 43:18-19). He saw a parallel between God bringing His people out of a place of bondage (first Egypt, then Babylon). The specific reference is to the times when God provided **water** to Israel in the wilderness (Ex 17:1-7; Nm 20:1-13).

48:22 Though God will bring salvation to His people, He will not back down from His judgment on **the wicked**.

49:1 **Coastlands** is the same word translated "islands" in 41:1. It refers to the distant places of the earth. The Servant (49:3) spoke here and addressed all the peoples of the earth. He began by recounting his calling that began even before he was born. The language is reminiscent of the description of the prophet Jeremiah's call (Jr 1:5).

49:2 The Servant was made to be a weapon in the arsenal

He made me like a sharpened arrow;
He hid me in His quiver.
3 He said to me, "You are
My Servant, Israel;[a]
I will be glorified in him."
4 But I myself said: I have labored
in vain,
I have spent my strength for nothing
and futility;
yet my vindication is with the LORD,
and my reward is with my God.
5 And now, says the LORD,
who formed me from the womb to be
His Servant,
to bring Jacob back to Him
so that Israel might be gathered
to Him;
for I am honored in the sight
of the LORD,
and my God is my strength—
6 He says,
"It is not enough for you to be
My Servant
raising up the tribes of Jacob
and restoring the protected ones
of Israel.
I will also make you a light
for the nations,[b]
to be My salvation to the ends
of the earth."[c]
7 This is what the LORD,
the Redeemer[d] of Israel,
his Holy One, says,
to one who is despised,
to one abhorred by people,[A,e]
to a servant of rulers:

"Kings will see and stand up,
and princes[B] will bow down,
because of the LORD, who is faithful,
the Holy One of Israel[f]—
and He has chosen you."[g]

8 This is what the LORD says:

I will answer you in a time of favor,
and I will help you in the day
of salvation.[h]
I will keep you, and I will appoint you
to be a covenant for the people,[i]
to restore the land,
to make them possess
the desolate inheritances,
9 saying to the prisoners: Come out,[j]
and to those who are in darkness:
Show yourselves.
They will feed along the pathways,
and their pastures will be on all
the barren heights.[k]
10 They will not hunger or thirst,
the scorching heat or sun will not
strike them;
for their compassionate One
will guide them,
and lead them to springs of water.[l]
11 I will make all My mountains
into a road,
and My highways will be raised up.[m]
12 See, these will come from far away,
from the north and from the west,[C,n]
and from the land of Sinim.[D,E]

13 Shout for joy, you heavens![o]
Earth, rejoice!

Cross references:
a 49:3 Is 41:8-9; 42:1; 49:5-7; 50:10; 52:13; 53:11; Ezk 34:23-24; Zch 3:8; Ac 3:13
b 49:6 Is 42:6; 51:4; Lk 2:32; Ac 13:47; 26:23
c Ac 13:47
d 49:7 Is 41:14; 43:14
e Ps 22:6-8; 69:7-9; Is 53:3
f Is 1:4
g Is 41:8-9; 42:1; 43:10,20; 44:1-2; 45:4; 65:9,15,22
h 49:8 Ps 69:13; 2Co 6:2
i Is 42:6
j 49:9 Is 42:7; 61:1; Lk 4:18
k Is 41:18
l 49:10 Ps 23:2; Is 40:11; Jn 4:10; Rv 7:16-17
m 49:11 Is 40:4
n 49:12 Is 43:5-6
o 49:13 Is 44:23

A 49:7 Or by the nation   B 49:7 Lit princes and they   C 49:12 Lit sea   D 49:12 DSS read of the Syenites   E 49:12 Perhaps modern Aswan in southern Egypt

of God the warrior to wage war against the chaos of the world. The language reminds the reader of the description of a son's relationship to his father in Psalm 127.

49:3 The **Servant** is identified as **Israel**. As in 42:1-9 (see note there, as well as note at 42:1), the more precise identification is the purified remnant within Israel (an alternative idea views the Servant as Isaiah himself). However, as with all the Servant Songs, the NT authors recognized a second and deeper identification of the Servant as they associated these texts with Jesus Christ (Mt 8:17; 12:17-21; Jn 12:38; Ac 8:30-35).

49:4 The experience of the exile will lead the Servant Israel to express its frustration before acknowledging that God brings meaning through His act of **vindication**—release from bondage.

49:5 In verse 3 the **Servant** identified himself as Israel; here the Servant speaks as if He is the agent of Israel's restoration. This seeming inconsistency is resolved once it is realized that it is the remnant, and ultimately the remnant of one—Jesus—who functions in this way (see note at 42:1).

49:6 The Servant will do more than restore Israel to its former glory. He will serve as an agent of **salvation** to the

nations, thus fulfilling the divine promise to Abraham that through his descendants God would be a blessing to "all the peoples on earth" (Gn 12:3).

49:7 The lowly state of the Servant is a characteristic more fully developed in the final Servant Song in 52:13–53:12. A reversal will take place when **kings** pay homage to the despised Servant.

49:8 As in 42:6 the Servant has entered into a **covenant for the people**, and as there the reference is to the Abrahamic covenant. However, while the emphasis in chapter 42 is on the promise that the nations will be blessed through Abraham, here the emphasis is on the promise of the **land**. God will restore His people to the land He gave them and which they forfeited.

49:9-10 The people of God have been in desperate straits, but God will deliver them.

49:11-12 The oracle again uses language drawn from the exodus and wilderness wandering traditions (see note at 48:21). **Sinim** is typically associated with modern Aswan, postexilic Elephantine in Egypt.

49:13 Isaiah began with an oracle calling on **heavens** and

Mountains break into joyful shouts!
For the Lord has comforted His people,[a]
and will have compassion
    on His afflicted ones.[b]

Zion Remembered

14 •Zion says, "The Lord
        has abandoned me;
    The Lord has forgotten me!"
15 "Can a woman forget her nursing child,
    or lack compassion for the child
        of her womb?
    Even if these forget,
        yet I will not forget you.
16 Look, I have inscribed you
        on the palms of My hands;[c]
    your walls are continually before Me.
17 Your builders[A] hurry;
    those who destroy and devastate you
        will leave you.
18 Look up, and look around.
    They all gather together; they come
        to you.[d]
    As I live"—
            this is the Lord's declaration—
    "you will wear all your children[B]
        as jewelry,
    and put them on as a bride does.
19 For your waste and desolate places
    and your land marked by ruins—
    will now be indeed too small
        for the inhabitants,[e]
    and those who swallowed you up
        will be far away.
20 Yet as you listen, the children
    that you have been deprived of will say,
    'This place is too small for me;
    make room for me so that
        I may settle.'[f]

21 Then you will say within yourself,
    'Who fathered these for me?
    I was deprived of my children
        and unable to conceive,
    exiled and wandering—
    but who brought them up?
    See, I was left by myself—
    but these, where did they
        come from?'"[c]

22 This is what the Lord God says:

    Look, I will lift up My hand
        to the nations,
    and raise My banner to the peoples.[g]
    They will bring your sons in their arms,
    and your daughters will be carried
        on their shoulders.[h]
23 Kings will be your foster fathers,
    and their queens[D]
        your nursing mothers.[i]
    They will bow down to you
    with their faces to the ground,
    and lick the dust at your feet.[j]
    Then you will know that
        I am •Yahweh;[k]
    those who put their hope in Me
    will not be put to shame.[l]

24 Can the prey be taken
        from the mighty,
    or the captives of the righteous[E]
        be delivered?
25 For this is what the Lord says:
    "Even the captives of a mighty man
        will be taken,
    and the prey of a tyrant
        will be delivered;
    I will contend with the one
        who contends with you,

Cross references (center column)

[a]49:13 Is 40:1
[b]Is 54:7-10; Mt 11:29
[c]49:16 Sg 8:6; Hg 2:23
[d]49:18 Is 60:4
[e]49:19 Is 54:1-2; Zch 10:10
[f]49:20 Is 54:1-3
[g]49:22 Is 11:10-12; 18:3; 62:10
[h]Is 14:2; 43:6; 60:4
[i]49:23 Is 60:3,10-11
[j]Is 14:1-2
[k]Is 41:20; 43:10; 60:16
[l]Ps 25:3; Is 45:17; Jl 2:27

Textual notes

A49:17 DSS, Aq, Theod, Vg; MT, Syr, Sym read *sons*   B49:18 Lit *all of them*   C49:21 Lit *where are they*   D49:23 Lit *princesses*
E49:24 DSS, Syr, Vg read *fearsome one*, or *tyrant*

Study notes

earth to serve as witnesses to testify that God's people deserved their punishment (1:2); now they rejoice in their restoration.

49:14 Zion, personified as a woman, represents Jerusalem. She complained or lamented that God had **abandoned** her. The verses that follow suggest that what she missed was her "children," or the inhabitants of Jerusalem. Their absence in exile led her to suggest that God had forgotten her.

49:15 God responded by reflecting on the persistent memory of a mother. Indeed, verse 18 may imply that God addressed Zion as a husband addresses a wife. He understood what she was going through and would soon address her complaints.

49:16 To inscribe something on one's **hands** (tattooing perhaps) placed the writing on a bodily location that would be readily seen. In particular the defensive **walls** of Jerusalem were a concern of the Lord.

49:18 Zion's children, the people of God, will soon gather as they return to Jerusalem. The picture of Zion wearing her children like wedding **jewelry** suggests that the passage understood God to be her husband. The returned **children** were a wedding gift.

49:19-20 The passage envisions a return so large that Jerusalem will not be big enough to hold all its inhabitants.

49:21 Mother Zion will be amazed and will wonder who has **fathered** all these **children**. The implied answer is none other than God Himself.

49:22-23 The deportation that began the exile saw the people of God dragged off in chains by foreign armies. The picture of the return views the **nations** carrying them back to their land and showing subservience.

49:24-26 The people of God will doubt that it is possible for them to be delivered from their bondage and oppression, but God will make it clear that He is able not only to rescue

and I will save your children.

26 I will make your oppressors eat
their own flesh,[a]
and they will be drunk
with their own blood
as with sweet wine.
Then all flesh will know
that I, Yahweh, am your Savior,[b]
and your Redeemer,[c] the Mighty One
of Jacob."[d]

50

This is what the LORD says:

Where is your mother's
divorce certificate
that I used to send her away?[e]
Or who were My creditors
that I sold you to?[f]
Look, you were sold
for your iniquities,[g]
and your mother was put away
because of your transgressions.

2 Why was no one there when I came?
Why was there no one to answer
when I called?
Is My hand too short to redeem?[h]
Or do I have no power to deliver?
Look, I dry up the sea by My rebuke;[i]
I turn the rivers into a wilderness;
their fish rot because of lack of water
and die of thirst.

3 I dress the heavens in black
and make *sackcloth their clothing.[j]

The Obedient Servant

4 The Lord GOD has given Me
the tongue of those who are instructed[k]
to know how to sustain the weary
with a word.

He awakens Me each morning;
He awakens My ear to listen like those
being instructed.[l]

5 The Lord GOD has opened My ear,
and I was not rebellious;
I did not turn back.[m]

6 I gave My back to those who beat Me,
and My cheeks to those who tore out
My beard.
I did not hide My face from scorn
and spitting.[n]

7 The Lord GOD will help Me;
therefore I have not been humiliated;
therefore I have set My face like flint,[o]
and I know I will not be put to shame.

8 The One who vindicates Me is near;[p]
who will contend with Me?
Let us confront each other.[A]
Who has a case against Me?[B]
Let him come near Me!

9 In truth, the Lord GOD will help Me;
who will condemn Me?[q]
Indeed, all of them will wear out
like a garment;
a moth will devour them.[r]

10 Who among you *fears the LORD,
listening to the voice of His Servant?[s]
Who among you walks in darkness,
and has no light?
Let him trust in the name of *Yahweh;
let him lean on his God.

11 Look, all you who kindle a fire,
who encircle yourselves
with[c] firebrands;
walk in the light of your fire
and in the firebrands you have lit!
This is what you'll get from My hand:
you will lie down in a place of torment.

[a]49:26 Is 9:20
[b]Is 43:3
[c]Is 41:14
[d]Gn 49:24; Ps 132:2,5; Is 60:16
[e]50:1 Dt 24:1-3; Jr 3:8
[f]Dt 32:30; 2Kg 4:1; Neh 5:5
[g]Is 13:11
[h]50:2 Gn 18:14; Nm 11:23; Is 59:1
[i]Ex 14:21; Is 43:16; 44:27
[j]50:3 Rv 6:12
[k]50:4 Is 8:16; 54:13
[l]Jn 4:34
[m]50:5 Jn 8:29; 14:31; 15:10; Php 2:8; Heb 5:8
[n]50:6 Mt 26:67; 27:26; Mk 14:65; 15:19; Lk 22:63; Jn 19:1-5
[o]50:7 Ezk 3:8-9
[p]50:8 Is 45:25
[q]50:9 Rm 8:33-34
[r]Jb 13:28; Is 51:8; Hs 5:12
[s]50:10 Is 42:1; 49:3-7; 52:13; 53:11; Ezk 34:23-24; Zch 3:8; Ac 3:13

[A]50:8 Lit *us stand*   [B]50:8 Lit *Who is lord of My judgment*   [C]50:11 Syr reads *who set ablaze*

---

them but also to subject their captors to the punishment they deserved.

50:1 Zion continues to be described as the mother of God's people. God is the father of His people. He put away Zion but did not divorce her (there is no **divorce certificate**; Dt 24:1-4). God **sold** His children, but not to settle a debt (so there are no **creditors**). Why did He do it? Because of their sins.

50:2 God expressed wonder, though, that the children, God's people, did not expect redemption. He did not divorce Zion and He did not sell His people to a creditor, so He could get them back. Further, God is certainly powerful enough to save them. The act of drying up the waters (**sea . . . rivers**) reflects an ancient Near Eastern understanding that the waters stood for the forces of chaos. God controlled them and could decimate them at will. His control of the waters and the reference to His redeeming **hand** recall the exodus.

50:3 Sackcloth was a very rough material, irritating to the skin, worn as part of mourning rites. The **heavens** mourned because of God's acts of judgment.

50:4 The first-person speaker (**Me**) is the Servant (v. 10).

For this reason, the HCSB capitalizes the pronoun since the Servant ultimately is identified with Christ, though the original audience probably identified the Servant as purified Israel (see note at 42:1-9). Alternatively, a number of scholars identify the Servant in this poem as Isaiah. The speaker is a student of God, trained to provide encouragement to those who are **weary**. Each morning God awakens Him with new insight.

50:6-7 Anticipating a fuller development in 52:13–53:12, the Servant is one who suffers, though God will keep Him from shame.

50:10 A human **fears the LORD** when he understands that God is far superior and that man is a mere creature. Such fear does not lead to flight but to a trust that can depend on God for protection. The person who fears the Lord listens to what the Servant of the Lord says.

50:11 Opposite of the one who fears the Lord and leans on Him is the self-reliant person who tries to create light by his own hand. He kindles his own fire to produce light. Such people will experience **torment** from God.

Salvation for Zion

51 Listen to Me, you
who pursue righteousness,
you who seek the LORD:
Look to the rock from which
you were cut,
and to the quarry from which
you were dug.

2 Look to Abraham your father,
and to Sarah who gave birth to you
in pain.
When I called him, he was only one;
I blessed him and made him many.[a]

3 For the LORD will comfort •Zion;[b]
He will comfort all her waste places,
and He will make her wilderness
like Eden,[c]
and her desert like the garden
of the LORD.[d]
Joy and gladness will be found in her,
thanksgiving and melodious song.

4 Pay attention to Me, My people,
and listen to Me, My nation;
for instruction will come from Me,
and My justice for a light
to the nations.[e]
I will bring it about quickly.

5 My righteousness is near,[f]
My salvation appears,
and My arms will bring justice
to the nations.[g]
The coastlands[A] will put their hope
in Me,
and they will look to My strength.[B]

6 Look up to the heavens,
and look at the earth beneath;
for the heavens will vanish like smoke,
the earth will wear out like a garment,
and its inhabitants will die like gnats.[C,h]

But My salvation will last forever,[i]
and My righteousness will never
be shattered.

7 Listen to Me, you who
know righteousness,
the people in whose heart is
My instruction:[j]
do not fear disgrace by men,
and do not be shattered by their taunts.

8 For the moth will devour them
like a garment,[k]
and the worm will eat them like wool.[l]
But My righteousness will last forever,
and My salvation for all generations.

9 Wake up, wake up!
Put on the strength of the LORD's power.
Wake up as in days past,
as in generations of long ago.
Wasn't it You who hacked •Rahab
to pieces,[m]
who pierced the sea monster?[n]

10 Wasn't it You who dried up the sea,[o]
the waters of the great deep,
who made the sea-bed into a road
for the redeemed to pass over?[p]

11 And the redeemed of the LORD
will return[q]
and come to Zion with singing,
crowned with unending joy.
Joy and gladness will overtake them,
and sorrow and sighing will flee.

12 I—I am the One who comforts you.
Who are you that you should fear man
who dies,[r]
or a son of man who is given up
like grass?[s]

13 But you have forgotten the LORD,
your Maker,

Cross-references (center column)

[a] 51:2 Gn 12:1; 15:5; Dt 1:10; Is 29:22; 41:8; 63:16; Ezk 33:24
[b] 51:3 Is 40:1
[c] Gn 2:8; Jl 2:3
[d] Gn 13:10
[e] 51:4 Is 42:6; 49:6
[f] 51:5 Is 46:13; 54:17
[g] Is 40:10
[h] 51:6 Ps 102:25-26; Is 34:4; Mt 24:35; Heb 1:10-12; 2Pt 3:10
[i] Is 45:17; 2Tm 2:10; Heb 5:9
[j] 51:7 Ps 37:31
[k] 51:8 Is 50:9
[l] Is 14:11
[m] 51:9 Jb 26:12; Ps 89:10; Is 30:7
[n] Ps 74:13; Is 27:1
[o] 51:10 Is 11:15-16; 50:2; 63:11-12
[p] 51:10 Ex 15:13
[q] 51:11 Is 35:10
[r] 51:12 Ps 118:6; Is 2:22
[s] Is 40:6-7; Jms 1:10-11; 1Pt 1:24

[A] 51:5 Or islands   [B] 51:5 Lit arm   [C] 51:6 Or die in like manner

---

51:1-2 The prophet called to the righteous among God's people and reminded them of their heritage. Abraham was the **rock** from which the people of God were cut and Sarah the **quarry** from which they were dug. From the one man Abraham came **many** descendants according to the promise of the Abrahamic covenant (Gn 12:1-3).

51:3 On the foundation of the ancient promises to Abraham, God will transform Zion's suffering and devastation (**her wilderness . . . her desert**) to joy and prosperity (**Eden . . . garden of the LORD**).

51:4-5 According to the Abrahamic promise, his descendants were to be a blessing to the **nations**. The **coastlands** represent the distant nations (49:1). Invoking them implies that all the nations of the world will put their **hope** in the Lord.

51:6 From a human perspective the **heavens** and the **earth** look permanent. People die but the heavens and earth endure. But God's **salvation** and **righteousness** make even the heavens and the earth appear temporary.

51:7-8 If the heavens and the earth are temporary, so are even shorter-lived human beings. Why then should anyone **fear** another? The only One who is the proper recipient of our fear is the Lord Himself.

51:9-10 God is encouraged to **wake up** from slumber and go about His redemptive work (Ps 44:23; 78:65). Past victories are then recounted in the form of the defeat of **Rahab**, a sea monster. The sea and its monsters represent the forces of chaos that are against God and His creation. Rahab in other texts clearly stands for Egypt. Here we have a poetic allusion to God's victory over the Egyptians at the time of the exodus. God, after all, dried up the **sea-bed** and made it a **road** at the Red Sea (Ex 14–15). God's past deliverance of His people from Egyptian bondage bodes well for their future deliverance from Babylonian captivity.

51:12 It is folly to **fear** humans who die rather than the Lord who endures forever.

51:13 God constructed the **heavens** and the **earth** like a per-

who stretched out the heavens
and laid the foundations of the earth.[a]
You are in constant dread all day long
because of the fury of the oppressor,
who has set himself to destroy.
But where is the fury of the oppressor?[b]

14 The prisoner[A] is soon to be set free;
he will not die and go to the •Pit,
and his food will not be lacking.

15 For I am •Yahweh your God
who stirs up the sea so that
  its waves roar[c]—
His name is Yahweh of •Hosts.

16 I have put My words in your mouth,[d]
and covered you in the shadow
  of My hand,[e]
in order to plant[B] the heavens,
to found the earth,
and to say to Zion, "You are My people."

17 Wake yourself, wake yourself up!
Stand up, Jerusalem,
you who have drunk the cup of His fury[f]
from the hand of the LORD;
you who have drunk the goblet
  to the dregs—
the cup that causes people to stagger.

18 There is no one to guide her
among all the children she has raised;
there is no one to take hold of her hand
among all the offspring
  she has brought up.

19 These two things have happened to you:[g]
devastation and destruction,
famine and sword.
Who will grieve for you?
How can I[C] comfort you?

20 Your children have fainted;
they lie at the head of every street
like an antelope in a net.
They are full of the LORD's fury,
the rebuke of your God.

21 So listen to this, afflicted
and drunken one—but not with wine.[h]

22 This is what your Lord says—
Yahweh, even your God,
who defends His people[i]—
"Look, I have removed
the cup of staggering from your hand;
that goblet, the cup of My fury.
You will never drink it again.

23 I will put it into the hands
  of your tormentors,
who said to you:[j]
Lie down, so we can walk over you.
You made your back like the ground,
and like a street for those who walk on it.

52 "Wake up, wake up;
put on your strength, •Zion!
Put on your beautiful garments,[k]
Jerusalem, the Holy City![l]
For the uncircumcised and the •unclean
will no longer enter you.[m]

2 Stand up, shake the dust off yourself!
Take your seat, Jerusalem.
Remove the bonds[D] from your neck,
captive Daughter Zion."

3 For this is what the LORD says:
"You were sold for nothing,
and you will be redeemed
  without silver."[n]

4 For this is what the Lord GOD says:

Cross references (center column):

[a]51:13 Is 44:24; 45:12; Am 9:6; Zch 12:1
[b]Is 49:26
[c]51:15 Ps 107:25; Jr 31:35
[d]51:16 Is 59:21
[e]Ex 33:22; Is 49:2
[f]51:17 Jb 21:20; Is 63:6; Jr 25:15; Mt 20:22; 26:39; Jn 18:1; Rv 14:10
[g]51:19 Is 47:9
[h]51:21 Is 29:9
[i]51:22 Is 3:12-13; 49:25; Jr 50:34
[j]51:23 Is 49:26; Jr 25:15-17,26,28; Zch 12:2
[k]52:1 Is 61:3
[l]Neh 11:1; Is 48:2
[m]Is 35:8; Rv 21:27
[n]52:3 Is 45:13; 1Pt 1:18

[A]51:14 Hb obscure   [B]51:16 Syr reads *to stretch out*   [C]51:19 DSS, LXX, Syr, Vg read *you? Who can*   [D]52:2 Alt Hb tradition reads *The bonds are removed*

---

son would build a tent (**stretched out**) or a house (**laid the foundations**).

51:14 The word **prisoner** refers to those who were exiled by the Babylonians. Some high-ranking officials were literally thrown into prisons (2Kg 25:27), but others were in a metaphorical prison by being removed from their land and forced to live in Babylon. The Israelites thought of the grave and the underworld as a large **Pit**.

51:15 God is in charge of the mighty waters. This shows metaphorically His ability to control the forces of evil.

51:17-23 In this section Isaiah called on God's people to wake up. They were slumbering under the influence of drinking God's cup of wrath, an image already cited (see note at 19:14).

51:18 In the ancient Near East, it was the duty of the children to care for a drunk parent. Noah's son Ham acted in a reprehensible manner when his father was drunk (Gn 9:18-29). Here Jerusalem's children, God's people, did not take hold of her hand when she was drunk after drinking the cup of God's fury.

51:21-23 Once Jerusalem has experienced the full force of God's judgment, once they have drunk of the **cup** of His **fury**, He will take it away and give it to their **tormentors**. Among the latter, Babylon is particularly in mind.

52:1 For the third time in this section, the call to **wake up** occurs (51:9,17; see also 50:4). This time it is addressed to Zion, again personified as a woman (49:14–50:4). The description is of a renewed, refreshed, and restored Jerusalem, no longer contaminated by the uncircumcised and the unclean.

52:2 In an obvious allusion to the exile, **Zion** is pictured as freed from bondage. She will rise from the dust to take her **seat**, perhaps implying a transition from dusty captive to dignified queen.

52:3 God was so anxious to get rid of sinful Zion that He **sold** her for **nothing**. Since He sold her for nothing, He can now redeem her for nothing.

52:4 The prophecy speaks from a prophetic perspective as if Isaiah were living at the time of the Babylonian captivity. From that time in the future, he looks back on two previous

"At first My people went down to Egypt
to live there,[a]
then Assyria oppressed them
without cause.[A]
5 So now what have I here"—
this is the LORD's declaration—
"that My people are taken away
for nothing?
Its rulers wail"—
this is the LORD's declaration—
"and My name is continually
blasphemed all day long.[b]
6 Therefore My people will know
My name;[c]
therefore they will know on that day
that I am He who says:
Here I am."

7 How beautiful on the mountains
are the feet of the herald,
who proclaims peace,
who brings news of good things,[d]
who proclaims salvation,
who says to Zion, "Your God reigns!"[e]
8 The voices of your watchmen[f]—
they lift up their voices,
shouting for joy together;
for every eye will see
when the LORD returns to Zion.
9 Be joyful, rejoice together,
you ruins of Jerusalem![g]
For the LORD has comforted
His people;[h]
He has redeemed Jerusalem.

10 The LORD has displayed His holy arm
in the sight of all the nations;[i]
all the ends of the earth will see
the salvation of our God.[j]
11 Leave, leave, go out from there![k]
Do not touch anything unclean;
go out from her, purify yourselves,[l]
you who carry the vessels of the LORD.
12 For you will not leave in a hurry,[m]
and you will not have to take flight;
because the LORD is going before you,[n]
and the God of Israel is
your rear guard.[o]

The Servant's Suffering and Exaltation

13 See, My Servant[B,p] will act wisely;[C]
He will be raised and lifted up
and greatly exalted.[q]
14 Just as many were appalled at You[D]—
His appearance was so disfigured
that He did not look like a man,
and His form did not resemble
a human being—
15 so He will sprinkle[E,F] many nations.[G,r]
Kings will shut their mouths
because of Him,
For they will see
what had not been told them,
and they will understand
what they had not heard.[s]

Cross references
[a]52:4 Gn 46:6
[b]52:5 Ezk 36:20; Rm 2:24
[c]52:6 Is 49:23
[d]52:7 Nah 1:15; Rm 10:15
[e]Ps 93:1; Is 24:23
[f]52:8 Is 62:6
[g]52:9 Is 44:26; 51:3; 61:4
[h]Is 40:1
[i]52:10 Ps 98:1-3; Is 51:9; 66:18-19
[j]Is 40:5; Lk 3:6
[k]52:11 Is 48:20; Jr 50:8; Ezk 20:34,41; Zch 2:6,7; 2Co 6:17
[l]2Co 6:17; 2Tm 2:19
[m]52:12 Ex 12:11,33; Dt 16:3
[n]Ex 23:23; Dt 1:30; 31:8; Is 45:2
[o]Jos 6:9,13; Is 58:8
[p]52:13 Is 42:1; 49:3-7; 50:10; 53:11; Ezk 34:23-24; Zch 3:8; Ac 3:13
[q]Php 2:9-11
[r]52:15 Nm 19:18-21; Ezk 36:25
[s]Rm 15:21; Eph 3:5

A52:4 Or *them at last*, or *them for nothing*   **B**52:13 Tg adds *the Messiah*   **C**52:13 Or *will be successful*   **D**52:14 Some Hb mss, Syr, Tg read *Him*   **E**52:15 Or *startle*   **F**52:15 As the blood of a sacrifice is sprinkled on the altar on behalf of the people   **G**52:15 LXX reads *so many nations will marvel at Him*

---

traumatic periods in Israelite history—the exodus from Egypt in the second millennium B.C. and the Assyrian invasion of the northern kingdom during Isaiah's lifetime (722 B.C.). The Babylonian captivity dates to 586–539 B.C.

52:5-6 God's **people** come to **know** Him through this process of punishment and restoration.

52:7 In the ancient world, news was carried by a **herald**. In this verse the herald announces the end of hostilities and the fact that **God reigns** as King over His people. A variation of this verse occurs in Nah 1:15.

52:8 Watchmen were posted on city walls to keep an eye out for attack, or in this case to be the first to witness the return of the Lord to His Holy City, Jerusalem.

52:10 The **salvation** referred to here is the conspicuous restoration of Jerusalem after it had been reduced to ruins by the Babylonians.

52:11 The priests (**who carry the vessels of the LORD**) are now encouraged to leave, presumably from Babylonian captivity (48:20-22). Ezekiel 1:5-11 recounts the return of the temple vessels under the leadership of Sheshbazzar. This oracle exhorts the priests not to defile themselves ritu-

ally because they are going back to a Zion that is not stained by impurity (v. 1).

52:13–53:12 See the note at 42:1-9 for the view that the Servant in this passage represents the purified remnant of Israel and ultimately the Messiah. The NT authors recognized that the description of a Suffering Servant, who "bore the sins of many," fit Jesus Christ, who died on the cross for the sins of His people. This chapter's description is the most individualistic of all the Servant Songs in the book of Isaiah, and thus most clearly points to application beyond Israel.

52:13 The poem begins with the end point—the exaltation of the Servant (53:11-12). Glory will be the end result of His suffering.

52:14 The suffering of the Servant will so disfigure Him that He will not appear human.

52:15 Much debate surrounds the meaning of the Servant sprinkling **many nations**. The main problem is that the verse does not specify what the Servant will use to **sprinkle** them. The best guess is that it refers to a ritual act like the sprinkling of blood (Lv 4:6,17; 16:14-15,19; Nm 19:4) or oil (Lv 8:11). The effect of this sprinkling is either to purify or to dedicate to a holy status.

53

Who has believed
    what we have heard?[A]
And who has the arm of the Lord[a]
    been revealed to?[b]
2 He grew up before Him
    like a young plant[c]
and like a root out of dry ground.
He didn't have an impressive form
    or majesty that we should look at Him,
no appearance that we should
    desire Him.[d]
3 He was despised and rejected
    by men,[e]
a man of suffering who knew
    what sickness was.[f]
He was like someone
    people turned away from;[B]
He was despised, and we didn't
    value Him.

4 Yet He Himself bore our sicknesses,
    and He carried our pains;[g]
but we in turn regarded Him stricken,
    struck down by God,[h] and afflicted.
5 But He was pierced because of
    our transgressions,[i]
crushed because of our iniquities;[j]
punishment[k] for our peace
    was on Him,
and we are healed by His wounds.[l]
6 We all went astray like sheep;[m]
we all have turned to our own way;
and the Lord has punished Him
    for[C] the iniquity[n] of us all.[o]

7 He was oppressed and afflicted,
    yet He did not open His mouth.

Like a lamb led to the slaughter
and like a sheep silent
    before her shearers,
He did not open His mouth.[p]
8 He was taken away because of
    oppression and judgment;
and who considered His fate?[D]
For He was cut off from the land
    of the living;
He was struck because of
    my people's rebellion.
9 They[E] made His grave
    with the wicked
and with a rich man
    at His death,[q]
although He had done no violence
and had not spoken deceitfully.[r]
10 Yet the Lord was pleased[s] to crush Him
    severely.[F,t]
When[G] You make Him
    a •restitution offering,[u]
He will see His •seed, He will prolong
    His days,
and by His hand, the Lord's pleasure
    will be accomplished.[v]
11 He will see it[H] out of His anguish,
and He will be satisfied
    with His knowledge.
My righteous[w] Servant[x]
    will justify many,[y]
and He will carry their iniquities.
12 Therefore I will give Him[I] the many
    as a portion,
and He will receive[J] the mighty
    as spoil,

[a]53:1 Is 30:30; 40:10; 48:14; 51:9; 52:10; Lk 1:51; Ac 13:17
[b]Jn 12:38; Rm 10:16
[c]53:2 Is 11:1
[d]Is 52:14
[e]53:3 Ps 22:6; Is 49:7; Lk 18:31-33
[f]Mk 8:31; Jn 1:10-11; Heb 4:15
[g]53:4 Mt 8:17; 1Pt 2:21
[h]Ps 69:26
[i]53:5 Is 53:8; Rm 4:25; 1Co 15:3; Heb 9:28
[j]Is 1:4
[k]Jr 2:30; Zph 3:2; Heb 5:8
[l]53:5-6 1Pt 2:24-25
[m]53:6 Mt 18:12
[n]Is 13:11
[o]2Co 5:21; Col 2:14
[p]53:7 Jr 11:19; Mt 26:63; 27:12-14; Lk 23:9; Jn 19:9; Ac 8:32-33; 1Pt 2:23
[q]53:9 Mt 27:57-60
[r]Heb 4:15; 1Pt 2:22; 1Jn 3:5
[s]53:10 Is 44:28; 55:11
[t]Dt 29:22; Is 17:11
[u]Lv 5:1-19
[v]Is 46:10
[w]53:11 1Jn 2:1
[x]Is 42:1
[y]Ac 13:39; Rm 5:18-19

[A]53:1 Or *believed our report* [B]53:3 Lit *And like a hiding of faces from Him* [C]53:6 Or *has placed on Him*; lit *with* [D]53:8 Or *and as for His generation, who considered Him?* [E]53:9 DSS; MT reads *He* [F]53:10 Or *Him; He made Him sick.* [G]53:10 Or *If* [H]53:11 DSS, LXX read *see light* [I]53:12 Or *Him with* [J]53:12 Or *receive with*

53:1 The speakers of these verses (**we**) are likely the prophet and the community that he represents. The **arm of the Lord** refers to His victorious power, ironically revealed through a Suffering Servant.

53:2-3 A **young plant** growing up in **dry ground** would be withered, thus providing an appropriate image of the **man of suffering**. Just like a withered plant is uprooted and thrown away, so the Suffering Servant was **rejected by men**.

53:4-6 For the first time the reader learns that the Servant suffered on behalf of others. Even so, people did not recognize it, and He was rejected as One **struck down by God** for His own supposed sins.

53:7 Though not suffering for His own sins, the Servant suffered silently and willingly. Philip used this passage to tell the Ethiopian eunuch the good news about Jesus, who silently bore His crucifixion (Ac 8:31-35; 1Pt 2:23).

53:8 For the first time the passage reveals that the Servant's suffering culminated in death.

53:9 The Servant died unjustly and was buried as if He were

an evil man. The pairing of the wicked with the rich man implies that the wealthy man got his riches by deceit. This may be confirmed by the final statement of the verse that the servant **had not spoken deceitfully**. Jesus was literally buried with a rich man when He was placed in the tomb of Joseph of Arimathea (Lk 23:50-56).

53:10-11 That God was **pleased to crush** the Servant sounds mean-spirited, but His pleasure is explained by the fact that the Servant's suffering **will justify many**. What seems harsh will turn out to be gracious. The Servant's pain, suffering, and death will function like a restitution offering (Lv 5:14–6:7; 7:1-10)—a sacrifice offered when there was a "transgression against the sacred things of the Lord" (Longman, *Immanuel in Our Place*, p. 99). The sin of God's people was such a transgression.

53:12 Returning to the theme at the beginning of the poem (52:13), the suffering of the Servant will give way to His exaltation. Jesus' suffering culminated in the crucifixion but gave way to the resurrection.

because He submitted Himself
    to death,[a]
and was counted
    among the rebels;[b]
yet He bore the sin of many[c]
and interceded for the rebels.[d]

Future Glory for Israel

54 "Rejoice, childless one, who did not
    give birth;
burst into song and shout,
you who have not been in labor![e]
For the children of the forsaken one
    will be more
than the children
    of the married woman,"[f]
says the Lord.

2 "Enlarge the site of your tent,
and let your tent curtains
    be stretched out;[g]
do not hold back;
lengthen your ropes,
and drive your pegs deep.

3 For you will spread out to the right
    and to the left,[h]
and your descendants
    will dispossess nations
and inhabit the desolate cities.

4 "Do not be afraid, for you will not
    be put to shame;[i]
don't be humiliated, for you will not
    be disgraced.
For you will forget the shame
    of your youth,
and you will no longer remember
the disgrace of your widowhood.[j]

5 Indeed, your husband is your Maker[k]—
His name is •Yahweh of •Hosts—

and the Holy One of Israel[l] is
    your Redeemer;[m]
He is called the God of all the earth.

6 For the Lord has called you,
like a wife deserted and wounded
    in spirit,[n]
a wife of one's youth[o]
    when she is rejected,"
says your God.

7 "I deserted you for a brief moment,[p]
but I will take you back
    with great compassion.

8 In a surge of anger
I hid My face[q] from you for a moment,
but I will have compassion on you
with everlasting love,"[r]
says the Lord your Redeemer.

9 "For this is like the days[A] of Noah
    to Me:
when I swore that the waters of Noah
would never flood the earth again,[s]
so I have sworn that I will not be angry
    with you
or rebuke you.[t]

10 Though the mountains move
and the hills shake,
My love will not be removed from you
and My covenant of peace[u] will not
    be shaken,"
says your compassionate Lord.

11 "Poor Jerusalem, storm-tossed,
    and not comforted,
I will set your stones in black mortar,[B]
and lay your foundations
    in sapphires.[C,v]

12 I will make your fortifications[D]
    out of rubies,

Cross references (center column):

[a] 53:12 Mt 26:42; Jn 10:14-18; Php 2:6-8
[b] Lk 22:37
[c] Heb 9:28
[d] Lk 23:34; Rm 8:34; Heb 7:25
[e] 54:1 Gl 4:27
[f] 1Sm 2:5; Is 62:4
[g] 54:2 Is 49:19-20
[h] 54:3 Gn 28:14; Is 43:5-6; 60:3
[i] 54:4 Is 45:17
[j] Is 4:1; 25:8; 51:7
[k] 54:5 Jr 3:14; Hs 2:19
[l] Is 1:4
[m] Is 41:14; 43:14
[n] 54:6 Is 49:14-21; 50:1-2; 62:4
[o] Mal 2:14
[p] 54:7 Is 26:20
[q] 54:8 Dt 31:17-18; Is 8:17
[r] Ps 100:5; Jr 31:3; 33:11
[s] 54:9 Gn 9:11
[t] Ezk 39:29
[u] 54:10 Nm 25:12; Ezk 34:25; Mal 2:5
[v] 54:11 Rv 21:19

[A]54:9 DSS, Cairo Geniza; MT, LXX read *waters*   [B]54:11 Lit *in antimony*   [C]54:11 Or *lapis lazuli*   [D]54:12 Lit *suns*; perhaps *shields*; Ps 84:11

54:1 A **childless** woman was often scorned in the ancient Near East and sometimes replaced by a secondary wife. With no sons to care for her in her old age, she was particularly vulnerable. Thus, barrenness is a frequent image of loneliness and helplessness. In this verse Jerusalem is a barren woman who will have a child (like Sarah, Rachel, or Hannah). Indeed she will have many **children**. Thus her sadness will turn to joy (Ps 113:9).

54:2-3 An enlarged family must have a larger place to live. Restored Jerusalem will teem with inhabitants, stretching its boundaries.

54:4-5 A worse fate than childlessness was being a widow. Such a woman had no husband to protect her and care for her. The oracle tells the widow Israel not to be afraid because God has married her. She has gone from nothing to everything, as the list of divine names makes clear.

54:6-8 The metaphor changes in this verse. Israel is no longer a widow; she is a divorcee. God, her husband, has aban-

doned her, but now He will take her back. The relationship between God and Israel as described here is like the relationship between Hosea and Gomer (Hs 1; 3) that typifies Israel's relationship with God. He rejected Israel because of her sin (**in a surge of anger**), but now He takes her back with **everlasting** covenant **love**.

54:9-10 After the flood, God promised, "Water will never again become a flood to destroy every creature" (Gn 9:15). God declares in these verses that though Israel may sin, He will not completely eradicate His people. He may make the **hills shake**, but He will not completely destroy them. Thus, God is **compassionate** in not treating Israel as they deserve because of their transgressions. The **covenant of peace** may be an allusion to the covenant with Noah, symbolized by the rainbow.

54:11-12 Jerusalem is now personified as a **storm-tossed** city that God will restore to unprecedented splendor, made of precious **stones** and metals, which anticipates new Jerusalem in Rv 21:15-21.

your gates out of sparkling stones,
and all your walls out of precious stones.
13 Then all your children will be taught
by the LORD,[a]
their prosperity will be great,
14 and you will be established
on a foundation of righteousness.
You will be far from oppression,
you will certainly not be afraid;
you will be far from terror,
it will certainly not come near you.
15 If anyone attacks you,
it is not from Me;
whoever attacks you
will fall before you.
16 Look, I have created the craftsman
who blows on the charcoal fire
and produces a weapon suitable
for its task;
and I have created the destroyer
to cause havoc.
17 No weapon formed against you
will succeed,
and you will refute any accusation[A]
raised against you in court.
This is the heritage
of the LORD's servants,[b]
and their righteousness is
from Me."[c]
            This is the LORD's declaration.

Come to the LORD

55 "Come, everyone who is thirsty,[d]
come to the waters;
and you without money,
come, buy, and eat!
Come, buy wine and milk
without money and without cost!

2 Why do you spend money on what
is not food,
and your wages on what
does not satisfy?
Listen carefully to Me, and eat
what is good,
and you will enjoy the choicest
of foods.[B]
3 Pay attention and come to Me;
listen, so that you will live.
I will make an everlasting covenant
with you,[e]
the promises assured to David.[f]
4 Since I have made him a witness
to the peoples,[g]
a leader and commander
for the peoples,[h]
5 so you will summon a nation
you do not know,[i]
and nations who do not know you
will run to you.[j]
For the LORD your God,
even the Holy One of Israel,[k]
has glorified you."[l]

6 Seek the LORD while He may be found;
call to Him while He is near.[m]
7 Let the wicked one abandon his way
and the sinful one his thoughts;[n]
let him return to the LORD,
so He may have compassion on him,
and to our God, for He will
freely forgive.[o]

8 "For My thoughts are not
your thoughts,
and your ways are not My ways."
            This is the LORD's declaration.
9 "For as heaven is higher than earth,[p]

Cross-references:
a 54:13 Jn 6:45
b 54:17 Is 41:8-9; Lk 1:54
c 55:1 Is 45:24; 46:13
d 55:1 Ps 42:1-2; 63:1; 143:6; Is 41:17; 44:3; Jn 4:14; 7:37; Rv 21:6
e 55:3 Gn 9:16; 17:7; 2Sm 23:5; Is 24:5; 59:21; 61:8
f Ac 13:34
g 55:4 Ps 18:43
h Ezk 34:24; 37:24-25; Dn 9:25; Mc 5:2
i 55:5 Is 45:14,22-24; 49:6
j Zch 8:22
k Is 1:4
l Is 60:9
m 55:6 Ps 32:6; Am 5:4
n 55:7 Ps 33:10; Is 32:7; 59:7; 65:2
o Is 1:18; 43:25; 44:22
p 55:9 Ps 103:11

A 54:17 Lit refute every tongue   B 55:2 Lit enjoy fatness

54:13 The **children** of Jerusalem are its inhabitants who will be taught by the Lord. The new covenant of Jr 31:31-34 anticipated a time when God's people would no longer need a teacher, "for they will all know Me."

54:15 Those who attacked Jerusalem (the Assyrians in 701 B.C. and the Babylonians in 605, 597, and 586 B.C.) did so with God's permission, but after the restoration, their enemies will not be God-sent and will fall for that reason.

54:16-17 Using both military (**weapon**) and legal (**accusation**) metaphors, God proclaims that His people will withstand all attacks because of His protection.

55:1-13 This chapter consists of an invitation to God's people to experience His forgiveness.

55:1 God will not only freely give water, but also the more substantial drinks of **milk** and **wine**. These drinks represent spiritual as well as physical nourishment.

55:2 God's people had not been accepting the free offer of salvation represented by water for the thirsty. They had been spending their resources on things that did not bring soul satisfaction.

55:3 The **promises** to **David** are found in 2 Samuel 7. They include the affirmation that David's dynasty would be established forever (2Sm 7:16). During the Babylonian captivity, though, the Davidic line of kings ruling in Jerusalem came to an end with Zedekiah. The NT understood the unconditional promise to be fulfilled in Jesus Christ, a descendant of David.

55:4-5 The promises to David are extended beyond God's people to include the **nations**. In fulfillment of the Abrahamic covenant (Gn 12:3), it envisions a time when the nations will come to God's people.

55:6 The call to repent has a tone of urgency. A person must repent before God withdraws His presence and begins His work of judgment.

55:8-9 God is far above humanity in thought and deed. God's people are called to turn from their sinful **thoughts** and deeds (v. 7) to God's exalted thoughts and deeds.

so My ways are higher than your ways,
and My thoughts than your thoughts.

10 For just as rain and snow fall
      from heaven
and do not return there
without saturating the earth
and making it germinate and sprout,
and providing seed to sow
and food to eat,[a]

11 so My word that comes from My mouth
will not return to Me empty,
but it will accomplish what I please
and will prosper in what I send it
   to do."[b]

12 You will indeed go out with joy
and be peacefully guided;
the mountains and the hills will break
   into singing before you,
and all the trees of the field will clap
   their hands.[c]

13 Instead of the thornbush, a cypress
   will come up,
and instead of the brier, a myrtle
   will come up;[d]
it will make a name for •Yahweh[e]
as an everlasting sign that will not
   be destroyed.

A House of Prayer for All

56 This is what the LORD says:

Preserve justice and do what is right,[f]
for My salvation is coming soon,
and My righteousness
   will be revealed.[g]

2 Happy is the man who does this,
anyone who maintains this,

Cross-reference column:

a55:10 2Co 9:10
b55:11 Is 45:23;
46:10; 53:10
c55:12 Ps 98:8;
Is 44:23
d55:13 Is 35:1-2;
41:19; 60:13
eIs 63:12-14;
Jr 33:9
f56:1 Gn 18:19;
Ps 106:3; Pr
21:3
g Ps 98:2; Is
46:13; 51:5; Rm
1:17; 3:21
h56:2 Is 58:13
i56:3 Is 14:1;
56:6
jDt 23:1
k56:5 Is 55:13;
Rv 2:17
l56:7 Is 2:2-3
mMal 1:11

---

who keeps the Sabbath
   without desecrating it,
and keeps his hand from doing
   any evil.[h]

3 No foreigner who has joined himself
      to the LORD
should say,
"The LORD will exclude me
   from His people";[i]
and the eunuch should not say,
"Look, I am a dried-up tree."[j]

4 For the LORD says this:
"For the eunuchs who keep
      My Sabbaths,
and choose what pleases Me,
and hold firmly to My covenant,

5 I will give them, in My house
      and within My walls,
a memorial and a name
better than sons and daughters.
I will give each of them
   an everlasting name
that will never be cut off.[k]

6 And the foreigners who join themselves
      to the LORD
minister to Him,
   love the name of •Yahweh
and become His servants,
all who keep the Sabbath
   without desecrating it
and who hold firmly to My covenant—

7 I will bring them to My holy mountain[l]
and let them rejoice in My house
   of prayer.
Their •burnt offerings and sacrifices
will be acceptable on My altar,[m]

55:10-11 Precipitation falls from sky to earth but then returns, but in the process it replenishes the earth and produces fertility. The same is true of God's word. It returns to Him but in the process causes spiritual growth in humanity.

55:12-13 Because of the redemption of God, His people and the rest of creation will break out in joyful **singing**, and wilderness terrain will turn into lush forests.

56:1 Salvation here is equivalent to victory or rescue since it envisions release from Babylonian bondage. This verse does not call for obedience that earns salvation. Obedience is a response to the promise of God's coming deliverance, not a way to earn His favor.

56:2 God pronounces **happy** (see Ps 1) those who are obedient and who avoid evil. The **Sabbath** commandment (Ex 20:8-11; Dt 5:12-15) is singled out because it was considered the epitome (the "sign") of the Mosaic covenant (Ex 31:13).

56:3 God reminds His people that foreigners who convert to the Lord are not excluded from worship. Isaiah is not at odds with Ezekiel (Ezk 44:6-9) or Ezra (Ezr 4:1-3), because they addressed the issue of foreigners who had not convert-

ed. Indeed, Ex 12:43 states in regard to the Passover meal that "no foreigner may eat it," but Ex 12:48-49 then makes it clear that if a foreigner converted and was circumcised, then he could partake of the Passover.

56:4 Eunuchs were typically excluded from worship, according to Dt 23:1: "No man whose testicles have been crushed or whose penis has been cut off may enter the LORD's assembly." That law pointed out that gender and sex were divine gifts that should not be intentionally altered. However, this verse describes an obedient eunuch and thus one who had become a eunuch accidentally or who had converted to worship of God after becoming a eunuch. Such devout eunuchs were invited to join in the worship of God.

56:5 Eunuchs could not have children and thus lacked progeny who would perpetuate their name. God proclaims that He will provide a **memorial** for them.

56:7 God will not turn away anyone who desires to worship Him, even foreigners and eunuchs. His house, the temple, will be a place where everyone can come to pray.

56:8 The **dispersed of Israel** refers to those Israelites who were removed from the land of Israel as a result of foreign

for My house will be called a house
of prayer
for all nations."[a]

[8] This is the declaration of the Lord GOD,
who gathers the dispersed of Israel:
"I will gather to them still others
besides those already gathered."[b]

Unrighteous Leaders Condemned

[9] All you animals of the field and forest,
come and eat!
[10] Israel's[A] watchmen are blind,
all of them,
they know nothing;
all of them are mute dogs,
they cannot bark;
they dream, lie down,
and love to sleep.
[11] These dogs have fierce appetites;
they never have enough.
And they are shepherds
who have no discernment;
all of them turn to their own way,
every last one for his own gain.[c]
[12] "Come, let me get some wine,
let's guzzle some beer;
and tomorrow will be like today,
only far better!"[d]

57 The righteous one perishes,
and no one takes it to heart;
faithful men are swept away,
with no one realizing
that the righteous one is swept away
from the presence[B] of evil.
[2] He will enter into peace—
they will rest on their beds[c]—
everyone who lives uprightly.

Pagan Religion Denounced

[3] But come here,
you sons of a sorceress,

Cross references (center column):
[a]56:7 Jr 7:11; Mt 21:13; Mk 11:17; Lk 19:46
[b]56:8 Is 11:12; 60:3-11; 66:18-21; Jn 10:16
[c]56:11 Jr 10:21; 23:1; 50:6; Ezk 34:2
[d]56:12 Lk 12:19; 1Co 15:32
[e]57:4 Is 30:1,9
[f]57:5 2Kg 16:4; Jr 2:20; 3:13
[g]2Kg 23:10; Ps 106:37-38; Jr 7:31; Ezk 16:20-21
[h]57:7 Jr 3:6; Ezk 16:16
[i]57:8 Ezk 23:17-18
[j]57:9 Ezk 16:26-29
[k]57:10 Jr 2:25; 18:12

---

offspring of an adulterer
and a prostitute![D]
[4] Who is it you are mocking?
Who is it you are opening your mouth
and sticking out your tongue at?
Isn't it you, you rebellious children,[e]
you race of liars,
[5] who burn with lust among the oaks,
under every green tree,[f]
who slaughter children in the •wadis
below the clefts of the rocks?[g]
[6] Your portion is
among the smooth stones of the wadi;
indeed, they are your lot.
You have even poured out
a •drink offering to them;
you have offered a •grain offering;
should I be satisfied with these?
[7] You have placed your bed
on a high and lofty mountain;[h]
you also went up there
to offer sacrifice.
[8] You have set up your memorial
behind the door and doorpost.
For away from Me, you stripped,
went up, and made your bed wide,[i]
and you have made a bargain[E]
for yourself with them.
You have loved their bed;
you have gazed on their genitals.[F,G]
[9] You went to the king with oil
and multiplied your perfumes;
you sent your couriers far away[j]
and sent them down even to •Sheol.
[10] You became weary
on your many journeys,
but you did not say, "I give up!"[k]
You found a renewal
of your strength;[H]
therefore you did not grow weak.
[11] Who was it you dreaded and feared,

[A]56:10 Or *His*, or *Its*   [B]57:1 Or *away because*   [C]57:2 Either their deathbeds or their graves   [D]57:3 Lit *and she acted as a prostitute*   [E]57:8 Lit *you cut*   [F]57:8 Lit *hand*   [G]57:8 In Hb, the word hand is probably a euphemism for "genitals."   [H]57:10 Lit *found life of your hand*

---

invasions (Assyrian and Babylonian) that God sent as punishment against His people.

56:9-10 Watchmen were supposed to keep wild animals away from the crops, but these watchmen—Israel's leaders—were ineffective, silent (**mute dogs**), and asleep.

56:11 In verse 10 the watchmen were called "mute dogs." This verse picks up on that image to describe their voracious **appetites**. The verse also compares the leaders to **shepherds**, but corrupt shepherds, exploiting their followers.

56:12 The leaders were totally self-indulgent. They were in it for themselves.

57:1-2 Retribution does not always happen in this life. Good things happen to bad people and, as these verses point out, bad things happen to good people. Even so, verse 2 hints at

future resolution of this problem when it talks about death for the righteous as an entering **into peace**.

57:3-13 In this section God blasts those who practice idolatry and warns them of coming judgment. In the last half of the section, He affirms the righteous.

57:3 God addresses those of His people who cannot be counted among the "righteous" (v. 1) and speaks of them in the harshest possible terms.

57:5 In ancient Israel illegitimate worship took place under trees, perhaps suggesting a fertility religion and sexual rites (Dt 12:2; Jr 2:20; 3:6,13). At times during the OT period, gruesome acts like child sacrifice were also included among the false religious practices of Israel (2Kg 23:10).

57:6-10 These verses describe idolatrous rituals, many

so that you lied and didn't
   remember Me
or take it to heart?
Have I not kept silent for such
   a long time[A,a]
and you do not •fear Me?
12 I will expose your righteousness,
   and your works—they will not
     profit you.
13 When you cry out,
   let your collection of idols deliver you!
The wind will carry all of them off,
   a breath will take them away.
But whoever takes refuge in Me
will inherit the land[b]
and possess My holy mountain.[c]

Healing and Peace

14 He said,
"Build it up, build it up,
   prepare the way,
remove every obstacle
   from My people's way."[d]
15 For the High and Exalted One
who lives forever, whose name is Holy[e]
   says this:
"I live in a high and holy place,
and with the oppressed and lowly
   of spirit,[f]
to revive the spirit of the lowly
and revive the heart of the oppressed.[g]
16 For I will not accuse you forever,
and I will not always be angry;[h]

for then the spirit would grow weak
   before Me,
even the breath of man,
   which I have made.
17 Because of his sinful greed
   I was angry,[i]
so I struck him; I was angry and hid;[B]
but he went on turning back
   to the desires of his heart.
18 I have seen his ways,
   but I will heal him;
I will lead him and restore comfort
to him and his mourners,[j]
19 creating words of praise."[C,k]
The LORD says,
"Peace, peace to the one who is far
   or near,[l]
and I will heal him.
20 But the wicked are like the
   storm-tossed sea,[m]
for it cannot be still,
and its waters churn up mire
   and muck.
21 There is no peace for the wicked,"
says my God.[n]

True Fasting

58 "Cry out loudly,[D] don't hold back!
   Raise your voice like a trumpet.
Tell My people their transgression
and the house of Jacob their sins.
2 They seek Me day after day
and delight to know My ways,
like a nation that does what is right

a57:11 Ps 50:21; Is 42:14
b57:13 Ps 37:3,9; Is 25:4
c Is 65:9
d57:14 Is 62:10; Jr 18:15
e57:15 Lk 1:49
f Ps 34:18; 51:17; Is 66:2
g Ps 147:3; Is 61:1-3
h57:16 Gn 6:3; Ps 103:9; Jr 3:12
i57:17 Is 2:7; 56:11; Jr 6:13
j57:18 Is 61:1-3
k57:19 Is 6:7; 51:16; 59:21; Heb 13:15
l Ac 2:39; Eph 2:17
m57:20 Ps 107:29
n57:21 Is 48:22; 59:8

A57:11 LXX reads *And I, when I see you, I pass by*   B57:17 Lit *him; hiding and I am angry*   C57:19 Lit *creating fruit of the lips*
D58:1 Lit *with throat*

---

features of which are obscure (e.g., **the smooth stones of the wadi**). Even so, the sexual nature of these practices comes through clearly at points (see references to **bed** and **genitals**), suggesting a connection with the fertility religion of ancient Canaan from which the Israelites were supposed to separate themselves.

57:11-12 Such idolatrous behavior was a result of a lack of **fear** of God, perhaps encouraged by His silence. He would be silent no more as He exposed His people's **righteousness**, which was no righteousness at all.

57:13 God warned His people that if they worshiped **idols**, they would have to depend on those idols in times of trouble. But the idols were not substantial, so the **wind** would blow them away. They will be of no help. On the other hand, God Himself is a refuge in trouble. The section ends with the promise that the truly righteous will possess God's **holy mountain**, Zion, in Jerusalem. This contrasts with the first part of this section that describes those who performed sexual rituals "on a high and lofty mountain" (v. 7).

57:14-21 Reversing the proportions of the previous oracle (vv. 3-13), this section has a long statement about God's good intentions toward the righteous, with a brief statement about the fate of the wicked at the end (vv. 20-21).

57:14-15 Again, Isaiah used the theme of removing ob-

stacles between God and His people in order to describe a restoration of intimate relationship (see note at 40:3-4). In this instance the road leads to God who lives in a **high and holy place**, so the road is one that goes up (**build it up**). God may live in a high place, but the **lowly of spirit**, not the exalted, are with Him.

57:16-18 God's punishment of His people's sins has a limit. He will not completely destroy them, but will punish them in a disciplinary way. He removed His presence from them, but still they continued to sin. Psalm 30 describes a person who grew presumptuous in his success and forgot about God. God turned His face from him, and he came running back. Here God's people do not break their sin pattern, but God in His grace still promises to **heal** them.

57:19-21 There is a distinction between those to whom God grants **peace** and those who remain wicked. The **wicked** will have no peace but will be like the turbulent **sea**. The sea is commonly a symbol of chaos and wickedness in ancient Near Eastern literature, including the Bible.

58:1 God spoke to Isaiah and told him to proclaim loudly and publicly (**like a trumpet**) the sin of His people. They had tried to put on a show of piety, so it was necessary to expose them for what they were—rebellious.

58:2-3a God acknowledged that His people appeared pious

and does not abandon the justice
of their God.
They ask Me for righteous judgments;
they delight in the nearness of God."[a]

3 "Why have we fasted,
but You have not seen?[b]
We have denied ourselves,
but You haven't noticed!"[A]
"Look, you do as you please on the day
of your fast,
and oppress all your workers.[c]

4 You fast with contention and strife
to strike viciously with your fist.
You cannot fast as you do today,
hoping to make your voice heard
on high.

5 Will the fast I choose be like this:
A day for a person to deny himself,
to bow his head like a reed,
and to spread out ·sackcloth
and ashes?[d]
Will you call this a fast
and a day acceptable to the LORD?

6 Isn't the fast I choose:
To break the chains of wickedness,[e]
to untie the ropes of the yoke,
to set the oppressed free,
and to tear off every yoke?[f]

7 Is it not to share your bread
with the hungry,[g]
to bring the poor and homeless
into your house,
to clothe the naked when you see him,[h]
and not to ignore[B] your own flesh
and blood?[i]

8 Then your light will appear
like the dawn,
and your recovery will come quickly.[j]
Your righteousness will go before you,[k]
and the LORD's glory will be
your rear guard.[l]

9 At that time, when you call, the LORD
will answer;[m]
when you cry out, He will say,
'Here I am.'
If you get rid of the yoke among you,[C]
the finger-pointing
and malicious speaking,[n]

10 and if you offer yourself[D] to the hungry,
and satisfy the afflicted one,
then your light will shine
in the darkness,[o]
and your night will be like noonday.

11 The LORD will always lead you,
satisfy you in a parched land,
and strengthen your bones.
You will be like a watered garden[p]
and like a spring whose waters
never run dry.[q]

12 Some of you will rebuild
the ancient ruins;[r]
you will restore the foundations laid
long ago;[E,s]
you will be called the repairer
of broken walls,
the restorer of streets
where people live.

13 "If you keep from desecrating[F]
the Sabbath,[t]

Cross-references

a 58:2 Ps 119:151; Is 29:13; 57:3; Jms 4:8
b 58:3 Mal 3:14; Lk 18:12
c Is 22:12-13; Zch 7:5-6
d 58:5 Est 4:3; Dn 9:3
e 58:6 Jb 36:8; Ps 107:10; Ec 7:26
f Neh 5:10-12; Is 58:9; Jr 34:8
g 58:7 Jb 31:19-20; Is 58:10; Ezk 18:7,16
h Mt 25:35-36; Lk 3:11
i Dt 22:1-4; Lk 10:31-32
j 58:8 Is 30:26; 33:24; Jr 30:17; 33:6
k Ps 85:13; Is 62:1
l Ex 14:19; Is 52:12
m 58:9 Ps 50:15; Is 55:6; 65:24
n Pr 6:13
o 58:10 Jb 11:17; Ps 37:6; Is 42:16; 58:8
p 58:11 Sg 4:15; Is 27:3; Jr 31:12
q Jn 4:14; 7:38
r 58:12 Ezr 6:14; Neh 4:6; Is 49:8; 61:4; Ezk 36:10
s 1Kg 6:37; Ezr 3:10-12
t 58:13 Ex 31:16-17; 35:2-3; Is 56:2-6; Jr 17:21-27

A 58:3 These are Israel's words to God.   B 58:7 Lit *not hide yourself from*   C 58:9 Lit *yoke from your midst*   D 58:10 Some Hb mss, LXX, Syr read *offer your bread*   E 58:12 Lit *foundations generation and generation*   F 58:13 Lit *keep your foot from*

---

on the surface. They made pretense that they wanted to know and follow God's will for their lives as expressed in the commands. They had even **fasted**, expecting God to do something for them. They claimed to have **denied** themselves before God, but God had not responded. They challenged God's silence. Fasts occur elsewhere in Scripture, but they are commanded by human rulers rather than God. Thus, the people of God complained about getting no divine response from their self-initiated fast, while they failed to observe the Sabbath, one of the OT's most important commands (vv. 13-14).

58:3b-5 God responded to His people's challenge. He did not respond to their fasting because it was superficial and inauthentic. It led to divisions in the community and exploitative behavior toward underlings, as well as self-absorption. God's idea of fasting extended far beyond public expressions of mourning.

58:6 After condemning the people's idea of fasting, God defined what He understood to be legitimate and effective fasting. The emphasis is on social justice. Fasting must be connected to behavior that helps the exploited find freedom. The **yoke** is often an image of exploitation and bondage.

58:7 Proper fasting is also connected to care for those in

need, including the **hungry** and those who needed shelter and clothing (cp. Mc 6:6-8). **Flesh and blood** is a reference to fellow Israelites.

58:8-9 The people began by complaining that God did not respond to their fasting (v. 3). Fasting seems self-denying, but God recognized that the fasting of His people had been manipulative. True self-denial means helping others, and behavior that is other-centered rather than self-directed will be rewarded. On **yoke**, see note at verse 6.

58:10 **Light** and **darkness** stand for prosperity and need. True obedience and a turning from evil will transform darkness into light.

58:11-12 The oracle looks forward to the restoration when God's people will leave their captivity and return to the land, but the land and its cities, especially Jerusalem, will be in **ruins**. Obedience will lead to prosperity and fertility. The **parched land** will turn into a **watered garden**. Obedience and true piety will also lead to the strength needed to rebuild the city of Jerusalem and its defenses.

58:13-14 While God's people kept fasts not commanded in the Bible, they flouted **Sabbath** observance, which was one of the central commands of the OT. It was the fourth

from doing whatever you want
  on My holy day;
if you call the Sabbath a delight,
and the holy day of the Lord honorable;
if you honor it, not going
  your own ways,[a]
seeking your own pleasure, or talking
  too much;[A]
14 then you will delight yourself
  in the Lord,[b]
and I will make you ride
  over the heights of the land,[c]
and let you enjoy the heritage
  of your father Jacob."
For the mouth of the Lord has spoken.[d]

Sin and Redemption

59 Indeed, the Lord's hand is not
    too short to save,[e]
and His ear is not too deaf to hear.
2 But your iniquities[f] have built barriers
  between you and your God,
  and your sins have made Him
    hide His face from you[g]
  so that He does not listen.[h]
3 For your hands are defiled with blood
  and your fingers, with iniquity;
  your lips have spoken lies,
  and your tongues mutter injustice.
4 No one makes claims justly;
  no one pleads honestly.
  They trust in empty
    and worthless words;
  they conceive trouble and give birth
    to iniquity.[i]
5 They hatch viper's eggs
  and weave spider's webs.

Whoever eats their eggs will die;
crack one open, and a viper is hatched.
6 Their webs cannot become clothing,
  and they cannot cover themselves
    with their works.
  Their works are sinful works,
  and violent acts are in their hands.
7 Their feet run after evil,[j]
  and they rush to shed innocent blood.[k]
  Their thoughts are sinful thoughts;[l]
  ruin and wretchedness are
    in their paths.
8 They have not known the path
    of peace,[m]
  and there is no justice in their ways.
  They have made their roads crooked;
  no one who walks on them
    will know peace.[n]
9 Therefore justice is far from us,
  and righteousness does not reach us.
  We hope for light,
    but there is darkness;
  for brightness, but we live in the night.
10 We grope along a wall like the blind;
  we grope like those without eyes.[o]
  We stumble at noon as though
    it were twilight;
  we are like the dead among those
    who are healthy.
11 We all growl like bears
  and moan like doves.[p]
  We hope for justice, but there is none;
  for salvation, but it is far from us.
12 For our transgressions have multiplied
    before You,[q]
  and our sins testify against us.[r]

Cross references
[a] 58:13 Is 55:8
[b] 58:14 Jb 22:26; Ps 37:4
[c] Dt 32:13; 33:29; Is 33:16; Hab 3:19
[d] Is 1:20; 40:5
[e] 59:1 Nm 11:23; Is 50:2; Jr 32:17
[f] 59:2 Is 13:11
[g] Dt 31:17-18; 32:20; Is 50:6; Ezk 39:29; Mc 3:4
[h] Dt 3:26; 23:5; Jb 35:13; Is 1:15
[i] 59:4 Jb 15:35; Ps 7:14; Is 33:11
[j] 59:7-8 Rm 3:15-17
[k] 59:7 Pr 1:16; 6:17
[l] Mk 7:21-22
[m] 59:8 Lk 1:79
[n] Is 57:20-21
[o] 59:10 Dt 28:29; Jb 5:14
[p] 59:11 Is 38:14; Ezk 7:16
[q] 59:12 Ezr 9:6
[r] Is 3:9; Jr 14:7; Hs 5:5

[A]58:13 Lit *or speak a word*

commandment, considered the sign of the Mosaic covenant (see note at 56:2). To observe the Sabbath meant turning away from self-absorbed behavior (see note at 58:8-9).

59:1 This oracle begins with an affirmation that God can hear and act, characteristics that contrast with the powerless idols that tempted Israel (44:6-23).

59:3-4 A selection of the sins that separated God from His people is listed. The list begins with acts of violence and moves on to deceit and **injustice**. They were guilty in thought and action (**they conceive trouble and give birth to iniquity**).

59:5-6 These sinners produced **viper's eggs**. Eggs promise life, but these eggs produced death. Thus, the works of God's people may look promising, but they kill. In a similar vein, God's people produce **spider's webs**. They may look beautiful in their intricacy, but they have no practical value.

59:7 Again (v. 4), the oracle emphasizes that the people are sinful in thought and deed. Indeed, they do not merely walk in "the advice of the wicked" (Ps 1:1), they show their eagerness when they **run after evil**.

59:8 Isaiah used the words **path** and **roads** to refer to the

course of a person's life. Proverbs 1–9 talks about two paths, a straight path that leads to God and life, and a crooked path that leads to death. Isaiah described God's people as choosing the latter and thus they were headed toward death (they will not **know peace**).

59:9 Note the transition from third person plural speech ("they") to first person (**we**) that begins in this verse and continues until verse 15a. The prophet included himself along with the people. Since the content of these verses acknowledges the people's sinfulness, it may be that the righteous are among those who are speaking here.

59:10 Chapter 58 has already described the way to light in obedience to God (see note at 58:10), but they appear incapable of getting there on their own.

59:11 Bears growl out of anger, and **doves** make a sound like the groans to a suffering person. These metaphors suggest that God's people were angry and sad about their present state.

59:12-15a The people had no one but themselves to blame for their lamentable situation, and they knew it. They had

For our transgressions are with us,
and we know our iniquities:[a]
13 transgression and deception
   against the LORD,
turning away from following our God,
speaking oppression and revolt,
conceiving and uttering lying words
   from the heart.
14 Justice is turned back,
and righteousness stands far off.
For truth has stumbled
   in the public square,
and honesty cannot enter.
15 Truth is missing,
and whoever turns from evil
   is plundered.

The LORD saw that there was no justice,
and He was offended.
16 He saw that there was no man—
He was amazed that there was
   no one interceding;[b]
so His own arm brought salvation,
and His own righteousness
   supported Him.
17 He put on righteousness
   like a breastplate,
and a helmet of salvation on His head;[c]
He put on garments of vengeance
   for clothing,
and He wrapped Himself in zeal
   as in a cloak.[d]
18 So He will repay according to
   their deeds:[e]

[a]59:12 Is 13:11
[b]59:16 Is 41:28;
63:5; Ezk 22:30
[c]59:17 Eph
6:14,17; 1Th 5:8
[d]Is 9:7; 37:32;
Zch 1:14
[e]59:18 Jr 25:14;
Rv 22:12
[f]59:19 Ps 113:3
[g]Is 30:28; 66:12
[h]59:20 Is 41:14;
43:14
[i]59:20-21 Ezk
18:30-31; Rm
11:26-27
[j]59:21 Jr
31:31-34
[k]Is 51:16
[l]60:1 Is 9:2;
26:19; 30:26;
51:17; 52:2; Eph
5:14
[m]Is 40:5; 58:8;
Mal 4:2
[n]60:3 Is 42:6;
49:6; Rv 21:24

fury to His enemies,
retribution to His foes,
and He will repay the coastlands.
19 They will *fear the name of *Yahweh
   in the west
and His glory in the east;[f]
for He will come like a rushing stream[g]
driven by the wind of the LORD.
20 "The Redeemer[h] will come to *Zion,
and to those in Jacob who turn
   from transgression."[i]
                This is the LORD's declaration.

21 "As for Me, this is My covenant with
them,"[j] says the LORD: "My Spirit who is on
you, and My words that I have put in your
mouth,[k] will not depart from your mouth, or
from the mouth of your children, or from the
mouth of your children's children, from now
on and forever," says the LORD.

The LORD's Glory in Zion

60 Arise, shine, for your light has come,[l]
   and the glory of the LORD shines
      over you.[A,m]
2 For look, darkness covers the earth,
   and total darkness the peoples;
but the LORD will shine over you,
   and His glory will appear over you.
3 Nations will come to your light,
   and kings to the brightness
      of your radiance.[n]
4 Raise your eyes and look around:
   they all gather and come to you;

sinned against God by perverting justice in their society (in
the public square).

59:15b-21 The chapter concludes with a description of God's
reaction to the sin and helplessness of His people. He will
intercede and rescue His people in spite of their sin and
helplessness.

59:15b-16 The section begins with a statement of God's recognition of human injustice and the offense that He takes at
it. It also goes on to describe His amazement that no human
was interceding on behalf of the people. Perhaps the intercession of Moses (Ex 33) or the other prophets is what is in
mind here. In any case, God proclaims that in the absence
of such a human intercessor, He Himself will step into the
gap between His people and Himself. Indeed, God's hand is
not "too short" (Is 59:1). His **arm** reaches out to save His
people.

59:17 To save His people, God assumed the guise of a warrior. However, His armor and His weapons are not physical
but spiritual. The description of God's armor and weapons
remind believers of Paul's description of the spiritual weapons available to Christians as they wage battle against "the
spiritual forces of evil in the heavens" (Eph 6:12).

59:18-19 God's **enemies** do not get off without punishment.
The mention of the **coastlands** indicates that the far-flung
nations, indeed the whole world (**west** and **east**), are in

mind here. The whole world will **fear the name of Yahweh**
after His work of retribution.

59:20-21 The climax of this oracle announces the future
arrival of God **the Redeemer** at **Zion**, God's holy mountain
in Jerusalem. He had abandoned Zion in anticipation of its
destruction at the Babylonian captivity (Ezk 11–19), but His
war against sin will result in His return. It is specifically to
the repentant that He will come. He will reestablish His
covenant with them. God's Spirit will be given to His people
to cleanse their mouths (reminiscent of Isaiah's cleansing
at his prophetic commission; chap. 6) so they will proclaim
the glory of God to future generations.

60:1-2 In 59:9 the righteous among God's people expressed
their desire for light, though they lived in darkness. Now God
announces the arrival of the **light**, whose source is the glory
of God. **Darkness** still **covers the earth** (a reference to pervasive sin), but God's hovering glory will illuminate the way for
His people. How has light penetrated the darkness? Through
the action of the divine warrior described in 59:17-21.

60:3 Though the light comes to God's people, the **nations**
will share in it by coming to the light. The idea that the
nations will respond favorably to God is a fulfillment of the
promise to Abraham that he would be a blessing to the nations (Gn 12:3).

60:4 Among the arriving nations will be the dispersed of

your sons will come from far away,
and your daughters will be carried
on the hip.[a]
5 Then you will see and be radiant,[b]
and your heart will tremble
and rejoice,[A]
because the riches of the sea
will become yours
and the wealth of the nations will come
to you.[c]
6 Caravans of camels will cover
your land[B]—
young camels of Midian and Ephah—
all of them will come from Sheba.[d]
They will carry gold
and frankincense[e]
and proclaim the praises of the LORD.
7 All the flocks of Kedar will be gathered
to you;
the rams of Nebaioth will serve you[f]
and go up on My altar
as an acceptable sacrifice.[g]
I will glorify My beautiful house.[h]
8 Who are these who fly like a cloud,

like doves to their shelters?[i]
9 Yes, the islands will wait for Me[j]
with the ships of Tarshish in the lead,[k]
to bring your children from far away,[l]
their silver and gold with them,
for the honor of the LORD your God,
the Holy One of Israel,[m]
who has glorified you.[n]
10 Foreigners will build up your walls,[o]
and their kings will serve you.[p]
Although I struck you in My wrath,
yet I will show mercy to you
with My favor.[q]
11 Your gates will always be open;
they will never be shut day or night
so that the wealth of the nations
may be brought into you,[r]
with their kings being led in procession.
12 For the nation and the kingdom
that will not serve you will perish;
those nations will be annihilated.[s]
13 The glory of Lebanon will come
to you[t]—
its pine, fir, and cypress together[u]—

---

a 60:4 Is
49:18-22
b 60:5 Ps 34:5
c Is 61:6
d 60:6 Gn 25:3;
Ps 72:10
e Mt 2:11
f 60:7 Gn 25:13
g Is 19:19; 56:7
h Is 60:13; Hg
2:7,9
i 60:8 Hs 11:11
j 60:9 Is 51:5
k Ps 48:7; Is 2:16
l Is 14:2; 43:6;
49:22
m Is 1:4; 60:14
n Is 55:5
o 60:10 Is 14:1-2;
61:5; Zch 6:15
p Is 49:7,23; Rv
21:24
q Hab 3:2
r 60:11 Rv
21:25-26
s 60:12 Zch
14:17-19
t 60:13 Is 35:2
u Is 41:19

A 60:5 Lit expand   B 60:6 Lit cover you

Israel (**your sons . . . your daughters**), who will also return to Zion.

60:5-6 As they return to their homeland, the people will bring the **wealth of the nations**, just as their father Abraham returned from his sojourn in Egypt with increased wealth (Gn 12:10-20). **Camels** carried freight on the caravan trails of the ancient Near East. Here they are described as carrying precious items like **gold and frankincense**. The camels will come from **Midian**, a nomadic Arabic tribe. **Ephah** was associated with Midian by way of genealogy (Gn 25:4; 1Ch 1:33), but not much else is known about it. **Sheba** was also an Arabian kingdom. It was famous because of the queen of Sheba, whose wealth flowed to Israel because of her admiration for Solomon's wisdom (1Kg 10:1-10).

tiph'ereth

Hebrew Pronunciation	[tif EH ret]
HCSB Translation	beauty, glory
Uses in Isaiah	17
Uses in the OT	49
Focus Passage	Isaiah 60:7,19

Tiph'ereth is *beauty* (Ex 28:2), *glory* (Dt 26:19), *honor* (Jdg 4:9), *splendor* (Is 28:1), or *finery* (Is 3:18). It is one's *pride* (Jr 13:20), *boast* (Is 20:5), or *virtue* (Pr 19:11). It suggests *rejoicing* (Pr 28:12). Adjectivally it implies *glorious* (Is 62:3), *beautiful* (Is 44:13), or *magnificent* (Ps 89:17) and especially modifies objects like *jewelry* and *crowns* (Ezk 23:26,42). *Tiph'ereth* derives from the verb *pe'ar* (13x), which reflexively indicates *glorify* (Is 44:23) or *exalt* (Is 10:15) *oneself*. *Pe'ar* means *brag* (Jdg 7:2) and can take a passive sense of *be glorified* (Is 49:3). Intensive verbs denote *glorify* (Is 60:7) or *adorn* (Ps 149:4). *Tiph'ereth* and *pe'ar* together describe God *glorifying* His *beautiful* house (Is 60:7). The noun *pe'er* (7x) is *crown of beauty* (Is 61:3), *turban* (Is 61:10), *headdress* (Is 3:20), or *headband* (Ex 39:28). *Tiph'arah* indicates a *glorious* staff (Jr 48:17) or *crown* of *splendor* (Is 28:5)

60:7 The theme of the "wealth of the nations" streaming to Zion continues. Sacrificial animals that will be offered at the temple (**My beautiful house**) are described. On **Kedar**, see note at 21:13-17 **Nebaioth** is elsewhere in the Bible a personal name, the son of Kedar, showing a relationship between these two nomadic tribes (Gn 25:13; 36:3; 1Ch 1:29).

60:8 A **cloud** travels through the sky unobstructed by mountains or ravines. **Doves** fly above such obstacles to their homes. The rhetorical question has "God's people" as the implied answer. The oracle looks forward to the time when the scattered peoples of Israel will come back to the promised land.

60:9 The **islands** refer to distant lands and thus represent all the nations of the world. The **ships of Tarshish**, thought to be what is today Spain (Tartessus), were particularly impressive since they traveled so far between Tyre and Iberia. Again, the passage refers to the return of God's people to their land and not just any return, since they will be wealthy, bringing **silver and gold with them**.

60:10 In the past, foreign nations and their kings had exploited Israel, but the future will see them serve God's people. One thinks of Nehemiah, who received the permission of the Persian king Artaxerxes to rebuild the **walls** of Jerusalem. This reversal of fortunes is due to God, who had expressed His anger toward His people by allowing foreign nations to defeat and oppress them, but now in His favor He will allow them to rebuild.

60:11 Open **gates** indicated that a city felt secure. When an enemy threatened, all the people in the surrounding villages sought refuge behind the city walls, and the gates were locked down. But the gates will also be open because the **wealth of the nations** is flowing into Jerusalem.

60:13 The trees (**glory**) of Lebanon were renowned for their

to beautify the place of My sanctuary,
and I will glorify My dwelling place.[A]

14 The sons of your oppressors
will come and bow down to you;[a]
all who reviled you
will fall facedown at your feet.[b]
They will call you the City of the Lord,
•Zion of the Holy One of Israel.[c]

15 Instead of your being deserted
and hated,
with no one passing through,[d]
I will make you an object
of eternal pride,[e]
a joy from age to age.

16 You will nurse on the milk of nations,
and nurse at the breast of kings;[f]
you will know that I, •Yahweh,
am your Savior[g]
and Redeemer,[h] the Mighty One
of Jacob.[i]

17 I will bring gold instead of bronze;
I will bring silver instead of iron,
bronze instead of wood,
and iron instead of stones.
I will appoint peace as your guard
and righteousness as your ruler.

18 Violence will never again be heard of
in your land;[j]
devastation and destruction
will be gone from your borders.
But you will name
your walls salvation[k]
and your gates, praise.

19 The sun will no longer be your light
by day,
and the brightness of the moon
will not shine on you;
but the Lord will be
your everlasting light,[l]
and your God will be your splendor.

20 Your sun will no longer set,
and your moon will not fade;
for the Lord will be
your everlasting light,
and the days of your sorrow
will be over.[m]

21 Then all your people will be righteous;[n]
they will possess the land forever;[o]
they are the branch I planted,
the work of My[B] hands,
so that I may be glorified.[p]

22 The least will become a thousand,
the smallest a mighty nation.
I am Yahweh;
I will accomplish it quickly in its time.

Messiah's Jubilee

61 The Spirit of the Lord God is on Me,[q]
because the Lord has anointed Me
to bring good news to the poor.[r]
He has sent Me to heal[C]
the brokenhearted,
to proclaim liberty to the captives
and freedom to the prisoners;[s]
2 to proclaim the year of the Lord's favor,[t]
and the day of our God's vengeance;[u]

Cross references: [a]60:14 Is 14:1-2; Zch 8:23 [b]Is 49:23; Rv 3:9 [c]Is 1:26 [d]60:15 Is 34:10 [e]Is 65:18 [f]60:16 Is 49:23; 66:11-12 [g]Is 43:3; 49:26 [h]Is 41:14; 43:14 [i]Gn 49:24; Ps 132:2,5; Is 49:26 [j]60:18 Is 11:9 [k]Is 26:1 [l]60:19 Zch 14:6-7; Rv 21:23; 22:5 [m]60:20 Is 35:10; 65:19; Rv 21:4 [n]60:21 Is 52:1 [o]Ps 37:9; Ezk 37:25 [p]Is 61:3 [q]61:1-2 Is 11:2; 42:1; 48:16; Lk 4:18-19 [r]61:1 Lk 7:22 [s]Is 42:7; 49:9 [t]61:2 Is 49:8 [u]Is 2:12; 13:6; 34:2,8

[A]60:13 Lit *glorify the place of My feet*   [B]60:21 LXX, DSS read *His*   [C]61:1 Lit *bind up*

---

beauty and quality. The oracle envisions their use in the temple of the Lord.

60:14 As part of the reversal from humiliation to glory, the **sons** of those who had previously oppressed God's people will show their subservience and indicate their acknowledgment of the sacred character of Jerusalem.

60:15 Throughout the OT period, Jerusalem was not a major city of the ancient Near East. At best it was a provincial capital. In the future its status will exceed those of other major cities because of the presence of God.

60:16 Rather than oppressed Israel providing sustenance to the nations through forced labor, the resources of the nations (their **milk**) will succor Israel.

60:17 God will increase the quality of the provision that comes to His people. But the good things coming to Jerusalem will far exceed mere wealth. **Peace** and **righteousness** will abound, indicating a new quality of spirituality in the city.

60:19-20 The oracle returns to the theme with which it began: God's people will experience **light**, not darkness. This is a supernatural light provided by God, not the **sun**. God will be perpetually present with His people.

60:21 God had promised Abraham that his descendants would inherit the land. God's judgment had removed His

people from the land for a time, but now they will return to possess it again. They are the **branch** that God labored to plant.

60:22 Because of God's grace, His chosen people will multiply rapidly.

61:1-3 Much debate surrounds the identity of the first-person speaker of the first three verses of this chapter. He identified Himself as having the **Spirit**. This reference provides a connection to the Servant on whom God had placed His Spirit (see note at 42:1-9). Isaiah 11:2 states of the Messiah that "the Spirit of the Lord will rest on Him." It is significant that 61:1-3 uses the language of anointing from which the word *Messiah* ("anointed one") comes. Thus, it is best to consider the first-person speaker in this oracle to be none other than the Messiah-Servant. Jesus identified Himself as the embodiment of this passage when He read these verses in a synagogue, to the amazement of all who heard Him (Lk 4:16-30).

61:1 The description of this future day as one in which **prisoners** will be freed and the **poor** will receive **good news** associates this time with the Jubilee, where slaves were freed and land reverted to the original owners (Lv 25).

61:2 The same act can be designated as displaying the **Lord's favor** as well as **God's vengeance**, depending on whether a person is on God's side or not.

to comfort[a] all who mourn,

3   to provide for those who mourn
    in •Zion;
    to give them a crown of beauty
      instead of ashes,
    festive oil instead of mourning,[b]
    and splendid clothes instead of despair.[A]
    And they will be called righteous trees,
    planted by the LORD
    to glorify Him.[c]

4   They will rebuild the ancient ruins;[d]
    they will restore
      the former devastations;
    they will renew the ruined cities,
    the devastations of many generations.

5   Strangers will stand and feed
      your flocks,
    and foreigners will be your plowmen
      and vinedressers.[e]

6   But you will be called the LORD's priests;[f]
    they will speak of you as ministers
      of our God;
    you will eat the wealth of the nations,
    and you will boast in their riches.

7   Because your shame was double,[g]
    and they cried out,
      "Disgrace is their portion,"
    therefore, they will possess double
      in their land,[h]
    and eternal joy will be theirs.

8   For I •Yahweh love justice;[i]
    I hate robbery and injustice;[B]
    I will faithfully reward them
    and make an everlasting covenant[j]
    with them.

9   Their descendants will be known
      among the nations,
    and their posterity among the peoples.
    All who see them will recognize
    that they are a people the LORD
      has blessed.

10 I greatly rejoice in the LORD,
    I exult in my God;
    for He has clothed me
      with the garments of salvation
    and wrapped me in a robe
      of righteousness,[k]
    as a groom wears a turban
    and as a bride adorns herself
      with her jewels.[l]

11 For as the earth produces its growth,
    and as a garden enables what is sown
      to spring up,
    so the Lord GOD
      will cause righteousness and praise
    to spring up before all the nations.[m]

Zion's Restoration

62 I will not keep silent
      because of •Zion,
    and I will not keep still
      because of Jerusalem,[n]
    until her righteousness shines
      like a bright light[o]
    and her salvation, like a flaming torch.
2   Nations will see your righteousness[p]
    and all kings, your glory.
    You will be called by a new name
    that the LORD's mouth will announce.[q]
3   You will be a glorious crown
      in the LORD's hand,

Cross references (center column)

[a]61:2 Is 40:1
[b]61:3 Ps 45:7; Heb 1:9
[c]Is 60:21; Jr 17:7-8
[d]61:4 Is 49:8; 58:12; Ezk 36:33; Am 9:14
[e]61:5 Is 14:2; 60:10
[f]61:6 Ex 19:6; Is 66:21; 1Pt 2:5,9
[g]61:7 Is 54:4
[h]Is 40:2; Zch 9:12
[i]61:8 Ps 11:7; Is 59:15
[j]Is 24:5; 55:3
[k]61:10 Is 49:18; 52:1; 59:17
[l]Rv 21:2
[m]61:11 Is 45:23-24; 60:18,21
[n]62:1 Ps 83:1; Is 64:12; 65:6
[o]Is 1:26; 58:8; 61:11
[p]62:2 Is 60:3
[q]Is 60:14; Rv 2:17; 3:12

A61:3 Lit *a dim spirit*   **B**61:8 Some Hb mss, DSS, LXX, Syr, Tg, Vg; other Hb mss read *robbery with a burnt offering*

61:3 This verse emphasizes the reversal of fortune (from suffering to restoration) expressed in chapter 60. The reference to God's people as **righteous trees** is reminiscent of Psalm 1 and the opposite of what is said of them in Isaiah 1:30-31.

61:4 The Babylonians devastated Jerusalem and its surrounding towns and villages in 587 B.C. The oracle looks to the future when the **cities** will be restored and rebuilt.

61:5-6 Like chapter 60, this oracle repeats the themes of **foreigners** serving rather than oppressing the people of God as well as **the wealth of the nations** flowing to Jerusalem. The idea that all of God's people will function as **priests** toward the nations points back to Ex 19:6 where God told Moses that the Israelites would be "My kingdom of priests and My holy nation." Because of their failure to function in this way, God had brought judgment against His people.

61:8 According to 24:5, God's devastating judgment had come on Israel because it had broken the **everlasting covenant**, but now God will establish it anew with His restored people.

61:9 In the Abrahamic covenant, God promised that Abraham's descendants would enjoy great blessing, which pointed to happiness and prosperity.

61:10 Isaiah broke out in a hymn of praise in response to the oracle he had just delivered. He used the theme of clothing to describe his taking on God's salvation and righteousness. These were not just any clothes but the clothes of a bride. This image implies the metaphor of God as husband of His people.

62:1-12 The theme of the transformation of God's people continues in this chapter. From shame, they will rise up in glory—thanks to their God.

62:1 The first-person speaker here is either the Servant-Messiah of 61:1-3 or the prophet Isaiah. He will speak until Jerusalem's spiritual transformation is complete. **Light** is an important theme describing God's work among His people (58:10; 60:1-13). It is also connected with the Messiah (10:17; 42:6).

62:2 Names and their meaning often were connected with a person's character or reputation. **Name** changes were not uncommon. For instance, Naomi ("pleasant") changed her name to Mara ("bitter") when her fortunes turned bad (Ru 1:20). Israel's **new** divinely given name indicates a change of condition for the people of God (vv. 4,12).

62:3 Israel's future elevated status is compared to a **crown**.

and a royal diadem in the palm
of your God.[a]

4 You will no longer be called Deserted,[b]
and your land will not
be called Desolate;
instead, you will be called My Delight
is in Her,[A]
and your land Married;[B,c]
for the LORD delights in you,
and your land will be married.

5 For as a young man marries
a young woman,
so your sons will marry you;
and as a groom rejoices[c] over his bride,
so your God will rejoice over you.[d]

6 Jerusalem,
I have appointed watchmen
on your walls;[e]
they will never be silent, day or night.
There is no rest for you,
who remind the LORD.

7 Do not give Him rest
until He establishes
and makes Jerusalem
the praise of the earth.[f]

8 The LORD has sworn
with His right hand
and His strong arm:
I will no longer give your grain
to your enemies for food,[g]
and foreigners will not drink
your new wine
you have labored for.

9 For those who gather grain will eat it
and praise the LORD,

and those who harvest the grapes
will drink the wine
in My holy courts.

10 Go out, go out through the gates;
prepare a way for the people!
Build it up, build up the highway;[h]
clear away the stones!
Raise a banner for the peoples.[i]

11 Look, the LORD has proclaimed
to the ends of the earth,
"Say to Daughter Zion:[j]
Look, your salvation is coming,
His reward is with Him,[k]
and His gifts accompany Him."

12 And they will be called[D]
the Holy People,[l]
the LORD's Redeemed;
and you will be called Cared For,
A City Not Deserted.

The LORD's Day of Vengeance

63 Who is this coming from Edom[m]
in crimson-stained garments
from Bozrah—
this One who is splendid in His apparel,
rising up proudly[E] in His great might?

It is I, proclaiming vindication,[F]
powerful to save.

2 Why are Your clothes red,
and Your garments like one who treads
a winepress?[n]

3 I trampled the winepress alone,
and no one from the nations was
with Me.

Cross references

[a]62:3 Is 28:5; Zch 9:16; 1Th 2:19
[b]62:4 Is 54:6-7; 60:15,18
[c]Hs 2:19-20
[d]62:5 Is 65:19
[e]62:6 Is 52:8; Jr 6:17; Ezk 3:17; 33:7
[f]62:7 Is 60:18; Jr 33:9; Zph 3:19-20
[g]62:8 Lv 26:16; Dt 28:31,33; Jdg 6:3-6; Is 1:7; Jr 5:17
[h]62:10 Is 11:16; 19:23; 35:8; 49:11; 57:14
[i]Is 11:10,12; 49:22
[j]62:11 Mt 21:5; Zch 9:9
[k]Is 40:10; Rv 22:12
[l]62:12 Dt 7:6; Is 4:3; 1Pt 2:9
[m]63:1 Ps 137:7; Is 34:5-6; Ezk 25:12-14; 35:1-15; Ob 1-14; Mal 1:2-5
[n]63:2 Rv 19:13-15

A62:4 Or Hephzibah   B62:4 Or Beulah   C62:5 Lit and the rejoicing of the groom   D62:12 Lit will call them   E63:1 Syr, Vg read apparel, striding forward   F63:1 Or righteousness

---

62:4-5 Israel's names are changed from ones that indicated her loneliness (**Deserted** and **Desolate**) to those that show intimate relationship (**My Delight is in Her** and **Married**). The metaphor of God married to His people as a husband is to his bride communicates the intimacy and exclusivity of the relationship (see note at 61:10). As a bride can have only one husband, so Israel can have only one God.

62:6-7 The **watchmen** on the **walls** (see note at 52:8) were those who kept an eye out to alert the inhabitants of the city about news or danger. The leaders of God's people are compared to watchmen whose responsibilities included the encouragement of the people's relationship with God. Isaiah urged them to keep after God to maintain His efforts at restoring Jerusalem until it was truly "the joy of the whole earth" (Ps 48:1).

62:8-9 Attacking armies would steal the crops of people they conquered. God had allowed a succession of foreign powers to invade His people because of their sin (Assyria and Babylon most notably), but their plundering will be brought to an end.

62:10 A **highway** is a frequent image in Isaiah for the remov-

al of barriers between God and His people (11:16; 19:23; 33:8; 35:8; 40:3; 49:11). A **banner** marked a gathering place for the regathered remnant (see note at 11:10) and a rallying point for an army (see note at 13:2).

62:12 Again (vv. 2,4), God speaks of Israel's new name. These names indicate the restored status of God's people as well as the care that God displays toward them.

63:1-6 This passage is similar to 59:15b-20. Both passages describe God as a warrior going to battle to defeat the forces of evil.

63:1 The verse opens with a question from the watchman, and God responds. The warrior God has waged war and is returning blood stained and victorious. Perhaps **Edom**, with its capital city of **Bozrah**, is representative of all the nations that had exploited God's people through the years (which may also explain its role in 34:5-17).

63:3 God responded to the watchman's second question by describing His work of anger against the foes (identified as "the nations" in v. 6). He described His killing work as trampling the enemy underfoot like a winemaker tramples on

I trampled them in My anger
and ground them underfoot in My fury;
their blood spattered My garments,
and all My clothes were stained.

4 For I planned the day of vengeance,[A,a]
and the year of My redemption[B] came.

5 I looked, but there was no one to help,[b]
and I was amazed that no one assisted;
so My arm accomplished victory
for Me,
and My wrath assisted Me.

6 I crushed nations in My anger;
I made them drunk with My wrath[c]
and poured out their blood
on the ground.[d]

Remembrance of Grace

7 I will make known
the Lord's faithful love
and the Lord's praiseworthy acts,
because of all the Lord has done
for us—
even the many good things
He has done for the house of Israel
and has done for them based on
His compassion
and the abundance of His faithful love.

8 He said, "They are indeed My people,
children who will not be disloyal,"
and He became their Savior.

9 In all their suffering, He suffered,[C,e]
and the Angel of His Presence
saved them.
He redeemed them
because of His love and compassion;[f]
He lifted them up and carried them
all the days of the past.[g]

10 But they rebelled
and grieved His Holy Spirit.[h]
So He became their enemy
and fought against them.

11 Then He[D] remembered the days
of the past,

a 63:4 Is 34:8;
61:2; Jr 46:10
b 63:5 Is 59:16
c 63:6 Is 29:9;
51:17; Jr 51:39
d Rv 14:20
e 63:9 Jdg 10:16
f Dt 7:7-8
g Dt 1:31; 32:10-
12; Is 46:3
h 63:10 Ps 51:11;
78:40; 106:33; Is
48:16; Ac 7:51;
Eph 4:30
i 63:12 Ex 14:21;
Ps 74:13
j 63:15 Dt 26:15;
Ps 80:14
k 63:16 Is 41:14;
43:14
l 63:17 Is 6:10
m 63:18 Ps 74:3-
7; Is 64:11

the days of Moses and his people.
Where is He who brought them
out of the sea
with the shepherds[E] of His flock?
Where is He who put His Holy Spirit
among the flock?

12 He sent His glorious arm
to be at Moses' right hand,
divided the waters before them[i]
to obtain eternal fame for Himself,

13 and led them through the depths
like a horse in the wilderness,
so that they did not stumble.

14 Like cattle that go down
into the valley,
the Spirit of the Lord gave them[F] rest.
You led Your people this way
to make a glorious name for Yourself.

Israel's Prayer

15 Look down from heaven and see[j]
from Your lofty home—
holy and beautiful.
Where is Your zeal and Your might?
Your yearning[G] and Your compassion
are withheld from me.

16 Yet You are our Father,
even though Abraham does not
know us
and Israel doesn't recognize us.
You, •Yahweh, are our Father;
from ancient times,
Your name is our Redeemer.[k]

17 Why, Yahweh, do You make us stray
from Your ways?
You harden our hearts so we do not
•fear[H] You.[l]
Return, because of Your servants,
the tribes of Your heritage.

18 Your holy people had a possession[l]
for a little while,
but our enemies have trampled down
Your sanctuary.[m]

A 63:4 Lit For day of vengeance in My heart   B 63:4 Or blood revenge   C 63:9 Alt Hb tradition reads did not suffer   D 63:11 Or he, or
they   E 63:11 LXX, Tg, Syr read shepherd   F 63:14 Lit him   G 63:15 Lit The agitation of Your inward parts   H 63:17 Lit our heart from
fearing   I 63:18 Or Your people possessed Your holy place

grapes. This image is picked up by the book of Revelation to describe Jesus as warrior at the final battle in Rv 19:13.

63:6 Finally, the object of God's warring anger is explicitly identified as the **nations**. The description of the nations as **drunk** with God's wrath invokes the metaphor of the cup of God's anger (see note at 19:14).

63:7-9 Isaiah looked to the distant past of Israel's history and remembered God's grace and **compassion**. These verses speak in general terms of God's **praiseworthy acts** and Israel's **suffering**. The later focus on the crossing of the sea (vv. 11-13) leads to the conclusion that even here the prophet alluded to Israel's bondage in Egypt and God's

rescue. The **Angel of His Presence** alludes to the Angel's role at the time of the Red Sea crossing (Ex 14:19).

63:11-14 God's grace was not eradicated, in spite of Israel's sin. These verses contemplate a second exodus where God again will deliver His people from their oppressors (cp. 4:5; 11:15-16; 40:3-5; 43:18-19; 48:21).

63:15 Isaiah began a lament that continues to 64:12. It bemoaned the fact that God had not yet enacted His exodus mercies (63:11-14). God seemed to be up in His heavenly home, distant from His people.

63:16 The appeal is made to God as a son makes an appeal to his father. God's fatherhood supersedes even that of fa-

19 We have become like those
    You never ruled over,
like those not called by Your name.*a*

64 *A* If only You would tear
    the heavens open
and come down,*b*
so that mountains would quake
    at Your presence*c*—
2*B* as fire kindles the brushwood,
    and fire causes water to boil—
to make Your name known
    to Your enemies,
so that nations will tremble
    at Your presence!
3 When You did awesome works*d*
    that we did not expect,
You came down,*e*
    and the mountains quaked
    at Your presence.
4 From ancient times no one has heard,
    no one has listened,
no eye has seen any God except You,
who acts on behalf of the one who waits
    for Him.*f*
5 You welcome the one who joyfully does
    what is right;
they remember You in Your ways.
But we have sinned, and You
    were angry.
How can we be saved if we remain in
    our sins?*c*
6 All of us have become
    like something •unclean,
and all our righteous acts are
    like a polluted*D* garment;*g*
all of us wither like a leaf,*h*
and our iniquities*i* carry us away
    like the wind.

7 No one calls on Your name,
    striving to take hold of You.
For You have hidden Your face from us*j*
and made us melt because of*E,F*
    our iniquity.

8 Yet LORD, You are our Father;*k*
we are the clay, and You are
    our potter;
we all are the work of Your hands.*l*
9 LORD, do not be terribly angry
    or remember our iniquity forever.*m*
Please look—all of us are Your people!
10 Your holy cities have become
    a wilderness;
•Zion has become a wilderness,
Jerusalem a desolation.*n*
11 Our holy and beautiful*G* temple,
where our fathers praised You,
has been burned with fire,
and all that was dear to us lies
    in ruins.*o*
12 LORD, after all this, will You
    restrain Yourself?
Will You keep silent
    and afflict severely?*p*

The LORD's Response

65 "I was sought by those
    who did not ask;*H*
I was found by those
    who did not seek Me.
I said: Here I am, here I am,
to a nation that was not called
    by*I* My name.*q*
2 I spread out My hands all day long
to a rebellious people*r*
who walk in the wrong path,
following their own thoughts.

*a*63:19 Dt 28:10; Is 43:7; 65:1 *b*64:1 Ex 19:18; Ps 18:9; 144:5 *c*Jdg 5:5; Ps 68:8; Nah 1:5 *d*64:3 Dt 10:21; 2Sm 7:23; Ps 65:5 *e*Mc 1:3-4; Hab 3:13 *f*64:4 1Co 2:9 *g*64:6 Is 61:10; Php 3:7-9 *h*Ps 90:5-6; Is 1:30 *i*Is 13:11 *j*64:7 Is 54:8 *k*64:8 Is 63:16 *l*Is 29:16; 45:9; Rm 9:20-21 *m*64:9 Is 43:25; 57:17; Mc 7:18 *n*64:10 Is 62:4 *o*64:11 2Kg 25:9; Ps 74:5-7; Is 63:18; Mt 23:38 *p*64:12 Is 42:14 *q*65:1 Is 63:19; Hs 1:10; Rm 10:20; Jms 2:7 *r*65:2 Rm 10:21

A64:1 Is 63:19b in Hb   B64:2 Is 64:1 in Hb   C64:5 Lit *angry; in them continually and we will be saved;* Hb obscure   D64:6 Lit *menstrual*   E64:7 LXX, Syr, Vg, Tg read *and delivered us into the hand of*   F64:7 Lit *melt by the hand*   G64:11 Or *glorious;* Is 60:7   H65:1 LXX, Syr, DSS, Tg read *ask for Me*   I65:1 LXX, Syr, DSS, Tg, Vg read *that did not call on*

ther Abraham as well as his son Jacob/Israel, who gave his name to his descendants.

64:1-2 Isaiah continued to pray and moved on to his request. God seemed to be up in heaven (see note at 63:15), and Isaiah asked that He **come down** to help them in their need. When God appears as a warrior, **mountains . . . quake** (see Nah 1:5) and **nations . . . tremble**.

64:3-4 The prophet's request was based on God's actions in the past. God had made the mountains quake in the past. Indeed, Isaiah's God is the only God who had acted for His people. The implication is that the rest of the gods are fakes. But God only acts **on behalf of the one who waits for Him.** Confidence in God is a prerequisite for experiencing His saving power.

64:5-7 Isaiah also confessed sin on behalf of the community, thus justifying God's judgment against them. Though they were like a **polluted garment**, they will now obey and experience God's salvation. "Polluted garment" means

clothes stained by menstrual blood and thus rendered ritually unclean (Lv 15:19-33).

64:8 Isaiah appealed to God as their **Father** (see note at 63:16). Only rarely and in extreme cases will a human father disown a delinquent child. The prophet also appealed to God as their Creator, using the image of the **potter** and his **clay** (see notes at 29:16; 45:9).

64:10-12 Isaiah foresaw the time when the Babylonians would destroy the city of Jerusalem and burn the temple in 586 B.C. Isaiah appealed to God to turn things around and restore the city and its **temple**.

65:1-2 In these and the following verses, God responded to the people's prayer uttered by Isaiah. God first described His total openness and accessibility to the people. Even more, He sought them out, though they should be the ones who were seeking Him out. God would **spread out** His hands in welcome to people who had passed Him by.

3 These people continually provoke Me
  to My face,
  sacrificing in gardens,[a]
  burning incense on bricks,
4 sitting among the graves,
  spending nights in secret places,
  eating the meat of pigs,[b]
  and putting polluted broth
    in their bowls.[A]
5 They say, 'Keep to yourself,
  don't come near me, for I am too holy
    for you!'
  These practices are smoke
    in My nostrils,
  a fire that burns all day long.
6 It is written before Me:
  I will not keep silent,[c] but I will repay;[d]
  I will repay them fully[B]
7 for your iniquities and the iniquities[e]
  of your[c] fathers together,"
  says the LORD.
  "Because they burned incense
    on the mountains
  and reproached Me on the hills,[f]
  I will reward them fully[D]
  for their former deeds."

8 The LORD says this:

  As the new wine is found in a bunch
    of grapes,
  and one says, 'Don't destroy it,
  for there's some good[E] in it,'
  so I will act because of My servants

and not destroy them all.
9 I will produce descendants from Jacob,[g]
  and heirs to My mountains from Judah;
  My chosen[h] ones will possess it,
  and My servants will dwell there.[i]
10 Sharon will be a pasture for flocks,[j]
  and the Valley of Achor a place
    for cattle to lie down,[k]
  for My people who have sought Me.[l]
11 But you who abandon the LORD,
  who forget My holy mountain,
  who prepare a table for Fortune
  and fill bowls of mixed wine
    for Destiny,[F]
12 I will destine you for the sword,
  and all of you will kneel down
    to be slaughtered,
  because I called and you did not answer,
  I spoke and you did not hear;
  you did what was evil in My sight
  and chose what I did not delight in.[m]

13 Therefore, this is what the Lord GOD says:

  My servants will eat,
  but you will be hungry;
  My servants will drink,
  but you will be thirsty;
  My servants will rejoice,
  but you will be put to shame.
14 My servants will shout for joy
    from a glad heart,
  but you will cry out
    from an anguished heart,

Cross-references
[a]65:3 Is 1:29; 66:17
[b]65:4 Lv 11:7; Is 66:3,17
[c]65:6 Ps 50:3,21; Is 42:14; 64:12
[d]Jr 16:18
[e]65:7 Is 13:11
[f]Ezk 20:27-28; Hs 9:10; Zch 8:14; Mal 3:7
[g]65:9 Jr 31:36-37
[h]Is 41:8
[i]Is 49:8; 60:21; Am 9:11-15
[j]65:10 Is 33:9; 35:2
[k]Jos 7:26; Hs 2:15
[l]Is 51:1
[m]65:12 2Ch 36:15-16; Pr 1:24; Is 41:28; 50:2; 66:4; Jr 7:13

[A]65:3-4 These vv. describe pagan worship.   [B]65:6 Lit *repay into their lap*   [C]65:7 LXX, Syr read *for their iniquities and the iniquities of their*   [D]65:7 Lit *reward into their lap*   [E]65:8 Or *there's a blessing*   [F]65:11 Pagan gods

---

65:3 The rebellion of the people is enumerated in terms of their false worship. False worship modeled on the pattern of Canaanite religion was carried on in garden areas. Canaanite worship was part of fertility worship, often featuring sacred **gardens** and trees. Such false religion was condemned in Dt 12:2; Jr 3:9; and Hs 4:13. **Incense** offerings are often associated with the worship of a god like Baal or a goddess like Asherah (17:8; 27:9; Ezk 6:6; Hs 11:2).

65:4 God's description of false religion continues with a mention of those who sat **among the graves**. The worship of departed ancestors was a feature of Canaanite religion. Eating the meat of **pigs** was particularly sinful because pork was considered an unclean food (Lv 11:7).

65:5 Ironically, these sinful people claimed to be holy, which God considered extremely irritating.

65:7 God accused His people of reproaching Him on the **mountains** and **hills**. False worship on "high places" was condemned (Dt 12:2; 2Kg 17:10; Jr 2:20-21; Ezk 6:13; 20:28; Hs 4:13).

65:8 Using the analogy of a **bunch of grapes**, God announced that He would not destroy the good grapes out of the bunch but would use them to make **new wine**. The analogy presents the idea that God will preserve a faithful remnant of His people after the judgment.

65:10 Sharon was the name of the foothills west of Jerusalem, famous for wildflowers. In 33:9 Sharon was described as a desert as a result of God's judgment (35:2). The **Valley of Achor** (lit "Valley of Trouble") received its name in the early days of the conquest of Canaan (Jos 7:16-26) when Achan stole some of the plunder from the city of Jericho. Because of his theft, Israel was defeated at the city of Ai. In Isaiah's vision of a restored remnant, Achor was a peaceful and prosperous place. See Hs 2:15 for a similar use of the name "Achor" in a positive prophetic context. Since the Valley of Achor was located in the east (near Jericho) and Sharon was in the west, the two together signified that all of Israel would be prosperous.

65:11-12 Fortune (Hb *gad*) and **Destiny** (Hb *meni*) are personified as objects of false worship. *Gad* is thought to be a minor Canaanite god, while *Meni* is more obscure but "thought to be venerated by the Arabs in the pre-Islamic period" (Childs, *Isaiah*, p. 536). While God had good things in store for the faithful remnant, those among His people who continued to worship false deities would meet a horrible end.

65:13-16 In this section God continued the distinction between those who followed Him and were His servants and those who rejected Him. The former will enjoy life; the latter will suffer.

and you will lament out of
a broken spirit.
15 You will leave your name behind
as a curse for My chosen ones,[a]
and the Lord God will kill you;
but He will give His servants
another name.[b]
16 Whoever is blessed in the land
will be blessed by the God of truth,[c]
and whoever swears in the land
will swear by the God of truth.
For the former troubles
will be forgotten
and hidden from My sight.

A New Creation

17 "For I will create a new heaven
and a new earth;[d]
the past events will not be remembered
or come to mind.
18 Then be glad and rejoice forever
in what I am creating;
for I will create Jerusalem to be a joy
and its people to be a delight.
19 I will rejoice in Jerusalem
and be glad in My people.
The sound of weeping and crying
will no longer be heard in her.[e]
20 In her, a nursing infant
will no longer live
only a few days,[A]
or an old man not live out his days.
Indeed, the youth will die
at a hundred years,
and the one who misses
a hundred years will be cursed.[f]
21 People will build houses and live
in them;
they will plant vineyards and eat
their fruit.[g]
22 They will not build and others live
in them;
they will not plant and others eat.
For My people's lives will be
like the lifetime of a tree.[h]
My chosen ones will fully enjoy
the work of their hands.
23 They will not labor without success[i]
or bear children destined for disaster,
for they will be a people blessed
by the Lord
along with their descendants.[j]
24 Even before they call, I will answer;[k]
while they are still speaking, I will hear.
25 The wolf and the lamb
will feed together,[B]
and the lion will eat straw like the ox,[l]
but the serpent's food will be dust![m]
They will not do what is evil or destroy
on My entire holy mountain,"[n]
says the Lord.

Final Judgment and Joyous Restoration

66 This is what the Lord says:

Heaven[o] is My throne,[p]
and earth is My footstool.[q]
What house could you possibly build
for Me?
And what place could be My home?[r]

[a]65:15 Jr 24:9; 25:18; Zch 8:13
[b]Is 62:2
[c]65:16 Ps 31:5; 2Co 1:20; Rv 3:7,14
[d]65:17 Is 66:22; 2Pt 3:13; Rv 21:1
[e]65:19 Is 25:8; 30:19; 35:10; 51:11; Rv 7:17; 21:4
[f]65:20 Ec 8:12-13; Is 3:11; 22:14
[g]65:21 Jos 24:13; Is 37:30; Jr 29:5,28; Ezk 28:26; Zph 1:13
[h]65:22 Ps 92:12-14
[i]65:23 Dt 28:3-12; Is 55:2
[j]Is 61:9
[k]65:24 Ps 91:15; Is 55:6; 58:9; Dn 9:20-23; 10:12
[l]65:25 Is 11:6-9
[m]Gn 3:14; Mc 7:17
[n]Is 11:9; 27:13; 56:7
[o]66:1-2 Ac 7:49-50
[p]66:1 Ps 11:4; Mt 5:34-35; 23:22
[q]1Ch 28:2; Ps 99:5
[r]2Sm 7:5; 1Kg 8:27; Jer 23:24

[A]65:20 Lit *her, no longer infant of days* [B]65:25 Lit *as one*

65:15 Because of their sin, the wicked have a bad reputation (**name**). What they do to create that reputation becomes a curse for God's people. On the other hand, God's people will get a new name (see note at 62:2), a new start after the judgment.

65:16 Blessing, a pleasant and prosperous life, comes only through God, not through false gods like Fortune and Destiny (see note at vv. 11-12).

65:17 Just as God will give His people a "new name" after His judgment and restoration (see notes at v. 15 and 62:2), so He will create a **new heaven and a new earth**. The **past events** are acts of sin by the people that resulted in God's judgment.

65:18-19 God's original intention for **Jerusalem** will be fulfilled (see Ps 48:1 where it is called "the joy of the whole earth"). Its sin and God's judgment had reduced it to the point where it was "a horror to all the earth's kingdoms" (Jr 34:17), but now it will be **a joy**.

65:20-21 The future blessing of Jerusalem includes long life for its inhabitants. Infant mortality rates will disappear and **old** people will survive even longer. If someone dies at age 100, it will be considered tragic because he was just a **youth** compared to others. Further blessing will come in the form of shelter and agricultural abundance.

65:23 In the past the **labor** of God's people had been enjoyed by others as He allowed foreign nations to take them over. Their **children** had been born to disaster since the enemy would either kill them or deport them. But this will change in God's "new heaven" and "new earth" (see note at v. 17). The blessing of work and of childbearing was first troubled at the time of the fall into sin (Gn 3:16-19). The language of this verse suggests a reversal of these curses.

65:25 The oracle uses language that suggests a restoration of Eden-like conditions. Wolves would normally eat lambs, but they will eat peacefully together. The **lion**, another predator, will **eat straw** rather than other animals. The serpent will eat **dust**, reminiscent of the serpent's role in Genesis 3. The similar language in Is 11:6-9 suggests a connection with the theme of the Messiah expressed in those verses.

66:1 One of the presumptions of the preexilic people of God was that the temple literally was the place where God lived (Jr 7:3-4). This attitude had no justification, especially in light of the speech King Solomon gave when he dedicated the temple (1Kg 8:27). Thus, God began the final oracle in

2 My hand made all these things,
and so they all came into being.
                This is the LORD's declaration.
I will look favorably on this kind
    of person:
one who is humble,[a]
    submissive[A] in spirit,[b]
and trembles at My word.
3 One slaughters an ox, one kills a man;
one sacrifices a lamb, one breaks
    a dog's neck;
one offers a •grain offering, one offers
    pig's blood;
one offers incense, one praises an idol—
all these have chosen their ways
and delight
    in their detestable practices.[c]
4 So I will choose their punishment,
and I will bring on them
    what they dread
because I called and no one answered;
I spoke and they didn't hear;
they did what was evil in My sight
and chose what I didn't delight in.[d]

5 You who tremble at His word,[e]
hear the word of the LORD:[f]
"Your brothers who hate
    and exclude you
because of Me have said,[g]
'Let the LORD be glorified
so that we can see your joy!'
But they will be put to shame."[h]

6 A sound of uproar from the city!
A voice from the temple—
the voice of the LORD,
paying back His enemies
    what they deserve![i]

7 Before •Zion was in labor, she gave birth;
before she was in pain, she delivered
    a boy.
8 Who has heard of such a thing?
Who has seen such things?
Can a land be born in one day
or a nation be delivered in an instant?
Yet as soon as Zion was in labor,
she gave birth to her sons.
9 "Will I bring a baby to the point
    of birth
and not deliver it?"
says the LORD;
"or will I who deliver, close the womb?"
says your God.
10 Be glad for Jerusalem and rejoice
    over her,
all who love her.[j]
Rejoice greatly with her,
all who mourn over her—
11 so that you may nurse and be satisfied
from her comforting breast
and drink deeply and delight yourselves
from her glorious breasts.

12 For this is what the LORD says:

I will make peace flow to her
    like a river,[k]
and the wealth[B] of nations like a flood;[l]
you will nurse and be carried
    on her hip[m]
and bounced on her lap.
13 As a mother comforts her son,
so I will comfort you,[n]
and you will be comforted
    in Jerusalem.

14 You will see, you will rejoice,
and you[c] will flourish like grass;[o]

Cross references (center column):
[a] 66:2 Ps 86:1; Pr 16:19; Mt 11:29
[b] Ps 34:18; Mt 5:3; 1Ti 2:11
[c] 66:3 Am 5:21-25
[d] 66:4 2Kg 21:2,6; Is 59:7; 65:12; Jr 7:30
[e] 66:5 Ezr 9:4; 10:3
[f] Is 28:14
[g] Mt 5:10-12; 10:22; Jn 9:34; 15:18-20
[h] Is 26:11; 44:9; 65:13
[i] 66:6 Is 59:18; 65:6; Jl 3:7
[j] 66:10 Ps 122:6; 137:6; Is 65:18
[k] 66:12 Ps 72:3,7; Is 48:18
[l] Is 61:6
[m] Is 60:4-5
[n] 66:13 Ps 86:17; Is 40:1; 49:13; 51:13; 52:9; 2Co 1:3-4
[o] 66:14 Ps 72:16; Pr 11:28; Is 58:11

A 66:2 Lit *broken*   **B** 66:12 Or *glory*   **C** 66:14 Lit *your bones*

---

the book of Isaiah by reminding His people that His presence fills heaven (**My throne**) and earth (**My footstool**).

66:2 God made everything. This means that people should honor and fear God, which will result in humility, submissiveness to God, and total obedience to His commands.

66:3 This verse links four legitimate ritual acts with four perverse acts. The people did both, rendering even the legitimate ritual acts **detestable practices**.

66:5-6 Trembling at God's word (v. 2) indicates the kind of submission to God that leads to obedience. The **brothers** (fellow Israelites) mocked the faithful by saying **Let the LORD be glorified** because they did not think that would happen. God will see that the mockers get **what they deserve**.

66:7-8 **Zion** or Jerusalem has been described as Israel's mother before (see notes at 49:14 and 50:1). Here the return to Judah after the exile is described as Zion giving **birth** painlessly (again reversing a punishment of the fall; see note at Gn 3:16) to many sons.

66:9 In previous passages (see note at 50:1) God is imagined to be the husband of Zion. That idea might also be operative here, but He is definitely pictured as the doctor who delivered Zion's babies.

66:11 Zion, the mother of the returned exiles, will not only give them birth but will succor them and give them life.

66:12 Zion (Jerusalem) will be a place of abundant (**like a river**) peace and overflowing (**like a flood**) wealth (on **the wealth of nations**, see 60:1–61:11). Zion, the mother, will care for and play with her children, the returned inhabitants of Jerusalem.

66:13 God, who is typically featured as the Father, speaks in the first person as the **mother** (a role typically played by Zion).

66:14-16 God will save His people and punish those who disobey Him. While God blesses and punishes in historical time, the ultimate expression of God's salvation and judgment will take place at the final judgment (pictured most graphically in the book of Revelation).

then the Lord's power will be revealed
   to His servants,
but He will show His wrath
   against His enemies.
15 Look, the Lord will come with fire[a]—
His chariots are like the whirlwind[b]—
to execute His anger with fury
and His rebuke with flames of fire.
16 For the Lord will execute judgment
   on all flesh[c] with His fiery sword,
and many will be slain by the Lord.

17 "Those who dedicate and purify themselves to enter the groves[d] following their leader,[A] eating meat from pigs, vermin, and rats, will perish together."

                  This is the Lord's declaration.
18 "Knowing[B] their works and their thoughts, I have come to gather all nations and languages;[e] they will come and see My glory. 19 I will establish a sign among them, and I will send survivors from them to the nations—to Tarshish, Put,[C] Lud (who are archers), Tubal, Javan,[f] and the islands far away—who have not heard of My fame or seen My glory. And they will proclaim My glory among the nations.[g]

20 They will bring all your brothers from all the nations as a gift to the Lord on horses and chariots, in litters, and on mules and camels, to My holy mountain Jerusalem,"[h] says the Lord, "just as the Israelites bring an offering in a •clean vessel to the house of the Lord. 21 I will also take some of them as priests and Levites,"[i] says the Lord.

22 "For just as the new heavens
      and the new earth,[j]
   which I will make,
   will endure before Me"—
            this is the Lord's declaration—
   "so your offspring and your name
      will endure.
23 All mankind will come to worship Me
   from one New Moon to another
   and from one Sabbath to another,"
   says the Lord.

24 "As they leave, they will see the dead bodies of the men who have rebelled against Me;[k] for their worm[l] will never die, their fire will never go out,[m] and they will be a horror to all mankind."[n]

Cross references (center column):
[a]66:15 Is 33:14; Mal 3:1-2; 2Th 1:7-8; 2Pt 3:7
[b]Ps 68:17; Is 5:28; Hab 3:8
[c]66:16 Gn 6:12; Jr 12:12; 25:31; Ezk 20:48; 21:4-5
[d]66:17 Is 65:3-5
[e]66:18 Is 45:22-25; Jr 3:17
[f]66:19 Gn 10:2,5; 1Kg 10:22; Jr 46:9; Ezk 27:10,13
[g]1Ch 16:24; Ps 96:3
[h]66:20 Ps 2:6; Is 56:7; Ezk 20:40; Jl 3:17
[i]66:21 Ex 19:6; Is 61:6; 1Pt 2:5,9; Rv 1:6
[j]66:22 Is 65:17; Heb 12:26-27; 2Pt 3:13; Rv 21:1
[k]66:24 Is 1:2; 5:25; 34:3
[l]Jb 7:5; Is 14:11
[m]Mk 9:44-48
[n]Dn 12:2

A 66:17 Hb obscure   B 66:18 LXX, Syr; MT omits *Knowing*   C 66:19 LXX; MT reads *Pul*

66:17 The wicked who receive the punishment described in verses 14-16 are those who entered illegitimate worship sites (**groves**; see note at 65:4). They ate the most unclean food, defiantly rejecting God's law for Israel.

66:18 God was never interested in Israel alone. His promise to Abraham extended to the **nations** (Gn 12:3). Isaiah looked forward to the day when the nations would recognize God's **glory**.

66:19 The survivors, the remnant of God's people who survive the judgment, will go out to **the nations** to speak of God's **glory**. Among the representative nations named are those at great distance. **Tarshish** is modern day Spain (likely Tartessus); **Put** (ancient Punt) is equivalent to modern Somaliland (though some think a part of Libya; Nah 3:9 lists Libya along with Put); **Tubal** is an area near the Black Sea; **Javan** is modern Greece. The **islands** refer to distant lands and thus represent all the nations of the world.

66:21 The most natural antecedent to **them** is the nations. Thus, Isaiah presented a remarkable picture of the nations producing people set apart for service to the Lord like **priests and Levites**.

66:22 On **new heavens** and **new earth**, see note at 65:17.

66:23 In this future day, no one will neglect the regular worship of the Lord. The **New Moon** festival was a monthly sacred observance (1:13; Nm 29:6; 2Kg 4:23; Ezr 3:5; Ps 81:3).

66:24 Isaiah ended his book with one last description of the fate of the wicked. If his intention was to describe a departure from Jerusalem, then perhaps he referred to the Hinnom Valley—a place where garbage was burned and bodies were left to rot. The purpose of this graphic image was to move people toward God and redemption.

Jeremiah
Introduction

The book and prophet Jeremiah hold at least two great distinctions among all the Old Testament prophets: (1) this is the longest Prophetic Book in the Bible (1,364 verses), and (2) Jeremiah's life is more fully described than any of the other 15 writing prophets. Into the tumultuous times of the last half of the seventh century and the first quarter of the sixth century B.C., came this prophet bearing a word from God for the stubborn people of Judah. The book's contents span roughly from 640 to 580 B.C.

Anathoth, the home of Jeremiah (1:1), was three miles northeast of Jerusalem. Though Jeremiah was opposed and threatened by his fellow citizens (11:21-23), he purchased a field there from his cousin Hanamel in obedience to the word of the Lord to symbolize ultimate hope after exile (32:6-15). Anathoth was overrun by the Babylonians but resettled following the exile (Neh 7:27; 11:32).

Circumstances of Writing

Author: Jeremiah was a priest from the town of Anathoth (1:1). At the Lord's command, he neither married nor had children because of the impending judgment that would come upon the next generation. His ministry as a prophet began in 626 B.C. and ended after 586 B.C. He was a contemporary of Habakkuk and possibly Obadiah.

Background: The book of Jeremiah discusses the last days of Judah. King Hezekiah reigned for 42 years (729–686 B.C.) and began to reverse Judah's spiritual bankruptcy. But when Hezekiah's son, Manasseh, came to the throne, idolatrous and superstitious cultic practices and rites came back like a flood. Manasseh's son Amon ruled for only two years (642–640 B.C.). He also reinstated idol worship as the official religion of Judah (2Ch 33:22-23).

Amon's eight-year-old son, Josiah, succeeded him on the throne. This lad walked in the ways of the former King David. When he was 18 years old (622 B.C.), he called for long-delayed repairs to be made to the temple. During this work, a copy of the law of Moses was found. On the basis of hearing this word, the young king and all his people renewed the covenant with the Lord. However, this reformation failed to overcome the effects of the wickedness Manasseh and Amon had instituted.

Message and Purpose

Jeremiah is the prophet of the "word of the LORD" (1:2). Of the 349 times the OT uses the phrase "thus says the LORD," Jeremiah accounts for 157 of them. But this prophetic word that Jeremiah spoke was more than an objective revelation from God to the nation; God's words were to be joy and food for Jeremiah's own soul. As 15:16 states, "Your words were found, and I ate them. Your words were a delight to me and the joy of my heart." However, God's word was sometimes a burden to the prophet. He sometimes grew tired of bringing God's message of judgment to an unresponsive people.

650 B.C.	625 B.C.
Under Ashurbanipal, Assyrians capture and destroy Babylon. 649	Second phase of Josiah's reforms when the book of the law is found in the temple 622
Birth of Jeremiah 640?	Under Nabopolassar (626–605), Asshur and Nineveh fall, marking the end of the Assyrian Empire. 612
Ashurbanipal (668–629) rules over a declining Assyrian Empire that experienced revolts (642) and contributed to the assassination of Amon of Judah (641) and the rise of Amon's son Josiah (641–609).	Babylonians and Medes take Harran from what remained of Assyrian forces. 610
	Jeremiah's temple sermon 609
Initial reforms of Josiah 631	Josiah killed by the Egyptians at Megiddo 609
Jeremiah is called to be a prophet; he warns of an invasion from the north. 626	Josiah's son, Jehoahaz II, succeeds him and is deposed; he's replaced by his brother, Jehoiakim. 609

The people felt immune to any threat of divine judgment, but Jeremiah repeatedly warned them about the vanity of their reliance on ritual and external formalism. The prophetic word of God was to make the people blush and turn away from meaningless outward piety.

Contribution to the Bible

The best known passage in Jeremiah is the new covenant text in 31:31-34. Not only is it the largest OT text quoted in the NT (Heb 8:8-12; 10:16-17), but arguably better than any other passage it links God's ancient promises to Eve (Gn 3:15), Abraham (Gn 12:1-3), and David (2Sm 7:16-19) with NT assurances that God in Christ grants believers new hearts, salvation, and fellowship with Him.

Structure

One date rings throughout the entire book of Jeremiah: "the fourth year of Jehoiakim son of Josiah king of Judah." That year, 605 B.C., brought major change to the political situation of the Near East. Both Egypt and Assyria were defeated at the battle of Carchemish (46:2-12; 2Kg 24:7; 2Ch 35:20). Nebuchadnezzar ascended the throne of Babylon. In that same year God instructed Jeremiah to put his prophecies into writing as a final test of King Jehoiakim's responsiveness to the word of God.

This significant dateline, "the fourth year of Jehoiakim," was placed at 25:1; 36:1; and 45:1, thereby dividing the prophet's book into three main sections: the prophet's faithfulness in carrying out God's commission (chaps. 2–24); the fierce opposition to his ministry (chaps. 25–35); and the collapse of Judah (chaps. 36–45).

The book of Jeremiah includes poetic sections (especially in chaps. 2–25) and prose accounts as well. Critical scholars generally say that the poetry is Jeremiah's and the prose is either the work of his friends or a person who is labeled a Deuteronomic writer (so designated because the prose sections are said to reflect the book of Deuteronomy). But we may ask, Could not Jeremiah have written in both poetic and prose form? There is no reason to suppose he was incapable of writing in both forms.

605–575 B.C.

Nebuchadnezzar attacks Jerusalem and leads citizens of Judah into exile. 605, 597, 586, 582

Jehoiakim makes a decision to turn from his alliance with Egypt and submit to Nebuchadnezzar. 604

Jehoiakim ignores Jeremiah's warning and turns back to Egypt for support after Egypt defeats Babylon at Migdol. 601

A reinforced Babylonian army approaches Judah; Jehoiakim dies. 598

Nebuchadnezzar suppresses a rebellion of exiles in Babylon. 593

575–525 B.C.

Cyrus the Great founds the Persian Empire. 559

Cyrus captures Babylon without resistance. 539

Cyrus issues an edict allowing the Jews to return to Judah. 538

Work begins on rebuilding the temple in Jerusalem. 537–536

Renewed work on the temple 520–518

New temple dedicated 515

Outline

1 The words of Jeremiah,[a] the son of Hilki-ah, one of the priests living in Anathoth[b] in the territory of Benjamin. ²The word of the LORD came to him in the thirteenth year of the reign of Josiah[c] son of Amon, king of Judah. ³It also came throughout the days of Jehoi-akim[d] son of Josiah, king of Judah, until the fifth month of the eleventh year of Zedekiah[e] son of Josiah, king of Judah, when the people of Jerusalem went into exile.

The Call of Jeremiah

⁴The word of the LORD came to me:

5 I chose you before I formed you
    in the womb;
  I set you apart
    before you were born.[f]
  I appointed you a prophet
    to the nations.[g]

⁶But I protested, "Oh no, Lord, GOD! Look, I don't know how to speak[h] since I am only a youth."[i]

⁷Then the LORD said to me:

Do not say, "I am only a youth,"[j]

for you will go to everyone
  I send you to
and speak whatever I tell you.[k]
8 Do not be afraid of anyone,[l]
  for I will be with you
    to deliver you.[m]
      This is the LORD's declaration.

⁹Then the LORD reached out His hand, touched my mouth,[n] and told me:

I have now filled your mouth
  with My words.[o]
10 See, I have appointed you today
  over nations and kingdoms
  to uproot and tear down,
  to destroy and demolish,[p]
  to build and plant.[q]

Two Visions

¹¹Then the word of the LORD came to me, asking, "What do you see, Jeremiah?"[r]

I replied, "I see a branch of an almond tree."

¹²The LORD said to me, "You have seen correctly, for I watch over My word to

ᵃ1:1 2Ch 35:25; 36:12; Ezr 1:1; Dn 9:2; Mt 2:17; 16:14; 27:9
ᵇJos 21:18; 1Kg 2:26; Jr 32:7
ᶜ1:2 2Kg 21:24; 22:1; Jr 25:3; 36:2; Zph 1:1
ᵈ1:3 2Kg 23:34; 24:2; 1Ch 3:15; Jr 22:18; 25:1; 35:1
ᵉ2Kg 24:17-20; 1Ch 3:16; Jr 21:1; 27:1; 39:2
ᶠ1:5 Ps 139:13-16; Is 44:2; 49:1-6; Lk 1:15; Gl 1:15
ᵍJr 25:15-26
ʰ1:6 Ex 4:10; 1Co 2:1-5
ⁱ1Kg 3:7
ʲ1:7 1Tm 4:12
ᵏDt 18:18; Jr 1:17; Ezk 2:7
ˡ1:8 Ezk 2:6
ᵐJr 15:20
ⁿ1:9 Is 6:7
ᵒIs 51:16
ᵖ1:10 2Co 10:4-5
ᵠJr 12:14-17; 18:7,9; 19:7; 24:6; 31:28; Col 2:6-7
ʳ1:11 Jr 24:3; Am 8:2; Zch 4:2

1:1-3 Jeremiah was the instrument through whom God spoke, but it was the divine **word** that **came to him**. This was a favorite expression of Jeremiah, indicating that God's word took possession of him and exerted deep influence in his life. Verse 4 repeats this favorite expression, assuring us that Jeremiah's words and God's word stand together, not in some ethereal or romantic way, but concretely as God gave Jeremiah specific words. God's word came to Jeremiah over many years, ending with the Babylonian exile. The revelations began during the reign of the Judean King **Josiah** (640–609 B.C.), and continued during the reigns of Jehoahaz (reigned for three months in 609 B.C.); **Jehoiakim** (609–597 B.C.); Jehoiachin (reigned for three months in 597 B.C.); and **Zedekiah** (597–586 B.C.). Jeremiah did not mention the brief reigns of Jehoahaz or Jehoiachin in his list (v. 3).

1:4 The word of the LORD came to me. The Hebrew expression for the "word" *(dabar)* means not only the spoken word, as it is frequently and correctly rendered, but also "thing," "action," or "event." Thus "word" and "event" in the OT often are treated as a single perception. A person's thoughts, plans, actions, and spoken or written words are seen as one complete act. Accordingly, Jeremiah both preached and acted out some of his messages in symbolic performances in order to bring the word of God home more forcibly to his audience.

1:5 The prophet was told that God **chose** him **before** He **formed** him **in the womb**. The verb for "to choose" is the Hebrew verb "to know." Similar concepts are used in the call of the Servant of the Lord (Is 49:5) and the apostle Paul (Gl 1:15). God had more than an intellectual knowledge of Jeremiah; He had a personal relationship with him. He was **set . . . apart** or separated (as in the root "to be holy," or "set apart" to the Lord) and **appointed** to be a **prophet to the nations**. If God is the Lord of the entire world, it is natural that His message would extend to all nations.

1:6 Jeremiah objected, saying **I am only a youth**. "Youth" (Hb *na'ar*) can refer to an infant (Ex 2:6), a child (1Sm 1:22), a boy (1Sm 3:1), or even a young man (Gn 22:3; 34:19).

1:7-8 The word **deliver** also means to "rescue." This was the same strong assurance God had given to His people in the exodus from Egypt (Ex 3:8; 12:27) and when He rescued David from a lion (1Sm 17:37).

1:9 The Lord touched the prophet's mouth and told him, **I have now filled your mouth with My words.** Almost identical words were spoken to Moses in Dt 18:18: "I will put My words in his mouth." Here is an anthropomorphism (description of God in human terms) that promises that God will personally be the source of His message. Later Jeremiah will speak of having eaten God's word (Jr 15:16). These words became like fire in his mouth (5:14). This same close relationship between God's word and the prophet who delivers them is graphically illustrated in the case of Moses (Ex 4:15-16; 7:1-2). The word of God in Jeremiah's mouth was "like a hammer that pulverizes rock" (Jr 23:29).

1:10 Six metaphors—**uproot . . . tear down . . . destroy . . . demolish . . . build**, and **plant**—will constitute Jeremiah's message to the nations; four negative and two positive. Some or all of these same words occur throughout Jeremiah's message (12:14-17; 16:19-21; 18:7-9; 24:6; 25:9-32; 31:28,40; 42:10; 45:4). God's word, Jeremiah understood from Dt 32:39, had the power to bring life or death, wounding or healing, and no one would be able to rescue these nations or individuals from God's hand.

1:11-12 In the first of two visions, God showed the prophet a **branch** of an **almond tree**, one of the first trees to blossom in the spring. In 1:12 the Lord interpreted this imagery by saying, **I watch over My word**. The "almond" is *shaqed* in Hebrew, and the verb "to watch" is *shoqed*, and so these verses involve a pun in the original language. Just as the almond tree blossoms early in Israel's springtime and

accomplish it."[a] [13]Again the word of the Lord came to me inquiring, "What do you see?"

And I replied, "I see a boiling pot,[b] its lip tilted from the north to the south."

[14]Then the Lord said to me, "Disaster will be poured out[A] from the north on all who live in the land. [15]Indeed, I am about to summon all the clans and kingdoms of the north."[c]

This is the Lord's declaration.

> They will come, and each king
> will set up his throne
> at the entrance to Jerusalem's gates.
> They will attack
> all her surrounding walls
> and all the other cities of Judah.

[16]"I will pronounce My judgments against them for all the evil they did when they abandoned Me to burn incense to other gods and to worship the works of their own hands.[d]

[17]"Now, get ready. Stand up and tell them everything that I command you. Do not be intimidated by them[e] or I will cause you to cower before them. [18]Today, I am the One who has made you a fortified city,[f] an iron pillar, and bronze walls[g] against the whole land—against the kings of Judah, its officials, its priests, and

[a] 1:12 Jr 31:28; Php 1:6
[b] 1:13 Ezk 24:3
[c] 1:15 Jr 25:9
[d] 1:16 Ex 20:3; Is 37:19; 44:15; Ac 7:41
[e] 1:17 Ezk 2:6-7; 1Th 2:2
[f] 1:18-19 Jr 15:20
[g] 1:18 Jr 6:27; Ezk 3:8-9
[h] 1:19 Ps 129:2
[i] Jr 1:6
[j] 2:2 Ezk 16:8,60; Hos 2:15; Rv 2:4
[k] 2:3 Dt 7:6
[l] Jms 1:18
[m] Gn 12:3; Ps 105:14-15; Is 41:11
[n] 2:5 Is 5:4; Mc 6:3
[o] 2Kg 17:15

the population. [19]They will fight against you but never prevail over you,[h] since I am with you to rescue you."[i]

This is the Lord's declaration.

Israel Accused of Apostasy

2 The word of the Lord came to me: [2]"Go and announce directly to Jerusalem that this is what the Lord says:

> I remember the loyalty of your youth,[j]
> your love as a bride—
> how you followed Me in the wilderness,
> in a land not sown.
> 3 Israel was holy to the Lord,[k]
> the *firstfruits of His harvest.[l]
> All who ate of it found
> themselves *guilty;[m]
> disaster came on them."

This is the Lord's declaration.

> 4 Hear the word of the Lord,
> house of Jacob
> and all families of the house of Israel.
> 5 This is what the Lord says:

> What fault did your fathers find in Me[n]
> that they went so far from Me,
> followed worthless idols,[o]

[A]1:14 LXX reads *will boil*

---

signifies the coming of a fruitful season, God told Jeremiah that He would soon cause him to "blossom" with fruitful words from God.

1:13-15 Next the prophet saw **a boiling pot** or cauldron, tilted toward the south, spilling its contents of disaster from the north. This was the direction from which foreign armies would come against Israel and Judah. This enemy is identified in 25:9 as Babylon, but the threat collectively came from **all the clans and kingdoms of the north**. Each northern king would **set up his throne**, symbolizing his conquest and rule over defeated Judah.

1:16 The reason for such a severe judgment was Judah's burning **incense to other gods**. This was a clear violation of God's covenant with Israel and the first and second of the Ten Commandments. They were worshiping **the works of their own hands**. The Hebrew verb shows these were repeated acts and that they were still going on.

1:17-19 Jeremiah was given three commands: (1) **stand up**, (2) **tell them everything that I command you**, and (3) **do not be intimidated by them**. The command to stand up is literally "gird your loins," or "brace yourself." It is used of getting ready for work, battle, debate, or for the tiring job of preaching to an unreceptive audience. The prophet was not to speak out of his own thoughts, but everything that God commanded him. The word for "to be intimidated" (also meaning "to be terrified," "to be confounded," or "to panic") plays on the word **to cower** (same Hb verb; "to ruin [you]" or "to make [you] a failure") **before them**. God would make Jeremiah **a fortified city, an iron pillar, and bronze walls against the whole land**. The prophet would be made strong, resistant, and as impregnable as these objects. There would be strong opposition to his message, but **kings . . . officials**, and **priests** would not prevail over God's prophet.

2:2-20 In this section God recalled the "honeymoon" He had enjoyed with Israel from the time of the exodus to the events at Mount Sinai (Ex 3–24). During that time the people believed the Lord and worshiped Him (Ex 4:29-31; 12:22-28; 14:31; see also Hs 2:15; 9:10). However, Israel soon murmured, grumbled, and complained (Ex 14:11; 15:24; 16:2; 17:2). These early "gripe sessions" illustrated a lack of faith, but full-fledged rebellion and apostasy were often the marks of Israel in the years following the establishment of the covenant at Mount Sinai (known as the Sinaitic covenant).

2:2 The **loyalty of your youth** uses the beautiful Hebrew word *chesed* for "loyalty" (see Ps 136). It occurs 248 times in the OT and speaks of the "loving-kindness" or "unfailing devotion" Israel (depicted as a bride) initially showed to her bridegroom, the Lord.

2:3 That Israel will be the **firstfruits of His harvest**, rather than the *only* fruits, anticipates other peoples and nations coming to the Lord. **Israel was holy to the Lord** in the same way that certain offerings were called "holy" or "hallowed." They were set aside from common or ordinary use to be reserved for the Lord (Nm 18:8-19,26-29). Israel was also called God's "firstborn" (Ex 4:22; Jr 31:9), meaning first in preeminence and rank.

2:5 The rhetorical **what fault did your fathers find in Me** uses the language of divorce proceedings (Dt 24:1), as if God had proven to be an unworthy marital partner. But God was not to blame for Israel's apostasy. God had remained faithful, but Israel departed from the covenant to follow **worthless idols**. The word for "worthless" is the same term used in Ecclesiastes for "vanity." These idols were mere fictions, the products of human imagination.

2:6 Forgetting the story of redemption, Israel soon forgot

and became worthless themselves?[a]

6 They stopped asking, "Where is
the LORD[b]
who brought us from the land of Egypt,
who led us through the wilderness,[c]
through a land of deserts and ravines,
through a land of drought
and darkness,[A]
a land no one traveled through
and where no one lived?"

7 I brought you to a fertile land[d]
to eat its fruit and bounty,
but after you entered, you defiled
My land;[e]
you made My inheritance[f] detestable.

8 The priests quit asking, "Where is
the LORD?"
The experts in the law no longer
knew Me,[g]
and the rulers[h] rebelled against Me.
The prophets prophesied by[B] •Baal[i]
and followed useless idols.[j]

9 Therefore, I will bring a case
against you again.
This is the LORD's declaration.

I will bring a case
against your children's children.[k]

10 Cross over to Cyprus[C,l] and take a look.
Send someone to Kedar[m]
and consider carefully;
see if there has ever been
anything like this:

11 Has a nation ever exchanged its gods?[n]
(But they were not gods![o])
Yet My people have exchanged
their[D] Glory
for useless idols.[p]

12 Be horrified at this, heavens;[q]
be shocked and utterly appalled.
This is the LORD's declaration.

13 For My people have committed
a double evil:
They have abandoned Me,[r]
the fountain of living water,[s]
and dug cisterns for themselves,
cracked cisterns that cannot
hold water.[t]

Consequences of Apostasy

14 Is Israel a slave?
Was he born into slavery?[E]

---

[a] 2:5 Ps 115:8; Rm 1:21 [b] 2:6 Jdg 6:13; Jb 35:10 [c] Dt 8:15; 32:10 [d] 2:7 Ex 3:8; Dt 8:7-10; Jr 4:26 [e] Nm 35:33; Ezk 36:17 [f] Jr 16:18 [g] 2:8 Hs 4:6; Mal 2:7; Lk 11:52 [h] Jr 23:1-4; Ezk 34 [i] Jr 2:23; 9:14 [j] Hab 2:8 [k] 2:9 Ex 20:5; Is 3:13; Mc 6:1-8 [l] 2:10 Gn 10:4; Nm 24:24; Is 23:1,12; Ac 13:4 [m] Ps 120:5 [n] 2:11 Mc 4:5 [o] Jr 16:20; Gl 4:8 [p] Ps 106:20; Hs 4:7; Rm 1:23; 1Pt 1:18 [q] 2:12 Dt 32:1; Is 1:2; Mc 6:1 [r] 2:13 Jdg 10:13 [s] Ps 36:9; Jr 17:13; Jn 4:10 [t] Is 55:2; Gl 1:6-7

[A] 2:6 Or shadow of death [B] 2:8 = in the name of [C] 2:10 Lit to the islands of Kittim [D] 2:11 Ancient Jewish tradition reads My [E] 2:14 Lit born of a house

---

about God Himself (**they stopped asking, "Where is the LORD . . . ?"**).

2:7 The words **fertile land** are literally "land of Carmel." Mount Carmel was renowned for its luxurious vegetation and crops (Am 1:2; Mc 7:14).

2:8 Four types of leaders are charged for failing to carry out their responsibilities and for allowing apostasy and unfaithfulness to take over in Israel: **priests . . . experts in the law . . . rulers** (lit "the shepherds," used metaphorically of political leaders in the OT), and false **prophets** who **prophesied by Baal**.

2:9 Therefore introduces a prophetic announcement about coming judgment. God will take His nation to court, and He will act as both plaintiff and judge.

2:10-12 Here is God's courtroom accusation: Israel had behaved ludicrously. They **exchanged their Glory for useless idols**. Though they alone among the nations knew the one true and living God, they left Him to worship mute objects of stone and wood. Look from Cyprus to **Kedar** in the desert east of Transjordan, God says, and nowhere will you find another nation making such a foolish exchange, for no other nation had the privilege of knowing the living God. What a privilege Israel had forsaken!

2:13 As the **fountain of living water**, or a flowing spring, God is the source of everlasting life (17:13; Is 55:1; Zch 13:1; Jn 4:10-14; 7:37-39). In defiance of God as the source of life, Judah had dug her own wells (metaphorically speaking) in the earth and plastered their sides to hold in stale rainwater, only to have the plaster crack, the **cisterns** fail, and the water escape. Such is the futility of false religion.

2:14-19 God asks six rhetorical questions. In contrast to the safety they enjoyed in their honeymoon days with the

Lord, now the nations attack Israel at will. She was not born a slave, so how did she become everyone else's prey?

A cistern (2:13) with a stone mortar in the foreground. The innumerable cisterns, wells, and pools that exist in Palestine are evidence of the efforts of ancient people to supplement the natural water supply. Here and in 14:3, broken cisterns symbolize pagan gods that could not give or sustain life.

Why else has he become a prey?
15 The young lions have roared at him;[a]
they have roared loudly.
They have laid waste his land.[b]
His cities are in ruins,
without inhabitants.
16 The men of Memphis and Tahpanhes[c]
have also broken your skull.
17 Have you not brought this on yourself[d]
by abandoning the LORD your God
while He was leading you
along the way?
18 Now what will you gain
by traveling along the way to Egypt[e]
to drink the waters of the Nile?[A]
What will you gain
by traveling along the way to Assyria[f]
to drink the waters of the Euphrates?[g]
19 Your own evil will discipline you;[h]
your own apostasies
will reprimand you.
Think it over and see how evil
and bitter[i] it is
for you to abandon the LORD
your God
and to have no •fear of Me.
    This is the declaration
    of the Lord GOD of •Hosts.

20 For long ago I[B] broke your yoke;[j]
I[B] tore off your chains.
You insisted, "I will not serve!"
On every high hill
and under every green tree[k]
you lie down like a prostitute.[l]
21 I planted you, a choice vine[m]
from the very best seed.
How then could you turn into
a degenerate, foreign vine?[n]
22 Even if you wash with lye
and use a great amount of soap,[o]
the stain of your sin is still
in front of Me.[p]
    This is
    the Lord GOD's declaration.
23 How can you protest, "I am not defiled;
I have not followed the Baals"?[q]
Look at your behavior in the valley;
acknowledge what you have done.[r]
You are a swift young camel
twisting and turning on her way,
24 a wild donkey[s] at home[c]
in the wilderness.
She sniffs the wind in the heat
of her desire.
Who can control her passion?

a 2:15 Is 5:29
b Is 1:7
c 2:16 Jr 44:1;
46:14,19; Ezk
30:13,16,18
d 2:17 Jr 4:18
e 2:18 Is 30:1-2;
31:1
f Hs 7:11
g Is 8:7
h 2:19 Is 3:9;
Hs 5:5
i Jr 4:18
j 2:20 Lv 26:13;
Is 10:27; Nah
1:13
k Dt 12:2; 1Kg
14:23; Is 57:5
l Ezk 16:28;
Hs 2:5
m 2:21 Gn 49:11;
Ps 80:8; Is 5:2
n Is 5:4
o 2:22 Ps 51:2,7;
Mal 3:2; Eph
5:26
p Ps 90:8
q 2:23 Jr 2:8;
9:14
r Gn 3:13; 1Sm
15:13; Pr 28:13;
Jr 3:13; 1Jn 1:8
s 2:24 Jb 39:5

A 2:18 Lit of Shihor   B 2:20 LXX reads you   C 2:24 Lit donkey taught

God says the **discipline** was a result of their **own evil** (v. 19).

2:15 The **young lions** figuratively designate Israel's enemies, especially the Assyrians (see note at Ps 7:1-2).

2:16 Memphis was the capital of Lower Egypt, approximately 13 miles south of Cairo. **Tahpanhes** was a fortress close to the northeastern boundary of Egypt. The Egyptians would become allies with the Assyrians in the destruction of Judah.

'azav

Hebrew Pronunciation	[ah ZAV]
HCSB Translation	leave, abandon, forsake
Uses in Jeremiah	25
Uses in the OT	216
Focus Passage	Jeremiah 2:13,17,19

'Azav, a transitive verb, means leave (Gn 2:24), abandon (Jr 17:13), and forsake (Ps 22:1). It is synonymous with natash ("leave," Ps 27:9) and raphah ("leave," Jos 1:5). 'Azav implies renounce (Pr 28:13), desert (Jos 22:3), or reject (1Kg 12:8). Levites could be neglected or forgotten (Dt 12:19; 14:27). One leaves something behind (Ex 2:20), gives it up (Ezk 23:8), withholds it (Gn 24:27), or stops it (Neh 5:10). Once 'azav is entrust oneself (Ps 10:14), and once change facial expression (Jb 9:27). "Leaving upon oneself" is expressing (Jb 10:1) complaints. Regular passive participles often contrast with "slave" as free (Dt 32:36). Twice 'azav means restore (Neh 3:8), and once help (Ex 23:5); some argue that these cases involve a homonym. God is the most frequent object of 'azav. Abandoning Him for idols (1Sm 12:10) was Israel's most dangerous sin. He might abandon in return (2Ch 15:2).

2:18 The Hebrew word translated **Nile** is shichor, meaning "blackness." Referring to the Nile River in this way denigrates its status as a god among the Egyptians. Hence, it was futile for Judah to trust Assyria or Egypt to rescue them from the coming threat.

2:19 Again and again Jeremiah pleaded with Judah "to turn back" (Hb shuv) to the Lord. Instead, Judah's ongoing **apostasies** (Hb meshuvah, from the same root as shuv) earned her **reprimand** from God. Apostasies are characterized as backsliding or rebellion (3:6-8,11-12,14-22; 5:6; 8:5; 14:7; 31:22).

2:20-28 Five images in this section describe Judah's breaking of the covenant with God: (1) a beast that has broken loose from its yoke, (2) choice grapes that have gone wild, (3) a stain that will not wash off, (4) a young female camel that cannot walk straight, and (5) a wild donkey in heat, sniffing the wind for a male companion.

2:21 The Sorek vine (**a choice vine**) grew in the Wadi al-Sarar and yielded a much-prized red wine. Israel was once this vine, but turned **degenerate** and yielded inferior grapes.

2:22 Lye is probably a reference to niter, a mineral alkali deposited on the shores of some lakes in Egypt. **Soap** was a vegetable alkali, made by pouring water through wood ashes (Laetsch, p. 41).

2:23 A **swift young camel** could cause a lot of damage if turned loose in a crowded place, for it would be reckless in its direction and unsteady in its gait.

2:24 This female **wild donkey** was frantic for a male in the time of her heat. She could not be diverted from her

All who look for her will not
        become tired;
they will find her
        in her mating season.^A

25 Keep your feet from going bare
and your throat from thirst.
But you say, "It's hopeless;^a
I love strangers,^b
and I will continue to follow them."

26 Like the shame of a thief
        when he is caught,
so the house of Israel has been
        put to shame.^c
They, their kings, their officials,
their priests, and their prophets^d

27 say to a tree, "You are my father,"
and to a stone, "You gave birth to me."
For they have turned their back to Me
and not their face,
yet in their time of disaster^e they beg,
"Rise up and save us!"

28 But where are your gods you made
        for yourself?
Let them rise up and save you^f
in your time of disaster if they can,
for your gods are as numerous
        as your cities, Judah.

Judgment Deserved

29 Why do you bring a case against Me?^g
All of you have rebelled against Me.
        This is the LORD's declaration.

30 I have struck down your children
        in vain;
they would not accept discipline.^h
Your own sword has devoured
        your prophets^i
like a ravaging lion.

31 Evil generation,
pay attention to the word of the LORD!
Have I been a wilderness to Israel

or a land of dense darkness?
Why do My people claim,
"We will go where we want;^B
we will no longer come to You"?

32 Can a young woman forget her jewelry^j
or a bride her wedding sash?
Yet My people have forgotten Me^k
for countless days.

33 How skillfully you pursue love;
you also teach evil women your ways.

34 Moreover, your skirts are stained
with the blood of the innocent poor.^l
You did not catch them breaking
        and entering.^m
But in spite of all these things

35 you claim, "I am innocent.^n
His anger is sure to turn away
        from me."
But I will certainly judge you
because you have said, "I have
        not sinned."^o

36 How unstable you are,^p
constantly changing your ways!
You will be put to shame by Egypt^q
just as you were put to shame
        by Assyria.

37 Moreover, you will be led out from here
with your hands on your head^r
since the LORD has rejected
        those you trust;^s
you will not succeed even with
        their help.^C

Wages of Apostasy

3 If^D a man divorces his wife
and she leaves him to marry another,
can he ever return to her?^t
Wouldn't such a land^E become
        totally defiled?
But you!
You have played the prostitute
        with many partners^u—

Cross references

^a 2:25 Jr 18:12
^b Dt 32:16; Jr 3:13
^c 2:26 Jr 2:36; 6:15; 8:9,12; Rm 6:21
^d Ezr 9:7
^e 2:27 Jdg 10:9-10; Is 26:16
^f 2:28 Dt 32:37-38; Jdg 10:14; Is 45:20
^g 2:29 Jr 2:9
^h 2:30 Pr 3:11; Is 1:5; 9:13; Jr 5:3; 17:23; 32:33; Am 4:10
^i Mt 23:34
^j 2:32 Is 61:10
^k Ps 106:21; Hs 8:14
^l 2:34 2Kg 21:16; 24:4; Ps 106:38; Jr 19:4; 22:3,17
^m Ex 22:2
^n 2:35 Jb 33:9
^o Pr 28:13; 1Jn 1:8,10
^p 2:36 Jms 1:8
^q Is 30:3
^r 2:37 2Sm 13:19
^s 1Sm 15:23,26; 2Kg 17:20; Jr 7:29
^t 3:1 Dt 24:1-4
^u Ezk 16:26,28

---

^A 2:24 Lit *her month*   ^B 2:31 Or *We have taken control*, or *We can roam*   ^C 2:37 Lit *with them*   ^D 3:1 One Hb ms, LXX, Syr; other Hb mss
read *Saying: If*   ^E 3:1 LXX reads *woman*

sexual goal. This image depicts Judah mindlessly lusting after foreign gods.

2:26-28 God satirically mocked His people's adoption of Canaanite worship by reversing the genders of the pagan gods. He depicts Judah saying to **a tree** (representing the goddess Asherah in the form of a standing pole), **You are my father**, and **to a stone** (probably the stone pillars representing the male Canaanite deity), **You gave birth to me.**

2:31 God guided Israel through the wilderness after the exodus from Egypt, but now the people declared, **We will go where we want**, which signifies the rejection of divine guidance.

2:32 No bride would forget her treasured **wedding sash**

(bride's gown) or bridal **jewelry**, but faithless Judah had forgotten her marriage vows to the Lord (v. 2).

2:33 Even prostitutes could learn a thing or two from Judah, so skilled was the nation at pursuing other lovers.

2:36 Judah will **be put to shame** by Egypt, just as they had been by Assyria. Pharaoh Psammetich II (663–610 B.C.) had gained Egypt's independence from Assyria while King Ashurbanipal of Assyria was fending off revolutionaries. Judah thought the time was right to form an alliance with Egypt against Assyria, but this was doomed to failure. Instead of seeking human alliances to gain security, they should have sought a right relationship with God.

3:1 The phrase **Wouldn't such a land become totally defiled?** alludes to the divorce law in Dt 24:1-4, where a man

can you return to Me?[a]

> This is the LORD's declaration.

2 Look to the barren heights[b] and see.
Where have you not been immoral?
You sat waiting for them
  beside the highways[c]
like a nomad in the desert.
You have defiled the land
with your prostitution and wickedness.[d]

3 This is why the showers
  haven't come[e]—
why there has been no spring rain.
You have the brazen look[f]
  of a prostitute[A]
and refuse to be ashamed.

4 Have you not lately called to Me,
"My Father.[g]
You were my friend in my youth.[h]

5 Will He bear a grudge forever?[i]
Will He be endlessly infuriated?"
This is what you have said,
but you have done the evil things
you are capable of.

Unfaithful Israel, Treacherous Judah

6 In the days of King Josiah the LORD asked me, "Have you seen what unfaithful Israel has done? She has ascended every high hill and gone under every green tree to prostitute herself there.[j]

7 I thought: After she has done all these things, she will return to Me.[k] But she didn't return, and her treacherous sister Judah[l] saw it. 8 I[B] observed that it was because unfaithful Israel had committed adultery that I had sent her away and had given her a certificate of divorce.[m] Nevertheless, her treacherous sister Judah was not afraid but also went and prostituted herself.[n] 9 Indifferent to[C] her prostitution, she defiled the land and committed adultery with stones[o] and trees.[p] 10 Yet in spite of all this, her treacherous sister Judah didn't return to Me with all her heart[q]—only in pretense."

> This is the LORD's declaration.

11 The LORD announced to me, "Unfaithful Israel has shown herself more righteous than treacherous Judah.[r] 12 Go, proclaim these words to the north, and say:

> Return, unfaithful Israel.[s]
>
> > This is the LORD's declaration.
>
> I will not look on you with anger,[D]
> for I am unfailing in My love.[t]
>
> > This is the LORD's declaration.
>
> I will not be angry forever.[u]

13 Only acknowledge your *guilt[v]—
you have rebelled against the LORD
  your God.
You have scattered your favors
  to strangers

Cross references

a 3:1 Hs 2:7
b 3:2 Dt 12:2
c Gn 38:14; Pr 7:10-12; Ezk 16:25
d Nm 14:33
e 3:3 Zch 14:7
f Ezk 3:7-8
g 3:4 Ex 4:22; Is 1:2; 64:8; Hs 11:1; Gl 4:6
h Ps 71:17; Hs 2:15
i 3:5 Lv 19:18; Ps 103:9; Is 57:16; Nah 1:2
j 3:6 Jr 2:20
k 3:7 Hs 14:1
l Ezk 16:46
m 3:8 Dt 24:1-4; Is 50:1; Hs 2:2
n Ezk 23:11
o 3:9 Is 57:6
p Dt 28:36; Jr 2:27; Ezk 20:32; Hab 2:19; Rv 9:20
q 3:10 Hs 7:14
r 3:11 Ezk 16:51-52; 23:11
s 3:12 Pr 28:13
t Ps 86:5; 145:17
u Ps 103:9; Is 57:16; Mc 7:18
v 3:13 Lv 26:40; 1Jn 1:9

A 3:3 Lit have a prostitute's forehead   B 3:8 One Hb ms, Syr read She fall on you   C 3:9 Lit From the lightness of   D 3:12 Lit not cause My face to

---

is not allowed to remarry his ex-wife if she has married and divorced another man. In a similar way, God asks Judah, **can you return to Me** after defiling the land by your infidelities with false gods?

3:2 Like a nomad compares lustful Judah to a Bedouin waiting in ambush to rob a caravan. Such acts **defiled the land**.

3:3 Sin in the moral order can have a devastating effect on the ecological order, just as the ground was cursed because of Adam and Eve's sin (Lv 26:18-19; Dt 11:13-17; Am 4:7-8). Ironically, the false god Baal whom Judah worshiped was thought to be the god of **rain**, dew, thunder, and fertility. The true God withheld these things, demonstrating the futility of false religion. God's bride showed no shame for her sins. Jeremiah used shame language more than any other prophet (vv. 24-25; 2:26,36; 6:15; 8:12; 9:19; 10:14).

3:6-7 Jeremiah 2–20 is often assigned to the time of **King Josiah**, and therefore to Jeremiah's earliest writings. But if this is the case, it is strange that the prophet did not mention the discovery of the book of the law in 621 B.C. or the reforms that followed. Apostate northern Israel **ascended every high hill** to practice the fertility cult. On "backsliding and unfaithful Israel," see verses 6,8,11,12,22; 2:19; 5:6; 8:5; 14:7. Both sisters, Israel and Judah, became so calloused that they did not repent and return (Hb *shuv*) to the Lord.

3:9 The phrase **indifferent to her prostitution** is literally "through the lightness of adultery." Judah regarded her sins lightly, in spite of what had happened in 722 B.C. to the

10 tribes of northern Israel when the capital city, Samaria, fell to the Assyrians.

3:10 Judah pretended to return to the Lord, but with **pretense** rather than **all her heart**.

3:12 I am unfailing in My love refers to God's loyalty, mercy,

---

shuv

Hebrew Pronunciation	[SHUV]
HCSB Translation	return, turn back
Uses in Jeremiah	115
Uses in the OT	1,075
Focus Passage	Jeremiah 3:1,7,10,12,14,19,22

Shuv means *turn* (Jos 19:12), *turn back* (Ex 14:2), or *return* (Gn 3:19). Anger *subsides* or *turns away* (Gn 27:44-45). Water *recedes* (Gn 8:3); messages *are revoked* (Is 45:23), promises *abandoned* (Ps 132:11). *Shuv* is *change* (Lv 13:16), *resume* (Jos 4:18), *reappear* (Lv 14:43), or *retire* (Nm 8:25). "*Returning* to your heart" is *keeping in mind* or *coming to one's senses* (Dt 4:39; 30:1). *Shuv* denotes *repent* (Ps 7:12) or *reconsider* (Jb 6:29). It accompanies other verbs to show repeated action (Zch 5:1). Causative verbs signify *bring* (take, drive, let go, pull, put) *back* (Gn 14:16), *restore* (Gn 40:13), *repay* (Gn 50:15), *pay* (Ex 21:34), or *avert* (Ezr 10:14). One *takes* vengeance (Dt 32:43) and *stops* (Jb 9:12) or *rejects* (Ps 132:10) another. "*Returning* words" is *answering* (Jdg 5:29). Intensive verbs indicate *turn back*, *return*, *turn around/away* (Jr 8:5; Ezk 38:4), *lead astray* (Is 47:10), *restore*, and *renew* (Ps 23:3).

under every green tree[a]
and have not obeyed My voice.
　　This is the Lord's declaration.

[14] "Return, you faithless children"[b]—this is the Lord's declaration—"for I am your master,[c] and I will take you,[d] one from a city and two from a family, and I will bring you to •Zion. [15] I will give you shepherds who are loyal to Me,[A,e] and they will shepherd you with knowledge and skill. [16] When you multiply and increase in the land,[f] in those days"—the Lord's declaration—"no one will say any longer, 'The ark of the Lord's covenant.'[g] It will never come to mind, and no one will remember or miss it. It will never again be made. [17] At that time Jerusalem will be called, •Yahweh's Throne,[h] and all the nations will be gathered to it,[i] to the name of Yahweh in Jerusalem.[j] They will cease to follow the stubbornness of their evil hearts. [18] In those days the house of Judah will join with the house of Israel,[k] and they will come together from the land of the north to the land I have given your ancestors to inherit."[l]

True Repentance

[19] I thought: How I long to make you
　　My sons
and give you a desirable land,
the most beautiful inheritance[m] of all
　　the nations.
I thought: You will call Me,
　　my Father,
and never turn away from Me.
[20] However, as a woman may betray
　　her lover,[B]

so you have betrayed[n] Me,
　　house of Israel.
　　This is the Lord's declaration.

[21] A sound is heard on the barren heights,
the children of Israel weeping
　　and begging for mercy,
for they have perverted their way;
they have forgotten the Lord
　　their God.[o]
[22] Return, you faithless children.
I will heal your unfaithfulness.[p]
"Here we are, coming to You,
for You are the Lord our God.
[23] Surely, falsehood comes from the hills,
commotion from the mountains,[q]
but the salvation of Israel
is only in the Lord our God.[r]
[24] From the time of our youth
the shameful one[c] has consumed
what our fathers have worked for—
their flocks and their herds,
their sons and their daughters.
[25] Let us lie down in our shame;
let our disgrace cover us.[s]
We have sinned against the Lord
　　our God,
both we and our fathers,
from the time of our youth
　　even to this day.[t]
We have not obeyed the voice
of the Lord our God."

Blessing or Curse

4 If you return,[D] Israel—
　　　this is the Lord's declaration—

Cross references (center column)

[a] 3:13 Dt 12:2
[b] 3:14 Hs 14:1
[c] Hs 2:16-17
[d] Hs 2:19-20
[e] 3:15 1Sm 13:14; Jr 23:4; Ezk 34:23; Ac 20:28; Eph 4:11
[f] 3:16 Gn 1:28; Ex 1:12
[g] Ex 37:1-9; Dt 31:24-29; 1Kg 8:6
[h] 3:17 Ezk 43:7
[i] Is 2:2-4; 56:6-7; Jr 16:19
[j] Dt 12:5
[k] 3:18 Is 11:12-13; Jr 50:4-5; Ezk 37:15-22; Hs 11:1
[l] Am 9:15
[m] 3:19 Dt 32:8-9; Ps 16:6; Lm 2:15; Ezk 20:6,15
[n] 3:20 Is 48:8; Hs 1:2
[o] 3:21 Is 17:10
[p] 3:22 Is 57:18; Hs 5:15-6:3; 14:1-3
[q] 3:23 Ps 121:1-2
[r] Ps 3:8; Jr 17:5-8
[s] 3:25 Jb 8:22; Ezr 9:6
[t] Ezr 9:7; Ezk 2:3

[A] 3:15 Lit shepherds according to My heart　[B] 3:20 Lit friend　[C] 3:24 = Baal　[D] 4:1 Or Repent

---

and grace. On the Hebrew word *chesed*, or "unfailing love," see note at 2:2.

3:14 God offered His **faithless children** the chance to **return** to **Zion** despite their stubborn refusal to follow the Lord.

3:15 The **shepherds** mentioned here do not refer to political rulers but to the spiritual leaders or pastors (Jeremiah himself was counted as such in 17:16).

3:16 The future messianic era is signaled by the introductory phrase **in those days** (see also "in time to come," 30:24; "the days are coming," 31:27,31,38; and "after those days," 31:33). Israel and Judah would **multiply and increase in the land** in this messianic era. The ark of the covenant, the most central and precious symbol at the heart of Israel's worship, will not even be remembered because something more significant will take its place.

3:17 At that time Jerusalem will be called **Yahweh's Throne**, replacing the ark of the covenant as the symbol of His presence (Lv 16:2,13; Ps 80:1). The result will be that **all the nations will be gathered** to Jerusalem and they will **cease to follow the stubbornness of their evil hearts**.

3:18 The return to Zion is predicted again. But it does not seem to be return from exile. This will be a time when Is-

rael and Judah are reunited as one in the land that God had promised to His people.

3:19 The land of promise is called **a desirable land**, or literally "a land of longing" (Ps 106:24; Zch 7:14). The divine pathos of **I thought: You will call Me, my Father, and never turn away from Me** is heartbreaking. Having been rejected as Israel's spouse and husband, God was now rejected by the people of Judah as their Father.

3:21-22 The entire nation will be moved to repentance. In response to such genuine confession of their sin, the Lord will heal their apostasy and rebellion.

3:23 The **falsehood** and **commotion** of orgiastic religious practices that were carried out on bare hilltops could earn no one salvation, for **the salvation of Israel is only in the Lord**.

3:24 Baal is designated by the derisive term often used for him: **the shameful one** (Hb *bosheth*, as found in names like Ish-bosheth, also known as Esh-baal; 2Sm 2:8; 1Ch 8:33).

4:1 The people's cry of repentance (3:21-25) is answered with the assurance of what will happen in the future when they genuinely **return** to the Lord. To this point they had not yet truly repented.

you will return to Me,[a]
if you remove your detestable idols[b]
from My presence
and do not waver,
2 then you can swear,
"As the LORD lives,"[c]
in truth,[d] in justice,
and in righteousness,[e]
then the nations will be blessed[A]
by Him
and will pride themselves in Him.[f]

³For this is what the LORD says to the men of Judah and Jerusalem:

Break up the unplowed ground;[g]
do not sow among the thorns.[h]
4 Circumcise yourselves to the LORD;
remove the foreskin of your hearts,[i]
men of Judah and residents
of Jerusalem.
Otherwise, My wrath will break out
like fire
and burn with no one to extinguish it[j]
because of your evil deeds.

Judgment from the North

⁵Declare in Judah, proclaim in Jerusalem, and say:

Blow the ram's horn
throughout the land.[k]
Cry out loudly and say:
Assemble yourselves,
and let's flee to the fortified cities.
6 Lift up a signal flag toward •Zion.[l]
Run for cover! Don't stand still!
For I am bringing disaster
from the north—
a great destruction.[m]
7 A lion has gone up from his thicket;[n]

a destroyer of nations has set out.
He has left his lair
to make your land a waste.
Your cities will be reduced
to uninhabited ruins.[o]
8 Because of this, put on •sackcloth;
mourn and wail,[p]
for the LORD's burning anger[q]
has not turned away from us.

⁹"On that day"—this is the LORD's declaration—"the king and the officials will lose their courage. The priests will tremble in fear, and the prophets will be scared speechless."
¹⁰I said, "Oh no, Lord GOD, You have certainly deceived[r] this people and Jerusalem, by announcing, 'You will have peace,'[s] while a sword is at[B] our throats."
¹¹"At that time it will be said to this people and to Jerusalem, 'A searing wind[t] blows from the barren heights in the wilderness on the way to My dear[C] people. It comes not to winnow or to sift; ¹²a wind too strong for this comes at My call.[D] Now I will also pronounce judgments against them.'"[u]

13 Look, he advances like clouds;[v]
his chariots are like a storm.[w]
His horses are swifter than eagles.[x]
Woe to us, for we are ruined!
14 Wash the evil
from your heart,[y] Jerusalem,
so that you will be delivered.
How long will you harbor
malicious thoughts within you?[z]
15 For a voice announces from Dan,
proclaiming malice
from Mount Ephraim.
16 Warn the nations: Look!
Proclaim to Jerusalem:

Cross references

[a]4:1 Zch 1:3
[b]Jr 7:30; 16:18; 32:34
[c]4:2 Dt 6:13; 10:20; Jr 5:2
[d]Is 65:16
[e]Hs 2:19
[f]Gn 12:1-3; 18:18; 22:18; 1Co 1:31
[g]4:3 Hs 10:12
[h]Mt 13:7
[i]4:4 Gn 17:14; Dt 10:16; Jr 9:25; Rm 2:28-29
[j]Is 1:31; Jr 21:12; Am 5:6; Mal 4:1
[k]4:5 Hs 5:8; Jl 2:1; 1Th 4:16-17
[l]4:6 Is 62:10
[m]Jr 4:20
[n]4:7 Is 5:29; Jr 2:15; 50:17
[o]Is 1:7; 6:11
[p]4:8 Jl 1:13
[q]Nm 25:4; Ps 78:49
[r]4:10 1Kg 22:22; Ezk 14:9; 2Th 2:11
[s]Jr 6:14; 23:17
[t]4:11 Ezk 17:10
[u]4:12 Jr 1:16; Ezk 5:8
[v]4:13 Rv 1:7
[w]Is 5:28; 66:15
[x]2Sm 1:23; Jb 9:26; Lm 4:19
[y]4:14 Ps 51:2,7; Is 1:16; Jr 2:22; Ti 3:5; Jms 4:8
[z]Ps 119:113

A4:2 Or will bless themselves   B4:10 Lit sword touches   C4:11 Lit to the daughter of My   D4:12 Lit comes for Me

---

4:2 When Judah and Israel truly repent, **then the nations will be blessed** by the Lord. The promises made to Israel were never meant to bless Israel alone; but through them all nations (Gn 12:3; 18:18; 22:18; 26:4; 28:14).

4:3 Unplowed ground was soil long untended and abandoned to wild growth. Hosea issued the same challenge (Hs 10:12). Ground that had lain fallow too long needed to be broken up and cultivated again. Jeremiah and Hosea used this image to picture the need for spiritual renewal.

4:4 A hard build-up around the **hearts** of the people had to be cut away (Dt 10:16; Rm 2:28-29). Circumcision was a sign of the covenant (Gn 17:10-14), but religious ritual without the right heart relationship to God was worthless.

4:5-31 In this section Jeremiah was so sure that God's judgment was imminent that he described it as already present.

4:7 Jeremiah used many animals, including the **lion**, to portray the furious warfare that would come from the north.

Add to this the eagle (v. 13), wolf, and leopard (5:6), plus images of the hot winds of the sirocco (4:11), or fire (v. 4), and the threatened disaster grows more frightening.

4:10 This is one of the most controversial verses in Jeremiah. Was Jeremiah accusing God of deceiving the nation? James 1:13 says God doesn't do that. The solution is to recall that God rules over history (Ps 22:28). Scripture is often silent about secondary causes, and since God rules history even things He merely *permits* can be attributed to Him. In the present case, God allowed false prophets to mislead the nation by saying peace was on the way. Understanding God's rule over history, Jeremiah felt justified in asking this question though he knew that God is not a deceiver. God both allowed this deception and protested against it.

4:15-17 The advances of the enemy from the north can be heard from **Dan**, at the northern limit of Israel and at the headwaters of the Jordan River, on down to **Mount Ephraim**, the highlands stretching from Shechem to Bethel.

Those who besiege are coming
from a distant land;[a]
they raise their voices
against the cities of Judah.
17 They have her surrounded[b]
like those who guard a field,
because she has rebelled against Me.[c]
This is the LORD's declaration.
18 Your way of life and your actions
have brought this on you.[d]
This is your punishment. It is
very bitter,
because it has reached your heart!

Jeremiah's Lament

19 My anguish, my anguish![A] I writhe
in agony!
Oh, the pain in[B] my heart![e]
My heart pounds;
I cannot be silent.
For you, my soul,
have heard the sound
of the ram's horn—
the shout of battle.
20 Disaster after disaster[f] is reported
because the whole land is destroyed.
Suddenly my tents are destroyed,
my tent curtains, in a moment.
21 How long must I see the signal flag
and hear the sound of the ram's horn?
22 "For My people are fools;
they do not know Me.
They are foolish children,
without understanding.[g]
They are skilled in doing what is evil,
but they do not know how to do
what is good."[h]
23 I looked at the earth,
and it was formless and empty.[i]
I looked to the heavens,
and their light was gone.[j]
24 I looked at the mountains,

and they were quaking;[k]
all the hills shook.
25 I looked, and no man was left;
all the birds of the sky had fled.[l]
26 I looked, and the fertile field[m] was
a wilderness.[n]
All its cities were torn down
because of the LORD
and His burning anger.[o]
27 For this is what the LORD says:

The whole land will be a desolation,[p]
but I will not finish it off.[q]
28 Because of this, the earth will mourn;[r]
the skies above will grow dark.[s]
I have spoken; I have planned,
and I will not relent or turn back
from it.[t]
29 Every city flees[u]
at the sound of the horseman
and the archer.
They enter the thickets
and climb among the rocks.[v]
Every city is abandoned;
no inhabitant is left.
30 And you, devastated one, what are
you doing[w]
that you dress yourself in scarlet,
that you adorn yourself
with gold jewelry,
that you enlarge your eyes with paint?
You beautify yourself for nothing.
Your lovers reject you;
they want to take your life.[x]
31 I hear a cry like a woman in labor,[y]
a cry of anguish like one bearing
her first child.
The cry of Daughter Zion
gasping for breath,
stretching out her hands:[z]
Woe is me, for my life is weary
because of the murderers!

a4:16 Is 39:3	
b4:17 2Kg	
25:1-4	
c Is 1:20	
d4:18 Ps 107:17;	
Pr 1:31	
e4:19 Is 16:11;	
Hab 3:16; Rm	
9:1-2	
f4:20 Ezk 7:26	
g4:22 Ps 82:5;	
Is 1:3	
hRm 16:19	
i4:23 Gn 1:2; Jb	
26:7; Is 45:18	
jIs 5:30; 13:10	
k4:24 Jdg 5:5;	
Ps 46:1-3	
l4:25 Zph 1:3	
m4:26 Jr 2:7	
nPs 107:34	
oPs 76:7	
p4:27 Is 6:11	
qNeh 9:31; Jr	
5:10,18; Rm	
11:1-7	
r4:28 Hs 4:3	
sIs 50:3	
tNm 23:19	
u4:29 2Kg 25:4	
vIs 2:19-21	
w4:30 Is 10:3	
xEzk 23:9-10,22	
y4:31 Is 13:8;	
1Th 5:3	
zIs 1:15	

A4:19 Lit *My inner parts, my inner parts*   B4:19 Lit *the walls of*

4:19-22 These verses contain the first of Jeremiah's "confessions" (see his other confessions at 11:18-23; 12:1-6; 15:10-11,15-21; 17:14-18; 18:18-23; 20:7-13,14-18; and possibly 5:3-5; 8:18–9:1). The confessions reflect the pain Jeremiah experienced about the calamity that awaited his people. The prophet was accused of being a traitor, but these verses reveal his patriotism and his sincere love for Judah. It gave him no joy or satisfaction to proclaim such devastating words; he was under divine obligation to do so.

4:23-28 This is one of the most haunting passages in all the prophets because of its vivid, realistic portrayal of God's coming wrath against sin. The judgment moves beyond the Babylonian conquest to the coming Day of the Lord at the end of history.

4:23 Jeremiah borrowed the phrase **the earth . . . was formless and empty** from Gn 1:2. The imagery portrays the reversal of God's acts of creation. Such will be the devastation of the coming Day of the Lord.

4:27 Though the earth will be laid waste, it will not come to an end. There is always the promise of a remnant of those who are faithful to the Lord.

4:30 Jeremiah depicted Jerusalem in her death agony still rejecting God as her husband. Instead of choosing repentance and mourning, she dressed in **scarlet**, adorned herself with **gold jewelry**, and enlarged her eyes with **paint**. This imagery plays off the fact that women of Bible times applied a silver-white metallic substance as a base for black kohl on the upper and lower eyelids. But Jerusalem prettied herself **for nothing**; her **lovers** would only take her life.

The Depravity of Jerusalem

5 Roam[a] through the streets
of Jerusalem.
Look and take note;
search in her squares.
If you find one person,[b]
any who acts justly,
who seeks to be faithful,
then I will forgive her.[c]

2 When they say, "As the LORD lives,"[d]
they are swearing falsely.[e]

3 LORD, don't Your eyes
look for faithfulness?[f]
You have struck them, but they felt
no pain.[g]
You finished them off,
but they refused to accept discipline.[h]
They made their faces harder
than rock,[i]
and they refused to return.

4 Then I thought:

They are just the poor;
they have played the fool.
For they don't understand the way
of the LORD,[j]
the justice of their God.[k]

5 I will go to the powerful
and speak to them.
Surely they know the way of the LORD,
the justice of their God.[l]
However, these also had broken
the yoke
and torn off the chains.[m]

6 Therefore, a lion from the forest
will strike them down.[n]
A wolf from an arid plain
will ravage them.

A leopard[o] keeps watch over their cities.
Anyone who leaves them will be torn
to pieces
because their rebellious acts
are many,[p]
their unfaithful deeds numerous.

7 Why should I forgive you?
Your children have abandoned Me
and sworn by those who are not gods.[q]
I satisfied their needs, yet they
committed adultery;
they gashed themselves[r]
at the[A] prostitute's house.

8 They are well-fed,[B] eager[C] stallions,[s]
each neighing[t] after
someone else's wife.[u]

9 Should I not punish them
for these things?[v]
          This is the LORD's declaration.
Should I not avenge Myself[w]
on such a nation as this?

10 Go up among her vineyard terraces
and destroy them,[x]
but do not finish them off.[y]
Prune away her shoots,
for they do not belong to the LORD.[z]

11 They, the house of Israel and the house
of Judah,
have dealt very treacherously with Me.[aa]
          This is the LORD's declaration.

12 They have contradicted the LORD
and insisted, "It won't happen.[D,ab]
Harm won't come to us;
we won't see sword or famine."

13 The prophets become only wind,
for the LORD's word is not in them.
This will in fact happen to them.

Cross-references

a 5:1 2Ch 16:9
b Ps 14:1-3; Ezk 22:30; Rm 3:10
c Gn 18:26-32
d 5:2 Jr 4:2
e Lv 19:12; Is 48:1; Jr 7:9
f 5:3 2Ch 16:9; Ps 51:6
g Pr 23:35
h Pr 27:22
i Ezk 3:7-9
j 5:4 2Kg 17:26; Ps 95:10; Jr 8:7; Hs 4:6
k Mc 3:1
l 5:5 Ps 103:7
m Ps 2:3; Jr 2:20
n 5:6 2Kg 17:26
o Hs 13:7; Rv 13:2
p Is 59:12
q 5:7 Dt 32:21; Jos 23:7; Gl 4:8
r 1Kg 18:24
s 5:8 Ezk 23:20
t Jr 13:27
u Ex 20:14; Ezk 22:11
v 5:9 Jr 5:29; 8:10; 9:9
w Dt 32:35; Heb 10:30
x 5:10 2Kg 24:2
y Jr 4:27
z Hs 1:9
aa 5:11 Hs 6:7
ab 5:12 Is 28:15; Jr 23:17

A5:7 Or adultery and trooped to the, or adultery and lodged at the; Hb obscure   B5:8 Lit well-equipped; Hb obscure   C5:8 Lit early-rising; Hb obscure   D5:12 Lit He does not exist

---

5:1 The phrase **find one person** is a hyperbole. Jeremiah and his scribe Baruch would certainly count as two righteous persons. This reminds us of the five cities of the plain, which would have been spared had just 10 righteous persons lived there (Gn 18:22-32). God still extends mercy to cities and nations on the grounds of the few righteous people they contain. To act **justly** is to act according to the norms of behavior that God has established. This is clear in Hab 2:4: "The righteous one shall live by his faith."

5:5 Jeremiah thought, **I will go to the powerful.** He was probably expressing irony because the prominent citizens of Judah were no more loyal to the covenant than were the poor people.

5:6 On **lion**, see note at 2:15.

5:7 The phrase **I satisfied their needs** is literally "I fed them to the full." **They gashed themselves** as in the Canaanite cultic practices (1Kg 18:28).

5:8 Jeremiah pictured the people of Judah as **well-fed, eager stallions** or "lusty stallions." Their sexual immorality at the brothels of pagan temples was like horses whinnying after a mate.

5:10 God will severely prune His **vineyard**, which has turned into a wild vine; but He will not completely **destroy** the nation (God's vine; cp. Is 5:1-7; Ezk 17:1-6). The branches will be pruned back, but the root and stock will remain much as Paul argued in Rm 11:17-24.

5:12 The phrase **it won't happen** is literally "not He," meaning the Lord will not punish Judah. This attitude mistakenly presumed that God's promises to bless Israel precluded the possibility of judgment for sins.

5:13 The false prophets of peace fostered in the people a belief that nothing bad would happen to them. Jeremiah's rejoinder was that these false prophets were "windbags" (lit "will become wind"). The Hebrew word ruah can mean "wind" or "spirit." Thus this verse forms a wordplay in which

Coming Judgment

14 Therefore, this is what the Lord God of
•Hosts says:

Because you have spoken this word,
I am going to make My words
become fire in your mouth.[a]
These people are the wood,
and the fire will consume them.[b]
15 I am about to bring a nation
from far away against you,
house of Israel.
This is the LORD's declaration.
It is an established nation,
an ancient nation,
a nation whose language
you do not know
and whose speech
you do not understand.[c]
16 Their quiver is like an open grave;[d]
they are all mighty warriors.
17 They will consume your harvest
and your food.[e]
They will consume your sons
and your daughters.
They will consume your flocks
and your herds.
They will consume your vines
and your fig trees.
They will destroy with the sword
your fortified cities[f] in which
you trust.

18 "But even in those days"—this is the
LORD's declaration—"I will not finish you off.[g]
19 When people ask, 'For what offense has the
LORD our God done all these things to us?' You
will respond to them: Just as you abandoned
Me[h] and served foreign gods in your land, so
will you serve strangers in a land that is not
yours.'[i]
20 "Declare this in the house of Jacob; proclaim it in Judah, saying:

21 Hear this,
you foolish and senseless[A] people.[j]
They have eyes, but they don't see.
They have ears, but they don't hear.[k]
22 Do you not •fear Me?
This is the LORD's declaration.
Do you not tremble before Me,
the One who set the sand
as the boundary of the sea,
an enduring barrier that
it cannot cross?[l]
The waves surge, but they
cannot prevail.
They roar but cannot pass over it.
23 But these people have stubborn
and rebellious hearts.[m]
They have turned aside
and have gone away.
24 They have not said to themselves,
'Let's fear the LORD our God,[n]
who gives the rain,[o] both early
and late,[p] in its season,[q]
who guarantees to us the fixed weeks
of the harvest.'
25 Your •guilty acts have diverted
these things from you.
Your sins have withheld My bounty
from you,[r]
26 for wicked men live among My people.
They watch like fowlers lying in wait.[B,s]
They set a trap;[t]
they catch men.
27 Like a cage full of birds,
so their houses are full of deceit.
Therefore they have grown powerful
and rich.
28 They have become fat[u] and sleek.
They have also excelled in evil matters.
They have not taken up cases,
such as the case of the fatherless,
so they might prosper,
and they have not defended the rights
of the needy.[v]
29 Should I not punish them
for these things?
This is the LORD's declaration.

[a]5:14 Hs 6:5; Rv 11:5 [b]Zch 12:6 [c]5:15 Dt 28:49; Is 28:11; 33:19; 1Co 14:21 [d]5:16 Ps 5:9; Rm 3:13 [e]5:17 Lv 26:16; Dt 28:31,33,51 [f]Hs 8:14 [g]5:18 Jr 4:27; Ezk 11:13; Rm 11:1-5 [h]5:19 Dt 29:24-25; 1Kg 9:8-9 [i]Dt 4:27-28; 28:47-48 [j]5:21 Dt 32:6 [k]Ps 115:5-6; 135:16-17; Is 6:9; 42:20; Ezk 12:2; Mt 13:14; Mk 8:18 [l]5:22 Jb 26:10; 38:10-11; Ps 104:9; Pr 8:29 [m]5:23 Dt 21:18,20; Ps 78:8; Is 1:5; Heb 3:12 [n]5:24 Pr 9:10; Hs 6:1 [o]Mt 5:45 [p]Jl 2:23 [q]Dt 11:14 [r]5:25 Is 59:2 [s]5:26 Pr 1:11 [t]Ps 10:9 [u]5:28 Dt 32:15 [v]Is 1:23; Zch 7:10

[A]5:21 Lit *without heart* [B]5:26 Hb obscure

the false prophets are said to be filled with wind rather than spirit.

5:14-17 In a solemn introduction, Jeremiah declared his message in the name of **the Lord God of Hosts**. God is the commander of the armies of heaven and earth (1Sm 17:45). In contrast to the words of false prophets, the **words** in Jeremiah's **mouth** would consume the unrepentant nation. An enemy nation would fall on the **house of Israel**. The description of that nation as being **established . . . ancient**, with an unintelligible **language**, and boasting **mighty warriors** fits Babylon.

5:18 On **I will not finish you off**, see note at verse 10. A remnant of faithful people will be preserved even as God's judgment falls.

5:21 The word for **hear this** is the same Hebrew word *(shema)* that introduces the great Shema of Dt 6:4. It called Israel to covenantal accountability.

5:24 The **fixed weeks of the harvest** were the seven weeks from Passover to Pentecost in which the barley harvest was gathered first, followed by the wheat harvest.

5:26-28 Those who had **grown powerful and rich** through dishonest gain and neglect of **the fatherless** were like **fowlers lying in wait**. As fowlers set a net with several tame

Should I not avenge Myself[a]
on such a nation as this?

30 A horrible, terrible thing
has taken place in the land.[b]

31 The prophets prophesy falsely,[c]
and the priests rule
by their own authority.
My people love it like this.
But what will you do at the end of it?[d]

Threatened Siege of Jerusalem

6 "Run for cover,[e] Benjaminites,
out of Jerusalem!
Sound the ram's horn in Tekoa;[f]
raise a smoke signal[g] over Beth-
haccherem,[A]
for disaster threatens from the north,
even great destruction.

2 Though she is beautiful and delicate,
I will destroy[B] Daughter •Zion.

3 Shepherds and their flocks will come
against her;
they will pitch their tents
all around her.[h]
Each will pasture his own portion.

4 Set them apart for war[i] against her;
rise up, let's attack at noon.
Woe to us, for the day is passing;
the evening shadows grow long.

5 Rise up, let's attack by night.
Let us destroy her fortresses."

6 For this is what the LORD of •Hosts says:

Cut down the trees;[j]
raise a siege ramp against Jerusalem.
This city must be punished.
There is nothing but oppression
within her.

7 As a well gushes out its water,
so she pours out her evil.[c]
Violence and destruction[k] resound
in her.
Sickness and wounds keep coming
to My attention.

8 Be warned, Jerusalem,
or I will turn away from you;[l]
I will make you a desolation,
a land without inhabitants.

Wrath on Israel

9 This is what the LORD of Hosts says:

Glean the remnant of Israel
as thoroughly as a vine.
Pass your hand once more
like a grape gatherer
over the branches.

10 Who can I speak to and give
such a warning[D]
that they will listen?
Look, their ear is uncircumcised,[E,m]
so they cannot pay attention.
See, the word of the LORD
has become contemptible to them—
they find no pleasure in it.

11 But I am full of the LORD's wrath;
I am tired of holding it back.[n]
Pour it out on the children
in the street,[o]
on the gang of young men as well.
For both husband and wife
will be captured,
the old with the very old.[F]

12 Their houses will be turned over
to others,[p]
their fields and wives as well,

Cross references (center column)

a 5:29 Jr 5:9;
8:19; Heb 10:30
b 5:30 Hs 6:10
c 5:31 Lm 2:14
d Dt 32:29; Is
10:3
e 6:1 Ex 9:19; Is
10:31; Jr 4:6
f 2Sm 14:2; 2Ch
11:6; 20:20
g Jdg 20:38,40;
Neh 3:14
h 6:3 Jr 4:17
i 6:4 Jr 51:27;
Mc 3:5
j 6:6 Dt 20:19-20
k 6:7 Jr 20:8; Am
3:10; Hab 1:3
l 6:8 Ezk 23:18;
Hs 9:12
m 6:10 Lv 26:41;
Jr 9:26; Ezk
44:7,9
n 6:11 Jr 20:9
o Jr 9:21
p 6:12 Jr 8:10-12

A 6:1 = House of the Vineyard   B 6:2 Or silence   C 6:7 Or well keeps its water fresh, so she keeps her evil fresh   D 6:10 Or and bear witness   E 6:10 They are unresponsive to God.   F 6:11 Lit with fullness of days

---

birds in the net to attract wild, unsuspecting birds, so too **wicked men** preyed upon innocent victims.

5:30 The word **horrible** is derived from a Hebrew stem meaning "filthiness" or "rottenness" (29:17; Hs 6:10). Here it describes the wickedness of the false prophets, priests, and people.

5:31 The phrase **priests rule by their own authority** is literally "rule by their hands," meaning either at the direction of the false prophets, or on the priests' own authority.

6:1 Hebrew has a play on words between **Tekoa** (teqo'a) and **sound** (tiq'u) **the ram's horn.** Tekoa, about five miles south of Bethlehem, was the hometown of the prophet Amos. **Beth-haccherem** was either 'Ain Karim, west of Jerusalem, or modern Ramat Rachel (ancient Khirbet Salih), located on the road from Jerusalem to Bethlehem. A **smoke signal** was sent to warn about the approach of an enemy (Jdg 20:38,40).

6:3 The enemy and his troops are called **shepherds** and **their flocks.**

6:6 Cut down the trees; raise a siege ramp refers to military actions which the Assyrians and Babylonians boasted about in their victory memorials. They carried dirt in baskets, pouring it against the city walls until the slope was halfway up the wall. Then they built towers from felled trees to hurl heavy stones and firebrands against the wall (2Sm 20:15; Ezk 29:18).

6:7 Evil was erupting so spontaneously in Judah by now that Jeremiah compared it to a gushing **well.** The invasion was justified because Judah was guilty of oppression (v. 6), **evil . . . violence,** and **destruction,** resulting in a society with **sickness and wounds.**

6:9 Jeremiah was to **pass** his **hand once more like a grape gatherer** to make sure every last grape had been gathered. This ensured that everyone heard the message and had a chance to repent.

6:10 An **uncircumcised** ear was closed, impervious to God's Spirit and word.

for I will stretch out My hand
against the inhabitants of the land.
           This is the Lord's declaration.

13 For from the least to the greatest
    of them,
everyone is making profit dishonestly.[a]
From prophet to priest,
everyone deals falsely.
14 They have treated
    My people's brokenness superficially,
claiming, "Peace, peace,"
when there is no peace.
15 Were they ashamed when they acted
    so abhorrently?
They weren't at all ashamed.
They can no longer feel humiliation.
Therefore, they will fall
    among the fallen.
When I punish them, they will collapse,[b]
says the Lord.

Disaster because of Disobedience

16 This is what the Lord says:

Stand by the roadways and look.
Ask about the ancient paths:
Which is the way to what is good?
Then take it
and find rest for yourselves.[c]
But they protested, "We won't!"
17 I appointed watchmen over you[d]
and said: Listen for the sound
    of the ram's horn.
But they protested, "We won't listen!"

18 Therefore listen, you nations
and you witnesses,
learn what the charge is against them.
19 Listen, earth!
I am about to bring disaster
    on these people,

the fruit of their own plotting,[e]
for they have paid no attention
    to My word.
They have rejected My instruction.
20 What use to Me is frankincense
    from Sheba
or sweet cane[f] from a distant land?
Your *burnt offerings
    are not acceptable;
your sacrifices do not please Me.[g]
21 Therefore, this is what the Lord says:
I am going to place stumbling blocks
    before these people;
fathers and sons together will stumble
    over them;[h]
friends and neighbors will also perish.

A Cruel Nation from the North

22 This is what the Lord says:

Look, an army is coming
    from a northern land;
a great nation will be awakened
from the remote regions of the earth.[i]
23 They grasp bow and javelin.
They are cruel and show no mercy.
Their voice roars like the sea,[j]
and they ride on horses,
lined up like men in battle formation
against you, Daughter Zion.

24 We have heard about it,
and we are discouraged.[A]
Distress has seized us—
pain like a woman in labor.[k]
25 Don't go out to the fields;
don't walk on the road.
For the enemy has a sword;
terror is on every side.[l]

26 My dear[B] people, dress yourselves
    in *sackcloth

Cross references (center column)

[a] 6:13 Pr 1:19; 15:27; Hab 2:9
[b] 6:13-15 Jr 8:10-12
[c] 6:16 Mt 11:29
[d] 6:17 Is 21:11; 58:1
[e] 6:19 Pr 1:31
[f] 6:20 Ex 30:23; Is 43:24; Ezk 27:19
[g] Is 43:23; 66:3; Hs 9:4
[h] 6:21 Is 8:15; Jr 31:9; Ezk 7:19
[i] 6:22 Jr 25:32; 31:8
[j] 6:23 Is 5:30; 17:12
[k] 6:22-24 Jr 50:41-43
[l] 6:25 Ps 31:13; Jr 20:3,10; 49:29

A 6:24 Lit and our hands fail   B 6:26 Lit Daughter of My

6:14 Soothing words of **peace, peace** did no good when the stage was already set for calamity.

6:15 On **weren't at all ashamed**, see note at 3:3.

6:16 The ancient paths were the ones followed by Noah and the patriarchs, who believed God's promises and walked with God.

6:17 God **appointed watchmen** or sentinels (metaphors for true prophets), who would **sound** the **ram's horn** to warn of impending trouble (Ezk 3; 33).

6:19 The **fruit of their own plotting** represents destruction growing from the nation's sin and iniquity; they will harvest what they have sown (Pr 1:31). **My word** is paralleled by **My instruction**. The nation had ignored God's teaching through His prophet and disregarded the law Moses had delivered centuries earlier.

6:20 Frankincense came from southern Arabia. It was an

aromatic resin from trees used in perfume and incense. **Sheba** was a country in southwestern Arabia, the center of incense and spices trade. Incense and **burnt offerings** were no substitute for obeying God (7:21-24; Is 1:11-15; Am 5:21; Mc 6:6-8).

6:21 The **stumbling blocks** in this verse are undefined. God will allow events such as the Babylonian invasion because of the failure of His people to heed His calls to repent.

6:23 The word **javelin** probably refers to a sword.

6:25 The phrase **terror is on every side** (Hb magor missabib) is a favorite saying of Jeremiah. He used it to warn Pashhur the evil priest (20:3,10). But the people turned Jeremiah's saying around and used it against him, saying that all he saw were terrors coming from every direction.

6:26 The death of **an only son** (Hb yachid) meant that hope for descendants was gone (Gn 22:2).

and roll in the dust.[a]
Mourn as you would for an only son,[b]
a bitter lament,
for suddenly the destroyer will come
on us.

Jeremiah Appointed as an Examiner

27 I have appointed you to be an assayer
among My people—
a refiner[A]—
so you may know and assay their way
of life.[c]
28 All are stubborn rebels
spreading slander.[d]
They are bronze and iron;
all of them are corrupt.[e]
29 The bellows blow,
blasting the lead with fire.
The refining is completely in vain;
the evil ones are not separated out.
30 They are called rejected silver,
for the LORD has rejected them.[f]

False Trust in the Temple

7 This is the word that came to Jeremiah from the LORD: [2]"Stand in the gate of the house of the LORD[g] and there call out this word: Hear the word of the LORD, all you people of Judah who enter through these gates to worship the LORD. [3]"This is what the LORD of •Hosts, the God of Israel, says: Correct your ways and your deeds,[h] and I will allow you to live in this place. [4]Do not trust deceitful words, chanting: This is the temple of the LORD, the temple of the LORD,

the temple of the LORD. [5]Instead, if you really change your ways and your actions, if you act justly toward one another,[B,i] [6]if you no longer oppress the foreigner, the fatherless, and the widow[j] and no longer shed innocent blood in this place or follow other gods, bringing harm on yourselves, [7]I will allow you to live in this place, the land I gave to your ancestors[k] long ago and forever. [8]But look, you keep trusting in deceitful words that cannot help.

[9]"Do you steal, murder, commit adultery, swear falsely, burn incense to •Baal, and follow other gods that you have not known?[l] [10]Then do you come and stand before Me in this house[m] called by My name and say, 'We are delivered,' so we can continue doing all these detestable acts'? [11]Has this house, which is called by My name, become a den of robbers[n] in your view? Yes, I too have seen it."[o]

This is the LORD's declaration.

Shiloh As a Warning

[12]"But return to My place that was at Shiloh, where I made My name dwell at first.[p] See what I did to it because of the evil of My people Israel. [13]Now, because you have done all these things"—this is the LORD's declaration—"and because I have spoken to you time and time again[c] but you wouldn't listen,[q] and I have called to you, but you wouldn't answer,[r] [14]what I did to Shiloh I will do to the house that is called by My name[s]—the house in which you trust—the place that I gave you and your ancestors. [15]I will drive you from My

---

[a]6:26 Jr 25:34; Ezk 27:30; Mc 1:10
[b]Am 8:10
[c]6:27 1Ch 29:17; Ps 7:9; Pr 17:3
[d]6:28 Lv 19:16; Pr 11:13; 20:19
[e]2Ch 27:2; Is 1:4
[f]6:30 1Sm 15:23,26; Jr 2:37; 7:29
[g]7:2 Jr 26:2
[h]7:3 Jr 18:11; 26:13
[i]7:5 Jr 22:3
[j]7:6 Dt 27:19; Ps 146:9; Jr 22:3
[k]7:7 Gn 12:7; Jos 1:2; Jr 30:3
[l]7:9 Ezk 18:5-9,14-18; 22:6-12; Hs 4:2
[m]7:10 Jr 32:34
[n]7:11 Is 56:7; Mt 21:13; Mk 11:17; Lk 19:46
[o]Ps 33:13-15; Ezk 8:12; Am 9:1-4
[p]7:12 Dt 12:11; 14:23; 16:6,11
[q]7:13 Jr 7:25
[r]Pr 1:24; Is 65:12
[s]7:14 Dt 12:5; 1Kg 9:7; Mk 13:2

[A]6:27 Text emended; MT reads fortress   [B]7:5 Lit justly between a man and his neighbor   [C]7:13 Lit you rising early and speaking

---

6:27 Jeremiah was to act as **an assayer** among the people (cp. 9:7). An assayer was a metallurgist who tested the quality of ore (in this case, the quality of the people).

6:28 The people are described as **stubborn rebels** ("rebel of rebels," or "the most stubborn of rebels"), active in **spreading slander**.

6:29 To refine silver, **lead** and silver were heated together so that the oxidized lead would bind impurities (dross), leaving pure silver (Ps 66:10). However, here the ore (the people of Judah) was so impure that the alloys remained. The refining process failed. The **evil ones** were the dross that could not be **separated** from the pure silver.

7:1 Jeremiah's temple gate sermon from this chapter is repeated in chapter 26.

7:2 The Hebrew verb translated **worship** is a picturesque metaphor. It means "to cause oneself to bow down and prostrate oneself before one of high estate to whom allegiance is owed."

7:3 The phrase **I will allow you to live in this place** can also mean, "I will dwell or live with you" (cp. v. 7).

7:4 **This** refers not only to the temple itself, but to the complex of buildings around the temple. God had promised David an eternal dynasty in the chosen city of Zion, or Je-

rusalem (2Sm 7:12-13; Ps 132:13-14). The people came to believe that the temple was a talisman (good luck charm) that would never be destroyed.

7:9 The sins of the people included violations of the Eighth, Sixth, Seventh, Ninth, First, and Second of the Ten Commandments.

7:10 All that is **called** by God's **name** is the personal property of the Lord to which He lays claim (vv. 11,14,30).

7:11 Just as robbers steal and then lie low until the heat of pursuit is over, so the people were participating in all kinds of evil and then fleeing to the house of God for safety. They were making God's house **a den of robbers**, or literally "a cave" used by bandits.

7:12,14 **Shiloh**, 18 miles north of Jerusalem, near modern Seilun, was where the tabernacle and the ark of the covenant were set up after the conquest of Canaan (Jos 18:1; 22:12; Jdg 21:19). This place was destroyed by the Philistines in 1050 B.C. (Ps 78:60-64) after the battle of Ebenezer (1Sm 4:1-11), as confirmed by Danish excavations in 1922-31.

7:13 **I have spoken to you time and time again** is a unique anthropomorphism (description of God in human terms) that Jeremiah used repeatedly (v. 25; 11:7; 25:3-4; 26:5;

presence, just as I drove out all of your brothers, all the descendants of Ephraim.[a]

Do Not Pray for Judah

[16]"As for you, do not pray for these people.[b] Do not offer a cry or a prayer on their behalf, and do not beg Me,[c] for I will not listen to you. [17]Don't you see how they behave in the cities of Judah and in the streets of Jerusalem? [18]The sons gather wood, the fathers light the fire, and the women knead dough to make cakes for the queen of heaven,[A,d] and they pour out •drink offerings to other gods so that they provoke Me to anger. [19]But are they really provoking Me?"[e] This is the Lord's declaration. "Isn't it they themselves being provoked to disgrace?"

[20]Therefore, this is what the Lord God says: "Look, My anger—My burning wrath—is about to be poured out on this place,[f] on man and beast, on the tree of the field, and on the produce of the land. My wrath will burn and not be quenched."

Obedience Over Sacrifice

[21]This is what the Lord of Hosts, the God of Israel, says: "Add your •burnt offerings to your other sacrifices, and eat the meat yourselves,[g] [22]for when I brought your ancestors out of the land of Egypt, I did not speak with them[h] or command them concerning burnt offering and sacrifice. [23]However, I did give them this command: Obey Me, and then I will be your God, and you will be My people. You must follow every way I command you so that it may go well with you.[i] [24]Yet they didn't listen or pay attention[j] but followed their own advice and according to the stubborn, evil heart. They went backward and not forward.[k] [25]Since the day your ancestors came out of the land of Egypt until this day, I have sent all My servants the prophets to you time and time again.[B,l] [26]However, they wouldn't listen to Me or pay attention but became obstinate;[C,m] they did more evil than their ancestors.

A Lament for Disobedient Judah

[27]"When you speak all these things to them, they will not listen to you. When you call to them, they will not answer you. [28]You must therefore declare to them: This is the nation that would not listen to the voice of the Lord their God and would not accept discipline. Truth[D] has perished—it has disappeared from their mouths. [29]Cut off the hair of your sacred vow[E,n] and throw it away. Raise up a dirge on the barren heights,[o] for the Lord has rejected and abandoned the generation under His wrath.

[30]"For the Judeans have done what is evil in My sight." This is the Lord's declaration. "They have set up their detestable things[p] in the house that is called by My name and defiled it. [31]They have built the •high places of •Topheth[F,q] in the Valley of Hinnom[G,r] in order to burn their sons and daughters in the fire, a thing I did not command; I never entertained the thought.[H]

Cross references
[a]7:15 Dt 29:28; 2Kg 17
[b]7:16 Jr 11:14; 14:11-12; 15:1
[c]Gn 23:8; Ru 1:16; Jr 27:18
[d]7:18 Jr 44:17-19,25
[e]7:19 Jb 35:6
[f]7:20 Jr 42:18; Lm 4:11
[g]7:21 Dt 12:4-28; Ps 50:13
[h]7:22 Hs 6:6
[i]7:23 Dt 5:33
[j]7:24 Ps 81:11
[k]Jr 15:6
[l]7:25 2Ch 36:15-16; Jr 25:4
[m]7:26 2Kg 17:14; Jr 17:23; 19:15
[n]7:29 Nm 6:1-8
[o]Jr 3:2,21
[p]7:30 Jr 4:1; 16:18; 32:34
[q]7:31 2Kg 23:10; Jr 19:6,11-14
[r]Jos 15:8; Jr 19:5; 32:35

A7:18 = a pagan goddess   B7:25 Lit you, each day rising early and sending   C7:26 Lit but stiffened their neck   D7:28 Or Faithfulness
E7:29 Lit off your consecration   F7:31 Lit of the fireplace   G7:31 A valley south of Jerusalem   H7:31 Lit command, and it did not arise on My heart

---

29:19; 32:33; 35:14-15; 44:4). It depicts the Lord "rising up early and speaking."

7:16 The Lord commanded the prophet, **Do not pray for these people**. The nation had passed the point of no return (11:14; 14:11; 15:1). God would no longer listen to intercessions on behalf of the people of Judah.

7:18 The **queen of heaven** was the Assyrian-Babylonian goddess Ishtar, parallel to the Canaanite goddess Astarte. Both were astral deities (perhaps Venus) linked with love, fertility, and warfare. The women made **cakes**, perhaps in the shape of stars (44:15-19) as part of her worship ritual. King Manasseh introduced this false worship (2Kg 21:1-9), and it revived after King Josiah's death.

7:20 God was directly affected by what His people did, but **anger** is not one of His primary qualities or attributes. Rather, it is a response to injustices, which strike against His holy nature. Jeremiah referred to God's anger many times (v. 18; 8:19; 11:17; 25:6-7; 32:29-32; 44:3,8).

7:22 The phrase **I did not speak with them . . . concerning burnt offering and sacrifice** does not show, as some critics have assumed, that the laws about the cult and sacrifices originated in the era after the prophets rather than back in Moses' day. The word "concerning" (Hb 'al dibre) is best rendered "for the sake of," "in the interest of," or "out of concern for" (Dt 4:21; 2Sm 18:5; 2Kg 22:13). The point is that God never commanded His people to perform empty rituals. Rather, their offerings and sacrifices were to be heartfelt and born of a desire for obedience.

7:29 Judah is addressed as a former virgin or bride of the Lord. The undefiled Nazirites were required to cut and burn their hair when the term of their vow was fulfilled (Nm 6:13-18). Now Judah is told that she must **cut off the hair of your sacred vow and throw it away** not because she has completed her vow, but rather because she has violated it. She is no longer consecrated to the Lord, having become a prostitute physically and spiritually.

7:31 **Topheth** is an Aramaic word meaning "firepit," "fireplace," or "hearth," which was pronounced with the vowels from the Hebrew word bosheth, meaning "shame." This high place was located in the **Valley of Hinnom**, south of Jerusalem. Kings Ahaz (2Kg 16:3) and Manasseh (2Kg 21:5-6) instituted pagan sacrifices here, including the offering of Judah's children to the god Baal or Molech. Child sacrifice was forbidden by Mosaic law (Lv 18:21; 20:2-5; Dt 18:10). This practice was abolished under King Josiah (2Kg 23:10).

³²"Therefore, take note! Days are coming"—the Lord's declaration—"when this place will no longer be called Topheth and the Valley of Hinnom, but the Valley of Slaughter.ᵃ Topheth will become a cemetery,ᴬ because there will be no other burial place. ³³The corpses of these people will become food for the birds of the sky and for the wild animals of the land, with no one to scare them away.ᵇ ³⁴I will remove from the cities of Judah and the streets of Jerusalem the sound of joy and gladness and the voices of the groom and the bride,ᶜ for the land will become a desolate waste.

Death over Life

8 "At that time"—this is the Lord's declaration—"the bones of the kings of Judah, the bones of her officials, the bones of the priests, the bones of the prophets, and the bones of the residents of Jerusalem will be brought out of their graves. ²They will be exposedᵈ to the sun, the moon, and the whole heavenly •host,ᵉ which they have loved, served, followed, consulted, and worshiped. Their bones will not be collected and buried but will become like manure on the surface of the soil.ᶠ ³Death will be chosen over lifeᵍ by all the survivors of this evil family, those who remain wherever I have banished them." This is the declaration of the Lord of Hosts.

⁴"You are to say to them: This is what the Lord says:

Do people fall and not get up again?ʰ
If they turn away, do they not return?
⁵ Why have these people turned away?

Cross references (center column):
ᵃ7:32 Jr 19:6
ᵇ7:33 Dt 28:26
ᶜ7:34 Jr 16:9; 25:10; 33:11
ᵈ8:2 2Sm 21:12-14; Ps 53:5; Ezk 6:5
ᵉDt 4:19; 2Kg 17:16; 23:4-5
ᶠPs 83:10; Jr 9:22; 16:4
ᵍ8:3 Dt 30:11-20
ʰ8:4 Is 24:20; Jr 25:27; Am 5:2
ⁱ8:5 Jr 14:14; 23:26; Zph 3:13
ʲJr 5:3; Hs 11:5
ᵏ8:6 Jb 39:19-25
ˡ8:7 Jr 5:4
ᵐ8:8 Jb 19:24; Ps 45:1; Jr 17:1
ⁿ8:10-12 Jr 6:13-15

Why is Jerusalem always turning away?
They take hold of deceit;ⁱ
they refuse to return.ʲ
⁶ I have paid careful attention.
They do not speak what is right.
No one regrets his evil,
asking, 'What have I done?'
Everyone has stayed his course
like a horse rushing into battle.ᵏ
⁷ Even the stork in the sky
knows her seasons.
The turtledove, swallow, and craneᴮ
are aware of their migration,
but My people do not know
the requirements of the Lord.ˡ

Punishment for Judah's Leaders

⁸ "How can you claim, 'We are wise;
the law of the Lord is with us'?
In fact, the lying pen of scribesᵐ
has produced falsehood.
⁹ The wise will be put to shame;
they will be dismayed and snared.
They have rejected the word
of the Lord,
so what wisdom do they really have?
¹⁰ Therefore, I will giveⁿ their wives
to other men,
their fields to new occupants,
for from the least to the greatest,
everyone is making profit dishonestly.
From prophet to priest,
everyone deals falsely.
¹¹ They have treated superficially
the brokenness
of My dearᶜ people,

ᴬ7:32 Lit *They will bury in Topheth*   ᴮ8:7 Hb obscure   ᶜ8:11 Lit *of the daughter of My*

During Jeremiah's days the sacrifices appear to have been revived. Later generations dumped their garbage in the Valley of Hinnom (Hb *gey-hinnom*), perhaps in protest to the atrocities that had been enacted there. Understandably, this place became a symbol for the place of future judgment called Gehenna (Mt 5:22).

7:33-34 So devastating will be the invasion of Judah that corpses will lie everywhere (see note at Ps 79:2). But worst of all, **no one** will be left **to scare** scavengers **away**. The land will fall silent and **become a desolate waste**.

8:1 At that time links what follows with Jeremiah's temple gate sermon in chapter 7. The exhuming of **bones** (here of kings, officials, priests, prophets, and residents) **out of their graves** will be the ultimate insult to the defeated people. Judah will be unable to guard the remains of their ancestors, much less themselves.

8:2 In an ironic demonstration of the futility of false religion, the bones (v. 1) will be exposed to **the sun, the moon, and the whole heavenly host, which they have loved, served, followed, consulted, and worshiped**. The astral deities Judah worshiped will look down, powerless to prevent this desecration.

8:4-5 Once again the emphasis is on the word "to turn/return" or "repent" (Hb *shuv*). Jeremiah made a play on the words, saying: **If they turn away, do they not return? Why have these people turned away?** Normally, those who **fall** try to **get up again**. So why was this people acting so contrary to nature? The answer is they've taken **hold of deceit**.

8:6 The phrase **no one regrets** [or repents of] **his evil** (Hb *niham*) fits with the repeated (Hb) *shuv*, "turn/return," as a call for repentance.

8:7 The **stork . . . turtledove . . . swallow, and crane** are migratory birds. They instinctively obey the laws of nature set by their Creator. This contrasts with God's rational and intelligent beings who saw the impending signs of disaster but decided to do nothing to correct their path.

8:8-9 The people of Judah thought that mere possession of the law of God was all they needed to be secure and right with God. But they had falsified its words and intentions. Verse 8 literally says, "Verily, behold, it is to a delusion [that] it has been given; the pen of the scribes is deceitful." In the hands of the scribes, God's law was twisted into a covering for corruption.

claiming, 'Peace, peace,'
when there is no peace.
12 Were they ashamed when they acted
so abhorrently?
They weren't at all ashamed.
They can no longer feel humiliation.
Therefore, they will fall
among the fallen.
When I punish them,
they will collapse,"ᵃ
says the Lᴏʀᴅ.

13 I will gather them and bring them
to an end.ᴬ,ᵇ
This is the Lᴏʀᴅ's declaration.
There will be no grapes on the vine,
no figs on the fig tree,
and even the leaf will wither.
Whatever I have given them will be lost
to them.

God's People Unrepentant

14 Why are we just sitting here?
Gather together; let us enter
the fortified cities
and perish there,ᴮ
for the Lᴏʀᴅ our God
has destroyedᶜ us.
He has given us poisoned water
to drink,ᶜ
because we have sinned
against the Lᴏʀᴅ.
15 We hoped for peace, but there was
nothing good;
for a time of healing, but there was
only terror.ᵈ

16 From Dan the snorting of horses
is heard.
At the sound of the neighing
of mighty steeds,ᵉ
the whole land quakes.

They come to devour the land
and everything in it,
the city and all its residents.
17 Indeed, I am about to send snakes
among you,
poisonous vipersᶠ that cannot
be charmed.ᵍ
They will bite you.
This is the Lᴏʀᴅ's declaration.

Lament over Judah

18 My joy has flown away;
grief has settled on me.
My heart is sick.ʰ
19 Listen—the cry of my dearᴰ people
from a far away land,
"Is the Lᴏʀᴅ no longer in •Zion,ⁱ
her King not within her?"
Why have they provoked me to anger
with their carved images,
with their worthless foreign idols?ʲ
20 Harvest has passed, summer has ended,
but we have not been saved.
21 I am broken by the brokenness
of my dearᴰ people.ᵏ
I mourn; horror has taken hold of me.
22 Is there no balm in Gilead?ˡ
Is there no physician there?
So why has the healing
of my dearᴰ people
not come about?

9 ᴱ If my head were a spring of water,
my eyes a fountain of tears,
I would weep day and nightᵐ
over the slain of my dearᶠ people.
2ᴳ If only I had a traveler's lodging place
in the wilderness,
I would abandon my people
and depart from them,
for they are all adulterers,ⁿ

Cross-refs: ᵃ8:12 Jr 10:15; 49:8; 51:18 ᵇ8:13 Zph 1:2 ᶜ8:14 Jr 9:15 ᵈ8:15 Jr 14:19; 33:9 ᵉ8:16 Jdg 5:22; Jr 47:3; 50:11 ᶠ8:17 Nm 21:6-9; Dt 32:24 ᵍPs 58:4-5; Ec 10:11 ʰ8:18 Lm 5:17 ⁱ8:19 Ps 99:2; 102:21; Jl 3:17,21 ʲJr 2:5 ᵏ8:21 Jr 6:14; 8:11 ˡ8:22 Gn 37:25; Jr 46:11 ᵐ9:1 Ps 42:3; Jr 13:17; Lm 2:11; Lk 19:41 ⁿ9:2 Jr 23:10; Hs 7:4; Mal 3:5

ᴬ8:13 Lit Gathering I will end them ᴮ8:14 Or there be silenced ᶜ8:14 Or silenced ᴰ8:19,21,22 Lit of the daughter of my ᴱ9:1 Jr 8:23 in Hb ᶠ9:1 Lit slain among the daughter of my ᴳ9:2 Jr 9:1 in Hb

8:12 On **they weren't at all ashamed**, see note at 3:3.

8:13–9:23 This section spells out the doom of Judah and its inhabitants.

8:14 God will give Judah **poisoned water** to drink. This metaphor occurs again in 9:15 and 23:15 as a judgment on the people. The waters may symbolize the cities to which Judah will flee in futile search of peace, wells and springs that the enemy has salted with poison, or the "cup of God's wrath" (25:15-16).

8:16 The city of **Dan**, to the far north and bordering on Phoenicia, marked the route that the enemy from the east will take. The desert to the east was virtually impassable.

8:17 The battle metaphors change from the speed of the horse to the creeping terror of the snake. God will send poisonous **snakes** among the people. The point is that if death does not come from warriors on horse, it will come by some other means God appoints. There will be no escape.

8:20 The phrase **harvest has passed, summer has ended, but we have not been saved** is a proverbial saying meaning that all opportunities have passed and no hope of rescue exists.

8:22 **Gilead** was a territory in Transjordan, north of Moab, where its northern regions were heavily wooded. It was well known for its medicinal **balm**, a resin from the balsam tree that was applied to wounds, but neither healing nor healer could cure the hurt of the people.

9:2 The prophet longed for **a traveler's lodging place** so he could take a break and get some rest from his ministry to the people. This emotion here is just as strong as it was in

a solemn assembly
of treacherous people.[a]

3 They bent their tongues like their bows;
lies and not faithfulness prevail
in the land,
for they proceed from one evil
to another,
and they do not take Me into account.[b]
This is the LORD's declaration.

Imminent Ruin and Exile

4 Everyone has to be on guard
against his friend.
Don't trust any brother,
for every brother will certainly deceive,
and every friend spread slander.[c]
5 Each one betrays his friend;
no one tells the truth.
They have taught their tongues
to speak lies;
they wear themselves out doing wrong.
6 You live in a world of deception.[A]
In their deception they refuse
to know Me.[d]
This is the LORD's declaration.

7 Therefore, this is what the LORD of •Hosts
says:

I am about to refine them
and test them,[e]
for what else can I do
because of My dear[B] people?[C]
8 Their tongues are deadly arrows—
they speak deception.[f]
With his mouth
a man speaks peaceably with his friend,
but inwardly he sets up an ambush.
9 Should I not punish them
for these things?
This is the LORD's declaration.
Should I not avenge Myself[g]
on such a nation as this?

10 I will raise weeping and a lament
over the mountains,
a dirge over the wilderness
grazing land,
for they have been so scorched
that no one passes through.
The sound of cattle is no longer heard.
From the birds of the sky
to the animals,[h]
everything has fled—they have
gone away.
11 I will make Jerusalem a heap of rubble,[i]
a jackals' den.[j]
I will make the cities of Judah
a desolation,
an uninhabited place.

12 Who is the man wise enough to understand this?[k] Who has the LORD spoken to, that
he may explain it? Why is the land destroyed
and scorched like a wilderness, so no one can
pass through?
13 The LORD said, "It is because they abandoned My instruction[l] that I set in front of
them and did not obey My voice or walk according to it. 14 Instead, they followed the
stubbornness of their hearts[m] and followed
after the •Baals as their fathers taught them."[n]
15 Therefore, this is what the LORD of Hosts, the
God of Israel, says: "I am about to feed this
people •wormwood[o] and give them poisonous
water to drink.[p] 16 I will scatter them among
the nations[q] that they and their fathers have
not known. I will send a sword after them until I have finished them off."

Mourning over Judah

17 This is what the LORD of Hosts says:

Consider, and summon the women
who mourn;[r]
send for the skillful women.
18 Let them come quickly to raise
a lament over us
so that our eyes may overflow
with tears,

[a]9:2 Is 24:16; 33:1; Jr 12:1 [b]9:3 Jr 4:22 [c]9:4 Jr 6:28 [d]9:6 Rm 1:17 [e]9:7 Is 1:25; Jr 6:27 [f]9:8 Ps 28:3 [g]9:9 Jr 5:9,29 [h]9:10 Jr 4:25; 12:4 [i]9:11 2Kg 19:25; Is 25:2; Jr 51:37 [j]Jr 10:22; 49:33; 51:37 [k]9:12 Ps 107:43; Ec 8:1; Hs 14:9 [l]9:13 2Ch 12:1 [m]9:14 Dt 29:19; Ps 81:12 [n]Jr 2:8,23 [o]9:15 Dt 29:18; Jr 23:15; Lm 3:19 [p]Jr 8:14; 23:15 [q]9:16 Lv 26:33; Dt 4:27; 28:64 [r]9:17 Ec 12:5; Am 5:16

[A]9:6 LXX reads *Oppression on oppression, deceit on deceit* [B]9:7 Lit *of the daughter of My* [C]9:7 LXX, Tg read *because of their evils*

verse 1, which shows the depths of Jeremiah's grief over Judah's resistance to the word of God.

9:4 Every brother will certainly deceive, Jeremiah argued, punning on Jacob's name (Gn 27:36), here also rendered correctly as "will certainly deceive" (Hb *'aqov ya'qov*; lit "will deceive [like] the deceiver/Jacob"; cp. Hs 12:2-4).

9:7 Amazingly, God is still not ready to reject His people; He will once more attempt to **refine** and **test** them (17:10; Ps 66:10; Pr 17:3). The furnace of trials will determine if God can take away the dross of their sin. God declared, **what else can I do** in view of the fact that Judah was the daughter of **My dear people**.

9:10-11 The whole ecosystem will collapse, leaving only scavengers (jackals).

9:15 Wormwood belonged to the aster family. It had a bitter taste and the same effect as the **poisonous water**.

9:16 God's declaration **I will scatter them among the nations** is just what Moses had warned would happen if the people abandoned the Lord (Lv 26:33; Dt 28:36,64).

9:17-22 This section is a poem about death, the grim reaper. Death is personified as an intruder who sneaks in through the window at night.

9:17 The **women who mourn** were professional mourners whose dirges would start the mourning process for the conquered nation.

our eyelids soaked with weeping.
19 For a sound of lamentation is heard
   from *Zion:
How devastated we are.
We are greatly ashamed,[a]
for we have abandoned the land;
our dwellings have been torn down.

20 Now hear the word of the LORD,
   you women.
Pay attention to[A] the word
   of His mouth.
Teach your daughters a lament
and one another a dirge,
21 for Death[b] has climbed
   through our windows;
it has entered our fortresses,
cutting off children from the streets,
young men from the squares.

22 Speak as follows:
This is what the LORD says:

Human corpses will fall
like manure on the surface of the field,
like newly cut grain[c] after the reaper
with no one to gather it.

Boast in the LORD
23 This is what the LORD says:

The wise man must not boast
   in his wisdom;
the strong man must not boast
   in his strength;
the wealthy man must not boast
   in his wealth.
24 But the one who boasts should boast
   in this,
that he understands and knows Me[d]—

a9:19 Jr 2:26;
6:15; 8:12
b9:21 Jb 18:13;
28:22; Ps 49:14
c9:22 Am 2:13;
Mc 4:12; Zch
12:6
d9:24 Ps 34:2;
64:10; 105:3;
1Co 1:31; 2Co
10:17
e9:25 Jr 4:4; Rm
2:28-29
f9:26 Lv 19:27;
Jr 25:23; 49:32;
Ezk 44:7,9
g10:2 Jr 2:23,36
h10:4 Is 40:19
iIs 41:7
j10:5 Ps 115:5;
1Co 12:2
kPs 115:7; Is
46:7

that I am *Yahweh,
   showing faithful love,
justice, and righteousness on the earth,
   for I delight in these things.
      This is the LORD's declaration.

25 "The days are coming"—the LORD's declaration—"when I will punish all the circumcised yet uncircumcised:[e] 26 Egypt, Judah, Edom, the Ammonites, Moab, and all the inhabitants of the desert who clip the hair on their temples.[B] All these nations are uncircumcised, and the whole house of Israel is uncircumcised in heart."[f]

False Gods Contrasted with the Creator
10 Hear the word that the LORD has spoken to[C] you, house of Israel. 2 This is what the LORD says:

Do not learn the way of the nations[g]
or be terrified by signs in the heavens,
although the nations are terrified
   by them,
3 for the customs of the peoples
   are worthless.
Someone cuts down a tree
   from the forest;
it is worked by the hands of a craftsman
   with a chisel.
4 He decorates it with silver and gold.[h]
It is fastened with hammer and nails,[i]
so it won't totter.
5 Like scarecrows
   in a cucumber patch,
their idols cannot speak.[j]
They must be carried[k] because
   they cannot walk.

A9:20 Lit *Your ears must receive*   B9:26 Or *who live in distant places*   C10:1 Or *against*

9:23-24 Two contrasting ways are described in two triads of values. **Wisdom . . . strength**, and **wealth** are the values that **the wise . . . the strong**, and **the wealthy** aspire to. But the person who **understands and knows** the Lord sets his highest values on the fact that God alone is **the LORD**. He shows **faithful love** (Hb *chesed*; used 248 times in the OT, meaning "loyalty, steadfast love, grace"), **justice**, and **righteousness**. God's people should note what He delights in and order their priorities accordingly. The supreme goal and glory of humanity is to know and enjoy God.

9:25 The **circumcised yet uncircumcised** lumps Judah in with four other nations that practiced circumcision of the flesh but neglected circumcision of the heart (4:4; Gl 5:2-5). Circumcision of the flesh was merely an outward symbol. If that alone were enough to please God, the pagan nations mentioned here would enjoy God's favor.

9:26 The phrase **inhabitants . . . who clip the hair on their temples** refers to Arabian tribes that cut hair from the cor-

ners of their temples to honor Bacchus, the pagan god of wine. Israel was forbidden to do this (Lv 19:27; Dt 14:1) out of respect for the Lord.

10:1 Even though the 10 northern tribes had been in exile for more than a century, this message is addressed to the whole **house of Israel**.

10:2-3 The warning **do not learn** suggests the idea of not "becoming a disciple" of these idols. **The way of the nations** involved their religious practices and customs. Those ways were **worthless** (Hb *hevel*; "fog, mist, or breath"). This word is used almost 40 times in the book of Ecclesiastes and is usually rendered "vanity" or "worthless."

10:4 The idol makers used **silver** from Tarshish (often linked with Spain) and **gold** from Uphaz (perhaps the same city as Ophir, which may have been located in Africa or Arabia), to beautify and overlay the carved wooden form.

10:5 The idols are compared to **scarecrows**, though the

Do not fear them for they can do
  no harm[a]—
and they cannot do any good.[b]

6 •Yahweh, there is no one like You.[c]
You are great;
Your name is great in power.[d]

7 Who should not •fear You,
King of the nations?[e]
It is what You deserve.
For among all the wise people
  of the nations
and among all their kingdoms,
there is no one like You.

8 They are both stupid and foolish,
instructed by worthless idols
made of wood!

9 Beaten silver is brought from Tarshish,[f]
and gold from Uphaz[A,g]
from the hands of a goldsmith,
the work of a craftsman.
Their clothing is blue and purple,
all the work of skilled artisans.

10 But Yahweh is the true God;[h]
He is the living God[i] and eternal King.[j]
The earth quakes at His wrath,[k]
and the nations cannot endure
  His rage.

11 You are to say this to them, "The gods that
did not make the heavens[l] and the earth will
perish from the earth[m] and from under these
heavens."[B]

12 He made the earth by His power,
established the world[n] by His wisdom,[o]
and spread out the heavens
  by His understanding.[p]

13 When He thunders,[C]
the waters in the heavens
  are in turmoil,[q]
and He causes the clouds to rise
from the ends of the earth.
He makes lightning for the rain

and brings the wind
  from His storehouses.[r]

14 Everyone is stupid and ignorant.
Every goldsmith is put to shame
by his carved image,[s]
for his cast images are a lie;[t]
there is no breath in them.[u]

15 They are worthless, a work
  to be mocked.
At the time of their punishment
they will be destroyed.[v]

16 Jacob's Portion[D] is not like these
because He is the One who formed
  all things.[w]
Israel is the tribe of His inheritance;[x]
Yahweh of •Hosts is His name.[y]

Exile After the Siege

17 Gather up your belongings[E]
  from the ground,[z]
you who live under siege.

18 For this is what the LORD says:

Look, I am slinging out[aa]
the land's residents at this time
and bringing them such distress
that they will feel it.

Jeremiah Grieves

19 Woe to me because of my brokenness—
I am severely wounded![ab]
I exclaimed, "This is
  my intense suffering,
but I must bear it."

20 My tent is destroyed;[ac]
all my tent cords are snapped.
My sons have departed from me and are
  no more.
I have no one to pitch my tent again
or to hang up my curtains.

21 For the shepherds are stupid:
they don't seek the LORD.[ad]
Therefore they have not prospered,

a10:5 Is 41:23-24
b10:3-5 Is 44:9-20
c10:6 Ex 15:11; 2Sm 7:22; 1Kg 8:23
d Ps 76:1; 86:10; Mal 1:11
e10:7 Ps 22:28; 47:7-8; Jr 8:19
f10:9 Ezk 27:12,25; 38:13
g Dn 10:5
h10:10 2Ch 15:3
i Dt 5:26; 1Sm 17:26,36; 2Kg 19:4,16
j Ex 15:18; Ps 10:16; 29:10
k 2Sm 22:8; Ps 18:7; Is 13:13
l10:11 Ps 96:5
m Is 2:18
n10:12 Jb 38:4; Ps 93:1; 96:10
o Pr 3:19-20; 8:22-29
p Jb 9:8; Ps 104:2; Is 45:12
q10:13 Jr 5:22; 31:35
r Jb 38:25-30,34-38; Ps 135:7
s10:14 Is 40:18-31; 46:1-7
t Is 41:29
u Hab 2:19
v10:15 Jr 8:12; 51:18
w10:16 Gn 2:7-8,19; Ps 94:9; 95:5
x Dt 4:20; 32:8-9; Ps 74:2
y10:12-16 Jr 51:15-19
z10:17 Ezk 12:3
aa10:18 1Sm 25:29
ab10:19 Jr 14:17; 30:12; Nah 3:19
ac10:20 Jr 4:20
ad10:21 2Ch 16:12; Is 9:13; 31:1

word can be rendered "palm tree" (as in the KJV and ASV) or "pillar."

10:6-8 The majesty and incomparability of the Lord (**there is no one like You**) are contrasted with the uselessness and impotence of idols.

10:9 On **Tarshish** and **Uphaz**, see note at verse 4.

10:11 This is the only verse in the book of Jeremiah that is in Aramaic, a language similar to Hebrew. These idol merchants probably could understand Aramaic very well since their business dealings required that they know this language.

10:12-16 This section is repeated in 51:15-19.

10:16 Jacob's Portion refers to the Lord Himself, because

He had given Himself as Israel's **inheritance**. Usually the people made this claim for themselves, but in this mutual belonging, God is as much a possession of Israel as their land is. Since idols are lifeless, imaginary gods, they were unable to commit themselves to anyone.

10:17 The word for **belongings** comes from the same stem as "Canaan." These people were the merchants of their day and a symbol of commercialism.

10:21 The imagery of **shepherds** (Judah's leaders) who were **stupid** and a **flock** that was **scattered** is expanded in Ezekiel 34. Ezekiel described a good shepherd who would gather in the scattered flock. If the people would **seek** the Lord and His word, things would turn out differently.

10:22 A **great commotion** would announce the arrival of

and their whole flock is scattered.
²² Listen! A noise—it is coming—
a great commotion[a] from the land
  to the north.
The cities of Judah will be
  made desolate,
a jackals' den.[b]

²³ I know, Lord,
that a man's way of life is not his own;
no one who walks determines
  his own steps.[c]
²⁴ Discipline me, Lord, but with justice—
not in Your anger,[d]
or You will reduce me to nothing.
²⁵ Pour out Your wrath on the nations
that don't recognize You
and on the families
that don't call on Your name,
for they have consumed Jacob;
they have consumed him and finished
  him off
and made his homeland desolate.[e]

Reminder of the Covenant

11 This is the word that came to Jeremiah
from the Lord: ²"Listen to the words of
this covenant[f] and tell them to the men of Judah and the residents of Jerusalem. ³You must
tell them: This is what the Lord, the God of
Israel, says: 'Let a curse be on the man who
does not obey the words of this covenant,[g]
⁴which I commanded your ancestors when I
brought them out of the land of Egypt,[h] out
of the iron furnace.'[i] I declared: 'Obey Me, and
do everything that I command you, and you

will be My people, and I will be your God,'[j]
⁵in order to establish the oath I swore to your
ancestors,[k] to give them a land flowing with
milk and honey, as it is today.'"
I answered, "•Amen, Lord."[l]
⁶The Lord said to me, "Proclaim all these
words in the cities of Judah and in the streets
of Jerusalem: Obey the words of this covenant
and carry them out. ⁷For I strongly warned
your ancestors when I brought them out of
the land of Egypt until today, warning them
time and time again,[A,m] 'Obey My voice.' ⁸Yet
they would not obey or pay attention; each
one followed the stubbornness of his evil
heart.[n] So I brought on them all the curses
of this covenant, because they had not done
what I commanded them to do."
⁹The Lord said to me, "A conspiracy has been
discovered among the men of Judah[o] and the
residents of Jerusalem. ¹⁰They have returned
to the sins of their ancestors[p] who refused to
obey My words and have followed other gods
to worship them.[q] The house of Israel and the
house of Judah broke My covenant I made
with their ancestors.
¹¹"Therefore, this is what the Lord says: I
am about to bring on them disaster that they
cannot escape.[r] They will cry out to Me, but I
will not hear them. ¹²Then the cities of Judah
and the residents of Jerusalem will go and cry
out to the gods they have been burning incense to, but they certainly will not save them
in their time of disaster.[s] ¹³Your gods are indeed as numerous as your cities, Judah,[t] and
the altars you have set up to Shame[B,u]—altars

Cross references:
[a]10:22 Jr 4:29; 6:22-23
[b]Jr 9:11
[c]10:23 Ps 37:23; Pr 3:5-6; 16:9
[d]10:24 Ps 6:1; 38:1
[e]10:25 Ps 79:6-7
[f]11:2 Dt 29:9
[g]11:3 Dt 27:26; Gl 3:10
[h]11:4 Dt 29:25; Jr 7:22; 34:13
[i]Dt 4:20; 1Kg 8:51
[j]Dt 29:13; Jr 24:7; 30:22
[k]11:5 Gn 26:3; Dt 7:8
[l]Dt 27:15-16
[m]11:7 2Ch 36:15; Jr 7:25
[n]11:8 Jr 3:17; 7:24; 16:12
[o]11:9 Ezk 22:25; Hs 6:9
[p]11:10 Lv 26:39-40; Neh 9:2; Is 65:7
[q]Dt 28:14; Jr 13:10; 35:15
[r]11:11 Jr 39:4-7; Am 9:1-4
[s]11:12 Dt 32:35-37
[t]11:13 Jr 2:28
[u]Jr 3:24; Hs 9:10

---

^A11:7 Lit today, rising early and warning   ^B11:13 = Baal

---

the Babylonian army in 587 b.c. The imagery of being **made
desolate** and becoming **a jackals' den** is often used to describe the total destruction of conquered cities (51:37; Zph
2:13-15).

10:23-25 This is a personal prayer by Jeremiah, but it applied to the entire nation of Judah.

10:24 Discipline me, Lord, is a verb used frequently in the
wisdom literature of the OT for educational or corrective
punishment. Jeremiah, like the prophet Daniel (Dn 9:4-
19), prayed in the first person, identifying himself with his
people. But neither the prophet nor the nation wanted God
to deal with them according to what they really deserved.
Jeremiah may have reasoned that if God disciplined **with
justice,** there would be a chance that He would offer mercy.
If He disciplined **in . . . anger,** however, He would certainly
destroy them.

10:25 The prayer ends with a request for God to **pour out**
His **wrath** on the **nations** and devour them as they had
consumed Judah. This request is granted in 30:16, but
only after Judah had been devoured due to her refusal to
repent.

11:2 The phrase **listen** (pl) **to the words of this covenant and
tell** (pl) **them** is difficult in Hebrew, because Jeremiah is

addressed personally, yet the verbs are plural. Perhaps the
problem is solved by emphasizing the "words" or terms of
the covenant. The covenant is the main subject in verses 2,
3, and 6 where Jeremiah addressed the people.

11:3 At the heart of the covenant given by the Lord at Sinai
were two terms: a **curse** and the call to **obey** the words of
the covenant. Obedience would bring blessing, disobedience a curse.

11:4 You will be My people, and I will be your God were two
parts of the oft-repeated promise of God.

11:5 A **land flowing with milk and honey** was a figure of
speech indicating the fruitfulness of Canaan (32:22; Ezk
20:6,15). Its plentiful grass was turned into milk by grazing
livestock, and the nectar of flowering plants was changed
into honey by bees.

11:7 Until today shows that this warning had been issued
year after year, even up to "today" (the time of Jeremiah),
all to no avail.

11:9 There appears to have been a general **conspiracy** and
revolt against King Josiah's call for reform and revival in Judah. But it did not escalate into political action (e.g., a coup).
Instead, it was a revolt against God.

to burn incense to •Baal—as numerous as the streets of Jerusalem.

¹⁴"As for you, do not pray for these people. Do not raise up a cry or a prayer on their behalf,^a for I will not be listening when they call out to Me at the time of their disaster.

¹⁵   What right does My beloved have
to be in My house,^b
having carried out so many
evil schemes?
Can holy meat^{A,c} prevent your disaster^B
so you can rejoice?
¹⁶   The LORD named you
a flourishing olive tree,^d
beautiful with well-formed fruit.
He has set fire to it,
and its branches are consumed^{C,e}
with a great roaring sound.^f

¹⁷"The LORD of •Hosts who planted you^g has decreed disaster against you, because of the harm the house of Israel and the house of Judah brought on themselves, provoking Me to anger by burning incense to Baal."

¹⁸   The LORD informed me, so I knew.
Then You helped me to see their deeds,
¹⁹   for I was like a docile^D lamb led
to slaughter.^h
I didn't know that they had
devised plots against me:
"Let's destroy the tree with its fruit;^E
let's cut him off from the land
of the livingⁱ
so that his name will no longer
be remembered."
²⁰   But, LORD of Hosts,
who judges righteously,
who tests^j heart^F and mind,^k

let me see Your vengeance on them,
for I have presented my case to You.^l

²¹Therefore, here is what the LORD says concerning the people of Anathoth^m who want to take your life. They warn, "You must not prophesy in the name of •Yahweh, or you will certainly die at our hand." ²²Therefore, this is what the LORD of Hosts says: "I am about to punish them. The young men will die by the sword; their sons and daughters will die by famine.ⁿ ²³They will have no remnant, for I will bring disaster on the people of Anathoth^o in the year of their punishment."

Jeremiah's Complaint

¹² You will be righteous, LORD,^p
even if I bring a case against You.
Yet, I wish to contend with You:^q
Why does the way of the wicked
prosper?^r
Why do all the treacherous live at ease?
²   You planted them,^s and they
have taken root.
They have grown and produced fruit.
You are ever on their lips,^G
but far from their conscience.^{F,t}
³   As for You, LORD, You know me;<sup>
You see me.^u
You test whether my heart is with You.^v
Drag the wicked away like sheep
to slaughter^w
and set them apart for the day
of killing.
⁴   How long will the land mourn^x
and the grass of every field wither?
Because of the evil of its residents,
animals and birds have been
swept away,

^a11:14 Jr 7:16; 14:11	
^b11:15 Jr 7:1-15	
^cHg 2:12	
^d11:16 Ps 52:8; 128:3	
^eEzk 31:12	
^fEzk 1:24	
^g11:17 Is 5:2,7; Jr 2:21	
^h11:19 Ps 44:11,22; Is 53:7; Jr 12:3	
ⁱPs 27:13; Is 53:8; Ezk 26:20	
^j11:20 Jr 9:7; 12:3	
^kPs 7:9; 17:3; 26:2	
^lJr 20:12	
^m11:21 Jr 1:1; 32:7-9	
ⁿ11:21-22 Am 7:16-17	
^o11:23 Jr 23:12	
^p12:1 Ezr 9:15; Neh 9:8,33; Ps 119:137	
^qJb 9:14-15; 13:13-28; 23:2-17	
^rPs 73	
^s12:2 Ps 1:3; Jr 17:7-8	
^tPs 28:3; Is 29:13	
^u12:3 Ps 139; Jr 1:5	
^vPs 7:9; Jr 11:20	
^wJr 11:19	
^x12:4 Is 24:4-7; Jr 4:28; 23:10	

---

^A11:15 = sacrificial meat   ^B11:15 LXX; MT reads *meat pass from you*   ^C11:16 Vg; MT reads *broken*   ^D11:19 Or *pet*   ^E11:19 Lit *bread*
^F11:20; 12:2 Lit *kidneys*   ^G12:2 Lit *are near in their mouth*

11:14 Again as in 7:16 (see note there), God did not permit Jeremiah to pray for the people. It was now too late (14:11-12; 15:1).

11:15 My "beloved" (Hb *yadid*) is the same name the prophet Nathan gave to Solomon—Jedidiah, "The LORD's Beloved one." Judah had been the Lord's "beloved" (12:7; Ps 78:68-72; 82:2). God asked, **What right does My beloved have to be in My house?** This same point was made in Jeremiah's temple gate sermon (7:3-11). Like a son or daughter expelled for bad behavior, Judah's sin caused her to lose her privileges.

11:16-17 In another metaphor that depicted the nation as a thing created by God, Jeremiah declared the Lord had **planted** the **flourishing olive tree** (2:21; 5:10; 6:9; Ps 52:8; 92:12-15; Hs 14:7).

11:19 Because Jeremiah had not suspected all the plots and schemes arrayed against him, he was like **a docile lamb led to slaughter**. His enemies planned to **destroy the tree with its fruit** (lit "its bread"), a proverbial expression indi-

cating that they would destroy both him and whatever he produced ("food" or "bread"). Jeremiah was not married, so this refers to the destruction of his life's work, not a wife or children.

11:20 Out of a desire for justice, Jeremiah prayed for God's **vengeance** on his enemies.

11:21-23 Jeremiah's hometown of **Anathoth** plotted against him, presumably because his own family thought he had brought disgrace on them. Or did they regard him as a traitor because his pronouncements seemed to favor Babylon over Judah?

12:1-4 This is another of Jeremiah's "confessions" (see note at 4:19-22).

12:1 Even though God is **righteous** in all His actions and judgments, Jeremiah pressed the age-old question, **Why does the way of the wicked prosper?** Asaph wanted the same question answered (Ps 73), and so did David (Ps 37).

for the people have said,
"He cannot see what our end will be."[A,a]

The Lord's Response

5 If you have raced with runners
and they have worn you out,
how can you compete with horses?
If you stumble[B] in a peaceful land,
what will you do in the thickets
of the Jordan?[b]

6 Even your brothers—
your own father's household—
even they were treacherous to you;[c]
even they have cried out loudly
after you.[d]
Do not have confidence in them,
though they speak well of you.

7 I have abandoned My house;[e]
I have deserted My inheritance.
I have given the love of My life
into the hands of her enemies.

8 My inheritance has acted
toward Me
like a lion in the forest.
She has roared against Me.
Therefore, I hate her.[f]

9 Is My inheritance like a hyena[c]
to Me?
Are birds of prey circling her?
Go, gather all the wild animals;[g]
bring them to devour her.

10 Many shepherds have destroyed
My vineyard;
they have trampled My plot
of land.[h]
They have turned My desirable plot
into a desolate wasteland.

11 They have made it a desolation.
It mourns, desolate, before Me.

All the land is desolate,
but no one takes it to heart.[i]

12 Over all the barren heights
in the wilderness
the destroyers have come,
for the Lord has a sword
that devours
from one end of the earth to the other.
No one has peace.[j]

13 They have sown wheat
but harvested thorns.[k]
They have exhausted themselves
but have no profit.[l]
Be put to shame by your harvests
because of the Lord's burning anger.[m]

14 This is what the Lord says: "Concerning all My evil neighbors who attack the inheritance that I bequeathed to My people, Israel, I am about to uproot them[n] from their land, and I will uproot the house of Judah from them. 15 After I have uprooted them, I will once again have compassion[o] on them and return each one to his inheritance and to his land. 16 If they will diligently learn the ways of My people[p]—to swear by My name, 'As ᵃYahweh lives,' just as they taught My people to swear by ᵃBaal—they will be built up among My people. 17 However, if they will not obey, then I will uproot and destroy that nation."[q]
This is the Lord's declaration.

Linen Underwear

13 This is what the Lord said to me: "Go and buy yourself a linen undergarment[r] and put it on,[D] but do not put it in water." 2 So I bought underwear as the Lord instructed me and put it on.

3 Then the word of the Lord came to me a second time: 4 "Take the underwear that you

Cross-references (center column)

a 12:4 Dt 32:20; Jb 22:13; Jr 29:11
b 12:5 Jr 50:44
c 12:6 Jn 1:11
d Jr 11:19
e 12:7 Ezk 8:1–11:25
f 12:8 Hs 9:15; Am 6:8
g 12:9 Is 56:9; Jr 7:33
h 12:10 Is 63:18
i 12:11 Is 42:25
j 12:12 2Ch 15:5; Is 48:22; Ezk 13:16
k 12:13 Lv 26:16; Dt 28:38; Mc 6:15; Hg 1:6
l Is 55:2
m Jr 4:26; 25:37-38
n 12:14 Jr 1:10; 18:7-8
o 12:15 Jr 48:47; 49:6
p 12:16 Is 2:2-4; Mc 4:1-5
q 12:17 Is 60:12
r 13:1 Ex 39:27-29; Lv 16:4; Ezk 44:17-18

A 12:4 LXX reads *see our ways*   B 12:5 Or *you are secure*   C 12:9 Hb obscure   D 13:1 Lit *around your waist*

12:5-6 The Lord responded to Jeremiah's complaint (see vv. 1-4). If running refers to the false prophets who "ran" even though the Lord did not send them (23:21), how did Jeremiah hope to **compete with horses**? This may be an allusion to the Babylonian horses that would soon descend on Judah and the prophet. Or it may be that if Jeremiah thought his family and friends in Anathoth were hard to deal with, what would he do when the wicked (riders on horses) were turned loose on him?

12:7 God still referred to the nation of Judah as **My house . . . My inheritance**, and **the love of My life**. But these descriptions He must now abandon and give Judah into the hands of her **enemies**. The word **inheritance** or "heritage" occurs five times in this chapter, usually of God's gift of the land of Canaan to Israel (vv. 7,9,14-15), but in verse 8 it refers to the people.

12:10-11 Similar to the picture of 2:6-8, the good land will be **desolate**, suffering from drought, neglect, invaders, and divine judgment.

12:13 The image of planting and harvesting **thorns** is both literal and metaphorical. Thorns grow up on neglected land, and Judah will experience the "thorny" effect of an invasion.

12:14-17 This section deals with Israel's **evil neighbors**, who will be **uprooted** (cp. 1:10) just as Judah will be. The nations that ransack Israel will themselves be overrun by the Lord. But like Judah, God will build them up (cp. Jr 10) if they will repent and turn to the Lord.

13:1 The Lord told Jeremiah to purchase a new **linen undergarment**. This item of clothing extended from the waist to the thighs. The Hebrew word *'ezor* has been translated as "girdle" (KJV, NEB), "waistcloth" (RSV), and "loincloth" (JB). But it was made of valuable linen, material usually reserved for priests (Lv 16:4).

13:3-5 Jeremiah was then instructed to take the **underwear** he had **bought** and was **wearing** and hide it in a rocky crevice along the Euphrates River, which lay about 350 miles

bought and are wearing,[A] and go at once to the Euphrates[B] and hide it in a rocky crevice."[a] [5]So I went and hid it by the Euphrates, as the LORD commanded me.

[6]A long time later the LORD said to me, "Go at once to the Euphrates and get the underwear that I commanded you to hide there." [7]So I went to the Euphrates and dug up the underwear and got it from the place where I had hidden it, but it was ruined—of no use at all.

[8]Then the word of the LORD came to me: [9]"This is what the LORD says: Just like this I will ruin the great pride of both Judah and Jerusalem.[b] [10]These evil people, who refuse to listen to Me, who follow the stubbornness of their own hearts,[c] and who have followed other gods to serve and worship—they will be like this underwear, of no use at all. [11]Just as underwear clings to one's waist, so I fastened the whole house of Israel and of Judah to Me"[d]—this is the LORD's declaration—"so that they might be My people for My fame, praise, and glory,[e] but they would not obey.

The Wine Jars

[12]"Say this to them: This is what the LORD, the God of Israel, says: Every jar should be filled with wine. Then they will respond to you, 'Don't we know that every jar should be filled with wine?' [13]And you will say to them: This is what the LORD says: I am about to fill all who live in this land—the kings who reign for David on his throne, the priests, the proph-

[a]13:4 Jr 51:63
[b]13:9 Lv 26:19
[c]13:10 Jr 16:12
[d]13:11 Dt 4:3-4; 10:20
[e]Dt 26:19; Ezk 16:8-14
[f]13:14 Lm 2:2,17,21; 3:43
[g]13:16 Jos 7:19; 1Sm 6:5; Ps 29:1-2
[h]13:17 Ps 80:1; 95:7; Jr 23:1-4
[i]13:18 2Kg 24:12; Jr 22:26

ets and all the residents of Jerusalem—with drunkenness. [14]I will smash them against each other, fathers and sons alike"—this is the LORD's declaration. "I will allow no mercy, pity, or compassion to keep Me from destroying them."[f]

The LORD's Warning

[15] Listen and pay attention.
　　Do not be proud,
　　for the LORD has spoken.
[16] Give glory to the LORD your God[g]
　　before He brings darkness,
　　before your feet stumble
　　on the mountains at dusk.
　　You wait for light,
　　but He brings darkest gloom[c]
　　and makes thick darkness.
[17] But if you will not listen,
　　my innermost being will weep in secret
　　because of your pride.
　　My eyes will overflow with tears,
　　for the LORD's flock[h] has been
　　　taken captive.

[18] Say to the king and the queen mother:[i]
　　Take a humble seat,
　　for your glorious crowns
　　have fallen from your heads.
[19] The cities of the •Negev are
　　　under siege;
　　no one can help them.
　　All of Judah has been taken into exile,
　　taken completely into exile.

---

northeast of Anathoth—a round trip journey of 700 miles. The Hebrew word for the Euphrates is *perath*. Another site, using the same word, *perath*, was a spring at Wadi Farah, about four miles northeast of doomed Anathoth. Since the Hebrew names for both sites are the same, each suggests that destruction (symbolized by the ruined underwear, v. 7) would come from the region of the Euphrates River.

13:8-10 God's interpretation of this symbolic action was: **Just like this I will ruin the great pride of both Judah and Jerusalem**. Thus, the nation had gone from being untarnished when she was called as God's bride (2:2-3) to being rotten and useless because of her sinfulness.

13:11 The nation of Judah had previously clung to the Lord's **waist** as people whom He called **My people for My fame, praise, and glory**. But they would be removed just as Jeremiah's **underwear** was taken into Babylonian-controlled territory and ruined.

13:12-14 God had Jeremiah announce a common proverb: **Every jar should be filled with wine**. The people's derisive reply was essentially, "Why of course, what do you think those jars are for anyway?" But the metaphor meant that the people themselves were the earthen jars that should be filled with wine. Everyone from the top of society to the bot-

tom would be filled with **drunkenness**, or the wrath of God (25:15-16,27). God would **smash** these jars.

13:15-17 The word **pride** ties this section together with the two parables in verses 1-11, even though two different Hebrew words are used with the same meaning. Judah was guilty of self-exaltation, haughtiness, and high-mindedness. She would not heed God's directives.

13:16 The nation of Judah is depicted as a weary traveler on a mountain caught in the dark, stumbling about, anxious for the dawn, and accepting directions from no one, not even God. The command to **give glory to the LORD your God** occurs frequently in the OT as a call to confess one's sins (Jos 7:19; Jn 9:24). Unless Judah confessed, even darker days lay ahead.

13:18 The Lord commanded Jeremiah to address the **king** (Jehoiachin) and his **queen mother**, Queen Nehushta, who were deported to Babylon by Nebuchadnezzar in 597 B.C. (2Kg 24:8-15). Jehoiachin was only 18 years old when he ascended the throne for a short rule of three months. His mother probably exerted a lot of influence over him. Neither of them were receptive to God's call through the prophet.

13:19 Nebuchadnezzar of Babylon will strike the cities of south Judah, the **Negev** first. But eventually **all of Judah**

20 Look up and see
   those coming from the north.*a*
   Where is the flock entrusted to you,
   the sheep that were your pride?

The Destiny of Jerusalem

21 What will you say when He appoints
   close friends as leaders over you,
   ones you yourself trained?
   Won't labor pains seize you,*b*
   as they do a woman in labor?
22 And when you ask yourself,
   "Why have these things happened
      to me?"
   It is because of your great •guilt*c*
   that your skirts have been stripped off,*d*
   your body exposed.*A*
23 Can the •Cushite change his skin,
   or a leopard his spots?
   If so, you might be able to do
      what is good,*e*
   you who are instructed in evil.
24 I will scatter you*B* like drifting chaff*f*
   before the desert wind.
25 This is your lot,
   what I have decreed for you—
         this is the Lord's declaration—
   because you have forgotten Me
   and trusted in Falsehood.*C,g*
26 I will pull your skirts up over your face
   so that your shame might be seen.*h*
27 Your adulteries and
   your lustful neighing,*i*

your heinous prostitution
   on the hills, in the fields—
I have seen your detestable acts.
Woe to you, Jerusalem!
You are •unclean—
   for how long yet?*j*

The Drought

14 The word of the Lord that came to Jeremiah concerning the drought:*k*

2 Judah mourns;
   her gates languish.*l*
   Her people are on the ground
      in mourning;
   Jerusalem's cry rises up.*m*
3 Their nobles send their servants*D*
      for water.
   They go to the cisterns;
   they find no water;
   their containers return empty.
   They are ashamed and humiliated;
   they cover their heads.*n*
4 The ground is cracked
   since no rain has fallen on the land.
   The farmers are ashamed;*o*
   they cover their heads.
5 Even the doe in the field
   gives birth and abandons her fawn
   since there is no grass.
6 Wild donkeys stand
      on the barren heights*p*
   panting for air like jackals.

---

*a*13:20 Jr 1:13-15; 4:6; 10:22   *b*13:21 Is 13:8   *c*13:22 Jr 5:6; 30:15   *d*Ezk 16:37-39; Hs 2:3,10; Nah 3:5   *e*13:23 Ec 5:1; Jr 4:22; Hs 5:4   *f*13:24 Jb 13:25; Ps 83:13; Is 40:24   *g*13:25 Jr 3:23   *h*13:26 Is 47:2-3; Jr 49:10; Nah 3:5   *i*13:27 Jr 2:23-24; 5:8   *j*Hs 8:5   *k*14:1 Jr 17:8   *l*14:2 Is 3:26   *m*1Sm 5:12   *n*14:3 Est 6:12; 7:8   *o*14:4 Jl 1:11   *p*14:6 Jr 2:24

---

*A*13:22 Lit *your heels have suffered violence*   *B*13:24 Lit *them*   *C*13:25 = Baal   *D*14:3 Lit *little ones*

---

will be **taken into exile**. The words "all" and "taken completely into exile" are hyperbolic. The Babylonians did leave a remnant along with Jeremiah in the land (39:9-10).

13:20 The verbs **look up** and **see** are feminine imperatives. They are addressed to Jerusalem, who as a shepherd had abandoned her **flock** and **sheep**, misleading the people.

13:21 The Hebrew word for **leaders** (ro'sh) has a twofold sense—"head/chief" and "a poisonous plant/poison." Accordingly, Judah's self-chosen allies will become not just their chiefs but their poison as well.

13:22 In answer to Jerusalem's question about why **these things happened**, God pointed to their **great guilt**. Speaking euphemistically, God promised to expose Judah's secret parts (politely expressed as **your skirts have been stripped off**, i.e., they will be sexually attacked; see Lv 18:6-19; 20:17; Dt 22:30). **Your body exposed** is literally "your heels have suffered violence," another euphemism for sexual attack.

13:23-24 The question **Can the Cushite** (a Nubian or an Ethiopian) **change his skin, or a leopard his spots?** anticipates a negative answer. It was unlikely that Judah would change after centuries of acting in such an evil way.

13:25 **Lot** or "inheritance" is most commonly used for the portion of the land each family of Israel was to receive after the conquest of Canaan (Nm 26:55-56). But no portion was reserved for this rebellious generation. Instead God scattered them abroad in exile (Jr 13:24).

13:25 Judah had **trusted in Falsehood** or "the Lie." The article "the" goes with "Lie" (Hb *bashsheqer*). Therefore, "the Lie" is a derisive term for the pagan gods, especially Baal.

13:26 On **I will pull your skirts up over your face**, see note at verse 22. Judah's **shame** will be exposed.

13:27 This verse cites three sexual descriptions of Judah's wickedness: **adulteries . . . lustful neighing**, and **prostitution**. These refer to the people's practices out in the open as they went after sex with an animal passion in their worship of Canaanite gods.

14:1–17:27 The message in this long section was delivered during a severe drought (Hb *batstsaroth*) that hit Judah. The plural in the Hebrew may indicate the intensive nature of the drought.

14:2-6 This section is a lament with the devastation pictured as a crisis where there was **no water . . . no grass**, and **no green plants**.

14:2 **Her gates** represents the cities of Judah.

14:3-4 One indication of Judah's grief and sorrow was that the people covered their **heads** in shame (2Sm 15:30).

Their eyes fail
because there are no green plants.
7 Though our •guilt testifies against us,
•Yahweh, act for Your name's sake.
Indeed, our rebellions[a] are many;
we have sinned against You.
8 Hope of Israel,[b]
its Savior in time of distress,
why are You like a foreigner
in the land,
like a traveler stopping only
for the night?
9 Why are You like a helpless man,
like a warrior unable to save?[c]
Yet You are among us, Yahweh,[d]
and we are called by Your name.
Don't leave us!

[10]This is what the LORD says concerning these people:

Truly they love to wander;[e]
they never rest their feet.
So the LORD does not accept them.
Now He will remember their guilt
and punish their sins.[f]

False Prophets to be Punished

[11]Then the LORD said to me, "Do not pray for the well-being of these people.[g] [12]If they fast, I

will not hear their cry of despair. If they offer •burnt offering and •grain offering, I will not accept them. Rather, I will finish them off by sword, famine, and plague."[h]

[13]And I replied, "Oh no, Lord GOD! The prophets are telling them, 'You won't see sword or suffer famine. I will certainly give you true peace in this place.'"[i]

[14]But the LORD said to me, "These prophets are prophesying a lie in My name. I did not send them, nor did I command them or speak to them. They are prophesying to you a false vision, worthless •divination, the deceit[j] of their own minds.

[15]"Therefore, this is what the LORD says concerning the prophets who prophesy in My name, though I did not send them, and who say, 'There will never be sword or famine in this land.' By sword and famine these prophets will meet their end. [16]The people they are prophesying to will be thrown into the streets of Jerusalem because of the famine and the sword. There will be no one to bury them[k]—they, their wives, their sons, and their daughters. I will pour out their own evil on them."

Jeremiah's Request

[17] You are to speak this word to them:

[a]14:7 Jr 2:19; 3:6,22; 5:6
[b]14:8 Jr 17:13; 50:7
[c]14:9 Is 59:1
[d]Ex 29:45
[e]14:10 Jr 5:31; Am 8:12
[f]Hs 8:13
[g]14:11 Jr 7:16; 11:14; 15:1
[h]14:12 Jr 5:12
[i]14:13 Jr 4:10; 6:13-14; 8:10-12
[j]14:14 Ps 119:118; Jr 8:5; 23:26
[k]14:16 Jr 7:33; 9:22

14:7 Either Jeremiah, acting on behalf of the people, or the nation itself acknowledged that the drought had struck as a result of their sin. They appealed to God to **act for Your name's sake**. Since God's name expressed His character, and since His glory was known among the peoples of earth chiefly through His covenant people, the people asked God to act for the sake of His reputation and honor.

14:8 Yahweh is described in one of the prophet's favor-

ite names for the Lord: **Hope of Israel** (see 17:7,13; 50:7; Ps 71:5; Ac 28:20; Col 1:27; 1Tm 1:1). The complaint was that God seemed to show no more interest in Judah than a **foreigner** or a **traveler** who was just passing through the land.

14:9 How could God be **like a warrior unable to save?** Jeremiah knew God had the power to deliver His people if He wanted. Thus he knew the issue was not a lack of power on God's part, but a decree to punish. **We are called by Your name** means "we belong to you, Lord."

14:10 God explained His judgments on Judah. This verse reminds us of Hs 8:13; 9:9.

14:11-12 Once again the prophet was forbidden to pray for the people of Judah (see notes at 7:16 and 15:1). The Lord would not accept any of the ritual that had no meaning, including a **fast**, a **burnt offering**, or a **grain offering**. Instead, God **will finish them off by sword, famine, and plague**.

14:13-16 The false prophets are blamed for Judah's resistance to the word of God. More than any other prophet, Jeremiah dealt with false prophets (23:9-22; 28). Though they had been called to be revivalists who turned the people back to God, they instead flattered and promised peace.

14:14 This verse cites four methods the false prophets were using: (1) they were **prophesying a lie** in the Lord's name; (2) they were using **false** visions (3) and **worthless divination**; and (4) they were speaking **the deceit of their own minds**.

14:17 Judah is called **the virgin daughter of my people** because she had been guarded and protected from pagan nations and their gods.

meshuvah

Hebrew Pronunciation	[meh shu VAH]
HCSB Translation	turning away, rebellion
Uses in Jeremiah	10
Uses in the OT	13
Focus Passage	Jeremiah 14:7

Meshuvah is the most frequent of the nouns that derive from *shuv* (*turn, return*). Three nouns emphasize the idea of a *turning away* from God. *Meshuvah*, which occurs (4x) with *shuv*, suggests *apostasies* (Jr 2:19), *rebellions* (Jr 14:7), *infidelity* (Hs 14:4), or *waywardness* (Pr 1:32). It appears as *unfaithful, unfaithfulness*, or *unfaithful deeds* (Jr 3:6,22; 5:6). It involves *turning away* (Jr 8:5) or *from* (Hs 11:7). *Shovav* (4x) is being *faithless* (Jr 3:14) or *turning back* to sinful desires (Is 57:17). *Shovev* (3x) connotes *faithless* (Jr 31:22) or *pagan* (Mc 2:4). Two other nouns from *shuv* have the opposite implication. *Shuvah* is *returning* to God (Is 30:15), and *shiybah* implies *restoration* to favor (Ps 126:1). One noun from *shuv, teshuvah* (8x), is neutral. It indicates a physical *return* (1Sm 7:17), *spring* as "the *turning* of the year" (2Sm 11:1), or an *answer* (Jb 21:34).

Let my eyes overflow with tears;
day and night may they not stop,[a]
for the virgin daughter of my people
has been destroyed by a great disaster,[b]
an extremely severe wound.[c]

18 If I go out to the field,
look—those slain by the sword!
If I enter the city,
look—those ill[d] from famine!
For both prophet and priest
travel to a land they do not know.

19 Have You completely rejected Judah?
Do You detest[e] 'Zion?
Why do You strike us
with no hope of healing for us?
We hoped for peace,
but there was nothing good;
for a time of healing,
but there was only terror.[f]

20 We acknowledge our wickedness, LORD,
the guilt of our fathers;[g]
indeed, we have sinned against You.

21 Because of Your name, don't despise us.
Don't disdain Your glorious throne.[h]
Remember Your covenant[i] with us;
do not break it.

22 Can any of the worthless idols
of the nations[j] bring rain?
Or can the skies alone give showers?
Are You not the LORD our God?
We therefore put our hope in You,[k]
for You have done all these things.

The LORD's Negative Response

15 Then the LORD said to me: "Even if[l] Moses and[m] Samuel should[n] stand before

---

Me,[o] My compassions would not reach out to these people. Send them from My presence, and let them go. ²If they ask you, 'Where will we go?' you must tell them: This is what the LORD says:

Those destined for death,[p] to death;
those destined for the sword,
to the sword.
Those destined for famine, to famine;
those destined for captivity, to captivity.

³"I will ordain four kinds[A] of judgment for them"—this is the LORD's declaration—"the sword to kill, the dogs to drag away,[q] and the birds of the sky and the wild animals of the land[r] to devour and destroy. ⁴I will make them a horror to all the kingdoms of the earth because of Manasseh[s] son of Hezekiah, the king of Judah, for what he did in Jerusalem.

5 Who will have pity on you, Jerusalem?[t]
Who will show sympathy toward you?[u]
Who will turn aside
to ask about your welfare?
6 You have left Me.
This is the LORD's declaration.
You have turned your back,
so I have stretched out My hand
against you
and destroyed you.
I am tired of showing compassion.
7 I scattered them
with a winnowing fork
at the gates of the land.
I made them childless; I destroyed
My people.

---

a 14:17 Jr 9:1,10; 13:17
b Jr 4:6; 6:1
c Jr 10:19; 30:12
d 14:18 Dt 29:22
e 14:19 Lv 26:11,30,43-44
f Jr 8:15; 33:9
g 14:20 Jr 3:25; 11:10; 16:12-13
h 14:21 Jr 17:12
i Lv 26:44; Jdg 2:1; Is 33:8
j 14:22 Jr 8:19; 10:8,15; 16:19
k Is 8:17; 25:9
l 15:1 Ps 99:6; Ezk 14:14
m Ex 32:11-14; Ps 106:23
n 1Sm 7:9; 12:23
o Jr 15:19; 35:19
p 15:2 Jr 14:12; 43:11; Ezk 5:12; Zch 11:9
q 15:3 Jr 22:19; 49:20-50:45
r Is 18:6; Jr 7:33; 19:7
s 15:4 2Kg 21:1-18; 2Ch 33:1-20
t 15:5 Lm 1:1-2; Am 5:2
u Is 51:19; Nah 3:7

A 15:3 Lit families

14:18 The word **travel** means "to go about" as a herdsman, or "to travel about" as a merchant or tradesperson, or even in Syriac, "to go about as a beggar." The false prophets and priests could practice their illegitimate trade in exile, Jeremiah declared.

14:19-22 Finally, the people admitted that it was their **wickedness** that had brought this trouble, but in desperation they pleaded for God's help for three reasons: (1) Your **name**, (2) **Your glorious throne**, and (3) **Your covenant**. God's throne was Jerusalem, particularly the temple (2Kg 19:15; Ps 99:1).

14:22 Jeremiah returned to the rain theme that began in 14:3. The astral deities could not bring rain; the only hope for relief from the drought was action from the Lord.

15:1 Even if great prayer warriors such as **Moses** and **Samuel** came before Him, they could not persuade God to change His decision. The people had gone so far in sin that no prayer would help them. Moses successfully interceded for Israel numerous times (Ex 32:7-14,30-32; Nm 14:13-19; Dt 9:13-29) as did Samuel (1Sm 7:8-9; 12:17-25). But Judah was now beyond all hope.

15:3 The fourfold curses (death, sword, famine, captivity) appear frequently in Jeremiah and Ezekiel. The same afflictions appear with the four horseman of Revelation (Rv 6:1-8).

15:4 Judah would be made **a horror to all the kingdoms of the earth**, just as Moses had predicted in Dt 28:37 (Jr 24:9; 29:18; 34:17). This verse contains the only reference to King Manasseh (696–642 B.C.) in the book of Jeremiah. He is listed here as the reason for the terrible state of affairs in Judah. So far-reaching was the evil Manasseh introduced that Judah was still bound for destruction, even after the revival introduced by his grandson, King Josiah, in 621 B.C. (2Kg 23:26).

15:6 You (emphatically, "It was *you* who") **have left Me** first, declared the Lord; this is why God rejected them.

15:7 God will use a **winnowing fork** to toss the nation of Judah like grain into the wind so the chaff will be blown away. The metaphor suggests that the destruction would not be total. A remnant of faithful people would be spared.

15:7 The phrase **gates of the land** refers to the outlying towns of Judah.

They would not turn from their ways.[a]

8 I made their widows more numerous
than the sand of the seas.[b]
I brought a destroyer at noon
against the mother of young men.
I suddenly released on her
agitation and terrors.

9 The mother of seven grew faint;[c]
she breathed her last breath.
Her sun set while it was still day;
she was ashamed and humiliated.
The rest of them I will give over
to the sword
in the presence of their enemies."
     This is the Lord's declaration.

Jeremiah's Complaint

10 Woe is me, my mother,
that you gave birth to me,[d]
a man who incites dispute and conflict
in all the land.
I did not lend or borrow,
yet everyone curses me.[e]

The Lord's Response

11 The Lord said:

I will certainly set you free and care
for you.[A]
I will certainly intercede for you
in a time of trouble,
in your time of distress,
with the enemy.

12 Can anyone smash iron,
iron from the north, or bronze?

13 I will give up your wealth
and your treasures as plunder,
without cost,[f] for all your sins
in all your borders.

14 Then I will make you serve
your enemies[B]
in a land you do not know,
for My anger will kindle a fire
that will burn against you.[g]

Jeremiah's Prayer for Vengeance

15 You know,[h] Lord;
remember me and take note of me.
Avenge me against my persecutors.[i]
In Your patience,[C] don't take me away.
Know that I suffer disgrace
for Your honor.[j]

16 Your words were found,
and I ate them.[k]
Your words became a delight to me
and the joy of my heart,
for I am called by Your name,[l]
•Yahweh God of •Hosts.

17 I never sat with the band of revelers,
and I did not celebrate with them.
Because Your hand was on me,
I sat alone,[m]
for You filled me with indignation.

18 Why has my pain become unending,
my wound incurable,[n]
refusing to be healed?
You truly have become like a mirage
to me—
water that is not reliable.

Jeremiah Told to Repent

19 Therefore, this is what the Lord says:

If you return, I will restore you;
you will stand in My presence.
And if you speak noble words,
rather than worthless ones,
you will be My spokesman.[o]

a 15:7 Jr 18:11; 25:5; 35:15
b 15:8 Gn 22:17; 32:12; 41:49
c 15:9 Ru 4:15; 1Sm 2:5; Jb 42:13
d 15:10 Jb 3:1-10
e Is 53:3
f 15:13 Ps 44:12; Is 52:3
g 15:13-14 Jr 17:3-4
h 15:15 Jr 12:3
i Jr 11:20
j Ps 69:7-9
k 15:16 Ezk 3:3
l Jr 14:9
m 15:17 Ps 102:7; Lm 3:28
n 15:18 Jr 19:8; 30:12,14,17
o 15:19 Ex 4:16

A 15:11 Lit free for good   B 15:14 Some Hb mss, LXX, Syr, Tg; other Hb mss read you pass through   C 15:15 Lit In the slowness of Your anger

15:10-12 This is another "confession" of Jeremiah (see note at 4:19-22). Here he wished he had never been born. He was tempted to reject his call and mission.

15:10 The prophet felt he had incited **dispute** and **conflict**—words for legal strife and legal contention—always taking his people to court.

15:10 Jeremiah insisted he had not done any lending or borrowing, which were often associated with ill-gotten gain through charging outrageous interest (Dt 23:19).

15:12 **Anyone** may actually refer to the false prophet Hananiah. He had broken the wooden yoke around Jeremiah's neck, but he would not be able to break the yoke of iron (28:10-13). Neither would he be able to stop the **iron from the north**—Babylon.

15:15-18 This is another of Jeremiah's "confessions" (see note at 4:19-22). God's answer occurs in 15:19-21.

15:15 **Avenge me**, Jeremiah cried. He did not seek his own

retribution but left it to God. His enemies were actually opposing God, not His prophet.

15:16 Both Jeremiah and Ezekiel (Ezk 2:8–3:3) initially found God's words delightful. In the expression **Your words were found**, there may be an allusion to the discovery of the book of the law in the temple in King Josiah's time (2Kg 22:13; 23:2).

15:18 Jeremiah accused God of being **a mirage**, or "a deceitful brook"—a stream that went dry in the summer and could not be depended on to supply water. Contrast this image with 2:13, where the prophet described God as a "fountain of living water."

15:19 God startled the prophet by calling on him to **return** (Hb shuv; "turn, repent"). God wanted him to stop talking this way so He could **restore** (Hb shuv, hiphil; "cause to turn") him to **stand in** His **presence** once again. God called Jeremiah's words in verses 15-18 **worthless**. The prophet must repent if he is to continue to serve as the Lord's **spokesman**.

It is they who must return to you;
you must not return to them.
20 Then I will make you a fortified wall
of bronze
to this people.
They will fight against you
but will not overcome you,
for I am with you
to save you and deliver you.[a]
This is the LORD's declaration.
21 I will deliver you from the power
of evil people
and redeem you from the control
of the ruthless.

No Marriage for Jeremiah

16 The word of the LORD came to me: [2]"You must not marry or have sons or daughters in this place. [3]For this is what the LORD says concerning sons and daughters born in this place as well as concerning the mothers who bear them and the fathers who father them in this land: [4]They will die from deadly diseases. They will not be mourned or buried but will be like manure on the face of the earth.[b] They will be finished off by sword and famine. Their corpses will become food for the birds of the sky and for the wild animals of the land.[c]

[5]"For this is what the LORD says: Don't enter a house where a mourning feast is taking place.[A] Don't go to lament or sympathize with them, for I have removed My peace from these people"—this is the LORD's declaration—"as well as My faithful love and compassion.[d] [6]Both great and small will die in this land without burial. No lament will be made for them, nor will anyone cut himself or[e] shave his head for them.[B] [7]Food won't be provided for the mourner[f] to comfort him because of

[a]15:20 Jr 1:8,19; 30:11; 42:11
[b]16:4 Jr 8:2; 9:22; 25:33
[c]Dt 28:26; Is 18:6; Jr 7:33
[d]16:5 Ps 25:6; 40:11; 69:16
[e]16:6 Dt 14:1
[f]16:7 Dt 26:14; Ezk 24:17; Hs 9:4
[g]16:9 Jr 7:34; 25:10; 33:11
[h]16:10 Jr 5:19
[i]16:11 Dt 29:25; Jr 22:9
[j]Dt 29:26
[k]16:12 Jr 7:26
[l]16:13 Jr 15:14; 17:4; 22:26
[m]Dt 4:28; 28:36,64
[n]16:14-15 Jr 23:7-8
[o]16:15 Jr 3:18
[p]Jr 23:8
[q]16:16 Am 4:2; Hab 1:14-15

the dead. A cup of consolation won't be given him because of the loss of his father or mother. [8]You must not enter the house where feasting is taking place to sit with them to eat and drink. [9]For this is what the LORD of *Hosts, the God of Israel, says: I am about to eliminate from this place, before your very eyes and in your time, the sound of joy and gladness, the voice of the groom and the bride.[g]

Abandoning the LORD and His Law

[10]"When you tell these people all these things, they will say to you, 'Why has the LORD declared all this great disaster against us?[h] What is our *guilt? What is our sin that we have committed against the LORD our God?' [11]Then you will answer them: Because your fathers abandoned Me'[i]—this is the LORD's declaration—"and followed other gods, served them, and worshiped them.[j] Indeed, they abandoned Me and did not keep My instruction. [12]You did more evil than your fathers.[k] Look, each one of you was following the stubbornness of his evil heart, not obeying Me. [13]So I will hurl you from this land into a land that you and your fathers are not familiar with.[l] There you will worship other gods[m] both day and night, for I will not grant you grace.[C]

[14]"However, take note! The days are coming"—the LORD's declaration—"when it will no longer be said, 'As the LORD lives who brought the Israelites from the land of Egypt,'[n] [15]but rather, 'As the LORD lives who brought the Israelites from the land of the north[o] and from all the other lands where He had banished them.' For I will return them to their land that I gave to their ancestors.[p]

Punishment of Exile

[16]"I am about to send for many fishermen"[q]

[A]16:5 Lit house of mourning   [B]16:6 This custom demonstrated pagan mourning rituals.   [C]16:13 Or compassion

---

15:20-21 These words amount to a recommissioning service for Jeremiah (1:18-19). God would make him a **fortified wall of bronze** (see note at 1:17-19) in the presence of his people who had become his enemies. The three verbs of deliverance, featured also in the exodus story, emphasize several sides of God's salvation/deliverance: Hebrew *hoshia'*, to bring out from bondage into a wide place; Hebrew *hitstsil*, to snatch a person from a predator or a powerful oppressor; and Hebrew *padah*, to liberate a person by paying a ransom to set him free.

16:2 Jeremiah **must not marry**. This call to celibacy was unusual for an Israelite. Already the prophet was isolated from his own citizens (15:10) and lonely (15:17); now he must face celibacy and restrictions against going to funeral feasts (16:5) or times of festivity (v. 8). He became a social outcast.

16:4 Deadly diseases, apparently of epidemic proportions, awaited the rebellious nation of Judah.

16:5 A **mourning feast** was like a funeral wake.

16:6 According to the pagan mourning customs of that time, people **cut** themselves or shaved their heads (cp. 41:5; 47:5; 48:37; Is 15:2-3; 22:12; Ezk 7:18; Am 8:10; Mc 1:16). Since these were pagan customs, Israel was forbidden to practice them (Lv 21:5; Dt 14:1).

16:7 Neighbors apparently brought food and drink for the relatives of the deceased (**food** and **a cup of consolation**). The "bread/food of the mourners" is mentioned in Dt 26:14 and Hs 9:4, but not the "cup." In later Judaism, a special cup of wine was drunk by the chief mourner.

16:13 The Hebrew verb for **worship** is the same stem as the noun "servant" or "vassal." Worship, then, is "service." The expression **day and night** means "all the time."

16:16-17 The double imagery of God sending out **many fishermen** and **many hunters** was a frequent metaphor in Israel (Ezk 12:13; 29:4-5; Am 4:2; 9:1-4; Hab 1:14-17).

—this is the Lᴏʀᴅ's declaration—"and they will fish for them. Then I will send for many hunters, and they will hunt them down on every mountain and hill and out of the clefts of the rocks, [17]for My gaze takes in all their ways.[a] They are not concealed from Me, and their guilt is not hidden from My sight. [18]I will first repay them double for their guilt[b] and sin because they have polluted My land. They have filled My inheritance with the lifelessness of their detestable and abhorrent idols."

[19] Lᴏʀᴅ, my strength and my stronghold,
　my refuge in a time of distress,[c]
　the nations will come to You
　from the ends of the earth,
　　and they will say,
　"Our fathers inherited only lies,
　worthless idols[d] of no benefit at all."
[20] Can one make gods for himself?
　But they are not gods.[e]
[21] "Therefore, I am about to inform them,
　and this time I will make them know
　My power and My might;
　then they will know that My name
　　is ˙Yahweh."[f]

The Persistent Sin of Judah

17 The sin of Judah is written
　　with an iron stylus.[g]
　With a diamond point
　it is engraved on the tablet
　　of their hearts[h]
　and on the horns of their[A] altars,

[2] while their children remember
　their altars
　and their ˙Asherah poles,
　by the green trees
　on the high hills—
[3] My mountains in the countryside.
　I will give up your wealth
　and all your treasures as plunder
　because of the sin of your ˙high places[B]
　in all your borders.[i]
[4] You will, on your own, relinquish
　　your inheritance
　that I gave you.
　I will make you serve your enemies
　in a land you do not know,[j]
　for you have set My anger on fire;[k]
　it will burn forever.

Curse and Blessing

[5]This is what the Lᴏʀᴅ says:

　The man who trusts in mankind,[l]
　who makes human flesh his strength[m]
　and turns his heart from the Lᴏʀᴅ
　　is cursed.
[6] He will be like a juniper
　　in the ˙Arabah;[n]
　he cannot see when good comes
　but dwells in the parched places
　　in the wilderness,
　in a salt land where no one lives.[o]
[7] The man who trusts in the Lᴏʀᴅ,
　whose confidence indeed is the Lᴏʀᴅ, is
　　blessed.[p]
[8] He will be like a tree planted by water:[q]

[a]16:17 Jr 32:19; 2Ch 16:9; Jb 34:21; Ps 90:8; Pr 5:21
[b]16:18 Jr 17:18
[c]16:19 Ps 37:39; Nah 1:7
[d]Jr 8:19; 10:8,15; 14:22
[e]16:20 Jr 2:11
[f]16:21 Jr 33:2
[g]17:1 Jb 19:24
[h]Pr 3:3; 7:3; Jr 31:33-34
[i]17:3 Jr 15:13
[j]17:4 Jr 16:13; 22:28; Ezk 32:9
[k]Dt 32:22; Jr 15:14
[l]17:5 Ps 146:3
[m]2Ch 32:8
[n]17:6 Jr 48:6
[o]Gn 19:24-26; Ps 107:34
[p]17:7 Ps 40:4
[q]17:8 Ps 1:3; Ezk 17:5-8

[A]17:1 Some Hb mss, Syr, Vg; other Hb mss read *your*　　[B]17:3 Lit *plunder, your high places because of sin*

16:18 The Hebrew word *mishneh* usually means "twofold" or **double** (cp. Is 40:2), but tablets from Alalakh contain a similar word meaning "equivalent." If "double" is the correct translation, it means "ample, full, or complete" punishment. If "equivalent" is the correct rendering, the sentence means God would repay them the equivalent of their sinful iniquity. In either case, the Israelites reaped what they sowed.

17:1-27 There is no central theme in this chapter. It is a collection of wise sayings on how life should be lived.

17:1 The **iron stylus with a diamond point** (cp. Jb 19:24) was an iron engraver's tool that chiseled the sin of Judah onto their hard **hearts** and the **horns of their altars**. These horns were the projections at the four stone corners on top of the altar (Ex 27:2; 29:12; 30:1-3,10; Lv 4:7). Archaeologists have found such altars at Arad and Tel Sheba. The **tablet** of Judah's heart listed her sins, a far contrast to what would happen when God placed His law on hearts in the new covenant (31:33).

17:2 Asherah poles were upright carved wooden objects representing the fertility mother goddess of the Canaanites (2Kg 13:6; 17:16; 18:4; 21:3; 23:6,15).

17:3 High places were elevated platforms on top of a mountain or hill. An altar to a pagan god and a carved pole for the

fertility goddess Asherah were located on these sites (2Kg 21:3; 2Ch 14:3). They also featured a stone pillar symbolizing the male deity (2Kg 3:2), along with other deities and perhaps a shelter (1Kg 12:31; 16:32-33).

17:4 Just as Jeremiah predicted a 70-year captivity in 25:11 and 29:10, so his statement **relinquish your inheritance** in this verse may hint of that impending judgment. The Hebrew word for "relinquish" (*shamat*; "lose") is used in connection with the sabbatical year. Later, Jeremiah explained that Judah's exile would last 70 years to make up for the seven sabbatical years she had failed to observe.

17:5-13 The poem in these verses has close parallels with Ps 1 and the wisdom literature of Job, Proverbs, and Ecclesiastes. It focuses on two ways of death and two ways of life.

17:5-6 In these verses there is a play on the words for **man . . . mankind** and **flesh**. In Hebrew, the first word is *gever*, meaning "strong one," man as male. The second is *'adam*, "man made of dust." The third is *basar*, "flesh." Put together, these indicate a poor substitute for trusting in the Lord. The people's misplaced trust is like **a juniper in the Arabah**, a bush that shriveled in the scorching heat. The Arabah, part of the Great Rift Valley that stretches from the south end of the Dead Sea to the Gulf of Aqabah, is desertlike.

it sends its roots out toward a stream,
it doesn't fear when heat comes,
and its foliage remains green.
It will not worry in a year of drought
or cease producing fruit.

The Deceitful Heart

9 The heart is more deceitful
than anything else,
and incurable—
who can understand it?[a]
10 I, •Yahweh, examine the mind,
I test the heart[A,b]
to give to each according to his way,
according to what
his actions deserve.[c]
11 He who makes a fortune unjustly
is like a partridge that hatches eggs
it didn't lay.
In the middle of his days
his riches will abandon him,
so in the end he will be a fool.[d]
12 A throne of glory[e]
on high[f] from the beginning
is the place of our sanctuary.[g]
13 LORD, the hope of Israel,[h]
all who abandon You
will be put to shame.
All who turn away from Me
will be written in the dirt,
for they have abandoned
the LORD, the fountain
of living water.[i]

Jeremiah's Plea

14 Heal me, LORD, and I will be healed;
save me, and I will be saved,
for You are my praise.[j]
15 Hear how they keep challenging me,[k]
"Where is the word of the LORD?
Let it come!"

16 But I have not run away from being
Your shepherd,
and I have not longed for the fatal day.
You know my words were spoken
in Your presence.
17 Don't become a terror to me.
You are my refuge[l] in the day
of disaster.
18 Let my persecutors be put to shame,[m]
but don't let me be put to shame.
Let them be terrified, but don't let me
be terrified.
Bring on them the day of disaster;[n]
shatter them with total[B] destruction.

Observing the Sabbath

19 This is what the LORD said to me, "Go and
stand at the People's Gate, through which the
kings of Judah enter and leave, as well as at all
the gates of Jerusalem. 20 Announce to them:
Hear the word of the LORD, kings of Judah, all
Judah, and all the residents of Jerusalem who
enter through these gates. 21 This is what the
LORD says: Watch yourselves; do not pick up a
load and bring it in through the gates of Jerusalem on the Sabbath day.[o] 22 You must not
carry a load out of your houses on the Sabbath
day or do any work,[p] but you must consecrate
the Sabbath day, just as I commanded your
ancestors.[q] 23 They wouldn't listen or pay attention but became obstinate,[r] not listening
or accepting discipline.

24 "However, if you listen to Me, says the
LORD, and do not bring loads through the
gates of this city on the Sabbath day and consecrate the Sabbath day and do no work on
it, 25 kings and princes will enter through the
gates of this city. They will sit on the throne of
David, riding in chariots and on horses[s] with
their officials, the men of Judah, and the residents of Jerusalem. This city will be inhabited

---

[a]17:9 Jr 15:18; Mc 1:9
[b]17:10 Dt 8:2; Ps 17:3; 26:2
[c]Jr 32:19; Rm 2:6
[d]17:11 Lk 12:20
[e]17:12 Is 6:1-3; Jr 14:21; Ezk 1:26-28
[f]Ps 102:19; Jr 25:30
[g]Ps 68:33-35; Is 60:13
[h]17:13 Jr 14:8; 50:7
[i]Jr 2:13
[j]17:14 Ps 22:25; 71:6; 109:1
[k]17:15 Is 5:19; 2Pt 3:4
[l]17:17 Ps 46:1; 61:3; 62:7-8
[m]17:18 Ps 35:4
[n]Ps 35:8
[o]17:21 Neh 13:15-21; Jn 5:9-12
[p]17:22 Ex 20:8-10; Dt 5:12-14; Is 56:2-6
[q]Ezk 20:12
[r]17:23 Jr 7:26
[s]17:25 Jr 22:4

A17:10 Lit kidneys   B17:18 Lit double

17:9-11 These verses contain three wisdom sayings: (1)
The heart is more deceitful than anything and is **incurable** (lit "perverse" or "beyond cure"; 13:23). (2) **I, Yahweh,
examine the mind** (Hb "heart"), **I test the heart** (lit "kidneys"). The "mind" and the "heart" are hidden elements of
a human personality, but God sees them perfectly. (3) The
partridge (perhaps a sand grouse) **hatches eggs it didn't
lay.** Some people amass wealth via the sweat of others, but
like these birds, they will discover that their wealth does
not last forever (Pr 23:4-5).

17:12 The phrase **a throne of glory** refers to the temple
where the Lord dwelled, and thus to His rule (Lm 5:19).

17:13 On **LORD, the hope of Israel,** see note at 14:8. Judah
had turned her back on her hope and had **abandoned the
LORD, the fountain of living water** (see note at 2:13).

17:14 The Lord is described as Jeremiah's **praise** or hope.
He trusted the Lord to heal and save him.

17:16 Jeremiah took no delight in announcing God's coming
judgment, nor did he shrink away from the unpleasant task.

17:17 Jeremiah feared God might desert him and leave him
alone before his enemies.

17:19 The **People's Gate** was not the gate of the temple. The
gate Jeremiah referred to is unknown, but it was apparently
a place where people commonly gathered.

17:22-27 The **Sabbath day**, mentioned several times in these
verses, testifies to the fact that God was the Creator of the
seventh day and that He had a covenant with Israel. If the
Sabbath law was observed, the Davidic line of kings would
continue to sit on the throne and Jerusalem would continue
to be the center of worship.

forever. 26 Then people will come from the cities of Judah and from the area around Jerusalem, from the land of Benjamin and from
the Judean foothills, from the hill country and
from the •Negev[a] bringing •burnt offerings
and sacrifice, •grain offerings and frankincense, and thank offerings to the house of the
LORD. 27 If you do not listen to Me to consecrate
the Sabbath day by not carrying a load while
entering the gates of Jerusalem on the Sabbath day, I will set fire to its gates,[b] and it will
consume the citadels[c] of Jerusalem[d] and not
be extinguished."[e]

Parable of the Potter

18 This is the word that came to Jeremiah from the LORD: 2 "Go down at once
to the potter's house;[f] there I will reveal My
words to you." 3 So I went down to the potter's
house, and there he was, working away at the
wheel.[A] 4 But the jar that he was making from
the clay became flawed in the potter's hand, so
he made it into another jar, as it seemed right
for him to do.[g]
5 The word of the LORD came to me: 6 "House
of Israel, can I not treat you as this potter
treats his clay?"—this is the LORD's declaration. "Just like clay in the potter's hand, so are
you in My hand, house of Israel.[h] 7 At one moment I might announce concerning a nation
or a kingdom that I will uproot, tear down,
and destroy it.[i] 8 However, if that nation I have
made an announcement about turns from its
evil, I will relent concerning the disaster I had
planned to do to it.[j] 9 At another time I announce that I will build and plant a nation or
a kingdom.[k] 10 However, if it does what is evil
in My sight by not listening to My voice, I will
relent concerning the good I had said I would
do to it.[l] 11 So now, say to the men of Judah and
to the residents of Jerusalem: This is what the
LORD says: I am about to bring harm to you and
make plans against you. Turn now, each from
your evil way, and correct your ways and your
deeds.[m] 12 But they will say, 'It's hopeless.[n] We
will continue to follow our plans, and each of
us will continue to act according to the stubbornness of his evil heart.'"

Deluded Israel

13 Therefore, this is what the LORD says:

Ask among the nations,
Who has heard things like these?
Virgin Israel has done
a most terrible thing.[o]
14 Does the snow of Lebanon ever leave
the highland crags?
Or does cold water flowing
from a distance ever fail?
15 Yet My people have forgotten Me.[p]
They burn incense to false idols
that make them stumble in their ways
on the ancient roads[q]

[a]17:26 Jr 32:44; 33:13 [b]17:27 Lm 4:11 [c]Jr 49:27; Am 1:14 [d]2Kg 25:9 [e]Jr 7:20 [f]18:2 Jr 19:1-2 [g]18:4 Rm 9:21 [h]18:6 Gn 2:7-8; Is 43:1; 64:8 [i]18:7 Jr 1:10; 24:6; 31:28 [j]18:8 2Sm 24:1; Jr 42:10; Jnh 3:10 [k]18:9 Jr 1:10 [l]18:10 Ezk 18:25-29; 33:12-13 [m]18:11 Jr 7:3 [n]18:12 Jr 2:25 [o]18:13 Jr 5:30; Hs 6:10 [p]18:15 Jr 2:32; 3:21; 13:25 [q]Jr 6:16

[A]18:3 Lit *pair of stones*

17:26 The **land of Benjamin** was north of Judah; the **Judean foothills** were the western lowlands, west and southwest of Judah; the **hill country** was the central part of the country; and the **Negev** was the dry, arid land south of Judah. **Frankincense** was not the incense offering, but the incense that was added *to* the offerings (Ex 30:7-9). **Thank offerings** were a type of peace or fellowship offering (Lv 7:11).

18:2 Like the episode with the underwear (see note at 13:3-5), the trip to the **potter's house** provided Jeremiah with a symbolic action message. Pottery making was very common in the ancient Near East. Potters commonly used a wheel, turned by foot, as they shaped a lump of clay with their hands. The vessel was then fired in a kiln to make it hard.

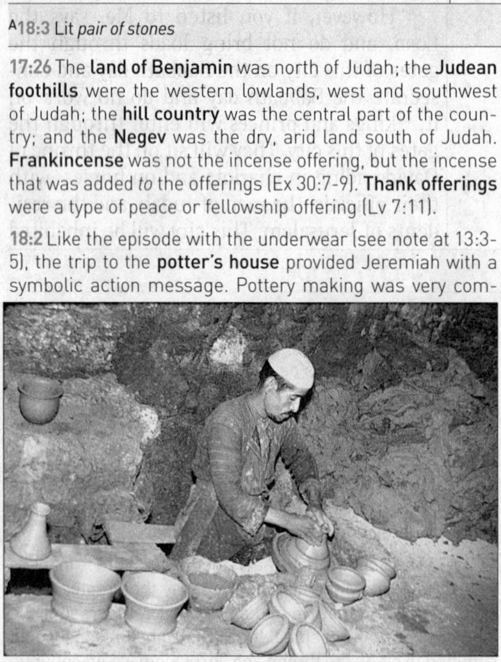

A Middle Eastern potter (18:1-6) fashioning pottery in the same manner as in Jeremiah's time.

18:4 The **jar** the potter was working on was **flawed**, but how or why this happened is not stated.

18:5-6 The Lord was the **potter**, and Israel (later the nations as well) were the **clay**.

18:7-10 The lesson of the potter illustrates God's grace for all who will repent and turn back to Him. Both alternatives are given: God threatened to **uproot, tear down, and destroy** Judah, but He promised to **build and plant** others (cp. 1:10). God never changes His character, nature, or being (Nm 23:19), but He changes in His actions toward humans when they change their response to Him.

18:11 The Lord used the same word for **about to bring harm to you** that He had used for "potter," or "One forming [harm] against you." The word choice was deliberate so Judah would grasp the connection.

18:13 God called on the nations to verify that Judah had done a **most terrible** thing by defecting from Him. On **virgin Israel**, see note at 14:17.

18:14 Nature is a lot more dependable and constant than Judah had been.

18:16 Judah had become a land of **horror** and an **object of scorn**, or of "hissing" or "whistling." This was the ultimate

and walk on new paths,
    not the highway.
¹⁶ They have made their land a horror,^a
    a perpetual object of scorn;^{A,b}
    everyone who passes by it
      will be horrified^c
    and shake his head.^d
¹⁷ I will scatter them before the enemy
    like the east wind.^e
    I will show them^B My back and not
      My face
    on the day of their calamity.

Plot against Jeremiah

¹⁸ Then certain ones said, "Come, let's make plans against Jeremiah,^f for instruction will never be lost from the priest,^g or counsel from the wise, or an *oracle from the prophet.^h Come, let's denounce him^C and pay no attention to all his words."

¹⁹ Pay attention to me, LORD.
    Hear what my opponents are saying!ⁱ
²⁰ Should good be repaid with evil?
    Yet they have dug a pit for me.^j
    Remember how I stood before You
    to speak good on their behalf,
    to turn Your anger from them.
²¹ Therefore, hand their children
      over to famine,^k
    and pour the sword's power on them.
    Let their wives become childless
      and widowed,
    their husbands slain by deadly disease,^D
    their young men struck down
      by the sword in battle.
²² Let a cry be heard from their houses

when You suddenly bring raiders
      against them,
    for they have dug a pit to capture me
    and have hidden snares for my feet.^l
²³ But You, LORD, know
    all their deadly plots against me.
    Do not wipe out their *guilt;^m
    do not blot out their sin before You.
    Let them be forced to stumble
      before You;
    deal with them in the time
      of Your anger.

The Clay Jar

19 This is what the LORD says: "Go, buy a potter's clayⁿ jar. Take^E some of the elders of the people and some of the leading priests^o ² and go out to the Valley of Hinnom^p near the entrance of the Potsherd Gate. Proclaim there the words I speak to you. ³ Say: Hear the word of the LORD, kings of Judah and residents of Jerusalem.^q This is what the LORD of *Hosts, the God of Israel, says: I am going to bring such disaster on this place that everyone who hears about it will shudder^{F,r} ⁴ because they have abandoned Me and made this a foreign place. They have burned incense in it to other gods that they, their fathers, and the kings of Judah have never known. They have filled this place with the blood of the innocent.^s ⁵ They have built *high places to *Baal on which to burn their children in the fire as burnt offerings to Baal, something I have never commanded or mentioned; I never entertained the thought.^{G,t}

⁶ "Therefore, take note! The days are coming"—this is the LORD's declaration—"when

---

^a18:16 Jr 25:9; 50:13
^bLm 2:15
^cJr 19:8; 49:17
^dPs 22:7
^e18:17 Jr 13:24
^f18:18 Jr 11:19
^gJr 2:8
^hJr 5:13
ⁱ18:19 Ps 55:2-3; 142:6
^j18:20 Ps 35:7; 57:6
^k18:21 Ps 109:9-20
^l18:22 Ps 140:5; 142:3
^m18:23 Neh 4:5
ⁿ19:1 Jr 18:2
^o2Kg 19:2
^p19:2 2Kg 23:10; 2Ch 28:3; Jr 7:31-32
^q19:3 Jr 17:20
^r1Sm 3:11
^s19:4 2Kg 21:6,16; Jr 2:34
^t19:5 Jr 7:31; 32:35

---

^A18:16 Lit *hissing*   ^B18:17 LXX, Lat, Syr, Tg; MT reads *will look at them*   ^C18:18 Lit *let's strike him with the tongue*   ^D18:21 Lit *by death*   ^E19:1 Syr, Tg; MT omits *Take*   ^F19:3 Lit *shudder their ears*; 1Sm 3:11; 2Kg 21:12   ^G19:5 Lit *mentioned, and it did not arise on My heart*

---

expression in the Near Eastern "loss of face." People would make a hissing sound at a guilty person and shake their heads in scorn and disbelief.

18:17 The **east wind** was the hot wind or sirocco from the desert (4:11; 13:24; Hs 13:15), the same direction from which Babylon would come. Instead of the Aaronic benediction of Nm 6:24-26 with the Lord smiling on Judah, He had turned His back—a universal symbol of rejection (Hs 5:15).

18:18 The people foolishly believed that divine revelations would continue and life would go on as usual despite Jeremiah's gloomy predictions.

18:19-23 This is another of Jeremiah's "confessions" (see note at 4:19-22). His accusers said, "Come, let's denounce him" (18:18), or literally, "Let us smite him with the tongue." Jeremiah charged his opponents with the following: (1) paying "no attention to all his words" (v. 18), (2) digging **a pit** for him (vv. 20,22), (3) hiding **snares** for his **feet** (v. 22), and (4) planning to kill him (v. 23).

19:1 The Lord told Jeremiah to buy a **potter's clay jar** as his next symbolic action. This was probably a narrow-necked

water jar (Hb *baqbuq*). In verse 7, "I will spoil" (Hb *baqqotih*; "to empty out, cancel, spoil") is a wordplay on "jar."

19:2 Along with some elders, Jeremiah was told to go to the **Valley of Hinnom** (later Gehenna; see note at 7:31) **near the entrance of the Potsherd Gate**. This gate, south of the Jerusalem wall, was the gate through which broken pottery and other trash were transported to the city dump. The Valley of Hinnom is the modern Wadi er-Rababi. It runs along the western side of Jerusalem toward the south where it joins the Wadi Kidron on the southeastern corner of the city.

19:3 The ears of those who heard about the coming destruction **will shudder** or "tingle" (1Sm 3:11; 2Kg 21:12).

19:4 The **blood of the innocent** refers to the practice of offering children as burnt offerings to Baal or Molech (see note at 7:31). Human sacrifice is well attested in Canaan and Phoenicia, especially during the days of kings Ahaz (2Kg 16:3) and Manasseh (2Kg 21:6).

19:6-7 Though the **plans of Judah and Jerusalem** included expectation of God's ongoing favor, in reality the covenant

this place will no longer be called Topheth and the Valley of Hinnom, but the Valley of Slaughter.[a] [7]I will spoil the plans of Judah and Jerusalem in this place. I will make them fall by the sword before their enemies, by the hand of those who want to take their life. I will provide their corpses as food for the birds of the sky and for the wild animals of the land.[b] [8]I will make this city desolate, an object of scorn. Everyone who passes by it will be horrified and scoff because of all its wounds.[c] [9]I will make them eat the flesh of their sons and their daughters, and they will eat each other's flesh in the siege and distress that their enemies, those who want to take their life, inflict on them.[d]

[10]"Then you are to shatter the jar in the presence of the people traveling with you, [11]and you are to proclaim to them: This is what the LORD of Hosts says: I will shatter these people and this city, like one shatters a potter's jar that can never again be mended. They will bury the dead in Topheth because there is no other place for burials.[e] [12]I will do so to this place"—this is the declaration of the LORD—"and to its residents, making this city like Topheth. [13]The houses of Jerusalem and the houses of the kings of Judah will become impure like that place Topheth—all the houses on whose rooftops they have burned incense to the whole heavenly host[f] and poured out ·drink offerings to other gods."

[14]Jeremiah came back from Topheth, where the LORD had sent him to prophesy, stood in the courtyard of the LORD's temple,[g] and proclaimed to all the people, [15]"This is what the LORD of Hosts, the God of Israel, says: 'I am about to bring on this city—and on all its dependent villages—all the disaster that I spoke against it, for they have become obstinate, not obeying My words.'"[h]

Jeremiah Beaten by Pashhur

20 Pashhur the priest, the son of Immer[i] and chief official in the temple of the LORD, heard Jeremiah prophesying these things. [2]So Pashhur had Jeremiah the prophet beaten and put him in the stocks at the Upper Benjamin Gate in the LORD's temple. [3]The next day, when Pashhur released Jeremiah from the stocks, Jeremiah said to him, "The LORD does not call you Pashhur, but Magor-missabib,[A] [4]for this is what the LORD says, 'I am about to make you a terror to both yourself and those you love.[j] They will fall by the sword of their enemies before your very eyes. I will hand Judah over to the king of Babylon, and he will deport them to Babylon and put them to the sword. [5]I will give away all the wealth of this city, all its products[k] and valuables. Indeed, I will hand all the treasures of the kings of Judah over to their enemies. They will plunder them, seize them, and carry them off to Babylon. [6]As for you, Pashhur, and all who live in your house, you will go into captivity. You will go to Babylon. There you will die, and there you will be buried, you and all your friends that you prophesied falsely[l] to.'"

Cross-references

[a]19:6 Jr 7:32
[b]19:7 Dt 28:26; Jr 7:33; 15:3
[c]19:8 Jr 18:16; Mc 1:9; Nah 3:19
[d]19:9 Dt 28:53-57; Ezk 5:10; Lm 4:10
[e]19:11 Jr 7:32
[f]19:13 Dt 4:19; 2Kg 17:16; 23:4-5
[g]19 14 2Ch 20:5; Jr 26:2
[h]19:15 Jr 7:26
[i]20:1 1Ch 24:14; Ezr 2:37-38
[j]20:4 Jr 6:25
[k]20:5 Dt 28:33; Ezk 23:29
[l]20:6 Jr 14:14

[A]20:3 = Terror Is on Every Side; Jr 6:25; 20:10; 46:5

---

curses would be enacted (Dt 28:15ff). **Topheth** (see note at 7:31) and the **Valley of Hinnom** would then be called **Valley of Slaughter** to reflect God's judgment. The corpses of Judah's dead would remain unburied, a sign of judgment as **birds of the sky** and **wild animals** fed on their remains (7:33; 16:4; 34:20; Dt 28:26).

19:9 So severe would be the conditions of the siege that Judah's survivors would **eat the flesh of their sons** and **daughters**. This cannibalism is attested in the siege of Samaria (2Kg 6:26-29) and in the Babylonian siege in 587 B.C. (Lm 2:20; 4:10). According to Josephus in *Wars of the Jews*, this also happened in A.D. 70 when Jerusalem fell to the Romans.

19:10-11 As the prophet shattered the clay jar, he announced that God would **shatter these people and this city** as well. This was a symbolic act of warning to Judah. So many corpses would be gathered that there would be no place left to bury the dead but **Topheth**.

19:13 The city will become **impure** (ritually unclean) and a place where the Lord will no longer stay, **like that place Topheth** (see note at 7:31).

19:15 Judgment will fall on **this city** (Jerusalem) and **its dependent villages**, meaning the rest of Judah's cities.

20:1 Ironically, **Pashhur**, the **chief official** or "overseer" of **the temple of the LORD**, came against Jeremiah, the true prophet whom God had set "over nations and kingdoms" as an overseer (1:10). This Pashhur is probably the same as the father of Gedaliah (38:1), but not the same as another official named Pashhur in 21:1; 38:1. Jeremiah predicted Pashhur would go into exile in Babylon (20:6).

20:2 Pashhur ordered that Jeremiah be **beaten**. This was the first act of violence against the prophet. The **Upper Benjamin Gate** (built by King Jotham; 2Kg 15:35) was the northern gate of the upper temple court and the most prominent gate in the city.

20:3 By God's commission, Jeremiah changed Pashhur's name to **Magor-missabib**, meaning "terror all around." This name appears five times in Jeremiah (v. 10; 6:25; 46:5; 49:29) and in Lm 2:22. Elsewhere the term is found only in Ps 31:13 and Is 31:9.

20:4 This is the first time the **king of Babylon** is mentioned in the book of Jeremiah. His inclusion here prompts some scholars to date this prophecy after the battle of Carchemish in 605 B.C. This was roughly the halfway mark of Jeremiah's 40-year ministry.

20:6 Even though **Pashhur** was a priest, he had apparently prophesied falsely along with his **friends**. For this sin he would face captivity and death in a foreign land.

Jeremiah Compelled to Preach

7 You deceived me, LORD,
    and I was deceived.
You seized me and prevailed.
I am a laughingstock all the time;*a*
    everyone ridicules me.
8 For whenever I speak, I cry out,
I proclaim, "Violence and destruction!"*b*
because the word of the LORD
    has become for me
constant disgrace and derision.
9 If I say, "I won't mention Him
or speak any longer in His name,"
His message becomes a fire burning
    in my heart,*c*
shut up in my bones.
I become tired of holding it in,
    and I cannot prevail.
10 For I have heard the gossip
    of many people,
"Terror is on every side!*A,d*
Report him; let's report him!"
Everyone I trusted*B* watches
    for my fall.*e*
"Perhaps he will be deceived
so that we might prevail against him
and take our vengeance on him."
11 But the LORD is with me
    like a violent warrior.*f*
Therefore, my persecutors will stumble
    and not prevail.
Since they have not succeeded,
    they will be utterly shamed,
an everlasting humiliation that will
    never be forgotten.

a 20:7 Lm 3:14
b 20:8 Jr 6:7
c 20:9 Jb 32:18-20; Ps 39:3
d 20:10 Jr 6:25; 46:5
e Ps 35:15; 41:9; 56:6
f 20:11 Ex 15:3
g 20:12 Jr 11:20
h 20:14 Jb 3:3
i 20:16 Gn 19:25
j Jr 18:22
k 20:17 Jb 3:10-11
l 20:18 Jb 3:20; Lm 3:1

12 LORD of •Hosts, testing the righteous
and seeing the heart*c* and mind,
let me see Your vengeance on them,
for I have presented my case to You.*g*
13 Sing to the LORD!
Praise the LORD,
for He rescues the life of the needy
from the hand of evil people.

Jeremiah's Lament

14 May the day I was born
    be cursed.*h*
May the day my mother bore me
    never be blessed.
15 May the man be cursed
who brought the news
    to my father, saying,
"A male child is born to you,"
bringing him great joy.
16 Let that man be like the cities
the LORD demolished
    without compassion.*i*
Let him hear an outcry in the morning*j*
and a war cry at noontime
17 because he didn't kill me in the womb*k*
so that my mother might have been
    my grave,
her womb eternally pregnant.
18 Why did I come out of the womb
to see only struggle and sorrow,*l*
to end my life in shame?

Zedekiah's Request Denied

21 This is the word that came to Jeremiah from the LORD when King Zedekiah

---

A 20:10 Hb *Magor-missabib*; Jr 20:3   *B* 20:10 Lit *Every man of my peace*   *C* 20:12 Lit *kidneys*

20:7-18 This is the last of Jeremiah's "confessions" (see note at 4:19-22). As his saddest and most bitter complaint, it is one of his most revealing self-disclosures.

20:7 Jeremiah cried, **You deceived me, LORD**. So bold, offensive, and verging on blasphemous were these words that many have tried to soften them by translating them as "enticed," or "persuaded." Jeremiah did not accuse God of lying. But the Hebrew verb *pathah* means "to seduce" as a virgin is seduced (Ex 22:16). Thus, he thought God had "twisted his arm" in calling him to prophetic ministry. Jeremiah's audiences made him a **laughingstock**.

20:8 People characterized the prophet's message as "doom and gloom," or in his words **violence and destruction** (see note at 6:7).

20:9 Whenever Jeremiah decided to quit and no longer speak in God's name, the divine message became **a fire burning** in his **heart, shut up** in his **bones**. Thus he felt compelled to speak, no matter how unpopular his message.

20:10 A gossip campaign began to build against Jeremiah as they nicknamed him Mr. **Terror . . . on every side**.

20:11 Jeremiah believed that God would turn the tables on his persecutors. God had promised him that He would

be with him **like a violent warrior** or "a mighty champion" (1:8,18; 15:20-24).

20:12 This verse is virtually the same as 11:20, bracketing the first and the last of the prophet's "confessions."

20:13 Some question the genuineness of this verse because they find it hard to imagine Jeremiah singing for joy in these circumstances. But his heart understandably fluctuated with conflicting emotions. His task was hard and doom surrounded him, yet God was with him.

20:14-15 Whereas a messenger who brought **news** of a birth was usually rewarded in that culture, Jeremiah said the man who announced his birth should have been **cursed**. Notice that Jeremiah did not curse his parents for bringing him into the world. Cursing one's parents was forbidden (Ex 21:17).

20:16 Jeremiah wished the messenger's demise would be like that of **the cities the LORD demolished**. Those cities, Sodom and Gomorrah (Gn 19:24-25), were examples of God's sudden destruction.

20:18 Because of all the criticism Jeremiah had to take, he struggled inwardly. But he never wavered in fulfilling his mission.

21:1-14 This chapter contains three messages that God

sent Pashhur[a] son of Malchijah and the priest Zephaniah[b] son of Maaseiah to Jeremiah, asking, [2]"Ask the LORD on our behalf, since Nebuchadnezzar[A,c] king of Babylon is making war against us. Perhaps the LORD will perform for us something like all His past wonderful works so that Nebuchadnezzar will withdraw from us."

[3]But Jeremiah answered, "This is what you are to say to Zedekiah: [4]'This is what the LORD, the God of Israel, says: I will repel the weapons of war in your hands,[d] those you are using to fight the king of Babylon and the Chaldeans[B] who are besieging you outside the wall, and I will bring them into the center of this city.[e] [5]I will fight against you[f] with an outstretched hand and a mighty arm,[g] with anger, rage, and great wrath. [6]I will strike the residents of this city, both man and beast. They will die in a great plague. [7]Afterward'"—this is the LORD's declaration—"'King Zedekiah of Judah, his officers, and the people—those in this city who survive the plague, the sword, and the famine—I will hand over to King Nebuchad-

nezzar of Babylon,[h] to their enemies, yes, to those who want to take their lives. He will put them to the sword; he won't spare them or show pity or compassion.'[i]

A Warning for the People

[8]"But you must say to this people, 'This is what the LORD says: Look, I am presenting to you the way of life and the way of death.[j] [9]Whoever stays in this city will die by the sword, famine, and plague, but whoever goes out and surrenders to the Chaldeans who are besieging you will live and will retain his life like the spoils of war.[k] [10]For I have turned[c] against this city to bring disaster[l] and not good'"—this is the LORD's declaration. "'It will be handed over to the king of Babylon, who will burn it down.'[m]

[11]"And to the house of the king of Judah say this: 'Hear the word of the LORD! [12]House of David, this is what the LORD says:

Administer justice every morning,
and rescue the victim of robbery
from the hand of his oppressor,[n]

Cross references

[a]21:1 1Ch 9:12; Neh 11:12; Jr 38:1
[b]Jr 29:24-29; 37:3; 52:24-27
[c]21:2 2Kg 24:11; 25:22; 2Ch 36:6-13
[d]21:4 Jr 32:5; 37:8-10
[e]Is 13:4
[f]21:5 1Sm 4:1-5:12; Lm 2:5
[g]Dt 5:15; 26:8; Ps 136:12
[h]21:7 Jr 37:17; 39:5-9; 52:9
[i]2Ch 36:17
[j]21:8 Dt 30:15-19; Pr 12:28; Jr 8:3
[k]21:9 Jr 38:2; 39:18; 45:5
[l]21:10 Jr 44:11
[m]Jr 34:2,22; 37:8; 38:18
[n]21:12 Dt 28:29; Ec 4:1; Jr 22:3

[A]21:2 Lit Nebuchadrezzar   [B]21:4 = Babylonians   [C]21:10 Lit set My face

---

revealed to Jeremiah: (1) a message to King Zedekiah of Judah, (2) a message to the people of Jerusalem, and (3) a message to **the house of the king of Judah**.

21:1 This **Pashhur** is not the same person as the Pashhur in 20:1. **Zephaniah** was the successor of Jehoiada the priest (29:25-26; 37:3; 52:24) and second in rank behind the high priest.

21:2 King Zedekiah of Judah depended on Pharaoh Hophra of Egypt to take care of Nebuchadnezzar, king of Babylon. Zedekiah sent Pashhur to Jeremiah to foretell what the outcome of his foolish rebellion against Babylon would be. He was hopeful that the Lord would perform **wonderful works**

dever

Hebrew Pronunciation	[DEH ver]
HCSB Translation	plague, pestilence
Uses in Jeremiah	17
Uses in Prophetic Writings	31
Uses in the OT	48
Focus Passage	Jeremiah 21:6-7,9

Dever is plague (Ex 5:3) or pestilence (Lv 26:25) that strikes animals, people, or both (Ex 9:3,15; Jr 21:6). Some suppose it was specifically bubonic plague and see the Philistines' outbreak of tumors in the presence of mice as evidence (1Sm 5:9; 6:4). Yet debate exists whether bubonic plague struck the Near East so early. Dever most often pertains to Israel, whom God threatened to inflict with a curse for disobedience (Lv 26:25). But it was the subject of prophecies about many lands (Jr 28:8) and is even part of a description characterizing God (Hab 3:5). So others seem correct in regarding dever as applicable to any pestilence that causes death. With few exceptions dever is usually a divine judgment. It seems to follow defeat in battle (Jr 21:9) and in 24 verses accompanies sword and famine (Jr 14:12). God delivers the godly from it (Ps 91:3,6).

for Judah, just as He had done in the days of Hezekiah (2Kg 18-19) and Jehoshaphat (2Ch 20).

21:2 The spelling of Nebuchadnezzar's name (in the Hebraized form) as Nebuchadrezzar in some translations more closely approximates ancient Babylonian inscriptions. The full Akkadian form is Nabu-kudurri-usur, meaning "Nebo [a god], do protect the crown."

21:4 Chaldeans is the normal term for Babylonians. The Assyrians gave the name Kaldu to the area between the Tigris and Euphrates rivers and between the city of Babylon and the Persian Gulf. Thus the tribal groups living there were called Chaldeans. A Chaldean dynasty was started under Nabopolassar, whose son Nebuchadnezzar organized many nationalities under the name of "Chaldeans" or "Babylonians."

21:5 An **outstretched hand** and a **mighty arm** are routine metaphors describing God's miraculous intervention in times past, such as at the exodus (Dt 4:34).

21:6 During military sieges, the possibility of an epidemic or **great plague** is heightened. Such illness would further weaken the people's ability to defend against attackers.

21:8-10 Jeremiah turned to address the **people** of Judah.

21:8 The phrase **the way of life and the way of death** is reminiscent of Dt 30:19. But here it has the opposite twist of its usage in Deuteronomy.

21:9 The prophet counseled desertion for the citizens of Judah. In other circumstances this would have been considered treason, but Jeremiah's authority was from God. The people were faced with a choice of obeying God or humans. The person who surrendered to Babylon would **retain his life like the spoils of war**. This is an idiomatic expression meaning literally "his soul will be to him for booty" (38:2; 39:18; 45:5).

21:11-14 The message to the **house of the king of Judah** in

or My anger will flare up like fire
and burn unquenchably
because of their evil deeds.
¹³ Beware! I am against you,^a
you who sit above the valley,
you atop the rocky plateau—
    this is the LORD's declaration—
you who say, "Who can come down
against us?^b
Who can enter our hiding places?"
¹⁴ I will punish you according to
what you have done^c—
    this is the LORD's declaration.
I will kindle a fire in its forest^d
that will consume everything
around it.'"^e

Judgment against Sinful Kings

22 This is what the LORD says: "Go down to the palace of the king of Judah and announce this word there. ²You are to say: Hear the word of the LORD, king of Judah, you who sit on the throne of David—you, your officers, and your people who enter these gates. ³This is what the LORD says: Administer justice and righteousness.^f Rescue the victim of robbery from the hand of his oppressor.^g Don't exploit or brutalize the foreigner, the fatherless, or the widow. Don't shed innocent blood in this place. ⁴For if you conscientiously carry out this word, then kings sitting on David's throne will enter through the gates of this

^a21:13 Ezk 13:8
^bJr 49:4
^c21:14 Is 3:10
^dEzk 20:47
^eJr 50:32
^f22:3 2Sm 8:15;
2Ch 9:8; Jr 23:5
^gDt 28:29; Ec
4:1; Jr 21:12
^h22:4 Jr 17:25
ⁱ22:5 Jr 17:27
^j22:8-9 Dt
29:24-25
^k22:9 Dt 30:17

palace^h riding on chariots and horses—they, their officers, and their people. ⁵But if you do not obey these words, then I swear by Myself"—this is the LORD's declaration—"that this house will become a ruin."ⁱ

⁶For this is what the LORD says concerning the house of the king of Judah:

You are like Gilead to Me,
or the summit of Lebanon,
but I will certainly turn you
    into a wilderness,
uninhabited cities.
⁷ I will appoint destroyers against you,
each with his weapons.
They will cut down the choicest
    of your cedars
and throw them into the fire.

⁸"Many nations will pass by this city and ask one another, 'Why did the LORD do such a thing to this great city?' ⁹They will answer, 'Because they abandoned the covenant^j of •Yahweh their God and worshiped and served other gods.'"^k

A Message Concerning Shallum

¹⁰ Do not weep for the dead;
do not mourn for him.
Weep bitterly for the one^A
    who has gone away,
for he will never return again
and see his native land.

---

^A22:10 = Shallum (Jehoahaz) in v. 11

---

these verses must have come at a time when repentance and righteousness would still reverse the threatened judgment of God. "House" refers to the dynasty of the king.

21:12 The task of the king and his officials was to **administer justice every morning**, presumably before the heat of the day (2Sm 4:5). This is how the ideal king would operate (Jr 23:5-6). Likewise, **the victim of robbery** called for action not only against common thieves, but also against all sorts of economic thievery, such as cheating on wages, land-grabbing, and other types of oppression.

21:13 The phrases **you who sit above the valley** and **you atop the rocky plateau** refer to the city of Jerusalem as well as the king. The city, with its palace complex, was surrounded by valleys. There is irony and sarcasm in these designations because the king and the people had a false sense of security. Complacently and proudly the people asked, **Who can come down against us?** The short answer: God Himself.

21:14 The word **forest** is used here figuratively for the royal palace (1Kg 7:2; 10:21).

22:1 Jeremiah was to **go down** from the temple or Mount Zion to the king's **palace**, which was south of the temple (26:10; 36:12).

22:3 The sins mentioned here fit the reigns of all the Judean kings of this period, but they were especially fitting for Jehoiakim's time (2Kg 23:35). These themes appear frequent-

ly in the law, especially Dt 10:18-19; 24:17-22; 27:19 and Ex 22:21-24.

22:4 The conditional prospect of blessing and prosperity was once again offered to the king with the words **if you conscientiously carry out this word**. The Davidic dynasty would be continued and the people would live securely in the land as God had promised David (2Sm 7).

22:5 To underline the solemnity of this message, the Lord declared, **I swear by Myself**, giving the strongest possible authentication to Jeremiah's words.

22:6-9 These verses refer not to the Davidic line, but to the royal palace. The regions of **Gilead** and **Lebanon** were noted for trees such as **cedars** (1Kg 5:6,8-10; 7:2-5; 10:27). However, the lofty and startling cedar columns of the palace would be burned up in the fall of Jerusalem.

22:9 The phrase **they abandoned the covenant of Yahweh** occurs only here and at Dt 29:25. It refers to the Sinaitic covenant, not God's covenant with David (2Sm 7).

22:10 Instead of weeping for **the dead** King Josiah, who was killed at the Battle of Megiddo in 609 B.C. (2Kg 23:29-35; 2Ch 35:24-25), Jeremiah told the people to reserve their tears for Josiah's son, King Shallum. This king was also known as Jehoahaz. After a short reign of three months, Jehoahaz would be exiled to Egypt, where he would die (2Kg 23:34). In

¹¹ For this is what the LORD says concerning Shallum^a son of Josiah, king of Judah, who became king in place of his father Josiah: "He has left this place—he will never return here again, ¹²but he will die in the place where they deported him, never seeing this land again."

A Message concerning Jehoiakim

¹³   Woe for the one who builds his palace
        through unrighteousness,^b
        his upper rooms through injustice,
        who makes his fellow man serve
            without pay
        and will not give him his wages,^c
¹⁴   who says, "I will build myself
            a massive palace,
        with spacious upper rooms."
        He will cut windows^A in it,
        and it will be paneled with cedar
        and painted with vermilion.
¹⁵   Are you a king because you excel
            in cedar?
        Didn't your father eat and drink
        and administer justice
            and righteousness?^d
        Then it went well with him.

¹⁶   He took up the case of the poor
            and needy,
        then it went well.
        Is this not what it means to know Me?
                This is the LORD's declaration.
¹⁷   But you have eyes and a heart
            for nothing
        except your own dishonest profit,
        shedding innocent blood
        and committing extortion
            and oppression.

¹⁸ Therefore, this is what the LORD says concerning Jehoiakim^e son of Josiah, king of Judah:

        They will not mourn for him, saying,
        "Woe, my brother!" or "Woe,
            my sister!"
        They will not mourn for him, saying,
        "Woe, lord! Woe, his majesty!"
¹⁹   He will be buried like a donkey,^f
        dragged off and thrown
        outside the gates of Jerusalem.
²⁰   Go up to Lebanon and cry out;
        raise your voice in Bashan;

^a22:11 2Kg 23:32-35; 1Ch 3:15
^b22:13 Mc 3:10
^cLv 19:13; Jms 5:4
^d22:15 Jr 22:3
^e22:18 2Kg 23:34-24:6; 2Ch 36:4-8
^f22:19 Jr 36:30

^A22:14 Lit My windows

that sense, Josiah would be better off than his son. Jehoahaz would be the first Judean king to die in exile.

22:13-16 Jeremiah denounced King Jehoiakim more severely than he denounced any other king. In a manic building campaign that was typical of Near Eastern kings, Jehoiakim violated Mosaic law (Lv 19:13; Dt 24:14-15) by forcing Judean laborers to build and remodel his palace without paying them any wages. Meanwhile he continued paying enormous sums as tribute to Pharaoh Neco of Egypt. By his love of luxury and his tyranny over Judah, he imitated King Manasseh (2Kg 24:3-4). History had taught Jehoiakim very little.

22:15 Jehoiakim thought that luxurious buildings made a man a king, but Jeremiah asked sarcastically, **Are you a king because you excel in cedar?**

22:16 Concern for the **poor and needy** demonstrates **what it means to know** the Lord. More than head knowledge is required. What is needed is a personal relationship with the Lord that results in justice and righteousness for all. To know God in this manner is to do His will.

22:17 Not only was Jehoiakim tyrannical, covetous, and oppressive; he was also guilty of shedding **innocent blood**. For example, because the prophet Uriah had prophesied against him, the king brought Uriah back from Egypt and had him executed (26:20-23).

22:18-19 A humiliating death awaited evil King Jehoiakim. His own family (**brother . . . sister**) and friends would not mourn his death, but he would be buried like a **donkey, dragged off and thrown outside the gates of Jerusalem**. This meant no burial at all, which was considered a curse (Dt 28:26). Some have questioned the fulfillment of this prophecy, because 2Kg 24:6 says that Jehoiakim "rested with his fathers." But "resting" with one's fathers is not the

same thing as being buried (see 2Kg 15:38; 16:20). The fact that Scripture does not describe the later fulfillment of this prophecy in no way indicates that it did not happen. Second Kings 24:6 does not contradict this prophecy because 1Kg 21:19; 22:30-38,40 uses the same wording for King Ahab's similarly disgraceful death.

22:18 This call to mourning may have come on the eve of Nebuchadnezzar's 597 B.C. attack on Jerusalem.

22:20 The people are told to pick a mountain in the north, **Lebanon**, for example, or **Bashan** in northern Transjordan, or **Abarim**, the mountains of Moab, east of the Dead Sea.

ne'um

Hebrew Pronunciation	[neh OOM]
HCSB Translation	declaration, oracle
Uses in Jeremiah	176
Uses in the OT	376
Focus Passage	Jeremiah 22:5,16,24

The history of *ne'um* is uncertain. Many compare an Arabic word meaning "growl, roar, or sigh." The related verb *na'am*, *deliver* (Jr 23:31), occurs once, probably developed from *ne'um*, and takes *ne'um* as its object. *Ne'um* regularly (365x) stands in a formula indicating a *declaration* from the Lord. Otherwise, it appears six times in the Balaam *oracles* (Nm 22–24), three times of David (2Sm 23:1; Ps 36:1), and once of false prophets of God (Jr 23:31). *Ne'um* occurs only 19x outside the Prophets. So it implies a prophetic *declaration* or *oracle* (Nm 24:3). Once it is *oration*, describing Agur's words (Pr 30:1). But since Agur's words are Scripture, they may have prophetic authority. The words "*declaration* of the LORD" usually open or close divine messages but can occur in the middle (Am 2:11). Such words emphasize the divine source of the *oracle* and add solemnity to it.

cry out from Abarim,[a]
for all your lovers[A] have been crushed.[b]

21 I spoke to you when you were secure.
You said, "I will not listen."
This has been your way since youth;[c]
indeed, you have never listened to Me.

22 The wind will take charge of[B] all
your shepherds,
and your lovers[A] will go into captivity.
Then you will be ashamed
and humiliated[d]
because of all your evil.

23 You residents of Lebanon,
nestled among the cedars,
how you will groan[c] when labor pains
come on you,
agony like a woman in labor.[e]

A Message concerning Coniah

24 "As I live," says the LORD, "though you, Coniah[D,f] son of Jehoiakim, the king of Judah, were a signet ring[g] on My right hand, I would tear you from it. 25 In fact, I will hand you over to those you dread,[h] who want to take your life, to Nebuchadnezzar king of Babylon and the Chaldeans. 26 I will hurl you and the mother who gave birth[i] to you into another land,[j] where neither of you were born, and there you will both die. 27 They will never return to the land they long to return to."

28 Is this man Coniah
a despised, shattered pot,[k]

[a]22:20 Nm 27:12; Dt 32:49
[b]Jr 3:1
[c]22:21 Jr 3:25
[d]22:22 Is 41:11
[e]22:23 Jr 6:24
[f]22:24 2Kg 24:6-17; Jr 37:1; 52:31
[g]Gn 38:18; 1Kg 21:8; Hg 2:23
[h]22:25 Jr 34:20-21
[i]22:26 2Kg 24:15
[j]2Kg 24:8
[k]22:28 Ps 31:12; Jr 48:38; Hs 8:8
[l]22:30 1Ch 3:17; Mt 1:12
[m]Jr 36:30
[n]23:1 Ps 100:3; Ezk 34:31
[o]23:2 Ps 8:4; Is 23:16
[p]23:3 Gn 1:26-28; 9:1-7; 35:11
[q]23:4 Ezk 34:23; Mc 5:2-6

a jar no one wants?
Why are he and his descendants
hurled out
and cast into a land
they have not known?

29 Earth, earth, earth,
hear the word of the LORD!

30 This is what the LORD says:

Record this man as childless,[l]
a man who will not be successful
in his lifetime.
None of his descendants will succeed
in sitting on the throne of David[m]
or ruling again in Judah.

The LORD and His Sheep

23 "Woe to the shepherds who destroy and scatter the sheep of My pasture!"[n] This is the LORD's declaration. 2 "Therefore, this is what the LORD, the God of Israel, says about the shepherds who shepherd My people: You have scattered My flock, banished them, and have not attended to them.[o] I will attend to you because of your evil acts"—this is the LORD's declaration. 3 "I will gather the remnant of My flock from all the lands where I have banished them, and I will return them to their grazing land. They will become fruitful and numerous.[p] 4 I will raise up shepherds over them who will shepherd them.[q] They will no longer be afraid or dismayed, nor will any be missing." This is the LORD's declaration.

A22:20,22 Or friends, or allies   B22:22 Lit will shepherd   C22:23 LXX, Syr, Vg; MT reads will be pitied   D22:24 = Jehoiachin

From these heights they could broadcast their lament over what was about to happen. The words **your lovers** refer to the faithful patriots in Judah, the leaders of the nation, or perhaps Egypt and those countries to whom King Jehoiakim had looked for help against Babylon.

22:22-23 There is a play on words in the expression **the wind will take charge of** [or "will shepherd"] **all your shepherds**. The coming doom is also likened to childbirth. The people **will groan when labor pains come on you, agony like a woman in labor**.

22:24-30 In these verses Jehoiachin (son of Jehoiakim) is condemned. He reigned for only three months. Jehoiachin was also called **Coniah** (vv. 24,28), which is an abbreviated form of Jeconiah, the alternate of the throne name Jehoiachin. See textual footnote at 37:1.

22:24 A **signet ring** contains the king's official seal, which he used to stamp official documents. Such documents bore the sign of royal authority (Hg 2:23). Because of his sins, God says in figurative language that, were Jehoiachin a signet ring on His right hand, He would rip that privilege away from him. Jehoiachin was exiled to Babylon in 597 B.C. (2Kg 24:8-17; 25:27-30).

22:26 Jehoiachin's **mother** was Nehushta (2Kg 24:8).

22:29 The repetition of **earth** gives a strong and solemn emphasis to the message God was about to deliver.

22:30 The words **record this man as childless** are startling since Jehoiachin had seven sons (1Ch 3:17). This is an allusion to the fact that **none of his descendants** would ascend to the throne. Isaiah 39:7 predicted that some of Hezekiah's descendants (Jehoiachin and his sons fell into this category) would "be carried off to Babylon" to become "eunuchs in the palace of the king of Babylon." The Weidner Tablets verify that Jehoiachin and his sons received a daily ration of oil while captive in Babylon. Jehoiachin's uncle, Zedekiah, reigned after him, but he died before Jehoiachin died in Babylon. Thus Jehoiachin was the last living Judean king in the line of David.

23:1-2 The shepherds were not only Zedekiah and the three godless Judean kings mentioned in chapter 22, but all leaders of Judah, including spiritual and civil leaders. The phrases **the sheep of My pasture . . . My people**, and **My flock** are used by Jeremiah more than 40 times to designate the close relationship between God and the people of Judah. There is a play on words for **not attended to** ["My flock"] and **I will attend to** ["shepherds"]. The Hebrew word is pagad, meaning "to care for" or "to chastise." God will discipline the shepherds for not taking care of His flock.

23:3-4 The upcoming exile was a sure thing, but so too the future regathering was sure to happen. The good **shepherds** that God would raise up were not only Zerubbabel, Ezra, and Nehemiah, but leaders far into the future. God

The Righteous Branch of David

5 "The days are coming"[a]—this is
the Lord's declaration—
"when I will raise up a Righteous
Branch of David.[b]
He will reign wisely as king
and administer justice and
righteousness in the land.[c]
6 In His days Judah will be saved,
and Israel will dwell securely.[d]
This is what He will be named:
·Yahweh Our Righteousness.[e]

7 "The days are coming"—the Lord's declaration—"when it will no longer be said, 'As the
Lord lives who brought the Israelites from the
land of Egypt,'[f] 8 but, 'As the Lord lives, who
brought and led the descendants of the house
of Israel from the land of the north and from
all the other countries where I[A] had banished
them.' They will dwell once more in their own
land."[g]

False Prophets Condemned

9 Concerning the prophets:

My heart is broken within me,[h]
and all my bones tremble.
I have become like a drunkard,
like a man overcome by wine,
because of the Lord,
because of His holy words.
10 For the land is full of adulterers;[i]
the land mourns because of the curse,

and the grazing lands in the wilderness
have dried up.
Their way of life[B] has become evil,
and their power is not rightly used
11 because both prophet and priest
are ungodly,[j]
even in My house I have found
their evil.
This is the Lord's declaration.
12 Therefore, their way will be to them
like slippery paths in the gloom.[k]
They will be driven away
and fall down there,
for I will bring disaster on them,
the year of their punishment.
This is the Lord's declaration.

13 Among the prophets of Samaria
I saw something disgusting:
They prophesied by[c] ·Baal
and led My people Israel astray.[l]
14 Among the prophets of Jerusalem also
I saw a horrible thing:
They commit adultery and walk in lies.
They strengthen the hands of evildoers,
and none turns his back on evil.
They are all like Sodom[m] to Me;
Jerusalem's residents are
like Gomorrah.

15 Therefore, this is what the Lord of ·Hosts
says concerning the prophets:

I am about to feed them ·wormwood

---

[a]23:5-6 Jr 33:14-16
[b]23:5 Zch 3:8; 6:12
[c]Is 11:1-9
[d]23:6 Dt 33:12
[e]Ps 4:1
[f]23:7 Jr 16:14
[g]23:8 Jr 16:15
[h]23:9 Hab 3:16
[i]23:10 Jr 9:2; Hs 7:4; Mal 3:5
[j]23:11 Jr 6:13; Zph 3:4
[k]23:12 Ps 35:6; 73:18
[l]23:13 Pr 12:26; Is 3:12; Jr 50:6
[m]23:14 Gn 13:10-13; 18:16-19:28; Is 1:10-17

[A]23:8 LXX reads He   [B]23:10 Lit Their manner of running   [C]23:13 = in the name of

---

would bring Judah and Israel back from **all the lands where**
He had banished them.

23:5 The expression **the days are coming** points to messianic times. It is used 15 times in the book of Jeremiah. **Branch**
of David refers to the Messiah. It appears five times in the
Prophets (v. 5; 33:15; Is 4:2; Zch 3:8; 6:12). Four pictures of
Jesus the Messiah, often compared to the emphasis given
in each of the four Gospels, are: "the Branch of David" (Jr
23:5), compared to Matthew's presentation (Mt 1:1) of Jesus
the King; "My Servant, the Branch" (Zch 3:8), compared to
Mark's depiction (Mk 10:45) of Jesus as the Servant; "a man
whose name is Branch" (Zch 6:12), compared to Luke's
presentation (Lk 23:47) of Jesus in His human aspects; and
"the branch of the Lord" (Is 4:2), compared to John's presentation (Jn 20:31) of Jesus as being from God. **He will**
reign wisely speaks of the manner of the Messiah's reign
(see also Is 52:13).

23:6 In contrast to the name of Zedekiah, meaning "The Lord
is righteousness" (a name given to Mattaniah by Nebuchadnezzar in 2Kg 24:17), the coming Messiah will be named
Yahweh Our Righteousness. Zedekiah was nothing like the
Messiah in his character or actions.

23:7-8 God's deliverance of His people from **Egypt** will be
surpassed in a future worldwide regathering of Israel, exceeding even the return orchestrated by King Cyrus of Persia.

23:9 Jeremiah's words refer back to his laments and "confessions" in chapters 11–20.

23:10 The physical and spiritual immorality of a **land . . . full**
of adulterers has yielded a godless society.

23:11-31 Both **prophet** and **priest** were accomplices in
corrupting and misleading the people. Jeremiah had
more to say against false prophets than any other OT
writer (vv. 9-40; 2:8; 5:30-31; 6:13-14; 8:10-11; 14:13-
15; 18:18-23; 26:8,11,16; 27:1–28:16). His four charges
against them were: (1) low morals and character (23:14),
(2) they invented their own messages (v. 16), (3) they did
not have a call from God (vv. 21-22), and (4) they were
plagiarists (v. 30).

23:13 The **something disgusting** ("offensive thing") that
Jeremiah saw was Israel being **led . . . astray** as prophets
prophesied in Baal's name. Their polluted lives were hindrances to legitimate proclamation of God's message.

23:14 To God the false prophets had become as bad as the
cities of **Sodom** and **Gomorrah**. They encouraged moral
laxity and sin rather than repentance.

23:15 What the false prophets were about to experience
would be like eating **wormwood**—a shrub with a bitter
taste—and drinking **poisoned water** (9:15).

23:16-17 These **peace** prophets created messages as fig-

and give them poisoned water
   to drink,[a]
for from the prophets of Jerusalem
ungodliness[A] has spread
   throughout the land.

[16] This is what the LORD of Hosts says: "Do not listen to the words of the prophets who prophesy to you. They are making you worthless. They speak visions from their own minds, not from the LORD's mouth. [17] They keep on saying to those who despise Me, 'The LORD has said: You will have peace.'[b] They have said to everyone who follows the stubbornness of his heart, 'No harm will come to you.'"

[18] For who has stood in the council[c]
      of the LORD
   to see and hear His word?
   Who has paid attention to His word
      and obeyed?
[19] Look, a storm from the LORD![d]
   Wrath has gone out,
   a whirling storm.
   It will whirl about the heads
      of the wicked.
[20] The LORD's anger will not turn back
   until He has completely fulfilled
      the purposes of His heart.
   In time to come you will
      understand it clearly.[e]
[21] I did not send these prophets,[f]
   yet they ran with a message.
   I did not speak to them,
   yet they prophesied.
[22] If they had really stood in My council,
   they would have enabled My people
      to hear My words
   and would have turned them back
      from their evil ways
   and their evil deeds.

[23] "Am I a God who is only near"[g]—this is the LORD's declaration—"and not a God who is far away? [24] Can a man hide himself in secret places where I cannot see him?"[h]—the LORD's declaration. "Do I not fill the heavens and the earth?"[i]—the LORD's declaration.

[25] "I have heard what the prophets who prophesy a lie in My name have said, 'I had a dream! I had a dream!' [26] How long will this continue in the minds of the prophets prophesying lies, prophets of the deceit of their own minds? [27] Through their dreams that they tell one another, they plan to cause My people to forget My name as their fathers forgot My name through Baal worship.[j] [28] The prophet who has only a dream should recount the dream, but the one who has My word should speak My word truthfully, for what is straw compared to grain?"—this is the LORD's declaration. [29] "Is not My word like fire"—this is the LORD's declaration—"and like a hammer that pulverizes rock? [30] Therefore, take note! I am against the prophets"[k]—the LORD's declaration—"who steal My words from each other. [31] I am against the prophets"—the LORD's declaration—"who use their own tongues to make a declaration. [32] I am against those who prophesy false dreams"[l]—the LORD's declaration—"telling them and leading My people astray with their falsehoods and their boasting. It was not I who sent or commanded them, and they are of no benefit at all[m] to these people"—this is the LORD's declaration.

The Burden of the LORD

[33] "Now when these people or a prophet or a priest asks you, 'What is the burden of the LORD?' you will respond to them: What is the burden? I will throw you away"—this is the LORD's declaration. [34] "As for the prophet, priest, or people who say, 'The burden of the

---

[a]23:15 Jr 8:14; 9:15
[b]23:17 Jr 4:10
[c]23:18 Jb 15:8; Ps 25:14; 89:7
[d]23:19 Ps 83:15; Is 29:6; Zch 9:14
[e]23:19-20 Jr 30:23-24
[f]23:21 Jr 14:14
[g]23:23 Ps 139:1-10
[h]23:24 Gn 3:8; 4:14; Jb 34:22
[i]Ps 139:7-12; Am 9:2-4
[j]23:27 Jdg 3:7; 8:33-34
[k]23:30 Dt 18:20; Jr 14:14-15; Ezk 13:8
[l]23:32 Dt 18:20
[m]Is 30:5-6; Jr 2:8,11

[A]23:15 Or pollution

---

ments of their **own minds**. They deceived the people by promising peace, prosperity, and success. The false prophets were **making** the people **worthless**, a word reflecting the Hebrew noun *hevel* ("vapor," "vanity," "transitoriness"), as used in the book of Ecclesiastes.

23:18 Some understand the **council of the LORD** to be a gathering of divine beings over whom God presided or consulted, as was believed in Near Eastern polytheism. But the biblical concept is different. The "council of the LORD" referred to God's desire to share His teaching with His prophets, as Amos declared (Am 3:7).

23:19-20 This announcement of judgment is repeated almost identically in 30:23-24. The **storm** (4:11-12; 13:24; 18:17; 25:32) unleashes the **purposes** of God's **heart** for judgment.

23:21-22 Even though God **did not send these prophets, yet**

they ran (cp. 2Sm 18:19). They had no authority as God's courier and no understanding of God's purposes.

23:23-24 God is not a pagan local god confined to His shrine or temple. He is both immanent (**near**) and transcendent (**far**).

23:25-29 Jeremiah did not deny that God sometimes uses dreams. He used them with Joseph (Gn 37; 41) and with authentic prophets (Nm 12:6). But the dreams to which the prophet referred here were fabricated and preyed on the gullible. The dreams of the false prophets were like **straw**, not **grain**. God's word, by contrast, was **like a hammer that pulverizes rock**.

23:30 Since they did not truly speak from God, God said the false prophets could only plagiarize **My words from each other** as they made up false messages in God's name.

23:33-38 The word **burden** comes from the Hebrew verbal

LORD,' I will punish that man and his household. ³⁵This is what each man is to say to his friend and to his brother, 'What has the LORD answered?' or 'What has the LORD spoken?' ³⁶But no longer refer toᴬ the burden of the LORD, for each man's word becomes his burden and you pervert the words of the living God, the LORD of Hosts, our God. ³⁷You must say to the prophet: What has the LORD answered you? and What has the LORD spoken? ³⁸But if you say, 'The burden of the LORD,' then this is what the LORD says: Because you have said, 'The burden of the LORD,' and I specifically told you not to say, 'The burden of the LORD,' ³⁹I will surely forget youᴮ and throw away from My presence both you and the city that I gave you and your fathers. ⁴⁰I will bring on you everlasting shame and humiliationᵃ that will never be forgotten."

The Good and the Bad Figs

24 After Nebuchadnezzar king of Babylon had deported Jeconiahᶜ son of Jehoiakim king of Judah, the officials of Judah, and the craftsmen and metalsmithsᵇ from Jerusalem and had brought them to Babylon, the LORD showed me two baskets of figsᶜ placed before the temple of the LORD. ²One basket contained very good figs, like early figs,ᵈ but the other basket contained very bad figs, so bad they were inedible. ³The LORD said to me, "What do you see, Jeremiah?" I said, "Figs!

The good figs are very good, but the bad figs are extremely bad, so bad they are inedible."

⁴The word of the LORD came to me: ⁵"This is what the LORD, the God of Israel, says: Like these good figs, so I regard as good the exiles from Judah I sent away from this place to the land of the Chaldeans. ⁶I will keep My eyes on them for their good and will return them to this land. I will build them up and not demolish them; I will plant them and not uproot them.ᵉ ⁷I will give them a heart to know Me,ᶠ that I am •Yahweh. They will be My people, and I will be their God because they will return to Me with all their heart.ᵍ

⁸"But as for the bad figs, so bad they are inedible,ʰ this is what the LORD says: in this way I will deal with king Zedekiah of Judah, his officials, and the remnant of Jerusalem—those remaining in this land and those living in the land of Egypt.ⁱ ⁹I will make them an object of horrorʲ and disaster to all the kingdoms of the earth, a disgrace, an object of scorn, ridicule,ᵏ and cursing, wherever I have banished them. ¹⁰I will send the sword, famine, and plagueˡ against them until they have perished from the land I gave to them and their ancestors."

The Seventy-Year Exile

25 This is the word that came to Jeremiah concerning all the people of Judah in the fourth year of Jehoiakimᵐ son of Josiah, king of Judah (which was the first year of Neb-

Cross references (center column)
ᵃ 23:40 Ps 78:66; Jr 20:11
ᵇ 24:1 2Kg 24:14,16; Jr 29:2
ᶜ Am 8:1
ᵈ 24:2 Is 28:4; Hs 9:10; Mc 7:1
ᵉ 24:6 Jr 1:10
ᶠ 24:7 Dt 30:6; Jr 31:33; 32:40
ᵍ 2Ch 6:38; Jr 29:13
ʰ 24:8 Jr 29:17
ⁱ Jr 44:1
ʲ 24:9 2Ch 29:8; Jr 15:4; 29:18
ᵏ Dt 28:37; 1Kg 9:7; 2Ch 7:20
ˡ 24:10 Jr 14:12; 21:9; 29:17-18
ᵐ 25:1 2Kg 23:34-24:6; 2Ch 36:4-8

ᴬ23:36 Or *longer remember*   ᴮ23:39 Some Hb mss; other Hb mss, LXX, Syr, Vg read *surely lift you up*   ᶜ24:1 = Jehoiachin

---

root *nasa'*, meaning "to lift up." All instances of the Hebrew noun *massa'* imply a "burden," for all are judgment passages. So when the people or the false prophets asked, **What is the burden of the LORD?** (v. 33), the answer was the short retort given in the Latin Vulgate and the Greek Septuagint (LXX): "You are the burden." The pun of the two senses of "burden" (prophetic burden of judgment and the burden of trying to speak to stubborn people) recurs throughout this section.

23:39-40 Because of the deceptive words of the false prophets, God would **surely forget** them and **throw** them **away from** His **presence**—a drastic measure for a serious offense.

24:1-10 In this vision Jeremiah saw **two baskets of figs**, one good and one bad. These images seem to fit poorly with Jeremiah's pessimistic estimate that all Jerusalem was wicked (chap. 5) and his attitude toward the exiles (chap. 29). Those who remain true to God in the midst of mass compromise often mistakenly think they are all alone in devotion to God (see 1Kg 19:14-18).

24:1 The phrase **the LORD showed me** marks a supernatural revelation to the prophet, much like that in Am 7:1,4,7. This happened in a vision and not in reality, because bad figs could not be offered to the Lord (Dt 26:2).

24:2 The **early figs**, which ripened in May–June, were very juicy and were considered a delicacy. Their Hebrew name

was *bakkuroth* ("newly ripe," "early ripening"), suggesting the similar Hebrew word for "firstfruits."

24:5 God regarded as **good the exiles from Judah** that He **sent away** to Babylon in 597 B.C. They were the pride of the nation in skills, leadership, and craftsmanship. Some of the leaders in that deportation had intervened on Jeremiah's behalf on several occasions (chaps. 26, 36).

24:6 In keeping with the call of Jeremiah in 1:10, God promised these good figs that He would **build them . . . plant them . . . not demolish**, and **not uproot** them.

24:7 Two parts of the tripartite formula for the promise of God appear in this verse: **They will be My people, and I will be their God**. God would **give them a heart to know** Him **because they will return to Me with all their heart**. The new heart did not depend on the people returning to God, because He had already given them a heart to know Him. The new heart of 32:37-41 was also an unconditional promise of God.

24:8-10 The **bad figs** were **inedible**. This describes those who were still living in the land or those who had fled to Egypt. Their disobedience to God led them into ever greater sin as they hardened their hearts. As He had done with Pharaoh, God responded by further hardening their hearts.

25:1-38 This chapter describes a critical year in the history of the Near East. In this year Jeremiah dictated his prophecies to his scribe Baruch (36:1-6), the battle of Carche-

uchadnezzar king of Babylon). ²The prophet Jeremiah spoke concerning all the people of Judah and all the residents of Jerusalem as follows: ³"From the thirteenth year of Josiah son of Amon,ᵃ king of Judah, until this very day—23 years—the word of the LORD has come to me, and I have spoken to you time and time again,ᴬ·ᵇ but you have not obeyed. ⁴The LORD sent all His servants the prophets to you time and time again,ᴮ but you have not obeyed or even paid attention.ᶜ·ᶜ ⁵He announced, 'Turn, each of you, from yourᴰ evil way of life and from your evil deeds.ᵈ Live in the land the LORD gave to you and your ancestors long ago and forever. ⁶Do not follow other gods to serve them and to worship them,ᵉ and do not provoke Me to anger by the work of your hands.ᶠ Then I will do you no harm.

⁷"But you would not obey Me'—this is the LORD's declaration—'in order that you might provoke Me to anger by the work of your hands and bring disaster on yourselves.'

⁸"Therefore, this is what the LORD of •Hosts says: 'Because you have not obeyed My words, ⁹I am going to send for all the families of the north'ᵍ—this is the LORD's declaration—'and send for My servantʰ Nebuchadnezzar king of Babylon, and I will bring them against this land, against its residents, and against all these surrounding nations, and I will •completely destroy them and make them a desolation,ⁱ a derision, and ruins forever. ¹⁰I will eliminate the sound of joy and gladness from them—the voice of the groom and the bride,ʲ

the sound of the millstones and the light of the lamp. ¹¹This whole land will become a desolate ruin, and these nations will serve the king of Babylon for 70 years.ᵏ ¹²When the 70 years are completed, I will punish the king of Babylon and that nation'—this is the LORD's declaration—'the land of the Chaldeans, for their •guilt, and I will make it a ruin forever.ˡ ¹³I will bring on that land all My words I have spoken against it, all that is written in this book that Jeremiah prophesied against all the nations. ¹⁴For many nations and great kings will enslave them, and I will repay them according to their deedsᵐ and the work of their hands.'"

The Cup of God's Wrath

¹⁵This is what the LORD, the God of Israel, said to me: "Take this cup of the wine of wrath from My hand and make all the nations I am sending you to, drink from it.ⁿ ¹⁶They will drink, stagger,ᴱ and go out of their minds because of the sword I am sending among them."

¹⁷So I took the cup from the LORD's hand and made all the nations drink from it, everyone the LORD sent me to. ¹⁸These included:

Jerusalem and the other cities of Judah, its kings and its officials, to make them a desolate ruin, an object of scorn and cursing—as it is today; ¹⁹Pharaoh king of Egypt, his officers, his leaders, all his people,

ᵃ 25:3 Jr 1:2
ᵇ Jr 11:7; 26:5
ᶜ 25:4 Jr 7:25-26
ᵈ 25:5 Jr 18:11; 35:15
ᵉ 25:6 Dt 8:19; Jr 13:10
ᶠ Dt 31:29; 1Kg 16:7; Jr 44:8
ᵍ 25:9 Jr 1:13
ʰ Is 45:1
ⁱ Jr 4:7; 18:16; 19:8
ʲ 25:10 Jr 7:34; 16:9; 33:11
ᵏ 25:11 2Ch 36:21; Jr 29:10; Dn 9:2
ˡ 25:12 Is 13:19
ᵐ 25:14 Jr 50:29
ⁿ 25:15 Ps 75:8; Is 51:17; Jr 49:12

ᴬ 25:3 Lit *you; rising early and speaking*   ᴮ 25:4 Lit *prophets, rising early and sending*   ᶜ 25:4 Lit *even inclined your ears*   ᴰ 25:5 Lit *his*   ᴱ 25:16 Or *vomit*

---

mish unfolded, and Nebuchadnezzar ascended the throne of Babylon (see notes at 36:1 and 45:1-5).

25:1 That the **first year of Nebuchadnezzar** paralleled the **fourth year** of King Jehoiakim of Judah is not in conflict with Dn 1:1, which says Nebuchadnezzar laid siege in Jehoiakim's "third year." The two countries used different methods of reckoning the initiation of a king's reign. Judah used the accession-year principle, where the portion of the calendar year that remained when the king came to power was called his first year of reign. Babylon used the non-accession-year principle, where the first year of reign was calculated only with the advent of the new calendar year (hence, a king who took the throne on January 2 would begin his first year of reign on January 1 of the next calendar year).

25:3 Jeremiah had ministered in Judah for **23 years**, but he had to conclude that the people had **not obeyed**. Jeremiah was not the only prophet sent by God during this time (Uriah, Zephaniah, and Habakkuk). In spite of his efforts, four times in verses 3-8 Judah's disobedience is emphasized.

25:5-7 The imperatives **turn** and **live** are highlighted, but little success resulted from these urgent messages from God.

25:9 All the families of the north meant Babylon's allies or

the many nations and tribes within the Babylonian Empire. **Nebuchadnezzar** is called **My servant** three times in Jeremiah (v. 9; 27:6; 43:10), just as King Cyrus of Persia was called God's servant or shepherd in Is 44:28; 45:1. Both were called by God as instruments of His plan to **completely destroy** Judah and the surrounding nations. "Completely destroy" is related to the Hebrew noun *cherem*, where the enemy was "put under the ban" and set apart for destruction.

25:11 The **70 years** is often regarded as a round number, but here it is the literal period of time between 606/605 B.C. when Daniel was taken captive, and 536 B.C. when Zerubbabel led the first group of resettlers back to Judah.

25:12-14 At the end of the 70 years, God would **punish the king of Babylon and that nation**, not for carrying out His will but for her own sins (50:11-13).

25:15-16 The **cup of the wine of wrath** is a common biblical image indicating God's wrath (49:12; 51:7; Ps 60:3; Is 51:17,22; Ezk 23:31; Hab 2:16; Rv 14:8,10; 16:19; 18:6). The prophet did not physically take the cup to all the nations, but all nations would experience that cup in the tragedies of the future.

25:19-22 All the nations listed in chapters 46–51 except

20 and all the mixed peoples;
all the kings of the land of Uz;
all the kings of the land of the
Philistines—Ashkelon, Gaza, Ekron,
and the remnant of Ashdod;
21 Edom, Moab, and the Ammonites;
22 all the kings of Tyre,
all the kings of Sidon,
and the kings of the coastlands across
the sea;
23 Dedan, Tema, Buz, and all those who
shave their temples;[A,a]
24 all the kings of Arabia,
and all the kings of the mixed peoples
who have settled in the desert;
25 all the kings of Zimri,
all the kings of Elam,
and all the kings of Media;
26 all the kings of the north, both near
and far from one another;
that is, all the kingdoms of the world
which are on the face of the earth.
Finally, the king of Sheshach[B] will
drink after them.

27 "Then you are to say to them: This is what
the LORD of Hosts, the God of Israel, says:
Drink,[b] get drunk, and vomit. Fall down and
never get up again, as a result of the sword
I am sending among you. 28 If[c] they refuse to
take the cup from you and drink, you are to say
to them: This is what the LORD of Hosts says:
You must drink! 29 For I am already bringing
disaster on the city that bears My name,[c] so
how could you possibly go unpunished? You
will not go unpunished, for I am summoning a sword against all the inhabitants of the
earth"—this is the declaration of the LORD of
Hosts.[d]

Judgment on the Whole World

30 "As for you, you are to prophesy all these
things to them, and say to them:

The LORD roars from heaven;
He raises His voice
from His holy dwelling.[e]
He roars loudly over His grazing land;
He calls out with a shout, like those
who tread grapes,
against all the inhabitants of the earth.
31 The tumult reaches to the ends
of the earth
because the LORD brings a case
against[f] the nations.
He enters into judgment with all flesh.
As for the wicked, He hands them over
to the sword—
this is the LORD's declaration.

32 "This is what the LORD of Hosts says:

Pay attention! Disaster spreads
from nation to nation.
A great storm is stirred up
from the ends of the earth."[g]

33 Those slain by the LORD[h] on that day will be
spread from one end of the earth to the other.
They will not be mourned,[i] gathered, or buried. They will be like manure on the surface
of the ground.

34 Wail, you shepherds, and cry out.
Roll in the dust,[D,j] you leaders
of the flock.
Because the days of your slaughter
have come,
you will fall and become shattered
like a precious vase.
35 Flight will be impossible
for the shepherds,
and escape, for the leaders of the flock.
36 Hear the sound of the shepherds' cry,
the wail of the leaders of the flock,
for the LORD is destroying their pasture.
37 Peaceful grazing land
will become lifeless

a 25:23 Lv 19:27; Jr 9:26; 49:32
b 25:27 Jr 25:16; Hab 2:16
c 25:29 Dn 9:18
d 25:28-29 Jr 49:12-13
e 25:30 Dt 26:15; 2Ch 30:27; Ps 76:2; Am 1:2; Jl 3:16
f 25:31 Hs 4:1; 12:3; Mc 6:2
g 25:32 Jr 23:19; 30:23
h 25:33 Is 66:16 Jr 16:4
i 25:34 Jb 2:8,12; Jr 6:26; Ezk 27:30

A 25:23 Or who live in distant places   B 25:26 Probably a name for Babylon   C 25:28 Or When   D 25:34 This custom demonstrated mourning.

Damascus are included in this section. Judah heads the list
and then comes Pharaoh of Egypt, perhaps because he instigated the alliance of Judah against Babylon. The list runs
from south to north.

25:20 The land of Uz is mentioned in Jb 1:1. It was probably
east and northeast of Edom. The remnant of Ashdod is singled out because Pharaoh Psammetik I of Egypt (663–609
B.C.) took the city after a 29-year siege.

25:25 The location of Zimri is unknown, though the name
appears in Nm 25:14 and elsewhere. Elam and Media were
east of the Tigris River.

25:26 Sheshach is probably a cipher code for Babylon, written in what the Hebrews called Atbash, where letters of the

Hebrew alphabet are substituted for their opposite (see
note at 51:1). Here the letters bet-bet-lamed of Babylon are
changed to shin-shin-khet.

25:29 The Lord asked, How could the nations possibly go
unpunished? The same principles that governed Judah
must also govern the world.

25:30-33 The imagery changes from a cup of wine to a lion.
This signals the Lord's voice from on high. It changes again
to an image of the Lord treading out grapes in the winepress (Is 63:3; Rv 14:19-20; 19:15), and once more to the
image of a great storm as nation after nation succumbs to
Babylon's advances.

25:34-38 Three times in these verses Jeremiah used the

because of the LORD's burning anger.[a]

38 He has left His den like a lion,
for their land has become a desolation
because of the sword[A] of the oppressor,[b]
because of His burning anger.

Jeremiah's Speech in the Temple

26 At the beginning of the reign of Jehoiakim[c] son of Josiah, king of Judah, this word came from the LORD: [2]"This is what the LORD says: Stand in the courtyard of the LORD's temple and speak all the words I have commanded you to speak to all Judah's cities that are coming to worship there. Do not hold back a word.[d] [3]Perhaps they will listen and return—each from his evil way of life—so that I might relent[e] concerning the disaster that I plan to do to them because of the evil of their deeds. [4]You are to say to them: This is what the LORD says: If you do not listen to Me by living according to My instruction that I set before you[f] [5]and by listening to the words of My servants the prophets[g] I have been sending you time and time again,[B] though you did not listen, [6]I will make this temple like Shiloh.[h] I will make this city an object of cursing for all the nations of the earth."

Jeremiah Seized

[7]The priests, the prophets, and all the people heard Jeremiah speaking these words in the temple of the LORD. [8]He finished the address the LORD had commanded him to deliver to all the people. Then the priests, the prophets, and all the people took hold of him, yelling, "You must surely die! [9]How dare you prophesy in the name of •Yahweh, 'This

temple will become like Shiloh and this city will become an uninhabited ruin'!" Then all the people assembled against Jeremiah at the LORD's temple.

[10]When the officials of Judah heard these things, they went from the king's palace to the LORD's temple and sat at the entrance of the New Gate.[C,i] [11]Then the priests and prophets said to the officials and all the people, "This man deserves the death sentence because he has prophesied against this city, as you have heard with your own ears."[j]

Jeremiah's Defense

[12]Then Jeremiah said to all the officials and the people, "The LORD sent me to prophesy all the words that you have heard against this temple and city. [13]So now, correct your ways and deeds[k] and obey the voice of the LORD your God so that He might relent concerning the disaster that He warned about. [14]As for me, here I am in your hands; do to me what you think is good and right. [15]But know for certain that if you put me to death, you will bring innocent blood[l] on yourselves, on this city, and on its residents, for it is certain the LORD has sent me to speak all these things directly to you."

Jeremiah Released

[16]Then the officials and all the people told the priests and prophets, "This man doesn't deserve the death sentence, for he has spoken to us in the name of Yahweh our God!"

[17]Some of the elders of the land stood up[m] and said to all the assembled people, [18]"Micah the Moreshite[n] prophesied in the days of

Cross references (center column)

a 25:37 Nm 32:14; 2Ch 28:11; Zph 2:2
b 25:38 Jr 46:16
c 26:1 2Kg 23:34–24:6; 2Ch 36:4-8
d 26:2 Dt 4:2; Ec 3:14
e 26:3 Ex 32:12,14; Am 7:3,6; Jnh 3:9-10
f 26:4 Lv 26:14
g 26:5 Jr 25:3-4
h 26:6 Jos 18:1,8-10; 21:2; 1Sm 1:3
i 26:10 Jr 36:10; Ezk 46:1,3
j 26:11 Jr 38:4
k 26:13 Jr 7:3-5; 18:11
l 26:15 Dt 19:10; 2Kg 24:4; Jr 22:17
m 26:17 Ac 5:34
n 26:18 Mc 1:1,14

[A]25:38 Some Hb mss, LXX, Tg; other Hb mss read *burning*　[B]26:5 Lit *you, rising early and sending*　[C]26:10 Some Hb mss, Syr, Tg, Vg add *of the house*

---

shepherd metaphor and then switched over to describe the nations' impending disaster. They will be **shattered like a precious vase**. The nations will be shattered by the One who is Lord over all the earth.

26:1-24 This chapter is connected with chapter 7, the prophet's famous temple gate sermon.

26:1 The date for this event is set as **the beginning of the reign of Jehoiakim** (609 B.C.). This is chronologically earlier than 25:1, Jehoiakim's "fourth year." King Josiah had died that year, and Jehoahaz had ruled only three months.

26:2 Nothing of God's revelation was to be held back, not even **a word**.

26:3 A repentance that delivers nations must start with individuals. God has called **each** to return **from his evil way of life**.

26:4-6 This is a summary of the more complete message in chapter 7 with three emphases: (1) the call to obey God's law, (2) the alignment of Jeremiah's message with **My servants the prophets**, and (3) the seriousness of the impending threat against the city of Jerusalem and the temple.

26:6,9 On **Shiloh**, see note at 7:12,14.

26:7-8 The **priests**, the **prophets**, and **all the people** listened until Jeremiah finished his address, but then their pent-up fury broke loose as they **took hold of him**, yelling, **You must surely die!** They thought Jeremiah had spoken blasphemy (Lv 24:16; Dt 18:20). How could God destroy the city and temple, which they considered invincible because of God's promise to David?

26:9 The people **assembled against** (lit "thronged about") Jeremiah in a hostile manner.

26:10 The **New Gate** is thought to be the gate leading to the inner court of the temple (36:10). This was the place where trials were held. King Jotham built it (2Kg 15:35).

26:12-15 Jeremiah defended himself with great courage, unusual brevity, and straightforward accounting for his 20 years of ministry among them (cp. 25:3, three years earlier). His message originated with God, and he had stayed on message.

26:18 Micah the Moreshite alludes to Mc 1:1. The quoted verse is from Mc 3:12. Moresheth was a village 23 miles

Hezekiah king of Judah[a] and said to all the people of Judah, 'This is what the LORD of •Hosts says:

> •Zion will be plowed like a field,
> Jerusalem will become ruins,
> and the temple mount a forested hill.'[b]

[19] Did Hezekiah king of Judah and all the people of Judah put him to death? Did he not •fear the LORD and plead for the LORD's favor,[A,c] and did not the LORD relent concerning the disaster He had pronounced against them?[d] We are about to bring great harm on ourselves!"

The Prophet Uriah

[20] Another man was also prophesying in the name of Yahweh—Uriah son of Shemaiah from Kiriath-jearim.[e] He prophesied against this city and against this land in words like all those of Jeremiah. [21] King Jehoiakim, all his warriors, and all the officials heard his words, and the king tried to put him to death. When Uriah heard, he fled in fear and went to Egypt. [22] But King Jehoiakim sent men to Egypt: Elnathan son of Achbor[f] and certain other men with him went to Egypt. [23] They brought Uriah out of Egypt and took him to King Jehoiakim, who executed him with the sword and threw his corpse into the burial place of the common people.[B]

[24] But Ahikam[g] son of Shaphan supported

Jeremiah, so he was not handed over to the people to be put to death.

The Yoke of Babylon

27 At the beginning of the reign of Zedekiah[c] son of Josiah, king of Judah, this word came to Jeremiah from the LORD:[D] [2] "This is what the LORD said to me: Make chains and yoke bars[h] for yourself and put them on your neck. [3] Send word to the king of Edom, the king of Moab, the king of the Ammonites, the king of Tyre, and the king of Sidon[i] through messengers who are coming to Zedekiah king of Judah in Jerusalem. [4] Command them to go to their masters, saying: This is what the LORD of •Hosts, the God of Israel, says: This is what you must say to your masters: [5] By My great strength and outstretched arm,[j] I made the earth,[k] and the people, and animals on the face of the earth. I give it to anyone I please.[E,l] [6] So now I have placed all these lands under the authority of My servant[m] Nebuchadnezzar,[n] king of Babylon. I have even given him the wild animals to serve him. [7] All nations will serve him, his son, and his grandson until the time for his own land comes, and then many nations and great kings will enslave him.[o]

[8] "As for the nation or kingdom that does not serve Nebuchadnezzar king of Babylon and does not place its neck under the yoke of the king of Babylon, that nation I will punish by

[a] 26:18 2Kg 16:20; 18:4–21:3; Is 36:1–39:8
[b] Mc 3:12
[c] 26:19 2Ch 32:26
[d] Ex 32:14; 2Sm 24:16
[e] 26:20 Jos 9:17; 1Sm 6:21; 7:2
[f] 26:22 Jr 36:12
[g] 26:24 2Kg 22:12,14; Jr 39:14; 40:5–43:6
[h] 27:2 Jr 28:10-13
[i] 27:3 Jr 25:21-22
[j] 27:5 Dn 4:17
[k] Is 45:12
[l] Ps 115:15-16
[m] 27:6 Jr 25:9
[n] 2Kg 24:11; 25:22; 2Ch 36:6-13
[o] 27:7 Jr 25:12

<hr>

[A] 26:19 Or and appease the LORD   [B] 26:23 Lit the sons of the people   [C] 27:1 Some Hb mss, Syr, Arabic; other Hb mss, DSS read Jehoiakim   [D] 27:1 LXX omits this v.   [E] 27:5 Lit to whomever is upright in My eyes

<hr>

southwest of Jerusalem. Micah's warnings were heeded, and the nation was delivered because the people responded with repentance. This argument from the past was effective, and Jeremiah was released.

26:20-23 These verses show that **Uriah son of Shemaiah** did not fare as well as Micah did. Why some faithful servants are delivered and others are not is in God's hands.

26:20 Kiriath-jearim was about eight miles northwest of Jerusalem where the ark of the covenant was kept after it was returned by the Philistines (1Sm 7:1-2).

26:22 Elnathan son of Achbor might have been one of the sons of Achbor son of Micaiah, an official of King Josiah (2Kg 22:12,14). Elnathan tried to stop King Jehoiakim from burning Jeremiah's scroll (Jr 36:25).

26:23 Uriah was **brought . . . out of Egypt** by King Jehoiakim of Judah. As a vassal nation under Egypt, Jehoiakim had rights of extradition in accordance with international treaties.

26:24 Ahikam son of Shaphan supported Jeremiah. Shaphan was the scribe of King Josiah's reform (2Kg 22:3-14). Gemariah, another son of Shaphan, argued that King Jehoiakim should not burn Jeremiah's scroll (Jr 36:10,25). A third son of Shaphan, Gedaliah, was appointed governor of Judah after the fall of Jerusalem (39:14; 40:5-16).

27:1 The **beginning of the reign of Zedekiah** was in 594 B.C. (28:1). The LXX may preserve the more accurate reading: "in

the fourth year of Zedekiah." Nebuchadnezzar of Babylon had just put down an uprising by some of his troops. News of this palace revolt may have stirred false hopes, especially in Judah.

27:2 Jeremiah was commanded by God to **make chains and yoke bars** for himself. Palestinian yokes consisted of a beam across the shoulders of oxen, with parallel pegs coming out of the beam on either side of the ox's neck and tied with thongs under the neck.

27:3 The phrase **send word** (in Hb, "send them") implies that Jeremiah made a separate yoke for each king of the five nations mentioned here, apparently giving an appropriate message for each ambassador. The enumeration of the nations from the south to the north may indicate that they were prompted by Pharaoh Psammetik II of Egypt to revolt when it appeared Babylon was going through internal troubles.

27:6 Revolt was futile because God had already assigned Babylon to execute judgment over these nations on His behalf. Again, Nebuchadnezzar is called **My servant** or instrument (see note at 25:9; cp. Cyrus in Is 44:28).

27:7 Nebuchadnezzar, **his son, and his grandson** were given power over all the mentioned nations. Their dominance lasted for three generations, including the kings Nebuchanezzar, Evil-Merodach (52:31; 2Kg 25:27) and Belshazzar (Dn 5:2). God appoints power and determines its duration as well; the exile would not be over quickly as some false prophets had promised.

sword, famine, and plague"—this is the LORD's declaration—"until through him I have destroyed it. ⁹But as for you, do not listen to your prophets, diviners,ᵃ dreamers, fortune-tellers,ᵇ or sorcerersᶜ who say to you, 'Don't serve the king of Babylon!' ¹⁰for they prophesy a lie to you so that you will be removed from your land. I will banish you, and you will perish. ¹¹But as for the nation that will put its neck under the yoke of the king of Babylon and serve him, I will leave it in its own land, and that nation will cultivateᴬ it and reside in it." This is the LORD's declaration.

Warning to Zedekiah

¹²I spoke to Zedekiah king of Judahᵈ in the same way: "Put your necks under the yoke of the king of Babylon, serve him and his people, and live! ¹³Why should you and your people dieᵉ by the sword, famine, or plague as the LORD has threatened against any nation that does not serve the king of Babylon? ¹⁴Do not listen to the words of the prophets who are telling you, 'You must not serve the king of Babylon,' for they are prophesying a lie to you.ᶠ ¹⁵'I have not sent them'—this is the LORD's declaration—'and they are prophesying falsely in My name; therefore, I will banish you, and you will perish—you and the prophets who are prophesying to you.'"

¹⁶Then I spoke to the priests and all these people, saying, "This is what the LORD says: 'Do not listen to the words of your prophets. They are prophesying to you, claiming, "Look, very soon now the articles of the LORD's temple will be brought back from Babylon."ᵍ They are prophesying a lie to you. ¹⁷Do not listen to them. Serve the king of Babylon and live! Why

should this city become a ruin?ʰ ¹⁸If they are indeed prophets and if the word of the LORD is with them, let them intercede with the LORD of Hosts not to let the articles that remain in the LORD's temple, in the palace of the king of Judah, and in Jerusalem go to Babylon.' ¹⁹For this is what the LORD of Hosts says about the pillars, the sea, the water carts,ⁱ and the rest of the articles that still remain in this city, ²⁰those Nebuchadnezzar king of Babylon did not take when he deported JeconiahᴮBson of Jehoiakim, king of Judah, from Jerusalem to Babylon along with all the nobles of Judahʲ and Jerusalem. ²¹Yes, this is what the LORD of Hosts, the God of Israel, says about the articles that remain in the temple of the LORD, in the palace of the king of Judah, and in Jerusalem: ²²'They will be brought to Babylon and will remain there until I attend to them again.'ᵏ This is the LORD's declaration. 'Then I will bring them up and restore them to this place.'"ˡ

Hananiah's False Prophecy

28 In that same year, at the beginning of the reign of King Zedekiah of Judah,ᵐ in the fifth month of the fourth year, the prophet Hananiah son of Azzur from Gibeonⁿ said to me in the temple of the LORD in the presence of the priests and all the people, ²"This is what the LORD of •Hosts, the God of Israel, says: 'I have broken the yoke of the king of Babylon.ᵒ ³Within two years I will restore to this place all the articles of the LORD's templeᵖ that King Nebuchadnezzar of Babylon took from here and transported to Babylon. ⁴And I will restore to this place JeconiahᴮBson of Jehoiakim, king of Judah, and all the exiles from Judahᑫ who

ᵃ27:9 Dt 18:10,14; Jr 14:14; 29:8
ᵇLv 19:26; Dt 18:10,14; 2Ch 33:6
ᶜEx 7:11; Dt 18:10; 2Ch 33:6
ᵈ27:12 Jr 28:1; 38:17
ᵉ27:13 Ezk 18:31
ᶠ27:14 Jr 14:14
ᵍ27:16 2Kg 24:13; 2Ch 36:7,10; Jr 28:3
ʰ27:17 Jr 7:34
ⁱ27:19 2Kg 25:13,16; Jr 52:17,20
ʲ27:20 Neh 6:17; 13:17; Jr 39:6
ᵏ27:22 Jr 29:10; 32:5
ˡEzr 1:7-11; 5:13-15; 7:19
ᵐ28:1 Jr 27:12
ⁿJos 9:3
ᵒ28:2 Jr 27:12
ᵖ28:3 Jr 27:16
ᑫ28:4 2Kg 24:10-17

ᴬ27:11 Lit work   ᴮ27:20; 28:4 = Jehoiachin

27:9-11 Five different types of false foretellers are listed here: false **prophets, diviners** (prophesied from the way arrows fell), **dreamers, fortune-tellers** (or "enchanters" who interpreted various signs), and **sorcerers** (conjurers). All these were banned from Israel (Dt 18:9-13). Their message (**don't serve the king of Babylon**) was nothing but falsehood.

27:12 King **Zedekiah**, his advisers, and all the people were to **put** their **necks under the yoke** in submission to Babylon.

27:16 The **articles** (not just "vessels," "utensils," or "furnishings") from the Lord's temple would not be coming back to Judah soon. Nothing was returned until the beginning of the reign of Cyrus of Persia in 536 B.C.

27:18 The primary task of a genuine prophet was to **intercede with the LORD.**

27:19 The **pillars**, made of bronze and placed in front of the temple, were called Jachin and Boaz (1Kg 7:15-22). These would be broken up, because they were too big to be taken away intact. The **sea** was a massive cast basin sitting on the backs of 12 cast oxen. It was used as a wash basin by

the priests (1Kg 7:23-26). The **water carts** were stands on wheels that supported the lavers (1Kg 7:27-37). The same three items are singled out in Jr 52:17.

28:1-17 The phrase **in that same year** places the incident in this chapter not long after the events in chapter 27.

28:1 Hananiah son of Azzur, whom the LXX calls a "false prophet," was a native of **Gibeon**, a city of priests five miles northwest of Jerusalem (modern el-Jib). He publicly contradicted Jeremiah's prophecy about the yoke (chap. 27).

28:2 I have broken the yoke refers to the prophecy Jeremiah had just delivered in chapter 27. Hananiah had the audacity to use the same introductory formula for a divine message that God had given Jeremiah, His genuine prophet.

28:3 Within two years, Hananiah predicted, everything would be restored. Such specificity must have made him look credible. But when his prophecy failed, he deserved the penalty prescribed in Dt 18:21-22.

28:4 Jeconiah is another name for King Jehoiachin of Judah (27:20).

went to Babylon'—this is the LORD's declaration—'for I will break the yoke of the king of Babylon.'"

Jeremiah's Response to Hananiah

[5] The prophet Jeremiah replied to the prophet Hananiah in the presence of the priests and all the people who were standing in the temple of the LORD. [6] The prophet Jeremiah said, "*Amen![a] May the LORD do so. May the LORD make the words you have prophesied come true and may He restore the articles of the LORD's temple and all the exiles from Babylon to this place! [7] Only listen to this message I am speaking in your hearing and in the hearing of all the people. [8] The prophets who preceded you and me from ancient times prophesied war, disaster,[A] and plague against many lands and great kingdoms. [9] As for the prophet who prophesies peace—only when the word of the prophet comes true will the prophet be recognized as one the LORD has truly sent."[b]

Hananiah Breaks Jeremiah's Yoke

[10] The prophet Hananiah then took the yoke bar from the neck of Jeremiah the prophet and broke it.[c] [11] In the presence of all the people Hananiah proclaimed, "This is what the LORD says: 'In this way, within two years I will break the yoke of King Nebuchadnezzar of Babylon from the neck of all the nations.'" Jeremiah the prophet then went on his way.

The LORD's Word against Hananiah

[12] The word of the LORD came to Jeremiah after Hananiah the prophet had broken the yoke bar from the neck of Jeremiah the

prophet: [13] "Go say to Hananiah: This is what the LORD says, 'You broke a wooden yoke bar, but in its place you will make an iron yoke bar.' [14] For this is what the LORD of Hosts, the God of Israel, says, 'I have put an iron yoke on the neck of all these nations that they might serve King Nebuchadnezzar of Babylon,[d] and they will serve him.[e] I have also put the wild animals under him.'"[f]

[15] The prophet Jeremiah said to the prophet Hananiah, "Listen, Hananiah! The LORD did not send you, but you have led these people to trust in a lie.[g] [16] Therefore, this is what the LORD says: 'I am about to send you off the face of the earth. You will die this year because you have spoken rebellion against the LORD.'"[h] [17] And the prophet Hananiah died that year in the seventh month.

Jeremiah's Letter to the Exiles

29 This is the text of the letter[i] that Jeremiah the prophet sent from Jerusalem to the rest of the elders of the exiles, the priests, the prophets, and all the people Nebuchadnezzar[j] had deported from Jerusalem to Babylon. [2] This was after King Jeconiah,[B,k] the queen mother, the court officials, the officials of Judah and Jerusalem, the craftsmen, and the metalsmiths had left Jerusalem. [3] The letter was sent by Elasah son of Shaphan and Gemariah son of Hilkiah[l] whom Zedekiah king of Judah had sent to Babylon to Nebuchadnezzar king of Babylon. The letter stated:

[4] This is what the LORD of *Hosts, the God of Israel, says to all the exiles I deported from Jerusalem to Babylon: [5] "Build

---

Cross references:
[a] 28:6 1Kg 1:36
[b] 28:9 Dt 18:20-22
[c] 28:10 Jr 27:2
[d] 28:14 Dt 28:48
[e] Jr 25:11
[f] Jr 27:6
[g] 28:15 Jr 29:31; Ezk 13:22
[h] 28:16 Dt 13:5; Is 59:13; Jr 29:32
[i] 29:1 2Sm 11:14-15; 1Kg 21:8-11
[j] 2Kg 24:11; 25:22; 2Ch 36:6-13
[k] 29:2 Jr 24:1; 27:20; 28:4
[l] 29:3 1Ch 6:13

[A]28:8 Some Hb mss, Vg read *famine*   [B]29:2 = Jehoiachin

28:6 Jeremiah responded to Hananiah's brazen prediction with an **Amen**. Whether he did so sarcastically or because he was thrown off balance since Hananiah's prophecy disputed everything God had shown him up to this point, we cannot say for sure.

28:8-9 Jeremiah reminded Hananiah that the prophets who had preceded them spoke of **war, disaster, and plague**. Prophets who prophesied **peace** had to show they were genuine by the fulfillment of their words (Dt 13:1-5; 18:15-22). So Hananiah was running against the grain not only of Jeremiah's words but of the messages of all the prophets from the past.

28:13 The Lord told Jeremiah to **make an iron yoke bar**, because Hananiah had made Jeremiah's word about God's judgment all the more certain and hardened.

28:15-17 In another wordplay the Lord declared that since He had not sent Hananiah to prophesy, He would **send** him **off the face of the earth**. Two months later Hananiah died. We are not told how this happened or if God caused his death, but the reason for his death is that he had **spoken rebellion against the LORD** (see Dt 13:5).

29:1 The **rest of the elders** appears to be those who had survived deportation to Babylon.

29:2 King Jeconiah is another name for King Jehoiachin (see note at 22:24-30). The Hebrew form of **queen mother** is a feminine ending on the same masculine form for "a mighty man of valor" or a "hero" (Hb *haggevirah*). The **court officials** (Hb *hassarisim*) is usually rendered "eunuchs," but it was also a title for palace officers (52:25; Gn 37:36; 40:2; 1Sm 8:15).

29:3 Jeremiah sent his letter by an emissary that King **Zedekiah** of Judah was sending to **Babylon**, which accompanied tribute he was paying to **Nebuchadnezzar**. The two men who carried the letter were **Elasah** son of Shaphan and **Gemariah** son of Hilkiah. Shaphan was a sort of secretary of state under King Josiah (2Kg 22:8-14), and Gemariah was the high priest under Josiah (2Ch 34–35). Despite a crooked government and priesthood, these men show that some people remained faithful to the Lord, even during the worst of times.

29:4-7 Jeremiah's letter must have arrived in Babylon shortly after the **exiles** did. It warned that this would not be a short exile.

houses and live in them.[a] Plant gardens and eat their produce. [6]Take wives and have sons and daughters. Take wives for your sons and give your daughters to men in marriage so that they may bear sons and daughters. Multiply there; do not decrease. [7]Seek the welfare of the city I have deported you to. Pray to the LORD on its behalf,[b] for when it has prosperity, you will prosper."

[8]For this is what the LORD of Hosts, the God of Israel, says: "Don't let your prophets who are among you[c] and your diviners deceive you,[d] and don't listen to the dreams you elicit from them, [9]for they are prophesying falsely to you in My name. I have not sent them."[e] This is the LORD's declaration.

[10]For this is what the LORD says: "When 70 years for Babylon are complete,[f] I will attend to you and will confirm My promise concerning you to restore you to this place. [11]For I know the plans I have for you"[g]—this is the LORD's declaration—"plans for your welfare, not for disaster, to give you a future and a hope. [12]You will call to Me and come and pray to Me, and I will listen to you.[h] [13]You will seek Me[i] and find Me when you search for Me with all your heart. [14]I will be found by you"—this is the LORD's declaration—"and I will restore your fortunes[A,j] and gather you from all the nations and places where I banished you"—this is the LORD's declaration. "I will restore you to the place I deported you from."[k]

[15]You have said, "The LORD has raised up prophets for us in Babylon!" [16]But this is what the LORD says concerning the king sitting on David's throne and concerning

[a]29:5 Jr 29:28
[b]29:7 Ezr 6:10; 1Tm 2:1-2
[c]29:8 Jr 27:9
[d]Jr 27:15
[e]29:9 Jr 29:31
[f]29:10 Jr 25:12; Dn 9:2
[g]29:11 Ps 33:10; Jr 26:3; 36:3
[h]29:12 Dt 30:1-10; Jr 3:12
[i]29:13 Dt 4:29; 1Ch 28:9; 2Ch 15:2
[j]29:14 Jb 42:10; Jr 32:44
[k]Dt 30:3; Jr 30:3
[l]29:17 Jr 14:12; 21:9; 24:10
[m]29:18 Dt 30:1; Jr 8:3; 16:15
[n]29:19 Jr 26:5
[o]29:20 Jr 24:5
[p]29:21 Jr 14:14; 29:9
[q]29:22 Is 65:15
[r]Dn 3:6
[s]29:23 Gn 34:7; Dt 22:21; Jos 7:15

all the people living in this city—that is, concerning your brothers who did not go with you into exile. [17]This is what the LORD of Hosts says: "I am about to send against them sword, famine, and plague[l] and will make them like rotten figs that are inedible because they are so bad. [18]I will pursue them with sword, famine, and plague. I will make them a horror to all the kingdoms of the earth—a curse and a desolation, an object of scorn and a disgrace among all the nations where I have banished them.[m] [19]I will do this because they have not listened to My words"—this is the LORD's declaration—"that I sent to them with My servants the prophets time and time again.[B,n] And you too have not listened." This is the LORD's declaration.

[20]Hear the word of the LORD, all you exiles I have sent from Jerusalem to Babylon.[o] [21]This is what the LORD of Hosts, the God of Israel, says to Ahab son of Kolaiah and to Zedekiah son of Maaseiah, the ones prophesying a lie to you in My name:[p] "I am about to hand them over to Nebuchadnezzar king of Babylon, and he will kill them before your very eyes. [22]Based on what happens to them, all the exiles of Judah who are in Babylon will create a curse[q] that says, 'May the LORD make you like Zedekiah and Ahab, whom the king of Babylon roasted in the fire!'[r] [23]because they have committed an outrage[s] in Israel by committing adultery with their neighbors' wives and have spoken a lie in My name, which I did not command them. I am He who knows, and I am a witness." This is the LORD's declaration.

[24]To Shemaiah the Nehelamite you are to say, [25]"This is what the LORD of Hosts,

---

[A]29:14 Or will end your captivity   [B]29:19 Lit prophets, rising up early and sending

29:7 Jeremiah's advice to the exiles was remarkable. He urged them to **pray** for Babylon and its prosperity. By doing this the exiles would **prosper** as well (1Tm 2:1-2).

29:10 The **70 years for Babylon** are also noted in 25:11. The duration of the Babylonian kingdom is linked with the length of the exile (see note at 25:11). From Nebuchadnezzar's accession to the throne in 605 B.C. to the fall of Babylon in 539 B.C. was 66 years.

29:12-13 These verses are a renewal of God's promise in Dt 30:3-5.

29:15-19 Many interpreters think these verses are misplaced since Jeremiah was so critical of Zedekiah in a letter carried by his ambassadors. But verses 4-23 may not be a single letter. Verses 15-19 could be a second letter not carried to Babylon by the king's officials.

29:17 The people left in Jerusalem who were not among the initial exiles will be made like **rotten figs**. This same imagery appears in chapter 24.

29:21-23 **Ahab son of Kolaiah** and **Zedekiah** son of Maaseiah were two prophets singled out for **committing adultery with their neighbors' wives** as well as prophesying lies. There is a wordplay here. The name Kolaiah is related to the Hebrew term *qelalah* ("curse") and *qalah* ("to burn"). Thus they would roast in the **fire**. So heinous were their lying prophecies that the king of Babylon would charge them with treason and condemn them to death by burning (Dn 3:6,20,23).

29:24-25 **Shemaiah** the Nehelamite was another false prophet. He had apparently ordered **the priest Zephaniah** to silence Jeremiah. Zephaniah was warden over police regulations in the temple (21:1; 37:3; 52:24).

the God of Israel, says: You[A] in your own name have sent out letters to all the people of Jerusalem, to the priest Zephaniah[a] son of Maaseiah, and to all the priests, saying: [26]"The LORD has appointed you priest in place of Jehoiada the priest to be the chief officer[b] in the temple of the LORD, responsible for every madman[c] who acts like a prophet. You must confine him in the stocks[d] and an iron collar. [27]So now, why have you not rebuked Jeremiah of Anathoth who has been acting like a prophet among you?[e] [28]For he has sent word to us in Babylon, claiming, "The exile will be long. Build houses and settle down. Plant gardens and eat their produce.""[f]

[29]Zephaniah the priest read this letter in the hearing of Jeremiah the prophet.

A Message about Shemaiah

[30]Then the word of the LORD came to Jeremiah: [31]"Send a message to all the exiles, saying: This is what the LORD says concerning Shemaiah the Nehelamite. Because Shemaiah prophesied to you, though I did not send him, and made you trust a lie,[g] [32]this is what the LORD says: I am about to punish Shemaiah the Nehelamite and his descendants. There will not be even one of his descendants living among these people,[h] nor will any ever see the good that I will bring to My people"—this is the LORD's declaration—"for he has preached rebellion against the LORD."[i]

Cross references
[a]29:25 Jr 21:1; 37:3; 52:24-27
[b]29:26 2Ch 31:13; Jr 20:1
[c]2Kg 9:11; Hs 9:7
[d]2Ch 16:10; Jr 20:2
[e]29:27 Jr 1:1
[f]29:28 Jr 29:5
[g]29:31 Jr 27:10,14-16; 28:15; 29:9,21,23
[h]29:32 Jr 17:6
[i]Jr 28:16
[j]30:2 Hab 2:2
[k]30:3 Ezk 37:15-23
[l]30:7 Jl 2:11; Zph 1:14
[m]Dn 12:1
[n]30:8 Jr 2:20
[o]Jr 27:2
[p]30:8 Ezk 34:27
[q]30:9 Is 55:3-5; Ezk 34:23-24; 37:24-25; Hs 3:5; Lk 1:69; Ac 13:23,34
[r]30:10 Is 41:8; 44:2; 45:4

Restoration from Captivity

30 This is the word that came to Jeremiah from the LORD. [2]This is what the LORD, the God of Israel, says: "Write down on a scroll all the words that I have spoken to you,[j] [3]for the days are certainly coming"—this is the LORD's declaration—"when I will restore the fortunes[B] of My people Israel and Judah"[k]—the LORD's declaration. "I will restore them to the land I gave to their ancestors and they will possess it."

[4]These are the words the LORD spoke to Israel and Judah. [5]Yes, this is what the LORD says:

We have heard a cry of terror,
of dread—there is no peace.
[6] Ask and see
whether a male can give birth.
Why then do I see every man
with his hands on his stomach
like a woman in labor
and every face turned pale?
[7] How awful that day will be![l]
There will be none like it![m]
It will be a time of trouble for Jacob,
but he will be delivered out of it.

[8]"On that day"—this is the declaration of the LORD of •Hosts—"I will break his yoke from your neck[n] and tear off your chains[o] so strangers will never again enslave him.[p] [9]They will serve the LORD their God and I will raise up David their king for them."[q]

[10] As for you, My servant Jacob,[r]

[A]29:25 Lit Because you   [B]30:3 Or will end the captivity

29:26 Shemaiah charged Jeremiah with being a **madman**.

29:29-32 Zephaniah the priest read Shemaiah's **letter** to Jeremiah, who responded with another letter from the Lord to the exiles. He exposed Shemaiah's hypocrisy and set his punishment—that he would have no **descendants** and he would not live to see the restoration God had predicted. No harm, however, came to Jeremiah, in fulfillment of God's promise (1:8,19; 15:20).

30:1-33:26 These chapters were written during the final days of the siege of Jerusalem (the last 18 months of that siege; 32:1-2); yet they foretell a bright future. Jeremiah was in prison and the city was in dire straits; nevertheless, he foresaw in the distant future the restoration of the nation to its land, the new covenant of redemption, the rule of a purified Davidic king over a purified Zion, and a large number of Gentiles coming to the Messiah.

30:2 The command from the Lord to Jeremiah to **write down on a scroll all the words that I have spoken** introduces chapters 30-31, and probably 32-33 as well.

30:3 The days are . . . coming announces eschatological times (3:16; 16:14; 23:5; 31:27,31). It is the distant future that Jeremiah had in mind. The phrase **I will restore the fortunes** (lit "turn the turnings" or "reverse the fortunes")

appears often in these chapters. **Restore them to the land I gave to their ancestors** looks to a time beyond the future return from the exile. The exiles, when they returned, retook only a small portion of the ancestral lands. Thus the restoration God promised here looks beyond this event.

30:7-8 Much debate revolves around the phrase **on that day**. Was this the day Cyrus captured Babylon? If so, why would it be so horrendous for Israel? Cyrus was their liberator. "That day" therefore must be the time when God will judge all nations. "That day" is used in Scripture to introduce the "Day of the LORD" (Am 5:18-20; Zph 1:14-18). All oppression (**his** understood collectively of all Israel's oppressors) of Israel will be overcome on that future day.

30:9 God **will raise up David their king for them** refers to the future ideal king, a so-called "second David." This messianic person in the line of David is paired with **the LORD their God**. The Jewish Targum correctly interprets this line as "Messiah, the son of David."

30:10 Judah and Israel are called **My servant Jacob**. Elsewhere diverse persons such as Nebuchadnezzar, Cyrus, and the Messiah are said to be God's servants or shepherds (e.g., 25:9; Is 44:28). God promised to regather Israel from all the lands where He had scattered them (**Jacob**

do not be afraid—
      this is the Lord's declaration—
and do not be dismayed, Israel,
   for without fail I will save you
     from far away,
   your descendants, from the land
     of their captivity!
Jacob will return and have calm
     and quiet
   with no one to frighten him.[a]
11 For I will be with you—
      this is the Lord's declaration—
   to save you![b]
I will bring destruction
   on all the nations
where I have scattered you;
however, I will not bring destruction
   on you.
I will discipline you justly,
   and I will by no means
     leave you unpunished.[c]

Healing Zion's Wounds

12 For this is what the Lord says:

Your injury is incurable;
   your wound most severe.[d]
13 No one takes up the case
     for your sores.[e]
There is no healing for you.
14 All your lovers have forgotten you;
   they no longer look for you,
for I have struck
   you as an enemy would,

with the discipline[f] of someone cruel,[g]
because of your enormous *guilt
   and your innumerable sins.
15 Why do you cry out about your injury?
   Your pain has no cure!
I have done these things to you
   because of your enormous guilt
   and your innumerable sins.
16 Nevertheless, all who devoured you
     will be devoured,[h]
and all your adversaries—all of them—
   will go off into exile.
Those who plunder you
     will be plundered,
and all who raid you will be raided.
17 But I will bring you health[i]
   and will heal you of your wounds—
      this is the Lord's declaration—
for they call you Outcast,
*Zion whom no one cares about.

Restoration of the Land

18 This is what the Lord says:

I will certainly restore the fortunes[A]
   of Jacob's tents[j]
and show compassion on his dwellings.
Every city will be rebuilt on its mound;
every citadel will stand
   on its proper site.
19 Thanksgiving will come out of them,
   a sound of celebration.
I will multiply them,
   and they will not decrease;[k]

Cross references:
- [a] 30:10 Jr 46:27; Ezk 39:26
- [b] 30:11 2Kg 19:34; Is 37:35; Jr 15:20
- [c] 30:10-11 Jr 46:27-28
- [d] 30:12 Jr 10:19; 15:18; 17:9
- [e] 30:13 Hs 5:13
- [f] 30:14 Jr 2:30; 5:3; 7:28
- [g] Is 13:9
- [h] 30:16 Jr 10:25
- [i] 30:17 Is 58:8; Jr 8:22; 33:6
- [j] 30:18 Jr 30:3
- [k] 30:19 Jr 29:6

A 30:18 Or certainly end the captivity

---

will return). Their condition will be one of **calm and quiet**, a pastoral metaphor, like sheep resting **with no one to frighten** them.

shever

Hebrew Pronunciation	[SHEH ver]
HCSB Translation	brokenness, destruction, injury
Uses in Jeremiah	15
Uses in the OT	44
Focus Passage	Jeremiah 30:12,15

Shever, from the verb *shavar (break)*, has many of its connotations. Jeremiah especially likes both words. *Shever* describes a *broken* foot (Lv 21:19), spirit (Is 65:14), or people (Jr 6:14). It denotes *fracture* (Lv 24:20) or *injury* (Jr 30:12). It is a personal *downfall* (Pr 18:12) and a people's *brokenness* (Jr 6:14), *ruin* (Am 6:6), or *wretchedness* (Is 59:7). It suggests land *fissures* (Ps 60:2), *collapse* of a wall (Is 30:13), or *shattering* of a jar (Is 30:14). *Shever* mostly implies *disaster* (Jr 4:20) or *destruction* (Is 15:5); it occurs with terms for "devastation" (*shod*, Jr 48:3; *she'th*, Lm 3:47). *Shever* indicates dream *interpretation* (Jdg 7:15). It connotes a *crashing* (Zph 1:10) or *thrashing* (Jb 41:25). It can be translated by verbs like *destroy* (Is 1:28). Related *shibbaron* indicates *destruction* (Jr 17:18) and *bitter* groaning (Ezk 21:6).

30:11 God will chasten and destroy all the nations that oppress Israel. But He **will not bring destruction** on Israel, even though no one will be left **unpunished**.

30:12-17 Israel's wounds will be beyond human help, but the Lord will serve as their physician (**but I will bring you health**, see also 3:22 and 33:6). Israel's sad condition appears in three metaphors: no medicine, no physician, and no lovers.

30:15-16 Some argue that there is a radical change in God's attitude between these two verses. But God remains the same. His judgment must fall to bring Israel to the point where He can restore them. Israel's best hope was that God remains constant in spite of human fickleness. Israel's enemies will experience the same things Israel went through: (1) The nations **who devoured you will be devoured**, (2) those who sent Israel into captivity **will go off into exile**, (3) the plunderers **will be plundered**, and (4) those who raided Israel **will be raided**.

30:18-20 In these verses a whole new day, not just a restoration, is promised for Israel. Jerusalem will be rebuilt, repopulated, and ruled by a new leader who is responsive to God.

30:18 **Every city will be rebuilt on its mound** or "tel." The Arabic word *tell* (Hb *tel*) denotes a mound that stands on the ruins of a destroyed or abandoned town.

I will honor them, and they will not
   be insignificant.
20 His children will be as in past days;
   his congregation will be established
     in My presence.
I will punish all his oppressors.^a
21 Jacob's leader will be one of them;
   his ruler will issue from him.
I will invite him to Me, and he will
   approach Me,^b
for who would otherwise risk his life
   to approach Me?
       This is the LORD's declaration.
22 You will be My people,
   and I will be your God.^c

The Wrath of God

23 Look, a storm from the LORD!^d
Wrath has gone out,
a churning storm.
It will whirl about the heads
   of the wicked.
24 The LORD's burning anger will not
   turn back
until He has completely fulfilled
   the purposes of His heart.
In time to come you will
   understand it.^e

God's Relationship with His People

31 "At that time"—this is the LORD's declaration—"I will be the God of all the
families of Israel,^f and they will be My people."
2 This is what the LORD says:

They found favor in the wilderness^g—
the people who survived the sword.
When Israel went to find rest,

Cross references (center column):

a 30:20 Jdg 10:12; Is 19:20-25
b 30:21 Nm 16:5
c 30:22 Jr 11:4; 24:7; 31:33
d 30:23 Ps 83:15; Is 29:6; Zch 9:14
e 30:23-24 Jr 23:19-20
f 31:1 Jr 30:22
g 31:2 Ex 33:12-17
h 31:3 Ps 36:10; 109:12
i 31:4 Ex 15:20; Jdg 11:34; 1Sm 18:6
j 31:5 Lv 19:23,25; Dt 20:6; 28:30
k 31:6 Is 2:3
l 31:7 Ps 28:9; Hab 3:13; Zch 8:7
m 31:8 Jr 6:22; 25:32; 50:41

---

3 the LORD appeared to him^A
   from far away.
I have loved you
   with an everlasting love;
therefore, I have continued to extend
   faithful love to you.^h
4 Again I will build you so that you will
   be rebuilt,
Virgin Israel.
You will take up
   your tambourines againⁱ
and go out in joyful dancing.
5 You will plant vineyards again
on the mountains of Samaria;
the planters will plant and will enjoy
   the fruit.^j
6 For there will be a day when watchmen
   will call out
in the hill country of Ephraim,
"Get up, let's go up to •Zion,^k
to •Yahweh our God!"

God's People Brought Home

7 For this is what the LORD says:

Sing with joy for Jacob;
shout for the chief of the nations!
Proclaim, praise, and say,
"LORD, save Your people,^l
the remnant of Israel!"
8 Watch! I am going to bring them
   from the northern land.
I will gather them from remote regions
   of the earth^m—
the blind and the lame will be
   with them,
along with those who are pregnant
   and those about to give birth.

---

^A31:3 LXX; MT reads *me*

30:21-22 This messianic prophecy emphasizes three functions: (1) the Messiah will be a native (**one of them**), not a foreigner; (2) He will carry the priestly prerogative, which allows him to **approach** the Lord like Melchizedek (Heb 5:5-6); and (3) He will declare **You will be My people, and I will be your God**.

30:23-24 To forestall any false security from the promises just delivered in verses 17-22, judgment must be poured out on the guilty. God's judgment will be like a sudden windstorm. His wrath will continue until **the purposes of His heart** are **completely fulfilled**. His purposes cannot be enacted until the sins of Israel and her adversaries have been addressed.

31:1-6 In these verses God declared that He will reunify all Israel. His words of comfort are addressed to **all the families of Israel**.

31:2 The combining of **the wilderness** with those who **survived the sword** links the exodus and wilderness experience with the return from exile in Assyria. Survivors of both events enjoy God's favor and grace.

31:3 God's love for Israel has continued up to the present (Dt 7:8; 10:15; Hs 11:1). It is an **everlasting** and a **faithful love**.

31:4-5 With a threefold repetition of **again**, Israel's future will parallel her past. God pictures His love for Israel by calling her His **virgin** bride (2:1-3; Hs 2:14-23), recalling the early days in the wilderness.

31:6 The assumption is that the temple will be rebuilt in Jerusalem. **Ephraim**, standing for the 10 northern tribes of Israel, will again **go up to Zion** to worship.

31:7 Israel is called the **chief of the nations** (cp. Dt 26:19; Am 6:1) because they are God's elect. Five imperatives (**sing . . . shout . . . proclaim, praise . . . say**) are given to Israel to celebrate the great deliverance of God for the **remnant of Israel**.

31:8 God's future restoration will come not only from the **northern land** (Assyria and Babylon), but it will come from **remote regions of the earth**. This refers to a worldwide regathering in which no one will be excluded.

31:9 The phrase **Ephraim is My firstborn** means not first in

They will return here
as a great assembly![a]
9 They will come weeping,
but I will bring them back
with consolation.[A,b]
I will lead them to •wadis filled
with water
by a smooth way where
they will not stumble,[c]
for I am Israel's Father,
and Ephraim is My firstborn.
10 Nations, hear the word of the LORD,
and tell it among the
far off coastlands![d]
Say: The One who scattered Israel
will gather him.
He will watch over him as a shepherd
guards his flock,
11 for the LORD has ransomed Jacob
and redeemed him from the power
of one stronger than he.[e]
12 They will come and shout for joy
on the heights of Zion;
they will be radiant with joy[f]
because of[g] the LORD's goodness,
because of the grain, the new wine,
the fresh oil,[h]
and because of the young of the flocks
and herds.
Their life will be
like an irrigated garden,
and they will no longer grow weak
from hunger.
13 Then the young woman will rejoice
with dancing,
while young and old men
rejoice together.
I will turn their mourning into joy,[i]

give them consolation,
and bring happiness out of grief.
14 I will refresh the priests
with an abundance,[B,j]
and My people will be satisfied
with My goodness.
This is the LORD's declaration.

Lament Turned to Joy
15 This is what the LORD says:

A voice was heard in Ramah,
a lament with bitter weeping—
Rachel weeping for her children,
refusing to be comforted
for her children
because they are no more.[k]

16 This is what the LORD says:

Keep your voice from weeping
and your eyes from tears,
for the reward for your work
will come—
this is the LORD's declaration—
and your children will return
from the enemy's land.
17 There is hope for your future[l]—
this is the LORD's declaration—
and your children will return
to their own territory.
18 I have heard Ephraim moaning,
"You disciplined me,
and I have been disciplined
like an untrained calf.
Restore me, and I will return,
for you, LORD, are my God.[m]
19 After I returned, I repented;
After I was instructed, I struck
my thigh in grief.[n]

Cross references (center column):
[a]31:8 Ezk 38:15
[b]31:9 Jb 15:11
[c]Pr 4:12; Is 63:13; Ezk 36:15
[d]31:10 Is 40:15; Jr 25:22; 47:4
[e]31:11 Is 44:23; 48:20
[f]31:12 Ps 34:5; Is 60:5
[g]Is 2:2; Jr 51:44; Mc 4:1
[h]Nm 18:12; Dt 7:13; Hg 1:11
[i]31:13 Ps 105:43; Is 35:10; 51:3,11
[j]31:14 Dt 31:20; Ps 36:8; Is 30:23
[k]31:15 Mt 2:18
[l]31:17 Jr 5:31; 23:20; 29:11
[m]31:18 Ps 40:5; Jr 3:22
[n]31:19 Ezk 21:12

[A]31:9 LXX; MT reads *supplications*   [B]31:14 Lit *fatness*

---

chronology (Ephraim was Joseph's second son), but first in rank and priority just as Israel was called God's "firstborn" (Ex 4:22). Jacob (Israel) was God's "firstborn," even though he was Isaac's second son. David, eighth son of Jesse, is called a "firstborn" in Ps 89:27, and Jesus is called "the firstborn of all creation (Col 1:15; Rv 1:5), both signifying first in rank and importance, not chronology.

31:10 The **nations**, all Gentiles, are to be told that the **One who scattered Israel will gather** them.

31:11 The Lord **ransomed Jacob**, as if He had paid the ransom price (Hb *padah*; cp. Ex 13:13,15; 34:20). The words **redeemed him** recalls the practice of a family redeemer (Hb *ga'al*; cp. Lv 25:25,48; Nm 35:12,19; Ru 2:20; 3:9,8,14), a man who was expected to rescue a close relative from danger or hardship.

31:12-14 The harvests will grow, with the result that the priests' portion will increase **with an abundance**.

31:15 Rachel, Joseph's mother, is pictured as **weeping in Ramah**, a town five miles north of Jerusalem. Ramah

served as the staging grounds for the deportation to Babylon (40:1-4). Rachel was Jacob's favorite wife. She died giving birth to Benjamin (Gn 35:18). She is also referred to as the mother of all 10 northern tribes of Israel since her descendants Ephraim and Manasseh were heads of the two leading tribes in that region. The citation in Mt 2:17-18 depicts Rachel as the embodiment of all Israel's mothers weeping for their slain children, a tragedy that Herod's atrocities called to mind once more.

31:16 The **reward for** Rachel's **work** is that her children will come back from exile from all over the world, just as Jacob and Rachel returned from serving Laban with all their children as their "reward."

31:16-17 Rachel is twice told to stop weeping, because **your children will return**.

31:18-20 Ephraim, representing the 10 northern tribes, finally saw how he had acted as **an untrained** (or "undisciplined") **calf** (cp. Hs 10:11) and as a rebel against God. But now chastened and repentant, he **struck** his **thigh...ashamed and humiliated**. Ephraim will be forgiven

I was ashamed and humiliated
because I bore the disgrace
      of my youth."
20 Isn't Ephraim a precious son to Me,
a delightful child?
Whenever I speak against him,
I certainly still think about him.
Therefore, My inner being yearns
      for him;
I will truly have compassion on him.
            This is the Lord's declaration.

Repentance and Restoration
21 Set up road markers[a] for yourself;
establish signposts!
Keep the highway in mind,
the way you have traveled.
Return, Virgin Israel!
Return to these cities of yours.
22 How long will you turn here and there,
faithless daughter?[b]
For the Lord creates something new
      in the land[A]—
a female[B] will shelter[c] a man.

23 This is what the Lord of 'Hosts, the God of
Israel, says: "When I restore their fortunes,[D]
they will once again speak this word in the
land of Judah and in its cities, 'May the Lord
bless you, righteous settlement,[c] holy mountain.'[d] 24 Judah and all its cities will live in it

together—also farmers and those who move[E]
with the flocks— 25 for I satisfy the thirsty person and feed all those who are weak."
26 At this I awoke and looked around. My
sleep had been most pleasant to me.
27 "The days are coming"—this is the Lord's
declaration—"when I will sow the house of
Israel[e] and the house of Judah with the seed of
man and the seed of beast. 28 Just as I watched
over them to uproot and to tear them down,
to demolish and to destroy, and to cause disaster, so will I be attentive to build and to plant
them,"[f] says the Lord. 29 "In those days, it will
never again be said:

The fathers have eaten sour grapes,
and the children's teeth are set
      on edge.[g]

30 Rather, each will die for his own wrongdoing.[h] Anyone who eats sour grapes—his own
teeth will be set on edge.

The New Covenant
31 "Look, the days are coming"—this is the
Lord's declaration—"when I will make a new
covenant[i] with the house of Israel and with the
house of Judah. 32 This one will not be like the
covenant I made with their ancestors when
I took them by the hand to bring them out
of the land of Egypt—a covenant they broke
even though I had married them"[j]—the Lord's

Cross references (center column)
a 31:21 2Kg 23:17; Ezk 39:15
b 31:22 Jr 3:14,22; 49:4
c 31:23 Jb 8:6; Jr 50:7
d Ps 2:6; 3:4; 48:1; 99:9
e 31:27 Ezk 36:9,11; Hs 2:23
f 31:28 Jr 1:10; 18:7-10; 44:27
g 31:29 Ezk 18:2
h 31:30 Dt 24:6; Ezk 18:20
i 31:31 Ezk 37:26; Lk 22:20; 1Co 11:25; 2Co 3:6; Heb 9:15; 12:24
j 31:32 Is 54:4; 62:4; Mal 2:11

A 31:22 Or new on earth   B 31:22 Or woman   C 31:22 Or female surrounds, or female courts; Hb obscure   D 31:23 Or I end their captivity
E 31:24 Tg, Vg, Aq, Sym; MT reads and they will move

---

and, like the prodigal, will return home. God's love will triumph over Israel's rebellion (Hs 11:1-11).

31:21 These **road markers** and **signposts** would lead Israel
back home from Babylon and function as signposts of the
"ancient paths" they had traveled with God (6:16).

31:22 Virgin Israel is called a **faithless daughter**—an apostate, backsliding turnabout. The phrase **a female will shelter a man** is perhaps the most obscure phrase in all of
Jeremiah. Some see this as a prophecy of the virgin birth
of Christ. But the word "female" does not have a definite
article with it, and such a general word for "woman" cannot
be made to mean a virgin. Further, "to shelter" does not
mean conceiving, nor does any of this fit the context. No
one interpretation satisfies all difficulties since the intention of the verb "to shelter" is uncertain. **Something new**
may mean that "woman" refers to Israel and "man" to the
Lord, so that a new relationship between Israel and her God
will arise in the latter days.

31:26 Some people take this verse to be a contradiction of
23:25, where Jeremiah criticized revelatory dreams. But
there he spoke only of the dreams of false prophets (see
note at 23:25-29).

31:29-30 The proverb about the **fathers** eating **sour grapes,
and the children's teeth** being **set on edge** reflects the
widespread belief that they were being unfairly punished
for the sins of the previous generation, but Moses taught

that this was not true (Dt 24:16). Ezekiel also refuted this
proverb (Ezk 18:2-4).

31:31-34 The NT frequently used this passage about the new
covenant (Lk 22:20; 1Co 11:25; 2Co 3:5-14; and Heb 8:8-12,
the longest quote from the OT in the NT). It is a classic text
that has shaped much of Christian theological reflection.

31:31 The new covenant is set in eschatological times of
the Messiah and the consummation of history (**the days
are coming**). The name of this **new covenant** suggests a
radical break from past covenants. But the word for "new"
in Hebrew can also mean "renewed covenant," especially
since three-fourths of the contents of this covenant recall
the Abrahamic-Davidic covenants. The principal parties
of the covenant are **the house of Israel** and **the house of
Judah**. While there has been a cleavage between the 10
northern tribes and the two southern tribes, both parts are
included here, suggesting a rejoining of the two parts. This
new covenant also applies to the church, because Gentiles
were part of this continuing Abrahamic-Davidic new covenant when God promised that in Abraham's seed all nations
would be blessed. Among the other names given to this new
covenant in the OT is "Everlasting Covenant," which speaks
to its duration.

31:32 The problem with the old covenant was not with its
maker or its contents, but with God's people who **broke**
their marriage vows to Him (cp. 11:10). God said this covenant would **not be like the covenant I made with their**

declaration. [33] "Instead, this is the covenant I will make with the house of Israel after those days"—the LORD's declaration. "I will put My teaching within them and write it on their hearts. I will be their God, and they will be My people. [34] No longer will one teach his neighbor or his brother, saying, 'Know the LORD,'[a] for they will all know Me, from the least to the greatest of them"—this is the LORD's declaration. "For I will forgive their wrongdoing[b] and never again remember their sin."[c]

[35] This is what the LORD says:

The One who gives the sun for light
   by day,
the fixed order of moon and stars
   for light by night,
who stirs up the sea and makes
   its waves roar[d]—
Yahweh of Hosts is His name:
[36] If this fixed order departs
   from My presence—
      this is the LORD's declaration—
then also Israel's descendants
   will cease
to be a nation before Me forever.[e]

[37] This is what the LORD says:

If the heavens above can be measured
and the foundations
   of the earth below explored,
I will reject all of Israel's descendants

because of all they have done—
   this is the LORD's declaration.

[38] "Look, the days are coming"—the LORD's declaration—"when the city[A] from the Tower of Hananel[f] to the Corner Gate[g] will be rebuilt for the LORD. [39] A measuring line will once again stretch out straight to the hill of Gareb[h] and then turn toward Goah. [40] The whole valley—the corpses, the ashes, and all the fields as far as the Kidron Valley[i] to the corner of the Horse Gate[j] to the east—will be holy to the LORD. It will never be uprooted or demolished again."

Jeremiah's Land Purchase

32 This is the word that came to Jeremiah from the LORD in the tenth year of Zedekiah[k] king of Judah, which was the eighteenth year of Nebuchadnezzar. [2] At that time, the army of the king of Babylon was besieging Jerusalem, and Jeremiah the prophet was imprisoned in the guard's courtyard[m] in the palace of the king of Judah. [3] Zedekiah king of Judah had imprisoned him, saying: "Why are you prophesying, 'This is what the LORD says: Look, I am about to hand this city over to Babylon's king, and he will capture it. [4] Zedekiah king of Judah will not escape from the Chaldeans; indeed, he will certainly be handed over to Babylon's king. They will speak face to face[B] and meet eye to eye.[n] [5] He will take Zedekiah to Babylon where he will stay until I

Cross references (center column):
[a]31:34 Jdg 2:10; 1Sm 3:7; Hs 2:20
[b]Nm 14:19; Ps 103:3; Jr 36:3
[c]31:31-34 Heb 8:8-12; 10:16-17
[d]31:35 Ps 46:3; Is 51:15; Jr 5:22
[e]31:36 Jr 33:18; 35:19
[f]31:38 Neh 3:1; 12:39
[g]2Kg 14:13; 2Ch 26:9; Zch 14:10
[h]31:39 Zch 2:1
[i]31:40 2Kg 23:4 /Neh 3:28
[k]32:1 2Kg 24:17-20; 2Ch 36:10-12; Jr 27:1-11
/Jr 29:1
[m]32:2 Neh 3:25; Jr 33:1; 37:21; 38:6; 39:14
[n]32:4 Jr 34:3

[A]31:38 = Jerusalem   [B]32:4 Lit *His mouth will speak with his mouth*

---

ancestors at the exodus or on Sinai, but it would be made "after those days" (v. 33) when the people of Israel are restored to their land.

31:33 God will still place His law **within them and write it on their hearts**. This law or instruction is a point of continuity between the old and new covenants, only this time God would write the law internally rather than externally on tablets. Gone would be the evil will and heart of the people, which had characterized Israel in the past (13:10; 18:12; 23:17).

31:34 Once the merely external law is a thing of the past, **no longer will one teach his neighbor or his brother, saying, 'Know the LORD,' for they will all know Me**. Teaching will also be a thing of the past. **From the least to the greatest of them** indicates all people no matter their social class ("great" to the "poor," cp. 5:4-5) or age ("youngest" to the "oldest," cp. 6:13). The phrase **I will forgive . . . and never again remember their sin** reflects the grace of God that forgives sin and the omniscience of God that chooses not to call it to mind or to hold it against us.

31:36-37 The permanence of God's promise to Israel is compared to the durability of the cosmos: **If this fixed order departs . . . then also Israel's descendants will cease . . . I will reject all of Israel's descendants**. It is impossible for Israel to disappear, or to cease existing.

31:38 Once again in days connected to the consummation of history, Jerusalem will be rebuilt **from the Tower of Han-**

anel to the Corner Gate. The Tower of Hananel was in the northeast corner of Jerusalem (Neh 3:1; 12:39; Zch 14:10), and the Corner Gate was probably at the northwest corner of the city wall (2Kg 14:13; 2Ch 26:9).

31:39 The **hill of Gareb** and **Goah** are unknown to us today. Since the other places mentioned were on the north side of Jerusalem, it may be assumed that these unknown places were on the south.

31:40 The **valley**, presumably composed of **corpses** and **ashes**, must be the Hinnom Valley (see note at 7:31), where Israel buried the dead. The **Horse Gate** apparently was on the eastern wall of the city at the northern end of the Kidron Valley (Neh 3:28).

32:1-2 The promise of a bright future was given during one of Judah's darkest moments in 588 B.C. when Jeremiah was **imprisoned in the guard's courtyard** (33:1), in the **tenth year of Zedekiah king of Judah** and the **eighteenth year of Nebuchadnezzar**. This dating is correct if Nebuchadnezzar's reign is based on his accession year in the fall of 605 B.C. (see note at 25:1). His first official full year as king was 604 B.C. (52:29). Otherwise, his eighteenth by Jewish reckoning was his seventeenth year by Babylonian reckoning.

32:3-5 The Babylonian siege, which began in King Zedekiah's ninth year (39:1), was temporarily lifted when news came that the Egyptian army was approaching (37:5). Jeremiah was arrested during this lull in the siege on the

attend to him'—this is the LORD's declaration. 'You will fight the Chaldeans, but you will not succeed'?"[a]

[6] Jeremiah replied, "The word of the LORD came to me: [7] Watch! Hanamel, the son of your uncle Shallum, is coming to you to say, 'Buy my field in Anathoth[b] for yourself, for you own the right of redemption[c] to buy it.'

[8] "Then my cousin Hanamel came to the guard's courtyard as the LORD had said and urged me, 'Please buy my field in Anathoth in the land of Benjamin, for you own the right of inheritance and redemption. Buy it for yourself.' Then I knew that this was the word of the LORD. [9] So I bought the field in Anathoth from my cousin Hanamel, and I weighed out to him the money[d]—17 •shekels[A] of silver. [10] I recorded it on a scroll,[e] sealed it, called in witnesses, and weighed out the silver in the scales. [11] I took the purchase agreement—the sealed copy with its terms and conditions and the open copy— [12] and gave the purchase agreement to Baruch[f] son of Neriah, son of Mahseiah. I did this in the sight of my cousin[B] Hanamel, the witnesses who were signing the purchase agreement, and all the Judeans sitting in the guard's courtyard.

[13] "I instructed Baruch in their sight, [14] 'This is what the LORD of •Hosts, the God of Israel, says: Take these scrolls—this purchase agreement with the sealed copy and this open copy—and put them in an earthen storage jar so they will last a long time. [15] For this is what the LORD of Hosts, the God of Israel, says: Houses, fields, and vineyards will again be bought in this land.'[g]

[16] "After I had given the purchase agreement to Baruch, son of Neriah, I prayed to the LORD: [17] Oh, Lord GOD! You Yourself made the heavens and earth[h] by Your great power[i] and with Your outstretched arm. Nothing is too difficult for You! [18] You show faithful love to thousands but lay the fathers' sins on their sons' laps after them,[j] great and mighty God[k] whose name is •Yahweh of Hosts, [19] the One great in counsel and mighty in deed, whose eyes are on all the ways of the sons of men in order to give to each person according to his ways and the result of his deeds.[l] [20] You performed signs and wonders in the land of Egypt[m] and do so to this very day both in Israel and among mankind. You made a name[n] for Yourself, as is the case today. [21] You brought Your people Israel out of Egypt with signs and wonders,

[a]32:3-5 Jr 21:3-7; 27:22; 34:2-3
[b]32:7 1Kg 2:26; Jr 1:1; 11:21,23
[c]Lv 25:24-52; Ru 4:1-7
[d]32:9 Gn 23:16; Zch 11:12
[e]32:10 Jr 32:44
[f]32:12 Jr 36:4-32; 43:3,6; 45:1-2
[g]32:15 Jr 32:43
[h]32:17 2Kg 19:15; 2Ch 2:12; Is 37:16
[i]Dt 4:37; Neh 1:10; Jr 27:5
[j]32:18 Ex 20:5-6; 34:7; Nm 14:18; Dt 5:9-10
[k]Neh 9:32
[l]32:19 Jr 17:10
[m]32:20 Ex 1-15; Dt 6:22; Neh 9:10
[n]Is 63:12,14; Dn 9:15

[A]32:9 About 7 ounces   [B]32:12 Some Hb mss, LXX, Syr; other Hb mss read *uncle*

---

grounds that he was trying to escape and because he was encouraging Judah to surrender to Babylon (37:11-14). It was God who would **hand this city over to Babylon's king**, but it would be Nebuchadnezzar who would **capture it**, showing that God's overarching plan for history is fulfilled by human choices. Zedekiah would be left in Babylon until God attended to him. **Attend** in this context connotes a sense of threat.

32:6 After the parenthetical explanation in verses 2-5, verse 6 picks up from verse 1 with a first-person description of what is about to take place.

32:7 Jeremiah was given symbolic evidence for the hope he had just preached about Israel's future. His cousin, **Hanamel**, would offer him **the right of redemption** for family property in his hometown of **Anathoth**. The legal precedent for this action is found in Lv 25:25-28. In the event of poverty or debt, the next of kin had the right to purchase the property, keeping it in the family. This same type of transaction is demonstrated in the Ruth story (Ru 3:9-13; 4:1-12).

32:8 Jeremiah had **the right of inheritance and redemption** in relation to the property.

32:9 The prophet purchased the land for **17 shekels of silver**. This refers to the weight of the silver. Coins were not used until the Persian period in the seventh century B.C. Monetary values were set by weighing ingots of precious metals. Silver was one of the chief forms of payment. A hoard of such ingots was found in a cooking pot beneath the floor in En-gedi from Jeremiah's time and another in Tel Miqne-Ekron from the same period.

32:10-11 Four steps were involved in this real estate transaction: Jeremiah **recorded** the transaction **on a scroll, sealed it, called in witnesses**, and stored it in two copies: a

sealed copy and an **open copy**. The sealed copy was rolled up with a seal placed on the outside as a backup copy to verify that no tampering had taken place. The open copy was a duplicate.

32:12 Jeremiah's scribe was **Baruch son of Neriah, son of Mahseiah**. A number of seal impressions (known as bullae) used to seal documents on parchments or papyrus have been discovered. One says, "Berekyahu son of Neriyahu the scribe." This seal's origin is unknown, but the names inscribed on it fit this verse, for the divine name (Yahweh, or the "LORD") is indicated by Yahu, which appears as a suffix to the names Baruch and Neriah. Baruch, meaning "blessed," is the shortened form of the proper name on this seal impression.

32:14 The **earthen storage jar** that Jeremiah used was the kind the Dead Sea Scrolls were sealed in. Other such jars have been found at Elephantine, Egypt.

32:15 Jeremiah's purchase of the field at Anathoth symbolized Israel's future restoration to the land.

32:17 Only twice in his book is Jeremiah recorded as praying—here and in 42:4. In this prayer the prophet declared, **Nothing is too difficult for You**. His emphasis was not on the difficulty of what God does, but on the "wondrous" (Hb *pele'*) nature of the divine work in creation and history (Gn 18:14; Ex 3:20; 15:11).

32:18 The phrase **You show faithful love to thousands** occurs also in Ex 20:6; Dt 5:10; compare Ex 34:7; Dt 7:9. God's retribution is just and fair, not capricious. He only lays **the fathers' sins on their sons' laps** when they themselves repeat those sins.

32:21-22 You brought Your people Israel out of Egypt repeats the language of Dt 26:8-9.

with a strong hand and an outstretched arm,
and with great terror.[a] 22 You gave them this
land You swore to give to their ancestors, a
land flowing with milk and honey.[b] 23 They entered and possessed it, but they did not obey
Your voice or live according to Your instructions.[c] They failed to perform all You commanded them to do,[d] and so You have brought
all this disaster on them. 24 Look! Siege ramps[e]
have come against the city to capture it, and
the city, as a result of the sword, famine, and
plague, has been handed over to the Chaldeans who are fighting against it. What You have
spoken has happened. Look, You can see it!
25 Yet You, Lord GOD, have said to me: Buy the
field with silver and call in witnesses—even
though the city has been handed over to the
Chaldeans!"

26 Then the word of the LORD came to Jeremiah:
27 "Look, I am •Yahweh, the God of all flesh.[f] Is
anything too difficult for Me? 28 Therefore, this is
what the LORD says: I am about to hand this city
over to the Chaldeans,[g] to Babylon's king Nebuchadnezzar, and he will capture it. 29 The Chaldeans who are going to fight against this city
will come, set this city on fire, and burn it along
with the houses where incense has been burned
to •Baal on their rooftops and where •drink offerings have been poured out to other gods to
provoke Me to anger.[h] 30 From their youth, the
Israelites and Judeans have done nothing but
what is evil in My sight! They have done nothing but provoke Me to anger by the work of
their hands"[i]—this is the LORD's declaration—
31 "for this city has caused My wrath and fury
from the day it was built until now. I will therefore remove it from My presence,[j] 32 because of
all the evil the Israelites and Judeans have done
to provoke Me to anger—they, their kings,[k]
their officials, their priests, and their prophets,
the men of Judah, and the residents of Jerusalem. 33 They have turned their backs to Me and
not their faces. Though I taught them time
and time again,[A,l] they do not listen and receive
discipline. 34 They have placed their detestable
things[m] in the house that is called by My name
and have defiled it. 35 They have built the •high
places of Baal in the Valley of Hinnom to make
their sons and daughters pass through the fire
to •Molech[n]—something I had not commanded
them. I had never entertained the thought[B]
that they do this detestable act causing Judah
to sin!

36 "Now therefore, this is what the LORD, the
God of Israel, says to this city about which you
said, 'It has been handed over to Babylon's
king through sword, famine, and plague': 37 I
am about to gather them from all the lands
where I have banished them in My anger, rage
and great wrath, and I will return them to this
place and make them live in safety.[o] 38 They will
be My people, and I will be their God. 39 I will
give them one heart[p] and one way so that for
their good and for the good of their descendants after them, they will •fear Me always.

40 "I will make an everlasting covenant with
them:[q] I will never turn away from doing good
to them, and I will put fear of Me in their
hearts so they will never again turn away from
Me. 41 I will take delight in them to do what
is good for them, and with all My heart and
mind I will faithfully plant them in this land.[r]

42 "For this is what the LORD says: Just as I
have brought all this great disaster on these
people,[s] so am I about to bring on them all
the good I am promising them. 43 Fields will
be bought in this land about which you are
saying,[t] 'It's a desolation[u] without man or
beast; it has been handed over to the Chaldeans!' 44 Fields will be purchased with silver,
the transaction written on a scroll and sealed,[v]
and witnesses will be called on in the land of
Benjamin,[w] in the areas surrounding Jerusalem, and in Judah's cities—the cities of the
hill country, the cities of the Judean foothills,

[a]32:21 Dt 4:34; 26:8
[b]32:22 Ex 3:8,17; Lv 20:24; Nm 13:27; Dt 26:9
[c]32:23 Ps 78:10; Is 42:24; Jr 44:10
[d]Jr 11:8
[e]32:24 2Kg 25:1; Jr 6:6; Ezk 4:2
[f]32:27 Nm 16:22
[g]32:28 Jr 32:3
[h]32:29 Jr 11:17; 44:3,8
[i]32:30 Jr 25:7
[j]32:31 2Kg 23:27; 24:3
[k]32:32 Jr 2:26
[l]32:33 Jr 25:3
[m]32:34 Jr 4:1; 7:30; Ezk 5:11
[n]32:35 Lv 20:2-5; Dt 18:10; 2Kg 23:10; Jr 7:31
[o]32:37 Dt 12:10; Ezk 28:26; 34:25,28
[p]32:39 Ezk 11:19
[q]32:40 Gn 17:7,13,19; Is 55:3; Jr 50:5
[r]32:41 Jr 24:6
[s]32:42 Jr 31:28
[t]32:43 Jr 32:15
[u]Jr 33:10
[v]32:44 Jr 32:10
[w]Jr 17:26

[A]32:33 Lit *them, rising up early and teaching* [B]32:35 Lit *them, and it did not arise on My heart*

32:27 On **is anything too difficult for Me**, see note at verse 17.

32:29-35 The first-person pronoun appears 10 times in these verses. God's anger is real, but its expression is always contingent on Israel's repentance.

32:33 Once again, Israel had **turned their backs** to God and **not their faces** (see note at 18:17).

32:35 The idolatrous worship of **Baal** and **Molech**, in which Israel caused **their sons and daughters** to **pass through the fire** (see notes at 7:31 and 19:4) is also banned in Lv 18:21 and 20:2-5.

32:36-44 In six remarkable promises in these verses, God declared that He will: (1) **gather** His people from all lands (23:3; 29:14; 30:10; 31:8-14; Is 11:12; Ezk 11:17; 36:24); (2) **make them live in safety**; (3) declare that **they will be My people, and I will be their God**; (4) **give them one heart and one way so . . . they will fear Me always**; (5) **make an everlasting covenant with them** (Is 55:3; 61:8; Ezk 16:60; 37:26); and (6) **take delight in them** and **faithfully plant them in this land**.

32:41 God pledges to carry this out with all His **heart and mind**. This is the only place in the OT where this expression is used of God.

32:42-44 The last verses of this chapter return to Jeremiah's purchase of the field in Anathoth. This was a sure sign that fields in Judah would once again belong to Hebrews in the future. This will include all the geographical areas in Israel,

and the cities of the ·Negev—because I will
restore their fortunes."[A]
This is the LORD's declaration.

Israel's Restoration

33 While he was still confined in the
guard's courtyard,[a] the word of the LORD
came to Jeremiah a second time: 2 "The LORD
who made the earth,[B] the LORD who forms it to
establish it, ·Yahweh is His name,[b] says this:
3 Call to Me and I will answer you[c] and tell you
great and incomprehensible things you do not
know.[d] 4 For this is what the LORD, the God of
Israel, says concerning the houses of this city
and the palaces of Judah's kings, the ones torn
down for defense against the siege ramps and
the sword:[e] 5 The people coming to fight the
Chaldeans will fill the houses with the corpses
of their own men that I strike down in My
wrath and rage. I have hidden My face[f] from
this city because of all their evil. 6 Yet I will
certainly bring health[g] and healing to it and
will indeed heal them. I will let them experience the abundance[C] of peace and truth.[h] 7 I
will restore the fortunes[D] of Judah and of Israel and will rebuild them as in former times.[i]
8 I will purify them from all the wrongs they
have committed against Me,[j] and I will forgive
all the wrongs they have committed against
Me, rebelling against Me. 9 This city will bear
on My behalf a name of joy, praise, and glory[k]
before all the nations of the earth, who will
hear of all the good I will do for them. They
will tremble with awe because of all the good
and all the peace[l] I will bring about for them.
10 "This is what the LORD says: In this place,
which you say is a ruin,[m] without man or
beast—that is, in Judah's cities and Jerusalem's streets that are a desolation without man, without inhabitant, and without
beast—there will be heard again 11 a sound of
joy and gladness, the voice of the groom and
the bride,[n] and the voice of those saying,

Praise the LORD of ·Hosts,
for the LORD is good;
His faithful love endures forever

as they bring thank offerings to the temple of
the LORD. For I will restore the fortunes[D] of
the land as in former times, says the LORD.
12 "This is what the LORD of Hosts says: In this
desolate place—without man or beast—and
in all its cities there will once more be a grazing land where shepherds may rest flocks.[o]
13 The flocks will again pass under the hands
of the one who counts them[p] in the cities of
the hill country,[q] the cities of the Judean foothills, the cities of the ·Negev, the land of Benjamin—the cities surrounding Jerusalem and
Judah's cities, says the LORD.

God's Covenant with David

14 "Look, the days are coming"—
this is the LORD's declaration—
"when I will fulfill the good promises
that I have spoken
concerning the house of Israel
and the house of Judah.[r]
15 In those days and at that time
I will cause a Righteous Branch[s]
to sprout up for David,
and He will administer justice
and righteousness in the land.
16 In those days Judah will be saved,
and Jerusalem will dwell securely,[t]
and this is what she will be named:
Yahweh Our Righteousness.

[a]33:1 Jr 32:2
[b]33:2 Ex 6:3
[c]33:3 Ps 91:15; Jr 29:12
[d]Is 48:6
[e]33:4 Jr 32:24
[f]33:5 Dt 31:17; 32:20; Is 54:8
[g]33:6 Is 58:8; Jr 8:22; 30:17
[h]2Kg 20:19; Est 9:30; Is 39:8
[i]33:7 Is 1:26
[j]33:8 Ps 51:2; Ezk 36:25; Heb 9:11-14
[k]33:9 Dt 26:19; Jr 13:11; Zph 3:19-20
[l]Jr 8:15; 14:19
[m]33:10 Jr 32:43
[n]33:11 Jr 7:34; 16:9; 25:10
[o]33:12 Is 65:10; Ezk 34:12-15
[p]33:13 Lv 27:32
[q]Jr 17:26
[r]33:14 Jos 21:45; Jr 23:5-6
[s]33:15 Is 4:2; Zch 3:8
[t]33:16 Dt 33:12

[A]32:44 Or *will end their captivity* [B]33:2 LXX; MT reads *made it* [C]33:6 Or *fragrance*; Hb obscure [D]33:7,11 Or *will end the captivity*

from **Benjamin**, where Jeremiah's purchase was made, to **Jerusalem . . . Judah**, and all the way south to the **Negev**.

33:1 The phrase **a second time** links verses 1-13 with the previous chapter.

33:3 The things that God will reveal are **incomprehensible**, or "inaccessible." The Hebrew word is *betsuroth*, used of "walled up" cities that were "fortified."

33:4-5 The sense of these verses seems to be that all efforts to rescue Jerusalem will fail. These actions include tearing down houses for stones to plug up holes in the city wall and to set up barricades. The **corpses** will be citizens of Judah, not Babylonian soldiers.

33:6 The word for **health** is literally "new flesh" (8:22). Thus the exile will have a healing effect on Judah. The word **abundance** occurs only here. Related to the Hebrew word for "crown" or "diadem," it means "treasures."

33:8 This emphasis on forgiveness picks up the theme of the new covenant (see note at 31:31-34). Three key Hebrew words for sin are used in this verse.

33:13 The Jewish Targum substitutes the word "Messiah" for **the one who counts them**, but this is not necessary. The word refers to a person who counted sheep as they came into the sheepfold at night to make sure that none were missing.

33:14-26 These verses are not in the LXX. Some think the promises are too exaggerated in their predictions since none of them have happened so far, but the time when this will happen is in **the days . . . coming**, meaning the distant future (v. 14). The perpetuity of the Davidic dynasty and Levitical priesthood are promised, keeping with the revelation in chapters 23 and 30–33.

33:15 On the **Righteous Branch**, see notes at 23:5 and 23:6.

33:16 The name **Yahweh Our Righteousness** was formerly a name applied to the Messiah. In this verse it is applied to Jerusalem (see note at 23:6).

[17] "For this is what the LORD says: David will never fail to have a man sitting on the throne of the house of Israel.[a] [18] The Levitical priests will never fail to have a man always before Me to offer •burnt offerings, to burn •grain offerings, and to make sacrifices."[b]

[19] The word of the LORD came to Jeremiah: [20] "This is what the LORD says: If you can break My covenant with the day and My covenant with the night so that day and night cease to come at their regular time,[c] [21] then also My covenant with My servant David[d] may be broken so that he will not have a son reigning on his throne, and the Levitical priests will not be My ministers.[e] [22] The hosts of heaven cannot be counted; the sand of the sea cannot be measured.[f] So, too, I will make the descendants of My servant David and the Levites who minister to Me innumerable."

[23] The word of the LORD came to Jeremiah: [24] "Have you not noticed what these people have said? They say, 'The LORD has rejected the two families He had chosen.'[g] My people are treated with contempt and no longer regarded as a nation among them. [25] This is what the LORD says: If I do not keep My covenant with the day and with the night and fail to establish the fixed order of heaven and earth,[h] [26] then I might also reject the •seed of Jacob and of My servant David—not taking from his descendants rulers over the descendants of Abraham,

Isaac, and Jacob. Instead, I will restore their fortunes[A] and have compassion on them."[i]

Jeremiah's Word to King Zedekiah

34 This is the word that came to Jeremiah from the LORD when Nebuchadnezzar, king of Babylon,[j] all his army, all the earthly kingdoms under his control,[k] and all other nations were fighting against Jerusalem and all its surrounding cities: [2] "This is what the LORD, the God of Israel, says: Go, speak to Zedekiah, king of Judah, and tell him: This is what the LORD says: I am about to hand this city over to the king of Babylon,[l] and he will burn it down. [3] As for you, you will not escape from his hand but are certain to be captured and handed over to him. You will meet the king of Babylon eye to eye and speak face to face;[B,m] you will go to Babylon.

[4] "Yet hear the LORD's word, Zedekiah, king of Judah. This is what the LORD says concerning you: You will not die by the sword; [5] you will die peacefully. There will be a burning ceremony for you just like the burning ceremonies for your fathers, the former kings who preceded you.[n] 'Our king is dead!'[C] will be the lament for you, for I have spoken this word." This is the LORD's declaration.

[6] So Jeremiah the prophet related all these words to Zedekiah king of Judah in Jerusalem [7] while the king of Babylon's army was attacking Jerusalem and all of Judah's remaining

Cross references (center column):

a33:17 1Kg 2:4; 8:25; 9:5
b33:18 Jr 31:36; 35:19
c33:20 Gn 8:22; Is 54:9-10; Jr 31:35-37
d33:21 2Sm 7:11-16; 2Ch 21:7; Ps 89:3
e33:18 Is 61:6; Ezk 45:4-5; Jl 1:9,13
f33:22 Gn 22:17
g33:24 Dt 7:6; 14:2
h33:25 Ps 74:16-17
i33:26 Jr 33:7
j34:1 2Kg 25:1; Jr 39:1; 52:4
k Jr 1:15
l34:2 Jr 32:3,28
m34:3 Jr 32:4
n34:5 2Ch 16:14; 21:19

A33:26 Or Instead, I will end their captivity   B34:3 Lit and his mouth will speak to your mouth   C34:5 Lit Alas, lord

---

33:17-18 These verses do not literally promise the constant presence of a Davidic king and a Levitical priesthood (history shows this did not happen). Rather, it means that there will be no cessation of David's dynasty or of the office of the priesthood (**will never fail to have a man always before Me**). Jesus fulfilled the offices of King and Priest (Ps 110:4). Christ's priesthood does not follow Levi's line, but the line of Melchizedek, the priest of Salem (Gn 14:17-20).

33:19-22 God compared the irrevocability of His promises to David (2Sm 7) and Levi's lines (Nm 17) with His unbreakable covenant with **day and night**. God would break His covenant with David and the Levites no sooner than day and night would **cease to come at their regular time**. The promise given to the whole nation (Gn 15:5; 22:17)—that they would be **innumerable**—is extended to **the descendants of My servant David and the Levites**.

33:24 Some disbelieving Israelites were saying that **the LORD** had **rejected the two families He had chosen**. These families were not the royal and priestly families referred to in verses 21-22, but the northern and southern kingdoms of Israel. The verb "to choose" is used uniquely here in Jeremiah. It is often used elsewhere of God's election of Israel (Ex 19:5-6; Am 3:2).

33:25-26 Even after the nation of Israel ceases to exist, the promises made to **Abraham, Isaac, and Jacob** are guaranteed by God and are as sure as His **covenant with the day**

and with the night. Count on the natural order collapsing and going out of existence before God's promises to David, Levi, and the nation evaporate.

34:1 The attack against Jerusalem and **all its surrounding cities** is spoken of in hyperbolic, global terms—**all the earthly kingdoms**, or literally "all the kingdoms of the earth." It was as if the whole world was lined up against Judah.

34:3 King Zedekiah would meet the Babylonian king **eye to eye and speak face to face**. There his eyes would be put out after he was forced to watch the execution of his sons (39:5-7; 52:8-11).

34:5 Zedekiah would not be killed. He would die in Babylon and have **a burning ceremony** just like the "funeral fire" at other royal funerals (2Ch 16:14; 21:19). This ceremony involved burning spices on the coffins, but it did not necessarily involve cremation.

34:7 Only **Lachish and Azekah** remained of all of Judah's cities as the siege of Jerusalem continued. Lachish was a fortified city 30 miles southwest of Jerusalem. Azekah, likewise fortified, was northeast of Lachish. Discovered among the ruins of Lachish were letters written on pottery. One contained the words of a sentinel: "We are watching for the signals of Lachish . . . because we do not see Azekah." Presumably, Azekah had already fallen when these words were written.

cities—against Lachish and Azekah,[a] for they were the only ones left of Judah's fortified cities.

The People and Their Slaves

[8] This is the word that came to Jeremiah from the LORD after King Zedekiah made a covenant with all the people who were in Jerusalem to proclaim freedom[b] to them, [9] so each man would free his male and female Hebrew slaves and no one would enslave his Judean brother.[c] [10] All the officials and people who entered into covenant to free their male and female slaves—in order not to enslave them any longer—obeyed and freed them. [11] Afterward, however, they changed their minds and took back their male and female slaves they had freed and forced them to become slaves again.

[12] Then the word of the LORD came to Jeremiah from the LORD: [13] "This is what the LORD, the God of Israel, says: I made a covenant[d] with your ancestors when I brought them out of the land of Egypt, out of the place of slavery, saying: [14] At the end of seven years, each of you must free his Hebrew brother who sold himself[A] to you. He may serve you six years, but then you must send him out free from you.[e] But your ancestors did not obey Me or pay any attention. [15] Today you repented and did what pleased Me, each of you proclaiming freedom for his neighbor. You made a covenant before Me[f] at the temple called by My name.[g] [16] But you have changed your minds[h] and profaned My name.[i] Each has taken back his male and

female slaves who had been freed to go wherever they wanted, and you have again subjugated them to be your slaves.

[17] "Therefore, this is what the LORD says: You have not obeyed Me by proclaiming freedom, each man for his brother and for his neighbor. I hereby proclaim freedom for you"[j]—this is the LORD's declaration—"to the sword, to plague, and to famine! I will make you a horror to all the earth's kingdoms. [18] As for those who disobeyed My covenant,[k] not keeping the terms of the covenant they made before Me, I will treat them like the calf they cut in two in order to pass between its pieces.[l] [19] The officials of Judah and Jerusalem, the court officials, the priests, and all the people of the land who passed between the pieces of the calf [20] will be handed over to their enemies, to those who want to take their life. Their corpses will become food for the birds of the sky and for the wild animals of the land.[m] [21] I will hand Zedekiah king of Judah and his officials over to their enemies, to those who want to take their lives, to the king of Babylon's army that is withdrawing. [22] I am about to give the command"—this is the LORD's declaration—"and I will bring them back to this city. They will fight against it, capture it, and burn it down.[n] I will make Judah's cities a desolation,[o] without inhabitant."

The Rechabites' Example

35 This is the word that came to Jeremiah from the LORD in the days of Jehoiakim[p] son of Josiah, king of Judah: [2] "Go to the house

---

Cross references:
a 34:7 Jos 10:3-35
b 34:8 Lv 25:10; Is 61:1; Ezk 46:17
c 34:9 Lv 25:39
d 34:13 Jr 31:32
e 34:14 Ex 21:2-6; Dt 15:12-17
f 34:15 2Kg 23:3
g Jr 7:10-11
h 34:16 Jr 34:11
i Lv 19:12
j 34:17 Mt 7:2
k 34:18 Jos 7:11; 2Kg 18:12
i Gn 15:10,17-18
m 34:20 Dt 28:26; Is 18:6; Jr 7:33
n 34:22 Jr 37:8
o Jr 4:7; 9:11
p 35:1 2Kg 23:34–24:19; 2Ch 36:4-8

A 34:14 Or *who was sold*

34:8-10 King Zedekiah's **covenant with all the people** was not the same as the Lord's covenant (v. 18), that all **male and female Hebrew slaves** should be set free. The motivation for issuing this proclamation of emancipation is not given. It seems to have come just before the temporary lifting of Nebuchadnezzar's siege against Jerusalem in late spring or early summer of 588 B.C. due to a rumor about the approach of the Egyptian army. All the king's officials and the people agreed **to free their male and female slaves** and to release them from their debts.

34:11 When the siege was lifted, the people abandoned their panic-inspired piety, with the result that slave owners repudiated their solemn oath to God in violation of the provisions in Ex 21:2-6; Dt 15:12-18.

34:14 At the end of seven years is actually "at the end of six years" as the passage makes clear and as the Sinaitic law specified (Ex 21:2-6). However, Dt 15:1,12 states, "at the end of seven years."

34:15-16 The king, his officials, and the people made a covenant before the Lord at the temple, only to change their minds, thus profaning God's **name**.

34:17 With a devastating play on words and an irony of ironies, God would take Judah's revoked proclamation of

emancipation and make His own proclamation: Judah would experience **freedom** from His protection, thus falling to **sword, to plague, and to famine**.

34:18-20 In a covenant ceremony, a **calf** was **cut** (Hb *karath*; "to cut," "to make a covenant") **in two in order** that the parties to the covenant could **pass between its pieces**. This is similar to Gn 15:10,17, where only God walked between the pieces, figuratively vowing His own destruction if He failed to keep His word. Parties who passed between the pieces were in effect saying, "If I do not keep the terms of this covenant, may I die like this slaughtered animal."

34:19-20 Everyone who passed between the pieces would be **handed over to their enemies**.

34:21-22 Nebuchadnezzar's army had withdrawn briefly, but God would give the command to **bring them back to this city** (Jerusalem). Archaeologists have not found a single town in Judah that was occupied from the time of this destruction up to the Hebrew return from exile.

35:1-19 After devoting several chapters to King Zedekiah, Jeremiah in this chapter skips back to approximately 10 years earlier, the time of **Jehoiakim son of Josiah** (609-598 B.C.).

35:2 The **house** (household) **of the Rechabites** is known

of the Rechabites, speak to them,[a] and bring them to one of the chambers[b] of the temple of the Lord to offer them a drink of wine."

[3] So I took Jaazaniah son of Jeremiah, son of Habazziniah, and his brothers and all his sons—the entire house of the Rechabites—[4] and I brought them into the temple of the Lord to a chamber occupied by the sons of Hanan son of Igdaliah, a man of God,[c] who had a chamber near the officials' chamber, which was above the chamber of Maaseiah son of Shallum the doorkeeper. [5] I set jars filled with wine and some cups before the sons of the house of the Rechabites and said to them, "Drink wine!"

[6] But they replied, "We do not drink wine, for Jonadab,[d] son of our ancestor Rechab, commanded: 'You and your sons must never drink wine. [7] You must not build a house or sow seed or plant a vineyard. Those things are not for you. Rather, you must live in tents your whole life, so you may live a long time on the soil where you stay as a temporary resident.'[e] [8] We have obeyed the voice of Jonadab, son of our ancestor Rechab, in all he commanded us. So we haven't drunk wine our whole life—we, our wives, our sons, and our daughters. [9] We also have not built houses to live in and do not have vineyard, field, or seed. [10] But we have lived in tents and have obeyed and done as our ancestor Jonadab commanded us. [11] However, when Nebuchadnezzar king of Babylon marched into the land,[f] we said: Come, let's go into Jerusalem to get away from the Chaldean and Aramean armies. So we have been living in Jerusalem."

[12] Then the word of the Lord came to Jeremi-

ah: [13] "This is what the Lord of 'Hosts, the God of Israel, says: Go, say to the men of Judah and the residents of Jerusalem: Will you not accept discipline[g] by listening to My words?"—this is the Lord's declaration. [14] "The words of Jonadab, son of Rechab, have been carried out. He commanded his sons not to drink wine, and they have not drunk to this very day because they have obeyed their ancestor's command. But I have spoken to you time and time again,[A,h] and you have not obeyed Me! [15] Time and time again[B] I have sent you all My servants the prophets, proclaiming: Turn, each one from his evil way of life,[i] and correct your actions. Stop following other gods to serve them.[j] Live in the land that I gave you and your ancestors. But you would not pay attention or obey Me.[k] [16] Yes, the sons of Jonadab son of Rechab carried out their ancestor's command he gave them, but these people have not obeyed Me. [17] Therefore, this is what the Lord, the God of Hosts, the God of Israel, says: I will certainly bring to Judah and to all the residents of Jerusalem all the disaster I have pronounced against them because I have spoken to them, but they have not obeyed, and I have called to them, but they would not answer."

[18] Jeremiah said to the house of the Rechabites: "This is what the Lord of Hosts, the God of Israel, says: 'Because you have obeyed the command of your ancestor Jonadab and have kept all his commands and have done all that he commanded you, [19] this is what the Lord of Hosts, the God of Israel, says: Jonadab son of Rechab will never fail to have a man to always stand before Me.'"[l]

---

[a]35:2 1Ch 2:55
[b]1Kg 6:5,8; 1Ch 9:26,33
[c]35:4 Dt 33:1
[d]35:6 2Kg 10:15,23
[e]35:7 Ex 20:12; Eph 6:2-3
[f]35:11 2Kg 24:1-2
[g]35:13 Jr 31:18; 32:33
[h]35:14 Jr 25:3
[i]35:15 Jr 18:11
Jr 7:6
[k]Jr 34:14
[l]35:19 Jr 31:36; 33:18

---

largely from this chapter. Their founder was Jonadab or Jehonadab, son of Rechab, who lived under King Jehu of the northern kingdom. Jehonadab apparently supported the king's radical reform movements (2Kg 10:15-23), which included demolishing the Baal cult and other elements of Canaanite culture. The Rechabites also promised their ancestor that they would not build houses or plant vineyards, apparently so they would be able to remain mobile. They were devout worshipers of the Lord. The Lord told Jeremiah to invite the Rechabites into the temple **to offer them a drink of wine.**

35:3-4 Jaazaniah and **Habazziniah** are not mentioned elsewhere. The father of Jaazaniah, identified here as Jeremiah, is not the prophet. Jaazaniah must have been the head of the Rechabites at this time.

35:4 The **chamber** Jeremiah used for this occasion was **near the officials' chamber, which was above the chamber of Maaseiah son of Shallum the doorkeeper.** Maaseiah may have been the father of the priest Zephaniah (21:1; 29:25; 37:3).

35:5 The **jars filled with wine** were large drinking bowls with dipping **cups. Drink wine,** Jeremiah invited them.

35:6-11 The Rechabites declined the offer of wine, making it clear that they had **obeyed the voice of Jonadab, son of . . . Rechab, in all he commanded us.** Their rejecting a sedentary culture and its trappings, such as wine cultivation and indulgence, was just the illustration Jeremiah needed to teach obedience to the Lord's commands.

35:14-16 Three times in these verses Jeremiah contrasted the Rechabites' obedience to a human command with Judah's disobedience to the living God.

35:17-19 Disaster would be Judah's lot because of her persistent disobedience, but the Rechabites would **never fail to have a man to always stand before Me.** The phrase "to stand before the Lord" is used for those who serve Him (7:10; 15:19; Dt 4:10; 10:8; 1Kg 17:1; 18:15; 2Kg 3:14). What happened to the Rechabites after 587 b.c. is unknown except for Malchijah son of Rechab. He repaired the Dung Gate in the days of Nehemiah (Neh 3:14).

Jeremiah Dictates a Scroll

36 In the fourth year of Jehoiakim son of Josiah,[a] king of Judah, this word came to Jeremiah from the LORD: [2] "Take a scroll,[b] and write on it all the words I have spoken to you concerning Israel, Judah, and all the nations from the time I first spoke to you during Josiah's reign until today. [3] Perhaps when the house of Judah hears about all the disaster I am planning to bring on them, each one of them will turn from his evil way. Then I will forgive their wrongdoing[c] and their sin."

[4] So Jeremiah summoned Baruch[d] son of Neriah. At Jeremiah's dictation,[A] Baruch wrote on a scroll all the words the LORD had spoken to Jeremiah. [5] Then Jeremiah commanded Baruch, "I am restricted;[e] I cannot enter the temple of the LORD, [6] so you must go and read from the scroll—which you wrote at my dictation[B]—the words of the LORD in the hearing of the people at the temple of the LORD on a day of fasting. You must also read

them in the hearing of all the Judeans who are coming from their cities. [7] Perhaps their petition will come before the LORD,[f] and each one will turn from his evil way, for the anger and fury that the LORD has pronounced against this people are great." [8] So Baruch son of Neriah did everything Jeremiah the prophet had commanded him. At the LORD's temple he read the LORD's words from the scroll.

Baruch Reads the Scroll

[9] In the fifth year of Jehoiakim son of Josiah, king of Judah, in the ninth month,[g] all the people of Jerusalem and all those coming in from Judah's cities into Jerusalem proclaimed a fast before the LORD.[h] [10] Then at the LORD's temple, in the chamber of Gemariah son of Shaphan the scribe,[i] in the upper courtyard at the opening of the New Gate[j] of the LORD's temple, in the hearing of all the people, Baruch read Jeremiah's words from the scroll.

[11] When Micaiah son of Gemariah, son of

Cross references (margin):
a 36:1 Jr 25:1; 45:1
b 36:2 Ps 40:7; Ezk 2:9
c 36:3 Jr 31:34; 33:8; 36:31
d 36:4 Jr 32:12-16; 43:3,6; 45:1-2
e 36:5 Jr 32:2; 33:1
f 36:7 1Kg 8:28,45,49; Ps 119:170
g 36:9 Jr 36:22
h 2Ch 20:3
i 36:10 2Kg 22:3-14; 2Ch 34:8-20; Jr 29:3
j Jr 26:10

A36:4 Lit *From Jeremiah's mouth*   B36:6 Lit *wrote from my mouth*

36:1 This **fourth year of Jehoiakim** in 605–604 B.C. was a critical time (25:1; 45:1). Nebuchadnezzar of Babylon had defeated the Assyrian forces at Carchemish on the Euphrates River and had begun his move south to Syria and Israel. Everything was heading toward the finale that Jeremiah had warned about for many years.

36:2-3 The prophet was instructed to **take a scroll**, which in Hebrew was called a *megillath sepher*, "a book-scroll," made of goat skins or papyrus. This word occurs only here; verse 4; Ps 40:7; and Ezk 2:9. Was it a scroll of book length? Modern book or codex formats did not appear until the first century A.D. Jeremiah was to write on this scroll all the words God had spoken **concerning Israel, Judah, and all the nations**. Some object to "Israel" in this verse, but Jeremiah did address his words to the now-banished northern part of the nation from time to time (3:6-11). His

call in 1:10 had been to "all the nations." The scroll was to cover **the time I first spoke to you during Josiah's reign until today**. The hope was that when Judah heard about **the disaster I am planning to bring on them**, each would turn from his **evil way**. The hope on which all preaching is based is God's willingness to **forgive . . . wrongdoing and . . . sin** in response to repentance.

36:4 Baruch son of Neriah came from a well-known family (see note at 32:12). Baruch's function is literally described: "Baruch wrote from the mouth of Jeremiah all the words the LORD had spoken to him on a book-scroll." Jeremiah claimed that the source of his words was God Himself and that Baruch just acted as his secretary.

35:5 Jeremiah had been **restricted** ("shut up," "confined," "imprisoned") from going to the temple, so he sent Baruch to read the scroll there.

36:6 When Baruch had transcribed all the words Jeremiah spoke to him from God, he was to give a public reading of the scroll on a **day of fasting**. Public fasts were often declared in Israel, especially during times of calamity (Jl 2:12,15) or war. This public reading might recall a similar day in which the public reading of the Torah sparked Josiah's revival (2Kg 23:1-3). A number of months passed between the writing of the scroll and its public reading, as seen from the dates in Jr 36:1,9,22.

36:9 The **fifth year of Jehoiakim** was 604 B.C., and the **ninth month** (December 604) was when the Babylonians sacked the Philistine city of Ashkelon. This event may have forced Jehoiakim to switch his allegiance from Egypt to Babylon.

36:9-10 Gemariah was the **son of Shaphan the scribe**. Shaphan was King Josiah's secretary of state (2Kg 22:3,8,12). Gemariah was the brother of Ahikam, one of Jeremiah's few friends (Jr 26:24), but he was not the Gemariah mentioned in 29:3. Gemariah allowed Baruch to use his room in the temple's inner court, which provided a setting in which the assembled people could hear Baruch's reading.

36:11 When **Micaiah son of Gemariah** and grandson of

---

megillah

Hebrew Pronunciation	[meh gil LAH]
HCSB Translation	scroll
Uses in Jeremiah	14
Uses in the OT	21
Focus Passage	Jeremiah 36:2,4,6,14,20-21

Megillah, from the verb *galal* ("roll"), refers to *scrolls*, which were unrolled from side to side (not top to bottom). Vertical lines might mark columns, with writing placed on horizontal lines. *Megillah* could be a late word, the earlier term being *sepher* ("writing, book"); both refer to Scripture in Ps 40:7. An Egyptian tomb held a papyrus scroll dating to about 3,000 B.C. Many Dead Sea Scrolls are leather; they are up to 12 inches high and 29 feet long, the Isaiah Scroll being 17 sheepskin sheets sewn together by linen. But some Dead Sea Scrolls are papyrus. The *scroll* Jehoiakim burnt indoors during winter might have made the room uninhabitable had it been leather (Jr 36:23). Ezekiel ate a divine *scroll* to picture his mission of sharing God's Word (Ezk 3:1-3). A visionary flying *scroll* 30 by 15 feet, written front and back, detailed God's laws (Zch 5:1-4).

Shaphan, heard all the words of the LORD from the scroll, [12]he went down to the scribe's chamber in the king's palace. All the officials were sitting there—Elishama the scribe, Delaiah son of Shemaiah, Elnathan son of Achbor,[a] Gemariah son of Shaphan, Zedekiah son of Hananiah, and all the other officials. [13]Micaiah reported to them all the words he had heard when Baruch read from the scroll in the hearing of the people. [14]Then all the officials sent word to Baruch through Jehudi son of Nethaniah, son of Shelemiah, son of Cushi, saying, "Bring the scroll that you read in the hearing of the people, and come." So Baruch son of Neriah took the scroll and went to them. [15]They said to him, "Sit down and read it in our hearing." So Baruch read it in their hearing.

[16]When they had heard all the words, they turned to each other in fear and said to Baruch, "We must surely tell the king all these things." [17]Then they asked Baruch, "Tell us—how did you write all these words? At his dictation?"[A]

[18]Baruch said to them, "At his dictation.[A] He recited all these words to me while I was writing on the scroll in ink."

Jehoiakim Burns the Scroll

[19]The officials said to Baruch, "You and Jeremiah must hide yourselves and tell no one where you are." [20]Then they came to the king at the courtyard, having deposited the scroll in the chamber of Elishama the scribe, and reported everything in the hearing of the king. [21]The king sent Jehudi to get the scroll, and he took it from the chamber of Elishama the scribe. Jehudi then read it in the hearing of the king and all the officials who were standing by the king. [22]Since it was the ninth month, the king was sitting in his winter quarters[b] with a fire burning in front of him. [23]As soon as Jehudi would read three or four columns, Jehoiakim would cut the scroll[B] with a scribe's knife and throw the columns into the blazing fire until the entire scroll was consumed by the fire in the brazier. [24]As they heard all these words, the king and all of his servants did not become terrified[c] or tear their garments. [25]Even though Elnathan, Delaiah, and Gemariah had urged the king not to burn the scroll, he would not listen to them. [26]Then the king commanded Jerahmeel the king's son, Seraiah son of Azriel, and Shelemiah son of Abdeel to seize Baruch the scribe and Jeremiah the prophet, but the LORD had hidden them.

Jeremiah Dictates Another Scroll

[27]After the king had burned the scroll with the words Baruch had written at Jeremiah's dictation,[c] the word of the LORD came to Jeremiah: [28]"Take another scroll, and once again write on it the very words that were on the original scroll that Jehoiakim king of Judah burned. [29]You are to proclaim concerning Jehoiakim king of Judah: This is what the LORD says: You have burned the scroll, saying, 'Why have you written on it:[d] The king of Babylon will certainly come and destroy this land and cause it to be without man or beast?' [30]Therefore, this is what the LORD says concerning Jehoiakim king of Judah: He will have no one to sit on David's throne, and his corpse will be thrown out to be exposed to the heat of day and the frost of night.[e] [31]I will punish him, his descendants, and his officers for their wrongdoing. I will bring on them, on the residents of Jerusalem, and on the men of Judah all the disaster, which I warned them about but they did not listen."

Cross references
[a] 36:12 Jr 26:22
[b] 36:22 Am 3:15
[c] 36:24 Jr 36:16
[d] 36:29 Jr 26:9
[e] 36:30 Gn 31:40

A 36:17,18 Lit *From his mouth*　　**B** 36:23 Lit *columns, he would tear it*　　**C** 36:27 Lit *written from Jeremiah's mouth*

Shephan—a family supportive of Jeremiah—heard what Baruch read, he repeated the words to all the king's officials (v. 12).

36:14 As Baruch read, he sat down in the typical Oriental manner of teaching (Lk 4:20). These cabinet ministers treated Baruch with respect and kindness (Jr 36:15,19).

36:16-19 The officials seemed to believe what Jeremiah had written. It must have been the opposite of what they were being told by the king and his counselors. Knowing the danger Jeremiah and Baruch were in, they urged them to **hide** themselves **and tell no one** where they were. This precaution was understandable because of what had happened to Uriah the prophet (26:20-23).

36:20-21 Fearing what the king's response might be, the officials **deposited the scroll in the chamber of Elishama the scribe**. But the king ordered **Jehudi** to retrieve it and read it for him.

36:22-25 Despite urgings from a few officials not to burn the scroll, King Jehoiakim **cut the scroll** up and threw the pieces into a **blazing fire** as he reclined in his **winter quarters**. This was a warm section of the palace apparently facing the winter sun (Am 3:15). The court officials were indifferent and irreverent as the king acted with defiance and blasphemy against the Word of God.

36:26 The king also ordered the arrest of Baruch and Jeremiah, but the Lord had provided protection for them through loyal friends.

36:28 God ordered Jeremiah to write on another scroll **the very words that were on the original scroll**. God's Word would not be so easily destroyed.

36:30 As punishment for his brazen act, Jehoiakim would **have no one to sit on David's throne**, and his corpse would be thrown out to the **heat of day and the frost of night**. Some assume that Jehoiakim died in a palace uprising or a revolution of the people (v. 31; cp. 22:18-19).

³²Then Jeremiah took another scroll and gave it to Baruch son of Neriah, the scribe, and he wrote on it at Jeremiah's dictation^A all the words of the scroll that Jehoiakim,^a Judah's king, had burned in the fire. And many other words like them were added.

Jerusalem's Last Days

37 Zedekiah son of Josiah^b reigned as king in the land of Judah^c in place of Jehoiachin^B,d son of Jehoiakim, for Nebuchadnezzar king of Babylon made him king. ²He and his officers and the people of the land did not obey the words of the Lord^e that He spoke through Jeremiah the prophet.

³Nevertheless, King Zedekiah sent Jehucal^f son of Shelemiah and Zephaniah^g son of Maaseiah, the priest, to Jeremiah the prophet, requesting, "Please pray to the Lord our God for us!" ⁴Jeremiah was going about his daily tasks^c among the people, for they had not yet put him into the prison.^h ⁵Pharaoh's army had left Egypt,^i and when the Chaldeans, who were besieging Jerusalem, heard the report, they withdrew from Jerusalem.

⁶The word of the Lord came to Jeremiah the prophet: ⁷"This is what the Lord, the God of Israel, says: This is what you will say to Judah's king,^j who is sending you to inquire of Me: Watch: Pharaoh's army, which has come out to help you,^k is going to return to its own land of Egypt. ⁸The Chaldeans will then return and fight against this city. They will capture it and burn it down.^l ⁹This is what the Lord says: Don't deceive yourselves by saying, 'The Chaldeans will leave us for good,' for they will not leave. ¹⁰Indeed, if you were to strike down the entire Chaldean army that is fighting with you,^m and there remained among them only the badly wounded^D men, each in his tent, they would get up and burn this city down."

Jeremiah's Imprisonment

¹¹When the Chaldean army withdrew from Jerusalem because of Pharaoh's army, ¹²Jeremiah started to leave Jerusalem to go to the land of Benjamin to claim his portion there^n among the people. ¹³But when he was at the Benjamin Gate,^o an officer of the guard was there, whose name was Irijah son of Shelemiah, son of Hananiah, and he apprehended Jeremiah the prophet, saying, "You are deserting to the Chaldeans."

¹⁴"That's a lie," Jeremiah replied. "I am not deserting to the Chaldeans!" Irijah would not listen to him but apprehended Jeremiah and took him to the officials. ¹⁵The officials were angry at Jeremiah and beat him and placed him in jail in the house of Jonathan^p the scribe, for it had been made into a prison. ¹⁶So Jeremiah went into a cell in the dungeon^q and stayed there many days.

Jeremiah Summoned by Zedekiah

¹⁷King Zedekiah later sent for him and re-

---

^a 36:32 Jr 36:4,18
^b 37:1 2Kg 24:17; 2Ch 36:10
^c Ezk 17:12-21
^d Jr 22:24
^e 37:2 2Ch 36:12-16
^f 37:3 Jr 38:1
^g 2Kg 25:18-21; Jr 21:1; 29:24-29
^h 37:4 Jr 32:2-3
^i 37:5 Ezk 17:15
^j 37:7 Jr 21:1-2
^k Lm 4:17
^l 37:8 Jr 21:10; 34:2,22; 38:18
^m 37:10 Jr 21:4-5
^n 37:12 Jr 32:1-15
^o 37:13 Jr 38:7; Zch 14:10
^p 37:15 Jr 38:26
^q 37:16 Gn 40:15; Is 24:22; Zch 9:11

---

^A 36:32 Lit *it from Jeremiah's mouth*   ^B 37:1 = Coniah   ^C 37:4 Lit *was coming in and going out*   ^D 37:10 Lit *the pierced*

36:32 In creating the replacement scroll, Jeremiah dictated to Baruch the words that had been on the first scroll plus **many other words like them**. Presumably, these new words dealt with the fulfillment of his prophecies about Judah as events unfolded after the burning of the first scroll.

37:1-21 Eighteen years passed between the events of chapter 36 and those of chapter 37.

37:1 In fulfillment of Jeremiah's prophecy in 36:30, **Zedekiah** (a brother of Jehoiakim) was placed on the throne **in place of Jehoiachin** (also known as Coniah), **son of Jehoiakim**. Nebuchadnezzar of Babylon had **made** Zedekiah **king**. This is an unusual expression until we remember that Jehoiachin was deported to Babylon after only three months as king, and Zedekiah was installed in his place by the Babylonian king.

37:2 Judah's problems were never just political; they were mostly spiritual problems shared by the newly installed king, **his officers and the people of the land**. They had no desire to heed the word from the Lord.

37:3 For the second time (21:1-2), Zedekiah sent messengers to Jeremiah requesting, **Please pray to the Lord our God for us**.

37:4 Jeremiah was free to come and go as he pleased, but this would soon change.

37:5 The phrase **Pharaoh's army had left Egypt** probably refers to Pharaoh Hophra (44:30) or Apries of Herodotus (2.161; 4.159). This caused Babylon to withdraw temporarily from the siege of Jerusalem in the summer of 588 b.c. The Babylonians soon defeated the Egyptians, and the siege of Jerusalem resumed.

37:6-10 Jeremiah's answer to Zedekiah's prayer request was that the Egyptian army would return home to Egypt and the Babylonians would resume their siege and sack Jerusalem. This was hardly a morale booster for Zedekiah and the people of Judah.

37:12 Jeremiah was arrested as he set out to inspect and **claim his portion** of the property in his native town of Anathoth (1:1; 32:8). He had just purchased this property from his cousin Hanamel (chap. 32).

37:13 An **officer of the guard** presumed Jeremiah was deserting to the enemy. After all, the prophet had encouraged others to surrender to the Babylonians (see note at 21:9).

37:15 The house of Jonathan the scribe **had been made into a prison**. Officer's homes often served as prisons in the ancient Near East.

37:16 Jeremiah was placed in **a cell in the dungeon** (lit "the house of a cistern-pit"). This was a vault adjoining an underground dungeon, where he could have been left to die (v. 20).

37:17 King Zedekiah called for Jeremiah a third time, but this

ceived him, and in his house privately asked him, "Is there a word from the LORD?"[a]

"There is," Jeremiah responded, and he continued, "You will be handed over to the king of Babylon."[b] [18] Then Jeremiah said to King Zedekiah, "How have I sinned against you or your servants or these people that you have put me in prison? [19] Where are your prophets who prophesied to you, claiming, 'The king of Babylon will not come against you and this land'?[c] [20] So now please listen, my lord the king. May my petition come before you.[d] Don't send me back to the house of Jonathan the scribe, or I will die there."

[21] So King Zedekiah gave orders, and Jeremiah was placed in the guard's courtyard.[e] He was given a loaf of bread each day from the baker's street until all the bread was gone from the city. So Jeremiah remained in the guard's courtyard.

Jeremiah Thrown into a Cistern

38 Now Shephatiah son of Mattan, Gedaliah son of Pashhur, Jucal[A] son of Shelemiah,[f] and Pashhur son of Malchijah heard the words Jeremiah was speaking to all the people: [2] "This is what the LORD says: 'Whoever stays in this city will die by the sword, famine, and plague, but whoever surrenders to the Chaldeans will live. He will keep his life like the spoils of war and will live.'[g] [3] This is what the LORD says: 'This city will most certainly be

handed over to the king of Babylon's army,[h] and he will capture it.'"

[4] The officials then said to the king, "This man ought to die, because he is weakening the morale of the warriors who remain in this city and of all the people by speaking to them in this way. This man is not seeking the well-being of this people, but disaster."[i]

[5] King Zedekiah said, "Here he is; he's in your hands since the king can't do anything against you." [6] So they took Jeremiah and dropped him into the cistern of Malchiah the king's son, which was in the guard's courtyard, lowering Jeremiah with ropes. There was no water in the cistern, only mud, and Jeremiah sank in the mud.[j]

[7] But Ebed-melech, a •Cushite court official employed in the king's palace, heard Jeremiah had been put into the cistern. While the king was sitting at the Benjamin Gate,[k] [8] Ebed-melech went from the king's palace and spoke to the king: [9] "My lord the king, these men have been evil in all they have done to Jeremiah the prophet. They have dropped him into the cistern where he will die from hunger, because there is no more bread in the city."[l]

[10] So the king commanded Ebed-melech, the Cushite, "Take from here 30 men under your authority and pull Jeremiah the prophet up from the cistern before he dies."

[11] So Ebed-melech took the men under his authority and went to the king's palace to a

---

[a] 37:17 Jr 38:14-16
[b] Jr 21:7
[c] 37:19 Jr 28:1-17
[d] 37:20 Jr 38:26
[e] 37:21 Jr 32:2
[f] 38:1 Jr 37:3
[g] 38:2 Jr 21:9; 39:18; 45:5
[h] 38:3 Jr 32:3-5
[i] 38:4 Jr 29:11
[j] 38:6 Gn 37:20-24
[k] 38:7 Jr 20:2; Ezk 48:32; Zch 14:10
[l] 38:9 Jr 37:21

A 38:1 = Jehucal in Jr 37:3

---

time in secrecy. Perhaps he hoped this would encourage a good word from the Lord. But the word from the prophet was not good. He, the king of Judah, would be **handed over to the king of Babylon**.

37:18-20 These verses show Jeremiah's humanity as he asked for humane treatment from Zedekiah and a bill of particulars to specify the crimes for which he had been imprisoned.

37:21 Zedekiah reversed his officials' decision and transferred Jeremiah to the **guard's courtyard**. Here he was given **a loaf of bread each day from the baker's street**. Streets of Near Eastern cities were often named after those whose businesses were on that street, hence Baker's Street—the only street name in Jerusalem known to us.

38:1 **Jucal** and **Pashhur**, already mentioned in 21:1 and 37:3, were among the four persons who heard Jeremiah's messages from the guard's courtyard (37:21).

38:2 The **Chaldeans** derived their name from an ancient name *Chaldai*, which referred to a group of Aramean tribes that moved into lower Mesopotamia somewhere around 1000 to 900 B.C. After they moved from their tribal settlements to urban settings, they acquired the name Babylonians, or more precisely, Neo-Babylonians. Thus "Chaldeans" and "Babylonians" are used interchangeably.

38:3 Jeremiah repeated the substance of this message over and over again (21:7; 37:8).

38:4 The prophet was charged with **weakening the morale** (lit "the hands") **of the warriors**. In Lachish Letter VI, one of 21 letters written on potsherds left during the siege of Jerusalem and Judah, this very expression is used of certain nobles in Jerusalem (see ANET, 16, pp. 321-22).

38:5 This verse portrays King Zedekiah as a weakling without moral fiber who was controlled by his officials.

38:6 **Malchiah the king's son** was not one of Zedekiah's sons, but a royal prince (see 36:26 for a similar expression).

38:7-9 **Ebed-melech, a Cushite court official**, whose name means "servant of the king," was a royal official of Ethiopian descent. He told Zedekiah what the officials had done and how desperate Jeremiah's situation was. It took real courage for him to oppose those who were determined to stop Jeremiah's proclamations.

38:10 Ebed-melech was authorized to take 30 men to **pull Jeremiah . . . up from the cistern before he dies**. One Hebrew manuscript and the Greek Septuagint read "three" for "thirty," but this is not enough evidence to overrule the Hebrew text as it stands. Perhaps 30 were needed for the total task: some for protection and some for pulling the prophet out of the pit.

38:11-13 The **old rags and worn-out clothes** were needed to protect Jeremiah from the ropes, since he was mired down in mud (v. 6). The narrative in 37:17-21 does not include all

place below the storehouse.[A] From there he took old rags and worn-out clothes and lowered them by ropes to Jeremiah in the cistern. [12]Ebed-melech the Cushite cried out to Jeremiah, "Place these old rags and clothes between your armpits and the ropes." Jeremiah did so, [13]and they pulled him up with the ropes and lifted him out of the cistern, but he continued to stay in the guard's courtyard.

Zedekiah's Final Meeting with Jeremiah

[14]King Zedekiah sent for Jeremiah the prophet and received him at the third entrance of the LORD's temple. The king said to Jeremiah, "I am going to ask you something; don't hide anything from me."

[15]Jeremiah replied to Zedekiah, "If I tell you, you will kill me, won't you? Besides, if I give you advice, you won't listen to me anyway."

[16]King Zedekiah swore to Jeremiah in private,[a] "As the LORD lives, who has given us this life,[b] I will not kill you or hand you over to these men who want to take your life."

[17]Jeremiah therefore said to Zedekiah, "This is what the LORD, the God of ⋅Hosts, the God of Israel, says: 'If indeed you surrender to the officials of the king of Babylon,[c] then you will live, this city will not be burned down, and you and your household will survive. [18]But if you do not surrender to the officials of the king of Babylon, then this city will be handed over to the Chaldeans. They will burn it down, and you yourself will not escape from them.'"

[19]But King Zedekiah said to Jeremiah, "I am worried about the Judeans who have deserted to the Chaldeans. They may hand me over to the Judeans to abuse me."[d]

[20]"They will not hand you over," Jeremiah replied. "Obey the voice of the LORD in what I am telling you, so it may go well for you and you can live. [21]But if you refuse to surrender, this is the verdict[B] that the LORD has shown me: [22]'All the women[C] who remain in the palace of Judah's king will be brought out to the officials of the king of Babylon and will say:

> Your trusted friends[D] misled[E] you
> and overcame you.
> Your feet sank into the mire,
> and they deserted you.

[23]All your wives and sons will be brought out to the Chaldeans.[e] You yourself will not escape from them, for you will be seized by the king of Babylon and this city will burn down.'"

[24]Then Zedekiah warned Jeremiah, "Don't let anyone know about these things or you will die. [25]If the officials hear that I have spoken with you[f] and come and demand of you, 'Tell us what you said to the king; don't hide anything from us and we won't kill you. Also, what did the king say to you?' [26]then you will tell them, 'I was bringing before the king my petition that he not return me to the house of Jonathan to die there.'"[g] [27]When all the officials came to Jeremiah and questioned him, he reported the exact words to them the king had commanded, and they quit speaking with him because nothing had been heard. [28]Jeremiah remained in the guard's courtyard until the day Jerusalem was captured, and he was there when it happened.[F]

The Fall of Jerusalem to Babylon

39 In the ninth year of Zedekiah king of Judah, in the tenth month, King Nebuchadnezzar of Babylon advanced against

---

a 38:16 Jr 37:17
b Is 57:16
c 38:17 2Kg 24:12; Jr 27:12; 38:2; 39:3
d 38:19 Jdg 19:25; 1Sm 31:4
e 38:23 Jr 39:6; 41:10
f 38:25 Jr 38:4-6
g 38:26 Jr 37:20

[A] 38:11 Or *treasury*   [B] 38:21 Or *promise;* lit *word*   [C] 38:22 Or *wives*   [D] 38:22 Lit *The men of your peace*   [E] 38:22 Or *incited*   [F] 38:28 Or *captured. This is what happened when Jerusalem was captured:*

---

these details about Jeremiah's rescue, but both record the prophet's plea not to be sent back to this cistern (37:20; 38:26).

38:14 The **third entrance**, where this secret discussion between Jeremiah and the king took place, is otherwise unknown. Could it have been the king's private entrance to the temple?

38:16 Zedekiah swore (**as the LORD lives**) to the prophet that he would not kill him or turn him over to his enemies.

38:19 Apparently a few citizens of Judah had already **deserted** to the Babylonians (see note at v. 2). The king feared these deserters might **abuse** him if he fell into the hands of the Babylonians.

38:21 The vision the Lord had shown Jeremiah (**the verdict that the LORD has shown me**) was the basket of figs (24:1-10), and it still foretold the same dire consequences.

38:22 Zedekiah feared the ridicule of Judah's defectors (v.

19). But he was even more frightened of the **women** (his own harem) who would **remain in the palace of Judah's king**. They might shower insult and ridicule on him for being so gullible that he trusted weak allies and false prophets. The women would try to curry favor with their new Babylonian overlords.

38:27 What Jeremiah told **all the officials** of the king was the truth. The prophet had requested that he not be sent back to his cistern prison again. Some argue that this was not the whole truth but only a half-truth. However, some persons give up their right to know the full truth. For example, the Lord instructed Samuel to tell Saul that he had come to offer a sacrifice, not revealing that he had also come to anoint David as king. Saul by his actions had forfeited his right to know the full truth (1Sm 16:1-4).

39:1-2 The siege of Jerusalem began in January of 588 B.C. and lasted until July of 587 B.C., except for a brief interlude in the summer of 588 (52:4-6).

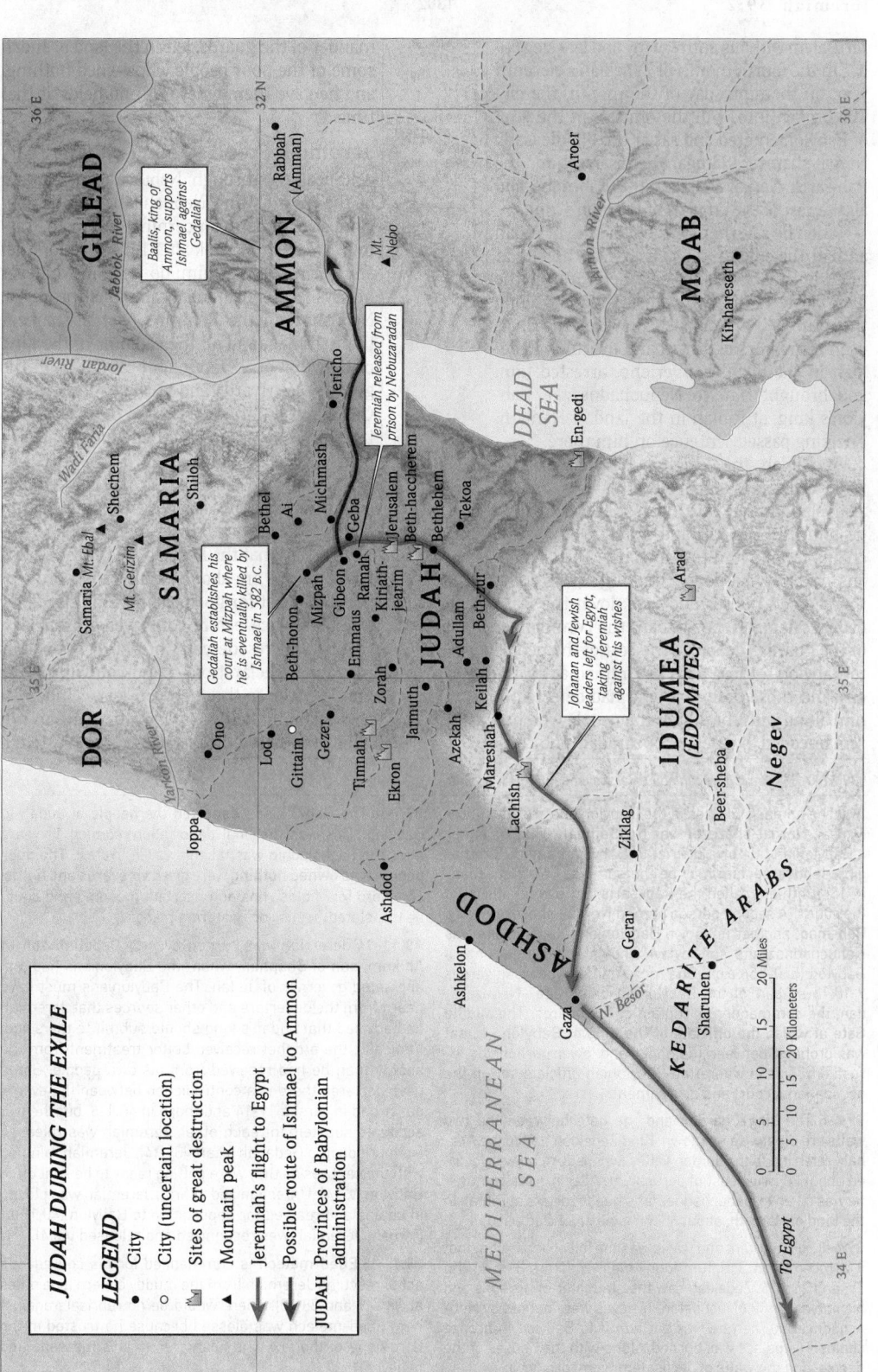

JUDAH DURING THE EXILE

LEGEND

• City
○ City (uncertain location)
⌂ Sites of great destruction
▲ Mountain peak
↓ Jeremiah's flight to Egypt
↓ Possible route of Ishmael to Ammon
JUDAH Provinces of Babylonian administration

Baalis, king of Ammon, supports Ishmael against Gedaliah

Jeremiah released from prison by Nebuzaradan

Gedaliah establishes his court at Mizpah where he is eventually killed by Ishmael in 582 B.C.

Johanan and Jewish leaders left for Egypt, taking Jeremiah against his wishes

GILEAD

SAMARIA

AMMON

MOAB

DOR

JUDAH

IDUMEA
(EDOMITES)

Negev

KEDARITE ARABS

DEAD SEA

MEDITERRANEAN SEA

Jordan River
Jabbok River
Wadi Fara
Yarkon River
Arnon River
N. Besor

Rabbah (Amman)
Aroer
Mt. Nebo
Kir-hareseth
Jericho
Shiloh
Shechem
Samaria Mt. Ebal
Mt. Gerizim
Bethel
Ai
Michmash
Geba
Jerusalem
Beth-haccherem
Bethlehem
Tekoa
En-gedi
Mizpah
Gibeon
Ramah
Kiriath-jearim
Beth-zur
Ono
Lod
Gittaim
Gezer
Timnah
Ekron
Zorah
Jarmuth
Azekah
Adullam
Keilah
Mareshah
Lachish
Arad
Joppa
Ashdod
Ashkelon
Gaza
Ziklag
Gerar
Beer-sheba
Sharuhen

ASHDOD

Beth-horon
Emmaus

To Egypt

36 E
35 E
34 E
32 N

0   5   10   15   20 Miles
0   5 10 15 20 Kilometers

Jerusalem with his entire army and laid siege to it. ²In the fourth month of Zedekiah's eleventh year, on the ninth day of the month, the city was broken into. ³All the officials of the king of Babylon entered and sat at the Middle Gate: Nergal-sharezer, Samgar, NebusarsechimᴬAthe Rab-saris, Nergal-sharezer the Rab-mag, and all the rest of the officials of Babylon's king.

⁴When he saw them, Zedekiah king of Judah and all the soldiers fled. They left the city at night by way of the king's garden through the gate between the two walls. They left along the route to the *Arabah.ᵃ ⁵However, the Chaldean army pursued them and overtook Zedekiah in the plainsᴮ of Jericho, arrested him, and brought him to Nebuchadnezzar, Babylon's king, at Riblah in the land of Hamath. The king passed sentence on him there.

⁶At Riblah the king of Babylon slaughtered Zedekiah's sons before his eyes, and he also slaughtered all Judah's nobles. ⁷Then he blinded Zedekiah and put him in bronze chains to take him to Babylon.ᵇ ⁸The Chaldeans next burned down the king's palace and the people's houses and tore down the walls of Jerusalem. ⁹Nebuzaradan, the commander of the guards,ᶜ deported the rest of the people to Babylon—those who had remained in the city and those deserters who had defected to him along with the rest of the people who had remained. ¹⁰However, Nebuzaradan, the com-

mander of the guards, left in the land of Judah some of the poor people who owned nothing, and he gave them vineyards and fields at that time.ᵈ

Jeremiah Freed by Nebuchadnezzar

¹¹Speaking through Nebuzaradan, captain of the guard, King Nebuchadnezzar of Babylon gave orders concerning Jeremiah, saying: ¹²"Take him, look after him, and don't let any harm come to him; do for him whatever he says." ¹³Nebuzaradan, captain of the guard, Nebushazban the Rab-saris, Nergal-sharezer the Rab-mag, and all the captains of the king of Babylon ¹⁴had Jeremiah brought from the guard's courtyardᵉ and turned him over to Gedaliahᶠ son of Ahikam,ᵍ son of Shaphan, to take him home. So he settled among his own people.

¹⁵Now the word of the Lᴏʀᴅ had come to Jeremiah when he was confined in the guard's courtyard:ʰ ¹⁶"Go tell Ebed-melech the *Cushite:ⁱ This is what the Lᴏʀᴅ of *Hosts, the God of Israel, says: I am about to fulfill My words for harm and not for good against this city. They will take place before your eyes on that day. ¹⁷But I will rescue you on that day"—this is the Lᴏʀᴅ's declaration—"and you will not be handed over to the men you fear. ¹⁸Indeed, I will certainly deliver you so that you do not fall by the sword. Because you have trusted in

---

ᵃ 39:4 Dt 2:8; 2Sm 4:7
ᵇ 39:1-7 2Kg 25:1-7; Jr 52:4-11
ᶜ 39:9 2Kg 25:8-20; Jr 52:12-30; Dn 2:14
ᵈ 39:8-10 2Kg 25:9-12; Jr 52:13-16
ᵉ 39:14 Jr 38:28; 40:1-6
ᶠ Jr 40:5
ᵍ 2Kg 22:12
ʰ 39:15 Jr 33:1
ⁱ 39:16 Jr 38:1-13

ᴬ39:3 LXX; MT reads *Samgar-nebu, Sarsechim*   ᴮ39:5 Lit *Arabah*

39:3 The names and titles of the Babylonians are not entirely clear. **Nergal-sharezer** was the **Samgar**, which is either a Babylonian title or a district in Babylon named "Simmagir." **Nebusarsechim** may be the same as "Nebushazban" (v. 13). Both are called the **Rab-saris**, or "a chief official of the court." A second person named **Nergal-sharezer** was a **Rab-mag**, another unknown Babylonian title. This one was Nebuchadnezzar's son-in-law who later became king of Babylon (560–556 B.C.). One more name appears in verses 9-10,13 as part of the Babylonian entourage—Nebuzaradan, the commander or captain of the guards. The **Middle Gate** at which **the officials of the king of Babylon . . . sat** was probably between the upper and lower portions of Jerusalem. This is where the Babylonian officials set up the occupational court and government.

39:4-5 The **king's garden** and the **gate between the two walls** are otherwise unknown. King Zedekiah fled to the **Arabah**, referring to the Jordan Valley, where **Jericho** was located about 20 miles east of Jerusalem. After he was captured he was taken to Nebuchadnezzar's headquarters at **Riblah in the land of Hamath**, about 65 miles north of Damascus.

39:6-8 So important and tragic was the fall of Jerusalem that it is recorded in Scripture four times: chapters 39; 52; 2Kg 25; and 2Ch 36. Zedekiah saw the slaughter of his sons and his nobles (Jr 39:6) just before his eyes were put out by Nebuchadnezzar. Then he was carted off to Babylon in **bronze chains**. His palace was burned, along with the houses of the people, and the **walls of Jerusalem** were torn down.

39:9-10 The Babylonians **deported** the people of Judah to Babylon. This was the final deportation, coming 11 years after King Jehoiachin was taken away in 598 B.C. **The poor people who owned nothing** were given **vineyards and fields**. The word for "fields" has an uncertain meaning and could be translated "wells" or "watering places."

39:11-14 Jeremiah was turned over to **Gedaliah son of Ahikam, son of Shaphan**, whom the Babylonians had just appointed governor of Judah. The Babylonians must have heard from the deserters and other sources that Jeremiah had advised that Judah's king should submit to the siege. Ironically, the prophet received better treatment from the enemy than he had received from his own people. Some have declared there is a contradiction between the events described in verses 11-14 and those in 40:1-6, but the two accounts supplement each other. Jeremiah was released from prison into Gedaliah's care (39:14). Jeremiah mingled with the captives as they were getting ready to be sent off to Babylon (v. 14). Unrecognized at first, Jeremiah was placed in chains and readied for deportation to Babylon (40:1). At Ramah, Jeremiah was recognized and released (40:4).

39:15-18 **Ebed-melech** is commended for his courageous act of rescuing Jeremiah from the muddy cistern (see notes at 38:7-9 and 38:10). There would be no reprisals against him. Ebed-melech was blessed because he **trusted** in the Lord—one of the few who heard Jeremiah's message and believed.

Me, you will keep your life like the spoils of war."[a] This is the Lord's declaration.

Jeremiah Stays in Judah

40 This is the word that came to Jeremiah from the Lord after Nebuzaradan, captain of the guard, released him at Ramah.[b] When he found him, he was bound in chains with all the exiles of Jerusalem and Judah who were being exiled to Babylon. [2]The captain of the guard took Jeremiah and said to him, "The Lord your God decreed this disaster on this place,[c] [3]and the Lord has fulfilled it. He has done just what He decreed. Because you people have sinned against the Lord[d] and have not obeyed Him, this thing has happened. [4]Now pay attention: Today I am setting you free from the chains that were on your hands.[e] If it pleases you to come with me to Babylon, come, and I will take care of you. But if it seems wrong to you to come with me to Babylon, go no farther.[A] Look—the whole land is in front of you.[f] Wherever it seems good and right for you to go, go there." [5]When Jeremiah had not yet turned to go, Nebuzaradan said to him: "Return[B] to Gedaliah son of Ahikam, son of Shaphan, whom the king of Babylon has appointed over the cities of Judah, and stay with him among the people or go wherever you want to go." So the captain of the guard gave him a ration[g] and a gift[h] and released him. [6]Jeremiah therefore went to Gedaliah son of Ahikam at Mizpah,[i] and he stayed with him among the people who remained in the land.

Gedaliah Advises Peace

[7]When all the commanders of the armies in the field—they and their men—heard that the king of Babylon had appointed Gedaliah son of Ahikam over the land and that he had put him in charge of the men, women, and children from the poorest of the land who had not been deported to Babylon, [8]they came to Gedaliah at Mizpah. The commanders included Ishmael[j] son of Nethaniah, Johanan and Jonathan the sons of Kareah, Seraiah son of Tanhumeth, the sons of Ephai the Netophathite, and Jezaniah son of the Maacathite—they and their men.

[9]Gedaliah son of Ahikam, son of Shaphan, swore an oath to them and their men, assuring them, "Don't be afraid to serve the Chaldeans. Live in the land and serve the king of Babylon, and it will go well for you.[k] [10]As for me, I am going to live in Mizpah to represent[C] you before the Chaldeans[l] who come to us. As for you, gather wine, summer fruit, and oil, place them in your storage jars, and live in the cities you have captured."

[11]When all the Judeans in Moab[m] and among the Ammonites and in[n] Edom and in all the other lands[o] also heard that the king of Babylon had left a remnant in Judah and had appointed Gedaliah son of Ahikam, son of Shaphan, over them, [12]they all returned from all the places where they had been banished[p] and came to the land of Judah, to Gedaliah at Mizpah, and harvested a great amount of wine and summer fruit.

---

a 39:18 Jr 21:9; 38:2; 45:5
b 40:1 1Kg 15:17-22; 2Ch 16:1-6
c 40:2 Dt 29:24-28
d 40:3 Dn 9:10-12
e 40:4 Jr 39:12
f Gn 20:15
g 40:5 2Kg 25:30; Jr 52:34
h 2Sm 11:8
i 40:6 Jdg 20:1-3; 1Sm 7:5-16; Jr 41:1-16
j 40:8 Jr 41:1,9
k 40:7-9 2Kg 25:22-24
l 40:10 Dt 1:38
m 40:11 Nm 22:1
n 1Sm 11:1; 12:12
o Gn 36:8
p 40:12 Jr 23:3,8; 29:14; 32:37

A 40:4 Lit Babylon, stop   **B** 40:5 LXX reads But if not, run, return; Hb obscure   **C** 40:10 Lit to stand

---

40:1-6 This passage amplifies and supplements 39:11-14 (see note there).

40:1 The **word that came to Jeremiah from the Lord** does not seem to be given until 42:9. The captain of the Babylonian guard released Jeremiah at **Ramah**, modern er-Ram, about five miles north of Jerusalem, a staging area for the deportation. Apparently, the Babylonians had mistakenly put Jeremiah in chains to be deported.

40:2-3 Some doubt that Nebuzaradan, a Babylonian, could have spoken such high Hebrew theology. But it is clear from 2Kg 18:22 that the Assyrians paid close attention to the beliefs of enemy nations in order to wage psychological warfare against them. This captain of the guard may also have been acquainted with some of Jeremiah's teachings. Perhaps he had heard them from messages sent by ambassadors, from Jeremiah's letters to those in exile, and from deserters.

40:5 Jeremiah was told to return to **Gedaliah son of Ahikam, son of Shaphan**. In 1935, James Starkey, the excavator of Lachish, found a stamp-seal with these words: "Gedalyahu, the one over the house," i.e., palace governor (Is 36:22). This could be the same Gedaliah mentioned here, even though the name was common. The Hebrew title "[the one] who is over the house" designates a royal administrative official.

40:6 **Mizpah** was perhaps present-day Tell en-Nasbeh, about eight miles north of Jerusalem. Others locate it four miles southwest of Ramah at present-day Nabi Samwil. Gedaliah made this site his headquarters or administrative center.

40:8 In the absence of leaders, guerrilla bands emerged from hiding after the Babylonians took their captives back to Babylon. Most of the population of Judah was from the underprivileged class, with a few royal princesses who were left behind (43:6). Netophah (the **Netophathite**) was a Judean town between Bethlehem and Tekoa. Maacah (the **Maacathite**) was southeast of Hermon.

40:9 The guerrilla bands were pacified by Governor Gedaliah with an oath and the advice to settle down in the land. Gedaliah would be the mediator with the Babylonians.

40:11-12 Refugee Jews started returning from all over **Moab**, Ammon, **Edom**, and **all the other lands**. Summer was coming to an end, so it was necessary to gather the harvest (consisting of **a great amount of wine and summer fruit**) for the winter and to pay the Babylonian taxes. Apparently, the conquerors did not use a scorched-earth policy.

¹³Meanwhile, Johanan son of Kareah and all the commanders of the armies in the field came to Gedaliah at Mizpah ¹⁴and warned him, "Don't you realize that Baalis, king of the Ammonites, has sent Ishmael son of Nethaniah[a] to kill you?" But Gedaliah son of Ahikam would not believe them. ¹⁵Then Johanan son of Kareah suggested to Gedaliah in private at Mizpah, "Let me go kill Ishmael son of Nethaniah. No one will know it. Why should he kill you and scatter all of Judah that has gathered to you so that the remnant of Judah would perish?"[b]

¹⁶But Gedaliah son of Ahikam responded to Johanan son of Kareah, "Don't do that! What you're saying about Ishmael is a lie."

Gedaliah Assassinated by Ishmael

41 In the seventh month, Ishmael son of Nethaniah, son of Elishama, of the royal family and one of the king's chief officers, came with 10 men to Gedaliah son of Ahikam at Mizpah. They ate a meal together there in Mizpah, ²but then Ishmael son of Nethaniah and the 10 men who were with him got up and struck down Gedaliah son of Ahikam, son of Shaphan, with the sword; he killed the one the king of Babylon had appointed in the land. ³Ishmael also struck down all the Judeans who were with Gedaliah at Mizpah, as well as the Chaldean soldiers who were there.[c]

⁴On the second day after he had killed Gedaliah, when no one knew yet, ⁵80 men came from Shechem, Shiloh,[d] and Samaria[e] who had shaved their beards,[f] torn their garments, and gashed themselves, and who were carrying •grain and incense offerings to bring to the temple of the LORD.[g] ⁶Ishmael son of Nethaniah came out of Mizpah to meet them, weeping as he came. When he encountered them, he said: "Come to Gedaliah son of Ahikam!" ⁷But when they came into the city, Ishmael son of Nethaniah and the men with him slaughtered them and threw them into[A] a cistern.

⁸However, there were 10 men among them who said to Ishmael, "Don't kill us, for we have hidden treasure in the field—wheat, barley, oil, and honey!" So he stopped and did not kill them along with their companions. ⁹Now the cistern where Ishmael had thrown all the corpses of the men he had struck down was a large one[B] that King Asa had made in the encounter with Baasha king of Israel.[h] Ishmael son of Nethaniah filled it with the slain.

¹⁰Then Ishmael took captive all the remnant of the people of Mizpah including the daughters of the king—all those who remained in Mizpah over whom Nebuzaradan, captain of the guard, had appointed Gedaliah son of Ahikam. Ishmael son of Nethaniah took them captive and set off to cross over to the Ammonites.[i]

The Captives Rescued by Johanan

¹¹When Johanan son of Kareah and all the commanders of the armies[j] with him heard

Cross references

a 40:14 Jr 41:10
b 40:15 Jr 42:2
c 41:1–3 2Kg 25:25
d 41:5 Jos 18:1
e 1Kg 16:24
f Dt 14:1
g 2Kg 25:9
h 41:9 1Kg 15:16-22
i 41:10 Jr 40:14
j 41:11 Jr 40:7-8,13-16

A 41:7 Syr; MT reads *slaughtered them in*   B 41:9 LXX; MT reads *down by the hand of Gedaliah*

40:13-14 Johanan warned Gedaliah that **Baalis, king of the Ammonites,** had sent **Ishmael** to kill the newly appointed governor.

40:15-16 Despite Johanan's offer to make a preemptive strike against Ishmael, Gedaliah refused to do so. He felt the rumors about Ishmael were **a lie.**

41:1 Gedaliah was assassinated in the **seventh month,** our month of October. This occurred either in 587 B.C., three months after the fall of Jerusalem, or five years later in 582 B.C. in connection with another deportation of Jews mentioned in 52:30. The year cannot be fixed with certainty. **Ishmael son of Nethaniah . . . of the royal family,** was a member of the Davidic line and one of King Zedekiah's chief officers. He did not agree with Jeremiah's advice to surrender to the Babylonians either before or after the fall of Jerusalem.

41:2-3 Ishmael came with his **10 men** and sat down for a meal with Gedaliah, who did not suspect treachery. In a breach of Eastern hospitality, they killed both **Judeans** and **Chaldean soldiers** on the spot.

41:4-5 Ishmael continued his slaughter by killing 70 of the **80 men** who came from **Shechem, Shiloh, and Samaria,** carrying **grain and incense offerings . . . to the temple.** Though the temple was destroyed (note that these were bloodless sacrifices), the plot of ground it had occupied was still regarded as sacred, just like the Western Wall in Jerusalem today. Even though these men lived in pagan northern Israel, they continued to worship God in Jerusalem.

41:5 Though the 80 pilgrims were genuine worshipers of the Lord, syncretism was evident in the fact that they **gashed themselves,** a cultic practice adopted from Baal worship yet forbidden in the law of God (5:7; Dt 14:1; 1Kg 18:28).

41:8 Ishmael spared **10 men** among the 80 because they offered him **hidden treasure in the field.** Ishmael's greed and deceit showed his true character. He had no good reason for killing the 70 men.

41:9 The **cistern** into which Ishmael stuffed the bodies of the slain was **a large one** from the time of **King Asa.** Three hundred years previously, Asa had built a fortress at Mizpah from the material he had dragged off from Baasha's construction of a fortress at Ramah (1Kg 15:22; 2Ch 16:6). Excavations at Tel en-Nasbeh may have uncovered this very cistern.

41:10 The phrase **daughters of the king** is puzzling. There are no references anywhere else to Zedekiah's daughters, so they may have been women of royal descent. Did the Babylonian garrison at Mizpah not know about their existence? Were they released after they were blinded? Did Nebuchadnezzar offer clemency to some of the royal princesses? We do not know.

41:11-18 **Johanan,** who opposed Ishmael, apparently re-

of all the evil that Ishmael son of Nethaniah had done, [12]they took all their men and went to fight with Ishmael son of Nethaniah and found him by the great pool in Gibeon.[a] [13]When all the people with Ishmael saw Johanan son of Kareah and all the commanders of the army with him, they rejoiced, [14]and all the people whom Ishmael had taken captive from Mizpah turned around and rejoined Johanan son of Kareah. [15]But Ishmael son of Nethaniah escaped from Johanan with eight men and went to the Ammonites. [16]Johanan son of Kareah and all the commanders of the armies with him then took from Mizpah all the remnant of the people whom he had recovered from Ishmael son of Nethaniah after Ishmael had killed Gedaliah son of Ahikam—men, soldiers, women, children, and court officials whom he brought back from Gibeon. [17]They left, stopping in Geruth Chimham,[b] which is near Bethlehem, in order to make their way into Egypt, [18]away from the Chaldeans. For they feared them because Ishmael son of Nethaniah had struck down Gedaliah son of Ahikam, whom the king of Babylon had appointed in the land.[c]

The People Seek Jeremiah's Counsel

42 Then all the commanders of the armies, along with Johanan son of Kareah,[d] Jezaniah son of Hoshaiah, and all the people from the least to the greatest,[e] approached [2]Jeremiah the prophet and said, "May our petition come before you;[f] pray to the LORD your God on our behalf,[g] on behalf of this entire remnant (for few of us remain out of the many,[h] as you can see with your own eyes), [3]that the LORD your God may tell us the way we should walk and the thing we should do."

[4]So Jeremiah the prophet said to them, "I have heard. I will now pray to the LORD your God according to your words, and every word that the LORD answers you I will tell you; I won't withhold a word from you."[i]

[5]And they said to Jeremiah, "As for every word the LORD your God sends you to tell us, if we don't act accordingly, may the LORD be a true and faithful witness against us.[j] [6]Whether it is pleasant or unpleasant, we will obey the voice of the LORD our God to whom we are sending you so that it may go well with us.[k] We will certainly obey the voice of the LORD our God!"

Jeremiah's Advice to Stay

[7]Now at the end of 10 days, the word of the LORD came to Jeremiah, [8]and he summoned Johanan son of Kareah, all the commanders of the armies who were with him, and all the people from the least to the greatest. [9]He said to them, "This is what the LORD says, the God of Israel to whom you sent me to bring your petition before Him: [10]'If you will indeed stay in this land, then I will rebuild and not demolish you,[l] and I will plant and not uproot you, because I relent concerning the disaster[m] that I have brought on you. [11]Don't be afraid of the king of Babylon[n] whom you now fear; don't be afraid of him'—this is the LORD's declaration—'because I am with you to save you[o]

[a]41:12 2Sm 2:13
[b]41:17 2Sm 19:37-38
[c]41:18 2Kg 25:26; Jr 40:5
[d]42:1 Jr 40:13; 41:11
[e]Jr 6:13
[f]42:2 Jr 36:7
[g]1Sm 7:8; 12:19; Is 37:4; Jr 42:20
[h]Lv 26:22
[i]42:4 1Sm 3:17-18
[j]42:5 Gn 31:50; Jdg 11:10
[k]42:6 Jr 7:23
[l]42:10 Jr 24:6
[m]Jr 18:7-8
[n]42:11 Jr 41:18
[o]Rm 8:31

---

turned to Mizpah, where he learned about Ishmael's treachery. Johanan tracked Ishmael with all the captives he had taken from Mizpah to **the great pool in Gibeon**, about three miles away. This large pit, hewn out of rock, is about 82 feet deep. Twelve of Abner's men fought 12 of Joab's men (2Sm 2:12-16) near this pool at what is today the city of el-Jib. Johanan rescued the captives, and Ishmael escaped with **eight men**. Johanan feared what the Babylonians might do as reprisals for Ishmael's killing spree, so he was determined to take the remnant of people left in Judah off to Egypt.

42:1-2 The commanders and all the people came to Jeremiah to pray for guidance on what to do. They wanted Jeremiah to plead to **the LORD your God** so He would direct them. The prophet agreed to do so. How Jeremiah reached this group—or whether he had been living in Mizpah when Ishmael's attack happened—is not revealed. This **Jezaniah** is not the same as the Jezaniah of 40:8, but he is the same as the Azariah of 43:2; the Greek Septuagint reads Azariah in both 42:1 and 43:2. As then as now, men could go by more than one name, as did King Uzziah (aka Azariah, 2Kg 15:1). **Hoshaiah** may be the same man mentioned in the Lachish Letters, inscribed potsherds that tell about the last moments before the city's fall to Nebuchadnezzar.

42:5-6 Three times the people affirmed that they would do whatever the Lord told Jeremiah. They would **certainly** (lit "yes, indeed") **obey the voice of the LORD.**

42:7-9 Jeremiah was unwilling to speak until he had the Lord's answer, so it took **10 days**. This must have caused more jitters about reprisals from the Babylonians. Perhaps the delay was part of God's test of the people. Would they be willing to wait for the Lord's answer despite their anxiety?

42:8-12 Once again Jeremiah delivered an unpopular message. God said He would **not uproot** them if they stayed in the land. This message disappointed them, for they wished to flee to Egypt rather than remain. God decided to **relent concerning the disaster** that He had brought on Judah (v. 10). This does not mean God changed His being, character, person, or purpose. The Hebrew verb is *niham* ("to be sorry," "to regret," "to relent"), which here means God "grieves" over Judah and changes His actions due to a change in Judah's response now that judgment had been meted out in the fall of Jerusalem. This verb with this meaning also occurs in 4:18; 18:8,10; 26:3,13,19 (see note at 18:7-10).

and deliver you from him. ¹²I will grant you compassion,ᵃ and heᴬ will have compassion on you and allow you to return to your own soil. ¹³But if you say, 'We will not stay in this land,'ᵇ so as not to obey the voice of the Lᴏʀᴅ your God, ¹⁴and if you say, 'No, instead we'll go to the land of Egyptᶜ where we will not see war or hear the sound of the ram's hornᵈ or hunger for food, and we'll live there,' ¹⁵then hear

the word of the Lᴏʀᴅ, remnant of Judah! This is what the Lᴏʀᴅ of •Hosts, the God of Israel, says: If you are firmly resolved to go to Egyptᵉ and live there for a while, ¹⁶then the swordᶠ you fear will overtake you there in the land of Egypt, and the famine you are worried about will follow on your heelsᴮ there to Egypt, and you will die there. ¹⁷All who resolve to go to Egypt to live there for a while will die by the

ᵃ42:12 Neh 1:11
ᵇ42:13 Jr 44:16-17
ᶜ42:14 Jr 41:17
ᵈJr 4:19,21
ᵉ42:15 Dt 17:16; Jr 44:12-14
ᶠ42:16 Ezk 11:8

ᴬ42:12 LXX reads *I*   ᴮ42:16 Lit *will cling after you*

42:13-17 If the remnant of Judah's citizens trusted in humans and not in God, terrifying consequences awaited them in Egypt—**sword . . . famine**, and death. Though Egypt was defeated at the battle of Carchemish in 605, she had not experienced warfare in her own country. Indeed Egypt was the only country that had escaped this scourge. Judah

had experienced war almost constantly since the battle of Megiddo in 609 B.C. when King Josiah was killed. The **remnant of Judah** are those who remained after the city's fall in 587 B.C.

42:18-22 The disobedient refugees would become **an object**

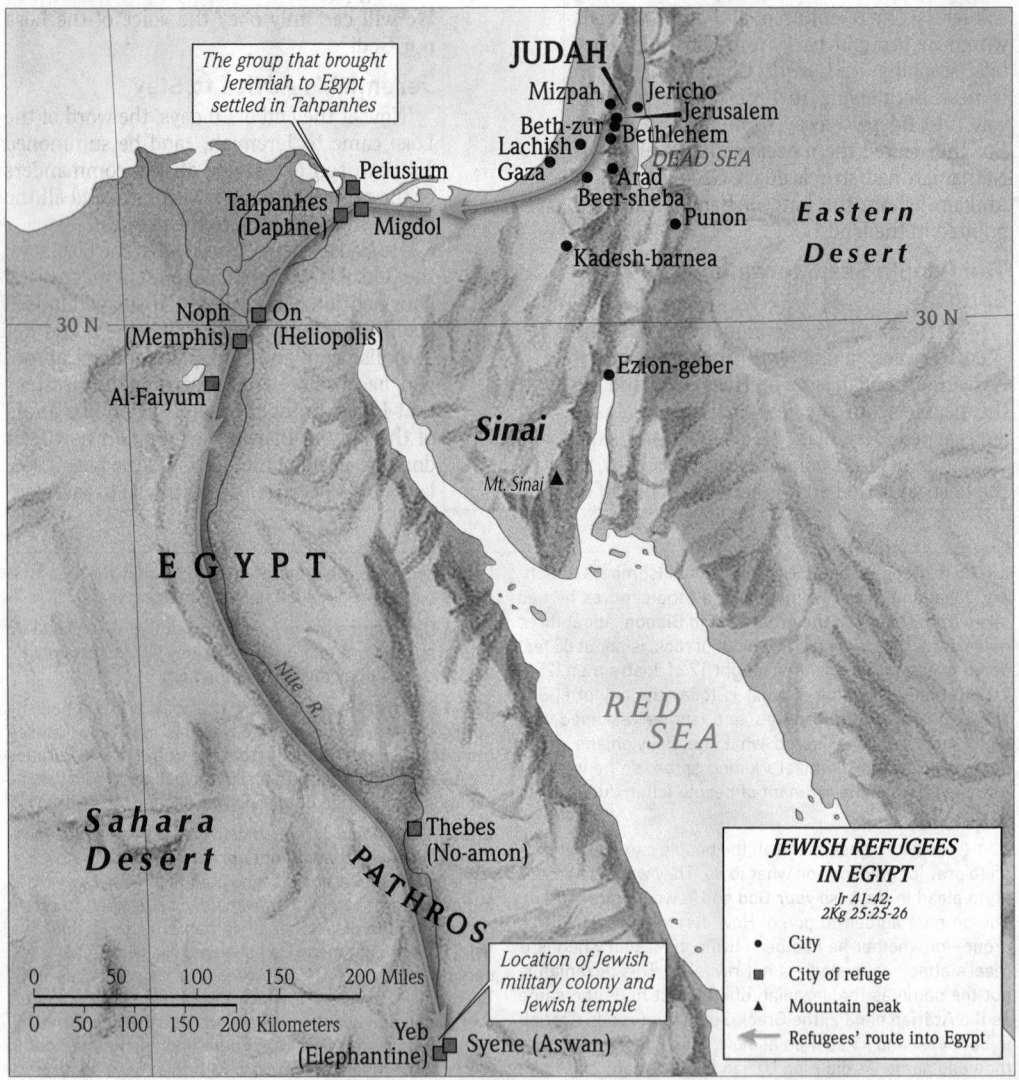

The group that brought Jeremiah to Egypt settled in Tahpanhes

JUDAH

Mizpah

Jericho

Jerusalem

Beth-zur

Bethlehem

Lachish

DEAD SEA

Gaza

Arad

Beer-sheba

Punon

Eastern Desert

Kadesh-barnea

Pelusium

Tahpanhes (Daphne)

Migdol

Noph (Memphis)

On (Heliopolis)

30 N   30 N

Al-Faiyum

Ezion-geber

Sinai

Mt. Sinai ▲

E G Y P T

Nile R.

RED SEA

Sahara Desert

PATHROS

Thebes (No-amon)

| 0 | 50 | 100 | 150 | 200 Miles |

| 0 | 50 | 100 | 150 | 200 Kilometers |

Location of Jewish military colony and Jewish temple

Yeb (Elephantine)

Syene (Aswan)

JEWISH REFUGEES IN EGYPT
Jr 41-42;
2Kg 25:25-26

• City

■ City of refuge

▲ Mountain peak

← Refugees' route into Egypt

⁵⁶ You hear my plea:
  Do not ignore my cry for relief.
⁵⁷ You come near when I call on You;
  You say: "Do not be afraid."

ר Resh

⁵⁸ You defend my cause, Lord;^a
  You redeem my life.^b
⁵⁹ Lord, You see the wrong done to me;
  judge my case.
⁶⁰ You see all their malice,
  all their plots against me.^c

ש Sin/ ש Shin

⁶¹ Lord, You hear their insults,^d
  all their plots against me.
⁶² The slander^A and murmuring
  of my opponents
  attack me all day long.
⁶³ When they sit and when they rise, look,
  I am mocked by their songs.^e

ת Tav

⁶⁴ You will pay them back
  what they deserve, Lord,
  according to the work of their hands.^f
⁶⁵ You will give them a heart
  filled with anguish.^{B,g}
  May Your curse be on them!
⁶⁶ You will pursue them in anger
  and destroy them
  under Your heavens.^{C,D,h}

Terrors of the Besieged City

א Alef

⁴ How the gold has become tarnished,
  the fine gold become dull!
  The stones of the temple^E lie scattered
  at the corner of every street.ⁱ

^a3:58 Ps 43:1;
Pr 23:11; Jr
50:34
^bPs 103:4;
119:154
^c3:60 Jr 11:19
^d3:61 Lm 5:1
^e3:63 Jb 30:9;
Ps 69:12; Lm
3:14
^f3:64 Ps 28:4;
Rm 2:6; Rv
20:12-13
^g3:65 Is 6:10
^h3:66 Ps 8:3
ⁱ4:1 Ezk 7:19-20
^j4:2 Is 62:3; Zch
9:16
^k4:3 Jb 39:13-18
^l4:4 Ps 22:15
^m4:5 Jdg 8:26;
Est 8:15
ⁿ4:6 Gn 18–19;
Is 3:9; Jr 23:14

ב Bet

² •Zion's precious people—
  once worth their weight in pure gold^j—
  how they are regarded as clay jars,
  the work of a potter's hands!

ג Gimel

³ Even jackals offer their breasts
  to nurse their young,
  but my dear people
  have become cruel
  like ostriches^k in the wilderness.

ד Dalet

⁴ The nursing infant's tongue
  clings to the roof of his mouth
  from thirst.^l
  Little children beg for bread,
  but no one gives them any.

ה He

⁵ Those who used to eat delicacies
  are destitute in the streets;
  those who were reared
  in purple garments^m
  huddle in garbage heaps.

ו Vav

⁶ The punishment of my dear people
  is greater than that of Sodom,ⁿ
  which was overthrown in an instant
  without a hand laid on it.

ז Zayin

⁷ Her dignitaries were brighter
  than snow,
  whiter than milk;

---

^A3:62 Lit lips   ^B3:65 Or them an obstinate heart; Hb obscure   ^C3:66 LXX, Syr, Vg read heavens, Lord   ^D3:66 Lit under the Lord's heavens   ^E4:1 Or The sacred gems

---

3:55 Like the psalmist, Jeremiah called on God's name **from the depths of the Pit** (see Ps 130:1).

3:56-57 God heard Jeremiah's **plea**. His words of assurance were, **Do not be afraid**.

3:58-60 There was no better judge for Jeremiah's case than the Lord, who saw all and yet was able to defend the prophet's cause and **redeem** his **life**.

3:61-63 The Lord, the Omniscient One, heard and saw everything. Jeremiah and Israel could be sure they were in good hands.

3:64-66 Sufferers must leave revenge (**pay them back**) in the hands of the Lord. Jeremiah never raised his own hand to seek personal vengeance for all he had suffered.

4:1-2 God's people were **worth their weight** in gold. The prophet used three terms for gold: the general term **gold**,

fine gold, and **pure gold**. That is what the holy nation was before God, but now smeared with sin, they were regarded as **clay jars**, like pieces of broken pottery.

4:3-4 The **jackals** offer their **breasts to nurse their young**, but Israel's parents neglected their young during the crisis. They are like **ostriches**, which are legendary for their habit of laying eggs and then leaving them (Jb 39:13-18).

4:5 Those who had been raised on delicacies and clothed in **purple** now had to go hungry and **huddle in garbage heaps**.

4:6 Greater privilege (revelation from God) brought greater responsibility to God and thus greater degrees of guilt for wrongdoing. Thus Judah's guilt was **greater** than that of **Sodom**.

4:7-8 The phrase **her dignitaries** is often rendered as "her

their bodies[A] were more ruddy
  than coral,
their appearance like sapphire.[B]

ח Khet

8 Now they appear darker than soot;[a]
they are not recognized in the streets.
Their skin has shriveled on their bones;
it has become dry like wood.

ט Tet

9 Those slain by the sword are better off
than those slain by hunger,
who waste away, pierced with pain
because the fields lack produce.

י Yod

10 The hands of compassionate women
have cooked their own children;[b]
they became their food
during the destruction
  of my dear people.[c]

כ Kaf

11 The LORD has exhausted His wrath,
poured out His burning anger;
He has ignited a fire in Zion,
and it has consumed her foundations.[d]

ל Lamed

12 The kings of the earth
and all the world's inhabitants
did not believe

that an enemy or adversary
could enter Jerusalem's gates.[e]

מ Mem

13 Yet it happened because of the sins
  of her prophets
and the *guilt of her priests,
who shed the blood of the righteous
within her.[f]

נ Nun

14 Blind, they stumbled in the streets,[g]
defiled by this blood,[h]
so that no one dared
to touch their garments.

ס Samek

15 "Stay away! *Unclean!" people shouted
  at them.
"Away, away! Don't touch us!"[i]
So they wandered aimlessly.[j]
It was said among the nations,
"They can stay here no longer."

פ Pe

16 The LORD Himself
  has scattered them;
He regards them no more.
The priests are not respected;
the elders find no favor.

ע Ayin

17 All the while our eyes were failing

a 4:8 Jb 30:30; Lm 5:10
b 4:10 Dt 28:53; 2Kg 6:9
c Jr 8:11,21; Lm 2:11; 3:48
d 4:11 Lm 2:3-4
e 4:12 2Sm 5:6-8; Ps 48:1-5
f 4:13 Ps 106:38-39; Ezk 22:1-5
g 4:14 Dt 28:29; Is 59:10; Zph 1:17
h Lv 21:11
i 4:15 Lv 13:45-46
j Gn 4:12

A 4:7 Lit bones   B 4:7 Or lapis lazuli

Nazirites." But Gn 49:26 and Dt 33:16 use it of a person who is "separated" by rank and task from his contemporaries.

kalah

Hebrew Pronunciation	[kah LAH]
HCSB Translation	end, finish, destroy, exhaust
Uses in Lamentations	5
Uses in the OT	207
Focus passage	Lamentations 4:11,17

Kalah means come to an end (Gn 41:53) or end. Things are gone, spent, or empty. They fade away (Ps 37:20), vanish, and disappear. People are destroyed (Ezk 13:14), consumed, finished off, or confounded. Eyes fail or grow weary. Flesh wastes away; people perish. Things are finished (Ru 2:23), concluded, fulfilled, done, or completed. Events are determined (1Sm 20:33) or certain. Individuals intend (1Sm 20:7), plan, yearn (Ps 84:2), or long. The intensive, often a helping verb, means finish (Nm 4:15). One brings about or to an end (Dn 9:24), puts or makes an end, and ends. Kalah is complete (Ezk 4:6) or fill. One spends (Is 49:4), uses up, exhausts, or strips. He has enough. People exterminate, consume, finish off, annihilate, wipe off or out, and (completely) destroy (Jos 24:20). They let go blind (Jb 31:16) or cause eyes to fail. They resolve (Ru 3:18) or deal.

Hence, these dignitaries, once **ruddy** and glamorous, were **darker than soot** and their skin was **shriveled on their bones**.

4:9 A swift death by the **sword** was better than a slow death by starvation.

4:10 So horrific were the effects of the famine during the siege of Jerusalem that even **compassionate women**, who under normal circumstances would never think of such a thing, **cooked their own children** for **food**.

4:11 All the miseries that had befallen Jerusalem were allowed by the Lord. **Exhausted His wrath** means His planned judgment was fulfilled, not that He became weary and thus relented.

4:12 What many **kings of the earth** and **all the world's inhabitants** had thought impossible had happened: Jerusalem had fallen.

4:13-14 The reason for this tragedy was the **sins** of the **prophets and the guilt** of the **priests** (as Jeremiah had warned time and again; Jr 6:13; 8:8-12; 23:11-36; 26:7-24; 28:1-17). Now **no one dared to touch their garments**. They were the outcasts of society.

4:15-16 The survivors, who once cheered the false prophets

as we looked in vain
  for assistance;[a]
we watched from our towers
  for a nation[A] that refused to help.

‫צ‬ Tsade

18 Our steps were closely followed
  so that we could not walk
    in our streets.
Our end drew near;[b] our time
  ran out.
Our end had come!

‫ק‬ Qof

19 Those who chased us were swifter
  than eagles in the sky;[c]
they relentlessly pursued us
  over the mountains
and ambushed us in the wilderness.

‫ר‬ Resh

20 The Lord's anointed,[B] the breath
  of our life,[C,d]
was captured in their traps.
We had said about him,
"We will live under his protection
  among the nations."

‫ש‬ Sin

21 So rejoice and be glad,
  Daughter Edom,[e]

---

[a]4:17 Jr 37:7-8
[b]4:18 Ezk 7:2-12; Am 8:2
[c]4:19 Jr 4:13; Hab 1:8
[d]4:20 Gn 2:7; 2Kg 25:7
[e]4:21 Ezk 35:15; Ob 12
[f]Jr 25:20
[g]Is 51:17; Jr 25:15-16; Hab 2:16
[h]4:22 Ps 137:7; Ezk 25:12-14; Jl 3:19
[i]5:1 Ps 74:18,22; 89:50-51
[j]5:6 Hs 12:1
[k]5:8 Pr 30:21-23; Ec 10:7

---

you resident of the land of Uz![f]
Yet the cup[g] will pass to you as well;
you will get drunk
  and expose yourself.

‫ת‬ Tav

22 Daughter Zion, your punishment
  is complete;
He will not lengthen your exile.[D]
But He will punish your iniquity,
  Daughter Edom,
and will expose your sins.[h]

Prayer for Restoration

5 ·Yahweh, remember what has happened
  to us.
Look, and see our disgrace![i]
2 Our inheritance has been turned over
  to strangers,
our houses to foreigners.
3 We have become orphans, fatherless;
our mothers are widows.
4 We must pay for the water we drink;
our wood comes at a price.
5 We are closely pursued;
we are tired, and no one offers us rest.
6 We made a treaty with[E] Egypt
and with Assyria, to get enough food.[j]
7 Our fathers sinned;
  they no longer exist,
but we bear their punishment.
8 Slaves rule over us;[k]
no one rescues us from their hands.

A4:17 Probably Egypt   B4:20 = King Zedekiah   C4:20 Lit nostrils   D4:22 Or not deport you again   E5:6 Lit We gave the hand to

---

and priests, now yelled at them: **Unclean! . . . Away, away! Don't touch us!** They were now homeless, aimless, and despised.

4:17 They looked **in vain** for **a nation** to come to their **assistance**. No human could overturn the judgment God had handed down.

4:20 Likewise, their trust in the heir of the Davidic line (**The Lord's anointed, the breath of our life**) proved futile. He was also **captured in their traps**. King Zedekiah was chained, blinded after watching his sons being massacred, and exiled to Babylon.

4:21-22 The nation of Edom might jeer for the moment, but the **cup** of God's wrath would fall on them also (Jr 25:15-29; Hab 2:15-16).

5:1 To **remember** in Scripture is never just calling something to mind. It involves a corresponding action.

5:2-4 Israel's **inheritance** had been **turned over to strangers**. Though they once owned everything, now even **water** and **wood** had to be purchased from foreigners.

5:5 The people of God were without **rest**, implying spiritual and physical troubles (Heb 3:16–4:11).

5:6 Israel lost her inheritance and suffered unrest because she made alliances with **Egypt** and **Assyria**. These policies

showed that Israel was placing her trust in man rather than God (Jr 2:18,36).

5:7 It was no use repeating the old cynical proverb from

haphak

Hebrew Pronunciation	[hah FAK]
HCSB Translation	turn, change
Uses in Lamentations	5
Uses in the OT	95
Focus passage	Lamentations 5:2,15

Haphak means *turn into* (Dt 23:5), *change* (Ex 10:19), *transform*, *pervert* (Jr 23:36), or *restore* (Zph 3:9). People *return*, *turn back*, or *turn around*. Haphak denotes *overthrow* (Gn 19:25), *overturn*, or *overwhelm*. It connotes *healing* (Ps 41:3) or *destruction* (Jb 12:15). People *retrace* steps; they *get down* from chariots (2Kg 5:26). Passive-reflexive forms imply *becoming* (Is 60:5) or *having a change* (Hs 11:8). Labor pains *come* (1Sm 4:19). Hearts *are broken* (Lm 1:20). Faces *grow pale*. The opposite happens (Est 9:1). Things *become warped*, *drained* (Ps 32:4), *turned over*, or *turned loose*. Speech is *deceitful* (Pr 17:20). Reflexive-passive verbs mean *whirl* (Gn 3:24) and *tumble* (Gn 3:24). Tahpuchah (10x) implies *perversity* (Pr 2:14), *contrariness*, *deception*, and *absurdity*. Mahpechah (5x) signifies *overthrow* (Jr 50:40) or *fall*. Hephek (3x) denotes *the opposite* (Ezk 16:34) or *turning* things *around*. Haphekah is *overthrow* (Gn 19:29). Haphakpak means *crooked* (Pr 21:8).

9 We secure our food at the risk
  of our lives
  because of the sword
  in the wilderness.
10 Our skin is as hot[A] as an oven[a]
   from the ravages of hunger.
11 Women are raped in •Zion,
   girls in the cities of Judah.
12 Princes are hung up by their hands;
   elders are shown no respect.[b]
13 Young men labor at millstones;[c]
   boys stumble under loads of wood.
14 The elders have left the city •gate,
   the young men, their music.[d]
15 Joy has left our hearts;[e]
   our dancing has turned to mourning.
16 The crown has fallen from our head.[f]

Woe to us, for we have sinned.[g]
17 Because of this, our heart is sick;
   because of these, our eyes grow dim:[h]
18 because of Mount Zion,
   which lies desolate
   and has jackals prowling in it.[i]
19 You, Lord, are enthroned forever;
   Your throne endures from generation
   to generation.[j]
20 Why have You forgotten us forever,[k]
   abandoned us for our entire lives?
21 Lord, restore us to Yourself, so we
   may return;[l]
   renew our days as in former times,
22 unless You have completely
   rejected us
   and are intensely angry with us.

a 5:10 Lm 4:8
b 5:12 Lm 4:16
c 5:13 Ex 11:5; Jdg 16:21; Is 47:2
d 5:14 Is 24:8
e 5:15 Am 8:10
f 5:16 Jb 19:9; Is 28:3; Jr 13:18
g Jr 8:14; 14:20; Dn 9:11
h 5:17 Ps 69:23; Ec 12:3
i 5:18 Is 13:19-22; 34:11-15
j 5:19 Ps 9:7; 45:6; 102:12; Ezk 43:7; Heb 1:8; Rv 4:9-10; 5:13
k 5:20 Ps 13:1
l 5:21 Jr 15:19; 31:18

A 5:10 Or *black*; Hb obscure

Jr 31:29, "The fathers have eaten sour grapes, and the children's teeth are set on edge." The people must admit, "We have sinned" (Lm 5:16).

5:9 Even the scanty harvests were subject to predatory raids by desert tribes.

5:10 Figuratively speaking, the people's skin was as **hot as an oven** as they suffered from the fever of extreme **hunger**.

5:11-14 Hardly anyone in Jerusalem was left unscathed. **Women** and **girls** were **raped** . . . **princes** were **hung up by their hands** . . . **elders** were **shown no respect**, young men and boys labored under enormous loads, and the **elders**, normally a fixture at the city gate, had all left.

5:15 All joy and merriment had **turned to mourning**.

5:16 The fallen **crown** symbolized Israel's loss of honor and glory. The reason was clear: **we have sinned**.

5:18 The once-magnificent city of Zion had become the haunt of **jackals**.

5:19 Though the city was wrecked and ruined, God's people could always find comfort and security in Him because His throne endures **from generation to generation**.

5:20 Jeremiah asked the Lord, **have You forgotten us forever**? But His goodness and mercy (3:22-24; Ps 23:6) argued just the opposite.

5:21 Only if the Lord restored the people would they enjoy life as it used to be. Such restoration is God's to give in response to repentance (turning from sin) and faith (trust in God).

5:22 One final question remained: Had God been so **intensely angry** with His people that He had **completely rejected** them? No. He would restore and renew them as He had done in the past.

Ezekiel

Introduction

The book of Ezekiel contains the divinely inspired prophecies of the prophet with the same name. These prophecies consist of oracles in the first person, giving the reader a sense of access to Ezekiel's private memoirs. Written primarily to the exiles in Babylon, the prophecies equally emphasize judgment of sins and the promise of hope and restoration.

Ezekiel settled with a group of Jewish exiles near the city of Nippur by the Chebar River. Shown here are ruins of a temple in Nafur, Iraq (ancient Nippur), a city that was most important for its religion. Various gods controlled every aspect of life. The chief deity was En-lil, also occasionally called Bel ("the lord"). He was thought of as god of the terrestrial world and the father of other gods. In this setting Yahweh, the sovereign God, appeared to Ezekiel and called him to prophesy both judgment and hope.

Background

Author: There is sufficient reason for maintaining that the prophet Ezekiel composed the book of Ezekiel in Babylon. The work demonstrates such homogeneity and literary coherence that it is reasonable to conclude that all editorial work was carried out by a single person, the prophet himself.

The inclusion of historical dates at the beginning of many of the oracles and prophecies in Ezekiel is another important unifying factor. The book is one of the most chronologically ordered books of the Bible. Thirteen times a passage is introduced by an indication of time. The common point of orientation for the dates given in Ezekiel is the exile of King Jehoiachin of Judah in 598/597 B.C.

The occurrence of visions throughout the book (chaps. 1; 8–11; 40–48) is another strong argument in favor of its overall unity. Finally, stylistic features throughout the book strengthen the unity argument.

Background: Ezekiel, son of Buzi, was among the approximately 10,000 citizens of Judah deported to Babylon when King Nebuchadnezzar invaded Jerusalem in 598/597 B.C. (2Kg 24:10-17). His prophetic call came to him five years later (the fifth year of King Jehoiachin's exile), in 593. He received his call at the age of 30 (1:1), the year he should have begun his duties as a priest (Nm 4:3). The last dated oracle in the book occurs in the twenty-seventh year of King Jehoiachin (29:17), thus indicating that Ezekiel's ministry lasted 22 or 23 years. The prophet lived during the greatest crisis in Israel's history—the destruction of Jerusalem and its temple, plus the exile of Judah's leading citizens to Babylon.

Message and Purpose

The message of the book revolves around the pivotal event in the history of Israel—the fall of Jerusalem in 586 B.C. Prior to the announcement of Jerusalem's fall, Ezekiel's message was characterized by judgment. In his scathing review of Israelite history, Ezekiel exposed the nation's moral depravity and absence of spiritual concern (2:1-8; 8:7-18; 13:1-23; 17:1-21; 20:1-32). After the destruction of Jerusalem was complete and the

---

625–590 B.C.

Year of Ezekiel's birth 623

First siege of Jerusalem by the Babylonians and first wave of exiles, including Daniel, taken to Babylon 605

Babylonians' second siege of Jerusalem; King Jehoiachin and 10,000 citizens of Judah, including Ezekiel, exiled to Babylon 597

God calls Ezekiel, then 30 years old, to prophesy. 593

Ezekiel prophesies against pagan practices at the temple in Jerusalem. 592

Elders of Israel seek a word of the Lord from Ezekiel. 591

590–585 B.C.

The Lord tells Ezekiel to let the captives know that the king of Babylon has once again laid siege to Jerusalem. 588

Ezekiel prophesies Egypt's ruin and the destruction of Pharaoh and his army. 587

Ezekiel prophesies the downfall of Tyre. 586

After a two-year siege, the walls of Jerusalem and the temple are destroyed; a third wave of exiles is taken to Babylon. 586

A messenger from Jerusalem comes to Ezekiel to announce the downfall of the city. 586/585

Ezekiel's lament for Pharaoh 585

nation was in exile, his message changed. He turned to a proclamation of hope, which is what the people now needed most. God would provide a new heart and a new spirit to enable the people to be faithful and avoid a future judgment (11:17-20; 36:26-28). The Lord would establish a new temple (chaps. 40–48) and a new way of worship for the people once they were restored.

The arrangement of the book (the announcement of judgment in the beginning and the declaration of restoration at the end) suggests that Ezekiel's message was ultimately one of hope and encouragement.

Six major theological statements are affirmed on behalf of Israel in the book: (1) The Lord will regather His scattered people (11:16-17; 16:1-63; 20:41; 34:11-13; 36:24; 37:21). (2) The Lord will bring the nation back to their land and will cleanse them from defilement (11:17-18; 20:42; 34:13-15; 36:24; 37:21). (3) The Lord will give His people a new heart and a new spirit so they might walk in His ways (11:19-20; 16:62; 34:30-31; 36:25-28; 37:23-24. (4) The Lord will restore the Davidic dynasty (34:23-24; 37:22-25). (5) The Lord will bless Israel with unprecedented prosperity and security in their land (34:25-29; 36:29-30; 37:26). (6) The Lord will establish His permanent residence in the midst of Israel (37:26-28; 40:1–48:35). All the covenants made with Israel will be fulfilled when she is restored to the promised land and the messianic kingdom is established.

Contribution to the Bible

There are not many quotations of the book of Ezekiel in the NT, but there are some notable correlations. For instance, the structure of the book of Revelation, which begins with a vision of Christ, corresponds to the appearances of God in Ezekiel's visions. The end of the book of Revelation also reflects the end of Ezekiel, where the river flows from the presence of God (Ezk 47:1-12; Rv 21:1–22:6). Finally, the depiction of the return of the exiles as resurrected from the dead is analogous to Paul's concept of regeneration (Eph 2:5).

Structure

The prophet Ezekiel displayed a distinct style throughout his prophetic work. The phrase "son of man" occurs

575–550 B.C.	550–500 B.C.
The Lord gives Ezekiel a vision of the new temple. 573	Cyrus captures Babylon without resistance. 539
The Lord shows Ezekiel that Egypt will be given over to the Babylonians. 571	Cyrus issues decree allowing the Jews to return to Judah. 538
Nebuchadnezzar invades Egypt in fulfillment of both Jeremiah's and Ezekiel's prophecies. 569	Work begins on rebuilding the temple in Jerusalem. 536
Evil-Merodach, Nebuchadnezzar's son, succeeds him as king of Babylon. 562	Renewed work on the temple 520–518
Evil-Merodach releases Judean King Jehoiachin from prison. 561	New temple dedicated 515
Nergal-sharezer becomes king of Babylon. 560	The Greek thinker Hecataeus of Miletus draws the first recognizable map of the Mediterranean basin and writes the first known geography book. 500
Cyrus the Great founds the Persian Empire. 559	

93 times as a title for Ezekiel, focusing on the prophet's human nature. The expression "the hand of the LORD was on me," which is said elsewhere only of Elijah (1Kg 18:46) and Elisha (2Kg 3:15), occurs in the various major sections of Ezekiel (1:3; 3:22; 33:22; 37:1). The so-called recognition formula "that you (or they) may know that I am Yahweh," a characteristic phrase of the exodus narrative (Ex 6:6-8; 7:5; 10:1-2; 14:4,18), occurs about 60 times in Ezekiel. The introductory oracle phrase "the word of the LORD came to me" occurs 46 times in the book and alerts the reader to the beginning of a separate section. The phrase "I, Yahweh, have spoken" also occurs frequently in Ezekiel (5:13,15,17; 17:21,24; 22:14; 24:14; 26:14; 30:12; 36:36; 37:14).

Another feature for which Ezekiel is well known is his performance of symbolic, dramatic actions. Accounts of this method of communication occur throughout the book. He also used the literary technique of allegory to communicate his prophecies. His allegories include: Jerusalem as a vine (chap. 15) and majestic eagles (17:1-21), the Davidic dynasty as a lioness (19:1-9) and a vineyard (19:10-14), a sword as judgment (21:1-17), and Oholah and Oholibah as corrupt sisters (23:1-35).

A final characteristic of the book is the citation of previously written Scripture in Ezekiel's prophecies. This is evident in the judgment oracles of chapters 4–5 that depend heavily on the curses listed in Leviticus 26. Ezekiel also references other portions of canonical Scripture, including Numbers 18:1-7,22-23 (in Ezk 44:9-16) and Zephaniah 3:1-4 (in Ezk 22:25-29).

Outline

I. **Israel, a Rebellious House, Will Fall (1:1–24:27)**
   A. Ezekiel sent as God's spokesman (1:1–3:27)
   B. First series of symbolic actions (4:1–7:27)
   C. Vision of Israel's doom (8:1–11:25)
   D. Second series of symbolic actions (12:1–14:23)
   E. Parables of doom (15:1–19:14)
   F. Rebukes and threats (20:1–22:31)
   G. Two final parables and last symbolic action (23:1–24:24)
   H. News of the fall of the rebellious house (24:25-27)

II. **Pagan Foreign Nations Will Be Destroyed (25:1–32:32)**
   A. Amon (25:1-7)
   B. Moab (25:8-11)
   C. Edom (25:12-14)
   D. Philistia (25:15-17)
   E. Tyre (26:1–28:19)
   F. Sidon (28:20-26)
   G. Egypt (29:1–32:32)

III. **Disciplined Israel Will Be Restored (33:1–48:35)**
   A. Basis of this message of hope (33:1-20)
   B. News of Jerusalem's fall arrives (33:21-33)
   C. The promises of restoration (34:1–39:29)
   D. The vision of restoration (40:1–48:35)

1 In the thirtieth year, in the fourth month, on the fifth day of the month, while I was among the exiles by the Chebar Canal,ᵃ the heavens openedᵇ and I saw visions of God.ᶜ ²On the fifth day of the month—it was the fifth year of King Jehoiachin's exile— ³the word of the LORD came directly to Ezekiel the priest, the son of Buzi, in the land of the Chaldeans by the Chebar Canal. And the LORD's hand was on him there.ᵈ

Vision of the LORD's Glory

⁴I looked and there was a whirlwind coming from the north,ᵉ a great cloud with fire flashing back and forth and brilliant light all around it. In the center of the fire, there was a gleam like amber.ᶠ ⁵The form of four living creatures came from it.ᵍ And this was their appearance: They had human form, ⁶but each of them had four faces and four wings. ⁷Their legs were straight, and the soles of their feet were like the hooves of a calf, sparkling like the gleam of polished bronze.ʰ ⁸They had human hands under their wings on their four sides.ⁱ All four of them had faces and wings.ʲ ⁹Their wings were touching. The creatures did not

ᵃ1:1 Ezk 3:15,23; 10:15,20,22
ᵇMt 3:16; Mk 1:10; Lk 3:21; Ac 7:56; 10:11
ᶜEzk 8:3; 11:24; 40:2
ᵈ1:3 1Kg 18:46; 2Kg 3:15; Ezk 3:14-22
ᵉ1:4 Jr 23:19
ᶠEzk 1:27; 8:2
ᵍ1:5 Ezk 10:14,21; Rv 4:6-8
ʰ1:7 Dn 10:6; Rv 1:15
ⁱ1:8 Ezk 1:17; 10:11
ʲEzk 10:8,21

1:1 The Targum, an Aramaic translation of the Hebrew OT, connects this date—**in the thirtieth year**—with Josiah's reforms in 621 B.C., but it is not easy to see any connection between the events in Josiah's reign and the time of this prophecy (2Kg 22:8-13). A rabbinic tradition understands the number as a reference to the Year of Jubilee. The editorial explanation (Ezk 1:2-3) takes "the thirtieth year" as equivalent to the fifth year of Jehoiachin's exile. Thirty was the age at which priests qualified for induction into their office (Nm 4:30). Just as Ezekiel was 30 and saw heaven open at the banks of a river, Jesus was 30 when He saw heaven open at His baptism in the Jordan River (Mt 3:16; Lk 3:21-23).

Ezekiel was among the 8,000 soldiers and nobility who had been sent into exile along with the king (2Kg 24:14-16) in 597 B.C. The **Chebar**, a river in Babylonia where the Jewish exiles settled, was the site of Ezekiel's visions (vv. 1,3; 3:15,23; 10:15,20,22; 43:3). The Hebrew *nehar kevar* corresponds to Akkadian *nar kabari/u* "the Kabaru Canal," a body of water mentioned twice in Akkadian documents from the Babylonian city of Nippur in the fifth century B.C. In the land of exile, God tore the heavens open and invited Ezekiel to see His glory, which was the grounding of both Israel's judgment and hope. The only other reference in the OT to the opening of **the heavens** occurs in Gn 7:11, although Is 64:1 speaks of the Lord rending the heavens. In the NT, the heavens were opened at Christ's baptism (Mt 3:16). Stephen saw the heavens open and was given supernatural perception of heavenly realities (Ac 7:56). Similar cases of the heavens opening are found in Rv 4:1; 19:11.

There are important similarities between the visions given to Isaiah and Ezekiel. Both prophets saw heavenly winged creatures serving God. Both underwent symbolic preparation for the prophetic ministry—Isaiah's lips were cleansed by fire; Ezekiel ate the scroll. Both men were commissioned to go to a people who would not respond to the prophetic message.

While Ezekiel was physically present with the exiles throughout his vision, he was so overwhelmed that he was oblivious to his surroundings. The initiative for Ezekiel's vision and prophecies lay solely with God, as was so with all true prophets.

1:2 The date given in verse 1 is anchored in verse 2 by the time of **King Jehoiachin's exile**. In fact all the dates in Ezekiel are figured in relation to this. Jehoiachin reigned only three months and ten days (2Kg 24:8; 2Ch 36:9). His removal and deportation provided the reference point for Ezekiel's prophecies. A king's accession to the throne was the normal time-marker by which prophecies were dated (2Kg 25:27; Jr 52:31). According to the Babylonian Chronicle, the date of Jehoiachin's captivity was April 22, 597 B.C.

1:3 The name **Ezekiel** means "may El strengthen or toughen." The other person in the OT known as Ezekiel was also a priest from the Levitical line (1Ch 24:16). Since foreign lands were considered unclean (Ezk 4:13; Am 7:17), it is not surprising that Israelite exiles would seek communion with God close to running water (Lv 14:5,50; 15:13; Nm 19:17; see Ac 16:13). In Ezekiel the name **Chaldeans** is interchanged with "Babylonians" (12:13; 23:15,23). God's **hand** is a manifestation of His power (Ex 9:3; Dt 2:15; 1Sm 5:9; Is 41:20). The power of the Spirit of God on the prophets enabled them to communicate divine truth.

1:4 The Babylonian army is described as an atmospheric storm. Storms and clouds were often associated with appearances of God (Jb 38:1; Ps 18:7-15; 29:3-9; 104:3; Is 29:6). The phrase **fire flashing back and forth** occurs elsewhere only in Ex 9:24 in the account of the plague of hail. The pillar of fire and the pillar of cloud led the Hebrews in the wilderness (Ex 13:17-22). God's appearance on Mount Sinai was characterized by lightning, smoke, and fire (Ex 19:16-18). God is characterized elsewhere as a consuming fire (Dt 4:24; Heb 12:28-29).

1:5 The prominence of the number four in Ezekiel's vision (**four living creatures**) is related to the ancient custom of envisioning earth in four parts (cp. "four corners of the earth" in Is 11:12) or four directions ("north and south, east and west" in Gn 13:14). Ezekiel's use of "four" symbolizes the divine capacity to control the entire world. From Ezekiel 10 we know that the four creatures were cherubim (10:5,20). Cherubim were embroidered on the curtain of the tabernacle (Ex 26:31). They were placed on top of the ark of the covenant in the holy of holies, where the tablets of covenant were kept (Ex 25:18-22). They were enforcers of divine judgment. When Adam and Eve were thrown out of the garden of Eden, cherubim were appointed to prohibit their entry back into the garden (Gn 3:24). Elsewhere God is said to be He who "dwells between the cherubim" (1Sm 4:4; 2Sm 6:2; Ps 99:1).

1:6 In the description of the living creatures, the gender of the creatures vacillates. Out of 45 descriptions, only 12 take the grammatically proper feminine plural, while the others are all masculine plural. In many ways the vision defies the capacity of human speech to provide description. Words cannot do justice to the vision of God. While we can know true things about God, He is ultimately beyond our full comprehension.

1:9 The outspread **wings** of the cherub in the holy of holies "touched" one another (1Kg 6:27); the verb used here occurs in Ex 26:3 and elsewhere for the interlinking of cloth strips that made up the curtains of the desert tabernacle. Whatever direction the four living creatures wished to take

turn as they moved; each one went straight ahead.[a] [10]The form of each of their faces was that of a man,[b] and each of the four had the face of a lion on the right, the face of an ox on the left, and the face of an eagle.[c] [11]That is what their faces were like. Their wings were spread upward; each had two wings touching that of another and two wings covering its

body.[d] [12]Each creature went straight ahead.[e] Wherever the Spirit[A] wanted to go, they went without turning as they moved.[f]

[13]The form of the living creatures was like the appearance of burning coals of fire and torches.[g] Fire was moving back and forth between the living creatures; it was bright, with lightning coming out of it. [14]The creatures

[a] 1:9 Ezk 10:22
[b] 1:10 Rv 4:7
[c] Ezk 10:14-21
[d] 1:11 Is 6:2; Ezk 1:23
[e] 1:12 Ezk 10:11,22
[f] Ezk 1:20
[g] 1:13 Ps 104:4; Rv 4:5

[A]1:12 Or *spirit*

was **straight ahead** for one of the four. Thus, all directions were "straight ahead."

1:10 The **lion** was considered the fiercest of beasts (Nm 23:24; 24:9; Jdg 14:18; 2Sm 1:23; 17:10), while the **eagle** was the most magnificent of birds (Dt 28:49; 2Sm 1:23; Jb 39:27; Jr 48:40; Lm 4:19). The **ox** was the most valued of domestic animals (Jb 21:10; Pr 14:4; cp. Ex 21:36). Humans were given dominion over all the creatures God made (Gn 1:28; Ps 8:6-7).

1:11 Each creature had one pair of **wings** raised upward,

touching the wing tips of the adjacent creature. This feature is identical to the cherubim over the ark of the covenant in the holy of holies. The cherub in the holy of holies also functioned as a symbolic footstool for the invisible throne of God (Ex 25:18-22; 1Sm 4:4; 2Sm 6:2; 2Kg 19:15; Ps 80:1; 99:1).

1:13 The fiery character of the living creatures (**burning coals of fire**) is reminiscent of the seraphim of Is 6 who were also fiery winged creatures. Fire will figure in the punishment of Jerusalem in Ezk 10:2 (Ps 50:3; 97:3).

1:14 In Nah 2:4, the chariots appear "like torches; they dart

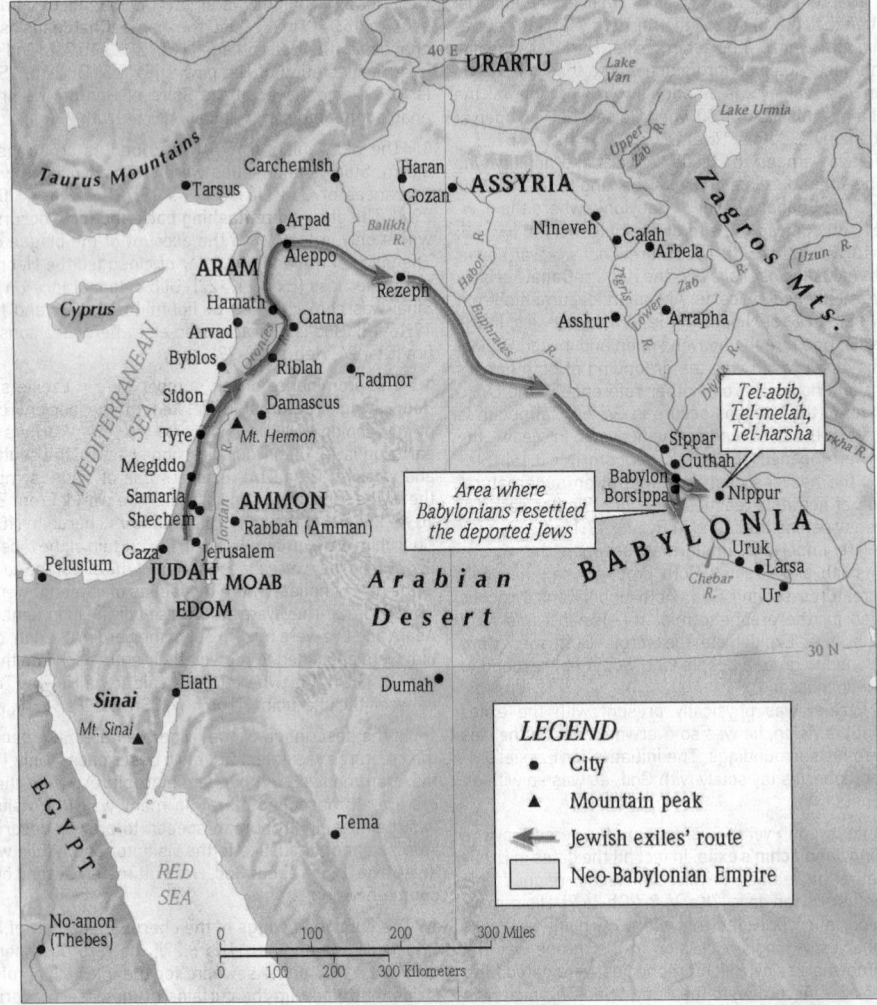

Jewish Exiles in Babylon

were darting back and forth[a] like flashes of lightning.[b]

[15]When I looked at the living creatures, there was one wheel on the ground beside each creature that had four faces. [16]The appearance of the wheels[c] and their craftsmanship was like the gleam of beryl,[d] and all four had the same form. Their appearance and craftsmanship was like a wheel within a wheel. [17]When they moved, they went in any of the four directions, without pivoting as they moved. [18]Their rims were large and frightening. Each of their four rims were full of eyes[e] all around. [19]So when the living creatures moved,[f] the wheels moved beside them, and when the creatures rose from the earth, the wheels also rose. [20]Wherever the Spirit[A] wanted to go, the creatures went in the direction the Spirit was moving. The wheels rose alongside them, for the spirit of the living creatures was in the wheels. [21]When the creatures moved, the wheels moved; when the creatures stood still, the wheels stood still; and when the creatures rose from the earth, the wheels rose alongside them, for the spirit of the living creatures was in the wheels.

[22]The shape of an expanse,[g] with a gleam like awe-inspiring crystal,[h] was spread out over the heads of the living creatures.[i] [23]And under the expanse their wings extended one toward another. Each of them also had two wings covering their bodies. [24]When they moved, I heard the sound of their wings like the roar of mighty waters,[j] like the voice of the •Almighty,[k] and a sound of commotion like the noise of an army.[l] When they stood still, they lowered their wings.

[25]A voice came from above the expanse over their heads; when they stood still, they lowered their wings. [26]The shape of a throne with the appearance of sapphire[B] stone was above the expanse.[C,m] There was a form with the appearance of a human on the throne high above.[n] [27]From what seemed to be His waist up, I saw a gleam like amber, with what looked like fire enclosing it all around.[o] From what seemed to be His waist down, I also saw what looked like fire. There was a brilliant light all around Him. [28]The appearance of the brilliant light all around was like that of a rainbow in a cloud on a rainy day.[p] This was the appearance of the form of the LORD's glory.[q] When I saw it, I fell facedown and heard a voice speaking.[r]

Mission to Rebellious Israel

2 He said to me, "Son of man, stand up on your feet[s] and I will speak with you." [2]As He spoke to me, the Spirit entered me and set me on my feet,[t] and I listened to the One who was speaking to me. [3]He said to me: "Son of man, I am sending you to the Israelites, to[D] the rebellious pagans[E] who have rebelled

---

Cross references (center column):

[a]1:14 Zch 4:10
[b]Mt 24:27; Lk 17:24
[c]1:16 Ezk 10:9-11
[d]Dn 10:6
[e]1:18 Ezk 10:12; Rv 4:6,8
[f]1:19-21 Ezk 10:16-17,19
[g]1:22 Gn 1:6-8
[h]Rv 4:6
[i]Ezk 10:1
[j]1:24 Ezk 43:2; Rv 1:15; 19:6
[k]Ezk 10:5
[l]Dn 10:6
[m]1:26 Ezk 10:1
[n]Is 6:1; Ezk 24:10
[o]1:27 Ezk 1:4; 8:2
[p]1:28 Gn 9:13; Rv 4:3; 10:1
[q]Ex 24:16; Ezk 8:4; 11:22-23; 43:4-5
[r]Gn 17:3; Ezk 3:23; Dn 8:17; Rv 1:17
[s]2:1 Dn 10:11
[t]2:2 Ezk 3:24; Dn 8:18

A1:20 Or *spirit*   B1:26 Or *lapis lazuli*   C1:26 Lit *expanse that was over their head*   D2:3 Or *Israelites and to*   E2:3 LXX omits *to the rebellious pagans*

---

back and forth like lightning." Matthew 24:27 depicts lightning going from one part of the world to the other.

1:16 The Septuagint took **beryl** to refer to a bright yellow precious stone, probably topaz.

1:18 The **rims** were the circumferences of the wheels. The eyes in the rims symbolized divine omniscience and watchfulness (2Ch 16:9; Pr 15:3; Zch 3:9; 4:10; Rv 4:6).

1:26 Made of lapis lazuli, the **sapphire stone** was one of the most prized stones in the ancient world.

1:27 Fire is often associated with the appearance of God (Ex 3:2-15; 24:17; Rv 4:1-4). The vision of the throne is similar to what Moses and the 70 elders observed on Mount Sinai (Ex 24:9-11). Numerous features of Ezekiel's vision are repeated in John's portrayal of the heavenly throne (Rv 4:2-8).

1:28 The **rainbow** in Ezekiel's vision recalls the ancient covenant God made with Noah and the human race (Gn 9). The **glory** of the Lord is a visible manifestation of God (Ex 16:7; 24:16-17; 40:34-35). The glory of the Lord also refers to the "pillar of fire" that accompanied the Israelites in their desert wanderings (Ex 16:10; Nm 14:14). Clouds, like fire, are frequently associated with the appearance of God (Ex 19:16; Jdg 5:4). Ezekiel declared that he **fell facedown**. This is the posture a person assumed before a king in ancient times. The Bible teaches that man cannot see God and live (Ex 33:18,20). Thus God must reveal Himself in a way that dims His full glory. What Ezekiel saw was not God in His essence, but a representation. Hence words like "likeness" and "appearance" pervade descriptions of God throughout the chapter. God did not manifest His full glory, but revealed as much as could be beheld by a mortal man. Even this partial unveiling of God's glory was enough to overwhelm Ezekiel. When God visibly manifests Himself, reverence and worship must follow, as biblical testimony from Moses onward makes clear (Ex 3:6; cp. Mt 17:1-9). The sound of God's **voice** was like the voice John heard in his vision (Rv 1:15).

2:1 The expression **son of man** occurs about 90 times in the book of Ezekiel. It should be distinguished from the same phrase in Dn 7:13, where it reflects a messianic title that was used in intertestamental Judaism and in the Gospels. Unlike the usage in Dn 7:13, Ezekiel's usage of the phrase can mean simply a "member of humanity." On **stand up on your feet**, see Dn 10:11; Ac 26:16.

2:2 The same **Spirit** of God that activated the chariot wheels (1:12,19; 10:16-17) and the living beings now **entered** Ezekiel. The Spirit would supply the strength to accomplish Ezekiel's prophetic ministry. It is not in our power to obey what God commands us. He must supply the power. In OT times, the Holy Spirit did not indwell all believers but came upon selected persons temporarily for a specific service (3:24; Ex 31:1-11; 1Sm 10:9-11; Ps 51:11).

2:3 Normally in the OT the Israelites are referred to as a "people" (Hb *'am*) and Gentiles as "nations" (Hb *goyim*).

against Me. The Israelites and their ancestors have transgressed against Me to this day.[a] [4]The children are obstinate[A] and hardhearted.[b] I am sending you to them, and you must say to them, 'This is what the Lord GOD says.' [5]Whether they listen or refuse to listen[c]—for they are a rebellious house—they will know that a prophet has been among them.[d]

[6]"But you, son of man, do not be afraid of them or their words,[e] though briers and thorns are beside you and you live among scorpions.[f] Don't be afraid of their words or be discouraged by the look on their faces, for they are a rebellious house. [7]But speak My words to them whether they listen or refuse to listen,[g] for they are rebellious.

[8]"And you, son of man, listen to what I tell you: Do not be rebellious like that rebellious house. Open your mouth and eat what I am giving you."[h] [9]So I looked and saw a hand reaching out to me,[i] and there was a written scroll in it.[j] [10]When He unrolled it before me, it was written on the front and back; words of lamentation, mourning, and woe were written on it.

3 He said to me: "Son of man, eat what you find here. Eat this scroll,[k] then go and speak to the house of Israel." [2]So I opened my mouth, and He fed me the scroll. [3]"Son

[a] 2:3 Ezk 20:18,30
[b] 2:4 Ezk 3:7
[c] 2:5 Ezk 3:11,27
[d] Ezk 33:33
[e] 2:6 Jr 1:8,17; Ezk 3:9
[f] 2Sm 23:6; Ezk 28:24; Mc 7:4
[g] 2:7 Jr 1:7,17
[h] 2:8 Jr 15:16; Ezk 3:3; Rv 10:9
[i] 2:9 Ezk 8:3
[j] Jr 36:2; Ezk 3:1
[k] 3:1 Ezk 2:8-9
[l] 3:3 Jr 15:16
[m] Ps 19:10; 119:103; Rv 10:9-10
[n] 3:6 Mt 11:21,23
[o] 3:7 Jn 15:20
[p] 3:8 Jr 1:18; 5:3
[q] 3:11 Ezk 2:5,7
[r] 3:12 Ezk 8:3; Ac 8:39

of man," He said to me, "eat[B] and fill your stomach with this scroll I am giving you." So I ate it,[l] and it was as sweet as honey in my mouth.[m]

[4]Then He said to me: "Son of man, go to the house of Israel and speak My words to them. [5]For you are not being sent to a people of unintelligible speech or difficult language but to the house of Israel. [6]You are not being sent to many peoples of unintelligible speech or difficult language, whose words you cannot understand. No doubt, if I sent you to them, they would listen to you.[n] [7]But the house of Israel will not want to listen to you because they do not want to listen to Me.[o] For the whole house of Israel is hardheaded and hardhearted. [8]Look, I have made your face as hard as their faces and your forehead as hard as their foreheads.[p] [9]I have made your forehead like a diamond, harder than flint. Don't be afraid of them or discouraged by the look on their faces, even though they are a rebellious house."

[10]Next He said to me: "Son of man, listen carefully to all My words that I speak to you and take them to heart. [11]Go to your people, the exiles, and speak to them. Tell them, 'This is what the Lord GOD says,' whether they listen or refuse to listen."[q]

[12]The Spirit then lifted me up,[r] and I heard a

[A]2:4 Lit hard of face   [B]3:3 Lit feed your belly

Here the designations are reversed. The traditional language of election has been turned on its head, so that the Gentiles have become an 'am (Hb for a "people") while Israel has become goyim (pagans). The Scriptures characteristically call foreigners goyim, a sign of disgrace and reproach. The people of God have become no different than the pagan people around them. According to 3:5-7, the problem was not intellectual but spiritual. The phrase who have rebelled against Me is used of subjects who refused to be loyal to their king (17:15; 2Kg 18:7).

2:4 The term obstinate often occurs in the phrase "stiff of neck, stubborn." It was used to describe Pharaoh's disposition (Ex 7:3) and thus emphatically illustrates the resistance of the people to Ezekiel's message. The Israelites had become the open enemies of God. The obstinate nature of the nation was later illustrated by their rejection of the Messiah (Ac 7:51-52).

2:5 The phrase a rebellious house occurs frequently in Ezekiel; instead of the "house of Israel," a common phrase describing God's people, they have become the "house of rebellion." The phrase they will know contains a shortened version of what is known as the recognition formula: "They will know that I am the Lord." The recognition formula occurs 92 times in Ezekiel. It is an intentional link to the frequent occurrence of the phrase in the book of Exodus. The criterion of true prophecy lies in the prophet's certainty that God had sent him (Is 6:8-10; Jr 1:4-10; Am 7:15). God's Word is absolutely true, no matter how it is received (Is 55:11; 2Co 2:15-16).

2:6 The word thorns was a standard figure of speech for hostility (28:24; Mc 7:4).

2:9 Some scrolls could be very long; one of the famous Dead Sea Scrolls measured approximately 24 feet in length. Normally scrolls were written on only one side, but papyrus scrolls in ancient Egypt and later in the Greco-Roman period could be written on both sides. The scroll and Ezekiel's consumption of it in the vision are reminiscent of references in the book of Revelation (Rv 5; 6; 10:9-10).

2:10 The lament or dirge is thought to derive from the mournful dirges that were wailed at funerals. See the lament over the deaths of Saul and Jonathan (2Sm 1:17), as well as the lament over Josiah's death (2Ch 35:25). Ezekiel will later lament for the princes of Israel (19:2-14). The scroll was saturated with words of judgment. See Zch 5:3 and Rv 5:1 for the same figure.

3:1 To eat this scroll signifies devouring the words written on it. After Ezekiel consumed the scroll, he would proclaim the words to the people.

3:3 The words as sweet as honey show that an encounter with the Word of God is a pleasant experience (Ps 19:10; 119:103).

3:5 The phrase unintelligible speech or difficult language reminds us of Moses' excuses in Ex 4:10 (cp. Is 33:19).

3:7 God warned Moses that Pharaoh would not listen to him (Ex 3:19). God told Isaiah that his prophetic ministry would only show the spiritual insensitivity of a corrupted people (Is 6:9-10). The refusal-to-listen theme is also prominent in Jeremiah (Jr 3:25; 7:13; 9:12; 11:8; 16:12; 17:23; 18:10; 19:15; 22:5; 25:3-4,7). Jesus' comment that a prophet receives honor everywhere but his hometown (Mt 13:57) par-

great rumbling sound behind me—praise the glory of the LORD in His place!— [13]with the[A] sound of the living creatures' wings brushing against each other[a] and the sound of the wheels beside them,[b] a great rumbling sound. [14]So the Spirit lifted me up and took me away. I left in bitterness and in an angry spirit, and the LORD's hand was on me powerfully.[c] [15]I came to the exiles at Tel-abib, who were living by the Chebar Canal, and I sat there among them stunned for seven days.[d]

Ezekiel as a Watchman

[16]Now at the end of seven days the word of the LORD came to me:[e] [17]"Son of man, I have made you a watchman over the house of Israel.[f] When you hear a word from My mouth, give them a warning from Me.[g] [18]If I say to the wicked person,[h] 'You will surely die,' but you do not warn him—you don't speak out to warn him about his wicked way in order to save his life—that wicked person will die for his iniquity. Yet I will hold you responsible for

his blood. [19]But if you warn a wicked person and he does not turn from his wickedness or his wicked way, he will die for his iniquity, but you will have saved your life.[i] [20]Now if a righteous person turns from his righteousness and practices iniquity,[j] and I put a stumbling block in front of him, he will die.[k] If you did not warn him, he will die because of his sin and the righteous acts he did will not be remembered. Yet I will hold you responsible for his blood. [21]But if you warn the righteous person that he should not sin, and he does not sin, he will indeed live because he listened to your warning, and you will have saved your life."

[22]Then the hand of the LORD was on me there, and He said to me, "Get up, go out to the plain,[l] and I will speak with you there."[m] [23]So I got up and went out to the plain. The LORD's glory was present there,[n] like the glory I had seen by the Chebar Canal,[o] and I fell facedown. [24]The Spirit entered me and set me on my feet.[p] He spoke with me and said: "Go, shut yourself inside your house. [25]And

Cross references:
[a]3:13 Ezk 1:24
[b]Ezk 1:15; 10:16-17
[c]3:14 2Kg 3:15
[d]3:15 Jb 2:13; Ps 137:1
[e]3:16 Jr 42:7
[f]3:17 Is 52:8; 56:10; 62:6; Jr 6:17; Ezk 33:7-9
[g]2Ch 19:10; Is 58:1
[h]3:18-19 Ezk 33:3,6,8-9
[i]3:19 Ezk 14:14,20; Ac 18:6; 1Tm 4:16
[j]3:20 Ezk 18:24
[k]Jr 6:21
[l]3:22 Ezk 8:4
[m]Ac 9:6
[n]3:23 Ezk 1:28; Ac 7:55
[o]Ezk 1:1
[p]3:24 Ezk 2:2

[A]3:12-13 Some emend to *behind me as the glory of the LORD rose from His place;* [13] *the*

---

allels Ezekiel's experience. Even when there was little hope of bringing about repentance, God still sent prophets so the people would realize that His word had been among them.

3:15 In the Akkadian language, the phrase **Tel-abib** literally means "mound of the flood," indicating that the location was well known as a ruined site. Mourning for the dead lasted **seven days** (Gn 50:10; Jb 2:13). The consecration ceremony for admission into the priesthood, which Ezekiel had anticipated for himself before the exile, also lasted seven days (Lv 8:33).

3:16 The phrase **the word of the LORD came to me** occurs almost 50 times in Ezekiel. It is also used to report a revelation experience with reference to Samuel (1Sm 15:10), Nathan (2Sm 7:4), Gad (2Sm 24:11), the Bethel prophet (1Kg

zahar

Hebrew Pronunciation	[zah HAR]
HCSB Translation	warn, instruct
Uses in Ezekiel	15
Uses in the OT	21
Focus passage	Ezekiel 3:17-21

Other languages do not show this root meaning *warn*, and debate exists whether *zahar, warn,* is identical with *zahar, shine* (Dn 12:3). An Arabic word "be clear" relates to *zahar, shine. Warning* does make something clear. *Zahar* occurs mostly in Ezk 3:17-21 and 33:3-9. As watchmen *warned* cities against attack (2Kg 6:10), so Ezekiel was a prophetic watchman *warning* about divine judgment against sin. *Zahar* once means *instruct* (Ex 18:20), perhaps as "enjoin." Judges *warned* litigants to avoid guilt before God over the law (2Ch 19:10); so Moses' *instruction* (Ex 18:20) may have *warned* about the law's implications. The passive-reflexive of *zahar* denotes objectively *being warned* (Ezk 33:6) but also subjectively *taking warning* (Ezk 33:5), that is, *listening to* (Ezk 3:21) and *paying attention to warnings* (Ec 4:13). The negative is *ignoring warning* (Ezk 33:4). The root in Aramaic involves *warning* against negligence in obeying orders (Ezr 4:22).

13:20), Jehu (1Kg 16:1), Elijah (1Kg 17:2,8; 18:1; 21:17,28), and Isaiah (2Kg 20:4; cp. Is 38:4).

3:17 In order to give a timely warning of approaching danger, lookouts or watchmen were posted on high places such as roofs of gatehouses (2Sm 18:24) or towers (2Kg 9:17). God gave His commandments for the people's good (Dt 5:28-33; 6:25; 10:12-13). If they were obedient to the stipulations, they would experience God's blessing (Lv 26:1-13; Dt 16:20; 28:1-14; Mal 3:10-12). If the people disobeyed these ordinances, the Lord promised that He would bring curses upon them. These statutes were designed to lead them to repentance (Lv 26:14-39; Dt 28:15-68).

3:18 Ezekiel's failure to deliver God's message would render him guilty of murder (**I will hold you responsible for his blood**) and thus subject to capital punishment (Gn 9:5-6). Thus whether Ezekiel lived or died depended on his "righteousness"—his faithfulness to the holy commission he had received. Ezekiel's commission as son of man/Adam can be compared to the first Adam and to the tree of the knowledge of good and evil (Gn 2:17). If Ezekiel was obedient he would live and would bring the possibility of life to those who heard him, but if he failed, he and his hearers would "surely die" (Ezk 3:18; Gn 2:17; 2Sm 4:11-12; Ac 18:6).

3:20 To lay a **stumbling block** before a person was to expose him to danger (Jr 6:21).

3:21 On **warn the righteous person**, see a similar warning in 1Co 10:12. Those who responded faithfully to the watchman's proclamation would **live**. This signified not just physical life but the fullness of fellowship with the Lord that flows from obedience.

3:24 Being **shut** in the **house** illustrates the siege of Jerusalem. This does not mean that Ezekiel was literally never to leave his house (cp. 5:2; 12:3); instead he was to refrain from open fellowship with others. Leaders often came to him at his house to receive God's word (8:1; 14:1; 20:1). General confinement to his home is reflected in all the

you, son of man, they will put ropes on you[a] and bind you with them so you cannot go out among them. [26]I will make your tongue stick to the roof of your mouth,[b] and you will be mute[c] and unable to rebuke them, for they are a rebellious house. [27]But when I speak with you, I will open your mouth,[d] and you will say to them, 'This is what the Lord GOD says.' Let the one who listens, listen, and let the one who refuses, refuse—for they are a rebellious house.

Jerusalem's Siege Dramatized

4 "Now you, son of man, take a brick, set it in front of you, and draw the city of Jerusalem on it. [2]Then lay siege against it:[e] construct a siege wall, build a ramp, pitch military camps, and place battering rams against it on all sides. [3]Take an iron plate and set it up as an iron wall between yourself and the city. Turn your face toward it so that it is under siege, and besiege it. This will be a sign for the house of Israel.[f]

[4]"Then lie down on your left side and place the iniquity[A] of the house of Israel on it. You will bear their iniquity for the number of days you lie on your side. [5]For I have assigned you the years of their iniquity according to the number of days you lie down, 390 days; so you will bear the iniquity of the house of Israel.[g]

[6]When you have completed these days, lie down again, but on your right side, and bear the iniquity of the house of Judah. I have assigned you 40 days, a day for each year. [7]You must turn your face toward the siege of Jerusalem with your arm bared, and prophesy against it. [8]Be aware that I will put cords on you so you cannot turn from side to side until you have finished the days of your siege.[h]

[9]"Also take wheat, barley, beans, lentils, millet, and spelt. Put them in a single container and make them into bread for yourself. You are to eat it during the number of days you lie on your side, 390 days. [10]The food you eat each day will be eight ounces[B] by weight; you will eat it from time to time.[C] [11]You are also to drink water by measure, a sixth of a gallon,[D] which you will drink from time to time. [12]You will eat it as you would a barley cake and bake it over dried human excrement in their sight." [13]The LORD said, "This is how the Israelites will eat their bread—ceremonially ‘unclean—among the nations where I will banish them."[i]

[14]But I said, "Oh, Lord GOD, I have never been defiled. From my youth until now I have not eaten anything that died naturally or was mauled by wild beasts,[j] And impure meat has never entered my mouth."[k]

Cross-references

[a]3:25 Ezk 4:8
[b]3:26 Ps 22:15
[c]Lk 1:20,22
[d]3:27 Ezk 24:27; 33:22
[e]4:2 Jr 6:6; Ezk 21:22
[f]4:3 Is 8:18; 20:3; Ezk 12:6,11; 24:24-27
[g]4:5 Nm 14:34
[h]4:8 Ezk 3:25
[i]4:13 Dn 1:8; Hs 9:3
[j]4:14 Lv 17:15; 22:8; Ezk 44:31
[k]Ac 10:14

A4:4 Or *punishment*   B4:10 Lit *20 shekels*   C4:10 Or *it at set times*   D4:11 Lit *hin*

---

locations of prophesying mentioned in the book (8:1; 14:1; 20:1; 33:30).

3:26 The expression **tongue stick to the roof of your mouth** is an idiomatic way of saying that a person cannot talk (Jb 29:10; Ps 137:6). Ezekiel's speechlessness lasted seven years (Ezk 33:21-22). He remained silent, except when God instructed him to deliver a message. There may be a correlation between the seven days that Ezekiel sat among his fellow exiles (3:15), and his seven-year speechlessness: one year of divinely imposed speechlessness for each day of hardened resistance.

3:27 Ezekiel remained unable to speak in the intervals between God's addresses. These lapses into muteness finally stopped when it was announced that Jerusalem had fallen (1Co 9:16; Col 1:24-29).

4:1 Sketching a city plan on a clay **brick** was not an uncommon practice in the ancient world. Ezekiel was instructed to sketch the siege of **Jerusalem**. Nebuchadnezzar's construction of the siege wall around Jerusalem is described in 2Kg 25:1 and Jr 52:4.

4:2 The purpose of a **siege** was to wear enemies down by halting their flow of food and supplies. Battering rams were pushed up siege ramps to attack the city walls.

4:3 The hiding of God's **face** indicated that He could no longer look favorably upon the people. The people would experience the covenant curses for their disobedience (Lv 26:17; Dt 31:17-18; 32:20). War (**it is under siege**), along with its repercussions, is included in the list of covenantal curses (Dt 28:52-57).

4:5-6 One popular view accounting for the periods of 390 days or years and 40 days or years is to calculate the 390 years backwards from 586 B.C., placing the starting point for the period of Israel's iniquity in 976 B.C., the year when the construction of the temple began. This would indicate that the nation was characterized by rebellion during the entire time the temple was standing. However, the best conclusion is that the 430-year period was chosen to represent the period of Israel's stay in Egypt. By depicting the total period of sin and judgment in terms of a renewed Egyptian bondage, the prophet invited the hope that the end of the appointed time of punishment would result in a new exodus and a new entry into the promised land. An ancient Jewish tradition noted that the number 390 derived from the Hebrew numerical value of *ymy msr*, the consonants of the phrase "the days of the siege" (v. 8; 5:2).

4:8 The **siege** that Ezekiel was predicting lasted two years (2Kg 25:1-8).

4:9 The food products mentioned in this verse, all native to Mesopotamia, constitute a siege diet. According to an experiment recorded in Jewish tradition, no one would touch Ezekiel's **bread**, not even a dog.

4:12 Because Ezekiel was aware of the laws regarding the removal of **human excrement**, he reacted with disgust (Dt 23:11-13). Land outside of Israel was considered unclean (Jos 22:19; Am 7:17).

4:14 Eating flesh that had been **mauled by wild beasts** disqualified a priest from priestly service (44:31; Lv 22:8). **Impure meat** was sacrificial meat that had not been eaten

[15]He replied to me, "Look, I will let you use cow dung instead of human excrement, and you can make your bread over that." [16]Then He said to me, "Son of man, I am going to cut off the supply of bread in Jerusalem.[a] They will anxiously eat bread rationed by weight and in dread drink water by measure.[b] [17]So they will lack bread and water; everyone will be devastated and waste away because of their iniquity.[c]

Ezekiel Dramatizes Jerusalem's Fall

5 "Now you, son of man, take a sharp sword,[d] use it as you would a barber's razor, and shave your head and beard. Then take a set of scales and divide the hair. [2]You are to burn up a third of it in the city when the days of the siege have ended;[e] you are to take a third and slash it with the sword all around the city; and you are to scatter a third to the wind, for I will draw a sword to chase after them. [3]But you are to take a few strands from the hair and secure them in the folds of your robe.[f] [4]Take some more of them, throw them into the fire, and burn them in it.[g] A fire will spread from it to the whole house of Israel.

[5]"This is what the Lord God says: I have set this Jerusalem in the center of the nations,

with countries all around her. [6]But she has rebelled against My ordinances with more wickedness than the nations, and against My statutes more than the countries that surround her. For her people have rejected My ordinances and have not walked in My statutes.

[7]"Therefore, this is what the Lord God says: Because you have been more insubordinate than the nations around you[h]—you have not walked in My statutes or kept My ordinances; you have not even kept the ordinances of the nations around you— [8]therefore, this is what the Lord God says: See, I am against you, Jerusalem, and I will execute judgments within you in the sight of the nations. [9]Because of all your detestable practices, I will do to you what I have never done before and what I will never do again.[i] [10]As a result, fathers will eat their sons[j] within Jerusalem,[A] and sons will eat their fathers. I will execute judgments against you and scatter all your survivors to every direction of the wind.

[11]"Therefore, as I live"—this is the declaration of the Lord God—"I am going to cut you off and show you no pity, because you have defiled My sanctuary[k] with all your detestable

Cross references

a[4:16] Lv 26:26; Ezk 5:16; 14:13
b[Ezk 12:19]
c[4:17] Lv 26:39; Ezk 24:23; 33:10
d[5:1] Lv 21:5; Is 7:20; Ezk 44:20
e[5:2] Ezk 4:2-8
f[5:3] Jr 40:6; 52:16
g[5:4] Jr 44:14
h[5:7] Jr 2:10-11
i[5:9] Dn 9:12; Am 3:2
j[5:10] Lv 26:29; Dt 28:53-57; Jr 19:9
k[5:11] Jr 7:9-11; Ezk 8:5-6,16

A[5:10] Lit you

by the third day after the animal was slaughtered (Lv 7:18; 19:7).

4:16 The expression **supply of bread** indicates the destruction of the whole food supply (Lv 26:26; Is 3:1).

4:17 To be defeated or **devastated** in war was to experience a covenant curse (Lv 26:17,37; Dt 28:25,49,52; 32:23-24,30,42).

5:1 Shaving one's **head** was often associated with mourning rites (7:18; 27:31; Jb 1:20; Is 7:20; 15:2,2-3; Jr 7:29; 48:37). Mourning for the dead in this way was prohibited for the Israelites (Dt 14:1). Weighing on **scales** was a symbol of evaluation for impending judgment (Pr 21:2; Dn 5:27).

5:3 From the last third of **hair** that was consigned to dispersion, Ezekiel was to take and bind some in the **folds** of his **robe**. This portrayed survival of only a remnant of exiles. From the ancient perspective, exile was a fate from which people never returned. Hair scattered to the wind would be impossible to retrieve. By tucking the remnants of hair into his garment, Ezekiel indicated that the future of the people of God lay with the Babylonian exiles (Lv 26:36-39; Hg 2:12). There would never be a complete end of Israel brought about by God's judgment.

5:5 According to Ps 132:13-14, the Lord's oath to the Davidic house was specifically linked to His choice of Zion or **Jerusalem** as His special dwelling place (Dt 12:5; 1Kg 8:41-43; Ps 48:1-14).

5:6 According to Dt 4:7-8, Israel's covenantal obligations to the Lord gained the admiration of the **nations** of the world. If Israel had obeyed these laws, she would have been the light of the world.

5:7 Ezekiel accused Israel of being worse than the **nations** (16:27; cp. 2Kg 21:11; Jr 2:11).

5:10 Cannibalism was prohibited in the law of Moses (Lv 26:29; Dt 28:53-57) and was denounced by the prophets (Is 9:19-21; Jr 19:9; Zch 11:9). Tragically, the Israelites resorted to cannibalism in Jerusalem during the siege and the subsequent fall to Babylon's forces in 588-586 B.C. (Lm 1:7-14; 2:20-22; 4:4-10).

5:11 The expression **show you no pity** was used to discourage

miqdash

Hebrew Pronunciation	[mik DAHSH]
HCSB Translation	sanctuary
Uses in Ezekiel	31
Uses in the OT	75
Focus passage	Ezekiel 5:11

Miqdash, from *qadash (be holy)*, is a noun designating a thing or place as holy or consecrated. *Miqdash* generally means *sanctuary* and refers to Israel's tabernacle (Ex 25:8) or temple (Is 63:18). Sometimes the plural of *miqdash* connotes the temple's various parts, its *sanctuaries* (Ezk 21:2), *holy places* (Jr 51:51), or *sacred places* (Ezk 7:24). "The *sanctuary (miqdash)* of the *sanctuary (qodesh)*" is the *most holy place* (Lv 16:33), where the ark was. *Miqdash* can indicate the *holy objects* carried by Kohathites (Nm 10:21). The Levites presented the *consecrated part* of Israel's offerings to God, a tenth of the tenth (Nm 18:29). Once *miqdash* appears as *temple* (Dn 11:31). *Miqdash* has modifiers indicating God's ownership of the *temple*: *God's* (Ps 73:17), *My* (Ezk 44:7-9), *His* (Ps 96:6), *Your* (Ps 74:7). The *temple* also belongs to Jerusalem (Lm 1:10) and the Israelites (2Ch 36:17). God Himself is a *sanctuary* (Is 8:14).

practices and abominations.[a] Yes, I will not spare you. [12]A third of your people will die by plague and be consumed by famine within you;[b] a third will fall by the sword all around you; and I will scatter a third to every direction of the wind, and I will draw a sword to chase after them.[c] [13]When My anger is spent and I have vented My wrath on them, I will be appeased.[d] Then after I have spent My wrath on them, they will know that I, •Yahweh, have spoken in My jealousy.[e]

[14]"I will make you a ruin and a disgrace among the nations around you, in the sight of everyone who passes by. [15]So you[A] will be a disgrace and a taunt, a warning and a horror, to the nations around you when I execute judgments against you in anger,[f] wrath, and furious rebukes. I, Yahweh, have spoken. [16]When I shoot deadly arrows of famine at them, arrows for destruction that I will send to destroy you, inhabitants of Jerusalem, I will intensify the famine against you and cut off your supply of bread. [17]I will send famine and dangerous animals against you. They will leave you childless, Jerusalem. Plague and bloodshed will sweep through you, and I will bring a sword against you. I, Yahweh, have spoken."[g]

Prophecy against Israel's Idolatry

6 The word of the LORD came to me: [2]"Son of man, turn your face toward the mountains of Israel[h] and prophesy against them.

Cross references (center column)
[a]5:11 Ezk 7:20; 11:18,21
[b]5:12 Jr 15:2; 21:9; Ezk 5:17; 6:11-12
[c]Jr 15:2; 43:10-11; 44:27
[d]5:13 Is 1:24
[e]Ezk 36:5-6; 38:19
[f]5:15 Ps 79:3-10; Ezk 22:4
[g]5:17 Lv 26:6; Dt 32:23-25
[h]6:2 Ezk 36:1
[i]6:3-4 Lv 26:30
[j]6:8 Jr 44:14,28; Ezk 7:16
[k]6:9 Dt 4:29
[l]Ps 78:40
[m]Ezk 20:43; 36:31

[3]You are to say: Mountains of Israel, hear the word of the Lord GOD! This is what the Lord GOD says to the mountains and the hills, to the ravines and the valleys: I am about to bring a sword against you, and I will destroy your •high places.[i] [4]Your altars will be desolated and your incense altars smashed. I will throw down your slain in front of your idols. [5]I will lay the corpses of the Israelites in front of their idols and scatter your bones around your altars. [6]Wherever you live the cities will be in ruins and the high places will be desolate, so that your altars will lie in ruins and be desecrated,[B] your idols smashed and obliterated, your incense altars cut down, and your works wiped out. [7]The slain will fall among you, and you will know that I am •Yahweh.

[8]"Yet I will leave a remnant when you are scattered among the nations, for throughout the countries there will be some of you who will escape the sword.[j] [9]Then your survivors will remember Me among the nations where they are taken captive,[k] how I was crushed by their promiscuous hearts that turned away from Me and by their eyes that lusted after their idols.[l] They will loathe themselves because of the evil things they did,[m] their detestable practices of every kind. [10]And they will know that I am the LORD; I did not threaten to bring this disaster on them without a reason.

Lament over the Fall of Jerusalem

[11]"This is what the Lord GOD says: Clap your

[A]5:15 DSS, LXX, Syr, Tg, Vg; MT reads she   [B]6:6 Hb obscure

---

leniency in criminal cases (Dt 7:16; 13:8; 19:13,21; 25:12). The defilement of the holy **sanctuary** is the sole issue in 8:1-18.

5:12 Famine and **plague** often accompanied the siege of a city. These were also numbered among the covenant curses of Lv 26:25-26.

5:15 The nation that was chosen for honor (Dt 26:19) now became the moral spectacle of the nations (**you will be a disgrace and a taunt**). The role of the nations here contrasts with the original blessing which Israel was supposed to bring them. She failed at this task (Lk 12:48).

5:16 The phrase **when I shoot deadly arrows of famine at them** begins a list of judgments. These are identical to the standard types of covenant curses associated with disobedience of God's law (famine, Lv 26:26,29; wild animals, Lv 26:22; Dt 32:24; disease, Dt 28:21; bloodshed, Dt 32:42).

6:2 The idiom **turn your face** reflects the Lord's adverse attitude toward His people, here identified as the **mountains of Israel**. The phrase "mountains of Israel" does not occur outside the book of Ezekiel. Mountains represent the whole land because the land of Israel was mountainous and hilly (Dt 11:12). Mountains were often centers of idolatrous worship, and thus reference to Israel as mountainous is a reference to Israel's apostasy (Ezk 6:13; 18:6,11; 22:9).

6:3 The translation of the Hebrew word *bamah* as **high places** goes back at least to the Latin Vulgate, which trans-

lated the word *excelsus*. These man-made installations were elevated platforms where sacrifices were performed. They existed in the land of Canaan before the Israelite conquest and were supposed to have been destroyed (Nm 33:52). After Shiloh was destroyed (Jr 7:12), but before the temple in Jerusalem was built, the high place was used as a place of legitimate worship.

6:4 For the Hebrews, burning corpses on **altars** defiled the altars (1Kg 13:2; 2Kg 23:16). Ezekiel's favorite word for idol (Hb *gillulim*) is based on the root *gll*, which means "to roll." Many believe the term is associated with round dung pellets, which would graphically express Ezekiel's disposition toward useless idols.

6:6 The Hebrew verb *machah* ("to wipe out") is used in Gn 6:7 and 7:4,23 to describe the decimation of the human race by the flood (2Kg 21:13).

6:7 The phrase **you will know that I am Yahweh** is known as a recognition formula. It is a characteristic way of closing oracles or sections within oracles (some 60 times in Ezekiel) and expresses the intended effect of the event predicted in the oracle. It was frequently used in the context of the exodus from Egypt (Ex 7:5; 14:4).

6:10 The expression **threaten to bring this disaster on them** occurs outside this passage only in the account of the golden calf (Ex 32:14).

hands, stamp your feet,[a] and cry out over all the evil and detestable practices of the house of Israel, who will fall by the sword, famine, and plague.[b] [12]The one who is far off will die by plague; the one who is near will fall by the sword; and the one who remains and is spared[A] will die of famine. In this way I will exhaust My wrath on them.[c] [13]You will all know that I am Yahweh when their slain lie among their idols around their altars,[d] on every high hill,[e] on all the mountaintops, and under every green tree and every leafy oak—the places where they offered pleasing aromas to all their idols.[f] [14]I will stretch out My hand against them,[f] and wherever they live I will make the land a desolate waste, from the wilderness to Diblah.[B] Then they will know that I am Yahweh."

Announcement of the End

7And the word of the Lord came to me: [2]"Son of man, this is what the Lord God says to the land of Israel:

An end! The end has come
on the four corners of the land.[g]
[3] The end is now upon you;
I will send My anger against you
and judge you according to your ways.
I will punish you for all
your detestable practices.
[4] I will not look on you with pity
or spare you,[h]
but I will punish you for your ways[i]
and for your detestable practices
within you.
Then you will know that I am *Yahweh."[j]

[5]This is what the Lord God says:

Look, one disaster after another
is coming![k]

[6] An end has come; the end has come!
It has awakened against you.
Look, it is coming!
[7] Doom[c] has come on you,[l]
inhabitants of the land.
The time has come; the day is near.
There will be panic on the mountains
and not celebration.[m]

[8] I will pour out My wrath on you
very soon;[n]
I will exhaust My anger against you
and judge you according to your ways.
I will punish you for all your
detestable practices.
[9] I will not look on you with pity
or spare you.
I will punish you for your ways
and for your detestable practices
within you.
Then you will know
that it is I, Yahweh, who strikes.

[10] Look, the day is coming!
Doom has gone out.[o]
The rod has blossomed;[p]
arrogance has bloomed.[q]
[11] Violence has grown into a rod
of wickedness.[r]
None of them will remain:
none of their multitude,
none of their wealth,
and none of the eminent[D] among them.

[12] The time has come; the day has arrived.
Let the buyer not rejoice[s]
and the seller not mourn,
for wrath is on all her masses.[t]
[13] The seller will certainly not return
to what was sold

Cross references

a 6:11 Ezk 21:14,17; 25:6
b Ezk 5:12
c 6:12 Ezk 5:13
d 6:13 Ezk 6:4-7
e Is 57:5-7; Jr 2:20; Ezk 20:28; Hs 4:13
f 6:14 Is 5:25
g 7:2 Am 8:2,10
h 7:4 Ezk 5:11
i Ezk 11:21
j Ezk 6:7,14
k 7:5 2Kg 21:12-13
l 7:7 Ezk 7:10
m Jl 2:1-2; Am 5:18-20; Zph 1:14-15
n 7:8 Ezk 20:8,21
o 7:10 Ezk 7:7
p Nm 17:8
q Is 10:5; Mt 24:32-33
r 7:11 Ps 73:8; 125:3
s 7:12 Pr 20:14
t Is 24:2

A 6:12 Or *besieged*　B 6:14 Some Hb mss, some LXX mss read *Riblah*; 2Kg 23:33; Jr 39:5　C 7:7 Hb obscure　D 7:11 Some Hb mss, Syr, Vg read *and no rest*

6:11 Ezekiel was commanded to sing a number of taunt songs against Israel's enemies (e.g., chaps. 27; 28; 31; and 32).

6:13 The phrases **on every high hill, on all the mountaintops, and under every green tree and every leafy oak** echo Dt 12:2 and Hs 4:13 (1Kg 14:23; Jr 2:20). In the pagan belief system of the ancient Near East, people sought the assistance of gods and goddesses of nature to bless themselves and make themselves productive.

6:14 On desolation as punishment, see Lv 26:32-35,43; Dt 29:23. Most of the Hebrew manuscripts read **Diblah** here, although a minority, including the Septuagint, read Riblah, which represented the northern border of Israel (47:15-17). If the reading "Diblah" is correct, this is the only reference to this city in the Bible. The Hebrew name may mean "cake of figs." Riblah was a city in Syria (2Kg 23:33; 25:21; Jr 39:5; 52:9,27) that served as the headquarters of Nebuchadnezzar of Babylon during his third expedition against Jerusalem in 588–586 B.C.

7:2 The Hebrew expression *'admat yisra'el* (the **land of Israel**) occurs only in Ezekiel. The more common expression for the "land of Israel" translates a Hebrew phrase *'erets yisra'el*. In the use of the term here, the emphasis is on the ground or soil rather than the land of the nation. The expression **the end has come** does not refer to the end of the latter days but the end of great tribulation, as in Gn 6:13. Just as in the days of Noah's flood (Gn 6), the sins of the people had reached such a point that it was time for the land to be wiped clean of them.

7:7 The Day of the Lord refers to a time of God's intervention in history to deliver or to judge (Is 2:12-22; chap. 13). But in some ways the Day of the Lord focuses on an event rather than a definite extent of time. Beginning with Amos the day was viewed as a time of great judgment (Am 5:18-20). The nearness of the Day of the Lord is a common theme in prophetic literature (Ezk 30:3; Jl 1:15; 2:1; Zph 1:7,14).

7:13 After the seventh sabbatical year (49 years) the Year of Jubilee took place, during which each person who had lost

as long as he and the buyer
  remain alive.[A]
For the vision concerning all its people
will not be revoked,
and none of them will preserve
his life because of his iniquity.

14 They have blown the trumpet[a]
and prepared everything,
but no one goes to war,
for My wrath is on all her masses.

15 The sword is on the outside;[b]
plague and famine are on the inside.
Whoever is in the field will die
  by the sword,
and famine and plague will devour
whoever is in the city.

16 The survivors among them will escape[c]
and live on the mountains
like doves of the valley,
all of them moaning,
each over his own iniquity.

17 All their hands will become weak,[d]
and all their knees will turn to water.

18 They will put on •sackcloth,
and horror will overwhelm them.
Shame will cover all their faces,
and all their heads will be bald.[e]

19 They will throw their silver
  into the streets,
and their gold will seem like
  something filthy.[f]
Their silver and gold will be unable
  to save them
in the day of the Lord's wrath.[g]
They will not satisfy their appetites
or fill their stomachs,
for these were the stumbling blocks[h]
that brought about their iniquity.

20 He appointed His beautiful ornaments
for majesty,

but[B] they made their abhorrent images
  from them,
their detestable things.[i]
Therefore, I have made these
into something filthy for them.

21 I will hand these things over
to foreigners as plunder[j]
and to the wicked of the earth as spoil,
and they will profane them.

22 I will turn My face from the wicked
as they profane My treasured place.
Violent men will enter it and profane it.

23 Forge the chain,[k]
for the land is filled with crimes
  of bloodshed,
and the city is filled with violence.[l]

24 So I will bring the most evil of nations[m]
to take possession of their houses.
I will put an end to the pride
  of the strong,
and their sacred places
  will be profaned.[n]

25 Anguish is coming!
They will seek peace,
  but there will be none.

26 Disaster after disaster will come,[o]
and there will be rumor after rumor.[p]
Then they will seek a vision
  from a prophet,[q]
but instruction will perish
  from the priests
and counsel from the elders.[r]

27 The king will mourn;
the prince will be clothed in grief;
and the hands of the people of the land
  will tremble.
I will deal with them according to
  their own conduct,
and I will judge them
  by their own standards.[s]
Then they will know that I am Yahweh.

---

a 7:14 Nm 10:9
b 7:15 Jr 14:18; Ezk 6:11-12
c 7:16 Ezk 6:8; 14:22
d 7:17 Is 13:7; Ezk 21:7
e 7:18 Is 15:2-3; Am 8:10
f 7:19 Is 2:20; 30:22
g Pr 11:4; Zph 1:18
h Ezk 14:3
i 7:20 Jr 7:30; Ezk 16:17
j 7:21 2Kg 24:13
k 7:23 Jr 27:2
l Ezk 8:17; 9:9
m 7:24 Ezk 21:31; 28:7
n 2Ch 7:20; Ezk 24:21
o 7:26 Is 47:11; Jr 4:20
p Ezk 21:7
q Jr 21:2; 37:17
r Ps 74:9; Mc 3:6
s 7:27 Mt 7:2

A 7:13 Lit sold, while still in life is their life   B 7:20 Or They turned their beautiful ornaments into objects of pride, and

---

or sold his land received back his personal property (Lv 25:8-22). The year began on the Day of Atonement of this fiftieth year. This generous attitude was to be displayed because the land actually belonged to the Lord; it had been given to the Israelites through an extended lease (Lv 25:23).

7:19 On something filthy, see Is 2:20 and Zph 1:18 for parallel phrases. The filthy thing (Hb niddah) was the technical term used for the ceremonial impurity that resulted from menstruation (Lv 15:19-33) and the touching of a corpse (Nm 19:13-21). Wealth had become the people's stumbling block (Mt 6:19-24; Lk 6:24-25; 1Tm 6:6-10,17-19; Jms 5:1-6).

7:20 Jewish medieval commentators as well as the Aramaic Targum translation indicate that the phrase beautiful ornaments is an allusion to the temple, as in verse 22 (cp. Dn 1:2; 5:3-4).

7:21 The phrase I will hand these things over to foreigners refers to a fulfillment of Dt 28:49-57.

7:22 Many Israelites considered themselves invincible because the presence of God resided in Jerusalem (My treasured place)—they thought that God would never let His holy dwelling be destroyed (Jr 7:1-5)—but even the temple would not escape God's judgment (Mc 3:12).

7:23 The phrase the city is filled with violence clearly echoes Gn 6:11.

7:26 Like the series of catastrophes that struck Job (cp. Jb 1:13-19), no sooner would one disaster be reported than word of another would come.

8:1 The words in the sixth year, in the sixth month, on the fifth day of the month show that Ezekiel had reflected on

Visionary Journey to Jerusalem

8 In the sixth year, in the sixth month, on the fifth day of the month, I was sitting in my house and the elders of Judah were sitting in front of me,[a] and there the hand of the Lord God came down on me.[b] [2]I looked, and there was a form that had the appearance of a man.[A] From what seemed to be His waist down was fire, and from His waist up was something that looked bright,[c] like the gleam of amber.[d] [3]He stretched out what appeared to be a hand and took me by the hair of my head. Then the Spirit lifted me up between earth and heaven and carried me in visions of God[e] to Jerusalem, to the entrance of the inner gate that faces north, where the offensive statue that provokes jealousy[f] was located. [4]I saw the glory of the God of Israel[g] there, like the vision I had seen in the plain.[h]

Pagan Practices in the Temple

[5]The Lord said to me, "Son of man, look toward the north." I looked to the north, and there was this offensive statue north of the altar gate, at the entrance. [6]He said to me, "Son of man, do you see what they are doing here, more detestable things that the house of Israel is committing,[i] so that I must depart from My sanctuary? You will see even more detestable things."

[7]Then He brought me to the entrance of the court, and when I looked there was a hole in the wall. [8]He said to me, "Son of man, dig through the wall." So I dug through the wall, and there was a doorway. [9]He said to me, "Go in and see the terrible and detestable things

they are committing here." [10]I went in and looked, and there engraved all around the wall was every form of detestable thing, crawling creatures and beasts, as well as all the idols of the house of Israel.[j]

[11]Seventy elders from the house of Israel were standing before them, with Jaazaniah son of Shaphan[k] standing among them. Each had a firepan in his hand, and a fragrant cloud of incense was rising up. [12]Then He said to me, "Son of man, do you see what the elders of the house of Israel are doing in the darkness, each at the shrine of his idol? For they are saying, 'The Lord does not see us. The Lord has abandoned the land.'"[l] [13]Again He said to me, "You will see even more detestable things, which they are committing."

[14]So He brought me to the entrance of the north gate of the Lord's house, and I saw women sitting there weeping for Tammuz. [15]And He said to me, "Do you see this, son of man? You will see even more detestable things than these."

[16]So He brought me to the inner court of the Lord's house, and there were about 25 men at the entrance of the Lord's temple, between the portico and the altar,[m] with their backs to the Lord's temple and their faces turned to the east.[n] They were bowing to the east in worship of the sun.[o] [17]And He said to me, "Do you see this, son of man? Is it not enough for the house of Judah to commit the detestable things they are practicing here, that they must also fill the land with violence[p] and repeatedly provoke Me to anger,[q] even putting the branch to their nose?[B,C] [18]Therefore I will

[a]8:1 Ezk 14:1; 20:1 [b]Ezk 1:3 [c]8:2 Ezk 1:27 [d]Ezk 1:4,27 [e]8:3 Ezk 11:1,24; 40:2; 2Co 12:1-4 [f]Ex 20:4; Dt 32:16 [g]8:4 Ezk 9:3 [h]Ezk 1:28; 3:22-23 [i]8:6 Ezk 5:11; 8:9,17; 23:4-5 [j]8:10 Ex 20:4; Dt 4:16-18; Rm 1:23 [k]8:11 Nm 11:16,25; Lk 10:1 [l]8:12 Ps 14:1; Is 29:15; Ezk 9:9 [m]8:16 Jl 2:17 [n]Jr 2:27; 32:33 [o]Dt 4:19; 17:3 [p]8:17 Ezk 7:11,23; 9:9 [q]Jr 7:18-19

[A]8:2 LXX; MT, Vg read of fire   [B]8:17 Ancient Jewish tradition reads My nose   [C]8:17 Possibly a pagan ritual or a euphemism for offensive behavior

---

his first vision for 14 months. The actions of the **elders of Judah** provide a shocking contrast to the 70 elders of Israel in the Pentateuch. Israel's leaders in the desert period, who had the privilege of seeing God (Ex 24:1-11), were endowed with the same spirit as Moses (Nm 11:16-30).

8:3 The nearest analogies to Ezekiel's experience occurred with Elijah, who was carried about by the **Spirit** (1Kg 18:12; 2Kg 2:1-12,16-18); and with Elisha, who was given astonishing extrasensory powers (2Kg 5:26; 6:17,32-33). The term translated **offensive statue** (Hb semel) occurs elsewhere only in Dt 4:16 and 2Ch 33:7,15. Scholars believe the term may be a foreign word and thus appropriate to associate with the worship of a foreign god. This image may have been one of the Asherahs set up in the temple by Manasseh (2Kg 21:7; 2Ch 33:7,15). This conclusion is suggested by the use of the same word (Hb semel) in reference to Manasseh's idol in 2Ch 33:7,15. God is a jealous God who accepts no rival; He will not share His glory with idols (Is 42:8).

8:10 The phrase **every form of detestable thing** is reminiscent of Rm 1:23.

8:11 The **seventy elders** were probably the leaders of the

nation whose position was established by Moses' appointment of officials to assist him in governing God's people (Ex 24:1,9; Nm 11:16-25). The prophet echoed the critical moment in the Day of Atonement ceremonies when the **cloud of incense** screened the ark from the vision of the high priest (Lv 16:2,13).

8:14 Wailing for **Tammuz** was a Babylonian ritual marking the death and descent into the underworld of the Sumerian god Dumuzi. The mythological course of death and return for Dumuzi (Tammuz) was thought to be parallel to the annual rhythm of nature.

8:16 The final and supreme act of idolatry took place within the **inner court** of the **temple** itself, where **25 men** bowed toward the **east**, worshiping the sun. According to 2Kg 21:5, worship of the sun god appears to have gained sponsorship during the reign of Manasseh, who built altars for foreign gods in the courts of the temple. The area between **the portico and the altar** was probably for use by priests alone, and was where they prayed to God on a fast day (Jl 2:17)).

8:17 The phrase **putting the branch to their nose** may have

respond with wrath.[a] I will not show pity or spare them.[b] Though they cry out in My ears with a loud voice,[c] I will not listen to them."

Vision of Slaughter in Jerusalem

9 Then He called to me directly with a loud voice, "Come near, executioners of the city, each of you with a destructive weapon in his hand." [2]And I saw six men coming from the direction of the Upper Gate,[d] which faces north, each with a war club in his hand. There was another man among them, clothed in linen,[e] with writing equipment at his side. They came and stood beside the bronze altar.

[3]Then the glory of the God of Israel[f] rose from above the •cherub where it had been, to the threshold of the temple. He called to the man clothed in linen with the writing equipment at his side. [4]"Pass throughout the city of Jerusalem," the Lord said to him, "and put a mark on the foreheads[g] of the men who sigh and groan[h] over all the detestable practices committed in it."

[5]He spoke as I listened to the others, "Pass through the city after him and start killing; do not show pity or spare them![i] [6]Slaughter the old men, the young men and women, as well as the older women and little children,[j] but do not come near anyone who has the mark.[k] Now begin at My sanctuary."[l] So they began with the elders who were in front of the temple. [7]Then He said to them, "Defile the temple and fill the courts with the slain.[m] Go!" So they went out killing people in the city.

[8]While they were killing, I was left alone. And I fell facedown and cried out, "Oh, Lord God![n] Are You going to destroy the entire remnant of Israel when You pour out Your wrath on Jerusalem?"

[9]He answered me: "The iniquity of the house of Israel and Judah is extremely great; the land is full of bloodshed,[o] and the city full of perversity. For they say, 'The Lord has abandoned the land;[p] He does not see.'[q] [10]But as for Me, I will not show pity or spare them.[r] I will bring their actions down on their own heads."[s] [11]Then the man clothed in linen with the writing equipment at his side reported back, "I have done as You commanded me."

God's Glory Leaves the Temple

10 Then I looked, and there above the expanse over the heads[t] of the •cherubim was something like sapphire[A] stone resembling the shape of a throne that appeared above them. [2]The Lord spoke to the man clothed in linen and said, "Go inside the wheelwork beneath the cherubim. Fill your hands with hot coals from among the cherubim and scatter them over the city."[u] So he went in as I watched.

[3]Now the cherubim were standing to the south of the temple when the man went in, and the cloud[v] filled the inner court.[w] [4]Then the glory of the Lord rose from above the cherub to the threshold of the temple.[x] The temple was filled with the cloud,[y] and the court was filled with the brightness of the Lord's glory.[z] [5]The sound of the cherubim's wings could be heard as far as the outer court; it was like the voice of •God Almighty when He speaks.

[6]After the Lord commanded the man clothed

a 8:18 Ezk 5:13
b Ezk 5:11
c Mc 3:4
d 9:2 2Kg 15:35; Jr 20:2
e Lv 16:4
f 9:3 Ezk 10:4,18; 11:22-23
g 9:4 Rv 7:2-3; 9:4; 14:1
h Ps 119:53,136; Jr 13:17
i 9:5 Ezk 5:11
j 9:6 2Ch 36:17
k Rv 9:4
l Jr 25:29
m 9:7 Ezk 7:20-22
n 9:8 Ezk 11:13
o 9:9 2Kg 21:16
p Ezk 8:12
q Is 29:15
r 9:10 Ezk 5:11; 7:4; 8:18
s Ezk 11:21
t 10:1 Ezk 1:22,26
u 10:2 Ezk 1:13; Rv 8:5
v 10:3 1Kg 8:10-11
w Ezk 8:3,16
x 10:4 Ezk 9:3; 10:18; 11:22-23; 43:2-5; 44:4
y Ex 40:34-35; Is 6:1-4; Rv 15:8
z Ezk 1:28; Hg 2:7

[A] 10:1 Or *lapis lazuli*

referred to an idolatrous practice, or possibly it is an idiomatic expression indicating contempt for God.

9:2 Linen was often worn by angelic messengers (Dn 10:5; Rv 15:6), but it was also the fabric for priestly garments (Ex 28:42); linen thus portrays purity and holiness. The **bronze altar**, originally built by Solomon (2Ch 4:1), was relocated during the reign of Ahaz to the northeast corner of the temple to make room for his own pagan altar (2Kg 16:14).

9:4 It is possible that those to be spared received the sign of the cross (**put a mark on the foreheads**), like those sealed for deliverance in Rv 7:3-4 and 14:1.

9:6 This deliverance from judgment (**do not come near anyone who has the mark**) resembles the Passover story, where the household was spared if the blood of a sacrificial lamb was placed above the door (Ex 12:7,13).

9:7 The historical fulfillment of this event (**fill the courts with the slain**) is depicted in 2Ch 36:17-19.

9:9 This verse is an apparent echo of the flood (Gn 6:11). The saying of the lawless (**the Lord has abandoned the land; He does not see**) repeats in inverted form what the idolatrous elders had said in 8:12.

10:1 The inner curtains and the veil that closed off the holy of holies in the tabernacle were adorned with **cherubim** (Ex 26:1,31; 36:8,35). Two golden cherubim with extended wings were part of the covering of the ark of the covenant within the holy of holies of the tabernacle (Ex 25:18-22; 37:7-9). Cherubim were also carved in the walls of the Jerusalem temple and covered with gold (1Kg 6:29; 2Ch 3:7; Ezk 41:18-20). In both the tabernacle and the temple, the cherubim constituted a throne for God's invisible presence and glory (1Sm 4:4; 2Sm 6:2; 2Kg 19:15; Ps 18:10; 80:1; 99:1). The creatures in the vision in Ezekiel 1 were not named. Ezekiel recognized these creatures to be cherubim.

10:2 The image of a **city** burned with fire came true for Jerusalem in 586 b.c. (2Kg 25:9).

10:3 All the time that the glory of the Lord dwelt in the temple, the **cloud** that accompanied it to reveal the glory of the Lord **filled** the **court** (see Ex 19:9; Lv 16:2).

10:6 Fire in the Bible is often associated with God's judgment against wickedness and sin (Gn 19:24; Dt 32:22; Am 1–2). According to Ezekiel, the same fire from God that purified the mouth of Isaiah (Is 6:6) and brought destruction to

in linen, saying, "Take fire from inside the wheelwork, from among the cherubim," the man went in and stood beside a wheel. [7]Then the cherub reached out his hand to the fire that was among them. He took some, and put it into the hands of the man clothed in linen, who took it and went out. [8]The cherubim appeared to have the form of human hands under their wings.[a]

[9]I looked, and there were four wheels beside the cherubim,[b] one wheel beside each cherub. The luster of the wheels was like the gleam of beryl.[c] [10]In appearance, all four had the same form, like a wheel within a wheel. [11]When they moved, they would go in any of the four directions,[d] without pivoting as they moved. But wherever the head faced, they would go in that direction,[A] without pivoting as they went. [12]Their entire bodies,[e] including their backs, hands, wings, and the wheels that the four of them had, were full of eyes all around.[f] [13]As I listened the wheels were called "the wheelwork." [14]Each one had four faces:[g] the first face was that of a cherub, the second that of a man, the third that of a lion, and the fourth that of an eagle.

[15]The cherubim ascended; these were the living creatures I had seen by the Chebar Canal.[h] [16]When the cherubim moved, the wheels moved beside them, and when they lifted their wings to rise from the earth, even then the wheels did not veer away from them. [17]When the cherubim stood still,[i] the wheels stood still, and when they ascended, the wheels ascended with them, for the spirit of the living creatures was in them.

[18]Then the glory of the LORD moved away from the threshold of the temple[j] and stood above the cherubim.[k] [19]The cherubim lifted their wings and ascended from the earth right before my eyes;[l] the wheels were beside them as they went. The glory of the God of Israel was above them, and it stood at the entrance to the eastern gate of the LORD's house.

[20]These were the living creatures I had seen[m] beneath the God of Israel by the Chebar Canal,[n] and I recognized that they were cherubim. [21]Each had four faces and each had four wings,[o] with the form of human hands under their wings. [22]Their faces looked like the same faces I had seen[p] by the Chebar Canal. Each creature went straight ahead.

Vision of Israel's Corrupt Leaders

11 The Spirit then lifted me up[q] and brought me to the eastern gate of the LORD's house, which faces east, and at the gate's entrance were 25 men. Among them I saw Jaazaniah son of Azzur, and Pelatiah son of Benaiah, leaders of the people. [2]The LORD said to me, "Son of man, these are the men who plan evil[r] and give wicked advice in this city. [3]They are saying, 'Isn't the time near to build houses?[B,s] The city is the pot,[t] and we are the meat.' [4]Therefore, prophesy against them. Prophesy, son of man!"

[5]Then the Spirit of the LORD came on me, and He told me, "You are to say: This is what the LORD says: That is what you are thinking, house of Israel; and I know the thoughts that arise in your mind.[u] [6]You have multiplied your slain in this city,[v] filling its streets with the dead.

[7]"Therefore, this is what the Lord GOD says: The slain you have put within it are the meat,[w] and the city is the pot, but I[c] will remove you from it.[x] [8]You fear the sword,[y] so I will bring the sword against you."[z] This is the declaration

Cross references (center column)

[a]10:8 Ezk 1:8
[b]10:9 Ezk 1:15-17
[c]Dn 10:6
[d]10:11 Ezk 1:17
[e]10:12 Rv 4:6,8
[f]Ezk 1:18
[g]10:14 Ezk 1:6,10; 10:21
[h]10:15 Ezk 1:3,5
[i]10:17 Ezk 1:21
[j]10:18 Ezk 10:4
[k]Ps 18:10
[l]10:19 Ezk 11:22
[m]10:20 Ezk 1:5,22,26; 10:15
[n]Ezk 1:1
[o]10:21 Ezk 1:6,8; 10:14; 41:18-19
[p]10:22 Ezk 1:10
[q]11:1 Ezk 3:12,14; 8:3
[r]11:2 Gn 6:5; Ps 36:4; Pr 14:2; Mc 2:1
[s]11:3 Jr 29:28; Am 3:15; Zph 1:13
[t]Jr 1:13; Ezk 24:3,6
[u]11:5 Jr 17:10; Ezk 2:2
[v]11:6 Ezk 7:23; 22:2-6,9,12,27
[w]11:7 Ezk 24:3-13; Mc 3:2-3
[x]Ezk 11:9
[y]11:8 Pr 10:24; Is 66:4
[z]Jb 3:25; Is 24:17-18

A10:11 Lit *go after it*   B11:3 Or *The time is not near to build houses.*   C11:7 Some Hb mss, LXX, Syr, Tg, Vg; other Hb mss read *He*

Sodom and Gomorrah (Gn 19:24) would now purge the city of Jerusalem in judgment.

10:12 In 1:18 only the wheels were "full of eyes all around," whereas here the creatures in their entirety were **full of eyes.** The four creatures John saw around God's throne were also covered with eyes (Rv 4:8).

10:18 In this verse Ezekiel set forth the fulfillment of the warning uttered by Moses (Dt 31:17) that was later repeated by Hosea (Hs 9:12). God had determined to forsake His sanctuary. His **temple** was supposed to be the place of His rest and dwelling (Ps 132:14; Is 66:1).

10:19 The movement of God's glory to the **eastern gate** anticipated its ultimate departure from the temple complex and Jerusalem (11:22-23). The east gate would also be the site of the final judgment for Jews (Zch 14:1-9). Jesus went to the mountain east of the city, the Mount of Olives, and ascended to the Father (Ac 1:9-12). God's presence among His people was an indication of His favor toward them (Dt

4:29,31). His absence, on the other hand, was a sign of His rejecting them (Dt 31:17-18). The ultimate privilege of faith is access to the presence of God.

11:1 This verse mentions the same **25 men** who had been described earlier (see note at 8:16).

11:3 In 24:3-5 Jerusalem is portrayed as a pot being filled with the choicest morsels. The people thought they could go ahead and build houses (Jr 32:6-15) because they belonged in Jerusalem, whereas the exiles were like the entrails that were discarded as unfit for the cooking pot. Jeremiah 29:5 may address this same concern from the context of those in exile and the elders in captivity.

11:5 On **the Spirit of the LORD came on me,** see note at 2:2.

11:6 This accusation of the leaders of Judah is illustrated in 19:3,6, where kings are charged with devouring humans, and in 22:27, where Ezekiel portrays Israel's leaders as ravenous, violent animals.

of the Lord God. [9]"I will bring you out of the city and hand you over to foreigners; I will execute judgments against you.[a] [10]You will fall by the sword,[b] and I will judge you at the border of Israel.[c] Then you will know that I am 'Yahweh. [11]The city will not be a pot for you,[d] and you will not be the meat within it. I will judge you at the border of Israel, [12]so you will know that I am Yahweh, whose statutes you have not followed and whose ordinances you have not practiced. Instead, you have acted according to the ordinances of the nations around you."[e]

[13]Now while I was prophesying, Pelatiah son of Benaiah died.[f] Then I fell facedown and cried out with a loud voice: "Oh, Lord God![g] Will You bring to an end the remnant of Israel?"

Promise of Israel's Restoration

[14]The word of the Lord came to me again: [15]"Son of man, your own relatives, those who have the right to redeem you,[A,B] and the entire house of Israel, all of them, are those that the residents of Jerusalem have said this to, 'Stay away from the Lord; this land has been given to us as a possession.'

[16]"Therefore say: This is what the Lord God says: Though I sent them far away among the nations and scattered them among the countries, yet for a little while I have been a sanc-

tuary for them[h] in the countries where they have gone.

[17]"Therefore say: This is what the Lord God says: I will gather you from the peoples[i] and assemble you from the countries where you have been scattered, and I will give you the land of Israel.

[18]"When they arrive there, they will remove all its[j] detestable things[k] and practices from it. [19]And I will give them one heart[l] and put a new spirit within them; I will remove their heart of stone[m] from their bodies[C] and give them a heart of flesh,[n] [20]so they may follow My statutes,[o] keep My ordinances, and practice them. Then they will be My people, and I will be their God.[p] [21]But as for those whose hearts pursue their desire for detestable things and practices, I will bring their actions down on their own heads."[q] This is the declaration of the Lord God.

God's Glory Leaves Jerusalem

[22]Then the 'cherubim, with the wheels beside them, lifted their wings,[r] and the glory of the God of Israel was above them. [23]The glory of the Lord[s] rose up from within the city and stood on the mountain[t] east of the city.[D,u] [24]The Spirit lifted me up[v] and brought me to Chaldea and to the exiles in a vision from the Spirit of God. After the vision I had seen left me, [25]I spoke to the exiles about all the things the Lord had shown me.

Cross references (center column)

[a]11:9 Ezk 5:8
[b]11:10 Jr 39:6; 52:9-10
[c]2Kg 14:25
[d]11:11 Ezk 11:3,7
[e]11:12 Ezk 8:10,14,16
[f]11:13 Ac 5:5 Ezk 9:8
[h]11:16 Is 8:14
[i]11:17 Ezk 20:34,41-42; 28:25
[j]11:18 Ezk 37:23
[k]Ezk 5:11
[l]11:19 Jr 32:39
[m]Zch 7:12
[n]Ps 51:10; Jr 31:33; Ezk 36:26; 2Co 3:3
[o]11:20 Ps 105:45; Ezk 36:27
[p]Ezk 36:28
[q]11:21 Ezk 9:10
[r]11:22 Ezk 10:19
[s]11:23 Ezk 8:4
[t]Zch 14:4
[u]11:22-23 Ezk 10:4
[v]11:24 Ezk 8:3

[A]11:15 LXX, Syr read *your relatives, your fellow exiles*　　[B]11:15 Or *own brothers, your relatives*　　[C]11:19 Lit *flesh*　　[D]11:23 = the Mount of Olives

---

11:9 The judgments that had once fallen on Egypt (Ex 6:6; 12:12) would now fall on the inhabitants of Jerusalem. They would be handed over to **foreigners**.

11:11 This prophecy **I will judge you at the border of Israel** was literally fulfilled at Riblah (2Kg 25:18-21; Jr 52:24-27).

11:15 God had given Israel the **land**, but He had also threatened to remove them from it because of their disobedience (Dt 28:36,64-68). God would spare a remnant, but the remnant would not include the corrupt leadership (Ezk 6:8; 12:16).

11:16 The temple was a symbol of the Lord's presence among the Israelites. With the coming of Jesus, the presence of God is no longer located in the physical, man-made temple, but the presence once again dwelt among the people (Jn 1:14), just as it had during the desert period and, according to Ezk 11:16, during the exile. In other words, with the coming of Jesus there is a fundamental redemptive-historical change in the demonstration of God's glory and presence. The closest parallels are found in the NT, with Jesus' appropriation of the term "sanctuary" to Himself (Jn 2:19-22) and His statement that true worship will occur in spirit and truth (Jn 4:21-24). But here the Lord promised personally to be for the exiles what the temple had been for them in Jerusalem.

11:17 The Lord may abandon His land, but He will not per-

manently forsake the people. The regathering (**I will gather you from the peoples**) refers to the end of the Babylonian exile but also may refer to a future gathering of Israel at the beginning of the millennial kingdom (36:24-38; 37:11-28).

11:18 The new inhabitants will remove the **detestable** idols and vile images that once filled the land (7:20; 8:3-17). Some scholars believe the historical fulfillment of these actions occurred in Ezra 6–10.

11:19 The **heart of stone** is that of the unregenerate, those who refuse to submit to the will of God (Zch 7:12). The stony heart is another way of referring to the "hardhearted" (Ezk 2:4; 3:7). The radical spiritual transformation of the people and the associated physical blessings promised in this and other prophecies of the new covenant (34:20-31; 36:24-38; 37:15-28; Jr 31:31-34) will take place in the future messianic age.

11:20 The restoration of Israel's relationship with God (**they will be My people, and I will be their God**) will fulfill the goal of the first exodus (Ex 6:7; cp. Gn 17:7-8; 2Co 6:16; Rv 21:3).

11:23 The **glory** of God, leaving the city, took the direction of King David's flight from Absalom, **on the mountain** (Mount of Olives) **east of the city** (see 2Sm 15:23). Jesus Christ ascended to heaven from the Mount of Olives and promised to return to the same place (cp. Zch 14:4; Ac 1:9-12).

Ezekiel Dramatizes the Exile

12 The word of the LORD came to me: [2]"Son of man, you are living among a rebellious house.[a] They have eyes to see but do not see, and ears to hear but do not hear,[b] for they are a rebellious house.[c]

[3]"Son of man, get your bags ready for exile and go into exile in their sight during the day. You will go into exile from your place to another place while they watch; perhaps they will understand, though they are a rebellious house. [4]During the day, bring out your bags like an exile's bags while they look on. Then in the evening go out in their sight like those going into exile. [5]As they watch, dig through the wall and take the bags out through it. [6]And while they look on, lift the bags to your shoulder and take them out in the dark; cover your face so that you cannot see the land. For I have made you a sign to the house of Israel."[d]

[7]So I did just as I was commanded. In the daytime I brought out my bags like an exile's bags. In the evening I dug through the wall by hand; I took them out in the dark, carrying them on my shoulder in their sight.

[8]Then the word of the LORD came to me in the morning: [9]"Son of man, hasn't the house of Israel, that rebellious house,[e] asked you, 'What are you doing?'[f] [10]Say to them: This is what the Lord GOD says: This •oracle is about the prince[A] in Jerusalem and all the house of Israel who are living there.[B] [11]You are to say, 'I am a sign for you. Just as I have done, so it

will be done to them; they will go into exile,[g] into captivity.' [12]The prince who is among[h] them will lift his bags to his shoulder in the dark and go out. They[c] will dig through the wall to bring him out through it. He will cover his face so he cannot see the land with his eyes. [13]But I will spread My net over him, and he will be caught in My snare. I will bring him to Babylon, the land of the Chaldeans, yet he will not see it,[i] and he will die there. [14]I will also scatter all the attendants who surround him and all his troops to every direction of the wind,[j] and I will draw a sword to chase after them. [15]They will know that I am •Yahweh[k] when I disperse them among the nations and scatter them among the countries.[l] [16]But I will spare a few of them from the sword,[m] famine, and plague so they can tell about all their detestable practices among the nations where they go. Then they will know that I am Yahweh."

Ezekiel Dramatizes Israel's Anxiety

[17]The word of the LORD came to me: [18]"Son of man, eat your bread with[n] trembling and drink your water with shaking and anxiety. [19]Then say to the people of the land: This is what the Lord GOD says about the residents of Jerusalem in the land of Israel: They will eat their bread with anxiety and drink their water in dread, for their[D,E] land will be stripped of everything[o] in it because of the violence of all who live there. [20]The inhabited cities will be

a12:2 Ezk 2:3,5
b Jr 5:21
c Ezk 2:5-8
d12:6 Ezk 4:3; 24:24
e12:9 Ezk 2:5-8
f Ezk 17:12; 20:49; 24:19
g12:11 Jr 15:2; 52:15,28-30
h12:12 2Kg 25:1-7; Jr 39:4; 52:7
i12:13 Jr 39:7; 52:11
j12:14 Ezk 5:2; 17:21
k12:15 Ezk 6:7,14
l Ezk 22:15; 29:12; 30:23
m12:16 Ezk 6:8-9
n12:18 Ezk 4:16
o12:19 Zch 7:14

A12:10 = King Zedekiah   B12:10 Lit are among them   C12:12 LXX, Syr read He   D12:19 Lit its   E12:19 = Jerusalem's

12:2 Blindness (unseeing **eyes**) and deafness (unhearing **ears**) often indicate disobedience or disbelief (Dt 29:1-4; Is 6:9-10; 43:8; Jr 5:21; Mt 13:13-15; Mk 8:18; Jn 12:39-40; Ac 28:26-27). The phrase **rebellious house** occurs in the prophetic commissioning of Ezekiel (2:5-8; 3:9), but it also occurs in 3:26-27.

12:5 Ezekiel's readers understood that breaking through a wall indicated exile, since the conquering armies would **dig through the wall** at strategic points in order to enter the city (Am 4:3).

12:7 The **exile's bags** symbolize the remnant that will be led out of the homeland as captives.

12:12 The covering of King Zedekiah's **face** was Ezekiel's symbolic prophecy of the blinding of the king of Judah by Nebuchadnezzar and his exile to Babylon (2Kg 25:7).

12:13 The phrase **I will spread My net over him** uses the image of a bird hunter (Hs 7:12) or animal hunter (Ezk 19:8). The words **yet he will not see it** refer to the ancient Near Eastern custom of gouging out the eyes of captives.

12:16 The statement **I will spare a few of them** refers to a remnant that will be preserved by the Lord. They will realize their guilt and turn to the Lord in heathen lands (6:8-10). God promised that there would always be a few people who remained loyal to Him (Lv 26:42-45; cp. Ex 32:10; Dt 4:30-31).

12:19 The phrase **because of the violence** reflects the rationale for the judgment of the earth by the flood (Gn 6:11,13).

'adam

Hebrew Pronunciation	[ah DAHM]
HCSB Translation	man, mankind, person
Uses in Ezekiel	132
Uses in the OT	561
Focus passage	Ezekiel 12:2-3,9,18,22,27

'Adam, which never occurs in the plural, broadly signifies man (Gn 1:27), encompassing male and female as mankind (Gn 6:1), humanity (Is 5:15), or mortal man (Ps 39:5). It is a collective indicating individuals (Jb 34:29), men (Ps 22:6), or people (Jr 47:2), often translated as the adjective human (Ex 4:11). But it specifies Adam (Gn 4:1) and a single man in contrast to a woman (Ec 7:28). It denotes one, someone, anyone, or everyone (Neh 2:10,12; Pr 17:18; Zch 11:6) and means person (Lv 6:3). "Son of man" is synonymous with other words for "man" ('iysh: Nm 23:19; 'enosh: Is 51:12; gever: Jb 16:21). "Sons of man" appears as human race (Dt 32:8), men (Ps 45:2), people (Ps 36:7), and descendants of Adam (Ps 90:3). 'Adam often contrasts with animals (Nm 31:26) or God (Is 31:3). "Sons of 'adam" opposes "sons of 'iysh" as low versus high (Ps 49:2).

destroyed, and the land will become a desolation. Then you will know that I am Yahweh."

A Deceptive Proverb Stopped

[21] Again the word of the LORD came to me: [22] "Son of man, what is this proverb you people have about the land of Israel,[a] which goes:

The days keep passing by,[b]
and every vision fails?

[23] Therefore say to them: This is what the Lord GOD says: I will put a stop to this proverb, and they will not use it again in Israel.[c] But say to them: The days draw near,[d] as well as the fulfillment of every vision. [24] For there will no longer be any false vision or flattering ·divination[e] within the house of Israel. [25] But I, Yahweh, will speak whatever message I will speak, and it will be done.[f] It will no longer be delayed.[g] For in your days, rebellious house, I will speak a message and bring it to pass." This is the declaration of the Lord GOD.

[26] The word of the LORD came to me: [27] "Son of man, notice that the house of Israel is saying, 'The vision that he sees concerns many years from now;[h] he prophesies about distant times.' [28] Therefore say to them: This is what the Lord GOD says: None of My words will be delayed any longer. The message I speak will be fulfilled." This is the declaration of the Lord GOD.

Israel's False Prophets Condemned

13 The word of the LORD came to me: [2] "Son of man, prophesy against the prophets of Israel who[i] are prophesying. Say to those who prophesy out of their own imagination:[j] Hear the word of the LORD! [3] This is what the Lord GOD says: Woe to the foolish prophets who follow their own spirit and have seen nothing. [4] Your prophets, Israel, are like jackals among ruins. [5] You did not go up to the gaps[k] or restore the wall around the house of Israel so that it might stand in battle on the

day of the LORD. [6] They see false visions and speak lying ·divinations.[l] They claim, 'This is the LORD's declaration,' when the LORD did not send them,[m] yet they wait for the fulfillment of their message. [7] Didn't you see a false vision and speak a lying divination when you proclaimed, 'This is the LORD's declaration,' even though I had not spoken?

[8] "Therefore, this is what the Lord GOD says: I am against you because you have spoken falsely and had lying visions." This is the declaration of the Lord GOD. [9] "My hand will be against the prophets who see false visions and speak lying divinations.[n] They will not be present in the fellowship of My people or be recorded in the register of the house of Israel, and they will not enter the land of Israel. Then you will know that I am the Lord ·Yahweh.

[10] "Since they have led My people astray saying, 'Peace,'[o] when there is no peace, for when someone builds a wall they plaster it with whitewash,[p] [11] therefore, tell those who plaster it that it will fall. Torrential rain will come,[q] and I will send hailstones plunging[A] down, and a windstorm will be released. [12] Now when the wall has fallen, will you not be asked, 'Where is the coat of whitewash that you put on it?'

[13] "So this is what the Lord GOD says: I will release a windstorm in My wrath. Torrential rain will come in My anger, and hailstones will fall in destructive fury. [14] I will tear down the wall you plastered with whitewash and knock it to the ground so that its foundation is exposed.[r] The city will fall, and you will be destroyed within it. Then you will know that I am Yahweh. [15] After I exhaust My wrath against the wall and against those who plaster it with whitewash, I will say to you: The wall is no more and neither are those who plastered it— [16] those prophets of Israel who prophesied to Jerusalem and saw a vision of peace for her when there was no peace."[s] This is the declaration of the Lord GOD.

[17] "Now, son of man, turn[B] toward the women

Cross-references
a 12:22 Ezk 16:44; 18:2-3
b Jr 5:12; Ezk 11:3; 12:27; 2Pt 3:4,9
c 12:23 Ezk 18:3
d Zph 1:14
e 12:24 Ezk 13:6,23
f 12:25 Is 14:24
g Is 7:16
h 12:27 Ezk 12:22; Dn 10:14
i 13:2 Ezk 22:25,28
j Jr 23:16,26
k 13:5 Ps 106:23; Ezk 22:30
l 13:6 Ezk 22:28
m Jr 14:14; 23:21; 28:15
n 13:9 Jr 20:3-6; 28:15-17
o 13:10 Jr 6:14; 8:11; 14:13; Mc 3:5
p Ezk 22:28; Mt 23:27; Ac 23:3
q 13:11 Ezk 38:22; Mt 7:27
r 13:14 1Co 3:10-15
s 13:16 Jr 6:14; 8:11

A13:11 One Hb ms, LXX, Vg; other Hb mss read *and you, hailstones, will plunge*   **B**13:17 Lit *set your face*

12:22 The expression **the days keep passing by, and every vision fails** reflects the test of true prophecy (Dt 18:20-22). If a prophecy did not come true, the person who made the prediction was a false prophet.

12:24 Even King Hezekiah succumbed to the influential reassurances of **false** prophets (2Kg 20:19). In Ezekiel's day false prophets opposed the claims of God's true messengers in Jerusalem (Jr 28:1-4) and Babylon (Jr 29:1,8-9).

13:3 In no sense were these people prophets of God. The source of their message was **their own spirit**. This is also true of modern false teachers (2Pt 2:1-2). According to Dt 18:18, genuine prophets receive their messages directly from God and speak for Him.

13:4 The sight of **jackals** scavenging in the **ruins** of the city pictures the despair of the people after the fall of Jerusalem (Lm 5:18).

13:8 The phrase **I am against you** is addressed to Israel one other time in Ezekiel (21:3). It was normally directed toward foreign nations.

13:10 Paul used this image—**plaster it with whitewash**—when he called the high priest a "whitewashed wall" (Ac 23:3).

13:17 Women practiced magic in Jerusalem (Jr 7:18; 44:17,19) as well as in Babylon. The Mosaic law condemned witches and necromancers (Lv 20:27; 1Sm 28:9; cp. Lv 19:31). There were a number of legitimate prophet-

of your people who prophesy[a] out of their own imagination. Prophesy against them[b] [18]and say: This is what the Lord God says: Woe to the women who sew magic bands on the wrist of every hand and who make veils for the heads of people of every height in order to ensnare lives. Will you ensnare the lives of My people but preserve your own?[c] [19]You profane Me in front of My people for handfuls of barley[d] and scraps of bread; you kill those who should not die and spare those who should not live, when you lie to My people, who listen to lies.

[20]"Therefore, this is what the Lord God says: I am against your magic bands that you ensnare people with like birds, and I will tear them from your arms. I will free the people you have ensnared like birds. [21]I will also tear off your veils and deliver My people from your hands,[e] so that they will no longer be prey in your hands. Then you will know that I am Yahweh. [22]Because you have disheartened the righteous person with lies, even though I have not caused him grief,[f] and because you have encouraged the wicked[g] person not to turn from his evil way to save his life, [23]therefore you will no longer see false visions or practice divination.[h] I will deliver My people from your hands. Then you will know that I am Yahweh."

Idolatrous Elders Punished

14 Some of the elders of Israel came[i] to me and sat down in front of me.[j] [2]Then the word of the Lord came to me: [3]"Son of man, these men have set up idols in their hearts and

have put sinful stumbling blocks before their faces.[k] Should I be consulted by them at all?[l]

[4]"Therefore, speak to them and tell them: This is what the Lord God says: When anyone from the house of Israel sets up idols in his heart, puts a sinful stumbling block before his face, and then comes to the prophet, I, •Yahweh, will answer him appropriately.[A] I will answer him according to his many idols, [5]so that I may take hold of the house of Israel by their hearts. They are all estranged from Me because of their idols.

[6]"Therefore, say to the house of Israel: This is what the Lord God says: Repent and turn away[m] from your idols; turn your faces away from all your detestable things. [7]For when anyone from the house of Israel or from the foreigners who reside in Israel separates himself from Me, setting up idols in his heart and putting a sinful stumbling block before his face, and then comes to the prophet to inquire of Me,[B] I, Yahweh, will answer him Myself. [8]I will turn against that one and make him a sign and a proverb; I will cut him off from among My people.[n] Then you will know that I am Yahweh.

[9]"But if the prophet is deceived and speaks a message, it was I, Yahweh, who deceived that prophet.[o] I will stretch out My hand against him and destroy him from among My people Israel.[p] [10]They will bear their punishment—the punishment of the one who inquires will be the same as that of the prophet— [11]in order that the house of Israel may no longer stray from following Me and no longer defile themselves[q] with all their

Cross references (center column)

[a]13:17 Jdg 4:4; 2Kg 22:14; Ac 21:9
[b]Ezk 13:2
[c]13:18 2Pt 2:14
[d]13:19 Pr 28:21; Mc 3:5
[e]13:21 Ps 91:3; 124:7
[f]13:22 Jr 28:15
[g]Jr 23:14
[h]13:23 Mc 3:5-6
[i]14:1 Ezk 8:1; 20:1
[j]Ezk 33:31-32
[k]14:3 Ezk 7:19
[l]Ezk 20:3,31
[m]14:6 1Sm 7:3; Neh 1:9; Is 2:20; 30:22; 55:6-7; Ezk 18:30
[n]14:8 Is 65:15; Jr 44:11; Ezk 5:15; 15:7
[o]14:9 Jdg 9:23; 1Sm 16:14; 1Kg 22:23; Jr 20:7; 2Th 2:11
[p]Jr 6:14-15; 14:15
[q]14:11 Ezk 11:18; 37:23

[A]14:4 Alt Hb tradition reads *him who comes*   [B]14:7 Lit *Me for himself*

---

esses in the OT, including Miriam (Ex 15:20), Deborah (Jdg 4:4), Huldah (2Kg 22:14), and Noadiah (Neh 6:14). Prophetesses are also mentioned in the NT (Lk 2:36-38; Ac 21:9; 1Co 11:5).

13:23 God will bring **false** prophecy and sorcery to an end (Am 8:11; Mc 3:6-7; Zch 13:1-6). Jeremiah 23:16-32 is very similar to this chapter. There were false prophets both in the exile and in Jerusalem. Counterfeit prophets attempted to thwart the prophets of God who announced the coming doom. The false prophets were motivated by self-interest. The Christian is to test every spirit (1Jn 4:1) and examine everything in light of Scripture (Ac 17:11).

14:3 The phrase **set up idols in their hearts** literally means "to raise on one's heart," conveying the notion of commitment to the service of an idol. This word for idols (Hb *gillulim*) was used in 6:4-6,13. It literally denotes "dung pellets," thus indicating what the prophet thought of idols. Greed was an inherent motivation for idolatry since worshipers believed the idols were bound to repay generous worship with prosperity. This is why the NT associates idolatry with greed (Eph 5:5). While the idolatry in Jerusalem was openly displayed (Ezk 8), the idolatry practiced by Hebrew exiles in

Babylon was more subtle, as revealed by the people's heart convictions.

14:4 God's answer and judgment against those who worshiped **idols** was for their own good so His people might not continue to be alienated from Him.

14:7 The word **foreigners** refers to non-Israelites who had identified themselves with the people of God and who sometimes became proselytes to the true faith.

14:8 To be **cut . . . off** refers to experiencing premature death, perhaps by means of the death penalty (Lv 20:2-5).

14:9 If the people continued to refuse to listen to prophets whom God sent to tell them the truth, the Lord would judge them by sending lying prophets to tell them what they wanted to hear rather than what they needed to hear. The Lord eventually abandons people to their corrupt passions (Rm 1:18-32).

14:10 The expression **they will bear their punishment** is a legal phrase from Lv 20:17. In that passage as here, the concept of being "cut off" accompanies this statement of judgment.

14:11 The formula **then they will be My people and I will be**

transgressions. Then they will be My people and I will be their God."[a] This is the declaration of the Lord GOD.

Four Devastating Judgments

[12] The word of the LORD came to me: [13] "Son of man, if a land sins against Me by acting faithlessly, and I stretch out My hand against it to cut off its supply of bread,[b] to send famine through it, and to wipe out both man and animal from it, [14] even if these three men[c]—Noah,[d] Daniel,[e] and Job[f]—were in it, they would deliver only themselves by their righteousness." This is the declaration of the Lord GOD.

[15] "If I allow dangerous animals[g] to pass through the land and depopulate it so that it becomes desolate, with no one passing through it for fear of the animals, [16] even if these three men were in it, as I live"—the declaration of the Lord GOD—"they could not deliver their sons or daughters. They alone would be delivered, but the land would be desolate.[h]

[17] "Or if I bring a sword[i] against that land and say: Let a sword pass through it, so that I wipe out both man and animal from it,[j] [18] even if these three men were in it, as I live"—the declaration of the Lord GOD—"they could not deliver their sons or daughters, but they alone would be delivered.

[19] "Or if I send a plague into that land[k] and pour out My wrath on it with bloodshed to wipe out both man and animal from it, [20] even if Noah, Daniel, and Job were in it, as I live"—the declaration of the Lord GOD—"they could not deliver their son or daughter. They would deliver only themselves by their righteousness.

[21] "For this is what the Lord GOD says: How much worse will it be when I send My four[l] devastating judgments against Jerusalem—sword, famine, dangerous animals, and plague—in order to wipe out both man and animal from it! [22] Even so, there will be survivors left in it, sons and daughters who will be brought out. Indeed, they will come out to you, and you will observe their conduct and actions.[m] Then you will be consoled about the devastation I have brought on Jerusalem, about all I have brought on it. [23] They will bring you consolation when you see their conduct and actions, and you will know that it was not without cause that I have done what I did to it."[n] This is the declaration of the Lord GOD.

Parable of the Useless Vine

15 Then the word of the LORD came to me: [2] "Son of man, how does the wood of the vine,[o] that branch among the trees of the forest, compare to any other wood? [3] Can wood be taken from it to make something useful? Or can anyone make a peg from it to hang things on? [4] In fact, it is put into the fire as fuel.[p] The fire devours both of its ends, and the middle is charred. Can it be useful for anything? [5] Even when it was whole it could not be made into a useful object. How much less can it ever be made into anything useful when the fire has devoured it and it is charred!

[6] "Therefore, this is what the Lord GOD says: Like the wood of the vine among the trees of the forest, which I have given to the fire as fuel, so I will give up the residents of Jerusalem. [7] I will turn against them.[q] They may have escaped from the fire, but it will still consume

a14:11 Ezk 36:28
b14:13 Lv 26:26;
Is 3:1; Ezk 4:16
c14:14 Jr 15:1
dGn 6:8
eEzk 28:3;
Dn 1:6
fJb 1:1,5; 42:8-9
g14:15 Lv 26:22;
Nm 21:6; 2Kg
17:25; Ezk 5:17
h14:16 Gn 19:29;
Ezk 18:20
i14:17 Lv 26:25;
Ezk 5:12; 21:3-4
jEzk 25:13;
Zph 1:3
k14:19 2Sm
24:15; Ezk 38:22
l14:21 Ezk 5:17;
33:27; Am 4:6-
10; Rv 6:8
m14:22 Ezk 6:8;
12:16; 20:43;
36:20
n14:23 Jr 22:8-9
o15:2 Ps 80:8-
16; Is 5:1-7; Hs
10:1
p15:4 Jn 15:6
q15:7 Ezk 14:8

---

their God has its origin in Ex 6:7 in connection with the establishment of the covenant relationship between God and His people. It recurs in the description of the ultimate bliss in the covenantal blessings (Lv 26:12).

14:14 Some people of Judah must have wondered whether the impending judgment on Jerusalem might be diverted if some well-known righteous man or men (**Noah, Daniel, and Job**) could be found (Gn 18). The biblical Daniel was exiled to Babylon in 605 B.C. (Dn 1:1). He would have had time to establish a reputation as a wise and righteous man by the time Ezekiel ministered. Daniel was well known for his righteousness (Dn 1:17-21; 2:14,48; 5:12). All of these men—Noah, Daniel, and Job—were recognized for their righteous behavior in the midst of corrupt generations and prevailed in difficult situations because of their righteousness. Ezekiel's reference to these men affirmed that moral responsibility is not transferable; it is individual.

14:15 The threat of **dangerous animals** devouring the land and destroying the people is mentioned in the Mosaic law (Lv 26:22; Dt 32:24).

14:21 Sword curses (predictions of punishment by war) occur in Lv 26:25,33; Dt 32:41-42. On **famine** curses, see Lv 26:26,29,45; Dt 28:53-56; 32:24. **Dangerous** animal curses appear in Lv 26:22; Dt 32:24. Pestilence or **plague** curses are found in Lv 26:14; Dt 28:21-22; 32:24. These four curses are also mentioned in Ezekiel 5.

14:22 When the exiles saw the wicked behavior of the survivors of the perilous judgments (**you will observe their conduct and actions**), they would be assured of God's justice—that He had acted righteously in His judgment. The exiles would regard the destruction of Judah's capital as well deserved.

15:6 The **vine** as an image of Israel goes back to Nm 13:23 where it appears as a symbol of the richness of Canaan, the land promised to Israel. The image of the vine portrays God's loving care for the nation as a vinedresser taking care of what He had planted (Ps 80:8-9; Is 5:1-7). It is clear from Mt 21:33-41 that God desires fruit (good works) from His vine. Unless people come into vital relationship with the true Vinedresser, there can be no fruit. **Fire** is a frequent

them.[a] And you will know that I am •Yahweh when I turn against them. [8] I will make the land desolate because they have acted unfaithfully." This is the declaration of the Lord God.

Parable of God's Adulterous Wife

16 The word of the Lord came to me again: [2] "Son of man, explain Jerusalem's detestable practices to her.[b] [3] You are to say: This is what the Lord God says to Jerusalem: Your origin and your birth were in the land of the Canaanites. Your father was an Amorite and your mother a Hittite.[c] [4] As for your birth, your umbilical cord wasn't cut on the day you were born,[d] and you weren't washed •clean[A] with water. You were not rubbed with salt or wrapped in cloths.[e] [5] No one cared enough about you to do even one of these things out

of compassion for you. But you were thrown out into the open field because you were despised on the day you were born.

[6] "I passed by you and saw you lying in your blood, and I said to you as you lay in your blood: Live! Yes, I said to you as you lay in your blood: Live![B] [7] I made you thrive[C] like plants of the field.[f] You grew up and matured and became very beautiful.[D] Your breasts were formed and your hair grew, but you were stark naked.

[8] "Then I passed by you and saw you, and you were indeed at the age for love. So I spread the edge of My garment over you and covered your nakedness.[g] I pledged Myself to you,[h] entered into a covenant with you, and you became Mine."[i] This is the declaration of the Lord God. [9] "I washed you with water, rinsed

Cross references column:
[a]15:7 Is 24:18
[b]16:2 Is 58:1; Ezk 20:4; 22:2
[c]16:3 Dt 7:1; Jdg 3:5; 1Kg 9:20-21; Ezk 16:45
[d]16:4 Hs 2:3
[e]Lk 2:12
[f]16:7 Ex 1:7
[g]16:8 Ru 3:9; Jr 2:2
[h]Gn 22:16-18
[i]Ex 19:5; 24:7-8

[A]16:4 Hb obscure   [B]16:6 Some Hb mss, LXX, Syr omit *Yes, I said to you as you lay in your blood: Live!*   [C]16:7 LXX reads *Thrive; I made you*   [D]16:7 Or *matured and developed the loveliest of ornaments*

---

figure for destruction in Ezekiel (5:2,4; 10:2; 16:41; 23:47; 24:10-11). The burning of the **wood** accompanied the destruction of **Jerusalem**. In Babylonian invasions fire accompanied annihilation (2Kg 25:9; 2Ch 36:19). Fire will be a prominent feature of the great tribulation (Rv 14:18).

16:1-63 This chapter is similar in purpose to 20:3-31, where a review of Israel's past history set the context for its coming judgment.

16:1 Jerusalem had a centuries-old, pre-Israelite history (Gn 14:18), and the city resisted Israelite conquest in the days of Joshua (Jos 15:63). It became an Israelite city only after David's conquest (2Sm 5:6-9).

16:3 In biblical ethnography **Canaanites**, Amorites, and Hittites were closely related. Moreover, these three were related to the Jebusites, the pre-Israelite inhabitants of Jerusalem (Gn 10:15-18; Jdg 19:11; 2Sm 5:6). The Amorites were pre-Israelite, Semitic inhabitants of Palestine (Gn 48:22; Jos 5:1; 10:5; Jdg 1:34-36). The Hittites were non-

Semitic residents of Canaan who earlier had flourished in Asia Minor during the second millennium B.C. (Gn 23:10-20; 26:34; 2Sm 11:3-27; 1Kg 11:1). By going back to the people's origin, Ezekiel emphasized that the people had always been characterized by rebellion. They were sinners like all peoples of the earth, and they often allowed themselves to be led astray into idol worship.

16:4 Exposure of unwanted babies, especially girls, was common in the ancient world. In this description the infant was abandoned, apparently still attached to the placenta, and left to die (**you were not rubbed with salt or wrapped in cloths**). Contemporary Arab midwives in Palestine commonly coat a baby's body with a mixture of salt and oil after cutting the umbilical cord.

16:5 God finding His people in the **open field** resembles the description in Dt 32:10 where God found Israel "in a desolate land, in a barren, howling wilderness."

16:6 The phrase **saw you lying in your blood** emphasizes that Israel was abandoned by her mother. The expression **I said to you as you lay in your blood: Live!** may refer to God's basic desire for all people to live, summed up by this one word (18:23,32; 1Tm 2:4). The command is reminiscent of the mandate to be fruitful and multiply (Gn 1:22,28), which was repeated to Jacob (Gn 28:3; 35:11; cp. Gn 17:2,6).

16:8 The special word for **love** (Hb *dodim*) in this verse refers to the love that leads to sexual relations (23:17; Sg 1:2,4; 4:10; 5:1; 7:13). Spreading a **garment** over a person was a proposal of marriage (Ru 3:9). The portrayal of Israel as the Lord's wife (**you became Mine**) derives from the first of the Ten Commandments, which says we must worship God alone. A wife's obligation to remain true to her husband offered a fitting parallel to Israel's obligations to God. In the Hebrew Torah, Yahweh is called *qanna'* ("passionate, jealous") toward those who broke faith with Him (Ex 20:5; 34:14). Ezekiel inherited a prophetic tradition in which sexual infidelity was used as a metaphor for Israel's adoption of Canaanite religion (Jr 2:20; Hs 1:2; 2:5-13; 3:1) and for its political alliances with foreign powers (Jr 2:33,36; Hs 8:9).

16:9 The expression **rinsed off your blood** may be associated with bleeding that occurs with the first experience of

---

to'evah

Hebrew Pronunciation	[toh ay VAH]
HCSB Translation	detestable thing, abomination, abhorrent
Uses in Ezekiel	43
Uses in the OT	118
Focus passage	Ezekiel 16:2,22,36,43,47,50-51,58

To'evah means *abomination* (Ezk 16:22) and *abhorrent* (Dt 7:26) or *detestable* (Dt 12:31) *thing*. Context may indicate *detestable practices* (Ezr 9:1) or *acts* (Jr 7:10) and *abhorrent idols* (Jr 16:18). *To'evah* describes what is culturally (Gn 43:32), ethically, or religiously *abhorrent* (Gn 43:34), *detestable* (Ex 8:26), and *repulsive* (Ps 88:8). The wicked and righteous are *detestable* to one another (Pr 29:27). God *detests* idolatry (Dt 27:15), related practices (Dt 18:10-12), prostitution (Dt 23:18), transvestism (Dt 22:5), homosexuality (Lv 18:22), child sacrifice (Dt 12:31), false prophecy (Jr 6:15), empty religious ritual (Is 1:13), and other sins (Pr 6:16-19). *Ta'av* (22x), apparently from *to'evah*, means *abhor* (Dt 7:26), *despise* (Dt 23:7), or *loathe* (Ps 107:18). Passive-reflexive verbs denote *be detestable* (1Ch 21:6), *worthless* (Is 14:19), or *revolting* (Jb 15:16). Causative verbs signify *commit a detestable act* (1Kg 21:26) or *what is vile* (Ps 14:1) and *commit abhorrently* (Ezk 16:52).

off your blood, and anointed you with oil. [10]I clothed you in embroidered cloth and provided you with leather sandals. I also wrapped you in fine linen and covered you with silk. [11]I adorned you with jewelry, putting bracelets on your wrists and a chain around your neck. [12]I put a ring in your nose,[a] earrings on your ears, and a beautiful tiara on your head. [13]So you were adorned with gold and silver,[b] and your clothing was made of fine linen, silk, and embroidered cloth. You ate fine flour, honey, and oil. You became extremely beautiful and attained royalty. [14]Your fame spread among the nations because of your beauty, for it was perfect through My splendor,[c] which I had bestowed on you." This is the declaration of the Lord GOD.

[15]"But you were confident in your beauty and acted like a prostitute because of your fame.[d] You lavished your sexual favors on everyone who passed by.[e] Your beauty became his.[A] [16]You took some of your garments and made colorful •high places for yourself, and you engaged in prostitution on them. These places should not have been built, and this should never have happened![A] [17]You also took your beautiful jewelry made from the gold and silver I had given you,[f] and you made male images so that you could engage in prostitution with them. [18]Then you took your embroidered garments to cover them, and set My oil and incense before them. [19]You also set before them as a pleasing aroma the food I gave you—the fine flour, oil, and honey that I fed you.[g] That is what happened." This is the declaration of the Lord GOD.

[20]"You even took your sons and daughters

you bore to Me and sacrificed them to these images as food.[h] Wasn't your prostitution enough? [21]You slaughtered My children and gave them up when you passed them through the fire[i] to the images. [22]In all your detestable practices and acts of prostitution, you did not remember the days of your youth[j] when you were stark naked and lying in your blood.

[23]"Then after all your evil—Woe, woe to you!"—the declaration of the Lord GOD— [24]"you built yourself a mound and made yourself an elevated place in every square.[k] [25]You built your elevated place at the head of every street[l] and turned your beauty into a detestable thing. You spread your legs to everyone who passed by and increased your prostitution. [26]You engaged in promiscuous acts with Egyptian men, your well-endowed neighbors, and increased your prostitution[m] to provoke Me to anger.

[27]"Therefore, I stretched out My hand against you and reduced your provisions. I gave you over to the desire of those who hate you, the Philistine women,[n] who were embarrassed by your indecent behavior. [28]Then you engaged in prostitution with the Assyrian men because you were not satisfied.[o] Even though you did this with them, you were still not satisfied. [29]So you extended your prostitution to Chaldea,[p] the land of merchants, but you were not even satisfied with this!

[30]"How your heart was inflamed with lust"—the declaration of the Lord GOD— "when you did all these things, the acts of a brazen prostitute, [31]building your mound at the head of every street and making your elevated place in every square. But you were

[a]16:11-12 Gn 24:22,47
[b]16:13 Dt 32:13-14; Ps 45:13-14
[c]16:14 Lm 2:15
[d]16:15 Is 57:8; Jr 2:20
[e]Pr 7:8-13
[f]16:17 Ex 12:35; 32:2-4
[g]16:19 Hs 2:8
[h]16:20 Jr 7:31; 19:5; Ezk 23:37
[i]16:21 Lv 18:21; Dt 18:10; 2Kg 17:17; Ezk 20:31
[j]16:22 Jr 2:2
[k]16:24 Jr 11:13
[l]16:25 Pr 9:14
[m]16:26 Ezk 23:19-20
[n]16:27 Ezk 16:57
[o]16:28 2Kg 16:7,10-18; 2Ch 28:16,20-23; Jr 2:18,36
[p]16:29 Ezk 23:14-16

[A]16:15,16 Hb obscure

sexual intercourse (Dt 22:13-21). Or it may refer to menstrual blood, indicating sexual maturity.

16:10 Jerusalem is **clothed** in materials that are elsewhere used in decorating the tabernacle (**embroidered cloth**). This is a subtle suggestion that Jerusalem was the home of the temple (Ps 48:2; 50:2; Lm 2:15).

16:15 The accusation (**acted like a prostitute**) referred both to a spiritual turning away from the Lord and to physical involvement with the fertility rites of Canaanite paganism (Jr 3:1-5; Hs 4:13-14; 9:1; cp. Gn 38:14-16). The infidelity of the city began with Solomon's introduction of idolatry and his creation of multiple shrine sites for idol worship (1Kg 11:1-10). Jerusalem played the harlot; she committed the sin of idolatry (Jms 4:4). Her pride led her astray (Dt 32:15; Jr 7:4; Mc 3:11).

16:17 The fabrication of objects of false worship from **jewelry** recalls the episode of the golden calf on Mount Sinai (Ex 32:2-4,24).

16:18 Putting clothing on idols is also mentioned in Jr 10:9.

16:20 The practice of child sacrifice (**your sons and daugh-**

ters you . . . sacrificed) occurred during the reigns of Ahaz (2Kg 16:3) and Manasseh (2Kg 21:6), and it was even more widely practiced during the time of Jeremiah (Jr 7:31; 19:5; 32:35). Child sacrifice is also further mentioned in Ezekiel (20:26; 23:37). By sacrificing her offspring Jerusalem proved that she was a moral descendant of Canaanite ancestry. The Mosaic law prohibited this practice (Lv 18:21; 20:2; Dt 12:31; 18:10).

16:22 The same concept and image (**you did not remember the days of your youth**) is conveyed in Hs 2:4-14.

16:26 Spiritual prostitution involved illicit worship of idols. It also included choosing and developing political and military alliances for security (**promiscuous acts with Egyptian men**; see Is 23:17-18). To reflect God's revulsion over these alliances, Ezekiel described these illicit lovers as "having oversized organs." He referred to them as **your well-endowed neighbors**.

16:31 Prostitutes normally engaged in illicit sexual relations as a means of earning income, but Jerusalem had descended so far into sin that she **scorned** the **payment** a prostitute normally received (1Co 7:22-23).

unlike a prostitute because you scorned payment.[a] [32] You adulterous wife, who receives strangers instead of her husband! [33] Men give gifts to all prostitutes, but you gave gifts to all your lovers. You bribed them to come to you from all around for your sexual favors. [34] So you were the opposite of other women in your acts of prostitution; no one solicited you. When you paid a fee instead of one being paid to you, you were the opposite.

[35] "Therefore, you prostitute, hear the word of the LORD! [36] This is what the Lord GOD says: Because your lust was poured out and your nakedness exposed by your acts of prostitution with your lovers, and because of all your detestable idols and the blood of your children that you gave to them,[b] [37] I am therefore going to gather all the lovers you pleased[c]—all those you loved as well as all those you hated. I will gather them against you from all around and expose your nakedness[d] to them so they see you completely naked. [38] I will judge you the way adulteresses and those who shed blood are judged.[e] Then I will bring about your bloodshed in wrath and jealousy.[f] [39] I will hand you over to them, and they will level your mounds and tear down your elevated places. They will strip off your clothes,[g] take your beautiful jewelry, and leave you stark naked. [40] They will bring a mob against you[h] to stone you and cut you to pieces with their swords. [41] Then they will burn down your houses and execute judgments against you in the sight of many women. I will stop you from being a prostitute,[i] and you will never again pay fees for lovers. [42] So I will satisfy My wrath against you,[j] and My jealousy will turn away from you. Then I will be silent and no longer angry. [43] Because you did not remember the days[k] of your youth but enraged Me with all these things, I will also bring your actions down on your own head."[l] This is the declaration of the Lord GOD. "Haven't you

committed immoral acts in addition to all your detestable practices?

[44] "Look, everyone who uses proverbs will say this proverb about you:

Like mother, like daughter.

[45] You are the daughter of your mother, who despised her husband and children. You are the sister of your sisters,[m] who despised their husbands and children. Your mother was a Hittite and your father an Amorite.[n] [46] Your older sister was Samaria,[o] who lived with her daughters to the north of you, and your younger sister was Sodom, who lived with her daughters to the south of you. [47] Didn't you walk in their ways and do their detestable practices? It was only a short time before you behaved more corruptly than they did.[A,p]

[48] "As I live"—the declaration of the Lord GOD—"your sister Sodom and her daughters have not behaved as you and your daughters have.[q] [49] Now this was the iniquity of your sister Sodom: she and her daughters had pride, plenty of food,[r] and comfortable security, but didn't support the poor and needy. [50] They were haughty and did detestable things before Me, so I removed them when I saw this.[B,s] [51] But Samaria did not commit even half your sins. You have multiplied your detestable practices beyond theirs and made your sisters appear righteous by all the detestable things you have committed. [52] You must also bear your disgrace, since you have been an advocate for your sisters. For they appear more righteous than you because of your sins, which you committed more abhorrently than they did. So you also, be ashamed and bear your disgrace, since you have made your sisters appear righteous.

[53] "I will restore their fortunes,[t] the fortunes of Sodom and her daughters and those of Samaria and her daughters. I will also restore[c] your fortunes among them,[u] [54] so you will bear your disgrace and be ashamed of all you did

a16:31 Is 52:3
b16:36 Jr 2:34
c16:37 Jr 13:22,26; Ezk 23:9,22
d Is 47:3
e16:38 Ezk 23:45
f Gn 9:6; Ezk 23:25
g16:39 Ezk 23:26; Hs 2:3
h16:40 Ezk 23:47
i16:41 Ezk 23:48
j16:42 Ezk 5:13; 21:17
k16:43 Ps 78:42
l Ezk 11:21; 22:31
m16:45 Ezk 23:2
n Ezk 16:31
o16:46 Ezk 23:4,33
p16:47 Ezk 5:6
q16:48 Mt 10:15; 11:23-24
r16:49 Gn 13:10
s16:50 Gn 18:20-21
t16:53 Is 1:9
uJr 20:16

A16:47 Lit they in all your ways   B16:50 Or them as you have seen   C16:53 LXX, Vg; MT reads Samaria and her daughters and the fortunes of

---

16:36 The public humiliation of a prostitute by exposing her **nakedness** is mentioned in Jr 13:22,26; Hs 2:10; and Nah 3:5. According to the law, this degradation was to be followed by stoning and sometimes by burning (Dt 22:22; Ezk 16:40).

16:39 Contracts discovered from Nuzi (fifteenth century B.C., northern Iraq) specified that if a wife divorced her husband, she would "go out naked."

16:41 This form of punishment (**they will burn down your houses**) was not uncommon in the OT (Jdg 12:1; 15:6).

16:45 Jerusalem was like her mother, a **Hittite**, who was

married to an **Amorite**, the people who were removed from Canaan by the Israelites because their sins had reached an intolerable level (Gn 15:16). God's justice now seemed to require that Israelites left in their land should also be removed.

16:46-47 The Israelites had become worse than **Sodom**, the city infamous for its corruption (Dt 32:32; Is 1:10; Jr 23:14). Sodomy is a sexual act named after the homosexual perversions at Sodom (Gn 19:5-29). Sodomy is "detestable" according to Lv 18:22; 20:13. The Bible frequently compares cities or peoples to Sodom, which was taken to be the epitome of evil and degradation (Dt 29:23; 32:32; Is 1:9-10; 3:9; Lm 4:6; Mt 10:15; 11:23-24; Jd 7).

when you comforted them.[a] [55] As for your sisters, Sodom and her daughters and Samaria and her daughters will return to their former state. You and your daughters will also return to your former state. [56] Didn't you treat your sister Sodom as an object of scorn when you were proud, [57] before your wickedness was exposed? It was like the time you were scorned by the daughters of Aram[A,b] and all those around her, and by the daughters of the Philistines—those who treated you with contempt from every side. [58] You yourself must bear the consequences of your indecency and detestable practices"[c]—this is the Lord's declaration.

[59] "For this is what the Lord God says: I will deal with you according to what you have done, since you have despised the oath by breaking the covenant.[d] [60] But I will remember the covenant I made with you in the days of your youth, and I will establish an everlasting covenant with you.[e] [61] Then you will remember your ways[f] and be ashamed when you[B] receive your older and younger sisters. I will give them to you as daughters, but not because of your covenant. [62] I will establish My covenant with you,[g] and you will know that I am *Yahweh, [63] so that when I make *atonement for all you have done, you will remem-

ber and be ashamed,[h] and never open your mouth again because of your disgrace."[i] This is the declaration of the Lord God.

Parable of the Eagles

17 The word of the Lord came to me: [2] "Son of man, pose a riddle and speak a parable to the house of Israel.[j] [3] You are to say: This is what the Lord God says:

> A great eagle with great wings,[k]
>   long pinions,
> and full plumage of many colors
> came to Lebanon and took the top
>   of the cedar.[l]
> [4] He plucked off its topmost shoot,
>   brought it to the land of merchants,
>   and set it in a city of traders.
> [5] Then he took some of the land's seed
>   and put it in a fertile field;[m]
> he set it like a willow,[n]
>   a plant[c] by abundant waters.
> [6] It sprouted and became
>   a spreading vine,
> low in height with its branches turned
>   toward him,[o]
> yet its roots stayed under it.
> So it became a vine,
> produced branches,
>   and sent out shoots.

Cross references

a16:54 Ezk 14:22-23
b16:57 2Kg 16:5-7
c16:58 Ezk 23:49
d16:59 Ezk 17:19
e16:60 Is 55:3; Jr 32:38-41
f16:61 Ezk 6:9
g16:62 Hs 2:19-20
h16:63 Ezk 36:31-32
iRm 3:19
j17:2 Ezk 20:49; 24:3
k17:3 Jr 48:40
lEzk 17:12
m17:5 Dt 8:7-9
nIs 44:4
o17:6 Ezk 17:14

A16:57 Some Hb mss, Syr read *Edom*   B16:61 Some LXX mss, Syr read *I*   C17:5 Hb obscure

---

16:56 The phrase **when you were proud** refers to the golden days of Jerusalem during the reign of David and the beginning of Solomon's reign.

16:59 Jerusalem's contempt toward the oath and the **breaking of the covenant** would be answered by the suspension of God's own covenant obligations. Judah's sin was especially grievous because she had despised the oath of obedience she made to the Lord at Sinai (Ex 19:6). The current generation had reached the limit of God's forbearance. In some sense God severed His relationship with that generation, though without breaking His covenant promises.

16:60 References to the Lord remembering His **covenant** occur only in relationship to the patriarchal covenants (Gn 9:15-16; Ex 2:24; 6:5; Lv 26:42,45; Ps 105:8). The mention of God remembering His covenant is contrasted with Jerusalem's forgetting the terms of her relationship with God (Ezk 16:22,43). When this new relationship is established, the people will remember their ways and be ashamed. The **everlasting covenant** is the new covenant spoken of in Is 59:21; 61:8; and Jr 31:31-34, but it should be viewed as closely related to the Abrahamic covenant. The features of the new covenant were actually the outworking of the basic elements of God's promises to Abraham (Is 55:3; Jr 32:40).

16:62 Prophetic passages that announce the restoration of Israel (**I will establish My covenant with you**) reflect the teaching of Dt 30:3. The letters to the churches in the book of Revelation illustrate how God acts in a similar way by disciplining His church (Rv 2:14,20).

17:2 A **riddle** (Hb *chidah*) is an obscure and mysterious saying. It hides the truth it imparts, while a **parable** (Hb *mashal*)

elucidates the truth that underlies it by putting it in fresh light. Judges 14:12-19 offers an example of how a riddle might be developed and handled in popular usage.

17:3 The **great eagle** in this verse is Nebuchadnezzar of Babylon (v. 12). He was a brilliant military strategist and succeeded his father, Nabopolassar, in 602 B.C. The fulfillment of the riddle came in Nebuchadnezzar's campaign against Jerusalem in 597 B.C. and his deportation of Jehoiachin (and Ezekiel) as part of the second deportation to Babylon (2Kg 24:10-12). The historical background behind this passage may be found in 2Kg 24:8-20; 2Ch 36:9-13; Jr 37; 52:1-17. **Lebanon** refers to Jerusalem (v. 12). In ancient times the Lebanon mountain range was covered with cedars. The **cedar** refers to David's dynasty, his royal family. The top of the cedar removed by the king of Babylon was Jehoiachin, who was taken into exile in 597 B.C. (2Kg 24:8-16).

17:4 The phrase **land of merchants** may be translated as "land of Canaan." Merchants and Canaanites can be interchanged due to the affinity of the Phoenicians for trade (Zph 1:11). The term is occupational rather than geographical. Here the phrase refers to Babylon (Ezk 16:29), the great center of commerce in all Asia.

17:5 The **land's seed** in this verse is King Zedekiah of Judah, son of Josiah (2Kg 23–34).

17:6 This image (**low in height with its branches turned toward him**) represents Zedekiah turning toward Nebuchadnezzar to whom he owed his power. The spreading vine may be of low stature to represent the loss of thousands of Judah's leading citizens to deportation (2Kg 24:15-16; Jr 52:28).

7 But there was another great eagle
with great wings and thick plumage.
And this vine bent its roots toward him!
It stretched out its branches to him
from its planting bed,[a]
so that he might water it.
8 It had been planted
in a good field by abundant waters
in order to produce branches,
bear fruit, and become a splendid vine.

9 You are to say: This is what the Lord GOD
says:

Will it flourish?
Will he not tear out its roots[b]
and strip off its fruit
so that it shrivels?
All its fresh leaves will wither!
Great strength and many people
will not be needed to pull it
from its roots.
10 Even though it is planted,
will it flourish?
Won't it completely wither
when the east wind strikes it?[c]
It will wither on the bed
where it sprouted."

11 The word of the LORD came to me: 12 "Now say to that rebellious house:[d] Don't you know what these things mean? Tell them: The king of Babylon came to Jerusalem, took its king and officials,[e] and brought them back with him to Babylon. 13 He took one of the royal family[f] and made a covenant with him, putting him under oath.[g] Then he took away the leading men of the land, 14 so the kingdom might

be humble and not exalt itself[h] but might keep his covenant in order to endure. 15 However, this king revolted against him[i] by sending his ambassadors to Egypt so they might give him horses and a large army.[j] Will he flourish? Will the one who does such things escape? Can he break a covenant and still escape?

16 "As I live"—this is the declaration of the Lord GOD—"he will die in Babylon, in the land of the king who put him on the throne,[k] whose oath he despised and whose covenant he broke. 17 Pharaoh will not help him with his great army and vast horde in battle,[l] when ramps are built and siege walls constructed to destroy many lives. 18 He despised the oath by breaking the covenant. He did all these things even though he gave his hand in pledge.[m] He will not escape!"

19 Therefore, this is what the Lord GOD says: "As I live, I will bring down on his head My oath that he despised and My covenant that he broke. 20 I will spread My net over him,[n] and he will be caught in My snare.[o] I will bring him to Babylon and execute judgment on him there for the treachery he committed against Me.[p] 21 All the fugitives[A] among his troops will fall by the sword, and those who survive will be scattered to every direction of the wind.[q] Then you will know that I, •Yahweh, have spoken."

22 This is what the Lord GOD says:

I will take a sprig
from the lofty top of the cedar
and plant it.[r]
I will pluck a tender sprig
from its topmost shoots,
and I will plant it
on a high towering mountain.

Cross references (center column):

a 17:7 Ezk 31:4
b 17:9 2Kg 25:7
c 17:10 Gn 41:6; 2Kg 19:26; Ezk 19:12; Hs 13:15; Jnh 4:8
d 17:12 Ezk 2:3-5; 12:9-11
e 2Kg 24:11-15
f 17:13 2Kg 24:17
g 2Ch 36:13
h 17:14 Ezk 29:14
i 17:15 2Kg 24:20; 2Ch 36:13
j Dt 17:16
k 17:16 Ezk 12:13
l 17:17 Jr 37:5,7
m 17:18 1Ch 29:24
n 17:20 Ezk 12:13
o 2Kg 25:5-6; Jr 39:5
p Ezk 20:35-36
q 17:21 Ezk 5:10
r 17:22 Ps 2:6

A 17:21 Some Hb mss, LXX, Syr, Tg read *choice men*

17:7 While the first eagle represents the king of Babylon, the second **great eagle** is Egypt. This eagle is the Egyptian pharaoh, either Psammetichus II (595–589 B.C.) or Hophra (589–570 B.C.). King Zedekiah of Judah attempted to seek Egypt's aid in an attempt to break free from the Babylonian yoke. For the details of these events, see 2Ch 36:13; Jr 35:5-7; 44:30; 52:11.

17:9 Taking up the **roots** signifies the abolition of national existence (Am 2:9). In this specific case, it refers to the deportation of Judah to Babylon.

17:10 The **east wind** is the hot, dry wind known in Hebrew as the *chamsin*. The east wind is an instrument of God's will. Note the effect of the east wind in the exodus narratives (Ex 10:13; 14:21; cp. Ps 78:26), as well as in Jonah (Jnh 4:8) and Hs 13:15. King Zedekiah was violating Dt 17:16.

17:13 The phrase **he took one of the royal family and made a covenant with him** describes Nebuchadnezzar's installation of his own puppet king, Mattaniah, whom he renamed Zedekiah after Jehoiachin was removed from the throne.

The people of the upper class of the land were carried away with Jehoiachin to Babylon (2Kg 24:15).

17:16 This prophecy (**he will die in Babylon**) was fulfilled in 2Kg 25:7.

17:19 Nebuchadnezzar had forced his vassal **covenant** on King Zedekiah of Judah (2Ch 36:13). The **oath** had been sworn to the God of Israel, so a violation of the agreement would bring the anger of the Lord. The king's most serious transgression was not against Nebuchadnezzar but against his responsibility and loyalty to God. As a consequence, God would carry out the impending punishment of exile and imprisonment in Babylon (2Kg 25:7,11-21).

17:22 Other prophets used a variety of horticultural expressions—including "shoot," "sprout," and "branch"—to designate the messianic figure who would revive the Davidic line (Is 4:2; 11:1; Jr 23:5; 33:15; Zch 3:8; 6:12). In this context, a **sprig** (Hb *yoneqeth*) serves as a forerunner of the messianic figure mentioned in later salvation oracles. God would replant a king from the line of David on the **mountain** heights of Israel. The mountain on which the

23 I will plant it on Israel's
    high mountain[a]
so that it may bear branches,
    produce fruit,
and become a majestic cedar.
Birds of every kind will nest under it,[b]
taking shelter in the shade
    of its branches.
24 Then all the trees of the field will know
    that I am Yahweh.
I bring down the tall tree,
and make the low tree tall.[c]
I cause the green tree to wither
and make the withered tree thrive.[d]
I, Yahweh, have spoken
and I will do it.[e]

Personal Responsibility for Sin

18 The word of the LORD came to me: 2 "What do you mean by using this proverb concerning the land of Israel:

The fathers eat sour grapes,[f]
    and the children's teeth are set
        on edge?[g]

[a]17:23 Ezk 20:40
[b]Dn 4:12
[c]17:24 Is 40:4
[d]Am 9:11
[e]Nm 14:35; Ps 33:9; Is 46:11; 55:11; Ezk 17:24; 22:14; 24:14; 36:36; 37:14
[f]18:2 Lm 5:7
[g]Jr 31:29
[h]18:3 Ezk 12:23
[i]18:4 Nm 16:22; 27:16
[j]Dt 24:16; Ezk 18:20; Rm 6:23
[k]18:6 Ezk 22:9
[l]Ex 20:17-18; Lv 20:10
[m]Lv 18:19-20
[n]18:7 Ex 22:21
[o]Dt 24:12-13
[p]Mt 25:35-40
[q]18:8 Ex 22:25; Lv 25:35-37
[r]Zch 8:16
[s]18:9 Am 5:4
[t]18:10 Nm 35:31

3 As I live"—this is the declaration of the Lord GOD—"you will no longer use this proverb in Israel.[h] 4 Look, every life belongs to Me.[i] The life of the father is like the life of the son—both belong to Me. The person who sins is the one who will die.[j]

5 "Now suppose a man is righteous and does what is just and right: 6 He does not eat at the mountain shrines[k] or raise his eyes to the idols of the house of Israel. He does not defile his neighbor's wife[l] or come near a woman during her menstrual impurity.[m] 7 He doesn't oppress anyone[n] but returns his collateral to the debtor.[o] He does not commit robbery, but gives his bread to the hungry[p] and covers the naked with clothing. 8 He doesn't lend at interest or for profit[q] but keeps his hand from wrongdoing and carries out true justice between men.[r] 9 He follows My statutes and keeps My ordinances, acting faithfully. Such a person is righteous; he will certainly live."[s] This is the declaration of the Lord GOD.

10 "Now suppose the man has a violent son, who sheds blood[t] and does any of these things,

---

cedar will be planted is the symbol of a mighty kingdom (Is 2:2; Mc 4:1).

17:23 Birds thriving under a leader's protection is a repeated biblical theme (Dn 4:20-22; Hs 14:5-7). The expression **birds of every kind** recalls the flood story (Gn 7:14). God's plan includes all the peoples of the world.

17:24 The concept of the Messiah as the **low tree** or "dry tree" awaiting glorification fits with the view of the Messiah as Suffering Servant. This passage should be correlated with Is 2:2-4 and Mc 4:1-4 where it is said that in messianic times the entire world will recognize the Lord and be subject to His will on Mount Zion. A new sprig will be planted and will flourish under the blessing of the Lord's protection. The fulfillment of this prophecy awaited the arrival of a greater son of David, Jesus the Messiah, who would claim the world as His kingdom (Jn 12:32; cp. Rv 22:16-17).

18:2 The Hebrew word for **set on edge** describes the effect on the **teeth** that results from eating **grapes**. The word appears elsewhere only in Ec 10:10, where it is used of blunted or worn iron. It may indicate the sensation of eating something bitter or sour. In the Ten Commandments, God said He would visit sin on the third and fourth generations of those who rebel against Him (Ex 20:5). This was intended to warn adults that their sins would have ominous influence on their children's lifestyle choices and thus on their relations to God. Following the model of their parents, they would choose sin and thus earn God's punishment. The people in Ezekiel's day misconstrued this reality, as reflected in this proverb accusing God of unfairness. A person's sin may outlive him and have negative repercussions on other people (Ezk 18:19-32), but God does not punish the innocent for the sins of others. This misinterpretation of God's justice is also reflected in Lm 5:7: "Our fathers sinned; they no longer exist, but we bear their punishment." The proverb was current in Jerusalem as well (Jr 31:29-30); see Dt 24:16.

18:3 God demanded that the people not recite this false **proverb**. It not only misconstrued God's conduct and character, but those who recited it regarded themselves as completely innocent (Pr 26:9).

18:5 The **righteous** person's actions are described largely in accordance with the Holiness Code (Lv 17-26).

18:6 In OT times, mountains were often the location for idolatrous sacrifices (20:28; 34:6; Hs 4:13). This verse affirms that the righteous person would not be involved in idolatrous practices (**does not eat at the mountain shrines**). An Aramaic translation of this verse suggests that what was forbidden was "eating sacrifices of the dead." To draw **near a woman** is a euphemism for sexual intercourse (Lv 18:14; Dt 22:14; Is 8:3).

18:7 On **returns his collateral to the debtor**, see Ex 22:26; Dt 24:12-13. **Robbery** refers to the seizure of property, usually by the rich (Is 3:14; 10:2; Mc 2:2).

18:8 This moral statute not to **lend at interest** is based on Lv 25:36-37. The law prohibited charging interest on loans made to fellow Israelites (Ex 22:25; Lv 25:35-37; Dt 23:19-20). Deuteronomy 23:20 allowed an Israelite to charge interest to a foreigner.

18:9 Because a person was called **righteous** in the OT does not mean that he was sinless or that he kept the law in every detail. It does affirm that he was a willing member of the covenant community who obeyed the ordinances of community life and sought atonement through the sacrificial system when he violated a law (Jb 1:1; Php 3:6). For the righteous person in the OT, to **live** refers to life in all its fullness. A meaningful life is one that enjoys the fullness of relationship with God and thus includes communion with God (Ps 63:3; 73:27-28). The expression of Ezk 18:9 does not advocate "works righteousness." Salvation has always been by faith (Hab 2:4). However, there is no real faith where there are no real works of righteousness (Jms 2:17). God

¹¹though the father has done none of them. Indeed, when the son eats at the mountain shrines and defiles his neighbor's wife, ¹²and when he oppresses the poor and needy, commits robbery, and does not return collateral, and when he raises his eyes to the idols, commits detestable acts,ª ¹³and lends at interest or for profit, will he live? He will not live! Since he has committed all these detestable acts, he will certainly die. His blood will be on him.ᵇ

¹⁴"Now suppose he has a son who sees all the sins his father has committed, and though he sees them, he does not do likewise. ¹⁵He does not eat at the mountain shrines or raise his eyes to the idols of the house of Israel. He does not defile his neighbor's wife. ¹⁶He doesn't oppress anyone, hold collateral, or commit robbery. He gives his bread to the hungry and covers the naked with clothing. ¹⁷He keeps his hand from harming the poor, not taking interest or profit on a loan. He practices My ordinances and follows My statutes. Such a person will not die for his father's iniquity. He will certainly live.

¹⁸"As for his father, he will die for his own iniquity because he practiced fraud, robbed his brother, and did what was wrong among his people.ᶜ ¹⁹But you may ask, 'Why doesn't the son suffer punishment for the father's iniquity?'ᵈ Since the son has done what is just and right, carefully observing all My statutes, he will certainly live. ²⁰The person who sins is the one who will die.ᵉ A son won't suffer punishment for the father's iniquity, and a father won't suffer punishment for the son's iniquity.ᶠ The righteousness of the righteous person will be on him,ᵍ and the wickedness of the wicked person will be on him.ʰ

²¹"Now if the wicked person turns from all

ª18:12 Ezk 8:6,17
ᵇ18:13 Lv 20:9,11
ᶜ18:18 Ezk 3:18
ᵈ18:19 Ex 20:5
ᵉ18:20 Ezk 18:4
ᶠDt 24:16; Jn 9:2
ᵍIs 3:10-11
ʰRm 2:6-9
ⁱ18:21 Ezk 33:12,19
ʲ18:22 Ezk 33:16
ᵏPs 18:20-24
ˡ18:23 Ezk 33:11
ᵐ18:24 Ezk 3:20; 33:18
ⁿ2Pt 2:20
ᵒ18:25 Ezk 18:29; 33:17,20
ᵖ18:30 Ezk 7:3,8; 33:20

the sins he has committed,ⁱ keeps all My statutes, and does what is just and right, he will certainly live; he will not die. ²²None of the transgressions he has committed will be held against him.ʲ He will live because of the righteousness he has practiced.ᵏ ²³Do I take any pleasure in the death of the wicked?"ˡ This is the declaration of the Lord GOD. "Instead, don't I take pleasure when he turns from his ways and lives? ²⁴But when a righteous person turns from his righteousnessᵐ and practices iniquity, committing the same detestable acts that the wicked do, will he live? None of the righteous acts he did will be remembered.ⁿ He will die because of the treachery he has engaged in and the sin he has committed.

²⁵"But you say, 'The Lord's way isn't fair.'ᵒ Now listen, house of Israel: Is it My way that is unfair? Instead, isn't it your ways that are unfair? ²⁶When a righteous person turns from his righteousness and practices iniquity, he will die for this. He will die because of the iniquity he has practiced. ²⁷But if a wicked person turns from the wickedness he has committed and does what is just and right, he will preserve his life. ²⁸He will certainly live because he thought it over and turned from all the transgressions he had committed; he will not die. ²⁹But the house of Israel says, 'The Lord's way isn't fair.' Is it My ways that are unfair, house of Israel? Instead, isn't it your ways that are unfair?

³⁰"Therefore, house of Israel, I will judge each one of you according to his ways."ᵖ This is the declaration of the Lord GOD. "Repent and turn from all your transgressions, so they will not be a stumbling block that causes your punishment. ³¹Throw off all the transgressions you have committed, and get yourselves

---

intends for good works to characterize His people. They are created in Christ for this purpose (Eph 2:10).

18:10 The phrase **sheds blood** occurs often in Ezekiel (16:38; 22:3,27; 23:45; 33:25). Its frequency indicates that human life was not valued among the Israelites at the time of the exile.

18:12 The **poor** and **needy** are often mentioned together in the OT (Dt 24:14; Jr 22:16; Ps 35:10; 37:14).

18:13 The expression **his blood will be on him** indicated that the one who performed a justified capital punishment (i.e., the executioner) was free of any guilt. The blame lay with the offender.

18:20 God's judgment does not recognize fathers and sons, only those who are **righteous** and those who are **wicked**.

18:21 True repentance involves confession, sorrow for sin, and a pledge to live an obedient life (Ps 51:1-12).

18:22 God will forgive and receive anyone who turns to Him

in repentance and faith, no matter the degree of his past rebellion (v. 21; Rm 5:6-11; Eph 2:1-8; Col 1:20-22; 2Pt 3:9). There is no reason for a person to live under condemnation for past sins if he is truly repentant and has experienced the new birth (Rm 8:1-17).

18:24 On turning from **righteousness** to **iniquity**, see Heb 2:3 and 2Pt 2:20-22. These verses contain warnings against those who knowingly and willfully turn from God. Those who are right with God will persevere to the end (Mt 10:22; 22:13; Mk 4:1-20).

18:30 Every person will face a final judgment in which obedience to God's commands will be fairly and justly evaluated.

18:31 What had been promised earlier in the book (11:19) is viewed now as attainable but not inevitable. Later in the book of Ezekiel (36:26-27) the people of Israel are promised **a new heart and a new spirit**. In this verse the people are commanded to obtain these new qualities. In similar fashion, Dt 10:16 commands God's people to circumcise

a new heart and a new spirit.[a] Why should you die, house of Israel? [32] For I take no pleasure in anyone's death." This is the declaration of the Lord God. "So repent and live!

A Lament for Israel's Princes

19 "Now, lament for the princes of Israel[b] [2] and say:

> What was your mother? A lioness!
> She lay down among the lions;
> she reared her cubs
>   among the young lions.
> [3] She brought up one of her cubs,
> and he became a young lion.[c]
> After he learned to tear prey,
> he devoured people.
> [4] When the nations heard about him,
> he was caught in their pit.
> Then they led him away with hooks
> to the land of Egypt.[d]
>
> [5] When she saw that she waited in vain,
> that her hope was lost,
> she took another of her cubs
> and made him a young lion.
> [6] He prowled among the lions,[e]
> and he became a young lion.
> After he learned to tear prey,
> he devoured people.
> [7] He devastated their strongholds[A]
> and destroyed their cities.

> The land and everything
>   in it shuddered
> at the sound of his roaring.
> [8] Then the nations from
>   the surrounding provinces
> set out against him.[f]
> They spread their net over him;
> he was caught in their pit.
> [9] They put a wooden yoke on him[B]
>   with hooks[g]
> and led him away to the king
>   of Babylon.
> They brought him into the fortresses
> so his roar could no longer be heard
> on the mountains of Israel.[h]
>
> [10] Your mother was like a vine
>   in your vineyard,[C,i]
> planted by the water;
> it was fruitful and full of branches[j]
> because of plentiful waters.
> [11] It had strong branches, fit for
>   the scepters of rulers;
> its height towered among the clouds.[D]
> So it was conspicuous for its height
> as well as its many branches.
> [12] But it was uprooted in fury,[k]
> thrown to the ground,
> and the east wind dried up its fruit.
> Its strong branches were torn off
>   and dried up;[l]
> fire consumed them.

---

*a*18:31 Jr 32:39
*b*19:1 Ezk 26:17; 27:2
*c*19:3 2Kg 23:31-32
*d*19:4-5 2Kg 23:34
*e*19:6 Jr 22:13-17
*f*19:8 2Kg 24:2,11
*g*19:9 2Ch 36:6
*h*Ezk 6:2
*i*19:10 Ps 80:8-11
*j*Dt 8:7-9
*k*19:12 Jr 31:28
*l*Hs 13:15

A19:7 Tg, Aq; MT reads *knew their widows*   **B**19:9 Or *put him in a cage*   **C**19:10 Some Hb mss; other Hb mss read *blood*   **D**19:11 Or *thick foliage*

---

the whole heart, which Dt 30:6 says is accomplished by the Lord. This same tension between human obligation and divine grant is also found in the NT (Php 2:12-13).

18:32 In every generation the church must be warned of a coming future judgment. This warning is meant to affect how we live (Rm 14:10,12; 2Co 5:10; Gl 6:7-8). Though believers are spared from eternal punishment, there are consequences for ongoing disobedience (Rm 11:22; 1Co 15:2; Col 1:23; Heb 3:14).

19:1 Sad songs of the type found in chapter 19 are known in Hebrew by the name *qinah*, which means "funeral dirge" or "funerary **lament**." They have a unique meter, and their content is similar to modern eulogies (2Sm 1:19-27). The switch of subjects from Ezekiel 18 seems to indicate that the emphasis on individual responsibility also applies to the monarchy of Judah. This chapter would therefore indicate that the house of David fell not because of the sins of past kings (Josiah was righteous), but because of the sins of the kings during the time leading up to the exile. The pronouncement of this rejection in the form of the funeral lament suggests that the house of David had been overwhelmed by the powers of death.

19:2 The **mother** in this allegory is the nation of Israel, who had produced the kings of the nation.

19:3 Genesis 49:9 seems to be the background for Judah, the royal line, being compared to a **lion**. In the Balaam ora-

cles, the nation itself is compared to a lion (Nm 23:24; 24:9). The first cub-king represents Jehoahaz, son of Josiah. He was crowned by the people after Josiah's death but was almost immediately deposed by Pharaoh Neco. He was then brought in fetters to Egypt after reigning only three months (2Kg 23:30-34).

19:4 The expression **they led him away with hooks** is also found in an Assyrian inscription that describes captives being led away during the reign of King Ashurbanipal.

19:5-9 This **lion** displayed greater power than the first by tearing down strongholds and devastating towns. The nations trapped him also, leading him with hooks to the land of Babylon. This second lion appears to refer to Jehoiachin. After a reign of only three months and ten days (2Ch 36:9), Jehoiachin was imprisoned in Babylon for 37 years until the Babylonian king Evil-Merodach released him. Jehoiakim died in Jerusalem, so he was not included in this lament (2Kg 25:27-30; Jr 52:31-34).

19:10 Ezekiel used the vine metaphor in 15:1-8 and 17:5-10 with reference to the decline and fall of Judah (Is 24:7; Jr 2:21; 6:9). But this imagery of the **vine** typifies the nation of Israel as a whole (Ps 80:8-16; Is 5:1-7; 27:2-6). The combination of lion and vine may be derived from Gn 49:9-11.

19:12 The **east wind** represents Nebuchadnezzar of Babylon and his army. The image refers to the capture and death

¹³ Now it is planted in the wilderness,^a
in a dry and thirsty land.
¹⁴ Fire has gone out from its
main branch^A
and has devoured its fruit,
so that it no longer has
a strong branch,
a scepter for ruling.^b

This is a lament and should be used as a lament."

Israel's Rebellion

20 In the seventh year, in the fifth month, on the tenth day of the month, some of Israel's elders came to consult the Lord,^c and they sat down in front of me. ²Then the word of the Lord came to me: ³"Son of man, speak with the elders of Israel and tell them: This is what the Lord God says: Are you coming to consult Me? As I live, I will not be con-

^a19:13 2Kg 24:12-16; Hs 2:3
^b19:14 Lm 2:5
^c20:1 Ezk 8:1,11-12; 14:1
^d20:3 Ezk 14:3
^e20:4 Ezk 16:2; 22:2
^f20:5 Ex 6:6-8
^gEx 6:2-3
^h20:6 Jr 32:22
ⁱEx 3:8
^jPs 16:6; 48:2; 50:2; Jr 3:19
^k20:7 Lv 18:3
^lEx 20:2

sulted by you."^d This is the declaration of the Lord God.

⁴"Will you pass judgment against them, will you pass judgment, son of man? Explain the detestable practices of their fathers to them.^e ⁵Say to them: This is what the Lord God says: On the day I chose Israel, I swore an oath^{B,f} to the descendants of Jacob's house and made Myself known to them in the land of Egypt. I swore to them, saying: I am •Yahweh your God.^g ⁶On that day I swore^c to them that I would bring them out^h of the land of Egypt into a land I had searched out for them, a land flowing with milk and honey,ⁱ the most beautiful of all lands.^j ⁷I also said to them: Each of you must throw away the detestable things that are before your eyes and not defile yourselves with the idols of Egypt.^k I am Yahweh your God.^l

⁸"But they rebelled against Me and were unwilling to listen to Me. None of them threw

---

^A19:14 Lit *from the branch of its parts*　^B20:5 Lit *I lifted My hand*　^C20:6 Lit *lifted My hand*

---

of King Zedekiah and the destruction of Jerusalem in the siege of 586 B.C.

19:13 Zedekiah was captured in the desert (**wilderness**) near Jericho, blinded, bound in chains, and taken to Babylon (2Kg 25; Jr 52).

19:14 Fire destroying the **fruit** of the vine recalls the image of Jotham's fable, in which the worthless bramble caused a fire that consumed the cedars of Lebanon (Jdg 9:20). The Davidic dynasty and the Israelite monarchy appear to come to a sudden end in Zedekiah. Fire is alternatively a symbol for annihilation or ongoing punishment (Gn 19:24; Jr 50:32; Am 1:4,7,10,12,14; 2:2,5; 7:4; Mt 25:41; Rv 20:14). The **scepter** will be temporarily removed from Judah as a punishment for sins. In the person of Christ, however, God's promise that the scepter will not depart from the line of Judah (Gn 49:10) will be ultimately fulfilled.

20:1 As in 8:1 and 14:1, a delegation of **elders** came to Ezek-

chemah

Hebrew Pronunciation	[khay MAH]
HCSB Translation	wrath, anger, fury
Uses in Ezekiel	33
Uses in the OT	125
Focus passage	Ezekiel 20:8,13,21,33-34

The Hebrew meanings for this root match those found in other languages. *Chemah* seems related to *yacham* (6x), to be sexually hot and *conceive* (Ps 51:5) or *breed* (Gn 30:38), and *chamam* (23x), *to be warm* or *grow hot* (Ex 16:21). Similarly *chammah* (6x) means *heat* (Ps 19:7) or *sun* (Sg 6:10). *Chemah* is the word most commonly translated *wrath* (Nm 25:11), over 60 times. It describes God's *wrath*, six times in the phrase "*chemah* of the Lord" (Jr 6:11), but also human *wrath*. *Chemah* often appears as *fury* (Dt 29:28), *rage* (2Kg 5:12), and *anger* (Gn 27:44). It occurs (38x) alongside nearly synonymous *ap* ("anger"; Ezk 22:20). *Chemah* signifies *heat* (Hs 7:5), *poison* (Jb 6:4), or *venom* (Dt 32:33). It implies *burning* (Ezk 36:6), *venomous* (Dt 32:24), *fierce* (Dt 9:19), *hot-tempered* (Pr 15:18), or *furious* (Lv 26:28). Once it is *burning wrath* (Jr 7:20).

iel's home seeking an oracle from the Lord. It had been almost 11 months since the vision of the abominations of the temple in 8:1.

20:4 Like chapters 16 and 23, chapter 20 presents a negative view of Israel's history, but unlike them, it does not use allegory.

20:5 The phrase **I swore an oath** is literally "I raise my hand in oath." The uplifted hand (vv. 5,15,23,42) was apparently a gesture used when a person made an oath (36:7; 44:12; 47:14; Ex 6:8; Neh 9:15; Ps 106:26). The phrase **descendants of Jacob's house** is a reference to all Israel (i.e., Israel and Judah; see 37:25). The statement **made Myself known to them in the land of Egypt** recalls the Lord's encounter with Moses in Ex 6:3, where God swore by oath and revealed the meaning of His name. Ezekiel portrayed the Israelites in Egypt, not the patriarchs, the recipients of the oath. Israel's history as a nation began in Egypt where God chose her. He took an oath to bring His people into the fruitful and glorious land that He had promised Abraham (Gn 12:7; Ex 3:8,13-18; 6:1-8; Jr 3:19).

20:6 Though one would expect the Hebrew term *nathan* ("give") in the phrase **a land I had searched out for them**, the verb *tur* ("search") is used instead. This term is taken from the desert wandering accounts, where the Lord went before the Israelites, scouting places for them to rest or camp (Dt 1:33; Nm 10:33). The phrase **a land flowing with milk and honey** occurs in Ex 3:8,17; 13:5; 33:3; Lv 20:24; Nm 13:27; Dt 6:3; 11:9; 26:9; 27:3; Jos 5:6; Jr 11:5; 32:22 (cp. Dt 1:25; 8:7-9). Deuteronomy 8:7-10 and Jr 3:19 describe the natural beauty of the land of Israel. Its true significance, however, was its designation as God's dwelling place (Dt 12:5,11).

20:7 The **idols of Egypt** became Israel's idols as well. Joshua 24:14 also mentions that the Israelites had worshiped foreign gods. On Israel's idolatry in Egypt, see Lv 17:7; 18:3; Ps 106:7; Ezk 23:3; Am 5:25-27.

20:8 Their act of ignoring the word of the Lord (**unwilling to listen to Me**) demonstrated the inward attitude of the people toward God.

away the detestable things that were before their eyes, and they did not forsake the idols of Egypt. So I considered pouring out My wrath on them,[a] exhausting My anger against them within the land of Egypt. [9] But I acted because of My name,[b] so that it would not be profaned in the eyes of the nations they were living among, in whose sight I had made Myself known to Israel by bringing them out of Egypt.

[10] "So I brought them out of the land of Egypt and led them into the wilderness.[c] [11] Then I gave them My statutes and explained My ordinances to them—the person who does them will live by them.[d] [12] I also gave them My Sabbaths to serve as a sign between Me and them,[e] so they will know that I am Yahweh who sets them apart as holy.

[13] "But the house of Israel rebelled against Me in the wilderness.[f] They did not follow My statutes and they rejected My ordinances—the person who does them will live by them.[g] They also completely profaned My Sabbaths.[h] So I considered pouring out My wrath on them in the wilderness to put an end to them.[i] [14] But I acted because of My name, so that it would not be profaned in the eyes of the nations in whose sight I had brought them out. [15] However, I swore[A] to them[j] in the wilderness that I would not bring them into the land I had given them—the most beautiful of all lands, flowing with milk and honey— [16] because they rejected My ordinances, profaned My Sabbaths, and did not follow My statutes.

For their hearts went after their idols.[k] [17] But I spared them from destruction and did not bring them to an end in the wilderness.[l]

[18] "Then I said to their children in the wilderness: Don't follow the statutes of your fathers, defile yourselves with their idols, or keep their ordinances.[m] [19] I am Yahweh your God. Follow My statutes, keep My ordinances, and practice them.[n] [20] Keep My Sabbaths holy,[o] and they will be a sign between Me and you, so you may know that I am Yahweh your God.

[21] "But the children rebelled against Me.[p] They did not follow My statutes or carefully keep My ordinances—the person who does them will live by them. They also profaned My Sabbaths. So I considered pouring out My wrath on them and exhausting My anger against them in the wilderness. [22] But I withheld My hand and acted because of My name, so that it would not be profaned in the eyes of the nations in whose sight I brought them out. [23] However, I swore[A] to them in the wilderness that I would disperse them among the nations and scatter them among the countries.[q] [24] For they did not practice My ordinances but rejected My statutes and profaned My Sabbaths, and their eyes were fixed[r] on their fathers' idols. [25] I also gave them statutes that were not good and ordinances[s] they could not live by. [26] When they made every firstborn pass through the fire,[t] I defiled them through their gifts in order to devastate them so they would know that I am Yahweh.[u]

[27] "Therefore, son of man, speak to the house

a 20:8 Ezk 5:13; 7:8
b 20:9 Ezk 36:21-22
c 20:10 Ex 13:18,20
d 20:11 Lv 18:5; Rm 10:5; Gl 3:12
e 20:12 Ex 31:13
f 20:13 Nm 14:11-12,22
g Lv 18:5
h Ezk 22:8; 23:38; 44:24
i Ex 32:10; Dt 9:8
j 20:15 Nm 14:28-30
k 20:16 Ezk 11:21; 14:3-7
l 20:17 Ezk 11:13
m 20:18 Mt 15:1-3
n 20:19 Dt 5:32-33
o 20:20 Jr 17:22
p 20:21 Nm 21:5; 25:1-3
q 20:23 Lv 26:33
r 20:24 Ezk 6:9
s 20:25 Ps 81:12; Rm 1:21-25,28
t 20:26 Lv 18:21
u Ezk 6:7

A 20:15,23 Lit lifted My hand

20:9 God's **name** would be degraded if He did not perform what He had proposed for the nation of Israel. Moses had used this same argument effectively in His intercession for Israel after the golden calf incident and in the wilderness (Ex 32:12; Nm 14:16).

20:10 The reference to **the wilderness** evokes the judgments God had to execute upon His rebellious people (Ex 32:15-35; Nm 11; 14:10-38; 16:31-50; Ps 106:7-48).

20:11 The phrase **the person who does them will live by them** appears to come from Lv 18:5. Deuteronomy 30:15-19 states forcefully that to follow the commandments is to choose life and blessing; not to follow them is to choose death and curse. Obedience of the law was the response of a person who realized how much God loved him. This truth is similar to Jesus' statement, "If you love Me, you will keep My commands" (Jn 14:15).

20:12 The prophet, in harmony with Is 58:13-14 and with Moses himself (Ex 20:8-11), commanded the Israelites to sanctify the Sabbath. The Sabbath was a visible manifestation of the Mosaic covenant (Is 56:1-8). With its regular one-day-in-seven observance, the Sabbath was at cross-purposes with the nature-based calendars of the pagans, which revolved around the seasons and phases of the moon. The Sabbath was a perpetual reminder of Yahweh's covenant with His people.

20:13 The Sabbath was **profaned** if it was not observed (Jr 17:21-23) or was improperly observed (Am 8:5).

20:15 The phrase **I swore to them** is literally "I lifted up my hand." The upraised hand was used earlier in reference to God's oath to bring the chosen people into the promised land (v. 5). Now the expression is used to refer to the solemn oath that this generation would never enter (v. 15). Later, Ezekiel used the formula to describe God's announcement that the people would go into exile (v. 23).

20:16 Israel failed at one point to enter the land of Canaan because of unbelief (Nm 14) expressed in four specific violations: they **rejected My ordinances, profaned My Sabbaths . . . did not follow My statutes . . . went after their idols**.

20:21 The rebellion of the second generation refers to acts of apostasy following the incident of the spies, particularly the events at Meribah (Nm 20) and Baal Peor (Nm 25).

20:23 The Pentateuch is silent about this remarkable oath (**I swore**) to exile the people, but it is alluded to in Ps 106:27. God made this oath before His people had even entered the land.

20:25-27 One of the ways that God punishes sin is to abandon people to it, so that they suffer its consequences. Thus the **statutes** and **ordinances** in this verse refer to the futile and blameworthy commandments of the pagan religions to

of Israel, and tell them: This is what the Lord God says: In this way also your fathers blasphemed Me by^a committing treachery against Me: ²⁸When I brought them into the land that I swore^A to give them and they saw any high hill or leafy tree,^b they offered their sacrifices and presented their offensive offerings there. They also sent up their pleasing aromas and poured out their ˙drink offerings there. ²⁹So I asked them: What is this ˙high place you are going to? And it is called High Place to this day.

³⁰"Therefore say to the house of Israel: This is what the Lord God says: Are you defiling yourselves the way your fathers did,^c and prostituting yourselves with their detestable things? ³¹When you offer your gifts, making your children pass through the fire,^d you continue to defile yourselves with all your idols to this day. So should I be consulted by you, house of Israel? As I live"—this is the declaration of the Lord God—"I will not be consulted by you!

Israel's Restoration

³²"When you say, 'Let us be like the nations, like the peoples of other countries, worshiping wood and stone,'^e what you have in mind will never happen.^f ³³As I live"—the declaration of the Lord God—"I will rule over you with a strong hand, an outstretched arm,^g and outpoured wrath. ³⁴I will bring you from the peoples and gather you from the countries where you were scattered,^h with a strong hand, an outstretched arm,ⁱ and outpoured wrath. ³⁵I will lead you into the wilderness of the peoples^j and enter into judgment with you there face to face. ³⁶Just as I entered into judgment with your fathers in the wilderness of the land of Egypt,^k so I will enter into judgment with you." This is the declaration of the Lord God. ³⁷"I will make you pass under the rod^l and will bring you into the bond of the covenant. ³⁸And I will also purge you of those who rebel and transgress against Me.^m I will bring them out of the land where they live as foreign residents, but they will not enter the land of Israel. Then you will know that I am Yahweh.

³⁹"As for you, house of Israel, this is what the Lord God says: Go and serve your idols, each of you. But afterward you will surely listen to Me, and you will no longer defile My holy name with your gifts and idols.ⁿ ⁴⁰For on My holy mountain, Israel's high mountain"—the declaration of the Lord God—"there the entire house of Israel, all of them,^o will serve

---

^a20:27 Rm 2:24
^b20:28 Ezk 6:13
^c20:30 Jdg 2:19;
Jr 7:26; 16:12
^d20:31 Ezk
16:20
^e20:32 Dt 4:28;
2Kg 19:18; Rv
9:20
^fEzk 11:5
^g20:33 Jr 21:5
^h20:34 Jr 31:8;
Ezk 36:24; 37:21
ⁱEx 6:6; Dt 4:34
^j20:35 Ezk 19:13
^k20:36 Nm
14:21-23,28
^l20:37 Lv 27:32;
Jr 33:13
^m20:38 Ezk
34:17-22
ⁿ20:39 Is 1:13-
15; Ezk 23:38-39
^o20:40 Ezk
37:22,24

---

^A20:28 Lit *lifted My hand*

---

which Israel had turned. These laws "required" the Israelites to sacrifice every firstborn (v. 26), a practice condemned by God (Lv 20:1-5). These statutes and ordinances devastated rather than blessed the people who obeyed them. In Ezk 14:9 God said He intentionally deceived false prophets. Similarly, the present passage says God gave the rebellious people worthless and unprofitable statutes (cp. Is 63:17). Ongoing disobedience leads to ever greater sin, until God finally turns people over to deception (Ps 81:12; Ezk 14:9; Ac 7:42; Rm 1:24-25; 2Th 2:11). Even in judgment, the rebellious came to **know** that God is **Yahweh**. The phrase **they made every firstborn pass through the fire** refers to the child sacrifices made by followers of the pagan god Molech. According to pagan perception, sacrifices made to a god put that god in your debt, such that he or she was bound to act favorably toward you.

20:28 These practices were common in pagan worship (Dt 12:2; 2Kg 16:4; Jr 3:6; 17:2; Hs 4:13).

20:30 The primary apostasy of the nation of Israel was idolatry—violation of the first commandment. This transgression demonstrated Israel's rebelliousness, and it was a clear violation of the covenant. The history of Israel from its very beginnings is a history of turning from God. All humans, no matter their nationality or ethnicity, share in the same sin nature that leads to this rebellion.

20:32 Here we find an allusion to the account of the choice of the initial Israelite king in 1 Samuel 8. This led to the election of Saul as Israel's first king. The designation of the heathen gods as **wood and stone** should have been enough to signal that these heathen gods were mere fictions. The same expression occurs in Dt 4:28; 28:36.

20:33 The phrase **as I live** recalls the language of Ex 6:6, which describes God's opposition to Egypt and its pharaoh. A **strong hand** and **outstretched arm** calls to mind God's strength in delivering His people from Egypt (Dt 4:34; 5:15; 7:19; 11:2; 26:8; Ps 136:12). Ironically, now His hand and arm will bring wrath rather than deliverance for His people.

20:34 The phrase **I will bring you from the peoples** that describes Israel's exodus from Egypt is now given a new twist. The ferocity that was once unleashed upon Egypt will now be turned against rebellious Israel to force her to accept God's kingship over her in the land.

20:35 Israel's exile among the nations is compared to the **wilderness** tradition in the book of Numbers. God's restoration of Israel would be like a return to the desert through which she journeyed on her way to the promised land (Hs 2:14).

20:37 The phrase **pass under the rod** appears to be an allusion to the Levitical law of counting animals for the tithe (Lv 27:32-33). While the selection in Leviticus was for dedication, here it is for destruction. God uses this metaphor to portray the purge of Israel that will take place when the temple is destroyed.

20:39 Desecrations of the **holy name** are recorded in Lv 18:21; 20:3; 21:6; 22:32.

20:40 The phrase **on My holy mountain** occurs only here in the book of Ezekiel. It refers to Jerusalem or Zion (Ps 2:6; 3:4; 15:1; Is 11:9; 56:7; 57:13; 65:11; Ob 16; Zph 3:11). The reference to the high mountain of Israel in Ezk 17:22-23 and 40:2 also relates to Jerusalem, anticipating a renewed Israel at worship on a high mountain in chapters 40–48. The

Me in the land. There I will accept them and will require your contributions and choicest gifts,[a] all your holy offerings. [41]When I bring you from the peoples and gather you from the countries where you have been scattered, I will accept you as a pleasing aroma. And I will demonstrate My holiness through you in the sight of the nations.[b] [42]When I lead you into the land of Israel, the land I swore[A] to give your fathers, you will know that I am Yahweh.[c] [43]There you will remember your ways and all your deeds that you have defiled yourselves with,[d] and you will loathe yourselves for all the evil things you have done.[e] [44]You will know that I am Yahweh,[f] house of Israel, when I have dealt with you because of My name[g] rather than according to your evil ways and corrupt acts." This is the declaration of the Lord GOD.

Fire in the South

[45B] The word of the LORD came to me: [46]"Son of man, face the south and preach against it. Prophesy against the forest land in the •Negev,[h] [47]and say to the forest there: Hear the word of the LORD! This is what the Lord GOD says: I am about to ignite a fire in you, and it will devour every green tree and every dry tree in you. The blazing flame will not be extin-

[a]20:40 Is 60:7; Ezk 43:27
[b]20:41 Is 5:16; Ezk 28:25; 2Co 6:17
[c]20:42 Ezk 36:23; 38:23
[d]20:43 Ezk 6:9; 16:61,63
[e]Ezk 36:31
[f]20:44 Ezk 24:24
[g]Ezk 36:22
[h]20:46 Ezk 21:2
[i]20:48 Jr 21:14
[j]20:49 Ezk 17:2
[k]21:2 Ezk 20:46
[l]21:3 Ezk 5:8
[m]21:4 Ezk 7:2; 20:47
[n]21:5 Ezk 21:30
[o]21:7 Ezk 7:26

guished, and every face from the south to the north will be scorched by it. [48]Then all people will see that I, Yahweh, have kindled it.[i] It will not be extinguished."

[49]Then I said, "Oh, Lord GOD, they are saying of me, 'Isn't he just posing riddles?'"[j]

God's Sword of Judgment

21[c] The word of the LORD came to me again: [2]"Son of man, turn your face toward[k] Jerusalem and preach against the sanctuaries. Prophesy against the land of Israel, [3]and say to it: This is what the LORD says: I am against you.[l] I will draw My sword from its sheath and cut off both the righteous and the wicked from you. [4]Since I will cut off[D] both the righteous and the wicked, My sword will therefore come out of its sheath against everyone from the south to the north.[m] [5]So all the people will know that I, •Yahweh, have taken My sword from its sheath—it will not be sheathed again.[n]

[6]"But you, son of man, groan! Groan bitterly with a broken heart[E] right before their eyes. [7]And when they ask you, 'Why are you groaning?' then say: Because of the news that is coming.[o] Every heart will melt, and every hand will become weak. Every spirit will be discouraged, and every knee will turn to wa-

---

[A]20:42 Lit *lifted My hand*   [B]20:45 Ezk 21:1 in Hb   [C]21:1 Ezk 21:6 in Hb   [D]21:4 Lit *off from you*   [E]21:6 Lit *with broken loins*

---

term *serve* is a technical word for priestly ministry. Thus this expression (**serve Me in the land**) is in harmony with the goal established at Mount Sinai—that the created nation would be a kingdom of priests (Ex 19:6).

20:41 The Lord will accept the people as a soothing or **pleasing aroma**, an expression used of God's response to an animal sacrifice. Only here in the OT is the expression used in reference to people as a "soothing aroma." This paves the way for Paul's application of the expression to the church in 2Co 2:14-16. In Eph 5:2 the term refers to Christ.

20:43 Ezekiel's expression **you will loathe yourselves for all the evil things you have done** describes a thorough repentance (6:9; 16:63; 36:31; Lk 15:17-19). Such a humiliating experience was the surest antidote against the pride that had led Israel again and again to rebel against God. Perceiving God in His holiness and majesty causes one to abhor one's sinful ways (Jb 42:5-6; Is 6:5).

20:44 The first fulfillment of this promise (**when I have dealt with you because of My name**) took place immediately after the exile. It also awaits a future fulfillment, according to Paul in Rm 11:25. When used in application to morality, the term **corrupt acts** occurs elsewhere only in Gn 6:11-12 where it describes the corruption of the human race before the flood.

20:46 The orientation in the phrase **face the south and preach against it** would be from the north, the direction of a Babylonian invasion.

20:47 The prophetic image of **fire** for judgment is particularly evident in Amos 1-2. It has already been used by Ezekiel in connection with the covenant metaphor of the vine (Ezk 15:4-

7; cp. 19:12,14). Fire is routinely a means of divine punishment in the Bible (Gn 14:23-28; Dt 28:24; 32:22; Rv 20:15).

21:2 Every time the phrase **son of man, turn your face toward** appears, it is in a judgment context. In Lk 9:51 the Son of Man, Jesus, "determined (lit "turned His face") to go to Jerusalem" against which He soon announced judgment (Lk 19:41; 21:20-24).

21:3 God's opposition to His people is expressed by the image of the drawn **sword**, the common way of referring to warfare in the OT. History would prove that God's drawn sword was King Nebuchadnezzar of Babylon and his armies. The sword refers to divine judgment in Is 31:8; 34:6; and 66:16.

21:4 No one will survive the coming invasion, not even the **righteous**. The Bible advocates corporate responsibility. The principle is illustrated in the case of Achan (Jos 7:1-26; see Ezk 18:1-4). For Judah as a nation, it was too late to repent; destruction was decreed. Individuals could repent and have assurance of eternal life, but many righteous people were going to be swept up in the coming destruction. Even today, Christians should not assume that God will preserve the righteous from general disasters or judgments against nations.

21:5 Ezekiel's prophecies against foreign nations declared repeatedly that they would be annihilated "that they may **know** that I am **Yahweh**" (25:7,11,17; 26:6; 39:6). The same paradox occurs in the exodus story. For example, in Ex 14:4 God declared that He would destroy Pharaoh and his army so that the Egyptians would know that He was Lord. God will not bring upon His people a partial defeat and exile this

ter. Yes, it is coming and it will happen." This is the declaration of the Lord God.

[8] The word of the Lord came to me: [9] "Son of man, prophesy: This is what the Lord says! You are to proclaim:

A sword![a] A sword is sharpened
and also polished.[b]
[10] It is sharpened for slaughter,
polished to flash like lightning!
Should we rejoice?
The scepter of My son,
the sword despises every tree.[A]
[11] The sword is given to be polished,
to be grasped in the hand.
It is sharpened, and it is polished,
to be put in the hand of the slayer.[c]
[12] Cry out and wail, son of man,
for it is against My people.
It is against all the princes of Israel!
They are given over to the sword
with My people.
Therefore strike your thigh in grief.[d]
[13] Surely it will be a trial!
And what if the sword despises
even the scepter?
The scepter will not continue.[A]
This is the declaration
of the Lord God.
[14] Therefore, son of man, prophesy
and clap your hands together.[e]
Let the sword strike two times,
even three.
It is a sword for massacre,
a sword for great massacre—
it surrounds[B] them!

[15] I have appointed a sword[f]
for slaughter[A]
at all their gates,
so that their hearts may melt
and many may stumble.
Yes! It is ready to flash like lightning;[g]
it is drawn[A] for slaughter.
[16] Slash to the right;
turn to the left—
wherever your blade is directed.
[17] I also will clap My hands together,
and I will satisfy My wrath.[h]
I, Yahweh, have spoken."

[18] Then the word of the Lord came to me: [19] "Now you, son of man, mark out two roads that the sword of Babylon's king can take. Both of them should originate from the same land. And make a signpost at the fork in the road to each city. [20] Mark out a road that the sword can take to Rabbah of the Ammonites[i] and to Judah into fortified Jerusalem. [21] For the king of Babylon stands at the split in the road, at the fork of the two roads, to practice •divination: he shakes the arrows, consults the idols, and observes the liver. [22] The answer marked[c] Jerusalem appears in his right hand, indicating that he should set up battering rams,[j] give the order to[D] slaughter, raise a battle cry, set battering rams against the gates, build a ramp, and construct a siege wall. [23] It will seem like false divination in the eyes of those who have sworn an oath to the Babylonians,[E,k] but it will draw attention to their •guilt so that they will be captured.

[24] "Therefore, this is what the Lord God says: Because you have drawn attention to

[a]21:9 Dt 32:41
[b]Jr 46:4
[c]21:11 Ezk 21:19
[d]21:12 Jr 31:19
[e]21:14 Nm 24:10
[f]21:15 Ezk 32:20
[g]Ezk 21:28
[h]21:17 Ezk 5:13
[i]21:20 Jr 49:2
[j]21:22 Ezk 4:2; 26:9
[k]21:23 Ezk 17:16,18

[A]21:10,13,15 Hb obscure   [B]21:14 Or penetrates   [C]21:22 Lit The divination for   [D]21:22 Lit rams, open the mouth in
[E]21:23 Lit them

time, as was the case in 598 b.c. when Ezekiel was exiled. This time, God will finish the job through His agent, the Babylonians.

21:10 The **scepter** symbolized the Lord's covenant promise to David that his house would have eternal title to the throne of Jerusalem (2Sm 7). This promise was rooted in the blessing spoken by Jacob, which said that the scepter would never pass from Judah (Gn 49:10). This interpretation is reinforced by the Hebrew phrase beni (**My son**), an echo of Gn 49:9 and 2Sm 7:14. Judah's hope in the midst of judgment was that the ultimate "scepter of Judah," the Messiah, would never be extinguished.

21:14 In verse 17 the act of clapping the **hands together** is associated with God's wrath. It should also be viewed here as an expression of anger (6:11). The mention of **three** strikes of the **sword** may refer to the three attacks and deportations that the Babylonians launched against Jerusalem in 605, 597, and 588–586 b.c.

21:20 Rabbah was the capital of Ammon (Jr 49:2). It is the location of modern Amman, the capital of Jordan. The com-

bined conspiracy of Judah and Ammon against Babylonia in 589 b.c. undoubtedly precipitated this coming of the Babylonian army (Jr 27:3).

21:21 The practice of shaking marked **arrows** in a quiver, letting them fall to the ground or shooting them into the distance and then interpreting the pattern, was known as belomancy (2Kg 13:15-19). It was a form of casting lots. The **idols** (Hb teraphim) appear to have been miniature household gods that were consulted even by Israelites (Gn 31:30; Hs 3:4; Zch 10:2). The examination of the **liver** of a sacrificial animal—called hepatoscopy and the best known of these practices in Mesopotamian literature—is mentioned only here in the OT. Though God did not condone divination in any form, as sovereign over the earth He controls all things. Thus in some sense even pagan practices could, by God's choice, reveal His will (Jnh 1:7).

21:23 Divination is expressly prohibited in Dt 18:10 and 2Kg 17:17. The phrase **sworn an oath to the Babylonians** probably refers to the treaty oaths made by Babylonia and Judah.

your guilt, exposing your transgressions, so that your sins are revealed in all your actions, since you have done this, you will be captured by them.

25 And you, profane and wicked prince of Israel,[A,a]
the day has come[b]
for your punishment."[B]

26 This is what the Lord God says:

Remove the turban, and take off
the crown.
Things will not remain as they are;[C]
exalt the lowly and bring down
the exalted.[c]
27 A ruin, a ruin,
I will make it a ruin!
Yet this will not happen
until He comes;[d]
I have given the judgment to Him.[D]

28 "Now prophesy, son of man, and say: This is what the Lord God says concerning the Ammonites and their contempt. You are to proclaim:

A sword! A sword
is drawn for slaughter,
polished to consume,[e] to flash
like lightning.
29 While they offer false visions[f]
and lying divinations about you,
the time has come to put you
to the necks of the profane
wicked ones;
the day has come
for your punishment.[B]

30 Return it to its sheath![g]

I will judge you[E]
in the place where you were created,
in the land of your origin.
31 I will pour out My indignation on you;
I will blow the fire of My fury on you.[h]
I will hand you over to brutal men,
skilled at destruction.
32 You will be fuel for the fire.
Your blood will be spilled in the land.
You will not be remembered,[i]
for I, Yahweh, have spoken."

Indictment of Sinful Jerusalem

22 The word of the Lord came to me: 2 "As for you, son of man, will you pass judgment? Will you pass judgment against the city of blood? Then explain all her detestable practices to her.[j] 3 You are to say: This is what the Lord God says: A city that sheds blood[k] within her walls so that her time of judgment has come and who makes idols for herself so that she is defiled. 4 You are •guilty of the blood you have shed,[l] and you are defiled from the idols you have made. You have brought your judgment days near and have come to your years of punishment. Therefore, I have made you a disgrace to the nations and a mockery to all the lands. 5 Those who are near and those far away from you will mock you, you infamous one full of turmoil.

6 "Look, every prince of Israel[m] within you has used his strength to shed blood. 7 Father and mother are treated with contempt,[n] and the foreign resident is exploited within you. The fatherless and widow are oppressed in

Cross references (center column):
a 21:25 2Kg 24:20
b Ezk 21:29
c 21:26 Ezk 17:24; Lk 1:52
d 21:27 Jr 23:5-6
e 21:28 Is 31:8; Jr 12:12; 46:10,14
f 21:29 Ezk 13:6-9; 22:28
g 21:30 Jr 47:6-7
h 21:31 Ezk 22:20-21
i 21:32 Ezk 25:10
j 22:2 Ezk 16:2; 20:4
k 22:3 Ezk 22:6,27; 23:37,45
l 22:4 2Kg 21:16
m 22:6 Is 1:23
n 22:7 Ex 20:12; Lv 20:9; Dt 27:16

A 21:25 = King Zedekiah   B 21:25,29 Lit come in the time of the punishment of the end   C 21:26 Lit This not this   D 21:27 Or comes to whom it rightfully belongs, and I will give it to Him   E 21:30 = the Ammonites

---

21:26 The **turban** was worn by priests, but it also served as a setting for the **crown** (Ex 28:36-37; 29:6; 39:31; Lv 8:9). The removal of these signs of dignity signifies degradation, as in Jb 19:9 and Lm 5:16. The removal of the priesthood and the kingship from Judah is symbolized by the removal of the high priest's turban (Ex 28:4,37,39; 29:6) and the king's crown.

21:27 The turban and the crown would not be worn again **until He comes**—a clear reference to Gn 49:10 and the king-priest Messiah (cp. Heb 5-7). Ezekiel used this reference with its messianic overtones to emphasize that the kingship (and priesthood) would be removed in judgment but returned ultimately in the Messiah's coming in accord with Gn 49:10 (Ps 2:6; Jr 23:5-6; Ezk 37:24; Zch 6:12-15).

21:31 The **fire** of the Lord's **fury** reflects the covenant curses. Fire was a symbol of divine judgment (Dt 28:24; 32:22).

22:2 Seven times in this prophecy (vv. 1-16) the words **blood** or "bloodshed" occur, suggesting that the crimes against God's covenant were routine as well as thoroughgoing in

Jerusalem. Rabbinic tradition relates this oracle to Manasseh's shedding of innocent blood in Jerusalem (2Kg 21:6). As in Ezekiel 18, the catalogue of crimes listed here derives especially from the Holiness Code in Leviticus 17–26. The **city** is personified as a person violating the Mosaic law. Verses 1-16 are very similar to Is 1:2-31 and may be an allusion to that prophetic text.

22:3 These two sins (**sheds blood . . . makes idols**) summarize the violation of the Ten Commandments which legislated stipulations about a person's relationship to God as well as to his fellow man. Rather than loving God, the city had turned to idolatry. Love for fellow Israelites had been replaced by treachery. The city's pouring out of blood is countered by God's pouring out of wrath (v. 22).

22:5 As a result of their lack of obedience, God had made them a reproach and a mockery to all the nations. Paul had the same concept in mind when he addressed Israel in Rm 2:24.

22:6 The indictment of verses 6-12 contains a catalogue of

you.[a] 8 You despise My holy things and profane
My Sabbaths.[b] 9 There are men within you
who slander in order to shed blood.[c] People
who live in you eat at the mountain shrines;
they commit immoral acts within you. 10 Men
within you have sexual intercourse with their
father's wife and violate women during their
menstrual impurity.[d] 11 One man within you
commits a detestable act with his neighbor's
wife;[e] another wickedly defiles his daughter-
in-law; and yet another violates his sister, his
father's daughter.[f] 12 People who live in you accept bribes in order to shed blood.[g] You take
interest and profit on a loan and brutally extort your neighbors.[h] You have forgotten Me."[i]
This is the declaration of the Lord GOD.
13 "Now look, I clap My hands together
against the dishonest profit you have made[j]
and against the blood shed among you. 14 Will
your courage endure[k] or your hands be strong
in the days when I deal with you? I, •Yahweh,
have spoken, and I will act.[l] 15 I will disperse
you among the nations and scatter you among
the countries;[m] I will purge your uncleanness.[n] 16 You[A] will be profaned in the sight of
the nations. Then you will know that I am
Yahweh."[o]

Jerusalem as God's Furnace

17 The word of the LORD came to me: 18 "Son
of man, the house of Israel has become dross
to Me.[p] All of them are copper, tin, iron, and
lead inside the furnace;[q] they are the dross of
silver. 19 Therefore, this is what the Lord GOD
says: Because all of you have become dross, I
am about to gather you into Jerusalem. 20 Just
as one gathers silver, copper, iron, lead, and
tin into the furnace to blow fire[r] on them and
melt them, so I will gather you in My anger
and wrath, put you inside, and melt you.
21 Yes, I will gather you together and blow on
you with the fire of My fury, and you will be
melted within the city. 22 As silver is melted inside a furnace, so you will be melted inside the
city. Then you will know that I, Yahweh, have
poured out My wrath on you."[s]

Indictment of a Sinful Land

23 The word of the LORD came to me: 24 "Son
of man, say to her: You are a land that has not
been cleansed,[t] that has not received rain in
the day of indignation. 25 The conspiracy of
her prophets[u] within her is[B] like a roaring
lion tearing its prey: they devour people, seize
wealth and valuables, and multiply the widows within her. 26 Her priests do violence to
My instruction and profane My holy things.[v]
They make no distinction between the holy
and the common, and they do not explain the
difference between the •clean and the •un-
clean.[w] They disregard[C] My Sabbaths, and I
am profaned among them.
27 "Her officials within her are like wolves
tearing their prey, shedding blood, and

[a] 22:7 Ex 22:22
[b] 22:8 Lv 19:30; Ezk 20:13
[c] 22:9 Lv 19:16
[d] 22:10 Lv 18:7-8,19
[e] 22:11 Ex 20:17; Ezk 18:11
[f] Lv 18:9,15; 20:17
[g] 22:12 Ex 23:8
[h] Lv 19:13; 25:36; Dt 23:19
[i] Ezk 23:35
[j] 22:13 Ezk 21:14,17
[k] 22:14 Ezk 21:7
[l] Ezk 17:24
[m] 22:15 Dt 4:27; Ezk 12:15
[n] Ezk 23:27,48
[o] 22:16 Ps 83:18; Ezk 6:7
[p] 22:18 Ps 119:119; Is 1:22
[q] Pr 17:3
[r] 22:20 Is 1:25
[s] 22:22 Ezk 20:8,33
[t] 22:24 Ezk 24:13
[u] 22:25 Jr 11:9; Hs 6:9
[v] 22:26 1Sm 2:12-17,22
[w] Lv 10:10

[A] 22:16 One Hb ms, LXX, Syr, Vg read *I* [B] 22:24-25 LXX reads *indignation,* [25] *whose princes within her are* [C] 22:26 Lit *close their eyes from*

sins based on the regulations in Leviticus 18–20. The kings are specifically indicted because it was their responsibility to make sure justice was administered in the community, especially by protecting the poor and weak (Ps 72:1-4).

22:7 The lack of concern for those in need (**fatherless and widow**) was a clear violation of the Mosaic covenant (Ex 22:20; 23:9,12; Dt 14:29; 16:11,14; 24:19-21; 26:12-19).

22:9 Leviticus 19:16 contains the only other occurrence of the legal word **slander** (Hb *rakil*) in the Bible. There it is also associated with bloodshed. Thus it is clear that Ezekiel was alluding to a legal stipulation that would have been well known to his audience. Ezekiel's use of the Hebrew word *zimmah* (**immoral acts**) to denote unchastity (vv. 9,11; 16:27,58; 23:21,27,35,44,48) followed the tradition in the Mosaic law (Lv 18:17-18; 19:29; 20:14).

22:10 The reference to **their father's wife** means stepmother rather than birthmother. Lewdness with one's stepmother is a violation of the law in Lv 20:11 (cp. 1Co 5:1; see Dt 22:30; Am 2:7).

22:11 All the sins mentioned in this verse were specifically forbidden in the law (Lv 18:7-20; 20:10-21; Dt 22:22-23,30; 27:22).

22:12 You have forgotten Me is the explanation for all the listed violations. Forgetting God is another way of saying that they have rejected His covenant (Dt 4:23; 8:19).

22:15 The residents of Jerusalem will be scattered all over the world (**among the countries**) if they continue to pursue disobedience. Moses had warned Israel that continual national disobedience would lead to dispersion (Lv 26:27-39; Dt 28:64-68).

22:18 Just as precious metals are melted to remove **dross**, Israel will be purified by fire to remove sins and impurities. Now the city will once again be melted by the heat of God's wrath in the **furnace** of Jerusalem. The Babylonians would execute this fire of God's wrath when they burned and sacked Jerusalem.

22:21 The phrase **will be melted within the city** may refer to the misery of being besieged by foreign enemies, which in itself was a divine punishment (Dt 28:52-57). The image of the smelter's fire was used by Ezekiel to represent the final purge that God planned for Judah. It is also an eschatological picture, referring to the time when God will purge His creation of sin (2Pt 3:9-14; Rv 20:15).

22:24 Ezekiel's combination of **rain** and judgment goes back to the account of the biblical flood in Genesis (Gn 6–8). Just as the purpose of this flood was to cleanse the world of human wickedness and violence (Hb *chamas*; Gn 6:5,11), the Lord declared that a similar kind of cleansing was now overdue for the land of Israel (Ezk 13:11; 38:22). The withholding of rain was a covenant curse (Lv 26:19).

22:26-27 Government **officials** were supposed to protect

destroying lives in order to make profit dishonestly. ²⁸Her prophets plaster with whitewash for them by seeing false visions and lying ·divinations,ᵃ and they say, 'This is what the Lord GOD says,' when the LORD has not spoken. ²⁹The people of the land have practiced extortion and committed robbery.ᵇ They have oppressed the poor and needy and unlawfully exploited the foreign resident. ³⁰I searched for a man among them who would repair the wallᶜ and stand in the gap before Me on behalf of the land so that I might not destroy it,ᵈ but I found no one. ³¹So I have poured out My indignation on them and consumed them with the fire of My fury. I have brought their actions down on their own heads."ᵉ This is the declaration of the Lord GOD.

The Two Immoral Sisters

23 The word of the LORD came to me again: ²"Son of man, there were two women,ᶠ daughters of the same mother, ³who acted like prostitutes in Egypt,ᵍ behaving promiscuously in their youth. Their breasts were fondled there, and their virgin nipples caressed.

⁴The older one was named Oholah,ᴬ and her sister was Oholibah.ᴮ They became Mine and gave birth to sons and daughters. As for their names, Oholah represents Samaria and Oholibah represents Jerusalem.

⁵"Oholah acted like a prostitute even though she was Mine. She lusted after her lovers, the Assyrians:ʰ warriors ⁶dressed in blue, governors and prefects, all of them desirable young men, horsemen riding on steeds. ⁷She offered her sexual favors to them; all of them were the elite of Assyria. She defiled herself with all those she lusted after and with all their idols. ⁸She didn't give up her promiscuity that began in Egypt,ⁱ when men slept with her in her youth, caressed her virgin nipples, and poured out their lust on her. ⁹Therefore, I handed her over to her lovers,ʲ the Assyrians she lusted for. ¹⁰They exposed her nakedness, seized her sons and daughters, and killed her with the sword. Since they executed judgment against her, she became notorious among women.

¹¹"Now her sister Oholibah saw this, but she was even more depraved in her lust than Oholah, and made her promiscuous acts worse

ᵃ22:28 Ezk 13:10-15
ᵇ22:29 Ezk 9:9; 22:7
ᶜ22:30 Ezk 13:5
ᵈEx 32:11-14; Ps 106:23
ᵉ22:31 Ezk 7:3,8-9; 9:10
ᶠ23:2 Ezk 16:46
ᵍ23:3 Lv 17:7; Jr 3:9
ʰ23:5 2Kg 15:19; 16:7; 17:3; Ezk 16:28; Hs 5:13; 8:9-10
ⁱ23:8 Ex 32:4; 1Kg 12:28; 2Kg 10:29; 17:16
ʲ23:9 Ezk 16:37; 23:22

ᴬ23:4 = Her Tent   ᴮ23:4 = My Tent Is in Her

---

people, the first function of government being the establishment of justice for everyone (Rm 13). The denunciation of the leadership in Ezk 22:25-28 has such close affinities to the denunciation of leaders in Zph 3:1-4 that there may be some kind of relationship between these two texts. For instance, each passage contains a nearly identical list of leaders. Even more striking is the fact that both passages describe the officials as **wolves** (Zph 3:3) and the priests as those who **do violence to My instruction** (Zph 3:4). It is possible that Ezekiel knew this oracle from the prophet Zephaniah.

22:30 This proposal (**I searched for a man among them who would repair the wall**) is reminiscent of Gn 18:22-33, where God promised to spare Sodom and Gomorrah if only 10 righteous persons were found there. Although we normally think of a prophet as one who represented God and delivered His word to the people, it is also true that the Bible includes intercession (**stand in the gap**) as part of a prophet's task (1Sm 12:23; Jr 37:3; 42:2). Compare the task of the prophetic "watchman" (Ezk 3:17-21; 33:1-6).

23:2 Since Israel was often portrayed as the wife of God (Jr 2-3; Hs 1-3), Ezekiel used the metaphor of harlotry (**two women**) to describe Samaria and Jerusalem. While chapter 16, another allegorical passage, focuses on Judah's idolatry, chapter 23 emphasizes Judah's illicit foreign alliances in addition to her idolatry. In chapter 16 the issue is Israel's trust in other gods; here she trusts in other nations.

23:3 Adultery and prostitution were both odious to God and punishable by death, according to numerous legal passages in Leviticus (Lv 19:29; 20:10; 21:9) and Deuteronomy (Dt 23:17). The adulterous cities will be destroyed.

23:4 Samaria, **the older one**, embraced idolatry and international alliances much earlier than Jerusalem. She would also precede Jerusalem in captivity. The phrase **they be-**

came Mine recalls marriage rituals described in 16:8-13. The two names **Oholah** and **Oholibah** relate to the Hebrew noun 'ohel (tent), corresponding to the cities they represent. The names recall the period when Israel lived in tents in the desert, reinforcing the notion of long-standing harlotry since that was a time in which Israel suffered punishment for its idolatries. Both names may have a connection to the tabernacle where God "met" with His people in the wilderness. The meaning of "Oholibah" (Jerusalem), "my tent is in her," may indicate that God's house, the temple, in fact resided in Jerusalem (2Sm 6:17; 1Kg 8:4; Ps 48:1-14). The mention of the mother of the sisters emphasizes their common origin from the united nation of Israel that existed for a time. The cities were the capital cities of the northern and southern kingdoms, respectively.

23:5 Prostitution here represents political alliances with pagan powers—not idolatry as in chapter 16 (v. 15). The graphic language underscores God's disgust with Israel for playing the game of international politics rather than relying on Him for security and support. Samaria's (**Oholah**) relations with the officers of Assyria presupposes the earlier alliance under Jehu's descendants Menahem (2Kg 15:17-22) and Hoshea (2Kg 17:1-6). The Black Obelisk of the Assyrian king Shalmaneser III (dated ca 841 B.C.) mentions "Jehu son of Omri" and actually shows him bowing to the Assyrian king, paying homage. This is one of the most significant archaeological finds related to biblical studies because it provides extrabiblical evidence for Jehu's submission to an Assyrian ruler.

23:10 The expression **they exposed her nakedness** refers to the fall of Samaria in 722 B.C.

23:11 Rather than embracing her God-given mission to bring the message of salvation to the nations (Gn 12:1-3), as a prostitute Jerusalem used the nations for her own advantage. Judah allied with Assyria (2Kg 16:7-9) and then

than those of her sister.[a] [12]She lusted after the Assyrians:[b] governors and prefects, warriors splendidly dressed, horsemen riding on steeds, all of them desirable young men. [13]And I saw that she had defiled herself; both of them had taken the same path. [14]But she increased her promiscuity when she saw male figures carved on the wall,[c] images of the Chaldeans, engraved in vermilion,[d] [15]wearing belts on their waists and flowing turbans on their heads; all of them looked like officers, a depiction of the Babylonians in Chaldea, the land of their birth. [16]At the sight of them[A] she lusted after them and sent messengers to them in Chaldea.[e] [17]Then the Babylonians came to her,[f] to the bed of love, and defiled her with their lust. But after she was defiled by them, she turned away from them in disgust. [18]When she flaunted her promiscuity and exposed her nakedness, I turned away from her in disgust just as I turned away from her sister.[g] [19]Yet she multiplied her acts of promiscuity, remembering the days of her youth when she acted like a prostitute in the land of Egypt [20]and lusted after their lovers, whose sexual members were like those of donkeys and whose emission was like that of stallions. [21]So you revisited the indecency of your youth, when the Egyptians caressed your nipples to enjoy your youthful breasts.[h]

[22]"Therefore Oholibah, this is what the Lord God says: I am going to incite your lovers against you, those you turned away from in disgust. I will bring them against you from every side: [23]the Babylonians and all the Chaldeans; Pekod, Shoa, and Koa;[i] and all the Assyrians with them—desirable young men, all of them governors and prefects, officers and administrators, all of them riding on horses. [24]They will come against you with an alliance of nations and with weapons, chariots, and[B]

[a]23:11 Jr 3:8-11; Ezk 16:51
[b]23:12 2Kg 16:7-20
[c]23:14 Ezk 8:10
[d]Ezk 16:29
[e]23:16 Is 57:9
[f]23:17 2Kg 24:17
[g]23:18 Ps 78:59; 106:40; Jr 12:8
[h]23:21 Ezk 16:26
[i]23:23 Jr 50:21
[j]23:25 Ex 34:14; Ezk 5:13; 8:17-18; Zph 1:18
[k]23:26 Ezk 16:39
[l]23:29 Ezk 16:7,22,39
[m]23:30 Ezk 6:9
[n]23:31 2Kg 21:13; Jr 7:14-15
[o]23:32 Ps 75:8; Is 51:17; Jr 25:15; Lm 4:21; Hab 2:16; Zch 12:2; Mt 20:22; 26:39; Rv 14:10
[p]Ezk 22:4-5

wagons. They will set themselves against you on every side with shields, bucklers, and helmets. I will delegate judgment to them, and they will judge you by their own standards. [25]When I vent My jealous rage on you,[j] they will deal with you in wrath. They will cut off your nose and ears, and your descendants will fall by the sword. They will seize your sons and daughters, and your descendants will be consumed by fire. [26]They will strip off your clothes and take your beautiful jewelry.[k] [27]So I will put an end to your indecency and sexual immorality, which began in the land of Egypt, and you will not look longingly at them or remember Egypt anymore.

[28]"For this is what the Lord God says: I am going to hand you over to those you hate, to those you turned away from in disgust. [29]They will treat you with hatred, take all you have worked for, and leave you stark naked,[l] so that the shame of your debauchery will be exposed, both your indecency and promiscuity. [30]These things will be done to you because you acted like a prostitute with the nations,[m] defiling yourself with their idols. [31]You have followed the path of your sister, so I will put her cup in your hand."[n]

[32]This is what the Lord God says:

> You will drink your sister's cup,[o]
> which is deep and wide.
> You will be an object of[C] ridicule
>   and scorn,
> for it holds so much.[p]
> [33] You will be filled with drunkenness
>   and grief,
> with a cup of devastation
>   and desolation,
> the cup of your sister Samaria.
> [34] You will drink it and drain it;
> then you will gnaw its broken pieces,

[A]23:16 Lit of her eyes   [B]23:24 LXX reads nations, from the north, chariots and; Hb obscure   [C]23:32 Or It will bring

Babylon (Ezk 17:13; 2Kg 24:1,17; cp. Is 39:1-8). Ezekiel may also have had in mind the disastrous political move of King Ahaz, who willingly made Judah Assyria's vassal. Rather than trusting God for deliverance (as Isaiah urged him to do), Ahaz enlisted Assyria's aid. With that act Judah became a vassal of Assyria for the next century (2Kg 16:5-9; Is 7).

23:14 Like the idols of the house of Israel in 8:10, these **male** images were **carved** on a **wall**. Visual art in Bible times was often painted on walls.

23:20 The reference to relations with Egypt (**lusted after their lovers**) may recall Solomon's early alliance with Egypt (1Kg 3:1) and Jehoiakim's support from Pharaoh Neco before he turned to Babylonia (2Kg 23:31–24:7).

23:23 The word **Chaldeans**, often interchanged with Babylonians, initially referred to the people living north of the Persian Gulf. **Pekod, Shoa, and Koa** were Aramean tribes

east of the Tigris River that were allied with Babylonia. Ezekiel may have mentioned such obscure, distant lands and peoples in order to convey to Israel the idea that "the whole world" was against them (chaps. 38–39).

23:31 The **cup** in the Bible is a neutral metaphor, based apparently on the custom of the host to pour wine into the cup of each of his guests (Ps 16:5). It was most frequently used, however, to refer to a toxic or intoxicating drink (Ps 75:8; Jr 25:15-16; Lm 4:21; Hab 2:15-16)—a cup of judgment or a cup of wrath (Is 51:17; Jr 51:7; Rv 17:3-4; 18:6). The motif of the cup was to culminate in Jesus, who absorbed in His own person the fullness of God's judgment, accepting it willingly from His hand (Mk 14:36).

23:34 Beating the breast was the customary response to a crisis (Is 32:12; Nah 2:7). The tearing of breasts intensified the image.

and tear your breasts.
For I have spoken.

This is the declaration
of the Lord God.

[35] Therefore, this is what the Lord God says: "Because you have forgotten Me[a] and cast Me behind your back,[b] you must bear the consequences of your indecency and promiscuity."

[36] Then the Lord said to me: "Son of man, will you pass judgment against Oholah and Oholibah?[c] Then declare their detestable practices to them.[d] [37] For they have committed adultery, and blood is on their hands; they have committed adultery with their idols. They have even made the children they bore to Me pass through the fire as food for the idols.[e] [38] They also did this to Me: they defiled My sanctuary[f] on that same day and profaned My Sabbaths.[g] [39] On the same day they slaughtered their children for their idols, they entered My sanctuary to profane it.[h] Yes, that is what they did inside My house.

[40] "In addition, they sent for men who came from far away when a messenger was dispatched to them. And look how they came! You bathed, painted your eyes,[i] and adorned yourself with jewelry for them.[j] [41] You sat on a luxurious couch with a table spread before it,[k] on which you had set My incense and oil. [42] The sound of a carefree crowd was there. Drunkards[A] from the desert were brought in, along with common men. They put bracelets on the women's hands and beautiful crowns on their heads. [43] Then I said concerning this woman worn out by adultery: Will they now have illicit sex with her, even her? [44] Yet they had sex with her as one does with a prosti-

tute. This is how they had sex with Oholah and Oholibah, those obscene women. [45] But righteous men will judge them the way adulteresses[l] and those who shed blood are judged, for they are adulteresses and blood is on their hands.

[46] "This is what the Lord God says: Summon[B] an assembly against them and consign them to terror and plunder.[m] [47] The assembly will stone them and cut them down with their swords.[n] They will kill their sons and daughters and burn their houses with fire. [48] So I will put an end to indecency in the land, and all the women will be admonished not to imitate your indecent behavior. [49] They will repay you for your indecency,[o] and you will bear the consequences for your sins of idolatry. Then you will know that I am the Lord ·Yahweh."

Parable of the Boiling Pot

24 The word of the Lord came to me in the ninth year, in the tenth month, on the tenth day of the month: [2] "Son of man, write down today's date, this very day. The king of Babylon has laid siege to Jerusalem this very day.[p] [3] Now speak a parable[q] to the rebellious house. Tell them: This is what the Lord God says:

Put the pot[r] on the fire—
put it on,
and then pour water into it!
[4]   Place the pieces of meat in it,
every good piece—
thigh and shoulder.
Fill it with choice bones.
[5]   Take the choicest of the flock
and also pile up the fuel[c] under it.

[a]23:35 Is 17:10; Jr 3:21; Ezk 22:12; Hs 8:14; 13:6
[b]1Kg 14:9; Jr 2:27; 32:33
[c]23:36 Jr 1:10; Ezk 20:4; 22:2
[d]Is 58:1; Ezk 16:2; Mc 3:8
[e]23:37 Ezk 16:20-21; 20:26,31
[f]23:38 2Kg 21:4,7
[g]Ezk 20:13
[h]23:39 Jr 7:9-11
[i]23:40 2Kg 9:30; Jr 4:30
[j]Is 3:18-23; Ezk 16:13-16
[k]23:41 Is 57:7
[l]23:45 Ezk 16:38
[m]23:46 Jr 15:4; 24:9; 29:18
[n]23:47 Lv 20:10; Ezk 16:40
[o]23:49 Is 59:18; Ezk 7:4,9; 9:10
[p]24:2 2Kg 25:1
[q]24:3 Ezk 17:2; 20:49
[r]Jr 1:13-14; Ezk 11:3,7,11

[A]23:42 Or *Sabeans*   [B]23:46 Or *I will summon*   [C]24:5 Lit *bones*

23:38 The defiling of God's **sanctuary** in Jerusalem was documented in chapter 8. Samaria, by its practice of worship at the illegal sanctuary of Bethel, defiled God's true sanctuary (1Kg 12:25-30).

23:41 Incense and **oil** not only belonged to the Lord, but they were products used in the offering of sacrifices.

23:42 The word **drunkards** may also be rendered as "men from Sheba." Sheba was located at the southwest corner of the Arabian Peninsula (modern Yemen) and was known for trading (27:22; 38:13; 1Kg 10:1-10; Jb 6:19).

23:46 Terror and **plunder** were standard types of covenant punishments (Lv 26:16-17; Dt 28:31,66-67; 32:25).

23:47 Stoning was the prescribed punishment for idolatry, child sacrifice, and adultery (Lv 20:2; Dt 13:10; 17:5; 22:21,24). These are the same judgments Ezekiel had pronounced earlier (16:40-41).

23:48 The actions of the Israelites and the consequences they suffer will provide a warning to other nations.

24:1 The date of this prophecy is significant. This was the

day that Nebuchadnezzar's siege of Jerusalem began in January of 588 b.c. Later in Israel's history the date became an appointed fast day and was observed as early as the time of the prophet Zechariah (Zch 8:19). This was the day Ezekiel had been pointing to for more than four years. The date was so significant that it was also mentioned by the writer of 1 and 2 Kings (2Kg 25:1) and by the prophet Jeremiah (Jr 39:1; 52:4).

24:3 This is the last occurrence of the phrase **the rebellious house**, which is unique to Ezekiel (2:5-6,8; 3:9,26-27; 12:2-3,9,25; 17:12). Those left in Jerusalem were like the choice meat intended for the **pot**, as opposed to the discarded by-products that represented the people taken away into exile. Now Ezekiel will utter a parable based on the same sort of imagery, once again (11:11) condemning rather than reassuring Jerusalem.

24:4 The phrase **every good piece** refers to choice offerings (Nm 18:12), including the breast and thigh (Gn 32:32; Ex 29:26-28; Lv 7:28-36; 10:12-15; Nm 18:18).

24:5 The **flock** elsewhere in Ezekiel represents the people

Bring it to a boil
and cook the bones in it."

⁶Therefore, this is what the Lord God says:

Woe to the city of bloodshed,ᵃ
the pot that has rust inside it,
and whose rust will not come off!
Empty it piece by piece;
lots should not be cast for its contents.
⁷ For the blood she shedᴬ is still
within her.
She put it out on the bare rock;
she didn't pour it on the ground
to cover it with dust.ᵇ
⁸ In order to stir up wrath
and take vengeance,ᶜ
I have put her blood on the bare rock,
so that it would not be covered.

⁹Therefore, this is what the Lord God says:

Woe to the city of bloodshed!ᵈ
I Myself will make the pile
of kindling large.
¹⁰ Pile on the logs and kindle the fire!
Cook the meat well
and mix in the spices!ᴮ,ᶜ
Let the bones be burned!
¹¹ Set the empty pot on its coals
so that it becomes hot
and its copper glows.
Then its impurity will melt inside it;
its rust will be consumed.ᵉ
¹² It has frustrated every effort;ᴰ
its thick rust will not come off.
Into the fire with its rust!
¹³ Because of the indecency
of your uncleanness—
since I tried to purify you,

but you would not be purified
from your uncleanness—
you will not be pure again
until I have satisfied My wrath on you.ᶠ
¹⁴ I, •Yahweh, have spoken.
It is coming, and I will do it!ᵍ
I will not refrain, I will not show pity,
and I will not relent.
Iᴱ will judge you
according to your ways and deeds.ʰ
This is the declaration
of the Lord God.

The Death of Ezekiel's Wife: A Sign

¹⁵Then the word of the Lord came to me:
¹⁶"Son of man, I am about to take the delight
of your eyesⁱ away from you with a fatal blow.
But you must not lament or weep or let your
tears flow.ʲ ¹⁷Groan quietly; do not observe
mourning rites for the dead.ᵏ Put on your turban and strap your sandals on your feet; do
not cover your mustache or eat the bread of
mourners."ᶠ,ˡ

¹⁸I spoke to the people in the morning, and
my wife died in the evening. The next morning I did just as I was commanded. ¹⁹Then
the people asked me, "Won't you tell us what
these things you are doing mean for us?"

²⁰So I answered them: "The word of the
Lord came to me: ²¹'Say to the house of Israel:
This is what the Lord God says: I am about
to desecrate My sanctuary, the pride of your
power, the delight of your eyes, and the desire of your heart. Also, the sons and daughters you left behind will fall by the sword.ᵐ
²²Then you will do just as I have done: You
will not cover your mustache or eat the bread
of mourners.ᶠ ²³Your turbans will remain on

Cross references (center column):
- ᵃ 24:6 Ezk 22:2-3,27
- ᵇ 24:7 Lv 17:13-14; Dt 12:16,24
- ᶜ 24:8 Is 26:21
- ᵈ 24:9 Hab 2:12
- ᵉ 24:11 Ezk 22:15; 23:27
- ᶠ 24:13 Ezk 5:13; 8:18
- ᵍ 24:14 Ezk 17:24
- ʰ Ezk 18:30; 36:19
- ⁱ 24:16 Pr 5:18; Ec 9:9; Sg 7:10
- ʲ Jr 16:5; 22:10
- ᵏ 24:17 Lv 21:10-12
- ˡ Jr 16:7; Hs 9:4
- ᵐ 24:21 Jr 6:11; 16:3-4; Ezk 23:25,47

ᴬ24:7 Lit *For her blood*   ᴮ24:10 Some Hb mss read *well; remove the broth*; LXX reads *fire so that the meat may be cooked and the broth may be reduced*   ᶜ24:10 Or *and stir the broth*   ᴰ24:12 Hb obscure   ᴱ24:14 Some Hb mss, LXX, Syr, Tg, Vg; other Hb mss read *They*   ᶠ24:17,22 Lit *men*

---

of Israel (chap. 34). Thus the pieces of meat (**choicest of the flock**) probably picture Jerusalem's inhabitants, who would be "boiled" in the judgment fire of Nebuchadnezzar's siege.

24:6 Jerusalem is called the **city of bloodshed**, just as the pagan city of Nineveh is in Nah 3:1. **Rust** represents injustice and bloodguilt (22:6-12).

24:7 Uncovered blood evoked God's vengeance (Gn 4:10; Is 26:21).

24:16 A **blow** resulted in a sudden death either from combat (1Sm 4:17; 2Sm 18:7) or from plague or disease (Ex 9:14; Nm 14:37; 17:13; 25:8-9). The statement **take the delight of your eyes away from you** is reminiscent of God's command to Abraham (Gn 22) to offer his son as a sacrifice.

24:17 In this passage five of the typical gestures of ancient Israelite mourning are alluded to: groaning (Is 24:7; Mal 2:13), removing one's **turban** or **sandals** (2Sm 15:30), cov-

ering one's lips (Mc 3:7), and eating special mourning **bread** (Hs 9:4). In addition, dust was often thrown atop the head (Jos 7:6; 1Sm 4:12). These practices were never prescribed in the law, but they became standard responses to tragedy.

24:21 The destruction of the **sanctuary** included the fall of the city. God's destruction of the people's sanctuary is one of the covenant punishments prescribed for national disobedience in the Mosaic law (Lv 26:31). Jerusalem died (as did Ezekiel's wife), and with it the temple and the prescribed methods of worship. This created a first-rate identity crisis for Hebrews who wished to remain faithful to God.

24:22 The people were not permitted to mourn; Jerusalem's fall was foretold and yet they persisted in sin. Thus they should have expected this judgment. The Mosaic law did not call for mourning over those who were justly executed for their crimes, and in like manner the citizens of Jerusalem had no right to mourn for the just execution of their city. Besides,

your heads and your sandals on your feet. You will not lament or weep[a] but will waste away[b] because of your sins and will groan to one another. 24 Now Ezekiel will be a sign for you.[c] You will do everything that he has done. When this happens, you will know that I am the Lord Yahweh.

25 "Son of man, know that on the day I take their stronghold from them, their pride and joy, the delight of their eyes and the longing of their hearts, as well as their sons and daughters, 26 on that day a fugitive will come to you and report the news.[d] 27 On that day your mouth will be opened to talk with him; you will speak and no longer be mute.[e] So you will be a sign for them, and they will know that I am Yahweh.'"

PROPHECIES AGAINST THE NATIONS

Judgment against Ammon

25 Then the word of the LORD came to me: 2 "Son of man, turn your face toward the Ammonites and prophesy against them.[f] 3 Say to the Ammonites: Hear the word of the Lord GOD: This is what the Lord GOD says: Because you said, 'Good!'[g] about My sanctuary when it was desecrated, about the land of Israel when it was laid waste, and about the house of Judah when they went into exile, 4 therefore I am about to give you to the people of the east as a possession. They will set up their en-

a24:23 Jb 27:15; Ps 78:64
b Lv 26:39
c24:24 Ezk 4:3; Lk 11:29-30
d24:26 Ezk 33:21-22
e24:27 Ezk 3:26-27
f25:2 Jr 49:1-6
g25:3 Ezk 21:28; 26:2
h25:5 Jr 49:2; Ezk 21:20
i25:6 Jb 27:23; Nah 3:19
j25:7 Zph 1:4
k25:8 Is 15:1; Jr 48:1; Am 2:1-2
l25:9 Jr 48:23
m25:12 2Ch 28:17; Ps 137:7; Jr 49:7-22

campments and pitch their tents among you. They will eat your fruit and drink your milk. 5 I will make Rabbah a pasture[h] for camels and Ammon a sheepfold. Then you will know that I am °Yahweh."

6 For this is what the Lord GOD says: "Because you clapped your hands,[i] stamped your feet, and rejoiced over the land of Israel with wholehearted contempt, 7 therefore I am about to stretch out My hand against you[j] and give you as plunder to the nations. I will cut you off from the peoples and eliminate you from the countries. I will destroy you, and you will know that I am Yahweh."

Judgment against Moab

8 This is what the Lord GOD says: "Because Moab and Seir said,[k] 'Look, the house of Judah is like all the other nations,' 9 therefore I am about to expose Moab's flank beginning with its[A] frontier cities, the pride of the land: Beth-jeshimoth, Baal-meon,[l] and Kiriathaim. 10 I will give it along with Ammon to the people of the east as a possession, so that Ammon will not be remembered among the nations. 11 So I will execute judgments against Moab, and they will know that I am Yahweh."

Judgment against Edom

12 This is what the Lord GOD says: "Because Edom acted vengefully against the house of Judah[m] and incurred grievous °guilt by taking revenge on them, 13 therefore this is what the Lord GOD says: I will stretch out My hand

---

A 25:9 Lit with the cities, with its

---

they would not have time to mourn in any event since they would immediately be taken as captives to Babylon.

24:26 This prophecy, which says a **fugitive** arriving from fallen Jerusalem will mark the end of Ezekiel's silence, is fulfilled in 33:21-22.

24:27 Ezekiel's ability to **speak** again will signal that his six-year ministry of announcing judgment is over and a new ministry of consolation will begin.

25:1–32:32 This section of Ezekiel bridges the book's message of doom and its message of hope. Doom for Israel's antagonists spells hope for Israel itself. The placement of these oracles at this point disrupts the flow of the book and heightens the tension as the destruction of the temple is imminent. God's judgment on these nations is based on the Abrahamic covenant, which said that those who cursed Israel would be cursed by God (Gn 12:1-3). All the nations named in the oracle had either taken part in Jerusalem's destruction or had rejoiced over it. The audience for these oracles was Judean, and so they had cause for future hope.

25:2 Ammon, Moab, and Edom are mentioned in the order of their geographic location, from north to south. The **Ammonites** are perhaps mentioned first in this section of oracles because the only previous oracle against a foreign nation was also about Ammon (21:28-32). The Ammonites

were descendants of Abraham's nephew, Lot (Gn 19:30-38). The Ammonites were known for their idolatry (1Kg 11:7,33), cruelty (Am 1:13), pride (Zph 2:9-10), and opposition to God's people (Dt 23:3-4; Jdg 3:13; 1Sm 11:1-3; 2Sm 10:1-14; 2Kg 24:2; Neh 4:3,7-8).

25:7 With ironic justice, the nation that rejoiced over the destruction of Judah (v. 3) will suffer the same fate. They will be conquered and oppressed by their enemies, a standard covenant punishment (Lv 26:16-17; Dt 28:31,33,43).

25:8-9 Like the Ammonites, the people of **Moab** were descendants of Lot and one of his daughters (Gn 19:30-38). Shortly after the Israelites were released from Egyptian bondage, the Moabites caused a great setback for the young Israelite nation by introducing them to Baal worship (Nm 21:1-25; 31:16). Judah went on to dominate Moab both politically and militarily throughout much of its history. During Ezekiel's time, however, Moabite troops joined forces with Nebuchadnezzar and attacked King Jehoiakim of Jerusalem (2Kg 24:2). When Judah was defeated the Moabites responded with delight (Jr 48:29; Zph 2:8-9).

25:12 The struggle between **Edom** and **Judah** began when their respective patriarchs were born as twin brothers. Jacob, who went on to father the Israelites, grabbed the heel of Esau, who fathered the Edomites, as they struggled to emerge from Rebekah's womb (Gn 25:21-34). Centuries

against Edom and cut off both man and animal from it. I will make it a wasteland; they will fall by the sword from Teman to Dedan. [14] I will take My vengeance[a] on Edom through My people Israel, and they will deal with Edom according to My anger and wrath. So they will know My vengeance." This is the declaration of the Lord GOD.

Judgment against Philistia

[15] This is what the Lord GOD says: "Because the Philistines acted in vengeance and took revenge with deep contempt,[b] destroying because of their ancient hatred, [16] therefore this is what the Lord GOD says: I am about to stretch out My hand against the Philistines,[c] cutting off the Cherethites and wiping out what remains of the coastal peoples.[A,d] [17] I will execute great vengeance against them with furious

rebukes. They will know that I am Yahweh[e] when I take My vengeance on them."

The Downfall of Tyre

26 In the eleventh year, on the first day of the month, the word of the LORD came to me: [2] "Son of man, because Tyre[f] said about Jerusalem, 'Good![g] The gateway to the peoples is shattered. She has been turned over to me. I will be filled now that she lies in ruins,' [3] therefore this is what the Lord GOD says: See, I am against you, Tyre![h] I will raise up many nations against you, just as the sea raises its waves. [4] They will destroy the walls of Tyre and demolish her towers. I will scrape the soil from her and turn her into a bare rock. [5] She will become a place in the sea to spread nets, for I have spoken." This is the declaration of the Lord GOD. "She will become plunder for

Cross references (center column):
a 25:14 Is 11:14
b 25:15 Is 14:29-31
c 25:16 Jr 25:20; 47:1-7
d 1Sm 30:14; Zph 2:5
e 25:17 Ps 9:16
f 26:2 2Sm 5:11; Jl 3:4
g Ezk 25:3
h 26:3 Is 23:3; Ezk 26:17; 28:2; Am 1:9; Zch 9:2; Mt 11:22

A 25:16 Lit *the seacoast*

later, shortly after the Israelites emerged from bondage in Egypt, Edom refused to let them pass through their land en route to Canaan (Nm 20:14-21). This was the beginning of a long adversarial relationship between Israel and Edom. There were conflicts between Israel and Edom during the reigns of Saul (1Sm 14:47), Solomon (1Kg 11:14-22), Jehoshaphat (2Ch 20:1-23), Jehoram (2Kg 8:20-21), and Ahaz (2Ch 28:17). The most blatant example of Edom's opposition to the people of God was Edom's role in the destruction of the Jerusalem temple (Ps 137:7; Lm 4:21-22; Ob 1-14). Like the Moabites and Ammonites, the Edomites were a warring (Gn 27:39-40), idolatrous (2Ch 25:14,20), cruel (Am 1:11-12), and vengeful (Ezk 25:12-14) people. Ezekiel and other prophets declared that Israel would possess Edom in the end time (35:1-36:15; Is 11:14; Dn 11:41; Am 9:12; Ob 18-19). This prophecy was fulfilled when Edom was defeated by the Maccabees and incorporated into the Jewish state.

25:14 God announced His verdict on **Edom**, and this judgment is further expanded in 35:1-36:15. Edom is always included in oracles against nations by the Major Prophets.

25:15 The **Philistines** migrated to the coast of Palestine from the Greek coasts and islands of the Aegean Sea (Jr 47:4; Am 9:7; Zph 2:5). As early as the time of the judges they were constant adversaries of Israel (Jdg 3:31; 10:7; 13-16; 1Sm 4; 13; 31; 2Sm 5; 2Kg 18:8; 2Ch 21:16-17; 28:18). David was credited with the final subjugation of the Philistines during his reign (2Sm 5:17-25). Though there is virtually no record of the existence of the Philistines after the time of the Maccabees (second century B.C.), the region of Canaan came to be called Palestine (Philistine = Palestine).

25:16 The **Cherethites** (possibly Cretans) were presumably an ethnic group of Aegean origin that settled along the southwestern coast of Canaan. By David's time they had such a positive relationship with Israel that David chose many Cherethites as his personal guardsmen (1Sm 30:14; 2Sm 8:18). They are frequently mentioned along with the Pelethite forces that together formed a mercenary unit during the time of David (2Sm 8:18; 20:23). The Pelethites and Cherethites accompanied David on his flight from Absalom (2Sm 15:18).

26:2 The Phoenicians represented the remnants of the original population that occupied Canaan before the Israelites arrived. As the most powerful city on the Phoenician coast, **Tyre** dominated not only other coastal cities but much of the Phoenician inland areas as well. Tyre's Hebrew name is *tsur*, which means "rock." Built atop an island off the Phoenician coast, Tyre was virtually impregnable by sea or land. The Assyrians conquered the northern kingdom of Israel (722 B.C.) but were forced to withdraw from their siege of Tyre after five years of effort. Relations between Israel and Tyre were often cordial (1Kg 5; 7). Tyre, the preeminent maritime power of the ancient world, joined Judah in revolt against the Babylonian Empire (Jr 27:3). After Nebuchadnezzar defeated Jerusalem he besieged Tyre for 13 years (585-572 B.C.) but was unsuccessful in his campaign to conquer the offshore rock fortress. In the fourth century B.C., Alexander built a causeway of stone, timber, and rubble a half mile long and 200 feet wide from the mainland to the island. By this means Tyre was finally conquered, thus fulfilling Ezekiel's prophecy (27:36).

haras

Hebrew Pronunciation	[hah RAS]
HCSB Translation	tear down, demolish
Uses in Ezekiel	8
Uses in the OT	43
Focus passage	Ezekiel 26:4,12

The root in other languages denotes "attack," "tear down," "destroy," and "break to pieces." *Haras* describes *tearing down* fortresses (Mc 5:11), altars (Jdg 6:25), or foundations (Ezk 30:4). Sixteen times it indicates *demolishing* objects: towers (Ezk 26:4), walls, idols, cities, and nations. Ten times it is the antonym of *banah* ("build, build up"; Pr 11:11). Five times it occurs with synonymous *natats* ("tear down"; Jr 1:10). God *overthrows* adversaries (Ex 15:7) and *knocks out* teeth (Ps 58:6). People *destroy* cities (2Kg 3:25) and *level* mounds (Ezk 16:39). Mountains *are thrown down* (Ezk 38:20). *Haras* can indicate states rather than actions: graineries *are broken down* (Jl 1:17), and walls *are ruined* (Pr 24:31). *Haras* connotes secondary ideas: someone *is ousted* from his position (Is 22:19). If Israelites *break through* to look at God, He will *break out* against them (Ex 19:21,24). *Hariysah* (Am 9:11) and *hariysuth* (Is 49:19) denote *ruins*.

the nations,[a] [6]and her villages on the mainland will be slaughtered by the sword.[b] Then they will know that I am •Yahweh."

[7]For this is what the Lord God says: "See, I am about to bring King Nebuchadnezzar of Babylon, king of kings,[c] against Tyre from the north with horses, chariots, cavalry, and a vast company of troops. [8]He will slaughter your villages on the mainland with the sword. He will set up siege works against you,[d] and will build a ramp[A] and raise a wall of shields against you. [9]He will direct the blows of his battering rams against your walls and tear down your towers with his iron tools. [10]His horses will be so numerous that their dust will cover you. When he enters your gates as an army entering a breached city, your walls will shake from the noise of cavalry, wagons, and chariots. [11]He will trample all your streets with the hooves of his horses.[e] He will slaughter your people with the sword, and your mighty pillars will fall to the ground. [12]They will take your wealth as spoil and plunder your merchandise.[f] They will also demolish your walls and tear down your beautiful homes. Then they will throw your stones, timber, and soil into the water. [13]I will put an end to the noise of your songs,[g] and the sound of your lyres will no longer be heard. [14]I will turn you into a bare rock, and you will be a place to spread nets. You will never be rebuilt, for I, Yahweh, have spoken."[h] This is the declaration of the Lord God.

[15]This is what the Lord God says to Tyre: "Won't the coasts and islands quake at the sound of your downfall,[i] when the wounded groan and slaughter occurs within you? [16]All the princes of the sea will descend from their thrones,[j] remove their robes, and strip off their embroidered garments. They will clothe themselves with trembling; they will sit on the ground, tremble continually, and be appalled[k] at you. [17]Then they will lament[l] for you and say of you:

How you have perished, city of renown, you who were populated from the seas![B] She who was powerful on the sea, she and all of her inhabitants inflicted their terror.[c]

[18] Now the coastlands tremble[m] on the day of your downfall; the islands in the sea are alarmed by your demise."

[19]For this is what the Lord God says: "When I make you a ruined city like other deserted cities, when I raise up the deep against you so that the mighty waters cover you, [20]then I will bring you down to be with those who descend to the •Pit,[n] to the people of antiquity. I will make you dwell in the underworld[D] like[E] the ancient ruins, with those who descend to the Pit, so that you will no longer be inhabited or display your splendor[F] in the land of the living.[o] [21]I will make you an object of horror, and you will no longer exist.[p] You will be sought but will never be found again." This is the declaration of the Lord God.

The Sinking of Tyre

27 The word of the Lord came to me: [2]"Now, son of man, lament for Tyre.[q] [3]Say to Tyre, who is located at the entrance of the sea, merchant of the peoples[r] to many coasts and islands: This is what the Lord God says:

Tyre, you declared,
'I am perfect in beauty.'
[4] Your realm was in the heart of the sea;
your builders perfected your beauty.
[5] They constructed all your planking
with pine trees from Senir.[G,s]
They took a cedar from Lebanon
to make a mast for you.
[6] They made your oars of oaks
from Bashan.
They made your deck of cypress wood

[a] 26:5 Ezk 25:7; 29:19
[b] 26:6 Ezk 16:46,53; 26:8
[c] 26:7 Jr 52:32; Dn 2:37,47
[d] 26:8 Ezk 21:22
[e] 26:11 Hab 1:8
[f] 26:12 Ezk 27:3-27
[g] 26:13 Is 23:16; 24:8-9; Am 6:5
[h] 26:14 Is 14:27
[i] 26:15 Jr 49:21
[j] 26:16 Jnh 3:6
[k] Ezk 27:35
[l] 26:17 Ezk 27:2,32; 28:12
[m] 26:18 Ezk 26:15
[n] 26:20 Jb 33:28; Ps 28:1; 30:3; Is 14:15; Ezk 28:8; 31:14; 32:18-30
[o] Jr 33:9; Zch 2:8
[p] 26:21 Ezk 27:36; 28:19
[q] 27:2 Ezk 28:12; 32:2
[r] 27:3 Is 23:2
[s] 27:5 Dt 3:9

[A]26:8 Lit ramp against you   [B]26:17 Some LXX mss read How you were destroyed from the seas, city of renown!   [C]26:17 Lit and all her inhabitants who put their terror on all her inhabitants; Hb obscure   [D]26:20 Lit the lower parts of the earth   [E]26:20 Some Hb mss, LXX; other Hb mss, Syr read in   [F]26:20 LXX reads or appear   [G]27:5 = Mount Hermon

26:6 It was not until Tyre's conquest by Alexander the Great that this prophecy (**her villages on the mainland will be slaughtered by the sword**) was fulfilled. Alexander built a causeway from the mainland to the island and took the city after seven months.

26:14 Nebuchadnezzar besieged Tyre for 13 years. After the siege ended Nebuchadnezzar had political control over Tyre for many years.

26:19 With these words (**when I raise up the deep against you so that the mighty waters cover you**) the Lord threatened Tyre with a judgment reminiscent of the Genesis flood (Gn 6-8).

26:20 The phrase **the Pit** is a figurative way of expressing death. It is virtually synonymous with the grave (Pr 1:12; Is 14:15; 38:18).

27:3 Ezekiel portrayed Tyre as a well-built ship. This symbolizes the way Tyre achieved wealth through maritime trade. The inhabitants of Tyre thought the city was indestructible. The warning here is that such pride is the prelude to destruction (Pr 6:17; 8:13; 16:18).

27:5 **Cedar from Lebanon** was prized for its height and strength (1Kg 4:33; 5:6; 1Ch 17:1-6; Ezr 3:7; Is 2:13). The material was often imported into Israel from Lebanon for building projects.

from the coasts of Cyprus,[a]
inlaid with ivory.

7 Your sail was made of
fine embroidered linen from Egypt,
and served as your banner.
Your awning was of blue
and purple fabric
from the coasts of Elishah.

8 The inhabitants of Sidon and Arvad[b]
were your rowers.
Your wise men were within you, Tyre;
they were your captains.

9 The elders of Gebal and its wise men[c]
were within you, repairing your leaks.

All the ships of the sea and their sailors
came to[A] you to barter for your goods.

10 Men of Persia, Lud, and Put[d]
were in your army, serving
as your warriors.
They hung shields and helmets in you;
they gave you splendor.

11 Men of Arvad and Helech
were stationed on your walls
all around,
and Gammadites were in your towers.
They hung their shields[B] all around
your walls;
they perfected your beauty.

12 "Tarshish[e] was your trading partner because of your great wealth of every kind. They exchanged silver, iron, tin, and lead for your merchandise. [13] Javan, Tubal, and Meshech[f] were your merchants. They exchanged slaves[C] and bronze utensils for your goods. [14] Those from Beth-togarmah[g] exchanged horses, war horses, and mules for your merchandise. [15] Men of Dedan[D,h] were also your merchants;

many coasts and islands were your regular markets. They brought back ivory tusks[i] and ebony as your payment. [16] Aram[E,F] was your trading partner because of your numerous products. They exchanged turquoise,[G] purple and embroidered cloth, fine linen, coral,[G] and rubies[G] for your merchandise. [17] Judah and the land of Israel were your merchants. They exchanged wheat from Minnith,[j] meal,[H] honey, oil, and balm, for your goods. [18] Damascus was also your trading partner because of your numerous products and your great wealth of every kind, trading in wine from Helbon and white wool.[I] [19] Vedan[J] and Javan from Uzal[G,k] dealt in your merchandise; wrought iron, cassia,[I] and aromatic cane were exchanged for your goods. [20] Dedan[m] was your merchant in saddlecloths for riding. [21] Arabia and all the princes of Kedar were your business[K] partners, trading with you in lambs, rams, and goats. [22] The merchants of Sheba[n] and Raamah traded with you. They exchanged gold, the best of all spices, and all kinds of precious stones for your merchandise.[o] [23] Haran, Canneh, Eden,[p] the merchants of Sheba, Asshur,[q] and Chilmad traded with you. [24] They were your merchants in choice garments, cloaks of blue and embroidered materials, and multicolored carpets,[G] which were bound and secured with cords in your marketplace. [25] Ships of Tarshish[r] were the carriers for your goods.

So you became full and heavily loaded[L]
in the heart of the sea.

26 Your rowers have brought you
onto the high seas,[s]
but the east wind has shattered you
in the heart of the sea.

27 Your wealth, merchandise, and goods,

[a]27:6-7 Gn 10:4; 1Ch 1:7
[b]27:8 Gn 10:18
[c]27:9 1Kg 5:18
[d]27:10 Ezk 30:5; 38:5
[e]27:12 Gn 10:4; Ezk 38:13
[f]27:13 Gn 10:2; Ezk 38:2; 39:1
[g]27:14 Gn 10:3; Ezk 38:6
[h]27:15 Ezk 38:13
[i]1Kg 10:22
[j]27:17 Jdg 11:33
[k]27:19 Gn 10:27
[l]Ex 30:24
[m]27:20 Ezk 38:13
[n]27:22 Gn 10:7; Ezk 38:13
[o]1Kg 10:1-2; Rv 18:12
[p]27:23 2Kg 19:12; Is 37:12
[q]Gn 25:3
[r]27:25 1Kg 10:22; 22:48; Is 2:16
[s]27:26 Ezk 26:19

A27:9 Lit *sailors were with*   B27:11 Or *quivers*; Hb obscure   C27:13 Lit *souls of men*   D27:15 LXX reads *Rhodes*   E27:16 Some Hb mss, Aq, Syr read *Edom*   F27:16 = Syria   G27:16,19,24 Hb obscure   H27:17 Or *resin*; Hb obscure   I27:18 Or *and wool from Zahar*   J27:19 Or *Dan*   K27:21 Lit *trading*   L27:25 Or *and very glorious*

27:7 Egypt was known for its fine **linen** cloth (Gn 41:42; Pr 7:16).

27:12 There is much debate about the exact location of **Tarshish**. While the place cannot be identified with certainty, it has often been linked with Tartessus—a Phoenician colony in western Spain. The nation of Spain was a source of metals in the ancient world.

27:16 Phoenicia was known for trade in **purple** dye derived from shellfish. Both names for the country, Phoenicia (Gk *Phoinikos*) and Canaan, mean "purple."

27:23 In ancient Near Eastern sources, **Eden** was considered to be a district south of Haran, mentioned in connection with Haran in 2Kg 19:12. See Beth-eden in Am 1:5.

27:26 Tyre's ruin came in the very element where she was most at home—the open **seas**.

27:27 The demise of another world system, Babylon the Great, is described in the book of Revelation. The articles of

The ruins of the ancient seaport city of Gebal (27:9) or Byblos, located in present-day Lebanon

your sailors and captains,
those who repair your leaks,
those who barter for your goods,
and all the warriors within you,
with all the other people on board,[A]
sink into the heart of the sea
on the day of your downfall.

28 The countryside shakes
at the sound of your sailors' cries.[a]

29 All those who handle an oar
disembark from their ships.
The sailors and all the captains
of the sea
stand on the shore.

30 They raise their voices over you
and cry out bitterly.
They throw dust on their heads;[b]
they roll in ashes.

31 They shave their heads because of you
and wrap themselves in *sackcloth.
They weep over you
with deep anguish
and bitter mourning.

32 In their wailing they lament for you,[c]
mourning over you:
Who was like Tyre,
silenced[B] in the middle of the sea?

33 When your merchandise was unloaded
from the seas,
you satisfied many peoples.
You enriched the kings of the earth
with your abundant wealth and goods.

34 Now you are shattered by the sea
in the depths of the waters;
your goods and the people within you

have gone down.

35 All the inhabitants of the coasts
and islands
are appalled[d] at you.
Their kings shudder with fear;
their faces are contorted.

36 Those who trade among the peoples
mock[C,e] you;
you have become an object of horror
and will never exist again."[f]

The Fall of Tyre's Ruler

28 The word of the LORD came to me: 2"Son of man, say to the ruler of Tyre: This is what the Lord GOD says:

Your[D] heart is proud,
and you have said, 'I am a god;[g]
I sit in the seat of gods
in the heart of the sea.'
Yet you are a man and not a god,
though you have regarded your heart
as that of a god.

3 Yes, you are wiser than Daniel;[h]
no secret is hidden from you!

4 By your wisdom and understanding
you have acquired wealth for yourself.
You have acquired gold and silver
for your treasuries.[i]

5 By your great skill in trading
you have increased your wealth,
but your heart has become proud
because of your wealth."

6Therefore this is what the Lord GOD says:

Because you regard your heart as that
of a god,

Cross references (center column)
[a] 27:28 Ezk 26:10,15
[b] 27:30 Rv 18:17-19
[c] 27:32 Ezk 26:17
[d] 27:35 Ezk 26:15-16
[e] 27:36 1Kg 9:8; Jr 19:8; Zph 2:15
[f] Ezk 26:21; 28:19
[g] 28:2 Is 14:14; Ac 12:22-23; 2Th 2:4
[h] 28:3 Dn 1:20; 2:20-23,28; 5:11-12
[i] 28:4 Ezk 27:33; Zch 9:2-3

[A]27:27 Lit *with all your assembly among you*   [B]27:32 Hb obscure   [C]27:36 Lit *hiss*   [D]28:2 Lit *Because your*

Babylon's worldwide commerce (Rv 18:12-13) are similar to what is mentioned here in the description of Tyre's fall.

28:2 This **ruler of Tyre** may be identified as Ittobaal II, whose name meant "Baal is with him," or Ethbaal III. Possibly the language was kept vague so that the condemnation could aptly describe any Tyrian king. Like the inhabitants of Tyre, the ruler of this city was guilty of pride (27:1-9; Pr 6:17–8:13; 16:18).

28:3 The fame of the prophet **Daniel** had spread in the exile, even beyond the bounds of his own people (14:14,20; Dn 1:20; 2:48; 4:18-27; 5:11-12; 6:3). Daniel's character was just the opposite of the pride and self-sufficiency of the king of Tyre.

28:10 In his disgraceful **death**, the king of Tyre will join the ranks of the **uncircumcised**. Since Phoenicians as well as most other ancient Near Eastern males practiced circumcision, Ezekiel's use of the term must be figurative. The point is that the king will be assigned to the most undesirable compartment of the netherworld, along with other degraded and unclean persons (31:18; 32:17-32).

28:13 The prideful king of Tyre is compared either to a guardian angel at the "mountain of God" (v. 14) or to errant

gavah

Hebrew Pronunciation	[gah VAH]
HCSB Translation	be high, be proud, make tall
Uses in Ezekiel	10
Uses in the OT	34
Focus passage	Ezekiel 28:2,5,17

Gavah means *be high* (Ps 103:11). Trees *tower, being great in height* (Ezk 19:11; 31:5). Comparatively, *gavah* denotes *stand taller* (1Sm 10:23) or *be higher* (Is 55:9). *Gavah* describes character, negatively signifying *be haughty* (Is 3:16) or *proud* (Jr 13:15). People *grow arrogant* (2Ch 26:16). *Gavah* positively is *rejoice* (2Ch 17:6) or *be exalted* (Is 5:16). The causative is *make tall* (Ezk 17:24). People *build high* (Pr 17:19), *exalt* (Ezk 21:26), *heighten* (2Ch 33:14), or *elevate* (Jr 49:16) things. Birds *soar* (Ob 4). *Gavoah* (41x) is *high* (Gn 7:19), *tall, lofty,* or *long* (Gn 15:15), *proud,* or *exalted*. *Govah* (17x) is *height* (Ezk 19:11) or *raised platform* (Ezk 41:8), appearing as *high, tall,* or *large* (Ezk 1:18). It is *pride* (2Ch 32:26), *arrogance* (Ps 10:4), or *insolence* (Jr 48:29), but also *majesty* (Jb 40:10). *Gavhuth* is *pride* (Is 2:11,17).

7 I am about to bring strangers
   against you,
ruthless men from the nations.
They will draw their swords
against your magnificent wisdom
and will defile your splendor.[a]
8 They will bring you down to the •Pit,[b]
and you will die a violent death
in the heart of the sea.
9 Will you still say, 'I am a god,'
in the presence of those who kill[A] you?
Yet you will be only a man, not a god,
in the hands of those who kill you.
10 You will die the death
   of the uncircumcised[c]
at the hands of strangers.[d]
For I have spoken.

This is the declaration
of the Lord GOD.

A Lament for Tyre's King

[11] The word of the LORD came to me: [12] "Son of man, lament[e] for the king of Tyre and say to him: This is what the Lord GOD says:

You were the seal[B] of perfection,[c]
full of wisdom and perfect in beauty.[f]
13 You were in Eden,[g] the garden of God.
Every kind of precious stone
   covered you:
carnelian, topaz, and diamond,[c]
beryl, onyx, and jasper,
sapphire,[D] turquoise[E] and emerald.[F]
Your mountings and settings
   were crafted in gold;[h]
they were prepared on the day
   you were created.
14 You were an anointed guardian cherub,[i]
for[G] I had appointed you.
You were on the holy mountain of God;
you walked among the fiery stones.
15 From the day you were created
you were blameless in your ways
until wickedness was found in you.

[a] 28:7 Ezk 30:11; 31:12; 32:12
[b] 28:8 Ezk 26:20
[c] 28:10 Ezk 31:18; 32:30
[d] Ezk 30:12
[e] 28:12 Ezk 27:2
[f] Ezk 27:3
[g] 28:13 Gn 2:8; Ezk 31:9,16,18; 36:35
[h] Ex 39:10-13
[i] 28:14 Ex 25:18-22
[j] 28:17 Ezk 28:2
[k] 28:18 Ezk 19:14
[l] 28:19 Ezk 26:21; 27:36
[m] 28:21 Gn 10:19; Is 23:2; Jl 3:4
[n] 28:22 Ezk 26:3; Zch 9:2; Mt 11:22
[o] Ezk 30:19
[p] 28:23 Ezk 38:22

16 Through the abundance of your trade,
you were filled with violence,
   and you sinned.
So I expelled you in disgrace
from the mountain of God,
and banished you, guardian cherub,[H]
from among the fiery stones.
17 Your heart became proud because of
   your beauty;[j]
For the sake of your splendor
you corrupted your wisdom.
So I threw you down to the earth;
I made you a spectacle before kings.
18 You profaned your sanctuaries
by the magnitude of your iniquities
in your dishonest trade.
So I made fire come from within you,
and it consumed you.[k]
I reduced you to ashes on the ground
in the sight of everyone watching you.
19 All those who know you
   among the nations
are appalled at you.
You have become an object of horror
and will never exist again."[l]

A Prophecy against Sidon

[20] The word of the LORD came to me: [21] "Son of man, turn your face toward Sidon[m] and prophesy against it. [22] You are to say: This is what •Yahweh GOD says:

Look! I am against you, Sidon,[n]
and I will display My glory within you.
They will know that I am •Yahweh
when I execute judgments against her[o]
and demonstrate My holiness
   through her.
23 I will send a plague against her[p]
and bloodshed in her streets;
the slain will fall within her,
while the sword is against her[l]
   on every side.
Then they will know that I am Yahweh.

[A] 28:9 Some Hb mss, LXX, Syr, Vg; other Hb mss read *of the one who kills*   [B] 28:12 Or *sealer*   [C] 28:12,13 Hb obscure   [D] 28:13 Or *lapis lazuli*   [E] 28:13 Or *malachite, or garnet*   [F] 28:13 Or *beryl*   [G] 28:14 Or *With an anointed guardian cherub*   [H] 28:16 Or *and the guardian cherub banished you*   [I] 28:23 Or *within her by the sword*

Adam in the **garden** of **Eden**. Nine of the twelve **precious** gemstones listed here were included on the high priest's breastpiece (Ex 28:15-20; 39:10-13).

28:14 Though the context is an oracle against the king of Tyre, many believe that this **anointed . . . cherub** should ultimately be identified as Satan himself. In that case the passage would have double reference. As an angel, Satan had continuous and unhindered access to the glorious presence of God before he rebelled.

28:17 The primary fault of the Tyrian king was greed. This may explain why there are numerous allusions to the gar-

den of Eden in the account. As Adam and Eve attempted to obtain equality with God (Gn 3:4), so also did the king of Tyre (Ac 12:20-23). Also, the description is similar to that which is given for the serpent in Rv 12:9.

28:21 **Sidon** was another key Phoenician port city. It was located 25 miles north of Tyre. Sidon and Tyre often are mentioned together (Jr 27:3; 47:4; Jl 3:4). During times when Tyre was in decline, Sidon would increase in prominence. In the Persian period, Sidon stood at the head of the Phoenician cities.

28:23 As in the account of the exodus, God will gain glory

²⁴"The house of Israel will no longer be hurt by^A prickly briers or painful thorns^a from all their neighbors who treat them with contempt. Then they will know that I am the Lord Yahweh.

²⁵"This is what the Lord GOD says: When I gather the house of Israel^b from the peoples where they are scattered and demonstrate My holiness through them in the sight of the nations, then they will live in their own land, which I gave to My servant Jacob. ²⁶They will live there securely,^c build houses, and plant vineyards.^d They will live securely when I execute judgments^e against all their neighbors who treat them with contempt. Then they will know that I am Yahweh their God."

A Prophecy of Egypt's Ruin

29 In the tenth year, in the tenth month on the twelfth day of the month, the word of the LORD came to me: ²"Son of man, turn your face toward Pharaoh king of Egypt and prophesy against him and against all of Egypt.^f³ Speak to him and say: This is what the Lord GOD says:

Look, I am against you, Pharaoh
    king of Egypt,
the great monster^B,g lying in the middle
    of his Nile,
who says, 'My Nile is my own;
I made it for myself.'
⁴ I will put hooks in your jaws^h
and make the fish of your streams
    cling to your scales.
I will haul you up
from the middle of your Nile,
and all the fish of your streams
    will cling to your scales.
⁵ I will leave you in the desert,^i
you and all the fish of your streams.
You will fall on the open ground
and will not be taken away
or gathered for burial.^j
I have given you
to the beasts of the earth
and the birds of the sky as food.^k

⁶ Then all the inhabitants of Egypt
will know that I am •Yahweh,
for they^c have been a staff made of reed

Cross references (center column):

^a 28:24 Nm 33:55
^b 28:25 Ps 106:47; Ezk 20:41; 34:13
^c 28:26 Jr 23:6; Ezk 34:25,28; 38:8
^d Jr 32:15; Ezk 11:3
^e Ezk 25:11
^f 29:2 Is 19:1-17; Jr 46:2-26; Ezk 30-32
^g 29:3 Ps 74:13; Is 27:1; Ezk 32:2
^h 29:4 Jb 41:2; Ezk 38:4
^i 29:5 Ezk 32:4-6 Jr 8:2; 25:33
^k Ezk 39:4

---

^A 28:24 Lit *longer have*   ^B 29:3 Or *crocodile*   ^C 29:6 LXX, Syr, Vg read *you*

Hypostyle Hall in the Temple of Amun-Re at Thebes, Egypt (29:9)

from the execution of judgment on the enemies of His people (Ex 14:4,17-18).

28:25 The gathering of God's people is a common theme in Ezekiel and later biblical books (11:17; 20:34,41-42; 29:13; 34:13; 36:24; 37:21; 38:8; 39:27; Neh 1:9; Zch 10:8,10). Another common theme in Ezekiel is the demonstration of God's **holiness** (vv. 22,25; 20:41; 36:23; 38:16; 39:27).

28:26 Once the nations that treated Israel with **contempt** are destroyed, the exiles will return to the land of Israel (Gn 12; 28; 35) and rebuild their community. Then they will exhibit God's holiness in the world.

29:2 Egypt was Israel's constant foe after keeping the nation in bondage for 400 years during its early history. This oracle against Egypt is somewhat unique insomuch as God promises to restore the pagan nation to its land after a period of 40 years. If Egypt fell to the Babylonians about 568 B.C., as implied in the chronicles of the Babylonian kings, then a 40-year "captivity" of Egypt would have ended under the Persians, who famously encouraged exiled peoples to return to their homelands (2Ch 36:22-23). Though she was restored to her land, Egypt never returned to her former position of preeminence in the international arena. Moreover, her "restoration" may not have been an act of divine grace for Egypt's sake so much as it was a reminder of Israel's past faithlessness, which earned them a 40-year penalty (Nm 32:13). When Christ returns, the positions of Israel and Egypt will be reversed. Israel will rule over Egypt, and the Egyptians will no longer be idolaters but will worship the one true God (Is 18–19).

29:3 In ancient Near Eastern literature, the word **monster** (Hb *tannin*) refers to the mythical sea monster, the chaos god, known elsewhere as Rahab or Leviathan. Ezekiel equates **Pharaoh** with *tannin*. Like the ruler of Tyre in chapter 28, Pharaoh dared to defy the Lord. Egypt is compared

to the house of Israel.

7 When Israel grasped you by the hand,
you splintered,[a] tearing all
their shoulders;
when they leaned on you,
you shattered and made all
their hips unsteady.[A]

8"Therefore this is what the Lord GOD says: I am going to bring a sword[b] against you and wipe out man and animal from you. 9The land of Egypt will be a desolate ruin.[c] Then they will know that I am Yahweh. Because you[B] said, 'The Nile is my own; I made it,' 10therefore, I am against you and your Nile. I will turn the land of Egypt into ruins, a desolate waste from Migdol to Syene, as far as the border of •Cush. 11No human foot will pass through it, and no animal foot will pass through it.[d] It will be uninhabited for 40 years. 12I will make the land of Egypt a desolation among[C] desolate lands, and its cities will be a desolation among[D] ruined cities[e] for 40 years. I will disperse the Egyptians among the nations and scatter them across the countries.[f]

13"For this is what the Lord GOD says: At the end of 40 years I will gather the Egyptians from the nations where they were dispersed.[g] 14I will restore the fortunes of Egypt and bring them back to the land of Pathros, the land of their origin. There they will be a lowly kingdom. 15Egypt will be the lowliest of kingdoms and will never again exalt itself over the nations. I will make them so small they cannot rule over the nations. 16It will never again be an object of trust[h] for the house of Israel,

a29:7 2Kg 18:21; Is 36:6
b29:8 Ezk 14:17
c29:9 Ezk 30:7-8
d29:11 Ezk 32:13
e29:12 Ezk 30:7
fEzk 12:15; 30:15,23,26
g29:13 Is 19:22-23
h29:16 Is 20:5; 30:1-3; Ezk 17:15
i29:18 Ezk 26:7-12
j29:19 Ezk 30:10,24-25; 32:11
k29:21 1Sm 2:10; Ps 92:10; 132:17
lEzk 3:27; 24:27; 33:22
m30:2 Is 13:6; Ezk 21:12; Jl 1:11,13
n30:3 Jl 2:1; Ob 15
oEzk 32:7; 34:12

drawing attention to their sin of turning to the Egyptians. Then they will know that I am the Lord Yahweh."

Babylon Receives Egypt as Compensation

17In the twenty-seventh year in the first month, on the first day of the month, the word of the LORD came to me: 18"Son of man, Nebuchadnezzar king of Babylon made his army labor strenuously against Tyre.[i] Every head was made bald and every shoulder chafed, but he and his army received no compensation from Tyre for the labor he expended against it. 19Therefore this is what the Lord GOD says: I am going to give the land of Egypt to Nebuchadnezzar king of Babylon,[j] who will carry off its wealth, seizing its spoil and taking its plunder. This will be his army's compensation. 20I have given him the land of Egypt as the pay he labored for, since they worked for Me." This is the declaration of the Lord GOD. 21"In that day I will cause a •horn to sprout[k] for the house of Israel, and I will enable you to speak out[l] among them. Then they will know that I am Yahweh."

Egypt's Doom

30 The word of the LORD came to me: 2"Son of man, prophesy and say: This is what the Lord GOD says:

Wail:[m] Woe for the day!
3 For a day is near;
a day belonging to the LORD is near.[n]
It will be a day of clouds,[o]

A29:7 LXX, Syr, Vg; MT reads *and you caused their hips to stand*   B29:9 LXX, Syr, Vg; MT reads *he*   C29:12 Or *Egypt the most desolate of*   D29:12 Or *be the most desolate of*

---

to a dragon in Is 30:7 (Jb 9:13; 26:12-13; Ps 89:9-10; Is 51:9-10).

29:7 Egypt's guilt stemmed from its pact to assist King Zedekiah of Judah in his defiance of Nebuchadnezzar, the agent of God's wrath against Judah. By resisting Nebuchadnezzar, Pharaoh Hophra was hindering the execution of God's plan. Over the centuries, Israel had repeatedly sought aid (military and otherwise) from Egypt against the counsel of God (Dt 17:16; 1Kg 10:28; Is 30:1-3). In Is 36:6 and 2Kg 18:21, placing trust in Pharaoh is portrayed as leaning on a staff no stronger than a reed. The reed will break and injure the hand that holds it. The phrase **you splintered, tearing all their shoulders; when they leaned on you** looks back to Hophra's unsuccessful attempt to give military support during the siege of Jerusalem. His attack against Nebuchadnezzar in the spring of 588 B.C. failed to relieve Jerusalem (Jr 37:5-10). God's people had once again turned elsewhere for the support they should have sought in Him alone (Is 36:6-7).

29:12 In the Bible **40 years** is a frequent expression for a complete and lengthy period of time (Nm 14:33; 1Kg 2:11). If Egypt fell to the Babylonians in 568 B.C., as most ancient

Near Eastern histories maintain, then this 40-year "captivity" of Egypt ended when the Persians came to power.

29:16 After the Babylonians were defeated and the Persians seized control, Egypt was **never again** a formidable world power.

29:21 **Horn** refers to the horn of an animal. Because animals used these during conflict, "horn" was used as a metaphor for strength or power (1Sm 2:1; 1Kg 22:11; Ps 92:10; Jr 48:25). Here the reference is to the strength of Messiah and the future restoration of the Davidic monarchy in the aftermath of Egypt's collapse (Ps 132:17; Is 11:1-16). The word "grow" or **sprout** is a specific messianic image. The ultimate fulfillment of this verse is found in Christ (17:22-24), who will come to the aid of Israel and defend her against the heathen world in the last days (Lk 1:69; Rv 5:6).

30:2 The Day of the Lord theme occurs in many prophetic books (Is 2:6-21; 13; 14; Jl 1–2; Am 5:18-20; Obadiah; Zph 1:2-18; 2:1-3).

30:3 **Clouds** often appear in texts that address the changes that take place in the end times (v. 18; 32:7-8; 34:12; Jl 2:2; Zph 1:15).

a time of doom for the nations.
⁴ A sword will come against Egypt,
and there will be anguish in •Cush
when the slain fall in Egypt,
and its wealth is taken away,
and its foundations are torn down.
⁵ Cush, Put, and Lud,ᵃ
and all the various foreign troops,ᴬ
plus Libyaᴮ and the men
   of the covenant landᶜ
will fall by the sword along with them.
⁶ This is what the LORD says:
Those who support Egypt will fall,
and its proud strength will collapse.
From Migdol to Syene
they will fall within it by the sword.
                This is the declaration
                      of the Lord GOD.
⁷ They will be desolate
amongᴰ desolate lands,
and their cities will lie
among ruinedᴱ cities.ᵇ
⁸ They will know that I am •Yahweh
when I set fire to Egyptᶜ
and all its allies are shattered.

⁹ On that day, messengers will go out from Me
in shipsᵈ to terrify confident Cush. Anguish
will come over them on the day of Egypt's
doom. For indeed it is coming."
¹⁰ This is what the Lord GOD says:

I will put an end to the hordesꜰ
   of Egypt
by the hand of Nebuchadnezzar
   king of Babylon.
¹¹ He along with his people,
ruthless men from the nations,
will be brought in to destroy the land.
They will draw their swords
   against Egypt
and fill the land with the slain.ᵉ
¹² I will make the streams dry
and sell the land into the hands
   of evil men.ᶠ
I will bring desolation
on the land and everything in it
by the hands of foreigners.
I, Yahweh, have spoken.

¹³ This is what the Lord GOD says:

I will destroy the idols and put an end
to the false gods in Memphis.ᵍ
There will no longer be
a prince from the land of Egypt.
So I will instill fear in that land.
¹⁴ I will make Pathrosʰ desolate,
set fire to Zoan,
and execute judgments on Thebes.
¹⁵ I will pour out My wrath on Pelusium,
the stronghold of Egypt,
and will wipe out the crowdsꜰ
   of Thebes.

ᵃ30:5 Jr 46:9
ᵇ30:7 Ezk 29:12
ᶜ30:8 Ezk 22:31
ᵈ30:9 Is 18:1-2
ᵉ30:11 Ezk 28:7;
31:12
ᶠ30:12 Is 19:4
ᵍ30:13 Jr
43:12-13
ʰ30:14 Jr
44:1,15; Ezk
29:14

ᴬ30:5 Or all Arabia   ᴮ30:5 Lit Cub; Hb obscure   ᶜ30:5 Probably Israel   ᴰ30:7 Or be the most desolate of   ᴱ30:7 Or will be the most ruined of   ꜰ30:10,15 Or pomp, or wealth

30:5 The phrase **men of the covenant land** is literally "sons of the land of the covenant." It contains an implied reference to Jewish mercenaries who fought with Pharaoh's forces.

30:13 The judgment that will be executed against Egypt (**I will destroy the idols and put an end to the false gods in Memphis**) recalls language of the exodus account (Ex 6:6), perhaps suggesting a reenactment of the exodus.

30:20 The date formula indicates that this oracle was announced shortly before the fall of Jerusalem. The date may allude to Pharaoh Hophra's attempt to intervene to deliver Judah from the crisis (Jr 37:5).

30:21 The figurative expression **I have broken the arm of Pharaoh** refers to Nebuchadnezzar's defeat of Hophra, who attempted to relieve Jerusalem in 588 B.C. (2Kg 24:7; Jr 37:5).

31:3 **Lebanon** was known for its cedars (vv. 15-18; Jdg 9:15; 1Kg 4:33; 5:6; 2Kg 14:9; Ezr 3:7; Ps 29:5; 92:12; 104:16). The **cedar** was a renowned ancient Near Eastern symbol of royalty and majesty. In the Bible it is frequently mentioned in texts describing the production of palaces and temples. The fall of **Assyria** forms the precedent and paradigm for the fall of Egypt. Isaiah 14:3-23 likewise portrays the demise of the Babylonian king, relating it to the downfall of Assyria (Is 14:24-27; see Nah 3:8-10 for a similar comparison of Egypt and Assyria). Similarly, Isaiah

portrayed the Assyrian monarch as a tall tree that would fall (Is 10:5-34).

31:4 This description of the cedar is reminiscent of the primeval **waters** of Gn 1:2 as well as the location of the **trees** in the garden of Eden in Genesis 3. These allusions may serve to heighten the origin and significance of the Pharaoh.

31:10 Because the tree representing the Pharaoh had become prominent (**great in height**), it would be cut down (Is 2:6-21; 10:5-34).

Valley of the Kings containing tombs of pharaohs, across the Nile from Luxor at ancient Thebes (30:21-24)

16 I will set fire to Egypt;
  Pelusium will writhe in anguish,
Thebes will be breached,
  and Memphis will face foes
    in broad daylight.^A
17 The young men of On^B and Pi-beseth
  will fall by the sword,
and those cities^C will go into captivity.
18 The day will be dark^D in Tehaphnehes,
  when I break the yoke of Egypt there
and its proud strength
  comes to an end in the city.
A cloud^a will cover Tehaphnehes,^E
  and its villages will go into captivity.
19 So I will execute judgments
    against Egypt,
and they will know that I am Yahweh.

Pharaoh's Power Broken

20 In the eleventh year, in the first month, on the seventh day of the month, the word of the Lord came to me: 21 "Son of man, I have broken the arm^b of Pharaoh king of Egypt. Look, it has not been bandaged—no medicine has been applied and no splint put on to bandage it so that it can grow strong enough to handle a sword. 22 Therefore this is what the Lord God says: Look! I am against Pharaoh king of Egypt. I will break his arms, both the strong one and the one already broken, and will make the sword fall from his hand. 23 I will disperse the Egyptians among the nations and scatter them among the countries.^c 24 I will strengthen the arms of Babylon's king and place My sword^d in his hand. But I will break the arms of Pharaoh, and he will groan before him as a mortally wounded man. 25 I will strengthen the arms of Babylon's king, but Pharaoh's arms will fall. They will know that I am Yahweh when I place My sword in the hand of Babylon's king and he wields it against the land of Egypt. 26 When I disperse the Egyptians among the nations and scatter them among the countries, they will know that I am Yahweh."

Downfall of Egypt and Assyria

31 In the eleventh year,^e in the third month, on the first day of the month, the word of the Lord came to me: 2 "Son of man, say to Pharaoh king of Egypt and to his hordes:

Who are you like in your greatness?
3   Think of Assyria, a cedar in Lebanon,^f

Cross references (center column)

^a 30:18 Ezk 34:12
^b 30:21 Ps 10:15; 37:17
^c 30:23 Ezk 29:12
^d 30:24 Zph 2:12
^e 31:1 Ezk 30:20
^f 31:3 Is 10:33-34; Ezk 17:3-4,22; 31:16
^g 31:5 Dn 4:11
^h Ezk 17:5
^i 31:6 Ezk 17:23; Dn 4:12,21; Mt 13:32
^j 31:8 Gn 2:8; Is 51:3; Ezk 28:13
^k 31:10 Ezk 28:17; Dn 5:20
^l 31:11 Ezk 30:10-11; Dn 5:18-19
^m 31:12 Ezk 28:7; 32:12

with beautiful branches
  and shady foliage
and of lofty height.
  Its top was among the clouds.^F
4 The waters caused it to grow;
  the underground springs made it tall,
directing their rivers all around
  the place where the tree was planted
and sending their channels
  to all the trees of the field.
5 Therefore the cedar became greater
    in height
than all the trees of the field.^g
  Its branches multiplied,
and its boughs grew long
  as it spread them out
because of the plentiful water.^h
6 All the birds of the sky
  nested in its branches,^i
and all the animals of the field
  gave birth beneath its boughs;
all the great nations lived in its shade.
7 It was beautiful in its greatness,
  in the length of its limbs,
for its roots extended
  to abundant water.
8 The cedars in God's garden could not
    rival it;^j
the pine trees couldn't compare
  with its branches,
nor could the plane trees match
  its boughs.
No tree in the garden of God
  could compare with it in beauty.
9 I made it beautiful with its many limbs,
  and all the trees of Eden,
which were in God's garden, envied it.

10 "Therefore this is what the Lord God says: Since it^G became great in height and set its top among the clouds,^F and it^H grew proud^k on account of its height, 11 I determined to hand it over to a ruler of nations;^l he would surely deal with it. I banished it because of its wickedness. 12 Foreigners, ruthless men from the nations,^m cut it down and left it lying. Its limbs fell on the mountains and in every valley; its boughs lay broken in all the earth's ravines. All the peoples of the earth left its shade and abandoned it. 13 All the birds of the sky nested on its fallen trunk, and all the animals of the field were among its boughs. 14 This happened so that no trees planted beside water would become great in height and set their tops among the clouds,^F and so that no other well-watered

---

trees would reach them in height. For they have all been consigned to death, to the underworld, among the •people who descend to the •Pit.[a]

[15] "This is what the Lord God says: I caused grieving on the day the cedar went down to •Sheol.[b] I closed off the underground deep because of it:[A] I held back the rivers of the deep, and its abundant waters were restrained. I made Lebanon mourn on account of it, and all the trees of the field fainted because of it. [16] I made the nations quake at the sound of its downfall, when I threw it down to Sheol to be with those who descend to the Pit. Then all the trees of Eden,[c] all the well-watered trees, the choice and best of Lebanon, were comforted[d] in the underworld. [17] They too descended with it to Sheol, to those slain by the sword. As its allies[B,C] they had lived in its shade among the nations.

[18] "Who then are you like in glory and greatness among Eden's trees? You also will be brought down to the underworld to be with the trees of Eden. You will lie among the uncircumcised with those slain by the sword.[e] This is Pharaoh and all his hordes"—the declaration of the Lord God.

A Lament for Pharaoh

32 In the twelfth year, in the twelfth month, on the first day of the month, the word of the Lord came to me: [2]"Son of man, lament[f] for Pharaoh king of Egypt and say to him:

You compare yourself to a lion
of the nations,
but[D] you are like a monster[g] in the seas.
You thrash about in your rivers,
churn up the waters with your feet,
and muddy the[E] rivers."

[3]This is what the Lord God says:

I will spread My net over you[h]
with an assembly of many peoples,

and they[F] will haul you up in My net.
[4] I will abandon you on the land
and hurl you on the open field.
I will cause all the birds of the sky
to settle on you
and let the beasts of the entire earth
eat their fill of you.[i]
[5] I will put your flesh on the mountains[j]
and fill the valleys with your carcass.
[6] I will drench the land
with the flow of your blood,
even to the mountains;
the ravines will be filled with your gore.

[7] When I snuff you out,
I will cover the heavens
and darken their stars.
I will cover the sun with a cloud,[k]
and the moon will not give its light.
[8] I will darken all the shining lights
in the heavens over you,
and will bring darkness on your land.
This is the declaration
of the Lord God.

[9] I will trouble the hearts
of many peoples,
when I bring about your destruction
among the nations,
in countries you do not know.
[10] I will cause many nations to be appalled
at you,
and their kings will shudder with fear
because of you[l]
when I brandish My sword
in front of them.
On the day of your downfall
each of them will tremble
every moment[m] for his life.

[11]For this is what the Lord God says:

The sword of Babylon's king
will come against you!
[12] I will make your hordes fall
by the swords of warriors,

[a]31:14 Ezk 26:20
[b]31:15 Ezk 32:22-23
[c]31:16 Ezk 26:15; 27:28; Hg 2:7
[d]Ezk 32:31
[e]31:18 Ezk 28:10; 32:19,21
[f]32:2 Ezk 19:1; 27:2; 28:12
[g]Is 27:1
[h]32:3 Ezk 12:13
[i]32:4 Ezk 29:3-5
[j]32:5 Ezk 31:12
[k]32:7 Jl 2:2,31; 3:15; Am 8:9; Mt 24:29; Rv 6:12; 8:12
[l]32:10 Ezk 27:35
[m]Ezk 26:16

[A]31:15 Or *I covered it with the underground deep*   [B]31:17 LXX, Syr read *offspring*   [C]31:17 Lit *arm*   [D]32:2 Or *Lion of the nations, you are destroyed;*   [E]32:2 Lit *their*   [F]32:3 LXX, Vg read *I*

31:15 Though in the OT the godly may express fear of being abandoned by God to **Sheol** (Ps 88:3), nowhere is a righteous person said actually to have gone to Sheol. The contrast between the destiny of the righteous and the unrighteous after death is most clearly apparent in Psalm 49.

31:18 The **trees** would die disgracefully as **uncircumcised** foreigners without a decent burial. This reality would be particularly poignant for Egyptian royalty because they built pyramids in the hopes of making themselves comfortable in the afterlife.

32:2 Many scholars see this as a portrayal of Pharaoh's defeat by God (**like a monster in the seas**), much like pas-

sages that figuratively speak of God defeating the mythical sea dragon Leviathan (Jb 38:8-11; Ps 74:12-17; 104:7-9; Is 27:1). God can lay any foe low, no matter his powers.

32:3 The Lord will cast His **net** over Pharaoh, a method by which hunters captured crocodiles and lions (19:8).

32:6 The image of flowing **blood** recalls the plague of blood, the first plague in the exodus account (Ex 7:19-24).

32:7 The darkness in this verse recalls the exodus plague of darkness against Egypt (Ex 10:21-29) as well as the darkness that will accompany the Day of the Lord. On the Day of the Lord the heavens will be darkened, and the **sun,**

all of them ruthless men
   from the nations.ᵃ
They will ravage Egypt's pride,
   and all its hordes will be destroyed.
¹³ I will slaughter all its cattle
   that are beside many waters.
No human foot will churn them again,
   and no cattle hooves
      will disturb them.ᵇ
¹⁴ Then I will let their waters settle
   and will make their rivers flow like oil.
            This is the declaration
               of the Lord Goᴅ.
¹⁵ When I make the land of Egypt
   a desolation,
so that it is emptied of everything in it,
   when I strike down all who live there,
   then they will know that
   I am •Yahweh.ᶜ

¹⁶"This is a lament that will be chanted;ᵈ the women of the nations will chant it. They will chant it over Egypt and all its hordes." This is the declaration of the Lord Goᴅ.

Egypt in Sheol

¹⁷In the twelfth year,ᴬ on the fifteenth day of the month, the word of the Lᴏʀᴅ came to me: ¹⁸"Son of man, wail over the hordes of Egypt and bring Egypt and the daughters of mighty nations down to the underworld,ᴮ to be with those who descend to the •Pit:ᵉ

¹⁹ Who do you surpass in loveliness?
   Go down and be laid to rest
      with the uncircumcised!
²⁰ They will fall among those slain
      by the sword.
   A sword is appointed!ᶠ
   They drag her and all her hordes away.
²¹ Warrior leaders will speak
   from the middle of •Sheol
   about himᶜ and his allies:
   They have come down;
   the uncircumcised lie
   slain by the sword.ᵍ

²² Assyria is there with all her company;
   her graves are all around her.

ᵃ32:12 Ezk 28:7; 31:12
ᵇ32:13 Ezk 29:11
ᶜ32:15 Ex 7:5
ᵈ32:16 2Sm 1:17; 2Ch 35:25; Jr 9:17; Ezk 26:17
ᵉ32:18 Ezk 26:20
ᶠ32:20 Ezk 21:15
ᵍ32:21 Is 14:9-11; Ezk 31:15-18

ᴬ32:17 LXX reads *year, in the first month,*   ᴮ32:18 Lit *the lower parts of the earth*   ᶜ32:21 Either Pharaoh or Egypt

---

moon, and **stars** will fail to give **light** (Jl 2:1-2; 3:15; Zph 1:15).

32:12-13 On the night of the first Passover, only firstborn humans and animals died (Ex 12:29). In this coming judgment on Egypt, all people and animals will be destroyed.

32:16 Women by custom served as mourners in the ancient Near East (Jr 9:17-18).

32:19 The reference to circumcision is a metaphor for uncleanness and vileness. It is a theological rather than a literal evaluation. The phrase **the uncircumcised** is used 10 times in chapter 32 (vv. 19,21,24-30,32), to emphasize that the death of the Pharaoh will be a death of shame and defeat. In this oracle, Egypt was the climactic seventh nation that occupied the underworld (v. 18).

The ruins at Haran, the last Assyrian stronghold, abandoned in 609 ʙ.ᴄ. when the Babylonians defeated the Assyrian army of Ashur-uballit II (the last Assyrian king), and captured Haran.

All of them are slain, fallen
　　by the sword.
23 Her graves are set
　　in the deepest regions of the Pit,
and her company is all around
　　her burial place.
All of them are slain, fallen
　　by the sword—
those who once spread terror
　　in the land of the living.

24 Elam[a] is there
with all her hordes around her grave.
All of them are slain, fallen
　　by the sword—
those who went down
　　to the underworld[A] uncircumcised,
who once spread their terror
　　in the land of the living.
They bear their disgrace
　　with those who descend to the Pit.

25 Among the slain
they prepare a resting place for Elam
　　with all her hordes.
Her graves are all around her.
All of them are uncircumcised,
　　slain by the sword,
although their terror was once spread
　　in the land of the living.
They bear their disgrace
　　with those who descend to the Pit.
They are placed among the slain.

26 Meshech and Tubal[B,b] are there,
with all their hordes.
Their graves are all around them.
All of them are uncircumcised,
　　slain by the sword,
although their terror was once spread
　　in the land of the living.

27 They do not lie down
with the fallen warriors
　　of the uncircumcised,[c]
who went down to Sheol
with their weapons of war,
whose swords were placed
　　under their heads.[D]
The punishment for their sins
rested on their bones,
although the terror of these warriors
was once in the land of the living.

28 But you will be shattered
and will lie down
　　among the uncircumcised,
with those slain by the sword.[c]

29 Edom[d] is there, her kings and all
　　her princes,
who, despite their strength,
　　have been placed
among those slain by the sword.
They lie down with the uncircumcised,
with those who descend to the Pit.

30 All the leaders of the north[e]
and all the Sidonians[f] are there.
They went down in shame
　　with the slain,
despite the terror
　　their strength inspired.
They lie down uncircumcised
with those slain by the sword.
They bear their disgrace
with those who descend to the Pit.

31 Pharaoh will see them
and be comforted[g] over all his hordes—
Pharaoh and all his army,
slain by the sword.
　　　This is the declaration
　　　　　of the Lord God.

32 For I will spread My[E] terror
in the land of the living,
so Pharaoh and all his hordes
will be laid to rest
　　among the uncircumcised,
with those slain by the sword."
　　　　　This is the declaration
　　　　　　of the Lord God.

Ezekiel as Israel's Watchman

33 The word of the Lord came to me: 2 "Son of man, speak to your people and tell them: Suppose I bring the sword against a land, and the people of that land select a man from among them, appointing him as their watchman, 3 and he sees the sword coming against the land and blows his trumpet[h] to warn the people. 4 Then, if anyone hears the sound of the trumpet but ignores the warning,[i] and the sword comes and takes him away, his blood will be on his own head. 5 Since he heard the sound of the trumpet but ignored the warning, his blood is on his own hands.[F] If he had taken warning, he would have saved his life. 6 However, if the watchman sees the sword coming but doesn't blow the trumpet, so that the people aren't warned, and the sword comes and takes away their lives, then they have been taken away because of their iniquity, but I will hold the watchman accountable for their blood.

a 32:24 Gn 10:22
b 32:26 Gn 10:2;
Ezk 27:13;
38:2-3
c 32:28 Is 14:18
d 32:29 Ezk 25:12-14
e 32:30 Ezk 38:6,15; 39:2
f Ezk 28:21-23
g 32:31 Ezk 31:16-18
h 33:3 Nm 10:9
i 33:4 Zch 1:4

A 32:24 Lit the lower parts of the earth　B 32:26 Lit Meshech-tubal　C 32:27 LXX reads of antiquity　D 32:27 Or Do they not . . . heads?
E 32:32 Alt Hb tradition, LXX, Syr read his　F 33:5 Lit on him

⁷"As for you, son of man, I have made you a watchman for the house of Israel.ᵃ When you hear a word from My mouth, give them a warning from Me. ⁸If I say to the wicked, 'Wicked one, you will surely die,'ᵇ but you do not speak out to warn him about his way, that wicked person will die for his iniquity, yet I will hold you responsible for his blood. ⁹But if you warn a wicked person to turn from his way and he doesn't turn from it, he will die for his iniquity, but you will have saved your life.

¹⁰"Now as for you, son of man, say to the house of Israel: You have said this, 'Our transgressions and our sins are heavy on us, and we are wasting away because of them!ᶜ How then can we survive?'ᵈ ¹¹Tell them: As I live"—the declaration of the Lord Goᴅ—"I take no pleasure in the death of the wicked, but rather that the wicked person should turn from his way and live.ᵉ Repent, repent of your evil ways! Why will you die, house of Israel?

¹²"Now, son of man, say to your people: The righteousness of the righteous person will not save him on the day of his transgression; neither will the wickedness of the wicked person cause him to stumble on the day he turns from his wickedness. The righteous person won't be able to survive by his righteousness on the day he sins. ¹³When I tell the righteous person that he will surely live, but he trusts in

his righteousness and commits iniquity, then none of his righteousness will be remembered, and he will die because of the iniquity he has committed.ᶠ

¹⁴"So when I tell the wicked person, 'You will surely die,' but he repents of his sin and does what is just and right— ¹⁵he returns collateral, makes restitution for what he has stolen, and walks in the statutes of lifeᵍ without practicing iniquity—he will certainly live; he will not die. ¹⁶None of the sins he committed will be held against him. He has done what is just and right; he will certainly live.ʰ

¹⁷"But your people say, 'The Lord's way isn't fair,'ⁱ even though it is their own way that isn't fair. ¹⁸When a righteous person turns from his righteousness and commits iniquity, he will die on account of this. ¹⁹But if a wicked person turns from his wickedness and does what is just and right, he will live because of this. ²⁰Yet you say, 'The Lord's way isn't fair.' I will judge each of you according to his ways, house of Israel."

The News of Jerusalem's Fall

²¹In the twelfth year of our exile, in the tenth month, on the fifth day of the month, a fugitive from Jerusalem came to me and reported, "The city has been taken!" ²²Now the hand of the Lᴏʀᴅ had been on me the evening before

---

ᵃ 33:7 Ezk 3:17-19
ᵇ 33:8 Ezk 18:4
ᶜ 33:10 Lv 26:39; Ezk 4:17; 24:23
ᵈ Ezk 37:11
ᵉ 33:11 Ezk 18:23,30-32; Hs 11:8; 1Tm 2:4; 2Pt 3:9
ᶠ 33:13 Ezk 3:20; 18:24,26
ᵍ 33:15 Lv 18:5; Dt 5:33; 1Kg 3:14; Ezk 20:11
ʰ 33:16 Is 1:18; 43:25; Ezk 18:21-22
ⁱ 33:17 Ezk 18:25-30

32:26 Meshech and **Tubal** (see Ezk 27:13) were probably located on the northern border of modern Turkey. They are the allies of Gog in chapters 38–39.

33:1-2 This announcement of a new oracle (**Son of man, speak to your people**) begins a transitional section in the book, bridging the oracles about the nations to prophecies of consolation that close the book.

33:2 In ancient times every major town had a **watchman** stationed at a high point, either at the city gate (2Sm 18:24) or on a lookout tower (2Kg 9:17). The task of the watchman may be seen in several biblical passages (Is 21:6-9; Jr 6:1,17; Hs 8:1; Am 3:6; Hab 2:1). The watchman was not responsible for the fate of the people in the city if he warned them of pending danger. Conversely, he was responsible if he failed to raise the alarm. The watchman is used here as a prophetic agent calling for repentance. The oracle is addressed to the people rather than to the prophet alone (Ezk 3:16-27). The metaphor of the lookout was first applied to Ezekiel in a private message at the start of his career. The prophet's role as sentinel explains how the intention behind Ezekiel's doom prophecy was not death but life—a warning call to repentance.

33:3 The **trumpet** was made from a ram's horn (Jos 6:4,6,13). It was used to **warn the people** of approaching danger (Neh 4:18-20; Jr 4:19; Am 3:6; 1Co 14:8) as well as to announce the beginnings of religious celebrations (Day of Atonement, Lv 25:9; New Moon festival, Ps 81:3).

33:6 Given its essential role in biological systems, **blood** is synonymous with life (see Gn 9:5; 42:22).

33:10 Earlier in chapter 18, charges announced from God through Ezekiel had aimed to convict the exiles of their sin and rebellion. Now that the judgment had become drastic reality (Lm 1:12; 2:13,20), the people felt that total destruction awaited them. But Ezekiel's theme of taking responsibility shows that a person's personal sinfulness is forgivable even if his nation is pressed hard under ongoing judgment. This section (33:10-20) in many ways paraphrases sections of 18:21-32. This is the first time the exiles expressed a consciousness of their **sins**. Previously they had placed the blame for their predicaments on their fathers (18:2) and even God (18:19,25).

33:12 This section (vv. 12-20) addresses the same subject as 18:21-29. Each person, whether **righteous** or wicked, has a choice to live faithfully each day.

33:13 Ezekiel 18:21-24 began by addressing the repentant wicked (vv. 21-23) and then moved to the backslidden righteous (v. 24). Here Ezekiel begins with the backslidden **righteous** and ends with the repentant wicked (vv. 14-16).

33:15 This description of the obedient life answers the question of verse 10: "How then can we survive?"

33:21 The six messages in 33:21–39:29 are dated in this verse. The time it took for the bearer of the news to reach Ezekiel was five to six months. When the exiles returned from Babylon, the journey took four or five months (Ezr 7:9). The siege of Jerusalem lasted two years and seven months (2Kg 25:8). Now that the prophet had been informed of Jerusalem's fall, the prophet would address

the fugitive arrived, and He opened my mouth before the man came to me in the morning. So my mouth was opened and I was no longer mute.[a]

Israel's Continued Rebellion

[23]Then the word of the LORD came to me: [24]"Son of man, those who live in the[A] ruins in the land of Israel are saying, 'Abraham was only one person,[b] yet he received possession of the land.[c] But we are many; the land has been given to us as a possession.'[d] [25]Therefore say to them: This is what the Lord GOD says: You eat meat with blood in it,[e] raise your eyes to your idols, and shed blood. Should you then receive possession of the land? [26]You have relied on your swords, you have committed detestable acts, and each of you has defiled his neighbor's wife. Should you then receive possession of the land?[f]

[27]"Tell them this: This is what the Lord GOD says: As surely as I live, those who are in the ruins will fall by the sword, those in the open field I have given to wild animals to be devoured, and those in the strongholds and caves will die by plague.[g] [28]I will make the land a desolate waste,[h] and its proud strength will come to an end.[i] The mountains of Israel[j] will become desolate, with no one passing

through. [29]They will know that I am •Yahweh when I make the land a desolate waste because of all the detestable acts they have committed.

[30]"Now, son of man, your people are talking about you near the city walls and in the doorways of their houses. One person speaks to another, each saying to his brother, 'Come and hear what the message is that comes from the LORD!' [31]So My people come to you in crowds,[B] sit in front of you, and hear your words, but they don't obey them. Although they express love with their mouths, their hearts pursue dishonest profit. [32]Yes, to them you are like a singer of love songs who has a beautiful voice and plays skillfully on an instrument. They hear your words, but they don't obey them. [33]Yet when it comes[k]—and it will definitely come—then they will know that a prophet has been among them."

The Shepherds and God's Flock

34 The word of the LORD came to me: [2]"Son of man, prophesy against the shepherds of Israel. Prophesy, and say to them: This is what the Lord GOD says to the shepherds: Woe to the shepherds of Israel, who have been feeding themselves![l] Shouldn't the shepherds feed their flock? [3]You eat the

a 33:22 Ezk 3:26-27; 24:26-27
b 33:24 Is 51:2
c Gn 15:7; 28:4
d Ezk 36:2
e 33:25 Lv 19:26
f 33:26 Ezk 18:6,10-11,15
g 33:27 Ezk 5:12
h 33:28 Ezk 35:3
i Ezk 7:24
j Ezk 6:2
k 33:33 Jr 28:9; Ezk 33:29
l 34:2 Jr 23:1

A33:24 Lit these   **B**33:31 Lit you like the coming of a people

---

the restoration of Israel (Ezk 33:21–39:29) and the temple (chaps. 40–48). Many of the prophecies of restoration reverse the earlier images of devastation and ruin. The fall of Jerusalem was a watershed, fulfilling the prophetic judgments; now was time for a message of hope and promise. The fulfillment of the prophecy from 24:26 displays God's sovereign power over history and marks a turning point in the prophet's relation to his listeners.

33:24 This saying (**Abraham was only one person . . .**) is based on a tradition represented in Genesis 15, in which Abraham, still childless, was promised innumerable descendants and possession of the land. Notice the similarity between this popular saying and one that was prevalent just six years earlier (Ezk 11:14-21). Those who remained behind were repeating their earlier claim to the land (11:15). The lack of heartfelt devotion, as well as the self-centeredness evident in the quotation, contrasts with Abraham's faithfulness and total dependence on God. Abraham is not only important historically, but he is also revered as the father of Judaism, Christianity, and Islam. Abraham was the first person in the Bible to be called a Hebrew (Gn 14:13), and he was the first to be designated as a prophet (Gn 20:7; cp. Ps 105:15). In the Genesis narratives, Abraham demonstrated a strong trust in God and His commands (Gn 12:4; 17:23; 21:14; 22:3). The NT appeals to Abraham as a model of what it means to trust God (Rm 4; Gl 3; Heb 11; Jms 2). Abraham is important not only for his faith but also because of the promises God made to him in a covenant that is central to God's plan for the ages. This covenant is known as the Abrahamic covenant (Gn 12).

33:25 The list of sins in this verse is similar to the basic pro-

hibitions for Gentile believers in Ac 15:29. The list is also similar to OT laws for strangers.

33:27 The dangers mentioned in this verse (**sword . . . wild animals . . . plague**) are also typical of Mosaic covenant punishment predictions (Lv 26:22; Dt 32:24; cp. 2Kg 17:25-26). Notice the threefold threat in Ezk 5:12; 7:15; 12:16 and the fourfold threat in 14:12-21. Ezekiel's strategy was deliberate. Those **who are in the ruins** are very unlike faithful Abraham, who received God's promise of land but was also enjoined to walk before God and be blameless (Gn 17:1-8).

33:29 Detestable acts denotes sexual violations of the Holiness Code, particularly Lv 18:26-30 (Ezk 5:17; 14:21). Because they disobeyed the Mosaic covenant stipulations, the Israelites failed to receive the Abrahamic covenant blessings, one of which was the blessing of occupying the promised land (Ex 20:4-5,13-14; Lv 17:10-14; 18:6; 19:26).

33:32 On **hear your words . . . don't obey them**, see Is 29:13; Mt 21:28-32; cp. Jms 1:22-25.

34:1 Ezekiel 34 is a self-contained literary unit. It begins with the introductory phrase **the word of the LORD came to me** and concludes with the recognition formula (vv. 30-31). The passage is similar to Jr 23:1-6.

34:2 The **shepherds of Israel** is a figurative expression referring to political leaders, perhaps primarily the kings. Kings and other leaders were commonly called "shepherds" (2Sm 7:7; Ps 78:70-72; Is 44:28; 63:11; Jr 10:21; 23:1-6; 25:34-38; Mc 5:4-5; Zch 11:4-17). Sheep are the most frequently mentioned animals in the Bible, and those who take care of them, "the shepherds," appear in approx-

fat, wear the wool, and butcher the fattened animals, but you do not tend the flock.*[a]* *[4]*You have not strengthened the weak, healed the sick, bandaged the injured, brought back the strays, or sought the lost.*[b]* Instead, you have ruled them with violence and cruelty. *[5]*They were scattered for lack of a shepherd;*[c]* they became food for all the wild animals*[d]* when they were scattered. *[6]*My flock went astray on all the mountains and every high hill.*[e]* They were scattered over the whole face of the earth, and there was no one searching or seeking for them.

[7]"Therefore, you shepherds, hear the word of the Lord. *[8]*As I live"—the declaration of the Lord God—"because My flock has become prey and food for every wild animal since they lack a shepherd, for My shepherds do not search for My flock, and because the shepherds feed themselves rather than My flock, *[9]*therefore, you shepherds, hear the word of the Lord!

[10]"This is what the Lord God says: Look, I am against the shepherds.*[f]* I will demand My flock from them*[A]* and prevent them from shepherding the flock. The shepherds will no longer feed themselves, for I will rescue My flock from their mouths so that they will not be food for them.

[11]"For this is what the Lord God says: See, I Myself will search for My flock and look for them. *[12]*As a shepherd looks for his sheep on the day he is among his scattered flock, so I will look for My flock. I will rescue them from all the places where they have been scattered*[g]* on a cloudy and dark day. *[13]*I will bring them out from the peoples, gather them from the countries, and bring them into their own land. I will shepherd them on the mountains of Israel, in the ravines, and in all the inhabited places of the land. *[14]*I will tend them with good pasture, and their grazing place will be on Israel's lofty mountains. There they will lie down in a good grazing place; they will feed in rich pasture on the mountains of Israel. *[15]*I will tend My flock and let them lie down."*[h]* This is the declaration of the Lord God. *[16]*"I will seek the lost,*[i]* bring back the strays, bandage the

---

[a] 34:3 Pr 27:23
[b] 34:4 Zch 11:16; Lk 15:4
[c] 34:5 Nm 27:17; 1Kg 22:17; Jr 10:21; 23:2; 50:6; Mt 9:36
[d] Ezk 34:28
[e] 34:6 1Pt 2:25
[f] 34:10 Jr 21:13; Ezk 5:8; 13:8
[g] 34:12 Jr 23:3
[h] 34:15 Ps 23:1-2
[i] 34:16 Ps 119:176; Lk 19:10

A34:10 Lit *their hand*

---

imately 100 biblical passages. Many of the most prominent individuals in the OT were shepherds, including Abraham (Gn 12:16), Isaac (Gn 26:14), Moses (Ex 3:1), David (2Sm 7:8), and Amos (Am 1:1). Because sheep are helpless if left to themselves, a person must have qualities such as care and compassion in order to be a good shepherd. Thus both civil and religious leaders are often spoken of as shepherds of the people, the flock. Just as the leaders of Israel were denounced for exploiting the sheep in Ezk 34:2,8,10, Peter warned elders against leading the church with self-serving motives (1Pt 5:2-3). On the positive side, the shepherd metaphor is used in the NT to describe how church pastors and elders should fulfill their responsibilities (Jn 21:15-17; Ac 20:28-29; 1Pt 5:1-5).

ra'ah

Hebrew Pronunciation	[rah AH]
HCSB Translation	shepherd, feed, graze
Uses in Ezekiel	32
Uses in the OT	168
Focus passage	Ezekiel 34:2-3,5,7-10,12-16

This root in many languages denotes *shepherd*. *Ra'ah* most often, as a participle, indicates a *shepherd* (Jr 51:23) or *herdsman* (Gn 13:7). The feminine is *shepherdess* (Gn 29:9). *Ra'ah* denotes *tending* (Gn 37:2) or *pasturing* (Gn 37:12) sheep or other animals (Gn 36:24). Animals *graze* (Gn 41:2) or *feed* (Sg 4:5). *Ra'ah* suggests *sustain* (Hs 9:2), *chase* (Hs 12:1), *live* (Ps 37:3), or *take charge of* (Jr 22:22). It describes people *feeding* themselves (Ezk 34:10), *eating* (Jnh 3:7), and *being well fed* (Is 14:30). Fire (Jb 20:26), animals (Ps 80:13), and people (Is 44:20) *feed on* things. *Ra'ah* metaphorically describes *God* (Gn 49:24) and *political leaders* (Ezk 34:2). *Ra'ah* connotes *ruler* (Jr 2:8). The related noun *re'iy* means *range* (1Kg 4:23). *Mir'eh* (13x) is *pasture* (Lm 1:6) or lions' *feeding ground* (Nah 2:11). *Mar'iyth* (10x) is *pasture* (Is 49:9) and once *flock* (Jr 10:21).

34:4 This characteristic feature of a shepherd (**sought the lost**) is mentioned in many biblical texts (Jr 50:6; Mt 18:12-14; Lk 15:4; 19:10). The word **cruelty** is the same word used to compare the oppression of the taskmasters who ruled brutally over the Israelites during their bondage in Egypt (Ex 1:13-14). This type of action was prohibited in the Mosaic law (Lv 25:43,46). A member of the community of Israel was not to be treated this way.

34:5 The verb **scattered** was often used by Ezekiel to describe Israel's exile and dispersion (11:16-17; 12:15; 20:23,34,41; 22:15; 28:25). Because the people were scattered they became food for wild animals and wandered over the mountains, but no **shepherd** searched for them (Mk 6:34).

34:6 This dispersion may allude to the Assyrian and Babylonian captivities, which scattered Israel and Judah among the nations. See the identical figure of a routed army in Micaiah's oracle (1Kg 22:17).

34:11 The verb to **look for** (Hb *biqqer*) is used in Leviticus to refer to the physical examination of a leper (Lv 13:36). In passages that address the offering of sacrifices, the verb describes the examination of a prospective sacrificial animal (Lv 27:33).

34:12 While most exiles were sent to Babylon, this was not the only foreign country that received displaced Israelites (Jr 43:1-7).

34:13 This promise of restoration (**I will bring them . . . into their own land**) is mentioned in 11:17 and repeated in 20:34,41-42; 28:25. The restoration of the nation is especially emphasized in Ezekiel 38-39 (see also 36:24; 37:21; 38:8; 39:27). These three phrases represent and reflect the exodus from Egypt. Hence, God's rescuing of Israel from Babylon and restoring her to Canaan follows the model of the formative saving event in the OT—the exodus from Egypt.

34:16 God is the good shepherd (Ps 23; Is 40:11; Jr 23:3;

injured,[a] and strengthen the weak, but I will destroy[A] the fat and the strong. I will shepherd them with justice.

[17]"The Lord GOD says to you, My flock: I am going to judge between one sheep and another, between the rams and male goats.[b] [18]Isn't it enough for you to feed on the good pasture? Must you also trample the rest of the pasture with your feet? Or isn't it enough that you drink the clear water? Must you also muddy the rest with your feet? [19]Yet My flock has to feed on what your feet have trampled, and drink what your feet have muddied.

[20]"Therefore, this is what the Lord GOD says to them: See, I Myself will judge between the fat sheep and the lean sheep. [21]Since you have pushed with flank and shoulder and butted all the weak ones with your horns until you scattered them all over, [22]I will save My flock, and they will no longer be prey for you. I will judge between one sheep and another. [23]I will appoint over them a single shepherd, My ser-

vant David, and he will shepherd them. He will tend them himself and will be their shepherd.[c] [24]I, *Yahweh, will be their God, and My servant David[d] will be a prince among them. I, *Yahweh, have spoken.

[25]"I will make a covenant of peace[e] with them and eliminate dangerous animals[f] in the land, so that they may live securely[g] in the wilderness and sleep in the forest. [26]I will make them and the area around My hill[h] a blessing: I will send down showers in their season[i]—showers[B] of blessing. [27]The trees of the field will give their fruit, and the land will yield its produce; My flock will be secure in their land. They will know that I am Yahweh when I break the bars of their yoke and rescue them from the hands of those who enslave them.[j] [28]They will no longer be prey for the nations, and the wild animals of the land will not consume them. They will live securely, and no one will frighten them. [29]I will establish for them a place renowned for its agriculture,[c]

---

[a]34:16 Ps 147:3; Is 30:26; Hs 6:1
[b]34:17 Mt 25:31-33
[c]34:23 Ps 78:70-71; Jn 10:11,16
[d]34:24 Jr 30:9; Ezk 37:24
[e]34:25 Ezk 37:26
[f]Is 11:6-9
[g]Ezk 28:26
[h]34:26 Ps 2:6; 15:1; 133:3; Is 27:13; Jr 31:23
[i]Dt 11:13-14; 28:12
[j]34:27 Lv 26:13; Is 52:2-3; Jr 30:8

[A]34:16 Some Hb mss, LXX, Syr, Vg read *watch over*   [B]34:26 Lit *season; they will be showers*   [C]34:29 LXX, Syr read *a plant of peace*

31:10; Mc 2:12; 4:6-8) who will gather the dispersed flock. This prophecy was not exhausted when Israel returned to her land after the Babylonian captivity. It still awaits future fulfillment in the millennium. Concern for social **justice** was a common topic for Ezekiel and other prophets (Is 3:13-15; 5:8; Am 5:12; 6:1-7; Mc 2:1-5). God will execute judgment against **the fat and the strong**, greedy sheep who trample good pasture and muddy clear waters, gorging themselves while depriving the needy of life's essential resources.

34:23 In addition to God becoming the **shepherd** for Israel, He also promised to appoint a ruler, the Messiah, from the line of **David** (see 2Sm 7:12-14a; Ps 89:4,20,29). Jeremiah equated the Messiah with the true Shepherd from the line of David, calling him "a righteous Branch," and "The Lord Is Our Righteousness." During His reign "Judah will be saved, and Israel will dwell securely" (Jr 23:5-6). This identity is also indicated elsewhere in the prophetic literature (Is 55:3-4; Jr 30:9; Ezk 37:24-25; Hs 3:5). David is referred to by name elsewhere in passages that look to the future restoration of Israel (Is 11:1-10; Jr 30:9; Ezk 37:24-25; Hs 3:5). Thus the Lord would be Israel's God; His servant David, the Messiah, would be Israel's ruler on earth after He restored Israel to her land. "My servant David" was a standing title of King David (1Kg 11:34,36,38; 2Kg 8:19; Ps 36:1; 78:70; see Is 55:3-4). David was important not just historically but theologically as well. This is evident from the covenant that God established with him (2Sm 7). This covenant was ultimately fulfilled in the person of Jesus, the Messiah. He is the Good Shepherd (Jn 10:11-18), who descended from the line of David to be King of Israel (Mt 1:1).

34:25 The archetype for this **covenant of peace** is the covenant with Noah in which the Lord swore after the flood to never again destroy all living things by water (Gn 9:8-17). This covenant should be equated with the new covenant relationship, which will provide peace (Nm 25:12; Jos 9:15; 10:1; Ps 29:11; 85:8; Is 54:10). Because of sin, man lost peace with God (Gn 3:15; 4:8), but peace was available through the Mosaic covenant as a result of obedience (Lv 26:6). The covenant of peace looks forward to the bless-

ings Israel will experience in the millennium. But even now peace may be experienced through relationship with Christ. It is only in Christ, the one true son of David, that this prophecy is fulfilled. Some of the benefits have begun already, such as the peace that surpasses understanding (Php 4:7; cp. Jn 14:27). Other benefits await full implementation at the time when Messiah (the promised Davidic king) comes again. The language used to describe Israel's future restoration (**live securely in the wilderness and sleep in the forest**) is cast in the language of the exodus, suggesting that the restoration of Israel will be a new exodus, reminiscent of the nation's earlier deliverance from Egyptian bondage.

34:26 In Israel autumn rains signaled the beginning of the rainy season, and spring rains the end (Jr 5:24). **Blessing** is a term that occurs frequently in the creation account, and this depends on the work of the Creator. God usually blesses His people by ensuring that natural processes work optimally rather than by circumventing them via miracles.

34:27 The term **yoke** occurs more than 50 times in the Bible. It refers to the wooden bar or frame that joined animals so they could carry or pull a heavier load. The **bars** consisted of wooden pegs inserted through holes in the yoke. Rope fastened the whole apparatus to the animal's neck, forming a collar (30:18; Lv 26:13; Jr 27:2; 28:10-13). The yoke became a symbol of bondage or of joining together for labor. Most occurrences of "yoke" in the Bible are figurative, as in Ezk 34:27, which represents foreign domination (Dt 28:48; Jr 27:8-12).

34:28 God will banish **wild animals**. Thus the people will live in safety (Lv 26:5-6). Ezekiel's idyllic picture of the messianic age as a time of universal peace, involving even the animal world, recalls Is 11:6-9 and Hs 2:18-23. The doom prophecies of Ezekiel 1–24 drew on the curses of the covenant documents (particularly Lv 26), and now the restoration visions draw on the language of blessings for covenant obedience (especially those of Lv 26) and present them as unconditional prophecies of future bliss.

34:29 The prophets declared that when Israel was finally

and they will no longer be victims of famine in the land. They will no longer endure the insults of the nations.[a] [30]Then they will know that I, Yahweh their God, am with them, and that they, the house of Israel, are My people."[b] This is the declaration of the Lord God. [31]"You are My flock, the human flock of My pasture, and I am your God." This is the declaration of the Lord God.[c]

A Prophecy against Edom

35 The word of the Lord came to me: [2]"Son of man, turn your face toward Mount Seir[d] and prophesy against it. [3]Say to it: This is what the Lord God says:

Look! I am against you, Mount Seir.
I will stretch out My hand against you
and make you a desolate waste.[e]
[4] I will turn your cities into ruins,
and you will become a desolation.
Then you will know that I am •Yahweh.

[5]"Because you maintained an ancient hatred[f] and handed over the Israelites to the power of the sword in the time of their disaster, the time of final punishment,[g] [6]therefore, as I live"—this is the declaration of the Lord

God—"I will destine you for bloodshed, and it will pursue you. Since you did not hate bloodshed, it will pursue you.[h] [7]I will make Mount Seir a desolate waste and will cut off from it those who come and go.[i] [8]I will fill its mountains with the slain;[j] those slain by the sword will fall on your hills, in your valleys, and in all your ravines. [9]I will make you a perpetual desolation; your cities will not be inhabited. Then you will know that I am Yahweh.

[10]"Because you said, 'These two nations and two lands will be mine, and we will possess them'—though the Lord was there[k]— [11]therefore, as I live"—the declaration of the Lord God—"I will treat you according to the anger and jealousy you showed in your hatred of them. I will make Myself known among them[A] when I judge you. [12]Then you will know that I, Yahweh, have heard all the blasphemies you uttered against the mountains of Israel, saying, 'They are desolate. They have been given to us to devour!' [13]You boasted against Me[l] with your mouth, and spoke many words against Me. I heard it Myself!

[14]"This is what the Lord God says: While the whole world rejoices, I will make you a desolation. [15]Just as you rejoiced over the

Cross references
a 34:29 Ezk 36:3,6,15
b 34:30 Ex 6:7; Lv 26:12; Dt 29:13; Jr 30:22; 31:33; Ezk 11:20; 36:28; 37:23,27; Zch 8:8; 2Co 6:16; Heb 8:10; Rv 21:3
c 34:31 Ps 100:3; Jr 23:1
d 35:2 Ezk 25:12-14
e 35:3 Ezk 6:14
f 35:5 Ps 137:7; Ezk 25:15
g Ezk 7:2; 21:25,29
h 35:6 Is 63:2-6; Ezk 16:38; 32:6
i 35:7 Ezk 33:28
j 35:8 Ezk 31:12; 32:4-5
k 35:10 Ps 48:1-3; Ezk 48:35
l 35:13 Jr 48:26,42; Ob 12; Zph 2:8

A 35:11 LXX reads you

---

obedient to the Lord, she would experience blessings on earth. This same theme occurs in Rm 11:25-27. Agricultural bounty is a standard way of describing the benefits of the restoration age (Dt 30:9; Am 9:13).

34:30 This conclusion (**they will know that I, Yahweh their God, am with them**) reflects covenant language, as seen in the establishment of Israel's relationship with God at the exodus (11:20; Ex 6:7; Hs 1:9).

34:31 This language (**You are My flock . . . I am your God**) is associated with reestablishment of the divine covenant established with Moses (Ex 6:7; Jr 7:23; Hs 2:23).

35:2 Mount Seir was the ancient name for the mountainous regions south of the Dead Sea on both sides of the Rift Valley. The Edomites inhabited the region and displaced the former residents, the Horites (Dt 2:12,22). Mount Seir was the central mountain of the Edomite nation and thus was synonymous with the country of Edom itself (Gn 32:3). In 126 B.C. Edom was subjugated by John Hyrcanus the Hasmonean. He compelled the Edomites to become Jews (1 Macc. 5:3,65). King Herod, who sought desperately to kill Jesus as a baby, was himself an Idumean, or Edomite. Edom disappeared following the sixth century A.D. as Arab nomads, who later became known as Nabateans, overran their territory. Mount Seir is used in this oracle as a foil for "the mountains of Israel" in Ezekiel 36. Most likely Edom was mentioned here to represent the judgment that God would inflict on all nations who opposed Israel.

35:4 This curse (**I will turn your cities into ruins**) echoes the covenant curse against Israel for its continual disobedience (Lv 26:31).

35:5 The bitter relations between Israel and Edom began in the womb of Rebekah (Gn 25:22-23) and continued with

Jacob's deception of Isaac for Esau's blessing (Gn 27). The phrase **ancient hatred** occurs elsewhere in the Bible only in 25:15 in reference to the actions of the Philistines. The theological significance of the word "hatred" (Hb 'ebah) is clear from its use in Gn 3:15 in reference to the perpetual hostility that exists between the serpent and Eve's descendants. "Hatred" here refers to the hostility between Jacob and Esau, as their personal rivalry (Gn 27:41) spilled over into a national conflict (Nm 20:14-21; 2Sm 8:13-14). When Nebuchadnezzar leveled Jerusalem, the Edomites stood by clapping their hands with joy at this **disaster** (Ps 137; Lm 4:21; Jl 3:19; Ob 1-14; Mal 1:2-5).

35:6 Twice it is stated in this verse that blood will **pursue** the Edomites. This is retribution in kind, as the punishment is commensurate with the crime (Ps 109:17; Mt 7:2; 26:52). "Disaster," "blood," and "Edom" sound similar in Hebrew and are thus interrelated in the passage.

35:11 This expression (**I will treat you according to**) indicates that punishment should be commensurate with the crime. It came to be known as the (Lat) *lex talionis*. The concept can be seen in principle in texts such as Gn 9:6: "Whoever sheds man's blood, his blood will be shed by man." In Exodus 21 we learn that the compensation had to fit the damage when a person accidentally injured a pregnant woman. The principle cited in the text is: "Life for life, eye for eye, tooth for tooth, hand for hand, foot for foot, burn for burn, bruise for bruise, wound for wound" (Ex 21:23-25). Simply put, the punishment should fit the crime. This guards against excessive punishment for a wrong committed. It also guards against personal revenge, which rarely matches the crime. As for Edom, her punishment will fit her crime.

35:15 As Edom **rejoiced** over Judah's fall (Ob 12), so the world would later rejoice over Edom's fall. When God

inheritance of the house of Israel because it became a desolation, so I will deal with you: you will become a desolation, Mount Seir, and so will all Edom in its entirety. Then they will know that I am Yahweh.

Restoration of Israel's Mountains

36 "Son of man, prophesy to the mountains of Israel and say: Mountains of Israel, hear the word of the LORD.[a] 2This is what the Lord GOD says: Because the enemy has said about you, 'Good![b] The ancient heights[c] have become our possession,' 3therefore, prophesy and say: This is what the Lord GOD says: Because they have made you desolate and have trampled you from every side, so that you became a possession for the rest of the nations and an object of people's gossip and slander,[d] 4therefore, mountains of Israel, hear the word of the Lord GOD. This is what the Lord GOD says to the mountains and hills, to the ravines and valleys, to the desolate ruins and abandoned cities, which have become plunder[e] and a mockery to the rest of the nations all around.

5"This is what the Lord GOD says: Certainly

in My burning zeal I speak against the rest of the nations and all of Edom,[f] who took[A] My land as their own possession with wholehearted rejoicing and utter contempt[g] so that its pastureland became[B] plunder. 6Therefore, prophesy concerning the land of Israel and say to the mountains and hills, to the ravines and valleys: This is what the Lord GOD says: Look, I speak in My burning zeal[h] because you have endured the insults of the nations. 7Therefore this is what the Lord GOD says: I swear[c] that the nations all around you will endure their own insults.[i]

8"You, mountains of Israel, will produce your branches[j] and bear your fruit for My people Israel, since their arrival is near. 9Look! I am on your side; I will turn toward you,[k] and you will be tilled and sown. 10I will fill you with people, with the whole house of Israel in its entirety.[l] The cities will be inhabited and the ruins rebuilt. 11I will fill you with people and animals,[m] and they will increase and be fruitful. I will make you inhabited as you once were and make you better off than you were before. Then you will know that I am •Yah-

a 36:1 Ezk 6:2
b 36:2 Ezk 25:3; 26:2
c Dt 32:13
d 36:3 Ezk 35:13
e 36:4 Ezk 34:8,28
f 36:5 Dt 4:24
g Ezk 35:10,15
h 36:6 Ps 74:10; 123:3-4
i 36:7 Ezk 20:5
j 36:8 Ezk 17:23
k 36:9 Lv 26:9
l 36:10 Ezk 37:21-22
m 36:11 Jr 33:12

A 36:5 Lit gave   B 36:5 Or contempt, to empty it of; Hb obscure   C 36:7 Lit lift up My hand

restores Israel's fortunes in the future, He will judge the other nations of the world based on their treatment of Israel (Gn 12:1-3; Mt 25:31-46). Edom declined steadily under Babylonian, Persian, Greek, and finally Roman rule. In the time of Roman rule it was designated as the region of Idumea. During the time between the testaments, an Arabic people, the Nabateans, occupied Edom. They made Petra their capital.

36:1 Chapter 36 is set in antithesis to chapter 35. When God intervenes on Israel's behalf, the "mountains" of Israel's enemies will be judged (35:1-3,8) but the **mountains of Israel** will be blessed. The terrain of Israel was an elevated region between the Jordan Valley and the Mediterranean Sea coast characterized by mountainous areas (Dt 32:13). Thus, this reference to the mountains of Israel should be understood as a reference to the entire nation.

36:3 That Israel would become the **object** of ridicule had been foretold in Dt 28:37 and reiterated in Jr 24:9. The term translated **slander** (Hb dbh) recalls the faithless Israelite scouts and their evaluation of the promised land (Nm 13:32). Now this appraisal was spoken from every side about the nation of Israel.

36:5 The phrase **burning zeal** occurs elsewhere only in verse 6. Formerly God's passion was kindled by Israel's rebellion against Him; now it flares against the arrogant Gentiles. **Edom** is once against pictured as representative of all nations that sought to harm Israel (Is 34; 63:1-6). The theological foundation of God's reaction is based on Gn 12:1-3 where God promised that all nations that opposed Israel would be cursed. God's personal identification with the land of Israel is demonstrated by the phrase **My land** (see Lv 25:23). The term for **possession** (Hb moresh) is from the same root as "take possession" in 35:10, connecting Edom to the current prophecy as well. Edom's claim of the promised land ridiculed Israel but also insulted God because the

land was His and He had given it to His people. In the legal prescriptions for the celebration of the Year of Jubilee, God announced, "The land . . . is Mine" (Lv 25:23).

36:6 The word translated "land" (Hb 'adamah) is not the normal term used in the expression **the land of Israel**. This term could be rendered "soil" in this context. It would be appropriate in this prophecy of renewal of the land's fertility (Gn 4:2; Pr 12:11).

36:7 The phrase **I swear** means literally "with uplifted hand." This gesture accompanied the taking of an oath (20:5,15,23; 47:14).

36:8 In the OT, agricultural abundance was seen as a blessing from God (Dt 30:9) and a preview of the blessings of the coming messianic age. The emphasis on **fruit**-bearing trees and arboriculture before agriculture shifts the focus to the narratives about the garden of Eden (Gn 2:15-16; 3:17-19). This oracle reverses the judgments on the mountains of Israel in Ezekiel 6.

36:9 The phrase **I will turn toward you** also occurs in Lv 26:9 in the context of the covenant blessings that would accompany obedience to the Mosaic law. Thus the renewed abundance of fruitfulness in the land will coincide with blessings that accompanied obedience to the Mosaic law (Lv 26:1-13).

36:10 The phrase **whole house of Israel** refers to the 12 tribes that had originally made up the nation, not just Judah alone. As in 37:15-23, Ezekiel was speaking of the restoration of all Israel.

36:11 The references to increased fertility and population growth (**increase and be fruitful**) refer back to the creation account where God's blessing upon animals (Gn 1:22) and humans (Gn 1:28) resulted in them filling the earth (Gn 9:1,7). What is promised in this verse is a return to Eden-like conditions, where blessings flow from God's presence

weh.[a] [12]I will cause people, My people Israel, to walk on you; they will possess you,[b] and you will be their inheritance. You will no longer deprive them of their children.

[13]"This is what the Lord GOD says: Because people are saying to you, 'You devour men and deprive your nation of children,'[c] [14]therefore, you will no longer devour men and deprive your nation of children."[A] This is the declaration of the Lord GOD. [15]"I will no longer allow the insults of the nations to be heard against you, and you will not have to endure the reproach of the peoples anymore;[d] you will no longer cause your nation to stumble."[B] This is the declaration of the Lord GOD.

Restoration of Israel's People

[16]The word of the LORD came to me: [17]"Son of man, while the house of Israel lived in their land, they defiled it with their conduct and actions.[e] Their behavior before Me was like menstrual impurity.[f] [18]So I poured out My wrath[g] on them because of the blood they had shed on the land, and because they had defiled it with their idols. [19]I dispersed them among the nations, and they were scattered

among the countries.[h] I judged them according to their conduct and actions.[i] [20]When they came to the nations where they went, they profaned My holy name,[j] because it was said about them, 'These are the people of Yahweh, yet they had to leave His land in exile.' [21]Then I had concern for My holy name,[k] which the house of Israel profaned among the nations where they went.

[22]"Therefore, say to the house of Israel: This is what the Lord GOD says: It is not for your sake that I will act,[l] house of Israel, but for My holy name,[m] which you profaned among the nations where you went. [23]I will honor the holiness of My great name, which has been profaned among the nations—the name you have profaned among them. The nations will know that I am Yahweh"—the declaration of the Lord GOD—"when I demonstrate My holiness through you in their sight.[n]

[24]"For I will take you from the nations and gather you from all the countries, and will bring you into your own land.[o] [25]I will also sprinkle clean water on you, and you will be ·clean.[p] I will cleanse you from all your impurities and all your idols.[q] [26]I will give you a

Cross references
a 36:11 Is 51:3
b 36:12 Ob 17
c 36:13 Nm 13:32
d 36:15 Ezk 34:29
e 36:17 Jr 2:7
f Lv 15:19
g 36:18 Ezk 16:36; 22:3
h 36:19 Dt 28:64; Ezk 22:15
i Rm 2:6
j 36:20 Is 52:5; Rm 2:24
k 36:21 Is 48:9; Ezk 20:44
l 36:22 Dt 9:5
m Ps 115:1; Is 43:25; 48:11; Ezk 20:9; Dn 9:18-19
n 36:23 Ezk 20:41; 38:23; 39:7,25
o 36:24 Ezk 34:13; 37:21
p 36:25 Ps 51:7; Heb 9:13,19; 10:22
q Jr 33:8

A 36:14 Alt Hb tradition reads *and cause your nation to stumble*   B 36:15 Some Hb mss, Tg read *no longer bereave your nation of children*

---

among His people. This new fertility will exceed anything the land had ever experienced (Lv 26:9).

36:12 God's **people** will be able to roam freely in the land of **Israel** because it will no longer be possessed by her enemies. Walking through land was a way to claim ownership (Gn 13:17; Jos 24:3; 1Kg 21:16). This promise reverses the desolation predicted in Ezk 6:14.

36:13 The threat of the land "devouring" (Hb 'klt) inhabitants not only recalls 5:13-17, but also echoes, for a second time, the statements of the faithless spies about the land of Canaan: "The land we passed through to explore is one that devours (Hb 'klt) its inhabitants" (Nm 13:32).

36:17 Since a woman's monthly **menstrual** period rendered her unclean under Jewish law (Lv 15:19-30; 18:19), God categorized the conduct of Israel as uncleanness or defilement. A woman in this condition was not eligible to take part in religious activities (Lv 15:19-24). Her **impurity** lasted seven days, after which she was considered clean and fit to return to the house of the Lord.

36:18 The dual offenses of **blood they had shed on the land** and idolatry summarize Israel's social injustices and idolatrous practices (22:3). The people have sinned against God and their fellow man—the two categories of sin outlined in the Ten Commandments.

36:19 To be faithful and loyal, God had no choice but to bring on His people the curses of the covenant they had broken, namely scattering them **among the nations** (see Dt 29:22-28). Moreover, by God's policy the homeland vomits out its inhabitants when it becomes defiled (Lv 18:25,28).

36:20 Though God expelled His people from the promised land for the purpose of chastening and eventually restoring them, their exile reflected unfavorably upon God among

foreign nations. The ancients believed that if a people were forced from their land—by conquest, famine, disease, etc.—it was a sign that their god was not strong enough to protect and care for them (2Kg 18:32-35; 19:10-12). Thus the Hebrew exile was taken as a sign that Israel's God was weaker than the gods of the nations that defeated Jerusalem. The nations **profaned** God's **holy name**, meaning they defamed His essence, character, and reputation.

36:22 In chapter 20 the expression **but for My holy name** states the reason for the withholding of divine punishment (20:9,14,22). Here it is the reason for divine restoration. In the NT, concern for God's name is a central theme—"Your name be honored as holy" (Mt 6:9; see Jn 1:12; 12:28).

36:23 The ultimate purpose of God's plans with Israel was that Israel and the whole world would **know** the true God.

36:25 Once the Israelites have arrived in the land, God will **sprinkle** them with **clean water** so they will be clean. This figurative language is based on water purification practices when the priest threw water on persons or objects to cleanse them of impurity (Nm 19:13,20). Sprinkling with water or blood symbolized the cleansing that comes through forgiveness (Ex 12:22; Lv 14:4-7; Ps 51:7; 1Co 6:11). The first order of business for the Israelites when they return to their homeland will be to pay attention to their spiritual condition (Ps 119:9; Is 4:4; Zch 13:1; Heb 10:22). The Lord Himself will sprinkle His people with clean water. On sprinkling with water as a ritual act of cleansing, see Ex 30:19-20; Lv 14:51; Nm 19:18; cp. Zch 13:1; Heb 10:22. The most significant use of water as a cleansing agent occurred during the biblical flood. God inundated the earth to remove the impurities and wickedness that had been caused by man.

36:26 The statement **I will give you a new heart and put a new spirit within you** reflects the teaching of Dt 30:6-8—

new heart and put a new spirit within you;[a] I will remove your heart of stone[A] and give you a heart of flesh.[b] [27]I will place My Spirit within you[c] and cause you to follow My statutes and carefully observe My ordinances.[d] [28]Then you will live in the land that I gave your fathers;[e] you will be My people, and I will be your God.[f] [29]I will save you from all your uncleanness. I will summon the grain and make it plentiful, and will not bring famine on you.[g] [30]I will also make the fruit of the trees and the produce of the field plentiful, so that you will no longer experience reproach among the nations on account of famine.

[31]Then you will remember your evil ways and your deeds that were not good,[h] and you will loathe yourselves for your iniquities and detestable practices.[i] [32]It is not for your sake that I will act"[j]—the declaration of the Lord God—"let this be known to you. Be ashamed and humiliated because of your ways, house of Israel!

[33]This is what the Lord God says: On the day I cleanse you from all your iniquities, I will cause the cities to be inhabited, and the ruins will be rebuilt.[k] [34]The desolate land will be cultivated instead of lying desolate in the sight of everyone who passes by. [35]Then they will say, 'This land that was desolate has become like the garden of Eden.[l] The cities that were once ruined, desolate, and destroyed are now fortified and inhabited.' [36]Then the nations that remain around you will know that I, Yahweh, have rebuilt what was destroyed and have replanted what was desolate. I, Yahweh, have spoken and I will do it.[m]

[37]This is what the Lord God says: I will respond to the house of Israel and do this for them:[n] I will multiply them in number like a flock.[B] [38]So the ruined cities will be filled with a flock of people, just as the flock of sheep for sacrifice[o] is filled[c] in Jerusalem during its appointed festivals. Then they will know that I am Yahweh."

The Valley of Dry Bones

37 The hand of the Lord was on me,[p] and He brought me out by His Spirit[q] and set me down in the middle of the valley; it was full of bones. [2]He led me all around them. There were a great many of them on the surface of the valley, and they were very dry.

Cross references (margin)

a 36:26 Ezk 18:31; Jl 2:28
b Dt 30:6; Ezk 11:19; 2Co 3:3
c 36:27 Ezk 37:14
d Jr 24:7; 31:33; 32:40
e 36:28 Ezk 37:23-25
f Ezk 34:30
g 36:29-30 Ezk 34:27,29
h 36:31 Ezk 16:61-63
i Ezk 6:9; 20:43
j 36:32 Dt 9:5
k 36:33 Ezk 36:10
l 36:35 Is 51:3; Jl 2:3
m 36:36 Ezk 17:24
n 36:37 Ezk 14:3
o 36:38 2Ch 35:7-9
p 37:1 Ezk 1:3
q Ezk 8:3; 11:24

A 36:26 Lit *stone from your flesh*   B 36:37 Lit *flock of people*   C 36:38 Lit *the flock of consecrated things, as the flock*

---

that the Lord will circumcise the hearts of His people so they may live in obedience. This radical new creation (Ezk 11:19; 18:31; Jr 31:31-34) was necessary to break the people's bondage to the cycle of sin and retribution emphasized in Ezekiel 20. Regeneration is a secret act of God by which He imparts new spiritual life to dead hearts. This is sometimes called being "born again" (Jn 3:3-8). Texts which address regeneration include Eph 2:5; Col 2:13; Jms 1:17-18; 1Pt 1:3. More than any other prophet, Ezekiel emphasizes the Holy Spirit's role in regeneration.

36:27 When God places His **Spirit** in His people, they will be able to follow His decrees and keep His laws. Thus, the people will be transformed, never again to profane God's holy name. This work of the Spirit is attested in many passages of Scripture (11:19-20; 18:31; 37:14; 39:29; Jl 2:28-29; Ac 2:17-18; 2Co 3:16-18; Gl 5:16-26). This work of God to transform lives through the implementation of a new heart and a new spirit is referred to in NT as the "new birth" or being "born again."

36:30 What is described in this passage (**you will no longer experience reproach among the nations**) does not refer to the return to Canaan under Zerubbabel, Ezra, and Nehemiah. Rather, it looks to a final and complete restoration under the Messiah in the end times.

36:31 God's unmerited grace causes sinners to **loathe** their ways, leading to reflection and repentance (**you will remember your evil ways**). This chapter moves beyond texts such as Lv 26:40-42 and Jr 31:18-20, where repentance is the driving motivation behind restoration.

36:35 In this prophecy for the land of Israel, God will restore the land to a "better than original" estate. It will become like **the garden of Eden**, the ultimate symbol of fertility and fruitfulness (28:13; 31:9; cp. Is 51:3; Jl 2:3). It will be paradise regained (Rm 8:19-22; 2Pt 3:13; Rv 21:1-4). Super-

natural fertility of the land is one of the characteristics of the messianic kingdom (Is 35:1-2; 55:13; Ezk 47:1-12; Zch 8:12). The replenishing of the land so that it resembles the garden of Eden (Gn 2–3) will reveal God to the nations. The mention of this idyllic state suggests a future fulfillment beyond that which occurred in the return from Babylon under the leadership of Zerubbabel, Ezra, and Nehemiah. These conditions will not be realized until the messianic age. Romans 8:18-25 indicates that creation still longs for complete deliverance from sin's curse.

36:38 The number of people is compared to the numerous **sheep** that passed through Jerusalem at the time of the appointed feasts (Lv 23). Through God's sovereign empowerment the people can now replenish the earth in harmony with God's purposes for creation—"Be fruitful, multiply, fill the earth" (Gn 1:28; cp. Gn 9:1,7). The phrase **a flock of people** conveys the idea of abundance (1Kg 8:63; 1Ch 29:21; 2Ch 35:7).

37:1 The introductory phrase **the hand of the Lord was on me** indicates a new subject. The hand is often used metaphorically for power in Scripture. The arrival of the hand of the Lord upon the prophet speaks of the overwhelming force with which the prophet was seized by God. On the "hand of the Lord" coming upon Ezekiel to overpower him, see 1:3; 3:14; 8:1; 40:1. The work of the Spirit in transporting Ezekiel to a different location occurs in 3:14; 8:3; 11:1,24; 43:5, indicating the beginning of a visionary revelation. As an Israelite trained in the priesthood, Ezekiel knew the importance of treating a human corpse properly. This vast array of skeletons left unburied (**it was full of bones**) reminded Ezekiel of the execution of the judgment curses for disobedience (Dt 28:26).

37:2 Bones that were **very dry** indicated that death had taken place long ago. Hence, life was obviously beyond resus-

3 Then He said to me, "Son of man, can these
bones live?"
I replied, "Lord GOD, only You know."[a]
4 He said to me, "Prophesy concerning these
bones and say to them: Dry bones, hear the
word of the LORD! 5 This is what the Lord GOD
says to these bones: I will cause breath to enter you, and you will live.[b] 6 I will put tendons
on you, make flesh grow on you, and cover
you with skin. I will put breath in you so that
you come to life. Then you will know that I
am •Yahweh."[c]
7 So I prophesied as I had been commanded.
While I was prophesying, there was a noise, a
rattling sound, and the bones came together,
bone to bone. 8 As I looked, tendons appeared
on them, flesh grew, and skin covered them,
but there was no breath in them. 9 He said to
me, "Prophesy to the breath,[A] prophesy, son of
man. Say to it: This is what the Lord GOD says:
Breath, come from the four winds and breathe
into these slain so that they may live!"[d] 10 So I
prophesied as He commanded me; the breath[A]
entered them,[e] and they came to life and stood
on their feet, a vast army.
11 Then He said to me, "Son of man, these
bones are the whole house of Israel.[f] Look
how they say, 'Our bones are dried up,[g] and
our hope has perished;[h] we are cut off.'[i]
12 Therefore, prophesy and say to them: This
is what the Lord GOD says: I am going to open
your graves and bring you up from them,[j] My
people, and lead you into the land of Israel.
13 You will know that I am Yahweh, My people,
when I open your graves and bring you up
from them.[k] 14 I will put My Spirit in you,[l] and
you will live, and I will settle you in your own
land. Then you will know that I am Yahweh.
I have spoken, and I will do it."[m] This is the
declaration of the LORD.

The Reunification of Israel

15 The word of the LORD came to me: 16 "Son
of man, take a single stick and write on it:[n]
Belonging to Judah and the Israelites associated with him. Then take another stick and
write on it: Belonging to Joseph—the stick
of Ephraim—and all the house of Israel associated with him.[o] 17 Then join them together
into a single stick so that they become one
in your hand.[p] 18 When your people ask you,
'Won't you explain to us what you mean by
these things?'[q]— 19 tell them: This is what the
Lord GOD says: I am going to take the stick of
Joseph, which is in the hand of Ephraim, and
the tribes of Israel associated with him, and

[a] 37:3 Dt 32:39; 1Sm 2:6
[b] 37:5 Gn 2:7; Ps 104:29-30
[c] 37:6 Jl 2:27; 3:17
[d] 37:9 Ps 104:30
[e] 37:10 Rv 11:11
[f] 37:11 Ezk 36:10
[g] Ps 141:7
[h] Eph 2:12
[i] Is 49:14; Lm 3:54
[j] 37:12 Is 26:19; 66:14; Hs 13:14; Rm 11:15
[k] 37:13 Jn 5:28-29; 1Co 15:21-22; Rv 20:4-5
[l] 37:14 Ezk 36:27
[m] Ezk 17:24
[n] 37:16 Nm 17:2-3
[o] 2Ch 11:11-17
[p] 37:17 Is 11:13; Hs 1:11
[q] 37:18 Ezk 12:9; 24:19

A 37:9,10 Or *wind*, or *spirit*

citation (1Kg 17:17-24; 2Kg 4:18-37; but see 2Kg 13:21). Dry bones are a metaphor for a downcast spirit in other biblical passages (Pr 15:30; 17:22).

37:3 Ezekiel was aware that God had the power to raise people from the dead (1Kg 17:17-24; 2Kg 4:18-37; Is 26:19; Dn 12:1-2). But these bones were dry, meaning that the flesh had decayed. This seemed to make resuscitation impossible (**can these bones live?**).

37:6 When the **breath** of life is breathed into a body, it comes alive (see Ps 119:25; Jn 6:63).

37:9 The **four winds** probably indicate the full power of the entering **breath** since the winds come from every direction. The picture reminds us of the creation event, where the Spirit of God hovered over the raw elements of the world, transforming it into a habitable earth (Gn 1:2).

37:10 The two-stage process of forming the physical body and filling it with the breath of life is patterned after the creation of Adam in Gn 2:7. The use of the same verb (Hb *naphach*) for "*breathe* into these slain" (37:9) and "*breathed* into his nostrils" (Gn 2:7) makes this correlation certain. In both cases the bodies did not come to **life** until they received an infusion of the Spirit (the words for "wind," "breath," and "spirit" are identical in Hebrew and Greek).

37:11 **These bones** symbolize the restoration of the **whole house of Israel** to its own land.

37:12 Continuing His explanation of the vision, God added a new dimension to the resurrection of the dry bones. He declared that He would **open** the **graves** of His people and take them from their place of burial, demonstrating the reality of national rebirth. Just as the events in the vision were miraculous, so will be Israel's restoration. The vision showed that Israel's new life depended on God's power.

37:14 Both Elijah and Elisha were involved in resurrection events (1Kg 17:17-24; 2Kg 4:18-37; 13:20-21). The focus on the work of the **Spirit** expands on the meaning of the statement of 36:27. **I will settle you in your own land** picks up the theme from the exodus and conquest. It also explains Paul's statement that the reincorporation of Israel into the community of faith was like "life from the dead" (Rm 11:15). The Jews who live in Israel today should not be viewed as fulfilling this prophecy. Rather, the prophecy will be fulfilled when God gathers believing Israelites to the land (Jr 31:33; 33:14-16) at the second coming of Christ (Mt 24:30-31).

37:16 The key word "one" (**single** in this verse) occurs 10 times in verses 15-28. On the use of a **stick** or staff to represent a tribe, see Nm 17:1-26.

37:17 By being placed end to end, the two sticks would appear to be a **single stick**. Ezekiel's contemporary, Jeremiah, shared Ezekiel's prophetic vision of a reunited Israel (Jr 3:12,14; 31:2-6; cp. Ezk 4:4-8; 16:53). Fundamental to all prophecy concerning Israel is the presupposition of a united people, a healing of the breach in the commonwealth of God's people (Is 11:12-13). The prophets recognized the northern tribes as still in existence and knew of no lost tribes (Is 43:5-7; 49:5-6; Jr 3:12-15). Israelites came from the northern kingdom into the kingdom of Judah particularly during the time of crisis (2Ch 15:9; 30:11,18).

37:19 God will reunite the two kingdoms that had been separated since Solomon's death (1Kg 12). For similar reunion prophecies, see Jr 3:18; 23:5-6; Hs 1:11; Am 9:11. Isaiah 11 also uses the image of a growing tree to symbolize the unification of Israel and Judah under a Davidic king.

put them together with the stick of Judah. I
will make them into a single stick so that they
become one in My hand.
20 "When the sticks you have written on are
in your hand and in full view of the people,[a]
21 tell them: This is what the Lord GOD says:
I am going to take the Israelites out of the
nations where they have gone.[b] I will gather
them from all around and bring them into
their own land. 22 I will make them one nation
in the land,[c] on the mountains of Israel, and
one king will rule over all of them.[d] They will
no longer be two nations and will no longer
be divided into two kingdoms. 23 They will not
defile themselves anymore with their idols,[e]
their detestable things, and all their transgressions.[f] I will save them from all their apostasies by which[A] they sinned,[g] and I will cleanse
them. Then they will be My people, and I will
be their God.[h] 24 My servant David will be king
over them, and there will be one shepherd for
all of them.[i] They will follow My ordinances,
and keep My statutes and obey them.[j]
25 "They will live in the land that I gave to My
servant Jacob,[k] where your fathers lived. They
will live in it forever with their children and
grandchildren, and My servant David will be
their prince forever.[l] 26 I will make a covenant
of peace with them;[m] it will be an everlasting
covenant[n] with them. I will establish and multiply them and will set My sanctuary among
them forever. 27 My dwelling place will be with
them;[o] I will be their God, and they will be My
people.[p] 28 When My sanctuary is among them
forever, the nations will know that I, Yahweh,
sanctify Israel."[q]

The Defeat of Gog

38 The word of the LORD came to me:
2 "Son of man, turn your face toward
Gog, of the land of Magog,[r] the chief prince
of[B] Meshech and Tubal.[s] Prophesy against him
3 and say: This is what the Lord GOD says: Look,
I am against you, Gog, chief prince of Meshech and Tubal. 4 I will turn you around, put
hooks in your jaws,[t] and bring you out with all
your army, including horses and riders,[u] who
are all splendidly dressed, a huge company
armed with shields and bucklers, all of them
brandishing swords. 5 Persia,[v] •Cush, and Put
are with them, all of them with shields and
helmets; 6 Gomer[w] with all its troops; and
Beth-togarmah[x] from the remotest parts of
the north along with all its troops—many
peoples are with you.
7 "Be prepared and get yourself ready, you
and all your company who have been mobilized around you; you will be their guard. 8 After a long time you will be summoned. In the
last years you will enter a land that has been
restored from war[C] and regathered from many
peoples to the mountains of Israel, which had
long been a ruin.[y] They were brought out
from the peoples, and all of them now live
securely. 9 You, all of your troops, and many

[a] 37:20 Ezk 12:3
[b] 37:21 Ezk 36:24
[c] 37:22 Jr 3:18
[d] Ezk 34:23-24
[e] 37:23 Ezk 36:25
[f] Ezk 36:28-29
[g] Rm 11:26
[h] Ezk 36:38
[i] 37:24 Ezk 34:23-24; Jn 10:16
[j] Ezk 36:27
[k] 37:25 Is 60:21
[l] Jn 12:34
[m] 37:26 Is 55:3; Ezk 34:25
[n] Is 55:3; Jr 32:40; Ezk 16:60; Heb 13:20
[o] 37:27 Jn 1:14
[p] Ezk 36:28
[q] 37:28 Ezk 20:12
[r] 38:2 Gn 10:2; Ezk 39:1; Rv 20:8
[s] Ezk 27:13
[t] 38:4 2Kg 19:28; Ezk 29:4
[u] Dn 11:40
[v] 38:5 Ezk 27:10
[w] 38:6 Gn 10:2
[x] Gn 10:3
[y] 38:8 Ezk 36:8-11

[A] 37:23 Some Hb mss, LXX, Sym; other Hb mss read *their settlements where* [B] 38:2 Or *the prince of Rosh,* [C] 38:8 Lit *from the sword*

37:24 The "servant" language (cp. Is 49; 53) is characteristic of messianic prophecies. The Davidic heritage, represented by such terms as **king** and **My servant David** (cp. 2Sm 7:5,8; Ps 89:20) will establish national unity and keep at bay abuses that were prevalent in Judah's preexilic history. The new ruler will embody the ideals established in Dt 17:14-20, submitting to the authority of the Lord. The reunification of the tribes is connected to the fostering of messianic hope (Ezk 37:25-28; cp. Rm 11:25-36).

38:1 The introductory phrase **the word of the LORD came to me** indicates a change of subject from the previous chapter. The message in chapters 38–39 should be seen as the sixth and last in Ezekiel's series of messages delivered the night before the news about the fall of Jerusalem arrived. The chapters describe the final attempt by foreigners to possess the land of Israel.

38:2 **Gog** may most immediately refer to Gyges, king of Lysia, from the seventh century B.C. Even so, the reference transcends this Gog's historical circumstances to refer to a leader who will oppose Israel in the far future. A modern parallel would be for us to speak of a prominent but vile leader as a "new Hitler." The only other occurrence of "Gog" is in Rv 20:8. Gog seems to transcend historical categories, serving as a symbol of the forces of antichrist. If so, Gog has become a transnational symbol of evil, much like Edom and Egypt (Ex 15; Is 34; 63:1-6; Mal 1:2-5). The references to the invasion of Gog in Revelation 19–20 allow for the view that Gog represents the "beast" as well as "Satan." Gog's being dragged and led around by hooks (Ezk 38:4; 39:2) may be analogous to or even parallel with God releasing Satan from prison in Rv 20:7. In Ezekiel 25–32 the prophet addressed nations that Judah was familiar with. Now, we read about the plan of God for distant, unknown nations. This is parallel to the book of Revelation's depiction of the battle of Armageddon. Revelation 20:8 identifies Gog and Magog as a figure for all the pagan foes of Israel and the Messiah. Magog is found elsewhere in the OT only in Gn 10:2 and its parallel in 1Ch 1:5, where Magog is identified as the second son of Japhetheh.

Because the Hebrew word for **chief** (Hb *ro'sh*) sounds similar to the name "Russia," many modern Bible students have attempted to identify Russia with the "chief" in this verse. This popular identification is based on a faulty etymology, the similarities in sound between Russia and Rosh being purely accidental. "Rosh" never appears as a nation in any biblical text. Furthermore, those who identify **Meshech** with Moscow and **Tubal** with Tobolsk likewise operate on faulty assumptions about the etymological evidence.

38:6 **Gomer** is mentioned as early as Gn 10:2-3. In 1Ch 1:6 he is listed as one of the sons of Japheth. According to Gn 10:3, Togarmah was one of the children of Gomer.

38:8-9 **After a long time** (lit "in the end of years") is a pro-

peoples with you will advance, coming like a thunderstorm; you will be like a cloud covering the land.

[10] "This is what the Lord God says: On that day, thoughts will arise in your mind, and you will devise an evil plan. [11] You will say, 'I will go up against a land of open villages; I will come against a tranquil people who are living securely,[a] all of them living without walls and without bars or gates[b]— [12] in order to seize spoil and carry off plunder,[c] to turn your hand against ruins now inhabited and against a people gathered from the nations, who have been acquiring cattle and possessions and who live at the center of the world.' [13] Sheba[d] and Dedan[e] and the merchants of Tarshish[f] with all its rulers[A] will ask you, 'Have you come to seize spoil? Have you assembled your hordes to carry off plunder, to make off with silver and gold, to take cattle and possessions, to seize great spoil?'

[14] "Therefore prophesy, son of man, and say to Gog: This is what the Lord God says: On that day when My people Israel are dwelling securely,[g] will you not know this [15] and come from your place in the remotest parts of the north[h]—you and many peoples with you, who are all riding horses—a mighty horde, a huge army? [16] You will advance against My people Israel like a cloud covering the land. It will happen in the last days, Gog, that I will bring you against My land so that the nations may know Me, when I show Myself holy through you in their sight.[i]

[17] "This is what the Lord God says: Are you the one I spoke about in former times

Cross-references:
[a] 38:11 Jdg 18:7
[b] Jr 49:31
[c] 38:12 Is 10:6; Ezk 29:19
[d] 38:13 Ezk 27:22
[e] Ezk 27:20
[f] Ezk 27:12
[g] 38:14 Jr 23:6
[h] 38:15 Ezk 39:2
[i] 38:16 Ezk 28:22
[j] 38:19 Ezk 36:6
[k] 38:21 Ezk 14:17
[l] 38:22 Rv 16:18-21
[m] 38:23 Ezk 37:28
[n] 39:1 Ezk 38:2-3
[o] 39:2 Ezk 38:4

through My servants, the prophets of Israel, who for years prophesied in those times that I would bring you against them? [18] Now on that day, the day when Gog comes against the land of Israel"—this is the declaration of the Lord God—"My wrath will flare up.[B] [19] I swear in My zeal and fiery rage:[j] On that day there will be a great earthquake in the land of Israel. [20] The fish of the sea, the birds of the sky, the animals of the field, every creature that crawls on the ground, and every human being on the face of the earth will tremble before Me. The mountains will be thrown down, the cliffs will collapse, and every wall will fall to the ground. [21] I will call for a sword against him on all My mountains"—the declaration of the Lord God—"and every man's sword will be against his brother.[k] [22] I will execute judgment on him with plague and bloodshed. I will pour out torrential rain, hailstones, fire, and brimstone on him, as well as his troops and the many peoples who are with him.[l] [23] I will display My greatness and holiness, and will reveal Myself in the sight of many nations.[m] Then they will know that I am •Yahweh.

The Disposal of Gog

39 "As for you, son of man, prophesy against Gog and say: This is what the Lord God says: Look, I am against you, Gog, chief prince of[c] Meshech and Tubal.[n] [2] I will turn you around, drive you on,[o] and lead you up from the remotest parts of the north. I will bring you against the mountains of Israel. [3] Then I will knock your bow from your left hand and make your arrows drop from

---

[A] 38:13 Lit *young lions,* or *villages*   [B] 38:18 Lit *up in My anger*   [C] 39:1 Or *Gog, prince of Rosh,*

---

phetic phrase that is sometimes applied to the end times (Jr 32:14; Dn 8:26). It alludes to the nearly identical phrase "end of days," which designates the time of the messianic kingdom (Gn 49:1; Is 2:2; Jr 23:20; 30:24; Hs 3:5; Mc 4:1). The attack will be so massive that the invading troops will appear to be **like a cloud covering the land.** The cloud and the storm are common images in biblical literature announcing prophetic threats (Jr 4:13).

38:11 In Zch 2:4-5 we find that the Lord alone is sufficient protection (Ezk 36:35-36). The phrase **living securely** describes messianic security after Israel's restoration.

38:12 The phrase **center of the world** may be translated "navel of the earth." Since the Hebrew word for land can also mean "earth," it could be argued that theologically Jerusalem will be both the center of the land of Israel and indeed of all the earth. The only other occurrence of this expression is in Jdg 9:37, but that text does not refer to Jerusalem.

38:13 **Sheba** (27:22), **Dedan** (25:13; 27:20), and **Tarshish** (27:12) are mentioned in chapter 27 as engaged in trade with Tyre. Sheba, located in the southwestern corner of the

Arabian Peninsula (modern Yemen), was known for its trading (Jb 6:19; see Ezk 27:22; 1Kg 10:1-2).

38:16 The phrase **so that the nations may know Me** refers to an important biblical theme (Ex 15; Pss 46-48; Is 2:1-4; Mc 4:1-5). This invasion will take place in the end times, after the people of Israel have been restored to the promised land and are living securely under the Messiah's rule and protection.

38:20 Such listings of **animals** are used to allude to the entire created order in the creation story (Gn 1) and elsewhere (Gn 9:2; 1Kg 4:33; Jb 12:7-8).

38:21 God will bring such confusion on those who oppose His people that they will kill one another (Lv 26:37; Dt 28:29). For a similar event in the time of King Jehoshaphat, see 2Ch 20:22-23.

38:22 These judgments against Gog are consistent with the covenant curses of **plague** (Dt 32:24), bloodshed (Dt 32:42), flood (Gn 6), hail, **fire,** and **brimstone** (Jos 10:11). The defeat of Gog by the sword and natural elements highlights God's role as Creator and Governor of nature. The destruction is also reminiscent of the destruction of Sodom and Gomorrah (Gn 18-19).

your right hand. ⁴You, all your troops, and the peoples who are with you will fall on the mountains of Israel. I will give you as food to every kind of predatory bird and to the wild animals. ⁵You will fall on the open field,ᵃ for I have spoken." This is the declaration of the Lord GOD.

⁶"I will send fire against Magogᵇ and those who live securely on the coasts and islands. Then they will know that I am ·Yahweh. ⁷So I will make My holy name known among My people Israel and will no longer allow it to be profaned. Then the nations will know that I am Yahweh, the Holy One in Israel.ᶜ ⁸Yes, it is coming, and it will happen." This is the declaration of the Lord GOD. "This is the day I have spoken about.

⁹"Then the inhabitants of Israel's cities will go out, kindle fires, and burn the weapons—the bucklers and shields, the bows and arrows, the clubs and spears. For seven years they will use them to make fires. ¹⁰They will not gather wood from the countryside or cut it down from the forests, for they will use the weapons to make fires. They will take the loot from those who looted them and plunder those who plundered them."ᵈ This is the declaration of the Lord GOD.

¹¹"Now on that day I will give Gog a burial place there in Israel—the Valley of the Travel-ersᴬ east of the Sea. It will block those who travel through, for Gog and all his hordes will be buried there. So it will be called the Valley of Hamon-gog.ᴮ ¹²The house of Israel will spend seven months burying them in order to cleanse the land.ᵉ ¹³All the people of the land will bury them and their fame will spreadᶠ on the day I display My glory."ᵍ This is the declaration of the Lord GOD.

¹⁴"They will appoint men on a full-time basis to pass through the land and bury the invadersᶜ who remain on the surface of the ground, in order to cleanse it. They will make their search at the end of the seven months. ¹⁵When they pass through the land and one of them sees a human bone, he will set up a marker next to it until the buriers have buried it in the Valley of Hamon-gog. ¹⁶There will even be a city named Hamonahᴰ there. So they will cleanse the land.

¹⁷"Son of man, this is what the Lord GOD says: Tell every kind of bird and all the wild animals: Assemble and come! Gather from all around to My sacrificial feast that I am slaughtering for you, a great feast on the mountains of Israel;ʰ you will eat flesh and drink blood. ¹⁸You will eat the flesh of mighty men and drink the blood of the earth's princes: rams,

ᵃ 39:5 Ezk 32:4
ᵇ 39:6 Am 1:4,7,10
ᶜ 39:7 Ezk 36:20-23
ᵈ 39:10 Is 14:2; 33:1
ᵉ 39:12 Dt 21:23
ᶠ 39:13 Jr 33:9; Zph 3:19-20
ᵍ Ezk 28:22
ʰ 39:17 Rv 19:17-18

ᴬ39:11 Hb obscure   ᴮ39:11 = Hordes of Gog   ᶜ39:14 Or basis, some to pass through the land, and with them some to bury those   ᴰ39:16 In Hb, Hamonah is related to the word "horde."

39:4 Ezekiel 39:4-9 is similar to Rv 19:17-18, perhaps referring to the same event.

39:6 The sending of **fire** (in this case, **against Magog**) is a common expression for divine judgment (Hs 8:14; Am 1:12).

39:7 God's name will be known among the nations. As a result of His actions against Gog and the coalition, His **holy name** will be made known among His people Israel. His name will never be **profaned** again (v. 25; 20:9; 36:20-23; 43:7-9).

39:9 Up to this point in the prophecy about the invasion of Gog, only God has defended His people against this enemy. Now for the first time Israel is called to act, but her role is to conduct a "mopping up" exercise. The carnage left in the aftermath of the defeat of Gog will be so massive that the Israelites will fuel their fires for **seven years** with the weapons of her slain enemies. Burning the war implements of a defeated foe recalls the burning of boots and blood-stained cloaks elsewhere in Scripture (Is 9:5; see Ps 46:9; 76:3). It also harkens back to when the Israelites burned all that belonged to the Canaanites at the time of the conquest (Dt 7:2; 20:16-18; Jos 6:24). In an ironic reversal, the Israelites will plunder those who had come to plunder them.

39:11 This **burial** project will be so massive that it will block travel through the land. The name of the valley will be changed to the **Valley of Hamon-gog**. The only major valley that ran in an east-west direction in Israel was the Jezreel Valley, a vital strategic link on the route from Egypt to Damascus in biblical times. This valley will be the location of

the great battle of the tribulation period known as Armageddon (Rv 16:13-16).

39:12 Because corpses were considered unclean (Lv 21:1,11; 22:4; Nm 5:2; 6:6-12; 31:19), the Mosaic law required all humans to be given a proper burial (Dt 21:22-23). Numbers 19:11-22 explains not only the contaminating effects of a corpse but also the process by which a person so defiled could be ceremonially cleansed.

39:17 This **sacrificial feast** (Is 34:6-8; Zph 1:7) will consist of the flesh and blood of the armies of Gog that had been killed. Birds and beasts will eat fat and drink blood, elements which were reserved exclusively for the Lord when the Hebrews made animal sacrifices (Lv 3:17). Mention of the fat and blood therefore may be a way of highlighting the Lord's participation in the annihilation of Israel's enemies. In standard sacrificial practices, the human worshiper slaughtered an animal before the Lord and partook of the food. For this present feast, the Lord will slaughter humans, and animals will devour their bodies, in contrast to the standard sacrificial procedure and the future banquet meal that Israel will celebrate on Mount Zion (Is 25:6-10). The feasting of wild animals and birds recalls the threatened covenant curse (Lv 26:22; Dt 28:26). Although humans were to have dominion over nature, in their pursuit of evil they become victims of the natural order.

39:18 The mention of the **fattened bulls of Bashan** is further confirmation that this is the Lord's sacrificial feast because fat and blood were normally reserved for Him (44:15; Lv 3:17). Bashan, east and northeast of the Sea of Galilee, was

lambs, male goats, and all the fattened bulls of Bashan. ¹⁹You will eat fat until you are satisfied[a] and drink blood until you are drunk, at My sacrificial feast that I have prepared for you. ²⁰At My table you will eat your fill of horses and riders, of mighty men and all the warriors." This is the declaration of the Lord GOD.

Israel's Restoration to God

²¹"I will display My glory among the nations,[b] and all the nations will see the judgment I have executed and the hand I have laid on them. ²²From that day forward the house of Israel will know that I am Yahweh their God. ²³And the nations will know that the house of Israel went into exile on account of their iniquity, because they dealt unfaithfully with Me.[c] Therefore, I hid My face from them and handed them over to their enemies, so that they all fell by the sword. ²⁴I dealt with them according to their uncleanness and transgressions, and I hid My face from them.

²⁵"So this is what the Lord GOD says: Now I will restore the fortunes of Jacob[d] and have compassion on the whole house of Israel,[e] and I will be jealous for My holy name. ²⁶They will

feel remorse for[A,B] their disgrace[f] and all the unfaithfulness they committed against Me, when they live securely in their land with no one to frighten them. ²⁷When I bring them back from the peoples and gather them from the countries of their enemies, I will demonstrate My holiness through them in the sight of many nations.[g] ²⁸They will know that I am Yahweh their God when I regather them to their own land after having exiled them among the nations. I will leave none of them behind.[c] ²⁹I will no longer hide My face from them, for I will pour out My Spirit on the house of Israel."[h] This is the declaration of the Lord GOD.

The New Temple

40 In the twenty-fifth year of our exile, at the beginning of the year, on the tenth day of the month in the fourteenth year after Jerusalem had been captured,[i] on that very day the LORD's hand was on me,[j] and He brought me there. ²In visions of God[k] He took me to the land of Israel and set me down on a very high mountain.[l] On its southern slope was a structure resembling a city. ³He brought me there, and I saw a man whose appearance was

---

Cross references (center column):

[a] 39:19 Rv 19:21
[b] 39:21 Ezk 36:23; 38:16,23
[c] 39:23 Ezk 36:18-20,23
[d] 39:25 Is 27:12-13; Jr 33:7; Ezk 34:13
[e] Ezk 36:10; 37:21-22; Hs 1:11
[f] 39:26 Ezk 16:53-54,63
[g] 39:27 Ezk 20:41; 38:23
[h] 39:29 Ezk 36:27; 37:14; Jl 2:28
[i] 40:1 2Kg 25:1-7; Jr 39:1-9; 52:4-11; Ezk 33:21
[j] Ezk 1:3; 3:14,22; 37:1
[k] 40:2 Ezk 1:1; 8:3; Dn 7:1,7
[l] Is 2:2-3; Ezk 17:23; 20:40; 37:22; Mc 4:1; Rv 21:10

A 39:26 Some emend to *will forget*   B 39:26 Lit *will bear*   C 39:28 Lit *behind there any longer*

---

famous for its fertile land and fat cows (Dt 32:14; Ps 22:12; Am 4:1).

39:24 The image of God hiding His **face**, turning away from Israel and choosing not to help them, also appears in Dt 31:17-18; Ps 13:1-2.

39:26 The remembrance which leads to shame (**they will feel remorse for their disgrace**) also occurs in 6:9; 20:43; and 36:31.

39:29 Before the destruction of Jerusalem God had promised to "pour out" (Hb *shaphak*) His wrath on Israel (7:8; 9:8;

goy

Hebrew Pronunciation	[GOY]
HCSB Translation	nation
Uses in Ezekiel	90
Uses in the OT	30
Focus passage	Ezekiel 39:7,21,23,27-28

Goy derives from a West Semitic word that means "people," but *goy* seems closer to the idea of *nation* (Gn 10:20), describing *peoples* according to political, territorial, and ethnic considerations. Israel was a *nation* descended from Abraham (Gn 12:2), existing as a *nation* before leaving Egypt (Ex 33:13) and after exile (Jr 31:36). *Goy* most often designates foreign *nations* outside Israel (Is 11:10,12), sometimes emphasizing their paganism (Dt 9:5). Idolatrous *nations* (Jr 14:22) are hostile to God and His people (Ps 59:5). *Goy* appears as *people* (Is 49:7) and *nationhood* (Jr 48:2). It mostly occurs in the plural (432x) and can be *peoples* (Gn 10:5), *foreigners* (Neh 5:8), or *Gentiles* (Ezr 6:21). *Goy* functions adjectivally as *foreign* (Neh 5:9), *Gentile* (Hg 2:22), and *national* (2Ch 32:13). *Goy* occurs in parallelism with (82x) *'am* ("people"), (23x) *mamlakah* ("kingdom"), (12x) *mishpochah* ("tribe"), and (7x) *le'om* ("people").

20:13,21; 22:22; 36:18). Now in restoring His people He will **pour out** (Hb *shaphak*) His **Spirit**. This reference to the Spirit of God connects the passage in its entirety to chapters 36–37 with its focus on the Spirit.

40:1 This date (**in the twenty-fifth year of our exile**) is the thirteenth and final date formula in Ezekiel. The tenth day of the first month marked the beginning of the Passover that was celebrated four days later. Moreover, the twenty-fifth year was the halfway point to the next Jubilee Year when freedom and release would be observed (Lv 25). Jubilee is mentioned in Ezk 46:17 in reference to the return of the prince's inheritance. But the number 25 has another significance in this vision. The dimensions of the temple are dominated by multiples of five, with the number 25 being most prominent. Whereas the opening vision of the heavenly King on His throne had been dated from the exile of the earthly king—Jehoiachin—this vision of the heavenly city is dated from the destruction of the earthly city, Jerusalem.

40:2 This vision provides a literary and conceptual envelope for the entire book. It complements especially the visions of God's departure and the temple's destruction in chapters 9–11. This vision is the longest vision in the Bible apart from the book of Revelation. As Ezekiel received legislation for the new age upon this **high mountain**, it is natural to compare the experience of Moses receiving the law on Mount Sinai. Indeed, Ezekiel is the only person in the OT except Moses who transmitted legislation that he received directly from God. As Ezekiel's vision was a vision of the city of Jerusalem, it is likely that this "very high mountain" is a reference to Mount Zion, often cited for its great height in the OT (17:22; Is 2:2; Mc 4:1; see Zch 14:10).

40:3 The **measuring rod** was used for short measurements. It was about 10 feet four inches in length.

like bronze,[a] with a linen cord and a measuring rod in his hand.[b] He was standing by the gate. [4]He spoke to me: "Son of man, look with your eyes, listen with your ears,[c] and pay attention to everything I am going to show you, for you have been brought here so that I might show it to you. Report everything you see to the house of Israel."[d]

The Wall and Outer Gates

[5]Now there was a wall surrounding the outside of the temple.[e] The measuring rod in the man's hand was six units of 21 inches;[A] each unit was the standard length plus three inches.[B] He measured the thickness of the wall structure; it was about 10 feet,[c] and its height was the same.[c] [6]Then he came to the gate that faced east and climbed its steps.[f] He measured the threshold of the gate; it was 10 feet deep—the first threshold was 10 feet deep. [7]Each recess was about 10 feet[c] long and 10 feet[D] deep, and there was a space of 8³/₄ feet[E] between the recesses. The inner threshold of the gate on the temple side next to the gate's portico was about 10 feet.[c] [8]Next he measured the portico of the gate; [9]it[F] was 14 feet,[G] and its pilasters were 3¹/₂ feet.[H] The portico of the gate was on the temple side.

[10]There were three recesses on each side of the east gate, each with the same measurements, and the pilasters on either side also had the same measurements. [11]Then he measured the width of the gate's entrance; it was 17¹/₂ feet,[I] while the width[J] of the gateway was 22³/₄ feet.[K] [12]There was a barrier of 21 inches[L] in front of the recesses on both sides, and the recesses on each side were 10¹/₂ feet[M] square. [13]Then he measured the gateway from the roof of one recess to the roof of the opposite

ᵃ40:3 Ezk 1:7; Dn 10:6; Rv 1:15
ᵇEzk 47:3; Zch 2:1-2; Rv 11:1; 21:15
ᶜ40:4 Ezk 2:1,3,6,8; 44:5
ᵈEzk 43:10
ᵉ40:5 Is 26:1; Ezk 43:10
ᶠ40:6 Ezk 43:1
ᵍ40:16 1Kg 6:4; Ezk 41:16,26
ʰ1Kg 6:29,32,35; 2Ch 3:5; Ezk 41:18-20,25-26
ⁱ40:17 Ezk 10:5; 42:1; 46:21; Rv 11:2
ʲ2Kg 23:11; 1Ch 9:26; 23:28; 2Ch 31:11

one; the distance was 43³/₄ feet.[N] The openings of the recesses faced each other. [14]Next, he measured the pilasters—105 feet.[O] The gate extended around to the pilaster of the court.[P] [15]The distance from the front of the gate at the entrance to the front of the gate's portico on the inside was 87¹/₂ feet.[Q] [16]The recesses and their pilasters had beveled windows all around the inside of the gateway.[g] The porticoes also had windows all around on the inside. Each pilaster was decorated with palm trees.[h]

[17]Then he brought me into the outer court,[i] and there were chambers and a paved surface laid out all around the court.[j] Thirty chambers faced the pavement, [18]which flanked the gates and corresponded to the length of the gates; this was the lower pavement. [19]Then he measured the distance from the front of the lower gate to the exterior front of the inner court; it was 175 feet.[R] This was the east; next the north is described.

[20]He measured the gate of the outer court facing north, both its length and width. [21]Its three recesses on each side, its pilasters, and its portico had the same measurements as the first gate: 87¹/₂ feet[Q] long and 43³/₄ feet[N] wide. [22]Its windows, portico, and palm trees had the same measurements as those of the gate that faced east. Seven steps led up to the gate, and its portico was ahead of them. [23]The inner court had a gate facing the north gate, like the one on the east. He measured the distance from gate to gate; it was 175 feet.[R]

[24]He brought me to the south side, and there was also a gate on the south. He measured its pilasters and portico; they had the same measurements as the others. [25]Both the gate and its portico had windows all around, like the other windows. It was 87¹/₂ feet[Q] long

ᴬ40:5 = a long cubit　ᴮ40:5 Lit six cubits by the cubit and a handbreadth　ᶜ40:5,7 Lit was one rod　ᴰ40:7 Lit and one rod　ᴱ40:7 Lit five cubits　ᶠ40:8-9 Some Hb mss, Syr, Vg; other Hb mss read gate facing the temple side; it was one rod. ⁹ Then he measured the portico of the gate; it　ᴳ40:9 Lit eight cubits　ᴴ40:9 Lit two cubits　ⁱ40:11 Lit 10 cubits　ᴶ40:11 Lit length　ᴷ40:11 Lit 13 cubits　ᴸ40:12 Lit one cubit　ᴹ40:12 Lit six cubits　ᴺ40:13,21 Lit 25 cubits　ᴼ40:14 Lit 60 cubits　ᴾ40:14 Hb obscure　Q40:15,21,25 Lit 50 cubits　ᴿ40:19,23 Lit 100 cubits

40:5 The dimensions of the **temple** and the city are dominated by multiples of five. The gate structure measured 25 by 50 cubits; the temple house with its adjoining structures, 50 by 100 cubits; the inner court and the quadrangles of the temple area, 100 by 100 cubits; and the entire temple complex, 500 by 500 cubits. The number of steps (7 + 8 + 10) leading to the temple adds up to 25. The length of the measuring rod (**six units of 21 inches**) followed the more common cubit length. The shorter cubit, 18 inches, was used in later times (2Ch 3:3).

40:7 The alcoves, guardrooms, or **recesses** inside the gates were one rod long and one rod wide (**10 feet long and 10 feet deep**; see also v. 10). The projecting walls between the alcoves were five cubits thick. Guardrooms were also a part of the Solomonic temple (2Ch 12:11). This pattern also oc-

curs at Solomon's fortified gates uncovered at the cities of Gezer, Hazor, and Megiddo. Each gate had an initial threshold, three recessed chambers on either side, and an inner vestibule.

40:16 Representations of the **palm** tree also decorated Solomon's temple (1Kg 6:29,32,35).

40:17-19 A **paved surface** functioned something like a border around the outside edges of the **outer court**. Along this pavement were 30 rooms used by the Levites (perhaps for meals) in other Israelite temples (Neh 13:4-14; Jr 35:2-4). The distance from the outer gate to the exterior of the inner court was 100 cubits, or **175 feet**. The dimensions of the northern and southern gates as well as the space between these gates to the inner court were identical to the dimensions of the east gate (vv. 17-27).

and 43³/₄ feet^A wide. ²⁶ Its stairway had seven steps, and its portico was ahead of them. It had palm trees on its pilasters, one on each side. ²⁷ The inner court had a gate on the south. He measured from gate to gate on the south; it was 175 feet.^B

The Inner Gates

²⁸ Then he brought me to the inner court through the south gate. When he measured the south gate, it had the same measurements as the others. ²⁹ Its recesses, pilasters, and portico had the same measurements as the others. Both it and its portico had windows all around. It was 87¹/₂ feet^C long and 43³/₄ feet^A wide. ³⁰ (There were porticoes all around, 43³/₄ feet long and 8³/₄ feet^D wide.^E) ³¹ Its portico faced the outer court, and its pilasters were decorated with palm trees. Its stairway had eight steps.

³² Then he brought me to the inner court on the east side. When he measured the gate, it had the same measurements as the others. ³³ Its recesses, pilasters, and portico had the same measurements as the others. Both it and its portico had windows all around. It was 87¹/₂ feet^C long and 43³/₄ feet^A wide. ³⁴ Its portico faced the outer court, and its pilasters were decorated with palm trees on each side. Its stairway had eight steps.

³⁵ Then he brought me to the north gate.^a When he measured it, it had the same measurements as the others, ³⁶ as did its recesses, pilasters, and portico. It also had windows all around. It was 87¹/₂ feet^C long and 43³/₄ feet^A wide. ³⁷ Its portico^F faced the outer court, and

its pilasters were decorated with palm trees on each side. Its stairway had eight steps.

Rooms for Preparing Sacrifices

³⁸ There was a chamber whose door opened into the portico of the gate.^G The •burnt offering was to be washed there.^b ³⁹ Inside the portico of the gate there were two tables on each side, on which to slaughter the burnt offering, •sin offering,^c and •restitution offering.^d ⁴⁰ Outside, as one approaches the entrance of the north gate, there were two tables on one side and two more tables on the other side of the gate's portico. ⁴¹ So there were four tables inside the gate and four outside, eight tables in all on which the slaughtering was to be done. ⁴² There were also four tables of cut stone for the burnt offering,^e each 31¹/₂ inches^H long, 31¹/₂ inches wide, and 21 inches^I high. The utensils used to slaughter the burnt offerings and other sacrifices were placed on them. ⁴³ There were three-inch^J hooks^K fastened all around the inside of the room, and the flesh of the offering was to be laid on the tables.

Rooms for Singers and Priests

⁴⁴ Outside the inner gate, within the inner court, there were chambers for the singers:^L,f one^M beside the north gate, facing south, and another beside the south^N gate, facing north. ⁴⁵ Then the man said to me: "This chamber that faces south is for the priests who keep charge of the temple.^g ⁴⁶ The chamber that faces north is for the priests who keep charge of the altar. These are the sons of Zadok,^h the ones from the sons of Levi who may approach

a40:35 Ezk 47:2
b40:38 2Ch 4:6
c40:39 Lv 1:3-4;
4:2-3
dLv 5:1-6
e40:42 Ex 20:25
f40:44 1Ch 6:31-
32; 16:41-43;
25:1-7
g40:45 1Ch 9:23;
Ps 134:1
h40:46 1Kg 2:35

^A40:25,29,33,36 Lit 25 cubits   ^B40:27 Lit 100 cubits   ^C40:29,33,36 Lit 50 cubits   ^D40:30 Lit five cubits   ^E40:30 Some Hb mss, LXX omit v. 30   ^F40:37 LXX; MT reads pilasters   ^G40:38 Text emended; MT reads door was by the pilasters, at the gates   ^H40:42 Lit one and a half cubits   ^I40:42 Lit one cubit   ^J40:43 Lit one handbreadth   ^K40:43 Or ledges   ^L40:44 LXX reads were two chambers   ^M40:44 LXX; MT reads singers, which was   ^N40:44 LXX; MT reads east

40:28 There was no western gate for this temple because the temple occupied the western side of the compound.

40:39 A **burnt offering** is mentioned in early texts such as Gn 8:20; Ex 10:25; and Jb 1:5. Burnt offerings were performed at momentous occasions in Israel's history (Jos 8:31; 1Kg 9:25). The purpose of burnt offerings was to honor God and attract His attention. Times of thankfulness (Gn 8:20) as well as times of crisis (Jdg 20:26) called for such offerings. The burnt offering may be considered the most important sacrifice since it was the most prominent sacrifice in the festivals (Nm 28–29). It was distinctive insomuch as the entire offering (apart from the skin) was offered, leaving none for the priest to eat. But even burnt offerings were inferior to the sacrifice of Jesus Christ, who offered Himself for sin once for all (Heb 10:1-4,10). The entire sacrificial system foreshadowed the death of Christ for the sins of the world.

For inadvertent sins, some were to be purified by the **sin offering** (Lv 4:1–5:13) while others required a **restitution offering** (Lv 5:14–6:7). In distinction to the sin offering, the restitution offering was required for offenses that cre-

ated a debt between humans or between a human and God, as for instance if someone had improperly handled one of God's "holy things," such as the implements in the temple. It is of great Christological significance that the offering of the Suffering Servant in Isaiah 53 is described as a restitution offering (Is 53:10). This passage was interpreted to be a prophecy of the suffering of the Christ by NT writers (see Mt 8:17; Lk 22:37; Jn 12:38; Rm 10:16; 1Pt 2:22,24-25), and thus Jesus' death is understood as a restitution offering that removed the debt we owe to God.

40:46 According to the book of Ezekiel, the Zadokites will be distinguished from the Levites in the coming age. The Zadokites were **sons of Zadok**, who traced his Levitical lineage to Aaron through Aaron's son Eleazar (1Ch 6:50-53). Zadok served as a priest under David, along with Abiathar (2Sm 8:17; 15:24-29; 20:25). Zadok was appointed chief priest during Solomon's reign because he supported Solomon as king (1Kg 1:32-35; 2:26-27,35). The Zadokites were elevated and the Levites demoted out of concern for ritual purity, a dominant subject in Ezekiel 40–46.

the LORD to serve Him."[a] [47]Next he measured the court. It was square, 175 feet[A] long and 175 feet wide. The altar[b] was in front of the temple.

[48]Then he brought me to the portico of the temple and measured the pilasters of the portico; they were 8¾ feet[B] thick on each side. The width of the gateway was 24½ feet,[c] and the side walls of the gate were[D] 5¼ feet[E] wide on each side. [49]The portico was 35 feet[F] across and 21[G] feet[H] deep, and 10 steps led[I] up to it.[c] There were pillars by the pilasters, one on each side.[d]

Inside the Temple

41 Next he brought me into the great hall and measured the pilasters;[e] on each side the width of the pilaster was 10½ feet.[J,K] [2]The width of the entrance was 17½ feet,[L] and the side walls of the entrance were 8¾ feet[B] wide on each side. He also measured the length of the great hall, 70 feet,[M] and the width, 35 feet.[F,f] [3]He went inside the next room and measured the pilasters at the entrance;[g] they were 3½ feet[N] wide. The entrance was 10½ feet[K] wide, and the width of the entrance's side walls on each side[o] was 12¼ feet.[P] [4]He then measured the length of the room adjacent to the great hall, 35 feet,[F] and the width, 35 feet.[h] And he said to me, "This is the most holy place."[i]

Outside the Temple

[5]Then he measured the wall of the temple; it was 10½ feet[K] thick. The width of the side rooms all around the temple was seven feet.[Q,j] [6]The side rooms were arranged one above another in three stories of 30 rooms each.[R] There were ledges on the wall of the temple all around to serve as supports for the side rooms, so that the supports would not be in the temple wall itself.[k] [7]The side rooms sur-

rounding the temple widened at each successive story, for the structure surrounding the temple went up by stages. This was the reason for the temple's broadness as it rose. And so, one would go up from the lowest story to the highest by means of the middle one.[S,l]

[8]I saw that the temple had a raised platform surrounding it; this foundation for the side rooms was 10½ feet high.[T,m] [9]The thickness of the outer wall of the side rooms was 8¾ feet.[B] The free space between the side rooms of the temple [10]and the outer chambers was 35 feet[F] wide all around the temple.[n] [11]The side rooms opened into the free space, one entrance toward the north and another to the south. The area of free space was 8¾ feet[B] wide all around.

[12]Now the building that faced the temple yard toward the west was 122½ feet[U] wide. The wall of the building was 8¾ feet[B] thick on all sides, and the building's length was 157½ feet.[V]

[13]Then the man measured the temple; it was 175 feet[A] long.[o] In addition, the temple yard and the building, including its walls, were 175 feet long. [14]The width of the front of the temple along with the temple yard to the east was 175 feet. [15]Next he measured the length of the building facing the temple yard to the west, with its galleries[W] on each side;[p] it was 175 feet.

Interior Wooden Structures

The interior of the great hall and the porticoes of the court— [16]the thresholds, the beveled windows,[q] and the balconies all around with their three levels opposite the threshold—were overlaid with wood on all sides.[r] They were paneled from the ground to the windows (but the windows were covered), [17]reaching to the top of the entrance, and as far as the inner temple and on the outside.

a 40:46 Lv 6:12-13; Ezk 43:19; 44:15
b 40:47 Ezk 43:13-17
c 40:49 1Kg 6:3
d 1Kg 7:15-22; 2Ch 3:17; Jr 52:17-23; Rv 3:12
e 41:1 Ezk 40:2-3,17
f 41:2 1Kg 6:2,17
g 41:3 Ezk 40:16
h 41:4 1Kg 6:20
i 1Kg 6:16
j 41:5 1Kg 6:5-10
k 41:6 1Kg 6:6
l 41:7 1Kg 6:8
m 41:8 Ezk 40:5
n 41:10 Ezk 40:17
o 41:13 Ezk 40:47
p 41:15 Ezk 42:3,5
q 41:16 1Kg 6:4; Ezk 40:16,25
r 1Kg 6:15

A40:47; 41:13 Lit 100 cubits   B40:48; 41:2,9,11,12 Lit five cubits   C40:48 Lit 14 cubits   D40:48 LXX; MT omits 24 1/2 feet, and the side walls of the gate were   E40:48 Lit three cubits   F40:49; 41:2,4,10 Lit 20 cubits   G40:49 LXX; MT reads 19 1/4   H40:49 Lit 12 cubits   I40:49 MT reads and it was on steps that they would go   J41:1 LXX; MT reads pilasters; they were 10 1/2 feet wide on each side—the width of the tabernacle   K41:1,3,5 Lit six cubits   L41:2 Lit 10 cubits   M41:2 Lit 40 cubits   N41:3 Lit two cubits   O41:3 LXX; MT reads width of the entrance   P41:3 Lit seven cubits   Q41:5 Lit four cubits   R41:6 Lit another three and 30 times   S41:7 Hb obscure   T41:8 Lit a full rod of six cubits of a joint; Hb obscure   U41:12 Lit 70 cubits   V41:12 Lit 90 cubits   W41:15 Or ledges

40:47 In Ezekiel's temple, **square** shapes (**175 feet long and 175 feet wide**) are often associated with holy places. The most holy place was a perfect cube (41:4).

41:6 There were three tiers or **stories** of **30 rooms** per tier on the sides of the temple (1Kg 6:5-10), yielding a total of 90 **side rooms**. The rooms widened as one went upward. They may have been designated for the storage of temple equipment and temple treasures (1Kg 6:5-10; 14:26; 2Kg 14:14).

41:18-19 **Cherubim** and **palm trees** were **carved** on the wall of the outer sanctuary and into the structure of Solomon's

temple (1Kg 6:29-30). Cherubim were associated with the appearance of God in the visions of Ezk 1:4-28 and chapter 10. Unlike the cherubim in the earlier visions, the cherubim in the temple had only two faces—a **human face** and a **lion's face**—instead of four faces. In the Genesis narrative, the cherubim served as guards of the garden (Gn 3:24). Here in the temple as well as in Ezekiel's earlier visions, the cherubim likewise served as guards over God's dwelling place. Palm trees may represent fruitfulness, but they also remind us of the trees in the garden of Eden.

On every wall all around, on the inside and outside, was a pattern [18] carved with *cherubim and palm trees.[a] There was a palm tree between each pair of cherubim.[b] Each cherub had two faces: [19] a human face turned toward the palm tree on one side,[c] and a lion's face turned toward it on the other. They were carved throughout the temple on all sides. [20] Cherubim and palm trees were carved from the ground to the top of the entrance and on the wall of the great hall.

[21] The doorposts of the great hall were square,[d] and the front of the sanctuary had the same appearance. [22] The altar was[A] made of wood, 5¼ feet[B] high and 3½ feet[C] long.[D] It had corners, and its length[E] and sides were of wood.[e] The man told me, "This is the table that stands before the LORD."[f]

[23] The great hall and the sanctuary each had a double door,[g] [24] and each of the doors had two swinging panels.[h] There were two panels for one door and two for the other. [25] Cherubim and palm trees were carved on the doors of the great hall like those carved on the walls. There was a wooden canopy[F,i] outside, in front of the portico. [26] There were beveled windows and palm trees on both sides,[j] on the side walls of the portico, the side rooms of the temple, and the canopies.[F]

The Priests' Chambers

42 Then the man led me out by way of the north gate into the outer court.[k] He brought me to the group of chambers opposite the temple yard and opposite the building[l] to the north. [2] Along the length of the chambers, which was 175 feet,[G,m] there was an entrance on the north; the width was 87½ feet.[H] [3] Opposite the 35 foot space[i] belonging to the inner court and opposite the paved surface[n] belonging to the outer court, the structure rose gallery by gallery[o] in three tiers. [4] In front of the chambers was a walkway toward the inside,[p] 17½ feet[J] wide and 175 feet[G] long,[K] and their entrances were on the north.

[5] The upper chambers were narrower because the galleries took away more space from them than from the lower and middle stories of the building. [6] For they were arranged in three stories and had no pillars like the pillars of the courts;[q] therefore the upper chambers were set back from the ground more than the lower and middle stories. [7] A wall on the outside ran in front of the chambers, parallel to them, toward the outer court; it was 87½ feet[H] long. [8] For the chambers on the outer court were 87½ feet long, while those facing the great hall were 175 feet[G] long.[r] [9] At the base of these chambers there was an entryway on the east side as one enters them from the outer court.[s]

[10] In the thickness of the wall of the court toward the south,[L] there were chambers facing the temple yard[t] and the western building, [11] with a passageway in front of them, just like the chambers that faced north.[u] Their length and width, as well as all their exits, measurements, and entrances, were identical. [12] The entrance at the beginning of the passageway, the way in front of the corresponding[M] wall as one enters on the east side, was similar to the entrances of the chambers that were on the south side.

[13] Then the man said to me, "The northern and southern chambers that face the temple yard are the holy chambers where the priests who approach the LORD will eat[v] the most holy offerings.[w] There they will deposit the most holy offerings—the *grain offerings, *sin offerings, and *restitution offerings—for the place is holy.[x] [14] Once the priests have entered, they must not go out from the holy area to the outer court until they have removed the clothes they minister in, for these are holy.[y] They are to put on other clothes before they approach the public area."[z]

Outside Dimensions of the Temple Complex

[15] When he finished measuring inside the

[a] 41:18 1Kg 6:29
[b] 2Ch 3:5; Ezk 40:16
[c] 41:19 Ezk 1:10; 10:14
[d] 41:21 1Kg 6:33; Ezk 40:9,14,16; 41:1
[e] 41:22 Ex 30:1-3; 1Kg 6:20; Rv 8:3
[f] Ex 25:23,30; Lv 24:6; Ezk 23:41; 44:16; Mal 1:7,12
[g] 41:23 1Kg 6:31-35
[h] 41:24 1Kg 6:34
[i] 41:25 1Kg 7:6
[j] 41:26 Ezk 40:16
[k] 42:1 Ezk 40:17,28,48; 41:1
[l] Ezk 41:12; 42:10,13
[m] 42:2 Ezk 41:13
[n] 42:3 Ezk 40:17
[o] Ezk 41:15-16
[p] 42:4 Ezk 46:19
[q] 42:6 Ezk 41:6
[r] 42:8 Ezk 41:13-14
[s] 42:9 Ezk 44:5; 46:19
[t] 42:10 Ezk 42:1
[u] 42:11 Ezk 42:4
[v] 42:13 Lv 10:3; Dt 21:5; Ezk 40:46
[w] Ex 29:31; Lv 7:6; 10:13-14,17
[x] Lv 6:25,29; 14:13; Nm 18:9-10
[y] 42:14 Ex 29:4-9; Lv 8:7,13; Is 61:10; Zch 3:4-5
[z] Ezk 44:19

A 41:21-22 Or and in front of the sanctuary was something that looked like [22] an altar   B 41:22 Lit three cubits   C 41:22 Lit two cubits   D 41:22 LXX reads long and 3 1/2 feet wide   E 41:22 LXX reads base   F 41:25,26 Hb obscure   G 42:2,4,8 Lit 100 cubits   H 42:2,7 Lit 50 cubits   I 42:3 Lit 20 cubits   J 42:4 Lit 10 cubits   K 42:4 LXX, Syr; MT reads wide, a way of one cubit   L 42:10 LXX; MT reads east   M 42:12 Or protective; Hb obscure

41:22 This **altar** stood outside the most holy place. This table was probably for the bread of the Presence (Ex 25:30; Lv 24:5-9; 1Kg 7:48).

42:13 It was customary for Israelite **priests** to eat a portion of the **most holy offerings** that the Israelites offered to the Lord (Lv 2:3; 5:13; 6:16,26,29; 7:6,10). The Hebrew word minchah, translated **grain offerings**, was probably borrowed from the administrative or political arena since the term was used to refer to gifts in the secular world (2Kg 8:8-9; 17:3-4). When used in the religious sphere, it referred to a gift presented by a worshiper to his Lord. The grain offering was usually offered with a burnt offering and often with the fellowship offering as well. The grain offering was a gift to the Lord that honored Him as the source of life and the land's fertility. The NT says that just as OT believers offered grain to God, Jesus Christ as the Bread of Life offered His life to God (Jn 6:32-35).

42:15 After the guide had finished measuring what was

temple complex, he led me out by way of the gate that faced east and measured all around the complex.[a]

[16] He measured the east side with a measuring rod;
it was 875 feet[A] by the measuring rod.[B]
[17] He[C] measured the north side;
it was 875 feet[A] by the measuring rod.[B]
[18] He[D] measured the south side;
it was 875 feet[A] by the measuring rod.[B]
[19] Then he turned to the west side and measured 875 feet[A] by the measuring rod.[B]

[20] He measured the temple complex on all four sides. It had a wall all around it,[b] 875 feet long and 875 feet[c] wide, to separate the holy from the common.[d]

Return of the Lord's Glory

43 He led me to the gate,[e] the one that faces east, [2] and I saw the glory of the God of Israel[f] coming from the east.[g] His voice sounded like the roar of mighty waters,[h] and the earth shone with His glory.[i] [3] The vision I saw[j] was like the one I had seen when He[E] came to destroy the city,[k] and like the ones I had seen by the Chebar Canal.[l] I fell face-down.[m] [4] The glory of the LORD entered the temple by way of the gate that faced east.[n] [5] Then the Spirit lifted me up[o] and brought me to the inner court, and the glory of the LORD filled the temple.[p]

[6] While the man was standing beside me, I heard someone speaking to me from the temple.[q] [7] He said to me: "Son of man, this is the place of My throne and the place for the soles of My feet,[r] where I will dwell among the Israelites forever.[s] The house of Israel and their kings will no longer defile My holy name by their religious prostitution and by the corpses[F,t] of their kings at their ·high places.[G,u] [8] Whenever they placed their threshold next to My threshold and their doorposts beside My doorposts, with only a wall between Me and them, they were defiling My holy name by the detestable acts they committed.[v] So I destroyed them in My anger. [9] Now let them remove their prostitution and the corpses[G,w] of their kings far from Me, and I will dwell among them forever.[x]

[10] "As for you, son of man, describe the temple to the house of Israel,[y] so that they may be ashamed of their iniquities.[z] Let them measure its pattern,[aa] [11] and they will be ashamed of all that they have done. Reveal[H] the design

Cross references
a 42:15 Ezk 40:6; 43:1
b 42:20 Is 60:18; Ezk 40:5; Zch 2:5
c Ezk 45:2; Rv 21:16
d Ezk 22:26; 44:23; 48:15
e 43:1 Ezk 10:19; 40:6; 42:15; 44:1
f 43:2 Is 6:3; Ezk 1:28; 3:23; 10:18-19
g Ezk 11:22-23
h Ezk 1:24; Rv 1:15
i Ezk 1:28; 10:4; Rv 18:1
j 43:3 Ezk 1:4-28
k Jr 1:10; Ezk 9:1
l Ezk 1:3
m Ezk 1:28; 3:23
n 43:4 Ezk 10:19
o 43:5 Ezk 3:14;
2Co 12:2-4
p Ezk 10:4
q 43:6 Ezk 1:26
r 43:7 Ps 47:8
s Ezk 37:26-28
t Lv 26:30; Ezk 6:5,13
u Ezk 6:3-5
v 43:8 Ezk 8:3
w 43:9 Ezk 18:30
x Ezk 37:26-28
y 43:10 Ezk 40:4
z Ezk 16:61-63
aa Ezk 28:12

Footnotes
A 42:16,17,18,19 Lit *500 in rods*   B 42:16,17,18,19 Lit *rod all around*   C 42:17 LXX reads *Then he turned to the north and*
D 42:18 LXX reads *Then he turned to the south and*   E 43:3 Some Hb mss, Theod, Vg; other Hb mss, LXX, Syr read *I*   F 43:7,9 Or
monuments   G 43:7 Some Hb mss, Theod, Tg read *their death*   H 43:10-11 LXX, Vg; MT reads *pattern.* [11] *And if they are ashamed . . . done, reveal*

---

inside the temple area, Ezekiel was brought outside to survey the temple from the outside.

42:20 The **temple complex** had a **wall all around it**, 875 feet long and 875 feet wide, a complete square. In the tabernacle only the most holy place was square.

43:2 God's **glory** as seen particularly in the exodus narrative, the Sinai legislation, and the wanderings in the wilderness was the visible manifestation of His presence among His people. In chapter 43 the return of the glory of God to the temple indicates a reversal of the tragedy described in chapters 10-11. God's glory is always described as radiant or very bright (10:4; Lk 2:9; Rv 21:11,23). The glory of the Lord returned through the **east** gate, the gate from which it had earlier departed (10:18-19; 11:23). The **roar of mighty waters** often accompanies a vision of God (1:24; Rv 1:15; 14:2; 19:6).

43:4 Chapters 40-42 focused on structures and spaces during temple construction. Now the focus is on filling those spaces. This is similar to the approach in Genesis 1, where spaces (domains such as water, land, and sky) are formed in Days 1-3, whereas Days 4-6 focus on filling those spaces with creatures. Israel's judgment began when God's glory departed from Solomon's temple in Jerusalem (Ezk 8-11). The climax to her restoration as a nation now took place as God's **glory** reentered the new **temple** in Jerusalem.

43:7 The filling of the temple with God's glory will begin with the most holy place (vv. 1-9) and end at the corners of the outer court, with the description of the activities in the kitchens (46:24). The **place for the soles of My feet** is another way

to describe the "footstool," the place for a king's feet when seated on a **throne** (1Ch 28:2; Ps 99:5; 132:7; Is 60:13-14; Lm 2:1). The phrase **I will dwell among the Israelites forever** indicates God's reason for entering the temple. This renews the promise of 37:26-28 (cp. 43:9; 1Kg 6:13; Zch 2:11). The

kalam

Hebrew Pronunciation	[kah LAM]
HCSB Translation	be humiliated, ashamed, humiliate
Uses in Ezekiel	6
Uses in the OT	38
Focus passage	Ezekiel 43:10-11

Kalam means be humiliated (Is 54:4). The root mostly indicates subjective *humiliation*: prostitutes refused to *be ashamed* (Jr 3:3). But it can also describe objective *humiliation*. *Kalam* in this sense relates to physical need (Jr 14:3), military defeat (Ps 44:9), and death (Is 41:11). People *are disgraced* (Is 41:11) or *embarrassed* (Ezr 9:6). They *remain in disgrace* (Nm 12:14). The participle suggests *in shame* (Ps 74:21). The causative verb means *humiliate* (Jb 19:3) or *harass* (1Sm 25:7). It suggests *feel humiliation* (Jr 6:15) or *behave shamefully* (1Sm 20:34). *Kalam* occurs with *bosh* ("be ashamed") 17 times (Jr 31:19). *Kelimmah* (30x) denotes *humiliation* (Is 45:16) and *disgrace* (Is 30:3). It connotes *scorn* (Is 50:6), *insults* (Ezk 34:29), *shame* (Mc 2:6), and *reproach* (Ps 35:26). It occurs 12 times with *nasa'* ("bear, endure") (Ps 69:7). *Cherpah* ("reproach") occurs with *kelimmah* five times (Ezk 36:15). *Kelimmuth* means *humiliation* (Jr 23:40).

of the temple to them—its layout with its exits and entrances[a]—its complete design along with all its statutes, design specifications, and laws. Write it down in their sight[b] so that they may observe its complete design and all its statutes and may carry them out.[c] [12] This is the law of the temple: all its surrounding territory on top of the mountain[d] will be especially holy. Yes, this is the law of the temple.

The Altar

[13] "These are the measurements of the altar[e] in units of length (each unit being the standard length plus three inches[f]):[A] the gutter is 21 inches[B] deep and 21 inches wide, with a rim of nine inches[c] around its edge. This is the base[D] of the altar. [14] The distance from the gutter on the ground to the lower ledge is 3½ feet,[E] and the width of the ledge is 21 inches.[B] There are seven feet[F] from the small ledge to the large ledge, whose width is also 21 inches. [15] The altar hearth[G] is seven feet[F] high, and four horns[g] project upward from the hearth. [16] The hearth is square, 21 feet[H] long by 21 feet wide.[h] [17] The ledge is 24½ feet[I] long by 24½ feet wide, with four equal sides.[i] The rim all around it is 10½ inches,[j] and its gutter is 21 inches[B] all around it. The altar's steps face east."[j]

[18] Then He said to me: "Son of man,[k] this is what the Lord God says: These are the statutes for the altar on the day it is constructed, so that •burnt offerings[l] may be sacrificed on it and blood may be sprinkled on it:[m] [19] You are to give a bull from the herd[n] as a •sin offering[o] to the Levitical priests who are from the offspring of Zadok,[p] who approach Me in order to serve Me."[q] This is the declaration of the Lord

God. [20] "You must take some of its blood and apply it to the four horns[r] of the altar, the four corners of the ledge, and all around the rim. In this way you will purify the altar and make •atonement for it.[s] [21] Then you must take away the bull for the sin offering, and it must be burned outside the sanctuary in the place appointed for the temple.[t]

[22] "On the second day you are to present an unblemished male goat as a sin offering. They will purify the altar just as they did with the bull. [23] When you have finished the purification, you are to present a young, unblemished bull[u] and an unblemished ram from the flock.[v] [24] You must present them before the Lord; the priests will throw salt on them and sacrifice them as a burnt offering to the Lord.[w] [25] You will offer a goat for a sin offering each day for seven days.[x] A young bull and a ram from the flock, both unblemished, must also be offered. [26] For seven days the priests are to make atonement for the altar and cleanse it. In this way they will consecrate it[K] [27] and complete the days of purification. Then on the eighth day[y] and afterward, the priests will offer your burnt offerings and •fellowship offerings on the altar, and I will accept you."[z] This is the declaration of the Lord God.

The Prince's Privilege

44 The man then brought me back toward the sanctuary's outer gate that faced east, and it was closed. [2] The Lord said to me: "This gate will remain closed. It will not be opened, and no one will enter through it, because the Lord, the God of Israel, has entered through it.[aa] Therefore it will remain closed. [3] The prince himself will sit in the gateway to

Cross references (center column)
[a] 43:11 Ezk 44:5
[b] Ezk 12:3
[c] Ezk 11:20
[d] 43:12 Ezk 40:2
[e] 43:13 Ex 27:1-8; 2Ch 4:1
[f] Ezk 40:5
[g] 43:15 Ex 27:2; Lv 9:9; 1Kg 1:50; Ps 118:27
[h] 43:16 Ex 27:1
[i] 43:17 Ex 20:26
[j] Ezk 40:6
[k] 43:18 Ezk 2:1
[l] Ex 40:29
[m] Lv 1:5,11; Heb 9:21-22
[n] 43:19 Lv 4:3
[o] Ezk 45:19; Heb 7:27
[p] 1Kg 2:35; Ezk 40:46
[q] Nm 16:5
[r] 43:20 Lv 8:15; 9:9
[s] Lv 16:19
[t] 43:21 Ex 29:14; Lv 4:12; Heb 13:11
[u] 43:23 Ex 29:1,10; Ezk 45:18
[v] Ex 29:1
[w] 43:24 Lv 2:13; Nm 18:19; Mk 9:49-50; Col 4:6
[x] 43:25 Ex 29:35-37; Lv 8:33
[y] 43:27 Lv 9:1
[z] Ezk 20:40
[aa] 44:2 Ezk 43:2-4

[A] 43:13 Lit *in cubits (a cubit being a cubit plus a handbreadth)*   [B] 43:13,14,17 Lit *one cubit*   [C] 43:13 Lit *one span*   [D] 43:13 LXX reads *height*   [E] 43:14 Lit *two cubits*   [F] 43:14,15 Lit *four cubits*   [G] 43:15 Hb obscure   [H] 43:16 Lit *12 cubits*   [I] 43:16 Lit *14 cubits*   [J] 43:17 Lit *one-half cubit*   [K] 43:26 Lit *will fill its hands*

---

corpses of their kings refers to the burial of kings near the temple. The proximity of these graves to the temple defiled the temple (1Kg 2:10; 11:43; 2Kg 21:18,26).

43:13 After the return of the glory of the Lord to the temple, the first issue to be addressed is the **altar**, the place of sacrifice. The altar was mentioned in 40:47, but now becomes the focus of temple activities. Because of the altar's size and height, it was necessary that steps lead up to it on the east side (Ex 20:26).

43:18 On **blood . . . sprinkled on it**, see Ex 29:16; Lv 4:6; 5:9.

43:20 When material objects were atoned for, they were purified and cleansed from the impurities that had resulted from sin (Lv 8:14-15). The purification of the altar with blood is analogous to the sprinkling of blood on the priests at their ordination (Ex 29:16), on the altar on the Day of Atonement to make atonement for the people (Lv 16:18-19), and on the people to seal the covenant (Ex 24:1-8).

43:21 Some sacrificial animals were taken **outside the sanc-**

tuary (Ex 29:14; Lv 4:12,21; 8:17; 9:11; 16:27). This action foreshadows one aspect of Christ's sacrifice (Heb 13:11-13).

43:26 The consecration of the **altar** for **seven days** was performed at the Festival of Tabernacles (1Kg 8:65-66; Ezr 3:1-7). It resembled the ordination of **priests** (Ex 29:1-37; Lv 8).

43:27 The **fellowship** offering was prescribed on three specific occasions: the Feast of Weeks (Lv 23:19-20), the completion of the Nazirite vow (Nm 6:17-20), and the installation of the priests (Lv 9:18,22). This offering appears to have been closely associated with the burnt offering which it followed. Like the burnt offering and often in association with it, the fellowship offering was offered on momentous occasions in Israel's history (Ex 24:5; Lv 23:19; Dt 27:7; 1Sm 11:15; 1Kg 8:63-65). What was distinctive about the fellowship offering was that the offerer could share in the sacrifice. As such it expressed the joy of fellowship around a shared meal. In this regard it resembles the celebration of the Lord's Supper.

44:1-2 After the ceremony for the consecration of the

eat a meal before the LORD.[a] He must enter by
way of the portico[b] of the gate and go out the
same way."
4Then the man brought me by way of the
north gate to the front of the temple. I looked,
and the glory of the LORD filled His temple.[c]
And I fell facedown.[d] 5The LORD said to me:
"Son of man, pay attention;[e] look with your
eyes and listen with your ears to everything
I tell you about all the statutes and laws of
the LORD's temple.[f] Take careful note of the
entrance of the temple along with all the exits
of the sanctuary.

The Levites' Duties and Privileges

6"Say to the rebellious people,[g] the house
of Israel: This is what the Lord GOD says: I
have had enough[h] of all your detestable practices, house of Israel. 7When you brought in
foreigners,[i] uncircumcised in both heart and
flesh,[j] to occupy My sanctuary, you defiled My
temple while you offered My food—the fat
and the blood. You[A] broke My covenant by
all your detestable practices. 8You have not
kept charge of My holy things[k] but have appointed others to keep charge of My sanctuary for you.
9"This is what the Lord GOD says: No foreigner, uncircumcised in heart and flesh, may
enter My sanctuary, not even a foreigner who
is among the Israelites. 10Surely the Levites
who wandered away from Me when Israel
went astray, and who strayed from Me after
their idols,[l] will bear the consequences of
their sin.[m] 11Yet they will occupy My sanctuary, serving as guards at the temple gates[n] and
ministering at the temple. They will slaughter
the •burnt offerings[o] and other sacrifices for
the people and will stand before them to serve
them.[p] 12Because they ministered to the house
of Israel before their idols and became a sinful
stumbling block to them, therefore I swore an
oath[B] against them"[q]—this is the declaration
of the Lord GOD—"that they would bear the
consequences of their sin. 13They must not
approach Me to serve Me as priests[r] or come
near any of My holy things or the most holy
things. They will bear their disgrace and the
consequences of the detestable acts they committed. 14Yet I will make them responsible for
the duties of the temple[s]—for all its work and
everything done in it.

The Priests' Duties and Privileges

15"But the Levitical priests descended from
Zadok,[t] who kept charge of My sanctuary when
the Israelites went astray from Me, will approach Me to serve Me. They will stand before
Me to offer Me fat and blood." This is the declaration of the Lord GOD. 16"They are the ones
who may enter My sanctuary[u] and draw near
to My table to serve Me.[v] They will keep My
mandate. 17When they enter the gates of the
inner court they must wear linen garments;[w]
they must not have on them anything made
of wool when they minister at the gates of the
inner court and within it. 18They must wear
linen turbans on their heads and linen undergarments around their waists.[x] They are not
to put on anything that makes them sweat.
19Before they go out to the outer court,[C] to
the people, they must take off the clothes they

[a]44:3 Gn 31:54; Ex 24:9-11
[b]Ezk 46:2,8-10
[c]44:4 Is 6:3; Ezk 3:23; 43:5
[d]Ezk 1:28; 43:3
[e]44:5 Dt 32:46; Ezk 40:4
[f]Dt 12:32; Ezk 43:10-11
[g]44:6 Ezk 2:5-7; 3:9
[h]Ezk 45:9; 1Pt 4:3
[i]44:7 Lv 22:25
[j]Lv 26:41; Dt 10:16; Jr 4:4; 9:26
[k]44:8 Lv 22:2; Nm 18:7
[l]44:10 2Kg 23:8-9
[m]Nm 18:23
[n]44:11 1Ch 26:1-19
[o]2Ch 29:34; 30:17
[p]Nm 16:9
[q]44:12 Ps 106:26
[r]44:13 2Kg 23:9
[s]44:14 Nm 18:4; 1Ch 23:28-32
[t]44:15 Ezk 40:46
[u]44:16 Nm 18:5,7-8
[v]Ezk 41:22
[w]44:17 Ex 28:42-43; 39:27-29
[x]44:18 Ex 28:40

[A]44:7 LXX, Syr, Vg; MT reads *They* [B]44:12 Lit *I lifted My hand* [C]44:19 Some Hb mss, LXX, Syr, Vg; other Hb mss read *court, to the outer court*

altar had ended, the guide brought Ezekiel back to the **outer gate** of the sanctuary, the one that faced **east**. Then the Lord informed the prophet that the gate was to remain **closed** because the God of Israel had entered through, giving it a special degree of holiness. Today in Jerusalem the east gate, known as the "Golden Gate," is likewise sealed.

44:5 Ezekiel is depicted here as the new Moses. After the entrance of God into the temple (as God descended on Mount Sinai), God revealed **statutes and laws** to His prophet.

44:6 A **rebellious . . . house** is a common phrase in the book of Ezekiel (2:5-6,8; 3:9,26-27; 12:3,9,25; 17:12; 24:3).

44:7 This description of the defilement of the **temple** may refer to the practice of using **foreigners** as guards in the temple (2Kg 11:14-15; see Jos 9:23,27). Nehemiah carried out this statute when he dismissed Tobiah (Neh 13:8), an Ammonite (Neh 2:10; cp. Dt 23:3).

44:10 This event (**Levites who wandered away from Me when Israel went astray**) may refer to the rebellion of the Israelites during Israel's wilderness wanderings (Nm 16–18).

44:11 This restriction regarding **sacrifices** goes beyond the earlier stipulations that allowed laymen to present and sacrifice their offerings (Lv 1:1-5,11).

44:12 The specific violation described in this verse (**ministered to the house of Israel before their idols**) is not clear. Suggestions include the sins of the priesthood during the incident of the golden calf (Ex 32) and the announced judgment against the house of Eli during the days of Samuel (1Sm 2).

44:15 The priest **Zadok** traced his Levitical lineage to Aaron through Aaron's son Eleazar (1Ch 6:50-53). He served as priest under David, along with Abiathar (2Sm 8:17; 15:24-29; 20:25). He supported Solomon and thus secured for himself and his descendants the privilege of serving in the Jerusalem temple (1Kg 1). Zadok was appointed chief priest during Solomon's reign (and hence over the first temple) because he supported Solomon as king (1Kg 1:32-35; 2:26-27,35).

44:17 When the Zadokites entered the sanctuary, they had to be appropriately dressed for service to God. Clothes **made of wool** were forbidden because this material caused

have been ministering in, leave them in the holy chambers, and dress in other clothes[a] so that they do not transmit holiness to the people through their clothes.[b] [20] "They may not shave their heads[c] or let their hair grow long,[d] but must carefully trim their hair. [21] No priest may drink wine before he enters the inner court.[e] [22] He is not to marry a widow or a divorced woman, but must marry a virgin from the offspring of the house of Israel,[f] or a widow who is the widow of a priest. [23] They must teach My people the difference between the holy and the common, and explain to them the difference between the •clean and the •unclean.[g] [24] "In a dispute, they will officiate as judges and decide the case according to My ordinances.[h] They must observe My laws and statutes regarding all My appointed festivals, and keep My Sabbaths holy.[i] [25] A priest may not come near a dead person so that he becomes defiled.[j] However, he may defile himself for a father, a mother, a son, a daughter, a brother, or an unmarried sister. [26] After he is cleansed, he is to count off seven days for himself.[k] [27] On the day he goes into the sanctuary, into the inner court[l] to minister in the sanctuary, he must present his •sin offering." This is the declaration of the Lord GOD.

[28] "This will be their inheritance: I am their inheritance.[m] You are to give them no possession in Israel: I am their possession. [29] They will eat the •grain offering, the sin offering,[n] and the •restitution offering. Everything in Israel that is permanently dedicated to the LORD will belong to them.[o] [30] The best of all the •firstfruits of every kind and contribution of every kind from all your gifts will belong to the priests.[p] You are to give your first batch of dough to the priest[q] so that a blessing may

rest on your homes.[r] [31] The priests may not eat any bird or animal that died naturally or was mauled by wild beasts.[s]

The Sacred Portion of the Land

45 "When you divide the land by lot as an inheritance,[t] you must set aside a donation to the LORD, a holy portion of the land,[u] $8^1/_3$ miles[A] long and $6^2/_3$ miles[B] wide. This entire tract of land will be holy. [2] In this area there will be a square section[C] for the sanctuary, 875 by 875 feet,[D,v] with $87^1/_2$ feet[E] of open space all around it. [3] From this holy portion,[F] you will measure off an area $8^1/_3$ miles[A] long and $3^1/_3$ miles[G] wide, in which the sanctuary, the most holy place,[w] will stand.[H] [4] It will be a holy area of the land to be used by the priests who minister in the sanctuary, who draw near to serve the LORD.[x] It will be a place for their houses, as well as a holy area for the sanctuary. [5] There will be another area $8^1/_3$ miles[A] long and $3^1/_3$ miles[G] wide for the Levites who minister in the temple;[y] it will be their possession for towns to live in.[I]

[6] "As the property of the city, you must set aside an area $1^2/_3$ of a mile[J] wide and $8^1/_3$ miles[A] long, adjacent to the holy donation of land.[z] It will be for the whole house of Israel. [7] And the prince will have the area on each side of the holy donation of land and the city's property, adjacent to the holy donation and the city's property, stretching to the west on the west side and to the east on the east side.[aa] Its length will correspond to one of the tribal portions from the western boundary to the eastern boundary. [8] This will be his land as a possession in Israel. My princes will no longer oppress My people[ab] but give the rest of the land to the house of Israel according to their tribes.

[9] "This is what the Lord GOD says: You have

a44:19 Ezk 42:14
bLv 6:27
c44:20 Lv 21:5
dNm 6:5
e44:21 Lv 10:9
f44:22 Lv 21:7,13-14
g44:23 Lv 10:10; Ezk 22:26
h44:24 Dt 17:8-9; 2Ch 19:8
iEzk 20:20; 22:26
j44:25 Lv 21:1-4
k44:26 Nm 19:11-19
l44:27 Lv 5:3,6
m44:28 Nm 18:20; Dt 18:2; Jos 13:33
n44:29 Nm 18:9,14; Jos 13:14
o Lv 27:21,28
p44:30 Nm 18:8-13; Neh 10:35-37
qNm 15:20-21
rMal 3:10
s44:31 Lv 22:8
t45:1 Ezk 47:21; 48:29
uEzk 48:8-9
v45:2 Ezk 42:20
w45:3 Ezk 43:12
x45:4 Ezk 48:10-11
y45:5 Ezk 48:13
z45:6 Ezk 48:15-18
aa45:7 Ezk 48:21
ab45:8 Ezk 19:7; 22:27

A45:1,3,5,6 Lit 25,000 cubits   B45:1 LXX reads 20,000 cubits; MT reads 10,000 cubits   C45:2 Lit square all around   D45:2 Lit 500 by 500 cubits   E45:2 Lit 50 cubits   F45:3 Lit this measured portion   G45:3,5 Lit 10,000 cubits   H45:3 Lit be   I45:5 LXX; MT, Syr, Tg, Vg read possession—20 chambers   J45:6 Lit 5,000 cubits

the wearer to perspire. Sweat, like other bodily excretions, was considered defiling (Dt 23:11-13).

44:23 On **teach . . . the difference between the holy and the common**, see a similar purpose for priests in Lv 10:10-11.

44:24 Priests functioned as **judges** early in Israel's history (1Sm 4:18; see also 2Ch 19:8-11).

44:25 The same requirements for priests (**may not come near a dead person**) are found in the Mosaic law (Lv 21:1-3).

44:28 The statement that priests were not to own land (**I am their inheritance**) is identical to the Mosaic legislation (Nm 18:20,23-24; Dt 10:9; Jos 13:14,33; 18:7).

44:31 The **priests** were not allowed to **eat** anything that had

been torn by a wild animal or was found dead (Lv 22:8; Dt 14:21).

45:1 In Ezekiel the allotments of the **land** were aligned with the east-west orientation of the temple. This differed from the divisions after the conquest in Joshua's time. These divisions did not follow any pattern. The allotment of the land is outlined in greater detail in 47:13-48:35.

45:5 The designation of the Levite settlements as **towns** or cities (Hb 'arim) recalls the Levitical cities prescribed in Nm 35:1-8. The centralization of the priests in this new arrangement contrasts with the rest of OT history when priests and Levites were scattered throughout the land.

45:9 Israel's political leaders had disregarded the rights of others throughout their history (19:1-9; 22:6,25; 34:1-10).

gone too far,[A,a] princes of Israel! Put away violence and oppression and do what is just and right.[b] Put an end to your evictions of My people." This is the declaration of the Lord GOD. [10]"You must have honest scales, an honest dry measure,[B] and an honest liquid measure.[C,c] [11]The dry measure[D] and the liquid measure[E] will be uniform, with the liquid measure containing 5½ gallons[F] and the dry measure holding half a bushel.[F] Their measurement will be a tenth of the standard larger capacity measure.[G] [12]The ·shekel will weigh 20 *gerahs*.[d] Your mina will equal 60 shekels.

The People's Contribution to the Sacrifices

[13]"This is the contribution you are to offer: Three quarts[H] from five bushels[I] of wheat and[J] three quarts from five bushels of barley. [14]The quota of oil in liquid measures[K] will be one percent of every[L] cor. The cor equals 10 liquid measures or one standard larger capacity measure,[M] since 10 liquid measures equal one standard larger capacity measure. [15]And the quota from the flock is one animal out of every 200 from the well-watered pastures of Israel. These are for the ·grain offerings, ·burnt offerings, and ·fellowship offerings, to make ·atonement for the people."[e] This is the declaration of the Lord GOD. [16]"All the people of the land must take part in this contribution for the prince in Israel. [17]Then the burnt offerings, grain offerings, and ·drink offerings for the festivals, New Moons, and Sabbaths—for all the appointed times of the house of Israel—will be the prince's responsibility. He will provide the ·sin offerings, grain offerings, burnt offerings, and fellowship offerings to make atonement on behalf of the house of Israel.

[18]"This is what the Lord GOD says: In the first month, on the first day of the month, you are to take a young, unblemished bull and purify the sanctuary. [19]The priest must take some of

[a]45:9 Ezk 44:6
[b]Jr 22:3
[c]45:10 Lv 19:36; Dt 25:15
[d]45:12 Ex 30:13; Lv 27:25
[e]45:15 Lv 1:4; 6:30
[f]45:19 Ezk 43:20
[g]45:20 Lv 4:2; 5:17
[h]45:21 Ex 12:18; Lv 23:4-8; Nm 28:16-17; Dt 16:1
[i]45:25 Lv 23:33-43; Dt 16:13-15
[j]46:1 Ex 20:9-10

the blood from the sin offering and apply it to the temple doorposts, the four corners of the altar's ledge, and the doorposts of the gate to the inner court.[f] [20]You must do the same thing on the seventh day of the month for everyone who sins unintentionally or through ignorance.[g] In this way you will make atonement for the temple.

[21]"In the first month, on the fourteenth day of the month, you are to celebrate the ·Passover, a festival of seven days during which unleavened bread will be eaten.[h] [22]On that day the prince will provide a bull as a sin offering on behalf of himself and all the people of the land. [23]During the seven days of the festival, he will provide seven bulls and seven rams without blemish as a burnt offering to the LORD on each of the seven days, along with a male goat each day for a sin offering. [24]He will also provide a grain offering of half a bushel[N] per bull and half a bushel per ram, along with a gallon[O] of oil for every half bushel. [25]At the festival that begins on the fifteenth day of the seventh month,[P,i] he will provide the same things for seven days—the same sin offerings, burnt offerings, grain offerings, and oil.

Sacrifices at Appointed Times

46 "This is what the Lord GOD says: The gate of the inner court that faces east must be closed during the six days of work, but it will be opened on the Sabbath day[j] and opened on the day of the New Moon. [2]The prince should enter from the outside by way of the gate's portico and stand at the doorpost of the gate while the priests sacrifice his ·burnt offerings and ·fellowship offerings. He will bow in worship at the threshold of the gate and then depart, but the gate must not be closed until evening. [3]The people of the land will also bow in worship before the LORD at the entrance of that gate on the Sabbaths and New Moons.

[4]"The burnt offering that the prince pre-

[A]45:9 Lit *Enough of you*   [B]45:10 Lit *an honest ephah*   [C]45:10 Lit *and an honest bath*   [D]45:11 Lit *the ephah*   [E]45:11 Lit *the bath*
[F]45:11 Lit *one-tenth of a homer*   [G]45:11 Lit *be based on the homer*   [H]45:13 Lit *One-sixth of an ephah*   [I]45:13 Lit *a homer*
[J]45:13 LXX, Vg; MT reads *and you are to give*   [K]45:14 Lit *oil, the bath, the oil*   [L]45:14 Lit *be a tenth of the bath from the*   [M]45:14 Lit
10 baths, a homer   [N]45:24 Lit *an ephah*   [O]45:24 Lit *a hin*   [P]45:25 = the Festival of Booths

45:10 The law warned against cheating people with false weights and measures (Lv 19:35-36; Dt 25:13-16; Mc 6:10-12). Holiness in the temple required just, standardized, **honest** measures as well (Pr 11:1; 20:10; Am 8:5).

45:22 The fact that the **prince** will make a sin offering for **himself** shows that he was not the promised Messiah.

45:23 The offering of **seven bulls and seven rams** daily conflicts with the offerings for the Passover Festival in Nm 28:19.

46:1 While the east gate of the outer court was permanent-

ly closed (44:2), the east **gate of the inner court** could be opened during special days like the Sabbath and the New Moon festival.

46:2 On the Sabbath and the New Moon festival, the prince was to enter from the outside through the portico of the temple, and the priests were to sacrifice his **burnt offerings** and his **fellowship offerings**. In the preexilic period, a king sometimes performed priestly functions (1Kg 8:63; 2Kg 16:12-13).

46:4 The Mosaic law called for two **lambs** and no **ram** for the offering on the Sabbath (Nm 28:9).

sents to the LORD[a] on the Sabbath day is to be six unblemished lambs[b] and an unblemished ram. [5]The •grain offering will be half a bushel[A] with the ram,[c] and the grain offering with the lambs will be whatever he wants to give, as well as a gallon[B] of oil for every half bushel. [6]On the day of the New Moon, the burnt offering is to be a young, unblemished bull, as well as six lambs and a ram without blemish. [7]He will provide a grain offering of half a bushel[A] with the bull, half a bushel with the ram, and whatever he can afford with the lambs, together with a gallon[B] of oil for every half bushel. [8]When the prince enters,[d] he must go in by way of the gate's portico and go out the same way.

[9]"When the people of the land come before the LORD at the appointed times,[C,e] whoever enters by way of the north gate to worship must go out by way of the south gate, and whoever enters by way of the south gate must go out by way of the north gate. No one must return through the gate by which he entered, but must go out by the opposite gate. [10]When the people enter, the prince will enter with them, and when they leave, he will leave. [11]At the festivals and appointed times, the grain offering will be half a bushel[A] with the bull, half a bushel with the ram, and whatever he wants to give with the lambs, along with a gallon[B] of oil for every half bushel.

[12]"When the prince makes a freewill offering, whether a burnt offering or a fellowship offering as a freewill offering to the LORD,[f] the gate that faces east must be opened for him. He is to offer his burnt offering or fellowship offering just as he does on the Sabbath day. Then he will go out, and the gate must be closed after he leaves.

[13]"You must offer an unblemished year-old male lamb as a daily burnt offering to the LORD; you will offer it every morning.[g] [14]You must also prepare a grain offering every morning along with it: three quarts,[D] with one-third of a gallon[E] of oil to moisten the fine flour—a grain offering to the LORD. This is a permanent

a 46:4 Ezk 45:17
b Nm 28:9
c 46:5 Nm 28:12; Ezk 45:24
d 46:8 Ezk 44:3
e 46:9 Ex 23:14-17
f 46:12 Lv 23:38
g 46:13 Ex 29:38
h 46:17 Lv 25:10
i 46:18 Ezk 45:8-9
j 46:19 Ezk 42:9
k 46:20 2Ch 35:13; Ezk 44:29
l Lv 2:4-7

statute to be observed regularly. [15]They will offer the lamb, the grain offering, and the oil every morning as a regular burnt offering.

Transfer of Royal Lands

[16]"This is what the Lord GOD says: If the prince gives a gift to each of his sons as their inheritance, it will belong to his sons. It will become their property by inheritance. [17]But if he gives a gift from his inheritance to one of his servants, it will belong to that servant until the year of freedom,[h] when it will revert to the prince. His inheritance belongs only to his sons; it is theirs. [18]The prince must not take any of the people's inheritance, evicting them from their property.[i] He is to provide an inheritance for his sons from his own property, so that none of My people will be displaced from his own property."

The Temple Kitchens

[19]Then he brought me through the entrance[j] that was at the side of the gate, into the priests' holy chambers, which faced north. I saw a place there at the far western end. [20]He said to me, "This is the place where the priests will boil the •restitution offering and the •sin offering,[k] and where they will bake the grain offering,[l] so that they do not bring them into the outer court and transmit holiness to the people." [21]Next he brought me into the outer court and led me past its four corners. There was a separate court in each of its corners. [22]In the four corners of the outer court there were enclosed[F] courts, 70 feet[G] long by 52½ feet[H] wide. All four corner areas had the same dimensions. [23]There was a stone wall[I] around the inside of them, around the four of them, with ovens built at the base of the walls on all sides. [24]He said to me: "These are the kitchens where those who minister at the temple will cook the people's sacrifices."

The Life-Giving River

47 Then he brought me back to the entrance of the temple and there was water flowing from under the threshold of the

---

A 46:5,7,11 Lit an ephah   B 46:5,7,11 Lit a hin   C 46:9 Or the festivals   D 46:14 Lit one-sixth of an ephah   E 46:14 Lit one-third of a hin   F 46:22 Hb obscure   G 46:22 Lit 40 cubits   H 46:22 Lit 30 cubits   I 46:23 Or a row

---

46:16 The fact that the **prince** had **sons** argues against identifying him with the Messiah.

46:17 Unlike the time when Israel was ruled by a king, the land that belonged to the prince was to be carefully regulated. The sons of the prince could inherit lands from him, but if the prince made a gift from his inheritance to one of his **servants**, the servant must return the property in the Year of Jubilee, or **year of freedom** (see Lv 25:8-15).

46:18 Because the prince's land will remain in his family,

he was prohibited from seizing the property of his fellow Israelites. Adherence to this law would prevent some of the abuses of previous times (34:3-4; 1Kg 21:1-16; Mc 2:1-2).

47:1 By its correlation with the book of Revelation, Ezekiel 47–48 addresses the consummation of all human history. This is perhaps best seen in this river of life **flowing** from the **temple** to bring healing to the land (vv. 1-12). In Gn 2:8-10 God provided a river that gave life to the land. When sin entered, the garden and its river were hidden or

temple toward the east, for the temple faced east. The water was coming down from under the south side of the threshold of the temple, south of the altar.[a] [2]Next he brought me out by way of the north gate and led me around the outside to the outer gate that faced east; there the water was trickling from the south side. [3]As the man went out east with a measuring line in his hand,[b] he measured off a third of a mile[A] and led me through the water. It came up to my ankles. [4]Then he measured off a third of a mile[A] and led me through the water. It came up to my knees. He measured off another third of a mile[A] and led me through the water. It came up to my waist. [5]Again he measured off a third of a mile,[A] and it was a river that I could not cross on foot. For the water had risen; it was deep enough to swim in, a river that could not be crossed on foot.

[6]He asked me, "Do you see this, son of man?" Then he led me back to the bank of the river. [7]When I had returned, I saw a very large number of trees along both sides of the riverbank.[c] [8]He said to me, "This water flows out to the eastern region and goes down to the 'Arabah. When it enters the sea, the sea of foul water,[B,C] the water of the sea becomes fresh.[d] [9]Every kind of living creature that swarms will live wherever the river flows,[D] and there will be a huge number of fish because this water goes there. Since the water will become fresh, there will be life everywhere the river

goes. [10]Fishermen will stand beside it from En-gedi to En-eglaim.[E] These will become places where nets are spread out to dry. Their fish will consist of many different kinds, like the fish of the Mediterranean Sea.[e] [11]Yet its swamps and marshes will not be healed; they will be left for salt. [12]All kinds of trees providing food will grow along both banks of the river. Their leaves will not wither, and their fruit will not fail.[f] Each month they will bear fresh fruit because the water comes from the sanctuary. Their fruit will be used for food and their leaves for medicine."[g]

The Borders of the Land

[13]This is what the Lord God says: "This is[F] the border you will use to divide the land[h] as an inheritance for the 12 tribes of Israel. Joseph will receive two shares.[i] [14]You will inherit it in equal portions, since I swore[G] to give it to your ancestors.[j] So this land will fall to you as an inheritance.

[15]"This is to be the border of the land:

On the north side[k] it will extend from the Mediterranean Sea by way of Hethlon and Lebo-hamath to Zedad,[H] [16]Berothah, and Sibraim (which is between the border of Damascus and the border of Hamath), as far as Hazer-hatticon, which is on the border of Hauran. [17]So the border will run from the sea to Hazar-enon at the border[l] of Damascus, with the terri-

Cross references (center column):
[a]47:1 Ps 46:4; Zch 14:8; Rv 22:1
[b]47:3 Ezk 40:3
[c]47:7 Rv 22:2
[d]47:8 Ex 15:26; 2Kg 2:21
[e]47:10 Nm 34:3; Ezk 48:28
[f]47:12 Ps 1:3
[g]Rv 22:2
[h]47:13 Nm 34:2-12
[i]Gn 48:15-16
[j]47:14 Dt 1:8; Ezk 20:6
[k]47:15 Nm 34:7-9; Ezk 48:1
[l]47:17 Nm 34:9

A47:3,4,5 Lit *1,000 cubits*   **B**47:8 Or *enters the sea, being brought out to the sea*; Hb obscure   **C**47:8 = the Dead Sea   **D**47:9 LXX, Vg; MT reads *the two rivers flow*   **E**47:10 Two springs near the Dead Sea   **F**47:13 Tg, Vg; Syr reads *The valley of*   **G**47:14 Lit *lifted My hand*   **H**47:15 LXX; MT reads *and Lebo to Zedad, Hamath*; Ezk 48:1

---

withdrawn, but when God concludes His redemptive program and brings full salvation to humankind with eternal life through Jesus Christ, the river of eternal life will again flow to provide healing for the earth. Ezekiel's program of restoration is, in part, an attempt to realize the promise of Eden without canceling the importance of Zion and David.

47:7 The abundance of **trees** in this vision correlates to the fruitfulness of the garden of Eden, suggesting that Ezekiel was shown a new creation for the coming age (Gn 2:9). Here as in the garden account, the surplus is possible because a marvelous stream, the river of life, flows in its midst (Gn 2:10-14). Since the river now comes from the temple and not the garden, the temple is the new center of creation (Ps 46:4).

47:8 The **sea of foul water** is another way of referring to the Dead Sea. The future blessing on this region is the subject of other prophetic passages (Is 35:1-2,6-7; Jl 3:18). The Dead Sea is approximately six times saltier than the ocean.

47:9 This scene is reminiscent of Gn 1:20-21.

47:12 Like the trees in the garden (Gn 2:15-17), these **trees** will remain perpetually green and provide an endless supply of food for nourishment. The fruit trees will **bear . . . fruit** every **month** (34:27; 36:30) because they draw nourishment from the water that comes from **the sanctuary**. Thus the

trees will resemble those in Eden that remain green and supply a constant source of food (Gn 2:15-17). The fruit of these trees will be for food, but their leaves will be for healing (Zch 13:1; Rv 22:1-2).

47:13 The boundaries of the land will differ from the less-than-ideal borders of the tribes during the days of Joshua. The land will be divided equally among the tribes, fulfilling the promise given to the Israelite forefathers (20:6; 36:28; Gn 12:1-3; 15:9-21; 17:8). Ezekiel's promised new exodus and settlement (20:33-38) will result in a new allotment of **the land** with boundaries similar to those of the Davidic empire and that of Jeroboam II (2Sm 8:5-12; 2Kg 14:25; cp. Nm 34). Strikingly absent from the land is the territory of Transjordan (Nm 34).

47:14 A sworn promise made under oath (20:5,15,42; 36:7-8; Neh 9:15) was accompanied by the gesture of an uplifted hand. For OT writers, it was inconceivable that anything could happen apart from the will of God. The God who had created the world was seen as directing history, and history was the unfolding of God's eternal plan to fellowship with a people created for Himself. As a result, the prophets spoke with absolute certainty when God revealed to them His future plans.

tory of Hamath to the north. This will be the northern side.

[18] On the east side it will run between Hauran and Damascus, along the Jordan between Gilead and the land of Israel; you will measure from the northern border to the eastern sea.[A] This will be the eastern side.

[19] On the south side it will run from Tamar to the waters of Meribath-kadesh,[B] and on to the Brook of Egypt[a] as far as the Mediterranean Sea.[b] This will be the southern side.

[20] On the west side the Mediterranean Sea will be the border, from the southern border up to a point opposite Lebo-hamath. This will be the western side.

[21] "You are to divide this land among yourselves according to the tribes of Israel.[c] [22] You will allot it as an inheritance for yourselves and for the foreigners living among you,[d] who have fathered children among you. You will treat them[c] like native-born Israelites; along with you, they will be allotted an inheritance among the tribes of Israel. [23] In whatever tribe the foreigner lives, you will assign his inheritance there." This is the declaration of the Lord GOD.

The Tribal Allotments

48 "Now these are the names of the tribes:

From the northern end, along the road of Hethlon, to Lebo-hamath as far as Hazar-enon, at the northern border of Damascus, alongside Hamath and extending from the eastern side to the sea, will be Dan—one portion. [2] Next to the territory of Dan, from the east side to the west, will be Asher—one portion.

a47:19 Nm 34:5;
1Kg 8:65; Is
27:12
bEzk 48:28
c47:21 Ezk 45:1
d47:22 Ac 11:18;
15:9; Eph 2:12-
14; 3:6; Col 3:11
e48:8-9 Ezk
45:1-5
f48:11 Ezk
44:10,15
g48:13 Ezk 45:1

[3] Next to the territory of Asher, from the east side to the west, will be Naphtali—one portion. [4] Next to the territory of Naphtali, from the east side to the west, will be Manasseh—one portion. [5] Next to the territory of Manasseh, from the east side to the west, will be Ephraim—one portion. [6] Next to the territory of Ephraim, from the east side to the west, will be Reuben—one portion. [7] Next to the territory of Reuben, from the east side to the west, will be Judah—one portion.

[8] "Next to the territory of Judah, from the east side to the west, will be the portion you donate to the LORD, 8 1/3 miles[D] wide, and as long as one of the tribal portions from the east side to the west.[e] The sanctuary will be in the middle of it.

[9] "The special portion you donate to the LORD will be 8 1/3 miles[D] long and 3 1/3 miles[E] wide. [10] This holy donation will be set apart for the priests alone. It will be 8 1/3 miles[D] long on the northern side, 3 1/3 miles[E] wide on the western side, 3 1/3 miles[E] wide on the eastern side, and 8 1/3 miles[D] long on the southern side. The LORD's sanctuary will be in the middle of it. [11] It is for the consecrated priests, the sons of Zadok, who kept My charge[f] and did not go astray as the Levites did when the Israelites went astray. [12] It will be a special donation for them out of the holy donation of the land, a most holy place adjacent to the territory of the Levites.

[13] "Next to the territory of the priests, the Levites will have an area 8 1/3 miles[D] long and 3 1/3 miles[E] wide. The total length will be 8 1/3 miles[D] and the width 3 1/3 miles.[E,g] [14] They must not sell or exchange any of it, and they must

---

A47:18 = the Dead Sea   B47:19 = Kadesh-barnea   C47:22 Lit They will be to you   D48:8,9,10,13 Lit 25,000 cubits   E48:9,10,13 Lit 10,000 cubits

47:15 Lebo-hamath was the northernmost location in the previous land divisions of Israel (Nm 13:21; 1Kg 8:65).

47:19 The **Brook of Egypt**, Wadi el-Arish, marked the southernmost extremity of Solomon's kingdom (1Kg 8:65).

47:20 The western boundary of the land would be the Great Sea, also known as the **Mediterranean Sea**. In the eternal state there will be no sea (Rv 21:1).

47:22 Aliens will be allotted **an inheritance** among the tribes of Israel. No matter which tribe the foreigner lives in, that will be his inheritance. While God had always instructed the Israelites to care for foreigners (Lv 19:33-34; 24:22; Nm 15:29), they will have even greater status in the coming age

(Is 56:3-8). The distinctions between foreigners and Israelites will be eliminated.

48:1 The tribal allotments of Israel in the coming age will begin at the northern frontier with **Dan**. Since the tribe of Levi was not to receive land (v. 28), Joseph's two sons Manasseh and Ephraim would inherit land just as they had done throughout Israel's history (Gn 48:8-22). The order of the tribes listed here has no conformity to any other such list in Israel's history. The tribes that originated through the handmaids of Jacob's wives' will be placed on the outer extremities. The tribes that originated from Jacob's wives Rachel and Leah will be given land in the center of the nation (cp. Gn 35:23-26). Judah and Benjamin will occupy the privileged positions next to the land's special sacred portion.

not transfer this choice part of the land, for it is holy to the LORD.[a]

[15] "The remaining area, 1²/₃ of a mile[A] wide and 8¹/₃ miles[B] long, will be for common use by the city,[b] for both residential and open space. The city will be in the middle of it. [16] These are the city's measurements:

1¹/₂ miles[c] on the north side;
1¹/₂ miles[c] on the south side;
1¹/₂ miles[c] on the east side;
and 1¹/₂ miles[c] on the west side.

[17] The city's open space will extend:

425 feet[D] to the north,
425 feet[D] to the south,
425 feet[D] to the east,
and 425 feet[D] to the west.

[18] "The remainder of the length alongside the holy donation will be 3¹/₃ miles[E] to the east and 3¹/₃ miles[E] to the west. It will run alongside the holy donation. Its produce will be food for the workers of the city. [19] The city's workers from all the tribes of Israel will cultivate it.[b] [20] The entire donation will be 8¹/₃ miles[B] by 8¹/₃ miles;[B] you are to set apart the holy donation along with the city property as a square area.

[21] "The remaining area on both sides of the holy donation and the city property will belong to the prince.[c] He will own the land adjacent to the tribal portions, next to the 8¹/₃ miles[B] of the donation as far as the eastern border and[F] next to the 8¹/₃ miles[B] of the donation as far as the western border. The holy donation and the sanctuary of the temple will be in the middle of it. [22] Except for the Levitical property and the city property in the middle of the area belonging to the prince, the area between the territory of Judah and that of Benjamin will belong to the prince.[d] [23] "As for the rest of the tribes:

From the east side to the west, will be Benjamin—one portion.

[24] Next to the territory of Benjamin, from the east side to the west, will be Simeon—one portion. [25] Next to the territory of Simeon, from the east side to the west, will be Issachar—one portion. [26] Next to the territory of Issachar, from the east side to the west, will be Zebulun—one portion. [27] Next to the territory of Zebulun, from the east side to the west, will be Gad—one portion.

[28] Next to the territory of Gad toward the south side, the border will run from Tamar to the waters[e] of Meribath-kadesh, to the Brook of Egypt, and out to the Mediterranean Sea. [29] This is the land you are to allot as an inheritance to Israel's tribes,[f] and these will be their portions." This is the declaration of the Lord GOD.

The New City

[30] "These are the exits of the city:

On the north side, which measures 1¹/₂ miles,[c] [31] there will be three gates facing north, the gates of the city being named for the tribes of Israel: one, the gate of Reuben; one, the gate of Judah; and one, the gate of Levi. [32] On the east side, which is 1¹/₂ miles,[c] there will be three gates: one, the gate of Joseph; one, the gate of Benjamin; and one, the gate of Dan. [33] On the south side, which measures 1¹/₂ miles,[c] there will be three gates: one, the gate of Simeon; one, the gate of Issachar; and one, the gate of Zebulun. [34] On the west side, which is 1¹/₂ miles,[c] there will be three gates: one, the gate of Gad; one, the gate of Asher; and one, the gate of Naphtali.

[35] The perimeter of the city will be six miles,[G] and the name of the city from that day on will be: •Yahweh Is There."[g]

ᵃ48:14 Lv 25:34; 27:28   ᵇ48:19 Ezk 45:6   ᶜ48:21 Ezk 34:24; 45:7   ᵈ48:22 Jos 18:21-28   ᵉ48:28 2Ch 20:2   ᶠ48:29 Ezk 47:13-20   ᵍ48:35 Is 12:6; 14:32; 24:23; Jr 3:17; 8:19; 14:9; Ezk 35:10; Jl 3:21; Zch 2:10; Rv 21:3; 22:3

A48:15 Lit *5,000 cubits*   B48:15,20,21 Lit *25,000 cubits*   C48:16,30,32,33,34 Lit *4,500 cubits*   D48:17 Lit *250 cubits*   E48:18 Lit *10,000 cubits*   F48:21 Lit *border, and to the west,*   G48:35 Lit *18,000 cubits*

48:15 The site of Jerusalem, with the surrounding **open** land, was exactly 50 times that of the temple (42:20).

48:21 What will belong to the **prince** includes 25,000 cubits from both the eastern and western borders. This area will lie between the border of Judah and Benjamin. The prince will have a higher rank than the average Israelite, yet his role will be below that of priests and Levites.

48:30 The names of the city gates adhere more to Israel's traditional genealogical traditions.

48:35 The city was square, as is the city in Revelation (specifically, it is a cube; Rv 21:16). They appear to be identical. In many ways the presence of God is the object of the final vision, and perhaps of the book of Ezekiel as a whole. It is the emphatic resolution to the tragic event of God leaving His people in Ezekiel 8–11 (esp. Ezk 10:18-19; see Is 60:14; Jr 23:6). It also fulfills the prophetic promises about the reality of God's presence among His people in Zion (Is 1:26; 62:2; Zch 8:3). The name **Yahweh Is There** reverses Ezk 10:18-19. This conclusion to chapters 40–48 communicates the truth that the meaning of human existence is found in the knowledge and worship of God.

Daniel

Daniel, whose name means "God Judges" or "God's Judge," was a sixth-century B.C. prophet living in exile in Babylon. Daniel recounts key events firsthand that occurred during the Jewish captivity and also shares visions that were given to him by God.

A view of the Tigris, "the great river" (10:4), as Daniel referred to it. On the banks of the Tigris a heavenly being appeared to Daniel. The source of the Tigris, several hundred miles north of Babylon, ran within 20 miles of Babylon on its way to the Persian Gulf. Daniel's exact location wasn't specified.

Circumstances of Writing

Author: The critical view of the book of Daniel suggests it was written by a second-century B.C. Jewish author, not the historical Daniel. This view is largely based on a naturalistic perspective that denies the possibility of the authentic foretelling found in Daniel. On the other hand, the traditional view maintains that Daniel the prophet did indeed write this book sometime shortly after the end of the Babylonian captivity (sixth century B.C.). Internal testimony supports this claim. In the text itself, Daniel claimed to have written down visions given by God (8:2; 9:2,20; 12:5). Passages which contain third-person references to Daniel do not disprove his authorship. After all, authors commonly refer to themselves in the third person, as for instance Moses does in the Pentateuch. Moreover, God speaks of Himself in the third person (Ex 20:2,7). The prophet Ezekiel referred to Daniel several times (Ezk 14:14,20; 28:3), a prominence that would befit the writing prophet. Finally, Jesus Christ attributed the book of Daniel to Daniel himself (Mt 24:15; Mk 13:14).

Background: The historical setting of the book of Daniel is the Babylonian captivity. The book opens after King Nebuchadnezzar's first siege of Judah (605 B.C.) when he brought Daniel and his friends to Babylon along with other captives among the Judean nobility. Nebuchadnezzar assaulted Judah again in 597 and brought 10,000 captives back to Babylon. In 586 he once again besieged Jerusalem, this time destroying the city, the holy temple, and exiling the people of Judah to Babylon. Daniel's ministry began in 605 when he arrived at Babylon with the first Jewish captives, extended throughout the Babylonian captivity (which ended in 539), and concluded sometime after the third year of Cyrus the Great, the Medo-Persian king who overthrew Babylonia (see Dn 1:21 and 10:1).

When was the book written? While the critical view maintains a date of 165 B.C. in the Maccabean period primarily because of the precise prophecies related to that time, the traditional view asserts that it was written just after the end of the Babylonian captivity in the late sixth century B.C. The book contains a factual recount-

---

650–620 B.C.

Under Ashurbanipal, Assyrians capture and destroy Babylon. 649

Birth of Jeremiah 640?

Jeremiah's call to be a prophet; warns of invasion from the north 626

Birth of Ezekiel 623

Birth of Daniel 620

620–605 B.C.

Under Nabopolassar (626–605) Asshur and Nineveh fall, marking the end of the Assyrian Empire. 612

Babylonians and Medes take Harran from what remained of Assyrian forces. 610

Jeremiah's temple sermon 609

Josiah killed by the Egyptians at Megiddo 609

Babylonians defeat Pharaoh Neco of Egypt at Carchemish. The Babylonians hold the balance of power in the region. 605

ing of events from the life of Daniel, supernatural prediction of events that took place during the intertesta-mental period, and prophecies that are yet to be fulfilled.

Manuscript evidence supports the early date. Fragments from Daniel were found among the Dead Sea Scrolls, a collection that included other books of the Bible that were written well before the second century. Linguistic evidence demonstrates that the use of Aramaic in Daniel fits a fifth- to sixth-century B.C. date because it parallels the Aramaic of Ezra as well as the Elephantine Papyrii and other secular works of that period. Historical evidence also supports the early date. For example, Daniel accurately described Belshazzar as co-regent with another king (Nabonidus), a fact that was not known until modern times. In summary, the late-date view is driven by a presuppositional rejection of supernatural prophecy and not objective evidence.

Message and Purpose

The theme of the book of Daniel is the hope of the people of God during the times of the Gentiles. The phrase, "the times of the Gentiles," used by Jesus (Lk 21:24), refers to the time between the Babylonian captivity and Jesus' return. It is a time when God's people live under ungodly world dominion. The book promotes hope by teaching that at all times "the Most High God is ruler over the kingdom of men" (5:21). Daniel's purpose was to exhort Israel to be faithful to the sovereign God of Israel during the times of the Gentiles. He accomplished this by recounting examples of godly trust and prophecies of God's ultimate victory.

Contribution to the Bible

Daniel's book establishes the validity of predictive prophecy and lays the foundation for understanding end-times prophecy, especially the book of Revelation in the NT. But most importantly, it emphasizes that the Lord has dominion over all the kingdoms of the earth, even in evil days when wicked empires reign. Two key words in the book are "king" (used 183 times) and "kingdom" (used 55 times). Above all, Daniel teaches that the God

605–560 B.C.

The Babylonians siege Jerusalem; King Jehoiakim, his family and nobles, including Daniel, are taken to Babylon. 605

Daniel and his Hebrew companions are trained to serve Nebuchadnezzar. 604–603

Nebuchadnezzar's dream of the colossal statue and Daniel's interpretation 602

Jerusalem falls to the third Babylonian siege and the temple is destroyed. 586

Nebuchadnezzar's seven years of insanity 573–566

Evil-Merodach, Nebuchadnezzar's son, succeeds him as king of Babylon. 562

560–525 B.C.

Daniel interprets the handwriting on the wall for Belshazzar. Cyrus captures Babylon without resistance. 539

Gabriel visits Daniel with the message of 70 weeks. 539

Cyrus issues a decree allowing the Jews to return to Judah. 538

Daniel, now 84 years old, is thrown into the lions' den. 536

Daniel receives vision of future events 535

of Israel is the Sovereign of the universe, "for His dominion is an everlasting dominion, and His kingdom is from generation to generation" (4:34).

Structure

The genre of the book of Daniel is narrative, recounting historical events for the purpose of present and future instruction. The narrative contains history, prophecy, and apocalyptic visions. Apocalyptic literature refers to revelation by God given through visions and symbols with a message of eschatological (end-time) triumph. Although Daniel contains apocalyptic elements, it is not an apocalyptic book. Rather it is a narrative that includes apocalyptic visions.

Noting that the book of Daniel contains both history (chaps. 1–6) and prophecy (chaps. 7–12), some divide the book into two sections. A better way to view the book's structure is based on the two languages it uses: 1:1–2:3 (Hebrew); 2:4–7:28 (Aramaic); and 8:1–12:13 (Hebrew). The Hebrew sections pertain primarily to the people of Israel, which is fitting since Hebrew was Israel's national language. Aramaic was the international language of that time. Fittingly, the Aramaic section of Daniel demonstrates God's dominion over the international Gentile nations.

Outline

I. The Godly Remnant in the Times of the Gentiles (1:1-21)
    A. Daniel and his friends in the Babylonian captivity (1:1-7)
    B. Daniel and the king's food (1:8-16)
    C. Daniel and the Lord's reward (1:17-21)

II. God's Sovereignty over the Times of the Gentiles (2:1–7:28)
    A. Daniel and the king's dream (2:1-49)
    B. Daniel's friends and the fiery furnace (3:1-30)
    C. Nebuchadnezzar's pride, madness, and repentance (4:1-37)
    D. Belshazzar's feast and the writing on the wall (5:1-30)
    E. Daniel in the lions' den (6:1-28)
    F. Daniel's vision of the four beasts, the ancient of days, and the Son of Man (7:1-28)

III. God's People in the Times of the Gentiles (8:1–12:13)
    A. Daniel's vision of the ram and the male goat (8:1-27)
    B. Daniel's prayer and vision of the 70 weeks (9:1-27)
    C. Daniel and his final visions (10:1–12:13)

Daniel's Captivity in Babylon

1 In the third year of the reign of Jehoiakim[a] king of Judah, Nebuchadnezzar[A,b] king of Babylon came to Jerusalem and laid siege to it. [2] The Lord handed Jehoiakim king of Judah over to him, along with some of the vessels from the house of God.[c] Nebuchadnezzar carried them to the land of Babylon,[B,d] to the house of his god,[c] and put the vessels in the treasury of his god.

[3] The king ordered Ashpenaz, the chief of his court officials,[D] to bring some of the Israelites from the royal family[e] and from the nobility— [4] young men without any physical defect, good-looking, suitable for instruction in all wisdom,[f] knowledgeable, perceptive, and capable of serving in the king's palace[g]—and to teach them the Chaldean language[h] and literature. [5] The king assigned them daily provisions from the royal food and from the wine that he drank.[i] They were to be trained for three years, and at the end of that time they were to serve in the king's court.[E,j] [6] Among them, from the descendants of Judah, were Daniel,[k] Hananiah, Mishael, and Azariah. [7] The chief official gave them other names: he gave the name Belteshazzar to Daniel, Shadrach to Hananiah, Meshach to Mishael, and Abednego to Azariah.[l]

Faithfulness in Babylon

[8] Daniel determined that he would not defile himself with the king's food[m] or with the wine he drank. So he asked permission from the chief official not to defile himself.[n] [9] God had granted Daniel favor and compassion from the chief official,[o] [10] yet he said to Daniel, "My lord the king assigned your food and drink. I'm afraid of what would happen if he saw your faces looking thinner than those of the other young men your age. You would endanger my life[F] with the king."

[11] So Daniel said to the guard whom the chief official had assigned to Daniel, Hananiah, Mishael, and Azariah, [12] "Please test your servants for 10 days. Let us be given vegetables to eat and water to drink. [13] Then examine our appearance and the appearance of the young men who are eating the king's food, and deal with your servants based on what you see." [14] He agreed with them about this and tested them for 10 days. [15] At the end of 10 days they looked better and healthier[G] than all the young men who were eating the king's food.[p] [16] So the guard continued to remove their food and the wine they were to drink and gave them vegetables.

Faithfulness Rewarded

[17] God gave these four young men knowledge and understanding[q] in every kind of literature and wisdom. Daniel also understood visions and dreams[r] of every kind. [18] At the end of the time that the king had said to present them, the chief official presented them to Nebuchadnezzar. [19] The king interviewed them, and among all of them, no one was found equal to Daniel, Hananiah, Mishael, and Azariah.[s] So they began to serve in the king's court. [20] In every matter of wisdom and understanding that the king consulted them about,

Cross references

a1:1 2Kg 24:1-2; 2Ch 36:5-6
bJr 25:1;
52:12,28-30
c1:2 2Kg 24:13;
2Ch 36:7-10; Ezr 5:14; Jr 27:19-22; Dn 5:2
dGn 10:10; 11:2;
Is 11:11; Zch 5:11
e1:3 2Kg 20:18;
24:15; Is 39:7;
Dn 1:9
f1:4 Dn 9:22
gIs 39:7
hJr 5:15
i1:5 2Kg 25:30;
Dn 11:26
jGn 41:46; 1Sm 16:22
k1:6 Ezk 14:14,20; 28:3
l1:7 2Kg 23:34;
24:17; Dn 4:8,19;
5:12; 10:1
m1:8 Pr 23:1-2
nLv 3:17; 11:47;
Ps 141:4; Ezk 4:13; Hs 9:3; Ac 10:11-15
o1:9 Gn 39:21;
1Kg 8:50; Jb 5:15; Ps 106:46;
Pr 16:7; Ac 7:10
p1:15 Ex 23:25
q1:17 Jb 32:8; Ac 7:22; Jms 1:5
r1Kg 3:10-12; Dn 2:19,30; 4:18-19;
7:1
s1:18-19 Gn 41:37-39

A1:1 Or *Nebuchadrezzar*   B1:2 Lit *Shinar*   C1:2 Or *gods*   D1:3 Or *his eunuchs*   E1:5 Lit *to stand before the king*   F1:10 Lit *would make my head guilty*   G1:15 Lit *fatter of flesh*

1:1 Although Daniel recorded these events as taking place **in the third year of . . . Jehoiakim**, Jeremiah wrote that it was in the fourth year (Jr 25:1,9; 46:1). Daniel probably used the Babylonian system which did not count a king's year of accession, while Jeremiah used the Israelite system of counting, which did include the accession year. The events took place during the accession year of **Nebuchadnezzar king of Babylon**, probably when he was still co-regent with his father and just after the battle of Carchemish (605 B.C.).

1:2 Although Nebuchadnezzar viewed his defeat of Judah as a victory for his gods, Daniel's perspective was that it was **the LORD** who **handed Jehoiakim** over to the Babylonians. The historian Berosus mentioned these events when he wrote that Nebuchadnezzar conquered Hattiland (referring to Syro-Palestine). At that time, Nebuchadnezzar took **vessels from the house of God**, in fulfillment of Isaiah's prediction when Hezekiah showed them to the Babylonian king a century beforehand (Is 39:2,6).

1:3 Chief of his court officials means literally "chief of the eunuchs," but since "eunuch" had come to mean "royal official," most likely **Ashpenaz** was not a eunuch, nor did Daniel and his friends become thus.

1:4 The Hebrew word for **young men** here literally means "children" or "boys" and probably refers to teenagers, a good estimate being around age 15. **Chaldean language and literature** refers to an ancient university-style education in Sumerian, Akkadian, and Aramaic.

1:7 Daniel and his friends, whose original names honored the God of Israel, were given **other names** that intended to honor the false gods of Babylon. **Daniel** ("God is My Judge") became **Belteshazzar** ("Bel Protect Him"); **Hananiah** ("God Has Been Gracious") became **Shadrach** ("The Command of Akku"); **Mishael** ("Who Is What God Is?") became **Meshach** ("Who Is What Aku Is?"); **Azariah** ("The Lord Has Helped") became **Abednego** ("Servant of Nebo").

1:8 The word **determined** means literally "set upon his heart," referring to inner resolve. Daniel decided that he **would not defile himself** with a diet that included non-Kosher meat such as horseflesh and pork, or drink **wine** that had been offered to Babylonian gods.

1:15 The fact that Daniel and his friends **looked better and healthier** is not a biblical endorsement of vegetarianism (Gn 9:3). Rather, God in His providence made them healthy and strong.

1:20 Throughout the book of Daniel, there are six different expressions for the king's counselors. The first two, used here,

ANCIENT
BABYLON

1. Summer Palace
2. Hanging Gardens
3. North Citadel
4. Reservoir
5. Sin Gate
6. Ishtar Gate
7. South Citadel
   (royal palace)

8. Emah Temple
9. Ishtar Temple
10. Nabu-sha-hare
    Temple
11. Marduk Gate
12. Zababa Gate
13. Elil Gate

14. Urash Gate
15. Ninurta Temple
16. Gula Temple
17. Esagila
    (Marduk Temple)
18. Etemananki
    Ziggurat

19. Processional Way
20. Lugalgirra Gate
21. Adad Gate
22. Shamash Gate
23. Shamash Temple
24. Adad Temple

he found them 10 times[A,a] better than all the diviner-priests and mediums[b] in his entire kingdom. [21] Daniel remained there until the first year of King Cyrus.[c]

Nebuchadnezzar's Dream

2 In the second year of his reign, Nebuchadnezzar had dreams[d] that troubled him, and sleep deserted him.[e] [2] So the king gave orders to summon the diviner-priests, mediums, sorcerers, and Chaldeans[B,f] to tell the king his dreams. When they came and stood before the king, [3] he said to them, "I have had a dream and am anxious to understand it."

[4] The Chaldeans spoke to the king (Aramaic[C,g] begins here): "May the king live forever.[h] Tell your servants the dream, and we will give the interpretation."

[5] The king replied to the Chaldeans, "My word is final: If you don't tell me the dream and its interpretation, you will be torn limb from limb,[D] and your houses will be made a garbage dump.[i] [6] But if you make the dream and its interpretation known to me, you'll receive gifts, a reward, and great honor from

me.[j] So make the dream and its interpretation known to me."

[7] They answered a second time, "May the king tell the dream to his servants, and we will give the interpretation."

[8] The king replied, "I know for certain you are trying to gain some time, because you see that my word is final. [9] If you don't tell me the dream, there is one decree for you.[k] You have conspired to tell me something false or fraudulent until the situation changes. So tell me the dream and I will know you can give me its interpretation."

[10] The Chaldeans answered the king, "No one on earth can make known what the king requests.[l] Consequently, no king, however great and powerful, has ever asked anything like this of any diviner-priest, medium, or Chaldean. [11] What the king is asking is so difficult that no one can make it known to him except the gods, whose dwelling is not with mortals."[m] [12] Because of this, the king became violently angry[n] and gave orders to destroy all the wise men of Babylon. [13] The decree was issued that the wise men were to be executed,

---

a1:20 Gn 31:7; Nm 14:22; Jb 19:3
b Pr 3:13-18; Dn 5:11-12
c1:21 Ezr 1:1-2; Is 45:1; Dn 6:28; 10:1
d2:1 Gn 40:5-8; Dn 4:5; 5:9
e Gn 41:1,8; Est 6:1; Dn 6:18
f2:2 Dt 18:10,11; 2Ch 33:6; Is 47:9,12
g2:4 Ezr 4:7; Is 36:11
h 1Kg 1:31; Dn 3:9; 5:10; 6:6,21
i2:5 Ezr 6:11; Dn 3:29
j2:6 Dn 5:7,16
k2:9 Is 41:23
l2:10 Dn 5:11-16
m2:11 Ex 29:45; Is 57:15
n2:12 Ps 76:10; Dn 2:24; 3:13,19

A1:20 Lit hands   B2:2 In this chap. Chaldeans are influential Babylonian wise men.   C2:4 Dn 2:4–7:28 is written in Aram.
D2:5 Lit be made into limbs

---

are **diviner-priests and mediums**. The word "diviner priests" comes from a root that means "engraver." It refers to those who engraved Babylonian religious activities and astrological movements of the stars on clay tablets. The word "mediums" means "conjurers." It refers to those who used spells and incantations to communicate with the spirit world.

1:21 Daniel saw the end of the exile, living until **the first year of King Cyrus** (539 B.C.) and even beyond that time (see 10:1, where "third year" dates to 536).

2:1 Nebuchadnezzar's dreams took place **in the second year of his reign**, which might appear to conflict with the claim that Daniel's three-year training program (1:5) began in Nebuchadnezzar's first year (1:1). However, by Babylonian reckoning Daniel's second year of training occurred during what was considered the first year of Nebuchadnezzar's reign (604–603 B.C.; see note at 1:1 about reckoning time). Therefore, the king sought interpretation of his dreams in 602 B.C., shortly after Daniel had completed his three-year education.

2:2 On **diviner-priests** and **mediums**, see note at 1:20. The Hebrew word for **sorcerers** comes from an Akkadian word that can also mean witchcraft. **Chaldeans** is both a general ethnic term for the Babylonian people and, as used here, a specific term for priests who served as astrologers, soothsayers, and wise men in the king's government.

2:4–7:28 The narrative switches from Hebrew to **Aramaic** in verse 4 and continues in Aramaic until 7:28. Chapters 2 through 7 pertain to God's revelations about the Gentile nations. The structure is chiastic (ABCCBA).

2:5 Some versions translate the phrase **my word is final** as "the dream is forgotten." It is better to translate it as referring to the certainty and finality of the king's demand. Nebuchadnezzar withheld the facts of the dream not because

he could not remember them but because he wanted to test his wise men.

2:11 This candid confession by the wise men admits that despite all their incantations, magic, and astrology, they were not capable of receiving supernatural revelation.

2:12 Wise men is a general term for all the king's counselors, who gained their knowledge through occult practices.

2:13 Daniel and his friends were subject to execution because they were in the class of wise men; they had not participated in any of the discussions with the king.

---

peshar

Hebrew Pronunciation	[peh SHAR]
HCSB Translation	interpretation
Uses in Daniel	32
Uses in the OT	32
Focus passage	Daniel 2:4-7,9,16,24

The Aramaic noun *peshar*, occurring only in Daniel, relates to an Akkadian word for *interpreting* dreams and omens, one connected with divination and magic and that could describe one's profession. True *interpretation* of dreams and divine messages requires God's enablement (Dn 2:30). The Aramaic verb *peshar* (2x) denotes *interpret* or *give interpretations* (Dn 5:12,16). These words link with two Hebrew word families. Similar-sounding *pesher* means *interpretation* (Ec 8:1) and need not involve divine messages. Ecclesiastes 8:1 is the only OT passage where the root lacks that association. Genesis 40–41 uses the verb *patar* (9x), which varies in spelling due to standard differences occurring between languages. It suggests Joseph's *interpreting* (8x) or *explaining* (Gn 40:8,22) of dreams. The related noun *pithron* (5x) in that narrative signifies *interpretation* (Gn 40:8) or *meaning* (Gn 40:5; 41:11). Commentaries among the Dead Sea Scrolls use this root of interpreting Scripture.

and they searched for Daniel and his friends, to execute them.

[14] Then Daniel responded with tact and discretion to Arioch, the commander of the king's guard,[A,a] who had gone out to execute the wise men of Babylon. [15] He asked Arioch, the king's officer, "Why is the decree from the king so harsh?"[B,b] Then Arioch explained the situation to Daniel. [16] So Daniel went and asked the king to give him some time, so that he could give the king the interpretation.

[17] Then Daniel went to his house and told his friends Hananiah, Mishael, and Azariah about the matter, [18] urging them to ask the God of heaven[c] for mercy[d] concerning this mystery, so Daniel and his friends would not be killed with the rest of Babylon's wise men.[e] [19] The mystery was then revealed to Daniel in a vision[f] at night, and Daniel praised the God of heaven [20] and declared:

> May the name of God
> be praised forever and ever,[g]
> for wisdom[h] and power belong to Him.
> [21] He changes the times and seasons;
> He removes kings
>   and establishes kings.[i]
> He gives wisdom to the wise
> and knowledge to those
> who have understanding.[j]
> [22] He reveals the deep and hidden things;
> He knows what is
>   in the darkness,[k]
> and light dwells with Him.[l]
> [23] I offer thanks and praise to You,
> God of my fathers,[m]
> because You have given me
> wisdom and power.
> And now You have let me know
> what we asked of You,

for You have let us know[n]
the king's mystery.[c]

[24] Therefore Daniel went to Arioch,[o] whom the king had assigned to destroy the wise men of Babylon. He came and said to him, "Don't kill the wise men of Babylon! Bring me before the king, and I will give him the interpretation."[p]

[25] Then Arioch quickly brought Daniel before the king and said to him, "I have found a man among the Judean exiles[q] who can let the king know the interpretation."

[26] The king said in reply to Daniel, whose name was Belteshazzar,[r] "Are you able to tell me the dream I had and its interpretation?"[s]

[27] Daniel answered the king: "No wise man, medium, diviner-priest, or astrologer[t] is able to make known to the king the mystery he asked about. [28] But there is a God in heaven who reveals mysteries, and He has let King Nebuchadnezzar know what will happen in the last days.[u] Your dream and the visions that came into your mind as you lay in bed[v] were these: [29] Your Majesty, while you were in your bed, thoughts came to your mind about what will happen in the future.[D,w] The revealer of mysteries[x] has let you know what will happen. [30] As for me, this mystery has been revealed to me,[y] not because I have more wisdom than anyone living, but in order that the interpretation might be made known to the king, and that you may understand the thoughts of your mind.[z]

The Dream's Interpretation

[31] "My king, as you were watching, a colossal statue appeared. That statue, tall and dazzling, was standing in front of you, and its appearance was terrifying. [32] The head of the statue was pure gold, its chest and arms were silver, its stomach and thighs were bronze, [33] its legs

Cross references (center column)

[a] 2:14 Gn 37:36
[b] 2:15 Dn 3:22
[c] 2:18 Mt 18:19
[d] Jr 33:3
[e] Mal 3:18
[f] 2:19 Nm 12:6; Jb 33:15-16; Am 3:7
[g] 2:20 1Ch 29:10; Ps 72:18; Lk 1:68
[h] Jb 12:13; Is 28:29
[i] 2:21 1Ch 29:11-12; Dn 4:17; Rm 13:1
[j] Jb 12:16-22
[k] 2:22 Jb 12:22; Ps 139:12; Jr 23:24; Am 4:13; Heb 4:13
[l] Jn 1:4-5; 1Tm 6:16; Jms 1:17; 1Jn 1:5
[m] 2:23 Gn 31:42; Ex 3:15; Dt 26:7; 1Ch 12:17; 29:18
[n] Dn 1:17-18
[o] 2:24 Dn 2:14-15
[p] Ac 27:24
[q] 2:25 Ezr 4:1; 6:16,19-20; 10:7,16; Dn 5:13
[r] 2:26 Dn 1:7; 5:12
[s] Dn 5:16
[t] 2:27 Dn 1:20; 4:7; 5:7,11
[u] 2:28 Is 2:2; Dn 10:14; Hs 3:5; Mc 4:1
[v] Dn 4:5; 7:15
[w] 2:29 Rv 1:1
[x] Jb 12:20-22; Dn 2:45
[y] 2:30 Eph 3:3
[z] Gn 41:16; Ec 3:18; Am 4:13; Ac 3:12

[A] 2:14 Or executioners   [B] 2:15 Or urgent   [C] 2:23 Lit matter   [D] 2:29 Lit happen after this

---

2:18 **This mystery** refers to a secret that can only be known by divine revelation.

2:20-23 Daniel's song of praise includes the two key ideas of the chapter: First, that God is sovereign over the political affairs of humanity because **He removes kings and establishes kings**. Second, that God alone can give revelation by giving **wisdom to the wise** and by revealing **the deep . . . hidden things**, even **the king's mystery** that had stumped the wise men.

2:27 Daniel asserted that no pagan soothsayer could solve **the mystery**. Rather, he attributed revelation to God alone. The word translated **astrologer** expresses the idea of cutting or determining, referring to a person who is able to determine another's fate.

2:28 **In the last days** indicates that the king's dream would find its complete fulfillment only in the end times.

2:31-45 Daniel interpreted the parts of the **colossal statue** to represent four empires in historical succession. The **head** represented the kingdom of Babylon (605–539 B.C.). The **chest and arms** symbolized the Medo-Persian Empire (539–331 B.C.). The **stomach and thighs** stood for the Greek Empire (331–146 B.C.). The **legs** referred to the Roman Empire (146 B.C.–A.D. 1476 in the West and 1453 in the East). The feet were mixed of **iron** and **clay** and represented a future continuation or revival of Rome. The material of each section of the statue decreased in value but increased in strength. The decreased value may symbolize the moral decline of each succeeding kingdom. The increased strength refers to the harsher domination each successive kingdom would impose on its subjects. Daniel also described a **stone** that would shatter the final kingdom and grow into a mountain that **filled the whole earth**. This "stone" is the kingdom of God.

Primarily because they disbelieve in the possibility of predictive prophecy, critical scholars assume that Daniel

were iron, and its feet were partly iron and partly fired clay. [34] As you were watching, a stone broke off without a hand touching it,[A,a] struck the statue[b] on its feet of iron and fired clay, and crushed them.[c] [35] Then the iron, the fired clay, the bronze, the silver, and the gold were shattered and became like chaff[d] from the summer threshing floors. The wind carried them away, and not a trace of them could be found. But the stone that struck the statue became a great mountain and filled[e] the whole earth.

[36] "This was the dream; now we will tell the king its interpretation. [37] Your Majesty, you are king of kings.[f] The God of heaven has given you sovereignty, power,[g] strength, and glory. [38] Wherever people live—or wild animals, or birds of the air—He has handed them over to you and made you ruler over them all.[h] You are the head of gold.

[39] "After you, there will arise another kingdom, inferior to yours, and then another, a third kingdom, of bronze, which will rule the whole earth.[i] [40] A fourth kingdom will be as strong as iron; for iron crushes and shatters everything, and like iron that smashes, it will crush and smash all the others.[B,j] [41] You saw the feet and toes, partly of a potter's fired clay and partly of iron—it will be a divided kingdom, though some of the strength of iron will be in it. You saw the iron mixed with clay, [42] and that the toes of the feet were partly iron and partly fired clay—part of the kingdom will be strong, and part will be brittle. [43] You saw the iron mixed with clay—the peoples will mix with one another[c] but will not hold together, just as iron does not mix with fired clay.

[44] "In the days of those kings, the God of heaven will set up a kingdom that will never be destroyed,[k] and this kingdom will not be left to another people. It will crush all these kingdoms[l] and bring them to an end, but will itself endure forever. [45] You saw a stone[m] break off from the mountain without a hand touching it,[D,n] and it crushed the iron, bronze, fired clay, silver, and gold. The great God has told the king what will happen in the future.[E,o] The dream is true, and its interpretation certain."

Nebuchadnezzar's Response

[46] Then King Nebuchadnezzar fell down, paid homage to Daniel, and gave orders to present an offering and incense to him.[p] [47] The king said to Daniel, "Your God is indeed God of gods, Lord of kings,[q] and a revealer of mysteries,[r] since you were able to reveal this mystery." [48] Then the king promoted Daniel and gave him many generous gifts. He made him ruler over the entire province of Babylon and chief governor over all the wise men of Babylon.[s] [49] At Daniel's request, the king appointed Shadrach, Meshach, and Abednego[t] to manage the province of Babylon. But Daniel remained at the king's court.[u]

Nebuchadnezzar's Gold Statue

3 King Nebuchadnezzar made a gold statue,[v] 90 feet high and nine feet wide.[F] He set it up on the plain of Dura in the province of Babylon.[w] [2] King Nebuchadnezzar sent word to assemble the satraps, prefects, governors, advisers, treasurers, judges, magistrates, and all the rulers[x] of the provinces to attend the dedication of the statue King Nebuchadnezzar had set up. [3] So the satraps, prefects, governors, advisers, treasurers, judges, magistrates, and all the rulers of the provinces assembled

Cross-references (center column)

[a]2:34 Jb 34:20; Lm 4:6; Dn 8:25; 2Co 5:1
[b]Mt 21:44; Lk 20:18
[c]Ps 2:9; Is 60:12
[d]2:35 Ps 1:4; Is 17:13; 41:15,16; Hs 13:3
[e]Is 2:2; Mc 4:1
[f]2:37 Is 47:5; Jr 27:6,7; Ezk 26:7
[g]Pr 8:15
[h]2:38 Ps 50:10; Jr 27:6; 28:14; Dn 4:21
[i]2:39 Dn 5:28,31; 7:6
[j]2:40 Dn 7:7,23
[k]2:44 Ps 145:13; Ezk 37:25; Dn 4:3; 6:26; 7:14; Lk 1:33
[l]Ps 2:9; Mt 21:44
[m]2:45 Is 28:16
[n]Dn 2:34
[o]Jr 32:18-19; Dn 2:29; Mal 1:11
[p]2:46 Mt 8:2; Ac 10:25; 14:13; Rv 19:10; 22:8
[q]2:47 Dt 10:17; Ps 136:2,3; 1Tm 6:15; Rv 17:14; 19:16
[r]Am 3:7
[s]2:48 Gn 41:41; Dn 3:1,12,30
[t]2:49 Dn 1:17; 3:12
[u]Est 2:19,21; Am 5:15
[v]3:1 1Kg 12:28; Is 46:6; Jr 16:20; Hs 2:8; 8:4; Hab 2:19
[w]Gn 11:2; Dn 2:48-49
[x]3:2 Ezr 8:36; Dn 2:48; 6:1-7

[A]2:34 Lit off not by hands   [B]2:40 Lit all these   [C]2:43 Lit another in the seed of men   [D]2:45 Lit mountain, not by hands   [E]2:45 Lit happen after this   [F]3:1 Lit statue, its height 60 cubits, its width six cubits

---

was written in 165 B.C. and therefore is looking backward rather than forward at the rise of earthly kingdoms such as the Roman Empire. They divide the four kingdoms into Babylon, Media, Persia, and Greece. On the other hand, most interpreters who accept the reality of predictive prophecy in Scripture believe Daniel was written in the late sixth century and view the fourth kingdom as Rome. They hold different opinions about the meaning of the stone, however. Some view it as a spiritual kingdom, embodied in the church, which gradually conquered the Roman Empire. Others more accurately view it as a future kingdom, when Messiah Jesus will return and establish His physical rule that will govern the whole earth and **never be destroyed**.

2:47 King Nebuchadnezzar responded to Daniel's remarkable revelation by recognizing the God of Israel as part of the pantheon of gods, though he did not recognize the God of Israel as the one and only true God.

3:1 The events of Daniel 3 probably took place shortly after Daniel explained the king's dream (cp. Dn 2), although some estimate that it could have been 10 or even 20 years later. Babylonian records indicate that there was a revolt against Nebuchadnezzar during the tenth year of his reign, so this may have led to the king's desire for the loyalty test described here. The **gold statue** was not likely solid gold but was instead overlaid with it. Nebuchadnezzar probably decked the entire thing in gold to negate the message conveyed by the statue of his dream, wherein only the head was gold and signaled that the Babylonian Empire would only be temporary. The location of the **the plain of Dura** has not been conclusively identified. Daniel was not involved in the events here since he remained in the capital city "at the king's court" (2:49) while other officials—including his three friends Shadrach, Meshach, and Abednego—were called to Dura to show their loyalty. Had Daniel been there he too would have refused to bow to the image.

3:2 The exact meaning of these seven positions is unclear other than that they are listed in descending order of rank.

for the dedication of the statue the king had set up. Then they stood before the statue Nebuchadnezzar had set up.

⁴A herald loudly proclaimed, "People of every nation and language, you are commanded: ⁵When you hear the sound of the horn, flute, zither,ᴬ lyre,ᴮ harp, drum,ᶜ and every kind of music, you are to fall down and worshipᵃ the gold statue that King Nebuchadnezzar has set up. ⁶But whoever does not fall down and worship will immediately be thrown into a furnace of blazing fire."ᵇ

⁷Therefore, when all the people heard the sound of the horn, flute, zither, lyre, harp, and every kind of music, people of every nation and language fell down and worshiped the gold statue that King Nebuchadnezzar had set up.

The Furnace of Blazing Fire

⁸Some Chaldeans took this occasion to come forward and maliciously accuseᴰ,ᶜ the Jews. ⁹They said to King Nebuchadnezzar, "May the king live forever. ¹⁰You as king have issued a decreeᵈ that everyone who hears the sound of the horn, flute, zither, lyre, harp, drum, and every kind of music must fall down and worship the gold statue. ¹¹Whoever does not fall down and worship will be thrown into a furnace of blazing fire. ¹²There are some Jews you have appointed to manage the province of Babylon: Shadrach, Meshach, and Abednego.ᵉ These men have ignored you,ᶠ the king; they

do not serve your gods or worship the gold statue you have set up."

¹³Then in a furious rageᵍ Nebuchadnezzar gave orders to bring in Shadrach, Meshach, and Abednego. So these men were brought before the king. ¹⁴Nebuchadnezzar asked them, "Shadrach, Meshach, and Abednego, is it true that you don't serve my gods or worship the gold statueʰ I have set up? ¹⁵Now if you're ready, when you hear the sound of the horn, flute, zither, lyre, harp, drum, and every kind of music, fall down and worship the statue I made. But if you don't worship it, you will immediately be thrown into a furnace of blazing fire—and who is the god who can rescue you from my power?"ⁱ

¹⁶Shadrach, Meshach, and Abednego replied to the king, "Nebuchadnezzar, we don't need to give you an answer to this question. ¹⁷If the God we serve exists,ᴱ then He can rescueʲ us from the furnace of blazing fire, and He can rescue us from the power of you, the king. ¹⁸But even if He does not rescue us,ᶠ we want you as king to know that we will not serveᵏ your godsˡ or worship the gold statue you set up."

¹⁹Then Nebuchadnezzar was filled with rage,ᵐ and the expression on his face changed toward Shadrach, Meshach, and Abednego. He gave orders to heat the furnace seven times more than was customary, ²⁰and he commanded some of the strongest soldiers in his army to tie up Shadrach, Meshach, and Abednego and throw them into the furnace of

---

ᵃ3:5 Dn 2:46
ᵇ3:6 Jr 29:22; Mt 13:42,50; Rv 9:2
ᶜ3:8 Ezr 4:12-16; Est 3:8-9; Dn 6:12,24
ᵈ3:10 Dn 4:6; 6:26
ᵉ3:12 Dn 1:7
ᶠDn 6:13
ᵍ3:13 Dn 2:12
ʰ3:14 Jr 50:2
ⁱ3:15 Ex 5:20; 2Kg 18:35; Is 36:18
ʲ3:17 1Sm 17:37; Jb 5:19; Jr 15:20,21; 2Co 1:10
ᵏ3:18 Heb 11:25
ˡJos 24:15
ᵐ3:19 Est 7:7

ᴬ3:5 Or *lyre*   ᴮ3:5 Or *sambuke*   ᶜ3:5 Or *pipe*   ᴰ3:8 Lit *and eat the pieces of*   ᴱ3:17 They do not doubt God's existence as 3:18 shows. The "if" is part of an argument used to defend their refusal to serve Babylonian gods.   ᶠ3:18 Lit *But if not*

3:4-5 Three of the instruments mentioned—**zither . . . harp**, and **drum**—are the only Greek loan words in Daniel. The presence of Greek words does not require that Daniel was written later in the Greek period. Even Assyrian inscriptions that predate the Babylonian period refer to Greek instruments and musicians (Archer, Expositor's: *Daniel*, VII, p. 21). Although some conjecture that the **gold statue** was of Nebuchadnezzar himself, this is unlikely because the Babylonians did not believe their king was divine. More likely, the image was of a Babylonian god, perhaps Nebuchadnezzar's patron Nabu or the chief Babylonian god Marduk. Nebuchadnezzar made this demand as some form of loyalty oath to him personally.

3:6 Incineration in **a furnace of blazing fire**—a punishment that Nebuchadnezzar had also used on two Judean false prophets, Zedekiah and Ahab (Jr 29:22)—was a normal Babylonian penalty as seen in the Code of Hammurabi, Sections 25, 110, and 157. Perhaps this furnace was built to smelt the gold for the image Nebuchadnezzar had made.

3:8 Chaldeans is both a general ethnic term for the Babylonian people and, as used here, a specific term for priests who served as astrologers, soothsayers, and wise men in the king's government. Their motive in denouncing the three faithful Jewish men was not devotion to the king's de-

mand but rather a hatred for the Jewish people. Hatred of the Jewish people is often on display in the Bible, as with Haman (Est 3:5-6). It reflects a hatred of the God of Israel and is expressed through oppression and attempted genocide of His people (Ps 83:2-5).

3:17-18 The king offered Daniel's friends a second chance to worship the idol, but they persistently refused. The Aramaic imperfect verb *yeseziv* ("He can **rescue**") in this context indicates possibility and not certainty. They were saying that God might deliver them or He might choose not to do so. Their faith in God did not rest on the belief that He would perform a miracle, but that their sovereign God could be trusted. They asserted that if God chose not to deliver them from this punishment but instead allowed them to become martyrs for Him, they would still refuse to serve the king's **gods or worship the gold statue**. This is one of the strongest examples of steadfast faith in the Bible.

3:19 The enraged king gave orders to **heat the furnace seven times more than was customary**, an idiom for "as hot as possible."

3:23 The furnace was built on a small hill or mound with openings at the top and side (Miller, *Daniel*, p. 122). So the three men **fell . . . into the furnace** from the top, and the

blazing fire. [21] So these men, in their trousers, robes, head coverings,[A] and other clothes, were tied up and thrown into the furnace of blazing fire. [22] Since the king's command was so urgent[B,a] and the furnace extremely hot, the raging flames[c] killed those men who carried Shadrach, Meshach, and Abednego up. [23] And these three men, Shadrach, Meshach, and Abednego fell, bound, into the furnace of blazing fire.

Delivered from the Fire

[24] Then King Nebuchadnezzar jumped up in alarm.[b] He said to his advisers, "Didn't we throw three men, bound, into the fire?"

"Yes, of course, Your Majesty," they replied to the king.

[25] He exclaimed, "Look! I see four men, not tied, walking around in the fire unharmed;[c] and the fourth looks like a son of the gods."[D,d]

[26] Nebuchadnezzar then approached the door of the furnace of blazing fire and called: "Shadrach, Meshach, and Abednego, you servants of the *Most High God—come out!" So Shadrach, Meshach, and Abednego came out of the fire.[e] [27] When the satraps, prefects, governors, and the king's advisers gathered around, they saw that the fire had no effect[f] on[E] the bodies of these men: not a hair of their heads was singed, their robes were unaffected, and there was no smell of fire on them. [28] Nebuchadnezzar exclaimed, "Praise to the God of Shadrach, Meshach, and Abednego! He sent His angel[F,g] and rescued His servants who trusted in Him.[h] They violated the king's command and risked their lives rather than serve or worship any god except their own God.[i] [29] Therefore I issue

a decree[j] that anyone of any people, nation, or language who says anything offensive against the God of Shadrach, Meshach, and Abednego will be torn limb from limb and his house made a garbage dump.[k] For there is no other god who is able to deliver like this." [30] Then the king rewarded Shadrach, Meshach, and Abednego in the province of Babylon.[l]

Nebuchadnezzar's Proclamation

4 [G] King Nebuchadnezzar,

To those of every people, nation, and language, who live in all the earth:[m]

May your prosperity increase.[n] [2] I am pleased to tell you about the miracles and wonders[o] the *Most High God has done for me.

[3] How great are His miracles,
     and how mighty His wonders![p]
     His kingdom is an eternal kingdom,[q]
     and His dominion is from generation
         to generation.

The Dream

[4][H] I, Nebuchadnezzar, was at ease in my house and flourishing in my palace.[r] [5] I had a dream, and it frightened me; while in my bed, the images and visions in my mind alarmed me.[s] [6] So I issued a decree[t] to bring all the wise men of Babylon to me in order that they might make the dream's interpretation known to me.[u] [7] When the diviner-priests, mediums, Chaldeans, and astrologers came in, I told them the dream, but they could not make its interpretation known to me.[v]

Cross-references

a3:22 Dn 2:15
b3:24 Dn 4:19
c3:25 Ps 91:3-9;
Is 43:2
d Mt 14:33; Mk
1:1; Lk 1:35; Jn
3:18; Ac 9:20
e3:26 Dn 4:2
f3:27 Heb 11:34
g3:28 Heb 1:14
h Ps 34:7; Is
37:36; Ac 5:19;
12:7
i Ps 22:4-5; Is
12:2; 26:3-4;
Jr 17:7
j3:29 Dn 4:6
k Ezr 6:11; Dn
2:5
l3:30 Dn 2:48-49
m4:1 Dn 6:25
n 2Pt 1:2
o4:2 Dn 6:27;
Jn 4:48
p4:3 Ps 105:27;
Is 25:1
q Dn 2:44
r4:4 Ps 30:6; Is
47:7-8
s4:5 Dn 2:28;
7:15
t4:6 Dn 3:10,29
u Gn 41:8; Dn
2:12
v4:7 Dn 2:2

A3:21 The identity of these articles of clothing is uncertain.   B3:22 Or harsh   C3:22 Lit the flame of the fire   D3:25 Or of a divine being   E3:27 Lit fire had not overcome   F3:28 Or messenger   G4:1 Dn 3:31 in Hb   H4:4 Dn 4:1 in Hb

---

king was able to see four men in the furnace (v. 25) as he looked in through the side opening.

3:25 The king saw in the furnace a **fourth** figure who looked **like a son of the gods**. This may have been an angel or even a preincarnate appearance of God the Son.

3:27 When Shadrach, Meshach, and Abednego came out of the furnace, Nebuchadnezzar and all his government officials **saw that the fire had no effect on the bodies of these men**. Not only did the fire fail to burn their hair and clothing, but they did not even have the **smell of fire** on them. Hebrews 11:34 cites this miracle of faith, referring to those who "quenched the raging of fire."

3:28-29 After Shadrach, Meshach, and Abednego were spared, Nebuchadnezzar saw that the God of Israel was greater than all other gods. Even so, he remained a worshiper of many gods, falling short of full devotion to the one and only true God.

4:4-36 The text does not indicate when King Nebuchadnezzar had his **dream**, nor does it matter for the interpreta-

tion of the passage, but it was likely some 10 years before the end of his 43-year reign. Then God in His grace allowed him one year to repent followed by seven years of madness. Once he came to his senses, Nebuchadnezzar lived another two or three years before dying in 562 B.C. No doubt, the king did indeed write the letter. But it was Daniel, as author of the book, who most likely wrote the section that speaks of the king in the third person (vv. 28-33) and records his time of mental illness. The chapter is structured in three sections: (1) A prologue in which the king praises the true God (4:1-3); (2) a narrative body (4:4-34a) that recounts the king's dream, Daniel's interpretation, the king's illness and repentance; and (3) a concluding epilogue in which the king declares the sovereignty of the true God (4:34b-37). The story covers a period of eight years, beginning with the dream, the year afterwards, and then the king's seven-year period of mental illness.

4:7 Nebuchadnezzar called the four classes of wise men to interpret his dream. Unlike the dream of Daniel 2, the king **told them the dream**. But similarly **they could not make its interpretation known** to him.

[8]Finally Daniel, named Belteshazzar[a] after the name of my god—and the spirit of the holy gods is in him[b]—came before me. I told him the dream: [9]"Belteshazzar, head of the diviners, because I know that you have a spirit of the holy gods[c] and that no mystery puzzles you,[d] explain to me the visions of my dream that I saw, and its interpretation. [10]In the visions of my mind as I was lying in bed, I saw this:

There was a tree in the middle
    of the earth,
and its height was great.
[11] The tree grew large and strong;
    its top reached to the sky,
and it was visible to the ends
    of the[A] earth.
[12] Its leaves were beautiful, its fruit
        was abundant,
and on it was food for all.
Wild animals found shelter under it,
the birds of the air[e] lived in its branches,
and every creature was fed from it.[f]

[13]"As I was lying in my bed, I also saw in the visions of my mind an observer, a holy one,[B,g] coming down from heaven. [14]He called out loudly:

Cut down the tree and chop off
    its branches;
strip off its leaves and scatter its fruit.
Let the animals flee from under it,
and the birds from its branches.[h]
[15] But leave the stump with its roots
        in the ground,[i]
and with a band of iron and bronze
        around it,
in the tender grass of the field.
Let him be drenched with dew
    from the sky

and share the plants of the earth[j]
    with the animals.
[16] Let his mind be changed from that
        of a man,
    and let him be given the mind
        of an animal
    for seven periods of time.[C,D,k]
[17] This word is by decree of the observers;
    the matter is a command
        from the holy ones.
This is so the living will know
    that the Most High is ruler
    over the kingdom of men.
He gives it to anyone He wants
    and sets the lowliest of men over it.[l]

[18]This is the dream that I, King Nebuchadnezzar, had. Now, Belteshazzar, tell me the interpretation, because none of the wise men of my kingdom can make the interpretation known to me.[m] But you can, because you have the spirit of the holy gods."

The Dream Interpreted

[19]Then Daniel, whose name is Belteshazzar, was stunned for a moment, and his thoughts alarmed him. The king said, "Belteshazzar, don't let the dream or its interpretation alarm you."

Belteshazzar answered, "My lord, may the dream apply to those who hate you, and its interpretation to your enemies![n] [20]The tree you saw, which grew large and strong, whose top reached to the sky and was visible to all the earth, [21]whose leaves were beautiful and its fruit abundant—and on it was food for all, under it the wild animals lived, and in its branches the birds of the air lived— [22]that tree is you, the king. For you have become great and strong: your greatness has grown and even reaches the sky, and your dominion extends to the ends of the earth.[o]

Cross references

[a]4:8 Dn 1:7
[b]Gn 41:38; Dn 2:11
[c]4:9 Dn 5:11
[d]Ezk 28:3
[e]4:12 Ezk 17:23; Mt 13:32; Lk 13:9
[f]Ezk 31:3-6
[g]4:13 Dt 33:2; Ps 89:7; Zch 14:5; Jd 14
[h]4:14 Ezk 31:10-14
[i]4:15 Jb 14:7-9
[j]Gn 3:18
[k]4:16 Dn 7:25
[l]4:17 1Sm 2:8; Ps 9:16; Jr 27:5-7; Dn 5:21
[m]4:18 Gn 41:8; Dn 5:8
[n]4:19 2Sm 18:32
[o]4:22 Jr 27:6-8; Ezk 31:3

A4:11 Lit of all the   B4:13 = an angel   C4:16 Lit animal as seven times pass over him   D4:16 Perhaps 7 years

---

4:8 The king recognized that **the spirit of the holy gods** was in Daniel. The HCSB translation reflects the fact that Nebuchadnezzar persisted in believing in a plurality of gods. But since he had recently been chastened (3:24-30) and knew that God alone could reveal what was hidden (2:47), it is possibly correct to translate the phrase alternatively as "the spirit of the Holy God is in him." Beginning in this verse and throughout the chapter, Daniel is most frequently called by his Babylonian name **Belteshazzar**, seemingly because this section is written from the perspective of the Babylonian king, not a Hebrew exile.

4:10-12 The king's dream was of a **tree** whose **top reached to the sky**. A similar expression was used in Gn 11:4 for the tower of the city of Babylon, the top of which was to reach "the sky." The tree provided food and shelter for all the creatures of the earth.

4:13 The **observer, a holy one**, was an angel.

4:14-17 The fact that **the stump with its roots** would remain **in the ground**, indicated the continuation of life. The **band of iron and bronze** pointed to the protection of the stump. The tree plainly represents a man (the king) because the angel declared that **his mind** would **be changed from that of a man** to **an animal for seven periods of time** or for seven years.

4:19 As a loyal servant of the king, Daniel was alarmed about the dreadful discipline that would befall the king.

4:22-25 The **tree** represented King Nebuchadnezzar, who would be struck with a mental illness that would cause him to live outdoors **with the wild animals** (or animals of the field) **for seven** years until he repented of his pride and acknowledged that **the Most High is ruler over the kingdom of men**.

²³"The king saw an observer, a holy one, coming down from heaven and saying, 'Cut down the tree and destroy it, but leave the stump with its roots in the ground and with a band of iron and bronze around it, in the tender grass of the field. Let him be drenched with dew from the sky, and share food with the wild animals for seven periods of time.' ²⁴This is the interpretation, Your Majesty, and this is the sentence of the Most High that has been passed against my lord the king:ᵃ ²⁵You will be driven away from people to live with the wild animals. You will feed on grass like cattleᵇ and be drenched with dew from the sky for seven periods of time, until you acknowledge that the Most High is ruler over the kingdom of men, and He gives it to anyone He wants.ᶜ ²⁶As for the command to leave the tree's stump with its roots, your kingdom will be restoredᴬ to you as soon as you acknowledge that Heavenᴮ rules.ᵈ ²⁷Therefore, may my advice seem good to you my king. Separate yourself from your sins by doing what is right,ᵉ and from your injustices by showing mercy to the needy.ᶠ Perhaps there will be an extension of your prosperity."ᵍ

The Sentence Executed

²⁸All this happened to King Nebuchadnezzar.ʰ ²⁹At the end of 12 months, as he was walking on the roof of the royal palace in Babylon, ³⁰the king exclaimed, "Is this not Babylon the Great that I have built by my vast power to be a royal residence and to display my majestic glory?"ⁱ ³¹While the words were still in the king's mouth, a voice came from heaven: "King Nebuchadnezzar, to you it is declared that the kingdom has departed from you.ʲ ³²You will be driven away from people to live with the wild animals, and you will feed on grass like cattle for seven periods of time, until you acknowledge that the Most High is ruler over the kingdom of men, and He gives it to anyone He wants." ³³At that moment the sentence against Nebuchadnezzar was executed. He was driven away from people. He ate grass like cattle, and his body was drenched with dew from the sky, until his hair grew like eagles' feathers and his nails like birds' claws.ᵏ

Nebuchadnezzar's Praise

³⁴But at the end of those days, I, Nebuchadnezzar, looked up to heaven, and my sanity returned to me. Then I praised the Most High and honored and glorified Him who lives forever:ˡ

For His dominion is
    an everlasting dominion,
and His kingdom is from generation
    to generation.ᵐ
35   All the inhabitants of the earth
    are counted as nothing,
and He does what He wantsⁿ
    with the army of heaven

Cross references (center column):
ᵃ4:24 Jb 40:11-12; Ps 107:40
ᵇ4:25 Ps 106:20; Jr 27:5
ᶜPs 83:18; Dn 5:21
ᵈ4:26 Dn 2:37
ᵉ4:27 Pr 28:13; Ac 8:22
ᶠPs 41:1-3; Is 58:6,7; Ezk 18:7
ᵍJr 18:8; Jn 3:10
ʰ4:28 Nm 23:19; Zch 1:6
ⁱ4:30 Hab 2:4
ʲ4:31 Lk 12:20
ᵏ4:32-33 Dn 5:21
ˡ4:34 Dn 6:26; 12:7; Rv 4:10
ᵐPs 145:13; Jr 10:10; Mc 4:7
ⁿ4:35 Jb 9:12; 42:2; Ps 115:3; 135:6; Rm 9:20

ᴬ4:26 Lit *enduring*   ᴮ4:26 = God

4:26 This is the only place in the OT where **Heaven** is used as a euphemism for God. This usage became commonplace in intertestamental literature, the NT, and rabbinic literature.

4:27 Daniel advised the king to repent (**doing what is right**) with the hope that this might prevent God's discipline.

4:29-30 Nebuchadnezzar had no less than three palaces in the city of Babylon. He was **walking on the roof** of one of them when he was overcome with the glory of the city and was consumed with pride. In his exclamation **Is this not Babylon the Great that I** (lit "I, myself") **have built by my vast power . . . to display my majestic glory**, Nebuchadnezzar emphasized himself as the source of majesty. He failed to give God the credit and glory as the ultimate Giver of all good gifts. Many years later, the apostle Paul scolded the Corinthians for their pride by asking, "What do you have that you didn't receive? If, in fact, you did receive it, why do you boast as if you hadn't received it?" (1Co 4:7).

4:31 Having delayed the execution of his sentence against Nebuchadnezzar for a year (v. 28), God disciplined him the instant he became fully consumed with his pride, even **while the words were still in the king's mouth**.

4:33 Nebuchadnezzar may have suffered from boanthropy, a rare mental illness in which people believe they are actually cattle. One modern case of boanthropy resulted in the patient growing long matted hair and thickened fingernails, much like Nebuchadnezzar, whose **hair grew like eagles' feathers and his nails like birds' claws**. Critics contend that secular history has no record of Nebuchadnezzar's mental illness. However, it is questionable as to whether an ancient Near Eastern despot would mention his bout with insanity in official court records which were typically devoted to highlighting his accomplishments. Silence about an embarrassing episode is understandable. Moreover, the church historian Eusebius cited Abydenus, a third-century B.C. Greek historian who referred to a time when Nebuchadnezzar was "possessed by a god." Also, the third-century B.C. historian Berosus possibly referred to these events when he spoke of an illness that befell Nebuchadnezzar just before his death.

4:34 Boanthropy does not render its victims entirely unable to reason or understand what has happened to them, so it was possible for the king to realize that his own pride had caused his insanity. Realizing the cause of his state, **Nebuchadnezzar** repented of his pride and acknowledged the Most High God. His **sanity returned** to him instantly, a signal that God had lifted his sentence.

4:34-36 As an epilogue to the narrative, Nebuchadnezzar glorified God, using words that describe his realization that God's **dominion is an everlasting dominion** and also aptly summarize the theme of the book of Daniel.

and the inhabitants of the earth.
There is no one who can hold back
His hand
or say to Him, "What have You done?"[a]

[36] At that time my sanity returned to me, and my majesty and splendor returned to me for the glory of my kingdom. My advisers and my nobles sought me out, I was reestablished over my kingdom, and even more greatness came to me.[b] [37] Now I, Nebuchadnezzar, praise, exalt, and glorify the King of heaven, because all His works are true and His ways are just.[c] He is able to humble[d] those who walk in pride.[e]

Belshazzar's Feast

5 King Belshazzar[f] held a great feast for 1,000 of his nobles and drank wine in their presence. [2] Under the influence of[A] the wine, Belshazzar gave orders to bring in the gold and silver vessels[g] that his predecessor[B] Nebuchadnezzar had taken from the temple in Jerusalem, so that the king and his nobles, wives, and concubines could drink from them. [3] So they brought in the gold[C] vessels that had been taken from the temple, the house of God in Jerusalem, and the king and his nobles, wives, and concubines drank from them. [4] They drank the wine and praised their gods made of gold and silver, bronze, iron, wood, and stone.[h]

Cross references
a4:35 Is 40:17; 43:13; 45:9; Rm 9:20
b4:36 2Ch 33:12-13; Pr 22:4
c4:37 Dt 32:4; Ps 33:4; Rv 15:3
dEx 18:11; Jb 40:11-12
ePs 18:27; Pr 16:18; Jms 4:6
f5:1 Dn 7:1; 8:1
g5:2 1Kg 7:51; Jr 52:19
h5:4 Is 46:6
i5:7 Gn 41:42
j5:9 Dn 2:1; 5:6; 7:28
k5:11 Dn 4:8-9,18

The Handwriting on the Wall

[5] At that moment the fingers of a man's hand appeared and began writing on the plaster of the king's palace wall next to the lampstand. As the king watched the hand[D] that was writing, [6] his face turned pale,[E] and his thoughts so terrified him that his hip joints shook and his knees knocked together. [7] The king called out to bring in the mediums, Chaldeans, and astrologers. He said to these wise men of Babylon, "Whoever reads this inscription and gives me its interpretation will be clothed in purple, have a gold chain around his neck,[i] and have the third highest position in the kingdom." [8] So all the king's wise men came in, but none could read the inscription or make its interpretation known to him. [9] Then King Belshazzar became even more terrified, his face turned pale,[F] and his nobles were bewildered.[j]

[10] Because of the outcry of the king and his nobles, the queen[G] came to the banquet hall. "May the king live forever," she said. "Don't let your thoughts terrify you or your face be pale.[H] [11] There is a man in your kingdom who has the spirit of the holy gods in him.[k] In the days of your predecessor he was found to have insight, intelligence, and wisdom like the wisdom of the gods. Your predecessor, King Nebuchadnezzar, appointed him chief of the

---

A5:2 Or When he tasted　B5:2 Or father, or grandfather　C5:3 Theod, Vg add and silver　D5:5 Lit part of the hand　E5:5-6 Lit writing, [6] the king's brightness changed　F5:9 Lit his brightness changed on him　G5:10 Perhaps the queen mother　H5:10 Lit your brightness change

---

4:37 The very last sentence of the chapter summarizes the message of the story—that God is **able to humble those who walk in pride**. Some disbelieve that the pagan King Nebuchadnezzar actually came to a saving knowledge of the true God, but possibly he did.

5:1 The developments in Daniel 5 occurred about 23 years after the events in the previous chapter. Nebuchadnezzar had died in 562 B.C., shortly after his time of madness and subsequent repentance (see note at 4:37). After his death, a series of intrigues and assassinations resulted in several obscure kings ruling Babylon until Nabonidus took the throne (556–539 B.C.). Beginning in A.D. 1914, 37 separate archival texts have been discovered documenting the existence of Belshazzar as crown prince. **King Belshazzar held a great feast for 1,000 of his nobles**, probably to bolster morale after Nabonidus had experienced a crushing defeat at the hands of the Persians. The Greek historians Herodotus and Xenophon confirm that Babylon fell while a great feast was in progress (v. 30). Excavations have uncovered a throne room that could accommodate 1,000 nobles.

5:2-4 By drinking libations to Babylonian gods with the **vessels . . . taken from the temple** devoted to the true God of Israel, Belshazzar was acting in an unusually aggressive and blasphemous way. **Nebuchadnezzar** is called Belshazzar's **predecessor** (lit "his father"). Most likely, Belshazzar's father, Nabonidus, married Nebuchadnezzar's daughter to establish his own claim to the throne of Babylon, mak-

ing Nebuchadnezzar the grandfather of Belshazzar. The Aramaic word "father" is flexible, capable of referring to a grandfather, ancestor, or even a predecessor to a king without any lineal tie.

5:5 The appearance of **a man's hand** beginning to write was not a vision seen by Belshazzar alone, but a miracle seen by everyone present. Afterward, the wise men called to interpret could still see the words written on the plaster wall. According to the archaeologist who excavated it, the throne room (see v. 1) had walls covered with white gypsum or plaster.

5:7 The king **called** for his wise men to come and offered great honor to anyone who could interpret the words on the wall. He even offered to give the successful wise man the **third highest position in the kingdom** after Nabonidus and Belshazzar.

5:8 None of the wise men of Babylon were able to interpret the inscription on the wall, showing the futility of their pagan religion. Only Daniel, prophet of the one true God, could discern its meaning (1:17).

5:10 The **queen** who **came to the banquet hall** was the queen mother, not the wife of King Belshazzar since all his wives were already present (cp. v. 3).

5:11-12 Daniel was approximately 80 years old at this point and was either retired or forgotten. The queen mother, being the daughter of Nebuchadnezzar, remembered Daniel's

diviners, mediums, Chaldeans, and astrologers. Your own predecessor, the king, [12] did this because Daniel, the one the king named Belteshazzar, was found to have an extraordinary spirit, knowledge and perception, and the ability to interpret dreams, explain riddles, and solve problems.[a] Therefore, summon Daniel, and he will give the interpretation."

Daniel before the King

[13] Then Daniel was brought before the king. The king said to him, "Are you Daniel, one of the Judean exiles that my predecessor the king brought from Judah?[b] [14] I've heard that you have the spirit of the gods in you, and that you have insight, intelligence, and extraordinary wisdom. [15] Now the wise men and mediums were brought before me to read this inscription and make its interpretation known to me, but they could not give its interpretation. [16] However, I have heard about you that you can give interpretations and solve problems. Therefore, if you can read this inscription and give me its interpretation, you will be clothed in purple, have a gold chain around your neck, and have the third highest position in the kingdom."[c]

[17] Then Daniel answered the king, "You may keep your gifts, and give your rewards to someone else;[d] however, I will read the inscription for the king and make the interpretation known to him. [18] Your Majesty, the 'Most High God gave sovereignty,[e] greatness, glory, and majesty to your predecessor Nebuchadnezzar.[f] [19] Because of the greatness He gave him, all peoples, nations, and languages[g] were terrified and fearful of him. He killed anyone he wanted and kept alive anyone he wanted; he exalted anyone he wanted and humbled anyone he wanted. [20] But when his

heart was exalted and his spirit became arrogant,[h] he was deposed from his royal throne and his glory was taken from him.[i] [21] He was driven away from people,[j] his mind was like an animal's, he lived with the wild donkeys,[k] he was fed grass like cattle, and his body was drenched with dew from the sky until he acknowledged that the Most High God is ruler over the kingdom of men and sets anyone He wants over it.[l]

[22] "But you his successor, Belshazzar, have not humbled your heart,[m] even though you knew all this. [23] Instead, you have exalted yourself against the Lord of heaven. The vessels from His house were brought to you, and as you and your nobles, wives, and concubines drank wine from them,[n] you praised the gods made of silver and gold, bronze, iron, wood, and stone, which do not see or hear or understand.[o] But you have not glorified the God who holds your life-breath in His hand and who controls the whole course of your life.[A] [24] Therefore, He sent the hand, and this writing was inscribed.

The Inscription's Interpretation

[25] "This is the writing that was inscribed:

MENE, MENE, TEKEL, PARSIN.

[26] This is the interpretation of the message:

MENE[B] means that God has numbered the days of your kingdom and brought it to an end.
[27] TEKEL[C] means that you have been weighed in the balance and found deficient.
[28] PERES[D,E] means that your kingdom has been divided and given to the Medes and Persians."

[a]5:12 Gn 41:11-15; Dn 6:3
[b]5:13 Dn 1:3-4; 2:25
[c]5:16 Gn 40:8; Dn 5:7,29
[d]5:17 2Kg 5:15-16
[e]5:18 Dn 4:2
[f]Jr 27:5-7
[g]5:19 Dn 2:12-13; 3:6
[h]5:20 Ex 9:17; Jb 15:25; Dn 4:30-31
[i]Jr 13:18
[j]5:21 Ex 9:17; Jb 15:25
[k]Jb 39:5-8
[l]Dn 4:30-31
[m]5:22 Ex 10:3; 2Ch 33:23; 36:12
[n]5:23 Jr 51:39,57
[o]Dn 5:3-4; Is 2:12; 37:23; Jr 50:29

A5:23 Lit and all your ways belong to Him   B5:26 Or a mina   C5:27 Or a shekel   D5:28 Or half a shekel   E5:28 In Aram, the word peres is the sg form of "parsin" in v. 25.

extraordinary spirit and ability to interpret dreams during her father's reign.

5:13-29 When Daniel was brought before the king, he did not demonstrate the same level of respect that he had consistently shown Nebuchadnezzar. Instead, he rebuked Belshazzar for his brazen attitude and failure to learn from Nebuchadnezzar.

5:16-17 Daniel refused to accept any reward for interpreting the inscription not because he was rude or arrogant but because he was indignant at the king's disregard for Nebuchadnezzar's experiences with God and the blasphemous use of the temple vessels.

5:18-24 Writers of historical narrative frequently communicate the essential message of a text through dialogue. In this case, Daniel's words served as a rebuke of Belshazzar for his failure to learn from the experience of Nebuchadnezzar (as described in Dn 4). Daniel reprimanded

Belshazzar because he had not humbled his heart, even though he knew what had happened to Nebuchadnezzar. According to ancient Babylonian texts, Belshazzar had served in the government of King Neriglissar in 560 B.C. This indicates that he had been old enough to be aware of the events at the end of Nebuchadnezzar's life. Instead of learning to submit to the Almighty, he exalted himself against God by using the temple vessels to blaspheme God. The specific sins Daniel cited were pride, blasphemy, idolatry, and failure to glorify the true God. For this reason, the writing was inscribed on the wall with a message of judgment and doom.

5:25 The three Aramaic words on the wall were: MENE (numbered), TEKEL (weighed), and PARSIN (divided).

5:28 Although the third word was written in the plural form (parsin), Daniel explained its meaning by using the singular form (PERES). The prediction that Belshazzar's kingdom

²⁹Then Belshazzar gave an order, and they clothed Daniel in purple, placed a gold chain around his neck,ᵃ and issued a proclamation concerning him that he should be the third ruler in the kingdom.

³⁰That very night Belshazzar the king of the Chaldeans was killed, ³¹ᴬ and Darius the Medeᵇ received the kingdom at the age of 62.

The Plot against Daniel

6 Darius decidedᴮ to appoint 120 satraps over the kingdom, stationed throughout the realm, ²and over them three administrators, including Daniel.ᶜ These satraps would be accountable to them so that the king would not be defrauded.ᵈ ³Danielᶜ distinguished himself above the administrators and satraps because he had an extraordinary spirit,ᵉ so the king planned to set him over the whole realm.ᶠ ⁴The administrators and satraps, therefore, kept trying to find a charge against Danielᵍ regarding the kingdom. But they could find no charge or corruption,ʰ for he was trustworthy,

and no negligence or corruption was found in him. ⁵Then these men said, "We will never find any charge against this Daniel unless we find something against him concerning the law of his God."ⁱ

⁶So the administrators and satraps went together to the king and said to him, "May King Darius live forever.ʲ ⁷All the administrators of the kingdom,ᵏ the prefects, satraps, advisers, and governors have agreed that the king should establish an ordinance and enforce an edict that for 30 days, anyone who petitions any god or man except you, the king, will be thrown into the lions' den.ˡ ⁸Therefore, Your Majesty, establish the edictᵐ and sign the document so that, as a law of the Medes and Persians, it is irrevocable and cannot be changed."ⁿ ⁹So King Darius signed the document.ᵒ

Daniel in the Lions' Den

¹⁰When Daniel learned that the document had been signed, he went into his house. The windows in its upper room opened toward Je-

ᵃ5:29 Dn 5:7,16
ᵇ5:31 Dn 6:1; 9:1; 11:1
ᶜ6:2 Dn 2:48-49; 5:16,29
ᵈEzr 4:22; Est 7:4
ᵉ6:3 Dn 5:12,14; 9:23
ᶠGn 41:40; Est 10:3
ᵍ6:4 Gn 43:18; Jdg 14:4; Jr 20:10; Dn 3:8; Lk 20:20
ʰDn 6:22; Lk 20:26; 23:14; Php 2:15; 1Pt 2:12; 3:16
ⁱ6:5 Ac 24:13-16,20-21
ʲ6:6 Neh 2:3; Dn 2:4; 5:10; 6:21
ᵏ6:7 Dn 3:2,27
ˡPs 10:9; Dn 3:6; 6:16
ᵐ6:8 Est 3:12; 8:10; Is 10:1
ⁿEst 1:9; 8:8; Dn 6:12,15
ᵒ6:9 Ps 118:9; 146:3

ᴬ5:31 Dn 6:1 in Hb   ᴮ6:1 Lit It was pleasing before Darius   ᶜ6:3 Lit Now this Daniel

has been divided does not indicate that the Babylonian Empire would be divided equally by two kingdoms (**Medes** and **Persians**) but rather that Babylon would be destroyed or dissolved and taken over by the Medo-Persian Empire. The third word on the wall (Parsin) has the same letters as the Aramaic word for "Persian." It was a play on words, indicating that the kingdom would fall to the Persian army.

5:30 Having lost a brief skirmish outside the walls of Babylon, Belshazzar retreated to the city and made light of the coming Persian siege. The Babylonians had 20 years of provisions, and the city was a seemingly impregnable fortress. Nevertheless, Darius diverted the waters of the Euphrates River so his forces could enter through the channel, passing below the water gates. He took the city **that very night** without a battle and killed Belshazzar, who was engaged in a drunken feast. The kingdom of Babylon fell just as foretold by Daniel (Dn 2:39). The colossus's head of gold (Babylon) had fallen. It was replaced by the chest and arms of silver, representing Medo-Persia (see 2:40).

5:31 The identity of **Darius the Mede**, who **received the kingdom at the age of 62**, is uncertain. Some believe he was Gubaru, the governor of Babylon, called Darius, an honorific title meaning "royal one." Others maintain that "Darius the Mede" was an alternate title for the Persian emperor, Cyrus the Great, also viewing the word "Darius" as a royal title.

6:1 In one of the best-known stories in the book, Daniel was cast into the lions' den for his faith. Since Daniel was about 15 years old in 605 B.C. when the Babylonians brought him as a captive to Babylon, and since the events in Daniel 6 most likely took place in the second or third year after the Medo-Persian conquest of Babylon in 539 B.C., Daniel would have been approximately 82 years old when he was thrown to the lions, not a teenager as is often pictured in Bible story books. Darius began organizing the newly conquered Babylonian Empire and immediately **decided to appoint 120 satraps over the kingdom**. These 120 satraps were lower tier officials who helped rule the entire empire or just over the part of the empire that was formerly under Babylonian control.

6:2 The king appointed **three administrators** over the 120 satraps to assure that taxes would be properly collected without any embezzlement or corruption by the 120 government officials. For these positions, the king needed men with trustworthy reputations. So he chose **Daniel** as one of these officials. He must have heard of Daniel's reputation; perhaps he was even aware of Daniel's interpretation of the writing that had appeared on the wall the night Babylon fell.

6:3 Daniel proved to be a superlative administrator because of his **extraordinary spirit**, a phrase used previously to describe his character (5:12). Therefore, **the king planned to set him over the whole realm** as prime minister.

6:4-5 The king's choice of Daniel created jealousy among the other court officials, and they wished to denounce Daniel. Since Daniel was both diligent and honest in his work, they could find no **corruption** in him. Therefore, they sought to trap him by creating a law to ban Daniel from worshiping his God.

6:6-7 When these corrupt officials approached the king, they falsely claimed that **all** government officials supported the proposal that for 30 days, **anyone** who petitioned **any god or man** except the **king** would be **thrown into the lions' den**. By agreeing to this law, Darius probably had not claimed deity but rather adopted the role of a priestly mediator (see note at 3:4-5). His goal was to unite the Babylonian realm under the authority of the new Persian Empire.

6:8 The irrevocability of **a law of the Medes and Persians** is confirmed elsewhere in Scripture (Est 1:19; 8:8) and secular literature (Diodorus of Sicily, XVII:30).

6:10 Even though the law prohibiting prayer had gone into effect, Daniel still prayed with his windows **opened toward Jerusalem**. Jewish people in exile always pray toward Jerusalem—even today—just as Solomon had instructed in his prayer of dedication for the temple (1Kg 8:44-49). Daniel prayed not out of rebellion toward the king but out of obedience to the greater command of God. As the apostles would

rusalem,[a] and three times a day he got down on his knees, prayed, and gave thanks to his God,[b] just as he had done before. [11] Then these men went as a group and found[c] Daniel petitioning and imploring his God. [12] So they approached the king[d] and asked about his edict: "Didn't you sign an edict that for 30 days any man who petitions any god or man except you, the king, will be thrown into the lions' den?"

The king answered, "As a law of the Medes and Persians, the order stands and is irrevocable."[e]

[13] Then they replied to the king, "Daniel, one of the Judean exiles, has ignored you,[f] the king, and the edict you signed, for he prays three times a day." [14] As soon as the king heard this, he was very displeased; he set his mind on rescuing Daniel[g] and made every effort until sundown to deliver him.

[15] Then these men went to the king and said to him, "You as king know it is a law of the Medes and Persians that no edict or ordinance the king establishes can be changed."[h]

[16] So the king gave the order, and they brought Daniel and threw him into the lions' den.[i] The king said to Daniel, "May your God, whom you serve continually,[j] rescue you!" [17] A stone was brought and placed over the mouth of the den.[k] The king sealed it with his own signet ring and with the signet rings of his nobles, so that nothing in regard to Daniel could be changed. [18] Then the king went to his palace and spent the night fasting.[l] No diversions[A] were brought to him, and he could not sleep.[m]

Daniel Released

[19] At the first light of dawn the king got up and hurried to the lions' den. [20] When he reached the den, he cried out in anguish to Daniel. "Daniel, servant of the living God," the king said,[B] "has your God whom you serve continually been able to rescue you[n] from the lions?"

[21] Then Daniel spoke with the king: "May the king live forever. [22] My God sent His angel[o] and shut the lions' mouths. They haven't hurt me, for I was found innocent before Him. Also, I have not committed a crime against you my king."

[23] The king was overjoyed and gave orders to take Daniel out of the den. So Daniel was taken out of the den, uninjured, for he trusted in his God.[p] [24] The king then gave the command, and those men who had maliciously accused Daniel[C,q] were brought and thrown into the lions' den—they, their children, and their wives.[r] They had not reached the bottom of the den before the lions overpowered them and crushed all their bones.

Darius Honors God

[25] Then King Darius wrote to those of every people, nation, and language who live in all the earth: "May your prosperity abound.[s] [26] I issue a decree[t] that in all my royal dominion, people must tremble in fear before the God of Daniel:[u]

> For He is the living God,
> and He endures forever;
> His kingdom will never be destroyed,[v]
> and His dominion has no end.
> [27] He rescues and delivers;
> He performs signs and wonders
> in the heavens and on the earth,[w]
> for He has rescued Daniel
> from the power of the lions."

Cross references (center column):

[a]6:10 1Kg 8:44-49; Ps 5:7; Jnh 2:4
[b]Ps 34:1; Dn 9:4-19; Php 4:6; 1Th 5:17-18
[c]6:11 Ps 37:32,33; Dn 6:6
[d]6:12 Dn 3:8-12; Ac 16:19-21
[e]Est 1:19; Dn 6:8,15
[f]6:13 Est 3:8; Dn 3:12; Ac 5:29
[g]6:14 Mk 6:26
[h]6:15 Est 8:8; Ps 94:20,21; Dn 6:8,12
[i]6:16 2Sm 3:39; Jr 38:5; Dn 6:7
[j]Jb 5:19; Ps 37:39-40; Is 41:10; 2Co 1:10
[k]6:17 Lm 3:53; Mt 27:66
[l]6:18 2Sm 12:16,17
[m]Est 6:1; Ps 77:4; Dn 2:1
[n]6:20 Gn 18:14; Nm 11:23; Jr 32:17; Dn 3:17
[o]6:22 Nm 20:16; Is 63:9; Dn 3:28; Ac 12:11; Heb 1:14
[p]6:23 1Ch 5:20; 2Ch 20:20; Ps 118:8,9; Is 26:3; Dn 3:17-18
[q]6:24 Dn 3:8; 6:12-13
[r]Dt 24:16; 2Kg 14:6; Est 9:10
[s]6:25 Ezr 4:17; 1Pt 1:2
[t]6:26 Ezr 6:8-12; 7:13,21; Dn 3:29; 4:6
[u]Dn 5:19
[v]Ps 93:1,2; Dn 2:44; 7:14; Mal 3:6
[w]6:27 Dn 4:2,3

[A]6:18 Hb obscure   [B]6:20 Lit said to Daniel   [C]6:24 Lit had eaten his pieces

---

later say, "We must obey God rather than men" (Ac 5:29). So great was Daniel's reputation for spiritual commitment that even his enemies knew he would obey God rather than bow to the king's edict.

6:14 The king was **very displeased** not because Daniel had defied him but because he came to understand that the true purpose of the law was to trap Daniel, whom he respected.

6:16 The Persians used mutilation by lions as one of several brutal forms of execution. It was Daniel's continual service to God that caused him to be cast into the lions' den; now the king hoped that this devotion would cause God to deliver Daniel. The word for **den** can also be translated as "pit."

6:17-18 Daniel was cast into a pit over which **a stone** was placed and sealed with the **signet rings** of the king and his nobles. King Darius then spent the night **fasting** and presumably praying for Daniel.

6:22-23 God uses angels to accomplish His purposes, including protection of His people (Ps 34:7; 91:11; Heb 1:14).

He had done so for Daniel's three friends in the furnace many years earlier (Dn 3:25). As on that occasion, this may have been an angel or even the angel of the Lord (i.e., a preincarnate appearance of the Messiah). Daniel was not claiming perfection in declaring that he was **found innocent** before God. Rather, Daniel claimed that his allegiance to God made him guiltless in this matter. It was Daniel's faith in God, not his works, that brought him deliverance from the lions.

6:24 Although executing family members is exceptionally cruel, this was a common Persian practice according to Herodotus (*Histories,* 3.119).

6:25-27 Just as King Nebuchadnezzar before him, King Darius issued a decree to **every people, nation, and language** (cp. 4:2), declaring praise to the God of Daniel. Darius recognized the greatness of God: that He is **living** and eternal, sovereign, all-powerful, and able to deliver His people. Nevertheless, it is unlikely that Darius came to a saving faith here. He instead accepted the God of Israel as just one of many gods.

[28] So Daniel prospered[a] during the reign of Darius and[A] the reign of Cyrus the Persian.[b]

Daniel's Vision of the Four Beasts

7 In the first year of Belshazzar king of Babylon, Daniel had a dream with visions in his mind[c] as he was lying in his bed. He wrote down the dream,[d] and here is the summary[B] of his account. [2] Daniel said, "In my vision at night I was watching, and suddenly the four winds of heaven[e] stirred up the great sea. [3] Four huge beasts[f] came up from the sea,[g] each different from the other.

[4] "The first was like a lion[h] but had eagle's wings. I continued watching until its wings were torn off. It was lifted up from the ground, set on its feet like a man, and given a human mind.

[5] "Suddenly, another beast appeared, a second one, that looked like a bear.[i] It was raised up on one side, with three ribs in its mouth between its teeth. It was told, 'Get up! Gorge yourself on flesh.'

[6] "While I was watching, another beast appeared. It was like a leopard[j] with four wings of a bird on its back. It had four heads[k] and was given authority to rule.

[7] "While I was watching in the night visions, a fourth beast[l] appeared, frightening and dreadful, and incredibly strong, with large iron teeth. It devoured and crushed, and it trampled with its feet whatever was left. It was different from all the beasts before it, and it had 10 horns.[m]

[8] "While I was considering the horns, suddenly another horn,[n] a little one, came up among them, and three of the first horns were uprooted before it. There were eyes in this horn like a man's, and it had a mouth that spoke arrogantly.[o]

The Ancient of Days and the Son of Man

[9] "As I kept watching,

thrones were set in place,[p]
and the Ancient of Days took His seat.

Cross references column:
[a]6:28 Dn 1:21
[b]2Ch 36:22,23; Dn 10:1
[c]7:1 Jb 33:14-16; Dn 1:17; 2:1; 4:5-9; Jl 2:28
[d]Jr 36:4,32
[e]7:2 Ezk 37:9; Zch 2:6; Rv 7:1
[f]7:3 Dn 7:17
[g]Rv 13:1; 17:8
[h]7:4 Jr 4:7; 25:9; Rv 13:2
[i]7:5 Rv 13:2
[j]7:6 Hab 1:8; Rv 13:2
[k]Dn 8:22
[l]7:7 Dn 7:19,23
[m]Dn 7:20,24; Rv 12:3; 13:1
[n]7:8 Dn 7:11,20-26; 8:9
[o]Rv 13:5,6
[p]7:9 Mt 19:28; Rv 20:4

A6:28 Or Darius, even   B7:1 Lit beginning

6:28 Some maintain that this verse draws a distinction between **Darius** and **Cyrus**, such that Darius could only be identified with Gubaru and not with Cyrus the Persian (see note at 5:31). But it is also possible to translate this verse as "during the reign of Darius, *even* Cyrus the Persian."

7:1-28 This chapter of Daniel is one of the most important in the entire OT, an essential guide to biblical prophecy. Moreover, the vision of the Son of Man is the centerpiece of OT revelation concerning the Messiah. The Aramaic section of Daniel begins in chapter 2 with Nebuchadnezzar's dream of the colossus and ends at the end of chapter 7. One reason for repeating the similar information in chapters 2 and 8 is that chapter 2 presents the world kingdoms from a Gentile perspective, while chapter 8 views the Gentile empires from the perspective of the Jewish people. Another reason for the repetition is to confirm the certainty of the predictions. As Joseph said, Pharaoh's dreams were repeated because "the matter has been determined by God, and He will carry it out soon" (Gn 41:32). The vision was included to give hope to Israel in captivity, informing the nation that life in the times of the Gentiles would get worse for God's covenant people, but ultimately the messianic kingdom would be established.

7:1 **Belshazzar** became co-regent with Nabonidus in 553 B.C. Assuming Daniel was about 15 when he was exiled to Babylon, he would have received this vision when he was approximately 67 years old. The events described in this chapter precede those of Daniel 5.

7:2 The **four winds** stirring up **the great sea** refers to the convulsions of the Gentile nations in the times of the Gentiles. The chapter later indicates that the sea represents "the earth" (v. 17) from which the four kingdoms arise. Moreover, "the sea" is frequently symbolic of Gentile humanity in other biblical passages (Is 17:12-13; 57:20; Rv 13:1; 17:1,15).

7:3 The **four huge beasts** represent the four nations previously identified in the vision of the colossus in Daniel 2 (see note at 2:31-45). These four beasts are increasingly violent,

perhaps indicating the growing moral degeneracy of the respective kingdoms they represent.

7:4 The **lion** with **eagle's wings** represents the Babylonian Empire. The winged lion was a fitting symbol because some biblical passages represent Nebuchadnezzar as a lion (Jr 4:7; 49:19; 50:17,44) and others as an eagle (Jr 49:22; Lm 4:19; Ezk 17:3; Hab 1:8). The Babylonian Empire used lions to represent itself, and statues with winged lions were common there. Perhaps the **wings** being **torn off** represents Nebuchadnezzar's madness, and the lion's being **set on its feet like a man** indicates his restoration.

7:5 The **bear . . . with three ribs in its mouth** represents the Medo-Persian Empire and its three main conquests: Babylon (539 B.C.), Lydia (546 B.C.), and Egypt (525 B.C.). Its lopsided nature expresses the Persian dominance in this joint empire.

7:6 The **leopard** represents the Greek Empire. Its **four wings** refer to the great speed of Alexander's conquests and its **four heads** represent the four principle sections of the empire: Greece and Macedonia, Thrace and Asia Minor, Syria and Babylon, and Egypt and Israel.

7:7 The terrifying **fourth beast** represents the Roman Empire. It was **different** from the previous three because it was more powerful and had longer dominion. **Horns** commonly represent kings or kingdoms in Scripture (Ps 132:17; Zch 1:18; Rv 13:1; 17:12), as the angel's later interpretation plainly indicates (Dn 7:24).

7:8 A **little . . . horn** represents a king who starts small in power but becomes dominant. The little horn's **eyes . . . like a man's** indicates its shrewdness and its **mouth that spoke arrogantly** points to its boasting blasphemously against God (cp. v. 25). This little horn is a future world ruler whom Scripture also calls "the coming prince" (9:26); the king who "will do whatever he wants" (11:36); "the man of lawlessness," "the son of destruction," (2Th 2:3); "the beast," (Rv 13:1-10); and the "Antichrist" (1Jn 2:18).

7:9-10 The phrase **the Ancient of Days** refers to God's eternal nature.

His clothing was white like snow,[a]
and the hair of His head
    like whitest wool.[b]
His throne was flaming fire;[c]
its wheels were blazing fire.[d]
10 A river of fire was flowing,
    coming out from His presence.
Thousands upon thousands[e]
    served Him;
ten thousand times ten thousand[f]
    stood before Him.
The court was convened,[g]
and the books were opened.[h]

11 "I watched, then, because of the sound of the arrogant words the horn was speaking. As I continued watching, the beast was killed and its body destroyed and given over to the burning fire.[i] 12 As for the rest of the beasts, their authority to rule was removed, but an extension of life was granted to them for a certain period of time.[j] 13 I continued watching in the night visions,

    and I saw One like a son of man[k]
    coming with the clouds of heaven.[l]
He approached the Ancient of Days
    and was escorted before Him.
14 He was given authority to rule,[m]
    and glory, and a kingdom;
so that those of every people,
    nation, and language[n]
    should serve[o] Him.
His dominion is
    an everlasting[p] dominion
    that will not pass away,
    and His kingdom is one
    that will not be destroyed.

Interpretation of the Vision

15 "As for me, Daniel, my spirit was deeply distressed within me,[A] and the visions in my mind terrified me.[q] 16 I approached one of those who were standing by and asked him[r] the true meaning of all this. So he let me know the interpretation of these things:[s] 17 'These huge beasts, four in number, are four kings who will rise from the earth. 18 But the holy ones of the 'Most High will receive the kingdom and possess it forever, yes, forever and ever.'[t]

19 "Then I wanted to know the true meaning of the fourth beast,[u] the one different from all the others, extremely terrifying, with iron teeth and bronze claws, devouring, crushing, and trampling with its feet whatever was left. 20 I also wanted to know about the 10 horns[v] on its head and about the other horn that came up, before which three fell—the horn that had eyes, and a mouth that spoke arrogantly,[w] and that was more visible than the others. 21 As I was watching, this horn waged war[x] against the holy ones and was prevailing over them 22 until the Ancient of Days arrived and a judgment[y] was given in favor of the holy ones of the Most High, for the time had come, and the holy ones took possession of the kingdom.

23 "This is what he said: 'The fourth beast will be a fourth kingdom on the earth, different from all the other kingdoms. It will devour the whole earth, trample it down, and crush it. 24 The 10 horns[z] are 10 kings who will rise from this kingdom. Another, different from the previous ones, will rise after them and subdue three kings. 25 He will speak words against the Most High[aa] and oppress[B] the holy ones[ab] of the Most High. He will intend to change religious

Cross references

[a]7:9 Mk 9:3
[b]Is 1:18; Rv 1:14
[c]Ezk 1:13,26
[d]Ezk 10:2,6
[e]7:10 Dt 33:2; 1Kg 22:19; Rv 5:11
[f]Ps 96:11-13; Rv 9:16
[g]Dn 7:26
[h]Dn 12:1; Rv 20:11-15
[i]7:11 Dn 7:26; Rv 19:20; 20:10
[j]7:12 Ps 75:6-7; Dn 2:21
[k]7:13 Mt 16:27-28; 24:30; Lk 21:27; Ac 7:56; Rv 1:7,13; 14:14
[l]Mt 26:64; Mk 13:26; 14:62
[m]7:14 Jn 3:35; 1Co 15:27; Eph 1:20-22; Php 2:9; Rv 1:6; 11:15
[n]Ps 72:11; 102:22; Rv 10:11
[o]Dn 3:14,17-18,28; 6:17,21; 7:27
[p]Heb 12:28
[q]7:15 Dn 4:19; 7:1,28
[r]7:16 Zch 1:9,19; Rv 5:5; 7:13-14
[s]Dn 7:3
[t]7:18 Ps 149:5-9; Is 60:12-14; Rv 2:26-27; 11:15; 22:5
[u]7:19 Dn 7:7-8
[v]7:20 Rv 12:3
[w]Dn 7:8; 2Th 2:9-10
[x]7:21 Rv 11:7; 13:7
[y]7:22 Dn 7:10; 1Co 6:2-3
[z]7:24 Dn 7:7; Rv 17:12
[aa]7:25 Dn 11:36; Rv 13:1-6
[ab]Rv 13:7; 18:24

[A]7:15 Lit was distressed in the middle of its sheath   [B]7:25 Lit wear out

---

7:11-12 The destruction of the **beast** by **burning fire** refers to the end of the fourth kingdom, the revived Roman Empire. The **rest of the beasts**, meaning the previous three kingdoms, would continue to exist but without their earlier dominance, until the coming of the messianic kingdom.

7:13-14 Although some have maintained that the **son of man** is the archangel Michael or a collective personification of the "holy ones of the most high" (v. 18), this One is none other than the divine Messiah Himself, who will fulfill the destiny of humanity (Ps 8; Heb 2:5-18). Jesus understood it to be a messianic title (Mk 14:61-62), and He used it to speak of Himself. Later rabbis saw it as one of the names of the Messiah.

7:18 The **holy ones of the Most High** is most likely a reference to Israel when the nation turns in faith to their Messiah Jesus (Zch 12:10; Rm 11:26). The literal covenant people will **receive the kingdom**, emphasizing that Messiah's final kingdom will be a literal kingdom on earth.

7:23-24a After a summary of the vision's meaning (vv. 19-

22), the angel explains that the fourth kingdom, in its future state, will **devour the whole earth**, indicating world domination. The **10 kings** could be a metaphor for completeness. More likely, it refers to an empire with a literal confederation of 10 kings (cp. Rv 17:12-13).

7:24b-26 **Another** king, the antichrist (cp. vv. 7-8), described in the vision as the little horn, will arise and take control of this last human empire by subduing **three kings**. He will be characterized by blasphemy (**words against the Most High**), anti-Semitism (he will **oppress the holy ones of the Most High**), religious corruption (he will **intend to change religious festivals and laws**). He will oppress the Jewish people for **time, times, and half a time**, meaning three and one-half years, or the second half of the future tribulation (cp. Rv 7:14). Some conclude that this was fulfilled when Antiochus oppressed the Jewish people from 167-164 B.C. This is unlikely since that period was for only three years and not three and one-half years. It is better to view this oppression as yet future. When the heavenly **court will convene**, the antichrist will **be completely destroyed forever**.

festivals^A and laws,^a and the holy ones will be handed over to him for a time, times, and half a time.^B,b ^26 But the court will convene,^c and his dominion will be taken away, to be completely destroyed forever.^d ^27 The kingdom, dominion, and greatness of the kingdoms under all of heaven will be given to the people, the holy ones of the Most High. His kingdom will be an everlasting kingdom,^e and all rulers will serve and obey Him.'

^28 "This is the end of the interpretation. As for me, Daniel, my thoughts terrified me greatly,^f and my face turned pale,^C but I kept the matter to myself."^g

The Vision of a Ram and a Goat

8 In the third year of King Belshazzar's^h reign, a vision appeared to me, Daniel, after the one that had appeared to me earlier.^i ^2 I saw the vision, and as I watched, I was in the fortress city of Susa,^j in the province of Elam.^k I saw in the vision that I was beside the Ulai Canal. ^3 I looked up,^D and there was a ram^l standing beside the canal. He had two horns. The two horns were long, but one was longer than the other, and the longer one came up last. ^4 I saw the ram charging to the west, the

north, and the south.^m No animal could stand against him, and there was no rescue from his power. He did whatever he wanted^n and became great.

^5 As I was observing, a male goat appeared, coming from the west across the surface of the entire earth without touching the ground. The goat had a conspicuous horn^E between his eyes.^o ^6 He came toward the two-horned ram I had seen standing beside the canal and rushed at him with savage fury. ^7 I saw him approaching the ram, and infuriated with him, he struck the ram, shattering his two horns, and the ram was not strong enough to stand against him. The goat threw him to the ground and trampled him, and there was no one to rescue the ram from his power. ^8 Then the male goat became very great,^p but when he became powerful, the large horn was shattered.^q Four conspicuous horns came up in its place, pointing toward the four winds of heaven.^r

The Little Horn

^9 From one of them a little horn^s emerged and grew extensively toward the south and the east and toward the beautiful land.^F,t ^10 It grew

Cross references
^a 7:25 Dn 2:21 ^b Dn 12:7; Rv 11:2; 12:14 ^c 7:26 Dn 7:10 ^d Rv 17:14; 19:20 ^e 7:27 Ps 145:13; Is 9:7; Lk 1:33; Rv 11:15; 22:5 ^f 7:28 Dn 4:19 ^g Lk 2:19,51 ^h 8:1 Dn 5:1 ^i Dn 7:1 ^j 8:2 Ezr 4:9; Neh 1:1; Est 1:2; 2:8 ^k Gn 10:22; 14:1; Is 11:11; Jr 25:25; Ezk 33:24 ^l 8:3 Dn 8:20 ^m 8:4 Dt 33:17; 1Kg 22:11; Ezk 34:21 ^n Dn 11:3 ^o 8:5 Dn 8:21 ^p 8:8 2Ch 26:16; Dn 5:20 ^q Dn 8:22 ^r Dn 7:2; Rv 7:1 ^s 8:9 Dn 7:8; 8:23 ^t Ps 48:2; Dn 11:16,41

^A 7:25 Lit change times   ^B 7:25 Or for three and a half years   ^C 7:28 Lit my brightness changed on me   ^D 8:3 Lit I lifted my eyes and looked   ^E 8:5 Lit a horn of a vision   ^F 8:9 = Israel

7:27 The Son of Man will take His throne and rule over His **everlasting kingdom**. Then **the people**—the believing remnant of Israel, also called **holy ones**—will receive this kingdom under the authority of their Messiah, the Son of Man.

8:1-27 Daniel 8:1–12:13 was written in Hebrew, focusing on God's people during the times of the Gentiles. The vision in Daniel 8 predicted events that involved the second and third world empires within a time frame from the sixth to second centuries B.C.

8:1 Belshazzar became co-regent with Nabonidus in 553 B.C. Assuming Daniel was about 15 when he was exiled to Babylon, he would have received this **vision** in 550 B.C. when he was about 70 years old. Although the events in this chapter precede those described in Daniel 5, they are included here because of the literary focus on Israel in the times of the Gentiles.

8:3 As in the previous chapter, Daniel saw a vision of animals that stood for world empires. First, he saw **a ram**, representing the Medo-Persian Empire (v. 20). It had **two horns**, representing the two nations in this confederated empire. **One was longer than the other, and the longer one came up last**, signifying the dominant status of Persia in the empire, even though it originally was the weaker kingdom.

8:5 Daniel also saw **a male goat**, representing the Greek Empire. The goat's **conspicuous horn** represents Alexander the Great (v. 21). The goat crossed **the surface of the entire earth** so rapidly that it did not touch **the ground**. This refers to Alexander the Great's speedy conquest of the entire Near East in only three years.

8:7 The goat **struck the ram** and shattered **his two horns**, indicating the Greek Empire's crushing defeat of Medo-Persia (331 B.C.).

8:8 Although **the male goat became very great**, at the height of his power **the large horn was shattered**. This refers to Alexander's sudden death at the peak of his greatness (323 B.C.). His kingdom was divided by four of his generals (Cassander over Macedon and Greece, Lysimachus over Thrace and Asia Minor, Seleucus over Syria and Babylon, Ptolemy over Egypt), described in the vision as **four conspicuous horns** that replaced him.

8:9-12 As opposed to the little horn that will come from the

tsalach

Hebrew Pronunciation	[tsah LAKH]
HCSB Translation	succeed, prosper, rush
Uses in Daniel	5
Uses in the OT	67
Focus passage	Daniel 8:12,24-25

Tsalach has several meanings but probably involves only one root. It means succeed (Is 53:10), be successful (Jr 22:30), or prosper (Jr 12:1). Plants and people flourish (Ezk 17:9,15). Things are useful (Ezk 15:4) or of use (Jr 13:7). Tsalach suggests attain (Ezk 16:13) or avail (Dn 11:27). Modifying another verb, tsalach connotes triumphantly (Ps 45:4). The Spirit controls someone (1Sm 10:6) or takes control of him (Jdg 14:6). God spreads fire (Am 5:6). People rush somewhere (2Sm 19:17). Causative verbs also mean succeed (1Ch 22:11), be successful (Dt 28:29), or prosper (Ps 1:3). They denote make a success or successful (Gn 24:40,42), cause to prosper (Dn 8:25), or give/grant success (Neh 1:11; 2:20). In narrative, tsalach often indicates political and military success (2Ch 14:7; 18:11). The rushing motion of fire and hastening people might resemble the Spirit's controlling people. People succeeding are "getting somewhere."

as high as the heavenly •host, made some of the stars and some of the host fall to the earth,[a] and trampled them.[b] [11]It made itself great,[c] even up to the Prince of the host;[d] it removed His daily sacrifice[e] and overthrew the place of His sanctuary. [12]Because of rebellion, a host, together with the daily sacrifice, will be given over. The horn will throw truth to the ground and will be successful[f] in whatever it does.

[13]Then I heard a holy one speaking,[g] and another holy one said to the speaker, "How long will the events of this vision last[h]—the daily sacrifice, the rebellion that makes desolate, and the giving over of the sanctuary and of the host to be trampled?"[i]

[14]He said to me,[A] "For 2,300 evenings and mornings; then the sanctuary will be restored."

Interpretation of the Vision

[15]While I, Daniel, was watching the vision and trying to understand it, there stood before me someone who appeared to be a man.[j] [16]I heard a human voice calling from the middle of the Ulai: "Gabriel,[k] explain the vision to this man."

[17]So he approached where I was standing; when he came near, I was terrified and fell facedown.[l] "Son of man," he said to me, "understand that the vision refers to the time of the end."[m] [18]While he was speaking to me, I fell into a deep sleep,[n] with my face to the ground. Then he touched me, made me stand

up,[o] [19]and said, "I am here to tell you what will happen at the conclusion of the time of wrath, because it refers to the appointed time of the end.[p] [20]The two-horned ram[q] that you saw represents the kings of Media and Persia. [21]The shaggy goat represents the king of Greece, and the large horn between his eyes represents the first king.[B] [22]The four horns that took the place of the shattered horn represent four kingdoms. They will rise from that nation, but without its power.

23 Near the end of their kingdoms,
    when the rebels have reached
    the full measure of their sin,[C]
    an insolent king, skilled in intrigue,[D]
    will come to the throne.
24 His power will be great,
    but it will not be his own.
    He will cause terrible destruction[r]
    and succeed in whatever he does.
    He will destroy the powerful
    along with the holy people.[s]
25 He will cause deceit to prosper
    through his cunning
      and by his influence,
    and in his own mind he will
      make himself great.
    He will destroy many in a
      time of peace;
    he will even stand against the Prince
      of princes.
    Yet he will be shattered—not by
      human hands.[t]

Cross references

[a] 8:10 Is 14:13; Jr 48:26; Rv 12:4
[b] Dn 7:7
[c] 8:11 2Kg 19:22-23; 2Ch 32:15-17; Is 37:23; Dn 11:36-37
[d] Jos 5:13-15
[e] Ezk 46:14; Dn 11:31; 12:11
[f] 8:12 Is 59:14; Dn 11:36
[g] 8:13 Dn 4:13,23; 1Pt 1:12
[h] Ps 74:10; 79:5; Is 6:11; Dn 12:6,8; Rv 6:10
[i] Is 63:18; Jr 12:10; Lk 21:24; Heb 10:29; Rv 11:2
[j] 8:15 Dn 7:13; 10:16,18
[k] 8:16 Dn 9:21; Lk 1:19,26
[l] 8:17 Ezk 1:28; 44:4; Dn 2:46; Rv 1:17
[m] Dn 11:35,40
[n] 8:18 Dn 10:9; Lk 9:32
[o] Ezk 2:2; Dn 10:10,16,18
[p] 8:19 Mt 13:7
[q] 8:20 Dn 8:3
[r] 8:24 Dn 11:36; 12:7
[s] Dn 7:27
[t] 8:25 Jb 34:20; Dn 2:34,45

[A] 8:14 LXX, Theod, Syr, Vg read him   [B] 8:21 = Alexander the Great   [C] 8:23 Lit have become complete   [D] 8:23 Lit king, and understanding riddles

fourth kingdom (Rome) described in Dn 7:8, a different **little horn** emerged out of one of the four kingdoms that divided the Greek Empire. This one was Antiochus IV (175–163 B.C.), ruler of the Seleucid dynasty, who conquered surrounding areas to **the south** and to **the east** but especially dominated **the beautiful land** of Israel. He brutally **trampled** and persecuted the Jewish people from 170–164 B.C. Antiochus blasphemously presented himself as **the Prince of the host**, God Himself (called the Prince of princes in 8:25), stopping **daily sacrifice** and defiling the holy temple (**His sanctuary**) in Jerusalem (167 B.C.). He will **be successful**, but only temporarily.

8:13-14 An angel announced that Antiochus's defilement of Israel would last only **2,300 evenings and mornings**, until the temple was rededicated by Judas Maccabeus in 164 B.C. This event is still celebrated by Jewish people today during the festival of *Chanukah* (Eng "Dedication," see Jn 10:22-23).

8:15-16 Daniel received the interpretation of the vision from the angel **Gabriel**, only one of two angels (along with Michael) who are named in Scripture. Gabriel would also give the message of Daniel's 70 weeks (9:24-27) and announce the birth of John the Baptist to Zechariah (Lk 1:19) and the birth of the Messiah Jesus to Mary (Lk 1:26).

8:17 Gabriel addressed Daniel as **son of man**, but he did not use the Hebrew equivalent of the Aramaic title given to the Messiah, which points to Messiah's divinity (7:13). The phrase used here emphasizes the human weakness and mortality of Daniel. Gabriel also indicated that the vision referred **to the time of the end**. This is surprising because all the events predicted took place between the sixth and second centuries B.C. and do not appear to be end-time events. Readers through the ages have identified Antiochus as the little horn of chapter 8 but also have recognized that he typifies the coming end-time antichrist. So, although this chapter does directly refer to Antiochus, it also pertains to the end times. Thus there is a double-fulfillment of this vision.

8:23-25 After his summary explanation of Daniel's vision, Gabriel expanded his description of Antiochus. He would take the throne through deceit against the rightful heir, his nephew Demetrius. His great power would **not be his own** but would have a satanic source. He would **succeed** at first, defeating **powerful** rulers and generals and destroying many of God's **holy people** Israel and deceive himself, thinking **himself great** enough to oppose God. Nevertheless, he would ultimately and suddenly be **shattered**, not through assassination or battle but through some ailment sent by God.

26 The vision of the evenings
    and the mornings
that has been told is true.
Now you must seal up the vision[a]
because it refers to many days
    in the future."

27 I, Daniel, was overcome and lay sick for days.[b] Then I got up and went about the king's business.[c] I was greatly disturbed by the vision and could not understand it.

Daniel's Prayer

9 In the first year of Darius,[d] the son of Ahasuerus, a Mede by birth, who was ruler over the kingdom of the Chaldeans: 2 In the first year of his reign, I, Daniel, understood from the books according to the word of the LORD to Jeremiah the prophet that the number of years for the desolation of Jerusalem would be 70.[e] 3 So I turned my attention to the Lord God to seek Him by prayer and petitions, with fasting, •sackcloth, and ashes.[f]

4 I prayed to the LORD my God and confessed:

Ah, Lord—the great and awe-inspiring God[g] who keeps His gracious covenant[h] with those who love Him[i] and keep His commands[j]— 5 we have sinned,[k] done

wrong, acted wickedly, rebelled,[l] and turned away from Your commands and ordinances.[m] 6 We have not listened to Your servants the prophets,[n] who spoke in Your name to our kings, leaders, fathers, and all the people of the land.

7 Lord, righteousness belongs to You,[o] but this day public shame belongs to us: the men of Judah, the residents of Jerusalem, and all Israel—those who are near and those who are far, in all the countries where You have dispersed them because of the disloyalty they have shown toward You. 8 Lord, public shame[p] belongs to us, our kings, our leaders, and our fathers, because we have sinned against You.[q] 9 Compassion and forgiveness belong to the Lord our God, though we have rebelled against Him 10 and have not obeyed the voice of the LORD our God by following His instructions that He set before us through His servants[r] the prophets.

11 All Israel has broken Your law and turned away,[s] refusing to obey You. The promised curse[A] written in the law of Moses,[t] the servant of God, has been poured out on us because we have sinned against Him. 12 He has carried out His words[u] that

Cross references (center column):

a 8:26 Ezk 12:27; Dn 12:4,9; Rv 10:4; 22:10
b 8:27 Dn 7:28; 8:17; Hab 3:16
c Dn 2:48
d 9:1 Dn 5:31; 6:1; 11:1
e 9:2 2Ch 36:21; Ezr 1:1; Jr 25:11-12; 29:10; Zch 7:5
f 9:3 Neh 1:4; Jb 2:8; Is 61:3; Lk 10:13
g 9:4 Dt 7:21; Neh 9:32
h Dt 7:9
i 1Jn 4:20
j Dt 7:9; Neh 1:5
k 9:5 1Kg 8:48; Neh 9:33; Ps 106:6; Is 64:5-7; Jr 14:7
l Lm 1:18,20
m Ps 119:176; Is 53:6; Dn 9:11
n 9:6 2Ch 36:16; Jr 44:4-5
o 9:7 Jr 23:6; 33:16; Dn 9:18
p 9:8 Ps 37:1-2
q Ps 78:56-64
r 9:10 2Kg 17:13-15; 18:12
s 9:11 Is 1:3-4; Jr 8:5-10
t Dt 28:15-68; 29:16-30:20; Lk 2:22
u 9:12 Is 44:26; Jr 44:2-6; Lm 2:17; Zch 1:6

A 9:11 Lit The curse and the oath

8:26 Gabriel instructed Daniel to **seal up the vision** not for the purpose of hiding its meaning from faithful readers of Scripture but rather to secure the document for safekeeping into the distant future, meaning the time of Antiochus (some 400 years after the vision was given) and the time of the antichrist which is yet future and is typified by Antiochus.

Antiochus IV as a Type of the Antichrist

Antiochus (8:9) and antichrist (7:8) are symbolized by horns that were "little" or small at the beginning.

Antiochus was "an insolent king" (8:23); antichrist will have an imposing look (7:20).

Antiochus was a master of intrigue (8:23); the brilliance of antichrist is suggested by the "eyes" of the horn (7:8,20).

Antiochus had great power (8:24); antichrist will have even greater power (11:39; 2Th 2:9; Rv 13:7-8).

Antiochus was energized by Satan (8:24), just as antichrist will be empowered by Satan (2Th 2:9; Rv 13:2).

Antiochus destroyed thousands (8:25); antichrist will destroy more (Rv 13:15; 16:13-16).

Antiochus prospered for a short time (8:25); likewise with antichrist (11:36; Rv 13:7).

Antiochus persecuted the Jews (8:24), as will antichrist (7:21,25; Rv 12:13).

Antiochus was a deceiver (8:25); antichrist will be a master deceiver (2Th 2:9; Rv 13:4,14; 19:11).

Antiochus was proud (8:25); antichrist will be a megalomaniac (7:8,11,20,25; Rv 13:5).

Antiochus blasphemed God (8:25); as will antichrist (7:25; 11:36).

Antiochus was not killed by human hands (8:25); the antichrist will not be either (2Th 2:8; Rv 19:19-20).

9:1 If Daniel was approximately 15 when he went into captiv-

ity, he would have been about 81 years old at the time of this vision. The name **Ahasuerus** was probably a Persian royal title rather than a personal name. It refers to an ancestor of Cyrus the Great or Governor Gubaru (see note at 5:31), not Ahasuerus (485–465 B.C.), the king mentioned in the book of Esther (Est 1:1).

9:2 Although the book of **Jeremiah** was completed only a generation before the events described in Daniel 9, Daniel already recognized it as Scripture. Jeremiah predicted that **the desolation of Jerusalem** would endure for 70 years (Jr 25:11-13; 29:10). Daniel calculated that since the first captives had been taken to Babylon in 605 B.C., the 70 years were nearly complete.

9:3 Daniel's prayer was with **fasting, sackcloth, and ashes**, three customary ways to express sorrow and contrition (Ezr 8:23; Neh 9:1; Est 4:1,3,16; Jb 2:12; Jnh 3:5-6).

9:4-19 In this section Daniel prayed to the Lord, using the Hebrew name Yahweh (translated "LORD" in English). Since Daniel's prayer emphasized the faithfulness of God, it was appropriate to use the name Yahweh because it was associated with the covenant-keeping nature of the God of Israel (Ex 6:2-8).

9:4 One **who keeps His gracious covenant** refers to the Abrahamic covenant in which God promised to preserve the Jewish people and provide them with a land (Gn 12:1-7; 15:18-21).

9:11 Daniel realized that it was Israel's disobedience that resulted in God sending the nation into exile, as **the law of Moses** had warned (Lv 26:27-33; Dt 29:63-68).

He spoke against us and against our rulers[A][a] by bringing on us so great a disaster that nothing like what has been done to Jerusalem has ever been done[b] under all of heaven. [13]Just as it is written in the law of Moses,[c] all this disaster has come on us, yet we have not appeased[d] the LORD our God by turning from our iniquities and paying attention to Your truth.[e] [14]So the LORD kept the disaster in mind and brought it on us, for the LORD our God is righteous in all He has done. But we have not obeyed Him.

[15]Now, Lord our God, who brought Your people out of the land of Egypt with a mighty hand[f] and made Your name renowned[g] as it is this day, we have sinned, we have acted wickedly. [16]Lord, in keeping with all Your righteous acts, may Your anger and wrath[h] turn away from Your city Jerusalem, Your holy mountain;[i] for because of our sins and the iniquities of our fathers, Jerusalem and Your people have become an object of ridicule to all those around us.

[17]Therefore, our God, hear the prayer and the petitions of Your servant. Show Your favor[j] to Your desolate sanctuary[k] for the Lord's sake. [18]Listen,[B] my God, and hear. Open Your eyes and see our desolations and the city called by Your name. For we are not presenting our petitions before You based on our righteous acts, but based on Your abundant compassion. [19]Lord, hear! Lord, forgive! Lord, listen and act! My God, for Your own sake, do not delay,[l] because Your city and Your people are called by Your name.

The 70 Weeks of Years

[20]While I was speaking, praying, confessing my sin and the sin of my people Israel,[m] and presenting my petition before *Yahweh my God concerning the holy mountain of my God— [21]while I was praying, Gabriel,[n] the man I had seen in the first vision,[o] came to me in my extreme weariness, about the time of the evening offering.[p] [22]He gave me this explanation: "Daniel, I've come now to give you understanding.[q] [23]At the beginning of your petitions an answer went out, and I have come to give it, for you are treasured by God.[r] So consider the message and understand the vision:[s]

[24] Seventy weeks[C] are decreed[t]
　　about your people and your holy city—
　　to bring the rebellion to an end,
　　to put a stop to sin,
　　to wipe away iniquity,
　　to bring in everlasting righteousness,[u]
　　to seal up vision and prophecy,
　　and to anoint the most holy place.
[25] Know and understand this:
　　From the issuing of the decree
　　to restore and rebuild Jerusalem[v]
　　until *Messiah[w] the Prince[D]
　　will be seven weeks and 62 weeks.[E]
　　It will be rebuilt with a plaza
　　　and a moat,
　　but in difficult times.
[26] After those 62 weeks[F]

Cross references (center column):
[a]9:12 Jb 12:17; Ps 82:2-7; 148:11
[b]Lm 1:12; 2:13; Ezk 5:9
[c]9:13 Lv 26:14-45; Dt 28:15-68; Dn 9:11
[d]Jb 36:13; Is 9:13; Jr 2:30; 5:3; Mal 1:9
[e]Jr 31:18
[f]9:15 Dt 5:15
[g]Neh 9:10; Jr 32:20
[h]9:16 Jr 32:31-32
[i]Ps 87:1-3; Dn 9:20; Jl 3:17; Zch 8:3
[j]9:17 Nm 6:25; Ps 31:17; 67:2
[k]Lm 5:18
[l]9:19 Ps 44:23; 74:10-11
[m]9:20 Ps 145:18; Is 58:9; Dn 9:3; 10:12
[n]9:21 Dn 8:16; Lk 1:19,26
[o]Dn 8:1,15
[p]Ex 29:39; 1Kg 18:36; Ezr 9:4
[q]9:22 Dn 8:16; 10:21; Zch 1:9
[r]9:23 Dn 10:11,19
[s]Mt 24:15
[t]9:24 Lv 25:8; Nm 14:34; Ezk 4:5-6
[u]Is 51:6,8; 56:1; Jr 23:5-6; Rm 3:21-22
[v]9:25 Ezr 4:24; 6:1-15; Neh 2:1-8; 3:1
[w]Mt 1:17; Jn 1:41; 4:25

[A]9:12 Lit *against rulers who ruled us*　[B]9:18 Lit *Stretch out Your ear*　[C]9:24 = 490 years　[D]9:25 Or *until an anointed one, a prince*
[E]9:25 = 49 years and 434 years　[F]9:26 = 434 years

9:17-18 Despite God's justice in sending Israel into exile, Daniel appealed to God not on the basis of Israel's **righteous acts** but on God's **abundant compassion**. God's forgiveness was an act of grace.

9:21 The angel **Gabriel** appears for a second time in Daniel (8:16), here called a **man** because he appeared in human form. Had the temple still stood, the **time of the evening offering** would have been between 3:00 and 4:00 p.m.

9:24 **Seventy weeks** probably refers to 70 periods of seven years, or 490 years, during which six objectives would be accomplished. The first three pertain to bringing **rebellion...sin**, and **iniquity** to an end. The final three relate to consummating prophetic events by bringing in a kingdom of **everlasting righteousness**, fulfilling **vision and prophecy** and setting apart **the most holy place** (lit "the holy of holies"), referring to a yet future, literal, millennial temple (cp. Ezk 40-48).

9:25 Those who advocate a symbolic interpretation of this verse identify it with Cyrus's decree allowing the captives to return to their homeland (2Ch 36:22-23; Ezr 1:1-3) in 539-538 B.C. Others hold a literal view of this verse and suggest that the starting point is Artaxerxes' first decree in 457 B.C. (Ezr 7:11-26). Since neither of these decrees pertains to the restoration of Jerusalem, it is more likely that the beginning point is Artaxerxes' second decree in 444 B.C., authorizing Nehemiah to rebuild the walls of Jerusalem (Neh 2:1-8). There will be a period of **seven weeks** of years (49 years) followed by **62 weeks** of years (434 years), making a total of 69 weeks of years or 483 years from the decree until the coming of **Messiah the Prince**. The starting point of the prophecy would have begun on Nisan 1 (March 5), 444 B.C., followed by 69 weeks of 360-day biblical/prophetic years or 173,880 days, and culminated on Nisan 10 (March 30), A.D. 33, the date of Jesus the Messiah's triumphal entry into Jerusalem (Lk 19:28-40).

9:26 Several events are said to follow the seven weeks and the **62 weeks** (or the 69 weeks). First, **the Messiah** would **be cut off**, a prediction of the death of the Messiah Jesus. Thus, the book of Daniel, written in the sixth century B.C., predicted not only the precise date of the Messiah's coming (v. 25) but also that the Messiah would be put to death some time before the destruction of Jerusalem in A.D. 70. This was

the Messiah will be cut off[a]
and will have nothing.
The people of the coming prince
will destroy the city[b] and the sanctuary.
The[A] end will come with a flood,[c]
and until the end there will be[B] war;
desolations are decreed.
27 He will make a firm covenant[c]
with many for one week,[D]
but in the middle of the week
he will put a stop to sacrifice and offering.
And the abomination of desolation[d]
will be on a wing[e] of the temple[E,F]
until the decreed destruction[f]
is poured out on the desolator."

Vision of a Glorious One

10 In the third year of Cyrus king of Persia,[g] a message was revealed to Daniel,

who was named Belteshazzar.[h] The message was true and was about a great conflict. He understood the message and had understanding of the vision.[i]

[2] In those days I, Daniel, was mourning for three full weeks.[j] [3] I didn't eat any rich food,[k] no meat or wine entered my mouth, and I didn't put any oil on my body until the three weeks were over. [4] On the twenty-fourth day of the first month,[G] as I was standing on the bank of the great river,[l] the Tigris, [5] I looked up, and there was a man dressed in linen,[m] with a belt of gold[n] from Uphaz[H,o] around his waist. [6] His body was like topaz,[l] his face like the brilliance of lightning, his eyes like flaming torches,[p] his arms and feet like the gleam of polished bronze, and the sound of his words like the sound of a multitude.[q]

Cross references
a 9:26 Is 53:8; Mk 9:12; Lk 24:26
b Mt 24:2; Mk 13:2; Lk 19:43-44
c Nah 1:8
d 9:27 Dn 11:31; Mt 24:15; Mk 13:14; Lk 21:20
e Is 7:7-8; Mt 4:5
f Is 10:23; 28:22
g 10:1 Dn 1:21; 6:28
h Dn 1:7
i Dn 1:17; 2:21
j 10:2 Ezr 9:4-5; Neh 1:4
k 10:3 Dn 6:18; Am 6:6; Mt 6:17
l 10:4 Ezk 1:3; Dn 8:2
m 10:5 Ezk 9:2; Dn 12:6-7
n Rv 1:13; 15:6
o Jr 10:9
p 10:6 Rv 1:14; 2:18; 19:12
q Rv 19:6

A 9:26 Lit Its, or His   B 9:26 Or end of a   C 9:27 Or will enforce a covenant   D 9:27 = 7 years   E 9:27 LXX; MT reads of abominations   F 9:27 Or And the desolator will be on the wing of abominations, or And the desolator will come on the wings of monsters (or of horror); Hb obscure   G 10:4 = Nisan (March–April)   H 10:5 Some Hb mss read Ophir   I 10:6 The identity of this stone is uncertain.

fulfilled when Jesus was crucified in A.D. 33 (A.D. 30 according to some interpreters). Second, **the people of the coming prince** would **destroy the city** of Jerusalem and the second temple. The "coming prince" probably is a reference to the future ruler described as the little horn in Daniel 7, also known as the beast or the antichrist. He is not said to be the one to destroy Jerusalem and the temple; rather it is *his people* who will do it. Since Daniel 7 clearly viewed this ruler as coming from the fourth major world power, or Rome, this prophecy predicts that the Romans would destroy Jerusalem, as they did in A.D. 70. Third, there appears to be a significant time gap from the end of the sixty-ninth week to the beginning of the seventieth week.

9:27 The final seven-year period, or the seventieth week, will begin when **he** (the coming prince) **will make a firm covenant** of peace **with many** in the leadership of Israel. Although some consider the prince to be Messiah, he is more accurately identified as the antichrist, who will desecrate the future temple and put a stop to worship there. This covenant is yet future and will mark the beginning of a time of oppression of the Jewish people called "a time of trouble

for Jacob" (Jr 30:7) or the tribulation period (Mt 24:29; Mk 13:24). **In the middle of the week**, or after the first three and one-half years, the antichrist will break his covenant with Israel, leading to a time of unprecedented persecution of the Jewish people (Mt 24:21; Mk 13:19) and followers of Jesus (Rv 7:14) that will last for another three and one-half years (Dn 7:25; Rv 11:2-3; 12:14; 13:5). When the antichrist breaks his covenant, he will also **put a stop to sacrifice** in the rebuilt temple (7:25) and will commit **the abomination of desolation** (Mt 24:15), desecrating the temple and declaring himself to be God (2Th 2:4; Rv 13:5-7). The antichrist's oppression and abominations will continue until God's **decreed destruction is poured out on the desolator** (11:45; Rv 19:20).

10:1 Daniel received this vision in 536 B.C. Assuming Daniel was about 15 when taken captive, he was approximately 84 years old at the time. The vision was about **a great conflict** in the future, recounted in 11:2–12:3. The last three chapters of Daniel are about the same vision.

10:2 Daniel may have been **mourning** because of the poor conditions of the returned captives. The Samaritans were opposing reconstruction of the temple, and the work had been stopped (Ezr 4:5,24). The Hebrew text contains the words "weeks of days" in describing Daniel's mourning period to distinguish it from the weeks of years in the previous chapter (Dn 9:24-27).

10:3 Daniel engaged in a semi-fast, not because the food had been offered to the gods but to give priority to prayer.

10:4 The **Tigris** River was some 20 miles from Babylon. At the advanced age of 84, Daniel had not made the difficult and demanding journey to Israel with the other Jewish returnees, but he remained instead in government service in Babylon.

10:5-6 Despite his similarity to Christ's appearance as described in Rv 1:12-16, the angel in the form of **a man dressed in linen** cannot have been the preincarnate Messiah because Christ would not need help from the angel Michael.

10:7 The Hebrew for **only I, Daniel, saw the vision** is emphatic: "I saw, I, Daniel, I alone." His companions sensed a

charats

Hebrew Pronunciation	[khah RATZ]
HCSB Translation	decide, decree, determine
Uses in Daniel	3
Uses in the OT	11
Focus passage	Daniel 9:26-27

This root in several languages suggests *cutting*, and in Akkadian also indicates *determining*. The former concept appears in the idiom "*sharpening* the tongue," which suggests dogs *snarling* (Ex 11:7) or people *saying something against* others (Jos 10:21). Otherwise *charats* denotes *decide* (1Kg 20:40) and *determine* (Jb 14:5). Once it means *act decisively* (2Sm 5:24). In Isaiah and Daniel it implies judgments *decreed* by God against someone in the future (Is 10:22-23). The noun *charuts* represents *threshing board/sledge* (4x) (Jb 41:30; Is 28:27), *verdict* (Jl 3:14), *moat* (Dn 9:25), and *maimed* animal (Lv 22:22).

⁷Only I, Daniel, saw the vision.ᵃ The men who were with me did not see it,ᵇ but a great terror fell on them,ᶜ and they ran and hid. ⁸I was left alone, looking at this great vision.ᵈ No strength was left in me; my face grew deathly pale,^(A,e) and I was powerless. ⁹I heard the words he said, and when I heard them I fell into a deep sleep,^(B,f) with my face to the ground.

Angelic Conflict

¹⁰Suddenly, a hand touched me and raised me to my hands and knees. ¹¹He said to me, "Daniel, you are a man treasured by God.ᵍ Understand the words that I'm saying to you. Stand on your feet,ʰ for I have now been sent to you."ⁱ After he said this to me, I stood trembling.

¹²"Don't be afraid,ʲ Daniel," he said to me, "for from the first day that you purposed to understand and to humble yourself before your God,ᵏ your prayers were heard. I have come because of your prayers.ˡ ¹³But the prince of the kingdom of Persia opposed me for 21 days. Then Michael,ᵐ one of the chief princes, came to help me after I had been left there with the kings of Persia.ⁿ ¹⁴Now I have come to help you understand what will happen to your people in the last days,ᵒ for the vision refers to those days."ᵖ

¹⁵While he was saying these words to me,

I turned my face toward the ground and was speechless.ᵠ ¹⁶Suddenly one with human likenessʳ touched my lips.ˢ I opened my mouth and said to the one standing in front of me, "My lord, because of the vision, anguish overwhelms me and I am powerless.ᵗ ¹⁷How can someone like me,ᵘ your servant,ᶜ speak with someone like you, my lord? Now I have no strength, and there is no breath in me."

¹⁸Then the one with human likeness touched me again and strengthened me.ᵛ ¹⁹He said, "Don't be afraid,ʷ you who areᴰ treasured by God.ˣ Peace to you; be very strong!"ʸ

As he spoke to me, I was strengthened and said, "Let my lord speak, for you have strengthened me."ᶻ

²⁰He said, "Do you know why I've come to you? I must return at once to fight against the prince of Persia, and when I leave, the prince of Greece will come.ᵃᵃ ²¹No one has the courage to support me against them except Michael,ᵃᵇ your prince. However, I will tell you what

11 is recorded in the book of truth. ¹In the first year of Darius the Mede,ᵃᶜ I stood up to strengthen and protect him. ²Now I will tell you the truth.ᵃᵈ

Cross references
ᵃ10:7 2Kg 6:17-20
ᵇAc 9:7
ᶜEzk 12:18
ᵈ10:8 Gn 32:24
ᵉDn 7:28; 8:27; Hab 3:16
ᶠ10:9 Gn 15:12; Jb 4:13; Dn 8:18
ᵍ10:11 Dn 9:23; 10:19
ʰEzk 2:2; Dn 8:18
ⁱHeb 11:14
ʲ10:12 Is 41:10,14; Dn 10:19
ᵏDn 9:2-23; 10:2-3
ˡAc 10:30-31
ᵐ10:13 Dn 10:21; 12:1; Jd 9; Rv 12:7
ⁿDn 7:17; 8:21
ᵒ10:14 Dt 31:29; Dn 2:28
ᵖDn 8:26; 12:4,9
ᵠ10:15 Ezk 3:26; 24:27; Lk 1:20
ʳ10:16 Dn 8:15
ˢIs 6:7; Jr 1:9
ᵗDn 7:15,28; 8:17,27; 10:8-9
ᵘ10:17 Ex 24:10-11; Is 6:1-5
ᵛ10:18 Is 35:3-4
ʷ10:19 Jdg 6:23; Is 43:1; Dn 10:12
ˣDn 9:23; 10:11
ʸJos 1:6-7,9; Is 35:4
ᶻPs 138:2; 2Co 12:9
ᵃᵃ10:20 Dn 8:21; 11:2
ᵃᵇ10:21 Dn 10:13; Rv 12:7
ᵃᶜ11:1 Dn 5:31; 9:1
ᵃᵈ11:2 Dn 8:26; 10:1,21

Footnotes
^A 10:8 Lit *my splendor was turned on me to ruin*   ^B 10:9 Lit *a sleep on my face*   ^C 10:17 Lit *Can I, a servant of my lord*   ^D 10:19 Lit *afraid, man*

---

powerful and terrifying presence but saw nothing, so **they ran and hid** (cp. Ac 9:7).

10:12-13 The Persian **prince** had to be supernatural to oppose this angel and he had to be evil to oppose God's purposes. Therefore, we conclude that he was a demonic spirit seeking to influence the political affairs of Persia and oppose God's purposes. Other Scriptures also teach that there are unseen spiritual forces influencing principalities and world powers (Ezk 28:11-19; 2Co 10:3-4; Eph 6:12). The unnamed angel was able to prevail over the demon associated with Persia only because the angel **Michael . . . came to help** him. Michael (whose name means "who is like God") is the guardian angel of Israel (cp. v. 21; 12:1; Rv 12:7), and he is designated an archangel in the NT (Jd 9).

10:14 The angel revealed that the first purpose of the vision was to reveal what would happen to Israel **in the last days**.

10:15-19 The angel not only came to reveal the future but to strengthen Daniel, first by his touch (v. 18) and secondly with his words of encouragement (v. 19).

10:20-21 The **prince of Greece** is an allusion to the prediction that Greece would follow Persia as the next major world power (8:4-8,20-22). The angel's final purpose was to reveal **what is recorded in the book of truth** (lit "the writings of truth"), a reference not to a particular earthly book but to God's heavenly decrees about the future of all nations.

11:1-45 This chapter contains some of the most precise predictions in the entire Bible. These predictions are so precise that many scholars claim this chapter was written as a pseudo-prophecy after the events actually took place. But if

God is omniscient, and if He chooses to foretell select future events, there is no problem with predictive prophecy or acceptance that this chapter was written long before the events occurred.

11:1 Although the angel visited Daniel "In the third year of Cyrus king of Persia" (10:1), he revealed to Daniel that he had **stood up to strengthen and protect** Darius since the first year of his reign (539 B.C.). God is active in the political affairs of the world.

11:2 The **three . . . kings** in Persia were Cambyses (530–522

Tomb of Cyrus the Great (10:1), near Pasargadae, oldest capital of the Achaemenid Empire, founded by Cyrus. It bore the inscription: "Mortal! I am Cyrus, son of Cambyses, who founded the Persian Empire and was Lord of Asia."

Prophecies about Persia and Greece

"Three more kings will arise in Persia, and the fourth will be far richer than the others. By the power he gains through his riches, he will stir up everyone against the kingdom of Greece.[a] [3]Then a warrior king will arise; he will rule a vast realm and do whatever he wants.[b] [4]But as soon as he is established, his kingdom will be broken up and divided to the four winds of heaven,[c] but not to his descendants; it will not be the same kingdom that he ruled, because his kingdom will be uprooted and will go to others besides them.[d]

Kings of the South and the North

[5]"The king of the South[e] will grow powerful, but one of his commanders will grow more powerful and will rule a kingdom greater than his. [6]After some years they will form an alliance, and the daughter of the king of the South will go to the king of the North[f] to seal the agreement. She will not retain power, and his strength will not endure. She will be given up, together with her entourage, her father,[A] and the one who supported her during those times. [7]In the place of the king of the South, one from her family[B] will rise up, come against the army, and enter the fortress of the king of the North. He will take action against them and triumph. [8]He will take even

their gods captive to Egypt, with their metal images and their precious articles of silver and gold.[g] For some years he will stay away from the king of the North, [9]who will enter the kingdom of the king of the South and then return to his own land.

[10]"His sons will mobilize for war and assemble a large number of armed forces. They will advance, sweeping through like a flood,[C,h] and will again wage war as far as his fortress. [11]Infuriated, the king of the South will march out to fight with the king of the North who will raise a large army but they will be handed over to his enemy. [12]When the army is carried off, he will become arrogant and cause tens of thousands to fall, but he will not triumph. [13]The king of the North will again raise a multitude larger than the first. After some years[D,i] he will advance with a great army and many supplies.

[14]"In those times many will rise up against the king of the South. Violent ones among your own people will assert themselves to fulfill a vision, but they will fail. [15]Then the king of the North will come, build up an assault ramp,[j] and capture a well-fortified city. The forces of the South will not stand; even their select troops will not be able to resist. [16]The king of the North who comes against him will do whatever he wants,[k] and no one can oppose

a 11:2 Dn 8:21; 10:20
b 11:3 Dn 5:19; 8:4; 11:16,36
c 11:4 Jr 49:36; Ezk 37:9; Dn 7:2; 8:8; Zch 2:6; 6:5; Rv 7:1
d Jr 12:15,17; 18:7
e 11:5 Dn 11:9,11,14,25,40
f 11:6 Dn 11:13,15,40
g 11:8 Is 37:19; 46:1-2; Jr 43:12-13
h 11:10 Is 8:8; Jr 46:7,8; 51:42; Dn 11:26,40
i 11:13 Dn 4:16; 12:7
j 11:15 Jr 6:6; Ezk 4:2; 17:17
k 11:16 Dn 5:19; 11:3,36

A 11:6 Some Hb mss, Theod read *the child*; Syr, Vg read *her children*   B 11:7 Lit *from the shoot of her roots*   C 11:10 Lit *advance and overflow and pass through*   D 11:13 Lit *At the end of the times*

B.C.), Pseudo-Smerdis (522 B.C.), and Darius I Hystaspes (522–486 B.C.). Ahasuerus was **the fourth** king who would be **far richer than the others**.

11:3-4 The **warrior king** predicted here was Alexander the Great (336–323 B.C.). As prophesied, his kingdom was **divided to the four winds of heaven**, referring to the division of his empire among his four generals rather than **his descendants** (see note at 8:8).

11:5 The **king of the South** is Ptolemy I Soter of Egypt (323–285 B.C.), who was outstripped by **one of his commanders**, Seleucus I Nicator (311–280 B.C.), who had abandoned Ptolemy I to become ruler of Babylonia, Media, and Syria, and establish the Seleucid kingdom that grew to be **greater than** that of Ptolemy's Egypt.

11:6 The **king of the South**, Ptolemy II Philadelphus (285–246 B.C.), would make **an alliance** with the **king of the North**, Antiochus II Theos (261–246 B.C.), sealing the agreement by giving his daughter, the Ptolemaic princess Berenice, to marry Antiochus. Yet Berenice would not **retain power**, as Antiochus's former wife Laodice would murder Antiochus, Berenice, and their child.

11:7-8 **One** from Berenice's **family**, her brother Ptolemy III Euergetes (246–221 B.C.), would avenge her murder by storming Antioch, **the fortress** of **the king of the North**, Seleucus II Callinicus (246–226 B.C.), and killing Laodice.

Ptolemy III would even seize Seleucid **gods** and valuables, bringing them back to **Egypt**.

11:10 The **sons** of Seleucus II—Seleucus III Ceraunus (226–223 B.C.) and Antiochus III (223–187 B.C.)—would **wage war** as far as the Ptolemaic **fortress** Raphia in southern Israel.

11:11-12 The **king of the South**, Ptolemy IV Philopator (221–203 B.C.) of Egypt, would counterattack **the king of the North**, Antiochus III (219–218 B.C.). Although both would command large armies, the result would be a great victory for the Ptolemies. As a result of his success, Ptolemy IV would **become arrogant** and slaughter **tens of thousands** of Seleucid troops, yet he would not be able to maintain his dominance over the Seleucid kingdom.

11:13-15 Fifteen years later, **the king of the North**, Antiochus III, would raise an even greater army and attack the Ptolemies in Phoenicia and Israel. Antiochus III would receive support against **the king of the South**, Ptolemy V Epiphanes (203–181 B.C.), and the Ptolemies. This support would come from Jewish rebels, here called **violent ones among your own people**. Antiochus III's forces would win a resounding victory, even capturing the **well-fortified city** of Sidon (199–198 B.C.).

11:16-17 The **king of the North**, Antiochus III, would make **the beautiful land** of Israel a possession of the Seleucid kingdom in 198 B.C. and force a peace agreement on the Ptolemies. Antiochus III would **give** his **daughter** Cleopatra

him. He will establish himself in the beautiful land[A,a] with total destruction in his hand. [17]He will resolve[b] to come with the force of his whole kingdom and will reach an agreement with him.[B] He will give him a daughter in marriage[c] to destroy it,[D] but she will not stand with him or support him. [18]Then he will turn his attention to the coasts and islands[E,c] and capture many. But a commander will put an end to his taunting; instead, he will turn his taunts against him.[d] [19]He will turn his attention back to the fortresses of his own land, but he will stumble, fall,[e] and be no more.[f]

[20]"In his place one will arise who will send out a tax collector[g] for the glory of the kingdom; but within a few days he will be shattered, though not in anger[F] or in battle.

[21]"In his place a despised[h] person will arise; royal honors will not be given to him, but he will come during a time of peace[G,i] and seize the kingdom by intrigue. [22]A flood of forces will be swept away before him; they will be shattered, as well as the covenant prince. [23]After an alliance is made with him, he will act deceitfully. He will rise to power with a small nation.[H] [24]During a time of peace,[i] he will come into the richest parts of the province[j] and do

what his fathers and predecessors never did. He will lavish plunder, loot, and wealth on his followers, and he will make plans against fortified cities, but only for a time.

[25]"With a large army he will stir up his power and his courage against the king of the South. The king of the South will prepare for battle with an extremely large and powerful army, but he will not succeed, because plots will be made against him. [26]Those who eat his provisions[k] will destroy him; his army will be swept away, and many will fall slain. [27]The two kings, whose hearts are bent on evil, will speak lies[l] at the same table but to no avail, for still the end will come at the appointed time.[m] [28]The king of the North will return to his land with great wealth, but his heart will be set against the holy covenant;[j] he will take action, then return to his own land.

[29]"At the appointed time he will come again to the South, but this time[K] will not be like the first. [30]Ships of Kittim[L,n] will come against him, and being intimidated, he will withdraw. Then he will rage against the holy covenant and take action. On his return, he will favor those who abandon the holy covenant. [31]His forces will rise up and desecrate the temple

[a]11:16 Dn 8:9; 11:41
[b]11:17 2Kg 12:17; Ezk 4:3,7
[c]11:18 Gn 10:5; Is 66:19; Jr 2:10; 31:10; Zph 2:11
[d]Hs 12:14
[e]11:19 Ps 27:2; Jr 46:6
[f]Jb 20:8; Ps 37:36; Ezk 26:21
[g]11:20 2Kg 23:35
[h]11:21 Is 53:3
[i]Dn 8:25; 11:24
[j]11:24 Nm 13:20; Neh 9:25; Ezk 34:14
[k]11:26 Dn 1:5,8,13,15
[l]11:27 Ps 12:2; Jr 9:3-5; 41:1-3
[m]Dn 8:19; 11:35,40; Hab 2:3
[n]11:30 Gn 10:4; Nm 24:24; 1Ch 1:7; Is 23:1,12; Jr 2:10

[A]11:16 = Israel　　[B]11:17 = the king of the South　　[C]11:17 Lit *him the daughter of women*　　[D]11:17 Perhaps the kingdom　　[E]11:18 of the Mediterranean　　[F]11:20 Or *not openly*　　[G]11:21 Or *come without warning*　　[H]11:23 Or *a few people*　　[I]11:24 Or *Without warning*　　[J]11:28 Or *the Jewish people and religion*　　[K]11:29 Lit *but the last*　　[L]11:30 = the Romans

to Ptolemy V as a wife, hoping to control the Ptolemaic kingdom through her. This failed because Cleopatra helped her Ptolemaic husband and did **not stand with . . . or support** her father Antiochus III.

11:18-19 Antiochus III would then **turn his attention** to the lands around the Mediterranean Sea but would be defeated by the Roman **commander** Lucius Cornelius Scipio at Thermopylae (191 B.C.) and then Magnesia (190 B.C.). This would force Antiochus to focus on his own country where he would **stumble, fall, and be no more**, being killed by a mob defending the temple of Zeus in Elymais as Antiochus tried to pillage it.

11:20 The king who would arise **in his place** was Seleucus IV Philopator (187-175 B.C.), who would send his **tax collector**, Heliodorus, to collect money with which to pay the heavy indemnity he owed to Rome. After his short reign, Seleucus IV was killed **not in anger or in battle** but by poison from his tax collector.

11:21-35 Antiochus IV Epiphanes (175-163 B.C.), the little horn in 8:9-12,23-25 (cp. notes there), is emphasized in this section because he would have a terrible and oppressive effect on the Jewish people in the near term, and his reign is a picture of the future world ruler (the antichrist) who will also oppress the Jewish people.

11:21 Antiochus IV was not of the **royal** line, but took control by **intrigue** while the rightful heir, Demetrius, was held in Rome. The prediction called him **a despised person** because of his hatred of the Jewish people, his attempt to destroy Judaism, his desecration of the temple, and his megalomania displayed in calling himself Epiphanes

["Manifest One, Illustrious One"]. People of that time also called him Epimanes ["madman"].

11:22 Despite Ptolemy VI Philometor (181-146 B.C.) attacking with **a flood of forces**, Antiochus IV would be able to defeat them and depose **the covenant prince**, the Jewish high priest Onias III.

11:23-24 Antiochus IV would increase in **power** by sharing the wealth of his conquests, lavishing **plunder, loot, and wealth on his followers**.

11:25-26 These verses refer back to the war with Ptolemy VI (v. 22), predicting that not only would the power of Antiochus IV defeat Ptolemy VI, but also that **plots . . . against him** would cause **his army** to **be swept away**.

11:27-28 After the defeat of Ptolemy VI, Ptolemy VII took control of Egypt. Then the other **two kings**, Antiochus IV and Ptolemy VI, would meet, speaking **lies at the same table**, to plot Ptolemy VI's restoration to the throne. After initial limited success, they would eventually fail. Then Antiochus IV (**the king of the North**), having plundered Egypt, would return to his land, with his **heart . . . set against the holy covenant**. On the way home, he would attack Israel, kill 80,000 Jewish men, women, and children, and plunder the holy temple (169 B.C.).

11:29-30 Antiochus IV would launch another attack against Egypt, but this time **ships of Kittim** (cp. Nm 24:24)—the Roman fleet led by Gaius Popilius Laenas—would force him to **withdraw** in humiliation.

11:31-32 Antiochus IV would once again attack Israel (167 B.C.) while returning to Syria, this time desecrating **the**

fortress. They will abolish the daily sacrifice[a] and set up the abomination of desolation.[b] [32]With flattery he will corrupt those who act wickedly toward the covenant, but the people who know their God will be strong and take action.[c] [33]Those who are wise among the people[d] will give understanding to many, yet they will die by sword and flame,[e] and be captured and plundered for a time. [34]When defeated, they will be helped by some, but many others will join them insincerely.[f] [35]Some of the wise will fall so that they may be refined,[g] purified, and cleansed[h] until the time of the end, for it will still come at the appointed time.

[36]"Then the king will do whatever he wants.[i] He will exalt and magnify himself above every god,[j] and he will say outrageous things against the God of gods.[k] He will be successful until the time of wrath is completed,[l] because what has been decreed will be accomplished. [37]He will not show regard for the gods[A] of his fathers, the god longed for by women, or for any other god,[m] because he will magnify himself above all. [38]Instead, he will honor a god of fortresses—a god his fathers did not know—with gold, silver, precious stones, and riches. [39]He will deal with the strongest fortresses with the help of a foreign god. He will greatly honor those who acknowledge him,[B] making them rulers over many and distributing land as a reward.

[40]"At the time of the end, the king of the

South will engage him in battle, but the king of the North will storm against him[n] with chariots, horsemen, and many ships. He will invade countries and sweep through them like a flood.[o] [41]He will also invade the beautiful land,[p] and many will fall. But these will escape from his power: Edom, Moab, and the prominent people[C] of the Ammonites.[q] [42]He will extend his power against the countries, and not even the land of Egypt will escape. [43]He will get control over the hidden treasures of gold and silver and over all the riches of Egypt. The Libyans and *Cushites will also be in submission.[D,r] [44]But reports from the east[s] and the north will terrify him, and he will go out with great fury to annihilate and *completely destroy many. [45]He will pitch his royal tents between the sea and[E] the beautiful holy mountain,[t] but he will meet his end with no one to help him.

12 At that time
    Michael[u] the great prince
      who stands watch over your people
        will rise up.
    There will be a time of distress[v]
    such as never has occurred[w]
    since nations came into being
      until that time.[x]
    But at that time all your people

[a]11:31 Dn 8:11-13; 12:11
[b]Dn 9:27; 12:11; Mt 24:15; Mk 13:14
[c]11:32 Mc 5:7-9; Zch 9:13-16; 10:3-6
[d]11:33 Mal 2:7
[e]Mt 24:9; Jn 16:2; Heb 11:36-38
[f]11:34 Dn 11:21,32; Mt 7:15; Ac 20:29,30; Rm 16:18
[g]11:35 Dt 8:16; Pr 17:3; Dn 12:10; Zch 13:9; Mal 3:2-3
[h]Dn 12:10
[i]11:36 Dn 5:19; 11:3,16
[j]Is 14:13; Dn 5:20; 8:11,25; 2Th 2:4
[k]Rv 13:5-6
[l]Is 10:25; 26:20; Dn 8:19
[m]11:37 1Co 8:5-6
[n]11:40 Is 5:28; Jr 4:13
[o]Dn 11:10,26; Zch 9:14
[p]11:41 Is 11:14; Dn 8:9; 11:16
[q]Jr 48:47; 49:6
[r]11:43 2Ch 12:3; Ezk 30:4; Nah 3:9
[s]11:44 Rv 16:12
[t]11:45 Is 11:9; 27:13; 65:25; 66:20; Dn 9:16,20
[u]12:1 Dn 10:13,21; Jd 9; Rv 12:7
[v]Mt 24:21; Mk 13:19
[w]Jr 30:7; Ezk 5:9; Dn 9:12
[x]Rv 16:18

A11:37 Or *God*   B11:39 Or *those he acknowledges*   C11:41 Lit *the first*   D11:43 Lit *Cushites at his steps*   E11:45 Or *the seas at*

---

temple in Jerusalem. Antiochus would prefigure the future antichrist's actions (9:27; 12:11) by abolishing the **daily sacrifice** and committing **the abomination of desolation**. In response, **the people who know their God will . . . take action**, as expressed in the Maccabean revolt (see note at 8:13-14).

11:33-35 The Maccabees would experience suffering in their battle with Antiochus. In **the end**, the Maccabees would defeat Antiochus, rededicate the holy temple in Jerusalem, and establish the festival of *Chanukah* (Eng "Dedication") which the Lord Jesus celebrated (Jn 10:22) and which Jewish people still observe today.

11:36-45 At this point, the predictions shift away from Antiochus IV and focus on the end of days. **The king** mentioned in this section is the future antichrist, already identified as "the little horn" (7:8,20,24-25) and "the coming prince" (9:26).

11:36-39 These verses provide a clear description of the future antichrist. **The god longed for by women** (lit "the desire of women") may be a reference to the longing of Jewish women to give birth to the Messiah.

11:40-44 During the great tribulation, the antichrist will be attacked in a pincer movement from both the north and the south. Yet he will be successful, sweeping through **like a flood**. He will also invade Israel, **the beautiful land**, ignoring some nations that are in alliance with him but

conquering others, including **Egypt**, Libya, and Sudan (the **Cushites**). Reports of nations from **the east and the north** coming to attack will both **terrify** and infuriate him, leading him to pursue a course of genocidal warfare against his enemies, especially many of the Jewish people (cp. Zch 13:8-9).

11:45 The antichrist will establish his military capital in Israel, pitching **his royal tents** between the Mediterranean Sea and the city of Jerusalem, situated on **the beautiful holy mountain**. There the nations of the earth will gather (Zch 14:2) at Mount Megiddo to begin the campaign of Armageddon (Rv 16:13-16). At that time, when the nation of Israel calls on the Messiah Jesus, He will return (Mt 23:37-39) to deliver them, and the antichrist **will meet his end with no one to help him**.

12:1 At that time refers to the events predicted in the previous paragraph (11:36-45), which details the antichrist's furious attempt to destroy and annihilate the Jewish people (11:44). Then the archangel **Michael . . . who stands watch** over the Jewish people will rise to their defense to preserve them (see note at 10:12-13; cp. Rv 12:7). This will be necessary because the great tribulation (the second half of Daniel's seventieth week; Dn 9:27) will be a time of unprecedented **distress**. Despite the horrific nature of the persecution of Israel, the result will be that the surviving remnant of the Jewish nation will turn in faith to their Messiah Jesus (Zch 12:10; Rm 11:25-27) and He will deliver

who are found written in the book[a] will escape.[b]

2 Many of those who sleep in the dust[c] of the earth will awake,
some to eternal life,[d]
and some to shame
and eternal contempt.[e]

3 Those who are wise will shine
like the bright expanse of the heavens,[f]
and those who lead many
to righteousness,[g]
like the stars forever and ever.

4 "But you, Daniel, keep these words secret[h] and seal the book[i] until the time of the end.[j] Many will roam about,[k] and knowledge will increase."[A]

5 Then I, Daniel, looked, and two others were

standing there, one on this bank of the river and one on the other. 6 One of them said to the man dressed in linen,[l] who was above the waters of the river,[m] "How long until the end[n] of these extraordinary things?" 7 Then I heard the man dressed in linen, who was above the waters of the river. He raised both his hands[B,o] toward heaven and swore by Him who lives eternally[p] that it would be for a time, times, and half a time.[q] When the power of the holy people is shattered, all these things will be completed.

8 I heard but did not understand. So I asked, "My lord, what will be the outcome of these things?"[r]

9 He said, "Go on your way, Daniel, for the words are secret[s] and sealed until the time of

*a*12:1 Dn 7:10; 10:21; Rv 20:12
*b*Php 4:3; Rv 20:12; 21:27
*c*12:2 Is 26:19; Ezk 37:12-14
*d*Mt 25:46; Jn 5:28-29
*e*Is 66:24
*f*12:3 Gn 1:6; Ps 19:1; Jn 5:35
*g*Is 53:11; Dn 11:33
*h*12:4 Dn 8:26; 12:9; Rv 10:4
*i*Is 8:16; Jr 32:9-12; Rv 22:10
*j*Dn 8:17; 12:9,13
*k*2Ch 16:9; Jr 5:1; Am 8:12
*l*12:6 Ezk 9:2; Dn 10:5
*m*Dn 8:16
*n*Dn 8:13; Mt 24:3; Mk 13:4
*o*12:7 Ezk 20:5; Rv 10:5-6   *p*Dn 4:34   *q*Dn 7:25; Rv 11:2; 12:14   *r*12:8 1Th 5:10; 2Pt 3:10-14   *s*12:9 Rv 10:4

A12:4 LXX reads *and the earth will be filled with unrighteousness*   B12:7 Lit *raised his right and his left*

them. **The book** refers to the heavenly Book of Life in which the names of the elect are listed (Ps 69:28; Php 4:3; Rv 13:8; 17:8; 20:15).

12:2 Following the deliverance of Israel, there will be a resurrection of **those who sleep in the dust**. This verse does not imply any kind of soul sleep before the resurrection since the faithful go to be with God instantly upon dying (2Co 5:8; Php 1:21-23) and the faithless go to a place of suffering also immediately upon dying (Lk 16:22-23). The word "sleep" is used as a metaphor to emphasize the temporary state of bodily death before being physically raised at the resurrection (cp. Jn 11:11-15). Although telescoped together here (as is common in prophecy), the resurrection of the faithful and the unfaithful are two distinct events separated by the one-thousand-year messianic kingdom (Rv 20:4-6). Daniel 12:2 contains the clearest statement of resurrection in the OT, but by no means is it the only one (cp. Jb 19:25-27; Is 26:19).

12:3 The phrase **those who are wise** refers to those with the wisdom to turn in faith to the Messiah Jesus. As a result, they will **lead many** others to faith and **righteousness**.

12:4 Although it is possible that Daniel was told to keep these words of the vision **secret**, an alternative rendering of the Hebrew is to "close up the words" **and seal the book**, a reference to preservation of the text of Daniel **until the time of the end**. Preserving Daniel's prophecy was necessary because in the end of days, **many will roam about** seeking answers that will be found in the book of Daniel. Moreover, in that day, **knowledge will increase**, possibly referring to the understanding of Daniel's prophecies as informed observers recognize the fulfillment of his predictions.

12:5-7 Daniel saw **two others**, meaning angels, who served as witnesses for the oath of the linen-dressed angel (10:5). Two was the minimum number of witnesses necessary for an oath (Dt 19:15). One of the witnessing angels asked **how long until the end** of the predicted time of distress. The angel dressed in linen answered that the time of the great tribulation (the second half of Daniel's seventieth week) would be for **a time, times, and half a time**, or three and one-half years (7:25; Rv 12:7). By the end of the great tribulation, **the power of the holy people** Israel will be **shattered**, causing them to turn in faith to their long-rejected Messiah

Jesus (Zch 12:10). At that time, He will return and deliver them (Zch 14:1-21) and **all these things will be completed**.

12:8-10 Daniel's statement that he **heard but did not understand** does not mean that he did not comprehend his prophecy was about the end of days but rather that he did not understand precisely how these events would happen. Daniel was told to go on his way, because **the words are secret** (or "closed") **and sealed until the time of the end**, meaning they would not be fully recognized until their fulfillment at the end of days. At that time, the wicked will fail to comprehend their situation **but the wise will understand** the fulfillment of Daniel's words and turn in faith to the God of Israel and His Messiah Jesus.

Courtyard at site purported to be the tomb of Daniel in Susa, Iran

the end.[a] [10]Many will be purified,[b] cleansed, and refined,[c] but the wicked will act wickedly;[d] none of the wicked will understand, but the wise will understand.[e] [11]From the time the daily sacrifice is abolished and the abomination of desolation[f] is set up,[g] there will

be 1,290 days. [12]The one who waits[h] for and reaches 1,335 days is blessed. [13]But as for you, go on your way to the end;[A] you will rest, then rise[i] to your destiny at the end of the days."

[a]12:9 Dn 12:4
[b]12:10 Zch 13:9;
Ac 1:6-7; 2Th
2:7-12
[c]Dn 11:35
[d]Is 32:6-7; Rv
22:11
[e]Dn 12:3; Hs 14:9;
Jn 7:17; 8:47

[f]12:11 Dn 9:27　[g]Dn 11:31; Mt 24:15; Mk 13:14　[h]12:12 Is
30:18　[i]12:13 Is 57:2; Rv 14:13

[A]12:13 LXX omits *to the end*

12:11-12 Two periods of time were revealed to Daniel. First, from the middle of the tribulation when the antichrist stops **daily sacrifice** and commits **the abomination of desolation** until the end, **there will be 1,290 days**. The great tribulation is said to be three and one-half years (v. 7) or 1,260 days (Rv 12:6; 13:5). Here it is 30 days longer, probably to include time for the judgment of the nations (Mt 25:31-46). Second, a blessing awaits **the one who . . . reaches 1,335 days**, a period that includes not only the 30 days for judging

the nations but an additional 45 days, perhaps to establish the government of the messianic kingdom. Those who enter that kingdom are said to be **blessed** because they will be part of the most glorious world, governed by its greatest King, the Lord Jesus Himself.

12:13 The angel told Daniel that he was to continue **to the end** of his life, at which point he would **rest**, a euphemism for death. Yet he was given the promise that he too would **rise** from the dead **at the end of the days** (v. 2).

Hosea

Introduction

Hosea is one of the most autobiographical of the Prophetic Books in that the opening account of Hosea's own marriage and family form a vital part of his unique message. God's word of grace and His call to repent are dramatically portrayed and punctuated by Hosea's scorned but constant love for his wife Gomer and by the odd names of his three children. Apart from this information about his immediate family, hardly anything is known about Hosea. His divinely commissioned marriage to the promiscuous Gomer, which brought Hosea such heartache, seems to have been the beginning of his long career. But rather than ministering in spite of personal sorrow, his troublesome marriage was the foundation stone of his ministry.

The growing Assyrian threat to both the northern and southern kingdoms is a historical reality that forms the background against which Hosea prophesied (11:5). Assyrian cruelty is attested in both writing and graphic art. In this relief fragment from Nineveh, Assyrian soldiers are deporting Chaldean women. The artist has captured the pathos of the moment by portraying one woman stopping to give water to an exhausted child while an Assyrian guard threatens to beat stragglers.

Circumstances of Writing

Author: According to the first verse, Hosea's prophetic career spanned at least 40 years. It began some time during the reign of Jeroboam II, who ruled Israel, the northern kingdom, as co-regent with his father Jehoash from 793 to 782 B.C., then independently until 753 B.C. Hosea's ministry ended sometime during the reign of Hezekiah, who ruled Judah from 716 to 686 B.C.

Although the southern kingdom of Judah was not neglected in Hosea's prophecy (e.g., 1:7,11; 6:11; 12:2), his messages were directed primarily to the northern kingdom of Israel, often referred to as "Ephraim" (5:3,12-14; 6:4; 7:1), and represented by the royal city, Samaria (7:1; 8:5-6; 10:5,7; 13:16). Hosea apparently lived and worked in or around Samaria, probably moving to Jerusalem at least by the time Samaria fell to the Assyrians in 722 B.C.

Background: The reign of Jeroboam II, the northern kingdom's greatest ruler by worldly standards, was a time of general affluence, military might, and national stability. The economy was strong, the future looked bright, and the mood of the country was optimistic, at least for the upper class (Hs 12:8; Am 3:15; 6:4-6). Syria was a constant problem to Israel, but Adad-nirari III of Assyria had brought Israel relief with an expedition against Damascus, the Syrian capital, in 805 B.C.

Then after Adad-nirari's death in 783 B.C. Israel and Judah expanded during a time of Assyrian weakness (the time of Jonah). But after Jeroboam's death in 753 B.C. Israel sank into near anarchy, going through six kings in about 30 years, four of whom were assassinated (Zechariah, Shallum, Pekahiah, and Pekah). Since Assyria also regained power during this time, Israel was doomed. Of course the real reason Israel crumbled was God's determination to judge the people for their sins, as Hosea and Amos made clear. Most of Hosea's messages were probably delivered during these last 30 years of Israel's nationhood.

---

850 B.C.

Jehu, king of Northern Kingdom 841–814

Jehoahaz, king of Northern Kingdom 814–798

Jehoash, king of Northern Kingdom 798–782

Jeroboam II, king of Northern Kingdom 793–753

Uzziah, king of Southern Kingdom 792–740

Amos is called to prophetic ministry. 783

750 B.C.

Zechariah, king of Northern Kingdom 753–752, assassinated by Shallum

Shallum, king of Northern Kingdom 752, assassinated by Menahem

Menahem, king of Northern Kingdom 752–742

Pekah, king of Northern Kingdom 752–732, assassinated by Hoshea

Micah is called to be a prophet. 750

Jotham, king of Southern Kingdom 750–732

Hosea's prophetic ministry 750–710?

Pekahiah, king of Northern Kingdom 742–740, assassinated by Pekah

Message and Purpose

Indictment: According to Hosea, Israel sinned in four ways. First, they were violating basic covenant requirements of faithfulness and kindness, rejecting knowledge of God and His law. They had become self-satisfied and proud and had forgotten God's grace. They even spoke contemptuously against Him. Second, they were engaging in idolatry and harlotry or cult prostitution. Third, they were trusting in human devices (kings, princes, warriors, and foreign covenants) rather than in God. Finally, they were guilty of injustice and violence, including murder, theft, lying, and oppression of the defenseless.

Instruction: Through Hosea the Lord told the people of Israel to stop their promiscuity, idolatry, and iniquity and to return to Him in humility and faithfulness toward the law of the covenant.

Judgment: Hosea informed Israel that their present distress was because the Lord had abandoned them and that further discipline would come. This would include foreign domination, exile, destruction, desolation, and death.

Hope: Hosea reminded Israel of the Lord's grace and love in making them a people, and in blessing them in the past with His attentive and patient care and His abundant provision. He was their only hope, and His ways were right. The Lord also assured them that in response to their repentance and faith He would again have compassion on them and redeem them; He would remove unrighteousness and restore the covenant, bringing righteousness and the knowledge of God; and He would rebuild and beautify Israel.

Structure

The first three chapters of the book establish a parallel between the Lord and Hosea. Both were loving husbands of unfaithful wives. Hosea's three children, whose names served as messages to Israel, represent an overture to the second main division of the book, which presents its accusations and the call to repent in groups of three. Just as chapter 1—a third-person account of Hosea's family—is balanced by chapter 3—a

---

740 B.C.

730 B.C.

Isaiah is called to be a prophet. 740

Ahaz, king of Southern Kingdom 735–716

Damascus and Israel attack Jerusalem hoping to replace Ahaz with a king favorable to their alliance. 735

Tiglath-pileser's continued expansion takes territory along the Mediterranean coast, destroys Damascus, and captures most of the the Northern Kingdom. 733–732

Hoshea, last king of Northern Kingdom 732–722

Tiglath-pileser III's successor, Shalmaneser V besieges Samaria. 725–722

Samaria falls to the hands of Shalmaneser's successor, Sargon II. 722

Sargon's inscriptions say that nearly 28,000 captives were deported from Israel. 722

Hezekiah, king of Southern Kingdom 716–686

first-person account—so the final main division of the book alternates between first-person announcements of God's message and third-person reports from the prophet.

Contribution to the Bible

Hosea compared the relationship between God and His people to that of a husband and his wife, drawing a parallel between spiritual and marital unfaithfulness. "The Bible is very clear in its moral code that the sexual act can only legitimately take place within the context of the marriage relationship. Thus the image of marriage and sex, a relationship that is purely exclusive and allows no rivals, is an ideal image of the relationship between God and his people" (*Dictionary of Biblical Imagery*, p. 778). Yet nothing can quench God's love for His covenant people. Like a marriage partner, God is deeply involved in our lives and is pained when we go our own way. God demands love and loyalty from His own. Often God's people have failed to demonstrate whole-hearted love for Him. But He stands ready to forgive and restore those who turn to Him in repentance. In buying Gomer's freedom, Hosea pointed ahead to God's love perfectly expressed in Christ, who bought the freedom of His bride, the church, with His own life.

Outline

I.   **The Pain and Persistence of Divine Love (1:1–3:5)**
    A.   **God's message to Israel through Hosea's family (1:1–2:23)**
    B.   **Hosea's testimony to his restored marriage (3:1-5)**

II.   **Threefold Accusation and Call to Repent (4:1–7:16)**
    A.   **Indictment and warning (4:1–5:15)**
    B.   **Call to repent and God's grief at Israel's refusal (6:1–7:16)**

III.   **Alternating Lament of the Lord and Hosea (8:1–14:9)**
    A.   **Failure of false hopes (8:1–10:15)**
    B.   **Israel's punishment for rebellion (11:1–13:16)**
    C.   **Final call to repent (14:1-9)**

1 The word of the Lord that came to Hosea son of Beeri during the reigns of Uzziah,[a] Jotham,[b] Ahaz,[c] and Hezekiah,[d] kings of Judah, and of Jeroboam[e] son of Jehoash, king of Israel.

Hosea's Marriage and Children

[2] When the Lord first spoke to Hosea, He said this to him:

Go and marry a promiscuous wife[f]
and have children of promiscuity,
for the land is committing
    blatant acts of promiscuity
by abandoning the Lord.

[3] So he went and married Gomer daughter of Diblaim, and she conceived and bore him a son.[g] [4] Then the Lord said to him:

Name him Jezreel,[h] for in a little while
I will bring the bloodshed of Jezreel[i]
on the house of Jehu[j]
and put an end to the kingdom
    of the house of Israel.
[5] On that day I will break the bow
    of Israel[k]
in the Valley of Jezreel.[A,l]

[6] She conceived again and gave birth to a daughter, and the Lord said to him:

Name her No Compassion,[B]
for I will no longer have compassion
on the house of Israel.
I will certainly take them away.
[7] But I will have compassion
    on the house of Judah,[m]
and I will deliver them by
    the Lord their God.[n]
I will not deliver them by bow, sword,
    or war,
or by horses and cavalry.[o]

[8] After Gomer had weaned No Compassion, she conceived and gave birth to a son. [9] Then the Lord said:

Name him Not My People,[C]
for you are not My people,
and I will not be your God.[D,p]
[10E] Yet the number of the Israelites
will be like the sand of the sea,[q]
which cannot be measured or counted.
And in the place where they were told:
You are not My people,
they will be called:
    Sons of the living God.[r]
[11] And the Judeans and the Israelites
will be gathered together.[s]
They will appoint for themselves
    a single ruler[t]

Cross references

[a]1:1 2Ch 26:1-23; Is 1:1; Am 1:1
[b]2Kg 15:5; 2Ch 27:1-9
[c]2Kg 16:1-20; 2Ch 28:1-27; Is 1:1; 7:1-17; Mc 1:1
[d]2Kg 18:1-20:21; 2Ch 29:1-32:33; Mc 1:1
[e]2Kg 13:13; 14:23-29; Am 1:1
[f]1:2 Hs 3:1
[g]1:3 Ezk 23:4
[h]1:4 Hs 2:22
[i]2Kg 9:24-10:11
[j]2Kg 9:7; 10:30; 15:10
[k]1:5 Gn 49:24; Jb 29:20; Jr 49:35
[l]Jos 17:16; Jdg 6:33
[m]1:7 Is 30:18
[n]Jr 25:5-6; Zch 9:9-10
[o]Ps 44:3-7
[p]1:9 Ex 6:7; Lv 26:12; Jr 7:23; 11:4; 30:22; Ezk 36:28
[q]1:10 Gn 22:17; Jr 33:22
[r]Rm 9:25-27
[s]1:11 Jr 23:5-6; 50:4-5; Ezk 37:18-25; Hs 3:5
[t]Jr 30:21; Hs 3:5

A1:5 = God sows   B1:6 Or *Lo-ruhamah*   C1:9 Or *Lo-ammi*   D1:9 Lit *not be yours*   E1:10 Hs 2:1 in Hb

---

1:2 Hosea's initial call to the prophetic ministry began with perplexing instructions to find a wife among the promiscuous women of Israel (of which there were apparently many; 4:14). This was no mere parable or vision but an actual command to enter a literal marriage that would vividly portray God's perspective on Israel. **Promiscuous wife** (lit "wife of promiscuity") describes her behavior and character when Hosea married her. She is not called a prostitute, but she almost certainly used her sexuality for her livelihood (2:5). Hosea, like the Lord, would have a wayward wife and a broken heart. **Children of promiscuity** indicates that the paternity of Gomer's children would be questioned. They would bear the shame of their mother's behavior and at the same time represent the shameful behavior and divine condemnation of the children of Israel. The reason the prophet had to invite such pain into his life was the flagrancy with which Israel, Yahweh's wife, had been selling herself to other gods and **abandoning the Lord**. Each idolatrous act had driven them further from Him. The Hebrew verb *zanah* ("be a harlot, act promiscuously") occurs far more in Hosea (13 times; 60 times in the OT) than in any other book but Ezekiel (17 times). These two books also account for about 50 percent of the uses of the root word in the OT (22 times in Hosea, 28 times in Ezekiel, 115 times in the OT), which includes words for "promiscuity" and "prostitute."

1:4 Jehu had carried out God's judgment (2Kg 9:7) by putting the last of Omri's dynasty to the sword at the city of **Jezreel** (2Kg 9:24-10:11). God commended him for this (2Kg 10:30). Hosea named his first child Jezreel, symbolizing that Jehu's dynasty, which had proved to be just as

wicked as Omri's (2Kg 10:31), would likewise suffer annihilation at Jezreel. Jehu's dynasty began in violence and would end in the same, but as the recipient rather than the instrument of divine judgment. Zechariah, Jehu's last royal descendant, was assassinated by Shallum in 752 B.C., probably at Ibleam in Jezreel (2Kg 15:10).

1:6 Hosea's second child, a **daughter**, was given the pathetic Hebrew name *Lo-ruhamah*, meaning **No Compassion**, symbolic of the fact that by her continual unfaithfulness Israel had forfeited God's love. **Take them away** could also be rendered "forgive them," although the context favors the present translation.

1:9 The Hebrew name of Hosea's third child, *Lo-ammi*, meaning **Not My People**, was a symbolic proclamation that Israel had broken covenant with God (Ex 6:7; Lv 26:12). **I will not be your God** is literally "and I will not be to you." This could also be rendered "and I am not 'I AM' to you" (Ex 3:14-15). God's statement amounted to a decree of divorce.

1:10-11 Allusion to the Abrahamic covenant in the phrase **like the sand of the sea** (cp. Gn 22:17) indicates that God's "divorce" of Israel was not final but applied only to that generation—the nation or leadership of that time. Eternal promise is placed profoundly beside final judgment, reconcilable only because **the living God** could bring life out of death. This is affirmed by the name **Jezreel**, which symbolized not only judgment but also life insomuch as the name meant "God plants" (cp. Ezk 36:9-11). The division between Israel and Judah was temporary, a theme to be repeated later (Ezk 37:18-25; Hs 3:5).

and go up from[A] the land.
For the day of Jezreel[a] will be great.

2[B]   Call[C] your brothers: My People
and your sisters: Compassion.

Israel's Adultery Rebuked

2 Rebuke your mother; rebuke her.[b]
For she is not My wife and I am not
her husband.[c]
Let her remove the promiscuous look
from her face[d]
and her adultery
from between her breasts.

3 Otherwise, I will strip her naked[e]
and expose her as she was on the day
of her birth.
I will make her like a desert[f]
and like a parched land,
and I will let her die of thirst.[g]

4 I will have no compassion
on her children[h]
because they are the children
of promiscuity.

5 Yes, their mother is promiscuous;
she conceived them
and acted shamefully.[i]

For she thought, "I will go
after my lovers,[j]
the men who give me my food
and water,
my wool and flax, my oil and drink."[k]

6 Therefore, this is what I will do:
I will block her[D] way[l] with thorns;[m]
I will enclose her with a wall,
so that she cannot find her paths.[n]

7 She will pursue her lovers
but not catch them;[o]
she will seek them but not find them.
Then she will think,
"I will go back to my former husband,[p]
for then it was better for me
than now."[q]

8 She does not recognize[r]
that it is I who gave her the grain,[s]
the new wine, and the oil.
I lavished silver and gold on her,
which they used for •Baal.

9 Therefore, I will take back My grain
in its time[t]
and My new wine in its season;
I will take away My wool and linen,
which were to cover her nakedness.

---

a 1:11 Ezk 36:9-11
b 2:2 Ezk 23:45
c Is 50:1
d Jr 3:1,9,13
e 2:3 Ezk 16:7,22,39
f Is 32:13-14; Hs 13:15
g Jr 14:3; Am 8:11-13
h 2:4 Jr 13:14
i 2:5 Is 1:21; Hs 3:1
j Jr 2:25
k Jr 44:17-18
l 2:6 Jb 19:8
m Hs 9:6; 10:8
n Jr 18:15
o 2:7 Hs 5:13
p Jr 2:2; 3:1; Ezk 16:8; 23:4
q Jr 14:22; Hs 13:6
r 2:8 Is 1:3
s Ezk 16:19
t 2:9 Hs 8:7; 9:2

A 1:11 Or *and flourish in*; Hb obscure   B 2:1 Hs 2:3 in Hb   C 2:1 Lit *Say to*   D 2:6 LXX, Syr; MT reads *your*

2:1-23 These verses elaborate on the "Not My People" oracle in 1:9-11. They open with the divorce formula in verse 2 that begins the rebuke in verses 1-13: "She is not My wife and I am not her husband." The forgiveness section in verses 14-23 announces the restoration of Israel. The Lord again becomes "My husband" (v. 16), and Israel becomes "My wife" (v. 19); "No Compassion" also receives compassion, and "Not My People" becomes "My people" (v. 23).

2:2 Here is the first command to repent in the book (4:15;

6:1; 10:12; 12:6; 14:1-2,9), followed by alternating verses of judgment (2:3-4,6-7,9-11) and indictment (vv. 5,8,12-13). The children, representing the common people of Israel, are urged to **rebuke** their mother, representing Israel's leadership. So Israel's divorce is not the end of hope and her punishment is not the last word (vv. 3,19-20).

2:3 Israel is portrayed in utter humiliation and deprivation. Captured exiles are often depicted in antiquity as being led away **naked** (Is 20:1-6).

2:4 The people would suffer individually because of the nation's idolatry. Therefore they must do what they could to "rebuke" their nation (v. 2).

2:5 The nation's **lovers** were other gods (idols), which she **thought** (lit "said"; cp. vv. 7,12) could meet her needs.

2:7 The purpose of God's punishment of Israel for abandoning Him (1:2) was to restore them.

2:8 The leaders had led the people to trust and seek **Baal** (6 times in Hs; 74 times in the OT) rather than Yahweh, the true God. Yahweh had not only created Israel and delivered them from Egyptian bondage but had also blessed them with the necessities of **grain . . . new wine**, and **oil** and even the luxuries of **silver** and **gold**. The verb translated **recognize** (lit "know") is used 16 times in Hosea, more than any of the Minor Prophets (v. 20; 5:4; 6:3; 8:2; 9:7; 11:3; 14:9). The Hebrew verb *ba'al* can mean "marry, rule over, possess" and is related to the noun "husband, lord, owner" and the name of the Canaanite god "Baal" as well as places such as Baal-peor where he was worshiped. These various terms occur 229 times in the OT. The name occurs 7 times in Hosea, all but one for the Canaanite god.

2:9 The word for **I will take back** is essentially the same Hebrew word as "I will go back" in verse 7. If Israel did not

---

racham

Hebrew Pronunciation	[rah KHAM]
HCSB Translation	love, have compassion, pity
Uses in Hosea	7
Uses in the OT	47
Focus passage	Hosea 2:1,4,23

Racham derives from *rechem* (26x: *womb*), and related languages associate "womb" and "compassion." *Racham* means *love* (Ps 18:1). Intensive verbs signify *have/show compassion* (Ex 33:19; Dt 13:17), *pity* (Hs 2:23), *have pity on* (Hs 1:6), or *show mercy* (Is 60:10). Their participle denotes *compassionate* (Ps 116:5), and their infinitive indicates *mercy* (Hab 3:2). Their passive conveys *receive compassion* (Hs 2:23) or *find mercy* (Pr 28:13). *Rachamiym* (40x) indicates *mercy* (Dt 13:17) or *compassion* (Is 54:7). It is *merciful acts* (Pr 12:10), *mercies* (Lm 3:22), and *merciful* (Gn 43:14). It suggests *emotion* (Gn 43:30), *pity* (Ps 106:46), and, in a prepositional phrase, *graciously* (Zch 1:16). The same words imply *abundant compassion* (Neh 9:31) or *great . . . mercies* (1Ch 21:13). *Rachum* (13x) means *compassionate* (Dt 4:31) or *merciful* (2Ch 30:9). Eleven times *rachum* occurs alongside "gracious" *(chanun)* (Ex 34:6). *Rachamaniy* is *compassionate woman* (Lm 4:10).

10 Now I will expose her shame[a]
   in the sight of her lovers,
   and no one will rescue her
      from My hands.
11 I will put an end to all
      her celebrations:[b]
   her feasts,[c] New Moons,[d]
      and Sabbaths—
   all her festivals.
12 I will devastate her vines and fig trees.[e]
   She thinks that these are her wages
   that her lovers have given her.
   I will turn them into a thicket,[f]
   and the wild animals will eat them.[g]
13 And I will punish her for the days
      of the Baals[h]
   when she burned incense to them,[i]
   put on her rings and jewelry,[j]
   and went after her lovers,
   but forgot Me.[k]
      This is the Lord's declaration.

Israel's Adultery Forgiven

14 Therefore, I am going to persuade her,
   lead her to the wilderness,[l]
   and speak tenderly to her.[A]
15 There I will give her vineyards
      back to her[m]
   and make the Valley of Achor[B,n]
   into a gateway of hope.

There she will respond as she did
   in the days of her youth,[o]
   as in the day she came out of the land
      of Egypt.
16 In that day—
            this is the Lord's declaration—
   you will call Me, "My husband,"[p]
   and no longer call Me, "My Baal."[c]
17 For I will remove the names
      of the Baals
   from her mouth;
   they will no longer be remembered
      by their names.
18 On that day I will make a covenant
      for them
   with the wild animals, the birds
      of the sky,
   and the creatures that crawl
      on the ground.[q]
   I will shatter bow, sword,
   and weapons of war in the land[D,r]
   and will enable the people
      to rest securely.[s]
19 I will take you to be My wife forever.[t]
   I will take you to be My wife
      in righteousness,
   justice, love, and compassion.[u]
20 I will take you to be My wife
      in faithfulness,

Cross references (center column):
a 2:10 Ezk 16:37
b 2:11 Jr 7:34; 16:9
c Hs 3:4; Am 5:21; 8:10
d Is 1:13-14
e 2:12 Jr 5:17; 8:13
f Ps 80:12; Is 5:5; 7:23
g Is 32:13-15
h 2:13 Hs 4:13; 11:2
i Jr 7:9
j Ezk 16:12,17; 23:40
k Hs 4:6; 8:14; 13:6
l 2:14 Ezk 20:33-38
m 2:15 Ezk 28:25-26
n Jos 7:26
o Jr 2:1-3
p 2:16 Is 54:5
q 2:18 Jb 5:23; Is 11:6-9; Ezk 34:25
r Ezk 39:1-10
s Ezk 34:25
t 2:19 Is 62:4-5
u Is 1:27; 54:6-8

A 2:14 Lit *speak to her heart*   B 2:15 = Trouble   C 2:16 Or *My master*   D 2:18 Or *war on the earth*

---

return to her husband, the Lord, He would take back His blessings.

2:10 On **expose her shame**, compare verse 3; Is 47:1-3; Jr 13:22; Ezk 16:36-37; 23:29; Nah 3:5. The noun translated "shame" refers literally to a woman's private parts. Israel's punishment would include the disgrace of having her sins exposed for everyone to see.

2:11 In spite of Israel's idolatry, they had continued the hypocrisy of "worship" in Yahweh's name. Outward religious activity can outlive the death of true faith.

2:12 This verse echoes verse 5 in exposing the lie Israel believed—that their blessings from Yahweh (v. 8) were just payment earned from their service to idols.

2:13 The words of rebuke (vv. 1-13) conclude with the common prophetic refrain **This is the Lord's declaration**, then God's promised eventual redemption and restoration in verses 14-23 follow.

2:14-15 The word **therefore** commonly begins an announcement of judgment following an indictment for sin in the writings of the prophets. It is so used in verses 6 and 9. But here, following the indictment in verses 12-13, begins an announcement of salvation. Israel's sin will not only result in judgment, but because of God's covenant promises it will also result in salvation. The Hebrew word *midbar* can mean "desert" (v. 3) or **wilderness**. The place of judgment, "the desert," will also be the place of salvation. **Speak tenderly** is literally "speak to her heart." It occurs elsewhere of Joseph's comforting assurance of favor and forgiveness to his brothers, who had done evil to him (Gn 50:21; cp. Gn 34:3;

Jdg 19:3; Is 40:2). Although Israel had forgotten Yahweh, He would carry her back to the wilderness where He would renew and restore her faith as it had been in **her youth** (cp. 13:5). **Achor** means "trouble" and alludes to the trouble that Achan caused Israel (Jos 7:24-26; see Is 65:10).

2:16-20 These verses are parallel to verse 2. Although Yahweh declared that Hosea's generation was no longer His wife and He was no longer her husband, a time would come when He would renew the covenant. A converted Israel would again declare Yahweh to be her **husband**, and He would assure her of His permanent commitment to her as His **wife**.

2:16-17 The phrase **the Lord's declaration** is repeated in verses 16 and 21 to echo its use in verse 13 and highlight Israel's radical change from Baal's mistress to Yahweh's restored wife. The Hebrew noun *ba'al* could mean "husband" as well as the name of the Canaanite deity (see note at v. 8; Dt 24:4). Israel's popular religion often merged concepts and practices of Baal worship with Yahweh worship, an idolatrous practice that angered God because it defiled His name (Lv 18:21; 20:3; Ezk 20:39). In the future day of Israel's final conversion, God would **remove** Israel's promiscuity (v. 2) when He removed any reference to **the Baals** (the plural indicates that Baal worship occurred at various locations) from her vocabulary (Zch 13:2).

2:18 **Wild animals . . . birds**, and **creatures** alludes to Gn 1:20-25; 8:17-19 as well as Hs 2:12. The **covenant** refers figuratively to the peace God will bring between man and beast (Jb 5:23; Is 11:6-9; Ezk 34:25).

and you will know •Yahweh.[a]

21 On that day I will respond[b]—
this is the LORD's declaration.
I will respond to the sky,
and it will respond to the earth.

22 The earth will respond to the grain,[c]
the new wine, and the oil,
and they will respond to Jezreel.

23 I will sow her[A] in the land for Myself,[d]
and I will have compassion[e]
on No Compassion;[f]
I will say[f] to Not My People:[g]
You are My people,[h]
and he will say, "You are My God."

Waiting for Restoration

3 Then the LORD said to me, "Go again; show love to a woman who is loved by another man and is an adulteress,[i] just as the LORD loves the Israelites though they turn to other gods and love raisin cakes."[j]

[2] So I bought her for 15 •shekels of silver and five bushels of barley.[B,C,k] [3] I said to her, "You must live with me many days. Don't be promiscuous or belong to any man, and I will act the same way toward you."

[4] For the Israelites must live many days without king or prince,[l] without sacrifice[m] or sacred pillar,[n] and without •ephod[o] or household idols.[p] [5] Afterward, the people of Israel will return[q] and seek the LORD their God and David their king.[r] They will come with awe to the LORD[s] and to His goodness in the last days.

God's Case against Israel

4 Hear the word of the LORD,[t]
people of Israel,
for the LORD has a case[u]
against the inhabitants of the land:
There is no truth,[v] no faithful love,[w]
and no knowledge of God[x] in the land!

2 Cursing,[y] lying,[z] murder,[aa] stealing,[ab]
and adultery[ac] are rampant;
one act of bloodshed follows another.[ad]

3 For this reason the land mourns,[ae]
and everyone who lives
in it languishes,
along with the wild animals[af]
and the birds of the sky;

Cross references
a 2:20 Hs 6:6; 13:4
b 2:21 Is 55:10; Zch 8:12; Mal 3:10-11
c 2:22 Jr 31:12; Jl 2:19
d 2:23 Jr 31:37
e Hs 1:6
f Rm 9:25
g Hs 1:9
h Hs 2:1
i 3:1 Hs 1:2
j 2Sm 6:19; 1Ch 16:3; Sg 2:5
k 3:2 Ru 4:10
l 3:4 Hs 13:10-11
m Dn 9:27; 11:31; 12:11; Hs 2:11
n Hs 10:1-2
o Ex 28:4-12; 1Sm 23:9-12
p Gn 31:19,34; Jdg 17:5; 18:14,17
q 3:5 Jr 50:4-5
r Is 11:1-10; Jr 23:5-6; 33:15-16; Ezk 34:24; Rm 11:23
s Jr 31:9
t 4:1 Hs 5:1
u Hs 12:2; Mc 6:2
v Is 59:4; Jr 7:28
w Hs 6:6
x Hs 5:4
y 4:2 Hs 10:4
z Hs 7:3; 10:13; 11:12
aa Hs 6:9
ab Hs 7:1
ac Hs 7:4
ad Hs 6:8; 12:14
ae 4:3 Is 24:4; 33:9
af Jr 4:25

A 2:23 = Israel   B 3:2 LXX reads barley and a measure of wine   C 3:2 Lit silver, a homer of barley, and a lethek of barley

---

2:21-23 These verses are parallel to 1:3–2:1 in that they refer back to Hosea's three children. God will **respond** to Israel's cries for help and the earth's need for rain. **Jezreel** generally meant bloodshed, but here it means "God plants" (cp. 1:10) and refers to Israel.

3:1 Even though Gomer, like Israel, had joined herself to **another man** (lit "a neighbor"; cp. Dt 5:21; Jr 3:1,20) and so committed adultery, Hosea was told to take her back. She is called **a woman** rather than "your wife" because she had broken the covenant and had no claim on him. Like Hosea, God would show love to Israel even though she had forfeited her right to His love. **Raisin cakes** were apparently used in Canaanite religious rites, possibly as an aphrodisiac. With its four uses of the word "love," this verse graphically depicts the foolishness of Israel's attitude toward God. Their relationship was best portrayed by "a marriage that is to all appearances senseless and grotesque" (A. Richardson). Gomer rejected Hosea's genuine love of her for the selfish "love" of another man. In the same way, Israel preferred ("loved") raisin cakes to the faithful love Yahweh had for her.

3:2-3 Why Hosea had to buy Gomer is not stated. Perhaps she had sold herself to someone as a personal slave. Hosea's instructions to Gomer probably mean they would refrain from conjugal relations for a time after she returned to him. Verses 4-5 compare this to Israel's coming time of exile when they would be without ruler or worship. During this time the Lord would be expecting Israel to seek Him (5:15). The time would end "in the last days" when Israel would seek their messianic king (descended from David, 3:5) in repentance and faith (Is 11:1-10; Jr 23:5-6; 33:15-16; Mt 1:1; 21:9; Rm 11:23). It is apparently the same time that believing Israel will be reunited (Hs 1:11).

4:1–5:15 This section is centered on the commands in 4:15.

Three repetitions of indictment plus judgment both precede and follow these commands.

4:1-3 The prophetic call to **hear the word of the LORD** is found 29 times in the OT (13 times in Jeremiah, 6 times in Ezekiel, 4 times in Isaiah, 3 times in 1 and 2 Kings), but only twice in the Minor Prophets—here and in Am 7:16. This central indictment section begins with a summary of the Lord's charges and a call to the true **people** (lit "sons") **of Israel** to recognize the moral and spiritual corruption of the rest of their countrymen who have abandoned their God and

kachash

Hebrew Pronunciation	[kah KHASH]
HCSB Translation	deceive, deny
Uses in Hosea	2
Uses in the OT	22
Focus passage	Hosea 4:2

This root may first appear in Hebrew. Debate exists whether two or more homonyms exist. Kachash means deny (Gn 18:15) or contradict (Jr 5:12). It involves speech contrary to the truth, entails denying God (Jb 31:28), and was a practice of false prophets (Zch 13:4). Kachash denotes deceive, lie, and act deceptively (Lv 6:2-3; 19:11). Infinitives imply deception (Is 59:13) or lying (Hs 4:2). Synonyms include shaqar ("betray, lie") and kazav ("lie"). Used of enemies surrendering, kachash connotes cringe (Dt 33:29), submit grudgingly (2Sm 22:45), or pretend submission (Ps 81:15). An element of deception seems present. A homonym implying leanness may be used of crops like olives (Hab 3:17) and new wine (Hs 9:2) failing. People are emaciated (Ps 109:24). The noun kachash (6x) signifies lie (Hs 7:3), lies (Ps 59:12), and deceitful (Nah 3:1) but once indicates frailty (Jb 16:8). The noun kechash appears as deceptive (Is 30:9).

even the fish of the sea disappear.[a]

4 But let no one dispute;[b]
   let no one argue,
 for My case is against you priests.[A,B,c]

5 You will stumble by day;[d]
 the prophet will also stumble with you
   by night.
 And I will destroy your mother.[e]

6 My people are destroyed for lack
   of knowledge.[f]
 Because you have rejected knowledge,[g]
 I will reject you[h] from serving
   as My priest.
 Since you have forgotten the law
   of your God,[i]
 I will also forget your sons.

7 The more they multiplied,[j]
 the more they sinned against Me.
 I[C] will change their honor[D]
   into disgrace.[k]

8 They feed on the sin[E] of My people;[l]
 they have an appetite
   for their transgressions.[m]

9 The same judgment will happen
   to both people and priests.[n]
 I will punish them for their ways[o]
 and repay them for their deeds.

10 They will eat but not be satisfied;[p]
 they will be promiscuous[q]
   but not multiply.
 For they have abandoned their devotion
   to the LORD.[r]

11 Promiscuity,[s] wine, and new wine
   take away one's understanding.[t]

12 My people consult their wooden idols,[u]
 and their divining rods inform them.
 For a spirit of promiscuity
   leads them astray;[v]
 they act promiscuously[w]
 in disobedience to[F] their God.

13 They sacrifice on the mountaintops,[x]
 and they burn offerings on the hills,[y]
 and under oaks, poplars,
   and terebinths,[z]
 because their shade is pleasant.
 And so your daughters
   act promiscuously
 and your daughters-in-law
   commit adultery.

14 I will not punish your daughters
 when they act promiscuously
 or your daughters-in-law
 when they commit adultery,
 for the men themselves go off
   with prostitutes[aa]
 and make sacrifices
   with cult prostitutes.[ab]
 People without discernment
   are doomed.[ac]

Warnings for Israel and Judah

15 Israel, if you act promiscuously,
   don't let Judah become *guilty!
 Do not go to Gilgal[ad]
   or make a pilgrimage to Beth-aven,[G,ae]

Cross references

[a] 4:3 Gn 1:20-25
[b] 4:4 Ezk 3:26; Am 5:10,13
[c] Dt 17:12-13
[d] 4:5 Ezk 14:3; Hs 5:5
[e] Hs 2:2,5
[f] 4:6 Is 5:13
[g] Mal 2:7-8
[h] Zch 11:8-9, 15-17
[i] Hs 2:13; 8:14; 13:6
[j] 4:7 Hs 10:1; 13:6
[k] Hab 2:16
[l] 4:8 Hs 10:13
[m] Is 56:11; Mc 3:11
[n] 4:9 Is 24:2; Jr 5:31
[o] Hs 8:13; 9:9
[p] 4:10 Lv 26:26; Is 65:13; Mc 6:14
[q] Hs 7:4
[r] Hs 9:17
[s] 4:11 Hs 5:4
[t] Is 5:12; 28:7
[u] 4:12 Is 44:19; Jr 2:27
[v] Hs 5:4
[w] Hs 9:1
[x] 4:13 Jr 3:6
[y] Hs 2:13; 11:2
[z] Jr 2:20
[aa] 4:14 Hs 4:18; 7:4
[ab] Dt 23:17
[ac] Hs 5:4
[ad] 4:15 Hs 9:15; 12:1
[ae] 1Kg 12:28-29; Hs 5:8; 10:5,8

[A] 4:4 Text emended; MT reads *argue, and your people are like those contending with a priest*   [B] 4:4 Hb obscure   [C] 4:7 Alt Hb tradition, Syr, Tg read *They*   [D] 4:7 Ancient Jewish tradition reads *My honor*   [E] 4:8 Or *sin offerings*   [F] 4:12 Lit *promiscuously from under*   [G] 4:15 = House of Wickedness

---

forfeited their right to be called His people. These adulterous **inhabitants** have abandoned (1) **truth** or integrity, the quality of being reliable and genuine; (2) **faithful love** or kindness and mercy to friends and associates; and (3) the **knowledge of God**. They had ceased to care about knowing Him or the truth about Him (Rm 1:18-32). As a result they were violating the Ten Commandments (Hs 4:2) and suffering the consequences (v. 3).

4:4-7 The common people are identified as guilty, but especially guilty were the priests who were responsible for teaching the people. Leaders of God's people who shirk or violate that responsibility invite special punishment (Mal 2:1-9; Mt 18:6; Jms 3:1).

4:8 The term for **sin** can also mean "sin offering," which the priests were to eat (Lv 6:25-26). The priests were using Israel's sin and the sacrificial system for their own advantage.

4:10 The fertility religion that had infected apostate Israel, even the priesthood, was about prosperity, but Yahweh would see to it that the opposite results occurred. They would **not multiply**. More references to promiscuity occur in verses 10-15 and 18 than anywhere else in the book (10 of the 22 times in Hosea).

4:14 God's statement that He would **not punish your daugh-**

ters must be understood as a rhetorical way of saying that God placed heavier blame on the men who supported the vile practice of cult prostitution. All would suffer when God brought judgment against Israel.

4:15 This verse contains the first of three exhortations (cp. 5:1,8) that divide this section into three warnings. Although the warnings are mainly directed against Israel, Judah was also in danger of following Israel in apostasy and punishment (5:5,10,12-14). Although there was a Benjaminite city **Beth-aven** (Jos 18:12), Hosea used it as a derogatory term for Bethel, which meant "house of God" (Hs 5:8; 10:5; cp. "Aven" in 10:8; Am 1:5). Beth-aven meant "house of disaster, wickedness, nothingness, or idolatry." Another Hebrew word with the same consonants as ʾaven but different vowels meant "wealth, strength" (12:3,8). **Gilgal** and Bethel had become centers of Israelite apostate religion (Am 5:5). The name of God continued to be used, but its attachment to idolatry made its utterance not only hypocritical but blasphemous. The Hebrew verb ʾasham ("be guilty") occurs here for the first of five times in the book (Hs 5:15; 10:2; 13:1,16), more than in any other book except Leviticus (11 times). The related noun usually meaning "restitution offering" occurs an additional 46 times in the OT, mostly in Leviticus. "Guilty" is the legal condition of unpunished lawbreakers regardless

and do not swear an oath:
As the LORD lives![a]
16 For Israel is as obstinate
as a stubborn cow.[b]
Can the LORD now shepherd them
like a lamb in an open meadow?[c]
17 Ephraim is attached to idols;[d]
leave him alone![e]
18 When their drinking is over,
they turn to promiscuity.
Israel's leaders[A] fervently love disgrace.[B]
19 A wind with its wings will
carry them off,[C,f]
and they will be ashamed
of their sacrifices.

5 Hear this, priests![g]
Pay attention, house of Israel!
Listen, royal house!
For the judgment applies to you
because you have been a snare
at Mizpah[h]
and a net spread out on Tabor.
2 Rebels[i] are deeply involved
in slaughter;[j]
I will be a punishment for all of them.[B]
3 I know Ephraim,[k]
and Israel is not hidden from Me.
For now, Ephraim,[l]
you have acted promiscuously;
Israel is defiled.
4 Their actions do not allow them
to return to their God,[m]
for a spirit of promiscuity
is among them,[n]
and they do not know the LORD.[o]
5 Israel's arrogance testifies
against them.[D,p]
Both Israel and Ephraim stumble
because of their wickedness;[q]
even Judah will stumble with them.[r]
6 They go with their flocks and herds
to seek the LORD[s]
but do not find Him;[t]
He has withdrawn from them.[u]
7 They betrayed the LORD;[v]
indeed, they gave birth
to illegitimate children.[w]
Now the New Moon[x] will devour them
along with their fields.[y]

8 Blow the horn in Gibeah,[z]
the trumpet in Ramah;[aa]
raise the war cry in Beth-aven:[ab]
After you, Benjamin![ac]
9 Ephraim will become a desolation[ad]
on the day of punishment;[ae]
I announce what is certain
among the tribes of Israel.[af]
10 The princes of Judah are like those

[a] **4:15** Jr 5:2; 44:26
[b] **4:16** Ps 78:8
[c] Is 5:17; 7:25
[d] **4:17** Hs 13:2
[e] Ps 81:12; Hs 4:4
[f] **4:19** Hs 12:1; 13:5
[g] **5:1** Hs 4:1
[h] Hs 9:8
[i] **5:2** Hs 9:15
[j] Hs 4:2; 6:9
[k] **5:3** Hs 6:4; 7:1; Am 3:2; 5:12
[l] Hs 6:10
[m] **5:4** Hs 4:11
[n] Hs 4:12
[o] Hs 4:6,11,14
[p] **5:5** Hs 7:10
[q] Hs 4:5
[r] Ezk 23:31-35
[s] **5:6** Hs 8:13; Mc 6:6-7
[t] Is 1:15; Jr 14:12
[u] Ezk 8:6
[v] **5:7** Is 48:8; Hs 6:7
[w] Hs 2:4
[x] Hs 2:11
[y] Is 1:14
[z] **5:8** Hs 9:9; 10:9
[aa] Is 10:29; Jr 31:15
[ab] Hs 4:15
[ac] Jdg 5:14
[ad] **5:9** Is 28:1-4; Hs 9:11-17
[ae] Is 37:3
[af] Is 46:10; Zch 1:6

[A] **4:18** Lit *Her shields*; Ps 47:9; 89:18 [B] **4:18; 5:2** Hb obscure [C] **4:19** Lit *wind will bind it in its wings* [D] **5:5** Lit *against his face*

of their emotional state, although shame was the appropriate emotional response (Ezr 9:6).

4:17 This verse has the first of 37 references to **Ephraim** in Hosea, more than in any other book (185 times in the OT). The name was given to Joseph's second son, then to the tribe he fathered, then to the northern hill country where they lived. It was popularly derived from the Hebrew word *parah*, "be fruitful" (Gn 41:52), a verb used ironically in Hs 13:15. "Fruitful" Ephraim would no longer be fruitful because of their foolish pursuit of fruitless pagan fertility rites.

4:19 Because of Israel's adulterous idolatry, arrogance, and stubbornness, they were warned that God would blow them away as with a whirlwind, the first of three metaphors used in this section to make vivid the coming judgment. He would also eat away at them like rot or a moth (5:12) and tear them to pieces like a lion (5:14).

5:1-2 Verses 1-7 contain a second exhortation directed against the corrupt leaders. **House of Israel** probably refers to unofficial leaders of society (Jr 2:26). **Mizpah** and Mount **Tabor** are described as **a snare** and **a net** respectively because of the unauthorized sanctuary at Mizpah (Jr 41:4-6) and a high place on Mount Tabor, where false religion was practiced. The words translated **rebels are deeply involved in slaughter** stem from unusual Hebrew words. D. Garrett suggests that the text should perhaps be emended to read, "and a pit they have dug at Shittim" (see textual footnote at Jos 2:1).

5:3-4 Although God knew all about **Ephraim**, they did not **know** Him (4:1). Israel's many evil **actions** (cp. Hs 7:2; 9:15; Dt 28:20; Jdg 2:19; Neh 9:35; Jr 4:18) had so enslaved them to sin that they were unable to repent (Rm 6:16-20).

5:6 Although unable to repent (v. 4), Israel sought God's favor with **flocks and herds** (1Sm 15:14-15; 2Ch 18:2; Ps 50:7-15). Some people **seek the LORD** and do not find Him because they come with gifts and labor rather than a "broken and humbled heart" (Ps 51:17; see Is 1:10-15; Am 5:21-24).

5:7 Israel's leaders had produced a generation of **illegitimate children** who did not know God and were therefore "not My people." The **New Moon** refers to the monthly festival held when the moon first appeared. This signaled the beginning of each month, thus establishing the chronology for all the festivals according to the lunar calendar. It was accompanied by trumpets and special offerings of animals, grain, and wine (Nm 28:11-15; Ps 81:3). Rather than grateful celebrations of Yahweh's blessings, Israel had turned all the festivals into hypocritical, idolatrous drains on the economy (Is 1:13-14; Hs 2:11). In return, God would end the feasts with destruction (Am 8:10). The sense may be that with every "new moon" God would send another wave of judgments.

5:8 These cities were in Benjamin between Ephraim (the northern kingdom of Israel) and Judah. The battle alarm would be sounded because a battle would be fought there. The outcome would be desolation for Israel (v. 9) and divine fury for Judah (v. 10).

5:10 On the imagery of God's **fury** like **water**, see Is 8:6-10.

5:12-13 **Rot** and **decay** are striking similes for God to use of Himself. The term for "rot" can also mean "maggot" or

who move boundary markers;[a]
I will pour out My fury[b] on them
    like water.[c]
11 Ephraim is oppressed,
    crushed in judgment,[d]
for he is determined to follow
    what is worthless.[A]
12 So I am like rot to Ephraim[e]
and like decay to the house of Judah.
13 When Ephraim saw his sickness
and Judah his wound,
Ephraim went to Assyria[f]
and sent a delegation
    to the great king.[B,g]
But he cannot cure you or heal
    your wound.[h]
14 For I am like a lion to Ephraim[i]
and like a young lion to the house
    of Judah.
Yes, I will tear them to pieces
    and depart.[j]
I will carry them off,
and no one can rescue them.[k]
15 I will depart and return to My place
until they recognize their *guilt
    and seek My face;[l]
they will search for Me
    in their distress.[m]

A Call to Repentance

6 Come, let us return to the LORD.[n]
For He has torn us,[o]

Footnote/cross-reference column:

[a] 5:10 Dt 27:17
[b] Ezk 7:8
[c] Ps 32:6; 93:3-4
[d] 5:11 Hs 9:16
[e] 5:12 Ps 39:11;
Is 51:8
[f] 5:13 Hs 7:11;
8:9; 12:1
[g] Hs 10:6
[h] Hs 14:3
[i] 5:14 Ps 7:2; Hs
13:7; Am 3:4
[j] Ps 50:22
[k] Mc 5:8
[l] 5:15 Is 64:7-9;
Jr 3:13-14
[m] Ps 50:15,
78:34; Jr 2:27;
Hs 3:5
[n] 6:1 Jr 50:4-5
[o] Hs 5:14
[p] Hs 14:4
[q] Is 30:26
[r] 6:2 Ps 30:5
[s] Dt 32:39
[t] 6:3 Is 2:3;
Mc 4:2
[u] Ps 19:6; Mc 5:2
[v] Jl 2:23
[w] 6:4 Hs 7:1;
11:8
[x] Ps 78:34-37
[y] 6:5 1Sm 15:32-
33; Jr 1:10,18;
5:14
[z] 6:6 Hs 4:1
[aa] Mt 9:13; 12:7
[ab] 6:7 Hs 8:1
[ac] Hs 5:7
[ad] 6:8 Hs 12:11
[ae] Hs 4:2

---

and He will heal us;[p]
He has wounded us,
    and He will bind up our wounds.[q]
2 He will revive us after two days,[r]
and on the third day He will raise us up
so we can live in His presence.[s]
3 Let us strive to know the LORD.[t]
His appearance is as sure as the dawn.[u]
He will come to us like the rain,[v]
like the spring showers that water
    the land.

The LORD's First Lament

4 What am I going to do
    with you, Ephraim?[w]
What am I going to do with you, Judah?
Your loyalty is like the morning mist[x]
and like the early dew that vanishes.
5 This is why I have used the prophets
    to cut them down;[C,y]
I have killed them with the words
    of My mouth.
My judgment strikes like lightning.[D]
6 For I desire loyalty and not sacrifice,
the knowledge of God[z] rather than
    *burnt offerings.[aa]

7 But they, like Adam,[E] have violated
    the covenant;[ab]
there they have betrayed Me.[ac]
8 Gilead is a city of evildoers,[ad]
tracked with bloody footprints.[ae]

[A] 5:11 Or *follow a command*; Hb obscure   [B] 5:13 Or *to King Yareb*   [C] 6:5 Or *have cut down the prophets*   [D] 6:5 LXX, Syr, Tg; MT reads *Your judgments go out as light*   [E] 6:7 Or *they, as at Adam,* or *they, like men,*

"pus." It pictures a man whose festering wounds were divinely inflicted. Israel's efforts to heal these wounds through

'ashaq

Hebrew Pronunciation	[ah SHACK]
HCSB Translation	oppress, defraud, extort
Uses in Hosea	2
Uses in the OT	38
Focus passage	Hosea 5:11

Similar languages indicate the root involves acting with violence. *Ashaq* means *oppress* (Lv 19:13). It appears seven times with *gazal* ("rob"; Dt 28:29) and five with *ratsats* ("crush"; Dt 28:33). Monetarily oriented meanings are *defraud* (Lv 6:2), *extort* (Hs 12:7), *exploit* (Ezk 22:29), and *deprive* (Mc 2:2). People *wrong* others (1Sm 12:3). Rivers *rage* (Jb 40:23). Women are *ravished* (Is 23:12) and consciences *burdened* (Pr 28:17). Similar *'asaq* ("contend"; Gn 26:20) may be related. *Ashaq* occurs three times with related *'osheq* (15x) as *practice fraud/extortion* (Ezk 18:18; 22:29) and *what . . . he defrauded* (Lv 6:4). *'Osheq* denotes *oppression* (Is 30:12) but can imply *extortion* (Jr 22:17) or *exploitation* (Ezk 22:7). Nominal *'oshqah* and *'ashoq* appear respectively as *oppressed* (Is 38:14) and *oppressor* (Jr 22:3). *'Ashuqiym* (2x) signifies *(acts of) oppression* (Jb 35:9; Am 3:9). *Ma'ashaqqoth* (2x) suggests *extortion* (Is 33:15) and *oppressive* (Pr 28:16).

human means would be futile. This is the first of nine references to **Assyria** in Hosea.

5:15 My place continues the imagery of God as a lion carrying its prey to its den. This picture of God's departure is parallel to the message of verse 6.

6:1-3 This exhortation to repent is accompanied by the assurance that all God's punishments—even death—would be reversed. After a short time in exile, Israel would be resurrected. Hosea 6:2 may be the verse Paul had in mind in 1Co 15:4. The NT viewed as messianic fulfillment certain events in Israel's history which Jesus paralleled or completed (Hs 11:1).

6:4 The Lord was to Israel like a father whose heart was broken by a rebellious child (11:3).

6:6 Quoted by Jesus in Mt 9:13 and 12:7, this verse does not reject **sacrifice** but rather ritualism and worship that is not accompanied by faithfulness and love and is not based on the **knowledge of God** (4:1). This section describes a nation full of violence and immorality. The king and national leadership neglected the nation and devoted themselves to debauchery and striving for power. As a result, the nation was decaying around them and being assimilated and swallowed up by surrounding nations. A remedy for the crisis was sought everywhere but in the Lord.

6:7 A place called **Adam** is known from Jos 3:16, but no sin

9 Like raiders who wait in ambush
    for someone,[a]
  a band of priests murders on the road
    to Shechem.[b]
  They commit atrocities.[c]
10 I have seen something horrible[d]
    in the house of Israel:
  Ephraim's promiscuity is there;[e]
    Israel is defiled.
11 A harvest is also appointed
    for you, Judah.[f]

  When I[A] return My people
    from captivity,[g]

7 [1]when I heal Israel,[h]
  the sins of Ephraim[i] and the crimes
    of Samaria[j]
  will be exposed.
  For they practice fraud;[k]
  a thief breaks in;
  a raiding party pillages outside.[l]
2 But they never consider
    that I remember all their evil.[m]
  Now their sins are all around them;[n]
  they are right in front of My face.

Israel's Corruption

3 They please the king with their evil,[o]
    the princes with their lies.[p]
4 All of them commit adultery;[q]
  they are like an oven heated by a baker
  who stops stirring the fire
  from the kneading of the dough
    until it is leavened.

5 On the day of our king,
    the princes are sick with the heat
    of wine[r]—
  there is a conspiracy with traitors.[B]
6 For they—their hearts like an oven—
    draw him into their oven.
  Their anger smolders all night;
    in the morning it blazes
    like a flaming fire.
7 All of them are as hot as an oven,[s]
    and they consume their rulers.[t]
  All their kings fall;
    not one of them calls on Me.[C]

8 Ephraim has allowed himself
    to get mixed up with the nations.
  Ephraim is unturned bread
    baked on a griddle.
9 Foreigners consume his strength,[u]
    but he does not notice.[v]
  Even his hair is streaked with gray,
    but he does not notice.
10 Israel's arrogance testifies
    against them,[D,w]
  yet they do not return to •Yahweh
    their God,[x]
  and for all this, they do not seek Him.

11 So Ephraim has become like a silly,
    senseless dove;[y]
  they call to Egypt,[z] and they go
    to Assyria.[aa]
12 As they are going, I will spread My net
    over them;[ab]

a 6:9 Hs 7:1
b Jr 7:9-10;
  Hs 4:2
c Ezk 22:9; 23:27;
  Hs 2:10
d 6:10 Jr 5:30-
  31; 23:14
e Hs 5:3
f 6:11 Jr 51:33;
  Jl 3:13
g Zph 2:7
h 7:1 Ezk 24:13;
  Hs 6:4; 7:13;
  11:8
i Hs 5:3
j Hs 8:5-6;
  10:5,7; 13:16
k Hs 4:2
l Hs 6:9
m 7:2 Ps 25:7;
  Jr 14:10; 17:1;
  Am 8:7
n Jr 2:19; 4:18;
  Hs 4:9
o 7:3 Jr 28:1-4;
  Mc 7:3
p Hs 4:2; 11:12
q 7:4 Jr 9:2;
  23:10
r 7:5 Is 28:1,7-8
s 7:7 Ps 21:9
t Hs 13:10
u 7:9 Is 1:7
v Hs 4:6
w 7:10 Hs 5:5
x Hs 5:4
y 7:11 Hs
  4:6,11,14; 5:4
z Hs 8:13; 9:3,6
aa Hs 5:13; 8:9;
  12:1
ab 7:12 Ezk 12:13

A 6:11 Or you, Judah, when I   B 7:5 Lit wine—he stretches out his hand to scorners; Hb obscure   C 7:3-7 These vv. may refer to a king's assassination; Hb obscure.   D 7:10 Lit against his face

or **covenant** violation is known to have occurred there. The reference is probably to the first man. Although the term "covenant" is not used in Genesis 1–3, the relation between God and the first man is often described as covenantal. The covenant is sometimes called the "covenant of works," in which Adam's divinely bestowed life would be maintained in return for obedience. The significance of Adam's sin for the human race is clarified in Rm 5:15-17. The word **there** is either a wordplay alluding to idolatry being practiced at or near Adam or is a vague reference to places where such betrayal was occurring.

6:11 Judgment approaching **Judah** is here described as a coming **harvest** because the people were growing ripe with wickedness (Jr 51:33; Jl 3:13; Rv 14:14-16).

7:3-7 Several parallels unite these verses with a chiastic (a-b-b-a) structure. The king cared nothing for God but loved to hear of evil, deceptive schemes, for which reason he would **fall. All of them** in the government burned with passions like a baker's **oven**. The king's conspiratorial counselors lured him into drunkenness, passion, and death. **Their anger smolders** may also be rendered "their baker sleeps." The **baker** may be an image of the king whose debauchery allowed evil to flourish.

7:8-10 Ephraim's leaders were negligent in allowing the people to become like the other nations. They were like careless cooks who failed to turn the **bread**, allowing it to burn on one side. Yet they did not even **notice** what was hap-

pashat

Hebrew word	[pah SHAT]
HCSB Translation	strip, raid, pillage, rush
Uses in Hosea	2
Uses in the OT	43
Focus passage	Hosea 7:1

This root in cognate languages usually means "spread/stretch out" but in Akkadian denotes "extirpate, eradicate." *Pashat* involves *taking off* (Ezk 44:19), *removing* (1Sm 19:24), or *stripping off* (Ezk 26:16) one's own clothes. One *strips oneself* (Is 32:11). *Pashat* also means *raid* (1Sm 23:27) or *make a raid* (Jb 1:17). It indicates the action of *charging* or *rushing (forward)* that is involved in a raid (Jdg 9:33,44). Locusts *strip* the land or *shed* their skin (Nah 3:16). Gangs *pillage* (Hs 7:1). Intensive verbs denote *stripping* or *plundering* the dead (1Sm 31:8; 2Sm 23:10). Causative verbs concern *stripping off* (Gn 37:23) or *removing* (Nm 20:26) the clothes from another person. Somebody *strips* another (Hs 2:3) or *strips* him of honor (Jb 19:9). People *strip* skin from people (Mc 3:3) and *skin* animals (Lv 1:6). The reflexive-passive also describes *removing* one's own clothes (1Sm 18:4)

I will bring them down like birds
  of the sky.
I will discipline them in accordance
with the news that reaches[A]
  their assembly.

The Lord's Second Lament

13 Woe to them,[a] for they fled from Me;[b]
destruction to them, for they rebelled
  against Me!
Though I want to redeem them,[c]
they speak lies against Me.

14 They do not cry to Me
  from their hearts;
rather, they wail on their beds.
They slash themselves[B,d] for grain
  and new wine;[e]
they turn away from Me.

15 I trained and strengthened their arms,[f]
but they plot evil against Me.[g]

16 They turn, but not to what is above;[C]
they are like a faulty bow.[h]
Their leaders will fall by the sword
because of the cursing of their tongue.[i]
They will be ridiculed for this
  in the land of Egypt.[j]

Israel's False Hopes

8 Put the horn to your mouth![k]
One like an eagle comes
against the house of the Lord,[l]
because they transgress My covenant[m]

and rebel against My law.[n]

2 Israel cries out to Me,[o]
"My God, we know You!"

3 Israel has rejected what is good;[p]
an enemy will pursue him.

4 They have installed kings,[q]
but not through Me.
They have appointed leaders,
but without My approval.
They make their silver and gold[r]
into idols for themselves
for their own destruction.[D]

5 Your calf-idol[E,s] is rejected, Samaria.[t]
My anger burns against them.
How long will they be incapable
  of innocence?[u]

6 For this thing is from Israel—
a craftsman made it,[v] and it is not God.
The calf of Samaria will be smashed
  to bits!

7 Indeed, they sow the wind[w]
and reap the whirlwind.[x]
There is no standing grain;
what sprouts fails to yield flour.[y]
Even if they did,
foreigners would swallow it up.

8 Israel is swallowed up![z]
Now they are among the nations
like discarded pottery.[aa]

9 For they have gone up to Assyria[ab]

a 7:13 Hs 9:12
b Jr 14:10; Hs 9:17
c Jr 51:9; Hs 7:1; Mt 23:37
d 7:14 1Kg 18:28
e Am 2:8
f 7:15 Hs 11:3
g Nah 1:9
h 7:16 Ps 78:57
i Ps 12:3-4; 17:10; Dn 7:25; Mal 3:13-14
j Ezk 23:32
k 8:1 Hs 5:8
l Dt 28:49
m Hs 6:7
n Hs 4:6; 8:12
o 8:2 Hs 7:14
p 8:3 Hs 3:5
q 8:4 Hs 13:10-11
r Hs 2:8; 13:1-2
s 8:5 Hs 10:5; 13:2
t 1Kg 12:28-29; Hs 7:1
u Ps 19:13; Jr 13:27
v 8:6 Hs 13:2
w 8:7 Hs 10:13
x Is 66:15; Nah 1:3
y Hs 2:9
z 8:8 Jr 51:34
aa Jr 25:34; Hs 13:15
ab 8:9 Hs 7:11

A 7:12 Lit news to   B 7:14 Some Hb mss, LXX; other Hb mss read They stay   C 7:16 Some emend to turn to what is useless   D 8:4 Lit themselves that it might be cut off   E 8:5 Lit calf

---

pening. For similar uses of **return** or "turn" and **seek**, see 3:5; 5:15; 2Ch 7:14; Is 9:13; Dn 9:3; Zph 1:6.

7:11-12 Israel was like a bird that had forgotten its way home. The **news that reaches their assembly** was probably news that their efforts to find security in foreign governments had failed.

7:13 The section that begins in 6:1 with a call to return to Yahweh and be healed ends here with a lament that Israel had done just the opposite. **Woe to them** is a declaration of coming judgment (9:12; Is 3:9; Jr 50:27; Jd 11). The term for **fled** is often used of birds (Is 16:2; Jr 4:25) and can also refer to restless wandering (Pr 27:8). Israel could flee from God in rebellion, but they could not escape **destruction**. The phrase **I want to redeem** can also be translated "I redeemed," referring to the exodus (Dt 7:8; 9:26; Mc 6:4). God's deliverance should cause His people to declare the truth about Him.

7:14 Israel's wailing and slashing probably involved pagan rituals (1Kg 18:28; Ezk 8:14).

7:15 Here is the second of two contrasts between "I" and "they" in the passage (cp. v. 13). God had **trained** Israel to be a mighty nation, but they had turned their might **against** Him.

7:16 Israel's **leaders** were as helpful as a faulty bow that could not send arrows to hit the mark (Ps 78:57). Israel's **cursing** may be their bitter words against God or the prophets (2Ch 36:16). The consequent ridicule may be what they

would experience when they sought help from Egypt (Hs 7:11) or when they were destroyed (v. 13).

8:1-3 God speaks in verses 1-14. An alarm was to sound because God was sending an army to swoop down on Israel like an **eagle** on its prey (Dt 28:49; Lm 4:19; Hab 1:8). Israel was treating their covenant with God (**we know You**) as if it were a blank check for sin. **House of the Lord** may refer to Israel (9:8) rather than the temple.

8:4-6 Samaria, Israel's capital, refers here to the entire northern kingdom (Is 10:10-11). Israel had arrogantly sought success and security through idolatry, military might, and political power ("two crimes" in the summary passage in Hs 10:10 probably refers to the military and politics). All their efforts would produce just the opposite of what they desired.

8:7 Idols were worshiped because they were thought to grant fertility. But the "planting" of idolatry would be like planting **wind**, and the harvest would be nothing but a **whirlwind**— a storm representing divine judgment (Pr 1:27; 10:25; Is 17:13; 29:6; 66:15; Nah 1:3). Whatever sprouted would be blown away. Foreigners would take everything the people produced. Israel's idols, temples, and fortresses would be destroyed, and military alliances would drain them dry, enslave them, and carry them away. For their wickedness and rebellion in trusting in the fertility cult of Baal, Yahweh would reject them and make the land barren.

like a wild donkey going off on its own.
Ephraim has paid for love.[a]

10 Even though they hire lovers
  among the nations,
  I will now round them up,
  and they will begin to decrease
  in number[b]
  under the burden of the king
  and leaders.[c]

11 When Ephraim multiplied his altars
  for sin,[d]
  they became his altars for sinning.

12 Though I were to write out for him
  ten thousand points of My instruction,[e]
  they would be[A] regarded
  as something strange.

13 Though they offer sacrificial gifts[B,f]
  and eat the flesh,[g]
  the LORD does not accept them.
  Now He will remember their •guilt[h]
  and punish their sins;[i]
  they will return to Egypt.[j]

14 Israel has forgotten his Maker[k]
  and built palaces;[l]
  Judah has also multiplied
  fortified cities.
  I will send fire on their cities,[m]
  and it will consume their citadels.

The Coming Exile

9 Israel, do not rejoice jubilantly
  as the nations do,[n]
  for you have acted promiscuously,[o]
  leaving your God.
  You have loved the wages
  of a prostitute
  on every grain-threshing floor.[p]

2 Threshing floor and wine vat will not
  sustain them,[q]
  and the new wine will fail them.

3 They will not stay in the land
  of the LORD.
  Instead, Ephraim will return
  to Egypt,[r]
  and they will eat •unclean food[s]
  in Assyria.[t]

4 They will not pour out
  their wine offerings to the LORD,[u]
  and their sacrifices will not please Him.
  Their food will be like the bread
  of mourners;
  all who eat it become defiled.[v]
  For their bread will be
  for their appetites alone;
  it will not enter the house of the LORD.

5 What will you do on a festival day,[w]
  on the day of the LORD's feast?[x]

6 For even if they flee from devastation,
  Egypt will gather them, and Memphis
  will bury them.[y]
  Thistles will take possession
  of their precious silver;
  thorns will invade their tents.[z]

7 The days of punishment have come;[aa]
  the days of retribution have come.[ab]
  Let Israel recognize it!
  The prophet is a fool,[ac]
  and the inspired man is insane,[ad]
  because of the magnitude
  of your •guilt and hostility.[ae]

8 Ephraim's watchman is with my God.
  The prophet encounters a fowler's snare
  on all his ways.[af]
  Hostility is in the house of his God!

9 They have deeply
  corrupted themselves[ag]
  as in the days of Gibeah.[ah]
  He will remember their guilt;
  He will punish their sins.[ai]

---

a 8:9 Ezk 16:33
b 8:10 Jr 42:2
c Is 10:8
d 8:11 Hs 10:1; 12:11
e 8:12 Hs 4:6
f 8:13 Hs 5:6; 9:4
g Jr 6:20; 7:21
h Hs 7:2; Lk 12:2; 1Co 4:5
i Hs 4:9; 9:7
j Hs 9:3,6
k 8:14 Is 2:13; 4:6; 13:6
l Is 9:9-10
m Jr 17:27
n 9:1 Is 22:12-13; Hs 10:5
o Hs 4:12
p Hs 7:14
q 9:2 Hs 2:9
r 9:3 Hs 7:16; 8:13
s Ezk 4:13
t Hs 11:7
u 9:4 Nm 15:5,7,10
v Nm 19:11-14; Dt 26:12-14; Jr 16:5-7
w 9:5 Is 10:3; Jr 5:31
x Hs 2:11; Jl 1:13
y 9:6 Is 19:13; Jr 2:16; 44:1; 46:14,19; Ezk 30:13,16
z Is 5:6; 7:23; Hs 10:8
aa 9:7 Is 10:3; Jr 10:15; Mc 7:4
ab Is 34:8; Jr 16:18; 25:14
ac Lm 2:14
ad Is 44:25
ae Ezk 14:9-10
af 9:8 Pr 29:5-6; Hs 5:1
ag 9:9 Is 31:6
ah Jdg 19–21; Hs 5:8; 10:9
ai Hs 7:2; 8:13

A 8:12 Or *Though I wrote out . . . instruction, they are*   B 8:13 Hb obscure

---

8:11-12 Israel built altars to cleanse them from **sin** (Lv 4:35), but the altars only increased Israel's sinning, perhaps by giving them a false sense of security. Their hypocritical sacrifices only added to their sin (Is 1:14; Jr 7:11; Am 5:21; Mk 11:17). Having God's written **instruction** likewise did them no good because they disregarded it as **something strange** and adopted Baal worship as their native religion.

8:13 The first line of this verse is difficult. The literal rendering is something like "as for My sacrifices of *havhav,* they sacrifice flesh." The Hebrew word *havhav* occurs only here and seems to refer to a type of offering, perhaps "roasted" or "choice." **Return to Egypt** is probably not literal but indicates the people would have to start over in foreign slavery (9:3). The northern kingdom fell to Assyria in 722 B.C. (2Kg 18:9-12), but Hosea did not neglect Judah, which was to suffer invasion by the Assyrians in 701 B.C. (2Kg 18:13).

9:1-3 Hosea speaks in verses 1-9. Israel was seeking prosperity by serving pagan fertility gods as the **nations** did, just as a woman would seek **the wages of a prostitute.** They could not **rejoice jubilantly** at "the LORD's feast" (v. 5), however, because Yahweh had withheld the harvest, causing deprivation that would increase during Israel's exile (v. 3).

9:4-6 Israel's failed harvest would leave the people with barely enough to eat, with nothing for **offerings** and **sacrifices.** The **bread of mourners** was food defiled by association with death. It could not be offered to God. Israel would seek refuge from **devastation** in Egypt, but they would die there outside their land.

9:7-9 God had sent prophets to warn the people, but their **guilt** and **hostility** were such that they considered God's **inspired** messengers to be **insane** fools. Nevertheless, God was with them. **Watchman** is a common biblical image for prophets (Jr 6:17; Ezk 3:17; 33:2). The **fowler's snare** may

Ephraim Bereaved of Offspring

10 I discovered Israel
　　like grapes in the wilderness.[a]
　I saw your fathers
　　like the first fruit of the fig tree
　　　in its first season.[b]
　But they went to Baal-peor,[c]
　consecrated themselves to Shame,[A,d]
　and became detestable,[e]
　　like the thing they loved.

11 Ephraim's glory will fly away
　　like a bird:[f]
　no birth, no gestation,
　　no conception.[g]

12 Even if they raise children,
　I will bereave them of each one.
　Yes, woe to them when I depart
　　from them![h]

13 I have seen Ephraim like Tyre,[i]
　planted in a meadow,
　so Ephraim will bring out his children
　to the executioner.

14 Give them, LORD—
　What should You give?
　Give them a womb that miscarries
　and breasts that are dry![j]

15 All their evil appears at Gilgal,[k]
　for there I came to hate them.
　I will drive them from My house

because of their evil, wicked actions.[l]
I will no longer love them;
　all their leaders are rebellious.[m]

16 Ephraim[n] is struck down;
　their roots are withered;
　they cannot bear fruit.[o]
　Even if they bear children,
　I will kill the precious offspring
　　of their wombs.[p]

17 My God will reject them
　because they have not listened to Him;[q]
　they will become wanderers
　　among the nations.[r]

The Vine and the Calf

10 Israel is a lush[B] vine;[s]
　　it yields fruit for itself.
　The more his fruit increased,
　the more he increased the altars.[t]
　The better his land produced,
　the better they made the sacred pillars.[u]

2 Their hearts are devious;[C,v]
　now they must bear their •guilt.[w]
　The LORD will break down their altars[x]
　and demolish their sacred pillars.

3 In fact, they are now saying,
　"We have no king!
　For we do not •fear the LORD.[y]
　What can a king do for us?"

4 They speak mere words,

Cross-references

a9:10 Mc 7:1
bJr 24:2
cNm 25:1-9
dJr 11:13; Hs 4:18
eEzk 20:8
f9:11 Hs 4:7; 10:4
gHs 4:10
h9:12 Hs 7:13
i9:13 Ezk 27:3-4
j9:14 Gn 49:25
k9:15 Hs 4:15; 12:11
lHs 4:9; 7:2; 12:2
mHs 5:2
n9:16 Hs 5:11
oHs 8:7
pEzk 24:21
q9:17 Hs 4:10
rHs 7:13
s10:1 Is 5:1-7; Ezk 15:1-6
t10:1 Hs 8:11; 12:11
u1Kg 14:23; Hs 3:4
v10:2 1Kg 18:21; Zph 1:5
wHs 13:16
xMc 5:13
y10:3 Ps 12:4; Is 5:19

A9:10 = Baal　B10:1 Or *ravaged*　C10:2 Or *divided*

be what the prophet was to the **ways** of foolish Israel (Is 8:14; 2Co 2:16). On **the days of Gibeah**, see note at 10:9.

9:10 God speaks in verses 10-17. Israel initially brought God as much pleasure as **grapes** found in the **wilderness** or the **first fruit of the fig tree**, but that changed with the incident of pagan sexuality at **Baal-peor** (Nm 25:1-9; Ps 106:28-30) where the people tried to ensure fertility by worshiping Baal, here referred to as **Shame**. The point is that Israel was now repeating its foolish behavior.

9:11-12 **Ephraim's glory** was the Lord, whose departure would end their fertility and cause them **woe**.

9:13 God had placed both Ephraim and Tyre in surroundings in which they should have flourished (**meadow** is figurative; Ezk 17:5-8), but both had turned to Baal worship and practiced child sacrifice. Both Tyre and Samaria were besieged by the Assyrian king Shalmaneser V. Both cities fell to Sargon II of Assyria in 722 B.C.

9:15-17 Just as verses 10-14 begin with an allusion to Baal-peor, these verses begin with an allusion to **Gilgal** (cp. 4:15; 12:11), a town so full of evil that God had rejected them (**hate** in v. 15 = **reject** in v. 17).

10:1-4 Hosea speaks in verses 1-8. Although once a **lush vine** (cp. Is 5; Jn 15), Israel only yielded **fruit for itself**. They had turned the Lord's blessings into gifts for the calf idols of Baal. The word rendered "lush" more often means "ravaging" (Nah 2:2), which it may mean here. Rather than producing fruit for harvest, they were **devious** and acted like **poisonous weeds** (cp. Dt 32:32; 2Kg 4:39; Jr 2:21). They recognized no external authority (**no king**), but pretended to

Canaanite altar (10:2) at Tel Hazor in Galilee

taking false oaths
　　while making covenants.[a]
So lawsuits break out
like poisonous weeds in the furrows
　　of a field.[b]

5　The residents of Samaria[c]
　　will have anxiety
over the calf[d] of Beth-aven.[e]
Indeed, its idolatrous priests rejoiced
　　over it;
the people will mourn over it,
over its glory.[f]
It will certainly depart from them.
6　The calf itself will be taken to Assyria[g]
as an offering to the great king.[A,h]
Ephraim will experience shame;[i]
Israel will be ashamed of its counsel.[j]
7　Samaria's king will disappear[B,k]
like foam[C] on the surface of the water.
8　The •high places[l] of Aven,
　　the sin of Israel,[m]
will be destroyed;
thorns and thistles will grow
　　over their altars.[n]
They will say to the mountains,[o]
　　"Cover us!"
and to the hills, "Fall on us!"[p]

Israel's Defeat because of Sin

9　Israel, you have sinned
since the days of Gibeah;[q]
they have taken their stand there.
Will not war against the unjust
overtake them in Gibeah?
10　I will discipline[r] them at My discretion;[s]

---

nations will be gathered against them
to put them in bondage[D]
for their two crimes.[t]

11　Ephraim is a well-trained calf[u]
　　that loves to thresh,
but I will place a yoke on[E] her
　　fine neck.[v]
I will harness Ephraim;[w]
Judah will plow;
Jacob will do the final plowing.
12　Sow righteousness for yourselves[x]
　　and reap faithful love;
break up your unplowed ground.[y]
It is time to seek the LORD[z]
until He comes[aa]
　　and sends righteousness
on you like the rain.[ab]

13　You have plowed wickedness
　　and reaped injustice;[ac]
you have eaten the fruit of lies.[ad]
Because you have trusted
　　in your own way[F]
and in your large number of soldiers,[ae]
14　the roar of battle will rise
　　against your people,
and all your fortifications
　　will be demolished[af]
in a day of war,
like Shalman's destruction
　　of Beth-arbel.
Mothers will be dashed to pieces
along with their children.[ag]
15　So it will be done to you, Bethel,[ah]
because of your extreme evil.

Cross references

[a] 10:4 Ezk 17:13-19; Hs 4:2
[b] Dt 31:16-17; 2Kg 17:3-4
[c] 10:5 Hs 7:1
[d] Hs 8:5-6
[e] Hs 4:15; 5:8
[f] Hs 9:11
[g] 10:6 Hs 11:5
[h] Hs 5:13
[i] Hs 4:7
[j] Is 30:3; Jr 7:24
[k] 10:7 Hs 13:11
[l] 10:8 Dt 12:2; Hs 4:13
[m] 1Kg 12:28-30; 13:34
[n] Is 32:13; Hs 9:6
[o] Lk 23:30; Rv 6:16
[p] Rv 6:16
[q] 10:9 Hs 5:8; 9:9
[r] 10:10 Hs 4:9
[s] Ezk 5:13
[t] Jdg 19-21; 1Kg 12:28-30
[u] 10:11 Jr 5:11; Hs 4:16
[v] Jr 28:14
[w] Ps 66:12
[x] 10:12 Pr 11:18
[y] Jr 4:3
[z] Hs 4:1; 12:6
[aa] Hs 6:3
[ab] Is 44:3; 45:8
[ac] 10:13 Jb 4:8; Gl 6:7
[ad] Hs 4:2; 7:3; 11:12
[ae] Ps 33:16
[af] 10:14 Is 17:3
[ag] Hs 13:16
[ah] 10:15 Hs 4:15; 10:5

---

worship Yahweh with **false oaths**. **Lawsuits** can also be rendered "justice," the fruit God was looking for.

10:5 Will have anxiety indicates that the **residents of Samaria** feared the **calf of Beth-aven**. This refers to the calf god worshiped at Bethel (see note at 4:15). The mourning (possibly over the mythological "death" of the god in the dry season) and rejoicing (possibly over his rising again) were likely part of the fertility worship. **Depart** could also be "go into exile" and is explained by verse 6.

10:6 For an account of Israel's troubles with **Assyria**, see 2Kg 15:19-20,29; 17:3-6.

10:8 When the **high places** were destroyed, the people would cry out to be buried by the very places of their idolatry (Dt 12:2; Lk 23:30).

10:9 God speaks in verses 9-15. Allusions to **Gibeah** in 9:9 and 10:9 (see also 5:8) recall the civil war occasioned by a Levite's concubine being raped, murdered, and cut into pieces (Jdg 19-21). Like Samaria, Gibeah was a hill with a fortress; it served as Saul's capital during his kingship but was later deserted. So it represents both depravity and militarism and may have figuratively referred to Samaria.

10:10 On the **two crimes**, see note at 8:4-6.

10:11 Calves were sometimes allowed to walk atop fresh grain stalks that had been laid out on the ground in order to separate the husks from the kernels (Mc 4:13). Little effort was involved, and the calves could eat some of the grain (Dt 25:4; 1Co 9:9; 1Tm 5:18). Israel would cease to be like the calf and would have to plow with the yoke of discipline.

10:12-13 The exhortations to **sow . . . reap**, and **seek** are essentially identical in meaning. Israel was to seek **righteousness . . . faithful love**, and **the LORD**. This recalls the threefold charge against Israel in 4:1 and is the summary of a life that pleases God (2:19; Ps 33:5; 36:10; 89:14; 103:17; Pr 21:21; Jr 9:24). But Israel had sought **wickedness . . . injustice**, and **the fruit of lies**. The latter is probably the "false fruit" of idolatry and military power, which looks good (Gn 3:6) but is unsatisfying and poisonous (Hs 10:4). **Sends . . . like the rain** renders the Hebrew verb yarah ("to rain, water") also found in 6:3 and related to the noun for the "early rains" that fell in Palestine in the fall.

10:14-15 The identities of Shalman and **Beth-arbel** are uncertain, but Shalman may refer to the Assyrian king Shal-

At dawn the king of Israel will be
  totally destroyed.

The Lord's Love for Israel

11 When Israel was a child, I loved him,[a]
     and out of Egypt I called My son.[b]
2 The more they[A] called them,[B,c]
     the more they[B] departed from Me.[C]
   They kept sacrificing to the *Baals[d]
     and burning offerings to idols.[e]
3 It was I who taught Ephraim to walk,[f]
     taking them[D] in My arms,[g]
   but they never knew
     that I healed them.[h]
4 I led them with human cords,
     with ropes of love.[i]
   To them I was like one
     who eases the yoke from their jaws;[j]
   I bent down to give them food.[k]
5 Israel will not return to the land
     of Egypt
   and Assyria will be his king,[l]
   because they refused to repent.[m]
6 A sword will whirl through his cities;[n]
   it will destroy and devour the bars
     of his gates,[E,o]

because of their schemes.[p]
7 My people are bent on turning
     from Me.[q]
  Though they call to Him on high,
  He will not exalt them at all.

8 How can I give you up, Ephraim?[r]
  How can I surrender you, Israel?
  How can I make you like Admah?[s]
  How can I treat you like Zeboiim?[t]
  I have had a change of heart;
  My compassion is stirred!
9 I will not vent the full fury
     of My anger;[u]
  I will not turn back
     to destroy Ephraim.[v]
  For I am God and not man,
  the Holy One among you;[w]
  I will not come in rage.[F]
10 They will follow the Lord;[x]
  He will roar like a lion.[y]
  When He roars,
  His children will come trembling
     from the west.[z]

a11:1 Dt 4:37; 7:6-8; 10:14-15; Ps 78:68; Is 41:8; Am 3:2; Mal 1:2 bEx 4:22-23; Dt 32:5-6,18-20; Ps 103:13; Jr 3:19; Hs 1:10; Mt 2:15 c11:2 2Kg 17:13-15 dHs 2:13; 4:13 eIs 65:7; Jr 18:15 f11:3 Hs 7:15 gDt 1:31; 32:10-11 hEx 15:26 i11:4 Jr 31:2-3 jHs 10:11 kEx 16:32 l11:5 Hs 7:16; 8:13; 9:3; 10:6 mHs 7:16 n11:6 Hs 13:16 oLm 2:9 pHs 4:16-17 q11:7 Jr 8:5 r11:8 Hs 6:4; 7:1 sGn 14:8; Dt 29:23 tGn 14:2; 19:1-29; Dt 29:23 u11:9 Dt 13:17 vJr 26:3; 30:11 wIs 5:24; 12:6; 41:14,16 x11:10 Hs 3:5; 6:1-3 yIs 31:4; Jl 3:16; Am 1:2 zIs 66:2-5

A11:2 Perhaps the prophets   B11:2 = Israel   C11:2 LXX; MT reads them   D11:3 LXX, Syr, Vg; MT reads him   E11:6 Or devour his empty talkers, or devour his limbs; Hb obscure   F11:9 Or come into any city; Hb obscure

maneser. Hosea's hearers were apparently familiar with the incident. **At dawn** would be when the battle started.

11:1-4 In these verses the Lord alternates between "I did this" and "but Israel did that."

11:1 A. Richardson notes that Hosea 11 comes close to saying that God *is* love, just as the NT says (1Jn 4:7-8). **I loved him** speaks of Yahweh's drawing Israel into His affectionate heart and of His faithfulness to His covenant with the patriarchs in redeeming Israel and choosing them for a covenant relationship (Dt 7:7-8). As a loving Father (Ex 4:22; Mal 2:10) God had brought (where "brought" is a strong use of the word "call"; cp. Ex 2:7; Is 41:4; Am 5:8) Israel to Himself and to a destiny. But now He grieved as a father abandoned by his son (Hs 6:4). Like 6:2, 11:1 is understood in the NT to have messianic significance in that Jesus, God's Son like Israel, was also brought out of Egypt in the context of hatred (Mt 2:15; cp. Ex 4:22). Jesus came as Israel's representative to fulfill the righteousness that the people lacked (Mt 3:15). Whereas Israel was freed from Egypt but became slaves to sin, Jesus followed through in righteousness so that He could die as their substitutionary atoning sacrifice.

11:2-3 The expression **the more . . . the more** occurs also in 4:7 and 10:1, speaking of Israel's sin increasing as God's blessing increased. The Hebrew of 11:2 begins literally "They called to them; thus they went from them." The first "they" may refer to God's prophets, but this seems doubtful since the prophets have not previously been introduced in the current context. The LXX reading may be original, and it seems to make sense: "As I called to them, so they went from My presence." The second line of verse 3 may be Hosea's parenthetic comment: "He took them in His arms." Israel's not knowing their own God, not recognizing Him

at work in their lives, and not praising His faithfulness but instead attributing the effects of His grace to other causes, is a major theme in Hosea, where the Hebrew verb *yada'* ("know") occurs 16 times. Reference to God healing Israel is also found in 5:13; 6:1; 7:1; 14:4.

11:5-7 In these verses the Lord announces the penalty for Israel's ingratitude. Israel would be delivered to Assyria, who would oppress them as Egypt had done (7:16; 10:6). Returning to Egypt is mentioned in 8:13; 9:3,6, so the first line here should probably be understood as a rhetorical question, "Will he not return?"

11:8-11 Yahweh refused to annihilate Israel but promised a new exodus for a believing remnant. T. McComiskey declared, "The drastic change of emotion" between verses 5-7 and verses 8-11 "is one of the most significant aspects of Hosea's prophetic message . . . We see the grace of God here as we have not yet seen it in the whole prophecy."

11:8-9 I **have had a change of heart** is literally "My heart has turned upon Me" (Ex 14:5). Unlike man, God's anger and compassion may not be manipulated but are subject only to His infinite wisdom, His holy intentions, and His perfect will. The point of God's manner of speaking here is that nothing stands in the way of the deserved abandonment and destruction of Israel but God's gracious compassion. Rather than a change of heart, what may be in view here is a broken heart, as the verb is used in Lm 1:20.

11:10 Whereas the Lord is like a **lion** as Israel's fierce predator in 5:14 and 13:7, here the comparison is a positive one as the divine Lion is Israel's champion restoring them to the land. The **trembling** signifies submissive excitement at hearing the Lord's voice (Jb 37:1-4).

11:11 The phrase **this is the Lord's declaration** concludes

11 They will be roused like birds
　　from Egypt
　and like doves[a] from the land
　　of Assyria.[b]
　Then I will settle them in their homes.[c]
　　This is the LORD's declaration.

12A Ephraim surrounds me with lies,[d]
　the house of Israel, with deceit.
　Judah still wanders with God
　and is faithful to the holy ones.[B,C]

God's Case against Jacob's Heirs

12 Ephraim chases[D] the wind[e]
　and pursues the east wind.[f]
　He continually multiplies lies
　　and violence.
　He makes a covenant with Assyria,[g]
　and olive oil is carried to Egypt.[h]

2 The LORD also has a dispute with Judah.
　He is about to punish Jacob
　　according to his ways;[i]
　He will repay him based on his actions.
3 In the womb he grasped
　　his brother's heel,[j]
　and as an adult he wrestled with God.[k]
4 Jacob struggled with the Angel
　　and prevailed;
　he wept and sought His favor.[l]
　He found him[E] at Bethel,[m]
　and there He spoke with him.[F,n]
5 ·Yahweh is the God of ·Hosts;
　Yahweh is His name.[o]
6 But you must return to your God.[p]
　Maintain love and justice,[q]
　and always put your hope in God.[r]

7 A merchant loves to extort[s]
　with dishonest scales in his hands.[t]

8 But Ephraim says:
　"How rich I have become;[u]
　I made it all myself.
　In all my earnings,
　no one can find any crime in me[v]
　that I can be punished for!"[G]

Judgment on Apostate Israel

9 I have been Yahweh your God
　ever since[H] the land of Egypt.[w]
　I will make you live in tents again,[x]
　as in the festival days.
10 I spoke through the prophets[y]
　and granted many visions;
　I gave parables
　　through the prophets.[z]
11 Since Gilead is full of evil,[aa]
　they will certainly come to nothing.
　They sacrifice bulls in Gilgal;[ab]
　even their altars will be like heaps
　　of rocks[ac]
　on the furrows of a field.

Further Indictment of Jacob's Heirs

12 Jacob fled to the land of Aram.[ad]
　Israel worked to earn a wife;[ae]
　he tended flocks for a wife.[af]
13 The LORD brought Israel from Egypt
　　by a prophet,[ag]
　and Israel was tended by a prophet.

14 Ephraim has provoked
　　bitter anger,[ah]
　so his Lord will leave his bloodguilt
　　on him[ai]
　and repay him for his contempt.[aj]

13 When Ephraim spoke,[ak]
　　there was trembling;
　he was exalted in Israel.[al]

[a]11:11 Is 60:8; Hs 7:11
[b]Is 11:11
[c]Ezk 34:27-28
[d]11:12 Hs 4:2; 7:3
[e]12:1 Jr 22:22; Hs 4:19
[f]Gn 41:6; Ezk 17:10
[g]Hs 5:13; 7:11; 8:9
[h]2Kg 17:4
[i]12:2 Hs 4:9; 7:2
[j]12:3 Gn 25:26; 27:36
[k]Gn 32:24-28
[l]12:4 Gn 32:26
[m]Gn 28:13-15; 35:10-15
[n]Gn 28:10-22; 35:1-14
[o]12:5 Ex 3:15
[p]12:6 Hs 6:1-3; 10:12
[q]Hs 6:6
[r]Mc 7:7
[s]12:7 Hs 7:14
[t]Pr 11:1; Am 8:5; Mc 6:11
[u]12:8 Ps 62:10; Hs 13:6
[v]Hs 4:8; 14:1; Am 3:15; 6:4-6
[w]12:9 Hs 11:1; 13:3
[x]Lv 23:42
[y]12:10 Jr 7:25
[z]Ezk 17:2; 20:49
[aa]12:11 Hs 6:8
[ab]Hs 4:15; 9:15
[ac]Hs 8:11; 10:1-2
[ad]12:12 Gn 28:5
[ae]Gn 29:20
[af]Gn 29:1-20
[ag]12:13 Ex 14:19-22; Is 63:11-14
[ah]12:14 2Kg 17:7-18
[ai]Ezk 18:10-13
[aj]Dn 11:18; Mc 6:16
[ak]13:1 Jb 29:21-22
[al]Jdg 8:1; 12:1

A11:12 Hs 12:1 in Hb　　B11:12 Or to the Holy One; Hb obscure　　C11:12 Possibly angels, or less likely, pagan gods or idols
D12:1 Or feeds on, or tends　　E12:4 Or Him　　F12:4 LXX, Syr; MT reads us　　G12:8 Lit crime which is sin　　H12:9 LXX reads God who brought you out of

the promise of restoration in verses 8-11 and echoes its use in a similar blessing passage in 2:16,21.

11:12 The section ends by declaring that both **Ephraim** or Israel and **Judah** were grieving the Lord. The last two lines of this verse are difficult. The Hebrew term for God is not the usual *Elohim* but *El*, which can refer to God but also to the Canaanite god of that name. The term for **wanders** is rare but suggests rebellion (Gn 27:40; Jr 2:31). **Holy ones** elsewhere refers to godly people or to angels (Ps 16:3; 89:5; Dn 7:18; 8:13), but it could refer in this context to Canaanite deities or cult prostitutes.

12:1-8 Dependence on foreign alliances meant trusting in deceit and violence. In doing so, Israel was playing with fire (2Kg 18:21; Is 30:12-13).

12:3-5 Hosea rebuked Israel by pointing out that although their namesake **Jacob** (whose name God changed to Israel) had once been a faithless, self-centered conniver, he met

God first at Bethel and was later changed in the encounter at the Jabbok River. The people of Israel, on the other hand, met Baal at Bethel (Beth-aven) and, in effect, died (13:1).

12:6 Again Hosea exhorted a threefold repentance (cp. 6:1; 10:12; 14:2-3).

12:10-11 The second line of verse 10 can be rendered "and I am the one who caused visions to abound." But Israel disposed of God's revelation and pursued pagan sacrifices at **Gilead** and **Gilgal**, for which they would receive **nothing** but **heaps of rocks**.

12:12-13 The prophet took up here where he left off in verse 4 and compared Israel's experience in Egypt to that of **Jacob** in **Aram**. Both man and nation went seeking for refuge in a foreign land but ended up being enslaved instead. But whereas Jacob came out shepherding flocks (Gn 31:17-18), the nation was led like a flock by a shepherd (Moses; see Ex 13ff).

But he incurred •guilt through •Baal[a]
and died.

2 Now they continue to sin
and make themselves a cast image,[b]
idols skillfully made from their silver,[c]
all of them the work of craftsmen.[d]
People say about them,
"Let the men who sacrifice[A] kiss
the calves."[e]

3 Therefore, they will be
like the morning mist,[f]
like the early dew that vanishes,
like chaff blown from a threshing floor,[g]
or like smoke from a window.[h]

Death and Resurrection

4 I have been •Yahweh your God[i]
ever since[B] the land of Egypt;
you know no God but Me,[j]
and no Savior exists besides Me.[k]

5 I knew[C] you in the wilderness,[l]
in the land of drought.

6 When they had pasture,
they became satisfied;[m]
they were satisfied,
and their hearts became proud.[n]
Therefore they forgot Me.[o]

7 So I will be like a lion[p] to them;
I will lurk like a leopard[q] on the path.

8 I will attack them
like a bear robbed of her cubs
and tear open the rib cage
over their hearts.
I will devour them there like a lioness,[r]
like a wild beast that would rip
them open.

9 I will destroy you, Israel;
you have no help but Me.[D,s]

10 Where now is your king,[E,t]
that he may save you in all your cities,
and the[F] rulers[G,u] you
demanded, saying,
"Give me a king and leaders"?

11 I give you a king in My anger[v]
and take away a king in My wrath.[w]

12 Ephraim's guilt is preserved;
his sin is stored up.[x]

13 Labor pains come on him.[y]
He is not a wise son;[z]
when the time comes,
he will not be born.[H,aa]

14 I will ransom them from the power
of •Sheol.
I will redeem[I] them from death.[ab]
Death, where are your barbs?
Sheol, where is your sting?[ac]
Compassion is hidden from My eyes.[ad]

The Coming Judgment

15 Although he flourishes
among his brothers,[J,ae]
an east wind will come,[af]
a wind from the LORD rising up
from the desert.
His water source will fail,
and his spring will run dry.[ag]
The wind[K] will plunder the treasury[ah]
of every precious item.

16[L] Samaria[ai] will bear her guilt[aj]
because she has rebelled
against her God.[ak]
They will fall by the sword;[al]
their little ones will be dashed
to pieces,[am]
and their pregnant women
ripped open.[an]

A Plea to Repent

14 Israel, return to •Yahweh your God,[ao]
for you have stumbled in your sin.[ap]
2 Take words of repentance with you[aq]
and return to the LORD.
Say to Him: "Forgive all our sin
and accept what is good,
so that we may repay You
with praise[M] from our[N] lips.[ar]

---

a13:1 Hs 2:8-17; 11:2
b13:2 Is 46:6; Jr 10:4; Hs 2:8
cIs 44:17-20
dHs 8:6
eHs 8:5-6; 10:5
f13:3 Hs 6:4
gPs 1:4; Is 17:13; Dn 2:35
hPs 68:2
i13:4 Hs 12:9
jEx 20:3; 2Kg 18:35
kIs 43:11; 45:21-22
l13:5 Dt 32:10
m13:6 Dt 8:12,14; 32:13-15; Jr 5:7
nHs 7:14
oHs 2:13; 4:6; 8:14
p13:7 Hs 5:14
qJr 5:6
r13:8 Ps 50:22
s13:9 Jr 2:17,19; Hs 6:1-2; Mal 1:12-13
t13:10 2Kg 17:4; Hs 8:4
uHs 7:7
v13:11 1Sm 8:7
w1Kg 14:7-10; Hs 10:7
x13:12 Dt 32:34-35; Jb 14:17; Rm 2:5
y13:13 Mc 4:9-10
zDt 32:6; Hs 5:4
aaIs 37:3; 66:9
ab13:14 Hs 6:1-2
ac1Co 15:55
adJr 20:16; 31:35-37
ae13:15 Gn 49:22; Hs 10:1
afGn 41:6; Jr 4:11-12; Ezk 17:10; 19:12
agJr 51:36
ahJr 20:5
ai13:16 Hs 7:1
ajHs 10:2
akHs 7:14
alHs 11:6
amHs 10:14
an2Kg 15:16
ao14:1 Hs 6:1; 10:12; 12:6
apHs 4:8; 5:5; 9:7
aq14:2 Mc 7:18-19
arHeb 13:15

A13:2 Or *Those who make human sacrifices*   B13:4 DSS, LXX read *God who brought you out of*   C13:5 LXX, Syr read *fed*   D13:9 LXX reads *At your destruction, Israel, who will help you?*   E13:10 LXX, Syr, Vg; MT reads *I will be your king*   F13:10 Lit *your*   G13:10 Or *judges*   H13:13 Lit *he will not present himself at the opening of the womb for sons*   I13:14 Or *Should I ransom . . . Should I redeem . . . ?*   J13:15 Or *among reeds*   K13:15 Probably the Assyrian king   L13:16 Hs 14:1 in Hb   M14:2 LXX reads *with the fruit*
N14:2 Lit *repay the bulls of our*

12:14–13:1 Ephraim had preeminence among the northern tribes but threw it away through their **contempt** of God's law. Their worship of **Baal** is called **bloodguilt** or murder because that was a capital offense.

13:2 This verse echoes God's judgment in 12:11 to bring the people "to nothing."

13:7-9 Those who are lulled into believing God is indulgent of our sins are shocked into reality by this picture of God being like a **lion** (cp. 11:10), a **leopard**, or a **bear**, tearing, ripping, and devouring. **Israel** had **no help** but God, and

God Himself had come to **destroy**. Thus was the fate of a people who continually turned their backs on God.

13:14 As in 6:1-2, although Israel was doomed, the Lord is able to bring life out of death. As Paul declared in 1Co 15:55, God's power makes personal, bodily resurrection possible, as well as national renewal.

13:15 On the punishment of Ephraim, see note at 4:17.

14:2-3 This final invitation to repent (6:1-3) even gives a "sinner's prayer."

3 Assyria will not save us,[a]
  we will not ride on horses,[b]
  and we will no longer proclaim,
    'Our gods!'[c]
  to the work of our hands.[d]
  For the fatherless receives compassion
    in You."[e]

A Promise of Restoration

4 I will heal their apostasy;[f]
  I will freely love them,[g]
  for My anger will have turned
    from him.[h]
5 I will be like the dew to Israel;[i]
  he will blossom like the lily[j]
  and take root like
    the cedars of Lebanon.[k]
6 His new branches will spread,
  and his splendor will be
    like the olive tree,[l]
  his fragrance, like
    the forest of Lebanon.[m]

7 The people will return and live
    beneath his shade.[n]
  They will grow grain[o]
  and blossom like the vine.
  His renown will be like the wine
    of Lebanon.

8 Ephraim, why should I[A] have
    anything more
  to do with idols?[p]
  It is I who answer and watch
    over him.
  I am like a flourishing pine tree;[q]
  your fruit comes from Me.[r]

9 Let whoever is wise[s] understand
    these things,
  and whoever is insightful
    recognize them.
  For the ways of the LORD are right,[t]
  and the righteous walk in them,[u]
  but the rebellious stumble in them.[v]

[a] 14:3 Hs 5:13	
[b] Is 31:1	
[c] Hs 4:12	
[d] Hs 8:6; 13:2	
[e] Ps 68:5	
[f] 14:4 Is 57:18; Hs 6:1	
[g] Zph 3:17	
[h] Is 12:1	
[i] 14:5 Is 26:19	
[j] Sg 2:1; Mt 6:28	
[k] Is 35:2	
[l] 14:6 Jr 11:16	
[m] Sg 4:11	
[n] 14:7 Ezk 17:23	
[o] Hs 2:21-22	
[p] 14:8 Jb 34:32	
[q] Is 41:19	
[r] Ezk 17:13	
[s] 14:9 Ps 107:43; Jr 9:12	
[t] Ps 111:7-8; Zph 3:5	
[u] Is 26:7	
[v] Is 1:28	

A 14:8 LXX reads he

Allat, the moon goddess of Syria and later of Northern Arabia

14:4 A believing remnant will experience restoration and blessing. God's promise to **heal their apostasy**, as Garrett noted, "implies that apostasy is more than an act of the will, but is also a kind of mental derangement . . . that God himself must cure."

14:6-7 The first three lines of verse 7 are literally "those who live in his shade will return/they will sustain like grain/ and blossom like the vine." God promised to restore life and beauty to Israel as to a dead, abandoned garden. Israel would again be a blessing to the nations as they were originally intended to be (Gn 12:1-3; Is 2:2-4), signified by the fragrant **olive tree** furnishing not only food, fuel, and medicine but also shade (Lk 13:18-19). **His renown** is literally "his memory," probably referring to God's remembrance of Israel that will prompt Him to restore them by His grace (Gn 8:21). **Lebanon** is referred to three times in verses 5-7 but nowhere else in the book. The reason may be that flourishing Lebanon had been the origin of Israel's Baal cult (1Kg 16:31-33).

14:9 Hosea concluded by exhorting readers to persevere in the study of his prophecy, so as to **understand** and **recognize** the things he had communicated.

Joel

Introduction

The book of Joel is one of the shortest in the Old
Testament. The first part (1:1–2:17) describes a terrible
locust plague concluding with a plea for confession of
sins. The second part (2:18–3:21) proclaims hope for
the repentant people coupled with judgment upon their
enemies.

"What the devouring locust has left, the swarming locust has eaten; what the
swarming locust has left, the young locust has eaten; and what the young locust
has left, the destroying locust has eaten" (1:4).

Circumstances of Writing

Author: Joel ("Yahweh is God") is identified as the son of Pethuel. He is not easily identified with the other Joels of Scripture (1Sm 8:2; 1Ch 4:35; 6:33; 11:38; 15:7; Ezr 10:43; Neh 11:9), leaving us only his book to know him, his calling from God, and his work. The book itself gives no biographical information other than his father's name.

Background: Dating the book of Joel has always been difficult and mainly conjecture, with suggestions ranging as widely as premonarchial Israel to the postexilic period, sometimes well into the Hellenistic period.

Message and Purpose

What is striking about the book of Joel is that it has no indictment section listing the offenses of the people. The only clue as to what sins called forth the prophet's message is found in the instruction of 2:12-13 to repent, that is, to "turn to Me with all your heart" and "tear your hearts, not just your clothes." All the other prophets (except Jonah, who does not use the prophetic genre) have at least some explicit indication of what behavior needed to be changed. Joel was concerned mainly with motivation, with messages of judgment and hope.

There are many exhortations in the book, but they are almost all formal rather than ethical or moral. Joel calls readers to hear (1:2-3), to war (2:1; 3:9-13), to lamentation (1:5,8,11,13-14; 2:15-16; though some interpreters understand these as indirect calls for repentance), and to celebration (2:21-23). The only true instruction message in Joel occurs in 2:12-13, the call to repentance.

Joel's message was concerned primarily with motivating repentance by proclaiming the Day of the Lord, which is "at the same time one event and many events" and "refers to a decisive action of Yahweh to bring His plans for Israel to completion" (D. A. Garrett). The locust plague is understood as judgment from God and a

725 B.C.	700 B.C.	600 B.C.
Alliance between Syria and Israel collapses with the fall of Damascus (732) and the fall of Samaria (722).	Philistines and Phoenicians sell the people of Judah and Jerusalem as slaves to the Greeks. 700	Nebuchadnezzar's three invasions of Judah 605, 597, 586
Joel's prophecy likely occurred between 722 and 605 or after the Babylonian exile. (See events under 450 for possible later date.)	God delivers Jerusalem from the Assyrian forces. 701	Temple of Solomon destroyed 586
	Ashurbanipal (668–631) rules over a declining Assyrian Empire that experiences revolts in 642, contributing to the assassination of Amon of Judah (641) and the rise of his son Josiah. 641–609	Events in Ezekiel 593–571
Greeks establish trading posts in Philistine territory along the Mediterranean coast. 700		Cyrus the Elder, founder of the Persian Empire, is born. 581
		Fall of Babylon and rise of Persia 539
	Josiah killed by the Egyptians at Megiddo 609	Cyrus's decree allows return of Jews from exile. 538
	Babylonians defeat Pharaoh Neco of Egypt at Carchemish. 605	

harbinger of the Day of the Lord (1:2-20, especially v. 15). Then Joel announced that a worse judgment was coming through a human army (2:1-11). This is also called the Day of the Lord (2:1,11).

Joel insisted that the only hope for God's people was through repentance (2:12-17). He assured Judah that repentance would be rewarded with physical (2:18-27) and spiritual (2:28-32) restoration associated with the Day of the Lord (2:31). He concluded by promising a Day of the Lord that would bring judgment against the nations opposing the Lord and His people (3:14).

Locusts: The book of Joel contains four specific words translated "locusts" in English. In both 1:4 and 2:25 "locust" is modified by four different adjectives: "devouring," "swarming," "young," and "destroying."

Interpreters have long asked what relationship exists between the locusts and the army that is mentioned later in Joel. Are they distinct from each other? Is one a metaphor for the other? Or are they two aspects of God's judgment against Israel and the nations? Are the locusts actual, metaphorical, or typological?

It is important to note that both the army of invading locusts and the foreign army came as judgments of God. Also, locusts can be described as an invading army, and an army of men could aptly be called a plague of destructive locusts.

The Day of the Lord: The phrase "Day of the LORD" figures prominently in the book of Joel. This describes the judgment day of God. That judgment could be directed both against the nation of Israel and against the "nations." The specific phrase occurs in the OT in Is 13:6,9; Ezk 13:5; Jl 1:15; 2:1,11; 4:14; Am 5:18,20; Ob 15; Zph 1:7,14; and Mal 3:2. The concept itself may also be found in Jr 46:10 and several other passages.

The "Day of the LORD" has several adjectives attached to it: "darkness and not light" (Am 5:18,20), "great and awesome" (Mal 4:5), "great and remarkable" (Ac 2:20). Associated with it are cosmic calamities; the sun will be turned to darkness and the moon to blood (Ac 2:20; Rv 6:12).

Extended descriptions of the Day of the Lord are found in Isaiah 13; 34; Ezekiel 7; and Joel 2. In Ezekiel 7 we

---

550 B.C.

Second temple construction begins under Zerubbabel's and Joshua's leadership. 536

Haggai and Zechariah encourage the people to finish rebuilding the temple. 520–518

Second temple is dedicated. 515

Events in Esther 486–465

Greek victory over Persians in Battle of Salamis, 480, and Plain of Plataea, 479, thwarted Persian expansion into Europe and were keys to Greek hegemony in the Mediterranean Basin and Europe.

Ezra goes to Jerusalem. 458

450 B.C.

Joel's prophecy occurred sometime after 445 when Jerusalem's walls had been rebuilt. (See events under 725 for a different view of when Joel prophesied.)

Events in Nehemiah 445–430

Nehemiah's ministry 445–420?

Nehemiah in Jerusalem 445–432

Jerusalem's walls rebuilt 445

The Peloponnesian War between Sparta and Athens 431–404

Greek philosopher Plato born 430

find that the Lord will send His anger against the land of Israel and judge it according to its ways. He will punish it for all its abominations. Disasters are coming, one after another. The judgment theme is prominent in Joel, as is the idea that the day is near when God will make Himself known through His judgments. In a move that shocked the Hebrews, God brought the most evil of nations to take possession of Judah and Israel.

Contribution to the Bible

The book of Joel shows us the Creator and Redeemer God of all the universe in complete control of nature. Joel made it clear that the God of judgment also is a God of mercy who stands ready to redeem and restore when His people come before Him in repentance. Joel points to a time when the Spirit of God would be present upon all people. On the day of Pentecost, Peter proclaimed that the new day of Spirit-filled discipleship, foretold by Joel, had arrived (Ac 2:17-21).

Structure

Joel's use of repetition gives the book the appearance of a series of folding doors, in some cases doors within doors. As Garrett has shown, the overall structure balances the section on God's judgment through the locust plague (1:1-20) with a section on the land's physical restoration (2:21-27). The prophecy of an invading army (2:1-11) is balanced by a prophecy on the destruction of this army (2:20). In the center is the highly prominent call to repent and the promise of renewal (2:12-19). But this balanced structure overlaps with another. The prophecy of the destruction of the invading army (2:20) is also balanced with the final prophecy of the Lord's vengeance against all the nations (3:1-21). Finally, the assurance of the land's physical restoration through rain (2:21-27) is balanced by the promise of the people's spiritual restoration through the outpouring of God's Spirit (2:28-32).

Outline

I. The Locust Plague (1:1-20)

II. An Invading Northern Army (2:1-11)

III. Repentance and Renewal (2:12-19)

IV. Northern Army Destroyed (2:20)

V. Physical Restoration of the Land (2:21-27)

VI. Spiritual Revival of the People (2:28-32)

VII. Vengeance on the Nations (3:1-21)

1

The word of the Lord that came[a] to Joel son of Pethuel:

A Plague of Locusts

2 Hear this,[b] you elders;
   listen, all you inhabitants of the land.
   Has anything like this ever happened
      in your days[c]
   or in the days of your ancestors?

3 Tell your children about it,[d]
   and let your children tell their children,
   and their children the next generation.

4 What the devouring locust[e] has left,
   the swarming locust has eaten;
   what the swarming locust has left,
   the young locust[f] has eaten;
   and what the young locust has left,
   the destroying locust[g] has eaten.

5 Wake up, you drunkards,[h] and weep;
   wail, all you wine drinkers,
   because of the sweet wine,
   for it has been taken from your mouth.

6 For a nation has invaded My land,[i]
   powerful and without number;
   its teeth are the teeth of a lion,
   and it has the fangs of a lioness.[j]

7 It has devastated My grapevine
   and splintered My fig tree.
   It has stripped off its bark
      and thrown it away;
   its branches have turned white.

8 Grieve like a young woman dressed
      in *sackcloth,[k]
   mourning for the husband
      of her youth.

9 *Grain and *drink offerings have been
      cut off[l]
   from the house of the Lord;
   the priests, who are ministers
      of the Lord, mourn.[m]

10 The fields are destroyed;[n]
   the land grieves;
   indeed, the grain is destroyed;
   the new wine is dried up;[o]
   and the olive oil fails.[p]

11 Be ashamed, you farmers,[q]
   wail, you vinedressers,[A]
   over the wheat and the barley,
   because the harvest of the field
      has perished.[r]

12 The grapevine is dried up,[s]
   and the fig tree is withered;
   the pomegranate,[t] the date palm,[u]
      and the apple[v]—
   all the trees
      of the orchard—have withered.
   Indeed, human joy has dried up.[w]

13 Dress in sackcloth and lament,[x]
      you priests;[y]
   wail,[z] you ministers of the altar.
   Come and spend the night
      in sackcloth,[aa]

Cross references (center column):
a1:1 Hs 1:1; Mc 1:1; Zph 1:1
b1:2 Hs 4:1; 5:1
cDt 4:32; Jr 2:10; Mk 2:12
d1:3 Ex 10:2; Jos 4:22; Ps 78:4
e1:4 Ex 10:4; Jl 2:25; Am 4:9
fPs 105:34; Nah 3:15-16
g Ps 78:46; Is 33:4
h1:5 Jl 3:3
i1:6 Jl 2:2,11,25
jRv 9:7-8
k1:8 Is 22:12; Jr 4:8; 6:26
l1:9 Hs 9:4; Jl 2:14
mHs 10:5; Jl 2:17
n1:10 Is 24:4
oHs 9:2
pDt 28:51; Hs 2:8-13; Hg 1:11
q1:11 Jr 14:4; 51:23; Am 5:16
rIs 17:11; Jr 9:12
s1:12 Hab 3:17
tHg 2:19
uSg 7:8
vSg 2:3
wIs 16:10; 24:11
x1:13 Jr 4:8; Ezk 7:18
yJl 2:17
zJr 9:10
aa1Kg 21:27

A1:11 Or *The farmers are dismayed, the vinedressers wail*

1:2-3 Joel addressed both the **elders** and the **inhabitants of the land** with a question designed to arrest their attention. A unique locust plague had come to the land. It was so unusual that it served as a warning of two future events: a coming war and the Day of the Lord.

1:4 The use of four different Hebrew words for "locusts" in this verse emphasizes the totality of their destruction.

1:5 Joel addressed a third group—the **drunkards**. Their wine-induced stupor kept them from realizing what was happening around them. Now out of wine, they sobered up and faced the devastation.

1:6-7 Grapevines and figs were two of the principle crops of the land. They were damaged during wars or plague, impacting the food supply and the economy.

1:8 The proper response to this catastrophe was grief, symbolized by donning **sackcloth**, a rough, uncomfortable fabric that chaffed and irritated the skin.

1:9 The **priests** lamented the fact that **offerings were cut off** not just because the temple would lack its sacrifices, but also because they would lack the food portion they took from these offerings. Empty altars also meant empty stomachs.

1:10-12 The farm workers were to mourn and wail because the agricultural economy had been ruined. The crops that sustained both humans and animals were gone. Even the fruit trees were destroyed. Starvation was imminent.

1:13-14 The **priests** were to take the lead in mourning rituals by dressing in **sackcloth** and spending the night at the temple. The whole assembly was to gather together and **cry out to the Lord**, an expression of their corporate guilt before God.

'arbeh

Hebrew Pronunciation	[ar BEH]
HCSB Translation	locust
Uses in Joel	3
Uses in the OT	24
Focus passage	Joel 1:4

'Arbeh is the common term for *locust*, used of Moses' plague against Egypt (Ex 10:4). It is the mature *swarming locust* (Nah 3:15). Human armies are compared to the 'arbeh (Jdg 7:12). 'Arbeh stands in figures about people shaken off like *locusts* (Ps 109:23) or horses leaping like them (Jb 39:20). Joel 1:4 mentions either varieties of *locust* or stages of *locust* life. *Chasiyl* (6x) may indicate the *caterpillar* stage (Jl 1:4). It is also translated *locust* (Is 33:4) and *grasshopper* (2Ch 6:28). *Yeleq* (9x) is *young locust* (Jl 2:25) or *locust* (Jr 51:14). These could hop but not yet fly. *Gazam* (3x) is the *devouring locust* (Jl 1:4) or *locust* (Am 4:9); this was a particularly destructive stage. *Govai* (2x) means *swarm of locusts* (Am 7:1). *Gov* (Nah 3:17), translated *cloud*, seems a synonym. *Sol'am* may indicate *katydid*, and *chargol* suggests *cricket* (Lv 11:22).

you ministers of my God,
because grain and drink offerings
are withheld from the house
    of your God.
14 Announce a sacred fast;[a]
proclaim an assembly!
Gather the elders[b]
and all the residents of the land
at the house of the LORD your God,[c]
and cry out to the LORD.[d]

The Day of the LORD

15 Woe because of that day![e]
For the Day of the LORD is near
and will come as devastation
    from the •Almighty.[f]
16 Hasn't the food been cut off
before our eyes,[g]
joy and gladness[h]
from the house of our God?
17 The seeds lie shriveled in their casings.[A,i]
The storehouses are in ruin,
and the granaries are broken down,
because the grain has withered away.
18 How the animals groan![j]
The herds of cattle wander in confusion
since they have no pasture.
Even the flocks of sheep
    suffer punishment.
19 I call to You, LORD,[k]
for fire has consumed
the pastures of the wilderness,[l]
and flames have devoured
all the trees of the countryside.
20 Even the wild animals cry out to[B] You,[m]
for the river beds are dried up,[n]

and fire has consumed
the pastures of the wilderness.

2 Blow the horn in •Zion;[o]
sound the alarm on My holy mountain!
Let all the residents of the land tremble,
for the Day of the LORD is coming;[p]
in fact, it is near—
2 a day of darkness and gloom,[q]
a day of clouds and dense overcast,[r]
like the dawn spreading
    over the mountains;
a great and strong people[s] appears,
such as never existed in ages past[t]
and never will again
in all the generations to come.[u]
3 A fire destroys[C] in front of them,[v]
and behind them a flame devours.
The land in front of them
is like the Garden of Eden,[w]
but behind them,
it is like a desert wasteland;[x]
there is no escape from them.
4 Their appearance is like that
    of horses,[y]
and they gallop like war horses.
5 They bound on the tops
    of the mountains.
Their sound is like the sound
    of chariots,[z]
like the sound of fiery flames
    consuming stubble,[aa]
like a mighty army deployed for war.
6 Nations writhe in horror before them;[ab]
all faces turn pale.

---

[a]1:14 Jl 2:15-16
[b]Jl 1:2
[c]2Ch 20:3; Neh 9:1; Jr 36:6,9
[d]Jnh 3:8
[e]1:15 Jr 30:7; Am 5:16
[f]Is 13:6,9; Ezk 30:2-3; Jl 2:1-2,11,31
[g]1:16 Is 3:7
[h]Is 16:10; Jr 48:33
[i]1:17 Is 17:10-11
[j]1:18 1Kg 18:5; Jr 12:4; 14:5-6; Hs 4:3
[k]1:19 Ps 50:15; Mc 7:7
[l]Jr 9:10; Am 7:4
[m]1:20 Ps 104:21; 147:9
[n]1Kg 17:7; 18:5
[o]2:1 Jl 2:15; Jr 4:5; 51:27
[p]Jl 1:15; 2:11,31; 3:14
[q]2:2 Jl 2:31; Zph 1:15
[r]Is 60:2; Zph 1:15
[s]Jl 1:6; 2:11,25
[t]Lm 1:12; Dn 9:12; 12:1; Jl 1:2
[u]Ex 10:14
[v]2:3 Ps 97:3; Is 9:18-19
[w]Gn 2:8-15; Ezk 36:35
[x]Ex 10:5,15; Ps 105:34-35
[y]2:4 Rv 9:7
[z]2:5 Rv 9:9
[aa]Is 5:24; 30:30
[ab]2:6 Is 13:8; Nah 2:10

A1:17 Or clods; Hb obscure   B1:20 Or animals pant for; Hb obscure   C2:3 Lit consumes

---

1:15-20 The people gathered at the temple for a communal lament. These verses give the content of their prayer. The major theme of the book is the **Day of the LORD**, and the people were terrified as they considered that coming day. It would be a time when Yahweh punished sin and judged the nations. The people knew they were sinners. They were out of food and could not offer fellowship offerings to commune with God. The **storehouses** for grain were empty. The plague appears to be compounded with a drought and perhaps with a **fire**, so the **pastures** were ruined. Even **sheep** that could survive in barren lands were suffering. The speaker in verse 19 expressed the community's complaint and petition for mercy. The **animals**, domestic and wild, also joined in crying out to Yahweh, who controlled the elements. Without water, death would soon come to man and beast.

2:1 Commentators are divided over the identity of the invading northern army (see note at v. 20) described in chapter 2. (1) Some see it as a figurative description of the locust invasion of chapter 1. (2) Some see literal enemy troops coming from the north, described as invading locusts. (3) Revelation 9:3-11 compares demonic forces to locusts. Whether this army was man or insect, it represented the judgment force of Yahweh. Joel as a spiritual watchman sounded

the alarm, just as other prophets did. Yahweh warned the people through His spokesman Joel **on My holy mountain**. This and the reference to **Zion** are the first geographical indicators in Joel. The prophet was called to **sound the alarm** to the nation from Jerusalem, from the place where the temple stood.

2:2 The people of God have often longed for the coming of Yahweh. Isaiah declared, "If only You would tear the heavens open and come down, so that the mountains would quake at Your presence" (Is 64:1). But Joel insisted that this day would be a day of **darkness . . . gloom**, blackness, and destruction (Zph 1:14-17).

2:3 The coming destructive army would be like a forest **fire** or a locust invasion. Paradise would be turned into a **desert**.

2:4-5 An attack of war horses and **chariots** was the ancient equivalent to blitzkrieg—the lightning war. As Germany overran entire countries in World War II, so this army of locusts would **gallop like war horses**. The deafening **sound** of their charge and the roaring of a forest fire are compared to the sounds heard on the coming Day of the Lord.

2:6 As in Ps 96:9 and 97:4, all the peoples or **nations** will be terrified by the appearance of the Lord.

7 They attack as warriors attack;
　　they scale walls as men of war do.
　　Each goes on his own path,[a]
　　and they do not change their course.
8 They do not push each other;
　　each man proceeds on his own path.
　　They dodge the arrows, never stopping.
9 They storm the city;
　　they run on the wall;
　　they climb into the houses;[b]
　　they enter through the windows
　　　　like thieves.[c]
10 The earth quakes before them;[d]
　　the sky shakes.
　　The sun and moon grow dark,[e]
　　and the stars cease their shining.[f]
11 The Lord raises His voice[g]
　　in the presence of His army.[h]
　　His camp is very large;
　　Those who carry out His command
　　　　are powerful.[i]
　　Indeed, the Day of the Lord is terrible
　　and dreadful[j]—
　　who can endure it?[k]

God's Call for Repentance

12 Even now—
　　　　this is the Lord's declaration—
　　turn to Me with all your heart,[l]
　　with fasting, weeping,
　　and mourning.[m]
13 Tear your hearts,[n]
　　not just your clothes,[o]
　　and return to the Lord your God.
　　For He is gracious and compassionate,
　　slow to anger, rich in faithful love,
　　and He relents from sending disaster.[p]

14 Who knows? He may turn and relent[q]
　　and leave a blessing behind Him,[r]
　　so you can offer grain and wine
　　to the Lord your God.[s]
15 Blow the horn in Zion![t]
　　Announce a sacred fast;[u]
　　proclaim an assembly.
16 Gather the people;
　　sanctify the congregation;[v]
　　assemble the aged;[A,w]
　　gather the children,
　　even those nursing at the breast.
　　Let the groom leave his bedroom,[x]
　　and the bride her honeymoon chamber.
17 Let the priests,[y] the Lord's ministers,
　　weep between the portico
　　　　and the altar.[z]
　　Let them say:
　　"Have pity on Your people, Lord,[aa]
　　and do not make Your inheritance
　　　　a disgrace,[ab]
　　an object of scorn among the nations.
　　Why should it be said
　　　　among the peoples,
　　'Where is their God?'"[ac]

God's Response to His People

18 Then the Lord became jealous for His land[ad] and spared His people.[ae] 19 The Lord answered His people:

　　Look, I am about to send you
　　grain, new wine, and olive oil.[af]
　　You will be satiated with them,
　　and I will no longer make you
　　a disgrace among the nations.[ag]

a 2:7 Pr 30:27
b 2:9 Ex 10:6
c Jr 9:21
d 2:10 Ps 18:7; Nah 1:5
e Is 13:10; 34:4; Jr 4:23; Ezk 32:7-8; Mt 24:29; Rv 8:12
f Jl 3:15
g 2:11 Ps 46:6; Is 13:4
h Jl 2:25
i Jr 50:34; Rv 18:8
j Jl 1:15; 2:31; 3:14
k Ezk 22:14
l 2:12 1Kg 8:35-40; 2Ch 7:14
m Est 4:3
n 2:13 Ps 51:17; Is 57:15
o Jr 41:5
p Ex 34:6; Nm 14:18; 1Ch 21:15; Neh 9:17; Ps 86:15; 103:8; 145:8; Jr 18:8; Jnh 4:2
q 2:14 Jnh 3:9
r Hg 2:19
s Jl 1:9,13
t 2:15 Jl 2:1
u 2Kg 10:20
v 2:16 1Sm 16:5; 2Ch 29:5
w 2:15-16 2Ch 20:3; Neh 9:1; Jr 36:6,9
x 2:16 Ps 19:5
y 2:17 Jl 1:9
z Hs 10:5; Jl 1:13
aa Is 37:20; Am 7:2,5
ab Ps 44:13; 74:10
ac Ps 42:3,10; 79:10; 115:2
ad 2:18 Ezk 36:5,6; Zch 1:14; 8:2
ae Is 60:10; 63:9,15
af 2:19 Jr 31:12; Hs 2:21-22
ag Ezk 34:29; 36:15

A2:16 Or elders

2:7-8 In many biblical passages (e.g., Jdg 6:5; Is 33:4; Jr 51:14) armies are compared to locusts and sometimes locusts are compared to armies (Pr 30:27).

2:9-11 Joel continued the interplay of soldiers with the imagery and actions of a locust plague. The swarming locusts ate everything in the fields and then came into the **city** and finally into the **houses**. So also invading armies breached the city walls and then plundered the houses. Joel used end-time language and moved beyond what happens in normal locust or military invasions. The very heavens were now engaged; Yahweh and His heavenly armies were ready to wreak havoc. Judgment day had come.

2:12-13 The tone of the prophet changes from this verse to the end of his message. The phrase **even now—this is the Lord's declaration** announces a wonderful possibility. Yahweh is a God of mercy and compassion to repentant sinners. Even the worst king of Judah, Manasseh, who sinned more heinously than all the rest, repented and received forgiveness (2Ch 33:10-13). "The Lord's declaration" is a solemn promise. This is the only place where this phrase appears in Joel. Solomon's prayer was answered by Yahweh, who

promised that He would forgive and heal the land from a locust plague (2Ch 7:12-16), but Yahweh required genuine and sincere repentance from the people for this to happen.

2:14 The question **who knows?** expresses hope based on the fact that God is free to choose pardon or punishment. There is always hope for repentant persons, for God knows our hearts (Jnh 3:9).

2:15-17 The trumpet call summoned the people to a solemn **assembly** for worship and petition. This contrasts with the trumpet call of verse 1, which heralded war. This time everyone was to come, even those who normally were exempt from such gatherings. The **priests** were given special instructions because they were to lead the expression of the national lament and petition. Some take verse 17 to mean "why should the nations rule over us?" This view fits the interpretation of a northern army invasion better than a literal locust invasion.

2:18-19 Joel announced the Lord's decision to turn away His judgment and spare the nation. Starting in verse 19 Yahweh speaks directly to the people. His covenant blessings will be restored, and the people will be protected from their enemies.

20 I will drive the northerner
   far from you[a]
and banish him to a dry
   and desolate land,
his front ranks into the Dead Sea,[b]
and his rear guard
   into the Mediterranean Sea.[c]
His stench will rise;
yes, his rotten smell will rise,[d]
   for he has done catastrophic things.

21 Don't be afraid, land;[e]
rejoice and be glad,
   for the Lord has done great things.[f]
22 Don't be afraid, wild animals,
for the wilderness pastures
   have turned green,[g]
the trees bear their fruit,
and the fig tree and grapevine yield
   their riches.
23 Children of Zion,[h] rejoice and be glad
in the Lord your God,[i]
because He gives you the autumn rain
for your vindication.[A,j]
He sends showers for you,
both autumn and spring rain[k] as before.

24 The threshing floors will be full of grain,[l]
and the vats will overflow
   with new wine and olive oil.

25 I will repay you for the years
that the swarming locust ate,[m]
the young locust, the destroying locust,
   and the devouring locust—
My great army that I sent against you.
26 You will have plenty to eat
   and be satisfied.[n]
You will praise the name
   of •Yahweh your God,[o]
who has dealt wondrously with you.[p]
My people will never again be put
   to shame.[q]
27 You will know that I am present
   in Israel[r]
and that I am Yahweh your God,
and there is no other.[s]
My people will never again be put
   to shame.[t]

God's Promise of His Spirit

28[B] After this[u]
I will pour out My Spirit[v]
   on all humanity;[w]

---

a 2:20 Jr 1:14-15
b Zch 14:8
c Dt 11:24
d Is 34:3; Am 4:10
e 2:21 Jl 1:10
f Ps 126:2-3
g 2:22 Ps 65:12; Jr 9:10; Jl 1:19
h 2:23 Ps 149:2
i Is 12:2-6
j Dt 11:13-15
k Hs 6:3; Zch 10:1
l 2:24 Lv 26:10; Am 9:13; Mal 3:10
m 2:25 Jl 1:4-7; 2:2-11
n 2:26 Dt 11:15; Is 62:9
o Ps 113:1; 135:1; 148:5,13
p Ps 126:2; Is 25:1
q Is 45:17
r 2:27 Jl 3:17,21
s Dt 4:35,39; 1Kg 8:60; Is 45:5-6
t Is 49:23
u 2:28-32 Ac 2:17-21
v 2:28 Is 32:15; 44:3; Ezk 39:29
w Is 40:5; 49:26

A 2:23 Or *righteousness*   B 2:28 Jl 3:1 in Hb

2:20 Who was this northern army? Though some interpreters say it was an army of locusts, the language of the passage makes this view difficult. Almost every military invasion of Is-

The Dead Sea (2:20)

rael came from the north, so it would be hard to identify a specific army. The best approach is to interpret the enemy from the north as a reference to the end-time attack of the nations against God's people (Is 34:1-7; Ezk 38; Dn 11:36-45).

2:21-22 The destruction caused by the locust invasion (or the invading army) is now reversed. Both **land** and **animals** will participate in the salvation of God's people (Rm 8:19-23; Rv 21). Covenant blessings will be restored to the land (Dt 11:13-15).

2:23-24 Israel was dependent on **autumn** and **spring** rains for the prosperity of the land. Egypt could irrigate their crops from the Nile River, but Israel needed the Lord's special provision. They must depend on Him. The phrase **autumn rain for your vindication** can also be translated as "teacher of or for righteousness." Some scholars link this phrase to the "teacher of righteousness" at the Qumran community. This could be a veiled allusion to a coming Davidic leader-teacher who would bring righteousness to the believing remnant (Dt 18:15; Jr 33:14-17).

2:25-27 The locusts served as symbols of all the invading armies that had attacked Israel and decimated the land. Several ancient interpreters listed the nation's enemies; any one of them could be in view in the book of Joel. That God would say **My great army** of a pagan military force reminded Israel that Yahweh is the sovereign Lord of history. He is in control of all nations and they ultimately serve His purposes no matter their intentions (Is 45:1-7). Our food comes from the Lord who is Lord of all nature. Thus when we have **plenty to eat**, we should **praise** God. As important as food is, the greatest blessing of all is the presence of the Lord and our knowledge of Him (Is 45:4-7).

2:28-29 The OT prophets looked forward to the day when Yahweh would enable His people to keep the covenant and

then your sons and your daughters
will prophesy,
your old men will have dreams,
and your young men will see visions.

29 I will even pour out My Spirit
on the male and female slaves
in those days.[a]

30 I will display wonders
in the heavens and on the earth:[b]
blood, fire, and columns of smoke.

31 The sun will be turned to darkness
and the moon to blood[c]
before the great and awe-inspiring Day
of the Lord comes.[d]

32 Then everyone who calls
on the name of Yahweh will be saved,[e]
for there will be an escape
for those on Mount Zion
and in Jerusalem,
as the Lord promised,[f]
among the survivors the Lord calls.

Judgment of the Nations

3[A] Yes, in those days and at that time,
when I restore the fortunes of Judah
and Jerusalem,[g]

2 I will gather all the nations[h]
and take them to the Valley
of Jehoshaphat.[B,i]
I will enter into judgment
with them there[j]
because of My people,
My inheritance Israel.

The nations have scattered
the Israelites
in foreign countries[k]
and divided up My land.[l]

3 They cast lots for My people;[m]
they bartered a boy for a prostitute
and sold a girl for wine to drink.[n]

4And also: Tyre,[o] Sidon, and all the territories of Philistia[p]—what are you to Me? Are you paying Me back or trying to get even with Me? I will quickly bring retribution on your heads.[q] 5For you took My silver and gold and carried My finest treasures[r] to your temples. 6You sold the people of Judah and Jerusalem to the Greeks[s] to remove them far from their own territory. 7Look, I am about to rouse them up from the place where you sold them;[t] I will bring retribution on your heads. 8I will sell your sons and daughters into the hands of the people of Judah,[u] and they will sell them to the Sabeans,[C,v] to a distant nation, for the Lord has spoken.

9 Proclaim this among the nations:[w]
Prepare for holy war;[x]
rouse the warriors;[y]
let all the men of war advance
and attack!

10 Beat your plows into swords
and your pruning knives into spears.[z]
Let even the weakling say, "I am
a warrior."

Cross-references
[a] 2:29 1Co 12:13 [b] 2:30 Lk 21:11,25-26 [c] 2:31 Is 13:9-10; 34:4; Mt 24:29; Mk 13:24 [d] Zph 1:14-16; Mal 4:1,5 [e] 2:32 Rm 10:13 [f] Ob 17 [g] 3:1 Jr 32:44; 33:7,11; Ezk 39:25 [h] 3:2 Is 66:18; Mc 4:12 [i] Jl 3:12,14 Is 66:16; Jr 25:31 [j] Jr 50:17; Ezk 34:6 [k] Ezk 35:10; 36:1-5 [l] 3:3 Ob 11; Nah 3:10 [m] Am 2:6 [n] 3:4 Am 1:9; Zch 9:2-4 [o] Am 1:6-8; Zch 9:5-7 [p] Ps 28:4 [q] 3:5 1Kg 20:6; 2Ch 36:19; Lm 1:10-11 [r] 3:6 Is 66:19; Ezk 27:13 [s] 3:7 Zch 9:13 [t] 3:8 Is 14:2; 60:14 [u] Jb 1:15; Ps 72:10; Ezk 38:13 [v] 3:9 Jr 51:27-28 [w] Jr 6:4; Mc 3:5 [x] Is 8:9-10; Jr 46:3-4; Zch 14:2-3 [y] 3:10 Is 2:4; Mc 4:3

[A]3:1 Jl 4:1 in Hb [B]3:2 = The Lord Will Judge [C]3:8 Probably the south Arabian kingdom of Sheba (modern Yemen)

His laws by giving them a new heart and mind (Is 32:15-20; Jr 31:33; Ezk 36:26-30). The giving of His **Spirit** would take place at the time of the forgiveness of their sins. Peter on the day of Pentecost announced the gift of the Spirit and the forgiveness of sins by calling on God's name (Ac 2:21,38-40). If the people accepted Jesus as Messiah and Savior, they would receive this gift of the Holy Spirit. Yahweh's promise of the Spirit in Joel was not reserved for a few but for anyone who would believe from **all humanity**. Peter saw that this gift was not limited to Israel, but was for "all who are far off, as many as the Lord our God will call" (Ac 2:39). This prophecy from Joel was partly fulfilled in the days of Pentecost as well as in the "Gentile Pentecost" (Ac 10), and the fulfillment has continued throughout the church age (Rm 10:13). The final fulfillment will take place at the conversion of the Jewish people (Rm 11:26-27). Moses was glad when Joshua told him that others gave evidence of having God's Spirit by prophesying. Said Moses, "If only all the Lord's people were prophets, and the Lord would place His Spirit on them" (Nm 11:29).

2:30-31 The cosmic signs that are part of the Day of the Lord inspire awe for believers and terror for unbelievers. This day is one of salvation as well as judgment (Rv 6:12-17).

2:32 This verse shows the human obligation (**calls on the name of Yahweh**) and the divine role in salvation (**among the survivors the Lord calls**). Both "calls" are necessary for salvation. God does not save those who do not call on Him, and none call whom He has not called.

3:1-2 Moses predicted that the Jewish people would be scattered among the nations, and that when they came to their senses and returned to God, He would restore them to their land and cause them to prosper (Dt 30:1-10). Sometime after this the Lord will gather and judge the nations (Is 66:18; Zph 3:8; Rv 16:14-16; 19:11-16). The **Valley of Jehoshaphat** is literally "the valley where Yahweh judged," but no valley by this name is known. Most likely this is the valley of Jezreel near Megiddo where the battle of Armageddon will take place (Rv 16:16).

3:3-4 When Israel lost wars, their children would be sold by their enemies as slaves. **Tyre** and **Sidon** were trading hubs for slaves. The Lord is the defender of widows and orphans and will bring retribution on the guilty.

3:5-6 The crimes of these enemies were not only against Israel but against Yahweh. It was God's **silver and gold** that they took. The slaves were sent as far away as Greece.

3:7-8 The (Lat) *lex talionis* (Dt 19:21) will be applied, where punishment for wrongdoing is meted out "life for life, eye for eye," etc. The Jews were sent in exile to the northwest, and so those who exiled them would be sent to the southeast. The **Sabeans** dominated the trade routes to the south.

3:9-12 The nations are summoned to battle (in Rv 16:14

11 Come quickly,^A all
   you surrounding nations;
gather yourselves.^a
Bring down Your warriors there, Lord.^b

12 Let the nations be roused
and come to the Valley of Jehoshaphat,
for there I will sit down
to judge all the surrounding nations.^c

13 Swing the sickle
because the harvest is ripe.^d
Come and trample the grapes
because the winepress is full;^e
the wine vats overflow
because the wickedness of the nations
   is great.^f

14 Multitudes, multitudes^g
in the valley of decision!
For the Day of the Lord is near^h
in the valley of decision.

15 The sun and moon will grow dark,
and the stars will cease their shining.^i

16 The Lord will roar from •Zion^j
and raise His voice from Jerusalem;^k
heaven and earth will shake.^l
But the Lord will be a refuge
   for His people,^m
a stronghold for the Israelites.^n

Israel Blessed

17 Then you will know
that I am •Yahweh your God,^o
who dwells in Zion, My holy mountain.^p
Jerusalem will be holy,^q
and foreigners will never
   overrun it again.^r

18 In that day
the mountains will drip
   with sweet wine,^s
and the hills will flow with milk.^t
All the streams of Judah will flow
   with water,^u
and a spring will issue
   from the Lord's house,^v
watering the Valley of Acacias.^B,w

19 Egypt will become desolate,
and Edom a desert wasteland,
because of the violence done
   to the people of Judah^x
in whose land they shed
   innocent blood.

20 But Judah will be inhabited forever,^y
and Jerusalem from generation
   to generation.

21 I will pardon their bloodguilt,^C,z
which I have not pardoned,
for the Lord dwells in Zion.

---

*a*3:11 Ezk 38:15-16   *b* Is 13:3   *c*3:12 Ps 7:6; 98:9; Is 3:13   *d*3:13 Jr 51:33; Hs 6:11   *e* Is 63:3; Lm 1:15   *f* Gn 18:20; Rv 19:14-16   *g*3:14 Is 34:2-8   *h* Jl 1:15; 2:1,11   *i*3:15 Jl 2:10,31   *j*3:16 Hs 11:10; Am 1:2   *k* Jr 25:30; Am 1:2   *l* Ezk 38:19; Jl 2:10; Hg 2:6   *m* Ps 46:1; 62:8; Pr 14:26   *n* Jr 16:19; Nah 1:7   *o*3:17 Ex 6:7; 29:46; Ezk 20:20   *p* Is 11:9; 56:7; Ezk 20:40   *q* Is 4:3; Ob 17   *r* Is 52:1; Nah 1:15   *s*3:18 Am 9:13   *t* Ex 3:8   *u* Is 30:25; 35:6   *v* Ezk 47:1-12   *w* Nm 25:1; Ezk 47:8   *x*3:19 Ob 10   *y*3:20 Ezk 37:25; Am 9:15   *z*3:21 Is 4:4

---

^A3:11 LXX, Syr, Tg read *Gather yourselves and come*; Hb obscure   ^B3:18 Or *Shittim*   ^C3:21 LXX, Syr read *I will avenge their blood*

---

demonic spirits are used to motivate the nations for the final battle). The nations are to mobilize for war (cp. the opposite in Is 2:4; Mc 4:3).

3:13 The Lord will trample His enemies like **grapes** in a **winepress** (Is 63:1-6; Rv 14:14-20).

3:14-17 Multitudes, multitudes are hordes of people in the valley of judgment. The **decision** is the verdict that Yahweh is pronouncing on an unbelieving world, not a decision that people are making to follow God. It is too late because it is

judgment day for Israel's enemies but salvation day for the people of God—**a refuge . . . a stronghold**. This will be a time of revelation to Israel and the nations because Yahweh will be known as He is.

3:18-21 Joel summarized the result of the Day of the Lord. The land of Israel will have miraculous fertility and fruitfulness. Traditional enemies will be punished. Yahweh will dwell with His people, and they will receive pardon for their sins.

Valley of Jehoshaphat (Kidron Valley) in Jerusalem (3:12)

Amos
Introduction

Amos is the first of the four eighth-century B.C. prophets, which also included Hosea, Isaiah, and Micah. Along with Hosea, Amos's ministry was to Israel even though he was from Judah. He was a layman who did not consider himself a professional prophet (7:14-15). Through words and visions, Amos spoke against the superficial religious institutions of his day.

"The Lord God showed me this: The Lord God was calling for a judgment by fire. It consumed the great deep and devoured the land" (7:4).

Circumstances of Writing

Author: Amos was a shepherd from Tekoa, a village about 10 miles south of Jerusalem. He received a call from God to go north and prophesy against Samaria and the kingdom of Israel probably around 760 B.C. We do not know how long he actually was in the north; it appears to have been a fairly short time. He provoked a great deal of opposition and anger, as illustrated by his encounter with Amaziah, the priest of Bethel (7:10-17). Apparently he wrote his book, a summary of his prophecies, after his return to Judah. He probably wrote it with the aid of a scribe.

Background: Amos prophesied during the reigns of Uzziah of Judah (792–740 B.C.) and Jeroboam II of Israel (793–753 B.C.). This was a time of great prosperity and military success for both nations, as all their traditional enemies were in a weakened condition. Samaria, the capital city of Israel, enjoyed enormous wealth, and luxuries flowed into the city.

At the same time, decades of struggle with Damascus had left the population exhausted. Many farmers were reduced to poverty. Their more affluent neighbors, and especially the aristocracy, swooped in with loans that the poor could not repay and then reduced the debtors to slavery and seized their lands. The leaders of society believed they had no reason to fear for the future. Their city had high walls and fortified citadels, and their army was everywhere victorious. They were the chosen people of God, and they considered themselves immune from judgment.

Message and Purpose

Several key teachings make up the message of Amos.

1. God is impartial and fair, judging each nation appropriately. Neither Jew nor Gentile is exempted from divine judgment. The Gentiles are punished for moral outrages that we would now call "crimes against humanity," while the Jews are judged by the demands of the Mosaic law (see 1:3–2:3; cp. with 2:4-5).

800–760 B.C.

Adad-Nirari III led his Assyrian army to victory over Syria and the destruction of Damascus. 802

For half a century after the fall of Damascus, Assyrian expansion was thwarted by internal problems. 802–745

Jeroboam II, king of Northern Kingdom, enjoyed an era of peace, expansion, increased trade, and increased affluence. 793–753

Uzziah, king of Southern Kingdom 792–740

Eclipse of the sun visible in Judah/Israel June 15, 763

Earthquake at Hazor between 765 and 760

760–750 B.C.

Amos is called to travel from Judah to Israel to prophesy in Samaria. 760

Zechariah, king of Northern Kingdom 753–752, assassinated by Shallum

Shallum, king of Northern Kingdom 752, assassinated by Menahem

Menahem, king of Northern Kingdom 752–742

Hosea's prophetic ministry 750–722?

Micah called to be a prophet 750

2. God despises human pride, especially when it is demonstrated through confidence in military power, wealth, and indifference toward other people (6:1-8).

3. God is especially harsh against anyone who abuses or cheats the poor (8:4-6).

4. God is not impressed by worship services with music and celebration if the people have unrepentant hearts (4:4-5; 5:21-24).

5. Religious leaders who oppose a genuine work of God are subject to special judgment (7:10-17).

6. People who are blinded by their confidence in their special status before God assume that they have no reason to fear divine judgment, but they are totally misguided (5:18-20).

7. When troubles begin to mount up against a nation, the people should see this as a warning from God and repent before it is too late (4:6-12).

8. Even after judgment, when it seems that all hope is lost (9:1-4), God is able to bring about redemption and salvation (9:13-15).

9. Israel's hope (and humanity's hope) is in the line of David, which God will raise up to establish His kingdom (9:11-12). We now know that this hope is fulfilled in David's descendant, Jesus Christ.

Contribution to the Bible

Amos reminds us of the sovereignty of God in His involvement with His people. God will bring His judgment, a reality that certainly came to pass. Amos's emphasis on the Day of the Lord had implications for Amos's contemporaries, but it also reminds the modern reader of a coming day referred to repeatedly in the NT—the day of Christ's return.

Structure

After the superscript (1:1), the book of Amos is divided into seven parts. The first part, the introduction, is a

---

750–740 B.C.

Assyrian aggressions were thwarted by internal problems until 745 when Tiglath-pileser III came to power.

Pekahiah, king of Northern Kingdom 742–740, assassinated by Pekah

Death of King Uzziah of Judah 740

Isaiah's call to be a prophet 740

Other states in the region pay tribute to the growing power of Assyria. 740

740–600 B.C.

Tiglath-pileser III's invasions of Israel 734–732

Pekah of Israel and Rezin of Damascus form a mutual defense alliance against Assyria and invite Ahaz of Judah to join them. 734

Ahaz refuses Isaiah's counsel and seeks protection from Assyria by paying tribute to them, creating a heavy financial burden on Judah for years to come. 734

Alliance between Syria and Israel collapses with the fall of Damascus (732) and the fall of Samaria (722)

Pekah, king of Northern Kingdom 752–732, assassinated by Hoshea, last king of Northern Kingdom 732–722

single verse (1:2). This is followed by six major divisions: 1:3–2:16; 3:1-15; 4:1-13; 5:1–6:14; 7:1–8:3; 8:4–9:15. Remarkably, formulas of divine speech (statements such as, "the LORD says," "the LORD has spoken," and "the LORD's declaration") are evenly distributed in these sections. Amos 1:3–2:16 has 14 such formulas, and each of the following sections have seven each, for a total of 49. The basic structure and content of each section is described in the notes.

Outline

I. Prophecies Against the Nations (1:1–2:16)
    A. Superscription and proclamation (1:1-2)
    B. Indictment of neighboring nations (1:3–2:3)
    C. Indictment of Judah (2:4-5)
    D. Indictment of Israel (2:6-16)

II. Three Discourses Against Israel (3:1–6:14)
    A. A declaration of judgment (3:1-15)
    B. The depravity of Israel (4:1-13)
    C. A lamentation for Israel's sin and doom (5:1–6:14)

III. Five Symbolic Visions of Israel's Condition (7:1–9:10)
    A. Devouring locusts (7:1-3)
    B. A flaming fire (7:4-6)
    C. A plumb line (7:7-17)
    D. A basket of ripe fruit (8:1-14)
    E. The Lord at the altar inflicting discipline (9:1-10)

IV. Promises of Israel's Restoration (9:11-15)

1 The words of Amos, who was one of the sheep breeders^{A,a} from Tekoa^b—what he saw regarding Israel in the days of Uzziah,^c king of Judah, and Jeroboam^d son of Jehoash, king of Israel, two years before the earthquake.^e

² He said:

> The LORD roars^f from *Zion
> and raises His voice from Jerusalem;
> the pastures of the shepherds mourn,^{B,g}
> and the summit of Carmel^h withers.

Judgment on Israel's Neighbors

³ The LORD says:

> I will not relent
>   from punishing Damascusⁱ
> for three crimes, even four,^j
> because they threshed Gilead
>   with iron sledges.
> ⁴ Therefore, I will send fire
>   against Hazael's palace,

> and it will consume
>   Ben-hadad's^k citadels.
> ⁵ I will break down the gates^{C,l}
>   of Damascus.
> I will cut off the ruler
>   from the Valley of Aven,
> and the one who wields the scepter
>   from Beth-eden.
> The people of Aram will be exiled
>   to Kir.^m
> The LORD has spoken.

⁶ The LORD says:

> I will not relent from punishing Gazaⁿ
> for three crimes, even four,
> because they exiled
>   a whole community,
> handing them over to Edom.
> ⁷ Therefore, I will send fire
>   against the walls of Gaza,
> and it will consume its citadels.
> ⁸ I will cut off the ruler from Ashdod,^o

Cross-references

ᵃ1:1 2Kg 3:4; Am 7:14-15
ᵇ 2Sm 14:2; Jr 6:1
ᶜ 2Kg 15:1-7; 2Ch 26:1-23; Is 1:1; Hs 1:1
ᵈ 2Kg 14:23-29
ᵉ Zch 14:5
ᶠ1:2 Is 42:13; Jr 25:30; Jl 3:16; Am 3:8
ᵍ Is 24:4-7; Jr 12:4; 23:10; Jl 1:10,18-19
ʰ Am 9:3
ⁱ1:3 Is 17:1-3
ʲPr 30:15-29; Am 2:1,4,6
ᵏ1:4 2Kg 8:11-15; 13:3,22,24
ˡ1:5 Gn 22:17; Neh 1:3; Lm 2:9; Hs 11:6; Nah 3:13
ᵐ 2Kg 16:9; Am 9:7
ⁿ1:6 Jr 47:1,4-5; Ezk 25:15-17
ᵒ1:8 2Ch 26:6; Am 3:9; Zch 9:6

1:1 Some believe that Amos was a very poor man, being no more than a day laborer who tended livestock and worked in orchards (7:14), but **sheep breeders** may imply that Amos owned sheep and cattle and that he was in the middle or upper-middle class. The book does not tell us anything about his economic status. Although Amos was from Judah, his message was primarily designated for **Israel**, the northern kingdom. The **earthquake** was evidently of such severity that other events were dated relative to it. Lacking a single fixed point for their calendar (as our calendar has, being fixed relative to the birth of Christ), the Israelites dated events relative to the reigns of kings or to other significant events. In addition, the earthquake, coming two years after Amos's ministry, symbolically confirmed his message (9:5). The fact that the book is precisely dated to **two years**

before the earthquake suggests that Amos's preaching career was fairly short.

1:2 This verse sets the theme of the book: God is like a roaring lion. This symbolically portrays His giving a message to His prophets and His readiness to pounce and attack (3:4-8).

1:3–2:16 The first section of Amos is a series of oracles against the nations: Damascus (or Syria; 1:3-5), Gaza (or Philistia; 1:6-8), Tyre (or Phoenicia; 1:9-10), Edom (1:11-12), Ammon (1:13-15), Moab (2:1-3), Judah (2:4-5), and Israel (2:6-16). The focus is on Israel, which is last and is given by far the longest oracle. There are six Gentile nations followed by Judah, the seventh. One would think that this creates a complete list, with seven oracles in all, but Israel comes as the eighth, and thus the tally of her sin is in effect greater than the number seven, which symbolized completion. That is, Israel is the quintessentially wicked nation. Also, the order of the nations slowly tightens around Israel. First is Damascus, to the northeast; then Gaza, to the southwest; then Tyre, to the northwest; then Edom, to the southeast; and next come Ammon and Moab, across the Jordan River to the east; and finally before Israel comes Judah, located immediately south of Israel.

1:3 The significance of the expression **for three crimes, even four** is debated. But it could be translated as "for three crimes, and for [another] four," implying that the number of offenses had reached seven and was therefore complete, requiring judgment. **Damascus** regularly struggled with Israel for control of **Gilead**, east of the Sea of Galilee. It used brutal military tactics there, symbolically described as going over the countryside with **iron sledges**.

1:4 Hazael and Ben-hadad were throne names used by all the kings of Damascus.

1:6 The Philistines captured villages in order to sell the entire populace into slavery.

1:7-8 All the major cities of the Philistines (**Gaza . . . Ekron . . . Ashkelon**, and **Ashdod**) are mentioned except Gath,

---

pesha'

Hebrew Pronunciation	[PEH shah]
HCSB Translation	rebellion, transgression, crime
Uses in Amos	10
Uses in the OT	93
Focus passage	Amos 1:3,6,9,11,13

Pesha' occurs alongside (23x) chatta'th ("sin") and (19x) 'awon ("iniquity") as a synonym stressing rebellion (Ex 34:7) against authority in a breach of relationships. Pesha' is wrongdoing that violates law (Ex 22:9), so also transgression (Gn 50:17) and crime (Am 1:3). It is sin (Pr 10:19), often provoking outrage as offense (Pr 10:12). Pesha' appears as rebellious (Is 57:4). The plural denotes acts of rebellion (Ps 25:7). The verb pasha' (41x) has similar meanings and accompanies the noun as commit (Ezk 18:31). Pasha' denotes rebel (Is 1:2) or be in rebellion (1Kg 12:19). Marah ("rebel"; Lm 3:42) is a synonym. Pasha' means transgress (Ezk 2:3) and sin (Pr 28:21). Participles imply rebels (Is 1:28), transgressors (Is 46:8), or the rebellious (Hs 14:9). The infinitive indicates transgression (Is 59:13). Pasha' occurs with prepositions meaning "against" (be; 'al; Hs 7:13; 8:1). The passive-reflexive participle signifies offended (Pr 18:19).

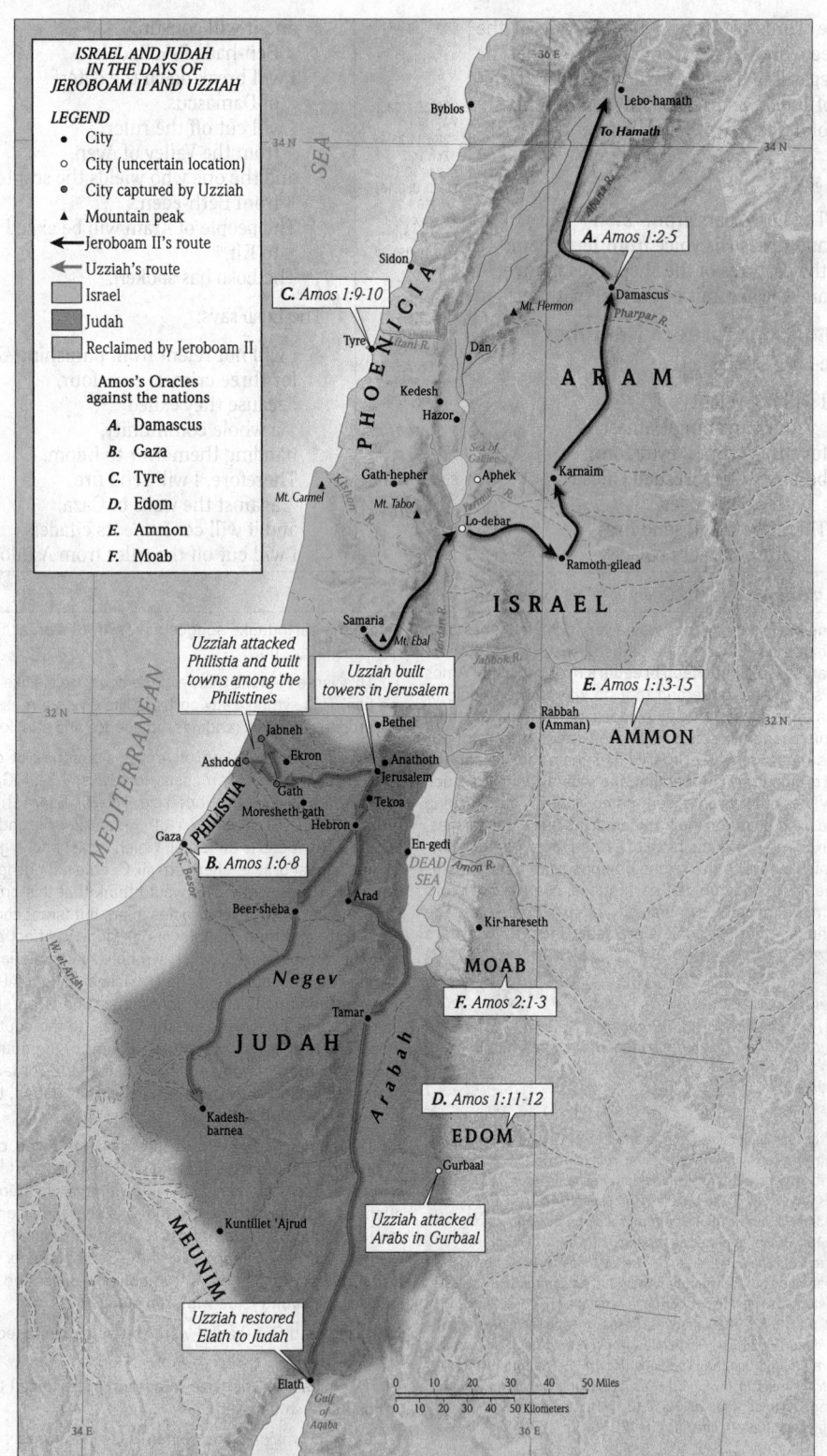

ISRAEL AND JUDAH
IN THE DAYS OF
JEROBOAM II AND UZZIAH

LEGEND

- • City
- ◦ City (uncertain location)
- ● City captured by Uzziah
- ▲ Mountain peak
- ← Jeroboam II's route
- ← Uzziah's route
- Israel
- Judah
- Reclaimed by Jeroboam II

Amos's Oracles
against the nations

- A. Damascus
- B. Gaza
- C. Tyre
- D. Edom
- E. Ammon
- F. Moab

A. Amos 1:2-5

C. Amos 1:9-10

E. Amos 1:13-15

B. Amos 1:6-8

F. Amos 2:1-3

D. Amos 1:11-12

Uzziah attacked
Philistia and built
towns among the
Philistines

Uzziah built
towers in Jerusalem

Uzziah attacked
Arabs in Gurbaal

Uzziah restored
Elath to Judah

MEDITERRANEAN SEA

PHOENICIA

ARAM

ISRAEL

PHILISTIA

JUDAH

AMMON

MOAB

EDOM

MEUNIM

Negev

Arabah

DEAD SEA

Sea of Galilee

Gulf of Aqaba

Byblos
Lebo-hamath
To Hamath
Sidon
Damascus
Mt. Hermon
Tyre
Dan
Kedesh
Hazor
Karnaim
Gath-hepher
Aphek
Mt. Carmel
Mt. Tabor
Lo-debar
Ramoth-gilead
Samaria
Mt. Ebal
Bethel
Rabbah (Amman)
Jabneh
Ashdod
Ekron
Anathoth
Gath
Jerusalem
Moresheth-gath
Tekoa
Gaza
Hebron
En-gedi
Beer-sheba
Arad
Kir-hareseth
Tamar
Kadesh-barnea
Gurbaal
Kuntillet 'Ajrud
Elath

0   10   20   30   40   50 Miles
0 10 20 30 40 50 Kilometers

and the one who wields the scepter
    from Ashkelon.[a]
I will also turn My hand against Ekron,
and the remainder of the Philistines[b]
    will perish.
The Lord God has spoken.

[9] The Lord says:

I will not relent from punishing Tyre[c]
    for three crimes, even four,
because they handed over
a whole community of exiles to Edom
and broke[A] a treaty of brotherhood.[d]

[10] Therefore, I will send fire[e]
    against the walls of Tyre,
and it will consume its citadels.

[11] The Lord says:

I will not relent from punishing Edom[f]
    for three crimes, even four,
because he pursued his brother
    with the sword.[g]
He stifled his compassion,
his anger tore at them[h] continually,
and he harbored his rage incessantly.

[12] Therefore, I will send fire against Teman,[i]
and it will consume the citadels
    of Bozrah.

[13] The Lord says:

I will not relent from punishing
    the Ammonites[j]
for three crimes, even four,
because they ripped open
the pregnant women of Gilead[k]
in order to enlarge their territory.[l]

[14] Therefore, I will set fire to the walls
    of Rabbah,[m]
and it will consume its citadels.
There will be shouting on the day
    of battle[n]
and a violent wind on the day
    of the storm.[o]

[15] Their king and his princes
    will go into exile together.[p]
The Lord has spoken.

2 The Lord says:

I will not relent from punishing Moab[q]
    for three crimes, even four,
because he burned the bones
of the king of Edom to lime.[r]

[2] Therefore, I will send fire against Moab,
and it will consume the citadels
    of Kerioth.[s]
Moab will die with a tumult,[t]
with shouting and the sound
    of the ram's horn.

[3] I will cut off the judge[u] from the land
and kill all its officials[v] with him.
The Lord has spoken.

Judgment on Judah

[4] The Lord says:

I will not relent from punishing Judah[w]
    for three crimes, even four,
because they have rejected
    the instruction of the Lord[x]
and have not kept His statutes.[y]
The lies[z] that their ancestors followed[aa]
have led them astray.

[5] Therefore, I will send fire[ab]
    against Judah,
and it will consume the citadels
    of Jerusalem.

Judgment on Israel

[6] The Lord says:

I will not relent from punishing Israel[ac]
    for three crimes, even four,
because they sell a righteous person
    for silver
and a needy person for a pair of sandals.[ad]

[7] They trample the heads of the poor[ae]
on the dust of the ground
and block the path of the needy.[af]

[a] 1:8 Jr 47:5; Zph 2:4
[b] Is 14:29-31; Ezk 25:16
[c] 1:9 Is 23; Ezk 26:1–28:19
[d] 1Kg 5:1,12; 9:11-14
[e] 1:10 Zch 9:4
[f] 1:11 Jr 49:8-22; Ezk 25:12-14
[g] Nm 20:14; Dt 2:4; 23:7; Ob 10-14
[h] Gn 37:33; Ps 7:2; Hs 5:14
[i] 1:12 Jr 49:7,20
[j] 1:13 Jr 49:1-6; Ezk 25:1-7; Zph 2:8-11
[k] 2Kg 8:12; 15:16; Hs 13:16
[l] Is 5:8; Ezk 35:10
[m] 1:14 1Ch 20:1; Jr 49:2
[n] Ezk 21:22; Am 2:2
[o] Is 29:6; 30:30
[p] 1:15 Jr 49:3
[q] 2:1 Is 15–16; Jr 48; Ezk 25:8-11
[r] Lv 20:14; 21:9
[s] 2:2 Jr 48:24,41
[t] Jr 48:45
[u] 2:3 Ps 2:10; 141:6
[v] Jb 12:21; Is 40:23
[w] 2:4 2Kg 17:19; Hs 2:12; Am 3:2
[x] Jdg 2:17-20; 2Kg 22:11-17; Jr 6:19; 8:9
[y] Jr 44:10; Ezk 5:7
[z] Is 9:15-16; Jr 11:10-13; 23:14,21-22
[aa] Jr 9:14; 16:11-12; Ezk 20:18,24,30
[ab] 2:5 Jr 17:27; 21:10
[ac] 2:6 2Kg 18:12
[ad] Dt 16:18-20; Am 5:12; 8:6
[ae] 2:7 Am 5:11; 8:4; Mc 2:2,9
[af] Jb 24:4

[A]1:9 Lit *and did not remember*

which by the time of Amos had already been substantially wiped out.

1:9 Tyre also raided towns to sell the people into slavery, and it did so in violation of treaty obligations.

1:11 Edom committed border raids (probably against Judah) in which they exterminated entire populations.

1:13 The Ammonites sought to exterminate the population of **Gilead** by slaughtering the **pregnant women**.

2:1 Interpreters puzzle over the charge that Moab **burned the bones of the king of Edom to lime**. Some say the act displayed simple disrespect for a human body, and others that it was motivated by a belief that burning the bones would prevent the victim from participating in the resurrec-

tion (but there is no evidence for such a belief). Lime was used for plastering walls, and an ancient Jewish interpretation says that the king of Moab used the lime to plaster his palace walls. Assyrian kings often decorated their walls with scenes depicting their atrocities against their enemies.

2:4 All the Gentile nations are accused of crimes against humanity, but **Judah** is charged with unfaithfulness to its covenant with God as described in the law. The **lies** mentioned here are idols.

2:6 Selling **a needy person for a pair of sandals** probably refers to selling a debtor into slavery over a trifling sum of money.

2:7-8 This text describes outrages committed at the religious shrines. Men had sexual relations with shrine prostitutes, even going to the point of **a man and his father** sharing the

A man and his father
  have sexual relations
with the same girl,*a*
profaning My holy name.*b*

8 They stretch out beside every altar*c*
on garments taken as collateral,*d*
and in the house of their God,
they drink wine obtained
  through fines.*e*

9 Yet I destroyed the Amorite*f*
  as Israel advanced;
his height*g* was like the cedars,
and he was as sturdy as the oaks;
I destroyed his fruit*h* above
  and his roots beneath.

10 And I brought you from the land
  of Egypt*i*
and led you 40 years in the wilderness*j*
in order to possess the land
  of the Amorite.*k*

11 I raised up some of your sons
  as prophets*l*
and some of your young men
  as Nazirites.*m*
Is this not the case, Israelites?
        This is the LORD's declaration.

12 But you made the Nazirites drink wine
and commanded the prophets,
"Do not prophesy."*n*

13 Look, I am about to crush*A* you
  in your place*o*
as a wagon full of sheaves
  crushes grain.

14 Escape will fail the swift,*p*
the strong one will not prevail
  by his strength,*q*
and the brave will not save his life.

15 The archer will not stand
  his ground,*r*
the one who is swift of foot
  will not save himself,
and the one riding a horse will not save
  his life.*s*

16 Even the most courageous
  of the warriors
will flee naked on that day*t*—
        this is the LORD's declaration.

God's Reasons for Punishing Israel

3 Listen to this message that the LORD has
spoken against you, Israelites, against the
entire clan that I brought from the land of
Egypt:*u*

2 I have known only you*v*
  out of all the clans of the earth;
therefore, I will punish you for all
  your iniquities.*w*

3 Can two walk together*x*
  without agreeing to meet?*B*

a 2:7 Hs 4:14
b Lv 18:21;
Pr 30:9; Ezk
36:20-23
c 2:8 Am 3:14
d Ex 22:26
e Am 4:1; 6:6
f 2:9 Jos 10:12
g Nm 13:28-33
h Ezk 17:9; Mal
4:1
i 2:10 Ex 20:2;
Am 3:1; 9:7
j Dt 2:7
k Nm 21:25
l 2:11 Dt 18:18-
19; Jr 1:4-5; Am
7:14-15
m Nm 6:1-21;
Jdg 13:2-5; 1Sm
1:11
n 2:12 Jr 11:21;
Am 7:13,16
o 2:13 Jl 3:13
p 2:14 Is
30:16-17
q Jr 9:23
r 2:15 Jr 51:56;
Ezk 39:3
s Is 31:3
t 2:16 Jdg 4:17
u 3:1 Am 2:10
v 3:2 Ex 19:5-6;
Dt 4:32-37
w Jr 14:10; Ezk
20:36; Dn 9:12
x 3:3 Lv 26:23-24

A 2:13 Or *hinder*; Hb obscure   *B* 3:3 LXX reads *without meeting*

---

same woman; they did this while lying on **garments** that they had taken from poor people as **collateral** for loans; they did this at pagan altars all over the countryside; and they combined this with drinking bouts at the shrines, using **wine** they had taken from powerless people.

2:9-12 In this section God gives a historical retrospective, comparing His favors toward Israel with Israel's impudent rejection of Him.

2:9-10 Disregarding historical sequence, the conquest of Canaan (v. 9) is mentioned before the exodus and wilderness wandering (v. 10). This is probably because the focus here is on how Israel occupied the land by virtue of God's grace, thus implying that God could just as easily expel them from the land.

2:11-12 The **prophets**, as exponents of God's will, and the **Nazirites**, as examples of great devotion to God, came to the Israelites as representatives sent by God to turn the people to righteousness. The Israelite rejection of both groups represents their rejection of God Himself.

2:13 The Hebrew of this verse is difficult. An alternative translation is, "Behold I am weighed down beneath you, just as a cart that is filled with sheaves is weighed down." If this is correct, it expresses God's frustration with Israel's stubborn attitude.

2:14-16 The Israelite army will be routed in battle. Soldiers are described in terms of their prowess and their military specialization. In verse 14, **swift** refers to any soldier who runs fast and therefore would normally escape defeat, and

strong refers to anyone who would normally prevail in battle. At the end of verse 14 and in verse 15, we have four military specializations: the **brave** (lit the "warrior," referring to the heavy infantry in the main line of battle), the **archer**, the **swift of foot** (light infantry), and the **one riding a horse** (the cavalry). Finally, in verse 16, **the most courageous of the warriors** (who would be expected to stand fast in the face of an onslaught) will **flee naked** (cast away their armor, shields, and weapons).

3:1-15 In this chapter Amos answered those who claimed that he had no right to prophesy against Israel because they were the chosen people of God. Against this charge, Amos made three claims: (1) their election guaranteed that they will be judged rather than escape judgment (vv. 1-3); (2) God has spoken, therefore His prophet must speak (vv. 4-8); (3) Israel was so wicked that even pagan nations could sit in judgment against them (vv. 9-11). This passage concludes with a portrait of Israel's destruction (vv. 12-15).

3:2 The Israelites thought their election as God's special people made them immune from judgment, but it actually made their liability to judgment all the more severe.

3:3 The phrase **without agreeing to meet** means "without coming to terms." The idea is that two people cannot walk together (that is, be closely associated with each other) unless they have come to terms and are in substantial agreement. In marriage, for example, two people must agree to certain commitments and have mutual values. Errant Israel could not walk with God because the two parties had substantial differences regarding their values and expectations.

4 Does a lion roar[a] in the forest
  when it has no prey?
  Does a young lion growl from its lair
  unless it has captured something?
5 Does a bird land in a trap on the ground
  if there is no bait for it?
  Does a trap spring from the ground
  when it has caught nothing?
6 If a ram's horn[b] is blown in a city,
  aren't people afraid?[c]
  If a disaster[d] occurs in a city,
  hasn't the LORD done it?[e]
7 Indeed, the Lord GOD does nothing
  without revealing His counsel
  to His servants the prophets.[f]
8 A lion has roared;[g]
  who will not fear?
  The Lord GOD has spoken;[h]
  who will not prophesy?[i]

9 Proclaim on the citadels in Ashdod[j]
  and on the citadels in the land of Egypt:
  Assemble on the mountains of Samaria[k]
  and see the great turmoil in the city
  and the acts of oppression within it.[l]
10 The people are incapable
   of doing right[m]—
          this is the LORD's declaration—
   those who store up violence
   and destruction[n]
   in their citadels.

11 Therefore, the Lord GOD says:

   An enemy[o] will surround the land;
   he will destroy[p] your strongholds
   and plunder your citadels.[q]

12 The LORD says:

   As the shepherd snatches two legs
   or a piece of an ear
   from the lion's mouth,[r]
   so the Israelites who live in Samaria
   will be rescued
   with only the corner of a bed[s]
   or the[A] cushion[B] of a couch.[C,t]

13 Listen and testify[u] against the house
   of Jacob—
                    this is the declaration
                          of the Lord GOD,
                        the God of •Hosts.
14 I will punish the altars of Bethel[v]
   on the day I punish Israel
     for its crimes;
   the horns of the altar[w] will be cut off
   and fall to the ground.[x]
15 I will demolish the winter house[y]
   and the summer house;[z]
   the houses inlaid with ivory[aa]
     will be destroyed,
   and the great houses[ab] will come
     to an end.
                 This is the LORD's declaration.

Social and Spiritual Corruption

4 Listen to this message, you cows
  of Bashan[ac]
  who are on the hill of Samaria,
  women who oppress the poor
  and crush the needy,[ad]
  who say to their husbands,
  "Bring us something to drink."[ae]

Cross references

a 3:4 Ps 104:21; Hs 5:14; 11:10
b 3:6 Jr 4:5,19,21; 6:1; Hs 5:8; Zph 1:16
c Nm 10:9; Jr 4:19; Jl 2:1
d Is 14:24-27; 45:7
e Lm 3:37-39
f 3:7 Gn 18:17; Jr 23:18,22; Jnh 1:2
g 3:8 Am 1:2
h Jnh 1:1-3; 3:1-3
i Jr 6:10-11; 20:9
j 3:9 1Sm 5:1; Am 1:8
k Am 4:1; 6:1
l Am 5:11; 6:8
m 3:10 Ps 14:4; Jr 4:22; Am 5:7; 6:12
n Hab 2:8-10; Zph 1:9; Zch 5:3-4
o 3:11 Am 6:14
p Am 2:14
q 2Kg 17:5-6; 18:9-12
r 3:12 1Sm 17:34-37
s Ps 132:3
t Est 1:6; 7:8; Am 6:4
u 3:13 Ezk 2:7
v 3:14 Hs 10:5-8,14-15; Am 4:4; 5:5-6; 7:10,13
w Lv 8:15; 16:18-19; 1Kg 1:50-51; 2:28; Ps 118:27
x Hs 10:1-2
y 3:15 Jr 36:22
z Jdg 3:20
aa 1Kg 22:39; 2Ch 9:17; Am 6:4
ab Am 2:5; 6:11
ac 4:1 Ps 22:12; Ezk 39:18
ad Ex 23:3,6; Lv 19:15; 25:35; Dt 15:4-11; Am 5:11; 8:6
ae Am 2:8; 6:6

A 3:12 Or Israelites will be rescued, those who sit in Samaria on a corner of a bed or a   B 3:12 Hb obscure   C 3:12 LXX, Aq, Sym, Theod, Syr, Tg, Vg read or in Damascus

---

3:4-8 These verses include a short epigram, a series of poetic verses that teach some kind of lesson and may contain a riddle (vv. 4-6). After this there is a short commentary on the epigram (vv. 7-8). The epigram makes the point that when one thing is true (for example, that a **lion** roars), it is reasonable that something else is also true (he has **prey**). The commentary in verses 7-8 tells us that because God has **roared**, disaster must come and His prophets must **prophesy**. Notice that all the examples in the epigram are violent in nature.

3:9-10 **Ashdod** (the Philistines) and **Egypt** were two traditional oppressors of Israel, but even they did not oppress the Israelites as cruelly as the Israelites oppressed themselves through their rebellion against God. Thus these pagans could sit in judgment on Israel.

3:11-15 Israel's punishment is described in this section.

3:12 Behind this verse one can detect a common viewpoint among the people of Israel: that if an enemy should attack, the Israelites would be **rescued** by God. Amos responded sarcastically by saying that they would be "rescued" like **a piece of an ear from the lion's mouth**. When only pieces of an ear or legs are snatched from a lion's mouth, obviously

the lamb is dead. The main point is that Israel will be completely destroyed, not that a remnant will survive. Even so, there may be a remnant theology in the idea that God can raise the dead nation back to life.

3:14-15 The phrase **altars of Bethel** refers to Israel's religious sins, and the **winter house** and the **summer house** refer to the destruction of the oppressive upper classes.

4:1-13 This chapter has two major parts, and each is an accusation followed by a religious statement used in an ironic and threatening manner. The first part (vv. 1-5) includes an accusation against the aristocratic women of Samaria (vv. 1-3) followed by an ironic benediction (actually a malediction) upon the pilgrims going to the religious shrines (vv. 4-5). The second part (vv. 6-13) accuses Israel of having disregarded all preliminary judgments sent against them, and it asserts that they must be ready for final judgment (vv. 6-12). After this, Amos gives a doxology that is threatening rather than encouraging, describing the power of God (v. 13).

4:1 The expression **cows of Bashan** derisively refers to the upper-class women of Samaria. Bashan, located east of the Sea of Galilee, was famous for its lush pasture and fine

² The Lord God has sworn^a by His holiness:^b

> Look, the days are coming^A
> when you will be taken away
>   with hooks,^c
> every last one of you with fishhooks.^d

³ You will go through breaches
>   in the wall,^e
> each woman straight ahead,
> and you will be driven along
>   toward Harmon.
>   This is the Lord's declaration.

⁴ Come to Bethel and rebel;
> rebel even more at Gilgal!^f
> Bring your sacrifices every morning,^g
> your tenths every three days.
⁵ Offer leavened bread as
>   a thank offering,^h
> and loudly proclaim
>   your freewill offerings,ⁱ
> for that is what you Israelites
>   love to do!^j
>   This is the Lord's declaration.

God's Discipline and Israel's Apostasy

⁶ I gave you absolutely nothing to eat^{B,k}
>   in all your cities,
> a shortage of food in all
>   your communities,
> yet you did not return to Me.^l
>   This is the Lord's declaration.

⁷ I also withheld the rain from you^m
> while there were still three months
>   until harvest.
> I sent rain on one city

> but no rain on another.ⁿ
> One field received rain
> while a field with no rain withered.^o
⁸ Two or three cities staggered
>   to another city to drink water^p
> but were not satisfied,^q
> yet you did not return^r to Me.
>   This is the Lord's declaration.

⁹ I struck you with blight and mildew;^s
>   the locust devoured^t
> your many gardens and vineyards,
> your fig trees and olive trees,^u
> yet you did not return to Me.^v
>   This is the Lord's declaration.

¹⁰ I sent plagues like those of Egypt;^w
> I killed your young men
>   with the sword,^x
> along with your captured horses.^y
> I caused the stench of your camp
>   to fill your nostrils,^z
> yet you did not return to Me.^{aa}
>   This is the Lord's declaration.

¹¹ I overthrew some of you
>   as I^C overthrew Sodom and Gomorrah,^{ab}
> and you were like a burning stick
>   snatched from a fire,^{ac}
> yet you did not return to Me^{ad}—
>   this is the Lord's declaration.

¹² Therefore, Israel, that is what I will do
>   to you,
> and since I will do that to you,
> Israel, prepare to meet your God!^{ae}
¹³ He is here:
>   the One who forms the mountains,^{af}

Cross references (center column):

a4:2 Am 6:8; 8:7
bPs 89:35
cIs 37:29; Ezk 38:4
d2Kg 19:28; 2Ch 33:10-11
e4:3 Jr 52:7
f4:4 Am 5:5
gAm 5:21-22
h4:5 Lv 7:12
iLv 22:18-21
jJr 7:9-10; Hs 9:1,10
k4:6 Is 3:1; Jr 14:18
lIs 9:13; Jr 5:3; Hg 2:17
m4:7 Jr 3:1-3; 5:23-25
nEx 9:4,26; 10:22-23
oLv 26:18-19; Jl 1:10-12
p4:8 1Kg 18:5; Jr 14:4
qEzk 4:16; Hg 1:6
rJr 3:7
s4:9 Dt 28:22; Hg 2:17
tJl 1:4; Am 7:1-2
uDt 28:38-42; Jl 1:4-7,12
vJr 3:10
w4:10 Ex 11:4-5; Dt 28:27,60
xJr 11:22; 18:21; 48:15
y2Kg 13:3,7
zIs 34:3
aaIs 9:13
ab4:11 Gn 19:24-25
acZch 3:1-2
adIs 9:13
ae4:12 Is 32:11; 64:2; Jr 5:22
af4:13 Jb 38:4-7; Ps 65:6; Is 40:12

A4:2 Lit *coming on you*   B4:6 Lit *you cleanness of teeth*   C4:11 Lit *God*

---

livestock (Dt 32:14; Ezk 39:18). Like the cattle of that region, these aristocratic women were well-fed and pampered. The word "cows" is not necessarily an insult in every case. Being a pastoral people, the Israelites often described beauty using imagery related to things that were valued in their culture. For instance, Sg 4:1 compares a beautiful woman's hair to a flock of goats. But the women spoken of by Amos were cruel and unfeeling, as shown by their indifference to the suffering of the poor. Their arrogance was apparent in how they treated even their husbands as household slaves.

4:2-3 The Hebrew of this verse is difficult. The word translated as **taken away** literally means to "lift up," and the words translated **hooks** and **fishhooks** are obscure and may not refer to hooks at all. But if "hooks" is correct, the metaphor may describe the bodies of the "cows" being hoisted on meat hooks. Also, the location of **Harmon** is unknown, and it may be that a scribal error has garbled the text. Still, the main point is clear: many people will be slaughtered, and those who survive will file out of the ruined walls of the city into exile.

4:4-5 A priest or prophet would normally pronounce a benediction on pilgrims going to a shrine, encouraging them to go to God with their offerings. Amos asserted sarcastically that when the Israelites went to their shrines, it only increased their guilt.

4:6-12 Behind this passage stand the warnings of Dt 28:15-68, which told the Israelites that if they refused to obey the laws of the covenant, they would be beset with diseases, droughts, crop failures, and military defeats. Should they refuse to repent, they would suffer national destruction and exile. Amos's point is that they did not repent and thus now must get ready for the judgment of God (Am 4:12). The partial drought that Amos described (vv. 7-8) was evidently of recent occurrence and was fresh in the people's minds. The **plagues** on **Egypt** in the exodus and the destruction of **Sodom** were prototypical acts of divine judgment; the comparison implied that Israel was as evil in God's eyes as those nations were.

4:13 This doxology may be an example of the kind of hymns the Israelites sang at their shrines and on their pilgrimages. Here, however, the lofty power of God is turned against them. This is also a fitting conclusion to the previous passage. Amos had told the Israelites to be ready to meet their God, and this is the kind of God they will meet.

creates the wind,[a]
and reveals His[A] thoughts to man,[b]
the One who makes the dawn
   out of darkness
and strides on the heights of the earth.[c]
•Yahweh, the God of •Hosts,
   is His name.[d]

Lamentation for Israel

5 Listen to this message that I am singing
for you, a lament,[e] house of Israel:

2   She has fallen;
    Virgin Israel[f] will never rise again.[g]
    She lies abandoned on her land,
    with no one to raise her up.[h]

3 For the Lord GOD says:

    The city that marches out
       a thousand strong
    will have only a hundred left,[i]
    and the one that marches out
       a hundred strong
    will have only ten left[j] in the house
       of Israel.

Seek God and Live

4 For the LORD says to the house of Israel:

    Seek Me and live![k]
5   Do not seek Bethel[l]
    or go to Gilgal[m]
    or journey to Beer-sheba,[n]
    for Gilgal will certainly go into exile,
    and Bethel will come to nothing.
6   Seek •Yahweh[o] and live,
    or He will spread like fire[p]
    throughout the house of Joseph;
    it will consume everything,

with no one at Bethel to extinguish it.[q]
7   Those who turn justice
       into •wormwood[r]
    throw righteousness to the ground.

8   The One who made the Pleiades
       and Orion,[s]
    who turns darkness[B] into dawn[t]
    and darkens day into night,[u]
    who summons the waters of the sea[v]
    and pours them out over the face
       of the earth[w]—
    Yahweh is His name.[x]
9   He brings destruction[C] on the strong,[D,y]
    and it falls on the stronghold.[z]

10 They hate the one who convicts
       the •guilty[aa]
    at the city •gate
    and despise[ab] the one who speaks
       with integrity.
11 Therefore, because you trample on
       the poor[ac]
    and exact a grain tax from him,
    you will never live in the houses
       of cut stone[ad]
    you have built;
    you will never drink the wine
    from the lush vineyards
    you have planted.[ae]
12 For I know your crimes are many
    and your sins innumerable.
    They oppress the righteous,[af]
       take a bribe,
    and deprive the poor of justice[ag]
       at the gates.
13 Therefore, the wise person
       will keep silent[E,ah]

Cross references

a 4:13 Ps 135:7
b Ps 139:2; Dn 2:30
c Mc 1:3
d Am 5:8-9,27; 9:5-6
e 5:1 Jr 7:29; 9:10,17; Ezk 19:1
f 5:2 Jr 14:17; 31:4,21
g Am 8:14
h Is 51:18
i 5:3 Is 6:13
j Am 6:9
k 5:4 Dt 4:29; 32:46-47
l 5:5 1Kg 12:28-29
m 1Sm 7:16; 11:14
n Gn 21:31-33
o 5:6 Is 55:3,6-7
p Dt 4:24; 32:22; Heb 12:29
q Is 33:14; 66:24; Jr 4:4
r 5:7 Am 6:12
s 5:8 Jb 9:9; 38:31
t Gn 1:2-3; Jb 38:12
u Am 8:9
v Ps 104:6-9; Jr 10:13
w Jb 36:27-30
x Am 4:13; 9:5-6
y 5:9 Is 29:5
z Mc 5:11
aa 5:10 Is 29:21
ab Is 59:15
ac 5:11 Am 3:9; 8:6; Jms 1:27
ad Am 3:15; 6:11
ae Dt 28:30; Mc 6:15; Zph 1:13
af 5:12 Is 1:23; 5:23
ag Am 2:6-7
ah 5:13 Ec 3:7; Hs 4:4

A 4:13 Or *his*   B 5:8 Or *turns the shadow of death*   C 5:9 Hb obscure   D 5:9 Or *stronghold*   E 5:13 Or *the prudent will perish*

5:1–6:14 This lengthy and complex passage presents the core of the accusation against Israel. The passage begins with the lament in 5:2 that there was no one to **raise . . . up** fallen **Israel**, and it ends in 6:14 with God **raising up** an enemy against Israel. The idea of lamentation dominates the passage, appearing as a lament over Israel's doom (5:1-3), in the predicted laments of 5:16-17, and in the funerary situation at 6:9-10. The main accusations are given in 5:4-6:7 in two sets of verses (5:4-15 and 5:18-6:7), and these two sets are similar to each other. In the first set, Israel presumptuously assumed that its pilgrimages satisfied God (5:4-7), even while they were oppressing the poor (5:10-15). In the second set, Israel again assumed its worship and festivals satisfied God, presumptuously certain that the Day of the Lord would bring them no trouble (5:18-24) even while they lived in arrogant luxury in Samaria (6:1-7). In both sets, therefore, their religious arrogance is placed alongside their arrogant indifference toward the poor. Also, in the first set, God is praised as Maker of the heavens (5:8-9), while in the second set, ironically, Israel worships the sky gods (5:25-27). Amos 6:8-11 pictures the judgment that is com-

ing to Israel. Finally, 6:12-14 summarizes the whole with a proverb (v. 12), an accusation (v. 13), and a judgment (v. 14).

5:2 Israel is lamented as a **virgin** because the land should have been kept secure but now had been raped by invading armies.

5:5 Bethel . . . Gilgal, and Beer-sheba were three pilgrimage shrines. Bethel was where Jacob had his vision of the stairway into heaven (Gn 28:12-19), but it was also one of the places where King Jeroboam I of Israel set up calf idols (1Kg 12:28-29). Gilgal was the embarkation point for the crossing of the Jordan River and the invasion of Canaan, and Joshua set up a memorial there (Jos 4:19-20). Beersheba, far to the south, is closely associated with the sojourns of Abraham (Gn 21:14), and we know from archaeology that there was a shrine there.

5:8 The focus here is on God's power over the skies; this is important in light of the accusation in verse 26.

5:13 Because the people with power were so hostile to anyone who told the truth in the courts of law (v. 10), honest and decent people were being silenced.

at such a time,
for the days are evil.

14 Seek good and not evil
so that you may live,
and the Lord, the God of •Hosts,
will be with you,
as you have claimed.[a]

15 Hate evil and love good;[b]
establish justice in the gate.[c]
Perhaps the Lord, the God of Hosts,
will be gracious[d]
to the remnant of Joseph.[e]

16 Therefore Yahweh, the God of Hosts, the Lord, says:

There will be wailing in all
the public squares;[f]
they will cry out in anguish[A] in all
the streets.
The farmer will be called on to mourn,[g]
and professional mourners[B,h] to wail.

17 There will be wailing in all
the vineyards,[i]
for I will pass among you.[j]
The Lord has spoken.

The Day of the Lord

18 Woe to you who long for the Day
of the Lord![k]
What will the Day of the Lord be for you?
It will be darkness and not light.[l]

19 It will be like a man who flees
from a lion[m]
only to have a bear confront him.
He goes home and rests his hand
against the wall
only to have a snake bite him.

20 Won't the Day of the Lord
be darkness rather than light,[n]
even gloom without any brightness
in it?[o]

a 5:14 Is 48:1-2
b 5:15 Rm 12:9
c Is 1:17
d Jl 2:14
e Mc 3:5,7-8
f 5:16 Jr 9:10,18-20; Am 8:3
g Jl 1:11
h Jr 9:17
i 5:17 Is 16:10; Jr 48:33
j Ex 12:12
k 5:18 Is 5:19; Jl 1:15; 2:1,11,31
l Is 5:30
m 5:19 Jb 20:24; Is 24:17; Jr 15:2-3
n 5:20 Is 13:10; Zph 1:15
o Jl 2:2; Zph 1:15
p 5:21 Is 1:11-16; 66:3; Am 6:8
q Lv 26:31; Jr 14:12; Hs 5:6
r 5:22 Mc 6:6-7
s Jr 14:12
t Lv 7:11-15
u 5:23 Is 5:12
v 5:21-24 Mc 6:6-8
w 5:25 Dt 32:17; Jos 24:14; Neh 9:18-21; Ac 7:42-43
x 5:26 Is 44:12-20
y 5:25-27 2Kg 17:5-6; Ac 7:42-43
z 5:27 Am 4:13
aa 6:1 Is 32:9-11; Zph 1:12
ab 6:2 Gn 10:10; Is 10:9
ac 1Kg 8:65; 2Kg 18:34; Is 10:9
ad 1Sm 5:8; 2Ch 26:6
ae 6:3 Am 9:10
af Am 3:10

21 I hate, I despise your feasts![p]
I can't stand the stench
of your solemn assemblies.[q]

22 Even if you offer Me
your •burnt offerings
and •grain offerings,[r]
I will not accept them;[s]
I will have no regard
for your •fellowship offerings
of fattened cattle.[t]

23 Take away from Me the noise
of your songs!
I will not listen to the music
of your harps.[u]

24 But let justice flow like water,
and righteousness,
like an unfailing stream.[v]

25 "House of Israel, was it sacrifices and grain offerings that you presented to Me during the 40 years in the wilderness?[w] 26 But you have taken up[C] Sakkuth[D,E] your king[F] and Kaiwan[G] your star god, images you have made for yourselves.[x] 27 So I will send you into exile beyond Damascus."[y] Yahweh, the God of Hosts, is His name.[z] He has spoken.

Woe to the Complacent

6 Woe to those who are at ease in •Zion[aa]
and to those who feel secure on the hill
of Samaria—
the notable people in this first
of the nations,
those the house of Israel comes to.

2 Cross over to Calneh[ab] and see;
go from there to great Hamath;[ac]
then go down to Gath[ad] of the Philistines.
Are you better than these kingdoms?
Is their territory larger than yours?

3 You dismiss any thought
of the evil day[ae]
and bring in a reign of violence.[af]

A 5:16 Lit will say, "Alas! Alas!"   B 5:16 Lit and those skilled in lamentation   C 5:26 Or you will lift up   D 5:26 LXX, Sym, Syr, Vg read the tent; Ac 7:43   E 5:26 Probably a Mesopotamian war god also called Adar or Ninurta   F 5:26 LXX reads up the tent of Molech and Rephan; Ac 7:43   G 5:26 Probably a Mesopotamian god identified with Saturn

5:16-17 The focus on the **farmer** and the **vineyards** in these verses suggests that the lamentation came about because of crop failure.

5:18-19 The Israelites assumed that because they were the chosen people, they would be exempt from judgment on the **Day of the Lord**.

5:25-26 This text is the source of great confusion because it appears to teach that the Israelites made no **sacrifices** during the **wilderness** period, contrary to what is recorded in the Pentateuch (Ex 24:5). Probably Am 5:25 should be joined to verse 26, as follows: "Did you offer sacrifices and grain offerings to Me 40 years in the wilderness, House of Israel, while you were taking up Sakkuth your king?" Read this way, Israel did make sacrifices to God while in the wil-

derness, but the people also carried images of the **Sakkuth** and other gods. During Amos's time, however, they were more brazenly combining the worship of the Lord with the worship of these pagan gods. Sakkuth and **Kaiwan** were names of the sky deity of the planet Saturn.

6:2 **Calneh** (Calno, Is 10:9) was in Syria. It had been destroyed by the Assyrians in the mid-ninth century. **Hamath**, another Syrian city, was conquered by Jeroboam II, the king of Israel during the ministry of Amos (2Kg 14:28; it may be that Calneh also was subdued by Jeroboam II). **Gath**, a Philistine city, was destroyed by another contemporary of Amos, King Uzziah of Judah (2Ch 26:6). These fallen cities served as warnings to the people of Samaria, who assumed their city was indestructible.

4 They lie on beds inlaid with ivory,[a]
     sprawled out on their couches,[b]
     and dine on lambs from the flock[c]
     and calves from the stall.
5 They improvise songs[A] to the sound
        of the harp[d]
     and invent[B] their own
        musical instruments like David.[e]
6 They drink wine by the bowlful[f]
     and anoint themselves with the finest oils
     but do not grieve over the ruin
        of Joseph.[g]
7 Therefore, they will now go into exile
     as the first of the captives,[h]
     and the feasting[i] of those
        who sprawl out
     will come to an end.

Israel's Pride Judged

8 The Lord God has sworn by Himself[j]—this
is the declaration of •Yahweh, the God of
•Hosts:

     I loathe Jacob's pride[k]
       and hate his citadels,[l]
     so I will hand over the city[m]
       and everything in it.

9 And if there are 10 men left in one house,
they will die.[n] [10] A close relative[C] and burner[D,o]
will remove his corpse[E] from the house. He
will call to someone in the inner recesses of
the house, "Any more with you?"
     That person will reply, "None."
     Then he will say, "Silence, because Yahweh's
name must not be invoked."[p]
11 For the Lord commands:

     The large house will be smashed
       to pieces,
     and the small house to rubble.[q]

Cross references (center column):
[a] 6:4 Am 3:15
[b] Am 3:12
[c] Ezk 34:2-3
[d] 6:5 Am 5:23; 8:10
[e] 1Ch 15:16
[f] 6:6 Am 2:8; 4:1
[g] Jr 8:21; Lm 2:11
[h] 6:7 Am 7:11,17
[i] 1Kg 20:16-21; Dn 5:4-6,30
[j] 6:8 Gn 22:16; Jr 22:5; 51:14
[k] Lv 26:30; Dt 32:19; Ps 106:40
[l] Am 3:10-11
[m] Hs 11:6
[n] 6:9 Am 5:3
[o] 6:10 1Sm 31:12; 2Ch 16:14; 2Ch 16:14; Jr 34:5
[p] Is 48:1; Jr 44:26; Hs 4:15
[q] 6:11 Am 1:1; 9:9

[A] 6:5 Hb obscure   [B] 6:5 Or *compose on*   [C] 6:10 Lit *His uncle*   [D] 6:10 A burner of incense, a memorial fire, or a body; Hb obscure
[E] 6:10 Lit *remove bones*

6:4-6 The Israelite aristocracy enjoyed what the Greeks would call a "symposium" (lit "drinking together"), in which participants lounged on **couches**, drank **wine**, and listened to music.

6:8 The **pride** of Israel is described in this verse as its **citadels**, the walls and towers that seemed to make the city of Samaria impregnable.

6:9-10 The meaning of this difficult text seems to be as follows. Casualties in the city will be so numerous that a household containing **10 men** will be wiped out. A **relative** will be designated to retrieve the bodies and conduct funeral rites, and he and his party will look for any survivors. Informed that there are none, he will declare that **Yahweh's name must not be invoked**. That is, instead of giving the normal

An eighth-century B.C. Hebrew house (3:15; 6:11). Archaeological excavations in the area bear out the society of Samaria and the Northern Kingdom in the eighth century. Houses in the tenth-century strata are uniform. The eighth-century strata shows great contrast between large houses of the affluent and small structures in which the poor lived.

12 Do horses gallop on the cliffs;
does anyone plow there with oxen?[A]
Yet you have turned justice
into poison[a]
and the fruit of righteousness
into •wormwood[b]—
13 you who rejoice over Lo-debar[c]
and say, "Didn't we capture Karnaim
for ourselves by our own strength?"[d]
14 But look, I am raising up a nation
against you, house of Israel[e]—
this is the declaration
of the Lord,
the God of Hosts—
and they will oppress you
from the entrance of Hamath[B,f]
to the Brook of the •Arabah.[c]

First Vision: Locusts

7 The Lord God showed me this: He was forming a swarm of locusts[g] at the time the spring crop first began to sprout—after the cutting of the king's hay. **2** When the locusts finished eating the vegetation of the land,[h] I said, "Lord God, please forgive![i] How will Jacob survive since he is so small?"[j]

3 The Lord relented concerning this.[k] "It will not happen," He said.

Second Vision: Fire

4 The Lord God showed me this: The Lord God was calling for a judgment by fire.[l] It consumed the great deep and devoured the land. **5** Then I said, "Lord God, please stop![m] How will Jacob survive since he is so small?"

6 The Lord relented concerning this.[n] "This will not happen either," said the Lord God.

Third Vision: A Plumb Line

7 He showed me this: The Lord was standing there by a vertical wall with a plumb line in His hand. **8** The Lord asked me, "What do you see, Amos?"[o]

I replied, "A plumb line."

Then the Lord said, "I am setting a plumb line among My people Israel;[p] I will no longer spare them:[q]

9 Isaac's •high places[r] will be deserted,
and Israel's sanctuaries will be in ruins;[s]
I will rise up
against the house of Jeroboam
with a sword."

a6:12 1Kg 21:7-13; Is 59:13-14
b Is 5:20; Am 5:7; Rv 8:11
c6:13 Jb 8:14-15; Ps 2:2-4; Lk 12:19-20
d Ps 75:4; Is 28:14-15
e6:14 Am 3:11
f Nm 34:7-8; 2Kg 14:25
g7:1 Ex 10:12-15; Dt 28:38,42; Jl 1:4
h7:2 Ex 10:15
i Jr 14:7,20-21; Ezk 9:8; 11:13
j Is 37:4; Jr 42:2
k7:3 Jr 26:19; Hs 11:8
l7:4 Am 1:3–2:5
m7:5 Ps 85:4; Jl 2:17
n7:6 Ps 106:45; Jnh 3:10
o7:8 Jr 1:11; Am 8:2
p Is 28:17; 34:11; Lm 2:8
q Am 8:2
r7:9 2Kg 17:9-13; Hs 10:8
s Lv 26:31; Is 63:18; Jr 51:51

A6:12 Some emend to *plow the sea*   **B**6:14 Or *from Lebo-hamath*   **C**6:14 Probably the Valley of Zared at the southeast end of the Dead Sea

---

funeral dirges and laments—which may have included invocations of Israel's God (Lm 1:20)—God's name will not be mentioned at all (probably because God's name should not be mentioned in the midst of so much carnage, and also because the dead were evidently under God's curse). Thus, where there ought to be a lament (Am 5:1-2), the situation will be so bad that even this will be denied to the people.

6:12-13 Verse 12 is a proverb concerning absurd, irrational behavior. The point is that the boasting of verse 13 is equally absurd. **Lo-debar** was a city east of the Sea of Galilee that the Israelites boasted about capturing, but the name "Lo-debar" sounds like the Hebrew for the word, "nothing." **Karnaim**, another town in Transjordan, means "two horns." In other words, the people boasted of having conquered "nothing" and "two horns."

6:14 The **entrance of Hamath** (also called Lebo-hamath) was the northern limit of Israel's domain. The **Brook of the Arabah** is only mentioned here, but it may be the same as the Brook of Egypt, the traditional southern border of Israel (Jos 15:4). The point is that the Israelites will be driven from all the lands that had been allotted to them by the Lord.

7:1–8:3 This section contains four visions (locusts, 7:1-3; fire, 7:4-6; plumb line, 7:7-9; basket of summer fruit, 8:1-3). Between the third and fourth vision is a biographical unit describing a confrontation between Amos and Amaziah, the chief priest of the Bethel shrine.

7:1-3 In the Bible **locusts** are a common image of God's wrath. Locusts were one of the plagues of Egypt (Ex 10:1-19). A locust plague struck Judah and became emblematic for the Day of the Lord in Joel 1. In this case, however, Israel was not actually struck with a locust plague; Amos merely saw it in a vision and, in response to his pleas, God relented and no actual locust plague came.

7:3 The phrase, **The Lord relented**, here and in verse 6 distresses and confuses some readers because it implies that God changed His mind. The same expression is used in Ex 32:14, where God relented in response to the intercession of Moses after He had announced His intention to wipe out Israel and make a new nation from Moses' descendants. Readers wonder how an omniscient God could change His mind. Two errors must be avoided. First, the conclusion that God is not fully omniscient and that there are things in the future that He cannot know. Second, the conclusion that God's relenting (or changing His mind) is only a pretense and that Amos's and Moses' acts of intercession did not really change anything God was planning to do. God is fully omniscient, and our prayers do matter. These two truths are certain even if they seem mysterious. Additionally, the "change" of God's mind would of course be something He foreknew He would do in response to intercession by prayerful men such as Moses and Amos.

7:4 The vision of **fire** is probably symbolic of a ferocious, all-consuming drought. Amos tells us that the land had endured a partial drought (4:7-8), but this was evidently a drought so severe that the whole land would become like a desert. But in response to Amos's intercession, it did not happen.

7:7 The Hebrew text does not contain a word meaning **vertical**, and the word translated as **plumb line** is an enigma; no one really knows what this Hebrew word means. Medieval interpreters proposed the translation "plumb line"; the Greek Septuagint translated it as "adamant" around 200 b.c. and the Latin Vulgate, around a.d. 400, translated it as "plaster." Many scholars today, on the basis of an Akkadian parallel, argue that it means "tin," but it is difficult to see why God would hold tin in His hand. Our confusion

Amaziah's Opposition

[10] Amaziah the priest[a] of Bethel sent word to Jeroboam king of Israel, saying, "Amos has conspired against you[b] right here in the house of Israel. The land cannot endure all his words, [11] for Amos has said this: 'Jeroboam will die by the sword, and Israel will certainly go into exile from its homeland.'"[c]

[12] Then Amaziah said to Amos, "Go away, you seer![d] Flee to the land of Judah. Earn your living[A] and give your prophecies there, [13] but don't ever prophesy[e] at Bethel again, for it is the king's sanctuary[f] and a royal temple."

[14] So Amos answered Amaziah, "I was[B] not a prophet or the son of a prophet;[C,g] rather, I was[B] a herdsman,[h] and I took care of sycamore figs. [15] But the LORD took me from following the flock[i] and said to me, 'Go, prophesy to My people Israel.'"[j]

[16] Now hear the word of the LORD. You say:

Do not prophesy[k] against Israel;
do not preach[l] against the house
of Isaac.

[17] Therefore, this is what the LORD says:

Your wife will be a prostitute
in the city,[m]
your sons and daughters will fall
by the sword,[n]

and your land will be divided up
with a measuring line.
You yourself will die on pagan[D] soil,[o]
and Israel will certainly go into exile[p]
from its homeland.

Fourth Vision: A Basket of Summer Fruit

8 The Lord GOD showed me this: A basket of summer fruit. [2] He asked me, "What do you see, Amos?"[q]

I replied, "A basket of summer fruit."[r]

The LORD said to me, "The end has come for My people Israel;[s] I will no longer spare them.[t] [3] In that day the temple[E] songs[u] will become wailing"[v]—this is the Lord GOD's declaration. "Many dead bodies, thrown everywhere!"[w] Silence!"[x]

[4] Hear this, you who trample
   on the needy[y]
and do away with the poor of the land,[z]
[5] asking, "When will the New Moon
   be over
so we may sell grain,[aa]
and the Sabbath,
so we may market wheat?[ab]
We can reduce the measure
while increasing the price[F]
and cheat with dishonest scales.[ac]
[6] We can buy the poor with silver

Cross references (center column)
a7:10 1Kg 12:31-32; 13:33
bJr 26:8-11; 38:4
c7:11 Am 5:27
d7:12 Mt 8:34
e7:13 Am 2:12; Ac 4:18
f1Kg 12:29; Am 7:9
g7:14 2Kg 2:3; 4:38; 2Ch 19:2
h Am 1:1
i7:15 2Sm 7:8
j Jr 1:7; Ezk 2:3-4
k7:16 Am 2:12
l Mc 2:6
m7:17 Hs 4:13-14
n Jr 14:16
o2Kg 17:6; Ezk 4:13; Hs 9:3
pJr 36:29-31
q8:2 Am 7:8
rJr 24:3
sEzk 7:2-3,6
tAm 7:8
u8:3 Am 5:23; 6:4-5
vAm 5:16
wIs 34:3; Jr 33:5; Nah 3:3
xAm 6:10
y8:4 Am 2:7; 5:11-12
zIs 10:2
aa8:5 Nm 28:11; 2Kg 4:23
abEx 31:13-17
acDt 25:13-15; Pr 20:23; Hs 12:7

A7:12 Lit *Eat bread*   B7:14 Or *am*   C7:14 = a prophet's disciple or a member of a prophetic guild   D7:17 Lit *unclean*   E8:3 Or *palace*   F8:5 Lit *reduce the ephah and make the shekel great*

---

about the meaning of this key word makes verses 7-8 difficult to interpret.

7:10-17 The account of Amos's confrontation with Amaziah in this section interrupts the sequence of visions. Amaziah represented the Israelite hierarchy, who considered Amos to be either a charlatan or a conspirator against King Jeroboam. Ironically, Amaziah called Amos a **seer** (someone who had visions; v. 12), and the context shows that Amos did in fact have visions from God and that he was a genuine seer. In addition, Amaziah accused Amos of plotting against Israel and the king (v. 10), but in fact Amos was interceding for Israel (vv. 2,5).

7:14 The Hebrew for **I was not a prophet** is ambiguous; it could be past tense, as here in the HCSB, or it could be present tense, "I am not a prophet." Both the past and present tenses are appropriate. On the one hand, Amos was not a prophet until God called him and gave him a message (v. 15). On the other hand, Amos is not a prophet in the sense that Amaziah meant it: a hireling who peddles his messages for gain (v. 12). Amos earned his bread as a herdsman, not by his prophesying. A **son of a prophet** refers not to a prophet's biological son but to a member of a prophetic guild.

Sycamore figs had to be scraped or split in order to ripen properly. Apparently one part of Amos's occupation was cutting such figs, but we do not know if he did it as a day laborer and was therefore poor or if he actually owned a grove of fig trees.

8:1-3 The Hebrew word for **summer fruit** (*qayits*) sounds almost identical to the word translated as **end** (*qets*) in verse 2. Just as the fruit in the basket had ripened, so also Israel was ripe for judgment.

8:4-9:15 This, the last major segment of Amos, is in four sections. First, God accused the merchants and the wealthy class of cheating people in the sale of grain and of enslaving people for the sake of trifling debts (8:4-6). Next, there is a judgment in which God swears an oath, the land heaves like the Nile River, people mourn, and there is a famine for the Word of God (8:7-14). For the third section, another judgment passage follows: God stands by the altar (in effect swearing another oath), the Israelites are hunted down, and the land again heaves like the Nile River (9:1-6). In the final section, Israel is compared to the nations to which it must go in exile, but abruptly the judgment is reversed, and Israel becomes predominant among all the nations and very prosperous (9:7-15). Other parallels also bind this passage together. There is, for example, a focus on food and crops. In 8:5 the merchants deceitfully sell grain, in 8:11-14 there is a famine, and finally in 9:13 there is a great harvest. Also, in 9:1-4 God hunts down and kills every last Israelite, but in 9:14-15 there is an abundant population. Finally, 8:9 and 9:6 both refer to God's power over the heavens.

8:5-6 Three accusations are combined here: contempt for the Sabbath, cheating customers when selling them food, and enslaving people who could not pay even the smallest of debts.

and the needy for a pair of sandals[a]
and even sell the chaff!"

[7] The LORD has sworn[b] by the Pride of Jacob:[A,c]

I will never forget all their deeds.[d]
[8] Because of this, won't the land quake[e]
and all who dwell in it mourn?[f]
All of it will rise like the Nile;[g]
it will surge and then subside
like the Nile in Egypt.[h]

[9] And in that day—
this is the declaration
of the Lord GOD—
I will make the sun go down at noon;[i]
I will darken the land in the daytime.[j]
[10] I will turn your feasts into mourning[k]
and all your songs into lamentation;[l]
I will cause everyone[B]
to wear *sackcloth[m]
and every head to be shaved.[n]
I will make that grief
like mourning for an only son[o]
and its outcome like a bitter day.

[11] Hear this! The days are coming—
this is the declaration
of the Lord GOD—
when I will send a famine
through the land:
not a famine of bread or a thirst
for water,
but of hearing the words of the LORD.[p]
[12] People will stagger from sea to sea
and roam from north to east,
seeking the word of the LORD,[q]
but they will not find it.
[13] In that day the beautiful young women,[r]
the young men also, will faint
from thirst.[s]

[14] Those who swear by the *guilt
of Samaria[t]
and say, "As your god lives, Dan,"[u]
or "As the way[C,D] of Beer-sheba lives"[v]—
they will fall, never to rise again.[w]

Fifth Vision: The LORD beside the Altar

[9] I saw the Lord standing beside the altar,[x]
and He said:

Strike the capitals of the pillars[y]
so that the thresholds shake;
knock them down on the heads of all
the people.
Then I will kill the rest of them
with the sword.[z]
None of those who flee will get away;[aa]
none of the fugitives will escape.
[2] If they dig down to *Sheol,[ab]
from there My hand will take them;
if they climb up to heaven,[ac]
from there I will bring them down.
[3] If they hide themselves
on the top of Carmel,
from there I will track them down[ad]
and seize them;
if they conceal themselves
from My sight on the sea floor,[ae]
from there I will command
the sea serpent to bite them.[af]
[4] And if they are driven
by their enemies into captivity,[ag]
from there I will command
the sword to kill them.[ah]
I will fix My eyes on them
for harm and not for good.[ai]

[5] The Lord, the GOD of *Hosts—
He touches the earth;[aj]
it melts, and all who dwell in it mourn;

---

[a] 8:6 Am 2:6
[b] 8:7 Am 4:2; 6:8
[c] Dt 33:26,29; Ps 47:4
[d] Ps 10:11; Hs 7:2; 8:13
[e] 8:8 Ps 18:7; 60:2; Is 5:25; Am 1:1
[f] Hs 4:3
[g] Jr 46:7-8
[h] Am 9:5
[i] 8:9 Is 13:10; Ezk 32:7; Jl 2:10,31
[j] Is 59:9-10; Am 4:13; 5:8; Mt 27:45
[k] 8:10 Jb 20:23; Am 5:21
[l] Lm 5:15; Hs 2:11; Jms 4:9
[m] Ezk 7:18
[n] Is 22:12; Jr 48:37; Ezk 7:18
[o] Zch 12:10-14
[p] 8:9-11 Mc 3:6-7
[q] 8:12 Ezk 20:3,31
[r] 8:13 Lm 1:18; 2:21
[s] Is 41:17; Hs 2:3
[t] 8:14 Hs 8:5
[u] 1Kg 12:28-29
[v] Am 5:5
[w] Am 5:2; Jr 25:27
[x] 9:1 Am 3:14
[y] Zph 2:14
[z] Jos 5:13-15; Am 7:9,17
[aa] Jr 11:11
[ab] 9:2 Ps 139:8
[ac] Jr 51:53; Ob 4
[ad] 9:3 Jb 34:22; Ps 139:9-10
[ae] Jnh 2:2-6
[af] Is 27:1
[ag] 9:4 Lv 26:33
[ah] 9:2-4 Jb 34:21-22; Ps 139:7-12; Jr 23:24
[ai] 9:4 Jr 21:10; 44:27
[aj] 9:5 Ps 104:32; 144:5; Is 64:1

[A] 8:7 = the LORD or the promised land   [B] 8:10 Lit every loin   [C] 8:14 LXX reads god   [D] 8:14 Or power

---

8:7 It is odd that God swears in this verse by the **Pride of Jacob**. In 6:8, He said that He hated "Jacob's pride," and in that case the pride of Jacob was the citadels and wealth of Israel. It is not likely that God would swear by something He hated. In 4:2 God swore by His "holiness," and in 6:8 He swore by "Himself." In this verse, therefore, the "Pride of Jacob" is probably again God Himself. The implication, comparing 6:8 to 8:7, is that the Israelites ought to boast in their God, but instead they were boasting in their military and economic power.

8:8 The **Nile** River flooded every year. The upheaval, overflow, and subsidence of the river are metaphorical for an earthquake.

8:9 The darkening of the **sun** implies the coming of the Day of the Lord.

8:11-12 The **famine** for **hearing the words of the LORD** suggests the time of Israel's exile and Diaspora, when Jewish people would wander through the nations, alienated from their God and Messiah.

8:14 The **guilt of Samaria** is the shrines the people made throughout the land, but especially at Dan and Bethel. The **way of Beer-sheba** probably refers to the pilgrimage devotees made to Beer-sheba and by extension to the pagan god they worshiped there.

9:1 The phrase **knock them down on the heads of all the people** could be translated as "sever them at the head—all of them!" The shrines, fortresses, and palaces will come down. Also, the leaders of the people are described here metaphorically as the **pillars** that will be cut down. The common people are called **the rest of them**. The point is that no one, whether of high or low status, will escape God's judgment.

9:2-4 None of the Israelites will be able to **hide** from God (v. 3). The language here is hyperbole (exaggeration for rhetor-

all of it rises like the Nile
and subsides like the Nile of Egypt.[a]
6 He builds His upper chambers
in the heavens[b]
and lays the foundation of His vault
on the earth.[c]
He summons the waters of the sea
and pours them out on the face
of the earth.[d]
·Yahweh is His name.[e]

Announcement of Judgment

7 Israelites, are you not like the ·Cushites
to Me?[f]
This is the LORD's declaration.
Didn't I bring Israel from the land
of Egypt,
the Philistines from Caphtor,[A,g]
and the Arameans from Kir?[h]
8 Look, the eyes of the Lord GOD
are on the sinful kingdom,[i]
and I will destroy it
from the face of the earth.[j]
However, I will not totally destroy
the house of Jacob[k]—
this is the LORD's declaration—
9 for I am about to give
the command,
and I will shake the house of Israel[l]
among all the nations,
as one shakes a sieve,
but not a pebble will fall
to the ground.
10 All the sinners among My people[m]
who say: "Disaster will never overtake[B]
or confront us,"[n]
will die by the sword.

Announcement of Restoration

11 In that day
I will restore the fallen booth[o]
of David:[p]
I will repair its gaps,
restore its ruins,[q]
and rebuild it as
in the days of old,[r]
12 so that they may possess
the remnant of Edom[s]
and all the nations
that are called by My name[C,t]—
this is the LORD's declaration—
He will do this.

[a]9:5 Am 8:8
[b]9:6 Ps 104:3,13
[c]Ps 102:25; Is 48:13; 51:13
[d]Ps 104:6
[e]Am 4:13; 5:8-9
[f]9:7 2Ch 14:9,12; Is 20:4; 43:3
[g]Dt 2:23; Jr 47:4
[h]2Kg 16:9; Is 22:6
[i]9:8 Am 9:4
[j]Am 3:12
[k]Jr 5:10; 30:11; 31:35-36; Jl 2:32
[l]9:9 Is 30:28; Lk 22:31
[m]9:10 Is 33:14; Zch 13:8
[n]Jr 5:12; 23:17; Am 6:3
[o]9:11 Lv 23:42-43; 2Sm 11:11; 1Kg 20:12; Is 4:6
[p]2Sm 7:11-16; Jr 23:5; Ezk 34:23-24; Zch 9:9-10; Lk 1:32; Rv 5:5
[q]Is 44:26
[r]Is 63:11; Jr 46:26
[s]9:12 Ezk 36:5; Ob 21
[t]9:11-12 Is 43:6-7; Mal 1:11; Ac 15:15-18

[A]9:7 Probably Crete [B]9:10 Or *You will not let disaster come near* [C]9:12 LXX reads *so that the remnant of man and all the nations . . . may seek Me*; Ac 15:17

ical effect). Obviously no one can literally climb into **heaven** or hide at the bottom of the **sea**.

9:7 The **Cushites** were people from Nubia, directly south of Egypt. **Caphtor** was either Crete or Cyprus, and it represented the Aegean Sea area from which the Philistines came. **Kir** was probably east of Mesopotamia, in the area of Elam. The point is that God had moved many nations, not just Israel, to their homelands. But it is astonishing that God would compare the exodus of Israel, the mighty act by which He claimed Israel for Himself, to the movements of other nations. This seems to be a terrible demotion of Israel, implying that it was no different than any other nation (rather than being a "holy nation"; Ex 19:6). Yet there is a positive side; if Israel is demoted to the level of the Gentiles, the Gentiles will be promoted to equality with Israel, and they will be included among God's people (Am 9:12; see also Eph 2:11-16).

9:8-10 The text moves abruptly from God's destruction of Israel to His restoration of the nation. Although He will scatter His people among the nations, not one person will be lost to Him, and one day He will bring them back.

9:11-12 The **fallen booth of David** refers to the dynasty and empire of David (normally called the "house" of David but here a "booth," symbolic of the pathetic condition of this once-mighty line of kings). The restoration will take place first at the resurrection of Christ but after that in the eternal kingdom of the new heaven and new earth (Rv 21:1). **Edom** is representative of the Gentiles that hated and persecuted Israel. The point is that some day all nations, however hostile they have been, will submit either willingly or unwillingly. Paul likewise declared that some day every knee will bow to Jesus (Php 2:10). But clearly Amos did not envision simple domination of the Gentiles. Many will be **called by My name**, implying that they will belong to God. This promise is fulfilled now, as Gentiles all over the world worship Israel's God and Messiah. James understood the passage in this way and cited it as being fulfilled in the mission to the Gentiles (Ac 15:14-18). James's citation of Am 9:12 in Ac 15:17 differs somewhat from the Hebrew because he seems to be loosely quoting from the Greek Septuagint translation of Amos. Also, the Hebrew word for "Edom" is similar to the word for "humanity" *(adam)*, which explains why Amos has "Edom" but James has "humanity."

shamad

Hebrew Pronunciation	[shah MAD]
HCSB Translation	destroy, annihilate, exterminate
Uses in Amos	5
Uses in the OT	90
Focus passage	Amos 9:8

This root appears in Aramaic (Dn 11:44) outside of Hebrew. *Shamad* means *destroy* (Am 2:9). It describes objects (Lv 26:30) and individuals (2Sm 14:11) but usually groups of people. *Shamad* suggests *demolish* (Nm 33:52) and *devastate* (Dt 9:3). It is *annihilate* (Dt 7:24), *exterminate* (1Kg 16:12), or *eliminate* (Ps 37:38). It connotes *wipe off* (Dt 6:15), *wipe out* (1Sm 24:21), and *remove* (Jos 7:12). Occurring 29 times in Deuteronomy, *shamad* describes God's destruction of earlier peoples (Dt 2:21-23) and intended destruction of Canaanites (Dt 7:23). *Shamad* often warns Israel of potential destruction (Dt 6:15), seven times in Deuteronomy 28 (Dt 28:51). *Shamad* appears 14 times with *'avad* ("perish, destroy"; Dt 28:20), 10 with *yarash* ("drive out, take possession"; Dt 2:12), six with *karath* ("cut off"; Is 10:7), five with *nachah* ("strike down"; Jos 11:14), four with *harag* ("kill"; Est 3:13), and three with *charam* ("annihilate"; Dn 11:44).

13 Hear this! The days are coming—
          this is the LORD's declaration—
    when the plowman will overtake
       the reaper[a]
    and the one who treads grapes,
    the sower of seed.
    The mountains will drip
       with sweet wine,
    and all the hills will flow with it.[b]
14 I will restore the fortunes
    of My people Israel.[A,c]

They will rebuild and occupy
    ruined cities,[d]
plant vineyards and drink
    their wine,
make gardens and eat
    their produce.[e]
15 I will plant them on their land,
    and they will never again
       be uprooted
    from the land I have given them.[f]
    Yahweh your God has spoken.

a9:13 Lv 26:5
bJl 2:24; 3:18
c9:14 Dt 30:3; Jr 31:23; 32:42-44
dJr 30:18; 33:10-11
eIs 65:21; Jr 31:5
f9:15 2Sm 7:10; Jr 24:6

A9:14 Or restore My people Israel from captivity

9:13-15 Just as God had promised to bring famine to Israel and nearly to exterminate the nation, He promises in these verses to give them abundant crops and a large population. The statement that **the plowman will overtake the reaper** is hyperbole for fruitfulness and served to assure the people that they would enjoy eternal well-being.

Obadiah

Introduction

Many Prophetic Books contain prophecies against several nations, but the book of Obadiah focuses exclusively on the nation of Edom. Obadiah's short message centers on the approaching Day of the Lord and the promise that Israel will possess the land of Edom.

"This is what the Lord God has said about Edom: . . . Your presumptuous heart has deceived you, you who live in clefts of the rock in your home on the heights, who say to yourself, 'Who can bring me down to the ground?' Though you seem to soar like an eagle and make your nest among the stars, even from there I will bring you down." (vv. 1,3,4)

Circumstances of Writing

Author: Presumably Obadiah (v. 1) was the author of this book, but nothing else is known about him. His common Hebrew name, denoting "servant of the Lord," is shared by at least a dozen persons in the Old Testament.

Background: The time of writing of Obadiah is disputed, with a wide variety of proposed dates from the tenth to the fifth centuries B.C., depending on when the invasion and plunder of Jerusalem (vv. 11-14) occurred. The two most popular views are during the reign of King Jehoram of Judah (ca 848–841 B.C.) and shortly after the final destruction of Jerusalem by the Babylonians (587/586 B.C.).

The former date (ca 845 B.C.) was when the Philistines and Arabs plundered Judah (2Ch 21:16-17) and the Edomites revolted (2Kg 8:20), presumably then becoming allies of the invaders. Since the text does not explicitly indicate the cooperation of the Edomites with the Philistines and Arabs, the latter date (mid-sixth or even fifth century B.C.) fits the biblical data better, including Ob 20 (the dispersed exiles of the Israelites and of Jerusalem to be restored), as opposed to dates before the dispersion of Israel (by 722 B.C.) or of Judah (605–586 B.C.). This postexilic view is also supported by the mention of Edomite involvement in Jerusalem's downfall (Ob 10-14, gloating over the fall of Jerusalem, as in other sixth-century B.C. texts—Lm 4:21a; Ezk 35:15; cp. Lm 2:15-17—and participating in the plunder) which would result in the Lord's promised justice ("As you have done, so it will be done to you" on their heads, Ob 15).

Message and Purpose

Judgment on Edom's arrogant presumption: Yahweh's judgment was predicted for Edom because of her arrogance in trusting geographical security (vv. 3-5), diplomatic treaties (v. 7), and the counsel of her famed wise men (v. 8; Jr 49:7) instead of the true God of Israel. Edom was doubly deceived, depending on their own human understanding (Ob 3,8) and believing in the loyalty of their human allies (v. 7). Thus God would bring them down from the lofty cliffs and caves of their mountains. He would cover the Edomites with shame be-

---

2000 B.C.

Edomites are descendants of Esau and seen as "brothers of Israel." 1900

The Edomites refused the Israelites' passage through their land as Israel journeyed from Egypt to Canaan. 1406

Egyptian texts from about 1300 to 1100 refer to Shasu, apparently semi–nomadic tribes, from Seir and Edom.

Saul delivers Israel from the hands of neighbors on almost all sides, including Edom. 1020

1000 B.C.

David resisted Edom's encroachment on Israel by striking down 18,000 Edomites in the region of the Dead Sea. To further secure Israel's southeastern flank, David builds garrisons throughout Edom, which are then subject to David. 982

Hadad, a member of Edom's royal family, fled to Egypt during the time David subjected Edom. When Solomon is king, God brings Hadad back as an enemy of Solomon, a disciplinary measure for Solomon's turning away from God. 940

cause of their arrogant gloating and gleeful participation in the downfall of their brother Jacob, the nation of Judah (vv. 10-14).

The Day of the Lord: Obadiah spoke of the nearness of the Day of the Lord (Is 13:6; Jl 1:15; 2:1; Zph 1:7,14), focusing on the darkness and gloom of Yahweh's wrath (Is 13:6-13; Jl 1:15; 2:1-3,10-11,31; Zph 1:7-18; 2:2; Mal 4:1-3,5). He emphasized the dual nature of the Day of the Lord in bringing retributive judgment on the historical nation Edom and "Edom" as symbolic of Israel's archenemies (payback on their heads; Ob 15) while, at the same time, bringing salvation (or restoration) for the nation of Israel (Jl 2:30-32; Zph 2:1-10; 3:8-16). In the OT, Edom was a historical entity whose people may have been completely wiped out by A.D. 70 (see notes at Ob 3,10,18). This historical entity blends with "Edom," a symbol for Israel's end-time enemies (cp. vv. 15-16; Is 63:1-6; Ezk 35; 36:2,5—the context of the Day of Lord against *all* the nations).

Israel's repossession of the land (vv. 17-21): In a second conquest motif, the Hebrew word meaning "possess by dispossessing" is used five times: four times of Israel (both north and south) dispossessing (v. 17) the inhabitants of the promised land (vv. 19-20) and once the same root (v. 17) describes those enemies (including "Esau") who had dispossessed them. Reminiscent of the conquest of Canaan, this Hebrew word was often used in Deuteronomy of God's instructions for conquering the promised land (Dt 1:8,21,39; 4:5,14,26) and also in Joshua (Jos 24:8). Thus as in Jr 49:2 (expected second conquest of Ammon in the last days), a second conquest motif (see usage of "Canaanites" in Ob 20) appears in Israel's possession of the hill country of "Edom" and the territories of other enemies (vv. 17-20).

Contribution to the Bible

Like the book of Revelation, which proclaims the downfall of the persecuting Roman Empire, the book of Obadiah sustains faith in God's moral government and hope in the eventual triumph of His just will. It brings a pastoral message to aching hearts that God is on His throne and He cares for His own.

---

850 B.C.

600 B.C.

During Jehoram's reign as king of the Southern Kingdom, Edom begins to rebel against domination by Judah and becomes an independent state with its own king. 848–841

Some interpreters place Obadiah's prophecy in the ninth century when Edom rebelled against Judah. 848–841

Edom puts aside its hostilities toward Judah during the reign of Zedekiah. 594

Edom becomes Judah's ally in resisting the Babylonians. 594

Edom soon commits an act of hostility against Judah that brings impassioned denunciation of Edom from Jeremiah, a psalmist (Ps 137), and Ezekiel. 586

The more likely setting of Obadiah's prophecy is in this era surrounding the Babylonian devastation of Jerusalem and the temple. 586

Structure

The text declares the book of Obadiah is a prophetic "vision" from the Lord (v. 1) which also appears to be a war oracle (v. 1) communicating Yahweh's imminent judgment upon Edom (vv. 2-9). As a subtype of the prophetic "oracle against foreign nations" (Is 13–23; Jr 46–51; Ezk 25–32; Am 1–2; Zph 2:4-15), it is typical in announcing judgment on a foreign power (specifically Edom; see also Lm 4:21-22) to bring deliverance for Judah (Ob 17-20; see Jr 46:25-28; Nah 1:1-15; Zph 3:14-20). Yet it, like Nahum and Jonah, is atypical in focusing solely on judgment for a foreign nation, rather than specifying judgment for Israel as well.

This shortest OT book consists of several parts. A war oracle from the Lord announces certain judgment on Edom for their arrogant presumption and self-deception (v. 3) that they were immune from divine intervention (vv. 1-9). Next is an explanation of the further cause for coming judgment on Edom (vv. 10-14)—a lack of brotherly commitment (vv. 10-11) in gloating over the day of disaster for God's people Judah (vv. 12-13) and cooperating with Judah's enemies in her destruction (vv. 10-11,13-14). Then the text focuses on the Day of the Lord (vv. 15-21) in which imminent judgment on the historical nation of Edom (vv. 15-16), followed by ultimate judgment on "Edom" as representative of Israel's end-time enemies (v. 16), would result in the deliverance of both Judah and Israel (vv. 17-21).

Outline

I.   An Oracle of the Lord Against Edom (vv. 1-9)

II. Esau's Sin Against His Brother Jacob (vv. 10-14)

III. The Wider Context: The Day of the Lord (vv. 15-18)

IV. House of Jacob Will Possess Edom's Territory (vv. 19-21)

The vision of Obadiah.

Edom's Certain Judgment

This is what the Lord God has said about Edom:[a]

We have heard a message from the Lord;[b]
a messenger has been sent[c]
  among the nations:
"Rise up,[d] and let us go to war
  against her."[A]

2 Look, I will make you insignificant[e]
among the nations;
you will be deeply despised.

3 Your presumptuous heart
  has deceived you,[f]
you who live in clefts of the rock[B,C,g]
in your home on the heights,
who say to yourself,
"Who can bring me down
  to the ground?"[h]

4 Though you seem to soar[D] like an eagle[i]
and make your nest among the stars,[j]
even from there I will bring you down.
                This is the Lord's declaration.

5 If thieves came to you,[k]
if marauders by night—
how ravaged you would be!—
wouldn't they steal only
  what they wanted?

If grape pickers came to you,
  wouldn't they leave some grapes?[l]

6 How Esau will be pillaged,[m]
his hidden treasures searched out![n]

7 Everyone who has a treaty with you[o]
will drive you to the border;
everyone at peace with you
will deceive and conquer you.
Those who eat your bread[p]
will set[E] a trap for you.
He will be unaware of it.[q]

8 In that day—
                this is the Lord's declaration—
will I not eliminate the wise ones
  of Edom[r]
and those who understand
from the hill country of Esau?

9 Teman,[F,s] your warriors[t] will be terrified
so that everyone
  from the hill country of Esau
will be destroyed by slaughter.[u]

Edom's Sins against Judah

10 You will be covered with shame
and destroyed forever
because of violence done
  to your brother Jacob.[v]

11 On the day you stood aloof,[w]
on the day strangers captured
  his wealth,[G]

Cross references

a1 Gn 25:30; Ps 137:7; Is 21:11-12; 34:1-17; 63:1-6; Ezk 25:12-14; Am 1:11-12; Mal 1:2-5
b1-4 Jr 49:14-16
c1 Is 18:2; 30:4
d Jr 6:4-5
e2 Nm 24:18; Is 23:9
f3 Is 16:6
g 2Kg 14:7; 2Ch 25:12
h Is 14:13-15
i4 Jb 20:6-7; Hab 2:9
j Is 14:12-15
k5 Jr 49:9
l Lv 19:10; 25:5,11
m6 Jr 49:10
n Mal 1:2-3
o7 Ps 55:20; Jr 30:14; Am 1:9
p Ps 41:9
q Jr 49:7
r8 Jb 4:1; 5:12-14
s9 Gn 36:11; 1Ch 1:45; Jb 2:11; Hab 3:3
t Jr 49:22
u Is 34:5-8; 63:1-3; Jr 49:7,20; Ezk 25:13; Am 1:12; Ob 5
v10 Ezk 25:12-14; Jl 3:19; Am 1:11
w11 Ps 83:5-6; 137:7; Am 1:6,9

A1 = Edom   B3 Or in Sela; probably = Petra   C3 Probably Petra   D4 Or to build high   E7 Some LXX mss, Sym, Tg, Vg; MT reads They will set your bread as   F9 = a region or city in Edom   G11 Or forces

---

1 The parallel passage in Jr 49:14 more clearly indicates that God is calling the nations together to **go to war against** Edom.

3 **Clefts of the rock** may also be translated as "clefts of Sela" (or Petra). The Nabateans, who built the famed rock-hewn temples at Petra, drove out the Edomites, who settled in southern Judah (Idumea in NT times). The Edomites may have been completely destroyed by about A.D. 70 (with "no survivor," v. 18), possibly suffering the same fate as many Jews when Jerusalem fell to the Romans.

5 **Thieves . . . grape pickers** is a twofold illustration of the thoroughness of the impending judgment (Jr 49:9). Even more completely than thieves pillaging from their victims' houses (cp. Ob 11, Edomites' ravaging of Israel's wealth) or farmers harvesting crops, this destruction would leave no remnant behind (v. 5; Jr 49:10). The mention of **grapes** (lit "gleanings of grapes or olives") alludes to the practice of leaving leftovers from the harvest in the corners of the field for widows, orphans, and aliens to gather (Lv 23:22; Ru 2). Whereas gleaning in the OT often entails a remnant (Is 17:6; Jr 6:9), Obadiah left no room for hope. No remnant would be left for Edom (cp. Ob 18).

6 **Esau**, the brother of Jacob (vv. 10,12), was the father of the Edomites. Thus his descendants the Edomites would be **pillaged** and destroyed like stubble (v. 18). In verses 9,21, everyone from the hill country of Esau would be destroyed so that it would become the possession of Jacob's descendants (vv. 17-18).

10 To harmonize the phrase **destroyed forever** with the seemingly contradictory statement in Am 9:12, see note at Ob 18.

11 Conquering soldiers who **cast lots** (Jl 3:2-3; Nah 3:10) probably did so by shaking a container of marked pebbles until one fell out. He whose stone fell out first picked the choice portions of **Jerusalem**.

sela'

Hebrew Pronunciation	[SEH lah]
HCSB Translation	rock, cliff
Uses in Obadiah	1
Uses in the OT	63
Focus passage	Obadiah 3

Sela' occurs alongside *tsur* (76x), which encompasses various kinds of *rock* (4x; Ps 71:3). *Sela'* often involves *rock* faces, particularly *cliffs* (Is 2:21), where eagles (Jb 39:28) and hyraxes (Pr 30:26) live. People are thrown off them (Ps 141:6). *Mountain goats* is literally "goats of the *sela'*" (Jb 39:1). *Sela'* identifies named *rocks* (Jdg 15:8) and *rock* columns (1Sm 14:4). Some think that Obadiah 3 specifies *Sela*, an Edomite fortress city, rather than *rock*. The Septuagint sometimes translates *sela'* (Is 42:11) as *Petra*, perhaps corresponding to *Petra* in Jordan. *Sela'* is associated with *crevices* and *clefts* (Jr 13:4; 49:16), also with *fortresses* (Is 33:16). God is our *sela'* (Ps 18:2). Tyre scraped of civilization is *sela'* (Ezk 26:14). Crypts were carved in *sela'* (Is 22:16). *Sela'* implies *stone* (Jdg 6:20); the plural suggests *rocks* (1Sm 13:6).

while foreigners entered his •gate
and cast lots for Jerusalem,[a]
you were just like one of them.[b]

12 Do not[A] gloat over your brother[c]
    in the day of his calamity;
  do not rejoice over the people of Judah[d]
    in the day of their destruction;
  do not boastfully mock[B,e]
    in the day of distress.[f]

13 Do not enter the gate of My people
    in the day of their disaster.[g]
  Yes, you—do not gloat
    over their misery
  in the day of their disaster
  and do not appropriate
    their possessions[h]
  in the day of their disaster.

14 Do not stand at the crossroads[C,i]
    to cut off their fugitives,
  and do not hand over their survivors
    in the day of distress.

Judgment of the Nations

15 For the Day of the Lord[j] is near,
    against all the nations.[k]
  As you have done,[l] so it will be done
    to you;
  what you deserve will return
    on your own head.[m]

16 As you have drunk
    on My holy mountain,[n]
  so all the nations will
    drink continually.[o]
  They will drink and gulp down
  and be as though they had never been.

17 But there will be a deliverance[a]
    on Mount •Zion,[p]
  and it will be holy;[q]
  the house of Jacob will dispossess[r]
    those who dispossessed them.[D,s]

18 Then the house of Jacob will be
    a blazing fire,[t]
  and the house of Joseph,
    a burning flame,
  but the house of Esau will be stubble;
  Jacob[E] will set them on fire
    and consume Edom.[F]
  Therefore no survivor will remain[u]
    of the house of Esau,
  for the Lord has spoken.

Future Blessing for Israel

19 People from the •Negev will possess[v]
    the hill country of Esau;[w]
  those from the Judean foothills
    will possess
  the land of the Philistines.[x]
  They[G] will possess
  the territories of Ephraim and Samaria,[y]
  while Benjamin will possess Gilead.

20 The exiles of the Israelites who are
    in Halah[H]
  and who are among the Canaanites
    as far as Zarephath[z]
  as well as the exiles of Jerusalem
    who are in Sepharad
  will possess the cities of the Negev.[aa]

21 Saviors[I] will ascend Mount Zion[ab]
    to rule over the hill country of Esau,
  but the kingdom will be the Lord's.[ac]

Cross references (center column):

[a] 11 Jl 3:3; Nah 3:10
[b] 2Ch 21:17; Ezk 35:10
[c] 12 Mc 4:11; 7:10
[d] Ps 83:1-6; 137:7-9; Lm 4:21-22; Ezk 35:15; 36:5
[e] Ps 31:18; Ezk 35:12
[f] Gn 35:3; Ps 50:15; Jr 16:19
[g] 13 Ezk 35:5
[h] Ezk 35:10; 36:2-3
[i] 14 Is 16:3-4
[j] 15 Jl 1:15; 2:1,11,31; Am 5:18,20
[k] Is 13:6; Jl 3:14; Zph 1:7,14
[l] Jr 50:29; 51:56
[m] Jr 50:15; Ezk 35:11
[n] 16 Jr 49:12
[o] Is 51:22-23
[p] 17 Is 4:2-3
[q] 16-17 Is 66:20; Jl 2:32
[r] 17 Is 14:1-2; Am 9:11-15
[s] Ezk 36:2-5
[t] 18 Is 5:24; 9:18-19; Am 1:12; Zch 12:6
[u] Jr 11:23
[v] 19 Is 11:14
[w] Am 9:11-12
[x] Is 11:14
[y] Jr 31:5; 32:44
[z] 20 1Kg 17:9-10; Lk 4:26
[aa] Jr 32:44; 33:13
[ab] 21 Neh 9:27; Is 4:5; 18:7; 24:23; Dn 2:44; Mc 4:7
[ac] Ps 22:28; 47:7-9; 67:4; Zch 14:9

[A] 12-14 Or You should not throughout vv. 12-14   [B] 12 Lit not make your mouth big   [C] 14 Hb obscure   [D] 17 DSS, LXX, Syr, Vg, Tg; MT reads Jacob will possess its inheritance   [E] 18 Lit they   [F] 18 Lit them   [G] 19 = The house of Jacob   [H] 20 Or of this host of the Israelites; Hb obscure   [I] 21 Or Those who have been delivered

---

12-14 The repetition of the **day** of their disaster emphasizes the calamity and suffering of Judah at the time of Edom's mistreatment. Ironically this preoccupation with distress and disaster prepared the way for the Day of the Lord (v. 15) when God would pay back Edom accordingly (cp. v. 8, "in that day").

15 The **Day of the Lord** was a time of retribution for the Edomites because of their cooperation with the conquering Babylonians in the day of Judah's distress (see note at vv. 12-14). **What you deserve** is literally "your payback or retribution." Retribution would come upon Babylon the ally of Edom (Ps 137:8) and all who had insulted Judah (Lm 3:61-64). The promise of "retribution on your heads" to all Israel's enemies will be fulfilled in the last days (Jl 3:4,7).

16 The initial occasion for the drinking bout (**as you have drunk on My holy mountain**) may have been the Edomite celebration over the recent demise of Judah (ca 586 B.C.). However, the reference to future drinking (**so all the nations will drink continually**) does not picture celebration but rather judgment against Edom. Drunken, they would stagger and "fall down and never get up again" as the sword swept through the land (Jr 25:27-29). "Edom" represents

not just the Edomites, but ultimately all the nations who oppose Israel in the end times. They will all fall under God's judgment.

17 This **deliverance** (lit "escape; escaped ones") for God's people in the last days is also prophesied in Jl 2:32 and Is 4:2-4. The surviving righteous remnant of Jerusalem will be **holy**.

18 God's burning anger will consume His enemies like grass or chaff. He will use Israel as a blazing fire consumes grass to destroy their enemies (Zch 12:6). The phrase **no survivor** (cp. Ob 10, "destroyed forever") is in tension with Am 9:12, which states that Israel will possess "the remnant of Edom." Will there or won't there be a remnant? The most likely solution is that "remnant of Edom" in Am 9:12 broadly represents Israel's remaining enemies in the end-times, not the Edomites specifically (see note at Ob 16).

19-21 The land of Edom will be given to the Israelites living in the **Negev**, or the southern section of the land. God's people, who were once **exiles**, will once again possess the land that they had taken originally from the **Canaanites**. **Saviors**, or deliverers, will rule the **hill country of Esau**, and the Lord will rule over the entire **kingdom**.

Jonah

Introduction

The book of Jonah, the fifth of the Minor Prophets, is more like the stories of the prophets found in the Historical Books in both form and content. The book gives us a brief glimpse into the life of Jonah, the "wrong-way prophet," who ran from God and was swallowed by a fish. Throughout the book, we see evidence of God's grace and His love for all people.

Restored gate at the site of the ancient city of Nineveh, located today on the left bank of the Tigris River. Nahum prophesied the fall of this city of unparalleled wealth and power that was designed to withstand a siege of 20 years. Nineveh's fall began when the Tigris overflowed its banks. The resulting flood destroyed part of the city's wall. The Babylonians entered the breach in the wall, invaded the city, and destroyed it by fire. From 612 B.C. to the A.D. 1800s, Nineveh was lost in accumulating layers of dust.

Circumstances of Writing

Author: The book is an anonymous narrative about Jonah.

Background: Jonah appears in 2Kg 14:25 as a prophet from Gath-hepher in the territory of Zebulun in northern Israel. He was active around the first half of the eighth century B.C. Jonah predicted the restoration of the northern kingdom's boundaries. This occurred during the reign of Jeroboam II (ca 793–753 B.C.). This book about Jonah could have been composed at any time from the eighth century to the end of the OT period.

Jonah preached to the city of Nineveh. Nineveh was a major city of the Assyrians, a cruel and warlike people who were longtime enemies of Israel. Assyrian artwork emphasizes war, including scenes of execution, impalement, flaying the skin off prisoners, and beheadings. This explains Jonah's reluctance to preach to the infamous city of Nineveh.

The key debate about the book of Jonah is the question of its genre. Is Jonah history or parable? The parable view argues that Jonah is a fictional story or fable made up to convey a theological point about God's attitude toward Gentiles. Proponents of the parable view argue that the ironic and fantastic events described by the book (e.g., Jonah living and praying in the stomach of a fish) is the author's way of tipping the reader off that this is not literal history. There are also historical difficulties that the fictional view would resolve: the exaggerated size of Nineveh (3:3) and the lack of extrabiblical, Assyrian evidence to confirm that the city ever repented.

Five considerations suggest taking the book of Jonah as genuine history. First, Jonah was a real historical figure, said to be a prophet in 2Kg 14:25. The book of Jonah portrays Jonah as a flawed character. Were the book of Jonah a piece of fiction, it would be guilty of slander, saying something derogatory and untrue about a real person who is elsewhere presented positively.

Second, Jonah is part of the collection of 12 Minor Prophets. All the other books of this collection convey

5000–1000 B.C.

Earliest settlement of Nineveh 5000

Three major Assyrian cities, Nineveh, Asshur, and Calah, engage in vigorous trading as far as Cappadocia. 1900

An expanding Assyria wars with Babylon's King Hammurabi shortly before breaking up into smaller city-states. 1700

Adad-nirari establishes the first Assyrian Empire. 1307

Tiglath-pileser I is monarch of the second Assyrian Empire. 1115–1077

At Tiglath-pileser's death the empire falls into a 166-year decline. 1077–911

1000–850 B.C.

Neo-Assyrian Empire established by Ashur-dan II, laying the foundation for a unified rule in the ancient Near East from Egypt to the Caspian Sea. 934

Adad-nirari II (911–891) and his grandson, Ashurnasirpal II (883–859) lead a resurgent Assyria.

Ashur-nasirpal's son, Shalmaneser III (859–824), fights a coalition of 12 kings including Ben-Hadad of Aram-Damascus and Ahab of Israel at Qarqar in north Syria. 853

prophecies by genuine, historical prophets. By placing Jonah in this collection, the compiler of the Minor Prophets signaled that he considered Jonah to be an historical account.

Third, the miracles in Jonah are not impossible for the God of the Bible. Presuming otherwise, some interpreters allow their antisupernaturalism to drive them to the parable view of Jonah.

Fourth, Jesus in Mt 12:39-41 and Lk 11:29-32 spoke of Jonah being in the fish and preaching in Nineveh as if these were real events. In particular, Jesus' statement that "the men of Nineveh will stand up at the judgment with this generation and condemn it, because they repented at Jonah's proclamation" (Mt 12:41; Lk 11:32) makes little sense if the people of Nineveh never actually repented due to Jonah's preaching. Unless one is willing to affirm that Jesus was wrong, it is best to say that the book of Jonah is historical.

Finally, the historical difficulties in Jonah can largely be resolved (see note at 3:1-3).

Message and Purpose

God's positive attitude toward Gentiles: In chapter 1, Gentile sailors learn to revere and worship Israel's God. Their reluctance to throw Jonah overboard shows that they were concerned to follow God's ethical demands by not taking innocent human life. In chapter 3, Nineveh's repentance shows that Gentiles can be saved too. God is interested in all people, a concern that anticipates the missionary mandate of the NT.

God's grace: God was "merciful and compassionate" (4:2) toward Nineveh, thus showing that the God of the OT is a God of grace.

God's sovereignty over nature: The book of Jonah portrays the sovereign power of God over the natural world. God can hurl a storm at people (1:4), raise up a plant miraculously and as well as a worm to kill it (4:6-7), and use a great fish to swallow and save Jonah (1:17). All this shows God's control over nature.

The futility of running from God: The trouble that Jonah got into when he tried to run from God's calling is a warning to readers that running from God is futile and only invites unnecessary hardship.

850–750 B.C.	750–700 B.C.
Shalmaneser defeats Hazael of Damascus and receives tribute from Israel's King Jehu. (841) This scene is carved in relief on the Black Obelisk of Shalmaneser, unearthed at Nimrud, Iraq, in A.D. 1846.	Tiglath-pileser III checks the aggression of the Kingdom of Urartu on Assyria's north and leads an expansion of Assyria, conquering Babylon and greatly reducing Israel's territory. 745–727
With the death of Shalmaneser III, Assyrian expansion is held in check. 824–745	Assyria's Shalmaneser V besieges Samaria. 725–722
Jonah prophesies that the Lord will restore the border of Israel from Lebo-hamath as far as the Sea of the Arabah.	Samaria falls to Assyria's Sargon II; nearly 28,000 Israelites are sent into exile, and Gentiles from Assyrian-controlled territories are resettled into what was the Northern Kingdom. 722
Jeroboam II strengthens Israel. 793–753	
God calls Jonah to go to Nineveh and preach repentance.	
During its time of weakness, Assyria experiences two severe plagues (765 and 759) and a total eclipse (763).	

Contribution to the Bible

The book of Jonah shows God's gracious concern for the whole world, His power over nature, and the futility of running from Him. In addition, it foreshadows Jesus' burial and resurrection. Matthew 12:38-45 and Lk 11:24-32 compare the ministry of Jesus with that of Jonah, Jesus being the greater. Both texts see Jonah's great fish as a foreshadowing of Jesus' burial in the tomb, making Jonah a "type" of Christ. If Jonah actually died in the fish (see note at Jnh 2:2), then his resurrection further parallels the resurrection of Jesus.

Structure

The book of Jonah exhibits a high degree of Hebrew literary excellence. Its style is rich and varied. It is considered by many as a masterpiece of rhetoric. There is symmetry and balance in the book, and it can be divided into two sections of two chapters each. The peak of the first discourse is marked by its poetic form, which has a higher prominence in narrative than prose. The peak in the second discourse is marked by the dialogue exchange between Jonah and God. The Lord and Jonah are indicated as the two main characters of the story by being the only ones who are named; the other characters are anonymous.

Phenomena of nature also serve in each half as props: wind, storm, sea, dry land, and fish in the first half; herd and flock, plant, worm, sun, and wind in the second half. When placed side by side, chapters 1 and 3 and chapters 2 and 4 can be seen as parallel. Finally, both chapters 1 and 3 begin with Jonah receiving a word from the Lord consisting of a call to go to Nineveh.

Outline

I. Jonah's Flight from God (1:1-17)
   A. The Lord calls; Jonah rebels (1:1-3)
   B. The Lord sends a storm (1:4-6)
   C. The sailors intervene (1:7-16)
   D. The Lord sends a big fish (1:17)

II. Jonah's Prayer of Thanksgiving from the Fish (2:1-10)
   A. Jonah prays (2:1-9)
   B. The Lord delivers Jonah (2:10)

III. Jonah's Preaching in Nineveh (3:1-10)
   A. Jonah obeys the call (3:1-4)
   B. King and Ninevites repent (3:5-9)
   C. The Lord withholds judgment (3:10)

IV. Jonah's Anger at God's Mercy (4:1-11)
   A. The Lord displeases Jonah (4:1-5)
   B. Jonah displeases the Lord (4:6-10)
   C. The Lord shows great pity (4:11)

Jonah's Flight

1 The word of the LORD came to Jonah son of Amittai:[a] [2]"Get up![b] Go to the great city[c] of Nineveh[d] and preach against it,[e] because their wickedness[f] has confronted[A] Me."[g] [3]However, Jonah got up to flee to Tarshish[h] from the LORD's presence.[i] He went down[j] to Joppa[k] and found a ship going to Tarshish. He paid the fare and went down into it to go with them to Tarshish, from the LORD's presence.

[4]Then the LORD hurled[l] a violent wind on the sea,[m] and such a violent storm arose on the sea that the ship threatened to break apart. [5]The sailors were afraid, and each cried out to his god.[n] They threw the ship's cargo into the sea to lighten the load.[o] Meanwhile, Jonah had gone down to the lowest part of the vessel and had stretched out and fallen into a deep sleep.[p]

[6]The captain approached him and said, "What are you doing sound asleep? Get up! Call to your god.[B,q] Maybe this god will consider us,[r] and we won't perish."

[7]"Come on!" the sailors said to each other.

"Let's cast lots.[s] Then we'll know who is to blame for this trouble we're in." So they cast lots, and the lot singled out Jonah.[t] [8]Then they said to him, "Tell us who is to blame for this trouble we're in.[u] What is your business[v] and where are you from? What is your country and what people are you from?"

[9]He answered them, "I'm a Hebrew.[w] I worship[C] •Yahweh,[x] the God of the heavens,[y] who made the sea[z] and the dry land."

[10]Then the men were even more afraid and said to him, "What is this you've done?" The men knew he was fleeing from the LORD's presence,[aa] because he had told them. [11]So they said to him, "What should we do to you to calm this sea that's against us?" For the sea was getting worse and worse.

[12]He answered them, "Pick me up and throw me into the sea[D] so it may quiet down for you, for I know that I'm to blame[ab] for this violent

Cross references

a1:1 2Kg 14:25; Jnh 3:1; Mt 12:39-41; 16:4; Lk 11:29-30,32
b1:2 Nm 22:20; Dt 10:11; Jos 7:10
c Jnh 3:2-3; 4:11
d Gn 10:11; 2Kg 19:36; Is 37:37; Nah 1:1; Zph 2:13
e Dt 15:9; 24:15; 2Kg 23:17; Is 58:1
f Jnh 3:8
g Gn 18:20; Hs 7:2
h1:3 Is 23:1,6,10; Jr 10:9
i Gn 4:16; Ps 139:7,9-10
j Jnh 2:6
k 2Ch 2:16; Ezr 3:7; Ac 9:36,43
l1:4 1Sm 18:11; 20:33; Is 22:17; Jr 22:26-28
m Ps 107:25-28; 135:7
n1:5 1Kg 18:26
o Ac 27:18-19,38
p Gn 2:21; 15:12; Jdg 4:21; Dn 8:18; 10:9; 1Th 5:6
q1:6 Ps 107:28
r2Sm 12:22; Am 5:15; Jnh 3:9   s1:7 Jos 7:14-18; 1Sm 10:20-21; 14:41-42; Pr 16:33; Ac 1:23-26   tNm 32:23; Pr 16:33   u1:8 Jos 7:19; 1Sm 14:43   vGn 47:3; 1Sm 30:13   w1:9 Gn 14:13; 39:14; Ex 1:15; 2:13; 1Sm 4:6   x2Kg 17:25,28,32-33   yGn 24:3,7; Ezr 1:2; Neh 1:4; Ps 136:26; Dn 2:18   zNeh 9:6; Ps 95:5; 146:6   aa1:10 Jb 27:22; Jnh 1:3   ab1:12 2Sm 24:17; 1Ch 21:17

A1:2 Or has come up to   B1:6 Or God   C1:9 Or fear   D1:12 Lit sea that's against you

---

1:1 Jonah in Hebrew means "dove." His father's name **Amittai** means "faithful [is Yahweh?]."

1:2 Nineveh on the east bank of the Tigris River became the Assyrian capital after 705 B.C., well after Jonah's day. Its ruins are found in the northern part of modern Iraq, opposite the city of Mosul 220 miles northwest of Baghdad. For Jonah, Nineveh was an arduous journey of over 500 miles to the northeast of Samaria. His probable route—first traveling north and then east—would have made the trip closer to 600 miles. God's holiness is offended by sin. He showed Himself judge of the world by holding these distant pagans accountable for **their wickedness**, though He also showed His mercy by commanding His prophet to warn them.

1:3 To flee . . . from the LORD's presence is to attempt the impossible since God is everywhere, though people still try. (See 4:2 for why he fled.) **Joppa** on the Mediterranean coast just south of modern Tel Aviv was one of Israel's few natural seaports. The location of **Tarshish** is uncertain. Its association with ships (1Kg 10:22) suggests it was near the sea. The "ships of Tarshish" used by King Jehoshaphat on the Red Sea were probably merchant ships of design similar to those used by sailors from Tarshish on the Mediterranean Sea. Tarshish has sometimes been identified with Paul's home of Tarsus in Cilicia or the city of Tharros on the island of Sardinia west of Italy. But the most probable identification of Tarshish is the Phoenician colony of Tartessus, located on the Guadalquivir River on the southwestern coast of Spain about 2,000 miles west of Palestine. This is about as far in the opposite direction from Nineveh that Jonah could have gone.

1:5-6 Jonah's spiritual decline is depicted in parallel with the descriptions of his response to God's call. He was told to "get up" (v. 2) to go to Nineveh, but instead he "went down to Joppa" (v. 3), "went down" to the ship (v. 3) and finally went **down to the lowest part of the vessel**. Eventually he will be swallowed by a fish and sink down to the foundations of the

mountains at the bottom of the sea (2:6). Only then did he hit bottom and begin to go back up. His **deep sleep** in the midst of a storm also symbolizes his spiritual condition. It may have been a symptom of depression stemming from his willful disobedience.

1:9 Worship is literally "fear." Fear of God in the OT is the respect that a person has for God, causing him to turn from evil and obey God's commandments (Gn 22:12; Jb 1:8; 28:28; Pr 8:13). Ironically God's prophet Jonah showed no such fear by his disobedience. It is also ironic that Jonah fled to avoid preaching to Gentiles in Nineveh, but now found himself preaching to Gentiles in the ship. **Yahweh** means "He is [present]!" and is God's personal name in the OT, ordinarily rendered in translation as LORD in small caps (as in vv. 1,3,4,10,16,17). The substitution in translation of the title LORD for the personal name Yahweh goes back to postexilic Jewish reluctance to pronounce the divine name. Neither Jonah nor these sailors had any qualms about using the term Yahweh at this time.

1:12-15 Rather than submitting to God, Jonah asked these

barach

Hebrew Pronunciation	[bah RACK]
HCSB Translation	flee, run through
Uses in Jonah	3
Uses in the OT	65
Focus passage	Jonah 1:3,10

Barach usually means *flee*, occurring four times with *malat* ("escape"; 1Sm 19:12) and once, translated *escape* (Jdg 9:21), with synonymous *nus* (160x; "flee"). *Barach* often portrays stealthy flight, while *nus* regularly depicts open flight. *Barach* describes slaves *running away* (1Kg 2:39). It suggests *go home* (Nm 24:11) or *go back* (Neh 13:10) when people *flee* homeward. As *hurry* (Sg 8:14), it connotes urgent speed rather than flight.

storm that is against you." [13]Nevertheless, the men rowed hard to get back to dry land, but they couldn't because the sea was raging against them more and more.

[14]So they called out to the LORD:[a] "Please, Yahweh, don't let us perish because of this man's life, and don't charge us with innocent blood! For You, Yahweh, have done just as You pleased."[b] [15]Then they picked up Jonah and threw him into the sea, and the sea stopped its raging.[c] [16]The men •feared the LORD[d] even more, and they offered a sacrifice to the LORD and made vows.[e]

[17]A Now the LORD had appointed a huge fish[f] to swallow Jonah, and Jonah was in[B] the fish three days and three nights.[g]

Jonah's Prayer

2 Jonah prayed to the LORD his God from in-side[C] the fish:[h]

[2] I called to the LORD in my distress,[i]
and He answered me.
I cried out for help in the belly
of •Sheol;[j]
You heard my voice.[k]
[3] You threw me into the depths,[l]
into the heart of the seas,[m]
and the current[D] overcame me.

All Your breakers and Your billows
swept over me.[n]
[4] But I said: I have been banished[o]
from Your sight,[p]
yet I will look once more[E]
toward Your holy temple.[q]
[5] The waters engulfed me up
to the neck;[F,r]
the watery depths overcame me;
seaweed was wrapped around my head.[s]
[6] I sank to the foundations
of the mountains;[t]
the earth with its prison bars closed
behind me forever![u]
But You raised my life[v] from the •Pit,
LORD my God![w]
[7] As my life was fading away,[x]
I remembered •Yahweh.[y]
My prayer came to You,[z]
to Your holy temple.[aa]
[8] Those who cling to worthless idols[ab]
forsake faithful love,[ac]
[9] but as for me, I will sacrifice[ad] to You
with a voice of thanksgiving.[ae]

a1:14 Ps 107:28
b Ps 51:18;
115:3; 135:6; Pr
21:1; Is 55:11;
Lm 3:37-39;
Dn 4:34-35; Mt
11:25
c1:15 Ps 65:7;
93:3-4; 107:29
d1:16 Is 59:19;
Mc 7:17; Zph
2:11; Mal 1:14;
Lk 8:22-25
e Ps 50:14;
66:13-14; 76:11;
116:17-18
f1:17 Gn 9:2;
Nm 11:22; 1Kg
4:33; Ps 8:8
g Mt 12:40; 16:4;
Lk 11:29-30; Jn
11:6,14
h2:1 Jb 13:15;
Ps 130:1-2; Lm
3:53-56
i2:2 1Sm 30:6;
Ps 18:4-6;
22:24; 120:1
j Ps 18:5-6;
86:13; 88:1-7; Is
28:15; 38:18
k Ps 34:7
l2:3 Ps 69:1-
2,14-15; Lm
3:54
m Neh 9:11
n Ps 42:7
o2:4 Lv 21:7
p Ps 31:22-23;
Jr 7:15
q 1Kg 8:38; 2Ch
6:38; Ps 5:7;
138:2

r2:5 Ps 69:1-2; 105:18; Pr 23:2; Lm 3:54   s Ps 18:4-5   t2:6 Ps 116:3   u Jb 38:10; Ps 9:13; Is 38:10; Mt 16:18   v Jb 33:28; Ps 16:10; 30:3; Is 38:17   w Ps 30:3; 86:13   x2:7 Ps 142:3   y 2Sm 14:11; Ps 77:10-11; 143:5   z 2Ch 30:27; Ps 18:6   aa Ps 11:4; 65:4; 88:2; Mc 1:2; Hab 2:20   ab2:8 Ezk 17:15; Ps 31:6; Jr 16:18   ac Ps 31:6   ad2:9 Ps 50:14,23; Jr 33:11; Hs 14:2   ae Ps 26:7

A1:17 Jnh 2:1 in Hb   B1:17 Lit *in the belly of*   C2:1 Lit *from the belly of*   D2:3 Lit *river*   E2:4 LXX reads *said: Indeed, will I look . . . ?*   F2:5 Or *me, threatening my life*

---

men to kill him by throwing him overboard. Yet despite Jonah's confession of guilt, these pagan Gentiles had moral scruples about sending a man to his death and tried to row ashore instead. Only after they saw no other option and had prayed that Yahweh would not hold them accountable for taking a human life did they throw Jonah into the sea. The integrity and spiritual sensitivity of these Gentiles would have shocked Israelite readers of this book, confronting their belief that non-Hebrews were unworthy of God's mercy. Certainly this is a lesson Jonah himself needed.

1:16 When the sea calmed, these Gentile sailors then **feared the LORD** in the sense of revering and worshiping Him (see note at 1:9). Jonah, who was fleeing from a mission to preach to Gentiles, had unintentionally converted an entire crew of Gentile sailors.

1:17 The **huge fish** that swallowed Jonah was not necessarily a whale. Yarns of a sailor surviving Jonah-like in a whale have been widely repeated in recent centuries, but no account has ever been authenticated. **Three days and three nights** parallels Christ's resurrection on the third day (Mt 12:40).

2:2 **Sheol** is the realm of the dead, often the grave. The fish's stomach is metaphorically like a tomb. Jonah thought he was dead, and perhaps he literally was at some point. If so, the parallel with Christ's resurrection (Mt 12:40) is even stronger. But God was present in Sheol (**You heard my voice**) to receive Jonah's prayer. Indeed, God is everywhere we go (Ps 139:8).

2:3-5 Verses 3 and 5 depict Jonah's dire circumstances. He sees both the **breakers** and the **billows** as judgment tools of God. But verse 4 sounds a note of faith and hope. Though

he had been **banished** from God's sight, he expected to **look once more toward** His **holy temple**, which means he expected he would live to pray again and perhaps even worship in the Jerusalem temple. Textual variations among Greek translations (LXX; Theodotion) make verse 4b into a question rather than a statement. For instance: "How will I look once more toward your holy temple?" The variations may have arisen because translators thought the optimism of verse 4 mixed poorly with the doom of verses 3,5. However, the contrast is a literary feature and is likely original. **Neck** (Hb *nephesh*) in verse 5 can also be rendered "life," but originally it meant "throat." The image of water up to the prophet's throat fits this context well.

2:6 Imagery for **foundations of the mountains** was provided by Israel's own Mount Carmel, whose base extends into the Mediterranean Sea, ending in unseen depths below. As **the earth** (or **the Pit**) permanently imprisons the dead, so Jonah thought the fish's body would trap him, but unexpectedly God was rescuing him. Both "earth" (Hb *'erets*) and "pit" could refer here to the underworld as the HCSB renders *'erets* in Ezk 26:20; 32:18.

2:7 Reminiscent of thanksgiving songs in the Psalms (Pss 18; 30), Jonah tells the story of answered prayer (see also Jnh 2:2).

2:8-9 Yahweh's miraculous deliverance shows that He exists, unlike pagan idols. **What I have vowed** refers to a promised gift to God if He should answer prayer (Nm 21:2; 1Sm 1:11). Jonah promised praise and animal sacrifice. A fellowship offering was used to worship God at the completion of a vow (Nm 6:21; 2Sm 15:7-8; Pr 7:14).

I will fulfill[a] what I have vowed.
Salvation[A] is from the LORD![b]

[10] Then the LORD commanded the fish,[c] and it vomited Jonah onto dry land.

Jonah's Preaching

3 Then the word of the LORD came to Jonah a second time:[d] [2] "Get up! Go to the great city of Nineveh[e] and preach[f] the message that I tell you." [3] So Jonah got up and went to Nineveh according to the LORD's command.

Now Nineveh was an extremely large city,[B,g] a three-day walk.[C] [4] Jonah set out on the first day of his walk in the city and proclaimed,[h] "In 40 days Nineveh will be demolished!" [5] The men of Nineveh believed in God.[D] They proclaimed a fast[i] and dressed in ˙sackcloth—from the greatest of them to the least.

[6] When word reached the king of Nineveh, he got up from his throne, took off his royal robe, put on sackcloth,[j] and sat in ashes. [7] Then he issued a decree[k] in Nineveh:

By order of the king and his nobles: No man or beast, herd or flock, is to taste

anything at all. They must not eat or drink water. [8] Furthermore, both man and beast must be covered with sackcloth, and everyone must call out earnestly to God.[l] Each must turn from his evil ways[m] and from the violence[E] he is doing.[F] [9] Who knows?[n] God may turn and relent; He may turn from His burning anger so that we will not perish.[o]

[10] Then God saw their actions—that they had turned from their evil ways[p]—so God relented from the disaster[q] He had threatened to do to them. And He did not do it.

Jonah's Anger

4 But Jonah was greatly displeased and became furious.[r] [2] He prayed to the LORD:[s] "Please, LORD, isn't this what I said while I was still in my own country? That's why I fled toward Tarshish in the first place.[t] I knew that You are a merciful and compassionate God,[u] slow to become angry, rich in faithful love, and One who relents from sending disaster.[v]

Cross references (center column)

[a]2:9 Jb 22:27; Ps 22:25; 116:14,18; Ec 5:4-5
[b]Ps 3:8; Is 12:2; 45:17; Rv 7:10
[c]2:10 Jnh 1:17
[d]3:1 Jnh 1:1
[e]3:2 Zph 2:13-15
[f]Jr 1:17; Ezk 2:7
[g]3:3 Gn 10:11-12; Jnh 1:2; 4:11
[h]3:4 2Kg 18:26-28; Mt 12:41; Lk 11:32
[i]3:5 Dn 9:3; Jl 1:14
[j]3:6 1Kg 21:27; Est 4:1-4; Jr 6:26; Ezk 27:30-31
[k]3:7 2Ch 20:3; Ezr 8:21
[l]3:8 Ps 130:1; Jnh 1:6,14
[m]Is 1:16-19; 55:6-7; Jr 18:11
[n]3:9 2Sm 12:22; Jl 2:14
[o]Jr 18:7-8
[p]3:10 1Kg 21:27-29; 2Kg 17:13; 2Ch 7:14; Jr 18:11; 31:18
[q]Ex 32:14; Am 7:3,6
[r]4:1 Jnh 4:9; Mt 20:15; Lk 15:28
[s]4:2 Jr 20:7
[t]Jnh 1:3
[u]Ex 34:6; Nm 14:18; Ps 86:5,15; Jl 2:13
[v]Neh 9:17

Textual footnotes

[A]2:9 Or *Deliverance*   [B]3:3 Or *was a great city to God*   [C]3:3 Probably the time required to cover the city on foot   [D]3:5 Or *believed God*   [E]3:8 Or *injustice*   [F]3:8 Lit *violence in their hands*

2:10 Vomited, an ignoble means of exiting the fish, perhaps symbolizes God's disgust at Jonah's prior disobedience or even his continued bad attitude, which the subsequent narrative unfolds.

3:1-3 Jonah went to Nineveh as God had commanded. **Extremely large city** (lit "a great city to God"; see textual footnote) may have a double meaning: great in size (where "God," Hb *elohim*, is used as a superlative for "extremely") and a city "important to God" even though inhabited by Gentiles. **Three-day walk** could refer to greater Nineveh that included the region around Nineveh proper, including

saq table

saq

Hebrew Pronunciation	[SACK]
HCSB Translation	sack, sackcloth
Uses in Jonah	3
Uses in the OT	48
Focus passage	Jonah 3:5-6,8

Saq denotes *sack* (6x; Gn 42:27), entering English through Greek and Latin. *Saq* was *sackcloth* (Is 15:3). The thick, rough, dark-colored material was goat hair (Is 50:3; Rv 6:12) or camel hair (Mt 3:4). It might provide blankets (2Sm 21:10). Akkadian, the Ninevite language, used the root similarly. Ninevites wore *sackcloth* to express repentance (Jnh 3:8), as did Israelites (Neh 9:1). *Sackcloth* was worn on the skin (2Kg 6:30; Jb 16:15) and involved self-humbling (1Kg 21:27-29). Mourning was the chief reason for wearing *sackcloth* (Gn 37:34; Jl 1:8). Ammonites (Jr 49:3) and Arameans (1Kg 20:32) wore *sackcloth*. Prophets called for it communally in the face of judgment (Jr 4:8). People might tear regular clothes and fast (Est 4:1,3), covering themselves with dust (4x; Jr 6:26) or ashes (7x; Jnh 3:6), perhaps shaving or cutting hair (Jr 48:37). *Sackcloth* could signal protest (Est 4:1).

modern Kuyunjik, Khorsabad, and Nimrud with a 60-mile perimeter. More likely, however, it refers to how long it took for Jonah to preach thoroughly throughout Nineveh itself, street corner by street corner. **Forty** often refers to a period of testing or judgment in the Bible (Lk 4:2; Heb 3:9), serving here to give Nineveh time to repent.

3:4 Jonah preached only on **the first day** of his three-day task (see note at 3:1-3), showing his half-hearted obedience. **Demolished** (Hb *haphak*) has a secondary meaning of "changed" which is not the sense Jonah meant, but ironically that is how the word of prophecy was actually fulfilled. Nineveh was not destroyed, but was instead changed.

3:5-8 After recounting that Nineveh repented and **believed** the deity whom Jonah represented (v. 5 uses the impersonal term **God**, not the personal name Yahweh/LORD), the text then explains that this overwhelming response was a result of a royal decree. The king led by example. **Sackcloth** was worn during times of mourning and repentance, usually while sitting atop ashes (Gn 37:34; 1Kg 21:27; Mt 11:21). **Man or beast** means even the animals fasted, bellowing miserably to heaven along with the people.

3:9 Who knows indicates that Jonah had not explicitly stated that judgment against the city could be averted by repentance. The king of Nineveh took a shot in the dark.

3:10 Prophecies of doom are often conditional warnings that can be averted through repentance (Jr 18:8-10).

4:1-2 The unexpected and overwhelming success of Jonah's preaching resulted in Nineveh's escape from calamity. However, this brought emotional calamity to the angry and self-pitying prophet, who wished he were dead. Jonah had initially fled from preaching to Nineveh because he feared that God, being excessively **merciful and compassionate** (see

³And now, Lᴏʀᴅ, please take my life from me,ᵃ for it is better for me to die than to live."ᵇ

⁴The Lᴏʀᴅ asked, "Is it right for you to be angry?"

⁵Jonah left the city and sat down east of it.ᶜ He made himself a shelter there and sat in its shade to see what would happen to the city. ⁶Then the Lᴏʀᴅ God appointed a plant,ᴬ and it grew up to provide shade over Jonah's head to ease his discomfort.ᴮ Jonah was greatly pleased with the plant. ⁷When dawn came the next day, God appointed a worm that attacked the plant, and it withered.ᵈ

⁸As the sun was rising, God appointed a scorching east wind.ᵉ The sun beat down so much on Jonah's headᶠ that he almost fainted, and he wanted to die. He said, "It's better for me to die than to live."ᵍ

⁹Then God asked Jonah, "Is it right for you to be angry about the plant?"

"Yes," he replied. "It is right. I'm angry enough to die!"

¹⁰So the Lᴏʀᴅ said, "You cared about the plant, which you did not labor over and did not grow. It appeared in a night and perished in a night. ¹¹Should I not care about the great city of Nineveh,ʰ which has more than 120,000 peopleᶜ who cannot distinguish between their right and their left,ⁱ as well as many animals?"ʲ

Cross references:
ᵃ 4:3 1Kg 19:4; Jb 6:8-9
ᵇ Jb 7:15-16; Ec 7:1
ᶜ 4:5 1Kg 19:9,13
ᵈ 4:7 Jl 1:12
ᵉ 4:8 Ezk 19:12; Hs 13:15
ᶠ Ps 121:6; Is 49:10
ᵍ Jnh 4:3
ʰ 4:11 Jnh 3:10
ⁱ Dt 1:39; Is 7:16
ʲ Ps 36:6

ᴬ4:6 A castor-oil plant or a climbing gourd ᴮ4:6 Lit *to deliver him from his evil* ᶜ4:11 Or *men*

Ex 34:6-7], would find some lame excuse to forgive these pagan, warlike Gentiles. Now his fears had come true.

4:3-4 Take my life echoes the words of the prophet Elijah (1Kg 19:4), who despaired over the failure of his mission, just as Jonah despaired over the success of his.

ra'ah

Hebrew Pronunciation	[rah AH]
HCSB Translation	evil, disaster, trouble
Uses in Jonah	9
Uses in the OT	354
Focus passage	Jonah 4:1-2,6

Feminine *ra'ah*, related to *ra'a'* (*be evil*), signifies *evil* (Jr 2:13), *disaster* (Dt 31:29), or *trouble* (Neh 2:17). Masculine *ra'*, either as noun or adjective (299x), has similar meanings. Feminine forms of adjectival *ra'* match *ra'ah*, so it is hard to differentiate them. *Ra'ah* more often means *disaster*; *ra'* more frequently concerns physical maladies. These words involve negatives, with the sense clarified by context.

4:5-8 Another factor behind Jonah's death wish was the blisteringly hot weather and the dry **east wind**, making him extremely uncomfortable as he sat watching to see what God would do to Nineveh. He was also upset over the withering of a **plant** (Hb *qiqayon*; perhaps a castor-oil plant or a climbing gourd) that had sprung up to give him temporary relief from the sun.

4:9-11 God used Jonah's emotional reaction to the death of the plant as an object lesson to rebuke him for being more concerned about a plant than the destruction of **120,000 people** who could not **distinguish between their right and their left**. This probably does not mean there were 120,000 small children in Nineveh, but rather that the people themselves were immature and uninformed morally and spiritually. God took their immaturity into consideration in His judgment. **As well as many animals** was a final rebuke. If Jonah could not feel compassion for Gentile people, he should at least feel sorry for the hungry livestock that were bellowing their misery (see 3:7-8). The book ends without telling us whether Jonah responded positively to the Lord's closing reprimand.

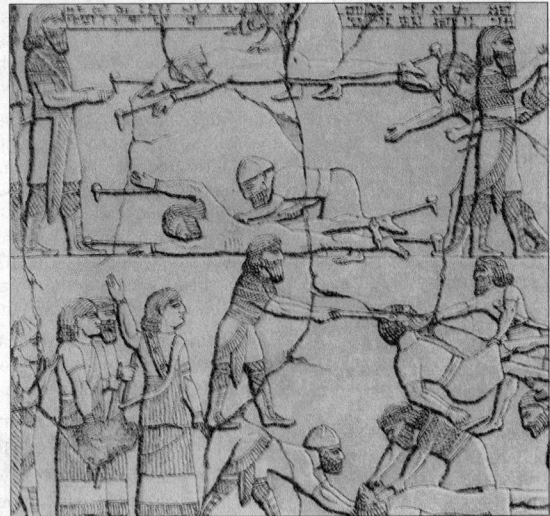

A relief from the palace of Ashurbanipal at Nineveh shows Assyrian soldiers subjecting captives to a series of tortures. In spite of the ruthlessness of the Assyrians, God sent His servant Jonah to offer them mercy (4:11).

Micah

Introduction

Micah's name "Who is like Yahweh?" found at the
beginning of the book (1:1; an abbreviation of
Micaiah, cp. Jr 26:18) and the question Micah asked at the
book's end, "Who is a God like You?" (Mc 7:18), sum up the
book's overall message: People should ponder the person,
acts, and character of the incomparable "Lord of all the
earth" (4:13). He is incomparable in His holiness, power,
and love. All people answer to this sovereign God for their
worship and the kind of lives they lead. The rebellious and
sinful will meet His judgment (1:5), but those who earnestly
watch and wait for Him will find His listening ear (7:7).

"Because of this I will lament and wail; I will walk barefoot and naked. I will
howl like the jackals and mourn like ostriches. For her wound is incurable and
has reached even Judah" (1:8-9).

Circumstances of Writing

Author: Micah's hometown of Moresheth-gath (1:1,14) in the lowlands of Judah was about 25 miles southwest of Jerusalem. The fact that his hometown is mentioned probably means that Micah ministered elsewhere, including Jerusalem, and since no genealogy is given we can probably assume that his family was not prominent. Though from the country, Micah was no bumpkin. He was a skilled orator, a master of metaphors with a genius for wordplay and blunt, vivid imagery. Few prophets saw the future more clearly. Micah prophesied the fall of Samaria (1:5-9), Jerusalem's destruction (1:1-16; 3:12), the Babylonian captivity and return from exile (4:6-10), as well as the birth of God's future Davidic ruler in Bethlehem (5:2).

Micah's ministry probably began late in Jotham's reign and ended early in Hezekiah's, dating between 730 and 690 B.C. His reference to the future judgment of Samaria (1:6) shows that his ministry began some time before 722 B.C. As such, Micah's ministry overlapped Isaiah's. The elders in Jeremiah's day remembered Micah's prophecy as having spurred Hezekiah's religious reform (Jr 26:17-19).

Background: Both Israel and Judah experienced affluence and material prosperity in the late eighth century B.C. In the south, King Uzziah's military victories brought wealth for some. A wealthy merchant class developed, and many poorer farmers found themselves at the mercy of government-supported businessmen. As business dealings became more corrupt, God's prophets spoke to the nation, confronting the ill-gotten wealth and accompanying godlessness. Amos and Hosea prophesied in the northern kingdom of Israel, and Isaiah and Micah prophesied in Judah to the south.

Judah's commercial and secular culture replaced God's covenant ideal. The rich became wealthy at the expense of the poor. Micah saw this as an indication of a rotten social fabric and crumbling national foundations. God's people were to be different socially and economically. They were stewards of God's land (Lv 25:23) that He had allotted to each family (Jos 13–19). God's law protected family property rights (Lv 25:1-55) and provided for the poor and less fortunate (Dt 14:28-29; 15:7-11). But growing affluence in Micah's day led to increasing cal-

---

750 B.C.

Jotham, king of Judah 750–732

Micah begins his prophetic ministry. 750

Tiglath-pileser III comes to power as king of Assyria and begins a program of expansion and domination of the region. 745

Death of King Uzziah of Judah 740

Isaiah's call to be a prophet 740

Ahaz, king of Judah 735–716

735 B.C.

Tiglath-pileser III's invasions of Israel 734–732

Pekah of Israel and Rezin of Damascus form a mutual defense alliance against Assyria and invite Ahaz of Judah to join them. 734

Ahaz refuses Isaiah's counsel and seeks protection from Assyria by paying tribute to them, creating a heavy financial burden on Judah for years to come. 734

Micah prophesies the fall of Samaria.

Alliance between Syria and Israel collapses with the fall of Damascus. 732

lousness toward the weak (Mc 2:1-2) and a blatant disregard for God's foundational laws (6:10-12). Judges and lawmakers became involved in conspiracy, bribery, and other corruption (3:1-3,9-11; 7:3). Religious leaders were concerned more about making money than teaching God's Word (3:11). The wealthy learned to separate their worship from everyday practice.

At this time the ancient Near East experienced an international power shift. Assyria was ascending, becoming one of the most evil, bloodthirsty, manipulative, and arrogant empires of the ancient world. Four Assyrian kings made military inroads into Palestine during Micah's ministry, taking Samaria in 722 B.C. and making Israel an Assyrian province. In 701 B.C. Sennacherib took 46 Judean towns and villages and besieged Jerusalem. King Hezekiah had allied with Egypt and Babylon against Assyria, for which both Micah and Isaiah urged him to repent. God miraculously spared Jerusalem (2Kg 19:35-36; 2Ch 32:22-23; Is 37:36-37), and according to Micah the Jerusalem siege was both an act of God's judgment and an occasion for God's deliverance.

Judah never learned its lesson. The people wavered between faith and apostasy and suffered many crises. Micah preached to people who had long since abandoned covenant loyalty, including the king, the royal court, judges, and religious leaders. As the rulers proved increasingly unfaithful, Micah prophesied Judah's destruction and exile by the Babylonians (586 B.C.). Beyond that, however, he saw a future restoration for a remnant of the people (539 B.C.).

Message and Purpose

Micah sought "to proclaim to Jacob his rebellion and to Israel his sin" (3:8). He pronounced God's judgment to call His people to repentance. Injustice was rampant (2:1-2; 3:1-3,9-11; 6:10-11), thus they would suffer destruction and exile (1:10-16), silence from God (3:6-7), and frustration (6:13-16). But Micah balanced his prophecy with hope of a remnant spared through God's judgment and a glorious future restoration (2:12-13; 4:1-5; 5:5-9; 7:8-20).

---

725 B.C.

5 B.C.

Assyria's Shalmaneser V besieges Samaria (725–722) which falls to Sargon II. 722

Hezekiah, king of Judah 716–687

Micah prophesies Jerusalem's destruction, the Babylonian captivity, the return from exile, and the birth of God's future Davidic ruler in Bethlehem.

Hezekiah's reforms 715

Assyria's King Sennacherib conquers 46 Judean towns and villages and besieges Jerusalem. 701

Micah's prophetic work ends about the time of Hezekiah's death. 686

Josiah's reforms 622

Nebuchadnezzar attacks Jerusalem and leads citizens of Judah into exile. The temple is destroyed. 605, 597, 586

Cyrus issues decree allowing the Jews to return to Judah. 538

Events in Ezra 538–457

Second temple construction under Zerubbabel's and Joshua's leadership. 536–515

Second temple dedicated 515

Jesus of Nazareth, son of David, is born in Bethlehem. 5

Contribution to the Bible

Micah's holy and just God demands holiness and justice from all people. This is the "good" He requires (6:8). The people had grown content with going through the religious motions while practicing very little genuine spiritual devotion. Even the religious leaders chose to speak popular messages in order to support their standard of living. Micah preached that true religion comes from a heart tuned to God, resulting in godly living. As such, religion and ethics are inseparable. People who refuse to repent will face His judgment, but the faithful will find His salvation and be led by God's King, who would usher in His peace and prosperity.

Structure

Structured thematically as a balanced chiasm, the book highlights the central and final sections. Each matching section reflects on the other. This literary structure emphasizes Micah's main themes of Judah's social sins, the moral failure of its leadership, and the establishment of God's kingship over the land.

Outline

I. Coming Defeat and Destruction (1:1-16)
   A. God's condemnation of His people (1:1-7)
   B. Micah's lament (1:8-16)

II. Corruption of the People (2:1-13)
   A. Judgment on greedy oppressors (2:1-5)
   B. Rejection of God's word (2:6-11)
   C. Hope after the judgment (2:12-13)

III. Corruption of the Leaders (3:1-12)
   A. Unjust rulers and judges (3:1-4)
   B. False prophets and the true prophet (3:5-8)
   C. Corrupt leaders and Jerusalem's fall (3:9-12)

IV. Hope for a Glorious Future Restoration (4:1–5:15)
   A. The Lord's rule over the nations (4:1-5)
   B. The remnant and the Lord's rule (4:6-10)
   C. The Lord's reversal of the present situation (4:11–5:1)
   D. The remnant and the Lord's ruler (5:2-9)
   E. The Lord's rule over the nations (5:10-15)

V. Corruption of the City and Its Leaders (6:1-16)
   A. God's lawsuit against His people (6:1-8)
   B. Accusations against Jerusalem (6:9-12)
   C. God's verdict of judgment (6:13-16)

VI. Corruption of the People (7:1-7)
   A. Lament over a decadent society (7:1-6)
   B. Waiting in hope (7:7)

VII. Future Reversal of Defeat and Destruction (7:8-20)
   A. God's anger over sin and His salvation (7:8-10)
   B. An exodus from exile (7:11-17)
   C. God's forgiveness of sin and His salvation (7:18-20)

1 The word of the Lord that came[a] to Micah[b] the Moreshite[c]—what he saw regarding Samaria and Jerusalem in the days of Jotham,[d] Ahaz,[e] and Hezekiah,[f] kings of Judah.

Coming Judgment on Israel

2 Listen, all you peoples;[g]
pay attention, earth[A] and everyone
   in it![h]
The Lord God will be a witness
   against you,[i]
the Lord, from His holy temple.[j]

3 Look, the Lord is leaving His place[k]
and coming down to trample
   the heights[B] of the earth.[l]

4 The mountains will melt beneath Him,
and the valleys will split apart,
like wax near a fire,[m]
like water cascading down
   a mountainside.

5 All this will happen because of
   Jacob's rebellion
and the sins of the house of Israel.
What is the rebellion of Jacob?
Isn't it Samaria?[n]
And what is the •high place of Judah?[o]
Isn't it Jerusalem?

6 Therefore, I will make Samaria
a heap of ruins[p] in the countryside,
a planting area[q] for a vineyard.
I will roll her stones[r] into the valley
and expose her foundations.[s]

7 All her carved images will be smashed[t]
   to pieces;
all her wages[u] will be burned in the fire,
and I will destroy all her idols.

Since she collected the wages
   of a prostitute,[v]
they will be used again for a prostitute.

Micah's Lament

8 Because of this I will lament and wail;
I will walk barefoot and naked.[w]
I will howl like the jackals[x]
and mourn like ostriches.[C]

9 For her wound is incurable[y]
and has reached even Judah;[z]
it has approached the gate
   of my people,[aa]
as far as Jerusalem.

10 Don't announce it in Gath,[ab]
don't weep at all.
Roll in the dust in Beth-leaphrah.

11 Depart in shameful nakedness,[ac]
you residents of Shaphir;
the residents of Zaanan[ad] will not
   come out.
Beth-ezel is lamenting;
its support[D] is taken from you.

12 Though the residents of Maroth
anxiously wait for something good,[ae]
disaster has come from the Lord[af]
to the gate of Jerusalem.

13 Harness the horses to the chariot,
you residents of Lachish.[ag]
This was the beginning of sin
   for Daughter •Zion,
because Israel's acts of rebellion[ah]
   can be traced to you.

---

*a*1:1 Hs 1:1; Jl 1:1; Zph 1:1   *b*2Ch 29:5-11; 32:24-26; Jr 26:18   *c*Mc 1:14   *d*2Kg 15:5,32-38; 2Ch 27:1-9; Is 1:1; Hs 1:1   *e*2Kg 16:1-20; 2Ch 28:1-27; Is 7:1-12   *f*2Kg 18:1-20; 2Ch 29:1-31   *g*1:2 1Kg 22:28; 2Ch 18:27; Jr 6:19; 22:29   *h*Ps 24:1; Is 34:1; Jr 47:2   *i*1Sm 12:5-6; Ps 50:7; Jr 42:5; Mal 3:5   *j*Ps 11:4; Hab 2:20   *k*1:3 Is 26:21   *l*Am 4:13   *m*1:4 Ps 97:5; Is 64:1-2; Nah 1:5   *n*1:5 Is 7:9; Am 8:14   *o*2Ch 34:3-4   *p*1:6 Mc 3:12   *q*Jr 31:5; Am 5:11   *r*Lm 4:1   *s*Ezk 13:14   *t*1:7 Dt 9:21; 2Ch 34:7   *u*Dt 23:18   *v*Dt 23:18   *w*1:8 Is 20:2-4; 32:11   *x*Is 13:21-22   *y*1:9 Is 3:26; Jr 30:12,15   *z*2Kg 18:13-16; 19:31-37; Is 8:7-8   *aa*Mc 1:12   *ab*1:10 2Sm 1:20   *ac*1:11 Ezk 23:29   *ad*Jos 15:37   *ae*1:12 Is 59:9-11; Jr 14:19   *af*Jdg 2:15; 2Kg 17:7; 21:12; Is 45:7; Mc 2:3   *ag*1:13 Jos 10:3; 2Kg 14:19; Is 36:2   *ah*Mc 1:5

A1:2 Or *land*   **B**1:3 Or *high places*   **C**1:8 Or *eagle owls*; lit *daughters of the desert*   **D**1:11 Lit *its standing place*; Hb obscure

---

1:1 Samaria and Jerusalem, the capitals of the northern and southern kingdoms, are representative of the entire nations of Israel and Judah respectively.

1:2-5 The Lord was **coming down** to judge the wickedness of Israel and Judah. **Rebellion** or "revolt" (Hb *pesha'*) denotes a willful, criminal breaking of a covenant (1Kg 12:19; Jr 2:29). **Sins** (Hb *chattoth*) are literally deviations from a target (Jdg 20:16; Pr 19:2), God's holiness in this case. Samaria's idolatry and immorality were so deep that God marked her for destruction (Mc 1:6-7). Micah compared worship in **Jerusalem** with pagan worship in the north. Hezekiah repented through Micah's preaching (Jr 26:19) and removed every **high place**, stone altar, and pagan Asherah pole (2Kg 18:1-6).

1:6-7 Assyria captured **Samaria** in 722 B.C. (2Kg 17:3-6). Israel's apostasy included participating in pagan cultic prostitution, which involved paying **wages** to prostitutes; Assyrian troops would pillage Samaria, steal these wages, and use the money yet again on prostitutes. Israel's sins were so bad that even the pagan armies that conquered her would do with her monies nothing worse than she herself had done.

1:8-16 This section declares that sinful Judah will also face God's wrath. Micah grieved over the towns of Judah facing

destruction, even his hometown (v. 14). Sennacherib of Assyria marched through Judah to Jerusalem in 701 B.C. (Is 10:28-32). He captured at least 46 Judean towns in this campaign but failed to take Jerusalem. Using vivid wordplay to evoke dread, Micah mentioned towns near his home to arouse the people from complacency and bring them to repent of their sin, perhaps preventing the upcoming judgment. Most astounding was the fact that behind this destruction would be the Lord Himself (Mc 1:12).

1:10-15 David lamented **Don't announce it in Gath** when Saul and Jonathan died in battle; for otherwise he knew the Philistines would gloat (2Sm 1:20). In the same spirit, Micah did not want the Assyrians to gloat in their success. **Beth-leaphrah** (lit "house of dust") would **roll in the dust** as a sign of humiliating defeat (Gn 3:14; Ps 44:25). Those living in **Shaphir** (lit "pleasant") would have the unpleasant experience of being stripped naked and led into exile. Neighboring **Zaanan** (wordplay with Hb *yatsa'*; "to go out") would not go out to help, and **Beth-ezel** (lit "house of taking away") would remove its support.

Maroth (sounds like Hb *mara'*; meaning "bitter") wanted something sweet but would instead face the Lord's **disaster**. This trouble would approach **the gate of Jerusalem**

14 Therefore, send farewell gifts[a]
    to Moresheth-gath;
the houses of Achzib[b] are a deception[c]
    to the kings of Israel.
15 I will again bring a conqueror
    against you who live in Mareshah.[d]
The nobility[A] of Israel will come
    to Adullam.[e]
16 Shave yourselves bald and cut off
    your hair[f]
in sorrow for your precious children;
make yourselves as bald as an eagle,
for they have been taken from you
    into exile.[g]

Oppressors Judged

2 Woe to those who dream up wickedness
and prepare evil plans[h] on their beds!
At morning light[i] they accomplish it
because the power is in their hands.[j]
2 They covet fields[k] and seize them;[l]
they also take houses.
They deprive a man of his home,[m]
a person of his inheritance.[n]

3 Therefore, the LORD says:

I am now planning[o] a disaster
    against this nation;[p]
you cannot free your necks from it.[q]
Then you will not walk so proudly[r]
because it will be an evil time.[s]

4 In that day one will take up[t] a taunt
    against you,
and lament mournfully,[u] saying,
"We are totally ruined![v]
He measures out the allotted land
    of my people.
How He removes it from me!
He allots our fields[w] to traitors."
5 Therefore, there will be no one
in the assembly of the LORD
to divide the land by casting lots.[B,x]

God's Word Rejected

6 "Quit your preaching,"[y] they[c] preach.
"They should not preach these things;[z]
shame will not overtake us."[D,aa]
7 House of Jacob, should it be asked,
"Is the Spirit of the LORD impatient?[ab]
Are these the things He does?"
Don't My words bring good[ac]
to the one who walks uprightly?[ad]
8 But recently My people have risen up
    like an enemy:[ae]
You strip off the splendid robe[af]
from those who are
    passing through confidently,[ag]
like those returning from war.
9 You force[ah] the women of My people
out of their comfortable homes,

Cross references
a 1:14 2Kg 16:8
b Jos 15:44
c Jr 15:18
d 1:15 Jos 15:44
e Jos 12:15; 15:35; 1Sm 22:1; 2Sm 23:13
f 1:16 Jb 1:20; Is 22:12; Jr 7:29
g 2Kg 17:6; Am 7:11,17
h 2:1 Ps 36:4; Is 32:7; Nah 1:11
i Hs 7:6-7
j Gn 31:29; Dt 28:32; Pr 3:27
k 2:2 Jr 22:17; Am 8:4
l Is 5:8
m 1Kg 21:1-15
n Ex 20:17; Is 5:8
o 2:3 Dt 28:48; Jr 18:11
p Jr 8:3; Am 3:1-2
q Lm 1:14; 5:5
r Is 2:11-12
s Am 5:13
t 2:4 Hab 2:6
u Jr 9:10,17-21; Mc 1:8
v Is 6:11; 24:3; Jr 4:13
w Jr 6:12; 8:10
x 2:5 Nm 34:13,16-29; Jos 18:4,10
y 2:6 Is 30:10; Am 2:12; 7:16
z Is 29:10; Mc 3:6
aa Mc 6:16
ab 2:7 Is 50:2; 59:1
ac Ps 119:65,68, 116; Jr 15:16
ad Ps 15:2; 84:11
ae 2:8 Jr 12:8   af Mc 3:2-3; 7:2-3   ag Ps 120:6-7   ah 2:9 Jr 10:20

A 1:15 Lit glory   B 2:5 Lit LORD stretching the measuring line by lot   C 2:6 = the prophets   D 2:6 Text emended; MT reads things. Shame will not depart.

---

but would not enter it. **Lachish**, a major fortification and military garrison (2Ch 11:9), would need riding steeds (Hb rekesh; Est 8:10; cp. Is 2:7; Mc 5:10) to power chariots in a fast getaway. Reliance on military might was **the beginning of sin** leading to **acts of rebellion** among God's

gazal

Hebrew Pronunciation	[gah ZAL]
HCSB Translation	rob, snatch
Uses in Micah	2
Uses in the OT	30
Focus passage	Micah 2:2

Originally this root probably meant "snatch away violently." Gazal particularly denotes steal (Lv 6:4) and rob (Lv 19:13). Abimelech's servants seized a well Abraham had dug (Gn 21:25). Laban might have taken Jacob's wives back by force (Gn 31:31). Something is taken away not to be returned (Dt 28:31). Benjaminites as kidnappers caught women (Jdg 21:23). Benaiah snatched a spear from an enemy's hand (2Sm 23:21). Infants were snatched as debt repayment (Jb 22:16). People deprive others of justice (Is 10:2). They seize fields (Mc 2:2) and houses (Jb 20:19), figuratively tearing off others' skin (Mc 3:2). Dry ground and heat snatch away melted snow (Jb 24:9). The passive participle connotes victim of robbery (Jr 21:12). Gazel (6x) denotes robbery (Ps 62:10) and perversion of justice (Ec 5:8). Gezelah (6x) indicates what is stolen (Lv 6:4) or plunder (Is 3:14). Gazal gezelah implies commit robbery (Ezk 18:7).

people (Is 30:15-17). Like a father giving away his betrothed daughter, Judah would have to give away **Moresheth-gath** (sounds like Hb meorashah; meaning "betrothed") to Assyria. Though it promised help, **Achzib** (lit "deception") would not come through. **Mareshah** (sounds like Hb hayyoresh; meaning "the conqueror") would be conquered. Israel's leaders would flee to **Adullam** to hide like David had done (1Sm 22:1; 2Sm 23:13).

2:1-13 Rich and powerful landlords had destroyed the Israelite community through their greed. According to Micah's declaration in this section, they believed that God's land (Lv 25:23) belonged to anyone with the power to take it.

2:1-5 Micah pronounced a "woe oracle" against wealthy men who devised wicked schemes to seize houses and lands from the weak. Their own lands would be seized by the Assyrians. Their covetousness led them to **seize . . . take**, and **deprive** people of their rightful **inheritance** (Gn 31:14; Lv 25:23-34; 1Kg 21:4). God's law prohibited such acts, even in cases where it was deemed legal (Lv 19:13). Thus the Lord was **planning a disaster** against this corrupt nation. With the exile God would distribute their land to other wicked people, and no one would be left **to divide the land by casting lots**, as in the time of Joshua (Jos 14:2; 18:8,10).

2:6-7 Popular false prophets rejected Micah's message of God's judgment. They told him to **quit your preaching**, because **shame will not overtake us**. Focusing only on God's love and patience, they lost sight of God's holiness and

and you take My blessing[A,a]
from their children forever.

10 Get up and leave,
for this is not your place of rest,[b]
because defilement[c]
brings destruction—
a grievous destruction![d]

11 If a man of wind[B] comes
and invents lies:[e]
"I will preach to you about wine
and beer,"[f]
he would be just the preacher
for this people![g]

The Remnant Regathered

12 I will indeed gather[h] all of you, Jacob;
I will collect the remnant of Israel.[i]
I will bring them together like sheep
in a pen,
like a flock in the middle of its fold.
It will be noisy with people.[j]

13 One who breaks open the way
will advance before them;
they will break out, pass
through the gate,
and leave by it.
Their King will pass through
before them,
the LORD as their leader.

Unjust Leaders Judged

3 Then I said, "Now listen,[k]
leaders of Jacob,
you rulers of the house of Israel.
Aren't you supposed to know
what is just?[l]

2 You hate good and love evil.
You tear off people's skin[m]
and strip their flesh from their bones.

3 You eat the flesh[n] of my people
after you strip their skin from them
and break their bones.
You chop them up[o]
like flesh for the cooking pot,
like meat in a cauldron."

4 Then they will cry out[p] to the LORD,
but He will not answer them.
He will hide His face from them
at that time[q]
because of the crimes
they have committed.

False Prophets Judged

5 This is what the LORD says
concerning the prophets
who lead my people astray,[r]
who proclaim[s] peace
when they have food to sink
their teeth into
but declare war against the one
who puts nothing in their mouths.

6 Therefore, it will be night[t] for you—
without visions;
it will grow dark for you—
without ˚divination.[u]
The sun will set[v] on these prophets,
and the daylight will turn black
over them.

7 Then the seers will be ashamed[w]
and the diviners disappointed.[x]
They will all cover their mouths[C,y]
because there will be no answer
from God.[z]

8 As for me, however, I am filled
with power[aa]
by the Spirit of the LORD,
with justice and courage,

Cross references (center column)

a 2:9 Ezk 39:21; Hab 2:14
b 2:10 Dt 3:19-20; 12:8-10
c Ps 106:38
d Lv 18:25-28
e 2:11 Jr 5:13,31
f Is 28:7
g Is 30:10-11
h 2:12 Mc 4:6-7
i 2Kg 19:31; Mc 5:7-8; 7:18
j Jr 23:3; Ezk 36:35-38
k 3:1 Is 1:10; Mc 3:9
l Ps 82:1-5; Jr 5:5
m 3:2 Ps 53:4; Ezk 22:27; Mc 2:8; 7:2-3
n 3:3 Ps 14:4; 27:2; Zph 3:3
o Ezk 11:3,6-7
p 3:4 Ps 18:41; Pr 1:28; Is 1:15; Jr 11:11
q Dt 31:17; Is 59:2
r 3:5 Is 3:12; 9:15-16; Jr 14:14-15
s Jr 6:14
t 3:6 Is 8:20-22; 29:10-12
u Dt 18:10; Jos 13:22
v Is 59:10
w 3:7 Zch 13:4
x Is 44:25; 47:12-14
y Lv 13:45; Lm 4:13-15; Ezk 24:17,22; Mc 7:16
z 1Sm 28:6; Is 29:9-12; Mc 3:4
aa 3:8 Is 61:1-2; Jr 1:18

A 2:9 Perhaps the land   B 2:11 Or spirit   C 3:7 Lit mustache

---

judgment (Ex 34:6-7). God responded that His word brings blessing to **the one who walks uprightly**, but not to those who are complacent in their sin.

2:8-11 Greedy oppressors were **an enemy** of the people, attacking innocent passersby, evicting **women** from their **homes**, and taking from them God's material **blessing**. God ordered these oppressors to **get up and leave**, a reference to the exile. With intense sarcasm Micah said the people deserved the false prophecy they received—**lies** of an easy life of **wine and beer** from God. They wanted a religion that satisfied their self-indulgence, not one that demanded righteousness and holiness.

2:12-13 False prophets preached that God's judgment would not fall, but Micah promised salvation beyond the judgment for a righteous remnant. God would **gather** them like a good shepherd (Is 40:11). **Their King . . . the LORD** Himself would lead them from exile and take them home (Ex 14:29-31; Dt 1:30-33; Is 63:9).

3:1-12 In this chapter Micah declared that corrupt rulers, prophets, and priests plagued God's people. Political and judicial leaders perverted justice, and the spiritual leaders perverted God's word.

3:1-4 Leaders should be **just**, putting things into a rightful state and restoring (Hb) shalom, or "wholeness." Instead, Micah saw rulers who hated **good** and loved **evil**. He described their sin in cannibalistic terms (**You eat the flesh of my people**), for such is the impact of false teaching about God. Because they offered no justice to others, they would find no solace in the Lord, who would **hide His face from them** (see Dt 31:17).

3:5-7 False prophets preached **peace** to those who supported them and **war** to those who did not (Jr 23:9-32; 28:1-17; Ezk 13:1-9; Zph 3:4). God would no longer speak to them in **visions** or otherwise. Having no word from the Lord, they would lose their position of honor and **be ashamed**.

3:8 But God had left a faithful witness distinctly different from the false prophets. Empowered by **the Spirit of the LORD**, Micah had a powerful voice of **justice** (see Is 58:1-2).

to proclaim to Jacob his rebellion
and to Israel his sin.[a]

Zion's Destruction

9 Listen to this, leaders of the house
  of Jacob,[b]
you rulers of the house of Israel,
who abhor justice[c]
and pervert everything that is right,
10 who build •Zion with bloodshed[d]
and Jerusalem with injustice.
11 Her leaders issue rulings for a bribe,[e]
her priests teach for payment,[f]
and her prophets practice divination
  for money.
Yet they lean on the Lord, saying,
"Isn't the Lord[g] among us?
No disaster will overtake us."
12 Therefore, because of you,
Zion will be plowed like a field,
Jerusalem will become ruins,[h]
and the hill of the temple mount[i]
  will be a thicket.[j]

The Lord's Rule from Restored Zion

4 In the last days[k]
  the mountain of the Lord's house[l]
will be established
at the top of the mountains
and will be raised above the hills.
Peoples will stream to it,[m]
2 and many nations will come and say,[n]
"Come, let us go up to the mountain
  of the Lord,[o]
to the house of the God of Jacob.
He will teach us about His ways[p]

a 3:8 Is 58:1
b 3:9 Mc 3:1
c Ps 58:1-2; Is 1:23
d 3:10 Jr 22:13,17; Hab 2:12
e 3:11 Is 1:23; Mc 7:3
f Jr 6:13
g Is 48:2
h 3:12 Jr 9:11
i Mc 4:1
j Jr 26:18
k 4:1-3 Is 2:2-4; Dn 2:28; 10:14; Hs 3:5; Mc 5:10
l 4:1 Ezk 43:12; Mc 3:12; Zch 8:3
m Ps 22:27; 86:9; Jr 3:17
n 4:2 Zch 2:11; 14:16
o Is 56:6-7; Jr 31:6
p Ps 25:8-9,12; Is 54:13
q Is 42:1-4; Zch 14:8-9
r 4:3 Is 11:3-5
s 4:4 1Kg 4:25; Zch 3:10
t Lv 26:6; Jr 30:10
u Is 1:20; 40:5
v 4:5 2Kg 17:29
w Zch 10:12
x Jos 24:15; Is 26:8,13
y 4:6 Is 35:6; Jr 31:8; Mc 2:12; Zph 3:19
z 4:7 Mc 5:7-8; 7:18; Mt 11:5; Lk 14:21
aa Is 24:23

so we may walk in His paths."
For instruction will go out of •Zion[q]
and the word of the Lord
  from Jerusalem.
3 He will settle disputes
  among many peoples[r]
and provide arbitration
  for strong nations
that are far away.
They will beat their swords into plows,
and their spears into pruning knives.
Nation will not take up the sword
  against nation,
and they will never again train for war.
4 But each man will sit
  under his grapevine[s]
and under his fig tree
with no one to frighten him.[t]
For the mouth of the Lord[u] of •Hosts
has promised this.
5 Though all the peoples each walk
in the name of their gods,[v]
we will walk[w] in the name
  of •Yahweh our God
forever and ever.[x]

6 On that day—
    this is the Lord's declaration—
I will assemble the lame
and gather the scattered,[y]
those I have injured.
7 I will make the lame into a remnant,[x]
those far removed into a strong nation.
Then the Lord will rule over them[aa]
  in Mount Zion

He preached about **rebellion** and **sin** (cp. 1:5,13), dealing with issues that would not be resolved until God's people confessed and abandoned their sin.

3:9-11 The corrupt leaders were known to **abhor justice** and **pervert everything that is right**. They were guilty of **bloodshed** and **injustice**, influenced by **a bribe . . . payment**, and **money**. Still they trusted in God's constant presence and blessing. Such false faith misinterpreted God's patience and grace as His approval of their actions. They saw Jerusalem and the temple as signs of an irreversible right standing with God, overlooking their responsibility for holiness (1Kg 6:12-13; 9:6-8; see note at Jr 7:4).

3:12 The Lord cannot look with favor upon sin (Hab 1:13), so the people faced God's judgment. **Jerusalem** would fall and the **temple mount** would be destroyed much like Samaria (1:5-7). Micah's sermon spurred King Hezekiah's reform (Jr 26:17-19; cp. 2Kg 18:1-6; 2Ch 29:1–31:21) and helped save Jeremiah's life a century later (Jr 26:7-19).

4:1–5:15 This central section portrays God establishing Himself as the true ruler over His people and all nations. He would replace Israel's wicked rulers with His own ruler, who would bring God's reign and peace to the world (5:4-5a).

4:1-4 This oracle (also in Is 2:1-4) refers to **the last days** when God's kingdom will be established. The temple mount, representing God's dwelling on earth, though previously destroyed (Mc 3:12), would **be established at the top of the mountains** and God would exalt Himself among the nations (Ps 46:10). Many peoples will be drawn to Him saying, **Come, let us go up to the mountain of the Lord**. They will want to learn **His ways**, and they will be changed by the truth of His **instruction** (Hb *torah*). God Himself will bring peace between **peoples** and **nations**, causing bloodshed to end (3:10) and instruments of death to be remade into implements promoting life. Nations will **never again train for war**. Peace and security are certain because **the mouth of the Lord of Hosts has promised this**.

4:5 Though outnumbered by unbelievers, faithful worshipers promised to **walk in the name of Yahweh our God forever**. Looking in hope, they would always follow His leadership, trusting Him to work out His plan in history.

4:6-8 Though **injured** by God's judgment, God would also **gather** His **lame** and **scattered** people once more (see note at 2:12-13). From this godly **remnant** He would build **a strong nation**. Thus God's people could expect to suffer before being redeemed. He **will rule over them . . . forever**.

from this time on and forever.

8 And you, watchtower for the flock,[a]
fortified hill[A] of Daughter Zion,
the former rule[b] will come to you,
sovereignty will come
to Daughter Jerusalem.

From Exile to Victory

9 Now, why are you shouting loudly?[c]
Is there no king with you?
Has your counselor perished[d]
so that anguish grips you like a woman
in labor?

10 Writhe and cry out,[B,e] Daughter Zion,
like a woman in labor,
for now you will leave the city[f]
and camp in the open fields.
You will go to Babylon;
there you will be rescued;[g]
there the LORD will redeem you[h]
from the power of your enemies!

11 Many nations have now assembled
against you;[i]
they say, "Let her be defiled,
and let us feast our eyes on Zion."

12 But they do not know
the LORD's intentions[j]
or understand His plan,
that He has gathered them
like sheaves to the threshing floor.

13 Rise and thresh,[k] Daughter Zion,
for I will make your horns iron
and your hooves bronze,
so you can crush many peoples.[l]
Then you[C] will •set apart their plunder[m]

to the LORD for destruction,
their wealth to the Lord of all
the earth.

From Defeated Ruler to Conquering King

5[D] Now, daughter who is under attack,
you slash yourself in grief;
a siege is set against us!
They are striking the judge[n] of Israel
on the cheek with a rod.

2[E] Bethlehem Ephrathah,[o]
you are small among the clans
of Judah;
One will come from you[p]
to be ruler over Israel for Me.[q]
His origin[F] is from antiquity,[r]
from eternity.[G]

3 Therefore, He will abandon them[s]
until the time
when she who is in labor[t]
has given birth;
then the rest of His brothers[u]
will return
to the people of Israel.[v]

4 He will stand and shepherd them[w]
in the strength of •Yahweh,
in the majestic name of Yahweh
His God.
They will live securely,
for then His greatness will extend
to the ends of the earth.[x]

5 He will be their peace.[y]
When Assyria invades our land,[z]
when it marches against our fortresses,

Cross-references (center column)
[a]4:8 Ps 48:3,12; 61:3
[b]Is 1:26; Zch 9:10
[c]4:9 Jr 8:19
[d]Is 3:1-3
[e]4:10 Mc 5:3
[f]2Kg 20:18; Hs 2:14
[g]Is 43:14; 45:13; Mc 7:8-12
[h]Is 48:20; 52:9-12
[i]4:11 Is 5:25-30; 17:12-14
[j]4:12 Ps 147:19-20
[k]4:13 Is 41:15
[l]Jr 51:20-23
[m]Is 60:9
[n]5:1 1Kg 22:24; Jb 16:10; Lm 3:30
[o]5:2 Gn 35:19; Ru 4:11; 1Sm 17:12; Mt 2:6
[p]Is 11:1; Lk 2:4
[q]2Ch 7:18; Is 11:1; Jr 30:21; Zch 9:9; Mt 2:6
[r]Ps 74:2; 102:25; Pr 8:22-23; Hab 1:12
[s]5:3 Hs 11:8; Mc 4:10; 7:13
[t]Mc 4:9-10
[u]Is 10:20-22; Mc 5:7-8
[v]Mc 4:6-7
[w]5:4 Is 40:11; 49:9; Ezk 34:13-15,23-24; Mc 7:14
[x]Is 45:22; 52:10
[y]5:5 Is 9:6
[z]Is 8:7-8; 10:24-27

The greatness of the Davidic empire in the past would return once more to *Migdal-eder* (**watchtower for the flock**), a location near Bethlehem (Gn 35:19-21).

4:9-10 But first (**now**) the people must face God's judgment. Zion's inhabitants were **shouting loudly** and in **anguish** much like **a woman in labor** before their enemies. They had forgotten the Lord, their **king** and **counselor** who would not abandon His People in their time of need. They would leave the city of Jerusalem, **camp in the open fields** on their way to exile, and go to **Babylon**. But God would not forget them, for they would be rescued and the Lord's power would **redeem** them.

4:11–5:1 Judah's oppressors did not **know** God's ultimate wisdom or **understand** the purpose of **His plan**. The Lord had actually **gathered** these oppressors to be threshed like **sheaves** of grain. His sovereign power will make His weak and frail people into a mighty army who will **rise and thresh** God's enemies and glorify **the Lord of all the earth**. But until that glorious day of deliverance, Jerusalem would suffer **attack** and **siege** and her ruler would be utterly humiliated. God always has a purpose for the seemingly random, difficult events of life (Gn 50:20; Rm 8:28). The Lord of all the

earth never loses control and can always bring good from evil.

5:2-5a God would raise up another **ruler** from David's hometown of **Bethlehem Ephrathah** (Ru 4:11) who would be His servant (**for Me**; cp. 1Sm 16:1). He would originate **from antiquity** (lit "from days long ago") and "ancient times," probably a reference to David's time (Neh 12:46; Am 9:11). God had not forgotten His promise of granting an eternal kingship to David (2Sm 7:4-17). This coming Davidic ruler would appear **when she who is in labor has given birth**. Varying interpretations of this woman include: (1) the mother of Messiah (i.e., Mary), (2) Bethlehem, the birthplace of Messiah, (3) a righteous remnant bringing forth salvation, and (4) a historical reference to the upcoming exile (4:10). The exiles would go forth as from the womb into captivity and **return** once more (v. 3). The ruler will **shepherd** His people like His ancestor David (2Sm 5:2; 7:7), serving with the authority and **strength of Yahweh**. His people will **live securely** in His kingdom that will extend to **the ends of the earth** (see Ps 2:8; 72:8). He would bring God's "wholeness" or **peace** (Hb *shalom*) with His righteous reign (Is 9:6).

we will raise against it
   seven shepherds,
even eight leaders of men.
6 They will shepherd[a] the land of Assyria
   with the sword,
   the land of Nimrod[b]
   with a drawn blade.[A]
So He will rescue us[c] from Assyria
   when it invades our land,
   when it marches against our territory.

The Glorious and Purified Remnant

7 Then the remnant of Jacob[d]
   will be among many peoples
   like dew from the LORD,[e]
   like showers on the grass,[f]
which do not wait for anyone
   or linger for •mankind.
8 Then the remnant of Jacob
   will be among the nations,
      among many peoples,
   like a lion among animals of the forest,[g]
   like a young lion among flocks
      of sheep,
   which tramples[h] and tears[i]
      as it passes through,
   and there is no one to rescue them.[j]
9 Your hand will be lifted up
   against your adversaries,[k]
   and all your enemies will be destroyed.

10 In that day—
            this is the LORD's declaration—
   I will remove your horses from you[l]

and wreck your chariots.
11 I will remove the cities of your land[m]
   and tear down all your fortresses.[n]
12 I will remove sorceries
      from your hands,[o]
   and you will not have
      any more fortune-tellers.
13 I will remove your carved images[p]
   and sacred pillars from you
   so that you will not bow down again
   to the work of your hands.
14 I will pull up the •Asherah poles[q]
      from among you[r]
   and demolish your cities.[B]
15 I will take vengeance in anger
      and wrath[s]
   against the nations that have not
      obeyed Me.

God's Lawsuit against Judah

6 Now listen to what the LORD is saying:

   Rise, plead your case
      before the mountains,
   and let the hills hear your voice.
2 Listen to the LORD's lawsuit,[t]
   you mountains
      and enduring foundations
      of the earth,[u]
   because the LORD has a case
      against His people,[v]
   and He will argue it against Israel.
3 My people,[w] what have I done to you,[x]
   or how have I wearied you?[y]

Cross-references (center column):

a 5:6 Nah 2:11-13; Zph 2:13
b Gn 10:8-12
c Is 14:25; 37:36-37
d 5:7 Is 10:21; Mc 2:12; 4:7; 7:18
e Dt 32:2; 2Sm 17:12; Ps 110:3; Hs 14:5
f Ps 72:6; Is 44:3
g 5:8 Gn 49:9; Nm 24:9
h Ps 44:5; Is 41:15-16; Mc 4:13; Zch 10:5
i Hs 5:14
j Ps 50:22
k 5:9 Ps 10:12; 21:8; Is 26:11
l 5:10 Dt 17:16; Is 2:7; Hs 14:3
m 5:11 Is 1:7; 6:11
n Is 2:12-17; Hs 10:14; Am 5:9
o 5:12 Dt 18:10-12; Is 2:6; 8:19
p 5:13 Is 2:18,20; 17:8; Ezk 6:9
q 5:14 Dt 16:21
r Ex 34:13; Is 27:9
s 5:15 Is 1:24; 65:12
t 6:2 Is 3:13; Jr 2:9
u 2Sm 22:16; Ps 104:5
v Is 1:18; Hs 4:1; 12:2
w 6:3 Ps 50:7
x Jr 2:5
y Is 43:22-23

A 5:6 Aq, Vg; MT, Sym read *Nimrod at its gateways*   B 5:14 Or *shrines*

5:5b-9 People confident in their own strength believed that they could **raise** up for themselves numerous **leaders** against their enemies, even ruling over **Assyria** and **Nimrod**, or Babylon. Micah asserted that only **He** (God's ruler) **will rescue us from Assyria**, not any human leaders. God would make the faithful **remnant . . . like dew** and rain **showers**, which are God-caused phenomena that humans cannot control (Jdg 6:36-40; Jb 38:28). People must not rely on human strength and initiative for their future but must

instead trust in God's power and wait for Him to act. He can make a feeble remnant become **like a young lion** to execute judgment on their **enemies**.

5:10-15 God revealed how He would bring about eschatological peace. He would purge His people of anything that hindered their relationship with Him, such as reliance on military might (vv. 10-11), divination (v. 12), and idolatry (vv. 13-14), judging any nation that refused to submit to His rule (v. 15). Objects of military strength hampered their faith. God would remove these hindrances, causing His people to rely on Him alone (Ps 20:7). **Sorceries . . . fortune-tellers**, and idolatrous worship were spiritual hindrances (Is 8:19-20). The people needed purification by God. All people (including Israel) must submit to Him or face His **anger and wrath** as the holy and sovereign ruler.

6:1-16 In this chapter Micah sealed God's indictment with a covenant lawsuit. He announced the case (vv. 1-2), defended God's benevolent actions (vv. 3-5), heard a response from the people (vv. 6-7), reported the basis for God's judgment (v. 8), brought specific accusations (vv. 9-12), and pronounced God's verdict and punishment (vv. 13-16).

6:1-5 Micah was to **plead** God's case, calling the **mountains** and **hills** as witnesses as he brought serious charges of covenant unfaithfulness against the people (v. 1). God reminded

---

darak

Hebrew Pronunciation	[dah RAK]
HCSB Translation	tread, guide, bend, march
Uses in Micah	4
Uses in the OT	63
Focus passage	Micah 5:5-6

Darak, related to *derek* (way), means *tread* (Dt 11:24), *trample* (Ps 91:13), *step* (1Sm 5:5), or *set foot* (Dt 1:36). One *strides* (Am 4:13), *walks* (Is 59:8), *comes* (Nm 24:17), *marches* (Mc 5:5), or *marches on* (Jdg 5:21). Eleven times *darak* refers to *treading* grapes in winepresses (Am 9:13), and *darak* alone connotes *treading/trampling* grapes (Jr 25:30; Is 16:10).

Testify against Me!
⁴ Indeed, I brought you up*a* from the land
  of Egypt
and redeemed you*b* from that place
  of slavery.*c*
I sent Moses,*d* Aaron, and Miriam*e*
ahead of you.
⁵ My people,
remember what Balak
  king of Moab*f* proposed,
what Balaam son of Beor
answered him,*g*
and what happened from
  the Acacia Grove*A,h* to Gilgal*i*
so that you may acknowledge
the LORD's righteous acts.*j*

⁶ What should I bring before the LORD*k*
when I come to bow before God
  on high?
Should I come before Him
with •burnt offerings,*l*
with year-old calves?

⁷ Would the LORD be pleased
  with thousands of rams*m*
or with ten thousand streams of oil?
Should I give my firstborn
  for my transgression,*n*
the child of my body for my own sin?

⁸ Mankind, He has told you what is good*o*
and what it is the LORD requires of you:*p*
to act justly,*q*
to love faithfulness,*r*
and to walk humbly with your God.*s*

Verdict of Judgment

⁹ The voice of •Yahweh calls out
  to the city*B*
(and it is wise to •fear Your name):
"Pay attention to the rod
and the One who ordained it.*C*
¹⁰ Are there still*D* the treasures
  of wickedness*t*
and the accursed short measure*u*
in the house of the wicked?

a 6:4 Ex 12:51; 20:2
b Dt 7:8
c Ex 20:2
d Ps 77:20
e Ex 15:20
f 6:5 Nm 22:5-6
g Nm 22-24
h Nm 25:1; Jos 2:1; 3:1
i Jos 4:19; 5:9-10
j 1Sm 12:7; Ps 103:6; Is 1:27
k 6:6 Ps 40:6-8
l Ps 51:16-17
m 6:7 Ps 50:9; Is 40:16
n Lv 18:21; 20:1-5; Jr 7:31
o 6:8 Dt 30:15
p Dt 10:12
q Is 56:1; Jr 22:3; Mt 23:23
r Hs 6:6
s Is 57:15; 66:2
t 6:10 Jr 5:26-27; Am 3:10
u Ezk 45:9-10; Am 8:5

---

^A^ 6:5 Or *Shittim*   ^B^ 6:9 = Jerusalem   ^C^ 6:9 Or *attention, you tribe. Who has ordained it?*; Hb obscure   ^D^ 6:10 Hb obscure

---

them of His righteous acts toward them in the past. He rescued them from **Egypt**, gave them trustworthy leaders such as Moses and Joshua, foiled the schemes of the enemy, and miraculously led them across the Jordan River. The people were to **remember** and **acknowledge** His **righteous acts**.

6:6-7 The people complained that God's demands were unreasonable. Even to bring **offerings**, sacrifices, or their **firstborn** son would not satisfy God's requirements.

6:8 The people already knew the **good** things that God re-

quired (see Ps 14:1,3; 37:3). God's interest was not in the offering but the offerer. A person's character and behavior mattered more to God than any gift they might bring. People were to **act justly** under God's standards. They were to **love faithfulness**, treating one another with love and mercy. They were to **walk humbly** with **God** as their constant companion (Gn 6:9), conforming their lives to His will.

6:9-12 The leaders of Jerusalem practiced violence and social injustice. They cheated people in their trade (Am 8:4-5).

Stairs up to Ahab's palace at Samaria (6:16)

11 Can I excuse wicked scales
    or bags of deceptive weights?[a]
12 For the wealthy of the city are full
    of violence,[b]
    and its residents speak lies;[c]
    the tongues in their mouths
    are deceitful.[d]
13 "As a result, I have begun to strike
    you severely,[A,e]
    bringing desolation because of
    your sins.[f]
14 You will eat but not be satisfied,[g]
    for there will be hunger within you.
    What you acquire, you cannot save,[h]
    and what you do save,
    I will give to the sword.[B]
15 You will sow but not reap;[i]
    you will press olives
    but not anoint yourself with oil;
    and you will tread grapes
    but not drink the wine.[j]
16 The statutes of Omri
    and all the practices of Ahab's house
    have been observed;
    you have followed their policies.[k]
    Therefore, I will make you
    a desolate place[l]
    and the city's[C] residents an object
    of contempt;[D,m]
    you will bear the scorn of My people."[E,n]

Israel's Moral Decline

7 How sad for me!
    For I am like one who—
    when the summer fruit
    has been gathered
    after the gleaning
    of the grape harvest[o]—
    finds no grape cluster to eat,
    no early fig, which I crave.[p]

2 Godly people have vanished
    from the land;[q]
    there is no one upright
    among the people.[r]
    All of them wait in ambush
    to shed blood;[s]
    they hunt each other with a net.[t]
3 Both hands are good[u]
    at accomplishing evil:
    the official and the judge demand
    a bribe;[v]
    when the powerful man communicates
    his evil desire,
    they plot it together.
4 The best of them is like a brier;[w]
    the most upright is worse than a hedge
    of thorns.[x]
    The day of your watchmen,
    the day of your punishment,
    is coming;[y]
    at this time their panic is here.[z]
5 Do not rely on a friend;[aa]
    don't trust in a close companion.
    Seal your mouth
    from the woman who lies in your arms.
6 Surely a son considers his father
    a fool,[ab]
    a daughter opposes her mother,
    and a daughter-in-law is
    against her mother-in-law;
    a man's enemies are the men
    of his own household.
7 But I will look to the LORD;[ac]
    I will wait for the God of my salvation.[ad]
    My God will hear me.[ae]

Zion's Vindication

8 Do not rejoice over me,[af] my enemy!
    Though I have fallen, I will stand up;[ag]
    though I sit in darkness,
    the LORD will be my light.[ah]

Cross references (center column):
a 6:11 Lv 19:36; Hs 12:7
b 6:12 Is 1:23; 5:7; Am 6:3-4; Mc 2:1-2
c Jr 9:2-6,8; Hs 7:13; Am 2:4
d Is 3:8
e 6:13 Mc 1:9
f Is 1:7; 6:11
g 6:14 Is 9:20
h Is 30:6
i 6:15 Dt 28:38-40; Jr 12:13
j Am 5:11; Zph 1:13
k 6:16 1Kg 16:25-34; 2Kg 21:3; 2Ch 21:6,13; Jr 7:24
l Jr 18:16
m Jr 19:8; 25:9,18; 29:18
n Ps 44:13; Jr 51:51; Hs 12:14
o 7:1 Is 24:13
p Is 28:4; Hs 9:10
q 7:2 Is 57:1
r 1Kg 19:10
s Is 59:7; Mc 3:10
t Jr 5:26; Hs 5:1
u 7:3 Pr 4:16-17
v Am 5:12; Mc 3:11
w 7:4 Ezk 2:6; 28:24
x Nah 1:10
y Is 10:3; Hs 9:7
z Is 22:5
aa 7:5 Jr 9:4
ab 7:6 Mt 10:21,35-36; Lk 12:53
ac 7:7 Hab 2:1
ad Ps 130:5; Is 25:9
ae Ps 4:3
af 7:8 Ob 12
ag Am 9:11
ah Ps 27:1; Is 9:2

A 6:13 LXX, Aq, Theod, Syr, Vg; MT reads *I have made you sick by striking you down*   B 6:14 Hb obscure   C 6:16 Lit *and its*   D 6:16 Lit *residents a hissing*   E 6:16 LXX reads *of the peoples*

The wealthy and powerful abused the weak through **violence** and practiced treachery through **lies** and deceit.

6:13-16 God's verdict of judgment for sins is certain. The Lord Himself would frustrate all of their best efforts. Because they had followed the example of the wicked and idolatrous kings **Omri** and Ahab (see 1Kg 16:25-33), God would make Jerusalem a **desolate place** and its inhabitants **an object of contempt**. Ahab had killed the Lord's prophets (1Kg 18:4) and stolen Naboth's family inheritance through greed, lying, and murder (1Kg 21:1-16).

7:1-6 As Micah's society disintegrated he responded with tears. Like a field already harvested, Micah found no fruit left in his ministry. No **godly** or **upright** people were left in the land, and the moral fabric of society was decayed. He saw bloodshed, evil, bribes, and wicked plots. It was a time of crisis and **panic**. Homes and family relationships had

disintegrated to the point that no man could trust **a friend** or even his wife. Children dishonored and rebelled against their parents, making family members their **enemies**.

7:7 Micah cried out to God, asking Him to transform his nation. Demonstrating personal intimacy with God, Micah declared that he would **look to the LORD** and **wait for the God** of his **salvation**, stating confidently that **my God will hear me**.

7:8-20 In these verses Micah's message looked past the coming defeat and destruction (1:1-16) to the future day when the Lord would reverse that judgment. Repentant people would be raised again (7:8-9). Enemies would be defeated and Israel would be rebuilt (vv. 10-11). The exiles would be gathered (v. 12), and a new exodus would take place (v. 15). Because of His promise to Abraham (v. 20), God would forgive sinners who deserved no mercy (vv. 18-19). God always keeps His promises.

9 Because I have sinned against Him,
I must endure the Lord's rage
until He argues my case[a]
and establishes justice for me.[b]
He will bring me into the light;[c]
I will see His salvation.[A,d]

10 Then my enemy will see,
and she will be covered with shame,
the one who said to me,
"Where is the Lord your God?"[e]
My eyes will look at her in triumph;
at that time she will be trampled
like mud in the streets.[f]

11 A day will come for rebuilding
your walls;[g]
on that day your boundary
will be extended.[h]

12 On that day people will come to you[i]
from Assyria and the cities of Egypt,
even from Egypt to the Euphrates River
and from sea to sea
and mountain to mountain.

13 Then the earth will become
a wasteland[j]
because of its inhabitants
and as a result of their actions.[k]

Micah's Prayer Answered

14 Shepherd Your people[l] with Your staff,[m]
the flock that is Your possession.
They live alone[n] in a woodland
surrounded by pastures.
Let them graze in Bashan and Gilead[o]
as in ancient times.[p]

15 I will perform miracles for them[B]
as in the days of your exodus
from the land of Egypt.[q]

16 Nations will see and be ashamed
of[C] all their power.
They will put their hands
over their mouths,[r]
and their ears will become deaf.

17 They will lick the dust like a snake;[s]
they will come trembling out of
their hiding places[t]
like reptiles slithering
on the ground.[u]
They will tremble in the presence
of •Yahweh our God;[v]
they will stand in awe of You.

18 Who is a God like You,[w]
removing iniquity and passing
over rebellion[x]
for the remnant
of His inheritance?[y]
He does not hold on
to His anger forever,[z]
because He delights in faithful love.[aa]

19 He will again have compassion
on us;
He will vanquish our iniquities.[ab]
You will cast all our[D] sins
into the depths of the sea.[ac]

20 You will show loyalty to Jacob[ad]
and faithful love to Abraham,
as You swore to our fathers[ae]
from days long ago.

---

[a]7:9 Jr 50:34
[b]Jb 23:3-7; Lm 3:58
[c]Ps 37:6; Is 42:7,16
[d]Is 46:13; 56:1
[e]7:10 Ps 42:3,10; 79:10; 115:2; Jl 2:17
[f]Ps 18:42; Zch 10:5
[g]7:11 Is 54:11; Am 9:11
[h]Zph 2:2
[i]7:12 Is 19:23-25; 60:4,9
[j]7:13 Jr 25:11; Mc 6:13
[k]Is 3:10-11; Mc 3:4
[l]7:14 Ps 95:7; Is 40:11; 49:10; Mc 5:4
[m]Lv 27:32; Ps 23:4
[n]Nm 23:9; Dt 33:28
[o]Jr 50:19
[p]Am 9:11
[q]7:15 Ex 3:20; 34:10; Ps 78:11-16
[r]7:16 Mc 3:7
[s]7:17 Ps 72:9; Is 49:23
[t]Ps 18:45
[u]Dt 32:24
[v]Is 25:3; 59:19
[w]7:18 Ex 15:11; Ps 71:19; Is 40:18
[x]Ex 34:7,9; Is 43:25; Rm 3:25
[y]Mc 2:12; 4:7; 5:7-8
[z]Ps 103:8-9,13
[aa]Jr 32:41
[ab]7:19 Jr 50:20
[ac]7:18-19 Ps 103:9-12; Is 38:17; 43:25; Jr 31:34
[ad]7:20 Gn 24:27; 32:10
[ae]Dt 7:8,12

[A]7:9 Or righteousness   [B]7:15 = Israel   [C]7:16 Or ashamed in spite of   [D]7:19 Some Hb mss, LXX, Syr, Vg; other Hb mss read their

---

7:8-10 As a representative of his people, Micah declared his faith and hope. **The Lord's rage** and judgment of sin would be temporary. God's anger was deserved and His punishment was just because the people had **sinned against Him.** One day the prophet would **stand up** and experience the Lord as his **light.** The Lord would defend him and establish justice for him. On that day the prophet would see His **salvation,** and enemies would see it and **be covered with shame.**

7:11-13 Judah would be rebuilt, and people would come from lands such as **Assyria** and **Egypt.** The earth would be made **a wasteland** because of the evil deeds of her **inhabitants.**

7:14-17 Using covenant language, Micah prayed for God to shepherd **Your people** and lead **Your possession** (cp. Ex 19:6) to the fertile lands that once belonged to Israel, much like God did in the first exodus from the land of Egypt. When this happened the nations would see God's power in sal-

vation and **be ashamed** of their own puny strength. They would cover **their mouths** in amazement, tremble in fear, and **stand in awe** in the presence of the Lord.

7:18-20 Hope is based on God's unchanging character. **Who is a God like You** is a question everyone should ponder. Only God can solve our greatest problem—sin. Micah described God's forgiveness as **removing iniquity** from His sight and **passing over rebellion** as no longer relevant. God would **vanquish** their **iniquities** like a conqueror, and cast their **sins** into the **depths of the sea.** God will deal with people's sins completely. The Lord is incomparable, gracious, merciful, compassionate, loyal, faithful, and loving (Ex 34:6-7). He covenanted with their forefathers **Jacob** and **Abraham** (Gn 22:17; 28:14) and would forever show **loyalty** and **faithful love** to the people of His covenant. Anyone in covenant relationship with Him may rest securely in hope because of His unchanging character.

Nahum

Introduction

The book of Nahum dramatically portrays God overwhelming Assyria to relieve His oppressed people. It was certainly a harsh message for Israel's enemies, but for the people of Judah it was a message of hope.

Relief (ca 728 B.C.) depicting Assyrian archers attacking a besieged city, most likely in Mesopotamia. An Assyrian soldier holds a large shield to protect two archers as they take aim. From the Central Palace in Nimrud and now in the British Museum, London. The Assyrian Empire brought down Israel (Samaria) in 722 B.C. In the next century, when Assyria was the dominant power in the ancient Near East, Nahum prophesied that, contrary to appearances, God would completely destroy Nineveh, the beautiful capital of Assyria (1:7-8).

Circumstances of Writing

Author: The presumed author Nahum (1:1) is the only person with that name in the OT. Like Jonah in the previous century, Nahum prophesied judgment upon Nineveh. The Ninevites in Jonah's time had repented (Jnh 3). But now that Nineveh's leaders had resumed their wicked actions, the Lord called Nahum to reaffirm His coming judgment. Ironically Nahum's Hebrew name means "comfort"—comfort for Judah (1:12-15) because its cruel overlord Assyria would be punished without any "comforters" (3:7). Except for the name of his hometown Elkosh (1:1), nothing certain is known about Nahum.

Two events circumscribe the earliest and latest possible dates for the composition of the book of Nahum: the capture and downfall of Thebes in about 663 B.C. and the announcements of Nineveh's certain destruction (1:1; 2:8; 3:7) which would happen in 612 B.C. The book's emphasis on the fall of Thebes, seemingly a recent event, would favor a date shortly after 663 B.C., during the reign of the notoriously wicked King Manasseh (ca 686–642 B.C.) and/or his evil son Amon (642–640 B.C.). Certainly Nah 1:12 (Assyria was still "strong [or at full strength] and numerous") suggests a time before the decline of that empire. This fits the reign of cruel Ashurbanipal (ca 668–627 B.C.) when Assyria was at the pinnacle of its power.

Background: The Assyrian capital Nineveh was located about 220 miles north of the modern Iraqi capital of Baghdad. By Nahum's time, Israel and Judah had experienced long and distressing affliction by the Assyrians. As early as Shalmaneser III (858–824 B.C.), King Jehu paid tribute to the Assyrians. The Lord often used Assyria as "the rod of My anger" (Is 10:5) to punish His people. Shalmaneser V (727–722 B.C.) and his successor Sargon II (722–705 B.C.) besieged and destroyed Samaria, taking the northern kingdom of Israel into captivity (2Kg 17:3-6). Similarly Sennacherib captured and devastated Judah, besieging Jerusalem by 701 B.C. (2Kg 18–19; Is 36–37). By Ashurbanipal's reign (ca 669–627 B.C.) Assyrian rulers were infamous for their cruelty (see notes at 3:10 and 3:19).

800–705 B.C.

At a time the Assyrian Empire is in decline, God calls Jonah to go to Nineveh and preach repentance. This was likely during the reigns of Uzziah of Judah (792–740) and Jeroboam II of Israel (793–753).

During its time of weakness, Assyria experiences two severe plagues (765 and 759) and a total eclipse (763).

Nineveh repents in response to Jonah's preaching and is spared God's judgment.

Assyria's Shalmaneser V besieges Samaria. 725–722

Samaria falls to Assyria's Sargon II; nearly 28,000 Israelites are sent into exile. 722

705–675 B.C.

Sennacherib establishes Nineveh as the capital of the Assyrian Empire. 705–681

Sennacherib captures and devastates Judah, besieging but not capturing Jerusalem. 701

When Babylon rebels against Sennacherib, he destroys the city. 689

Sennacherib is murdered by his two sons, one of whom, Esar-haddon (681–669), succeeds him as king. 681

Esar-haddon immediately begins the rebuilding of Babylon, an act that wins the allegiance of the local populace.

Message and Purpose

Judgment: The main theme of the book is the impending judgment of Nineveh by the Lord (1:1,8; 2:8-13; 3:7-19) by which he would deliver His people (1:12-15; cp. vv. 7-8). Yahweh would pay back Nineveh and the Assyrians in the same way they had mistreated their enemies. Since they were known for scattering their captives in brutal death marches, the Lord would send a scatterer (2:1) to disperse the Assyrians in retaliation for their cruelty (3:18-19; cp. 3:10). Since the Assyrians delighted in shedding blood and piling up the corpses of their foes, He would transform Nineveh into a city of blood with piles of its own corpses (3:1-3).

As the Assyrians had plucked the capital city Samaria like a first-ripe fig to devour her (fulfilling Is 28:4), so too the Lord would cause their capital Nineveh and other fortresses to fall into their enemies' hungry mouths (Nah 3:12). Though Nineveh (like Thebes) was seemingly impregnable because of its military strength (3:8) and its allies (3:9), the Assyrians would be exiled as they had exiled the Egyptians (3:10).

God, the caring warrior: The character of God, portrayed as a powerful but caring warrior (1:2-7), was the propelling force behind Nineveh's judgment. The Lord's jealousy for His people and His wrath toward His enemies (1:2-3), balanced by His compassion and longsuffering nature (1:3; Ex 34:6-7), seem to pivot on His great power (Nah 1:3) and goodness (1:7). Yahweh the warrior will take vengeance on His enemies (1:2,3-6). The portrait of a God of wrath is consistent with His promise to avenge the blood of His servants (Dt 32:35-36,42-43). Furthermore, God's goodness and compassion was not the doting love of a permissive or impotent grandparent (2Pt 3:9-10,12). He was "good" (or kind) to those who took refuge in Him (Nah 1:7) while bringing destruction on His unrepentant enemies, including Nineveh (1:8).

Contribution to the Bible

The book of Nahum provides a great view of a powerful, just God who maintains His absolute moral standards and offers hope to those who are despised and downtrodden. Nahum teaches us to trust God. Even when we despair of any help, we can know that God will stand with those who belong to Him.

675–610 B.C.

Nahum (675–612) prophesies that just as Assyria destroyed Thebes, Nineveh (Assyria's capital) will be destroyed.

Esar-haddon invades Egypt. 671

Egypt rebels (669) and Esar-haddon's son, Ashurbanipal (668–627), sets out to reconquer Egypt. 667

Egypt rebels again, so Ashurbanipal destroys Thebes. 665

Calah is destroyed and the combined armies of the Babylonians and the Medes lay siege to Nineveh. After two months, the city falls. 612

610–600 B.C.

An Assyrian general claims the throne and rallies what is left of the Assyrian army in Haran. An alliance with Egypt brings a few troops to Assyria's aid; but as the Babylonians approach, Haran is abandoned. 610

The last remnants of the battered Assyrian Empire, along with their recent Egyptian allies, are defeated at the Battle of Carchemish, bringing the Assyrian Empire to an end. 605

Structure

Nahum interweaved typical prophetic strands such as judgment songs against God's enemies (1:9-11,14; cp. 2:13; 3:5-7), a woe oracle or mock lament (3:1-7), salvation oracles for His people Judah (1:12-15), a victory hymn to Yahweh the divine warrior (1:2-8; cp. Ex 15; Ps 98), and a sarcastic "word vision" of imminent enemy invasion (Nah 2:1-10; cp. 3:2-3). He colored this literary tapestry with satirical "taunt songs" mocking Nineveh's soon-coming role reversal (2:11-12; 3:8-19; cp. 2:1-2; 3:4-5). He ridiculed Nineveh's practice of scattering of peoples to other nations by announcing that God's "scatterer" (2:1-2; 3:18-19) would pay her back in like manner. He taunted that her lion's lair of military booty would soon be looted (2:11-13). He also mocked her as a witch prostitute condemned to appropriate punishment: nakedness exposed with shame (3:4-7).

Using psychological warfare (as the Assyrians had used against Judah), Nahum taunted Nineveh's dependence on allies and other supposed defenses (3:8-10; cp. Is 36:4-20). Esar-haddon, father of Ashurbanipal, had threatened King Manasseh of Judah in 672 B.C. with treaty curses from the gods if they rebelled. As G. Johnston has argued, Yahweh converted borrowed treaty terminology to reverse this curse on Judah. It would not be Judah but Assyria's military men who would become defenseless like women (Nah 3:13). The Assyrians' ravaging of the land like a swarming army of locusts (cp. Jl 1:4-12; 2:4-9) was evoked and modified in order to mock Nineveh's merchants and military personnel, comparing them to harmless locusts on a wall, easily frightened and scattered (Nah 3:15-18). The incurable disease threatened from their gods would boomerang and inflict Assyria instead (3:19).

Yahweh as the caring warrior who would bring vengeance on His enemies, especially Nineveh, in order to save Judah, forms the backbone not only of Nahum's purpose statement but also of the book's literary structure.

Outline

I. Prelude (1:1-10)

II. Nineveh's Destruction as Part of God's Plan (1:11-15)
   A. Deliverance of Judah (1:12,13,15)
   B. Judgment against Assyria (1:11,14)

III. Nineveh's Destruction to Be Complete (2:1-13)
   A. Successful siege (2:1-9)
   B. Despair of the people (2:10-13)

IV. Nineveh's Destruction the Result of Sin (3:1-18)
   A. Inevitability of judgment (3:1-4)
   B. National annihilation (3:5-18)

V. Postlude (3:19)

1

The ·oracle concerning Nineveh.[a] The book of the vision of Nahum the Elkoshite.

God's Vengeance

2 The LORD is a jealous and avenging God;
the LORD takes vengeance
and is fierce in[A] wrath.
The LORD takes vengeance
against His foes;
He is furious with His enemies.[b]

3 The LORD is slow to anger but great
in power;
the LORD will never leave
the ·guilty unpunished.[c]
His path is in the whirlwind and storm,
and clouds are the dust
beneath His feet.

4 He rebukes the sea so that it dries up,
and He makes all the rivers run dry.[d]
Bashan and Carmel wither;[e]
even the flower of Lebanon withers.

5 The mountains quake before Him,
and the hills melt;
the earth trembles[B,C] at His presence—
the world and all who live in it.[f]

6 Who can withstand His indignation?
Who can endure His burning anger?[g]
His wrath is poured out like fire,
even rocks are shattered before Him.

Destruction of Nineveh

7 The LORD is good,
a stronghold in a day of distress;
He cares for those who take refuge[h]
in Him.

8 But He will completely destroy Nineveh[D]
with an overwhelming flood,[i]
and He will chase His enemies
into darkness.

9 Whatever you[E] plot against the LORD,
He will bring it to complete destruction;[j]

a1:1 Jnh 3:3-4;
4:11; Nah 2:8;
Zph 2:13
b1:2 Dt 6:15; Ps
94:1; Is 63:1-6;
Jr 46:10; 50:28-
29; Mc 5:15; Zph
1:18
c1:3 Ex 34:6-7;
Nm 14:18
d1:4 2Sm 22:16;
Ps 106:9; Is 50:2
e Is 33:9
f1:5 Ps 18:7; Jr
4:24; Am 8:8
g1:6 Ps 7:11;
69:24; 78:49
h1:7 2Sm 22:3;
Ps 17:7; 34:8
i1:8 Nah 2:6
j1:9 Ps 2:1-4
k1:10 Mal 4:1
l1:12 Is 10:5-34
m Ps 30:5; 103:9;
Is 54:8
n1:14 Lv 20:3;
1Sm 24:21; Ps
89:4; Is 48:19;
66:22
oDt 27:15; Jdg
18:14
p1:15 Is 52:7;
61:1; Rm 10:15

oppression will not rise up
a second time.

10 For they will be consumed
like entangled thorns,[k]
like the drink of a drunkard
and like straw that is fully dry.[F]

11 One has gone out from you,[G]
who plots evil against ·Yahweh,
and is a wicked counselor.

Promise of Judah's Deliverance

12 This is what the LORD says:

Though they are strong[H]
and numerous,
they will still be mowed down,
and he[I] will pass away.
Though I have afflicted you,[J,I]
I will afflict you no longer.[m]

13 For I will now break off his yoke
from you
and tear off your shackles.

The Assyrian King's Demise

14 The LORD has issued an order concerning
you:

There will be no offspring
to carry on your name.[K,n]
I will eliminate the carved idol
and cast image
from the house of your gods;[o]
I will prepare your grave,
for you are contemptible.

15 [L] Look to the mountains—
the feet of one bringing good news[p]
and proclaiming peace!
Celebrate your festivals, Judah;
fulfill your vows.
For the wicked one will never again
march through you;
he will be entirely wiped out.

A1:2 Lit *is a master of*   B1:5 Some emend to *earth is laid waste*   C1:5 Lit *lifts*   D1:8 Lit *her place*   E1:9 = Nineveh   F1:10 Hb obscure   G1:11 Possibly Nineveh   H1:12 Lit *intact*   I1:12 Either the king of Assyria or his army   J1:12 = Judah   K1:14 Lit *It will not be sown from your name any longer*   L1:15 Nah 2:1 in Hb

---

1:2-8 On this victory hymn to Yahweh, see Introduction.

1:2 Like a **jealous** (or zealous) husband, Yahweh would tolerate no rivals for Israel's affection, whether other so-called gods (Ex 34:14-16) or foreign nations and their kings.

1:3 That God was **slow to anger but great in power** indicates His wrath was not that of a hot-tempered tyrant. Neither was His compassion based on His inability to defeat those who oppressed His people. By no means would He **leave the guilty unpunished**, whether of His own people or their enemies (Ex 34:7).

1:4 Bashan and Carmel **wither** (and even the **flower of Lebanon**) because of a severe drought, parching the most fertile lands in Palestine (Is 33:9)—from the east, Bashan in Transjordan, to the northwest borders of the storm god

Baal's home territory near Mount Carmel and the Lebanon mountains. Actually Yahweh alone controlled the storm, rain, and fertility (drying up **the sea** and **all the rivers**). Bashan was famous for its lush pasturelands (Jr 50:19), fine cattle (Dt 32:14), and rich forests (Is 2:13; Ezk 27:6), and Carmel (lit "garden-land") was known for its verdant vegetation (Jr 50:19; Am 1:2). Both were withered by God's judgment.

1:11 The one who **plots evil against Yahweh, and is a wicked counselor** may be any Assyrian ruler (cp. v. 15, same Hb word "wicked") or even the demonic spirit that energizes him (Dn 10:13,20-21; contrast Messiah as Wonderful Counselor, Is 9:6). Sennacherib had plotted evil, but his objective to destroy Jerusalem (ca 701 B.C.) was thwarted (2Kg 19:20-28,32-34).

Attack against Nineveh

2 One who scatters is coming up
    against you.
Man the fortifications!
Watch the road!
Brace[A] yourself!
Summon all your strength![a]

2 For the LORD will restore the majesty
    of Jacob,
yes,[B] the majesty of Israel,
though ravagers have ravaged them
and ruined their vine branches.[b]

3 The shields of his[c] warriors are dyed red;
the valiant men are dressed in scarlet.[c]
The fittings of the chariot flash like fire
on the day of its battle preparations,
and the spears are brandished.

4 The chariots dash madly
    through the streets;
they rush around in the plazas.
They look like torches;
they dart back and forth like lightning.

5 He gives orders to his officers;
they stumble as they advance.
They race to its wall;
the protective shield is set in place.

6 The river gates are opened,
and the palace erodes away.[d]

7 Beauty[D] is stripped,[E]
she is carried away;
her ladies-in-waiting moan
like the sound of doves,[e]
and beat their breasts.

8 Nineveh has been like a pool of water
from her first days,[E]
but they are fleeing.
"Stop! Stop!" they cry,
but no one turns back.

9 "Plunder the silver! Plunder the gold!"
There is no end to the treasure,
an abundance of every precious thing.[f]

10 Desolation, decimation, devastation!
Hearts melt,[g]
knees tremble,
loins shake,
every face grows pale![h]

11 Where is the lions' lair,[i]
or the feeding ground
    of the young lions,
where the lion and lioness prowled,
and the lion's cub,
with nothing to frighten them away?[j]

12 The lion mauled whatever
    its cubs needed
and strangled prey for its lionesses.
It filled up its dens with the kill,
and its lairs with mauled prey.[k]

13 Beware, I am against you.[l]
                    This is the declaration
                    of the LORD of ˙Hosts.
I will make your chariots go up
    in smoke[F]
and the sword will devour
    your young lions.
I will cut off your prey from the earth,
and the sound of your messengers
will never be heard again.

Cross-references:
[a] 2:1 Am 2:14
[b] 2:2 Ps 80:12-15; Jr 12:10
[c] 2:3 Ezk 23:14
[d] 2:6 Nah 1:8
[e] 2:7 Is 38:14; 59:11
[f] 2:9 2Ch 32:27; 36:10; Dn 11:8; Nah 3:3
[g] 2:10 Dt 20:8; Jos 7:5; Is 13:7; 19:1; Ezk 21:7,15
[h] Is 21:3; Jl 2:6
[i] 2:11 Is 2:15; 5:26-29; Jr 4:7; 5:6; 50:17; 51:38; Jl 1:6; Am 3:12
[j] Lv 26:6; Dt 28:26; Jr 7:33
[k] 2:12 Jb 38:39-40
[l] 2:13 Jr 21:13; 50:31; 51:25; Nah 3:5

[A] 2:1 Lit *Strengthen*   [B] 2:2 Or *like*   [C] 2:3 = the army commander attacking Nineveh   [D] 2:7 Text emended; MT reads *Huzzab*
[E] 2:7,8 Hb obscure   [F] 2:13 Lit *will burn her chariots in smoke*

---

kashal

Hebrew Pronunciation	[kah SHAL]
HCSB Translation	stumble
Uses in Nahum	2
Uses in the OT	64
Focus passage	Nahum 2:5

Kashal often (13x) accompanies *naphal* ("fall") as *stumble* (Dn 11:19), implying physical (Lv 26:37) or spiritual (Is 3:8) *stumbling*. Truth *stumbles* (Is 59:14), strength *fails* (Neh 4:10), and knees *are weak* (Ps 109:24). The participle means *feeble* (2Ch 28:15) or *shaking* (Is 35:3). The passive signifies *be weak* (Zch 12:8) or *defeated* (Dn 11:34), *collapse* (Jr 6:15), *fall* (Dn 11:35), and *die* (Dn 11:33). The causative is *cause to* (Ezk 36:15) or *make* (2Ch 25:8) *stumble*. One *breaks* another's strength (Lm 1:14). The causative infinitive suggests *downfall* (2Ch 28:23). The causative passive signifies *forced to stumble* (Jr 18:23). *Mikshol* (14x) implies *obstacle* (Is 57:14) or *stumbling block* (Jr 6:21), *something that makes* people *stumble* (Ps 119:165). A conscience is *troubled* (1Sm 25:31). *Makshelah* is *stumbling block* (Zph 1:3) or *heap of rubble* (Is 3:6). *Kishshalon* is *fall* (Pr 16:18); *kashshiyl* is *hatchet* (Ps 74:6).

2:1 "Watchman" Nahum (**man the fortifications**) mockingly begins to cheer the Assyrians on as they prepared for siege warfare (3:14).

2:3-10 To heighten the suspense and surprise, **shields of his warriors . . . dyed red** and **valiant men . . . dressed in scarlet** initiate an intentionally ambiguous description of the battle's outcome. Were these uniforms dyed red or were they spattered with blood? Normally Nineveh's weapons would be stained with the blood of their enemies, but here it is unclear whether Nineveh or its attackers are so portrayed. Not until verse 8 is it clear that **Nineveh** is the defeated party, whose **hearts** would **melt** with fear.

2:11-13 The **lions' lair** with **lion** and **lioness** plays on two lion motifs commonly employed by Assyrian kings (G. Johnston). The kings described themselves as "lions" crushing their enemies. Ashurbanipal often portrayed himself killing literal lions single-handedly, with a weapon or even barehanded. Ironically reversing this imagery, Yahweh mocked Nineveh, the once-mighty lion who preyed on its enemies. Now Nineveh was being hunted and made prey. Its **young lions** (warriors) would be killed in battle.

Nineveh's Downfall

3 Woe to the city of blood,[a]
totally deceitful,
full of plunder,
never without prey.[b]

[2] The crack of the whip
and rumble of the wheel,
galloping horse
and jolting chariot![c]

[3] Charging horseman,
flashing sword,
shining spear;
heaps of slain,
mounds of corpses,
dead bodies without end[d]—
they stumble over their dead.

[4] Because of the continual prostitution
of the prostitute,
the attractive mistress of sorcery,
who betrays nations by her prostitution
and clans by her witchcraft,[e]

[5] I am against you.[f]

This is the declaration
of the LORD of •Hosts.
I will lift your skirts over your face
and display your nakedness to nations,
your shame to kingdoms.[g]

[6] I will throw filth on you
and treat you with contempt;
I will make a spectacle of you.

[7] Then all who see you will recoil
from you, saying,
"Nineveh is devastated;
who will show sympathy to her?"
Where can I find anyone
to comfort you?

[8] Are you better than Thebes[A,h]
that sat along the Nile
with water surrounding her,
whose rampart was the sea,
the river[B,C] her wall?

[9] •Cush and Egypt were
her endless source of strength;
Put and Libya were among her[D] allies.

[10] Yet she became an exile;
she went into captivity.
Her children were also dashed
to pieces[i]
at the head of every street.

They cast lots for her dignitaries,[j]
and all her nobles were bound
in chains.

[11] You[E] also will become drunk;
you will hide yourself.[F]
You also will seek refuge
from the enemy.

[12] All your fortresses are fig trees
with figs that ripened first;
when shaken, they fall—
right into the mouth of the eater!

[13] Look, your troops are like women
among you;
the gates of your land
are wide open to your enemies.
Fire will devour the bars of your gates.

[14] Draw water for the siege;
strengthen your fortresses.
Step into the clay and tread
the mortar;
take hold of the brick-mold!

[15] The fire will devour you there;
the sword will cut you down.
It will devour you
like the young locust.[k]
Multiply yourselves
like the young locust,
multiply like the swarming locust!

[16] You have made your merchants[l]
more numerous than the stars
of the sky.
The young locust strips[G] the land
and flies away.

[17] Your court officials are
like the swarming locust,
and your scribes like clouds
of locusts,
which settle on the walls
on a cold day;
when the sun rises, they take off,
and no one knows where they are.

[18] King of Assyria,
your shepherds slumber;
your officers sleep.
Your people are scattered
across the mountains
with no one to gather them together.[m]

---

[a] 3:1 Ezk 24:6,9
[b] Nah 2:9
[c] 3:2 Jdg 5:22; Jb 39:24; Jr 47:3
[d] 3:3 Nah 2:9
[e] 3:4 2Kg 9:22; Pr 7:10-23; Ezk 16:15; 23:1-21; Rv 17:3-6
[f] 3:5 Nah 2:13
[g] Jr 13:22,26; Ezk 16:37
[h] 3:8 Jr 46:25; Ezk 30:14-16
[i] 3:10 2Kg 8:12; Is 13:16; Hs 10:14
[j] Ob 11
[k] 3:15 Jl 1:4
[l] 3:16 Ezk 27:3,13,20,23-24
[m] 3:18 1Kg 22:17

A3:8 Or *No-amon*   B3:8 LXX, Syr, Vg read *water*   C3:8 Lit *sea from sea*   D3:9 Lit *your*   E3:11 = Nineveh   F3:11 Or *will be overcome*   G3:16 Or *sheds its skin*

3:1-3 Again, the author is initially vague (cp. note at 2:3-10) about the identity of the bloody city with its **mounds of corpses**, but the attentive reader knows that it is Nineveh, the once-formidable city, which God will now devastate (see note at v. 10; see also Introduction).

3:4-6 On a prostitute's punishment, see Introduction.

3:10 The Egyptian **children** were **dashed to pieces** by the Assyrians, just as Assyria had recently done to Israel in fulfillment of Hs 13:16 (cp. Ps 137:9; Hs 10:14-15). The atrocities included ripping pregnant women open. Such cruelty was not unique to the Assyrians (see note at Nah 3:19); other invading armies did similar things (see 2Kg 8:12; Is 13:16).

19 There is no remedy for your injury;
  your wound is severe.[a]
  All who hear the news about you

a 3:19 Jr 10:19;
14:17; 30:12

will clap their hands because of you,
  for who has not experienced
  your constant cruelty?

3:19 Assyrian rulers were infamous for their **cruelty** (see note at 3:10). Ashur-nasirpal II (858–824 B.C.) flayed captive kings alive and papered city walls with their skin. Impaling some on stakes, he gouged out their eyes and severed their hands, feet, and other body parts. Nahum's contempo-rary Ashurbanipal boasted of similar atrocities against the Egyptians. He also tore out the tongues of rebels who were uttering blasphemies against his god. He pulled a rope through an Arab king's jaw and chained him like a watch-dog at a city gate.

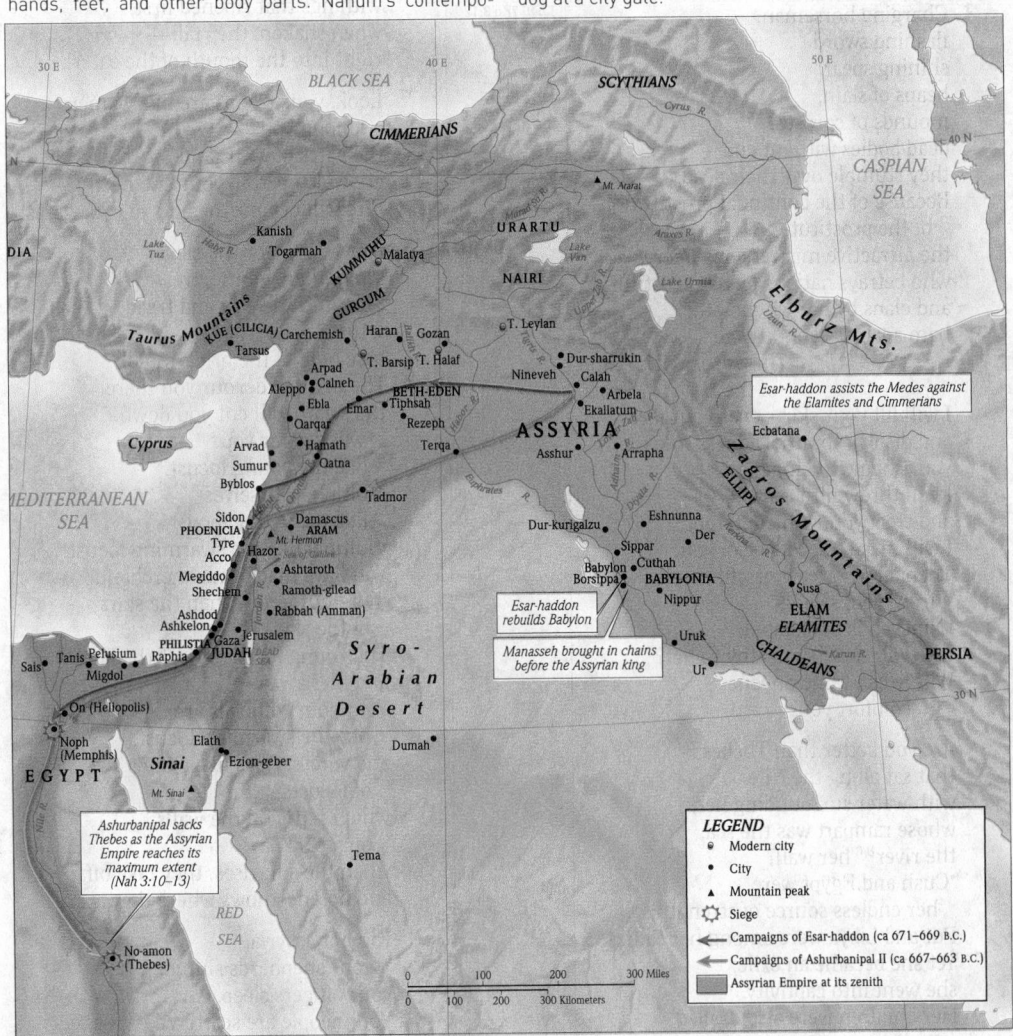

Assyrian Supremacy in the Seventh Century

Habakkuk

O ne of the Minor Prophets, the book of Habakkuk is
unique in its style. Rather than speaking to the people
on God's behalf, Habakkuk spoke to God on behalf of the
people. Habakkuk struggled with how to understand God's
actions in history, especially His use of an unrighteous
nation as the instrument of His justice. God's answer to
Habakkuk's objection was that "the righteous one will live
by his faith" (2:4).

"Look! I am raising up the Chaldeans, that bitter, impetuous nation that marches
across the earth's open spaces to seize territories not its own. They are fierce
and terrifying; their views of justice and sovereignty stem from themselves . . .
They fly like an eagle, swooping to devour" (1:6-8b).

Circumstances of Writing

Author: Habakkuk is not mentioned anywhere else in the Bible. His name is thought to derive from the Hebrew word *chabaq*, "to embrace," but its form appears non-Hebraic. More likely the name is related to *habbaququ*, a word found in the related Semitic language of Akkadian. It denotes a species of garden plant or fruit tree.

Background: Habakkuk predicted the invasion of Judah by the Chaldeans (1:6). The term Chaldean (Hb *kasdim*; Akk *kaldu*) was originally used of an ethnic group that appeared in southern Babylonia in the ninth century B.C. In the eighth century B.C., Chaldeans began to rise to power in Babylon. Among the early Chaldean kings was Merodach-baladan II (2Kg 20:12; Is 39:1), who twice in the late eighth century took (and lost) Babylon's throne. The Chaldean Nabopolassar (626–605 B.C.) began to dismantle the Assyrian Empire with help from the Medes and founded the Neo-Babylonian Empire. By the time of Habakkuk "Chaldean" had come to be a synonym for "Babylonian."

These world events came to affect Judah. Pharaoh Neco of Egypt passed through Palestine in an attempt to support the remnant of the Assyrians in northern Syria against Babylon. The godly King Josiah confronted him at Megiddo but was killed by Neco in 609 B.C. Judah then fell into the hands of Egypt from 609–605 B.C.

Judah's fortunes changed again when Nabopolassar's son Nebuchadnezzar II defeated Neco at the battle of Carchemish (May/June 605 B.C.) on the Euphrates River northeast of Aleppo and succeeded his father on the throne of Babylon in September of that year. The Babylonian army pursued Neco back to Egypt. This led to Judah falling under control of the Babylonians by 604 B.C.

Habakkuk predicted the Chaldean devastation of Judah (1:5-11), but that does not seem to have been fulfilled by the relatively bloodless Babylonian occupation in 604 B.C. But when Jehoiakim, whom Neco had placed on Judah's throne in 609 B.C., rebelled against Babylon in roughly 600 B.C., Nebuchadnezzar eventually invaded the land and besieged Jerusalem from 598 to 597 B.C. This led to Jehoiakim being deposed and killed in 598 B.C.

630–605 B.C.

Jeremiah is called to be a prophet; he warns of invasion from the north. 626

Second phase of King Josiah's reforms when the book of the law is found in the temple 622

Jeremiah's temple sermon 609

Judah's King Josiah seeks to block the movement of Pharaoh Neco II's Egyptian troops as they pass through territory north of Judah en route to join forces with Assyria. Josiah is killed by the Egyptians at Megiddo. 609

Josiah's son, Jehoahaz II, succeeds him and is deposed, replaced by his brother, Jehoiakim. 609

605–600 B.C.

Pharaoh Neco II presses on to engage the Babylonian army at Carchemish with the aim of saving what is left of the Assyrian Empire. Nebuchadnezzar leads the Babylonians to defeat Neco at Carchemish. 605

Habakkuk prophesies shortly before or after the battle at Carchemish to point out what the growing Babylonian strength means for Judah. 605

Jehoiakim makes a decision to turn from his alliance with Egypt and submit to Nebuchadnezzar. 604

Jehoiakim ignores Jeremiah's warning and turns back to Egypt for support after Egypt defeats Babylon at Migdol. 601

and his son Jehoiachin going into Babylonian exile in 597 B.C. The last king of Judah, Zedekiah, brought even more devastation upon Judah by rebelling against Babylon in 588 B.C. When Judah fell to the Babylonians in August of either 587 or 586 B.C., Nebuchadnezzar devastated Jerusalem and destroyed the temple. And yet as Habakkuk predicted (2:6-20), Babylon had its own day of reckoning in 539 B.C. when Cyrus of Persia conquered it.

These historical events help us to attach a date to the book of Habakkuk. Habakkuk probably wrote his prophecy during the time of trouble after the death of King Josiah of Judah in 609 B.C. but before the devastations of Judah in 598/597 B.C. and 587/586 B.C. by the Chaldeans. That places the prophecy during the reign of Jehoiakim (ca 609–599 B.C.), probably in the period of Egyptian domination before Babylon invaded Judah (609–605 B.C.).

Message and Purpose

Like the book of Job, Habakkuk deals with the problem of understanding God's ways: Why does God allow injustice to prevail (1:3)? How can God use the more wicked Babylonians to punish the less wicked Judeans (1:13)? How long will God allow evildoers to dominate the world (1:17)?

God did not give clear answers to the questions Habakkuk raised. Instead He called on the godly to have faith (2:4). When Habakkuk declared he would rejoice in God no matter what (3:17-19), he showed that he had accepted and appropriated this message to his own life.

God's sovereign greatness: Habakkuk shows the greatness of God. He is eternally alive (1:12), unlike dead idols of wood or stone (2:18-19). His prophecies come true (2:3). He can raise up nations to accomplish His purposes (1:6), and He shakes the world through pestilence and war (3:2-15).

God's hidden justice: Habakkuk's God is holy (1:12). The prophet expected Him to oppose injustice (1:2-4,13a), though sometimes it is hard to see the justice of God working through the events of human history (1:13b). But though God may use the wicked acts of men for His good purposes and allow evil to prevail for a

600–590 B.C.

Nebuchadnezzar attacks Jerusalem and leads the citizens of Judah into exile. 605, 597, 586

A reinforced Babylonian army approaches Judah; Jehoiakim dies. 598

Nebuchadnezzar plunders the temple, takes Jehoiachin and the royal family into exile, and Zedekiah becomes king. 597

Ezekiel begins to prophesy. 593

590–580 B.C.

Zedekiah rebels against Babylon and is taken to Riblah along with his family. At Riblah he witnesses the executions of his sons, before his own eyes are blinded. Then Zedekiah is taken to Babylon. He apparently dies in captivity. 587

Gedaliah is appointed governor of Judah by Nebuchadnezzar of Babylon in 587. He is soon assassinated.

As punishment for the uprising against Gedaliah, Nebuchadnezzar deports more citizens. 582

time, ultimately the wicked will pay for their crimes (2:6-14) and God will come to save His people and crush the wicked (3:13-15).

Faith: The key verse of Habakkuk is 2:4b: "The righteous one will live by his faith." Though we find it difficult to fathom the ways of God with man, we can learn, as Habakkuk did, to trust and exult in God's goodness despite our imperfect understanding (3:16-19).

Contribution to the Bible

The book of Habakkuk looks at an issue that often confronts people: trying to discern God's purposes in the midst of this world. There is a realization of the will of God for this world. This truth is seen throughout the Scripture: God's promises to Abraham; God's desire for us to have life abundantly; and God's will for a human community of joy, security, and righteousness. We ultimately triumph in the world and live abundantly only through faith. Habakkuk's message that the righteous will live by faith prepared the way for the greater understanding of this truth in the NT, which emphasizes salvation through faith in Christ (Rm 1:17; Gl 3:11; Heb 10:38-39).

Structure

The first two chapters consist of a dialogue between the prophet and God. Habakkuk first complained of injustice in Judah (1:2-4). God responded by announcing that He was sending the Chaldeans to punish Judah (1:5-11). Habakkuk then complained about God's answer, arguing that it seemed unfair for God to use the more wicked Babylonians to punish the less wicked Judeans (1:12–2:1). God responded that the Babylonians were indeed arrogant and would ultimately be punished; nonetheless, God would use the Babylonians just as He had determined (2:2-20). The final chapter consists of a psalm in which Habakkuk reflected on this dialogue with God.

Outline

I. Dialogue Between God and Habakkuk (1:1–2:20)
   A. Habakkuk's first complaint: injustice (1:1-4)
   B. God's first response: Chaldeans will invade (1:5-11)
   C. Habakkuk's second complaint: God seems unfair (1:12–2:1)
   D. God's second response: have faith, justice will prevail (2:2-20)

II. Habakkuk's Psalm (3:1-19)
   A. Habakkuk's fear (3:1)
   B. God's theophany (3:2-15)
   C. Habakkuk's faith (3:16-19)

1
The ˚oracle that Habakkuk the prophet saw.ᵃ

Habakkuk's First Prayer

2 How long,ᵇ Lord, must I call for helpᶜ
and You do not listen
or cry out to You about violence
and You do not save?

3 Why do You force me to look
at injustice?ᵈ
Why do You tolerateᴬ wrongdoing?
Oppression and violence are right
in front of me.
Strife is ongoing, and conflict escalates.

4 This is why the law is ineffective
and justice never emerges.
For the wicked restrictᵉ the righteous;
therefore, justiceᶠ comes out perverted.

God's First Answer

5 Look at the nationsᴮ,ᵍ and observeʰ—
be utterly astounded!ⁱ
For something is taking place
in your days
that you will not believeʲ
when you hear about it.ᵏ

6 Look! I am raising upˡ the Chaldeans,ᶜ
that bitter,ᵐ impetuous nation
that marches across
the earth's open spaces
to seize territories not its own.

7 They are fierceⁿ and terrifying;
their views of justice and sovereignty
stem from themselves.

8 Their horses are swifterᵒ than leopardsᵖ
and more fierceᴰ than wolves
of the night.
Their horsemen charge ahead;
their horsemen come
from distant lands.
They fly like an eagle,
swooping to devour. q

9 All of them come to do violence;
their facesʳ are set in determination.ᴱ
They gatherˢ prisoners like sand.ᵗ

10 They mockᵘ kings,
and rulers are a joke to them.
They laughᵛ at every fortress
and build siege ramps to captureʷ it.

11 Then they sweepˣ by like the wind
and pass through.
They are ˚guilty;ᶠ their strength
is their god.

Habakkuk's Second Prayer

12 Are You not from eternity,
˚Yahweh my God?
My Holy One,ʸ Youᴳ will not die.
Lord, You appointed them
to execute judgment;
my Rock,ᶻ You destined them
to punish us.

Cross references (center column):
ᵃ1:1 Nm 24:4; Jb 19:26; Is 13:1
ᵇ1:2 Ps 4:2; 6:3; 13:1
ᶜJb 19:7; Ps 5:2; Lm 3:8
ᵈ1:3 Jb 4:8; Ps 5:5; Is 5:7
ᵉ1:4 Jdg 20:43; Ps 22:12
ᶠEx 23:6
ᵍ1:5 Ps 2:1
ʰGn 15:5
ⁱGn 43:33; Ps 48:5; Ec 5:8
ʲGn 15:6
ᵏAc 13:41
ˡ1:6 Ru 4:5
ᵐJdg 18:25
ⁿ1:7 Sg 6:4,10
ᵒ1:8 2Sm 1:23
ᵖIs 11:6; Jr 5:6; 13:23; Hs 13:7
qDt 28:49
ʳ1:9 Gn 48:11
ˢDt 11:14
ᵗJos 11:4
ᵘ1:10 2Kg 2:23
ᵛ2Ch 30:10
ʷNm 21:32
ˣ1:11 Is 8:8
ʸ1:12 Is 1:4
ᶻDt 32:4; Ps 18:2

ᴬ1:3 Lit *observe*　　ᴮ1:5 DSS, LXX, Syr read *Look, you treacherous people*　　ᶜ1:6 = the Babylonians　　ᴰ1:8 Or *and quicker*　　ᴱ1:9 Hb obscure　　ᶠ1:11 Or *wind, and transgress and incur guilt*　　ᴳ1:12 Ancient Jewish tradition reads *we*

1:1 Oracle (Hb *massa'*) is a prophetic proclamation, literally a "lifting up [of voice]." "Burden" (KJV) is another meaning of *massa'*, though it does not fit the present context well (see note at Jr 23:33-38).

1:2-4 Habakkuk lamented to God (**how long**?) about overt **violence . . . injustice**, and **oppression** during Jehoiakim's reign. King Josiah (640–609 b.c.) promoted God's law (2Kg 23:24), but his son and successor Jehoiakim (609–598 b.c.) based his reign on injustice (Jr 22:13) so that God's **law** (Hb *torah*) ceased to be honored.

1:5-6 God responded that He would punish the sins of Judah through an invasion by the **Chaldeans** (the Babylonians).

1:7 The so-called **justice** of these invaders was human (**from themselves**) rather than divine.

1:8 Comparisons with predatory animals (**leopards . . . wolves**, and **an eagle**) illustrate the speed, brutality, and efficiency of the Babylonian military machine.

1:9 Violence (Hb *chamas*; see word study at Hab 2:8,17) is the punishment Judah will receive for its own violence (vv. 2-3).

1:10-11 The mighty Babylonian army scoffed at all opposition. The phrase **their strength is their god** suggests they worshiped their own military power (v. 16), though the verse possibly means that they attributed their strength to their national god Marduk (see note at 2:18-20).

1:12 Habakkuk reasoned that since God is holy, He must be using Babylon as an implement of his **judgment** on Judah. All manuscripts literally read "we will not die" (see textual footnote) rather than **You will not die**, but HCSB follows a Jewish tradition that says "You" was original and that this verse is one of 18 places where the Hebrew Bible was deliberately changed by scribes. If so, the change the scribes

---

navat

Hebrew Pronunciation	[nah VAT]
HCSB Translation	look
Uses in Habakkuk	5
Uses in the OT	70
Focus passage	Habakkuk 1:3,5,13

The root may basically mean "appear" or "come to light." Hebrew uses intensive (1x; Is 5:30) and causative verbs to denote *looking* in a direction. People *look* at the bronze snake (Nm 21:9). They *see* (Nm 12:8) and *perceive* (Is 5:12). *Navat* occurs 26 times with *ra'ah* ("see"). This may involve just physical vision (Gn 15:5) or include internal processes like approval (1Sm 16:7), trust (Is 22:8), or remembrance (Is 51:1). One *looks down* at defeated enemies (Ps 92:11) or *looks* in hope (Ps 34:5). Lot's wife *looks* back at Sodom (Gn 19:26). *Navat* implies *consider* (Ps 74:20), *think about* (Ps 119:15), *tolerate* (Hab 1:3), or *have regard* (Am 5:22). It suggests prolonged looking. Israelites *watched* Moses meet God (Ex 33:8). Eagles' eyes *penetrate* distances (Jb 39:29). God *gazes* earthward from heaven (Ps 102:19) and *observes* nations (Hab 1:5). *Mabbat* (3x) indicates *hope* or *reliance* (Is 20:5-6).

13 Your eyes[a] are too pure[b] to look on evil,
and You cannot tolerate wrongdoing.
So why do You tolerate those
who are treacherous?[c]
Why are You silent
while one[A] who is wicked swallows up
one[B] who is more righteous
than himself?

14 You have made mankind
like the fish of the sea,[d]
like marine creatures that have
no ruler.

15 The Chaldeans pull them all up
with a hook,
catch them in their dragnet,[e]
and gather them in their fishing net;

that is why they are glad and rejoice.

16 That is why they sacrifice
to their dragnet
and burn incense to their fishing net,
for by these things their portion is rich
and their food plentiful.[f]

17 Will they therefore empty their net[c]
and continually slaughter nations
without mercy?

Habakkuk Waits for God's Response

2 I will stand at my guard post
and station myself
on the lookout tower.[g]
I will watch to see what He will say
to me[h]

a 1:13 2Ch 6:20;
16:9
b Ex 25:11; Ps
12:6; 19:9; 51:10;
Pr 22:11; Ezk
36:25
c Jdg 9:23
d 1:14 Ec 9:12
e 1:15 Jr 16:16;
Am 4:2
f 1:16 Dt 8:17; Is
10:13; 37:24-25
g 2:1 Is 21:6-9
h Ps 85:8

A 1:13 = Babylon   B 1:13 = Judah   C 1:17 DSS read *sword*

---

made here aimed to avoid any hint of the unthinkable notion that God ("You") could die.

1:13 Habakkuk complained that rewarding the more wicked in order to punish the less wicked seemed inconsistent with God's **pure** goodness. As bad as the Jews were (see note at vv. 2-4), they were **more righteous** than the **wicked** Babylonian invaders.

1:14-16 Like fishermen who pull in a huge catch of **fish** from

the sea and as a result begin worshiping their **net**, so Babylon captured hordes of people and thus worshiped its own military strength (cp. v. 11).

1:17 How could a just God allow Babylon's merciless **slaughter** of the **nations**, much less their triumph against His people Judah?

2:1 Habakkuk braced himself for God's response. Hebrew *tokachath* ("reproof, reprimand") is probably stronger than

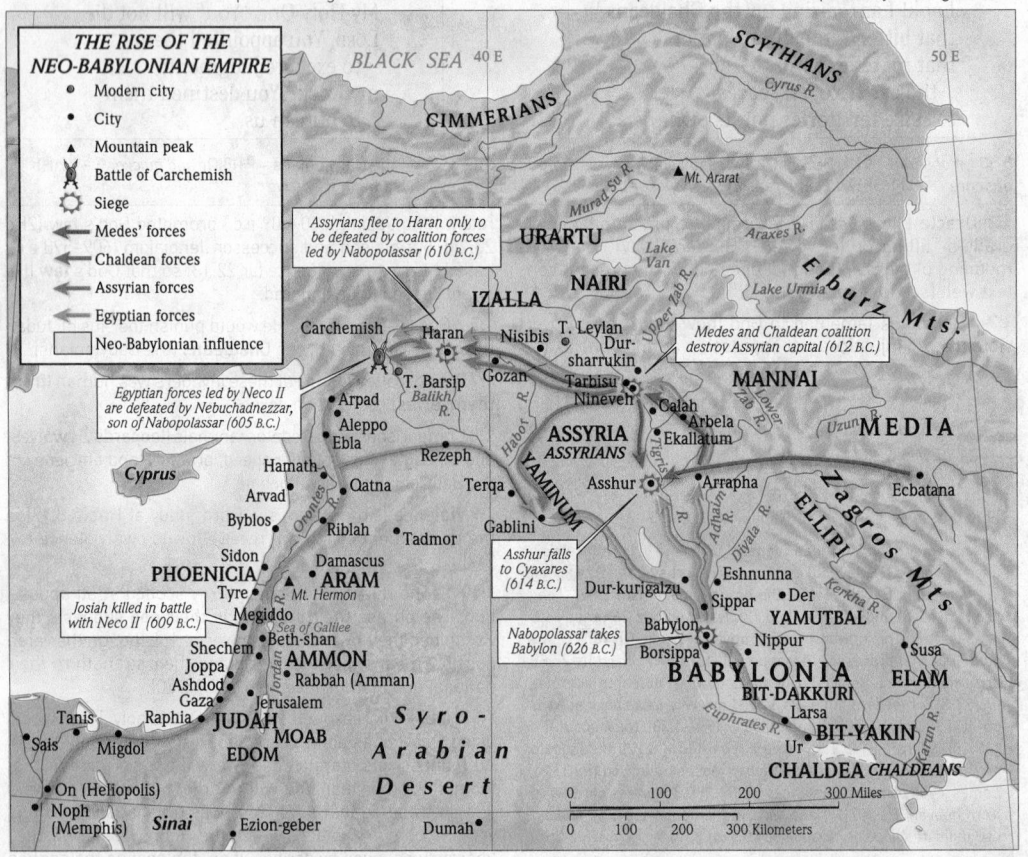

THE RISE OF THE NEO-BABYLONIAN EMPIRE

and what I should[A] reply
about my complaint.

God's Second Answer

[2] The LORD answered me:

Write down this vision;[a]
clearly inscribe it on tablets
so one may easily read it.[B]

[3] For the vision is yet
for the appointed time;
it testifies about the end
and will not lie.
Though it delays, wait for it,
since it will certainly come and not
be late.[b]

[4] Look, his ego is inflated;[C]
he is without integrity.
But the righteous one will live
by his faith.[D,c]

[5] Moreover, wine[E] betrays;
an arrogant man is never at rest.[F]
He enlarges his appetite like *Sheol,
and like Death he is never satisfied.[d]
He gathers all the nations to himself;
he collects all the peoples for himself.

The Five Woe Oracles

[6] Won't all of these take up a taunt
against him,
with mockery and riddles about him?
They will say:

Woe to him who amasses
what is not his—
how much longer?—
and loads himself with goods
taken in pledge.[e]

[7] Won't your creditors suddenly arise,
and those who disturb you wake up?
Then you will become spoil for them.[f]

[8] Since you have plundered
many nations,
all the peoples who remain
will plunder you—
because of human bloodshed
and violence against lands, cities,
and all who live in them.[g]

[9] Woe to him who dishonestly makes
wealth for his house[G]
to place his nest on high,
to escape from the reach of disaster![h]

[10] You have planned shame for your house
by wiping out many peoples
and sinning against your own self.

[11] For the stones will cry out[i]
from the wall,
and the rafters will answer them
from the woodwork.

[12] Woe to him who builds a city
with bloodshed
and founds a town with injustice![j]

[13] Is it not from the LORD of *Hosts
that the peoples labor only to fuel
the fire

Cross references
[a]2:2 1Sm 3:1; Ps 89:19; Pr 29:18; Is 1:1
[b]2:3 Dn 10:1,14; 11:35; Heb 10:36-37; 2Pt 3:9; Rv 22:10
[c]2:4 Rm 1:17; Gl 3:11
[d]2:5 Pr 27:20; 30:15-16; Is 5:14
[e]2:6 Dt 24:10-13
[f]2:7 2Kg 21:14; Is 42:22,24
[g]2:8 Is 33:1; Jr 25:12,14; Rv 13:10
[h]2:9 Pr 11:28; Jr 22:13; 49:16; Ob 4; Rv 18:7
[i]2:11 Lk 19:40
[j]2:12 Ezk 22:2-3; Mc 3:10

[A]2:1 Syr reads *what He will*   [B]2:2 Lit *one who reads in it may run*   [C]2:4 Hb obscure   [D]2:4 Or *faithfulness*   [E]2:5 DSS read *wealth*
[F]2:5 Or *man does not endure*; Hb obscure   [G]2:9 Or *dynasty*

---

the word **complaint** suggests: The prophet had presumed to correct God. Alternatively, it may refer to God's reproof of Habakkuk: "[His] reproof of me." The Syriac translation (see textual footnote) preserves another text for 2:1b that is possibly the original reading: "What He will reply about my reproof [of Him]."

2:2-3 God replied that the vision must be written down clearly for—in spite of Habakkuk's objections—the **vision** of the Babylonian invasion would come true.

2:4-5 The **arrogant** Babylonians were just as wicked as Habakkuk supposed. Yet verse 4b says **righteous** people such as Habakkuk must exercise **faith** in God's goodness despite His use of evil Babylon. This is similar to the answer Job received from God (Jb 38-41). God does not have to explain Himself to humans. We must let God be God and trust in His goodness even when we find His ways difficult to understand. This verse conveys the central message of the book. The NT cites it to show how the Christian life from beginning to end is based on faith (Rm 1:17; Gl 3:11; Heb 10:38).

2:6-8 Even though God used Babylon to punish Judah, Babylon would not go unpunished. Five woes in conjunction with **taunt** (or "proverb") are pronounced upon them. Babylon's plunder from the **nations** is like a debt from **creditors** that they must eventually repay.

2:9-14 Babylon built its **house** (empire; v. 9) with stolen **stones** and its **rafters** from stolen lumber. This involved

chamas

Hebrew Pronunciation	[chah MAHS]
HCSB Translation	violence
Uses in Habakkuk	6
Uses in the OT	60
Focus passage	Habakkuk 2:8,17

This root is slightly attested outside Hebrew. The noun usually denotes physical *violence* (Ezk 7:23). It suggests *crimes* (Jdg 9:24) or violent *wrong* (1Ch 12:17). *Chamas* provoked the Flood (Gn 6:13). It describes *suffering* that involves elements of violence (Gn 16:5). It appears (7x) with *shod* ("destruction"; Am 3:10). *Chamas* functions adjectivally as *violent* (Is 59:6), *vicious* (Gn 49:5), or *malicious* (Ex 23:1), and adverbially as *violently* (Ps 25:19). A malicious witness falsely accuses another (Dt 19:16). The verb *chamas* (8x) means *do violence*. Priests *did violence* to the law by disregarding and failing to teach it (Ezk 22:26). God *did violence* to the temple by destroying it (Lm 2:6). One *harms* himself (Pr 8:36) and *wrongs* (Jb 21:27) or *brutalizes* others (Jr 22:3). Vines *drop* unripe grapes (Jb 15:33). The passive phrase *body ravished* is literally "heels having *endured violence*"; it indicates physical abuse (Jr 13:22).

and countries exhaust themselves
  for nothing?[a]
14 For the earth will be filled
  with the knowledge of the Lord's glory,
  as the waters cover the sea.[b]

15 Woe to him who gives
  his neighbors drink,
  pouring out your wrath[A]
  and even making them drunk,
  in order to look at their nakedness!
16 You will be filled with disgrace
  instead of glory.
  You also—drink,
  and expose your uncircumcision![B]
  The cup in the Lord's right hand
  will come around to you,
  and utter disgrace will cover
  your glory.[c]
17 For your violence against Lebanon
  will overwhelm you;
  the destruction of animals
  will terrify you[c]
  because of your human bloodshed
  and violence
  against lands, cities, and all who live
  in them.

18 What use is a carved idol
  after its craftsman carves it?
  It is only a cast image, a teacher of lies.
  For the one who crafts its shape
  trusts in it
  and makes idols that cannot speak.
19 Woe to him who says to wood:
  Wake up!
  or to mute stone: Come alive!
  Can it teach?

Cross-references (center column):
[a] 2:13 Jr 51:58
[b] 2:14 Ps 72:19; Is 6:3; 11:9
[c] 2:15-16 Rv 14:8-10
[d] 2:20 Zph 1:7; Zch 2:13
[e] 3:1 Ps 7 title
[f] 3:3 Dt 33:2; Jdg 5:4-5
[g] Jb 37:22; Ps 148:13; Is 42:10

Look! It may be plated with gold
  and silver,
  yet there is no breath in it at all.
20 But the Lord is in His holy temple;
  let everyone on earth
  be silent in His presence.[d]

Habakkuk's Third Prayer

3 A prayer of Habakkuk the prophet. According to *Shigionoth.*[D,e]

2 Lord, I have heard the report
  about You;
  Lord, I stand in awe of Your deeds.
  Revive Your work in these years;
  make it known in these years.
  In Your wrath remember mercy!

3 God comes from Teman,
  the Holy One from Mount Paran.[f]
                                    ·*Selah*

  His splendor covers the heavens,
  and the earth is full of His praise.[g]
4 His brilliance is like light;
  rays are flashing from His hand.
  This is where His power is hidden.
5 Plague goes before Him,
  and pestilence follows in His steps.
6 He stands and shakes[E] the earth;
  He looks and startles the nations.
  The age-old mountains break apart;
  the ancient hills sink down.
  His pathways are ancient.
7 I see the tents of Cushan[F] in distress;
  the tent curtains of the land
  of Midian tremble.
8 Are You angry at the rivers, Lord?

[A] 2:15 Or *venom*   [B] 2:16 DSS, LXX, Aq, Syr, Vg read *and stagger*   [C] 2:17 DSS, LXX, Aq, Syr, Tg, Vg; MT reads *them*   [D] 3:1 Perhaps a passionate song with rapid changes of rhythm, or a dirge   [E] 3:6 Or *surveys*   [F] 3:7 = Midian

the **bloodshed** and **injustice** of slave labor. God in His **glory** would make it all **fuel** for the **fire** when Persia toppled Babylon in 539 B.C.

2:15-17 Babylon's shameless perversity foisted upon its **neighbors** such as **Lebanon** (whose famous forests provided much of the stolen lumber of v. 11) would come back in the form of **violence** against itself. By degrading and humiliating conquered peoples, the invaders sought to break their will and render them incapable of further resistance.

2:18-20 Though the Babylonians attributed their strength to their god Marduk (see note at 1:10-11), their god was only a lifeless **idol**, a piece of **wood** or **stone**, but Yahweh lives and will have the last word. There is an allusion here (**Wake up! . . . Come alive!**) to Egyptian and Mesopotamian rituals that were used to consecrate new idols. Called the "opening of the mouth," these rituals were supposed to prepare the idol for habitation by the god.

3:1 The **prayer** of Habakkuk 3 is a psalm to be sung to musical instruments and presented to a music director (v. 19). This psalm represents the prophet's response to God's mes-

sage to him. The Hebrew word *shigionoth* refers to a type of song. Like many musical terms in the Psalms, its precise meaning is unknown; "dirge" and "song of irregular beat" are educated guesses (see note at Ps 7 title). The meaning of Hebrew *selah* (in vv. 3,9,13 and 71 times in Psalms) is also obscure (see word study at Ps 46:3,7,11).

3:2 The **report about You** (or "what You have reported") perhaps alludes to the revelation that God was punishing Judah through Babylon (1:5-11). God's coming **deeds** made Habakkuk **stand in awe** (lit "fear") and beg for **mercy.**

3:3-7 This vision portrays God marching north in power and wrath from the direction of Mount Sinai (**Teman** was in Edom to the south; **Paran** was in the wilderness of Sinai; Dt 33:2). God was casting lightning bolts (Hab 3:4), and was accompanied front and back by personified **plague** and **pestilence.** Earthquakes associated with God's presence terrorized Bedouin peoples such as the **Cushan** and **Midian.**

3:8-15 Sea (Hb *yam*; vv. 8,15) is the name of the pagan god Yam, who was a symbol of chaos subdued by Baal in Ca-

Is Your wrath against the rivers?
Or is Your rage against the sea
when You ride on Your horses,
Your victorious chariot?

9 You took the sheath from Your bow;
the arrows are ready[A] to be used
    with an oath.[B,a]   *Selah*
You split the earth with rivers.

10 The mountains see You and shudder;[b]
a downpour of water sweeps by.
The deep roars with its voice[c]
and lifts its waves[c] high.

11 Sun and moon stand still
    in their lofty residence,[d]
at the flash of Your flying arrows,
at the brightness
    of Your shining spear.

12 You march across the earth
    with indignation;
You trample down the nations in wrath.

13 You come out to save Your people,
to save Your anointed.[D]
You crush the leader of the house
    of the wicked
and strip him from foot[E] to neck.   *Selah*

14 You pierce his head
with his own spears;
his warriors storm out to scatter us,

gloating as if ready to secretly devour
    the weak.

15 You tread the sea with Your horses,
stirring up the great waters.[e]

Habakkuk's Confidence in God Expressed

16 I heard, and I trembled within;[f]
my lips quivered at the sound.
Rottenness entered my bones;
I trembled where I stood.
Now I must quietly wait for the day
    of distress
to come against the people invading us.

17 Though the fig tree does not bud
and there is no fruit on the vines,
though the olive crop fails
and the fields produce no food,
though there are no sheep in the pen
and no cattle in the stalls,

18 yet I will triumph in •Yahweh;
I will rejoice in the God
    of my salvation![g]

19 Yahweh my Lord is my strength;
He makes my feet like those of a deer[h]
and enables me to walk
    on mountain heights![i]

For the choir director: on[F] stringed instruments.

Cross references:
a 3:9 Dt 32:40-43
b 3:10 Ps 77:16
c Ex 19:18
d 3:11 Jos 10:12-13
e 3:15 Ps 77:19
f 3:16 Dn 10:4-9; Rv 1:17
g 3:18 Ps 73:25
h 3:19 Ps 18:33
i 2Sm 22:34; Ps 18:33

A3:9 Or *set*   **B**3:9 Hb obscure   **C**3:10 Lit *hands*   **D**3:13 The Davidic king or the nation of Israel   **E**3:13 Lit *foundation*
F3:19 Lit *on my*

---

naanite mythology; similarly the watery **deep** (Hb *tehom*; v. 10) was the goddess Tiamat subdued by Marduk in Babylonian mythology. The purpose of God's march was to subdue His people's enemies, who were symbolized by elements of nature. He will punish the **wicked** Babylonians and **save** his **people** and their **anointed** Davidic lineage, thus preserving the promise of the coming Messiah.

3:16 The Hebrew of verse 16b is ambiguous. Did the prophet await **the day of distress to come against the people invading us** (HCSB) or "for the day of distress, for a people to come and attack us" (NJPS)? With the first rendering the prophet awaited a double distress: invasion of Judah and

judgment on Babylon (vv. 13-15; 2:6-20). With the second rendering the focus is on the predicted Babylonian invasion (1:5-11). In either case, Habakkuk's feeling of dread (**my lips quivered . . . I trembled**) best relates to the invasion of Judah that must come first.

3:17-19 But come what may, the prophet will trust in God, finding his **strength** and sure footing through faith. **Yahweh** is God's personal name in the OT. It is usually rendered LORD, though that rendering would be awkward here where Yahweh is also called **my Lord**. The prophet applied to his own life the message of 2:4: "The righteous one will live by his faith."

Zephaniah

Introduction

One of the Minor Prophets, Zephaniah focuses on the need to live in righteousness before God. Of all the prophets, Zephaniah probably gave the most forceful description of judgment, but he also lifted up the possibility of restoration for those who repented and turned to righteousness.

"Be silent in the presence of the Lord God, for the Day of the Lord is near. Indeed, the Lord has prepared a sacrifice; He has consecrated His guests . . . And at that time I will search Jerusalem with lamps and punish the men who settle down comfortably, who say to themselves: The Lord will not do good or evil" (1:7,12).

Circumstances of Writing

Author: Zephaniah's lengthy genealogy (1:1, four generations back to Hezekiah) suggests he was of royal lineage. Why list four generations (other prophets, at most, listed two generations; see Zch 1:1) unless this final name was significant? Perhaps because his father's name was "Cushi," people tended to suspect that Zephaniah was of mixed ancestry, including Cushite bloodlines. In fact Zephaniah twice mentions the Cushites/Cush ("Ethiopians") in his short prophecy (2:12; 3:10), possibly suggesting his Cushite roots.

Internal evidence indicates the book of Zephaniah was written sometime between 640 and 612 B.C. Zephaniah 1:1 refers to King Josiah's reign (ca 640–609 B.C.), and 2:13-15 prophesies Nineveh's fall. Since Nineveh fell in 612 B.C., Zephaniah's prophecy would have been given prior to that time. Furthermore, existing idolatrous practices in Judah (1:4-6) imply Zephaniah's ministry began before Josiah's reforms in roughly 621 B.C. (2Kg 23).

Background: King Josiah's father, King Amon (1:1), was a wicked man, as was his father before him, King Manasseh (2Kg 21:1-7,11,16,20-22). This heritage of wickedness helps explain the rampant idolatry in the land when Josiah inherited the throne in 640 B.C. Josiah struggled to squelch idolatry in Judah (Zph 1:4-9). Together pagan and "orthodox priests" led worship of Yahweh while also bowing before Baal, Molech, and other pagan gods (1:4-6). The public reading of the book of the law (ca 621 B.C.) helped spawn the reforms of Josiah as people repented and tore down the numerous altars (cp. Jr 11:13) and other idolatrous paraphernalia of Baal and Molech (2Kg 23:1-14; cp. Zph 1:3-4). This included abolishing the false priests (2Kg 23:5).

Message and Purpose

In view of the impending destruction of the "Day of the LORD" (1:7-18; 2:2-3), Zephaniah's primary purpose was to extend an urgent invitation. He urged the people of Judah to seek Yahweh alone in righteousness and humility (2:1-3). The immediate purpose was to warn idolatrous Judah of the Lord's imminent judgment (1:4-13). The ultimate purpose was to call out a "remnant" from all nations (Judah, 2:7-9; Israel, 3:12-13; all nations, 3:9-10) to trust in Yahweh because of the coming day of His judgment upon the earth (1:2-3,17-18).

---

800 B.C.

Amos is called to travel from Judah to Israel to prophesy in Samaria. 783

Jonah is called to go to Nineveh and preach repentance.

Hosea's prophetic ministry 750–722?

Micah begins his prophetic ministry. 750

Assyria emerges from years of decline as Tiglath-pileser III invades Israel and other territories in the region. 745–727

Isaiah is called to be a prophet. 740

740 B.C.

Assyria's Shalmaneser V besieges Samaria. 725–722

Samaria falls to Assyria's Sargon II, nearly 28,000 Israelites are sent into exile, and Gentiles from Assyrian-controlled territories are resettled into what was the Northern Kingdom. 722

Third temple reform under Hezekiah 715

Years of prophetic silence (698-626) in Judah coincides with some of Judah's darkest years under the rule of Manasseh (697-642) and Amon (642-640).

The Day of the Lord: In biblical times, capturing a city through siege warfare took months or even years; only a truly mighty warrior king (see Yahweh's titles, 3:15,17) would claim to win a battle or even a war in a single day. The Day of the Lord was any time He "visited" earth, whether to punish His enemies (1:7-9,12) or save His people (2:7; cp. 3:17). This would result in the salvation of His people from immediate hardships in some cases (2:7,9), but the ultimate Day of the Lord will come in the end times (3:11-20; cp. Jl 3:14-21; Zch 14:1-14).

The Remnant: Zephaniah emphasized that God's seemingly all-inclusive judgment (1:2-3,17-18; cp. 3:6; Am 9:1-4) was not inconsistent with preserving a few survivors, called the "remnant" or "remainder" of His people (see note at Zph 2:9). Although God would destroy the wicked of Judah and their foreign neighbors (2:4-9), He promised to preserve a remnant—including even foreign peoples—to worship Yahweh (3:9; cp. 2:11b).

God's titles: Yahweh is both God of Israel (2:9a) and LORD (lit "Yahweh") of Hosts (2:9a-10), sovereign ruler over all armies of heaven and earth. Yahweh, King of Israel (3:15), is both "warrior" and "Yahweh your God" who saves His people (3:17; cp. Ex 15:2-3,13-18). Second, "the Lord GOD" (Hb *'adonai Yahweh*), universal Master of the earth, pours out His wrath (overflowing anger) in the Day of the Lord (Zph 1:7,14-18) upon both idolatrous and complacent worshipers (1:4-13). Also "LORD of Hosts" focused on His punishment of nations that mistreated His people (2:8-10) and His "starving" of their false gods (2:11). Thus Yahweh's jealous anger is released (1:18; cp. Dt 4:23-27) not only against Judah (Zph 2:2-3) but upon all earthly kingdoms (3:8). Yahweh is a righteous God who executes justice (3:5) in the midst of rebellious Judah (3:1-4) by purging out haughty rebels (3:11). Yet because of His love (3:17), this warrior King (3:15,17) will thwart enemy oppressors to remove deserved punishment from His remnant and save them from harm (3:15-17,19).

Contribution to the Bible

The promise of a remnant illustrates God's amazing grace counterbalancing His jealous wrath and blazing fury against the wicked (Nah 1:2-8). He would judge the proud nations (Zph 2:8-11,13-15) and purge the haughty braggarts from His people (3:11) to preserve the humble. Thus Zephaniah invited everyone who

---

640 B.C.   **615 B.C.**

Josiah is placed on Judah's throne at the age of eight when his father, Amon, is assassinated. 640

Initial reforms of Josiah 631

Zephaniah's years of prophecy range between 626 and 612.

Jeremiah called to be a prophet; warns of invasion from the north 626

The book of the law is found and read publicly, spurring additional reform under Josiah. 621

Zephaniah and Nahum both prophesy the fall of Nineveh that occurred in 621.

With the fall of Nineveh, the Babylonian Empire succeeds the Assyrian Empire as the dominant force in the ancient Near East. 612

Josiah killed in battle by Pharaoh Neco 609

Habakkuk prophesies shortly before or after the battle at Carchemish (605) to point out what the growing Babylonian strength means for Judah.

Nebuchadnezzar attacks Jerusalem and leads citizens of Judah into exile. 605, 597, 586, 582

humbly obeyed the Lord to seek Him for possible deliverance (2:2-3). The NT highlights the wonderful truth that all of us can find salvation through faith in Christ. Paul underscored the idea of the Jewish remnant and reminded us that the remnant is "chosen by grace," not by works (Rm 11:5-6).

Structure

"The word of the LORD (lit Yahweh)" (1:1a) and "Yahweh has spoken" (3:20b) frame the whole book of Zephaniah to emphasize crucial complementary messages: imminent, universal judgment (1:1–3:8) but eventual blessing for the remnant (3:9-20). The chiastic first section, interlaced by the reinforcing refrain "this is the LORD's declaration" (see 1:2-3,10a; 2:9a; 3:8a; cp. 2:5, "word of the LORD"), highlights an all-inclusive judgment.

Zephaniah 3:8 is a transitional exhortation that looks both backward ("therefore," v. 8a) and forward (wait patiently for God to consummate judgment which will yield salvation for the remnant; vv. 9-13, introduced by Hebrew *ki*, "for/because" vv. 9,11). To offer hope during judgment in 3:8-13 may synthesize two exhortations: 1:7 (hush/wait for the Day of the Lord's "cutting off" the wicked) and 2:1-3 (pivotal invitation to seek Him for possible salvation).

Outline

I. Prophecy of God's Judgments (1:1–2:3)
   A. Identity of the prophet (1:1)
   B. Announcement of certain judgment (1:2-6)
   C. Announcement of the Day of the Lord (1:7-9)
   D. The Day of the Lord a day of woe (1:10-13)
   E. Judgment will not be delayed (1:14-18)
   F. Exhortation to repentance (2:1-3)

II. God's Judgment of the Nations (2:4–3:8)
   A. Destruction of Philistia announced (2:4-7)
   B. Moab and Ammon to be destroyed (2:8-11)
   C. Universality of the judgment (2:12-15)
   D. The corrupt city Jerusalem (3:1-8)

III. Promised Blessings (3:9-20)
   A. Salvation and deliverance (3:9-13)
   B. Salvation demands praise (3:14-20)

1 The word of the LORD that came to Zephaniah son of Cushi, son of Gedaliah, son of Amariah, son of Hezekiah, in the days of Josiah[a] son of Amon, king of Judah.

The Great Day of the LORD

2 I will completely
　sweep away everything
from the face of the earth[b]—
　　　　this is the LORD's declaration.
3 I will sweep away man and animal;[c]
I will sweep away the birds of the sky
　and the fish of the sea,
and the ruins[A] along with the wicked.[d]
I will cut off mankind
from the face of the earth.
　　　　This is the LORD's declaration.

4 I will stretch out My hand[e]
　against Judah
and against all the residents
　of Jerusalem.
I will cut off every vestige of ˙Baal[f]
from this place,
　the names of the pagan priests[g]
along with the priests;
5 those who bow in worship
　on the rooftops[h]
to the heavenly host;
those who bow and pledge loyalty
　to the LORD[i]
but also pledge loyalty to ˙Milcom;[B,j]
6 and those who turn back
　from following the LORD,
who do not seek the LORD or inquire
　of Him.
7 Be silent in the presence
　of the Lord GOD,[k]
for the Day of the LORD is near.[l]

Indeed, the LORD has prepared
　a sacrifice;[m]
He has consecrated His guests.[n]

8 On the day of the LORD's sacrifice
I will punish the officials,
　the king's sons,
and all who are dressed
　in foreign clothing.
9 On that day[o] I will punish
all who skip over the threshold,[C,p]
who fill their master's house
with violence and deceit.

10 On that day—
　　　this is the LORD's declaration—
there will be an outcry
　from the Fish Gate,[q]
a wailing from the Second District,[r]
and a loud crashing from the hills.
11 Wail, you residents of the Hollow,[D]
for all the merchants[E] will be silenced;
all those loaded with silver will be
　cut off.

12 And at that time I will search Jerusalem
　with lamps
and punish the men
　who settle down comfortably,[F,s]
who say to themselves:
The LORD will not do good or evil.
13 Their wealth will become plunder
and their houses a ruin.
They will build houses but never live
　in them,
plant vineyards but never drink
　their wine.[t]

14 The great Day of the LORD is near,[u]
near and rapidly approaching.

a 1:1 2Kg 22:1–23:30; 2Ch 34:1–36:1; Jr 1:2
b 1:2 Gn 6:7; 7:4
c 1:3 1Kg 14:10; Ezk 14:17
d 1:3 Is 13:9-12; Mt 13:41
e 1:4 Ex 3:20; Ps 138:7; Ezk 14:9; 25:7,16; Zph 2:13
f 1Kg 16:30-32
g 2Kg 23:5
h 1:5 Jr 19:13; 32:29
i Dt 6:13; Is 48:1
j 1Kg 11:5; 2Kg 23:13; Jr 49:1,3
k 1:7 Nm 13:30; Jdg 3:19; Hab 2:20; Zch 2:13
l Zph 1:14,18; 2:2-3
m Is 34:6; Jr 46:10
n Lv 7:11-21; 1Sm 16:5; 2Ch 35:5-13; Jr 22:17
o 1:9 Zph 1:10; 3:11,16
p 1Sm 5:5
q 1:10 2Ch 33:14; Neh 3:3; 12:39
r 2Kg 22:14; 2Ch 34:22
s 1:12 Ex 15:8; Is 25:6; Jr 48:11
t 1:13 Dt 28:30; Am 5:11; Mc 6:15
u 1:14 Is 13:6,9; Jl 1:15; 2:1,11,31; 3:14; Am 5:18,20; Ob 15; Zch 14:1; Mal 4:5

A 1:3 Perhaps objects connected with idolatry　　B 1:5 Some LXX mss, Syr, Vg; MT, other LXX mss read *their king*　　C 1:9 Hb obscure
D 1:11 Or *the market district*　　E 1:11 Or *Canaanites*　　F 1:12 Lit *who thicken on their dregs*

1:2 The prophetic **declaration**, God **will completely sweep away everything** on **earth**, is hyperbole. Though no one deserved to be spared, God would preserve a small remnant of Judah and of other peoples (2:7,9b; 3:9-10,12-13).

1:3 The judgment language—**sweep away man and animal** (lit "cattle, wild beasts") even **the birds of the sky** and the **fish of the sea**—is more comprehensive than Noah's flood (Gn 6:7, no fish mentioned). To underscore the gravity of their sins and the intensity of their deserved punishment, Zephaniah used prophetic hyperbole (Jr 4:23-29; 9:9-11) in which creation itself is reversed; here the creatures are listed in reverse order from Gn 1:20-28 (sea creatures, birds, beasts, and man). In the phrase **the ruins along with the wicked**, "ruins" (Hb *maksheloth*; lit "stumbling blocks") were apparently idol paraphernalia, including animals worshiped by depraved people such as in Egypt or Judah (see Ezk 8:10-12 for detestable animal images in the Jerusalem temple). The Lord would destroy those idols and their worshipers.

1:5 To **pledge loyalty to Milcom** involved religious syncretism, combining pseudo-worship of Yahweh with worship of a false god. Here and in Jr 49:1,3, "Milcom" is spelled "Milcam" (lit "their king") in the Masoretic Text, which some interpret as a reference to Baal worship (see Zph 1:4; cp. Jr 32; 35). Yet Milcom/Milcam was more likely the Ammonite god (Jr 49:1-3), interchangeable with "Molech" (1Kg 11:7; Jr 32:35). No consensus exists about the exact nature and spelling of this Ammonite deity; if equivalent to the Canaanite god of the underworld Molech, worship of this god apparently included child sacrifice (as in worship of Molech/Milcom; Lv 18:21; 20:2-5; 2Kg 23:10; Jr 32:35). This worship continued Manasseh's pagan practices which Josiah would disrupt (2Kg 23:10-13).

1:9 Since their leaders imitated foreign customs (v. 8), to **skip over the threshold** probably reflected a foreign, fearful superstition (similar to a Philistine custom; 1Sm 5:4-5).

1:14 The **Day of the LORD** was imminent (**near**, v. 7; cp. Is 13:6; Ezk 30:3; Jl 2:1; 3:14; Ob 15) and **rapidly approaching**.

Listen, the Day of the LORD—
then the warrior's cry is bitter.

15 That day is a day of wrath,
a day of trouble and distress,
a day of destruction and desolation,
a day of darkness*a* and gloom,
a day of clouds and blackness,*b*

16 a day of trumpet blast and battle cry
against the fortified cities,
and against the high corner towers.

17 I will bring distress on mankind,
and they will walk like the blind*c*
because they have sinned
against the LORD.
Their blood will be poured out like dust
and their flesh like dung.

18 Their silver and their gold
will not be able to rescue them
on the day of the LORD's wrath.*d*
The whole earth will be consumed
by the fire of His jealousy.*e*
For He will make a complete,
yes, a horrifying end
of all the inhabitants of the earth.

A Call to Repentance

2 Gather yourselves together;
gather together, undesirable*A* nation,

2 before the decree*f* takes effect
and the day passes like chaff,
before the burning of the LORD's anger
overtakes you,
before the day of the LORD's anger
overtakes you.

*a*1:15 Am
5:18-20
*b*Ps 97:2; Ezk
34:12; Jl 2:2
*c*1:17 Lm 4:14
*d*1:18 Ezk 7:19
*e*Ex 34:14
*f*2:2 Ps 2:7;
148:6
*g*2:3 Am 5:14
*h*Nm 12:3; Ps
25:9; 37:11;
76:9; Am 8:4
*i*Gn 4:14; Ex 3:6;
Ps 17:8
*j*2:4 Jr 25:20;
Am 1:6-8; Zch
9:5-7
*k*2:5 Ezk 25:16
*l*2:8 Am 1:13

3 Seek the LORD,*g* all you humble*h*
of the earth,
who carry out what He commands.
Seek righteousness, seek humility;
perhaps you will be concealed*i*
on the day of the LORD's anger.

Judgment against the Nations

4 For Gaza will be abandoned,
and Ashkelon will become a ruin.
Ashdod will be driven out at noon,
and Ekron will be uprooted.*j*

5 Woe, inhabitants of the seacoast,
nation of the Cherethites!*B,k*
The word of the LORD is against you,
Canaan, land of the Philistines:
I will destroy you until there is
no one left.

6 The seacoast will become pasturelands
with caves for shepherds and folds
for sheep.

7 The coastland will belong
to the remnant of the house of Judah;
they will find pasture there.
They will lie down in the evening
among the houses of Ashkelon,
for the LORD their God will return
to them
and restore their fortunes.

8 I have heard the taunting of Moab
and the insults of the Ammonites,*l*
who have taunted My people
and threatened their territory.

A2:1 Or *shameless*   B2:5 = Sea Peoples

On this day God would judge Judah for its rampant idolatry (vv. 4-7). On an impending day of wrath (vv. 15,18), God's rage would overflow to those who, by sinning against Him (v. 17), had become His enemies. He would unleash a storm of destruction (v. 15), primarily by enemy invaders (Ezk 38:9; cp. Jl 2:1-11). The Lord's destruction of Judah by the Babylonians in 586 B.C. (Lm 2:1-3,22; 4:11) partially fulfilled this day of His burning anger (Zph 1:18; 2:2-3) as He punished them for abominable idolatries (1:4-11; cp. Ezk 7:8-11,14-21; 8:5-18). Ultimately all earthly inhabitants would be judged (Jl 3:1-2,12-16; Zph 1:2-3) and consumed by His fiery anger (vv. 17-18; 3:8; cp. 2Pt 3:10-12).

2:3 The triple occurrence of **seek** prescribes an antidote for idolatry and self-sufficiency—humbly **seek the LORD** and **righteousness** (1:6b; cp. Am 5:14-15), while waiting on Him to respond (Zph 3:8). For God's people who have sinned, seeking is essential to finding Him (Dt 4:28-30; Hs 3:5; 10:12; cp. Zch 8:21-22).

2:4 In the Hebrew of this verse, similar sounding words (**Gaza** and **abandoned**) and puns (**Ekron** and **uprooted**) eloquently expressed judgment upon four of the five Philistine cities (Am 1:6-9; cp. Zph 2:5). An English approximation would be, "Gaza is a *gazing stock*; **Ashkelon** and **Ashdod** will be reduced to *ashes*."

2:7 Restore their fortunes is an OT technical formula (lit "restore the captivity") for total restoration, whether physical (cp. Jr 33:10-13) or spiritual (Ps 85:1-4; Jr 32:44; cp. Zph 3:20).

'evrah

Hebrew Pronunciation	[ev RAH]
HCSB Translation	rage, wrath, fury
Uses in Zephaniah	2
Uses in the OT	34
Focus passage	Zephaniah 1:15,18

'Evrah suggests extreme *anger* and sometimes human *arrogance* (Is 14:6; 16:6). The *fury* of brothers destroys an entire tribe for someone's rape of their sister (Gn 49:7). 'Evrah is *wrath* and *rage* (Is 9:19; 10:6), perhaps in *outbursts* (Jr 48:30). *Fury* is poured out (Hs 5:10). Adjectivally, 'evrah suggests *excessive* (Pr 21:24) and *raging* (Jb 40:11). 'Evrah occurs with synonyms *'aph* ("wrath") (12x) and *za'am* ("indignation"; Ps 78:49). Ezekiel mentions "fire of My 'evrah" (4x). "Rod of his 'evrah" (Lm 3:1) occurs twice. *Day* is modified by *wrath* five times (Jb 21:30), and *wrath* by *Lord* four times (Ezk 7:19). Related reflexive *'avar* (8x), different from *'avar* ("pass"), means *be angry* (Dt 3:26), *furious, enraged* (Ps 78:21,62), or *easily angered* (Pr 14:16). One *provokes* another (Pr 20:2) or *meddles* in quarrels (Pr 20:2; 26:17). Both noun and verb describe God more than twice as often as men.

9 Therefore, as I live—
　　　　this is the declaration
　　　of the LORD of •Hosts,
　　　　the God of Israel—
Moab will be like Sodom
and the Ammonites like Gomorrah[a]—
a place overgrown with weeds,
a salt pit, and a perpetual wasteland.
The remnant of My people
　　will plunder them;
the remainder of My nation
　　will dispossess them.
10 This is what they get for their pride,
because they have taunted
　　and acted arrogantly[b]
against the people of the LORD of Hosts.
11 The LORD will be terrifying to them
when He starves all the gods
　　of the earth.
Then all the distant coastlands
　　of the nations
will bow in worship to Him,
each in its own place.

12 You •Cushites will also be slain
　　by My sword.[c]

13 He will also stretch out His hand
　　against the north
and destroy Assyria;
He will make Nineveh a desolate ruin,[d]
dry as the desert.
14 Herds will lie down in the middle of it,
every kind of wild animal.[A]
Both the desert owl[B]
　　and the screech owl[C]
will roost in the capitals of its pillars.

Their calls will sound[D] from the window,
but devastation[E] will be
　　on the threshold,
for He will expose the cedar work.[F]
15 This is the self-assured[e] city
that lives in security,
that thinks to herself:
I exist, and there is no one else.
What a desolation she has become,
a place for wild animals to lie down!
Everyone who passes by her
jeers[G] and shakes his fist.

Woe to Oppressive Jerusalem

3 Woe to the city that is rebellious[H,f]
　　and defiled,[g]
　　the oppressive city!
2 She has not obeyed;[h]
she has not accepted discipline.[i]
She has not trusted[j] in •Yahweh;
she has not drawn near to her God.
3 The[i] princes within her are
　　roaring lions;[k]
her judges are wolves of the night,[l]
which leave nothing for[J] the morning.
4 Her prophets are reckless[m]—
treacherous men.
Her priests profane the sanctuary;
they do violence to instruction.[n]
5 The righteous LORD is in her;[o]
He does no wrong.[p]
He applies His justice morning
　　by morning;
He does not fail at dawn,
yet the one who does wrong
knows no shame.[q]

Cross references (center column):
a 2:9 Gn 19:24-25
b 2:10 Jr 48:42
c 2:12 Is 18:1-7
d 2:13 Nah 2:8; 3:7
e 2:15 Is 13:3; 22:2; 23:7; 24:8; 32:13; Zph 3:11
f 3:1 Ex 23:21; Dt 9:24; Ps 106:43
g Is 59:3
h 3:2 1Sm 15:22
i Jb 5:17
j Pr 3:5
k 3:3 Ezk 22:25
l Hab 1:8; Mt 7:15; Ac 20:29
m 3:4 Jdg 9:4
n Ezk 22:26
o 3:5 Ps 129:4
p Ps 92:15
q Jr 8:12

A 2:14 Lit every wild animal of a nation　B 2:14 Or the pelican　C 2:14 Or the hedgehog　D 2:14 Lit sing　E 2:14 LXX, Vg read ravens
F 2:14 Hb obscure　G 2:15 Or hisses　H 3:1 Or filthy　I 3:3 Lit Her　J 3:3 Or that had nothing to gnaw in

shemamah

Hebrew Pronunciation	[sheh mah MAH]
HCSB Translation	desolation, wasteland, ruin
Uses in Zephaniah	4
Uses in the OT	56
Focus passage	Zephaniah 2:4,9,13

Shemamah, from shamam (be desolate), denotes desolation or desolate (Jr 34:22). It means ruin (Jr 25:12) or wasteland (Mc 7:13). Shemamah connotes in grief (Ezk 7:27). It occurs with "make" (siym: Jr 12:11; nathan: Jr 34:22; ʾasah: Ezk 35:14): make desolate/a desolation, or destroy (Mc 1:7). Shemamah with shamam implies desolate waste (Ezk 33:28). Related shammah (39x) means devastation (Ezk 23:33) alongside shemamah. Shammah denotes desolate or desolation (Is 5:9). It suggests horrible thing, horror, or object of scorn (Jr 5:30; 42:18). With "make" (siym: Jr 4:7; shiyth: Jr 50:3; or nathan: Mc 6:16), shammah is lay waste or make desolate (Jr 2:15). Both nouns with chorbah ("ruin") imply desolate ruin. Related meshammah and shimmah (Ezk 33:29; 35:7) with shemamah indicate desolate waste. Meshammah (7x) elsewhere means desolate (Is 15:6) or horror (Ezk 5:15). Shamem (2x) means desolate (Jr 12:11). Shimmamon (2x) signifies dread (Ezk 4:16).

2:9 God's universal judgment (1:2-3,17-18) allowed for godly survivors—the remnant of My people or My nation (cp. Am 5:14-15; 9:8b). This remnant was primarily of Judah (Zph 2:7) and ultimately of all Israel (3:12-13). Remarkably, the two primary characteristics of this human remnant that was allowed to plunder enemies were meekness and humility (3:12). The Lord would give the godly remnant the territory of other nations (2:7,9), reversing the curse of Dt 28:62-66. He also promised to bless the eschatological remnant (Zph 3:14-17), including the lame and other outcasts (3:18-19; cp. Mc 4:6-7).

2:11 The phrase starves all the gods may indicate that Yahweh will literally cut off sacrifices (food and drink) to the "gods" (cult statues) by destroying (cp. Is 1:4; Jr 50:2-3; 51:43-44,52-53) or converting their worshipers (Zph 3:9).

2:15 God will judge each self-assured city (Assyria, v. 15; Babylon, Is 47:8-10) that makes God-like claims such as I exist, and there is no one else (cp. Is 45:5,6,19,21).

3:5 On in her (or "in her midst") cp. verses 15,17.

6 I have cut off nations;
  their corner towers[a] are destroyed.
I have laid waste their streets,
  with no one to pass through.
Their cities lie devastated,
  without a person,
    without an inhabitant.[b]

7 I thought: You will certainly •fear Me
and accept correction.
Then her dwelling place[A]
would not be cut off
based on all that I had allocated to her.
However, they became more corrupt
in all their actions.

8 Therefore, wait for Me[c]—
          this is the LORD's declaration—
until the day I rise up for plunder.[B]
For My decision is to gather nations,
to assemble kingdoms,
in order to pour out My indignation[d]
  on them,
all My burning anger;
for the whole earth will be consumed
by the fire of My jealousy.[e]

Final Restoration Promised

9 For I will then restore
pure[f] speech to the peoples
so that all of them may call
on the name of Yahweh
and serve Him with a single purpose.[C]

10 From beyond the rivers of •Cush[g]
My supplicants, My dispersed people,
will bring an offering to Me.

11 On that day you[D] will not be put
    to shame[h]
because of everything you have done
in rebelling[i] against Me.
For then I will remove
your proud,[j] arrogant people
  from among you,
and you will never again be haughty
on My holy mountain.[k]

12 I will leave
a meek and humble people[l] among you,
and they will take refuge in the name
of Yahweh.

13 The remnant[m] of Israel will no longer
do wrong or tell lies;
a deceitful tongue will not be found
in their mouths.
But they will pasture and lie down,
with nothing to make them afraid.[n]

14 Sing for joy, Daughter •Zion;
shout loudly, Israel!
Be glad and rejoice with all your heart,
Daughter Jerusalem!

15 The LORD has removed
  your punishment;
He has turned back your enemy.
The King of Israel, Yahweh,
  is among you;
you need no longer fear harm.

16 On that day it will be said to Jerusalem:
"Do not fear;
Zion, do not let your hands grow weak.[o]

17 Yahweh your God is among you,
a warrior[p] who saves.
He will rejoice over you[q] with gladness.
He will bring you quietness[E]
  with His love.
He will delight in you with shouts
  of joy."[r]

18 I will gather those
    who have been driven[s]
from the appointed festivals;
they will be a tribute from you[F]
and a reproach on her.[G]

19 Yes, at that time
I will deal with all who afflict you.
I will save the lame[t] and gather
    the scattered;[u]
I will make those who were disgraced
throughout the earth
receive praise and fame.

20 At that time I will bring you[H] back,
yes, at the time I will gather you.
I will give you fame and praise
among all the peoples of the earth,
when I restore your fortunes[v]
  before your eyes.
Yahweh has spoken.[H]

a 3:6 Zph 1:16
b Jr 44:2; Zph 2:5
c 3:8 Jb 3:21; Ps 33:20; Is 8:17; 30:18; 64:4
d Ps 69:24; Ezk 21:31; 22:31; Nah 1:6
e Dt 29:20; Ps 79:5; Zch 1:14; 8:2
f 3:9 Dn 12:10
g 3:10 Is 18:1-3
h 3:11 Gn 2:25; 2Sm 19:5; Ps 25:3
i Is 1:2
j Jr 48:29
k Is 11:9
l 3:12 Is 66:2
m 3:13 Gn 45:7; 2Kg 19:31; Jr 23:3
n Gn 42:28; Jr 50:19; Ezk 34:14; Mc 4:4; 7:14
o 3:16 Jr 6:24; 50:43
p 3:17 Jos 1:14; Jb 16:14; Ps 78:65
q Dt 28:63; 30:9
r Ps 30:5
s 3:18 Lm 1:4-5; 3:33
t 3:19 Ex 14:30
u Mc 4:6
v 3:20 Jb 42:10; Jr 29:14; Ezk 39:25; Hs 6:11; Jl 3:1

A 3:7 LXX, Syr read her eyes   B 3:8 LXX, Syr read for a witness; Vg reads up forever   C 3:9 Lit with one shoulder   D 3:11 = Israel
E 3:17 LXX, Syr read He will renew you   F 3:18 = Jerusalem   G 3:18 Hb obscure   H 3:20 = people of Israel

3:7 **You will certainly fear Me and accept correction** follows up verse 2, where Jerusalem neither "accepted discipline" nor "trusted in the LORD" (Pr 1:7; 3:5,7).

3:8 The **fire of My jealousy** may incorporate two OT themes: (1) Yahweh's fierce, jealous judgment of Israel by covenant curses (Dt 29:20-21) because they ignored warnings against idol worship (Dt 29:16-18); and (2) His zeal or jealousy for His people (cp. Zch 8:2), resulting in fire upon His enemies (Is 26:11) during earth's universal judgment (Is 24) to bring salvation to the remnant (Zch 8:6-8).

3:9 The phrase **restore pure speech to the peoples** may reflect a reversal of the Babel motif (cp. Is 2:2-4; 19:18-25) or international worship without language barriers. But its meaning apparently also involves genuine worship of Yahweh without deceit (Zph 3:13-14; cp. Rv 14:5).

Haggai

Introduction

Haggai challenged the discouraged people in Jerusalem to examine the way they were living and to set new priorities that would please God. They must remember that God was with them; He controls their future and wants His people to be holy.

"So on your account, the skies have withheld the dew and the land its crops. I have summoned a drought on the fields and the hills, on the grain, new wine, olive oil, and whatever the ground yields" (1:10-11a).

Circumstances of Writing

Author: There is no statement that strictly identifies who wrote this book, but the words recorded are repeatedly connected to what God spoke to the prophet Haggai (1:1,3,13; 2:1,10,14,20).

Background: In 587 B.C. Nebuchadnezzar came to Jerusalem for the third time, this time destroying the walls, the temple, and the city (2Kg 25:8-21; Jr 39–40). Most of the people were taken into Babylonian captivity for 70 years (Jr 25:11-12; 29:10), although Jeremiah and a few survivors stayed in Jerusalem (Jr 41–43). God predicted through Isaiah that the strong king named Cyrus (Is 44:24–45:2) would defeat Babylon and her gods (Is 46–47). After the Persian king Cyrus defeated Babylon, he issued a decree in 538 B.C. that allowed the exiled nations in Babylon to return to their homelands (Ezr 1:1-4; Cyrus Cylinder). Sheshbazzar (Ezr 1:8-11) led about 43,000 Jewish pilgrims back to the state of *Yehud* (Judah) to rebuild the temple in Jerusalem (Ezr 2:64-65). In the seventh month the governor Zerubbabel and the high priest Joshua led the people in building an altar to worship God (Ezr 3:1-7), then in their second year the people laid the foundation of the new temple (Ezr 3:8-10). But this effort was stopped for the next sixteen years because the Samaritan people who lived north of Jerusalem frustrated these rebuilding efforts, plus they hired lawyers to cause the Persian authorities to stop supporting the work on this temple (Ezr 4:1-5). This led to a period of great discouragement. Apathy set in because many of the hopes of the Jewish people were unfulfilled. The walls of the city were not repaired, the temple was not rebuilt, there was a famine in the land (Hag 2:9-11), and the people were still under Persian control. They could do nothing without the approval of Tattenai, the governor of the "region west of the Euphrates River," and his officials (Ezr 5:3-5). There seemed to be no way to move forward and rebuild the temple.

After the death of Cyrus, his son Cambyses became king (530–522 B.C.). He marched through Judah and conquered most of Egypt, but on his way home he died (possibly an assassination). A high army official named Darius took control of the Persian army, marched back to Babylon, defeated a rebel force led by Gaumata, and

---

605–540 B.C.

Babylonian campaign against Jerusalem begins; Daniel and others of Israelite nobility taken to Babylon. 605

A second deportation to Babylon includes the prophet Ezekiel. 597

Nebuchadnezzar's siege of Jerusalem begins. January, 588

Jerusalem and the temple are destroyed by the Babylonians; a third wave of exiles taken to Babylon. 586

Cyrus, who ruled the Persian Empire from 559 to 530, takes Babylon with little resistance. 539

540–525 B.C.

Cyrus issues a decree allowing the Jews to return to Judah and rebuild the temple. 538

Events in Ezra 538–457

Second temple construction begins under Zerubbabel's and Joshua's leadership. 536

Cyrus dies in battle and his son Cambyses succeeds him and rules from 530 to 522.

Discouragement reinforced by opposition from transplanted people brings work on the temple to a halt. 526

Darius succeeds Cambyses and rules from 522 to 486.

became king in 522 B.C. Darius put down several revolts and then reformed the satrapy administrative system, with the result that by 520 B.C. the Persian Empire was at peace.

In the second year of Darius (520 B.C.; Hag 1:1; Ezr 4:24–5:2) when the conflict over political control of the empire was over, God directed Haggai to encourage the leaders in Jerusalem to rebuild the temple. When governor Tattenai heard about this rebuilding, he questioned the plan's legitimacy and wrote to Darius to find out whether the government was sanctioning this project (Ezr 5:3-17). Darius approved the rebuilding campaign and even supported it through the royal treasury, as was confirmed by the discovery of Cyrus's original decree in a palace at Ecbatana (Ezr 6:1-12). Consequently, the temple rebuilding was completed in four years (Ezr 6:15).

Message and Purpose

Through his messages Haggai tried to persuade his audience to glorify God by rebuilding the temple. He argues that one should not: a) focus on one's own needs (1:4); b) be discouraged because the temple was not as glorious as Solomon's (2:3); c) be unclean and unholy (2:10-14); nor d) feel useless and powerless (2:20-23).

Contribution to the Bible

Throughout the Bible, there is a call and a reminder to place God first. The period following the return from exile was no exception. Haggai's challenge was to call the postexilic community of Jews living in Jerusalem not simply to focus on their own creature comforts but to honor God. This commitment would be reflected in their work on the temple. Haggai's call was later reflected in the words of Jesus: "Seek first the kingdom of God and His righteousness, and all these things will be provided for you" (Mt 6:33).

Haggai's call for the people to get their priorities in order and place God first by rebuilding His temple was of great importance. For the people to return to this task was a sign of their priorities. It also showed that God was with the remnant and that His promises of restoration had begun to be fulfilled. Their obedience in this

525–520 B.C.

Haggai and Zechariah encourage the people to resume construction of the temple. 520–518

Haggai's first message August 29, 520

Temple building resumes September 21, 520

Haggai's second message October 17, 520

520–515 B.C.

Haggai's third and fourth messages December 18, 520

Zechariah's night visions February 15, 519

Temple completed March 12, 515

matter declared God's glory and thus brought Him pleasure. It served to vindicate the Lord since the temple's destruction had disgraced the Lord's name. Finally, their obedience to Haggai's words served as a pledge of the new covenant and the messianic age. The restoration of the temple was a sign that God had not revoked His covenant with Levi or His covenant with David. He would provide cleansing and restoration through a glorious temple and a messianic ruler.

Structure

The book of Haggai contains four short confrontational speeches in chronological order that identify ways the leaders and people in Jerusalem should change their theological thinking and behavior. There is a logical progression in the structure. People must glorify God (1:1-15), stay committed to God's plans (2:1-9), please God by living holy lives (2:10-19), and serve Him faithfully (2:20-23).

Outline

I. Reprimand and Call to Rebuild the House of God (1:1-15)

II. Reminder of the Lord's Presence and Future Glory of the Temple (2:1-9)

III. Religious Principles About Holiness and Uncleanness (2:10-19)

IV. Restoration of Davidic Line Promised (2:20-23)

Command to Rebuild the Temple

1 In the second year of King Darius,[A,a] on the first day of the sixth month, the word of the LORD came through Haggai[b] the prophet to Zerubbabel son of Shealtiel,[c] the governor of Judah, and to Joshua son of Jehozadak, the high priest:[d]

2 "The LORD of •Hosts says this: These people say: The time has not come for the house of the LORD to be rebuilt."[e]

3 The word of the LORD came through Haggai the prophet: 4 "Is it a time for you yourselves to live in your paneled houses,[f] while this house[B] lies in ruins?" 5 Now, the LORD of Hosts says this: "Think carefully[g] about[C] your ways:

6 You have planted much
  but harvested little.
You eat
  but never have enough to be satisfied.
You drink
  but never have enough
    to become drunk.
You put on clothes
  but never have enough to get warm.
The wage earner puts his wages
  into a bag with a hole in it."[h]

7 The LORD of Hosts says this: "Think carefully about[c] your ways. 8 Go up into the hills, bring down lumber, and build the house. Then I will be pleased with it and be glorified," says the LORD. 9 "You expected much, but then it amounted to little. When you brought the harvest to your house, I ruined[D] it. Why?" This is the declaration of the LORD of Hosts. "Because My house still lies in ruins, while each of you is busy with his own house.

10 So on your account,[E]
    the skies have withheld the dew
    and the land its crops.[i]
11 I have summoned a drought
    on the fields and the hills,
    on the grain, new wine, olive oil,
    and whatever the ground yields,
    on man and beast,
    and on all that your hands produce."

The People's Response

12 Then Zerubbabel[j] son of Shealtiel, the high priest Joshua son of Jehozadak, and the entire remnant of the people[k] obeyed the voice of the LORD their God and the words of the prophet Haggai, because the LORD their God had sent him. So the people •feared the LORD.[l]

---

a1:1 Ezr 4:5; Neh 12:22; Dn 9:11; 11:1; Hg 1:15; 2:10; Zch 1:1,7; 7:1
bEzr 5:1; 6:14
c1Ch 3:19; Ezr 3:2,8; 5:2; Neh 12:1; Hg 1:12,14; 2:2,23; Lk 3:27
dHg 1:12,14; 2:2,4; Zch 3:1,8; 6:11
e1:2 Ezr 1:3
f1:4 1Kg 7:7; Jr 22:14
g1:5 Hg 2:15,18
h1:6 Lv 26:20; Dt 28:38-40
i1:10 Lv 26:20; Dt 11:17
j1:12 1Ch 13:9; Ezr 3:8; Neh 12:1; Hg 2:2; Zch 4:6
kIs 10:20-21; Jr 41:10; Hg 2:2
lEx 14:31; Dt 4:10; 1Sm 12:18

A1:1 King of Persia reigned 522–486 B.C.   B1:4 = the temple   C1:5,7 Lit *Place your heart on*   D1:9 Lit *blew on*   E1:10 Or *So above you*

1:1 The king named **Darius** is Darius I Hystaspes (522-486 B.C.), not the earlier Darius the Mede (Dn 5:31; 6:1,6,9) or the later Darius II Nothus (Neh 12:12). **Zerubbabel** is listed as the **governor** because under Persian control Judah (Hb *Yehud*) had no Hebrew king. His father **Shealtiel** was the son of the Davidic king Jehoiachin (1Ch 3:17). As leaders, Zerubbabel and **Joshua. . .the high priest** (1Ch 6:14-15; Ezr 3:2) carried the responsibility of guiding the people, so **the word of the LORD** was directed specifically to them.

1:2 A common name for God in Haggai is **the LORD of Hosts** (used 14 times). This title views God as the Divine Warrior in charge of the armies of heaven, thus He is all-powerful and directs the fiery forces of the armies of heaven (2Kg 6:16-17). Because He is sovereign, He can help the discouraged people of Jerusalem rebuild the temple. The people were saying to each other **the time has not come** to finish the work of building God's temple. Times were tough, and there was opposition, but God wanted His people to get on with the work.

1:4 **Your paneled houses** refers to the upper-income homes of Zerubbabel and Joshua. Their homes had expensive wood interior paneling to cover the ugly and uneven stones (similar to Solomon's palace in 1Kg 7:3,7). Why were these leaders spending lavishly on their own homes and giving no priority to building God's house?

1:5 **Think carefully about your ways** (lit "set your heart on your ways") is a call for serious thinking on the decisions the people were making and what these choices say about their priorities. Will they take the easy way out or will they follow God's ways?

1:6 **You have planted much but harvested little** indicates that God was not blessing the work of their hands. There

must be a theological reason why these people were not receiving what they needed.

1:8 God's desire was that the people **build the house** and give priority to worshiping God. Whatever one does, God should always **be pleased with it and be glorified** by it. These are two practical theological criteria that people can use to evaluate their life and set new priorities. Jesus set the example, for everything He did was aimed to please God (Jn 8:29). The reason He came to earth was to glorify the Father (Jn 12:27-28; 17:1,4).

1:9 **I ruined it** (lit "I blew on it") explains why the people never had enough in verse 6. God purposely frustrated their efforts by not blessing and multiplying their produce; instead, the fiery breath of His wrath consumed almost everything. Some might ask: Why would God be so judgmental? But a more appropriate question might be: Why would God not more quickly judge those who do not glorify Him? God's house was **in ruins** because each man was **busy with his own house.**

1:10 The covenant curses in Dt 28:38-39 indicate that when God's covenant people do not love and serve Him, He will neither bless their crops nor send rain (Dt 28:23-24). Thus these problems were **on your account**; you caused this to happen to yourselves.

1:11 **I have summoned a drought** indicates that God was personally responsible for this drought (cp. v. 9).

1:12 In response the **entire remnant of the people obeyed the voice of the LORD** and **feared the LORD**. When the leaders "obeyed" God, the people followed their example. One obeys God when one fears or reverences Him; that is the time when a person puts God first and determines to glorify Him.

¹³Haggai, the LORD's messenger, delivered the LORD's message to the people, "I am with you"ᵃ—this is the LORD's declaration.

¹⁴The LORD stirred up the spiritᵇ of Zerubbabel son of Shealtiel, governor of Judah, the spirit of the high priest Joshua son of Jehozadak, and the spirit of all the remnant of the people. They began work on the house of ˙Yahweh of Hosts, their God, ¹⁵on the twenty-fourth day of the sixth month, in the second year of King Darius.

Encouragement and Promise

2 On the twenty-first day of the seventh month,ᶜ the word of the LORD came through Haggai the prophet: ²"Speak to Zerubbabel son of Shealtiel, governor of Judah, to the high priest Joshua son of Jehozadak, and to the remnant of the people: ³Who is left among you who saw this house in its former glory? How does it look to you now? Doesn't it seem like nothing to you?ᴬ,ᵈ ⁴Even so, be strong, Zerubbabel"—this is the LORD's decla-

ration.ᵉ "Be strong, Joshua son of Jehozadak, high priest. Be strong, all you people of the land"—this is the LORD's declaration. "Work! For I am with you"ᶠ—the declaration of the LORD of ˙Hosts. ⁵"This is the promise I made to you when you came out of Egypt,ᵍ and My Spirit is present among you; don't be afraid."

⁶For the LORD of Hosts says this: "Once more, in a little while, I am going to shake the heavens and the earth,ʰ the sea and the dry land.ⁱ ⁷I will shake all the nations so that the treasures of all the nations will come, and I will fill this house with glory,ʲ says the LORD of Hosts. ⁸"The silver and gold belong to Me"—this is the declaration of the LORD of Hosts. ⁹"The final glory of this houseᴮ will be greater than the first,"ᵏ says the LORD of Hosts. "I will provide peace in this place"ˡ—this is the declaration of the LORD of Hosts.

From Deprivation to Blessing

¹⁰On the twenty-fourth day of the ninth month, in the second year of Darius, the

---

ᵃ1:13 Hg 2:4
ᵇ1:14 1Ch 5:26; Ezr 1:1,5; Is 13:17; 14:9; 41:10; 45:13; Jr 51:11
ᶜ2:1 Lv 23:33-43; 2Ch 7:8-10
ᵈ2:3 1Kg 5:13-16; 6:38; 1Ch 29:1-8; Ezr 3:10-13; Zch 4:10
ᵉ2:4 Jos 1:6-9; 1Ch 28:10,20
ᶠHg 1:13; Zch 8:9
ᵍ2:5 Ex 33:14-17
ʰ2:6 Hg 2:21
ⁱIs 64:2; Ezk 38:19-20; Heb 12:26-28
ʲ2:7 Ex 40:34-35; 1Kg 8:10-11; Is 60:1-13
ᵏ2:9 Mt 12:42
ˡIs 60:18

ᴬ2:3 Lit Is it not in your eyes?   ᴮ2:9 Or The glory of this latter house

---

1:13 Above all other responsibilities, a prophet is fundamentally God's spokesman, God's **messenger** who communicates the theological truth that God has revealed. **I am with you** is a foundational promise that God gives to His people (cp. 2:4). Things may be tough at times, but God is always there to care for the people He loves.

1:14 The LORD stirred up the spirit of the leaders and the people so that they would respond. Spiritual transformation happens when God stirs up the winds of change in people's hearts, convicts them of sin, and emboldens them to act in faith.

1:15 In the second year of King Darius is sometimes connected with the date in 2:1 (the dating system in 1:1 and 2:9

includes the month and year). On the other hand, since 2:20 and 2:1 do not give the year, a shortened formula is an acceptable way of identifying a date.

2:1 The twenty-first day of the seventh month was the last day of the Feast of Tabernacles/Shelters in which the people celebrated the blessings of a good harvest and commemorated the time when their ancestors lived in tents during their wilderness wanderings (Lv 23:33-43; Nm 29:12-40; Dt 16:13-17). There was a large crowd gathered for this feast, so it was a good time to address many people.

2:3 Saw this house in its former glory . . . Doesn't it seem like nothing to you? The prophet heard what people were saying about the temple rebuilding program during the feast. Many had a negative attitude, saying this temple would be greatly inferior to Solomon's gold-covered temple (1Kg 6:2-35).

2:4 Be strong (mentioned three times) is an encouragement for the leaders Zerubbabel and Joshua, as well as the rest of the people, to be bold and firmly committed. They should not question the worthiness of building a temple to glorify God.

2:5 My Spirit is present among you promises that the power that enabled the people to escape Egypt (cp. Ex 33:14-17) was still actively present to help in this crisis situation.

2:6 I am going to shake all parts of the earth describes God's sovereignty over what will happen.

2:7 The treasures of all the nations will come is not a messianic hope, but a promise that God will provide all the gold and silver that is needed (v. 8 says they **belong to Me**) to make the unimpressive temple glorious. Ezra 6:8 marks the fulfillment of this prophecy, for the Persians paid the full cost of reconstruction.

2:9 The final glory of this house will be greater may be an eschatological promise (cp. Is 60:1-9; Ezk 40:1—44:8).

2:12 Does it become holy asks if touching something holy can transfer holiness. The answer is no.

---

ra'ash

Hebrew Pronunciation	[rah ASH]
HCSB Translation	quake, tremble, shake
Uses in Haggai	3
Uses in the OT	30
Focus passage	Haggai 2:6-7,21

Ra'ash usually describes the earth *quaking* (Ps 18:7), *shaking* (Is 13:13), or *trembling* (Ps 68:8), perhaps at locust swarms (Jl 2:10) or kingdoms falling (Jr 10:10). Mountains (Ps 46:3), coasts, and islands (Ezk 26:15) *quake*; the skies (Jl 3:16), countryside (Ezk 27:28), and earth's foundations (Is 24:18) *shake*. Thresholds (Am 9:1) and walls (Ezk 26:10) *shake*. Every creature will *tremble* before God (Ezk 38:20). Grain *waves* (Ps 72:16). The causative shows God *shaking* kingdoms (Is 14:16), even heaven and earth (Hg 2:6). He *makes* nations *quake* (Ezk 31:16) and horses *leap* (Jb 39:20). The noun *ra'ash* (17x) signifies *earthquake* (Ezk 38:19), military *commotion* (Jr 10:22), or the *battle* (Is 9:5). It is *rumbling* of chariots (Jr 47:3), including God's chariot with angel wings and wheels (Ezk 3:12-13). *Ra'ash* indicates *rattling* of bones (Ezk 37:7) and *whirring* of javelins (Jb 41:29). It is people's *trembling* as they eat (Ezk 12:18).

word of the LORD came to Haggai the prophet: [11] "This is what the LORD of Hosts says: Ask the priests for a ruling.[a] [12] If a man is carrying consecrated meat in the fold of his garment, and it touches bread, stew, wine, oil, or any other food, does it become holy?"[b]

The priests answered, "No."

[13] Then Haggai asked, "If someone defiled by contact with a corpse touches any of these, does it become defiled?"[c]

The priests answered, "It becomes defiled."

[14] Then Haggai replied, "So is this people, and so is this nation before Me"—this is the LORD's declaration. "And so is every work of their hands; even what they offer there is defiled.

[15] "Now, reflect back from this day: Before one stone was placed on another in the LORD's temple, [16] what state were you in?[A] When someone came to a grain heap of 20 measures, it only amounted to 10; when one came to the winepress to dip 50 measures from the vat, it only amounted to 20. [17] I struck you—all the work of your hands—with blight, mildew,[d]

and hail,[e] but you didn't turn to Me"—this is the LORD's declaration. [18] "Consider carefully[f] from this day forward; from the twenty-fourth day of the ninth month, from the day the foundation of the LORD's temple was laid; consider it carefully. [19] Is there still seed left in the granary? The vine, the fig, the pomegranate, and the olive tree have not yet produced. But from this day on I will bless you."[g]

Promise to Zerubbabel

[20] The word of the LORD came to Haggai a second time on the twenty-fourth day of the month: [21] "Speak to Zerubbabel, governor of Judah: I am going to shake the heavens and the earth.[h] [22] I will overturn royal thrones and destroy the power of the Gentile kingdoms.[i] I will overturn chariots and their riders. Horses and their riders will fall, each by his brother's sword. [23] On that day"—this is the declaration of the LORD of Hosts—"I will take you, Zerubbabel son of Shealtiel, My servant"—this is the LORD's declaration—"and make you like My signet ring,[j] for I have chosen you."[k] This is the declaration of the LORD of Hosts.

---

[a] 2:11 Mal 2:7
[b] 2:12 Jr 11:15
[c] 2:13 Lv 11:39; 22:4-6; Nm 19:11-13,22
[d] 2:17 Dt 28:22; 1Kg 8:37; Am 4:9
[e] Ps 105:32-33
[f] 2:18 Hg 1:5,7
[g] 2:19 Zch 8:9-13
[h] 2:21 Ezk 38:19-20; Hg 2:6-7
[i] 2:22 Gn 19:25; Am 4:11
[j] 2:23 Est 8:8; Jr 22:23-25
[k] Mt 1:12-13

[A] 2:16 Hb obscure

2:13 Does it become defiled inquires about the transfer of uncleanness. The answer is yes (cp. Nm 19:11).

2:14 So is this people indicates that these people in Jerusalem will not become holy simply by touching the holy temple while rebuilding it. God wants people to have holy hearts; He is less concerned with the construction of holy buildings.

2:17 I struck you . . . but you didn't turn to Me describes past failures to repent and God's past discipline of them when He gave them poor crops (cp. 1:6,9-11).

2:18-19 Consider carefully from this day forward . . . I will bless you implies acts of confession and spiritual revival took place at this time. Because of this change God could richly bless their future crops and fill their empty granaries.

2:21-22 I will overturn royal thrones. Although Zerubbabel was discouraged with little power and few military resources, God promised to work on his behalf to determine who would win the wars at that time.

2:23 My servant identifies Zerubbabel not as an insignificant governor, but as a key obedient person who followed God's directions. **Make you like My signet ring** indicates that Zerubbabel will carry the authority to act as God's legitimate Davidic ruler, a right that God removed from the evil king Jehoiakim in Jr 22:24. This no doubt gave some hope about a future Davidic ruler who would some day rule on David's throne (Is 9:6-7; Jr 23:5-6).

Zechariah

Introduction

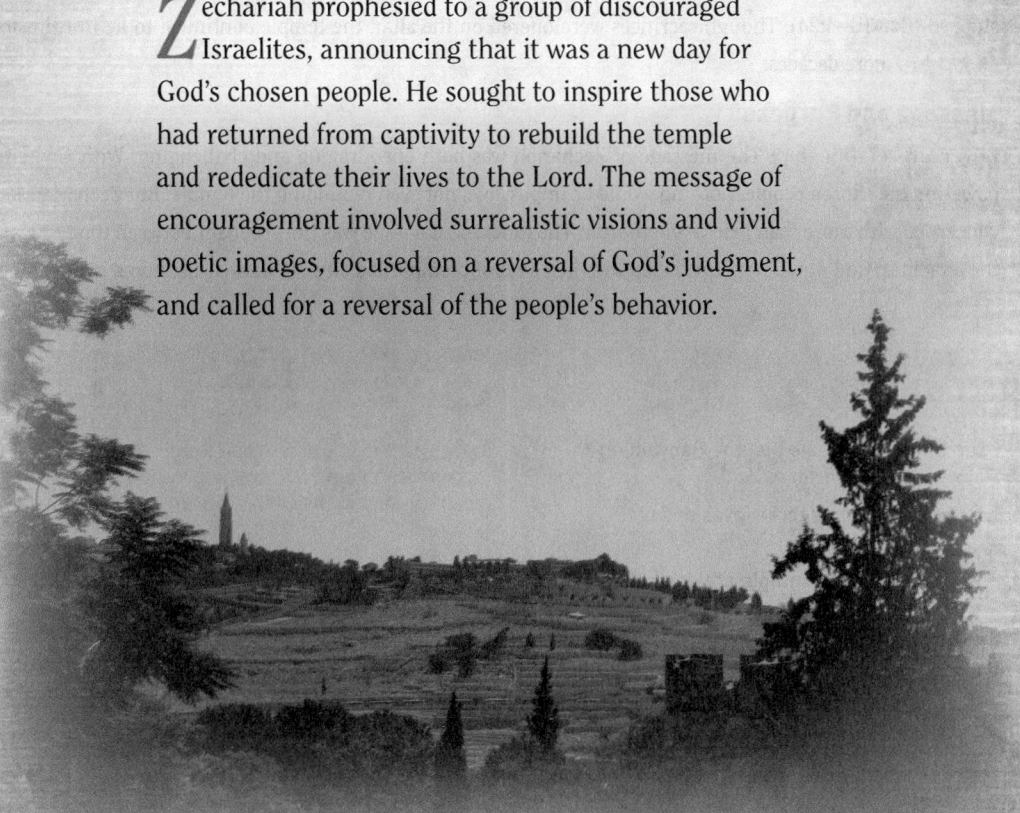

Zechariah prophesied to a group of discouraged Israelites, announcing that it was a new day for God's chosen people. He sought to inspire those who had returned from captivity to rebuild the temple and rededicate their lives to the Lord. The message of encouragement involved surrealistic visions and vivid poetic images, focused on a reversal of God's judgment, and called for a reversal of the people's behavior.

"Then the Lord will go out to fight against those nations as He fights on a day of battle. On that day His feet will stand on the Mount of Olives, which faces Jerusalem on the east. The Mount of Olives will be split in half from east to west, forming a huge valley, so that half the mountain will move to the north and half to the south" (14:3-4).

Circumstances of Writing

Author: Zechariah returned to Judah with the former exiles and was apparently a priest (Neh 12:16). He was a contemporary of Haggai. Though nothing is known of cooperation between the two prophets, they had similar missions and are credited with the successful reconstruction of the temple (Ezr 5:1-2; 6:14). Zechariah gave dates for two periods of his prophetic ministry (520 and 518 B.C.; Zch 1:1,7; 7:1). Whether he was the author of the entire book is debatable. Many scholars, impressed with the differences between chapters 1–8 and 9–14, conclude that Zechariah did not write the last six chapters. It is not a major issue. The concept of authorship at the time of the Bible was different from modern standards. In the OT, there is evidence of portions of books under a single author's name that were not written by that author (Nm 12:3; Dt 34:5-12; Jr 51:64c).

Background: A key moment in the history of the Israelites came after King Cyrus of Persia granted the captives permission to return to Palestine (538 B.C.). The chosen people had just come through one of the worst experiences possible in the ancient world. Their homeland was devastated by invading armies, their capital city and temple were plundered and flattened, many of their people and leaders were killed, and most of the rest were carried off into pagan lands. The returnees who made the long trek back to Judah were faced with the challenge of reestablishing Jerusalem and the temple. Based on the account in the book of Ezra, work began immediately. But after the altar was rebuilt and the foundation stones were laid, problems arose and the work stopped (Ezr 3:1–4:24). Though sacrifices were offered on the altar, the temple continued to lie in ruins for almost two more decades.

Message and Purpose

Covenant relationship: The message of Zechariah was both encouraging and challenging. With God empowering the chosen people, nothing would be impossible, not even rebuilding the temple. But Zechariah was concerned with more than bricks and mortar. The fundamental issue was the covenant between the Lord and the Israelites. God would not be satisfied with just a rebuilt temple and city. He wanted a restored relationship.

---

625 B.C.

Jeremiah prophesies that the Babylonian exile will last 70 years. 605

Nebuchadnezzar's three invasions of Judah 605, 597, 586

Jerusalem and the temple are destroyed. 586

Fall of Babylon and rise of Persia 539

Cyrus's decree allows return of Jews from exile; 42,360 returned initially. 538

Second temple construction begins under Zerubbabel's and Joshua's leadership. 536

Discouragement reinforced by opposition from transplanted peoples brought work on the temple to a halt. 526

525 B.C.

Aeschylus, (525–456) Greek tragedian, many of whose plays dealt with the Persian invasion of Greece. He participated in the Greek victories at Marathon and Salamis.

Haggai and Zechariah encourage the people to resume construction of the temple. 520–518

Haggai's first message August 29, 520

Temple building resumes September 21, 520

Haggai's second message October 17, 520

Zechariah's first prophetic message October/November 520

Because their ancestors had failed miserably in obeying the law—by not worshiping Him in spirit and in truth and by not acting justly toward one another—God called on the surrounding nations to punish His people. Now the question was whether the returnees had learned the hard lesson and would do any better at complying with the terms of the covenant.

Criticizing and energizing: Zechariah's message carried high stakes. The remnant that came out of the captivity was the only hope for the future of Israel. Based on the track record of previous generations, strong language would be necessary to penetrate the stubborn shoulders, closed ears, and rock-hard hearts of God's people (7:11-12). The method Zechariah adopted was to criticize the worldview that was dominant in the thinking of the Israelites and to energize them with the possibility of a completely new reality. Poetry served this purpose well because it allowed for language with the volume turned up.

Contribution to the Bible

The book of Zechariah is full of the language of judgment, but it is also full of God's promises. The Lord challenged His people to undertake an overwhelmingly difficult task, and He assured them of their success through His power. But the nature of these promises extended beyond rebuilding the temple. From beginning to end, the Bible tells the story of God's redemptive plan, culminating in God's triumph over evil and salvation for sinners. Zechariah's prophecies anticipate this grand culmination of history, describing a coming glorious king, a God who triumphs over all, and a world with all wrongs corrected. These promises set the stage for God's future kingdom, as evidenced by the quotes and allusions to Zechariah in the NT.

Structure

The book of Zechariah is complex, sometimes with seemingly disjointed units, like a series of snapshots that need to be put in order. The apparent lack of organization may reflect the oral origin of the book, a collection of sermons that were patched together in written form. But it may also have been intentional. With the goal of shocking the hearers and bringing them to their senses, rapid-fire movement from one thought to another

520 B.C.	**450 B.C.**
Haggai's third and fourth messages December 18, 520	Second group of exiles returns to Jerusalem under the leadership of Ezra. 458
Zechariah's night visions February 15, 519	Third group of exiles return under Nehemiah's leadership. 445
Zechariah's message on fasting December 7, 518	Jerusalem's walls rebuilt under Nehemiah's leadership 445
Temple completed March 12, 515	
Greeks, outnumbered almost five to one, defeat Persians in Battle of Marathon through superior military intelligence and strategy, forestalling Persian expansion into Europe. 490	Nehemiah returns to Persia. 432
	Peloponnesian Wars between Athens and other Greek city-states 431–404
Malachi's prophecy 460	Nehemiah returns to Jerusalem. 425

may have been part of Zechariah's technique. Chapters 1–8 contain carefully dated visions and sermons, while chapters 9–14 consist of undated poetic oracles and narrative descriptions of judgment and blessing.

Zechariah used a mix of genres. His sermons, poetry, and oracles of judgment and salvation were typical of the prophetic genre. But his visions had similarities with apocalyptic literature, best represented in the OT by the book of Daniel. The content of some of his oracles, describing divine intervention and a radically different world, are also typical of apocalyptic literature. Thus, Zechariah may represent a stage of development between a prophetic form and an apocalyptic form.

Outline

I. Call to Conversion (1:1-6)

II. Visionary Disclosure of God's Purposes (1:7–6:15)
    A. Vision one: appearances deceive (1:7-17)
    B. Vision two: the destroyers destroyed (1:18-21)
    C. Vision three: perfect safety of an open city (2:1-13)
    D. Vision four: Satan silenced (3:1-10)
    E. Vision five: the temple rebuilt (4:1-14)
    F. Vision six: the curse destroys sin (5:1-4)
    G. Vision seven: sin banished from the land (5:5-11)
    H. Vision eight: four chariots (6:1-8)
    I. Coronation scene (6:9-15)

III. A Prophetic Message to the People (7:1–8:23)
    A. Empty worship and judgment (7:1-14)
    B. Incredible blessings (8:1-23)

IV. The Emerging Kingdom (9:1–14:21)
    A. The King and His kingdom (9:1–11:3)
    B. Two shepherds (11:4-17)
    C. Jerusalem attacked and delivered (12:1-9)
    D. Inward blessings promised (12:10-14)
    E. Threefold purification (13:1-6)
    F. Death of the shepherd (13:7-9)
    G. The Day of the Lord (14:1-21)

A Plea for Repentance

1 In the eighth month, in the second year of Darius,[a] the word of the Lord came to the prophet Zechariah[b] son of Berechiah, son of Iddo: ²"The Lord was extremely angry with your ancestors. ³So tell the people: This is what the Lord of •Hosts says: Return to Me"—this is the declaration of the Lord of Hosts—"and I will return to you, says the Lord of Hosts. ⁴Do not be like your ancestors; the earlier prophets proclaimed to them: This is what the Lord of Hosts says: Turn from your evil ways and your evil deeds.[c] But they did not listen or pay attention to Me"—this is the Lord's declaration. ⁵"Where are your ancestors now? And do the prophets live forever? ⁶But didn't My words and My statutes that I commanded My servants the prophets overtake your ancestors? They repented and said: As the Lord of Hosts purposed to deal with us for our ways and deeds, so He has dealt with us."[d]

THE NIGHT VISIONS

⁷On the twenty-fourth day of the eleventh month, which is the month of Shebat, in the second year of Darius, the word of the Lord came to the prophet Zechariah son of Berechiah, son of Iddo:

First Vision: Horsemen

⁸I looked out in the night and saw a man riding on a red horse. He was standing among the myrtle trees in the valley. Behind him were red, sorrel, and white horses. ⁹I asked, "What are these, my lord?"

The angel who was talking to me replied, "I will show you what they are."

¹⁰Then the man standing among the myrtle trees explained, "They are the ones the Lord has sent to patrol the earth."

¹¹They reported to the Angel of the Lord standing among the myrtle trees, "We have patrolled the earth, and right now the whole earth is calm and quiet."[e]

¹²Then the Angel of the Lord responded, "How long, Lord of Hosts, will You withhold mercy from Jerusalem and the cities of Judah that You have been angry with these 70 years?"[f] ¹³The Lord replied with kind and

a1:1 Zch 7:1
bEzr 5:1; 6:14
c1:4 2Kg 17:13; 2Ch 7:14; Ezk 33:9,11
d1:6 Jr 51:12; Lm 2:17; Zch 8:14-15
e1:11 Jos 11:23; Jdg 5:31; Is 14:7
f1:12 Jr 25:11-12; 29:10

1:1 Zechariah and Haggai began their ministries only two months apart (Hg 1:1) in the fall of 520 B.C., 19 years after Cyrus, king of Persia, issued an edict giving the Israelites permission to return from exile to their homeland. Both prophets were instrumental in the temple being rebuilt, completed in 516/515 (Ezr 5:1-2; 6:14).

1:2 The Assyrians destroyed Samaria and the northern 10 tribes, and the Babylonians demolished Jerusalem and the southern two tribes (2Kg 17:5-23; 25:8-21; 2Ch 36:17-20). The pain and suffering, the loss of homes, lives, and cities, the deportation to foreign lands, and especially the destruction of the temple in Jerusalem raised troubling questions about God's covenant promises and justice. But the prophets were united in their assessment of the Lord's extreme anger. The blast of God's judgment was completely deserved.

1:3 Return (or "turn, repent"; Hb *shuv*) is a key motif throughout Zechariah (cp. v. 4, "turn"; v. 6, "repent"; v. 16, "return"; 8:3, "return"; 13:7, "turn"). It applied to the Israelites in two senses: a return from captivity (a spatial return) and a return to the Lord (a spiritual return). It applied to God in two senses. After withdrawing His presence and blessing from Jerusalem for a time, "return" referred to showing favor again. God's "turn" could also denote the change from judging the people to blessing them. God's offer to return was contingent on the people returning to Him, a consistent feature of the covenant (Gn 17:1-2,9; Jr 18:7-10).

1:4 They did not listen or pay attention to Me are some of the saddest words in the Bible. For more than 200 years the prophets described disobedience in all its ugliness (3:3-4; cp. Is 57:3-9). They pictured the blessings of faithfulness in fantastic images of a perfect world, though expressed more simply in Zch 1:3 as "I will return to you" (but see the expansion in vv. 16-17; 3:8-10). But nothing worked to penetrate the cold hearts of sinners (7:11-12; 2Kg 17:14-23; 2Ch 36:15-16; Jr 5:11-13; Mal 3:7).

1:5-6 By recalling the earlier **prophets** and their role, Zechariah placed himself on the same stage preaching the same sermon. It was a message with enduring significance because the chosen people had an ongoing challenge—living a life of faith. Shockingly he asked, **Where are your ancestors now?** The futility of disobedience could hardly be clearer. The wasted effort of heroes must not be repeated.

1:7 In a society that was reinventing itself—after its leaders, cities, and Jerusalem temple were destroyed, and after being in exile for many years—the need for vision and hope ran deep. A means to penetrate the very core of the human spirit and transform deepest feelings was necessary. The solution was pictures and visions. The string of visions that **came to the prophet Zechariah** brought to life the answer for people on the brink of despair: God is in control and is on your side.

1:8 I looked out in the night apparently introduces all eight of the prophet's visions. They offer a mix of the ordinary and the surreal—a world somewhere between heaven and earth. Like the apocalyptic visions of Daniel or Revelation, symbolism is commonplace, often requiring an interpreter.

1:8-11 The scene unfolds gradually, with clues appearing along the way and with the **angel** (or "messenger") interpreting certain details. The **man riding on a red horse** is the one **standing among the myrtle trees**, and he is the **Angel of the Lord**. **Horses** may suggest speed, but the Hebrew construction translated **patrol** (also "walk") suggests control (cp. 10:3). Finding the world calm and quiet underscored the contrast with the turbulence that Israel faced. Some details of the vision (myrtle trees **in the valley** and red, sorrel, and white horses) may have been included to enhance the sensory vividness of the scene rather than to convey symbolic meaning.

1:12-13 When Jerusalem was destroyed, God's glory departed (Ezk 10:1-19), and for nearly 70 years (likely a round

comforting words to the angel who was speaking with me.

[14] So the angel who was speaking with me said, "Proclaim: The LORD of Hosts says: I am extremely jealous[a] for Jerusalem and •Zion. [15] I am fiercely angry with the nations that are at ease, for I was a little angry, but they made it worse. [16] Therefore, this is what the LORD says: In mercy, I have returned to Jerusalem; My house will be rebuilt within it"—this is the declaration of the LORD of Hosts—"and a measuring line will be stretched out over Jerusalem.

[17] "Proclaim further: This is what the LORD of Hosts says: My cities will again overflow with prosperity; the LORD will once more comfort Zion and again choose Jerusalem."[b]

Second Vision: Four Horns and Craftsmen

[18A] Then I looked up and saw four •horns. [19] So I asked the angel who was speaking with me, "What are these?"

And he said to me, "These are the horns that scattered Judah, Israel, and Jerusalem."

[20] Then the LORD showed me four craftsmen. [21] I asked, "What are they coming to do?"

He replied, "These are the horns that scattered Judah so no one could raise his head. These craftsmen have come to terrify them, to cut off the horns of the nations that raised their horns against the land of Judah to scatter it."

Third Vision: Surveyor

2[B] I looked up and saw a man with a measuring line in his hand. [2] I asked, "Where are you going?"

He answered me, "To measure Jerusalem to determine its width and length."

[3] Then the angel who was speaking with me went out, and another angel went out to meet him. [4] He said to him, "Run and tell this young man: Jerusalem will be inhabited without walls because of the number of people and livestock in it."[c] [5] The declaration of the LORD: "I will be a wall[d] of fire around it, and I will be the glory within it."

[6] "Get up! Leave the land of the north"[e]—this is the LORD's declaration—"for I have scattered

---

a1:14 Ex 20:5; 34:14; Dt 5:9 **b**1:17 2Ch 6:6; Is 40:1; Zch 2:12 **c**2:4 Is 49:19; Jr 31:27; Ezk 36:11 **d**2:5 Is 26:1 **e**2:6 Jr 6:22; 10:22; 50:9

A1:18 Zch 2:1 in Hb   **B**2:1 Zch 2:5 in Hb

---

number) God's people had no temple to rally around or a central place of worship. Though the prophets had predicted that Jerusalem would become a wasteland (Is 32:14; Jr 9:11), they also painted images of restoration (Is 2:2-5; Ezk 40–48). Thus, the angel's question of how long the mercy of the Lord would be withheld was one that God's people were eager to have answered.

1:14-17 God being **extremely jealous for Jerusalem** suggests the intensity of His love as well as His high expectations for His people (Ex 20:5). News that the Lord's anger was turning against the **nations**, who had unjustly abused the chosen few, and that God was returning to **Jerusalem**, denoting the end of judgment and the resumption of blessing, would have been very encouraging to Zechariah's audience. The declaration that **My house will be rebuilt** suggests that the function of this vision and the ones to follow was to energize the people to unite in rebuilding God's temple. On a **measuring line**, see note at 2:1-5.

1:18-21 This scene continues the theme of reversal (v. 15). Whereas God had used the nations to judge Israel, now he turns against those nations (cp. Hab 2). The imagery of **four horns** that **scattered** the people so that **no one could raise his head** suggests the terrifying power and merciless ruin enacted by Israel's enemies. The **craftsmen** designate skilled artisans (blacksmiths, if the horns were iron) who could cut off or carve up horns for various purposes. With the horns in the vision removed, the chosen people could return to the promised land.

2:1-5 The third vision revisits the promise of Jerusalem being rebuilt but enlarges the scope dramatically. With **measuring line** (1:16)—a common tool of the building trade but in regard to sacred sites signifying divine commissioning—in hand, a surveyor set out to determine its **width and length**, apparently intending to measure from wall to wall (probably an allusion to Ezk 40:3–42:20). But an angelic messenger spoke with urgency: **Tell this young man** that the city could not be measured because there were no walls (for an opposite image, see note at Is 60:10). A wall-less city symbolized three ideas. (1) The city would be so vast that walls could not contain it, **because of the number of people and livestock**. An ingathering of people in Jerusalem was a common motif in the prophets' language of blessing (Is 2:2-5). (2) The city would be at peace,

---

gadol

Hebrew Pronunciation	[gah DOHL]
HCSB Translation	great, large, old
Uses in Zechariah	10
Uses in the OT	527
Focus passage	Zechariah 1:15

Gadol means *great* but has broader applications. *Gadol* is *old* (Gn 19:11), *large* (Neh 5:7), and *loud* (Gn 27:34). It is *high* (Ps 57:10), particularly regarding the *high* priest (Hg 1:14). *Gadol* connotes *wealthy* (2Sm 19:32), *famous* (Est 10:3), and *prominent* (2Kg 4:8), as well as *remarkable* (Ex 3:3), *significant* (Ec 9:13), and *important* (Ex 18:22). But it is *monstrous* (2Kg 8:13), *terrible* (1Sm 6:9), or *violent* (Jnh 1:4). Nominally, *gadol* signifies the *rich* (Lv 19:15), *noble* (Jr 52:13), and *powerful* (Jr 5:5). Speaking "*great things*" implies *boastfully* (Ps 12:3). *Gadol* suggests *fiercely* with respect to the literal phrase "angry with *great* anger" (Zch 1:15). A "thing small or *great*" is *anything* (1Sm 25:36). Like other adjectives, *gadol* can mean *greater* and *greatest* or *larger* and *largest*. According to context it denotes *severe* (Gn 12:17), *widespread* (Neh 5:1), *heavy* (Dt 25:13), or *broad* (Dt 29:7).

you like the four winds of heaven"—this is the Lord's declaration. [7]"Go, *Zion! Escape, you who are living with Daughter Babylon." [8]For the Lord of *Hosts says this: "He has sent Me[A] for His glory against the nations who are plundering you, for anyone who touches you touches the pupil[B] of His[C] eye. [9]I will move against them with My[D] power, and they will become plunder for their own servants.[a] Then you will know that the Lord of Hosts has sent Me.[A]

[10]"Daughter Zion, shout for joy and be glad, for I am coming to dwell among you"—this is the Lord's declaration. [11]"Many nations will join themselves to the Lord on that day and become My[E] people.[b] I will dwell among you, and you will know that the Lord of Hosts has sent Me[A] to you. [12]The Lord will take possession of Judah as His portion in the Holy Land, and He will once again choose Jerusalem.[c] [13]Let all people be silent[d] before the Lord, for He is coming from His holy dwelling."

Fourth Vision: High Priest and Branch

3 Then he showed me Joshua[e] the high priest standing before the Angel of the Lord,[f] with Satan[F,g] standing at his right side to accuse him. [2]The Lord[G] said to Satan: "The Lord rebuke you, Satan! May the Lord who has chosen Jerusalem rebuke you! Isn't this man a burning stick snatched from the fire?"[h]

[3]Now Joshua was dressed with filthy[H] clothes[i] as he stood before the Angel.[j] [4]So the Angel of the Lord[i] spoke to those[j] standing before Him, "Take off his filthy clothes!" Then He said to him, "See, I have removed your *guilt from you,[k] and I will clothe you with splendid robes."

[5]Then I said, "Let them put a *clean turban[l] on his head." So a clean turban was placed on his head, and they clothed him in garments while the Angel of the Lord was standing nearby.

---

[a]2:9 Is 11:15; 19:16
[b]2:10-11 Ps 47:9; Is 42:6; Mc 4:2
[c]2:12 2Ch 6:6; Zch 1:17; 3:2
[d]2:13 Hab 2:20
[e]3:1 Hg 1:1,12,14; 2:4; Zch 6:11
[f]Gn 16:7-13; 21:17; 22:11-16; 31:11-13
[g]1Ch 21:1; Jb 1:6-12; Rv 12:10
[h]3:2 Dt 4:20; Am 4:11
[i]3:3 Dt 23:13; Is 4:4
[j]Lv 22:3
[k]3:4 2Sm 24:10; Jb 7:21; Mc 7:18
[l]3:5 Ex 28:36-38

A2:8,9,11 Or me   B2:8 Or apple   C2:8 Ancient Jewish tradition reads My   D2:9 Or my   E2:11 LXX, Syr read His   F3:1 Or the adversary   G3:2 Syr reads The Angel of the Lord   H3:3 Probably stained with human excrement   I3:4 Lit He   J3:4 = the angels

---

and the only protection needed would be provided by God Himself. [3] **A wall of fire around it**, recalling God's fiery appearances associated with the miracle of deliverance from Egyptian captivity (Ex 3:2; 13:21-22; 19:18; Dt 4:24), makes clear that a physical wall would be unnecessary. His **glory within it** need not be an eschatological reference, but is more likely a reference to God's glory returning to the tabernacle or temple (Ex 40:34-35; Lv 9:23-24).

2:6-13 The extent of the divine declarations in these verses suggests that they are not a continuation of the vision in verses 1-5 but are a pause in the action. The progression of thought moves quickly. Instead of dwelling in Babylon, God called for a return to the land of promise where He would once again dwell with His people.

2:6 Continuing the theme of reversal (cp. 1:18-21), God appealed to exiles to return from **the land of the north**, the very people whom He had scattered **like the four winds of heaven**. The initial return in 537 B.C. preceded Zechariah's prophecies (Ezr 2:64-67; Neh 7:66-69). At least two more groups made the long journey (458 and 445 B.C.), while many remained behind in the dispersion.

2:7 Daughter Babylon may be a hint of tenderness toward this pagan nation, even with judgment impending (vv. 8-9). It anticipates "Daughter Zion" (v. 10) and suggests that God's love for the nation of Israel, though special, does not mean He does not love the other nations.

2:8 In contrast to judging His people, God reiterated judgment on the perpetrators of judgment (cp. 1:15,18-21). **Pupil of His eye** refers to the most valuable yet vulnerable part of the body and more accurately translates "gate of the eye" rather than the traditional "apple of the eye," though the poetic nature of the latter communicates more effectively. The metaphor functions to express God's deepest feelings for His chosen people (cp. Dt 32:10; Ps 17:8; Pr 7:2).

2:11 Many nations will . . . become My people under-

scores a paradox of unexpected double reversal. The nations that God had used to enact judgment—which in an act of reversal came under His judgment—have now come into His blessing, yet another act of reversal. This does not suggest indecision on God's part but the complexity of His mercy, shown to various people at different times, all of them sinners and none deserving. It is the miracle of grace.

3:1-10 The fourth vision signaled even more encouragement for the returnees to rebuild the temple. The priesthood, which did not operate during the exile, would be restored, and God would grant the chosen people the blessings of forgiveness, service, and peace. As the scene unfolds, the reader gradually discovers that the high priest is representative of the nation of Israel, an example of the literary device known as synecdoche, where one thing is singled out to represent the whole. The vision ends with God removing the guilt of this land and everyone inviting friends to fellowship under his vine and fig tree.

3:1-2 Joshua is the name of four different people mentioned in the OT (in the NT the equivalent name was "Jesus"). Joshua was the first high priest after the exile. He is mentioned numerous times in Ezra, Nehemiah, and Haggai. As in Jb 1:6-12; 2:1-6, **Satan** (or "the adversary") had access to God's courtroom and functioned as prosecutor. **A burning stick snatched from the fire** is the first clue that Joshua is symbolic for the chosen people, based on the prophet Amos using this same image for Israel (Am 4:11).

3:3-5 Patterned after the consecration of a high priest (Ex 29:1-9; cp. Lv 16:3-5), the forgiveness of sin is vividly portrayed by a change of apparel. The **filthy clothes** (lit "defiled by excrement") underscores the gruesome guilt of the people, which had resulted in the severity of God's judgment. In an unexpected reversal, which could only happen by divine decree, Joshua is vindicated and given clean clothes.

⁶Then the Angel of the LORD charged Joshua: ⁷"This is what the LORD of *Hosts says: If you walk in My ways and keep My instructions, you will both rule My house and take care of My courts; I will also grant you access among these who are standing here.

⁸"Listen, Joshua the high priest, you and your colleagues sitting before you; indeed, these men are a sign that I am about to bring My servant, the Branch.ᵃ ⁹Notice the stoneᵇ I have set before Joshua; on that one stone are seven eyes.ᶜ I will engrave an inscription on it"—this is the declaration of the LORD of Hosts—"and I will take away the guilt of this land in a single day. ¹⁰On that day, each of you will invite his neighbor to sit under his vine and fig tree."ᵈ This is the declaration of the LORD of Hosts.

Fifth Vision: Gold Lampstand

4 The angel who was speaking with me then returned and roused me as one awakened out of sleep. ²He asked me, "What do you see?"

I replied, "I see a solid gold lampstand there with a bowl on its top. It has seven lamps on it and seven channels for each ofᴬ the lamps on its top. ³There are also two olive trees beside it, one on the right of the bowl and the other on its left."

ᵃ3:8 Is 4:2; 11:1; Jr 23:5; 33:15; Ezk 17:22-24; Zch 6:12
ᵇ3:9 Ps 118:22-23; Is 8:14; 28:16; Dn 2:35,45; Zch 4:10; Rv 5:6
ᶜZch 4:10
ᵈ3:10 1Kg 4:25; 2Kg 18:31; Mc 4:1-8
ᵉ4:6 Hs 1:7; Hg 2:4-5
ᶠ4:7 Mt 17:20; 21:21; 1Co 13:2
ᵍIs 40:4
ʰ4:8 Zch 6:9
ⁱ4:9 Ezr 3:8-11; 5:16
ʲ4:10 Hg 2:3-4
ᵏ2Ch 16:9; Ps 34:15; Pr 15:3; Am 9:8; 1Pt 3:12
ˡ4:14 Jr 33:17-22

---

⁴Then I asked the angel who was speaking with me, "What are these, my lord?"

⁵"Don't you know what they are?" replied the angel who was speaking with me.

I said, "No, my lord."

⁶So he answered me, "This is the word of the LORD to Zerubbabel: 'Not by strength or by might, but by My Spirit,'ᵉ says the LORD of *Hosts. ⁷'What are you, great mountain?ᶠ Before Zerubbabel you will become a plain.ᵍ And he will bring out the capstone accompanied by shouts of: Grace, grace to it!'"

⁸Then the word of the LORD came to me:ʰ ⁹"Zerubbabel's hands have laid the foundation of this house,ⁱ and his hands will complete it. Then you will know that the LORD of Hosts has sent me to you. ¹⁰For who scorns the day of small things?ʲ These seven eyes of the LORD, which scan throughout the whole earth, will rejoice when they see the plumb lineᴮ in Zerubbabel's hand."ᵏ

¹¹I asked him, "What are the two olive trees on the right and left of the lampstand?" ¹²And I questioned him further, "What are the two olive branches beside the two gold conduits, from which golden oil pours out?"

¹³Then he inquired of me, "Don't you know what these are?"

"No, my lord," I replied.

¹⁴"These are the two anointed ones,"ᶜ·ˡ he

ᴬ4:2 Or seven lips to   ᴮ4:10 Lit the tin stone   ᶜ4:14 = Joshua and Zerubbabel

---

3:6-7 Lest the people become presumptuous on God's gift of forgiveness, **the Angel of the LORD charged** (or "admonished solemnly") **Joshua** that obedience was a prerequisite if he were to enjoy God's favor and perform his duties as high priest, including having access to God's presence.

3:8-10 Not only was the priesthood restored and forgiveness granted, but a descendant of David would become their ruler, as indicated by **My servant, the Branch**, probably a reference to Zerubbabel (Hg 2:23; see notes at Zch 4:11-14; 6:12-13; cp. Jr 33:15). The same is true for the **stone** of Zch 3:9 (see Is 8:14; 28:16). **Seven eyes** probably evoked an image of a foundation stone for a sacred site.

4:1-10 Faced with rebuilding their temple and city, the chosen people felt small, powerless, and overwhelmed. Opposition came from within and without—from the Samaritans accusing them of treason (Ezr 4:6-24), to some of their own people thinking the odds against the project were insurmountable (Ezr 3:12; Hg 2:3). But Zechariah saw things differently. God would empower the people and their leader Zerubbabel. The vision was particularly evocative: "For who scorns the day of small things?" (Zch 4:10).

4:2-3 Though the cumulative impact is evident, the vision is marked by complex imagery. Oil pressed from olives, with a wick to soak up the oil, provided the primary source of light in the ancient world. But the **lampstand** described here is surrealistic, with an inexplicable arrangement of containers of oil—**a bowl . . . seven lamps . . . seven channels**, and **two olive trees**—perhaps signifying an abundance of oil. On the lampstand in the tabernacle, see Ex 25:31-37.

4:4-6 The angel's question **don't you know what they are** heightens the anticipation of what the answer will be and underscores the necessity of supernatural insight. What the angel said to **Zerubbabel** about the **Spirit** provides insight into the interpretation of the lampstand. Oil was symbolic of God's Spirit (1Sm 16:13). Thus, while Zerubbabel would be instrumental in accomplishing God's purposes, it could only happen through the plentiful supply of God's Spirit. This understanding of the significance of the lampstand is supported by the angel's explanation at the end of the vision (Zch 4:14).

4:6-7 While **Zerubbabel** was a legitimate heir to David's throne, his role was apparently limited to governor, even though he is spoken of in elevated terms (Hg 2:21-23). In hyperbolic language, he would be able to move mountains. But since God deserved all the credit, shouts of **grace, grace** to the temple were very appropriate. Though God empowers human instruments, His intent is to negate any human claim to **strength** or **might**.

4:10 Typical of other visionary texts in the Bible, **these seven eyes of the LORD** involve symbolism that is left unexplained (cp. 3:9). Though it is often suggested that multiple eyes may signify wisdom or knowledge, uncertainty about such details reminds readers that God is transcendent and His ways are beyond human understanding.

4:11-14 Here the image of the **lampstand** (see note at vv. 2-3) becomes even more otherworldly. Given the placement of this vision next to the preceding one, it is likely that **the**

said, "who stand by the Lord of the whole earth."[a]

Sixth Vision: Flying Scroll

5 I looked up again and saw a flying scroll.[b] [2]"What do you see?" he asked me.

"I see a flying scroll," I replied, "30 feet[A] long and 15 feet[B] wide."[c]

[3]Then he said to me, "This is the curse[d] that is going out over the whole land, for every thief will be removed according to what is written on one side, and everyone who swears falsely will be removed according to what is written on the other side. [4]I will send it out,"[e]—this is the declaration of the Lord of •Hosts—"and it will enter the house of the thief and the house of the one who swears falsely by My name. It will stay inside his house and destroy it along with its timbers and stones."[f]

Seventh Vision: Woman in the Basket

[5]Then the angel who was speaking with me came forward and told me, "Look up and see what this is that is approaching."

[6]So I asked, "What is it?"

He responded, "It's a measuring basket[c]

that is approaching." And he continued, "This is their iniquity[D] in all the land." [7]Then a lead cover was lifted, and there was a woman[g] sitting inside the basket.[h] [8]"This is Wickedness," he said. He shoved her down into the basket and pushed the lead weight over its opening. [9]Then I looked up and saw two women approaching with the wind in their wings. Their wings were like those of a stork,[i] and they lifted up the basket between earth and sky.

[10]So I asked the angel who was speaking with me, "Where are they taking the basket?"

[11]"To build a shrine for it in the land of •Shinar,"[j] he told me. "When that is ready, the basket will be placed there on its pedestal."

Eighth Vision: Four Chariots

6 Then I looked up again and saw four chariots coming from between two mountains. And the mountains were made of bronze. [2]The first chariot had red horses,[k] the second chariot black horses,[l] [3]the third chariot white horses,[m] and the fourth chariot dappled[n] horses—all strong horses. [4]So I inquired of the angel who was speaking with me, "What are these, my lord?"

[5]The angel told me, "These are the four

Cross references
a4:14 Rv 11:3-4
b5:1 Ezk 2:9-10; Rv 5:1; 10:2
c5:2 Ex 26:15-25; 1Kg 6:3; 1Pt 4:17
d5:3 Dt 11:26-28; 28:15-68
e5:4 Ps 147:15; Is 55:11
f5:4 Ezr 6:11; Dn 2:5; 3:29
g5:7 Hs 9:15; Rv 17:1
h Lv 19:36; Dt 25:14; Pr 20:10; Ezk 45:10; Am 8:5
i5:9 Jr 8:7
j5:11 Gn 11:9
k6:2 Rv 6:4
l Rv 6:5-6
m6:3 Rv 6:2; 19:11
n Gn 31:10,12

A5:2 Lit 20 cubits　B5:2 Lit 10 cubits　C5:6 Lit It's an ephah　D5:6 One Hb ms, LXX, Syr; other Hb mss read eye

two anointed ones (Hb "two men of oil"; v. 14) are Joshua and Zerubbabel.

5:1-4 The sixth vision focuses on the Torah (the five books of the Law), which is a departure from the focus on Jerusalem and the temple in the preceding visions. The change involves a significant shift from encouragement to expectation, from revealing what God will do, to disclosing what He expects His people to do. Throughout the OT God's covenant with Israel was presented as a reciprocal relationship—blessings were dependent on compliance (Gn 17:1-2,9; Jr 18:7-10)—and that was no less true for the returnees. Though that point had already been made (Zch 1:3; 3:7), Zechariah developed it in this vision and the next.

5:2 The dimensions of the **scroll** are unusual, though the proportions suggest a partly unrolled scroll, as if it were waiting to be read.

5:3 The **curse** for disobedience is not unexpected (Dt 27:15-26; 28:15-68). The selection of two commandments (Ex 20:7,15) is probably representative of all 10 (for different selections, see Zch 7:4-14).

5:4 Everyone is held accountable to what the flying scroll says, with the consequences of disobedience expressed in vivid terms.

5:5-11 Idolatry was characteristic of Israel's disobedience, with memorable acts of idol worship recorded throughout their history (Ex 32:1-8; 1Kg 11:1-11). Yet God sent the Israelites into captivity in a land known for pagan deities. The seventh vision with "Wickedness" being transported in a basket back to Babylon signifies that idolatry belonged there, not in the promised land. But the basket held a woman, which may be an allusion to the Israelites. Hence, the imagery may also suggest that if the chosen people succumbed again to idolatry, they would be sent back into the captivity they had just escaped (see the same consequences announced for those who had come out of the captivity in Egypt; Dt 28:68).

5:7-8 God's chosen people are represented by a bride, or else by a prostitute when behaving in an idolatrous fashion (Ezk 16:8-19; Hs 1:2-3; 2:2-13). **This is Wickedness**, referring to the woman in a basket, was a shocking image, not intended to demean women but to symbolize anyone who was impure. The Hebrew word for "wickedness" is feminine in gender and may be connected with the Canaanite goddess Asherah.

5:11 Shinar is an older word for Babylon (Gn 11:1-2). If the chosen people were going to be idolatrous, they might as well do it in style back in Babylon, with a shrine in their honor.

6:1-8 The first and eighth visions functioned as bookends for the intervening visions and convey the same message: God is sovereign and is in control of the whole earth. However, there is a change of outcome between the two visions. While both picture four horses patrolling the earth, when the report came in the first vision that there was peace on earth, the angel asked a troubling question about the lack of peace in Jerusalem. Visions two through seven address this question. This eighth vision (vv. 1-8) provides the final resolution. God's Spirit is pacified.

6:1-3 The **mountains . . . made of bronze** may represent heaven or its gates since the **chariots** seem to originate there (v. 5).

6:5 The chariots are identified as **the four spirits of heaven**. The Hebrew term ruach can refer to spirit, breath, or wind (see note at 2:6). Combining both meanings—with the four

spirits[A,a] of heaven going out after presenting themselves to the Lord of the whole earth. [6]The one with the black horses is going to the land of the north, the white horses are going after them, but the dappled horses are going to the land of the south." [7]As the strong horses went out, they wanted to go patrol the earth, and the Lord said, "Go, patrol the earth." So they patrolled the earth. [8]Then He summoned me saying, "See, those going to the land of the north have pacified My Spirit in the northern land."

Crowning of the Branch

[9]The word of the Lord came to me:[b] [10]"Take an offering from the exiles, from Heldai, Tobijah, and Jedaiah, who have arrived from Babylon, and go that same day to the house of Josiah son of Zephaniah. [11]Take silver and gold, make crowns and place them on the head of Joshua son of Jehozadak, the high priest. [12]You are to tell him: This is what the Lord of •Hosts says: Here is a man whose name is Branch;[c] He will branch out from His place and build the Lord's temple. [13]Yes, He will build the Lord's temple; He will be clothed in splendor[d] and will sit on His throne and rule. There will also be a priest on His throne, and there will be peaceful counsel between the two of them.[e] [14]The crown will reside in the Lord's temple

as a memorial to Heldai, Tobijah, Jedaiah, and Hen[B] son of Zephaniah. [15]People who are far off will come and build the Lord's temple, and you will know that the Lord of Hosts has sent Me to you. This will happen when you fully obey the Lord your God."[f]

Disobedience and Fasting

[7] In the fourth year of King Darius,[g] the word of the Lord came to Zechariah on the fourth day of the ninth month, which is Chislev. [2]Now the people of Bethel had sent Sharezer, Regem-melech, and their men to plead for the Lord's favor[h] [3]by asking the priests who were at the house of the Lord of •Hosts as well as the prophets, "Should we mourn and fast in the fifth month as we have done these many years?"

[4]Then the word of the Lord of Hosts came to me: [5]"Ask all the people of the land and the priests: When you fasted and lamented in the fifth and in the seventh months for these 70 years, did you really fast for Me?[i] [6]When you eat and drink, don't you eat and drink simply for yourselves?[j] [7]Aren't these the words that the Lord proclaimed through the earlier prophets when Jerusalem was inhabited and secure,[c] along with its surrounding cities, and when the southern region and the Judean foothills were inhabited?"

[a]6:5 Jr 49:36; Rv 7:1-3
[b]6:9 Zch 4:8
[c]6:12 Zch 3:8
[d]6:13 1Ch 16:27; 29:25; Ps 96:6
[e]Ps 45:6-7; 110:1-7; Dn 7:9-14; Heb 1:3,13; Rv 5:6
[f]6:15 Dt 28:1
[g]7:1 Zch 1:1
[h]7:2 Zch 8:21-22
[i]7:5 Is 58:1-7
[j]7:6 1Co 10:31

[A]6:5 Or *winds*   [B]6:14 Probably Josiah   [C]7:7 Or *prosperous*

winds denoting the four directions of the compass—the point is that God's Spirit is present over **the whole earth**.

6:6-7 The horses going **to the land of the north** designate the nations that had destroyed Israel. The other direction in and out of Palestine was to the south. Thus the whole earth was **patrolled**.

6:8 Pacified My Spirit (or "My Spirit at rest") may be an allusion to the seventh day of creation.

6:9-15 This passage concludes the first section of Zechariah, presenting three prerequisites for rebuilding the temple. (1) There will need to be harmony between the civil and priestly leadership. (2) Israelites who have not returned from captivity should lend their support. (3) Everyone will need to be obedient to God's law.

6:10-11 The naming of specific individuals suggests that these are envoys representing Israelites still in exile in Babylon. Dedicating a memorial to them (v. 14) functioned as encouragement to those who had not returned. It was important to remain loyal to the homeland and to see themselves as part of God's chosen people.

6:12-13 On Zerubbabel as the **Branch**, see the fourth vision (see note at 3:8-10; cp. Hg 2:23). Joshua the high priest and Zerubbabel were previously identified as the key leaders in the building of the temple (see note at Zch 4:11-14; cp. Hg 2:2). Some see a reference to a messianic figure in this passage (see note at Zch 3:8-10).

6:15 People who are far off refers to exiles who had not returned but should have done so. Strengthening the call to

return, God's authority will be validated if they come back. **When you fully obey the Lord your God** is nearly an exact quote from Dt 28:1, which emphasizes contingency in the covenant. It also recalls Zechariah's introduction (Zch 1:3-6).

7:1-14 This second section of Zechariah begins in similar fashion to the first, looking back on the disobedient ancestors, their stubbornness, and the display of God's anger (1:4-6). The question still begged for an answer: Had the returnees learned the lesson of exile? Another issue under consideration was whether the temple in Jerusalem had regained its religious authority.

7:1 The second section of Zechariah is marked by a date two years later (cp. 1:1,7). Prophecies were commonly delivered first orally and written down later, sometimes many years later (Jr 36:2). In contrast to the first section of the book, which consists primarily of visions, this section is a sermon that develops themes introduced in the visions.

7:2-3 Bethel had been a center of worship for the northern 10 tribes (1Kg 12:29). Some Israelites who remained in the land during the exile worshiped there, but they were willing to defer to the authority of the religious leaders in Jerusalem as long as they found evidence of God's blessing being restored.

7:4-7 The answer to the question posed in verse 3 involved a series of convicting questions from the Lord of Hosts (v. 8), designed to accomplish three purposes: (1) to validate Zechariah as a true prophet of the Lord, for God was speaking through him as He did through the **earlier prophets**; (2) to demonstrate—by taking up the same concerns as the

⁸The word of the LORD came to Zechariah: ⁹"The LORD of Hosts says this: Make fair decisions.ᵃ Show faithful love and compassionᵇ to one another. ¹⁰Do not oppress the widow or the fatherless, the foreigner or the poor,ᶜ and do not plot evil in your hearts against one another.ᵈ ¹¹But they refused to pay attentionᵉ and turned a stubborn shoulder; they closed their ears so they could not hear.ᶠ ¹²They made their hearts like a rock so as not to obey the law or the words that the LORD of Hosts had sent by His Spirit through the earlier prophets.ᵍ Therefore great anger came from the LORD of Hosts. ¹³Just as He had called, and they would not listen, so when they called, I would not listen," says the LORD of Hosts. ¹⁴"I scattered them with a windstorm over all the nations that had not known them, and the land was left desolate behind them, with no one coming or going. They turned a pleasant land into a desolation."

Obedience and Feasting

8 The word of the LORD of •Hosts came: ²"The LORD of Hosts says this: I am extremely jealousʰ for •Zion; I am jealous for her

ᵃ7:9 Ex 18:19-23; Zch 8:16
ᵇJr 7:5-7; Hs 10:12; Mc 6:8
ᶜ7:10 Dt 14:29; 16:11
ᵈMt 22:39; Jms 3:5-6
ᵉ7:11 Zch 1:4
ᶠIs 6:10
ᵍ7:12 Jr 7:13,24
ʰ8:2 Zch 1:14
ⁱ8:3 Is 1:26
ʲ8:8 Is 11:11-12; Mc 2:12-13
ᵏGn 17:7-8; Dt 26:17-18; Rv 21:3

with great wrath." ³The LORD says this: "I will return to Zion and live in Jerusalem. Then Jerusalem will be called the Faithful City,ⁱ the mountain of the LORD of Hosts, and the Holy Mountain." ⁴The LORD of Hosts says this: "Old men and women will again sit along the streets of Jerusalem, each with a staff in hand because of advanced age. ⁵The streets of the city will be filled with boys and girls playing in them." ⁶The LORD of Hosts says this: "Though it may seem incredible to the remnant of this people in those days, should it also seem incredible to Me?"—this is the declaration of the LORD of Hosts. ⁷The LORD of Hosts says this: "I will save My people from the land of the east and the land of the west. ⁸I will bring them backʲ to live in Jerusalem. They will be My people, and I will be their faithful and righteous God."ᵏ

⁹The LORD of Hosts says this: "Let your hands be strong, you who now hear these words that the prophets spoke when the foundations were laid for the rebuilding of the temple, the house of the LORD of Hosts. ¹⁰For prior to those days neither man nor beast had wages. There was no safety from the enemy

---

prophets of the past (Jr 14:12; Am 5:21-23)—that God was endowing the returned community with the same authority it had before the exile; and (3) to underscore what God required in order to have His blessing.

7:8-10 The prophets typically took on the role of prosecutor, generally singling out three forms of disobedience: idolatry, empty worship, and social injustice. The latter is the focus here (cp. Is 1:17; 10:1-4; Mc 3:1-4; 6:8). Taking advantage of the poor earned the most severe punishment (Jr 5:28-29; Am 5:11-17).

7:11-12 **Stubborn shoulder . . . closed . . . ears**, and **hearts like a rock** are billboard-like metaphors for the insensitivity of the chosen people. They repeatedly refused to make Yahweh their God (see notes at 1:3; 1:4).

7:13-14 With the parade of sinfulness summarized in verses 4-12, God was justified in stirring up a **windstorm** that **scattered** the participants in all directions. Typical of prophetic language, judgment is expressed in hyperbole.

8:1-8 The sermon now turns dramatically from judgment to blessing, from complete dispersion to total restoration. Spectacular blessings from God had already been proclaimed in the visions (1:16-17; 2:4-5,11-12; 3:9-10), but here they are enlarged to hyperbolic proportions, seeking to change the hearers' perception of themselves. With the returnees barely existing in the land, Zechariah sought to energize them with the potential of becoming something magnificent, but it would occur only by an act of God (8:15).

8:2 The connection between a **jealous** God and a God of **wrath** is evident elsewhere in the Prophets (Ezk 16:38,42; Nah 1:2), suggesting that His deep desire for relationship was matched by decisive judgment against anything that

would interfere—whether from within or without (Zch 1:18-21; 2:9; 5:4; 7:12-14; cp. Heb 12:4-11).

8:3 In a remarkable reversal, God announced restoration instead of the dispersion just announced (7:14). Language of reversal is common in the Prophets (Ezk 16:59-60; Am 9:1-4,8-9,11-14). Whether announcing judgment or blessing, the object was the same—to enforce the covenant and encourage obedience. In the Prophets, **Jerusalem** was generally the centerpiece of God's blessing, with special emphasis on the **Holy Mountain** (Is 2:2-3; Mc 4:1-5). Calling Jerusalem the **Faithful City** was another reversal; it had previously been referred to as a harlot (Is 1:21; Jr 3:1-2; Lm 1:8-9).

8:4-5 In times of hostility a city's population could be decimated and the streets made unsafe, with the young and old being the first to suffer. The scene here offers an idyllic alternative.

8:6 Though the **incredible** blessings described may stagger the imagination, since God was the designer they were not too much to hope for (Jr 32:17,27). Several Hebrew terms suggest an allusion to Sarah's equally incredible experience—a miraculous pregnancy after years of barrenness (Gn 18:13-14). The reference to the **remnant** identifies the returnees as the true community of restoration, as promised in the Prophets (Is 10:21-22; 11:11,16; Jr 23:3).

8:7-8 **They will be My people and I will be their . . . God** indicates full restoration of the covenant relationship, in contrast to God's stunning declaration, "You are not My people and I will not be your God" (Hs 1:9).

8:9 Zechariah's sermon was presented approximately halfway between laying the foundation and the completion of the temple. **Let your hands be strong** (cp. v. 13; Hg 2:4)

for anyone who came or went, for I turned everyone against his neighbor. ¹¹But now, I will not treat the remnant of this people as in the former days"—this is the declaration of the LORD of Hosts. ¹²"For they will sow in peace: the vine will yield its fruit, the land will yield its produce, and the skies will yield their dew. I will give the remnant of this people all these things as an inheritance.ᵃ ¹³As you have been a curse among the nations,ᵇ house of Judah and house of Israel, so I will save you, and you will be a blessing.ᶜ Don't be afraid; let your hands be strong." ¹⁴For the LORD of Hosts says this: "As I resolved to treat you badly when your fathers provoked Me to anger, and I did not relent," says the LORD of Hosts, ¹⁵"so I have resolved again in these days to do what is good to Jerusalem and the house of Judah.ᵈ Don't be afraid. ¹⁶These are the things you must do: Speak truth to one another; make true and sound decisions within your *gates. ¹⁷Do not plot evilᵉ in your hearts against your neighbor,ᶠ and do not love perjury,ᵍ for I hate all this"—this is the LORD's declaration.

¹⁸Then the word of the LORD of Hosts came to me: ¹⁹"The LORD of Hosts says this: The fast of the fourth month,ʰ the fast of the fifth, the fast of the seventh, and the fast of the tenthⁱ will become times of joy, gladness, and cheerful festivals for the house of Judah. Therefore, love truth and peace." ²⁰The LORD of Hosts says this: "Peoples will yet come, the residents of many cities; ²¹the residents of one city will go to another, saying: Let's go at once to plead for the LORD's favor and to seek the LORD of Hosts. I am also going. ²²Many peoples and strong nations will come to seek the LORD of Hosts in Jerusalem and to plead for the LORD's favor."ʲ ²³The LORD of Hosts says this: "In those days, 10 men from nations of every language will grab the robe of a Jewish man tightly, urging: Let us go with you,ᵏ for we have heard that God is with you."

Judgment of Zion's Enemies

9   An *Oracle

The word of the LORD
is against the land of Hadrach,
and Damascusˡ is its resting place—
for the eyes of men
and all the tribes of Israel
are on the LORDᴬ—

ᵃ8:12 Dt 31:7; Jos 1:6; Is 49:8
ᵇ8:13 Dt 21:23; 2Kg 22:19
ᶜGn 12:2-3
ᵈ8:15 Dt 8:16; Jr 32:40-41; Ezk 36:11
ᵉ8:17 Mc 2:1
ᶠDt 10:12-22; Mt 22:39
ᵍLv 5:4; Nm 30:2; Jr 5:2
ʰ8:19 2Kg 25:3-4; Jr 39:2
ⁱ2Kg 25:1; Jr 39:1
ʲ8:20-22 Is 2:2-3; Jr 16:19; Mc 4:1-3; Mal 1:11-14
ᵏ8:23 Is 4:1
ˡ9:1 Gn 15:2; 1Kg 11:24; Sg 7:4; Is 7:8; Am 1:3

ᴬ9:1 Or *eyes of the LORD are on mankind—*

---

suggests that the sermon included encouragement for persistence in the work of rebuilding.

8:12 Everything the returnees could have hoped for was addressed in this sermon which was rich with blessings (cp. Ezk 34:25-29). The **peace . . . fruit . . . produce**, and **dew** were the opposite of their experience in the land during the previous two decades (Hg 1:6-11; 2:15-19).

8:16-17 The terms of the covenant made it clear that people determine their own destiny, while God responds accordingly (Jr 18:7-10). **These are things you must do** reveals that the function of the sermon was more than simply rebuilding the walls (v. 9). In order for the returnees to enjoy the incredible blessings that God offered, they would need to obey the covenant's standard of social justice (7:8-10).

8:19 In response to the question that initiated the sermon—whether it was necessary to continue fasting and mourning the destruction of Jerusalem (7:3,5)—the Lord announced a reversal. Fasts of lamentation were to be transformed into **times of joy, gladness, and cheerful festivals**.

8:20-22 The idea that **residents of many cities** of the world would come to Jerusalem is well attested in the OT (2:11; 14:16-19; 2Sm 22:45-46; 1Kg 10:23-25; 2Ch 9:22-24; Is 2:2-3; 27:13; 45:20; 60:3). As with Solomon, such an ingathering was a sign of greatness, both of Jerusalem and of God's presence. The image was a fitting conclusion to Zechariah's sermon. The seemingly insignificant city of Jerusalem was now seen as the most important city in the world.

8:23 In the ancient Near East, grabbing the hem of a garment was an act of submission and supplication. Since the Israelites spent years under foreign domination, to have Gentiles show submission to them would be an astonishing reversal (Gn 27:29).

9:1-17 The third section of Zechariah is different in many ways from the first and second sections, leading many commentators to conclude that it was written by a different person (see Introduction). It is an extended poem, beginning with a description of God as victorious Conqueror and King, and follows the pattern of oracles against the nations (see note at Am 1:3-2:16). Since poetry is often characterized by piling on images to emphasize a point, it is not surprising to find God's overpowering strength expressed in numerous ways and against many different

---

qatsaph

Hebrew Pronunciation	[kah TSAFF]
HCSB Translation	be angry, enraged, provoke to anger
Uses in Zechariah	4
Uses in the OT	34
Focus passage	Zechariah 8:14

Qatsaph means *be angry* (Gn 40:2). People *are furious* (Nm 31:14), *enraged* (Is 8:21), or *infuriated* (Est 2:21). God *grows angry* (Dt 1:34), *directs* fierce *anger* (Dt 9:19), or *vents wrath* (Nm 16:22). The causative verb denotes *provoke* (Dt 9:7), *provoke to anger* (Zch 8:14), or *anger* (Ps 106:32). *Qetseph* (28x) signifies divine *wrath* (21x: Nm 18:5) or *anger* (Is 54:8) and twice indicates human *anger* (Ec 5:17) or *fury* (Est 1:18). *Qatsaph* with *qetseph* implies being extremely angry (Zch 1:2). While Zch 1:15 mentions *being* a little *angry*, this root seems one of the strongest words for anger. *Qetseph* is synonymous with *chemah* ("wrath, fury"), but in a pair or series *qetseph* appears last, sometimes modified by "great," as the most intense word: God uprooted people in His anger, fury, and great *wrath* (Dt 29:28). Aramaic counterparts of the verb (Dn 2:12) and noun (Ezr 7:23) occur.

² and also against Hamath,^a
    which borders it,
as well as Tyre^b and Sidon,^c
    though they are very shrewd.
³ Tyre has built herself a fortress;
    she has heaped up silver like dust
    and gold like the dirt of the streets.
⁴ Listen! The Lord will impoverish her
    and cast her wealth into the sea;
    she herself will be consumed by fire.^d
⁵ Ashkelon will see it and be afraid;
    Gaza too, and will writhe in great pain,
    as will Ekron, for her hope will fail.
    There will cease to be a king in Gaza,
    and Ashkelon will become uninhabited.
⁶ A mongrel people will live in Ashdod,
    and I will destroy the pride
      of the Philistines.^e
⁷ I will remove the blood
    from their mouths
    and the detestable things^f
    from between their teeth.
    Then they too will become a remnant
      for our God;
    they will become like a clan in Judah
    and Ekron like the Jebusites.^g

⁸ I will set up camp at My house
      against an army,^A
    against those who march
      back and forth,
    and no oppressor will march
      against them again,
    for now I have seen with My own eyes.

The Coming of Zion's King

⁹ Rejoice greatly, Daughter •Zion!
    Shout in triumph, Daughter Jerusalem!
    Look, your King is coming to you;
    He is righteous and victorious,^B
    humble and riding on a donkey,
    on a colt, the foal of a donkey.^h
¹⁰ I will cut off the chariot from Ephraim
    and the horse from Jerusalem.
    The bow of war will be removed,
    and He will proclaim peace
      to the nations.
    His dominion will extend from sea
      to sea,
    from the Euphrates River
    to the ends of the earth.ⁱ
¹¹ As for you,
    because of the blood of your covenant,^j

Cross references (center column):
^a9:2 2Kg 14:25
^bJos 19:29; Is 23:1
^cGn 10:15
^d9:4 Ezk 26:4-6; 27:27
^e9:6 Am 1:6-8; Zph 2:4-6
^f9:7 Lv 11:10; Dt 29:17; Dn 11:31
^g2Sm 5:6-10; 24:16-25
^h9:9 Is 62:11; Mt 21:5; Jn 12:15
ⁱ9:10 Ps 72:8; Mc 7:12
^j9:11 Heb 10:29; 13:20

---

^A9:8 Or *house as a guard*   ^B9:9 Or *and has salvation*

---

enemies. The poet included obscure cities and regions not mentioned elsewhere in the Bible (Zch 9:1-2), with little archaeological or literary data preserved about them. The intent was to underscore the contrast between the enemies who would be consumed by God's power and the new king ruling from Jerusalem.

9:1 **Oracle** denotes a message from God, often language of judgment, here marking the beginning of a new section. For **the eyes of men and all the tribes of Israel** to be on the Lord would be a remarkable reversal, suggesting the reuniting of the 12 tribes (Judah and Israel, cp. 8:13) and the inclusion of Gentiles.

ga'on

Hebrew Pronunciation	[gah OWN]
HCSB Translation	pride
Uses in Zechariah	3
Uses in the OT	49
Focus passage	Zechariah 9:6

Ga'on, part of a large word family, denotes good (Is 4:2) or bad (Lv 26:19) *pride*. It is *majesty* (Ex 15:7) or *splendor* (Is 14:11) but also *arrogance* (Hs 5:5). *Ga'on* means *thicket* (Jr 12:5). Adjectivally, it is *proud* (Jb 38:11) or *majestic* (Mc 5:4). The verb *ga'ah* (7x) signifies *be exalted* (Ex 15:1) or *proud* (Jb 10:16), *rise* (Ezk 47:5), and *grow* (Jb 8:11). *Ga'awah* (19x) is good (Jb 41:15) and bad (Is 9:9) *pride*. It is *majesty* (Dt 33:26), positive *boasting* (Dt 33:29), and *triumph* (Is 13:3) but also *haughtiness* (Is 16:6), *arrogance* (Ps 10:2), and *turmoil* (Ps 46:3). The adjective *ge'eh* (8x), *proud* (Is 2:12), functions nominally as *pride* (Jr 48:29) or *proud person* (Jb 40:11). *Ge'wah* (3x) and *ge'ah* (Pr 8:13) denote *pride* (Jb 33:17). Once *ge'wah* imperatively requests *lifting up* (Jb 22:29). *Ga'ayon* (Ps 123:4) and *ge'* (Is 16:6) signify *proud*.

9:3-4 **Tyre** was well known as a naval and commercial power with an impregnable fortified island one-half mile off the Mediterranean coast. Alexander the Great and his army spent seven months dismantling the city on the mainland and building a causeway to the island. Tyre came under frequent prophetic judgment in the Prophets (Is 23; Jr 25:17-22; Ezk 26–28; Am 1:9-10).

9:5-7 The cities of Philistia represented the archenemy of the Israelites in the days of the monarchy. Removing **blood from their mouths** suggests judgment that was also an act of cleansing, bringing the people into conformity with God's law (Lv 17:11-12). Announcing that **they too will become a remnant** is a striking reversal, an extraordinary measure of divine compassion granted to enemies (cp. 2:11; 8:20-23).

9:8 The preceding verses denote the conqueror's movement through Palestine, from north to south, eventually arriving in Jerusalem—the path followed by Alexander the Great (332 B.C.). Some see the statement that **no oppressor will march against them again** as fulfilled when Alexander spared Jerusalem, but the city's subsequent destruction by the Romans in A.D. 70 suggests that it is better to understand the statement as poetic language for God's general protection (Is 45:17; Jr 17:25).

9:9 Since the days of David and Solomon the chosen people had longed for a king of similar stature, but none had come forth until the announcement of this **King** who is **righteous**. Instead of riding a mule, which was common for kings (see note at 2Sm 13:29), he would ride a **donkey**—signifying unexpected humility. This prophecy was recognized by early Christians as applying to Jesus' triumphal entry into Jerusalem (Mt 21:5; Jn 12:15).

9:10-15 The image of God as Divine Warrior is common in

I will release your prisoners
from the waterless cistern.[a]
12 Return to a stronghold,
you prisoners who have hope;
today I declare that I will restore
double to you.[b]
13 For I will bend Judah as My bow;
I will fill that bow with Ephraim.
I will rouse your sons, Zion,
against your sons, Greece.[A,c]
I will make you like a warrior's sword.
14 Then the LORD will appear over them,
and His arrow will fly like lightning.
The Lord GOD will sound the trumpet
and advance with the southern storms.[d]
15 The LORD of •Hosts will defend them.
They will consume and conquer
with slingstones;
they will drink and be rowdy as if
with wine.[e]
They will be as full as
the sprinkling basin,[f]
like those at the corners of the altar.[g]
16 The LORD their God will save them
on that day
as the flock of His people;[h]
for they are like jewels in a crown,[i]
sparkling over His land.
17 How lovely and beautiful they will be!
Grain will make
the young men flourish,
and new wine, the young women.

The LORD Restores His People

10 Ask the LORD for rain
in the season of spring rain.
The LORD makes the rain clouds,
and He will give them showers of rain
and crops in the field for everyone.[j]
2 For the idols speak falsehood,
and the diviners[k] see illusions;
they relate empty dreams
and offer empty comfort.
Therefore the people wander like sheep;
they suffer affliction because there is
no shepherd.
3 My anger burns against the shepherds,
so I will punish the leaders.[B]
For the LORD of •Hosts has tended
His flock,
the house of Judah;
He will make them
like His majestic steed in battle.
4 The cornerstone[l] will come from
Judah.[C]
The tent peg[m] will come from them
and also the battle bow[n] and
every[D] ruler.
Together 5 they will be like warriors
in battle
trampling down the mud of the streets.
They will fight because the LORD is
with them,
and they will put horsemen to shame.
6 I will strengthen the house of Judah
and deliver the house of Joseph.[E]
I will restore[F] them
because I have compassion on them,
and they will be
as though I had never rejected them.[o]
For I am •Yahweh their God,
and I will answer them.
7 Ephraim[p] will be like a warrior,
and their hearts will be glad as if
with wine.
Their children will see it and be glad;[q]
their hearts will rejoice in Yahweh.
8 I will whistle[r] and gather them
because I have redeemed[s] them;
they will be as numerous as
they once were.

[a]9:11 Gn 37:24; Jr 38:6 [b]9:12 Jb 42:10; Is 61:7; Jr 16:18 [c]9:13 Dn 8:21; 10:20 [d]9:14 Ps 83:15 [e]9:15 Nm 23:24 [f]Ex 27:3 [g]Lv 1:5,11; 3:2 [h]9:16 Ezk 36:38 [i]Lv 8:9 [j]10:1 Dt 28:12; Is 30:23; Jr 51:16 [k]10:2 Jr 27:9; Mc 3:7 [l]10:4 Jdg 20:2; 1Sm 14:38; Ps 118:22; Is 28:16 [m]Jdg 4:21 [n]2Kg 13:15-17; Rv 6:2 [o]10:6 Ps 103:12 [p]10:7 Is 7:8 [q]Ex 4:14; Ps 16:9 [r]10:8 Is 5:26; 7:18 [s]Ex 13:13; 21:8; 34:20; Jb 5:20; Ps 130:8; Is 51:11; Mc 6:4

[A]9:13 Lit *Javan* [B]10:3 Lit *male goats* [C]10:4 Lit *them* [D]10:4 Lit *also from them the . . . , from them every* [E]10:6 = the northern kingdom [F]10:6 Other Hb mss, LXX read *settle*

the OT (Ex 15:3-12; Jos 5:13-15; Hab 3:9-15). In this passage His actions are typical of a victorious conqueror, cutting down **chariot . . . horse**, and **bow**, extending the kingdom's **dominion**, releasing **prisoners**, and taking on distant enemies (**Greece**).

10:1-2 With a lack of leadership (referred to as shepherds, probably designating the leaders of the community), the Israelites had been turning to false sources of blessings. Zechariah rebuked them, instructing them to **ask the LORD for rain** (see Jr 14:22; Jl 2:23) instead of appealing to household deities (**idols**) and false prophets (**diviners**), which was forbidden in the Law (Dt 18:9-14).

10:3-5 The phrase **My anger burns against the shepherds** reflects a common concern of the prophets about inept and misguided leadership (Ezk 34:1-10; Mc 3:1-4). Conversely, when God **tended His flock**, they became like a **majestic steed**, a **cornerstone**, a **tent peg**, a **battle bow**, or as "jewels in a crown, sparkling over His land" (9:16). They will even **put horsemen to shame**. Such poetic images are designed to evoke desire among readers to be empowered in similar ways. "Cornerstone" can be a metaphor for leader (Is 19:13). It is used as a metaphor for Jesus in the NT (Ac 4:11; 1Pt 2:6-8).

10:6-9 Judah refers to the southern two tribes, while the northern 10 tribes can be denoted by **Joseph**, his son **Ephraim**, or Israel. When the chosen people were marched hundreds of miles into exile (Israel into Assyria and Judah into Babylonia), it seemed impossible that they could ever return (see note at 1:2). Once some exiles from Judah had returned, the lingering question concerned Israel. After almost 200 years in Assyria, was restoration to their land even possible? The answer was yes. God would **whistle and**

⁹ Though I sow^a them
      among the nations,
they will remember^b Me
      in the distant lands;
they and their children will live
      and return.
¹⁰ I will bring them back from the land
      of Egypt
and gather them from Assyria.
I will bring them to the land of Gilead^c
      and to Lebanon,
but it will not be enough for them.
¹¹ Yahweh^A will pass through the sea
      of distress
and strike the waves of the sea;
all the depths of the Nile will dry up.^d
The pride of Assyria will be
      brought down,
and the scepter of Egypt will come
      to an end.
¹² I will strengthen^e them in Yahweh,
and they will march^f in His name—
            this is Yahweh's declaration.

Israel's Shepherds: Good and Bad

11 Open your gates, Lebanon,
and fire will consume your cedars.^g
² Wail, cypress,^h for the cedar has fallen;
the glorious trees are destroyed!
Wail, oaks of Bashan,ⁱ
for the stately forest has fallen!
³ Listen to the wail^j of the shepherds,
for their glory is destroyed.
Listen to the roar of young lions,^k

for the thickets of the Jordan^l
are^B destroyed.

⁴ •Yahweh my God says this: "Shepherd the flock intended for slaughter. ⁵ Those who buy them slaughter them but are not punished.^m Those who sell them say: Praise the LORD because I have become rich! Even their own shepherds have no compassion for them. ⁶ Indeed, I will no longer have compassion on the inhabitants of the land"—this is the LORD's declaration. "Instead, I will turn everyone over to his neighbor and his king. They will devastate the land, and I will not deliver it from them."ⁿ

⁷ So I shepherded the flock intended for slaughter, the afflicted of the flock.^C I took two staffs, calling one Favor^o and the other Union, and I shepherded the flock. ⁸ In one month I got rid of three shepherds. I became impatient with them, and they also detested me. ⁹ Then I said, "I will no longer shepherd you. Let what is dying die, and let what is going astray go astray; let the rest devour each other's flesh." ¹⁰ Next I took my staff called Favor and cut it in two, annulling the covenant I had made with all the peoples. ¹¹ It was annulled on that day, and so the afflicted of the flock^D who were watching me knew that it was the word of the LORD. ¹² Then I said to them, "If it seems right to you, give me my wages; but if not, keep them." So they weighed my wages, 30 pieces of silver.^p

¹³ "Throw it to the potter,"^E the LORD said to

Cross references: ⁹10:9 Gn 26:12; Ex 23:16; Ps 126:5 ᵇGn 40:23; Jos 1:13 ᶜ10:10 Gn 31:21; Dt 34:1; Ps 60:7 ᵈ10:11 Gn 8:7; Jos 2:10; 4:23; 1Kg 17:7; Jb 12:15; Ps 74:15; Pr 17:22 ᵉ10:12 Zch 10:6 ᶠJos 6:3; Ps 68:7; Jr 46:9 ᵍ11:1 Jdg 9:15; 2Kg 19:23; Ps 29:5; Sg 5:15; Is 2:13 ʰ11:2 Is 14:8 ⁱIs 2:13; Ezk 27:6 ʲ11:3 Is 15:8; Zph 1:10 ᵏJb 4:10; Ps 34:10; Is 5:29; Nah 2:11 ˡJr 49:19 ᵐ11:5 Ps 34:22 ⁿ11:6 Jr 13:14; Lm 2:2,17,21; Ezk 7:4,9 ᵒ11:7 Ps 90:17; Zch 11:10 ᵖ11:12 Ex 21:32

A10:11 Lit *He*   B11:3 Lit *for the majesty of the Jordan is*   C11:7 LXX reads *slaughter that belonged to the sheep merchants*
D11:11 LXX reads *and the sheep merchants*   e11:13 Syr reads *treasury*

gather them and reverse His rejection of them (Ezk 37:15-28; Hs 1:10-11). However, there is no biblical evidence that this was fulfilled. Today, after thousands of years and with the people now completely absorbed by intermarriage into other cultures, a return seems improbable (Zch 11:14). Interpreters are divided on how the ultimate fulfillment will come about and what it will look like.

10:10-12 Egypt and **Assyria** were representative of various nations where the chosen people went into captivity. Even though the promised land is expanded to include outlying regions (**Gilead** and **Lebanon**), even that **will not be enough** for the number of returnees.

11:1-11 The rich symbolism in this scene recalls the visions in the first section of the book, though here the form is more like a parable. Given the failure of the shepherds to lead the people in the right paths (see note at 10:3-5), God appointed the prophet as an imaginary shepherd. When the people failed to follow him, the Lord canceled His relationship with them and turned them over to worthless leaders.

11:1-3 Some commentators think this poem—an imaginary portrayal of the humbling of the **stately forest** of Lebanon—belongs with the preceding chapter, as a continuation of judgment on Israel's enemies, but it more likely introduces the judgment and humbling of Israel's leaders in chapter

11. Open your gates, Lebanon may be a symbolic reference to the temple and its gates (timbers from Lebanon were used in the building of the temple), which suggests that the leadership in view is that of the religious authorities. Thus, the emphasis on the temple in earlier chapters continues.

11:4-6 The temple precinct was full of sheep **intended for slaughter**, which was their proper purpose in the sacrificial system. But they had become objects for personal gain, and with **their own shepherds** having **no compassion for them**, God withdrew and turned neighboring kingdoms loose on the chosen people and their land. As is often true, sin can overturn God's stated purposes and intended blessings (Gn 3:14-24).

11:7-9 The shepherd named one of his staffs **Favor** (or Grace) and the other **Union** (or Unity), the former symbolizing the covenant (v. 10) and the latter representing reunited Israel (v. 14). But the failure of the shepherds to be good leaders resulted in letting the people self-destruct. The phrase **three shepherds** probably does not refer to anyone in particular.

11:12-13 The **30 pieces of silver** may be an allusion to the value of a slave (Ex 21:32). Throwing the **magnificent price** (probably sarcastic) to the **potter** in the temple was an act of desecration. Matthew used some of this wording in

me—this magnificent price I was valued by them. So I took the 30 pieces of silver and threw it into the house of the Lord, to the potter.[A,a] [14]Then I cut in two my second staff, Union, annulling the brotherhood between Judah and Israel.

[15]The Lord also said to me: "Take the equipment of a foolish shepherd. [16]I am about to raise up a shepherd in the land who will not care for those who are going astray, and he will not seek the lost[B] or heal the broken. He will not sustain the healthy,[c] but he will devour the flesh of the fat sheep[b] and tear off their hooves.

[17] Woe to the worthless shepherd
who deserts the flock![c]
May a sword strike[D] his arm
and his right eye!
May his arm wither away
and his right eye go completely blind!"

Judah's Security

12

An •Oracle

The word of the Lord concerning Israel.
A declaration of the Lord,
who stretched out the heavens,[d]
laid the foundation of the earth,[e]
and formed the spirit of man
within him.

[2]"Look, I will make Jerusalem a cup that causes staggering[f] for the peoples who surround the city. The siege against Jerusalem will also involve Judah. [3]On that day I will make Jerusalem a heavy stone for all the peoples; all who try to lift it will injure them-

selves severely when all the nations of the earth gather against her.[g] [4]"On that day"—this is the Lord's declaration—"I will strike every horse with panic and its rider with madness.[h] I will keep a watchful eye on[i] the house of Judah but strike all the horses of the nations with blindness. [5]Then each of the leaders of Judah will think to himself: The residents of Jerusalem are my strength through the Lord of •Hosts, their God. [6]On that day I will make the leaders of Judah like a firepot in a woodpile, like a flaming torch among sheaves; they will consume all the peoples around them on the right and the left, while Jerusalem continues to be inhabited on its site, in Jerusalem. [7]The Lord will save the tents of Judah first, so that the glory of David's house and the glory of Jerusalem's residents may not be greater than that of Judah. [8]On that day the Lord will defend the inhabitants of Jerusalem, so that on that day the one who is weakest among them will be like David on that day, and the house of David will be like God, like the Angel of the Lord, before them. [9]On that day I will set out to destroy all the nations that come against Jerusalem.

Mourning for the Pierced One

[10]"Then I will pour out a spirit[E,j] of grace and prayer on the house of David and the residents of Jerusalem, and they will look at[F] Me whom they pierced. They will mourn for Him as one mourns for an only child and weep bitterly for Him as one weeps for a firstborn.[k] [11]On that day the mourning in Jerusalem will be as great as the mourning of Hadad-rimmon in the plain of Megiddo. [12]The land will mourn,

Cross references (center column)

a11:13 Mt 26:15; 27:3-10
b11:16 Ezk 34:3-4
c11:17 Jr 23:2
d12:1 Is 45:12; 51:13; Jr 10:12; 51:15
eJb 38:4; Heb 1:10
f12:2 Is 51:22-23; Jr 25:15-16; Rv 16:19
g12:3 Jl 3:1-2
h12:4 Dt 28:28
iIs 37:17; Jr 32:19
j12:10 Ezk 39:29; Jl 2:28-29; Zch 4:6
kJn 19:37; Rv 1:7

---

reference to Judas (Mt 27:9-10), though stating that it was Jeremiah's prophecy that was fulfilled (Jr 32:6-9).

11:14 The hoped-for reunification of Israel and Judah was canceled (see note at 10:6-9).

11:15-16 If the people were not going to follow a good shepherd, they might as well follow a bad one, so God responded in satire and appointed the prophet as a **foolish shepherd**.

12:1 Oracle marks the beginning of the fourth section of Zechariah (see note at 9:1), which recapitulates themes treated earlier in the book. God's great power—highlighted by reference to creation—is now focused on Jerusalem, which God promised to protect and exalt so it would be bigger and more significant than all other nations.

12:2-8 A cup that causes staggering recalls other prophets' descriptions of the cup of God's wrath (Jr 25:15-17,27-29; cp. Is 51:17; Ezk 23:32-34). What may taste good at first—when the nations attack Jerusalem—will leave them staggering around helplessly. Jerusalem's destruction would involve moving **heavy** stones, but in this case the stones would be too big, resulting in severe injury to anyone who attempted

it. Placing a **firepot in a woodpile** or a **flaming torch among sheaves** would result in a quick conflagration, signaling the ease with which Jerusalem's enemies would be defeated. An especially vivid picture is seeing **the one who is weakest** transformed into a superior fighter **like David**. To declare that Jerusalem would become the **house of David** and that it would be **like God** is the highest exaltation possible—an amazing reversal from God forsaking His people (11:9-10).

12:3 On that day may be translated "in the future." **When all the nations of the earth gather against her** may be a hyperbolic statement and not necessarily a reference to a final epic battle, even as it would be possible to refer to the many nations that had attacked Jerusalem in the past as "all the nations of the world." However, some commentators think this language refers to a specific battle in the end times (Armageddon). In either case, Zechariah's intent was to energize the current inhabitants of Jerusalem by looking ahead to God's blessings.

12:10-14 The announcement of God's blessing on Jerusalem shifts to spiritual reconciliation, which is dependent on divine grace and human contrition. The interpretive crux

every family by itself: the family of David's house by itself and their women by themselves; the family of Nathan's[A,a] house by itself and their women by themselves; [13]the family of Levi's house by itself and their women by themselves; the family of Shimei[B,b] by itself and their women by themselves; [14]all the remaining families, every family by itself, and their women by themselves.

God's People Cleansed

13 "On that day a fountain will be opened for the house of David and for the residents of Jerusalem, to wash away sin and impurity.[c] [2]On that day"—this is the declaration of the LORD of •Hosts—"I will erase the names of the idols from the land, and they will no longer be remembered. I will remove the prophets[c] and the •unclean spirit from the land. [3]If a man still prophesies, his father and his mother who bore him will say to him: You cannot remain alive because you have spoken falsely in the name of •Yahweh. When he prophesies, his father and his mother who bore him will pierce him through.[d] [4]On that day every prophet will be ashamed of his vision when he prophesies; they will not put on a hairy cloak[e] in order to deceive. [5]He will say: I am not a prophet; I work the land, for a man purchased[D] me as a servant since my youth.[f] [6]If someone asks him: What are these wounds[g] on your chest?[E]—then he will an-

swer: I received the wounds in the house of my friends.

[7]　Sword, awake against My shepherd,
　　against the man who is My associate—
　　　　this is the declaration
　　　　　of the LORD of Hosts.
　　Strike the shepherd, and the sheep
　　　will be scattered;[h]
　　I will also turn My hand
　　　against the little ones.
[8]　In the whole land—
　　　　this is the LORD's declaration—
　　two-thirds[F] will be cut off and die,
　　but a third will be left in it.
[9]　I will put this third through the fire;
　　I will refine them as silver is refined
　　and test them as gold is tested.
　　They will call on My name,
　　and I will answer them.
　　I will say: They are My people,
　　and they will say: Yahweh is our God."

The LORD's Triumph and Reign

14 A day of the LORD is coming when your plunder will be divided in your presence. [2]I will gather all the nations against Jerusalem for battle.[i] The city will be captured, the houses looted, and the women raped. Half the city will go into exile, but the rest of the people will not be removed from the city. [3]Then the LORD will go out to fight against

[a]12:12 2Sm 5:14; Lk 3:31
[b]12:13 Ex 6:17; Nm 3:18; 1Ch 6:17
[c]13:1 Zch 3:1-10
[d]13:3 Dt 13:5; 18:20; Jr 14:14
[e]13:4 1Kg 19:13,19; 2Kg 2:8
[f]13:5 Am 7:14
[g]13:6 1Kg 18:28
[h]13:7 Mt 26:31; Mk 14:27
[i]14:2 Jl 3:2; Zch 12:2-3

A12:12 = a son of David　　B12:13 = a descendant of Levi　　C13:2 = false prophets　　D13:5 Or sold　　E13:6 Lit wounds between your hands　　F13:8 Lit two-thirds in it

---

is the identity of **Me whom they pierced**, especially when the prophet declared, **They will mourn for Him**. The best explanation is that God's true followers will recognize that by their disobedience and rejection of the divine Shepherd, they in effect pierced God's soul. In their remorse, family after family will weep with the deepest bitterness imaginable. This verse also anticipates Jesus' crucifixion, as indicated by the quotation in Jn 19:37.

13:1-6 Continuing the theme of reconciliation begun in 12:10 (cp. 5:5-11), the oracle turns to two of the most heinous sins that needed to be washed away—worshiping other gods and prophesying falsely in God's name. False prophecy is so detestable that a counterfeit prophet's own parents would kill him.

13:2 Sin as defilement of **the land** (see Ezk 36:17-19; Hs 1:2) signifies the cancellation of the covenant relationship since the land was an integral element in the covenant promises (Gn 13:15-17; 15:18; 17:8).

13:4-6 A **hairy cloak** is an allusion to Elijah's clothes (2Kg 1:8), not necessarily an indication that all prophets dressed this way. The attempt of false prophets to hide their identity involved displaying **wounds** that were probably self-inflicted (1Kg 18:28). Claiming that the "wounds" were routine from a scuffle with **friends** would lead to more suspicion because the Hebrew word translated "friends" may denote illicit lovers.

13:7-9 Though the identity of the **shepherd** is ambiguous, the overall point of the passage is clear: to purge and refine, separating the true from the false. God desires followers worthy of the affirmation that **they are My people** (see note at 8:7-8). God **scattered** them and cut off **two-thirds** in order to gain a remnant that would sincerely say, **Yahweh is our God**. Possibilities for the meaning of "My shepherd" being struck include a flashback to striking the arm of the worthless shepherd (11:17). Alternatively, Jesus' quote of the lines with regard to His death and His disciples falling away (Mt 26:31) suggests that "shepherd" may have anticipated the messianic king. However, it is possible that Jesus was using the verse proverbially rather than declaring the fulfillment of Zechariah's prediction.

14:1-21 The book of Zechariah ends in classic prophetic fashion. The nations attack Jerusalem, God intervenes and blesses Jerusalem miraculously, God announces curses for Jerusalem's enemies, and the peoples of the world go up to Jerusalem to worship. Everything from cooking pots to horses' bells is set apart as **HOLY TO THE LORD**, a privilege previously extended only to the temple and priests (Ex 28:36-38) but actually intended for the entire nation of Israel (Ex 19:6). For the prophet's audience, this would have been unimaginable, yet invigorating.

14:3-5 The venue for God's great triumph is the city of Jerusalem under severe duress, not only being plundered but with the enemy dividing up belongings in the presence of

those nations as He fights on a day of battle.[a] [4]On that day His feet will stand on the •Mount of Olives,[b] which faces Jerusalem on the east. The Mount of Olives will be split in half from east to west, forming a huge valley, so that half the mountain will move to the north and half to the south. [5]You will flee by My mountain valley,[A] for the valley of the mountains will extend to Azal. You will flee as you fled[B] from the earthquake in the days of Uzziah king of Judah.[c] Then the Lord my God will come and all the holy ones with Him.[C,d]

[6]On that day there will be no light; the sunlight and moonlight[D] will diminish.[E,e] [7]It will be a day known only to •Yahweh,[f] without day or night, but there will be light at evening.

[8]On that day living water will flow out from Jerusalem,[g] half of it toward the eastern sea[F] and the other half toward the western sea,[G] in summer and winter alike. [9]On that day Yahweh will become King over all the earth[h]—Yahweh alone, and His name alone.[i] [10]All the land from Geba[j] to Rimmon[k] south of Jerusalem will be changed into a plain. But Jerusalem will be raised up and will remain[H] on its site from the Benjamin Gate[l] to the place of the First Gate,[I] to the Corner Gate, and from the Tower of Hananel to the royal winepresses.[m] [11]People will live there, and never again will there be a curse of •complete destruction. So Jerusalem will dwell in security.

[12]This will be the plague the Lord strikes all the peoples with, who have warred against Jerusalem: their flesh will rot while they stand on their feet, their eyes will rot in their sockets, and their tongues will rot in their mouths.

[13]On that day a great panic from the Lord will be among them, so that each will seize the hand of another, and the hand of one will rise against the other. [14]Judah will also fight at Jerusalem, and the wealth of all the surrounding nations will be collected: gold, silver, and clothing in great abundance.[n] [15]The same plague as the previous one will strike[J] the horses, mules, camels, donkeys, and all the animals that are in those camps.

[16]Then all the survivors from the nations that came against Jerusalem will go up year after year to worship the King, the Lord of •Hosts, and to celebrate the Festival of Booths.[o] [17]Should any of the families of the earth not go up to Jerusalem to worship the King, the Lord of Hosts, rain will not fall on them. [18]And if the people[K] of Egypt will not go up and enter, then rain will not fall on them; this will be the plague the Lord inflicts on the nations who do not go up to celebrate the Festival of Booths. [19]This will be the punishment of Egypt and all the nations that do not go up to celebrate the Festival of Booths.

[20]On that day, the words

HOLY TO THE LORD

will be on the bells of the horses.[p] The pots in the house of the Lord will be like the sprinkling basins before the altar. [21]Every pot in Jerusalem and in Judah will be holy to the Lord of Hosts. Everyone who sacrifices will come and take some of the pots to cook in. And on that day there will no longer be a Canaanite[L] in the house of the Lord of Hosts.

[a]14:3 Rv 19:11-21
[b]14:4 Ezk 11:23; Ac 1:11-12
[c]14:5 Am 1:1
[d]Ps 89:5-7; Mt 25:31
[e]14:6 Is 13:10; Jl 2:10; 3:15
[f]14:7 Mt 24:36
[g]14:8 Ezk 41:7; 47:1-12; Jl 3:18; Rv 8:8-9; 16:3
[h]14:9 Mt 25:31
[i]Dt 4:35,39; 6:4; Is 45:5
[j]14:10 2Kg 23:8
[k]Neh 11:29
[l]Jr 37:13
[m]Neh 3:1; 12:39; Jr 31:38-40
[n]14:14 Mc 4:13; Hg 2:7
[o]14:16 Lv 23:33-36
[p]14:20 Ex 28:36; 39:30

[A]14:5 Some Hb mss, LXX, Sym, Tg read *You will be blocked—the valley of My mountains—*   [B]14:5 LXX reads *It will be blocked as it was blocked*   [C]14:5 Some Hb mss, LXX, Vg, Tg, Syr; other Hb mss read *you*   [D]14:6 Lit *light; the precious things*   [E]14:6 LXX, Sym, Syr, Tg, Vg read *no light or cold or ice*   [F]14:8 = the Dead Sea   [G]14:8 = the Mediterranean Sea   [H]14:10 Or *will be inhabited*   [I]14:10 Or *the former gate*   [J]14:15 Lit *be on*   [K]14:18 Lit *family*   [L]14:21 Or *merchant*

the inhabitants (vv. 1-2). Yet the victory involved a **huge valley** providing a miraculous way of escape. On God as Divine Warrior, see note at 9:10-15. **Holy ones** refers to angelic forces from heaven (Ps 89:5,7; Jd 14).

14:6-7 The otherworldliness of these events is underscored by the absence of ways to keep track of time.

14:8 Since water was a premium in Palestine, and Jerusalem was not near a river, the picture of a year-round source of **living water** flowing from the city with sufficient quantity to reach the Dead Sea and the Mediterranean Sea was inspiring. It would require supernatural redesign of the geography of the region. "Living water" refers to fresh spring water as opposed to water stored in cisterns.

14:9 Yahweh alone, and His name alone is the starting point for true faith, the opposite of idolatry (Dt 6:4).

14:10 Isaiah envisioned **Jerusalem** to be the highest mountain on the world, with people streaming to it from all over the earth (Is 2:2-3; cp. Mc 4:1-2). Here the picture is of people coming to Jerusalem for the Feast of Tabernacles (Dt 16:13-15).

14:11 Never again is likely standard hyperbolic language for God's protection (see note at 9:8).

14:17-19 Along with the promises of God's blessings comes a reminder that humans may choose a path that will lead them away from what God offers. **Rain will not fall on them** is stock language of judgment.

14:21 Canaanite was a pejorative term since the Israelites considered the Canaanites vile and morally reprehensible. But the Israelites had become "Canaanites" by their disobedience. The announcement that there would be no Canaanite in the temple signified the purity of God's chosen people.

Malachi

Introduction

Malachi is the last prophetic message from God before the close of the Old Testament period (although non-prophetic books such as Ezra-Nehemiah and Chronicles may have been written later). This small book captures the essential message of the Old Testament and shows the reader the nature of God and our relationship and responsibility to Him and to others in the covenant community.

"For My name will be great among the nations, from the rising of the sun to its setting" [1:11].

Circumstances of Writing

Author: Nothing is known about the author except his name. The book emphasizes the message rather than the messenger; God is the speaker in about 47 of the 55 verses. The one prophesied in 3:1 to "clear the way" for God to come to His temple is identified as (Hb) *malakiy*, "My messenger," a word identical to the name of the book's author.

Background: Although the book is not dated by a reference to a ruler or a specific event, internal evidence, as well as its position in the canon, favors a postexilic date. Reference to a governor in 1:8 favors the Persian period when Judah was a province or sub-province of the Persian satrapy Abar Nahara, which included Palestine, Syria, Phoenicia, Cyprus, and, until 485 B.C., Babylon. The temple had been rebuilt (515 B.C.) and worship reestablished there (1:6-11; 2:1-3; 3:1,10). But the excitement and enthusiasm for which the prophets Haggai and Zechariah were the catalysts had waned. The social and religious problems that Malachi addressed reflect the situation portrayed in Ezra 9 and 10 and Nehemiah 5 and 13, suggesting dates not long before Ezra's return to Judah (ca 460 B.C.) or Nehemiah's second term as governor of Judah (Neh 13:6-7; ca 435 B.C.). Linguistic data favors the earlier date.

Message and Purpose

Like Nahum (Nah 1:1) and Habakkuk (Hab 1:1), this book is called an "oracle" (Mal 1:1). This Hebrew word *massa* is found 20 times in the OT (e.g., 2Kg 9:25; Is 13:1; Zch 9:1; 12:1). Once thought to mean "burden," it is now understood to refer to a divine pronouncement through God's prophet.

Indictment: Malachi presented Judah's sins largely by quoting their own words, repeating their own thoughts, and describing their own attitudes (1:2,6-7,12-13; 2:14,17; 3:7-8,13-15). Malachi was faced with the failure of the priests to fear God and to serve the people conscientiously during difficult times. This had contributed to Judah's indifference toward God. Blaming their economic and social troubles on His supposed unfaithfulness,

---

625 B.C.

The Assyrian Empire comes to an end when the Babylonians and Medes destroy Nineveh. **612**

The Babylonians level Jerusalem and the temple. **586**

Cyrus, founding ruler of the Medo-Persian Empire, captures Babylon with little resistance. **539**

Cyrus's decree allows return of Jews from exile; 42,360 returned initially. **538**

Second temple construction begins under Zerubbabel's and Joshua's leadership. **536**

Cambyses, son of Cyrus, rules Persian Empire. **530–522**

525 B.C.

Discouragement reinforced by opposition from transplanted people brings work on the temple to a halt. **526**

Darius I (Darius the Great) succeeds Cambyses. **521–486**

Haggai and Zechariah encourage the people to resume construction of the temple. **520–518**

Temple completed **March 12, 515**

Xerxes (Ahasuerus) ascends the throne of Persia upon the death of his father, Darius I. **486**

the people were treating one another faithlessly (especially their wives) and were profaning the temple by marrying pagan women. They were also withholding their tithes.

Instruction: God commanded sincere worship with genuine faith and humility. This included honoring Him with pure offerings, being faithful to human covenants, especially marriage covenants, and renewing the tithe of all they acquired to signify their recognition of Yahweh as their God and King.

Judgment: If the priests would not change their behavior, God would curse them and remove them from service. Malachi also announced a coming day when the "God of justice" would come to judge the wicked and refine His people (Mt 3:12; 13:24-30).

Hope: As other incentives to obedience, Malachi pointed to (1) God's demonstrations of love for Israel (1:2); (2) their spiritual and covenant unity with God and with one another (2:10); and (3) a coming day of salvation and blessing for those who fear Him (3:1-6; 3:16–4:3).

Contribution to the Bible

Malachi was the last prophetic message from God before the close of the OT period. This book is a fitting conclusion to the OT and a transition for understanding the kingdom proclamation in the NT. Malachi spoke to the hearts of a troubled people whose circumstances of financial insecurity, religious skepticism, and personal disappointments were similar to those often experienced by God's people today. The book contains a message that must not be overlooked by those who wish to encounter God and His kingdom and to lead others to a similar encounter. We have a great, loving, and holy God, who has unchanging and glorious purposes for His people. Our God calls us to genuine worship, fidelity to Himself and to one another, and to expectant faith in what He is doing and says He will do in this world and for His people.

God's love is paramount. It is expressed in Malachi in terms of God's election and protection of Israel above all the nations of the world. Since God had served the interests of Judah out of His unchanging love, He required

500 B.C.

460 B.C.

Greek victory over Persians in Battle of Salamis (480) and Plain of Plataea (479), thwart Persian expansion into Europe and are keys to Greek hegemony in the Mediterranean Basin and Europe.

Esther becomes queen of Persia. 479

Esther intercedes with Xerxes for her people. 474

First celebration of Purim 473

Xerxes I (Ahasuerus), husband of Esther, assassinated 465

Artaxerxes I succeeds his father. 465–423

Malachi's prophecy 460

Ezra leads second group of Jewish exiles to Jerusalem. 458

Events in Nehemiah 445–430

Jerusalem's walls rebuilt under Nehemiah's leadership 445

Nehemiah returns to Persia. 432

Peloponnesian Wars between Athens and other Greek city-states 431–404

Nehemiah returns to Jerusalem. 425

Judah to live up to its obligations by obedience, loyalty, and sincere worship. This love relationship between God and Judah is the model for how people were expected to treat other members of the redeemed community. They were required to be faithful in all their dealings with one another.

As a community devoted to God, His people enjoy His protection and provision. But failure to live right before God and one another will bring God's judgment. Thus, God's people could not expect the joy of His blessings if they continued to fail in their duties to Him and to one another. Before God would hold Judah in the balance of judgment, He would grant one last call for repentance. A forerunner would precede the fearsome Day of the Lord and herald the coming of God's kingdom on earth.

Structure

Malachi's message is communicated in three interrelated addresses. Each address contains five sections arranged in a mirror-like repetitive structure surrounding a central section (a-b-c-b-a). The first two addresses begin with positive motivation or hope (1:2-5; 2:10a) and end with negative motivation or judgment (2:1-9; 3:1-6). In between is God's indictment (1:6-9 and 1:11-14; 2:10b-15a and 2:17) surrounding His commands (1:10; 2:15b-16). The final climactic address begins and ends with commands to repent (3:7-10a; 4:4-6). In between are sections of motivation (3:10b-12; 3:16–4:3) surrounding the indictment (3:13-15).

Outline

I. Priests Exhorted to Honor Yahweh (1:1–2:9)
   A. Positive motivation: the Lord's love (1:2-5)
   B. Situation: failure to honor the Lord (1:6-9)
   C. Command: stop the vain offerings (1:10)
   D. Situation: priests profane the Lord's name (1:11-14)
   E. Negative motivation: results of disobedience (2:1-9)

II. Judah Exhorted to Faithfulness (2:10–3:6)
   A. Positive motivation: spiritual kinship among Israel (2:10a)
   B. Situation: faithlessness against a covenant member (2:10b-15a)
   C. Command: stop acting faithlessly (2:15b-16)
   D. Situation: complaints of the Lord's injustice (2:17)
   E. Negative motivation: coming messenger of judgment (3:1-6)

III. Judah Exhorted to Return to the Lord (3:7–4:6)
   A. Command: return to the Lord with tithes (3:7-10a)
   B. Positive motivation: future blessing (3:10b-12)
   C. Situation: complacency in serving the Lord (3:13-15)
   D. Motivation: the coming Day of the Lord (3:16–4:3)
   E. Command: remember the law (4:4-6)

The Lord's Love for Israel

1 An *oracle:[a] The word of the Lord[b] to Israel through[c] Malachi.[A]

[2] "I have loved you,"[d] says the Lord.

But you ask: "How have You loved us?"

"Wasn't Esau Jacob's brother?"[e] This is the Lord's declaration. "Even so, I loved Jacob, [3] but I hated Esau.[f] I turned his mountains into a wasteland, and gave his inheritance to the desert jackals."[g]

[4] Though Edom says: "We have been devastated, but we will rebuild[B] the ruins," the Lord of *Hosts says this: "They may build, but I will demolish. They will be called a wicked country[h] and the people the Lord has cursed[c] forever.[i] [5] Your own eyes will see this, and you yourselves will say, 'The Lord is great, even beyond[D] the borders of Israel'.[j]

Disobedience of the Priests

[6] "A son honors his father, and a servant his master. But if I am a father, where is My honor? And if I am a master, where is your *fear of Me?[k] says *Yahweh of Hosts to you priests, who despise My name."

Yet you ask: "How have we despised Your name?"

[7] "By presenting defiled food on My altar." You ask: "How have we defiled You?"[l] When you say: "The Lord's table is contemptible."[m]

[8] "When you present a blind animal for sacrifice, is it not wrong? And when you present a lame or sick animal, is it not wrong?[n] Bring it to your governor! Would he be pleased with you or show you favor?" asks the Lord of Hosts. [9] "And now ask for God's favor. Will He be gracious to us?[o] Since this has come from your hands, will He show any of you favor?"[p] asks the Lord of Hosts. [10] "I wish one of you would shut the temple doors,[q] so you would no longer kindle a useless fire on My altar![r] I am not pleased with you," says the Lord of Hosts, "and I will accept[s] no offering from your hands.

[11] "For My name will be great among the nations,[u] from the rising of the sun to its setting. Incense[E] and pure offerings will be presented in My name in every place because My name will be great among the nations,"[F] says Yahweh of Hosts.

[12] But you are profaning it[v] when you say:

a1:1 Is 13:1; Zch 9:1; 12:1
b1:1 Hs 1:1; Jl 1:1; Mc 1:1; Zph 1:1
c1:1 Jr 37:2; Hg 1:1
d1:2 Dt 4:37; 7:6-8; 10:14-15; Neh 13:26; Ps 78:68
e1:2 Gn 25:25-26; 36:19
f1:3 Gn 25:23; Rm 9:10-13
g1:3 Is 34:5-17; Jr 49:7-22; Ezk 35:1-15
h1:4 Mal 3:12,15
i1:4 Is 34:5-17; Jr 49:17-18; Mal 1:14; 2:2; 3:9; 4:6
j1:5 Ps 67:1-7; 72:8-11; Ezk 39:7; Zch 12:1-10; Rm 11:11-12
k1:6 1Sm 2:30; Dn 5:23; Hg 1:8
l1:7 Ezk 22:26
m Ezk 41:22; 44:16
n1:8 Lv 22:18-25; Dt 15:21; 17:1
o1:9 1Sm 13:12; Pr 19:6; Dn 9:13
p Nm 6:25-26
q1:10 2Ch 28:24
r Pr 1:17; Is 1:14
s Lv 22:19-21
t Is 1:10-17; Jr 6:20; Am 5:21-23; Mc 6:6-8
u1:11 Ps 113:3; Is 45:6; 59:19; Mt 8:11　　v1:12 Lv 22:2; Ezk 13:19; 22:26; 36:20-23; Mal 2:10-11

A1:1 = My Messenger　　B1:4 Or *will return and build*　　C1:4 Or *Lord is angry with*　　D1:5 Or *great over*　　E1:11 Or *Burnt offerings*
F1:11 Or *is great . . . are presented . . . is great*

1:2 To motivate God's demand for proper worship (vv. 6-14), for marital faithfulness (2:10b-17), and for wholehearted commitment to God signified by acknowledging His ownership of all they had (3:7–4:6), the Lord reminded the people in 1:2-5 of His faithful love throughout their history (Jr 31:3). But Judah disputed God's love, showing they had allowed life's trials to blind them to His faithfulness and loving presence. Such spiritual depletion was at the root of not only Israel's insulting religious rites (Mal 1:6-14), but also the moral decay and spiritual indifference that Malachi described.

1:3-5 God's love had been abundantly demonstrated in recent history, in contrast to His dealings with the nation of **Edom** (descended from Jacob's twin brother; Gn 25). Someday Israel would no longer doubt His love (Mal 1:5; cp. Jr 31:33-34; 33:8-11; Zch 12:10). God had demonstrated His love by choosing Israel out of all the nations for an intimate relationship (Ex 19:4; Dt 7:6) and by His subsequent faithfulness. "I loved Jacob" refers to God's choosing him over Esau as recipient and instrument of His blessing (Gn 25:23; Rm 9:10-13) as well as to God's enduring love for Jacob's descendants. God **hated Esau** insomuch as He did not choose to make a covenant of blessing with him and his descendants (the Edomites) but instead destroyed them for their rebellion. That nation was noted for its pride, treachery, greed, and violence (Jr 49:7-22; Am 1:9-12; Obadiah). Although God disciplined Israel severely, He did not destroy them completely (Neh 9:31; Jr 31:3) as He had done with Edom.

1:6 The only appropriate response to God's holiness is **fear**, which is essential to wisdom (Pr 1:7; Mc 6:9) and true faith (Is 33:6; 50:10), as well as wholehearted devotion and obedience.

1:7 The temple **altar** is compared to a divinely hosted dinner **table**, a symbol of hospitality and relationship (Ezk 44:16). Their casual attitude toward the altar betrayed how little the people valued their relationship with God.

1:10 King Ahaz in earlier years had **shut the temple doors** to pursue the worship of idols (2Ch 28:24). Religious activity not rooted in humble adoration of God as the source of all goodness and authority is not only useless "fig-leaf religion" but is repulsive to Him because it slanders His character (Pr 15:8; Is 1:10-17; Am 5:21-23; Rm 14:23; Heb 11:6).

1:11-14 A time is coming when even Gentiles everywhere

nagash

Hebrew Pronunciation	[nah GASH]
HCSB Translation	approach, bring
Uses in Malachi	6
Uses in the OT	125
Focus passage	Malachi 1:7-8,11

Nagash denotes *approach* (Jr 30:21) and in that sense *come near* (Gn 45:4), *come* (2Kg 4:27), or *go* (Ex 24:14). One *steps forward* (Gn 18:23) and *comes up* or *closer* (Gn 19:9; 27:21). Priests *come near* God and *approach* the altar; Levites *come near* holy objects (Nm 4:19). People *advance* or *draw near* for battle (2Sm 10:13). They *go* to judges (Ex 24:14) and to court (Dt 25:1). "*Approaching* women" involves *having sexual relations* (Ex 19:15). *Nagash* suggests *making room* (Is 49:20). "*Draw near* there" implies *get out of the way* (Gn 19:9). The causative is *bring* (Gn 27:25) or *bring near* (Lv 8:14). One *presents* sacrifices (Am 5:25), arguments (1Sm 41:21), or cases (Is 45:21). People *serve* (1Sm 28:25) or *offer* (Jdg 6:19) food, and *offer* tribute (1Kg 4:21). The passive describes *being placed* in shackles (2Sm 3:34) or *being presented* (Mal 1:11).

"The Lord's table is defiled, and its product, its food, is contemptible." [13]You also say: "Look, what a nuisance!" "And you scorn[A] it,"[B,a] says the LORD of Hosts. "You bring stolen,[C,b] lame, or sick animals. You bring this as an offering! Am I to accept that from your hands?" asks the LORD.

[14]"The deceiver is cursed who has an acceptable male in his flock and makes a vow but sacrifices a defective animal to the Lord.[c] For I am a great King," says Yahweh of Hosts, "and My name[D] will be feared among the nations.

Warning to the Priests

2 "Therefore, this decree[d] is for you priests: [2]If you don't listen, and if you don't take it to heart[e] to honor My name," says •Yahweh of •Hosts, "I will send a curse among you, and I will curse your blessings.[f] In fact, I have already begun to curse them because you are not taking it to heart.

[3]"Look, I am going to rebuke your descendants,[g] and I will spread animal waste[E] over your faces, the waste from your festival sacrifices,[h] and you will be taken away with it. [4]Then you will know that I sent you this decree so My covenant with Levi[i] may continue," says the LORD of Hosts. [5]"My covenant with him was one of life and peace,[j] and I gave these to him;

it called for reverence, and he revered Me and stood in awe of My name.[k] [6]True instruction was in his mouth, and nothing wrong was found on his lips. He walked with Me[l] in peace and fairness and turned many from sin.[m] [7]For the lips of a priest should guard knowledge, and people should seek instruction from his mouth, because he is the messenger of the LORD of Hosts.[n]

[8]"You, on the other hand, have turned from the way.[o] You have caused many to stumble[p] by your instruction. You have violated[F] the covenant of Levi," says the LORD of Hosts. [9]"So I in turn have made you despised[q] and humiliated before all the people because you are not keeping My ways but are showing partiality in your instruction."[r]

Judah's Marital Unfaithfulness

[10]Don't all of us have one Father?[s] Didn't one God create us?[t] Why then do we act treacherously against one another,[u] profaning[v] the covenant of our fathers?[w] [11]Judah has acted treacherously, and a detestable[x] thing has been done in Israel and in Jerusalem. For Judah has profaned[y] the LORD's sanctuary,[G,z]

a1:13 1Sm 2:29
b2Sm 24:24
c1:14 Lv 22:18-25; 27:9-10; Nm 30:2; Dt 23:21-23; Ec 5:4-7
d2:1 Nah 1:14
e2:2 Is 42:25; 57:1; Jr 12:11
fDt 28:20; Pr 3:33; 28:27; Mal 3:9
g2:3 Hs 4:6-8
hEx 29:14; Lv 16:27
i2:4 Nm 25:11-13; Dt 10:8; 33:8-11; Neh 13:29; Jr 33:17-22
j2:5 1Sm 25:6; Pr 3:2
kMal 1:6
l2:6 Gn 5:22,24; 6:9; Mc 6:8
mIs 53:6; Jr 23:22; Ezk 3:19-20
n2:7 2Ch 36:15-16; Hg 1:13
o2:8 Ex 32:8; Dt 31:29; Mal 3:7
pPr 4:16; Is 8:14-15; Hs 14:1
q2:9 Mal 1:6-7
rLv 19:15; Dt 10:17; Ps 82:2; Mt 22:16; 1Tm 5:21; Jms 2:1,9
s2:10 Ex 4:22-23; Is 63:16; Hs 11:1; Mal 1:6; Jn 8:41
tDt 32:6; Is 43:1-7; 64:8
uEx 21:8; Jdg 9:23; Jb 6:15; Is 21:2; Jr 3:20
vNm 30:2; Ps 55:20; 89:34; Mal 1:12
w1Kg 8:21
x2:11 Lv 18:22-30; Ezr 9:1-14; Neh 13:4-9
yJr 16:18; Ezk 44:7
zEx 36:1-6; Zph 3:4

A1:13 Lit blow at   B1:13 Ancient Jewish tradition reads Me   C1:13 Or injured   D1:14 Or Because I am . . . Yahweh of Hosts, My name   E2:3 Dung or entrails   F2:8 Lit corrupted   G2:11 Or profaned what is holy to the LORD

will recognize Yahweh's greatness and worship Him (Is 59:19; Ezk 36:20-36; 39:7; Mt 8:11-12; Rm 11:11-12). But God's own children, His kingdom of priests who were to mediate His grace to the nations, were **profaning** His **name**. God's "name" is His nature, character, and worth as He reveals it in His words and acts (Gn 16:13; 17:5; 22:14; Ex 33:19; 1Kg 8:43). Those who claim to belong to Him ("are called by [His] name"; Dt 28:10; 2Ch 7:14; Is 43:7) proclaim His character in both their worship (the phrase "call on the name of Yahweh" [Gn 4:26; 21:33] refers to praise or worship [Gn 12:8; Dt 32:3] as well as petition) and their behavior. If their worship or behavior misrepresents God's holy character, it "profanes" His name. This desecrates Him, damages His reputation, brings Him disgrace, and will not be tolerated (Lv 22). This is what Israel had done before the exile and was doing again.

2:1-3 In addition to the positive motivation of 1:2-5, God decreed that if the priests' attitude and behavior did not change, He would treat them with contempt (as they had treated Him) and would remove them from service (Lv 10:1-3; 1Sm 2:29-36; Ezk 44:6-14; Hs 4:6-8). The **waste** consisted of the dung and unclean sacrificial remains after a temple festival that were disposed of "outside the camp" (Ex 29:14; Lv 16:27-28). God had entrusted the priests with the spiritual well-being of Israel (Nm 25:11-13; Dt 33:8-11). By the time of Jesus the Jerusalem priesthood was under God's curse (Mt 16:21; 21:23-46). But the promise of a lasting Levitical priesthood was still in effect (Jr 33:17-22; Mal 3:3-4).

2:4-9 The **covenant with** or of **Levi** in verses 4 and 8 refers

not to a covenant with the son of Jacob but to the "covenant of peace" that God made with the Levite Phinehas, Aaron's grandson. God promised Phinehas and his descendants a "perpetual priesthood" in return for his zeal in protecting Israel from the corruption of idolatry (Nm 25:1-13). The entire tribe of Levi had earlier been set apart by God after a similar act of faithfulness at Mount Sinai (Ex 32:26-29). They were assigned responsibility for the sanctuary and worship (Dt 10:8-9; Neh 13:29). The tribe's function was to teach the law to Israel (and in that sense to be God's **messenger** and to officiate at the altar (Lv 10:8-11; Dt 33:8-11). The Levitical covenant was renewed in Jr 33:14-22 in connection with the Davidic covenant, though it was narrowed in Ezk 44:10-16 to the descendants of Zadok (1Sm 2:35; 1Kg 2:27). Although the priests had **violated** the covenant, 3:3-4 shows it would remain in effect. That teachers of God's Word could be described as "messengers" implies the ongoing relevance of God's past instructions and shows the continuing importance of the role of biblical teachers among God's people.

2:10 The people were failing to honor their covenant relationships with one another. The word **act treacherously** (Hb bagad) that occurs in verses 10,11,14,15,16 designates failure to fulfill one's promised obligations—i.e., to betray another. A person who does this is a traitor (Is 21:2). The **covenant of our fathers** is the Mosaic covenant (Jdg 2:20; 1Kg 8:21). To "profane" it meant to treat it with contempt (Mal 1:12; 2:11) by violating it.

2:11-12 The most obvious way Judah was violating the covenant was by intermarriage with women who worshiped for-

which He loves,[a] and has married the daughter of a foreign god.[A,b] [12]To the man who does this, may the LORD cut off[c] any descendants[B,C,d] from the tents of Jacob, even if they present an offering to the LORD of Hosts.

[13]And this is another thing you do: you cover the LORD's altar with tears, with weeping and groaning,[e] because He no longer respects your offerings or receives them gladly from your hands.[f]

[14]Yet you ask, "For what reason?" Because the LORD has been a witness[g] between you and the wife of your youth.[h] You have acted treacherously against her, though she was your marriage partner[i] and your wife by covenant.[j] [15]Didn't the one God make us with a remnant of His life-breath? And what does the One seek?[D] A godly •offspring. So watch yourselves carefully,[E,k] and do not act treacherously against the wife of your youth.

[16]"If he hates[l] and divorces his wife,[m]" says the LORD God of Israel, "he[F] covers his garment with injustice,"[n] says the LORD of Hosts.

Therefore, watch yourselves carefully,[G] and do not act treacherously.

Judgment at the LORD's Coming

[17]You have wearied the LORD[o] with your words.

Yet you ask, "How have we wearied Him?"

When you say, "Everyone who does what is evil is good in the LORD's sight, and He is pleased with them,"[p] or "Where is the God of justice?"[q]

3 "See, I am going to send My messenger,[r] and he will clear the way before Me.[s] Then the Lord you seek[t] will suddenly come to His temple,[u] the Messenger of the covenant you desire—see, He is coming," says the LORD of •Hosts. [2]But who can endure the day of His coming? And who will be able to stand when He appears?[v] For He will be like a refiner's fire[w] and like cleansing lye.[x] [3]He will be like a refiner and purifier of silver; He will purify

---

[a]2:11 Ps 78:68-69 [b]Dt 7:3-4; Ezr 9:1-2,10-14; Neh 13:23-30 [c]2:12 Ex 12:19; 31:14 [d]Ru 4:10; 1Sm 24:21 [e]2:13 Ps 6:6-10 [f]1Kg 8:28-30; Is 56:7 [g]2:14 Gn 31:50-53; Jdg 11:10; 1Sm 12:5 [h]Pr 2:16-17; 5:18; Is 54:6 [i]Ec 4:10 [j]Ezk 16:8,59-62; Hs 2:16-20 [k]2:15 Ex 23:13; Jos 23:11 [l]2:16 Gn 29:31; Dt 21:15-17; 22:13,16; Jdg 15:2; Pr 30:23 [m]Dt 24:1-4 [n]Gn 6:11,13; Ps 73:6; Jr 22:3; Hab 1:2-3 [o]2:17 Is 43:22-24 [p]Dt 25:16; Mal 3:15

[q]Neh 9:33; Is 40:27 [r]3:1 Ex 23:20; 33:2; 2Ch 36:15-16 [s]Is 40:3; Mk 1:2; Lk 1:76 [t]Hs 5:6 [u]Ps 24:7-10 [v]3:2 Rv 6:17 [w]Dt 4:24; Is 1:25; Zch 13:9 [x]Jr 2:22

[A]2:11 = a woman who worshiped a foreign god   [B]2:12 One Hb ms, LXX, DSS read off one witnessing or answering   [C]2:12 Lit off one waking or answering; Hb obscure   [D]2:15 Or Did the One not make them? So their flesh and spirit belong to Him, or No one who does this even has a remnant of the Spirit in him; Hb obscure   [E]2:15 Lit So guard yourselves in your spirit   [F]2:16 Or The LORD God of Israel says that He hates divorce and the one who   [G]2:16 Lit Therefore, guard yourselves in your spirit

---

eign gods, thus introducing a spiritually destructive element into the covenant community (Ex 34:11-16; Dt 7:3-4; Ezr 9:1-2; Neh 13:26; 2Co 6:14-17). A **detestable** act was one that caused such serious defilement that destruction or death was required (Lv 18:29; Dt 7:25; 13:15; Jr 44:22-23). Anyone who did this was cursed (Mal 2:12). **Descendants** is a reasonable rendering of a difficult phrase on the basis of parallels in 1Kg 14:10; Is 14:22; Jr 44:7. The last clause (lit "and presenting an offering to Yahweh of hosts") probably explains more precisely why their sin profaned the sanctuary: they were continuing to sacrifice to God despite their sin.

2:13-14 To marry pagan women, some men were divorcing their Jewish wives to whom they had sworn faithfulness before God. **Another thing you do** is not the **weeping** of verse 13, but introduces the issue of divorce in verse 14 (**you cover** could be rendered "while covering"). Divorce was the second detestable act of treachery that was profaning the sanctuary (v. 11). The verb forms in verses 13-14 are different from those in verses 11-12. This may suggest that Malachi was even more concerned with divorce than with intermarriage. Divorce profaned the sanctuary because the people continued to offer their sacrifices (v. 13) despite their marital betrayals. God's refusal to respond favorably to their offerings (hence their tears; see Gn 4:4-5; Ps 6:6-9) was probably linked to their continuing economic and social troubles (Neh 9:32-37; Hg 1:6,9-11; 2:16-19). Persistent sin renders worship meaningless. **Marriage partner** renders a word for someone with whom one is bound by friendship, common goals and commitments, kinship, or covenant, the latter being the case here. On marriage as covenantal, see Pr 2:17; Ezk 16:8,59-62; Hs 2:16-20.

2:15 The translation and point of verse 15a is unclear, but it seems to indicate that the marriage bond is not only earthly and easily dissolved, but that it is the product of God's Spirit, whose purpose is to produce **godly offspring**.

2:16 This verse ends by repeating verse 15b with one significant change. After speaking to "you" in verses 13-15a, verse 15b switches back to third person "he" as in verses 11-12, ending literally, "and with the wife of your youth let *him* not act treacherously." Then after a conjunction opening verse 16 (meaning "because," "if," "when," "that," or "indeed") is a verb that clearly means "*he* hates," although most translations change it to "*I* hate." But the subject apparently is the one who "acts treacherously," and who also **covers his garment with injustice**. The one speaking is **the LORD God of Israel**, and contrary to KJV, NKJV, etc., there is no indication of indirect discourse ("says that"), so God cannot be the subject of "he hates." This verse specifies how wives were being betrayed. Their husbands were "hating" so as to "divorce" (a Hb infinitive) them for no legitimate reason (Dt 24:3), which was a heinous injustice. Such a cold-blooded and unscrupulous traitor to his marital responsibilities, who would deny his wife the very things he had pledged to provide—devotion, care, companionship, protection, intimacy, peace, justice (Gn 2:24; Ex 21:10; Dt 22:13-19; Pr 5:15-20)—stood condemned by God, and he wore the stain of his crime like a garment for all to see (Ps 73:6).

2:17 The people's treachery against one another (v. 10) was a form of injustice (failing to give someone his due), but they accused God of injustice for not coming to their aid and punishing people they considered "evil" (1:2; 3:15). God's ironic reply was to announce in 3:1-6 a coming messenger of "judgment" (3:5; the same Hb word as "justice") who would purge and purify God's people, including the priests.

3:1-5 God's **messenger** here is the "voice . . . in the wilderness" of Is 40:3, which the NT interprets as the "Elijah" of Mal 4:5, fulfilled (conditionally) by John the Baptist (Mt 3:3; 11:14; 17:10-13). His goal would be to exhort the people to repent and prepare for God's other **Messenger** (see Jn 1:14-17). This "Messenger" is distinguished from God by

the sons of Levi and refine them like gold and silver.[a] Then they will present offerings to the LORD in righteousness. [4]And the offerings of Judah and Jerusalem will please the LORD as in days of old[b] and years gone by.

[5]"I will come to you in judgment, and I will be ready to witness against sorcerers and adulterers; against those who swear falsely; against those who oppress the widow and the fatherless, and cheat the wage earner; and against those who deny justice to the foreigner.[c] They do not •fear Me,"[d] says the LORD of Hosts. [6]"Because I, •Yahweh, have not changed,[e] you descendants of Jacob have not been destroyed.[f]

Robbing God

[7]"Since the days of your fathers, you have turned from My statutes; you have not kept them.[g] Return to Me,[h] and I will return to you,"[i] says the LORD of Hosts.

But you ask: "How can we return?"

[8]"Will a man rob[j] God? Yet you are robbing Me!"

You ask: "How do we rob You?"

"By not making the payments of the tenth and the contributions.[k] [9]You are suffering under a curse, yet you—the whole nation—are still robbing Me. [10]Bring the full tenth into the storehouse[l] so that there may be food in My house.[m] Test Me in this way,"[n] says the LORD of Hosts. "See if I will not open the floodgates of heaven[o] and pour out a blessing for you without measure.[p] [11]I will rebuke the devourer[A,q] for you, so that it will not ruin the produce of your land and your vine in your field will not fail to produce fruit," says the LORD of Hosts. [12]"Then all the nations will consider you fortunate, for you will be a delightful land," says the LORD of Hosts.

The Righteous and the Wicked

[13]"Your words against Me are harsh,"[r] says the LORD.

Yet you ask: "What have we spoken against You?"

[14]You have said: "It is useless to serve God. What have we gained by keeping His requirements[s] and walking mournfully[t] before the LORD of Hosts? [15]So now we consider the arrogant[u] to be fortunate.[v] Not only do those who

[a]3:3 Ps 12:6; Pr 17:3; Ezk 22:22
[b]3:4 Am 9:11
[c]3:5 Ex 20:14,16; 22:18-24; Dt 18:10; 24:14,17; Jr 5:2,7; 7:6,9
[d]Dt 10:17-20; Mal 2:5
[e]3:6 Nm 23:19; 1Sm 15:29; Ps 33:11; 119:89-91; Rm 11:29; Heb 6:17-18; Jms 1:17
[f]Ps 124; Hs 11:9
[g]3:7 Jos 1:7; 23:6; 1Kg 8:58; 2Kg 17:15; Ezr 9:7; Am 2:4; Mal 2:8
[h]Dt 4:30; 30:2; 2Ch 30:6,9; Is 55:7; Jl 2:13; Zch 1:3
[i]1Kg 8:33; Jr 15:19; 24:7
[j]3:8 Pr 22:22-23
[k]Lv 7:14,32-33; 27:30-32; Nm 18:8-24; Dt 12:5-19; 14:22-29; 26:12
[l]3:10 Jos 6:19,24; 1Kg 7:51
[m]2Ch 31:4-10; Neh 10:34-39; Ezk 44:28-31
[n]Ex 4:1-9; Jdg 6:36-40
[o]Gn 7:11; 8:2; Dt 11:16-17
[p]Dt 28:12; Is 41:18-20; Jl 2:18-32; Am 9:13-15
[q]3:11 Jl 1:4; 2:25
[r]3:13 Ps 119:23; Ezk 35:13
[s]3:14 Lv 8:35; Dt 11:1
[t]Ps 35:14; 38:6
[u]3:15 Ps 119:21,85; Is 13:11; Jr 43:2
[v]Gn 30:13; Ps 72:17; Pr 31:28

[A]3:11 Perhaps locusts

referring to Him as **He**, and yet also identified with God by calling Him **the Lord** in verse 1 and **I** in verse 5. The divine-human nature of this messianic bearer of a new covenant (Heb 9:15) may also be seen in other passages such as Zch 12:10-13:9.

3:6 In reply to charges that He had been unfaithful, God declared that if He were not the immutable God who did not lie, was not capricious, and whose purposes and promises were irrevocable (Nm 23:19; Ps 89:33-34; Is 46:3-4; Rm 11:26-29; Heb 6:17-18), Israel's rebellion would have destroyed them long ago (like Edom's in Mal 1:2-5; cp. Ps 124; Hs 11:9).

3:7-10a The final, climactic address begins with a command to **return** (Jr 3:22-4:4; 24:7; Hs 14:1-2; Zch 1:3) to Yahweh, and it ends with a command to "remember" His instructions (Mal 4:4). Evidence of the people's return to God would be to resume bringing tithes and other **contributions** to support the priests, Levites, and landless poor (Lv 27:30-33; Nm 18:8-32; Dt 12:5-19; 14:22-29; 26:12-15; Neh 10:38; 13:10). Such offerings would demonstrate a proper attitude toward their possessions as God's gifts (Dt 6:10-12; 8:17-18).

3:10b-12 Although testing God with complaining, rebellion, and unbelief is wrong (v. 15; Ex 17:2-7; Ps 95:8-9), testing His faithfulness with our obedience is not. The phrase rendered **without measure** may also mean "only what you need" (Pr 25:16). The Mosaic covenant promised material blessings or curses (Dt 28) to the nation as a whole, not necessarily to the individual. The book of Job and later Jesus (Mt 19:23-25; Jn 9:3) spoke against such an individual application.

3:13-15 On the **harsh** words, see Jd 14-15. Judah's current difficulties, in light of their perverse understanding of God's

demands and of having a relationship with Him, had led them to conclude there was no advantage in serving God (Is 5:20; Mal 2:17). The word for **gained** refers to dishonest gain (see Is 56:11).

3:16-18 The **book of remembrance** was the royal archives where the most significant events of a king's reign were recorded (Ezr 4:15; 5:17). As Mordecai was rewarded on the basis of the royal archives (Est 2:23; 6:1-3), so it will be

shicheth

Hebrew Pronunciation	[shih KHAYT]
HCSB Translation	destroy, act corruptly, ruin
Uses in Malachi	3
Uses in the OT	152
Focus passage	Malachi 3:11

Shicheth in passive-reflexive forms means *be corrupt* (Gn 6:11), *ruined*, or *flawed* (Jr 18:4). The participle involves *corrupt acts* (Ezk 20:44). Intensive and causative verbs share the meanings *destroy* (Gn 6:13), *ruin*, and *act corruptly* (Ex 32:7). Intensive verbs also connote *ravage* (Jos 22:33), *bring loss, waste* (Jdg 6:5), *corrupt* (Ezk 28:17), and *corrupt oneself* (Hs 9:9). One *violates* covenants (Mal 2:8), *stifles* compassion (Am 1:11), and wastefully *releases* semen (Gn 38:9). Causative verbs also suggest *annihilate* (Dt 9:26), *slaughter, devastate* (Jr 51:25), *mar*, and *batter* (2Sm 20:15). People *are depraved* or *become corrupt* in actions (Zph 3:7). Participles denote *destroyer, destructive, corrupt, depraved, ravaging, raiding parties* (1Sm 13:17), and *trap* (Jr 5:26). Passive participles signify *polluted* (Pr 25:26) and a *defective animal* (Mal 1:14). *Mashchiyth* (10x; Ezk 5:16) means *destruction*, and *mashcheth* conveys *destructive* (Ezk 9:1). *Mashchath* suggests *deformity* (Lv 22:25), and *mishchath*, *disfigurement* (Is 52:14).

commit wickedness prosper, they even test God[a] and escape."[b]

[16]At that time those who feared the Lord spoke to one another. The Lord took notice and listened. So a book of remembrance[c] was written before Him for those who feared Yahweh and had high regard for His name. [17]"They will be Mine," says the Lord of Hosts,[d] "a special possession on the day I am preparing. I will have compassion on them as a man has compassion on his son who serves him.[e] [18]So you will again see the difference between the righteous and the wicked, between one who serves God and one who does not serve Him.

The Day of the Lord

4 [A]"For indeed, the day is coming, burning like a furnace, when all the arrogant and everyone who commits wickedness will be come stubble. The coming day will consume them," says the Lord of *Hosts, "not leaving them root or branches. [2]But for you who *fear My name, the sun of righteousness will rise with healing in its wings,[f] and you will go out and playfully jump like calves from the stall.[B] [3]You will trample the wicked, for they will be ashes under the soles of your feet on the day I am preparing," says the Lord of Hosts.

A Final Warning

[4]"Remember the instruction of Moses My servant, the statutes and ordinances I commanded him at Horeb[g] for all Israel. [5]Look, I am going to send you Elijah the prophet[h] before the great and awesome Day of the Lord comes.[i] [6C]And he will turn the hearts of fathers to their children and the hearts of children to their fathers.[j] Otherwise, I will come and strike the land[D] with a curse."

[a]3:15 Ps 78:18,41,56; 95:9
[b]Ezk 17:15
[c]3:16 Ex 32:32; Est 6:1; Dn 12:1
[d]3:17 Ex 19:5; Dt 7:6; 14:2; 26:18; Ps 135:4
[e]Ps 103:13; Jl 2:18; Zch 11:5-6
[f]4:2 Ps 37:6; Is 58:8
[g]4:4 Dt 4:10,15; 5:2
[h]4:5 Mt 11:13-14 Jl 2:31; Ac 2:20
[i]4:6 Lk 1:17

[A]4:1 Mal 3:19 in Hb　[B]4:2 Or *like stall-fed calves*　[C]4:6 Mal 3:24 in Hb　[D]4:6 Or *earth*

for all who fear God and treasure His name. Whether such heavenly records exist literally, the many biblical references to them show that God knows and will reward those who belong to Him (1Kg 19:18; Ps 56:8; Is 34:16; Dn 7:10; 2Co 5:10; Rv 20:12). God has already marked a day on His calendar when He will come with compassion to retrieve His **special possession** (see Ex 19:5; Dt 7:6; 14:1-2; 26:18; Ps 135:4), all who serve Him in faith (Ezk 34:11-31; Gl 1:4; Eph 1:14).

4:1 The fiery element of the coming day echoes similar images in eschatological passages such as Jl 2:3-5 (see Ps 21:9; Is 31:9). The wicked may seem powerful, but they will be removed, both **root** and **branches**, from the earth like dry **stubble** thrown into a **furnace**.

4:2-3 Darkness in the Bible often symbolizes earthly life full of evil, ignorance, pain, and death (Gn 1:4; 1Sm 2:9; Is 8:22–9:2). God promises to invade this world with **righteousness** as the **sun** invades the night, driving the darkness away (Dt 33:2; 2Sm 23:3-4; Is 60:1-3,19-21). Other texts clarify that this image represents the Messiah, whose coming will be celebrated like the dawn (Lk 1:76-79), often pictured as the **wings** of the sun (Ps 139:9). As a bird's wings offer protection (Dt 32:11), God's "wings" will bring healing to His chil-

dren (Ps 91:4; Is 53:5; 57:18-19), who will never again fear **the wicked**.

4:4-6 The people of Israel wore tassels as constant reminders of God's instructions (Nm 15:38-40). Malachi called them to **remember**—not to be guided by human wisdom, ambition, or societal expectations, but by the application of God's **instruction** through **Moses** (see Ps 119:16). On the **great and awesome Day of the Lord**, see Jl 2:31 (the only other place where this phrase occurs). This will be a day of blessing for God's people as well as a time of judgment on His enemies. **Elijah**, mentioned 28 times in the NT, was viewed as the preeminent prophet of repentance. He appeared with Moses on the mountain of Jesus' transfiguration to testify that Jesus is the Messiah (Lk 9:29-31). Both Moses and Elijah were connected with **Horeb**, God's mountain (Ex 3:1; 1Kg 19:8). Although this prophecy was provisionally fulfilled by John the Baptist (Mal 3:1-5), it will be further fulfilled at Jesus' return (Mt 11:14; 17:11; Rv 11:3) and it will be accompanied by a great revival of faith in Israel (Dt 30:1-2). Malachi 4:6, quoted in Lk 1:16-17, describes a time of reconciliation when "the disobedient" will accept the wisdom of "the righteous" and when **fathers** and their **children** will no longer live self-serving lives but will regard one another with compassion and respect (2:15; Ezk 5:10; Rm 1:30).

The Origin, Transmission, and Canonization
of the New Testament Books

Jeremy Royal Howard

The term *canon* is the term used to describe the list of books approved for inclusion in the Bible. It stems from a Greek word meaning "rod," as in a straight stick that serves as a standard for measuring. Hence, to speak of the biblical canon is to speak of authoritative books, given by God, the teachings of which define correct belief and practice. Obviously, only books inspired by God should be received as canonical. The Bible before you includes 27 books in the New Testament (NT). Are these the right books? Do they reliably convey truth about Jesus Christ? This essay argues that the 27 books of the NT canon are the correct books and are fully reliable in recounting truth about Jesus and His earliest followers.

Origin and Reliability of the New Testament Writings

The reliability of the NT books rests on questions about their origin: Were they written by eyewitnesses and men closely linked to them? Were the authors inspired by God as they wrote? Historic Christianity has answered yes to these questions. While skeptics maintain that the books were written by men who were inheritors of a legend that had slipped the bonds of reality, Christian confidence in the NT is well founded. Following are some lines of evidence supporting the reliability of the NT.

(1) *Jesus personally groomed twelve disciples.* At the outset of His ministry, Jesus did what many gifted teachers of the ancient world did: He chose a small group of men to be His official students. For approximately three years they listened closely to Jesus' teachings and witnessed His actions. Jesus was intentional in His efforts to teach them; He used effective teaching tools such as parables, repetition, and visual aids. He also taught them *how* to spread His message (Mk 6:7-11) and then commanded them to give their lives to this task after His resurrection (Mt 28:18-20).

Despite many halts and hitches on the path to understanding, the disciples were dedicated to the tasks of comprehending Jesus' teachings and remembering them with precision. But how much could they remember decades later when they and their associates wrote the four Gospels? Three considerations suggest the disciples would have had no trouble remembering Jesus' teachings.

First, note that from the time they last walked with Jesus to the time the Gospels were written, the disciples gave unbroken attention to spreading the word about Jesus. This became their purpose in life. Hence, Jesus' teachings stayed fresh in their minds through the years as they preached in city after city and were continually challenged to defend their claims.

Second, most of us today have lost touch with the potential powers of the human memory. We store reams of data not in our minds, but in books and computers. Lack of such tools forced the ancients to make better use of the brain's storage capacities. The Jews in particular were impressive in this regard. As a people to whom God had revealed His will in spoken and written words, Jewish students of religion were motivated to achieve herculean feats of memorization. It was said that advanced students were like baskets full of books; they kept *everything* in their heads. Though Jesus' disciples lacked this level of training, it is certain that from the moment they were called to be Jesus' students they knew that they were expected to comprehend and remember His teachings. To do anything less would be to disrespect their teacher, especially since they believed He was the Messiah.

Third, it is likely that the disciples wrote down key portions of Jesus' teachings many years before the full Gospels were written. These deposits would have been available to refresh the memory, and they possibly served as handy source material for the writing of the Gospels (see Lk 1:1-4).

(2) *The Holy Spirit helped the disciples understand and remember.* Jesus sent the Spirit to help His disciples comprehend and remember His teachings (Jn 14:26). Thus they were not left to their own efforts when speaking and writing about Jesus. Internal testimony in the NT shows that the disciples became aware of the Spirit's role in each other's writings. The Jews stressed the difference between inspired Scripture and ordinary writing. Rabbis even said the Scriptures "defiled the hands," a surprising phrase that encouraged Jews to consider carefully their intentions before handling Scripture and to decide if these justified the trouble of becoming ceremonially unclean. This teaching discouraged flippant handling of the Scriptures. To claim that a document is from God would be blasphemous if untrue, and yet this is the very claim made by the NT itself. In 1 Timothy 5:18 Paul quotes Luke 10:7 as Scripture. Similarly, Peter affirms that Paul's writings are Scripture in 2 Peter 3:15-16. Peter's writings were in turn received as Scripture on the basis of his apostleship. While it is doubtful that NT authors were conscious at the time of writing that what they wrote was inspired Scripture (for example, see Luke's purpose statement in Lk 1:1-4), they were aware that they bore God-given authority as chosen

Reliability of the New Testament Writings

WERE THE NT BOOKS WRITTEN BY EYEWITNESSES?

YES   NO

UNREASONABLE CONCLUSION
The conclusion goes squarely against the claims of the NT itself as well as early Christian testimony about the NT authors.

The NT documents and early Christian writers affirm that the writings derive from eyewitnesses and/or their close associates.

DID THE WRITERS LIE OR TELL THE TRUTH ABOUT WHAT THEY SAW?

TRUTH   LIE

BY THIS DID THEY GAIN WORLDY GOODS?

UNREASONABLE CONCLUSION
Why would eyewitnesses lie about what they saw and thus fraudulently create a religion when all it earned them was suffering and death?

BY THIS DID THEY GAIN WORLDY GOODS?

YES   NO

NO   YES

UNREASONABLE CONCLUSION
But the NT authors did **not** earn any worldly gain on the basis of their teachings. In fact, they suffered much.

WHAT DROVE THEIR BEHAVIOR?

Mental Illness?
Delusion?
Hype?

UNREASONABLE CONCLUSION
The NT accounts show every evidence of being written by men of sound mind and high ethic. It is unreasonable to suggest that they poured their lives out to tell false tales they mistakenly believed to be truth.

Commitment to truth coupled with a desire to serve God and people.

REASONABLE CONCLUSION
It is most reasonable to conclude that the NT is a truthful account of the remarkable life of Jesus and the early church.

messengers, and the church swiftly received their writings as authoritative, inspired words from God.

(3) *The NT writings stress the importance of eyewitnesses and hard facts.* The NT authors emphasize the role of eyewitnesses and hang their truth claims on the reality of the events they describe. For instance, when Luke discloses his methods and purposes at the beginning of his Gospel (Lk 1:1-4), he says his book is about "the events that have been fulfilled among us" as recounted by "the original eyewitnesses and servants" of Christ. He also says he researched these matters carefully before writing and that his reason for doing this was so his reader could "know the certainty" on which the Christian faith is based. Here is a man who has no place for legends, half-truths, or shots in the dark. His focus is on the real Jesus and on world-altering events that cannot be doubted. John similarly emphasizes the importance of *fact*. He is sure of what he has written and says he has included only a small fraction of Jesus' doings (Jn 20:30 and 21:24-25). And like Luke, John wants his readers to know Jesus as Lord and thus gain eternal life (Jn 20:31 and 1Jn 5:13). Far from passing on shady legends, his goal is to convey assured truth.

Luke and John impress us with their insistence on truth, but the most striking assertion that the NT witness is truthful comes from the apostle Paul. Paul bitterly opposed the young church as it spread from Jerusalem like wildfire. As a zealot for Pharisaic doctrines and all the old ways, he wanted to eradicate Christianity. This all changed when the risen Lord appeared to him on the road to Damascus. In a stunning reversal, Paul then poured the rest of his life into spreading truth about Jesus. The foundation of Paul's preaching was Jesus' resurrection. More than just a snappy preaching point, Paul understood that the literal resurrection of Christ was the absolute basis of Christianity. For this reason, in 1 Corinthians 15:12-19 Paul said that if Christ's resurrection was not a real historical event, Christianity is a myth and Christians are liars. How could Paul dare lay his faith and personal integrity on the line like this? The answer is obvious. Like John, Luke, and every other NT author, Paul knew that Christianity is fixed on the sure foundation of historical reality. Be assured, reader of the NT, that God the Son came in flesh, dwelt among humans, trained disciples for His service, died for us on the cross, rose on the third day and then ascended to heaven, from which He will someday return in power.

Summing up, the NT is to be received as reliable on the basis of the following facts: Jesus trained a group of disciples to comprehend and spread His teachings. Following the established pattern among Jewish students of religion, they would have taken this task with great seriousness, including the memorization of Jesus' key teachings. For a decade or so after Christ's resurrection, these men kept His teachings alive by preaching incessantly and by grooming avid disciples such as Luke and Mark. They also accepted Paul as a bona fide apostle after his miraculous conversion (Ac 9). Then, starting in the mid 40s, the apostles and their approved associates began writing authoritative, Spirit-inspired letters, which they circulated among the churches. Paul's writings came first, and later the Gospels. These writings were received as Scripture by the earliest churches and became the standards by which doctrine and practice were judged.

Factors in the Formation of the New Testament Canon

If one asks when and how the canon formed, the first thing to note is that the canon, being a list of books and not the books themselves, necessarily came into existence *after* the books were written. Thus the authoritative books were inspired Scripture prior to a list identifying them as such. Second, the canon formed as a matter of widespread consensus, not executive pronouncement. Third, in keeping with the first two points, it was several centuries before the canon emerged as a widely acknowledged fact. Critics take this relatively late emergence as proof that the books were not initially received as Scripture and that they came to be regarded as holy books only because later Christians lost sight of how they originated. In reality, however, the piecemeal development of canon consensus was a natural reflection of four conditions:

(1) *The gradual creation and dissemination of the NT books*. The books of the canonical NT were written over a span of approximately fifty years (A.D. 45-95). Before winning universal acceptance, each newly written book had to be circulated, copied, examined, and discussed among the churches. This was not a quick process. Books that were written relatively late underwent the sort of treatment that is common for newcomers: they were vetted with especially great care before being granted a seat among the old guard. Also, the Christian faith multiplied rapidly in the early centuries, with new churches cropping up in far-flung regions at a pace that outstripped the dissemination of the Scriptures. Thus, many early churches had access to only a few NT books. Naturally, when new books came to their attention they were cautious about embracing them as biblical, and they accepted them only after careful consideration and consultation with churches that had been founded by the apostles.

(2) *Apostolic authority and the NT canon*. All the earliest churches were founded by the apostles and their associates as they fanned out from Jerusalem in the years after Jesus' resurrection. Naturally, the churches depended on these men to teach them about Jesus and the Christian life. At first these teachings were strictly oral, but over time the apostles began writing letters and Gospels for the churches, thus providing early Christians with authoritative "books" to guide them in their beliefs and practices. These apostolic churches were among

the first to receive the Scriptures as they were written, and so they were in a good position to help guide newer churches into the correct identification of a NT canon.

(3) *The relative independence of each local church.* Apostolic authority was honored by all true churches at the advent of Christianity, and yet each local church was relatively independent from any centralized ecclesiastical authority. One practical result of this was that no central office pronounced the identities of the NT books or forced their use in worship abroad. Understandably, it took several centuries for churches sprawled all over the map to forge communicative ties and common consensus on the canon.

(4) *The rise of heresy.* When someone came into the churches pushing ideas contrary to what had been received from the apostles, their teachings were recognized as unauthorized innovation. This is the very thing that happened in the second century with the advent of so-called Gnostic Christianity. Gnosticism was a popular dualistic Greek philosophy which held that the material world was created by an evil God. Hence, Gnostics stressed meditation on the secrets of a pure invisible realm, and they denied that God could take on material flesh as Christ did. A man named Marcion wedded Gnosticism with Christian elements and petitioned the church in Rome to adopt his views. Among other perversions, Marcion tried to convince Christians to reject the Old Testament Scriptures and adhere only to the writings of Paul plus a heavily edited version of Luke's Gospel that did not mention Christ's birth. As inheritors of the apostolic teachings, Christians in Rome and elsewhere knew that Marcion's teachings did not square with genuine Christian doctrines. As churches marked the distinction between authorized apostolic writings and the heretical innovations of men such as Marcion, and as Christians all across the Roman Empire endured periodic persecutions that threatened death to anyone harboring Christian Scriptures, the NT began to emerge as a defined and defended body of books. So-called "alternative Christianities," represented in second- and third-century works such as *The Gospel of Thomas* and *The Gospel of Judas,* were never considered for adoption into the NT canon because they were written long after the apostles, and their teachings did not match the Old Testament or the apostolic traditions.

Authoritative Witnesses to the Canon in the Early Church

Though it took several centuries for the canon to emerge as a definite collection of books that were agreed upon by the majority of churches, it is certain that many of the books were widely recognized as Scripture from early on. For example, in A.D. 96 Clement of Rome quoted from Jesus' Sermon on the Mount (Mt 5-7) and treated it as Scripture. As a member of a church founded by an apostle, Clement probably had access to all or nearly all 27 canonical books at this time. In A.D. 110 Ignatius of Antioch, who was a disciple of John, claimed the Gospel materials were Scripture. By A.D. 180, the famed apologist Irenaeus defended Christianity by appealing to the authority of many NT writings. In total, scholars who have examined Irenaeus's surviving works believe he used 22 of our 27 NT books, including all four Gospels. A short time after Irenaeus an apologist named Tertullian charged Gnostic Christians with misusing "the instrument," by which he meant the collection of authoritative NT books. That he would refer to the collection of NT books in this way proves that by this time the leading churches had identified a well-defined set of books as canonical. Only James, 2 Peter, and 2 and 3 John go unnamed by Tertullian. A few decades later the church father Origen named all 27 books and noted that six of them (Hebrews, James, 2 Peter, 2 and 3 John, and Jude) were disputed by some. These disputed books went on to be the subject of debate for many centuries more, though their revered position among most churches was never shaken.

It was in the fourth century that the NT canon clearly emerged as a widely accepted set of holy books. First, Eusebius of Caesarea, known as the father of church history since he was the first to write a comprehensive history of Christianity, named 27 books that were commonly accepted as NT Scripture by the churches. He had reservations about the Book of Revelation, but all in all he names the same canon as we use today. In A.D. 367 the Bishop of Alexandria, a stalwart man named Athanasius, wrote a festal letter in which he listed all 27 NT books as Scripture. He made no note about disputed books—an indication that the disputes mentioned by Origen and Eusebius had diminished in importance by this time. A little more than a decade later the renowned scholar Jerome translated all 27 NT books into Latin and included them in his Bible, which is commonly called the Vulgate. As for the disputed books, he was convinced that their long-standing acceptance in the churches proved that they were indeed Scripture. Augustine, Bishop of Hippo, agreed that the 27 were all canonical. Of the disputed books he said they are to be accepted because the majority of churches, especially those accorded great authority due to their apostolic origins, have long accepted them. Finally, in 393 and 397 the Councils of Hippo and Carthage concluded that the NT canon properly includes 27 books, no more and no less.

The Canon from the Reformation to the Present

The Reformation era was a time in which many beliefs and practices were reexamined in the light of Scripture. Men such as Luther and Calvin desired to peel away the traditions of men and take their cues only from God's

authoritative Word. This emphasis highlighted the need to be certain about which books were from God and which were not. When Luther published a German translation of the NT in 1522, he included all 27 books of the traditional canon even though he sounded a few notes of disapproval over the disputed books. In the table of contents he listed them separately from the undisputed books. For Luther, it seems, the books of the NT were divided into first-class and second-class canons. All 27 books were from God, but he did not believe Hebrews, James, Jude, and Revelation measured up to the others. Despite Luther's reservations, Christianity's long-standing acceptance of a 27-book NT canon was not seriously questioned. In 1546 the Roman Catholic Church affirmed all 27 books at the Council of Trent, and a hundred years later the Protestants did the same in the Westminster Confession of Faith. No sustained challenge to the canon has arisen in the churches since that era.

Preservation of the Manuscripts through the Centuries

It has become popular in recent decades for skeptics to claim that the NT books have evolved beyond all recognition since the days when they were written. Amateur copyists, hapless monks, rogue theologians, sly politicians—folk from many quarters are said to have had a turn at corrupting the text by adding, deleting, and modifying at will. One popular critic famously says that the total number of variations found in the existing manuscripts exceeds the number of words in the entire NT! Technically his claim is true, but the conclusions to be drawn from it are far less drastic than he would have us believe. The fact is the vast majority of all changes are easily detected, and they amount to nothing more than simple misspellings and other minor alterations that have no impact whatsoever on the meaning of the NT. In the few places where the changes potentially have theological importance, scholars are often able to trace the text back to its original reading with confidence. In cases where the original reading is in greater dispute, textual scholars have rightly said that you could eliminate all such verses from the NT and not detract from a single vital doctrine of Christianity. In other words, none of the corrupted verses serve as the sole basis for any NT doctrine. So even if we dropped such verses from the Bible, we could always point to undisputed verses elsewhere in the NT as support for the doctrine in question. In this light we see that the variants are not very important. A fair assessment of the evidence reveals that the NT manuscripts have been preserved remarkably well through centuries of transmission. Aside from inconsequential alterations, the NT manuscripts on which our translation is based are very close replications of the original writings.

Conclusion

The churches that initially received the letters and Gospels written by the apostles and their commissioned associates understood that the writings were Scripture, for they came from men who were recognized as the authorized exponents of Jesus' life and message. These writings were copied with care and circulated to other churches. Awareness of the approved books among Christians increased as the decades clicked away, for slowly the copies reached churches that sprang up far from the point of Christian origins in Israel. It is nevertheless true that many sincere Christian devotees in the early centuries would have been unaware of several or even many of the inspired works since many newer churches had little or no access to Scripture. Hence, the fact that the canon was not widely described until the fourth century does not mean the canon itself was an open question among those who were in a good position to judge the matter. After all, we find clear references to most of the canonical books in the writings of the early church fathers, and certainly Christians who worshiped at churches founded by the apostles had an early grasp of the NT canon since their churches were among those that received the original writings in the first century. It is no exaggeration to say that once the practical obstacles to travel, communication, and dissemination of the manuscripts were alleviated, the 27-book NT canon quickly became the consensus position in Christendom.

Looking back, it is apparent that all the books that were admitted into the canon met the following criteria: (a) they were written either by an apostle or a sanctioned associate of the apostles; (b) they had enjoyed wide and long-standing usage in the churches, especially churches that were founded by the apostles; (c) they reflected high praise for Jesus, were true to the apostolic tradition that had been handed down to the churches, and fit with the overall theology of the other biblical books in both testaments.

In summary, church history shows that great care was taken when candidate books were assessed; the fact that a number of the books in our canon were repeatedly quizzed for their merits proves this beyond all doubt. Our NT canon is a well-proven, carefully protected heritage in which Christians can rejoice and place their full confidence.

New Testament

Matthew

It seems fitting that the first book of the New Testament—the Gospel of Matthew—begins with these words: "the historical record of Jesus Christ." This Gospel was written from a strong Jewish perspective to show that Jesus truly is the Messiah promised in the Old Testament.

"After they were gone, an angel of the Lord suddenly appeared to Joseph in a dream, saying, 'Get up! Take the child and His mother, flee to Egypt, and stay there until I tell you. For Herod is about to search for the child to destroy Him'. . . He stayed there until Herod's death, so that what was spoken by the Lord through the prophet might be fulfilled: Out of Egypt I called My Son" (2:13,15).

Circumstances of Writing

Author: The author did not identify himself in the text. However, the title that ascribes this Gospel to Matthew appears in the earliest manuscripts and is possibly original. Titles became necessary to distinguish one Gospel from another when the four Gospels began to circulate as a single collection. Many early church fathers (Papias, Irenaeus, Pantaenus, and Origen) acknowledged Matthew as the author. Papias also contended that Matthew first wrote in Hebrew, implying that this Gospel was later translated into Greek.

Many modern scholars dispute these traditional claims. For instance, against Papias they argue that this Gospel was not originally written in Hebrew since the Greek of Matthew does not appear to be translation Greek. They further argue that if the early church, following Papias's opinion, was wrong about the original language, they were likely incorrect about the author as well. However, the excellent Greek of Matthew could have been produced by a skilled translator of an original Hebrew text. Furthermore, there are many hints of Hebraic influence in this Gospel (see notes at 1:17, 1:21, and 2:22-23). Finally, since Hebrew quickly ceased to be the dominant language of early Christians as the church expanded into Gentile territories, requiring the Gospel to circulate in a Greek translation, the absence of ancient Hebrew texts of Matthew is not surprising.

Even if Papias was wrong about the original language of the Gospel of Matthew, this does not imply that he and other early church leaders were wrong to identify Matthew as the author of this Gospel. In fact the early church unanimously affirmed that the Gospel of Matthew was authored by the apostle Matthew. It would require impressive evidence to overturn this early consensus.

Clues from the Gospel itself support its ascription to Matthew. First, both Mark 2:14 and Luke 5:27 identify the tax collector whom Jesus called to be His disciple as "Levi." This Gospel, however, identifies Levi as "Matthew." Matthew, a Hebrew name meaning "Gift of God," appears to be the apostolic name that Jesus gave to Levi after he chose to follow Christ, much like Simon was named "Peter" by Jesus after his confession of faith

---

2200–1800 B.C.

From Abraham to David

Abraham 2166–1991

Isaac 2066–1886

Jacob 2006–1859

Joseph 1915–1805

1526–1000 B.C.

Moses 1526–1406

Exodus 1446

Joshua 1490?–1380?

Destruction of Jericho 1406

Judges 1380?–1060?

Ruth 1175?–1125?

Samuel 1105?–1025?

Saul 1080?–1010

1000–586 B.C.

From David to the Babylonian Exile

David 1050?–970

Solomon 990?–931

Rehoboam 971?–913

Jeroboam 971–909

Fall of the Northern Kingdom 722

Fall of the Southern Kingdom 586

(16:18). The use of "Matthew" in this Gospel may be Matthew's personal touch, a self-reference that gives us a clue about authorship.

Background: Determining the date of composition of Matthew's Gospel depends largely on the relationship of the Gospels to one another. Most scholars believe that Matthew utilized Mark's Gospel in writing his own gospel. If this is correct, Matthew's Gospel must postdate Mark's. However, the date of Mark's Gospel is also shrouded in mystery. Irenaeus (ca A.D. 180) seems to claim that Mark wrote his Gospel after Peter's death in the mid-60s. However, Clement of Alexandria, who wrote only 20 years after Irenaeus, claimed that Mark wrote his Gospel while Peter was still alive. Given the ambiguity of the historical evidence, a decision must be based on other factors.

The date of composition for Mark is best inferred from the date of Luke and Acts. The abrupt ending of Acts which left Paul under house arrest in Rome implies that Acts was written before Paul's release. Since one of the major themes of Acts is the legality of Christianity in the Roman Empire, one would have expected Luke to mention Paul's release by the emperor if it had already occurred. This evidence dates Acts to the early 60s. Luke and Acts were two volumes of a single work, as the prologues to these books demonstrate. Luke was written before Acts. Given the amount of research that Luke invested in the book and the travel that eyewitness interviews probably required, a date in the late 50s is reasonable. If Luke used Mark in writing his own Gospel, as seems likely, by implication Mark was written some time before the late 50s, perhaps the early to mid-50s. Thus, despite Matthew's dependence on Mark, Matthew may have been written any time beginning in the mid-50s once Mark was completed. The earliest historical evidence is consistent with this opinion, since Irenaeus (ca A.D. 180) claimed that Matthew wrote his Gospel while Peter and Paul were preaching in Rome (early 60s).

Message and Purpose

Matthew probably wrote his Gospel in order to preserve written eyewitness testimony about the ministry of Jesus. Matthew's Gospel emphasizes certain theological truths. First, Jesus is the Messiah, the long-awaited

586–63 B.C.	5 B.C.–A.D. 33
From the Exile to the Messiah	**Messiah**
Babylonian Exile 586–538	Jesus' birth Winter 5 B.C.
Temple completed 516	Herod the Great's death 4 B.C.
Greeks thwart Persian expansion into Europe with victories at Plataea and Mycale. 479	John the Baptist's ministry begins A.D. 29
	Jesus' ministry begins A.D. 29
Jerusalem's walls completed 445	Jesus' final week March 28–April 3, A.D. 33
Alexander the Great invades Persia. 334	Jesus' resurrection April 5, A.D. 33
Greek control of Palestine 323–167	Jesus' ascension May 14, A.D. 33
Years of Jewish independence 167–63	Feast of Pentecost May 24, A.D. 33
Roman dominance begins. 63	

King of God's people. Second, Jesus is the new Abraham, the founder of a new spiritual Israel consisting of all people who choose to follow Him. This new Israel will consist of both Jews and Gentiles. Third, Jesus is the new Moses, the deliverer and instructor of God's people. Fourth, Jesus is the Immanuel, the virgin-born Son of God who fulfills the promises of the OT.

Contribution to the Bible

As the first book in the NT, the Gospel of Matthew serves as a gateway between the two testaments. Of the NT books, and certainly of the four Gospels, Matthew has the strongest connections to the OT. Matthew gave us God's entire plan from Genesis to Revelation. Matthew looked back and referred to Hebrew prophecies about 60 times ("was fulfilled" and "so that what was spoken . . . might be fulfilled"). He also looked forward by dealing not only with Messiah's coming and His ministry, but also His future plan for His church and kingdom.

Structure

Matthew divided his Gospel into three major sections. He introduced new major sections with the words "from then on Jesus began to" (4:17; 16:21). These transitional statements divide the Gospel into the introduction (1:1–4:16), body (4:17–16:20), and conclusion (16:21–28:20). Matthew also divided his Gospel into five major blocks of teaching, each of which concludes with a summary statement (8:1; 11:1; 13:53; 19:1; 26:1). Some scholars believe these five major discourses were meant to correspond to the five books of Moses and to confirm Jesus' identity as the new Moses.

Outline

I. Birth and Infancy of Jesus (1:1–2:23)
   A. Genealogy (1:1-17)
   B. Birth narratives (1:18–2:18)
   C. Settlement in Nazareth (2:19-23)

II. Beginning of Jesus' Ministry in Galilee (3:1–4:25)
   A. Ministry of John the Baptist (3:1-12)
   B. Baptism of Jesus (3:13-17)
   C. Temptation of Jesus (4:1-11)
   D. Summary of Galilean ministry (4:12-25)

III. Discourse One: The Sermon on the Mount (5:1–7:29)
   A. The Beatitudes (5:1-16)
   B. Character of kingdom righteousness (5:17-48)
   C. Practice of kingdom righteousness (6:1–7:12)
   D. Choice of the kingdom (7:13-27)
   E. Manner of Jesus' teaching (7:28-29)

IV. Jesus' First Miracles (8:1–9:38)
   A. A series of miracles (8:1–9:8)
   B. The kingdom and the old order (9:9-17)
   C. More miracles (9:18-38)

V. Discourse Two: Ministry of Jesus' Disciples (10:1-42)
   A. The preachers and their mission (10:1-15)
   B. The response to be expected (10:16-42)

The Genealogy of Jesus Christ

1 The[a] historical record[A,b] of Jesus Christ, the Son of David,[c] the Son of Abraham:[d]

From Abraham to David

2 Abraham fathered[B] Isaac,
   Isaac fathered Jacob,
   Jacob fathered Judah and his brothers,[e]
3 Judah fathered Perez and Zerah
   by Tamar,
   Perez fathered Hezron,
   Hezron fathered Aram,[f]
4 Aram fathered Amminadab,
   Amminadab fathered Nahshon,
   Nahshon fathered Salmon,
5 Salmon fathered Boaz by Rahab,
   Boaz fathered Obed by Ruth,
   Obed fathered Jesse,[g]
6 and Jesse fathered King David.

From David to the Babylonian Exile

Then[c] David fathered Solomon
   by Uriah's wife,[h]
7 Solomon fathered Rehoboam,
   Rehoboam fathered Abijah,
   Abijah fathered Asa,[D]
8 Asa[D] fathered Jehoshaphat,
   Jehoshaphat fathered Joram,[E]

Joram fathered Uzziah,[i]
9 Uzziah fathered Jotham,
   Jotham fathered Ahaz,
   Ahaz fathered Hezekiah,
10 Hezekiah fathered Manasseh,
   Manasseh fathered Amon,[F]
   Amon fathered Josiah,[j]
11 and Josiah fathered Jechoniah
   and his brothers
   at the time of the exile to Babylon.[k]

From the Exile to the Messiah

12 Then after the exile to Babylon
   Jechoniah fathered Shealtiel,
   Shealtiel fathered Zerubbabel,
13 Zerubbabel fathered Abiud,
   Abiud fathered Eliakim,
   Eliakim fathered Azor,[l]
14 Azor fathered Zadok,
   Zadok fathered Achim,
   Achim fathered Eliud,
15 Eliud fathered Eleazar,
   Eleazar fathered Matthan,
   Matthan fathered Jacob,
16 and Jacob fathered Joseph the husband
   of Mary,
   who gave birth to[G] Jesus who is called
   the *Messiah.[m]

Cross-references

a 1:1-6 Ru 4:18-22; 2Sm 7:12-16; 1Ch 2:1-15; Lk 3:32-34
b 1:1 Mk 12:26; Lk 3:4; Ac 1:20; Php 4:3; Rv 3:5
c Ps 89:3; Is 9:6; Lk 1:32,69
d Gn 22:18; Mt 9:7; Rm 1:3; Gl 3:16
e 1:2 Gn 29:35; Ps 14:7; 105:9; Mt 8:11; 22:32; Jms 2:21
f 1:3 Gn 38:29-30; 46:12; Lk 3:33
g 1:5 Ru 1:4; 2:1; Lk 3:32
h 1:6 1Sm 16:1; 17:12; 2Sm 11:27; 12:24
i 1:7-8 1Kg 11:43; 14:31; 15:8,24; 22:50; 2Kg 14:21
j 1:9-10 2Kg 15:5,38; 16:20; 20:21; 21:18,24
k 1:11 2Kg 24:6,14; Is 5:13; Jr 27:20; Ezk 1:1; Mt 1:17
l 1:12-13 Gn 10:10; 1Ch 3:17; Lk 3:27,30
m 1:16 Mt 27:17,22; Lk 2:11; Jn 1:45; 4:25

A 1:1 Or *The book of the genealogy*   B 1:2 In vv. 2-16 either a son, as here, or a later descendant, as in v. 8   C 1:6 Other mss add *King*   D 1:7,8 Other mss read *Asaph*   E 1:8 = Jehoram   F 1:10 Other mss read *Amos*   G 1:16 Lit *Mary, from whom was born*

1:1 The title of this genealogy introduces several important themes in Matthew. Jesus is identified as the **Christ**, Messiah, the King anointed by God to rule over His people. This is reiterated by identifying Jesus as **Son of David** (v. 20; 2:2; 9:27; 12:3,23; 15:22; 20:30-31; 21:9,15). OT prophecies like 2Sm 7:16 and Is 9:2-7 foretold that Messiah (the "anointed one") would be a descendant of King David. Jesus' Davidic lineage shows that He meets this qualification. Though the genealogy is otherwise arranged in chronological order, Matthew shifted "Son of David" ahead of **Son of Abraham** to lay emphasis on the royal title.

The title "Son of Abraham" implies that just as Abraham was the father of national Israel, Jesus will be the founder of a new spiritual Israel. The phrase the **historical record of Jesus** is unusual. OT genealogies are consistently named after the earliest ancestor in the lineage because the Jews considered that person to be most significant since everyone else derived from them. That Matthew names his genealogy after Jesus, the final descendant in the lineage, implies that Jesus is more important than anyone who preceded Him.

1:2-6 Matthew mentioned four women in his genealogy, all of them Gentiles. **Tamar** was a Canaanite. **Rahab** was from Jericho. **Ruth** was a Moabitess. **Uriah's wife** Bathsheba was probably a Hittite. The mention of these women signals God's intention to include Gentiles and women in His redemptive plan. Several kings are named also, but only David is explicitly given the title **King**. This highlights that the Son of David (Jesus) will likewise be a kingly figure.

1:7-16 Matthew's genealogy agrees with the genealogies of 1Ch 1-3 and Lk 3:23-38 from the generation of Abraham down to David. After David, Matthew's genealogy agrees with that of 1 Chronicles except for a few intentional gaps, but departs significantly from Luke's. Some interpreters argue from this, that one or both of the NT genealogies is inaccurate. However, Jews in David's line carefully preserved their genealogies because they knew from the OT prophecies that one of their descendants would be Messiah. David's descendants also had the privilege of providing firewood for the altar in Jerusalem (*m. Ta'an.* 4:5). Naturally, they kept careful records to demonstrate their Davidic descent and preserve their privileges. Evidence in Josephus (*Life* 1) and rabbinic texts suggests that genealogical archives were kept in public registers.

Scholars suggest several ways in which the genealogies of Matthew and Luke may be harmonized. First, one may preserve the genealogy of Jesus through Mary and the other through Joseph. Second, the custom of levirate marriage resulted in a child having different biological and legal fathers. Perhaps one genealogy follows the biological line while the other follows the legal. Third, one genealogy may trace David's legal descendants who would have reigned if the Davidic kingdom had continued while the other lists descendants in Joseph's specific line. A combination of these approaches is also possible.

In English, it is difficult to identify the antecedent of the first occurrence of the pronoun **who** in verse 16. However, in Matthew's Greek, the pronoun is feminine. Thus, although the rest of the genealogy focuses on fathers and only rarely mentions mothers, Matthew identified a human mother but not a human father of Jesus, thus implying Jesus' virginal conception.

¹⁷So all the generations from Abraham to David were 14 generations; and from David until the exile to Babylon, 14 generations; and from the exile to Babylon until the Messiah, 14 generations.ᵃ

The Nativity of the Messiah

¹⁸The birth of Jesus Christ came about this way: After His mother Mary had been •engaged to Joseph, it was discovered before they came together that she was pregnant by the Holy Spirit.ᵇ ¹⁹So her husband Joseph, being a righteous man,ᶜ and not wanting to disgrace her publicly, decided to divorce her secretly.ᵈ

²⁰But after he had considered these things, an angel of the Lord suddenly appeared to him in a dream, saying, "Joseph, son of David, don't be afraid to take Mary as your wife, because what has been conceived in her is by the Holy Spirit.ᵉ ²¹She will give birth to a son, and

you are to name Him Jesus,ᴬᶠ because He will save His people from their sins."ᵍ

²²Now all this took place to fulfill what was spoken by the Lord through the prophet:

²³ **See, the virgin will become pregnant**
   and give birth to a son,
   and they will name Him Immanuel,ᴮ

which is translated "God is with us."ʰ

²⁴When Joseph got up from sleeping, he did as the Lord's angel had commanded him. He married herⁱ ²⁵but did not know her intimately until she gave birth to a son.ᶜ And he named Him Jesus.ʲ

Wise Men Seek the King

2 After Jesus was born in Bethlehem of Judea in the days of King •Herod, •wise

Cross references (center column)
ᵃ1:17 2Kg 24:14; Jr 27:20; Dn 9:25-26; Mk 8:29; Ac 2:31,36,38
ᵇ1:18 Mt 12:46; Lk 1:27,35
ᶜ1:19 Mt 13:17; Mk 10:12; Lk 2:36; 1Co 14:35; 2Co 11:2; Gl 4:27
ᵈ Dt 22:20-24; 24:1-4; Mt 2:7; Lk 16:18; Jn 8:4-5
ᵉ1:20 2Ch 1:1; Mt 13:49; 27:19; Jn 6:20; Rm 1:3
ᶠ1:21 Lk 1:31; 2:21; Jn 10:25; 1Jn 2:12
ᵍ Lk 2:11; Jn 1:29; Ac 4:12; 5:31; 13:23,38-39
ʰ1:22-23 Is 7:14; Mt 21:1-4; Lk 24:44; Rm 1:2-4
ⁱ1:24 Mt 1:6; 13:49; Lk 1:1;
19:32; Jd 5   ʲ1:25 Gn 4:1,17; Ex 13:2; Jdg 11:39; 1Sm 1:19; Lk 2:7,21

ᴬ1:21 *Jesus* is the Gk form of the Hb name "Joshua," which = "The LORD saves" or "Yahweh saves."   ᴮ1:23 Is 7:14   ᶜ1:25 Other mss read *to her firstborn son*

1:17 Matthew's arrangement of Jesus' genealogy into three sets of **14 generations** is probably an example of gematria, a system that assigns numerical value to letters of the alphabet (e.g. A = 1, B = 2, etc.) in order to communicate a subtle message. In Hebrew, the numerical value of the letters composing the name "David" is 14. Thus Matthew's artistic arrangement probably highlights Jesus' Davidic lineage. If Matthew did intentionally use gematria, this supports the view that he originally wrote his Gospel in Hebrew, for the gematria functions in the Hebrew version of the genealogy but not the Greek.

1:18 The words **of Jesus Christ** are in an emphatic position in the Greek text, implying that the circumstances of Jesus' birth differed from those of everyone else in the genealogy. Although several of those people were conceived by miracles, they all had a human father. Only Jesus was born of a virgin. **Before they came together** means that Joseph and Mary had not yet had intercourse. Joseph thus assumed that Mary had been unfaithful. **Pregnant by the Holy Spirit** means that Mary's pregnancy was a miracle performed by the Spirit, not that God assumed material form and physically impregnated her. This makes Jesus' conception dramatically different from Greek myths that speak of children born to gods who lay with women.

1:19 Joseph did not want to humiliate Mary publicly because he was a **righteous man**. His peers most likely expected him to expose her apparent sin, but true righteousness is characterized by compassion and mercy, an important theme for Matthew (5:6-7,21-26,38-48).

1:20 God spoke to Joseph through dreams, just as He did to his OT namesake (Gn 37:1-11). The title **son of David** reminded Joseph of his royal lineage and prepared him for the announcement of Messiah's birth. On **conceived . . . by the Holy Spirit**, see note at verse 18.

1:21 **Jesus** is the Greek form of the Hebrew name *Joshua* which means "Yahweh saves." The angel explained that Jesus' name revealed His purpose: He would rescue sinners from the punishment they deserve. This salvation would be experienced by **His people**, identified as those who follow Jesus.

1:22 **Spoken by the Lord through the prophet** implies that God was the ultimate author of the messages spoken and

written by the prophets. The grammar that Matthew uses to introduce the quote from Is 7:14 (see Mt 1:23) suggests that the angel quoted this verse to Joseph during his announcement. Some interpreters argue that Matthew mishandled Isaiah 7:14, but he seems to have handled it just as the angel did, which means his usage is backed by angelic authority.

1:23 The name **Immanuel** (God with us) implies Jesus' deity. Mary's virgin-born Son would be God Himself living among His people. The Immanuel of Is 7:14 is to be identified with the person described in Is 9:2-7 and 11:1-9.

1:24-25 These verses emphasize Joseph's absolute obedience to the angel's instructions, a prevalent theme in these early chapters (2:13-15,19-21). Joseph is a model of the obedience that should characterize Jesus' disciples (5:19-20). **Did not know her intimately** confirms again that Jesus was the product of a virginal conception.

2:1 The **wise men** were magi. Eastern magi mixed

magos

Greek Pronunciation	[MAH gahss]
HCSB Translation	wise man, sorcerer
Uses in Matthew	4
Uses in the NT	6
Focus passage	Matthew 2:1,7,16

In the Greek OT, *magos* occurs only in Daniel 2:2,10 and describes a group of people possessing knowledge of Babylonian religious and magical arts, whom Nebuchadnezzar summoned to interpret his dream. In Matthew 2:1,7,16, *magos* refers to those who have wisdom through investigation and interpretation of the movements of heavenly bodies (i.e., *wise men/astrologers*). It is likely (though not certain) these *astrologers* were from Babylon, since there they would have had contact with Jewish exiles and obtained an interest in the Jewish Messiah. The irony in the passage is difficult to miss: The Jewish King Herod in Jerusalem attempted to slaughter baby Jesus born in nearby Bethlehem, while pagan devotees of a foreign religion recognized Messiah's star, traveled a great distance to find Him, presented Him with valuable gifts, and paid homage to Him. Elsewhere in the NT, *magos* refers to Elymas the *sorcerer* (Ac 13:6,8).

men from the east arrived unexpectedly in Jerusalem,[a 2] saying, "Where is He who has been born King of the Jews?[b] For we saw His star in the east[A,c] and have come to worship Him."[B]

[3] When King Herod heard this, he was deeply disturbed, and all Jerusalem with him. [4] So he assembled all the •chief priests and •scribes[d] of the people and asked them where the •Messiah would be born.

[5] "In Bethlehem of Judea," they told him, "because this is what was written by the prophet:

[6]   **And you, Bethlehem,** in the land
        of Judah,
      are by no means **least**
        among the leaders of Judah:
      because out of you will come a leader
      who will shepherd My people Israel."[C,e]

[7] Then Herod secretly summoned the wise men and asked them the exact time the star appeared. [8] He sent them to Bethlehem and said, "Go and search carefully for the child. When you find Him, report back to me so that I too can go and worship Him."[D,f]

[9] After hearing the king, they went on their way. And there it was—the star they had seen in the east![E] It led them until it came and stopped above the place where the child was. [10] When they saw the star, they were overjoyed beyond measure. [11] Entering the house, they saw the child with Mary His mother, and falling to their knees, they worshiped Him.[F] Then they opened their treasures and presented Him with gifts: gold, frankincense, and myrrh.[g] [12] And being warned[h] in a dream not to go back to Herod, they returned to their own country by another route.

Cross references:
[a]2:1 Gn 25:6; 1Kg 4:30; Lk 1:5; 2:4-7
[b]2:2 Jr 23:5; 30:9; Zch 9:9; Mt 27:11; Lk 19:38; Jn 1:49
[c] Nm 24:17; Rv 22:16
[d]2:4 Mt 16:21; 20:18; 21:15; 27:41; Lk 9:22
[e]2:6 2Sm 5:2; Mc 5:2; Jn 7:42; 21:16
[f]2:7-8 Mk 5:6; Lk 1:7; Ac 13:6; Rv 1:16
[g]2:11 Ps 72:10; Is 60:6; Mt 1:18; 12:46; Mk 5:6
[h]2:12 Mt 27:19; Lk 2:26; Ac 10:22; Heb 8:5; 11:7

A2:2 Or *star at its rising*   B2:2 Or *to pay Him homage*   C2:6 Mc 5:2   D2:8 Or *and pay Him homage*   E2:9 Or *star . . . at its rising*
F2:11 Or *they paid Him homage*

Zoroastrianism with astrology and black magic. They are described in Dn 2:2,4-5,10, where they are associated with diviner-priests, mediums, and sorcerers. The term "magus" (sg of "magi") appears only once in the NT. It describes the sorcerer whom Paul portrayed as a "son of the Devil, full of all deceit and all fraud, enemy of all righteousness" (Ac 13:6-10). The magus of whom Paul spoke would have held beliefs that were similar to those of the wise men. Thus, the summons of the magi to visit Jesus demonstrates God's intention to save Gentiles from their futile religions. As an adult, Jesus cast out demons and broke Satan's grip on beleaguered people. Here we see that even in His infancy, Christ plundered Satan's kingdom and set captives free. The **east** may refer to Babylonia or Persia.

2:2 The question posed by the wise men was an unintentional challenge to Herod's reign. Jesus was **born King** in the sense that He was from David's line and thus King by birthright. Herod, however, was neither a full Jew nor a descendant of David and thus was not genuinely qualified to reign as king. The word translated **star** can indicate many different astronomical phenomena, including comets, meteors, or planetary conjunctions. Matthew later (2:9) described the star as moving through the sky in order to point the magi to Jesus' precise location. This indicates that it was no ordinary star. **In the east** probably means "at its rising," indicating that the star mysteriously appeared in the eastern sky to signal Messiah's birth. The interest of the magi in astrology, a practice condemned in the Bible (Is 47:13-15), probably first directed their attention to Messiah's star. In another profound display of grace, God condescended to use the magi's pagan superstitions to draw them to Jesus.

2:3 Herod was **disturbed** by reports of the birth of a legitimate claimant to his throne. The people of **Jerusalem** were equally disturbed because they feared Herod's paranoid and delusional rages. In the past he had killed even his favorite wife and sons in order to protect his rule.

2:4 Herod summoned expert scribes to learn where the OT said Messiah would be born. To this point the star had guided the wise men near to Jesus, but now the witness

of the Scriptures was necessary before God caused the star to reappear and pinpoint Messiah's exact location. Thus the value of biblical revelation was upheld even as new revelations unfolded.

2:5-6 The chief priests and scribes (v. 3) knew Scripture well enough to identify **Bethlehem** as Messiah's birthplace (Mc 5:2; Jn 7:42), but nevertheless they later opposed His teachings. Knowledge of Scripture does not guarantee that your heart is right with God. The priestly opposition to Jesus is foreshadowed here by the fact that they made no effort to go visit Him even as the magi undertook the last leg of a long journey to do so. Micah 5:2 foretold that Bethlehem would be the birthplace of a king, a ruler who would **shepherd . . . Israel**. Although Micah said that the promised prince would "rule" over Israel, Matthew's translation says that Messiah will "shepherd" Israel. Matthew likely chose this word to reflect Micah's use in 5:4 and thus show that the entirety of Mc 5 applies to Jesus. This indicates that Jesus is eternal since Micah says "His origin is from antiquity, from eternity." Micah's prophecy also said that the shepherd's "greatness will extend to the ends of the earth."

2:7-8 Herod questioned the magi about the **exact time** of the star's appearance under the assumption that the star first appeared at the time of the child's birth. On the basis of this date, he ordered the execution of all male children in Bethlehem two years of age and under (2:16). This implies that the magi's journey was lengthy and involved great sacrifice. Herod's pretended desire to worship Messiah highlights his deceitfulness.

2:11 In contrast to the stable in which Jesus was born (Lk 2), Jesus' family now lived in a **house**. This shows that the magi visited Jesus after the visit of the shepherds described by Luke. The magi worshiped Jesus openly, as did many other people during His lifetime (8:2; 9:18; 14:33; 15:25; 20:20; 28:9,17). Jesus' reception of worship reinforces His identity as Immanuel, "God with us" (1:23).

2:13-14 The angel called Jesus **the child** rather than "your child" when speaking to Joseph because Joseph was not

The Flight into Egypt

¹³ After they were gone, an angel of the Lord suddenly appeared to Joseph in a dream, saying, "Get up! Take the child and His mother, flee to Egypt, and stay there until I tell you. For Herod is about to search for the child to destroy Him."ᵃ ¹⁴ So he got up, took the child and His mother during the night, and escaped to Egypt. ¹⁵ He stayed there until Herod's death, so that what was spoken by the Lord through the prophet might be fulfilled: **Out of Egypt I called My Son.**ᴬ,ᵇ

The Massacre of the Innocents

¹⁶ Then Herod, when he saw that he had been outwitted by the wise men, flew into a rage. He gave orders to massacre all the male children in and around Bethlehem who were two yearsᴮ old and under, in keeping with the time he had learned from the wise men.ᶜ ¹⁷ Then what was spoken through Jeremiah the prophet was fulfilled:

¹⁸ A voice was heard in Ramah,
weeping,ᶜ and great mourning,
Rachel weeping for her children;
and she refused to be consoled,
because they were no more.ᴰ,ᵈ

The Holy Family in Nazareth

¹⁹ After Herod died, an angel of the Lord suddenly appeared in a dream to Joseph in Egypt,ᵉ ²⁰ saying, "Get up! Take the child and His mother and go to the land of Israel, because those who sought the child's life are dead." ²¹ So he got up, took the child and His mother, and entered the land of Israel. ²² But when he heard that Archelausᴱ was ruling over Judea in place of his father Herod, he was afraid to go there. And being warned in a dream, he withdrew to the region of Galilee.ᶠ ²³ Then he went and settled in a town called Nazareth to fulfill what was spoken through the prophets, that He will be called a •Nazarene.ᵍ

ᵃ2:13 Mt 1:20; 13:49; Mk 11:18; Jms 4:7 ᵇ2:15 Ex 4:22; Nm 24:8; Hs 11:1 ᶜ2:16 Is 59:7; Mk 10:34; Ac 13:6; 25:3; Rv 12:4 ᵈ2:18 Gn 35:19; Jdg 4:5; Jr 31:15; Ac 8:2; 2Co 7:7 ᵉ2:19 Mt 1:20; 13:49; Lk 1:11; Jd 5 ᶠ2:22 Mt 17:22; Lk 1:5; Ac 27:29; Col 3:21; Heb 8:5 ᵍ2:23 Mk 1:24; Lk 1:26; Jn 1:45-46

ᴬ2:15 Hs 11:1   ᴮ2:16 Lit *were from two years*   ᶜ2:18 Other mss read *Ramah, lamentation, and weeping,*   ᴰ2:18 Jr 31:15
ᴱ2:22 A son of Herod the Great who ruled a portion of his father's kingdom 4 B.C.–A.D. 6

Jesus' biological father. Similarly, he described Mary as **His mother** rather than "your wife" because he wished to identify her in relation to the greater (Jesus) rather than the lesser (Joseph). Joseph promptly obeyed when he was told to **flee to Egypt.** See note at 1:24-25.

2:15 That **what was spoken** had to be fulfilled indicates that the Bible is inspired by God and authoritative over history. In its original context, the calling of the son **out of Egypt** in Hs 11 is a reference to Israel's exodus from Egypt, not young Messiah's trip back home. Matthew understood this, but under the Spirit's direction he recognized Jesus as the new Moses who will lead a new and climactic exodus. Just as Moses delivered his people from slavery to Pharaoh, Jesus will deliver people from slavery to Satan. Thus Matthew rightly regarded Hs 11:1 and other portions of the OT as foreshadows of Jesus and events in His life.

2:16-17 Skeptics deny that Herod ever slaughtered the boys of Bethlehem since no extrabiblical source documents this horrific event. However, the murders are consistent with his documented dealings, such as his murdering his own family. The Jewish historian Josephus reported that Herod arranged for many Jewish nobles to be murdered upon his death in order to ensure that the land mourned his passing (*Ant.* 17:167-69). Herod's behavior is reminiscent of Pharaoh's around the time of Moses' birth (Ex 1:15-22). This and other striking similarities to Moses' birth narrative strengthen Matthew's presentation of Jesus as the new Moses whom God promised in Dt 18:15-19. Ancient Jews thought of Moses as a deliverer (Ac 7:25,35). By highlighting parallels between Moses and Jesus, Matthew shows that Jesus was the promised Deliverer who would save His people from their sins (see notes at Mt 1:7-16 and 2:20-21). Herod killed all boys **two years old and under** in Bethlehem because the star had appeared to the magi two years previously, presumably at the moment of Jesus' birth.

2:17-18 Once again Matthew introduces a quotation in a way that implies that the OT author (Jeremiah in this case) was used by God to proclaim His message. This was the unquestioned view among religious Jews from the day of the prophets down to Jesus' day. In verse 18 Matthew quotes Jr 31:15 which originally expressed the lament of mothers who grieved over sons who were sent into exile. Matthew's application here implies that Israel was again in exile, estranged from God, and in need of redemption. Since Jr 31 includes the weeping and then climaxes with the joyous promise that God would establish a new covenant with His people, one in which He would forgive their sins and write His law on their hearts, Matthew likely intends to call this to mind and apply it to the Bethlehem massacre and the coming of Jesus. Just as the weeping of mothers preceded the promise of the new covenant in Jr 31, so now the **weeping** of mothers preceded the establishment of the new covenant through Jesus (see note at 26:28).

2:19 Since **Herod died** in 4 B.C., and since Jesus was born roughly two years before Herod ordered the massacre of the Bethlehem boys, it seems that Jesus was born in 5 or 6 B.C. It also seems likely that the shameless Bethlehem massacre was one of Herod's final acts. A fitting close to a life of infamous violence.

2:20-21 The angel's words are almost identical to the words Yahweh spoke to Moses from the burning bush (Ex 4:19, LXX). This allusion to the Moses narrative again identifies Jesus as the new Moses (see notes at 2:15 and 2:16-17). Jesus, now perhaps three years old, returns from Egypt with his family.

2:22-23 Archelaus, son of Herod the Great, inherited his father's violent traits. His rule over Judea signaled that the holy family should settle elsewhere, and so Joseph led his family to resettle in the obscure Galilean village of **Nazareth,** where Joseph and Mary had previously lived (Lk 1:26). Matthew states that the decision was a fulfillment of an OT prophecy that Messiah **will be called a Nazarene.** No specific OT text explicitly prophesies this, and so Matthew was appealing to a prominent OT theme rather than a particular text. Specifically, he was probably alluding to

Differences in the Gospels

Robert H. Stein

Serious readers of the Gospels notice various differences between them. One difference involves geographical arrangement. In the Synoptic Gospels (Matthew, Mark, and Luke), Jesus visits Jerusalem only once during His entire ministry. For instance, all of the events in Mark 1:1–11:10 take place either in Galilee (1:1–8:21) or on the way to Jerusalem (8:22–11:10). Only from 11:11 forward is Jesus recorded as entering Jerusalem. The Gospel of John takes a different approach. John records Jesus visiting Jerusalem several times throughout His ministry (2:13–4:45; 5:1-47; 7:1–10:40; and 12:12–20:31), including an early temple cleansing (John 2:13-22). The Synoptics say nothing about an early temple cleansing, and John in turn says nothing about the later cleansing that the Synoptics recount (Mt 21:12-13; Mk 11:15-18; Lk 19:45-48). It seems the authors chose different ways of using geography as a tool for arranging their accounts of Jesus' life. Mark, whose Gospel likely predated and influenced Matthew and Luke, chose not to discuss any of Jesus' doings in Jerusalem until the climactic events beginning in 11:11. This literary approach builds a steady tension that finally explodes with Jesus' crucifixion in the sacred city. John, writing years after the Synoptics, took a different approach, sprinkling Jerusalem throughout his account.

Another literary consideration that helps account for differences among the Gospels is how the authors chose to group Jesus' teachings. Matthew is organized around alternating blocks of Stories of Jesus and Teachings of Jesus. Here is the arrangement: chapters 1–4 (S); 5–7 (T); 8–9 (S); 10 (T); 11–12 (S); 13 (T); 14–17 (S); 18 (T); 19–22 (S); 23–25 (T); 26–28 (S). Luke, on the other hand, places the teachings of Jesus in two large sections: 6:20–8:3; and 9:51–18:14. Different approaches such as this explain why the Gospel authors often place sayings of Jesus in different contexts, as for instance when Matthew records the Lord's Prayer early in Jesus' ministry (6:9-13) while Luke places it later (11:1-4). The Gospel writers arranged much of their material on topical and logical grounds rather than chronological. The earliest reference to any Gospel was made by Papias, a church father who in the first decade of the second century stated that Mark wrote accurately but *not in chronological order* the traditions he learned from Peter. Thus early readers noticed the differences between the Gospels, understood some of the basic causes of the differences, and did not regard them as problematic.

Another reason for differences involves the literary style of individual evangelists. In Matthew 8:5-13 and Luke 7:1-10 we have two accounts of Jesus healing a centurion's servant. In Luke the conversation takes place between Jesus and Jewish elders who speak on behalf of the centurion. In Matthew the conversation is directly between Jesus and the centurion. There is no conflict in these accounts when we realize that Matthew has abbreviated the story (103 words compared to 186 words in Luke). Matthew omitted material unessential to the story, and the elders (serving as go-betweens) are the least important element in the story. Thus, just as modern-day journalists report on meetings between heads of state without mentioning the go-betweens, Matthew makes no mention of the elders.

Furthermore, the evangelists understood themselves to be inspired interpreters, not mere stenographers of Jesus' acts and teachings. They felt free to clarify and add explanatory comments to the traditions they were recording. For example, whereas Matthew in 7:11 records Jesus as saying God the Father gives "good things" to those who ask, Luke has Jesus saying God gives "the Holy Spirit." In this case, Luke has done some interpretive extension: of all the good things God gives, the Holy Spirit is the best of them. Other examples of inspired editorial work include:

The Baptism of Jesus

- In Matthew 3:17 the voice from heaven states, "This is My beloved Son."
- In Mark 1:11 and Luke 3:22 the voice states, "You are My beloved Son."
- Explanation: In Mark and Luke, God's voice addresses Jesus. Matthew shifts the audience to the bystanders in order to make clear to his readers that God would have them know that Jesus is His Son. The overall meaning is unchanged.

The Beatitudes

- In Matthew 5:3 the first beatitude reads, "The poor in spirit are blessed . . ."
- Luke 6:20 has, "You who are poor are blessed . . ."
- Explanation: Matthew gives a "thought for thought" rather than "word for word" translation of the original. He adds "in spirit" to help his readers understand that in this context "poor" refers to spiritual

The Messiah's Herald

3 In those days John the Baptist came,[a] preaching in the Wilderness of Judea[b 2] and saying, "Repent, because the kingdom of heaven has come near!"[c 3] For he is the one spoken of through the prophet Isaiah, who said:

**A voice of one crying out
in the wilderness:**

**Prepare the way
for the Lord;
make His paths straight![A,d]**

[4] John himself had a camel-hair garment with a leather belt around his waist, and his food was locusts and wild honey. [5] Then people from Jerusalem, all Judea, and all the vicinity of the Jordan were flocking to him, [6] and they

[a]3:1-12 Mk 1:3-8; Lk 3:2-17; Jn 1:6-8,19-28
[b]3:1 Jos 15:61; Jdg 1:16
[c]3:2 Dn 2:44; Mt 4:17; 6:10; 10:7; Mk 1:15; Lk 10:9; 11:20; 21:31
[d]3:3 Is 40:3; Lk 1:17,76; Jn 1:23

A3:3 Is 40:3

the "Branch prophecies" since the Hebrew consonants *nzr* (which make up the word "branch") are shared by the words "Nazareth" and "Nazarene." These prophecies (Is 4:2; 11:1; Jr 23:5; 33:15) told of a righteous descendant of David whose wise and just rule would be empowered by the Spirit and who would bring salvation to Judah. Matthew thus saw Jesus' hometown as a subtle clue to His identity as Messiah.

3:1 In those days means "during the time of Jesus' residence in Nazareth" rather than "during the reign of Archelaus." After all, Archelaus reigned from 4 b.c. to a.d. 6, too early for **John the Baptist** to have begun his ministry since he would have been under age 12. In OT usage, "in those days" often referred to a time of prophetic fulfillment (Is 10:20; Am 9:11; Zph 1:15; Zch 12:3-4). Matthew probably used the phrase in conjunction with his references to fulfilled prophecy to emphasize that God's promises were being fulfilled through Jesus and John the Baptist, herald and predecessor of Messiah. The location of John's ministry (**Wilderness of Judea**) is reminiscent of the ministry of the prophet Elijah (1Kg 17:3; 19:3-18; 2Kg 2:1-12), whom many Jews believed would appear again to prepare the way for Messiah (Mt 17:10-13). Josephus described

John's ministry in a way that closely matches the Gospel accounts (Ant. 18.114-119).

3:2 John's message focused on repentance and the coming **kingdom of heaven**. Jesus emphasized the same thing from the outset of His ministry (see note at 4:17). The kingdom is defined as the rule which God exercises through the person, work, and teachings of Jesus. The call to **repent** means we must abandon sinful lifestyles and express sorrow for sins.

3:3 Matthew's application of Is 40:3 to John the Baptist tells us as much about Jesus as it does about John. After all, in its original context the prophecy spoke of one who prepared the way for the coming of Yahweh, God Himself. By using a text about the coming of Yahweh to describe the coming of Jesus, Matthew proclaimed that Jesus is divine.

3:4 John's **garment** was similar to Elijah's (2Kg 1:8) and his ministry and lifestyle paralleled Elijah's also, including his residence in the Judean wilderness, his austere diet, his call for Israel to repent, and his confrontation with an evil king and his wife. Jesus explained the significance of these parallels in Mt 11:14; 17:12-13.

3:6 Although Jews required Gentiles to immerse themselves in water in order to convert from paganism to Judaism,

humility. A similar usage of "poor" occurs in Psalm 86:1, where King David (who was financially wealthy) speaks of being "poor and needy."

Hour of the Crucifixion

- In Mark 15:25 Jesus is crucified at "nine in the morning" (the third hour).
- In John 19:14 Jesus is crucified at "about six in the morning."
- Explanation: There are twenty-three time designations in the New Testament referring to a particular hour. Twenty of them refer to the third, sixth, or ninth hour. Only three designate other hours (the seventh, tenth, and eleventh). In an era when timekeeping was imprecise, a mid-morning crucifixion (occurring at, say, 10:30 a.m.) could very reasonably have been referred to as taking place at either the third or sixth hours since it fell between these times.

Peter's Denial of Christ

- Mark tells his readers of Peter's denial in Mk 14:53-54 and 14:66-72. Wedged between this two-part account is the story of Jesus' trial.
- Luke completes the entire account of Peter's denial before telling of Jesus' trial.
- Explanation: Rather than a chronological discrepancy, these are two different ways of telling two separate stories. Mark follows one of his favored stylistic techniques and "sandwiches" Jesus' trial between the two halves of the story of Peter's denial. Luke chooses to treat them separately.

We have avoided such terms as "discrepancy" and "contradiction" when discussing differences among the Gospels. When we seek to understand what the evangelists are doing as interpreters of Jesus' life, we often find that their different approaches help clarify and draw out implications from Jesus' acts and teachings. This often entails sharing the stories of Jesus' life in a topical or logical order, not chronological. In this light, alleged "discrepancies" and "contradictions" are seen as mere "differences."

were baptized by him in the Jordan River as they confessed their sins.[a]

[7] When he saw many of the •Pharisees and •Sadducees[b] coming to the place of his baptism,[A] he said to them, "Brood of vipers! Who warned you to flee from the coming wrath?[c] [8] Therefore produce fruit[d] consistent with[B] repentance. [9] And don't presume to say to yourselves, 'We have Abraham as our father.'[e] For I tell you that God is able to raise up children for Abraham from these stones! [10] Even now the ax is ready to strike the root of the trees! Therefore, every tree that doesn't produce good fruit will be cut down and thrown into the fire.[f]

[11] "I baptize you with[C] water for repentance,[D,g] but the One who is coming after me is more powerful than I. I am not worthy to remove[E] His sandals. He Himself will baptize you with[c] the Holy Spirit and fire.[h] [12] His winnowing shovel[F] is in His hand, and He will clear His threshing floor and gather His wheat into the barn. But the chaff He will burn up with fire that never goes out."[i]

The Baptism of Jesus

[13] Then Jesus came from Galilee to John at the Jordan, to be baptized by him.[j] [14] But John tried to stop Him, saying, "I need to be baptized by You, and yet You come to me?" [15] Jesus answered him, "Allow it for now, because this is the way for us to fulfill all

[a]3:5-6 Mt 23:37; Mk 1:5; Lk 3:3; Jn 15:22; Ac 19:18 [b]3:7 Mt 16:1; 22:23; 23:15; Ac 4:1; 5:17; 23:6 [c]Mt 12:34; 23:33; Rm 5:9; 1Th 1:10 [d]3:8 Mt 3:10; 12:33; 13:8,26; 21:19,34,41,43; Mk 11:14 [e]3:9 Lk 3:8; Jn 8:33,39; Ac 13:26; Rm 4:1 [f]3:10 Mt 7:19; Lk 13:7,9; Jn 15:2,6 [g]3:11 Mk 1:4,8; Jn 1:26; Ac 1:5 [h]Is 4:4; Jn 1:33; Ac 2:3-4; 11:16; Ti 3:5 [i]3:12 Is 30:24; Mt 13:30; Mk 9:43,48; Lk 3:17 [j]3:13-17 Mk 1:9-11; Lk 3:21-22; Jn 1:31-34

[A]3:7 Lit to his baptism [B]3:8 Lit fruit worthy of [C]3:11 Or in [D]3:11 Baptism was the means by which repentance was expressed publicly. [E]3:11 Or to carry [F]3:12 A wooden farm implement used to toss threshed grain into the wind so the lighter chaff would blow away and separate from the heavier grain

John demanded that repentant Jews be **baptized** as well. This bold move implied that Jews did not belong to God merely by virtue of their descent from Abraham (see note at vv. 7-9). Like anyone else, ethnic Jews needed to repent in order to enter the coming kingdom. Unlike the repetitive ritual washings of other religious groups, John's baptism appears to have been a one-time event associated with a permanent repentance and a transformed life.

3:7-9 In Mt 2:4 the chief priests and scribes identified the place of Messiah's birth but made no effort to visit Him. Their attention was on worldly power instead. That negative portrayal is now followed by John's charge that the leading priests of the Jews were a **brood of vipers** (see 12:34; 23:33) fleeing from God's **coming wrath**. John stressed that the coming kingdom would be accompanied by blessing for God's people and by punishment for the unrepentant. John knew that the **Pharisees and Sadducees** had no intention of confessing their sins because they presumed that descent from Abraham guaranteed that they would escape God's wrath. This belief was reflected in the Mishnah, which stated: "All Israel will have a share in the world to come." John's statement about raising up **children for Abraham from these stones** involves a wordplay in Aramaic. The word child [ben] sounds similar to the word stone [eben]. A stone has no intrinsic value, yet Almighty God can transform worthless rock into a person and include him in His covenant people if He so chooses (Is 51:1-2). Consequently, descent from Abraham gave the Jews no grounds for boasting. John's warning foreshadows the incorporation of believing Gentiles into the people of God, an important theme in Matthew's Gospel.

3:10 Just as the owner of an orchard laid **the ax** to barren trees, so too God will punish those who fail to produce "fruit consistent with repentance" (v. 8). In the teachings of John and Jesus, **fruit** represents good works that result from a miraculous inner transformation (7:15-20; 12:33; 13:23). Later, the cursing of the fig tree and the parable of the wicked tenants illustrated the consequences of failing to produce good fruits (21:18-22,33-43).

3:11 Removing the master's **sandals** was a task so menial that Hebrew slave owners could not require it of Hebrew slaves. John, however, saw himself as unworthy to perform for Jesus the very task that slaves were spared from performing. John expressed this deep humility because Jesus was **more powerful** than he, and this greater power expressed itself through a new baptism that was vastly superior to John's. John's baptism was a public expression of **repentance**, but his baptism could not change a person's heart. Jesus, however, baptized the repentant **with the Holy Spirit**, making them holy through inner transformation. Matthew's quotation from Jr 31:15 in Mt 2:18 was probably intended to remind his readers of the promise of the new covenant (Jr 31:31-34). The reference to baptism with the Spirit recalls the related promise in Ezk 36:24-27 in which God declared, "I will place My Spirit within you and cause you to follow My statutes and carefully observe My ordinances." This work of the Spirit was highlighted again at Jesus' baptism (3:16). Jesus would have the power to transform human character in a way that John could not. Jesus would also baptize people with **fire**, a reference to divine judgment against unrepentant sinners.

3:12 A **winnowing shovel** was used to toss grain into the air. The wind would blow the useless husks (called **chaff**) aside while the heavier grain kernels fell to the threshing floor. The chaff would then be gathered up and burned. John's parable thus described a coming divine judgment in which all people are sifted, with the result that Messiah's followers will be preserved by God while the unrepentant are gathered for punishment. Though chaff is highly flammable and burns away quickly, possibly giving the impression that divine judgment is only temporary, John made clear that the fire which awaits the unrepentant will never go out. God's punishment against unrepentant sinners is eternal.

3:13 Apparently Jesus and His family still lived in Nazareth (in **Galilee**) at this time.

3:14 John **tried to stop Him** because he recognized Jesus' superiority. By his protest John further identified Jesus as the holy One who would come after him (v. 11). John knew that he needed Jesus' baptism, the baptism of the Spirit, but he also understood that sinless Jesus did not seek water baptism as an expression of repentance.

3:15 Jesus explained that baptism was essential to His perfection. Jesus wished to please His Father by obeying the

righteousness." Then he allowed Him to be baptized.

[16] After Jesus was baptized, He went up immediately from the water. The heavens[a] suddenly opened for Him,[A] and He saw the Spirit of God descending like a dove and coming down on Him.[b] [17] And there came a voice from heaven:

> This is My beloved Son.
> I take delight in Him![c]

The Temptation of Jesus

4 Then[d] Jesus was led up by the Spirit into the wilderness to be tempted by the Devil.[e]

[2] After He had fasted 40 days and 40 nights,[f] He was hungry. [3] Then the tempter approached Him and said, "If You are the Son of God, tell these stones to become bread."[g]

[4] But He answered, "It is written:

> **Man must not live on bread alone**
> **but on every word that comes**
> **from the mouth of God."[B,h]**

[5] Then the Devil took Him to the holy city,[C] had Him stand on the pinnacle of the temple,[i] [6] and said to Him, "If You are the Son of God, throw Yourself down. For it is written:

Cross references
[a]3:16 Mt 24:35; Lk 2:33; Ac 17:24; Eph 6:9; Rv 21:10
[b]Is 11:2; Jn 1:32; Ac 7:56; 2Pt 1:17
[c]3:17 Ps 2:7; Is 42:1; Lk 9:35; Jn 12:28
[d]4:1-11 Mk 1:12-13; Lk 4:1-13
[e]4:1 Jos 15:61; Jdg 1:16; Jn 1:6-7; Jms 1:14
[f]4:2 Ex 34:28; 1Kg 19:8; Jn 9:4
[g]4:3 Mk 3:11; 5:7; Lk 1:35; 4:41; Jn 1:34,49; Ac 9:20
[h]4:4 Dt 8:3   [i]4:5 Neh 11:1,18; Dn 9:24; Mt 27:53

[A]3:16 Other mss omit *for Him*   [B]4:4 Dt 8:3   [C]4:5 = Jerusalem

commands of the prophets (John was the greatest of the prophets; 11:9-13) and by identifying with God's righteous cause among the people. If He had refused to participate in John's baptism, Jesus would have seemed like a rebel rather than One who came to **fulfill all righteousness**.

3:16 The opening of the **heavens** demonstrates that both the voice and the descending **Spirit** came from heaven and were divine. First-century Jews associated the **dove** with the Spirit since Gn 1:2 describes the Spirit as hovering over the primeval waters. The Hebrew verb translated "hover" is the same word used to describe a bird rapidly fluttering its wings. Consequently, both the Qumran Scrolls and the Talmud associated God's Spirit in Gn 1:2 with the dove. The descent of the Spirit thus alludes to Gn 1 and identifies Jesus not only as One empowered by the Spirit but also as One who brings new creation (2Co 5:17; Gl 6:15).

3:17 The Father speaks directly only twice in Matthew—here at Jesus' baptism and later at the transfiguration. On both occasions He identified Jesus as His **Son** and expressed approval of Him (see 17:5). The Father's words at Jesus' baptism blend together two important OT texts: Ps 2:7 and Is 42:1. Psalm 2 was a song sung at the crowning of Israel's kings. The Father's application of this text to Jesus identified Him as a divinely appointed King who would rule with divine authority and whose kingdom would extend to the ends of the earth (Ps 2:1-12). The allusion to Is 42 identified Jesus as the Servant, the messianic figure whom Is 53:5 promised would be "pierced because of our transgressions, crushed because of our iniquities." Matthew 12:18-21 explicitly applies Is 42 to Jesus, and Mt 8:17 explicitly applies Is 53 to Jesus. With this OT background in mind, we see that the Father's words identify Jesus as King and Savior.

4:1-2 The temptation of Christ highlights numerous parallels between Jesus and OT Israel. Deuteronomy 8:2-3 says that the Lord led Israel into the wilderness to be tested for 40 years. Similarly, **Jesus was led up by the Spirit into the wilderness** to be tested for **40 days**. The three temptations Jesus faced parallel the tests Israel faced in the wilderness, and every Scripture that Jesus quoted in response to His temptations were drawn from God's message to the Israelites about their wilderness test (Dt 6–8). Israel failed its tests, but Jesus passed His and in doing so "fulfilled all righteousness" (Mt 3:15). Thus He is qualified to create a new spiritual Israel. Several features of Matthew confirm Jesus' intention to gather a new people for God. He chose 12 disciples to parallel Israel's 12 tribes. This was a con-

scious effort to identify His followers as the new Israel. The fact that Jesus **was hungry** shows that He was truly human as well as divine.

4:3 The **stones** that littered the wilderness floor resembled small round loaves of **bread** in shape, size, and color. Interpreters disagree as to why it would have been wrong for Jesus to transform and eat the stones. Most suggest that He was tempted to exercise supernatural power rather than depend on God's provision. Clues in the text suggest that the Spirit, who led Jesus into the wilderness, commanded this fast. Thus, breaking the fast prematurely would have been an act of disobedience, preventing Jesus from fulfilling every act of righteousness (3:15). Jesus aimed to end His fast when the test was over and no sooner. God would signal the end by providing food. Matthew 4:11 shows that at fast's end, angels came and "began to serve" Jesus. The verb "serve" means "to serve as a table-waiter" and implies that the angels fed Jesus. During their wilderness wanderings, Israel failed to trust God to provide food and water. Jesus, the embodiment of the new Israel, had unwavering trust in God's care. On **Son of God**, see note at 3:17.

4:4 Jesus is quoting Dt 8:3. His reference to **every word that comes from the mouth of God** recalls the OT theme that God's words are not idle, but are to be received as commands. Deuteronomy 8:1,6 emphasize the need to obey God's commands, and Dt 8:1 teaches that man lives by following God's commandments just as 8:3 says that man lives by what comes from God's mouth (Dt 6:24). Thus the OT text which Jesus quoted teaches that obeying God is more important than being well-fed. Israel struggled to learn this truth (Ex 16:3; Nm 11:4-5). In contrast, Jesus hungered for righteousness more than bread and thirsted for obedience more than water. He urged His disciples to have the same priority (Mt 5:6).

4:5-7 Satan quoted Ps 91:11-12 out of context, trying to convince Jesus that the Father would supernaturally protect Him even if He gambled with His life. Jesus responded by quoting Dt 6:16 which refers to the time when Israel, angry and thirsty, questioned God's presence until He miraculously produced a stream of water from a rock: "They tested the LORD saying, 'Is the LORD among us or not?'" (Ex 17:7). Had Jesus succumbed to Satan's temptation, it would indicate that His faith was frail and depended on God's miraculous action. Jumping from the **pinnacle of the temple** would test God by attempting to force Him to perform a miracle.

Satan implied that God is trustworthy only when He rescues us from suffering and danger. Jesus knew better. God is

He will give His angels[a] orders
　　concerning you,
and they will support you
　　with their hands
so that you will not strike
　　your foot against a stone."[A,b]

[7] Jesus told him, "It is also written: Do not test the Lord your God."[B,c]

[8] Again, the Devil took Him to a very high mountain and showed Him all the kingdoms of the world and their splendor. [9] And he said to Him, "I will give You all these things if You will fall down and worship me."[c]

[10] Then Jesus told him, "Go away,[D] Satan! For it is written:

Worship the Lord your God,
　　and serve only[d] Him."[E]

[11] Then the Devil left Him, and immediately angels came and began to serve Him.[e]

Ministry in Galilee

[12] When He heard that John had been arrested,[f] He withdrew into Galilee.[g] [13] He left Nazareth behind and went to live in Capernaum[h] by the sea, in the region of Zebulun and Naphtali. [14] This was to fulfill what was spoken through the prophet Isaiah:

[15] 　Land of Zebulun and land
　　　of Naphtali,
　along the sea road,
　　beyond the Jordan,
　Galilee of the Gentiles!
[16] 　The people who live in darkness
　have seen a great light,
　and for those living in the shadowland
　　of death,
　light has dawned.[F,G,i]

[17] From then on Jesus began to preach, "Repent, because the kingdom of heaven[j] has come near!"

Cross references (center column)
a 4:6 Gn 16:7; Mt 13:49; Lk 1:11; Ac 5:19; Rv 14:6
b Ps 91:11-12; 1Pt 2:8
c 4:7 Dt 6:16; 1Sm 7:3; 1Ch 21:1
d 4:10 Dt 6:13; 1Ch 21:1
e 4:11 Mt 26:53; Lk 22:43; Heb 1:14
f 4:12 Mt 14:3; Mk 1:14; Lk 3:20; Jn 3:24
g Lk 4:14; Jn 1:43; 2:11
h 4:13 Mk 1:21; 2:1; Lk 4:23; Jn 2:12; 4:46
i 4:15-16 Is 9:1-2; 42:7; Lk 2:32
j 4:17 Mt 3:2; 5:3,10,19-20; 7:21; 8:11; Mk 1:14

Text notes
A 4:6 Ps 91:11-12　B 4:7 Dt 6:16　C 4:9 Or and pay me homage　D 4:10 Other mss read Get behind Me　E 4:10 Dt 6:13　F 4:16 Lit dawned on them　G 4:15-16 Is 9:1-2

---

trustworthy even when He allows us or even causes us to suffer. True faith recognizes this and perseveres through hard times. When Jesus suffered on the cross (27:41-44), those who tormented Him used arguments similar to that of the Devil: "If You are the Son of God, come down from the cross." They even quoted Ps 22:8 to argue that Jesus would be rescued if God really loved Him, much as Satan quoted Ps 91:11-12 to argue that God would rescue Jesus from a deadly fall if He were really God's Son. Again, Jesus knew better. He trusted God even through a brutal scourging, even when nails were driven through His limbs, and even when God let Him suffer a horrible death.

4:8-9 Although Satan exercises some authority over the world (Lk 4:6; Jn 12:31), the **kingdoms of the world** belong to God, and He promised to give them to Messiah (Ps 2:8).

4:10-11 Jesus responded to Satan by quoting from Dt 6:14 and 10:20. If Jesus had worshiped Satan in order to gain worldly power, it would have indicated that He valued creation more than the Creator and the kingdoms of the earth more than the kingdom of God. Jesus insisted that **only** God is worthy of **worship**. After citing Dt 6:13, Jesus' reception of worship later in this Gospel (8:2; 9:18; 14:33; 15:25; 20:20; 28:9,17) without rebuking the worshiper (cp. Ac 10:25-26; 14:11-15) strongly implies His deity. That the **angels came** to serve Jesus further implies His superior status.

4:12 John the Baptist **had been arrested** because he dared to say that Herod Antipas's marriage to his brother's wife was immoral. As tetrarch of Galilee and Perea (Lk 3:1), Herod did not have jurisdiction over Judea, the locale of Jesus' baptism and wilderness temptation. Thus Jesus fearlessly marched into the heart of Herod's territory when He heard of John's arrest. In Lk 13:31-33, the Pharisees urged Jesus to leave Galilee in order to escape arrest by Herod. Jesus replied by calling Herod "that fox" and insisted that He would travel to Jerusalem only because it was necessary for Him to die there, not to flee Herod. Jesus caused kings to tremble (2:3; 14:1-2), but He Himself feared no man.

4:13 At this point Jesus made an important strategic move

by shifting his headquarters from **Nazareth** to **Capernaum**. Nazareth was an obscure village, but Capernaum was a much larger fishing center on the shores of Lake Galilee. It boasted a tax collection station and a Roman garrison of at least 100 soldiers. **By the sea** alludes to Isaiah's prophecies, which describe the area as "the Way of the Sea," ancient trade route stretching from Damascus down to Caesarea Maritima on the coast of the Mediterranean Sea. By the time of Christ, the Romans had built a stone road along the route, allowing caravans to travel from Syria and pass through Capernaum on the way to Caesarea. Since Capernaum was on the coast of the Sea of Galilee, it also provided easy access to every other city along the Galilean coast. Thus by choosing high-traffic Capernaum as His headquarters, Jesus was able to reach many Jews and Gentiles.

4:14-16 Matthew's quotation of Is 9:1-2 highlights the international focus of Jesus' ministry by describing Galilee as **Galilee of the Gentiles**. Second Kings 15:29 and 17:24-27 show that after the Jews were deported from the northern kingdom of Israel, foreigners flooded into Galilee. For instance, reports from the geographer Strabo and first-century Jewish historian Josephus show that Egyptians, Arabians, Phoenicians, and Greeks lived in Galilee. The Apocrypha (1 Maccabees 5) says Galilee's population was largely Gentile and heathen. Jesus' move to Galilee and the strategically located city of Capernaum shows His intention to save Gentiles as well as Jews. Matthew's application of Is 9 also shows that Jesus was the great King called "Mighty God" who would reign from David's throne over a universal and eternal kingdom, liberate God's people from spiritual slavery, and bring peace and joy to the world (Is 9:3-7).

4:17 On the significance of the words **from then on Jesus began to**, see "Structure" in the Introduction to Matthew. Jesus' message was identical to the message proclaimed by John the Baptist before his arrest. This identifies Jesus as the One who came after John (3:11) whom John had identified from Is 40:3 as the Lord God Himself (see note at Mt 3:2).

The First Disciples

[18] As[a] He was walking along the Sea of Galilee,[b] He saw two brothers, Simon, who was called Peter, and his brother Andrew. They were casting a net into the sea, since they were fishermen. [19] "Follow Me," He told them, "and I will make you fish for[A] people!" [20] Immediately they left their nets and followed Him.

[21] Going on from there, He saw two other brothers, James the son of Zebedee, and his brother John. They were in a boat with Zebedee their father, mending their nets, and He called them. [22] Immediately they left the boat and their father and followed Him.

Teaching, Preaching, and Healing

[23] Jesus was going all over Galilee,[c] teaching in their •synagogues, preaching the good news of the kingdom, and healing every[B] disease

a4:18-22 Mk 1:16-20; Lk 5:2-11; Jn 1:40-42
b4:18 Mn 15:29; Mk 7:31; Lk 5:1; Jn 6:1
c4:23-25 Mk 1:35-39; Lk 4:42-44
d4:23 Mt 13:54; 24:14; Ac 10:38
e4:24 Lk 2:2; Ac 15:23; Gl 1:21
f Mt 8:16; 9:32; Mk 5:15; Jn 10:21
g4:25 Mk 3:7; 5:20; Lk 6:17
h5:1 Mk 3:13; Lk 9:28; Jn 6:3,15
i5:2 Ac 8:35; 10:34; 18:14
j5:3 Is 57:15; 66:2
k Mt 19:14; 25:34; Mk 10:14; Lk 6:20

and sickness among the people.[d] [24] Then the news about Him spread throughout Syria.[e] So they brought to Him all those who were afflicted, those suffering from various diseases and intense pains, the demon-possessed, the epileptics, and the paralytics.[f] And He healed them. [25] Large crowds followed Him from Galilee, •Decapolis, Jerusalem, Judea, and beyond the Jordan.[g]

THE SERMON ON THE MOUNT

5 When He saw the crowds, He went up on the mountain,[h] and after He sat down, His disciples came to Him. [2] Then[C] He began to teach them, saying:[i]

The Beatitudes

[3]   "The poor in spirit are blessed,[j]
       for the kingdom of heaven[k] is theirs.

A4:19 Lit *you fishers of*   B4:23 Or *every kind of*   C5:2 Lit *Then opening His mouth*

4:18-22 Jesus' command, **Follow Me**, urged the disciples not just to accompany Him on His travels but to follow His example and emulate His character. Following Jesus involved significant sacrifice for **Simon . . . Andrew . . . James**, and **John**. They abandoned their careers as fishermen. The words **they left . . . their father** indicate that following Jesus also required the disciples to place commitment to Jesus above commitment to their own families (10:37; 19:29).

4:23 Jesus' ministry in the **synagogues** shows that He initially focused His ministry on the Jewish population of Galilee, but this focus then widened to include Gentiles from there and beyond. The **good news of the kingdom**, the primary topic of Jesus' preaching, was that the long-awaited Messiah, the human ruler through whom God would establish His reign on earth, had come at last. This was the message proclaimed by John the Baptist (3:2), preached by Jesus (4:17), and emphasized by Matthew through his mention of Jesus' Davidic lineage, the account of His miraculous birth, and his record of the visit of the magi. Jesus healed **every disease and sickness among the people**. The adjective "every" shows that no type of ailment was beyond Jesus' power

to heal. In the Greek text, the adjective "every" is repeated, placing emphasis on Jesus' unlimited power to heal (9:35).

4:24 Syria was located just north of Galilee. Not surprisingly, word of Jesus' healings quickly **spread** to that region, crossing geographical and language barriers. Soon Syrians began bringing their sick for Jesus to heal. By consenting to this, Jesus distinguished Himself from some later Jewish interpreters who urged Jews to give no aid to a drowning Gentile or a Gentile woman giving birth (Maimonides). Matthew says Jesus healed **demon-possessed** people, but some scholars argue that these people were just epileptics. However, this verse distinguishes epilepsy from demon possession, which proves that the ancients differentiated between the two conditions.

4:25 Jesus' earliest followers hailed from Jewish and Gentile regions. **Jerusalem** and **Judea** were Jewish regions, **Galilee** had a mixture of Jews and Gentiles, and **Decapolis** was a group of predominantly Gentile cities. These geographical references and the diverse peoples entailed by them demonstrate Jesus' desire to serve, heal, teach, and save all the nations of the earth (28:18-20). He came as the world's Messiah.

5:1 Jesus ascended a mountain **when He saw the crowds** because He deemed the mountainside to be a better setting for teaching a large group. As the new Moses, His delivery of God's message from a mountaintop provides yet another parallel with the ancient Moses. The Greek words translated **He went up on the mountain** are used three times in the Greek OT (Ex 19:3; 24:18; 34:42), and all three fall in the section describing Moses' ascent of Mount Sinai. This fits with Matthew's repeated theme of drawing out parallels between Moses and Jesus. For instance, Jesus' birth paralleled several events surrounding Moses' birth. Herod attempted to kill the infant Christ by ordering the slaughter of Bethlehem's boys (Mt 2:16-18) much as Pharaoh ordered the execution of newborn male Israelites (Ex 1:15-18,22). Furthermore, the angel's pronouncement that danger had passed ("Those who sought the child's life are dead," Mt 2:20) is a clear echo of Ex 4:19, "All the men who wanted to kill you are dead" (see note at Mt 2:15).

5:3 Since Matthew introduces the Sermon on the Mount by highlighting the connection between Jesus and Moses,

makarios

Greek Pronunciation	[mah KAH ree ahss]
HCSB Translation	blessed
Uses in Matthew	13 (Lk, 15; Jn, 2)
Uses in the NT	50
Focus passage	Matthew 5:3-12

Makarios occurs 30 times in the Gospels, all but two on the lips of Jesus (Lk 1:45; 11:27). The OT Hebrew term *ashrey* stands behind the NT usage of *makarios*. Both terms are normally translated "blessed" or "happy." *Makarios* has two main nuances in the NT. It predominantly refers to God's *blessing* upon His people, and secondarily to God's people *blessing* Him. In the latter sense, *makarios* is basically synonymous with *praise*. When a person is *blessed* by God, he is approved by God. The opposite of *makarios* is "woe" (*ouai*), the status of one who is not approved by God and is thus the object of impending judgment (Mt 23:13-32; Lk 6:24-26). God's *blessing* does not necessarily include material prosperity in this life (Mt 19:23-24; Lk 6:24; 16:19-31)—the contrary is actually quite possible (Lk 6:20)—but it does anticipate full, uninterrupted prosperity in the future kingdom (Mt 5:4-9,11-12; 25:34).

⁴ Those who mourn
  are blessed,ᵃ
for they will be comforted.
⁵ The gentle are blessed,ᵇ
  for they will inherit the earth.
⁶ Those who hunger and thirst
  for righteousness are blessed,ᶜ
for they will be filled.
⁷ The merciful are blessed,

for they will be shown mercy.ᵈ
⁸ The pure in heart
  are blessed,
for they will see God.ᵉ
⁹ The peacemakers are blessed,
  for they will be called sons
  of God.ᶠ

ᵃ 5:4 Is 61:2; Mt 11:29; 21:5; Jn 16:20; Rv 7:17
ᵇ 5:5 Ps 37:11; Rm 4:13; Rv 21:7
ᶜ 5:6 Is 55:1-2; Jn 4:14; 6:48; 7:37
ᵈ 5:7 Pr 11:17; Mt 18:33; Lk 6:36; 2Tm 1:16
ᵉ 5:8 Ps 24:4; Heb 12:14; 1Jn 3:2; Rv 22:4
ᶠ 5:9 Mt 5:45; Lk 6:35; Rm 8:14; Jms 3:18; 1Jn 3:1

the Beatitudes (Mt 5:3-12) should probably be read against the backdrop of Moses' teachings. The only time the adjective "Blessed" (Gk *makarios*) was used by Moses was in his blessing on Israel (Dt 33:29): "How happy you are, Israel! Who is like you, a people saved by the LORD? He is the shield that protects you, the sword you boast in. Your enemies will cringe before you, and you will tread on their backs." Israel's blessing had both a historical and future focus. "Saved by the LORD" referred to Israel's exodus from Egypt. The remainder of the blessing assured the Israelites of success in their conquest of the promised land. Against this backdrop, the blessings of the new Moses identify Jesus' disciples as the new Israel who will enjoy a new exodus and conquest. The new Moses is a spiritual deliverer rather than a political one, and His promises must be understood in that light. In the Beatitudes, the new Moses pronounces spiritual salvation (exodus from slavery to sin) and promises spiritual victory (conquest and inheritance of a new promised land) to the new Israel. This background is confirmed by the allusion to Israel's exodus and conquest in the promise that the meek will "inherit the earth" (5:5).

In the OT, the **poor** were those who cried out for God's help, depended entirely on Him for their needs, had a humble and contrite spirit, experienced His deliverance, and enjoyed His undeserved favor (Ps 86:1-5). In light of this background, Jesus was describing His disciples as unworthy sinners who depend on God's grace for salvation. Although the promises in Mt 5:4-9 are expressed in the future tense, the affirmation **the kingdom of heaven is theirs** is in the present tense (5:3,10). This suggests that the kingdom had already arrived through the coming of Jesus but that the fulfillment of many kingdom promises will occur only in the future. This future fulfillment awaits Christ's second coming. The statement "the kingdom of heaven is theirs" appears at the beginning and end of the main body of the Beatitudes (5:3,10). This bracketing device suggests that the Beatitudes constitute promises only to those who belong to the kingdom. Isaiah 61:1 promised that Messiah would bring good news to the poor. This beatitude serves as a fulfillment of that prophecy (Lk 4:16-21).

5:4 This beatitude is also dependent on Is 61: "He has sent Me to heal the brokenhearted . . . to comfort all who mourn, to provide for those who mourn in Zion; to give them a crown of beauty instead of ashes, festive oil instead of mourning, and splendid clothes instead of despair" (vv. 1-3). The context of Is 61 portrays mourning as expressive of Israel's sorrow over the exile which their sins had caused. In this light, Mt 5:4 expresses the grief of those suffering the consequences of sin. Theirs is an attitude of repentance.

5:5 Like the preceding Beatitudes, this one parallels Is 61. Isaiah 61:7 (LXX) uses the words "they will inherit the land," an exact parallel to Mt 5:5b. The first three Beatitudes thus confirm Jesus' identity as the Servant of Is 61. This identification is important for understanding the sacrificial nature

of Jesus' death since Is 52:14–53:12 describes the Servant as suffering the punishment that sinners deserved (see Mt 8:17 and 12:17-21 which appeal to Is 53:4 and 42:1-4). The beatitude also echoes Ps 37:11 in the which the **gentle** are those who stubbornly trust God and surrender to His authority even when they cannot make sense of their circumstances. **Inherit the earth** (land) in the OT refers to inheriting the promised land of Canaan. Thus most of Jesus' hearers recognized that His disciples were a new Israel that would inherit the land promised to Abraham. In the context of the Sermon on the Mount and the Gospel of Matthew as a whole, "inheriting the earth" involves more than the promise of living in Palestine. It refers to living in a recreated earth over which Christ rules eternally. Matthew 19:28 anticipates the renewal of earth and assures Jesus' disciples that they will enjoy great reward in the eternal kingdom.

5:6 **Hunger** and **thirst** are metaphors for a disciple's fervent desire for **righteousness**. The words **they will be filled** are in the passive voice, indicating that righteousness is not something that disciples can achieve by their own efforts. The verb here, like those in the promises of Mt 5:4,6–7 (and possibly 9), is a "divine passive" that describes an act of God. He alone imparts the righteousness for which disciples hunger and thirst. This is crucial to understanding the theology of the Sermon on the Mount, where Jesus required His disciples to keep the least of the commandments (5:19), surpass the righteousness of the scribes and Pharisees (5:20), and to "be perfect . . . as your heavenly Father is perfect" (5:48). Such demands can be twisted into a false theology in which righteousness is achieved by works, but the righteousness Jesus demands of us is actually a divine gift given to His followers.

5:7 The **merciful** are those who relate to others with a forgiving and compassionate spirit (6:2-4; 18:21-35). God will show mercy to the merciful.

5:8 The words **pure in heart** refer to someone who is authentically righteous in their inner person. Righteousness can be faked, as was the case with the Pharisees (23:25-28). Jesus said true purity is attained when God grants it to the person who hungers and thirsts for it. Complete fulfillment of this divine promise will occur at Jesus' return, but the identification of His disciples as those who are pure shows that dramatic transformation occurs even in this lifetime. The promise that Jesus' disciples **will see God** looks forward to the time when they will literally behold God in all His glory. The words are not to be interpreted figuratively as if they refer merely to special insight into God's nature or to a visionary experience. The new Moses promises His followers access to God that not even the ancient Moses was allowed to experience (Ex 33:12-23).

5:9 The ministry of peacemaking involves resolving conflict by making prompt apologies and acts of restitution, refusing

¹⁰ Those who are persecuted
    for righteousness are blessed,
  for the kingdom of heaven^a is theirs.

¹¹"You are blessed when they insult and persecute you and falsely say every kind of evil against you because of Me. ¹²Be glad and rejoice, because your reward is great in heaven. For that is how they persecuted^b the prophets who were before you.^c

Believers Are Salt and Light

¹³"You are the salt of the earth. But if the salt should lose its taste, how can it be made salty? It's no longer good for anything but to be thrown out and trampled on by men.^d ¹⁴"You are the light of the world. A city situated on a hill cannot be hidden.^e ¹⁵No one lights a lamp^f and puts it under a basket,^A but rather on a lampstand, and it gives light for all who are in the house.^g ¹⁶In the same way, let your light shine^B before men, so that they may

see your good works and give glory to your Father in heaven.^h

Christ Fulfills the Law

¹⁷"Don't assume that I came to destroy the Law or the Prophets. I did not come to destroy but to fulfill.ⁱ ¹⁸For *I assure you: Until heaven and earth pass away, not the smallest letter^C or one stroke of a letter will pass from the law until all things are accomplished. ¹⁹Therefore, whoever breaks one of the least of these commands and teaches people to do so will be called least in the kingdom of heaven. But whoever practices and teaches these commands will be called great in the kingdom of heaven.^j ²⁰For I tell you, unless your righteousness surpasses that of the *scribes and *Pharisees, you will never enter the kingdom of heaven.

Murder Begins in the Heart

²¹"You have heard that it was said to our

Cross references (center column):
^a 5:10 Mt 19:14; 25:34; Mk 10:14; Lk 6:20; 22:29
^b 5:12 Mt 2:23; 2Tm 3:12
^c Mt 23:37; Ac 7:52; 1Th 2:15
^d 5:13 Mk 9:50; Lk 14:34
^e 5:14 Pr 4:18; Jn 8:12; Php 2:15
^f 5:15 Jn 5:35; Rv 21:23
^g Mk 4:21; Lk 8:16; 11:33
^h 5:16 Mt 9:8; Jn 15:8; 1Pt 2:12
ⁱ 5:17 Mt 7:12; Rm 3:31; 10:4; 13:8; Gl 3:24
^j 5:18-19 Mt 11:11; 24:35; Lk 16:17; Jms 2:10

---

^A5:15 A large basket used to measure grain   ^B5:16 Or *way, your light must shine*   ^C5:18 Or *not one iota; iota* is the smallest letter of the Gk alphabet.

---

to seek revenge, and humbly serving and loving one's enemies (5:21-26,38-41,43-48). The promise that **peacemakers . . . will be called sons of God** probably means that Jesus' authentic disciples emulate God by undertaking the ministry of reconciliation. Thus at the final judgment they shall be accepted as the sons (and daughters) of God.

5:10 The purest form of **righteousness** is pursued by disciples who know that their good deeds will demand great sacrifice and will result in pain rather than immediate reward. This is the epitome of the kingdom righteousness demanded by the Sermon on the Mount. Jesus pronounced that the kingdom of heaven belongs to those who suffer for righteousness. In the Greek text, **theirs** is shifted from its normal position at the end of the clause to the beginning instead. This gives the pronoun a special emphasis indicating that the kingdom belongs to righteous sufferers and to them alone. Those who always endeavor to evade persecution are not true disciples and will not have a share in the kingdom because true disciples follow Jesus even at the cost of their lives (16:24-27). The **kingdom of heaven** is the reign of God in the person of Jesus the Messiah. Righteous sufferers are subjects of God's rule through their submission to Jesus' authority. Jesus inaugurated this kingdom during His ministry, but it will be consummated in the end times.

5:11-12 Jesus' words show that persecution is typically either verbal or violent. Verbal forms include insult and slander. The word persecute includes acts of physical violence like the slap of Mt 5:39. Jesus promised that the cost of discipleship will be offset by the enormity of the **reward** the disciple enjoys **in heaven**. Jewish leaders rejected and vehemently **persecuted** the OT **prophets**, and Jesus repeatedly denounced this persecution (21:34-36; 23:29-37). By treating Jesus' followers in the same way they had treated the prophets, Jewish persecutors unwittingly bestowed on them a prophet's honor.

5:13 Salt has many uses, but in the OT it is most often a purifying agent (Ex 30:35; Lv 2:13; 2Kg 2:21; Ezk 16:4). As

the salt of the earth, Jesus' disciples are to purify a corrupt world through their example of righteous living and their proclamation of the gospel. However, contaminated salt does not promote purity. The verb translated **lose its taste** indicates foolish and immoral behavior. It refers to a professing disciple whose unrighteous lifestyle promotes destruction rather than purification. Such salt is only good for spreading over ground where you want to kill vegetation. Such is the fatal effect of an unrighteous disciple's lifestyle. Nothing grows where they go. The verb **thrown out** describes the disposal of something worthless, and the verb **trampled** alludes to the treatment an immoral disciple receives from the world.

5:14-16 You are the light of the world is an allusion to Is 9:1-2; 42:6; 49:6—texts that describe the ministry of Messiah, Servant of the Lord. This indicates that Jesus' disciples are to be extensions of His ministry, carrying salvation to the ends of the earth. Such ministry is intrinsic to true discipleship. A disciple should no more conceal his righteousness or the gospel message than a glowing **city** should douse its light at night. The reference to giving light **for all** combines with the reference to **the world** to show that Christ's ministry is intended for all people. This anticipates the Great Commission of Mt 28:18-20.

Jesus' words make clear that the disciple is not the ultimate author of his good works. If the disciple were the author of his good works, he would justly receive praise. However, Jesus taught that only the **Father in heaven** is to be praised for a disciple's good works, for He is the true source of such works (see note at v. 6). This must not be overlooked. The righteousness demanded by the Sermon on the Mount is a divine gift that God imparts to Jesus' followers.

5:17-20 Jesus defended Himself against charges that He defied the law (9:3,11,14; 12:2,10; 15:1-2; 17:24; 19:3; 22:34-36) by insisting that He came to **fulfill** both the **Law** and the **Prophets**, which together amount to the entire OT. The word "fulfill" may refer to fulfillment of OT prophecies (1:22; 2:15,17,23; 4:14; 8:17; 12:17; 13:35; 21:4; 26:54,56;

ancestors,^A **Do not murder**,^B,a and whoever murders will be subject to judgment.^b ²²But I tell you, everyone who is angry with his brother ^C will be subject to judgment. And whoever says to his brother, 'Fool!'^D will be subject to the •Sanhedrin. But whoever says, 'You moron!' will be subject to •hellfire.^E,c ²³So if you are offering your gift on the altar, and there you remember that your brother has something against you, ²⁴leave your gift there in front of the altar. First go and be reconciled with your brother, and then come and offer your gift. ²⁵Reach a settlement quickly with your adversary while you're on the way with him, or your adversary will hand you over to the judge, the judge to^F the officer, and you will be thrown into prison.^d ²⁶I assure you: You will never get out of there until you have paid the last penny!^G

Adultery in the Heart

²⁷"You have heard that it was said, **Do not commit adultery**.^H,e ²⁸But I tell you, everyone

who looks at a woman to lust for her has already committed adultery with her in his heart.^f ²⁹If your right eye •causes you to sin,^g gouge it out and throw it away. For it is better that you lose one of the parts of your body than for your whole body to be thrown into hell.^h ³⁰And if your right hand causes you to sin, cut it off and throw it away. For it is better that you lose one of the parts of your body than for your whole body to go into hell!

Divorce Practices Censured

³¹"It was also said, **Whoever divorces**^i **his wife must give her a written notice of divorce.**^i,j ³²But I tell you, everyone who divorces his wife, except in a case of sexual immorality,^j causes her to commit adultery. And whoever marries a divorced woman commits adultery.^k

Tell the Truth

³³"Again, you have heard that it was said to our ancestors,^A **You must not break your oath,**

Cross references (center column):
a 5:21 Ex 20:13; Dt 5:17
b Mt 19:18; 23:31,35; Mk 10:19; Lk 18:20; Rm 13:9; Jms 2:11
c 5:22 Mt 18:9; Mk 9:43; Jms 3:6; 1Jn 3:15
d 5:25 Pr 25:8; Lk 12:58
e 5:27 Ex 20:14; Dt 5:18
f 5:28 2Sm 11:2; Jb 31:1; Pr 6:25
g 5:29 Mt 18:9; Mk 9:47
h Mt 10:28; 23:15,33; Lk 12:5
i 5:31 Jr 3:1; Mt 19:7; Mk 10:4
j Dt 24:1
k 5:32 Mt 19:9; Mk 10:11; Lk 16:18; Rm 7:3; 1Co 7:11

---

^A5:21,33 Lit *to the ancients*   ^B5:21 Ex 20:13; Dt 5:17   ^C5:22 Other mss add *without a cause*   ^D5:22 Lit *Raca*, an Aram term of abuse similar to "airhead"   ^E5:22 Lit *the gehenna of fire*   ^F5:25 Other mss read *judge will hand you over to*   ^G5:26 Lit *quadrans*, the smallest and least valuable Roman coin, worth 1/64 of a daily wage   ^H5:27 Ex 20:14; Dt 5:18   ^I5:31 Dt 24:1   ^J5:32 Gk *porneia* = fornication, or possibly a violation of Jewish marriage laws

---

27:9). This is suggested by the words **all things are accomplished**. However, it can also refer to obedience to God's commands (3:15). This additional meaning is implied by the reference to practicing **these commands**. Consequently, Jesus' words imply that He would fulfill all of the OT promises and obey all its commandments. The **smallest letter** of the Hebrew alphabet is the *yod*, which resembles an English apostrophe. The **stroke of a letter** is a slight pen stroke that distinguishes similar letters. Jesus' statement shows that He regarded the OT as accurate and reliable down to the smallest detail. In keeping with this conviction, Jesus taught that fidelity to the OT witness determines a disciple's stature in His kingdom. True fidelity to God's commands is made possible by God's miraculous work in a disciple's heart (see note at v. 6).

5:21-22 Matthew 5:21 begins a section of the Sermon on the Mount generally known as the "Six Antitheses." The title may seem to imply that Jesus opposed the OT in some way, but in reality He always upheld its authority. Rather than contradicting or overturning OT teachings, Jesus opposed the misguided interpretations of the scribes and Pharisees. These men were concerned only with superficial matters, but Jesus went deeper. He argued that the law prohibits not just actual murder but murderous attitudes as well. Similarly, violent temperaments are condemned just as surely as violent deeds.

5:23-24 Disciples must attempt at their earliest opportunity to reconcile with a brother or sister who **has something against** them, even if doing so interrupts important business. Speaking to the context of His day, Jesus said disciples should seek reconciliation even if it meant halting in the middle of offering sacrifices at the Jerusalem temple. This interruption was significant since Jesus' original audience (located away from Jerusalem) would have to abandon their **gift** at the **altar**, travel for days to reach Galilee and

seek reconciliation, and then return to Judea to complete the sacrifice. Such is the priority of reconciliation.

5:25-26 A person can typically pay a smaller penalty for their offense by seeking an out-of-court settlement rather than waiting for the issue to be settled in court. This illustrates that reconciliation is urgent because the longer it is postponed, the more severe the consequences.

5:27-28 Jesus said that gazing on a member of the opposite sex for the purpose of arousing illicit sexual desire is **adultery** of the **heart**. True righteousness therefore seeks to avoid not only adulterous acts but also adulterous thoughts.

5:29-30 Self-mutilation and amputation are not effective ways to overcome sin. After all, sin arises from a corrupt heart rather than flesh and bone (15:19). Jesus here uses hyperbole (intentional exaggeration for the sake of making a point) and allegory (in which the **eye** represents a lustful perspective and the **hand** represents an immoral deed) in order to convey a vital requirement of discipleship. Disciples should put a stop to thoughts and behaviors that contribute to immorality.

5:31-32 Jesus challenged a loose rabbinic paraphrase of Dt 24:1 that distorted the original meaning of the text. In the hands of the rabbis, Dt 24:1 greatly multiplied the number of offenses that could justify **divorce**. For instance, rabbinic commentaries on Dt 24 cited minor complaints such as a wife's fading beauty or her tendency to burn food as legitimate grounds for divorce. However, Jesus kept true to Dt 24:1 and insisted that **sexual immorality** is the legitimate grounds for divorce. People who divorce for frivolous reasons and remarry are guilty of adultery since their original marriage covenant has not been genuinely dissolved.

5:33-37 Oaths to the Lord (i.e., "I swear to God") were considered binding, but since Jews avoided use of God's personal

but you must keep your oaths to the Lord.[A,a] [34] But I tell you, don't take an oath at all: either by heaven, because it is God's throne; [35] or by the earth, because it is His footstool; or by Jerusalem, because it is the city of the great King.[b] [36] Neither should you swear by your head, because you cannot make a single hair white or black. [37] But let your word 'yes' be 'yes,' and your 'no' be 'no.'[B] Anything more than this is from the evil one.[c]

Go the Second Mile

[38] "You have heard that it was said, **An eye for an eye** and **a tooth for a tooth.**[C,d] [39] But I tell you, don't resist[D] an evildoer. On the contrary, if anyone slaps you on your right cheek, turn the other to him also.[e] [40] As for the one who wants to sue you and take away your shirt,[E] let him have your coat[F] as well. [41] And if anyone forces[G] you to go one mile, go with him two. [42] Give to the one who asks you, and don't turn away from the one who wants to borrow from you.[f]

Love Your Enemies

[43] "You have heard that it was said, **Love your neighbor**[H,g] and hate your enemy. [44] But I tell you, love your enemies[i] and pray for those who[j] persecute you,[h] [45] so that you may be[K] sons of your Father in heaven. For He causes His sun to rise on the evil and the good, and sends rain on the righteous and the unrighteous.[i] [46] For if you love those who love you, what reward will you have? Don't even the tax collectors do the same? [47] And if you greet only your •brothers, what are you doing out of the

Cross references (center column):
a5:33 Lv 19:12; Nm 30:2; Dt 23:21; Mt 23:16
b5:34-35 Ps 48:2; Is 66:1; Mt 23:22; Ac 7:49; Jms 5:12
c5:37 Mt 6:13; 13:19,38; Jn 17:15; 2Th 3:3
d5:38 Ex 21:24; Lv 24:20; Dt 19:21
e5:39 Lk 6:29-30; Rm 12:17; 1Co 6:7; 1Pt 3:9
f5:42 Dt 15:8; Lk 6:34
g5:43 Lv 19:18; Dt 23:6; Lk 10:29
h5:44 Lk 6:27; 23:34; Ac 7:60; Rm 12:20; 1Co 4:12; 1Pt 2:23
i5:45 Jb 25:3; Mt 5:9; Lk 6:35; Ac 14:17

A5:33 Lv 19:12; Nm 30:2; Dt 23:21   B5:37 Say what you mean and mean what you say   C5:38 Ex 21:24; Lv 24:20; Dt 19:21   D5:39 Or *don't set yourself against, or don't retaliate against*   E5:40 Lit *tunic*; = inner garment   F5:40 Or *garment*; lit *robe*; = outer garment   G5:41 Roman soldiers could require people to carry loads for them.   H5:43 Lv 19:18   I5:44 Other mss add *bless those who curse you, do good to those who hate you,*   J5:44 Other mss add *mistreat you and*   K5:45 Or *may become*, or *may show yourselves to be*

---

name and instead used reverent substitutions, clever liars could take an oath that seemed to appeal to God without technically doing so (23:16-22). Jesus taught that swearing oaths is wrong since oaths call for the destruction of an object or person if the oath is broken. Thus, swearing by **heaven . . . earth . . . Jerusalem,** or even one's own **head** is inappropriate because it implies that we have the authority to destroy things over which God alone has authority. Swearing against God or His belongings aligns us with the **evil one** who attempted to assume God's position as Ruler of the universe.

5:38-39 Jesus explained that **eye for an eye** (Ex 21:24; Lv 24:20; Dt 19:21) was given not as a mandate for personal vengeance but as a principle to guide courts in determining appropriate punishments. The slap on **your right cheek** was a back-handed slap that was both insulting and injurious. For this act Jewish law imposed a fine that was double the one for an open-palmed blow on the left cheek. Thus we see that Jesus urged His disciples not to seek vengeance even against the most offensive kind of blow. The words **don't resist an evildoer** do not indicate, however, that we should not seek justice or defend ourselves when threatened with serious bodily harm.

5:40 Frivolous lawsuits were rare in first-century Israel, and so the suit described here was probably a legitimate one which the plaintiff was likely to win. Ordinarily, defendants are upset if the judgment goes against them, but Jesus commanded His disciples to seek reconciliation with their opponents by going above and beyond the legal requirements in order to make amends. Jewish law permitted an opponent to sue for possession of an offender's inner garment, the **shirt.** Typically it was a sleeved tunic that extended to the ankles and was made of wool or linen. These could be valuable and were frequently used for bartering or making payments. The **coat** was an outer robe or wrap. It was the more essential piece of clothing since it provided warmth and could double as a blanket for the poor. Based on OT texts such as Ex 22:26-27 and Dt 24:12-13, Jewish law insisted that the coat was exempt from seizure by the courts (*m. B. Qam.* 8:6). Taking the coat was too severe a punishment. Jesus thus commanded His disciples to do even more than the courts allowed when seeking reconciliation with an opponent.

5:41 Jesus likely had in mind the much-resented practice of compulsion, in which Roman officials could force their subjects to perform menial tasks such as hauling a load on their backs (27:32). It is often said that soldiers could legally compel a subject to carry a load for only one mile before letting them go, but no surviving text establishes this as law. Most likely compulsion was usually limited to a mile simply out of common sense: people are tired after hauling a load for a mile, and soldiers who pressed for more than this risked fostering dangerous resentment among subjugated peoples. In contrast to this, Jesus said His disciples should carry their oppressor's pack out of obligation for the first mile, but then exceed all expectations by going a second mile as an act of love and service.

5:42 Since this entire paragraph is devoted to Jesus' teaching against retaliation, this verse probably prohibits disciples from seeking vengeance against opponents by refusing to help them in a time of need. By giving the necessities of life to an enemy, disciples may restore broken relationships (Rm 12:19-21).

5:43 The words **love your neighbor** appear in Lv 19:18. However, the command **hate your enemy** does not appear anywhere in the OT. Evidently some of Jesus' contemporaries argued that the command to love your neighbor also implied the opposite—that a person was to hate everyone who was not his neighbor.

5:44-45 Loving **enemies** and praying for one's persecutors does not make a person God's child. Only rebirth does that. However, the sort of forgiving love Jesus mentions displays your family resemblance to the heavenly Father, and thus serves as a sign to your true identity. God blesses both **the evil and the good** with **sun** and **rain.**

5:46-47 **Tax collectors** were despised because they often collected more than the legal tax and served Rome at the expense of their downtrodden fellow Jews. Jesus taught that selfish behavior and loving only **those who love you** resembles the behavior of tax collectors and pagan **Gentiles,** not the character of the heavenly Father.

ordinary?[A,a] Don't even the Gentiles[B] do the same? [48]Be perfect,[b] therefore, as your heavenly Father is perfect.

How to Give

6 "Be careful not to practice your righteousness[c] in front of people, to be seen by them. Otherwise, you will have no reward from your Father in heaven. [2]So whenever you give to the poor, don't sound a trumpet before you, as the hypocrites do in the •synagogues and on the streets, to be applauded by people. •I assure you: They've got their reward![c] [3]But when you give to the poor, don't let your left hand know what your right hand is doing, [4]so that your giving may be in secret. And your Father who sees in secret will reward you.[D,d]

How to Pray

[5]"Whenever you pray, you must not be like the hypocrites, because they love to pray standing in the synagogues and on the street corners to be seen by people. I assure you: They've got their reward![e] [6]But when you pray, go into your private room, shut your door, and pray to your Father who is in secret. And your Father who sees in secret will reward you.[E,f] [7]When you pray, don't babble like the idolaters,[F] since they imagine they'll be heard for their many words.[g] [8]Don't be like them, because your Father knows the things you need before you ask Him.[h]

The Model Prayer

[9]"Therefore, you should pray like this:[i]

Our Father in heaven,
Your name be honored as holy.[j]
[10] Your kingdom come.
Your will be done
on earth as it is in heaven.[k]
[11] Give us today
our daily bread.[G]

a 5:47 Mt 5:37; Mk 6:51; Jn 10:10; Rm 3:1; 2Co 9:1
b 5:48 Gn 17:1; Lv 19:2; Php 3:15; Col 4:12; Jms 1:4; 1Pt 1:15
c 6:1-2 Mt 23:5; Lk 6:24
d 6:4 Jr 17:10; Lk 14:14; Col 3:23-24; Heb 4:13
e 6:5 Mt 6:16; Mk 11:25; Lk 6:24; 18:11
f 6:6 2Kg 4:33; Is 26:20; Mt 6:18
g 6:7 1Kg 18:26; Ec 5:2
h 6:8 Mt 9:12; Mk 2:17; Lk 5:31; 9:11; 10:42; Ac 2:45
i 6:9-13 Lk 11:1-13
j 6:9 Lk 11:2; 1Co 7:14
k 6:10 Ps 103:20; Mt 3:2; 4:17; 26:42; Lk 22:42; Ac 21:14

A 5:47 Or doing that is superior; lit doing more   B 5:47 Other mss read tax collectors   C 6:1 Other mss read charitable giving   D 6:4 Other mss read will Himself reward you openly   E 6:6 Other mss add openly   F 6:7 Or Gentiles, or nations, or heathen, or pagans   G 6:11 Or our necessary bread, or our bread for tomorrow

---

5:48 Much as a child resembles his biological parents, spiritual children bear close resemblance to their **heavenly Father**. Consequently, Jesus' disciples are commanded to exhibit moral perfection. The close connection between this verse and Jesus' teaching about love (vv. 43-47) suggests that unconditional love is the most crucial expression of God's character in the life of His followers.

6:1 Jesus did not prohibit public acts of righteousness (see note at 5:16), but He warned that the motivation for such acts is more important than the bare fact of performing them. All such deeds must be done for God's glory, not human reputation. Those who seek human acclaim when performing good works will receive no heavenly reward. In Mt 6:2-18, Jesus supplies general principles for performing righteous acts.

6:2-4 The words **whenever you give** assume that disciples will regularly assist needy people. The prohibition **don't sound a trumpet** stems from the fact that the offering chests in the temple (shofar chests or trumpet chests) were trumpet-shaped with a wide opening where coins were deposited and a winding, ever-narrower funnel that, at its narrowest point, exits into the chest. This arrangement prevented thieves from sticking their hands into the chest (m. Shek. 2:1; 6:1,5). Thus, "sounding the trumpet" is likely a reference to tossing coins noisily into the trumpet-shaped coffer and thereby calling attention to one's generosity. Jesus described such conduct as hypocritical. The word **hypocrites** (Gk hupocrites) originally referred to actors who performed in Greek or Roman theaters. The hypocrites to whom Jesus referred are spiritual actors who pretend to have piety in order to win human approval. The instructions about the **left hand** and the **right hand** prohibit a person from celebrating their own acts of righteousness. Give liberally, but never dwell on the fact that you do so.

6:5 **Standing in the synagogues** (gathering places for Jewish worship) or **on the street corners** when praying ensures that many people saw the hypocrites praying, but Jesus taught that God has no regard for such actions.

6:6 A **private room** (Gk tameion) was a room that did not have doors or windows to the building's exterior. Closing the **door** granted total privacy. Since the true disciple prays for a heavenly rather than a human audience, privacy is ideal for genuine prayer. Jesus described the Father as the One **who is in secret**. God is ever-present. The disciple can encounter Him in the most obscure locations.

6:7 The babbling of **idolaters** may refer to the meaningless gibberish that appears in Greek magical papyri. Like the familiar "abracadabra," these formulas were nonsensical combinations of sounds that were believed to have special power. Ancient texts show that Jews sometimes embraced these practices.

6:9 By commanding His disciples to **pray like this** rather than simply "pray this," Jesus demonstrated that this prayer was offered as a model rather than a mantra to be recited. The first person plural pronoun **Our** implies that Jesus intended this prayer to be a model for corporate prayer, i.e., a prayer for when disciples gather as a group. This confirms that Mt 6:5 was not intended to prohibit disciples from praying together publicly in the synagogue or other gatherings but instead prohibited prayers that were motivated by religious showmanship. **Your name be honored as holy** suggests that Jesus expected His disciples to live righteous lives that honor rather than profane God's name (5:16; Lv 22:31-32). This is an important precondition for successful prayer.

6:10 In light of parallels with contemporary Jewish prayers and Jesus' teaching that the kingdom of God is a present reality but also awaits a fuller future consummation, the petition **Your kingdom come** has a present and a future focus. The petition asks that disciples submit more fully to God's **will** as subjects of His reign through Jesus. We should daily pray for the future consummation of God's rule in which He will reign fully and completely over the world.

6:11 **Daily bread** was the amount of bread necessary to sur-

¹² And forgive us our debts,
    as we also have forgiven our debtors.^a
¹³ And do not bring us into^A temptation,^b
    but deliver us from the evil one.^{B,c}
    [For Yours is the kingdom and the power
    and the glory forever. •Amen.]^C

¹⁴"For if you forgive people their wrongdoing,^D your heavenly Father will forgive you as well.^d ¹⁵But if you don't forgive people,^E your Father will not forgive your wrongdoing.^D

How to Fast

¹⁶"Whenever you fast, don't be sad-faced like the hypocrites. For they make their faces unattractive^{F,e} so their fasting is obvious to people. I assure you: They've got their reward! ¹⁷But when you fast, put oil on your head, and wash your face,^f ¹⁸so that you don't show your fasting to people but to your Father who is in secret. And your Father who sees in secret will reward you.^G

God and Possessions

¹⁹"Don't collect for yourselves treasures^H on earth, where moth and rust destroy and where thieves break in and steal.^g ²⁰But collect for yourselves treasures in heaven,^h where neither moth nor rust destroys, and where thieves don't break in and steal. ²¹For where your treasure is, there your heart will be also.

²²"The eye is the lamp of the body. If your eye is good, your whole body will be full of light. ²³But if your eye is bad, your whole body will be full of darkness. So if the light within you is darkness—how deep is that darkness!ⁱ

²⁴"No one can be a •slave of two masters, since either he will hate one and love the other, or be devoted to one and despise the other. You cannot be slaves of God and of money.^j

The Cure for Anxiety

²⁵"This is why I tell you:^k Don't worry about your life, what you will eat or what you will drink; or about your body, what you will wear. Isn't life more than food and the body more than clothing?^l ²⁶Look at the birds of the sky: They don't sow or reap or gather into barns, yet your heavenly Father feeds them. Aren't you worth more than they?^m ²⁷Can any of you add a single •cubit to his height^l by worrying? ²⁸And why do you worry about clothes? Learn how the wildflowers of the field grow: they don't labor or spin thread. ²⁹Yet I tell you that not even Solomon in all his splendor was adorned like one of these! ³⁰If that's how God clothes the grass of the field, which is here today and thrown into the furnace tomorrow, won't He do much more for you—you of little faith?ⁿ ³¹So don't worry, saying, 'What will we eat?' or 'What will we drink?' or 'What will we wear?' ³²For the idolaters^J eagerly seek all these things, and your heavenly Father knows that you need them. ³³But seek first the kingdom of God^{K,o} and His righteousness,^p

Cross references (center column)

^a6:11-12 Pr 30:8; Rm 4:4; Gl 5:3
^b6:13 Mt 26:41; 1Co 10:13; 2Pt 2:9
^cMt 5:37; Jn 17:15; 2Th 3:3; 2Tm 4:18
^d6:14 Mk 11:25; Eph 4:32; Col 3:13
^e6:15-16 Is 58:5; Mt 18:35; Jms 2:13
^f6:17 Ru 3:3; 2Sm 12:20; Dn 10:3
^g6:19 Pr 23:4; Heb 13:5
^h6:20 Mt 19:21; Lk 12:33; 18:22; 1Tm 6:19
ⁱ6:23 Mt 4:16; 8:12; 22:13; 25:30; 27:45
^j6:24 Lk 16:13; Gl 1:10; Jms 4:4
^k6:25-33 Lk 12:22-31
^l6:25 Lk 10:41; Php 4:6; 1Pt 5:7
^m6:26 Jb 38:41; Ps 147:9; Mt 10:29-31
ⁿ6:29-30 1Kg 10:4-7; Mt 8:26; 14:31; 16:8
^o6:33 Mk 1:15; Ac 20:25
^pMt 27:19; Lk 7:29; 23:41,47; Jn 5:30; 17:25; Ac 3:14

---

^A6:13 Or *do not cause us to come into*   ^B6:13 Or *from evil*   ^C6:13 Other mss omit bracketed text   ^D6:14,15 Or *trespasses*   ^E6:15 Other mss add *their wrongdoing*   ^F6:16 Or *unrecognizable*, or *disfigured*   ^G6:18 Other mss add *openly*   ^H6:19 Or *valuables*   ^I6:27 Or *add one moment to his life-span*   ^J6:32 Or *Gentiles*, or *nations*, or *heathen*, or *pagans*   ^K6:33 Other mss omit *of God*

---

vive for a day. The request is reminiscent of Pr 30:8-9. Jesus wanted His disciples to live in a state of constant dependence on God and His provision.

6:12 The Greek grammar indicates that the disciple prays for forgiveness from God only after having first expressed forgiveness to others.

6:14-15 God forgives those who are truly repentant. True repentance results in a willingness to **forgive** others.

6:16 They make their faces unattractive refers to the Jewish practice of smearing ashes on the face and wearing grim expressions during times of fasting. Although these acts originally expressed true repentance, hypocrites adopted them as a mask of false piety.

6:19-20 Jesus emphasized the fleeting value of worldly wealth. The larvae of the **moth** could quickly destroy valuable fabrics that were treasured by the ancients. The word **rust** is literally "eating." It can refer to the pitting of metal coins or to vermin that ruin valuable food stores.

6:21 Jesus taught that a person's **heart** truly belongs to what it most treasures. Since a disciple is to love God with all his heart (22:37; Dt 6:4), love for material possessions and riches is a subtle form of idolatry (Col 3:5).

6:22-23 In Jewish writings, a good eye represented a generous attitude and a bad eye a stingy, miserly attitude. The bad eye (an improper perspective on wealth) results in a deep internal darkness, a moral blindness that diminishes the ability to see and pursue what is good.

6:25 Isn't life more than food is a rabbinic style of argument. It reasons that if God does a greater thing for us, He will also do lesser things. Specifically, if God created you (the greater accomplishment), He is certainly capable of feeding you (a lesser accomplishment).

6:26 Jesus here reversed His previous argument and reasoned that if God bothers to do a lesser thing (feed **the birds**), He will assuredly accomplish the greater thing of feeding humans.

6:27 The words translated as **add a single cubit to his height** probably refer to longevity (see textual note, "add one moment to his life-span"). Worry is futile and cannot prolong your life.

6:30 Jesus revealed that the real cause of anxiety is when disciples have **little faith**, meaning doubt about God's power and disbelief in His desire to provide for His children.

6:32 Obsession with material possessions displays the warped priorities of **idolaters** (Col 3:5).

6:33 The disciple who values the reign of God over his life

and all these things will be provided for you.[a] [34] Therefore don't worry about tomorrow, because tomorrow will worry about itself. Each day has enough trouble[b] of its own.

Do Not Judge

7 "Do not judge, so that you won't be judged.[c] [2] For with the judgment you use,[A] you will be judged, and with the measure you use,[B] it will be measured to you.[d] [3] Why do you look at the speck in your brother's eye but don't notice the log in your own eye?[e] [4] Or how can you say to your brother, 'Let me take the speck out of your eye,' and look, there's a log in your eye? [5] Hypocrite! First take the log out of your eye, and then you will see clearly to take the speck out of your brother's eye. [6] Don't give what is holy to dogs or toss your pearls before pigs,[f] or they will trample them with their feet, turn, and tear you to pieces.

Keep Asking, Searching, Knocking

[7] "Keep asking,[C,g] and it will be given to you.[h] Keep searching,[D] and you will find. Keep knocking,[E] and the door[F] will be opened to you. [8] For everyone who asks receives, and the one who searches finds,[i] and to the one who knocks, the door[G] will be opened. [9] What man among you, if his son asks him for bread, will give him a stone? [10] Or if he asks for a fish, will give him a snake? [11] If you then, who are evil,[j] know how to give good gifts to your children, how much more will your Father in heaven give good things to those who ask Him! [12] Therefore, whatever you want others to do for you, do also the same for them—this is the Law and the Prophets.[H,k]

Entering the Kingdom

[13] "Enter through the narrow gate.[l] For the gate is wide and the road is broad that leads to destruction,[m] and there are many who go through it. [14] How narrow is the gate and

---

a6:33 1Kg 3:13; Mt 19:28; Mk 10:29; Lk 18:29; 1Tm 4:8
b6:34 Mt 6:25; Lk 10:41; Php 4:6; 1Pt 5:7
c7:1-5 Mk 4:24-25; Lk 6:37-42
d7:2 Mk 4:24; Lk 6:38; Rm 2:1; 14:10; Jms 2:13
e7:3 Lk 6:41; Jn 8:7-9
f7:6 Pr 9:7-8; 23:9; Mt 15:26
g7:7-11 Lk 11:9-13
h7:7 Mt 18:22; Mk 11:24; Jn 14:13-14; 15:7; 16:24; Jms 1:5; 1Jn 3:22; 5:14
i7:8 Pr 8:17; Is 55:6; Jr 29:12-13
j7:11 Gn 6:5; 8:21
k7:12 Mt 22:40; Lk 6:31; Rm 13:8; Gl 5:14
l7:13-14 Lk 13:23-24
m7:13 Mt 26:8; Mk 14:4; Jn 17:12; Ac 8:20; Rm 9:22; Php 1:28

A7:2 Lit *you judge*　B7:2 Lit *you measure*　C7:7 Or *Ask*　D7:7 Or *Search*　E7:7 Or *Knock*　F7:7 Lit *and it*　G7:8 Lit *knocks, it*
H7:12 When capitalized, the Law and the Prophets = the OT

---

and who diligently pursues righteous living can trust God to satisfy his needs.

6:34 Jesus did not prohibit planning for the future, but He did prohibit worrying about it. He urged His disciples instead to focus on the challenges of the present.

7:1 Jesus did not intend to prohibit all acts of judgment. Elsewhere He commanded believers to discern the actions of others (v. 15; 18:15-20). What Jesus condemned is hypocritical judgment that focuses on the faults of others while excusing one's own sins.

7:2 Jesus warned that those who use a harsh standard of **judgment** when evaluating others can expect God to use the same harsh standard when they face His judgment.

7:3-5 The **speck**, perhaps a piece of sawdust, represents a small fault. The **log**, a piece of large timber, represents a major moral fault. He who corrects the minor faults of others without attending to his own more serious faults is a hypocrite. Believers do have a responsibility to help one another repent of sins, but only after first dealing with their own serious sins.

7:6 **What is holy** probably refers to sacrificial meat. **Dogs** would devour it insensibly without appreciating its sacredness. In Jesus' allegory, this sacrificial meat symbolizes His own sacred teachings. The dogs symbolize the wicked who disregard the value of His teachings. First-century teachers referred to **pearls** symbolically to speak of insightful and valuable teaching. Consequently, the pearls here symbolize Jesus' teachings given by the disciples. **Pigs** were ritually unclean animals. They symbolize the wicked and unclean. Pigs eat spoiled food but have no appreciation for pearls, just as the wicked consume wicked pleasures but disregard the gospel. This contempt for the gospel is pictured by the pig trampling the pearls underfoot. That pigs may turn against the one offering the pearls shows that contempt for the gospel message can become contempt for the gospel messenger, as has often happened in history.

7:7-8 While some people interpret these verses as a promise that God will give disciples whatever they pray for, linguistic connections between these verses and other portions of the Sermon on the Mount suggest that Jesus promised that those who ask, search, and knock will be invited to enter His kingdom. The command to **keep asking** is tied to the promise of "good things" to those who ask in verse 11. In the Lukan parallel, these good things are interpreted as the Holy Spirit who transforms the disciple and makes him fit for the kingdom. **Keep searching** uses the same Greek verb as 6:33, "Seek first the kingdom of God and His righteousness." Since the word **door** is not in the Greek text of verse 7, and because ancient people knocked on gates as well as doors to request entrance (Ac 12:13), **keep knocking** likely refers to knocking on the gate of the kingdom (mentioned in vv. 13-14).

7:9-10 Round loaves of bread resemble smooth, brown stones. Certain **fish** in the Sea of Galilee resemble snakes.

7:11 Jesus' description of humans as **you . . . who are evil** disproves the modern concept that people are basically good. Although Jesus acknowledged that humans may perform gracious acts like providing for their children, He insisted that they do so contrary to their sinful nature. God's gracious acts, on the other hand, express our heavenly Father's perfect nature.

7:12 The word **therefore** suggests that the "Golden Rule" of this verse draws an application from the preceding section. Since the preceding verse describes God's gracious and loving provision for others, the conjunction probably implies that following the Golden Rule shows the disciple's resemblance to the heavenly Father (see notes at 5:44-45; 5:48).

7:13-14 The **narrow gate** symbolizes the exclusive nature of Christ's kingdom. Entrance requires the disciple to do the will of the Father in heaven (v. 21). The **gate** that is **wide** indicates that hell grants unrestricted entrance and that many will enter through its gates. The **difficult** (lit "narrow") . . . **road** may symbolize the life of hardship and persecution that the disciple must face. However, since Jewish literature

difficult the road that leads to life, and few
find it.
15 “Beware of false prophets[a] who come to
you in sheep's[b] clothing[c] but inwardly are
ravaging wolves.[d] 16 You'll recognize them by
their fruit.[e] Are grapes gathered from thornbushes or figs from thistles?[f] 17 In the same
way, every good tree produces good fruit, but
a bad tree produces bad fruit. 18 A good tree
can't produce bad fruit; neither can a bad tree
produce good fruit. 19 Every tree that doesn't
produce good fruit is cut down and thrown
into the fire.[g] 20 So you'll recognize them by
their fruit.[h]
21 “Not everyone who says to Me, ‘Lord,
Lord!’ will enter the kingdom of heaven,[i] but
only the one who does the will[j] of My Father
in heaven.[k] 22 On that day many will say to
Me, ‘Lord, Lord, didn't we prophesy in Your
name, drive out demons[l] in Your name, and do
many miracles in Your name?’[m] 23 Then I will
announce to them, ‘I never knew you! **Depart
from Me, you lawbreakers!**’[A,B,n]

The Two Foundations

24 “Therefore,[o] everyone who hears these
words[p] of Mine and acts on them will be like a
sensible man who built his house on the rock.
25 The rain fell, the rivers rose, and the winds
blew and pounded that house. Yet it didn't collapse, because its foundation was on the rock.
26 But everyone who hears these words of Mine
and doesn't act on them will be like a foolish
man who built his house on the sand. 27 The
rain fell, the rivers rose, the winds blew and
pounded that house, and it collapsed. And its
collapse was great!”
28 When Jesus had finished this sermon,[C,q]
the crowds were astonished at His teaching,[r]
29 because He was teaching them like one who
had authority, and not like their •scribes.

A Man Cleansed

8 When He came down from the mountain,
large crowds[s] followed Him. 2 Right away[t]
a man with a serious skin disease came up and
knelt before Him,[u] saying, “Lord, if You are
willing, You can make me •clean.”
3 Reaching out His hand He touched
him, saying, “I am willing; be made clean.”

[a] 7:15 Mt 24:11,24; Mk 13:22; Lk 6:26; Ac 13:6; 2Pt 2:1 [b] Mt 9:36; 10:6,16; 12:11-12; 15:24; 18:12-13 [c] Mc 3:5; 2Tm 3:5 [d] Ezk 22:27; Jn 10:12; Ac 20:29 [e] 7:16-21 Pr 11:30; Mt 12:33; Lk 6:43-44; Jn 4:36; Jms 3:12 [f] 7:16 Mt 13:7; Heb 6:8 [g] 7:19 Jr 11:19; Mt 3:10; Lk 3:9; 13:7; Jn 15:2; Jd 12 [h] 7:20 Mt 7:16; 12:33; Lk 6:44; Jms 3:12 [i] 7:21 Mt 3:2; 18:3; Mk 9:43 [j] Ps 143:10; Pr 16:9; Mt 12:50; Gl 1:4; Eph 1:9; 1Jn 2:17 [k] Hs 8:2; Mt 25:11; Lk 6:46; Rm 2:13; Jms 1:22 [l] 7:22 Mk 3:15; Rv 9:20; 18:2 [m] Nm 24:4; Mt 10:15; Lk 13:25; Jn 11:51; 1Co 13:2 [n] 7:23 Ps 5:5; 6:8; Mt 25:12,41; Lk 13:25-27 [o] 7:24-27 Lk 6:47-49; Jms 1:22-25 [p] 7:24 Mt 12:36; Mk 4:14; Lk 6:47; 8:21; Jn 1:1; 2:22 [q] 7:28 Mt 11:1; 13:53; 19:1; 26:1 [r] Mt 13:54; 22:23; Mk 1:22; 6:2; 11:18; Lk 4:32; Jn 7:46 [s] 8:1 Mt 5:1; Lk 3:7 [t] 8:2-4 Mk 1:40-44; Lk 5:12-14 [u] 8:2 Mt 9:18; 15:25; 18:26; 20:20; Jn 9:38; Ac 10:25

[A] 7:23 Lit *you who work lawlessness* [B] 7:23 Ps 6:8 [C] 7:28 Lit *had ended these words*

often used the symbol of the road to represent a moral path (Jdg 2:22; Is 30:21; Jr 6:16; 2Jn 6) and because the law was portrayed as a narrow road from which a person was not to deviate (Dt 5:32; 17:20; 28:14; Jos 1:7; 2Kg 22:2), the narrow road probably represents Jesus' morally restrictive teaching. The wide road permits travelers to meander and pursue worldly desires, but the narrow path requires travelers to stick to God's will (Mt 7:21).

7:15-20 **False prophets** don **sheep's clothing** to disguise the fact that they are **ravaging wolves** masquerading as true disciples. However, a prophet's character and behavior (his **fruit**) indicates whether he is true or false. Other NT texts insist that a teacher's doctrine must also be examined (1Jn 4:2-3). True disciples bear the fruit of good works, and this confirms their identity as Jesus' disciples (Mt 7:21-23). The image of cutting down and burning a bad **tree** portrays the judgment and eternal punishment of false disciples.

7:21-23 By referring to Himself as **Lord** and depicting Himself as the ultimate Judge of humanity, Jesus implied His deity. True disciples affirm Jesus' lordship, submit to His authority, and obey His commands. Jesus insisted that a person is confirmed as a true disciple not by prophecy, exorcism, or working miracles but by living a transformed life made possible by God. The disobedient lifestyles of **lawbreakers** are inconsistent with genuine discipleship. Jesus' words, **I never knew you**, show that these were never truly disciples.

7:24-27 The adjectives **sensible** and **foolish** describe a person's spiritual and moral state, not his intellect. Whether one is considered sensible or foolish is determined by his response to Jesus' teaching. Since OT writers described God's wrath using the image of a great storm (Is 28:16-17; Ezk 13:10-13), the storm that destroys the **house on the sand** is a picture of divine judgment. Hence, the person who **hears** and **acts** on Jesus' teaching is prepared for judgment. The one who **hears** but doesn't **act** on Jesus' **words** will be destroyed in the storm of judgment.

7:28-29 Jesus amazed the crowds with an **authority** that surpassed that of other teachers. First-century Jewish teachers appealed to the authority of their rabbinic predecessors. However, Jesus introduced His teachings with the contrast, "You have heard that it was said . . . but I tell you" (5:21,27,31,33,38,43). By this Jesus made clear that He had the authority to interpret the law independent from and even contrary to the Jewish oral tradition and the most esteemed rabbis. The words **when Jesus had finished** are important for understanding the structure of Matthew's Gospel. See "Structure" in the Introduction to Matthew.

8:2 The **serious skin disease** is difficult to identify. The Greek term can refer to several conditions, ranging from fungal infections to Hansen's Disease. The OT law required lepers to be isolated from society (Lv 13:45-46). By kneeling before Jesus and addressing Him as Lord (Gk *kurios*, the Greek translation of the Hebrew name Yahweh), the man recognized Jesus as far more than just a man. His confidence in Jesus' ability to heal his condition hints that his act of worship involved full recognition of Jesus' deity. After all, only God was capable of healing lepers in the OT (Ex 4:6-7; Nm 12:10-16; 2Kg 5:1-15, esp. v. 7). The man's qualification, **if You are willing**, may indicate that other so-called healers had mistreated or failed him.

8:3 Although Jesus frequently healed by touch (v. 15; 9:20,25), He could heal by command and even at great distance from the sufferer (8:5-13; 9:6). Touching a leper was

Immediately his disease was healed.^A ⁴Then Jesus told him, "See that you don't tell anyone;^a but go, show yourself to the priest, and offer the gift that Moses prescribed, as a testimony to them."^b

A Centurion's Faith

⁵When He entered Capernaum,^c a •centurion came to Him, pleading with Him, ⁶"Lord, my servant is lying at home paralyzed, in terrible agony!"

⁷"I will come and heal him," He told him.

⁸"Lord," the centurion replied, "I am not worthy to have You come under my roof. But only say the word, and my servant will be cured.^d ⁹For I too am a man under authority,^B having soldiers under my command.^B I say to this one, 'Go!' and he goes; and to another, 'Come!' and he comes; and to my •slave, 'Do this!' and he does it."

¹⁰Hearing this, Jesus was amazed and said to those following Him, "•I assure you: I have not found anyone in Israel with so great a faith! ¹¹I tell you that many will come from

east and west, and recline at the table with Abraham, Isaac, and Jacob in the kingdom of heaven.^e ¹²But the sons of the kingdom will be thrown into the outer darkness. In that place there will be weeping and gnashing of teeth."^f

¹³Then Jesus told the centurion, "Go. As you have believed,^g let it be done for you." And his servant was cured that very moment.^C

Healings at Capernaum

¹⁴When Jesus went into Peter's house,^h He saw his mother-in-law lying in bed with a fever. ¹⁵So He touched her hand, and the fever left her. Then she got up and began to serve Him. ¹⁶When evening came, they brought to Him many who were demon-possessed. He drove out the spirits^i with a word and healed all who were sick,^j ¹⁷so that what was spoken through the prophet Isaiah might be fulfilled:

**He Himself took our weaknesses
and carried our diseases.**^D,k

Following Jesus

¹⁸When Jesus saw large crowds^E,l around

Cross-reference column:
^a 8:4 Mt 9:30; 17:9; Mk 5:43; 7:36; 8:30
^b Lv 14:3-4,10; Lk 5:14; 17:14
^c 8:5-13 Lk 7:1-10; Jn 4:46-54
^d 8:8 Ps 107:20; Lk 15:19,21
^e 8:11 Is 49:12; 59:19; Mk 1:11; Lk 13:29; Eph 3:6
^f 8:12 Mt 13:42,50; 22:13; 24:51; 25:30; Lk 13:28
^g 8:13 Mt 9:22,29; Jn 4:53
^h 8:14-16 Mk 1:29-34; Lk 4:38-41
^i 8:16 Mk 3:15; 1Tm 4:1; 1Jn 4:1
^j Mt 4:24; 8:33; Ac 19:12
^k 8:17 Is 53:4; Mt 1:22
^l 8:18 Mt 14:22; Mk 4:35; Lk 8:22; Jn 6:15-17

---

^A 8:3 Lit *cleansed*   ^B 8:9 Lit *under me*   ^C 8:13 Or *that hour*; lit *very hour*   ^D 8:17 Is 53:4   ^E 8:18 Other mss read *saw a crowd*

---

an expression of boldness and deep compassion since doing so was prohibited by OT law (Lv 5:3).

8:4 By being inspected and declared clean by the priest, the healed man could authenticate the miracle that Jesus performed.

8:5 A **centurion** was an officer of the Roman army who commanded about 100 soldiers.

8:7-8 Jesus' willingness to enter the home of a Gentile shocked the centurion, for Jewish law banned Jews from doing this (Ac 10:28). God's grace to Gentiles and His intention to include them in His redemptive plan is a prominent theme in Matthew. The centurion was confident that Jesus had the authority to heal his servant even though the servant was in another location.

8:11 The **kingdom of heaven** is open to anyone who places their faith in Jesus. Believing Gentiles will be equal even to the great Jewish patriarchs **Abraham, Isaac, and Jacob**.

8:12 The **sons of the kingdom** refers to Jews to whom the kingdom was originally promised but who will be excluded because they rejected Jesus. **Outer darkness** is a metaphor for damnation in ancient Jewish texts. **Weeping and gnashing of teeth** denotes anguish expressed by those who suffer eternal torment.

8:14 Mention of Peter's **mother-in-law** confirms that Peter was married. His marriage was foundational to Paul's argument that apostles had the right to marry and to have their wives accompany them in their missionary labors (1Co 9:5).

8:15 The woman's ability to get up immediately and serve a meal indicates that her healing was instant and complete.

8:16 Jesus' ability to drive out **spirits** by command stands in contrast to the drastic measures used by Jewish exorcists. These included using offensive odors to drive demons away or nose rings to hook them (Tob 6:7-8,16-17;

Josephus, *Ant.* 8:45-49). That Jesus could heal **all who were sick** indicates that no disease could thwart His healing powers.

8:17 In one sense Jesus was able to heal physical illnesses because His impending sacrificial death purchased spiritual atonement from sin. All sickness is ultimately a consequence of Adam's sinful choice. Jesus could remove these consequences because He would bear the full penalty for sin on the cross. Matthew's application of Is 53:4 shows that he understood Jesus' death as an act of substitution, an atonement in which Jesus was "pierced because of our transgressions" and bore punishment "for the iniquity of us all" (Is 53:5-6).

---

pleroo

Greek Pronunciation	[play RAH oh]
HCSB Translation	fulfill
Uses in Matthew	16 (Mk, 2; Lk, 9; Jn, 15)
Uses in the NT	86
Focus passage	Matthew 8:17

Pleroo (to fill) refers to the action of *filling up* an item with some object (Mt 13:48; Ac 2:2; 5:28], and metaphorically to the *filling* of persons with certain qualities or powers (Lk 2:40; Ac 2:28; Rm 15:13-14; 2Tm 1:4) or to the completion (i.e., *filling up*) of some time period (Mk 1:15; Ac 9:23) or activity (Lk 7:1; Ac 12:25; 13:25). By extension, *pleroo* may also mean *to fulfill* and often indicates the *fulfillment* of OT prophecies. Prophecies may be directly prophetic (a predicted event is *fulfilled*; e.g., Jesus' Galilean ministry; Mt 4:13-16; cp. Is 9:1-7), or they may be indirectly *fulfilled* by the correspondence of two historical events (the first event foreshadows the second; Mt 27:9; cp. Jr 32:6-9; Zch 11:12-13), or they may be based on parallels between Israel's history and Jesus' life (Israel and Jesus being called out of Egypt; Mt 2:15; cp. Hs 11:1)

Him, He gave the order to go to the other side of the sea.[A] [19]A •scribe approached Him and said,[a] "Teacher, I will follow You wherever You go!"

[20]Jesus told him, "Foxes have dens and birds of the sky have nests, but the Son of Man[b] has no place to lay His head."

[21]"Lord," another of His disciples said, "first let me go bury my father."[B]

[22]But Jesus told him, "Follow Me, and let the dead bury their own dead."

Wind and Wave Obey the Master

[23]As He got into the[c] boat,[c] His disciples[d] followed Him. [24]Suddenly, a violent storm arose on the sea, so that the boat was being swamped by the waves. But He was sleeping. [25]So the disciples came and woke Him up, saying, "Lord, save us! We're going to die!"

[26]But He said to them, "Why are you fearful, you of little faith?" Then He got up and rebuked the winds and the sea.[e] And there was a great calm.

[27]The men were amazed and asked, "What kind of man is this?—even the winds and the sea obey[f] Him!"

Demons Driven Out by the Master

[28]When He had come to the other side,[g] to the region of the Gadarenes,[D] two demon-possessed men met Him as they came out of the tombs. They were so violent that no one could pass that way. [29]Suddenly they shouted, "What do You have to do with us,[E,F] Son of God? Have You come here to torment us before the time?"[h]

[30]Now a long way off from them, a large herd of pigs was feeding. [31]"If You drive us out," the demons begged Him, "send us into the herd of pigs."

[32]"Go!" He told them. So when they had come out, they entered the pigs. And suddenly the whole herd rushed down the steep bank into the sea and perished in the water. [33]Then the men who tended them fled. They went into the city and reported everything—especially what had happened to those who were demon-possessed. [34]At that, the whole town went out to meet Jesus. When they saw Him, they begged Him to leave their region.[i]

The Son of Man Forgives and Heals

9 So He got into a boat, crossed over, and came to His own town.[j] [2]Just then[k] some men[G] brought to Him a paralytic lying on a mat. Seeing their faith, Jesus told the paralytic, "Have courage, son, your sins are forgiven."[l]

Cross references (center column):

[a] 8:19-22 Lk 9:57-60
[b] 8:20 Dn 7:14; Mt 9:6; 12:8; 13:41; Mk 8:31
[c] 8:23-27 Mk 4:36-41; Lk 8:22-25; Jn 6:16-21
[d] 8:23 Mt 10:1; 26:56; Mk 3:7; 16:20; Lk 6:13; Jn 12:16
[e] 8:26 Ps 65:7; 89:9; 107:29; Mt 6:30; Lk 4:39
[f] 8:27 Mk 1:27; Lk 5:9
[g] 8:28-34 Mk 5:1-17; Lk 8:26-37
[h] 8:29 Jdg 11:12; 2Sm 16:10; Mk 1:24; Lk 4:34; Jn 2:4; Ac 8:7
[i] 8:34 1Kg 17:18; Lk 5:8; Ac 16:39
[j] 9:1 Mt 4:13; Mk 5:21
[k] 9:2-8 Mk 2:3-12; Lk 5:18-26
[l] 9:2 Mt 4:24; 8:10,13; 9:22; Lk 7:48; Jn 16:33

[A] 8:18 = Sea of Galilee   [B] 8:21 Not necessarily meaning his father was already dead   [C] 8:23 Other mss read to a   [D] 8:28 Other mss read Gergesenes   [E] 8:29 Other mss add Jesus   [F] 8:29 Lit What to us and to You   [G] 9:2 Lit then they

---

8:20 Following Jesus can involve sacrificing the comforts of home. Jesus is more than worthy of such sacrifice because He is the **Son of Man**. This title was drawn from Dn 7:13-14 where it described a ruler of heavenly origin who would reign over a universal and eternal kingdom. This was Jesus' favorite self-designation. It is used 28 times in Matthew.

8:21-22 Jesus' demand seems harsh to modern readers, for today funerals would only briefly delay a commitment to follow Him. However, ancient Jewish burials stretched over an entire year. A year after the initial interment, the eldest son was obligated to gather the skeletal remains and place them in an ossuary for second burial. Many Jews regarded the commandment to honor father and mother as the supreme commandment, and they also viewed giving parents an honorable burial as its most important implication. Jesus insisted that following Him was to be an even higher priority. Since obligation to God supersedes obligation to parents (Dt 13:5-6), Jesus assumed a divine prerogative in this teaching.

8:23-27 Jesus' authority over **winds** and **sea** identified Him as the Creator and Ruler of nature.

8:28 Early manuscripts of Matthew describe this event as occurring in **the region of the Gadarenes**. In contrast, early manuscripts of Mark and Luke describe it as occurring in "the region of the Gerasenes" (Mk 5:1; Lk 8:26). Gadara and Gerasa were located in the same province. The different readings mean very little in this light, and they likely arose due to transcription errors rather than disagreement between the original texts of the Gospels. These regions were Gentile lands, as confirmed by the large herd of pigs nearby.

The **tombs** were burial caves in which fugitives sometimes hid. The presence of the **demon-possessed** among the tombs indicates their obsession with things profane and unclean.

8:29 Although Jesus' disciples were slow to recognize His divine Sonship, the demons were not. Jesus was first identified as God's Son by the Father during His baptism (3:17). Later, Satan acknowledged Jesus' divine sonship (4:3,6). Now demons reiterated Jesus' identity. **Son of God** was a messianic title drawn from Ps 2:7,12 (see note at Mt 3:17). The demons also recognized Jesus as the One who would judge and punish them.

8:30-32 No longer able to continue their destructive and violent work in the lives of the two men, the demons begged for permission to enter the **herd of pigs** where the demons' deceptive and murderous nature was clearly displayed in the senseless destruction of the entire herd. Here is a picture of Satan's ultimate aim for the world.

8:34 Gentiles from the nearby town may have thought that Jesus personally destroyed the herd as a statement against Gentile idolatry and uncleanness, and they naturally feared destruction of other valuable herds (see note at v. 28).

9:1 Jesus' **own town** was Capernaum, the headquarters of His ministry (see note at 4:13).

9:2 Jesus elsewhere insisted that illness is not necessarily a direct consequence of a person's sin (Jn 9:1-3). **Seeing their faith** implies that personal faith ("their" included the paralytic and his friends) was necessary to receive Jesus' healing and forgiveness. On the association of personal

³At this, some of the *scribes said among themselves, "He's blaspheming!"ᵃ

⁴But perceiving their thoughts,ᵇ Jesus said, "Why are you thinking evil things in your hearts?ᴬ ⁵For which is easier: to say, 'Your sins are forgiven,' or to say, 'Get up and walk'? ⁶But so you may know that the *Son of Man has authority on earth to forgive sins"—then He told the paralytic, "Get up, pick up your mat, and go home." ⁷And he got up and went home. ⁸When the crowds saw this, they were awestruckᴮ,ᶜ and gave gloryᶜ to God who had given such authority to men.

The Call of Matthew

⁹As Jesus went on from there,ᵈ He saw a man named Matthew sitting at the tax office, and He said to him, "Follow Me!" So he got up and followed Him.ᵉ

¹⁰While He was reclining at the table in the house, many tax collectors and sinners came as guests to eatᴰ with Jesus and His disciples.ᶠ ¹¹When the *Pharisees saw this, they asked His disciples, "Why does your Teacher eat with tax collectors and sinners?"ᵍ

¹²But when He heard this, He said, "Those who are well don't need a doctor, but the sick do.ʰ ¹³Go and learn what this means: **I desire mercy and not sacrifice.**ᴱ,ʲ For I didn't come to call the righteous, but sinners."ᶠ

A Question about Fasting

¹⁴Then John's disciples came to Him, saying, "Why do we and the Pharisees fast often, but Your disciples do not fast?"ʲ ¹⁵Jesus said to them, "Can the wedding guestsᴳ be sad while the groom is with them? The timeᴴ will come when the groom will be taken away

Cross references (center column):
ᵃ9:3 Mt 26:65; Jn 10:36
ᵇ9:4 Mt 12:25; Lk 6:8; 9:47; 11:17
ᶜ9:8 Mt 5:16; 15:31; Lk 7:16; 13:13; Jn 15:8; Ac 4:21
ᵈ9:9-17 Mk 2:14-22; Lk 5:27-38
ᵉ9:9 Mt 10:3; Mk 2:14; 3:18; Lk 6:15; Ac 1:13
ᶠ9:10 Mt 10:42; 28:19; Lk 14:26; Jn 8:31; 13:35; 15:8; Ac 6:1
ᵍ9:11 Mt 11:19; Lk 5:30; 15:2; Gl 2:15
ʰ9:12 Mk 2:17; Lk 5:31
ⁱ9:13 Hs 6:6; Mc 6:6-8; Mt 12:7
ʲ9:14 Mt 11:2; 14:12; 15:2; Lk 11:1; 18:12

ᴬ9:4 Or *minds* ᴮ9:8 Other mss read *amazed* ᶜ9:8 Lit *afraid* ᴰ9:10 Lit *came, they were reclining* (at the table); at important meals the custom was to recline on a mat at a low table and lean on the left elbow. ᴱ9:13 Hs 6:6 ᶠ9:13 Other mss add *to repentance* ᴳ9:15 Lit *the sons of the bridal chamber* ᴴ9:15 Lit *days*

---

faith with Jesus' miracles, see verses 22,28-29; 8:13. In chapter 9, Jesus healed people who were lame (vv. 1-8), blind (vv. 27-31), and unable to speak (vv. 32-34). A Jewish audience who knew OT prophecies would recognize these miracles as the fulfillment of Is 35:5-6.

9:3 Scribes were a guild of scholars skilled in copying and interpreting the OT. They viewed themselves as guardians of Jewish traditions. The scribes considered Jesus' pronouncement of forgiveness to be blasphemous since only God can forgive sins. By asserting this divine right, Jesus put Himself in God's place (Mk 2:7).

9:4 Jesus' ability to know the scribes' secret **thoughts** implies supernatural knowledge.

9:5 Jesus proved His authority to forgive sins by removing the physical consequences of sin.

9:6 Jesus associated His **authority** to forgive sins with His identity as the **Son of Man** (see note at 8:20). Although first-century Jews did not associate forgiveness of sin with Messiah, Is 53 showed that Messiah would offer the sacrifice that accomplished atonement for sin. Matthew alludes to this in Mt 8:17 (see also 20:28).

9:8 Although other individuals do not share Jesus' authority to forgive sins, Jesus did impart to His disciples the authority to heal sickness and disease (10:1). The amazement of the **crowds** shows that the scribes were incapable of performing such miracles even though they claimed to be God's authoritative spokespersons.

9:9 Parallel texts (Mk 2:14; Lk 5:27) identify this tax collector as Levi. Most Jews had two or three names. Matthew means "Gift of Yahweh," and it may have been a nickname given to Levi by Jesus (cp. Mt 16:17-18) to remind him that his conversion and call were gifts from God. Many interpreters believe this verse identifies Matthew as the author of this Gospel.

9:11 Tax collectors were detested by many first-century Jews because they served the oppressive Roman government and often abused their authority for their own financial gain.

9:13 Hosea 6:6 is an important text in Matthew, since it is quoted twice (see 12:7). In its original context, the verse meant that sacrifice would not secure atonement for anyone who sought God's mercy but did not extend it to others. Jesus often insisted that those who seek forgiveness from God must also offer it to others (5:23-24; 6:14-15; 18:21-35). The two Hs 6:6 citations are the only times that Matthew uses the term **sacrifice**. Elsewhere when he refers to sacrifice, he uses the term "gift" (Gk *doron*). This is likely because Jesus' death was the one true sacrifice that secured atonement for sins (8:17; 20:28). Matthew wanted Jewish Christians who continued to practice temple rituals to view their sacrifices as gifts expressing gratitude for forgiveness already received through Jesus rather than acts that accomplish atonement.

9:15 The presence of Messiah gave the disciples an irrepressible joy that was inconsistent with fasting.

---

eleos

Greek Pronunciation	[EH leh ahss]
HCSB Translation	mercy
Uses in Matthew	3 (Lk, 6)
Uses in the NT	27
Focus Passage	Matthew 9:13

Eleos is one of several NT words meaning *mercy*. Each of the three times that this word appears in Matthew, Jesus uses it to refer to principles established in the OT, where God clearly required that His people show *mercy*. Twice Jesus quotes from Hosea 6:6, "I desire *mercy* and not sacrifice" (Mt 9:13; 12:7). The Hebrew term *(chesed)* underlying the Greek translation combines the ideas of love, *mercy*, and faithful loyalty. The Pharisees condemned Jesus for fraternizing with social outcasts (Mt 9:11), but He reminded them that God expected His people to show *mercy* before giving sacrifice. In Matthew 23 Jesus rebuked the Pharisees even more harshly, and one of His grievances was their neglect of the more important aspects of the law ("justice, *mercy*, and faith") even while they meticulously tithed their mint, dill, and cumin.

from them, and then they will fast. [16] No one patches an old garment with unshrunk cloth, because the patch pulls away from the garment and makes the tear worse. [17] And no one puts[A] new wine into old wineskins. Otherwise, the skins burst, the wine spills out, and the skins are ruined. But they put new wine into fresh wineskins, and both are preserved."

A Girl Restored and a Woman Healed

[18] As He was telling them these things,[a] suddenly one of the leaders[B] came and knelt down before Him, saying, "My daughter is near death,[C] but come and lay Your hand on her, and she will live."[b] [19] So Jesus and His disciples got up and followed[c] him.

[20] Just then, a woman who had suffered from bleeding for 12 years approached from behind and touched the •tassel on His robe,[d] [21] for she said to herself, "If I can just touch His robe, I'll be made well!"[D,e]

[22] But Jesus turned and saw her. "Have courage, daughter," He said. "Your faith has made you well."[E,f] And the woman was made well from that moment.[F]

[23] When Jesus came to the leader's house, He saw the flute players and a crowd lamenting loudly.[g] [24] "Leave," He said, "because the girl isn't dead, but sleeping."[h] And they started laughing at Him. [25] But when the crowd had been put outside, He went in and took her by the hand, and the girl got up.[i] [26] And this news spread throughout that whole area.[j]

Healing the Blind

[27] As Jesus went on from there, two blind men followed Him, shouting, "Have mercy on us, Son of David!"[k]

[28] When He entered the house, the blind men approached Him, and Jesus said to them, "Do you believe[l] that I can do this?"

"Yes, Lord," they answered Him.

[29] Then He touched their eyes, saying, "Let it be done for you according to your faith!" [30] And their eyes were opened. Then Jesus warned them sternly, "Be sure that no one finds out!"[G,m] [31] But they went out and spread the news about Him throughout that whole area.

Driving Out a Demon

[32] Just as they were going out, a demon-possessed man who was unable to speak was brought to Him.[n] [33] When the demon had been driven out, the man[H] spoke. And the crowds were amazed, saying, "Nothing like this has ever been seen in Israel!"

[34] But the Pharisees said, "He drives out demons by the ruler of the demons!"[o]

The Lord of the Harvest

[35] Then Jesus went to all the towns and villages, teaching in their •synagogues, preaching the good news of the kingdom,[p] and healing every[I] disease and every sickness.[J] [36] When He saw the crowds, He felt compassion for them, because they were weary and worn out,[q] like sheep without a shepherd.[r] [37] Then He said to His disciples,[s] "The harvest is abundant, but the workers are few. [38] Therefore, pray to the Lord of the harvest to send out workers into His harvest."

Cross-reference column

[a] 9:18-26 Mk 5:22-43; Lk 8:41-56
[b] 9:18 Mt 8:2-3; Mk 5:23
[c] 9:19 Lk 5:11; Jn 8:12
[d] 9:20 Lv 15:25; Nm 15:38; Dt 22:12; Mt 14:36; 23:5
[e] 9:21 Mt 14:36; Mk 3:10; Lk 6:19
[f] 9:22 Mt 15:28; Mk 10:52; Lk 7:50; 17:19; 18:42
[g] 9:23 2Ch 35:25; Jr 9:17; 16:6; Ezk 24:17; Rv 18:22
[h] 9:24 Jn 11:13; Ac 20:10
[i] 9:25 Mk 9:27; Ac 3:7; 9:40-41
[j] 9:26 Mt 4:24; 9:31; 14:1; Mk 1:28; Lk 4:14
[k] 9:27 Mt 1:1; 12:23; 15:22; 20:30-31; Mk 10:47; Lk 18:38-39
[l] 9:28 Mk 11:24; Jn 3:16; Ac 10:43; Rm 10:9; 1Pt 1:8-10
[m] 9:29-30 Mt 8:4,13; 9:22; Mk 8:25; Jn 9:26
[n] 9:32-34 Mt 12:22-24; Lk 11:14-15
[o] 9:34 Mk 3:22; Jn 7:20
[p] 9:35 Mt 4:23; Mk 1:15
[q] 9:36 Mt 14:14; 15:32; Mk 6:34; 8:2
[r] Nm 27:17; 1Kg 22:17; Ezk 34:5; Zch 10:2
[s] 9:37 Mt 10:1; 26:56; Mk 3:7; 16:20; Lk 6:13; Jn 12:16

[A] 9:17 Lit And they do not put   [B] 9:18 A leader of a synagogue; Mk 5:22   [C] 9:18 Lit daughter has now come to the end   [D] 9:21 Or be delivered   [E] 9:22 Or has saved you   [F] 9:22 Lit hour   [G] 9:30 Lit no one knows   [H] 9:33 Lit the man who was unable to speak   [I] 9:35 Or every kind of   [J] 9:35 Other mss add among the people

---

9:16-17 The images of a shrinking **patch** tearing the **garment** that it was intended to repair and brittle **wineskins** rupturing from the gases released by fermenting wine picture the incompatibility of traditional Jewish teaching and Jesus' teaching.

9:20 This woman's condition left her perpetually unclean (Lv 25:15-31; Is 64:6). The penalty for entering the temple while unclean ranged from 40 lashes to death by stoning (m. Ker. 1.1). The **tassel** attached to the four corners of the outer cloak was prescribed in Nm 15:38-39 and Dt 22:12 as a reminder of God's commandments.

9:24 The presence of mourners and **flute players** indicate that the girl had been dead for a while and that her funeral had begun (m. Ketub. 4.4). The word **sleeping** implies that death is a state from which believers will be awakened at the resurrection (1Th 4:13-14).

9:27 On the meaning of **Son of David**, see note at 1:1. The healing of the **blind** recalls Is 35:5-6 and confirms Jesus' identity as Messiah.

9:28-29 On the relationship between **faith** and Jesus' healing miracles, see note at 9:2.

9:32 The healing of a man who was **unable to speak** recalls Is 35:5-6 and confirms Jesus' identity as Messiah (see notes at vv. 2 and 27).

9:34 Because they were unable to deny Jesus' repeated exorcisms, the Pharisees attempted to dismiss them as evidence of His alliance with Satan. Jesus later showed how unreasonable this accusation was (12:25-32).

9:35 On Jesus' ministry in the region of Galilee, see note at 4:23. These two very similar verses bracket Mt 4:23-9:34 as a single literary unit.

9:36 The words **like sheep without a shepherd** recall Ezk 34. They imply that Israel's spiritual condition reflected the failures of its spiritual shepherds. By showing **compassion** for the abused and neglected sheep of God's flock, Jesus identified Himself as the Shepherd of God's people, Lord and Servant of David (Ezk 34:11-16,20-24). See also Mt 25:32; 26:31.

9:38 By sending out the Twelve in Mt 10:5, Jesus identified

Commissioning the Twelve

10 Summoning His 12 disciples,[a] He gave them authority over *unclean spirits, to drive them out and to heal every[A] disease and sickness.[b] [2]These are the names of the 12 apostles:[c]

First, Simon, who is called Peter,
   and Andrew his brother;
James the son of Zebedee,
   and John his brother;
[3] Philip and Bartholomew;[B]
Thomas and Matthew the tax collector;
James the son of Alphaeus,
   and Thaddaeus;[c]
[4] Simon the Zealot,[D] and Judas Iscariot,[E]
   who also betrayed Him.[d]

[5]Jesus sent out these 12 after giving them instructions: "Don't take the road leading to other nations, and don't enter any *Samaritan[e] town. [6]Instead, go to the lost sheep[f] of the house of Israel.[g] [7]As you go, announce this: 'The kingdom of heaven has come near.'[h] [8]Heal the sick, raise the dead, cleanse those with skin diseases, drive out demons.[i] You have received free of charge; give free of charge. [9]Don't take along gold, silver, or copper for your moneybelts.[j] [10]Don't take a traveling bag for the road, or an extra shirt, sandals, or a walking stick, for the worker[k] is worthy of his food.

[11]"When you enter any town or village, find out who is worthy, and stay there until you leave. [12]Greet a household when you enter it,[l] [13]and if the household is worthy, let your peace be on it. But if it is unworthy, let your peace return to you.[m] [14]If anyone will not welcome you or listen to your words, shake the dust off your feet[n] when you leave that house or town. [15]*I assure you: It will be more tolerable on the day of judgment[o] for the land of Sodom and Gomorrah than for that town.[p]

Persecutions Predicted

[16]"Look, I'm sending you out like sheep among wolves. Therefore be as shrewd as serpents and as harmless as doves.[q] [17]Because people will hand you over to sanhedrins[F] and flog you in their *synagogues,[r] beware of them. [18]You will even be brought before governors and kings because of Me, to bear witness to them and to the nations.[s] [19]But when they hand you over, don't worry about how or what you should speak.[t] For you will be given what to say at that hour, [20]because you are not speaking, but the Spirit[u] of your Father is speaking through you.[v]

[21]"Brother will betray brother to death, and a father his child. Children will even rise up against their parents and have them put to death.[w] [22]You will be hated by everyone because of My name.[x] But the one who endures

a10:1-4 Mk 3:13-19; 6:13-16 b10:1 Mt 9:35; Mk 6:7; Lk 9:1 c10:2 Mt 4:18,21; 16:18; Jn 1:42 d10:4 Mt 26:14; Lk 22:3; Jn 6:71; 13:2,26 e10:5 2Kg 17:24; Lk 9:52; 17:16; Jn 4:9; Ac 8:25 f10:6 Ps 119:36; Is 53:6; Jr 50:6; Mt 9:36; 18:12 gAc 2:36; 7:42; Heb 8:8,10 h10:7 Mt 3:2-3; 4:17; Lk 10:9 i10:8 Mk 3:15; Rv 9:20; 18:2 j10:9-15 Mk 6:6-8; Lk 9:3-5; 10:4-12 k10:10 Lk 10:7; 1Co 9:14; 1Tm 5:18 l10:12 1Sm 25:6; 1Ch 12:18; Ps 122:7-8 m10:13 Ps 35:13; Mt 8:8; Ac 16:15 n10:14 Neh 5:13; Lk 10:11; Ac 13:51 o10:15 Mt 12:36; Ac 17:31; Heb 10:25; 2Pt 2:9; 1Jn 4:17 p Mt 11:22,24; 2Pt 2:6; Jd 6-7 q10:16 Gn 3:1; Lk 10:3; Rm 16:19; Php 2:15 r10:17 Mk 13:9,11; Lk 12:11-12; Ac 5:40; 26:11 s10:18 Mt 28:19; Rm 1:5; Gl 1:16 t10:19 Ex 4:12; Nm 23:5; Dt 18:18; Mt 6:25 u10:20 Ps 51:11; Jn 1:33; Ac 2:4; Rm 8:9; Gl 5:25; Ti 3:5 v Lk 12:12; Ac 4:8; 13:9; 2Co 13:3 w10:21 Mc 7:6; Mt 10:35-36; Mk 13:12 x10:22 Mt 24:9; Lk 21:17; Jn 15:18

A10:1 Or every kind of   B10:3 Probably the Nathanael of Jn 1:45-51   C10:3 Other mss read and Lebbaeus, whose surname was Thaddaeus   D10:4 Lit the Cananaean   E10:4 Iscariot is probably "a man of Kerioth," a town in Judea.   F10:17 Local Jewish courts or local councils

Himself as **Lord of the harvest**. Since OT texts and rabbinic parables presented Yahweh as Master of the harvest in portrayals of eschatological judgment (Is 18:4-5; 27:12; Hs 6:11; Jl 3:13), this identification strongly implies Jesus' deity (3:11-12; 13:39,41).

10:1 The emphasis on Jesus' selection of **12 disciples** (cp. 11:1) reminds readers of the 12 tribes of Israel (Mt 19:28) and identifies Jesus' followers (the church) as the new and true Israel, the beneficiaries of God's promises to Abraham (Gn 12:1-3; 15:6; see note at Mt 1:1).

10:5-6 Jesus prioritized the mission to Israel. Although He had already served Gentiles (8:5-13) and would do so again (15:21-28), Jews were the main focus of the earliest Christian missions (see Acts).

10:9-10 Jesus prohibited His disciples from carrying the provisions normally taken on lengthy trips. This invited utter dependence on God. The disciples trusted that God would provide for them just as He had for OT Israel (Dt 8:3-4). Some suggest that the prohibition against a **walking stick** here contradicts the permission to carry one in Mk 6:8. However, the texts can be harmonized by several explanations. For example, Matthew may prohibit acquiring a staff while Mark allows those who already own one to take it along.

10:11-14 Those who were **worthy** would welcome the disciples and their message (see note at 7:6). Those who were unworthy would neither welcome them nor listen. The typical Jewish greeting Shalom ("Peace be unto you") pronounced a blessing, but those who rejected the gospel were unworthy of such a greeting. Jews shook the **dust off** their **feet** when they returned to Israel from pagan lands. By doing this when rejected, Jesus' disciples marked those who rejected the gospel as pagans who did not truly belong to Israel.

10:15 God destroyed **Sodom and Gomorrah** because of their wickedness (Gn 19:24-29). Jesus declared in Mt 11:23-24 that even these notorious cities would have repented if they had heard the message the disciples announced and had witnessed the miracles they performed.

10:16 Just as **wolves** stalk and destroy **sheep**, persecutors will attempt to hunt and destroy Jesus' disciples. **Serpents** are **shrewd** because they flee from danger (see note at 3:7-9). Similarly, Jesus' disciples must be prepared to take strategic action when persecution threatens (10:23). However, like **doves**, they should be **harmless** and not use violent means to answer persecution.

10:17-18 The references to **sanhedrins** and **synagogues** show that Jews sponsored the first anti-Christian persecution. Jewish persecutors appealed to **governors** and **kings**

to the end will be delivered.[A,a] [23]When they persecute you in one town, escape to another.[b] For I assure you: You will not have covered the towns of Israel before the •Son of Man comes. [24]A disciple[B] is not above his teacher, or a •slave above his master.[c] [25]It is enough for a disciple to become like his teacher and a slave like his master. If they called the head of the house "•Beelzebul,' how much more the members of his household![d]

Fear God

[26]"Therefore,[e] don't be afraid of them, since there is nothing covered that won't be uncovered and nothing hidden that won't be made known.[f] [27]What I tell you in the dark, speak in the light. What you hear in a whisper,[C] proclaim on the housetops.[g] [28]Don't fear those who kill the body but are not able to kill the soul;[h] rather, fear Him who is able to destroy both soul and body in •hell.[i] [29]Aren't two sparrows sold for a penny?[D] Yet not one of them falls to the ground without your Father's[j] consent.[E] [30]But even the hairs of your head have all been counted.[k] [31]So don't be afraid therefore; you are worth more than many sparrows.[l]

Acknowledging Christ

[32]"Therefore, everyone who will acknowl-

edge Me before men, I will also acknowledge him before My Father in heaven.[m] [33]But whoever denies Me before men,[n] I will also deny him before My Father in heaven. [34]Don't assume that I came to bring peace on the earth. I did not come to bring peace, but a sword.[o] [35]For I came to turn

> **a man against his father,**
> **a daughter against her mother,**
> **a daughter-in-law**
>   **against her mother-in-law;**
> [36] **and a man's enemies will be**
>   **the members of his household.[F,p]**

[37]The person who loves father or mother more than Me is not worthy of Me;[q] the person who loves son or daughter more than Me is not worthy of Me. [38]And whoever doesn't take up his cross and follow[G] Me is not worthy of Me. [39]Anyone finding[H] his life will lose it,[r] and anyone losing[I] his life because of Me will find it.[s]

A Cup of Cold Water

[40]"The one who welcomes you welcomes Me,[t] and the one who welcomes Me welcomes Him who sent Me.[u] [41]Anyone who[J] welcomes a prophet[K] because he is a prophet[K] will receive a

Cross references (center column)

[a]10:22 Mt 24:13; Mk 13:13; Jn 12:12-13
[b]10:23 Mt 12:15; Ac 8:1; 9:25; 14:6; 17:10
[c]10:24 Lk 6:40; Jn 13:16; 15:20
[d]10:25 2Kg 1:2; Mt 12:24,27; Mk 3:22; Lk 11:15,18-19
[e]10:26-33 Lk 12:2-9
[f]10:26 Mk 4:22; Lk 8:17; 12:3
[g]10:27 Mt 24:17; Lk 5:19; 12:3; Ac 5:20
[h]10:28 Is 8:12-13; 51:12-13; Jr 1:8; 1Pt 3:14
[i]Mt 5:22; Lk 12:5; Heb 10:31; Jms 4:12
[j]10:29 Mt 5:16; 11:27; Lk 11:13; Jn 8:42
[k]10:30 1Sm 14:45; 2Sm 14:11; Lk 21:18; Ac 27:34
[l]10:31 Mt 6:26; 12:12
[m]10:32 Lk 12:8; Rm 10:9-10; Rv 3:5
[n]10:33 Mk 8:38; Lk 9:26; 2Tm 2:12; 2Pt 2:1
[o]10:34-36 Lk 12:51-53
[p]10:36 Mic 7:6; Jn 13:18
[q]10:37-39 Lk 14:25-27 [r]10:39 Mt 16:25; Mk 8:35; Lk 9:24; 17:33; Jn 12:25 [s]Mt 9:9; Jn 8:12; 12:26; 21:19 [t]10:40 Mt 18:5; Lk 10:16; Jn 13:20; Gl 4:14 [u]Mk 9:37; Lk 9:48; Jn 12:44 [v]10:41 1Kg 17:10-15; 18:4; 2Kg 4:8; 3Jn 5-8

Footnotes

[A]10:22 Or saved [B]10:24 Or student [C]10:27 Lit in the ear [D]10:29 Gk assarion, a small copper coin [E]10:29 Lit ground apart from your Father [F]10:35-36 Mc 7:6 [G]10:38 Lit follow after [H]10:39 Or The one who finds [I]10:39 Or and the one who loses [J]10:41 Or The one who [K]10:41 Lit prophet in the name of a prophet

---

because only Roman officials had the authority to order executions. However, persecution by the highest levels of government gave the disciples opportunity to **bear witness . . . to the nations**.

10:23 The phrase **you will not have covered the towns of Israel before the Son of Man comes** may mean that Chris-

phobeo

Greek Pronunciation	[fah BEH oh]
HCSB Translation	fear
Uses in Matthew	18 (Mk, 12; Lk, 23; Jn, 5)
Uses in the NT	95
Focus Passage	Matthew 10:28

Like the English term *fear*, Greek *phobeo* covers a broad spectrum of meanings, including *worry* (Mt 1:20), *discomfort* at potential circumstances (Mt 2:22; 10:31; 14:5; 21:26,46), and feelings of *awe* and/or *terror*, especially in the presence of the supernatural (Mt 9:8; 10:28; 14:27; 17:6-7; 27:54; 28:5,10). *Phobeo* has two main applications in the NT: *fear* of God and *fear* of man or circumstances. In regard to the former, *fear* can be understood as a healthy understanding of who God is, His power, and what He demands from us (cp. Pr 1:7; 9:10). The unbeliever should tremble in *terror* before such a God, for He is the one who can "destroy both soul and body in hell" (Mt 10:28). For the believer, however, such *fear* is replaced by a relationship in which perfect love can flourish (1Jn 4:18; cp. Rm 8:15), though *awe* of God's greatness remains (2Co 5:11; 7:1).

tian disciples will not complete their mission to the Jewish people before the second coming of Christ. The towns of Israel likely include the far-flung cities of the world where Jews settled down after several dispersions from Israel. However, Jesus' promise is closely linked to the first half of the verse by the conjunction **for** and by the repetition of the word **town**. Thus "will not have covered the towns" primarily means that the disciples will not have run out of Jewish towns to which to escape before Messiah comes. The mission to the nations in Mt 28:19-20 augments rather than replaces the mission to Israel.

10:25 On the meaning of **Beelzebul**, see note at 12:24.

10:29-30 If God must consent to the fall of **sparrows**, no disciple can suffer persecution without His consent. The God who has numbered **even the hairs of your head** has also numbered the days of your life. His plan for His disciples cannot be cut short by persecution.

10:34 Jesus' words do not imply that His disciples should take up the **sword** in violent reprisal against persecutors. The sword is merely a symbol for conflict and division (Lk 12:51).

10:38 Taking up a cross does not refer to evangelism. Instead, Jesus refers here to the death march that leads to crucifixion. The point is that disciples must be prepared to die (literally and figuratively) as martyrs for Christ.

10:40-42 The person who welcomes a persecuted disciple **welcomes** Jesus and the One who sent Him. He can expect

prophet's reward. And anyone who[A] welcomes a righteous person because he's righteous[B] will receive a righteous person's reward. [42] And whoever gives[a] just a cup of cold water to one of these little ones because he is a disciple[C,b]—I assure you: He will never lose his reward!"

In Praise of John the Baptist

11 When Jesus had finished giving orders to His 12 disciples, He moved on from there to teach and preach in their towns.[c] [2] When John heard in prison what the •Messiah was doing, he sent a message by his disciples[d] [3] and asked Him, "Are You the One who is to come, or should we expect someone else?"[e]

[4] Jesus replied to them, "Go and report to John what you hear and see: [5] the blind see, the lame walk, those with skin diseases are healed,[D] the deaf hear, the dead are raised, and the poor are told the good news.[f] [6] And if anyone is not •offended because of Me, he is blessed."[g]

[7] As these men went away, Jesus began to speak to the crowds about John: "What did you go out into the wilderness to see? A reed swaying in the wind?[h] [8] What then did you

go out to see? A man dressed in soft clothes? Look, those who wear soft clothes are in kings' palaces. [9] But what did you go out to see? A prophet? Yes, I tell you, and far more than a prophet.[i] [10] This is the one it is written about:

> Look, I am sending My messenger
>   ahead of You;[E]
> he will prepare Your way before You.[F,j]

[11] "I assure you: Among those born of women no one greater than John the Baptist has appeared,[G] but the least in the kingdom of heaven is greater than he. [12] From the days of John the Baptist until now, the kingdom of heaven has been suffering violence,[H] and the violent have been seizing it by force. [13] For all the prophets and the Law prophesied until John; [14] if you're willing to accept it, he is the Elijah who is to come.[k] [15] Anyone who has ears[i] should listen![l]

An Unresponsive Generation

[16] "To what should I compare this generation? It's like children sitting in the marketplaces who call out to each other:

[17]   We played the flute for you,

Cross references (center column)

[a]10:42 Mt 25:40; Mk 9:41; Heb 6:10
[b]Mt 28:19; Lk 14:26; Jn 8:31; 13:35; 15:8; Ac 6:1
[c]11:1 Mt 7:28; 9:35; Lk 23:5
[d]11:2-19 Lk 7:18-35
[e]11:3 Ps 118:26; Jn 6:14; 11:27; Heb 10:37
[f]11:5 Is 35:5; 61:1; Lk 4:18; Jms 2:5
[g]11:6 Is 8:14-15; Mt 13:21; Jn 6:61; 16:1
[h]11:7 Mt 3:1; Eph 4:14
[i]11:9 Mt 14:5; 21:26; Lk 1:76
[j]11:10 Mal 3:1; Mk 1:2
[k]11:14 Mal 4:5; Mt 17:10-13; Mk 9:11-13; Lk 1:17; Jn 1:21
[l]11:15 Mt 13:9; Mk 4:23; Lk 8:8; 14:35; Rv 2:7

Textual notes

[A]10:41 Or And the one who   [B]10:41 Lit person in the name of a righteous person   [C]10:42 Lit little ones in the name of a disciple   [D]11:5 Lit cleansed   [E]11:10 Lit messenger before Your face   [F]11:10 Mal 3:1   [G]11:11 Lit arisen   [H]11:12 Or has been forcefully advancing   [I]11:15 Other mss add to hear

---

to receive a heavenly **reward**, just as the person who welcomes a prophet or righteous person receives the reward that a prophet or **righteous person** deserves.

11:1 The words **when Jesus had finished** are important for understanding the structure of the Gospel. See "Structure" in the Introduction to Matthew.

11:2-3 John the Baptist previously expressed faith in Jesus as **Messiah** (3:14; Jn 2:29-37; 3:22-30). John's doubts here were likely the result of his prolonged imprisonment and his disappointment that a "baptism of fire" had not yet occurred (Mt 3:11-12). Jesus identified Himself as the One anointed by the Spirit in Is 61:1-3. However, Is 61:1 promised that the Anointed One would "proclaim liberty to the captives, and freedom to the prisoners." John probably interpreted the prophecy literally and thus mistakenly expected a miraculous release from prison.

11:4-5 Jesus confirmed His identity as the Christ by appealing to His miraculous and gracious works (Is 29:18-19; 35:5-6; 61:1).

11:6 Jesus pronounced blessing on those who were willing to suffer without being **offended** at Him. John thus serves as a model for those who persevere in faith despite suffering.

11:7 A **reed swaying in the wind** is a metaphor for someone who lacks conviction and is easily swayed by public opinion (1Kg 14:15; 2Kg 18:21).

11:8 Unlike false prophets, John did not allow himself to be bought off by a king who wished to purchase favorable prophecies (see 1Kg 22:13-28).

11:10 On John the Baptist in Isaiah's prophecy, see note at 3:3.

11:11 John was imprisoned and executed before Jesus' reign was established through His death and resurrection (Ac 2:32-36; Rm 1:4). Thus, disciples who enjoy the present reign of Christ enjoy blessings that John yearned for but did not experience (Mt 13:17). The description of the OT prophets in 1Pt 1:10-12 accurately portrays the experience of John. These men did not live to see the messianic sufferings and the glories that followed.

11:12 The arrest, imprisonment, and eventual execution of John and the Jewish leaders' violent opposition to Jesus were attempts to seize and control the unfolding **kingdom of heaven**. The words **until now** hint that the kingdom will someday break free from the grip of those who seek to restrain it (see note at v. 14).

11:14 Malachi 4:5 promised that the Day of the Lord, a time of divine judgment for the wicked but healing and joy for God's people, would be preceded by the sending of **Elijah**. Jesus explained that John the Baptist fulfilled this role and that his ministry signaled the dawn of the Day of the Lord. Malachi 4:3 promised that the Day of the Lord would be a time when God's people "will trample the wicked, for they will be ashes under the soles of your feet." This signals that violent suppression of the kingdom will soon end (see note at Mt 11:12).

11:16-19 Jesus portrayed His unbelieving contemporaries as spoiled children who whined when they did not get their way. In an ancient version of the game "Simon says," if a designated child **played** a pretend **flute** the other children

but you didn't dance;
we sang a lament,
but you didn't mourn!A

[18] For John did not come eating or drinking, and they say, 'He has a demon!'[a] [19] The •Son of Man came eating and drinking, and they say, 'Look, a glutton and a drunkard,[b] a friend of tax collectors and sinners!'[c] Yet wisdom is vindicated[B] by her deeds."[c]

[20] Then He proceeded to denounce the towns where most of His miracles were done, because they did not repent: [21] "Woe to you, Chorazin![d] Woe to you, Bethsaida![e] For if the miracles that were done in you had been done in Tyre and Sidon,[f] they would have repented in •sackcloth and ashes long ago! [22] But I tell you, it will be more tolerable for Tyre and Sidon on the day of judgment[g] than for you. [23] And you, Capernaum, will you be exalted to heaven? You will go down to •Hades.[h] For if the miracles that were done in you had been done in Sodom, it would have remained until today. [24] But I tell you, it will be more tolerable for the land of Sodom on the day of judgment than for you."

The Son Gives Knowledge and Rest

[25] At that time Jesus said,[i] "I praise[D] You, Father, Lord of heaven and earth, because You have hidden these things from the wise and learned and revealed them to infants.[j] [26] Yes, Father, because this was Your good pleasure.[E] [27] All things have been entrusted to Me by My

Father. No one knows[F] the Son except the Father, and no one knows the Father except the Son and anyone to whom the Son desires[G] to reveal Him.[k]

[28] "Come to Me, all of you who are weary and burdened, and I will give you rest.[l] [29] All of you, take up My yoke and learn from Me,[m] because I am gentle and humble in heart, and you will find rest for yourselves.[n] [30] For My yoke is easy and My burden is light."

Lord of the Sabbath

12 At that time Jesus passed through the grainfields on the Sabbath.[o] His disciples[p] were hungry and began to pick and eat some heads of grain. [2] But when the •Pharisees saw it, they said to Him, "Look, Your disciples are doing what is not lawful[q] to do on the Sabbath!"

[3] He said to them, "Haven't you read what David did when he and those who were with him were hungry— [4] how he entered the house of God, and they ate[H] the •sacred bread, which is not lawful for him or for those with him to eat, but only for the priests?[r] [5] Or haven't you read in the Law[I] that on Sabbath days the priests in the temple violate the Sabbath and are innocent?[s] [6] But I tell you that something greater than the temple is here![t] [7] If you had known what this means: **I desire mercy and not sacrifice,**[j,u] you would not have

---

Cross references (center column):

[a]11:18 Mt 3:4; Lk 1:15
[b]11:19 Mt 9:10; Lk 7:36; 14:1; Jn 2:1; 12:2
[c]Mt 9:11; 18:17; Lk 15:2; 19:7
[d]11:21-24 Lk 10:12-15
[e]11:21 Mk 6:45; Lk 9:10; Jn 12:21
[f]Mt 15:21; Lk 6:17; Ac 12:20
[g]11:22 Ezk 28:2-4; Am 1:9-10; Mt 10:15; 15:21; Mk 3:8
[h]11:23 Is 14:13,15; Mt 4:13
[i]11:25-27 Lk 10:21-22
[j]11:25 Ps 8:2; Lk 22:42; Jn 11:41; 1Co 1:26; 2Co 3:14
[k]11:27 Mt 28:18; Jn 1:18; 7:29; 8:19; 10:15; 17:25-26
[l]11:28 Jr 31:25; Jn 7:37
[m]11:29 Jn 13:15; Eph 4:20; Php 2:5; 1Pt 2:21; 1Jn 2:6
[n]Jr 6:16; Zch 9:9; 2Co 10:1; Php 2:7-8
[o]12:1-8 Mk 2:23-28; Lk 6:1-5
[p]12:1 Mt 10:1; 26:56; Mk 3:7; 16:20; Lk 6:13; Jn 12:16
[q]12:2 Mt 12:10; Lk 13:14; 14:3; Jn 5:10; 7:23; 9:16
[r]12:4 Ex 25:30;

Lv 24:5-9; 1Sm 21:6   [s]12:5 Nm 28:9-10; 1Ch 9:32; Jn 7:22-23   [t]12:6 2Ch 6:18; Mal 3:1; Mt 12:41-42   [u]12:7 Hs 6:6; Mc 6:8; Mt 9:13

A11:17 Or *beat your breasts*   B11:19 Or *declared right*   C11:19 Other mss read *children*   D11:25 Or *thank*   E11:26 Lit *was well-pleasing in Your sight*   F11:27 Or *knows exactly*   G11:27 Or *wills*, or *chooses*   H12:4 Other mss read *he ate*   I12:5 = The Torah (the Pentateuch)   J12:7 Hs 6:6

---

were supposed to **dance**. If he **sang a lament** they were supposed to **mourn**. However, like unresponsive children, Israel did not pay heed to the ministries of Jesus and John the Baptist. The reference to wisdom's **deeds** parallels the reference to Messiah's deeds (v. 2) and implies that Jesus' claims were vindicated by the acts described in verses 4-6. Between the time of the OT and the NT, Jewish interpreters elaborated on Pr 8:32-36 and taught that Wisdom was an eternal being who served as God's agent in the creation of the world. By identifying Himself with personified wisdom, Jesus hinted that He is the eternal One through whom the Father created everything (Jn 1:3).

11:20-24 These verses remind us that the Gospels are not exhaustive accounts of Jesus' life. Jesus performed most of His **miracles in Chorazin . . . Bethsaida**, and **Capernaum**, and yet the Gospels do not describe His miracles at Chorazin and mention only two that were performed at Bethsaida (Mk 6:45; 8:22; Lk 9:10). God's judgment against sin is **more tolerable** for people to whom little revelation is given. On the other hand, those who have received much revelation bear greater responsibility and thus incur greater judgment for their unbelief.

11:27 Jesus' statement resembles those attributed to Him in John's Gospel (Jn 7:29; 10:14-15; 17:25). This shows how

substantially John and the Synoptic Gospels agree on the portrait of Jesus.

11:28-30 Jesus' words recall a statement made by personified Wisdom in a Jewish document dating to several hundred years before Christ (Sir 6:18-31; 51:23-27). When combined with Mt 11:19, this suggests that Jesus portrayed Himself as personified Wisdom, the One who exists eternally and acted on Yahweh's behalf to create the world. (1Co 1:24; see note at Mt 11:16-19). Jesus' teaching provided an easy **yoke** in contrast to the heavy, suppressive yoke of rabbinic teaching (23:4; Ac 15:10).

12:1-2 Work was prohibited on the **Sabbath**. First-century rabbis divided work into 39 categories, each having many subcategories. Three prohibited categories were picking, threshing, and winnowing. The disciples picked **grain** and rubbed it between their hands to remove the husks and thus broke the highly restrictive rabbinic law on three different counts. Handpicking grain from a neighbor's field was not considered stealing (Dt 23:25).

12:3-7 Jesus taught that **Sabbath** law was overridden by priorities such as (1) genuine human need (1Sm 21:1-6); (2) worship (Nm 28:9-10); and (3) acts of kindness (Hs 6:6).

condemned the innocent. ⁸For the •Son of Man is Lord of the Sabbath."^a

The Man with the Paralyzed Hand

⁹Moving on from there, He entered their •synagogue.^b ¹⁰There He saw a man who had a paralyzed hand. And in order to accuse Him they asked Him, "Is it lawful to heal on the Sabbath?"^c

¹¹But He said to them, "What man among you, if he had a sheep^A that fell into a pit on the Sabbath, wouldn't take hold of it and lift it out?^d ¹²A man is worth far more than a sheep,^e so it is lawful to do what is good on the Sabbath."

¹³Then He told the man, "Stretch out your hand." So he stretched it out, and it was restored,^f as good as the other. ¹⁴But the Pharisees went out and plotted against Him, how they might destroy Him.^g

The Servant of the Lord

¹⁵When Jesus became aware of this, He withdrew from there. Huge crowds^B followed Him, and He healed them all.^h ¹⁶He warned them not to make Him known,ⁱ ¹⁷so that what was spoken through the prophet Isaiah might be fulfilled:

¹⁸	Here is My Servant
	whom I have chosen,
	My beloved in whom My soul delights;
	I will put My Spirit on Him,
	and He will proclaim justice
	to the nations.^j
¹⁹	He will not argue or shout,
	and no one will hear His voice
	in the streets.
²⁰	He will not break a bruised reed,
	and He will not put out
	a smoldering wick,
	until He has led justice to victory.^C
²¹	The nations will put their hope
	in His name.^{D,k}

A House Divided

²²Then a demon-possessed man^l who was blind and unable to speak was brought to Him. He healed him, so that the man^E could both speak and see.^m ²³And all the crowds were astounded and said, "Perhaps this is the Son of David!"ⁿ

²⁴When the Pharisees heard this, they said, "The man drives out demons only by •Beelzebul, the ruler of the demons."^o

²⁵Knowing their thoughts,^p He told them:

---

a 12:8 Mt 8:20; 9:6; 12:32,40   *b* 12:9-14 Mk 3:1-6; Lk 6:6-11   *c* 12:10 Mt 12:2; Lk 13:14; 14:3; Jn 9:16   *d* 12:11 Ex 23:4-5; Dt 22:4; Lk 14:5   *e* 12:12 Mt 6:26; 10:31   *f* 12:13 1Kg 13:4; Mt 8:3; Ac 28:8   *g* 12:14 Mt 26:4; 27:1; Mk 3:6; Lk 6:11; Jn 10:39; 11:53   *h* 12:15 Mt 4:23; 10:23; 19:2; Mk 3:7   *i* 12:16 Mt 8:4; 9:30   *j* 12:18 Mt 3:17; 17:5; Lk 4:18; Jn 3:34   *k* 12:18-21 Is 42:1-4; Jn 10:25   *l* 12:22-24 Lk 11:14-15   *m* 12:22 Mt 4:24; 9:32-34   *n* 12:23 2Ch 1:1; Mt 1:1; Rm 1:3   *o* 12:24 Mt 9:34; 10:25; Mk 3:22   *p* 12:25-29 Mk 3:23-27; Lk 11:17-22

---

^A12:11 Or *had one sheep*   ^B12:15 Other mss read *Many*   ^C12:20 Or *until He has successfully put forth justice*   ^D12:18-21 Is 42:1-4   ^E12:22 Lit *mute*

12:8 Son of Man was Jesus' favorite self-designation. **Lord of the Sabbath** refers to Yahweh since He instituted the Sabbath (Gn 2:1-3), commanded the Sabbath (Ex 20:10), and was the Lord for whom the Sabbath was observed (Lv 23:3). By calling Himself "Lord of the Sabbath," Jesus clearly meant to identify Himself as God Almighty.

12:10 Many rabbis permitted healing on the Sabbath only when a life was at risk (*m. Yoma* 8:6). Otherwise, it was illegal to tie a bandage, set a broken bone, or administer medicine. Some rabbis even banned prayer for the sick on the Sabbath.

12:11-12 With the exception of the Essenes (CD 11.13-14), most Jews believed it was permissible to rescue a beast of burden (e.g., a donkey) on the Sabbath. It was inconsistent to refuse the same privilege to humans since God values people more than animals. The Sabbath was to be kept holy (Ex 20:8-11), but a ban on good deeds is unholy and dishonors God.

12:13 The man's paralyzed **hand** had wasted away from disuse. Jesus **restored** the hand's function and also renewed the wasted muscle. Thus, this miracle was an act of creation. Since the Creator God had instituted the Sabbath (Gn 2:1-3), the miracle confirmed Jesus' self-confessed identity as Lord of the Sabbath.

12:15-21 Matthew recognized Jesus as the fulfillment of Is 42:1-4. This implies: (1) He is God's Son/**Servant**; (2) He is **chosen** and loved by God; (3) He pleases God with His obedience; (4) He bears God's **Spirit**; (5) He will rule over a universal kingdom that includes all **nations**; (6) He is humble and nonviolent; and (7) He will include Gentiles in His redemptive plan. Matthew's identification of Jesus as "Servant" is closely connected to his interpretation of Is 53 (see note at 8:17).

12:23 On **Son of David**, see note at 1:1.

12:24 Beelzebul was probably an ancient name for Baal, a Canaanite storm/fertility god. Worship of Baal competed with worship of Yahweh in the OT. Although gods were nonexistent, demonic spirits were at work in the pagan religions (Ps 106:28,36-39; 1Co 10:19-20). Satan himself was deemed to be the spirit at work in Baal worship. Consequently, Beelzebul became an alternate name for Satan.

12:25-27 Jesus argued that Satan is too smart to undermine his own kingdom. Also, the objection of the Pharisees (v. 24) indicted their own disciples, for they too claimed to cast out demons.

Reconstruction of a typical first-century synagogue.

"Every kingdom divided against itself is headed for destruction, and no city or house divided against itself will stand. [26] If Satan[a] drives out Satan, he is divided against himself. How then will his kingdom stand? [27] And if I drive out demons by Beelzebul, who is it your sons drive them out by? For this reason they will be your judges.[b] [28] If I drive out demons by the Spirit of God, then the kingdom of God has come to you.[c] [29] How can someone enter a strong man's house and steal his possessions unless he first ties up[d] the strong man? Then he can rob his house. [30] Anyone who is not with Me is against Me,[e] and anyone who does not gather with Me scatters. [31] Because of this,[f] I tell you, people will be forgiven every sin and blasphemy,[g] but the blasphemy against[A] the Spirit will not be forgiven.[B] [32] Whoever speaks a word against the Son of Man,[h] it will be forgiven him. But whoever speaks against the Holy Spirit, it will not be forgiven him, either in this age or in the one to come.[i]

A Tree and Its Fruit

[33] "Either make the tree good and its fruit good, or make the tree bad[C] and its fruit bad; for a tree is known by its fruit.[j] [34] Brood of vipers! How can you speak good things when you are evil? For the mouth speaks from the overflow[k] of the heart. [35] A good man produces good things from his storeroom of good,[D] and an evil man produces evil things from his storeroom of evil.[l] [36] I tell you that on the day of judgment[m] people will have to account[n] for every careless word they speak.[E] [37] For by your words you will be acquitted, and by your words you will be condemned."

The Sign of Jonah

[38] Then some of the •scribes and Pharisees said to Him, "Teacher, we want to see a sign from You."[o]

[39] But He answered them,[p] "An evil and adulterous generation demands a sign, but no sign will be given to it except the sign of the prophet Jonah.[q] [40] For as Jonah was in the belly of the huge fish three days and three nights,[r] so the Son of Man will be in the heart of the earth three days and three nights. [41] The men of Nineveh will stand up at the judgment with this generation and condemn it,[s] because they repented at Jonah's proclamation; and look—something greater than Jonah is here![t] [42] The queen of the south[u] will rise up at the judgment with this generation and condemn it, because she came from the ends

Cross references

a 12:26 Mt 4:1,10; 13:19; Ac 13:10
b 12:27 2Kg 2:7; Ac 19:13
c 12:28 Lk 17:21; 1Jn 3:8
d 12:29 Is 49:24; 53:12
e 12:30 Mk 9:40; Lk 9:50; 11:23
f 12:31-32 Mk 3:28-30; Lk 12:10
g 12:31 Heb 6:4-6; 10:26; 1Jn 5:16
h 12:32 Mt 11:19; Mk 2:10; Jn 7:12; 9:24
i 12:32 Mk 10:30; Lk 12:10; 20:34-35; Eph 1:21; Ti 2:12; Heb 6:5
j 12:33 Mt 7:18-19,23; Lk 6:43-44; Jn 15:4-7
k 12:34 1Sm 24:13; Mt 3:7; 23:33; Lk 6:45; Eph 4:29
l 12:35 Mt 13:52; Col 4:6
m 12:36 Mt 12:41; Jn 5:29; 1Jn 4:17
n Lk 16:2; Ac 19:40; Rm 14:12; Heb 13:17; 1Pt 4:5
o 12:38 Mt 16:1; Mk 8:11-12; Lk 11:16; Jn 2:18; 6:30; 1Co 1:22
p 12:39 Mk 8:11-12; Lk 11:29-32
q 12:39 Is 57:3; Mt 16:4; Mk 8:38
r 12:40 Jnh 1:17
s 12:41 Jr 3:11; Ezk 16:51; Rm 2:27
t Jnh 1:2; 3:5
u 12:42 1Kg 10:1; 2Ch 9:1

Footnotes

A 12:31 Or of   B 12:31 Other mss add people   C 12:33 Or decayed; lit rotten   D 12:35 Other mss read from the storehouse of his heart   E 12:36 Lit will speak

Study notes

12:28-29 Jesus' power to cast out **demons** proved that the **kingdom of God** was overthrowing Satan's kingdom. Jesus was tying up the **strong man** (Satan) so He could **rob his house**, or claim Satan's captives as citizens of His own kingdom.

12:31-32 Jesus claimed to cast out demons "by the Spirit of God" (v. 28). By refuting this and attributing His exorcisms to Satan's power instead, Jesus' opponents were guilty of **blasphemy against the Spirit** in whose power Jesus worked the miracles. Their attempt to dismiss Jesus' supernatural power would **not be forgiven** because it expressed a resolute, permanent rejection of Jesus.

12:33-37 The evil words spoken by the Pharisees divulged the true nature of their hearts.

12:38 The Jewish leaders had already witnessed several of Jesus' miracles (vv. 9-14; 9:1-8).

12:39-40 The word **adulterous** refers to the scribes' and Pharisees' spiritual adultery exhibited by their rejection of Jesus. Mention of the **sign of . . . Jonah** is Jesus' first explicit prediction of His death in Matthew. Jonah was as good as dead for **three days and three nights** (Jnh 1:17). His prayer compared his experience to being in the grave. Thus, Jonah's experience was analogous to Jesus' experience of being interred for three days. Since Jesus' resurrection occurred on Sunday, some have argued that the reference to three days and three nights requires a Thursday or Wednesday crucifixion. However, 1Sm 30:12-13 suggests that "three days and three nights" could be idiomatic for a span of time that covered all of one day and parts of two others. Thus Jesus' interment late on Friday and His resurrection early on Sunday counts as three days.

12:41-42 Ninevites and the queen of Sheba were pagan Gentiles who repented and sought the truth. Jesus is greater than **Jonah** and **Solomon**, whom these pagans heard and obeyed.

blasphemia

Greek Pronunciation	[blahss fay MEE uh]
HCSB Translation	blasphemy
Uses in Matthew	4 (Mk, 3; Lk, 1; Jn, 1)
Uses in the NT	18
Focus Passage	Matthew 12:31

The Greek noun *blasphemia* comes from a compound verb (*blasphemeo*) meaning *to speak evil against* (*blas*-evil; *phemi*-to speak), *slander*, or *revile*. In the NT, *blasphemy* is an extremely serious offense and primarily directed against God (Mt 9:3; 26:65), Christ (Lk 22:65), or anything related to either Person (1Tm 6:1; Ti 2:5; Jms 2:7). *Blasphemy* can also be directed against angels (2Pt 2:10; Jd 8) and human beings (Rm 3:8; 1Co 4:13; 10:30; Ti 3:2). Jesus told the Jewish religious leaders that the most grievous sin, one that cannot be forgiven, is *blasphemy* against the Holy Spirit (Mt 12:31-32). Apparently, they were in danger of committing this sin, or perhaps already had, for Jesus' warning was in response to their claim that He cast out demons through the power of Satan (Mt 12:24) and that Jesus Himself was demon-possessed (Mk 3:30).

of the earth to hear the wisdom of Solomon; and look—something greater than Solomon is here!

An Unclean Spirit's Return

[43] "When an *unclean spirit comes out of a man, it roams through waterless places looking for rest but doesn't find any.[a] [44] Then it says, 'I'll go back to my house that I came from.' And returning, it finds the house vacant, swept, and put in order. [45] Then off it goes and brings with it seven other spirits more evil than itself, and they enter and settle down there. As a result, that man's last condition is worse than the first.[b] That's how it will also be with this evil generation."

True Relationships

[46] He[c] was still speaking to the crowds when suddenly His mother and brothers were standing outside wanting to speak to Him.[d] [47] Someone told Him, "Look, Your mother and Your brothers are standing outside, wanting to speak to You."[A]

[48] But He replied to the one who told Him, "Who is My mother and who are My brothers?" [49] And stretching out His hand toward His disciples,[e] He said, "Here are My mother and My brothers! [50] For whoever does the will of My Father in heaven, that person is My brother and sister and mother."[f]

The Parable of the Sower

13 On that day Jesus went out of the house and was sitting by the sea.[g] [2] Such large crowds gathered around Him that He got into a boat and sat down, while the whole crowd stood on the shore.[h]

[3] Then He told them many things in parables,[i] saying: "Consider the sower who went out to sow. [4] As he was sowing, some seed fell along the path, and the birds came and ate them up. [5] Others fell on rocky ground, where there wasn't much soil, and they sprang up quickly since the soil wasn't deep. [6] But when the sun came up they were scorched, and since they had no root, they withered. [7] Others fell among thorns, and the thorns came up and choked them. [8] Still others fell on good ground and produced a crop: some 100, some 60, and some 30 times what was sown.[j] [9] Anyone who has ears[B] should listen!"[k]

Why Jesus Used Parables

[10] Then the disciples[l] came up and asked Him, "Why do You speak to them in parables?"[m]

[11] He answered them, "Because the *secrets of the kingdom of heaven have been given for you to know,[n] but it has not been given to them. [12] For whoever has, more will be given to him, and he will have more than enough. But whoever does not have, even what he has will be taken away from him.[o] [13] For this reason I speak to them in parables, because looking they do not see,[p] and hearing they do not listen or understand.[q] [14] Isaiah's prophecy is fulfilled in them, which says:

> You will listen and listen,
> yet never understand;
> and you will look and look,
> yet never perceive.[r]
> [15] For this people's heart
>   has grown callous;
> their ears are hard of hearing,
> and they have shut their eyes;
> otherwise they might see
>   with their eyes
> and hear with their ears,

Cross references (center column)

[a] 12:43-45 Lk 11:24-26
[b] 12:45 Heb 6:4; 2Pt 2:20
[c] 12:46-50 Mk 3:31-35; Lk 8:19-21
[d] 12:46 Mt 13:55; Mk 6:3; Jn 2:12; Ac 1:14; 1Co 9:5; Gl 1:19
[e] 12:49 Mt 10:42; 28:19; Lk 14:26; Jn 8:31; 13:35; 15:8; Ac 6:1
[f] 12:50 Mt 6:1; 7:21; Jn 15:14; Heb 2:11
[g] 13:1-15 Mk 4:1-12; Lk 8:4-10
[h] 13:2 Mk 3:9; Lk 5:3
[i] 13:3 Mt 13:10,34-36; 15:15; 21:33,45; 22:1; 24:32; Mk 4:2
[j] 13:8 Gn 26:12; Mt 13:23
[k] 13:9 Mt 11:15; 13:43; Lk 8:8; 14:35; Rv 2:7,11,17,29; 3:6,13,22
[l] 13:10 Mt 9:10; Mk 10:10; Lk 6:1; Jn 6:3; Ac 6:1
[m] Mt 13:35; 15:15; 21:33,45; 22:1; 24:32
[n] 13:11 Mt 11:25; 19:11; Jn 6:65; 1Co 2:10; Col 1:27; 1Jn 2:20,27
[o] 13:12 Mt 25:29; Lk 8:18; 19:26; Jn 15:2; Jms 4:6
[p] 13:13 Dt 29:4; Is 42:19-20; Jr 5:21; Ezk 12:2
[q] Mt 15:10; 16:12; 17:13; Mk 8:21
[r] 13:14 Is 6:9; Mk 4:12; Lk 8:10; Jn 12:40; Ac 28:26-27; Rm 11:8

A12:47 Other mss omit this v.   B13:9 Other mss add *to hear*

12:43-45 The words **that's how it will also be with this evil generation** show that this discussion functioned like a parable. Jesus cast evil spirits out of afflicted people, but the Jewish leaders discouraged them from accepting God's help and rule through the person of Jesus. This left them empty and vulnerable to even greater evil.

12:48-50 Jesus valued His spiritual relationship with His disciples above His physical relationship with His family. Later, once faith had dawned in their hearts, His family members understood and adopted this value system (Jms 1:1; Jd 1).

13:3-9 The word **parables** can refer to a wide variety of figurative speech. Although many interpreters insist that Jesus' parables were simple metaphors that teach only one main truth, Jesus' interpretation of His own parables may suggest that many of them were allegories that carried multiple points of symbolism, teaching several related truths (see note at vv. 18-23).

13:10-13 Jesus' parables had two distinct purposes: (1) to reveal truth to those who were willing to hear and believe, and (2) to conceal truth from those who willingly rejected truth because of their calloused hearts (v. 15). The hiddenness component of Jesus' teaching may seem harsh, but since greater exposure to truth increases one's accountability to God in judgment (11:20-24), the concealment may represent God's graciousness toward those whom He knew would be unresponsive.

13:14-16 Matthew frequently explained how Jesus' ministry fulfilled prophecy. Here Jesus Himself described the fulfillment of Is 6:9-10. The application of this text to Jesus' contemporaries probably implies that Israel's hardened rejection of Jesus was not permanent, since Is 6:11-13 showed that the hearts of the people would someday be softened and that God would preserve a righteous remnant in Israel. The word "never" (Gk *ou me*) in the phrases **never understand** and **never perceive** means "will absolutely not" rather than "never will." Thus the picture is of stony resistance, not permanent resistance.

understand with their hearts
and turn back—
and I would cure them.[A,a]

[16]"But your eyes are blessed[b] because they do see, and your ears because they do hear![c] [17]For •I assure you: Many prophets and righteous people longed to see the things you see yet didn't see them; to hear the things you hear yet didn't hear them.[d]

The Parable of the Sower Explained

[18]"You, then, listen to the parable of the sower:[e] [19]When anyone hears the word[B] about the kingdom and doesn't understand it, the evil one comes and snatches away what was sown in his heart. This is the one sown along the path.[f] [20]And the one sown on rocky ground—this is one who hears the word and immediately receives it with joy.[g] [21]Yet he has no root in himself, but is short-lived. When pressure or persecution[h] comes because of the word, immediately he stumbles. [22]Now the one sown among the thorns—this is one who hears the word, but the worries of this age[i] and the seduction[C] of wealth[j] choke the word, and it becomes unfruitful. [23]But the one sown on the good ground—this is one who hears and understands the word, who does bear fruit and yields: some 100, some 60, some 30 times what was sown."

The Parable of the Wheat and the Weeds

[24]He presented another parable to them: "The kingdom of heaven may be compared to a man who sowed good seed in his field.[k] [25]But while people were sleeping, his enemy came, sowed weeds[D] among the wheat, and left. [26]When the plants sprouted and produced grain, then the weeds also appeared. [27]The landowner's •slaves[l] came to him and

said, 'Master, didn't you sow good seed in your field? Then where did the weeds come from?' [28]"'An enemy did this!' he told them.

"'So, do you want us to go and gather them up?' the slaves asked him.

[29]"'No,' he said. 'When you gather up the weeds, you might also uproot the wheat with them. [30]Let both grow together until the harvest. At harvest time I'll tell the reapers: Gather the weeds first and tie them in bundles to burn them, but store the wheat in my barn.'"

The Parables of the Mustard Seed and of the Yeast

[31]He[m] presented another parable to them: "The kingdom of heaven[n] is like a mustard seed that a man took and sowed in his field. [32]It's the smallest of all the seeds, but when grown, it's taller than the vegetables and becomes a tree, so that the birds of the sky come and nest in its branches."[o]

[33]He told them another parable: "The kingdom of heaven is like yeast that a woman took and mixed into 50 pounds[E] of flour until it spread through all of it."[F,p]

Using Parables Fulfills Prophecy

[34]Jesus told the crowds all these things in parables, and He would not speak anything to them without a parable,[q] [35]so that what was spoken through the prophet might be fulfilled:

I will open My mouth in parables;
I will declare things kept secret
from the foundation of the world.[G,r]

Jesus Interprets the Wheat and the Weeds

[36]Then He dismissed the crowds and went into the house. His disciples approached Him

Cross-references (center column)

[a]13:15 Is 6:10; Mt 15:8; Heb 5:11
[b]13:16-17 Lk 10:23-24
[c]13:16 Mt 16:17; Jn 20:29
[d]13:17 Jn 8:56; Heb 11:13; 1Pt 1:10-12
[e]13:18-23 Mk 4:13-20; Lk 8:11-15
[f]13:19 Mk 4:23; 5:37; 6:13
[g]13:20 Is 58:2; Ezk 33:31-32; Mk 6:20; Jn 5:35
[h]13:21 Mk 4:17; 10:30; Ac 8:1; 13:50; Rm 8:35; 2Co 12:10
[i]13:22 Rm 12:2; 2Tm 4:10; 1Jn 2:15
[j]Mt 19:23; Mk 10:23; 1Tm 6:9-10; 2Tm 4:10
[k]13:24 Mt 18:23; 20:1; 25:1; Mk 4:26,30
[l]13:27 Mt 10:24; Col 3:11; 4:1; Rv 1:1
[m]13:31-32 Mk 4:30-32; Lk 13:18-19
[n]13:31 Mt 13:24; 17:20; Lk 17:6
[o]13:32 Ps 104:12; Ezk 17:23; 31:6; Dn 4:12
[p]13:33 Gn 18:6; Lk 13:21; Gl 5:9
[q]13:34 Mk 4:34; Jn 10:6; 16:25
[r]13:35 Ps 78:2; Rm 16:25-26; 1Co 2:7; Eph 3:9; Col 1:26

[A]13:14-15 Is 6:9-10 [B]13:19 Gk logos = word, or message, or saying, or thing [C]13:22 Or pleasure, or deceitfulness [D]13:25 Or darnel, a weed similar in appearance to wheat in the early stages [E]13:33 Lit 3 sata; about 40 quarts [F]13:33 Or until all of it was leavened [G]13:35 Ps 78:2

13:17 The OT prophets and saints had eagerly awaited Messiah's coming (see 1Pt 1:10-12).

13:18-23 The four types of soil represent types of people and their differing responses to Jesus. The first three types represent those who reject Jesus outright (7:26-27) and those who falsely claim to be His disciples (7:15-23; 10:35-39). These are all unfruitful. Only the last type does bear fruit. Since bearing the fruit of good deeds is an essential expression of discipleship (3:8,10; 7:16-20; 12:33; 21:18-19,33-41), only the last type is a true disciple. A harvest of 10 to 20 times what was sown was considered a bumper crop, given the primitive agricultural technology of the period. The amazing harvest described by Jesus' parable (100 ... 60 ... 30) shows that true disciples bear fruit in a miraculous quantity.

13:24-30 The weeds were probably darnel. This plant is related to wheat and resembles it during the early stages of

growth, but darnel is actually a poisonous weed. Roman law prohibited sowing darnel in another's field, which suggests Jesus' story was realistic. The root systems of wheat and darnel become intertwined as the crop matures and makes it difficult to uproot the weeds without damaging the wheat. For the interpretation of this parable, see note at verses 36-43.

13:31-32 Like the mustard seed, the kingdom of heaven began as something small and seemingly insignificant but later grew to be large.

13:33 The image of a pinch of yeast permeating 50 pounds of dough parallels the great impact the kingdom would have despite its small beginnings.

13:34-35 Like Asaph in Ps 78, Jesus taught in parables and revealed to His disciples truths that had not previously been understood.

and said, "Explain the parable of the weeds in the field to us."[a]

[37]He replied: "The One who sows the good seed is the •Son of Man; [38]the field is the world; and the good seed—these are the sons of the kingdom. The weeds are the sons of the evil one,[b] [39]and the enemy who sowed them is the Devil. The harvest is the end of the age, and the harvesters are angels.[c] [40]Therefore, just as the weeds are gathered and burned in the fire, so it will be at the end of the age.[d] [41]The Son of Man will send out His angels, and they will gather from His kingdom everything that causes sin[A] and those •guilty of lawlessness.[B,e] [42]They will throw them into the blazing furnace[f] where there will be weeping and gnashing of teeth.[g] [43]Then the righteous will shine like the sun in their Father's kingdom. Anyone who has ears[c] should listen![h]

The Parables of the Hidden Treasure and of the Priceless Pearl

[44]"The kingdom of heaven is like treasure, buried in a field, that a man found and reburied. Then in his joy he goes and sells everything he has and buys that field.[i]

[45]"Again, the kingdom of heaven is like a merchant in search of fine pearls. [46]When he found one priceless[D] pearl, he went and sold everything he had, and bought it.[j]

The Parable of the Net

[47]"Again, the kingdom of heaven is like a large net thrown into the sea. It collected every kind of fish,[k] [48]and when it was full, they dragged it ashore, sat down, and gathered the good fish into containers, but threw out the worthless ones. [49]So it will be at the end of the age. The angels will go out, separate the evil people from the righteous,[l] [50]and throw them into the blazing furnace. In that place there will be weeping and gnashing of teeth.[m]

The Storehouse of Truth

[51]"Have you understood all these things?"[E]

"Yes," they told Him.

[52]"Therefore," He said to them, "every student of Scripture[F] instructed in the kingdom of heaven is like a landowner who brings out of his storeroom what is new and what is old."[n] [53]When Jesus had finished these parables, He left there.

Rejection at Nazareth

[54]He went to His hometown[o] and began to teach them in their •synagogue, so that they were astonished and said, "How did this wisdom and these miracles come to Him?[p] [55]Isn't this the carpenter's son?[q] Isn't His mother called Mary, and His brothers James,[r] Joseph,[G] Simon, and Judas?[s] [56]And His sisters, aren't they all with us? So where does He get all these things?" [57]And they were •offended by Him.

But Jesus said to them, "A prophet is not without honor except in his hometown and in his household."[t] [58]And He did not do many miracles there because of their unbelief.

John the Baptist Beheaded

14 At that time[u] •Herod the tetrarch[v] heard the report about Jesus. [2]"This is

Cross references (center column)

[a] 13:36 Mt 13:3; 15:15; 21:33,45; 22:1; 24:32
[b] 13:38 Mt 8:12; Jn 8:44; Ac 13:10; 1Jn 3:10
[c] 13:39 Jl 3:13; Heb 9:26; Rv 14:15
[d] 13:40 Mt 24:3; 28:20
[e] 13:41 Zph 1:3; Mt 8:20; 18:7; 24:31
[f] 13:42 Rv 1:15; 9:2
[g] Mt 8:12; Rv 19:20; 20:10
[h] 13:43 Dn 12:3; Mt 11:15; 1Co 15:42
[i] 13:44 Is 55:1; Php 3:7-8; Rv 3:18
[j] 13:46 Pr 2:4; Mt 7:6
[k] 13:47 Mt 3:2; 13:44; 22:10
[l] 13:49 Mt 13:39-40; 25:32
[m] 13:50 Mt 8:12; 13:42
[n] 13:52 Mt 12:35; 28:19
[o] 13:54-58 Mk 6:1-6; Lk 4:16-30
[p] 13:54 Mt 2:23; 4:23; 7:28
[q] 13:55 Mt 13:55; Mk 6:3; Lk 3:23; Jn 6:42
[r] Jms 1:1; Jd 1
[s] Mt 12:46; Jn 7:5
[t] 13:57 Jr 11:21; 12:6; Lk 4:24; Jn 4:44
[u] 14:1-12 Mk 6:14-29; Lk 9:7-9
[v] 14:1 Mk 8:15; Lk 3:19; 13:31; 23:7; Ac 4:27; 12:1; 13:1

[A]13:41 Or *stumbling*   [B]13:41 Or *those who do lawlessness*   [C]13:43 Other mss add *to hear*   [D]13:46 Or *very precious*   [E]13:51 Other mss add *Jesus asked them*   [F]13:52 Or *every scribe*   [G]13:55 Other mss read *Joses*; Mk 6:3

13:36-43 This parable is frequently interpreted as if the wheat represents true disciples and the weeds false disciples. But Jesus' interpretation shows that the subject is not the mixture of true and false disciples in the church but rather the presence of both good and evil people in the broader world. Many Jews expected Messiah to immediately destroy evildoers and vindicate the righteous. Thus they were puzzled as to why Jesus didn't do this if He truly were the **Son of Man** (see Dn 7:13-14). In this parable Jesus demonstrated (1) that He is not the source of evil (13:27-28,36-39); (2) that the entire world belongs to the Son of Man and the Devil had no right to bring evil into it; and (3) the Son of Man would assert His kingship over the world by punishing the wicked and blessing the righteous at an appropriate future time.

13:44-46 These parables teach that the **kingdom of heaven** is so valuable that the wise are willing to sacrifice anything in order to gain it (19:21-26).

13:47-50 The parable of the net closely parallels the parable of the wheat and weeds (vv. 24-30,38-43). It describes the final judgment in which the righteous (Jesus' disciples) are separated from those who reject Him and His rule and are sentenced to everlasting punishment.

13:51-52 Because of their exposure to Jesus' teaching, which disclosed what had previously been hidden (vv. 34-35), Jesus' disciples were better qualified than the scribes and Pharisees to serve as teachers of the law. In their storeroom of instruction, they had **old** treasures (the OT) and **new** treasures (the teachings of Jesus).

13:53 The words **when Jesus had finished** are important for understanding the structure of the Gospel. See "Structure" in the Introduction to Matthew.

13:54 Jesus' **hometown** was Nazareth (see note at 2:22-23).

13:55 This verse and its parallels (Mk 6:3; Lk 4:22) are the only references to Joseph's and Jesus' trade in the NT. Jewish tradition dictated that fathers teach their trade to their sons. The word "carpenter" (Gk *tekton*) was occasionally used to describe stone masons, but normally referred to woodworkers. One early tradition says that Jesus primarily made yokes and plows. Both **James** and **Judas** later became followers of Jesus and authored NT books.

13:57 Jesus identified Himself as a prophet, but also more than a prophet (12:41). Prophets were typically rejected (23:37).

14:1 **Herod** Antipas ruled as **tetrarch** of Galilee and Perea

John the Baptist!" he told his servants. "He has been raised from the dead, and that's why supernatural powers are at work in him."[a]

[3]For Herod had arrested John, chained[A] him, and put him in prison on account of Herodias, his brother Philip's wife,[b] [4]since John had been telling him, "It's not lawful[c] for you to have her!" [5]Though he wanted to kill him, he feared the crowd, since they regarded him as a prophet.[d]

[6]But when Herod's birthday celebration came, Herodias's daughter danced before them[B] and pleased Herod. [7]So he promised with an oath to give her whatever she might ask. [8]And prompted by her mother, she answered, "Give me John the Baptist's head here on a platter!" [9]Although the king regretted it, he commanded that it be granted because of his oaths and his guests. [10]So he sent orders and had John beheaded in the prison. [11]His head was brought on a platter and given to the girl, who carried it to her mother. [12]Then his disciples came, removed the corpse,[c] buried it, and went and reported to Jesus.

Feeding 5,000

[13]When Jesus heard about it,[e] He withdrew from there by boat to a remote place to be alone. When the crowds heard this, they followed Him on foot from the towns. [14]As He stepped ashore,[D] He saw a huge crowd, felt compassion for them, and healed their sick.[f]

[15]When evening came, the disciples[g] approached Him and said, "This place is a wilderness, and it is already late.[E] Send the crowds away so they can go into the villages and buy food for themselves."

[16]"They don't need to go away," Jesus told them. "You give them something to eat."

[17]"But we only have five loaves and two fish here," they said to Him.

[18]"Bring them here to Me," He said. [19]Then He commanded the crowds to sit down[F] on the grass. He took the five loaves and the two fish, and looking up to heaven, He blessed them. He broke the loaves and gave them to the disciples, and the disciples gave them to the crowds.[h] [20]Everyone ate and was filled. Then they picked up 12 baskets full of leftover pieces![i] [21]Now those who ate were about 5,000 men, besides women and children.

Walking on the Water

[22]Immediately[j] He[G] made the disciples get into the boat and go ahead of Him to the other side, while He dismissed the crowds. [23]After dismissing the crowds, He went up on the mountain by Himself to pray. When evening came, He was there alone.[k] [24]But the boat was already over a mile[H] from land,[l] battered by the waves, because the wind was against them. [25]Around three in the morning,[J] He came toward them walking on the sea.[l] [26]When the

---

[column notes between columns]
[a]14:2 Mt 16:14; Mk 6:14; Lk 9:7
[b]14:3 Mt 4:12; 11:2; Jn 3:24
[c]14:4 Lv 18:16; 20:21
[d]14:5 Mt 11:9; 21:26,46
[e]14:13-21 Mk 6:32-44; Lk 9:10-17; Jn 6:1-13
[f]14:14 Mt 4:23; 9:36
[g]14:15 Mt 10:1, 26:56; Mk 3:7; 16:20; Lk 6:13; Jn 12:16
[h]14:19 1Sm 9:13; Mt 26:26; Mk 8:7; 14:22; Lk 24:30; Ac 27:35
[i]14:20 Mt 16:9; Mk 6:43; 8:19; Lk 9:17; Jn 6:13
[j]14:22-33 Mk 6:45-51; Jn 6:15-21
[k]14:23 Lk 6:12; 9:48
[l]14:25 Mt 24:23; Mk 13:35

[A]14:3 Or *bound*   [B]14:6 Lit *danced in the middle*   [C]14:12 Other mss read *body*   [D]14:14 Lit *Coming out* (of the boat)   [E]14:15 Lit *and the time* (for the evening meal) *has already passed*   [F]14:19 Lit *to recline*   [G]14:22 Other mss read *Jesus*   [H]14:24 Lit *already many stadia*; 1 *stadion* = 600 feet   [I]14:25 Other mss read *already in the middle of the sea*   [J]14:25 Lit *fourth watch of the night* = 3 to 6 a.m.

---

from about 4 B.C. until he was banished for seeking the kingship in A.D. 39 (Josephus, *Ant.* 18.252-54). In general, a tetrarch was one step below an ethnarch which was in turn a step below king.

14:3 The explanatory conjunction **for** (Gk *gar*) shows that Herod's belief that **John** had been resurrected and possessed supernatural powers was a product of paranoia fed by his guilty conscience. John was arrested because he criticized Herod's illicit marriage to his brother's wife.

14:6-11 Herodias's daughter Salome danced erotically for her uncle Herod. This seems to have enticed a drunken Herod to make an oath he would later regret. Herodias preferred beheading as the means of execution so she could display John's head as a trophy. The Gospel accounts of this event were probably dependent on an informant in Herod's court, possibly Joanna or Manaen (Lk 8:3; 24:10; Ac 13:1).

14:14 On Jesus' **compassion** for the **crowd**, see note at 9:36.

14:17 Loaves of bread and small **fish** were staple foods in Galilee. The loaves were the size of dinner rolls. John's description of the fish (Gk *opsarion*) indicates that they were either dried or pickled (Jn 6:9). He also identified the loaves as made of barley, the food of the poor. He implied that the loaves and fish were small since they were sufficient for only one boy's lunch.

14:18-21 This is the only miracle of Jesus recorded by all

four Gospels. A true miracle is clearly expressed by the words **everyone ate and was filled**. Normally, a few small loaves and fish divided among so many people would only provide each person with a very tiny crumb. However, everyone ate to satisfaction and the disciples collected in leftovers more food than was originally available. Collecting these **baskets full of leftover pieces** served as a powerful reminder of Jesus' ability to provide abundance for His disciples (6:11,25-33). John's Gospel shows that many bystanders compared Jesus' miracles to God's provision of manna in the wilderness (Jn 6:22-33). The miracle also closely resembles a miracle of Elisha (2Kg 4:42-44). Although the miracle is referred to as the "Feeding of the 5,000," the **5,000 men, besides women and children** might equal a total of 15,000 people. Thus Jesus' miracle was far greater than that performed by Elisha.

14:24 Whether the original text stated that the disciples' boat was "in the middle of the sea" or "many stadia (a stadia equaling about 600 feet) from the land," the location of the boat is roughly the same. John noted that the boat was 25 or 30 stadia from the land, a distance ranging from about 2.8 to 3.5 miles. The Sea of Galilee is about eight miles wide at its widest point.

14:25 Around three in the morning is literally "during the fourth watch of the night." The Romans divided the period from 6:00 p.m. to 6:00 a.m. into four watches of three hours

disciples saw Him walking on the sea, they were terrified. "It's a ghost!" they said, and cried out in fear.

²⁷Immediately Jesus spoke to them. "Have courage! It is I. Don't be afraid."ᵃ

²⁸"Lord, if it's You," Peter answered Him, "command me to come to You on the water."

²⁹"Come!" He said.

And climbing out of the boat, Peter started walking on the water and came toward Jesus. ³⁰But when he saw the strength of the wind,ᴬ he was afraid. And beginning to sink he cried out, "Lord, save me!"

³¹Immediately Jesus reached out His hand, caught hold of him, and said to him, "You of little faith, why did you doubt?"ᵇ ³²When they got into the boat, the wind ceased. ³³Then those in the boat worshiped Him and said, "Truly You are the Son of God!"ᶜ

Miraculous Healings

³⁴Once they crossed over,ᵈ they came to land at Gennesaret.ᵉ ³⁵When the men of that place recognized Him, they alertedᴮ the whole vicinity and brought to Him all who were sick. ³⁶They were begging Him that they might only touch the ˙tassel on His robe. And as many as touched it were made perfectly well.ᶠ

The Tradition of the Elders

15 Thenᵍ ˙Pharisees and ˙scribes came from Jerusalem to Jesus and asked,ʰ ²"Why do Your disciplesⁱ break the tradition of the elders? For they don't wash their hands when they eat!"ᶜ,ʲ

³He answered them, "And why do you break God's commandment because of your tradition? ⁴For God said:ᴰ

**Honor your father
    and your mother;ᴱ,ᵏ and,
The one who speaks evil of father
    or mother
must be put to death.ᶠ,ˡ**

⁵But you say, 'Whoever tells his father or mother, "Whatever benefit you might have received from me is a gift committed to the temple"— ⁶he does not have to honor his father.'ᴳ In this way, you have revoked God's wordᴴ because of your tradition. ⁷Hypocrites! Isaiah prophesied correctly about you when he said:

⁸   **These peopleⁱ honor Me with their lips,
        but their heart is far from Me.**
⁹   **They worship Me in vain,
        teaching as doctrines the commands
        of men."ʲ,ᵐ**

Cross references (center column)

ᵃ14:27 Dt 31:6; Is 41:13; 43:1-2; Mt 17:7; Lk 2:10; Rv 1:17
ᵇ14:31 Mt 6:30; 8:26; 16:8
ᶜ14:33 Ps 2:7; Mt 16:16; 26:63; Mk 1:1; Lk 4:41; Jn 11:4
ᵈ14:34-36 Mk 6:53-56; Jn 6:24-25
ᵉ14:34 Mk 6:5; Lk 5:1
ᶠ14:36 Mt 9:20; Mk 3:10; Lk 6:19; Ac 5:15
ᵍ15:1-20 Mk 7:1-23
ʰ15:1 Mk 3:22; Jn 1:19
ⁱ15:2 Mt 10:1; 26:56; Mk 3:7; 16:20; Lk 6:13; Jn 12:16
ʲLk 11:38; Gl 1:14; Col 2:8; Heb 11:2
ᵏ15:4 Ex 20:12; Dt 5:16; Eph 6:2
ˡEx 21:17; Lv 20:9
ᵐ15:8-9 Is 29:13; Ezk 33:31; Col 2:22; Ti 1:14

ᴬ14:30 Other mss read *saw the wind*   ᴮ14:35 Lit *sent into*   ᶜ15:2 Lit *eat bread* = eat a meal   ᴰ15:4 Other mss read *commanded, saying*   ᴱ15:4 Ex 20:12; Dt 5:16   ᶠ15:4 Ex 21:17; Lv 20:9   ᴳ15:6 Other mss read *then he does not have to honor his father or mother*   ᴴ15:6 Other mss read *commandment*   ⁱ15:8 Other mss add *draw near to Me with their mouths, and*   ʲ15:8-9 Is 29:13 LXX

---

each. Thus the fourth watch lasted from 3:00 a.m. to 6:00 a.m.

14:26 The word **ghost** (Gk *phantasma*) was used in Greek literature to describe dream visions or spirit apparitions. In the OT a closely related term referred to a dream or vision in which one saw something that was not real (Is 28:7; Jb 20:8 [LXX]). Matthew's usage may imply that the disciples thought their eyes were deceiving them. The language of the text does not imply that the Bible supports the belief that spirits of the dead roam the earth.

14:27 The words **It is I** are literally "I am." The statement is Jesus' purposeful echo of OT texts like Ex 3:14 and identifies Him as Yahweh God.

14:33 The disciples' confession of Jesus as **Son of God** is not surprising in light of close connections between this miracle and important OT parallels. The title "Son of God" often serves as a messianic title in the NT (see note at 3:17), but here it also implies Jesus' deity. The disciples likely interpreted the miracle in light of Jb 9:8 (LXX) which states that Yahweh walked on the sea as if it were dry land. Their worship of Jesus also confirmed their growing recognition of His divine nature (see note at Mt 4:10-11).

14:34 Gennesaret was located on the northwestern shore of the Sea of Galilee about five miles south of Capernaum.

14:36 The people of Gennesaret appeared to be aware of the healing of the woman in Mt 9:20. This miracle occurred in nearby Capernaum and set a precedent for

healing by touching the tassel of Jesus' robe (see note at 9:20).

15:1-2 The Mishnah devotes an entire tractate of Jewish law to a discussion on how the **hands** should be washed. Good Jews were expected to perform ritual hand washing before, during, and after each meal. A person would first pour water over his hands with the fingers pointing up and with the water reaching the wrist, then he would point the fingers down and pour the water again, this time allowing the water to drip off the fingers. If one mixed up this order or poured the water both times with the hands pointed down or up, the hands were still ritually unclean. Each hand had to be rubbed with the other, but this could not be done until the other hand was clean. To neglect the first or third washing was considered a serious sin, possibly a deadly one. Such washing was not prescribed by OT law, but was a **tradition** passed down to first-century Jews by their **elders**. Many teachers gave these human traditions an authority equal to that of OT commandments.

15:3 Jesus taught that the authority of the Scriptures trumps all human **tradition**, and He condemned the Pharisees and scribes for valuing human tradition above Scripture.

15:5-6 Jewish law required sons to care for their aging parents (1Tm 5:8). However, corrupt priests allowed sons who were tired of caring for their parents to take a vow of Corban. This vow dedicated to God and the Jerusalem temple the resources they would otherwise have used to support their parents. Since one's obligation to God truly outweighs

Defilement Is from Within

[10] Summoning the crowd, He told them, "Listen and understand: [11] It's not what goes into the mouth that defiles[a] a man, but what comes out of the mouth, this defiles a man."[b]

[12] Then the disciples came up and told Him, "Do You know that the Pharisees took offense when they heard this statement?"

[13] He replied, "Every plant that My heavenly Father didn't plant will be uprooted.[c] [14] Leave them alone! They are blind guides.[A] And if the blind guide the blind, both will fall into a pit."[d]

[15] Then Peter replied to Him, "Explain this parable to us."[e]

[16] "Are even you still lacking in understanding?" He[B] asked. [17] "Don't you realize[c] that whatever goes into the mouth passes into the stomach and is eliminated?[D] [18] But what comes out of the mouth comes from the heart, and this defiles a man.[f] [19] For from the heart come evil thoughts, murders, adulteries, sexual immoralities, thefts, false testimonies,[g] blasphemies.[h] [20] These are the things that defile a man, but eating with unwashed hands does not defile a man."[i]

Cross references

a15:11 Mt 15:18; Mk 7:15; Ac 21:28; Heb 9:13
b Ac 10:14-15; 1Tm 4:3
c15:13 Is 60:21; 61:3; Jn 15:2; 1Co 3:9
d15:14 Mal 2:8; Mt 23:16,24; Lk 6:39
e15:15 Mt 13:36; Mk 7:17
f15:18 Mt 12:34; Jms 3:6
g15:19 Eph 4:31; Col 3:8; 1Tm 6:4
h Ex 20:13-16; Gl 5:19-21; Jms 2:4
i15:20 Mt 11:18; Mk 7:2,5; 1Co 6:9-10
j15:21-28 Mk 7:24-30
k15:21 Mt 11:21; Mk 7:24
l15:22 Gn 10:15,19; Jdg 1:30-33; Mt 4:24; 9:27
m15:23 Mt 10:1; 26:56; Mk 3:7; 16:20; Lk 6:13; Jn 12:16
n15:24 Mt 10:6,23; Jn 4:22; Rm 15:8
o15:26 Ex 22:31; 2Kg 9:10; Mt 8:2; Php 3:2
p15:28 Mt 9:22;17:18; Jn 4:52-53
q15:29-31 Mk 7:31-37

A Gentile Mother's Faith

[21] When Jesus left there,[j] He withdrew to the area of Tyre and Sidon.[k] [22] Just then a Canaanite woman from that region came and kept crying out,[E] "Have mercy on me, Lord, Son of David! My daughter is cruelly tormented by a demon."[l]

[23] Yet He did not say a word to her. So His disciples[m] approached Him and urged Him, "Send her away because she cries out after us."[F]

[24] He replied, "I was sent only to the lost sheep of the house of Israel."[n]

[25] But she came, knelt before Him, and said, "Lord, help me!"

[26] He answered, "It isn't right to take the children's bread and throw it to their dogs."[o]

[27] "Yes, Lord," she said, "yet even the dogs eat the crumbs that fall from their masters' table!"

[28] Then Jesus replied to her, "Woman, your faith is great. Let it be done for you as you want." And from that moment[G] her daughter was cured.[p]

Healing Many People

[29] Moving on from there,[q] Jesus passed along

A15:14 Other mss add for the blind   B15:16 Other mss read Jesus   C15:17 Other mss add yet   D15:17 Lit and goes out into the toilet   E15:22 Other mss read and cried out to Him   F15:23 Lit she is yelling behind us or after us   G15:28 Lit hour

---

all other obligations, the priests taught that such a maneuver was righteous. Jesus strongly condemned it, however.

15:11-12 The laws regarding purification of the hands were concerned with ritual purity, not sanitation. After all, Jewish law permitted the water to be drawn from vessels made of cow manure. Further, it permitted the water to be so filthy that cattle refused to drink it (m. Ta'an. 1). Jesus argued that food consumed with unpurified hands does not spiritually defile a person. The words that proceed from the **mouth** defile a person because they show the sinful condition of the heart (v. 18). That the **Pharisees took offense** at Jesus' teaching suggests that they understood that He was referring to their hypocritical speech, which honored God even as their hearts refused to worship Him (vv. 8-9).

15:13 Based on texts like Is 60:21 and 61:3, first-century Jews described themselves as the "plant of the Lord." **Every plant that My heavenly Father didn't plant** represents national Jews who neither understood nor practiced true righteousness. Like the weeds in the parable of Mt 13:24-30, these imposters would be **uprooted** and destroyed.

15:14 Jewish teachers like the Pharisees and scribes prided themselves on being **guides** for the blind (Rm 2:19). In ironic reversal, Jesus claimed the guides themselves were blind.

15:16-20 Jesus taught that the human **heart** is innately corrupt, but He also described His followers as "pure in heart" (5:8). From this we conclude that following Jesus results in a transformation of the heart that greatly diminishes our love of sin.

15:21 Tyre and Sidon were port cities on the coast of the

Mediterranean Sea north of Galilee. Because these cities were denounced in Is 23 and Ezk 28, first-century Jews viewed them as notoriously wicked and deserving of divine wrath (11:21).

15:22 By labeling the woman a **Canaanite** (cp. Mk 7:26), Matthew associates her with the most notorious pagan enemy of Israel. Like the magi of Mt 2, her role shows that Gentiles may follow Christ and be blessed by Him (see note at 2:1). Her use of the title **Son of David** indicates that she recognized Jesus as the Jewish Messiah (see note at 1:1).

15:24 Matthew emphasized Jesus' intention to include Gentiles in His kingdom, but he also stressed that Jesus focused His earthly ministry on Israelites who had been abused by their spiritual leaders (10:5-6).

15:26-27 Comparison of the Canaanite woman to a dog sounds like a racial slur to modern readers, but the word **dogs** (Gk kunarion) was a diminutive used as a term of endearment. It typically referred to house dogs that slept in the master's lap. Jesus' metaphorical statement merely implies that He had a higher obligation to serve His fellow Jews, not that He despised Gentiles. The woman replied that Jesus need not neglect Jews by meeting Gentile needs any more than children go hungry because **crumbs** that fall from their **table** are eaten by their pets.

15:28 The faith that Jesus most highly commended in Matthew was expressed by Gentiles (see notes at 8:7-8 and 8:11). The faith of the Canaanite woman even compared favorably to that of the 12 disciples (14:31).

15:29-31 The location is apparently the northern shores of

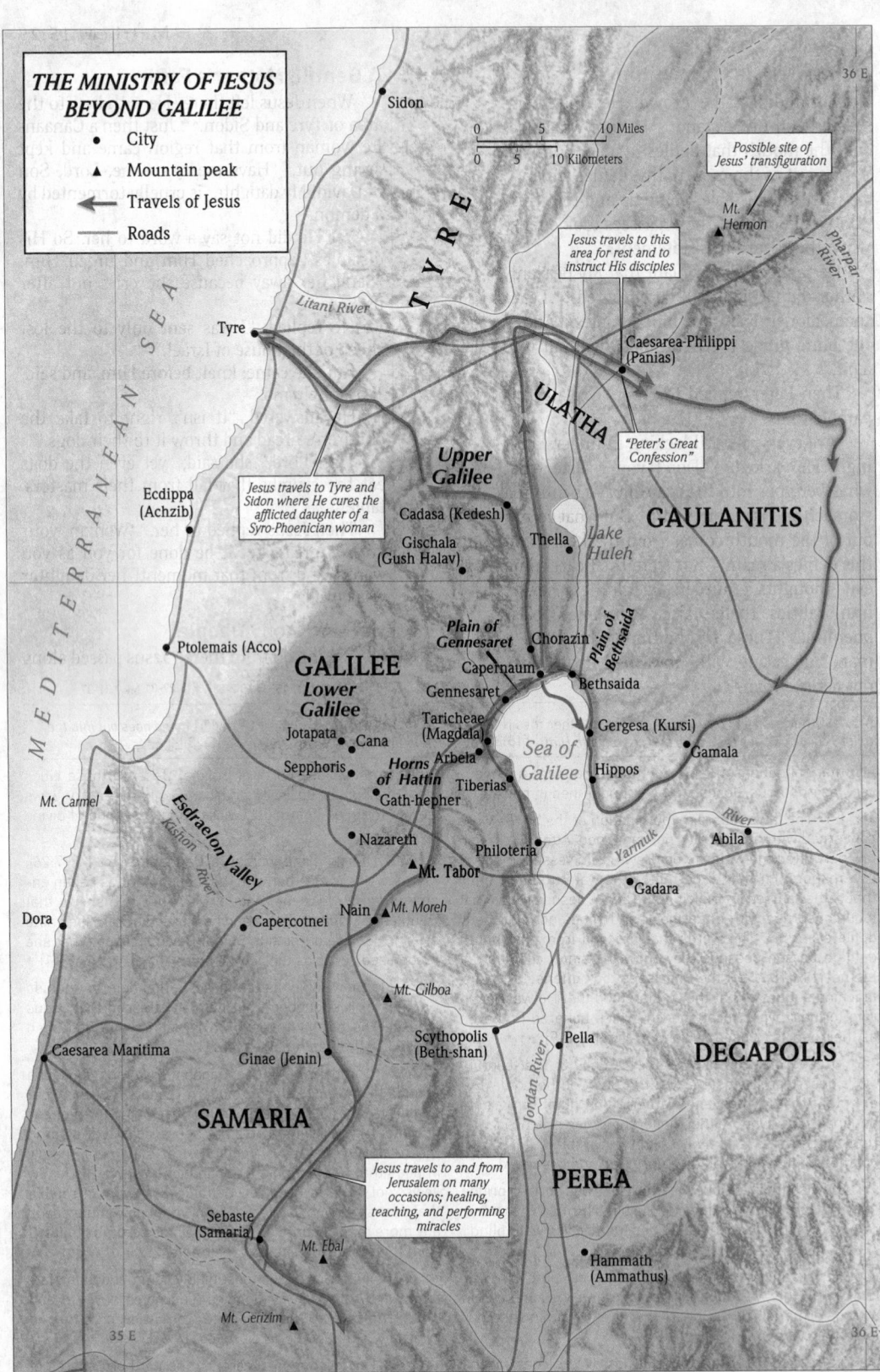

THE MINISTRY OF JESUS BEYOND GALILEE

- ● City
- ▲ Mountain peak
- ← Travels of Jesus
- ─ Roads

0   5   10 Miles
0   5   10 Kilometers

36 E

Possible site of Jesus' transfiguration

Mt. Hermon ▲

Pharpar River

Sidon

Jesus travels to this area for rest and to instruct His disciples

Litani River

T Y R E

Tyre

ULATHA

Caesarea-Philippi (Panias)

"Peter's Great Confession"

GAULANITIS

Upper Galilee

Cadasa (Kedesh)

Thella

Lake Huleh

Gischala (Gush Halav)

Jesus travels to Tyre and Sidon where He cures the afflicted daughter of a Syro-Phoenician woman

Ecdippa (Achzib)

M E D I T E R R A N E A N   S E A

Ptolemais (Acco)

GALILEE

Lower Galilee

Plain of Gennesaret

Chorazin

Plain of Bethsaida

Capernaum

Gennesaret

Bethsaida

Taricheae (Magdala)

Jotapata   Cana

Horns of Hattin

Arbela

Sea of Galilee

Gergesa (Kursi)

Gamala

Sepphoris

Gath-hepher

Tiberias

Hippos

Mt. Carmel ▲

Gath-hepher

Philoteria

River

Abila

Nazareth

▲ **Mt. Tabor**

Yarmuk

Dora

Nain   ▲ *Mt. Moreh*

Gadara

Capercotnei

Esdraelon Valley

Kishon River

Mt. Gilboa ▲

Caesarea Maritima

Scythopolis (Beth-shan)

Pella

DECAPOLIS

Ginae (Jenin)

Jordan River

SAMARIA

PEREA

Jesus travels to and from Jerusalem on many occasions; healing, teaching, and performing miracles

Sebaste (Samaria)

Mt. Ebal ▲

Hammath (Ammathus)

Mt. Gerizim ▲

35 E

36 E

the Sea of Galilee.[a] He went up on a mountain and sat there, [30]and large crowds came to Him, having with them the lame, the blind, the deformed, those unable to speak, and many others. They put them at His feet, and He healed them. [31]So the crowd was amazed when they saw those unable to speak talking, the deformed restored, the lame walking, and the blind seeing.[b] And they gave glory to the God of Israel.

Feeding 4,000

[32]Now Jesus summoned His disciples and said,[c] "I have compassion on the crowd, because they've already stayed with Me three days and have nothing to eat. I don't want to send them away hungry; otherwise they might collapse on the way."

[33]The disciples said to Him, "Where could we get enough bread in this desolate place[d] to fill such a crowd?"

[34]"How many loaves do you have?" Jesus asked them.

"Seven," they said, "and a few small fish."

[35]After commanding the crowd to sit down on the ground, [36]He took the seven loaves and the fish, and He gave thanks, broke them, and kept on giving them to the disciples, and the disciples gave them to the crowds.[e] [37]They all ate and were filled. Then they collected the leftover pieces—seven large baskets full. [38]Now those who ate were 4,000 men, besides women and children. [39]After dismissing the crowds, He got into the boat and went to the region of Magadan.[A,f]

The Yeast of the Pharisees and the Sadducees

16 The *Pharisees and *Sadducees approached,[g] and as a test, asked Him to show them a sign from heaven.[h]

[2]He answered them: "When evening comes you say, 'It will be good weather because the sky is red.' [3]And in the morning, 'Today will be stormy because the sky is red and threatening.' You[B] know how to read the appearance of the sky, but you can't read the signs of the times.[C] [4]An evil and adulterous generation demands a sign, but no sign will be given to it except the sign of[D] Jonah."[i] Then He left them and went away.

[5]The disciples reached the other shore,[E] and they had forgotten to take bread.

[6]Then Jesus told them, "Watch out and

Cross references (center column):

[a] 15:29 Mt 9:8; 18:8; Mk 9:43
[b] 15:31 Is 29:23; Lk 1:68; Ac 13:17
[c] 15:32-39 Mt 14:14-21; Mk 8:1-10
[d] 15:33 Mk 8:4; 2Co 11:26; Heb 11:38
[e] 15:36 Mt 26:27; Lk 22:17; Jn 6:11,23; Ac 27:35; Rm 14:6; 1Co 10:30
[f] 15:39 Mk 3:9; 8:10
[g] 16:1-12 Mt 12:38-39; Mk 8:11-21; Lk 12:54-56
[h] 16:1 Lk 11:16; 1Co 1:22
[i] 16:4 Mt 4:13; 21:17; Lk 11:29

[A]15:39 Other mss read *Magdala*   [B]16:3 Other mss read *Hypocrites! You*   [C]16:2-3 Other mss omit *When* (v. 2) through end of v. 3
[D]16:4 Other mss add *the prophet*   [E]16:5 Lit *disciples went to the other side*

---

the **Sea of Galilee**, still in Gentile territory. The list of ailments that Jesus cured is reminiscent of Is 35:5-6 and identifies Jesus as Messiah (Mt 11:1-6). The people's praise to **the God of Israel** shows that Jesus' ministry pointed Gentiles to the one true God.

15:32-38 This miracle is similar to the previous feeding (Mt 14:13-21). In both cases Jesus was moved with **compassion**, utilized **loaves** and **fish**, and satisfied the people so completely that **leftover pieces** were collected. One notable

difference is the audience. The first miracle was performed for Israelites, the second for Gentiles.

15:39 The **Magadan** mentioned here was probably ancient Magdala on the northwestern shore of the Sea of Galilee.

16:1 The **Pharisees** and **Sadducees** disagreed on major theological and political views. They unite only because of their joint opposition to John the Baptist and Jesus (3:7).

16:2-3 Jesus' opponents could skillfully read signs for the coming weather but they missed the more obvious signs (Jesus' miracles) about the coming kingdom of God (see note at 16:4).

16:4 Jesus' description of Israel's religious leaders is reminiscent of Dt 32:5, where Moses rebuked Israel for rejecting Yahweh. Jesus thus compared Israel's rejection of God with its rejection of Himself. By doing this, He equated Himself with God. The context of Dt 32:5 uses meteorological terms like heavens, rain, dew, and showers (Dt 32:1-2) and Moses elsewhere calls "heaven and earth as witnesses" against rebellious Israel (Dt 4:26; 30:19). Jesus used a meteorological illustration in order to tie in the OT text. On the **sign of Jonah**, see note at 12:39-40.

16:5-7 The disciples should have collected leftovers from Jesus' feeding miracle in order to sustain them on their next journey. Their failure to do so may have been an act of carelessness, but it may also indicate that they expected Jesus to perform signs and wonders at every turn, as did the sect leaders (vv. 1-4). The verb **had forgotten** (Gk *epilanthanomai*) often implies willful neglect (Ezk 23:35, LXX). **Yeast** was a metaphor for something seemingly insignificant that could have enormous influence (see note at 13:33). It could be used to indicate positive influence, but

---

splanchnizomai

Greek Pronunciation	[splahnk NIH zah migh]
HCSB Translation	feel compassion for
Uses in Matthew	5 (Mk, 4; Lk, 3)
Uses in the NT	12
Focus Passage	Matthew 15:32

Splanchnizomai (*to feel compassion for*) is related to the noun *splanchnon*, which in the plural literally means *bowels* (insides; Ac 1:18). In the ancient world, internal organs served as referents for psychological aspects (cp. modern English usage of *heart*). Thus, the *bowels* were considered the seat of love, sympathy, affection, and *compassion* (Lk 1:78; 2Co 6:12; 7:15; Php 2:1; Col 3:12). By extension, *splanchnon* became synonymous with the feeling itself (i.e., *love, affection, compassion*; Php 1:8; Phm 12). The verb *splanchnizomai* occurs only in the Synoptic Gospels and apart from appearing in Jesus' parables (Mt 18:27; Lk 10:33; 15:20), the word refers to Jesus Himself. His *compassion* led Him to provide the crowds with leadership (Mt 9:36 = Mk 6:34), to feed people (Mt 15:32 = Mk 8:2), and to heal them (Mt 14:14; 20:34; Mk 1:41; Lk 7:13).

beware of the yeast[A] of the Pharisees and Sadducees."[a]

[7] And they discussed among themselves, "We didn't bring any bread."

[8] Aware of this, Jesus said, "You of little faith![b] Why are you discussing among yourselves that you do not have bread? [9] Don't you understand yet? Don't you remember the five loaves for the 5,000 and how many baskets you collected? [10] Or the seven loaves for the 4,000 and how many large baskets you collected?[c] [11] Why is it you don't understand that when I told you, 'Beware of the yeast of the Pharisees and Sadducees,' it wasn't about bread?"[d] [12] Then they understood that He did not tell them to beware of the yeast in bread, but of the teaching of the Pharisees and Sadducees.[e]

Peter's Confession of the Messiah

[13] When Jesus came to the region of Caesarea Philippi,[B,f] He asked His disciples, "Who do people say that the •Son of Man is?"[c]

[14] And they said, "Some say John the Baptist; others, Elijah; still others, Jeremiah or one of the prophets."[g]

[15] "But you," He asked them, "who do you say that I am?"

[16] Simon Peter answered, "You are the •Messiah, the Son of the living God!"[h]

[17] And Jesus responded, "Simon son of Jonah,[D,i] you are blessed because flesh and blood did not reveal this to you, but My Father in heaven.[j] [18] And I also say to you that you are Peter,[E] and on this rock[F] I will build My church,[k] and the forces[G] of •Hades will not overpower it. [19] I will give you the keys of the kingdom of heaven,[l] and whatever you bind on earth is already bound[H] in heaven, and whatever you loose on earth is already loosed[I] in heaven."

[20] And He gave the disciples orders to tell no one that He was[J] the Messiah.[m]

His Death and Resurrection Predicted

[21] From[n] then on Jesus began to point out to His disciples that He must go to Jerusalem and suffer many things from the elders, •chief priests, and •scribes, be killed, and be raised the third day.[o] [22] Then Peter took Him aside and began to rebuke Him, "Oh no,[K] Lord! This will never happen to You!"

[23] But He turned and told Peter, "Get behind Me, Satan! You are an offense to Me because

---

[a]16:6 Mt 3:7; 8:15; Lk 12:1; 1Co 5:6-8; Gl 5:9
[b]16:8 Mt 6:30; 8:26; 14:31; Lk 12:28
[c]16:9-10 Mt 14:17-21; 15:34-38
[d]16:11 Mt 3:7; 16:6; Mk 8:15; Lk 12:1
[e]16:12 Mt 5:20; 17:13; 23:3
[f]16:13-16 Mk 8:27-29; Lk 9:18-20
[g]16:14 Mt 14:2; 17:10; Mk 6:15; Lk 9:8; Jn 1:21
[h]16:16 Mt 1:16; Jn 11:27
[i]16:17 Jn 1:42; 21:15-17
[j]1Co 15:50; Gl 1:16; Eph 6:12; Heb 2:14
[k]16:18 Mt 18:17; Ac 5:11; 7:38; 8:1,3; 9:31; 11:22,26
[l]16:19 Is 22:22; Mt 18:18; Jn 20:23; Rv 1:18; 3:7
[m]16:20 Mk 8:30; Lk 9:21
[n]16:21-28 Mk 8:31-9:1; Lk 9:22-27
[o]16:21 Mt 17:9; 20:18; 27:63; Lk 24:7; Jn 2:19

[A]16:6 Or *leaven*   [B]16:13 A town north of Galilee at the base of Mount Hermon   [C]16:13 Other mss read *that I, the Son of Man, am*   [D]16:17 Or *son of John*   [E]16:18 *Peter* (Gk *Petros*) = a specific stone or rock   [F]16:18 *Rock* (Gk *petra*) = a rocky crag or bedrock   [G]16:18 Lit *gates*   [H]16:19 Or *earth will be bound*   [I]16:19 Or *earth will be loosed*   [J]16:20 Other mss add *Jesus*   [K]16:22 Lit *Mercy to You* = *May God have mercy on You*

---

here it is used negatively. **The Pharisees and Sadducees** disagreed about many doctrines, so reference to their common teaching likely meant their joint skepticism regarding Jesus' messiahship.

16:8-12 The disciple's memory of Jesus' feeding miracles should have been enough to sustain their faith. Their constant desire for miracles paralleled the Pharisees' and Sadducees' demand for a "sign from heaven" (v. 1) and demonstrated that they were people **of little faith**.

16:13 Two cities in ancient Israel were named Caesarea. Caesarea Maritima was located on the coast of the Sea of Galilee. **Caesarea Philippi** was an inland city located approximately 25 miles north of the Sea of Galilee. This was the site of worship for a nature god known as Pan and the home of a temple dedicated to Augustus Caesar. That Jesus' identity as Messiah was announced here demonstrates that Jesus' kingdom is superior to Caesar's and that He is likewise superior to all idols and mythical gods. On the meaning of **Son of Man**, see note at 8:20.

16:14 Many of Jesus' contemporaries recognized His prophetic role. Herod suspected He was **John the Baptist** resurrected (14:2). Some of Jesus' miracles were similar to those of **Elijah** (cp. 1Kg 17:9-16 and Mt 14:13-21; 1Kg 17:17-24 and Mt 9:18-19,23-26), leading people to believe He was the fulfillment of Elijah's promised return (Mal 4:5). Like **Jeremiah**, Jesus was a much-rejected preacher of judgment.

16:16 On the titles **Messiah** and **Son of the living God**, see notes at 1:1 and 3:17. Although Matthew called Jesus Messiah earlier (1:1,16), this is the first time the disciples called Him this. Peter used the title "living God" to contrast Yahweh with lifeless pagan deities, such as the false god Pan who was represented in a nearby pagan temple.

16:17-18 Simon understood Jesus' identity due to divine revelation (11:25-27), which is why Jesus nicknamed him **Peter**. Although Matthew previously referred to Simon as Peter, this is the first time in the Gospel that Jesus did so. Jesus identified Peter as the **rock** on which His church would be founded. Peter and the other apostles' proclamation of Jesus' messiahship laid the foundation for the church (Eph 2:19-20; Rv 21:14). **I will build** demonstrates that Jesus is ultimately responsible for the growth and expansion of the church. The word **church** was the word used in the OT to describe sacred Jewish assemblies. Jesus' use of the word implies that His followers constitute the new Israel, the true people of God who submit to His kingly reign.

16:19 The **keys** are a symbol of authority. The rabbis used the words **bind** and **loose** to denote decisions about what was or was not permitted. Note that Peter will permit or prohibit only what had already been permitted or prohibited in heaven. Peter was an agent of divine revelation.

16:20 Jesus' contemporaries, even His disciples, were slow to understand the nature of His messiahship.

16:21-22 On the significance of the words **from then on Jesus began to**, see "Structure" in the Introduction to Matthew. Jesus referred to His death and resurrection earlier (12:40), but now He did so more persistently and clearly. Peter could not accept the warning because his messianic expectations did not include a suffering, executed Messiah.

16:23 The cross was central to Jesus' purposes on earth.

you're not thinking about God's concerns,[A] but man's."[a]

Take Up Your Cross

[24] Then Jesus said to His disciples, "If anyone wants to come with Me, he must deny himself, take up his cross, and follow Me.[b] [25] For whoever wants to save his •life will lose it, but whoever loses his life because of Me will find it.[c] [26] What will it benefit a man if he gains the whole world yet loses his life? Or what will a man give in exchange for his life?[d] [27] For the Son of Man is going to come with His angels in the glory of His Father,[e] and then He will reward each according to what he has done. [28] •I assure you: There are some standing here who will not taste death until they see the Son of Man coming in His kingdom."[f]

The Transfiguration

17 After six days[g] Jesus took Peter, James, and his brother John and led them up on a high mountain by themselves.[h] [2] He was transformed[B] in front of them, and His face shone like the sun. Even His clothes became as white as the light.[i] [3] Suddenly, Moses and Elijah appeared to them, talking with Him. [4] Then Peter said to Jesus, "Lord, it's good for us to be here! If You want, I will make[C] three •tabernacles here: one for You, one for Moses, and one for Elijah."[j] [5] While he was still speaking, suddenly a bright cloud covered[D] them, and a voice from the cloud said:

> This is My beloved Son.
> I take delight in Him.
> Listen to Him![k]

a16:23 2Sm 19:22; Rm 8:5,7; Php 2:5; 3:19; Col 3:2 b16:24 Mt 10:38; Lk 14:27 c16:25 Mt 10:39; Jn 12:25 d16:26 Ps 49:7-8; Lk 12:20 e16:27 Mt 26:64; Mk 8:38; Ac 1:11; 1Th 1:10; 4:16; Rv 1:7 f16:28 Mt 4:23; 10:23; Ac 20:25 g17:1-8 Mk 9:2-8; Lk 9:28-36 h17:1 Mt 26:37; Mk 5:37 i17:2 Ps 104:2; Dn 7:9; Mt 28:3; 2Co 3:18; Rv 1:16; 10:1 j17:4 Mk 9:5; Lk 9:33 k17:5 Is 42:1; Mt 3:17; Mk 1:11; Lk 3:22; Ac 3:22; 2Pt 1:16-18

A16:23 Lit *about the things of God* B17:2 Or *transfigured* C17:4 Other mss read *wish, let's make* D17:5 Or *enveloped*; Ex 40:34-35

Because Peter's statement essentially tempted Jesus to evade the cross, he unwittingly became a spokesman for **Satan**.

16:24 Take up his cross refers to the death march of the Christian disciple, who is figuratively sentenced to crucifixion over his decision to follow Christ. The Christian must be prepared to give his life for Jesus. **Follow me** requires the disciple to follow the example of his Master, emulating Jesus' character and behavior.

16:27 Jesus applied to Himself Ps 62:12 and Zch 14:5, statements which referred to Yahweh God. On the title **Son of Man**, see note at 8:20.

16:28 This promise refers to Jesus' transfiguration which foreshadowed His resurrection and glorification (2Pt 1:16-18).

17:1-6 The reference to **six days** indicates the rapidity of the fulfillment of Jesus' promise in Mt 16:28, but it also may draw a parallel between Jesus' transfiguration and God's revelation of Himself to **Moses** in Ex 24:13-18. Other parallels include the reference to a **cloud**, a brilliant **light**, a **mountain**, and the separation of a small number of men from the larger group. Moses' face shone brilliantly after he met with God (Ex 34:29-35), so Jesus' transfiguration serves to identify Him as the new Moses. This seems confirmed by the words **listen to Him** which echo Dt 18:15, a text from the prophet-like-Moses prophecy (Dt 18:15-19). On the new Moses theme, see notes at Mt 2:15 and 2:16-17. However, the description of Jesus transcends OT descriptions of the glorified Moses. In Ex 34:29-35, only Moses' face was radiant and this radiance was concealed by his veil. Jesus' face had radiance too glorious to conceal and **even His clothes became as white as the light**. The description of Jesus parallels the description of the Ancient of Days in Dn 7:9-10 and shows that Jesus possessed the glory of His Father (Mt 16:27).

The presence of Moses and Elijah indicates that the

Mount Tabor, in lower Galilee, is the traditional site of Jesus' transfiguration, but it is not a high mountain (1,850 ft.) and was probably fortified and inaccessible in Jesus' day. The more likely site is Mount Hermon, shown in the photo. Mount Hermon is 9,100 feet and is north of Caesarea Philippi where Peter confessed that Jesus was the Messiah.

⁶When the disciplesᵃ heard it, they fell face-down and were terrified.

⁷Then Jesus came up, touched them, and said, "Get up; don't be afraid."ᵇ ⁸When they looked up they saw no one except Himᴬ—Jesus alone. ⁹As they were coming down from the mountain, Jesus commanded them,ᶜ "Don't tell anyone about the vision until the ˙Son of Man is raisedᴮ from the dead."

¹⁰So the disciples questioned Him, "Why then do the ˙scribes say that Elijah must come first?"ᵈ

¹¹"Elijah is comingᶜ and will restore everything," He replied.ᴰ,ᵉ ¹²"But I tell you: Elijah has already come, and they didn't recognize him. On the contrary, they did whatever they pleased to him. In the same way the Son of Man is going to suffer at their hands."ᴱ,ᶠ ¹³Then the disciples understood that He spoke to them about John the Baptist.

The Power of Faith over a Demon

¹⁴When they reached the crowd,ᵍ a man approached and knelt down before Him. ¹⁵"Lord," he said, "have mercy on my son,

because he has seizuresᶠ and suffers severely. He often falls into the fire and often into the water. ¹⁶I brought him to Your disciples, but they couldn't heal him."ʰ

¹⁷Jesus replied, "You unbelieving and rebelliousᴳ generation! How long will I be with you? How long must I put up with you? Bring him here to Me."ⁱ ¹⁸Then Jesus rebuked the demon,ᴴ and itᴵ came out of him,ʲ and from that momentʲ the boy was healed.

¹⁹Then the disciples approached Jesus privately and said, "Why couldn't we drive it out?"

²⁰"Because of your little faith," Heᴷ told them. "For ˙I assure you: If you have faith the size ofᴸ a mustard seed, you will tell this mountain, 'Move from here to there,' and it will move.ᵏ Nothing will be impossible for you.ᴸ [²¹However, this kind does not come out except by prayer and fasting.]"ᴹ

The Second Prediction of His Death

²²Asᵐ they were meetingᴺ in Galilee, Jesus told them, "The Son of Man is about to be betrayed into the hands of men. ²³They will kill

---

Cross-references (center column):
ᵃ17:6 Mt 10:1; 26:56; Mk 3:7; 16:20; Lk 6:13; Jn 12:16
ᵇ17:7 Dn 8:18; 9:21; 10:10; Mt 14:27
ᶜ17:9-13 Mk 9:9-13
ᵈ17:10 Mal 4:5; Mt 11:14
ᵉ17:11 Mal 4:6; Lk 1:16-17
ᶠ17:12 Mt 14:3,10; 16:21
ᵍ17:14-21 Mk 9:14-29; Lk 9:37-43
ʰ17:16 Mt 10:1; Mk 6:7; Lk 10:17
ⁱ17:17 Jn 14:9; 20:27; Php 2:15
ʲ17:18 Zch 3:2; Mt 8:26; Mk 1:25; Lk 4:35; Jd 9
ᵏ17:20 Mt 21:21-22; Mk 11:23; Lk 17:6; Jn 11:40; 1Co 13:2
ᴸMk 9:23; 13:31
ᵐ17:22-23 Mt 16:21; 20:17; Mk 8:31; 9:30-32; Lk 9:44-45

ᴬ17:8 Other mss omit *Him*   ᴮ17:9 Other mss read *Man has risen*   ᶜ17:11 Other mss add *first*   ᴰ17:11 Other mss read *Jesus said to them*   ᴱ17:12 Lit *suffer by them*   ᶠ17:15 Lit *he is moonstruck*; thought to be a form of epilepsy   ᴳ17:17 Or *corrupt,* or *perverted,* or *twisted*; Dt 32:5   ᴴ17:18 Lit *rebuked him* or *it*   ᴵ17:18 Lit *the demon*   ʲ17:18 Lit *hour*   ᴷ17:20 Other mss read *your unbelief,"* Jesus   ᴸ17:20 Lit *faith like*   ᴹ17:21 Other mss omit bracketed text; Mk 9:29   ᴺ17:22 Other mss read *were staying*

---

necessary conditions for Messiah's coming had been fulfilled (v. 10; Dt 18:15-19; Mal 4:5). Peter's request to build **tabernacles** unjustly suggested equal treatment for Jesus and His guests. The Father's voice from heaven showed Jesus' superiority to Moses and Elijah. Jesus is God's **beloved Son**, the object of His **delight**, and the focus of true disciples. God spoke from heaven only twice in Matthew, both times to express His love for Jesus and His delight in His works (v. 5; 3:17). On the meaning of **Son**, see note at 3:17. The disciples' reaction is understandable, for the OT

shows that direct encounters with God inspire fright (e.g., Is 6:1-5).

17:9 The disciples could report the transfiguration only after the resurrection when the nature of Jesus' messianic reign became clear. This is Jesus' third mention of His resurrection in this Gospel.

17:10-13 The view of the **scribes** was prompted by Mal 4:5. John the Baptist was the fulfillment of the Elijah prophecy since his ministry had many similarities to Elijah's. See notes at Mt 3:1,4, and 11:14.

17:14-16 Like the magi (2:11), the leper (8:2), the father of the deceased daughter (9:18), and Jesus' disciples (14:33), this father worshiped Jesus (cp. 4:10). The **seizures** were probably the result of epilepsy. Epilepsy is distinguished from demon possession in Mt 4:24. However, Jesus recognized in this rare instance that the seizures were the result of demonic activity. The apparent suicidal tendencies described in verse 15 show the destructive influence of demons.

17:17-18 Jesus' description of His own disciples as an **unbelieving and rebellious generation** is similar to His description of the Jewish leaders who rejected Him (11:16; 12:39,45).

17:20-21 Moving a **mountain** was a metaphor for accomplishing an impossible task (1Co 13:2). Nothing that Christ authorizes His followers to do will be **impossible**. Verse 21 does not appear in the oldest and best manuscripts of Matthew. It was probably incorporated into the text by later scribes who were familiar with the parallel text in Mk 9:29.

17:22-23 This is Jesus' fourth prediction of His death in Matthew (v. 12; 12:40; 16:21). Each prediction adds additional

---

metamorphoo

Greek Pronunciation	[meh tah mohr FAH oh]
HCSB Translation	transform
Uses in Matthew	1 (Mk, 1)
Uses in the NT	4
Focus Passage	Matthew 17:2

Metamorphoo means *to change* or *transform* and occurs only in the passive (*to be changed, transformed,* or *transfigured*) in the NT. *Metamorphoo* may refer to outward physical change (e.g., Jesus' *transfiguration*) or to an inward spiritual transformation. Jesus was *transformed* (Mt 17:1-2 = Mk 9:2) on the "holy mountain" (2Pt 1:18) while Peter, James, and John looked on. He temporarily assumed the form of His heavenly glory, permitting His disciples to see Him as He will appear in His kingdom. Paul employs *metamorphoo* in reference to the inward spiritual transformation occurring in Christians. As believers gaze upon the Lord's glory, they are *transformed* into His image through the work of the Spirit (2Co 3:18), reattaining the fullness of the divine image, which they shared at creation. On the basis of their status in Christ, Paul commands believers to be inwardly *transformed* through the renewing of their minds (Rm 12:2).

Him, and on the third day He will be raised up." And they were deeply distressed.

Paying the Temple Tax

²⁴When they came to Capernaum, those who collected the double-drachma tax^A approached Peter and said, "Doesn't your Teacher pay the double-drachma tax?"^a

²⁵"Yes," he said.

When he went into the house, Jesus spoke to him first,^B "What do you think, Simon? Who do earthly kings collect tariffs or taxes from? From their sons or from strangers?"^C,b

²⁶"From strangers," he said.^D

"Then the sons are free," Jesus told him. ²⁷"But, so we won't •offend them, go to the sea, cast in a fishhook, and take the first fish that you catch. When you open its mouth you'll find a coin.^E Take it and give it to them for Me and you."^c

Who Is the Greatest?

18 At that time^F,d the disciples^e came to Jesus and said, "Who is greatest in the kingdom of heaven?"^f

²Then He called a child to Him and had him stand among them. ³"'I assure you," He said, "unless you are converted^G and become like

children,^g you will never enter the kingdom of heaven.^h ⁴Therefore, whoever humbles himself like this child—this one is the greatest in the kingdom of heaven. ⁵And whoever welcomes^H one child like this in My name welcomes Me.

⁶"But whoever •causes the downfall of one of these little ones who believe in Me—it would be better for him if a heavy millstone^I were hung around his neck and he were drowned in the depths of the sea!^i ⁷Woe to the world because of •offenses. For offenses must come, but woe to that man by whom the offense comes.^j ⁸If your hand or your foot causes your downfall, cut it off and throw it away. It is better for you to enter life maimed or lame, than to have two hands or two feet and be thrown into the eternal fire.^k ⁹And if your eye causes your downfall, gouge it out and throw it away. It is better for you to enter life with one eye, rather than to have two eyes and be thrown into •hellfire!^J,l

The Parable of the Lost Sheep

¹⁰"See that you don't look down on one of these little ones,^m because I tell you that in heaven their angels^n continually view the face of My Father in heaven.^o [¹¹For the •Son of

^a17:24 Ex 30:13; 38:26; Mk 9:33
^b17:25 Mt 22:17,19; Mk 12:14; Rm 13:7
^c17:27 Mt 5:29; Jn 6:61
^d18:1-5 Mk 9:33-37; Lk 9:46-48
^e18:1 Mt 9:10; Mk 10:10; Lk 6:1; Jn 6:3; Ac 6:1
^f Mt 22:24; Jn 3:35; 13:20
^g18:3 Mt 19:14; Mk 10:15; Lk 18:17; 1Co 14:20; 1Pt 2:2
^h Mt 5:20; 7:21; 19:23-24; Mk 9:47; Jn 3:5
^i18:6 Mk 9:42; Lk 17:2; 1Co 8:12
^j18:7 Mt 26:24; Lk 17:1; 1Co 11:19
^k18:8 Mt 5:30; 25:41; Mk 9:43
^l18:9 Mt 5:22,29; Mk 9:47
^m18:10 Est 1:14; Lk 1:19; Rv 8:2
^n Ps 34:7; 91:11; Heb 1:14
^o Mt 6:29; 25:40,45; Lk 15:7,10

^A17:24 Jewish men paid this tax to support the temple; Ex 30:11-16. A double-drachma could purchase 2 sheep.   ^B17:25 Lit Jesus anticipated him by saying   ^C17:25 Or foreigners   ^D17:26 Other mss read Peter said to Him   ^E17:27 Gk stater, worth 2 double-drachmas   ^F18:1 Lit hour   ^G18:3 Or are turned around   ^H18:5 Or receives   ^I18:6 A millstone turned by a donkey   ^J18:9 Lit gehenna of fire

details. This prophecy adds that Jesus will be thrust **into the hands of men** by an act of betrayal.

17:24 On **Capernaum**, see note at 4:13. The **double-drachma tax** was collected from every Jewish male over the age of 20 and used for the upkeep of the Jerusalem temple (Ex 30:13; 38:25-26; Josephus, *Ant.* 18.9.1 and *War* 7.6.6). This episode is recorded only in Matthew and provides evidence for the pre-A.D. 70 date of Matthew. See "Date" in the Introduction to Matthew.

17:25-26 Because Jesus' disciples were children of the true King, they were exempt from the obligation to support the temple. This had enormous implications for Jewish Christians. If temple taxes were no longer obligatory, sacrifices and other offerings were also now optional. See the discussion of Matthew's view of sacrifice under "Date" in the Introduction to Matthew.

17:27 Though Jesus insisted that the temple tax was not obligatory for His disciples, He gladly paid it to avoid offending His fellow Jews. His action provided an important model for believers who dealt with issues of ritual later in the early church (Rm 14:13-23). Several ancient texts refer to fishermen discovering valuable items inside fish. Through supernatural knowledge, Jesus knew that a nearby **fish** had swallowed an amount of money that was sufficient to pay the tax. He also exercised authority over nature, ensuring that the fish would take the bait Peter offered.

18:1-5 These verses are commonly said to promote childlike innocence or naivety, but Jesus' statement actually urged disciples to adopt childlike humility. The desire to be the

greatest in the kingdom displayed a pride that was inconsistent with genuine discipleship. Humility is the path to true greatness. Jesus urged kind and gracious treatment of children by teaching that anyone welcoming a **child** in His **name** would be rewarded as if they had received Messiah Himself.

18:6-7 Jesus shifted the topic from literal children to spiritual **little ones who believe in** Him, meaning His disciples. The **heavy millstone** was a large round stone turned by a donkey rather than the much smaller stone used to pound grain by hand. Drowning was a particularly horrifying way to die in the mind-set of first-century Jews, for Israel was not a seafaring nation.

18:8-9 Those who cause Jesus' disciples to sin will face severe punishment. Nevertheless, disciples are responsible for their own actions and must commit to purity (see note at 5:29-30).

18:10 Daniel 10:10-14 teaches that **angels** are assigned to represent and protect the nations. In similar fashion, Jesus appears to teach that angels are assigned to represent believers to God. Jesus said that these angels **continually view the face of My Father**, meaning they have access to the heavenly throne and constantly present the needs of believers to God.

18:11-14 Sinful believers who are restored to church fellowship should not be received begrudgingly or hesitantly but with the jubilation of a shepherd who finds a **sheep** that **goes astray**. The heavenly Shepherd cannot accept the loss

Man[a] has come to save the lost.][A] [12]What do you think?[b] If a man has 100 sheep, and one of them goes astray, won't he leave the 99 on the hillside and go and search for the stray?[c] [13]And if he finds it, I assure you: He rejoices over that sheep[B] more than over the 99 that did not go astray. [14]In the same way, it is not the will of your Father in heaven that one of these little ones perish.

Restoring a Brother

[15]"If your brother sins against you,[C] go and rebuke him in private.[D] If he listens to you, you have won your brother.[d] [16]But if he won't listen, take one or two more with you, so that **by the testimony**[E] of two or three witnesses every fact may be established.[F,e] [17]If he pays no attention to them, tell the church.[G,f] But if he doesn't pay attention even to the church, let him be like an unbeliever[H] and a tax collector to you.[g] [18]I assure you: Whatever you bind on earth is already bound[I] in heaven, and whatever you loose on earth is already loosed[J] in heaven.[h] [19]Again, I assure you: If two of you on earth agree about any matter that you[K] pray

for, it will be done for you[L] by My Father in heaven. [20]For where two or three are gathered together in My name, I am there among them."

The Parable of the Unforgiving Slave

[21]Then Peter came to Him and said, "Lord, how many times could my brother sin against me and I forgive him? As many as seven times?"[i]

[22]"I tell you, not as many as seven," Jesus said to him, "but 70 times seven.[M] [23]For this reason, the kingdom of heaven can be compared to a king who wanted to settle accounts with his 'slaves. [24]When he began to settle accounts, one who owed 10,000 talents[N] was brought before him. [25]Since he had no way to pay it back, his master commanded that he, his wife, his children, and everything he had be sold to pay the debt.[j]

[26]"At this, the slave fell facedown before him and said, 'Be patient with me, and I will pay you everything!' [27]Then the master of that slave had compassion, released him, and forgave him the loan.

---

a 18:11 Mk 2:10; Jn 2:25
b 18:12-14 Lk 15:1-7
c 18:12 Mt 17:25; 21:28
d 18:15 Lv 19:17; Lk 17:3; Gl 6:1; 2Th 3:15; Jms 5:19; 1Pt 3:1
e 18:16 Nm 35:30; Jn 8:17; 2Co 13:1; 1Tm 5:19; Heb 10:28
f 18:17 Mt 16:18; 1Co 14:4; Rv 1:4
g Rm 16:17; 1Co 5:9; 6:1-6; 2Th 3:6,14; 2Jn 10
h 18:18 Mt 16:19; Jn 20:23
i 18:21 Lk 17:3-4; Col 3:13
j 18:25 Ex 21:2; Lv 25:39; 2Kg 4:1; Neh 5:5,8; Lk 7:42

---

of even a single believer. Like the shepherd of this parable, He will rescue His stray sheep.

18:15-17 These verses outline the process by which disciples demonstrate the Great Shepherd's concern for stray sheep. The words **against you** do not appear in the earliest and best manuscripts of verse 15. Thus the process is not intended merely for dealing with personal grievances but rather for any sinful conduct on the part of a Christian **brother** (or sister) that indicates they are straying from Christ. The purpose of the process is not to punish, but to restore the sinful disciple (**you have won your brother**). If, at the final step of the process, the professing disciple refuses to heed the church's call to repentance, the **church** must assume that they are not a true believer and must exclude them from fellowship (see 1Co 5:1-13).

18:18 On binding and loosing, see note at 16:19. The decisions made by the church about what behavior is permissible or unacceptable reflect decisions already made by God in heaven.

18:19-20 A common but mistaken interpretation holds that these verses promise that God will do whatever two or more believers ask. This violates the context. There is a clear connection with the immediately preceding discussion about restoring a sinning disciple. Verses 18 and 19 relate the restoration/disciplinary actions of Jesus' disciples **on earth** to the decisions of the Father **in heaven**. The word **again** at the beginning of verse 19 suggests that this verse restates the principle of verse 18. The **two or three** mentioned in verse 20 are thus the two or three witnesses first mentioned in verse 16. Christ is present with His disciples when they gather and seek His leadership about troubling behavior among disciples. He will answer their prayer for the sinning believer's restoration.

18:21-22 Although forgiving someone only **seven times** seems stingy, this standard was generous considering the fact that some rabbis required their students to forgive offenders only three times. Interpreters dispute whether Jesus demanded forgiving one's **brother** 77 times or 490 times (70 times 7), but Jesus' point was that forgiveness should be unlimited when true repentance is present.

18:23-27 In Jewish parables, a king symbolizes God and to **settle accounts** symbolizes divine judgment. The **10,000 talents** was equivalent to a billion day's worth of peasant wages. This was more money than was circulating in all

aphiemi

Greek Pronunciation	[ah FEE ay mee]
HCSB Translation	forgive
Uses in Matthew	47 (Mk, 34; Lk, 31; Jn, 15)
Uses in the NT	143
Focus Passage	Matthew 18:27

Aphiemi exhibits a broad range of nuances in the NT. It can mean to *send away/dismiss* (Mt 13:36) and in a legal sense *to leave/divorce* (1Co 7:11-13). It may also mean *to leave/depart* (Mk 1:20,31) or *to tolerate* (Rv 2:20). Another important meaning is *to pardon/forgive*. In this sense, *aphiemi* may describe the *cancellation* of a loan or debt (Mt 18:27,32), but it more commonly means *to forgive* sins (Mt 6:12,14-15; Mk 2:5,7,9-10; 3:28; Lk 7:47-49; Jn 20:23; Rm 4:7). The related noun *aphesis* almost always refers to God's *forgiveness* of human sins. The resurrected Lord told the disciples that this *forgiveness* would be preached in His name, and the apostles were the first to do exactly that (Ac 2:38; 5:31; 10:43; 13:38; 26:18). Paul employed *aphiemi* and *aphesis* to describe the *cancellation* of sin's infinite debt to God (Rm 4:7; Eph 1:7; Col 1:14).

Church Discipline

Mark Dever

Jesus Christ founded and purchased the church with His blood (Ac 20:28), and He builds it upon acknowledgment and faith in Him as Messiah (Mt 16:18). This means the church belongs to Jesus and represents Him to the nations. In this light, the purity of the church is vital. Rightly practiced, church discipline helps ensure that purity.

Two Categories of Church Discipline

Two categories of church discipline describe ways a church may teach its members right living and right beliefs.

- *Formative Discipline:* Formative discipline is a preventative measure. It includes the positive, direct teaching of biblical truth through sermons and Sunday school lessons. It also includes modeling godliness and mentoring new believers.
- *Corrective Discipline:* Corrective discipline is used when trouble arises. It can include contradicting, challenging, rebuking, and excommunicating a member for unrepentance or erroneous teachings.

Corrective discipline may seem controversial, but Jesus clearly taught that if a believer continues to sin despite the call to repentance, the church should treat him as if he were "an unbeliever and a tax collector" (Mt 18:17). This exclusion from church membership is generically called "church discipline." It is also called "excommunication" because those under discipline are not permitted to participate in Communion (the Lord's Supper).

Correcting Misconceptions about Church Discipline

Excommunication is the *final* stage of church discipline. It is undertaken only if other corrective measures fail to bring the sinner to repentance. Though painful and traumatic, excommunication is not an unloving act. One of the obligations of love is to not leave someone in their sin. "Better an open reprimand than concealed love. The wounds of a friend are trustworthy, but the kisses of an enemy are excessive" (Pr 27:5-6).

Excommunication does not mean that the person should stop attending church. Except in rare cases, the congregation desires the disciplined sinner to continue attending and sitting under the preaching of God's Word. By this the sinner is confronted by Scripture and his life is observed by the faith community that has disciplined him.

Church discipline need not be permanent. One goal is the repentance of the sinner. Paul rebuked the Corinthian church for not readmitting into membership repentant members whom they had disciplined (2Co 2:6-7). Finally, church discipline is not an infallible assessment of the eternal state of the person disciplined. It is instead a fallible but serious warning about an evident lack of regeneration.

Why Church Discipline Is Important

Church discipline presents to the world and believers a clarifying picture of what it means to follow Christ. It is important to make sinners aware of their sin (e.g., 1Co 5). By confronting persistent sin, the church may reveal hypocrites—both to themselves so that they might repent, and to the church so that the church might distinguish sheep from wolves (see Mt 7).

The practice of church discipline is also an important part of glorifying God, for the church is to reflect God's holy character in a fallen world (1Pt 1:14-16). God is both merciful and holy. To neglect either aspect of His character is to distort His image and lie about Him.

²⁸ "But that slave went out and found one of his fellow slaves who owed him 100 •denarii.^{A,a} He grabbed him, started choking him, and said, 'Pay what you owe!' ²⁹ At this, his fellow slave fell down^B and began begging him, 'Be patient with me, and I will pay you back.' ³⁰ But he wasn't willing. On the contrary, he went and threw him into prison until he could pay what was owed. ³¹ When the other slaves saw what had taken place, they were deeply distressed and went and reported to their master everything that had happened.

³² "Then, after he had summoned him, his master said to him, 'You wicked slave! I forgave you all that debt because you begged me. ³³ Shouldn't you also have had mercy on your fellow slave, as I had mercy on you?'^b ³⁴ And his master got angry and handed him over to the jailers to be tortured until he could pay everything that was owed. ³⁵ So My heavenly Father will also do to you if each of you does not forgive his brother^C from his^D heart."^c

The Question of Divorce

19 When Jesus had finished this instruction,^d He departed from Galilee and went to the region of Judea across the Jordan.^e ² Large crowds followed Him, and He healed them there.^f ³ Some •Pharisees approached Him to test Him. They asked, "Is it lawful for a man to divorce his wife on any grounds?"^g

⁴ "Haven't you read," He replied, "that He who created^E them in the beginning **made them male and female**,"^{F,h} ⁵ and He also said:

> "**For this reason a man will leave
> his father and mother
> and be joined to his wife,
> and the two will become one flesh**?^{G,i}

⁶ So they are no longer two, but one flesh. Therefore, what God has joined together, man must not separate."

⁷ "Why then," they asked Him, "did Moses command us to give divorce papers^j and to send her away?"

⁸ He told them, "Moses permitted you to divorce your wives because of the hardness of your hearts. But it was not like that from the beginning. ⁹ And I tell you, whoever divorces his wife, except for sexual immorality, and marries another, commits adultery."^{H,k}

¹⁰ His disciples^l said to Him, "If the relationship of a man with his wife is like this, it's better not to marry!"

¹¹ But He told them, "Not everyone can accept this saying, but only those it has been given^m to. ¹² For there are eunuchs who were born that way from their mother's womb, there are eunuchs who were made by men,

Cross references (center column):
^a18:28 Mt 20:2; 22:19; Mk 6:37; 14:5; Lk 7:41; 10:35; Jn 6:7
^b18:33 Mt 6:12; Eph 4:32; Col 3:13; 1Jn 4:11
^c18:35 Pr 21:13; Mt 6:14; Jms 2:13
^d19:1-9 Mk 10:1-12
^e19:1 Mt 7:28; Lk 9:51; Jn 10:40
^f19:2 Mt 4:23; 12:15
^g19:3 Mt 5:31; Jn 8:6
^h19:4 Gn 2:18; Mt 21:16
ⁱ19:5 Gn 2:24; Mal 2:15; 1Co 6:16; Eph 5:31
^j19:7 Dt 24:1-4; Mt 5:31
^k19:9 Mt 5:32; Lk 16:18
^l19:10 Mt 10:1; 26:56; Mk 3:7; 16:20; Lk 6:13; Jn 12:16
^m19:11 Mt 13:11; 1Co 7:7

A18:28 A small sum compared to 10,000 talents   **B**18:29 Other mss add *at his feet*   **C**18:35 Other mss add *his trespasses*   **D**18:35 Lit *your*   **E**19:4 Other mss read *made*   **F**19:4 Gn 1:27; 5:2   **G**19:5 Gn 2:24   **H**19:9 Other mss add *Also whoever marries a divorced woman commits adultery*; Mt 5:32

---

of Palestine. The talent was the largest unit of currency (equivalent to approximately 6,000 days' worth of wages) and 10,000 is the highest single number that can be expressed in Greek. Thus we see that in this allegory the sum represents the sinner's hopeless debt to God. Selling the debtor, his family, and possessions would hardly begin to recoup this debt. Forgiving such a loan is an astounding act of grace.

18:28-31 One hundred denarii was equivalent to three months of wages. This was negligible compared to the first slave's debt to the king. The contrast between the 10,000 talents and the **100 denarii** shows that the sins of others against us are trivial in comparison to the enormity of our own sins against God. The drudge begged the slave to **be patient** just as the slave had begged before the king, but the drudge was more honest in his pleas and promises since his debt was actually manageable.

18:32-35 The parable's point is now revealed. Since God has shown believers such great mercy by pardoning their sins, they should in turn forgive the sins of others from their heart. The word **jailers** literally means "torturers." The debtor's torture would continue until the debt was paid in full. Since the debt could not possibly be repaid, the torture symbolizes eternal punishment.

19:1 For the importance of **when Jesus had finished**, see "Structure" in the Introduction to Matthew.

19:3 First-century Pharisees who associated themselves with Hillel's school were liberal toward **divorce**. They permitted it for virtually any reason, including such ridiculous grounds as the wife burning her husband's supper or having physical defects like bushy eyebrows.

19:4-6 God ordained marriage both by creation and command. He created two complimentary genders, **male and female**, and commanded one man and one woman to unite in marriage. Since God ordained marriage, human efforts to dissolve it constitute an attack on God's own work.

19:7-9 Although the Pharisees described divorce as something **Moses** commanded, Jesus described it as something Moses merely **permitted**. No provision for divorce was given at **the beginning**. Only after human **hearts** were hardened by sin was divorce permitted. The hearts of Jesus' disciples are transformed (5:8), enabling them to be faithful to their marital covenant. Jesus permitted divorce and remarriage for marital unfaithfulness because sexual infidelity effectively destroys the one-flesh union of marriage.

19:10-12 The disciples rashly concluded that if marriage covenants are permanent, lifelong celibacy is the wisest option. Jesus upheld the value of marriage, but in this case He affirms those who chose celibacy in order to devote themselves wholly to God. **Eunuchs who have made themselves that way** are those who voluntarily abstain from marriage. Jesus did not condone self-emasculation.

and there are eunuchs who have made themselves that way because of the kingdom of heaven. Let anyone accept this who can."

Blessing the Children

[13] Then children were brought to Him so He might put His hands on them and pray. But the disciples rebuked them.[a] [14] Then Jesus said, "Leave the children alone, and don't try to keep them from coming to Me, because the kingdom of heaven is made up of people like this."[A,b] [15] After putting His hands on them, He went on from there.

The Rich Young Ruler

[16] Just then someone came up and asked Him,[c] "Teacher, what good must I do to have eternal life?"[d]
[17] "Why do you ask Me about what is good?"[B] He said to him. "There is only One who is good.[C] If you want to enter into life, keep the commandments."[e]
[18] "Which ones?" he asked Him. Jesus answered:

> **Do not murder;**
> **do not commit adultery;**
> **do not steal;**
> **do not bear false witness;**[f]
> [19] **honor your father and your mother;**
> **and love your neighbor as yourself.**[D,g]

[20] "I have kept all these,"[E] the young man told Him. "What do I still lack?"
[21] "If you want to be perfect,"[F] Jesus said to him, "go, sell your belongings and give to the poor,[h] and you will have treasure in heaven. Then come, follow Me."
[22] When the young man heard that command, he went away grieving, because he had many possessions.

Possessions and the Kingdom

[23] Then Jesus said to His disciples, "'I assure you: It will be hard for a rich person to enter the kingdom of heaven![i] [24] Again I tell you, it is easier for a camel to go through the eye of a needle than for a rich person to enter the kingdom of God."[j]
[25] When the disciples heard this, they were utterly astonished and asked, "Then who can be saved?"
[26] But Jesus looked at them and said, "With men this is impossible, but with God all things are possible."[k]
[27] Then Peter responded to Him, "Look, we have left everything and followed You. So what will there be for us?"
[28] Jesus said to them, "I assure you: In the Messianic Age,[G,l] when the •Son of Man sits on His glorious throne,[m] you who have followed Me will also sit on 12 thrones, judging the 12 tribes of Israel. [29] And everyone who has left houses, brothers or sisters, father or mother,[H] children, or fields because of My name will receive 100 times more and will inherit eternal life.[n] [30] But many who are first will be last, and the last first.[o]

The Parable of the Vineyard Workers

20 "For the kingdom of heaven is like a landowner who went out early in the morning to hire workers for his vineyard.[p] [2] After agreeing with the workers on one •denarius for the day, he sent them into his vineyard. [3] When he went out about nine in the morning,[l] he saw others standing in the marketplace doing nothing. [4] To those men he said, 'You also go to my vineyard, and I'll give you whatever is right.' So off they went. [5] About noon and at three,[j] he went out again and did

---

Cross references (center column):

[a]19:13-15 Mk 10:13-16; Lk 18:15-17
[b]19:14 Mt 18:3; 1Pt 2:2
[c]19:16-29 Mk 10:17-30; Lk 10:25-28; 18:18-30
[d]19:16 Mk 10:17; Jn 12:25; Ac 13:48
[e]19:17 Lv 18:5; Neh 9:29; Ezk 20:21
[f]19:18 Ex 20:13-16; Dt 5:17-20
[g]19:19 Ex 20:12; Lv 19:18; Dt 5:16; Mt 5:43; 22:39; Gl 5:14; Jms 2:8
[h]19:21 Lk 12:33; 16:9; Ac 2:45; 4:35; 1Tm 6:18
[i]19:23 Mt 13:22; Mk 10:23; 1Co 1:26; 1Tm 6:9
[j]19:24 Mt 12:28; Mk 10:25; Lk 18:25
[k]19:26 Gn 18:14; Jb 42:2; Jr 32:17; Zch 8:6; Mk 10:27; Lk 18:27
[l]19:28 Is 65:17; 66:22; 2Pt 3:13; Rv 21:1
[m]Ps 45:6; Mt 25:31; Heb 1:8; Rv 3:21; 22:1,3
[n]19:29 Mt 6:33; Mk 10:29; Lk 18:29
[o]19:30 Mt 20:16; 21:31; Mk 10:31; Lk 13:30
[p]20:1 Mt 13:24; 21:28,33

[A]19:14 Lit heaven is of such ones   [B]19:17 Other mss read Why do you call Me good?   [C]19:17 Other mss read No one is good but One—God   [D]19:18-19 Ex 20:12-16; Lv 19:18; Dt 5:16-20   [E]19:20 Other mss add from my youth   [F]19:21 Or complete   [G]19:28 Lit the regeneration   [H]19:29 Other mss add or wife   [I]20:3 Lit about the third hour   [J]20:5 Lit about the sixth hour and the ninth hour

---

19:13-15 On Jesus' blessing of children, see note at 18:1-5.

19:16-17 This question wrongly assumed that **eternal life** can be earned through good deeds. The statement **there is only One who is good** was intended to shatter the man's deluded notion of attaining a personal goodness that merited salvation.

19:18-22 Jesus' command to **sell your belongings . . . Then come, follow Me** was designed to show the young man that (1) his covetousness defied the spirit of the tenth commandment, (2) his neglect of the poor defied the commandment to love his neighbor, and possibly (3) his love for his possessions surpassed his love for God, thus breaking the commandment against idolatry.

19:24-26 The image of the largest animal in Palestine, a **camel**, passing through a small opening was an oft-used metaphor for impossible events. The salvation of rich people (tempted as they are to trust themselves and their possessions) is possible only by divine miracle.

19:28-29 The **Messianic Age** is literally the "regeneration," the renewal of all creation. This renewal will take place **when the Son of Man sits on His glorious throne**, reigning over the new heaven and new earth. The reign of the 12 disciples over Israel demonstrates that Jesus' disciples constitute the new Israel, the chosen people of God who will benefit from His covenant with Abraham. In a great divine reversal in which the first become last and the last become first, those who made personal sacrifices for Christ will enjoy enormous blessings and those like the rich young ruler, who loved wealth more than Christ, will be punished.

20:1-2 In Jewish parables, authority figures like a wealthy **landowner** typically represent God. A **denarius** was the wage for a day's work in the first century.

the same thing. [6]Then about five[A] he went and found others standing around,[B] and said to them, 'Why have you been standing here all day doing nothing?'

[7]"Because no one hired us,' they said to him.

"'You also go to my vineyard,' he told them.[C] [8]When evening came, the owner of the vineyard told his foreman, 'Call the workers and give them their pay,[a] starting with the last and ending with the first.'[D]

[9]"When those who were hired about five[A] came, they each received one denarius. [10]So when the first ones came, they assumed they would get more, but they also received a denarius each. [11]When they received it, they began to complain to the landowner: [12]'These last men put in one hour, and you made them equal to us who bore the burden of the day and the burning heat!'[b]

[13]"He replied to one of them, 'Friend, I'm doing you no wrong. Didn't you agree with me on a denarius?[c] [14]Take what's yours and go. I want to give this last man the same as I gave you. [15]Don't I have the right to do what I want with my business?[E] Are you jealous[F] because I'm generous?'[G,d]

[16]"So the last will be first, and the first last."[H,e]

The Third Prediction of His Death

[17]While going up to Jerusalem,[f] Jesus took the 12 disciples aside privately and said to them on the way: [18]"Listen! We are going up to Jerusalem. The *Son of Man will be handed over to the *chief priests and *scribes, and they will condemn Him to death.[g] [19]Then they will hand Him over to the Gentiles[h] to be mocked, flogged,[i] and crucified, and He will be resurrected[j] on the third day."

Suffering and Service

[20]Then the mother of Zebedee's sons approached Him with her sons.[i] She knelt down to ask Him for something.[j] [21]"What do you want?" He asked her.

"Promise,"[K] she said to Him, "that these two sons of mine may sit, one on Your right and the other on Your left, in Your kingdom."[k]

[22]But Jesus answered, "You don't know what you're asking. Are you able to drink the cup[L] that I am about to drink?"[M,l]

"We are able," they said to Him.

[23]He told them, "You will indeed drink My cup.[N] But to sit at My right and left is not Mine to give; instead, it belongs to those for whom it has been prepared by My Father."[m] [24]When the 10 disciples heard this, they became indignant with the two brothers. [25]But Jesus

---

Cross references (center column):

[a]20:8 Lv 19:13; Dt 24:15
[b]20:12 Jnh 4:8; Lk 12:55; Jms 1:11
[c]20:13 Mt 22:12; 26:50
[d]20:15 Dt 15:9; Pr 23:6; Mt 6:23; Mk 7:22
[e]20:16 Mt 19:30; Mk 10:31; Lk 13:30
[f]20:17-19 Mk 10:32-34; Lk 18:31-33
[g]20:18 Mt 16:21; 26:66; Jn 19:7
[h]20:19 Mt 27:2; Ac 2:23; 3:13; 4:27; 21:11
[i]20:20-28 Mk 10:35-45; Lk 22:24-27
[j]20:20 Mt 4:21; 8:2
[k]20:21 Mt 16:28; 19:28; 25:31,34; Lk 23:42
[l]20:22 Is 51:22; Jr 49:12; Mk 14:36
[m]20:23 Ac 12:2; Rv 1:9

A[20:6,9] Lit about the eleventh hour   B[20:6] Other mss add doing nothing   C[20:7] Other mss add 'and you'll get whatever is right.'
D[20:8] Lit starting from the last until the first   E[20:15] Lit with what is mine   F[20:15] Lit Is your eye evil; an idiom for jealousy or
stinginess   G[20:15] Lit good   H[20:16] Other mss add For many are called, but few are chosen."   I[20:19] Or scourged   J[20:19] Other
mss read will rise again   K[20:21] Lit Say   L[20:22] Figurative language referring to His coming suffering; Mt 26:39; Jn 18:11
M[20:22] Other mss add and (or) to be baptized with the baptism that I am baptized with?"   N[20:23] Other mss add and be baptized
with the baptism that I am baptized with.

20:8 The words **starting with the last and ending with the first** recall 19:30 and show that this parable is an illustration of the principle taught there.

20:9-12 Since those who worked only **one hour** received a **denarius**, a full day's wage, other workers expected to be paid proportionally—one denarius an hour.

20:13-15 The workers had no right to protest their pay since their wage was the normally accepted sum and since they had agreed to work for this wage in the first place (v. 2). Just as the landowner was free to dispense his wealth as he saw fit, God is free to dispense His grace as He determines. The first workers hired represent people who consider themselves to be of greater importance to God, like the self-righteous man in 19:16-26. The last workers hired represent people like the 12 disciples, who live sacrificially but will be rewarded far more generously than they expect or deserve.

20:16 This repeats 19:30. Since this is repeated immediately before and after the parable of the vineyard workers, it is the key to interpreting the parable. The conjunction at the beginning of 19:30 links this discussion with the one about the unexpected reward of Jesus' disciples.

20:17-19 This is Jesus' fifth prediction of His death in Matthew's Gospel (12:40; 16:21; 17:12,22-23). Each prediction

adds additional details. This time He added that He would be **mocked, flogged, and crucified** at the hands of **Gentiles**.

20:20 **Zebedee's sons** were James and John (see note at 4:18-22).

20:21 Jesus had promised that His disciples would sit on 12 thrones ruling over Israel in the Messianic Age (19:28-29). Now James and John sought, through their mother, to gain prominence over their fellows. Along with Peter, they were members of Jesus' inner circle. Because Jesus rebuked Peter in 16:23, they may have aspired to usurp Peter's position of prominence as well.

20:22-23 The **cup** was a metaphor for suffering (26:39). Jesus' question probed the disciples' willingness to suffer for Him like He would suffer for them. **You will indeed drink My cup** foretells the martyrdom of James (Ac 12:1-2) and John. The parable in Mt 20:1-16 demonstrated that the Father distributes reward as He chooses, not according to merit. Jesus confirmed again the principle of the Father's freedom to determine who will enjoy heaven's greatest blessings.

20:24-28 The competition between the disciples exposed their pride. Jesus called His disciples to the same humble servitude that He modeled. The ultimate expression of His humility was His own sacrificial death that served as a **ran-**

called them over and said, "You know that the rulers of the Gentiles dominate them, and the men of high position exercise power over them. 26It must not be like that among you. On the contrary, whoever wants to become great among you must be your servant,*ª 27and whoever wants to be first among you must be your *slave; 28just as the Son of Man did not come to be served, but to serve,*b and to give His life—a ransom for many."*c

Two Blind Men Healed

29As they were leaving Jericho, a large crowd followed Him.*d 30There were two blind men sitting by the road. When they heard that Jesus was passing by, they cried out, "Lord, have mercy on us, Son of David!" 31The crowd told them to keep quiet, but they cried out all the more, "Lord, have mercy on us, Son of David!"*e

32Jesus stopped, called them, and said, "What do you want Me to do for you?"

33"Lord," they said to Him, "open our eyes!" 34Moved with compassion, Jesus touched their eyes. Immediately they could see, and they followed Him.

The Triumphal Entry

21 When they approached Jerusalem*f and came to Bethphage at the *Mount of

Olives,*g Jesus then sent two disciples, 2telling them, "Go into the village ahead of you. At once you will find a donkey tied there, and a colt with her. Untie them and bring them to Me. 3If anyone says anything to you, you should say that the Lord needs them, and immediately he will send them."

4This took place so that what was spoken through the prophet might be fulfilled:

5　　**Tell Daughter *Zion,**
　　　"Look, your King is coming to you,
　　　gentle, and mounted on a donkey,
　　　even on a colt,
　　　the foal of a beast of burden."*A,h

6The disciples went and did just as Jesus directed them. 7They brought the donkey and the colt; then they laid their robes on them, and He sat on them. 8A very large crowd spread their robes on the road; others were cutting branches from the trees and spreading them on the road. 9Then the crowds who went ahead of Him and those who followed kept shouting:

　　Hosanna **to the Son of David!**
　　He who comes in the name
　　of the Lord is the blessed One!*B
　　Hosanna **in the highest heaven!*i**

Cross references (center column)

ª20:26 Mt 23:11; Mk 9:35
b20:28 Lk 22:27; Jn 13:13-15; 2Co 8:9; Php 2:7
c Mt 26:28; 1Tm 2:6; Ti 2:14; Heb 9:28
d20:29-34 Mk 10:46-52; Lk 18:35-43
e 20:30-31 Mt 9:27; 21:9; 22:42
f21:1-9 Mk 11:1-10; Lk 19:28-38; Jn 12:12-19
g21:1 Zch 14:4; Mt 24:3; 26:30; Lk 19:29,37; 21:37; Jn 8:1; Ac 1:12
h21:5 Is 62:11; Zch 9:9
i21:9 Ps 118:25; Mt 9:27; 23:39; Lk 2:14

A21:5 Is 62:11; Zch 9:9　　B21:9 Ps 118:25-26

---

som for believers. Jesus' words echo the themes of Is 53 which Matthew applied to Jesus in Mt 8:17.

20:29-31 The parallel passage in Mk 10:46-52 refers to only one blind man, not **two blind men**. However, since Mark gives the name of the blind man he mentions, he was probably known to Mark's original readers. Mark did not mention the other blind man because he wished to focus attention only on the man with whom his readers were familiar. On **Son of David**, see note at 1:1.

21:1 The **Mount of Olives** was a large hill on the eastern side of Jerusalem. It was mentioned in Zch 14:4 and ancient rabbis interpreted the text as referring to Messiah (Mt 24:3). **Bethphage** was a small village on the slopes of the hill.

21:2-3 Jesus may have made previous arrangements to use the animals mentioned here, but since Matthew often refers to Jesus' supernatural knowledge (17:27; 20:17-19), it is also possible that Jesus used supernatural knowledge here, in which case He has commandeered the animals in a show of messianic authority.

21:4-5 The formula that Matthew used to introduce the OT quotation affirms that God spoke through the OT prophets. The quotation is a combination of one line from Is 62:11 and excerpts from Zch 9:9. The first text refers to the coming of the Lord while the second refers to the approach of the divine King. Both texts imply Jesus' deity and messiahship.

21:7 The mother **donkey** was led alongside her untamed **colt** in order to calm it. The **robes** of bystanders were draped across the backs of both animals, serving as make-

shift decorative saddles. The words **He sat on them** refer to Jesus sitting atop the robes, not to His riding both animals simultaneously.

21:8 The scattering of **robes** and **branches** in Jesus' path recalls the way in which kings entered their royal cities (2Kg 9:13).

21:9 These words of celebration echo Ps 118:25-26. The people pleaded for salvation from God and blessed God for sending a deliverer who came in the **name of the Lord**.

hosanna

Greek Pronunciation	[hoh sahn NAH]
HCSB Translation	Hosanna
Uses in Matthew	3 (Mk, 2; Jn, 1)
Uses in the NT	6
Focus Passage	Matthew 21:9,15

Hosanna derives from two Hebrew words hoshi'ah na' via Aramaic hosha' na', meaning "Please save!" The phrase first occurs in Psalm 118:25 (similar expressions occur in Ps 12:1; 20:9; 28:9; 60:5; 108:6), and by the time of Jesus it had become a fixed liturgical expression used as a prayer for help, an exclamation of praise, and a shout of celebration. Sometimes, the phrase was interpreted messianically, and in this sense, the Gospels highlight Jesus' triumphal entry by noting the crowds shouting Hosanna (Mt 21:9 = Mk 11:9-10 = Lk 19:38 = Jn 12:13) as well as the cheering of the children in praise of Jesus (Mt 21:15).

[10] When He entered Jerusalem, the whole city was shaken, saying, "Who is this?" [11] And the crowds kept saying, "This is the prophet Jesus[a] from Nazareth in Galilee!"

Cleansing the Temple Complex

[12] Jesus went into the *temple complex[A,b] and drove out all those buying and selling in the temple. He overturned the money changers' tables and the chairs of those selling doves.[c] [13] And He said to them, "It is written, **My house will be called a house of prayer.**[B] But you are making it **a den of thieves!**"[C,d]

Children Praise Jesus

[14] The blind and the lame came to Him in the temple complex, and He healed them. [15] When the *chief priests and the *scribes saw the wonders that He did and the children shouting in the temple complex, "*Hosanna* to the Son of David!" they were indignant [16] and said to Him, "Do You hear what these children are saying?"

"Yes," Jesus told them. "Have you never read:

> **You have prepared[D] praise[e]**
> **from the mouths of children**
> **and nursing infants?"[E]**

[17] Then He left them, went out of the city to Bethany,[f] and spent the night there.

The Barren Fig Tree

[18] Early in the morning,[g] as He was returning to the city, He was hungry. [19] Seeing a lone fig tree by the road, He went up to it and found

nothing on it except leaves. And He said to it, "May no fruit ever come from you again!" At once the fig tree withered.

[20] When the disciples saw it, they were amazed and said, "How did the fig tree wither so quickly?"

[21] Jesus answered them, "I assure you: If you have faith and do not doubt, you will not only do what was done to the fig tree, but even if you tell this mountain, 'Be lifted up and thrown into the sea,' it will be done.[h] [22] And if you believe, you will receive[i] whatever you ask for in prayer."

Messiah's Authority Challenged

[23] When He entered the temple complex,[j] the chief priests and the elders of the people came up to Him as He was teaching and said, "By what authority are You doing these things? Who gave You this authority?"[k]

[24] Jesus answered them, "I will also ask you one question, and if you answer it for Me, then I will tell you by what authority I do these things. [25] Where did John's baptism come from? From heaven or from men?"

They began to argue among themselves, "If we say, 'From heaven,' He will say to us, 'Then why didn't you believe him?'[l] [26] But if we say, 'From men,' we're afraid of the crowd,[m] because everyone thought John was a prophet."[n] [27] So they answered Jesus, "We don't know."

And He said to them, "Neither will I tell you by what authority I do these things.

The Parable of the Two Sons

[28] "But what do you think? A man had two

---

[a] 21:11 Mk 6:15; Lk 7:16; 13:33; 24:19; Jn 1:21; 4:19; 6:14
[b] 21:12-16 Mk 11:15-18; Lk 19:45-47; Jn 2:14-16
[c] 21:12 Ex 30:13; Lv 1:14; 5:7; 12:8; Dt 14:25
[d] 21:13 Jr 7:11
[e] 21:16 Ps 8:2; Mt 11:25; 12:3,5; 19:4; 22:31
[f] 21:17 Mt 26:6; Mk 11:1; Lk 19:29; 24:50; Jn 11:18
[g] 21:18-22 Mk 11:12-14,20-24
[h] 21:21 Mt 17:20; Lk 17:6; 1Co 13:2; Jms 1:6
[i] 21:22 Mt 7:7-8; Jn 11:22
[j] 21:23-27 Mk 11:27-33; Lk 20:1-8
[k] 21:23 Ex 2:14; Mt 26:55; Ac 4:7; 7:27
[l] 21:25 Mt 13:54; Lk 7:30; 15:18,21; Jn 3:27
[m] 21:26 Mt 14:5; 21:46; Mk 11:32; 12:12
[n] Mt 11:9; Mk 6:20

A21:12 Other mss add *of God*   B21:13 Is 56:7   C21:13 Jr 7:11   D21:16 Or *restored*   E21:16 Ps 8:2

21:12 Since Roman currency had idolatrous images stamped on it, the temple accepted only idol-free Tyrian currency. **Money changers** exchanged pagan coins for acceptable currency for a fee. Merchants sold sacrificial animals to those who had traveled long distances. **Doves** were sacrificed by poor pilgrims who could not afford lambs (Lv 5:7). Although the merchants and money changers normally performed their services outside the temple precincts, they occasionally set up shop in the court of the Gentiles.

21:13 Jesus' quote is from Is 56:7 and Jr 7:11. The commotion in the Court made the temple unsuitable as a **house of prayer**. Zechariah 6:12-13 foretold that Messiah would purify the temple. See also Zch 14:21.

21:14 Evidence suggests that first-century Jews extended the demands of Lv 21:16-20 to exclude handicapped persons from entering the temple (2Sm 5:8, LXX). By healing the **blind** and **lame**, Jesus identified Himself as Messiah (Is 35:5-6). By doing so in the **temple complex**, He demonstrated that the handicapped were welcomed by a gracious God.

21:15-16 Both the wonders performed by Jesus and the words spoken by the **children** identified Jesus as the Son of David and Messiah (see notes at v. 14 and 1:1). Jesus argued

from Ps 8:2 that the children's celebration was appropriate and divinely inspired. After all, God had **prepared praise from the mouths of children**.

21:17-19 On His way from **Bethany** to Jerusalem, Jesus passed again through Bethphage, "the House of Unripe Figs" (v. 1). In light of Mc 5:7, the fruitless **fig tree** symbolized Israel's moral barrenness. The cursing of the tree forewarned of God's coming judgment against Jerusalem and its temple.

21:20-22 Jesus' disciples apparently overlooked the symbolic significance of Jesus' miracle and simply focused on the power of His command. Although **this mountain** could be a reference to the Mount of Olives (Zch 14:4) or the temple mount, it probably referred to God's power to do humanly impossible things in response to prayer (1Co 13:2).

21:23-27 John the Baptist said that Messiah would pour out the transforming Spirit on His disciples and punish the unrepentant with fiery judgment (see note at 3:11). John also identified Jesus as the promised Messiah (see note at 3:14). Admission that John was a prophet would require the Jewish leaders to acknowledge Jesus' authority also.

21:28-32 The father here symbolizes God. The **first** son symbolizes notorious sinners like **tax collectors** and **prostitutes**

sons. He went to the first and said, 'My son, go, work in the vineyard today.'[a]

[29] "He answered, 'I don't want to!' Yet later he changed his mind and went. [30] Then the man went to the other and said the same thing.

"'I will, sir,' he answered. But he didn't go. [31] "Which of the two did his father's will?"

"The first," they said.

Jesus said to them, "I assure you: Tax collectors and prostitutes are entering the kingdom of God before you! [32] For John came to you in the way of righteousness,[b] and you didn't believe him. Tax collectors and prostitutes did believe him, but you, when you saw it, didn't even change your minds then and believe him.

The Parable of the Vineyard Owner

[33] "Listen[c] to another parable:[d] There was a man, a landowner, who planted a vineyard, put a fence around it, dug a winepress in it, and built a watchtower.[e] He leased it to tenant farmers and went away.[f] [34] When the grape harvest[A] drew near, he sent his •slaves to the farmers to collect his fruit. [35] But the farmers took his slaves, beat one, killed another, and stoned a third.[g] [36] Again, he sent other slaves, more than the first group, and they did the same to them. [37] Finally, he sent his son to them. 'They will respect my son,' he said.

[38] "But when the tenant farmers saw the son, they said among themselves, 'This is the heir. Come, let's kill him and take his inheritance!'[h] [39] So they seized him, threw him out of the vineyard, and killed him. [40] Therefore, when the owner of the vineyard comes, what will he do to those farmers?"

[41] "He will completely destroy those terrible men," they told Him, "and lease his vineyard to other farmers who will give him his produce at the harvest."[B,i]

[42] Jesus said to them, "Have you never read in the Scriptures:

**The stone that the builders rejected
has become the cornerstone.[C]
This came from the Lord
and is wonderful in our eyes?[D,j]**

[43] Therefore I tell you, the kingdom of God will be taken away from you and given to a nation producing its[E] fruit. [[44] Whoever falls on this stone will be broken to pieces;[k] but on whoever it falls, it will grind him to powder!]"[F]

[45] When the chief priests and the •Pharisees heard His parables,[l] they knew He was speaking about them. [46] Although they were looking for a way to arrest Him, they feared the crowds, because they[G] regarded Him as a prophet.[m]

The Parable of the Wedding Banquet

22 Once more Jesus spoke to them in parables: [2] "The kingdom of heaven[n] may be compared to a king who gave a wedding banquet for his son.[o] [3] He sent out his •slaves to summon those invited to the banquet,[p] but they didn't want to come. [4] Again, he sent out other slaves, and said, 'Tell those who are invited: Look, I've prepared my dinner; my oxen and fattened cattle have been slaughtered, and everything is ready. Come to the wedding banquet.'[q]

[5] "But they paid no attention and went away, one to his own farm, another to his business.

Cross references (center column):

[a] 21:28 Mt 20:1
[b] 21:32 Pr 8:20; Mt 3:8-12; 2Pt 2:21
[c] 21:33-46 Mk 12:1-12; Lk 20:9-19
[d] 21:33 Mt 13:3,34-36; 15:15; 22:1; 24:32
[e] Is 5:1-2; Lk 14:28
[f] Ps 80:8; Sg 8:11-12; Mt 25:14
[g] 21:35 2Ch 24:21; Neh 9:26; Mt 5:12; 23:34,37; Ac 7:52; 1Th 2:15; Heb 11:36-37
[h] 21:38 Ps 2:8; Heb 1:2
[i] 21:41 Mt 8:11; Ac 13:46; 18:6; 28:28
[j] 21:42 Ps 118:22-23; Ac 4:11; Rm 9:33; 1Pt 2:7
[k] 21:44 Is 8:14-15; Rm 9:32-33; 1Pt 2:8
[l] 21:45 Mt 13:3,35; 15:15; 21:33; 22:1; 24:32
[m] 21:46 Mt 26:4; Mk 11:18; Lk 19:47-48; Jn 7:25,30,44
[n] 22:2-14 Lk 14:16-24
[o] 22:2 Mt 13:24; Lk 12:36; Jn 2:2; Rv 19:7
[p] 22:3 Est 6:14; Pr 9:3,5
[q] 22:4 Pr 9:2; Mt 21:36

A 21:34 Lit *the season of fruits* B 21:41 Lit *him the fruits in their seasons* C 21:42 Lit *the head of the corner* D 21:42 Ps 118:22-23 E 21:43 = the kingdom's F 21:44 Other mss omit bracketed text G 21:46 = the crowds

---

who initially rebel against the Father's will but later repent and obey. The other son represents the chief priests and elders who promised obedience to God but never fulfilled their commitment.

21:33-41 The **landowner** represents God; the **vineyard** stands first for Israel (Is 5:1-7), then Jerusalem, then the kingdom; the **tenant farmers** represent the Jewish leaders; the **slaves**, the OT prophets; the **son**, Jesus. Because the Jewish leaders refused to give God the fruits of righteousness that He demanded and because they rejected and murdered His Son, God would destroy them, take His kingdom away from them, and entrust it to Jesus' disciples.

21:42-44 Jesus quoted Ps 118:22-23, the same psalm from which the people described in Mt 21:9 drew their expressions of praise. The image of a **stone** that was **rejected** as worthless by builders but later used as the **cornerstone**—the most important part of the structure—foreshadowed the fact that though Jesus was rejected by the Jewish leaders, He would be vindicated by God and would become the focal point of God's kingdom. Verse 43 interprets and

applies the parable of the vineyard owner: God would take His **kingdom** away from the Jewish leaders and entrust it to Jesus' disciples. Verse 44 alludes to Is 8:14-15 and Dn 2:34,44-45. In Isaiah, the stone is Yahweh over whom the people of Israel stumble, fall, and are broken. By identifying Himself as the stone, Jesus strongly implied His deity. In Daniel, the stone symbolized a powerful kingdom that would destroy all others and endure forever. The OT allusion thus describes Jesus' deity and kingship and the destruction of all who reject Him.

22:1-7 This parable is an allegory of Israel's history. The **king** represents God; the **son**, Jesus; the **slaves**, the prophets and possibly Jesus' disciples; and the **wedding banquet** symbolized the great messianic feast that Jews expected to share with Messiah at the beginning of His rule. Those who rejected, persecuted, and murdered the slaves represent OT Israel and their rejection of the prophets. The destruction of the **city** represents God's judgment on those who refuse to honor His Son. This destruction, like the penalty described in verse 13, portrays eternal punishment but may also hint at the destruction of Jerusalem in A.D. 70.

⁶And the others seized his slaves, treated them outrageously and killed them. ⁷The king^A was enraged, so he sent out his troops, destroyed those murderers, and burned down their city.

⁸"Then he told his slaves, 'The banquet is ready, but those who were invited were not worthy.^a ⁹Therefore go to where the roads exit the city and invite everyone you find to the banquet.'^b ¹⁰So those slaves went out on the roads and gathered everyone they found, both evil and good. The wedding banquet was filled with guests.^B ¹¹But when the king came in to view the guests, he saw a man there who was not dressed for a wedding.^c ¹²So he said to him, 'Friend,^d how did you get in here without wedding clothes?' The man was speechless.

¹³"Then the king told the attendants, 'Tie him up hand and foot,^C and throw him into the outer darkness, where there will be weeping and gnashing of teeth.'

¹⁴"For many are invited, but few are chosen."^e

God and Caesar

¹⁵Then the *Pharisees went and plotted how to trap Him by what He said.^D,f ¹⁶They sent their disciples to Him, with the *Herodians.^g "Teacher," they said, "we know that You are truthful and teach truthfully the way of God. You defer to no one, for You don't show par-

tiality.^E,h ¹⁷Tell us, therefore, what You think. Is it lawful to pay taxes to Caesar^i or not?"

¹⁸But perceiving their malice, Jesus said, "Why are you testing Me, hypocrites? ¹⁹Show Me the coin used for the tax." So they brought Him a *denarius. ²⁰"Whose image and inscription is this?" He asked them.

²¹"Caesar's," they said to Him.

Then He said to them, "Therefore give back to Caesar the things that are Caesar's, and to God the things that are God's."^j ²²When they heard this, they were amazed. So they left Him and went away.

The Sadducees and the Resurrection

²³The same day some *Sadducees,^k who say there is no resurrection, came up to Him and questioned Him:^l ²⁴"Teacher, Moses said, **if a man dies, having no children, his brother is to marry his wife and raise up offspring for his brother.**^F,m ²⁵Now there were seven brothers among us. The first got married and died. Having no offspring, he left his wife to his brother. ²⁶The same happened to the second also, and the third, and so to all seven.^G ²⁷Then last of all the woman died. ²⁸In the resurrection, therefore, whose wife will she be of the seven? For they all had married her."^H

²⁹Jesus answered them, "You are deceived, because you don't know the Scriptures or the power of God. ³⁰For in the resurrection they

Cross references
^a 22:8 Mt 10:11; Ac 13:46
^b 22:9 Ezk 21:21; Ob 14
^c 22:11 Rv 19:8; 22:14
^d 22:12 Mt 20:13; 26:50
^e 22:14 Mt 20:16; Rv 17:14
^f 22:15-22 Mk 12:13-17; Lk 20:20-26
^g 22:16 Mk 2:8; 3:6; 8:15
^h Jn 3:2; Ac 10:34; 13:10; 18:26
^i 22:17 Mk 12:14,16-17; Lk 2:1; 3:1; 20:22,24-25; Jn 19:12,15
^j 22:21 Mt 17:25; Rm 13:7
^k 22:23-32 Mk 12:18-27; Lk 20:27-38
^l 22:23 Mt 3:7; Ac 4:1; 23:8
^m 22:24 Dt 25:5

---

^A 22:7 Other mss read *But when the (that) king heard about it he*   ^B 22:10 Lit *those reclining* (to eat)   ^C 22:13 Other mss add *take him away*   ^D 22:15 Lit *trap Him in a word*   ^E 22:16 Lit *don't look on the face of men*; that is, on the outward appearance   ^F 22:24 Dt 25:5   ^G 22:26 Lit *so until the seven*   ^H 22:28 Lit *all had her*

22:8-12 The **guests** represent Jesus' disciples who are invited into the kingdom despite their unworthiness. The improperly dressed guest represents a false disciple (7:15-23). His presence seems initially to honor the Son, but his refusal to wear festive garments dishonors Him. Similarly, many false disciples appear to honor Jesus by calling Him "Lord," but their lack of true faith and repentance offends Him.

22:13-14 On the guest's punishment, see note at 8:12. Many people are **invited** to God's kingdom, but only those who repent and honor the Son are **chosen** to enter.

22:15-17 The question was a trap. Jesus would have seemed to support the Roman occupation if He expressed approval, and had He disapproved it would have counted as treason against Rome. Matthew mentioned the **Herodians** only here. Little is known about them. They were probably Jews who preferred the rule of the Herodian dynasty over the rule of Roman procurators.

22:18 On **hypocrites**, see note at 6:2-4.

22:19 The parallel texts in Mark and Luke refer to the coin as a **denarius** (see notes at vv. 20-22 and 20:1-2), but Matthew also uses the more precise term "state coin" (Gk *nomisma*). This may reflect his background as a tax collector.

22:20-22 The denarius was a Roman silver coin that bore a portrait of Emperor Tiberius, a Latin superscription that said "Tiberius Caesar, son of the Divine Augustus," an image of a goddess, and superscripted titles of the Roman high priest. Thus the coins were loaded with propaganda for the worship of emperors and pagan gods, and the Jews considered them to be idolatrous. Jesus approved the payment of taxes to Rome. However, He said that coins ultimately belong to the one whose **image** it bears, which implied that all a person is and has belongs to God since we bear God's image and likeness (Gn 1:26-27).

22:23 The **Sadducees** believed that humans cease to exist at the moment of physical death (Ac 23:6-8; Josephus, *Ant.* 18:16; *War* 2.164-65).

22:24-28 The Sadducees appealed to the law of levirate marriage (Dt 25:5) in an attempt to disprove the doctrine of **resurrection**. Although many first-century Jews practiced polygamy, they generally rejected polyandry (a woman having multiple husbands). The Sadducees tried to force Jesus either to reject the doctrine of resurrection or admit the legitimacy of polyandry.

22:29-32 Like **angels**, resurrected people will not marry because they are eternal and have no need to procreate. This shows that the dilemma described by the Sadducees is false. The Sadducees accepted only the Pentateuch (Genesis-Deuteronomy) as Scripture, and so they dismissed resurrection texts like Is 26:19 and Dn 12:2. In order to convince them of the resurrection, Jesus needed to appeal to

neither marry nor are given in marriage but are like^A angels in heaven.^a ³¹Now concerning the resurrection of the dead, haven't you read what was spoken to you by God: ³²**I am the God of Abraham and the God of Isaac and the God of Jacob**?^B,b He^c is not the God of the dead, but of the living."

³³And when the crowds heard this, they were astonished at His teaching.

The Primary Commandments

³⁴When^c the Pharisees heard that He had silenced the Sadducees, they came together. ³⁵And one of them, an expert in the law, asked a question to test Him:^d ³⁶"Teacher, which command in the law is the greatest?"^D

³⁷He said to him, "**Love the Lord your God with all your heart, with all your soul, and with all your mind.**^E,e ³⁸This is the greatest and most important^F command. ³⁹The second is like it: **Love your neighbor as yourself.**^G,f ⁴⁰All the Law and the Prophets depend^H on these two commands."^g

The Question about the Messiah

⁴¹While the Pharisees were together, Jesus questioned them,^h ⁴²"What do you think about the •Messiah? Whose Son is He?"

"David's," they told Him.

⁴³He asked them, "How is it then that David, inspired by the Spirit,^i calls Him 'Lord':

The Lord declared to my Lord,
'Sit at My right hand
until I put Your enemies
under Your feet'?^J,K,j

⁴⁵"If David calls Him 'Lord,' how then can the Messiah be his Son?" ⁴⁶No one was able to answer Him at all,^L and from that day no one dared to question Him anymore.^k

Religious Hypocrites Denounced

23 Then^l Jesus spoke to the crowds and to His disciples:^m ²"The •scribes and the •Pharisees are seated in the chair of Moses.^M,n ³Therefore do whatever they tell you, and observe it. But don't do what they do,^N because they don't practice what they teach.^o ⁴They tie up heavy loads that are hard to carry^o and put them on people's shoulders, but they themselves aren't willing to lift a finger^P to move them.^p ⁵They do everything^Q to be observed by others: They enlarge their phylacteries^R,q and lengthen their •tassels.^S,r ⁶They love the place of honor at banquets, the front seats in the •synagogues,^s ⁷greetings in the marketplaces, and to be called "Rabbi" by people.

⁸"But as for you, do not be called 'Rabbi,' because you have one Teacher,^T and you are all •brothers.^t ⁹Do not call anyone on earth your father, because you have one Father, who is

Cross references (center column)

^a 22:30 Mt 24:38; Lk 17:27
^b 22:32 Ex 3:6; Ac 7:32
^c 22:34-40 Mk 12:28-33; Lk 10:25-28
^d 22:35 Lk 7:30; 10:25; 11:45; 14:3
^e 22:37 Dt 6:5; Lk 10:27
^f 22:39 Lv 19:18; Mt 19:19
^g 22:40 Mt 7:12; Rm 13:8-10; Gl 5:14
^h 22:41-46 Mk 12:35-37; Lk 20:41-44
^i 22:43 2Sm 23:2; Rv 1:10; 4:2
^j 22:44 Ps 110:1; Ac 2:34-35; 1Co 15:25; Heb 1:13; 10:13
^k 22:46 Mk 12:34; Lk 14:6; 20:40
^l 23:1-7 Mk 12:38-39; Lk 20:45-46
^m 23:1 Mt 10:42; 28:19; Lk 14:26; Jn 8:31; 13:35; 15:8; Ac 6:1
^n 23:2 Ezr 7:6,25; Neh 8:4
^o 23:3 Mt 5:20; 15:3-9; Rm 2:17-23
^p 23:4 Lk 11:46; Ac 15:10; Gl 6:13
^q 23:5 Ex 13:9; Dt 6:8; 11:18; Mt 6:1,5,16
^r 23:5 Mt 9:20; 14:36; Mk 6:56; Lk 8:44
^s 23:6 Lk 11:43; 14:7; 20:46
^t 23:7-8 Mk 9:5; 10:51; Jn 1:38,49; 11:8; Jms 3:1

---

^A 22:30 Other mss add *God's*   ^B 22:32 Ex 3:6,15-16   ^C 22:32 Other mss read *God*   ^D 22:36 Lit *is great*   ^E 22:37 Dt 6:5   ^F 22:38 Lit *and first*   ^G 22:39 Lv 19:18   ^H 22:40 Or *hang*   ^I 22:43 Lit *David in Spirit*   ^J 22:44 Other mss read *until I make Your enemies Your footstool*   ^K 22:44 Ps 110:1   ^L 22:46 Lit *answer Him a word*   ^M 23:2 Perhaps a special chair for teaching in synagogues, or a metaphorical phrase for teaching in synagogues, or Moses' authority   ^N 23:3 Lit *do according to their works*   ^O 23:4 Other mss omit *that are hard to carry*   ^P 23:4 Lit *lift with their finger*   ^Q 23:5 Lit *do all their works*   ^R 23:5 Small leather boxes containing OT texts, worn by Jews on their arms and foreheads   ^S 23:5 Other mss add *on their robes*   ^T 23:8 Other mss add *the Messiah*

---

the books they revered. Thus He cited Ex 3:6,15-16, where God spoke to Moses from the burning bush and He referred to the dead patriarchs in a manner that implied that they still existed, i.e., **I am the God of Abraham** rather than "I was the God of Abraham."

22:37 Deuteronomy 6:4-5, known as the Shema, was recited several times daily by faithful Jews.

22:40 Deuteronomy 6:4 and Lv 19:18 summarized the essence of God's demands in Scripture by calling individuals to love God and their fellow man (Mt 5:43-47).

22:41-42 After having been questioned by His opponents repeatedly (vv. 17,23-28,34-36), Jesus entrapped them with a question of His own.

22:42 **Son** was used in ancient Greek and Hebrew to describe any male descendant. Due to several OT prophecies, Messiah was expected to be **David's** descendant (see note at 1:1).

22:43-46 Psalm 110:1 describes Yahweh's command to David's **Lord** (Gk *kurios*; Hb *adon*). "Lord" was a title of authority and/or deity that portrayed **Messiah** as David's divine superior, not just his descendant. Psalm 110:1-4 is quoted more often in the NT than any other OT passage.

23:2 **Chair of Moses** may figuratively identify the scribes

and **Pharisees** as representatives of Moses as they taught the OT. Several centuries after Jesus, seats reserved for teachers in synagogues were regularly called "Moses' seat."

23:3 Jesus did not intend to impose all the teachings of the Pharisees on His disciples. After all, He criticized many of their beliefs. His command meant "Obey the Pharisees' teachings whenever they accurately interpret the Scriptures."

23:4 The Pharisees sought to "build a fence around the law," i.e., establish rules so strict that people would not even come close to breaking God's law (Ac 15:10).

23:5 **Phylacteries** were small boxes containing tiny scrolls of Ex 13:2-16 and Dt 6:4-9; 11:13-21. They were worn by faithful Jewish men on one arm and on the forehead (Dt 6:8; 11:18). **Tassels** made of blue or white threads were worn at the four corners of the outer garment (Nm 15:38-39; Dt 22:12). The Pharisees enlarged the phylacteries and lengthened the tassels in a bid to appear more pious.

23:8-10 Jesus prohibited the use of honorific titles for spiritual leaders that might encourage a sense of superiority in them or detract from the reverence that is properly due the **Father** and **Messiah**.

in heaven.[a] [10] And do not be called masters either, because you have one Master,[A] the •Messiah. [11] The greatest among you will be your servant.[b] [12] Whoever exalts himself will be humbled, and whoever humbles himself will be exalted.[c]

[13] "But woe to you, scribes and Pharisees, hypocrites! You lock up the kingdom of heaven from people. For you don't go in, and you don't allow those entering to go in.[d]

[[14] "Woe to you, scribes and Pharisees, hypocrites! You devour widows' houses and make long prayers just for show.[B] This is why you will receive a harsher punishment.][C]

[15] "Woe to you, scribes and Pharisees, hypocrites! You travel over land and sea to make one •proselyte,[e] and when he becomes one, you make him twice as fit for •hell[D] as you are!

[16] "Woe to you, blind guides,[f] who say, 'Whoever takes an oath by the sanctuary, it means nothing. But whoever takes an oath[g] by the gold of the sanctuary is bound by his oath.'[E] [17] Blind fools![F] For which is greater, the gold or the sanctuary that sanctified the gold? [18] Also, 'Whoever takes an oath by the altar, it means nothing. But whoever takes an oath by the gift that is on it is bound by his oath.'[E] [19] Blind people![G] For which is greater, the gift or the altar that sanctifies the gift?[h] [20] There-

fore, the one who takes an oath by the altar takes an oath by it and by everything on it. [21] The one who takes an oath by the sanctuary takes an oath by it and by Him who dwells[i] in it. [22] And the one who takes an oath by heaven takes an oath by God's throne[j] and by Him who sits on it.[k]

[23] "Woe to you, scribes and Pharisees, hypocrites! You pay a tenth of[H] mint, dill, and cumin,[i] yet you have neglected the more important matters of the law—justice,[i] mercy, and faith. These things should have been done without neglecting the others. [24] Blind guides![m] You strain out a gnat, yet gulp down a camel!

[25] "Woe to you, scribes and Pharisees, hypocrites! You •clean the outside of the cup and dish, but inside they are full of greed[J] and self-indulgence![n] [26] Blind Pharisee! First clean the inside of the cup,[K] so the outside of it[L] may also become clean.

[27] "Woe to you, scribes and Pharisees, hypocrites! You are like whitewashed tombs,[o] which appear beautiful on the outside, but inside are full of dead men's bones and every impurity. [28] In the same way, on the outside you seem righteous to people, but inside you are full of hypocrisy and lawlessness.

[29] "Woe to you, scribes and Pharisees, hypocrites! You build the tombs of the prophets

---

[a] 23:9 Mal 1:6; Mt 6:9; 7:11
[b] 23:11 Mt 20:26-27; Mk 9:35; 3Jn 9
[c] 23:12 Pr 29:23; Ezk 21:26; Lk 14:11; 18:14; Jms 4:6,10; 1Pt 5:5-6
[d] 23:13 Mt 23:15,23,25; Lk 11:52
[e] 23:15 Ac 2:11; 6:5; 13:43
[f] 23:16 Mt 15:14; 23:24; Ac 1:16; Rm 2:19
[g] Lv 19:12; Nm 30:2; Dt 23:21; Mt 5:33; 14:7; 26:63,72
[h] 23:19 Ex 29:37; 30:29
[i] 23:21 1Kg 8:13; 2Ch 6:2; Ps 26:8; 132:14
[j] 23:22 Ex 17:16; Ps 11:4; Mt 5:34; Heb 8:1
[k] Ps 47:8; Mt 19:28; Rv 4:2
[l] 23:23 1Sm 15:22; Ps 33:5; Jr 5:1; Mc 6:8; Zch 7:9; Lk 11:42
[m] 23:24 Mt 15:14; 23:16
[n] 23:25 Mk 7:4; Lk 11:39
[o] 23:27 Lk 11:44; Ac 23:3

[A] 23:10 Or Teacher   [B] 23:14 Or prayers with false motivation   [C] 23:14 Other mss omit bracketed text   [D] 23:15 Lit twice the son of gehenna   [E] 23:16,18 Lit is obligated   [F] 23:17 Lit Fools and blind   [G] 23:19 Other mss read Fools and blind   [H] 23:23 Or You tithe   [I] 23:23 A plant whose seeds are used as a seasoning   [J] 23:25 Or full of violence   [K] 23:26 Other mss add and dish   [L] 23:26 Other mss read of them

---

23:13 **Woe** was a term used by OT prophets to express condemnation (Is 5:8-23; Hab 2:6-9). Pharisees prevented people from **entering** the **kingdom of heaven** by discouraging them from following Jesus.

23:16-22 First-century laws declared some oaths to be valid and others invalid. The system was corrupt insomuch as it allowed loopholes that justified lies and manipulated naive or credulous people. See note at 5:33-37.

23:23-24 In accordance with Lv 27:30; Nm 18:21-32; and Dt 14:22, the scribes and Pharisees meticulously tithed a **tenth** of everything, including their tiny garden herbs. Jesus did not discourage this since **these things should have been done**. However, He rebuked the Jewish leaders for obsessing with ritual matters while overlooking the true essence of religion as described in Mc 6:8. Like those who strain a **gnat** out of their drink but leave a **camel** floating in it, they were obsessed with tiny matters but overlooked important ones.

23:25-26 Some first-century rabbis debated whether cleansing the **outside** or **inside** of vessels was more important. Jesus cited this to illustrate their obsession with ritual purity and their neglect of inner spiritual purity.

23:27-28 First-century Jews **whitewashed** the **tombs** in Jerusalem to alert people to their location so they would not unintentionally draw too near and thus defile themselves. The whitewash also beautified the tombs. Despite this outer beauty, Jewish purity laws regarded the inside of tombs as

defiled. Jesus said this resembled individuals whose outer piety (the whitewash) masks an inner corruption (spiritual defilement).

hupokrites

Greek Pronunciation	[hoo pah krih TAYSS]
HCSB Translation	hypocrite
Uses in Matthew	13 (Mk, 1; Lk, 3)
Uses in the NT	17
Focus Passage	Matthew 23:13-36

Hupokrites (hypocrite) is derived from the verb hupokrinomai meaning to interpret or play the part. Hupokrinomai was often used to describe what actors accomplished on stage, and hupokrites referred to an actor, as one who interprets the words of a poet and plays a part. Though not originally a negative term, hupokrites metaphorically assumed a negative sense in Jewish and Christian literature, referring to one who pretends or who misinterprets truth and subsequently plays a part contrary to reality (e.g., the Jewish leaders of Jesus' day misinterpreted the relationship between written Law and interpretive tradition and subsequently played the part of properly interpreting the Law when they were actually not properly interpreting it). Jesus uses hupokrites 17 times to denounce the Jewish leaders' fraudulent claim to spirituality. Perhaps His most scorching declamation comes in Matthew 23:13-36.

and decorate the monuments of the righteous, [30] and you say, 'If we had lived in the days of our fathers, we wouldn't have taken part with them in shedding the prophets' blood.'[A] [31] You, therefore, testify against yourselves that you are sons of those who murdered the prophets. [32] Fill up, then, the measure of your fathers' sins![B,a]

[33] "Snakes! Brood of vipers! How can you escape being condemned to hell?[C,b] [34] This is why I am sending you prophets,[c] sages, and scribes. Some of them you will kill and crucify, and some of them you will flog in your synagogues[d] and hound from town to town. [35] So all the righteous blood shed on the earth will be charged to you,[D] from the blood of righteous Abel to the blood of Zechariah,[e] son of Berechiah, whom you murdered between the sanctuary and the altar.[f] [36] I assure you: All these things will come on this generation![g]

Jesus' Lamentation over Jerusalem

[37] "Jerusalem, Jerusalem![h] She who kills the prophets and stones those who are sent to her. How often I wanted to gather your children together, as a hen gathers her chicks[E] under her wings, yet you were not willing![i] [38] See, your house is left to you desolate.[j] [39] For I tell you, you will never see Me again until you say, **'He who comes in the name of the Lord is the blessed One'!**"[F,k]

Reference column

a23:31-32 Gn 15:16; Ac 7:51; 1Th 2:15-16
b23:33 Mt 3:7; 5:22; 12:34
c23:34 Ac 13:1; 1Co 12:28
d2Ch 36:15-16; Mt 10:17; Ac 22:19
e23:35 2Ch 24:21; Zch 1:1
fGn 4:8; Heb 11:4; 1Jn 3:12; Rv 18:24
g23:36 Mt 10:23; 16:28; 24:34
h23:37-39 Lk 13:34-35
i23:37 Dt 32:11-12; Ru 2:12; Mt 5:12
j23:38 1Kg 9:7; Is 64:11; Jr 12:7; 22:5
k23:39 Ps 118:26; Mt 21:9
l24:1-51 Mk 13:1-37; Lk 21:5-36
m24:1 Mt 9:10; Mk 10:10; Lk 6:1; Jn 6:3; 12:16
n24:3 Mt 21:1; 24:27,37,39
o24:4 Jr 29:8; Eph 5:6; Col 2:8; 2Th 2:3
p24:5 Mt 1:17; Eph 5:2
q24:7 Ac 11:28; Rv 6:8
r2Ch 15:6; Is 19:2
s24:8-20 Lk 21:12-24
t24:9 Mt 10:17,22; Jn 16:2

Destruction of the Temple Predicted

24 As Jesus left and was going out of the temple complex,[l] His disciples[m] came up and called His attention to the temple buildings. [2] Then He replied to them, "Don't you see all these things? I assure you: Not one stone will be left here on another that will not be thrown down!"

Signs of the End of the Age

[3] While He was sitting on the Mount of Olives, the disciples approached Him privately and said, "Tell us, when will these things happen? And what is the sign of Your coming and of the end of the age?"[n]

[4] Then Jesus replied to them: "Watch out that no one deceives[o] you. [5] For many will come in My name, saying, 'I am the Messiah,' and they will deceive many.[p] [6] You are going to hear of wars and rumors of wars. See that you are not alarmed, because these things must take place, but the end is not yet. [7] For nation will rise up against nation, and kingdom against kingdom. There will be famines[G,q] and earthquakes in various places.[r] [8] All these events are the beginning of birth pains.[s]

Persecutions Predicted

[9] "Then they will hand you over for persecution,[H] and they will kill you. You will be hated by all nations because of My name.[t] [10] Then many will take offense, betray one another and hate one another. [11] Many false

---

A23:30 Lit *have been partakers with them in the blood of the prophets*   B23:32 Lit *the measure of your fathers*   C23:33 Lit *escape from the judgment of gehenna*   D23:35 Lit *will come on you*   E23:37 Or *as a mother bird gathers her young*   F23:39 Ps 118:26   G24:7 Other mss add *epidemics*   H24:9 Or *tribulation, or distress*

23:32 By persecuting God's representatives (John the Baptist, Jesus, the disciples), the scribes and Pharisees continued the rebellion of their ancestors and probed the limits of God's patience.

23:33 On **snakes** and **brood of vipers**, see note at 3:7-9.

23:35-36 Jesus, in an apparent allusion to the coming destruction of the temple in A.D. 70, warned that His generation would suffer God's wrath for its abuse of the **righteous**. Abel's murder is recorded in Genesis 4, while Zechariah's is recorded in 2Ch 24:20-21. Second Chronicles was the final book of the OT in the typical order of the Hebrew Bible, so the martyrdoms of **Abel** and **Zechariah** were recorded in the first and last books of the Hebrew OT. Thus Jesus apparently meant to cite the whole span of martyrdom in the OT. Some interpreters argue that He confused the Zechariah of 2 Chronicles (identified as the son of Jehoiada) with the prophet Zechariah (described as the son of Berechiah in Zch 1:1). However, the Hebrew phrase **son of** was used to identify sons, grandsons, and even remote descendants. Consequently, Jesus probably identified the Zechariah of 2 Chronicles by an earlier or later ancestor. It is not unreasonable to suggest that both Zechariahs had ancestors ("fathers") named **Berechiah**.

23:37 In Ps 17:8; 91:4; and Is 31:5, the image of a **hen** sheltering her **chicks** portrayed Yahweh's protection of Israel. By rejecting Jesus, Jerusalem rejected God's protection. The image implies Jesus' identity as Yahweh.

23:38-39 The word **desolate** means "abandoned." It denotes God's abandonment of His **house**, the temple. This occurred when Jesus departed from the temple with the words **you will never see Me again. Is the blessed one** quotes Ps 118:26 and echoes the jubilant greeting that welcomed Jesus into Jerusalem in Mt 21:9 before His rejection by the people.

24:2 This remarkable prophecy must have stunned the disciples. Josephus (*Ant.* 15.392) stated that the temple was constructed of blocks of white limestone that measured 37.5 feet long, 12 feet high, and 18 feet wide. Some of the remaining blocks weigh nearly 400 tons.

24:3 The separate questions imply that Jesus' disciples understood that the destruction of the temple and His second coming would be separate events.

24:4-14 These verses describe events that will happen between Jesus' prophecy and the end of the age.

prophets[a] will rise up and deceive many. [12]Because lawlessness[b] will multiply, the love of many will grow cold. [13]But the one who endures to the end will be delivered.[A] [14]This good news of the kingdom will be proclaimed in all the world[B] as a testimony to all nations.[c] And then the end will come.[d]

The Great Tribulation

[15]"So when you see **the abomination that causes desolation**,[C,D] spoken of by the prophet Daniel,[e] standing in the holy place"[f] (let the reader understand[E]), [16]"then those in Judea

must flee to the mountains! [17]A man on the housetop[F] must not come down to get things out of his house.[g] [18]And a man in the field must not go back to get his clothes. [19]Woe to pregnant women and nursing mothers in those days! [20]Pray that your escape may not be in winter or on a Sabbath. [21]For at that time there will be great tribulation,[h] the kind that hasn't taken place from the beginning of the world until now and never will again! [22]Unless those days were limited, no one

[a] 24:11 Is 44:25; Mt 7:15; 24:24; Mk 13:22; Lk 6:26; Ac 13:6; 2Pt 2:1; 1Jn 4:1
[b] 24:12 Mt 13:41; 2Th 2:3
[c] 24:14 Mt 4:23; Rm 10:18; Col 1:6,23; 1Th 1:8
[d] Lk 2:1; 4:5; Ac 11:28; 17:6; Rv 3:10; 16:14
[e] 24:15 Dn 9:27; 11:31; 12:11; Mk 13:14; Lk 21:20
[f] Ac 6:13; 21:28
[g] 24:17 1Sm 9:25; Mt 10:27; Lk 5:19; 12:3; 17:31; Ac 10:9
[h] 24:21 Dn 12:1; Jl 2:2; Mt 24:29; Rv 7:14

A 24:13 Or *be saved*   B 24:14 Or *in all the inhabited earth*   C 24:15 Or *abomination of desolation*, or *desolating sacrilege*   D 24:15 Dn 9:27   E 24:15 These are, most likely, Matthew's words to his readers.   F 24:17 Or *roof*

24:15-22 These verses probably describe events related to the destruction of Jerusalem that occurred in A.D. 70. However, Mt 24:29 closely associates this tribulation period with the second coming of Jesus. This implies that these events closely parallel things that will occur immediately before Jesus' return (2Th 2:3-4). The entire period ranging

TITUS'S CAMPAIGNS

Titus assembles two legions to attack Jerusalem

DECAPOLIS

35 E

MEDITERRANEAN SEA

Caesarea Maritima

Scythopolis (Beth-shan)

Pella

SAMARIA

Sebaste (Samaria)

Gerasa (Jerash)

Mt. Ebal

Neapolis (Shechem)

Jordan R.

Jabbok R.

Mt. Gerizim

Coreae

Antipatris (Aphek)

Acrabeta

Alexandrium

Joppa

Yarkon R.

Thamna

Bethel

Gadara

PEREA

32 N

Lydda

Gophna

Legions from Jericho and Emmaus join Titus

Esbus (Heshbon)

JUDEA

Jericho

Azotus (Ashdod)

Jamnia

Emmaus

Gibeah

Cyprus

Mt. Nebo

Roman troops torch the temple August 28, A.D. 70 and gain complete control by late September

Jerusalem

Qumran

Hyrcania

Herodium

Ascalon (Ashkelon)

Capharabis

Caphartobas

Anthedon

Betogabris

Hebron

Judean Wilderness

DEAD SEA

Machaerus

Gaza

Caparorsa

En-gedi

NABATEA

IDUMEA

Arnon R.

LEGEND
- • City
- ○ City (uncertain location)
- ▲ Mountain peak
- ✿ Siege
- ← Titus' campaign
- ◄ Roman pressure
- □ Area of Jewish revolt

Masada falls A.D. 73–74

Masada

36 E

35 E

0   10   20   30   40 Miles
0   10   20   30   40 Kilometers

As Jesus left the temple He prophesied, "Not one stone will be left here on another that will not be thrown down!" (24:2). This part of Jesus' prophecy was fulfilled in A.D. 70 when the Roman general (and later emperor) Titus led in the destruction of Jerusalem.

would[A] survive.[B] But those days will be limited because of the elect.[a]

[23]"If anyone tells you then, 'Look, here is the Messiah!'[b] or, 'Over here!' do not believe it![c] [24]False messiahs[c] and false prophets will arise and perform great signs and wonders to lead astray,[d] if possible, even the elect. [25]Take note: I have told you in advance. [26]So if they tell you, 'Look, He's in the wilderness!' don't go out; 'Look, He's in the inner rooms!' do not believe it. [27]For as the lightning comes from the east and flashes as far as the west, so will be the coming of the •Son of Man.[e] [28]Wherever the carcass is, there the vultures[D] will gather.[f]

The Coming of the Son of Man

[29]"Immediately after the tribulation[g] of those days:

The sun will be darkened,
and the moon will not shed its light;
the stars will fall from the sky,
and the celestial powers will be shaken.

[30]"Then the sign of the Son of Man will appear in the sky, and then all the peoples of the earth[E] will mourn;[F] and they will see the Son of Man coming on the clouds of heaven with power and great glory.[h] [31]He will send out His angels with a loud trumpet,[i] and they will gather His elect from the four winds,[j] from one end of the sky to the other.

The Parable of the Fig Tree

[32]"Now learn this parable[k] from the fig tree: As soon as its branch becomes tender and sprouts leaves, you know that summer is near. [33]In the same way, when you see all these things, recognize[G] that He[H] is near—at the door![l] [34]I assure you: This generation will certainly not pass away until all these things take place.[m] [35]Heaven and earth will pass away,[n] but My words will never pass away.[o]

No One Knows the Day or Hour

[36]"Now concerning that day and hour no one knows—neither the angels in heaven, nor the Son[I]—except the Father only.[p] [37]As the days of Noah were, so the coming of the Son of Man will be. [38]For in those days before the flood they were eating and drinking, marrying and giving in marriage, until the day Noah boarded the ark.[q] [39]They didn't know[J] until the flood came and swept them all away. So this is the way the coming of the Son of Man will be: [40]Then two men will be in the

---

[a]24:22 Mt 22:14; 24:24,31; Mk 13:20,22,27; 1Tm 5:21; 2Tm 2:10; Rv 17:14
[b]24:23 Lk 17:3; 21:28
[c]Mk 11:24; Jn 6:64
[d]24:24 Dt 13:1-3; Mt 24:11; Ac 8:9; 2Th 2:9-11; Rv 13:13-14; 16:14; 19:20
[e]24:27 Zch 9:14; Mt 8:20; 24:3,37,39; Lk 17:24
[f]24:28 Jb 39:30; Lk 17:37
[g]24:29 Is 13:10; 24:23; Ezk 32:7; Jl 2:10,31; 3:15; Zph 1:15; Rv 6:12-13
[h]24:30 Dn 7:13; Zch 12:12; Mt 24:3; Rv 1:7
[i]24:31 Is 27:13; 1Co 15:52; 1Th 4:16; Rv 8:2; 11:15
[j]Dn 7:2; Zch 2:6; Rv 7:1
[k]24:32 Mt 13:3,34-36; 15:15; 21:33,45; 22:1
[l]24:33 Jms 5:9; Rv 3:20
[m]24:34 Mt 10:23; 16:28; 23:36
[n]24:35 Ps 102:26; Is 51:6; Mt 5:18; Heb 12:27; 2Pt 3:10
[o]Ps 119:89; Is 40:8; Mk 13:31; Lk 21:33; 1Pt 1:23,25
[p]24:36 Zch 14:7; Mk 13:32; Ac 1:7; 1Th 5:1-2
[q]24:37-38 Gn 6:5; 7:6-23; Mt 22:30; Lk 17:26

[A]24:22 Lit short, all flesh would not   [B]24:22 Or be saved or delivered   [C]24:24 Or False christs   [D]24:28 Or eagles   [E]24:30 Or all the tribes of the land   [F]24:30 Lit will beat; that is, beat their breasts   [G]24:33 Or things, you know   [H]24:33 Or it; that is, summer   [I]24:36 Other mss omit nor the Son   [J]24:39 They didn't know the day and hour of the coming judgment.

---

from the destruction of the temple to the events preceding Christ's return may be described as a period of **great tribulation** for Christ's followers. The **abomination that causes desolation** is an idolatrous object that will desecrate the Jerusalem temple as foretold in Dn 9:27. Though Josephus identified it as the shedding of priestly blood in the sanctuary several years before the destruction of the temple (*War* 4.147-201; 4.343; 5.17-18; cp. Mt 23:29-36), Jesus' description of the abomination as **standing** in the temple implies that it is an object, not an event.

24:24 God protects and preserves the faith of the **elect**. Those who truly believe in Jesus as God, Savior, and King will persevere in their faith to the end.

24:27 The second coming will be visible to everyone on earth.

24:28 Some interpreters believe this verse refers to eagles that were emblazoned on the standards carried by Roman soldiers as they destroyed Jerusalem, but it is probably a reference to birds of carrion descending upon the corpses of those destroyed during this judgment (Dt 28:26; Jb 39:30; Ezk 39:17-20).

24:29 Jesus' words combine allusions to Is 13:10, which describes the fall of Babylon, and Is 34:4, which describes the judgment of Edom and the nations. In the OT context, the words were metaphorical. Jesus may also have used the words in a symbolic portrayal of the judgment and destruction of people and nations who opposed His rule.

24:30 The **sign of the Son of Man** may resemble military

banners that signal the onset of battle, calling all who belong to Christ to gather around Him (Is 13:2-4). Such a sign would parallel the function of the trumpet in Mt 24:31. However, since Is 11:10 figuratively identified Messiah Himself as a military banner, His own appearance may be the sign about which He spoke. Matthew 24:30b is an allusion to Zch 12:10-14 in which the Jews will mourn for the One they pierced (crucified). The reference to the **Son of Man coming on the clouds** is an allusion to Dn 7:13. It identifies Jesus as the King who will descend from heaven to establish an eternal reign over the earth.

24:31 This verse combines Dt 30:4; Is 27:13, and Zch 2:6 (LXX). The Messiah will gather the elect, His followers both living and dead, from heaven and earth. The angels are **His** **angels** because He has absolute authority over them (see note at 4:10-11).

24:33-34 All these things refers to the tribulation that will precede Jesus' return, not the second coming itself. **He is near** means that Messiah is prepared to return at any moment, not that He must return immediately after these events unfold. All of these events occurred within Jesus' **generation**, particularly in the circumstances surrounding the fall of Jerusalem in A.D. 70. Thus Christ's followers must always be ready for His return.

24:35 Jesus' **words** have the same reliability and enduring quality as the OT itself (5:18).

24:36-44 Close observation of world events will not enable

field: one will be taken and one left. [41] Two women will be grinding at the mill: one will be taken and one left.[a] [42] Therefore be alert, since you don't know what day[A] your Lord is coming.[b] [43] But know this: If the homeowner had known what time[B] the thief was coming, he would have stayed alert and not let his house be broken into.[c] [44] This is why you also must be ready, because the Son of Man is coming at an hour you do not expect.[d]

Faithful Service to the Messiah

[45] "Who then is a faithful and sensible *slave,[e] whom his master has put in charge of his household, to give them food at the proper time?[f] [46] That slave whose master finds him working[g] when he comes will be rewarded. [47] I assure you: He will put him in charge of all his possessions. [48] But if that wicked slave says in his heart, 'My master is delayed,' [49] and starts to beat his fellow slaves, and eats and drinks with drunkards,[h] [50] that slave's master will come on a day he does not expect and at an hour he does not know. [51] He will cut him to pieces[c] and assign him a place with the hypocrites. In that place there will be weeping and gnashing of teeth.

The Parable of the 10 Virgins

25 "Then the kingdom of heaven will be like 10 virgins[D] who took their lamps and went out to meet the groom.[i] [2] Five of them were foolish and five were sensible.[j] [3] When the foolish took their lamps, they didn't take olive oil with them. [4] But the sensible ones took oil in their flasks with their lamps. [5] Since the groom was delayed, they all became drowsy and fell asleep.

[6] "In the middle of the night there was a shout: 'Here's the groom! Come out to meet him.'

a24:41 Ex 11:5; Is 47:2; Lk 17:35
b24:42 Mt 25:13; Lk 12:40; 21:36
c24:43 Lk 12:39; 1Th 5:2; Rv 3:3
d24:44 Mt 25:10; 1Th 5:6
e24:45-51 Lk 12:42-46
f24:45 Mt 7:24; 10:16; 25:2,21
g24:46 Jn 13:17; Rv 16:15
h24:49 Ac 2:15; 1Co 11:21; 1Th 5:7; Rv 17:6
i25:1 Mt 13:24; Ac 20:8; Rv 4:5; 19:7; 21:2,9
j25:2 Mt 7:24; 10:16; 24:45
k25:10 Mt 22:2; Lk 13:25
l25:14-30 Lk 19:12-27
m25:15 Mt 18:24; Lk 19:13; Rm 12:6; 1Co 12:11; Eph 4:7

[7] "Then all those virgins got up and trimmed their lamps. [8] But the foolish ones said to the sensible ones, 'Give us some of your oil, because our lamps are going out.'

[9] "The sensible ones answered, 'No, there won't be enough for us and for you. Go instead to those who sell, and buy oil for yourselves.'

[10] "When they had gone to buy some, the groom arrived. Then those who were ready went in with him to the wedding banquet, and the door was shut.[k]

[11] "Later the rest of the virgins also came and said, 'Master, master, open up for us!'

[12] "But he replied, "I assure you: I do not know you!'

[13] "Therefore be alert, because you don't know either the day or the hour.[E]

The Parable of the Talents

[14] "For it is just like a man going on a journey.[l] He called his own *slaves and turned over his possessions to them. [15] To one he gave five talents;[F] to another, two; and to another, one—to each according to his own ability. Then he went on a journey.[m] [16] Immediately the man who had received five talents went, put them to work, and earned five more. [17] In the same way the man with two earned two more. [18] But the man who had received one talent went off, dug a hole in the ground, and hid his master's money.

[19] "After a long time the master of those slaves came and settled accounts with them. [20] The man who had received five talents approached, presented five more talents, and said, 'Master, you gave me five talents. Look, I've earned five more talents.'

[21] "His master said to him, 'Well done, good and faithful slave! You were faithful over a

---

A24:42 Other mss read *hour*; = time   B24:43 Lit *watch*; a division of the night in ancient times   C24:51 Lit *him in two*   D25:1 Or *bridesmaids*   E25:13 Other mss add *in which the Son of Man is coming.*   F25:15 Worth a very large sum of money; a talent = 6,000 *denarii

---

us to predict the time of Christ's return. Rather, Jesus' followers should live in a state of constant preparation. The words **one will be taken and one left** likely refers to the fact that some will be gathered by Messiah at His return while others will be left behind. On **Son of Man**, see note at 8:20.

24:45-51 We must not take advantage of the delay in Messiah's return by pursuing sinful pleasures. Rather, we must live each day as if it were the day of His return.

25:1-5 Whereas the previous parable warned against postponing preparation for Messiah's coming, this one warns against making preparations that are inadequate for the lengthy delay that precedes His second coming.

25:6-9 The **virgins** least expected the groom to arrive in the **middle of the night**. This signifies the suddenness of Jesus'

return (24:36,42). The **shout** announcing the groom's arrival parallels the trumpet blast in 24:31.

25:10-13 The foolish **virgins** represent those who fail to persevere by waiting for Jesus' return with constant vigilance. The cry **Master, master** (Gk *kurie, kurie*) is identical to that of the false disciples in 7:21. **I do not know you** echoes 7:23 and expresses exclusion from Messiah's kingdom. The parable does not describe a true disciple who loses his salvation, but a false one whose commitment to Jesus was deficient from the start. By portraying Himself as a spiritual bridegroom, Jesus implied His deity. God was often portrayed as a bridegroom in the OT (Is 54:4-6; Ezk 16:7-34; Hs 2:19).

25:14-30 The **man** on the long **journey** symbolizes Jesus and the lengthy delay that will precede His second com-

few things; I will put you in charge of many things. Share your master's joy!'[a]

[22] "Then the man with two talents also approached. He said, 'Master, you gave me two talents. Look, I've earned two more talents.'

[23] "His master said to him, 'Well done, good and faithful slave! You were faithful over a few things; I will put you in charge of many things. Share your master's joy!'

[24] "Then the man who had received one talent also approached and said, 'Master, I know you. You're a difficult man, reaping where you haven't sown and gathering where you haven't scattered seed.[b] [25] So I was afraid and went off and hid your talent in the ground. Look, you have what is yours.'

[26] "But his master replied to him, 'You evil, lazy slave![c] If you knew that I reap where I haven't sown and gather where I haven't scattered, [27] then[A] you should have deposited my money with the bankers. And when I returned I would have received my money[B] back with interest.

[28] "'So take the talent from him and give it to the one who has 10 talents. [29] For to everyone who has, more will be given, and he will have more than enough. But from the one who does not have, even what he has will be taken away from him.[d] [30] And throw this good-for-nothing slave into the outer darkness.[e] In that place there will be weeping and gnashing of teeth.'

The Sheep and the Goats

[31] "When the •Son of Man comes in His glory, and all the angels[C,f] with Him, then He will sit on the throne of His glory.[g] [32] All the nations[D,h] will be gathered before Him, and He will separate them one from another, just as a shepherd separates the sheep from the goats.[i] [33] He will put the sheep on His right and the goats on the left. [34] Then the King will say to those on His right, 'Come, you who are blessed by My Father, inherit the kingdom[j] prepared for you from the foundation of the world.[k]

[35] For I was hungry
and you gave Me something to eat;
I was thirsty
and you gave Me something to drink;
I was a stranger and you took Me in;
[36] I was naked and you clothed Me;
I was sick and you took care of Me;
I was in prison and you visited Me.'[l]

[37] "Then the righteous will answer Him, 'Lord, when did we see You hungry and feed You, or thirsty and give You something to drink? [38] When did we see You a stranger and take You in, or without clothes and clothe You? [39] When did we see You sick, or in prison, and visit You?'

[40] "And the King will answer them, 'I assure you: Whatever you did for one of the least of these •brothers of Mine, you did for Me.'[m] [41] Then He will also say to those on the left, 'Depart from Me, you who are cursed, into the eternal fire prepared for the Devil and his angels![n]

[42] For I was hungry
and you gave Me nothing
    to eat;
I was thirsty
and you gave Me nothing
    to drink;
[43] I was a stranger
and you didn't take Me in;
I was naked
and you didn't clothe Me,
sick and in prison
and you didn't take care
    of Me.'

[44] "Then they too will answer, 'Lord, when did we see You hungry, or thirsty, or a stranger, or without clothes, or sick, or in prison, and not help You?'

[45] "Then He will answer them, 'I assure you: Whatever you did not do for one of the least of these, you did not do for Me either.'[o]

[46] "And they will go away into eternal punishment, but the righteous into eternal life."[p]

Cross-reference column:

[a] 25:21 Mt 24:45,47; Lk 12:44; 22:28; Heb 12:2
[b] 25:24 1Sm 25:3; 2Co 8:12
[c] 25:26 Pr 20:4; Mt 18:32; Rm 12:11
[d] 25:29 Mt 13:12; Mk 4:25; Lk 8:18; 19:26; Jn 15:2
[e] 25:30 Mt 8:12; 22:13; Lk 13:28
[f] 25:31 Gn 16:7; Mt 5:34; 13:49; Lk 1:11; Ac 5:19; Rv 14:6
[g] Mt 16:27; 19:28; 2Th 1:7; Jd 14; Rv 1:7
[h] 25:32 Jl 3:12; Mt 24:14; 28:19; Rm 1:5; Gl 1:16
[i] Ezk 34:17,20; Mt 13:49
[j] 25:34 Mt 19:29; Lk 12:32; 1Co 15:50; Gl 5:21; Jms 2:5; 1Pt 3:9; Rv 21:7
[k] Mt 13:35; 20:23; 1Co 2:9; Heb 4:3; 9:26; 11:16; Rv 13:8; 17:8
[l] 25:35-36 Jb 31:32; Is 58:7; Ezk 18:7; 2Tm 1:16; Heb 13:2; Jms 1:27; 2:15-16
[m] 25:40 Pr 19:17; Mt 10:42; 25:34; Heb 6:10
[n] 25:41 Mt 7:23; 13:40,42; Mk 9:48; 2Pt 2:4; Jd 6-7
[o] 25:45 Pr 14:31; 17:5; Ac 9:5
[p] 25:46 Dn 12:2; Jn 5:21; Ac 24:15; Rm 2:7

[A]25:26-27 Or *So you knew . . . scattered? Then* (as a question)　[B]25:27 Lit *received what is mine*　[C]25:31 Other mss read *holy angels*　[D]25:32 Or *the Gentiles*

---

ing. The **talents** (Greek coins whose value equaled 6,000 days of wages) represent the financial resources, gifts, privileges, and opportunities that Jesus entrusts to His disciples. The **faithful** servants (true disciples) used their gifts and resources responsibly and were generously rewarded. The **evil, lazy** servant (a false disciple) failed to use the resources and was severely punished. He attempted to excuse his failure by assaulting the character of his **master** (v. 24). However, the master's treatment of the other servants demonstrates that the wicked servant's slander was unfair.

25:31-46 This passage uses figurative language (**shepherd . . . sheep . . . goats**) drawn from Ezk 34:17-19 in Mt 25:32-33, but the rest is too literal to be classified as a parable. The passage is therefore best taken as a literal description of the final judgment. Verses 31 and 34 define the title **Son of Man** as **King** (see note at 8:20). The King, Jesus, will judge people based on their reception and treatment of **the least of** His **brothers**. In light of 12:50, the words refer to Jesus' followers who seek to do God's will. Humble and compassionate treatment of Jesus' followers necessarily accompanies acceptance of the gospel that they proclaim

The Plot to Kill Jesus

26 When Jesus had finished saying all this,[a] He told His disciples, [2]"You know[A] that the •Passover takes place after two days, and the •Son of Man will be handed over to be crucified."[b]

[3]Then the •chief priests[B] and the elders of the people assembled in the palace of the high priest, who was called Caiaphas,[c] [4]and they conspired to arrest Jesus in a treacherous way and kill Him.[d] [5]"Not during the festival," they said, "so there won't be rioting among the people."

The Anointing at Bethany

[6]While Jesus was in Bethany at the house of Simon,[e] a man who had a serious skin disease, [7]a woman approached Him with an alabaster jar of very expensive fragrant oil. She poured it on His head as He was reclining at the table. [8]When the disciples[f] saw it, they were indignant. "Why this waste?" they asked. [9]"This might have been sold for a great deal and given to the poor."

[10]But Jesus, aware of this, said to them, "Why are you bothering this woman? She has done a noble thing for Me. [11]You always have the poor with you, but you do not always have Me.[g] [12]By pouring this fragrant oil on My body, she has prepared Me for burial. [13]•I assure you: Wherever this gospel[h] is proclaimed in the whole world, what this woman has done will also be told in memory of her."

[14]Then[i] one of the Twelve—the man called Judas Iscariot—went to the chief priests[j] [15]and said, "What are you willing to give me if I hand Him over to you?" So they weighed out 30 pieces of silver for him.[k] [16]And from that time he started looking for a good opportunity to betray Him.

Betrayal at the Passover

[17]On the first day of •Unleavened Bread[l] the disciples came to Jesus and asked, "Where do You want us to prepare the Passover so You may eat it?"

[18]"Go into the city to a certain man," He said, "and tell him, 'The Teacher says: My time is near; I am celebrating the Passover at your place[C] with My disciples.'"[m] [19]So the disciples did as Jesus had directed them and prepared the Passover. [20]When evening came, He was reclining at the table with the Twelve. [21]While they were eating, He said, "I assure you: One of you will betray Me."[n]

[22]Deeply distressed, each one began to say to Him, "Surely not I, Lord?"

[23]He replied, "The one who dipped his hand with Me in the bowl—he will betray Me. [24]The Son of Man will go just as it is written about Him,[o] but woe to that man by whom the Son of Man is betrayed! It would have been better for that man if he had not been born." [25]Then Judas, His betrayer, replied, "Surely not I, •Rabbi?"[p]

"You have said it," He told him.

The First Lord's Supper

[26]As they were eating,[q] Jesus took bread,

Cross references (center column)

a 26:1-5 Mk 14:1-2; Lk 22:1-2; Jn 11:47-53
b 26:2 Jn 11:55; 13:1
c 26:3 Ps 2:2; Mt 26:57; Lk 3:2; Jn 11:47; 18:13,15; Ac 4:6
d 26:4 Mt 21:46; Jn 11:53
e 26:6-13 Mk 14:3-9; Jn 12:1-8
f 26:8 Mt 10:1; 26:56; Mk 3:7; 16:20; Lk 6:13; Jn 12:16
g 26:11 Dt 15:11; Jn 12:8
h 26:13 Mt 24:14; Mk 1:1; 13:10
i 26:14-16 Mk 14:10-11; Lk 22:3-6
j 26:14 Mt 10:4; Jn 6:71; 12:4; 13:30; Ac 1:16
k 26:15 Ex 21:32; Zch 11:12-13; Mt 27:3
l 26:17-19 Mk 14:12-16; Lk 22:7-13
m 26:18 Jn 7:6,8; 8:20; 13:1; 17:1
n 26:21-24 Mk 14:17-21; Lk 22:21-23; Jn 13:21-26
o 26:24 Dn 9:26; Mk 9:12; Lk 24:25-27; Ac 17:2-3; 26:22-23; 1Co 15:3; 1Pt 1:10
p 26:25 Lk 22:70; Jn 1:38
q 26:26-29 Mk 14:22-25; Lk 22:17-20; 1Co 11:23-25

A 26:2 Or Know (as a command)   B 26:3 Other mss add and the scribes   C 26:18 Lit Passover with you

---

(10:40-42). **Whatever you did for one of** the least of **these** brothers **of Mine, you did for Me** means that a person's treatment of Jesus' representatives expresses their love for and commitment to Jesus Himself. Those who show no compassion to Jesus' followers betray their lack of devotion to Him. As in 7:21-23, Jesus identifies Himself as the final Judge, a role that Jews expected Yahweh to fulfill.

26:1-2 Passover was a celebration that commemorated the Israelites' flight from Egypt in the days of Moses (Ex 12). The timing of Jesus' death (at Passover) confirms His identity as the new Moses who will lead His disciples on a new spiritual exodus. On **Son of Man**, see note at 8:20. The temporal reference Passover **takes place after two days** means that Jesus' prophecy was given on Tuesday.

26:3 Joseph **Caiaphas** served as high priest from A.D. 18 to 36, after he replaced his father-in-law, Annas. His burial cave was discovered in 1990 south of Abu Tor.

26:5 The fear of **rioting** during Passover was well-founded since riots had previously occurred (Josephus, War 1.88). A riot would cause the Romans to strengthen their grip on Jerusalem and the Jewish leadership.

26:6 Jesus had apparently healed **Simon** of his **serious skin disease** at a previous date since he now lived in a house (rather than a leper colony) and entertained Jewish guests before the Passover.

26:7 The unnamed **woman** was Mary (Jn 12:3). Her **fragrant oil** was **very expensive**, worth a year's wages. Since Jesus was Messiah (a title meaning "anointed One"), anointing His head was especially meaningful. It recalled the anointing of OT kings (1Sm 10:1; 2Kg 9:3,6).

26:12 Corpses were perfumed in first-century Palestine to mask the odor of putrefaction. Jesus interpreted Mary's act as preparation for His **burial**. Messiah was beginning His reign, but, to the surprise of His disciples, His throne would be a cross and His diadem a crown of thorns.

26:14-16 If the **30 pieces of silver** are 30 shekels, the amount was equal to 120 days' wages. Thus by his traitorous act Judas earned an amount of money that equaled only one-third of the value of Mary's lavish gift (see note at v. 7). On the significance of this amount, see note at 27:9.

26:17 The feast of **Unleavened Bread** was a seven- or eight-day feast associated with the one-day **Passover**. During this feast, the Jews refused to eat anything containing yeast in order to commemorate the speed with which God delivered them from Egypt (Ex 13:7-8; Dt 16:3-4). The feast began on the day before Passover, Thursday of Passion Week.

blessed and broke it, gave it to the disciples,[a] and said, "Take and eat it; this is My body."[b] [27]Then He took a cup, and after giving thanks, He gave it to them and said, "Drink from it, all of you. [28]For this is My blood that establishes the covenant;[A] it is shed for many for the forgiveness of sins.[c] [29]But I tell you, from this moment I will not drink of this fruit of the vine until that day when I drink it in a new way[B] in My Father's kingdom[d] with you." [30]After singing psalms,[c] they went out to the •Mount of Olives.[e]

Peter's Denial Predicted

[31]Then Jesus said to them, "Tonight all of you will run away[D] because of Me, for it is written:

> **I will strike the shepherd,**
> **and the sheep of the flock**
> **will be scattered.**[E,f]

[32]But after I have been resurrected, I will go ahead of you to Galilee."[g]

[33]Peter told Him, "Even if everyone runs away because of You, I will never run away!"

[34]"I assure you," Jesus said to him, "tonight, before the rooster crows, you will deny Me three times!"[h]

[35]"Even if I have to die with You," Peter told

Him, "I will never deny You!" And all the disciples said the same thing.

The Prayer in the Garden

[36]Then Jesus came with them to a place called Gethsemane,[F,i] and He told the disciples, "Sit here while I go over there and pray." [37]Taking along Peter and the two sons of Zebedee, He began to be sorrowful and deeply distressed.[j] [38]Then He said to them, "My soul is swallowed up in sorrow[G]—to the point of death.[H] Remain here and stay awake with Me."[k] [39]Going a little farther,[i] He fell facedown and prayed, "My Father! If it is possible, let this cup pass from Me. Yet not as I will, but as You will."[l]

[40]Then He came to the disciples and found them sleeping. He asked Peter, "So, couldn't you[j] stay awake with Me one hour? [41]Stay awake and pray, so that you won't enter into temptation. The spirit is willing, but the flesh is weak."

[42]Again, a second time, He went away and prayed, "My Father, if this[K] cannot pass[L] unless I drink it, Your will be done."[m] [43]And He came again and found them sleeping, because they could not keep their eyes open.[M]

[44]After leaving them, He went away again and prayed a third time, saying the same thing once more. [45]Then He came to the disciples

Cross references (center column)

[a] 26:26 Mt 10:1; 26:56; Mk 3:7; 16:20; Lk 6:13; Jn 12:16
[b] Mt 14:19; 1Co 10:16
[c] 26:28 Ex 24:8; Mt 20:28; Mk 1:4; Heb 9:20
[d] 26:29 Mt 4:23; Mk 1:15; Ac 20:25
[e] 26:30 Mt 21:1; Lk 22:39; Jn 18:1
[f] 26:31 Zch 13:7; Mt 11:6; Jn 16:32
[g] 26:32 Mt 28:7,10,16; Mk 16:7
[h] 26:34 Mt 26:75; Lk 22:34; Jn 13:38
[i] 26:36-46 Mk 14:32-42; Lk 22:40-46
[j] 26:37 Mt 4:21; 17:1
[k] 26:38 Ps 42:5-6; Mt 24:42; Jn 12:27
[l] 26:39 Mt 20:22; Jn 5:30; 6:38; Php 2:8; Heb 5:7
[m] 26:42 Mt 26:39; Mk 14:36; Lk 22:42; Jn 6:38

A 26:28 Other mss read *new covenant*   B 26:29 Or *drink new wine*; lit *drink it new*   C 26:30 Pss 113–118 were sung during and after the Passover meal.   D 26:31 Or *stumble*   E 26:31 Zch 13:7   F 26:36 A garden east of Jerusalem at the base of the Mount of Olives; Gethsemane = olive oil press   G 26:38 Or *I am deeply grieved*, or *I am overwhelmed by sorrow*; Ps 42:6,11; 43:5   H 26:38 Lit *unto death*   I 26:39 Other mss read *Drawing nearer*   J 26:40 = all 3 disciples because the verb in Gk is pl   K 26:42 Other mss add *cup*   L 26:42 Other mss add *from Me*   M 26:43 Lit *because their eyes were weighed down*

26:18-19 Mark's account of this event more clearly implies that Jesus' instructions to His disciples indicate that He had used supernatural knowledge (Mk 14:13-16).

26:24 **Just as it is written** indicates that Jesus' sufferings were foretold in the OT. Jesus probably had in mind texts such as Is 53 and Ps 22.

26:26 The Passover meal was rich with symbolic meaning. Jews ate lamb to commemorate the lamb whose blood protected firstborn Israelites from the death plague before the exodus. Bitter herbs were reminiscent of their enslavement. Unleavened bread symbolized the haste of their departure from Egypt (Ex 12). Jesus invested the meal with new symbolism: the unleavened **bread** symbolized His own **body** which would be torn by scourging and crucifixion. His sacrifice would begin a new exodus in which people were liberated from slavery to sin.

26:28 The making of a **covenant** was normally accompanied by an act of sacrifice. The slaughter of the animal signified the consequences that would befall anyone who broke the covenant. The old covenant was sealed by such a sacrifice (Ex 24:8). Now, Jesus' sacrifice enacted the new covenant that had been promised in the OT (Jr 31:31-34). In this covenant God vowed to forgive and forget His people's sins. He also promised to write His law on the hearts of His people so that they will fulfill His righteous demands.

26:29 Many Jews expected Messiah to begin His reign by

sharing a great banquet with His subjects. The final cup of the meal anticipated that great messianic feast and encouraged Jesus' disciples to eagerly wait "until He comes" (1Co 11:26).

26:30 Jews typically sang portions of OT **psalms** like Pss 113–118 during the Passover meal.

26:31 Many Jews regarded Zch 13:7, which Jesus quoted here, as a prophecy about Messiah. Jesus' quote implied that the Father Himself would **strike** Him. Although His crucifixion involved the conspiracy of religious leaders, Roman officials, and the betrayal of a friend, Jesus viewed His death ultimately as the fulfillment of God's righteous plan.

26:34 For the fulfillment of Jesus' prophecy, see verses 69-75.

26:38 Jesus' **sorrow** resulted from His anticipation of His physical, emotional, and spiritual suffering, especially His alienation from His Father as He bore the sins of the world on the cross.

26:39 In the OT, the **cup** is often an image of divine wrath and judgment (Ps 75:7-8; Is 51:17). The cup that Jesus faced was God's wrath against sin. With the words **if it is possible, let this cup pass**, Jesus asked His Father to provide forgiveness by some means other than His sacrificial death. Jesus knew that God's power made it possible for Him to evade the power of Jewish and Roman executioners (see note at v. 53), but He did not want to reject the Father's plan to provide salvation to His people.

26:42 Jesus' second petition in Gethsemane assumed that

and said to them, "Are you still sleeping and resting?[A] Look, the time is near. The Son of Man is being betrayed into the hands of sinners.[a] [46]Get up; let's go! See, My betrayer is near."

The Judas Kiss

[47]While He was still speaking, Judas, one of the Twelve, suddenly arrived.[b] A large mob, with swords and clubs, was with him from the chief priests and elders of the people. [48]His betrayer had given them a sign: "The One I kiss, He's the One; arrest Him!" [49]So he went right up to Jesus and said, "Greetings, Rabbi!" and kissed Him.

[50]"Friend,"[c] Jesus asked him, "why have you come?"[B]

Then they came up, took hold of Jesus, and arrested Him. [51]At that moment one of those with Jesus reached out his hand and drew his sword. He struck the high priest's *slave and cut off his ear.[d]

[52]Then Jesus told him, "Put your sword back in its place because all who take up a sword will perish by a sword.[e] [53]Or do you think that I cannot call on My Father, and He will provide Me at once with more than 12 legions[c] of angels?[f] [54]How, then, would the Scriptures be fulfilled[g] that say it must happen this way?"

[55]At that time Jesus said to the crowds, "Have you come out with swords and clubs, as if I were a criminal,[D] to capture Me? Every day

I used to sit, teaching in the *temple complex, and you didn't arrest Me.[h] [56]But all this has happened so that the prophetic Scriptures[E,i] would be fulfilled." Then all the disciples[j] deserted Him and ran away.

Jesus Faces the Sanhedrin

[57]Those[k] who had arrested Jesus led Him away to Caiaphas[l] the high priest, where the *scribes and the elders had convened. [58]Meanwhile, Peter was following Him at a distance right to the high priest's courtyard.[F] He went in and was sitting with the temple police[G] to see the outcome.[H,m]

[59]The chief priests and the whole *Sanhedrin were looking for false testimony against Jesus so they could put Him to death.[n] [60]But they could not find any, even though many false witnesses[o] came forward.[I] Finally, two who came forward [61]stated, "This man said, 'I can demolish God's sanctuary[p] and rebuild it in three days.'"

[62]The high priest then stood up and said to Him, "Don't You have an answer to what these men are testifying against You?" [63]But[q] Jesus kept silent.[r] Then the high priest said to Him, "By the living God I place You under oath:[s] tell us if You are the *Messiah, the Son of God!"[t]

[64]"You have said it,"[K] Jesus told him. "But I tell you, in the future[L] you will see **the Son of**

Cross references
[a] 26:45 Jn 12:27; 13:1
[b] 26:47-56 Mk 14:43-50; Lk 22:47-53; Jn 18:3-11
[c] 26:50 Mt 20:13; 22:12
[d] 26:51 Lk 22:38; Jn 18:10
[e] 26:52 Gn 9:6; Rv 13:10
[f] 26:53 2Kg 6:17; Dn 7:10; Mt 4:11; Lk 8:30
[g] 26:54 Mt 1:22; 26:24
[h] 26:55 Mk 12:35; Lk 21:37; Jn 7:19; 8:2; 18:20
[i] 26:56 Mt 26:54; Rm 1:2; 2Pt 1:20
[j] Mt 10:1; 26:56; Mk 3:7; 16:20; Lk 6:13; Jn 12:16
[k] 26:57-68 Mk 14:53-65; Jn 18:12-13,19-24
[l] 26:57 Mt 26:3; Jn 11:49
[m] 26:58 Jn 7:32; 18:15
[n] 26:59 Mt 5:22; Ac 6:11
[o] 26:60 Dt 19:15; Ps 27:12; 35:11; Ac 6:13
[p] 26:61 Mt 27:40; Jn 2:19; Ac 6:14
[q] 26:63-66 Lk 22:67-71
[r] 26:63 Is 53:7; Mt 27:12,14; Jn 19:9
[s] Lv 19:12; Nm 30:2; Dt 23:21;
Mt 5:33; 14:7; 23:16 [t] Lv 5:1; 1Sm 14:24,26; Mt 16:16

Footnotes
[A] 26:45 Or *Sleep on now and take your rest.* [B] 26:50 Or *Jesus told him, "do what you have come for."* (as a statement) [C] 26:53 A Roman legion contained up to 6,000 soldiers. [D] 26:55 Lit *as against a criminal* [E] 26:56 Or *the Scriptures of the prophets* [F] 26:58 Or *high priest's palace* [G] 26:58 Or *the officers,* or *the servants* [H] 26:58 Lit *end* [I] 26:60 Other mss add *they found none* [J] 26:60 Other mss add *false witnesses* [K] 26:64 Or *That is true,* an affirmative oath; Mt 27:11; Mk 15:2 [L] 26:64 Lit *you, from now*

His sacrificial death was necessary. Matthew 26:54 shows that God had predicted Jesus' death in the OT. The Scriptures, being God's Word, had to be fulfilled. This second petition closely parallels the Model Prayer of 6:9-13. Both prayers address God as **Father** and contain the petition **Your will be done**.

paradidomi

Greek Pronunciation	[pah rah DIHD oh mee]
HCSB Translation	betray, hand over, entrust
Uses in Matthew	31 (Mk, 20; Lk, 17; Jn, 15)
Uses in the NT	119
Focus Passage	Matthew 26:46

In a positive sense, *paradidomi* (entrust, hand down) may describe commendation for service (Ac 14:26) or the passing on of traditions (Lk 1:2; Ac 6:14; Rm 6:17; 1Co 11:2,23; 15:3; 2Pt 2:21; Jd 3). It also describes the Father *entrusting* all things to the Son (Mt 11:27 = Lk 10:22) and the Son *handing over* all things to the Father (1Co 15:24), as well as Jesus being *offered up* by the Father (Rm 8:32) and *giving* His own life as a sacrifice (Jn 19:30; Gl 2:20; Eph 5:2,25). Negatively, *paradidomi* describes arrest and/or imprisonment (Mt 4:12; 10:19; 18:34; Ac 8:3; 22:4; 2Pt 2:4), Jesus being *handed over* to death by His enemies (Mt 26:2; 27:2,26; Ac 3:13), believers being *persecuted* (Mt 10:21; 24:9; Ac 21:11), people being *turned over* to Satan (1Co 5:5; 1Tm 1:20), and God *delivering* people over to their sin (Rm 1:24,26,28).

26:47-49 Jewish men did not **kiss** one another publicly except on formal occasions. Such a kiss expressed respect and affection. Thus Judas's kiss was an act of shameful hypocrisy.

26:51 The servant was named Malchus (Jn 18:10). Jesus restored his severed **ear** (Lk 22:51).

26:53 A Roman legion consisted of 6,000 soldiers. A roughly equal number of auxiliary troops supported each legion. Thus **12 legions** of angels would be equivalent to 72,000 or even 144,000 angels, more than enough to defend Jesus against arrest and crucifixion.

26:54-56 Jesus expressed the same view of the **Scriptures** that He taught in the Sermon on the Mount (5:17-20).

26:59-60 The **Sanhedrin** was obligated to interview witnesses separately and then compare their testimonies to determine if they were consistent (Mk 14:55-59). Inconsistent testimonies were considered invalid.

26:61-63 The testimony was based on a confused understanding of Jesus' statement in Jn 2:19. Since both 2Sm 7:13-14 and Zch 6:12 portrayed Messiah as One who would build a temple for God, the high priest regarded the statement about

Man seated at the right hand of the Power and coming on the clouds of heaven."[A,a]

[65]Then the high priest tore his robes and said, "He has blasphemed![b] Why do we still need witnesses? Look, now you've heard the blasphemy![c] [66]What is your decision?"[B]

They answered, "He deserves death!"[d] [67]Then they spit in His face[e] and beat Him; others slapped Him [68]and said, "Prophesy to us, Messiah! Who hit You?"[f]

Peter Denies His Lord

[69]Now Peter was sitting outside in the courtyard.[g] A servant approached him and she said, "You were with Jesus the Galilean too."

[70]But he denied it in front of everyone: "I don't know what you're talking about!"

[71]When he had gone out to the gateway, another woman saw him and told those who were there, "This man was with Jesus the •Nazarene!"[h]

[72]And again he denied it with an oath,[i] "I don't know the man!"

[73]After a little while those standing there approached and said to Peter, "You certainly are one of them, since even your accent[c] gives you away."

[74]Then he started to curse[D] and to swear with an oath, "I do not know the man!" Immediately a rooster crowed, [75]and Peter remembered the words Jesus had spoken, "Before the rooster crows, you will deny Me three times."[j] And he went outside and wept bitterly.

Jesus Handed Over to Pilate

27 When daybreak came, all the •chief priests and the elders of the people plotted against Jesus to put Him to death.[k] [2]After tying Him up, they led Him away and handed Him over to •Pilate,[E] the governor.[l]

Judas Hangs Himself

[3]Then Judas, His betrayer, seeing that He had been condemned, was full of remorse and returned the 30 pieces of silver to the chief priests and elders.[m] [4]"I have sinned by betraying innocent blood," he said.

"What's that to us?" they said. "See to it yourself!"

[5]So he threw the silver into the sanctuary[n] and departed. Then he went and hanged himself.

[6]The chief priests took the silver and said, "It's not lawful[o] to put it into the temple treasury,[F] since it is blood money."[G] [7]So they

Cross references (center column)
[a] 26:64 Ps 110:1; Dn 7:13; Mt 16:27; 24:30; Rv 1:7
[b] 26:65 Mk 3:29; Jn 10:33
[c] Nm 14:6; Mk 14:63; Ac 14:14
[d] 26:66 Lv 24:16; Jn 19:7
[e] 26:67 Mt 27:30; Mk 10:34; Lk 22:63-65; Jn 18:22
[f] 26:68 Mk 14:65; Lk 22:64
[g] 26:69-75 Mk 14:66-72; Lk 22:55-62; Jn 18:16-18,25-27
[h] 26:71 Mk 14:67; Ac 6:14
[i] 26:72 Lv 19:12; Nm 30:2; Dt 23:21; Mt 5:33; 14:7; 23:16
[j] 26:75 Mt 26:34; Jn 13:38; Ac 3:13-14
[k] 27:1 Mk 15:1; Lk 22:66; Jn 18:28
[l] 27:2 Mt 20:19; Lk 13:1; Ac 3:13; 1Tm 6:13
[m] 27:3 Mt 21:29; 26:14-15
[n] 27:5 2Sm 17:23; Lk 1:19,21; Ac 1:18
[o] 27:6 Mk 2:24; Jn 18:31

[A]26:64 Ps 110:1; Dn 7:13   [B]26:66 Lit *What does it seem to you?*   [C]26:73 Or *speech*   [D]26:74 To call down curses on himself if what he said weren't true   [E]27:2 Other mss read *Pontius Pilate*   [F]27:6 See Mk 7:11 where the same Gk word (*Corban*) means a gift pledged to the temple.   [G]27:6 Lit *the price of blood*

---

building the temple in **three days** as a claim to messiahship. The high priest appears to use the titles **Messiah** and **Son of God** interchangeably, suggesting that many Jews saw the title "Son of God" as messianic in light of Ps 2.

26:64 Jesus' confession acknowledged that He is Messiah and the Son of God. However, He countered confused interpretations of His messianic role by describing Himself as the **Son of Man**. Both "Son of Man" and the phrase **coming on the clouds** of heaven were drawn from Dn 7:13. Jesus' words confirmed that He intended this title to express not just His humanity but His identity as a King of heavenly origin who would reign over an eternal kingdom. The words **seated at the right hand** echo Ps 110:1 (see note at Mt 22:43-46). Jesus' application of Ps 110:1 to Himself gave the impression that He was claiming to be God's equal. The unbelieving Jewish leaders regarded this as blasphemy, a crime worthy of death (Lv 24:10-23).

26:65 Tearing one's **robes** was a common expression of deep grief and was the customary Jewish response to blasphemy. However, because the robes of the high priest were sacred, Lv 21:10 prohibited "the priest who is highest among his brothers" from tearing his garments. Thus the high priest's anger at Jesus' statement prompted him to commit an act of sacrilege.

26:66 Execution by stoning was the prescribed OT penalty for blasphemy (Lv 24:10-23).

26:67-68 Mark 14:65 shows that the men covered Jesus' face before they beat Him. Thus Jesus was expected to identify His abusers by name without seeing their faces or hearing their voices. This mock test of messiahship was probably based on a misinterpretation of Is 11:3 which said that Messiah "will not judge by what He sees with His eyes . . . [or] by what He hears with His ears." A century later Bar Kochba was executed after his claims to be Messiah were disproved by his inability to judge by smell.

26:69-71 The emphasis on Jesus' identity as a **Galilean** and a **Nazarene** may imply that one of the arguments used to refute His messianic claims was that He did not come from Bethlehem, the city of David. This city is identified as the birthplace of Messiah in Mc 5:2. Thus, this argument against Jesus' messiahship confused His hometown with His birthplace (Mt 2:4-11).

26:73 Galileans spoke with an **accent** that distinguished them from the inhabitants of Judah.

26:75 This event fulfilled Jesus' prophecy in verse 34.

27:1-2 This early morning meeting of the Sanhedrin was convened to compensate for the illegal procedures of the previous night. According to Jewish law, judges had to conduct and conclude capital trials during daylight hours (*m. Sanh.* 4:1). The law also prohibited conducting trials on the eve of the Sabbath. The Jewish leaders also needed to plot and secure Roman approval for the intended execution of Jesus. Pontius **Pilate** was the Roman prefect of Judea from A.D. 26-36. The title **governor** (Gk *hegemon*) was an acceptable Greek translation of the Latin title "prefect" and was also used of Pilate by Josephus (*Ant.* 18.55).

27:4 Betraying **innocent blood** is a heinous offense that results in a divine curse (Dt 27:25). The reaction of the chief priests and elders shows that they realized that Jesus was innocent.

27:5 Some Jews believed that criminals received atonement

conferred together and bought the potter's field with it as a burial place for foreigners. [8]Therefore that field has been called "Blood Field" to this day. [9]Then what was spoken through the prophet Jeremiah was fulfilled:

They took the 30 pieces of silver, the price of Him whose price was set by the Israelites, [10]and they gave them for the potter's field, as the Lord directed me.[A,a]

Jesus Faces the Governor

[11]Now Jesus stood before the governor.[b] "Are You the King of the Jews?" the governor asked Him.

Jesus answered, "You have said it."[B,c] [12]And while He was being accused by the chief priests and elders, He didn't answer.[d] [13]Then Pilate said to Him, "Don't You hear how much they are testifying against You?" [14]But He didn't answer him on even one charge, so that the governor was greatly amazed.[e]

Jesus or Barabbas

[15]At the festival[f] the governor's custom was to release to the crowd a prisoner they wanted. [16]At that time they had a notorious prisoner called Barabbas.[c] [17]So when they had gathered together, Pilate said to them, "Who is it you want me to release for you—Barabbas,[c] or Jesus who is called •Messiah?"[g] [18]For he knew they had handed Him over because of envy.

[19]While he was sitting on the judge's bench, his wife sent word to him, "Have nothing to do with that righteous man, for today I've suffered terribly in a dream because of Him!"[h] [20]The chief priests and the elders, however, persuaded the crowds to ask for Barabbas and to execute Jesus. [21]The governor asked them, "Which of the two do you want me to release for you?"

"Barabbas!" they answered.

[22]Pilate asked them, "What should I do then with Jesus, who is called Messiah?"

They all answered, "Crucify Him!"[D,i]

[23]Then he said, "Why? What has He done wrong?"

But they kept shouting, "Crucify Him!" all the more.[j]

[24]When Pilate saw that he was getting nowhere,[E] but that a riot was starting instead, he took some water, washed his hands in front of the crowd, and said, "I am innocent of this man's blood.[F] See to it yourselves!"[k] [25]All the people answered, "His blood be on us[l] and on our children!" [26]Then he released Barabbas to them. But after having Jesus flogged,[G] he handed Him over to be crucified.[m]

Mocked by the Military

[27]Then[n] the governor's soldiers took Jesus into •headquarters and gathered the whole •company around Him.[o] [28]They stripped Him and dressed Him in a scarlet military robe.[p] [29]They twisted together a crown of thorns, put it on His head, and placed a reed in His

Cross references (center column)

[a] 27:9-10 Jr 32:6-9; Zch 11:12-13; Mt 1:22
[b] 27:11-14 Mk 15:2-5; Lk 23:2-3; Jn 18:29-38
[c] 27:11 Mt 2:2; 1Tm 6:13
[d] 27:12 Mt 26:63; Jn 19:9
[e] 27:14 Mk 15:5; Lk 23:9
[f] 27:15-26 Mk 15:6-15; Lk 23:16-25; Jn 18:39-40; 19:16
[g] 27:17 Mt 1:16; 27:22
[h] 27:19 Gn 20:6; Nm 12:6; Jb 33:14-16; Mt 2:12; Jn 19:13
[i] 27:22 Mt 1:16; Ac 13:28
[j] 27:23 Lk 23:41; Jn 8:46
[k] 27:24 Dt 21:6-8; Ps 26:6; Mt 26:5; 27:4,19
[l] 27:25 Jos 2:19; Ac 5:28
[m] 27:26 Is 53:5; Mk 15:15; Lk 23:16; Jn 19:1
[n] 27:27-31 Mk 15:16-20; Jn 19:2-3
[o] 27:27 Jn 18:28,33; 19:9; Ac 10:1
[p] 27:28 Lk 23:11; Jn 19:2

[A]27:9-10 Jr 32:6-9; Zch 11:12-13   [B]27:11 Or *That is true*, an affirmative oath; Mt 26:64; Mk 15:2   [C]27:16,17 Other mss read *Jesus Barabbas*   [D]27:22 Lit *"Him—be crucified!"*   [E]27:24 Lit *that it availed nothing*   [F]27:24 Other mss read *this righteous man's blood*   [G]27:26 Roman flogging was done with a whip made of leather strips embedded with pieces of bone or metal that brutally tore the flesh.

---

from God through their execution (*m. Sanh* 6:3). Once he realized the horror of his crime, guilt-stricken Judas ended his life, perhaps hoping to earn atonement. But only one death brings atonement: that of Jesus Christ.

27:8 This verse hints that Matthew wrote his Gospel before the destruction of Jerusalem in A.D. 70. That such a burial field could be located and recognized by name decades after the utter destruction of Jerusalem is unlikely.

27:9-10 Matthew's appeal to the OT blends themes from Zch 11:12-13 and Jr 32:6-9. The first text describes Israel's rejection of its spiritual Shepherd, the low estimation they had of Him (worth only **30 pieces of silver**, the price of a slave; Ex 21:32), and destruction of Jerusalem by the Romans. The second text assures that Israel will be restored after its devastation by the Babylonians. The two prophecies do more than just foretell the events surrounding Judas's actions. By merging these texts, Matthew showed that Jerusalem's rejection of Messiah would result in its destruction, but that God would restore the city in due time.

27:11-14 According to Roman law, the refusal to offer a defense counted as an admission of guilt.

27:15 The custom of releasing a **prisoner** for Passover

seems to be attested in one Jewish text (*m. Pes.* 8:6: "they may slaughter a Passover lamb for one . . . whom they have promised to bring out of prison").

27:16 Mark 15:7 describes **Barabbas** as a murderous rebel. Some ancient manuscripts of Matthew and some important figures in the early church mention that Barabbas's full name was Jesus Bar Abbas, which might indicate that he was the son of a renowned teacher ("son of Rabba"). Thus Pilate apparently offered the Jews a choice between a Jesus who was the son of a teacher and a Jesus who was the Son of God.

27:24-25 Both Judas (vv. 3-5) and **Pilate** (v. 24) feared being accountable for Jesus' death, but the people gladly accepted responsibility. Many later Christians speculated that the destruction of Jerusalem was the penalty for this self-confessed guilt.

27:26 Roman flogging utilized an instrument of torture called the (Gk) *flagellum*, a leather whip that had thongs laced with sharp pieces of iron or bone. Although beatings in the Jewish synagogue were limited to 39 blows, no limit was imposed on Roman flogging. Ancient writers described victims being disemboweled or having their bones laid bare by the *flagellum*.

right hand. And they knelt down before Him and mocked Him: "Hail, King of the Jews!" [30]Then they spit on Him, took the reed, and kept hitting Him on the head. [31]When they had mocked Him, they stripped Him of the robe, put His clothes on Him, and led Him away to crucify Him.[a]

Crucified Between Two Criminals

[32]As they were going out, they found a Cyrenian man named Simon. They forced this man to carry His cross.[b] [33]When they came to a place called *Golgotha*[c] (which means Skull Place), [34]they gave Him wine[A] mixed with gall to drink. But when He tasted it, He would not drink it. [35]After crucifying Him they divided His clothes by casting lots.[B,d] [36]Then they sat down and were guarding Him there. [37]Above His head they put up the charge against Him in writing:

THIS IS JESUS
THE KING OF THE JEWS.

[38]Then two criminals[c] were crucified with Him, one on the right and one on the left.[e]

[39]Those who passed by were yelling insults at[D] Him, shaking their heads[f] [40]and saying, "The One who would demolish the sanctuary and rebuild it in three days, save Yourself! If You are the Son of God, come down from the cross!"[g] [41]In the same way the chief priests, with the •scribes and elders,[E] mocked Him and said, [42]"He saved others, but He cannot save Himself! He is the King of Israel![h] Let Him[F] come down now from the cross, and we will believe in Him. [43]He has put His trust in God; let God rescue Him now—if He wants Him![G] For He said, 'I am God's Son.'" [44]In the same way even the criminals who were crucified with Him kept taunting Him.[i]

The Death of Jesus

[45]From noon until three in the afternoon[H] darkness came over the whole land.[i,j] [46]About three in the afternoon Jesus cried out with a loud voice, ***"Elí, Elí, lemá[j] sabachtháni?"*** that is, **"My God, My God, why have You forsaken[K] Me?"**[L,k] [47]When some of those standing there heard this, they said, "He's calling for Elijah!" [48]Immediately one of them ran and got a

Cross references (center column):
[a]27:30-31 Is 53:7; Mt 26:67
[b]27:32 Nm 15:35; Mk 15:21; Lk 23:26; Heb 13:12
[c]27:33-44 Mk 15:22-32; Lk 23:33-43; Jn 19:17-24
[d]27:34-35 Ps 22:17; 69:21
[e]27:38 Is 53:12; Mt 20:21; Jn 18:40
[f]27:39 Jb 16:4; Ps 22:7; 109:25; Lm 2:15; Mk 15:29
[g]27:40 Mt 4:3,6; 26:61,63; Jn 2:19
[h]27:42 Jn 1:49; 12:13
[i]27:43-44 Ps 22:8; Lk 23:39-43
[j]27:45-56 Mk 15:33-41; Lk 23:44-49; Jn 19:28-30
[k]27:46 Ps 22:1; Heb 5:7

---

^A27:34 Other mss read *sour wine* ^B27:35 Other mss add *that what was spoken by the prophet might be fulfilled: "They divided My clothes among them, and for My clothing they cast lots."* ^C27:38 Or *revolutionaries* ^D27:39 Lit *passed by blasphemed or were blaspheming* ^E27:41 Other mss add *and Pharisees* ^F27:42 Other mss read *If He . . . Israel, let Him* ^G27:43 Or *if He takes pleasure in Him* ^H27:45 Lit *From the sixth hour to the ninth hour* ^I27:45 Or *whole earth* ^J27:46 Some mss read *lama;* other mss read *lima* ^K27:46 Or *abandoned* ^L27:46 Ps 22:1

27:28-29 With their mock royal **robe . . . crown**, and scepter, the soldiers ridiculed Jesus' messianic claims.

27:32 Crucifixion victims normally carried the cross's (Gk) *patibulum* (crossbeam) to the execution site. Having lost much blood, Jesus was too weak to carry it beyond the city walls. The soldiers impressed (see note at 5:41) **Simon**, a **Cyrenian**, to carry the beam the rest of the way. Simon's sons were later known in the early church (Mk 15:21). This

suggests that Simon became a disciple of Jesus. Cyrene was situated near the Mediterranean coast in northern Africa. Simon was probably an ethnic Jew visiting Jerusalem for the Passover (Ac 6:9).

27:34 This **wine** was probably intended to dull the pain of crucifixion or hasten death. Jesus' refusal to drink it expressed His determination to suffer the full agony of the cross.

27:35 Crucifixion was a horrifying and torturous means of execution. Naked victims were tied or nailed (Jn 20:25) to a cross. The victim might remain alive for days, and after death they were often consumed by dogs, carrion birds, or insects. Josephus described crucifixion as "the most wretched of all ways of dying" (*War* 7.5.4). Cicero (106–43 B.C.) said that crucifixion so frightened Roman citizens that they refused to speak the word "cross."

27:37 A wooden placard called a *titulus* was often tied around the criminal's neck as he marched to death. This sign announced the reason for his crucifixion. When Jesus arrived at Golgotha, the placard was nailed over His head. Although Roman crosses were sometimes shaped like X or T, the placement of the *titulus* on Jesus' cross shows that it was shaped like a lowercase letter "t."

27:45 The bystanders naturally interpreted the **darkness** as God's judgment (Am 8:9). While they likely thought the judgment was against Jesus (as if He were a heretic), in light of His later resurrection they came to see the darkness as judgment against the sin that Jesus became on our behalf (2Co 5:21).

27:46 Jesus' lament quotes Ps 22:1. The psalm reads like

---

stauroo

Greek Pronunciation	[stow RAH oh]
HCSB Translation	crucify
Uses in Matthew	10 (Mk, 8; Lk, 6; Jn, 11)
Uses in the NT	46
Focus Passage	Matthew 27:31

Stauroo originally referred to building a fence by driving stakes into the ground. Stakes could easily be used as instruments of death, and impalement became an early form of execution. Through the Roman practice of *crucifixion*, *stauroo* eventually came to refer primarily to the common form of execution—tying or nailing someone to a cross and leaving them hanging until they died. The vast majority of the occurrences of *stauroo* refer to the manner of Jesus' death, though the NT mentions others who died by *crucifixion* (Mt 23:34; 27:38). *Crucifixion* was occasionally used as a metaphor for the Christian life (Mt 16:24; Gl 5:24; 6:14), an image emphasizing the believers' identification with Christ and His suffering and death. It thus became a subject of boasting among Christians (Gl 6:14), for their *crucified* Savior was also the risen Lord and Messiah (Ac 2:36; 4:10; 1Co 1:23; 2:2; 2Co 13:4).

sponge, filled it with sour wine, fixed it on a reed, and offered Him a drink.[a] [49]But the rest said, "Let's see if Elijah comes to save Him!"

[50]Jesus shouted again with a loud voice and gave up His spirit.[b] [51]Suddenly, the curtain of the sanctuary[A,c] was split in two from top to bottom; the earth quaked and the rocks were split. [52]The tombs were also opened[d] and many bodies of the •saints who had fallen •asleep were raised. [53]And they came out of the tombs after His resurrection, entered the holy city, and appeared to many.

[54]When the •centurion and those with him, who were guarding Jesus, saw the earthquake and the things that had happened, they were terrified and said, "This man really was God's Son!"[B,e]

[55]Many women who had followed Jesus from Galilee and ministered to Him were there, looking on from a distance.[f] [56]Among them were •Mary Magdalene, Mary the mother of James and Joseph, and the mother of Zebedee's sons.[g]

---

a 27:48 Ps 69:21; Mk 15:36; Lk 23:36; Jn 19:29
b 27:50 Mk 15:37; Lk 23:46; Jn 10:18; 19:30
c 27:51 Ex 26:31-33; 2Ch 3:14; Heb 9:3
d 27:52 Ezk 37:12
e 27:54 Jn 5:19; Heb 1:2
f 27:55 Ps 38:11; Lk 8:2-3; Jn 19:25
g 27:56 Mt 20:20; Mk 15:40; Jn 19:25

A 27:51 A heavy curtain separated the inner room of the temple from the outer.   B 27:54 Or *the Son of God*

---

it was written by someone standing near the cross (see especially Ps 22:7-8,14-18). Jesus' cry expressed the alienation from God that He endured as He bore the Father's wrath against sin. Although Jesus elsewhere addressed God as "Father," He addressed Him merely as **My God** in this verse.

27:51 Jesus' death at 3:00 p.m. coincided with the afternoon sacrifice. Thus the priests were present in the temple to observe the rending of the curtain. The **curtain of the sanctuary** separated the holy of holies from the rest of the temple. According to the Mishnah, it was 60 feet long, 30 feet wide, and as thick as a man's palm. It was so heavy that it took 300 men to lift it when it was wet (*m. Shek.* 8:5). That it **split in two from top to bottom** shows that it was torn by God. This signified that Jesus'

death granted sinners new access to God (Heb 6:19-20; 10:19-20).

27:52-53 Although the **tombs** were ruptured at the time of Jesus' death, the **saints** did not depart from them until after Jesus' resurrection. This demonstrated that Jesus' victory over death guaranteed that God would also raise His people (1Co 15:20).

27:54 Gentiles again recognized and confessed Jesus' true identity. This hints at God's worldwide plan for salvation (see note at 28:19).

27:56 Mary **the mother of James and Joseph** was probably the mother of two of Jesus' lesser known disciples (Mk 15:40).

27:57-60 Joseph, a member of the Sanhedrin (Mk 15:43),

Gordon's Calvary, one of two sites consider to be the location of Jesus' crucifixion. This site was named for British General Charles Gordon who argued that this was the site of Jesus' crucifixion. It is located just north and east of the Damascus Gate and conforms closely to the details of the Gospels. The second site is the Church of the Holy Sepulchre within the walls of the modern city. It has the weight of tradition on its side (from about the fourth century).

The Burial of Jesus

[57]When it was evening,[a] a rich man from Arimathea named Joseph came, who himself had also become a disciple[b] of Jesus. [58]He approached Pilate and asked for Jesus' body. Then Pilate ordered that it[A] be released. [59]So Joseph took the body, wrapped it in *clean, fine linen, [60]and placed it in his new tomb, which he had cut into the rock. He left after rolling a great stone against the entrance of the tomb.[c] [61]Mary Magdalene and the other Mary were seated there, facing the tomb.

The Closely Guarded Tomb

[62]The next day, which followed the preparation day, the chief priests and the *Pharisees gathered before Pilate[d] [63]and said, "Sir, we remember that while this deceiver was still alive He said, 'After three days I will rise again.'[e] [64]Therefore give orders that the tomb be made secure until the third day. Otherwise, His disciples[f] may come, steal Him, and tell the people, 'He has been raised from the dead.' Then the last deception will be worse than the first."

[65]"You have[B] a guard of soldiers,"[C] Pilate told them. "Go and make it as secure as you know how." [66]Then they went and made the tomb secure by sealing the stone and setting the guard.[D,g]

Resurrection Morning

28 After the Sabbath,[h] as the first day of the week was dawning, *Mary Magdalene and the other Mary went to view the tomb. [2]Suddenly there was a violent earthquake, because an angel of the Lord descended from heaven and approached the tomb. He rolled back the stone and was sitting on it.[i] [3]His appearance was like lightning, and his robe was as white as snow.[j] [4]The guards were so shaken from fear of him that they became like dead men.

[5]But the angel told the women, "Don't be afraid, because I know you are looking for Jesus who was crucified.[k] [6]He is not here! For He has been resurrected, just as He said. Come and see the place where He lay.[l] [7]Then go quickly and tell His disciples,[m] 'He has been raised from the dead. In fact, He is going ahead of you to Galilee; you will see Him there.' Listen, I have told you."[n]

[8]So, departing quickly from the tomb with fear and great joy, they ran to tell His disciples the news. [9]Just then[E] Jesus met them and said, "Good morning!" They came up, took hold of His feet, and worshiped Him.[o] [10]Then Jesus told them, "Do not be afraid. Go and tell My brothers to leave for Galilee, and they will see Me there."[p]

The Soldiers Are Bribed to Lie

[11]As they were on their way, some of the guards came into the city and reported to the *chief priests everything that had happened. [12]After the priests[F] had assembled with the elders and agreed on a plan, they gave the soldiers a large sum of money [13]and told them,

Cross references

a 27:57-61 Mk 15:42-47; Lk 23:50-56; Jn 19:38-42
b 27:57 Mt 10:42; 28:19; Lk 14:26; Jn 8:31; 13:35; 15:8; Ac 6:1
c 27:60 Is 53:9; Mt 27:66; 28:2; Mk 16:4
d 27:62 Mk 15:42; Lk 23:54; Jn 19:14,31,42
e 27:63 Mt 16:21; 17:22-23; 20:19; Mk 8:31; 10:34; Lk 9:22; 18:33
f 27:64 Mt 10:1, 26:56; Mk 3:7; 16:20; Lk 6:13; Jn 12:16
g 27:66 Dn 6:17; Mt 28:2,11
h 28:1-8 Mk 16:1-8; Lk 24:1-10; Jn 20:1-8
i 28:2 Lk 24:4; Jn 20:12
j 28:3 Dn 7:9; 10:6; Mk 9:3; Jn 20:12; Ac 1:10
k 28:5 Mt 14:27; 28:10; Rv 1:17
l 28:6 Mt 12:40; 16:21; 27:63
m 28:7 Mt 10:1; 26:56; Mk 3:7; 16:20; Lk 6:13; Jn 12:16
n Mt 26:32; Mk 16:7
o 28:9 Mk 16:9; Jn 20:14
p 28:10 Jn 20:17; Rm 8:29; Heb 2:11-12,17

A 27:58 Other mss read *that the body*   B 27:65 Or *"Take*   C 27:65 It is uncertain whether this guard consisted of temple police or Roman soldiers.   D 27:66 Lit *stone with the guard*   E 28:9 Other mss add *as they were on their way to tell the news to His disciples*   F 28:12 Lit *After they*

had opposed their condemnation of Jesus (Lk 23:50-51). Though Jesus taught that rich people cannot enter God's kingdom by their own efforts, Joseph is proof that God can save anyone by His grace (Mt 19:24-26). The bodies of crucified victims were normally allowed to rot on the cross, but Pilate respected Jewish scruples and allowed the dead to be buried.

27:65 Pilate sent a detachment of soldiers to protect the tomb from disciples who might attempt to stage a fake resurrection. The Greek term for the detachment (Gk *koustodia*) does not specify the number of soldiers in the unit.

27:66 The seal consisted of wax bearing the imprint of an official Roman seal. This ensured that no one could tamper with the tomb without being detected. Any unauthorized persons who broke the seal defied the authority of Rome and could be punished by death.

28:1 These events occurred early Sunday morning. For the identity of **the other Mary**, see note at 27:56. Since the ancients did not view women as trustworthy, a writer who made up an account designed to convince readers of Jesus' resurrection would not have made women the first witnesses of the resurrection. That Matthew included the women

confirms that he was faithful to record actual events, even if they would be seen as discreditable by society.

28:3 The angel's **appearance** identified him as a heavenly being (see Dn 7:9; 10:6).

28:4 The soldiers lost consciousness and fell to the ground.

28:6 The words **just as He said** recall Jesus' prophecies about His resurrection (12:40; 16:21; 17:23; 20:19). Jesus taught that the OT prophecies had to be fulfilled since they came from God (5:18; 26:54,56).

28:9 During His wilderness temptation (4:10), Jesus quoted Dt 6:13, "Worship the Lord your God, and serve only Him" (Mt 4:10). By accepting worship here, Jesus identified Himself as "the Lord your God."

28:13-14 Wide circulation of this story probably led to the emperor's edict in the Nazareth Inscription (likely dated ca A.D. 41-54) that threatened death to anyone who removed an entombed body. Several aspects of the soldiers' story make no sense. If the soldiers were all asleep, they could not have known that it was Jesus' disciples who removed His body. Furthermore, it is extremely unlikely that all of the soldiers would have slept at the same time. Finally, soldiers were severely punished or even executed for sleeping on duty.

"Say this, 'His disciples came during the night and stole Him while we were sleeping.' [14]If this reaches the governor's ears,[A] we will deal with[B] him and keep you out of trouble."[a] [15]So they took the money and did as they were instructed. And this story has been spread among Jewish people to this day.[b]

The Great Commission

[16]The 11 disciples traveled to Galilee, to the mountain where Jesus had directed them.[c] [17]When they saw Him, they worshiped,[c] but some doubted. [18]Then Jesus came near and said to them, "All authority has been given to Me in heaven and on earth.[d] [19]Go, therefore, and make disciples[e] of[D] all nations,[f] baptizing[g] them in the name of the Father and of the Son and of the Holy Spirit, [20]teaching them to observe everything I have commanded you. And remember,[E] I am with you always,[F] to the end of the age."[h]

[a] 28:14 Mt 27:2; Ac 12:20 [b] 28:15 Mt 9:31; 27:8; Mk 1:45 [c] 28:16 Mt 26:32; 28:7 [d] 28:18 Dn 7:13-14; Jn 17:2; Rm 14:9; Eph 1:20-22; Php 2:9-10; Col 2:10; 1Pt 3:22 [e] 28:19 Mt 10:42; 28:19; Lk 14:26; Jn 8:31; 13:35; 15:8; Ac 6:1 [f] Mk 16:15; Lk 24:47 [g] Ac 2:38; 8:16 [h] 28:20 Mt 13:39; 18:20; Ac 1:2; 2:42; 18:10

[A] 28:14 Lit this is heard by the governor [B] 28:14 Lit will persuade [C] 28:17 Other mss add Him [D] 28:19 Or and disciple; lit and instruct [E] 28:20 Lit look [F] 28:20 Lit all the days

28:17 On the significance of the disciples' worship, see note at verse 9. The lingering confusion among them about Jesus' resurrection undermines the skeptical theory that the disciples shared a hallucination of Jesus' resurrection because they all expected Him to arise.

28:18 Before the resurrection, Jesus had authority (7:29; 9:6,8; 11:27; 21:23). However, through the resurrection, the Father granted Him **all authority** over **heaven and . . . earth,** an authority far greater than that which Satan had vainly promised Him (see note at 4:8-9).

28:19 The command to extend their mission worldwide brings to a climax Matthew's repeated theme of Gentile participation in God's salvation. The inclusion of four Gentile women in Jesus' genealogy and the summons of the magi to worship the infant Christ foreshadowed the disciples' mission of making disciples of all nations. Baptism marked a person's entrance into the faith community. **In the name of the Father and of the Son and of the Holy Spirit** is a reference to the Trinity. Matthew's language shows that a clear understanding of Jesus' nature and identity as God was required before baptism.

28:20 The Great Commission (vv. 19-20) is preceded by a reference to Jesus' authority and followed by the promise of Jesus' spiritual presence among us. Both are necessary if we are to fulfill our God-given mission.

matheteuo

Greek Pronunciation	[mah they TYOO oh]
HCSB Translation	make disciples
Uses in Matthew	3
Uses in the NT	4
Focus Passage	Matthew 28:19

The verb *matheteuo* (to make disciples) is derived from the noun *mathetes,* which occurs over 250 times, entirely in the Gospels and Acts. *Mathetes* means *disciple, pupil, one who learns* from another, and typically indicates a person whose life is bound up with that of Jesus, his Master. *Matheteuo* means *to become a disciple* (Mt 27:57) or *to be instructed* (Mt 13:52). In another two occurrences it means *to make disciples* (Mt 28:19; Ac 14:21). In the Great Commission (Mt 28:18-20), the particular Greek construction (aorist participle followed by aorist imperative; this construction is relatively common in Matthew, Luke, and Acts) indicates that the primary weight of Jesus' command in the Great Commission is to *make disciples,* while the act of "going" is a necessary prerequisite to accomplishing this task.

The Biblical Basis for Missions

M. David Sills

Not only is there a biblical basis for missions, it is accurate to see a missionary purpose for the entire Bible. If God had not revealed Himself in Scripture, we would only know that there is a Creator God (Ps 19; Rm 1:18-20) and that we are sinners (Rm 2:14-15). Such general revelation is not sufficient to lead us to saving knowledge of God.

The Bible teaches that Jesus is the only answer to humanity's need for holiness and salvation (Jn 3:16; 14:6; Ac 4:12; 2Co 5:21). We are all sinners by birth and choice (Rm 3:23). Therefore, everyone must repent and be spiritually born again because sin separates us from God (Rm 3:2). People are not spiritually neutral until they hear the gospel and reject it; as sinners, they are already condemned and hopeless. Therefore, God gave us the Bible that we might know Him and make Him known. Making God known is what missions is all about.

The Bible teaches that God has a missionary heart. After their fall into sin, God came to Adam and Eve and announced the *protoevangelion* (first gospel), that One was coming to destroy the work of the evil one (Gn 3:15). When God later called Abram, He told him that He would bless all the families of the earth through him (Gn 12:3). Many of the Psalms also reveal God's desire that all nations know and glorify Him (Pss 67; 96). In Isaiah 49:6, God says that it is too small a thing for the Christ to raise up only the tribes of Israel; He would also make Him a light to the Gentiles. Simeon quoted this passage when he held the baby Jesus at the temple (Lk 2:29-32). The book of Jonah reveals God's missionary heartbeat, for God sent Jonah to pagan Nineveh. Jesus' disciples were surprised when some Greeks wanted to see Him, but He announced that He would draw all people to Himself (Jn 12:32). Throughout the Bible God led people from many nations to join with His people. We even see this on display in the lineage of Jesus, which includes Gentile ancestors (Mt 1:1-17; Lk 3:3-38).

We see God's missionary purpose and heartbeat in three key elements of the Gospels: the Great Commission, the Great Commandments, and the Great Compassion. In the Great Commission, Jesus charges His followers to make disciples of all nations by going to them, winning and baptizing them, and teaching them to obey all He has commanded (Mt 28:19-20). In Matthew 22:33-40, the Great Commandments teach us to love God and our neighbor. If we love God, we will obey His commands and strive to see the whole world worship Him. If we love our neighbor, we will want him to have eternal life. As we seek to imitate Jesus, the Great Compassion that characterized His life will shape ours also. Mark 6:34 shows that Jesus had compassion for the crowds who were like sheep without a shepherd. He said in Luke 19:10 that He came to seek and save those who were lost. Our compassion should lead us to go to them and preach the gospel, disciple believers, teach leaders, and plant New Testament churches among them.

The gospel is God's power to save all who believe (Rm 1:16; 10:13), and Christ calls every Christian to participate in global missions (Mt 28:19-20). While all who call on Jesus will be saved, Paul reasons that no one can call on Him if they do not believe, believe unless they hear, hear unless someone goes to preach, or go to preach unless they are sent. The Bible teaches that we all have a role in missions, either as "goers" or as "senders." Neither is more biblical than the other and neither is possible without the other (Rm 10:13-15).

Mark

Mark's Gospel emphasizes actions and deeds. Jesus is on the go—healing, casting out demons, performing miracles, hurrying from place to place, and teaching. In Mark everything happens "immediately." As soon as one episode ends, another begins. The rapid pace slows down when Jesus enters Jerusalem (11:1). Thereafter, events are marked by days, and His final day by hours.

"Who then is this?" is the central question of Mark's Gospel. Jesus' disciples asked this question to each other just after Jesus spoke to and calmed what seemed a life-threatening storm on the Sea of Galilee (4:35-41).

Circumstances of Writing

Author: The Gospel of Mark is anonymous. Eusebius, the early church historian, writing in A.D. 326, preserved the words of Papias, an early church father. Papias quoted "the elder," probably John, as saying that Mark recorded Peter's preaching about the things Jesus said and did, but not in order. Thus, Mark was considered the author of this Gospel even in the first century.

The Mark who wrote this Gospel was John Mark, the son of a widow named Mary, in whose house the church in Jerusalem sometimes gathered (Ac 12:12-17) and where Jesus possibly ate the Last Supper with His disciples. Mark was the cousin of Barnabas (Col 4:10), and he accompanied Barnabas and Paul back to Antioch after their famine relief mission to Jerusalem (Ac 12:25). Mark next went with Barnabas and Paul on part of the first missionary journey as an assistant (Ac 13:5), but at Perga, Mark turned back (Ac 13:13).

When the apostle Peter wrote to the churches in Asia Minor shortly before his martyrdom, he sent greetings from Mark, whom he called "my son" (1Pt 5:13). Then shortly before his execution, Paul asked Timothy to "Bring Mark with you, for he is useful to me in the ministry" (2Tm 4:11). After Paul's execution, Mark is said to have moved to Egypt, established churches, and served them in Alexandria (Eusebius, *Eccl. Hist.*, 2:16). Some have suggested the young man in Mark 14:51-52 was Mark himself.

Background: According to the early church fathers, Mark wrote his Gospel in Rome just before or just after Peter's martyrdom. Further confirmation of the Roman origin of Mark's Gospel is found in Mark 15:21 where Mark noted that Simon, a Cyrenian who carried Jesus' cross, was the father of Alexander and Rufus, men apparently known to the believers in Rome.

Because Mark wrote primarily for Roman Gentiles, he explained Jewish customs, translated Aramaic words and phrases into Greek, used Latin terms rather than their Greek equivalents, and rarely quoted from the OT. Most Bible scholars are convinced that Mark was the earliest Gospel and served as one of the sources for Matthew and Luke.

---

75 B.C.

Spartacus, the Roman gladiator, leads a slave revolt based near Mount Vesuvius. **73**

Pompey conquers Jerusalem. **63**

Rome's Gallic wars (58–51) begin after Julius Caesar became Roman governor of Gaul.

Pompey builds first stone amphitheater in Rome. **55**

Julius Caesar invades Britain. **55–54**

50 B.C.

Circus Maximus built in Rome **50**

Mark Antony controls Rome; Julius Caesar assassinated. **44**

Parthians conquer Jerusalem. **40–37**

Herod becomes "king of the Jews." **37**

Qumran abandoned **31**

Message and Purpose

Mark's Gospel is a narrative about Jesus. Mark identified his theme in the first verse: "the gospel of Jesus Christ, the Son of God." That Jesus is the divine Son of God is the major emphasis of his Gospel. God announced it at Jesus' baptism in 1:11. Demons and unclean spirits recognized and acknowledged it in 3:11 and 5:7. God reaffirmed it at the transfiguration in 9:7. Jesus taught it parabolically in 12:1-12, hinted at it in 13:32, and confessed it directly in 14:61-62. Finally, the Roman centurion confessed it openly and without qualification in 15:39. Thus Mark's purpose was to summon people to repent and respond in faith to the good news of Jesus Christ, the Messiah, the Son of God (1:1,15).

Contribution to the Bible

Many concepts of the Messiah existed in Jesus' day, and several individuals laid claim to the title. What Mark contributes is a clarification of the concept of Messiah and a redefining of the term. Peter's insightful confession at Caesarea Philippi in 8:29 became the turning point at which Jesus began to explain that the divine conception of the Messiah involved rejection, suffering, death, and then resurrection (8:31). Mark also shows us the human side of Jesus. In fact, more than the other Gospel writers, Mark emphasizes Jesus' human side and His emotions. Thus Mark gives us a strong picture of both the humanity and the divinity of Jesus.

Structure

Mark's Gospel begins with a Prologue (1:1-13), which is then followed by three major sections. The first (1:14–8:21) tells of Jesus' Galilean ministry. There Jesus healed and cast out demons and worked miracles. The second section (8:22–10:52) is transitional. Jesus began His journey that would take Him to Jerusalem. The final section (11:1–16:8) involves a week in Jerusalem. From the time Jesus entered the city He was at odds with the religious leaders, who quickly brought about His execution. A brief appendix (16:9-20) in which some of Jesus' appearances, His commissioning of His disciples, and His ascension are recorded is attached to the Gospel.

A.D. 25

A.D. 30

Jesus visits the temple at the age of 12. 9

Tiberius, Rome's second emperor 14–37

Caiaphas, Jewish high priest 18–36

Jesus baptized and begins calling disciples. 29

Jesus' early ministry in Judea Autumn 29 to Spring 30 (John 2–4)

Jesus' Galilean ministry Summer 30 to Spring 32 (all four Gospels)

Jesus travels with disciples and engages in intensive training. Summer and early Autumn 32 (Matthew, Mark, and Luke)

Jesus' later ministry in Judea late Autumn and early Winter 32 (Luke and John)

Jesus' Perean ministry late Winter and early Spring 33 (Luke and John)

Jesus' crucifixion, resurrection, exaltation 33 (all four Gospels)

Outline

The Messiah's Herald

1 The beginning[a] of the gospel[b] of Jesus Christ, the Son of God.[c] [2] As it is written in Isaiah[d] the prophet:[A,e]

> Look, I am sending My messenger[f]
>   ahead of You,
> who will prepare Your way.[B]
> [3] A voice of one crying out
>   in the wilderness:[g]
> Prepare the way for the Lord;[h]
> make His paths straight![C,i]

[4] John came baptizing[D,j] in the wilderness[k] and preaching a baptism of repentance[E,l] for the forgiveness[m] of sins.[n] [5] The whole Judean countryside and all the people of Jerusalem[o] were flocking to him, and they were baptized by him in the Jordan[p] River as they confessed[q] their sins.[r] [6] John wore a camel-hair garment with a leather belt around his waist and ate locusts[s] and wild honey.[t] [7] He was preaching: "Someone more powerful[u] than I will come after me.[v] I am not worthy[w] to stoop down and untie the strap of His sandals.[x] [8] I have baptized you with[F] water,[y] but He will baptize you with the Holy Spirit."[z]

The Baptism of Jesus

[9] In[aa] those days Jesus came from Nazareth[ab] in Galilee[ac] and was baptized in the Jordan by John. [10] As soon as He came up out of the water, He saw the heavens[ad] being torn open and the Spirit descending to Him like a dove. [11] And a voice[ae] came from heaven:[af]

> You are My beloved[ag] Son;[ah]
> I take delight[ai] in You![G]

[a]1:1 Jn 1:1; Php 4:15
[b]1:1-8 Mt 3:1-12; Lk 3:1-18
[c]1:1 Jn 5:19; Heb 1:2
[d]1:2 Mt 3:3; 4:14; 12:17
[e]Lk 16:29
[f]Mt 13:49
[g]1:3 Jn 1:23
[h]Lk 10:1; 17:5
[i]1:2-3 Is 40:3; Mal 3:1
[j]1:4 Lk 7:29; Ac 22:16
[k]Rv 12:6
[l]Lk 3:3; Ac 13:24; 19:4; 26:20
[m]Mt 9:2; Lk 24:47
[n]Jn 15:22; Ac 26:18
[o]1:5 Mt 23:37; Jn 11:36
[p]Gn 13:10; Ps 114:3; Lk 3:3
[q]Ac 19:18
[r]Jn 15:22; Rm 6:23; 1Pt 4:1
[s]1:6 Rv 9:3,7
[t]Rv 10:9-10
[u]1:7 Rv 18:8
[v]Jn 1:15
[w]Mt 3:11
[x]Lk 3:16; Ac 13:23-25
[y]1:8 Jn 1:26,31,33; Ac 1:5; 8:36; 11:16
[z]Jn 1:33
[aa]1:9-11 Mt 3:13-17; Lk 3:21-23
[ab]1:9 Mt 2:23; 4:13; 21:11; Lk 1:26; 2:4,39,51; 4:16; Jn 1:45-46
[ac]Mt 17:22
[ad]1:10 Mt 24:35; Lk 12:33; Ac 17:24; Eph 6:9; Rv 21:10
[ae]1:11 Jn 5:37
[af]Rv 14:13
[ag]Lk 20:13; Eph 1:6; Phm 1
[ah]Ps 2:7
[ai]Is 42:1

[A]1:2 Other mss read *in the prophets*   [B]1:2 Other mss add *before You*   [C]1:2-3 Is 40:3; Mal 3:1   [D]1:4 Or *John the Baptist came*, or *John the Baptizer came*   [E]1:4 Or *a baptism based on repentance*   [F]1:8 Or *in*   [G]1:11 Or *In You I am well pleased*

1:1 Mark's Gospel starts at **the beginning** (Gk *arché*) **of the gospel** (Gk *euangelion*, meaning "good news"). The name **Jesus** is the NT equivalent of the OT name Joshua, meaning "Yahweh is salvation." Jesus is identified as **Christ** or Messiah and **Son of God**. Jesus is often identified as God's Son in Mark: at His baptism (v. 11), by demons (3:11; 5:7), the transfiguration (9:7), His trial (14:61), and the centurion's confession (15:39).

1:2-3 As it is written is a formulaic expression indicating the authoritative character of the OT (7:6; 9:13; 11:17; 14:21,27). The phrase **in Isaiah the prophet** introduces a mixed quotation from Ex 23:20; Is 40:3; and Mal 3:10. Hence some manuscripts read "in the prophets." In its original context, **Lord** refers to Yahweh. The **messenger** announces the coming of God Himself. The Gospel writers applied the words to Jesus, who is God in flesh (Jn 1:14).

1:4 Mark does not mention John's birth (Lk 1) but instead introduces him as **baptizing in the wilderness**, a place that recalled Israel's disobedience (Jos 5:6) and God's redemption. John called for **a baptism of repentance for the forgiveness of sins**. "Repentance" means "to change one's mind." It involves a deliberate turn from sins.

1:5 That John attracted **the whole Judean countryside and all the people of Jerusalem** indicates his appeal among both country folk and urbanites.

1:6 John's dress was like Elijah's (2Kg 1:8) and other prophets (Zch 13:4). Mark's description suggests that John was the Elijah who was expected to return and call the nation to repent before the day of the Lord (Mal 4:5-6).

1:7-8 John announced that the coming One was **more powerful** and that he was **not worthy to stoop down and untie the strap of His sandals**—a task for Gentile slaves. The coming One was also superior in His work: **He will baptize you with the Holy Spirit** (Ac 11:16; see notes at Ac 1:5 and 1:8). John's baptism was symbolic; Jesus' baptism would introduce the reality. Only here and in Mk 3:29 and 13:11 does Mark mention the Holy Spirit.

1:9-11 Nazareth is mentioned only here in Mark (cp. 6:1).

Three things occurred **as soon as** Jesus **came up out of the water**. The **heavens** were **torn open . . . the Spirit** descended, and God's **voice** came **from heaven**. "As soon as" or "immediately" (Gk *euthus*) occurs over 40 times in Mark. **My beloved Son** indicates the Son's uniqueness and recalls Abraham's love for Isaac (Gn 22:2,12,16). Only Israel (Ex 4:23) and Israel's king (Ps 2:7) were called God's son in

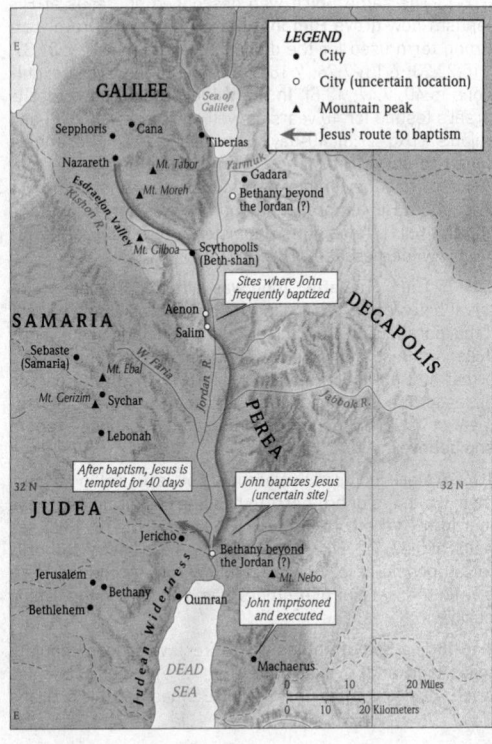

The Temptation of Jesus

[12] Immediately[a] the Spirit[b] drove[c] Him into the wilderness.[d] [13] He was in the wilderness 40 days, being tempted[e] by Satan.[f] He was with the wild animals,[g] and the angels[h] began to serve Him.

Ministry in Galilee

[14] After[i] John was arrested,[j] Jesus went to Galilee,[k] preaching[l] the good news[A,B,m] of God:[C,n] [15] "The time[o] is fulfilled, and the kingdom of God[p] has come[q] near.[r] Repent[s] and believe[t] in the good news!"

The First Disciples

[16] As[u] He was passing along by the Sea of Galilee,[v] He saw Simon[w] and Andrew,[x] Simon's brother. They were casting a net into the sea,[y] since they were fishermen. [17] "Follow Me,"[z] Jesus told them, "and I will make you fish for[D,aa] people!"[ab] [18] Immediately they left their nets and followed[ac] Him.[ad] [19] Going on a little farther, He saw James[ae] the son of Zebedee[af] and his brother John.[ag] They were in their boat mending their nets. [20] Immedi-

ately He called them, and they left their father Zebedee in the boat with the hired men and followed Him.[ah]

Driving Out an Unclean Spirit

[21] Then[ai] they went into Capernaum,[aj] and right away He entered the *synagogue[ak] on the Sabbath[al] and began to teach.[am] [22] They were astonished[an] at His teaching[ao] because, unlike the *scribes,[ap] He was teaching them as one having authority.

[23] Just then a man with an *unclean[aq] spirit[ar] was in their synagogue.[as] He cried out,[E] [24] "What do You have to do with us,[F] Jesus—Nazarene?[at] Have You come to destroy[au] us? I know who You are—the Holy[av] One of God!"[aw] [25] But Jesus rebuked[ax] him and said, "Be quiet,[G,ay] and come out of him!" [26] And the

---

[a]1:12-13 Mt 4:1-11; Lk 4:1-13 [b]1:12 Jn 1:33 [c]3Jn 10 [d]Mt 3:1; Rv 12:6 [e]1:13 Jms 1:13 [f]Mt 4:1,10; Ac 13:10 [g]Rv 6:8 [h]Mt 13:49; Ac 5:19; Rv 14:6 [i]1:14-15 Mt 4:17; Jn 4:45 [j]1:14 Mt 3:12; Lk 3:20; 9:7-9; Jn 3:24 [k]Mt 17:22 [l]Mk 13:10 [m]Mk 1:1 [n]Rm 15:16; 1Th 2:2,8-9 [o]1:15 Ps 37:39; Lk 20:10; Jn 7:8 [p]Mt 3:2; 6:33; 12:28; 19:24; 21:31,43; Mk 4:11; 9:1; 10:14; 12:34; 14:25; 15:43 [q]Mk 9:1 [r]Rm 13:11; 1Pt 4:7 [s]Ac 3:19; 26:20 [t]Mk 11:24; Jn 3:16; Ac 10:43; Rm 10:9; 1Pt 1:8-10
[u]1:16-20 Mt 4:18-22; Lk 5:1-11 [v]1:16 Mt 4:18; 15:29; Jn 6:1 [w]Mt 16:17 [x]Jn 6:8 [y]Mk 7:31 [z]1:17 Mt 4:19 [aa]Mt 4:18-19; Lk 5:2 [ab]Mt 4:19 [ac]1:18 Lk 5:11; Jn 8:12 [ad]Lk 18:28 [ae]1:19 Ac 12:2 [af]Jn 21:2 [ag]Jn 21:7 [ah]1:20 Lk 18:28 [ai]1:21-26 Lk 4:31-35 [aj]1:21 Lk 10:15 [ak]Mk 3:1; Jms 2:2 [al]Mk 2:23; Lk 13:10 [am]Mt 28:20; Ac 4:2; 2Tm 4:11 [an]1:22 Mk 6:2 [ao]Mt 7:28; 22:33; Mk 11:18; Lk 4:32; Ac 2:42; 17:19 [ap]Mt 2:4 [aq]1:23 2Co 6:17 [ar]Lk 11:24 [as]Jms 2:2 [at]1:24 Mk 14:67 [au]Jn 6:27 [av]1Co 7:14 [aw]Lk 4:34; Jn 6:69; Eph 4:30 [ax]1:25 2Tm 4:2 [ay]Mt 22:12

A1:14 Other mss add *of the kingdom* **B**1:14 Or *gospel* **C**1:14 Either *from God* or *about God* **D**1:17 Lit *you to become fishers of* **E**1:23 Other mss add to the beginning of v. 24: *"Leave us alone.* **F**1:24 Lit *What to us and to You* **G**1:25 Or *Be muzzled*

---

the OT. The divine declaration in Mk 1:11 announced Jesus' eternal relationship to God. All three persons of the Trinity were represented at Jesus' baptism.

1:12-13 The same **Spirit** who descended on Jesus at His baptism now **drove Him into the wilderness**. "Drove" is a strong term used for the driving out of demons (vv. 34,39; 3:15,22,23; 6:13; 7:26; 9:18,28,38) and other forced expulsions (5:40; 9:47; 12:8). **In the wilderness 40 days** recalls Israel's testing for 40 years as well as Moses' (Dt 9:18) and Elijah's (1Kg 19:8) 40-day wilderness fasts. **The angels began to serve Him** is in the imperfect tense. This may indicate that they ministered to Jesus in unstated ways throughout His temptation, though He was not fed until the end (Mt 4:11). Angels also ministered to Elijah during his 40-day wilderness fast (1Kg 19:1-8).

1:14-15 The words **after John was arrested** indicate an interval between verses 13 and 14, possibly as long as a year if this parallels Jn 4:3,43. Mark did not include Jesus' early Judean ministry (Jn 3:22-36). Further details about John's arrest and execution appear in Mk 6:17-29. In the person of Jesus, the **kingdom of God** was so near that announcement of its arrival demanded immediate response—**repent and believe**.

1:16-20 Mark included two accounts of Jesus calling fishermen, two pairs of brothers, to become His disciples. These four formed the core of the group (v. 29; 3:16-18; 13:3; see notes at 5:37; 9:2; 14:33). Mark emphasized Jesus' authority to call people to leave all and follow Him. According to Lk 5:7-10, the two pair of brothers were partners in the fishing business.

1:16-18 The **Sea of Galilee** was a freshwater lake about 12 miles long and 7 miles wide that lay 700 feet below sea level. Also known as the Sea of Gennesaret (Lk 5:1) and

the Sea of Tiberias (Jn 21:1), it hosted a thriving fishing industry. Brothers **Simon** and **Andrew** hailed from Bethsaida, across the northern end of the lake (Jn 1:44), but they now lived in Capernaum (Mk 1:29). **Follow Me** is the heart of NT discipleship. It involves adopting Jesus' values and lifestyle. **I will make you fish for people** expands on their former profession. The words also point to a second aspect of discipleship—the call to serve the Lord and people through ministry.

1:19-20 The phrase **going on a little farther** links the call of the second pair of brothers—**James** and **John**—in time and place to the first pair. The fact that **hired men** were present implies their fishing business was prosperous. Leaving this to follow Jesus meant leaving a nice living. Like the first pair of brothers in verse 18, these **followed** Jesus. Mark's words in the Greek directly link their response in verse 20 to Jesus' command in verse 17.

1:21-22 Capernaum, on the northwestern shore of the Sea of Galilee, became Jesus' home (2:1) and headquarters (Mt 4:13). Mark did not record what Jesus **began to teach** in the **synagogue**, but he did say that the people were **astonished**. This was a regular reaction to Jesus' teachings (6:2; 7:37; 10:26; 11:18). What impressed listeners was the **authority** with which Jesus taught. His authority contrasted with that of **the scribes** who mastered the Torah and treasured traditional interpretations (oral traditions). In Mark the scribes were Jesus' fiercest opponents (2:6,16; 11:27) and were among the main instigators leading to His death (8:31; 10:33; 11:18; 14:1,43,53; 15:1,31).

1:23-24 Just then links this event to verses 21-22. Mark used **unclean spirit** to denote a demonic spirit. "Unclean spirit" contrasts with the demons' identification of Jesus as **the Holy One of God**. The man's shout **What do You have to do with us**

unclean spirit convulsed him,[a] shouted with a loud voice, and came out of him.

[27] Then they were all amazed,[b] so they began to argue[c] with one another, saying, "What is this? A new teaching[d] with authority![A,e] He commands even the unclean[f] spirits,[g] and they obey Him." [28] News about Him then spread throughout the entire vicinity of Galilee.[h]

Healings at Capernaum

[29] As[i] soon as they left the synagogue,[j] they went into Simon[k] and Andrew's[l] house[m] with James[n] and John.[o] [30] Simon's mother-in-law was lying in bed with a fever, and they told Him about her at once. [31] So He went to her, took her by the hand, and raised her up.[p] The fever[q] left her,[B] and she began to serve[r] them.[s]

[32] When[t] evening came, after the sun had set, they began bringing to Him all those who were sick[u] and those who were demon-possessed.[v] [33] The whole town was assembled at the door, [34] and He healed[w] many who were sick with various diseases[x] and drove out[y] many demons.[z] But He would not permit the demons to speak, because they knew Him.[aa]

Preaching in Galilee

[35] Very[ab] early in the morning, while it was still dark, He got up, went out, and made His way to a deserted place.[ac] And He was praying[ad] there. [36] Simon[ae] and his companions went searching for Him. [37] They found Him and said, "Everyone's looking for You!"

[38] And He said to them, "Let's go on to the neighboring villages so that I may preach[af] there too. This is why I have come." [39] So He went into all of Galilee,[ag] preaching in their synagogues[ah] and driving out demons.

A Man Cleansed

[40] Then[ai] a man with a serious skin disease[aj] came to Him and, on his knees,[C,ak] begged Him: "If You are willing, You can make me *clean.*"[al]

[41] Moved with compassion,[am] Jesus reached out His hand and touched[an] him. "I am willing," He told him. "Be made clean." [42] Immediately the disease[ao] left him, and he was healed.[D] [43] Then He sternly warned[ap] him and sent him away[aq] at once, [44] telling him, "See

Cross references:
a 1:26 Mk 9:26; Lk 9:39
b 1:27 Mk 10:24,32
c Mk 8:11
d Mk 11:18; Ac 2:42
e Jd 25
f 2Co 6:17
g Lk 11:24
h 1:28 Mt 17:22
i 1:29-31 Mt 8:14-15; Lk 4:38-39
j 1:29 Jms 2:2
k Mt 16:17
l Jn 6:8
m Mk 9:33
n Ac 12:2
o Jn 21:7
p 1:31 Mk 5:41
q Lk 4:38
r Phm 13
s Rm 12:13
t 1:32-34 Mt 8:16-17; Lk 4:40-41
u 1:32 Lk 5:31
v Mt 9:32
w 1:34 Ac 8:7
x Ac 19:12
y 3Jn 10
z Rv 9:20; 18:2
aa Mk 3:11-12; 5:7
ab 1:35-38 Mt 4:23-25; Lk 4:42-44
ac 1:35 Mt 14:13; Mk 6:31-32; Lk 4:42; 9:12;
Rv 12:6
ad Mt 5:44; Ac 12:12
ae 1:36 Mt 16:17
af 1:38 Mk 1:4
ag 1:39 Mt 17:22
ah Mk 3:1
ai 1:40-44 Mt 8:2-4; Lk 5:12-14
aj 1:40 Mt 11:5
ak Mt 17:14
al 1Jn 1:7
am 1:41 Lk 15:20
an Jn 20:17
ao 1:42 Lk 5:12
ap 1:43 Mt 9:30; Mk 14:5; Jn 11:33,38
aq 3Jn 10

A 1:27 Other mss read *What is this? What is this new teaching? For with authority* **B** 1:31 Other mss add *at once* **C** 1:40 Other mss omit *on his knees* **D** 1:42 Lit *made clean*

echoes Jephthah's words to the Ammonite king (Jdg 11:12) and those of the widow of Zarephath to Elijah (1Kg 17:18).

1:25-26 On the basis of the authority of His word, Jesus **rebuked** and expelled the spirit, commanding it to **be quiet,** (lit "be muzzled") **and come out of him.** The **spirit convulsed** the man (see note at 9:26-27) and **shouted** its desperate but futile resistance to Jesus.

1:27-28 The people were **amazed** to see an exorcism, especially given the authoritative manner in which Jesus accomplished it. Their statement that **the unclean spirits . . . obey Him** indicates their belief that what He did to one spirit, He could do to all. The word **then** (Gk *euthus,* "immediately") indicates how quickly the story of these events traveled **throughout . . . Galilee.**

1:29-31 As soon as they left the synagogue connects verses 29-34 to the same Sabbath day as verses 21-28. **Simon and Andrew's house** was large enough to host Jesus and His followers. Archaeologists have identified such a house near the synagogue in Capernaum. **Simon's mother-in-law** indicates that Peter was married. First Corinthians 9:5 suggests Peter's wife was supportive of his ministry. Jesus did not speak any words to heal Peter's mother-in-law, He simply **took her by the hand.** The phrase **raised her up** is a common expression for Jesus' healings in Mark (2:9,11; 3:3; 5:41; 9:27; 10:49).

1:32-34 The expressions **when evening came** and **after the sun had set** emphasize that the Sabbath prohibitions against work were over since the Sabbath ended at sunset. The phrases **those who were sick . . . those who were demon-possessed** recall the two types of healings Jesus

performed earlier that day (vv. 23-26 and 30-31). That there is a difference between disease and demon possession is affirmed by Mark's description of Jesus' actions: He **healed** the **sick** but **drove out** the **demons** (3:10-11; 6:13). That Jesus healed **various diseases** points to the comprehensive nature of His healing powers.

1:35-39 **Very early in the morning** and **while it was still dark** together indicate that Jesus did not rest much after the previous evening's activity. The early hour explains how He got out of town undetected. The motion verbs **got up, went out, and made His way** describe Jesus' search for **a deserted place,** the same word used for the wilderness where John preached (v. 4) and where Jesus was tempted (v. 12). **Simon and his companions** refers to the four disciples Jesus called. This is the first time Mark depicted Peter as the leading disciple. **Went searching** implies an unwelcome intrusion. Apparently everyone expected more miracles, but Jesus intended to **preach,** thus returning the focus to the start of His ministry (vv. 14-15).

1:40-45 Legislation related to **serious skin disease** appears in Lv 13-14. This account (and parallels in Mt 8:1-4 and Lk 5:12-16) and that of the 10 men (Lk 17:11-19) are the only stories of healing skin diseases in the NT. **Came to Him** shows the sick man initiated the action and that he broke protocol in doing so. His words **if You are willing, You can make me clean** affirmed Jesus' ability while submitting to His willingness. That Jesus was **moved with compassion** is a detail only Mark recorded. To touch someone with a skin disease violated OT law and rendered a person unclean. Nevertheless, **Jesus reached out His hand and touched him,** healing the man immediately. Jesus told him to follow

that you say nothing to anyone;[a] but go and show[b] yourself to the priest,[c] and offer[d] what Moses prescribed for your cleansing,[e] as a testimony[f] to them." [45] Yet he went out and began to proclaim[g] it widely and to spread the news,[h] with the result that Jesus could no longer enter a town openly. But He was out in deserted places, and they would come to Him from everywhere.

The Son of Man Forgives and Heals

2 When[i] He entered Capernaum[j] again after some days, it was reported that He was at home. [2] So many people gathered together that there was no more room, not even in the doorway, and He was speaking the message[k] to them. [3] Then they came to Him bringing a paralytic,[l] carried by four men. [4] Since they were not able to bring him to[A] Jesus because of the crowd, they removed the roof above where He was. And when they had broken through, they lowered the mat on which the paralytic was lying.

[5] Seeing their faith,[m] Jesus told the paralytic, "Son, your sins[n] are forgiven."[o]

[6] But some of the •scribes[p] were sitting there, thinking[q] to themselves:[B] [7] "Why does He speak like this? He's blaspheming![r] Who can forgive[s] sins[t] but God alone?"[u]

[8] Right away[v] Jesus understood in His spirit[w] that they were thinking like this within themselves and said to them, "Why are you thinking these things in your hearts?[C] [9] Which is easier:[x] to say to the paralytic,[y] 'Your sins are forgiven,' or to say, 'Get up, pick up your mat, and walk'?[z] [10] But so you may know that the •Son of Man[aa] has authority[ab] on earth to forgive sins,"[ac] He told the paralytic, [11] "I tell you: get up,[ad] pick up your mat, and go home."

[12] Immediately he got up, picked up the mat, and went out in front of everyone. As a result, they were all astounded[ae] and gave glory[af] to God,[ag] saying, "We have never seen anything like this!"[ah]

---

[a]1:43 Mk 5:43; 7:36; 8:26,30; 9:9; 16:8; Lk 5:14
[b]Rv 1:1
[c]Ac 4:1
[d]Heb 5:1; 8:3
[e]Lv 13-14; Heb 1:3
[f]Mk 6:11; 1Tm 2:6
[g]1:45 Mk 1:4; Jn 18:32
[h]Mk 4:14
[i]2:1-12 Mt 9:1-8; Lk 5:17-26
[j]2:1 Lk 10:15
[k]2:2 Mk 4:14; Jn 18:32
[l]2:3 Mt 4:24; 8:6; 9:2,6; Mk 2:3-10
[m]2:5 Mt 8:10; Ac 3:16; Rm 1:8; 1Co 2:5; Gl 2:16; 1Tm 1:2; Heb 4:2
[n]Jn 15:22
[o]Mt 9:2,5; Lk 5:20,23; 7:48
[p]2:6 Mt 2:4
[q]Mk 9:33
[r]2:7 Ex 22:28; Mk 3:29; Rv 13:6
[s]Ps 25:11; Mt 9:2
[t]Jn 15:22
[u]Ex 34:6-7; Is 43:25; 44:2
[v]2:8 Mk 10:52
[w]Lk 5:22; 16:15; Jn 2:25
[x]2:9 Lk 16:17; 18:25
[y]Mk 2:3
[z]Mt 11:5
[aa]2:10 Ps 8:4; Lk 5:24; Ac 7:56
[ab]Mt 28:18; Mk 1:22
[ac]Jn 15:22
[ad]2:11 Mk 5:41
[ae]2:12 Ac 10:45
[af]Jn 11:4; 17:1; 1Pt 2:12
[ag]Lk 2:14
[ah]Mt 9:33

[A]2:4 Other mss read *able to get near*   [B]2:6 Or *thinking in their hearts*   [C]2:8 Or *minds*

---

the requirements of Lv 13:47–14:54 **as a testimony** to the priests of his cure. We do not know whether he completed the prescribed rites, but he disobeyed Jesus' command to **say nothing to anyone** about his healing.

2:1–3:6 This section contains five conflict stories relating to Jesus' authority. In each, Jesus was accused of blasphemy, challenged about His association with sinners, rebuked for neglecting religious customs, and accused of breaking Sabbath laws.

2:1 He was at home probably refers to Peter's house (see note at 1:29-31).

2:2 The message (lit "the [Gk] *logos*," see also 4:33; 8:32) was later used to refer to Christian missionary preaching (Ac 6:4; 8:4; 17:11; Gl 6:6; Col 4:3). Here, it refers to the good news (Mk 1:14-15).

2:3 This is the only time Mark mentioned **a paralytic** (cp. Mt 8:6).

2:4 Removed the roof literally translates "unroofed the roof." Most houses in Palestine were single-story, flat-roofed structures with an outside staircase. The roof was used for work, drying laundry, sleeping, or prayer. Over the crossbeams small poles or branches were placed and covered with thatch and mud. **Broken through** (lit "digging it out") suggests debris must have fallen on the people below. A **mat** (vv. 4,9,11-12) was a poor person's pallet (6:55; Jn 5:8-11; Ac 5:15).

2:5 Their faith refers to those who carried the paralyzed man as well as the paralytic himself. Rather than a word of healing, Jesus spoke forgiveness over the paralytic after addressing him as **son. Your sins** is plural and possibly specific. The Greek word "sin" refers to missing the mark. Only here did Jesus link sin and infirmity. Possibly there was a direct relationship between this man's sins and his paralysis.

2:6-7 The scribes supposed Jesus was **blaspheming** when they heard Him declare the man's sins forgiven. Death by stoning was the prescribed penalty for blasphemy (Lv 24:16; Jn 10:33), and it was the charge on which Jesus was eventually executed (Mk 14:64).

2:8-11 The answer to Jesus' question **which is easier** is of course the unverifiable claim to have forgiven the paralytic's sins. After all, forgiveness of sins is a quality that cannot be checked against visible evidence, and so anyone can claim to forgive sins. Actually having the authority to do it is another thing altogether. To prove His right to forgive sins, Jesus undertook the more verifiable (yet still remarkable) task of healing the man. **Son of Man** was Jesus' favorite self-designation. It derives from Dn 7:13-14, where the messianic Son of Man is given **authority** (see note at 1:21-22).

2:12 This proved that Jesus could forgive sins. On **immediately**, see note at 1:9-11. **They were all astounded** recalls 1:27. The scribes accused Jesus of usurping God's prerogatives (2:7), but the crowd **gave glory to God** because of Jesus.

2:13-14 Sea refers to the Sea of Galilee. Only Mark identified the tax collector as **Levi the son of Alphaeus** (cp. Mt 9:9; Lk 5:27, from which we learn that Levi was another name for Matthew; Mt 10:3). The **tax office** was probably a local customs booth. Tax collectors were regarded as no better than thieves or Gentiles. **Follow Me** recalls 1:17-18. This is the standard term in the Gospels for discipleship. **He got up and followed Him** shows Levi's response to Jesus' call was immediate.

2:15-17 Reclining at the floor-level **table** on an elbow with the feet extended across the floor was the traditional dining posture. Levi invited Jesus and His disciples to a banquet that included notorious figures—**tax collectors and sinners** (cp. Lk 5:29). "Sinners" refers to those who deliberately

The Call of Matthew

[13] Then[a] Jesus went out again beside the sea. The whole crowd was coming to Him, and He taught[b] them. [14] Then, moving on, He saw Levi[c] the son of Alphaeus sitting at the tax office,[d] and He said to him, "Follow Me!"[e] So he got up and followed[f] Him.

Dining with Sinners

[15] While He was reclining at the table in Levi's house, many tax collectors[g] and sinners[h] were also guests[A,i] with Jesus and His disciples, because there were many who were following Him. [16] When the scribes[j] of the •Pharisees[B,k] saw that He was eating[l] with sinners[m] and tax collectors,[n] they asked His disciples, "Why does He eat[C] with tax collectors and sinners?"

[17] When Jesus heard this, He told them, "Those who are well don't need[o] a doctor,[p] but the sick[q] do need one. I didn't come to call the righteous,[r] but sinners."[s]

A Question about Fasting

[18] Now[t] John's[u] disciples[v] and the Pharisees[D,w] were fasting.[x] People came and asked Him, "Why do John's disciples and the Pharisees' disciples fast, but Your disciples do not fast?"

[19] Jesus said to them, "The wedding guests[E]

cannot fast while the groom[y] is with them, can they? As long as they have the groom with them, they cannot fast. [20] But the time[F] will come[z] when the groom is taken away from them,[aa] and then they will fast[ab] in that day. [21] No one sews a patch of unshrunk cloth on an old garment. Otherwise, the new patch pulls away from the old cloth,[ac] and a worse tear is made. [22] And no one puts new wine[ad] into old wineskins. Otherwise, the wine will burst[ae] the skins, and the wine is lost as well as the skins.[G] But new wine is for fresh wineskins."

Lord of the Sabbath

[23] On[af] the Sabbath He was going through the grainfields, and His disciples[ag] began to make their way picking some heads of grain. [24] The Pharisees[ah] said to Him, "Look, why are they doing what is not lawful[ai] on the Sabbath?"

[25] He said to them, "Have you never read what David[aj] and those who were with him did when he was in need[ak] and hungry[al]— [26] how he entered the house of God in the time of Abiathar[am] the high priest[an] and ate the •sacred bread[ao]—which is not lawful for anyone to eat except the priests[ap]—and also gave some to

Cross references
a2:13-17 Mt 9:9-13; Lk 5:27-32 b2:13 Mt 28:20; Ac 4:2; 2Tm 4:11 c2:14 Lk 5:27,29 dLk 5:27 eLk 5:27 fLk 5:11; Jn 8:12 g2:15 Lk 3:12; 18:13 hMt 9:10; 1Tm 1:15 iMt 14:9; Rm 12:13 j2:16 Mt 2:4 kMk 7:3 lMt 11:18 m1Tm 1:15 nLk 3:12 o2:17 Mt 6:8 pCol 4:14 qLk 5:31 rMt 13:17; Rm 1:17 sLk 5:32 t2:18-22 Mt 9:14-17; Lk 5:33-39 u2:18 Mk 1:4 vJn 3:25 wMk 7:3 xLk 18:12; Ac 13:2 y2:19 Jn 2:9 z2:20 Mk 13:24 aaLk 17:22; Jn 16:16-20 abLk 18:12 ac2:21 Lk 19:36 ad2:22 Lk 5:37 aeJn 6:27 af2:23-28 Mt 12:1-8; Lk 6:1-5 ag2:23 Mk 10:10 ah2:24 Mk 7:3 aiLk 6:2 aj2:25 Lk 1:27 akAc 2:45 alRv 7:16 am2:26 1Sm 21:1-6 anLv 16:32 aoEx 25:30 apAc 4:1

A2:15 Lit reclining (at the table); at important meals the custom was to recline on a mat at a low table and lean on the left elbow. B2:16 Other mss read scribes and Pharisees C2:16 Other mss add and drink D2:18 Other mss read the disciples of John and of the Pharisees E2:19 Lit The sons of the bridal chamber F2:20 Lit the days G2:22 Other mss read the wine spills out and the skins will be ruined

violate God's laws. By dining with such people, Jesus in some sense identified with them. Far from condoning their sins, Jesus dwelt among them because He had come to save sinners. On **scribes**, see note at 1:21-22. Most scribes were **Pharisees**. Pharisees ("separated ones") strictly observed the written and oral law, believed in angels and resurrection, opposed Greek influence, and were esteemed by the people. They were constantly in conflict with Jesus. **The righteous** whom Jesus says He **didn't come to call** is an ironical reference to the self-righteous Pharisees.

2:18 The question about **fasting** arose because the behavior of Jesus' disciples contrasted with that of disciples who belonged to John the Baptist and the Pharisees. Fasting was only required on the Day of Atonement (Lv 16:29-30, but see Est 9:31 and Zch 8:19 for fasts originating in the postexilic period). In NT times, the Pharisees fasted on Mondays and Thursdays (Lk 18:12). It was considered an act of piety (Mt 6:16-18).

2:19-20 A **wedding** typically lasted seven days. **Guests** (lit "sons of the bridal chamber") may refer to wedding guests or the groom's attendants. **The groom** recalls John the Baptist's designation of Jesus (Jn 3:29). **Is taken away** suggests forcible removal and shifts the focus to Jesus' coming death. Jesus stated that after He had been violently "taken away" as John the Baptist had been (1:14), His disciples would fast as John's disciples were doing now.

2:21-22 These are Jesus' first parables in Mark. **Wineskins** were made from soft, pliable goatskins. Old wineskins that already had been used to ferment wine lost their elasticity, became brittle, and would burst if used again, resulting in the loss of the containers and the new wine. Both sayings indicate the impossibility of integrating Jesus' teachings (the **new**) with the religious structures and practices of traditional Judaism (the **old**).

2:23-24 **What is not lawful** does not specify what regulations were broken. The controversy was that they did this **on the Sabbath**, a day of rest on which no work was permitted (Ex 20:8-11; Dt 5:12-15). Harvesting and threshing grain on the Sabbath was specifically forbidden (Ex 34:21). The ripened grain places this narrative in late spring or early summer. On **the Pharisees**, see note at verses 15-17.

2:25-26 Jesus defended His disciples by appealing to David's flight from King Saul (1Sm 21:1-6). **In the time of Abiathar the high priest** is peculiar to Mark (cp. Mt 12:3; Lk 6:3) and is debated because the event actually happened when Abiathar's father Ahimelech was high priest. However, Abiathar was the only high priest to escape Saul's slaughter of the priests (1Sm 22:19-20), and he was well-known throughout David's era. Thus Mark's reference is a fitting approximation. The **sacred bread** refers to 12 loaves of unleavened bread placed in the temple's holy place to represent Israel's 12 tribes. These were replaced every Sabbath, and only priests could eat them (Lv 24:5-9). **Which is not lawful** is

his companions?" [27]Then He told them, "The Sabbath was made for[A] man and not man for[A] the Sabbath.[a] [28]Therefore, the Son of Man[b] is Lord[c] even of the Sabbath."[d]

The Man with the Paralyzed Hand

3 Now[e] He entered the *synagogue[f] again, and a man was there who had a paralyzed[g] hand. [2]In order to accuse[h] Him, they were watching Him closely[i] to see whether He would heal[j] him on the Sabbath.[k] [3]He told the man with the paralyzed hand, "Stand before us."[B] [4]Then He said to them, "Is it lawful[l] on the Sabbath to do what is good[m] or to do what is evil,[n] to save life[o] or to kill?"[p] But they were silent.[q] [5]After looking around at them with anger[r] and sorrow at the hardness[s] of their hearts, He told the man, "Stretch out your hand." So he stretched it out, and his hand was restored.[t] [6]Immediately the *Pharisees[u] went out and started plotting[v] with the *Herodians[w] against Him, how they might destroy[x] Him.

Ministering to the Multitude

[7]Jesus[y] departed with His disciples to the sea, and a large crowd followed from Galilee,[z] Judea,[aa] [8]Jerusalem,[ab] Idumea, beyond the Jordan,[ac] and around Tyre[ad] and Sidon.[ae] The large crowd came to Him because they heard about everything He was doing. [9]Then He told His disciples to have a small boat[af] ready for Him, so the crowd would not crush Him. [10]Since He had healed[ag] many, all who had diseases were pressing toward Him to touch[ah] Him. [11]Whenever the *unclean[ai] spirits[aj] saw Him, those possessed fell down[ak] before Him and cried out, "You are the Son of God!"[al] [12]And He would strongly warn[am] them not to make Him known.[an]

The 12 Apostles

[13]Then[ao] He went up the mountain[ap] and summoned those He wanted, and they came

Cross-references

a 2:27 Col 2:16
b 2:28 Mk 2:10
c Rm 7:25; 1Co 8:6; Col 3:22
d Lk 6:5
e 3:1-6 Mt 12:9-14; Lk 6:6-11
f 3:1 Mk 1:21,39; Jms 2:2
g Mk 4:6; 5:29; 9:18; 11:20-21
h 3:2 Rv 12:10
i Lk 6:7; 14:1; 20:20
j Ac 8:7
k Mk 2:23; Lk 13:10; 14:3
l 3:4 Jn 18:31
m Ps 34:14; Lk 18:18
n Ps 34:12-16; 1Pt 3:17
o Php 2:12; Jms 5:20
p Lk 20:15
q Lk 1:20; 19:40
r 3:5 Jms 1:19
s Ex 7:13; Rm 11:25
t Mk 8:25
u 3:6 Mk 7:3
v Mt 12:14; Mk 15:1
w Mt 22:16; Mk 12:13
x Mk 11:18; Jn 5:18; 6:27   y 3:7-12 Mt 4:24-25; 12:15-16; Lk 6:17-19   z 3:7 Mt 17:22   aa Lk 1:5   ab 3:8 Mt 23:37   ac Lk 3:3   ad Ac 21:7   ae Gn 49:13   af 3:9 Jn 21:8   ag 3:10 Ac 8:7   ah Jn 20:17   ai 3:11 2Co 6:17   aj Lk 11:24   ak Lk 8:47   al Lk 4:34,41   am 3:12 2Tm 4:2   an Mk 1:34   ao 3:13-19 Mt 10:2-4; Lk 6:12-16   ap 3:13 Mt 4:8

A 2:27 Or because of   B 3:3 Lit Rise up in the middle

---

a repetition of the Pharisees' phrase in verse 24, allowing Jesus to declare that while David's actions were technically a violation of OT law they were not condemned.

2:27-28 Mark alone recorded Jesus' declaration about God's priorities regarding the Sabbath and humans. On **Son of Man**, see note at verses 8-11. **Lord even of the Sabbath** turned the issue to Jesus' authority and affirmed His status.

3:1-2 The **synagogue** that Jesus **entered . . . again** was probably the one in Capernaum. A **paralyzed hand** is literally "withered." **To accuse** is a legal term for bringing a charge against someone (cp. 15:3-4). The Pharisees are almost certainly the ones who were **watching Him closely** (v. 6). **To see whether He would heal** indicates they did not question Jesus' ability to heal. They only wanted to know whether He would dare to do so **on the Sabbath**. Only life-saving medical treatment and preventive medical measures were regarded as legal on the Sabbath.

3:3-4 **Stand before us** (lit "rise up into the middle") indicates that Jesus was about to heal the man (1:31; 2:9,11-12; 5:41; 10:49). **Is it lawful** recalls the previous exchange (2:24,26).

3:5 Mark alone mentioned Jesus' **anger** (Gk orge). It can mean righteous indignation. **Sorrow** is an intensive form of the same word. The reason for Jesus' emotion was **the hardness of their hearts**, an expression describing willful rejection of God's truth. Mark used this phrase twice of the disciples (6:52; 8:17).

3:6 Only Mark mentions **the Herodians** here (cp. Mt 12:14; Lk 6:11). They are also mentioned in Mk 12:13 and Mt 22:16, and possibly alluded to in Mk 8:15. The Herodians were Jewish supporters of Herod the Great and his family, here specifically Herod Antipas of Galilee. The Herodians are allied with the Pharisees in the NT, which is ironic because the Herodians supported Hellenism (Greek influence) while the Pharisees opposed it. The linking of these groups indi-

cates that opposition to Jesus involved the unlikely unification of diverse political and religious factions.

3:7-8 **Galilee** and **Judea**, including **Jerusalem**, were Jewish areas. **Idumea** was the OT Edomite area south of Judea in the Negev. Its population was mixed Jewish-Gentile. **Beyond the Jordan** refers to the Jewish area of Perea, east of the Jordan River. **Tyre** and **Sidon** were in the old Phoenician area north of Galilee and were largely Gentile, but they included a Jewish presence. The phrase **large crowd** emphasizes the large area over which Jesus' fame had spread.

3:11-12 On **You are the Son of God**, compare 1:1,11,24. To this point in Mark, only the Father and the unclean spirits fully understood Jesus' identity. **Not to make Him known** recalls 1:25,34,44.

apostolos

Greek Pronunciation	[ah PAHSS tah lahss]
HCSB Translation	apostle
Uses in Mark's Gospel	2
Uses in the NT	80
Focus Passage	Mark 3:14

The Greek noun apostolos comes from the common verb apostello and literally means "one sent forth with a message." The noun did not attain the significance of being sent with authority until its adoption by Jesus and the NT writers. The original 12 disciples were chosen and named apostles by Jesus (Mt 10:2; Mk 3:14; Lk 6:13); they were trained by Him (see Ac 1:15-26) and were invested with His authority to lead the church to accomplish the task He gave it (Mt 28:18-20). Apostles had to be eyewitnesses of Jesus' resurrection (Ac 1:22; 1Co 9:1; 15:8-9). Together with prophets, apostles were foundational for the early church (Eph 2:20), particularly in being responsible for giving divine revelation to God's people (Eph 3:5). Only 15 people are clearly referred to as apostles in the NT: the original 12, Matthias (Ac 1:26), Paul, and Barnabas (Ac 14:14).

to Him. ¹⁴He also appointed 12—He also named them apostles^A,a—to be with Him, to send them out to preach,^b ¹⁵and to have authority to^B drive out demons.

¹⁶He appointed the Twelve:^C,c

To Simon,^d He gave the name Peter;^e
¹⁷ and to James^f the son of Zebedee,^g
and to his brother John,^h
He gave the name "Boanerges"
(that is, "Sons of Thunder");
¹⁸ Andrew;^j
Philip^k and Bartholomew;
Matthew^l and Thomas;^m
James the son of Alphaeus,
and Thaddaeus;
Simon the Zealot,^D
¹⁹ and Judas Iscariot,^E,n
who also betrayed Him.

A House Divided

²⁰Then He went home, and the crowd gathered again so that they were not even able to eat.^F ²¹When His family^o heard this, they set

out to restrain Him, because they said, "He's out of His mind."^p

²²The *scribes^q who had come down from Jerusalem said, "He has *Beelzebul^r in Him!" and, "He drives out^s demons^t by the ruler^u of the demons!"^v

²³So He summoned^w them and spoke to them in parables:^x "How can Satan^y drive out Satan?^z ²⁴If a kingdom^aa is divided against itself, that kingdom cannot stand. ²⁵If a house is divided against itself, that house cannot stand. ²⁶And if Satan rebels against himself and is divided, he cannot stand but is finished!^G

²⁷"On the other hand, no one can enter a strong man's house and rob his possessions unless he first ties up^ab the strong man. Then he will rob his house. ²⁸•I assure you: People will be forgiven for all sins^H and whatever blasphemies^ac they may blaspheme. ²⁹But whoever blasphemes^ad against the Holy Spirit never has forgiveness,^ae but is •guilty^af of an eternal

Cross references (center column)

^a 3:14 Ac 1:2; Jd 17
^b Mk 1:4
^c 3:16 Mk 11:11; Jn 1:35-51
^d Mt 16:17
^e Ac 10:32
^f 3:17 Ac 12:2
^g Jn 21:2
^h Jn 21:7
^i Rv 6:1
^j 3:18 Jn 6:8
^k Jn 1:43-48; 6:5,7; 12:21-22; 14:8-9
^l Ac 1:13
^m Jn 11:16; 14:5; 20:24,26-28; 21:2
^n 3:19 Mk 14:10,43; Ac 1:16,25
^o 3:21 Jn 7:3
^p Lk 2:48; Jn 2:3-4; 7:3-5
^q 3:22 Mt 2:4
^r Mt 10:25; 12:24,27; Lk 11:15-19
^s 3 Jn 10
^t Rv 9:20; 18:2
^u Lk 12:58
^v Mt 9:34; 12:24; Lk 11:15
^w 3:23 Lk 18:16
^x Mk 12:1
^y Mk 1:13; 4:15; 8:33
^z 3:23-27 Mt 12:25-29; Lk 11:17-22
^aa 3:24 Lk 4:5
^ab 3:27 Mk 15:1
^ac 3:28-30 Mt 12:31-32; Lk 12:10
^ad 3:29 Ac 7:51
^ae Heb 6:4-6; 10:26-29; 1 Jn 5:16
^af Mk 14:64

Footnotes

^A 3:14 Other mss omit *He also named them apostles*   ^B 3:15 Other mss add *heal diseases, and to*   ^C 3:16 Other mss omit *He appointed the Twelve*   ^D 3:18 Lit *the Cananaean*   ^E 3:19 *Iscariot* is probably "a man of Kerioth," a town in Judea.   ^F 3:20 Or *eat a meal*; lit *eat bread*   ^G 3:26 Lit *but he has an end*   ^H 3:28 Lit *All things will be forgiven the sons of men*

Study notes

3:13-15 The **mountain** here is not identified. Jesus spent the night praying (Lk 6:12). **Summoned those He wanted** seems to indicate more than just the 12 disciples (cp. Lk 6:13). The number **12** recalls the 12 tribes of Israel (cp. Mt 19:28; Lk 22:30). Two purpose clauses identify the apostles' functions. They were **to be with Him** and learn His message, then go **out to preach**.

3:16-17 Verses 16-19 identify **the Twelve** men whom Jesus appointed as apostles. The NT contains three other such lists (Mt 10:2-4; Lk 6:14-16; Ac 1:13), and these contain variations in names and order. **Peter** is first in all lists. Only Mark says that Jesus nicknamed **James** and **John** the **Sons of Thunder**, possibly because of their temperament (Lk 9:54). Peter, James, and John made up Jesus' inner circle (Mk 5:37; 9:2; 14:33).

3:18-19 On **Andrew**, Peter's brother, see note at 1:16-18. **Philip** (lit "lover of horses") is not mentioned again in Mark. **Bartholomew** may be Nathaniel (Jn 1:45-46), otherwise he is not mentioned in the Gospels again. **Matthew** is mentioned only here in Mark, but he is the same person as Levi the tax collector (2:14; Mt 9:9; 10:3). **Thomas** appears in Jn 11:16; 20:24. **James the son of Alphaeus** is not mentioned again. He is distinguished from James who was the son of Zebedee. **Thaddaeus** is not mentioned again in the NT and is not in Luke's lists (Lk 6:14-16; Ac 1:13). Possibly he is the same as "Judas the son of James" (Lk 6:16; Ac 1:13). **Simon the Zealot** (cp. Lk 6:15) is literally "Simon the Cananean," an Aramean rendering of "zealous" and not an indication that he was a Canaanite. The term was used of religious and political zealots but here likely refers to Simon's piety (cp. Ac 21:20; 22:3; Gl 1:14) and distinguishes him from Simon Peter. Nothing more is said about him in the NT. **Judas Iscariot** appears last in each list. "Judas" is the Greek form of "Judah." "Iscariot" probably indicates

that he hailed from Kerioth and thus may identify him as the only Judean among the group.

3:20-21 Home probably refers to Capernaum (1:29; 2:1). To this point Mark has not mentioned Jesus' **family**, and after this extended section they are mentioned only in 6:3. After introducing them in 3:21, Mark picks them up again in verses 31-35. **To restrain Him** is the same verb used for "arrest" in 6:17; 12:12; 14:1,44. Mark hinted that Jesus' family tried to do what the Jewish authorities sought to do. Neither Matthew nor Luke mention that Jesus' family thought He was **out of His mind** (cp. Ps 69:8).

3:22 Between the introduction of Jesus' family (v. 21) and discussing their actions (vv. 31-35), Mark placed an incident with the scribes (v. 22) and two parabolic sayings (vv. 23-26,27-30). The description of **the scribes** as those **who had come down from Jerusalem** indicates they were an official delegation (cp. 7:1). **Said** is an imperfect tense, indicating continuous action. What they were saying repeatedly was that **He has Beelzebul in Him** (see notes at Mt 12:24; Lk 11:14-15) and **He drives out demons by the ruler of the demons** (see note at Mt 9:34). The scribes and Pharisees did not deny Jesus' power; instead, they attributed His power to Satan (Mk 1:13; cp. Mt 10:25; 12:24,27; Lk 11:15,18-19).

3:23-27 This is the first mention of **parables** in Mark, though Jesus had already used them (2:17,21-22). A parable is an analogy or comparison that includes proverbial sayings, allegories, or narrative. Jesus used parables to reject the scribes' logic of 3:22. Neither a **kingdom** nor a **house** is strengthened by internal divisions. Attacks on Satan's kingdom came not from within but from God's kingdom. In Jesus' reference to external attack on **a strong man's house** and tying him up, Satan was the strong man (v. 27; cp. Is 49:24-26; Rv 20:1-3).

3:28-30 I assure you is a declaration of Jesus' authority to

sin"A,a— 30because they were saying, "He has an unclean spirit."b

True Relationships

31Thenc His motherd and His brotherse came, and standing outside, they sent word to Him and called Him. 32A crowd was sitting around Him and told Him, "Look, Your mother, Your brothers,f and Your sistersB are outside asking for You."

33He replied to them, "Who are My mother and My brothers?" 34And looking about at those who were sitting in a circle around Him, He said, "Here are My mother and My brothers!g 35Whoever does the will of Godh is My brother and sister and mother."

The Parable of the Sower

4 Againi He began to teachj by the sea, and a very large crowd gathered around Him. So He got into a boat on the sea and sat down, while the whole crowd was on the shore facing the sea. 2He taught them many things in parables,k and in His teachingl He said to them: 3"Listen! Consider the sower who went out to sow.m 4As he sowed, this occurred: Some seed fell along the path,n and the birds came and ateo it up. 5Other seed fell on rocky ground where it didn't have much soil, and it sprang up right away,p since it didn't have deep soil. 6When the sun came up, it was scorched, and since it didn't have a root, it withered.q 7Other seed fell among thorns, and the thorns came up and choked it, and it didn't produce a crop. 8Still others fell on good ground and produced a crop that increasedr 30, 60, and 100 times what was sown."s 9Then He said, "Anyone who has ears to hear should listen!"t

Why Jesus Used Parables

10When He was alone with the Twelve,u those who were around Him asked Him about the parables.v 11He answered them, "The ·secretw of the kingdom of Godx has been given to you, but to those outside,y everything comes in parables 12so that

**they may look and look,
yet not perceive;
they may listen and listen,**

Cross references (center column)

a3:29 1Jn 5:16
b3:30 Lk 11:24
c3:31-35 Mt 12:46-50; Lk 8:19-21
d3:31 Mt 1:16
eJn 2:12
f3:32 Mk 6:3
g3:34 Ac 9:30
h3:35 Rm 8:27; Gl 1:4; Eph 1:9; 1Jn 2:17
i4:1-12 Mt 13:1-15; Lk 8:4-10
j4:1 Mt 28:20; Ac 4:2; 2Tm 4:11
k4:2 Mk 12:1
lMk 11:18; Ac 2:42; 17:19
m4:3 Gl 6:7
n4:4 Mk 8:27
o Gl 5:15
p4:5 Mk 10:52
q4:6 Mk 3:1
r4:8 1Pt 2:2
sJn 15:5; Col 1:6
t4:9 Is 6:9; Jr 5:21; Ezk 12:2; Mk 8:18; Lk 14:35
u4:10 Mk 11:11
vMk 12:1
w4:11 1Co 2:7
xMk 1:15
yRm 9:27

A3:29 Other mss read *is subject to eternal judgment*   B3:32 Other mss omit *and Your sisters*

---

declare truth. This is the first time it appears in Mark (8:12; 9:1,41; 10:15,29; 11:23; 13:30; 14:25,30). **All sins** that people commit, including blasphemies (see note at 2:6-7), can be **forgiven—except whoever blasphemes against the Holy Spirit**. This person **never has forgiveness**, and **is guilty of an eternal sin** (a sin with eternal consequences). Blasphemy against the Holy Spirit is attributing Jesus' works to Satan, claiming that Jesus was empowered by evil.

3:31-35 This completes the account begun in verses 20-21. Mark did not name Jesus' **mother**, His **brothers**, or His **sisters** (cp. 6:3). Possibly Joseph was dead by now. The phrases **standing outside** and **sent word** indicate there was no direct contact between Jesus and His family, only messages exchanged. **Whoever** signifies that being part of Jesus' most significant family, His spiritual family, is a possibility for all people.

4:1-20 Between the parable (vv. 3-9) and its interpretation (vv. 13-20), Mark placed Jesus' explanation for why He spoke in parables (vv. 10-12). For Mark, the parable of the seeds and soils was the key to understanding the rest of Jesus' parables (v. 13).

4:1 Again recalls 2:13 and 3:1. **The sea** refers to the Sea of Galilee (see note at 1:16-18). **He got into a boat** to use it as a floating platform from which to **teach**.

4:3 The imperative **listen** calls for obedience to what is taught, not mere comprehension. **The sower** represents Jesus.

4:4-7 Three failures based on soil type and circumstances are pictured. The seed that **fell along the path** did not have time to germinate (profess faith) before **birds** (Satan) **came and ate it up**. The seed that **fell on rocky ground . . . sprang up**, meaning there was early evidence of faith, but it quickly **withered** when the **sun** (pressure, persecution) came. The seed that **fell among thorns** (worries) was **choked** and didn't produce a crop.

4:8 The seed that **fell on good ground . . . produced a crop that increased**. Jesus pointed to the productive nature of the good soil versus the unproductive or transitory yield of the others. He reinforced this by specifying a bountiful increase (cp. Gn 26:12) of **30, 60, and 100 times what was sown**.

4:9 The phrase **anyone who has ears to hear should listen** ("should listen" is imperative) recalls His initial admonition ("Listen!") in verse 3 and prepares His listeners for the important information in verses 10-12 (cp. v. 23; 7:14; 8:18).

4:10-12 These verses, among the most difficult in the NT, give Jesus' rationale for teaching in **parables**. Interpreters are divided as to their meaning. It may be that one of Jesus' purposes in using parables was to deliver judgment against hard-hearted listeners.

4:10 Verses 10-12 were not part of Jesus' lakeside teaching but were spoken **when He was alone**. This is the first mention of **the Twelve** since they were chosen in 3:14. **Those who were around Him** were not just the Twelve. The Greek reads, "those around Him with the Twelve" (cp. 3:34), indicating a larger group.

4:11 Jesus distinguished two audiences: **you** (pl) to whom revelation **has been given** (by God) and **those outside**. Outsiders only heard **parables**; insiders learned **the secret**. "Secret" is literally "mystery" (Gk *musterion*). In the NT, *musterion* refers not to esoteric knowledge or secret rites that are discoverable by human effort, but to truth that is hidden and can only be known if God reveals it (Dn 2:18-19,27-30,47). The secret relates to **the kingdom of God**, which is what Jesus came to announce (1:15) and what He will begin to explain in 4:26-32.

4:12 So that (Gk *hina*) can indicate purpose or result. Thus Jesus' quotation of Is 6:9-10 either offers the reason for His teaching in parables or describes the result. Matthew 13:13 reads "because" (Gk *hoti*), and thus states the result of the

yet not understand;[a]
otherwise, they might turn back—
and be forgiven."[A,B,b]

The Parable of the Sower Explained

[13] Then[c] He said to them: "Don't you understand this parable?[d] How then will you understand any of the parables? [14] The sower sows[e] the word.[f] [15] These[C] are the ones along the path[g] where the word is sown: when they hear, immediately Satan[h] comes and takes away the word[i] sown in them.[D] [16] And these are[E] the ones sown on rocky ground: when they hear the word, immediately they receive it with joy.[j] [17] But they have no root in themselves; they are short-lived. When pressure[k] or persecution comes because of the word, they immediately •stumble.[l] [18] Others are sown among thorns; these are the ones who hear the word, [19] but the worries[m] of this age,[n] the seduction[F,o] of wealth,[p] and the desires[q] for other things enter in and choke the word, and it becomes unfruitful.[r] [20] But the ones sown on good ground are those who hear the word,[s] welcome it, and produce a crop:[t] 30, 60, and 100 times what was sown."

Using Your Light

[21] He[u] also said to them, "Is a lamp brought in to be put under a basket or under a bed?[v] Isn't it to be put on a lampstand?[w] [22] For nothing is concealed except to be revealed,[x] and nothing hidden except to come to light. [23] If anyone has ears to hear, he should listen!"[y] [24] Then He said to them, "Pay attention to what you hear. By the measure[z] you use,[G,aa] it will be measured and added[ab] to you. [25] For to the one who has, it will be given, and from the one who does not have, even what he has will be taken away."[ac]

The Parable of the Growing Seed

[26] "The kingdom of God[ad] is like this," He said. "A man scatters seed on the ground; [27] he sleeps[ae] and rises[af]—night[ag] and day, and the seed sprouts and grows—he doesn't know how. [28] The soil produces a crop[ah] by itself—first the blade, then the head, and then the ripe grain[ai] on the head. [29] But as soon as the crop is ready, he sends for the sickle,[aj] because the harvest[ak] has come."

The Parable of the Mustard Seed

[30] And[al] He said: "How can we illustrate the kingdom of God,[am] or what parable[an] can we use to describe it? [31] It's like a mustard seed[ao] that, when sown in the soil, is smaller than all the seeds on the ground. [32] And when

---

[a]4:12 Mk 7:18
[b]Is 6:9-10
[c]4:13-20 Mt 13:18-23; Lk 8:9-15
[d]4:13 Mk 12:1
[e]4:14 Gl 6:7
[f]Mk 16:20
[g]4:15 Mk 8:27
[h]Mt 4:10
[i]Lk 6:47
[j]4:16 Jn 5:43; 15:11
[k]4:17 2Co 1:4
[l]Jn 16:1
[m]4:19 1Pt 5:7
[n]Lk 16:8; Eph 1:21
[o]Mt 13:22
[p]Mt 13:22; Lk 8:14
[q]2Pt 1:4; 2:10
[r]Rm 1:13; Ti 3:14; Jd 12
[s]4:20 Lk 6:47
[t]Col 1:10
[u]4:21-25 Lk 8:16-18
[v]4:21 Lk 5:18
[w]Rv 1:12
[x]4:22 2Co 4:11
[y]4:23 Mk 4:9
[z]4:24 2Co 10:13
[aa]Mt 7:2; Lk 6:38
[ab]Lk 17:5
[ac]4:25 Mt 25:29; Lk 19:26
[ad]4:26 Mk 1:15
[ae]4:27 Mt 9:24
[af]Mk 5:41
[ag]Jn 9:4
[ah]4:28 Col 1:10
[ai]Lk 16:7
[aj]4:29 Jl 3:13; Rv 14:14-19
[ak]Rv 14:15
[al]4:30-34 Mt 13:31-35; Lk 13:18-21   [am]4:30 Mk 1:15   [an]Mk 12:1
[ao]4:31 Mt 17:20; Lk 17:6

[A]4:12 Other mss read *and their sins be forgiven them*   [B]4:12 Is 6:9-10   [C]4:15 Some people   [D]4:15 Other mss read *in their hearts*
[E]4:16 Other mss read *are like*   [F]4:19 Or *pleasure*, or *deceitfulness*   [G]4:24 Lit *you measure*

---

hearers' unwillingness, not its cause. Mark's abbreviated quotation of Is 6:9-10 reverses the first two clauses, drops the first half of verse 10, and changes "and be healed" to **and be forgiven**. **Turn back** expresses repentance. "Be forgiven" is a divine passive, meaning "be forgiven by God."

4:13-20 Jesus responded to the question of verse 10 and interpreted His own parable.

4:13 For Mark this verse is key: Whoever does not **understand this parable** will not understand **any of the parables** of Jesus.

4:14-20 In Jesus' explanation, the seed sown (cp. 1Co 3:5-9) is **the word** (cp. 2:2); the birds become **Satan**; the sun and its scorching become **pressure or persecution** (i.e., religious persecution); withered becomes **stumble**; the choking from the thorns is specified as **the worries of this age, the seduction of wealth, and the desires for other things** (i.e., from misplaced priorities, see Mt 6:24-34); and the good ground is identified as **those who hear the word, welcome it, and produce a crop**. Clearly Jesus' emphasis was on **the word** (Gk *logos*)—used eight times in these verses—and on **hear**—used four times. Those who hear the word, welcome it, and produce a crop are true disciples, even though they produce varying results (Mt 25:14-30).

4:21-34 Mark concluded his section on Jesus teaching in parables with four epigrams (vv. 21-25), two parables about the kingdom of God (vv. 26-29,30-32), and a brief explanation of Jesus' parabolic teaching method (vv. 33-34).

4:21-23 Lamp refers to a small clay lamp that was placed on a **lampstand** to maximize illumination. The lamp represents Jesus. A **basket** refers to a grain container that would hold about two gallons. The rhetorical questions assume that light should not be hidden. The sayings in verse 22 are an example of synonymous parallelism which emphasizes that Jesus is only temporarily to be concealed.

4:24-25 Pay attention to what you hear reinforces verses 9 and 23 and the emphasis on hearing in verses 13-20. Jesus' words to His disciples are almost the opposite of those given to outsiders in verse 12. Hearing is vital (Rm 10:17), and God will grant more revelation and understanding to those who listen to and respond. Some will neither hear nor benefit from revelation (Mk 4:25).

4:26-29 Mark included two parables related to **the kingdom of God** (vv. 26-29,30-32; cp. 1:15). Like **seed**, God's kingdom contains within itself the power to grow. The only human role is planting. Once planted, seeds grow and become a **harvest**. The **sickle** is a symbol of the final judgment (Jl 3:13; Rv 14:15).

4:30-32 Mark's second kingdom parable (cp. Mt 13:31-32 and Lk 13:18-19) contrasts a small beginning with disproportionate growth. Technically **a mustard seed** is not **smaller than all the seeds on the ground**, but it was apparently the smallest seed used in Jesus' time and thus was metaphorical for very small things (Mt 17:20; Lk 17:6). The mustard seed produces a bush up to six feet tall with **large branches** on which **the birds of the sky can nest**. The OT used this image for Gentiles finding a place among God's people (Ps 104:12; Ezk 17:22-23; 31:6; Dn 4:9-21).

sown,[a] it comes up and grows taller than all the vegetables,[b] and produces large branches, so that the birds of the sky[c] can nest in its shade."

Using Parables

[33] He would speak the word[d] to them with many parables[e] like these, as they were able to understand.[f] [34] And He did not speak to them without a parable. Privately, however, He would explain everything to His own disciples.[g]

Wind and Wave Obey the Master

[35] On[h] that day, when evening had come, He told them, "Let's cross over to the other side of the sea." [36] So they left the crowd and took Him along since He was already in the boat. And other boats were with Him. [37] A fierce windstorm[i] arose, and the waves[j] were breaking over the boat, so that the boat was already being swamped. [38] But He was in the stern, sleeping[k] on the cushion. So they woke Him up[l] and said to Him, "Teacher! Don't You care that we're going to die?"[m]

[39] He got up, rebuked[n] the wind, and said to

the sea, "Silence![o] Be still!" The wind ceased, and there was a great calm. [40] Then He said to them, "Why are you fearful?[p] Do you still have no faith?"

[41] And they were terrified[q] and asked one another, "Who then is this? Even the wind and the sea obey[r] Him!"[s]

Demons Driven Out by the Master

5 Then[t] they came to the other side of the sea, to the region of the Gerasenes.[A] [2] As soon as He got out of the boat, a man with an •unclean[u] spirit[v] came out of the tombs[w] and met Him. [3] He lived in the tombs.[x] No one was able to restrain him anymore—even with chains[y]— [4] because he often had been bound with shackles and chains, but had snapped off the chains and smashed[z] the shackles. No one was strong enough to subdue[aa] him. [5] And always, night[ab] and day, he was crying out among the tombs[ac] and in the mountains[ad] and cutting himself with stones.

[6] When he saw Jesus from a distance, he ran

Cross references (center column)

[a] 4:32 Gl 6:7
[b] Lk 11:42
[c] Mt 24:35; Lk 12:33; Ac 17:24; Eph 6:9; Rv 21:10
[d] 4:33 Lk 6:47; Jn 18:32
[e] Mk 12:1
[f] Jn 16:12
[g] 4:34 Mt 9:10; Mk 10:10; Lk 6:1; Jn 6:3; Ac 6:1
[h] 4:35-41 Mt 8:23-27; Lk 8:22-25
[i] 4:37 Ps 107:25; Jnh 1:5-6; Jd 13
[k] 4:38 Mt 9:24
[l] Mk 5:41
[m] Jn 6:27
[n] 4:39 2Tm 4:2
[o] Mt 22:12; Mk 3:4
[p] 4:40 Mt 8:26; Rv 21:8
[q] 4:41 Rv 11:11
[r] Mk 1:27
[s] Jnh 1:10,16; Mk 6:50-51
[t] 5:1-20 Mt 8:28-34; Lk 8:26-39
[u] 5:2 2Co 6:17
[v] Lk 11:24
[w] Jn 5:28
[x] 5:3 Lk 23:53
[y] Mk 15:1
[z] 5:4 Rm 16:20; Rv 2:27 [aa] Jms 3:7-8 [ab] 5:5 Jn 9:4 [ac] Lk 23:53 [ad] Mt 4:8

[A] 5:1 Some mss read Gadarenes; other mss read Gergesenes

4:33-34 Mark concluded his section on Jesus' parabolic teaching with a final explanation. **Would speak** is imperfect tense, denoting customary action. **With many parables like these** indicates Mark (and the other Gospel writers) included only a selection of Jesus' parables (cp. v. 2). **As they were able to understand** is literally "as they were able to hear." **He did not speak to them without a parable** indicates that parables were Jesus' regular method of public teaching, but in private **He would explain everything to His own disciples.**

4:35 On that day refers to the same day that Jesus delivered His teaching in verses 1-34. **When evening had come** is typical of Mark's dual references in which the second time marker is more specific than the first. In this case the words indicate that Jesus had been teaching all day and they help build suspense for what follows since a storm on the water at night is more frightening. **The other side of the sea** refers to the eastern side, which was Gentile territory.

4:37 The Greek term for "furious squall" is used here and in Lk 8:23 to describe the **fierce windstorm**, whereas Mt 8:24 used a phrase that means "sea-quake." The Sea of Galilee lies almost 700 feet below sea level. It is surrounded by highlands. To the northeast is Mount Hermon, which rises over 9,000 feet above sea level. When the cold air from Mount Hermon meets the rising warm air from the sea, it often results in a storm that sweeps down on to the lake from the heights. Because fishing boats of the day had low sides, **the boat was already being swamped.**

4:38 The **stern** (rear) of the boat had a raised deck on which fishermen could sit or lay. **The cushion** was for the helmsman. For the only time recorded in the Gospels, Jesus was **sleeping**. Exhausted from teaching, He entrusted Himself to God (cp. v. 27; Ps 3:5; 4:8). **Don't You care that we're going to die** was softened in Mt 8:25 and Lk 8:24. The words recall Jnh 1:14.

4:39 The phrase **Silence! Be still!** recalls the exorcism of 1:25 in which Jesus rebuked and silenced the demon. The use of the perfect tense means "be still, and stay still." Nature responded immediately. The **great calm** of verse 39 contrasts with the great storm of verse 37. This transformation was accomplished by just a word from Jesus.

4:40 Jesus' rebuke of His disciples was not as harsh in Mt 8:26 and Lk 8:25. **Fearful** refers to timidity and lack of confidence in God. **Faith** is trust in God. Lack of faith thus made them fearful in the crisis.

4:41 They were terrified is literally "they feared a great fear." The great storm that Jesus turned into great calm now led to great fear. Their terror is understandable in light of the teaching that only God can make **the wind and the sea obey Him** (cp. Ps 65:7; 89:8-9).

5:1-20 The healing of the demoniac is recorded in Mt 8:28-34 in shortened form and in Lk 8:26-39. Jesus brought calm to a raging man just as He brought calm to the raging sea.

5:1 The region where Jesus and His disciples landed is unclear.

5:2 A man is reported as "two demon-possessed men" in Mt 8:28. On **unclean spirit**, see note at 1:23-24.

5:3-5 Mark's description is the most detailed in the Gospels. Three times he mentioned **the tombs** where the demoniac lived. They were cut from rock or were natural mountain caves. Tombs, burial places, and items associated with the dead were unclean for Jews. Though **shackles and chains** were repeatedly used, **no one was able to restrain or subdue him.** "Subdue" can refer to taming a wild animal (Jms 3:7). The man's supernatural strength is indicated by the fact that he **snapped off the chains and smashed the shackles.** The man was **always . . . crying out**, his shrieks echoing among **the tombs and in the mountains**. He was a danger to himself and others.

and knelt down before Him. [7]And he cried out with a loud voice, "What do You have to do with me,[A] Jesus, Son[a] of the Most High God?[b] I beg[B] You before God, don't torment[c] me!" [8]For He had told him, "Come out of the man, you unclean[d] spirit!"[e]

[9]"What is your name?" He asked him.

"My name is Legion,"[C,f] he answered Him, "because we are many." [10]And he kept begging Him not to send them out of the region.

[11]Now a large herd of pigs[g] was there, feeding[h] on the hillside. [12]The demons[D] begged Him, "Send us to the pigs, so we may enter them." [13]And He gave them permission. Then the unclean[i] spirits[j] came out and entered the pigs, and the herd of about 2,000 rushed down the steep bank into the sea and drowned there. [14]The men who tended them[E] ran off[k] and reported it in the town and the countryside, and people went to see what had happened. [15]They came to Jesus and saw the

man who had been demon-possessed[l] by the legion,[m] sitting there, dressed and in his right mind;[n] and they were afraid.[o] [16]The eyewitnesses described to them what had happened to the demon-possessed[p] man and told about the pigs. [17]Then they began to beg Him to leave their region.

[18]As He was getting into the boat, the man who had been demon-possessed kept begging Him to be with Him. [19]But He would not let him; instead, He told him, "Go back home to your own people, and report to them how much the Lord[q] has done[r] for you and how He has had mercy on you." [20]So he went out and began to proclaim[s] in the *Decapolis[t] how much Jesus had done for him, and they were all amazed.[u]

A Girl Restored and a Woman Healed

[21]When[v] Jesus had crossed over again by

Cross references (center column)

[a]5:7 Jn 5:19; Heb 1:2
[b]Ps 78:35
[c]Rv 20:10
[d]5:8 2Co 6:17
[e]Lk 11:24
[f]5:9 Mt 26:53; Lk 8:30
[g]5:11 Mt 7:6; 8:30-32; Lk 8:32-33; 15:15-16
[h]Jn 21:15
[i]5:13 2Co 6:17
[j]Lk 11:24
[k]5:14 Jms 4:7
[l]5:15 Mt 9:32
[m]Mk 5:9
[n]1Pt 4:7
[o]Ps 147:11; Pr 1:7; Rv 14:7
[p]5:16 Mt 9:32
[q]5:19 Col 4:1; Jd 5
[r]Lk 1:25; 8:39; Ac 15:17; Rm 9:28
[s]5:20 Mk 1:4
[t]Mt 4:25; Mk 7:31
[u]Rv 17:6
[v]5:21-43 Mt 9:18-26; Lk 8:40-56

[A]5:7 Lit *What to me and to You*   [B]5:7 Or *adjure*   [C]5:9 A Roman legion contained up to 6,000 soldiers; here legion indicates a large number.   [D]5:12 Other mss read *All the demons*   [E]5:14 Other mss read *tended the pigs*

5:6 From a distance does not indicate discrepancy between verses 2 and 6. Verse 6 resumes the story from verse 2 after Mark's description of the demon-possessed man.

5:7 What do You have to do with me virtually repeats the unclean spirit's words from 1:24. The demoniac's identification of **Jesus** as **Son of the Most High God** answered the disciples' question from 4:41 and underscored that the spirits knew who Jesus was. Ironically the spirits asked Jesus not to **torment** them as they had tormented the possessed man.

5:9 My name is Legion indicated the strength of the demons. A Roman military legion consisted of about 6,000 soldiers (cp. the number of pigs in v. 13). The name "Legion" thus serves to indicate a large number (**because we are many**), explains the supernatural strength of the man,

and magnifies the fact that Jesus was the "more powerful" One (1:7) who could "enter a strong man's house" and tie him up (3:27).

5:10 Out of the region may refer to the false idea that demons were territorial.

5:11 Pigs were unclean to Jews. Herding them was forbidden (Lv 11:7; Dt 14:8). The **large herd** reminds us that this event took place in a Gentile area.

5:12 In verse 10 the unclean spirits begged Jesus not to send them out of the region. In this verse they **begged** to be sent into unclean animals.

5:13 Drowned refers to the **pigs**, not the spirits (cp. Mt 12:43-44). None of the Gospel authors comment on the loss of animal life or its economic impact. The action of the demon-possessed pigs reemphasizes the self-destructive impulse caused by demon possession (Mk 5:5).

5:15 Sitting ... dressed ... in his right mind proved the man's healing. **They were afraid** echoes the reaction of the disciples in 4:41. Ironically, the people were more afraid of the One who cast out demons than they were of the demoniac.

5:17-18 The spirits begged Jesus (vv. 10,12), the people of the region begged Jesus (v. 17), and now the healed man **kept begging** to stay with Jesus.

5:19-20 Jesus told the man to tell his **own people ... how much the Lord** had done for him. People changed by Jesus must tell the world about His miraculous works. **The Decapolis** (lit "Ten Cities") refers to a league of 10 Greek cities spread throughout Syria, Jordan, and Palestine. They were predominantly Gentile and were largely independent from Rome.

5:21-43 The intertwined miracles involving Jairus's daughter and the bleeding woman occur in all three Synoptic Gospels (cp. Mt 9:18-26; Lk 8:40-56). Both miracles involved uncleanness.

5:21 The other side refers to the western side of the Sea

---

daimonizomai

Greek Pronunciation	[digh mah NEE zah migh]
HCSB Translation	be demon-possessed
Uses in Mark's Gospel	4
Uses in the NT	13
Focus Passage	Mark 5:1-20

The Greek verb *daimonizomai* comes from the noun *daimonion*, meaning "demon," or "evil spirit." The verb literally means to "be demonized" and refers to the activities of *demons* in harassing, oppressing, and even *possessing* people. Though possession is not always in view when the NT mentions demonic activity, this is the case in Mark 5 where a man is described with a "Legion" of demons that Jesus cast into a herd of pigs. The loss of 2,000 pigs implies an incredibly high *demon possession* that explains the man's bizarre behavior and astounding strength. The word *daimonion* was used in the ancient world to refer to pagan gods and lesser deities (such as stars), but the NT reveals that they are actually Satan's followers. The verb is used only in the Gospels to demonstrate both the reality of the unseen world of spirit beings and Jesus' absolute power over demons, regardless of the evil they cause.

boat to the other side, a large crowd[a] gathered around Him while He was by the sea. [22] One of the •synagogue leaders, named Jairus,[b] came, and when he saw Jesus, he fell at His feet[c] [23] and kept begging Him, "My little daughter is at death's door.[A] Come and lay Your hands on[d] her so she can get well[e] and live."

[24] So Jesus went with him, and a large crowd was following and pressing against Him. [25] A woman suffering from bleeding[f] for 12 years [26] had endured[g] much under many doctors.[h] She had spent everything she had and was not helped at all. On the contrary, she became worse. [27] Having heard about Jesus, she came behind Him in the crowd and touched[i] His robe.[j] [28] For she said, "If I can just touch His robes, I'll be made well!"[k] [29] Instantly her flow of blood ceased, and she sensed in her body that she was cured[l] of her affliction.

[30] At once Jesus realized in Himself that power[m] had gone out from Him. He turned around in the crowd[n] and said, "Who touched My robes?"[o]

[31] His disciples said to Him, "You see the crowd pressing against You, and You say, 'Who touched Me?'"

[32] So He was looking around to see who had done this. [33] Then the woman, knowing what had happened to her, came with fear and trembling, fell down[p] before Him, and told Him the whole truth.[q] [34] "Daughter," He said to her, "your faith[r] has made you well.[B,s] Go in peace and be free[C,t] from your affliction."[u]

[35] While He was still speaking, people came from the synagogue leader's house and said, "Your daughter is dead. Why bother the Teacher[v] anymore?"

[36] But when Jesus overheard what was said, He told the synagogue leader, "Don't be afraid.[w] Only believe." [37] He did not let anyone accompany Him except Peter,[x] James,[y] and John,[z] James's brother. [38] They came to the leader's house, and He saw a commotion—people weeping and wailing loudly. [39] He went in and said to them, "Why are you making a commotion and weeping?[aa] The child[ab] is not dead but asleep."[ac] [40] They started laughing at Him, but He put them all outside. He took the child's father,[ad] mother, and those who were with Him, and entered the place where the child was. [41] Then He took the child[ae] by the hand and said to her, *"Talitha koum!"*[D] (which is translated,

Cross references

[a]5:21 Mk 2:4
[b]5:22 Lk 8:41
[c]Rv 19:10
[d]5:23 1Tm 5:22
[e]Mk 6:56
[f]5:25 Lk 8:43
[g]5:26 Php 1:29
[h]Col 4:14
[i]5:27 Jn 20:17
[j]Lk 19:36
[k]5:28 Mk 6:56;
Ac 16:31
[l]5:29 Lk 7:7
[m]5:30 Lk 5:17;
6:19; 8:46
[n]Mk 2:13
[o]Lk 19:36
[p]5:33 Lk 8:47
[q]Jn 14:6
[r]5:34 Mt 8:10
[s]Mt 9:22; Mk 6:56
[t]Ac 4:10
[u]Mk 5:29
[v]5:35 Mk 4:38;
Eph 4:11
[w]5:36 Jn 6:20
[x]5:37 Lk 6:14
[y]Ac 12:2
[z]Jn 21:7
[aa]5:39 Mt 9:23
[ab]Lk 1:7
[ac]Mt 9:24
[ad]5:40 Col 3:21
[ae]5:41 Lk 1:7

[A]5:23 Lit *My little daughter has it finally*; = to be at the end of life expression   [B]5:34 Or *has saved you*   [C]5:34 Lit *healthy*   [D]5:41 An Aram

---

of Galilee. Mark has already recorded key ministry events **by the sea** (1:16-20; 2:13-15; 4:1-34). Mark's description of Jesus' return is virtually identical to that given in 4:1 before He crossed the lake.

5:22-23 Synagogue leaders such as Jairus were respected laymen responsible for synagogue oversight and activities. **Fell at His feet and kept begging Him** shows Jairus's desperate concern for his **little daughter.** Luke recorded that she was his only daughter (Lk 8:42). The ruler's request **lay Your hands on her** shows awareness of Jesus' method in other healings (1:31,41; 6:5; 7:32; 8:23,25). Jairus's word for **get well** also means "be saved." The same word was used of the woman in verse 28 and in Jesus' proclamation in verse 34.

5:25-26 The implication is that the **woman suffering from bleeding** was beset with vaginal bleeding, making her unclean according to OT law (Lv 15:19-33). That this had gone on for **12 years** (cp. v. 42) and that she had been treated by **many doctors** but **not helped at all** indicates an illness that was beyond the help of current medicine.

5:27-29 The climax that has been building since verse 25 is finally reached with **touched**. The woman fulfilled her intent to reach out and touch Jesus. **His robe** is clarified in Mt 9:20 and Lk 8:44 as "the tassel." Many Jews wore tassels on the corners of their outer garments (Nm 15:38-39; Dt 22:12). On **instantly**, see note at 1:9-11.

5:30-31 At once are the same words as "instantly" (v. 29). As soon as the woman was healed, Jesus knew that **power** (Gk *dunamis*) **had gone out from Him**. This reaction is not reported in His other healings.

5:32-33 Fell down before Him recalls the actions of Jairus (v. 22) and the demoniac (v. 6).

5:34 Only here did Jesus address someone as **daughter**. It reassured the trembling woman. **Your faith has made you well** recalls the healing of the paralytic in 2:5 and anticipates 10:52. **Go in peace** was the usual Hebrew blessing at dismissal (Ex 4:18; Jdg 18:6; 1Sm 1:17; 25:35; 2Kg 5:19; Lk 7:50; Ac 16:36; Jms 2:16). Jesus used the word **affliction** (v. 29) to assure the woman that her cure was permanent.

5:35 This resumes Jairus's story (vv. 21-24) after the interruption. Precious time had been lost, with the result that the girl had died.

5:36 Jesus' words to Jairus (**only believe**) are a present tense imperative, "Keep believing."

5:37 On other important occasions (9:2; 14:33), **Peter, James, and John** accompanied Jesus while the other disciples waited behind (see note at 1:16-20).

5:38-39 The **commotion** and **people weeping and wailing** were typical of Middle Eastern funerals. Flute players were also present (Mt 9:23). The mourners could have been friends or hired professionals. Before even seeing the girl, Jesus declared she was **not dead but asleep**. This earned Him much derision. He meant that her sleep was not the sleep of final death.

5:40 The **laughing** indicates skepticism and mockery. **Those who were with Him** refers to Peter, James, and John (v. 37).

5:41 Taking the girl's body **by the hand** technically made Jesus unclean. *Talitha koum* (lit "little lamb, arise!") is Aramaic. Her spirit returned at this command (Lk 8:55).

5:42-43 That Jesus arranged for the girl to get **something to eat** proves His practical concern for her.

"Little girl, I say to you, get up!"*a*). [42] Immediately the girl got up*b* and began to walk.*c* (She was 12 years old.) At this they were utterly astounded.*d* [43] Then He gave them strict orders that no one should know about this*e* and said that she should be given something to eat.

Rejection at Nazareth

6 He*f* went away from there and came to His hometown,*g* and His disciples*h* followed Him. [2] When the Sabbath*i* came, He began to teach*j* in the •synagogue,*k* and many who heard Him were astonished. "Where did this man get these things?" they said. "What is this wisdom*l* given to Him, and how are these miracles*m* performed by His hands? [3] Isn't this the carpenter,*n* the son of Mary,*o* and the brother of James,*p* Joses, Judas,*q* and Simon? And aren't His sisters here with us?" So they were •offended*r* by Him.

[4] Then Jesus said to them, "A prophet*s* is not without honor*t* except in his hometown, among his relatives, and in his household." [5] So He was not able to do any miracles*A,u*

there, except that He laid His hands on*v* a few sick*w* people and healed*x* them. [6] And He was amazed*y* at their unbelief.*z*

Commissioning the Twelve

Now He was going around the villages in a circuit, teaching.*aa* [7] He*ab* summoned*ac* the Twelve*ad* and began to send*ae* them out in pairs and gave them authority over •unclean*af* spirits.*ag* [8] He instructed them to take nothing for the road except a walking stick: no bread, no traveling bag,*ah* no money in their belts. [9] They were to wear sandals, but not put on an extra shirt.*ai* [10] Then He said to them, "Whenever you enter a house, stay there until you leave that place. [11] If any place does not welcome*aj* you and people refuse to listen to you, when you leave there, shake the dust off your feet*ak* as a testimony*al* against them."*B*

[12] So they went out and preached*am* that people should repent.*an* [13] And they were driving

---

*a*5:41 Mk 1:31; 2:11; 4:27,38; 9:27; 14:41-42 *b*5:42 Mk 9:27 *c*Mt 11:5 *d*Mk 16:8; Ac 10:45 *e*5:43 Mk 1:44; Lk 8:56 *f*6:1-6 Mt 13:53-58 *g*6:1 Mk 1:9 *h*Mt 9:10; Mk 10:10; Lk 6:1; Jn 6:3; Ac 6:1 *i*6:2 Mk 2:23; Lk 13:10 *j*Mt 28:20; Ac 4:2; 2Tm 4:11 *k*Jms 2:2 *l*Pr 3:19; Ac 7:22; 1Co 1:21 *m*Ac 19:11 *n*6:3 Mt 13:55 *o*Mt 1:16 *p*Jms 1:1; Jd 1 *q*Mt 13:55; Jd 1 *r*Jn 16:1 *s*6:4 Mt 2:23 *t*Mt 13:57; 1Co 4:10; 12:23 *u*6:5 Ac 19:11 *v*1Tm 5:22 *w*1Co 11:30 *x*Ac 8:7 *y*6:6 Rv 17:6

*z*Heb 3:12,19 *aa*Mt 28:20; Ac 4:2; 2Tm 4:11 *ab*6:7-13 Mt 10:5-42; Lk 9:1-6 *ac*6:7 Lk 18:16 *ad*Mk 11:11 *ae*Mk 3:14 *af*2Co 6:17 *ag*Lk 11:24 *ah*6:8 Lk 10:4 *ai*6:9 Jn 19:23 *aj*6:11 Ac 17:11 *ak*Mt 10:14; Lk 9:5; 10:11; Ac 13:51 *al*1Tm 2:6 *am*6:12 Mk 1:4 *an*Ac 3:19; 26:20

---

*A*6:5 Lit *miracle*   *B*6:11 Other mss add *I assure you, it will be more tolerable for Sodom or Gomorrah on judgment day than for that town.*

6:1 Jesus' **hometown** was Nazareth (see note at 1:9-11).

6:2 The words **He began to teach** assume Jesus was invited to do so. Unlike Luke (Lk 4:16-21), Mark did not focus on the content of Jesus' teaching. In Galilee Jesus regularly taught (Mk 1:21-22,39) or performed miracles (1:23-28,39; 3:1-6) in the synagogues. After His rejection at Nazareth, there is no record of Jesus entering a synagogue again. Synagogues are only mentioned again in Mark as places of hypocrisy and persecution (12:39; 13:9). As was true in Capernaum (1:22), people in Nazareth **were astonished** by Jesus' teaching.

6:3 This is the only place in the NT where Jesus is called a **carpenter**. The parallel in Mt 13:55 reads, "Isn't this the carpenter's son?" Luke 4:22 has, "Isn't this Joseph's son?" A carpenter (Gk *tekton*) was a craftsman in wood and stone. **Son of Mary** may hint at Jesus' supposed illegitimacy or indicate that Joseph had died (no mention is made of him in v. 4 or elsewhere in Mark, but see Jn 6:42). This is the only time Jesus' mother is mentioned by name in Mark. Jesus' brother **James** later became leader of the Jerusalem church and was killed on orders from the high priest in A.D. 62 (Josephus, *Ant.*, 20.9.1). He authored the book of James. **Judas** probably was the author of the book of Jude. **Joses** ("Joseph") and **Simon** are not named again in the NT (but see Jn 2:12; 7:5; Ac 1:14; 1Co 9:5). Jesus' **sisters** are not named, but the plural indicates He had more than one.

6:4 Jesus used this self-applied proverb elsewhere (Jn 4:44). In Mark's version (cp. parallels in Mt 13:57; Lk 4:24) Jesus named three settings where **a prophet** is dishonored—**in his hometown, among his relatives** (referring to 3:20-21,31-35), **and in his household**.

6:5-6a Matthew treats **He was not able** not as a statement about limitations of power but as a statement of fact ("He did not do," Mt 13:58). The reason was the people's **unbelief**. Previously they were astonished at Jesus (v. 2). In an

ironic twist, Mark alone ended the narrative (cp. Lk 4:25-30) with Jesus being **amazed** at *them*. What amazed Him was their "lack of faith." The people of Nazareth did not refer to Jesus by name but only as "this man," a sign of contempt.

6:6b This is the third time Jesus went on a preaching **circuit** in Galilee (1:14,39).

6:7 He summoned the Twelve recalls 3:13. **To send them out** recalls 3:14. **Authority over unclean spirits** recalls 3:15. **In pairs** reflects common-sense wisdom (Ec 4:9-10) and was Jesus' usual practice (Mk 11:1; 14:13; Lk 10:1), which was followed in the early church (Ac 8:14; 9:38; 11:30; 12:25; 13:2; 15:39-40). The practice ensured companionship and mutual support, and it fulfilled the OT requirement of two witnesses (Dt 17:6; 19:15; 2Co 13:1). "The Twelve" are called "apostles" after they returned (Mk 6:30).

6:8-9 According to Mark, the disciples were to take **a walking stick . . . belts . . . sandals . . . shirt**. These were the same items God told the Israelites to take on their departure from Egypt (Ex 12:11). Matthew and Luke's accounts prohibited the walking stick (Mt 10:10; Lk 9:3) and Matthew also forbade sandals (Mt 10:10; cp. Lk 10:4). According to Mark, they were not to take **bread**, a **traveling bag . . . money**, or **an extra shirt**.

6:10-11 The disciples were to **stay** in one home until they left a given town and not look for better lodging. If they were not welcomed, they were **to shake the dust off** their feet. Jesus elaborated more on this when He sent out the 70 (Lk 10:10-11), and it was the practice of the earliest missionaries (Ac 13:51; cp. Ac 18:6). **As a testimony against them** can be rendered "as a witness to them," signifying a call to repentance (cp. Mk 1:44; 13:9).

6:12-13 That people should repent was the content of their preaching, modeling the messages of John the Baptist (1:4) and Jesus (1:15). The ministry of the Twelve is summarized as preaching and teaching (6:30), exorcism, and healing.

out many demons,[a] anointing[b] many sick[c] people with olive oil,[d] and healing them.[e]

John the Baptist Beheaded

[14] King[f] •Herod[g] heard of this, because Jesus' name[h] had become well known. Some[A] said, "John the Baptist[i] has been raised from the dead,[j] and that's why supernatural powers[k] are at work[l] in him." [15] But others said, "He's Elijah."[m] Still others said, "He's a prophet[B]—like one of the prophets."[n]

[16] When Herod[o] heard of it, he said, "John,[p] the one I beheaded, has been raised!"[q] [17] For[r] Herod himself had given orders to arrest John and to chain[s] him in prison on account of Herodias,[t] his brother Philip's wife, whom he had married.[u] [18] John had been telling Herod, "It is not lawful[v] for you to have your brother's wife!"[w] [19] So Herodias held a grudge against him and wanted to kill[x] him. But she could not, [20] because Herod was in awe[y] of[C] John and was protecting him, knowing he was a righteous[z] and holy[aa] man. When Herod heard him he would be very disturbed,[D,ab] yet would hear him gladly.[ac]

[21] Now an opportune time came on his birthday, when Herod gave a banquet[ad] for his nobles,[ae] military commanders,[af] and the leading men of Galilee.[ag] [22] When Herodias's own daughter[E] came in and danced,[ah] she pleased Herod and his guests. The king said to the girl, "Ask me whatever you want, and I'll give it to you." [23] So he swore[ai] oaths[aj] to her: "Whatever you ask me I will give you, up to half my kingdom."[ak]

[24] Then she went out and said to her mother, "What should I ask for?"

"John the Baptist's[al] head!" she said.

[25] Immediately she hurried to the king and said, "I want you to give me John the Baptist's[am] head on a platter[an]—right now!"

[26] Though the king was deeply distressed,[ao] because of his oaths[ap] and the guests[F] he did not want to refuse[aq] her. [27] The king immediately sent for an executioner and commanded him to bring John's head. So he went and beheaded him in prison, [28] brought his head on a platter, and gave it to the girl. Then the girl gave it to her mother. [29] When his disciples[G,ar] heard about it, they came and removed his corpse and placed it in a tomb.[as]

Feeding 5,000

[30] The[at] apostles[au] gathered around Jesus and reported to Him all that they had done

a6:13 Mk 3:15; Rv 9:20; 18:2
bMk 16:1
c1Co 11:30
dJms 5:14
eAc 8:7
f6:14-16 Lk 9:7-9
g6:14 Mt 14:1
hJn 10:25
iMk 1:4
jMt 17:9; Jn 21:14
kMk 5:30
l1Co 12:6
m6:15 Mk 8:28
nMt 2:23; Ac 7:52
o6:16 Mt 14:1
pMk 1:4
qMt 26:32
r6:17-29 Mt 14:6-12
s6:17 Mk 15:1
tMt 14:3,6; Lk 3:19
u1Tm 5:14
v6:18 Mk 2:24; Jn 18:31
wLv 18:16; 20:21
x6:19 Lk 20:15
y6:20 Ps 147:11; Pr 1:7; Rv 14:7
zMt 13:17
aaPs 20:6; 1Co 7:14
abLk 24:4; Jn 13:22; Ac 25:20; 2Co 4:8; Gl 4:20
ac2Co 11:19
ad6:21 Jn 13:2
aeRv 6:15
afAc 21:31
agMt 17:22

ah6:22 Mt 11:17
ai6:23 Heb 6:16
ajMt 5:34
akLk 4:5
al6:24 Mk 1:4
am6:25 Lk 7:20
anMt 14:8
ao6:26 Mt 26:38; Mk 14:34
apMt 5:33
aq1Th 4:8
ar6:29 Mk 10:10; Jn 3:25
asJn 5:28
at6:30-44 Mt 14:13-21; Lk 9:10-17; Jn 6:1-15
au6:30 Ac 1:2; Jd 17

A6:14 Other mss read He   B6:15 Lit Others said, "A prophet   C6:20 Or Herod feared   D6:20 Other mss read When he heard him, he did many things   E6:22 Other mss read When his daughter Herodias   F6:26 Lit and those reclining at the table   G6:29 = John's disciples

Anointing . . . sick people with olive oil is mentioned only here, in a parable in Luke 10:34, and in James 5:14.

6:14-15 The story of Herod Antipas, Herodias, and John is similar to that of Ahab, Jezebel, and Elijah in 1Kg 21. In fact, Elijah's name is closely tied to this story (Mk 6:15). **King Herod** was Herod Antipas (born 20 B.C.), a son of Herod the Great. He ruled Galilee and Perea from 4 B.C. to A.D. 39. Jesus **had become well known** because of His circuit preaching and the mission of the Twelve. The three opinions about Jesus' identity (that He was **John the Baptist . . . Elijah**, or **a prophet**) are given again in 8:28 as reflections of popular opinion.

6:16-17 Herod's belief that Jesus was John the Baptist resurrected prompted him to reflect fearfully on **the one** he had **beheaded** (see Josephus, Ant., 18.5.2). John was imprisoned (1:14) **on account of Herodias**. Herodias was formerly married to Herod's half-**brother**, Herod Philip, and had a daughter with him named Salome. Herod Antipas convinced Herodias to leave Philip and marry him instead. To clear the way, Herod Antipas had to divorce his own wife.

6:18 John the Baptist repeatedly condemned this marriage as **not lawful** (Lv 18:16; 20:21).

6:19-20 These verses contrast Herodias's and Herod Antipas's conflicting opinions about John the Baptist. Herodias **held a grudge . . . wanted to kill him**, and asked for a way to do so (all imperfect tense verbs). Antipas, on the other hand, **was in awe of John . . . was protecting him**, and considered him **a righteous and holy man**.

6:21 It is ironic that wicked Herod's **birthday** became the death day for righteous John.

6:22 Mark did not name Salome, but the Jewish historian Josephus did (Josephus, Ant., 18.5.4). **Girl** (vv. 22,28) is the same word Jesus used of the 12-year-old in 5:41. **Danced** and **pleased** do not necessarily carry a nuance of sensuousness, though it is possible.

6:23 Herod's oath recalls King Ahasuerus's words to Esther (Est 5:3,6; 7:2). Since Antipas was only an underlord to Rome, the promise was a hyperbolic figure of speech, not a literal promise (cp. 1Kg 13:8).

6:24-25 From this point the story moves quickly to conclusion. Note the double reference to **immediately** (vv.25,27) and the words **hurried** and **right now** in verse 25. Salome was a pawn in her mother's hands. When she sought to fulfill her mother's wish, she literally said to the king, "I desire that at once you may give to me upon a platter the head of John the Baptist."

6:26-28 Herod was **deeply distressed**. The only other time Mark used this word was concerning Jesus in the garden of Gethsemane (14:33).

6:30-31 Mark referred to the Twelve as **the apostles** only here and in 3:14 when they were appointed. **Reported to Him all that they had done and taught** refers to the mission of verses 7-13. **A remote place** recalls 1:3-5,12-13,35,45 and provides the ideal setting for the miracle that echoes the provision of bread in the wilderness. **They**

and taught. [31] He said to them, "Come away by yourselves to a remote place and rest for a while." For many people were coming and going, and they did not even have time to eat. [32] So they went away in the boat by themselves to a remote place, [33] but many saw them leaving and recognized them. People ran there by land from all the towns and arrived ahead of them.[A] [34] So as He stepped ashore, He saw a huge crowd and had compassion[b] on them, because they were like sheep[b] without a shepherd. Then He began to teach them many things.

[35] When it was already late, His disciples[c] approached Him and said, "This place is a wilderness,[d] and it is already late! [36] Send them away, so they can go into the surrounding countryside and villages to buy themselves something to eat."

[37] "You give them something to eat," He responded.

They said to Him, "Should we go and buy 200 •denarii[e] worth of bread and give them something to eat?"

[38] And He asked them, "How many loaves do you have? Go look."

When they found out they said, "Five, and two fish."

[39] Then He instructed them to have all the people sit down[B] in groups on the green grass. [40] So they sat down in ranks of hundreds and fifties. [41] Then He took the five loaves and the two fish, and looking up to heaven, He blessed and broke the loaves. He kept giving them to His disciples to set before the people. He also divided the two fish among them all. [42] Everyone ate and was filled.[f] [43] Then they picked up 12 baskets full of pieces of bread and fish. [44] Now those who ate the loaves were 5,000 men.

Walking on the Water

[45] Immediately[g] He made His disciples get into the boat and go ahead of Him to the other side, to Bethsaida,[h] while He dismissed the crowd. [46] After He said good-bye to them, He went away to the mountain[i] to pray.[j] [47] When evening came, the boat was in the middle of the sea, and He was alone on the land. [48] He saw them being battered[k] as they rowed,[C] because the wind was against them. Around three in the morning[D] He came toward them

Cross references (center column):
[a]6:34 Lk 15:20
[b]Mt 7:15
[c]6:35 Mk 10:10
[d]Jn 1:23; Rv 12:6
[e]6:37 Mt 18:28
[f]6:42 Mt 5:6
[g]6:45-56 Mt 14:22-36; Jn 6:16-21
[h]6:45 Jn 12:21
[i]6:46 Mt 4:8
[j]Mt 5:44; Ac 12:12
[k]6:48 Rv 20:10

A6:33 Other mss add *and gathered around Him*   B6:39 Lit *people recline*   C6:48 Or *them struggling as they rowed*   D6:48 Lit *Around the fourth watch of the night* = 3 to 6 a.m.

---

did not even have time to eat recalls 3:20 and prepares the way for the story that follows.

6:32 Mark did not name the **remote place** (cp. Lk 9:10). In Mark this was Jesus' third journey by **boat** (4:35–5:1,21-22).

6:34 The word for **compassion** refers to intestinal organs, which were thought to be the seat of the emotions. The word is only used of Jesus in the NT (see note at 1:40-45). Jesus saw the people as leaderless and needy (**like sheep without a shepherd**). In fulfillment of Is 40:11, Jesus cared for His flock.

6:35-44 The feeding of the 5,000 is the only miracle recorded in all four Gospels (Mt 14:13-21; Lk 9:10-17; Jn 6:1-15).

6:35-36 The words **this place is a wilderness** mark the third mention of the remoteness of the place (vv. 31-32,35). After pointing out it was **already late**, the disciples commanded Jesus to **send them away**.

6:37 Jesus responded with a command of His own. **You** is emphatic. Two hundred **denarii** would be about a year's salary. Obviously the disciples did not have that much money since they had just returned from a mission on which they had taken no bread or money (v. 8). Feeding this many people was a big challenge. (Cp. Moses' wilderness situation in Ex 16:1-35; Nm 11:13,22; and Elijah's in 2Kg 4:42-44.)

6:38 The disciples focused on what they lacked, but Jesus focused on what they had—**five . . . loaves** and **two fish**. The loaves were probably small, round, flat barley biscuits; the fish were probably dried.

6:39-40 Sit down is literally "recline," the traditional position for dining. Matthew (14:19) and John (6:10) mentioned

the **grass** on which the people sat, but only Mark said it was **green**, indicating springtime.

6:41 Looking **up to heaven** was a position of prayer (cp. 7:34). The Gospel writers did not record Jesus' prayer, but the traditional Jewish blessing over bread would have been appropriate: "Blessed art Thou, Lord our God, King of the world, who bringeth forth bread from the earth."

6:42 The word **was filled** is used of fattening animals. Thus Jesus provided abundance, not just sustenance.

6:43 The **12 baskets** matches the number of apostles and tribes of Israel. The word for "baskets" denotes large, heavy containers.

6:44 A total of **5,000 men** were fed. Mark's word (Gk) *andres* ("males") is gender specific. Matthew added "besides women and children" (Mt 14:21) which mean that considerably more than 5,000 people were fed.

6:45 The word **immediately** is characteristic of Mark's style (see note at 1:9-11). **Made** is a strong verb that carries the sense of "compelled." Mark did not say why Jesus rushed His disciples away, but Jn 6:14-15 indicates that the people wanted to make Him king.

6:46 After He said good-bye to them refers to the disciples. For the second time in Mark, Jesus went off by Himself **to pray**.

6:48 The phrases **being battered** (lit "tormented") **as they rowed** and **the wind was against them** do not picture the same situation as 4:35-41 when Jesus calmed wind and sea. **Around three in the morning** (lit "around the fourth watch of the night") reflects the Roman method of dividing the night into four watches. The fourth was from 3:00 a.m.

walking on the sea and wanted to pass by them. [49] When they saw Him walking on the sea, they thought it was a ghost[a] and cried out; [50] for they all saw Him and were terrified.[b] Immediately He spoke with them and said, "Have courage![c] It is I.[d] Don't be afraid."[e] [51] Then He got into the boat with them, and the wind ceased. They were completely astounded,[A] [52] because they had not understood about the loaves. Instead, their hearts were hardened.[f]

Miraculous Healings

[53] When they had crossed over, they came to land at Gennesaret[g] and beached the boat. [54] As they got out of the boat, people immediately recognized Him. [55] They hurried throughout that vicinity and began to carry the sick[h] on mats to wherever they heard He was. [56] Wherever He would go, into villages, towns, or the country, they laid the sick in the marketplaces and begged Him that they might touch just the *tassel[i] of His robe.[j] And everyone who touched it was made well.

The Traditions of the Elders

7 The[k] *Pharisees[l] and some of the *scribes[m] who had come from Jerusalem[n] gath-

ered around Him. [2] They observed that some of His disciples were eating their bread with *unclean[o]—that is, unwashed—hands. [3] (For the Pharisees, in fact all the Jews, will not eat unless they wash their hands ritually, keeping the tradition of the elders. [4] When they come from the marketplace,[p] they do not eat unless they have washed.[q] And there are many other customs they have received and keep, like the washing of cups, jugs, copper utensils, and dining couches.[B,r]) [5] Then the Pharisees[s] and the scribes[t] asked Him, "Why don't Your disciples live according to the tradition of the elders,[u] instead of eating bread with ritually unclean[C] hands?"

[6] He answered them, "Isaiah[v] prophesied[w] correctly about you hypocrites,[x] as it is written:[y]

> These people honor[z] Me
>   with their lips,
> but their heart is far from Me.
> [7] They worship Me in vain,
>   teaching[aa] as doctrines[ab]
>   the commands[ac] of men.[D,ad]

[8] Disregarding the command of God, you keep the tradition of men."[E] [9] He also said to them, "You completely invalidate God's command in

Cross references
[a]6:49 Mt 14:26
[b]6:50 Jn 5:7
[c]Jn 16:33
[d]Ex 3:14; Ps 45:8; Jn 8:24
[e]Jn 6:20
[f]6:52 Mk 8:17; Heb 3:8
[g]6:53 Mt 14:34; Lk 5:1
[h]6:55 Lk 5:31
[i]6:56 Mt 23:5
[j]Mt 9:20; 14:36; Lk 8:44; 19:36
[k]7:1-23 Mt 15:1-20
[l]7:1 Mk 7:3
[m]Mt 2:4
[n]Mt 23:37
[o]7:2 Ac 10:28
[p]7:4 Mk 6:56
[q]Heb 6:2; 9:10
[r]Lk 5:18
[s]7:5 Mk 7:3
[t]Mt 2:4
[u]3 Jn 1
[v]7:6 Mk 3:3; 4:14; 12:17
[w]Jn 11:51
[x]Lk 6:42
[y]Ac 15:15
[z]1 Tm 5:3
[aa]7:7 Mt 28:20; Ac 4:2; 2 Tm 4:11
[ab]Rm 15:4
[ac]Col 2:22
[ad]7:6-7 Is 29:13

[A]6:51 Lit *were astounded in themselves*   [B]7:4 Other mss omit *and dining couches*   [C]7:5 Other mss read *with unwashed*
[D]7:6-7 Is 29:13   [E]7:8 Other mss add *The washing of jugs, and cups, and many other similar things you practice.*

---

to 6:00 a.m. **Walking on the sea** is meant literally and is verbally parallel to "on the land" (v. 47).

6:49 The disciples thought Jesus was a **ghost** (Gk *phantasma*), which expresses the idea of illusion.

6:50 Jesus reassured the disciples with two commands: **Have courage** and **don't be afraid**. The words **It is I** are literally "I AM" (Gk *Ego Eimi*), the divine name of God in Ex 3:14 (cp. Is 41:4; 43:10-11; 48:12). Jesus did what God alone could do and used God's name to identify Himself.

6:51 In 4:35-41 **the wind ceased** when Jesus commanded it to stop; here it stopped when **He got into the boat**. "Astounded" was the usual reaction to Jesus' power (1:22,27; 2:12; 5:15,20,42].

6:52 Mark diagnosed a twofold problem: the disciples **had not understood** and **their hearts were hardened**. Hard hearts (spiritual insensitivity) characterized the Pharisees at the synagogue in Capernaum (3:5).

6:53-56 This is Mark's third summary of Jesus' ministry (cp. 1:35-39; 3:7-12).

6:53 Gennesaret was a fertile plain on the western shore of the Sea of Galilee between Capernaum and Tiberius.

6:54 The **people immediately recognized** Jesus. This contrasts with the disciples, who had failed to recognize Him (v. 49).

6:55 The **mats** on which **the sick** were carried were the same type used by the paralytic (2:2-12).

6:56 Villages, towns, and **country** sum up the entire region of Galilee. **Marketplaces** (Gk *agora*) were the busiest centers of local life. The statement that **the sick . . . begged**

Jesus to heal them recalls the man with skin disease (1:40], the demoniac (5:10,12,17-18), and the synagogue ruler (5:23) where the same word is used. Their desire to **touch just the tassel of His robe** recalls the desire of the bleeding woman (5:28).

7:1-23 This is Jesus' longest conflict speech in the Gospel of Mark.

7:1 On the **Pharisees** and **scribes**, see notes at 1:21-22; 2:15-17; and 3:22.

7:2 As in 2:18,24, the dispute occurred over the actions of Jesus' disciples. **Unclean . . . hands** refers to ritual cleansing, not hygiene.

7:3-4 These verses are an explanatory parenthesis. This is Mark's only reference to **the Jews** as a group. **Wash their hands ritually** (lit "wash their hands with the fist") could refer to washing with a fistful of water, or washing up to the wrist. **The tradition of the elders** (cp. vv. 5,8-9,13) refers to oral traditions which had grown up around the written law. Such traditions became the heart of rabbinic Judaism. Apparently when the Pharisees returned from the **marketplace** they did more than just ritually wash their hands; they thoroughly purified themselves.

7:5 Jesus replied in verse 8 that the **tradition of the elders** is merely "the tradition of men."

7:6-7 The word for **hypocrites** referred to an actor who hid behind a mask. Thus the word meant "pretender." Jesus' quotation from Is 29:13 clearly defined what a hypocrite was and focused on God's condemnation of those who taught **as doctrines the commands of men**.

7:8-9 Jesus accused the scribes and Pharisees of **disre-**

order to maintain[A] your tradition! [10] For Moses[a] said:

> **Honor your father**
> **and your mother;**[B,b] **and**
> **Whoever speaks evil of father**
> **or mother**
> **must be put to death.**[C,c]

[11] But you say, 'If a man tells his father or mother: Whatever benefit[d] you might have received from me is Corban'" (that is, a gift[e] committed to the temple), [12] "you no longer let him do anything for his father or mother. [13] You revoke God's word[f] by your tradition that you have handed[g] down. And you do many other similar things." [14] Summoning[h] the crowd again, He told them, "Listen to Me, all of you, and understand:[i] [15] Nothing that goes into a person from outside can defile him, but the things that come out of a person are what defile him. [[16] If anyone has ears to hear, he should listen!]"[D]

[17] When He went into the house away from the crowd, the disciples asked Him about the parable. [18] And He said to them, "Are you also as lacking in understanding? Don't you realize that nothing going into a man from the outside can defile him? [19] For it doesn't go into his heart but into the stomach[j] and is eliminated."[E] (As a result, He made all foods •clean.[F,k]) [20] Then He said, "What comes out of a person—that defiles him. [21] For from within, out of people's hearts, come evil thoughts, sexual immoralities,[l] thefts, murders,[m] [22] adulteries,[n] greed,[o] evil actions, deceit,[p] promiscuity,[q] stinginess,[G] blasphemy,[r] pride,[s] and foolishness.[t] [23] All these evil things come from within and defile a person."

A Gentile Mother's Faith

[24] He got up and departed from[u] there to the region of Tyre[v] and Sidon.[H,w] He entered a house and did not want anyone to know it, but He could not escape notice. [25] Instead, immediately after hearing about Him, a woman whose little daughter had an unclean spirit[x] came and fell at His feet.[y] [26] Now the woman was Greek,[z] a Syrophoenician by birth, and she kept asking Him to drive the demon[aa] out of her daughter. [27] He said to her, "Allow the children to be satisfied first, because it isn't right to take the children's bread and throw it to the dogs."[ab]

[28] But she replied to Him, "Lord,[ac] even

Cross references:
[a]7:10 Ps 77:20; Mt 8:4; Heb 3:2
[b]Ex 20:12; Dt 5:16
[c]Ex 21:17; Lv 20:9
[d]7:11 Mk 5:26
[e]Heb 5:1; 9:9; 11:4
[f]7:13 Mk 4:14; Lk 8:21; Jn 18:32
[g]Jd 3
[h]7:14 Lk 18:16
[i]Mt 13:13
[j]7:19 Php 3:19
[k]1Jn 1:7
[l]7:21 1Th 4:3
[m]Pr 1:16
[n]7:22 Nm 5:11
[o]Eph 5:3
[p]Ps 10:7
[q]Rm 13:13; 2Co 12:21; Gl 5:19; Eph 4:19; 1Pt 4:3; 2Pt 2:2,7,18
[r]Jn 10:33; Rv 13:6
[s]Ps 17:10
[t]2Co 11:1
[u]7:24-30 Mt 15:21-28
[v]7:24 Ac 21:7
[w]Gn 49:13
[x]7:25 Lk 11:24
[y]Lk 8:47
[z]7:26 Ac 17:12
[aa]Mk 3:15; Rv 9:20; 18:2
[ab]7:27 Ex 22:31
[ac]7:28 Lk 10:1

[A]7:9 Other mss read *to establish*   [B]7:10 Ex 20:12; Dt 5:16   [C]7:10 Ex 21:17; Lv 20:9   [D]7:16 Other mss omit bracketed text
[E]7:19 Lit *goes out into the toilet*   [F]7:19 Other mss read *is eliminated, making all foods clean."*   [G]7:22 Lit *evil eye*   [H]7:24 Other mss omit *and Sidon*

---

garding the command of God while keeping **the tradition of men**. They made their oral traditions more important than God's law.

7:10 By quoting the fifth commandment (Ex 20:12; Dt 5:16) and Ex 21:17 (Lv 20:9), Jesus introduced a specific example of what He charged in Mk 7:8-9.

7:11-13 You say is emphatic and pits the rabbis' teaching against **God's word**. The rabbinic custom of **Corban** (modified from Lv 27:28; Nm 18:14) allowed a person to devote all his material goods to the Lord. The rabbis shamefully allowed Corban to excuse sons from meeting the material needs of their aging parents. **You do many other similar things** emphasized that the Corban practice was representative of other hypocritical Pharisaic practices.

7:14-16 Jesus broadened His audience to **the crowd** and expanded His topic to true defilement. Verse 15 is the heart of His teaching. A person is defiled by what comes out, not what goes in.

7:17-18 The disciples asked Jesus privately about **the parable** of verse 15. Jesus repeated what He had said and rebuked them for their lack of **understanding**.

7:19 What goes into a person's stomach doesn't defile because it is digested and **eliminated**. Recall that Mark was written under Peter's influence and that Peter learned in Ac 10:15 that all foods are clean. Thus the parenthetical statement of Mk 7:19 indicates that Mark, Peter, and others looked back afresh on Jesus' saying and realized that He had pronounced all foods clean. They failed fully to grasp this when Jesus originally uttered it.

7:20-23 Jesus listed 13 moral problems to illustrate His point about internal defilement. The first seven are plural and indicate repeated acts. **Sexual immoralities** (Gk *porneia*) includes all illicit sexual practices outside marriage. **Evil actions** is a term for maliciousness. The last six evils are all singular, indicating attitudes. **Stinginess** is literally "the evil eye." It refers to jealousy, envy, covetousness, and a grudging attitude. **Blasphemy** includes slander of others (cp. 2Tm 3:2). The word for **pride** refers to exalting oneself above others. **Foolishness** is lack of moral judgment.

7:24-8:10 These verses describe Jesus' ministry in the Gentile areas of Tyre, Sidon, and the Decapolis.

7:24 Tyre was on the Mediterranean coast northwest of Galilee. Jesus went to **the region of Tyre**, which refers to the administrative district around Tyre and not to the city itself. **Sidon** was about 20 miles north of Tyre. Persons from these areas had earlier traveled to Galilee to hear Jesus (3:8).

7:25-26 This woman was not ethnically **Greek**. Rather, she was a Gentile who lived according to Greek culture. **A Syrophoenician** (a Phoenician from Syria) reflects Mark's use of double expression, with the second term being more specific. **Fell at His feet** recalls the actions of Jairus (5:23) and the Gerasene demoniac (5:6).

7:27 In Jesus' curt statement, **the children** refers to the Jews (cp. Mt 15:24). Jews typically referred to Gentiles as **dogs**. Since Jews considered dogs unclean (Ex 22:31; 1Kg 21:23; 22:38; 2Kg 9:36; Pr 26:11; Mt 7:6; 2Pt 2:22), calling someone a dog was an insult (1Sm 17:43; 24:14; 2Sm 16:9; Is 56:10-11).

7:28 Lord can be a divine title or just a polite address. The woman asserted that even though dogs did not eat with the

the dogs under the table eat the children's crumbs."

²⁹ Then He told her, "Because of this reply, you may go. The demon has gone out of your daughter." ³⁰ When she went back to her home, she found her child lying on the bed, and the demon was gone.

Jesus Does Everything Well

³¹ Again, leaving the region of Tyre,ᵃ He went by way of Sidon to the Sea of Galilee,ᵇ throughᴬ the region of the ˙Decapolis.ᶜ ³² They brought to Him a deafᵈ man who also had a speech difficulty,ᵉ and begged Jesus to lay His hand onᶠ him. ³³ So He took him away from the crowd privately. After putting His fingers in the man's ears and spitting,ᵍ He touched his tongue. ³⁴ Then, looking up to heaven,ʰ He sighed deeply and said to him, *"Ephphatha!"*ᴮ (that is, "Be opened!"). ³⁵ Immediately his ears were opened,ⁱ his speech difficulty was removed,ᶜ and he began to speak clearly.ʲ ³⁶ Then He ordered them to tell no one,ᵏ but the more He would order them, the more they would proclaimˡ it.

³⁷ They were extremely astonished and said, "He has done everything well!ᵐ He even makes deafⁿ people hear, and people unable to speak,ᵒ talk!"

Feeding 4,000

8 Inᵖ those days there was again a large crowd, and they had nothing to eat. He summonedᑫ the disciplesʳ and said to them, ²"I have compassionˢ on the crowd, because they've already stayed with Me three days and have nothing to eat. ³ If I send them home hungry,ᴰ they will collapse on the way,ᵗ and some of them have come a long distance."

⁴ His disciples answered Him, "Where can anyone get enough bread here in this desolate place to fillᵘ these people?"

⁵ "How many loaves do you have?" He asked them.

"Seven," they said. ⁶ Then He commanded the crowd to sit down on the ground. Taking the seven loaves, He gave thanks, brokeᵛ the loaves, and kept on giving them to His disciples to set before the people. So they served the loaves to the crowd. ⁷ They also had a few small fish, and when He had blessed them, He said these were to be served as well. ⁸ They ate and were filled. Then they collected seven large baskets of leftover pieces. ⁹ About 4,000 men were there. He dismissed them ¹⁰ and immediately got into the boat with His disciples and went to the district of Dalmanutha.ᴱ

ᵃ7:31 Ac 21:7
ᵇMt 4:18; 15:29; Mk 1:16; Jn 6:1
ᶜMt 4:25; Mk 5:20
ᵈ7:32 Lk 7:22
ᵉEx 4:11; Is 35:6; 56:10
ᶠ1Tm 5:22
ᵍ7:33 Jn 9:6
ʰ7:34 Mt 24:35; Lk 12:33; Ac 17:24; Eph 6:9; Rv 21:10
ⁱ7:35 Phm 10
ʲLk 20:21
ᵏ7:36 Mk 1:44; Lk 8:56
ˡMk 1:4
ᵐ7:37 Gn 1:31
ⁿLk 7:22
ᵒMk 9:17
ᵖ8:1-10 Mt 15:29-38
ᑫ8:1 Lk 18:16
ʳMt 9:10; Mk 10:10; Lk 6:1; Jn 6:3; Ac 6:1
ˢ8:2 Lk 15:20
ᵗ8:3 Mk 8:27
ᵘ8:4 Mt 5:6; 15:33
ᵛ8:6 Mk 14:22

ᴬ7:31 Or *into*   ᴮ7:34 An Aram expression   ᶜ7:35 Lit *opened, the bond of his tongue was untied*   ᴰ8:3 Or *fasting*   ᴱ8:10 Probably on the western shore of the Sea of Galilee

---

children at the table, they did eat the **crumbs** that fell to the floor (cp. Lk 16:21). She accepted the priority of Jesus' mission to the Jews but pointed out that Israel's privileges did not exclude Gentiles from enjoying the overflow.

7:29-30 The narrative returns to the exorcism, which was the occasion for the woman's coming to Jesus. His words **because of this reply** in Matthew's account focused on the greatness of the woman's faith (Mt 15:28).

7:31-37 This account is likely part of a larger healing ministry in the Decapolis that Matthew summarized (Mt 15:29-31). Jesus' reception this time contrasts with that of His first visit (cp. Mk 5:17) and possibly hints at the success of the Gerasene demoniac's proclamation (5:20).

7:31 By way of Sidon . . . the Decapolis indicates Jesus traveled more than 20 miles farther north before turning southeast. The entire journey was more than 120 miles. On the Decapolis, see note at 5:19-20.

7:32 A speech difficulty is also used in the Greek version of Is 35:5-6, a passage that Jesus fulfilled with this miracle.

7:33-34 Only here and in 8:22-26 did Jesus take the person He healed aside **privately**. **Spitting** (cp. 8:23) probably means Jesus spit into His hand and applied saliva to the man's tongue (Jn 9:6). **Looking up to heaven** is a sign of prayer (see note at 6:41). **Sighed deeply** indicates Jesus' deep emotional involvement. Mark translates the Aramaic word *Ephphatha* parenthetically (cp. 5:41).

7:35 His speech difficulty was removed is literally "the chain of his tongue was broken." **He began to speak clearly** indicates that, like many deaf people, he was previously able to make sounds but not form coherent words.

7:36 Proclaim is the word Mark used for telling others about Jesus (Gk *kerysso*). The people of the Decapolis now responded as the Gerasene demoniac had done (5:20).

7:37 While Jesus' other healing miracles brought astonishment and amazement (1:22,27; 2:12; 5:20,42; 6:2,6,51), this is the only time that **extremely** or "beyond all measure" appears. **He has done everything well** echoes the Septuagint wording of Gn 1:31. Once again, Jesus had done what only God could do (Ex 4:11).

8:1-10 The feeding of the 4,000 fulfilled the request of the Syrophoenician woman in 7:28 for the Gentiles to eat the children's crumbs.

8:1 In those days refers to the time Jesus spent in the Decapolis (7:31).

8:7 The phrase **a few small fish** can refer to sardines or fish scraps.

8:8 Were filled is literally "were satisfied." **Seven large baskets** corresponds to the number of loaves (v. 5). The Greek word for "baskets" differs from the Jewish term in 6:43. This term refers to a hamper large enough to hold a person (Ac 9:25).

8:9 The number **4,000 men** is not gender specific as in 6:44. It implies men, women, and children (as Mt 15:38 makes clear).

8:10 The **district of Dalmanutha** is only mentioned here in the NT and in ancient literature. Matthew identified the place as Magadan.

8:11 Back on the western side of the lake, Jesus was again accosted by the Pharisees. On **Pharisees**, see note at 2:15-

The Yeast of the Pharisees and Herod

[11] The[a] •Pharisees[b] came out and began to argue with Him, demanding of Him a sign[c] from heaven[d] to test[e] Him. [12] But sighing deeply in His spirit,[f] He said, "Why does this generation[g] demand a sign? •I assure you:[h] No sign will be given to this generation!" [13] Then He left them, got on board the boat again, and went to the other side.

[14] They had forgotten to take bread and had only one loaf with them in the boat. [15] Then[i] He commanded them: "Watch out! Beware of the yeast[j] of the Pharisees and the yeast of •Herod."[k]

[16] They were discussing among themselves that they did not have any bread. [17] Aware of this, He said to them, "Why are you discussing that you do not have any bread? Don't you understand or comprehend? Is your heart hardened?[l] [18] **Do you have eyes, and not see, and do you have ears, and not hear?**[A,m] And do you not remember?[n] [19] When I broke the five loaves for the 5,000, how many baskets full of pieces of bread did you collect?"

"Twelve," they told Him.

[20] "When I broke the seven loaves for the 4,000, how many large baskets full of pieces of bread did you collect?"

"Seven," they said.

[21] And He said to them, "Don't you understand yet?"[o]

Healing a Blind Man

[22] Then they came to Bethsaida.[p] They brought a blind[q] man to Him and begged Him to touch him. [23] He took the blind man by the hand and brought him out of the village. Spitting[r] on his eyes and laying His hands on[s] him, He asked him, "Do you see anything?"

[24] He looked up and said, "I see people—they look to me like trees walking."[t]

[25] Again Jesus placed His hands on the man's eyes, and he saw distinctly. He was cured and could see everything clearly. [26] Then He sent[u] him home, saying, "Don't even go into the village."[B,v]

Peter's Confession of the Messiah

[27] Jesus[w] went out with His disciples to the villages of Caesarea Philippi. And on the road He asked His disciples, "Who do people say that I am?"

[28] They answered Him, "John the Baptist;[x] others, Elijah; still others, one of the prophets."[y]

[29] "But you," He asked them again, "who do you say that I am?"

Peter[z] answered Him, "You are the •Messiah!"[aa]

Cross references (center column):

[a] 8:11-12 Mt 16:1-4
[b] 8:11 Mk 7:3
[c] Mk 13:22; Jn 2:11; Heb 2:4
[d] Mt 24:35; Lk 12:33; Ac 17:24; Eph 6:9; Rv 21:10
[e] Jms 1:13
[f] 8:12 Ps 51:12
[g] Lk 11:29
[h] Rv 22:21
[i] 8:15-21 Mt 16:5-12
[j] 8:15 Lk 13:21; Gl 5:9
[k] Mt 14:1
[l] 8:17 Mk 6:52; Jn 12:40; Rm 11:7; 2Co 3:14
[m] 8:18 Jr 5:21; Ezk 12:2; Mk 4:9,40
[n] Rv 2:5
[o] 8:21 Mk 4:40
[p] 8:22 Jn 12:21
[q] Mt 15:14
[r] 8:23 Mk 7:33; 8:23; Jn 9:6
[s] 1Tm 5:22
[t] 8:24 Mt 11:5
[u] 8:26 Mk 3:14
[v] Mk 1:44
[w] 8:27-30 Mt 16:13-20; Lk 9:18-20
[x] 8:28 Mk 1:4; Lk 7:20
[y] Mt 2:23; Ac 7:52
[z] 8:29 Lk 6:14
[aa] Mt 1:17; Eph 5:2

A8:18 Jr 5:21; Ezk 12:2   B8:26 Other mss add *or tell anyone in the village*

---

17. A sign from heaven could refer to "a sign from God" or to "a cosmic phenomenon." The Pharisees demanded further divine confirmation to **test** Jesus. They were trying to discredit Him and His authority.

8:12 The word for **sighing deeply** points to despair rather than anger. **In His spirit** (cp. 2:8) refers to Jesus' inner being and the depth of His dismay.

8:13 He left them marks Jesus' break with the Pharisees. After verse 15 they are mentioned only in 10:2 and 12:13. **The other side** where Jesus went was Bethsaida on the northeastern shore of the Sea of Galilee (see note at v. 22).

8:14 One loaf of bread was not enough to feed those in the boat.

8:15 Jesus' double warning indicates strong admonition. **Yeast** permeates, spreads, and grows. It is a symbol for evil or corruption (1Co 5:6-8; Gl 5:9). In Matthew the yeast is identified as the teaching of the Pharisees (Mt 16:6), while in Luke it is their hypocrisy (Lk 12:1). After this, nothing more is said about yeast or Pharisees.

8:16-20 Jesus used the disciples' discussion about bread to rebuke them. His reference to deafness recalled His healing of a deaf man (7:32-37); His reference to blindness anticipated His next miracle (8:22-26). He was disappointed that His disciples lacked spiritual perception.

8:21 This repeats the question of verse 17. The disciples still did not get it. This is Jesus' most severe rebuke of the disciples in the Gospel of Mark, but there was a bright spot. They didn't understand **yet** what Jesus was about.

8:22–10:52 In this section, Jesus completed His ministry in Galilee and began His journey to Jerusalem. It was time to leave the crowds, limit His miracles, and teach the disciples about His impending death.

8:22 Bethsaida, on the northeastern shore of the Sea of Galilee, was the hometown of Philip, Andrew, and Peter (Jn 1:44; 12:21). Mark did not record Jesus' previous visit to Bethsaida, but Luke associated it with the feeding of the 5,000 (Lk 9:10). **They brought** presumably refers to the blind man's friends (cp. 2:3-5; 7:32). This is Mark's first account about the healing of **a blind man** (cp. 10:46-52).

8:23 Jesus' taking the blind man **out of the village** and then **spitting** on him recalls 7:33 (cp. Jn 9:6-7). **Laying His hands on him** recalls 5:23; 6:2,5.

8:24 After Jesus' first action, the man's vision was only partially restored. This is the only miracle of Jesus in which healing did not occur immediately and completely.

8:26 No reason is given for Jesus' command to avoid **the village**.

8:27-30 Peter's confession near Caesarea Philippi is the watershed of Mark's Gospel.

8:27-28 Caesarea Philippi was 25 miles north of Bethsaida in the foothills of Mount Hermon. Caesar Augustus gave the city to Herod the Great. Herod's son Philip rebuilt and enlarged it and renamed it in honor of Caesar Augustus. **The villages** refers to surrounding settlements. Jesus' question and the disciples' response recall the opinions voiced to Antipas in 6:14-15.

8:29 The words **but you** are emphatic and call for a deeper answer. Jesus asked His disciples to state their own belief.

³⁰And He strictly warned[a] them to tell no one about Him.

His Death and Resurrection Predicted

³¹Then[b] He began to teach them that the *Son of Man[c] must suffer many things and be rejected[d] by the elders,[e] the *chief priests, and the *scribes,[f] be killed, and rise[g] after three days.[h] ³²He was openly talking about this. So Peter took Him aside and began to rebuke Him.

³³But turning around and looking at His disciples, He rebuked Peter and said, "Get behind Me, Satan,[i] because you're not thinking about God's concerns,[A] but man's!"

Take Up Your Cross

³⁴Summoning the crowd along with His disciples, He said to them, "If anyone wants to be My follower, he must deny himself,[j] take up his cross,[k] and follow Me.[l] ³⁵For whoever wants to save[m] his *life will lose it,[n] but whoever loses[o] his life[p] because of Me[q] and the gospel[r] will save it.[s] ³⁶For what does it benefit[t] a man to gain[u] the whole world[v] yet lose[w] his life?[x] ³⁷What can a man give in exchange for his life?[y] ³⁸For whoever is ashamed[z] of Me and of My words[aa] in this adulterous and sinful[ab] generation,[ac] the Son of Man will also be ashamed of him when He comes in the glory[ad] of His Father[ae] with the holy[af] angels."[ag]

9 Then He said to them, "'I assure you:[ah] There are some standing here who will not taste death[ai] until they see the kingdom of God come in power."[aj]

ᵃ8:30 2Tm 4:2
ᵇ8:31–9:1 Mt 16:21-28; Lk 9:21-27
ᶜ8:31 Mk 2:10
ᵈMt 21:42; Mk 12:10; Lk 9:22; 17:25; 20:17; Heb 12:17; 1Pt 2:4,7
ᵉ3Jn 1
ᶠMt 2:4
ᵍMt 16:21; Lk 18:33; Ac 2:24
ʰLk 9:22
ⁱ8:33 Mt 4:1,10; Ac 13:10
ʲ8:34 Mk 10:45
ᵏLk 9:23
ˡJn 8:12; 3Jn 9
ᵐ8:35 Ac 16:30; Jms 5:20; Jd 23
ⁿ1Jn 3:16
ᵒMt 16:26
ᵖMt 10:39
ᑫMk 10:29; Rm 8:36
ʳMk 1:1; Php 1:5
ˢMt 16:25; Lk 9:24

ᵗ8:36 Mk 5:26 ᵘMt 16:26 ᵛMt 13:38 ʷ1Co 3:15; Php 3:7
ˣRm 15:1 ʸ8:37 Mt 20:28 ᶻ8:38 Rm 1:16 ᵃᵃMk 4:14; Jn 18:32 ᵃᵇ1Tm 1:15 ᵃᶜMt 12:39; Lk 11:29 ᵃᵈMt 9:32; Jn 17:24; 2Co 3:18; 2Pt 3:18 ᵃᵉMt 5:16; 11:27; Jn 8:42 ᵃᶠ1Co 7:14 ᵃᵍMt 13:49; Ac 5:19; Jd 14; Rv 14:6 ᵃʰ9:1 Ps 72:19; Rv 22:21 ᵃⁱMk 13:28-32; 14:25; Jn 21:22-23; 2Pt 3:4 ᵃʲLk 6:19

A8:33 Lit about the things of God

Peter responded, **You are the Messiah.** This is the first time in Mark's Gospel that a person made this identification. To this point, only God (1:11) and demons (1:24,34; 3:11; 5:7) had testified to Jesus' true identity. The word "Messiah" (Christ) means "anointed one," and refers to God's appointed deliverer and King.

8:30 Strictly warned is the same Greek verb Jesus used (1:25; 3:12) to silence unclean spirits. His command to **tell no one** was a response to the popular misunderstanding that Messiah would be a military conqueror. Jesus had to teach His disciples that Messiah would actually suffer and die.

8:31 This is the first of three times in Mark that Jesus predicted His death (see notes at 9:31; 10:33-34). On **Son of**

The disciples earlier asked each other who Jesus was (4:35-41). Later, in the vicinity of the Banias waterfall near Caesarea Philippi, Jesus asked His disciples this question (8:27-30).

Man, see note at 2:8-11. Jesus will now use this title often, including in His death predictions. **Must suffer** points to the necessity of His suffering and death. The **elders**, the **chief priests**, and the **scribes** were the three power groups of the Sanhedrin, the ruling Jewish body. Jesus would **be killed**, not by a lawless mob but by Israel's religious leaders.

8:32 Peter could not accept a suffering Messiah. He took Jesus **aside** in a bid to convince Him to stop speaking of His death.

8:33 Get behind Me, Satan are the same words Jesus spoke to the Devil during the wilderness temptation (Mt 4:10).

8:34 The kind of Messiah Jesus was had implications for **anyone** who wanted to be His **follower.** An incorrect understanding of Jesus' messiahship leads to an incorrect understanding of discipleship. **Deny himself** is found only here and in the parallels (Mt 16:24; Lk 9:23). It refers to a denial of self-centered interests. To **take up** a **cross** referred to the fact that crucifixion victims were made to carry the crossbeam to the site of their execution.

8:35-37 The words **save** and **lose** show that Jesus was speaking not merely of physical life but of the essence of humanity: the soul. The sure way to save the soul is to lose it (entrust it to Jesus). There is no exchange rate high enough for the soul; money cannot buy it. Jesus' words echo Ps 49:7-9.

8:38 The phrase **My words** refers to the gospel. **This adulterous and sinful generation** is used only here in the NT (cp. Mt 12:39; 16:4) and is based on the language of OT prophets (Is 1:4; 57:3-13; Ezk 16:32-41; Hs 2:2-6). Jesus' present rejection contrasts with His future **glory.** His coming **with the holy angels** is spelled out in 13:26-27.

9:1 Jesus previously used this solemn introductory formula (**I assure you**) in 3:28 and 8:12. **Some standing here** is clarified by verse 2. **Until they see the kingdom of God come in power** is clarified by Jesus' transfiguration in verses 2-13. This saying precedes the transfiguration in all three Synoptic Gospels (Mt 16:28; Lk 9:27).

9:2 Six days appears to refer to the time between Peter's confession and Jesus' transfiguration. It may also tie Jesus' experience to Moses' (Ex 24:15-17). On **Peter, James, and**

The Transfiguration

[2] After[a] six days[b] Jesus took Peter, James, and John[c] and led them up on a high mountain[d] by themselves to be alone. He was transformed[A,e] in front of them, [3] and His clothes[f] became dazzling—extremely white[g] as no launderer on earth could whiten[h] them. [4] Elijah[i] appeared to them with Moses,[j] and they were talking with Jesus.

[5] Then Peter said to Jesus, "•Rabbi,[k] it's good[l] for us to be here! Let us make three •tabernacles:[m] one for You, one for Moses, and one for Elijah"— [6] because he did not know what he should say,[n] since they were terrified.[o]

[7] A cloud[p] appeared, overshadowing[q] them, and a voice[r] came from the cloud:[s]

> This is My beloved[t] Son;[u]
> listen to Him![v]

[8] Then suddenly, looking around, they no longer saw anyone with them except Jesus alone.

[9] As[w] they were coming down from the mountain,[x] He ordered them to tell no one what they had seen[y] until the •Son of Man[z] had risen[aa] from the dead.[ab] [10] They kept this word[ac] to themselves, discussing what "rising from the dead" meant.

[11] Then they began to question Him, "Why do the •scribes[ad] say that Elijah must come first?"[ae]

[12] "Elijah does come first and restores[af] everything,"[ag] He replied. "How then is it written[ah] about the Son of Man that He must suffer[ai] many things and be treated with contempt?[aj] [13] But I tell you that Elijah really has come, and they did whatever they pleased to him, just as it is written[ak] about him."

The Power of Faith over a Demon

[14] When[al] they came to the disciples, they saw a large crowd around them and scribes disputing[am] with them. [15] All of a sudden, when the whole crowd saw Him, they were amazed[B] and ran to greet Him. [16] Then He asked them, "What are you arguing with them about?"

[17] Out of the crowd, one man answered Him, "Teacher,[an] I brought my son to You. He has a spirit[ao] that makes him unable to speak.[ap] [18] Wherever it seizes him, it throws him down, and he foams at the mouth, grinds his teeth, and becomes rigid. So I asked Your disciples to drive it out, but they couldn't."

Cross references

[a]9:2-8 Mt 17:1-8; Lk 9:28-36
[b]9:2 Ex 24:15-18; Hs 6:2
[c]Mt 10:2; Mk 5:37; 13:3; 14:33; Ac 1:13
[d]Mt 4:8; 2Pt 1:18
[e]Rm 12:2; 2Co 3:18
[f]9:3 Lk 19:36
[g]Rv 3:4
[h]Rv 7:14
[i]9:4 Mk 8:28
[j]Ps 77:20; Mt 8:4; Heb 3:2
[k]9:5 Jn 11:8
[l]Gn 1:31
[m]Ex 25:9
[n]9:6 Mk 14:40
[o]Heb 12:21
[p]9:7 Ex 24:15; Mt 26:64
[q]Lk 1:35
[r]Jn 5:37
[s]2Pt 1:16-18
[t]Eph 1:6; Phm 1
[u]Lk 20:13; Jn 5:19
[v]Dt 18:15
[w]9:9-13 Mt 17:9-13
[x]9:9 Mt 4:8
[y]Lk 8:56
[z]Mk 2:10
[aa]Mt 16:21; Lk 18:33
[ab]Jn 20:9
[ac]9:10 Mk 4:14
[ad]9:11 Mt 2:4
[ae]Mal 4:5
[af]9:12 Mk 8:25
[ag]Lk 1:17
[ah]Ac 15:15
[ai]Mk 8:31
[aj]Lk 23:11
[ak]9:13 Mk 1:2
[al]9:14-29 Mt 17:14-21; Lk 9:37-42
[am]9:14 Mk 8:31; Eph 4:11
[an]9:17 Mk 4:38; Eph 4:11
[ao]Lk 11:24; 1Tm 4:1; 1Jn 4:1
[ap]Mk 7:37

A9:2 Or transfigured   B9:15 Or surprised

John as Jesus' inner circle, see note at 1:16-20. The **high mountain** is often identified as Mount Tabor, but Mount Hermon or Mount Meron may be better candidates. **Transformed** is from the Greek verb from which our word *metamorphosis* comes (Mt 17:2; Rm 12:2; 2Co 3:18). Jesus' nature was not changed but unveiled.

9:3 Dazzling connotes extreme whiteness that is beyond natural explanation (Mt 17:2 describes them as "white as the light"). Matthew (17:2; cp. Lk 9:29) added that Jesus' face glowed like the sun (cp. Ex 34:35).

9:4 Mark probably intended to indicate Moses as the greater OT figure by saying Elijah appeared **with Moses**. Luke said they **were talking** about Jesus' death (Lk 9:31, lit "Jesus' exodus").

9:5 The **three tabernacles** Peter mentioned relate to the Jewish custom of building booth-like shelters during the Feast of Tabernacles (Lv 23:39-43). Perhaps Peter wished to prolong this experience, but his words wrongly implied equality among the three persons.

9:6 Peter proves that when you don't know what to say, it's best to keep quiet. But he was not alone in his uncertainty; all the disciples were **terrified**.

9:7 A cloud is often a symbol of God's presence in the OT (Ex 40:34-38). The **voice** from within echoes Ex 24:15-18. **Them** probably refers to all six persons on the mountain. The divine announcement recalls the divine words at Jesus' baptism (see note at 1:9-11). This time Jesus' Sonship is confirmed to others, not just to Jesus, and the hearers are told to **listen to Him** (cp. Dt 18:15). God's words affirmed Jesus' teaching in Mk 8:31-38 about His suffering and the requirements for discipleship.

9:8 Not even Moses or Elijah can compare with Jesus. The spotlight was on Him and Him **alone**.

9:9 Nine times in Mark's Gospel Jesus enjoined people to be quiet about His messiahship. This is the only time when He put a time limit on the injunction. Jesus' prohibition indicated that His glory and mission could not be understood fully until after His death and resurrection.

9:10 This verse indicates continued lack of understanding among Jesus' inner circle (cp. 8:31).

9:11 On **the scribes**, see note at 1:21-22. The question here was based on Mal 4:5-6.

9:12-13 Jesus affirmed the scribal teaching about Elijah and his role, but Elijah's coming did not change the fact that **the Son of Man . . . must suffer many things** (cp. 8:31). Jesus then made two startling statements: **Elijah** had **come** already, and he suffered because the people **did whatever they pleased to him**. Jesus was identifying Elijah with John the Baptist. The treatment John received (6:16-29) foreshadowed the way Jesus would be treated.

9:14-29 These verses reveal what the other disciples were doing while Jesus and His inner circle were on the Mount of Transfiguration. Mark's account is twice as long as the parallels (Mt 17:14-20; Lk 9:37-43).

9:14 The **scribes**, again showing hostility toward the disciples (cp. 2:6,16; 3:22; 7:1), have no further role in Mark's account.

9:15 Only Mark in the entire NT used the verb for **were amazed** (cp. 14:33; 16:5-6). It refers to intense emotion.

9:17-18 That the disciples couldn't **drive . . . out** this demon

19 He replied to them, "You unbelieving[a] generation! How long will I be with you? How long
must I put up with you? Bring him to Me." 20 So
they brought him to Him. When the spirit saw
Him, it immediately convulsed the boy. He fell
to the ground and rolled around, foaming at
the mouth. 21 "How long has this been happening to him?" Jesus asked his father.
"From childhood," he said. 22 "And many
times it has thrown him into fire or water to
destroy[b] him. But if You can do anything, have
compassion[c] on us and help us."
23 Then Jesus said to him, "'If You can'?[A,B] Everything is possible[d] to the one who believes."[e]
24 Immediately the father of the boy cried
out, "I do believe! Help my unbelief."
25 When Jesus saw that a crowd was rapidly
coming together, He rebuked[f] the •unclean[g]
spirit, saying to it, "You mute and deaf[h] spirit,[C]
I command you: come out of him and never
enter him again!"
26 Then it came out, shrieking and convuls-
ing[i] him[D] violently. The boy became like a
corpse, so that many said, "He's dead." 27 But
Jesus, taking him by the hand, raised him,[j]
and he stood up.
28 After He went into a house, His disciples
asked Him privately, "Why couldn't we drive
it out?"
29 And He told them, "This kind can come
out by nothing but prayer[k] [and fasting]."[E,l]

The Second Prediction of His Death

30 Then[m] they left that place and made their
way through Galilee, but He did not want anyone to know it.[n] 31 For He was teaching[o] His
disciples and telling them, "The Son of Man[p]
is being betrayed[F] into the hands of men. They
will kill Him, and after He is killed, He will
rise[q] three days later."[r] 32 But they did not understand this statement, and they were afraid
to ask Him.[s]

Who is the Greatest?

33 Then[t] they came to Capernaum.[u] When
He was in the house,[v] He asked them, "What
were you arguing about on the way?"[w] 34 But
they were silent,[x] because on the way they had
been arguing with one another about who was
the greatest.[y] 35 Sitting down, He called the
Twelve[z] and said to them, "If anyone wants to
be first, he must be last of all and servant of
all."[aa] 36 Then He took a child,[ab] had him stand
among them, and taking him in His arms, He
said to them, 37 "Whoever welcomes[G] one little
child such as this in My name[ac] welcomes Me.
And whoever welcomes Me does not welcome
Me, but Him who sent[ad] Me."[ae]

[a] 9:19 Lk 12:46
[b] 9:22 Jn 6:27
[c] Lk 15:20
[d] 9:23 Mt 17:20; Jn 11:40
[e] Jn 3:16; Ac 10:43; Rm 10:9; 1Pt 1:8-10
[f] 9:25 2Tm 4:2
[g] 2Co 6:17
[h] Lk 7:22
[i] 9:26 Mk 1:26
[j] 9:27 Mk 1:31
[k] 9:29 Ac 12:5; 16:13; Phm 22
[l] Lk 18:12
[m] 9:30-32 Mt 17:22-23; Lk 9:43-45
[n] 9:30 Mk 1:44
[o] 9:31 Mt 28:20; Ac 4:2; 2Tm 4:11
[p] Mk 2:10
[q] Mt 16:21; Lk 18:33; Ac 2:24
[r] Mk 8:31; Lk 9:22
[s] 9:32 Mk 4:40; Lk 2:50
[t] 9:33-50 Mt 18:1-11; Lk 9:46-50
[u] 9:33 Lk 10:15
[v] Mk 1:29
[w] Mk 8:27
[x] 9:34 Mk 3:4
[y] Lk 22:24-27; Ac 8:9
[z] 9:35 Mk 11:11
[aa] Mt 20:16-27; 23:11; Mk 10:43-44; Lk 22:26
[ab] 9:36 Lk 1:7
[ac] 9:37 Jn 10:25
[ad] Mt 15:24; Mk 12:6; Jn 3:16-17
[ae] Mt 10:40

[A] 9:23 Other mss add *believe* [B] 9:23 Jesus appears to quote the father's words in v. 22 and then comment on them. [C] 9:25 A spirit that caused the boy to be deaf and unable to speak [D] 9:26 Other mss omit *him* [E] 9:29 Other mss omit bracketed text [F] 9:31 Or *handed over* [G] 9:37 Or *Whoever receives*

is surprising because Jesus had commissioned them to do this (3:15; 6:7) and they had previously succeeded in doing so (6:13). The symptoms were similar to epilepsy, but Mark said they were the result of unclean spirits (9:17,20,25).

9:19 Jesus' words **you unbelieving generation** recalls 8:38.

9:20 The reaction of **the spirit** when it **saw** Jesus was similar to that of other demonic spirits (see notes at 1:25-26 and 5:7).

9:22 To destroy him shows the evil intention of demons. The father asked for **help** based on Jesus' **compassion** (see notes at 1:40-45 and 6:34). **If You can** was an appropriate qualifier, considering the disciples' failure to cast out the demon.

9:23 At issue was not Jesus' ability but the father's faith—**everything is possible to the one who believes** (cp. 5:36; 10:27).

9:24 Both faith and unbelief resided in the father's heart. Mark previously used **unbelief** when describing the people of Nazareth (see note at 6:5-6a).

9:25 The demonic spirit was **mute and deaf**, rendering the boy mute (v. 17). When Jesus issued the **command** to **come out of him**, He used a word that emphasized His authority. The demon was able to resist the disciples, but not the Lord. Jesus' command to **never enter him again** is unique in all the exorcisms in the Gospels.

9:26-27 The unclean spirit responded like one that Jesus had cast out earlier (see note at 1:25-26).

9:28-29 To the disciples' question **why**, Jesus told them **this kind** (apparently a very resistant and powerful evil being) required spiritual preparation on the part of the exorcist, specifically **prayer and fasting**.

9:30 This is the last reference in Mark to **Galilee** until after Jesus' resurrection (see 14:28; 16:7 and notes there).

9:31 Jesus' second death prediction is the briefest of the three (see notes at 8:31; 10:33-34), and has much in common with the others. The new element in this prediction is that He would be **betrayed**. The words **teaching** and **telling** are imperfect tenses, indicating repeated instruction.

9:32 Luke explained why the disciples **did not understand**: "It was concealed from them so that they could not grasp it" (Lk 9:45).

9:33 This is the last time Jesus returned to **Capernaum**. The **house** may have been Peter's (see note at 1:29-31).

9:34 They were silent also described the people in the Capernaum synagogue (3:4).

9:35 Sitting down was the posture assumed by a teacher (4:1-2; Mt 5:1). Jesus' teaching reversed human thinking. In His value system, being **first** did not come through aggressiveness and privilege but through humility (Mt 18:4) and by being **servant of all**.

9:36-37 Jesus used **a child** as an object lesson. He did not command His disciples to become like children but to **welcome** those who are like a **little child**. A child is an example of a person with no status and no rights.

In His Name

[38] John[a] said to Him, "Teacher,[b] we saw someone[A] driving out demons[c] in Your name,[d] and we tried to stop him because he wasn't following us."[e]

[39] "Don't stop him," said Jesus, "because there is no one who will perform a miracle[f] in My name who can soon afterward speak evil of Me. [40] For whoever is not against us is for us.[g] [41] And whoever gives you a cup of water to drink[h] because of My name,[B] since you belong to the •Messiah[i]—I assure you:[j] He will never lose his reward.[k]

Warnings from Jesus

[42] "But whoever •causes the downfall of one of these little ones who believe in Me[l]—it would be better for him if a heavy millstone[C,m] were hung around his neck and he were thrown into the sea. [43] And if your hand causes your downfall, cut it off.[n] It is better for you to enter life maimed[o] than to have two hands and go to •hell—the unquenchable fire,[p] [[44] where

**Their worm does not die,
and the fire is not quenched.**][D,E,q]

[45] And if your foot causes your downfall,[r] cut it off. It is better for you to enter life lame[s] than to have two feet and be thrown into hell—[the unquenchable fire,[t] [46] where

**Their worm does not die,
and the fire is not quenched.**][D,E,u]

[47] And if your eye causes your downfall, gouge it out. It is better for you to enter the kingdom of God[v] with one eye than to have two eyes and be thrown[w] into hell,[x] [48] where

**Their worm does not die,
and the fire is not quenched.**[E]

[49] For everyone will be salted with fire.[F,G,y] [50] Salt is good, but if the salt should lose its flavor, how can you make it salty?[z] Have salt[aa] among yourselves and be at peace[ab] with one another."

The Question of Divorce

10 He[ac] set out from there and went to the region of Judea[ad] and across the Jordan.[ae] Then crowds converged on Him again and, as

Cross references (center column)

[a]9:38 Jn 21:7
[b]Mk 4:38
[c]Mk 3:15; Rv 9:20
[d]Jn 10:25; 14:13
[e]Nm 11:26-30
[f]9:39 Ac 19:11
[g]9:40 Mt 12:30; Lk 11:23
[h]9:41 Mt 10:42; 25:35-42; Rm 12:20
[i]Mt 1:17; Eph 5:2
[j]Rv 22:21
[k]Mt 10:42; 2Pt 2:13
[l]9:42 Ex 23:33; Jn 6:35
[m]Jdg 9:53; Mt 24:41; Rv 18:22
[n]9:43 Mt 5:29-30
[o]Mt 15:30-31
[p]Mt 3:12; 5:22; 25:41; 2Th 1:8
[q]9:44 Is 66:24
[r]9:45 Jn 16:1
[s]Jn 5:3
[t]2Th 1:8
[u]9:46 Is 66:24
[v]9:47 Mk 1:15
[w]3Jn 10
[x]Jms 3:6
[y]9:49 Lv 2:13; Ezk 43:24
[z]9:50 Mt 5:13; Lk 14:34
[aa]Ex 30:35; 2Kg 2:19-23; Col 4:6
[ab]Mt 5:9;
Rm 12:18; 14:13; 2Co 13:11; 1Th 5:13; Heb 12:14
19:1-2
[ac]10:1-12 Mt 19:1-2
[ad]10:1 Lk 1:5
[ae]Mt 4:15,25; Lk 3:3; Jn 1:28; 3:26; 10:40

Translation footnotes

[A]9:38 Other mss add *who didn't go along with us* [B]9:41 Lit *drink in the name* [C]9:42 A millstone turned by a donkey
[D]9:44,46 Other mss omit bracketed text [E]9:44,46,48 Is 66:24 [F]9:49 Other mss add *and every sacrifice will be salted with salt* [G]9:49 Lv 2:13; Ezk 43:24

9:38 It is ironic that the disciples told this man to stop **driving out demons** when they had failed at the same task (vv. 14-29). Apparently they thought they were the only ones authorized to do this (3:14-15; 6:7,13). The episode recalls Nm 11:26-29.

9:39-41 Jesus gave three reasons not to stop the man. First, anyone who performed **a miracle in** Jesus' **name** wouldn't turn and **speak evil** of Him. Second, there is no middle ground. A person is either **against** or **for** Jesus. Third, anyone who extends a kind gesture (giving **a cup of water** was a

skandalizo

Greek Pronunciation	[skahn dah LEE zoh]
HCSB Translation	cause the downfall of
Uses in Mark's Gospel	8
Uses in the NT	29
Focus Passage	Mark 9:42-50

The Greek verb *skandalizo* means "to entrap" and is related to the noun *skandalon*, meaning "trap" or "snare." Symbolically, *skandalizo* can mean to cause [someone] to *stumble* or in a passive sense to *take offense*. Similarly, the noun *skandalon* can mean *offense* or *stumbling block*. In the NT, both *skandalizo* and *skandalon* always refer to *offenses* either given or taken in spiritual matters. Paul used *skandalizo* three times (1Co 8:13 [2x]; 2Co 11:29) and *skandalon* once (Rm 14:13) in connection with a Christian's responsibility to other Christians. Every other use of *skandalizo* occurs in the Gospels. Jesus often warned about *offending* people, that is, doing spiritual harm to others (Mk 9:42-50; see Jn 16:1). Incredibly, Jesus Himself was often the cause of the *offense*, for those who did not believe in Him often misunderstood His words and actions (see Mt 11:6; 13:57; 15:12; 17:27; Mk 6:3; 14:27; Jn 6:61).

basic Eastern courtesy) **because of My name . . . will never lose his reward**. Except for two objective uses in 12:35 and 13:21, this is the only time in Mark's Gospel that Jesus used the name **Messiah** of Himself.

9:42 The words **causes the downfall** refer to hindering discipleship or causing someone to sin. **Little ones** refers to immature disciples. A **heavy millstone** was the one donkeys turned to grind wheat. As terrible as drowning was, Jesus said it would be **better** than suffering the punishments of verses 43-48.

9:43-48 The body parts and admonitions are figures of speech that warn disciples to guard their sight and actions against participation in evil, for recklessness here can lead to spiritual downfall (cp. Jb 31:1,5,7). This is the only place where Mark used the word for **hell** (Gk *gehenna*). The imagery for hell developed from the Hinnom Valley southwest of Jerusalem. This valley was used for pagan human sacrifice (2Kg 16:3; 21:6; Jr 7:31) and as a garbage dump, hence the association with **unquenchable fire** and perpetual rot (**their worm does not die**).

9:49-50 Jesus' puzzling statement in verse 49 probably drew on the association of fire and salt in the sacrificial context of Lv 2:13. The first salt saying of Mk 9:50 occurs elsewhere (Mt 5:13; Lk 14:34) and focuses on the **good** uses of salt, which disciples must reflect on (Mt 5:13). Salt from deposits around the Dead Sea could **lose its flavor** since it was not pure sodium chloride. Disciples who lose their saltiness are no longer effective witnesses. The second "salt saying" of verse 50 draws on the OT custom of using salt in making covenants of peace (Lv 2:13; Nm 18:19; 2Ch 13:5; cp. Col 4:6).

10:1 The words **from there** probably refer to Capernaum

He usually did, He began teaching[a] them once more. [2] Some *Pharisees[b] approached Him to test[c] Him. They asked, "Is it lawful[d] for a man to divorce[e] his wife?"[f]

[3] He replied to them, "What did Moses[g] command you?"

[4] They said, "Moses permitted us to write divorce papers[h] and send her away."[i]

[5] But Jesus told them, "He wrote this command for you because of the hardness of your hearts.[j] [6] But from the beginning[k] of creation[l] God[A] **made them male and female**.[B,m]

[7]   **For this reason a man will leave[n]
his father and mother
[and be joined to his wife],[C]**

[8]   **and the two will become
one flesh.[D,o]**

So they are no longer two, but one flesh. [9] Therefore what God has joined together, man must not separate."[p]

[10] Now in the house the disciples questioned Him again about this matter. [11] And He said to them, "Whoever divorces his wife[q] and marries[r] another commits adultery[s] against her. [12] Also, if she divorces her husband[t] and marries another, she commits adultery."

Blessing the Children

[13] Some[u] people were bringing little children[v] to Him so He might touch them, but His disciples rebuked[w] them. [14] When Jesus saw it, He was indignant[x] and said to them, "Let the little children come to Me.[y] Don't stop[z] them, for the kingdom of God[aa] belongs to such as these. [15] *I assure you:[ab] Whoever does not welcome[E,ac] the kingdom of God like a little child[ad] will never enter it." [16] After taking them in His arms, He laid His hands on[ae] them and blessed[af] them.

The Rich Young Ruler

[17] As[ag] He was setting out on a journey,[ah] a man ran up, knelt down[ai] before Him, and asked Him, "Good[aj] Teacher,[ak] what must I do to inherit[al] eternal life?"[am]

Cross references
[a]10:1 Mt 28:20; Ac 4:2; 2Tm 4:11
[b]10:2 Mk 7:3
[c]Jms 1:13
[d]Jn 18:31
[e]Lv 21:7
[f]1Pt 3:1
[g]10:3 Ps 77:20; Mt 8:4; Heb 3:2
[h]10:4 Mt 5:31
[i]Dt 24:1,3
[j]10:5 Mk 16:14
[k]10:6 Jn 1:1; Ac 26:4
[l]Jn 1:3; Rv 3:14
[m]Gn 1:27; 5:2
[n]10:7 Lk 15:4
[o]10:7-8 Gn 2:24
[p]10:9 1Co 7:10-15; Heb 7:26
[q]10:11 1Pt 3:1
[r]1Tm 5:14
[s]Mt 5:27-28
[t]10:12 Mt 1:19
[u]10:13-16 Mt 19:13-15; Lk 18:15-17
[v]10:13 Lk 1:7
[w]2Tm 4:2
[x]Lk 13:14
[y]10:14 Lk 14:26
[z]1Co 14:39
[aa]Mk 1:15
[ab]10:15 Ps 72:19; Rv 22:21
[ac]Ac 17:11
[ad]Lk 1:7
[ae]10:16 1Tm 5:22
[af]Gn 48:15
[ag]10:17-31 Mt 19:16-30; Lk 18:18-30
[ah]10:17 Mk 8:27
[ai]Mt 17:14; 27:29; Mk 1:40
[aj]Gn 1:31
[ak]Mk 4:38; Eph 4:11
[al]Rv 21:7
[am]Lk 10:25-28; Jn 12:25; Ac 13:48

A10:6 Other mss omit *God*   **B**10:6 Gn 1:27; 5:2   **C**10:7 Other mss omit bracketed text   **D**10:7-8 Gn 2:24   **E**10:15 Or *not receive*

(9:33). **Judea** was south; **across the Jordan** refers to Perea or Transjordan. This latter area was under the jurisdiction of Antipas and may explain the reason for the question in verse 2.

10:2 Two major schools of thought differed on the justifications for divorce (Mt 19:3). Shammai's school was strict, Hillel's liberal. The Pharisees' motive was to **test** Jesus (8:11; 12:15). Perhaps if this encounter occurred in Antipas's territory, they hoped Jesus would answer as John the Baptist had done and suffer the same fate (see note at 6:16-17).

10:3-4 Jesus asked, **What did Moses command you?** They responded based on Dt 24:1-4, but this passage did not command divorce. It only acknowledged it, protected the woman's rights, and prohibited a husband from remarrying his original wife if he married another woman in between. Once again the Pharisees were misusing Scripture.

10:5 The phrase **hardness of your hearts** refers to closing one's heart to God's truths. Moses allowed divorce as a concession to spiritual hardness.

10:6-8 Jesus moved from Moses' concession to God's intention **from the beginning of creation**. By quoting Gn 1:27 Jesus established that marriage is between a **male and female**.

10:9 Jesus emphasized that marriage is a divinely established institution. His final statement, **man must not separate**, refers to the husband, not a judicial court (cp. v. 11). Thus Jesus answered the question of verse 2 and ruled out divorce.

10:10 Jesus' disciples were stunned by His teaching and asked what He meant.

10:11-12 Though Jesus appeared to associate remarriage with **adultery**, He did not rule out all remarriage but emphasized that if a divorce is not grounded in biblically valid reasons, subsequent marriage is adulterous. Mark did not include the exception clauses of Mt 5:32 and 19:9. This is a reminder that this passage does not contain all of Jesus' teaching on divorce and remarriage.

10:13 The phrase **some people** probably refers to parents. **Little children** was clarified by Luke as "infants" (Lk 18:15). **Touch them** is clarified in verse 16 as "blessed them."

10:14 This is the only place in the Gospels where Jesus was **indignant** (cp. 3:5). The word indicates strong anger. Jesus allowed the children to come to Him, but the real point related to **such as these**. This saying pertains to the kind of people to whom God's kingdom **belongs**.

10:15 Jesus' second saying relates to how a person welcomes and enters **the kingdom of God**. A little child accepts what is given as a gift without asserting his rights or claims (cp. Mt 18:3). To **enter** God's kingdom a person must accept it as a gracious gift.

10:16 The phrase **taking them in His arms** is one word in Greek. Jesus not only received the children, He also **blessed** them. The word for "blessed" is intensified, conveying Jesus' sincerity.

10:17 The **journey** language continues, reminding readers that Jesus was on His final sweep toward Jerusalem (v. 1; 8:27; 9:2,30,33). Matthew (Mt 19:22) stated that this man who approached Jesus was "young," and Luke (Lk 18:18) that he was "a ruler." Mark indicated that he was wealthy (Mk 10:22). Hence the man is referred to as "the rich young ruler." His actions—**ran up, knelt down**—suggest earnestness and respect. He knew he was not entitled to life after death. Verse 23 shows that **eternal life** and "the kingdom of God" are synonymous.

10:18 Jesus' rebuff directed the man to **God**. In asserting that only God is **good**, Jesus did not deny His own deity. He only indicated that human judgment cannot serve as ultimate judge of good and bad.

[18] "Why do you call Me good?" Jesus asked him. "No one is good but One—God.[a] [19] You know the commandments:

Do not murder;[b]
do not commit adultery;[c]
do not steal;[d]
do not bear false witness;[e]
do not defraud;[f]
honor[g] **your father and mother."**[A,h]

[20] He said to Him, "Teacher,[i] I have kept all these from my youth."

[21] Then, looking at him, Jesus loved him[j] and said to him, "You lack one thing: Go, sell all you have and give to the poor,[k] and you will have treasure[l] in heaven.[m] Then come,[B] follow Me."[n] [22] But he was stunned[C] at this demand, and he went away grieving,[o] because he had many possessions.[p]

Possessions and the Kingdom

[23] Jesus looked around and said to His disciples, "How hard it is for those who have wealth[q] to enter the kingdom of God!"[r] [24] But the disciples were astonished at His words. Again Jesus said to them, "Children,[s] how hard it is[D] to enter the kingdom of God! [25] It is easier for a camel to go through the eye of a needle than for a rich[t] person to enter the kingdom of God."

[26] So they were even more astonished, saying to one another, "Then who can be saved?"[u]

[27] Looking at them, Jesus said, "With men it is impossible,[v] but not with God, because all things are possible with God."

[28] Peter[w] began to tell Him, "Look, we have left everything and followed You."

[29] "I assure you,"[x] Jesus said, "there is no one who has left house, brothers or sisters, mother or father,[E] children, or fields because of Me and the gospel,[y] [30] who will not receive 100 times[z] more, now at this time[aa]—houses, brothers and sisters, mothers and children, and fields, with persecutions[ab]—and eternal life[ac] in the age to come.[ad] [31] But many who are first will be last, and the last first."[ae]

The Third Prediction of His Death

[32] They[af] were on the road, going up to Jerusalem,[ag] and Jesus was walking ahead of them. They were astonished, but those who followed Him were afraid.[ah] Taking the Twelve aside again, He began to tell them the things that would happen to Him.[ai]

[33] "Listen! We are going up to Jerusalem. The •Son of Man[aj] will be handed over to the •chief priests and the •scribes,[ak] and they will condemn Him to death. Then they will hand

---

[a]10:18 Ps 69:16
[b]10:19 Mt 5:21
[c]Mt 5:27-28
[d]Eph 4:28
[e]Pr 6:19
[f]1Co 6:7-8; 7:5; 1Tm 6:5; Jms 5:4
[g]1Tm 5:3
[h]Ex 21:15
[i]10:20 Mk 4:38; Eph 4:11
[j]10:21 Lk 6:35; 2Th 2:13; Heb 12:6
[k]Mk 14:7; Rm 15:26
[l]2Co 4:7
[m]Mt 6:20; 13:44; Lk 12:33
[n]Jn 8:12
[o]10:22 2Co 2:2
[p]Ac 2:45; 5:1
[q]10:23 Ac 4:37; 8:18,20; 24:26
[r]Mk 1:15
[s]10:24 Lk 1:7
[t]10:25 Gn 24:35; Rv 2:9
[u]10:26 Ac 16:30; Eph 2:8
[v]10:27 Heb 6:4
[w]10:28 Lk 6:14; Ac 10:32
[x]10:29 Rv 22:21
[y]Mk 1:1; Php 1:5
[z]10:30 Lk 21:8
[aa]Lk 20:10
[ab]Mt 13:21
[ac]Jn 12:25; Ac 13:48
[ad]Mt 12:32; Lk 20:35; Eph 1:21; 2:7
[ae]10:31 Mk 9:35
[af]10:32-34 Mt 20:17-19; Lk 18:31-34
[ag]10:32 Ps 79:1; Mt 23:37; Pr 1:7; Rv 14:7
[ah]Ps 147:11;
[ai]Jn 6:61
[aj]10:33 Mk 2:10
[ak]Mt 2:4

[A]10:19 Ex 20:12-16; Dt 5:16-20   [B]10:21 Other mss add *taking up the cross, and*   [C]10:22 Or *he became gloomy*   [D]10:24 Other mss add *for those trusting in wealth*   [E]10:29 Other mss add *or wife*

10:19 The **commandments** were from the second tablet of the law, those that focused on behavior and relationships (Ex 20:12-16; Dt 5:16-20).

10:20 The young man again addressed Jesus as **Teacher**, but this time he did not add "good."

10:21 Looking at him is an intensified form of the verb, indicating close scrutiny. Only Mark stated that **Jesus loved him.** The phrase **you lack one thing** shows that perfect obedience to the law does not merit eternal life. The "one thing" involved divesting himself of his possessions and becoming a disciple (1:17; 2:14). In exchange for earthly possessions, he would have **treasure in heaven.**

10:22 He was stunned is a descriptive verb used only here in Mark. It means "shocked" or "appalled." The effect of Jesus' **demand** must have been visible on the young man's face. Rather than following Jesus (v. 21), he **went away**, choosing his **many possessions** over Jesus. He is an example of 4:19 (see note at 4:14-20).

10:23 How hard it is refers to extreme difficulty. Rather than an advantage, possessions are a hindrance to entering God's kingdom.

10:24 On **were astonished**, see note at 1:21-22. Perhaps the disciples understood wealth as a sign of God's blessing (Dt 28:1-14).

10:25 Jesus used a proverb for impossibility. The **camel** was the largest animal in Palestine, and one certainly could not squeeze through **the eye of a needle**.

10:26 The astonishment of Jesus' disciples increased from "astonished" (Gk *thambein*) in verse 24 to **even more astonished** (Gk *perissos ekplessesthai*) in verse 26. **Be saved** (Gk *sozo*) is equivalent to "enter the kingdom of God" (vv. 23-25), "eternal life" (vv. 17,30), "heaven" (v. 21), and "the age to come" (v. 30).

10:27 The phrase **looking at** connotes great intensity. It recalls how Jesus looked at the young man (v. 21).

10:28 As usual, **Peter** served as spokesman for the disciples (8:29,32; 9:5; 11:21). In his judgment, he and the disciples had done what Jesus commanded the rich man to do (10:21).

10:29 I assure you was Jesus' solemn oath formula. He placed equal importance on Himself and **the gospel.**

10:30 The promised compensation (**100 times more**) covered **this time** (see 3:34-35) and **the age to come**. Following Jesus provides no protection against suffering, but the reward includes **eternal life**. The rich ruler sought this (v. 17) but walked away from it (v. 22).

10:31 Jesus emphasized the reversal of values that is so prominent in Christian discipleship (cp. Mt 19:30; 20:16; Lk 13:30).

10:32 The road trip continues (vv. 1,17; 8:27; 9:2,30,33-34). The eastern approach to Jerusalem goes **up** because of the city's elevation. Jesus was **walking ahead of them**, showing He was not afraid of what awaited Him.

10:33-34 On **listen**, see note at 4:3. Jesus' use of **we** must have frightened the disciples even further. In this final

Him over to the Gentiles,[a] [34]and they will mock Him, spit on Him, flog[A] Him, and kill Him, and He will rise[b] after three days."[c]

Suffering and Service

[35]Then[d] James[e] and John,[f] the sons of Zebedee,[g] approached Him and said, "Teacher,[h] we want You to do something for us if we ask You."

[36]"What do you want Me to do for you?" He asked them.

[37]They answered Him, "Allow us to sit at Your right and at Your left in Your glory."[i]

[38]But Jesus said to them, "You don't know what you're asking.[j] Are you able to drink the cup[k] I drink or to be baptized with the baptism[l] I am baptized with?"[m]

[39]"We are able," they told Him.

Jesus said to them, "You will drink the cup I drink, and you will be baptized with the baptism I am baptized with.[n] [40]But to sit at My right or left is not Mine to give; instead, it is for those it has been prepared for."[41]When the other 10 disciples heard this, they began to be indignant with James and John.[o]

[42]Jesus called them over and said to them, "You know that those who are regarded as rulers of the Gentiles dominate[p] them, and their men of high positions exercise power over them. [43]But it must not be like that among you.[q] On the contrary, whoever wants to become great among you must be your servant,[r]

[44]and whoever wants to be first among you must be a •slave[s] to all. [45]For even the Son of Man[t] did not come to be served, but to serve,[u] and to give His life[v]—a ransom[w] for many."[B,x]

A Blind Man Healed

[46]They[y] came to Jericho.[z] And as He was leaving Jericho with His disciples and a large crowd, Bartimaeus (the son of Timaeus), a blind[aa] beggar,[ab] was sitting by the road.[ac] [47]When he heard that it was Jesus the •Nazarene,[ad] he began to cry out, "Son of David,[ae] Jesus, have mercy[af] on me!"[ag] [48]Many people told him to keep quiet, but he was crying out all the more, "Have mercy on me,[ah] Son of David!"

[49]Jesus stopped and said, "Call him."

So they called the blind man and said to him, "Have courage![ai] Get up; He's calling for you." [50]He threw off his coat,[aj] jumped up, and came to Jesus.

[51]Then Jesus answered him, "What do you want[ak] Me to do for you?"

"*Rabbouni,*"[C,al] the blind man told Him, "I want to see!"

[52]"Go your way," Jesus told him. "Your faith has healed you."[am] Immediately he could see and began to follow Him on the road.

Cross references (center column)

a10:33-34 Mk 8:31; 9:31
b10:34 Mt 16:21; Ac 2:24
cLk 9:22
d10:35-45 Mt 20:20-28
e10:35 Ac 12:2
fJn 21:7
gJn 21:2
hMk 4:38; Eph 4:11
i10:37 Mt 19:28; Lk 9:26
j10:38 Jn 11:22
kPs 75:8
lLk 12:50; Ac 22:16
mLk 12:50; Rm 6:3; 2Co 4:10-11; Gl 2:20
n10:39 Ac 12:2; Rv 1:9
o10:41 Jn 21:7
p10:42 Ac 19:16; 1Pt 5:3
q10:43 Mk 9:35; 10:45
r10:43-44 Lk 22:26
s10:44 Mt 10:24; Php 2:7; Rv 1:1
t10:45 Mk 2:10
uJn 13:13-15; Php 2:7
vJn 6:51; 10:15; Gl 2:20
wLv 27:31; Ps 49:8; Mt 26:28; Eph 1:7
xIs 52:13-53:12; Mt 20:28
y10:46-52 Mt 20:29-34; Lk 18:35-43
z10:46 Nm 22:1
aaMt 15:14
abJn 9:8 acMk 8:27 ad10:47 Mk 14:67 ae2Ch 1:1; Mt 1:1; Rm 1:3 afMt 5:7; Mk 5:19; Lk 1:50 ag Mt 15:22; 17:15; Mk 10:48; Lk 16:24 ah10:48 Mk 10:47 ai10:49 Jn 16:33 aj10:50 Lk 19:36 ak10:51 Mk 1:40 alJn 20:16 am10:52 Mk 9:22; Mk 6:56; Lk 5:20

A10:34 Or *scourge*   B10:45 Or *in the place of many*; Is 53:10-12   C10:51 Hb word for *my teacher*

---

prediction, Jesus declared that the **chief priests** and the **scribes** would **condemn** Him to **death** (see notes at 14:53 and 14:64) and **hand Him over to the Gentiles** since they lacked authority to carry out the sentence (15:1-2).

10:35-45 James and John failed to realize the implications of Jesus' suffering and death.

10:35-36 This is the only time in Mark that James and John acted on their own apart from the other disciples, and they did so selfishly. Most likely they asked Jesus to grant their request even before they spelled it out because they knew they were being selfish.

10:37 The **right** side was the highest position of honor, the **left** the second. James and John caught a glimpse of Jesus' **glory** in the transfiguration (9:2-13), now they wanted more. It was their mother who suggested they make this request (Mt 20:20-21).

10:38 The cup and **baptism** refer to Jesus' suffering and death (14:36).

10:39-40 You will may predict James's martyrdom (Ac 12:2) and John's exile (Rv 1:9). **It is for those it has been prepared for** is a divine passive, indicating that God would decide who would receive places of honor.

10:41 The other disciples became **indignant**, the same verb used of Jesus in verse 14.

10:42 That Jesus instructed all His apostles in this lesson shows that all of them struggled with the same greed that led James and John to seek places of honor.

10:43-44 Becoming **great** in Christian leadership means becoming a **servant**. The Greek word *diakonos* refers to a person who waits on tables. But even more is required of

doulos

Greek Pronunciation	[DOO lahss]
HCSB Translation	slave
Uses in Mark's Gospel	5
Uses in the NT	126
Focus Passage	Mark 10:44

Several Greek words in the NT convey the idea of one person being the servant of another. By far the most common is *doulos*, best conveyed by the English word *slave*. Other types of servants had various responsibilities, privileges, and rights, but under Roman law the *doulos* had no rights. He belonged completely to his master and had only those responsibilities and privileges granted by his master. In the NT, *doulos* is normally used literally (14:47; Mt 8:9; Lk 17:7-10; Jn 13:16; Eph 6:5-9; Phm 16), but a figurative meaning describing someone who serves God and His people is also common (Mk 10:44; Ac 2:18; 4:29; Rm 1:1; 2Co 4:5; 1Pt 2:16; Rv 2:20). Paul has two significant uses of *doulos*, one about Christ and the other about Christians: (1) Php 2:6 refers to Jesus' condescension in the incarnation, and (2) Rm 6:16-18 refers to being *slaves* of righteousness instead of *slaves* of sin.

The Triumphal Entry

11 When they approached Jerusalem,^b at Bethphage and Bethany^c near the •Mount of Olives, He sent two of His disciples [2] and told them, "Go into the village ahead of you. As soon as you enter it, you will find a young donkey tied there, on which no one has ever sat. Untie it and bring it here. [3] If anyone says to you, 'Why are you doing this?' say, 'The Lord needs it and will send it back here right away.'"

[4] So they went and found a young donkey outside in the street, tied by a door. They untied it, [5] and some of those standing there said to them, "What are you doing, untying the donkey?" [6] They answered them just as Jesus had said, so they let them go. [7] Then they brought the donkey to Jesus and threw their robes on it, and He sat on it. [8] Many people spread their robes on the road,^d and others spread leafy branches cut from the fields.^{A [9]} Then those who went ahead and those who followed kept shouting:

> •*Hosanna!*
> **He who comes in the name^e**
> **of the Lord is the blessed One!**^{B,f}
> [10] The coming kingdom^g
> of our father David^h is blessed!
> *Hosannaⁱ* in the highest heaven!

[11] And He went into Jerusalem^j and into the •temple complex.^k After looking around at everything, since it was already late, He went out to Bethany^l with the Twelve.

The Barren Fig Tree Is Cursed

[12] The^m next day when they came out from Bethany, He was hungry. [13] After seeing in the distance a figⁿ tree with leaves, He went to find out if there was anything on it. When He came to it, He found nothing but leaves, because it was not the season for figs. [14] He said to it,

Cross references (center column):
^a11:1-11 Mt 21:1-11; Lk 19:28-44; Jn 12:12-19
^b11:1 Mt 23:37; Ac 8:1
^cMt 26:6; Lk 24:50; Jn 11:1,18; 12:1
^d11:8 Mk 8:27
^e11:9 Jn 10:25
^fLk 1:42; Heb 6:14
^g11:10 Mk 1:15; 9:1
^hLk 1:27; Ac 2:29; 4:25
ⁱMk 11:9
^j11:11 Mt 23:37
^kAc 21:26
^lMk 11:1
^m11:12-19 Mt 21:12-19; Lk 19:45-48
ⁿ11:13 Lk 6:44; Jn 1:48

A11:8 Other mss read *others were cutting leafy branches from the trees and spreading them on the road*   **B**11:9 Ps 118:26

---

a disciple: **Whoever wants to be first among you must be a slave to all.** A "slave" (Gk *doulos*) is lower than a servant, has no rights, and does only his master's bidding.

10:45 The greatest example of servant leadership is **the Son of Man**. Giving is the essence of servanthood, and Jesus gave **His life** as **a ransom for many** (cp. Is 53:10-12). "Ransom" refers to the price paid to release a slave.

10:46-52 Mark concluded the "on the road" section just as he began it—with the story of a blind man (8:22-26). This account contrasted what the blind man could see with what the disciples could not (10:35-45).

10:46 The city of **Jericho** lay 17 miles northeast and 3,500 feet below Jerusalem. The **large crowd** was made up of Passover pilgrims.

10:47-48 This is the second time Mark identified Jesus as **the Nazarene** (1:24), and the only time in Mark that someone addressed Jesus as **Son of David**, a messianic designation based on 2Sm 7:1-14 (cp. Mk 11:10; 12:35-37).

10:52 In contrast to His healing of the blind man in 8:22-25, Jesus simply announced Bartimaeus's healing. **Healed** is the Greek word *sozo*. It can refer to physical healing and spiritual salvation. Bartimaeus experienced both.

11:1-11 Jesus' royal procession into Jerusalem took place on what is now called "Palm Sunday."

11:1 This is Jesus' first recorded visit to **Jerusalem** in Mark. (Luke 2:41-52 records Jesus' visit as a boy and John's Gospel indicates several visits.) **Bethphage** (lit "house of unripe figs") was located on the slope of the **Mount of Olives**, a large hill east of Jerusalem. **Bethany** was two miles east of Jerusalem.

11:2 **The village ahead of you** was probably Bethphage.

11:4 **Outside in the street** indicates the **donkey** was in plain sight.

11:6 This verse may indicate that Jesus arranged in advance to borrow the donkey.

11:7 The two unnamed disciples **threw their robes** on the donkey to create a makeshift saddle. Even though Mark did not quote Zch 9:9 in this account (as did Mt 21:5; Jn 12:15), the messianic symbolism of Jesus' action is clear.

11:8 **Robes** and **leafy branches** were traditionally draped across the road to receive a king (cp. 2Kg 9:13).

11:9 The two groups (**those who went ahead . . . those who followed**) may refer to fellow pilgrims traveling with Jesus (10:46) and those who came out of Jerusalem to meet them (Jn 12:9; cp. Mt 21:10-11). The crowd's shouts were recitations from Ps 118:25-26, the last of the Hallel psalms sung at Passover. *Hosanna* is Hebrew for "save us."

11:10 Only Mark recorded this shout from the crowd. The words echo Bartimaeus's cry (10:47-48).

11:11 The **temple complex** included several buildings and courtyards. Herod's temple was being reconstructed, a project that had been going on for more than 45 years (13:1; Jn 2:20). **Bethany**, two miles east of Jerusalem, was where Jesus apparently lodged during Passover.

11:12-26 Matthew recorded the temple clearing (Mt 21:12-17) and the cursing of the fig tree (Mt 21:18-20) as distinct events. Mark divided the cursing of the fig tree (Mk 11:12-14) from its withering (vv. 20-21) and placed the clearing of the temple in between (vv. 15-19). Thus he meant for readers to see the connection between the barren fig tree (symbolic for Israel) and the barren temple. Jesus' cursing of the fig tree was an acted-out parable of God's judgment on Jerusalem and the temple.

11:12 The **next day** was Monday of Holy Week.

11:13 Jesus spotted a **fig tree** that bore **nothing but leaves**. Even though **it was not the season for figs**, the leafy tree should have been covered with edible buds (Gk *paggim*).

11:14 Jesus' words express a curse (v. 21). This is the last of Jesus' miracles recorded in Mark and the only miracle of destruction in the Gospels. In the OT, the fig tree was a symbol of Israel (Jr 24:1-10; Hs 9:10; cp. Lk 13:6-9). The episode recalls Jr 8:13; Hs 2:12; and Mc 7:1.

"May no ever eat fruit[a] from you again!"[b] And His disciples[c] heard it.

Cleansing the Temple Complex

[15]They came to Jerusalem,[d] and He went into the temple complex[e] and began to throw out those buying and selling in the temple. He overturned the money changers'[f] tables and the chairs of those selling doves, [16]and would not permit anyone to carry goods through the temple complex.

[17]Then He began to teach them: "Is it not written,[g] **My house**[h] **will be called a house of prayer**[i] **for all nations?**[A] But you have made it **a den of thieves!**"[B,j] [18]Then the •chief priests and the •scribes[k] heard it and started looking for a way to destroy Him. For they were afraid[l] of Him, because the whole crowd was astonished by His teaching.

[19]And whenever evening came, they would go out of the city.

The Barren Fig Tree Is Withered

[20]Early[m] in the morning, as they were passing by, they saw the fig tree withered from the roots up. [21]Then Peter[n] remembered and said to Him, "•Rabbi,[o] look! The fig tree that You cursed[p] is withered."

[22]Jesus replied to them, "Have faith in God.[q] [23]•I assure you:[r] If anyone says to this mountain, 'Be lifted up and thrown into the sea,' and does not doubt[s] in his heart, but believes[t] that what he says will happen, it will be done for him.[u] [24]Therefore I tell you, all the things you pray[v] and ask for[w]—believe that you have received[C,x] them, and you will have them. [25]And whenever you stand[y] praying, if you have anything against anyone, forgive[z] him, so that your Father[aa] in heaven[ab] will also forgive[ac] you your wrongdoing. [[26]But if you don't forgive, neither will your Father in heaven[ad] forgive your wrongdoing.]"[D,E]

Messiah's Authority Challenged

[27]They[ae] came again to Jerusalem.[af] As He was walking in the temple complex,[ag] the chief priests, the scribes,[ah] and the elders[ai] came [28]and asked Him, "By what authority[aj] are You doing these things? Who gave You this authority to do these things?"

[29]Jesus said to them, "I will ask you one question;[ak] then answer Me, and I will tell you

---

[a]11:14 Mt 3:8; 7:16-21
[b]Jr 8:13
[c]Mk 10:10
[d]11:15 Mt 23:37
[e]Ac 21:26
[f]Jn 2:15
[g]11:17 Mk 1:2; Ac 15:15
[h]Lk 11:51; Jn 2:17
[i]Ac 12:5; 16:13
[j]Jr 7:11
[k]11:18 Mt 2:4
[l]Ps 147:11; Pr 1:7; Rv 14:7
[m]11:20-26 Mt 21:19-22
[n]11:21 Lk 6:14; Ac 10:32
[o]Jn 11:8
[p]Jms 3:9
[q]Mt 17:20
[r]11:23 Ps 72:19; Rv 22:21
[s]Ac 10:20
[t]Jn 3:16; Ac 10:43; Rm 10:9; 1Pt 1:8-10
[u]Mk 9:23; Jn 11:22
[v]11:24 Mt 5:44; Ac 12:12
[w]Jn 14:13; Jms 1:5
[x]Mt 7:8
[y]11:25 Lk 18:11
[z]Mt 6:12; 9:2
[aa]Mt 5:16; Lk 11:13
[ab]Mt 6:1; Lk 12:33
[ac]Ps 25:11; Mt 9:2
[ad]11:26 Mt 24:35; Ac 7:24; Eph 6:9; Rv 21:10
[ae]11:27-33 Mt 21:23-27; Lk 20:1-8
[af]11:27 Mt 23:37
[ag]Ac 21:26
[ah]Mt 2:4
[ai]3Jn 1
[aj]11:28 Mk 1:22
[ak]11:29 Mk 4:14

[A]11:17 Is 56:7   [B]11:17 Jr 7:11   [C]11:24 Some mss read *you receive*; other mss read *you will receive*   [D]11:26 Other mss omit bracketed text   [E]11:25-26 These are the only uses of this word in Mk. It means "the violation of the Law" or "stepping over a boundary" or "departing from the path" or "trespass."

11:15-18 Scripture prophesied Messiah would purify the temple (Ezk 37:26-28; Mal 3:1-4). Jesus' temple cleansing is clearly messianic. John recorded a cleansing at the beginning of his Gospel (Jn 2:13-17).

11:15 Having noted all that went on in the **temple complex** the day before, Jesus now returned, probably to the Court of the Gentiles, where most **buying and selling** occurred. People who traveled from afar needed to purchase pure, unblemished animals once they arrived for Passover. **Money changers** exchanged idol-engraved Greek and Roman coinage for imageless Tyrian or Jewish temple coins that could be used to buy sacrificial items or pay the temple tax (Ex 30:11-16). **Doves** were offered by women after childbirth (Lv 12:6-8; Lk 2:22-24), by cleansed lepers (Lv 14:22), by those healed of bodily discharges (Lv 15:14,29), and by those who could not afford more expensive sacrifices (Lv 5:7,11). Sheep and cattle were sold also (Jn 2:14). The Court of the Gentiles had become a virtual stockyard.

11:16 Only Mark added the information in this verse, indicating further inappropriate use of the temple as a thoroughfare or shortcut.

11:17 Only Mark added **for all nations**. The **den of thieves** quotation is from Jr 7:11, part of Jeremiah's sermon in which he condemned temple goers for their attitudes and behaviors and predicted the temple's destruction (Jr 7:12-15).

11:18 Jesus' last word in verse 17, "thieves" (Gk *lestes*), involved foreshadowing since within three days He would be arrested as if He were a thief (14:48) and within four days

would be crucified between two thieves (15:27). The words **a way to destroy Him** recall the plot in 3:6 by the Pharisees and Herodians.

11:19-20 The destruction of the fig tree echoes Hs 9:10,16.

11:21 This is the second time Mark recorded Peter addressing Jesus as **Rabbi** (9:5). Peter served as spokesman for the disciples (8:29,32; 9:5; 10:28).

11:22 The proper object of **faith** is **God**, not the temple.

11:23 Jesus' saying on faith and impossibilities (cp. 1Co 13:2) began with His solemn formula, **I assure you** (cp. 3:28; 8:12; 9:1,41; 10:15,29). He gave a negative condition (**does not doubt in his heart**) and a positive condition (**but believes**) for fulfillment of this promise (cp. Jms 1:6).

11:24 For more about the role of faith in prayer, see 1Jn 5:14-15 and note there.

11:25 A second condition to petitions being granted is to **forgive** others. Standing while **praying** was the usual Jewish posture for public prayers (cp. Lk 18:9-14). **If you have anything against anyone** recalls Mt 5:23-24 (cp. Mt 18:21-35).

11:27–12:44 In this section Mark recorded a series of conflict stories with the religious leaders.

11:27 The **chief priests**, the **scribes**, and the **elders** made up the Sanhedrin, the 70-member governing body of the Jews. These were representatives, not the whole body. In His first death prediction, Jesus named these groups as those who would put Him to death (see note at 8:31).

11:28 The questions focused on the nature (**by what**) of Jesus' **authority** (Gk *exousia*) and on **who gave** it to Him.

by what authority I am doing these things. ³⁰Was John's baptism*a* from heaven or from men? Answer Me."

³¹They began to argue among themselves: "If we say, 'From heaven,' He will say, 'Then why didn't you believe*b* him?' ³²But if we say, 'From men'"—they were afraid of the crowd, because everyone thought that John was a genuine prophet.*c* ³³So they answered Jesus, "We don't know."

And Jesus said to them, "Neither will I tell you by what authority I do these things."

The Parable of the Vineyard Owner

12 Then*d* He began to speak to them in parables: "A man planted a vineyard,*e* put a fence around it, dug out a pit for a winepress, and built a watchtower. Then he leased it to tenant farmers and went away. ²At harvest time he sent*f* a •slave*g* to the farmers to collect some of the fruit*h* of the vineyard from the farmers. ³But they took him, beat*i* him, and sent him away empty-handed.*j* ⁴Again he sent another slave to them, and they*A* hit him on the head and treated him shamefully.*B* ⁵Then he sent another, and they killed that one. He also sent many others; they beat some and they killed some.

⁶"He still had one to send, a beloved*k* son.

a11:30 Lk 7:29;
Ac 18:25; 19:3
b11:31 1Jn 5:10
c11:32 Mt 2:23;
Ac 7:52
d12:1-12 Mt
21:33-46; Lk
20:9-19
e12:1 Gn 9:20
f12:2 Mk 3:14
gMt 10:24
hMt 3:8; 7:16
i12:3 Lk 22:63
jCol 2:8
k12:6 Eph 1:6;
Phm 1
lHeb 1:1-2
m12:9 Col 3:22
n12:10 Mt 26:54;
2Pt 1:20
o12:10-11 Ps
118:22-23
p12:10 Ac 4:11;
1Pt 2:7
q12:11 Col 4:1;
Jd 5
r12:13-17 Mt
22:15-22; Lk
20:20-26
s12:13 Mk 7:3
tMk 3:6
uLk 11:54
v12:14 Dt 1:17
wMt 17:25

Finally*l* he sent him to them, saying, 'They will respect my son.'

⁷"But those tenant farmers said among themselves, 'This is the heir. Come, let's kill him, and the inheritance will be ours!' ⁸So they seized him, killed him, and threw him out of the vineyard.

⁹"Therefore, what will the owner*C,m* of the vineyard do? He will come and destroy the farmers and give the vineyard to others. ¹⁰Haven't you read this Scripture:*n*

The*o* stone that
    the builders rejected
has become the cornerstone.*D,p*
¹¹ This came from the Lord*q*
    and is wonderful in our eyes?"*E*

¹²Because they knew He had said this parable against them, they were looking for a way to arrest Him, but they were afraid of the crowd. So they left Him and went away.

God and Caesar

¹³Then*r* they sent some of the •Pharisees*s* and the •Herodians*t* to Him to trap Him by what He said.*F,u* ¹⁴When they came, they said to Him, "Teacher, we know You are truthful and defer to no one, for You don't show partiality*G,v* but teach truthfully the way of God. Is it lawful to pay taxes*w* to Caesar or not? ¹⁵Should we pay, or should we not pay?"

A12:4 Other mss add *threw stones and* **B**12:4 Other mss add *and sent him off* **C**12:9 Or *lord* **D**12:10 Lit *the head of the corner* **E**12:10-11 Ps 118:22-23 **F**12:13 Lit *trap Him in (a) word* **G**12:14 Lit *don't look on the face of men*; that is, on the outward appearance

---

Jesus' authority had been at issue since the beginning (1:22,27; 2:10). **These things** probably refer to His temple clearing and His royal entry into the city.

11:30 John's baptism encapsulates John the Baptist's entire ministry. **From heaven** means "from God." Jesus' question turned the tables on the Pharisees. If they admitted that John was sent by God, they would have to admit the same about Jesus.

11:31-33 A **genuine prophet** has authority from heaven. If John was a prophet from God, Jesus was even more so. Unwilling to admit this, the authorities refused to answer Jesus.

12:1 The phrase **a man planted a vineyard** points to the song of Is 5:1-7 in which Israel is symbolized by a vineyard. **Tenant farmers** and absentee landlords stand for Israel's leaders.

12:2-5 Harvest time for a vineyard might be as late as the fifth year after the vines were planted (Lv 19:23-25). The mistreated slaves stand for the prophets.

12:6 The **beloved son** in this parable is Jesus.

12:7 Come, let's kill him were the words spoken by Joseph's brothers (Gn 37:20).

12:8 Matthew (Mt 21:39) and Luke (Lk 20:15) reported that the son was cast out before being killed. Mark's order

(seized him, killed him, and threw him out) indicates they did not give the son a proper burial.

12:9 The man who planted the vineyard (v. 1) and sent his servants and son is identified as **the owner**. The word is literally "lord" (Gk *kyrios*), which is also a title for God. **Give the vineyard to others** alludes to the upcoming gospel mission to the Gentiles.

12:10-11 Jesus concluded by quoting Ps 118:22-23, the first verse of which is also quoted elsewhere (Lk 20:17; Ac 4:11; Rm 9:33; 1Pt 2:6-8). Only Mark and Matthew (Mt 21:42) included Ps 118:23, which adds a strong providential element. **Cornerstone** (lit "head of the corner") may refer to a foundation cornerstone, the capstone on a column, or the keystone in an arch.

12:13 The fact that **the Pharisees** (see note at 2:15-17) and **the Herodians** (see note at 3:6) were **sent** indicates an approved delegation. The same groups are united in 3:6 in the plot against Jesus in Galilee. They hoped to **trap** Jesus with a trick question.

12:14 The specific tax the Pharisees and Herodians had in mind was the Roman poll tax imposed when Judea became a Roman province in A.D. 6. This tax represented Jewish subjugation to Rome.

12:15 If Jesus answered "yes," He would be seen as pro-Roman and would alienate the crowds. If He said "no," the Pharisees and Herodians would denounce Him as a

But knowing their hypocrisy,[a] He said to them, "Why are you testing[b] Me? Bring Me a •denarius[c] to look at." [16]So they brought one. "Whose image[d] and inscription[e] is this?" He asked them.

"Caesar's," they said.

[17]Then Jesus told them, "Give back to Caesar the things that are Caesar's, and to God the things that are God's."[f] And they were amazed[g] at Him.

The Sadducees and the Resurrection

[18]Some[h] •Sadducees,[i] who say there is no resurrection,[j] came to Him and questioned Him: [19]"Teacher,[k] Moses[l] wrote for us that **if a man's brother dies**, leaves his wife behind, and **leaves no child,**[m] **his brother should take the wife**[n] **and produce •offspring for his brother.**[A,o] [20]There were seven brothers. The first took a wife, and dying, left no offspring. [21]The second also took her, and he died, leaving no offspring. And the third likewise. [22]So the seven[B] left no offspring. Last of all, the woman died too. [23]In the resurrection, when they rise,[c] whose wife will she be, since the seven had married her?"[D]

[24]Jesus told them, "Are you not deceived because you don't know the Scriptures[p] or the power[q] of God?[r] [25]For when they rise[s] from the dead,[t] they neither marry nor are given in marriage[u] but are like angels[v] in heaven. [26]Now concerning the dead being raised—haven't you read in the book of Moses, in the passage about the burning bush, how God spoke to him: **I**[w] **am the God of Abraham**[x] **and the God of Isaac**[y] **and the God of Jacob?**[E,z] [27]He is not God of the dead but of the living. You are badly deceived."

The Primary Commandments

[28]One[aa] of the •scribes[ab] approached. When he heard them debating and saw that Jesus answered them well, he asked Him, "Which command is the most important of all?"[F] [29]"This is the most important,"[G] Jesus answered:

Listen, Israel! The Lord[ac] **our God, the Lord**[ad] **is One.**[H] [30]**Love**[ae] **the Lord your God**[af] **with all your heart, with all your**

Cross references (center column)

[a]12:15 Mt 23:28; Lk 12:1; Gl 2:13; 1Tm 4:2; 1Pt 2:1
[b]Jms 1:13
[c]Mt 18:28
[d]12:16 Rv 13:14
[e]Mk 15:26; Lk 23:38
[f]12:17 Rm 13:7
[g]Rv 17:6
[h]12:18–27 Mt 22:23-33; Lk 20:27-40
[i]12:18 Ac 23:6
[j]Ac 1:22
[k]12:19 Mk 4:38; Eph 4:11
[l]Ps 77:20; Mt 8:4; Heb 3:2
[m]Lk 1:7
[n]Mt 1:6
[o]Gn 38:8; Dt 25:5-10
[p]12:24 Mt 26:54; 2Pt 1:20
[q]Lk 1:35; 6:19
[r]2Co 13:4; Rv 11:17
[s]12:25 Lk 18:33
[t]Jn 5:25; 20:9
[u]1Tm 5:14
[v]Mt 13:49; Ac 5:19; Rv 14:6
[w]12:26 Ex 3:6,15-16
[x]Gl 3:6
[y]Jms 2:21
[z]Mt 1:2; Lk 1:33
[aa]12:28-34 Mt 22:34-40
[ab]12:28 Mt 2:4
[ac]12:29 Col 4:1; Jd 5
[ad]Dt 6:4
[ae]12:30 Lk 6:35
[af]Dt 6:5; Lk 10:27

Text notes

[A]12:19 Gn 38:8; Dt 25:5   [B]12:22 Other mss add *had taken her and*   [C]12:23 Other mss omit *when they rise*   [D]12:23 Lit *the seven had her as a wife*   [E]12:26 Ex 3:6,15-16   [F]12:28 Lit *Which command is first of all?*   [G]12:29 Other mss add *of all the commandments*   [H]12:29 Or *The Lord our God is one Lord.*

Study notes

revolutionary (Lk 20:20). Jesus was not fooled. He saw their **hypocrisy** and realized they were **testing** Him. A **denarius** was the equivalent of a day's wages (Mt 20:9-10).

12:16-17 The denarius bore an **image** of Tiberius Caesar (reigned A.D. 14–37) with an **inscription** professing his divinity. Since Jesus was asked about giving (vv. 14-15), He replied with a lesson about ownership. **Give back** has the nuance of obligation. The coin had Caesar's image, so it belonged to Caesar. Jesus supported the legitimacy of human government, but He raised the issue to a higher level. He did not identify **the things that are God's**, but since humans bear God's image (Gn 1:27), we have an obligation to give to God that which bears His image—ourselves.

12:18 The **Sadducees** arose in the second century B.C. during the Maccabean revolt. They were closely associated with aristocratic and priestly classes; accepted only the books of Moses (the Pentateuch) as Scripture; denied bodily resurrection, future judgment, the existence of angels, demons,

and spirits; and affirmed human free will (v. 18; Ac 23:6-8; Josephus, *Ant.*,18.1.4).

12:19-23 The Sadducees approached Jesus with a situation based on the books of **Moses**. Specifically, the case involved the levirate (or brother-in-law) marriage law (Dt 25:5-6). This law obligated a male sibling to marry his deceased brother's widow in order to preserve the family name and inheritance. Based on this, the Sadducees presented a scenario designed to make the doctrine of resurrection look absurd. Their question assumed that the future life will be like the temporal life.

12:24-27 Jesus declared that the afterlife will be different from life on earth. In heaven people will not **marry** or be **given in marriage**. By going to **the book of Moses**, specifically Ex 3 and the passage about **the burning bush**, Jesus used the part of the OT that the Sadducees recognized as Scripture. The point of the OT quotation is that **Abraham . . . Isaac**, and **Jacob** were long dead by the time God spoke to Moses, but God declared He was their God. Since God **is not God of the dead but of the living**, they must still be alive in the afterlife.

12:28-40 This section describes three encounters with the scribes. The scribes were allies of the chief priests and elders (see note at 11:27).

12:28 The phrase **one of the scribes** may indicate that others were standing by ready to challenge Jesus (cp. Mt 22:34-35). This is the first time an individual scribe **approached** Jesus. He wanted to know which **command** was **most important**. The rabbis had counted 613 commandments in the books of Moses. They classified 365 as prohibitions and 248 as commands. They further divided the commandments into weightier and lesser ("least" in Mt 5:19).

Roman denarius bears the image of Tiberius Caesar who reigned A.D. 14–37.

soul, with all your mind,[a] and with all your strength.[A,B,b]

[31]"The second is: **Love your neighbor[c] as yourself**.[C,d] There is no other command[e] greater than these."

[32]Then the scribe said to Him, "You are right, Teacher! You have correctly said that He is One, and there is no one[f] else except Him.[g] [33]And to love[h] Him with all your heart, with all your understanding,[D] and with all your strength, and to love your neighbor as yourself, is far more important than all the burnt offerings and sacrifices."[i]

[34]When Jesus saw that he answered intelligently, He said to him, "You are not far from the kingdom of God."[j] And no one dared[k] to question Him any longer.

The Question about the Messiah

[35]So[l] Jesus asked this question as He taught in the 'temple complex,[m] "How can the scribes[n] say that the 'Messiah[o] is the Son of David?[p] [36]David[q] himself says by the Holy Spirit:[r]

The Lord[s] declared to my Lord,
'Sit at My right hand[t]

until I put Your enemies
under Your feet.'[E,u]

[37]David himself calls Him 'Lord'; how then can the Messiah be his Son?" And the large crowd was listening to Him with delight.

Warning against the Scribes

[38]He[v] also said in His teaching, "Beware of the scribes, who want to go around in long robes,[w] and who want greetings in the marketplaces,[x] [39]the front seats[y] in the 'synagogues,[z] and the places of honor[aa] at banquets.[ab] [40]They devour[ac] widows'[ad] houses and say long prayers[ae] just for show. These will receive harsher punishment."

The Widow's Gift

[41]Sitting[af] across from the temple treasury,[ag] He watched how the crowd dropped money into the treasury. Many rich[ah] people were putting in large sums. [42]And a poor[ai] widow came and dropped in two tiny coins worth very little.[F] [43]Summoning His disciples,[aj] He said to them, "'I assure you:[ak] This poor

---

[a]12:30 Jn 5:20
[b]Dt 6:4-5; Jos 22:5
[c]12:31 Lk 10:29
[d]Lv 19:18; 1Jn 4:21
[e]Mk 7:8
[f]12:32 Rm 3:30
[g]Dt 4:35,39; 6:4; Is 37:20; 43:10; 44:6; 45:21
[h]12:33 Lk 6:35
[i]1Sm 15:22; Ps 51:16; Hs 6:6; Am 5:22; Mc 6:6-8
[j]12:34 Mk 1:15
[k]Lk 20:40
[l]12:35-37 Mt 22:41-46; Lk 20:41-44
[m]12:35 Ac 21:26
[n]Mt 2:4
[o]Mt 1:17; Eph 5:2
[p]2Ch 1:1; Mt 1:1; Rm 1:3
[q]12:36 Lk 1:27
[r]Jn 1:33; Ac 19:21
[s]Lk 17:5
[t]Mt 20:21
[u]Ps 110:1
[v]12:38-40 Mt 23:1-36; Lk 20:45-47
[w]12:38 Rv 7:14
[x]Mk 6:56
[y]12:39 Lk 11:43
[z]Jms 2:2
[aa]Lk 14:7-8 [ab]Jn 13:2 [ac]12:40 Gl 5:15 [ad]Jms 1:27 [ae]Mt 5:44; Ac 12:12 [af]12:41-44 Lk 21:1-4 [ag]12:41 Jn 8:20 [ah]Gn 24:35; Pr 2:9 [ai]12:42 Mk 14:7 [aj]12:43 Mt 9:10; Mk 10:10; Lk 6:1; Jn 6:3; Ac 6:1 [ak]Ps 72:19; Rv 22:21

12:29-30 Jesus quoted the Shema (Dt 6:4-5), a Scripture passage that pious Jews recited every morning and evening. The words affirmed monotheistic orthodoxy (**the Lord is One**), identified the primary affection with which people were to relate to God (**love**), and emphasized the necessity to do so with one's total being: **heart** (affections); **soul** (spirit); **mind** (intelligence); and **strength** (the will).

12:31 The scribe asked Jesus for one commandment, but Jesus gave him two. Love for neighbors is rooted in love for God, the First Commandment. No one before Jesus had combined these commandments (Lv 19:18; Dt 6:5), but it became standard for His followers (Rm 13:8-10; Gl 5:14; Jms 2:8-11; 1Jn 4:11,19-20).

12:32-33 Only Mark recorded the scribe's response and Jesus' praise. He saw that the love Jesus spoke of was far more **important** than all the **burnt offerings and sacrifices**.

12:34 Jesus told the scribe that he had **answered intelligently**, a word meaning "wisely." Ironically the scene ended with Jesus judging the scribe rather than vice versa. Having foiled all questioners, Jesus now posed His own question (v. 35).

12:35 Jesus' question related to **the scribes** and their understanding of **Messiah** (1:1; 8:29) as **Son of David** (see note at 10:47-48). This identification, based on God's promise in 2Sm 7:12-16, was commonplace in Jesus' time.

12:36-37 Jesus quoted Ps 110:1, the OT text quoted and alluded to most frequently in the NT (33 times). Jesus affirmed the psalm's Davidic authorship and inspiration by **the Holy Spirit** (cp. 2Sm 23:2; Ac 1:16). The scribes identi-

fied **Messiah** as David's **Son** (vv. 35-36), but David identified Messiah as his **Lord**. Therefore, Messiah was not just a descendant of David. He was David's Lord.

12:38-39 The phrase **He also said** indicates that Mark's summary in verses 38-40 is only a brief part of the extensive condemnations of the scribes and Pharisees (cp. Mt 23, Lk 11:37-54). Naming four examples of what the scribes took pleasure in, Jesus first condemned them for showmanship. Their **long robes** (Gk *stole*) were festive garments that were unreasonable for everyday wear. **Greetings in the marketplaces** refers to the fact that people were expected to rise in the presence of scribes. The **front seats** faced the congregation, identifying those seated as teachers and distinguished persons. The **places of honor at banquets** literally reads "the first (or best) couches." See Jesus' comments on this in Lk 14:7-11.

12:40 Jesus condemned the scribes for dishonesty and hypocrisy. **Widows** were among the most vulnerable people. To defraud them was despicable (Is 1:17,23; 10:2; Jr 7:6; Ezk 22:7; Zch 7:10). The phrase **these will receive harsher punishment** refers to God's eschatological judgment (cp. 9:42-48).

12:41 Previously Jesus was in the Court of the Gentiles. The **temple treasury** was in the Court of the Women, so named because that was as close as women could come to the sanctuary. The treasury consisted of 13 trumpet-shaped chests into which worshipers deposited their freewill offerings. Apparently the trumpet shape of the collection boxes amplified the sound of coins when they were dropped in, making it obvious when **rich people** deposited **large sums**.

12:42-44 The **two tiny coins** are identified as *lepta*—copper

widow has put in more than all those giving to the temple treasury.*a* *44* For they all gave out of their surplus,*b* but she out of her poverty*c* has put in everything she possessed*d*—all she had to live on."*e*

Destruction of the Temple Predicted

13 As*f* He was going out of the •temple complex,*g* one of His disciples said to Him, "Teacher,*h* look! What massive stones! What impressive buildings!"*i*

2 Jesus said to him, "Do you see these great buildings?*j* Not one stone will be left here on another that will not be thrown down!"

Signs of the End of the Age

3 While He was sitting on the •Mount of Olives*k* across from the temple complex,*l* Peter,*m* James,*n* John,*o* and Andrew*p* asked Him privately, *4* "Tell us, when will these things happen? And what will be the sign when all these things are about to take place?"

5 Then Jesus began by telling them: "Watch out that no one deceives you. *6* Many will come

in My name,*q* saying, 'I am He,'*r* and they will deceive*s* many. *7* When you hear of wars and rumors of wars,*t* don't be alarmed;*u* these things must take place,*v* but the end is not yet. *8* For nation will rise up against nation, and kingdom against kingdom.*w* There will be earthquakes in various places, and famines.*A* These are the beginning*x* of birth pains.*y*

Persecutions Predicted

9 "But you, be on your guard! They will hand you over to sanhedrins,*B,z* and you will be flogged*aa* in the •synagogues.*ab* You will stand before governors and kings*ac* because of Me,*ad* as a witness*ae* to them.*af* *10* And the good news*C,ag* must first be proclaimed to all nations. *11* So when they arrest you and hand you over, don't worry beforehand what you will say. On the contrary, whatever is given to you in that hour—say it. For it isn't you speaking, but the Holy Spirit. *12* Then brother will betray*ah* broth-

*a*12:43 Jn 8:20
*b*12:44 1Co 15:58
*c*Php 4:11
*d*Lk 15:12
*e*1Jn 3:17
*f*13:1-37 Mt 24:1-51; Lk 21:5-38
*g*13:1 Ac 21:26
*h*Mk 4:38
*i*1Co 14:3
*j*13:2 Mk 14:58
*k*13:3 Mt 21:1
*l*Ac 21:26
*m*Lk 6:14; Ac 10:32
*n*Ac 12:2
*o*Jn 21:7
*p*Jn 6:8
*q*13:6 Jn 10:25; 14:13
*r*Ex 3:14; Ps 45:8; Jn 8:24
*s*1Jn 4:6
*t*13:7 Jr 51:46; Dn 11:44
*u*2Th 2:2
*v*Dn 2:28-29
*w*13:8 Is 19:2
*x*Ac 26:4
*y*Gl 4:19
*z*13:9 Mt 10:17
*aa*Lk 22:63; Ac 5:40; 16:19-23,37
*ab*Jms 2:2 *ac*Ac 24:10-27; 25:1-12,23-27 *ad*Rm 8:36 *ae*Mk 6:11; 1Tm 2:6 *af*Php 1:12 *ag*13:10 Mk 1:1; Php 1:5 *ah*13:12 Jn 13:21

A13:8 Other mss add *and disturbances* **B**13:9 Local Jewish courts or local councils **C**13:10 Or *the gospel*

---

coins of little value. The widow's gift meant more than the larger gifts of rich people because she gave in spite of her poverty. The phrase **all she had to live on** meant she would not have enough for her next meal.

13:1-37 This chapter is often called Jesus' Olivet Discourse (cp. Mt 24-25; Lk 21). The themes of the destruction of Jerusalem and the temple by the Romans in A.D. 70 seem to be interwoven with the final tribulation and Jesus' return. Some interpreters assign all of Mk 13 to the destruction of Jerusalem and the temple. Most believe Jesus used the earlier destruction to foreshadow the end times. Some who hold this latter view assign verses 1-13 to the first-century events and verses 14-37 to earth's last days. Others assign verses 1-31 to the first century and verses 32-37 to the end times. Still others find an A¹-B¹-A²-B² pattern and assign verses 1-13 and 28-31 to the first century and verses 14-27 and 32-37 to the end times.

13:1 The **massive stones** and **buildings** of the temple complex were truly impressive. Herod's temple had been under construction for almost 50 years, and the Jewish historian Josephus said some of the stones were 60 feet long. Archaeologists have found stones 42 feet long, 11 feet high, and 14 feet deep, weighing over a million pounds.

13:2 Jesus prophesied (announced, not merely predicted) the destruction of the **great buildings**. Symbolically in the withering of the fig tree (11:12-14,20-21) Jesus had already prophesied their end. Some question the accuracy of **not one stone will be left here on another** because some stones remain today in the Western Wall, but this was not part of the temple itself but the foundation that supported the platform on which the temple stood.

13:3 The **Mount of Olives** rose 300 feet above Jerusalem, across the Kidron Valley. It provided a panoramic view of the **temple complex** and Jerusalem.

13:4 **These things** and **all these things** refer to Jesus' comment in verse 2 and the temple's destruction. According

to Mark and Luke (Lk 21:7), the disciples asked a double question. Their first question was about **when** the destruction would occur; their second asked what **sign** would precede it.

13:5-13 Jesus began His discourse by warning that His followers would experience persecution **because of** Him.

13:5 It is the responsibility of disciples to **watch out** and not be deceived.

13:6 False claimants and false teachers can be popular. The phrase **in My name** may mean these imposters would claim to teach in Jesus' name or that they would claim to be Messiah (cp. Mt 24:5).

13:7 **Wars** and **rumors of wars** are not signs of **the end** but characterize the entire age. Jesus said **these things must take place**, meaning they are part of God's plan.

13:8 Natural disasters are not signs of the end, only **the beginning of birth pains**. Though troubling, these pains are harbingers of hope and new life.

13:9 **Hand you over** refers to betrayal. **Sanhedrins** (cp. Mt 10:17) and **synagogues** were local Jewish councils (not the Sanhedrin in Jerusalem that conducted Jesus' trial; Mk 14:53-65). On being **flogged**, see 2Co 11:24-25. **Governors and kings** referred to Roman political authorities.

13:10 Persecution is the context in which universal proclamation of the good news will take place.

13:11 Jesus admonished His disciples against anxiety that would distract them from their witness. God would give the appropriate response through His **Holy Spirit**. This is the last reference to the Spirit in Mark (1:8,10,12; 3:29; 12:36) and the only one that pictures His role with believers. On the Holy Spirit as Counselor, see Jn 14:16,26; 15:26; 16:7; 1Jn 2:1.

13:12 Some Christians will experience betrayal by family members, even to the point of **death** (cp. Mt 10:34-36).

er to death,[a] and a father his child. Children will rise up against parents and put them to death. [13] And you will be hated by everyone because of My name.[b] But the one who endures to the end will be delivered.[A,c]

The Great Tribulation

[14] "When you see the **abomination that causes desolation**[B,d] standing where it should not" (let the reader understand[C]), "then those in Judea[e] must flee to the mountains! [15] A man on the housetop must not come down or go in to get anything out of his house.[f] [16] And a man in the field must not go back to get his clothes.[g] [17] Woe[h] to pregnant women and nursing mothers in those days! [18] Pray[i] it[D] won't happen in winter. [19] For those will be days of tribulation,[j] the kind that hasn't been from the beginning[k] of the world,[E,l] which God created, until now and never will be again! [20] Unless the Lord[m] limited those days,[n] no one would survive.[F] But He limited those days because of the elect,[o] whom He chose.[p]

[21] "Then if anyone tells you, 'Look, here is the •Messiah![q] Look—there!' do not believe it!

[22] For false messiahs[G] and false prophets will rise up and will perform signs and wonders[r] to lead astray, if possible, the elect. [23] And you must watch! I have told you everything in advance.

The Coming of the Son of Man

[24] "But in those days, after that tribulation:[s]

The sun will be darkened,
   and the moon will not shed its light;
[25]   the stars[t] will be falling from the sky,
   and the celestial powers
      will be shaken.[u]

[26] Then they will see the •Son of Man[v] coming[w] in clouds[x] with great power[y] and glory.[z] [27] He will send out the angels[aa] and gather His elect[ab] from the four winds, from the end of the earth to the end of the sky.[ac]

The Parable of the Fig Tree

[28] "Learn[ad] this parable[ae] from the fig[af] tree: As

Cross references:
[a]13:12 Is 19:2; Mc 7:6
[b]13:13 Mt 10:22; Lk 6:22; Jn 15:18-21
[c]1Co 4:12; 2Th 1:4; 2Tm 2:12; Jms 1:12
[d]13:14 Dn 9:27; 11:31; 12:11
[e]Lk 1:5
[f]13:15 Lk 17:22-36
[g]13:16 Lk 19:36
[h]13:17 Rv 9:12
[i]13:18 Mt 5:44; Ac 12:12
[j]13:19 1Co 1:4
[k]Ac 26:4
[l]Jn 1:3; Rv 3:14
[m]13:20 Col 4:1; Jd 5
[n]Is 60:21-22
[o]Mt 24:22
[p]Eph 1:4
[q]13:21 Mt 1:17; Eph 5:2
[r]13:22 Ex 7:3; Dn 6:27; Jn 4:48; Ac 4:30; Rm 15:19; 2Th 2:9; Heb 2:4
[s]13:24 2Co 1:4
[t]13:25 Rv 1:16
[u]13:24-25 Is 13:10; 34:4; Jl 2:10,31; 3:15
[v]13:26 Mk 2:10
[w]Mk 8:38; 1Th 4:16
[x]Dn 7:13-14
[y]Lk 6:19
[z]Mk 10:37; Lk 9:32
[aa]13:27 Mt 13:49; Ac 5:19; Rv 14:6
[ab]Mt 22:14,22
[ac]Zch 2:6
[ad]13:28 Jn 7:15
[ae]Mk 12:1
[af]Jn 1:48

[A]13:13 Or *saved* **[B]**13:14 Dn 9:27 **[C]**13:14 These are, most likely, Mark's words to his readers. **[D]**13:18 Other mss read *pray that your escape* **[E]**13:19 Lit *creation* **[F]**13:20 Lit *days, all flesh would not survive* **[G]**13:22 Or *false christs*

13:13 You will be hated indicates the animosity unbelievers often feel toward Christians because of the **name** of Jesus (cp. 1Pt 4:16). Jesus did not warn His followers so they could seek safety but so they would endure faithfully.

13:14 The abomination that causes desolation is drawn from Dn 9:27; 11:31; 12:11 (cp. Mt 24:15) and was used to describe the desecration of the temple by Antiochus Epiphanes in 167 B.C. (see the Apocryphal book, 1Macc 1:54). Jesus' reference may be to some event prior to A.D. 70 or to the "man of lawlessness" (2Th 2:3-10; Rv 13:1-10,14-15). Mark did not identify the location for **standing where it should not**, but Matthew (Mt 24:15) said "in the holy place," meaning the temple's sanctuary (cp. 2Th 2:4).

SOZO

Greek Pronunciation	[SOH zoh]
HCSB Translation	deliver
Uses in Mark's Gospel	15
Uses in the NT	106
Focus Passage	Mark 13:13

The Greek verb *sozo* literally means "to preserve" or "to keep safe" with an underlying idea of "making whole." The term can refer to saving someone from physical harm (Mt 8:25) or death (Mt 14:30; 15:30-31; Ac 27:20,31), healing (Mk 5:23,28,34; 6:56; Jms 5:15), exorcism (Lk 8:36), or *deliverance* from a severe ordeal (Jn 12:27; Heb 5:7; Jd 5). The most common use of *sozo* in the NT, especially in Acts and the Epistles, is to describe the various aspects of salvation. Two important nouns are derived from *sozo*: (1) *soteria*, which means salvation (in the redemptive sense) or *deliverance* from physical death or danger (see Ac 7:25; 27:34); and (2) *soter*, which means "Savior" and is always a reference to either the Father or Jesus Christ in the work of redemption.

13:15-16 On **housetop**, see note at 2:4.

13:17 Woe is not a condemnation as in Mt 23:13-32 but a cry of pity for **pregnant women** and **nursing mothers** unable to move quickly.

13:18 Winter weather along with swollen streams that could not be crossed would add to the difficulty of their flight (cp. Mt 24:20).

13:19 This verse is drawn from Dn 12:1. The intensity of these **days of tribulation** (cp. Rv 7:14) will exceed what was experienced in the destruction of Jerusalem in A.D. 70.

13:20 The Lord will curtail the tribulation for the sake of **the elect** (lit "the elect whom He elected"), emphasizing God's sovereign choice.

13:21-22 Many messianic pretenders and **false prophets** will come throughout the final age.

13:24-25 Just as Jesus warned of earthly signs occurring before the tribulation, He also spoke of cosmic signs occurring **after that tribulation**. He declared that **the celestial powers will be shaken** as if with a heavenly earthquake (cp. Heb 12:26-29). His language is drawn from Is 13:9-10; Jl 2:10-11,30-31; 3:14-16.

13:26 Jesus drew the wording for this verse from Dn 7:13. **They will see** refers to those living when these events occur. The **clouds** are a reference to God's presence (9:7; 14:62; Ex 19:9; 1Kg 8:10-11; Ps 97:2; Dn 7:13). The phrase **with great power and glory** contrasts with the Son of Man's first coming in weakness and humility.

13:27 The **angels** are regularly pictured as accompanying Christ on His return (8:38; Mt 13:39-41; 16:27; 25:31).

13:28 For Jesus' previous use of a **fig tree**, see notes at 11:13 and 11:19-20. When the fig tree **sprouts**, usually in March or April around Passover, **summer is near**.

soon as its branch becomes tender and sprouts leaves, you know that summer is near.[a] [29]In the same way, when you see these things happening, know[A] that He[B] is near—at the door! [30]•I assure you:[b] This generation will certainly not pass away until all these things take place. [31]Heaven and earth[c] will pass away,[d] but My words will never pass away.[e]

No One Knows the Day or Hour

[32]"Now concerning that day[f] or hour no one knows—neither the angels[g] in heaven nor the Son[h]—except the Father.[i] [33]Watch! Be alert![C] For you don't know when the time[j] is coming.[k] [34]It is like[l] a man on a journey, who left his house, gave authority to his •slaves,[m] gave each one his work, and commanded the doorkeeper to be alert. [35]Therefore be alert,[n] since you don't know when the master[o] of the house is coming—whether in the evening or at midnight or at the crowing of the rooster or early in the morning. [36]Otherwise, he might come suddenly and find you sleeping.[p] [37]And what I say to you, I say to everyone: Be alert!"

The Plot to Kill Jesus

14 After[q] two days it was the •Passover[r] and the Festival[s] of •Unleavened Bread.[t] The •chief priests and the •scribes[u] were looking

for a treacherous[v] way to arrest and kill Him.[w] [2]"Not during the festival," they said, "or there may be rioting among the people."

The Anointing at Bethany

[3]While[x] He was in Bethany[y] at the house of Simon who had a serious skin disease,[z] as He was reclining at the table,[aa] a woman came with an alabaster jar of pure and expensive fragrant oil of nard. She broke the jar and poured it on His head.[ab] [4]But some were expressing indignation to one another: "Why has this fragrant oil been wasted? [5]For this oil might have been sold for more than 300 •denarii[ac] and given to the poor."[ad] And they began to scold her.

[6]Then Jesus said, "Leave her alone. Why are you bothering her? She has done a noble thing[ae] for Me. [7]You always have the poor[af] with you, and you can do what is good for them whenever you want, but you do not always have Me.[ag] [8]She has done what she could; she has anointed My body[ah] in advance for burial.[ai] [9]•I assure you:[aj] Wherever the gospel[ak] is proclaimed in the whole world,[al] what this woman has done will also be told in memory of her."

a 13:28 Rv 1:1
b 13:30 Ps 72:19; Rv 22:21
c 13:31 Lk 10:21
d 2Pt 3:10
e Ps 102:25-27; Is 40:6-8; 51:6; Mt 5:18; Lk 16:17
f 13:32 Mt 25:13
g Mt 13:49
h Jn 5:19; Heb 1:2
i Mt 5:16; 11:27; Jn 8:42
j 13:33 Lk 20:20
k Ac 1:7; 1Th 5:1-2; 1Pt 5:6
l 13:34 Lk 12:35-40
m Mt 10:24
n 13:35 Rv 16:15
o Col 3:22
p 13:36 Pr 6:4
q 14:1-2 Mt 26:1-5; Lk 22:1-2
r 14:1 Ex 12:11
s Jn 5:1
t Ex 23:15
u Mt 2:4
v Ps 10:7
w Jn 5:18
x 14:3-9 Mt 26:6-13; Jn 12:2-8
y 14:3 Mk 11:1
z Mt 11:5
aa Lv 19:34
ab Rm 12:13
ac 14:5 Mt 18:28
ad Rm 15:26
ae 14:6 1Pt 2:12
af 14:7 Dt 15:11
ag Lk 10:38-42
ah 14:8 Lk 12:4
ai Jn 19:40   aj 14:9 Ps 72:19; Rv 22:21   ak Mk 1:1; Php 1:5   al Mt 13:38; 1Jn 2:2

A 13:29 Or *you know*   B 13:29 Or *it*; = summer   C 13:33 Other mss add *and pray*

13:29 Just as Jesus' followers knew how to read the signs of the coming summer, so also when they saw **these things happening** they were to know that a cataclysmic event was near. It is unclear whether Jesus was referring to Jerusalem's fall or His return in the end time.

13:30 I assure you was Jesus' standard indication of a solemn pronouncement. The **generation** that will **not pass away** until **all these things take place** is either Jesus' contemporary generation that would live to see the destruction of Jerusalem and the temple (cp. 8:12,38; 9:19) or the eschatological generation that will be alive when the end begins.

13:31 Heaven and earth will pass away because they are temporal by nature. Jesus' **words**, however, will **never pass away**. Only God can make this claim (Is 40:8; 51:6). Jesus' words are as sure and permanent as God's Word (Mt 5:18; Lk 16:17).

13:32 That day or hour indicates Jesus was speaking of the eschatological future. When the end will come is unknown to **angels** or even **the Son**. Only the Father knows (Ac 1:7).

13:33 Be alert expresses the idea of staying awake and watchful. Even though Jesus' disciples **don't know when the time is coming**, they are to be ready and faithful.

13:35-37 Jesus' followers are to be like the doorkeeper (v. 34), always on the alert for the master's **coming**.

14:1 After two days points to the start of the Jewish **Passover** and the **Festival of Unleavened Bread**. This means the Sanhedrin plotted Jesus' death some time between sunset on Tuesday and sunset on Wednesday.

14:2 The Sanhedrin hesitated to act because of Jesus' popularity among **the people** who had flooded into town for Passover.

14:3 On Bethany, see notes at 11:1 and 11:11. An **alabaster jar** was a long-necked perfume vase that was considered a luxury item. A woman (Mary of Bethany, according to Jn 12:2-3) poured **expensive fragrant oil of nard** on Jesus' head.

14:4-5 Some people expressed **indignation** at the waste of expensive perfume. A denarius was a day's wage for a common laborer (Mt 20:2). Hence the perfume's value of **300 denarii** was about a year's wages.

14:6 Jesus rebuked the critics of this woman. What they considered wasteful was actually **a noble thing** (lit "a good work"). Her act was noble because she did it for the Son of God, who is worthy of great sacrifices.

14:7 Christ's followers could **always** minister to the poor, but they would **not always** have the chance to serve Jesus in person. On concern for the poor, see Dt 15:1-11.

14:8 The phrase **she has done what she could** is almost identical to what Jesus said about the poor widow's donation (see note at 12:42-44). The widow gave almost nothing of monetary value; this woman gave a wealthy gift, but Jesus commended both equally. Jesus interpreted the perfume as a makeshift anointing oil for His coming **burial**.

14:9 Jesus anticipated that **the gospel** would be **proclaimed** in the **whole world** (cp. 13:10). When this happened, this woman's act would be told **in memory of her** (cp. Mt 26:13). Your reading of this verse fulfills this promise.

¹⁰Then^a Judas Iscariot,^b one of the Twelve,^c went to the chief priests^d to hand Him over^e to them. ¹¹And when they heard this, they were glad and promised to give him silver.^{A,f} So he started looking for a good opportunity to betray^g Him.

Preparation for Passover

¹²On^h the first day of Unleavened Bread, when they sacrifice the Passover lamb,ⁱ His disciples^j asked Him, "Where do You want us to go and prepare the Passover so You may eat it?"

¹³So He sent two of His disciples and told them, "Go into the city, and a man carrying a water jug will meet you. Follow him. ¹⁴Wherever he enters, tell the owner of the house, 'The Teacher^k says, "Where is the guest room for Me to eat the Passover with My disciples?"' ¹⁵He will show you a large room upstairs, furnished and ready. Make the preparations for us there." ¹⁶So the disciples^l went out, entered the city, and found it just as He had told them, and they prepared the Passover.

Betrayal at the Passover

¹⁷When^m evening came, He arrived with the Twelve.ⁿ ¹⁸While they were reclining and eating, Jesus said, "I assure you: One of you will betray Me—one who is eating with Me!"

¹⁹They began to be distressed and to say to Him one by one, "Surely not I?"

²⁰He said to them, "It is one of the Twelve—the one who is dipping bread with Me in the bowl. ²¹For the •Son of Man^o will go just as it is written^p about Him,^q but woe^r to that man by whom the Son of Man is betrayed! It would have been better for that man if he had not been born."

The First Lord's Supper

²²As^s they were eating, He took bread,^t blessed and broke^u it, gave it to them,^v and said, "Take it;^B this is My body."^w

²³Then He took a cup, and after giving thanks,^x He gave it to them, and so they all drank from it. ²⁴He said to them, "This is My blood that establishes the covenant;^{C,y} it is shed^z for many.^{aa} ²⁵I assure you:^{ab} I will no longer drink of the fruit of the vine^{ac} until that day

---

^a14:10-11 Mt 26:14-16; Lk 22:3-6　^b14:10 Mk 3:19　^cMk 11:11　^dMt 2:4　^eMk 9:31　^f14:11 Lk 19:15　^gJn 13:21　^h14:12-16 Mt 26:17-19; Lk 22:7-13　ⁱ14:12 Ex 12:21　^jMt 9:10; Mk 10:10; Lk 6:1; Jn 6:3; Ac 6:1　^k14:14 Mk 4:38; Eph 4:11　^l14:16 Mk 10:10　^m14:17-21 Mt 26:20-25; Lk 22:21-23; Jn 13:21-30　ⁿ14:17 Mk 11:11　^o14:21 Mk 2:10　^pMk 1:2; Ac 15:15　^qDn 7:21,25; 9:26　^rRv 9:12　^s14:22-26 Mt 26:26-30; Lk 22:17-20; 1Co 11:23-25　^t14:22 1Co 10:16　^uMt 14:19; 15:36; Ac 2:46; 20:7,11; 27:35　^vLk 24:30　^wLk 12:4; Jn 2:21; 6:51　^x14:23 Mk 8:6　^y14:24 Ex 24:8; Zch 9:11; Heb 9:18-20; 10:29; 13:20　^zGn 4:11; Nm 35:33; Lm 4:13; Mt 23:35　^{aa}Is 52:13–53:12　^{ab}14:25 Rv 22:21　^{ac}Is 32:12; Hab 3:17; Jms 3:12

---

^A14:11 Or *money*; in Mt 26:15 it is specified as 30 pieces of silver; see Zch 11:12-13　^B14:22 Other mss add *eat*;　^C14:24 Other mss read *the new covenant*

14:10 Mark mentions **Judas Iscariot** here, in the account of Jesus' arrest (vv. 43-45), and in the listing of the Twelve (3:19). The phrase **went to** places the initiative for Jesus' betrayal clearly on Judas; he wasn't recruited by the authorities. **Hand Him over** is used of John the Baptist (1:14), of Jesus (9:31; 10:33; 14:10-11,18,21,41-42,44; 15:1,10,15), and of Jesus' disciples after Him (13:9,11-12).

14:11 Only Matthew (Mt 26:15) indicated how much **silver** Judas was given. The phrase **a good opportunity** recalls the Sanhedrin's hope to arrest Jesus "when the crowd was not present" (Lk 22:6) so they would not cause a riot (Mk 14:1-2).

14:12 Jesus decided where they would observe the Passover, but His disciples were responsible to **prepare** it. Preparations included obtaining and preparing a lamb, bitter herbs, unleavened bread, wine, crushed fruit, etc.

14:13-14 Luke (Lk 22:8) identified the **two . . . disciples** as Peter and John. **Go into the city** indicates they were outside Jerusalem, probably at Bethany. **A man carrying a water jug** was unusual. Normally women carried water in earthenware pitchers whereas men used animal skins. **Meet** could mean either "encounter" or that the man was looking for them. He apparently knew Jesus since the disciples identified Jesus cryptically as **the Teacher**.

14:15-16 The "guest room" (v. 14) was **a large room upstairs**, probably the spacious roof chamber of a wealthy man. The room was **ready** to accommodate a large group.

14:17 When evening came marked the start of a new day by Jewish reckoning. According to Ex 12:8, the Passover meal had to be eaten at night and be finished by midnight.

14:18 Jesus had said earlier that He would be betrayed (9:31; 10:33). Now He added that the betrayer would be one of His disciples. The words **one who is eating with Me** did not immediately identify the betrayer since all of the disciples were dining together.

14:19 No one attempted to refute Jesus or make accusations. Apparently Judas was above all suspicion at this point. The disciples' statement **surely not I** expected both a negative response and a word of reassurance from Jesus.

14:20 That the betrayer was **dipping bread** with Jesus meant he was seated nearby (Mt 26:25; Jn 13:23-30).

14:21 On **Son of Man**, see note at 2:8-11. Previously Jesus had stated His betrayal was predicted by Scripture (9:12). This verse unites God's prophesied plan (**just as it is written**) with human actions and responsibility.

14:22 Mark did not specify at what point in the traditional course of the Passover meal Jesus instituted the Last Supper. **This is My body** is metaphorical.

14:23 They **all drank from** one cup. "Eucharist" derives from the word for **giving thanks**.

14:24 The phrase **blood that establishes the covenant** recalls the institution of the Mosaic covenant at Sinai when the Israelites were sprinkled with blood (Ex 24:1-8; cp. Heb 9:19-20; 10:28-30). Jesus' blood established a new covenant. **Shed for many** recalls Jesus' words in 10:45 and Isaiah's words (Is 53:11-12) about Messiah dying on behalf of others.

14:25 Jesus' solemn formula **I assure you** focused the group's attention on the eschatological future. Even though Jesus had explained His death and its meaning, it would not be the end for Him. The day (cp. 13:17,19-20,24,32) would come when He would **drink** with them in the **kingdom of God** (cp. 15:43-46).

when I drink it in a new[a] way[A] in the kingdom of God."[b] [26]After singing psalms,[B] they went out to the •Mount of Olives.[c]

Peter's Denial Predicted

[27]Then[d] Jesus said to them, "All of you will run away,[C,D] because it is written:[e]

I will strike the shepherd,
and the sheep[f] will be scattered.[E,g]

[28]But after I have been resurrected,[h] I will go ahead of you to Galilee."[i]

[29]Peter[j] told Him, "Even if everyone runs away, I will certainly not!"

[30]"I assure you," Jesus said to him, "today, this very night, before the rooster crows twice, you will deny Me three times!"[k]

[31]But he kept insisting, "If I have to die with You, I will never deny You!" And they all said the same thing.

The Prayer in the Garden

[32]Then[l] they came to a place named Gethsemane, and He told His disciples,[m] "Sit here while I pray."[n] [33]He took Peter,[o] James,[p] and John[q] with Him, and He began to be deeply distressed and horrified. [34]Then He said to them, "My soul is swallowed up in sorrow[F]—to the point of death. Remain here and stay awake."[r] [35]Then He went a little farther, fell to the ground, and began to pray that if it were possible, the hour[s] might pass from Him. [36]And He said, "•Abba,[t] Father![u] All things are possible[v] for You. Take this cup[w] away from Me. Nevertheless, not what I will, but what You will."

[37]Then He came and found them sleeping. "Simon,[x] are you sleeping?" He asked Peter.[y] "Couldn't you stay awake one hour? [38]Stay awake and pray[z] so that you won't enter into temptation.[aa] The spirit[ab] is willing, but the flesh[ac] is weak."

[39]Once again He went away and prayed, saying the same thing. [40]And He came again and found them sleeping, because they could not

Cross-references

[a]14:25 Is 25:6; Lk 13:28-29; 14:15-24
[b]Mk 1:15
[c]14:26 Mt 21:1
[d]14:27-31 Mt 26:31-35; Lk 22:31-38; Jn 13:31-38
[e]14:27 Ac 15:15
[f]Mt 7:15
[g]Zch 13:7
[h]14:28 1Co 15:4
[i]Mt 17:22
[j]14:29 Lk 6:14; Ac 10:32
[k]14:30 Mk 14:72
[l]14:32-42 Mt 26:36-46; Lk 22:39-46
[m]14:32 Mk 10:10
[n]Mt 5:44; Ac 12:12
[o]14:33 Lk 6:14
[p]Ac 12:2
[q]Jn 21:7
[r]14:34 Rv 16:15
[s]14:35 Jn 2:4
[t]14:36 Rm 8:15; Gl 4:6
[u]Mt 5:16; 11:27; Jn 8:42
[v]Mt 19:26; Mk 9:23
[w]Ps 11:6; Is 51:17,22; Lm 4:21; Ezk 23:32-34; Mk 10:38-39; Jn 18:11
[x]14:37 Mt 16:17
[y]Lk 6:14
[z]14:38 Mt 5:44
[aa]Mt 6:13; Lk 4:13
[ab]Ps 51:12
[ac]Php 3:3

[A]14:25 Or *drink new wine;* lit *drink it new*   [B]14:26 Pss 113–118 were sung during and after the Passover meal.   [C]14:27 Other mss add *because of Me this night*   [D]14:27 Or *•stumble*   [E]14:27 Zch 13:7   [F]14:34 Or *I am deeply grieved*

14:26 The Passover meal traditionally ended with **singing** the Hallel **psalms** (Pss 115–118).

14:27 Jesus told His disciples, **All of you will run away.** The Greek word *skandalizein* means literally "to stumble." **It is written** grounds Jesus' prediction in OT Scripture, specifically Zch 13:7.

14:28 Jesus referred to His resurrection and added that He would gather His disciples again in **Galilee** for a new mission (cp. 16:7).

14:29-31 Quick-tongued Peter declared his steadfastness, but Jesus infallibly foreknew that Peter would cower in the face of opposition.

14:32 Gethsemane means "olive press." Located across the Kidron Valley on the western slope of the Mount of Olives, it was Jesus' regular meeting place with His disciples (Jn 18:2).

Located across the Kidron Valley on the western slope of the Mount of Olives, Gethsemane was Jesus' regular meeting place with His disciples (Jn 18:2). It means "olive press" (Mk 14:32).

14:33 Peter, James, and John were the inner circle of Jesus' disciples (5:37; 9:2; 13:3). Each had pledged his willingness to die with Jesus (10:38-39; 14:29,31). Mark used two rare words to describe Jesus' emotions. **Deeply distressed** occurs only in Mark (v. 33; 9:15; 16:5-6) and has the nuance of "greatly alarmed." The word for **horrified** expresses extreme anxiety, and it occurs elsewhere in Mt 26:37 and Php 2:26.

14:34 The phrase **to the point of death** indicates the depth of Jesus' distress (cp. Jnh 4:9). Luke 22:44 added that "His sweat became like drops of blood falling to the ground."

14:35 Fell to the ground pictures Jesus collapsing under His burden (Mt 26:39; cp. Lk 22:41). **The hour** refers to Jesus' divinely appointed death (Jn 7:30; 8:20; 12:23,27; 13:1; 17:1). **If it were possible** was a request for God to change His divine plan.

14:36 Abba is Aramaic for "father." Jesus' words **all things are possible for You** affirmed God's power and recalled His teaching (10:27). **This cup** refers to personal suffering and death (cp. 10:38-39) but also to God's judgment on sin (14:24; cp. Jr 25:15-16; 2Co 5:21; 1Pt 2:24). **Not what I will, but what You will** recalls Jesus' Model Prayer (Mt 6:10). Not His personal desire but the Father's will defined Jesus' life (Jn 5:30; 6:38).

14:37 Peter was singled out for his failure to stay awake because of his bold claims earlier in the evening (vv. 29-31). **One hour** may be idiomatic rather than literal.

14:38 Jesus' acknowledgment that the **flesh** is weak may have applied to Himself also that night, given His suffering. Natural human weaknesses (hunger, fatigue, etc.) can pose great spiritual danger.

14:39-40 The stupefied disciples **did not know what to say to Him.** This recalls Peter's experience on the Mount of Transfiguration (9:6) and the disciples' silence in 9:34.

keep their eyes open.^A They did not know what to say to Him.^a ^41 Then He came a third time and said to them, "Are you still sleeping and resting? Enough! The time has come. Look, the Son of Man^b is being betrayed into the hands of sinners.^c ^42 Get up;^d let's go! See—My betrayer is near."

The Judas Kiss

^43 While^e He was still speaking, Judas,^f one of the Twelve,^g suddenly arrived. With him was a mob, with swords and clubs, from the chief priests, the scribes,^h and the elders.^i ^44 His betrayer had given them a signal. "The One I kiss," he said, "He's the One; arrest Him and take Him away under guard." ^45 So when he came, he went right up to Him and said, "•Rabbi!"^j—and kissed Him. ^46 Then they took hold of Him and arrested Him. ^47 And one of those who stood by drew his sword, struck the high priest's •slave, and cut off his ear.

^48 But Jesus said to them, "Have you come out with swords and clubs, as though I were a criminal,^B to capture Me? ^49 Every day I was among you, teaching in the •temple complex,^k and you didn't arrest Me. But the Scriptures^l must be fulfilled."^m ^50 Then they all deserted Him and ran away.^n

^51 Now a certain young man,^c having a linen cloth wrapped around his naked body, was following Him. They caught hold of him, ^52 but he left the linen cloth behind and ran away naked.^o

Jesus Faces the Sanhedrin

^53 They^p led Jesus away to the high priest,^q and all the chief priests, the elders, and the scribes^r convened.^s ^54 Peter^t followed Him at a distance, right into the high priest's courtyard. He was sitting with the temple police,^D,u warming himself by the fire.^E

^55 The chief priests and the whole •Sanhedrin^v were looking for testimony against Jesus to put Him to death,^w but they could find none. ^56 For many were giving false testimony^x against Him, but the testimonies did not agree. ^57 Some stood up and were giving false testimony against Him, stating, ^58 "We heard Him say, 'I will demolish this sanctuary made by human hands,^y and in three days I will build another not made by hands.'" ^59 Yet their testimony did not agree^z even on this.

^60 Then the high priest stood up before them all and questioned Jesus, "Don't You have an answer to what these men are testifying

^a 14:40 Mk 4:40	
^b 14:41 Mk 2:10	
^c Mk 8:31; 9:31; 10:33-34	
^d 14:42 Mk 5:41	
^e 14:43-52 Mt 26:47-56; Lk 22:47-53; Jn 18:1-2	
^f 14:43 Mk 3:19	
^g Mk 11:11	
^h Mt 2:4	
^i 3Jn 1	
^j 14:45 Jn 11:8	
^k 14:49 Ac 21:26	
^l 2Pt 1:20	
^m Mt 1:22; Mk 9:12	
^n 14:50 Mk 4:40; Jms 4:7	
^o 14:52 Am 2:16	
^p 14:53-65 Mt 26:57-68; Lk 22:54,63-65; Jn 18:24	
^q 14:53 Mt 26:3	
^r Mt 2:4	
^s Mk 8:31; 10:33	
^t 14:54 Lk 6:14	
^u Jn 18:18	
^v 14:55 Mk 13:9	
^w Mt 10:21	
^x 14:56 Pr 6:19; 1Jn 5:10	
^y 14:58 Col 2:11	
^z 14:59 Nm 35:30; Dt 17:6; 19:15; Php 2:6	

---

^A 14:40 Lit *because their eyes were weighed down*　^B 14:48 Lit *as against a criminal*　^C 14:51 Perhaps John Mark who later wrote this Gospel　^D 14:54 Or *the officers*; lit *the servants*　^E 14:54 Lit *light*

14:41-42 Enough was a cry of exasperation and served to awaken the sleepers. **The time has come** literally is "the hour is come." Jesus had prayed "that if it were possible, the hour might pass from Him" (v. 35), but God did not grant that request. **Get up; let's go** was a call to meet the mob head-on, not an encouragement to flee (cp. Jn 14:31). The words **look** and **see** indicate they could see the torches of the approaching throng.

14:43 In fulfillment of Jesus' prediction in 8:31, the **mob** hailed from the **chief priests**, the **scribes**, and the **elders**— the three parties of the Sanhedrin. This was an officially sanctioned arrest party.

14:44 Signal refers to a sign agreed on in advance. The specific signal was a **kiss** (probably on the cheek). While a kiss was a common greeting (Lk 7:45; Ac 20:37; Rm 16:16), this is the only time a disciple is recorded as greeting Jesus this way (cp. 2Sm 20:9-10).

14:45 Rabbi means "my great one." It was an address of honor to one's teacher.

14:47 The attack on **the high priest's slave** is recorded in all four Gospels (Mt 26:51-52; Lk 22:49-51; Jn 18:10-11). John identifies the attacker as Peter and the slave as Malchus (Jn 18:10). Apparently Jesus' disciples asked if they should defend Him with swords (Lk 22:49), but Peter didn't wait for a reply. On Jesus' disciples carrying swords, see note at Lk 22:35-38. Jesus restored Malchus's ear (Lk 22:51).

14:48-50 The **Scriptures** that **must be fulfilled** are not identified, but verse 50 points to Zch 13:7 as one of them. **They all deserted Him** refers to the fleeing disciples.

14:51-52 The **young man** is unidentified, but many have suggested he was John Mark, the author of this Gospel.

14:53-65 No single Gospel comprehensively records Jesus' trials, and each emphasizes different perspectives and events. It is clear, however, that both Roman political authorities and Jewish religious leaders were involved in handing down Jesus' death sentence.

14:53 They refers to those who arrested Jesus (vv. 43,46). Matthew said **the high priest** was Caiaphas, who served from A.D. 18–36 (Mt 26:57). That all three parties **convened** indicates this was a meeting of the Sanhedrin (vv. 43,55).

14:54 Peter followed the arrest party and ended up **warming himself** (cp. Jn 18:18) in the high priest's courtyard.

14:55-56 The entire Sanhedrin, especially **the chief priests**, had already decided to put Jesus to death, so they went looking for evidence to justify their plan. Many witnesses gave **false testimony** that **did not agree** under cross-examination. The OT required the agreement of two witnesses in a capital case (Nm 35:30; Dt 17:6; 19:15).

14:57-58 Some who gave **false testimony** claimed firsthand experience. Apparently they distorted Jesus' remark in 13:2 where the same word for **demolish** was used.

14:59 Only Mark noted that the accusers **did not agree even on this** (cp. Mt 26:60). The Jews took threats against the temple seriously (cp. Jr 26:7-24). This charge was issued against Jesus again while He hung on the cross (Mk 15:29).

14:60 Frustrated with the ineptitude of the proceedings, Caiaphas **stood up** and questioned Jesus himself.

against You?" [61] But He kept silent and did not answer anything.[a] Again the high priest questioned Him, "Are You the •Messiah,[b] the Son[c] of the Blessed[d] One?"

[62] "I am,"[e] said Jesus, "and all of you[A] will see **the Son of Man[f] seated at the right hand**[g] of the Power and **coming with the clouds**[h] **of heaven.**"[B,i]

[63] Then the high priest[j] tore his robes[k] and said, "Why do we still need witnesses?[l] [64] You have heard the blasphemy![m] What is your decision?"[C]

And they all condemned Him to be deserving of death.[n] [65] Then some began to spit on Him, to blindfold Him, and to beat Him, saying, "Prophesy!"[o] The temple police[p] also took Him and slapped Him.

Peter Denies His Lord

[66] While[q] Peter[r] was in the courtyard below, one of the high priest's servants came. [67] When she saw Peter warming himself, she looked at him and said, "You also were with that •Nazarene,[s] Jesus."

[68] But he denied it: "I don't know or understand what you're talking about!" Then he went out to the entryway, and a rooster crowed.[D]

[69] When the servant saw him again she began to tell those standing nearby, "This man is one of them!"

[70] But again he denied it. After a little while those standing there said to Peter again, "You certainly are one of them, since you're also a Galilean!"[E,t]

[71] Then he started to curse[F] and to swear with an oath,[u] "I don't know this man you're talking about!"

[72] Immediately a rooster crowed a second time,[v] and Peter remembered when Jesus had spoken the word to him, "Before the rooster crows twice, you will deny Me three times." When he thought about it, he began to weep.[G]

Jesus Faces Pilate

15 As[w] soon as it was morning, the •chief priests had a meeting with the elders,[x] •scribes,[y] and the whole •Sanhedrin.[z] After tying Jesus up, they led Him away and handed Him over to •Pilate.[aa]

[2] So Pilate asked Him, "Are You the King[ab] of the Jews?"[ac]

Cross-references

[a]14:61 Is 53:7; Mt 27:12,14; Mk 15:5; Lk 23:9; Jn 19:9
[b]Mt 1:17; Eph 5:2
[c]Jn 5:19; Heb 1:2
[d]Lk 1:68; Rm 1:25; 9:5; 2Co 1:3; 11:31; Eph 1:3; 1Pt 1:3
[e]14:62 Ex 3:14; Ps 45:8; Jn 8:24
[f]Mk 2:10; Ac 7:56
[g]Mt 20:21
[h]Mt 26:64; Mk 13:26
[i]Ps 110:1; Dn 7:13
[j]14:63 Mt 26:3
[k]Lv 10:6; 21:10; Nm 14:6; Jn 19:23
[l]Heb 12:1
[m]14:64 Jn 10:33; Rv 13:6
[n]Mk 10:33
[o]14:65 Jn 11:51
[p]Jn 18:18
[q]14:66-72 Mt 26:69-75; Lk 22:54-62; Jn 18:15-18,25-27
[r]14:66 Lk 6:14
[s]14:67 Mk 1:24; 10:47; 16:6; Lk 4:34; 24:19
[t]14:70 Jn 4:45
[u]14:71 Mt 5:34
[v]14:72 Mk 14:30

[w]15:1-5 Mt 27:2,11-14; Lk 23:25; Jn 18:28-38　[x]15:1 3Jn 1　[y]Mt 2:4　[z]Mk 13:9　[aa]1Tm 6:13　[ab]15:2 Lk 19:38　[ac]Jn 19:21

Footnotes

[A]14:62 Lit *and you*　[B]14:62 Ps 110:1; Dn 7:13　[C]14:64 Lit *How does it appear to you?*　[D]14:68 Other mss omit *and a rooster crowed*　[E]14:70 Other mss add *and your speech shows it*　[F]14:71 To call down curses on himself if what he said weren't true
[G]14:72 Or *he burst into tears*, or *he broke down*

Study notes

14:61-62 Throughout Mark's Gospel Jesus had shied away from the title *Messiah* to avoid misunderstanding, but here He embraced it. **I am** (cp. Mt 26:64; Lk 22:67) echoes the divine name (Ex 3:14). Jesus then switched to His favorite self-designation **Son of Man** and quoted from Ps 110:2 and Dn 7:13. To be **seated at the right hand** was an honor (cp. 10:37,40). **Coming with the clouds of heaven** is often understood as a reference to the second coming, but **all of you will see** leads some interpreters to understand that Jesus was referring to His post-ascension enthronement in heaven.

14:63 Tearing one's clothes symbolized grief (Gn 37:34; Jos 7:6; 2Sm 1:11-12; 2Kg 2:12) or horror at blasphemy (2Kg 18:37; 19:1). **Witnesses** were no longer needed since Jesus had incriminated Himself by claiming He was the Messiah.

14:64 Deserving of death indicates death by stoning for blasphemy (Lv 24:10-16).

14:65 To **spit** in a person's face (Mt 26:67) was the ultimate insult (Nm 12:14; Dt 25:9; Jb 30:9-10). Jesus predicted this would happen (Mk 10:34; cp. 15:19). Isaiah described this as one of the sufferings of the Servant of the Lord (Is 50:6).

14:66 This picks up from verse 54. The phrase **the courtyard below** indicates Jesus' hearing was held in the hall above the entry level to the high priest's house.

14:67 As Peter stood in the courtyard of the high priest's house (see note at v. 54), a servant said she had seen him with **that Nazarene** (a contemptuous usage, as is "the Galilean," Mt 26:69).

14:68 Many manuscripts do not include **and a rooster crowed**. Only Mark recorded Jesus as predicting a rooster would crow twice (vv. 29-31). This is a logical place for the

first crowing even though it apparently escaped Peter's notice.

14:69 The phrase **when the servant saw him again** seems to imply that the same servant confronted Peter again, but Matthew said it was a different person (Mt 26:71). This time **those standing nearby** were made aware of Peter's identity.

14:70 The tense of the word **denied** suggests Peter repeatedly denied knowing Jesus. Peter's accent identified him as a **Galilean** (Mt 26:73).

14:71 Peter's denials escalated. **To curse** (Gk *anathematize*) means to call down God's curse on oneself (cp. Ac 23:12,14,21). **To swear** refers to taking an oath in God's name. Peter's cursing and swearing backed his strongest denial—**I don't know this man**.

14:72 Immediately (see note at 1:9-11) links Peter's third denial to the fulfillment of Jesus' prophecy (14:26-31). Jesus turned and looked at Peter (Lk 22:61) and then he **remembered** Jesus' prediction and his own vow of steadfastness.

15:1 This verse is often seen as a third Jewish trial in which **the whole Sanhedrin** legalized their verdict in the **morning** (cp. Lk 22:66-71). Decisions reached at night were not binding. Being **handed . . . over** (Gk *paradidomi*) is repeatedly emphasized in this chapter (vv. 1,10,15) and throughout Mark. **Pilate** was a Roman official among the Jews from A.D. 26-36.

15:2 Pilate focused on whether Jesus claimed to be **King of the Jews**. This is the first use of this title in Mark's Gospel, but Pilate used it several times (vv. 2,9,12,26; cp. v. 32).

15:3-5 Pilate's question involves a double negative. It is matched by Mark's double negative that Jesus **did not**

He answered him, "You have said it."[A]

[3] And the chief priests began to accuse Him of many things. [4] Then Pilate[a] questioned Him again, "Are You not answering anything? Look how many things they are accusing You of!" [5] But Jesus still did not answer anything, so Pilate was amazed.

Jesus or Barabbas

[6] At[b] the festival[c] it was Pilate's[d] custom to release for the people a prisoner they requested. [7] There was one named Barabbas, who was in prison with rebels who had committed murder[e] during the rebellion.[f] [8] The crowd came up and began to ask Pilate to do for them as was his custom. [9] So Pilate answered them, "Do you want me to release the King[g] of the Jews[h] for you?" [10] For he knew it was because of envy[i] that the chief priests had handed Him over. [11] But the chief priests stirred up the crowd so that he would release Barabbas to them instead.

[12] Pilate asked them again, "Then what do you want me to do with the One you call the King of the Jews?"

[13] Again they shouted, "Crucify Him!"

[14] Then Pilate said to them, "Why? What has He done wrong?"

But they shouted, "Crucify Him!" all the more.

[15] Then, willing to gratify the crowd, Pilate released Barabbas to them. And after having Jesus flogged,[B] he handed Him over to be crucified.

Mocked by the Military

[16] Then[j] the soldiers led Him away into the courtyard (that is, *headquarters[k]) and called the whole *company together. [17] They dressed Him in a purple[l] robe, twisted together a crown[m] of thorns, and put it on Him. [18] And they began to salute Him, "Hail,[n] King[o] of the Jews!" [19] They kept hitting Him on the head with a reed and spitting on Him. Getting down on their knees,[p] they were paying Him homage. [20] When they had mocked[q] Him, they stripped Him of the purple robe, put His clothes on Him, and led Him out to crucify Him.

Crucified between Two Criminals

[21] They[r] forced a man coming in from the country, who was passing by, to carry Jesus' cross.[s] He was Simon, a Cyrenian,[t] the father of Alexander and Rufus.[u] [22] And[v] they brought Jesus to the place called *Golgotha* (which means Skull Place[w]). [23] They tried to give Him wine[x] mixed with myrrh,[y] but He did not take

Cross-references
[a]15:4 1Tm 6:13
[b]15:6-15 Mt 27:15-26; Lk 23:13-25; Jn 18:39-19:6
[c]15:6 Mk 14:1
[d]1Tm 6:13
[e]15:7 Pr 1:16
[f]Ac 23:7
[g]15:9 Lk 19:38
[h]Jn 19:21
[i]15:10 Ps 37:1
[j]15:16-20 Mt 27:27-31
[k]15:16 Jn 18:28,33; 19:9; Ac 23:35; Php 1:13
[l]15:17 Mk 15:20; Lk 16:19; Rv 18:12
[m]Jn 19:2,5; Rv 12:1
[n]15:18 Mt 26:49; Lk 1:28; Jn 19:3
[o]Lk 19:38
[p]15:19 Mk 5:6; Lk 22:41; Eph 3:14
[q]15:20 Mk 10:34
[r]15:21 Mt 27:32; Lk 23:26-31
[s]Lk 9:23
[t]Ac 6:9
[u]Rm 16:13
[v]15:22-26 Mt 27:33-37; Lk 22:32-34; Jn 19:17-24
[w]15:22 Jn 19:17
[x]15:23 Gn 9:21; Dt 7:13; Ps 4:7; Pr 3:10; Lk 5:37
[y]Ps 69:21

[A]15:2 Or *That is true,* an affirmative oath; Mt 26:64; 27:11   [B]15:15 Roman flogging was done with a whip made of leather strips embedded with pieces of bone or metal that brutally tore the flesh.

---

answer anything. Pilate was amazed at Jesus' silence because he could free Him if His answers were satisfactory.

15:6 Mark is silent about Pilate's attempt to extricate himself from the situation by sending Jesus to Herod Antipas (cp. Lk 23:5-12), the same Herod as in Mk 6:14-29. Here, in 15:6-15, Pilate tried another maneuver involving a **custom to release for the people a prisoner.** This custom is not documented outside the NT and was apparently done only at the Passover **festival** (Jn 18:39).

15:7 The **rebels** who were **in prison** with **Barabbas** probably included the two criminals who were crucified with Jesus. Mark gave no other details about **the rebellion,** which may indicate that his readers were familiar with it and thus did not need him to spell it out.

15:8-9 The crowd, coached by Jesus' enemies, asked Pilate to follow **his custom** of releasing a prisoner. Pilate instinctively offered them **the King of the Jews** (vv. 2,9,12,26). Thus Pilate unknowingly confessed Jesus' true status.

15:10 Pilate recognized that **envy** was why the **chief priests** wanted Jesus dead.

15:11-12 Again **the chief priests** (vv. 1,3,10) manipulated the course of events. **Stirred up** suggests they incited the crowd to riot. Ironically, the **crowd** chose **Barabbas** ("son of the father") over Jesus, the true Son of the Father.

15:13 This is Mark's first reference to crucifixion. None of Jesus' death predictions specifically mentioned crucifixion, though He had hinted at it (8:34).

15:15 Willing to gratify the crowd at the cost of justice, Pilate **handed** Jesus **over.**

15:16 Company reflects the Greek equivalent of the Latin "cohort," which totaled 600 soldiers. Mark did not use "company" in its technical sense, but he meant to indicate that a large group of soldiers mocked Jesus.

15:17 The soldiers used makeshift substitutes for the **robe . . . crown,** and scepter of a king. **Purple** was a royal color.

15:18 Hail, King of the Jews was a mocking corruption of the greeting, "Hail, Caesar."

15:19 The verbs in this verse are in the imperfect tense, indicating repeated action. They beat the King of the Jews **on the head** with his own scepter (**reed**) to indicate, as they believed, the weakness of His reign.

15:20 The phrase **led Him out to crucify Him** refers to the centurion and the execution squad, not to the company of soldiers.

15:21 Roman soldiers had the right to press citizens of subject nations into compulsory service (Mt 5:41), so they forced Simon to **carry Jesus' cross.** Simon was a Jewish **Cyrenian** from the north coast of Africa. He was **the father of Alexander and Rufus,** indicating that readers in Rome probably knew these men (Rm 16:13). Simon apparently became a Christian due to this experience.

15:22 *Golgotha* is Aramaic for **Skull Place.** The traditional site of the crucifixion is the Church of the Holy Sepulcher, located outside the city walls (Lv 24:14; Nm 15:35-36; Heb 13:12).

15:23 Wine mixed with myrrh was a primitive narcotic. The offer fulfilled Ps 69:21.

it. [24] Then they crucified Him and divided His clothes, casting lots[a] for them to decide what each would get. [25] Now it was nine in the morning[A] when they crucified Him. [26] The inscription of the charge written against Him was:

THE KING[b] OF THE JEWS.[c]

[27] They[d] crucified two criminals[B,e] with Him, one on His right and one on His left. [[28] So the Scripture was fulfilled that says: **And He was counted among outlaws.**][C,D,f] [29] Those[g] who passed by were yelling insults[h] at[E] Him, shaking their heads,[i] and saying, "Ha! The One who would demolish the sanctuary and build it in three days,[j] [30] save Yourself by coming down from the cross!"[k] [31] In the same way, the chief priests with the scribes[l] were mocking Him to one another and saying, "He saved others; He cannot save Himself! [32] Let the •Messiah,[m] the King[n] of Israel,[o] come down now from the

cross,[p] so that we may see and believe."[q] Even those who were crucified with Him were taunting Him.

The Death of Jesus

[33] When[r] it was noon,[F] darkness came over the whole land[G] until three in the afternoon.[H,s] [34] And at three[H] Jesus cried out with a loud voice, "*Eloi, Eloi, lemá[i] sabachtháni?*" which is translated, "**My God, My God, why have You forsaken Me?**"[J,t] [35] When some of those standing there heard this, they said, "Look, He's calling for Elijah!" [36] Someone ran and filled a sponge with sour wine, fixed it on a reed, offered Him a drink,[u] and said, "Let's see if Elijah comes to take Him down!" [37] But Jesus let out a loud cry and breathed His last. [38] Then the curtain[v] of the sanctuary[K]

---

a15:24 Ps 22:18
b15:26 Lk 19:38
c Jn 11:36
d15:27-28 Mt 27:38,44; Lk 23:39-43
e15:27 Mk 14:48
f15:28 Is 53:12
g15:29-32 Mt 27:39-43; Lk 23:35-38
h15:29 Ex 22:28; Mk 3:29; Rv 13:6
i Ps 22:7
j Jn 2:19
k15:30 Lk 23:26
l15:31 Mt 2:4
m15:32 Mt 1:17; Eph 5:2
n Lk 19:38
o Jn 1:49
p Lk 23:26
q Mk 8:11-12; 11:24; Jn 3:16; Ac 10:43; Rm 10:9; 1Pt 1:8-10
r15:33-39 Mt 27:45-54; Lk 23:44-48; Jn 19:28-30
s15:33 Am 8:9
t15:34 Ps 22:1
u15:36 Ps 69:21
v15:38 Ex 26:31-33; 2Ch 3:14; Heb 6:19; 9:3; 10:20

A15:25 Lit *was the third hour*   B15:27 Or *revolutionaries*   C15:28 Other mss omit bracketed text   D15:28 Is 53:12   E15:29 Lit *passed by blasphemed*   F15:33 Lit *the sixth hour*   G15:33 Or *whole earth*   H15:33,34 Lit *the ninth hour*   I15:34 Some mss read *lama*; other mss read *lima*   J15:34 Ps 22:1   K15:38 A heavy curtain separated the inner room of the temple from the outer.

15:24 They crucified Him is all Mark wrote about the main event of the gospel. The crucifixion took place on Friday, now known as Good Friday. That the four soldiers of the execution squad **divided His clothes** and cast lots for them fulfilled Ps 22:18 (cp. Jn 19:23-24).

15:25 Nine in the morning is literally "the third hour." Jews reckoned time of the daylight from sunrise.

15:26 The **charge** on which a person was condemned was often **written** on a placard and hung around his neck. In Jesus' case, it was nailed to His cross (Jn 19:19). All four Gospels record the words differently (cp. Mt 27:37; Lk 23:38; Jn 19:19), possibly because **the inscription** was trilingual (Jn 19:20). **THE KING OF THE JEWS** ironically proclaimed the truth about Jesus.

15:27 Criminals is the word used to describe Barabbas in Jn 18:40 (cp. Mk 14:48). Jesus' crucifixion between "criminals"

was meant as a parody of His kingship (as if He had attendants on either side) but by God's design the whole event really was His royal enthronement. The phrase **one on His right and one on His left** recalls the request of James and John (10:37,40).

15:29-30 Insults means "blasphemies." **Those who passed by** were thus guilty of the very thing for which the Sanhedrin had condemned Jesus (14:64). The bystanders' insults and **shaking** of their **heads** fulfilled Ps 22:7 and Lm 2:15.

15:31 Once again the **chief priests** led the mockery of Jesus. Their derision along with that of **the scribes** went to the heart of Jesus' mission: To save others, Jesus refused to **save Himself** (10:45).

15:32 On **Messiah**, see note at 8:29. The religious leaders' mockery recalls the second charge Jesus faced before the Sanhedrin (14:61). Mark reported that the two **crucified** with Jesus also taunted Him. One of them repented (Lk 23:39-43).

15:33 Noon was literally "the sixth hour," and **three in the afternoon** was "the ninth hour." The **darkness** was supernatural and represented God's judgment (Ex 10:21-23; Am 8:9-10).

15:34 At 3:00 p.m. Jesus **cried out with a loud voice** the Aramaic phrase, *Eloi, Eloi, lemá sabachtháni*. As usual, Mark provided a translation. Even when Jesus felt most **forsaken** by God, He affirmed His relationship with His Father—**My God, My God**, quoting the opening words of Ps 22:1. Jesus endured God's wrath as the sin-bearer.

15:35-36 Perhaps bystanders mistook *Eloi* for **Elijah** (Aram *Eli*) since there was a tradition in Judaism that Elijah would return (9:11-13; Mal 4:5). **Sour wine**, made with vinegar and water, was a drink of the soldiers, not the wine of verse 23. This action fulfilled Ps 69:21 (see note at Jn 19:28-29).

15:37 The content of Jesus' **loud cry** (reported by all three Synoptic Gospels) is specified in Jn 19:30—"It is finished." Luke recorded Jesus' final words (Lk 23:46).

---

enkataleipo

Greek Pronunciation	[en kah tah LIGH poh]
HCSB Translation	forsake
Uses in Mark's Gospel	1
Uses in the NT	10
Focus Passage	Mark 15:34

The Greek verb *enkataleipo* is a double compound that produces an intensive form of a verb meaning "to lack or leave" (*leipo*). With one exception (Rm 9:29), each occurrence of the term in the NT means *forsake* or "abandon." In Mk 15:34 and Mt 27:46, *enkataleipo* is used to translate the Aramaic word *sabach*, which in turn translates the original Hebrew *'azab* in Ps 22:1. Jesus' quote of this verse occurred toward the end of three hours of darkness (Mk 15:33) during which He endured God's wrath by being separated from the Father as payment for the sins of mankind. The word *enkataleipo* also occurs in Heb 13:5: "I will never . . . *forsake* you." Since this promise is addressed to believers, it indicates that while God was willing to *forsake* Jesus on the cross in order to redeem us, He is not now willing to *forsake* those whom He has redeemed.

was split in two from top to bottom. ³⁹ When the ˙centurion, who was standing opposite Him, saw the way He^A breathed His last, he said, "This man really was God's Son!"^{B,a}

⁴⁰ There^b were also women looking on from a distance. Among them were ˙Mary Magdalene,^c Mary the mother of James the younger and of Joses, and Salome. ⁴¹ When He was in Galilee,^d they would follow Him and help Him. Many other women had come up with Him to Jerusalem.^e

The Burial of Jesus

⁴² When^f it was already evening, because it was preparation day (that is, the day before the Sabbath), ⁴³ Joseph of Arimathea, a prominent member of the Sanhedrin who was himself looking forward^g to the kingdom of God,^h came and boldly went in to Pilateⁱ and asked for Jesus' body.^j ⁴⁴ Pilate was surprised that He was already dead. Summoning the centurion, he asked him whether He had already died. ⁴⁵ When he found out from the centurion, he gave the corpse to Joseph. ⁴⁶ Af-

ter he bought some fine linen, he took Him down and wrapped Him in the linen. Then he placed Him in a tomb^k cut out of the rock, and rolled a stone^l against the entrance to the tomb. ⁴⁷ Now^m Mary Magdalene and Mary the mother of Joses were watching where He was placed.

Resurrection Morning

16 Whenⁿ the Sabbath was over, ˙Mary Magdalene,^o Mary the mother of James, and Salome bought spices, so they could go and anoint Him. ² Very early in the morning, on the first day of the week,^p they went to the tomb^q at sunrise. ³ They were saying to one another, "Who will roll away the stone from the entrance to the tomb for us?" ⁴ Looking up, they observed that the stone—which was very large—had been rolled away. ⁵ When^r they entered the tomb,^s they saw a young man^{C,t} dressed^u in a long white^v robe sitting on the right side; they were amazed and alarmed.

^a15:39 Jn 5:19; Heb 1:2
^b15:40-41 Mt 27:55-56; Lk 23:49; Jn 19:25-27
^c15:40 Mt 28:1; Mk 16:1,9; Lk 8:2; 24:10; Jn 20:1-18
^d15:41 Mt 17:22
^eMt 23:37
^f15:42-46 Mt 27:57-60; Lk 23:50-54; Jn 19:38-42
^g15:43 Jd 21
^hMk 1:15
ⁱ1Tm 6:13
^jLk 12:4; Jn 2:21
^k15:46 Jn 5:28; 11:38; Ac 13:29
^lJn 20:1
^m15:47 Mt 27:61-66; Lk 23:55-56
ⁿ16:1-4 Mt 28:1; Lk 24:1-2
^o16:1 Mk 15:40
^p16:2 Ac 20:7; 1Co 16:2
^qJn 5:28
^r16:5-8 Mt 28:5-8; Lk 24:3-8; Jn 20:1-2
^s16:5 Jn 5:28 ^tLk 7:14 ^uLk 12:27 ^vRv 3:4

^A15:39 Other mss read *saw that He cried out like this and*   ^B15:39 Or *the Son of God*; Mk 1:1   ^C16:5 In Mt 28:2, the young man = an angel

15:38 The **curtain of the sanctuary** hung before the holy of holies in the temple. Its tearing symbolizes unhindered access to God, made possible because of Jesus' atonement for sin on the cross (Heb 6:19-20; 9:3; 10:19-22).

15:39 The Gentile **centurion** who presided over the execution was the first in Mark's Gospel to confess Jesus as **God's Son** (cp. 1:11,24; 3:11; 5:9; 9:7). His confession matched Mark's opening statement (1:1).

15:40 This is the first reference to **Mary Magdalene** in Mark. Jesus expelled seven demons from her (16:9; Lk 8:2). She came from Magdala on the western side of the Sea of Galilee. **Mary the mother of James the younger and of Joses** is called "the other Mary" in Mt 27:61. Possibly she was the mother of James the son of Alphaeus (Mk 3:18). **Salome** is named only in Mark (v. 40; 16:1). She was the mother of James and John, the sons of Zebedee (Mt 20:20; 27:56).

15:41 In Mark, only women (v. 41; 1:31) and angels (1:13) serve or help (Gk *diakoneo*) Jesus. The **many other women** who made the pilgrimage **to Jerusalem** did so for Passover.

15:42-47 Jesus' burial, an important element in early Christian proclamation (1Co 15:3-4), is recorded also in Mt 27:57-61; Lk 23:50-56; and Jn 19:38-42.

15:42 Jesus' burial was hastily performed because it was **already evening** on Friday. The Sabbath was soon to begin, a time when burial labors were not permitted. **Preparation day** (the day before the Sabbath) was when pious Jews prepared whatever they needed for the Sabbath.

15:43 **Joseph of Arimathea** was a secret follower of Jesus (Mt 27:57; Jn 19:38). That he was **a prominent member of the Sanhedrin** and opposed their verdict (Lk 23:51) shows that this group was not unanimous in its decision to execute Jesus (cp. Mk 14:55,64; 15:1). Joseph went **boldly** to Pilate to ask for Jesus' body. This contrasts with his formerly secret discipleship (Jn 19:38). The Romans often let criminals

rot on their crosses, but the Jews objected to leaving the dead hanging overnight (Dt 21:22-23).

15:44 Crucifixion victims often survived for days before dying. Jesus died in about six hours. Thus He **surprised** Pilate a second time (v. 5).

15:45 Pilate **gave** Joseph Jesus' body without demanding the bribe that families sometimes had to pay to retrieve the bodies of their loved ones.

15:46 To seal the tomb and prevent looting, they **rolled a stone against the entrance**. The large, circular, flat stone rolled in a track cut into the rock at the tomb entrance.

15:47 The women who witnessed Jesus' death also witnessed His burial.

16:1-8 Women were the first to know that Jesus was risen (Mt 28:1-8; Lk 24:1-8; Jn 20:1-2). Mary Magdalene's name heads the list in all four Gospels. The role of women in this account is astonishing since Judaism did not accept the testimony of women as legally valid.

16:1 The **Sabbath was over** at about 6:00 p.m. on Saturday. This allowed the women to buy more **spices** that evening. All three women had witnessed Jesus' crucifixion (15:40), and two of them had witnessed His burial (15:47). On **Mary the mother of James**, see note at 15:40. The Jews anointed bodies to cover the stench of decay.

16:2 The **first day of the week** was Sunday. **Very early in the morning** probably indicates when the women left for the tomb, whereas **at sunrise** indicates when they arrived.

16:3 That the women wondered who would **roll away the stone** reveals that they did not know that the tomb was sealed or guarded (Mt 27:62-66).

16:5 The stone was not moved to let Jesus out but to let witnesses enter. That the women **entered the tomb** confirms it was a large family tomb. The **young man dressed in a**

⁶"Don't be alarmed," he told them. "You are looking for Jesus the •Nazarene,ᵃ who was crucified. He has been resurrected!ᵇ He is not here! See the place where they put Him. ⁷But go, tell His disciples and Peter,ᶜ 'He is going ahead of you to Galilee;ᵈ you will see Him there just as He told you.'"

⁸So they went out and started running from the tomb,ᵉ because trembling and astonishment overwhelmed them. And they said nothing to anyone,ᶠ since they were afraid.

Appearances of the Risen Lord

[⁹Earlyᵍ on the first day of the week,ʰ after He had risen,ⁱ He appeared first to Mary Magdalene,ʲ out of whom He had driven seven demons.ᵏ ¹⁰She went and reported to those who had been with Him, as they were mourning and weeping. ¹¹Yet, when they heard that He was alive and had been seen by her, they did not believe it.ˡ ¹²Then after this, He appearedᵐ in a different form to two of them walking on their way into the country.ⁿ ¹³And they went and reported it to the rest, who did not believe them either.

The Great Commission

¹⁴Later, He appeared to the Elevenᵒ themselves as they were reclining at the table. He rebuked their unbelief and hardness of heart, because they did not believe those who saw Him after He had been resurrected.ᵖ ¹⁵Thenᵠ He said to them, "Go into all the worldʳ and preach the gospel to the whole creation.ˢ ¹⁶Whoever believesᵗ and is baptized will be saved,ᵘ but whoever does not believe will be condemned.ᵛ ¹⁷And these signs will accompany those who believe: In My name they will drive out demons; they will speak in new languages; ¹⁸they will pick up snakes;ᴬ,ʷ if they should drink anything deadly, it will never harmˣ them; they will lay hands onʸ the sick, and they will get well."

The Ascension

¹⁹Then after speaking to them, the Lord Jesusᶻ was taken up into heavenᵃᵃ and sat down at the right handᵃᵇ of God. ²⁰And they went out and preached everywhere, the Lord working with them and confirming the word by the accompanying signs.]ᴮ

ᵃ16:6 Mk 14:67
ᵇ1Co 15:4
ᶜ16:7 Lk 6:14
ᵈMt 17:22
ᵉ16:8 Jn 5:28
ᶠMk 1:44; 4:40
ᵍ16:9-11 Jn 20:11-18
ʰ16:9 Lk 24:1; Ac 20:7; 1Co 16:2
ⁱLk 18:33; Ac 2:24
ʲMk 15:40
ᵏMk 3:15; Lk 8:2
ˡ16:11 Lk 24:5,11,23
ᵐ16:12 Jn 21:1; 2Co 4:11
ⁿLk 24:13-35
ᵒ16:14 Lk 24:9
ᵖLk 24:38,41
ᵠ16:15-18 Mt 28:16-20
ʳ16:15 Mt 13:38; 1Jn 2:2
ˢRm 8:22
ᵗ16:16 Mk 11:24; Jn 3:16; Ac 10:43; Rm 10:9; 1Pt 1:8-10
ᵘAc 2:38; 22:16
ᵛMt 12:41; Jn 3:18,36; 5:11; 20:23
ʷ16:18 Lk 10:19; Ac 28:3-6
ˣAc 28:5
ʸAc 9:12,17; 1Tm 5:22
ᶻ16:19 Lk 24:3
ᵃᵃLk 24:51; Ac 1:2,11,22; 1Tm 3:16
ᵃᵇLk 22:69; Heb 10:12

ᴬ16:18 Other mss add *with their hands*   ᴮ16:9-20 Other mss omit bracketed text

long white robe (Mt 28:3; Ac 1:10; 10:30) was an angel (Mt 28:5; Lk 24:4).

16:6 The words of reassurance (**don't be alarmed**) are a standard feature in angelic manifestations (Dn 10:12,19; Mt 28:5; Lk 1:13,30; 2:10; Ac 27:24). **See the place where they put Him** recalls 15:47 (cp. Jn 20:6-7) and indicates the shelf inside the tomb on which Jesus' body was placed.

16:7 Go, tell are the two things that all followers of Jesus are to do. **Peter** is given special mention only in Mark as an encouragement following his denials of Jesus (14:66-72). The message for the disciples to meet Jesus in **Galilee** recalls Jesus' prophecy in 14:28.

16:8 Trembling and **astonishment** overwhelmed the women, whether from fear or excitement (cp. Mt 28:8). Most likely it was both. The phrase **they said nothing to anyone**, stated only by Mark, is a strong double negative. It does not imply that they forever kept silent but that they initially refused to speak about their bewildering experience (Mt 28:8; Lk 24:9-10).

16:9-20 These verses do not appear in the oldest and best manuscripts of Mark's Gospel.

16:9 This verse jumps abruptly from the topic of verses 1-8 to Jesus' appearance to **Mary Magdalene** (Jn 20:11-18). The description **out of whom He had driven seven demons** comes from Lk 8:2 and makes it appear that Mary Magdalene is being introduced by Mark for the first time, but in fact she was mentioned in Mk 15:40,47 and 16:1. This is another indication that this ending (vv. 9-20) of the Gospel was added at a later time by someone other than Mark, the author of this Gospel.

16:10 Those who had been with Him recalls 3:14.

16:11 They did not believe it recalls Lk 24:11.

16:12-13 These verses are a synopsis of Jesus' appearance

to the two disciples on the road to Emmaus (Lk 24:13-35). **In a different form** explains why they did not recognize Jesus (Lk 24:16). On the reaction of **the rest, who did not believe them either**, compare Lk 24:33-34.

16:14 Jesus' appearance to the **Eleven** (vv. 14-18) is based on Lk 24:36-49 and Jn 20:19-29. The reason for Jesus' **rebuke** is stated twice: **unbelief** (cp. vv. 11,13). They had not believed the eyewitness testimonies of Mary Magdalene or the Emmaus travelers.

16:15 This verse echoes the Great Commission (Mt 28:19; Lk 24:47). **All the world** and **the whole creation** are universal and inclusive. **Preach** is an imperative, indicating a binding responsibility.

16:16 Believes points to the acceptance of the gospel by faith. **Baptized** points to the outward testimony of one's conversion. These elements were closely related in apostolic preaching (Ac 2:38; 8:36-38; 16:30-33).

16:17-18 Jesus named five **signs** that would **accompany those who believe**, not just those who preach. **In My name** stands emphatically at the head of the list before any signs are enumerated. This emphasizes that the power to do these things comes from the risen Lord.

16:19 Jesus' ascension recalls Lk 24:50-51 and Ac 1:9-11. **Sat down at the right hand of God** draws from Ps 110:1. His exaltation and enthronement are also noted in Mt 26:64; Ac 2:33-35; 7:56; Heb 1:3; 8:1; 10:12; 12:2.

16:20 Preached everywhere is the fulfillment of verse 15. **The Lord working with them** fulfills the "in My Name" of verse 17 and Jesus' promise in Mt 28:20. **The word** is the gospel. The **signs** that accompanied their ministry (vv. 17-18) were for the purpose of **confirming** the word, or authenticating the message. Testimony to this is found in Ac 14:3 and Heb 2:4.

The Resurrection of Jesus as a Historical Event

Gary R. Habermas

In recent years, studies of Jesus' resurrection have taken surprisingly positive directions. This does not mean that contemporary critical scholars now accept exactly what Scripture states. However, there is a newfound respect for some of the New Testament (NT) reports. We will mention key areas leading to these developments and address their significance.

Early Traditions Embedded in the New Testament Writings

Arguably the most exciting development in recent decades is the almost unanimous recognition of scholars that the NT contains many items that predate the book in which they appear. This means the NT authors frequently made use of earlier sources—traditions, creeds, or confessions that they had gathered or received from others. Examples include a reliable statement received from others (1Co 11:23-26; 15:3ff), repeating the words of what was likely an early Christian hymn (Php 2:6-11) and summarizing an early sermon (such as Ac 1:21-22; 2:22-36; 3:13-16). These sources had different applications, such as keeping a reliable record, passing on doctrine, or serving liturgical functions like worship.

Of course, just because the NT authors *claimed* to have received accurate material from others does not make it so. But the growing consensus among critical scholars is that many of these traditions present ample indications that the material is in fact reliable. In the case of the resurrection traditions, the crucial portion of the data is taken from known church leaders who were actually present at the events themselves, and whose very lives depended on the veracity of their reports.

The Gospel Reports

Some New Testament writers claim to have witnessed personally the events that they record (Jn 19:35; Gl 1:20; 1Jn 1:1-3) or to have checked the existing sources for relevant information (Lk 1:1-4). Again, critical scholars do not take this testimony at face value, but there is a growing conviction in recent years that points to a positive verdict. The best critical example is that of influential scholar Richard Bauckham, whose work *Jesus and the Eyewitnesses* (Eerdmans, 2006) applies a startling array of checks and balances to the Gospels.

Scholars are increasingly convinced that particular tests, commonly termed "criteria," establish the credibility of many individual Gospel reports. For example, these tests emphasize material that is attested by multiple sources, is dissimilar from other Jewish or Christian literature, includes Palestinian or Aramaic background, is acknowledged even by ancient enemies of Christianity, or is embarrassing to report.

Test Case

For a variety of reasons, virtually all scholars, no matter how skeptical their orientation, agree that 1 Corinthians and Galatians are among the early, authoritative Christian writings that were written by the apostle Paul. In 1 Corinthians 15:3-7, Paul presents perhaps the earliest tradition of all. He probably acquired it from the apostles Peter and James the brother of Jesus when he visited them in Jerusalem about A.D. 35, a mere five or six years after Jesus' crucifixion (Gl 1:18-24). Paul inquired of these two witnesses (Gk *historeō*, 1:18), and, in the context of this chapter, discussed the gospel message, which unquestionably included the claim that Jesus had literally risen from the dead (Rm 10:9; 1Co 15:3-5).

Fourteen years later, Paul returned to Jerusalem to discuss the gospel once again with the apostles Peter, James, and John, to determine whether they all held to the same, central message of Christ's resurrection (Gl 2:2). None of the others added anything to Paul's message (Gl 2:6); rather, they agreed with him (Gl 2:9).

It is easy to miss the significance of the pre-Pauline tradition in 1 Corinthians 15:3-7. As he reported often, the most sacred proclamation of Christianity, the gospel, centered on the deity, death, and resurrection of Jesus Christ (Rm 1:3-4; 10:9-13). Therefore, Paul prefaced this creedal tradition by asserting that this message was of primary importance (1Co 15:3). Nothing was more central than the resurrection of Christ. In fact, whether or not we are Christians is determined by how we have responded to it (1Co 15:1-2).

Whenever we study history, we endeavor to uncover the past. Since the events cannot be repeated, the best method is to study the experiences of those who were there on those occasions. This is why Paul interviewed those who knew Jesus firsthand. Paul was especially interested in learning from those to whom Jesus had appeared after His death (1Co 15:9-11). Paul had also seen the risen Jesus personally, but His

appearance to Paul was somewhat distinctive (1Co 15:8). By traveling to Jerusalem more than once, he was able to chat with the other apostles about their own experiences of the risen Christ.

Not only did Paul discuss these matters with two of the original eyewitnesses of these events, Peter and James, but he did so almost immediately after the actual events. His initial trip to Jerusalem occurred a mere five years after the crucifixion. In the second visit, John was also present. These were the three most influential leaders in the early church, and their memories would have been fresh at the time Paul spoke with them.

While Paul heard the testimonies firsthand no more than several years after Jesus' death, Peter, James, and John had obviously experienced the appearances even earlier. Therefore we have an unbroken path here that stretches from Paul's hearing this early, eyewitness testimony back to the actual events themselves.

While witnesses may be mistaken, additional pointers attest to the truth of the resurrection testimony. For example, it is recognized that the early believers were more than willing to die for their proclamation. While this does not necessarily make it true, it does indicate that they certainly believed their testimony to be true and would rather suffer execution rather than deny what they knew to be true about the resurrection. Crucially, they were the only ones who were in a position to know whether or not their testimony was accurate, and they persisted in bearing testimony to the resurrection until their deaths.

No hypothesis has yet been able to viably explain the resurrection testimony in natural terms. Critics have tried often over the centuries, but today only a few scholars even make such suggestions. The evidence for Jesus' resurrection appearances is defensible and very compelling, and it stands as the best indicator of the believer's own future resurrection (1Co 15:53-57; 2Co 4:14-18; 1Pt 1:3-9)!

Luke

Introduction

The Gospel of Luke is the longest book in the New Testament. Focusing on the life and ministry of Jesus Christ, this Gospel is part one of a two-part history, the book of Acts being part two. Both were dedicated to "most honorable Theophilus" (Lk 1:3; Ac 1:1).

Emmaus or Imwas (24:13-35). According to the Sinai manuscript, Emmaus is thought to be the site of the house of Cleopas. Ruins of a Byzantine church now stand on the site of the house.

Circumstances of Writing

Author: The author of the Third Gospel is not named. Considerable evidence points to Luke as its author. Much of that proof is found in the book of Acts, which identifies itself as a sequel to Luke (Ac 1:1-3). A major line of evidence has to do with the so-called "we" sections of the book (Ac 16:10-17; 20:5-15; 21:1-18; 27:1-37; 28:1-16). Most of Acts is narrated in third-person plural ("they," "them"), but some later sections having to do with the ministry of the apostle Paul unexpectedly shift to first-person plural ("we," "us"). This indicates that the author had joined the apostle Paul for the events recorded in those passages. Since there are no "we" passages in the Gospel of Luke, that fits with the author stating that he used eyewitness testimony to the life of Jesus (1:2), indicating he was not such an eyewitness himself.

Among Paul's well-known coworkers, the most likely candidate is Luke, the doctor (see Col 4:14; Phm 24). That is also the unanimous testimony of the earliest Christian writers (e.g., Justin Martyr, the Muratorian Canon, and Tertullian). Since Luke is not named among the workers who were "of the circumcision" (i.e., a Jew; Col 4:11), he was almost certainly a Gentile. That explains the healthy emphasis on Gentiles in Luke (6:17; 7:1-10). Luke also reflects an interest in medical matters (e.g., 4:38; 14:2).

Background: Traditionally, the Gospel of Luke is believed to have been written after both Matthew and Mark. Those who date Matthew and Mark in the 60s or 70s of the first century A.D. have tended to push the dating of Luke back to the 70s or 80s.

Since Luke wrote both the Third Gospel and the book of Acts (Ac 1:1-3), it is relevant to consider the dating of both books together. The events at the end of Acts occurred around A.D. 62–63. That is the earliest point at which Acts could have been written. If Acts was written in the early 60s from Rome, where Paul was imprisoned for two years (Ac 28:30), the Third Gospel could date from an earlier stage of that period of imprisonment. The other reasonable possibility is during Paul's earlier two-year imprisonment in Caesarea

---

50 B.C.

Augustus Caesar's reign begins. **March 15, 44** B.C.

Roman Senate declares Herod king of the Jews. **39** B.C.

Herod assumes possession of the domain to which he had been named earlier. **37** B.C.

Herod begins thorough expansion of the temple in Jerusalem in **20** B.C. The inner sanctuary was completed in 1 ½ years and the rest of the temple was finished in A.D. **63**, only seven years before it was destroyed.

Imperial census in territory governed by Herod **6** TO **4** B.C.

5 B.C.–A.D. 9

Jesus' birth **5** B.C.

Eclipse of the moon just prior to Herod's death **March 12/13, 4** B.C.

Passover celebrated just after Herod's death **April 11, 4** B.C.

Herod's sons, Herod Phillip, Herod Antipas, and Archelaus divide Palestine and rule three territories under the aegis of Rome. **4** B.C.

Jesus travels with His parents from Nazareth to Jerusalem for the Passover Festival. A.D. **9**

(Ac 24:27). From that location, Luke would have been able to travel and interview the eyewitnesses to Jesus' life and ministry who were still alive.

The Third Gospel is addressed to "most honorable Theophilus" (Lk 1:3), about whom nothing else is known other than that he is also the recipient of the book of Acts (Ac 1:1). The Greek name Theophilus means "lover of God" or "friend of God" and implies that he was a Gentile, probably Greek. He seems to have been a relatively new believer, recently instructed about Jesus and the Christian faith (Lk 1:4). The title "most honorable" indicates that, at the least, he was a person of high standing and financial substance. It may also reflect that he was an official with some governmental authority and power.

Message and Purpose

The Gospel of Luke is a carefully researched (1:3), selective presentation of the person and life of Jesus Christ, designed to strengthen the faith of believers (1:3-4) and to challenge the misconceptions of unbelievers, especially those from a Greek background. Its portrait of Jesus is well-balanced, skillfully emphasizing His divinity and perfect humanity.

Contribution to the Bible

Nearly 60 percent of the material in the Gospel of Luke is unique. Thus, there is a great deal that readers of Scripture would not know if the Third Gospel were not in the Bible. Notable among the larger distinctive portions are: (1) much of the material in Luke 1–2 about the births of John the Baptist and Jesus, (2) the only biblical material on Jesus' childhood and pre-ministry adult life (2:40-52), (3) a genealogy for Jesus (3:23-38) that is significantly different from the one in Matthew 1:1-17, (4) most of the "travelogue" section about Jesus' journey to Jerusalem (Lk 9:51–19:44), (5) a considerably different slant on the destruction of the temple (21:5-38) from the Olivet Discourse in Matthew 24–25 and Mark 13, and (6) quite a bit of fresh material in the post-resurrection appearances, including the Emmaus Road, a distinctive statement of the Great Commission, and the only description in the Gospels of Jesus' ascension into heaven (Lk 24:13-53).

A.D. 10–30

Caiaphas is high priest. 18–36

Pontius Pilate is prefect of Judea. 26–36

John the Baptist's ministry begins. 29

Jesus' baptism 29

Jesus' wilderness temptations 29

Jesus' call of His first disciples 29

The first Passover of Jesus' ministry, an occasion on which it was said that the temple (inner sanctuary) had stood for 46 years 30

Jesus goes from Judea to Galilee when he learns of John the Baptist's death. 30

A.D. 31–33

Second Passover of Jesus' ministry; He comes under increasing scrutiny for plucking grain on the Sabbath. 31

Jesus feeds the 5,000 around the time of His third Passover. 32

Between Passover of 32 and 33 Jesus withdraws from public ministry and focuses on preparing His disciples. During this time period is Peter's confession at Caesarea Philippi and Jesus' transfiguration.

Jesus' trials, death, resurrection, and ascension Nisan 14-16 or April 3-5, 33

Structure

Luke's distinctive "narrative about the events" (1:1) of the life of Jesus is written in "orderly sequence" (1:3), though not strict chronological sequence in many cases (as the notes will explain at various points). Generally, after the key events leading up to the beginning of Christ's public ministry (1:5–4:13), the flow of the book is from His early ministry in and around Galilee (4:14–9:50), through an extended description of ministry related to His journey to Jerusalem (9:51–19:44), climaxing in the events of Passion Week and post-resurrection appearances in and around Jerusalem (19:45–24:53).

Outline

I. Preparation for the Ministry of Jesus (1:1–4:13)
   A. Formal prologue (1:1-4)
   B. Births of John the Baptist and Jesus (1:5–2:20)
   C. Childhood and early adulthood of Jesus (2:21-52)
   D. Ministry of John the Baptist (3:1-22)
   E. Genealogy of Jesus (3:23-38)
   F. Testing of Jesus by the Devil (4:1-13)

II. Jesus' Ministry in Galilee (4:14–9:50)
   A. Early preaching in Galilee (4:14-44)
   B. Calling of disciples, then apostles (5:1–6:16)
   C. The Sermon on the Plain (6:17-49)
   D. Faith issues; the sending out of the Twelve (7:1–9:17)
   E. Peter's confession and the transfiguration (9:18-50)

III. Jesus' Ministry in Judea and Perea (9:51–19:44)
   A. Setting out toward Jerusalem (9:51–13:21)
   B. Continuing toward Jerusalem (13:22–18:30)
   C. Final approach to Jerusalem (18:31–19:44)

IV. Climax of Jesus' Ministry in Jerusalem (19:45–24:53)
   A. Controversies and teaching (19:45–21:4)
   B. Prediction of the temple's destruction (21:5-38)
   C. Events of Jesus' final Passover (22:1-46)
   D. Betrayal, arrest, and trials (22:47–23:25)
   E. Crucifixion and burial (23:26-56)
   F. Resurrection, Great Commission, and ascension (24:1-53)

Herod the Great's Temple

ca A.D. 30 (ALL VIEWS SHOWN ARE LOOKING WEST)

Interior View

INTERIOR VIEW

1. Lampstand
2. Altar of Incense
3. Table of the Bread of the Presence
4. Veil (separating Holy Place from Most Holy Place)

EXTERIOR VIEWS

1. Temple
2. Altar of Burnt Offering
3. Golden Vine (mentioned by Josephus)
4. Lamp of Queen Helena of Adiabene
5. Veil at Entrance to Holy Place (mentioned by Josephus)
6. Council Chambers and Priests' Quarters
7. Nicanor Gate
8. Court of the Women
9. Chamber of the Lepers
10. Chamber of the Nazirites
11. Soreg (partition wall separating Court of the Gentiles from temple area)
12. Court of the Gentiles
13. Royal Stoa
14. Solomon's Porch
15. Beautiful Gate (Shushan Gate)
16. Muster Gate
17. Fortress of Antonia

Exterior View

Exterior View

The Dedication to Theophilus

1 Many have undertaken to compile a narrative about the events that have been fulfilled[A] among us,[a] [2] just as the original eyewitnesses[b] and servants of the word[c] handed them down to us. [3] It also seemed good to me, since I have carefully investigated everything from the very first, to write to you in an orderly sequence, most honorable[d] Theophilus,[e] [4] so that you may know the certainty of the things about which you have been instructed.[B,f]

Gabriel Predicts John's Birth

[5] In the days of King *Herod[g] of Judea, there was a priest of Abijah's division[C,h] named Zechariah. His wife was from the daughters of Aaron, and her name was Elizabeth. [6] Both were righteous in God's sight,[i] living without blame[j] according to all the commands and re-

quirements of the Lord. [7] But they had no children[D] because Elizabeth could not conceive,[E] and both of them were well along in years.[F]

[8] When his division was on duty[k] and he was serving as priest before God, [9] it happened that he was chosen by lot, according to the custom of the priesthood, to enter the sanctuary of the Lord and burn incense.[l] [10] At the hour of incense the whole assembly of the people was praying outside. [11] An angel of the Lord[m] appeared to him, standing to the right of the altar of incense. [12] When Zechariah saw him, he was startled and overcome with fear.[G] [13] But the angel said to him:

Do not be afraid,[n] Zechariah,
because your prayer has been heard.
Your wife Elizabeth will bear you a son,
and you will name him John.[o]

Cross references

[a] 1:1 Rm 4:21; 14:5; Col 2:2; 4:12; 1Th 1:5; 2Tm 4:17; Heb 6:11; 10:22
[b] 1:2 Jn 15:27; Ac 1:21; 2Pt 1:16; 1Jn 1:1
[c] Ac 26:16; 1Co 4:1; Heb 2:3
[d] 1:3 Ac 23:26; 24:3; 26:25
[e] Ac 1:1
[f] 1:4 Ac 18:25; Rm 2:18; 1Co 14:19; Gl 6:6
[g] 1:5 Mt 2:1
[h] 1Ch 24:10
[i] 1:6 Gn 7:1; Ac 2:25; 8:21
[j] Php 2:15; 3:6; 1Th 3:13
[k] 1:8 1Ch 24:19; 2Ch 8:14; 31:2
[l] 1:9 Ex 30:7-8
[m] 1:11 Mt 2:13-14; 28:2; Lk 2:9; Ac 5:19; 8:26; 12:7
[n] 1:13 Gn 15:1; Mt 14:27; Lk 1:30
[o] Gn 16:11; 17:19; Lk 1:60,63

Footnotes

A 1:1 Or events that have been accomplished, or events most surely believed   B 1:4 Or informed   C 1:5 One of the 24 divisions of priests appointed by David for temple service; 1Ch 24:10   D 1:7 Lit child   E 1:7 Lit Elizabeth was sterile or barren   F 1:7 Lit in their days   G 1:12 Lit and fear fell on him

---

1:1-4 Using elegant Greek, Luke began his **narrative about the events** of Jesus' life and ministry with a formal preface. This was a common practice in historical works of Luke's era. His prologue was (1) acknowledged previous treatments of the subject, (2) stated his methodology, (3) identified the recipient, and (4) articulated his purpose in writing.

1:1 Many have undertaken to compile a narrative means that a number of others had previously written about the life and works of Jesus. This may include the Gospels of Mark and Matthew since they preceded Luke's writing. **Events . . . fulfilled among us** speaks of how Jesus fulfilled many OT prophecies (see note at 24:44-45).

1:2 Original eyewitnesses included Mary, the mother of Jesus, about whom Luke wrote more than any other NT author. Mary may have still been alive when Luke wrote his Gospel. **Servants of the word** refers to the apostles of Jesus but may also include His brothers, James and Jude. Tradition says both brothers wrote NT books.

1:3 It also seemed good to me does not mean that Luke found the previous narratives (v. 1) to be erroneous or inadequate. Rather, he wrote his Gospel to complement what was already written. **Carefully investigated everything from the very first** means Luke studied the life and ministry of Jesus in meticulous detail ("carefully") and with comprehensive scope ("everything"), including many aspects related to the births of John the Baptist and Jesus ("from the very first") that are not found in the other Gospels. **Orderly sequence** does not mean strict chronological sequence, but in an orderly manner, whether chronological (generally) or topical. On **most honorable Theophilus**, see Introduction.

1:4 Luke's stated purpose in writing his Gospel was to provide historical **certainty** and theological clarity for Theophilus in regard to what he had been taught (**instructed**) about Jesus.

1:5 King Herod the Great was an Idumean appointed by the Roman emperor who ruled from 37–4 B.C. His realm covered not only **Judea**, but also Samaria, Galilee, and parts of Perea and Syria. **In the days of** indicates that the events

that immediately follow probably occurred in 7–6 B.C. The priesthood of Israel was made up of 24 divisions, including the house of Abijah (1Ch 24:10). **Daughters of Aaron** reveals that **Elizabeth** and her husband **Zechariah** were from priestly families. It is also the first instance of Luke's regular emphasis on the vital role that women played throughout Jesus' life.

1:6-7 The words **righteous . . . living without blame** refers to consistent obedience to God's **commands and requirements**, but more foundationally to living by faith. This is how Abraham was justified **in God's sight** (Gn 15:6; Gl 3:6-7,9). Like Abraham and Sarah, despite their godliness, Zechariah and Elizabeth **had no children** and were **well along in years** (past the age of child-bearing). It was considered a curse from God for a woman to be unable to bear children (see note at vv. 24-25).

1:8-9 Twice a year the priestly **division** of Abijah (see note at v. 5) was **on duty** at the Jerusalem temple for a week. Out of hundreds of priests in his division, Zechariah was **chosen** by the casting of a **lot** (see notes at Pr 16:33; Ac 1:24-26) to **burn incense** on the altar in front of the holy of holies (**the sanctuary**), a privileged duty that a priest could perform only once in his life. In fact, many never enjoyed this privilege because the lot never fell to them.

1:10 The **hour of incense** occurred at 9:00 a.m. and 3:00 p.m. daily. The presence of a sizeable **assembly of the people** makes it more likely that this incident took place in the afternoon.

1:11-12 On **an angel of the Lord**, see note at verse 19. To be **overcome with fear** upon seeing an angel is common in Luke (v. 29; 2:9) and elsewhere in Scripture (Jdg 6:22-23; Dn 8:16-17).

1:13 **Your prayer** may refer to Zechariah and Elizabeth praying to have a child (**your wife . . . will bear you a son**), or it could have been the prayer a priest was to offer at the altar for the redemption of Israel. **John** means "the Lord is gracious."

1:14-15 Joy is the prevailing mood of the first two chapters

14 There will be joy and delight for you,
   and many will rejoice at his birth.
15 For he will be great in the sight
   of the Lord
   and will never drink wine or beer.*a*
   He will be filled with the Holy Spirit
   while still in his mother's womb.*b*
16 He will turn many of the sons of Israel
   to the Lord their God.
17 And he will go before Him
   in the spirit and power of Elijah,
   to turn the hearts of fathers
   to their children,*c*
   and the disobedient
   to the understanding of the righteous,
   to make ready for the Lord
   a prepared people.*d*

18 "How can I know this?" Zechariah asked the angel. "For I am an old man, and my wife is well along in years."*A*

19 The angel answered him, "I am Gabriel,*e* who stands in the presence of God,*f* and I was sent to speak to you and tell you this good news. 20 Now listen! You will become silent and unable to speak until the day these things take place, because you did not believe my words, which will be fulfilled in their proper time."

21 Meanwhile, the people were waiting for Zechariah, amazed that he stayed so long in the sanctuary. 22 When he did come out, he could not speak to them. Then they realized that he had seen a vision in the sanctuary. He kept making signs to them*g* and remained speechless. 23 When the days of his ministry were completed, he went back home.

24 After these days his wife Elizabeth conceived and kept herself in seclusion for five months. She said, 25 "The Lord has done this for me. He has looked with favor in these days to take away my disgrace*h* among the people."

Gabriel Predicts Jesus' Birth

26 In the sixth month, the angel Gabriel*i* was sent by God to a town in Galilee called Nazareth,*j* 27 to a virgin •engaged*k* to a man named Joseph, of the house of David.*l* The virgin's

Cross references:
a 1:13-15 Nm 6:3; Jdg 13:3-5; Mt 11:18; Lk 7:33
b 1:15 Is 44:2; Lk 1:41,44
c 1:16-17 Mal 4:5-6
d 1:17 Lk 1:76
e 1:19 Dn 8:16; 9:21; Lk 1:26
f Mt 18:10
g 1:22 Lk 1:62
h 1:25 Gn 30:23; Is 4:1; 25:8
i 1:26 Lk 1:19
j Mt 2:23
k 1:27 Dt 21:23; Is 7:14; Mt 1:18,23
l Mt 1:20; Lk 2:4

A 1:18 Lit *in her days*

---

of Luke's Gospel (vv. 44,47,58; 2:10). As **great in the sight of the Lord** as John would be, he was still only the forerunner for the coming Messiah. **Never drink wine or beer** indicates that John the Baptist was under a lifelong Nazirite vow (Nm 6:1-21). On **filled with the Holy Spirit . . . in his mother's womb,** see note at verse 41. On the meaning of being filled with the Holy Spirit, see Eph 5:18.

1:16-17 **Turn . . . to the Lord their God** speaks of conversion, the result of repentance, which John the Baptist preached forcefully (3:3). **Go before Him . . . to make ready for the Lord a prepared people** echoes the essence of the prophecy in Is 40:3-5 (see Lk 3:4-6). Malachi 4:5-6 prophesied that an Elijah-like figure would come and **turn the hearts of fathers to their children.** That new "Elijah" would be John the Baptist.

1:18 Like Abraham (Gn 15:8) and Sarah (Gn 18:10-15), Zechariah had a difficult time believing God would fulfill His promise in his **old age.**

1:19 **Gabriel** means "(mighty) man of God." He is one of only two angels named in Scripture. The other is Michael (Dn 12:1; Rv 12:7).

1:20 As punishment for doubting the angel's pronouncement, Zechariah was rendered mute (**silent and unable to speak**) and possibly deaf as well (v. 62). **The day these things take place** was the time that began at John's birth and culminated at his circumcision (vv. 57-64).

1:21-22 The **people . . . waiting** for Zechariah to come out of the **sanctuary** were surprised because he did not emerge when expected. Since Gabriel had rendered him **speechless** (v. 20), Zechariah was unable to pronounce the traditional Aaronic blessing (Nm 6:24-26) upon the crowd. They realized **he had seen a vision,** likely because they noted his facial expressions and the excited **signs** he made with his hands.

1:23 Since each priest was only on duty for a week at a time, Zechariah would have been able to go **home** soon after his encounter with Gabriel (vv. 10-20). His home was located in the Judean hill country, not far from Jerusalem (v. 39).

1:24-25 **Elizabeth** withdrew and **kept herself in seclusion for five months** after she miraculously **conceived.** Why did she do this? Some speculate that she feared miscarrying during the early months of pregnancy. More likely she recognized that her unusual pregnancy would draw unwelcome attention if it became widely known. Better to have a restful start to a pregnancy that came so late in life.

1:26-38 Here the announcement of Jesus' coming birth is told from Mary's perspective. Matthew gives it from Joseph's vantage point (Mt 1:18-23).

1:26 In the **sixth month** of Elizabeth's pregnancy, **Gabriel,** the same angel who had appeared to Zechariah previously

parthenos

Greek Pronunciation	[pahr THEHN ahss]
HCSB Translation	virgin
Uses in Luke's Gospel	2
Uses in the NT	15
Focus passage	Luke 1:27,34

In the Greek NT, *parthenos* (*virgin*) connotes an unmarried female virgin of marriageable age. Once, the term refers to a male *virgin* (Rv 14:4). Both Matthew and Luke acknowledge that Mary was a *parthenos* at the time she conceived Jesus (Mt 1:20,23; Lk 1:27,34), and Matthew indicates that she remained a *virgin* while she carried the child to term (Mt 1:25). Both books mention the salvific significance of Jesus' birth (Mt 1:21; Lk 1:31-32). However, Matthew alone indicates the prophetic significance of Jesus' birth by a *virgin* (Mt 1:23). According to Matthew, Mary was the fulfillment of a prophecy given through the prophet Isaiah, who described a *virgin* (Is 7:14; *parthenos* occurs here in the Greek OT) who would give birth to a child to be named Immanuel. Matthew applies this prophecy to Messiah's birth.

name was Mary. [28] And the angel came to her and said, "Rejoice, favored woman! The Lord is with you."[A] [29] But she was deeply troubled[a] by this statement, wondering what kind of greeting this could be. [30] Then the angel told her:

Do not be afraid, Mary,[b]
for you have found favor with God.
[31] Now listen:
You will conceive and give birth to
a son,
and you will call His name Jesus.[c]
[32] He will be great
and will be called the Son of
the Most High,[d]
and the Lord God will give Him
the throne of His father David.[e]
[33] He will reign over the house of Jacob[f]
forever,
and His kingdom will have no end.[g]

[34] Mary asked the angel, "How can this be, since I have not been intimate with a man?"[B] [35] The angel replied to her:

"The Holy Spirit will come upon you,[h]

and the power of the Most High
will overshadow you.
Therefore, the holy One to be born
will be called the Son of God.[i]

[36] And consider your relative Elizabeth—even she has conceived a son in her old age, and this is the sixth month for her who was called childless. [37] For nothing will be impossible with God."[j] [38] "I am the Lord's •slave,"[c] said Mary. "May it be done to me according to your word." Then the angel left her.

Mary's Visit to Elizabeth

[39] In those days Mary set out and hurried to a town in the hill country of Judah [40] where she entered Zechariah's house and greeted Elizabeth. [41] When Elizabeth heard Mary's greeting, the baby leaped inside her,[D] and Elizabeth was filled with the Holy Spirit.[k] [42] Then she exclaimed with a loud cry:

"You are the most blessed of women,
and your child will be blessed![E]

[43] How could this happen to me, that the

Cross references
[a]1:29 Lk 1:12
[b]1:30 Mt 14:27; Lk 1:13
[c]1:31 Is 7:14; Mt 1:21,25; Lk 2:21
[d]1:32 Lk 1:76; 6:35; 8:28; Ac 7:48
[e]2Sm 7:12-13; 1Kg 2:12; Ps 132:11; Is 9:7; Jr 33:17
[f]1:33 Ex 19:3; Ps 114:1; Is 14:1; 29:22; 46:3
[g]Is 9:6 LXX; Dn 7:14
[h]1:35 Mt 1:18
[i]Mt 14:33; Lk 4:3,9,41; 22:70
[j]1:37 Gn 18:14; Lk 18:27
[k]1:41 Lk 1:67; Ac 2:4; 4:8; 9:17; 13:9

A1:28 Other mss add *blessed are you among women*   B1:34 Lit *since I do not know a man*   C1:38 Lit *Look, the Lord's slave*
D1:41 Lit *leaped in her abdomen* or *womb*   E1:42 Lit *and the fruit of your abdomen* (or *womb*) *is blessed*

(v. 19), was dispatched by God to **Nazareth**. This was a small village in **Galilee**, a region north of Judea and Samaria.

1:27 Virgin (Gk *parthenos*) may echo the prophecy of the virgin birth in Is 7:14 (Mt 1:18-25). According to Jewish law, being **engaged** was just as legally binding as being married (Mt 1:18-19). The **house of David** refers to the tribe of Judah, from which prophecies said the Messiah would come (Gn 49:9-10).

1:28-30 Mary was **favored** because **the Lord** set His undeserved grace upon her, not because she had earned good standing. Understandably, she was **deeply troubled** (Gk *diatarasso*; "confused, perplexed") by Gabriel's visit and greeting, **wondering** how she had come to receive such an honor. Gabriel's admonishment that Mary **not be afraid** was the same thing he said to Zechariah (v. 13).

1:31-33 The miracle that would cause Mary to **conceive and give birth to a son** would be a far greater miracle than the one that caused Elizabeth to conceive in old age (vv. 13,18) because, unlike Elizabeth, Mary was still a virgin (v. 34). The **name Jesus** (Gk *Iesous*) is equivalent to the Hebrew *Yehoshua* (Joshua), meaning "the Lord is salvation." Being **the Son of the Most High** means Jesus was the Son of God Himself (v. 35) because God created the life in Mary's womb without the aid of a human father (see note at vv. 34-35). Humanly speaking, though, Jesus' lineage would be traced legitimately through the royal family of **David** (see note at 3:23-28) because Joseph, Jesus' adoptive father, was a descendant of David. This made Jesus heir to David's **throne** according to God's eternal covenant (**forever . . . His kingdom will have no end**, v. 33; see 2Sm 7:13,16).

1:34-35 The difference between Mary's response (**how can this be**) and Zechariah's (v. 18) is that Mary asked her question not from unbelief but from puzzlement (v. 38; see note at v. 20). The answer to Mary's question about how she could get pregnant without being **intimate with a man** is that the **Holy Spirit** would **overshadow** (Gk *episkiazo*; "to fall upon [as a shadow]") her and cause her to conceive (see note at vv. 31-33). Because the Holy Spirit was the agent of conception, the child (**the holy One**; 2Co 5:21; Heb 4:15) would be **the Son of God**.

1:36-37 There is no way of knowing whether **your relative Elizabeth** means Elizabeth was Mary's aunt or cousin. On **she has conceived . . . the sixth month**, see note at verses 24-25. If ever Mary was tempted to doubt God's promise to her, she could recall Gabriel's words that **nothing will be impossible with God**, as had been shown in the lives of Abraham and Sarah (Gn 18:14).

1:38 Mary's response is a classic model of humble commitment (**I am the Lord's slave**) and willing obedience (**may it be done to me according to your word**).

1:39-40 Shortly after Gabriel left, Mary traveled to **Judah** to check on her relative, **Elizabeth**, whom she had just learned (from the angel) was pregnant (see note at vv. 36-37).

1:41-45 The baby (John) being **filled with the Holy Spirit** (v. 15) fulfilled Gabriel's prediction to Zechariah. But **Elizabeth** was filled with the Spirit also (v. 41), and the Spirit's revelations to her were apparently the source of her knowledge about the blessed roles and identities of Mary and her unborn child. When baby John **leaped** inside Elizabeth, she understood that he had experienced great **joy** at Mary's presence.

mother of my Lord should come to me? [44] For you see, when the sound of your greeting reached my ears, the baby leaped for joy inside me![A] [45] She who has believed is blessed because what was spoken to her by the Lord will be fulfilled!"

Mary's Praise

[46] And Mary said:

> My soul proclaims the greatness
>> of[B] the Lord,[a]
> [47] and my spirit has rejoiced[b] in God
>> my Savior,[c]
> [48] because He has looked with favor
> on the humble condition of His slave.
> Surely, from now on all generations
> will call me blessed,[d]
> [49] because the Mighty One[e]
> has done great things for me,[f]
> and His name[g] is holy.
> [50] His mercy is from generation
>> to generation[h]
> on those who fear Him.
> [51] He has done a mighty deed
>> with His arm;[i]
> He has scattered the proud
> because of the thoughts
>> of their hearts;
> [52] He has toppled the mighty
> from their thrones

and exalted the lowly.
> [53] He has satisfied the hungry
>> with good things[j]
> and sent the rich away empty.
> [54] He has helped His servant Israel,
>> mindful of His mercy,[c]
> [55] just as He spoke to our ancestors,
> to Abraham and his
>> descendants[D] forever.

[56] And Mary stayed with her about three months; then she returned to her home.

The Birth and Naming of John

[57] Now the time had come for Elizabeth to give birth, and she had a son. [58] Then her neighbors and relatives heard that the Lord had shown her His great mercy,[E,k] and they rejoiced with her.

[59] When they came to circumcise the child on the eighth day,[l] they were going to name him Zechariah, after his father. [60] But his mother responded, "No! He will be called John."[m]

[61] Then they said to her, "None of your relatives has that name." [62] So they motioned to his father[n] to find out what he wanted him to be called. [63] He asked for a writing tablet and wrote:

HIS NAME IS JOHN.

And they were all amazed. [64] Immediately his

---

a 1:46-53 1Sm 2:1-10; b 1:47 Ps 35:9; Hab 3:18; c 1Tm 1:1; 2:3; Ti 1:3; 2:10; 3:4; Jd 25; d 1:48 Lk 11:27; e 1:49 Ps 89:8; Zph 3:17; f Ps 71:19; 126:2-3; g Ps 99:3; 111:9; Is 57:15; h 1:50 Ps 100:5; 103:11,17; i 1:51 Ps 89:10; 98:1; 118:15; j 1:53 Ps 34:10; 107:9; Lk 6:21,24-25; k 1:58 Gn 19:19; l 1:59 Gn 17:12; Lv 12:3; Lk 2:21; Php 3:5; m 1:60 Lk 1:13,63; n 1:62 Lk 1:22

A 1:44 Lit *in my abdomen* or *womb*   B 1:46 Or *soul magnifies*   C 1:54 Because He remembered His mercy; Ps 98:3   D 1:55 Or *offspring*; lit *seed*   E 1:58 Lit *the Lord magnified His mercy with her*

1:46-55 Mary's hymn of praise is known as the "Magnificat," so named for the Latin term rendered as **proclaims the greatness** (Gk *megaluno*). It is similar in tone to the song of Hannah (1Sm 2:1-10).

1:46-49 There is a beautiful balance in Mary's hymn of praise. She expressed **humble** recognition of the **greatness** and **holy** nature of God and His grace (**favor**) on His voluntary slave, but also an awareness that God's unique calling on her life would result in all future generations calling her **blessed**. She viewed herself as both humbled and exalted.

1:50-53 These verses recall the descriptions of God's justice found throughout the Psalms (e.g., Ps 100:5; 103:11). **Those who fear Him** is an OT expression that is equivalent to the NT idea of faith. Fear of God is faith in God. **His arm** is figurative for God's power. God is a Spirit being (Jn 4:24) and does not have a physical body, but bodily metaphors are effective in communicating some of God's attributes and actions. God is against **the proud . . . the mighty**, and **the rich**, who imagine themselves self-sufficient. By contrast, He champions the cause of **the lowly** and **the hungry**, for they acknowledge their need for Him.

1:54-55 In sending Jesus to be born to Mary, God mercifully **helped . . . Israel**, in keeping with promises He had made centuries earlier to **Abraham** and **his descendants** (see Gn 12:1-3; 22:15-18).

1:56-57 Mary visited **Elizabeth** shortly after hearing she was "in the sixth month" of her pregnancy (vv. 36,39-40) and

stayed with her about three months. Mary may have returned to Nazareth either shortly before or after the birth of Elizabeth's son, John. Given their spiritual bond and the great roles their sons would play in God's plan, it seems likely that Mary stayed for John's birth.

1:58 Since Elizabeth remained secluded for the early months of her pregnancy (see note at vv. 24-25), it is possible that many of **her neighbors and relatives** first learned of God's **great mercy** toward her at or near the time of John's birth. The birth of a son was seen as favor from God.

1:59-63 In the OT, a child's name was more often given at birth. Perhaps Zechariah's inability to speak at John's birth caused the delay. Because Luke was writing for a Gentile audience that was unfamiliar with Jewish rites, he explained that Mosaic law (Lv 12:3) required parents to **circumcise** a male child (i.e., cut off the foreskin of his sex organ) **on the eighth day**. It was customary to name a boy baby after his father, in this case **Zechariah**, or his grandfather. Elizabeth had apparently already learned from Zechariah in writing that God wished for them to name the baby John. That neighbors and relatives **motioned** to Zechariah (rather than spoke) may imply that he was temporarily deaf as well as mute (vv. 20,22). A **writing tablet** was a small wooden board covered with wax. A wooden stylus was used to etch words into the wax.

1:64 That Zechariah was again able **to speak** fulfilled Gabriel's prediction (see note at v. 20).

mouth was opened[a] and his tongue set free, and he began to speak, praising God. [65]Fear came on all those who lived around them, and all these things were being talked about throughout the hill country of Judea. [66]All who heard about him[b] took it to heart, saying, "What then will this child become?" For, indeed, the Lord's hand was with him.

Zechariah's Prophecy

[67]Then his father Zechariah was filled with the Holy Spirit[c] and prophesied:[d]

[68]   Praise the Lord, the God of Israel,[e]

[a]1:64 Lk 1:20
[b]1:66 Ac 11:21
[c]1:67 Lk 1:41
[d]Jl 2:28
[e]1:68 Ps 41:13
[f]Lk 1:71; 2:38; Heb 9:12
[g]1:69 1Sm 2:1,10; Ps 18:2; 89:17; 132:17; Ezk 29:21
[h]2Sm 7:26; Ps 89:3,20; Ezk 34:23-24; 37:24-25
[i]1:70 Ac 3:21; Rm 1:2
[j]1:72 Mc 7:20
[k]Ps 105:8-9,42; 106:45

    because He has visited
    and provided ⋅redemption
        for His people.[f]
[69] He has raised up a ⋅horn of salvation[A]
        for us[g]
    in the house of His servant David,[h]
[70] just as He spoke by the mouth
    of His holy prophets in ancient times;[i]
[71] salvation from our enemies
    and from the clutches[B] of those
        who hate us.
[72] He has dealt mercifully with our fathers[j]
    and remembered His holy covenant[k]—

[A]1:69 = a strong Savior   [B]1:71 Lit *the hand*

1:65-66 The overall outcome of the preceding episode is that it was clear that **the Lord's hand** was with the newborn John in a remarkable way and that everyone living in the region continued to ponder (**took . . . to heart**) the question, **What . . . will this child become?**

1:67 On the meaning of **filled with the Holy Spirit**, see Eph 5:18. It is ironic that **Zechariah**, being a priest (v. 5) and having **prophesied**, set the stage for the ministry of his son, John the Baptist. Though John hailed from a priestly family, he was called to serve as a prophet of the Most High (v. 76).

1:68-79 Zechariah's prophecy is traditionally called the "Benedictus," from the first word (**praise**) of verse 68 in the Latin Vulgate Bible.

1:68-70 The births of John the Baptist, the forerunner (v. 17; Is 40:1-5; Mal 4:5-6), and Jesus, the Messiah, marked the initiation of the final stages of God's plan of **salvation** for His people. This salvation would require a payment of **redemption** on the cross by Jesus. An animal's **horn** symbolized strength or power (Dt 33:17). Jesus was from **the house of . . . David** (see v. 27; 3:30).

1:71-75 The ministries of John the Baptist and Jesus fulfilled God's covenant with David (v. 69; 2Sm 7:12-16) and **the oath that He swore to . . . Abraham** (see Gn 12:1-3). As a result, in the Messiah's future reign, Israel would have full salvation from their enemies and would serve God in **holiness and righteousness**.

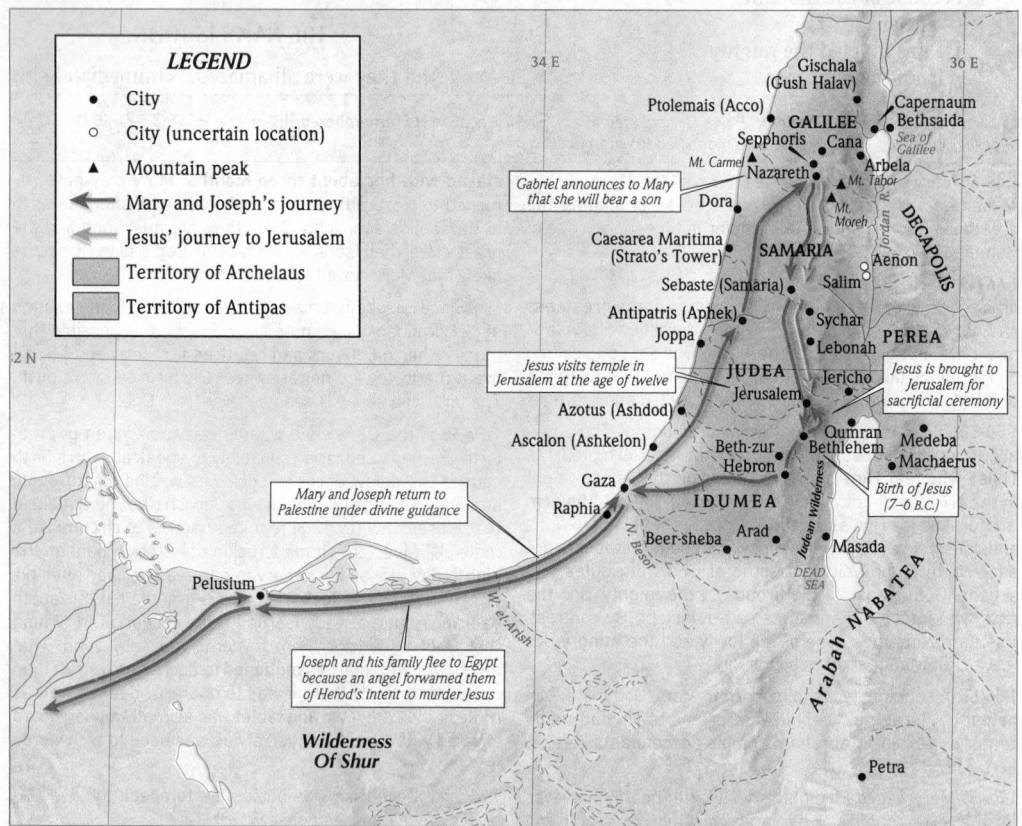

Jesus' Birth and Early Childhood

⁷³ the oath that He swore to our father
  Abraham.^a

He has given us the privilege,
⁷⁴ since we have been rescued
  from our enemies' clutches,^A
  to serve Him without fear
⁷⁵ in holiness and righteousness
  in His presence all our days.
⁷⁶ And child, you will be called
  a prophet of the Most High,^b
  for you will go before the Lord
  to prepare His ways,^c
⁷⁷ to give His people knowledge of salvation
  through the forgiveness of their sins.^d
⁷⁸ Because of our God's merciful
  compassion,
  the Dawn from on high^e will visit us
⁷⁹ to shine on those who live in darkness
  and the shadow of death,^f
  to guide our feet into the way of peace.

⁸⁰ The child grew up and became spiritually strong,^g and he was in the wilderness until the day of his public appearance to Israel.

Cross references (center column):
^a1:73 Gn 22:16-17; Heb 6:13
^b1:76 Mt 11:9
^cMal 3:1; Lk 1:17
^d1:77 Jr 31:34; Mk 1:4
^e1:78 Is 58:8; Jr 23:5; Zch 3:8; 6:12 LXX; Mal 4:2; Lk 24:49; Eph 4:8; 2Pt 1:19
^f1:79 Is 9:2; 60:2-3
^g1:80 Lk 2:40
^h2:1 Mt 22:17; Lk 3:1
ⁱ2:2 Mt 4:24
^j2:4 Lk 1:27
^k2:9 Lk 1:11; Ac 5:19
^lLk 24:4; Ac 12:7
^m2:10 Mt 14:27

The Birth of Jesus

2 In those days a decree went out from Caesar Augustus^{B,h} that the whole empire^c should be registered. ² This first registration took place while^D Quirinius was governing Syria.ⁱ ³ So everyone went to be registered, each to his own town.

⁴ And Joseph also went up from the town of Nazareth in Galilee, to Judea, to the city of David, which is called Bethlehem, because he was of the house and family line of David,^j ⁵ to be registered along with Mary, who was •engaged to him^E and was pregnant. ⁶ While they were there, the time came for her to give birth. ⁷ Then she gave birth to her firstborn Son, and she wrapped Him snugly in cloth and laid Him in a feeding trough—because there was no room for them at the lodging place.

The Shepherds and the Angels

⁸ In the same region, shepherds were staying out in the fields and keeping watch at night over their flock. ⁹ Then an angel of the Lord^k stood before^F them,^l and the glory of the Lord shone around them, and they were terrified.^G ¹⁰ But the angel said to them, "Don't be afraid,^m

---

^A1:74 Lit *from the hand of enemies*   ^B2:1 Emperor who ruled the Roman Empire 27 B.C.–A.D. 14; also known as Octavian, he established the peaceful era known as the *Pax Romana*; Caesar was a title of Roman emperors.   ^C2:1 Or *the whole inhabited world*   ^D2:2 Or *This registration was the first while*, or *This registration was before*   ^E2:5 Other mss read *was his engaged wife*   ^F2:9 Or *Lord appeared to*   ^G2:9 Lit *they feared a great fear*

1:76 John was to be the **prophet of the Most High** who would go before Jesus, "the Son of the Most High" (see note at vv. 31-33) to **prepare His ways** (see Is 40:3; Mal 3:1).

1:77 To give **knowledge of salvation** through the forgiveness of sins was the emphasis of John the Baptist's preaching (see note at 3:2-3).

1:78-79 **Dawn from on high** speaks of the coming of Messiah (Mal 4:2). The Lord's visitation began with John's birth. The next part of that **visit** would be Jesus' birth (2:1-20). The phrase **those who live in darkness and the shadow of death** probably echoes Is 9:1-2, which is cited in Mt 4:16. The **way of peace** with God is through faith in Christ (Rm 5:1).

1:80 This verse about John's upbringing is parallel to Lk 2:51-52, which is about Jesus' upbringing. Because Zechariah and Elizabeth were already quite old when John was born (see note at 1:6-7), they probably died while he was fairly young, which may explain why he **grew up . . . in the wilderness** of Judea, between Jerusalem and the Dead Sea. **The day of his public appearance** is recounted in 3:1-3. Since ministry for a Levite (which John was) began at 30 years old (Nm 4:46-47), this is probably when he launched his ministry, as did Jesus (3:23).

2:1 Augustus (meaning "Exalted," a title approved by the Roman Senate in 27 B.C.) was the Roman **Caesar** from 31 B.C. to A.D. 14. This **decree . . . that the whole empire should be registered** was a census for the purposes of taxation and military service.

2:2 It is thought that **Quirinius** served two terms as Roman governor of **Syria**: from 6-4 B.C., and then A.D. 6-9. Jesus was born during the period of the **first registration**. There

was also a census registration in Quirinius's second term (Ac 5:37).

2:3-4 His own town refers not to where Joseph presently lived (**Nazareth in Galilee**), but to the town of his ancestral roots (**Bethlehem in Judea**), which was called **the city of David** because King David grew up there (1Sm 16:1). Joseph was descended from David (1:27). The trip from Nazareth to Bethlehem would have taken three days and covered roughly 90 miles.

2:5-6 As months before in 1:27, **Mary** at this time was still only **engaged** to Joseph because they had not yet consummated their marriage via intercourse. Nevertheless, she was **pregnant** (see note at 1:31-33) and ready to **give birth.**

2:7 The words **her firstborn Son** naturally implies that Mary later had other children (Mt 13:55-56). In that day, a newborn was **wrapped . . . snuggly in cloth** to keep its arms and legs straight. That baby Jesus was **laid . . . in a feeding trough** indicates that the family was forced to stay in a stable, or perhaps a cave that served as a stable, because there was no other room available in Bethlehem.

2:8 The sheep used for temple sacrifices in Jerusalem were kept in fields outside Bethlehem. The work of **shepherds** was more important **at night** because of the threats from thieves and predators.

2:9-10 Though not named in the present passage, the **angel of the Lord** was Gabriel (1:11-20). The **glory of the Lord** was a bright light (in the midst of the darkness of night), indicating God's glorious presence. It is only natural to be **terrified** at the sight of an angel (see note at 1:11-12), not to mention a sudden, overwhelming light from the sky. The angel spoke to calm the shepherds and refocus their

for look, I proclaim to you good news of great joy that will be for all the people:[A] [11] Today a Savior,[a] who is •Messiah[b] the Lord,[c] was born for you in the city of David. [12] This will be the sign for you:[d] You will find a baby wrapped snugly in cloth and lying in a feeding trough."

[13] Suddenly there was a multitude of the heavenly host with the angel, praising God and saying:

[14]   Glory to God in the highest heaven,[e]
        and peace on earth[f] to people
        He favors![B,C,g]

[15] When the angels had left them and returned to heaven, the shepherds said to one another, "Let's go straight to Bethlehem and see what has happened, which the Lord has made known to us."

[16] They hurried off and found both Mary and Joseph, and the baby who was lying in the feeding trough. [17] After seeing them, they reported the message they were told about this child, [18] and all who heard it were amazed at what the shepherds said to them. [19] But Mary was treasuring up all these things[D] in her heart[h] and meditating on them. [20] The shep-

herds returned, glorifying and praising God[i] for all they had seen and heard, just as they had been told.

The Circumcision and Presentation of Jesus

[21] When the eight days were completed for His circumcision,[j] He was named Jesus[k]—the name given by the angel before He was conceived.[E] [22] And when the days of their purification according to the law of Moses were finished,[l] they brought Him up to Jerusalem to present Him to the Lord [23] (just as it is written in the law of the Lord: **Every firstborn male[F] will be dedicated[G] to the Lord[H,m]** and to offer a sacrifice (according to what is stated in the law of the Lord: **a pair of turtledoves or two young pigeons[l,n]**).

Simeon's Prophetic Praise

[25] There was a man in Jerusalem whose name was Simeon. This man was righteous and devout,[o] looking forward to Israel's consolation,[J,p] and the Holy Spirit was on him. [26] It had been revealed to him by the Holy Spirit[q] that he would not see death before he saw the Lord's Messiah.[r] [27] Guided by the Spirit, he en-

Cross references (center column)

[a] 2:11 Mt 1:21; Jn 4:42; Ac 5:31
[b] Mt 1:16; 16:16,20; Jn 11:27
[c] Lk 1:43; Ac 2:36; 10:36
[d] 2:12 1Sm 2:34; 2Kg 19:29; 20:8-9; Is 7:11,14
[e] 2:14 Mt 21:9; Lk 19:38
[f] Lk 12:51
[g] Lk 3:22; Eph 1:9; Php 2:13
[h] 2:19 Lk 2:51
[i] 2:20 Mt 9:8
[j] 2:21 Lk 1:59
[k] Lk 1:31
[l] 2:22 Lv 12:6-8
[m] 2:23 Ex 13:2,12
[n] 2:24 Lv 5:11; 12:8
[o] 2:25 Lk 1:6
[p] Mk 15:43; Lk 2:38; 23:51
[q] 2:26 Mt 2:12
[r] Ps 89:48; Jn 8:51; Heb 11:5

[A] 2:10 Or *the whole nation*   [B] 2:14 Other mss read *earth good will to people*   [C] 2:14 Or *earth to men of good will*   [D] 2:19 Lit *these words*   [E] 2:21 Or *conceived in the womb*   [F] 2:23 Lit *"Every male that opens a womb*   [G] 2:23 Lit *be called holy*   [H] 2:23 Ex 13:2,12   [I] 2:24 Lv 5:11; 12:8   [J] 2:25 The coming of the Messiah with His salvation for the nation; Is 40:1; 61:2; Lk 2:26,30

attention on the proclamation of the gospel (**good news). All the people** could refer to Israel, but given Luke's emphasis on the gospel spreading to the Gentiles, it probably means "all nations."

2:11-12 Savior (Gk *soter*) means "deliverer, redeemer." **Messiah** (Gk *christos*, equivalent to the Hb *meshiach*) means "anointed one," especially focusing on being anointed as king. **Lord** (Gk *kurios*) was used of secular rulers, but it is also the standard translation of the primary name of God in Hebrew, *Yahweh*. The shepherds would have been shocked to hear that a divine messianic ruler had been born, but to be told He was **lying in a feeding trough** and born to a man and woman of humble means would have seemed preposterous.

2:13-14 The hymn sung by the choir of angels (**heavenly host**) is well-known today as the "Gloria in Excelsis Deo," from the first words of verse 14 in the Latin Vulgate (**glory to God in the highest**). To give "glory to God" does not give Him something He otherwise lacks. Rather, it is a confession of the wondrous glory He forever possesses. The **peace** to be found **on earth** was not the *Pax Romana* (the "universal peace" of the Roman Empire), but peace with God through faith in Jesus Christ (Rm 5:1; see note at Lk 1:78-79). The people whom God **favors** are those who have found God's undeserved favor, or grace, through Christ.

2:15 What has happened refers to the birth of the Savior, who is Christ and Lord (see note at vv. 11-12).

2:16 On **lying in the feeding trough**, see note at verse 7.

2:17 On **the message they were told about this child**, see note at verses 9-10.

2:18 All who heard it included anyone in or around Bethlehem with whom the shepherds had the opportunity to share their story (vv. 8-14).

2:19 It is possible that Luke gained much of his knowledge about what happened in chapters 1 and 2 from talking to Mary, who recalled the things she had "treasured" (Gk *suntereo*; "to treasure, keep in mind") **in her heart.**

2:20 The **shepherds returned** to the fields outside Bethlehem to tend their flocks. They were **glorifying and praising God** because everything they found in Bethlehem was just as the angel said it would be (vv. 10-12).

2:21 On **eight days** and **circumcision**, see note at 1:59-63. On the name **Jesus**, see note at 1:31-33.

2:22-24 The **days of their purification** lasted another 33 days after the child's circumcision (Lv 12:2-8). **To present Him to the Lord** was what was done with **every firstborn male** in Israel (Ex 13:2,12). On the sacrifice of **turtledoves** or **pigeons**, see Lv 12:8 and note there.

2:25-26 Like Zechariah and Elizabeth (see note at 1:6-7), **Simeon** was a **righteous** person. **Israel's consolation** spoke of the comfort and hope the people had in regard to God's plan for His people, but, more specifically, it referred to Messiah's role in that plan. In the OT, the **Holy Spirit** came on a few selected people (Nm 24:2; 1Sm 10:10; 16:13). After the day of Pentecost, the Spirit has indwelt all believers (Jn 14:16-17; 1Co 3:16). The Holy Spirit filled Zechariah so he could prophesy about John (Lk 1:67-79). In this case, the Spirit assured Simeon that he would live long enough to see the Messiah, so that he would be in a position to do the same in regard to Jesus (2:29-32).

tered[A] the •temple complex. When the parents brought in the child Jesus to perform for Him what was customary under the law, [28] Simeon took Him up in his arms, praised God, and said:

[29]   Now, Master,
       You can dismiss Your •slave in peace,
       as You promised.
[30]   For my eyes have seen Your salvation.[a]
[31]   You have prepared it
       in the presence of all peoples—
[32]   a light for revelation to the Gentiles[B,b]
       and glory to Your people Israel.[c]

[33] His father and mother[c] were amazed at what was being said about Him. [34] Then Simeon blessed them and told His mother Mary: "Indeed, this child is destined to cause the fall and rise of many in Israel[d] and to be a sign that will be opposed[D]— [35] and a sword will pierce your own soul—that the thoughts[E] of many hearts may be revealed."

Anna's Testimony

[36] There was also a prophetess,[e] Anna, a daughter of Phanuel, of the tribe of Asher.[f] She was well along in years,[F] having lived with her husband seven years after her marriage,[G,g] [37] and was a widow for 84 years.[H] She did not leave the temple complex, serving God night and day with fasting and prayers.[h] [38] At that very moment,[I] she came up and began to thank God and to speak about Him to all who were looking forward to the •redemption of Jerusalem.[J,i]

The Family's Return to Nazareth

[39] When they had completed everything according to the law of the Lord, they returned to Galilee, to their own town of Nazareth.[j] [40] The boy grew up and became strong, filled with wisdom, and God's grace was on Him.[k]

In His Father's House

[41] Every year His parents traveled to Jerusalem for the •Passover Festival.[l] [42] When He was 12 years old, they went up according to the custom of the festival.[m] [43] After those days were over,[n] as they were returning, the boy Jesus stayed behind in Jerusalem, but His parents[K] did not know it. [44] Assuming He was in the traveling party, they went a day's journey. Then they began looking for Him among their relatives and friends. [45] When they did not find Him, they returned to Jerusalem to search for Him. [46] After three days, they found Him in the temple complex sitting among the teachers, listening to them and asking them questions. [47] And all those who heard Him were astounded at His understanding and

Cross references:
- [a] 2:30 Ps 119:166,174; Is 52:10; Lk 3:6
- [b] 2:32 Is 42:6; 49:6,9; Ac 13:47; 26:23
- [c] Is 46:13 LXX
- [d] 2:34 Mt 21:44; 1Co 1:23; 2Co 2:16; 1Pt 2:8
- [e] 2:36 Lk 2:38; Ac 21:9
- [f] Jos 19:24
- [g] 1Tm 5:9
- [h] 2:37 Lk 5:33; Ac 13:3; 14:23; 1Tm 5:5
- [i] 2:38 Is 52:9; Lk 1:68; 2:25
- [j] 2:39 Mt 2:23; Lk 1:26; 2:51; 4:16
- [k] 2:40 Lk 1:80; 2:52
- [l] 2:41 Ex 12:11; 23:15; Dt 16:1-6
- [m] 2:42 Dt 16:16-17
- [n] 2:43 Ex 12:15

[A]2:27 Lit *And in the Spirit, he came into*   [B]2:32 Or *the nations*   [C]2:33 Other mss read *But Joseph and His mother*   [D]2:34 Or *spoken against*   [E]2:35 Or *schemes*   [F]2:36 Lit *in many days*   [G]2:36 Lit *years from her virginity*   [H]2:37 Or *she was a widow until the age of 84*   [I]2:38 Lit *very hour*   [J]2:38 Other mss read *in Jerusalem*   [K]2:43 Other mss read *but Joseph and His mother*

2:27 The Holy Spirit **guided** Simeon to the right place (**the temple**) at the right time (when **the child Jesus** was brought to **perform ... what was customary under the law**). See notes at verses 21 and 22-24.

2:29-32 Simeon's words here are traditionally called the "Nunc Dimittis," from wording in the Latin Vulgate translation. Simeon's Divine **Master** had kept His promise that he would live to see Christ (i.e., **Your salvation**), so he could now die (**dismiss Your slave**). God's salvation in Christ (v. 30) is for **all peoples** (**the Gentiles** and **Israel**). The worldwide scope of the gospel is Luke's ongoing theme in both of his writings (his Gospel and the book of Acts).

2:33-35 Legally, Joseph was Jesus' **father** (see note at 3:23-38) even though it was the Holy Spirit who caused Mary to conceive (see note at 1:34-35). Jesus was a spiritual divider of society (**a sign ... opposed**). In considering the gospel about Christ, **many in Israel** "fell" eternally due to unbelief and others rose by faith to eternal life. Mary would suffer great pain in watching Jesus be rejected and executed. How people respond to Jesus is the difference between pardon and condemnation, eternity in heaven or hell.

2:36-38 The immediate shift of focus from Simeon, a male who prophesied, to **Anna**, the **prophetess**, fits with Luke's emphasis on women. The other prophetesses mentioned in the NT are Philip's daughters (Ac 21:8-9). If Anna had been married for **seven years** and a **widow for 84 years**, she was well over 100 years old. The Greek text can also be read to mean that she was a widow until age 84, but that reading does not fit the circumstances well. Besides being a prophetess, Anna's other ministry included devotion to prayer. Since Jerusalem was the Jewish capital, **the redemption of Jerusalem** means the redemption of all the people of Israel.

2:39 Luke did not include several of the well-known incidents that appear in the Gospel of Matthew, including the visit of the magi and the trip to Egypt to avoid an attempt by Herod the Great to kill the infant Messiah (Mt 2:1-23).

2:40 This description of Jesus as a young boy is similar to that of John the Baptist in Lk 1:80. The additional elements emphasized that Jesus was **filled with wisdom, and God's grace was on Him** (see the similar description of Stephen in Ac 6:8,10).

2:41-42 This is the only incident Scripture reports about Jesus' life between the time He was a small child and His baptism by John (3:21-22). Adult Jewish males and their families were expected to make a pilgrimage to **Jerusalem** for the annual feasts of **Passover**, Pentecost, and Tabernacles. The *Bar Mitzvah* (Hb "son of the commandment") ceremony at age 13 marked the time when a Jewish male was recognized as a man. Since Jesus was now **12 years old**, this was His last Passover before adulthood.

2:43-45 Joseph and Mary **went a day's journey** before worrying about Jesus because they assumed He was with the traveling party. It was completely out of character (see v. 51) for Him not to obey them in every respect.

2:46-47 **Three days** included one day traveling from

His answers. [48] When His parents saw Him, they were astonished, and His mother said to Him,[a] "Son, why have You treated us like this? Your father and I have been anxiously searching for You."[b]

[49] "Why were you searching for Me?" He asked them. "Didn't you know that I had to be in My Father's house?"[A] [50] But they did not understand what He said to them.[c]

In Favor with God and with People

[51] Then He went down with them and came to Nazareth and was obedient to them. His mother kept all these things in her heart.[d] [52] And Jesus increased in wisdom and stature, and in favor with God and with people.[e]

The Messiah's Herald

3 In the fifteenth year of the reign of Tiberius Caesar,[B] while Pontius •Pilate was governor of Judea,[f] •Herod was tetrarch[C] of Galilee,[g] his brother Philip tetrarch of the region of Iturea[D] and Trachonitis,[D] and Lysanias tetrarch of Abilene,[E] [2] during the high priesthood of Annas[h] and Caiaphas,[i] God's word

came to John the son of Zechariah in the wilderness.[j] [3] He went into all the vicinity of the Jordan,[k] preaching a baptism of repentance[F] for the forgiveness of sins, [4] as it is written in the book of the words of the prophet Isaiah:

> A voice of one crying out
>   in the wilderness:
> Prepare the way for the Lord;
>   make His paths straight!
> [5] Every valley will be filled,
>   and every mountain and hill will be
>   made low;[G]
>   the crooked will become straight,
>   the rough ways smooth,
> [6]   and everyone[H] will see the salvation
>   of God.[I]

[7] He then said to the crowds who came out to be baptized by him, "Brood of vipers![m] Who warned you to flee from the coming wrath? [8] Therefore produce fruit consistent with repentance. And don't start saying to yourselves, 'We have Abraham as our father,'[n] for I tell you that God is able to raise up children for Abra-

[a]2:48 Mt 12:46 [b]Lk 2:49; 3:23; 4:22 [c]2:50 Mk 9:32; Lk 9:45; 18:34 [d]2:51 Lk 2:19 [e]2:52 Lk 2:40 [f]3:1 Mt 27:2 [g]Mt 14:1 [h]3:2 Jn 18:13,24; Ac 4:6 [i]Mt 26:3 [j]3:2-10 Mt 3:1-10; Mk 1:3-5 [k]3:3 Mt 3:5 [l]3:4-6 Is 40:3-5 [m]3:7 Mt 12:34; 23:33 [n]3:8 Jn 8:33

[A]2:49 Or be involved in My Father's interests (or things), or be among My Father's people   [B]3:1 Emperor who ruled the Roman Empire A.D. 14–37   [C]3:1 Or ruler   [D]3:1 A small province northeast of Galilee   [E]3:1 A small Syrian province   [F]3:3 Or baptism based on repentance   [G]3:5 Lit be humbled   [H]3:6 Lit all flesh   [I]3:4–6 Is 40:3-5

Jerusalem, one coming back, and the third searching for Jesus in the city. The **teachers** were rabbis who were scholars of the Mosaic law. It was highly unusual for a boy to be welcomed by a group of rabbis, much less amaze them with brilliant scriptural **understanding**.

2:48-50 Joseph and Mary **did not understand** that Jesus was referring to His heavenly Father (**My Father's house**; i.e., the temple), whom He also had to obey even when such obedience entailed giving His parents' concerns less priority.

2:51 The phrase **kept all these things in her heart**, like verse 19, implies that Mary herself was Luke's source for much of the unique material in chapters 1 and 2.

2:52 During the years in which Jesus lived in obedience to Joseph and Mary, He continually increased in **wisdom** (intellect and practical holiness), **stature** (growing to adult size), **favor with God** (spiritual closeness to the Father) and favor with **people** (social respect). Jesus' wisdom was already noteworthy as a young boy (see note at v. 40), and the rabbis marveled at His understanding at age 12. His advancement would have been astounding by the time He began His ministry.

3:1 The **fifteenth year of...Tiberius Caesar** could be as early as A.D. 26 or as late as 29 because Tiberius had been delegated some of the authority of his stepfather, Augustus (see note at 2:1), several years before he died. **Pontius Pilate was governor of Judea**, Samaria, and Idumea (south of Judea, west of the Dead Sea), A.D. 26–36. He was responsible for regional administration and tax collection. At the death of Herod the Great (4 B.C.), his son, **Herod** Antipas, became **tetrarch** (a secondary prince) of **Galilee** and Perea (east of the Jordan River), while another son, Herod **Philip**, was tetrarch...**of Iturea and Trachonitis** (east and northeast of

the Sea of Galilee), A.D. 4–34. Nothing else is known about **Lysanius tetrarch of Abilene** (the area near Damascus).

3:2-3 Technically, the **high priesthood** of Annas ended by A.D. 18. However, he continued to use the title and exercise considerable influence while his son-in-law **Caiaphas** was high priest during most of the period until 37. **John** the Baptist lived in **the wilderness** of Judea for a number of years before this (see note at 1:80), then moved a few miles northeast to **the vicinity of the Jordan** River, probably not far north of the Dead Sea. John preached **repentance** (a change of mind and heart, in this case toward Jesus and one's personal sins) **for the forgiveness of sins**, with water **baptism** being the outer sign of inner cleansing.

3:4-6 The quotation from Is 40:3-5 shows that John was the forerunner of the Messiah (**prepare the way for the Lord**; see Mal 3:1; 4:5). The apocalyptic language figuratively depicts the earth becoming level (**every mountain...made low**) and all **paths straight** before the coming Christ. **Everyone** (lit "all flesh") indicates that both Gentiles and Jews would see God's salvation.

3:7 Some among **the crowds** who flocked to hear John preach (see note at vv. 2-3) and **be baptized** (Gk *baptizo*; "to wash, dip") were not sincere. John called them poisonous snakes and warned them to change their attitudes and **flee...the coming wrath** (judgment based on God's righteous anger). Jesus rescues believers from "the coming wrath" (1Th 1:10).

3:8-9 The **fruit** (behavioral impact) of **repentance** (see note at vv. 10-14), or the lack of it, proves whether or not a person has truly repented. At the time of judgment (**the ax is ready is strike**), the claim of Jewish lineage (**Abraham as our father**) will mean nothing unless a person's faith is genuine, like Abraham's (see Gn 15:6; Gl 3:6-7).

ham from these stones! ⁹Even now the ax is ready to strike[A] the root of the trees! Therefore, every tree that doesn't produce good fruit will be cut down and thrown into the fire."[a]

¹⁰"What then should we do?"[b] the crowds were asking him.

¹¹He replied to them, "The one who has two shirts[B] must share with someone who has none, and the one who has food must do the same."[c]

¹²Tax collectors also came to be baptized, and they asked him, "Teacher, what should we do?"[d]

¹³He told them, "Don't collect any more than what you have been authorized."

¹⁴Some soldiers also questioned him: "What should we do?"

He said to them, "Don't take money from anyone by force or false accusation; be satisfied with your wages."

¹⁵Now the people were waiting expectantly, and all of them were debating in their minds[c] whether John might be the •Messiah.[e] ¹⁶John answered them all,[f] "I baptize you with[D] water, but One is coming who is more powerful than I. I am not worthy to untie the strap of His sandals. He will baptize you with[D] the Holy Spirit and fire. ¹⁷His winnowing shovel[E,g] is in His hand to clear His threshing floor and gather the wheat into His barn, but the chaff He will burn up with a fire that never goes out."[h] ¹⁸Then, along with many other exhortations, he proclaimed good news to the people. ¹⁹But Herod the tetrarch,[i] being rebuked by him about Herodias, his brother's wife, and about all the evil things Herod had done,[j] ²⁰added this to everything else—he locked John up in prison.[k]

The Baptism of Jesus

²¹When all the people were baptized,[l] Jesus also was baptized. As He was praying,[m] heaven opened, ²²and the Holy Spirit descended on Him in a physical appearance like a dove. And a voice came from heaven:

You are My beloved Son.
I take delight in You![n]

The Genealogy of Jesus Christ

²³As He began His ministry, Jesus was about 30 years old and was thought to be[F] the

Cross references (center column):
a 3:9 Mt 7:19; Lk 13:6-9
b 3:10 Ac 2:37-38
c 3:11 Is 58:7
d 3:12 Mt 9:10-11; 21:31-32; Lk 5:29-30; 7:29; 15:1
e 3:15 Jn 1:19-20
f 3:16-17 Mt 3:11-12; Mk 1:7-8
g 3:17 Is 30:24
h Mk 9:43,48
i 3:19 Mt 14:3; Mk 6:17
j Mt 14:1; Lk 3:1
k 3:20 Jn 3:24
l 3:21-22 Mt 3:13-17; Mk 1:9-11
m 3:21 Mt 14:23; Lk 5:16; 9:18,28-29
n 3:22 Ps 2:7; Is 42:1; Mt 3:17; 17:5; Mk 1:11; Lk 9:35; 2Pt 1:17

A 3:9 Lit *the ax lies at*   B 3:11 Lit *tunics*   C 3:15 Or *hearts*   D 3:16 Or *in*   E 3:17 A wooden farm implement used to toss threshed grain into the wind so the lighter chaff would blow away and separate from the heavier grain   F 3:23 People did not know about His virgin birth; Mt 1:18-25; Lk 1:26-38

3:10-14 The question the crowds asked John (what then should we do?) is the same as the one addressed to Peter on the day of Pentecost (Ac 2:37). To the general population, John answered: be compassionate (share with someone who has none); to the tax collectors (who were allowed to raise taxes to cover "expenses"): don't collect any more than is owed; to the soldiers: don't abuse military power but instead be satisfied with your wages.

3:15-17 John knew that the throngs of people wondered if he was the long-awaited Messiah. He answered that there was no comparison between him baptizing with water and Messiah baptizing with the Holy Spirit (see Ac 1:5; 2:4; 1Co 12:13) and fire of judgment. On winnowing, see Ru 3:1-3. Chaff (symbolizing unbelievers) is the worthless husk that covers wheat (standing for believers); it is separated at harvest and burned. A fire that never goes out refers, ultimately, to the eternal lake of fire (Rv 20:10,14-15).

3:18 As well as preaching related to repentance (v. 3), John also proclaimed good news (Gk *euangelizo*; "to preach the gospel"), consistent with the message Messiah was prophesied to deliver (see note at 4:18).

3:19 On Herod Antipas, the tetrarch, see note at verse 1. Antipas divorced his wife, the daughter of King Aretas IV of Arabia, so he could marry the wife of his brother Philip (Mt 14:3; see note at Lk 3:1). Such a marriage was forbidden by Mosaic law (Lv 18:16; 20:21).

3:20 The events here are not given in chronological sequence, since John could not have baptized Jesus (see note at vv. 21-22) while he was in prison. Luke wrapped up his discussion of John's ministry before moving on to the beginning of Jesus' ministry. John was arrested at some point after Jesus began His public ministry (Jn 3:22-24). Josephus, the Jewish historian, stated John was held in the Machaerus prison, east of the Dead Sea.

3:21-22 Jesus was not baptized for the forgiveness of sins, as were all the other people whom John baptized. Rather, Jesus was baptized to identify Himself and His ministry with the ministry and message of His forerunner (see notes at vv. 4-6 and vv. 15-17). Prayer, especially Jesus' praying, is a strong emphasis of Luke's Gospel. This is the first of three times in the Gospels when a voice from heaven spoke about Jesus. The other two were at the transfiguration (see note at 9:34-35) and in the temple during Passion Week (Jn 12:28). This is a relatively rare scriptural passage in which all three persons of the Godhead are mentioned: (1) the Father who said, You are My beloved Son, (2) Jesus the Divine Son, who was being baptized, and (3) the Holy Spirit who was in physical appearance like a dove. The words "You are My beloved Son" echo Ps 2:7, while I take delight in You looks back to a key prophecy of the messianic Servant in Is 42:1.

3:23-38 The family tree of Jesus in the Gospel of Luke is considerably different from the one in Mt 1:1-17. Luke's genealogy traced Jesus' lineage all the way back to Adam, emphasizing Jesus' relation to all humankind, while Matthew's version started with Abraham and moved forward to Jesus, emphasizing Jesus' relation to Israel (i.e., that He was the Son of Abraham, fulfiller of the Abrahamic promises, and the messianic Son of David). In Luke, the family tree moved through Nathan, a younger son of David (Lk 3:30), while in Matthew it went through Solomon (Mt 1:6-7), inheritor of Israel's throne after David. Since Lk 1–2 narrates events from Mary's point of view, Lk 3:23-38 follows Jesus' physical line through Mary since verse 23 says Jesus was only "thought to be the son of Joseph." By contrast, Mt 1:1-17, in the midst of a section from Joseph's point of view (Mt 1–2), tracked Jesus' legal lineage. This demonstrated His right to the throne of David through His adoptive father, Joseph.

3:23 Jesus began His ministry at about 30 years old—the

son of Joseph,[a] son[A] of Heli,
[24] son of Matthat, son of Levi,
son of Melchi, son of Jannai,
son of Joseph, [25] son of Mattathias,
son of Amos, son of Nahum,
son of Esli, son of Naggai,
[26] son of Maath, son of Mattathias,
son of Semein, son of Josech,
son of Joda, [27] son of Joanan,
son of Rhesa, son of Zerubbabel,[b]
son of Shealtiel, son of Neri,
[28] son of Melchi, son of Addi,
son of Cosam, son of Elmadam,
son of Er, [29] son of Joshua,
son of Eliezer, son of Jorim,
son of Matthat, son of Levi,
[30] son of Simeon, son of Judah,
son of Joseph, son of Jonam,
son of Eliakim, [31] son of Melea,
son of Menna, son of Mattatha,
son of Nathan, son of David,
[32] son of Jesse,[c] son of Obed,
son of Boaz, son of Salmon,[B]
son of Nahshon, [33] son of Amminadab,
son of Ram,[C] son of Hezron,
son of Perez, son of Judah,
[34] son of Jacob, son of Isaac,
son of Abraham,[d] son of Terah,
son of Nahor, [35] son of Serug,
son of Reu, son of Peleg,
son of Eber, son of Shelah,
[36] son of Cainan, son of Arphaxad,

a3:23 Mt 1:16
b3:27 Mt 1:12
c3:32-34 Mt 1:1-6
d3:34-36 Gn 11:26-30; 1Ch 1:24-27
e3:36-38 Gn 5:3-32; 1Ch 1:1-4
f4:1-13 Mt 4:1-11; Mk 1:12-13
g4:1 Lk 3:3
h4:4 Dt 8:3
i4:6 1Jn 5:19
j4:8 Dt 6:13

son of Shem, son of Noah,[e]
son of Lamech,
[37] son of Methuselah,
son of Enoch, son of Jared,
son of Mahalaleel,
son of Cainan,
[38] son of Enos, son of Seth,
son of Adam, son of God.

The Temptation of Jesus

4 Then Jesus[f] returned from the Jordan,[g] full of the Holy Spirit, and was led by the Spirit in the wilderness [2] for 40 days to be tempted by the Devil. He ate nothing during those days, and when they were over,[D] He was hungry. [3] The Devil said to Him, "If You are the Son of God, tell this stone to become bread."

[4] But Jesus answered him, "It is written: **Man must not live on bread alone.**"[E,F,h]

[5] So he took Him up[G] and showed Him all the kingdoms of the world in a moment of time. [6] The Devil said to Him, "I will give You their splendor and all this authority, because it has been given over to me,[i] and I can give it to anyone I want. [7] If You, then, will worship me,[H] all will be Yours."

[8] And Jesus answered him,[I] "It is written:

**Worship the Lord your God,
and serve[j] Him only.**"[J]

[9] So he took Him to Jerusalem, had Him

[A]3:23 The relationship in some cases may be more distant than a son.   [B]3:32 Other mss read *Sala*   [C]3:33 Other mss read *Amminadab, son of Aram, son of Joram*; other mss read *Amminadab, son of Admin, son of Arni*   [D]4:2 Lit *were completed*   [E]4:4 Other mss add *but on every word of God*   [F]4:4 Dt 8:3   [G]4:5 Other mss read *So the Devil took Him up on a high mountain*   [H]4:7 Lit *will fall down before me*   [I]4:8 Other mss add "*Get behind Me, Satan!*   [J]4:8 Dt 6:13

---

age when a Levite began priestly service (Nm 4:46-47; see note at Lk 1:80). **Thought to be the son of Joseph** affirms the prophecy of the virgin birth of Jesus (see notes at 1:31-33 and 1:34-35). Jesus was not Joseph's *physical* son, as everyone around them mistakenly assumed (see note at 4:22).

3:38 Adam is called **son of God** in this genealogy because he was directly created by God (see Gn 2:7).

4:1-2 When Jesus returned from being baptized by John (see note at 3:21-22), He was full of the **Holy Spirit** and was led by the Spirit to His encounter with **the Devil** in **the wilderness**. The role of the Holy Spirit here is significant for at least three reasons: (1) the Spirit's role in driving Jesus to the wilderness shows Jesus' face-off with the Devil was ordained by God; (2) the Spirit's activity is a repeated emphasis in Luke's Gospel; (3) the Spirit's involvement in Jesus' life highlights Jesus' genuine humanity. The filling (Eph 5:18) and leading of the Spirit (Gl 5:18) are key aspects of empowerment for the Christian life. The wilderness is where Israel failed its test of faith before God (Nm 14). Jesus would pass the wilderness test that Israel could not. Also, Jesus was being tested as "the last Adam" (1Co 15:45), the One who would succeed where the first Adam failed. The Greek word translated **tempted** *(peirazo)* is more commonly rendered "tested."

4:3-4 Satan tested Jesus at the point of His physical weakness—hunger ("tell this stone to become bread," v. 2). The phrase **if you are the Son of God** expresses no doubt that Jesus is God, and is best understood as, "*Since* you are the Son of God." The Devil tried to bait Jesus into satisfying His extreme hunger by exercising His divine powers. Jesus' duty, however, was to suffer and patiently endure hardship as a perfectly obedient human who waited for God's deliverance and empowerment (v. 1). Jesus answered by citing the written Word of God (Dt 8:3). The context of this citation deals with Israel's needs being met in the wilderness for 40 years, physically through the manna and spiritually by the presence and Word of God.

4:5-12 The order of the second and third tests is reversed in Lk 4 from Mt 4. The obvious reason would be that the wider structure of the Gospel of Luke depicted Jesus moving toward Jerusalem, with the final test in Luke taking place on the pinnacle of the temple in Jerusalem.

4:5-8 As Messiah, Jesus will rule over **all the kingdoms of the world** at the end of the age (see Rv 11:15). The Devil tried to entice Jesus with a shortcut to that kind of worldwide authority. Even though Satan is called "the ruler of this world" (Jn 12:31), his claim that the world **was given over** to him and that he can **give it to anyone** he wants is untrue.

stand on the pinnacle of the temple, and said to Him, "If You are the Son of God, throw Yourself down from here. [10] For it is written:

> He will give His angels orders
>   concerning you,
> to protect you,[A,a] [11] and
> they will support you with their hands,
> so that you will not strike
>   your foot against a stone."[B,b]

[12] And Jesus answered him, "It is said: **Do not test the Lord your God.**"[C,c]

[13] After the Devil had finished every temptation, he departed from Him for a time.

Ministry in Galilee

[14] Then Jesus returned to Galilee in the power of the Spirit,[d] and news about Him spread throughout the entire vicinity.[e] [15] He was teaching in their *synagogues,[f] being acclaimed[D] by everyone.

Rejection at Nazareth

[16] He came to Nazareth, where He had been brought up.[g] As usual, He entered the synagogue on the Sabbath day[h] and stood up to read.[i] [17] The scroll of the prophet Isaiah was given to Him, and unrolling the scroll, He found the place where it was written:

> [18] **The Spirit of the Lord is on Me,**
>   **because He has anointed Me**
> **to preach good news to the poor.**
> **He has sent Me[E]**
> **to proclaim freedom[F] to the captives**
>   **and recovery of sight**
>   **to the blind,**
> **to set free the oppressed,**
>   [19] **to proclaim the year**
>   **of the Lord's favor.**[G,H,j]

[20] He then rolled up the scroll, gave it back to the attendant, and sat down.[k] And the eyes of everyone in the synagogue were fixed on Him. [21] He began by saying to them, "Today as you listen, this Scripture has been fulfilled."

[22] They were all speaking well of Him[I] and were amazed by the gracious words that came from His mouth, yet they said, "Isn't this Joseph's son?"[l]

[23] Then He said to them, "No doubt you will quote this proverb[J] to Me: 'Doctor, heal yourself.

Cross references

a4:10 Ps 91:11
b4:11 Ps 91:12
c4:12 Dt 6:16
d4:14 Mt 4:12
eMt 9:26; Lk 4:37
f4:15 Mt 4:23
g4:16 Lk 2:39,51
hMt 13:54; Mk 6:1-2
iAc 13:14-16
j4:18-19 Is 61:1-2; Mt 11:5; 12:18; Jn 3:34
k4:20 Mt 26:55
l4:22 Mt 13:55; Mk 6:3; Jn 6:42

Footnotes

A4:10 Ps 91:11   B4:11 Ps 91:12   C4:12 Dt 6:16   D4:15 Or *glorified*   E4:18 Other mss add *to heal the brokenhearted,*   F4:18 Or *release,* or *forgiveness*   G4:19 The time of messianic grace   H4:18-19 Is 61:1-2   I4:22 Or *They were testifying against Him*   J4:23 Or *parable*

The Devil is a usurper of God's realm. It is no surprise that he did not tell the truth here, for he is "a liar and the father of liars" (Jn 8:44). Jesus quoted Dt 6:13 to make clear that only God is worthy of **worship**, a point that echoes the first of the Ten Commandments (Ex 20:3).

4:9-12 After two failed tests (vv. 3-8), the Devil attempted to catch Jesus off balance by quoting Scripture. In challenging Jesus to **throw** Himself from **the pinnacle of the temple** (from which the fall may have been over 100 feet), the Devil referred to Ps 91:11-12, claiming that **angels** would rush to the rescue if Jesus jumped. Jesus did not deny the truth of the Scripture the Devil quoted, just the application he gave it. In clear contrast, He cited Dt 6:16, which recalls the tragedy of Israel's complaining and testing God at Meribah and Massah (Ex 17:1-7).

4:13 Only three tests are recorded in Mt 4 and Lk 4, but the wording **every temptation** may imply that there were more. The Devil was thwarted this time, but he **departed** from Jesus only to wait for the right **time** (Gk *kairos*; "time"—as an occasion or opportunity) to try again.

4:14-15 The same **power** of the Holy **Spirit** (see note at vv. 1-2) by which Jesus countered every test thrown at Him by the Devil, was present in His **teaching** in the **synagogues** throughout **Galilee**, bringing initial acceptance by virtually **everyone**.

4:16-17 Jesus lived (was **brought up**) in **Nazareth** in Galilee from the time He was a small boy (2:39,51) until He began His public ministry, when He was "about 30 years old" (see note at 3:23). When Jesus lived at His family home in Nazareth, He always worshiped in this **synagogue** on the **Sabbath** (the Sabbath lasted from Friday night at sundown to Saturday night at sundown). From what is known about synagogue services of that era, the reading from the Mosaic law (Hb *torah*) was usually prescribed, while the person

chosen to read from the books of the Prophets (Hb *nebi'im*) had the latitude to choose any passage he wished. When Jesus was given the **Isaiah** scroll, He unrolled it and began reading from Is 61:1.

4:18 Jesus' ministry throughout Galilee demonstrated that **the Spirit of the Lord** was on Him (v. 14). As Messiah, He was **anointed** as the rightful king of Israel. But here the anointing was as a prophet (**to preach good news**). Even though the message Jesus preached was first to those who were captivated by sin, the mention of **the poor . . . the captives . . . the blind**, and **the oppressed** is in keeping with Luke's emphasis on the poor and downtrodden.

4:19-21 Jesus stopped reading from Is 61 in the middle of verse 2 and **sat down** (the normal posture for reading Scripture was standing; teaching was done while sitting). He ended the reading precisely at the phrase **to proclaim the year of the Lord's favor** because this is exactly what His preaching proclaimed: the season of God's grace had come in Messiah's ministry. The very next phrase in Is 61:2, which Jesus did not read, is "and the day of our God's vengeance." This refers to the second coming of Christ and His judgment of the world (Rv 19:11-21). Thus Jesus read in the synagogue the part of Is 61:1-2 that was being **fulfilled** at that time, but held off on reading the portion that would not be fulfilled until the time of judgment.

4:22 The immediate response to Jesus' message in the synagogue was mostly positive, as it had been elsewhere in Galilee (see note at vv. 14-15). But knowing Is 61 was a messianic prophecy, it greatly troubled the people that the young preacher whom they thought of merely as **Joseph's son** (see note at 3:23-28) was claiming to be the long-awaited Messiah.

4:23-24 The people in Jesus' **hometown** of Nazareth, motivated by curiosity rather than genuine spiritual interest,

So all we've heard that took place in Capernaum,[a] do here in Your hometown also.'"

[24]He also said, "'I assure you: No prophet is accepted in his hometown.[b] [25]But I say to you, there were certainly many widows in Israel in Elijah's days,[c] when the sky was shut up for three years and six months while a great famine came over all the land. [26]Yet Elijah was not sent to any of them—but to a widow at Zarephath in Sidon. [27]And in the prophet Elisha's time, there were many in Israel who had serious skin diseases, yet not one of them was healed[A]—only Naaman the Syrian."[d]

[28]When they heard this, everyone in the synagogue was enraged. [29]They got up, drove Him out of town,[e] and brought Him to the edge[B] of the hill that their town was built on, intending to hurl Him over the cliff. [30]But He passed right through the crowd and went on His way.[f]

Driving Out an Unclean Spirit

[31]Then He went down to Capernaum,[g] a town in Galilee, and was teaching them on the Sabbath. [32]They were astonished at His teaching because His message had authority.[h] [33]In the synagogue there was a man with an •unclean demonic spirit who cried out with a loud voice,[i] [34]"Leave us alone![C] What do You have to do with us,[D] Jesus—•Nazarene? Have You come to destroy us? I know who You are—the Holy One of God!"

[35]But Jesus rebuked him[j] and said, "Be quiet and come out of him!"

And throwing him down before them, the demon came out of him without hurting him at all. [36]Amazement came over them all, and they kept saying to one another, "What is this message? For He commands the unclean spirits with authority and power, and they come out!" [37]And news about Him began to go out to every place in the vicinity.

Healings at Capernaum

[38]After He left the synagogue, He entered Simon's house.[k] Simon's mother-in-law was suffering from a high fever, and they asked Him about her. [39]So He stood over her and rebuked the fever, and it left her. She got up immediately and began to serve them.

[40]When the sun was setting, all those who had anyone sick with various diseases brought them to Him. As He laid His hands on each one of them, He would heal them.[l] [41]Also, demons were coming out of many, shouting and saying, "You are the Son of God!"[m] But He rebuked them and would not allow them to speak, because they knew He was the •Messiah.[n]

Preaching in Galilee

[42]When it was day, He went out and made His way to a deserted place.[o] But the crowds were searching for Him. They came to Him and tried to keep Him from leaving them.

Cross references (center column):
a 4:23 Mt 11:23; Mk 2:1-12; Jn 4:46-53
b 4:24 Mt 13:57; Mk 6:4; Jn 4:44
c 4:25 1Kg 17:1; 18:1; Jms 5:17
d 4:27 2Kg 5:1-14
e 4:29 Nm 15:35; Ac 7:58; Heb 13:12
f 4:30 Jn 10:39
g 4:31-37 Mk 1:21-28
h 4:32 Mt 7:28-29; Mk 1:22; Jn 7:46
i 4:33-37 Mk 1:23-28
j 4:35 Mt 8:26; Mk 4:39; Lk 4:39,41; 8:24
k 4:38-41 Mt 8:14-17; Mk 1:29-34
l 4:40 Mt 4:23; Mk 5:23
m 4:41 Mt 4:3
n Mt 8:16; Mk 1:34; 3:11-12
o 4:42-43 Mk 1:35-38

A 4:27 Lit cleansed   B 4:29 Lit brow   C 4:34 Or Ha!, or Ah!   D 4:34 Lit What to us and to You

---

expected to see Him **heal**, as they had heard about Him doing in nearby **Capernaum**. Instead of satisfying them, Jesus illustrated a principle that often proved true in OT times: A **prophet** (see 4:18; Is 61:1) is not **accepted** in his hometown.

4:25-27 Jesus' first example of a prophet being rejected by his own people was **Elijah**, who was so unpopular in Israel during the **three years and six months** of a drought that he had to seek refuge in the home of a widow in the Gentile town of **Zarephath** in Phoenicia, on the Mediterranean coast, northwest of Galilee (1Kg 17:1-24). The second example was the prophet Elisha, who skipped over all the lepers of Israel in his time and only **healed . . . Naaman the Syrian**, a Gentile general (2Kg 7:1-19).

4:28-30 The crowd in the synagogue **was enraged** because Jesus' examples implied God's acceptance of Gentiles and His rejection of Israel. Jesus foiled their attempt at mob violence by walking **right through the crowd**, an odd circumstance that may imply a miracle. Alternatively, it may only indicate that Jesus' presence was so forceful that the people, though angry, willingly stepped aside and let Him through.

4:31-32 Luke does not elaborate on the exact nature of the **authority** that Jesus demonstrated through His **teaching** in Capernaum on the **Sabbath**. Most likely the authority derived from the fact that Jesus' message was directly from

God, not merely from the religious authorities of earlier generations whom Jewish teachers typically cited.

4:33-36 This is an example of the far-reaching authority Jesus displayed in Capernaum. He cast out **an unclean demonic spirit** that had possessed a man in the synagogue. Jesus did this simply by the rebuke, **Be quiet and come out of him**. The crowds wondered about Jesus, His message, and His power over the demonic realm, but the demon knew exactly who Jesus was—**the Holy One of God**—a title that Simon Peter also used of Jesus (Jn 6:69).

4:38-40 Jesus' authority also extended to physical illness. As He had done with the demon, Jesus **rebuked the fever**, and Simon Peter's **mother-in-law** was immediately healed. As a result, word of Jesus' authority over sickness spread through Capernaum. He **laid His hands** on many people with **various diseases**, healing all of them.

4:41 As He healed the physical diseases of many people in Capernaum, Jesus also cast out more **demons**. This leaves the strong impression that demons were able to cause some diseases. As with the demon in the man in the synagogue (vv. 33-36), the demons identified Jesus as divine. Jesus **rebuked** the demons for revealing that He was **the Messiah** because they were attempting to assert control over Him by revealing who He was before the appropriate time.

4:42-44 This is the first of more than 30 times that **the king-**

[43] But He said to them, "I must proclaim the good news about the kingdom of God to the other towns also, because I was sent for this purpose." [44] And He was preaching in the synagogues of Galilee.[A,a]

The First Disciples

5 As the crowd was pressing in on Jesus to hear God's word,[b] He was standing by Lake Gennesaret.[B,c] [2] He saw two boats at the edge of the lake;[c] the fishermen had left them and were washing their nets. [3] He got into one of the boats,[d] which belonged to Simon, and asked him to put out a little from the land. Then He sat down and was teaching the crowds from the boat.

[4] When He had finished speaking, He said to Simon, "Put out into deep water and let down[D] your nets for a catch."[e]

[5] "Master,"[f] Simon replied, "we've worked hard all night long and caught nothing! But at Your word, I'll let down the nets."[E]

[6] When they did this, they caught a great number of fish, and their nets[E] began to tear. [7] So they signaled to their partners in the other boat to come and help them; they came and filled both boats so full that they began to sink.

[8] When Simon Peter saw this, he fell at Jesus' knees and said, "Go away from me, because I'm a sinful man, Lord!" [9] For he and all

*a*4:44 Mt 4:23; Mk 1:39
*b*5:1-11 Mt 4:18-22; Mk 1:16-20; Jn 1:40-42
*c*5:1 Nm 34:11; Dt 3:17; Jos 12:3; 13:27; Mt 4:18
*d*5:3 Mt 13:2; Mk 3:9-10; 4:1
*e*5:4-6 Jn 21:3-6
*f*5:5 Lk 8:24; 9:33,49; 17:13

A4:44 Other mss read *Judea*   B5:1 = Sea of Galilee   C5:2 Lit *boats standing by the lake*   D5:4 Lit *and you* (pl in Gk) *let down*   E5:5,6 Other mss read *net* (Gk sg)

---

dom of God is mentioned in Luke's Gospel. A full-blown concept of the kingdom includes: (1) the King (ruler), (2) the rule itself (sovereignty to rule), (3) the realm being ruled (this world), and (4) those ruled (individuals who believe the good news of Jesus Christ). In addition, some passages in the Gospels present the kingdom of God as already present in at least some senses (Mt 12:28) while others speak of it as being still future (Mt 6:10).

5:1-3 Lake Gennesaret was an alternate name for the Sea of Galilee, which is also called the Sea of Tiberias (Jn 6:1; 21:1). The boat Jesus chose belonged to **Simon** Peter, whose mother-in-law He had recently healed (4:38-39).

Jesus **sat down** in the boat; this was the normal posture for a teacher (see note at 4:19-21).

5:4-7 In spite of the fact that his night labors had been fruitless, at Jesus' command Peter responded in faith (**at Your word, I'll let down the nets**). His faith was rewarded with a catch so big that their nets tore and the boats almost sank.

5:8-11 Peter's realization of Jesus' divine power and holiness through **the catch of fish** was essentially the same as that of Job (Jb 42:6) and Isaiah (Is 6:5). **James and John**, along with Simon Peter, formed Jesus' inner circle (9:28; Mt 26:37). Jesus used the huge catch of fish to illustrate the kind of evangelistic impact Simon would have (**catching

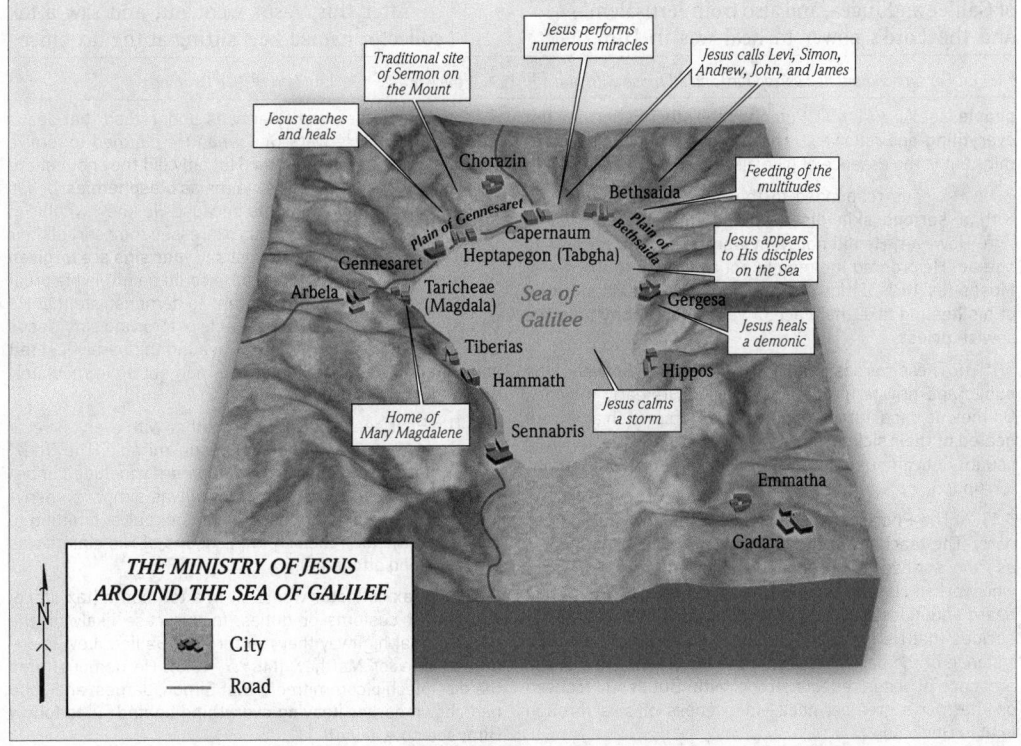

Jesus teaches and heals

Traditional site of Sermon on the Mount

Jesus performs numerous miracles

Jesus calls Levi, Simon, Andrew, John, and James

Chorazin

Bethsaida

Feeding of the multitudes

Plain of Gennesaret

Capernaum

Plain of Bethsaida

Gennesaret

Heptapegon (Tabgha)

Jesus appears to His disciples on the Sea

Arbela

Taricheae (Magdala)

Sea of Galilee

Gergesa

Jesus heals a demonic

Tiberias

Hippos

Hammath

Jesus calms a storm

Home of Mary Magdalene

Sennabris

Emmatha

Gadara

THE MINISTRY OF JESUS AROUND THE SEA OF GALILEE

N

City

Road

those with him were amazed^A at the catch of fish they took, ¹⁰and so were James and John, Zebedee's sons, who were Simon's partners.

"Don't be afraid,"^a Jesus told Simon. "From now on you will be catching people!"^b ¹¹Then they brought the boats to land, left everything, and followed Him.^c

A Man Cleansed

¹²While He was in one of the towns, a man was there who had a serious skin disease all over him.^d He saw Jesus, fell facedown, and begged Him: "Lord, if You are willing, You can make me •clean."

¹³Reaching out His hand, He touched him, saying, "I am willing; be made clean," and immediately the disease left him. ¹⁴Then He ordered him to tell no one: "But go and show yourself to the priest, and offer what Moses prescribed for your cleansing as a testimony to them."

¹⁵But the news^B about Him spread even more, and large crowds would come together to hear Him and to be healed of their sicknesses. ¹⁶Yet He often withdrew to deserted places and prayed.^e

The Son of Man Forgives and Heals

¹⁷On one of those days while He was teaching, •Pharisees and teachers of the law^f were sitting there who had come from every village of Galilee and Judea, and also from Jerusalem. And the Lord's power to heal was in Him.^g

¹⁸Just then some men came,^h carrying on a mat a man who was paralyzed. They tried to bring him in and set him down before Him. ¹⁹Since they could not find a way to bring him in because of the crowd, they went up on the roof and lowered him on the mat through the roof tiles into the middle of the crowd before Jesus.

²⁰Seeing their faith He said, "Friend,^c your sins are forgiven you."

²¹Then the •scribes and the Pharisees^i began to think: "Who is this man who speaks blasphemies? Who can forgive sins but God alone?"^j

²²But perceiving their thoughts, Jesus replied to them, "Why are you thinking this in your hearts?^D ²³Which is easier: to say, 'Your sins are forgiven you,' or to say, 'Get up and walk'? ²⁴But so you may know that the •Son of Man has authority on earth to forgive sins"—He told the paralyzed man, "I tell you: Get up, pick up your mat, and go home."

²⁵Immediately he got up before them, picked up what he had been lying on, and went home glorifying God. ²⁶Then everyone was astounded, and they were giving glory to God. And they were filled with awe^k and said, "We have seen incredible things today!"

The Call of Matthew

²⁷After this, Jesus went out and saw a tax collector named Levi sitting at the tax office,^l

Cross References

a 5:10 Mt 14:27
b 2Tm 2:26
c 5:11 Mt 4:20,22; 19:29; Mk 1:18,20; Lk 5:28
d 5:12-14 Mt 8:2-4; Mk 1:40-44
e 5:16 Mt 14:23; Mk 1:35; Lk 6:12
f 5:17 Ac 5:34; 1Tm 1:7
g Mk 5:30; Lk 6:19; 8:46
h 5:18-26 Mt 9:2-8; Mk 2:3-12
i 5:21 Mt 23:2; Lk 11:53; Jn 8:3
j Is 43:25
k 5:26 Lk 1:65; 7:16
l 5:27-39 Mt 9:9-17; Mk 2:14-22

---

^A 5:9 Lit For amazement had seized him and all those with him   ^B 5:15 Lit the word   ^C 5:20 Lit Man   ^D 5:22 Or minds

---

people; see Ac 2:41; 4:4). Peter and the other fishermen **left everything** and followed Jesus. This thoroughgoing commitment is the essence of true discipleship (14:26).

5:12-14 Jesus responded to the faith of a leper (a man with a **serious skin disease**) and **immediately** healed him. However, He did not want word about the miracle to spread. He ordered the man to act according to the law of **Moses** (Lv 14:1-32) for **cleansing** and let the visual proof of his healing take the place of verbal **testimony** before a Jewish **priest**.

5:15-16 These verses reflect the difference between the public and private life of Jesus during His early ministry. On the one hand, **large crowds** heard Him preach and were **healed of their sicknesses**. On the other hand, Jesus often sought out remote places where He could pray without interruption.

5:17-20 The **Pharisees** were the legalistic Jewish religious party. The **teachers of the law** of Moses were also known as "the scribes." They functioned essentially as lawyers who worked closely with the Pharisees. These leaders had heard about Jesus' preaching and **power to heal**, and they decided that He needed to be observed carefully. The persistence of the paralyzed man's friends to get him into the presence of Jesus reflects strong **faith**. But Jesus focused on the man's greatest need—forgiveness of sins through faith in God's Son.

5:21-25 The scribes and Pharisees understood that Jesus was acting as if He were God when He claimed to forgive the **sins** of the paralyzed man. Not only did they not believe He was God, they viewed His claims as **blasphemies**. Jesus was **perceiving their thoughts** because He knew what is in man (Jn 2:25). In verse 23 Jesus expressed the heart of their doubt. It was much easier to just say **your sins are forgiven** than to heal a paralytic since there could be no visible proof of whether sins had been forgiven. To demonstrate that He had power to do the invisible miracle of forgiving sins, Jesus performed the visible miracle of healing the paralytic: **I tell you: Get up . . . and go home**. The man got up immediately and went home **glorifying God**.

5:26 The Pharisees and scribes together with everyone else in the crowd were **astounded** at Jesus' miracle. The "they" of **they were giving glory to God** apparently included unbelieving scribes and Pharisees. There was simply no denying the wonder of what Jesus had done, but submitting to Jesus and the far-reaching implications of His claims was another thing altogether.

5:27-28 A **tax collector** would sit in a toll booth (**tax office**) and collect customs or duties, in this case likely on the international highway that ran through Galilee. **Levi** is another name for Matthew (Mt 9:9; 10:3). He demonstrated the discipleship commitment that Simon, James, and John had shown earlier (**leaving everything behind . . . to follow Him**; see note at vv. 8-11).

and He said to him, "Follow Me!" ²⁸So, leaving everything behind, he got up and began to follow Him.

Dining with Sinners

²⁹Then Levi hosted a grand banquet for Him at his house. Now there was a large crowd of tax collectors and others who were guests^A with them.^a ³⁰But the Pharisees and their scribes^b were complaining to His disciples, "Why do you eat and drink with tax collectors and sinners?"

³¹Jesus replied to them, "The healthy don't need a doctor, but the sick do. ³²I have not come to call the righteous, but sinners to repentance."

A Question about Fasting

³³Then they said to Him, "John's disciples fast often and say prayers, and those of the Pharisees do the same, but Yours eat and drink."^B

³⁴Jesus said to them, "You can't make the wedding guests^C fast while the groom is with them, can you? ³⁵But the time^D will come^c

*a*5:29 Lk 15:1
*b*5:30 Mk 2:16; Ac 23:9
*c*5:35 1Sm 2:31; Ps 37:13; Ec 2:16; 12:1; Lk 17:22
*d*6:1-5 Mt 12:1-8; Mk 2:23-28

when the groom will be taken away from them—then they will fast in those days."

³⁶He also told them a parable: "No one tears a patch from a new garment and puts it on an old garment. Otherwise, not only will he tear the new, but also the piece from the new garment will not match the old. ³⁷And no one puts new wine into old wineskins. Otherwise, the new wine will burst the skins, it will spill, and the skins will be ruined. ³⁸But new wine should be put into fresh wineskins.^E ³⁹And no one, after drinking old wine, wants new, because he says, 'The old is better.'"^F

Lord of the Sabbath

6 On a Sabbath,^G He passed through the grainfields.^d His disciples were picking heads of grain, rubbing them in their hands, and eating them. ²But some of the •Pharisees said, "Why are you doing what is not lawful on the Sabbath?"

³Jesus answered them, "Haven't you read what David and those who were with him did when he was hungry— ⁴how he entered the house of God, and took and ate the •sacred

---

^A5:29 Lit *were reclining* (at the table); at important meals the custom was to recline on a mat at a low table and lean on the left elbow.　^B5:33 Other mss read *"Why do John's . . . drink?"* (as a question)　^C5:34 Or *the friends of the groom;* lit *sons of the bridal chamber*　^D5:35 Lit *days*　^E5:38 Other mss add *And so both are preserved.*　^F5:39 Other mss read *is good*　^G6:1 Other mss read *a second-first Sabbath;* perhaps a special Sabbath

---

5:29-30 Levi's becoming a disciple was very open. He hosted a **grand banquet** in honor of Jesus, to which he invited his fellow **tax collectors**. The Pharisees and scribes (see note at vv. 17-20) were incensed because tax collectors were considered ritually unclean. Tax collectors and **sinners** (others who were ritually unclean) were socially off-limits to devout Jews. Although Levi was a fellow Jew, he was despised because he worked for the Roman government.

5:31-32 Jesus referred to the Pharisees and their allies as the **healthy** and **righteous**. In contrast, He labeled tax collectors and their associates as the **sick** and **sinners**. He did not mean that the Pharisees were actually righteous, but only that they saw themselves that way. By contrast, those whom the Pharisees viewed as sinners realized they were spiritually sick and desperately needed a spiritual **doctor** who could guide them to **repentance** (see note at 3:2-3). Thus Jesus had higher regard for the sick and sinners.

5:33 The Pharisees were offended at the behavior of Jesus' **disciples** as compared to their own disciples and those of John the Baptist. Jesus was not opposed to fasting (Mt 4:2; 6:16-18), but He also allowed His disciples to attend banquets (**eat and drink**), like that given by Levi (see note at vv. 29-30). This was in stark contrast to the Pharisees' rigid schedule of fasting. They fasted twice weekly (18:12), on the Day of Atonement (Lv 16:29), four times a year to remember the destruction of Jerusalem by the Babylonians (Zch 8:19), plus any other time it was deemed appropriate.

5:34-35 Jesus applied the issue of fasting to a **wedding**, as if He were the **groom**. It was not appropriate to fast during the joy of a wedding or before the divine groom was **taken away** (i.e., before the cross, resurrection, and ascension).

5:36-37 The first of Jesus' two parables applied the principle

that you cannot patch an **old garment** with **new** cloth. It will tear the new cloth and it won't match the old garment. On the heels of the controversy about fasting, Jesus illustrated the point that His message was radical (the new) and could not serve as a patch for the existing form of Judaism (the old garment).

5:38-39 Jesus' second parable initially made the same point as the first, but then proceeded further. **New** (not fully fermented) **wine** cannot be put into **old wineskins** because it will **burst** and ruin them. New wine (the message of Jesus) must be put into **fresh wineskins** (the church of Jesus Christ; see Mt 16:18). But there was a natural reason why many of Jesus' hearers continued to cling to Judaism: old (properly fermented and aged) wine (the established traditions of Judaism) tastes **better** (more familiar and comfortable).

6:1-2 The controversy with the **Pharisees** shifts to the issue of keeping the Sabbath day. Deuteronomy 23:25 permitted going through a neighbor's field and **picking . . . grain**, as long as a person did not use a sickle. The issue here was the permissibility of such behavior on the **Sabbath**.

6:3-5 Jesus' argument in answering the Pharisees was that there are exceptions even to important religious standards. He cited the example of **David** eating the **sacred bread** (the "bread of the Presence" of God, kept in the holy place of the temple; 2Ch 2:4), which only **priests** were **to eat**. David once used this consecrated bread to feed himself and **those who were with him** (1Sm 21:1-6) in a time of need. **Son of Man** is a messianic title (see Dn 7:13) that Jesus often used of Himself (Lk 5:24; 19:10). As Messiah, Jesus was the same **Lord** who instituted the **Sabbath** regulations. Thus He had full authority to make an exception to the observance of this special day.

bread, which is not lawful for any but the priests to eat?[a] He even gave some to those who were with him."[b] [5] Then He told them, "The *Son of Man is Lord of the Sabbath."

The Man with the Paralyzed Hand

[6] On another Sabbath[c] He entered the *synagogue and was teaching. A man was there whose right hand was paralyzed. [7] The *scribes and Pharisees were watching Him closely,[d] to see if He would heal on the Sabbath, so that they could find a charge against Him.[e] [8] But He knew their thoughts[f] and told the man with the paralyzed hand, "Get up and stand here."[A] So he got up and stood there. [9] Then Jesus said to them, "I ask you: Is it lawful on the Sabbath to do what is good or to do what is evil, to save life or to destroy it?"[g] [10] After looking around at them all,[h] He told him, "Stretch out your hand."[i] He did so, and his hand was restored.[B] [11] They, however, were filled with rage and started discussing with one another what they might do to Jesus.

The 12 Apostles

[12] During those days He went out to the mountain to pray[j] and spent all night in prayer to God. [13] When daylight came, He summoned His disciples,[k] and He chose 12 of them—He also named them apostles:[l]

[14] Simon, whom He also named Peter,
and Andrew his brother;
James and John;
Philip and Bartholomew;
[15] Matthew and Thomas;[m]
James the son of Alphaeus,
and Simon called the Zealot;
[16] Judas the son of James,
and Judas Iscariot, who became
a traitor.

Teaching and Healing

[17] After coming down with them, He stood on a level place with a large crowd of His disciples and a great number of people from all Judea and Jerusalem and from the seacoast of Tyre and Sidon.[n] [18] They came to hear Him and to be healed of their diseases; and those tormented by *unclean spirits were made well. [19] The whole crowd was trying to touch Him,[o] because power was coming out from Him and healing them all.[p]

Cross-references (center column):

[a]6:4 Ex 25:30; Lv 24:5-9
[b]1Sm 21:6
[c]6:6-11 Mt 12:9-14; Mk 3:1-6
[d]6:7 Mk 3:2; Lk 14:1; 20:20
[e]Jn 8:6
[f]6:8 Mt 9:4
[g]6:9 Lk 14:3
[h]6:10 Mk 3:5
[i]1Kg 13:4
[j]6:12 Mt 14:23; Lk 5:16; 9:18,28
[k]6:13-16 Mt 10:2-4; Mk 3:16-19; Ac 1:13
[l]6:13 Mk 6:30
[m]6:15 Mt 9:9
[n]6:17 Mt 11:21
[o]6:19 Mt 9:21; 14:36; Mk 3:10
[p]Lk 5:17

[A]6:8 Lit *stand in the middle* [B]6:10 Other mss add *as sound as the other*

6:6-7 The second **Sabbath** controversy occurred in a **synagogue** while Jesus was teaching and a man affected by paralysis (cp. 5:17-25) was present. The **scribes and Pharisees** began watching His every move. They saw this as an opportunity to have Jesus charged and arrested.

6:8-10 On **He knew their thoughts**, see note at 5:21-25. When Jesus had the man with the **paralyzed hand** get up and stand near Him, He thrust the man's situation into the spotlight and confronted the Pharisees and scribes head-on. The answer to Jesus' rhetorical question was obvious. Everyone should agree that it was **lawful** to **do . . . good** or **save life** on the Sabbath. Because healing was doing good, it would be wrong not to heal this man, even on the Sabbath. By stretching out his hand in obedience to Jesus' command, the man's hand was **restored**.

6:11 The Pharisees and scribes were **filled with rage** that Jesus had outwitted them again. The parallel passages in Mt 12:14 and Mk 3:6 state that they wanted to "destroy" Jesus.

6:12-13 Although this is another example of Luke's emphasis on prayer, it is the only time it is said that Jesus **spent all night in prayer**. That Jesus prayed all night indicates the importance of the choice of the **12 . . . apostles** from the wider group of **His disciples**. While disciple (Gk *mathetes*) means "learner, pupil, follower," the meaning of apostle (Gk *apostolos*) is literally "sent one," with the idea of being sent with a commission. It is not stated why He chose 12 apostles, though the fact that Israel had 12 tribes was likely the reason.

6:14-16 Other lists of the apostles appear in Mt 10:2-4; Mk 3:16-19; and Ac 1:13. Although certain details vary among the lists, **Simon . . . Peter** is always listed first and the trai-tor . . . **Judas Iscariot**, is listed last. "Iscariot" (Gk *iskarioth*) may be derived from Judas's hometown of Kerioth or an Aramaic word meaning "assassin." **Bartholomew** is probably another name for Nathanael (Jn 1:45). **Matthew** is an alternate name for Levi (5:27,29). **Judas the son of James** seems to be the same as Thaddaeus (Mt 10:3).

6:17-49 This section of Luke's Gospel is often referred to as the Sermon on the Plain. It has many similarities to the Sermon on the Mount in Mt 5-7, but it is much shorter. The two best explanations for the similarities and differences are: (1) after becoming acquainted with the material found in Matthew, Luke selected and shaped the content to fit his purposes in writing (see notes at Lk 1:1; 1:2; 1:3; and 1:4 in regard to Luke's editorial approach), or (2) since Jesus undoubtedly preached the same material in various locations, it is possible that the Sermon on the Mount and the Sermon on the Plain were presented on different occasions.

6:17 If this is the same event as the Sermon on the Mount (Mt 5-7), the **level place** would be a plateau on the side of a mountain where Jesus went up to pray in 6:12. In Matthew, the message is directed only to the disciples of Jesus (Mt 5:1), while Luke added two other groups: (1) **a great number of people from all Judea and Jerusalem** (i.e., where Jesus would minister later), and (2) many people from **the seacoast of Tyre and Sidon** (these were probably Gentile regions).

6:18-19 The crowd did not gather just to hear Jesus preach. Many came to be healed of physical **diseases** or spiritual oppression by **unclean spirits** (demons). Since **power** (Gk *dunamis*) **was coming out from Him**, all who touched Jesus were healed.

The Apostles and Their History

Name	Surname	Parents	Home	Business	Writings	Work	Death
Simon	Peter or Cephas = Rock	Jonah	Early life: Bethsaida; Later: Capernaum	Fisherman	1 & 2 Peter	Peter may have ministered in the provinces of Pontus, Galatia, Cappadocia, Asia, perhaps in Corinth, and finally in Rome.	According to tradition, attested by Tertullian and Origin, Peter was crucified "with his head downwards" in Rome. The date of his death is likely between A.D. 64–68.
Andrew = manhood or valor		Jonah	Early life: Bethsaida; Later: Capernaum	Fisherman		Uncertain but tradition says he ministered in Cappadocia, Galatia, Bithynia; later in the Sythian deserts and Byzantium; and finally in Thrace, Macedonia, Thessaly, and Achaia.	The traditional view is that he was crucified at Patrae in Achaia by order of the Roman governor Ageas.
James the greater or the elder	Boanerges or Sons of Thunder	Zebedee and Salome	Bethsaida, Capernaum, and Jerusalem	Fisherman		Preached in Jerusalem and Judea	Beheaded by Herod in A.D. 62 or 66 in Jerusalem
John, the beloved disciple	Boanerges or Sons of Thunder	Zebedee and Salome	Bethsaida, Capernaum, and Jerusalem	Fisherman	Gospel, three epistles, and Revelation	Labored among the churches of Asia Minor, especially in Ephesus	Banished to Patmos A.D. 95. Recalled; died a natural death
James the less		Alphaeus and Mary	Galilee			Preached in Judea and Egypt	According to tradition, he was martyred in Egypt.
Judas (not Iscariot)	Same as Thaddaeus and Lebbaeus	James	Galilee			Preached in Mesopotamia and Armenia	Was martyred in present day Iran and buried near Tabriz
Philip			Bethsaida			Preached in Phrygia	Was martyred in Phrygia; tradition says that he was buried in Hieropolis.
Bartholomew	Nathaniel		Cana of Galilee			One tradition says he preached in India. Others say he ministered in Mesopotamia, Persia, Egypt, Armenia, Lycaonia, Phrygia, and on the shores of the Black Sea.	One tradition says King Astyages of Babylon had him flayed and beheaded because the king's brother had been converted under Bartholomew's preaching.
Matthew	Levi		Galilee	Tax Collector	Gospel	There is strong consensus that he preached to his own people for nearly two decades. He is also associated with Ethiopia to the south of the Caspian Sea, Parthia, Macedonia, and Syria.	Some sources say Matthew was martyred; others say he died a natural death.
Thomas	Didymus		Galilee			Tradition says Thomas brought the gospel to India.	He is said to have been killed with a spear. Later his remains were taken to Edessa.
Simon	The Zealot		Galilee			Preached in Persia	Tradition says Simon was tortured and sawed in two.
Judas	Iscariot	Simon Iscariot	Kerioth of Judea			Betrayed Jesus	Suicide

The Beatitudes

20 Then looking up at[A] His disciples, He said:[a]

You who are poor are blessed,
because the kingdom of God is yours.
21 You who are now hungry are blessed,
because you will be filled.
You who now weep are blessed,
because you will laugh.
22 You are blessed when people hate you,
when they exclude you,[b] insult you,
and slander your name as evil[c]
because of the Son of Man.[d]

23 "Rejoice in that day and leap for joy! Take note—your reward is great in heaven, for this is the way their ancestors used to treat the prophets.[e]

Woe to the Self-Satisfied

24 But woe to you who are rich,
for you have received your comfort.
25 Woe to you who are now full,
for you will be hungry.
Woe to you[B] who are now laughing,
for you will mourn and weep.
26 Woe to you[B]
when all people speak well of you,
for this is the way their ancestors
used to treat the false prophets.[f]

Love Your Enemies

27 "But I say to you who listen: Love your enemies, do what is good to those who hate you,

28 bless those who curse you, pray for those who mistreat you.[g] 29 If anyone hits you on the cheek,[h] offer the other also. And if anyone takes away your coat, don't hold back your shirt either. 30 Give to everyone who asks you, and from one who takes your things, don't ask for them back. 31 Just as you want others to do for you, do the same for them.[i] 32 If you love those who love you, what credit is that to you? Even sinners love those who love them.[j] 33 If you do what is good to those who are good to you, what credit is that to you? Even sinners do that. 34 And if you lend to those from whom you expect to receive, what credit is that to you?[k] Even sinners lend to sinners to be repaid in full. 35 But love your enemies, do what is good, and lend, expecting nothing in return. Then your reward will be great, and you will be sons of the Most High.[l] For He is gracious to the ungrateful and evil. 36 Be merciful, just as your Father also is merciful.[m]

Do Not Judge

37 "Do not judge, and you will not be judged.[n] Do not condemn, and you will not be condemned. Forgive, and you will be forgiven.[o] 38 Give, and it will be given to you; a good measure—pressed down, shaken together, and running over—will be poured into your lap.[p] For with the measure you use,[c] it will be measured back to you."[q]

39 He also told them a parable: "Can the blind guide the blind? Won't they both fall into a pit?[r] 40 A disciple is not above his teacher, but

a6:20-23 Mt 5:3-12
b6:22 Jn 9:22; 16:2
cHeb 11:26; 1Pt 4:14
dJn 15:21
e6:23 Neh 9:26; Ezk 2:1-7; Ac 7:52
f6:26 Jr 5:12-13; 6:13-15; Mc 2:11
g6:28 Mt 5:44
h6:29-30 Mt 5:39-42
i6:31 Mt 7:12
j6:32 Mt 5:46
k6:34 Pr 19:17; Mt 5:42; Lk 14:12-14
l6:35 Mt 5:45; Lk 1:32
m6:36 Mt 5:7,48; Jms 5:11
n6:37-42 Mt 7:1-5
o6:37 Mt 6:14; 18:23-35; Lk 23:16; Ac 3:13
p6:38 Ps 79:12; Is 65:6-7; Jr 32:18
qMk 4:24
r6:39 Mt 15:14

A6:20 Lit *Then lifting up His eyes to*   B6:25,26 Other mss omit *to you*   C6:38 Lit *you measure*

6:20-26 Verses 24-26 in this section are the exact counterpart to verses 20-23 (**blessed** vs. **woe**; **poor** vs. **rich**; **hungry** vs. **full**; **when people hate you** vs. **when all people speak well of you**). In Matthew, it is "the poor in spirit" and "those who hunger . . . for righteousness" who are blessed. The same is true here, because the reward for the blessed ones is in heaven. Jesus noted that rejection was the way those in earlier generations **used to treat the prophets**, while speaking well was the way they treated **the false prophets**. The implication is that Jesus' growing rejection by the religious leaders is proof that He was a true prophet.

6:27-49 The remainder of the Sermon on the Plain in this section deals with the attitudes and actions of those who are followers of Jesus.

6:27-30 Christ's disciples are to be characterized by actions of **love** (loving **enemies**, doing good to **those who hate you**, blessing **those who curse you**, praying for **those who mistreat you**, not retaliating against violence) and generosity (lit "giving the **shirt** off your back," lending and not expecting repayment).

6:31 This verse is usually referred to as the Golden Rule. This is apparently a restatement of the second commandment: "Love your neighbor as yourself" (Lv 19:18).

6:32-34 Jesus discussed the logic of selfless **love**. It is not

the kind of love His disciples display if they just return the love someone has shown them, or **do . . . good** to someone as a sort of repayment, or **lend** when they are certain to be repaid. There is no spiritual **credit** in God's eyes for such behavior since even many unsaved **sinners** behave this way. Christians are to practice a deeper, selfless love.

6:35-36 The **reward** for obeying Jesus' command to **love your enemies, do . . . good** and **lend** without expecting repayment will be **great**, though much of it will not be in this life. But your selfless love will reflect that you are **sons of the Most High** (children of God). He is gracious and merciful to all people, and disciples of Jesus are to follow His example.

6:37 The problems here are hypocritical judgment, shortsighted condemnation, and an unforgiving spirit. These warnings do not mean that Jesus' followers should not practice careful discernment (judgment).

6:38 "Measure" involves weighing and judging. Be fair to others, because **the measure you use** will return to you. If you are generous, generosity will be returned to you in full measure. If you are stingy and uncharitable, such will be the standards by which you are judged.

6:39-40 This **parable** is a warning about following the wrong person. Spiritually blind leaders mislead disciples.

everyone who is fully trained will be like his teacher.ᵃ

⁴¹"Why do you look at the speck in your brother's eye, but don't notice the log in your own eye? Or how can you say to your brother, 'Brother, let me take out the speck that is in your eye,' when you yourself don't see the log in your eye? Hypocrite! First take the log out of your eye, and then you will see clearly to take out the speck in your brother's eye.

A Tree and Its Fruit

⁴³"A good tree doesn't produce bad fruit; on the other hand, a bad tree doesn't produce good fruit.ᵇ For each tree is known by its own fruit. Figs aren't gathered from thornbushes, or grapes picked from a bramble bush. ⁴⁵A good man produces good out of the good storeroom of his heart. An evil man produces evil out of the evil storeroom, for his mouth speaks from the overflow of the heart.

The Two Foundations

⁴⁶"Why do you call Me 'Lord, Lord,' and don't do the things I say?ᶜ ⁴⁷I will show you what someone is like who comes to Me, hears My words, and acts on them:ᵈ ⁴⁸He is like a man building a house, who dug deepᴬ and laid the foundation on the rock. When the flood came, the river crashed against that house and couldn't shake it, because it was well built. ⁴⁹But the one who hears and does not act is like a man who built a house on the ground without a foundation. The river crashed against it, and immediately it col-

lapsed. And the destruction of that house was great!"ᵉ

A Centurion's Faith

7 When He had concluded all His sayings in the hearing of the people, He entered Capernaum.ᶠ ²A ·centurion's ·slave, who was highly valued by him, was sick and about to die. ³When the centurion heard about Jesus, he sent some Jewish elders to Him, requesting Him to come and save the life of his slave. ⁴When they reached Jesus, they pleaded with Him earnestly, saying, "He is worthy for You to grant this, ⁵because he loves our nation and has built us a ·synagogue."ᵍ ⁶Jesus went with them, and when He was not far fromᴮ the house, the centurion sent friends to tell Him, "Lord, don't trouble Yourself, since I am not worthy to have You come under my roof. ⁷That is why I didn't even consider myself worthy to come to You. But say the word, and my servant will be cured.ᶜ,ʰ ⁸For I too am a man placed under authority, having soldiers under my command.ᴰ I say to this one, 'Go!' and he goes; and to another, 'Come!' and he comes; and to my slave, 'Do this!' and he does it."

⁹Jesus heard this and was amazed at him, and turning to the crowd following Him, He said, "I tell you, I have not found so great a faith even in Israel!" ¹⁰When those who had been sent returned to the house, they found the slave in good health.

A Widow's Son Raised to Life

¹¹Soon afterward He was on His way to a

6:41-42 A person is a **hypocrite** (Gk *hupokrites*; "one who pretends to be someone else") if he harshly criticizes a small weakness (a **speck**) in another person's life while overlooking a large fault (a **log**) in his own. We are in no position to criticize another person until we have dealt with our own shortcomings.

6:43-45 The type of **fruit** produced is determined by the type of **tree** that produces it. A person's actions and words come from the heart, whether good or evil.

6:46-49 The illustration of **building** on a solid **foundation** versus building **without a foundation** points out the necessity for a disciple's behavior to be consistent with his stated commitment. The difference between a life that can withstand storms and one that cannot depends not just on whether one comes to Christ and hears His words, but also whether one **acts** on His teachings.

7:1 **Capernaum** was Jesus' headquarters for His ministry in Galilee (4:14–9:50).

7:2-3 A **centurion** was a commander of 100 men in the Roman army. This centurion was apparently a compassionate man, deeply concerned about the illness of his servant.

He reached out to Jesus through some local **Jewish elders** (either recognized leaders in the community or respected older men). In the parallel passage in Mt 8:5-10, the centurion approached Jesus directly.

7:4-8 The Jewish elders were willing to intervene with Jesus because they considered the centurion a truly **worthy** man. Though he was a Gentile, he loved Israel and had spent time and money constructing **a synagogue** in Capernaum. The centurion did not consider himself worthy of being in Jesus' presence, but he had faith that Jesus could heal his **servant**, even at a distance. He understood the spiritual authority Jesus commanded because he understood military authority (**I . . . am . . . under authority, having soldiers under my command**).

7:9-10 Jesus was **amazed** that the **faith** of the Gentile centurion was greater than the faith of any He had found in Israel. The centurion's faith was rewarded; his slave was restored to **good health** by Jesus.

7:11-12 **Nain** was about six miles south of Nazareth, where Jesus grew up. Jesus' arrival coincided with a funeral procession for the **son** of a **widow**, who was left childless and without a means of financial support.

Messianic Expectations

Craig A. Evans

"Messianism" and "messianic expectation" are ways of describing the expectation that an anointed person will come to redeem Israel and/or the Church. Christians believe that Messiah has already come in the person of Jesus of Nazareth. The appearance of Messiah is understood to be part of a larger eschatological drama whereby human activity on earth is appreciably altered by the in-breaking of the "kingdom of God," a time when God's will on earth is more tangibly and permanently experienced. It is usually believed that this anointed figure is part of the climax of human history.

The word "messiah" comes from the Greek *messias* (cp. Jn 1:41; 4:25), which is itself a transliteration of the Hebrew *mashiach* (2Sm 22:51; 23:1), meaning one who is "smeared" or "anointed" (with oil). The Greek equivalent is *christos* (cp. LXX 2Sm 22:51; 23:1), which occurs some 500 times in the New Testament. The nominal form of *christos* is derived from the verbs *mashach* (Hebrew) and *chriein* (Greek), which means "to anoint" or "to smear (with oil)."

The Origin of Messianic Expectation

The messianic expectations in the Jewish and Christian faiths are traced back to God's covenant with King David (2Sm 7) and the aftermath of exile and cessation of the Davidic dynasty. Hope arose that God would someday restore a godly king to Israel. Some of Israel's prophets foretold the coming of a regal Davidic descendant, and their descriptions seem to portray him as far more than a mere mortal. Isaiah foretold the coming of a "child" and "son" who "will be named Wonderful Counselor, Mighty God, Eternal Father, Prince of Peace," and whose kingdom will never end (Is 9:6–7). Again Isaiah prophesied the coming of a Branch of David, on whom the Spirit of God will rest, who will rule the earth with justice and equity (Is 11:1–5). Descriptions such as these hinted that the coming anointed one, the Messiah, would be God Himself.

In the intertestament period (ca 400 B.C. to the birth of Christ) several passages of Old Testament Scripture are interpreted in the light of the messianic hope. Besides Isaiah 11:1–5, Genesis 49:10 ("The scepter will not depart from Judah or the staff from between his feet.") and Numbers 24:17 ("A star will come from Jacob, and a scepter will arise from Israel") are often appealed to. First-century philosopher Philo of Alexandria and Josephus, historian and survivor of the great rebellion (A.D. 66–70), both allude to these passages as pertaining to Messiah. Isaiah 11 is of special interest in the Dead Sea Scrolls. 1QSb 5 applies portions of Isaiah 11:2-5 to the awaited Messiah, while 4Q161, a major commentary on the book of Isaiah, interprets Isaiah 10:34–11:5 as a prophecy of the coming Messiah, called the "Branch of David," who will destroy Israel's enemies, the Romans (called the "Kittim"). 4Q285 quotes Isaiah 10:34–11:1 and interprets it as a reference to the coming Messiah, called the "Branch of David" and "leader of the community" (that is, the leader of the Qumran community). It is said that he will put to death the "king of the Kittim," or the Roman emperor (see also the parallel 11Q14).

Jesus and Messianic Expectation

Jesus' willingness to suffer and die stands in marked contrast to the widespread expectation of a coming Messiah who would slay His enemies. The fact that He did not attempt to overthrow the Roman occupiers and reclaim Israel's throne may explain in part why He was widely rejected by Jewish authorities. They wished for Him to pursue violent, military goals whereas He came instead to usher in the merciful, forgiving rule of God. As for Jesus' fulfillment of the Bible's messianic expectations, it must not be missed that He came first to suffer and die on behalf of sinners (as predicted in Is 52:13–53:12), but will come again as conquering King (2Th 1:7-10).

town called Nain. His disciples and a large crowd were traveling with Him. [12] Just as He neared the gate of the town, a dead man was being carried out. He was his mother's only son, and she was a widow.[a] A large crowd from the city was also with her. [13] When the Lord saw her, He had compassion on her[b] and said, "Don't cry." [14] Then He came up and touched the open coffin,[A] and the pallbearers stopped. And He said, "Young man, I tell you, get up!"[c]

[15] The dead man sat up and began to speak, and Jesus gave him to his mother.[d] [16] Then fear[B] came over everyone,[e] and they glorified God,[f] saying, "A great prophet has risen among us,"[g] and "God has visited[C] His people."[h] [17] This report about Him went throughout Judea and all the vicinity.

In Praise of John the Baptist

[18] Then John's disciples told him about all these things.[i] So John summoned two of his disciples [19] and sent them to the Lord, asking, "Are You the One[j] who is to come, or should we look for someone else?"

[20] When the men reached Him, they said, "John the Baptist sent us to ask You, 'Are You the One who is to come, or should we look for someone else?'"

[21] At that time Jesus healed many people of diseases,[k] plagues, and evil spirits,[l] and He granted sight to many blind people.[m] [22] He

replied to them, "Go and report to John the things you have seen and heard: The blind receive their sight, the lame walk, those with skin diseases are healed,[D] the deaf hear,[n] the dead are raised, and the poor are told the good news.[o] [23] And anyone who is not •offended because of Me is blessed." [24] After John's messengers left, He began to speak to the crowds about John: "What did you go out into the wilderness to see? A reed swaying in the wind? [25] What then did you go out to see? A man dressed in soft robes? Look, those who are splendidly dressed[E] and live in luxury are in royal palaces. [26] What then did you go out to see? A prophet?[p] Yes, I tell you, and far more than a prophet. [27] This is the one it is written about:

**Look, I am sending My messenger ahead of You;[F]
he will prepare Your way before You.[G,q]**

[28] I tell you, among those born of women no one is greater than John,[H] but the least in the kingdom of God is greater than he." [29] (And when all the people, including the tax collectors, heard this, they acknowledged God's way of righteousness,[i] because they had been baptized with John's baptism.[r] [30] But since the •Pharisees and experts in the law[s] had not been baptized by him, they rejected the plan of God for themselves.[t])

Cross references (center column)

[a]7:12 Jdg 11:34; Lk 8:42; 9:38; Heb 11:17
[b]7:13 Mt 20:34
[c]7:14 Mt 11:5; Mk 5:41; Lk 7:22; 8:54; Jn 11:43; Ac 9:40
[d]7:15 1Kg 17:23; 2Kg 4:36
[e]7:16 Lk 5:26
[f]Mt 5:16; Lk 2:20; 13:13; 23:47; Ac 4:21; 11:18
[g]Dt 18:15; Mt 21:11; Lk 7:39; Jn 7:40
[h]Lk 1:68
[i]7:18-35 Mt 11:2-19
[j]7:19 Jn 4:25; 6:14; 11:27; Rm 5:14; Heb 10:37
[k]7:21 Mt 4:23
[l]Mk 1:34
[m]Mt 9:30; 12:22; Mk 8:25; Lk 18:42; Jn 9:7
[n]7:22 Is 29:18; 35:5-6
[o]Is 61:1; Lk 4:18
[p]7:26 Mt 14:5; Lk 1:76; 20:6
[q]7:27 Mal 3:1; Mt 11:10; Mk 1:2; Lk 1:17
[r]7:29 Mt 21:32; Lk 3:12; Ac 18:25; 19:3
[s]7:30 Mt 22:35; Lk 10:25; 11:45-46,52; 14:3
[t]Mt 21:25,32; 23:13; Mk 7:9

[A]7:14 Or the bier　[B]7:16 Or awe　[C]7:16 Or come to help　[D]7:22 Lit cleansed　[E]7:25 Or who have glorious robes　[F]7:27 Lit messenger before Your face　[G]7:27 Mal 3:1　[H]7:28 Other mss read women is not a greater prophet than John the Baptist　[i]7:29 Lit they justified God

---

7:13-15 Jesus acted out of **compassion** for the widow in bringing her son back from the dead. By custom Jewish funerals included an **open coffin**, but anyone who touched the corpse became ceremonially unclean (Nm 19:11). This is the first of several times that Jesus raised a person from the dead (Lk 8:40-56; Jn 11:38-44).

7:16-17 The phrase **a great prophet has risen** probably refers to Elijah (1Kg 17:17-24) and Elisha (2Kg 4:18-37) raising people from the dead. **God has visited His people** does not necessarily mean that the people at this early date believed that God had become a man in the person of Jesus (Jn 1:14). It can mean simply that the power of God had been experienced among His people. The fact that the report about this miracle reached **Judea** looks ahead to Jesus' journey to Jerusalem (9:51-19:44).

7:18-20 John the Baptist had to be told **all these things** because he was in prison (see note at 3:20). John's question grew out of confusion more than doubt. On the one hand, Jesus certainly did the works of the Messiah. On the other hand, He had not acted to overturn Roman rule or free righteous prisoners, as the Jews expected Messiah to do. So John decided to send **two of his disciples** to clear up the confusion by asking Jesus, **Are you the One**?

7:21-23 Verse 21 is a summary of the miracles Jesus was

doing in His ministry, serving as a lead-in to His response to the question from John the Baptist's disciples. The things Jesus told John's disciples to **report** that they had **seen and heard** went beyond the prophecy of the Messiah in Is 61:1-2 (e.g., **the dead are raised**). **Blessed** looks back to 6:22.

7:24-28 The crowds were apparently asking Jesus why John the Baptist's **messengers** had come to Him. So Jesus explained the significance of John and his ministry. He was not one who fit in with current thought or comfortable surroundings, and he had nothing to do with royalty and its excesses. Instead, he was **a prophet** and, beyond that, the forerunner for Messiah (**My messenger ahead of You**; see Mal 3:1). No mere human to that point was **greater than John** the Baptist. However, even the **least** Christian of the new covenant era (the coming form of **the kingdom of God**), beginning with the day of Pentecost (Ac 2), would have greater spiritual resources than John due to the permanent indwelling of the Holy Spirit.

7:29-30 All of those who had repented and been baptized (see note at 3:2-3) by John acknowledged **God's way of righteousness** (John's message as forerunner to Jesus). But the **Pharisees and experts in the law**, who would not repent and humble themselves to be baptized by John, rejected the **plan of God** regarding salvation.

An Unresponsive Generation

31 "To what then should I compare the people of this generation, and what are they like? 32 They are like children sitting in the marketplace and calling to each other:

> We played the flute for you,
> but you didn't dance;
> we sang a lament,
> but you didn't weep!

33 For John the Baptist did not come eating bread or drinking wine,[a] and you say, 'He has a demon!' 34 The •Son of Man has come eating and drinking, and you say, 'Look, a glutton and a drunkard, a friend of tax collectors and sinners!'[b] 35 Yet wisdom is vindicated[A] by all her children."

Much Forgiveness, Much Love

36 Then one of the Pharisees invited Him to eat with him. He entered the Pharisee's house and reclined at the table.[c] 37 And a woman in the town who was a sinner found out that Jesus was reclining at the table in the Pharisee's house.[d] She brought an alabaster jar of fragrant oil 38 and stood behind Him at His feet, weeping, and began to wash His feet with her tears. She wiped His feet with the hair of her head, kissing His feet and anointing them with the fragrant oil.[e]

39 When the Pharisee who had invited Him saw this, he said to himself, "This man, if He were a prophet, would know who and what kind of woman this is who is touching Him—she's a sinner!"[f]

40 Jesus replied to him, "Simon, I have something to say to you."

"Teacher," he said, "say it."

41 "A creditor had two debtors. One owed 500 •denarii,[g] and the other 50. 42 Since they could not pay it back,[h] he graciously forgave them both. So, which of them will love him more?"

43 Simon answered, "I suppose the one he forgave more."

"You have judged correctly," He told him. 44 Turning to the woman, He said to Simon, "Do you see this woman? I entered your house; you gave Me no water for My feet,[i] but she, with her tears, has washed My feet and wiped them with her hair. 45 You gave Me no kiss,[j] but she hasn't stopped kissing My feet since I came in. 46 You didn't anoint My head with olive oil,[k] but she has anointed My feet with fragrant oil. 47 Therefore I tell you, her many sins have been forgiven; that's why[B] she loved much. But the one who is forgiven little, loves little." 48 Then He said to her, "Your sins are forgiven."[l]

49 Those who were at the table with Him began to say among themselves, "Who is this man who even forgives sins?"[m]

50 And He said to the woman, "Your faith has saved you.[n] Go in peace."[o]

Many Women Support Christ's Work

8 Soon afterward He was traveling from one town and village to another,[p] preaching and telling the good news of the kingdom of God.[q] The Twelve were with Him, 2 and also

Cross references

[a] 7:33 Lk 1:15
[b] 7:34 Mt 9:10-11; Lk 15:2; 19:7
[c] 7:36 Lk 11:37; 14:1
[d] 7:37-39 Mt 26:6-13; Mk 14:3-9; Jn 12:1-8
[e] 7:38 Jn 11:2
[f] 7:39 Lk 7:16; Jn 4:19
[g] 7:41 Mt 18:28; Mk 6:37
[h] 7:42 Mt 18:25
[i] 7:44 Gn 18:4; 19:2; 43:24; Jdg 19:21; 1Tm 5:10
[j] 7:45 2Sm 15:5; 19:39; 20:9
[k] 7:46 2Sm 12:20; Ps 23:5; Ec 9:8; Dn 10:3
[l] 7:48 Mt 9:2; Mk 2:5; Lk 5:20; Jms 5:15; 1Jn 2:12
[m] 7:49 Lk 5:21
[n] 7:50 Mt 9:22; Mk 10:52; Lk 17:19; 18:42
[o] 1Sm 1:17; Mk 5:34; Lk 8:48
[p] 8:1 Mk 6:6
[q] Mt 4:23; Lk 4:43

Footnotes

A 7:35 Or wisdom is declared right   B 7:47 Her love shows that she has been forgiven

---

7:31-35 Jesus declared that it was impossible to please the people of His generation. They would not respond to the playing of a **flute** (a happy sound) or the singing of a **lament** (a sad sound). John the Baptist led a very strict lifestyle, but he was accused of having **a demon**. By contrast, Jesus was accused of living loosely and eating with **sinners**, and thus was called a **glutton** and a **drunkard**.

7:35 The phrase **wisdom is vindicated by all her children** means that the teachings of John the Baptist and Jesus will be shown correct by all those who live (and live well) by following their teachings.

7:36-38 It is not clear whether the Pharisee who **invited** Jesus into his home wanted to learn from Him, as did Nicodemus (Jn 3:1-2), or was seeking to trap Him. The unnamed **woman** was probably a prostitute (**sinner**) who heard Jesus preach and repented. **Reclining** meant resting on your side, with your feet facing away from **the table**. Though she said nothing, her **tears** and her willingness to give the expensive **fragrant oil** to anoint Jesus' feet were an eloquent testimony of her gratitude to Jesus.

7:39 The Pharisee who had invited Jesus into his home could not conceive that a true **prophet** would associate with this kind of woman—a known sinner. Being a Phari-

see required him to be separated from sin and sinners like her.

7:40-43 Jesus showed that He knew what **Simon**, the Pharisee, was thinking. The point of Jesus' story was simple: a person who is forgiven **more** appreciates it more.

7:44-47 Jesus drew a contrast between the Pharisee and the woman. Simon had failed to provide **water** to wash His **feet**, had given Him **no kiss** of hospitality, and did not **anoint** His **head** with oil—all things she had done. Jesus did not mean that the Pharisee had little sin to be forgiven, but that he did not think of himself as a sinner while the woman was profoundly aware of her sinfulness.

7:48-50 Based on her actions, which reflected true repentance of sins, Jesus forgave the woman who anointed His feet. He made it clear that her **faith** had **saved** her (see Eph 2:8-9). Once again, His authority to **forgive sins** was questioned (see note at 5:21-25).

8:1-3 As Jesus was **traveling** and **preaching** in Galilee, He was accompanied by **the Twelve** (see note at 6:14-16) and several well-to-do **women** who, out of gratitude for being healed by Jesus, financially supported Him and the apostles. **Mary . . . Magdalene** (i.e., of the town of Magdala), who became a well-known follower (Mt 27:61), is introduced

some women who had been healed of evil spirits and sicknesses:[a] Mary, called •Magdalene (seven demons had come out[b] of her); [3] Joanna the wife of Chuza, •Herod's steward; Susanna; and many others who were supporting them from their possessions.

The Parable of the Sower

[4] As a large crowd was gathering, and people were flocking to Him from every town, He said in a parable:[c] [5] "A sower went out to sow his seed. As he was sowing, some fell along the path; it was trampled on, and the birds of the sky ate it up. [6] Other seed fell on the rock; when it sprang up, it withered, since it lacked moisture. [7] Other seed fell among thorns; the thorns sprang up with it and choked it. [8] Still other seed fell on good ground; when it sprang up, it produced a crop: 100 times what was sown."[d] As He said this, He called out, "Anyone who has ears to hear should listen!"[e]

Why Jesus Used Parables

[9] Then His disciples asked Him, "What does this parable mean?"[f] [10] So He said, "The •secrets of the kingdom of God have been given for you[g] to know, but to the rest it is in parables, so that

> **Looking they may not see,**
> **and hearing they may**
> **not understand. [A,h]**

The Parable of the Sower Explained

[11] "This is the meaning of the parable:[B,i] The seed is the word of God.[j] [12] The seed along the

[a] 8:2 Mt 27:55; Mk 15:40-41; Lk 23:49,55; Ac 1:14
[b] Mt 27:56,61; 28:1; Mk 16:9; Lk 24:10; Jn 19:25; 20:1,18
[c] 8:4-8 Mt 13:3-9; Mk 4:3-9
[d] 8:8 Gn 26:12
[e] Mt 11:15; Lk 13:34
[f] 8:9-10 Mt 13:10-11; Mk 4:10-11
[g] 8:10 Mt 19:11
[h] Is 6:9
[i] 8:11-15 Mt 13:18-23; Mk 4:13-20
[j] 8:11 Lk 8:21; 11:28; Ac 18:11; Jms 1:21; 1Pt 1:23
[k] 8:13 Ezk 33:31-32; Gl 1:6
[l] 8:14 Mt 6:25
[m] 8:15 Heb 10:36; Jms 5:7
[n] 8:16 Mt 5:15-16; Lk 11:33
[o] 8:16-18 Mk 4:21-25
[p] 8:17 Mt 10:26; Lk 12:2; 1Tm 5:25
[q] 8:18 Mt 13:12
[r] 8:19 Mt 13:55; Mk 6:3; Jn 2:12; 7:3,5,10; Ac 1:14; 1Co 9:5; Gl 1:19
[s] 8:19-21 Mt 12:46-50; Mk 3:31-35

path are those who have heard and then the Devil comes and takes away the word from their hearts, so that they may not believe and be saved. [13] And the seed on the rock are those who, when they hear, welcome the word with joy. Having no root, these believe for a while and depart in a time of testing.[k] [14] As for the seed that fell among thorns, these are the ones who, when they have heard, go on their way and are choked with worries, riches, and pleasures of life,[l] and produce no mature fruit. [15] But the seed in the good ground—these are the ones who,[c] having heard the word with an honest and good heart, hold on to it and by enduring,[m] bear fruit.

Using Your Light

[16] "No one, after lighting a lamp,[n] covers it with a basket or puts it under a bed, but puts it on a lampstand so that those who come in may see its light.[o] [17] For nothing is concealed that won't be revealed, and nothing hidden that won't be made known and come to light.[p] [18] Therefore take care how you listen. For whoever has, more will be given to him;[q] and whoever does not have, even what he thinks he has will be taken away from him."

True Relationships

[19] Then His mother and brothers[r] came to Him,[s] but they could not meet with Him because of the crowd. [20] He was told, "Your mother and Your brothers are standing outside, wanting to see You."

[21] But He replied to them, "My mother and

[A] 8:10 Is 6:9   [B] 8:11 Lit *But this is the parable:*   [C] 8:15 Or *these are the kind who*

---

here. **Joanna**, who is also mentioned in 24:10, was married to a man who held a responsible position under Herod Antipas, the tetrarch of Galilee (see note at 3:1). Nothing else is known about **Susanna**.

8:5-8 From this point forward, Jesus used the parable approach much more, the purpose of which is explained in verses 9-10. In an agricultural society, everyone would have understood what happened when a **sower** went out into a field to **sow his seed**. At least one **path** ran through most fields, and much of the terrain in Israel was rocky under a thin layer of topsoil. Dropping seeds along such paths was futile. Many fields had thorn bushes along the perimeters. Seeds falling there had no chance to grow and survive until harvest time. Others, however, did fall on fertile soil and produced a bumper crop (**100 times what was sown**). **Anyone who has ears to hear should listen** is a challenge to carefully consider the story and its hidden meaning and practical implications (Rv 2:7).

8:9-10 Jesus' disciples could not understand the point of the story, so they asked Him its meaning. Quoting from Is 6:9, Jesus explained that He used parables as a way to reveal the truths of **the kingdom of God** to believers but that the story by itself actually concealed the meaning from unbelievers.

8:11-12 The key to the parable is that the **seed** being sown stands for the preaching of **the word of God**. The seeds that fell on the hard dirt **along the path** did not penetrate the **hearts** of those who heard God's Word because the Devil stole the seed away. So they remained unsaved.

8:13-14 The seeds on the rocky soil seemed to flourish at first, but they could not put down roots, so they soon withered and died. **The seed . . . among thorns** that **produce no mature fruit** may be: (1) those whose unbelief is revealed by their response to **worries, riches,** and the **pleasures of life**, or (2) believers who are not fruitful (1Co 3:10-15).

8:15 The **seed in the good ground** represents fruitful believers (Jn 15:2) who receive God's **word** with an open heart and persevere in the faith.

8:16-18 How a person responds to God's revelation determines whether he will receive more **light** or lose what he has. In the end, God will bring everything to light.

8:19-21 Human relationships built upon mutual faith in Christ, spiritual openness to one another, and shared obedience to **the word of God** are more important than relationships with physical family members, especially if the family members are unbelievers.

My brothers are those who hear and do the word of God."[a]

Wind and Wave Obey the Master

[22] One day He and His disciples got into a boat,[b] and He told them, "Let's cross over to the other side of the lake."[c] So they set out, [23] and as they were sailing He fell asleep. Then a fierce windstorm came down on the lake; they were being swamped and were in danger. [24] They came and woke Him up, saying, "Master, Master, we're going to die!" Then He got up and rebuked the wind and the raging waves. So they ceased, and there was a calm.[d] [25] He said to them, "Where is your faith?"

They were fearful and amazed, asking one another, "Who can this be?[A,e] He commands even the winds and the waves, and they obey Him!"

Demons Driven Out by the Master

[26] Then they sailed to the region of the Gerasenes,[B,f] which is opposite Galilee. [27] When He got out on land, a demon-possessed man from the town met Him. For a long time he had worn no clothes and did not stay in a house but in the tombs. [28] When he saw Jesus, he cried out,[g] fell down before Him, and said in a loud voice, "What do You have to do with me,[C,h] Jesus, You Son of the Most High God?[i] I beg You, don't torment me!" [29] For He had commanded the •unclean spirit to come out of the man. Many times it had seized him, and though he was guarded, bound by chains and shackles, he would snap the restraints and be

driven by the demon into deserted places. [30] "What is your name?" Jesus asked him.

"Legion,"[j] he said—because many demons had entered him. [31] And they begged Him not to banish them to the •abyss.[k]

[32] A large herd of pigs was there, feeding on the hillside. The demons begged Him to permit them to enter the pigs, and He gave them permission. [33] The demons came out of the man and entered the pigs, and the herd rushed down the steep bank into the lake and drowned. [34] When the men who tended them saw what had happened, they ran off and reported it in the town and in the countryside. [35] Then people went out to see what had happened. They came to Jesus and found the man the demons had departed from, sitting at Jesus' feet,[l] dressed and in his right mind. And they were afraid. [36] Meanwhile, the eyewitnesses reported to them how the demon-possessed man was delivered.[m] [37] Then all the people of the Gerasene region[B] asked Him to leave them,[n] because they were gripped by great fear. So getting into the boat, He returned.

[38] The man from whom the demons had departed kept begging Him to be with Him. But He sent him away and said, [39] "Go back to your home, and tell all that God has done for you." And off he went, proclaiming throughout the town all that Jesus had done for him.

A Girl Restored and a Woman Healed

[40] When Jesus returned, the crowd welcomed Him,[o] for they were all expecting

Cross references (center column)

[a] 8:21 Lk 11:28; Jms 1:22
[b] 8:22-25 Mt 8:23-27; Mk 4:36-41; Jn 6:16-21
[c] 8:22 Lk 5:1
[d] 8:24 Ps 65:7; 104:7; Mt 14:32; Mk 6:51; Lk 4:39
[e] 8:25 Mt 21:10; Lk 1:66; 5:21; 7:49; 9:9
[f] 8:26-39 Mt 8:28-34; Mk 5:1-20
[g] 8:28 Lk 4:33-34; Ac 8:7
[h] Jn 2:4
[i] Gn 14:18; Ps 57:2; Dn 3:26; Lk 1:32; Ac 16:17
[j] 8:30 Mt 26:53
[k] 8:31 Ps 140:10; Rm 10:7; Rv 9:1-2,11; 11:7; 17:8; 20:1,3
[l] 8:35 Lk 8:41; 10:39
[m] 8:36 Mt 4:24
[n] 8:37 1Kg 17:18; Lk 5:8; Ac 16:39
[o] 8:40 Lk 9:11

[A] 8:25 Lit Who then is this?   [B] 8:26,37 Other mss read the Gadarenes   [C] 8:28 Lit What to me and to You

---

8:22-25 When a boat trip across the Sea of Galilee ran into **a fierce windstorm**, Jesus slept in the boat while His disciples faced the storm and feared they would die. When Jesus was awakened, He demonstrated full authority over **wind** and **waves** by calming the storm. He also chided His disciples for their lack of **faith**. Had they genuinely trusted Jesus, they would not have feared even the fiercest winds and waves.

8:26 The **region of the Gerasenes** was probably around the town of Gergesa (or Khersa), on the eastern coast of the Sea of Galilee. The name for this predominantly Gentile region came from the city of Gerasa, located about 35 miles to the southeast.

8:27 In the parallel account in Mt 8:28, *two* **demon-possessed** men are mentioned. Apparently, Luke chose to focus on the one who did the talking. The phrase **did not stay in a house but in the tombs** may refer to an outdoor burial ground, but since the man was naked, it is more likely this refers to a cave, several of which have been found in that area.

8:28-31 The demon who spoke identified Jesus, just as the demons had in 4:34 and Ac 16:17. **Son of the Most High** was the wording used by the angel in speaking to Mary (see note at 1:31-33). **Don't torment me** probably refers to sending the demon to the abyss, a place where some of the demons are

currently confined (Rv 9:1-2,11). Demons enabled people whom they possessed to perform feats of great strength (**he would snap the restraints**). It is not clear whether Jesus was asking the name of the man or the demon, but the demon answered. A **legion** of Roman soldiers was a force of 6,000. Thus, many demons possessed this man.

8:32-33 The presence of **a large herd of pigs** indicates that the region of the Gerasenes was heavily Gentile because Jews considered pigs to be unclean animals (Lv 11:7-8) and would never herd them. The cruel destructiveness of demons is seen in that, as soon as Jesus permitted them to enter the pigs, they caused them to drown in **the lake** (the Sea of Galilee).

8:34-37 Sitting at Jesus' feet is the position of a disciple (i.e., the pupil; see 10:38-42). The people were **afraid** when the demon-possessed man returned to normal, for Jesus had exercised a power that revealed His supernatural identity.

8:38-39 Because He had been asked to leave, Jesus told the healed man to stay in that region and testify to what God had done for him. The man obeyed by proclaiming **all that Jesus had done for him.**

8:40-42 Jesus **returned** to Galilee. He likely had met this **Jairus** before. He had spoken in most of the synagogues in

Him.[a] [41]Just then, a man named Jairus came. He was a leader of the •synagogue.[b] He fell down at Jesus' feet and pleaded with Him to come to his house, [42]because he had an only daughter[c] about 12 years old, and she was at death's door.[A]

While He was going, the crowds were nearly crushing Him.[d] [43]A woman suffering from bleeding[e] for 12 years,[f] who had spent all she had on doctors[B] yet could not be healed by any, [44]approached from behind and touched the •tassel of His robe.[g] Instantly her bleeding stopped.

[45]"Who touched Me?" Jesus asked.

When they all denied it, Peter[c] said, "Master,[h] the crowds are hemming You in and pressing against You."[D]

[46]"Someone did touch Me," said Jesus. "I know that power has gone out from Me."[i]

[47]When the woman saw that she was discovered,[E] she came trembling and fell down before Him. In the presence of all the people, she declared the reason she had touched Him and how she was instantly cured. [48]"Daughter," He said to her, "your faith has made you well.[F] Go in peace."[j]

[49]While He was still speaking,[k] someone came from the synagogue leader's house, say-

ing, "Your daughter is dead. Don't bother[l] the Teacher[m] anymore."

[50]When Jesus heard it, He answered him, "Don't be afraid. Only believe, and she will be made well." [51]After He came to the house, He let no one enter with Him except Peter, John, James,[n] and the child's father and mother. [52]Everyone was crying[o] and mourning for her.[p] But He said, "Stop crying, for she is not dead but asleep."[q]

[53]They started laughing at Him, because they knew she was dead. [54]So He[G] took her by the hand[r] and called out, "Child, get up!"[s] [55]Her spirit returned,[t] and she got up at once. Then He gave orders that she be given something to eat. [56]Her parents were astounded, but He instructed them to tell no one what had happened.[u]

Commissioning the Twelve

9 Summoning the Twelve,[v] He gave them power and authority over all the demons, and power to heal[H] diseases.[w] [2]Then He sent them to proclaim the kingdom of God and to heal the sick.[x]

[3]"Take nothing for the road,"[y] He told them, "no walking stick,[z] no traveling bag, no bread, no money; and don't take an extra shirt. [4]Whatever house you enter, stay there and

---

[a] 8:40-42 Mt 9:18-19; Mk 5:21-24
[b] 8:41 Lk 13:14; Ac 13:15; 18:8,17
[c] 8:42 Lk 7:12
[d] Mk 3:9
[e] 8:43 Lv 15:25
[f] 8:43-48 Mt 9:20-22; Mk 5:25-34
[g] 8:44 Nm 15:38-39; Dt 22:12; Mt 14:36; 23:5
[h] 8:45 Lk 5:5
[i] 8:46 Lk 5:17; 6:19; Ac 10:38
[j] 8:48 Lk 7:50
[k] 8:49-56 Mt 9:23-26; Mk 5:35-43
[l] 8:49 Lk 7:6
[m] Jn 11:28
[n] 8:51 Mk 3:17; 14:33; Lk 9:28
[o] 8:52 Lk 7:13
[p] Mt 11:17; Lk 23:27
[q] Jn 11:4,11; Ac 20:10
[r] 8:54 Mk 1:31
[s] 8:54 Mt 11:5; Lk 7:14,22; Jn 11:43
[t] 8:55 Jdg 15:19; 1Sm 30:12
[u] 8:56 Mt 8:4
[v] 9:1 Lk 6:12-16
[w] 9:1 Mt 10:1; Mk 3:13-15; 6:7
[x] 9:2 Mt 10:5,7-8; Lk 4:43; 9:11,60; 10:1,9
[y] 9:3-5 Mt 10:9-15; Mk 6:8-11; Lk 10:4-12; 22:35
[z] 9:3 Mk 6:8

[A]8:42 Lit she was dying   [B]8:43 Other mss omit who had spent all she had on doctors   [C]8:45 Other mss add and those with him   [D]8:45 Other mss add and You say, 'Who touched Me?'   [E]8:47 Lit she had not escaped notice   [F]8:48 Or has saved you   [G]8:54 Other mss add having put them all outside   [H]9:1 In this passage, different Gk words are translated as heal. In Eng, "to heal" or "to cure" are synonyms with little distinction in meaning. Technically, we do not heal or cure diseases. People are healed or cured from diseases.

Galilee, and Jairus was a **leader** (Gk archon, "ruler"; probably the chief elder who conducted the services) in the local **synagogue**.

8:43-46 The account of the **woman suffering from bleeding for 12 years** interrupts the narrative to show that delay during a critical hour of the girl's illness could not keep Jesus from healing her. As for the woman, her bleeding was probably menstrual hemorrhaging, which had made her ceremonially unclean for all this time (Lv 15:25-31). As a doctor, Luke was especially sensitive to the fact that this woman had **spent** all her resources on **doctors yet could not be healed**. Even with the crowd pressing against Jesus from all sides, He was immediately aware of the touch of the woman who was instantly healed of her bleeding. No explanation is given for how He knew that healing **power** had gone out from Him.

8:47-48 The woman was **instantly cured**, but she was understandably fearful when Jesus singled her out. After hearing her explanation, Jesus stated that her **faith** in Him had brought about her healing.

8:49-50 During the delay caused by Jesus' interaction with the bleeding woman, the **daughter** of the synagogue leader died. The natural conclusion was that she was now beyond the help of Jesus. However, He stated that the same kind of faith that had brought about the healing of the bleeding woman would bring the dead girl back to life.

8:51-53 In this passage **Peter, John**, and **James**, are set apart by Jesus as the inner circle of the apostles (9:28; Mt 26:37). The sense of finality by the child's parents and, apparently, even the apostles was so profound that the people in the house started **laughing** at Jesus when He seemingly denied that the girl was dead (**she is not dead but asleep**).

8:54-56 When Jesus commanded, **Child, get up**, her spirit returned to her body. Then **she got up** and had **something to eat**. It is not known why Jesus insisted that her parents not tell about Him raising their daughter from the dead. The crowd outside knew that the girl had genuinely died. Now she was alive just after Jesus went in to see her. There could be no hiding the fact that Jesus raised her.

9:1-2 After **the Twelve** had observed Jesus' ministry for several months, He delegated **power and authority** over **demons** and **diseases** to them (see note at 6:12-13). Their other mission (Gk apostello; "to send out") was to **proclaim the kingdom of God**. In the parallel passage in Mt 10, the apostles were specifically instructed to avoid the Samaritans and Gentiles and to go only to "the lost sheep of the house of Israel" (Mt 10:5-6), but Luke did not include this restriction.

9:3-5 The apostles were to be dependent on whom they lodged with (**take nothing**) and were to move on if a family or town did not **welcome** them. **Shake off the dust from**

leave from there. [5] If they do not welcome you, when you leave that town, shake off the dust from your feet as a testimony against them."[a] [6] So they went out and traveled from village to village, proclaiming the good news and healing everywhere.

Herod's Desire to See Jesus

[7] •Herod the tetrarch[b] heard about everything that was going on.[c] He was perplexed, because some said that John had been raised from the dead, [8] some that Elijah had appeared,[d] and others that one of the ancient prophets had risen.[e] [9] "I beheaded John," Herod said, "but who is this I hear such things about?" And he wanted to see Him.[f]

Feeding 5,000

[10] When the apostles returned,[g] they reported to Jesus all that they had done.[h] He took them along and withdrew privately to a[A] town called Bethsaida.[i] [11] When the crowds found out, they followed Him. He welcomed them,[j] spoke to them about the kingdom of God, and cured[B] those who needed healing.

[12] Late in the day,[C,k] the Twelve approached and said to Him, "Send the crowd away,[l] so they can go into the surrounding villages and

countryside to find food and lodging, because we are in a deserted place here."

[13] "You give them something to eat," He told them.

"We have no more than five loaves[m] and two fish," they said, "unless we go and buy food for all these people." [14] (For about 5,000 men were there.)

Then He told His disciples, "Have them sit down[D] in groups of about 50 each." [15] They did so, and had them all sit down. [16] Then He took the five loaves and the two fish, and looking up to heaven,[n] He blessed and broke them.[o] He kept giving them to the disciples to set before the crowd. [17] Everyone ate and was filled. Then they picked up[E] 12 baskets of leftover pieces.

Peter's Confession of the Messiah

[18] While He was praying in private[p] and His disciples were with Him, He asked them, "Who do the crowds say that I am?"

[19] They answered, "John the Baptist; others, Elijah; still others, that one of the ancient prophets has come back."[F,q]

[20] "But you," He asked them, "who do you say that I am?"

Peter answered, "God's •Messiah!"[r]

Cross references (center column)

a9:5 Neh 5:13; Ac 13:51; 18:6
b9:7 Lk 3:1,19; 13:31; 23:7; Ac 13:1
c9:7-9 Mt 14:1-2; Mk 6:14-16
d9:8 Mt 11:14; 16:14; 17:3-4,10-12; Lk 1:17; 4:26
e Mk 6:15
f9:9 Lk 23:8
g9:10-17 Mt 14:13-21; Mk 6:32-44; Jn 6:5-13
h9:10 Mk 6:30
i Mt 11:21; Mk 8:22; Jn 1:44; 12:21
j9:11 Lk 8:40
k9:12 Lk 24:29
l Mt 15:23
m9:13 Mt 16:9; Mk 8:19
n9:16 Mk 7:34; Jn 11:41; 17:1
o Mt 26:26; Mk 8:7; 14:22; Lk 24:30
p9:18-20 Mt 16:13-16; Mk 8:27-29
q9:19 Lk 9:7-8
r9:20 Mt 1:17; Lk 23:35; Ac 3:18; Rv 12:10

A9:10 Other mss add *deserted place near a*   B9:11 Or *healed*; in this passage, different Gk words are translated as heal. In Eng, "to heal" or "to cure" are synonyms with little distinction in meaning. Technically, we do not heal or cure diseases. People are healed or cured from diseases.   C9:12 Lit *When the day began to decline*   D9:14 Lit *them recline*   E9:17 Lit *Then were picked up by them*   F9:19 Lit *has risen*

---

your feet was a gesture of judgment against those who rejected the apostles and their message about Jesus.

9:6 **Proclaiming the good news** (Gk *euangelizo*; "to preach the gospel") is paralleled here with "proclaim the kingdom of God" in v. 2. The message of the gospel of Jesus Christ is the means of entry into the kingdom of God.

9:7-9 **Herod** Antipas (see note at 3:1) was at a loss (**perplexed**) to decide whether Jesus was John the Baptist raised from the dead. The parallel passages (Mt 14:2; Mk 6:16) indicate he decided that Jesus was indeed the risen John. Others around Antipas, however, thought Jesus was the prophet **Elijah** (see Mal 4:5). John himself had partially fulfilled this prophecy (Mt 11:14). Still others believed that some other OT prophet had come back.

9:10-11 After the apostles returned from their mission, they **reported** their deeds, and Jesus again took the lead over the ministry of preaching and healing. **Bethsaida** was a town on the northeastern coast of the Sea of Galilee that had recently been rebuilt by Herod Philip (see note at 3:1). The attempt to find a private place outside Bethsaida where the apostles could rest and confer with Jesus was foiled by the following **crowds**.

9:12-17 Other than His resurrection from the dead, the feeding of the 5,000 is the only miracle of Jesus that appears in all four Gospels (Mt 14:13-21; Mk 6:30-44; Jn 6:5-14).

9:12-14 According to John's Gospel, Jesus, already knowing what He was going to do, was the one who expressed concern initially over where the crowd would find **food and**

lodging so late in the day (Jn 6:5-6). Here in Luke, Jesus responded to the question by the Twelve by challenging them to **give them something to eat**. The apostles had already surveyed the crowd and found only **five loaves** of bread and **two fish** to feed about 5,000 men (who, with women and children, could easily have totaled 15,000 or more). To better manage distribution, Jesus had the apostles organize the huge crowd into **groups of about 50** people.

9:16-17 It is likely that when Jesus looked **up to heaven** and **blessed and broke** the loaves, He uttered the traditional Jewish mealtime prayer: "Blessed are You, Lord our God, King of the world, who brings out bread from the earth." The miracle of the multiplying of the loaves and fish took place in the hands of Jesus as He broke the food and **kept giving** it to the disciples to distribute. At the end, it appears that each of the 12 apostles picked up a full basket of **leftover pieces**, even after feeding thousands of people. The Jews were required to pick up scraps of food that fell during any meal.

9:18-20 These verses are another example of Luke's emphasis on prayer. The answers the disciples gave to Jesus' question about His identity prove that Herod Antipas was not the only person who was perplexed on this point (see note at vv. 7-9). When Jesus asked the disciples their personal opinion, **Peter** answered as spokesman for the group. His answer, that Jesus is **God's Messiah**, is the conclusion to which everything in Luke's Gospel points.

9:21-22 Jesus was not ready to present Himself openly as the Messiah. In popular Jewish views of that time, Messi-

His Death and Resurrection Predicted

[21] But He strictly warned and instructed them to tell this to no one,[a] [22] saying,[b] "The •Son of Man[c] must suffer many things[d] and be rejected[e] by the elders, •chief priests, and •scribes,[f] be killed, and be raised the third day."[g]

Take Up Your Cross

[23] Then He said to them all, "If anyone wants to come with[A] Me, he must deny himself,[h] take up his cross daily,[B] and follow Me.[i] [24] For whoever wants to save his •life will lose it, but whoever loses his life because of Me will save it.[j] [25] What is a man benefited if he gains the whole world, yet loses or forfeits himself?[k] [26] For whoever is ashamed of Me and My words,[l] the Son of Man will be ashamed of him when He comes in His glory[m] and that of the Father and the holy angels.[n] [27] I tell you the

truth: There are some standing here who will not taste death[o] until they see the kingdom of God."[p]

The Transfiguration

[28] About eight days after these words,[q] He took along Peter, John, and James[r] and went up on the mountain to pray.[s] [29] As He was praying, the appearance of His face changed,[t] and His clothes became dazzling white.[u] [30] Suddenly, two men were talking with Him—Moses and Elijah. [31] They appeared in glory and were speaking of His death,[c] which He was about to accomplish in Jerusalem.

[32] Peter and those with him were in a deep sleep,[D,v] and when they became fully awake,

---

Cross references (center column):

[a] 9:21 Mt 12:16; 16:20; Mk 7:36; 8:30; 9:9; Lk 5:14; 8:56
[b] 9:22-27 Mt 16:21-28; Mk 8:31-9:1
[c] 9:22 Lk 13:33; 18:31
[d] Mt 17:12,22-23; Lk 24:7
[e] Lk 17:25; 20:17; 1Pt 2:4
[f] Lk 20:1; 22:66
[g] Mt 27:63; Jn 2:19
[h] 9:23 2Tm 2:12-13
[i] Mt 10:38-39; Lk 14:27; 1Co 15:31
[j] 9:24 Lk 17:33; Jn 12:25
[k] 9:25 Lk 12:20
[l] 9:26 Mt 10:33; Rm 1:16; 2Tm 1:8; Heb 11:16; 1Jn 2:28
[m] Dn 7:10; Zch 14:5; Mt 24:30;

Jn 1:51; Ac 1:11; 1Th 1:10   [n] Lk 12:9; Rv 14:10   [o] 9:27 Jn 8:52; Heb 2:9   [p] Mt 10:23; 23:36; 24:34; Mk 13:30; Lk 21:31-32   [q] 9:28-36 Mt 17:1-8; Mk 9:2-8   [r] 9:28 Mk 14:33; Lk 8:51   [s] Mt 14:23; Lk 3:21; 5:16; 6:12; 9:18   [t] 9:29 Mk 16:12   [u] Ex 34:29; Dn 7:9; Mt 28:3   [v] 9:32 Gn 2:21; 15:12; 1Sm 26:12; Dn 8:18; 10:9; Mt 26:43

[A] 9:23 Lit *come after*   [B] 9:23 Other mss omit *daily*   [C] 9:31 Or *departure*; Gk *exodus*   [D] 9:32 Lit *were weighed down with sleep*

---

ah was expected to overthrow Roman rule and, in a wave of popularity, take over as king of Israel. Contrary to this, Jesus' mission was to **suffer** and **be rejected** by the Jewish leadership before being **killed** and **raised** from the dead. This was the first of several predictions by Jesus of His death and/or resurrection (v. 44; 12:50; 17:25; 18:31-33).

9:23 To be a true disciple of Jesus requires self-denial. The **cross** was the most painful and humiliating form of execution of the Roman era. Thus, to **take up** one's cross **daily** is to expect painful situations every day because of allegiance to Christ.

9:24 The principle that one must lose one's **life** to **save it** as opposed to living only for this world is Jesus' most common refrain in the Gospels (14:26-27; 17:33; Mt 10:38-39; 16:24-25; Mk 8:34-35; Jn 12:25). To follow Him, we must lay down our devotions to this world and live for Christ and His mission.

dei

Greek Pronunciation:	[DAY]
HCSB Translation:	must
Uses in Luke's Gospel:	18
Uses in the NT:	101
Focus passage:	Luke 9:22

The Greek word *dei* is a special form of the verb *deo*, meaning *to bind*, and refers to something that is a binding obligation upon someone. In the Gospels the term *dei* normally occurs in contexts related to some aspect of salvation, and the binding obligation comes from the decree of God—though this is not stated but is clearly implied. Thus, in Luke's Gospel *dei* indicates that Jesus *must* do the Father's will (2:49); preach (4:43); keep a divine appointment with a tax collector (19:5); suffer, die, and rise again (9:22; 17:25; 24:7,26; see Mt 16:21; Mk 8:31; Ac 17:3); and that the Scriptures *must* be fulfilled (Lk 24:44; see Jn 20:9; Ac 1:16). Luke continued the theme of divine necessity in Acts: Jesus *must* remain in heaven until the appointed time (Ac 3:21), everyone *must* believe in Jesus for salvation (Ac 4:12; 16:30-31), and believers *must* suffer for Jesus' sake (Ac 9:16; 14:22).

9:25 No matter how wealthy a person is in this life (**gains the whole world**), he will be bankrupt eternally (**forfeits himself**) if he dies without Christ.

9:26 To be **ashamed** of Christ and His **words** indicates unbelief, which will bring eternal judgment (12:9; 2Tm 2:12) at His second coming. It is also possible for believers to temporarily cower in fear around unbelieving peers and act "ashamed" of Jesus, as Peter did in his denials of Christ. In such cases a believer may suffer loss of heavenly reward (1Co 3:10-15; 2Co 5:10), but not suffer eternal punishment.

9:27 This cryptic statement refers to the next event in the book—the transfiguration of Jesus (vv. 28-35). **Some standing here** indicates Peter, James, and John, who were with Jesus at His transfiguration (v. 28). **See the kingdom of God** apparently means that the glorious appearance of Jesus (vv. 29,32) was a preview of the coming kingdom.

9:28-29 On **Peter, John, and James**, see note at 8:51-53. The traditional candidate for **the mountain** in these verses is Mount Tabor, six miles east of Nazareth and about 1,900 feet in elevation. However, it is more likely that it was Mount Hermon, located between Caesarea Philippi and Damascus, which rises to 9,000 feet above sea level. We are not told in what sense the **appearance** of Jesus' face **changed**. His clothes are described as **dazzling white** (gleaming, like a bolt of lightning). There may be an intended similarity here to Moses after he was with God on Mount Sinai (Ex 34:29-35) or to the vision of the Son of Man in Rv 1:13-16.

9:30-31 Jewish tradition expected **Moses** and **Elijah** (see Mal 4:5-6) to return before the arrival of the kingdom of God. Like Jesus, their appearances were almost blinding in this special appearance. The word translated **death** (Gk *exodos*) means "departure," though it can also refer to the OT exodus from Egypt. The choice of this word may be an association with the presence of Moses. **In Jerusalem** makes it clear that the "exodus" would be Jesus' death on the cross.

9:32-33 It is not clear whether Peter, James, and John were in a **deep sleep** because it was in the middle of the night, or if they were caused to fall asleep as Daniel was when angels came (Dn 8:18; 10:9). Peter spoke as Moses and Elijah **were departing** in an attempt to prolong the glorious scene.

they saw His glory and the two men who were standing with Him. ³³As the two men were departing from Him, Peter said to Jesus, "Master,^a it's good for us to be here! Let us make three *tabernacles: one for You, one for Moses, and one for Elijah"—not knowing what he said.^b

³⁴While he was saying this, a cloud appeared and overshadowed^c them. They became afraid as they entered the cloud. ³⁵Then a voice came from the cloud,^d saying:

This is My Son,^e the Chosen One;^{A,f} listen to Him!^g

³⁶After the voice had spoken, only Jesus was found. They kept silent, and in those days told no one what they had seen.

The Power of Faith over a Demon

³⁷The next day,^h when they came down from the mountain, a large crowd met Him. ³⁸Just then a man from the crowd cried out, "Teacher, I beg You to look at my son, because he's my only child.ⁱ ³⁹Often a spirit seizes him; suddenly he shrieks, and it throws him into convulsions until he foams at the mouth;^B wounding^c him, it hardly ever leaves him. ⁴⁰I begged Your disciples to drive it out, but they couldn't."^j

⁴¹Jesus replied, "You unbelieving and rebellious^D generation!^k How long will I be with you and put up with you?^l Bring your son here."

⁴²As the boy was still approaching, the de-

mon knocked him down and threw him into severe convulsions. But Jesus rebuked the *unclean spirit, cured the boy,^m and gave him back to his father.ⁿ ⁴³And they were all astonished at the greatness of God.^o

The Second Prediction of His Death

While everyone was amazed at all the things He was doing,^p He told His disciples, ⁴⁴"Let these words sink in:^E The Son of Man is about to be betrayed into the hands of men."^q

⁴⁵But they did not understand this statement;^r it was concealed from them so that they could not grasp it,^s and they were afraid to ask Him about it.^F

Who Is the Greatest?

⁴⁶Then an argument started among them about who would be the greatest of them.^t ⁴⁷But Jesus, knowing the thoughts of their hearts,^u took a little child and had him stand next to Him. ⁴⁸He told them, "Whoever welcomes^G this little child in My name welcomes Me. And whoever welcomes Me welcomes Him who sent Me.^v For whoever is least among you—this one is great."^w

In His Name

⁴⁹John responded,^x "Master, we saw someone driving out demons in Your name,^y and we tried to stop him because he does not follow us."^z

⁵⁰"Don't stop him," Jesus told him, "because whoever is not against you is for you."^{H,aa}

^a9:33 Lk 5:5; 9:49
^bMk 14:40
^c9:34 Lk 1:35; Ac 5:15
^d9:35 Ex 24:15-16; 2Pt 1:16-18
^eEx 4:23; Ps 2:7; Hs 11:1; Ac 13:33; Heb 1:5
^fPs 89:3; Is 42:1; Lk 23:35
^gAc 3:22
^h9:37-42 Mt 17:14-18; Mk 9:14-27
ⁱ9:38 Lk 7:12
^j9:40 Lk 9:1; 10:17
^k9:41 Php 2:15
^lJn 14:9
^m9:42 Zch 3:2; Mt 8:26; Mk 1:25; Lk 4:35,39; Jd 9
ⁿLk 7:15
^o9:43 2Pt 1:16
^p9:43-45 Mt 17:22-23; Mk 9:30-32
^q9:44 Lk 9:22
^r9:45 Mk 6:52; Lk 2:50; 18:34; 24:25; Jn 10:6; 12:16; 16:17-19
^sLk 18:34; 24:16
^t9:46-48 Mt 18:1-5; Mk 9:33-37; Lk 22:24
^u9:47 Mt 9:4
^v9:48 Mt 10:40,42; Lk 10:16; Jn 13:20
^wLk 22:26
^x9:49-50 Mk 9:38-40
^y9:49 Mt 7:22; 12:27; Mk 16:17; Lk 10:17; Ac 19:13
^zNm 11:28
^{aa}9:50 Mt 12:30; Lk 11:23

But his idea was shortsighted for two reasons: (1) to make **three** equal **tabernacles** (temporary structures for housing) was to place Moses and Elijah on a level with Jesus, and not to worship Him exclusively (Rv 19:10; 22:8-9); and (2) Jesus' discussion of His coming "exodus" in Jerusalem (see note at Lk 9:30-31) meant there was no room for delay in God's plan of redemption.

9:34-35 The **cloud** that **overshadowed** the scene recalls the cloud that came over the tabernacle in the wilderness (Ex 40:34-35). The **voice . . . from the cloud** combines an echo of 3:22, at Jesus' baptism, and an allusion to Dt 18:15, where Israel was told to **listen** to the prophet like Moses who would come (the Messiah).

9:36 Luke did not state why the three apostles were **silent** about what they had experienced, though Mt 17:9 states that Jesus commanded them to tell no one until after His resurrection. In 2Pt 1:16-18, Peter recalled his experience at the transfiguration.

9:38-42 It is not known whether the **disciples** who could not heal the boy afflicted with seizures by a demon were the nine apostles who did not see Jesus' transfiguration or some of the wider group of disciples. It is not explained whether it was just the onlookers, or also the disciples, who

were **unbelieving**. The boy was immediately **cured** when Jesus **rebuked** the demon.

9:44-45 In the aftermath of the healing of the demon-possessed boy (vv. 38-43), Jesus shifted gears and announced that He would soon be **betrayed** (Gk *paradidomi*; "to be handed over, delivered") and captured. The disciples were confused by Jesus' words. Luke stated that it was **concealed from them** until after Jesus' death and resurrection. Meanwhile, their fear of Jesus' talk about betrayal and death kept them from asking Him what He meant.

9:46-48 The question about **who would be the greatest** among the apostles came up more than once (22:24). Jesus knew the competitive pride that fostered the argument and was quick to point out that, spiritually, **whoever** was **least** (truly humble as a disciple of Christ) was **great**.

9:49-50 Apparently the man casting out **demons** in Jesus' **name** was a true disciple, even though he did not **follow** Jesus from town to town. The spiritual principle here is to be careful about judging, because certain people who are **not against you** may be on your side. The opposite point is made in 11:23.

9:51 The phrase **the days . . . for Him to be taken up** refers

The Journey to Jerusalem

[51] When the days were coming to a close for Him to be taken up,[A,a] He determined[B,b] to journey to Jerusalem.[c] [52] He sent messengers ahead of Him,[d] and on the way they entered a village of the •Samaritans[e] to make preparations for Him. [53] But they did not welcome Him, because He determined to journey to Jerusalem.[f] [54] When the disciples James and John saw this, they said, "Lord, do You want us to call down fire from heaven to consume them?"[C,g]

[55] But He turned and rebuked them,[D] [56] and they went to another village.

Following Jesus

[57] As they were traveling on the road someone said to Him,[h] "I will follow You wherever You go!"

[58] Jesus told him, "Foxes have dens, and birds of the sky[E] have nests, but the Son of Man has no place to lay His head." [59] Then He said to another, "Follow Me."

"Lord," he said, "first let me go bury my father."[F]

[60] But He told him, "Let the dead bury their own dead, but you go and spread the news of the kingdom of God."[i]

---

[a]9:51 Mk 16:19
[b]2Kg 12:17; Is 50:7; Jr 42:15
[c]Lk 13:22; 17:11; 18:31; 19:11,28
[d]9:52 Lk 10:1
[e]Mt 10:5
[f]9:53 Jn 4:9,20
[g]9:54 2Kg 1:9-16; Rv 13:13
[h]9:57-60 Mt 8:19-22
[i]9:60 Lk 8:1; 9:2; 16:16
[j]9:61 1Kg 19:20
[k]10:2 Mt 9:37-38; Jn 4:35
[l]Rv 14:15
[m]Mt 20:1
[n]2Th 3:1
[o]10:3 Mt 7:15; 10:16; Jn 10:12; Ac 20:29
[p]10:4 Lk 12:33; 22:35-36
[q]Mk 6:8; Lk 9:3; 22:35-36
[r]Mt 10:9-10
[s]10:5 Mt 11:26; Lk 10:21; 12:51
[t]10:6 Lk 7:50; 8:48; 24:36; Jn 20:19; Ac 15:33; 1Co 16:11; Jms 2:16
[u]10:7 Mt 10:10; 1Tm 5:18; 2Pt 2:13
[v]10:8 1Co 10:27
[w]10:9 Mt 10:8; 1Th 5:14

---

[61] Another also said, "I will follow You, Lord, but first let me go and say good-bye to those at my house."[j]

[62] But Jesus said to him, "No one who puts his hand to the plow and looks back is fit for the kingdom of God."

Sending Out the Seventy

10 After this, the Lord appointed 70[G] others, and He sent them ahead of Him in pairs to every town and place where He Himself was about to go. [2] He told them:[k] "The harvest[l] is abundant, but the workers[m] are few. Therefore, pray to the Lord of the harvest to send out workers into His harvest.[n] [3] Now go; I'm sending you out like lambs among wolves.[o] [4] Don't carry a money-bag,[p] traveling bag,[q] or sandals;[r] don't greet anyone along the road. [5] Whatever house you enter, first say, 'Peace[s] to this household.' [6] If a son of peace[H] is there, your peace[t] will rest on him; but if not, it will return to you. [7] Remain in the same house, eating and drinking what they offer, for the worker is worthy of his wages.[u] Don't be moving from house to house. [8] When you enter any town, and they welcome you, eat the things set before you.[v] [9] Heal the sick[w] who are there, and tell them, 'The kingdom of

---

[A]9:51 His ascension　[B]9:51 Lit He stiffened His face to go; Is 50:7　[C]9:54 Other mss add as Elijah also did　[D]9:55-56 Other mss add and said, "You don't know what kind of spirit you belong to. [56] For the Son of Man did not come to destroy people's lives but to save them,"　[E]9:58 Wild birds, as opposed to domestic birds　[F]9:59 Not necessarily meaning his father was already dead　[G]10:1 Other mss read 72　[H]10:6 A peaceful person; one open to the message of the kingdom

---

to Jesus' ascension to heaven and the events leading up to it. **Determined** means literally "to fix your face," a Hebrew expression for firmness of purpose in spite of danger. The mention of traveling to **Jerusalem** begins the third major section of Luke's Gospel (9:51–19:27).

9:52-56 The **Samaritans** would not **welcome** Jesus because He was headed to **Jerusalem** to worship in the temple and not to Mount Gerizim, their preferred site of worship (see Jn 4:20-21). In Mk 3:17, the apostles **James and John** were nicknamed by Jesus *Boanerges*, meaning "Sons of Thunder," likely indicating that they had fiery tempers. **Call down fire from heaven** recalls Elijah's action in 2Kg 1:9-16.

9:57-58 Jesus warned this would-be disciple to count the cost before committing to follow Him. After all, even Christ Himself had **no place** to call home. To follow Christ is to loosen your grip on the things that normally provide physical and emotional security.

9:59-60 It is doubtful that this man's **father** had already died. If he had, the man would have been involved in burial rites instead of talking to Jesus. Thus, the man's words were an excuse to delay, possibly for years, his responsibility to follow Jesus and **spread the news of the kingdom of God**.

9:61-62 In 14:26, Jesus made it clear that He must be the top priority in a disciple's life, even above one's family. **Puts his hand to the plow and looks back** means looking over your shoulder while plowing, making it impossible to plow a straight furrow. Christians cannot follow Christ by looking

back. We must focus on serving Him as we move ahead at His command.

10:1 Though not mentioned in 9:1-6, Jesus had apparently sent out the apostles previously **in pairs** (see Mk 6:7). In this verse He sent out 70 other followers to cover Judea with the message of good news in advance of His coming.

10:2 Christ seems to be saying that, as **abundant** as the spiritual **harvest** was, the 70 whom He sent out to preach were not enough. There was need for many more to take the message, and prayers must be offered to meet this need.

10:3 **Lambs among wolves** was a common metaphor in Judaism for being in a dangerous situation.

10:4 On items for the journey, see note at 9:3-5.

10:5-6 **Peace** (Hb *shalom*) was a traditional Jewish greeting. But the word actually speaks of wholeness or well-being. **Son of** is a Jewish expression meaning "one characterized by" (Ac 4:36). In this context, "son of peace" and **your peace** appear to relate to the 70 followers who were offering the message of peace with God through faith in Jesus Christ (Rm 5:1).

10:7 On **remain in the same house**, see note at 9:3-5. **The worker is worthy of his wages** is a basic principle of fairness. This was quoted by the apostle Paul in making his case for ministers of God's Word being paid for their work (1Tm 5:17-18).

10:8-9 If the 70 disciples were made **welcome** in a town, it indicated that the hearts of the people were open to the

God[a] has come near[b] you.' [10]When you enter any town, and they don't welcome you, go out into its streets and say, [11]'We are wiping off as a witness against you[c] even the dust of your town that clings to our feet. Know this for certain: The kingdom of God has come near.' [12]I tell you, on that day[d] it will be more tolerable for Sodom[e] than for that town.[f]

Unrepentant Towns

[13]"Woe[g] to you,[h] Chorazin![i] Woe to you, Bethsaida![j] For if the miracles[k] that were done in you had been done in Tyre and Sidon,[l] they would have repented long ago, sitting in •sackcloth and ashes![m] [14]But it will be more tolerable for Tyre and Sidon at the judgment[n] than for you. [15]And you, Capernaum,[o] will you be exalted to heaven?[p] No, you will go down to •Hades![q] [16]Whoever listens to you listens to Me.[r] Whoever rejects you rejects Me.[s] And whoever rejects Me rejects the One who sent Me."[t]

The Return of the Seventy

[17]The Seventy[A,u] returned with joy, saying,[v] "Lord, even the demons[w] submit to us in Your name."[x]

[18]He said to them, "I watched Satan[y] fall from heaven like a lightning flash.[z] [19]Look, I have given you the authority[aa] to trample[ab] on snakes[ac] and scorpions[ad] and over all the power of the enemy;[ae] nothing will ever harm you.[af] [20]However, don't rejoice that[B] the spirits[ag] submit to you,[ah] but rejoice that your names are written[ai] in heaven."

The Son Reveals the Father

[21]In that same hour[aj] He[C] rejoiced in the Holy[D] Spirit[ak] and said, "I praise[E] You, Father,[al] Lord of heaven and earth,[am] because You have hidden these things from the wise and the learned[an] and have revealed them to infants.[ao] Yes, Father, because this was Your good pleasure.[F,ap] [22]All things have[G] been entrusted to Me by My Father. No one knows who the Son

[a]10:9 Mt 12:28; Lk 11:20; 17:20 [b]Mt 10:7; Mk 1:15; 1Pt 4:7 [c]10:11 Mt 10:14; Mk 6:11; Lk 9:5; Ac 13:51; 18:6 [d]10:12 Mt 7:22; 23:1; Lk 17:31; 2Pt 3:10 [e]Rv 11:8 [f]Mt 10:15; 11:22,24; Lk 10:14 [g]10:13-15 Mt 11:20-24 [h]10:13 Ezk 16:23; Mt 23:13-16; Lk 6:24; Rv 9:12 [i]Mt 11:21 [j]Jn 12:21 [k]Ex 3:20; Lk 19:37; Ac 2:22 [l]Ezr 3:7; Jr 25:22; 47:4; Jl 3:4; Lk 6:17 [m]Est 4:1,3; Dn 9:3; Jnh 3:6 [n]10:14 Ps 1:5; Mt 12:41 [o]10:15 Mt 4:13; Lk 4:23,31; 7:1 [p]Ac 2:33 [q]Is 14:12-15; Ac 2:27 [r]10:16 Mt 10:40; Jn 13:20

[s]Mt 25:45; Lk 9:48; Jn 12:48 [t]Jn 5:23; 1Th 4:8 [u]10:17 Ezk 8:11 [v]10:17-20 Mk 16:17-18; Jn 12:31 [w]10:17 Rv 9:20 [x]Jn 10:25; 14:13 [y]10:18 Mt 4:1,10; Ac 13:10; Rv 12:9 [z]Mt 28:3; Col 2:15 [aa]10:19 Mk 1:22 [ab]Lk 21:24; Rv 11:2 [ac]Gn 3:16; Mt 23:33; Rv 9:19 [ad]Lk 11:12; Rv 9:3 [ae]Mt 13:39; 1Co 15:25 [af]Ps 91:13; Mk 16:18; Ac 28:5 [ag]1Tm 4:1; 1Jn 4:1 [ah]10:20 Mt 7:22-23 [ai]Ex 32:32; Neh 9:38; Mal 3:16 [aj]10:21-24 Mt 11:25-27; 13:16-17 [ak]10:21 Lk 2:27; 4:1; 19:21; Ac 2:4 [al]Mt 7:21; Lk 23:34,46; Jn 8:42; 11:41; 12:27-28; 17:1-25 [am]Gn 14:19; Ac 17:24 [an]Is 44:25; Jr 8:9; Ac 13:7; 1Co 1:19-27; 3:19-20 [ao]Ps 8:2; Mt 21:16 [ap]Lk 2:14

gospel message. In some sense, the present tense aspects of **the kingdom of God** were present in the preaching of the gospel and the healing ministry delegated by Jesus to the 70.

10:10-11 On wiping dust off the feet, see note at 9:3-5. On **the kingdom of God has come near**, see note at verses 8-9.

10:12 That day is the day of judgment. **Sodom** was destroyed by the Lord because of its sin (Gn 19:23).

10:13-14 Chorazin and Bethsaida were towns in Galilee near Capernaum. **Tyre** and **Sidon** were Gentile cities in Phoenicia on the Mediterranean coast northwest of Galilee. **Sackcloth and ashes** were worn by those in mourning, sometimes as an expression of repentance from sin (Neh 9:1; Jnh 3:5).

10:15 Jesus spent more time in ministry in **Capernaum** than anywhere else in Galilee. Yet, in their arrogance (**exalted to heaven**), the people of this city rejected Jesus and, as a result of their unbelief, would be sent to **Hades** (death, the realm of death or punishment beyond the grave).

10:16 The principle here is that rejection of the disciples is ultimately rejection of God the Father (**the One who sent Me**), for the Father sent the Son and the Son in turn sent out the 70 disciples to preach and heal (vv. 1,9). Since they were commissioned by Christ, to listen to the 70 was like listening to Jesus Himself. Likewise, to reject the 70 was to reject Jesus. Finally, to reject Jesus was to reject God the Father.

10:17-20 Part of the healing these **Seventy** disciples performed (v. 9) had to do with casting out **demons**. The phrase **Satan fall from heaven** is probably an echo of Ezk 28:16-17, speaking of the initial judgment upon the Devil after he rebelled against God. This passage speaks of a further defeat suffered by Satan as Jesus' disciples were victorious in ministry over the power of the enemy (Satan), symbolized

here by **snakes and scorpions**. As awesome as the power to cast out demons was, it was even more significant that the disciples' **names** were written in the listing of the elect of God—the Lamb's book of life **in heaven** (see Rv 13:8).

10:21-22 The mention of the **Holy Spirit** here is part of Luke's emphasis on the Spirit. The **wise** and **learned** people of the area had rejected the ministry of the 70 disciples, but the insignificant and children (**infants**) had accepted their message. This was part of the plan of God. In His **good pleasure** (see Eph 1:3-11), these things were hidden (Gk *apokrupto*; "to keep secret") from some and revealed to others. It is

The old Roman road from Jerusalem to Jericho was legendary for the dangers it posed to first-century travelers. The road is part of the precipitous drop from the east side of the Mount of Olives down to the Jordan Valley. A Roman aqueduct that is still used today is in the lower portion of the photo.

is except the Father, and who the Father is except the Son, and anyone to whom the Son desires[A] to reveal Him."[a]

[23] Then turning to His disciples He said privately, "The eyes that see the things you see are blessed! [24] For I tell you that many prophets and kings wanted to see the things you see yet didn't see them; to hear the things you hear yet didn't hear them."[b]

The Parable of the Good Samaritan

[25] Just[c] then an expert in the law[d] stood up to test[e] Him, saying, "Teacher,[f] what must I do to inherit eternal life?"[g]

[26] "What is written in the law?" He asked him. "How do you read it?"

[27] He answered:

Love the Lord your God[h] **with all your heart, with all your soul, with all your strength, and with all your mind;**[i] **and your neighbor as yourself.**[B,j]

[28] "You've answered correctly," He told him. "Do this and you will live."[k]

[29] But wanting to justify himself,[l] he asked Jesus, "And who is my neighbor?"[m]

[30] Jesus took up the question and said: "A man was going down from Jerusalem to Jer-

icho and fell into the hands of robbers. They stripped him, beat him up, and fled, leaving him half dead. [31] A priest happened to be going down that road. When he saw him, he passed by on the other side. [32] In the same way, a Levite, when he arrived at the place and saw him, passed by on the other side. [33] But a •Samaritan[n] on his journey came up to him, and when he saw the man, he had compassion.[o] [34] He went over to him and bandaged his wounds, pouring on olive oil[p] and wine. Then he put him on his own animal, brought him to an inn, and took care of him. [35] The next day[C] he took out two •denarii, gave them to the innkeeper, and said, 'Take care of him. When I come back I'll reimburse you for whatever extra you spend.'

[36] "Which of these three do you think proved to be a neighbor to the man who fell into the hands of the robbers?"

[37] "The one who showed mercy[q] to him," he said.

Then Jesus told him, "Go and do the same."

Martha and Mary

[38] While they were traveling, He entered a village, and a woman named Martha[r] welcomed Him into her home.[D] [39] She had a sister

Cross references (center column)

[a] 10:22 Jn 1:18; 6:46; 7:29; 8:19; 10:15; 17:25-26
[b] 10:24 Jn 8:56; Heb 11:13; 1Pt 1:10-12
[c] 10:25-28 Mt 22:34-40; Mk 12:28-34
[d] 10:25 Lk 7:30
[e] Mt 16:1; 19:3
[f] Mt 8:19; Lk 3:12; Jn 1:38
[g] Mt 19:29; Lk 18:18; Jn 12:25; Rv 21:7
[h] 10:27 Lk 4:8
[i] Dt 6:5
[j] Lv 19:18
[k] 10:28 Lv 18:5; Neh 9:29; Ezk 20:11; Rm 10:5; Gl 3:12
[l] 10:29 Lk 16:15
[m] Ex 20:16-17; Lv 6:2; 19:13-18; Pr 3:28-29; Mt 5:43; 19:19; Rm 13:9-10
[n] 10:33 Mt 10:5; Lk 9:52; Ac 1:8
[o] Lk 7:13; 15:20
[p] 10:34 Is 1:6; Jms 5:14
[q] 10:37 Mt 23:23; Lk 1:72; Jms 2:13
[r] 10:38 Jn 11:1,19-20; 12:2-3

[A] 10:22 Or *wills*, or *chooses*   [B] 10:27 Lv 19:18; Dt 6:5   [C] 10:35 Other mss add *as he was leaving*   [D] 10:38 Other mss omit *into her home*

---

impossible for spiritually dead humans to know God the **Father** or His **Son** unless the Son reveals both.

10:23-24 It was a truly **blessed** circumstance to see the ministry of Christ and even His delegated authority in healing and casting out demons. Peter stated that, beyond OT **prophets and kings**, even angels wanted to **see** and **hear** the things that Jesus was doing (see 1Pt 1:12).

10:25 Expert in the law refers to a scribe (11:45-46,52-53), many of whom were also Pharisees. The question asked was a standard one in Judaism and was intended to **test** Jesus. To **inherit** (Gk *kleronomeo*; "to receive an allotted share") **eternal life** shows that many Jews thought their eternal destiny was based on their Jewish bloodline and their good deeds.

10:26-28 Jesus turned the tables on the scribe by asking him to answer his own question, then complimented the man on correctly citing Lv 19:18 and Dt 6:5. Jesus did not say that it is possible to earn eternal life by loving **God** and **your neighbor**. No human other than Jesus has been able to love perfectly in every situation. Since **heart . . . soul**, and **mind** are sometimes used interchangeably in Scripture, the terms here are not intended to speak of separate aspects of human existence. Rather, they describe the total person.

10:29 Having correctly answered the first question, this man asked for an important clarification. Certain kinds of neighbors are of course easy to love, while others, being argumentative or of different religious and moral persuasions, can be very hard to love. It seems that the man hoped Jesus would justify his bias against certain kinds of neighbors.

10:30-32 The road **from Jerusalem to Jericho**, a distance of

17 miles with a descent of more than 3,000 feet in elevation, was a dangerous route through desert country. It had many places where **robbers** could lie in wait. It is possible that the **priest** and the **Levite . . . passed by on the other side** of the road because they thought the wounded man was dead and they would become ritually unclean by touching him, but it is more likely that they were afraid of being attacked by the same robbers or simply did not want to be bothered with the inconvenience of helping the man.

10:33-35 The Jews considered the Samaritans to be physical half-breeds who had intermarried with foreigners and who were guilty of false worship. For such a sworn enemy of the Jews to show **compassion** on an injured Jew and pay the expenses of his recuperation, while two Jewish religious officials did not, would deeply humiliate a Jew.

10:36-37 Now Jesus got back to the question with which this story began: Who is my neighbor? (see note at v. 29). His point was that the Samaritan **proved** he was a good **neighbor** by his gracious actions toward the man who had been attacked by robbers. It was impossible for the scribe to avoid acknowledging that it was the Samaritan who **showed mercy**. Jesus' reply to **go and do the same** emphasized that Jews should love their Samaritan neighbors even as the good Samaritan in the story had acted in love toward a Jew.

10:38-39 The **village** in v. 38 was Bethany, just over the Mount of Olives and two miles east of Jerusalem. **Martha** and **Mary** were the sisters of Lazarus, whom Jesus raised from the dead (Jn 11:1-44). **Sat at the Lord's feet . . . listening** was the posture of a committed disciple.

named Mary, who also sat at the Lord's[A] feet[a] and was listening to what He said.[B] 40 But Martha was distracted by her many tasks, and she came up and asked, "Lord, don't You care[b] that my sister has left me to serve alone? So tell her to give me a hand."[C,c]

41 The Lord[D] answered her, "Martha, Martha, you are worried and upset about many things,[d] 42 but one thing is necessary.[e] Mary has made the right choice,[E] and it will not be taken away from her."

The Model Prayer

11 He was praying[f] in a certain place, and when He finished, one of His disciples said to Him, "Lord, teach us to pray, just as John also taught his disciples."[g]

2 He said to them, "Whenever you pray, say:[h]

Father,[F,i]
Your name[j] be honored as holy.[k]
Your kingdom come.[G,l]
3 Give us each day our daily bread.[H,m]
4 And forgive us our sins,[n]
for we ourselves also forgive everyone
in debt to us.[I,o]
And do not bring us into temptation."[J,p]

Keep Asking, Searching, Knocking

5 He also said to them: "Suppose one of you[K] has a friend and goes to him at midnight and says to him, 'Friend, lend me three loaves of bread, 6 because a friend of mine on a journey has come to me, and I don't have anything to offer him.'[L] 7 Then he will answer from inside and say, 'Don't bother me! The door is already locked, and my children and I have gone to bed. I can't get up to give you anything.' 8 I tell you, even though he won't get up and give him anything because he is his friend, yet because of his friend's persistence,[M] he will get up and give him as much as he needs.[q]

9 "So[r] I say to you, keep asking,[N,s] and it will be given to you. Keep searching,[O,t] and you will find. Keep knocking,[P,u] and the door will be opened to you. 10 For everyone who asks receives, and the one who searches finds, and to the one who knocks, the door will be opened. 11 What father among you, if his son[Q] asks for a fish, will give him a snake instead of a fish? 12 Or if he asks for an egg, will give him a scorpion? 13 If you then, who are evil,[v] know how to give good gifts to your children, how much more will the heavenly Father[w] give[R] the Holy Spirit[x] to those who ask Him?"

A House Divided

14 Now[y] He was driving out a demon[z] that

Cross references (center column)

a 10:39 Lk 8:35; Ac 22:3
b 10:40 Mk 4:38; 1Pt 5:7
c Rm 8:26
d 10:41 Lk 12:22; 1Co 7:32; Php 4:6
e 10:42 Ps 16:5; 27:4; Jn 6:27
f 11:1 Lk 3:21
g Lk 5:33
h 11:2-13 Mt 6:9-13
i 11:2 Jn 20:17; 1Pt 1:17
j Ps 9:10; Jn 10:25; 17:6
k Is 29:23; Lk 1:49; 1Pt 3:15
l Mk 9:1
m 11:3 Pr 30:8
n 11:4 Lk 6:12; 7:48; 24:47
o Mt 18:23-35
p Mt 26:41; Lk 4:13; 22:40,46; 1Co 10:1
q 11:8 Lk 18:1-6
r 11:9-13 Mt 7:7-11; Jn 14:13-14; 15:7; 16:24
s 11:9 Mt 18:19; 21:22; Mk 11:24; Jms 1:5-6,17; 1Jn 3:22; 5:14-15
t Dt 4:29; 1Ch 28:9; 2Ch 15:2; Pr 8:17; Is 55:6; Jr 29:13
u Lk 11:10; 12:36; 13:25; Ac 12:13,16; Rv 3:20
v 11:13 Rm 12:17; 1Th 5:22; 2Tm 3:13
w Mt 5:48
x Ps 51:11; Jn 1:33; Ac 2:4,38; Rm 8:9
y 11:14-23 Mt 9:32-34; 12:22-30; Mk 3:22-27; Jn 7:20; 8:48,52; 10:20
z 11:14 Mk 7:26

Textual notes

A 10:39 Other mss read at Jesus' B 10:39 Lit to His word or message C 10:40 Or tell her to help me D 10:41 Other mss read Jesus E 10:42 Lit has chosen the good part F 11:2 Other mss read Our Father in heaven G 11:2 Other mss add Your will be done on earth as it is in heaven H 11:3 Or our bread for tomorrow I 11:4 Or everyone who wrongs us J 11:4 Other mss add But deliver us from the evil one K 11:5 Lit Who of you L 11:6 Lit I have nothing to set before him M 11:8 Or annoying persistence, or shamelessness N 11:9 Or you, ask O 11:9 Or Search P 11:9 Or Knock Q 11:11 Other mss read son asks for bread, would give him a stone? Or if he R 11:13 Lit the Father from heaven will give

Study notes

10:40-42 Martha was **distracted** from what should have been her highest priority—learning from Jesus. She was **worried and upset** about all the household chores that needed to be done and irritated with her sister Mary because it was the role of women to serve men in such a setting. Jesus indicated that Martha's exclusive focus should be the same as her sister's—discipleship, an eternally commendable choice (**it will not be taken away from her**).

11:1-4 This model prayer for Jesus' disciples is similar to the one in the Sermon on the Mount (Mt 6:9-13), but much shorter. Apparently, the **disciples** were motivated to learn to **pray** by both Jesus' example and that of John the Baptist and his disciples. It was unusual for Jews to refer to God as **Father**. Such an address would seem too personal and familiar. Even though Luke emphasized the offer of the kingdom of God (4:43) and the nearness of the kingdom in Jesus' ministry (10:9,11), some aspects of the kingdom are still future (**Your kingdom come**). All people are dependent on the Lord to meet their daily needs, as in **give us . . . our daily bread**. **In debt** refers to what is "owed" to us spiritually (i.e., having been sinned against). The phrase **do not bring us into temptation** is in contrast with Christ Himself, who was led by the Holy Spirit to be tested by Satan (see note at 4:1).

11:5-8 The point of this story is that bold **persistence** pays off. But, as with the story of the widow and the judge

in 18:1-8, it must not be understood that God is like the hesitant homeowner in the story. If bold persistence is rewarded even by someone who is disposed against granting our request, how much more so will God, who cares about His children, delight in responding generously to our persistent prayers.

11:9-10 Asking, searching, and knocking visualize different aspects of prayer, all of which are valid. **Keep asking . . . searching . . . knocking** reflects the persistence theme emphasized in the story of verses 5-8. The assurance that **everyone who asks receives** does not mean that every prayer is answered as we want it to be. Rather, it means that if we persist in prayer, our prayers will eventually be answered according to God's best for us.

11:11-12 No human **father** who really loved his child would be so uncaring as to give him a **snake** in place of a **fish** or a **scorpion** in place of an **egg**.

11:13 The parallel passage in Mt 7:11 reads, "Give good things to those who ask Him." If those good things are related to the **Holy Spirit**, the wording may be speaking of spiritual gifts (Rm 12; 1Co 12). This verse reflects Luke's emphasis on the Holy Spirit. Leading up to the day of Pentecost, the apostles and other believers waited in prayer (Ac 1:14) for the baptism of the Spirit to come. In that instance, **the heavenly Father** gave the Holy Spirit to those who asked Him.

was mute.[A,a] When the demon came out, the man who had been mute, spoke, and the crowds were amazed. [15] But some of them said, "He drives out demons by •Beelzebul,[b] the ruler[c] of the demons!"[d] [16] And others, as a test,[e] were demanding of Him a sign[f] from heaven.

[17] Knowing their thoughts,[g] He told them: "Every kingdom divided[h] against itself is headed for destruction, and a house divided against itself falls. [18] If Satan[i] also is divided against himself, how will his kingdom[j] stand? For you say I drive out demons by Beelzebul. [19] And if I drive out demons by Beelzebul, who is it your sons[B,k] drive them out by? For this reason they will be your judges. [20] If I drive out demons by the finger of God,[l] then the kingdom of God[m] has come to you. [21] When a strong man, fully armed, guards his estate, his possessions are secure.[C] [22] But when one stronger than he attacks and overpowers[n] him, he takes from him all his weapons[D,o] he trusted[p] in, and divides up his plunder.[q] [23] Anyone who is not with Me is against Me,[r] and anyone who does not gather with Me scatters.

An Unclean Spirit's Return

[24] "When[s] an •unclean spirit[t] comes out of a man, it roams through waterless places looking for rest,[u] and not finding rest, it then[E] says, 'I'll go back to my house where I came from.' [25] And returning, it finds the house swept and put in order. [26] Then it goes and brings seven

other spirits[v] more evil than itself, and they enter and settle down there. As a result, that man's last condition is worse than the first."[w]

True Blessedness

[27] As He was saying these things, a woman from the crowd[x] raised her voice and said to Him, "The womb that bore You and the one who nursed You[y] are blessed!"

[28] He said, "Even more, those who hear the word of God[z] and keep it[aa] are blessed!"

The Sign of Jonah

[29] As the crowds were increasing, He began saying: "This generation[ab] is an evil generation.[ac] It demands a sign,[ad] but no sign will be given to it except the sign of Jonah.[F,ae] [30] For just as Jonah became a sign to the people of Nineveh, so also the •Son of Man[af] will be to this generation. [31] The queen of the south[ag] will rise up at the judgment[ah] with the men of this generation and condemn[ai] them, because she came from the ends of the earth to hear the wisdom of Solomon,[aj] and look—something greater than Solomon is here! [32] The men of Nineveh will rise up at the judgment with this generation and condemn it, because they repented at Jonah's proclamation, and look—something greater than Jonah is here!

[a]11:14 Mk 7:37; 9:15-25; Lk 7:22
[b]11:15 2Kg 1:2; Mt 10:25
[c]Lk 12:58
[d]Jn 12:31; 14:30; 16:11; Eph 2:2
[e]11:16 Lk 10:25
[f]Jn 2:11; 8:6
[g]11:17 Lk 5:22; Php 2:6
[h]Dn 5:28; 11:4; Lk 12:52-53
[i]11:18 Mt 4:1,10; Ac 13:10
[j]Lk 4:5
[k]11:19 Gl 3:7; 1Pt 5:13
[l]11:20 Ex 8:19; 31:18; Dt 9:10; Ps 8:3
[m]Mt 19:24; 21:31,43; Lk 17:21
[n]11:22 Jn 16:33; 1Jn 2:13
[o]Eph 6:11,13
[p]Ac 26:28
[q]Is 49:24-26
[r]11:23 Mk 9:40; Lk 9:50
[s]11:24-26 Mt 12:43-45
[t]11:24 Mk 1:23-27; Lk 8:29; 9:42; Rv 18:2
[u]Mt 11:29; Rv 4:8; 14:11
[v]11:26 Lv 26:18-28; Dt 7:1; Pr 6:31; 26:25; Lk 8:2
[w]Jn 5:14; 2Pt 2:20-22
[x]11:27 Lk 12:3
[y]Lk 1:48; 23:29
[z]11:28 Lk 5:1; 8:21; Ac 13:7
[aa]Lv 22:31; Jn 13:17; Jms 1:22; Rv 1:3; 22:7
[ab]11:29 Lk 7:31; 17:25; 21:32
[ac]11:29-32 Mt 12:39-42; Mk 8:12
[ad]Lk 11:16
[ae]Jnh 1:1-4:9; Mt 16:4
[af]11:30 Mk 2:10; Lk 5:24
[ag]11:31 1Kg 10:1; 2Ch 9:1
[ah]Lk 10:14
[ai]Heb 11:7
[aj]1Kg 4:34; Pr 1:1

[A]11:14 A demon that caused the man to be mute   [B]11:19 Your exorcists   [C]11:21 Lit his possessions are in peace   [D]11:22 Gk panoplia, the armor and weapons of a foot soldier; Eph 6:11,13   [E]11:24 Other mss omit then   [F]11:29 Other mss add the prophet

---

11:14-16 Instead of praising God for Jesus' healing of the **mute** demon-possessed man, some in the crowd accused Him of casting out demons by the power of Satan. **Beelzebul**, the god worshiped by Philistines in Ekron, had become a nickname for Satan. Others were trying to trap Jesus by asking Him to perform a miraculous **sign**.

11:17-20 A **kingdom** or **house** divided against itself is self-destructive. Jesus made two key points in His defense: (1) It is nonsense to think that Satan would divide his own "house" by casting out his own **demons**, and (2) it is unlikely that Jewish exorcists were drawing on a different source of power than Jesus. Thus, the best explanation of what happened was that Jesus drove out **demons by the finger of God** (God's power active in the world).

11:21-22 The **stronger** man can usually overpower the weaker man and disarm him. The implication is that Jesus, being stronger than Satan, was in the process of disarming him. **Divides up his plunder** may refer to the same thing as the giving of gifts related to Christ's victory in Eph 4:8.

11:23 This is the opposite principle from what is stated in 9:50. Since the context has to do with demonic activity and power, anyone who did not believe that Jesus cast out demons by the power of God was **against** Christ. **Anyone who does not gather with Me scatters** is a reference to

a shepherd gathering or scattering a flock of sheep. This could refer to either Israel or the church as a flock since Luke wrote his Gospel after the church's beginning.

11:24-26 These verses warn that the exorcism of a demon is incomplete unless Christ enters by faith and indwells the person who is healed. Otherwise, there is nothing to prevent the demon and **seven other spirits** from reentering and possessing the person. In that case, this person's **last condition** is even **worse** than it was initially.

11:27-28 Jesus did not deny that His mother, Mary, was greatly **blessed**. Instead, He stated that a person who hears God's word and acts upon it in faith is even more blessed than anyone who has mere family ties to Him (Rv 1:3).

11:29-32 There are two possible meanings of **the sign of Jonah**. (1) Since Jonah's preaching prompted repentance by **the people of Nineveh** (Jnh 3), such preaching was the only sign Israel would receive from Jesus, or (2) Jonah's three days and nights in the large fish (Jnh 1:17) was a foreshadowing of Jesus' death and resurrection, which was the sign that would be given to that **evil generation**. The queen of Sheba (**queen of the south**) responded to the wisdom of **Solomon**, which was not equal to the wisdom and salvation offered by Jesus, **the Son of Man**. If Nineveh repented at Jonah's proclamation, how much more should the crowds repent at Jesus' preaching!

The Lamp of the Body

[33] "No[a] one lights a lamp[b] and puts it in the cellar or under a basket,[A] but on a lampstand, so that those who come in may see its light. [34] Your eye is the lamp of the body.[c] When your eye is good, your whole body is also full of light. But when it is bad,[d] your body is also full of darkness. [35] Take care then, that the light in you is not darkness. [36] If, therefore, your whole body is full of light, with no part of it in darkness, it will be entirely illuminated, as when a lamp shines its light on you."[B]

Religious Hypocrisy Denounced

[37] As He was speaking, a *Pharisee[e] asked Him to dine with him. So He went in and reclined at the table. [38] When the Pharisee saw this, he was amazed that He did not first perform the ritual washing[C,f] before dinner.[g] [39] But the Lord said to him: "Now you Pharisees *clean the outside of the cup and dish, but inside you are full of greed[h] and evil.[i] [40] Fools![j] Didn't He who made the outside make the inside too? [41] But give from what is within to the poor,[D,k] and then everything is clean[l] for you.

[42] "But woe[m] to you Pharisees! You give a tenth[E,n] of mint, rue, and every kind of herb, and you bypass[F] justice[o] and love for God.[G,p] These things you should have done without neglecting the others.

[43] "Woe to you Pharisees! You love the front seat[q] in the *synagogues[r] and greetings in the marketplaces.

[44] "Woe to you![H] You are like unmarked graves;[s] the people who walk over them don't know it."

[45] One of the experts in the law[t] answered Him, "Teacher, when You say these things You insult us too."

[46] Then He said: "Woe also to you experts in the law! You load people with burdens[u] that are hard to carry, yet you yourselves don't touch these burdens with one of your fingers.[v]

[47] "Woe to you! You build monuments[I] to the prophets,[w] and your fathers killed[x] them. [48] Therefore, you are witnesses[y] that you approve[J,z] the deeds of your fathers, for they killed them, and you build their monuments.[K] [49] Because of this, the wisdom of God[aa] said, 'I will send them prophets and apostles,[ab] and some of them they will kill and persecute,'[ac] [50] so that this generation[ad] may be held responsible for the blood of all the prophets shed since the foundation of the world[L,ae]— [51] from the blood of Abel[af] to the blood of Zechariah,[ag] who perished between the altar and the sanctuary.

"Yes, I tell you, this generation will be held responsible.[M]

[52] "Woe to you experts in the law! You have taken away the key of knowledge![ah] You didn't

[a]11:33 Mt 5:15; Mk 4:21
[b]Lk 8:16
[c]11:34-36 Mt 6:22-23
[d]11:34 Jr 24:8; Mt 7:17
[e]11:37 Lk 7:36
[f]11:38 Heb 6:2
[g]Mt 15:2; Mk 7:2-5
[h]11:39 Mt 23:25; Lk 12:20; 16:14; Heb 10:34
[i]Mk 7:22
[j]11:40 Mt 23:17; Lk 12:20
[k]11:41 Lk 12:33; Ac 24:17
[l]Ps 24:4; Ti 1:15
[m]11:42 Lk 10:13
[n]Dt 14:22; Lk 18:12
[o]Mc 6:8; Zch 7:9; Mt 12:18,20; Jn 7:24; Ac 8:33
[p]Dt 6:5; Lk 10:27; Jn 5:42; 2Th 3:5
[q]11:43 Mt 23:6; Mk 12:39; Lk 20:46
[r]Jms 2:2
[s]11:44 Mt 23:27
[t]11:45 Lk 7:30
[u]11:46 Mt 23:4; Ac 27:10; Gl 6:5
[v]Mt 11:28-30; Ac 15:10
[w]11:47 Mt 2:23; Ac 7:52
[x]Lk 20:15
[y]11:48 Mt 23:31
[z]Ac 22:20; Rm 1:32
[aa]11:49 Pr 1:20-33; 8:1-36; Mt 23:34
[ab]Lk 11:27;
13:1; 15:32; 21:9-10; Jn 13:16; Ac 1:2
[ac]1Th 2:15; 2Tm 3:12
[ad]11:50 Lk 11:29
[ae]Heb 9:26; Rv 18:24
[af]11:51 Gn 4:9-10; Heb 12:24; 1Jn 3:12
[ag]2Ch 24:20-22
[ah]11:52 1Co 14:6

A11:33 Other mss omit *or under a basket*   B11:36 Or *shines on you with its rays*   C11:38 Lit *He did not first wash*   D11:41 Or *But donate from the heart as charity*   E11:42 Or *a tithe*   F11:42 Or *neglect*   G11:42 Lit *the justice and the love of God*   H11:44 Other mss read *you scribes and Pharisees, hypocrites!*   I11:47 Or *graves*   J11:48 Lit *witnesses and approve*   K11:48 Other mss omit *their monuments*   L11:50 Lit *so that the blood of all . . . world may be required of this generation,*   M11:51 Lit *you, it will be required of this generation*

11:33-36 Jesus held forth the **light** of the gospel for all to see. Those who rejected Him and His message had **bad** spiritual eyes, which turned the light of Christ into **darkness**. But those who received Christ by faith were filled with light.

11:37-38 The **ritual washing** that took place before a meal was an ancient Jewish tradition, but it was not commanded in the Mosaic law (Mk 7:3).

11:39-41 Jesus declared that the problem of uncleanness on our **inside** is not taken care of by cleansing our **outside** (hands, feet, etc.). The way to make sure everything is **clean** in God's eyes is to give freely from a heart devoted to God.

11:42-44 The first **woe** pronounced by Jesus on the **Pharisees** was not because they tithed everything, but because they did not practice **justice and love**. The second woe was because they loved the spotlight, not the Lord. Regarding the third woe, if Jews walked over **unmarked graves**, they became defiled. Ironically, Jesus said that following the teachings of the Pharisees was like walking over an unmarked grave; you would become defiled without even knowing it. The teachings of the Pharisees seemed genuine and true, but in reality they were corrupted and misleading.

11:45-46 The scribe (expert **in the law**) standing by realized

that the three woes Jesus had just pronounced against the Pharisees also reflected negatively on the scribes. So Jesus leveled an additional **woe** on the scribes. They burdened the average Jew with a **load** that they themselves did not carry. This could mean that the scribes were hypocritical in their keeping of the law or that they had no compassion for the people who tried to live by their burdensome regulations.

11:47-48 Jesus' point in these verses is that the scribes and Pharisees were pleased to honor the **prophets** with **monuments**, now that the prophets were dead and silenced. The scribes and Pharisees were like their **fathers**, who **killed** God's prophets.

11:49-51 The Lord was not surprised when some of His **prophets and apostles** were persecuted or killed. Because of the presence of Jesus—who was far greater than prophets or apostles—that **generation** of Israel was held responsible (see the similar statement about Babylon the Great in Rv 18:20). The judgment for that responsibility was apparently the destruction of Jerusalem in A.D. 70. **Abel** was the victim of the first murder in Scripture (Gn 4:8), while Zechariah's murder is recorded in 2Ch 24:20-25. Since 2 Chronicles was the last book in the Hebrew Bible, that would make it the last murder in the Bible of Jesus' day.

11:52 In Mt 23:13, Jesus accused the scribes (**experts in the**

go in yourselves, and you hindered[a] those who were going in."

[53]When He left there,[A] the *scribes and the Pharisees began to oppose[b] Him fiercely and to cross-examine Him about many things; [54]they were lying in wait[c] for Him to trap Him in something He said.[B,d]

Beware of Religious Hypocrisy

12 In these circumstances,[c] a crowd of many thousands came together, so that they were trampling[e] on one another. He began to say to His disciples first:[f] "Be on your guard[g] against the yeast[D,h] of the *Pharisees, which is hypocrisy.[i] [2]There is nothing covered that won't be uncovered,[j] nothing hidden that won't be made known.[k] [3]Therefore, whatever you have said in the dark will be heard in the light, and what you have whispered in an ear in private rooms[l] will be proclaimed on the housetops.[m]

Fear God

[4]"And I say to you, My friends,[n] don't fear those who kill the body, and after that can do nothing more. [5]But I will show you the One to fear: Fear[p] Him who has authority to throw people into *hell[q] after death. Yes, I say to you, this is the One to fear! [6]Aren't five sparrows sold for two pennies?[E] Yet not one

of them is forgotten in God's sight.[r] [7]Indeed, the hairs of your head are all counted. Don't be afraid; you are worth more than many sparrows!

Acknowledging Christ

[8]"And I say to you, anyone who acknowledges[s] Me before men, the *Son of Man[t] will also acknowledge him before the angels of God,[u] [9]but whoever denies Me before men will be denied before the angels of God.[v] [10]Anyone who speaks a word against the Son of Man will be forgiven,[w] but the one who blasphemes against the Holy Spirit[x] will not be forgiven. [11]Whenever[y] they bring you before *synagogues and rulers and authorities,[z] don't worry[aa] about how you should defend[ab] yourselves or what you should say. [12]For the Holy Spirit will teach you at that very hour what must be said."[ac]

The Parable of the Rich Fool

[13]Someone from the crowd said to Him, "Teacher,[ad] tell my brother to divide the inheritance with me."

[14]"Friend,"[F] He said to him, "who appointed Me a judge or arbitrator over you?" [15]He

[a]11:52 1Co 14:39	
[b]11:53 Mk 6:19; Gl 5:1	
[c]11:54 Ac 23:21	
[d]Is 29:21; Mt 22:15; Mk 3:2; 12:13; Lk 20:20; Jn 8:6	
[e]12:1 Lk 8:5	
[f]Mt 16:5-6; Mk 8:14-15	
[g]Jr 9:4; Lk 17:3; Ac 20:28	
[h]Lk 13:21; Gl 5:9	
[i]Mt 23:28; Mk 12:15; Gl 2:13; 1Pt 2:1	
[j]12:2-9 Mt 10:26-33; Mk 4:22; Lk 8:17	
[k]12:2 Lk 6:44	
[l]12:3 Mt 6:6; 24:26; Lk 12:24	
[m]Ac 10:9	
[n]12:4 Ac 27:3	
[o]Is 8:13; 51:12; Jr 1:8; Jn 6:20	
[p]12:5 Ps 147:11; Pr 1:7; Ac 10:2; Rv 14:7	
[q]Mk 9:43; Jms 3:6	
[r]12:6 Ps 50:11	
[s]12:8 Mt 7:23; Jn 9:22	
[t]Lk 5:24; 11:30	
[u]Lk 15:10; Jn 1:51; Ac 10:3; Rm 10:9; Rv 3:5	
[v]12:9 Lk 9:26	
[w]12:10 Mt 12:31-32; Mk 3:28-30	
[x]Lk 1:15,35;	

[y]12:11-12 Mt 10:19-20; Mk 13:11; Lk 21:14-15
[z]12:11 Lk 20:20; Eph 3:10; Col 2:15 [aa]Php 4:6 [ab]Ac 26:24
[ac]12:12 Pr 1:23; Jn 14:26 [ad]12:13 Lk 11:45

[A]11:53 Other mss read *And as He was saying these things to them* [B]11:54 Other mss add *so that they might bring charges against Him* [C]12:1 Or *Meanwhile*, or *At this time*, or *During this period* [D]12:1 Or *leaven* [E]12:6 Lit *two assaria; the assarion* (sg) was a small copper coin [F]12:14 Lit *Man*

law] of locking up "the kingdom of heaven." Here in Luke, **the key of knowledge** is the Scriptures, which the scribes and Pharisees mishandled. Thus the people were locked out from understanding the things of God.

11:53-54 The **Pharisees** and **scribes** reacted with accusations and hostile questions. Their intent was to **trap** Jesus by some statement for which He could be arrested.

geenna

Greek Pronunciation:	[GEH ehn nah]
HCSB Translation:	hell
Uses in Luke's Gospel:	1
Uses in the NT:	12
Focus passage:	Luke 12:5

Geenna (hell) is the Greek form of Hb *gey'-hinnom* (Valley of Hinnom) via Aramaic *geyhinnam*, a valley located just south/southwest of Jerusalem's Old City. In the days of Ahaz and Manasseh, it was the location where children were dedicated and/or sacrificed to Molech (2Kg 23:10; 2Ch 28:3; 33:6; Jr 7:31), and by NT times it had become a place for burning trash. Because of its sordid history, the Hinnom Valley became associated in Jewish thought with *hell*, the place of final punishment. *Geenna* is described primarily with images of fire (Mt 5:22; 18:9; Mk 9:43,45,48), and though the term does not occur in Revelation, it is a prominent theme there (cp. the lake of fire; Rv 19:20; 20:10,14-15; 21:8). At the final resurrection, the souls of the ungodly (in Hades) will be reunited with their resurrected bodies, and thrown into *Geenna* (Mt 10:28).

12:1-3 In the NT, **yeast** is normally a symbol of corruption or evil (Mt 16:6,11; 1Co 5:6-8; Gl 5:9). Here the symbol is defined as the evil of **hypocrisy**. Hypocritical behavior fools many people, but it will eventually be **uncovered** and **made known** by God, who is never fooled. Everything said in **private** will become public knowledge.

12:4-5 There are many people who can **kill** you physically, but that is the limit of the harm they can do. As natural as it is to **fear** such people, it makes more sense to fear God, for He presides over not just life and death but eternity. Those who remain opposed to Him by their unbelief and unrepentant sins will be punished in **hell**.

12:6-7 If God does not overlook even the most insignificant birds (**sparrows**), He is aware of all the details of life (**the hairs of your head**) of every human being. **Pennies** translates the Greek word for a coin that was similar to a nickel.

12:8-9 These verses add a positive element to Jesus' statement in 9:26. There, if a person is "ashamed" of Jesus (here it is **denies Me before men**), he will face shame when Christ comes in judgment. Here, it is also stated that if a person **acknowledges** (Gk *homologeo*; "to confess") Christ, He will do likewise in heaven (in the presence of **the angels of God**).

12:10 Apparently, speaking against Jesus could be **forgiven** because of His human appearance (one aspect of the meaning of **Son of Man**). According to the parallel passage in Mk 3:28-30, blasphemy **against the Holy Spirit** is to attribute to Satan the works of the Spirit. That is the unforgivable sin.

then told them, "Watch out and be on guard[a] against all greed[b] because one's life is not in the abundance of his possessions."[c]

[16] Then He told them a parable:[d] "A rich[e] man's land was very productive. [17] He thought to himself, 'What should I do, since I don't have anywhere to store my crops? [18] I will do this,' he said. 'I'll tear down my barns and build bigger ones and store all my grain and my goods there. [19] Then I'll say to myself, "You[A] have many goods stored up for many years. Take it easy;[f] eat, drink, and enjoy yourself."'[g]

[20] "But God said to him, 'You fool![h] This very night your •life is demanded of you. And the things you have prepared—whose will they be?'[i]

[21] "That's how it is with the one who stores up treasure[j] for himself and is not rich toward God."[k]

The Cure for Anxiety

[22] Then He said to His disciples: "Therefore I tell you,[l] don't worry about your life, what you will eat; or about the body, what you will wear.[m] [23] For life is more than food and the body more than clothing. [24] Consider the ravens:[n] They don't sow or reap; they don't have a storeroom or a barn; yet God feeds them.[o] Aren't you worth much more than the birds? [25] Can any of you add a •cubit to his height[B] by worrying?[p] [26] If then you're not able to do even a little thing, why worry about the rest?

[27] "Consider how the wildflowers grow: They don't labor or spin thread. Yet I tell you, not even Solomon[q] in all his splendor was adorned like one of these! [28] If that's how God clothes the grass, which is in the field today and is thrown into the furnace tomorrow, how much more will He do for you—you of little faith?[r] [29] Don't keep striving for what you should eat and what you should drink, and don't be anxious. [30] For the Gentile world eagerly seeks[s] all these things, and your Father[t] knows that you need them.

[31] "But seek His kingdom,[u] and these things will be provided for you.[v] [32] Don't be afraid,[w] little flock,[x] because your Father delights[y] to give you the kingdom.[z] [33] Sell[aa] your possessions and give to the poor.[ab] Make money-bags[ac] for yourselves that won't grow old, an inexhaustible treasure[ad] in heaven, where no thief comes near and no moth destroys. [34] For where your treasure is, there your heart will be also.[ae]

Ready for the Master's Return

[35] "Be ready for service[C] and have your lamps lit.[af] [36] You must be like people waiting for their master[ag] to return[D] from the wedding banquet[ah] so that when he comes and knocks, they can open the door for him at once.[ai] [37] Those •slaves the master will find alert[aj] when he comes will be blessed. •I assure you: He will get ready,[E]

[a]12:15 1Tm 6:20; 2Tm 1:14; 4:15; 2Pt 3:17; 1Jn 5:21
[b]Eph 5:3
[c]Gn 12:5; Jb 20:20; 31:24; Ps 62:10
[d]12:16 Lk 5:36; 8:11
[e]Lk 6:24; 16:19; 18:23; 19:2; 21:1
[f]12:19 Mt 11:28; Mk 6:31; Rv 6:11; 14:13
[g]Ec 2:24
[h]12:20 Jr 17:11; Lk 11:40
[i]Ps 39:6; 49:10; Jr 17:11; Mt 16:26
[j]12:21 2Pt 3:7
[k]Mt 6:19-20
[l]12:22-32 Mt 6:25-34
[m]12:22 Pr 31:25
[n]12:24 1Kg 17:4,6; Jb 38:41; Ps 147:9; Pr 30:17
[o]Rv 12:6
[p]12:25 Php 4:6
[q]12:27 1Kg 10:4-7
[r]12:28 Mt 8:26; 14:31; 16:8
[s]12:30 Heb 11:14; 13:14
[t]Mt 5:16; 6:1; 11:27; Jn 8:42
[u]12:31 Mt 5:6,20; Lk 11:2
[v]1Kg 3:11-14; Mt 19:29; Mk 10:29-30
[w]12:32 Lk 12:4,7
[x]Is 40:11; Ac 20:28; 1Pt 5:2-3
[y]Mt 11:26; Lk

10:21; Eph 1:5,9; Php 2:13   [z]Mt 13:19; 25:34; Lk 22:29
[aa]12:33-34 Mt 6:19-21 [ab]12:33 Ac 24:17 [ac]Lk 10:4 [ad]Mk 10:21; 2Co 4:7   [ae]12:34 1Pt 1:4   [af]12:35-48 Mt 24:42-51; 25:1-13; Mk 13:33-37; Jn 13:4-5 [ag]12:36 2Pt 3:12 [ah]Jn 2:1 [ai] Rv 3:20
[aj]12:37 Rm 13:11

[A]12:19 Lit say to my soul, "Soul, you   [B]12:25 Or add one moment to his life-span   [C]12:35 Lit Let your loins be girded; an idiom for tying up loose outer clothing in preparation for action; Ex 12:11   [D]12:36 Lit master, when he should return   [E]12:37 Lit will gird himself

12:11-12 These verses speak of the persecution the apostles would face at the hands of **rulers and authorities**. Classic examples where the **Holy Spirit** did teach them **what must be said** are Ac 4:8-12; 5:29-32.

12:13-15 Disputes over family **inheritance** were normally handled by rabbis (teachers) in Jewish society, and Jesus was recognized as such. The person who approached Jesus was probably a younger brother who was upset because his older brother received twice the inheritance, the Jewish tradition. Jesus refused to be drawn into the matter, realizing that the man's motivation was **greed**.

12:16-20 This parable is about the danger of greed, measured by the abundance of possessions (v. 15). The rich man was infatuated with hoarding his **goods**. In his self-centered perspective (there are at least 10 self-references in vv. 17-19), he thought this was an effective strategy for a long life of leisure and pleasure. But God views such an outlook as foolish and short-sighted. When a person dies—which could be at any time—"you cannot take it with you."

12:21 Rich toward God is what verse 33 and Mt 6:20 refer to as "treasures in heaven." Being "rich toward God" means living to glorify God and investing our earthly assets to make an eternal difference.

12:22-26 Jesus' advice to His disciples was not to be over-

come with anxiety over the basic needs of life. Worrying won't change **even a little thing**. Since God feeds **the ravens**, who have no storeroom, will He not care for humans, His most valuable and beloved creatures?

12:27-32 If God "dresses" (**clothes**) nature so beautifully, He will certainly meet a disciple's basic needs. Unbelievers (the unsaved **Gentile world**) pursue provision and wealth as if life were all about these things and as if God is unconcerned about their needs, but this is not to be the focus of the Christian. In the parallel passage in Mt 6:33, Jesus declared, "Seek first the kingdom of God and His righteousness." Thus, at least a key part of seeking God's **kingdom** for the believer is to strive to live by His standards. In regard to other benefits of the kingdom, believers can rest assured that the Father will give them to His children with joy.

12:33-34 If a disciple is living for God's glory and His kingdom (v. 31), he or she will choose priorities for this life that are designed to reap **inexhaustible** heavenly dividends. These become the **treasure** of one's **heart**. Wealth on this earth can be stolen or destroyed, but heavenly treasures are eternally secure.

12:35-40 The point of this story is that we must practice constant readiness. **Waiting** for the **master to return** means waiting for Christ's second coming. It is not known

have them recline at the table, then come and serve them.[a] [38] If he comes in the middle of the night, or even near dawn,[A] and finds them alert, those slaves are blessed. [39] But know this: If the homeowner had known at what hour the thief was coming,[b] he would not have let his house be broken into. [40] You also be ready,[c] because the Son of Man[d] is coming at an hour that you do not expect."[e]

Rewards and Punishment

[41] "Lord," Peter asked, "are You telling this parable to us or to everyone?"

[42] The Lord said: "Who then is the faithful and sensible manager[f] his master will put in charge of his household servants to give them their allotted food[g] at the proper time? [43] That slave whose master finds him working when he comes will be rewarded. [44] I tell you the truth: He will put him in charge of all his possessions. [45] But if that slave says in his heart, 'My master is delaying his coming,'[h] and starts to beat the male and female slaves, and to eat and drink and get drunk, [46] that slave's master will come on a day he does not expect him and at an hour he does not know. He will cut him to pieces[B] and assign him a place with the unbelievers.[C] [47] And that slave who knew his master's will and didn't prepare himself or do it[D] will be severely beaten.[i] [48] But the one who did not know and did things deserving[j] of blows will be beaten lightly. Much will be required of everyone who has been given much. And even more will be expected of the one who has been entrusted with more.[E,k]

Not Peace but Division

[49] "I came[l] to bring fire on the earth, and how I wish it were already set ablaze! [50] But I have a baptism to be baptized with,[m] and how it consumes[n] Me until it is finished![o] [51] Do you think that I came here to give peace to the earth?[p] No, I tell you, but rather division! [52] From now on, five in one household will be divided: three against two, and two against three.

[53] **They will be divided,**
 father against son,
 son against father,
 mother against daughter,
 daughter against mother,
 mother-in-law against
 her daughter-in-law,
 and daughter-in-law
 against mother-in-law."[F,q]

Interpreting the Time

[54] He also said to the crowds:[r] "When you see a cloud rising in the west, right away you say, 'A storm is coming,' and so it does.[s] [55] And when the south wind is blowing, you say, 'It's going to be a scorcher!' and it is. [56] Hypocrites![t] You know how to interpret the appearance of the earth and the sky, but why don't you know how to interpret this time?[u]

Settling Accounts

[57] "Why don't you judge for yourselves what is right?[v] [58] As you are going with your adversary[w] to the ruler, make an effort to settle with him on the way. Then he won't drag you before the judge,[x] the judge hand you over to the

---

[a]12:37 Lk 17:8; 22:27
[b]12:39 1Th 5:2
[c]12:40 Lk 21:36
[d]Mk 2:10
[e]1Th 5:2; 2Pt 3:10; Rv 3:3; 16:15
[f]12:42 Lk 16:1
[g]1Tm 6:8
[h]12:45 1Jn 2:28
[i]12:47 Dt 25:2; Jms 4:17
[j]12:48 Lv 5:17; Nm 15:29
[k]Lv 5:17; Mt 13:12; Rm 1:20; 2:14; 1Tm 1:13
[l]12:49-53 Mt 10:34-36; Mk 10:38
[m]12:50 Ac 22:16; Rm 6:3; Eph 4:5
[n]2Co 5:14
[o]Jn 19:28; 19:30
[p]12:51 Lk 2:14
[q]12:53 Mc 7:6
[r]12:54-56 Mt 16:2-3
[s]12:54 1Kg 18:43-44
[t]12:56 Lk 6:42
[u]Lk 20:10; 21:8,30
[v]12:57-59 Mt 5:25-26
[w]12:58 1Pt 5:8
[x]2Tm 4:8

[A]12:38 Lit *even in the second or third watch*   [B]12:46 Lit *him in two*   [C]12:46 Or *unfaithful*, or *untrustworthy*   [D]12:47 Lit *or do toward his will*   [E]12:48 Or *much*   [F]12:53 Mc 7:6

---

when the return will take place, so it is necessary to be constantly vigilant. If a **thief** can come unexpectedly, how much more can the coming of Christ catch His servants by surprise?

12:41-44 Jesus previously told His disciples that His parables held secrets that were only for His followers (see note at 8:9-10). Jesus did not answer Peter's question directly. Instead, He told another story about a **master** and his **manager**. The story in verses 35-40 emphasized that the master's servant should be watching, but this story made it clear that the servant must also be **working**. Disciples who persevere in faithfulness will be rewarded by the master.

12:45-48 If a servant of the **master** does not faithfully watch and work, there will be severe consequences when the master comes. The reason for the difference in punishments is the principle of accountable stewardship. More is expected of those who have been **given much**.

12:49-50 **Fire** in these verses symbolizes judgment on the **earth** at the second coming of Christ. **A baptism to be baptized with** refers to the suffering of Christ, specifically His agony on the cross (Mk 10:38). **Consumes** (Gk *sunecho*; "to control, distress") expresses how focused Jesus was on

completing His mission. **It is finished** are the words Jesus used on the cross to signal that redemption was accomplished (Jn 19:30).

12:51-53 Jesus Christ made **peace** with God possible for anyone who will choose to follow as His disciple (Rm 5:1). Unbelievers, however, remain at odds with God and His requirements for holiness. There will be such division over the gospel of Christ that some families will be split down the middle. The spiritual family of God is more important than family bloodlines.

12:54-56 Storms in Palestine usually blow in from the west, off the Mediterranean Sea, or from the deserts to the south. A **cloud** coming from the west usually brought rain or a **storm**, while a **south wind** was dry and hot. In this context, **interpret** (Gk *dokimazo*) means "to discern." **Time** (Gk *kairos*) refers to "the opportune moment," in this case the presence of Messiah in their midst.

12:57-59 The need to **settle** accounts before undergoing judicial punishment pictures the need to be reconciled to God (Rm 5:10) before facing His judgment. At that point, it will be too late to seek reconciliation.

bailiff, and the bailiff throw you into prison.[a] [59] I tell you, you will never get out of there until you have paid the last cent."[A,b]

Repent or Perish

13 At that time,[c] some people came and reported to Him about the Galileans[d] whose blood •Pilate[e] had mixed with their sacrifices. [2] And He[B] responded to them, "Do you think that these Galileans were more sinful than all Galileans because they suffered these things?[f] [3] No, I tell you; but unless you repent, you will all perish as well! [4] Or those 18 that the tower in Siloam[g] fell on and killed—do you think they were more sinful than all the people who live in Jerusalem? [5] No, I tell you; but unless you repent, you will all perish as well!"

The Parable of the Barren Fig Tree

[6] And He told this parable:[h] "A man had a fig tree that was planted in his vineyard. He came looking for fruit on it and found none.[i] [7] He told the vineyard worker, 'Listen, for three years I have come looking for fruit on this fig tree and haven't found any. Cut it down![j] Why should it even waste the soil?'[k]

[8] "But he replied to him, 'Sir,[c] leave it this year also, until I dig around it and fertilize it.[l] [9] Perhaps it will bear fruit next year, but if not, you can cut it down.'"

Healing a Daughter of Abraham

[10] As He was teaching in one of the •syna-gogues on the Sabbath,[m] [11] a woman was there who had been disabled by a spirit[D,n] for over 18 years. She was bent over and could not straighten up at all.[E] [12] When Jesus saw her, He called out to her,[F] "Woman, you are free of your disability." [13] Then He laid His hands on her,[o] and instantly she was restored[p] and began to glorify God.[q]

[14] But the leader of the synagogue, indignant[r] because Jesus had healed on the Sabbath, responded by telling the crowd, "There are six days when work should be done;[s] therefore come on those days and be healed and not on the Sabbath day."

[15] But the Lord answered him and said, "Hypocrites![t] Doesn't each one of you untie his ox[u] or donkey from the feeding trough[v] on the Sabbath and lead it to water?[w] [16] Satan[x] has bound[y] this woman, a daughter of Abraham,[z] for 18 years—shouldn't she be untied from this bondage on the Sabbath day?"

[17] When He had said these things, all His adversaries[aa] were humiliated,[ab] but the whole crowd was rejoicing over all the glorious things He was doing.[ac]

The Parables of the Mustard Seed and of the Yeast

[18] He said, therefore, "What is the kingdom of God like,[ad] and what can I compare it to? [19] It's like a mustard seed that a man took

a 12:58 Pr 25:8
b 12:59 Lk 21:2
c 13:1 Mt 21:18-19; Mk 11:12-14
d Jn 4:45
e Mt 27:2
f 13:2 Jn 9:2
g 13:4 Jn 9:7
h 13:6 Lk 5:35; 12:16
i Mt 21:18-19; Mk 11:13
j 13:7 Mt 7:19; Lk 3:9; Jn 15:2; Rm 11:22
k Is 5:2
l 13:8 Lk 16:3
m 13:10 Lk 4:31; 6:6
n 13:11 Mt 8:17; Lk 4:33; 6:18; 7:21; 8:2,29; 9:39
o 13:13 Mt 19:15; Mk 5:23; 6:2,5; 8:23; Lk 4:40
p Ac 15:16; Heb 12:12
q Jn 11:4
r 13:14 Mt 20:24; 21:15; 26:8; Mk 10:14,41; 14:4
s Ex 20:9; Ezk 46:1
t 13:15 Lk 6:42
u Lk 14:5,19; 1Co 9:9
v Lk 2:7,12,16
w Mt 12:11; Lk 14:5
x 13:16 Mt 4:1,10; Ac 13:10
y Mk 5:3; 15:1; 2Tm 2:9
z Gn 16:15; Jn 8:37; Heb 2:16
aa 13:17 Lk 21:5; 1Co 16:9; Php 1:28; 1Tm 5:14
ab Ps 132:18; Is 45:16 LXX;
1Pt 3:16   ac Is 12:5   ad 13:18-19 Mt 13:31-32; Mk 4:30-32

A 12:59 Gk lepton, the smallest and least valuable copper coin in use   B 13:2 Other mss read Jesus   C 13:8 Or Lord   D 13:11 Lit had a spirit of disability   E 13:11 Or straighten up completely   F 13:12 Or He summoned her

13:1-5 It is not known why Pontius **Pilate** (see note at 3:1) killed the **Galileans** mentioned here. The mention of **their sacrifices** specifies that their deaths took place in the temple area, probably in relation to a major religious festival, when all Jewish men were required to make a pilgrimage to Jerusalem. Nor is anything else known about the 18 people killed by the collapse of **the tower in Siloam** in the southeastern part of Jerusalem. Jesus' questions about the sinfulness of the Galileans and those killed by the tower was apparently inspired by widespread opinion that such things happen only as punishment for specific sins. Jesus countered this notion but nevertheless emphasized that every person must **repent** (see note at 3:2-3) or else perish spiritually for eternity.

13:6-9 The **fig tree** is often used as a symbol for the nation of Israel (Mt 24:32-33; Mk 11:12-14). Though young fig trees are slow to begin bearing fruit, three years was a sufficient length of time for trees to become mature and thus fruitful. The extra **year** requested by the vineyard worker represented one final chance for the trees to become fruitful. Otherwise they would be **cut . . . down**. This parable thus referred to Israel's last chance before judgment. If they rejected Jesus' message and miracles, the time for patience would be ended. But a future hope for Israel remains (Rm 11).

13:10-13 The mention of the **Sabbath** as the time of this healing calls to mind the earlier controversy between Jesus and the religious leaders (6:1-11). The woman He healed had severe curvature of the spine, caused somehow by a demon (an evil **spirit**). The healing involved two acts: (1) the casting out of the demon, and (2) the straightening of the spine. This verse does not imply that deformities or illnesses are commonly caused by demons. This was apparently a very rare case, reflective of the heightened spiritual warfare during the time of Christ's earthly stay.

13:14-16 The **leader of the synagogue** rejected the healing as it was **work** done in violation of **the Sabbath day** (see note at Ex 20:8-11). Jesus' use of the plural **hypocrites** shows that He knew the leader spoke for many others who shared his view. He revealed their hypocrisy by showing that it was necessary for everyone to do some work on the Sabbath, notably related to the tending of farm animals. Should not a Jewish woman (**daughter of Abraham**) under bondage to Satan for such a long time also be **untied** on the Sabbath?

13:17 Those who had sided with the leader of the synagogue were **humiliated** because it made them look as if they had more compassion for animals than for a demonized, disfigured woman.

13:18-21 Both of these parables allude to the astonishing advancement of the **kingdom of God** (God's rule in this

and sowed in his garden. It grew and became a tree, and the birds of the sky nested in its branches."

²⁰Again He said, "What can I compare the kingdom of God[a] to? ²¹It's like yeast[b] that a woman took and mixed into 50 pounds[A] of flour until it spread through the entire mixture."[B]

The Narrow Way

²²He went through one town and village after another, teaching and making His way to Jerusalem.[c] ²³"Lord," someone asked Him, "are there few being saved?"[C,d]

He said to them, ²⁴"Make every effort to enter through the narrow door,[e] because I tell you, many will try to enter and won't be able ²⁵once the homeowner gets up and shuts the door.[f] Then you will stand[D] outside and knock on the door, saying, 'Lord, open up for us!' He will answer you, 'I don't know you or where you're from.' ²⁶Then you will say,[E] 'We ate and drank in Your presence, and You taught in our streets!' ²⁷But He will say, 'I tell you, I don't know you or where you're from. Get away from Me,[g] all you workers of unrighteousness!' ²⁸There will be weeping and gnashing of teeth[h] in that place,[i] when you see Abra-

ham, Isaac, Jacob, and all the prophets in the kingdom of God[j] but yourselves thrown out. ²⁹They will come from east and west, from north and south, and recline at the table[k] in the kingdom of God. ³⁰Note this: Some are last who will be first, and some are first who will be last."[l]

Jesus and Herod Antipas

³¹At that time some •Pharisees came and told Him, "Go, get out of here! •Herod[m] wants to kill You!"[n]

³²He said to them, "Go tell that fox, 'Look! I'm driving out demons and performing healings today and tomorrow, and on the third day[F] I will complete My work.'[G,o] ³³Yet I must[p] travel today, tomorrow, and the next day, because it is not possible for a prophet[q] to perish[r] outside of Jerusalem!

Jesus' Lamentation over Jerusalem

³⁴"Jerusalem, Jerusalem![s] She who kills the prophets and stones[t] those who are sent to her.[u] How often I wanted to gather your children[v] together, as a hen gathers her chicks under her wings,[w] but you were not willing![x]

Cross references (center column):

[a]13:20-21 Mt 13:33
[b]13:21 Mt 16:6,11-12; Mk 8:15; Lk 12:1; 1Co 5:6-8; Gl 5:9
[c]13:22 Lk 9:51
[d]13:23 Mt 22:14; Lk 18:26; Ac 2:21; Rm 9:27; Eph 2:8; 1Pt 3:20; Rv 3:4
[e]13:24 Mt 7:13-14
[f]13:25 Mt 7:22-23; 10:33; 25:12
[g]13:27 Ps 6:8; 2Tm 2:19; Heb 3:12
[h]13:28 Mt 13:42,50; 22:13; 24:51; 25:30
[i]13:28-29 Mt 8:11-12
[j]13:28 Mk 1:15; Lk 4:43
[k]13:29 Lk 12:37
[l]13:30 Mt 19:30; 20:16; Mk 10:31
[m]13:31 Mt 14:1
[n] Mt 14:5; Mk 6:19; Jn 7:19-25; Ac 5:33
[o]13:32 Heb 2:10; 5:9; 7:28
[p]13:33 Ac 3:21; 17:3
[q] Mt 2:23; 21:11
[r] Mk 8:31
[s]13:34-35 Mt 23:37-39; Lk 19:41-44
[t]Heb 11:37 [u]2Ch 24:20-22; Mt 21:35; Lk 20:15 [v]Ps 147:2; Is 62:1,4 [w]Dt 32:11; Ps 17:8; 36:7 [x]Jn 5:40

[A]13:21 Lit *3 sata*; about 40 quarts [B]13:21 Or *until all of it was leavened* [C]13:23 Or *are the saved few?* (in number); lit *are those being saved few?* [D]13:25 Lit *you will begin to stand* [E]13:26 Lit *you will begin to say* [F]13:32 Very shortly [G]13:32 Lit *I will be finished*

---

world) that Jesus initiated. The first story focused on the kingdom's small beginning (**like a mustard seed**, which was proverbially considered the smallest seed in the ancient world) and dramatic spread (**a tree . . . its branches**) through Jesus' ministry. The second parable reinforced the first, with the implication that the kingdom of God would eventually permeate the entire earth much as yeast can spread through even **50 pounds of flour**. While it is true that leaven, or yeast, often symbolizes evil in the Bible (1Co 5:6), this passage is a clear exception. Here leaven is used positively and calls to mind the potency of Jesus' message and works on behalf of humanity.

13:22-23 Luke structured his Gospel in a way that emphasizes that Jesus was **making His way to Jerusalem** in order to die on the cross. The question **are there few being saved?** may reflect two important realities about Jesus' ministry: (1) Many of His teachings insisted that true discipleship comes with many difficult challenges, and (2) though large crowds came to hear Jesus in every **town and village**, there were relatively few who authentically followed Him as disciples.

13:24-27 Jesus' story here answered the question in verse 23 about why so few people were being saved. It is because they were not entering by **the narrow door** (faith in Jesus) while the Lord gave them opportunity (in this case, while Jesus was present, preaching the gospel). Unbelievers may appeal that they knew Jesus in His social life (**we ate and drank**) and public ministry (**You taught in our streets**), but they don't know the Lord personally as Savior (**I don't know you or where you're from**). Because they had not been jus-

tified (declared righteous) through faith in Christ (Rm 5:1), they were ultimately **workers of unrighteousness**.

13:28-29 An irony of eternal life in the **kingdom of God** is that many Jews, though they were the original people of God's covenant, will be excluded due to their unbelief, while many believing Gentiles will **recline at the table** in full fellowship because they have accepted God's offer of reconciliation in Jesus. There will be much anguish (**weeping and gnashing of teeth**) among excluded Jews.

13:30 The kingdom of God reverses many of the world's values. In the present context, the inversion apparently refers to the fact that believing Gentiles, though they were historically not part of God's covenant people Israel, became the first to receive the Messiah *en masse*. By contrast, the Jews were chronologically first in God's plan, but they became spiritually last since the bulk of their numbers rejected Christ. Jews will only receive Jesus widely near the end of the age (Rm 11:25-27).

13:31-34 Jesus seemed to take the warning of these **Pharisees** at face value, though it is doubtful that they really wished to protect Jesus from **Herod** Antipas (see note at 3:1). Most likely they simply wanted Him to leave their region. Though verse 32 makes it seem that Jesus stayed put for three days more, the subsequent mention of **travel** to **Jerusalem** in order to die there makes it likely that this verse was a veiled reference to His coming resurrection. The mention of Jerusalem and His coming death as a prophet allowed Jesus to review the city's history of killing the **prophets** whom God **sent to her**. Jerusalem had repeatedly rejected God's compassionate outreach (pictured as a

³⁵See, your house[A] is abandoned to you.[a] And I tell you, you will not see Me until the time comes when you say, **'He who comes in the name of the Lord is the blessed One'**!"[B,b]

A Sabbath Controversy

14 One Sabbath, when He went to eat[C] at the house of one of the leading •Pharisees,[c] they were watching Him closely.[d] ²There in front of Him was a man whose body was swollen with fluid.[D] ³In response, Jesus asked the law experts[e] and the Pharisees, "Is it lawful to heal on the Sabbath or not?"[f] ⁴But they kept silent. He took the man, healed him, and sent him away. ⁵And to them, He said, "Which of you whose son or ox falls into a well, will not immediately pull him out on the Sabbath day?"[g] ⁶To this they could find no answer.

Teachings on Humility

⁷He told a parable[h] to those who were invited, when He noticed how they would choose the best places[i] for themselves: ⁸"When you are invited by someone to a wedding banquet, don't recline at the best place, because a more distinguished person[j] than you may have been invited by your host.[E] ⁹The one who invited both of you may come and say to you, 'Give your place to this man,' and then in humiliation, you will proceed to take the lowest place.

¹⁰"But when you are invited, go and recline

in the lowest place, so that when the one who invited you comes, he will say to you, 'Friend, move up higher.' You will then be honored[k] in the presence of all the other guests.[l] ¹¹For everyone who exalts himself will be humbled, and the one who humbles himself will be exalted."[m]

¹²He also said to the one who had invited Him, "When you give a lunch or a dinner, don't invite your friends, your •brothers, your relatives, or your rich neighbors, because they might invite you back, and you would be repaid. ¹³On the contrary, when you host a banquet,[n] invite those who are poor, maimed, lame, or blind.[o] ¹⁴And you will be blessed, because they cannot repay you; for you will be repaid[p] at the resurrection of the righteous."[q]

The Parable of the Large Banquet

¹⁵When[r] one of those who reclined at the table with Him heard these things, he said to Him, "The one who will eat bread in the kingdom of God[s] is blessed!"

¹⁶Then He told him: "A man was giving a large banquet and invited many. ¹⁷At the time of the banquet, he sent his •slave to tell those who were invited, 'Come, because everything is now ready.'

¹⁸"But without exception[F] they all began to make excuses. The first one said to him, 'I have bought a field, and I must go out and see it. I ask you to excuse me.'

---

[a]13:35 Is 64:11; Jr 12:7; 22:1-8
[b]Ps 118:26; Mt 21:9; Lk 19:38; Jn 12:13
[c]14:1 Lk 7:36; 11:37
[d]Mk 3:2; Lk 6:7; 20:20
[e]14:3 Lk 7:30; 14:30
[f]Mt 12:2; Mk 3:4; Lk 6:2,9; 13:14; Jn 5:10
[g]14:5 Ex 21:33; Dt 22:4; Mt 12:11; Lk 13:15
[h]14:7 Lk 5:36; 13:6
[i]Lk 11:43
[j]14:8 Lk 7:2; Php 2:29; 1Pt 2:4
[k]14:10 Jn 5:44; 7:18; Rm 2:7
[l]Pr 25:6-7; 29:23
[m]14:11 Ezk 21:26; Mt 18:4; 23:12; Lk 1:51; 3:5; 18:14; Jms 4:10; 1Pt 5:5-6
[n]14:13 Lk 5:29
[o]Lv 22:22; Lk 14:21
[p]14:14 Rm 11:35; 12:19; 1Th 3:9; 2Th 1:6; Heb 10:30
[q]Ac 24:15
[r]14:15-24 Mt 22:1-14
[s]14:15 Lk 13:29; 22:16,30; Rv 19:9

[A]13:35 Probably the temple; Jr 12:7; 22:5   [B]13:35 Ps 118:26   [C]14:1 Lit *eat bread*; = eat a meal   [D]14:2 Afflicted with dropsy or edema   [E]14:8 Lit *by him*   [F]14:18 Lit *And from one* (voice)

---

mother **hen** gathering her chicks). The city would soon do the same thing again by rejecting Jesus, God's Son.

13:35 Your house is abandoned (Gk *aphiemi*; "to forsake") reveals that God's blessing and protection would be removed, leading ultimately to judgment in the destruction of Jerusalem by the Romans in A.D. 70. **He who comes in the name of the Lord is the blessed One** quoted Ps 118:26 and was later cited in regard to Jesus' "triumphant entry" (see note at Lk 19:37-38). However, here it looks beyond that to the second coming of Christ (see Zch 12:10; Rv 1:7).

14:1-4 These verses continue the theme (see 6:1-11) of the Pharisees seeking to trap Jesus. **Swollen with fluid** describes a condition known as "dropsy," the major symptom of which was swollen limbs. Jesus performed five miracles on the Sabbath in Luke (vv. 1-4 ; 4:31,38; 6:6; 13:10,14). The probable reason why the scribes (**law experts**) and Pharisees refused to answer Jesus' question about whether it was **lawful to heal on the Sabbath** was that others had been humiliated previously when they tried to debate Jesus on this topic (see note at 13:17).

14:5 The commandment not to work on **the Sabbath day** (Dt 5:12-14) should not have been taken to mean that rescue efforts (for people or animals) were forbidden on the Sabbath.

14:7-10 The **best places** at a dinner were next to the host. Jesus' parable made the point that the danger of arrogantly

taking the best place at a banquet was that the person who invited you—here representing God—could ask you to move to the **lowest place** at the banquet table, causing humiliation rather than honor. It was wiser to sit in the seat of the humble and then be asked to **move up** to a seat of higher honor.

14:11 The principle that arrogance leads to humiliation appears repeatedly in the OT Wisdom Literature, especially Proverbs. That humility can lead to exaltation is a common theme in the NT (Lk 18:14; Jms 4:10; 1Pt 5:6).

14:12-14 True hospitality (hosting a dinner or a banquet) will be **blessed** by the Lord if you invite those who cannot return the favor. The **resurrection of the righteous** is the positive side of the resurrection mentioned in Dn 12:2 and Jn 5:28-29. It is probably the same thing as "the first resurrection" mentioned in Rv 20:4-6.

14:15 The statement about being **blessed** to **eat bread** in the coming **kingdom of God** is true. However, the person who said this probably assumed (wrongly) that many at the table in the Pharisee's home (v. 1) would experience this blessing. The story Jesus told next (vv. 16-24) reflected a different reality.

14:16-20 This story symbolizes being **invited** to the messianic **banquet** in the future kingdom of God (v. 15). Those who were initially invited (the religious leaders of the Jewish people) all made excuses about why they could not attend.

¹⁹"Another said, 'I have bought five yoke of oxen, and I'm going to try them out. I ask you to excuse me.'

²⁰"And another said, 'I just got married,[A,a] and therefore I'm unable to come.'

²¹"So the slave came back and reported these things to his master. Then in anger, the master of the house told his slave, 'Go out quickly into the streets and alleys of the city, and bring in here the poor, maimed, blind, and lame!'[b]

²²"'Master,' the slave said, 'what you ordered has been done, and there's still room.'

²³"Then the master told the slave, 'Go out into the highways and lanes and make them come in, so that my house may be filled. ²⁴For I tell you, not one of those men who were invited will enjoy my banquet!'"

The Cost of Following Jesus

²⁵Now[c] great crowds were traveling with Him. So He turned and said to them: ²⁶"If anyone comes to Me[d] and does not hate[e] his own father and mother, wife and children, brothers and sisters—yes, and even his own life—he cannot be My disciple. ²⁷Whoever does not bear his own cross[f] and come after Me cannot be My disciple.

²⁸"For which of you, wanting to build a tower, doesn't first sit down and calculate the

cost[g] to see if he has enough to complete it? ²⁹Otherwise, after he has laid the foundation and cannot finish it, all the onlookers will begin to make fun of him, ³⁰saying, 'This man started to build and wasn't able to finish.'

³¹"Or what king, going to war against another king, will not first sit down and decide if he is able with 10,000 to oppose the one who comes against him with 20,000? ³²If not, while the other is still far off, he sends a delegation and asks for terms of peace. ³³In the same way, therefore, every one of you who does not say good-bye to[B] all his possessions[h] cannot be My disciple.

³⁴"Now,[i] salt[j] is good, but if salt should lose its taste, how will it be made salty? ³⁵It isn't fit for the soil or for the manure pile; they throw it out. Anyone who has ears to hear should listen!"[k]

The Parable of the Lost Sheep

15 All[l] the tax collectors[m] and sinners were approaching to listen to Him. ²And the •Pharisees and •scribes were complaining, "This man welcomes sinners[n] and eats with them!"

³So He told them this parable:[o] ⁴"What man among you, who has 100 sheep and loses one of them,[p] does not leave the 99 in the open field[C] and go after the lost one until he finds

Cross references (center column):

a14:20 Dt 24:5
b14:21 Lk 14:13
c14:25-33 Mt 10:37-38
d14:26 Mt 11:28; Mk 10:14; Lk 6:47; Jn 5:40
eDt 21:15; 22:13; 24:3; Lk 16:13
f14:27 Jn 19:17
g14:28 Pr 24:27
h14:33 Mt 19:21; Php 3:7; Heb 11:26
i14:34-35 Mt 5:13; Mk 9:49-50
j14:34 Jdg 9:45; Mk 9:50
k14:35 Mt 11:15; 13:9; Mk 4:9
l15:1-7 Mt 18:12-14
m15:1 Mt 11:19; Lk 5:29
n15:2 Lk 5:30; 7:39; Ac 11:3; Gl 2:12
o15:3 Mk 12:1
p15:4 Ps 119:176; Jr 50:6; Zc 11:16; Mt 10:6; 15:24

A14:20 Lit *I have married a woman*   B14:33 Or *does not renounce* or *leave*   C15:4 Or *the wilderness*

14:21-24 After being rejected by those who symbolized the religious leaders, the unfortunate ones to whom Jesus came to minister (Is 61:1) were invited. However, there was **still room** for others. So a wider group (those from **the highways**) was also invited. These stand for Gentiles. Non-Jewish participation in the gospel is a common theme in Luke's Gospel.

14:26 Hate his own here hyperbolically expresses the same principle found in Matthew 10:37, where Jesus says, "The person who loves father or mother more than Me is not worthy of Me." Both Luke and Matthew convey the same point. Disciples must love Jesus more than they love their own family members.

14:27 On bearing a **cross**, see note at 9:23.

14:28-32 It is necessary to **calculate the cost** to be a disciple of Christ. Like a person who does not foresee the full cost of building **a tower** and suffers ridicule for starting something he cannot finish, a disciple must understand what it will take to complete the Christian life before he makes the commitment. Similarly, a **king** must soberly consider the odds before deciding between war and peace.

14:33 The essence of being a disciple of Christ is unreserved commitment to Him. This involves holding loosely the material things of this world.

14:34-35 Most **salt** of the ancient world was impure and lost its **taste** easily, making it unfit to use even as fertilizer or as a catalyst for burning **manure**. The danger for a person who lets his witness become "unsalty" is that he or she may

be discarded from the Lord's service. On **ears to hear**, see note at 8:5-8.

15:1-2 On **tax collectors** and **sinners**, see note at 5:29-30. Then and now, to share a meal with someone typically indicates that you accept them.

15:3-7 Though it might be considered reckless to leave a flock of **99** sheep to search for **the lost one**, Jesus' story

---

miseo

Greek Pronunciation:	[mih SEH oh]
HCSB Translation:	hate
Uses in Luke's Gospel:	7
Uses in the NT:	40
Focus passage:	Luke 14:26

The Greek verb *miseo* is the basic word meaning *to hate*, the exact antonym of love (*agapao*). The essence of love is caring more about others than about self, even to the point of great sacrifice—including death (Jn 15:13). *Hate*, on the other hand, is the opposite; it cares little or nothing about others and actually wishes them harm or even death (Mt 24:9). With only one exception (Lk 1:71), *miseo* in the Gospels is always used by Jesus. By far the most difficult occurrence of *miseo* is Luke 14:26—difficult both to understand and to practice. In this passage Jesus seems to demand *hatred*, even toward one's parents, wife, children, and siblings—those whom we are specifically told elsewhere in Scripture to honor, protect, and love. Jesus' statement is best understood as the willingness to choose Him above all else. The context is Jesus' challenge to measure the cost of being His disciple (see 14:26-35).

it? ⁵When he has found it, he joyfully puts it on his shoulders, ⁶and coming home, he calls his friends and neighbors together, saying to them, 'Rejoice with me, because I have found my lost sheep!' ⁷I tell you, in the same way, there will be more joy in heaven^a over one sinner who repents than over 99 righteous people who don't need repentance.

The Parable of the Lost Coin

⁸"Or what woman who has 10 silver coins,^A if she loses one coin, does not light a lamp, sweep the house, and search carefully until she finds it? ⁹When she finds it, she calls her women friends and neighbors together, saying, 'Rejoice with me, because I have found the silver coin I lost!' ¹⁰I tell you, in the same way, there is joy in the presence of God's angels^b over one sinner who repents."

The Parable of the Lost Son

¹¹He also said: "A man had two sons. ¹²The younger of them said to his father, 'Father, give me the share of the estate I have coming to me.' So he distributed the assets^B to them. ¹³Not many days later, the younger son gathered together all he had and traveled to a distant country, where he squandered^c his estate in foolish living.^d ¹⁴After he had spent everything, a severe famine struck that country, and he had nothing.^C ¹⁵Then he went to work for^D one of the citizens of that country, who sent him into his fields to feed pigs.^e ¹⁶He longed to eat his fill from^E the carob pods^F the pigs were eating, but no one would give him any. ¹⁷When he came to his senses,^G he said, 'How many of my father's hired hands have more than enough food, and here I am dying of hunger!^H ¹⁸I'll get up, go to my father, and say to him, Father, I have sinned^f against heaven^g and in your sight. ¹⁹I'm no longer worthy^h to be called your son. Make me like one of your hired hands.' ²⁰So he got up and went to his father. But while the son was still a long way off, his father saw him and was filled with compassion.ⁱ He ran, threw his arms around his neck,^I and kissed^j him. ²¹The son said to him, 'Father, I have sinned against heaven and in your sight. I'm no longer worthy to be called your son.'

²²"But the father told his •slaves, 'Quick! Bring out the best robe^k and put it on him; put a ring^l on his finger^J and sandals^m on his feet. ²³Then bring the fattened calfⁿ and

Cross-references:
^a15:7 Jr 51:48; Rv 18:20
^b15:10 Lk 2:10
^c15:13 Lk 16:1
^dRm 6:2; 8:12; Gl 2:14; Col 3:7
^e15:15 Lv 11:7; Dt 14:8
^f15:18 Ex 10:16
^gMt 21:25; Jn 3:27
^h15:19 Lk 7:6-7
ⁱ15:20 Mt 9:36; Mk 1:41; Lk 7:13; 10:33
^jGn 29:13; 33:4; 45:15; 2Sm 14:33
^k15:22 Zch 3:3-5
^lGn 41:42; Est 3:10; 8:2
^mEzk 16:10
ⁿ15:23 1Sm 28:24

---

^A15:8 Gk 10 drachmas; a drachma was a silver coin = a •denarius   ^B15:12 Or living; lit livelihood   ^C15:14 Lit and he began to be in need   ^D15:15 Lit went and joined with   ^E15:16 Other mss read to fill his stomach with   ^F15:16 Seed casings of a tree used as food for cattle, pigs, and sometimes the poor   ^G15:17 Lit to himself   ^H15:17 Or dying in the famine; v. 14   ^I15:20 Lit He ran, fell on his neck   ^J15:22 Lit hand

---

emphasizes how much God cares for every lost **sinner** and how **joyfully** He responds when each one is found.

15:8-10 To search for a lost **coin** (Gk drachma; worth about a day's wage for the average worker) indoors required lighting **a lamp** since very few homes had windows. This search also required sweeping **the house**, because the floor was earthen. **Joy in the presence of God's angels** speaks of God's joy over a repentant sinner.

15:11-12 Although this well-known parable (vv. 11-32) is

metanoeo

Greek Pronunciation:	[meh tuh nah EH oh]
HCSB Translation:	repent
Uses in Luke's Gospel:	9
Uses in the NT:	34
Focus passage:	Luke 15:7

The Greek verb for repent (metanoeo) and the related noun for repentance (metanoia) signify a change of mind (meta, meaning after or change; and nous, meaning mind). More than just an intellectual change of mind is in view; rather, both terms refer to a change in one's way of thinking that results in different beliefs and a change in the direction of one's life. The verb pisteuo (meaning believe) is much more common than metanoeo, though both words refer to concepts foundational to salvation (15:7,10; Mt 4:17; Jn 3:16). Repent and believe may be understood as opposite sides of the same coin. Repent means to turn from one's allegiance to sin and unbelief, whereas believe means to place one's trust in Christ. Thus, when one is mentioned the other is implied.

usually called the parable of the prodigal son, the other son and the father are also important characters. It was unusual, but not unheard of, for a father to settle his estate before his death. Since the older son got a double portion of his father's estate, the younger son's share (**share . . . I have coming to me**) would have been one-third of the estate.

15:13-15 The younger son had no intention of returning to his family. It is impossible to know whether his **foolish living** included "prostitutes" (v. 30), or if that was just an angry accusation made by the older brother. The irony of the penniless younger son's new job was that **pigs** were unclean animals to Jews (Lv 11:7). He was at rock bottom in his new life.

15:17-19 It took extreme poverty and **hunger** to prompt the younger son to come to his senses and realize that, in spite of all he had done, the correct course of action was to return and become one of his father's **hired hands**. To do so, however, it would be necessary to confess that he had sinned greatly and was not worthy to be called his son. This is a vivid picture of a person "hitting bottom" and finally realizing the magnitude of his sin.

15:20-23 That the father saw his son coming from **a long way off** indicates that he habitually looked for his return. Perhaps the normal parental reaction to the younger son's return would be anger or at least deep disappointment, but this father's response displayed: (1) **compassion**, (2) love (**threw his arms around his neck and kissed him**), (3) celebration (a **feast**), and (4) joyful restoration of status for his son (a **robe** of distinction, signet **ring** of family authority, **sandals** worn by a son, in contrast to barefoot slaves).

slaughter it, and let's celebrate with a feast, [24]because this son of mine was dead and is alive again;[a] he was lost and is found!' So they began to celebrate.

[25]"Now his older son was in the field; as he came near the house, he heard music and dancing. [26]So he summoned one of the servants and asked what these things meant. [27]'Your brother is here,' he told him, 'and your father has slaughtered the fattened calf because he has him back safe and sound.'[A]

[28]"Then he became angry and didn't want to go in. So his father came out and pleaded with him. [29]But he replied to his father, 'Look, I have been slaving many years for you, and I have never disobeyed your orders, yet you never gave me a young goat so I could celebrate with my friends. [30]But when this son of yours came, who has devoured your assets[B] with prostitutes,[b] you slaughtered the fattened calf for him.'

[31]"'Son,'[c] he said to him, 'you are always with me,[c] and everything I have is yours. [32]But we had to celebrate and rejoice, because this brother of yours was dead and is alive again; he was lost and is found.'"

The Parable of the Dishonest Manager

16 He also said to the disciples: "There was a rich[d] man who received an accusation

that his manager[e] was squandering[f] his possessions. [2]So he called the manager in and asked, 'What is this I hear about you? Give an account of your management,[g] because you can no longer be my manager.'

[3]"Then the manager said to himself, 'What should I do, since my master is taking the management away from me? I'm not strong enough to dig; I'm ashamed to beg. [4]I know what I'll do so that when I'm removed from management, people will welcome me into their homes.'

[5]"So he summoned each one of his master's debtors. 'How much do you owe my master?' he asked the first one.

[6]"'A hundred measures of olive oil,' he said.

"'Take your invoice,' he told him, 'sit down quickly, and write 50.'

[7]"Next he asked another, 'How much do you owe?'

"'A hundred measures of wheat,' he said.

"'Take your invoice,' he told him, 'and write 80.'

[8]"The master praised the unrighteous manager[h] because he had acted astutely. For the sons of this age[i] are more astute than the sons of light[j] in dealing with their own people.[D] [9]And I tell you, make friends[k] for yourselves by means of the unrighteous money[l] so that when it fails,[E] they may welcome you into

Cross references
[a]15:24 Lk 15:32; Rm 11:15; 2Co 4:10; Col 2:13
[b]15:30 Pr 29:3
[c]15:31 Jn 8:35
[d]16:1 Lk 16:19
[e]Lk 12:42
[f]Lk 15:13
[g]16:2 1Tm 1:4
[h]16:8 Lk 18:6
[i]Mt 12:32; Lk 20:34
[j]Jn 12:46; Eph 5:8; 1Th 5:5
[k]16:9 Lk 11:41
[l]Mt 6:24; 1Tm 6:10

[A]15:27 Lit *him back healthy*   [B]15:30 Lit *livelihood*, or *living*   [C]15:31 Or *Child*   [D]16:8 Lit *own generation*   [E]16:9 Other mss read *when you fail* or *pass away*

15:24 This is the point at which the parable ties in to the two previous stories about God's joy in saving the **lost**. The father's celebratory attitude depicts the way in which God the Father receives repentant sinners. This contrasts with the contempt the Pharisees and scribes displayed for sinners who came to Jesus (v. 2).

15:25-30 Instead of the story ending on a note of joy and celebration, as might be expected, the spotlight shifts to the older brother. Unlike the father's positive attitude, the older brother (1) was surprised at the return of his sinning brother, (2) was offended and jealous at the father's celebration, (3) became angry at the father's forgiving love, (4) declared his own self-righteousness, and (5) focused on his brother's sinfulness rather than his newfound repentance. Jesus' representation of the religious leaders in the character of the older brother was a scathing rebuke of their self-righteousness.

15:31-32 The rebuke of the religious leaders continues. They did not understand (1) the opportunity for a close relationship with God, (2) the generosity of His grace, (3) His joy at the salvation of sinners, or (4) the profound transformation of conversion. Perhaps most crucial of all, however, is the reminder of kinship to the sinners intended in the phrase **this brother of yours**. The religious leaders refused to accept their Jewish brethren, the "sinners," as the older brother in this story.

16:1-2 A **rich man** would often employ a **manager** (Gk *oikon-*

omos; "steward, administrator") who handled all the business affairs of his estate. The charge that this manager had squandered the rich man's **possessions**, indicating either neglectful management or criminal misconduct, must have been true. After all, the manager offered no defense when questioned. The landowner demanded a careful accounting of his assets, possibly so the next manager would have accurate data from the outset.

16:3-4 Realizing that he was being fired, the manager had to find a way to support himself. Since he was not in condition to do physical labor and too proud to **beg**, he focused on a way to make his former clients willing to offer him hospitality.

16:5-7 Four explanations are offered for the manager's tactics in lowering these debts: (1) He dropped the price enough to ingratiate himself with the debtors, (2) he removed the interest charges on the debt, (3) he removed his commission on the transactions, or (4) he reduced the debt back to what it should have been in the first place, after having overcharged them previously in a bid to cover his mismanagement. All four tactics are possible, but it should be remembered that the manager was required to present a full accounting to the landowner. Therefore, his tactics here must have been legitimate.

16:8-9 Because the Greek word translated **master** is *kurios* ("lord"), some have thought that it was God who **praised the unrighteous manager**. However, it is much more likely that

eternal dwellings. [10] Whoever is faithful[a] in very little[b] is also faithful in much, and whoever is unrighteous in very little is also unrighteous in much. [11] So if you have not been faithful with the unrighteous money, who will trust you with what is genuine? [12] And if you have not been faithful with what belongs to someone else, who will give you what is your own? [13] No[c] household slave can be the •slave of two masters, since either he will hate[d] one and love the other, or he will be devoted to one and despise the other. You can't be slaves to both God and money."

Kingdom Values

[14] The •Pharisees, who were lovers of money,[e] were listening to all these things and scoffing[f] at Him. [15] And He told them: "You are the ones who justify[g] yourselves in the sight of others, but God knows your hearts.[h] For what is highly admired by people is revolting[i] in God's sight.

[16] The[j] Law and the Prophets[k] were[A] until John; since then, the good news of the kingdom of God[l] has been proclaimed, and everyone is strongly urged to enter it.[B] [17] But it is easier[m] for heaven and earth to pass away than for one stroke of a letter in the law to drop out.

[18] "Everyone[n] who divorces[o] his wife and marries another woman commits adultery,[p] and everyone who marries a woman divorced from her husband commits adultery.

The Rich Man and Lazarus

[19] "There was a rich man who would dress in purple and fine linen,[q] feasting lavishly every day. [20] But a poor man named Lazarus, covered with sores, was left at his gate.[r] [21] He longed to be filled[s] with what fell from the rich man's table,[t] but instead the dogs[u] would come and lick his sores. [22] One day the poor man died and was carried away by the angels to Abraham's side.[C,v] The rich man also died and was buried. [23] And being in torment[w] in •Hades,[x] he looked up and saw Abraham a long way off, with Lazarus at his side. [24] 'Father Abraham!'[y] he called out, 'Have mercy on me and send Lazarus to dip the tip of his finger in water and cool my tongue, because I am in agony[z] in this flame!'

[25] "'Son,'[D] Abraham said, 'remember that during your life you received your good things,[aa]

Cross references (center column)

[a]16:10 Mt 25:21-23
[b]Lk 19:17
[c]16:13 Mt 6:24
[d]Lk 14:26
[e]16:14 2Tm 3:2
[f]Lk 23:35
[g]16:15 Lk 10:29; 18:9
[h]1Sm 16:7; Ps 17:3; Pr 21:2; Rm 8:27
[i]Dt 24:4
[j]16:16-17 Mt 5:18; 11:12-13; 24:35; Mk 13:31
[k]16:16 Mt 7:12; 22:40; Ac 13:15; Rm 3:21
[l]Mt 4:23
[m]16:17 Mt 5:18
[n]16:18 Mt 5:32; 19:9; Mk 10:11-12
[o]Mt 1:19; 19:9
[p]Ex 20:14; Lv 20:10; Pr 6:32; 2Pt 2:14
[q]16:19 Ex 28:6; 35:35; Est 8:15; Pr 31:22; Ezk 27:16; Rv 18:16
[r]16:20 Ac 3:2
[s]16:21 Lv 15:16
[t]Mt 15:27
[u]1Kg 21:19
[v]16:22 Jn 13:23
[w]16:23 Is 50:11
[x]Mt 11:23
[y]16:24 Lk 3:8; 16:30; 19:9; Jn 8:33,39,53
[z]Is 66:24; Mt 25:41 [aa]16:25 Lk 6:24

[A]16:16 Perhaps *were proclaimed*, or were in effect [B]16:16 Or *everyone is forcing his way into it* [C]16:22 Or *to Abraham's bosom*; lit to the fold of Abraham's robe; Jn 13:23 [D]16:25 Lit *Child*

---

the story ends in the middle of verse 8. Thus, it was the landowner rather than God who offered praise, and he did so only because the manager **acted astutely** (Gk *phronimos*; "shrewdly, wisely") in response to his errors. In the last half of verse 8 and all of verse 9, Jesus shares an implication of the story: the **sons of this age** (unbelievers) typically deal shrewdly with each other and win friends by this means, whereas the **sons of light** (believers) often fail to utilize their financial resources to win people to faith, who thus become friends forever (**welcome you into eternal dwellings**). Thus Jesus encouraged His followers to use their money shrewdly (but innocently) in order to advance God's kingdom.

16:10-12 A second lesson that this story teaches is the need to be **faithful** before the Lord. Spiritually, every believer is a steward of the gifts God has given. If you are faithful with small amounts of money, the Lord may trust you with **much** more, including things of priceless eternal value. If you cannot be trusted with only a **little**, you would also be a poor steward if more were entrusted to you.

16:13 On **slave of two masters**, see Mt 6:24.

16:14-15 The Pharisees, because they were **lovers of money**, were **scoffing** (Gk *ekmukterizo*; "to sneer at, show contempt") at Jesus, for they believed it was possible to serve both God and money (v. 13). In response, Jesus told the Pharisees that their desire to be **admired by people** was an abomination in **God's sight**, for He does not approve of the world's values.

16:16-17 The Law and the Prophets is a way of referring to the entire OT (v. 29; 24:27,44). The ministry of John the Baptist marked the end of the old covenant era. The ministry of Jesus began the offer of the gospel (**good news**), the new covenant era, and embodied the nearness of **the kingdom of God**. In this context, **everyone is strongly urged** probably refers to the urgency expressed by the evangelistic preaching efforts of John the Baptist, Jesus, and His apostles. On **one stroke of a letter**, see Mt 5:17-20.

16:18 Remarriage after divorce constitutes **adultery** if the former marriage was dissolved for illegitimate reasons or motivations; hence the strict terms of this verse. The parallel passages in Mt 5:31-32 and 19:9 are more detailed. They indicate that remarriage is legitimate in cases where the former marriage was dissolved due to sexual immorality.

16:19-21 The **rich man** (called *Dives*, Latin for "rich man") clearly did not use his wealth to make friends in the "eternal dwellings" (see note at vv. 8-9). **Covered with sores** (Gk *elkoo*; "to be ulcerated") is a medical term used only here in the NT, perhaps reflecting Luke's background as a physician (Col 4:14). It is ironic that the suffering **poor man** was named **Lazarus** since a man by that name would later rise from the dead (Jn 11:1-44). On **dress in purple**, see Ac 16:14.

16:22-24 The circumstances were reversed after both men **died**. The Jewish Talmud refers to both paradise (23:43; 2Co 12:4) and **Abraham's side** (or "bosom") as names for the place of blessedness beyond the grave. **Hades**, the Greek equivalent of the Hebrew *sheol*, is, generally, "the place of the dead." In this case, however, because of the mention of **being in torment**, Hades must be viewed as hell, the place of the unrighteous dead. **In this flame** refers to the eternal lake of fire (Mt 25:41).

16:25 This verse is an application of the principle in 13:30. The rich man had been "first" in this life, having enjoyed

just as Lazarus received bad things, but now he is comforted here,[a] while you are in agony. [26]Besides all this, a great chasm has been fixed between us and you, so that those who want to pass over from here to you cannot; neither can those from there cross over to us.'

[27]"'Father,' he said, 'then I beg you to send him to my father's house— [28]because I have five brothers—to warn[b] them, so they won't also come to this place of torment.'

[29]"But Abraham said, 'They have Moses and the prophets;[c] they should listen to them.'

[30]"'No, father Abraham,' he said. 'But if someone from the dead goes to them, they will repent.'

[31]"But he told him, 'If they don't listen to Moses and the prophets, they will not be persuaded if someone rises from the dead.'"[d]

Warnings from Jesus

17 He[e] said to His disciples, "Offenses[A] will certainly come,[B] but woe[f] to the one they come[g] through! [2]It would be better for him if a millstone[C] were hung around his neck and he were thrown into the sea than for him to cause one of these little ones to •stumble.[h] [3]Be[i] on your guard. If your brother sins,[D] rebuke[j] him, and if he repents, forgive[k] him. [4]And if he sins against you seven times in a day, and comes back to you seven times, saying, 'I repent,' you must forgive him."

Faith and Duty

[5]The[l] apostles[m] said to the Lord, "Increase our faith."[n]

[6]"If you have faith the size of[E] a mustard seed,"[o] the Lord said, "you can say to this mulberry tree, 'Be uprooted and planted in the sea,' and it will obey you.

[7]"Which one of you having a •slave tending sheep or plowing will say to him when he comes in from the field, 'Come at once and sit down to eat'? [8]Instead, will he not tell him, 'Prepare something for me to eat, get ready,[F] and serve me while I eat and drink; later you can eat and drink'?[p] [9]Does he thank that slave because he did what was commanded?[G] [10]In the same way, when you have done all that you were commanded, you should say, 'We are good-for-nothing[q] slaves; we've only done our duty.'"

Ten Men Healed

[11]While traveling to Jerusalem,[r] He passed between[H] Samaria and Galilee.[s] [12]As He entered a village, 10 men with serious skin diseases[t] met Him. They stood at a distance [13]and raised their voices, saying, "Jesus, Master,[u] have mercy on us!"

[14]When He saw them, He told them, "Go and show yourselves to the priests."[v] And while they were going, they were healed.[I]

[15]But one of them, seeing that he was healed, returned and, with a loud voice, gave glory to

Cross references

a16:25 Mt 11:28
b16:28 Ac 2:40; 8:25
c16:29 Lk 24:27,44; Jn 1:45; Ac 26:22; 28:23
d16:31 Mt 28:11-15; Jn 12:10-11
e17:1-3 Mt 18:6-7; Mk 9:42; 1Co 11:19
f17:1 Lk 22:22
g Mt 13:41
h17:2 1Co 8:9
i17:3-4 Mt 18:15,21-22
j17:3 Lv 19:17
k Mt 6:14
l17:5-6 Mt 17:19-21; Mk 9:28-29
m17:5 Lk 6:13
n Mk 9:24
o17:6 Mt 13:31; Mk 4:31; Lk 13:19
p17:8 Lk 12:35-37
q17:10 Jb 22:2-3; 35:7; Mt 25:30; Rm 11:35
r17:11 Lk 9:51
s Jn 4:3-4
t17:12 Lv 13:45-46
u17:13 Lk 5:5
v17:14 Lv 13:2-14:32; Mt 8:4; Lk 5:14

A17:1 Or *Traps*, or *Bait-sticks*, or *Causes of stumbling*, or *Causes of sin*   B17:1 Lit *It is impossible for offenses not to come*   C17:2 Large stone used for grinding grains into flour   D17:3 Other mss add *against you*   E17:6 Lit *faith like*   F17:8 Or *eat, gird yourself*; lit *eat, tuck in your robe*   G17:9 Other mss add *I don't think so*   H17:11 Or *through the middle of*   I17:14 Lit *cleansed*

---

many **good things**, but was now "last," referring to his **agony** in the afterlife. By contrast, Lazarus had been "last" during his earthly existence (vv. 20-21), but now was "first" (eternally **comforted**).

16:26 In the afterlife, there is a separation between believers and unbelievers which cannot be spanned. It is not possible to **cross over** from heaven to hell or hell to heaven.

16:27-29 Not being able to improve his own lot, the rich man finally showed concern for the eternal destiny of his **five brothers**. The phrase **Moses and the prophets** is another way of referring to the entire OT (see note at vv. 16-17).

16:30-31 The irony here is that Luke, writing from a time after Jesus' resurrection, knew that very few people would be persuaded to **repent** even through witnessing the miracle of someone rising **from the dead** (Lazarus or Jesus). They must listen with "ears to hear" to the message of salvation in the Scriptures. On **Moses and the prophets**, see notes at verses 16-17 and 27-29.

17:1-2 Offenses (Gk *skandalon*; "that which causes sin") are unavoidable in life. However, divine judgment awaits the person who causes a disciple of Christ (**one of these little ones**) to sin. A **millstone** was a large round stone used to grind grain. A large stone around the neck would cause a person thrown into the sea to sink and drown.

17:3-4 The purpose of rebuking a sinner is to get him to repent of his sin. If there is true repentance, there should be full forgiveness. **Seven** is the biblical number of completeness. To forgive "seven times" means to keep forgiving, no matter what (see Mt 18:21-22).

17:5-6 Genuine faith is powerful even in small quantities. The **mustard seed** was thought by farmers in Palestine to be the smallest of seeds. A **mulberry tree** has such an extensive and deep root system that it might live for several hundred years. It took a very powerful force to uproot such a tree.

17:7-10 A **slave** who only did his job, or what was **commanded**, got no special commendation since all he had done was to fulfill his responsibilities. Similarly, a disciple of Christ (v. 1) should not expect special commendation for doing what is required. We serve the Lord because this is what it means to follow Him as disciples. It is our **duty**.

17:11 Jesus apparently walked along the border **between Samaria and Galilee**, then crossed the Jordan River at the nearest point, proceeding down the eastern bank of the Jordan toward the crossing point opposite Jericho (see note at 19:1-2), which is the next location mentioned in the narrative (18:35).

17:12-14 On **show yourselves to the priests** after being healed from **serious skin diseases**, see note at 5:12-14.

God.[a] [16] He fell facedown[b] at His feet, thanking Him. And he was a •Samaritan.[c]

[17] Then Jesus said, "Were not 10 cleansed? Where are the nine? [18] Didn't any return[A] to give glory to God except this foreigner?" [19] And He told him, "Get up and go on your way. Your faith has made you well."[B,d]

The Coming of the Kingdom

[20] Being[e] asked by the •Pharisees when the kingdom of God will come,[f] He answered them, "The kingdom of God is not coming with something observable; [21] no one will say,[C] 'Look here!' or 'There!' For you see, the kingdom of God is among you."

[22] Then He told the disciples: "The days are coming[g] when you will long to see one of the days of the •Son of Man, but you won't see it.[h] [23] They will say to you,[i] 'Look there!' or 'Look here!' Don't follow or run after them.[j] [24] For as the lightning flashes from horizon to horizon and lights up the sky, so the Son of Man will be in His day.[k] [25] But first He must suffer many things and be rejected by this generation.[l]

[26] "Just as it was in the days of Noah,[m] so it will be in the days of the Son of Man: [27] People went on eating, drinking, marrying and giving in marriage[n] until the day Noah boarded the ark,[o] and the flood came and destroyed them all. [28] It will be the same as it was in the days of Lot:[p] People went on eating, drinking, buying, selling, planting, building. [29] But on the day Lot left Sodom, fire and sulfur rained from heaven and destroyed[q] them all. [30] It[r] will be like that on the day the Son of Man is revealed.[s]

[31] On that day, a man on the housetop, whose belongings are in the house, must not come down to get them. Likewise the man who is in the field must not turn back. [32] Remember Lot's wife![t] [33] Whoever tries to make his •life secure[D,E] will lose it, and whoever loses his life will preserve it.[u] [34] I tell you, on that night[v] two will be in one bed: One will be taken and the other will be left. [35] Two women will be grinding grain together: One will be taken and the other left. [[36] Two will be in a field: One will be taken, and the other will be left.]"[F]

[37] "Where, Lord?"[w] they asked Him.

He said to them, "Where the corpse is, there also the vultures[x] will be gathered."

The Parable of the Persistent Widow

18 He then told them a parable on the need for them to pray[y] always and not become discouraged:[z] "There was a judge in a certain town who didn't fear God[aa] or respect man. [2] And a widow[ab] in that town kept coming to him, saying, 'Give me justice against my adversary.'

[4] "For a while he was unwilling, but later he said to himself, 'Even though I don't fear God or respect man, [5] yet because this widow

a17:15 Mt 9:8; Mk 2:12; Lk 2:14; 5:26; Jn 9:24; Ac 4:21; 12:23; Rm 4:20
b17:16 1Sm 20:41; 2Sm 14:22; Mt 17:6; 1Co 14:25
c Mt 10:5; Jn 4:9
d17:19 Mt 9:22; Mk 10:52; Lk 5:20; 18:42
e17:20-21 Mt 24:23; Mk 13:21
f17:20 Lk 19:11; Ac 1:6
g17:22 Dt 32:35; Is 2:12; Jr 7:32; Am 4:2; Lk 5:35; 19:43; 21:6; 23:29
h Am 5:18
i17:23-24 Mt 24:23,27; Mk 13:21
j17:23 Lk 21:8
k17:24 1Co 1:8
l17:25 Mt 16:21; Lk 9:22
m17:26-27 Mt 24:37-38
n17:27 Lk 20:34-35
o Gn 6:14
p17:28 Gn 19:1-26
q17:29 Gn 19:24-25
r17:30-35 Mt 24:17,39-41; Mk 13:15
s17:30 Mt 16:27; 24:44; 1Co 1:7; 2Th 1:7; 1Pt 1:7; 4:13
t17:32 Gn 19:26
u17:33 Mt 10:39; Jn 12:25
v17:34 Lk
1:78-79 w17:37 Lk 17:20 x Ezk 29:5; 32:4; 39:17-20 y18:1 Lk 11:5-13; 21:36; 1Th 5:17 z 2Co 4:1 aa18:2 Ps 147:11; Pr 1:7; Ac 10:2; Rv 14:7 ab18:3 Lk 2:37; 4:26; 7:12; 21:2

A17:18 Lit *Were they not found returning*   B17:19 Or *faith has saved you*   C17:21 Lit *they will not say*   D17:33 Other mss read *to save his life*   E17:33 Or *tries to retain his life*   F17:36 Other mss omit bracketed text

17:15-19 It is striking that the only one of the 10 men healed who **returned** and thanked Jesus was a **foreigner . . . a Samaritan**. This is in keeping with Luke's theme of the universal outreach of the gospel. Jesus' statement **your faith has made you well** implies that the Samaritan was healed physically and spiritually.

17:20-21 The Jews were looking for a **kingdom of God** that would come with signs in the sky and miracles (Jl 2:28-32), but that was yet future. The aspect of God's kingdom that Jesus emphasized in His ministry was not **observable** in that sense. The presence of the King (Jesus) and His offer of the kingdom through the gospel meant that the kingdom was already **among** them.

17:22-24 Jesus' disciples must not be led astray by false predictions of His coming. Instead, when He comes, it will be as obvious as **the lightning** flashing across the sky.

17:25 This is one of numerous predictions Jesus made about His suffering and rejection in Luke's Gospel (5:35; 9:22,43-44; 13:32-33; 18:32; 24:7).

17:26-29 Before Christ comes back, there will be no clear-cut warning signs that signal the end. Rather, it will be like (1) **the days of Noah**, when business as usual was carried on until the unexpected destruction of the flood, and (2) **the days of Lot**, when the status quo continued until, suddenly, fire and sulfur rained down on Sodom.

17:30-33 When Jesus returns, those on earth must not be attached to their possessions and earthly comforts, as was **Lot's wife** (see Gn 19:26). Commitment to Christ involves attachment only to spiritual and eternal realities. These provide the greatest security available.

17:34-36 The three aspects of life mentioned here cover the normal routine in an agricultural society: sleeping, **grinding grain**, and working in **a field**. It is not certain whether the one who is **taken** will be a believer taken by the Lord (see 1Th 4:15-17) or an unbeliever taken in judgment (Mt 13:40-42).

17:37 Jesus answered the disciples' question about where His coming would take place with a proverbial saying. It is easy to find a **corpse** by noting where the **vultures** are circling. Similarly, there will be no hiding Christ's second coming. It will be obvious to the entire world.

18:1 This parable speaks to the common tendency to **become discouraged** and stop praying before receiving an answer from God.

18:2-3 This **judge** was not a religious or compassionate man. A **widow** in that culture was almost helpless. Her only hope was that her persistent plea for **justice** would be granted.

18:4-5 Though the judge was unprincipled and **unwilling** to grant the widow's request (perhaps he was waiting for the

keeps[a] pestering me,[A] I will give her justice, so she doesn't wear me out[B] by her persistent coming.'"

[6] Then the Lord said, "Listen to what the unjust judge says. [7] Will not God grant justice[b] to His elect[c] who cry out to Him day and night?[d] Will He delay[e] to help them?[C] [8] I tell you that He will swiftly grant them justice. Nevertheless, when the •Son of Man comes,[f] will He find that faith[D] on earth?"

The Parable of the Pharisee and the Tax Collector

[9] He[g] also told this parable to some who trusted in themselves[h] that they were righteous[i] and looked down[j] on everyone else: [10] "Two men went up to the •temple complex to pray,[k] one a •Pharisee and the other a tax collector. [11] The Pharisee took his stand[E,l] and was praying like this: 'God, I thank You that I'm not like other people[F]—greedy,[m] unrighteous,[n] adulterers,[o] or even like this tax collector. [12] I fast[p] twice a week; I give a tenth[G,q] of everything I get.'

[13] "But the tax collector, standing far off,[r] would not even raise his eyes to heaven[s] but kept striking his chest[H,t] and saying, 'God, turn Your wrath from me[I,u]—a sinner!'[v] [14] I tell you, this one went down to his house •justified[w] rather than the other; because everyone who exalts himself will be humbled, but the one who humbles himself will be exalted."[x]

Blessing the Children

[15] Some[y] people were even bringing infants to Him so He might touch them, but when the disciples saw it, they rebuked them. [16] Jesus, however, invited them: "Let the little children come to Me,[z] and don't stop them, because the kingdom of God belongs to such as these. [17] •I assure you:[aa] Whoever does not welcome[ab] the kingdom of God like a little child[ac] will never enter it."

The Rich Young Ruler

[18] A[ad] ruler[ae] asked Him, "Good Teacher, what must I do to inherit eternal life?"[af] [19] "Why do you call Me good?" Jesus asked him. "No one is good but One—God. [20] You know the commandments:

**Do not commit adultery;
do not murder;
do not steal;
do not bear false witness;
honor your father and mother."**[J,ag]

[21] "I have kept all these from my youth," he said.

[22] When Jesus heard this, He told him, "You still lack one thing: Sell all that you have and distribute it to the poor,[ah] and you will have treasure in heaven.[ai] Then come, follow Me."[aj]

[23] After he heard this, he became extremely sad,[ak] because he was very rich.

Possessions and the Kingdom

[24] Seeing that he became sad,[K] Jesus said,

---

[a]18:5 Lk 11:8
[b]18:7 Is 63:4; Rv 6:10
[c]Mt 24:22; Rm 8:33; 2Tm 2:10; Ti 1:1
[d]Ps 88:1
[e]2Pt 3:9
[f]18:8 Dn 7:13; Lk 9:26; 12:40
[g]18:9-14 Mt 18:4; 23:12; Lk 14:11
[h]18:9 Mt 5:20; 2Co 1:9
[i]Lk 16:15
[j]Lk 23:11; Ac 4:11; Rm 14:3,10
[k]18:10 1Kg 10:5; 2Kg 20:5,8; Ac 3:1
[l]18:11 Mt 6:5; Mk 11:25
[m]Mt 7:15; 1Co 5:10-11; 6:10
[n]Lk 16:10
[o]Ex 20:14; 1Co 6:9; Heb 13:4
[p]18:12 Lk 5:33-35; Ac 13:2-3
[q]Lk 11:42
[r]18:13 Lk 17:12
[s]Ezr 9:6
[t]Lk 23:48
[u]Heb 2:17
[v]1Tm 1:15
[w]18:14 Lk 16:15; Php 3:8
[x]Is 2:11; Lk 1:52; 3:5; 14:11
[y]18:15-17 Mt 18:3; 19:13-15; Mk 10:13-16
[z]18:16 Lk 14:26
[aa]18:17 Ps 72:19; Rv 22:21
[ab]Lk 8:13
[ac]1Co 14:20; 1Pt 2:2
[ad]18:18-30 Mt 19:16-30; Mk 10:17-31;
Lk 22:28-30 [ae]18:18 Lk 8:41; 12:58 [af]Lk 10:25; Jn 3:15
[ag]18:20 Ex 20:12-16; Dt 5:16-20 [ah]18:22 Lk 12:33; 19:8; Ac 2:45; 4:34 [ai]Mt 6:19-20; Lk 5:11; 12:33 [aj]Lk 5:27 [ak]18:23 Mt 26:38; Mk 6:26; 14:34

[A]18:5 Lit widow causes me trouble   [B]18:5 Or doesn't give me a black eye, or doesn't ruin my reputation   [C]18:7 Or Will He put up with them?   [D]18:8 Or faith, or that kind of faith, or any faith, or the faith, or faithfulness; the faith that persists in prayer for God's vindication   [E]18:11 Or Pharisee stood by himself   [F]18:11 Or like the rest of men   [G]18:12 Or give tithes   [H]18:13 = mourning   [I]18:13 Lit God, be propitious to me; = May Your wrath be turned aside by the sacrifice   [J]18:20 Ex 20:12-16; Dt 5:16-20   [K]18:24 Other mss omit he became sad

---

widow to offer a bribe) he eventually caved in and granted her **justice** because she was **persistent** and he knew she would soon wear him out.

18:6-8 Jesus intends to make a contrast between the **unjust judge** and **God**. Unlike the unjust judge, God will not only grant **justice** to His children who are praying consistently, but will act **swiftly** in doing so. The last part of verse 8 refers to the fact that at the time just before Christ's second coming, genuine faith will be rare on earth (Mt 24:12-13).

18:9 The following parable focuses on a Pharisee (vv. 10-11). The phrase **some who trusted in themselves** describes the self-righteous outlook of the average Pharisee (vv. 11-12,14).

18:10-14 There were times around the morning and evening sacrifices at **the temple** when people could **pray**, although private prayer at other times was allowed. The Pharisee apparently kept the requirements of the Mosaic law and beyond (giving a **tenth** of earnings was all that was required). He was proud of his actions and his religious superiority to people such as the **tax collector**. By con-

trast, the tax collector knew that, as a **sinner**, he deserved only God's wrath. Jesus emphasized that God's justification is available to the humble, while the self-exalting will be brought low.

18:15-17 Jesus' disciples apparently thought His time was too precious to be taken up with infants. Jesus responded that **little children** coming to Him demonstrate the kind of childlike faith that is necessary to **enter** the **kingdom of God**.

18:18-23 The ruler was under the impression that **eternal life** could be earned by works (**what must I do**). Jesus shifted the focus by asserting that goodness only comes from God. Either the ruler had kept all the commandments listed in verse 20 or Jesus preferred not to argue about that. The latter is most likely, especially since Jesus' follow-up command revealed that the man was more interested in wealth on earth than **treasure in heaven** (where he would have eternal life). His unwillingness to distribute his wealth to **the poor** kept him from becoming Jesus' disciple.

18:24-27 Jesus contradicted the conventional wisdom that

"How hard it is for those who have wealth to
enter the kingdom of God! 25For it is easier
for a camel to go through the eye of a needle
than for a rich person to enter the kingdom
of God."
26Those who heard this asked, "Then who
can be saved?"[a]
27He replied, "What is impossible with men
is possible with God."[b]
28Then Peter said, "Look, we have left what
we had and followed[c] You."
29So He said to them, "I assure you: There is
no one who has left a house, wife or •brothers,
parents or children because of the kingdom
of God, 30who will not receive many times
more at this time,[d] and eternal life in the age
to come."

The Third Prediction of His Death

31Then[e] He took the Twelve aside and told
them, "Listen! We are going up to Jerusalem.[f] Everything that is written[g] through the
prophets about the Son of Man will be accomplished.[h] 32For He will be handed over to the
Gentiles,[i] and He will be mocked,[j] insulted,
spit[k] on; 33and after they flog Him, they will
kill Him, and He will rise on the third day."[l]
34They understood none of these things.[m]
This saying[A,n] was hidden[o] from them, and
they did not grasp what was said.

A Blind Man Receives His Sight

35As[p] He drew near Jericho, a blind man was
sitting by the road begging. 36Hearing a crowd
passing by, he inquired what this meant.
37"Jesus the •Nazarene[q] is passing by," they
told him.
38So he called out,[r] "Jesus, Son of David,[s]
have mercy[t] on me!" 39Then those in front
told him to keep quiet,[B] but he kept crying
out all the more, "Son of David, have mercy
on me!"
40Jesus stopped and commanded that he be
brought to Him. When he drew near, He asked
him, 41"What do you want Me to do for you?"
"Lord," he said, "I want to see!"
42"Receive your sight!"[u] Jesus told him.
"Your faith has healed you."[C,v] 43Instantly he
could see, and he began to follow Him, glorifying God.[w] All the people,[x] when they saw it,
gave praise to God.

Jesus Visits Zacchaeus

19 He entered Jericho and was passing
through. 2There was a man named
Zacchaeus who was a chief tax collector, and
he was rich. 3He was trying to see who Jesus
was, but he was not able because of the crowd,
since he was a short man. 4So running ahead,
he climbed up a sycamore tree to see Jesus,
since He was about to pass that way. 5When
Jesus came to the place, He looked up and said
to him, "Zacchaeus, hurry and come down because today I must stay at your house."
6So he quickly came down and welcomed

[a] 18:26 Lk 18:42; Eph 2:8
[b] 18:27 Gn 18:14; Jb 42:2; Jr 32:17; Zch 8:6; Lk 1:37; Rm 4:21; 11:22
[c] 18:28 Lk 5:11; Jn 8:12
[d] 18:30 Jb 42:10; Mt 6:33; Lk 21:8
[e] 18:31-34 Mt 20:17-19; Mk 10:32-34
[f] 18:31 Lk 9:51
[g] Ps 22; Is 52:13–53:12; Mt 1:22; 26:24
[h] Lk 22:37; Jn 19:28
[i] 18:32 Mt 27:2; Jn 18:30-31; Ac 3:13
[j] Mt 27:26-31
[k] Mt 26:67; Mk 14:65; 15:19
[l] 18:33 Mt 16:21; Lk 9:22
[m] 18:34 Mk 9:32; Lk 2:50; 9:45
[n] Lk 1:29
[o] Lk 24:16
[p] 18:35-43 Mt 20:29-34; Mk 10:46-52
[q] 18:37 Mt 2:23; Jn 18:5; 19:19; Ac 2:22
[r] 18:38 Lk 18:7
[s] Mt 1:1; 9:27; Lk 1:32; Rm 1:3
[t] Lk 16:24
[u] 18:42 Lk 7:22; Jn 9:11; Ac 9:12
[v] Mt 9:22; Lk 5:20; 7:50; 8:48; 17:19; 18:26
[w] 18:43 Lk 7:16; 13:13
[x] Lk 2:10

[A] 18:34 The meaning of the saying [B] 18:39 Or *those in front rebuked him* [C] 18:42 Or *has saved you*

those with **wealth** were blessed by God and would certainly be in His kingdom. A **camel** trying to go through the **eye of a needle** was apparently a proverbial saying for what was impossible; this explains the question from Jesus' hearers. His response was that people cannot be **saved** by their own efforts, but only by salvation that comes by God's grace.

18:28-30 After hearing the earlier discussions, Peter—as spokesman for the apostles—indicated that they had done precisely what Jesus had instructed the rich ruler to do in verse 22. They had left everything and followed Him. Jesus replied that not only would they have **eternal life in the age to come**, but they would also be greatly blessed in this life. To leave **wife** and **children** means itinerant ministry, not divorce or abandonment of domestic responsibilities.

18:31-34 As is true through the entire middle portion of Luke's Gospel, the movement of the narrative is toward **Jerusalem**. The only passage in the OT prophets that deals with the **Son of Man** is found in Dn 7:13 and its context. However, there are several major prophecies about the sufferings of the Messiah, notably Ps 22 and Is 53. **Handed over** and **rise on the third day** give a preview of Luke's narrative from 22:63 to 24:12. The disciples did not understand what Jesus meant about these things until after His resurrection (24:25-27,44-46).

18:35-43 In Lk 17:11, Jesus apparently crossed the Jordan River to the east near the border between Galilee and Samaria. Now He crossed back to the west opposite **Jericho**. When the **blind man** inquired about the crowd, he was only told that **Jesus the Nazarene** (from Nazareth, in Galilee, a town of little significance) was near. There is nothing messianic about such an identification. However, when he cried out that Jesus was the **Son of David** (see Mt 1:1), he was confessing Jesus as Messiah. His faith became the basis for his healing. His cry, **Have mercy on me**, prompted Jesus to restore his sight. It is ironic that the formerly blind man, who now became a disciple of Jesus, could **see** immediately, while the 12 apostles had no insight into where Jesus and His ministry were headed (see note at vv. 31-34).

19:1-2 Jericho was one of the most ancient cities in the world. Today its ruins date back more than 10,000 years. It was located about five miles west of the Jordan River, 10 miles northwest of the Dead Sea, and about 17 miles by winding road from Jerusalem. **Chief tax collector** refers to a supervisor of other tax collectors in a certain tax district. **Zacchaeus** was rich because he had taken advantage of his position by extorting money (see note at vv. 5-9).

19:3-4 A **sycamore tree** might grow to be 30 to 40 feet tall. However, it had low, spreading branches that even **a short man** could climb and that would support his weight.

19:5-9 Must (Gk *dei*; "it is necessary") implies divine necessity in Jesus' statement about staying at Zacchaeus's

Him joyfully. [7] All who saw it began to complain,[a] "He's gone to lodge with a sinful man!"

[8] But Zacchaeus stood there and said to the Lord, "Look, I'll give[A] half of my possessions to the poor,[b] Lord! And if I have extorted[c] anything from anyone, I'll pay[B] back four times as much!"[d]

[9] "Today salvation[e] has come to this house," Jesus told him, "because he too is a son of Abraham.[f] [10] For the •Son of Man has come to seek and to save the lost."[C,g]

The Parable of the 10 Minas

[11] As[h] they were listening to this, He went on to tell a parable because He was near Jerusalem,[i] and they thought the kingdom of God was going to appear right away.[j]

[12] Therefore He said: "A nobleman traveled to a far country to receive for himself authority to be king[D] and then return. [13] He called 10 of his •slaves, gave them 10 minas,[E] and told them, 'Engage in business until I come back.'

[14] "But his subjects hated him and sent a delegation after him, saying, 'We don't want this man to rule over us!'

[15] "At his return, having received the authority to be king,[D] he summoned those slaves he had given the money to, so he could find out how much they had made in business. [16] The first came forward and said, 'Master, your mina has earned 10 more minas.'

[17] "'Well done, good[F] slave!' he told him. 'Because you have been faithful[k] in a very small matter, have authority over 10 towns.'

[18] "The second came and said, 'Master, your mina has made five minas.'

[19] "So he said to him, 'You will be over five towns.'

[20] "And another came and said, 'Master, here is your mina. I have kept it hidden away in a cloth [21] because I was afraid of you, for you're a tough man: you collect what you didn't deposit and reap what you didn't sow.'[l]

[22] "He told him, 'I will judge you by what you have said,[G] you evil slave! If you knew I was a tough man, collecting what I didn't deposit and reaping what I didn't sow, [23] why didn't you put my money in the bank? And when I returned, I would have collected it with interest!' [24] So he said to those standing there, 'Take the mina away from him and give it to the one who has 10 minas.'

[25] "But they said to him, 'Master, he has 10 minas.'

[26] "'I tell you, that to everyone who has,

Cross references (center column)

[a] 19:7 Lk 15:2
[b] 19:8 Lk 18:22
[c] Lk 3:14
[d] Ex 22:1; 2Sm 12:6
[e] 19:9 Lk 1:77
[f] Lk 3:8; 13:16; Gl 3:7,29
[g] 19:10 Ezk 34:16; Mt 9:13; 10:6; 15:24; 18:12; Lk 15:4
[h] 19:11-27 Mt 25:14-30; Mk 13:34
[i] 19:11 Lk 9:51
[j] Lk 17:20; Ac 1:6
[k] 19:17 Lk 16:10; 1Co 4:2
[l] 19:21 2Co 8:12

Footnotes

[A]19:8 Or I give [B]19:8 Or I pay [C]19:10 Or save what was lost [D]19:12,15 Lit to receive for himself a kingdom or sovereignty
[E]19:13 = Gk coin worth 100 drachmas or about 100 days' wages [F]19:17 Or capable [H]19:22 Lit you out of your mouth

Study notes

house. The Jews greatly resented tax collectors because they worked for the Roman government that had invaded Israel, turning her into a subject nation. Thus Jesus' decision to stay overnight with such a **sinful man** as Zacchaeus, who had sold out and mistreated his own people, seemed outrageous. But Zacchaeus's words and actions were those of a transformed man. It was considered extremely generous to give one-fifth of your possessions to the poor, but Zacchaeus stated he would give **half**. Also, while repayment for extortion was 20 percent over what had been extorted, Zacchaeus promised to repay **four times as much**. Zacchaeus had become a **son of Abraham** and gained **salvation** through faith in Jesus Christ (Gl 3:7).

19:10 Son of Man was both a messianic title for Jesus and a reflection of His full humanity. His mission was to **seek and to save** those who were **lost**.

19:11 In keeping with the messianic expectation of that day, Jesus' disciples believed that as soon as He arrived in **Jerusalem**, He would be declared ruler and overturn the Romans. Then **the kingdom of God** would appear in its glory.

19:12-13 This parable is similar to the one in Mt 25:14-30 in some respects, but different enough that it was almost certainly told at a time distinct from the Matthew account. Jesus told the story to emphasize that He must go away in order to receive full **authority** (see Mt 28:18). Only after this would He **return** in the fullness of His glory and kingdom. A mina was equivalent to 100 drachmas. A drachma was essentially a day's wages for an ordinary worker. So each mina

would be worth about 100 days' pay, roughly four months' wages. The command (**engage in business until I come back**) describes an undefined duration of absence by the nobleman (Jesus). This fits with the nearly 2,000 years that have elapsed since Jesus ascended to heaven (24:50-53).

19:14 Jesus warned about the dire consequences of the Jews rejecting His **rule** as Messiah.

19:15-19 Ten slaves had been entrusted with one mina each, but only three were questioned about how much they had earned while the new king was gone. The first earned **10 more minas**, and his faithfulness resulted in his being given authority over **10 towns** in the kingdom. The second earned **five minas** and was also granted wider authority. Both servants are examples of the principle of verse 26: "To everyone who has, more will be given."

19:20-25 The third slave hid his mina because he feared his Master. It is also possible that he hoped the king would not return. In that case the money would become his. The **Master** did not accept his excuses, saying that even the small **interest** earned in a bank account would have been more useful. That the **evil slave** had to hand over his mina to the slave who had 10 minas demonstrates the principle of verse 26: "From the one who does not have, even what he does have will be taken away."

19:26-27 There is great reward for faithfulness to the Lord. Conversely, poor stewardship is punished by great loss. Those who do not want the Lord to **rule** their lives will be severely punished. It is likely that **slaughter them** refers to the destruction of Jerusalem in A.D. 70.

more will be given; and from the one who
does not have, even what he does have will
be taken away.[a] 27 But bring here these enemies of mine,[b] who did not want me to rule
over them, and slaughter[A] them in my presence.'"

The Triumphal Entry

28 When[c] He had said these things, He went
on ahead, going up to Jerusalem.[d] 29 As He approached Bethphage and Bethany, at the place
called the •Mount of Olives,[e] He sent two of
the disciples 30 and said, "Go into the village
ahead of you. As you enter it, you will find a
young donkey tied there, on which no one has
ever sat. Untie it and bring it here. 31 If anyone
asks you, 'Why are you untying it?' say this:
'The Lord needs it.'"

32 So those who were sent left and found it
just as He had told them.[f] 33 As they were untying the young donkey, its owners said to them,
"Why are you untying the donkey?"

34 "The Lord needs it," they said. 35 Then[g]
they brought it to Jesus, and after throwing
their robes on the donkey, they helped Jesus
get on it.[h] 36 As He was going along, they were
spreading their robes on the road.[i] 37 Now He
came near the path down the Mount of Olives,
and the whole crowd of the disciples began to
praise God joyfully with a loud voice for all the
miracles they had seen:

38 **The King[j] who comes**
in the name of the Lord[B,C,k]
is the blessed One.
Peace in heaven
and glory[l] in the highest heaven![m]

39 Some of the •Pharisees from the crowd
told Him, "Teacher, rebuke Your disciples."

40 He answered, "I tell you, if they were to
keep silent, the stones would cry out!"[n]

Jesus' Love for Jerusalem

41 As He approached and saw the city, He
wept[o] over it, 42 saying, "If you knew[p] this
day what would bring peace—but now it is
hidden[q] from your eyes. 43 For the days will
come on you[r] when your enemies will build
an embankment against you, surround you,

[a]19:26 Mt 13:12; Mk 4:25; Lk 8:18
[b]19:27 Lk 19:14
[c]19:28-44 Mt 21:1-11; Mk 11:1-11
[d]19:28 Lk 9:51
[e]19:29 2Sm 15:30; Zch 14:4; Lk 21:37; 22:39
[f]19:32 Lk 22:13
[g]19:35-38 Jn 12:12-15
[h]19:35 Zch 9:9
[i]19:36 2Kg 9:13
[j]19:38 Mt 2:2; 25:34
[k]Ps 118:26; Lk 13:35
[l]Lk 2:14
[m]Jb 16:19; Ps 148:1; Mt 21:9; Mk 11:10; Lk 2:14
[n]19:40 Hab 2:11
[o]19:41 Lk 13:34-35; Jn 11:35; Heb 5:7
[p]19:42 Lk 23:34
[q]Lk 8:9-10; 10:21
[r]19:43 Lk 17:22

[A]19:27 Or *execute* [B]19:38 Luke substitutes "the King" for "He" in Ps 118:26. [C]19:38 Ps 118:26

19:28-44 These verses describe Jesus' "triumphal entry" into Jerusalem. Though He was not accepted as Messiah by most Jews, His entry was nevertheless "triumphant" insomuch as (1) the palm branches (Jn 12:13) that were waved and placed on the ground symbolized royalty and victory, and (2) His entry into Jerusalem represented the fulfillment of OT prophecy (Zch 9:9) and the triumph of God's plan of redemption.

19:28 Over the course of the 17 miles from Jericho (see note at vv. 1-2) to **Jerusalem**, the elevation rises about 3,300 feet. Thus, to travel that road was **going up** at the average rate of almost 200 feet per mile.

kurios

Greek Pronunciation:	[KUHR ee ahss]
HCSB Translation:	Lord
Uses in Luke's Gospel:	104
Uses in the NT:	717
Focus passage:	Luke 19:30-34

The word *kurios* is the twenty-second most common word in the Greek NT and the third most common noun (after the words for "God" and "Jesus"). *Kurios* can mean *lord, master* (both with reference to either deity or humans), and even *sir* (see Jn 4:11; 5:7). In the Greek OT, however, *kurios* was used to translate two significant Hebrew words: *Yahweh* (over six thousand times), the personal name for God (normally translated Lord or God); and *adonai* (over seven hundred times; over three hundred in reference to God), a title of respect and honor (normally translated *Lord/lord* or *Master/master*). Thus, two important ideas from the OT carry over into the NT's use of *kurios*: deity and lordship. *Yahweh* is God and demands absolute loyalty to Himself as *Master*. The NT teaches that Jesus, God's Son, is deity and demands loyalty to Himself as absolute *Lord*—His deity being the basis of His lordship.

19:29 Bethphage and **Bethany** were small villages near the road from Jericho to Jerusalem. Bethany, the hometown of Lazarus, Mary, and Martha (Jn 11:1) was only two miles east of Jerusalem, just over **the Mount of Olives**, a ridge across the Kidron Valley from the temple in Jerusalem. The **two . . . disciples** are not named in any of the Gospels.

19:30-34 Religious or political leaders in that time often borrowed property (**a young donkey**) for a short time, as here. Matthew 21:7 says that the mother donkey was also commandeered. This action fulfilled the prophecy of Zch 9:9: "Daughter Jerusalem . . . your King is coming to you . . . humble and riding on a donkey, on a colt, the foal of a donkey."

19:35-36 The **robes** (outer garments) were cast down by the two disciples and by the crowd. **Spreading their robes on the road** was a way to honor special dignitaries, as was done for Jehu when he was acclaimed king of Israel (2Kg 9:13).

19:37-38 As Jesus passed over the **Mount of Olives** (see note at v. 29) and began His descent into Jerusalem, the crowd of disciples praised God for **all the miracles they had seen**. The Gospel of John reports that the miracle of raising Lazarus from the dead had recently occurred in Bethany, near the beginning point of the triumphal entry (Jn 11:1-44). The crowd was shouting Ps 118:26, which is messianic. In addition, they added the word **King** to their recitation of the OT Scripture, showing that they believed Jesus was the Messiah.

19:39-40 The **Pharisees** asked Jesus to **rebuke** His disciples because they understood that the repetition of Ps 118:26 was a confession that Jesus was both Messiah and rightful king of Israel. Jesus replied that, even if His disciples were to **keep silent**, God would make the truth known some other way (**the stones would cry out**), even if it took a miracle.

19:41-44 Jesus wept before Lazarus's tomb (Jn 11:35), and

and hem you in on every side.[a] They will crush you and your children within you to the ground,[b] and they will not leave one stone on another[c] in you, because you did not recognize the time of your visitation."[d]

Cleansing the Temple Complex

He[e] went into the ˙temple complex and began to throw out those who were selling,[A] and He said, "It is written, **My house will be a house of prayer,**[f] but you have made it **a den of thieves!**"[B,g]

Every day He was teaching[h] in the temple complex. The ˙chief priests, the ˙scribes, and the leaders of the people were looking for a way to destroy[j] Him, but they could not find a way to do it, because all the people[j] were captivated by what they heard.[C]

The Authority of Jesus Challenged

20 One[k] day[D] as He was teaching[l] the people in the ˙temple complex and proclaiming the good news,[m] the ˙chief priests and the ˙scribes, with the elders,[n] came up and said to Him: "Tell us, by what authority are You doing these things? Who is it who gave You this authority?"

He answered them, "I will also ask you a question. Tell Me, was the baptism of John from heaven or from men?"

They discussed it among themselves: "If we say, 'From heaven,' He will say, 'Why didn't

you believe him?' But if we say, 'From men,' all the people[o] will stone us, because they are convinced that John was a prophet."[p]

So they answered that they did not know its origin.[E]

And Jesus said to them, "Neither will I tell you by what authority I do these things."

The Parable of the Vineyard Owner

Then[q] He began to tell the people this parable: "A man planted a vineyard,[r] leased it to tenant farmers, and went away for a long time. At harvest time he sent a ˙slave to the farmers so that they might give him some fruit from the vineyard. But the farmers beat him and sent him away empty-handed. He sent yet another slave, but they beat that one too, treated him shamefully, and sent him away empty-handed. And he sent yet a third, but they wounded this one too and threw him out.

"Then the owner of the vineyard said, 'What should I do? I will send my beloved[s] son. Perhaps[F] they will respect him.'

"But when the tenant farmers saw him, they discussed it among themselves and said, 'This is the heir. Let's kill him, so the inheritance will be ours!'[t] So they threw him out of the vineyard and killed him.

"Therefore, what will the owner of the vineyard do to them? He will come and destroy[u] those farmers and give the vineyard to others."

Cross-references (center column)

[a] 19:43 Is 29:3; Jr 6:6; Ezk 4:2; Lk 21:20
[b] 19:44 Mt 24:2; Mk 13:2
[c] Lk 21:6
[d] Ex 3:16; Lk 1:68; 7:16; 1Pt 2:12
[e] 19:45-48 Mt 21:12-19; Mk 11:12-19; Jn 2:13-17; 8:1-2; 11:45-53
[f] 19:46 Is 56:7
[g] Jr 7:11
[h] 19:47 Mt 26:55; Lk 20:1
[i] Lk 6:11; 11:53-54; 20:19
[j] 19:48 Lk 18:43; 20:6
[k] 20:1-8 Mt 21:23-27; Mk 11:27-33
[l] 20:1 Lk 19:47
[m] Lk 4:18; 8:1
[n] Lk 9:22; 22:66
[o] 20:6 Lk 19:48
[p] Mt 11:9; Lk 7:29-30
[q] 20:9-19 Mt 21:33-46; Mk 12:1-12
[r] 20:9 Is 5:1-7
[s] 20:13 Mt 17:5; Lk 3:22
[t] 20:14 Lk 16:16
[u] 20:16 Lk 19:27

A19:45 Other mss add *and buying in it*   B19:46 Is 56:7; Jr 7:11   C19:48 Lit *people hung on what they heard*   D20:1 Lit *It happened on one of the days*   E20:7 Or *know where it was from*   F20:13 Other mss add *when they see him*

---

here He wept at the thought of His rejection by the city of Jerusalem. True, lasting peace with God comes through faith in Jesus Christ (Rm 5:1). The Jews enjoyed a temporal though imperfect peace under Roman rule, but such a peace cannot be secured forever, as the destructive events of A.D. 70 proved. Due to their unbelief, many Jews did not open their eyes to see Christ as Messiah (2Co 4:4) or recognize His coming as the time (Gk *kairos*; "opportune time") of God's **visitation** and offer of salvation.

19:45-46 The court of the Gentiles in **the temple complex** was where sacrificial animals were sold for outrageously high prices. According to Is 56:7, the temple (**My house**) was to be **a house of prayer**. The other quote (**a den of thieves**) is from Jr 7:11, which reflects a time when the corruption of the nation and its religious system was about to be judged by God in the Babylonian captivity. Now, as Jesus beheld the corruption of the temple and the opposition arrayed against Him, the nation faced an even greater season of judgment.

19:47-48 The religious **leaders** of Israel were increasingly desperate to get rid of Jesus, but they were hesitant to act because Jesus had gained considerable popularity among the masses.

20:1-2 Luke did not specify which day of the Passion Week is in view here, but the parallel account in Mk 11:19-20,27-33 indicates it was Tuesday. **Chief priests . . . scribes**, and **elders** were part of the Jewish ruling council, the Sanhedrin

(see note at 22:66). The Jewish religious leaders questioned Jesus' **authority** for throwing the merchants out of the temple complex (19:45) because such an act was a direct attack on the heart of Jewish religion. To their mind, none but a blasphemer would dare do such a thing. Thus they sought to discredit Jesus in the eyes of the people gathered for Passover (see note at 19:47-48).

20:3-8 As He often did, Jesus turned the attention back on His questioners by asking them about the authority of John the Baptist's **baptism**. Finding themselves in a "no-win" situation, the religious leaders stated that **they did not know** the basis of John's authority. Having caught His opponents in a trap, Jesus also refused to answer their question.

20:9-12 The **vineyard** was a symbol of Israel (Is 5:7), and its owner was God. The **tenant farmers** stood for the people of Israel, notably its religious leaders. The successive slaves who suffered mistreatment from the tenants stood for the OT prophets who were sent from God but were rejected and even killed by Israel.

20:13-18 **My beloved son** stands for Jesus (see note at 3:21-22). The Jewish religious leaders did not kill Jesus to claim His inheritance, but rather to forcefully and finally reject Him as Messiah and heir to David's throne. The destruction of the **farmers** (Israel) by the **owner of the vineyard** (God) looks ahead to Gentiles being added to God's plan for His new covenant people, the church. This is one of Luke's

But when they heard this they said, "No—never!"[a]

[17] But He looked at them and said, "Then what is the meaning of this Scripture:[A,b]

> **The stone that the builders rejected— this has become the cornerstone?**[B,C,c]

[18] Everyone who falls on that stone will be broken to pieces, and if it falls on anyone, it will grind him to powder!"[d]

[19] Then the scribes and the chief priests[e] looked for a way to get their hands on Him[f] that very hour, because they knew He had told this parable against them, but they feared the people.[g]

God and Caesar

[20] They[D,h] watched closely[i] and sent spies[i] who pretended to be righteous,[E] so they could catch Him in what He said,[F,k] to hand Him[l] over to the governor's[m] rule and authority. [21] They questioned Him, "Teacher, we know that You speak and teach correctly,[n] and You don't show partiality,[G,o] but teach truthfully the way of God.[p] [22] Is it lawful[q] for us to pay taxes[r] to Caesar[s] or not?"

[23] But detecting their craftiness, He said to them,[H] [24] "Show Me a •denarius. Whose image and inscription does it have?"

"Caesar's," they said.

[25] "Well then," He told them, "give back to Caesar[t] the things that are Caesar's and to God the things that are God's."

[26] They were not able to catch Him in what He said[F] in public,[i] and being amazed at His answer, they became silent.[u]

The Sadducees and the Resurrection

[27] Some[v] of the •Sadducees, who say there is no resurrection,[w] came up and questioned Him: [28] "Teacher, Moses wrote for us that **if a man's brother** has a wife, and **dies childless, his brother should take the wife and produce •offspring for his brother.**[J,x] [29] Now there were seven brothers. The first took a wife and died without children. [30] Also the second[K] [31] and the third took her. In the same way, all seven died and left no children. [32] Finally, the woman died too. [33] In the resurrection, therefore, whose wife will the woman be? For all seven had married her."[L]

[34] Jesus told them, "The sons of this age[y] marry and are given in marriage.[z] [35] But those who are counted worthy[aa] to take part in that age[ab] and in the resurrection from the dead neither marry nor are given in marriage. [36] For they cannot die anymore,[ac] because they are like angels and are sons of God,[ad] since they are sons of the resurrection. [37] Moses even indicated in the passage about the burning

a 20:16 Rm 3:4; 1Co 6:15; Gl 2:17
b 20:17 Lk 4:17; 18:31; 21:22,37; 24:44
c Ps 118:22; Ac 4:11; Eph 2:20; 1Pt 2:4-7
d 20:18 Is 8:14-15; Dn 2:34-35,44-45; Rm 9:32-33; 1Pt 2:8
e 20:19 Mt 2:4; 20:18; 21:15; Lk 22:2; 23:10
f Lk 19:47; 21:12
g Lk 22:2
h 20:20-26 Mt 20:15-22; Mk 12:13-17
i 20:20 Lk 6:7; 14:1
j Mt 22:15-16
k Lk 11:54
l Lk 14:20; Ac 3:13; Rm 8:32
m Mt 27:2; Lk 21:12
n 20:21 Jn 3:2
o Dt 1:17; 10:17; Mal 2:9; Mt 22:16
p Ac 13:10; 18:25-26
q 20:22 Lk 6:9; 14:3
r Mt 17:25; Lk 23:2; Rm 13:6-7
s Lk 2:1; 3:1; 20:24-25; 23:2
t 20:25 Mt 22:21
u 20:26 Lk 9:36; 14:4
v 20:27-40 Mt 22:23-33,46; Mk 12:18-

27,34 w 20:27 Ac 23:6 x 20:28 Dt 25:5 y 20:34 Lk 16:8 z Lk 17:27 aa 20:35 Ac 5:41; 2Th 1:5 ab Mk 10:30 ac 20:36 1Co 15:54-55; Rv 21:4 ad Ps 82:6; Mt 5:45; Rm 8:14,19; Gl 3:26

A 20:17 Lit What then is this that is written   B 20:17 Lit the head of the corner   C 20:17 Ps 118:22   D 20:20 The scribes and chief priests of v. 19   E 20:20 Or upright; that is, loyal to God's law   F 20:20,26 Lit catch Him in a word   G 20:21 Lit You don't receive a face   H 20:23 Other mss add "Why are you testing Me?   I 20:26 Lit in front of the people   J 20:28 Dt 25:5   K 20:30 Other mss add took her as wife, and he died without children   L 20:33 Lit had her as wife

major focuses in his next book, the Acts of the Apostles. The people in the temple area who were listening to Jesus (vv. 1,9) could not imagine God doing such a thing. In this quote from Ps 118:22, Jesus is **the stone** and **cornerstone** (see Ac 4:11; Eph 2:20; 1Pt 2:7). The **builders** are not identified, but they were undoubtedly Israel's religious leaders (vv. 1,19).

20:19-21 The religious leaders (**scribes . . . chief priests**) understood that Jesus' preceding **parable** referred to them, and so they wanted to get rid of Him immediately. But in order not to anger the people, they sought to trap Him through a question that would allow them to turn Him over to the Roman authorities. So, while attempting to sound pious and respectful, they asked for Jesus' view on one of the most divisive issues of the day—the Roman poll tax.

20:22-26 The religious leaders thought they had found the perfect way to trap Jesus, no matter how He answered. If He said it was **lawful** to pay the poll tax to **Caesar**, it would turn the Jewish people against Him. If He said it was not lawful, it would provide grounds for the Romans to arrest Him for treason. But Jesus did not fall into their trap. By asking for a **denarius**, the specific coin used to pay the poll tax, Jesus demonstrated that the religious leaders themselves found it necessary to cooperate with the ruling Roman government. **Give back to Caesar the things that are Caesar's** was a proper recognition of the legitimate role of human gov-

ernment in God's plan (Rm 13:1-7). **To God the things that are God's** does not divide life into secular and sacred, which would imply that God is indifferent about some aspects of human existence. Rather, Jesus' statement demonstrates that all facets of life have reference to God, including the need to submit to governmental rule. This answer amazed the scribes and chief priests (v. 26), thwarting their efforts to catch Jesus in a self-condemning statement.

20:27-33 Another group among the religious leaders attempted to trap Jesus. The **Sadducees** did not believe in the **resurrection** from the dead because it was not taught in the Torah (Genesis through Deuteronomy). They asked Jesus a question that was designed to discredit the idea of resurrection by reducing it to absurdity. **If a man's brother . . . dies childless** refers to the law of levirate marriage in Dt 25:5. The Sadducees mistakenly assumed that life after **the resurrection** of the body would include the same basic structures as earthly life.

20:34-36 Jesus answered that **marriage** is confined to **this age**. **Those who are counted worthy** are those who place faith in Christ because faith in Messiah is the only means by which anyone can be accepted by God (Rm 5:1; Gl 2:16). In heaven we will be **like angels**, who enjoy many meaningful relationships but do not marry or reproduce. After the resurrection, the human life cycle (birth, marriage, reproduction, death) is forever changed.

bush that the dead are raised, where he calls the Lord **the God of Abraham and the God of Isaac and the God of Jacob.**[A,a] [38] He is not God of the dead but of the living, because all are living to[B] Him."[b]

[39] Some of the scribes answered, "Teacher, You have spoken well." [40] And they no longer dared to ask Him anything.

The Question about the Messiah

[41] Then[c] He said to them, "How can they say that the •Messiah is the Son of David?[d] [42] For David himself says in the Book of Psalms:[e]

> **The Lord declared
>   to my Lord,
> 'Sit at My right hand**
> [43] **until I make Your enemies
>   Your footstool.'**[C,f]

[44] David calls Him 'Lord'; how then can the Messiah be his Son?"[g]

Warning against the Scribes

[45] While[h] all the people were listening, He said to His disciples, [46] "Beware[i] of the scribes, who want to go around in long robes and who love greetings in the marketplaces, the front seats in the •synagogues, and the places of honor at banquets.[j] [47] They devour widows' houses and say long prayers just for show. These will receive greater punishment."[D]

The Widow's Gift

21 He[k] looked up and saw the rich dropping their offerings into the temple treasury.[l] [2] He also saw a poor widow dropping in two tiny coins.[E,m] [3] "I tell you the truth," He said. "This poor widow has put in more than all of them.[n] [4] For all these people have put in gifts out of their surplus, but she out of her poverty has put in all she had to live on."

Destruction of the Temple Predicted

[5] As[o] some were talking about the •temple complex, how it was adorned with beautiful stones and gifts dedicated to God,[F] He said, [6] "These things that you see—the days will come[p] when not one stone will be left on another that will not be thrown down!"[q]

Signs of the End of the Age

[7] "Teacher," they asked Him, "so when will these things be? And what will be the sign when these things are about to take place?"[r] [8] Then He said, "Watch out that you are not deceived.[s] For many will come in My name,[t] saying, 'I am He,'[u] and, 'The time is near.' Don't follow them.[v] [9] When you hear of wars and rebellions,[G] don't be alarmed. Indeed, these things must take place first, but the end won't come right away."

[10] Then He told them: "Nation will be raised up against nation, and kingdom against kingdom.[w] [11] There will be violent earthquakes,[x]

Cross references (center column):

a 20:37 Ex 3:6,15-16; 4:5; Mt 1:2; Ac 3:13; 7:30-32
b 20:38 Rm 6:10-11; 14:7-8; 2Co 5:14-15; Gl 2:19-20; 1Th 4:14; 5:10
c 20:41-44 Mt 22:41-46; Mk 12:34-37
d 20:41 Mt 1:1,17; Lk 1:27; Rm 1:3; Eph 5:2
e 20:42 Lk 24:44; Ac 1:20
f 20:42-43 Ps 110:1; Ac 2:34-35; 1Co 15:25; Heb 1:13; 10:13
g 20:44 Rm 1:3-4
h 20:45-47 Mt 23:1-36; Mk 12:37-40
i 20:46 Mt 16:6
j Lk 11:43
k 21:1-4 Mk 12:41-44
l 21:1 2Kg 12:9; Mt 27:6; Jn 8:20
m 21:2 Lk 12:59
n 21:3 2Co 8:2,12
o 21:5-38 Mt 24:1-51; Mk 13:1-37
p 21:6 Lk 17:22
q Lk 19:44
r 21:7 Ac 1:6-7
s 21:8 Jr 29:8; Eph 5:6; 2Th 2:3
t Jr 14:14; 1Jn 2:18
u Jn 8:24
v Lk 17:23
w 21:10 2Ch 15:6; Is 19:2
x 21:11 Is 29:6; Zch 14:5; Rv 6:12

A 20:37 Ex 3:6,15　B 20:38 Or *with*　C 20:42-43 Ps 110:1　D 20:47 Or *judgment*　E 21:2 Lit *two lepta*; the *lepton* was the smallest and least valuable Gk coin in use.　F 21:5 Gifts given to the temple in fulfillment of vows to God　G 21:9 Or *insurrections*, or *revolutions*

20:37-40 Jesus quoted Ex 3:1-6 to draw in the Sadducees, who revered the books of Moses. Jesus' logic is as follows: God could identify Himself to Moses as the **God of Abraham . . . Isaac**, and **Jacob** only if they were still living in Moses' day. Since these men had died many years previously, there must be an afterlife. The religious leaders **no longer dared** to bait Jesus after this because He had **spoken well** and made them look foolish.

20:41-44 Jesus then asked His own difficult theological question: how could the Christ (Messiah) be both **the Son of David** and the divine **Lord** of David? Though not given here, the answer is that Jesus, the Messiah, was both fully God (Lord) and fully human (Son of David).

20:45-47 The **long robes** of **the scribes** were of white linen and had a decorative fringe. The **front seats** were where a person could be seen by everyone in attendance at the synagogue. **Devour widows' houses** probably means that some scribes defrauded helpless widows of their homes and their limited resources. Matthew 23:1-36 is an extended parallel passage describing the sins for which the scribes and Pharisees would be judged by God.

21:1-4 There were 13 coffers shaped like inverted trumpets in the court of women in the temple and a **treasury** room nearby where supplicants could deposit their **offerings**. The **poor widow** did not have much to give, unlike **the rich** who made a great show of their offerings. **Tiny** copper **coins** called mites were the smallest Jewish currency at that time. Jesus commended the widow for giving sacrificially.

21:5 Herod the Great began renovating **the temple complex** in 20 B.C. The work was completed in A.D. 63, some 30 years after Jesus' crucifixion. Some of the stones used for the foundation were 40 feet long. Others were overlaid with gold.

21:6 Jesus hyperbolically declared that **not one stone will be left on another**. In A.D. 70, the Roman armies fulfilled this prophecy by leveling the temple and the city of Jerusalem. Many of the huge stones of the temple were toppled into lower areas surrounding the complex.

21:7 The parallel passages in Mt 24 and Mk 13 focus primarily on the end of the age, while Luke is concerned mostly about the near-term destruction of the temple (**these things**). But verses 25-28 do speak of the second coming of Christ. The events leading to the destruction of the temple in A.D. 70 foreshadow the later time that leads up to Jesus' return.

21:8-10 The appearance of false messiahs and date-setting schemes (**the time is near**), as well as widespread **wars**, will continue throughout the present age. However, these things must occur and are part of an expected delay before the **end** of the age.

21:11 Earthquakes . . . famines, and **plagues** of varied

and famines and plagues[a] in various places, and there will be terrifying sights and great signs from heaven.[b] [12]But before all these things, they will lay their hands on you[c] and persecute[d] you. They will hand you over to the *synagogues[e] and prisons,[f] and you will be brought before kings and governors[g] because of My name. [13]It will lead to an opportunity for you to witness.[A,h] [14]Therefore make up your minds[B] not to prepare your defense ahead of time,[i] [15]for I will give you such words[C,j] and a wisdom[k] that none of your adversaries will be able to resist or contradict.[l] [16]You will even be betrayed by parents, brothers, relatives, and

friends.[m] They will kill some of you. [17]You will be hated by everyone because of My name,[n] [18]but not a hair of your head will be lost.[o] [19]By your endurance gain[D] your *lives.[p]

The Destruction of Jerusalem

[20]"When you see Jerusalem surrounded by armies,[q] then recognize that its desolation[r] has come near. [21]Then those in Judea must flee[s] to the mountains![t] Those inside the city[E] must leave it, and those who are in the coun-

[a]21:11 Rv 6:8
[b]Lk 11:16; 12:33
[c]21:12-17 Mt 10:19-22; Mk 13:11-13
[d]21:12 Ps 119:84
[e]Ac 22:19; 26:11
[f]Ac 4:3; 5:18; 8:3; 12:4; 16:23
[g]Ac 17:6; 18:12; 24:1,27; 25:6; 27:24; 2Co 11:23
[h]21:13 Php 1:12-19
[i]21:14 Lk 12:11
[j]21:15 Ex 4:12
[k]Ac 6:10
[l]Ac 4:14
[m]21:16 Mt

10:35; Lk 12:53   [n]21:17 Lk 6:22; Jn 15:18-19   [o]21:18 1Sm 14:45; Mt 10:30; Lk 12:7; Jn 10:28   [p]21:19 Mt 10:22; 24:13; Rm 2:7; 5:3; Heb 10:36; Jms 1:3   [q]21:20 Lk 19:43   [r]Dn 9:27   [s]21:21 Lk 17:31   [t]Mt 4:8

[A]21:13 Lit *lead to a testimony for you*   [B]21:14 Lit *Therefore place (determine) in your hearts*   [C]21:15 Lit *you a mouth*   [D]21:19 Other mss read *endurance you will gain*   [E]21:21 Lit *inside her*

---

intensity will occur through history all the way to the end of the age. **Great signs from heaven** probably refer to such cosmic phenomena as that prophesied in Jl 2:28-32 and fulfilled in Rv 6:13-14.

21:12-15 These verses return to discussion of the immediate circumstances of the apostles and their co-laborers in the gospel. Persecution by Jews (**the synagogues**) and Gentiles (**kings and governors**) will lead to opportunities to **witness** for Christ (Ac 4; 7; 22-24; 26). **I will give you such words** basically repeats Jesus' earlier promise in 12:11-12.

21:16-19 When troubles came upon them after Jesus' death, the disciples would draw comfort from their recollection of

Jesus' forewarning that they would be **hated** and even **betrayed** by those closest to them. **Not a hair of your head** refers to spiritual security. **Endurance** (Gk *hupomone*; "patience, steadfastness") is not to be understood to mean that we earn salvation by our efforts to persevere. Rather, perseverance is required of every true believer in Jesus Christ. Ultimately the strength to endure is supplied by God.

21:20-22 The words **Jerusalem** and **its desolation** indicate that this is the point where the questions in verse 7 are answered. **Surrounded by armies** is the "sign" that the temple and the city are about to be destroyed. Matthew 24:15 refers to "the abomination of desolation" spoken of by Daniel (Dn 9:27; 11:31; 21:11) that will be set up in the holy place in

The Siege of Jerusalem, A.D. 70 (21:6).

"Where is this city that was believed to have God himself inhabiting therein? It is now demolished to the very foundations, and hath nothing but that monument of it preserved, I mean the camp of those that hath destroyed it, which still dwells upon its ruins. . . . I cannot but wish that we had all died before we had seen that holy city demolished by the hands of our enemies, or the foundations of our holy temple dug up after so profane a manner."

– Flavius Josephus, *The Wars of the Jews* VII.8.7

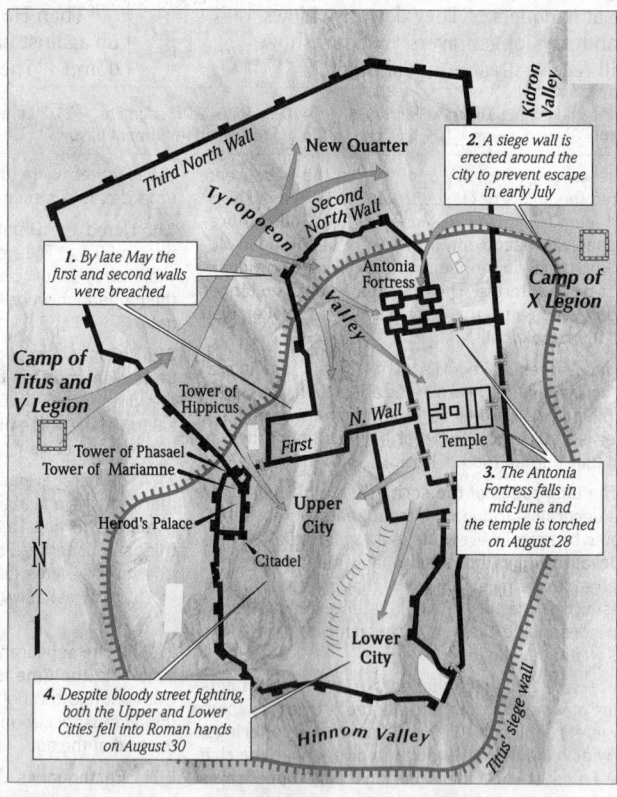

1. By late May the first and second walls were breached

2. A siege wall is erected around the city to prevent escape in early July

3. The Antonia Fortress falls in mid-June and the temple is torched on August 28

4. Despite bloody street fighting, both the Upper and Lower Cities fell into Roman hands on August 30

Third North Wall

New Quarter

Kidron Valley

Tyropoeon

Second North Wall

Antonia Fortress

Camp of X Legion

Camp of Titus and V Legion

Valley

Tower of Hippicus

N. Wall

Temple

First

Tower of Phasael

Tower of Mariamne

Upper City

Herod's Palace

Citadel

Lower City

Hinnom Valley

Titus' siege wall

N

try must not enter it, [22] because these are days of vengeance[a] to fulfill all the things that are written. [23] Woe to pregnant women and nursing mothers in those days,[b] for there will be great distress in the land[A] and wrath against this people. [24] They will fall by the edge of the sword[c] and be led captive into all the nations, and Jerusalem will be trampled by the Gentiles[B,d] until the times of the Gentiles[e] are fulfilled.

The Coming of the Son of Man

[25] "Then there will be signs in the sun, moon, and stars;[f] and there will be anguish on the earth among nations bewildered by the roaring sea and waves.[g] [26] People will faint from fear and expectation of the things that are coming on the world, because the celestial powers will be shaken.[h] [27] Then they will see the •Son of Man coming in a cloud[i] with power and great glory.[j] [28] But when these things begin to take place, stand up and lift up your heads, because your •redemption is near!"[k]

The Parable of the Fig Tree

[29] Then He told them a parable: "Look at the fig tree, and all the trees. [30] As soon as they put out leaves you can see for yourselves and recognize that summer is already near. [31] In the same way, when you see these things happening, recognize[c] that the kingdom of God is near. [32] •I assure you: This generation will certainly not pass away until all things take place.[l] [33] Heaven and earth will pass away,[m] but My words will never pass away.[n]

The Need for Watchfulness

[34] "Be on your guard,[o] so that your minds are not dulled[D] from carousing,[E] drunkenness,[p] and worries of life,[q] or that day will come on you unexpectedly[r] like a trap. For it will come on all who live on the face of the whole earth. [36] But be alert at all times,[s] praying that you may have strength[F] to escape[t] all

a21:22 Is 34:8; 63:4; Dn 9:24-27; Hs 9:7; Lk 18:7-8
b21:23 Lk 23:29
c21:24 Heb 11:34
dPs 79:1; Is 63:18; Dn 8:13; Rv 11:2
e Dn 12:7; Rm 11:25
f21:25 Is 13:10; 24:23; Ezk 32:7; Jl 2:10; 3:15; Ac 2:20; Rv 6:12-13
g Ps 46:2-3; 65:7; Is 17:12; Jl 2:30-31
h21:26 Is 34:4; Hg 2:6
i21:27 Dn 7:13; Rv 1:7
j Mt 16:27; 26:64; Mk 9:1
k21:28 Lk 2:38; 24:21; Rm 8:23; 13:11
l21:32 Lk 9:27
m21:33 Ps 102:26; Is 51:6; 2Pt 3:10
n Ps 119:89; Is 40:8; Mt 5:18; Lk 16:17; 1Pt 1:23,25
o21:34 Lk 17:3   pRm 13:13   qMt 13:22; Mk 4:19; 1Th 5:6-7; 1Pt 4:7   rLk 12:40; 1Th 5:3   s21:36 Mt 25:13; 26:41; Mk 14:34-38; Lk 12:37; Ac 20:31; 1Co 16:13; Eph 6:18; 1Th 5:6; 1Pt 5:8   tRm 2:3; 1Th 5:3; Heb 2:3

A21:23 Or the earth   B21:24 Or nations   C21:31 Or you know   D21:34 Lit your hearts are not weighed down   E21:34 Or hangovers
F21:36 Other mss read you may be counted worthy

the temple. Luke spoke only of the desolation of Jerusalem. When the city was surrounded, it was imperative that its inhabitants and those in the surrounding areas (**Judea**) flee for their lives because the siege of the city was part of God's planned **vengeance** (Gk *ekdikesis*; "rendering of justice, retribution") against Jerusalem.

21:23-24 Matthew 24:21 uses the phrase "great tribulation," taken from Dn 12:1, to refer to the intensity of the suffering during this time of judgment. Luke called it **great distress** (Gk *anagke*; "trouble"). **Wrath** is God's anger against sin expressed as righteous judgment. The survivors of the destruction of Jerusalem in A.D. 70 were spread all over the known world, even more extensively than the Diaspora

---

orge

Greek Pronunciation:	[ohr GAY]
HCSB Translation:	wrath
Uses in Luke's Gospel:	2
Uses in the NT:	36
Focus passage:	Luke 21:23

The most common Greek word in the NT to describe God's *wrath* is *orge*, normally translated *wrath* or *anger*. Only five occurrences of *orge* in the NT do not refer to God's *wrath* (Eph 4:31; Col 3:8; 1Tm 2:8; Jms 1:19,20). Mark alone refers specifically to the *orge* ("anger") of Jesus (3:5); Matthew refers to God's *orge* once (3:7); and Luke does so twice (3:7; 21:23).

A three-fold dynamic exists as an expression of God's *orge*: (1) His *wrath* is a present reality for everyone who does not believe in His Son (Jn 3:36; Rm 1:18-32), but unbelievers do not recognize God's *wrath* when they see it; (2) His *wrath* on unbelievers will intensify as the day of Christ's return approaches (1Th 5:9; Rv 6:16,17; 11:18; 16:19); and (3) the complete and final demonstration of His *wrath* is reserved for the time of Christ's personal presence on earth as King and Judge (Rv 14:10; 19:15).

which occurred during the Babylonian exile hundreds of years earlier. From 70 until the emergence of the modern state of Israel in the mid-twentieth century, Jerusalem was controlled by **Gentiles**. The **times** of the Gentiles refers to the current opportune time (Gk *kairoi*) in which Gentile nations embrace the gospel. Meanwhile, Israel is spiritually hardened and will remain so until near the end (Rm 11:25-26).

21:25-26 Signs in the sun, moon, and stars, probably referring to Jl 2:28,31, were mentioned earlier (Lk 21:11). These cosmic effects will cause great anxiety among the world population.

21:27 The second coming of Christ is described in words that echo the prophecy of Dn 7:13 (**the Son of Man coming . . . with . . . great glory**). This passage is also cited in relation to Christ's return in Rv 1:7.

21:28-31 Instead of cowering in the face of these signs, believers should be encouraged because they indicate that the divine plan for **redemption** is being completed and the advent of **the kingdom of God is near**. It is like watching **trees** sprouting **leaves** in the spring and knowing that **summer** is at hand.

21:32-33 This generation probably refers to those who will be alive when the various phenomena described by Jesus begin to take place in rapid succession. Since "generation" (Gk *genea*) occasionally means "family" or "posterity," some believe that it refers specifically to the people of Israel. On **heaven and earth . . . but My words**, see Mt 5:17-18.

21:34-36 That day refers to the time of Christ's return. Those caught up in a worldly lifestyle (**carousing, drunkenness**) or the **worries of life** will be caught off guard when Christ comes back. The proper outlook is prayerful alertness (18:8), which will prepare the believer to **stand** and not be ashamed **before the Son of Man** at His return (see 1Jn 2:28).

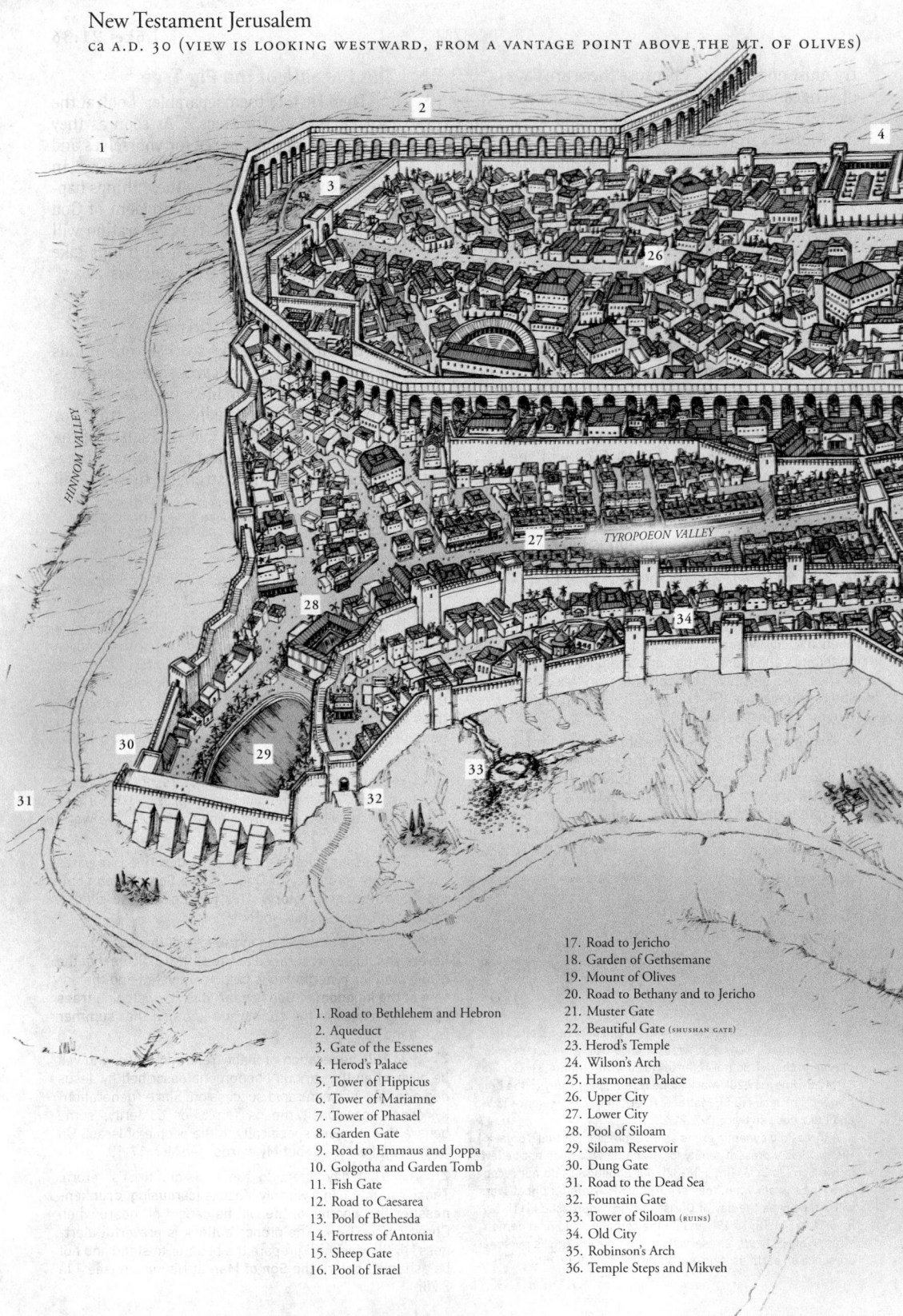

New Testament Jerusalem

ca A.D. 30 (VIEW IS LOOKING WESTWARD, FROM A VANTAGE POINT ABOVE THE MT. OF OLIVES)

HINNOM VALLEY

TYROPOEON VALLEY

1. Road to Bethlehem and Hebron
2. Aqueduct
3. Gate of the Essenes
4. Herod's Palace
5. Tower of Hippicus
6. Tower of Mariamne
7. Tower of Phasael
8. Garden Gate
9. Road to Emmaus and Joppa
10. Golgotha and Garden Tomb
11. Fish Gate
12. Road to Caesarea
13. Pool of Bethesda
14. Fortress of Antonia
15. Sheep Gate
16. Pool of Israel
17. Road to Jericho
18. Garden of Gethsemane
19. Mount of Olives
20. Road to Bethany and to Jericho
21. Muster Gate
22. Beautiful Gate (SHUSHAN GATE)
23. Herod's Temple
24. Wilson's Arch
25. Hasmonean Palace
26. Upper City
27. Lower City
28. Pool of Siloam
29. Siloam Reservoir
30. Dung Gate
31. Road to the Dead Sea
32. Fountain Gate
33. Tower of Siloam (RUINS)
34. Old City
35. Robinson's Arch
36. Temple Steps and Mikveh

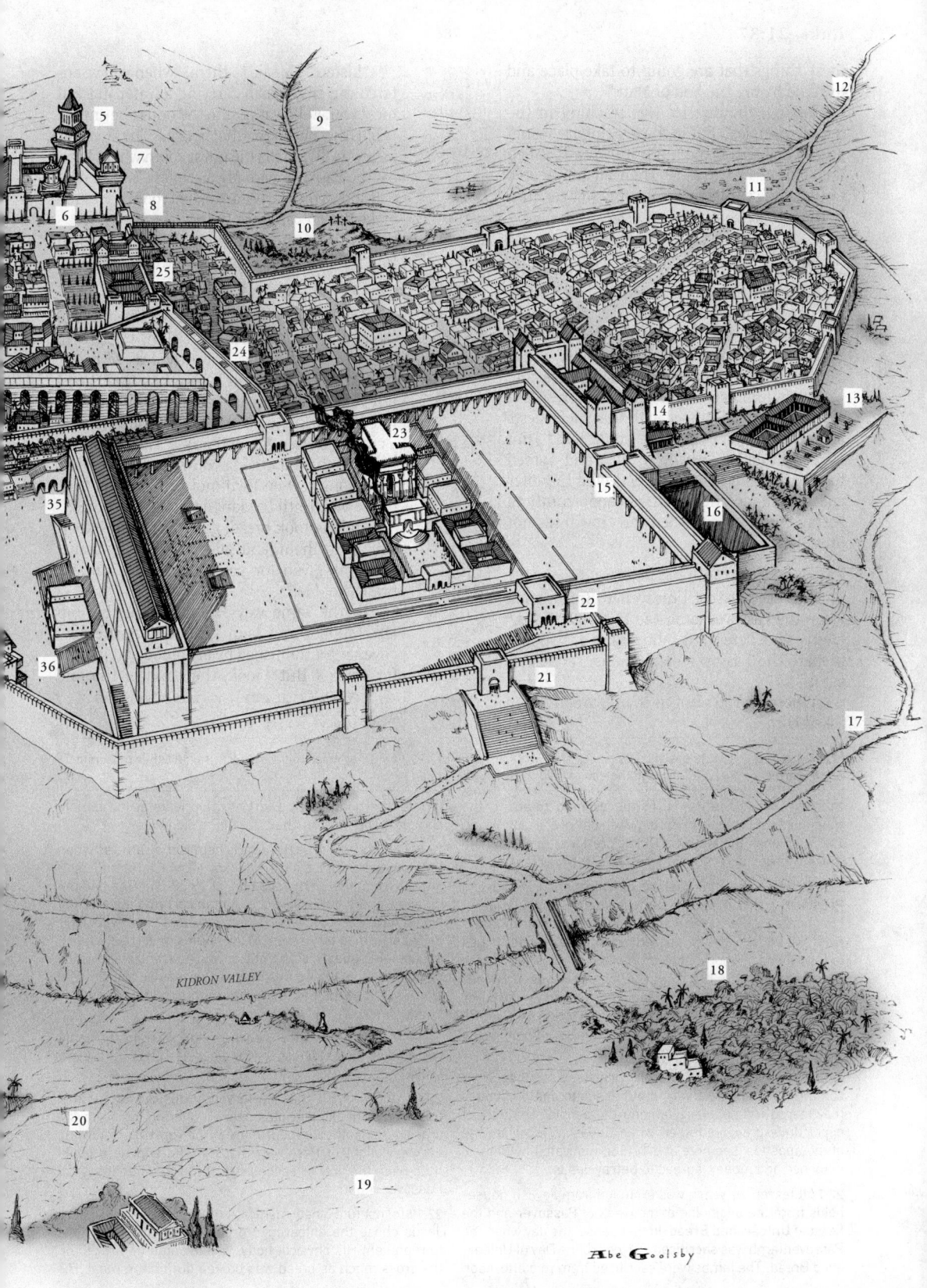

KIDRON VALLEY

Abe Goolsby

these things that are going to take place and to stand before the Son of Man."

[37] During[a] the day, He was teaching in the temple complex,[b] but in the evening He would go out and spend the night on what is called the •Mount of Olives.[c] [38] Then all the people would come early in the morning to hear Him in the temple complex.[d]

The Plot to Kill Jesus

22 The[e] Festival of •Unleavened Bread,[f] which is called •Passover,[g] was drawing near. [2] The •chief priests and the •scribes were looking for a way to put Him to death,[h] because they were afraid of the people.[i]

[3] Then[j] Satan entered Judas,[k] called Iscariot,[l] who was numbered among the Twelve. [4] He went away and discussed with the chief priests and temple police[m] how he could hand Him over[n] to them. [5] They were glad and agreed to give him silver.[A] [6] So he accepted the offer and started looking for a good opportunity to betray Him to them when the crowd was not present.

Preparation for Passover

[7] Then[o] the Day of Unleavened Bread came when the Passover lamb had to be sacrificed.[p] [8] Jesus sent Peter and John,[q] saying, "Go and prepare the Passover meal for us, so we can eat it."

[9] "Where do You want us to prepare it?" they asked Him.

[10] "Listen," He said to them, "when you've entered the city, a man carrying a water jug will meet you. Follow him into the house he enters. [11] Tell the owner of the house, 'The Teacher asks you, "Where is the guest room where I can eat the Passover with My disciples?"' [12] Then he will show you a large, furnished room upstairs.[r] Make the preparations there."

[13] So they went and found it just as He had told them,[s] and they prepared the Passover.

The First Lord's Supper

[14] When[t] the hour came, He reclined at the table, and the apostles with Him. [15] Then He said to them, "I have fervently desired to eat this Passover with you before I suffer. [16] For I tell you, I will not eat it again[B] until it is fulfilled in the kingdom of God."[u] [17] Then He took a cup,[v] and after giving thanks,[w] He said, "Take this and share it among yourselves. [18] For I tell you, from now on I will not drink of the fruit of the vine until the kingdom of God comes."

[19] And He took bread, gave thanks, broke it, gave it to them, and said, "This is My body,[x] which is given for you. Do this in remembrance[y] of Me."

[20] In the same way He also took the cup after supper and said, "This cup is the new covenant[z] established by My blood;[aa] it is shed for you.[C] [21] But[ab] look, the hand of the one

Cross references
[a]21:37-38 Jn 8:1-2
[b]21:37 Mt 26:55
[c]Mt 21:1; Lk 22:39; Jn 8:1; 18:2
[d]21:38 Jn 8:2
[e]22:1-2 Mt 26:1-5; Mk 14:1-2
[f]22:1 Ex 23:15
[g]Ex 12:11; Jn 6:4; 11:55; 13:1
[h]22:2 Mt 12:14; 21:46
[i]Lk 19:47-48; 20:19
[j]22:3-6 Mt 26:14-16; Mk 14:10-11
[k]22:3 Jn 13:2,27; Ac 5:3
[l]Lk 6:16
[m]22:4 Lk 22:52; Ac 4:1; 5:24,26; 16:20,22,35-36,38
[n]Mk 9:31
[o]22:7-13 Mt 26:17-19; Mk 14:12-16
[p]22:7 Ex 12:21; 1Co 5:7
[q]22:8 Ac 3:1; 8:14
[r]22:12 Ac 1:13
[s]22:13 Lk 19:32
[t]22:14 Mt 26:20; Mk 14:17
[u]22:16 Lk 14:15; Rv 19:9
[v]22:17-20 Mt 26:26-29; Mk 14:22-25; 1Co 11:23-25
[w]22:17 Mt 14:19; 15:36
[x]22:19 Jn 6:51-53
[y]Heb 10:3
[z]22:20 Ex 24:8; Jr 31:31; Zch 9:11; 1Co 11:25; 2Co 3:6; Heb 7:22; 8:8,13; 9:15; 12:24; 13:20   [aa]1Co 10:16   [ab]22:21-23 Mt 26:21-24; Mk 14:18-21; Jn 13:18-26

[A]22:5 Or *money*; Mt 26:15 specifies 30 pieces of silver; Zch 11:12-13   [B]22:16 Other mss omit *again*   [C]22:19-20 Other mss omit *which is given for you* (v. 19) through the end of v. 20

21:37-38 During the day...in the evening refers to the schedule that Jesus kept during each day of Passion Week. The mention of **the Mount of Olives** previews the incident in which He was betrayed and arrested (22:39,47-54).

22:1 By NT times, the **Festival of Unleavened Bread** and **Passover** had come to be almost interchangeable ideas. For the Jews, Passover was a meal commemorating the night the angel of death "passed over" those Jewish homes in Egypt whose doorposts were covered by the blood of a Passover lamb (Ex 12:1-14; Lv 23:5). "Unleavened Bread" was a week-long feast immediately following Passover that commemorated the exodus (Ex 12:14-20; Lv 23:6-8). These feasts were celebrated during our months of March or April.

22:2-6 The religious leaders (**chief priests...scribes**) were committed to finding a way to **put Jesus to death** because they feared His popularity among the people. The perfect opportunity presented itself when **Judas...Iscariot,** one of the apostles (see note at 6:14-16), motivated by Satanic influence and money, agreed to **betray** Jesus.

22:7 All leaven, or yeast, was excluded from Jewish households from the beginning of the week of **Passover** and the Feast of **Unleavened Bread**. In that sense, the day when the Passover lamb was **sacrificed** was called the Day of Unleavened Bread. The lambs were sacrificed from mid afternoon

to late afternoon in the court of the priests at the temple complex. This was on Thursday of Passion Week.

22:8-12 The effect of Jesus' words here is the same as when He sent two disciples for the donkey on which He rode during the triumphal entry (see note at 19:30-34). God had the details worked out in advance. **A man carrying a water jug** would have been a strange sight since that chore was typically performed by women. Many homes in Jerusalem had an upstairs **guest room** with an outside entrance which could be rented to pilgrims observing a feast in the city. The wording suggests that the owner of this room knew Jesus or was even a disciple.

22:14 The Passover meal began at sundown. Participants **reclined** on their sides on low couches, leaning over the low **table** to eat.

22:15-18 By saying that He **fervently desired to eat this Passover** with His disciples before suffering (going to the cross), Jesus encouraged them to interpret the following events in light of Passover imagery. The **cup** here could have been the first or second cup of the traditional Jewish Passover ritual.

22:19 To institute a new memorial meal (the Lord's Supper), Jesus chose the unleavened **bread** of the Passover meal to represent His physical **body,** which would be broken on the cross much as bread was broken during the meal. His

betraying Me is at the table with Me!ᵃ ²²For the ˙Son of Man will go away as it has been determined,ᵇ but woe to that man by whom He is betrayed!"

²³So they began to argueᶜ among themselves which of them it could be who was going to do this thing.

The Dispute over Greatness

²⁴Then a dispute also arose among them about who should be considered the greatest.ᵈ ²⁵But He said to them,ᵉ "The kings of the Gentiles dominate them, and those who have authority over them are calledᴬ 'Benefactors.'ᴮ But it must not be like that among you. On the contrary, whoever is greatest among you must become like the youngest,ᶠ and whoever leads, like the one serving. ²⁷For who is greater, the one at the table or the one serving? Isn't it the one at the table? But I am among you as the One who serves.ᵍ ²⁸You are the ones who stood by Me in My trials.ʰ ²⁹I bestow on you a kingdom,ⁱ just as My Father bestowed one on Me, ³⁰so that you may eat and drink at My table in My kingdom.ʲ And you will sit on thrones judging the 12 tribes of Israel.ᵏ

Peter's Denial Predicted

³¹"Simon, Simon,ᶜ look out! Satanˡ has asked to sift youᴰ like wheat.ᵐ ³²But I have prayedⁿ for youᴱ that your faith may not fail. And you, when you have turned back, strengthenᵒ your brothers."

³³"Lord,"ᵖ he told Him, "I'm ready to go with You both to prison and to death!"

³⁴"I tell you, Peter," He said, "the rooster will not crow today untilᶠ you deny three times that you know Me!"

Be Ready for Trouble

³⁵He also said to them, "When I sent you outᵠ without money-bag, traveling bag, or sandals, did you lack anything?"

"Not a thing," they said.

³⁶Then He said to them, "But now, whoever has a money-bag should take it, and also a traveling bag. And whoever doesn't have a sword should sell his robe and buy one. ³⁷For I tell you, what is written must be fulfilled in Me: **And He was counted among the outlaws.**ᴳʳ Yes, what is written about Me is coming to its fulfillment."ˢ

³⁸"Lord," they said, "look, here are two swords."

"Enough of that!"ᴴ He told them.

The Prayer in the Garden

³⁹He went out and made His wayᵗ as usualᵘ to the ˙Mount of Olives,ᵛ and the disciples followed Him. ⁴⁰When He reached the place,ʷ He

Cross References (center column)

ᵃ22:21 Ps 41:9
ᵇ22:22 Ac 2:23; 10:42; 17:26, 31
ᶜ22:23 Mt 21:25; Mk 9:10; Lk 24:15
ᵈ22:24 Mk 9:34; Lk 1:32
ᵉ22:25-27 Mt 20:25-28; Mk 10:42-45
ᶠ22:26 Lk 9:48; 1Pt 5:3
ᵍ22:27 Mt 20:28; Jn 13:1-17
ʰ22:28 Heb 2:18; 4:15
ⁱ22:29 Mt 25:34; 2Tm 2:12
ʲ22:30 Lk 22:16
ᵏMt 19:28
ˡ22:31 Mt 4:10
ᵐAm 9:9
ⁿ22:32 Jn 17:9-15; Rm 8:34
ᵒJn 21:15-17; 1Co 1:9; Php 1:6; 1Th 5:24; 2Tm 2:13
ᵖ22:33-34 Mt 26:33-35; Mk 14:29-31; Jn 13:37-38
ᵠ22:35 Mt 10:9-10; Mk 6:8; Lk 9:3; 10:4
ʳ22:37 Is 53:12
ˢJn 17:4; 19:30
ᵗ22:39 Mt 26:30; Mk 14:26; Lk 4:30; Jn 18:1
ᵘLk 21:37
ᵛMt 21:1
ʷ22:40-46 Mt 26:36-46; Mk 14:32-42

ᴬ22:25 Or *them call themselves*   ᴮ22:25 Title of honor given to those who benefited the public good   ᶜ22:31 Other mss read *Then the Lord said, "Simon, Simon*   ᴰ22:31 In Gk, the word you is pl   ᴱ22:32 In Gk, the word you is sg   ᶠ22:34 Other mss read *before*   ᴳ22:37 Is 53:12   ᴴ22:38 Or *It is enough!*

22:20 death would be offered (**given for you**) as a substitute for sinners, all of whom deserve to die for their sins.

22:20 The new memorial meal also lent fresh meaning to **the cup after supper** (probably the third of four cups in the Passover ritual). The cup was reinterpreted to refer to the **blood** of Christ, **shed** as a payment for sins by Jesus, the ultimate Lamb of God (Jn 1:29). The mention of the **new covenant** related to Christ's shed blood means that the prophesied new covenant (Jr 31:31-34) would be ratified by Jesus' death on the cross.

22:21-22 Judas was guilty as **the one betraying** Jesus (vv. 3-6), yet it remains the case that his actions were **determined** (planned, ordained) by God as part of the plan that would culminate in Jesus' crucifixion (Ac 2:23).

22:23-24 Luke is tenacious and honest about the immaturity of the disciples. After so great a spiritual experience as the Passover meal, conducted by the Lord Himself, they argued over who was **greatest** among them. Had they misunderstood everything?

22:25-27 The wording in these verses is significantly different than that in Mt 20:25-28, suggesting that the apostles argued about greatness more than once. Greatness in the world is based on power and public recognition, but Christ taught that spiritual greatness requires humility and self-sacrifice. Jesus is our example because He came among us as **the One who serves**.

22:28-30 Because the apostles **stood by** Jesus in His **trials** (i.e., His troubles generally, not the trials He would soon face before Roman and Jewish authorities), they would be rewarded by the rights and privileges of leadership in the coming **kingdom**, including close fellowship with the King and rulership over eschatological Israel (Mt 19:28).

22:31-34 In these verses Jesus addressed **Simon** Peter as the leader of the apostles and their spokesman. The plural **you** indicates **Satan** wanted to sift all the apostles like wheat, a rough action that symbolizes tempting them to spiritual ruin. Peter protested that nothing would cause him to deny Jesus, but Jesus knew better. **When you have turned back** demonstrates that Jesus also knew that Peter's denial would be temporary, and that he would play a significant role in church history.

22:35-38 On **when I sent you out without**, see notes at 9:1-2 and 9:3-5. Because of the rejection they would face, Jesus emphasized that the apostles must prepare to take care of their own needs (**money-bag, traveling bag**) and protect themselves physically (**a sword**). By arming themselves, Jesus' apostles unintentionally paved the way for Jesus to fulfill the **outlaws** prophecy of Is 53:12. Jesus' call for a sword was likely only figurative, but the apostles responded that they had **two swords** among them.

22:39-41 Throughout Passion Week, Jesus and the apostles spent the nights on **the Mount of Olives** (Lk 21:37). John

told them, "Pray that you may not enter into temptation."[a] [41]Then He withdrew from them about a stone's throw, knelt down, and began to pray,[b] [42]"Father, if You are willing, take this cup[c] away from Me—nevertheless, not My will, but Yours, be done."

[[43]Then an angel from heaven[d] appeared to Him, strengthening Him. [44]Being in anguish,[e] He prayed more fervently, and His sweat became like drops of blood falling to the ground.][A] [45]When He got up from prayer and came to the disciples, He found them sleeping, exhausted from their grief.[B] [46]"Why are you sleeping?" He asked them. "Get up and pray, so that you won't enter into temptation."

The Judas Kiss

[47]While[f] He was still speaking, suddenly a mob was there, and one of the Twelve named Judas was leading them. He came near Jesus to kiss Him, [48]but Jesus said to him, "Judas, are you betraying the Son of Man with a kiss?"

[49]When those around Him saw what was going to happen, they asked, "Lord, should we strike with the sword?" [50]Then one of them struck the high priest's *slave and cut off his right ear.

[51]But Jesus responded, "No more of this!"[C]

And touching his ear, He healed him. [52]Then Jesus said to the chief priests, temple police, and the elders who had come for Him, "Have you come out with swords and clubs as if I were a criminal?[D] [53]Every day while I was with you in the *temple complex,[g] you never laid a hand on Me. But this is your hour[h]—and the dominion of darkness."[i]

Peter Denies His Lord

[54]They seized Him, led Him away, and brought Him into the high priest's house. Meanwhile Peter[j] was following at a distance. [55]They[k] lit a fire in the middle of the courtyard[l] and sat down together, and Peter sat among them. [56]When a servant saw him sitting in the firelight, and looked closely at him, she said, "This man was with Him too."

[57]But he denied it: "Woman, I don't know Him!"

[58]After a little while, someone else saw him and said, "You're one of them too!"

"Man, I am not!" Peter said.

[59]About an hour later, another kept insisting, "This man was certainly with Him, since he's also a Galilean."

[60]But Peter said, "Man, I don't know what you're talking about!" Immediately, while he

---

a 22:40 Mt 6:13; Lk 4:13; 11:4
b 22:41 Lk 18:11
c 22:42 Jn 18:11
d 22:43 Mt 4:11; Heb 1:14
e 22:44 Heb 5:7
f 22:47-53 Mt 26:47-56; Mk 14:43-50; Jn 18:3-12
g 22:53 Lk 2:46; Jn 18:20
h Jn 12:27; 16:4
i Ac 26:18; Eph 6:12; Col 1:13
j 22:54 Mt 26:58; Mk 14:54; Jn 18:15
k 22:55-62 Mt 26:69-75; Mk 14:66-72; Jn 18:16-18,25-27
l 22:55 Mt 26:3

A22:43-44 Other mss omit bracketed text   B22:45 Lit sleeping from grief   C22:51 Lit Permit as far as this   D22:52 Lit as against a criminal

---

18:1 says the location of this incident was a garden and Mt 26:36 calls the place Gethsemane. On this occasion, Jesus instructed the apostles to linger in prayer so they would not be tempted by the Devil and so their faith would not fail (Lk 22:32). Jesus then met the Father in prayer in order to seek strength in a time of deep suffering.

22:42 This cup refers to Jesus' upcoming judicial trials and execution on the cross (Mt 20:22-23). Jesus addressed God as **Father**, just as He had instructed His disciples to do (see note at 11:1-4). **If you are willing, take** this cup shows that Jesus, fully aware of the suffering that awaited Him, struggled with going to the cross. He resolved His struggle in favor of doing God's **will**, which was always His focus (Jn 6:38).

22:43-44 Though God the Father would not allow Jesus to bypass the upcoming suffering (v. 42), He did send **an angel** to minister to Him. However, this did not eliminate Jesus' **anguish**. As He prayed, Jesus' **sweat** poured off His body as if He were bleeding. Some believe Luke is describing a condition called hematidrosis, in which sweat and blood mingle in extreme cases of anxiety, but most likely his language is only figurative.

22:45-46 Human physical weakness (hunger, fatigue, etc.) can lead to spiritual weakness and **temptation** (see note at vv. 39-41).

22:47-48 Knowing exactly where Jesus would be spending the night (see note at 21:37-38), **Judas** Iscariot led a group of Jesus' enemies to arrest Him. They are described as a **mob** because they carried swords and clubs. A **kiss** on the cheek was a common greeting between friends and family.

Thus Judas used his intimacy with Jesus and His disciples as a platform for betraying the **Son of Man**.

22:49-51 The apostles' earlier misunderstanding about wielding the **sword** (see note at vv. 35-38) now came to a climax. Luke did not name the apostle who cut off the **ear** of the high priest's slave, but Jn 18:10 discloses that it was Peter. Jesus immediately **healed** the man's ear, averting certain disaster if the mob had attacked Peter.

22:52-53 That Jesus was viewed as a **criminal** fulfilled Is 53:12 (see note at Lk 22:35-38). Jesus' prior awareness of the time (**this is your hour**) and place (not in **the temple complex**) of His arrest indicates that everything was according to God's design even though the **chief priests** and **elders** were in league with **the dominion of darkness** (Satan and the demons) in carrying out the arrest.

22:54 John 18:13 says that Jesus was first taken to the **house** of Annas, a former high priest who was the father-in-law of Caiaphas, the current high priest (see note at 3:2-3). Most of the apostles fled from Gethsemane, though **Peter** circled back and tracked down the arresting group, all the while careful to keep a safe **distance** in the darkness. John 18:15 indicates that "another disciple" (probably the apostle John) also followed.

22:55-62 In a period of only slightly over an **hour**, Peter disowned three years of discipleship. Jesus had predicted this only a few hours earlier (see note at vv. 31-34), and when **a rooster crowed** after Peter's denials, Jesus **turned and looked** at him. Immediately **Peter remembered** Jesus' prophecy and **wept** tears of shame and regret. Since Jesus was inside the high priest's house (v. 54), there must have

was still speaking, a rooster crowed. [61]Then the Lord turned and looked at Peter.[a] So Peter remembered the word of the Lord, how He had said to him, "Before the rooster crows today, you will deny Me three times."[b] [62]And he went outside and wept bitterly.

Jesus Mocked and Beaten

[63]The men who were holding Jesus started mocking and beating Him.[c] [64]After blindfolding Him, they kept[A] asking, "Prophesy! Who hit You?" [65]And they were saying many other blasphemous[d] things against Him.

Jesus Faces the Sanhedrin

[66]When daylight came,[e] the elders[B] of the people, both the chief priests and the scribes,[f] convened and brought Him before their •Sanhedrin.[g] [67]They said,[h] "If You are the •Messiah, tell us."

But He said to them, "If I do tell you, you will not believe. [68]And if I ask you, you will not answer. [69]But from now on, the Son of Man will be seated at the right hand of the Power of God."[i]

[70]They all asked, "Are You, then, the Son of God?"[j]

And He said to them, "You say that I am."[k]

[71]"Why do we need any more testimony," they said, "since we've heard it ourselves from His mouth?"

Jesus Faces Pilate

23 Then[l] their whole assembly rose up and brought Him before •Pilate. [2]They began to accuse Him, saying, "We found this man subverting our nation, opposing payment of taxes[m] to Caesar, and saying that He Himself is the •Messiah, a King."

[3]So Pilate asked Him,[n] "Are You the King of the Jews?"[o]

He answered him, "You have said it."[C]

[4]Pilate then told the •chief priests and the crowds, "I find no grounds[p] for charging this man."

[5]But they kept insisting, "He stirs up the people,[q] teaching throughout all Judea, from Galilee[r] where He started even to here."

Jesus Faces Herod Antipas

[6]When Pilate[s] heard this,[D] he asked if the man was a Galilean. [7]Finding that He was under •Herod's jurisdiction, he sent Him to Herod,[t] who was also in Jerusalem during those days. [8]Herod was very glad to see Jesus; for a long time he had wanted to see Him because he had heard about Him and was hoping

Cross references

a 22:61 Mk 10:21
b Lk 22:31-34; Ac 3:13-14
c 22:63-65 Mt 26:67-68; Mk 14:65; Jn 18:22-23
d 22:65 Mk 3:29
e 22:66 Mt 27:1; Mk 15:1; Jn 18:28
f Lk 9:22; 20:1
g Mk 13:9
h 22:67-71 Mt 26:63-66; Mk 14:61-64; Jn 18:19-21
i 22:69 Ps 110:1; Mk 16:19; Ac 7:56; Heb 1:3
j 22:70 Mt 4:3; Lk 1:32,35
k Mt 26:64; 27:11; Lk 23:3
l 23:1-5 Mt 27:1,11-14; Mk 15:1-5; Jn 18:28-38
m 23:2 Lk 20:22-25
n 23:3 Mt 27:11; Mk 15:2
o Mt 2:2; Lk 23:37-38; Jn 18:39; 19:3
p 23:4 Mt 27:24; Lk 23:14,22; Jn 19:4,6; 1Pt 2:22
q 23:5 Ac 17:5-8,13
r Mt 4:12,23; Lk 4:14; Jn 1:43; 2:11
s 23:6 1Tm 6:13
t 23:7 Lk 3:1; 9:7-9; 13:31

Textual notes

A 22:64 Other mss add *striking Him on the face and*   B 22:66 Or *council of elders*   C 23:3 Or *That is true*; an affirmative oath
D 23:6 Other mss read *heard "Galilee"*

---

been an open window or door through which He could look into **the courtyard** and catch Peter's eye.

22:63-65 Jesus' horrific treatment at the hands of the soldiers is also described in Mt 26:67; Mk 14:65.

22:66 By rule it had to be **daylight** outside for the Sanhedrin (ruling council of the Jews) to hold a trial in which they decided on the death penalty (which could only be carried out by the Roman government). This explains why they waited for daylight. However, in several other respects the trial was illegal: (1) No trial could be held on the morning of a feast day (i.e., Passover), (2) there was no formal defense offered for Jesus, and (3) the verdict was reached in one day, not the two days required for capital offenses.

22:67-69 In a tactical move that may have been designed to keep Rome from thinking Jesus intended to ascend Israel's vacant throne, Jesus did not give a direct answer to the question of whether He was **the Messiah**. Since He knew He could not expect fair treatment from the members of the Sanhedrin, Jesus identified Himself as **the Son of Man** who would sit as judge over them in a much higher court in heaven (**at the right hand**).

22:70-71 The Sanhedrin understood Jesus' previous claim to be Messiah, but they wanted to catch Him in what they thought was a more clear-cut blasphemy: the claim that He was **the Son of God**. Jesus' response seems vague to modern readers, but those present understood it as a clear confession. Having this in hand, they concluded there was no need for **any more testimony**.

23:1 On Pontius **Pilate**, see note at 3:1. Pilate's normal resi-

dence was in Caesarea Maritima, but he came to Jerusalem during the Jewish feasts to keep an eye on things. Since Jesus was crucified along with two criminals (vv. 32-33), a punishment that only the Romans could render, it seems that a couple of executions were already scheduled even before Jesus' sentencing. Thus Pilate came to town planning to execute criminals, but he left town having executed an innocent man.

23:2-4 The three charges the Jews brought against Jesus in Pilate's presence were fabrications. It was true that huge crowds had flocked to hear Jesus speak, but His teachings were not aimed at **subverting** Israel. The claim that He was **opposing payments of taxes to Caesar** was an outright lie (see note at 20:22-26). Jesus was **the Messiah**, but He carefully avoided giving the impression that He meant to topple Rome or ascend the throne as **King** of Israel. Pilate had undoubtedly heard about Jesus, and he saw right through the Sanhedrin's "rush to judgment."

23:5-7 When Pilate heard that Jesus was from **Galilee**, he saw a convenient way to excuse himself from the Sanhedrin's headhunt. He turned Jesus over to the proper **jurisdiction**, that of **Herod** Antipas, the ruler over Galilee (see note at 3:1). Like Pilate, Herod was in Jerusalem for the feasts of Passover and Unleavened Bread.

23:8-11 At an earlier **time**, Herod Antipas had been anxious to meet Jesus (9:7-9), and the Pharisees had claimed that Herod wanted to kill Jesus (13:31). Jesus' silence before Herod may have been designed to fulfill the prophecy in Is 53:7-8. In spite of the serious accusations of the Sanhedrin, Herod Antipas simply made sport of Jesus and **sent Him**

to see some miracle[A] performed by Him. [9] So he kept asking Him questions, but Jesus did not answer him.[a] [10] The chief priests and the ·scribes stood by, vehemently accusing Him. [11] Then Herod, with his soldiers, treated Him with contempt, mocked[b] Him, dressed Him in a brilliant robe,[c] and sent Him back to Pilate. [12] That very day Herod and Pilate became friends.[B,d] Previously, they had been hostile toward each other.

Jesus or Barabbas

[13] Pilate called together the chief priests, the leaders, and the people,[e] [14] and said to them, "You have brought me this man as one who subverts the people.[f] But in fact, after examining Him in your presence, I have found no grounds[g] to charge this man with those things you accuse Him of. [15] Neither has Herod, because he sent Him back to us. Clearly, He has done nothing to deserve death. [16] Therefore, I will have Him whipped[C,h] and then release Him." [[17] For according to the festival he had to release someone to them.][D,i]

[18] Then[j] they all cried out together, "Take this man away![k] Release Barabbas to us!" [19] (He had been thrown into prison for a rebellion that had taken place in the city, and for murder.)

[20] Pilate, wanting to release Jesus,[l] addressed them again, [21] but they kept shouting, "Crucify! Crucify Him!"

[22] A third time he said to them, "Why? What has this man done wrong?[m] I have found in Him no grounds[n] for the death penalty. Therefore, I will have Him whipped and then release Him."

[23] But they kept up the pressure, demanding with loud voices that He be crucified. And their voices[E] won out. [24] So[o] Pilate decided to grant their demand[p] [25] and released the one they were asking for, who had been thrown into prison for rebellion and murder. But he handed Jesus over to their will.[q]

The Way to the Cross

[26] As[r] they led Him away, they seized Simon, a Cyrenian,[s] who was coming in from the country, and laid the cross[t] on him to carry behind Jesus. [27] A large crowd of people followed Him, including women who were mourning and lamenting Him.[u] [28] But turning to them, Jesus said, "Daughters of Jerusalem,[v] do not weep for Me, but weep for yourselves and your children. [29] Look, the days are coming[w] when they will say, 'The women without children, the

Cross references (center column)

a 23:9 Is 53:7; Mt 27:12,14; Mk 15:4-5; Jn 19:9
b 23:11 Is 53:3; Mk 9:12; Lk 18:32; Ac 4:11
c Mt 27:28; Mk 15:17
d 23:12 Ps 2:2; Ac 4:27
e 23:13 Lk 23:35; 24:20; Jn 7:26,48; 12:42
f 23:14 Lk 23:2
g Lk 23:4
h 23:16 Jn 19:1; Ac 5:40
i 23:17 Mt 27:15; Mk 15:6; Jn 18:39
j 23:18-23 Mt 27:15-23; Mk 15:6-14; Jn 18:40
k 23:18 Ac 21:36; 22:22
l 23:20 Ac 3:13-14
m 23:22 Jn 8:46
n Lk 23:4
o 23:24-25 Mt 27:24-26; Mk 15:15; Jn 19:16
p 23:24 Php 4:6
q 23:25 Lk 24:20; Ac 4:24-28
r 23:26-32 Mt 27:31-32; Mk 15:20-21; Jn 19:17
s 23:26 Rm 16:3
t Lk 9:23; 14:27
u 23:27 Lk 8:52; Ac 8:2; Rv 1:7;
18:9   v 23:28 Sg 1:5; 2:7   w 23:29 Lk 17:22

A 23:8 Or sign   B 23:12 Lit friends with one another   C 23:16 Gk paideuo; to discipline or "teach a lesson"; 1Kg 12:11,14 LXX; 2Ch 10:11,14; perhaps a way of referring to the Roman scourging; Lat flagellatio   D 23:17 Other mss omit bracketed text
E 23:23 Other mss add and those of the chief priests

---

back to Pilate for final legal disposition. He dressed Jesus in **a brilliant robe** in order to ridicule Him as a fake king and irritate the Sanhedrin since they charged Him with claiming to be king (see note at vv. 2-4).

23:12-15 **Herod** Antipas and Pontius **Pilate** became friends because they both made the same assessment (**no grounds to charge this man**) of Jesus (vv. 14-15). Apparently they also shared the same low opinion of the Jewish Sanhedrin for pursuing a **death** sentence against Jesus.

23:16-19 In order to placate the Sanhedrin, Pilate was willing to have Jesus severely **whipped** and set free. It was his custom to release a prisoner in honor of Passover (Jn 18:39). However, the crowd demanded that a dangerous criminal named **Barabbas** be released instead.

23:20-25 Pilate tried two more times to release Jesus, finding no valid basis for the **death penalty**. But he was repeatedly shouted down by a chorus of **crucify Him**. Finally, Pilate caved in to the crowd's demand, releasing Barabbas and handing Jesus over to be executed.

23:26 **Simon** of Cyrene was staying outside Jerusalem and **coming in from the country** to worship each day during the feast of Unleavened Bread. Jesus was unable to carry the cross any farther after His earlier beating (22:63), so it was placed on Simon's back. Simon may have been part of the synagogue of the Cyrenians mentioned in Ac 6:9. Mark 15:21 mentions the names of Simon's sons (Rm 16:13 may refer to one of those sons).

23:27-31 Jesus told the crowds who were **mourning** His un-

just crucifixion that they should weep for their own families because of the future destruction of Jerusalem. It would be preferable not to have children in such awful times. Jesus then cited Hs 10:8, where it is said that people will request landslides to hide them from the military onslaught. The proverbial statement in Luke 23:31 implies that if things are this bad for an innocent man in a time of peace (**when the wood is green**), they will be much worse for those who deserve judgment during a time of war (**when it is dry**).

paradeisos

Greek Pronunciation:	[pah RAH day sahss]
HCSB Translation:	paradise
Uses in Luke's Gospel:	1
Uses in the NT:	3
Focus passage:	Luke 23:43

The word "paradise" in Luke 23:43 is transliterated directly from the Greek word paradeisos, which occurs in only two other places in the NT. In the Greek world paradeisos could refer to a garden, a grove, or a park; thus, it is the word found in the Greek OT for the Garden of Eden (11 times in Gn 2-3). Luke 23:43 and 2 Corinthians 12:4 use paradeisos to refer to the place where God especially manifests His presence, which we call heaven. Revelation 2:7 refers to paradeisos as the place where believers (those who "conquer") eat from "the tree of life," which is in the new Jerusalem (see Rv 22:2,14,19).

wombs that never bore and the breasts that never nursed, are fortunate!'[a] 30 Then they will begin **to say to the mountains, 'Fall on us!' and to the hills, 'Cover us!'**[A,b] 31 For if they do these things when the wood is green, what will happen when it is dry?"[c]

Crucified between Two Criminals

32 Two others—criminals[d]—were also led away to be executed with Him. 33 When[e] they arrived at the place called The Skull, they crucified Him there, along with the criminals, one on the right and one on the left. [34 Then Jesus said, "Father,[f] forgive[g] them, because they do not know what they are doing."[h]][B] And they divided His clothes and cast lots.[i]

35 The[j] people stood watching, and even the leaders kept scoffing:[k] "He saved others; let Him save Himself if this is God's Messiah, the Chosen One!"[l] 36 The soldiers also mocked Him. They came offering Him sour wine[m] 37 and said, "If You are the King of the Jews,[n] save Yourself!"

38 An inscription was above Him:[C]

THIS IS THE KING OF THE JEWS.

39 Then[o] one of the criminals hanging there began to yell insults at[D] Him: "Aren't You the Messiah? Save Yourself and us!"

40 But the other answered, rebuking him: "Don't you even fear God,[p] since you are undergoing the same punishment? 41 We are punished justly, because we're getting back what we deserve for the things we did, but this man has done nothing wrong."[q] 42 Then he said, "Jesus, remember me[E,r] when You come into Your kingdom!"[s]

43 And He said to him, "•I assure you: Today you will be with Me in paradise."[t]

The Death of Jesus

44 It[u] was now about noon,[F] and darkness came over the whole land[G] until three,[H] 45 because the sun's light failed.[I] The curtain[v] of the sanctuary was split down the middle. 46 And Jesus called out with a loud voice, "Father, **into Your hands I entrust My spirit.**"[J,w] Saying this, He breathed His last.

47 When the •centurion saw what happened, he began to glorify[x] God, saying, "This man really was righteous!" 48 All the crowds that had gathered for this spectacle, when they saw what had taken place, went home, striking their chests.[K,y] 49 But[z] all who knew Him, including the women who had followed Him from Galilee, stood at a distance,[aa] watching these things.

[a] 23:29 Mt 24:19; Mk 13:17; Lk 11:27; 21:23 [b] 23:30 Hs 10:8 [c] 23:31 Ezk 20:47; Lk 19:41 [d] 23:32 Is 53:12; Mt 27:38; Mk 15:27; Lk 22:37; Jn 19:18 [e] 23:33-34 Mt 27:33-38; Mk 15:22-27; Jn 19:17-24 [f] 23:34 Mt 5:16; 6:1; 11:27; Jn 8:42 [g] Mt 11:25; Lk 6:29,35; 22:42 [h] Ac 3:17; 1Co 2:6-8 [i] Ps 22:18 [j] 23:35-38 Mt 27:43,48; Mk 15:26,29-32; Jn 19:19,29 [k] 23:35 Ps 22:7,17; Lk 16:14; 23:13 [l] Is 42:1; Mt 1:17; 12:18; Lk 9:20,35; 1Pt 2:4 [m] 23:36 Ps 69:21 [n] 23:37 Lk 23:3 [o] 23:39-43 Mt 27:44; Mk 15:32 [p] 23:40 Ps 147:11; Pr 1:7; Ac 10:2; Rv 14:7 [q] 23:41 Lk 23:4 [r] 23:42 Jdg 16:28; 1Sm 25:31; Neh 5:19; Jb 14:13; Ps 106:4 [s] Mk 8:38; Ac 20:25 [t] 23:43 2Co 12:4; Rv 2:7 [u] 23:44-49 Mt 27:45-56; Mk 15:33-41 [v] 23:45 Ex 26:31-33; Heb 6:19 [w] 23:46 Ps 31:5; Is 53:12; Jn 19:30; 1Co 15:55; 1Pt 4:19 [x] 23:47 Lk 13:13 [y] 23:48 Lk 18:13 [z] 23:49 Mt 27:55-56; Mk 15:40-41; Jn 19:25 [aa] Ps 38:11; 88:8

[A] 23:30 Hs 10:8 [B] 23:34 Other mss omit bracketed text [C] 23:38 Other mss add *written in Greek, Latin, and Hebrew letters* [D] 23:39 Or *began to blaspheme* [E] 23:42 Other mss add *Lord* [F] 23:44 Lit *about the sixth hour* [G] 23:44 Or *whole earth* [H] 23:44 Lit *the ninth hour* [I] 23:45 Other mss read *three, and the sun was darkened* [J] 23:46 Ps 31:5 [K] 23:48 = mourning

23:32-33 Being **executed** between **two . . . criminals** fulfilled the prophecy of Is 53:12, as well as Jesus' words in Lk 22:37. The place where Jesus was crucified was called **The Skull**. In Aramaic, the name is *Golgotha*. The Latin equivalent is *Calvary*.

23:34 Jesus forgave His executioners because they acted in ignorance of who He really was. Some early manuscripts do not include the first part of this verse. The phrase **they divided His clothes and cast lots** fulfilled Ps 22:18.

23:35-39 Four different groups (the **people** in general, the **leaders**, the **soldiers**, and **one of the criminals** being crucified) scoffed at Jesus and challenged Him to save Himself. None of them believed that Jesus was **the Messiah . . . the King of the Jews**, even though the official inscription above His head on the cross charged Him with posing as "the King of the Jews."

23:40-43 In the midst of this display of unbelief and mockery, the other criminal came to understand the difference between his own guilt and Jesus' innocence (**this man has done nothing wrong**). He also realized that Jesus was the Messiah and asked to take part in His coming **kingdom**. Jesus assured him that, after death, he would immediately be reunited with Him in **paradise** (eternal life beyond the grave; see 2Co 12:4).

23:44-45 The three hours of darkness at midday (from **noon . . . until three**) was a sign of divine judgment against sin (which Jesus became on the cross) and the sinners who unjustly executed the Son of God. Matthew 27:51 explains that the splitting of **the curtain of the sanctuary** (between the holy place and the holy of holies in the temple) was caused by a great earthquake. The torn curtain symbolized open access to God, made possible by the death of Christ (see note at 22:20).

23:46 While expressing faith in God by reciting Ps 31:5, Jesus **breathed His last**. Jesus was placed on the cross at about 9:00 a.m. (Mk 15:25) and died after only six hours—an unusually short time. Crucifixion victims sometimes lingered for two or three days before death occurred.

23:47 Compared to the parallel accounts, Luke muted the centurion's confession. Here the centurion merely observed that Jesus was truly **righteous** (not a criminal in any respect), whereas in Mt 27:54 and Mk 15:39 he is reported as acknowledging that Jesus is the Son of God.

23:48-49 **Striking their chests** could be a sign of grief, though in Lk 18:13 it appears to reflect contrition before the Lord. Significantly, the **women** disciples from **Galilee**, who had generously supported Jesus' ministry financially (see note at 8:1-3), are spotlighted among those who were **watching** Him die on the cross. They stuck with Him even after the male disciples abandoned Him.

Christ in the Old Testament

Craig Blaising

In Luke 24 Jesus showed Himself alive to His disciples and explained that the cross and resurrection, and indeed much else in His life, were predicted in Scripture. Verse 27 states: "Then beginning with Moses and all the Prophets, He interpreted for them the things concerning Himself in all the Scriptures." Then in verse 44, He told them "that everything written about Me in the Law of Moses, the Prophets, and the Psalms must be fulfilled."

In the preaching of the apostles in Acts, the evidence given in the Gospels, and the rest of the New Testament, many (OT) texts are applied to Jesus. This practice likely reflects Jesus' own teachings about how the OT relates to Him. Furthermore, because themes are repeated and developed in Scripture, the application of a particular text to Jesus is suggestive of other texts that relate to or repeat that theme. In this way we can see a rich portrait of OT patterns, types, allusions, and predictions that present to us the Person and Work of Christ.

From beginning to end the OT exudes an expectation that someone is coming. Genesis 3:15 speaks of the "seed" of the woman who comes to crush the tempter's head (Gn 3:15). To Abraham the promise was made that through his "offspring" blessing or curse would come to all nations (Gn 12:1-3; 22:15-18). Among the descendants of Abraham many patterns and types pointed to a Coming One. Isaac, born of promise (Gn 15:3-6; 17:19), was offered to God as a sacrifice but was redeemed by a substitute (Gn 22:1-14). Joseph, raised up to bless all peoples, was first rejected by his brothers but later was sought by them for forgiveness (Gn 37; 41-48; 50:15-21). Judah offered himself in place of his brother and received a promise of a scepter and the obedience of all peoples (Gn 49:1,9-12). Moses failed to enter the promised land despite all his works, but it was said that a prophet like him would arise in the future (Dt 18:15-19). David, of the tribe of Judah, was raised up by God to deliver and shepherd Israel. God made a covenant to raise up David's son and seat him on his throne, establishing his kingdom forever (2Sm 7:8-17; 1Ch 17:7-15). God would be his Father, and he would be His son (2Sm 7:14).

The covenant with David is the key to messianic prophecy. It incorporates all former prophecies of a coming king, such as Balaam's prophecy that a star would arise from Jacob and exercise dominion (Nm 24:15-19; cp. 23:24; 24:7-9), plus it serves as the basis for later prophecies such as Isaiah 9:6-7 of a son who establishes the throne of David forever with peace, justice, and righteousness; Isaiah 11:1-10 of a "shoot . . . from the stump of Jesse" upon whom the Spirit rests and who destroys the wicked, brings peace, righteousness, and extends the knowledge of God to the entire earth; Jeremiah 23:5 and 33:15 of a righteous "Branch" of David who will reign with justice and wisdom; and Zechariah 9:9-10 of a humble, righteous king, bringing salvation, speaking peace to the nations and ruling from sea to sea.

David's experiences of suffering, deliverance, and exaltation become types and patterns replayed and brought to a higher level of fulfillment in the experiences of his later son (descendant), Jesus. These include the rejected stone that becomes the cornerstone (Ps 118); the suffering that becomes a literal depiction of the cross (Ps 22); and the soul not abandoned to Sheol, the flesh that does not see decay (Ps 16).

Key among the prophecies of Isaiah are predictions of a coming servant who will bring Israel to God and be a light for the nations (Is 49), who will bear *our* sorrows, *our* griefs, be wounded for *our* iniquities, be bruised for *our* transgressions, and by whose stripes we will be healed. He would be like a lamb led to slaughter, and yet resurrected (Is 53:3-12). Through this prophecy, we are able to see types and images of Christ in the sacrificial system, especially the Passover and Day of Atonement.

But we see more. In the house of David, One became incarnate whom we know across the pages of the OT: One who forgives sins and heals diseases (Ps 103:3), feeds bread to a multitude in the wilderness (Ex 16), stills the sea (Jb 26:12), and is coming to reign as King (Zch 14). That son of David, son of Abraham, seed of Eve, is none other than the eternal Son of God.

The Burial of Jesus

[50]There[a] was a good and righteous man named Joseph, a member of the *Sanhedrin, [51]who had not agreed with their plan[b] and action. He was from Arimathea, a Judean town, and was looking forward to the kingdom of God.[c] [52]He approached Pilate and asked for Jesus' body. [53]Taking it down, he wrapped it in fine linen and placed it in a tomb cut into the rock, where no one had ever been placed.[A,d] [54]It was preparation day, and the Sabbath was about to begin.[B] [55]The women[e] who had come with Him from Galilee followed along and observed the tomb and how His body was placed. [56]Then they returned and prepared spices and perfumes.[f] And they rested on the Sabbath according to the commandment.[g]

Resurrection Morning

24 On[h] the first day of the week,[i] very early in the morning, they[c] came to the tomb, bringing the spices they had prepared. [2]They found the stone rolled away from the tomb. [3]They went in but did not find the body[j] of the Lord Jesus.[k] [4]While they were perplexed about this, suddenly two men stood by them in dazzling[l] clothes. [5]So the women were terrified and bowed down to the ground.[D]

"Why are you looking for the living among the dead?" asked the men. [6]"He is not here, but He has been resurrected![m] Remember how He spoke to you when He was still in Galilee,[n] [7]saying, 'The *Son of Man must be betrayed[o] into the hands of sinful men, be crucified, and rise[p] on the third day'?" [8]And they remembered His words.

[9]Returning from the tomb, they reported all these things to the Eleven[q] and to all the rest. [10]*Mary Magdalene, Joanna, Mary the mother of James,[r] and the other women with them were telling the apostles[s] these things. [11]But these words seemed like nonsense to them, and they did not believe[t] the women. [12]Peter,[u] however, got up and ran to the tomb. When he stooped to look in, he saw only the linen cloths.[E,v] So he went home, amazed[w] at what had happened.

The Emmaus Disciples

[13]Now[x] that same day two of them were on their way to a village called[F] Emmaus, which was about seven miles[G,y] from Jerusalem.[z] [14]Together they were discussing everything that had taken place. [15]And while they were discussing and arguing, Jesus Himself came near and began to walk along with them.

---

[a]23:50-56 Mt 27:57-61; Mk 15:42-47; Jn 19:38-42 [b]23:51 Ac 2:23 [c]Lk 2:25,38 [d]23:53 Is 53:9; Mk 11:2 [e]23:55 Lk 1:42 [f]23:56 Mk 16:1; Lk 24:1 [g]Ex 20:10; Dt 5:14 [h]24:1-12 Mt 28:1-10; Mk 16:1-11; Jn 20:1-18 [i]24:1 Ac 20:7; 1Co 16:2 [j]24:3 Lk 12:4 [k]Lk 7:13; Ac 1:21 [l]24:4 Lk 2:9; 17:24; Ac 12:7 [m]24:6 Mt 26:32; Mk 5:41; 9:27; Jn 2:19; 1Co 15:4 [n]Mt 17:22-23; Mk 9:30-31; Lk 9:22,44 [o]24:7 Lk 9:22,31,44; 18:32-33; 23:21 [p]Mt 17:9,23; Mk 8:31; 9:31; 10:34; Lk 18:33; 24:46 [q]24:9 Ac 1:15-26; 2:14 [r]24:10 Mk 15:40; 16:1; Lk 8:2-3 [s]Lk 6:13 [t]24:11 Mt 28:17; Lk 24:41; Jn 20:25,27 [u]24:12 Lk 6:14; Ac 10:32 [v]Lk 23:53 [w]Lk 1:21,63; 2:18,33; 4:22; Ac 2:7; 3:12 [x]24:13 Mk 16:12-13 [y]Rv 21:16 [z]Mt 23:37; Ac 8:1

[A]23:53 Or interred, or laid [B]23:54 Lit was dawning; not in the morning but at sundown Friday [C]24:1 Other mss add and other women with them [D]24:5 Lit and inclined their faces to the ground [E]24:12 Other mss add lying there [F]24:13 Lit village, which name is [G]24:13 Lit about 60 stadia; 1 stadion = 600 feet

---

23:50-53 Even though **Joseph** of Arimathea was a **member of the Sanhedrin**, he had disagreed with their decision to execute Jesus (22:71–23:1). He was **a good and righteous man**, but he was also a secret disciple of Jesus (Jn 19:38). Jesus was laid in the **tomb** of the wealthy Joseph instead of the shallow common grave reserved for criminals. This fulfilled the prophecy of Is 53:9. Matthew (27:65-66) stated that soldiers were assigned to guard Jesus' tomb and that the stone rolled in front of the tomb was stamped with the Roman seal of authority.

23:54-56 **Preparation day** (from Thursday sundown to Friday sundown), was the last day before the **Sabbath** when preparations for the Sabbath were completed. Joseph of Arimathea and Nicodemus did much to prepare Jesus' body for burial (Jn 19:39-40), but the women disciples from Galilee planned to finish the task (**prepared spices and perfumes**). They had to wait for the Sabbath to pass before they could carry out their plan.

24:1 The **first day of the week** was Sunday. It was so **early** in the morning that it was still dark (Jn 20:1) when the women arrived at Jesus' tomb to anoint His body.

24:2 On their way to the **tomb**, the women pondered the difficultt the sealing stone would present. Who would move it for them (Mk 16:3)? However, when they arrived, they found the **stone rolled away** from the entrance. The stone had been moved by "a violent earthquake" (Mt 28:2).

24:3-8 Jesus' **body** was nowhere to be found, and the wom-

en had no answer for why it was missing. The **two men** who suddenly appeared and terrified them were angels (v. 23; Jn 20:12). Matthew 28:2-3 and Mk 16:5 mention only one angel. The angels announced the resurrection of Jesus to the women and reminded them that He had predicted this would happen. As soon as they were reminded of Jesus' assertion that He would **rise on the third day**, they **remembered His words**. Now they were better prepared to understand and believe the radical things Jesus had said.

24:9-12 In Jesus' day women were not considered to be credible witnesses. This is why **the Eleven** (the apostles who remained after Judas' act of betrayal) **did not believe** the women's report about what had happened at Jesus' tomb, viewing it as **nonsense**. However, Peter was curious enough to run to the tomb and look for himself. When he saw **only the linen cloths** in which Jesus had been wrapped (23:53), he was **amazed**, but still skeptical.

24:13-14 Of the two disciples traveling **from Jerusalem** to **Emmaus** that Sunday, one was named Cleopas (v. 18). He was possibly the husband of one of the women disciples who watched Jesus die on the cross (Jn 19:25). They had heard about the women's report and Peter's experience at the empty tomb (Lk 24:19-24) before leaving Jerusalem.

24:15-16 That the two men were **arguing** (Gk suzeteo; "to argue, question") about what had happened indicates that there was no agreement among Jesus' disciples about what had occurred and why. Like Peter at the tomb, many were amazed and yet unconvinced. It is not known how God

[16]But they[A] were prevented from recognizing Him.[a] [17]Then He asked them, "What is this dispute that you're having[B] with each other as you are walking?" And they stopped walking and looked discouraged.

[18]The one named Cleopas answered Him, "Are You the only visitor in Jerusalem who doesn't know the things that happened there in these days?"[b]

[19]"What things?" He asked them.

So they said to Him, "The things concerning Jesus the *Nazarene,[c] who was a Prophet[d] powerful in action and speech[e] before God and all the people,[f] [20]and how our *chief priests and leaders[g] handed Him over to be sentenced to death,[h] and they crucified Him.[i] [21]But we were hoping that He was the One who was about to *redeem[j] Israel. Besides all this, it's the third day[k] since these things happened. [22]Moreover, some women from our group astounded us. They arrived early at the tomb, [23]and when they didn't find His body, they came and reported that they had seen a vision of angels who said He was alive. [24]Some of those who were with us went to the tomb and found it just as the women had said, but they didn't see Him."[l]

[25]He said to them, "How unwise and slow you are to believe in your hearts all that the prophets have spoken![m] [26]Didn't the *Messiah have to suffer[n] these things and enter into His glory?"[o] [27]Then beginning with Moses[p] and all the Prophets,[q] He interpreted for them the things concerning Himself in all the Scriptures.[r]

[28]They came near the village where they were going, and He gave the impression that He was going farther.[s] [29]But they urged Him: "Stay with us, because it's almost evening, and now the day is almost over." So He went in to stay with them.

[30]It was as He reclined at the table with them that He took the bread, blessed and broke[t] it, and gave it to them. [31]Then their eyes were opened,[u] and they recognized Him, but He disappeared from their sight.[v] [32]So they said to each other, "Weren't our hearts ablaze within us while He was talking with us on the road and explaining the Scriptures[w] to us?" [33]That very hour they got up and returned to Jerusalem. They found the Eleven[x] and those with them gathered together, [34]who said,[C] "The Lord has certainly been raised, and has appeared to Simon!"[y] [35]Then they began to describe what had happened on the road and how He was made known to them in the breaking of the bread.[z]

The Reality of the Risen Jesus

[36]And[aa] as they were saying these things, He

Cross references:

[a]24:16 Lk 9:45; 18:34; Jn 20:14-15; 21:4
[b]24:18 Ac 26:26
[c]24:19 Lk 4:34; 18:37; Ac 2:22
[d]Dt 18:15; Lk 4:24
[e]Lk 4:14; Ac 1:1; 2:22
[f]Lk 18:43
[g]24:20 Lk 23:13
[h]Lk 9:44; 18:32; Ac 3:13; 13:27-28
[i]Lk 23:21,25; Ac 5:30
[j]24:21 Lk 22:20; Ac 1:6
[k]Lk 9:22; 13:32; 18:33
[l]24:24 Lk 24:12; Jn 20:2-10
[m]24:25 Lk 16:31; 18:31; Ac 26:27; 2Pt 1:21
[n]24:26 Lk 24:44-48; 1Co 15:3-5
[o]Lk 9:26,32; 21:27; 22:69; Ac 2:33; 7:55; 22:11
[p]24:27 Gn 3:15; 12:3; 22:18; Nm 21:9; 24:17
[q]2Sm 7:12-16; Is 7:14; 9:6; 52:13-53:12; Jr 23:5-6; Dn 7:13-14; Mc 5:2; Zch 9:9; 12:10
[r]Lk 16:16
[s]24:28 Mk 6:48
[t]24:30 Lk 9:16; 22:19
[u]24:31 2Kg 6:17; Lk 24:16
[v]Jn 20:19,26 [w]24:32 Ac 17:3; 1Co 15:3-8 [x]24:33 Lk 24:9 [y]24:34 Lk 22:32; 1Co 15:4-5 [z]24:35 Ac 2:42 [aa]24:36-44 Jn 20:19-20

[A]24:16 Lit *their eyes* [B]24:17 Lit *What are these words that you are exchanging* [C]24:34 Gk is specific that this refers to the Eleven and those with them.

---

prevented the two disciples from **recognizing** Jesus at this point, but He eventually "opened their eyes" to recognize Him (v. 31).

24:17-18 The men were **discouraged** (Gk *skuthropos*; "sad, sullen") and shocked that the stranger (Jesus) seemed to know nothing about what had happened the past few days, though it was the talk of all **Jerusalem**.

24:19-20 The description of Jesus by the two disciples is short on both insight and faith. Jesus is referred to in relation to His hometown (**the Nazarene**) and as a **Prophet** and miracle worker, but not as the Son of God. In addition, nothing is said about the unjust nature of Jesus' betrayal, trials, and crucifixion—just that the **chief priests and leaders** got Him **sentenced to death** and **crucified**. These disciples had not fully grasped Jesus' identity, nor had they understood the divine necessity of His death.

24:21-24 Jesus' death had dashed these men's hopes that He was the Messiah (**the One . . . to redeem Israel**), but the reports from the tomb that morning **astounded** them and made them wonder what was going on. The reports said: (1) the women disciples didn't find Jesus' body at the tomb, (2) the women had seen **a vision of angels** proclaiming His resurrection, and (3) some male disciples had verified that the tomb was indeed empty.

24:25-29 The stranger (Jesus) rebuked the two disciples for not believing the OT prophecies about **the Messiah**, particularly about His suffering and following **glory**. Then, during the remainder of the walk to Emmaus, Jesus worked His way through all the major messianic prophecies in the Hebrew Bible (**Moses and all the Prophets** refers to the entire OT), carefully interpreting their meaning to His hearers. Then, when Jesus **gave the impression** that He was not going to stop in Emmaus, they invited Him to spend the night with them, probably so they could hear more.

24:30-33 During the evening meal, Jesus **blessed** and **broke** the **bread**. At that point, the two disciples were allowed to recognize Jesus, but He immediately **disappeared** from sight. Their first thought was to recall the things He had taught them as they walked along the road to Emmaus. With **hearts ablaze**, they ventured to Jerusalem through the darkness of night to meet with the apostles and tell them about their experience.

24:34-35 Unknown to the two disciples, the risen Christ had **appeared** to **Simon** Peter (an appearance mentioned elsewhere only in 1Co 15:5) some time earlier in the day. This was a decisive event for Peter and the church because he led the apostles and the early church in the years to come. Now, in a room full of eager listeners, these men told about their experiences on the road to Emmaus and the meal that followed. It had been a day of many wonders, but an even greater wonder would soon visit them all.

24:36-37 It is ironic that the group of disciples was **startled**

Himself stood among them. He said to them, "Peace[a] to you!" [37]But they were startled and terrified[b] and thought they were seeing a ghost.[c] [38]"Why are you troubled?"[d] He asked them. "And why do doubts arise in your hearts? [39]Look at My hands and My feet, that it is I Myself![e] Touch Me and see,[f] because a ghost does not have flesh and bones as you can see I have." [40]Having said this, He showed them His hands and feet. [41]But while they still were amazed and unbelieving because of their joy, He asked them, "Do you have anything here to eat?" [42]So they gave Him a piece of a broiled fish,[A] [43]and He took it and ate in their presence.

[44]Then He told them, "These are My words[g] that I spoke to you while I was still with you—that everything written about Me in the Law of Moses, the Prophets,[h] and the Psalms[i] must be fulfilled." [45]Then He opened their minds[j] to understand[k] the Scriptures. [46]He also said to them, "This is what is written:[B]

The Messiah would suffer and rise from the dead the third day,[l] [47]and repentance for[C] forgiveness of sins[m] would be proclaimed in His name to all the nations,[n] beginning at Jerusalem.[o] [48]You are witnesses[p] of these things. [49]And look, I am sending you[D] what My Father promised.[q] As for you, stay in the city[E] until you are empowered[F,r] from on high."

The Ascension of Jesus

[50]Then He led them out as far as Bethany,[s] and lifting up His hands[t] He blessed them. [51]And while He was blessing them, He left them and was carried up into heaven.[u] [52]After worshiping Him,[v] they returned to Jerusalem with great joy.[w] [53]And they were continually in the *temple complex praising God.[G,x]

Cross references

a 24:36 Lk 2:14; 7:50; 8:48; 10:5; 19:38; Ac 10:36
b 24:37 Lk 24:5; Ac 10:4; 24:25
c Mt 14:26
d 24:38 Jn 14:1,27
e 24:39 Jn 20:25,27
f Mt 28:9; Ac 2:31; 17:18,31-32; 23:6-10; 24:15,21
g 24:44 Lk 9:22,44; 17:25; 18:31-33; 22:37
h Ac 13:15; 28:23
i Ps 2:6-9; 16:10; 22:1-18; 34:20; 41:9; 69:1-9,20-21,26; 110:1-7; 118:22-26
j 24:45 Lk 24:27,31
k Lk 9:45; 18:34
l 24:46 Ps 16:10; Lk 9:22,44; 17:25; 18:32; Ac 8:26-40; 1Co 15:3-4
m 24:47 Hs 14:2; Lk 3:3;
n Gn 12:3; Ps 22:27; Is 2:2; 49:6; Hs 2:23; Mal 1:11; Mt 28:19-20; Mk 16:15
o 24:47-49 Ac 1:4-8
p 24:48 Ac 4:20,33
q 24:49 Is 32:15; Jl 2:28-32; Jn 14:26; Ac 2:16-21; Eph 1:13
r Ac 4:33; Rm 15:13
s 24:50 Lk 19:29; Ac 1:12
t Lv 9:22; 1Tm 2:8
u 24:51 Mk 16:19; Jn 20:17; Ac 1:9-11
v 24:52 Mt 28:17
w Lk 2:10
x 24:53 Ac 2:46; 3:1; 5:42

Textual notes

A24:42 Other mss add *and some honeycomb*   B24:46 Other mss add *and thus it was necessary that*   C24:47 Other mss read *repentance and*   D24:49 Lit *upon you*   E24:49 Other mss add *of Jerusalem*   F24:49 Lit *clothed with power*   G24:53 Other mss read *praising and blessing God. Amen.*

Study notes

and terrified and thought they were seeing a ghost when the risen Christ suddenly appeared in their midst. After all, they had been rejoicing about His resurrection (v. 34) and swapping stories about His several appearances that day. But their fear is understandable since Jesus appeared suddenly in the middle of a crowd in what was surely a locked room. **Peace to you** was a traditional Jewish greeting.

24:38-40 Jesus calmed the fears and doubts of His disciples with evidence of His resurrection body. In His **hands** and **feet** the nail scars were clearly visible. The crowd of disciples could touch Him and verify that He had a human body and that He was not a **ghost**.

24:40-43 It is understandable that some were slow to believe. This was a highly unusual and unexpected event. Realizing their doubts, Jesus offered an additional piece of evidence. He showed them that He could eat food (**a piece of a broiled fish**), something no ghost could do.

24:44-45 The Law of Moses, the Prophets, and the **Psalms** represent the three major divisions of the Hebrew Bible. Jesus now did for the wider group of disciples essentially what He had already done for the two on the road to Emmaus. He explained the Scriptures (see note at vv. 25-29).

24:46-49 OT passages that clearly prophesy the suffering of **the Messiah** are Ps 22 and Is 53. A key OT passage for Messiah's resurrection, cited several times in the NT, is Ps 16:10. Significant OT passages that Jesus may have had in mind about **repentance . . . proclaimed . . . to all the nations, beginning at Jerusalem** are Is 2:1-4 and 49:6. Luke 24:47 is Luke's version of the Great Commission (Mt 28:19-20; Mk 16:15; Jn 20:21-22; Ac 1:8). These verses echo Ac 1:4-8. Since Luke wrote both this Gospel and the book of Acts, he skillfully intertwined the conclusion of his first volume with the beginning of his second volume. **The city** refers to Jerusalem.

24:50-51 Bethany was located just over the Mount of Olives, about two miles from Jerusalem. Acts 1:12 specifies that the ascension of Christ occurred at the Mount of Olives.

24:52-53 As Jesus had requested (v. 49), the disciples returned to Jerusalem and stayed there until the events of the day of Pentecost (Ac 2). Although at least some disciples were **continually in the temple complex praising God** during that time and later (Ac 2:46; 3:1), it should not be assumed that all of them were always there. Acts 1:13-14 also speaks of the apostles, some of the women disciples, and Jesus' brothers (the sons of Joseph and Mary) being "continually united in prayer" in an upper room in Jerusalem. Such devotion to prayer was a fitting prelude and precondition to the wonderful things God would do through Christ's earliest messengers. Christ's church was set to explode onto the scene as a beacon of light and hope in a spiritually dark world.

John

The Gospel of John is different from the Synoptic
Gospels—Matthew, Mark, and Luke—in that over 90
percent of its material is unique. John's Gospel does not
focus on the miracles, parables, and public speeches that
are so prominent in the other accounts. Instead, the Gospel
of John emphasizes the identity of Jesus as the Son of God
and how we, as believers, should respond to His teachings.

The Northern Lights above an alpine lake. "All things were created through Him,
and apart from Him not one thing was created that has been created" (1:3).

Circumstances of Writing

Author: A close reading of the Gospel of John suggests that the author was an apostle (1:14; cp. 2:11; 19:35); one of the Twelve ("the disciple Jesus loved": 13:23; 19:26; 20:2; 21:20; cp. 21:24-25); and, still more specifically, John, the son of Zebedee (note the association of "the disciple Jesus loved" with Peter in 13:23-24; 18:15-16; 20:2-9; 21; and in Lk 22:8; Ac 1:13; 3–4; 8:14-25; Gl 2:9). The church fathers, too, attested to this identification (e.g., Irenaeus). Since the apostolic office was foundational in the history of the church (Ac 2:42; Eph 2:20), the apostolic authorship of John's Gospel invests it with special authority as firsthand eyewitness (Jn 15:27; 1Jn 1:1-4).

Background: The most plausible date of writing is the period between A.D. 70 (the date of the destruction of the temple) and 100 (the end of John's lifetime), with a date in the 80s most likely. A date after 70 is suggested by the references to the Sea of Tiberias in 6:1 and 21:1 (a name widely used for the Sea of Galilee only toward the end of the first century); Thomas's confession of Jesus as "my Lord and my God" in 20:28 (possibly a statement against emperor worship in the time of Domitian); the reference to Peter's martyrdom, which occurred in 65 or 66 (21:19); the lack of reference to the Sadducees, who ceased to be a Jewish religious party after 70; and the comparative ease with which John equated Jesus with God (1:1,14,18; 10:30; 20:28).

The testimony of the early church also favors a date after A.D. 70. Clement of Alexandria (cited in Eusebius, *Hist. eccl.*, 6.14.7) stated, "Last of all, John, perceiving that the external facts had been made plain [in the other canonical Gospels] . . . composed a spiritual gospel." The most likely place of writing is Ephesus (Irenaeus, *Haer.*, 3.1.2; cp. Eusebius, *Hist. eccl.*, 3.1.1), one of the most important urban centers of the Roman Empire at the time, though the envisioned readership of John's Gospel transcends any one historical setting.

John's original audience was probably composed of people in the larger Greco-Roman world in Ephesus and beyond toward the close of the first century A.D. Hence John frequently explained Jewish customs and Palestinian geography and translated Aramaic terms into Greek.

A.D. 18–29

Caiaphas is high priest. 18–36

Pontius Pilate is prefect of Judea. 26–36

John the Baptist's ministry begins. 29

Jesus' baptism 29

Jesus' wilderness temptations 29

Jesus' call of His first disciples 29

A.D. 30–33

Jesus cleanses the temple at Passover. 30

Jesus' ministry in Galilee Autumn 30 to Spring 32

Jesus' feeding of the 5,000 during Passover 32

Jesus' teachings at the Festival of Tabernacles Autumn 32

Growing opposition to Jesus at the Festival of Dedication Winter 32/33

Message and Purpose

The purpose statement in 20:30-31 indicates that John wrote with an evangelistic purpose, probably seeking to reach unbelievers through Christian readers of his Gospel. If the date of composition was after 70, the time of the destruction of the Jerusalem temple, it is likely that John sought to present Jesus as the new temple and center of worship for God's people in replacement of the old sanctuary.

The deity of Jesus: John emphasized the deity of Jesus from the beginning of his Gospel. The prologue affirms that He is the eternal Word (Gk *logos*) who was with God and was God. Jesus used the significant phrase "I am" seven times in John, claiming the personal name of God as His own. In John, Jesus is always in charge and knows what will happen in advance.

Know and believe: Eternal life is knowing God and Jesus Christ (17:3). Further knowledge of God comes from believing and knowing Jesus. "Knowing" and "believing" are key terms for John. Both occur over 90 times in this Gospel and are always used as verbs. Jesus' teaching in John reminds us that knowing God and believing in Jesus are expressed in action.

Contribution to the Bible

Of all the Gospels and any of the New Testament books, the Gospel of John most clearly teaches the deity and preexistence of Christ (1:1-2,18; 8:58; 17:5,24; 20:28). Together with the Gospel of Matthew, it provides the most striking proofs of Jesus' messiahship. It does so by narrating seven messianic signs (see note at 2:11), by seven "I am" statements of Jesus (see note at 6:35,48), by specific fulfillment quotations, especially at Jesus' passion, and by showing how Jesus fulfilled the symbolism inherent in a variety of Jewish festivals and institutions. Jesus' messianic mission is shown to originate with God the Father, "the One who sent" Jesus (7:16,18,28,33; 8:26,29; 15:21), and to culminate in His commissioning of His new messianic community in the power of His Spirit (20:21-22). John's Trinitarian teaching is among the most overt presentations of the

---

A.D. **33**

Jesus raises Lazarus from death. Winter 33

Jesus' last journey to Jerusalem by way of Samaria and Galilee late Winter 33

Jesus' triumphal entry into Jerusalem Sunday, Nisan 9, 33

Jesus' second cleansing of the temple Monday, Nisan 10, 33

Jesus teaches in the temple and prophesies the destruction of Jerusalem. Tuesday, Nisan 11, 33

A.D. **33**

Judas bargains with the Jewish leaders to betray Jesus. Tuesday evening, Nisan 11, 33

Jesus celebrates Passover with His disciples. Thursday evening, Nisan 13, 33

Jesus' trials and crucifixion Friday, Nisan 14, 33

Jesus' resurrection Sunday, Nisan 16, 33

Jesus' ascension; forty days after His resurrection 33

Day of Pentecost; seven weeks following Jesus' resurrection Sivan 4, 33

tri-unity of the Godhead—Father, Son, and Spirit—in the entire NT and has provided much of the material for early Trinitarian and Christological formulations in the history of the church.

Structure

John is divided into two main parts. In the first section (chaps. 2–11) the focus is on both Jesus' ministry to "the world" and the signs He performed. Jesus performs seven signs that meet with varying responses. The second major section (chaps. 12–21) reveals Jesus' teaching to His disciples and the triumphant "hour" of His passion. John's record of the passion focuses on Jesus' control of the events. He had to instruct His adversaries on how to arrest Him (18:4-8). Pilate struggled with his decision, but Jesus knew what would happen. Jesus died as the Lamb and was sacrificed at the very time lambs were being sacrificed for Passover (19:14).

Outline

I. Prologue: Christ as the Eternal Word (1:1-18)
    A. The Word (1:1)
    B. The Word and creation (1:2-5)
    C. The Word and the world (1:6-18)

II. Presentation of Christ as the Son of God (1:19–12:50)
    A. By John the Baptist (1:19-34)
    B. To His disciples (1:35-51)
    C. Through miraculous signs (2:1–12:50)

III. Instruction of the Twelve by the Son of God (13:1–17:26)
    A. The Last Supper (13:1-38)
    B. The way to the Father (14:1-31)
    C. The true vine (15:1-27)
    D. The gift of the Spirit (16:1-33)
    E. Jesus' high-priestly prayer (17:1-26)

IV. Suffering of Christ as the Son of God (18:1–20:31)
    A. His arrest, trial, and death (18:1–19:42)
    B. His triumph over death (20:1-31)

V. Epilogue: The Continuing Work of the Son of God (21:1-25)
    A. Appearances to His disciples (21:1-14)
    B. Assignment to His disciples (21:15-25)

Prologue

1 In the beginning[a] was the Word,[A,b]
and the Word was with God,
and the Word was God.[c]

[2] He was with God in the beginning.[d]

[3] All things were created[e] through Him,[f]
and apart from Him not one thing
was created
that has been created.

[4] Life was in Him,[B,g]
and that life was the light[h] of men.

[5] That light shines[i] in the darkness,
yet the darkness did not overcome[C] it.[j]

[6] There was a man named John[k]
who was sent from God.

[7] He came as a witness
to testify about the light,
so that all might believe through him.[D]

[8] He was not the light,
but he came to testify[l] about the light.

[9] The true light,[m] who gives light
to everyone,
was coming into the world.[E,n]

[10] He was in the world,
and the world was created[o]
through Him,
yet the *world did not
recognize Him.

[11] He came to His own,[F]
and His own people[F]
did not receive Him.

[12] But to all who did receive[p] Him,[q]
He gave them the right[r] to be[G]
children[s] of God,[t]
to those who believe[u]
in His name,[v]

[13] who were born,[w]
not of blood,[H]
or of the will[x] of the flesh,[y]
or of the will of man,[I]
but of God.[z]

[14] The Word[aa] became flesh,[J,ab]
and took up residence[K] among us.
We observed His glory,[ac]

Cross-references

a1:1 Gn 1:1; Col 1:18
b Jn 1:14; 1Jn 1:1; Rv 19:13
c Jn 20:28; Php 2:6
d 1:2 Jn 8:38; 17:5; Ac 26:4
e 1:3 Col 1:16; Heb 1:2
f Rm 11:36
g 1:4 1Jn 2:5
h Ps 36:9; Jn 12:46
i 1:5 1Jn 2:8
j Php 3:12
k 1:6 Mk 1:4
l 1:8 Jn 15:26
m 1:9 Jn 12:46
n Jn 18:37; 1Jn 2:8
o 1:10 Jn 1:3
p 1:12 2Jn 10
q Jn 5:43
r Mk 1:22; Ac 9:14
s Lk 1:7
t Mt 5:9; Jn 11:52; Rm 8:16; 1Jn 3:1
u Jn 3:16
v Jn 10:25; 1Jn 3:23
w 1:13 1Pt 3:3
x 1Co 7:37;
16:12; Eph 2:3; 2Tm 2:26; 2Pt 1:21   y Php 3:3   z 1Pt 1:3; 1Jn 2:29
aa 1:14 Jn 1:1   ab Php 2:7; 1Jn 4:2; 5:20   ac Mk 10:37; Jn 17:24

Translation notes

A 1:1 The *Word* (Gk *Logos*) is a title for Jesus as the communication and the revealer of God the Father; Jn 1:14,18; Rv 19:13.
B 1:3-4 Other punctuation is possible: . . . *not one thing was created. What was created in Him was life*   C 1:5 Or *grasp*, or *comprehend*, or *overtake*; Jn 12:35   D 1:7 Or *through it* (the light)   E 1:9 Or *The true light who comes into the world gives light to everyone*, or *The true light enlightens everyone coming into the world*.   F 1:11 The same Gk adjective is used twice in this verse: the first refers to all that Jesus owned as Creator (*to His own*); the second refers to the Jews (*His own people*).   G 1:12 Or *become*   H 1:13 Lit *bloods*; the pl form of *blood* occurs only here in the NT. It may refer either to lineal descent (that is, blood from one's father and mother) or to the OT sacrificial system (that is, the various blood sacrifices). Neither is the basis for birth into the family of God.   I 1:13 Or *not of human lineage, or of human capacity, or of human volition*   J 1:14 The eternally existent Word (vv. 1-2) took on full humanity but without sin; Heb 4:15.   K 1:14 Or *and dwelt in a tent*; lit *and tabernacled*; this word occurs only here in John. A related word, referring to the Festival of Tabernacles, occurs only in 7:2; Ex 40:34-38.

1:1-18 John's prologue presents Jesus as the eternal, pre-existent Word-become-flesh (vv. 1,14) and as the one-of-a-kind Son of the Father who is Himself God (vv. 1,18). Jesus culminated God's plan of salvation. Previous to Jesus this plan included God giving the law through Moses (v. 17), His dwelling among His people in the tabernacle (v. 14), and the sending of John the Baptist (vv. 6-8,15). The prologue introduces several themes that are emphasized later in the Gospel, including Jesus as life, light, and truth, believers as God's children, and the world's rejection of Jesus.

1:1 In the beginning was the Word echoes Gn 1:1, "In the beginning God created the heavens and the earth." John located Jesus' existence in eternity past with God. "The Word" (Gk *logos*) conveys the notion of divine self-expression or speech (Ps 19:1-4). God's Word is effective. He speaks, and things come into being (Gn 1:3,9; Is 55:11-12).

1:4-5 The references to **life . . . light**, and **darkness** continue to draw on Genesis themes (cp. Gn 1:3-5,14-18,20-31; 2:7; 3:20). Light symbolism is also found in later OT messianic passages (Is 9:2; 42:6-7; 49:6; 60:1-5; Mal 4:2; cp. Lk 1:78-79).

1:7-8 On John as a witness to Jesus, see note at 5:31-47.

1:11 His own people did not receive Him refers to the Jewish people, the recipients of God's covenants, the law, and promises of a Messiah (Rm 9:4). Messiah's rejection by the Jews despite convincing proofs of His messiahship (esp. the "signs") is a major subject in the first half of John's Gospel (cp. 12:37).

1:12-13 Reference to **children of God** builds on the OT characterization of Israel as God's children (Dt 14:1; cp. Ex 4:22). **Born, not of blood . . . but of God** makes clear that true children of God come into being through faith in Messiah, not physical birth or ethnic descent (8:41-47; cp. 3:16). This opens the way for Gentiles to become God's children (11:51-52; cp. 10:16).

1:14 The Word continues the theme of 1:1. **Became flesh** does not mean the Word stopped being God; rather, the Word was made flesh. **Took up residence among us** literally

logos

Greek Pronunciation	[LAH gahss]
HCSB Translation	Word
Uses in John's Gospel	40
Uses in the NT	330
Focus Passage	John 1:1,14

Like the related verb *lego* (to speak), the noun *logos* most often refers to either oral or written communication. It means *statement* or *report* in some contexts, but most often in John's Gospel (and in the NT in general) *logos* refers to God's Word (that is, the Old Testament) or to Jesus' words. Thus, the primary use of *logos* is to denote divine revelation in some form or another. John used the term in its most exalted sense when he personified *logos* to refer to Christ. The *Logos* eternally existed as God (the Son) and with God (the Father)—He was in fact the Creator (Jn 1:1-3)—but He became a human being (v. 14), Jesus of Nazareth, so that He could reveal the Father and His will for humanity (v. 18).

Incarnation and Christology

Stephen J. Wellum

The word "incarnation" derives from a Latin word developed from *in* + *caro* [flesh], which literally means "in the flesh." In Christian theology the term refers to the supernatural act of God, effected by the Holy Spirit, whereby the eternal Son of God, the second person of the Triune Godhead, took into union with Himself a complete human nature apart from sin. As a result of that action, the Son of God became the God-man forever, the Word made flesh (Jn 1:1,14; Rm 1:3-4; 8:3; Gl 4:4; Php 2:6-11; 1Tm 3:16; Heb 2:5-18; 1Jn 4:2).

The means whereby the incarnation came about is the virgin conception, commonly known as the virgin birth—the miraculous action of the Holy Spirit in the womb of Mary—so that what was conceived was fully God and fully man in one person forever (Mt 1:18-25; Lk 1:26-38). He did this in order to become the Redeemer of the church, our Prophet, Priest, and King, and thus to save His people from their sins (Mt 1:21). By becoming one with us, the Lord of Glory not only shares our sorrows and burdens, He is also able to secure our redemption by bearing our sin on the cross as our substitute and being raised for our justification (see Rm 4:25; Heb 2:17-18; 4:14-16; 1Pt 3:18).

The Humanity and Deity of Jesus in Scripture

Biblical evidence for the full deity and humanity of Christ is abundant. In regard to His humanity, Jesus is presented as a Jewish man who was born, underwent the normal process of growth and development (Lk 2:52), experienced a full range of human experiences (e.g. Mt 8:10,24; 9:36; Lk 22:44; Jn 19:28), including growth in knowledge (Mk 13:32), and the experience of death (Jn 19:30). Apart from His sinlessness, which Scripture unequivocally affirms (Jn 8:46; 2Co 5:21; Heb 4:15; 1Pt 1:19), He is one with us in every way.

Scripture also affirms that the *man* Christ Jesus is also the eternal Son of God and thus God equal with the Father and Spirit. From the opening pages of the NT, Jesus is identified as the Lord: the One who establishes the divine rule and inaugurates the new covenant era in fulfillment of OT expectation—something only God can do (e.g. Is 9:6-7; 11:1-10; Jr 31:31-34; Ezk 34). That is why Jesus' miracles are not merely human acts empowered by the Spirit of God; rather they are demonstrations of His own divine authority over nature (e.g. Mt 8:23-27; 14:22-23), Satan and his hosts (Mt 12:27-28), and all things (Eph 1:9-10,19-23). Because He is God the Son, Jesus has the authority to forgive sin (Mk 2:3-12), call Himself the fulfillment of Scripture (Mt 5:17-19; 11:13), view His relationship with the Father as one of equality and reciprocity (Mt 11:25-27; Jn 5:16-30; 10:14-30), and do the very works of God in creation, providence, and redemption (Jn 1:1-18; Php 2:6-11; Col 1:15-20; Heb 1:1-3).

Theological Expression of Jesus' Natures

Later church reflection, especially at the Council of Chalcedon (A.D. 451), affirmed that we cannot do justice to Scripture without confessing that Jesus of Nazareth was fully God and fully man. God the Son, who gave personal identity to the human nature He had assumed and did so without putting aside or compromising His divine nature, must be confessed as one person who now exists in two natures. Additionally, Chalcedon affirmed that we must not think that the incarnation involved a change in the properties of each nature so that some kind of blending resulted which was neither divine nor human, as the Eutychians wrongly affirmed. Rather, we must affirm that the properties of each nature (human and divine) were preserved so that Jesus is all that God is in all of His perfections and all that we humans are except in terms of sin.

This affirmation entails at least two important points. First, *the man* Jesus from the moment of conception was personal by virtue of the union of the human nature in the person of the divine Son. At no point were there two persons or two centers of self-consciousness, as the Nestorians wrongly affirmed. That is why in our Lord Jesus Christ we come face-to-face with God. We meet Him, not subsumed under human flesh, not merely associated with it, but in undiminished moral splendor. The deity and humanity coincide, not because the human has grown into the divine, but because the divine Son has taken to Himself a human nature for our salvation. He is the divine Son who subsists in two natures, who has lived His life for us as

the glory as the •One and Only[a] Son[A]
from the Father,
full of grace and truth.

15 (John testified concerning Him
and exclaimed,
"This was the One of whom I said,
'The One coming after me[b],
has surpassed me,[c]
because He existed before me.'")[d]

16 Indeed, we have all received grace[e]
after grace
from His fullness,

17 for the law was given
through Moses,[f]

grace and truth[g] came
through Jesus Christ.

18 No one has ever seen God.[B]
The One and Only[h] Son[C]—
the One who is at the Father's[i] side[D]—
He has revealed Him.[j]

John the Baptist's Testimony

19 This is John's testimony when the •Jews from Jerusalem[k] sent priests[l] and Levites[m] to ask him, "Who are you?"

20 He did not refuse to answer, but he declared: "I am not the •Messiah."[n]

[a]1:14 Heb 11:17; 1Jn 4:9
[b]1:15 Mt 3:11; Mk 1:7; Jn 1:27,30
[c]Col 1:19
[d]Jn 3:13; 8:58; 10:30; 14:7-9,23; Php 2:6
[e]1:16 Ac 15:11; 2Pt 3:18
[f]1:17 Ps 77:20; Mt 8:4; Heb 3:2
[g]Ps 119:142; Jn 14:6; 2Th 2:10
[h]1:18 1Jn 4:9
[i]Mt 5:16; 11:27; Jn 8:42
[j]Mt 11:27; Lk 10:22; 1Jn 2:24
[k]1:19 Mt 23:37
[l]Ac 4:1 [m]Ex 6:19; Lk 10:32 [n]1:20 Mt 1:17; Eph 5:2

[A]1:14 Son is implied from the reference to the Father and from Gk usage. [B]1:18 Since God is an infinite being, no one can see Him in His absolute essential nature; Ex 33:18-23. [C]1:18 Other mss read God [D]1:18 Lit is in the bosom of the Father

means "pitched His tent" (Gk skenoo), an allusion to God's dwelling among the Israelites in the tabernacle (Ex 25:8-9; 33:7). In the past God demonstrated His presence to His people in the tabernacle and the temple. Now God has taken up residence among His people in the Word-made-flesh, Jesus Christ (Jn 1:17). The references to God's **glory** hark back to OT passages that describe the manifestation of God's presence and glory in theophanies (appearances of God), the tabernacle, or the temple (Ex 33:22; Nm 14:10; Dt 5:22). The Greek word monogenes underlying **One and Only Son from the Father** means "only child" (Jdg 11:34; Jr 6:26; Am 8:10; Zch 12:10). "Only" may mean "one of a kind," as in the case of Isaac, who is called Abraham's "one of a kind" son in Gn 22:2,12,16 (in contrast to Ishmael; cp. Heb 11:17). In the OT, the Son of David and Israel are called God's "firstborn" son (see Ps 89:27). The reference to God's "giving" of His "One and Only Son" in Jn 3:16,18 may allude to Abraham's willingness to sacrifice Isaac (Gn 22).

1:14 Full of grace and truth recalls "lovingkindness (Hb hesed) and truth (Hb emet)" in Ex 34:6 (cp. Ex 33:18-19), where the expression refers to God's covenant faithfulness to His people Israel. According to John, God's covenant faithfulness found ultimate expression in His sending of His **One and Only Son**, Jesus (see textual note at 1:14).

1:15 John the Baptist was six months older than Jesus (Lk 1:24,26), and he started his ministry earlier than Jesus (Lk 3:1-20). Usually, priority in time (such as being the first-born) implied preeminence, but Jesus' preexistence over-rode John's temporal precedence.

1:17 The contrast between the **law** and **grace and truth** is not that the law was bad and Jesus was good; rather, both the giving of the law and the coming of Jesus Christ mark stages in God's reaching out to humanity. Jesus, however, marks the final, definitive revelation of God's grace and truth. He is superior to Abraham (8:53), Jacob (4:12), and Moses (5:46-47; cp. 9:28).

1:18 The HCSB translation reads **Son** rather than "only God," which appears in many translations. Based on manuscript evidence, the Theos reading was judged to be an early transcriptional error in the Alexandrian manuscript tradition; hence the HCSB excludes it.

1:19–2:11 This introductory unit presents the first week of Jesus' ministry: Day 1, John's witness about Jesus (1:19-28); Day 2, John's encounter with Jesus (1:29-34); Day 3, John's referral of two of his disciples to Jesus (1:35-39); Day 4, Andrew's introduction of his brother Peter to Jesus (1:40-42); Day 5, the recruitment of Philip and Nathanael (1:43-51); and Day 7, the wedding at Cana (2:1-11). During this early stage Jesus was hailed by John the Baptist as the "Lamb of God" (1:29,36), gathered His first disciples, and performed His first "sign"—turning water into wine (2:11).

1:19-21 John denied being the Christ (cp. vv. 8,15; 3:28), **Elijah**, or **the Prophet**. "The Messiah" refers to the coming greater Son of David, predicted in the OT (2Sm 7:11-16; Hs 3:5). Elijah, who never died (2Kg 2:11), was expected to return in the end time (Mal 4:5) to "restore everything" (Mt 17:11; cp. Lk 1:17). John the Baptist resembled Elijah in his rugged lifestyle (Mt 3:4; cp. 2Kg 1:8) but denied being Elijah.

our representative head, died our death as our substitute, and been raised for our eternal salvation. This is why the Lord Jesus is utterly unique and without parallel and thus the only Lord and Savior. Second, since in the incarnation the eternal Son took to Himself a human nature, He can now live a fully human life. Yet He was not totally confined to that human nature as if for a period of time the divine nature was divested of its attributes or function. That is why Scripture affirms that even as the incarnate One, the divine Son continued to uphold and sustain the universe (Col 1:15-17; Heb 1:1-3) even while He lived out His life on earth as a man dependent upon the Father and empowered by the Spirit (Jn 5:19-27; Ac 10:38).

Our affirmation of the biblical Jesus is beyond our full comprehension, but it is only in such a Jesus that we have One who can meet our every need. Apart from Him as God the Son incarnate, we do not have a Redeemer who can stand on our behalf as a man, let alone satisfy God's own righteous demand upon us due to our sin. After all, it is only God who can save us. By becoming one with us, our Lord not only becomes our sympathetic Savior, He also accomplishes a work that saves us fully, completely, and finally.

21"What then?" they asked him. "Are you Elijah?"[a]

"I am not," he said.

"Are you the Prophet?"[A,b]

"No," he answered.

22"Who are you, then?" they asked. "We need to give an answer to those who sent us. What can you tell us about yourself?"

23He said, "I am a **voice of one crying out in the wilderness: Make straight the way of the Lord**[B,c]—just as Isaiah[d] the prophet said."

24Now they had been sent from the •Pharisees.[e] 25So they asked him, "Why then do you baptize if you aren't the Messiah, or Elijah, or the Prophet?"

26"I baptize with[c] water,"[f] John answered them. "Someone stands among you, but you don't know Him. 27He is the One coming after me,[D,g] whose sandal strap I'm not worthy to untie."

28All this happened in Bethany[E] across the Jordan,[F,h] where John was baptizing.

The Lamb of God

29The next day John saw Jesus coming toward him and said, "Here is the Lamb of God,[i] who takes away the sin[j] of the world! 30This is the One I told you about: 'After me comes a man who has surpassed me, because He existed before me.' 31I didn't know Him,[k] but I came baptizing with[c] water so He might be revealed[l] to Israel."

32And John testified, "I watched the Spirit[m] descending from heaven like a dove, and He rested on Him.[n] 33I didn't know Him, but He[G] who sent me to baptize with[c] water told me, 'The One you see the Spirit descending and resting on—He is the One who baptizes with[c] the Holy Spirit.'[o] 34I have seen and testified that He is the Son of God!"[H,p]

35Again the next day, John was standing with two of his disciples. 36When he saw Jesus passing by, he said, "Look! The Lamb of God!"

37The two disciples heard him say this and followed Jesus. 38When Jesus turned and noticed them following Him, He asked them, "What are you looking for?"

They said to Him, "•Rabbi"[q] (which means "Teacher"), "where are You staying?"

39"Come and you'll see," He replied. So they went and saw where He was staying, and they stayed with Him that day. It was about 10 in the morning.[I]

40Andrew,[r] Simon Peter's brother, was one of the two who heard John and followed Him. 41He first found his own brother Simon and told him, "We have found the Messiah!"[J,s]

a1:21 Mal 4:5; Mt 11:14; 17:10-13; Mk 8:28; Lk 1:17
b Dt 18:15; Mt 2:23
c 1:23 Is 40:3
d Mt 3:3; 4:14; 12:17
e 1:24 Mk 7:3
f 1:26 Mk 1:8
g 1:27 Jn 1:15
h 1:28 Mk 10:1; Lk 3:3
i 1:29 Is 53:7; Ac 8:32; 1Pt 1:19; Rv 5:6
j Jn 15:22; 1Jn 3:5
k 1:31 Jn 7:28
l 2Co 4:11; 1Jn 1:2
m 1:32 Ps 51:11; Jn 1:33; Ac 2:4; Rm 8:9; Gl 5:25; Ti 3:5; 1Jn 5:8; Rv 3:22
n Jms 4:5
o 1:33 Mt 3:11; Mk 1:8; Lk 3:16; Ac 11:16
p 1:34 Mt 3:17; 4:3; Jn 1:49; 5:19; Heb 1:2
q 1:38 Jn 11:8
r 1:40-42 Mt 4:18-22; Mk 1:16-20; Lk 5:2-11
s 1:41 Mt 1:17

A1:21 Probably the Prophet in Dt 18:15   B1:23 Is 40:3   C1:26,31,33 Or in   D1:27 Other mss add *who came before me*   E1:28 Other mss read *in Bethabara*   F1:28 Another Bethany, near Jerusalem, was the home of Lazarus, Martha, and Mary; Jn 11:1.   G1:33 He refers to God the Father, who gave John a sign to help him identify the Messiah. Vv. 32-34 indicate that John did not know that Jesus was the Messiah until the Spirit descended upon Him at His baptism.   H1:34 Other mss read *is the Chosen One of God*   I1:39 Lit *about the tenth hour*. Various methods of reckoning time were used in the ancient world. John probably used a different method from the other 3 Gospels. If John used the same method of time reckoning as the other 3 Gospels, the translation would be: *It was about four in the afternoon.*   J1:41 In the NT, the word Messiah translates the Gk word *Christos* ("Anointed One"), except here and in Jn 4:25 where it translates *Messias.*

Moses predicted the coming of "the Prophet" in Dt 18:15,18 (cp. Ac 3:22; 7:37), who was expected in Jesus' time (Jn 6:14; 7:40); John denied being this Prophet as well (though he was a prophet; see 10:40-41; Mt 11:11-14).

1:23 John was **a voice . . . crying out in the wilderness: Make straight the way of the Lord** in keeping with Isaiah's words (Is 40:3; cp. Mt 3:3; Mk 1:3; Lk 3:4). This messenger of God was to prepare the way for Yahweh's coming by preaching repentance and divine judgment. Isaiah's vision in Is 40–55 drew heavily on exodus typology and envisioned a new exodus of God's people in which God's glory would be revealed and His people delivered. This would be accomplished by the coming of the Servant of the Lord (see esp. Is 52:13–53:12).

1:28 John was baptizing at the Jordan River. Luke 3:1 places this event in the fifteenth year of the reign of Tiberius (A.D. 14–37), or A.D. 29. John would have been about 33 years old. The **Bethany across the Jordan** (cp. 10:40) was probably not the village near Jerusalem where Lazarus was raised (cp. 11:1,18) but the region of Batanea in the northeast (called Bashan in the OT).

1:29 On **the next day**, see note at 2:1-2. John the Baptist's references to Jesus as **the Lamb of God** may echo the lamb led to the slaughter mentioned in Is 53:7. John may also have proclaimed Jesus as the apocalyptic warrior lamb who would bring judgment (Rv 5:6,12; 7:17; cp. Mt 3:7-12; Lk 3:7-17). **Takes away the sin of the world** refers to Jesus' sacrificial, substitutionary death, which appeased God's wrath against sin and sinners (1Jn 2:2; 4:10).

1:31 By **I didn't know Him** John probably meant that he did not know Jesus was the Messiah until he saw the sign from God mentioned in verses 32-33.

1:32-34 The **Spirit** did not just descend on Jesus, He **rested** on Him (cp. 3:34)—a sign of Jesus' divine anointing. In the OT, the Spirit came upon people to enable them to accomplish specific tasks. Isaiah predicted that Messiah would be full of the Spirit at all times (Is 11:2; 61:1; cp. Lk 4:18; see note at 5:31-47).

1:35 In 1:35–4:42 John narrated events that fell between Jesus' baptism and the start of His Galilean ministry. On **the next day**, see note at 2:1-2.

1:38 Rabbi (which means Teacher) is one of six instances where John translated an Aramaic term for his readers. The others are "Messiah" (Christ, v. 41; 4:25); "Cephas" (Peter, 1:42); "Siloam" (Sent, 9:7); "Thomas" (Didymus, "Twin"; 11:16; 20:24; 21:2); and "Place of the Skull" (Golgotha, 19:17).

1:40 Andrew was **one of the two**; the other disciple is not named. He was probably John, the son of Zebedee.

(which means "Anointed[a] One"), [42] and he brought Simon to Jesus.

When Jesus saw him, He said, "You are Simon, son of John.[A] You will be called •Cephas"[b] (which means "Rock").

Philip and Nathanael

[43] The next day He[B] decided to leave for Galilee. Jesus found Philip[c] and told him, "Follow Me!"

[44] Now Philip was from Bethsaida,[d] the hometown of Andrew and Peter. [45] Philip found Nathanael[C,e] and told him, "We have found the One Moses wrote about in the Law (and so did the prophets[f]): Jesus the son of Joseph,[g] from Nazareth!"[h]

[46] "Can anything good[i] come out of Nazareth?" Nathanael asked him.

"Come and see," Philip answered.

[47] Then Jesus saw Nathanael coming toward Him and said about him, "Here is a true Israelite;[j] no deceit is in him."

[48] "How do you know me?" Nathanael asked.

"Before Philip called you, when you were under the fig tree, I saw you," Jesus answered.

[49] "Rabbi,"[k] Nathanael replied, "You are the Son[l] of God! You are the King of Israel!"[m]

[50] Jesus responded to him, "Do you believe only because I told you I saw you under the fig tree? You[D] will see greater things than this." [51] Then He said, "'I assure you: You[E] will see heaven opened and the angels of God[n] ascending and descending[o] on the •Son of Man."[p]

The First Sign: Turning Water into Wine

2 On the third day a wedding took place in Cana[q] of Galilee.[r] Jesus' mother[s] was there, and [2] Jesus and His disciples were invited to the wedding as well. [3] When the wine ran out, Jesus' mother told Him, "They don't have any wine."

[4] "What has this concern of yours to do with Me,[F,t] •woman?"[u] Jesus asked. "My hour[G] has not yet come."

[a]:41 Ex 29:29
[b]:42 1Co 1:12; 3:22; 9:5; 15:5; Gl 1:18; 2:9,11,14
[c]:43 Mk 3:18
[d]:44 Jn 12:21
[e]:45 Jn 1:46-49; 21:2
[f]Mt 2:23; Ac 7:52; Rm 3:21
[g]Mt 1:16; Lk 1:27; 2:4,16,33; 3:23; Jn 6:42
[h]Mk 1:9
[i]:46 Gn 1:31
[j]:47 2Co 11:22
[k]:49 Jn 11:8
[l]Jn 5:19
[m]Mt 27:42; Mk 15:32; Jn 12:13
[n]:51 Lk 12:8-9; 15:10; Ac 10:3
[o]Gn 28:12
[p]Mk 2:10
[q]2:1 Jn 2:11; 4:46; 21:2
[r]Mt 17:22
[s]Mt 1:16
[t]2:4 2Sm 16:10; 19:22
[u]Jn 19:26

A1:42 Other mss read *Simon, son of Jonah*　**B**1:43 Or *he*, referring either to Simon Peter (vv. 41-42) or Andrew (vv. 40-41)
C1:45 Probably the Bartholomew of the other Gospels and Acts　**D**1:50 In Gk, the word you is sg and refers to Nathanael.
E1:51 In Gk, the word you is pl and refers to Nathanael and the other disciples.　**F**2:4 Or *You and I see things differently*; lit
What to Me and you; Mt 8:29; Mk 1:24; 5:7; Lk 8:28　**G**2:4 The time of His sacrificial death and exaltation; Jn 7:30; 8:20;
12:23,27; 13:1; 17:1

1:41 On **Messiah . . . Anointed One**, see note at verse 38.

1:42 Cephas is an Aramaic word meaning "rock" (cp. Mt 16:16-18; see note at Jn 1:38). In OT times, God frequently changed people's names to indicate their special calling.

1:43 On **the next day**, see note at 2:1-2. Jesus' calling of His disciples (**follow Me**) differed from customary practice. Usually it was a disciple who took the initiative to follow a rabbi (15:16).

1:44 Most likely, **Andrew** and **Peter** grew up in **Bethsaida** and later moved to Capernaum (Mk 1:29; cp. Mk 1:21), located only a few miles west. Similarly, Jesus was born in Bethlehem, grew up in Nazareth (Jn 1:45), and later moved to Capernaum (Mt 4:13).

1:45 Nathanael is also mentioned in 21:2. Nathanael may be the personal name of Bartholomew (Bar-Tholomaios = son of Tholomaios), who is linked with Philip in all three Synoptic lists (Mt 10:3; Mk 3:18; Lk 6:14). Philip's reference to **the One Moses wrote about in the Law** may allude to predictions of a coming prophet in Dt 18:15,18 (see note at Jn 1:19-21). The expression "the Law and the Prophets" commonly referred to the OT in its entirety (Mt 5:17; 7:12).

1:46 Nathanael, who hailed from the small village of Cana in Galilee (21:2; cp. 2:1-11), used something of a double standard when he displayed prejudice toward insignificant **Nazareth**. Nazareth was a small town of no more than 2,000 people.

1:48 Jesus displayed supernatural knowledge (**I saw you**), identifying Himself as Messiah.

1:49 Son of God and **King of Israel** are both messianic titles. "Son of God" identifies Jesus as the prophesied Messiah (2Sm 7:14; Ps 2:7); "King of Israel" likewise is a common

OT designation for Messiah (Zph 3:15). The two terms also appear in Mt 27:42; Mk 15:32.

1:51 I assure you translates Hebrew *amen, amen*, a solemn affirmation emphasizing the authoritative nature of Jesus' pronouncement. The phrase appears 25 times in John's Gospel. **Heaven opened and the angels of God ascending and descending** recalls the story of Jacob in Gn 28:12-15. The greatness of the Son of Man will far surpass the vision of Jacob the patriarch (Jn 4:5-6,11-12). Jesus is the "new Bethel" where God is revealed, and the "new Israel." The expression **Son of Man** harks back to the mysterious figure of "One like a son of man" in Dn 7:13-14. The Son of Man would be "lifted up" by crucifixion (see note at Jn 3:14), provide divine revelation (6:27,53), and act with end-time authority (5:27; 9:39).

2:1-2 Third day is probably counted from Jesus' encounter with Nathanael. **Cana of Galilee** was later the site of Jesus' third sign ("the second sign" performed in Cana; 4:54). Jewish weddings were community events, a time of special focus not just on bride and groom but also on their extended families. **Jesus' mother** may have been a friend of the family, helping behind the scenes. Jesus' **disciples** probably included the five mentioned in 1:35-51.

2:3 The wedding party's running out of **wine** ironically calls to mind the spiritual barrenness of first-century Judaism.

2:4 Jesus' use of **woman** to address His mother established a polite but firm distance between them, as did His question, **What has this concern of yours to do with Me?** On Jesus' **hour has not yet come**, cp. 7:6,8,30; 8:20. Because of misconceptions about the coming Messiah, Jesus chose not to reveal Himself openly to Israel (though He did perform numerous messianic "signs"; see note at 2:11). John portrayed Jesus as the "elusive Christ" via Jesus' pattern of

5"Do whatever He tells you," His mother told the servants.

6Now six stone water jars had been set there for Jewish purification.[a] Each contained 20 or 30 gallons.[A]

7"Fill the jars with water," Jesus told them. So they filled them to the brim. 8Then He said to them, "Now draw some out and take it to the chief servant."[B] And they did.

9When the chief servant tasted the water (after it had become wine), he did not know where it came from—though the servants who had drawn the water knew. He called the groom 10and told him, "Everyone sets out the fine wine first, then, after people have drunk freely, the inferior. But you have kept the fine wine until now."

11Jesus performed this first sign[c] in Cana[b] of Galilee.[c] He displayed[d] His glory,[e] and His disciples believed in Him.

12After this, He went down to Capernaum,[f] together with His mother, His brothers,[g] and His disciples, and they stayed there only a few days.

Cleansing the Temple Complex

13The Jewish *Passover[h] was near, so Jesus went up to Jerusalem.[i] 14In the *temple complex[j] He found people selling oxen, sheep, and doves, and He also found the money changers sitting there. 15After making a whip out of cords,[k] He drove everyone out of the temple complex with their sheep[l] and oxen. He also poured out the money changers' coins and overturned the tables. 16He told those who were selling doves, "Get these things out of here! Stop turning My Father's[m] house[n] into a marketplace!"[D,o]

17And His disciples remembered that it is written: **Zeal[p] for Your house will consume[q] Me.**[E,r]

Cross references:
a 2:6 Lv 13–14; Heb 1:3
b 2:11 Jn 2:1; 21:2
c Mt 17:22
d 2Co 4:11; 1Jn 1:2
e Mk 10:37; Jn 17:24
f 2:12 Lk 10:15
g Mt 12:46–50; Mk 3:31–35; 6:3; Lk 8:19–21; Ac 1:14
h 2:13 Ex 12:11
i Mt 23:37
j 2:14–17 Mt 21:12–13; Mk 11:15–17; Lk 19:45–46
k 2:15 Ac 27:32
l Mt 7:15
m 2:16 Mt 5:16; 11:27; Jn 8:42
n Lk 11:51; Jn 2:17
o Jr 7:11; Zch 14:21; Mal 3:1-3
p 2:17 Nm 25:13
q Gl 5:15
r Ps 69:9

A 2:6 Lit 2 or 3 measures   B 2:8 Lit ruler of the table; perhaps master of the feast, or headwaiter   C 2:11 Lit this beginning of the signs; Jn 4:54; 20:30. Seven miraculous signs occur in John's Gospel and are so noted in the headings.   D 2:16 Lit a house of business   E 2:17 Ps 69:9

---

occasional withdrawal (7:6-9; 10:40-41; 11:56-57), His realism about people's true motives (2:23-25), and His ability to elude His opponents when charged with blasphemy (7:44; 8:59; 10:39). Jesus remained elusive until His time finally arrived (12:23,27; 13:1; 16:32; 17:1).

2:5 Mary's instructions, **Do whatever He tells you**, recalls Pharaoh's instructions in Gn 41:55.

2:6 The number of jars (**six**) may indicate incompleteness since seven represented fullness. Since **each contained 20 or 30 gallons**, this added up to as much as 180 gallons. The **Jewish purification** ritual may have involved the washing of the guests' hands and certain utensils used at the wedding.

2:7 Filled them to the brim points to the abundance of Jesus' messianic provision (3:34).

2:9 The **chief servant** may have been the head waiter in charge of catering. He supervised the serving of food and drink, and employed several servants.

2:11 The fact that Jesus' turning of water into wine at the wedding is called the **first sign in Cana of Galilee** leads the reader to expect more signs to follow. The corresponding reference in 4:54 is to Jesus' healing of the royal official's son again while at Cana, "the second sign Jesus performed after He came from Judea to Galilee." Beyond this, Jesus' signs include the non-miraculous but prophetic temple clearing (2:13-22; one of Jesus' Judean signs; cp. v. 23; 3:2); His healing of a lame man (5:1-15); the feeding of the crowds (6:1-15); the healing of the man born blind (chap. 9); and the raising of Lazarus (chap. 11).

In each case, the emphasis is on the way the "sign" revealed Jesus' messianic nature (12:37-40; 20:30-31) and on the striking nature of the feat. These signs pointed unmistakably to Jesus as Messiah—whether it be the large quantity and high quality of wine (2:6,10); the short span required by Jesus to "rebuild" the temple (vv. 19-20); the long-distance healing of the royal official's son (4:47,49-50); the lame man's 38 years as an invalid (5:5); the abundance of food Jesus produced (6:13); the man's congenital blindness (9:1-2); or Lazarus's four days in the tomb (11:17,39). The

phrases **He displayed His glory, and His disciples believed in Him** hark back to 1:14.

2:12 Jesus **went down** from Cana (in the hill country) to **Capernaum** (situated by the Sea of Galilee). Capernaum was about 15 miles northeast of Cana and could be reached in a day's journey. Capernaum served as Jesus' headquarters after John the Baptist's imprisonment (Mt 4:12-13; Lk 4:28-31; cp. Mt 9:1).

2:13-22 Jesus' first major confrontation with Jewish leaders in John's Gospel took place when He cleared the Jerusalem temple at Passover. The Synoptic Gospels record a later clearing, just before the crucifixion (Mk 11:15-19). By clearing the temple, Jesus displayed zeal for God's house (Jn 2:17; cp. Ps 69:9) and performed a sign of judgment on the Jewish leaders who had allowed worship to deteriorate into commerce. His action also prophetically foreshadowed His crucifixion and resurrection, which would establish Him as the new center of worship, replacing the old temple.

2:13 This is the first reference to a Jewish festival in John's Gospel and the first reference to **Passover**. Later, John referred to two more Passovers at 6:4 (Jesus in Galilee) and 11:55; 12:1 (Jesus' final Passover in Jerusalem). Beyond this, Mt 12:1 may refer to another Passover not recorded in John. If so, Jesus' ministry included four Passovers and extended over about three and one-half years, spanning from A.D. 29 to 33 (see note at Jn 1:28). Apart from these Passover references, John also mentioned Jesus' activities at an unnamed Jewish festival in 5:1 (possibly Tabernacles); at the Festival of Tabernacles (or Booths) in 7:2; and at the Festival of Dedication (or Hanukkah) in 10:22. People are described as traveling **up** to Jerusalem because it was located at a higher elevation than Galilee.

2:14 Temple complex (Gk hieron) denotes the area surrounding the temple, including the Court of the Gentiles, in distinction from the temple proper (Gk naos). Merchants (**selling oxen, sheep, and doves**) and **money changers** (exchanging idol-free coins for those tainted with pagan engravings) eased the logistical burden on pilgrims traveling

[18] So the *Jews replied to Him, "What sign of authority will You show us for doing these things?"

[19] Jesus answered, "Destroy this sanctuary,[a] and I will raise it up in three days."[b]

[20] Therefore the Jews said, "This sanctuary took 46 years to build, and will You raise it up in three days?"[c]

[21] But He was speaking about the sanctuary of His body.[d] [22] So when He was raised from the dead,[e] His disciples remembered that He had said this.[f] And they believed the Scripture[g] and the statement Jesus had made.

[23] While He was in Jerusalem[h] at the Passover Festival,[i] many trusted in His name[j] when they saw the signs He was doing. [24] Jesus, however, would not entrust Himself to them, since He knew them all [25] and because He did not need anyone to testify about man; for He Himself knew what was in man.[k]

Jesus and Nicodemus

3 There was a man from the *Pharisees[l] named Nicodemus,[m] a ruler[n] of the *Jews. [2] This man came to Him at night and said, "'Rabbi,[o] we know that You have come from God[p] as a teacher,[q] for no one could perform these signs You do unless God were with him."[r]

[3] Jesus replied, "'I assure you: Unless someone is born again,[A,s] he cannot see the kingdom of God.'"[t]

[4] "But how can anyone be born when he is old?" Nicodemus asked Him. "Can he enter his mother's womb a second time and be born?"

[5] Jesus answered, "I assure you: Unless someone is born[u] of water and the Spirit,[B,v] he cannot enter the kingdom of God. [6] Whatever is born of the flesh[w] is flesh, and whatever is born of the Spirit[x] is spirit. [7] Do not be amazed

Cross references
[a] 2:19 Lk 1:21
[b] Lk 9:22
[c] 2:20 Mk 15:29
[d] 2:21 Mt 26:26; 27:52,58; Mk 14:22; 15:43; Lk 12:4; 22:19; 23:52,55; Jn 19:31,38,40; 20:12; 1Co 10:16; 11:23-26; Heb 10:5,10; 1Pt 2:24
[e] 2:22 Mt 17:9; Rv 20:12
[f] Jn 14:26
[g] Mt 26:54; 2Pt 1:20
[h] 2:23 Mt 23:37
[i] Jn 5:1
[j] Jn 10:25; 1Jn 3:23
[k] 2:25 Jr 17:10
[l] 3:1 Mk 7:3
[m] Jn 3:4,9; 7:50; 19:39
[n] Lk 8:41; 12:58
[o] 3:2 Jn 11:8
[p] Mk 1:45
[q] Mk 4:38; Eph 4:11
[r] Ex 3:12; Jn 3:3

15:24; Ac 10:38; Rv 21:3   [s] 3:3 1Pt 1:3; 1Jn 2:29   [t] Mk 1:15; 9:1   [u] 3:5 Mk 9:43   [v] Ezk 36:25-27; Ac 22:16; Ti 3:5   [w] 3:6 Php 3:3   [x] Jn 1:33

A 3:3 The same Gk word can mean again or from above (also in v. 7).   **B** 3:5 Or spirit, or wind; the Gk word pneuma can mean wind, spirit, or Spirit, each of which occurs in this context.

---

to Jerusalem from afar by providing them with appropriate animals and coins for sacrifices and offerings. By conducting their business within the temple complex, however, they disrupted worship (esp. for Gentiles) and obstructed the temple's purpose.

2:17 Jesus' clearing of the temple reminded His disciples of the righteous sufferer in Ps 69:9. First-century Jews expected Messiah to purge and reconstitute the temple. Jesus was passionately concerned for the holiness and purity of God's **house**.

2:20 This sanctuary took 46 years to build seems to indicate that the reconstruction of the second temple had taken 46 years. Alternatively, it can be read: "This sanctuary was completed 46 years ago (and has stood since that time)." The Jews were amazed that Jesus claimed He could **raise it up in three days**, an impossibly short time. The misunderstanding is cleared up in verse 21.

2:22 The Scripture may be Ps 69:9 (cited in Jn 2:17). **The statement Jesus had made** refers to verse 19.

2:23-25 Trusted . . . would not entrust Himself is a wordplay in the original Greek. Jesus' knowledge of people's hearts was displayed in His encounters with Nicodemus and the Samaritan woman; see note at verse 4.

2:23-4:42 The bulk of chapters 3 and 4 is devoted to Jesus' encounters with Nicodemus, a representative of the Jewish religious establishment, and an unnamed woman representing Samaritan religion. Interspersed are explanatory sections (3:16-21,31-36) and a vignette on John the Baptist (3:22-30). The encounters with Nicodemus and the Samaritan woman are a study in contrasts. Nicodemus's status as a Sanhedrin member differs sharply from the lowly Samaritan woman who had a sinful past and present. Yet in both cases Jesus discerned deep spiritual need. He confronted Nicodemus about his need for regeneration and the woman about her sin.

3:1 Nicodemus was a common name in first-century Palestine. **Ruler of the Jews** refers to the Jewish governing body known as the Sanhedrin.

3:2 Nicodemus's coming to Jesus **at night** may have nega-

tive overtones ("night" is probably negative in 13:30 but not in 21:3; see also the reference to the present event without apparent negative connotation in 19:39). Coming from a "teacher of Israel" (3:10), the address **rabbi** denoted respect, especially since it was known that Jesus did not have formal rabbinic training (7:15). The **signs** mentioned in John's Gospel presumably included those performed in Jerusalem (2:23), possibly the temple clearing (cp. 2:18; see note at 2:11).

3:3-8 The discussion of the need for spiritual rebirth develops the reference to the "children of God" who are "born of God" in the prologue (1:12-13). On "children of God," see 8:39-58 and 11:51-52. The phrase **born of water and the Spirit** probably refers to spiritual birth that cleanses from sin and brings spiritual transformation (Ezk 36:25-27). The **kingdom of God**, a major topic in the other Gospels, is mentioned by John only in verses 3,5 (see the reference to Jesus' kingdom in 18:36).

3:7 You is plural, probably indicating Nicodemus and other Sanhedrin members (cp. vv. 1,11).

---

anothen

Greek Pronunciation	[AH noh thuhn]
HCSB Translation	again
Uses in John's Gospel	5
Uses in the NT	13
Focus Passage	John 3:3,7

The expression born again comes from Jn 3:3, where Jesus tells Nicodemus that he must be born (gennao, the term used for the genealogy in Mt 1:1-17) again (anothen). The term anothen can mean again or from above. The meaning again for anothen occurs in Gl 4:9, which is the only clear instance of this meaning in the NT. All other uses of the term mean from above (see Jn 3:31; 19:11; Jms 1:17; 3:15,17) or something similar (such as top in Mt 27:51; Mk 15:38; Jn 19:23). It is likely that Nicodemus misunderstood Jesus' use of anothen, thinking He meant again as in a second time. This is why Nicodemus responded the way he did, by a reference to physical birth (3:4). But Jesus went on to indicate that He was referring to the other meaning of anothen, a birth from above, a birth from the Spirit (vv.5,6,8).

that I told you that you[A] must be born[a] again. [8] The wind[B] blows where it pleases, and you hear its sound, but you don't know where it comes from or where it is going.[b] So it is with everyone born of the Spirit."[c]

[9] "How can these things be?" asked Nicodemus.

[10] "Are you a teacher[C] of Israel and don't know these things?" Jesus replied. [11] "I assure you:[d] We speak what We know and We testify to what We have seen, but you[D] do not accept Our testimony.[E] [12] If I have told you about things that happen on earth and you don't believe, how will you believe if I tell you about things of heaven? [13] No one has ascended[e] into heaven[f] except the One who descended from heaven[g]—the •Son of Man.[F,h] [14] Just as Moses[i] lifted up the snake in the wilderness,[j] so the Son of Man must be lifted up, [15] so that everyone who believes in Him will[G] have eternal life.[k]

[16] "For God loved[l] the world •in this way: He gave His •One and Only[m] Son,[n] so that everyone who believes in Him will not perish but have eternal life.[o] [17] For God did not send His Son into the world that He might condemn[p]

the world, but that the world might be saved through Him. [18] Anyone who believes in Him is not condemned, but anyone who does not believe is already condemned,[q] because he has not believed in the name[r] of the One and Only Son[s] of God.

[19] "This, then, is the judgment: The light[t] has come into the world,[u] and people loved darkness rather than the light because their deeds were evil. [20] For everyone who practices wicked things hates[v] the light and avoids it,[H] so that his deeds[w] may not be exposed. [21] But anyone who lives by[I] the truth comes to the light, so that his works[x] may be shown to be accomplished by God."[J]

Jesus and John the Baptist

[22] After this, Jesus and His disciples went to the Judean countryside, where He spent time with them and baptized. [23] John[y] also was baptizing in Aenon near Salim, because there was plenty of water there. People were coming and being baptized, [24] since John had not yet been thrown into prison.[z]

[a]3:7 1Pt 1:3
[b]3:8 Jn 8:14
[c]1Co 2:13-16
[d]3:11 1Jn 1:51; Rv 22:21
[e]3:13 Jn 20:17
[f]Dt 30:12; Jn 6:62; Ac 2:34; Rm 10:6; 1Co 15:47; Eph 4:8-10; Rv 11:12
[g]Jn 6:38; 8:23
[h]Mk 2:10
[i]3:14 Ps 77:20; Mt 8:4; Heb 3:2
[j]Nm 21:4-9
[k]3:15 Mk 10:17; Jn 12:25; Ac 13:48
[l]3:16 Jn 12:43; 1Co 13:1; Gl 2:20; Col 1:13; 3:12; 1Th 1:4; 2Th 2:13,16; 1Jn 4:7-12; Jd 1
[m]1Jn 4:9
[n]Jn 5:19; Heb 1:2
[o]Jn 12:25; Rm 5:8; 1Jn 3:16; 4:9-10
[p]3:17 Jn 8:11
[q]3:18 Mt 12:41; Mk 16:16
[r]Jn 10:25; 1Jn 3:23
[s]Jn 5:19
[t]3:19 Ps 36:9; Jn

3:10; Jms 2:14-26
12:46   [u]Jn 18:37; 1Jn 2:8   [v]3:20 Lk 6:27; 19:14   [w]Mk 14:6; Gl
[x]3:21 Jn 5:36   [y]3:23 Mk 1:4   [z]3:24 Mk 1:14

[A]3:7 The pronoun is pl in Gk.   [B]3:8 The Gk word *pneuma* can mean wind, spirit, or Spirit, each of which occurs in this context.   [C]3:10 Or *the teacher*   [D]3:11 In Gk, the word you is pl here and throughout v. 12.   [E]3:11 The pronouns we and our refer to Jesus and His authority to speak for the Father.   [F]3:13 Other mss add *who is in heaven*   [G]3:15 Other mss add *not perish, but*   [H]3:20 Lit *and does not come to the light*   [I]3:21 Lit *who does*   [J]3:21 It is possible that Jesus' words end at v. 15. Ancient Gk did not have quotation marks.

3:8 Jesus illustrated His pronouncement in verses 3-5 with an analogy between wind and a person born of the Spirit. **Wind** and **Spirit** translate the same Greek and Hebrew words (Gk *pneuma*; Hb *ruach*). While the wind's origin is invisible, its effects can be observed; it is the same with those born of the Spirit.

3:10 Jesus may here be "returning the compliment" (see

note at v. 2), though He chastised Nicodemus for his lack of understanding.

3:13 Jesus' statement may allude to Pr 30:4. Only Jesus **descended from heaven** and returned there (Lk 24:51; Ac 1:9).

3:14 The reference to the **Son of Man** being **lifted up** is the first of three "lifted up" sayings in John (8:28;12:32). All three speak of the future "lifting up" of the Son of Man in double meaning (possibly inspired by the language of Is 52:13). The reference in this verse invokes **Moses**' lifting up of a serpent in the **wilderness** so that everyone who had been bitten by a poisonous snake and looked at the serpent in faith was healed (Nm 21:8-9). The third and final "lifted up" saying (Jn 12:32) emphasizes that the lifting up of the Son of Man refers to Jesus' crucifixion (cp. 12:33 and the similar reference to Peter's martyrdom in 21:19).

3:16-18 God, out of love, **gave His One and Only Son** (cp. 1:14,18), so that everyone who believes in Him will **have eternal life** (see notes at 5:26 and 14:6). John's favorite designation for Jesus is the Son sent by the Father (3:34-36; 5:19-26; 6:40; 8:35-36; 14:13; 17:1), imagery taken from the Jewish concept of the *shaliach* (messenger), according to which the sent one is like the sender himself and faithfully pursues the sender's interests (13:16,20). Jesus is that "Sent One" par excellence (9:7), and He in turn sends His disciples (see note at 20:21-22). Being sent implies that the commission, charge, and message are issued by the sender rather than originating with the ones sent. The messengers' role is to fulfill their commission according to their sender's will.

3:19-21 On Jesus as the **light**, see note at 8:12.

monogenes

Greek Pronunciation	[mah nah gehn AYSS]
HCSB Translation	only
Uses in John's Gospel	4
Uses in the NT	9
Focus Passage	John 3:16,18

English translations have traditionally understood *monogenes* to be from *monos* (only) and *gennao* (beget), thus following the Latin Vulgate (*unigenitus*) and translating the word *only begotten*. This has caused great misunderstanding since God the Son did not have an origin and was not created by God. He is Himself an eternal being. It is best to understand *monogenes* to be from *monos* (only) and *genos* (kind, Latin *genus*), meaning *the only one of its kind*. This view is more consistent with John's five uses of the word, and support for this translation is found in Hb 11:17 where Isaac is called Abraham's *monogenes*. Isaac was not Abraham's *only begotten* son but he was the *only one* of his kind—the son of promise. In the Old Latin translation, *monogenes* was translated as *unicus*, from which we get our word *unique*. This is what is meant by *monogenes* in John's writings (Jn 1:14,18; 3:16,18; 1Jn 4:9): Jesus is God's *unique* Son in that His essential nature is the same as the Father's.

²⁵Then a dispute arose between John's disciples[a] and a Jew[A] about purification.[b] ²⁶So they came to John and told him, "Rabbi,[c] the One you testified about, and who was with you across the Jordan,[d] is baptizing—and everyone is flocking to Him."[e]

²⁷John responded, "No one can receive a single thing unless it's given to him from heaven. ²⁸You yourselves can testify that I said, 'I am not the •Messiah,[f] but I've been sent ahead of Him.' [g] ²⁹He who has the bride[h] is the groom. But the groom's friend, who stands by and listens for him, rejoices greatly[B] at the groom's voice. So this joy[i] of mine is complete. ³⁰He must increase, but I must decrease."

The One from Heaven

³¹The One who comes from above[j] is above all. The one who is from the earth is earthly and speaks in earthly terms.[C] The One who comes from heaven is above all.[k] ³²He testifies[l] to what He has seen and heard, yet no one accepts His testimony. ³³The one who has accepted His testimony has affirmed that God is true.[m] ³⁴For God sent Him, and He speaks

God's words, since He[D] gives the Spirit[n] without measure. ³⁵The Father loves the Son[o] and has given all things into His hands.[p] ³⁶The one who believes in the Son has eternal life, but the one who refuses to believe in the Son will not see life; instead, the wrath of God remains on him.[q]

Jesus and the Samaritan Woman

4 When Jesus[E] knew that the •Pharisees[r] heard He was making[s] and baptizing more disciples than John[t] ²(though Jesus Himself was not baptizing, but His disciples were), ³He left Judea[u] and went again to Galilee.[v] ⁴He had to travel through Samaria,[w] ⁵so He came to a town of Samaria called Sychar near the property[F] that Jacob[x] had given his son Joseph.[y] ⁶Jacob's well[z] was there, and Jesus, worn out from His journey, sat down at the well. It was about six in the evening.[G]

⁷A woman of Samaria came to draw water.[aa] "Give Me a drink," Jesus said to her, ⁸for His disciples had gone into town to buy food.

⁹"How is it that You, a Jew,[ab] ask for a drink

a 3:25 Mt 9:14; 11:2; 14:12; Mk 2:18; 6:29; Lk 5:33; 7:18-19; 11:1; Jn 1:35,37; 6:3
b Lv 13-14; Heb 1:3
c 3:26 Jn 11:8
d Mk 10:1; Lk 3:3
e Mk 1:45
f 3:28 Mt 1:17; Eph 5:2
g Lk 1:17
h 3:29 Rv 21:2
i Jn 15:11
j 3:31 Jms 1:17
k Jn 8:23; 1Jn 4:5-6
l 3:32 Jn 15:26; Ac 26:5
m 3:33 1Jn 5:20
n 3:34 Jn 1:33
o 3:35 Jn 5:20; 10:17; 1Co 13:1
p Jn 5:19
q 3:36 Mk 16:16
r 4:1 Mk 7:3
s Mt 28:19-20
t Mk 1:4
u 4:3 Lk 1:5
v Mt 17:22
w 4:4 Ac 1:8
x 4:5 Ps 22:23; Mt 1:2; Lk 1:33
y Gn 30:24; 33:19; 48:22; 49:22
z 4:6 Jms 3:11
aa 4:7 Gn 24:11-17; 29:2-12   ab 4:9 Jn 11:36; Ac 14:1; Rv 2:9

3:22 Jesus left the vicinity of Jerusalem and headed to the **Judean countryside**. In 4:3, Jesus left Judea altogether, returning to Galilee (2:12) by way of Samaria.

3:26 On John the Baptist as a witness to Jesus, see note at 5:31-47.

3:28 John's assertion that he had **been sent ahead** of the Messiah may allude to Mal 3:1 (cp. Mt 11:10; Mk 1:2; Lk 7:27).

3:29 John's reference to Jesus as the **groom** (cp. Mt 9:15) identified Jesus as Israel's long-awaited King and Messiah. In the OT, Israel is frequently depicted as God's "bride" (Is 62:4-5; Jr 2:2; Hs 2:16-20). John's role was that of **the groom's friend**, who selflessly rejoiced with the groom (1:6-9,15,19-36).

3:30 John the Baptist downplayed his disciples' concerns expressed in verse 26. Now that the Light had come (1:6-9), the "lamp" had done its work (see note at 5:35).

3:33 **Has affirmed** (Gk *sphragizo*) means literally "to seal" in the sense of confirming or authenticating something as true (see note at 6:27-29).

3:34 On Jesus as the recipient of God's Spirit, see note at 1:32-34 (see also Rv 3:1; 5:6).

3:36 **Has eternal life** indicates that eternal life is not just a future expectation but is already a present experience. **The wrath of God remains on him** makes it clear that unless a person believes in Jesus the Messiah, he remains under God's judgment (vv. 19-21).

4:1-42 Jesus' encounter with the Samaritan woman took place by divine necessity (v. 4). Unlike Nicodemus, the woman progressed in her understanding. She viewed Him first as a Jew (v. 9), then as someone who could make her life easier (v. 15), then as a prophet (v. 19), and then possibly as

Messiah (v. 29). The woman's fellow townspeople concluded that Jesus was the Savior of the world (v. 42).

4:1 The Pharisees had investigated John the Baptist's credentials (1:19,24); now they were looking into those of Jesus.

4:2 John the evangelist, author of this Gospel, here clarified the earlier statement in 3:26.

4:3 On Jesus going from **Judea** to **Galilee**, see note at 3:22.

4:4 **Had to travel** may indicate that Jesus' itinerary was set by the sovereign plan of God (9:4; 10:16; 12:34; 20:9). **Through Samaria** was the most direct route from Judea to Galilee, but strict Jews, wishing to avoid defilement, bypassed Samaria by taking a longer, less direct route. This involved crossing the Jordan River and traveling across from Samaria on the eastern side of the river.

4:5 **Sychar** was located just east of Mount Gerizim and Mount Ebal. The reference to **the property that Jacob had given his son Joseph** reflects the customary inference from Gn 48:21-22 and Jos 24:32 that Jacob gave his son Joseph the land at Shechem which he had bought from the sons of Hamor (Gn 33:18-19) and which later served as Joseph's burial place (Ex 13:19; Jos 24:32).

4:6 Jesus was **worn out from His journey**. This underscores His genuine, full humanity.

4:8 Jesus and His disciples usually carried little or nothing to eat on their journeys. Rather, they brought money to buy provisions along the way (12:6; 13:29). Purchasing food was a common assignment given to disciples. Jesus did not fear being defiled by **food** bought in a Samaritan village.

4:9 The author's aside that **Jews do not associate with Samaritans** explained to his Diaspora readership that

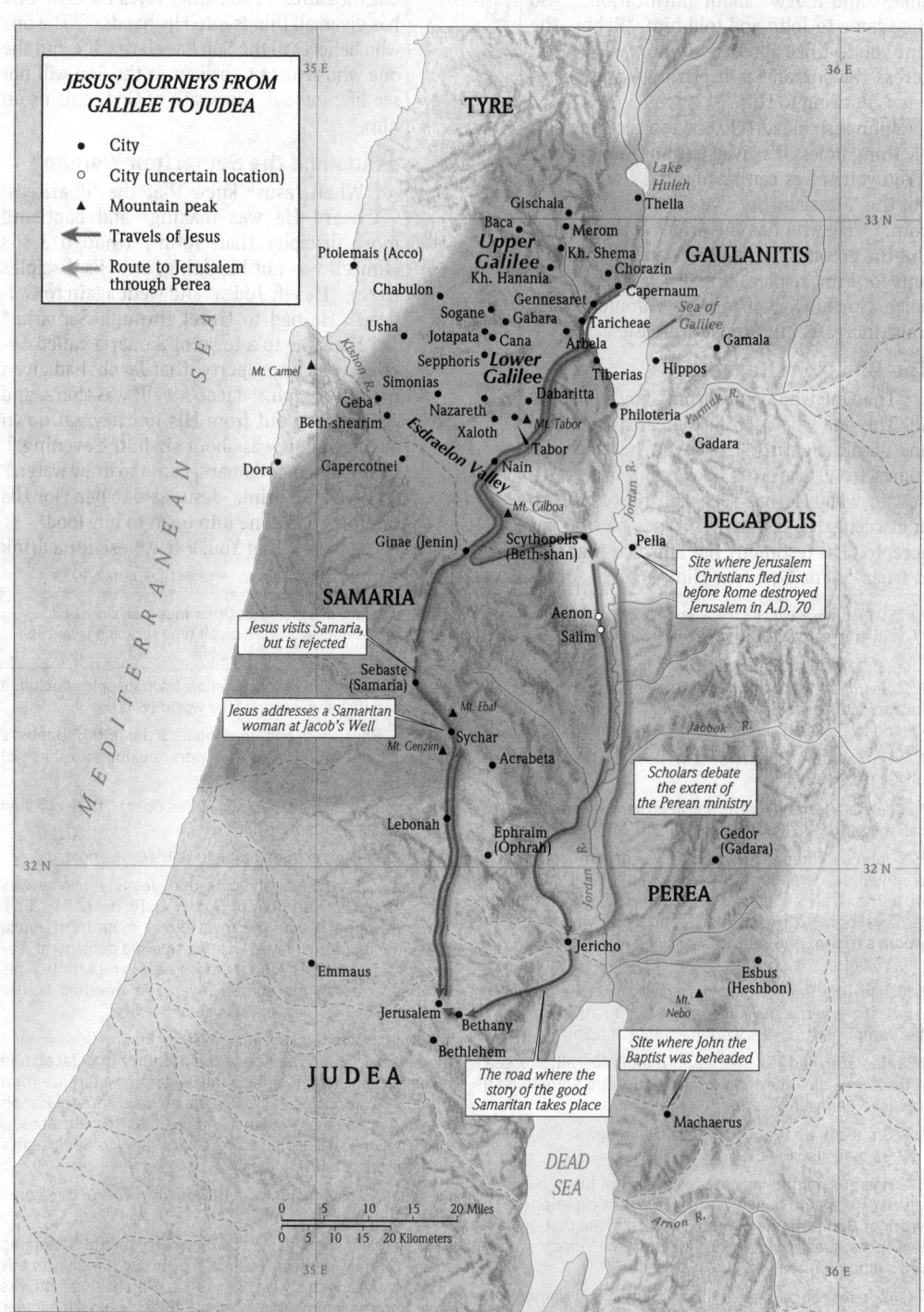

JESUS' JOURNEYS FROM GALILEE TO JUDEA

- ● City
- ○ City (uncertain location)
- ▲ Mountain peak
- ← Travels of Jesus
- ← Route to Jerusalem through Perea

TYRE

Lake Huleh

Gischala
Thella

Baca
Merom
Kh. Shema

Ptolemais (Acco)
Upper Galilee
Chorazin
GAULANITIS

Chabulon
Kh. Hanania
Capernaum

Sogane
Gennesaret
Sea of Galilee

Usha
Gabara
Taricheae
Gamala

Jotapata
Cana
Arbela

Sepphoris
Lower Galilee
Tiberias
Hippos

Mt. Carmel
Simonias
Dabaritta

Geba
Nazareth
Mt. Tabor
Philoteria

Beth-shearim
Xaloth
Tabor
Yarmuk R.

Esdraelon Valley
Nain
Gadara

Dora
Capercotnei
Mt. Gilboa

DECAPOLIS

Ginae (Jenin)
Scythopolis (Beth-shan)
Pella

SAMARIA

Site where Jerusalem Christians fled just before Rome destroyed Jerusalem in A.D. 70

Aenon
Salim

Jesus visits Samaria, but is rejected

Sebaste (Samaria)
Mt. Ebal

Jesus addresses a Samaritan woman at Jacob's Well

Sychar
Mt. Gerizim
Acrabeta

Jabbok R.

Scholars debate the extent of the Perean ministry

Lebonah

Ephraim (Ophrah)

Gedor (Gadara)

Jordan R.

PEREA

Jericho

Emmaus

Esbus (Heshbon)

Mt. Nebo

Jerusalem
Bethany

Bethlehem

Site where John the Baptist was beheaded

JUDEA

The road where the story of the good Samaritan takes place

Machaerus

DEAD SEA

Arnon R.

0   5   10   15   20 Miles
0 5 10 15 20 Kilometers

from me, a •Samaritan^a woman?" she asked Him. For Jews do not associate with^A Samaritans.^B

¹⁰ Jesus answered, "If you knew the gift of God,^b and who is saying to you, 'Give Me a drink,' you would ask Him, and He would give you living water."^c

¹¹ "Sir,"^d said the woman, "You don't even have a bucket, and the well is deep. So where do You get this 'living water'? ¹² You aren't greater than our father Jacob,^e are You? He gave us the well and drank from it himself, as did his sons and livestock."

¹³ Jesus said, "Everyone who drinks from this water will get thirsty again. ¹⁴ But whoever drinks from the water that I will give him will never get thirsty again—ever!^f In fact, the water I will give him will become a well^{C,g} of water springing up within him for eternal life."^h

¹⁵ "Sir," the woman said to Him, "give me this water so I won't get thirsty and come here to draw water."

¹⁶ "Go call your husband," He told her, "and come back here."

¹⁷ "I don't have a husband," she answered.

"You have correctly said, 'I don't have a husband,'" Jesus said. ¹⁸ "For you've had five husbands, and the man you now have is not your husband. What you have said is true."

¹⁹ "Sir," the woman replied, "I see that You are a prophet. ²⁰ Our fathers worshiped on this mountain,^{D,i} yet you Jews say that the place to worship is in Jerusalem."^j

²¹ Jesus told her, "Believe Me, •woman, an hour is coming when you will worship the Father neither on this mountain nor in Jerusalem. ²² You Samaritans^E worship what you do not know. We worship what we do know, because salvation is from the Jews.^k ²³ But an hour is coming, and is now here,^l when the true worshipers will worship the Father in spirit and truth. Yes, the Father wants such people to worship Him. ²⁴ God is spirit,^m and those who worship Him must worship in spirit and truth."ⁿ

²⁵ The woman said to Him, "I know that •Messiah^{F,o} is coming" (who is called Christ^p). "When He comes, He will explain everything to us."

²⁶ "I am He,"^q Jesus told her, "the One speaking to you."

The Ripened Harvest

²⁷ Just then His disciples arrived, and they were amazed that He was talking with a woman. Yet no one said, "What do You want?" or "Why are You talking with her?"

²⁸ Then the woman left her water jar, went into town, and told the men, ²⁹ "Come, see a man who told me everything I ever did! Could

---

^a4:9 Lk 9:52; Ac 1:8
^b4:10 Ac 8:20
^cGn 26:19; Ps 36:7-9; Is 49:10; 55:1; Jr 2:13; Zch 14:8; Jn 7:38; Rv 7:17; 21:6; 22:1,17
^d4:11 Lk 10:1
^e4:12 Mt 1:2; Lk 1:33
^f4:14 Jn 6:35; 7:37; 1Co 4:11; Rv 7:16; 21:6; 22:17
^gJms 3:11
^hJn 12:25; Ac 13:48; Rm 8:2; 1Jn 2:25
ⁱ4:20 Dt 11:29-12:14; 27:3; Jos 24:1
^jMt 23:37
^k4:22 Gn 12:1-7; Is 2:3; Mal 1:11; Mt 15:24; Jn 11:36; Rm 3:1-2; 9:4-5; 15:8-9
^l4:23 Jn 5:25-29; 16:32
^m4:24 Jn 1:33; 2Th 2:10; Jd 20
ⁿ2Th 2:10
^o4:25 Mt 1:17; Eph 5:2
^pEx 29:27; Jn 1:41
^q4:26 Ex 3:14; Ps 45:8; Jn 8:24

---

^A4:9 Or *do not share vessels with*   ^B4:9 Other mss omit *For Jews do not associate with Samaritans.*   ^C4:14 Or *spring*   ^D4:20 Mount Gerizim, where there had been a Samaritan temple that rivaled Jerusalem's   ^E4:22 *Samaritans* is implied since the Gk verb and pronoun are pl.   ^F4:25 In the NT, the word Messiah translates the Gk word *Christos* ("Anointed One"), except here and in Jn 1:41 where it translates *Messias.*

---

rabbis considered Samaritans to be in a continual state of uncleanness.

4:10-15 The references to Jesus as the giver of **living water** involve double meaning (see notes at 3:3-8 and 3:14). Literally, the phrase refers to fresh spring water (Gn 26:19; Lv 14:6). God was known as the source of life (Gn 1:11-12,20-31; 2:7) and "the spring of living water" (Jr 2:13; see Is 12:3). In Nm 20:8-11, water gushed out of the rock, a much-needed provision for the Israelites.

4:11 Jacob's **well** may have been the deepest well in Palestine. It is more than 100 feet **deep** today and was probably deeper in Jesus' day.

4:12 The woman's account of **Jacob** giving the Samaritans the **well** and drinking from it **himself** was based on tradition, not Scripture. The book of Genesis does not record Jacob digging a well, drinking from it, and giving it to his sons.

4:14 The phrase **will become a well of water springing up within him** is reminiscent of Is 12:3 (cp. Is 44:3; 55:1-3).

4:17 While technically truthful, the woman's statement was potentially misleading because it could be taken to imply that she was unattached. Jesus knew the full truth.

4:18 The woman had had **five husbands**—or five "men" (the Gk *aner* can mean "husband" or "man")—having engaged in a series of illicit relationships, and she was not married to her current lover. Sexual relations outside of marriage are forbidden in both Testaments.

4:19 The woman recognized that Jesus knew her life circumstances without apparently having been told by anyone—hence He must be **a prophet** (cp. Lk 7:39).

4:20-21 The **fathers** who worshiped on **this mountain**—a reference to Mount Gerizim (Dt 11:29; 27:12), the OT setting for the pronouncement of blessings for keeping the covenant, and the mountain on which Moses commanded an altar to be built (Dt 27:4-6)—included Abraham (Gn 12:7) and Jacob (Gn 33:20), who built altars in this region.

4:24 Because **God is spirit**, the Israelites were not to make idols "in the shape of anything" as the surrounding nations did (Ex 20:4). Jesus' point was that since God is Spirit, proper worship of Him is also a matter of spirit rather than physical location.

4:25 On **Christ** as a title of Jesus, see note at 1:38.

4:27 The disciples' amazement that Jesus was **talking with a woman** stemmed from the common Jewish teaching that talking too much to a woman, even one's wife, was a waste of time, diverting one's attention from the study of Scripture and reflection on God.

4:28 The woman's **water jar** was probably a large earthenware pitcher carried on the shoulder or hip. She abandoned her original purpose for coming to the well in order to tell her townspeople about Jesus.

4:29 Who told me everything I ever did was an exaggeration

this be the Messiah?"ᵃ ³⁰They left the town and made their way to Him.ᵇ

³¹In the meantime the disciples kept urging Him, "Rabbi,ᶜ eat something."

³²But He said, "I have food to eat that you don't know about."

³³The disciples said to one another, "Could someone have brought Him something to eat?"

³⁴"My food is to do the will of Himᵈ who sent Meᵉ and to finish His work,"ᶠ Jesus told them. ³⁵"Don't you say, 'There are still four more months, then comes the harvest'? Listen to what I'm telling you: OpenᴬA your eyes and look at the fields, for they are readyᴮB for harvest. ³⁶The reaper is already receiving pay and gathering fruit for eternal life,ᵍ so the sower and reaper can rejoice together. ³⁷For in this case the saying is true: 'One sows and another reaps.'ʰ ³⁸I sent you to reap what you didn't labor for; others have labored, and you have benefited fromᶜC their labor."

The Savior of the World

³⁹Now many Samaritansⁱ from that town be-

lieved in Him because of what the woman saidᴰD when she testified,ʲ "He told me everything I ever did." ⁴⁰Therefore, when the Samaritans came to Him,ᵏ they asked Him to stay with them, and He stayed there two days. ⁴¹Many more believed because of what He said.ᴱE ⁴²And they told the woman, "We no longer believe because of what you said, for we have heard for ourselves and know that this really is the Saviorˡ of the world."ᶠF

A Galilean Welcome

⁴³After two days He left there for Galilee.ᵐ ⁴⁴Jesus Himself testifiedⁿ that a prophet has no honor in his own country.ᵒ ⁴⁵Whenᵖ they entered Galilee, the Galileansᑫ welcomed Him because they had seen everything He did in Jerusalemʳ during the festival.ˢ For they also had gone to the festival.

The Second Sign: Healing an Official's Son

⁴⁶Then He went again to Canaᵗ of Galilee, where He had turned the water into wine.

a 4:29 Mt 1:17
b 4:30 Mk 1:45
c 4:31 Jn 11:8
d 4:34 Eph 1:9; 1 Jn 2:17
e Jn 5:30
f Jn 5:36
g 4:36 Mk 10:17; Jn 12:25; Ac 13:48
h 4:37 Lv 26:16; Dt 20:6; Jb 31:8; Mc 6:15; Mt 25:24; Lk 19:21
i 4:39 Lk 9:52; Ac 1:8
j Jn 15:26; Ac 26:5
k 4:40 Mk 1:45
l 4:42 2Pt 3:18
m 4:43 Is 9:1-2; Mt 17:22
n 4:44 Jn 15:26; Ac 26:5
o Mt 13:57; Mk 6:4; Lk 4:24
p 4:45 Mt 4:17; Mk 1:14-15
q Mt 26:69; Mk 14:70; Lk 13:1-2; 22:59; 23:6; Ac 1:11; 2:7; 5:37
r Mt 23:37
s Jn 2:23; 5:1
t 4:46 Jn 2:1,11; 21:2

A 4:35 Lit *Raise* B 4:35 Lit *white* C 4:38 Lit *you have entered into* D 4:39 Lit *because of the woman's word* E 4:41 Lit *because of His word* F 4:42 Other mss add *the Messiah*

—but understandable in light of her excitement. See note at verse 39.

4:31 Rabbi, eat something reflected the disciples' customary concern for their Master's well-being. Jesus had been worn out from His journey before His conversation with the Samaritan woman (see note at v. 6). He still had not had anything to eat.

4:32-34 The accomplishment of Jesus' mission was more important to Him than physical food (Mt 6:25; Mk 3:20-21). His statement may echo Dt 8:3 (cp. Mt 4:4; Lk 4:4). On Jesus' **work**, see note at 17:4.

4:35 In agriculture there is always a considerable separation in time between sowing and harvesting. The disciples needed to realize that with the coming of Jesus, sowing (preaching) and reaping (conversions) coincided. The immediate reference may be to the approaching Samaritans (vv. 39-42).

4:36 This saying is reminiscent of Am 9:13, which depicted the prosperity of the new age. Hence Jesus claimed that He was ushering in the messianic age, a time of swift, abundant harvest.

4:37 This saying may allude to Mc 6:15, "You will sow but not reap." Yet Jesus' adaptation left judgment unmentioned. The others who had labored were Jesus and His predecessors, most recently John the Baptist, the final prophet associated with the OT era. Jesus' followers were the beneficiaries of their work and would bring in the harvest.

4:39 That town refers to Sychar (see note at v. 5). Though people would naturally be skeptical about religious pronouncements made by an immoral woman such as this Samaritan, her sincerity (and perhaps a noticeable change in her morality) convinced her townspeople to take her seriously as she spoke about Jesus.

4:40 Jesus obviously did not share in the Jewish bias against

Samaritans since He spent **two days** with them (see notes at vv. 4 and 9).

4:41-42 As others had done (1:40-41,45), the woman brought people to Jesus so they could see for themselves. Ultimately, it was on the basis of a personal encounter with Jesus that they believed. His large harvest among the Samaritans marked the first sign of the universal scope of His saving mission (10:16; 11:51-52). The early church also undertook a Samaritan mission (Ac 8:4-25; cp. Ac 1:8). In fact, the pattern of Jesus' mission from Judea (Nicodemus, Jn 3), to Samaria (Jn 4), to the Gentiles (vv. 46-54; cp. 12:20-33), anticipated the post-Pentecost mission of the early church (Ac 1:8).

4:43-54 The healing of the royal official's son completes the "Cana cycle" in John's Gospel, which spans from 2:1 to 4:54 and begins and ends with a "sign" performed by Jesus in Cana of Galilee (2:11; 4:54; see note at 2:11). The present sign is a rare instance of a long-distance healing performed by Jesus. The story resembles that of the Gentile centurion in Mt 8:5-13 and Lk 7:2-10, but this is not the same incident. All three signs featured in the Cana cycle (the turning of water into wine, the temple clearing, and the healing of the royal official's son) set forth Jesus as the Messiah, who showed convincing proofs of His divine commission.

4:43 Jesus **left there** [Sychar] and entered **Galilee**. From Sychar to Cana was about 40 miles, a trip of two or three days.

4:44 On a prophet's lack of **honor in his own country**, compare Mt 13:57; Lk 4:24.

4:45 Jesus' Galilean welcome must be understood in light of verses 44 and 48 (cp. 2:23-25).

4:46 The **royal official** was probably a Gentile centurion, possibly in service to Herod Antipas (Mk 6:14). His son's illness involved fever (Jn 4:52) and appears to have been terminal (vv. 47,49).

There was a certain royal official whose son was ill at Capernaum.[a, 47] When this man heard that Jesus had come from Judea[b] into Galilee, he went to Him and pleaded with Him to come down and heal his son, for he was about to die.

[48] Jesus told him, "Unless you people see signs and wonders,[c] you will not believe."[d]

[49] "Sir,"[e] the official said to Him, "come down before my boy dies!"

[50] "Go," Jesus told him, "your son will live." The man believed what[A] Jesus said to him and departed.

[51] While he was still going down, his •slaves met him saying that his boy was alive. [52] He asked them at what time he got better. "Yesterday at seven in the morning[B] the fever left him," they answered. [53] The father[f] realized this was the very hour at which Jesus had told him, "Your son will live." Then he himself believed, along with his whole household.

[54] This, therefore, was the second sign[g] Jesus performed after He came from Judea to Galilee.[h]

The Third Sign: Healing the Sick

5 After this, a Jewish festival took place, and Jesus went up to Jerusalem.[i] [2] By the Sheep Gate[j] in Jerusalem there is a pool, called Bethesda[C] in •Hebrew, which has five colonnades.[D] [3] Within these lay a large number of the sick—blind, lame, and paralyzed [—waiting for the moving of the water, [4] because an angel would go down into the pool from time to time and stir up the water. Then the first one who got in after the water was stirred up recovered from whatever ailment he had].[E]

[5] One man was there who had been sick for 38 years. [6] When Jesus saw him lying there and knew he had already been there a long time,[k] He said to him, "Do you want to get well?"

[7] "Sir,"[l] the sick man answered, "I don't have a man to put me into the pool when the water is stirred up, but while I'm coming, someone goes down ahead of me."

[8] "Get up," Jesus told him, "pick up your mat and walk!" [9] Instantly the man got well, picked up his mat, and started to walk.

Now that day was the Sabbath,[m] [10] so the

a4:46 Lk 10:15
b4:47 Lk 1:5
c4:48 Ex 7:3-4; Mk 13:22; Jn 2:23-25; 6:26
d Jn 3:16; 6:64; 20:25
e4:49 Lk 10:1
f4:53 Lk 11:11; Col 3:21
g4:54 Jn 2:11
hMt 17:22
i5:1 Mt 23:37
j5:2 Neh 3:1,32; 12:39
k5:6 Is 46:10; Zch 14:7; Jn 5:6; 6:6; 8:14; 9:3; 11:11-15; 13:1-3,11
l5:7 Lk 10:1
m5:9 Mk 2:23

A4:50 Lit the word　　B4:52 Or seven in the evening; lit at the seventh hour; see note at Jn 1:39; an alt time reckoning would be at one in the afternoon　　C5:2 Other mss read Bethzatha; other mss read Bethsaida　　D5:2 Rows of columns supporting a roof
E5:3-4 Other mss omit bracketed text

4:47 The distance from Capernaum to Cana was about 15 miles. The journey was mostly uphill (see note at 2:12). Conversely, from Cana Jesus would **come down** to Capernaum.

4:48 The expression **signs and wonders** probably harks back to the series of miracles performed by Moses at the exodus. Jesus rebuked people for their dependence on the miraculous; for John, miracles were "signs" pointing to Jesus' messianic identity (see note at 2:11).

4:49-50 This is a rare instance of a long-distance miracle. A similar incident is described in Mt 8:5-13 and Lk 7:1-10. The words **your son will live** may recall Elijah's statement in 1Kg 17:23. If so, Jesus' messianic activity is compared with the healing ministry of Elijah (Lk 4:23-27).

4:54 The **second sign** refers to signs done in Cana (see note at 2:11); in the interim, Jesus had performed signs in Jerusalem (2:23; 3:2; 4:45). Thus John closed the cycle of Jesus' first ministry circuit, starting and ending in Cana of Galilee (see note at vv. 43-54).

5:1-47 The "festival cycle" in John's Gospel spans from 5:1 to 10:42 and is characterized by escalating conflict between Jesus and the Jewish authorities. This cycle begins with yet another sign—Jesus' healing of a lame man at a feast in Jerusalem (see note at 2:11). The fact that the healing took place on a Sabbath provoked a major controversy. Jesus was accused of breaking the law by telling the man to pick up his mat (5:8-10). The controversy escalated to the point where the Jewish leaders charged Jesus with blasphemy for claiming to continue the work of God (v. 18). This provided an occasion for Jesus to defend His ministry and enumerate evidences for His identity.

5:1 After this marks the passing of an indefinite period of time. Up to a year and a half may have passed after the last recorded festival, the Passover, when Jesus cleared the temple and met with Nicodemus. The unnamed **Jewish festival** may have been the Feast of Tabernacles. On Jesus **went up to Jerusalem**, see note at 2:13.

5:2 Bethesda may mean "house of mercy," a fitting term given the desperate state of the people who lay there hoping for a miraculous cure; see note at 1:38.

5:3 Most likely official Judaism did not approve of the superstition associated with the alleged healing powers of the pool of Bethesda (see note at v. 7).

5:5 Sick probably means "paralyzed" or "lame" here (the Gk word expresses "disabled"). We do not know the invalid's age or how long he had been lying there, but he had been crippled for **38 years**, which is longer than many people in antiquity lived and roughly as long as Israel's wilderness wanderings (Dt 2:14). On John's penchant for selecting "difficult" and striking miracles, see note at 2:11. For a similar healing, see Mt 9:1-8.

5:6 Knew probably indicates supernatural knowledge (see notes at 1:48 and 4:19). Jesus' conversation with the man may have been occasioned by his request for alms (Ac 3:1-5).

5:7 Superstition attributed the stirring of the **water** to the actions of an angel (see the addition of v. 4 in some later mss).

5:8-9 A **mat** (Gk krabattos; as distinguished from "bed," Gk klinarion, e.g., Ac 5:15) was the poor man's bedding. Made of straw, it could be rolled up and carried. We are not told this day was **the Sabbath** until the miracle was performed. This sets the context for the tensions with the unbelieving Jews (cp. 9:14).

5:10 In a petty display of religious legalism, the Jewish leaders objected to the man's picking up his **mat** on the

ʼJews[a] said to the man who had been healed, "This is the Sabbath![b] It's illegal for you to pick up your mat."

[11] He replied, "The man who made me well[c] told me, 'Pick up your mat and walk.'"

[12] "Who is this man who told you, 'Pick up your mat and walk'?" they asked. [13] But the man who was cured did not know who it was,[d] because Jesus had slipped away into the crowd that was there.[A]

[14] After this, Jesus found him in the •temple complex[e] and said to him, "See, you are well. Do not sin anymore, so that something worse doesn't happen to you." [15] The man went and reported to the Jews that it was Jesus who had made him well.[f]

Honoring the Father and the Son

[16] Therefore, the Jews began persecuting[g] Jesus[B] because He was doing these things on the Sabbath.[h] [17] But Jesus responded to them, "My Father[i] is still working, and I am working also." [18] This is why the Jews began trying all the more to kill Him.[j] Not only was He breaking the Sabbath, but He was even calling God His own Father, making Himself equal with God.

[19] Then Jesus replied, "'I assure you: The Son is not able to do anything on His own, but only what He sees the Father doing. For whatever the Father[c] does, the Son also does these things in the same way.[k] [20] For the Father loves the Son and shows Him everything He is doing, and He will show Him greater works[l] than these so that you will be amazed. [21] And just as the Father raises[m] the dead and gives them life, so the Son also gives life to anyone He wants to.[n] [22] The Father,[o] in fact, judges no one but has given all judgment to the Son, [23] so that all people will honor the Son just as they honor the Father.[p] Anyone who does not honor the Son does not honor the Father who sent Him.[q]

Life and Judgment

[24] "I assure you: Anyone who hears My word and believes Him who sent Me has eternal life[r] and will not come under judgment but has passed from death to life.

[25] "I assure you: An hour is coming, and is now here,[s] when the dead will hear the voice of the Son of God, and those who hear will live.[t] [26] For just as the Father has life in Himself, so also He has granted to the Son[u] to have life in

Cross references
[a] 5:10 Jn 11:36
[b] Lk 14:3
[c] 5:11 Ti 2:8
[d] 5:13 Jn 7:28
[e] 5:14 Ac 21:26
[f] 5:15 Ti 2:8
[g] 5:16 Lk 6:28; 2Tm 3:12
[h] Lk 13:10
[i] 5:17 Mt 5:16; 11:27; Jn 8:42
[j] 5:18 Mt 12:14; 26:4; 27:1; Mk 3:6; 14:1; Lk 6:11; Jn 7:1,19; 10:33; 11:53
[k] 5:19 Jn 3:35; 6:38; 7:16,28; 8:26-42; 10:18,30,36-38; 12:49-50; 14:9,24,31; 15:9-10; 16:15; 17:9-10
[l] 5:20 Heb 3:9; Rv 15:3
[m] 5:21 Mk 9:27; Jn 2:19
[n] Jn 11:25-26
[o] 5:22 Mt 11:27
[p] 5:23 Jn 15:23
[q] Lk 10:16
[r] 5:24 Jn 6:53; 12:25; Ac 13:48; 1Jn 2:25
[s] 5:25 Jn 4:23
[t] Php 1:21
[u] 5:26 Jn 5:19; Col 1:19

[A] 5:13 Lit slipped away, there being a crowd in that place   [B] 5:16 Other mss add and trying to kill Him   [C] 5:19 Lit whatever that One

---

Sabbath. While not actually breaking any biblical Sabbath regulations, the man was violating a rabbinical code that prohibited the carrying of an object "from one domain into another" (m. Sabb. 7:2). Hence Jesus was accused of enticing the man to sin.

5:14 Jesus met the man again in **the temple complex** (see note at 2:14), a short distance from the site of his healing. Jesus' words may imply that the man's suffering was due to sin but do not suggest that all suffering is caused by personal sin (see note at 9:2). **Something worse** may refer to eternal judgment for sin (vv. 22-30).

5:17 While Gn 2:2-3 teaches that God rested (Hb shabath) on the seventh day of creation, Jewish rabbis agreed that God continually upheld the universe, yet without breaking the Sabbath. If God was above Sabbath regulations, so was Jesus (Mt 12:1-14). What is more, even the Jews made exceptions to the rule prohibiting work on the Sabbath, most notably in cases where circumcision occurred on a Sabbath (Jn 7:23).

5:18 Making Himself equal with God seemed to violate the OT teaching that there is only one God (Dt 6:4). Thus the Jewish leaders accused Jesus of blasphemy, which became the primary charge leveled against Jesus before Pilate (Jn 19:7).

5:19-26 On Jesus' relationship to the **Father** in these verses, see note at 3:16-18.

5:19 Jesus' claim that **the Son is not able to do anything on His own** echoes Moses' affirmation that "the Lord sent me to do all these things and that it was not of my own will" (Nm 16:28).

5:21 Jesus' statement that **the Son also gives life to anyone He wants** is significant since raising the dead and giving life are the prerogatives of God alone (Dt 32:39; 1Sm 2:6; 2Kg 5:7).

5:22 Like life (v. 21), **judgment** is the exclusive prerogative of God (Gn 18:25; Jdg 11:27).

5:23 Jesus characterized Himself as God's authorized messenger. This is similar to Moses and the prophets, who served as God's agents and spokesmen. Of designated messengers (Hb shaliach), Jews held that "a man's agent is like the man himself" (m. Ber. 5:5). The statement **so that all people will honor the Son just as they honor the Father** in effect established Jesus' right to be worshiped and amounted to a claim of deity.

5:25 Jesus' words are reminiscent of Ezekiel's vision of the valley of dry bones (Ezk 37).

5:26 The claim that Jesus had **life in Himself** echoes the affirmation in the prologue of John's Gospel that "life was in Him [Jesus]" (1:4; see note at 14:6). It is further supported by Jesus' statement, "I am the resurrection and the life" (11:25). Because He is "the life" and has life in Himself, Jesus is able to give life (abundant life now; eternal life in the future) to all who place their trust in Him (3:16; 10:10).

5:27 Because He is the Son of Man echoes Dn 7:13.

5:28-29 Compare these verses with Dn 12:2.

5:30 On **I can do nothing on My own**, see notes at verses 19 and 23.

5:31-47 Jesus spoke of several witnesses who bore testimony about Him: John the Baptist (vv. 32-36; cp. 1:7-8,15,19,32-34; 3:26); His own works (5:36; cp. 10:25,32,37-38; 15:24); God the Father (5:37-38; 8:18); and the Scriptures (5:39), particularly those written by Moses (vv. 45-47). Elsewhere in this Gospel, reference is made to the witness of Jesus Himself (3:11,32; 8:14,18; 18:37), the Spirit (chaps. 14-16, esp. 15:26), the disciples (15:27), and the fourth evangelist (19:35; 21:24). The "witness" theme in John's Gospel is part of a larger "trial motif." This reverses the world's perspec-

Himself. [27] And He has granted Him the right to pass judgment,[a] because He is the ·Son of Man.[b] [28] Do not be amazed at this, because a time is coming when all who are in the graves will hear His voice [29] and come out—those who have done good things, to the resurrection of life, but those who have done wicked things, to the resurrection of judgment.

[30] "I can do nothing on My own. I judge only as I hear, and My judgment[c] is righteous,[d] because I do not seek My own will, but the will of Him who sent Me.[e]

Four Witnesses to Jesus

[31] "If I testify about Myself, My testimony is not valid.[A] [32] There is Another who testifies about Me, and I know that the testimony He gives about Me is valid.[B,f] [33] You have sent messengers to John, and he has testified to the truth.[g] [34] I don't receive man's testimony, but I say these things so that you may be saved. [35] John[C,h] was a burning and shining lamp,[i] and for a time you were willing to enjoy his light.[j]

[36] "But I have a greater testimony than John's because of the works that the Father has given Me to accomplish.[k] These very works I am doing testify about Me that the Father has sent[l] Me. [37] The Father who sent Me has Himself testified[m] about Me. You have not heard His voice

at any time, and you haven't seen His form.[n] [38] You don't have His word living in you, because you don't believe the One He sent. [39] You pore over[D] the Scriptures[o] because you think you have eternal life in them, yet they testify about Me.[p] [40] And you are not willing[q] to come to Me[r] so that you may have life.

[41] "I do not accept glory[s] from men, [42] but I know you—that you have no love for God[t] within you. [43] I have come in My Father's name,[u] yet you don't accept Me.[v] If someone else comes in his own name, you will accept him. [44] How can you believe? While accepting glory from one another, you don't seek the glory that comes from the only[w] God.[x] [45] Do not think that I will accuse you to the Father. Your accuser is Moses,[y] on whom you have set your hope. [46] For if you believed Moses, you would believe Me, because he wrote about Me. [47] But if you don't believe his writings,[z] how will you believe My words?"[aa]

The Fourth Sign: Feeding 5,000

6 After[ab] this, Jesus crossed the Sea of Galilee[ac] (or Tiberias[ad]). [2] And a huge crowd was

[a]5:27 2Th 1:5
[b]Mk 2:10; Heb 2:6; Rv 1:13; 14:14
[c]5:30 Mt 12:41; 2Th 1:5
[d]Mt 6:33; Jn 8:16
[e]Mt 26:39; Jn 4:34; 6:38; 7:16-18; 8:28; 14:10; Rm 8:27; Eph 1:9
[f]5:32 1Jn 5:20
[g]5:33 Ps 119:142; Jn 14:6
[h]5:35 Mk 1:4
[i]2Sm 21:17; Mt 5:14-15; Lk 12:35; 2Pt 1:19; Rv 21:23
[j]Ps 36:9; Jn 12:46
[k]5:36 Jn 15:24
[l]Mk 9:37; Jn 1:6,33
[m]5:37 1Jn 5:9
[n]Ex 33:11; Dt 4:12; Is 6:1; Lk 3:22; Jn 1:18; 6:46-47; 14:9; 1Tm 1:17
[o]5:39 Mt 26:54; 2Pt 1:20
[p]Lk 24:27,44; Ac 13:27
[q]5:40 Lk 13:34
[r]Lk 14:26
[s]5:41 Jn 17:24; Php 3:19; 1Pt 5:4
[t]5:42 Lk 10:27; 11:42; 1Jn 4:20

[u]5:43 Jn 10:25; 14:13; Ac 15:14; Rv 14:1　[v]Mk 4:16; Jn 1:12; 12:48; 13:20; 17:8　[w]5:44 Dt 6:4; Jn 17:3; Rm 3:30; 16:27; 1Tm 1:17; 6:15-16; Jd 25; Rv 15:4　[x]1Th 2:4　[y]5:45 Ps 77:20; Mt 8:4; Heb 3:2　[z]5:47 Mt 26:54; Rm 1:2　[aa]Lk 16:29-31　[ab]6:1-15 Mt 14:13-21; Mk 6:30-44; Lk 9:10-17　[ac]6:1 Mk 1:16　[ad]Jn 6:23; 21:1

[A]5:31 Or *not true*　[B]5:32 Or *true*　[C]5:35 Lit *That man*　[D]5:39 In Gk this could be a command: *Pore over . . .*

---

tive of Jesus being put on trial. It becomes clear that it is really the world, not Jesus, that is on trial, with a multitude of witnesses bearing testimony to His true identity as Messiah. This section also emphasizes the world's guilt for rejecting Jesus.

5:31 Jesus did not deny His reliability. He was alluding to the importance of having multiple witnesses (Dt 17:6; 19:15; cp. Nm 35:30).

5:32 Jesus was speaking of God the Father (v. 37) when He said, **There is Another who testifies about Me**. Avoiding God's name was a common way of showing reverence.

5:33 On Jesus as the **truth**, see note at 14:6 and the echo of this passage before Pilate (18:37). Compare 3Jn 3,12.

5:35 Jesus' characterization of John the Baptist as **a burning and shining lamp** seems to echo Ps 132:17 where God will "set up a lamp" for His Anointed One. John was a "lamp" but not the Light (Jn 1:7-9); his witness was comparatively small and temporary. The past tense may imply that John was now dead or imprisoned. See notes at 3:29 and 3:30.

5:37 The Father . . . has Himself testified may refer to the voice at Jesus' baptism (Mt 3:17), a passage not explicitly mentioned in John, though the primary reference may be to God's witness in Scripture (Jn 5:45-47; cp. Lk 24:27,44; Ac 13:27; 1Jn 5:9). Jesus' affirmation that His hearers had not **heard** God's **voice** or **seen His form** (cp. 1:18) seems to allude to wilderness Israel, which received the law at Mount Sinai without hearing God's voice or seeing His form.

5:38 Have His word living in you recalls the depiction of a God-fearing person who has the word of God living in his heart (Jos 1:8-9; Ps 119:11).

5:39 Scripture itself does not impart life, but it witnesses to the One who does—Jesus (cp. vv. 46-47).

5:43 Jesus predicted the proliferation of false Christs as a sign of the end times (Mt 24:5). The first-century Jewish historian Josephus reported a string of messianic pretenders in the years before A.D. 70.

5:45-47 Jesus' appeal to **Moses** prepares the way for chapter 6, where Jesus is presented as the new Moses providing the new "bread from heaven." The reference to Moses as a witness or **accuser** against the Jews may allude to Dt 31:26-27 where the law was invoked as a witness against the Israelites. The reference to Moses writing about Jesus in Jn 5:46 may allude to the Pentateuch (attributed to Moses) or to the prediction of a "prophet like" Moses in Dt 18:15.

6:1-71 The feeding of the crowds (cp. Mt 14:13-23; Mk 6:30-44; Lk 9:10-17) is yet another of Jesus' messianic "signs" (see note at Jn 2:11), aligning Jesus with God's provision of manna to wilderness Israel through Moses (6:30-31). In response to the people's demand that He perform a sign greater than Moses' signs at the exodus, Jesus claimed to be the "bread of life" that provides spiritual nourishment for all who believe in Him (eat and drink of Him). This controversial statement proved to be a watershed moment in Jesus' ministry, because many of His followers abandoned Him at this point (vv. 60-66). But the Twelve, through Peter their spokesman, reaffirmed their allegiance (vv. 68-69).

6:1 After this again indicates the passing of an indefinite period of time (5:1). Half a year may have passed since the previous event. Sea of **Tiberias** (cp. 21:1) was an alternate name for the Sea of Galilee. Herod Antipas founded Tiberias, the largest city on the Sea of Galilee, in honor of his

following Him because they saw the signs that He was performing by healing the sick. ³So Jesus went up a mountain and sat down there with His disciples.

⁴Now the *Passover, a Jewish festival, was near. ⁵Therefore, when Jesus looked up and noticed a huge crowd coming toward Him,ᵃ He asked Philip,ᵇ "Where will we buy bread so these people can eat?" ⁶ He asked this to test him,ᶜ for He Himself knew what He was going to do.

⁷Philip answered, "Two hundred *denariiᵈ worth of bread wouldn't be enough for each of them to have a little."

⁸One of His disciples, Andrew,ᵉ Simonᶠ Peter'sᵍ brother, said to Him, ⁹"There's a boy here who has five barley loaves and two fish—but what are they for so many?"

¹⁰Then Jesus said, "Have the people sit down."

There was plenty of grass in that place, so they sat down. The men numbered about 5,000.ʰ ¹¹Then Jesus took the loaves, and after giving thanks He distributed them to those who were seated—so also with the fish, as much as they wanted.ⁱ

¹²When they were full, He told His disciples, "Collect the leftovers so that nothing is wasted."ʲ ¹³So they collected them and filled 12 baskets with the pieces from the five barley loaves that were left over by those who had eaten.

¹⁴When the people saw the signᴬ He had done, they said, "This really is the Prophetᵏ who was to comeˡ into the world!"ᵐ ¹⁵Therefore, when Jesus knew that they were about to come and take Him by force to make Him king,ⁿ He withdrew againᴮ to the mountain by Himself.

The Fifth Sign: Walking on Water

¹⁶Whenᵒ evening came, His disciples went down to the sea, ¹⁷got into a boat, and started across the sea to Capernaum.ᵖ Darkness had already set in, but Jesus had not yet come to them. ¹⁸Then a high wind arose, and the sea began to churn. ¹⁹After they had rowed about three or four miles,ᶜ they saw Jesus walking on the sea. He was coming near the boat, and they were afraid.

²⁰But He said to them, "It is I.ᴰ,ᑫ Don't be

Cross-references:

ᵃ6:5 Mk 1:45
ᵇMk 3:18
ᶜ6:6 Ex 15:25
ᵈ6:7 Mt 18:28
ᵉ6:8 Mt 4:18; 10:2; Mk 1:16,29; 3:18; 13:3; Lk 6:14; Jn 1:40,44; 12:22; Ac 1:13
ᶠMt 16:17
ᵍLk 6:14; Ac 10:32
ʰ6:10 Mt 14:21
ⁱ6:11 2Kg 4:42-44
ʲ6:12 Lk 15:4
ᵏ6:14 Dt 18:15
ˡMt 11:3; Lk 7:19-20; Rm 5:14; Heb 10:37
ᵐJn 18:37
ⁿ6:15 Jn 19:21
ᵒ6:16-21 Mt 14:22-36; Mk 6:45-56
ᵖ6:17 Lk 10:15
ᑫ6:20 Ex 3:14; Ps 45:8; Jn 8:24

Footnotes:

ᴬ6:14 Other mss read *signs*   ᴮ6:15 A previous withdrawal is mentioned in Mk 6:31-32, an event that occurred just before the feeding of the 5,000.   ᶜ6:19 Lit *25 or 30 stadia*; 1 *stadion* = 600 feet   ᴰ6:20 Lit *I am*

Study notes:

patron, the Roman emperor Tiberius (A.D. 14–37). The name gained currency toward the end of the first century.

6:3 Mountain may not refer to a specific mountain. It could designate the hill country east of the lake, known today as the Golan Heights (Mt 14:23; Mk 6:46). Like other rabbis, Jesus **sat down** to teach (Mt 5:1; Mk 4:1; 9:35; Lk 4:20), although teaching is not mentioned here.

6:4 This is the second of three Passovers mentioned by John, and the only one Jesus spent in Galilee (see note at 2:13).

6:5 The **huge crowd** apparently walked several miles around the north side of the lake and caught up with Jesus and the disciples. **Philip** would be the natural choice for Jesus' question since he, like Andrew (v. 8) and Peter, was a native of nearby Bethsaida (see note at 1:44). Jesus' question echoes Moses' query in the wilderness: "Where can I get meat to give all these people?" (Nm 11:13). Other parallels between Jn 6 and Nm 11 are the people's grumbling (Nm 11:1; Jn 6:41,43); the description of the manna (Nm 11:7-9; Jn 6:31); the reference to the eating of meat/Jesus' "flesh" (Nm 11:13; Jn 6:51); and the overabundance of the provision (Nm 11:22; Jn 6:7-9).

6:7 Two hundred denarii was roughly eight months' wages, since one denarius was about one day's pay for a common laborer (12:5; Mt 20:2).

6:9 Boy may refer to a kid, a teenager, or even someone in his early twenties. The same word is used to refer to young Joseph in Gn 37:30 and Daniel and his friends in Dn 1. **Barley** was common food for the poor (the well-to-do preferred wheat bread); the **fish** were probably dried or preserved, perhaps pickled. In a similar account, Elisha fed 100 men with 20 barley loaves (2Kg 4:42-44).

6:10 The men numbered **about 5,000,** plus women and children (Mt 14:21), totaling perhaps as many as 15,000 people.

Plenty of grass may allude to the messianic age (10:9-10; Ps 23:2). Mark (Mk 6:39-40) mentioned that the grass was green, which points to springtime.

6:11 A common Jewish thanksgiving prayer was, "Blessed are you, O Lord our God, King of the universe, who brings forth bread from the earth."

6:12 Jesus' words echo Ruth 2:14: "She ate and was satisfied and had some left over." Jesus took the same care in providing for those whom the Father gave Him (Jn 10:28-29; 17:11-12,15).

6:13 The number of **baskets** may allude to Jesus' symbolic restoration of the 12 tribes of Israel.

6:14 The reference to **the Prophet who was to come into the world** alludes to Dt 18:15,18 (see notes at Jn 1:19-21 and 7:40-41).

6:15 On Jesus' withdrawal to the **mountain,** see note at v. 3.

6:16-24 Jesus' walking across the Sea of Galilee may echo Job 9:8 (LXX) where God is said to walk on the waters.

6:16-17 The disciples were on the eastern side of the lake, and they ventured to row the six or seven miles back **across the sea to Capernaum** on the western side.

6:19 They had rowed about **three or four miles.** If the feeding of the crowd occurred on the eastern shore, the shortest distance to Capernaum would have been five to six miles.

6:20 It is I may have overtones of epiphany (cp. Ex 3:14; see note at Jn 6:35,48). The statement may allude to Ps 77:16,19, describing God's manifestation to Israel during the exodus.

6:21 The reference to the boat reaching the shore **at once** may allude to Ps 107:23-32 (esp. 6:29-30).

6:23-24 Tiberias was and is the chief city on the western side of the lake (see note at v. 1). Whereas **Capernaum** was

afraid!" [21] Then they were willing to take Him on board, and at once the boat was at the shore where they were heading.

The Bread of Life

[22] The next day, the crowd that had stayed on the other side of the sea knew there had been only one boat.[A,a] They also knew that Jesus had not boarded the boat with His disciples, but that His disciples had gone off alone. [23] Some boats from Tiberias[b] came near the place where they ate the bread after the Lord gave thanks. [24] When the crowd saw that neither Jesus nor His disciples were there, they got into the boats and went to Capernaum looking for Jesus.

[25] When they found Him on the other side of the sea, they said to Him, "'Rabbi,[c] when did You get here?"

[26] Jesus answered, "'I assure you: You are looking for Me, not because you saw[B] the signs, but because you ate the loaves and were filled. [27] Don't work for the food that perishes[d] but for the food that lasts for eternal life,[e] which the •Son of Man[f] will give you, because God the Father[g] has set His seal of approval on Him."

[28] "What can we do to perform the works of God?" they asked.

[29] Jesus replied, "This is the work[h] of God —that you believe in the One He has sent."[i]

[30] "What sign then are You going to do so we may see and believe You?" they asked. "What are You going to perform? [31] Our fathers ate the manna[j] in the wilderness,[k] just as it is written: **He gave them bread from heaven to eat.**"[C,D,l]

[32] Jesus said to them, "I assure you: Moses[m] didn't give you the bread from heaven, but My Father gives you the real bread from heaven. [33] For the bread of God is the One who comes down from heaven and gives life to the world."

[34] Then they said, "Sir, give us this bread always!"

[35] "I am[n] the bread of life," Jesus told them. "No one who comes to Me[o] will ever be hungry,[p] and no one who believes in Me[q] will ever be thirsty[r] again. [36] But as I told you, you've seen Me,[E] and yet you do not believe. [37] Everyone the Father gives Me will come to Me, and the one who comes to Me I will never cast out.[s] [38] For I have come down from heaven,[t] not to do My will, but the will of Him[u] who sent Me. [39] This is the will of Him who sent Me: that I should lose none of those He has given Me but should raise[v] them up on the last day. [40] For this is the will of My Father:[w] that everyone who sees the Son[x] and believes in Him

Cross references

a 6:22 Jn 21:8
b 6:23 Jn 6:1; 21:1
c 6:25 Jn 11:8
d 6:27 Is 55:2
e Jn 12:25; Ac 13:48; 1Jn 2:25
f Dn 7:13; Mk 2:10; Jn 6:53,62
g 1Co 8:6; 15:24; Eph 5:20
h 6:29 Jn 5:36
i Mk 9:37; Jn 1:6
j 6:31 Ex 16:31
k Rv 12:6
l Ex 16:4,15; Ps 78:24
m 6:32 Ps 77:20; Mt 8:4; Heb 3:2
n 6:35 Jn 8:24
o Lk 14:26
p Jn 4:14; Rv 7:16
q Mt 18:6; Mk 9:42; Jn 6:35; 7:38; 11:25-26; 12:44,46; 14:12; 16:9
r Jn 7:37
s 6:37 Mt 24:22
t 6:38 Ex 3:8; Pr 30:4; Dn 4:13,23; Mt 28:2; Jn 1:51; 3:13; Eph 4:10; Rv 10:1; 18:1; 20:1
u Eph 1:9; 1Jn 2:17
v 6:39 Lk 18:33
w 6:40 Mt 11:27
x Jn 5:19

A 6:22 Other mss add *into which His disciples had entered*   B 6:26 Or *perceived*   C 6:31 Bread miraculously provided by God for the Israelites   D 6:31 Ex 16:4; Ps 78:24   E 6:36 Other mss omit *Me*

---

located on the northwestern edge of the lake, Tiberias is several miles to the south.

6:25 On the other side of the sea refers to the area in or around Capernaum (see note at vv. 23-24; cp. v. 59).

6:27-29 People misunderstood Jesus' statement and asked about the works God required. Jesus said the only "work" required by God is faith in Messiah. On **seal of approval**, see note at 3:33.

6:30 Again, the people misunderstood. They demanded a **sign** as evidence of Jesus' claims (cp. 1Co 1:22). Jesus pointed to the significance of the "sign" He had just performed—the feeding of the crowd (cp. 2:18). This revealed people's stubbornness, which led many of Jesus' disciples to leave (6:60-66) and prompted John to indict the Jews for unbelief at the close of Jesus' public ministry (12:37-40).

6:31 This verse links exodus and Passover motifs with Jesus as the Prophet like Moses and the expectation that God would again provide manna in the messianic age. The OT reference seems to involve several passages, with Ps 78:23-24 being most prominent (Ex 16:4,15; Neh 9:15; Ps 105:40).

6:35,48 I am the bread of life is the first of Jesus' seven "I am" sayings in John. Subsequently He said He is "the light of the world" (8:12; 9:5); "the door" of the sheep (10:7,9); the "good shepherd" (10:11,14); "the resurrection and the life" (11:25); "the way, the truth, and the life" (14:6); and "the true vine" (15:1). Apart from these sayings, there are statements where Jesus referred to Himself as "I am" (6:20; 8:24,28,58; 18:5), a clear allusion to God's identification as "I am" (Ex 3:14).

6:37,44 Jesus affirmed the twin themes of election and perseverance of the saints, prominent topics in John's Gospel. Those predestined by God will come to Jesus, and Jesus will preserve His own. No one can come to Jesus apart from the Father's drawing him. These themes continue in the Good Shepherd discourse (10:28-29) and Jesus' final prayer (17:6,9,11-12).

6:40 On Jesus' promise of **eternal life**, see note at 3:16-18.

pisteuo

Greek Pronunciation	[pihss TYEW oh]
HCSB Translation	believe
Uses in John's Gospel	98
Uses in the NT	241
Focus Passage	John 6:29-47

The Greek word *pisteuo* means *to believe, trust, rely upon,* and its related noun is *pistis (faith).* In his Gospel, John never used the words *repent, repentance,* or *faith* to describe the way people are saved. Instead, he used *believe* since this term included all these ideas. John preferred the verb form to emphasize the act that is necessary for someone to be saved—total dependence on the work of Another. John did indicate, however, that *believing* can be superficial; that is, it can be merely intellectual without resulting in true salvation (Jn 2:23-24; 12:42-43; see Jms 2:19). But John's main point is that complete *reliance* upon Jesus, the Messiah and Son of God (20:31), for salvation gives eternal life to the person who *believes* (3:16; 6:47). Jesus used a wordplay when He said that people must do "the work of God" for salvation, for His point was that we must not try to work for it at all. We must simply "*believe* in the One He has sent" (6:29).

may have eternal life, and I will raise[a] him up
on the last day."
41 Therefore the •Jews started complaining
about Him because He said, "I am the bread
that came down from heaven." 42 They were
saying, "Isn't this Jesus the son of Joseph,[b]
whose father and mother we know? How can
He now say, 'I have come down from heaven'?"
43 Jesus answered them, "Stop complaining
among yourselves. 44 No one can come to Me
unless the Father who sent Me draws[A] him,
and I will raise him up on the last day. 45 It is
written in the Prophets:[c] **And they will all be
taught by God.**[B,d] Everyone who has listened
to and learned from the Father[e] comes to
Me— 46 not that anyone has seen the Father[f]
except the One who is from God.[g] He has seen
the Father.[h]
47 "I assure you: Anyone who believes[C] has
eternal life. 48 I am the bread of life. 49 Your fathers ate the manna[i] in the wilderness,[j] and
they died. 50 This is the bread that comes down
from heaven so that anyone may eat of it and
not die.[k] 51 I am the living bread that came
down from heaven. If anyone eats of this bread
he will live[l] forever.[m] The bread that I will give
for the life[n] of the world is My flesh."[o]
52 At that, the Jews argued[p] among themselves,[q] "How can this man give us His flesh
to eat?"
53 So Jesus said to them, "I assure you: Unless you eat the flesh of the Son of Man[r] and
drink His blood,[s] you do not have life in yourselves. 54 Anyone who eats My flesh and drinks
My blood[t] has eternal life, and I will raise[u] him
up on the last day, 55 because My flesh is real
food and My blood is real drink. 56 The one
who eats My flesh and drinks My blood lives in
Me, and I in him.[v] 57 Just as the living[w] Father
sent Me and I live because of the Father, so
the one who feeds on Me will live[x] because of
Me. 58 This is the bread that came down from
heaven; it is not like the manna[D] your fathers
ate—and they died. The one who eats this
bread will live forever."[y]
59 He said these things while teaching in the
•synagogue[z] in Capernaum.[aa]

Many Disciples Desert Jesus

60 Therefore, when many of His disciples
heard this, they said, "This teaching is hard!
Who can accept[E] it?"
61 Jesus, knowing in Himself[ab] that His disciples were complaining about this, asked them,
"Does this •offend you? 62 Then what if you
were to observe the Son of Man[ac] ascending[ad] to
where He was before? 63 The Spirit[ae] is the One
who gives life. The flesh doesn't help at all. The
words that I have spoken to you are spirit and
are life. 64 But there are some among you who
don't believe." (For Jesus knew from the beginning[af] those who would not[F] believe and the
one who would betray[ag] Him.) 65 He said, "This
is why I told you that no one can come to Me[ah]
unless it is granted to him by the Father."
66 From that moment many of His disciples
turned back and no longer accompanied Him.
67 Therefore Jesus said to the Twelve,[ai] "You
don't want to go away too, do you?"
68 Simon Peter[aj] answered, "Lord, who will
we go to? You have the words of eternal life.
69 We have come to believe and know that You
are the Holy One of God!"[G,ak]
70 Jesus replied to them, "Didn't I choose you,
the Twelve?[al] Yet one of you is the Devil!"[am]

[a] 6:40 Mt 16:21 [b] 6:42 Jn 1:45 [c] 6:45 Mt 2:23; Ac 7:52 [d] Is 54:13 [e] 1Co 2:13; 1Th 4:9; 1Jn 2:20 [f] 6:46 Ex 33:20; Jn 5:47 [g] Jn 16:27 [h] Lk 10:22; Jn 8:38; 14:9 [i] 6:49 Ex 16:12-36 [j] Rv 12:6 [k] 6:50 Jn 11:26 [l] 6:51 Php 1:21 [m] Rv 4:9 [n] Jn 5:26; 6:53 [o] Php 3:3; Heb 10:10 [p] 6:52 2Tm 2:24 [q] Jn 9:16; 10:19 [r] 6:53 Mk 2:10 [s] Heb 9:12 [t] 6:54 Mt 26:26-29; Mk 14:22-25; Lk 22:15-20; 1Co 11:23-25 [u] Mt 16:21 [v] 6:56 Jn 15:4-5; 1Jn 3:24; 4:13-16 [w] 6:57 Mt 25:31-46; Heb 10:31 [x] Php 1:21; 1Pt 1:18 [y] 6:58 Rv 4:9 [z] 6:59 Jms 2:2 [aa] Lk 10:15 [ab] 6:61 Mk 10:32; Jn 1:47-48; 2:24-25; 4:17-18; 9:3; 11:4,11; 13:10-11,38 [ac] 6:62 Mk 2:10 [ad] Jn 3:13; 20:17; Ac 1:9 [ae] 6:63 Ps 51:11; Jn 1:33; Ac 2:4; Rm 8:9; Gl 5:25; Ti 3:5; Rv 3:22 [af] 6:64 Jn 16:30; Ac 26:4 [ag] Mt 10:4; Jn 13:21 [ah] 6:65 Lk 14:26 [ai] 6:67 Mk 11:11 [aj] 6:68 Lk 6:14 [ak] 6:69 Mk 1:24 [al] 6:70 Jn 13:18 [am] Mt 4:1,10; Jn 13:2,27; Ac 13:10

[A] 6:44 Or *brings*, or *leads*; see the use of this Gk verb in Jn 12:32; 21:6; Ac 16:19; Jms 2:6. [B] 6:45 Is 54:13 [C] 6:47 Other mss add *in Me* [D] 6:58 Other mss omit *the manna* [E] 6:60 Lit *hear* [F] 6:64 Other mss omit *not* [G] 6:69 Other mss read *You are the Messiah, the Son of the Living God*

6:41,43 The references to the **complaining** of the **Jews** highlights the parallel between Jews of Jesus' day and wilderness Israel (cp. Ex 16:2,8-9; Nm 11:4-23; see note at Jn 6:5). The Israelites complained about the first giver of bread, Moses. Now they griped against the second giver, Jesus.

6:42 People showed no awareness of Jesus' virginal conception (Mt 1:18-25). They objected to Jesus' claim of descent from **heaven** since He was clearly human and was, they believed, conceived in the standard way (4:44).

6:44 On the "raising up" ministry of Jesus, see note at 12:32.

6:45 Citing Is 54:13, Jesus affirmed that, while His ministry fulfilled the prophetic vision that one day all people would be taught by God, this applied only to those who were drawn by the Father and who came to believe in Jesus as Messiah.

6:53 The Hebrew idiom "flesh and blood" refers to the total person.

6:63 Unaided by the **Spirit**, human reason cannot discern spiritual truth. The Jews wrongly believed study of Scripture (see note at 5:39) and doing "works of the law" (see note at 6:27-29) were sufficient for spiritual understanding.

6:68 Who will we go to may refer to transferring allegiance to another rabbi (cp. 1:35-37).

6:69 Peter's confession of Jesus as **the Holy One of God** anticipates later references to Jesus being set apart for God (10:36; 17:19). In the OT, God was called "the Holy One of Israel" (Ps 71:22; Is 43:3; 54:5). See similar confessions of Jesus in Mt 16:16; Mk 8:29; Lk 9:20.

6:70 This is the first reference to **the Twelve** in John's Gospel. Their existence and appointment are assumed from the testimony in the Synoptic Gospels. See notes at 1:43 and 15:16.

71 He was referring to Judas,[a] Simon Iscariot's son,[A,B] one of the Twelve, because he was going to betray[b] Him.

The Unbelief of Jesus' Brothers

7 After this, Jesus traveled in Galilee,[c] since He did not want to travel in Judea[d] because the •Jews[e] were trying to kill Him.[f] 2 The Jewish Festival of Tabernacles[C,D,g] was near, 3 so His brothers[h] said to Him, "Leave here and go to Judea so Your disciples can see Your works[i] that You are doing. 4 For no one does anything in secret while he's seeking public recognition. If You do these things, show Yourself to the world." 5 (For not even His brothers believed in Him.)

6 Jesus told them, "My time[j] has not yet arrived, but your time is always at hand. 7 The world cannot hate[k] you, but it does hate Me because I testify about it—that its deeds are evil. 8 Go up to the festival yourselves. I'm not going up to the festival yet,[E] because My time has not yet fully come." 9 After He had said these things, He stayed in Galilee.

Jesus at the Festival of Tabernacles

10 After His brothers had gone up to the festival, then He also went up, not openly but secretly. 11 The Jews were looking for Him at the festival and saying, "Where is He?" 12 And there was a lot of discussion about Him among the crowds. Some were saying, "He's a good[l] man." Others were saying, "No, on the contrary, He's deceiving[m] the people." 13 Still, nobody was talking publicly about Him because they feared the Jews.

14 When the festival was already half over, Jesus went up into the •temple complex[n] and began to teach. 15 Then the Jews were amazed and said, "How does He know the Scriptures,[o] since He hasn't been trained?"

16 Jesus answered them, "My teaching isn't Mine but is from the One who sent Me.[p] 17 If anyone wants to do His will,[q] he will understand whether the teaching is from God or if I am speaking on My own. 18 The one who speaks for himself seeks his own glory.[r] But He who seeks the glory[s] of the One who sent Him is true,[t] and there is no unrighteousness in Him.[u] 19 Didn't Moses[v] give you the law? Yet none of you keeps the law![w] Why do you want to kill Me?"

20 "You have a demon!" the crowd responded. "Who wants to kill You?"

21 "I did one work,[x] and you are all amazed,"

[a] 6:71 Mk 3:19
[b] Mt 10:4; Jn 13:21
[c] 7:1 Mt 17:22
[d] Lk 1:5
[e] Jn 11:36
[f] Jn 5:18
[g] 7:2 Ex 23:16
[h] 7:3 Mk 3:21,31-35; 6:3; Lk 8:19
[i] Mk 6:28; Jn 5:36; Heb 3:9; Rv 15:3
[j] 7:6 Ps 37:39; Lk 20:10; Jn 7:8
[k] 7:7 Lk 6:27; 19:14
[l] 7:12 Gn 1:31
[m] Rv 20:10
[n] 7:14 Ac 21:26
[o] 7:15 Mt 26:54
[p] 7:16 Jn 5:19,30
[q] 7:17 Rm 8:27; Eph 1:9
[r] 7:18 Php 3:19
[s] Lk 9:32; Jn 17:24; 2Co 3:18; 1Pt 5:4; 2Pt 3:18
[t] Jn 8:14; 1Jn 5:20
[u] 1Jn 3:5
[v] 7:19 Ps 77:20; Mt 8:4; Heb 3:2
[w] Rm 2:12-29; 3:9-10,20-23, 27-28
[x] 7:21 Jn 5:36; Heb 3:9; Rv 15:3

[A] 6:71 Other mss read *Judas Iscariot, Simon's son* [B] 6:71 Lit *Judas, of Simon Iscariot* [C] 7:2 Or *Booths* [D] 7:2 One of 3 great Jewish religious festivals, along with Passover and Pentecost; Ex 23:14; Dt 16:16 [E] 7:8 Other mss omit *yet*

6:71 **Judas, Simon Iscariot's son**, likely was the only non-Galilean among the Twelve.

7:1–8:59 On the heels of the unbelief of many disciples (6:60-66), chapter 7 opens with the unbelief of Jesus' brothers and closes with the unbelief of the Jewish leaders (7:45-52). Chapters 7 and 8 convey Jesus' teaching at the Feast of Tabernacles in Jerusalem. Jesus' teaching is given in two cycles (7:10-24,37-39; 8:12-30), climaxing in His invitation to all who are thirsty to come to Him and drink. Once the Spirit was given, believers conveyed "streams of living water" (7:37-38). The second cycle begins with Jesus' startling affirmation that He is the "light of the world."

7:1 **Galilee** (under the jurisdiction of Herod Antipas) was safer than **Judea** (under the Roman prefect) for Jesus since **the Jews were trying to kill Him**.

7:2 The **Jewish Festival of Tabernacles** was celebrated in September or October, two months before the Feast of Dedication (see note at 10:22). It was also called the "Feast of Booths," because people temporarily lived in booths to remember God's faithfulness during Israel's wilderness wanderings (Lv 23:42-43; cp. Mt 17:4). See note at 2:13.

7:3-4 Jesus' **brothers** were naturally born sons of Mary. Their names were James, Joseph, Judas, and Simon (Mt 13:55 and Mk 6:3). Their poor advice stemmed from unbelief (Jn 7:5) and revealed a fundamental misunderstanding of Jesus' messianic identity (Mt 4:5-7).

7:6-10 On **My time has not yet arrived**, see note at 2:4. In 7:8, Jesus stated, **I'm not going up to the festival yet**. In verse 10, we learn that **He also went up, not openly but secretly** (see note at v. 1). It surprises many readers to realize that Jesus used craft and subterfuge to combat opposition and false expectations.

7:12 The charge that Jesus was **deceiving the people** may hark back to Dt 13:1-11 (cp. Mt 27:63; Lk 23:2). Later Jewish literature called Jesus a deceiver.

7:13 The phrase **they feared the Jews** (cp. 9:22; 19:38; 20:19) refers to Jerusalem authorities represented by the Sanhedrin (see note at 3:1).

7:14 On the **temple complex**, see note at 2:14.

7:15 **The Jews** may include Judean crowds and Jewish authorities. Jesus lacked formal rabbinic training (as did His disciples; Ac 4:13), but His teaching and authority came from God (Jn 7:16; 8:28; cp. Mt 5:21-26; 7:28-29).

7:16 Unlike other rabbis, Jesus claimed direct knowledge from God (8:28).

7:18-19 Jesus as authoritative source contrasted Himself with vain, false prophets (Dt 18:9-22). The Jews were proud of the fact that **Moses** had given them **the law** (cp. 9:28; Rm 2:17; 9:4).

7:20 This is one of several instances where Jesus was charged with **demon** possession (8:48; 10:20; Mt 12:24); the same charge was leveled against John the Baptist (Mt 11:18). Other charges against Jesus included breaking the Sabbath (Jn 5:16,18; 9:16), blasphemy (5:18; 8:58-59; 10:31,33,39; 19:7), deceiving the people (7:12,47), being a Samaritan (i.e., apostate, 8:48), madness (10:20), and criminal activity (18:30).

7:21 The **one work** Jesus referred to was probably the healing in 5:1-15.

Jesus answered. 22 "Consider this: Moses has
given you circumcision[a]—not that it comes
from Moses but from the fathers[b]—and you
circumcise a man on the Sabbath.[c] 23 If a man
receives circumcision on the Sabbath[d] so that
the law of Moses[e] won't be broken, are you angry at Me because I made a man entirely well
on the Sabbath? 24 Stop judging[f] according to
outward appearances; rather judge according
to righteous judgment."

The Identity of the Messiah

25 Some of the people of Jerusalem[g] were
saying, "Isn't this the man they want to kill?
26 Yet, look! He's speaking publicly and they're
saying nothing to Him. Can it be true that the
authorities[h] know He is the •Messiah?[i] 27 But
we know where this man is from.[j] When the
Messiah comes, nobody will know where He
is from."

28 As He was teaching in the temple complex,[k] Jesus cried out, "You know Me and you
know where I am from. Yet I have not come on
My own, but the One who sent Me[l] is true. You
don't know Him;[m] 29 I know Him because I am
from Him, and He sent Me."[n]

30 Then they tried to seize Him. Yet no one
laid a hand on Him because His hour[A] had not
yet come. 31 However, many from the crowd
believed in Him and said, "When the Messiah
comes, He won't perform more signs than
this man has done,[o] will He?"

32 The •Pharisees[p] heard the crowd muttering these things about Him, so the •chief
priests[q] and the Pharisees sent temple police
to arrest Him.

33 Then Jesus said, "I am only with you for a
short time.[r] Then I'm going to the One who sent
Me.[s] 34 You will look for Me, but you will not find
Me; and where I am, you cannot come."[t]

35 Then the Jews[u] said to one another, "Where
does He intend to go so we won't find Him?
He doesn't intend to go to the Dispersion[B,v]
among the Greeks[w] and teach the Greeks,
does He? 36 What is this remark He made: 'You
will look for Me, and you will not find Me; and
where I am, you cannot come'[x]?"

The Promise of the Spirit

37 On the last and most important day of
the festival,[y] Jesus stood up and cried out, "If
anyone is thirsty, he should come to Me[C,z] and
drink![aa] 38 The one who believes in Me,[ab] as the
Scripture[ac] has said,[D] will have streams of living water[ad] flow[ae] from deep within him." 39 He
said this about the Spirit.[af] Those who believed
in Jesus were going to receive the Spirit,[ag] for

[a] **7:22** Ac 15:1; Gl 6:15
[b] Gn 17:9-14; Lv 12:3
[c] Mk 2:23
[d] **7:23** Lk 13:10
[e] Lk 2:22
[f] **7:24** Lk 6:37; Heb 9:27
[g] **7:25** Mt 23:37
[h] **7:26** Lk 8:41; 12:58
[i] Mt 1:17; Eph 5:2
[j] **7:27** Mt 13:55; 21:11; Lk 4:22; Jn 6:42
[k] **7:28** Ac 21:26
[l] Jn 5:19
[m] Jn 1:26-33; 5:13; 8:14,19,55; 9:29-30; 12:35; 13:7; 14:5; 15:15,21; 20:14; Gl 4:8; 1Th 4:5; 2Th 1:8; Ti 1:16
[n] **7:29** Mk 9:37; Lk 10:22; Jn 1:6; 9:16
[o] **7:31** Jn 15:24
[p] **7:32** Mk 7:3
[q] Mt 2:4
[r] **7:33** Jn 12:35; 14:19; 16:5,16
[s] Jn 14:12; 16:5,10,17,28
[t] **7:34** Jn 8:21; 13:33
[u] **7:35** Jn 11:36
[v] Jms 1:1; 1Pt 1:1
[w] Gl 2:3
[x] **7:36** Jn 8:21
[y] **7:37** Lv 23:34-36; Nm 29:35; Dt 16:13-14; Neh 8:18; Jn 5:1
[z] Lk 14:26 [aa] Is 55:1; Rv 22:17 [ab] **7:38** Jn 6:35 [ac] Mt 26:54 [ad] Jn 4:10-14 [ae] Ex 17:1-6; Ps 78:15-16; 105:40-41; Pr 18:4; Is 12:3; Ezk 47:1-11; Zch 14:8; Rv 22:1-2 [af] **7:39** Ps 51:11; Jn 1:33; Ac 2:4; 8:15; Rm 8:9; Gl 5:25; Ti 3:5; Rv 3:22 [ag] Ac 2:33

[A] **7:30** The time of His sacrificial death and exaltation; Jn 2:4; 8:20; 12:23,27; 13:1; 17:1 [B] **7:35** Jewish people scattered throughout Gentile lands who spoke Gk and were influenced by Gk culture [C] **7:37** Other mss omit *to Me* [D] **7:38** Jesus may have had several OT passages in mind; Is 58:11; Ezk 47:1-12; Zch 14:8

7:22 **Circumcision** was given by **the fathers** (i.e., Abraham; Gn 17:9-14) and **Moses** (Ex 12:44,48-49; Lv 12:3). Jesus' argument was "from the lesser to the greater." The Jews were to **circumcise** their males on the eighth day even if that day fell on the **Sabbath** (the "lesser" issue). If "perfecting" one part of a human body on the Sabbath was legitimate, how much more the healing of an entire person?

7:24 Jesus' statement about judging may allude to Lv 19:15 (cp. Dt 16:18-19; Is 11:3-4; Zch 7:9).

7:25-44 The next three scenes (vv. 25-31,32-36,37-44) center on the question, "Is Jesus the Christ?" Representative queries (in some cases involving misunderstanding) from the crowd serve as foils for dealing with this issue (vv. 27,31,42), in turn focusing on the supposedly unknown origins of Messiah, His performance of signs, and Bethlehem as Messiah's birthplace.

7:26 **The authorities** probably refers to the Sanhedrin (v. 48; 12:42; see notes at 3:1 and 7:13).

7:27 Some rabbis taught that **Messiah** would be wholly unknown until He set out to procure salvation for Israel. Others felt His birthplace was foreknown (v. 42; cp. Mt 2:1-6).

7:28 On the **temple complex**, see note at 2:14.

7:30 On Jesus' ability to elude His enemies, see note at 2:4.

7:31 Since **Messiah** would be a prophet like Moses (Dt 18:15,18) and Moses performed many miraculous signs at the exodus (Ex 7–11), Messiah was expected to perform miracles as well (see notes at Jn 6:30 and 6:31). It would have been natural for people to wonder, after witnessing Jesus' miracles, if He was the Messiah.

7:32 The **chief priests and the Pharisees**, representing the Sanhedrin, deployed the **temple police** to arrest Jesus. The police were drawn from the Levites and were charged with maintaining order in the temple precincts. The **arrest** of Jesus implied that He was a criminal (but see note at vv. 45-52). The leaders hoped this would discourage people from following Him.

7:33 Six months after Jesus issued this prediction, He was crucified.

7:35 People misunderstood Jesus' statement in verse 34. Ever since the exile, many Jews had not returned to Palestine but continued to live in the Dispersion (Gk *diaspora*). **Greeks** is synonymous with "Gentiles."

7:37 While verse 14 referred to the festival being "already half over," this was now the last and greatest day of the Feast of Tabernacles. Jesus' invitation harks back to OT prophetic passages such as Is 55:1 (see Is 12:3).

7:38-39 **Streams of living water** flowing from **deep within** Jesus' followers fulfill the end-time blessings predicted in the OT. John noted in verse 39 that these streams are emblematic of the **Spirit**, who would be given after Jesus' exaltation with the Father (20:22).

7:40-41 **The Prophet** is the figure referred to in Dt 18:15-18

the Spirit[A] had not yet been received[B,C] because Jesus had not yet been glorified.

The People Are Divided over Jesus

[40] When some from the crowd heard these words, they said, "This really is the Prophet!"[D,a] [41] Others said, "This is the Messiah!" But some said, "Surely the Messiah doesn't come from Galilee, does He? [42] Doesn't the Scripture[b] say that the Messiah comes from David's[c] offspring[E] and from the town of Bethlehem,[d] where David once lived?" [43] So a division[e] occurred among the crowd because of Him. [44] Some of them wanted to seize Him,[f] but no one laid hands on Him.

Debate over Jesus' Claims

[45] Then the temple police[g] came to the chief priests[h] and Pharisees, who asked them, "Why haven't you brought Him?"

[46] The police answered, "No man ever spoke like this!"[F,i]

[47] Then the Pharisees responded to them: "Are you fooled[j] too? [48] Have any of the rulers[k] or Pharisees believed in Him? [49] But this crowd, which doesn't know the law, is accursed!"

[50] Nicodemus[l]—the one who came to Him previously, being one of them—said to them, [51] "Our law doesn't judge a man before it hears from him and knows what he's doing, does it?"[m]

[52] "You aren't from Galilee[n] too, are you?" they replied. "Investigate and you will see that no prophet arises from Galilee."[G,o]

8 [[53] So each one went to his house. [1] But Jesus went to the •Mount of Olives.[p]

An Adulteress Forgiven

[2] At dawn He went to the •temple complex[q] again, and all the people were coming to Him.[r] He sat down[s] and began to teach them. [3] Then the •scribes and the •Pharisees[t] brought a woman caught in adultery,[u] making her stand in the center. [4] "Teacher," they said to Him, "this woman was caught in the act of committing adultery.[v] [5] In the law Moses[w] commanded us to stone such women.[x] So what do You say?" [6] They asked this to trap Him,[y] in order that they might have evidence to accuse Him.

Jesus stooped down and started writing on the ground with His finger. [7] When they persisted in questioning Him, He stood up and said to them, "The one without sin[z] among you[aa] should be the first to throw a stone at her."[ab]

[8] Then He stooped down again and continued writing on the ground. [9] When they heard this, they left one by one, starting with the older men. Only He was left, with the woman in the center. [10] When Jesus stood up, He said to her, "•Woman, where are they? Has no one condemned you?"

[11] "No one, Lord,"[H] she answered.

Cross references (center column)

a 7:40 Jn 6:14
b 7:42 2Pt 1:20
c Lk 1:27
d Gn 35:19
e 7:43 Jn 9:16; 1Co 1:10
f 7:44 Jn 10:39
g 7:45 Jn 18:18
h Mt 2:4
i 7:46 Mt 7:28-29
j 7:47 Rv 20:10
k 7:48 Lk 8:41
l 7:50 Jn 3:1; 19:39
m 7:51 Dt 1:16; 17:6; 19:15
n 7:52 Mt 17:22
o 2Kg 14:25
p 8:1 Mt 21:1
q 8:2 Ac 21:26
r Mk 1:45
s Mk 9:35
t 8:3 Mk 7:3
u Nm 5:11
v 8:4 Mt 5:27-28
w 8:5 Ps 77:20; Mt 8:4; Heb 3:2
x Lv 20:10; Dt 22:22-24; Ezk 16:38-41
y 8:6 Lk 11:54
z 8:7 Rm 3:23; 6:23
aa Rm 2:1,22
ab Dt 17:7

(see note at Jn 1:19-21; cp. 6:14). This "Prophet" and the **Messiah** were thought to be different persons by some first-century Jews, but Jesus turned out to be both.

7:42 Bethlehem, south of Jerusalem in the heart of Judea, was foretold as Messiah's birthplace in Mc 5:2 (cp. Mt 2:5-6; see note at Jn 7:27). As David's city (1Sm 16:1,4; 20:6), Bethlehem had important messianic implications. In this verse the irony is apparent. Some people, knowing that Jesus hailed from Galilee, objected that **Messiah** was to be born in Bethlehem, not realizing that Bethlehem was in fact Jesus' birthplace.

7:44 On the right time for Jesus' death and resurrection, see note at 2:4.

7:45-52 The Sanhedrin's meeting highlighted the increasing threat that Jesus' popularity represented for the Jewish leadership. But Nicodemus's plea for fairness shows that the Sanhedrin was not yet united in opposition against Jesus.

7:45 On the attempt to arrest Jesus, see note at verse 32.

7:46 The temple **police** heard many people teach in the temple courts, but they recognized Jesus' teaching as unique (Mt 7:28-29; see note at Jn 7:15).

7:48 Rulers probably refers to members of the Sanhedrin (see note at 3:1).

7:49 The disparaging reference to **this crowd, which doesn't**

know the law reveals the arrogant contempt many rabbis had for the unschooled masses.

7:50 Jesus' previous encounter with Nicodemus is described in 3:1-15.

7:51 Old Testament law charged judges to investigate accusations fairly (Dt 1:16) and thoroughly (Jn 17:4; 19:18). Nicodemus's plea for fairness was later duplicated by the rabbi Gamaliel (Ac 5:34-39).

7:52 Contrary to the Pharisees' implication, prophets occasionally did arise from **Galilee**. These included Jonah (2Kg 14:25), possibly Elijah (1Kg 17:1), and Nahum (Nah 1:1).

7:53–8:11 The story of Jesus and the adulteress may be authentic, but it is doubtful that the account is part of John's original Gospel. Reasons include: (1) the account is absent from all the oldest copies of John; (2) where it does occur in later manuscripts, it is found at various places (after Jn 7:36,44,52; at the end of John's Gospel; or after Lk 21:38); (3) virtually every verse from 8:1-11 (except for 8:5) features words not elsewhere found in John's Gospel, and standard vocabulary used in John is conspicuously absent; (4) the account appears to interrupt the narrative flow from 7:52 to 8:12, breaking the literary unit 7:1–8:59; and (5) the account was virtually unknown by early church fathers before the fourth century.

"Neither do I condemn you,"[a] said Jesus. "Go, and from now on do not sin anymore."][A

The Light of the World

[12] Then Jesus spoke to them again: "I am[b] the light[c] of the world. Anyone who follows Me will never walk in the darkness but will have the light of life."[d]

[13] So the Pharisees said to Him, "You are testifying about Yourself. Your testimony is not valid."[B]

[14] "Even if I testify about Myself," Jesus replied, "My testimony is valid,[c] because I know where I came from and where I'm going. But you don't know where I come from or where I'm going.[e] [15] You judge[f] by human standards.[D,g] I judge no one.[h] [16] And if I do judge, My judgment is true, because I am not alone, but I and the Father who sent Me judge[i] together.[j] [17] Even in your law it is written that the witness of two men is valid.[k] [18] I am the One who testifies[l] about Myself, and the Father who sent Me testifies about Me."

[19] Then they asked Him, "Where is Your Father?"

"You know neither Me nor My Father,"[m] Jesus answered. "If you knew Me, you would also know My Father."[n] [20] He spoke these words by the treasury,[E,o] while teaching in the temple complex. But no one seized Him, because His hour[F] had not come.

Jesus Predicts His Departure

[21] Then He said to them again, "I'm going away;[p] you will look for Me, and you will die in your sin.[q] Where I'm going, you cannot come."[r]

[22] So the •Jews said again, "He won't kill Himself, will He, since He says, 'Where I'm going, you cannot come'[s]?"

[23] "You are from below," He told them, "I am from above.[t] You are of this world;[u] I am not of this •world.[v] [24] Therefore I told you that you will die in your sins. For if you do not believe that I am He,[G] you will die in your sins."

[25] "Who are You?" they questioned.

"Precisely what I've been telling you from the very beginning," Jesus told them. [26] "I have many things to say and to judge about you, but the One who sent Me[w] is true, and what I have heard from Him—these things I tell the world."[x]

[27] They did not know He was speaking to them about the Father. [28] So Jesus said to them, "When you lift up the •Son of Man,[y] then you will know that I am[z] He, and that I do nothing on My own.[aa] But just as the Father taught Me, I say these things. [29] The One who sent Me is with Me. He has not left Me alone,[ab] because I always do what pleases Him."

Truth and Freedom

[30] As He was saying these things, many believed

Cross references

[a]8:11 Jn 3:17
[b]8:12 Ex 3:14; Jn 8:24,58
[c]Ps 36:9; Jn 12:46; 1Jn 2:8
[d]Ex 13:21-22; 14:19-25; Is 42:6; 49:6; 60:19-22; Zch 14:5-8; Jn 9:5; 12:46
[e]8:14 Jn 3:8; 7:28; 9:29; 12:35; 13:3,36; 14:5; 16:5,28; 1Jn 2:11
[f]8:15 Lk 6:37; Rv 19:11
[g]Php 3:3
[h]Jn 3:17; 12:47
[i]8:16 Mt 12:41; 2Th 1:5
[j]Jn 16:32
[k]8:17 Nm 35:30; Jn 8:14
[l]8:18 1Jn 5:7,9
[m]8:19 Jn 7:28; 1Jn 2:23
[n]Lk 10:22; Jn 17:3; 1Jn 4:8
[o]8:20 Mk 12:41,43; Lk 21:1
[p]8:21 Jn 14:2; 16:5
[q]Dt 24:16; Ezk 3:18; 33:8; Jn 15:22; Rm 3:23; 6:23
[r]Jn 7:34,36; 8:22; 13:33
[s]8:22 Jn 8:21
[t]8:23 Jn 3:13,31; 18:36; Col 3:1-2
[u]1Jn 4:5
[v]Jn 15:19; 17:14-16; 18:36
[w]8:26 Jn 5:19
[x]Jn 3:32; 15:15
[y]8:28 Mk 2:10
[z]Jn 8:24
[aa]Mk 6:5; Jn 9:33; 15:5
[ab]8:29 Jn 16:32; Ac 10:38

Footnotes

[A]8:11 Other mss omit bracketed text   [B]8:13 The law of Moses required at least 2 witnesses to make a claim legally valid (v. 17).   [C]8:14 Or true   [D]8:15 Lit You judge according to the flesh   [E]8:20 A place for offerings to be given, perhaps in the court of women   [F]8:20 The time of His sacrificial death and exaltation; Jn 2:4; 7:30; 12:23,27; 13:1; 17:1   [G]8:24 Jesus claimed to be deity, but the Pharisees didn't understand His meaning.

8:12 Jesus as **the light of the world** (see note at 6:35,48) develops further the affirmation in the prologue that Jesus was "the light of men" and that "that light shines in the darkness" (1:4-5). On this basis, Jesus exhorted His hearers to put their trust in the light while they had Him with them, so they might become "sons of light" (12:35-36). Jesus' concluding testimony is that He came into the world as light so that no one who believes in Him should remain in darkness (12:46). Yet, according to the evangelist, the verdict is this: Light has come into the world, but people loved darkness rather than light because their deeds were evil (3:19-21).

phos

Greek Pronunciation	[FOHSS]
HCSB Translation	light
Uses in John's Gospel	23
Uses in the NT	73
Focus Passage	John 8:12

The word *phos* is seldom used in the literal sense in the NT. Most often it is a metaphor referring to holiness, purity, or godliness. Jesus used the term in the Sermon on the Mount to describe His disciples and the holy standard of conduct that He expected them to model to the world (Mt 5:14-16; 6:23). In John's Gospel, however, Jesus Himself is "the light," as stated in the Prologue (1:4-5) and in Jesus' own words (8:12; 9:5). In this case, *the light* is revelatory and reflects God's character or holiness. In other words, *the light* refers to God's revelation or disclosure of Himself to the world in the incarnation (1:4-9). Incredibly, those in darkness prefer the darkness, at least until they accept the truth of God's revelation in His Son and believe in *the light* (3:19-21; 8:12; 12:46)

8:13-14 The Pharisees' challenge and Jesus' response continue the acrimony of 5:31-47. Again, Mosaic stipulations were in view (Dt 17:6; 19:15).

8:14,18 On Jesus' testimony about Himself, see note at 5:31-47.

8:15 Jesus' statement may echo 1Sm 16:7. People rejected Jesus because He did not come with regal fanfare, but appearances can be deceiving (Is 53:2-3).

8:17 On the testimony of two witnesses, see notes at Dt 17:6-7; 19:15.

8:20 On the timing of Jesus' **hour**, see note at 2:4.

8:24,28 These statements hint at Jesus' deity (see note at 6:35,48).

8:28 On the lifting up of Jesus, see note at 3:14.

in Him. ³¹So Jesus said to the Jews who had believed Him, "If you continue in My word,^A,^a you really are My disciples. ³²You will know the truth,^b and the truth will set you free."

³³"We are descendants^B of Abraham,"^c they answered Him, "and we have never been enslaved to anyone. How can You say, 'You will become free'?"

³⁴Jesus responded, "•I assure you: Everyone who commits sin is a •slave of sin.^d ³⁵A slave does not remain in the household forever,^e but a son does remain forever.^f ³⁶Therefore, if the Son sets you free, you really will be free. ³⁷I know you are descendants^B of Abraham,^g but you are trying to kill Me because My word^A is not welcome among you. ³⁸I speak what I have seen^h in the presence of the Father;^C,^i therefore, you do what you have heard from your father."

³⁹"Our father is Abraham!" they replied.

"If you were Abraham's children," Jesus told them, "you would do what Abraham did.^j ⁴⁰But now you are trying to kill Me, a man who has told you the truth^k that I heard from God. Abraham did not do this! ⁴¹You're doing what your father does."^l

"We weren't born^m of sexual immorality,"^n they said. "We have one Father—God."^o

⁴²Jesus said to them, "If God were your Father, you would love Me,^p because I came from God^q and I am here. For I didn't come on My own, but He sent Me. ⁴³Why don't you understand what I say? Because you cannot listen to^D My word.^r ⁴⁴You are of your father the Devil,^s and you want to carry out your father's desires. He was a murderer^t from the beginning^u and has not stood in the truth,^v because there is no truth in him. When he tells a lie, he speaks from his own nature,^E because he is a liar and the fa-

ther of liars.^F ⁴⁵Yet because I tell the truth, you do not believe Me. ⁴⁶Who among you can convict Me of sin?^w If I tell the truth, why don't you believe Me? ⁴⁷The one who is from God listens to God's words. This is why you don't listen, because you are not from God."

Jesus and Abraham

⁴⁸The Jews responded to Him, "Aren't we right in saying that You're a •Samaritan^x and have a demon?"^y

⁴⁹"I do not have a demon," Jesus answered. "On the contrary, I honor My Father and you dishonor Me. ⁵⁰I do not seek My glory;^z the One who seeks it also judges. ⁵¹I assure you: If anyone keeps My word,^aa he will never see death—ever!"

⁵²Then the Jews said, "Now we know You have a demon. Abraham died and so did the prophets. You say, 'If anyone keeps My word, he will never taste death—ever!' ⁵³Are You greater than our father Abraham who died? Even the prophets died. Who do You pretend to be?"^G

⁵⁴"If I glorify Myself," Jesus answered, "My glory is nothing. My Father—you say about Him, 'He is our God'—He is the One who glorifies Me. ⁵⁵You've never known Him, but I know Him. If I were to say I don't know Him,^ab I would be a liar like you. But I do know Him,^ac and I keep His word. ⁵⁶Your father Abraham was overjoyed that he would see My day; he saw it^ad and rejoiced."

⁵⁷The Jews replied, "You aren't 50 years old yet, and You've seen Abraham?"^H

⁵⁸Jesus said to them, "I assure you: Before Abraham was, I am."^I,^ae

⁵⁹At that, they picked up stones^af to throw at

Cross references (center column)
^a 8:31 Jn 2:22; 18:32
^b 8:32 Ps 119:142; Jn 14:6; 2Th 2:10
^c 8:33 Gn 16:15; Jn 8:37; Heb 2:16
^d 8:34 Rm 6:17-20; 2Pt 2:19
^e 8:35 1Jn 2:17
^f Gn 21:10; Lk 15:31; Gl 4:30
^g 8:37 Lk 19:9; Jn 8:31-47; Ac 13:26; Rm 4:11,16; Gl 3:7
^h 8:38 Jn 3:32; 5:19; 6:46
^i Mt 5:16; 11:27; Lk 11:13; Jn 8:42
^j 8:39 Gl 3:7,9
^k 8:40 Ps 119:142; Jn 14:6
^l 8:41 2Jn 9
^m 1Jn 2:29
^n Hs 2:4; 1Th 4:3
^o Dt 32:6
^p 8:42 Dt 6:5; Lk 10:27; 1Jn 5:1
^q Jn 13:3; 16:27; 1Jn 5:20
^r 8:43 Lk 6:47; Jn 18:32
^s 8:44 Mt 4:1; Jn 13:2,27; Eph 2:1-3
^t 1Jn 3:15
^u Gn 3:1-4; 4:8-9; Ac 26:4; 2Co 11:3; 1Jn 3:8-15; Rv 12:9
^v Jn 14:6; Rm 3:7
^w 8:46 Jn 15:22; 1Jn 3:5
^x 8:48 Lk 9:52; Ac 1:8
^y Jn 7:20; 10:20; Rv 9:20; 18:2
^z 8:50 Jn 17:24; Php 3:19; 1Pt 5:4
^aa 8:51 Jn 8:52,55; 14:23-24; 15:20; 17:6; 18:32; 1Jn 2:5; Rv 1:3; 3:8,10; 22:7,9
^ab 8:55 Jn 7:28 ^ac Mt 11:27 ^ad 8:56 Lk 10:24; Heb 11:13-19 ^ae 8:58 Ex 3:14; Ps 45:8; Jn 1:15; 8:24; 17:5; Col 1:17 ^af 8:59 Jn 10:33

---

^A 8:31,37 Or *My teaching*, or *My message* ^B 8:33,37 Or *offspring*; lit *seed*; Jn 7:42 ^C 8:38 Other mss read *of My Father* ^D 8:43 Or *cannot hear* ^E 8:44 Lit *from his own things* ^F 8:44 Lit *of it* ^G 8:53 Lit *Who do You make Yourself?* ^H 8:57 Other mss read *and Abraham has seen You?* ^I 8:58 *I AM* is the name God gave Himself at the burning bush; Ex 3:13-14; see note at Jn 8:24.

8:33 The OT extols the blessings of being **descendants of Abraham** (Ps 105:6; Is 41:8).

8:35 The contrast between **son** and **slave** may allude to Abraham's sons through Sarah and Hagar (Gn 21:1-21; see Ex 21:2).

8:35-36 On Jesus as the life-giving **Son**, see note at 3:16-18.

8:37-38 Even in the OT, physical descent from **Abraham** was insufficient to establish one's lineage (Jr 9:25-26; cp. Rm 2:28-29; 9:7; Gl 4:21-31).

8:39-58 On children of God, see note at 3:3-8.

8:41 Though the OT calls the Israelites God's children (Ex 4:22; Dt 14:1-2; 32:6; Is 63:16; 64:8; Jr 31:9; Mal 2:10), John said only those born of God (through faith) are God's children (Jn 1:12-13; 3:3-8).

8:44 The Devil is **a murderer from the beginning**. He incited Cain to kill Abel (1Jn 3:15). He **has not stood in the truth** is a possible reference to Satan's fall (Is 14:12). At the fall of Adam and Eve, he blatantly contradicted God's word (Gn 3:3-4; cp. Gn 2:17).

8:46 Jesus always did what pleases God (v. 29; Is 53:9).

8:48,52 On the accusation that Jesus had a demon, see note at 7:20.

8:56 Jesus' statement refers to Abraham's joyful anticipation of the coming of the Messiah. See the later affirmation in 12:41 that Isaiah saw Jesus' glory.

8:58 On Jesus' **I am** statements, see note at 6:35,48.

8:59 Stoning was the prescribed punishment for blasphemy (Lv 24:16; cp. Dt 13:6-11; Jn 10:31-33; 11:8). However, this was never to be enacted by mob violence (Dt 17:2-7). In the

Him.[a] But Jesus was hidden[A,b] and went out of the temple complex.[B,c]

The Sixth Sign: Healing a Man Born Blind

9 As He was passing by, He saw a man blind from birth. [2]His disciples questioned Him: "Rabbi,[d] who sinned, this man[e] or his parents,[f] that he was born blind?"

[3]"Neither this man nor his parents sinned," Jesus answered. "This came about so that God's works[g] might be displayed in him. [4]We[C] must do the works[h] of Him who sent Me[D] while it is day.[i] Night is coming when no one can work. [5]As long as I am in the world, I am the light of the world."[j]

[6]After He said these things He spit on the ground, made some mud[k] from the saliva, and spread the mud on his eyes. [7]"Go," He told him, "wash in the pool of Siloam"[l] (which means "Sent"). So he left, washed, and came back seeing.[m]

[8]His neighbors and those who formerly had seen him as a beggar said, "Isn't this the man who sat begging?" [9]Some said, "He's the one."

"No," others were saying, "but he looks like him."

He kept saying, "I'm the one!"

[10]Therefore they asked him, "Then how were your eyes opened?"

[11]He answered, "The man called Jesus made mud, spread it on my eyes, and told me, 'Go to Siloam[n] and wash.' So when I went and washed I received my sight."[o]

[12]"Where is He?" they asked.

"I don't know," he said.

The Healed Man's Testimony

[13]They brought the man who used to be blind to the •Pharisees.[p] [14]The day that Jesus made the mud and opened his eyes was a Sabbath.[q] [15]So again the Pharisees asked him how he received his sight.

"He put mud on my eyes," he told them. "I washed and I can see."

[16]Therefore some of the Pharisees said, "This man is not from God,[r] for He doesn't keep the Sabbath!" But others were saying, "How can a sinful man[s] perform such signs?" And there was a division[t] among them.

[17]Again they asked the blind man,[E] "What

---

[a]8:59 Ex 17:4; Lv 24:16; 1Sm 30:6; 1Kg 21:10-13; Jn 10:31; 11:8
[b]Lk 4:30; Jn 12:36
[c]Ac 21:26
[d]9:2 Jn 11:8
[e]Ezk 18:20
[f]Ex 20:5; Jb 21:19
[g]9:3 Jn 5:36; 6:28-29; Rm 14:20; Heb 3:9; Rv 15:3
[h]9:4 Jn 5:17; 2Jn 8
[i]Jn 11:9; 12:35; Rm 13:12
[j]9:5 Mt 5:14; Jn 8:12; 12:46
[k]9:6 Gn 2:7
[l]9:7 Lk 13:4; Jn 9:11
[m]Is 35:5
[n]9:11 Jn 9:7
[o]Ac 9:12
[p]9:13 Mk 7:3
[q]9:14 Mk 2:23
[r]9:16 Jn 7:29
[s]Mt 26:45; Lk 24:7; Jn 9:24; Rm 5:19
[t]Jn 7:43; 10:19; 1Co 1:10

OT, righteous men like Moses (Ex 17:4), Joshua and Caleb (Nm 14:10), and David (1Sm 30:6) were nearly stoned. As on previous occasions, Jesus evaded arrest (Jn 7:30,44; 8:20; see note at 2:4). His withdrawal from the Jews strikes a note of judgment similar to the removal of God's favor from King Saul (1Sm 15:23).

9:1-41 Jesus' identity as "the light of the world" was illustrated in His sixth and penultimate "sign" recorded in John's Gospel—the healing of a man born blind (see note at 2:11). As in chapter 5, Jesus healed on the Sabbath and thus suffered persecution from the Jewish leaders. But in contrast to the lame man of chapter 5, who showed no faith and reported Jesus to the authorities, the formerly blind man showed a progression of faith and ended up worshiping Jesus (9:38). Jesus condemned the Pharisees for their spiritual blindness (vv. 40-41).

9:2 The disciples' question reflected the assumption, customary in ancient Judaism, that suffering could be traced to specific sins (cp. Jb 4:7). The underlying concern of this assumption is to clear God of wrongdoing against innocent people (Ex 20:5; Nm 14:18; Dt 5:9). Yet the NT makes it clear that suffering is not always a direct result of a person's sin (Lk 13:2-3; 2Co 12:7; Gl 4:13). We should not speculate about the cause of a person's suffering but realize that even evil can contribute to the greater glory of God (esp. the crucifixion; cp. Jn 12:28,37-41; 17:1,5).

9:5 On Jesus as **the light of the world**, see notes at 6:35,48 and 8:12.

9:7 Jesus' sending the man to **wash in the pool of Siloam** is reminiscent of Elijah's sending Naaman to wash in the Jordan River (2Kg 5:10-13). The words **which means "Sent"** may echo the messianic reference in Gn 49:10 (cp. Is 8:6); see notes at Jn 1:38 and 3:16-18). After 9:7, Jesus is not heard from again until verse 35.

9:14 The mention of the **Sabbath** here (cp. 5:9) resumes the earlier Sabbath controversy in chapter 5. Jesus had

A section of the Pool of Siloam discovered in 2005. Pottery indicates this section of the pool was in use in the first century.

do you say about Him, since He opened your eyes?"

"He's a prophet,"[a] he said.

[18] The *Jews did not believe this about him —that he was blind and received sight—until they summoned the parents of the one who had received his sight.

[19] They asked them, "Is this your son, the one you say was born blind? How then does he now see?"

[20] "We know this is our son and that he was born blind," his parents answered. [21] "But we don't know how he now sees, and we don't know who opened his eyes. Ask him; he's of age. He will speak for himself." [22] His parents said these things because they were afraid of the Jews, since the Jews had already agreed that if anyone confessed Him as *Messiah,[b] he would be banned from the *synagogue. [23] This is why his parents said, "He's of age; ask him."

[24] So a second time they summoned the man who had been blind and told him, "Give glory[c] to God.[A,d] We know that this man is a sinner!"

[25] He answered, "Whether or not He's a sinner, I don't know. One thing I do know: I was blind, and now I can see!"

[26] Then they asked him, "What did He do to you? How did He open your eyes?"

[27] "I already told you," he said, "and you didn't listen. Why do you want to hear it again? You don't want to become His disciples too, do you?"

[28] They ridiculed him: "You're that man's disciple, but we're Moses'[e] disciples. [29] We know that God has spoken to Moses. But this man—we don't know where He's from!"[f]

[30] "This is an amazing thing," the man told them. "You don't know where He is from, yet He opened my eyes! [31] We know that God doesn't listen to sinners,[g] but if anyone is God-fearing and does His will,[h] He listens to him.[i] [32] Throughout history[B] no one has ever heard of someone opening the eyes of a person born blind.[j] [33] If this man were not from God, He wouldn't be able to do anything."[k]

[34] "You were born entirely in sin,"[l] they replied, "and are you trying to teach us?" Then they threw him out.[C,m]

The Blind Man's Sight and the Pharisees' Blindness

[35] When Jesus heard that they had thrown the man out, He found him and asked, "Do you believe in the *Son of Man?"[D,n] [36] "Who is He, Sir,[o] that I may believe in Him?" he asked.

[37] Jesus answered, "You have seen Him; in fact, He is the One speaking with you."

Cross references column:
a 9:17 Jn 6:14
b 9:22 Mt 1:17; Eph 5:2
c 9:24 Jn 17:24
d Jos 7:19; 1Sm 6:5; Is 42:12; Jr 13:16; Lk 2:14; Rm 4:20
e 9:28 Ps 77:20; Mt 8:4; Heb 3:2
f 9:29 Jn 7:27-28; 8:14
g 9:31 Jb 27:9; Ps 66:18; Pr 28:9; Is 1:15; 1Jn 3:21
h Eph 1:9
i Ps 34:15,16; 145:19; Pr 15:20; Jms 5:16-18; 1Jn 5:14-15
j 9:32 Jn 15:24
k 9:33 Jn 8:28
l 9:34 Ps 51:5
m Is 66:5
n 9:35 Mk 2:10
o 9:36 Lk 10:1

A 9:24 *Give glory to God* was a solemn charge to tell the truth; Jos 7:19.   B 9:32 Lit *From the age*   C 9:34 = they banned him from the synagogue; v. 22   D 9:35 Other mss read *the Son of God*

moistened clay with His saliva and then kneaded it to make mud. Kneading dough, and by analogy kneading clay, was included among the 39 classes of work forbidden on the Sabbath by Jewish rabbinic tradition (m. Shabb. 7:2).

9:16 The **division** among the Pharisees follows the differing ways of reasoning observed by the schools of Shammai and Hillel. The former argued from foundational principles ("anyone who breaks the law is a sinner"), the latter from the established facts of a case ("Jesus has performed a good work").

9:22 On **the Jews** and their power, see note at 7:13.

9:24 The Pharisees' exhortation to the healed man, **Give glory to God**, was a solemn warning for him to tell the truth (Jos 7:19; 2Ch 30:8; Jr 13:16).

9:28 The Pharisees' claim of being **Moses' disciples** was undermined by their failure to listen to the One of whom Moses wrote (see note at 5:45-47).

9:29 The Pharisees' assertion, **We know that God has spoken to Moses**, harks back to God's giving Moses the law at Mount Sinai (Ex 33:11; Nm 12:2-8; cp. Jn 1:17).

9:31-33 The healed man's major premise, that **God doesn't listen to sinners**, is borne out by the OT (Ps 34:15; 66:20; 109:7; 145:19). His minor premise, that there was no precedent for **opening the eyes of a person born blind**, is also confirmed by the absence of such instances cited in OT or extrabiblical sources. The man's conclusion, **If this man**

were not from God, He wouldn't be able to do anything (cp. 3:2), fit with the common Jewish view that miracles were performed in answer to prayer.

9:34 The Pharisees' charge against the healed man may allude to Ps 51:5. **Threw him out** refers to expulsion from the synagogue (see note at v. 22). The way this was done

hamartolos

Greek Pronunciation	[hah mahr toh LAHSS]
HCSB Translation	sinner
Uses in John's Gospel	4
Uses in the NT	47
Focus Passage	John 9:16,24

One of the key doctrines of the Christian faith is that every person is a *sinner* and must believe in Jesus as Savior to have eternal life. This teaching is consistent with the use of the word *hamartolos (sinner)* in several places and with other related passages about sin (Rm 3:9-23; 5:12). A special use of the term *hamartolos* occurs in the Gospels and refers to those who have a reputation for being guilty of grievous sins, such as tax collectors, prostitutes, and pagans (see Mt 9:10-11; Lk 6:32-34; 7:36-39). In the aftermath of Jesus' miracle of healing the man born blind (Jn 9), Jewish leaders used the term *sinner* in this especially derisive sense to describe Jesus (v. 24). In doing so they hoped to undermine the clear implication of this miracle—that Jesus was the Messiah—and to keep people from following Him.

³⁸"I believe, Lord!" he said, and he worshiped Him.

³⁹Jesus said, "I came into this world[a] for judgment,[b] in order that those who do not see will see and those who do see will become blind."[c]

⁴⁰Some of the Pharisees who were with Him heard these things and asked Him, "We aren't blind too, are we?"

⁴¹"If you were blind," Jesus told them, "you wouldn't have sin.[A,d] But now that you say, 'We see'—your sin remains.

The Ideal Shepherd

10 "'I assure you: Anyone who doesn't enter the sheep pen by the door but climbs in some other way, is a thief and a robber.[e] ²The one who enters by the door is the shepherd[f] of the sheep.[g] ³The doorkeeper opens it for him, and the sheep hear his voice. He calls his own sheep by name and leads them out. ⁴When he has brought all his own outside, he goes ahead of them. The sheep follow him

Cross references column:
a 9:39 Jn 18:37
b Mk 12:40; Jn 5:22-30
c Lk 4:18; Jn 3:19; 12:47-50
d 9:41 Jn 15:22,24; 1Jn 1:8; 3:5
e 10:1 Jr 7:11; Hs 6:9; 1Th 5:2,4; 2Pt 3:10; Rv 3:3; 16:15
f 10:2 Gn 4:2; Ps 23:1
g Mt 7:15
h 10:6 Mk 9:32; Lk 2:50; 9:45; 18:34; Jn 2:24; 12:16
i 10:7 Ex 3:14; Ps 45:8; Jn 8:24
j Mt 7:15
k 10:10 Eph 4:28 Jn 6:27
m 10:11 Ps 23:1; Is 40:11; Ezk 34:12,23; 37:24; Zch 13:7; Jn 21:15-17; Heb 13:20; 1Pt 2:25; 5:4; Rv 7:17
n Mt 20:28; Mk 10:45; 2Co 5:21; Gl 3:13; 1Jn 3:16
o 10:12 Lk 10:3

because they recognize his voice. ⁵They will never follow a stranger; instead they will run away from him, because they don't recognize the voice of strangers."

⁶Jesus gave them this illustration, but they did not understand[h] what He was telling them.

The Good Shepherd

⁷So Jesus said again, "I assure you: I am[i] the door of the sheep.[j] ⁸All who came before Me[B] are thieves and robbers, but the sheep didn't listen to them. ⁹I am the door. If anyone enters by Me, he will be saved and will come in and go out and find pasture. ¹⁰A thief comes only to steal[k] and to kill and to destroy.[l] I have come so that they may have life and have it in abundance.

¹¹"I am the good shepherd.[m] The good shepherd lays down his life for the sheep.[n] ¹²The hired man, since he is not the shepherd and doesn't own the sheep, leaves them[c] and runs away when he sees a wolf[o] coming. The wolf

---

A 9:41 To *have sin* is an idiom that refers to guilt caused by sin. B 10:8 Other mss omit *before Me* C 10:12 Lit *leaves the sheep*

---

suggests an impulsive action rather than excommunication based on a formal procedure.

9:39-41 Giving sight to the righteous blind (Ps 146:8; Is 29:18; 35:5; 42:7,18) and blinding unrighteous persons who can see (Is 6:10; 42:19; Jr 5:21; cp. Mt 13:13-15; Jn 12:40) are common OT themes. Elsewhere, Jesus called the Pharisees "blind guides" (Mt 23:16; cp. 15:14; 23:26).

10:1-42 In this discourse, Jesus criticized the Jewish leaders for failing to give Israel proper spiritual guidance. By contrast, Jesus is the Good Shepherd who lays down His life for the sheep. Hence chapter 10 provides a commentary on the previous chapter which revealed the Jewish leadership's legal pettiness, rigidity, and hardness toward God. Not only is Jesus the Good Shepherd, He is also the door through which believers find abundant, eternal life (vv. 9-10). The following interchange, culminating in another attempt to stone Jesus for blasphemy, took place at the Feast of Dedication (vv. 22-39). It is followed by a final reference to John the Baptist, which closes out the "festival cycle" of chapters 5-10 and the entire section (1:19-10:42), which began with the ministry of John the Baptist and his witness to Jesus.

10:1 The **sheep pen** may have been a courtyard (18:15) near a house surrounded by a stone wall where several families kept their sheep. The gate would have been guarded by a hired doorkeeper (10:3). **Thief** may focus on the covert nature of entrance to the pen, and **robber** on violence (Lk 10:30,36).

10:2 The **shepherd** was the authorized caretaker of the flock.

10:3-4 On **doorkeeper**, see note at verse 1. The reference to the shepherd calling his **own sheep by name** and leading them out may allude to passages such as Nm 27:16-18 (esp. v. 17), possibly a messianic passage, or Ezk 34:13. Israel's exodus from Egypt is sometimes portrayed as a flock following its shepherd (Ps 77:20; Is 63:11,14; cp. Ps 78:52). Old Testament prophetic literature envisioned a similar end-time deliverance for God's people (Mc 2:12-13).

10:6 On **illustration**, see note at 16:21.

10:7,9 Jesus' reference to Himself as **the door** may hark back to messianic readings of passages such as Ps 118:20 (see notes at Jn 6:35,48 and 10:1).

10:8 All who came before Me may hint at messianic pretenders who promised their followers freedom but led them into armed conflict and doom instead (Ac 5:36-37; 21:38). The reference to **thieves and robbers** is reminiscent of the reference to Israel's shepherds "who have been feeding themselves" but not the flock (Ezk 34:2-4; see note at Jn 10:1).

10:9 Jesus is **the door** to salvation (cp. 14:6). The NT elsewhere speaks of "entering" God's kingdom as through a door (Mt 7:7,13; 25:10; Ac 14:22). **Will come in and go out** echoes covenant terminology, especially blessings for obedience (Dt 28:6; cp. Ps 121:8). It is also reminiscent of Moses' description of Joshua, who led Israel into the promised land (Nm 27:16-17). **Find pasture** depicts the assurance of God's provision (1Ch 4:40; Ps 23:2; Is 49:9-10; Ezk 34:12-15).

10:10 Jesus' promise of abundant life in the here and now brings to mind OT prophetic passages such as Ezk 34:12-15,25-31. See note at Jn 5:26.

10:11 Jesus is **the good shepherd** (see note at 6:35,48). In the OT, God as the true shepherd is contrasted with unfaithful shepherds whom God will judge (Jr 23:1-4; Ezk 34; Zch 11:4-17). David (or the Davidic Messiah) was also depicted as a good shepherd (2Sm 5:2; Ps 78:70-72; Ezk 37:24; Mc 5:4), as was Moses (Is 63:11; cp. Ps 77:20). The reference to the good shepherd who **lays down his life for the sheep** calls to mind young David (1Sm 17:34-37).

10:12 The **hired man** does not care for the sheep and abandons them in times of danger. The hired hands of Israel (Ezk 22:27) are contrasted with God and His Messiah, whose role is patterned after God's "good shepherd" par excellence, King David (1Sm 17:34-36).

then snatches and scatters them. ¹³This happens because he is a hired man and doesn't care about the sheep.

¹⁴"I am the good shepherd. I know My own sheep, and they know Me, ¹⁵as the Father knows Me, and I know the Father.ᵃ I lay down My lifeᵇ for the sheep. ¹⁶But I have other sheepᶜ that are not of this fold; I must bring them also, and they will listen to My voice. Then there will be one flock, one shepherd.ᵈ ¹⁷This is why the Father loves Me,ᵉ because I am laying down My lifeᶠ so I may take it up again. ¹⁸No one takes it from Me, but I lay it down on My own. I have the right to lay it down, and I have the right to take it up again. I have received this command from My Father."ᵍ

¹⁹Again a divisionʰ took place among the •Jews because of these words. ²⁰Many of them were saying, "He has a demonⁱ and He's crazy! Why do you listen to Him?" ²¹Others were saying, "These aren't the words of someone demon-possessed. Can a demon open the eyes of the blind?"ʲ

Jesus at the Festival of Dedication

²²Then the Festival of Dedicationᴬ took place in Jerusalem, and it was winter. ²³Jesus was walking in the •temple complex in Solomon's Colonnade.ᴮ,ᵏ ²⁴Then the Jews surrounded

Him and asked, "How long are You going to keep us in suspense?ᶜ If You are the •Messiah,ˡ tell us plainly."ᴰ,ᵐ

²⁵"I did tell you and you don't believe," Jesus answered them. "The worksⁿ that I do in My Father's name testify about Me. ²⁶But you don't believe because you are not My sheep.ᴱ,ᵒ ²⁷My sheep hear My voice, I know them, and they follow Me. ²⁸I give them eternal life,ᵖ and they will never perishᑫ—ever! No one will snatchʳ them out of My hand. ²⁹My Father,ˢ who has given them to Me, is greater than all. No one is able to snatch them out of the Father's hand. ³⁰The Father and I are one."ᶠ,ᵗ

Renewed Efforts to Stone Jesus

³¹Again the Jews picked up rocks to stone Him.ᵘ

³²Jesus replied, "I have shown you many good worksᵛ from the Father. Which of these works are you stoning Me for?"

³³"We aren't stoningʷ You for a good work," the Jews answered, "but for blasphemy, because You—being a man—make Yourself God."

³⁴Jesus answered them, "Isn't it written in

Cross references (center column)
ᵃ10:15 Mt 11:27; Lk 10:22
ᵇMt 20:28
ᶜ10:16 Is 56:8; Ezk 34:11-13; Mt 8:11,12; Jn 12:32; Ac 10:34-35; 1Pt 2:25
ᵈEzk 34:23; 37:24; Jn 11:52; 17:11,20-22; Eph 2:11-19
ᵉ10:17 Jn 3:35; 5:20
ᶠJn 3:16
ᵍ10:18 Jn 5:19
ʰ10:19 Jn 7:43; 9:16
ⁱ10:20 Jn 7:20; 8:48; Rv 9:20; 18:2
ʲ10:21 Ex 4:11; Ps 146:8; Jn 9:32-33
ᵏ10:23 Ac 3:11; 5:12
ˡ10:24 Mt 1:17; Eph 5:2
ᵐMt 26:63; Lk 22:67; 2Co 3:12
ⁿ10:25 Jn 5:36; 6:28-29; Rm 14:20; Heb 3:9; 2Jn 8; Rv 15:3
ᵒ10:26 Jn 6:37; 8:47
ᵖ10:28 Jn 12:25; Ac 13:48; 1Jn 2:25
ᑫMt 10:42; Mk 9:41; Lk 21:18; Jn 3:16; 6:27,39; 17:12; 18:9; 2Co 4:9; 2Jn 8
ʳ1Th 4:17 ˢ10:29 Mt 11:27 ᵗ10:30 Jn 1:15; 14:10; 17:11; 1Jn 2:24 ᵘ10:31 Jn 11:8 ᵛ10:32 Jn 5:36; 15:24 ʷ10:33 Lv 24:16; Mt 9:3; 26:62-66; Jn 5:18; 8:59

ᴬ10:22 Or *Hanukkah*, also called *the Feast of Lights*; this festival commemorated the rededication of the temple in 164 B.C.
ᴮ10:23 Rows of columns supporting a roof ᶜ10:24 Lit *How long are you taking away our life?* ᴰ10:24 Or *openly*, or *publicly*
ᴱ10:26 Other mss add *just as I told you* ᶠ10:30 Lit *I and the Father—We are one.*

10:14 On Jesus as **the good shepherd**, see note at verse 11.

10:16 The **other sheep . . . not of this fold** refers to Gentiles (Is 56:8). Jesus envisioned a future Gentile mission following His death on the cross. **One flock, one shepherd** alludes to Ezk 34:23; 37:24. Believing Jews and Gentiles will be united into one messianic community.

10:18 Received this command is covenantal language, relating Jesus' relationship with the Father to the OT depiction of God's relationship with Israel.

10:20-21 In ancient times insanity and demon possession were frequently linked. The reference to opening the **eyes of the blind** links the Good Shepherd discourse with the healing of the blind man in chapter 9. The charges of demon possession (which harks back to similar charges from earlier; see note at 7:20) and insanity were contradicted by OT teaching that it is the Lord who gives sight to the blind (Ps 146:8; cp. Ex 4:11).

10:22 The eight-day **Festival of Dedication** celebrated the rededication of the Jewish temple in December of 164 B.C. after its desecration by the Seleucid ruler Antiochus Epiphanes in 167 B.C. (1Macc 1:59). **It was winter** refers to December. See note at 2:13.

10:23 On the **temple complex**, see note at 2:14. Probably because of the cold winter weather, Jesus taught not out in the open but in the area called **Solomon's Colonnade**. The structure was commonly (though erroneously) thought to

date back to Solomon's time. Later it became the gathering place for the early church (Ac 3:11; 5:12).

10:24-25 The demand, **If you are the Messiah, tell us plainly** seems like double talk (Lk 22:67). If they had not understood Jesus' claim to be the Messiah, why did they repeatedly try to kill Him? (Jn 5:18; 7:25; 8:59). Indeed, Jesus responded that He did make this claim. On Jesus' **works** testifying about Himself, see note at 5:31-47.

10:26-29 Snatch (vv. 28-29) denotes the use of force (see note at v. 1). The comment contrasts with the figure of the hired man in verses 12-13 who abandoned the flock in times of danger, and recalls OT statements that no one can rob from God's hand (Is 43:13).

10:30 Jesus' claim that He and the Father **are one** (cp. vv. 33-38; 5:17-18) echoes the Shema, the basic confession of Judaism (Dt 6:4) and amounts to a claim to deity. Jesus' unity with the Father is later said to be the basis on which Jesus' followers are to be unified (Jn 17:22).

10:31 On the attempt to stone Jesus for blasphemy, see notes at 5:18 and 8:59.

10:32 On Jesus' works as a testimony to Himself, see note at 5:31-47.

10:33 The charge against Jesus appears to be grounded in Lv 24:16 (cp. Nm 15:30-31; Mk 14:61-64; see notes at Jn 8:59 and 19:7).

10:34 Jesus' point in quoting Ps 82:6 was that if human judges can in some sense be called "god" in the

your scripture,[A] **I said, you are gods?**[B,a] [35] If He called those whom the word[b] of God came to 'gods'—and the Scripture[c] cannot be broken— [36] do you say, 'You are blaspheming' to the One the Father set apart and sent into the world, because I said: I am the Son of God?[d] [37] If I am not doing My Father's works,[e] don't believe Me. [38] But if I am doing them and you don't believe Me, believe the works. This way you will know and understand[C] that the Father is in Me and I in the Father."[f] [39] Then they were trying again to seize Him,[g] yet He eluded their grasp.[h]

Many beyond the Jordan Believe in Jesus

[40] So He departed again across the Jordan[i] to the place where John[j] had been baptizing earlier, and He remained there. [41] Many came to Him[k] and said, "John never did a sign, but everything John said about this man was true." [42] And many believed in Him there.

Lazarus Dies at Bethany

11 Now a man was sick, Lazarus, from Bethany,[l] the village of Mary and her sister Martha.[m] [2] Mary was the one who anointed the Lord with fragrant oil and wiped His feet with her hair,[n] and it was her brother Lazarus who was sick. [3] So the sisters sent a message to Him: "Lord, the one You love is sick." [4] When Jesus heard it, He said, "This sickness will not end in death but is for the glory of God,[o] so that the Son of God[p] may be glori-

fied through it." [5] Now Jesus loved Martha, her sister, and Lazarus. [6] So when He heard that he was sick, He stayed two more days in the place where He was. [7] Then after that, He said to the disciples, "Let's go to Judea[q] again."

[8] "Rabbi,"[r] the disciples told Him, "just now the •Jews tried to stone You,[s] and You're going there again?"

[9] "Aren't there 12 hours in a day?" Jesus answered. "If anyone walks during the day, he doesn't stumble, because he sees the light of this world.[t] [10] If anyone walks during the night,[u] he does stumble, because the light is not in him." [11] He said this, and then He told them, "Our friend Lazarus has fallen •asleep,[v] but I'm on My way to wake him up."

[12] Then the disciples said to Him, "Lord, if he has fallen asleep, he will get well." [13] Jesus, however, was speaking about his death, but they thought He was speaking about natural sleep. [14] So Jesus then told them plainly, "Lazarus has died. [15] I'm glad for you that I wasn't there so that you may believe. But let's go to him."

[16] Then Thomas[w] (called "Twin") said to his fellow disciples, "Let's go so that we may die with Him."

The Resurrection and the Life

[17] When Jesus arrived, He found that Lazarus had already been in the tomb[x] four days. [18] Bethany was near Jerusalem[y] (about two

---

Cross references (center column):
a 10:34 Ps 82:6
b 10:35 Lk 8:21; Jn 2:22; 18:32
c Mt 26:54
d 10:36 Jn 5:19; Heb 1:2
e 10:37 Jn 5:36; 15:24; Heb 3:9; Rv 15:3
f 10:38 Jn 14:10; 1Jn 5:20
g 10:39 Jn 7:44
h Lk 4:30
i 10:40 Mk 10:1; Lk 3:3
j Mk 1:4
k 10:41 Mk 1:45
l 11:1 Mk 11:1
m Lk 10:38-39, 40-42
n 11:2 Lk 7:38; Jn 12:3
o 11:4 Lk 9:32; Jn 9:3; 10:38; 11:40; 17:24; 2Co 3:18; 2Pt 3:18
p Jn 5:19; Heb 1:2
q 11:7 Lk 1:5
r 11:8 Mt 23:7-8; 26:25,49; Mk 9:5; 11:21; 14:45; Jn 1:38,49; 3:2,26; 4:31; 6:25; 9:2
s Jn 10:31
t 11:9 Mt 5:14; Jn 8:12
u 11:10 Jn 9:4
v 11:11 Ac 13:36; 1Co 11:30
w 11:16 Mk 3:18
x 11:17 Jn 5:28
y 11:18 Mt 23:37

A 10:34 Other mss read *in the scripture*   **B** 10:34 Ps 82:6   **C** 10:38 Other mss read *know and believe*

Scriptures, this designation is even more appropriate for Himself.

10:35 Jesus' statement that **the Scripture cannot be broken** is evidence for His belief in the inviolability of God's written Word (in this case, the Hebrew Scriptures; cp. Mt 5:18). Jesus and many of His opponents upheld the authority of God's Word.

10:36 The reference to Jesus being **set apart** for His mission echoes language used of appointed men such as Moses the lawgiver, Jeremiah the prophet, and the Aaronic priests.

10:37-38 On Jesus' **works** testifying about Himself, see note at 5:31-47.

10:40-41 On the place where **John** was **baptizing**, see note at 1:28.

11:1-57 The raising of Lazarus is Jesus' seventh and climactic messianic sign in John's Gospel (see note at 2:11). This miracle (recorded only by John) anticipated Jesus' own resurrection and revealed Him as "the resurrection and the life" (11:25). Resurrections are rare in the OT (Elijah, 1Kg 17:17-24; Elisha, 2Kg 4:32-37; 13:21) and in the Gospels (Jesus' raising of Jairus's daughter, Mk 5:22-24,38-42; Jesus' raising of the widow's son at Nain, Lk 7:11-15). The raising of Lazarus served as the final event that triggered

the Jewish leaders' resolve to arrest Jesus and try Him for blasphemy (Jn 11:45-57).

11:1 The introduction of **Lazarus** is similar to 5:5. Lazarus (which means "whom God helps") was a common name. **Bethany**, called a **village** (Gk *kome*) as is Bethlehem (7:42), was not the Bethany mentioned in 1:28 and alluded to in 10:40-42. Bethany, where Lazarus lived, was located east of the Mount of Olives less than two miles from Jerusalem (11:18; cp. Mt 21:17; 26:6). The **village of Mary and her sister Martha** and the reference to Mary's anointing of Jesus anticipates chapter 12 and seems to presuppose that readers knew these women, perhaps from Luke's Gospel (Lk 10:38-42).

11:6 Jesus **stayed two more days . . . where He was**. Puzzling as this delay seems, it served to reveal God's glory (v. 4) since it enabled Jesus to perform an even "harder" miracle (v. 17).

11:9 Most people worked as long as there was daylight; once it was dark, work was over.

11:11 Fallen asleep means "died," as the following interchange makes clear (vv. 12-14). The OT equivalent is "slept with his fathers." Occasionally, death is depicted as a deep sleep from which we will be awakened (Dn 12:2).

11:16 On Thomas's designation as **Twin**, see note at 1:38.

11:17 By comforting Martha and Mary after Lazarus's death,

miles[A] away). [19] Many of the Jews had come to Martha and Mary to comfort them about their brother. [20] As soon as Martha heard that Jesus was coming, she went to meet Him. But Mary remained seated in the house.

[21] Then Martha said to Jesus, "Lord, if You had been here, my brother wouldn't have died. [22] Yet even now I know that whatever You ask from God, God will give You."

[23] "Your brother will rise[a] again," Jesus told her.

[24] Martha said, "I know that he will rise again in the resurrection at the last day."[b]

[25] Jesus said to her, "I am[c] the resurrection and the life. The one who believes in Me,[d] even if he dies, will live.[e] [26] Everyone who lives and believes in Me will never die—ever.[f] Do you believe this?"

[27] "Yes, Lord," she told Him, "I believe You are the •Messiah,[g] the Son[h] of God, who comes into the world."[i]

Jesus Shares the Sorrow of Death

[28] Having said this, she went back and called her sister Mary, saying in private, "The Teacher is here and is calling for you."

[29] As soon as she heard this, she got up quickly and went to Him.[j] [30] Jesus had not yet come into the village but was still in the place where Martha had met Him. [31] The Jews who were with her in the house consoling her saw that Mary got up quickly and went out. So

they followed her, supposing that she was going to the tomb[k] to cry there.

[32] When Mary came to where Jesus was and saw Him, she fell at His feet[l] and told Him, "Lord, if You had been here, my brother would not have died!"

[33] When Jesus saw her crying, and the Jews who had come with her crying, He was angry[B] in His spirit[m] and deeply moved. [34] "Where have you put him?" He asked.

"Lord," they told Him, "come and see."

[35] Jesus wept.[n]

[36] So the Jews said, "See how He loved[o] him!"

[37] But some of them said, "Couldn't He who opened the blind man's eyes[p] also have kept this man from dying?"

The Seventh Sign: Raising Lazarus from the Dead

[38] Then Jesus, angry[C] in Himself again, came to the tomb. It was a cave, and a stone was lying against it.[q] [39] "Remove the stone," Jesus said.

Martha, the dead man's sister, told Him, "Lord, he's already decaying.[D] It's been four days."

[40] Jesus said to her, "Didn't I tell you that if you believed you would see the glory[r] of God?"[s]

[41] So they removed the stone. Then Jesus raised His eyes and said, "Father, I thank[t] You that You heard Me.[u] [42] I know that You always

Cross references (center column)

[a]11:23 Mk 9:27
[b]11:24 Jn 2:4; 6:39; 1Pt 1:5; 3:3; 2Pt 3:3; Jd 18
[c]11:25 Ex 3:14; Jn 8:24,58
[d]Jn 6:35
[e]Php 1:21
[f]11:26 Jn 6:50; 8:51
[g]11:27 Mt 1:17; Eph 5:2
[h]Jn 5:19
[i]Jn 18:37
[j]11:29 Mk 1:45
[k]11:31 Jn 5:28
[l]11:32 Rv 19:10
[m]11:33 Ps 51:12
[n]11:35 Lk 19:41
[o]11:36 Mk 14:44; Jn 5:20
[p]11:37 Jn 9:6-7
[q]11:38 Mt 27:60; Mk 15:46; Lk 24:2; Jn 20:1
[r]11:40 Jn 17:24
[s]Mk 9:23; 1Jn 3:2
[t]11:41 Mk 8:6; Rm 1:8
[u]Jn 9:31

[A]11:18 Lit 15 stadia; 1 stadion = 600 feet   [B]11:33 The Gk word is very strong and probably indicates Jesus' anger against sin's tyranny and death.   [C]11:38 See note at 11:33.   [D]11:39 Lit he already stinks

---

Jesus fulfilled one of the most essential obligations in the Jewish culture of His day—mourning with those who mourn. Burial usually followed shortly after death, so Lazarus had been dead **four days**.

11:18 On **Bethany**, see note at v. 1.

11:19 If the many Jews who **had come to Martha and Mary to comfort them** were from Jerusalem, this would indicate that their family had considerable social standing.

anastasis

Greek Pronunciation	[ah NAH stah sihss]
HCSB Translation	resurrection
Uses in John's Gospel	4
Uses in the NT	42
Focus Passage	John 11:24-25

The Greek noun *anastasis* is derived from the verb *anistemi*, meaning literally *to stand up* and then by extension *"to rise up."* Both words could be used metaphorically. The word *anastasis* was common in the ancient Greek world; but it rarely referred to the *resurrection* of the dead, which is the dominant meaning of its occurrences in the NT. Two major events are described with the word *anastasis* in the NT: the physical, bodily *resurrection* of Jesus in the past (Rm 1:4; 1Co 15:12-13), and the physical, bodily *resurrection* of believers in the future (Jn 5:29; 11:24-25; 1Co 15:42; Php 3:11; Rv 20:5-6).

11:20 Seated in the house was the customary posture for those mourning a deceased loved one (Jb 2:8,13; Ezk 8:14).

11:24 Martha's belief in end-time **resurrection** agreed with Pharisaic beliefs (Ac 23:8), popular Jewish opinion, and Jesus' teaching (Jn 5:21,25-29; 6:39-44,54).

11:25 On **I am the resurrection and the life**, see notes at 5:26 and 6:35,48.

11:27 Martha's reference to the one who **comes into the world** took up the messianic expression derived from Ps 118:26 (cp. Jn 12:13).

11:28 The Teacher was a natural way for a disciple to refer to Jesus before His resurrection (v. 8; 1:38,49; 3:2; 4:31; 6:25; 9:2; 20:16).

11:33 Jesus was **angry in His spirit** (the Gk word for "angry," *embrimaomai*, connotes anger and snorting; cp. Lm 2:6; Dn 11:30). Jesus was upset in the face of human suffering and death (Jn 12:27; 13:21). **Deeply moved** means agitated and stirred up (Est 4:4).

11:35 Jesus wept, or perhaps even better, "burst into tears," as the term is regularly translated in extrabiblical sources.

11:39 While the Jews used spices at burials, this did not prevent decomposition of the body, as Martha pointed out.

11:41-42 Jesus' prayer finds an OT antecedent in Elijah's prayer (1Kg 18:37). Compare Jn 6:11.

hear Me, but because of the crowd standing here I said this, so they may believe You sent[a] Me." [43] After He said this, He shouted with a loud voice, "Lazarus, come out!" [44] The dead man came out bound hand and foot with linen strips and with his face wrapped in a cloth. Jesus said to them, "Loose him and let him go."

The Plot to Kill Jesus

[45] Therefore, many of the Jews who came to Mary and saw what He did believed in Him.[b] [46] But some of them went to the •Pharisees[c] and told them what Jesus had done.

[47] So the •chief priests and the Pharisees convened the •Sanhedrin[d] and said, "What are we going to do since this man does many signs? [48] If we let Him continue in this way, everyone will believe in Him! Then the Romans[e] will come and remove both our place[A] and our nation."

[49] One of them, Caiaphas,[f] who was high priest[g] that year, said to them, "You know nothing at all! [50] You're not considering that it is to your[B] advantage that one man should die for the people rather than the whole nation

perish."[h] [51] He did not say this on his own, but being high priest that year he prophesied that Jesus was going to die[i] for the nation, [52] and not for the nation only, but also to unite the scattered children[j] of God. [53] So from that day on they plotted to kill Him.[k] [54] Therefore Jesus no longer walked openly[l] among the Jews but departed from there to the countryside near the wilderness,[m] to a town called Ephraim. And He stayed there with the disciples.

[55] The Jewish •Passover[n] was near, and many went up to Jerusalem[o] from the country to purify[c] themselves before the Passover. [56] They were looking for Jesus and asking one another as they stood in the •temple complex:[p] "What do you think? He won't come to the festival,[q] will He?" [57] The chief priests[r] and the Pharisees had given orders that if anyone knew where He was, he should report it so they could arrest Him.

The Anointing at Bethany

12 Six days before the •Passover, Jesus came to Bethany[s] where Lazarus[D] was,

Cross references

a 11:42 Mk 9:37; Jn 1:6
b 11:45 Jn 2:23; 12:11
c 11:46 Mk 7:3
d 11:47 Mk 13:9
e 11:48 Ac 16:21
f 11:49 Mt 26:3,57; Lk 3:2; Jn 18:13-14,24,28; Ac 4:6
g Lv 16:32
h 11:50 Is 53:8; Jn 18:14
i 11:51 2Co 4:10
j 11:52 Lk 1:7
k 11:53 Jn 5:18
l 11:54 Jn 7:1
m Mt 3:1; Rv 12:6
n 11:55 Ex 12:11
o Mt 23:37
p 11:56 Ac 21:26
q Jn 2:23
r 11:57 Mt 2:4
s 12:1 Mk 11:1

A 11:48 The temple or possibly all of Jerusalem   B 11:50 Other mss read *to our*   C 11:55 The law of Moses required God's people to purify or cleanse themselves so they could celebrate the Passover. Jews often came to Jerusalem a week early to do this; Nm 9:4-11.   D 12:1 Other mss read *Lazarus who died*

11:43 Jesus raised Lazarus not by magic, incantations, or spells, but by the power of His word.

11:44 John did not record Lazarus's reaction or any of the aftermath of his raising. Instead, he immediately moved (v. 45) to focus on the plot against Jesus.

11:47 On the **Sanhedrin**, see notes at 3:1 and 7:45-52.

11:48 Our place almost certainly refers to the temple. Similar concerns resurface in Ac 6:13-14 and 21:28, where the temple is referred to as "this holy place" or "this place." **Remove . . . our nation** may refer to the feared removal of the Jews' semi-autonomous status by the Romans. Ironically, what the Sanhedrin sought to prevent by killing Jesus still came to pass when the Romans razed the temple and sacked Jerusalem in A.D. 70 (see note at 2:13-22).

11:49 That year need not imply that the high priestly office rotated annually. It simply indicates that Caiaphas happened to serve in this role the year Jesus was tried and crucified. In fact, Caiaphas was high priest for 18 years (A.D. 18–36), longer than any other first-century high priest.

11:50-51 Die for the people invokes memory of the Maccabean martyrs (2Macc 7:37-38). In the typical double meaning used in John's Gospel, Caiaphas's pronouncement anticipated the substitutionary atonement Jesus was to render. As the Jewish high priest, Caiaphas **prophesied**, speaking better than he knew.

11:52 The **scattered children of God** refers to the Gentiles (see note at 3:3-8).

11:55 This is the third and final **Passover** mentioned by John. See note at 2:13. People went **up** to **Jerusalem** early to **purify themselves** from any ceremonial uncleanness that would prevent them from celebrating Passover (Nm 9:4-14; 19:11-12).

11:56-57 On the timing of Jesus' arrest, see note at 2:4. On the **temple complex**, see note at 2:14.

The traditional site of Lazarus's tomb in Bethany.

the one Jesus had raised from the dead.[a] [2]So[b] they gave a dinner for Him there; Martha[c] was serving them, and Lazarus was one of those reclining at the table with Him. [3]Then Mary took a pound of fragrant oil—pure and expensive nard—anointed Jesus' feet, and wiped His feet with her hair.[d] So the house was filled with the fragrance of the oil.

[4]Then one of His disciples, Judas Iscariot[e] (who was about to betray Him), said, [5]"Why wasn't this fragrant oil sold for 300 •denarii[A,f] and given to the poor?" [6]He didn't say this because he cared about the poor but because he was a thief.[g] He was in charge of the money-bag and would steal part of what was put in it.

[7]Jesus answered, "Leave her alone; she has kept it for the day of My burial.[h] [8]For you always have the poor with you,[i] but you do not always have Me."

The Decision to Kill Lazarus

[9]Then a large crowd of the Jews learned He was there. They came not only because of Jesus, but also to see Lazarus the one He had raised from the dead.[j] [10]Therefore the •chief priests decided to kill Lazarus also [11]because

he was the reason many of the Jews were deserting them[B] and believing in Jesus.

The Triumphal Entry

[12]The[k] next day, when the large crowd that had come to the festival heard that Jesus was coming to Jerusalem, [13]they took palm branches[l] and went out to meet Him. They kept shouting: "'Hosanna![m] **He who comes in the name of the Lord is the blessed One**[C,n]—the King of Israel!"[o]

[14]Jesus found a young donkey[p] and sat on it, just as it is written: [15]**Fear no more,[q] Daughter •Zion. Look, your King is coming, sitting on a donkey's colt.**[D,r]

[16]His disciples did not understand these things at first. However, when Jesus was glorified, then they remembered that these things had been written about Him[s] and that they had done these things to Him. [17]Meanwhile, the crowd, which had been with Him when He called Lazarus out of the tomb[t] and raised him from the dead, continued to testify.[E] [18]This is also why the crowd met Him, because they heard He had done this sign.

[19]Then the •Pharisees said to one another,

Cross references (center column):

[a]12:1 Jn 11:43-44
[b]12:2-8 Mt 26:6-13; Mk 14:3-9
[c]12:2 Jn 11:1
[d]12:3 Mk 14:3; Jn 11:2
[e]12:4 Mt 26:14; Mk 3:19
[f]12:5 Mt 18:28
[g]12:6 Jn 10:1
[h]12:7 Jn 19:40
[i]12:8 Dt 15:11
[j]12:9 Jn 21:14
[k]12:12-19 Mt 21:1-11; Mk 11:1-11; Lk 19:28-44
[l]12:13 Lv 23:40; Rv 7:9
[m]Lk 1:42
[n]Ps 118:25-26
[o]Jn 1:49
[p]12:14 Lk 13:15
[q]12:15 Jn 6:20
[r]Zch 9:9
[s]12:16 Jn 2:22; 14:26
[t]12:17 Jn 5:28

[A]12:5 This amount was about a year's wages for a common worker.   [B]12:11 Lit *going away*   [C]12:13 Ps 118:25-26   [D]12:15 Zch 9:9   [E]12:17 Other mss read *Meanwhile the crowd, which had been with Him, continued to testify that He had called Lazarus out of the tomb and raised him from the dead.*

12:1-11 The anointing by Mary of Bethany foreshadowed Jesus' imminent arrest, trial, condemnation, crucifixion, and burial (vv. 7-8). The account is closely linked with the raising of Lazarus, whose presence served as proof of Jesus' miracle-working power and thus fueled the Jewish leaders' hostility toward Jesus. What is more, the anointing also revealed Judas's antagonism toward Jesus (vv. 4-8). While only verse 3 is devoted to Mary's act of devotion, five verses speak of Judas's objection and Jesus' rebuke of Judas (vv. 4-8).

12:1 On this Passover, see notes at 2:13 and 11:55. **Six days before the Passover** most likely refers to Saturday, which began Friday evening at sundown.

12:2 Dinner (Gk *deipnon*) refers to the main meal of the day, which was usually held toward evening (Lk 14:12). The term may also refer to a festive banquet (Mt 23:6; Mk 6:21). It is used later of the Last Supper (Jn 13:2,4; 21:20). **Reclining at the table** may imply a banquet rather than a regular meal (13:2-5,23).

12:3 A **pound** or half a liter was a large amount of **fragrant oil** or perfume (11:2). **Pure and expensive nard** was imported from northern India and used by the Romans for anointing the head. The Synoptic Gospels indicate that the perfume was kept in an alabaster jar (Mt 26:7; Mk 14:3). Attending to the **feet** of a guest was the work of servants (1:27; 13:5), so Mary's actions showed humility and devotion. Her wiping of Jesus' feet with her **hair** is remarkable since Jewish women rarely unbound their hair in public.

12:5 A total of **300 denarii** represents the modern-day equivalent of a year's wages (see note at 6:7). This was a lot of money for a jar of perfume and a lot of money to "waste" by breaking the jar, as Judas observed.

12:6 Judas's motivation was impure. Before he betrayed Jesus, he was already a **thief**.

12:8 Jesus' response may have been an allusion to Dt 15:11.

12:12-19 Jesus' triumphal entry, with people waving palm branches to greet Him, is celebrated in Christian tradition as Palm Sunday. Jesus' riding into Jerusalem on a donkey fulfilled OT Scripture (Zch 9:9; see Ps 118:25-26). The waving of palm branches, a symbolic act celebrating victory over one's enemy and/or reception of a king, may indicate that the people thought Jesus would take Israel's vacant throne and deliver the nation from Roman occupation and suppression. Yet Jesus' popular acclaim would not last; some people who now hailed Him as victor called for His crucifixion only a few days later.

12:12 The next day probably refers to Sunday of Passion Week, now known as Palm Sunday. The **festival** was the Passover celebration.

12:13 Palm branches were a Jewish national symbol. The people hailed Jesus as the Davidic king of Ps 118:26 (cp. Mt 21:4-9). Psalm 118 was part of the Hallel (Pss 113-118), sung by the temple choir at major Jewish festivals.

12:15 Jesus is depicted as the humble Shepherd-King of Zch 9:9 who came to the Holy City to take His rightful place. An early messianic prophecy spoke of a ruler from Judah who would command the obedience of nations and would ride on a donkey (Gn 49:10-11). **Fear no more** may be taken from Is 40:9, which refers to one who brings good tidings to Zion (Is 44:2).

12:19 The world was an obvious exaggeration, highlighting the Pharisees' frustration (Ac 17:6).

"You see? You've accomplished nothing. Look—the world has gone after Him!"[a]

Jesus Predicts His Crucifixion

[20] Now some Greeks were among those who went up to worship at the festival. [21] So they came to Philip,[b] who was from Bethsaida[c] in Galilee,[d] and requested of him, "Sir,[e] we want to see Jesus."

[22] Philip went and told Andrew;[f] then Andrew and Philip went and told Jesus. [23] Jesus replied to them, "The hour has come for the •Son of Man[g] to be glorified.

[24] "•I assure you: Unless a grain of wheat[h] falls to the ground and dies, it remains by itself. But if it dies, it produces a large crop.[A,i] [25] The one who loves his life will lose it,[j] and the one who hates[k] his life[l] in this world will keep it for eternal life. [26] If anyone serves Me, he must follow Me. Where I am, there My servant[m] also will be.[n] If anyone serves Me, the Father will honor[o] him.

[27] "Now My soul is troubled. What should I say—Father, save Me[p] from this hour? But that is why I came to this hour. [28] Father, glorify Your name!"[B,q]

Then a voice[r] came from heaven:[s] "I have glorified it, and I will glorify it again!"[t]

[29] The crowd standing there heard it and said it was thunder. Others said that an angel had spoken to Him.

[30] Jesus responded, "This voice came, not for Me, but for you.[u] [31] Now is the judgment of this world.[v] Now the ruler of this •world[w] will be cast out.[x] [32] As for Me, if I am lifted up[C] from the earth I will draw all people to Myself."[y] [33] He said this to signify what kind of death He was about to die.[z]

[34] Then the crowd replied to Him, "We have heard from the scripture that the •Messiah will remain forever.[aa] So how can You say, 'The Son of Man[ab] must be lifted up'?[C] Who is this Son of Man?"

[35] Jesus answered, "The light will be with you only a little longer.[ac] Walk while you have the light[ad] so that darkness doesn't overtake you.[ae] The one who walks in darkness doesn't know where he's going.[af] [36] While you have the light,[ag] believe in the light so that you may become sons of light." Jesus said this, then went away and hid from them.[ah]

Isaiah's Prophecies Fulfilled

[37] Even though He had performed so many

a12:19 Mk 15:6-15; Lk 19:39-44; Jn 11:47-48; 12:36-43; 19:15
b12:21 Mk 3:18
cMt 11:21; Mk 6:45; 8:22; Lk 9:10; 10:13; Jn 1:44
dMt 17:22
eCol 3:22
f12:22 Jn 6:8
g12:23 Mk 2:10
h12:24 Lk 16:7
i1Co 15:36
j12:25 Jn 10:28
kLk 6:27; 19:14
lMt 10:39
m12:26 1Co 3:5
nJn 14:3; 17:24; 2Co 5:8; Php 1:23; 1Th 4:17
o1Tm 5:3
p12:27 Ps 3:7
q12:28 Jn 10:25; Ac 15:14; Rv 14:1
rJn 5:37
sRv 14:13
tJn 11:4; 17:1; 1Pt 2:12
u12:30 Jn 11:42
v12:31 Lk 4:6
wJn 3:16; 14:30; 16:11
xCol 2:15; 1Jn 3:8
y12:32 Jn 11:51
z12:33 Jn 18:32
aa12:34 Ps 89:36; Jn 15:4; 1Jn 2:17
ab Mk 2:10
ac12:35 Ps 118:27; Jn 7:33; 9:4
adPs 36:9; Jn 12:46; 1Jn 2:8
aePhp 3:12
afJn 7:28; 8:14; 1Jn 2:11
ag12:36 Jn 7:33; 1Th 5:5
ahLk 4:30

A12:24 Lit *produces much fruit*   B12:28 Other mss read *Your Son*   C12:32,34 Or *exalted*

12:20-50 This section concludes the first major unit of John's Gospel, which narrates Jesus' mission to the Jews. The approach of some Greeks signaled that Jesus' mission was approaching the climax in which He would die and thus reach all nations. His "hour" was now at hand (vv. 23-26; see note at 2:4); the Son of Man would shortly be "lifted up" (crucified) by men and highly exalted by God the Father (12:32; see note at 3:14). After these things Jesus would be able to draw people (Jews and non-Jews) to Himself (12:32). Further, the Jewish nation would suffer judgment for rejecting Messiah, who had performed so many signs among them (vv. 37-40).

12:20 Greeks likely refers to Gentiles, not necessarily Grecians (see note at 7:35). They were "God-fearers" who came to Jerusalem to worship at the Passover festival.

12:21-22 On **Andrew** and **Philip**, see notes at 1:44 and 6:5. The Greeks may have singled out Philip (who in turn went to get Andrew) because he and Andrew were the only two members of the Twelve with Greek names.

12:23,27 On Jesus' **hour**, see note at 2:4.

12:24 The principle of life through death is illustrated by an agricultural example.

12:25 Following Christ involves self-sacrifice, shown supremely at the cross.

12:26 This truth extends beyond a disciple's earthly life to his eternal destiny (7:34,36; 14:3; 17:24).

12:27 Jesus' expression of anguish may invoke Davidic psalms such as Ps 6:3 or 42:5,11.

12:28 This is one of only three times during Jesus' earthly

ministry when a heavenly voice attested to His identity (cp. His baptism and His transfiguration, Mt 3:13-17 and 17:1-13 and parallels).

12:29 God's revelation through **thunder** and angels is well documented in the OT. Thunder was part of God's appearance at Mount Sinai (Ex 19:16,19). Angels (or the angel of the Lord) spoke to Hagar (Gn 21:17), Abraham (Gn 22:11), Moses (Ac 7:38), Elijah (2Kg 1:15), and Daniel (Dn 10:4-11).

12:31 The **ruler of this world** in its fallen, sinful state is Satan (14:30; 16:11; 1Jn 5:19). **Now**, at the cross, the Devil would be **cast out**, or decisively defeated (Lk 10:18; Col 2:14-15).

12:32 This most explicit "lifted up" saying completes the earlier references in 3:14 (see note there) and 8:28. Very likely, the terminology echoes Is 52:13. **All people**, in the present context, means "all kinds of people"—both Jews and Gentiles (10:16; 11:52; cp. 12:20-21).

12:33 On the **kind of death** Jesus was about to die, see note at 21:19.

12:34 This is the final of several messianic misunderstandings featured in John's Gospel (cp. 7:27,31,41-42; see note at 7:25-44). This reference may find its basis in passages such as Ps 89:4,36-37 (which in turn is grounded in 2Sm 7:12-16); Ps 110:1; Is 9:7; and Dn 7:14.

12:35-36,46 Jesus' answer was indirect. In light of the fact that the light would be with people **only a little longer**, His crucifixion was near (7:33; 16:16-19). He urged that they **believe in the light** (9:4; 11:10; see note at 8:12) while there was still time.

12:36 When Jesus **hid from them**, He illustrated God's

signs in their presence, they did not believe in Him. [38] But this was to fulfill[a] the word of Isaiah[b] the prophet, who said:[A]

> **Lord, who has believed our message?**
> **And who has the arm[c] of the Lord**
> **been revealed to?**[B,d]

[39] This is why they were unable to believe, because Isaiah also said:

> [40] **He has blinded[e] their eyes**
> **and hardened their hearts,[f]**
> **so that they would not see**
> **   with their eyes**
> **or understand with their hearts,**
> **and be converted,[g]**
> **and I would heal them.**[C,h]

[41] Isaiah said these things because[D] he saw His glory[i] and spoke about Him. [42] Nevertheless, many did believe in Him even among the rulers,[j] but because of the Pharisees they did not confess Him, so they would not be banned from the •synagogue. [43] For they loved praise from men[k] more than praise from God.[E,l]

A Summary of Jesus' Mission

[44] Then Jesus cried out, "The one who believes in Me[m] believes not in Me, but in Him who sent Me. [45] And the one who sees Me sees Him[n] who sent Me. [46] I have come as a light into the world, so that everyone who believes in Me would not remain in darkness. [47] If anyone hears My words and doesn't keep[o] them, I do not judge him; for I did not come to judge the world[p] but to save the world.[q] [48] The one who rejects Me[r] and doesn't accept My sayings has this as his judge:[F] The word I have spoken will judge him on the last day.[s] [49] For I have not spoken on My own, but the Father[t] Himself who sent Me has given Me a command as to what I should say and what I should speak. [50] I know that His command is eternal life.[u] So the things that I speak, I speak just as the Father has told Me."[v]

Jesus Washes His Disciples' Feet

13 Before the •Passover Festival, Jesus knew that His hour had come to depart from this world to the Father.[w] Having loved His own who were in the world,[x] He loved them to the end.[G]

[2] Now by the time of supper, the Devil[y] had already put it into the heart of Judas,[z] Simon Iscariot's son, to betray[aa] Him. [3] Jesus knew

Cross references (center column)

a 12:38 Mt 1:22
b Mt 3:3; 4:14; 12:17
c Ex 15:16
d Is 53:1
e 12:40 Jn 8:59
f Heb 3:8
g Is 56:3,6; Mt 18:3; 23:15; Ac 15:3; 28:27; Rm 16:5; 1Tm 3:6
h Is 6:10; 1Pt 2:24
i 12:41 Mk 10:37; Jn 17:24
j 12:42 Lk 8:41
k 12:43 Php 3:19
l Lk 9:32; 2Co 3:18; 1Th 2:4; 2Pt 3:18
m 12:44 Jn 6:35
n 12:45 Jn 14:9
o 12:47 Lk 11:28; 2Tm 1:14; 2Pt 3:17
p Lk 6:37; Jn 3:18; 8:15; Rv 6:10
q Jn 3:17; Ac 16:30; Eph 2:8
r 12:48 Lk 10:16
s Jn 2:4; 6:39; 1Pt 1:5; 3:3; 2Pt 3:3; Jd 18
t 12:49 Mt 11:27
u 12:50 Jn 5:26; 12:25; Ac 13:48; 1Jn 2:25
v Jn 5:19; 14:24
w 13:1 Jn 10:18; 12:23; 16:28
x Jn 1:11; 6:37
y 13:2 Mt 4:1,10; Jn 8:44; Ac 13:10
z Mk 3:19
aa Mt 10:4; Jn 12:4; 13:21

---

imminent judgment and completed His revelatory work to the people of Israel (1:18).

12:37-50 This indictment identified Israel's wilderness generation with the unbelieving Jews in Jesus' day. Just as the ancient Jews saw God's power (performed through Moses) at the exodus (Dt 29:2-4) and turned away, so the Jews in Jesus' day watched miraculous signs (performed by Jesus) and responded with grumbling (Jn 6:41,61; cp. Ex 17:3; Nm 11:1) and unbelief (Jn 12:39).

12:38-40 John cited Is 53:1 and 6:10 to indicate that the Jewish rejection of Jesus was predicted by Scripture and thus served to confirm rather than thwart God's plan. Isaiah 53:1 referred to the Servant of the Lord who was rejected by the people but exalted by God. Isaiah 6:10 attributed people's hardening ultimately to God Himself (similar to Pharaoh's; see notes at Rm 9:17 and 9:18). These verses are the first in a series of fulfillment quotations in the second half of John's Gospel.

12:41 The reference to Isaiah seeing **His** (Jesus') **glory** may indicate that Isaiah foresaw that God would be pleased with a Suffering Servant who would be "raised and lifted up and greatly exalted" (Is 52:13). Like Abraham, Isaiah saw "Jesus' day" (cp. Jn 8:58).

12:42 On fear of the Pharisees and the Sanhedrin, see notes at 7:13 and 9:22.

12:44-50 This section summarizes Jesus' message and conveys His final appeal, bringing closure to the first major section of John's Gospel. **Sent Me** presupposes the Jewish idea of representation, according to which a messenger's identity is indistinct from that of the one

who sent him. Verses 48-50 echo Deuteronomy (Dt 18:19; 31:19,26).

13:1-17:26 In the second major unit of John's Gospel, Jesus prepared His messianic community (represented by the Twelve, minus Judas) for the time following His exaltation to the Father. The community was first cleansed literally (foot-washing, 13:1-17), then figuratively through the removal of the betrayer (13:18-30). Jesus' farewell discourse (13:31–16:33) conveys instructions to His followers, particularly about the coming "Helping Presence" (Gk *parakletos*), the Holy Spirit, and the disciples' need to remain in Jesus spiritually after His physical departure from earth. The discourse (unique to John's Gospel) concludes with Jesus' final prayer (chap. 17).

13:1-17 With His crucifixion imminent, Jesus washed His disciples' feet as a final proof of His love and to give them an example of humility and service. In a striking demonstration of love for His enemies, Jesus washed *all* of His disciples' feet, including Judas's. Jesus' act is all the more remarkable because washing people's feet was considered a task so low it could only be performed by non-Jewish slaves. In a culture where people walked long distances on dusty roads in sandals, it was customary for the host to provide water for foot-washing. This was usually done upon arrival, not during the meal. The disciples probably felt guilty that none of them had thought to do this.

13:1 References to Jewish religious festivals and the coming of Jesus' **hour** (see note at 2:4) now converge. Jesus' **own** refers to the Twelve, the representatives of His new messianic community (1:11).

that the Father had given everything into His hands,[a] that He had come from God,[b] and that He was going back to God.[c] 4 So He got up from supper, laid aside His robe,[d] took a towel, and tied it around Himself.[e] 5 Next, He poured water into a basin and began to wash His disciples' feet and to dry them with the towel tied around Him.

6 He came to Simon Peter,[f] who asked Him, "Lord, are You going to wash my feet?"

7 Jesus answered him, "What I'm doing you don't understand now, but afterward you will know."[g]

8 "You will never wash my feet—ever!" Peter said.

Jesus replied, "If I don't wash you, you have no part with Me."

9 Simon Peter said to Him, "Lord, not only my feet, but also my hands and my head."

10 "One who has bathed," Jesus told him, "doesn't need to wash anything except his feet, but he is completely •clean. You are clean, but not all of you." 11 For He knew who would betray Him. This is why He said, "You are not all clean."

The Meaning of Footwashing

12 When Jesus had washed their feet and put on His robe, He reclined[A] again and said to them, "Do you know what I have done for you? 13 You call Me Teacher and Lord. This is well said, for I am. 14 So if I, your Lord and Teacher, have washed your feet, you also ought to wash one another's feet.[h] 15 For I have given you an example[i] that you also should do just as I have done for you.

16 "I assure you: A •slave is not greater than his master,[B,j] and a messenger is not greater than the one who sent him. 17 If you know these things, you are blessed if you do them.[k] 18 I'm not speaking about all of you; I know those I have chosen.[l] But the Scripture[m] must be fulfilled:[n] **The one who eats My bread**[C] has raised his heel against Me.[D,o]

19 "I am telling you now before it happens,[p] so that when it does happen you will believe[q] that I am He.[r] 20 I assure you: Whoever receives anyone I send receives Me, and the one who receives[s] Me receives Him who sent Me."

Judas's Betrayal Predicted

21 When[t] Jesus had said this, He was troubled in His spirit[u] and testified,[v] "I assure you: One of you will betray Me!"

22 The disciples started looking at one another—uncertain which one He was speaking about. 23 One of His disciples, the one Jesus loved,[w] was reclining close beside Jesus.[E] 24 Simon Peter motioned to him to find out who it was He was talking about. 25 So he leaned back against Jesus and asked Him, "Lord, who is it?"

26 Jesus replied, "He's the one I give the piece of bread to after I have dipped it."[x] When He had dipped the bread,[y] He gave it to Judas, Simon Iscariot's son.[F] 27 After Judas ate the piece of bread, Satan[z] entered him. Therefore Jesus told him, "What you're doing, do quickly." 28 None of those reclining at the table knew why He told him this. 29 Since Judas[aa] kept the money-bag, some thought that Jesus was telling him, "Buy what we need for the festival,"[ab]

Cross-references
[a] 13:3 Mt 11:27; 28:18; Jn 17:2
[b] Jn 8:42; 16:27; 17:8
[c] Jn 8:14; 14:12; 16:28; 17:11
[d] 13:4 Lk 19:36
[e] Lk 12:37
[f] 13:6 Mt 16:17
[g] 13:7 Jn 3:11; 7:28; 12:16
[h] 13:14 1Tm 5:10; 1Pt 5:5
[i] 13:15 1Tm 2:8; 1Pt 2:21
[j] 13:16 Jn 15:20
[k] 13:17 Mt 7:24-25; Lk 6:47; 11:28; Jms 1:22-25
[l] 13:18 Jn 6:70; Eph 1:4
[m] Mt 26:54
[n] Mt 1:22
[o] Ps 41:9
[p] 13:19 Jn 13:19
[q] Mk 11:24; Jn 3:16; Ac 10:43; Rm 10:9; 1Pt 1:8-10
[r] Ex 3:14; Jn 8:24,58
[s] 13:20 Jn 5:43; 2Jn 10
[t] 13:21-30 Mt 26:20-25; Mk 14:17-21; Lk 22:21-23
[u] 13:21 Ps 51:12
[v] Jn 15:26; Ac 26:5
[w] 13:23 Jn 19:26; 20:2; 21:7,20
[x] 13:26 Ps 41:9
[y] Mk 14:20
[z] 13:27 Mt 4:1,10; Jn 8:44; Ac 13:10
[aa] 13:29 Mk 3:19
[ab] Jn 2:23

A 13:12 At important meals the custom was to recline on a mat at a low table and lean on the left elbow.   B 13:16 Or *lord*
C 13:18 Other mss read *eats bread with Me*   D 13:18 Ps 41:9   E 13:23 Lit *reclining at Jesus' breast*; that is, on His right; Jn 1:18
F 13:26 Other mss read *Judas Iscariot, Simon's son*

13:4-5 The practice of foot-washing had a long OT tradition (Gn 18:4; 19:2; 24:32; 43:24; Jdg 19:21; 1Sm 25:41). Jesus' performance of this menial task exemplified His humility (Php 2:6-8).

13:16 On Jesus as the one **sent** as well as the sender, see note at 3:16-18.

13:18-30 Judas's betrayal of Jesus comes as no surprise to the alert reader. John repeatedly anticipated this treacherous act (vv. 10-11; 6:70-71; 12:4). It is shocking that one whom Jesus had chosen as an apostle would betray Him. But far from indicating that Jesus made a mistake, the betrayal actually fulfilled Scripture (13:18, citing Ps 41:9; see note at Jn 17:12). God's plan was right on track. This section also contains the first mention of "the one Jesus loved" (13:23). He is frequently featured side by side with Peter in the second half of John's Gospel.

13:18 Judas's treachery fulfilled OT typology. Jesus cited Ps 41:9, which dealt with Absalom's rebellion against King David. Judas's betrayal came as no surprise to Jesus (Jn 13:19). Eating someone's **bread** indicated close fellowship, and yet Judas **raised his heel** against Jesus, an idiom that describes betrayal. Not only did Jesus' public foes plot against Him; even His own disciples could not be trusted.

13:19 Jesus' statement is one of several references to His omniscience in this section (14:29; 16:1,4,32,33). **I am He**, as in 8:24,28 (see note there), very likely had overtones of deity.

13:21 Jesus' being **troubled in His spirit** (cp. 11:33; 12:27) parallels the emotions of David, who expressed anguish over the betrayal of a close friend (Ps 55:2-14; cp. Ps 31:9-10; 38:10).

13:23 The reference to one of His disciples, **the one Jesus loved . . . reclining close beside Jesus** (Gk *kolpos*) echoes the description of Jesus as "the One who is at the Father's side" (Gk *kolpos*) in 1:18. This disciple is mentioned again in 21:20. Clearly he was an integral member of Jesus' group. Tradition identifies him as John, author of this Gospel.

13:29 The supposition that Jesus may have sent Judas to **give something to the poor** harks back to 12:5, where Judas

or that he should give something to the poor. [30] After receiving the piece of bread, he went out immediately. And it was night.[a]

The New Commandment

[31] When[b] he had gone out, Jesus said, "Now the 'Son of Man[c] is glorified, and God is glorified[d] in Him.[e] [32] If God is glorified in Him,[A] God will also glorify Him in Himself and will glorify Him at once.

[33] "Children, I am with you a little while longer.[f] You will look for Me, and just as I told the 'Jews, 'Where I am going you cannot come,'[g] so now I tell you.

[34] "I give you a new command: Love one another. Just as I have loved you, you must also love one another. [35] By this all people will know that you are My disciples, if you have love[h] for one another."

Peter's Denials Predicted

[36] "Lord," Simon Peter said to Him, "where are You going?"

Jesus answered, "Where I am going[i] you cannot follow Me now, but you will follow later."

[37] "Lord," Peter asked, "why can't I follow You now? I will lay down my life[j] for You!"[k]

[38] Jesus replied, "Will you lay down your life for Me? I assure you: A rooster will not crow until you have denied Me three times.

The Way to the Father

14 "Your heart must not be troubled.[l] Believe[B] in God;[m] believe also in Me. [2] In My Father's house are many dwelling places;[C] if not, I would have told you. I am going away[n] to prepare a place for you. [3] If I go away and prepare a place for you, I will come back[o] and receive you to Myself, so that where I am you may be also.[p] [4] You know the way to where I am going."[D,q]

[5] "Lord," Thomas[r] said, "we don't know where You're going. How can we know the way?"

[6] Jesus told him, "I am[s] the way,[t] the truth, and the life. No one comes to the Father except through Me.

Jesus Reveals the Father

[7] "If you know Me, you will also know[E] My Father.[u] From now on you do know Him[v] and have seen Him."

[8] "Lord," said Philip,[w] "show us the Father, and that's enough for us."

[9] Jesus said to him, "Have I been among you

---

[a]13:30 Jn 9:4
[b]13:31-38 Mt 26:31-35; Mk 14:27-31; Lk 22:31-38
[c]13:31 Mk 2:10
[d]Jn 11:4; 17:1; 1Pt 2:12
[e]2Th 1:12; 1Jn 2:5
[f]13:33 Jn 7:33
[g]Jn 8:21-22; 14:2; 16:5
[h]13:35 1Co 13:1
[i]13:36 Jn 14:2; 16:5
[j]13:37 1Jn 3:16
[k]Mk 14:31
[l]14:1 Jn 14:27
[m]Ac 16:34; 27:25; Rm 4:3,17,24; Gl 3:6; Ti 3:8; Jms 2:23; 1Jn 5:10
[n]14:2 Jn 8:21-22; 13:33,36; 16:7
[o]14:3 Mk 8:38
[p]Jn 12:26
[q]14:4 Jn 7:28; 8:14; 16:5; 1Jn 2:11
[r]14:5 Mk 3:18
[s]14:6 Ex 3:14; Jn 8:24,58
[t]Heb 10:20
[u]14:7 Mt 11:27; 1Jn 2:23
[v]Jn 17:3; 1Jn 4:8
[w]14:8 Mk 3:18

A13:32 Other mss omit *If God is glorified in Him*   **B**14:1 Or *You believe*   **C**14:2 The Vg used the Lat term *mansio*, a traveler's resting place. The Gk word is related to the verb *meno*, meaning *remain* or *stay*, which occurs 40 times in John.   **D**14:4 Other mss read this verse: *And you know where I am going, and you know the way*   **E**14:7 Other mss read *If you had known Me, you would have known*

---

presented himself as a champion of charity. Almsgiving was an important part of Jewish piety (Mt 6:2-4).

13:30 The phrase **it was night** strikes an ominous note. Compare Lk 22:53: "This is your hour—and the dominion of darkness"; see Mt 26:20; Mk 14:17; 1Co 11:23.

13:31 This verse echoes Isaiah (Is 49:3; see note at Jn 2:4).

13:31–16:33 Jesus' farewell discourse in John's Gospel is patterned after Moses' farewell discourse in Deuteronomy 31–33. Such discourses typically include predictions of a person's death and departure; predictions of future challenges for his followers after his death; arrangements for succession; exhortations to moral behavior; a final commission; an affirmation and renewal of God's covenant promises; and a closing doxology. While Jesus' farewell discourse is generally true to this pattern, there are differences as well. Jesus' farewell was only temporary (His followers will see Him again after **a little while**, Jn 14:19), so His final words focused on the future rather than the past. Also, the vine allegory in John 15 is distinct from OT or second temple farewell discourses. Overall, Jesus made provision for the Holy Spirit to continue His mission through the disciples. Jesus Himself would continue to direct their mission from His exalted position with the Father.

13:34-35 Love must be the distinguishing mark of Jesus' disciples. Jesus' **new command** closely resembled the Mosaic commands to love the Lord (Dt 6:5) and one's neighbor as oneself (Lv 19:18; cp. Mk 12:28-33). Elsewhere Jesus said we must love even our enemies (Mt 5:43-48). While the command to love God and one's neighbor was thus not new,

Jesus' example (**as I have loved you**) was unparalleled, as was His insistence that we should love our enemies.

14:1 Jesus' words echo similar admonishments in the OT (Dt 1:21,29; 20:1,3; Jos 1:9; cp. Jn 11:33; 12:27; 13:21). **Believe** denotes personal, relational trust in keeping with OT usage (Is 28:16).

14:2-3 Jesus elsewhere said His followers would be welcomed into "eternal dwellings" (Lk 16:9). The disciples' homecoming will be comparable to a son's return to his father's **house** (Lk 15:11-32). The words **I will come back and receive you to Myself, so that where I am you may be also** echoes the terminology in Sg 8:2. Jesus, the messianic bridegroom (Jn 3:29), said He would **prepare a place** for His followers in His **Father's house** and then come to take them home to be with Him.

14:6 Jesus is **the way, the truth, and the life** (see note at 6:35,48), and **no one comes to the Father** except through Him. Jesus alone is able to provide access to God because He alone paid the penalty for our sins (Is 53:5; Heb 1:3). He is the truth (Jn 1:14,17; 5:33; 18:37; cp. 8:40,45-46), and all contrary claims are false. He alone is the life (1:4), having life in Himself (5:26). He is thus able to confer eternal life on all those who believe in Him (3:16). Jesus is truth and life, and He is the one and only way of salvation.

14:7 The emphasis on truly knowing Jesus and God the Father harks back to OT covenant language (Jr 24:7; 31:34; Hs 13:4).

14:8 Philip apparently wanted some sort of revelation of God. In the OT, Moses asked and was given a limited vision

all this time without your knowing Me, Philip? The one who has seen Me has seen the Father.[a] How can you say, 'Show us the Father'? [10]Don't you believe that I am in the Father and the Father is in Me?[b] The words I speak to you I do not speak on My own.[c] The Father who lives in Me does His works.[d] [11]Believe Me that I am in the Father and the Father is in Me. Otherwise, believe[A] because of the works themselves.[e]

Praying in Jesus' Name

[12]"I assure you: The one who believes in Me[f] will also do the works that I do. And he will do even greater works than these,[g] because I am

going to the Father.[h] [13]Whatever you ask in My name, I will do it so that the Father may be glorified[i] in the Son.[j] [14]If you ask Me[B] anything in My name,[k] I will do it.[C,l]

Another Counselor Promised

[15]"If you love Me, you will keep[D] My commands.[m] [16]And I will ask the Father, and He will give you another •Counselor[n] to be with you forever. [17]He is the Spirit[o] of truth.[p] The •world is unable to receive Him because it doesn't see Him or know Him. But you do

[a]14:9 Jn 5:19,37; 12:45
[b]14:10 Jn 10:30; 14:11,20; 1Jn 2:24; 4:17
[c]Jn 5:30
[d]Jn 5:36; 6:28; Heb 3:9; Rv 15:3
[e]14:11 Jn 10:38
[f]14:12 Jn 6:35
[g]Jn 5:20
[h]Jn 7:33; 13:1,3; 16:5,10,17,28; 17:11,13; 20:17
[i]14:13 Jn 11:4; 17:1; 1Pt 2:12
[j]Jn 5:19
[k]14:14 Jn 10:25
[l]Jn 11:22; 15:6; 16:23-24
[m]14:15 1Jn 5:3   [n]14:16 Lk 24:49; Jn 14:26; 15:26; 16:7; 1Jn 2:1; Ac 2:33   [o]14:17 Jn 1:33   [p]Ps 119:142; 2Th 2:10; 1Jn 4:6

[A]14:11 Other mss read *believe Me*   [B]14:14 Other mss omit *Me*   [C]14:14 Other mss omit all of v. 14   [D]14:15 Other mss read *If you love Me, keep* [as a command]

of God's glory (Ex 33:18; cp. Ex 24:10); Isaiah received a similar vision (Is 6:1; see note at Jn 12:41). In keeping with OT teaching, however, Jesus denied the possibility of a direct vision of God (1:18; 5:37; 6:46).

14:12 The disciples' **greater works** are made possible because Jesus was **going to the Father** after His work on the

cross (12:24; 15:13; 19:30). The works are greater because they are based on the totality of Jesus' work and will bear lasting fruit (Mt 11:11; Jn 15:8,16).

14:13 Praying in Jesus' **name** expresses alignment of one's desires and purposes with God (1Jn 5:14-15). See note at Jn 3:16-18.

Is Jesus the Only Way?

Robert M. Bowman, Jr.

Is faith in Jesus Christ the only way of salvation—the only way to gain eternal life? In thinking about this question, here are some fixed biblical teachings to keep in mind:

Not everyone will be saved. Some people will not make it to heaven (Mt 7:13-14; 25:41,46; 2Th 1:6-9; Heb 10:26-31; Rv 20:10-15).

People will be judged by their works. God does not condemn people who never heard of Jesus because they failed to believe in Him. Rather, God judges all people based on their works (Ps 62:12; Mt 16:27; Rm 2:6; Rv 2:23; 20:13). People who trust in Jesus are mercifully saved from God's just judgment by Jesus' death on their behalf.

None of us can be saved by doing good works. "For no one will be justified in His sight by the works of the law . . . For all have sinned and fall short of the glory of God" (Rm 3:20,23). Two important conclusions follow. First, God is not obliged to save anyone, for no sinner deserves eternal life. Second, everyone needs a Savior.

Jesus is the only Savior available. Only Jesus died to save us from our sins (Mt 1:21; 1Co 15:3; 1Tm 1:15; 2Tm 1:9-10). That is why Jesus is "the Savior of the world" (Jn 4:42; see 12:47; 1Jn 4:14). Jesus claimed to be the only way: "I am the way, the truth, and the life. No one comes to the Father except through Me" (Jn 14:6). Peter agreed: "There is salvation in no one else, for there is no other name under heaven given to people and we must be saved by it" (Ac 4:12).

Those who reject Jesus will be lost. Whatever may be said about those who have never heard the gospel, those who have *heard* and *rejected* it are in trouble. Jesus warned that those who reject Him are rejecting the Father (Lk 10:16; Jn 12:48). People who know that Christ died for them but refuse to follow Him face a terrifying judgment (Heb 10:26-27).

Does all this mean that no one who has not heard of Jesus can be saved? Not quite. We know that Old Testament believers were saved by trusting in God's mercy, even though they lived before Jesus came (Rm 4:1-7; Heb 11:4-32). The unborn, infants, young children, and people whose mental development is impaired are not capable of discerning good from evil or making moral choices (Is 7:15-16; Rm 9:11). We may presume that God does not condemn these souls even though they do not consciously choose to follow Jesus. Apart from these exceptions, it is clear that Jesus' command to take the gospel to all nations (Mt 28:19-20; Lk 24:47) assumes that people who do not know Christ as Savior are in spiritual darkness and need to hear and embrace the gospel (Ac 26:18; Eph 2:12). Every Christian should have a sense of urgency that all people everywhere need Jesus Christ as their Savior.

know Him, because He remains with you and will be[A] in you.[a] [18]I will not leave you as orphans; I am coming to you.

The Father, the Son, and the Holy Spirit

[19]"In a little while the world will see Me no longer,[b] but you will see Me.[c] Because I live, you will live[d] too. [20]In that day you will know that I am in My Father,[e] you are in Me, and I am in you. [21]The one who has My commands and keeps them is the one who loves Me.[f] And the one who loves Me will be loved by My Father.[g] I also will love him and will reveal Myself to him."

[22]Judas[h] (not Iscariot) said to Him, "Lord, how is it You're going to reveal Yourself to us and not to the world?"[i]

[23]Jesus answered, "If anyone loves Me, he will keep My word. My Father will love him, and We will come to him and make Our home with him.[j] [24]The one who doesn't love Me will not keep My words. The word that you hear is not Mine but is from the Father who sent Me.[k]

[25]"I have spoken these things to you while I remain with you. [26]But the Counselor, the Holy Spirit[l]—the Father will send[m] Him in My name—will teach you all things[n] and remind you of everything I have told you.[o]

Jesus' Gift of Peace

[27]"Peace I leave with you. My peace I give to you. I do not give to you as the world gives. Your heart must not be troubled or fearful.[p] [28]You have heard Me tell you, 'I am going away[q] and I am coming to you.' If you loved Me, you would have rejoiced that I am going to the Father,[r] because the Father is greater than I.[s] [29]I have told you now before it happens[t] so that when it does happen you may believe. [30]I will not talk with you much longer, because the ruler of the world[u] is coming. He has no power over Me.[B,v] [31]On the contrary, I am going away[C] so that the world may know that I love the Father. Just as the Father commanded Me, so I do.

"Get up; let's leave this place."

The Vine and the Branches

15 "I am[w] the true vine, and My Father is the vineyard keeper. [2]Every branch in

Cross references (center column)

[a]14:17 1Jn 4:4
[b]14:19 Jn 7:33
[c]Jn 16:16
[d]Php 1:21
[e]14:20 Jn 14:10
[f]14:21 Jn 8:31; 1Jn 2:5
[g]Dt 7:12-13; Jn 16:27
[h]14:22 Lk 6:16; Ac 1:13
[i]Ac 10:40-41
[j]14:23 Jn 14:2; 1Jn 2:24
[k]14:24 Jn 5:19; 7:16; 8:28; 12:49-50
[l]14:26 Ps 51:11; Jn 1:33; Ac 2:4; Rm 8:9; Gl 5:25; Ti 3:5; Rv 3:22
[m]Lk 24:49; Jn 14:16; 15:26; 16:7; Ac 2:33
[n]Jn 16:13; 1Co 2:10; 1Jn 2:27
[o]Jn 2:22; 2Pt 1:21
[p]14:27 2Tm 1:7
[q]14:28 Jn 16:5
[r]Jn 16:10
[s]Jn 10:29; 1Jn 3:20; 4:4
[t]14:29 Jn 13:19; 16:4
[u]14:30 Mt 4:1; Jn 12:31
[v]Lk 4:6
[w]15:1 Ex 3:14; Jn 8:24,58

[A]14:17 Other mss read *and is*   [B]14:30 Lit *He has nothing in Me*   [C]14:31 Probably refers to the cross

14:15 Jesus' words echo the demands of the Deuteronomic covenant (Dt 5:10; 6:5-6; 7:9; 10:12-13; 11:13,22).

14:16-17 **Another Counselor** or the **Spirit of truth** is the Holy Spirit (v. 26), who guides disciples into all truth (16:13). The Spirit replaces Jesus' physical presence by permanently indwelling His followers. Divine presence for Jesus' followers includes the Spirit (14:15-17), Jesus (vv. 18-21), and the Father (vv. 22-24).

14:18 The Spirit's presence within disciples essentially amounts to Jesus' own presence, because the Spirit testifies about Jesus (15:26) and helps disciples understand the significance of what Jesus has done (16:14). Jesus' assurance, **I will not leave you as orphans**, echoes Moses' parting words to Israel (Dt 31:6; cp. Jos 1:5). By saying this, Jesus likely had in mind both His resurrection and the coming of the Spirit at Pentecost.

14:21 The references to **the one who has My commands and keeps them** and the phrase **reveal Myself** hark back to the giving of the law at Mount Sinai and to other OT appearances of God (Ex 33:13).

14:22 This **Judas (not Iscariot)** is probably "Judas the son of James," mentioned in Lk 6:16 and Ac 1:13, not Jude, the half-brother of Jesus (Mt 13:55; Mk 6:3).

14:23 **Make Our home with him** recalls God's dwelling among His people in the tabernacle (Ex 25:8; 29:45; Lv 26:11-12) and the temple (1Kg 8:10-11; cp. Ac 7:46-47), and points forward to the time when the Spirit would come at Pentecost (Ac 2).

14:26 The **Holy Spirit** (1:33; 20:22) is mentioned infrequently in the OT (Ps 51:11; Is 63:9-10). Jesus' focus here was on the Spirit's future teaching ministry (1Jn 2:20,27).

14:27 The expression **peace** (Hb *shalom*) could serve as a greeting or announce blessing upon those who enjoyed a right relationship with God (Nm 6:24-26; cp. Ps 29:11; Hg 2:9). The OT prophesied a period of peace following Messiah's coming, for He is the "Prince of Peace" (Is 9:6), who would "proclaim peace to the nations" (Zch 9:10; cp. 9:9). There would be tidings of peace and salvation (Is 52:7; cp. 54:13; 57:19), and God would establish an everlasting "covenant of peace" with His people (Ezk 37:26). Jesus' parting encouragement for His followers not to be **troubled or fearful** echoes Moses' parting counsel (Dt 31:6,8).

14:30 On **the ruler of the world**, see note at 12:31. Satan has no legal claim or hold on Jesus.

14:31. Some scholars view the transition between 14:31 to 15:1 as a literary seam, which would indicate that John's Gospel was pieced together from different sources (one ending at 14:31; another beginning at 15:1). More likely, John is simply describing Jesus' transition (**Get up; let's leave this place**) from the upper room to the garden of Gethsemane, where He arrived in 18:1.

15:1-17 This allegory is at the heart of Jesus' farewell discourse to the disciples. The OT used the vineyard or vine as a symbol for Israel, God's covenant people, especially in two "vineyard songs" (Is 5:1-7; 27:2-6). However, Israel's failure to produce fruit issued in divine judgment. Jesus, by contrast, is the true vine, and His followers are to remain in Him and produce much fruit for God.

15:1 **I am the true vine** is the last of Jesus' seven "I am" sayings in John's Gospel (see note at 6:35,48). "True" contrasts Jesus with OT Israel (see note at 15:1-17). Joseph was called a "fruitful vine" in Gn 49:22. The reference to the Father as **the vineyard keeper** harks back to Isaiah's first vineyard song, where God is depicted as tending His vineyard, only to be rewarded with sour grapes (Is 5:1-7; cp. Ps 80:8-9).

15:2 To ensure maximal fruit production, the divine vineyard

Me that does not produce fruit He removes,[a] and He prunes every branch that produces fruit so that it will produce more fruit. [3]You are already •clean[b] because of the word I have spoken to you. [4]Remain in Me, and I in you. Just as a branch is unable to produce fruit by itself unless it remains on the vine, so neither can you unless you remain in Me.[c]

[5]"I am the vine;[d] you are the branches. The one who remains in Me and I in him produces much fruit,[e] because you can do nothing without Me. [6]If anyone does not remain in Me, he is thrown aside[f] like a branch and he withers. They gather them, throw them into the fire,[g] and they are burned.[h] [7]If you remain in Me and My words remain in you, ask whatever you want and it will be done for you.[i] [8]My Father is glorified[j] by this: that you produce much fruit and prove to be[A] My disciples.

Christlike Love

[9]"As the Father has loved Me, I have also loved you. Remain in My love.[k] [10]If you keep My commands you will remain in My love, just as I have kept My Father's commands and remain in His love.[l]

[11]"I have spoken these things to you so that My joy may be in you and your joy may be complete.[m] [12]This is My command: Love one another as I have loved[n] you. [13]No one has greater love than this, that someone would lay down his life[o] for his friends. [14]You are

My friends if you do what I command you. [15]I do not call you •slaves anymore, because a slave doesn't know what his master[B,p] is doing. I have called you friends, because I have made known to you everything I have heard from My Father. [16]You did not choose Me, but I chose you.[q] I appointed you that you should go out and produce fruit and that your fruit should remain, so that whatever you ask[r] the Father in My name,[s] He will give you.[t] [17]This is what I command you: Love one another.

Persecutions Predicted

[18]"If the •world hates[u] you, understand that it hated Me before it hated you. [19]If you were of the world, the world would love you as its own. However, because you are not of the world, but I have chosen[v] you out of it, the world hates you. [20]Remember the word I spoke to you: 'A slave is not greater than his master.'[w] If they persecuted Me, they will also persecute you. If they kept My word,[x] they will also keep yours. [21]But they will do all these things to you on account of My name,[y] because they don't know[z] the One who sent Me. [22]If I had not come and spoken to them, they would not have sin.[C,aa] Now they have no excuse for their sin. [23]The one who hates Me also hates My Father.[ab] [24]If I had not done the works[ac] among them that no one else has done,[ad] they would not have sin.[ae] Now they have seen and hated both Me and My Father. [25]But this happened so that the statement written in their

a15:2 Mt 3:10; 7:19; 15:13; Lk 3:9; 13:6-9; Jn 15:6; Rm 11:17,22
b15:3 Ps 24:4; Ti 1:15
c15:4 Jn 6:56; 8:28; 1Jn 2:5
d15:5 Jms 3:12
eMk 4:8
f15:6 Jn 15:2
g2Th 1:8
h1Th 1:8; 2Pt 3:7
i15:7 Jn 14:14
j15:8 Jn 11:4; 17:1; 1Pt 2:12
k15:9 Col 1:13; 1Jn 5:20; Jd 21
l15:10 Jn 5:19
m15:11 1Jn 1:4; 2Jn 12
n15:12 Jn 3:16
o15:13 Rm 5:8; 1Jn 3:16
p15:15 Col 3:22
q15:16 Mt 24:22
rJn 10:25
sJn 14:13
tJn 11:22; 16:23
u15:18 Lk 6:27; 19:14
v15:19 Eph 1:4
w15:20 Jn 13:16
xJn 8:51
y15:21 Mk 13:13; Jn 10:25
zJn 3:11; 7:28; 20:9
aa15:22 Ezk 2:5; 3:7; Jn 9:41; Rm 1:20; 2:1; 6:23
ab15:23 Jn 5:23
ac15:24 Jn 5:36; Heb 3:9; Rv 15:3
adJn 3:2; 7:31; 9:32; 10:32,37
aeJn 9:41

A15:8 Or and become　B15:15 Or lord　C15:22 To have sin is an idiom that refers to guilt caused by sin.

keeper **removes** dead branches and **prunes** all the others (Heb 6:7-8). In John's Gospel, Judas the betrayer is an example of the former scenario (Jn 13:10-11). Peter, who denied Jesus three times, is an example of the latter (18:15-18,25-27; 21:15-19).

15:3 On **you are already clean**, see 13:10-11.

15:4 The **in** terminology harks back to OT covenant theology, including prophetic texts about a future new covenant (Ex 25:8; 29:45; Lv 26:11-12; Ezk 37:27-28; 43:9).

15:4,5,8 The repeated reference to **fruit** underscores that fruitfulness is God's primary creative (Gn 1:11-12,22,28) and redemptive purpose (Jn 15:8,16). The OT prophets envisioned a time when God's people would "blossom and bloom and fill the whole world with fruit" (Is 27:6; cp. Hs 14:4-8).

15:6 This verse echoes Ezk 15:1-8, where a barren vine is said to be fit only for burning. **Fire** is a common symbol for divine judgment (Is 30:27; Mt 3:12; 5:22; 18:8; 25:41; see note at Jn 15:2).

15:10-11 Obedience is not all gloom and doom; rather, it's a source of **joy**. The OT prophets envisioned a period of great end-time rejoicing (Is 25:9; 35:10; 51:3; 61:10; 66:10; Zch 9:9).

15:12-17 On Jesus' "love commandment," see note at 13:34-35.

15:13-14 In the OT, only Abraham (2Ch 20:7; Is 41:8), and by implication Moses (Ex 33:11), are called "friends of God." Jesus extended this privilege to all obedient believers.

15:16 In first-century Palestine, disciples typically took the initiative in attaching themselves to a particular rabbi, not vice versa. As a well-known dictum declared, "Provide yourself with a teacher." Jesus broke with this custom and called His own disciples. **Appointed** recalls the OT description of God's appointment of Abraham (Gn 17:5; cp. Rm 4:17), the ordination of Levites (Nm 8:10), and Moses' commissioning of Joshua (Nm 27:18).

15:18–16:33 This final major unit in Jesus' farewell discourse deals with the world's hostility toward Himself and His followers and with the future ministry of the Holy Spirit.

15:18 Jesus' followers are to be known by their love (13:34-35 and note there).

15:24 On Jesus' **works** as a witness to Himself, see note at 5:31-47.

15:25 Jesus declared that the Jews' hatred of Him fulfilled OT Scripture, specifically Ps 69:4 (cp. Ps 35:19). This Davidic psalm depicts a righteous sufferer who is zealous for God but is persecuted by God's enemies **for no reason**. Thus Jesus saw David's experiences as a prefiguration of the hatred and rejection He suffered.

scripture might be fulfilled:[a] **They hated Me for no reason.**[A,b]

Coming Testimony and Rejection

[26] "When the *Counselor[c] comes, the One I will send to you from the Father[d]—the Spirit of truth[e] who proceeds from the Father—He will testify about Me. [27] You also will testify,[f] because you have been with Me from the beginning.

16 "I have told you these things to keep you from *stumbling. [2] They will ban you from the *synagogues.[g] In fact, a time is coming when anyone who kills you will think he is offering service[h] to God. [3] They will do these things because they haven't known[i] the Father or Me. [4] But I have told you these things so that when their time[B] comes you may remember[j] I told them to you. I didn't tell you these things from the beginning, because I was with you.

The Counselor's Ministry

[5] "But now I am going away[k] to Him who sent Me, and not one of you asks Me, 'Where are You going?'[l][6] Yet, because I have spoken these things to you, sorrow has filled your heart. [7] Nevertheless, I am telling you the truth.[m] It is for your benefit that I go away, because if I don't go away the *Counselor will not come to

you. If I go, I will send Him to you.[n][8] When He comes, He will convict the world about sin, righteousness, and judgment: [9] About sin, because they do not believe in Me; [10] about righteousness, because I am going to the Father[o] and you will no longer see Me; [11] and about judgment,[p] because the ruler of this *world[q] has been judged.[r]

[12] "I still have many things to tell you, but you can't bear them now.[s] [13] When the Spirit of truth[t] comes, He will guide you into all the truth.[u] For He will not speak on His own, but He will speak whatever He hears. He will also declare to you what is to come. [14] He will glorify Me, because He will take from what is Mine and declare it to you. [15] Everything the Father[v] has is Mine.[w] This is why I told you that He takes from what is Mine and will declare it to you.[x]

Sorrow Turned to Joy

[16] "A little while[y] and you will no longer see Me;[z] again a little while and you will see Me."[C]

[17] Therefore some of His disciples said to one another, "What is this He tells us: 'A little while and you will not see Me; again a little while and you will see Me'; and, 'because I am going to the Father'[aa]?" [18] They said, "What is

Cross references (center column)

[a]15:25 Jn 12:38; 13:18; 17:12; 18:9,32; 19:24,36
[b]Ps 69:4
[c]15:26 Jn 14:16
[d]Jn 14:26
[e]Ps 119:142; Jn 1:33; 14:17; 16:13; Rm 3:7; 1Jn 4:6
[f]15:27 Ac 4:20
[g]16:2 Jn 9:22; 12:42
[h]Ex 12:25
[i]16:3 Jn 7:28
[j]16:4 Jn 14:29; Rv 2:5
[k]16:5 Jn 7:33; 8:14,21-22; 13:3,33,36; 14:4-5,28; 16:10,17
[l]Jn 8:14
[m]16:7 Ps 119:142
[n]Jn 14:26
[o]16:10 Jn 14:12,28; 16:17
[p]16:11 Mt 12:41; Jn 5:22; 2Th 1:5; Rv 19:11
[q]Mt 4:1; Jn 12:31
[r]Col 2:15; Heb 2:14
[s]16:12 Mk 4:33
[t]16:13 Rm 3:7; 1Jn 4:6
[u]Jn 1:17; 14:6; 2Th 2:10
[v]16:15 Mt 11:27
[w]Jn 17:10
[x]Jn 5:19
[y]16:16 Jn 7:33
[z]Mk 2:20; 14:19
[aa]16:17 Jn 14:12; 16:10

[A]15:25 Ps 69:4   [B]16:4 Other mss read *when the time*   [C]16:16 Other mss add *because I am going to the Father*

15:26 On Jesus' promise of the Holy Spirit, see notes at 14:16-17 and 14:26.

15: 27 The call for Jesus' followers to serve as His witnesses recalls OT prophetic literature, where God's end-time people are called His "witnesses" to the nation (Is 43:10-12; 44:8). In the NT, believers are promised the Spirit's help in times of persecution (Mt 10:20; Mk 13:11; Lk 12:12), and the Spirit played a vital part in the church's mission (Ac 1:8; cp. Lk 24:48; Ac 5:32; 6:10).

16:2 The phrase **a time is coming** is reminiscent of prophetic or apocalyptic expressions such as "the days are coming" (Jr 7:32; 9:25; 16:14; 31:31,38; Am 9:13; Zch 14:1). On expulsion from the synagogue, see note at Jn 9:34.

parakletos

Greek Pronunciation	[pah RAH klay tahss]
HCSB Translation	Counselor
Uses in John's Gospel	4
Uses in the NT	5
Focus Passage	John 14:16,26; 15:26

The Greek word *parakletos* is derived from the verb *parakaleo* (lit *to call alongside;* basically *to comfort, counsel, exhort*). It is also related to the noun *paraklesis (comfort, exhortation).* Both are much more common than *parakletos* but do not occur in John's writings, while *parakletos* occurs only in John's writings. In all four occurrences of *parakletos* in John's Gospel, Jesus used the term to refer to the Holy Spirit as our *Counselor.* The idea is that the Spirit comes *alongside* to aid us in the tasks Jesus gave us as His disciples.

When anyone who kills you will think he is offering service to God most likely refers to Jewish rather than Roman persecution. Some rabbis believed that killing heretics was an act of divine worship.

16:7 Reference to **the Counselor** (see notes at 14:16-17 and 14:26) harks back to the anticipated coming of the Spirit and the inauguration of the age of the kingdom in OT prophetic literature (Is 11:1-10; 32:14-18; 42:1-4; 44:1-5; Jr 31:31-34; Ezk 11:17-20; 36:24-27; 37:1-14; Jl 2:28-32).

16:8-11 The Holy Spirit will judge the world's **sin** of unbelief on the basis of His **righteousness**. On **the ruler of this world**, see note at 12:31.

16:13 On the **Spirit of truth**, see note at 14:16-17. The Spirit's ministry of guiding Jesus' followers into **all the truth** will fulfill the psalmists' longing for divine guidance (Ps 25:4-5; 43:3; 86:11; 143:10). Isaiah recounted how God led His people in the wilderness by the Holy Spirit (Is 63:14) and predicted God's renewed guidance in the future (Is 43:19). The word **declare** (Gk *anangello*) occurs over 40 times in the book of Isaiah, where declaring things to come is said to be the exclusive domain of God (Is 48:14) and where God challenges pretenders to declare the things to come (Is 42:9; 44:7; 46:10; cp. Is 41:21-29, esp. vv. 22-23; 45:19).

16:16-19 A little while harks back to previous instances of this expression in John's Gospel (7:33; 12:35; 13:33; 14:19). Similar terms were used by OT prophets for announcing God's judgment (Is 10:25; Jr 51:33; Hs 1:4; Hg 2:6) and salvation (Is 29:17). In this situation the reference is to the brief period between Jesus' crucifixion and resurrection.

this He is saying,[A] 'A little while'? We don't know what He's talking about!"

[19] Jesus knew they wanted to question Him, so He said to them, "Are you asking one another about what I said, 'A little while and you will not see Me; again a little while and you will see Me'?

[20] "I assure you: You will weep and wail,[a] but the world will rejoice. You will become sorrowful,[b] but your sorrow will turn to joy. [21] When a woman is in labor she has pain[c] because her time has come. But when she has given birth to a child,[d] she no longer remembers the suffering because of the joy that a person has been born into the world. [22] So you also have sorrow[B] now. But I will see you again. Your hearts will rejoice,[e] and no one will rob you of your joy.[f] [23] In that day you will not ask Me anything.

"I assure you: Anything you ask the Father in My name, He will give you.[g] [24] Until now you have asked for nothing in My name.[h] Ask and you will receive,[i] so that your joy may be complete.[j]

Jesus the Victor

[25] "I have spoken these things to you in figures of speech. A time is coming when I will no longer speak to you in figures, but I will tell you plainly about the Father. [26] In that day

you will ask[k] in My name.[l] I am not telling you that I will make requests to the Father on your behalf. [27] For the Father Himself loves you, because you have loved[m] Me and have believed that I came from God.[C,n] [28] I came from the Father and have come into the world. Again, I am leaving the world and going to the Father."[o]

[29] "Ah!" His disciples said. "Now You're speaking plainly and not using any figurative language. [30] Now we know that You know everything[p] and don't need anyone to question You. By this we believe that You came from God."[q]

[31] Jesus responded to them, "Do you now believe? [32] Look: An hour is coming, and has come,[r] when each of you will be scattered to his own home, and you will leave Me alone. Yet I am not alone, because the Father is with Me.[s] [33] I have told you these things so that in Me you may have peace. You will have suffering in this world. Be courageous! I have conquered the world."

Jesus Prays for Himself

17 Jesus spoke these things, looked up to heaven, and said:

Father,
the hour has come.
Glorify Your Son
so that the Son[t] may glorify You,[u]

Cross references (center column):
- a 16:20 Mt 11:17; Lk 7:32; 23:27
- b Jn 16:6; 2Co 2:2
- c 16:21 Gl 4:19
- d Lk 1:7
- e 16:22 Jn 20:20
- f Jn 15:11
- g 16:23 Jn 11:22; 14:13-14; 15:16
- h 16:24 Jn 10:25
- i Mt 7:8
- j 1Jn 1:4; 2Jn 12
- k 16:26 Jn 14:16
- l Jn 10:25
- m 16:27 Jn 14:21
- n Jn 6:46; 8:42; 13:3; 16:30
- o 16:28 Jn 14:12
- p 16:30 Mk 2:8; Jn 1:48; 2:24-25; 6:64; 21:17
- q Jn 16:27
- r 16:32 Jn 4:23
- s Jn 8:16,29
- t 17:1 Jn 5:19; Heb 1:2
- u Jn 12:28

A 16:18 Other mss omit *He is saying*   B 16:22 Other mss read *will have sorrow*   C 16:27 Other mss read *from the Father*

16:20 Jesus' prediction that His disciples' **sorrow will turn to joy** echoes the experiences of God's people in OT times (Est 9:22) and marks the fulfillment of OT prophecies (Is 61:2-3; Jr 31:13).

16:21 Jesus' illustration of a woman in childbirth resonates with human experience. While the labor preceding birth is intense, all anguish is forgotten the moment the new child

is born. Jesus elsewhere spoke of the end-times as "the beginning of birth pains" and times of "great tribulation" (Mt 24:8,21,29).

16:28 The depiction of Jesus as having come **from the Father . . . into the world** and as **leaving the world and going to the Father** is patterned after the portrayal of the Word of God which is sent, accomplishes its purpose, and returns to the One who sent it (Is 55:11-12; see note at Jn 1:1).

16:32 Jesus' prediction of a coming **hour** at which His followers will be **scattered** (cp. 19:27) may allude to Zch 13:7 (quoted in Mt 26:31; cp. Mt 26:56; 1Kg 22:17). The sheep would desert the Shepherd and return home, and yet Jesus would not be **alone** due to the constant presence of His Father.

16:33 Jesus' farewell discourse ends on a note of triumph (1Jn 2:13-14; 4:4; 5:4-5).

17:1-26 In His final prayer in this chapter, Jesus gave an account of His earthly mission to the Father who sent Him. He prayed first for Himself (vv. 1-5), then for His disciples (vv. 6-19), and finally for all future believers (vv. 20-26). In His prayer, Jesus adopted the stance of one who has completed His mission (v. 4, cp. 4:34), having been sent by the Father and now preparing to return (13:1; 16:28). His prayer was fulfilled when He cried out from the cross, saying of the mission of redemption and revelation He had come to accomplish: "It is finished" (19:30).

17:1-5 The first unit in Jesus' prayer is His intercession for Himself.

17:1 Jesus **looked up to heaven**, striking a customary

---

kosmos

Greek Pronunciation	[KAHZ mahss]
HCSB Translation	world
Uses in John's Gospel	78
Uses in the NT	186
Focus Passage	John 16:11,28,33

The noun *kosmos* (English *cosmos, cosmic*), is normally translated *world* and most often has negative connotations, especially in John's writings. John provides the foundational verse about the *kosmos* in 1:10—"He [the Word] was in the *world*, and the *world* was created through Him, yet the *world* did not recognize Him." The *kosmos* is consistently described by John as hostile to Jesus and the things of God. The *world* needs the light (1:9; see 8:12) because it is in darkness (3:19). It is dead and needs life (6:33,51). The *world* hates Jesus (7:7) and His followers (15:18; 17:14), but it will be judged (9:39; 12:31), as will its prince (that is, Satan; 12:31; 16:11). But as "the Lamb of God, who takes away the sin of the *world*" (1:29), Jesus "conquered the *world*" (16:33). God loved the *world* (despite its sins) and gave His Son to redeem the *world* (3:16-17).

2 for You gave Him authority
over all flesh;^A,a
so He may give eternal life^b
to all You have given Him.^c
3 This is eternal life:
that they may know You,
the only^d true^e God,
and the One
You have sent^f—Jesus Christ.^g
4 I have glorified You on the earth
by completing the work You gave Me
to do.
5 Now, Father,^h glorify Me
in Your presence
with that glory^i I had with You
before the world existed.^j

Jesus Prays for His Disciples

6 I have revealed Your name^k
to the men You gave Me^l
from the world.^m
They were Yours, You gave them
to Me,^n
and they have kept Your word.^o
7 Now they know that all things
You have given to Me are from You,
8 because the words that You gave Me,^p
I have given them.
They have received them
and have known for certain
that I came from You.^q
They have believed that You sent Me.
9 I pray^B for them.
I am not praying for the •world
but for those You have given Me,^r
because they are Yours.
10 Everything I have is Yours,

and everything You have is Mine,^s
and I have been glorified in them.
11 I am no longer in the world,
but they are in the world,
and I am coming to You.^t
Holy^u Father,
protect^C them by Your name^v
that You have given Me,
so that they may be one^w
as We are^x one.
12 While I was with them,
I was protecting them by Your name
that You have given Me.
I guarded^y them and not one of them
is lost,
except the son of destruction,^D
so that the Scripture^z may be fulfilled.^aa
13 Now I am coming to You,
and I speak these things in the world
so that they may have My joy
completed in them.
14 I have given them Your word.
The world hated^ab them
because they are not of the world,^ac
as I am not of the world.^ad
15 I am not praying
that You take them out of the world
but that You protect them
from the evil one.^ae
16 They are not of the world,
as I am not of the world.^af
17 •Sanctify^E,ag them by the truth;^ah
Your word is truth.
18 As You sent Me into the world,^ai
I also have sent them into the world.
19 I sanctify Myself for them,

Cross-references:
a17:2 Php 3:3
b Jn 12:25; Ac 13:48; 1Jn 2:25
c Mt 24:22
d17:3 Jn 5:44; Rm 16:27
e Jn 4:23; 1Jn 5:20
f Mk 9:37; Jn 1:6
g Jn 5:38; 6:29
h17:5 Mt 11:27
i Mk 10:37; Jn 17:24; 1Pt 5:1
j Pr 8:23; Jn 1:1-2; 8:58
k17:6 Jn 10:25; Ac 15:14; Rv 14:1
l Mt 24:22; Jn 6:37
m Jn 8:23; 13:1; 15:19; 17:14-16; 18:36; 1Co 5:10; 1Jn 2:16; 4:5
n Jn 18:9
o Jn 8:51
P17:8 Jn 14:24
q Jn 5:43; 13:3
r17:9 Rm 9:11
s17:10 Jn 16:15
t17:11 Jn 13:3; 14:12
u Ps 20:6; 1Co 7:14
v Pr 18:10
w Jn 11:52
x Jn 10:16,30; 17:22; Gl 3:28
y17:12 2Tm 1:14
z Mt 26:54
aa Ps 41:9; Jn 13:18; 15:25; 19:24,36
ab17:14 Lk 6:22,27; 19:14
ac Jn 15:19
ad Jn 8:23; 18:36
ae17:15 2Th 3:3
af17:16 Jn 18:36; 1Jn 4:17
ag17:17 Lk 11:2
ah Ps 119:142; 2Th 2:10; 1Jn 5:20
ai17:18 1Jn 4:17

A17:2 Or *people* B17:9 Lit *ask* (throughout this passage) C17:11 Lit *keep* (throughout this passage) D17:12 The one destined for destruction, loss, or perdition E17:17 Set apart for special use

---

posture in prayer (Ps 123:1; Mk 7:34; Lk 18:13). On **the hour has come**, see note at 2:4. The opening petition, **Glorify Your Son so that the Son may glorify You**, is a claim to deity since the OT affirms that God will not give His glory to another (Is 42:8; 48:11). On Jesus as the sent Son, see note at Jn 3:16-18.

17:2 God's granting of **authority** to Jesus (5:27) marks the beginning of a new era (Is 9:6-7; Dn 7:13-14; see Mt 11:27; 28:18).

17:2-3 Eternal life comes from knowing God and Jesus the sent Son (1:4; 5:26; 20:31). Knowing God is not confined to intellectual knowledge; it involves living in fellowship with Him. That God is **the only true God** is affirmed in the Shema (Dt 6:4; cp. Jn 5:44; 1Jn 5:20). Jesus, in turn, is the One and Only sent by the Father (Jn 1:14,18; 3:16,18) and the only way to Him (14:6). The full name **Jesus Christ** is found only here and in 1:17, forming a literary inclusion. Note that in these verses Jesus referred to Himself in the third person.

17:4 The reference to Jesus' **work** in the singular harks back to 4:34, another inclusion.

17:5 Again, Jesus claimed preexistence (v. 24; 1:1,14; 3:13; 6:62; 8:58; 16:28).

17:6-19 The second unit of Jesus' prayer contains His intercession for His disciples, beginning with a rehearsal of His ministry to them (vv. 6-8). Jesus' prayer for His followers in verses 9-19 includes petitions for their protection (vv. 11-16) and for their consecration for service in the truth (vv. 17-19).

17:6 Jesus' revelation of God's **name** included making known the Father's works and words (1:18; 8:19,27; 10:38; 12:45; 14:9-11).

17:7-8 The portrayal of Jesus here is reminiscent of the description of the "prophet like" Moses in Dt 18:18.

17:12 Even Judas's betrayal happened in fulfillment of Scripture. The antecedent passage is probably Ps 41:9 (applied to Jesus in Jn 13:18; see note there). Other Scriptures fulfilled through Judas are Ps 69:25 and 109:8 (cited in Ac 1:20).

17:18 This verse looks forward to the commission that Jesus assigned His disciples after His resurrection (20:21).

so they also may be sanctified
by the truth.

Jesus Prays for All Believers

20 I pray not only for these,
but also for those who believe in Me
through their message.
21 May they all be one,[a]
as You, Father, are in Me and I am
in You.[b]
May they also be one[A] in Us,
so the world may believe
You sent Me.
22 I have given them the glory[c]
You have given Me.
May they be one as We are one.
23 I am in them and You are in Me.[d]
May they be made completely one,
so the world may know You have
sent Me
and have loved[e] them as
You have loved Me.[f]
24 Father,
I desire those You have given Me
to be with Me where I am.[g]
Then they will see My glory,
which You have given Me

because You loved Me
before the world's foundation.
25 Righteous Father!
The world has not known You.
However, I have known You,[h]
and these have known
that You sent Me.
26 I made Your name[i] known to them
and will make it known,
so the love You have loved Me with
may be in them and I may be in them.[j]

Jesus Betrayed

18 After[k] Jesus had said these things, He went out with His disciples across the Kidron Valley, where there was a garden, and He and His disciples went into it. [2]Judas,[l] who betrayed[m] Him, also knew the place, because Jesus often met there with His disciples. [3]So Judas took a *company of soldiers and some temple police from the *chief priests and the *Pharisees[n] and came there with lanterns, torches, and weapons. [4]Then Jesus, knowing everything that was about to happen to Him,[o] went out and said to them, "Who is it you're looking for?" [5]"Jesus the *Nazarene," they answered.

Cross references
a 17:21 Jn 11:52; 17:11
b 1Jn 2:24; 5:20
c 17:22 Mk 10:37; Jn 17:24; 1Pt 5:1,4
d 17:23 1Jn 4:4
e Jn 3:16; 12:43; 1Co 13:1; 2Th 2:13
f Jn 15:9
g 17:24 Jn 12:26
h 17:25 Mt 11:27; Lk 10:22
i 17:26 Jn 10:25
j 1Jn 4:4
k 18:1–12 Mt 26:47-56; Mk 14:43-52; Lk 22:47-53
l 18:2 Mk 3:19
m Mt 10:4; Mk 9:31; Jn 13:21
n 18:3 Mk 7:3
o 18:4 Jn 16:30

A 17:21 Other mss omit one

17:20-26 Jesus did not stop at praying for Himself (vv. 1-5) and His disciples (vv. 6-19); His vision transcended the present (Dt 29:14-15). Jesus was concerned for His followers' unity (Jn 17:21-23) and love (v. 26). The vision of a unified people of God was previously expressed in 10:16 and 11:52. Unity among believers results from the indivisible unity of God (10:38; 14:10-11,20,23; 15:4-5). Once unified, believers are able to bear witness to the true identity of Jesus as the One sent by God.

17:25 Jesus addressed God as **Righteous Father**. The OT teaches that God is righteous and just (Ps 116:5; 119:137; Jr 12:1). Though His betrayal, torture, and death were looming, Jesus affirmed the righteousness of God His Father.

17:26 The phrase **I may be in them** is filled with covenantal overtones (v. 23; 14:20). After the giving of the law at Sinai, God came to dwell in the midst of Israel in the tabernacle (Ex 40:34). As they moved toward the promised land, God frequently assured His people that He was in their midst (Ex 29:45-46; Dt 7:21; 23:14).

18:1–19:42 John's Passion Narrative appears in these chapters. The familiar sequence of events starts with Jesus' betrayal by Judas (18:1-11), His informal hearing before Annas (18:12-14,19-24), Peter's denials (18:15-18,25-27), Jesus' Roman trial before Pilate (18:28–19:16a), and His crucifixion and burial (19:16b-42). Only John among all the Gospels featured Jesus' appearance before Annas, and His Roman trial is covered in more detail in John. On the other hand, John did not provide an account of Jesus' formal Jewish trial before Caiaphas and the Sanhedrin.

18:1 The **Kidron Valley** is mentioned frequently in the OT (2Sm 15:23; 1Kg 2:37; 15:13; 2Kg 23:4,6,12). The **garden** is called "Gethsemane" in the Synoptic Gospels (Mt 26:36;

Mk 14:32). **Went into it** may suggest that it was a walled garden.

18:3 The **company of soldiers** was dispatched to prevent rioting. The **temple police from the chief priests and the Pharisees** were the primary arresting officers (see notes at 7:32 and 7:46). **Lanterns** and **torches** were needed to track down a suspect hiding in the dark garden. The presence of **weapons** shows that the arrest party anticipated resistance.

18:5 **I am He** connotes deity (see note at 6:35,48). This is shown by the soldiers' reaction in the following verse.

ego eimi

Greek Pronunciation	[eh GOH ay mee]
HCSB Translation	I am
Uses in John's Gospel	76
Uses in the NT	153
Focus Passage	John 18:5

The words *ego eimi* occur numerous times in the NT, but in John's Gospel they have a special meaning with two related connotations. First, *I am* often refers to Jesus' claim to be the Messiah. This is clear in John 4 where the woman at the well referred to the coming Messiah (v. 25) and Jesus responded, "I am He *[ego eimi]*" (v. 26). This meaning of *ego eimi* also occurs in Jesus' words to the disciples, "I am telling you now before it [Judas' betrayal] happens, so that when it does happen you will believe that I am He *[ego eimi]*" (13:19). Jesus' foreknowledge of Judas' betrayal provided evidence for the other disciples that He was indeed the Messiah. Second, *ego eimi* often refers to Jesus' claim to deity and probably reflects the burning bush episode when God revealed Himself to Moses as "I AM" (Ex 3:14).

"I am He,"[A,a] Jesus told them.

Judas, who betrayed Him, was also standing with them. [6]When He told them, "I am He," they stepped back and fell to the ground.

[7]Then He asked them again, "Who is it you're looking for?"

"Jesus the Nazarene," they said.

[8]"I told you I am He," Jesus replied. "So if you're looking for Me, let these men go." [9]This was to fulfill[b] the words He had said: "I have not lost one of those You have given Me."[c]

[10]Then Simon[d] Peter,[e] who had a sword,[f] drew it, struck the high priest's[g] •slave, and cut off his right ear. (The slave's name was Malchus.)

[11]At that, Jesus said to Peter, "Sheathe your sword! Am I not to drink the cup[h] the Father has given Me?"

Jesus Arrested and Taken to Annas

[12]Then the company of soldiers, the commander, and the Jewish temple police arrested Jesus and tied Him up. [13]First they led Him to Annas,[i] for he was the father-in-law of Caiaphas,[j] who was high priest that year. [14]Caiaphas was the one who had advised the •Jews that it was advantageous that one man should die for the people.[k]

Peter Denies Jesus

[15]Meanwhile, Simon Peter[l] was following Jesus, as was another disciple. That disciple was an acquaintance of the high priest; so he went with Jesus into the high priest's courtyard. [16]But Peter remained standing outside by the door. So the other disciple, the one known to the high priest, went out and spoke to the girl who was the doorkeeper and brought Peter in.

[17]Then the slave girl who was the doorkeeper said to Peter, "You aren't one of this man's disciples too, are you?"

"I am not!" he said. [18]Now the slaves and the temple police had made a charcoal fire, because it was cold. They were standing there warming themselves, and Peter was standing with them, warming himself.

Jesus before Annas

[19]The high priest[m] questioned Jesus about His disciples and about His teaching.

[20]"I have spoken openly to the world," Jesus answered him. "I have always taught in the •synagogue[n] and in the •temple complex,[o] where all the Jews congregate, and I haven't spoken anything in secret. [21]Why do you question Me? Question those who heard what I told them. Look, they know what I said."

[22]When He had said these things, one of the temple police standing by slapped Jesus, saying, "Is this the way you answer the high priest?"

Cross references

[a]18:5 Ex 3:14; Jn 8:24,58; [b]18:9 Mt 1:22; [c]Jn 17:6,12; [d]18:10 Mt 16:17; [e]Lk 6:14; Ac 10:32; [f]Mk 14:47; Heb 4:12; [g]Lv 16:32; [h]18:11 Is 51:22; Jr 49:12; Mt 20:22; 26:39,42; Mk 14:36; Lk 22:42; [i]18:13 Lk 3:2; Jn 18:24; Ac 4:6; [j]Mt 26:3; Jn 11:49; [k]18:14 Jn 11:50; [l]18:15 Lk 6:14; [m]18:19 Mt 26:3; [n]18:20 Jms 2:2; [o]Ac 21:26

A18:5 Lit I am; see note at Jn 8:58.

18:6 Falling to the **ground** was a common reaction to divine revelation (Ezk 1:28; 44:4; Dn 2:46; 8:18; 10:9; Ac 9:4; 22:7; 26:14; Rv 1:17; 19:10; 22:8).

18:8-9 Jesus' statement summarized 17:12, which harks back to 6:39 and 10:28. Jesus is portrayed as the Good Shepherd who chose death to save His sheep (10:11,15,17-18,28).

18:10 Peter's **sword** was short and could be hidden under his robe (Lk 22:38). The name **Malchus** (stated only in John) indicates a slave of Arabic origin.

18:11 **Drink the cup** is a metaphor for death.

18:12 On **temple police**, see note at verse 3. **Tied him up** is a customary expression in conjunction with arrest or imprisonment (Ac 9:2,14,21).

18:13 **Annas**, apart from being **the father-in-law of Caiaphas, who was high priest that year**, also had been high priest from A.D. 6–15. He continued to wield considerable influence.

18:14 On this description of Caiaphas, see notes at 11:49 and 11:50-51.

18:15-16 The **other disciple** was probably "the one Jesus loved" (20:2; see note at 13:23).

18:16-17 The **girl who was the doorkeeper** was probably one of the high priest's slaves.

18:18 The Roman soldiers had returned to their barracks, entrusting the task of guarding Jesus to the **temple police** (see note at v. 3). Another **charcoal fire** was lit at Peter's restoration in 21:9.

18:19 **High priest** refers to Annas (see note at v. 13). Questioning Jesus about **His disciples** and **His teaching** suggests that the primary concern was theological. Political charges were later added (19:7,12).

18:20 Jesus' words **I haven't spoken anything in secret** echo God's words in the book of Isaiah (Is 45:19; 48:16). Jesus did not mean that He never spoke in private with His disciples but that His message was the same in private as in public; He was not leading a conspiracy. John recorded instances of Jesus teaching both **in the synagogue** (cp. 6:59) and **in the temple complex** (Gk *hieron*; cp. 2:14-21; 7:14,28; 8:20; 10:23; see note at 2:14).

18:21 Jesus' response is understandable, especially if the questioning of prisoners was considered improper in His day. Note also the legal principle that a person's own testimony about himself was inadmissible (see note at 5:31).

18:22 **One of the temple police standing by** was probably one of those who helped arrest Jesus (vv. 3,12). The slapping was likely a sharp blow with the flat of one's hand (Is 50:6 LXX; cp. Mt 26:67; Ac 23:1-5). The phrase, **Is this the way you answer the high priest** may refer to Ex 22:28: "You must not blaspheme God or curse a leader among your people" (quoted by Paul in Ac 23:5).

23 “If I have spoken wrongly,” Jesus answered
him, “give evidence[A] about the wrong; but if
rightly,[a] why do you hit Me?”
24 Then[b] Annas[c] sent Him bound to Caiaphas
the high priest.

Peter Denies Jesus Twice More

25 Now Simon Peter was standing and warming himself. They said to him, “You aren’t one
of His disciples too, are you?”
He denied it and said, “I am not!”
26 One of the high priest’s slaves, a relative
of the man whose ear Peter had cut off, said,
“Didn’t I see you with Him in the garden?”
27 Peter then denied it again. Immediately a
rooster crowed.[d]

Jesus before Pilate

28 Then[e] they took Jesus from Caiaphas to
the governor’s •headquarters.[f] It was early
morning. They did not enter the headquarters
themselves; otherwise they would be defiled
and unable to eat the •Passover.
29 Then •Pilate[g] came out to them and said,
“What charge[h] do you bring against this
man?”
30 They answered him, “If this man weren’t a
criminal,[B] we wouldn’t have handed Him over
to you.”
31 So Pilate told them, “Take Him yourselves
and judge Him according to your law.”
“It’s not legal[C] for us to put anyone to
death,” the Jews declared. 32 They said this so
that Jesus’ words might be fulfilled signifying
what kind of death He was going to die.[i]
33 Then Pilate went back into the headquarters, summoned Jesus, and said to Him, “Are
You the King of the Jews?”[j]
34 Jesus answered, “Are you asking this on
your own, or have others told you about Me?”
35 “I’m not a Jew, am I?” Pilate replied. “Your
own nation and the chief priests handed You
over to me. What have You done?”
36 “My kingdom[k] is not of this •world,” said
Jesus. “If My kingdom were of this world,[l] My
servants[D,m] would fight, so that I wouldn’t be
handed over to the Jews. As it is, My kingdom
does not have its origin here.”[E,n]
37 “You are a king then?” Pilate asked.
“You say that I’m a king,” Jesus replied. “I
was born for this, and I have come into the
world[o] for this: to testify[p] to the truth.[q] Everyone who is of the truth listens to My voice.”
38 “What is truth?” said Pilate.

Jesus or Barabbas

After he had said this, he went out to the
Jews again and told them, “I find no grounds[r]
for charging Him. 39 You[s] have a custom that
I release one prisoner to you at the Passover.
So, do you want me to release to you the King
of the Jews?”

[a] 18:23 Gn 1:31
[b] 18:24-27 Mt 26:57-75; Mk 14:53-72; Lk 22:54,62-65
[c] 18:24 Jn 18:13
[d] 18:27 Jn 13:38
[e] 18:28-38 Mt 27:2,11-14; Mk 15:1-5; Lk 23:25
[f] 18:28 Mk 15:16
[g] 18:29 1Tm 6:13
[h] 1Tm 5:19; Ti 1:6
[i] 18:32 Jn 12:32-33
[j] 18:33 Jn 19:21
[k] 18:36 Mk 1:15; Ac 20:25
[l] Jn 17:6
[m] Lk 1:2; Jn 18:18; Ac 26:16; 1Co 4:1
[n] Jn 8:23; 17:14,16
[o] 18:37 Jn 1:9; 3:19; 6:14; 9:39; 11:27; 12:46; 16:28; 1Tm 1:15
[p] Jn 15:26; Ac 26:5
[q] Ps 119:142; 2Th 2:10
[r] 18:38 Mt 27:37; Mk 15:26; Jn 19:4,6; Ac 13:28; 23:28; 25:18; 28:18
[s] 18:39–19:6 Mt 27:15-26; Mk 15:6-15; Lk 23:13-25

[A] 18:23 Or *him, testify* [B] 18:30 Lit *an evil doer* [C] 18:31 According to Roman law [D] 18:36 Or *attendants*, or *helpers* [E] 18:36 Lit *My kingdom is not from here*

18:23 When challenged about His response to the high priest, Jesus alluded to the law of Ex 22:28 and denied having violated it.

18:24 Before Jesus could be brought to the Roman governor, charges had to be confirmed by the official high priest, Caiaphas, in his function as chairman of the Sanhedrin (see note at 3:1).

18:26 On **one of the high priest’s slaves**, see note at 18:10.

18:27 On the crowing of a **rooster**, compare 13:38.

18:28 The **governor’s headquarters** may refer to Herod’s palace on the western wall of the temple or the Fortress of Antonia northwest of the temple grounds. **Early morning** probably means shortly after sunrise, when the Sanhedrin met in formal session and pronounced its verdict (Mt 27:1-2). The reference to Passover may mean the entire Feast of Unleavened Bread, which lasted seven days (cp. Lk 22:1: “the Festival of Unleavened Bread, which is called Passover”). **Eat the Passover** probably means “celebrate the Feast” (see 2Ch 30:21).

18:29 Pilate was appointed by Emperor Tiberius, and he served as governor of Judea from A.D. 26 until 36/37. The famous “Pilate inscription,” discovered in Caesarea in 1961, identified Pilate as prefect of Judea.

18:31 Like Gallio after him (Ac 18:14-15), Pilate was not interested in judging internal Jewish disputes. The Sanhedrin did not have the power of capital punishment.

18:32 Crucifixion horrified Jewish sensibilities. It was considered to be the same as hanging (Ac 5:30; 10:39), for which Mosaic law enunciated the principle, “Anyone hung on a tree is under God’s curse” (Dt 21:23; cp. Gl 3:13). If Jesus had been put to death by the Sanhedrin, He would have been stoned, the method of execution for blasphemy (Lv 24:16; cp. Jn 10:33; Ac 7:57-58).

18:33 On **the headquarters**, see note at verse 28. **King of the Jews** had political overtones. Pilate’s question aimed at determining whether Jesus was a threat to Rome’s imperial power.

18:36 Jesus’ description of His kingdom echoes passages in Daniel (Dn 2:44; 7:14,27; cp. Jn 6:15).

18:37 On **testify** and **truth**, see notes at 5:31-47 and 14:6.

18:38 Ironically, the man charged with determining truth in the matter glibly dismissed the relevance of truth in the presence of the One who *is* truth incarnate (see note at 14:6). Pilate’s comment may reflect disillusionment, if not bitterness, and a pragmatic viewpoint. On **he went out to the Jews again**, see verses 28-29. Pilate exonerated Jesus three times (cp. 19:4,6), but Jewish pressures convinced him to press the prosecution (19:12-16).

18:39 **At the Passover** refers to the entire festival (see note at v. 28).

18:40 **Barabbas** means “son of the father” (Gk *bar-abbas*). Ironically, people wanted Barabbas released rather than the true Son of the Father—Jesus. **Revolutionary** refers to

⁴⁰ They shouted back, "Not this man, but Barabbas!"*a* Now Barabbas was a revolutionary.*A,b*

Jesus Flogged and Mocked

19 Then •Pilate took Jesus and had Him flogged. ²The soldiers also twisted together a crown*c* of thorns, put it on His head, and threw a purple robe around Him. ³And they repeatedly came up to Him*d* and said, "Hail, King of the Jews!" and were slapping His face.

⁴ Pilate went outside again and said to them, "Look, I'm bringing Him outside to you to let you know I find no grounds*e* for charging Him."

Pilate Sentences Jesus to Death

⁵Then Jesus came out wearing the crown of thorns and the purple robe.*f* Pilate said to them, "Here is the man!"*g*

⁶When the •chief priests and the temple police saw Him, they shouted, "Crucify! Crucify!"

Pilate responded, "Take Him and crucify Him yourselves, for I find no grounds for charging Him."

⁷ "We have a law," the •Jews replied to him, "and according to that law He must die,*h* because He made Himself*B* the Son of God."*i*

⁸When Pilate heard this statement, he was

more afraid than ever. ⁹He went back into the •headquarters*j* and asked Jesus, "Where are You from?" But Jesus did not give him an answer.*k* ¹⁰So Pilate said to Him, "You're not talking to me? Don't You know that I have the authority to release You and the authority to crucify You?"

¹¹ "You would have no authority over Me at all," Jesus answered him, "if it hadn't been given you from above. This is why the one who handed Me over to you has the greater sin."*C,l*

¹²From that moment Pilate made every effort*D* to release Him. But the Jews shouted, "If you release this man, you are not Caesar's friend. Anyone who makes himself a king opposes Caesar!"

¹³When Pilate heard these words, he brought Jesus outside. He sat down on the judge's bench in a place called the Stone Pavement (but in •Hebrew *Gabbatha*). ¹⁴It was the preparation day for the •Passover, and it was about six in the morning.*E* Then he told the Jews, "Here is your king!"

¹⁵But they shouted, "Take Him away! Take Him away! Crucify Him!"

Pilate said to them, "Should I crucify your king?"

*a*18:40 Mk 15:7
*b*Mk 14:48
*c*19:2 Mk 15:17
*d*19:3 Mk 1:45
*e*19:4 Jn 18:38
*f*19:5 Lk 19:36
*g*Zch 6:12
*h*19:7 Lv 24:16; Jn 10:33,36
*i*Jn 5:18; 19:12; Heb 1:2
*j*19:9 Mk 15:16
*k*Mk 14:61
*l*19:11 Jn 15:22; 18:13-14,19-24,28

A18:40 Or *robber*; see Jn 10:1,8 for the same Gk word used here   **B**19:7 He claimed to be   **C**19:11 To *have sin* is an idiom that refers to guilt caused by sin.   **D**19:12 Lit *Pilate was trying*   **E**19:14 Lit *the sixth hour*; see note at Jn 1:39; an alt time reckoning would be *about noon*

---

an insurrectionist or domestic terrorist, perhaps engaged in Zealot-style political extremism (Mk 15:7; Lk 23:19).

19:1 After the Jewish phase of the trial and Jesus' interrogation by Pilate, the sentencing stage of His trial began. On **Pilate**, see note at 18:29. The flogging weakened Jesus so much that He could not carry His crossbeam very far.

19:2 The **crown of thorns** represented a mock crown ridiculing Jesus' messiahship. The thorns would sink into His skull, bloodying and distorting His face. The **purple robe** (cp. Mt 27:28; Mk 15:17) represented a mock royal robe. Purple was the imperial color (1Macc 8:14).

19:3 **Hail, King of the Jews** mimicked the "Ave Caesar" ("Hail, Caesar!") extended to the Roman emperor. Roman soldiers customarily played "mock king" games during the Saturnalia festival.

19:5 **Here is the man** (Lat *ecce homo*) conveys a sense of, "Look at the poor fellow!" In His mock regal clothes, Jesus made a heartrending sight. In the context of John's Gospel, the statement may also highlight Jesus' humanity and invoke messianic passages such as Zch 6:12.

19:6 Pilate used sarcasm, being fully aware that the Jews did not have the authority to impose the death penalty (see note at 18:31).

19:7 The Jews' comment may refer to Lv 24:16: "Whoever blasphemes the name of Yahweh is to be put to death" (see note at Jn 5:18; cp. 8:59; 10:31,33).

19:8 Pilate was **more afraid than ever**. Earlier that morning his wife's dream had disturbed him (Mt 27:19).

19:9 Jesus' origin was frequently an issue with His opponents (7:27-28; 8:14; 9:29-30). For John, there were clear spiritual overtones to Pilate's question, **Where are You from?** (cp. 18:36-37). Jesus' silence before Pilate is reminiscent of Is 53:7; cp. Mk 14:61; 15:5; 1Pt 2:22-23].

19:10-11 In typical Jewish fashion, Jesus used **from above** to refer to God.

19:12 Unconvinced of Jesus' guilt, Pilate sentenced Him to die only after intense Jewish pressure (vv. 13-16). **Caesar**, originally the surname of Gaius Julius Caesar (d. 44 B.C.), became the title of subsequent Roman emperors (cp. v. 15; Mt 22:17,21). **Caesar's friend** was a semiformal status indicating a person favored by the emperor. Pilate feared losing this status.

19:13 The **judge's bench** served as the platform for the judge's formal verdict (Ac 25:6,17). The kind of **Stone Pavement** mentioned here has been excavated on the lower level of the Fortress of Antonia, one of the two possible sites for the governor's residence (see note at 18:28).

19:14 The **preparation day for the Passover** may refer to the day before the Sabbath of Passover week (Mt 27:62; Mk 15:42; Lk 23:54; see note at Jn 18:28). If so, all four Gospels concur that Jesus' Last Supper was a Passover meal eaten on Thursday evening (which, by Jewish reckoning, was the beginning of Friday).

19:15 By professing to acknowledge Caesar alone as their king, the Jewish leaders betrayed their national heritage and denied their own messianic expectations based on the promises of Scripture.

The Cross and the Gospel

Bruce A. Ware

The cross of Christ and the gospel of Christ are inextricably linked. Indeed, the gospel is the good news of what took place when Christ died on the cross. To understand what Jesus accomplished on the cross, then, is to understand the gospel. To believe personally that what Christ did on the cross He did for you, is to believe the gospel of Jesus Christ.

What Happened on the Cross?

What took place in Christ's death on the cross? The short answer is this: "Christ died for our sins" (1Co 15:3). Christ's death for our sin must be understood in two broad ways: First, when Jesus was nailed to the cross, the Father charged to Him all of our sin (2Co 5:21) and judged the full penalty of our sin in Jesus as He died (Col 2:14). Second, Jesus conquered the power of Satan, darkness, and death as He died for our sin (Col 2:15; Heb 2:14), thus establishing His supreme authority and power over everything in creation (Eph 1:20-23). To summarize, in His death on the cross Jesus fully paid the penalty for our sin, and He totally defeated the power of sin.

Jesus' subsequent resurrection from the dead was not just a nice ending to the story but rather necessary evidence that His death for sin really worked (1Co 15:17). The penalty of sin is death, and the greatest power that sin has over us is death. But since the penalty of sin is death, and since Christ paid the penalty of sin fully by His death on the cross, His resurrection from the dead demonstrated that the penalty had been paid in full. And since the greatest power of sin is death, and since Christ conquered all of sin's power in His death on the cross, His resurrection also demonstrated that the complete power of sin had been defeated as He arose victorious from the grave.

Erasing the Certificate of Debt

It is only because Christ paid sin's penalty that He was able also to liberate us from sin's power. That is, His payment of sin's penalty (sometimes called "penal substitution") is the basis for His conquering of sin's power (sometimes called "Christus Victor").

Consider one sample passage that shows this to be true. Colossians 2:13-14 teaches that believers are forgiven of all their trespasses through the death of Christ on the cross. The thrust here is on expiation: the liability we owed before a holy God to suffer the penalty for our violation of His law is removed because Christ took upon Himself our record of debt. Jesus "erased the certificate of debt, with its obligations, that was against us and opposed to us, and has taken it out of the way by nailing it to the cross" (v. 14).

The substitutionary death Christ died, in which He cancelled out the debt of sinners, then, is the backdrop for the next glorious truth found in Colossians 2:15. Here it is said that Jesus "disarmed the rulers and authorities and disgraced them publicly," putting them to shame and triumphing over them. The death by which Satan is disarmed and put to shame, then, is a death that cancels our sin. The disarming of Satan and the death that cancels our sin are theologically linked in this way: the basis of Satan's power over sinners is sin itself; the only way to overthrow this power was for sin to be paid for and forgiven. Christ's forgiveness through penal substitution, therefore, is the means by which we are freed from Satan's power.

An Analogy of Our Freedom

An analogy may assist in clarifying Scripture's teaching about the pardon Christ earned for believers on the cross. Under a just system of laws, a prisoner is jailed because he has been convicted of some crime whose penalty involves his incarceration. Notice, then, that his guilt forms the basis for his bondage. Only because he has been proven guilty of breaking the law does the state have the right to imprison him. Furthermore, if a prisoner can prove his actual innocence, such that the charge of guilt can be removed—e.g., if some forensic or DNA evidence available after his incarceration demonstrates his innocence—then the state is obligated to release him from prison. It is clear, then, that the power of the state to put criminals in bondage comes from the guilt they have incurred and the accompanying penalty directed at them as a result. Remove the guilt and its penalty, and you remove the just basis for the state's power to enforce bondage.

"We have no king but Caesar!" the chief priests answered.

[16] So then, because of them, he handed Him over to be crucified.

The Crucifixion

Therefore they took Jesus away.[A] [17] Carrying[a] His own cross,[b] He went out to what is called Skull Place, which in Hebrew is called *Golgotha*. [18] There they crucified Him and two others with Him, one on either side, with Jesus in the middle. [19] Pilate also had a sign lettered and put on the cross. The inscription was:

**JESUS THE NAZARENE
THE KING OF THE JEWS.**

[20] Many of the Jews read this sign, because the place where Jesus was crucified was near the

city,[c] and it was written in Hebrew,[B] Latin, and Greek. [21] So the chief priests of the Jews said to Pilate, "Don't write, 'The King of the Jews,'[d] but that He said, 'I am the King of the Jews.'"

[22] Pilate replied, "What I have written, I have written."

[23] When the soldiers crucified Jesus, they took His clothes and divided them into four parts, a part for each soldier. They also took the tunic, which was seamless, woven in one piece from the top. [24] So they said to one another, "Let's not tear it, but cast lots for it, to see who gets it." They did this to fulfill[e] the Scripture[f] that says: **They divided My clothes among themselves, and they cast lots for My clothing.**[C,g] And this is what the soldiers did.

Jesus' Provision for His Mother

[25] Standing[h] by the cross[i] of Jesus were His

Cross-references:
[a]19:17-24 Mt 27:33-37; Mk 15:22-26; Lk 23:32-34
[b]19:17 Lk 9:23; 23:26
[c]19:20 Heb 13:12
[d]19:21 Mt 2:2; 27:11,29,37; Mk 15:2,9,12,18,26; Lk 23:3,37-38; Jn 18:33,39; 19:3,19
[e]19:24 Mt 1:22
[f]Mt 26:54
[g]Ps 22:18
[h]19:25-27 Mt 27:55-56; Mk 15:40-41; Lk 23:49
[i]19:25 Lk 23:26

A19:16 Other mss add *and led Him out*　B19:20 Or *Aramaic*　C19:24 Ps 22:18

19:16 Upon pronouncement of the sentence, the person was scourged and then executed.

19:16b-42 The final unit in John's Passion Narrative describes Jesus' crucifixion and burial.

19:17 Jesus set out **carrying His own cross** until He collapsed. Simon of Cyrene was then pressed into service, and he carried it to the execution site (Mt 27:32). **He went out** means "out of the city," where Jewish custom prescribed that executions should take place (Lv 24:14,23; Nm 15:35-36; Dt 17:5; 21:19-21; 22:24; cp. Heb 13:12). **Skull Place** translates Hebrew *Golgotha;* the Latin equivalent used in the Vulgate is "Calvary" (see note at 1:38).

19:18 On crucifixion, see note at 18:32. Jesus' crucifixion between two criminals is reminiscent of Ps 22:16: "A gang of evildoers has closed in on me." The passage also echoes Is 53:12: "counted among the rebels."

19:19 The **inscription** on Jesus' cross specified the crime for which He was executed, probably to discourage others from committing similar acts.

19:20 On **the place . . . was near the city,** see note at verse 17. **Hebrew** or Aramaic was the language most widely understood by the Jewish population of Palestine; **Latin** was the official language of the Roman occupying force; and

Greek was the "international language" of the empire, understood by most Diaspora Jews as well as Gentiles. The trilingual inscription ensured that virtually anyone could read the crimes with which Jesus was charged.

19:22 Pilate was unwilling to give in to further Jewish pressures. For John, the inscription unintentionally confirmed Jesus' true kingship.

19:23 The **seamless** tunic may recall Joseph's robe (Gn 37:3,23). Similar to several later events at the crucifixion (Jn 19:28-37), the soldiers' division of Jesus' clothes and their casting of lots fulfilled Scripture (Ps 22:18). On other fulfillment quotations, see note at Jn 12:38-40.

19:24 Psalm 22, a lament psalm ascribed to David, is the most frequently quoted psalm in the NT. This is the first of several references to Jesus as the righteous sufferer in keeping with the experience of the psalmist (Jn 19:28,36-37). The soldiers did not want to tear Jesus' tunic because it was woven of one cloth (vv. 23-24). John may have purposefully shaped his account of Jesus' crucifixion in a way that highlighted the parallels and fulfillments between the experiences of David and Jesus. For instance, Ps 22:15-18 mentions the sufferer's thirst (v. 15), his pierced hands and feet (v. 16), and the preservation of all his bones (v. 17).

19:25 On Jesus' **mother**, see 2:1-5 and note at 19:26-27.

Similarly, Satan's power over sinners is tied specifically and exclusively to the sinner's guilt through sin. His hold on them is owing to their sinful rebellion against God. But remove the guilt through Christ's payment for their sin and you remove the basis for Satan's hold on them! So by His death Christ took upon Himself the sin of others and paid the full penalty for their sin. As a consequence, the hold that Satan had upon sinners is necessarily broken since the basis for this bondage is removed. Remove the guilt and you remove the bondage; accomplish penal substitution and you accomplish Christus Victor.

The Cross Is Good News

The gospel is the good news that in the cross of Christ, the penalty of our sin was paid fully by Christ. By this, sin's powerful hold on our lives, which leads ultimately to death, has been completely defeated. If we will trust fully Christ's accomplishment for us—that He paid sin's penalty and conquered sin's power—and not look to our own works or accomplishments as if they could commend us to God, we will be saved (Eph 2:8-9).

mother,[a] His mother's sister, Mary the wife of Clopas, and •Mary Magdalene.[b] [26]When Jesus saw His mother and the disciple He loved[c] standing there, He said to His mother, "•Woman, here is your son." [27]Then He said to the disciple, "Here is your mother." And from that hour the disciple took her into his home.

The Finished Work of Jesus

[28]After[d] this, when Jesus knew that everything was now accomplished[e] that the Scripture might be fulfilled, He said, "I'm thirsty!"[f] [29]A jar full of sour wine was sitting there; so they fixed a sponge full of sour wine on hyssop[A,g] and held it up to His mouth.

[30]When Jesus had received the sour wine, He said, "It is finished!"[h] Then bowing His head, He gave up His spirit.[i]

Jesus' Side Pierced

[31]Since it was the preparation day,[j] the Jews did not want the bodies[k] to remain on the cross[l] on the Sabbath[m] (for that Sabbath was a special[B] day). They requested that Pilate have the men's legs broken and that their bodies be taken away.[n] [32]So the soldiers came and broke the legs of the first man and of the other one who had been crucified with Him. [33]When they came to Jesus, they did not break His legs since they saw that He was already dead.[o] [34]But one of the soldiers pierced[p] His side[q] with a spear, and at once blood and water[r] came out. [35]He who saw this has testified[s] so that you also may believe. His testimony is true, and he knows he is telling the truth.[t] [36]For these things happened so that the Scripture would be fulfilled:[u] **Not one of His bones will be broken.**[C,v] [37]Also, another Scripture says: **They will look at the One they pierced.**[D,w]

Jesus' Burial

[38]After[x] this, Joseph of Arimathea, who was a disciple of Jesus—but secretly because of his fear of the Jews—asked Pilate that he might remove Jesus' body.[y] Pilate gave him permission, so he came and took His body away.

Cross-references

[a]19:25 Mt 1:16
[b]Mk 15:40
[c]19:26 Jn 13:23; 21:7
[d]19:28-30 Mt 27:45-54; Mk 15:33-39; Lk 23:44-48
[e]19:28 Lk 12:50; 18:31; 22:37; Jn 19:30; Ac 13:29; Heb 10:14; 11:40
[f]Ps 22:15; 69:21
[g]19:29 Ex 12:22
[h]19:30 Lk 12:50; Jn 4:34; 17:4; 19:28
[i]1Jn 5:8
[j]19:31 Jn 19:14
[k]Lk 12:4
[l]Lk 23:26
[m]Mk 2:23
[n]Dt 21:22-23; Jos 8:29; 10:26-27
[o]19:33 Ex 12:46; Nm 9:12; Ps 34:20
[p]19:34 Zch 12:10; Rv 1:7
[q]Jn 20:20
[r]1Jn 5:6-9
[s]19:35 Jn 1:14-15,34
[t]Jn 21:24
[u]19:36 Jn 13:18; 17:12; 19:24
[v]Ex 12:46; Nm 9:12; Ps 34:20
[w]Zch 12:10
[x]19:38-42 Mt 27:57-60; Mk 15:42-46; Lk 23:50-54
[y]19:38 Lk 12:4; Jn 2:21

[A]19:29 Or with hyssop [B]19:31 Lit great [C]19:36 Ex 12:46; Nm 9:12; Ps 34:20 [D]19:37 Zch 12:10

His mother's sister may be Salome, the mother of the sons of Zebedee mentioned in Matthew and Mark. On **Mary the wife of Clopas**, cp. Lk 24:18. On **Mary Magdalene**, see 20:1-18 (cp. Lk 8:2-3).

19:26-27 In keeping with biblical injunctions to honor one's parents (Ex 20:12; Dt 5:16), Jesus made provision for His mother, who was almost certainly widowed and probably in her early fifties, with little or no personal income. On the word **woman**, see note at 2:4.

19:28-29 The reference to Scripture being fulfilled builds on verse 24 (see note there), most likely in allusion to Ps 69:21: "They gave me vinegar to drink" (cp. Mt 27:34,48; see Ps 22:15). Soldiers and laborers used **sour wine** to quench their thirst (Mk 15:36). It is different from the "wine mixed with myrrh" Jesus refused on the way to the cross (Mk 15:23). **Hyssop** was a plant classified in 1Kg 4:33 as a humble shrub. It was used for the sprinkling of blood on the doorpost at the original Passover (Ex 12:22).

19:30 Gave up may echo "submitted Himself to death," which was prophesied of the Suffering Servant (Is 53:12).

19:31 On **preparation day**, see note at verse 14. That **Sabbath was . . . special** because it was the Sabbath of Passover week. For the Jews, bodies of hanged criminals were not to defile the land by remaining on a tree overnight (Dt 21:22-23; cp. Jos 8:29).

19:31-33 The **legs** of crucifixion victims were **broken** to hasten death. This prevented them from pushing themselves up with their legs to open the chest cavity and thus breathe better. Since the victims would now have to pull themselves up by the arms instead, suffocation occurred once their arm strength failed. See note at verse 36.

19:34 The flow of **blood and water** proved that Jesus was dead (1Jn 5:6-8). The passage may also allude to Ex 17:6: "Hit the rock, water will come out of it and the people will drink" (cp. Nm 20:11). The **spear** was about three and one-half feet long and consisted of an iron spearhead joined to a shaft of wood.

19:35 On John's witness about Jesus, see notes at 5:31-47; 13:23; and 21:24.

19:36 After verses 24 and 28-29 (see notes there), this is the third scriptural proof that shows that Jesus' death fulfilled Scripture (Ex 12:46; Ps 34:20). Jesus escaped having His legs broken since He died so quickly, and the spear did not damage any of His bones.

19:37 The Roman soldiers again fulfilled prophecy without knowing it: "They will look at Me whom they pierced" (Zch 12:10; also cited in Rv 1:7).

19:38 Joseph of Arimathea, a wealthy member of the Jewish ruling council (Mt 27:57), asked Pilate for Jesus' body. Thus Jesus was killed alongside criminals and was buried in a rich man's tomb. This fulfilled another Scripture: "They

teleo

Greek Pronunciation	[tehl EH oh]
HCSB Translation	finish
Uses in John's Gospel	2
Uses in the NT	28
Focus Passage	John 19:28-30

Just before His death on the cross, Jesus uttered a single word of victory: *tetelestai* [teh TEHL ehs tigh], "It is *finished!*" (Jn 19:30). The verb *teleo* is related to several other Greek words that refer to something being *finished*, accomplished, completed, or coming to an end. (The same verb is translated "accomplished" in v. 28.) The perfect tense of the Greek verb Jesus used indicates that He understood His death at this point in time to have abiding or lasting results. Jesus' death on the cross on our behalf was His purpose for coming into the world. It is not surprising that Revelation uses the term eight times, more than any other NT book, to describe various events related to Jesus' second coming (Rv 10:7; 11:7; 15:1,8; 17:17; 20:3,5,7).

Nicodemus[a] (who had previously come to Him at night) also came, bringing a mixture of about 75 pounds[A] of myrrh and aloes. [40]Then they took Jesus' body[b] and wrapped it in linen cloths[c] with the aromatic spices, according to the burial[d] custom of the Jews. [41]There was a garden in the place where He was crucified. A new tomb was in the garden; no one had yet been placed in it. [42]They placed Jesus there because of the Jewish preparation and since the tomb was nearby.

The Empty Tomb

20 On[e] the first day of the week[f] •Mary Magdalene[g] came to the tomb[h] early, while it was still dark. She saw that the stone[i] had been removed[B] from the tomb. [2]So she ran to Simon Peter[j] and to the other disciple, the one Jesus loved, and said to them, "They have taken the Lord out of the tomb,[k] and we don't know where they have put Him!"

[3]At that, Peter and the other disciple went out, heading for the tomb. [4]The two were running together, but the other disciple outran Peter and got to the tomb first. [5]Stooping down, he saw the linen cloths[l] lying there, yet he did not go in. [6]Then, following him, Simon Peter came also. He entered the tomb and saw the linen cloths lying there. [7]The wrapping[m] that had been on His head was not lying with the linen cloths[n] but was folded up in a separate place by itself. [8]The other disciple, who had reached the tomb first, then entered the tomb, saw, and believed. [9]For they still did not understand the Scripture[o] that He must rise[p] from the dead.[q] [10]Then the disciples went home again.

Mary Magdalene Sees the Risen Lord

[11]But[r] Mary stood outside facing the tomb,[s] crying. As she was crying, she stooped to look into the tomb. [12]She saw two angels[t] in white

a19:39 Jn 3:1-9; 7:50
b19:40 Jn 2:21; 19:40
cJn 20:5
dMk 14:8
e20:1-2 Mt 28:5-8; Mk 16:5-8; Lk 24:3-8
f20:1 Lk 24:1; Ac 20:7; 1Co 16:2
gMk 15:40
hJn 5:28
iMt 27:60,66; Mk 15:46
j20:2 Lk 6:14; Jn 21:7; Ac 10:32
kJn 5:28
l20:5 Lk 24:12; Jn 19:40; 20:5-7
m20:7 Lk 19:20;
Jn 11:44; Ac 19:12
nJn 20:5
o20:9 Mt 26:54
pLk 18:33; Ac 2:24
qMk 9:9-10; 12:25; Lk 16:31; 24:46; Ac 10:41; 13:34; 17:3,31
r20:11-18 Mk 16:9-11
s20:11 Jn 5:28   t20:12 Gn 16:7; Mt 13:49; Ac 5:19; Rv 14:6

A19:39 Lit 100 litrai; a Roman litrai = 12 ounces   B20:1 Lit She saw the stone removed

---

made His grave with the wicked and with a rich man at His death" (Is 53:9).

19:39-40 The amount of aromatic spices brought by Joseph and Nicodemus—**about 75 pounds of myrrh and aloes**—was considerable (2Ch 16:14). Myrrh was a fragrant resin used by Egyptians in embalming; aloes were a powder of aromatic sandalwood; the mixture cloaked the smell of decay.

19:41 On **the place where He was crucified**, see notes at verses 17 and 20. The **garden** was apparently somewhat elaborate; note the mention of a gardener in 20:15. Garden burials are recorded in the OT (Manasseh in 2Kg 21:18; Amon in 2Kg 21:26).

19:42 On the **Jewish** day of **preparation**, see note at verse 14. Sabbath was rapidly approaching, when all work ceased, including that of carrying spices or transporting a corpse. Thus we may see it as an instance of divine providence that the tomb was **nearby** (see note at 20:1).

20:1-21:25 The final two chapters of John's Gospel cover the aftermath of Jesus' crucifixion and burial, specifically the empty tomb, the risen Jesus' encounter with Mary Magdalene, three resurrection appearances to His disciples (21:14), the commissioning of the disciples (20:21), a special commissioning of Peter (21:15-23), conclusions to the Gospel proper (20:30-31), and the epilogue (21:24-25). The concluding statement in 20:30-31 rehearses some of the major themes of the Gospel, particularly Jesus' identity as Messiah and Son of God, His messianic "signs," the importance of believing in Jesus, and the gift of eternal life. The conclusion to the epilogue identifies the "disciple Jesus loved" (who was one of the Twelve; cp. 21:20; 13:23) as the writer of John's Gospel (21:24; cp. 19:35) and affirms the truth of his testimony about Jesus (21:24).

20:1 The **first day of the week** was Sunday. **Mary Magdalene** (and several other women) decided to attend to some matters that had been left undone because of the beginning of the Sabbath (see note at 19:42). The need to complete the care for the dead may have overridden the customary seven-day mourning period (see note at 11:20). On **while it was still dark**, compare the slightly different time frame depicted in Mt 28:1; Mk 16:2; and Lk 24:1.

20:2 At this point Mary had no thought of Jesus' resurrection. The Jewish charge that His disciples stole His body (Mt 27:62-66; 28:11-15) shows that grave robbery was not uncommon. The plural **we** suggests the presence of other women besides Mary. On **the other disciple**, see note at 18:15-16.

20:5 Apparently by now there was enough daylight to see inside the burial chamber through the small, low opening in the cave tomb. The other disciple **did not go in**, presumably in deference to Simon Peter, a leader among the Twelve.

20:7 Jesus' resurrection body apparently passed through the linen wrappings similar to the way in which He later appeared to His disciples in a locked room (vv. 19,26). The reference to the head wrapping being **folded up in a separate place by itself** counters the notion of grave robbers, who in their haste would not have taken the time to fold up this cloth.

20:8-9 The presence of two witnesses rendered the evidence admissible under Jewish law (Dt 17:6; 19:15). The **other disciple** believed based on what he saw, not on an understanding from Scripture that Jesus **must rise from the dead**. This lack of expectation of a resurrection shows that the disciples did not fabricate the resurrection story to fit their preconceived expectations. Rather, the resurrection shocked them and did not fit with what they understood from Scripture. Only later, aided by the Spirit's teaching (see notes at 14:26 and 16:13), did they come to see that Jesus' resurrection was foretold in the OT.

20:10 When **the disciples went home**, "the disciple Jesus loved" in all likelihood told the Lord's mother, whom he had taken "into his home" (19:27), that He was risen.

20:11 Mary was **crying**, not because Jesus had died, but because His body had vanished.

20:12 She saw **two angels in white**. Angels often appeared in pairs (Ac 1:10) and are often depicted as dressed in white (Ezk 9:2; Dn 10:5-6; Rv 15:6). The angels were **sitting . . . one at the head and one at the feet** of the burial shelf.

The Missional Church

Ed Stetzer

"Peace to you! As the Father has sent Me, I also send you" (Jn 20:21).

Most believers readily grasp the idea of Jesus being sent to the world. While speaking to His disciples at the well of Samaria, Jesus said, "My food is to do the will of Him who *sent* Me." In John chapters 4–8 Jesus spoke of being sent by His Father on 14 separate occasions, such as saying, "I have come down from heaven, not to do My will, but the will of Him who *sent* Me" (6:38) and "I am the One who testifies about Myself, and the Father who *sent* Me testifies about Me" (8:18). Paul wrote of the same truth in Romans 8:3 referring to God's "*sending* His own Son in flesh like ours." When Jesus says, "the Father has sent Me," it is not a surprise. The fact that Jesus was the "sent One" is one of the most fundamental identifications of Jesus. The incarnation of Christ is the definitive occurrence of being sent on mission— and a model for us to represent Christ in the world.

Believers know that they are sent on mission into the world. The word "sent" is replete through Paul's epistles as he mentions those such as Timothy and Titus who have been entrusted with a message and a mission. In the book of Acts, sending is a common occurrence as well. Ananias is sent to pray for Paul and open his eyes. Paul and Barnabas are sent out from the church in Antioch as missionaries with the gospel. "As they were ministering to the Lord and fasting, the Holy Spirit said, 'Set apart for Me Barnabas and Saul for the work that I have called them to.' Then, after they had fasted, prayed, and laid hands on them, they sent them off" (Ac 13:2-3). Most know that Jesus "sent" some, but often do not consider the breadth and depth of that sending (cp. Gn 12:1-3; Ex 19:5,6; Is 6:8; Mt 24:14; 28:18-20; Lk 24:46-48; Ac 1:8; 1Pt 2:9-10).

All of God's people are sent on mission, the only questions are "where?" and "among whom?" So, God has a kingdom mission and He entrusts that mission to the church—in other words, the church does not have a mission, but the mission has a church. Some are sent cross-culturally as missionaries (we call that missions), but all are sent (we call that being missional).

To understand the depth of this *sentness,* consider that the source of our missional identity is located in the nature of God. Further consider that this sending is as central to God's nature as His love, forgiveness, righteousness, and holiness. It must be since we are given example after example of it in His Word. Without God's sending nature we would know little else of His other attributes. Without His sending nature, we would not see the "groom coming from the bridal chamber" in creation (Ps 19:5) culminating in Jesus "present[ing] the church to Himself in splendor" in the gospel (Eph 5:27).

God's sending is as tangible as any other attribute of the Godhead. And sending does belong to the Godhead: The Father sent His Son and the Holy Spirit. The Father, Son, and Spirit in indivisible unity send the church. We are to be missional, we are to live *sent.* Our sent-and-sending identity is connected ontologically with the very existence of the church. That is, just as it is the nature of God, it is in the nature of the church. When Jesus proclaimed, "As the Father has sent Me, I also send you" (Jn 20:21), His mandate was a commissioning act for the disciples of that day. His command then develops into the missional task described by Peter in his first letter. "But you are a chosen race, a royal priesthood, a holy nation, a people for His possession, so that you may proclaim the praises of the One who called you out of darkness into His marvelous light" (1Pt 2:9).

The concept of a missional church is recognition that God is a sending God and we, the church and individual believers, are to live *sent.* The missional church is shaped by the idea that every believer is to live on mission. Being *sent* means that we move outside the walls of our church buildings and our Christian homes in order to engage all people with the gospel. The missional nature of the church calls for us to engage in and support the work of international missionaries to take the gospel across the world and the local mission-shaped believers to take the gospel and show the love of Christ across the street. There is a *sentness* inherent to being a follower of Jesus. It is the way of Jesus in us.

We are not sent on mission alone. God's people join Him on His mission. We are commanded and empowered to participate with Him. We know this because Jesus promised, "I am with you always, to the end of the age" (Mt 28:20). We are sent on a mission with the Sender. As believers, we don't decide if we are on mission. We are by our calling—and because of God's nature. The only question is whether or not we are living up to the calling we have been given. Is our identity (sent on mission) aligning with our life (living on mission)?

Missional churches engage the people with the redemptive message of the gospel. To do so, the church emulates Christ in the engagement of the mission. He came announcing that He would serve the hurting

sitting there, one at the head and one at the feet, where Jesus' body[a] had been lying. 13 They said to her, "•Woman, why are you crying?"

"Because they've taken away my Lord,"[b] she told them, "and I don't know where they've put Him." 14 Having said this, she turned around and saw Jesus standing there, though she did not know it was Jesus.[c]

15 "Woman," Jesus said to her, "why are you crying? Who is it you are looking for?"

Supposing He was the gardener, she replied, "Sir, if you've removed Him, tell me where you've put Him, and I will take Him away."

16 Jesus said, "Mary."

Turning around, she said to Him in •Hebrew, "Rabbouni!"[A]—which means "Teacher."[d]

17 "Don't cling to Me," Jesus told her, "for I have not yet ascended[e] to the Father.[f] But go to My brothers[g] and tell them that I am ascending to My Father[h] and your Father—to My God[i] and your God."

18 Mary Magdalene went and announced to the disciples, "I have seen the Lord!"[j] And she told them what[B] He had said to her.

The Disciples Commissioned

19 In the evening of that first day of the week,[k] the disciples were gathered together with the doors locked because of their fear of the •Jews. Then Jesus came, stood among them, and said to them, "Peace to you!"[l]

20 Having said this, He showed them His hands and His side.[m] So the disciples rejoiced when they saw the Lord.

21 Jesus said to them again, "Peace to you! As the Father has sent Me,[n] I also send you."[o]

22 After saying this, He breathed on them[p] and said,[C] "Receive the Holy Spirit.[q] 23 If you forgive the sins of any, they are forgiven them; if you retain the sins of any, they are retained."[r]

Thomas Sees and Believes

24 But one of the Twelve, Thomas[s] (called "Twin"), was not with them when Jesus came. 25 So the other disciples kept telling him, "We have seen the Lord!"

But he said to them, "If I don't see the mark of the nails in His hands, put my finger into

---

[a]20:12 Lk 12:4; Jn 2:21 [b]20:13 Lk 10:1; 1Co 8:6 [c]20:14 Jn 21:4 [d]20:16 Mk 4:38; Eph 4:11 [e]20:17 Lk 24:51; Jn 3:13; 6:62; Ac 1:9-11; 2:33-34; Rm 10:6; Eph 1:20-21; 4:8; 1Pt 3:22 [f]Mt 5:16; 11:27; Jn 8:42 [g]Ac 9:30 [h]Jn 14:12 [i]Mt 27:46 [j]20:18 Mk 16:10 [k]20:19 Lk 24:1; Ac 20:7; 1Co 16:2 [l]Jn 14:27; 16:33 [m]20:20 Lk 24:39-40; Jn 19:34; 20:25-29 [n]20:21 Jn 3:17; 17:18; Heb 3:1 [o]Jn 13:20; Ac 1:2 [p]20:22 Gn 2:7; Ezk 37:9 [q]Ps 51:11; Jn 1:33; 14:17; 16:7; Ac 2:4; 8:15; Rm 8:9; Gl 5:25; Ti 3:5; Rv 3:22 [r]20:23 Mt 16:19; 18:18; Jn 9:41 [s]20:24 Mk 3:18; Jn 11:16

[A]20:16 *Rabbouni* is also used in Mk 10:51   [B]20:18 Lit *these things*   [C]20:22 Lit *He breathed and said to them*

20:15 Mary mistook Jesus for **the gardener**, which suggests that Jesus was indistinguishable from an ordinary person. Gardeners often tend to their grounds in the early morning.

20:17 My Father and your Father maintains a distinction between how Jesus and the disciples relate to God. Even so, Jesus called believers His **brothers**.

20:19,21,26 The common Jewish greeting **Peace to you** (representing Hb *Shalom alekem*) is still used today. Peace was Jesus' gift to His followers by virtue of His sacrificial death on the cross. On the disciples' **fear of the Jews**, see note at 7:13.

20:21-22 These verses contain the Gospel of John's version of the Great Commission, which culminates in the presentation of Jesus as the One sent from the Father (see note at 3:16-18). Now the sent One (Jesus) had turned Sender, commissioning His followers to serve as His messengers and representatives (17:18). All three persons of the Godhead are involved in this commissioning. As Jesus was sent by God the Father, so He, the Son, was sending out His disciples (20:21), equipping them with the Holy Spirit (v. 22). John thus demonstrated that each member of the Godhead is involved in the redemption plan and the mission of spreading the gospel to the world. **The Holy Spirit** was given dramatically and permanently a short time later (Ac 2).

20:23 The reference to forgiveness or lack thereof may echo the reference to "the key of the House of David" in Is 22:22 (cp. Rv 3:7). Jesus bestowed on His followers authority to announce access or disbarment from God's kingdom based on reception or denial of the gospel message. For those who reject Jesus, His messengers are commissioned to say that they do not have forgiveness of sins.

20:24 On Thomas as **Twin**, see note at 1:38.

20:25 Apparently Thomas thought the disciples had seen a ghost (Mt 14:26). Yet John was careful to affirm that Jesus'

(Lk 4) and save the lost (Lk 19:10). We are called to join Him on that mission and show and share the good news of Jesus to a world Jesus loves. The missional church contends for the truth.

The missional church engages and inhabits the culture while seeking to remain separate from its sin and sinful structures. Jesus Christ was a thoroughly Jewish, first-century man who engaged believers, doubters, scoffers, friends, and foes, yet never sinned. He was truly in the world without being of the world. We can engage the greedy without becoming greedy, the hateful without becoming hateful, and the proud without becoming prideful. The existence of temptation should not hinder us from missional living. Instead, we are to be a culturally relevant, counter-culture community for the kingdom.

Last, being sent by Jesus as the Father sent Him means that the seed of the gospel will take root. The seed of the gospel must be sown in the soil of the culture, which necessitates Christians being engaged there. Scripture calls us salt and light and that requires presence and proclamation.

The sending nature of the Father, the commission by Christ, and the empowerment of the Spirit creates a missional church. As believers, we should revel in the invitation by Christ to join His missional people.

the mark of the nails,[a] and put my hand into His side,[b] I will never believe!"[c]

[26] After eight days His disciples were indoors again, and Thomas was with them. Even though the doors were locked, Jesus came and stood among them. He said, "Peace to you!"

[27] Then He said to Thomas, "Put your finger here and observe My hands. Reach out your hand and put it into My side. Don't be an unbeliever, but a believer."[d]

[28] Thomas responded to Him, "My Lord and my God!"

[29] Jesus said, "Because you have seen Me, you have believed.[A] Those who believe without seeing[e] are blessed."

The Purpose of This Gospel

[30] Jesus performed many other signs[f] in the presence of His disciples that are not written[g] in this book.[h] [31] But these are written so that you may believe Jesus is the *Messiah,[i] the Son[j] of God,[B,k] and by believing you may have life in His name.[l]

Jesus' Third Appearance to the Disciples

21 After this, Jesus revealed[m] Himself again to His disciples by the Sea of Tiberias.[C,n] He revealed Himself in this way:

[2] Simon Peter,[o] Thomas[p] (called "Twin"), Nathanael[q] from Cana of Galilee,[r] Zebedee's[s] sons, and two others of His disciples were together.

[3] "I'm going fishing," Simon Peter said to them.

"We're coming with you," they told him. They went out and got into the boat, but that night they caught nothing.[t]

[4] When daybreak came, Jesus stood on the shore. However, the disciples did not know it was Jesus.[u]

[5] "Men,"[D] Jesus called to them, "you don't have any fish, do you?"

"No," they answered.

[6] "Cast the net on the right side of the boat," He told them, "and you'll find some." So they did,[E] and they were unable to haul it in because of the large number of fish. [7] Therefore the disciple, the one Jesus loved, said to Peter, "It is the Lord!"[v]

When Simon Peter heard that it was the Lord, he tied his outer garment around him[F] (for he was stripped) and plunged into the sea. [8] But since they were not far from land (about 100 yards[G,w] away), the other disciples came in the boat,[x] dragging the net full of fish. [9] When they got out on land, they saw a charcoal fire there, with fish lying on it, and bread.

[10] "Bring some of the fish you've just caught," Jesus told them. [11] So Simon Peter got up and hauled the net ashore, full of large fish—153 of them. Even though there were so many, the net was not torn.[y]

[12] "Come and have breakfast," Jesus told them. None of the disciples dared ask Him, "Who are You?" because they knew it was the Lord. [13] Jesus came, took the bread, and gave it to them. He did the same with the fish.

[14] This was now the third time[H,z] Jesus ap-

---

[a]20:25 Ps 22:16
[b]Jn 20:20
[c]Dt 9:23; Mk 16:11; Lk 22:67; Jn 4:48; 6:64; Ac 13:41
[d]20:27 Nm 12:7
[e]20:29 2Co 5:7; 1Pt 1:8
[f]20:30 Jn 2:11; 21:25
[g]1Jn 1:4
[h]2Tm 4:13
[i]20:31 Mt 1:17; Ac 18:5; 1Jn 2:22; 5:1
[j]Jn 5:19
[k]Heb 1:2
[l]Jn 10:27; 1Jn 3:23
[m]21:1 Mk 16:12; Jn 21:14; 2Co 4:11; 5:10; 1Tm 3:16; Heb 9:26; 1Pt 1:10; 1Jn 1:2; 3:5,8
[n]Jn 6:1,23
[o]21:2 Lk 6:14; Ac 10:32
[p]Mk 3:18
[q]Jn 1:45-49
[r]Mt 17:22
[s]Mt 4:21; 10:2; 20:20; 26:37; 27:56; Mk 1:19-20; 3:17; 10:35; Lk 5:10; Jn 21:7; Ac 12:2
[t]21:3 Lk 5:5
[u]21:4 Jn 20:14, 19,26
[v]21:7 Lk 10:1; 1Co 8:6
[w]21:8 Lk 12:25
[x]Mk 3:9; Jn 6:22-24
[y]21:11 Lk 5:4-10
[z]21:14 Jn 20:19,26

[A]20:29 Or *have you believed?* (as a question)   [B]20:31 Or *that the Messiah, the Son of God, is Jesus*   [C]21:1 The Sea of Galilee; *Sea of Tiberias* is used only in John; Jn 6:1,23   [D]21:5 Lit *Children*   [E]21:6 Lit *they cast*   [F]21:7 Lit *he girded his garment*   [G]21:8 Lit *about 200 cubits*   [H]21:14 The other two are in Jn 20:19-29.

---

resurrection body was not that of a phantom or spirit apparition but a genuine (although glorified) human body (Jn 20:27).

20:26 **After eight days** refers to the following Sunday, one week after Easter (v. 19).

20:29 Readers of the Gospel of John may **believe without seeing** because John, by aid of the Holy Spirit, has written the truth about God's Son.

20:30-31 On Jesus' **signs** in John's Gospel, see note at 2:11.

21:1-25 This epilogue narrates Jesus' third and final resurrection appearance recorded in this Gospel and contrasts the callings of Peter and "the disciple Jesus loved."

21:1 With the week-long festival of Unleavened Bread now past, the disciples left Jerusalem and returned to Galilee (see note at 20:26; cp. Lk 2:43). On the **Sea of Tiberias**, see note at 6:1.

21:2 The names of **Zebedee's sons** are given in the Synoptic Gospels as James and John (Mt 4:21). Luke mentioned that they were "Simon's partners" in the fishing business before they were called to follow Jesus as disciples (see note at Jn 1:40).

21:3 **Night** was the preferred time for **fishing** in ancient

times (Lk 5:5). This schedule allowed fish caught at night to be sold fresh in the morning market.

21:7 The **disciple . . . Jesus loved** must be one of the seven mentioned in verse 2, which included Zebedee's sons, and was almost certainly John the son of Zebedee, author of this Gospel (see note at v. 24).

21:9 On the **charcoal fire**, see note at 18:18.

21:11 Various attempts have been made to interpret the number **153** symbolically, but most likely it simply represents the actual number of fish. Large numbers elsewhere in John are meant literally as well (2:6; 12:3).

21:13 By taking the **bread** and **fish** and giving them to His disciples, Jesus acted as a Jewish host pronouncing the blessing at a meal (6:11,23).

21:15 On **Simon, son of John**, see note at 1:42. Jesus' question **do you love Me more than these** probably meant, "Do you love Me more than these disciples do?" rather than, "Do you love Me more than these fish [i.e., his profession]?" or "Do you love Me more than you love these men?" though each of the three meanings is possible.

21:15-17 Peter had denied Jesus three times (18:15-18,25-

peared[A,a] to the disciples after He was raised from the dead.

Jesus' Threefold Restoration of Peter

[15] When they had eaten breakfast, Jesus asked Simon Peter, "Simon, son of John,[B] do you love[C] Me more than these?"

"Yes, Lord," he said to Him, "You know that I love You."

"Feed[b] My lambs,"[c] He told him.

[16] A second time He asked him, "Simon, son of John, do you love[d] Me?"[e]

"Yes, Lord," he said to Him, "You know that I love You."

"Shepherd[f] My sheep,"[g] He told him.

[17] He asked him the third time, "Simon, son of John, do you love[h] Me?"

Peter was grieved[i] that He asked him the third time, "Do you love Me?" He said, "Lord, You know everything![j] You know that I love You."

"Feed[k] My sheep," Jesus said. [18] "'I assure you:[l] When you were young, you would tie your belt and walk wherever you wanted. But when you grow old, you will stretch out your hands and someone else will tie you and carry you where you don't want to go." [19] He said this to signify by what kind of death[m] he would glorify God.[D,n] After saying this, He told him, "Follow Me!"[o]

Correcting a False Report

[20] So Peter turned around and saw the disciple Jesus loved[p] following them. That disciple was the one who had leaned back against Jesus at the supper and asked, "Lord, who is the one that's going to betray You?"[q] [21] When Peter saw him, he said to Jesus, "Lord—what about him?"

[22] "If I want him to remain until I come,"[r] Jesus answered, "what is that to you? As for you, follow Me."

[23] So this report[E] spread to the •brothers[F,s] that this disciple would not die.[t] Yet Jesus did not tell him that he would not die, but, "If I want him to remain until I come, what is that to you?"

Epilogue

[24] This is the disciple who testifies to these things and who wrote them down. We know that his testimony is true.

[25] And there are also many other things that Jesus did, which, if they were written one by one, I suppose not even the world itself could contain the books[G] that would be written.[u]

Cross references column:
[a] 21:14 Jn 21:1; 2Co 4:11; 1Jn 1:2
[b] 21:15 Mt 8:30,33; Mk 5:11,14; Lk 8:32,34; 15:15; Jn 21:17
[c] Rv 5:6
[d] 21:16 Lk 6:35; Rv 12:11
[e] Lk 10:27
[f] 1Pt 5:2
[g] Mt 7:15; Jn 10:11
[h] 21:17 Mk 14:44; Jn 5:20
[i] 2Co 2:2
[j] Jn 16:30
[k] Jn 21:15
[l] 21:18 Jn 1:51; Rv 22:21
[m] 21:19 2Pt 1:14
[n] Jn 11:4; 17:1; 1Pt 2:12
[o] Jn 1:43; 8:12; 10:27
[p] 21:20 Jn 21:7
[q] Jn 13:21,23-25
[r] 21:22 Mk 8:38
[s] 21:23 Ac 9:30
[t] Mk 9:1
[u] 21:25 Jn 20:30

[A] 21:14 Lit was revealed (see v. 1) [B] 21:15-17 Other mss read Simon, son of Jonah; Mt 16:17; Jn 1:42 [C] 21:15-17 Two synonyms are translated love in this conversation: agapao, the first 2 times by Jesus (vv. 15-16); and phileo, the last time by Jesus (v. 17) and all 3 times by Peter (vv. 15-17). Peter's threefold confession of love for Jesus corresponds to his earlier threefold denial of Jesus; Jn 18:15-18,25-27. [D] 21:19 Jesus predicts that Peter would be martyred. Church tradition says that Peter was crucified upside down. [E] 21:23 Lit this word [F] 21:23 The word brothers refers to the late first century Christian community. [G] 21:25 Lit scroll

---

27); now Jesus asked him three times to reaffirm his love for Him before recommissioning him for gospel service.

21:18 Stretch out your hands refers to crucifixion, where a person's hands and arms are spread out and nailed to the crossbeam. Tradition says Peter chose to be crucified up-side down because he felt himself unworthy of dying in the same exact manner as Jesus.

21:19 The reference **to signify by what kind of death he** [Peter] **would glorify God** echoes the reference "to signify what kind of death He [Jesus] was about to die" in 12:33. This verse therefore establishes a connection between the deaths of Jesus and Peter. As God's Lamb, Jesus died for the sins of the world (1:29,36); Peter died a martyr's death, giving his life as a witness to his faith in Jesus.

21:20 On **the disciple Jesus loved**, see note at 13:23.

21:21-23 Like the final chapter of Matthew, the closing verses of John's Gospel dispel a rumor. Matthew denied that Jesus' disciples stole His body (Mt 28:11-15; cp. Mt 27:62-66) while John sought to lay to rest the rumor that Christ had promised to return during John's lifetime.

21:24 This is the disciple is a third-person authorial self-reference. Again, this is "the disciple Jesus loved" (cp. v. 7; see note at 13:23), one of the Twelve (cp. 21:20), John the son of Zebedee, the apostle John, who referred to himself by the epithet "the beloved disciple." **We know** represents an instance of the authorial "we," by which the author included himself along with his audience.

21:25 John acknowledged that he had to be selective, choosing from a vast amount of material about Jesus (specifically, the "signs"; cp. 20:30-31).

---

phileo

Greek Pronunciation	[fihl EH oh]
HCSB Translation	love
Uses in John's Gospel	13
Uses in the NT	25
Focus Passage	John 21:15-17

Although agapao (verb) and agape (noun) are normally considered the Greek words for divine love, the verb phileo can be used in the same way. The phileo word family has over 30 terms in the NT, including philos (friend), philadelphia (brotherly love), and philema (kiss). But phileo is also used to describe the Father's love for the Son (Jn 5:20), the Father's love for believers (Jn 16:27), Jesus' love for believers (11:3; 20:2; Rv 3:19), and believers' love for the Lord (1Co 16:22) and for each other (Ti 3:15). Both agapao (Jn 13:23; 19:26; 21:7,20) and phileo (20:2) are used to describe "the disciple Jesus loved," and the meaning is the same. Thus, it is better not to make a sharp distinction in John 21:15-17 between agapao (Jesus' term in vv. 15,16) and phileo (Jesus' term in v. 17 and all three times by Peter). Peter's threefold confession of his love for Jesus, which corresponds to his earlier threefold denial of Him, should not be understood as a secondary form of love.

Acts
Introduction

The book of Acts provides a glimpse into the first three decades of the early church (ca A.D. 30–63) as it spread and multiplied after the ascension of Jesus Christ. It is not a detailed or comprehensive history. Rather, it focuses on the role played by apostles such as Peter, who ministered primarily to Jews, and Paul, the apostle to the Gentiles.

Roman aqueduct at Caesarea Maritima, one of Israel's principal port cities in the first century. In A.D. 6, Caesarea became the capital of the province of Judea and served as the official home of the Roman procurators. The city is a setting for several pivotal events in Acts (9:30; 10:1; 12:19-23; 18:22; 21:8; 23:23; 25:1-7).

Circumstances of Writing

Author: The book of Acts is formally anonymous. The traditional view is that the author was the same person who wrote the Gospel of Luke—Luke the physician and traveling companion of Paul (Col 4:14; 2Tm 4:11; Phm 24). As early as the second century A.D., church leaders such as Irenaeus wrote that Luke was the author of Acts. Irenaeus based his view on the "we" passages in Acts, five sections where the author changed from the third person ("he/she" and "they") to first-person plural ("we") as he narrated the action (16:10-17; 20:5-15; 21:1-18; 27:1-29; 28:1-16). Irenaeus and many scholars since his time have interpreted these passages to mean that the author of Acts was one of the eyewitness companions of Paul. Luke fits this description better than any other candidate, especially given the similar themes between the Gospel of Luke and the book of Acts.

Background: The date of composition of the book of Acts is to a large extent directly tied to the issue of authorship. A number of scholars have argued that Acts should be dated to the early 60s (at the time of Paul's imprisonment). Acts closes with Paul still in prison in Rome (28:30-31). Although it is possible that Luke wrote at a later date, a time when Paul had been released, it is more plausible to think that he completed this book while Paul was still in prison. Otherwise he would have ended the book by telling about Paul's release.

Message and Purpose

The book of Acts emphasizes the work of God through the Holy Spirit in the lives of people who devoted themselves to Jesus Christ, especially Paul as he led the Gentile missionary endeavor. It is no exaggeration to say that the Christian church was built through the dynamic power of the Spirit working through chosen vessels. Another important concept is the radial spread of the gospel from Jews to Gentiles, from Jerusalem to Judea, from Samaria and on to the rest of the world (1:8). Thus Christianity transformed from being a sect within Judaism to a world religion that eventually gained welcome everywhere, even in the heart of the pagan Roman Empire: Rome itself.

At the heart of the Christian movement was the work of the apostle Paul, a former skeptic who became Christianity's most vocal advocate. From his first appearance at the stoning of Stephen (where he concurred in the

A.D. 33–37

Jesus' trials, death, resurrection, and ascension Nisan 14-16 or April 3-5, 33

Pentecost 33

Saul's conversion on the Damascus Road October 34

Paul's years in Arabia 34–37

Paul's first visit to Jerusalem following his conversion 37?

A.D. 37–41

Paul returns to his native Tarsus. Summer 37-40

Caligula, Emperor of Rome 37-41

Barnabas travels from Antioch of Syria to find Paul. Summer 40

Conversion of Cornelius and his family 40

Barnabas and Saul serve together in Antioch. 41

decision to stone Stephen for his Christian preaching), to his final appearance while imprisoned in his own rented house at Rome (where he was active in spreading the gospel even as he faced a death sentence), Paul's work on behalf of the gospel is evident at almost every turn as he proclaimed the good news before "Gentiles, kings, and the Israelites" (9:15).

The book of Acts provides biographical glimpses of a few of the early apostles as they spread the gospel first in Jerusalem and then on to the rest of the world. Peter, Philip, and a few others were responsible for the spread of the gospel to Jerusalem, Judea, and Samaria. Paul was responsible for much of the rest of the world.

Paul's typical missionary strategy was to go to a familiar place in each city he visited, usually a synagogue, and proclaim the gospel first to local Jews. The speed with which he shifted his focus to Gentiles outside the synagogue depended on how Jews received him within the synagogue. Before leaving town, Paul united Jewish and Gentile converts alike to form a local church.

The early apostles are distinguished by their being filled by the Holy Spirit and empowered to proclaim the gospel under a variety of trying circumstances. These circumstances included theological, political, and physical oppression or a combination of these as they were marginalized, imprisoned, and stoned.

Nevertheless, through the power of the Holy Spirit they refused to stop proclaiming the message that the OT prophesied about a coming Savior which was fulfilled in the person and works of Jesus of Nazareth. As a result, many thousands of people in Jerusalem and abroad came to believe that the Lord Jesus was the Messiah, their one hope for salvation from their sins.

Contribution to the Bible

The book of Acts ties the other books of the NT together. It does so by first providing "the rest of the story" to the Gospels. The gospel and the message of the kingdom of God did not end with Jesus' ascension to heaven forty days after His resurrection, but continued on in the lives of His followers. Acts shows us how the words

A.D. 41–49

Claudius, Emperor of Rome 41–54

Believers respond to famine prophesied by Agabus. 44–47

Martyrdom of James, son of Zebedee 44

Death of Herod Agrippa 44

Paul, Barnabas, and John Mark make first missionary journey. 47–49

A.D. 49–62

Paul and Silas take second missionary journey. 49–52

Paul's third missionary journey 53–57

Paul's arrest in Jerusalem (57) and imprisonment at Caesarea 58–59

Paul's journey to Rome late 59

Paul's house arrest in Rome 60–62

and promises of Jesus were carried out by the apostles and other believers through the power of the Holy Spirit. Second, the book of Acts gives us the context for much of the rest of the NT, especially the letters Paul wrote to the churches he had helped establish during his missionary journeys.

Structure

So far as literary form is concerned, the book of Acts is an ancient biography that focuses on several central characters, especially Peter and Paul. Ancient biography was not concerned simply with narrating events but with displaying the character of the people involved, especially their ethical behavior. Other features included genealogies and rhetorical elements such as speeches. Ancient biographies also commonly drew from both written and oral sources for information.

Acts 1:8 provides the introduction and outline for the book. Once empowered by the Holy Spirit, the disciples proclaimed the gospel boldly in Jerusalem. As the book progresses, the gospel spread further into Judea and Samaria, and then finally into the outer reaches of the known world through the missionary work of Paul.

Outline

I. Empowerment for the Church (1:1–2:47)
    A. Waiting for power (1:1-26)
    B. The source of power (2:1-13)
    C. Pentecostal witness to the dispersion (2:14-47)

II. Early Days of the Church (3:1–12:25)
    A. In Jerusalem (3:1–7:60)
    B. In Samaria: the Samaritan Pentecost (8:1-25)
    C. To the ends of the earth: Philip's witness (8:26-40)
    D. Conversion and preparation of Paul (9:1-31)
    E. In Judea: Peter in Caesarea (9:32–11:18)
    F. To the ends of the earth (11:19–12:25)

III. Paul's First Missionary Journey (13:1–14:28)
    A. Cyprus (13:1-12)
    B. Pisidian Antioch (13:13-52)
    C. Iconium (14:1-7)
    D. Lystra, Derbe; return to Antioch (14:8-28)

IV. The Jerusalem Council (15:1-35)

V. Paul's Second Missionary Journey (15:36–18:22)
    A. Antioch to Troas (15:36–16:10)
    B. Troas to Athens (16:11–17:34)
    C. Corinth (18:1-22)

VI. Paul's Third Missionary Journey (18:23–21:16)
    A. The Ephesian Pentecost (18:23–19:41)
    B. Macedonia to Troas, Athens, Corinth, and return (20:1–21:16)

VII. Paul en Route to and in Rome (21:17–28:31)
    A. In Jerusalem (21:17–23:35)
    B. In Caesarea (24:1–26:32)
    C. Voyage to Rome (27:1–28:15)
    D. Ministry at Rome (28:16-31)

Prologue

1 I wrote the first narrative, Theophilus, about all that Jesus began to do and teach[a] [2] until the day He was taken up, after He had given orders through the Holy Spirit to the apostles He had chosen.[b] [3] After He had suffered, He also presented Himself alive to them by many convincing proofs, appearing to them during 40 days and speaking about the kingdom of God.[c]

The Holy Spirit Promised

[4] While He was together[A] with them, He commanded them not to leave Jerusalem, but to wait for the Father's promise.[d] "This," He said, "is what you heard from Me; [5] for John baptized with water, but you will be baptized with the Holy Spirit not many days from now."[e]

[6] So when they had come together, they asked Him, "Lord, are You restoring the kingdom to Israel at this time?"

[7] He said to them, "It is not for you to know times or periods that the Father has set by His own authority.[f] [8] But you will receive power when the Holy Spirit has come on you, and you will be My witnesses in Jerusalem, in all Judea and Samaria, and to the ends[B] of the earth."[g]

The Ascension

[9] After He had said this, He was taken up as they were watching, and a cloud took Him out of their sight. [10] While He was going, they were gazing into heaven, and suddenly two men in white clothes stood by them.[h] [11] They said, "Men of Galilee, why do you stand looking up into heaven? This Jesus, who has been taken from

---

Cross-references (center column):

[a] 1:1 Lk 1:3; 24:19
[b] 1:2 Mt 28:19-20; Lk 24:47; Jn 20:21
[c] 1:3 Mt 28:17; Mk 16:14; Lk 24:34,36; Jn 20:19; 1Co 15:5-7
[d] 1:4 Lk 24:49; Jn 14:1; Ac 2:33
[e] 1:5 Jl 3:18; Mt 3:11; Ac 11:16
[f] 1:7 Mt 24:36; Mk 13:32; 1Th 5:1
[g] 1:8 Lk 24:48; Ac 2:1,4; 4:33; 8:1,14; 13:47
[h] 1:10 Mt 28:13; Mk 16:5; Lk 24:4; Jn 20:12

A 1:4 Or He was eating, or He was lodging　**B** 1:8 Lit the end

---

1:1 The preface links the book of Acts explicitly with the **first narrative**, the Gospel of Luke (Lk 1:1-4). Though the books are separate in the NT canonical order, both were probably written by Luke, the traveling companion of Paul. The books are both large enough to fill a complete scroll, and so it is unlikely that they were ever joined as a single book.

The book of Acts was written after the Gospel of Luke, as is indicated by the preface (1:1; cp. Lk 1:1-4). Luke builds these companion narratives on a broad chronology that begins with the birth of Jesus, then extends through His life, death, resurrection, and ascension. He next shows the expansion of the church from Jerusalem to Rome. Acts closes with Paul awaiting trial in Rome. Like the first volume, the second is addressed to a person named **Theophilus**. Some speculate that Theophilus (Gk "lover of God") was a literary figure representing Christians generally, but more likely he was an actual historical person.

Some think on the basis of Lk 1:1-4 that Theophilus was a seeker after God and that Luke aimed to explain Christianity to him. Others think Theophilus was a recent convert who required instruction in his newfound faith. Still others suggest he was an early church leader for whom Luke provided a summary of events surrounding the rise of Christianity. In any of the above scenarios, it is possible that Theophilus was Luke's patron, financing the publication of Luke and Acts. Though only a maximum of 20 percent of urban men were literate, there was a distinct book culture in the ancient world. Publication involved hand copying an original document to make it available for others. The cost of materials for the initial document plus all subsequent drafts could be expensive, with each copy costing up to four days' wages. As a result, the patronage system was an important fact in making book publication possible in the ancient world.

1:2-3 Luke opened Acts by mentioning the Gospel of Luke, the narrative of Jesus' life and ministry up until His ascension. Before His ascension, Jesus **suffered** the agony of death and then **presented** Himself alive to His disciples (Lk 24). Jesus presented Himself by **many convincing proofs**, including appearing to the disciples during the **40 days** between His resurrection and ascension. During this time Jesus instructed them about **the kingdom of God**.

1:4 The **Father's promise** refers to the gift of the Holy Spirit, which would soon come (chap. 2).

1:5 John's baptism was a symbolic washing to purify and to indicate repentance of sin. Jesus' baptism of believers would be of greater impact and involved the indwelling of the Holy Spirit.

1:6-7 Restoration of the **kingdom** of **Israel** was something for which all first-century Jews longed. It was commonly believed that Messiah, son of David and heir to his throne, would accomplish this restoration. Jesus deflected the disciples' misguided question and repeated His command that they were to be His witnesses near and far (cp. Mt 28:19).

1:8 The major focus of the book of Acts is stated in this verse. Jesus said believers would **receive power** when the **Holy Spirit** came upon them, empowering them to be His **witnesses in Jerusalem** first and then spreading to **the ends of the earth**. Note three things about how this unfolds. First, the empowering presence is to be the Holy Spirit, not Jesus Himself. Jesus prepared His disciples for the transition when the Holy Spirit would come to be a constant presence in His bodily absence. Second, the growth of the church would come about through the witness of the disciples. From the beginning, the church is depicted as a community that actively witnesses to their faith in Jesus Christ. Third, the result of this witness will be measurable, geographical growth. This growth will begin in Jerusalem and then spread through ever-widening concentric circles to other Jewish areas (e.g., **Judea**), to areas on the edges of Judaism (e.g., **Samaria**), and eventually to "the ends of the earth," which may refer to the known world of that time, likely coextensive with the reach of the Roman Empire. As new lands and peoples were discovered in coming centuries, the church understood that it must keep expanding its witness to reach the newfound "ends of the earth."

1:9-11 Luke briefly told about Jesus' ascension in his Gospel (Lk 24:51), and now he provides a somewhat fuller account. **A cloud took Him out** recalls the presence of God depicted as a cloud elsewhere (e.g., Ex 13:21-22). Thus Jesus was received by the Father in fulfillment of His words in Jn 7:33-34. Jesus' final instructions and ascension to heaven provide overlap and transition between Luke's Gospel and the book of Acts. The ascension took place on the Mount of

Opportunities and Challenges in Global Missions

M. David Sills

The twenty-first century is a time of unprecedented challenge and opportunity for global missions. The terrorism of 9/11 was the first of many cataclysmic global changes that are reshaping our world. The surge of terrorism against Western powers, the growth of Islam, and the burgeoning global prominence of the Majority World (formerly called Third World) represent significant challenges facing Christian missions. The unprecedented worldwide interconnectivity due to globalization both facilitates and challenges missions work. Urbanization has resulted in more than half of the world's people living in major cities. In many global south countries, up to one-half of the population lives in the capital cities. The principle of acceleration, which means that something is not just true but is *increasingly* true, exacerbates the challenges. In order to meet new challenges, missionaries and their agencies must constantly monitor global trends in order to reshape strategies and methodologies.

Beginning in the mid-1970s, missionaries began to strategize to reach people groups rather than just nations. This led to a focus on unreached people groups and more recently to strategies for engaging groups where no one was seeking to plant churches. Missiologists call this the "Last Frontier"—unreached and unengaged people groups. Reaching areas where there is no Christian witness and no government permission to do so is one of the daunting challenges facing missions today. On average three countries per year legally close their doors to traditional missions.

As the world's economic center shifts toward the global south, there is also rapid growth in the Southern Church. The churches of Latin America, Africa, and Asia have produced record numbers of Christians and missionaries that dwarf their older sister Church of the North. Evangelical missionaries celebrate this growth cautiously because, sadly, aberrant doctrine and practice abound in many southern churches. Since the first missionaries to these areas often emphasized simply reaching groups with the gospel, they left once they had evangelized a number of people. This means they regularly left behind undiscipled believers, ill-equipped leadership, and churches that adopted syncretistic beliefs and practices.

Missionaries of the twenty-first century must find ways to disciple people who learn in differing ways. This will require returning to some areas to train biblical leadership in the churches. One reason why many areas of the world are unreached, as well as why many reached peoples were left untaught, is that the people are oral learners who do not read. Oftentimes, their languages have not even been reduced to writing. Although missionaries are developing methods to teach this 70-80 percent of the world, less than 10 percent of all evangelism and discipleship resources are currently designed for oral learners.

The growth of the Southern Church has also brought about an emerging mission movement. The Southern Church has heard the missionary call, and its members are following the Lord's guidance to fulfill it all over the world. The biblical principal that those who know should teach those who do not suggests that missionary training programs ought to be developed for this emerging missions force. Discipled and trained believers among the cultures of the world are the key to healthy, reproducing New Testament churches.

Modern missions history has witnessed pendulum swings ranging from the rejection of cultures to an uncritical acceptance of them. A healthy balance is one that is faithful to God's Word and sensitive to cultures so that they can embrace the pure gospel in culturally appropriate ways. Missionaries in Muslim and Hindu areas are facing challenges to this balance in the extreme forms of insider movements and uncritical contextualization models that fail to stress the exclusivity of Christ.

Answers to these challenges are not easy, and no single-solution strategy will fit every culture in all ages. We can be certain God will make a way, but we must be diligent and faithful no matter the challenges. Missionaries must stay in the Word, on their faces in prayer, and as close to Jesus as they can get in order to tread the narrow way through an ever-changing world, bringing the Good News to all nations.

you into heaven, will come in the same way that you have seen Him going into heaven."[a]

United in Prayer

[12]Then they returned to Jerusalem from the mount called the Mount of Olives, which is near Jerusalem—a Sabbath day's journey away. [13]When they arrived, they went to the room[b] upstairs where they were staying:

> Peter, John,
> James, Andrew,
> Philip, Thomas,
> Bartholomew, Matthew,
> James the son of Alphaeus,
> Simon the Zealot,
> and Judas the son of James.[c]

[14]All these were continually united[d] in prayer,[A] along with the women, including Mary[B] the mother of Jesus, and His brothers.[e]

Matthias Chosen

[15]During these days Peter stood up among the •brothers[c]—the number of people who were together was about 120—and said: [16]"Brothers, the Scripture had to be fulfilled that the Holy Spirit through the mouth of David spoke in advance about Judas, who became a guide to those who arrested Jesus.[f] [17]For he was one of our number and was allotted a share in this ministry."[g] [18]Now this man acquired a field with his unrighteous wages. He fell headfirst and burst open in the middle, and all his insides spilled out.[h] [19]This became known to all the residents of Jerusalem, so that in their own language that field is called

Hakeldama (that is, Field of Blood). [20]"For it is written in the Book of Psalms:

> **Let his dwelling become desolate;**
> **let no one live in it;[D] and**
> **Let someone else take his position.[E,i]**

[21]"Therefore, from among the men who have accompanied us during the whole time the Lord Jesus went in and out among us— [22]beginning from the baptism of John until the day He was taken up from us—from among these, it is necessary that one become a witness with us of His resurrection."[j] [23]So they proposed two: Joseph, called Barsabbas, who was also known as Justus, and Matthias.[k] [24]Then they prayed,[l] "You, Lord, know the hearts of all; show which of these two You have chosen[m] [25]to take the place[F] in this apostolic service[n] that Judas left to go to his own place." [26]Then they cast lots[o] for them, and the lot fell to Matthias. So he was numbered with the 11 apostles.

Pentecost

2 When the day of Pentecost had arrived, they were all together in one place.[p] [2]Suddenly a sound like that of a violent rushing wind[q] came from heaven, and it filled the whole house where they were staying.[r] [3]And tongues, like flames of fire that were divided, appeared to them and rested on each one of them. [4]Then they were all filled[s] with the Holy Spirit and began to speak in different •languages, as the Spirit gave them ability for speech.[t]

[a]1:11 Mt 16:27; Ac 2:7; 1Th 1:10; 2Th 1:10
[b]1:13 Ac 9:37,39; 20:8
[c]Mt 10:2-4; Mk 3:16-19; Lk 6:14-16
[d]1:14 Ac 2:46; 4:24; 5:12; 15:25; Rm 15:6
[e]Mt 12:46; Lk 23:49,55; Rm 12:12; Col 4:2
[f]1:16 Lk 22:37,47; 24:44; Jn 13:18; 18:3
[g]1:17 Jn 6:71; Ac 20:24; 21:19
[h]1:18 Mt 26:14-15; 27:5,7-8
[i]1:20 Ps 69:25; 109:8
[j]1:22 Mk 1:4; Ac 2:31; 4:2; 17:18; 23:6; 24:15; 26:23
[k]1:23 Ac 15:22; 18:7
[l]1:24 Ac 6:6; 13:3
[m]1Sm 16:7; Jr 17:10; Ac 15:8; Rv 2:23
[n]1:25 Rm 1:5; 1Co 9:2; Gl 2:8
[o]1:26 Mt 27:35; Mk 15:24; Lk 23:34; Jn 19:24; Ac 8:21; 26:18; Col 1:12; 1Pt 5:3
[p]2:1 Lv 23:15; Ac 1:14; 20:16
[q]2:2 1Kg 19:11; Jb 38:1; Ezk 1:4
[r]Ac 4:31; 16:26
[s]2:4 Ac 4:31; 13:52
[t]Mk 16:17; 1Co 12:10

[A]1:14 Other mss add *and petition*   [B]1:14 Or *prayer, with their wives and Mary*   [C]1:15 Other mss read *disciples*   [D]1:20 Ps 69:25
[E]1:20 Ps 109:8   [F]1:25 Other mss read *to share*

Olives outside Jerusalem (Ac 1:12). Jesus' return will be in the **same way** as He departed—bodily and visibly.

1:13 Luke 6:14-16 provides the same list of disciples. The lists in Mark and Matthew are similar, except for differences in the names of two disciples between Luke-Acts and Mark and Matthew. Several disciples had alternative names (Simon/Peter, Matthew/Levi; cp. v. 23), possibly accounting for differences between the lists. **Simon the Zealot** of Luke-Acts is probably Simon the Cananean, and **Judas the son of James** in Luke-Acts may be Thaddaeus.

1:18-19 The differences between the two NT accounts of Judas's death (here and Mt 27:3-8) should not be overemphasized. Both agree that he died a shameful death and that a field was named after his traitorous deed. Matthew 27:5 says Judas hanged himself, while the present passage says he fell **headfirst** and **burst open**. Possibly after he hanged himself, Judas's body decayed and fell from the rope, bursting open.

1:21-23 The person selected to take Judas's place had to have **accompanied** the disciples throughout the course of Jesus' ministry (from His **baptism** to His ascension), thus assuring that he could speak about things he had seen personally.

1:24-26 The disciples **prayed** for God to make clear to them which person He had **chosen** as a successor for Judas. The casting of **lots** was an acceptable method for making decisions in the era before the Holy Spirit was given. The sovereign Lord superintended the event, ensuring that the lot fell in such a way as to identify His chosen man.

2:1-12 The events of Pentecost, which mark the formal and public beginning of the church, involved a number of supernatural phenomena. These included the rush of violent wind from heaven, tongues like flames of fire, the infilling with the Holy Spirit, and speaking in languages as the Spirit gave believers the ability to do so.

2:4 One of the supernatural phenomena at Pentecost was speaking in **different languages** as the **Holy Spirit** gave the apostles **ability** to do so. The languages have been interpreted as (1) supernatural languages given specifically for the purpose of communicating with the people gathered from all over the Roman Empire, (2) human languages that were recognized by individuals from various lands, or (3) the Greek language that was common to all the people

⁵There were Jews living in Jerusalem, devout men from every nation*a* under heaven. ⁶When this sound occurred, a crowd came together and was confused because each one heard them speaking in his own language. ⁷And they were astounded and amazed, saying,*A* "Look, aren't all these who are speaking Galileans?*b* ⁸How is it that each of us can hear in our own native language? ⁹Parthians, Medes, Elamites; those who live in Mesopotamia, in Judea and Cappadocia, Pontus and •Asia,*c* ¹⁰Phrygia and Pamphylia, Egypt and the parts of Libya near Cyrene; visitors from Rome, both Jews and •proselytes,*d* ¹¹Cretans and Arabs—we hear them speaking the magnificent acts of God in our own languages." ¹²They were all astounded and perplexed, saying to one another, "What could this be?" ¹³But some sneered and said, "They're full of new wine!"*e*

Peter's Sermon

¹⁴But Peter stood up with the Eleven, raised his voice, and proclaimed to them: "Men of Judah and all you residents of Jerusalem, let me explain this*B* to you and pay attention to my words. ¹⁵For these people are not drunk, as you suppose, since it's only nine in the morning.*C* ¹⁶On the contrary, this is what was spoken through the prophet Joel:

¹⁷   **And it will be** in the last days, says God,
   that **I will pour out My Spirit**
      on all humanity;
   then your sons and your daughters
      will prophesy,

a 2:5 Mt 28:19; Rm 1:5; Gl 1:16
b 2:7 Ac 1:11; 2:12
c 2:9 Gn 14:9; 2Kg 17:6
d 2:10 Mt 23:15; Ac 13:13; 15:38; 16:6,21; 18:23
e 2:13 Ac 17:32; 1Co 14:23
f 2:17 Is 44:3; Jn 7:38; Ac 10:45; 21:9
g 2:18 Ac 21:10; 1Co 2:10
h 2:20 Mt 24:29; 1Th 5:2
i Is 58:13; Ezk 13:5; Am 5:18; Ob 15; Zph 1:14; Zch 14:1; Mal 4:5
j 2:17-21 Jl 2:28-32; Ac 16:31; Rm 10:13
k 2:22 Jn 3:2; 4:48; Ac 10:38; Heb 2:4
l 2:23 Mt 26:24; Lk 22:22; 24:20; Ac 3:18; 4:28; 5:30
m 2:24 Rm 8:11; 1Co 6:14; 2Co 4:14; Eph 1:20; Col 2:12; 1Th 1:10; Heb 13:20

   your young men will see visions,
   and your old men will dream dreams.*f*
¹⁸   I will even pour out My Spirit
      on My male and female •slaves
         in those days,
   and they will prophesy.*g*
¹⁹   I will display wonders
      in the heaven above
   and signs on the earth below:
   blood and fire and a cloud of smoke.
²⁰   The sun will be turned to darkness
      and the moon to blood*h*
   before the great and remarkable Day
      of the Lord*i* comes.
²¹   Then everyone who calls
      on the name of the Lord
      will be saved.*Dj*

²²"Men of Israel, listen to these words: This Jesus the •Nazarene was a man pointed out to you by God with miracles, wonders, and signs that God did among you through Him, just as you yourselves know.*k* ²³Though He was delivered up according to God's determined plan and foreknowledge, you used*E* lawless people*F* to nail Him to a cross and kill Him.*l* ²⁴God raised Him up, ending the pains of death,*m* because it was not possible for Him to be held by it. ²⁵For David says of Him:

   I saw the Lord ever before me;
   because He is at my right hand,
   I will not be shaken.
²⁶   Therefore my heart was glad,
   and my tongue rejoiced.

A 2:7 Other mss add *to one another*   *B* 2:14 Lit *let this be known*   *C* 2:15 Lit *it's the third hour of the day*   *D* 2:17-21 Jl 2:28-32
E 2:23 Other mss read *you have taken*   *F* 2:23 Or *used the hand of lawless ones*

gathered from throughout the Roman world. The second option seems to best fit the context.

2:8-11 Those present in Jerusalem for Pentecost included people from a wide variety of places and ethnic backgrounds. All the regions listed in verses 9-10 are known to have had Jewish populations. They encompassed the eastern Mediterranean area that ran from Rome to Libya. The gathering at Pentecost is thus inclusive, featuring Jews from throughout the eastern Roman Empire.

2:14 Acts is primarily a narrative punctuated by numerous speeches. Most of the speeches are summaries rather than word-for-word accounts. Just as he did in the Gospel that bears his name, Luke relied on "the original eyewitnesses and servants of the word" to report the essentials of speeches and events for which he was not present (Lk 1:2).

2:17-21 In his reply to the jeering crowd (v. 13), Peter cited three OT passages to demonstrate the biblical basis for the events of Pentecost. The first passage he cited was from Jl 2:28-32. The quote follows the Masoretic Text version almost verbatim. Peter identified Joel's prophecy with **the last days**, and said those days had now arrived with the coming of the Spirit. There may also yet be a future, fuller fulfillment of Joel's prophecy.

2:23 Peter's declaration articulates a major paradox of the Christian life: Jesus' death occurred as a result of the plan and foreknowledge of God, but it was the free (and sinful) acts of human beings that executed that plan. The Bible often affirms the reality of both divine sovereignty and genuine human choice without explaining how the two can possibly work together without conflict (e.g., 4:28; Gn 45:5).

2:24 The resurrection of Jesus Christ is the fundamental event of Christianity and the basis of the gospel. Peter made several important statements about the resurrection in this verse. First, it was **God** who **raised** Jesus from the dead. This pictures the resurrection as God the Father's vindication of God the Son. Second, Jesus was literally dead before the resurrection, not simply injured. Thus His resurrection was no mere resuscitation. Notice also that Peter personifies **death** as an actual force that holds the deceased in its embrace. Third, death's power was overcome by the resurrection, which means that believers should no longer fear it.

2:25-28 The second OT passage Peter cited is Ps 16:8-11. He recognized that Jesus was the one about whom David had prophesied, one who would not see the **decay** of death (also in v. 31).

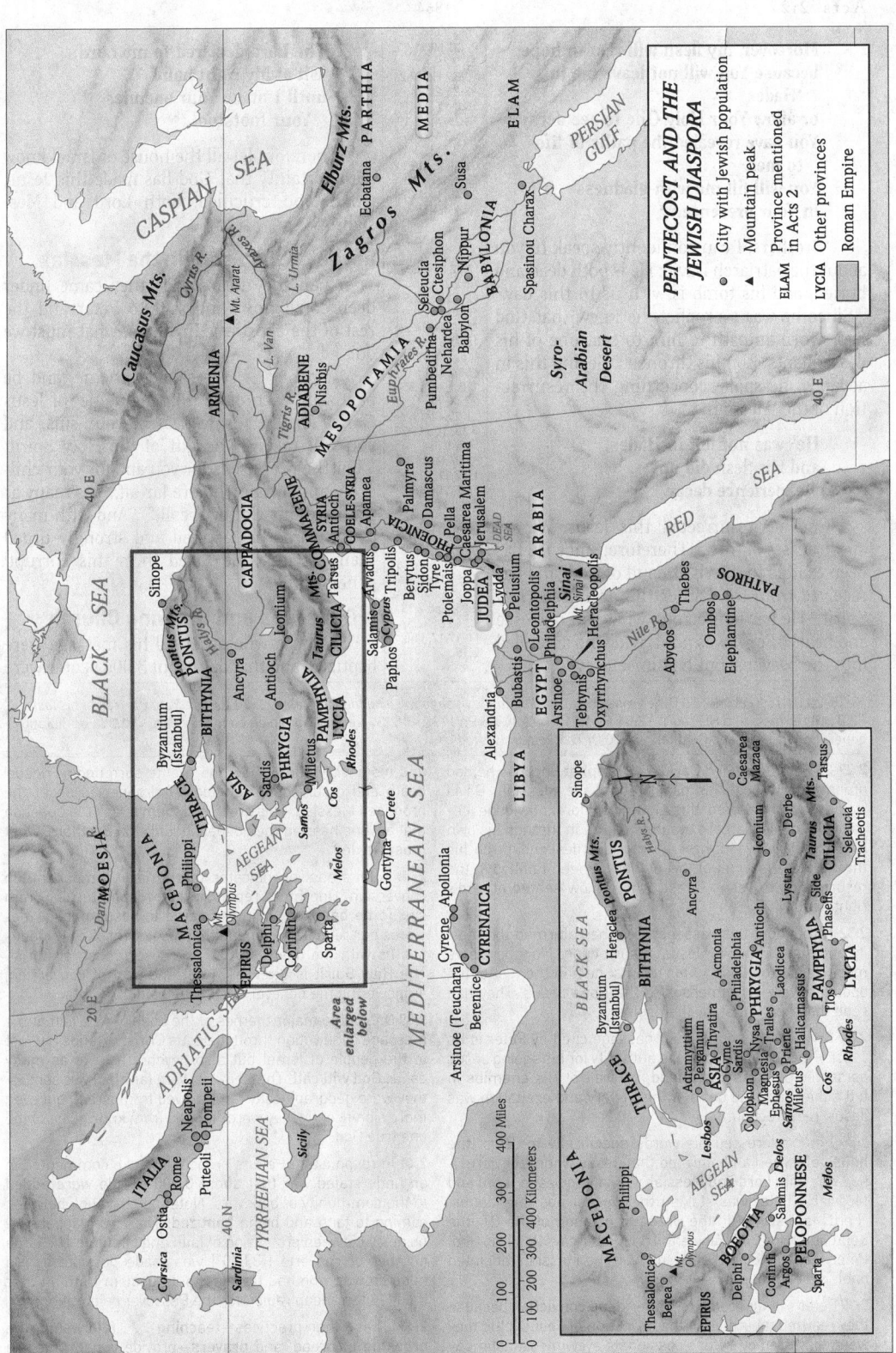

PENTECOST AND THE
JEWISH DIASPORA

- City with Jewish population
- ▲ Mountain peak
- ELAM Province mentioned in Acts 2
- LYCIA Other provinces
- Roman Empire

Moreover, my flesh will rest in hope,
27 because You will not leave me in
    ·Hades
    or allow Your Holy One to see decay.[a]
28 You have revealed the paths of life
    to me;
    You will fill me with gladness
    in Your presence.[A,b]

29 "·Brothers, I can confidently speak to you about the patriarch David: He is both dead and buried, and his tomb is with us to this day.[c] 30 Since he was a prophet, he knew that God had sworn an oath to him to seat one of his descendants[B,c] on his throne.[d] 31 Seeing this in advance, he spoke concerning the resurrection of the ·Messiah:

He[D] was not left in Hades,
and His flesh did not
    experience decay.[E,e]

32 "God has resurrected[f] this Jesus. We are all witnesses of this. 33 Therefore, since He has been exalted to the right hand of God[g] and has received from the Father the promised Holy Spirit,[h] He has poured out[i] what you both see and hear. 34 For it was not David who ascended into the heavens, but he himself says:

The Lord declared to my Lord,
    'Sit at My right hand
35 until I make Your enemies
    Your footstool.'[F,j]

36 "Therefore let all the house of Israel know with certainty that God has made this Jesus, whom you crucified, both Lord and Messiah!"[k]

Forgiveness through the Messiah

37 When they heard this, they came under deep conviction[G] and said to Peter and the rest of the apostles: "Brothers, what must we do?"[l]

38 "Repent,"[m] Peter said to them, "and be baptized,[n] each of you, in the name[o] of Jesus Christ for the forgiveness of your sins, and you will receive the gift of the Holy Spirit. 39 For the promise is for you and for your children, and for all who are far off,[H,p] as many as the Lord our God will call." 40 And with many other words he testified and strongly urged them, saying, "Be saved from this corrupt[I] generation!"[q]

A Generous and Growing Church

41 So those who accepted his message were baptized, and that day about 3,000 people were

Cross references

[a]2:27 Mt 11:23; Lk 2:26; Ac 13:35; Heb 7:26
[b]2:25-28 Ps 16:8-11
[c]2:29 1Kg 2:10; Neh 3:16; Ac 7:8-9; 13:36
[d]2:30 2Sm 23:2; Ps 132:11; Mt 22:43; Lk 1:32; Ac 1:8; Heb 11:32
[e]2:31 Ps 16:10; Ac 2:27
[f]2:32 Lk 18:33; Ac 2:24
[g]2:33 Php 2:9; Heb 10:12
[h]Jn 7:39; 14:26; 16:7,13
[i]Ac 2:17; 10:45
[j]2:34-35 Ps 110:1; Mt 5:35; 22:44; Mk 12:36; Lk 20:42-43; Jn 3:13; 1Co 15:25; Heb 1:13
[k]2:36 Mt 28:18; Lk 2:11; Rm 14:9; 2Co 4:5
[l]2:37 Lk 3:10; Ac 16:30
[m]2:38 Lk 24:47; Ac 3:19; 26:20
[n]Ac 8:12; 22:16
[o]Ac 3:16; 15:14
[p]2:39 Is 44:3; Ac 3:25; Eph 2:13
[q]2:40 Dt 32:5; Mt 17:17; Php 2:15

[A]2:25-28 Ps 16:8-11   [B]2:30 Other mss add *according to the flesh to raise up the Messiah*   [C]2:30 Lit *one from the fruit of his loin*   [D]2:31 Other mss read *His soul*   [E]2:31 Ps 16:10   [F]2:34-35 Ps 110:1   [G]2:37 Lit *they were pierced to the heart*   [H]2:39 For distant generations or perhaps Gentiles   [I]2:40 Or *crooked*, or *twisted*

2:29-30 Peter identified **David** as a **prophet** because he had prophesied through his psalm about the Messiah. David would have treasured this God-given foreknowledge because it entailed Israel's eventual salvation through his own progeny. David would have a victorious descendant **on his throne**. Peter saw all of this as having been fulfilled in the resurrection of Jesus Christ, who is now seated at God's right hand (v. 25; Eph 1:20).

2:32 Throughout this passage Peter has affirmed the reality and significance of Jesus' resurrection. Now he states most clearly the basis of his claims: he and the rest of the apostles were all **witnesses** to the risen Jesus. They had seen the risen Christ for themselves.

2:34-35 The third and final OT passage cited by Peter is Ps 110:1. Peter cited David as the authority for his seeing Jesus as seated at God's **right hand**, with all of His **enemies** in full subjection. The basis of this victory and exaltation was Jesus' resurrection.

2:36 Peter addressed his words specifically to Jews (**the house of Israel**) and affirmed that Jesus whom they crucified was **both Lord and Messiah**. By calling Jesus "Lord and Messiah," Peter was staking the biggest possible claims. "Lord" is reserved in the Greek translation of the OT (the Septuagint) for God (Yahweh). Thus Peter says Jesus is God. Peter further noted that Jesus was the Messiah (anointed one), Israel's hope for salvation.

2:37 Peter's audience **came under deep conviction** because they realized their guilt in the execution of Jesus, plus they were convinced by Peter's passionate eyewitness testimony

and his description of how the events surrounding Jesus' death and resurrection fulfilled OT prophecies about the promised Messiah. This prompted them to ask the question that anyone hearing the gospel should ask, **Brothers, what must we do?**

2:38 Peter's answer indicates three major components in conversion. One must **repent**, which means turning from sin. To **be baptized . . . in the name of Jesus** publicly declares our repentance and faith, plus it symbolically identifies us with the death, burial, and resurrection of Christ. The **Holy Spirit** is given as a gift and seal of conversion, empowering the believer for the life of faith.

2:39 One of the major themes of the book of Acts is that the message of salvation through Jesus Christ extends not just to the people of Israel but also beyond them to **as many as . . . God will call**. The Gentiles were **far off** in two senses: they were geographically far removed from Israel, but even more significantly they were "far off" from knowledge of the one true God.

2:41 In response to Peter's preaching, Luke commented in an understated way that **about 3,000 people were added** to the community of believers. Note the close link between coming to faith and being **baptized**. There was apparently no delay between profession of faith and baptism. The large number of converts ("3,000") was made possible by the huge crowds who had traveled to Jerusalem from all over the Mediterranean region for the Passover celebration.

2:42 These four practices—**teaching . . . fellowship**, the **breaking of bread**, and **prayers**—provide insight into the

added to them. ⁴²And they devoted themselves to the apostles' teaching,ª to the fellowship, to the breaking of bread, and to the prayers.ᵇ

⁴³Then fear came over everyone, and many wonders and signs were being performed through the apostles.ᶜ ⁴⁴Now all the believers were together and held all things in common.ᵈ ⁴⁵They sold their possessions and property and distributed the proceeds to all, as anyone had a need.ᴬ ⁴⁶Every day they devoted themselves to meeting together in the •temple complex, and broke bread from house to house. They ate their food with a joyful and humble attitude,ᵉ ⁴⁷praising God and having favor with all the people. And every day the Lord added to themᴮ those who were being saved.ᶠ

Healing of a Lame Man

3 Now Peter and John were going up together to the •temple complex at the hour of

prayerᵍ at three in the afternoon.ᶜ ²And a man who was lame from birth was carried there and placed every day at the temple gate called Beautiful, so he could beg from those entering the temple complex.ʰ ³When he saw Peter and John about to enter the temple complex, he asked for help. ⁴Peter, along with John, looked at him intently and said, "Look at us." ⁵So he turned to them,ᴰ expecting to get something from them. ⁶But Peter said, "I don't have silver or gold, but what I have, I give you: In the name of Jesus Christ the •Nazarene, get up and walk!"ⁱ ⁷Then, taking him by the right hand he raised him up, and at once his feet and ankles became strong. ⁸So he jumped up, stood, and started to walk, and he entered the temple complex with them—walking, leaping, and praising God.ʲ ⁹All the people saw him walking and praising God, ¹⁰and they recognized that he was the one who used to sit

ª2:42	Ac 5:28; 13:12; 17:19; 1Co 14:6
ᵇAc 1:14; Heb 10:25	
ᶜ2:43	Mk 16:17,20; Ac 5:12
ᵈ2:44	Mt 19:21; Ac 4:32
ᵉ2:46	Lk 24:53; Ac 5:42; 20:7
ᶠ2:47	Ac 5:14; 11:24; 16:5; Rm 14:18
ᵍ3:1	Ps 55:17; Mt 27:46; Ac 10:3,30
ʰ3:2	Lk 16:20; Jn 9:8; Ac 14:8
ⁱ3:6	Ac 4:10; 2Co 6:10
ʲ3:8	Is 35:4-6; Ac14:10

ᴬ2:45 Or to all, according to one's needs   ᴮ2:47 Other mss read to the church   ᶜ3:1 Lit at the ninth hour   ᴰ3:5 Or he paid attention to them

priorities of early Christianity. These same practices should be considered normative for the church today. The apostles' teaching was probably similar to Peter's message at Pentecost. That is to say, it focused on making Christ known by appealing to eyewitness testimony and the prophecies of the OT. Early Christians gathered together regularly for edification, prayer, and exhortation. The breaking of bread probably included fellowship meals and participation in the Lord's Supper (1Co 11:17-34).

2:44-45 As part of their fellowship, the early church practiced a community of goods for a short time. Distribution to members of the faith community took place according to individual **need**. This practice did not last long, likely because it was logistically difficult and fraught with potential abuse (see chaps. 4–6).

2:46 Early Christian gatherings took place in two places: **the temple complex** and the homes of individual believers.

2:47 The early church was an evangelizing church. Luke recounted that **every day** the Lord **added to those who were being saved**. He did not say how this took place, but it appears that evangelism took place primarily through the gathering of Christians in the temple and in individual houses. The crucifixion and resurrection of Christ were at the heart of early Christian preaching, which called for immediate response from anyone who listened.

3:1 Peter and John continued to participate in Jewish rituals and worship, and early Christians regularly gathered in the **temple complex** (2:46). This is fitting, for Christianity began as a form of contemporary Judaism that accepted Jesus as Messiah. The beginning stages of the church's separation from Judaism are recounted in Acts as Christian leaders such as Peter and Paul continued boldly to proclaim Jesus as Messiah. The full and final split of Christianity from Judaism came by the time of the first Jewish revolt against Rome (A.D. 66–70).

3:2 This is the first healing miracle in Acts. The man was **lame** from birth and was daily carried to the **temple gate called Beautiful** so he could beg for money. In the era be-

fore governmental aid for needy persons, it was the kindness of strangers and loved ones that kept men such as this alive.

3:6 It is good for the lame man that Peter and John had neither **silver or gold** to hand out, for what they did have to offer was of far greater value—healing power through **Jesus Christ**. Rather than a temporary fix, the man was given a permanent remedy for his physical and spiritual problems.

3:7 The book of Acts recounts several healing miracles (e.g., 9:32-34,36-42). During the Hellenistic period, knowledge of science and medicine was advanced enough that the bystanders recognized without a doubt that Peter had enacted a miracle. The mention of the strengthening of the lame man's **feet and ankles** may provide indirect support for the traditional view that the author, Luke, was a physician.

onoma

Greek Pronunciation	[AH nah mah]
HCSB Translation	name
Uses in Acts	60
Uses in the NT	231
Focus passage	Acts 3:6,16

The Greek noun onoma means name and has several uses, such as the following: (1) Used for proper names of persons and places. (2) In Revelation 3:1 onoma is rendered "reputation," as in the expression he has made a name for. (3) It also occurs in the sense of title, as in Matthew 10:41 (the literal in the name of a prophet means "because he is a prophet" or "because he has the title prophet"). In Hebrews 1:4 onoma refers to "Son" as the name or title that is more excellent than the angels' (see vv. 2,5,8), and in Philippians 2:9 the "name that is above every name" is the title "Lord" (kurios), as explained in verse 11. (4) Finally, the NT often demands that believers act for, or in the name of, Jesus Christ. The phrase "in Jesus' name" is not a mystical formula attached to the end of a prayer. It's an expression of faith that identifies the Person whom believers serve (Mt 18:20; Ac 2:38).

and beg at the Beautiful Gate of the temple complex. So they were filled with awe and astonishment at what had happened to him.^a

Preaching in Solomon's Colonnade

¹¹ While he^A was holding on to Peter and John, all the people, greatly amazed, ran toward them in what is called Solomon's Colonnade.^b ¹² When Peter saw this, he addressed the people: "Men of Israel, why are you amazed at this? Or why do you stare at us, as though we had made him walk by our own power or godliness? ¹³ The God of Abraham, Isaac, and Jacob, the God of our fathers,^c has glorified His Servant Jesus, whom you handed over and denied in the presence of *Pilate,^d when he had decided to release Him. ¹⁴ But you denied the Holy and Righteous One^e and asked to have a murderer given to you.^f ¹⁵ You killed the source^B of life, whom God raised from the dead; we are witnesses of this.^g ¹⁶ By faith in His name, His name has made this man strong, whom you see and know. So the faith that comes through Him has given him this perfect health in front of all of you.

¹⁷ "And now, *brothers, I know that you did it in ignorance, just as your leaders also did.^h ¹⁸ But what God predicted through the mouth of all the prophets—that His *Messiah would suffer—He has fulfilledⁱ in this way. ¹⁹ Therefore repent^j and turn back, so that your sins

may be wiped out,^k that seasons of refreshing may come from the presence of the Lord,^C ²⁰ and that He may send Jesus, who has been appointed^l for you as the Messiah. ²¹ Heaven must welcome^D Him until the times of the restoration of all things, which God spoke about by the mouth of His holy prophets from the beginning.^m ²² Moses said:^E

> **The Lord your God will raise up for you a Prophet like me from among your brothers. You must listen to Him in everything He will say to you.** ²³ **And everyone who will not listen to that Prophet will be completely cut off from the people.**^{F,n}

²⁴ "In addition, all the prophets who have spoken, from Samuel and those after him, have also announced these days. ²⁵ You are the sons of the prophets and of the covenant that God made with your ancestors, saying to Abraham, **And all the families of the earth will be blessed through your offspring.**^{G,o} ²⁶ God raised up His Servant^H and sent Him first to you to bless you by turning each of you from your evil ways."^p

Peter and John Arrested

4 Now as they were speaking to the people, the priests, the commander of the temple police, and the *Sadducees confronted them,^q ² because they were provoked that they were

^a3:10 Jn 9:8; Ac 3:2 ^b3:11 Lk 22:8; Jn 10:23; Ac 5:12 ^c3:13 Ac 5:30; 7:32; 22:14 ^dMt 27:2; Lk 23:4; Jn 19:15; Ac 13:28 ^e3:14 Mk 1:24; Ac 4:27; 7:52 ^fMk 15:11; Lk 23:18,25 ^g3:15 Ac 2:24; 5:31 ^h3:17 Lk 23:34; Ac 13:27 ⁱ3:18 Lk 24:27; Ac 2:23; 17:3; 26:23 ^j3:19 Ac 2:38; 8:22; 17:30; 26:20 ^kPs 51:1,9; Is 43:25; 44:22; Col 2:14 ^l3:20 Ac 22:14; 26:16 ^m3:21 Mt 17:10; Lk 1:70; Ac 1:11 ⁿ3:22-23 Dt 18:15-19; Ac 7:37 ^o3:25 Gn 22:18; Ac 2:39; Rm 9:4 ^p3:26 Ac 2:24; 13:46; Rm 1:16 ^q4:1 Mt 3:7; Lk 22:4; Ac 5:24

3:12 Recognizing that the onlookers were **amazed**, Peter seized the chance to testify about Jesus Christ. Signs of God's power can point to the truth about Jesus (Jn 3:2; 14:11).

3:13-15 Peter told his hearers in Solomon's Colonnade, which was part of the temple complex, that Jesus Christ was God's **Servant**. And yet the people had **handed** Him **over** to Pilate and **denied** Him even though Pilate had judged Him to be innocent (Lk 23:20-25). Peter emphasized the heinous nature of this deed by calling Jesus the **Holy and Righteous One** and by noting that they had asked Pilate to release a **murderer** in place of Jesus. Thus they killed the **source of life** instead of one who had taken life. But **God raised** Jesus **from the dead**, a fact to which both Peter and John were **witnesses**.

3:16 Peter and John had a chance to claim credit for the miraculous healing of the man, but instead insisted that it was **faith in His** [Jesus'] **name** that **made this man strong**. The apostles were merely God's chosen instruments for conveying the miracle.

3:18 The prophecy that the **Messiah** would suffer is an apparent reference to the Suffering Servant of Is 52:13–53:12. The suffering of the servant for sins (Is 53:10) had been fulfilled through Jesus.

3:19 On the basis of what he had said about who Jesus was, how He was treated by the Jewish people, and how God had

vindicated Him by raising Him from the dead, Peter called on his audience to **repent and turn back** to God so that their **sins may be wiped out**.

3:20-21 Early Christians looked with expectation to the second coming of Jesus and the **restoration of all things** that accompanies the establishment of His earthly kingdom. God had foretold the time of "restoration" through the prophets, starting as far back as Moses (v. 22; see also Rm 8:18-25).

3:22-24 Peter appealed to Dt 18:15-19, where Moses foretold Israel that **God will raise up for you a Prophet like me**. Over time this came to be recognized as a Messianic prophecy. Anyone who rejects Messiah **will be completely cut off** from God's people. Peter also appealed to **all the prophets** throughout Israel's history, for all of them had **announced these days**. Jesus Himself taught the apostles to recognize this about the OT (Lk 24:27).

3:25-26 The Jews listening to Peter were **sons of the prophets** and inheritors of the covenant God made with Abraham. Thus they had a personal stake in the words of the prophets and the Pentateuch, but so do all the peoples of earth. After all, God's **covenant** with Abraham promised that all the earth would be blessed through Abraham's seed, a reference ultimately to Jesus Christ, God's **Servant**.

4:1-3 The religious authorities **confronted** and ultimately arrested Peter and John for unauthorized teaching about **the resurrection from the dead** by using Jesus as the example.

teaching the people and proclaiming the resurrection from the dead, using Jesus as the example.[A,a] [3] So they seized them and put them in custody until the next day, since it was already evening. [4] But many of those who heard the message believed, and the number of the men came to about 5,000.

Peter and John Face the Jewish Leadership

[5] The next day, their rulers, elders, and •scribes assembled in Jerusalem [6] with Annas the high priest, Caiaphas, John and Alexander, and all the members of the high-priestly family.[B,b] [7] After they had Peter and John stand before them, they asked the question: "By what power or in what name have you done this?"

[8] Then Peter was filled with the Holy Spirit and said to them, "Rulers of the people and elders:[C,c] [9] If we are being examined today about a good deed done to a disabled man—by what means he was healed— [10] let it be known to all of you and to all the people of Israel, that by the name of Jesus Christ the •Nazarene—whom you crucified and whom God raised from the

dead—by Him this man is standing here before you healthy.[d] [11] This Jesus is

**the stone rejected by you builders,
which has become the cornerstone.**[D,E,e]

[12] There is salvation in no one else, for there is no other name under heaven given to people, and we must be saved by it."[f]

The Name Forbidden

[13] When they observed the boldness of Peter and John and realized that they were uneducated and untrained men, they were amazed and recognized that they had been with Jesus.[g] [14] And since they saw the man who had been healed standing with them, they had nothing to say in response. [15] After they had ordered them to leave the •Sanhedrin, they conferred among themselves, [16] saying, "What should we do with these men? For an obvious sign, evident to all who live in Jerusalem, has been done through them, and we cannot deny it![h] [17] However, so this does not spread any further among the people, let's threaten them against speaking to anyone in this name again." [18] So they called for them and ordered

*a*4:2 Ac 3:15; 17:18
*b*4:6 Mt 26:3; Lk 3:2; Jn 18:13
*c*4:8 Lk 23:13; Ac 4:5
*d*4:10 Ac 2:24; 3:6
*e*4:11 1Pt 2:7
*f*4:12 Mt 1:21; Ac 10:43; 1Tm 2:5
*g*4:13 Mt 11:25; Lk 22:8; Jn 7:15
*h*4:16 Jn 11:47; Ac 3:9-10

A4:2 Lit *proclaiming in Jesus the resurrection from the dead*   B4:6 Or *high-priestly class*, or *high-priestly clan*   C4:8 Other mss add *of Israel*   D4:11 Lit *the head of the corner*   E4:11 Ps 118:22

The Sadducees in particular were provoked by this, for they did not believe in resurrection because they did not think it was taught in the Pentateuch, the only portion of the Hebrew Bible they acknowledged as authoritative (Mt 22:23). The apostles were held **in custody** overnight because Sanhedrin trials were not conducted at night. Rome had granted the Sanhedrin legal authority over the temple area since disputes arising there were religious in nature rather than civic.

4:4 Repeated attempts to suppress the Christian message only caused it to spread more quickly. On Pentecost morning the believers in Jerusalem only numbered 120 (1:15). In response to Peter's sermon that day, another 3,000 were added (2:41). Now, with the healing of the lame man, Peter's sermon, and the arrest of the apostles, the church grew **to about 5,000.**

4:5-7 The parties listed in verses 5-6 represent all the most powerful players in the Jewish religious establishment. They made **Peter and John stand before them**, two men against all the powers of Israel. Ironic, therefore, that they asked the apostles **by what power** they had performed the miracle and preached the gospel. It was clear that the apostles, who shirked the traditional powers, considered themselves answerable to and empowered by a different authority.

4:8 Peter was **filled with the Holy Spirit**, a necessary prelude to his successful confrontation with the Jewish religious establishment.

4:9-10 Peter again emphasizes to a Jewish audience that **Jesus Christ the Nazarene**, whom the nation had **crucified**, was **raised from the dead** by God. This same Jesus is the power by which the lame man was made **healthy**.

4:11 Peter again identifies Jesus with OT testimony by citing Ps 118:22. Though Jesus was a **stone rejected** by the Jew-

ish leaders, God made Him **the cornerstone** (foundation) of the church.

4:12 Peter concluded by making clear the uncompromising claim of Christianity: There is **salvation in no one else** besides Jesus. This message rings throughout the NT. Jesus Himself said, "No one comes to the Father except through Me" (Jn 14:6).

4:16-18 Remarkably, the Sanhedrin admitted that **an obvious sign** had been done **through them** (the apostles), and yet rather than repent and believe they focused on damage

parresia

Greek Pronunciation	[pahr ray SEE ah]
HCSB Translation	boldness
Uses in Acts	5
Uses in the NT	31
Focus passage	Acts 4:13,29,31

The Greek noun *parresia* literally means *every word* and thus signifies the freedom to speak *openly*. Since such freedom of speech often provokes opposition, *parresia* also indicated fearlessness in speaking one's mind. Finally, *parresia* developed into a term meaning *boldness, openness*, or *confidence* (as an adverb, *openly* or *plainly*). The word was normally used in a positive sense, but a negative usage such as *bluntness* or *shamelessness* also occurs in ancient Greek literature.

All ten occurrences of *parresia* in the Gospels refer to speaking *openly* or *plainly*, either by Jesus or about Jesus (Mk 8:32; Jn 7:4,13,26; 10:24; 11:14,54; 16:25,29; 18:20). The uses of the term in Acts refer to three instances of *boldness* on the part of the apostles in proclaiming the gospel (2:29; 4:13,29,31; 28:31), something Paul referred to in his letters (2Co 3:12; Eph 6:19; Php 1:20).

them not to preach or teach at all in the name of Jesus.

[19] But Peter and John answered them, "Whether it's right in the sight of God for us to listen to you rather than to God, you decide;[a] [20] for we are unable to stop speaking about what we have seen and heard."[b]

[21] After threatening them further, they released them. They found no way to punish them, because the people were all giving glory to God over what had been done;[c] [22] for this sign of healing had been performed on a man over 40 years old.

Prayer for Boldness

[23] After they were released, they went to their own people and reported everything the •chief priests and the elders had said to them. [24] When they heard this, they all raised their voices to God and said, "Master, You are the One who made the heaven, the earth, and the sea, and everything in them.[d] [25] You said through the Holy Spirit, by the mouth of our father David Your servant:[A]

> Why did the Gentiles rage
> and the peoples plot futile things?
> [26] The kings of the earth took their stand
> and the rulers assembled together
> against the Lord and
> against His •Messiah.[B,e]

[27] "For, in fact, in this city both •Herod and Pontius •Pilate, with the Gentiles and the people[c] of Israel, assembled together against Your holy Servant Jesus, whom You anointed,[f] [28] to do whatever Your hand and Your plan had pre-

destined to take place. [29] And now, Lord, consider their threats, and grant that Your •slaves may speak Your message with complete boldness,[g] [30] while You stretch out Your hand for healing, signs, and wonders[h] to be performed through the name of Your holy Servant Jesus." [31] When they had prayed, the place where they were assembled was shaken, and they were all filled with the Holy Spirit and began to speak God's message with boldness.[i]

Believers Sharing

[32] Now the large group of those who believed were of one heart and mind, and no one said that any of his possessions was his own, but instead they held everything in common.[j] [33] And the apostles were giving testimony with great power to the resurrection of the Lord Jesus, and great grace was on all of them.[k] [34] For there was not a needy person among them, because all those who owned lands or houses sold them, brought the proceeds of the things that were sold,[l] [35] and laid them at the apostles' feet. This was then distributed for each person's basic needs.[D,m]

[36] Joseph, a Levite and a Cypriot by birth, the one the apostles called Barnabas, which is translated Son of Encouragement,[n] [37] sold a field he owned, brought the money, and laid it at the apostles' feet.[o]

Lying to the Holy Spirit

5 But a man named Ananias, with his wife Sapphira, sold a piece of property. [2] However, he kept back part of the proceeds with his wife's knowledge, and brought a portion of it and laid it at the apostles' feet.[p]

---

a4:19 Ac 4:13; 5:28
b4:20 Ac 22:15; 1Co 9:16; 1Jn 1:1,3
c4:21 Mt 9:8; 21:26; Lk 20:6,19; 22:2; Ac 5:26
d4:24 Ex 20:11; 2Ch 2:12; Neh 9:6; Ps 102:25; 124:8; 134:3; 146:6; Is 37:16
e4:25-26 Ps 2:1-2; Dn 9:24-25; Lk 4:18; Ac 1:16; 10:38; Heb 1:9
f4:27 Mt 14:1; 27:2; Lk 23:1,12
g4:29 Ac 9:27; 13:46; 14:3; 19:8; Php 1:14
h4:30 Jn 4:48; Ac 3:6
i4:31 Ac 2:2,4; 16:26; Php 1:14
j4:32 Ac 2:44; Php 1:27
k4:33 Lk 24:48; Ac 1:8,22
l4:34 Mt 19:21; Ac 2:45
m4:35 Ac 2:45; 4:37; 5:2; 6:1
n4:36 Ac 9:27; 1Co 9:6
o4:37 Ac 4:35; 5:2
p5:2 Ac 4:37; 5:3

A4:25 Other mss read *through the mouth of David Your servant*   B4:25-26 Ps 2:1-2   C4:27 Lit *peoples*   D4:35 Lit *person as anyone had need*

---

control **among the people**. They sought to halt the spread of Christianity at all costs, so they **ordered** the apostles **not to preach or teach** any more about Jesus. It seems they wished to guard their status as religious authorities even at the expense of obvious truth.

4:19-20 Peter and John's reference to what they had **seen and heard** included their experiences with Jesus plus what they had witnessed since the founding of the church at Pentecost. All told, they had been eyewitnesses to many of God's revelatory acts.

4:24-28 When Peter and John told the members of their fellowship what had happened, they all recognized this persecution as fulfillment of Ps 2:1-2. **Gentiles and the people of Israel** had united in opposition to God's **holy Servant Jesus** and His followers. Then and now, believers take comfort in knowing that Jesus' sufferings (as well as their own) are not by chance, but are **predestined** by God.

4:29 The early Christians recognized that just as Jesus had been promised trouble, they too would encounter persecution for proclaiming Him as Messiah. They asked God for

the power to speak with **complete boldness**, even if punishment should follow.

4:30 Besides boldness in testifying, the early Christians expected to receive power from God to perform **healing, signs, and wonders** through the **name of . . . Jesus**.

4:32-35 As long as there was complete unanimity of purpose and intention among them, the early Christians shared their **possessions** freely, such that **there was not a needy person among them**. They were able to do this not because of their own strength, but because **great grace was on all of them**. Therefore the generosity was above all a work of God. Yet trouble was coming (5:1-11).

4:36-37 **Joseph** (aka **Barnabas**) led by example, selling his **field** and donating all the proceeds to the church. Such charitable acts inspire others to do good, but also incite some to seek acclaim.

5:2 Not everyone shared in Joseph's liberality. **Ananias** and his wife **Sapphira** sold a piece of property but **kept back** part of the sale price despite claiming otherwise (v. 8).

³ Then Peter said, "Ananias, why has Satan filled your heart*ᵃ* to lie to the Holy Spirit and keep back part of the proceeds from the field? ⁴ Wasn't it yours while you possessed it? And after it was sold, wasn't it at your disposal? Why is it that you planned this thing in your heart? You have not lied to men but to God!" ⁵ When he heard these words, Ananias dropped dead, and a great fear came on all who heard.*ᵇ* ⁶ The young men got up, wrapped his body, carried him out, and buried him.*ᶜ*

⁷ There was an interval of about three hours; then his wife came in, not knowing what had happened. ⁸ "Tell me," Peter asked her, "did you sell the field for this price?"

"Yes," she said, "for that price."

⁹ Then Peter said to her, "Why did you agree to test the Spirit of the Lord? Look! The feet of those who have buried your husband are at the door, and they will carry you out!"*ᵈ*

¹⁰ Instantly she dropped dead at his feet. When the young men came in, they found her dead, carried her out, and buried her beside her husband. ¹¹ Then great fear came on the whole church and on all who heard these things.

Apostolic Signs and Wonders

¹² Many signs and wonders were being done among the people through the hands of the apostles.*ᵉ* By common consent they would all meet in Solomon's Colonnade.*ᶠ* ¹³ None of the rest dared to join them, but the people praised them highly.*ᵍ* ¹⁴ Believers were added to the Lord in increasing numbers—crowds of both men and women. ¹⁵ As a result, they would carry the sick out into the streets and lay them on cots and mats so that when Peter came by, at least his shadow*ʰ* might fall on some of them. ¹⁶ In addition, a large group came together from the towns surrounding Jerusalem, bringing sick people and those who were tormented by •unclean spirits, and they were all healed.

In and Out of Prison

¹⁷ Then the high priest took action. He and all his colleagues, those who belonged to the party of the •Sadducees, were filled with jealousy.*ⁱ* ¹⁸ So they arrested*ᴬ* the apostles and put them in the city jail.*ʲ* ¹⁹ But an angel of the Lord opened the doors of the jail during the night, brought them out, and said,*ᵏ* ²⁰ "Go and stand in the •temple complex, and tell the people all about this life."*ˡ* ²¹ In obedience to this, they entered the temple complex at daybreak and began to teach.

Cross references (center column)
*ᵃ*5:3 Mt 4:10; Lk 22:3; Jn 13:2,27
*ᵇ*5:5 Ezk 11:13; Ac 5:10-11
*ᶜ*5:6 Ezk 29:5; Jn 19:40; Ac 8:2
*ᵈ*5:9 Ac 5:3-4; 15:10; 1Co 10:9
*ᵉ*5:12 Ac 2:43; 14:3; 19:11; Rm 15:19; 2Co 12:12; Heb 2:4
*ᶠ*Jn 10:23; Ac 4:21,32
*ᵍ*5:13 Ac 2:47; 3:11
*ʰ*5:15 Mt 14:36; Ac 19:12
*ⁱ*5:17 Ac 4:1; 15:5
*ʲ*5:18 Lk 21:12; Ac 4:3
*ᵏ*5:19 Mt 1:20; Lk 1:11; Ac 8:26; 12:7; 16:26; 27:23
*ˡ*5:20 Jn 6:63,68; Php 2:16

ᴬ5:18 Lit *laid hands on*

5:3-4 Ananias and Sapphira assumed they were merely lying to men (the apostles), but in reality they had lied to the **Holy Spirit** who is ever-present in the church. Peter's wording indicates that the Holy Spirit is God. Peter's question (**wasn't it at your disposal?**) implies that Ananias and Sapphira would have been justified to sell the land and give only a portion to the church. Their sin lay in their deception and their desire to win praise.

5:9 The deception of Ananias and Sapphira, and in particular Sapphira's lie to Peter, was a test of the **Spirit of the Lord**. This is a powerful indication of the Spirit's role in the church and church leadership; Peter was a mere man, but he was God's man to lead this fellowship of believers.

5:12 Undaunted by their previous arrest at the temple (4:3), the apostles continued to perform **signs and wonders** among the people they encountered in **Solomon's Colonnade**.

5:15-16 The people came to believe that there was something magical about **Peter** and that even his **shadow** would be enough to heal them. There are a number of places in the NT, including Acts, where God healed people through surprising means. Besides Peter's shadow, these included the hem of Jesus' robe (Lk 8:44) as well as facecloths and aprons that the apostle Paul had touched (Ac 19:12). There was of course nothing special about these items; rather, it was the power of God working through the messengers with whom the objects were associated.

5:17 The **high priest** and his **colleagues** opposed the spread of Christianity not merely because they didn't believe in Jesus as Messiah, but because they were **filled with jealousy** at the following that was building around Him daily as the apostles preached and performed miracles.

5:19-20 Having been arrested again for their ministry in Jesus' name (v. 18), the apostles were set free by **an angel of the Lord** in such a way that aroused no attention. Some speculate that they were transported directly from the jail to the **temple complex**, but the fact that the angel **opened the doors of the jail** and told the apostles to **Go and stand** in the temple suggests otherwise. See 12:6-10 and note there for a similar episode.

5:21a Newly freed, we might expect the apostles to flee Jerusalem. Instead, they went to the **temple complex at**

---

ekklesia

Greek Pronunciation	[ehk lay SEE ah]
HCSB Translation	church
Uses in Acts	23
Uses in the NT	114
Focus passage	Acts 5:11

The Greek noun *ekklesia* is a compound from the preposition *ek*, meaning *out of*, and the verb *kaleo*, meaning *to call*; thus, *ekklesia* literally means *called out ones*. Despite the origin of the term *ekklesia*, its emphasis is not on a people called out but on a people gathered together, that is, an *assembly* or *congregation*. In secular Greek, *ekklesia* was commonly used for the *assembled citizens* of a city (see Ac 19:32,39-40).

In the NT, *ekklesia* is found in the Gospels only three times, all in Matthew (16:18; 18:17). It occurs in Acts more than any other book, and 62 times in Paul's letters. Jesus stated that He would build the *ekklesia* (Mt 16:18) and that the *ekklesia* must exercise discipline on members who sin (Mt 18:15-17). In the former passage Jesus used *ekklesia* in a corporate sense (all believers), and in the latter passage in the local sense (believers in a specific *assembly*).

The Apostles on Trial Again

When the high priest and those who were with him arrived, they convened the •Sanhedrin—the full Senate of the sons of Israel—and sent orders to the jail to have them brought.[a] [22]But when the temple police got there, they did not find them in the jail, so they returned and reported, [23]"We found the jail securely locked, with the guards standing in front of the doors, but when we opened them, we found no one inside!" [24]As[A] the commander of the temple police and the •chief priests heard these things, they were baffled about them, as to what could come of this.

[25]Someone came and reported to them, "Look! The men you put in jail are standing in the temple complex and teaching the people." [26]Then the commander went with the temple police and brought them in without force, because they were afraid the people might stone them.[b] [27]After they brought them in, they had them stand before the Sanhedrin, and the high priest asked, [28]"Didn't we strictly order you not to teach in this name?[c] And look, you have filled Jerusalem with your teaching and are determined to bring this man's blood on us!"[d]

[29]But Peter and the apostles replied, "We must obey God rather than men. [30]The God of our fathers raised up Jesus,[e] whom you had murdered by hanging Him on a tree.[f] [31]God exalted this man to His right hand as ruler and Savior, to grant repentance to Israel, and forgiveness of sins.[g] [32]We are witnesses of these things, and so is the Holy Spirit[h] whom God has given to those who obey Him."

Gamaliel's Advice

[33]When they heard this, they were enraged and wanted to kill them.[i] [34]A •Pharisee named Gamaliel, a teacher of the law who was respected by all the people, stood up in the Sanhedrin and ordered the men[B] to be taken outside for a little while.[j] [35]He said to them, "Men of Israel, be careful about what you're going to do to these men. [36]Not long ago Theudas rose up, claiming to be somebody, and a group of about 400 men rallied to him. He was killed, and all his partisans were dispersed and came to nothing.[k] [37]After this man, Judas the Galilean rose up in the days of the census and attracted a following.[c] That man also perished, and all his partisans were scattered. [38]And now, I tell you, stay away from these men and leave them alone. For if this plan or this work is of men, it will be overthrown;[l] [39]but if it is of God, you will not be able to overthrow them. You may even be found fighting against God." So they were persuaded by him.[m] [40]After they called in the apostles and had them flogged, they ordered them not to speak in the name of Jesus and released them.[n] [41]Then they went out from the presence of the Sanhedrin, rejoicing that

Cross references

[a]5:21 Mt 5:22; Ac 4:6; 5:27,34,41
[b]5:26 Ac 4:21; 5:13
[c]5:28 Jn 14:13; Ac 3:16; 1Jn 3:23
[d]Mt 27:25; Ac 2:23,36; 3:15; 4:10; 7:52
[e]5:30 Ac 2:24; 3:13
[f]Ac 10:39; 13:29; Gl 3:13; 1Pt 2:24
[g]5:31 Ac 2:33; 3:15
[h]5:32 Lk 24:48; Jn 15:26; Ac 15:28; Heb 2:4
[i]5:33 Ac 2:37; 7:54
[j]5:34 Lk 2:46; 5:17; Ac 22:3
[k]5:36 Ac 8:9; Gl 2:6; 6:3
[l]5:38 Mt 15:17; Mk 11:30
[m]5:39 Pr 21:30; Ac 7:51; 11:17
[n]5:40 Mt 10:17; Mk 13:9; Ac 4:18

A5:24 Other mss add *the high priest and*   B5:34 Other mss read *apostles*   C5:37 Lit *and drew people after him*

---

daybreak and began to do the very thing that had gotten them in trouble in the first place: **teach** about Jesus.

5:21b-23 The Sanhedrin convened in the morning, intent on taking decisive action to halt the growth of Christian faith. That the **temple police** found **the jail securely locked** and the **guards** standing duty proves that the jailbreak was both miraculous and secretive.

5:26 The temple police **were afraid the people might stone them** because Jerusalem was responding positively to the apostles. Meanwhile, the Jewish leaders saw their authority slipping away.

5:28 The Jewish leaders feared that the people would hold them responsible for Jesus' death. They were more concerned about maintaining their authority than embracing the truth.

5:29 Christians should obey the law of the land, but when human law conflicts with God's law, we must **obey God rather than men.**

5:30-32 If anything, Peter stepped up the pressure on the Sanhedrin (and endangered himself and the others more) by declaring that they had **murdered** Jesus, whom **God exalted . . . to His right hand as ruler and Savior.** Peter and the other apostles knew this to be true because they were **witnesses** of this, as was **the Holy Spirit.**

5:33-34 If the Jewish leaders had been willing to kill Jesus, much more were they prepared to **kill** the apostles, whose stubborn testimony was serving to prolong the Jesus controversy. But **Gamaliel** wisely cooled their rage. This was Gamaliel I, the teacher of Paul the apostle (22:3). It is uncertain whether he was the successor to the great rabbinic teacher Hillel or whether he founded his own school. In either case, he became a major rabbinic teacher. His conciliatory stance toward the apostles is consistent with what is known of his temperate attitude elsewhere.

5:36 Josephus, the Jewish historian, reported that many revolts against Roman rule occurred during the time of Jesus—some of them even having messianic overtones. He mentions a person named Theudas, who came after Judas the Galilean (v. 37). This is probably not the same person as the **Theudas** referred to here.

5:37 Judas the Galilean, or Judas of Gamala, rebelled against the census that Quirinius took in A.D. 6. He was mentioned by Josephus as teaching that the Israelites were not to give tribute to pagan rulers. His revolt ended in defeat.

5:39 Gamaliel's advice reflected the Pharisees' belief that if **God** has ordained a thing, it will come to pass. Thus Gamaliel felt it was prudent for the Sanhedrin to step back and see what God would do with the Christian movement.

5:41 Some people believe that suffering and hardships are signs that we are not in God's will. Contrast this with the apostles, who, after being flogged, went out of **the presence of the Sanhedrin, rejoicing** that they had been considered **worthy** to be **dishonored** on Christ's behalf.

6:1 The distinction between **Hellenistic** and **Hebraic Jews**

they were counted worthy to be dishonored on behalf of the Name.^A,a ^42Every day in the temple complex, and in various homes, they continued teaching and proclaiming the good news that Jesus is the *Messiah.

Seven Chosen to Serve

6 In those days, as the number of the disciples^b was multiplying, there arose a complaint by the Hellenistic Jews^B against the Hebraic Jews^c that their widows were being overlooked in the daily distribution.^c ^2Then the Twelve summoned the whole company of the disciples and said, "It would not be right for us to give up preaching about God to handle financial matters.^D ^3Therefore, *brothers, select from among you seven men of good reputation,^d full of the Spirit^e and wisdom, whom we can appoint to this duty. ^4But we will devote ourselves to prayer and to the preaching ministry." ^5The proposal pleased the whole company. So they chose Stephen,^f a man full of faith and the Holy Spirit, and Philip, Prochorus, Nicanor, Timon, Parmenas, and Nicolaus, a *proselyte from Antioch.^g ^6They had them stand before the apostles, who prayed^h and laid their hands on^i them.^E

^a5:41 Mt 5:12; Jn 15:21; 1Pt 4:13
^b6:1 Mt 9:10; Mk 10:10; Lk 6:1; Jn 6:3; Ac 9:1,10,19,25-36; 21:4,16
^c Ac 2:41; 4:4,35; 5:14; 9:29,39; 11:20
^d6:3 Dt 1:13; 1Tm 3:7
^e Lk 4:1; Ac 7:55; 11:19,24
^f6:5 Ac 6:8-9; 11:19; 22:20
^g Mt 23:15; Ac 8:5,26; 21:8
^h6:6 Ac 1:24; 8:17; 13:3; 2Tm 1:6
^i Nm 8:10; Ac 9:17; 1Tm 4:14
^j6:7 Ac 12:24; 19:20; Col 1:6
^k6:11 1Kg 21:10,13; Mt 26:59-60
^l6:13 Mt 24:15; Ac 7:58; 21:28; 25:8
^m6:14 Dn 9:26; Ac 15:1; 21:21; 26:3; 28:17

^7So the preaching about God flourished, the number of the disciples in Jerusalem multiplied^j greatly, and a large group of priests became obedient to the faith.

Stephen Accused of Blasphemy

^8Stephen, full of grace and power, was performing great wonders and signs among the people. ^9Then some from what is called the Freedmen's *Synagogue, composed of both Cyrenians and Alexandrians, and some from Cilicia and *Asia, came forward and disputed with Stephen. ^10But they were unable to stand up against his wisdom and the Spirit by whom he was speaking.

^11Then they persuaded some men to say, "We heard him speaking blasphemous words against Moses and God!"^k ^12They stirred up the people, the elders, and the *scribes; so they came, dragged him off, and took him to the *Sanhedrin. ^13They also presented false witnesses who said, "This man does not stop speaking blasphemous words against this holy place and the law.^l ^14For we heard him say that Jesus, this *Nazarene, will destroy this place and change the customs that Moses handed down to us."^m ^15And all who were sitting in the

---

^A5:41 Other mss add of Jesus, or of Christ   ^B6:1 Jews of Gk language and culture   ^C6:1 Jews of Aram or Hb language and culture   ^D6:2 Or to serve tables   ^E6:6 The laying on of hands signified the prayer of blessing for the beginning of a new ministry.

---

probably refers to their respective languages. Many Jews whose primary language was Greek were converted to Christianity (e.g., Paul; Ac 9; see note at 22:3). Needy Hellenistic believers felt they had been neglected in the early church's charity **distribution**. This imbalance may have arisen due simply to the logistical challenge caused by the rapid addition of Hellenistic Jewish Christians. The existing church structure proved unable to meet the growing demands. It was time for change.

6:2-4 The distinction between those responsible for **preaching** and those responsible for distribution of food marks the beginning of functional distinction of roles and responsibilities in the early church. The apostles (**the Twelve**) believed **prayer** and preaching were their primary duties. It is not that other roles were unimportant. In fact, the high requirements (**good reputation, full of the Spirit and wisdom**) that had to be met by the **seven men** who would take over the **duty** of food distribution signals the importance of all roles in Christian service. Each of the "seven men" filled a position that later came to be reserved for deacons. Informally, therefore, these men were the first Christian deacons. They were responsible for the practical needs of the congregation.

6:5-6 Stephen and six others (their Greek names probably identify them as Hellenistic believers) were selected as the first deacons. They were set apart for service by prayer and the laying on of **hands** by the apostles. The laying on of hands occurs in several contexts in Acts (8:17; 13:3; 19:6). Here, as in 13:3, it indicated the church's recognition that God had called these people to a particular ministry.

6:7 Bold **preaching about God** drove growth in the **number of the disciples** in the early church. Even **a large group of priests** became followers of Christ. Luke did not specify who the priests were, but they were probably those who per-

formed duties in connection with worship at the temple. This put them in a good position to hear the apostles preach on a regular basis.

6:8 A mark of the authenticity of Stephen's work is that it was distinguished by **great wonders and signs**. God often affirmed the apostolic message in this way (5:12).

6:9-10 Though Jews from several different backgrounds **disputed with Stephen**, he swept them aside by use of his human intellectual gifts (**wisdom**) and divine empowerment (**the Spirit**).

6:11 Stephen's supposedly **blasphemous words** on this occasion were probably similar to his speech in Ac 7, which emphasized Israel's disobedience and the fulfillment of the OT in the ministry of Jesus, including His replacing the temple and the law. This would have aroused resentment among those who revered Moses and rejected Jesus as Messiah.

6:12 Like the apostles before him, especially Peter and John, Stephen was taken before the **Sanhedrin** after those from the synagogues were unable to stand against him. The confrontation now elevated from informal dispute to a more formal legal interrogation.

6:13 The fact that Stephen had not actually spoken **blasphemous words** is confirmed by the fact that **false witnesses** were produced to sustain the charges against him.

6:14 The charge against Stephen was similar to the charges against Jesus—that He would **destroy** the temple. They were also concerned about preserving their **customs** or oral laws, which they believed they had inherited from **Moses**.

6:15 Stephen's facial expression reflected his innocence and the Spirit's role in his life.

Sanhedrin looked intently at him and saw that his face was like the face of an angel.

Stephen's Sermon

7 "Is this true?"[A] the high priest asked.
² "Brothers and fathers," he said, "listen: The God of glory appeared to our father Abraham when he was in Mesopotamia, before he settled in Haran,[a] ³ and said to him:

> Get out of your country
> and away from your relatives,
> and come to the land
> that I will show you.[B,b]

⁴ "Then he came out of the land of the Chaldeans and settled in Haran. From there, after his father died, God had him move to this land you now live in.[c] ⁵ He didn't give him an inheritance in it, not even a foot of ground, but He promised to give it to him as a possession, and to his descendants after him,[d] even though he was childless. ⁶ God spoke in this way:

> His descendants would be strangers
> in a foreign country,
> and they would enslave
> and oppress them 400 years.
> ⁷ I will judge the nation
> that they will serve as *slaves,
> God said.
> After this, they will come out
> and worship Me in this place.[C,e]

⁸ Then He gave him the covenant of circumcision. After this, he fathered Isaac and circumcised[f] him on the eighth day; Isaac did the same with Jacob, and Jacob with the 12 patriarchs.[g]

The Patriarchs in Egypt

⁹ "The patriarchs became jealous of Joseph and sold him into Egypt, but God was with him[h] ¹⁰ and rescued him out of all his troubles. He gave him favor and wisdom in the sight of Pharaoh, king of Egypt, who appointed him ruler over Egypt and over his whole household.[i] ¹¹ Then a famine and great suffering came over all of Egypt and Canaan,[j] and our ancestors could find no food. ¹² When Jacob heard there was grain in Egypt, he sent our ancestors the first time. ¹³ The second time, Joseph was revealed to his brothers, and Joseph's family became known to Pharaoh. ¹⁴ Joseph then invited his father Jacob and all his relatives, 75 people in all,[k] ¹⁵ and Jacob went down to Egypt. He and our ancestors died there,[l] ¹⁶ were carried back to Shechem, and were placed in the tomb that Abraham had bought for a sum of silver from the sons of Hamor in Shechem.[m]

Moses, a Rejected Savior

¹⁷ "As the time was drawing near to fulfill the promise that God had made to Abraham, the people flourished and multiplied in Egypt[n] ¹⁸ until a different king who did not know Joseph ruled over Egypt.[D] ¹⁹ He dealt deceitfully with our race and oppressed our ancestors by making them leave their infants outside, so they wouldn't survive.[E,o] ²⁰ At this time Moses was born, and he was beautiful in God's sight. He was cared for in his father's home three months, ²¹ and when he was left outside, Pharaoh's daughter adopted and raised him as her own son.[p] ²² So Moses was educated in all the wisdom of the Egyptians and was powerful in his speech and actions.[q]

²³ "As he was approaching the age of 40, he decided[F] to visit his brothers, the Israelites. ²⁴ When he saw one of them being mistreated,

Cross references (center column)

ᵃ7:2 Gn 11:31; 15:7; Ps 29:3; Ac 22:1; 1Co 2:8
ᵇ7:3 Gn 12:1
ᶜ7:4 Gn 11:31; 12:4-5
ᵈ7:5 Gn 12:7; 13:15; 15:18; 17:8; Gl 3:16; Heb 8:8-9
ᵉ7:6-7 Gn 15:13-14; Ex 3:12; 12:40
ᶠ7:8 Gn 17:9-11; 21:2-4
ᵍGn 25:26; 29:31; 30:5; 35:23
ʰ7:9 Gn 37:11,28; 39:2,21; 45:4; Ps 105:17
ⁱ7:10 Gn 41:37-43; 42:6; Ps 105:21
ʲ7:11 Gn 41:54; 42:5
ᵏ7:13-14 Gn 45:1-4,9-10, 16,27; 46:26-27; Ex 1:5; Dt 10:22
ˡ7:15 Gn 46:5; 49:33; Ex 1:6
ᵐ7:16 Gn 23:16; 33:19; 50:13; Ex 13:19; Jos 24:32
ⁿ7:17 Gn 15:13; Ex 1:7; Ps 105:24
ᵒ7:18-19 Ex 1:8-10,22; Ps 105:25
ᵖ7:20-21 Ex 2:2-10; Heb 11:23
ᑫ7:22 1Kg 4:30; Is 19:11; Lk 24:19

7:2-53 Stephen recited how God had been at work from earliest times with His appointed people, Israel. The authenticity of his speech has been called into question because the ideas he expressed about the temple—that God was not confined to a single spot (v. 48)—seem to reflect later thought, especially that which developed after the destruction of the temple in A.D. 70. But there was a tradition extending from the OT prophets (cp. vv. 49-50 citing Is 66:1-2, as one example) on to early Christian thinkers (e.g., Paul in Ac 17) that said God could not be confined to a particular location. Stephen's speech is similar to Paul's in Pisidian Antioch (13:16-41).

7:3 Stephen cited Gn 12:1, in which God directed Abraham to leave his home in Haran and go to the land that God would give him. In essence, this was the beginning of Israel.

7:5 Though Abraham had no children at the time, God promised to give his **descendants** land **as a possession**. Thus it

was fundamentally on an act of trust (faith) that the nation of Israel had its beginning.

7:6-7 Stephen recalled Gn 15:13-14, where God foretold Abraham that his descendants would be enslaved **in a foreign country** (Egypt) before they would **come out and worship** in the promised land. Thus God's promise of blessing came with an equally sure promise of suffering.

7:21-22 Moses, though born to Jewish parents, was reared by Pharaoh's daughter and **educated** in the wisdom of the **Egyptians**, becoming powerful in **his speech and actions**. When God called Moses (Ex 3:1-4:17), it was as if a non-Hebrew became a follower of the Hebrew God. Similarly, many non-Hebrews flooded into the early church, forsaking their pagan background (e.g., Ac 10).

7:23,30 Moses' life is divided into three periods of **40 years** each—40 in Egypt, 40 in Midian, and 40 in the wilderness.

7:27-28 The Israelites initially questioned Moses as their

he came to his rescue and avenged the oppressed man by striking down the Egyptian. [25]He assumed his brothers would understand that God would give them deliverance through him, but they did not understand. [26]The next day he showed up while they were fighting and tried to reconcile them peacefully, saying, 'Men, you are brothers. Why are you mistreating each other?'[a]

[27]"But the one who was mistreating his neighbor pushed him[A] away, saying:

Who appointed you a ruler and a judge over us? [28]**Do you want to kill me, the same way you killed the Egyptian yesterday?**[B,b]

[29]"At this disclosure, Moses fled and became an exile in the land of Midian, where he fathered two sons.[c] [30]After 40 years had passed, an angel[C] appeared to him in the wilderness of Mount Sinai, in the flame of a burning bush. [31]When Moses saw it, he was amazed at the sight. As he was approaching to look at it, the voice of the Lord came: [32]**I am the God of your fathers—the God of Abraham, of Isaac, and of Jacob.**[D,d] So Moses began to tremble and did not dare to look.

[33]"Then the Lord said to him:

Remove the sandals from your feet, for the place where you are standing is holy ground. [34]**I have observed the oppression of My people in Egypt; I have heard their groaning and have come down to rescue them. And now, come, I will send you to Egypt.**[E,e]

[35]"This Moses, whom they rejected when they said, **Who appointed you a ruler and a judge?**[B]—this one God sent as a ruler and a redeemer by means of the angel who appeared to him in the bush.[f] [36]This man led them out and performed wonders and signs in the land of Egypt,[g] at the Red Sea, and in the wilderness 40 years.[h]

Israel's Rebellion against God

[37]"This is the Moses who said to the Israelites, **God**[F] **will raise up for you a Prophet like me from among your brothers.**[G,i] [38]He is the one who was in the congregation in the wilderness together with the angel who spoke to him on Mount Sinai, and with our ancestors.[j] He received living oracles to give to us.[k] [39]Our ancestors were unwilling to obey him, but pushed him away, and in their hearts turned back to Egypt.[l] [40]They told Aaron:

Make us gods who will go before us. As for this Moses who brought us out of the land of Egypt, we don't know what's happened to him.[H,m]

[41]They even made a calf in those days, offered sacrifice to the idol, and were celebrating what their hands had made.[n] [42]Then God turned away[o] and gave them up to worship[p] the host of heaven, as it is written in the book of the prophets:

House of Israel, did you bring Me offerings and sacrifices 40 years in the wilderness? [43]**No, you took up the tent of Moloch**[I] **and the star of your god Rephan,**[J] **the images that you made to worship. So I will deport you beyond Babylon!**[K,q]

God's Real Tabernacle

[44]"Our ancestors had the tabernacle of the testimony in the wilderness, just as He who spoke to Moses commanded him to make it according to the pattern he had seen.[r] [45]Our ancestors in turn received it and with Joshua brought it in when they dispossessed the nations that God drove out before our fathers,[s] until the days of David. [46]He found favor in God's sight and asked that he might provide a dwelling place for the God[L] of Jacob.[t] [47]But it was Solomon who built Him a house.[u]

Cross references (center column):

[a]7:23-26 Ex 2:11-14; Heb 11:24-26
[b]7:27-28 Ex 2:14; Lk 12:14; Ac 7:35
[c]7:29 Ex 2:15,22; 18:3-4
[d]7:32 Ex 3:6; Mt 22:32; Mk 12:26; Lk 20:37
[e]7:33-34 Ex 3:5,7-8,10
[f]7:35 Ex 14:19; Nm 20:16
[g]7:36 Ex 12:41; 33:1; Heb 8:9
[h]Ex 14:21; 16:35; Nm 14:33; Ps 95:10; Ac 13:18
[i]7:37 Dt 18:15; Ac 3:22
[j]7:38 Ex 19:17; Is 63:9; Ac 7:53
[k]Dt 5:27; 32:47; Jn 1:17; Rm 3:2; Heb 4:12; 5:12; 1Pt 4:11
[l]7:39 Ex 16:3; Nm 11:4; 14:3-4; Ezk 20:8,24
[m]7:40 Ex 32:1,23
[n]7:41 Dt 9:16; Ps 106:19-20; Rv 9:20
[o]7:42 Jos 24:20; Is 63:10
[p]Dt 4:19; 2Kg 21:3; Jr 19:13; Zph 1:5
[q]7:42-43 1Kg 11:7; Am 5:25-27; Ac 7:36
[r]7:44 Ex 25:8-9,40; 38:21; Heb 8:5
[s]7:45 Jos 3:14; 18:1; 23:9; 24:18; Ps 44:2
[t]7:46 2Sm 7:1,8; 1Ch 22:7; Ps 89:19; 132:5
[u]7:47 1Kg 6:1-2; 8:17-20; 2Ch 3:1

[A]7:27 Moses   [B]7:27-28,35 Ex 2:14   [C]7:30 Other mss add *of the Lord*   [D]7:32 Ex 3:6,15   [E]7:33-34 Ex 3:5,7-8,10   [F]7:37 Other mss read *'The Lord your God*   [G]7:37 Dt 18:15   [H]7:40 Ex 32:1,23   [I]7:43 Canaanite or Phoenician sky or sun god   [J]7:43 Perhaps an Assyrian star god—the planet Saturn   [K]7:42-43 Am 5:25-27   [L]7:46 Other mss read *house*

---

ruler (Ex 2:14). Perhaps Stephen brought this up to provoke reconsideration of Israel's assessment and rejection of Jesus. They had been wrong about Moses. Might they have been wrong about Jesus too?

7:32 God revealed Himself to **Moses** as the God of his forefathers (Ex 3:6,15) at a time when, as a fugitive and exile, he desperately needed a sense of belonging and continuity.

7:33-34 Stephen and the early believers must have drawn comfort from the fact that God does not sit idly by when He sees His people being oppressed (Ex 3:5,7-8,10).

7:38 The **living oracles** to which Stephen referred were the Ten Commandments given by God to Moses for His people.

7:40 Though God accompanied the Hebrews in highly visible, powerful ways during their journey out from Egypt, they defied Him and asked Aaron to **make . . . gods** for them (Ex 32:1). Much the same thing occurred when the nation rejected Jesus, who likewise came among them as God in highly visible, powerful ways.

7:42-43 Stephen's citation of Am 5:25-27 was perhaps intended to convey that just as the Hebrews rejected God in the desert, suffering exile and spiritual estrangement as

48 However, the Most High does not dwell in sanctuaries made with hands, as the prophet says:[a]

49 **Heaven is My throne,
and earth My footstool.
What sort of house will you build
for Me?
says the Lord,
or what is My resting place?**
50 **Did not My hand make all
these things?[A,b]**

Resisting the Holy Spirit

51 "You stiff-necked[c] people with uncircumcised hearts and ears![d] You are always resisting the Holy Spirit; as your ancestors did, so do you. 52 Which of the prophets did your fathers not persecute?[e] They even killed those who announced beforehand the coming of the Righteous One, whose betrayers and murderers[f] you have now become. 53 You received the law under the direction of angels[g] and yet have not kept it."

The First Christian Martyr

54 When they heard these things, they were

enraged in their hearts[B] and gnashed their teeth at him. 55 But Stephen, filled by the Holy Spirit, gazed into heaven. He saw God's glory, with[c] Jesus standing at the right hand of God,[h] and he said, 56 "Look! I see the heavens opened and the •Son of Man standing at the right hand of God!"[i]

57 Then they screamed at the top of their voices, covered their ears, and together rushed against him. 58 They threw him out of the city and began to stone[j] him. And the witnesses laid their robes at the feet of a young man named Saul.[k] 59 They were stoning Stephen as he called out: "Lord Jesus, receive my spirit!"[l] 60 Then he knelt down and cried out with a loud voice,[m] "Lord, do not charge them with this sin!" And saying this, he fell •asleep.[n]

Saul the Persecutor

8 Saul agreed with putting him to death. On that day a severe persecution broke out against the church in Jerusalem, and all except the apostles were scattered throughout the land of Judea and Samaria.[o] 2 Devout men buried Stephen and mourned deeply over him.

Cross-references

a7:48 1Kg 8:27; 2Ch 2:6
b7:49-50 Is 66:1-2; Mt 5:34-35
c7:51 Ex 32:9; Dt 10:16; Heb 3:13
d Lv 26:41; Jr 4:4; 6:10; 9:26
e7:52 2Ch 36:16; Mt 5:12; 21:35; 23:31,37; 1Th 2:15
f Ac 3:14; 5:28
g7:53 Ac 7:38; Gl 3:19; Heb 2:2
h7:55 Jn 12:41; Ac 6:5
i7:56 Mt 3:16; Jn 1:51
j7:58 Lv 24:14-16; Dt 13:9; Heb 13:12
k Ac 8:1; 22:20
l7:59 Ps 31:5; Lk 23:46; Ac 9:14
m7:60 Mt 5:44; Lk 22:41; 23:34; Ac 9:40
n Jn 11:11; 1Co 11:30; 1Th 4:13-15
o8:1 Ac 9:31; 11:19

A7:49-50 Is 66:1-2 B7:54 Or were cut to the quick C7:55 Lit and

---

a consequence, so too contemporary Israel was inviting similar consequences by rejecting Jesus.

7:48-50 Though God does not **dwell in sanctuaries made with hands**, He allowed a house to be built for Him by Solomon (Is 66:1-2). God accommodates Himself to us in order to make human-divine relationship possible.

7:51 The descriptors Stephen used to condemn Israel for unbelief and disobedience (**stiff-necked people** with **uncircumcised hearts and ears**) were commonly used by OT prophets (Lv 26:41; Jr 4:4; 6:10; 9:26; Ezk 44:7,9). This language was also adopted by Paul (Rm 2; Gl 5) where he said unbelieving Jews relied on outward signs rather than transformed hearts. Possibly Paul was influenced by Stephen's speech since he was present (Ac 7:58; 8:1), but the OT was the more obvious influence.

7:52 Stephen's words would either raise the ire of his audience or break their hearts, leading to repentance. The OT prophets had delivered messages similar to his own, and **your fathers**, Stephen said, persecuted and **killed** them. Worse, his audience had made themselves the **betrayers and murderers** of the **Righteous One** whom God promised through the prophets.

7:53 Even though the OT does not explicitly state that the **law** was given by **angels**, Stephen, Paul (Gl 3:19), and the author of Hebrews (Heb 2:2) stated that angels were involved in the process of lawgiving. This likely implied that the law was especially important since God entrusted its deliverance to angels.

7:54 Stephen's audience expressed displeasure both inwardly (**enraged in their hearts**) and outwardly (**gnashed their teeth at him**). They took themselves to be Israel's religious leaders, pious men of God, and yet Stephen charged them with deep spiritual corruption.

7:55 Stephen was a stark contrast to his audience. They were fuming with rage, but he was filled with the **Holy Spirit** and **gazed** peacefully into **heaven** even as he knew death was coming.

7:56-57 Son of Man was Jesus' favorite self-designation. Each use of this expression in the NT came from the lips of Jesus, except where people quoted His words back to Him (Jn 12:34) and in this verse. Jesus' enthronement beside God in heaven implies His divine status and equality with God the Father, which is why the members of the Sanhedrin became enraged.

7:58 The Romans allowed the Jewish leaders to maintain the sanctity of the temple area, but not carry out the death penalty. That is why Jesus was taken to Pilate, a Roman official, for trial. In this instance, however, Stephen was killed illegally by an enraged mob. This is the first reference in Scripture to **Saul** (later called Paul). It is disputed whether he was a member of the Sanhedrin or just a young rabbinic student who was zealous for traditional Jewish faith. Whether he was formally involved in the Sanhedrin or not, he "agreed" with the decision to stone Stephen (8:1).

7:59-60 Both of Stephen's requests are remarkable. His first, **Lord Jesus, receive my spirit!**, proclaims that Jesus is Judge and Savior. Stephen's second request, that God **not charge** his executioners with **sin** in this matter, illustrates the nonvindictive spirit of one who understands that his own sins have been forgiven by grace. **Fell asleep** is a common expression for death in the Bible (Jn 11:11; 1Co 11:30).

8:1 Events surrounding Stephen's testimony and murder led to **severe persecution** of the **church in Jerusalem**. All believers **except the apostles** were **scattered** to nearby regions. Hence the persecution helped spread the gospel to surrounding areas such as **Judea** and **Samaria**. The facts that the apostles were not the focus of the persecution and

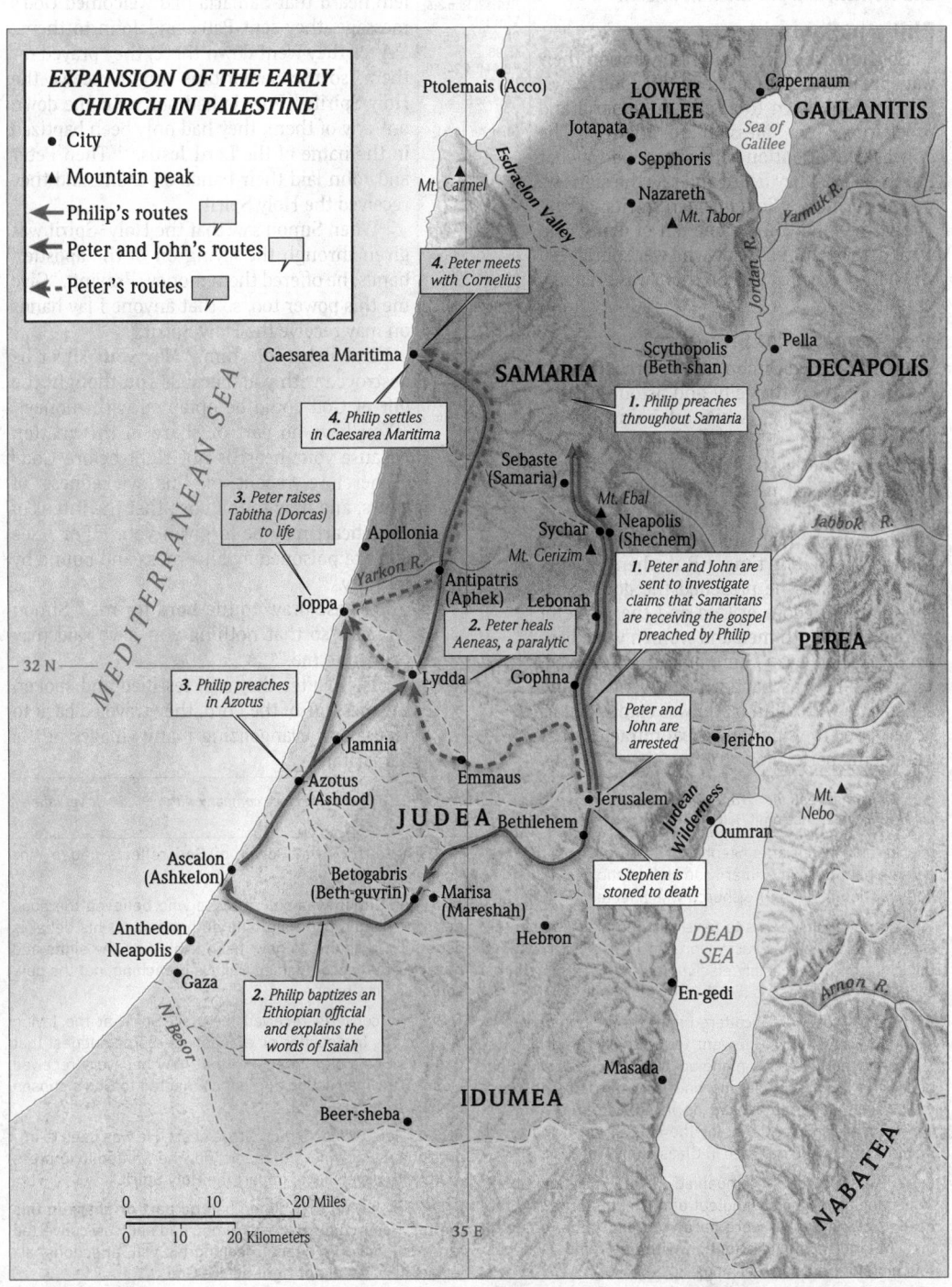

EXPANSION OF THE EARLY CHURCH IN PALESTINE

- • City
- ▲ Mountain peak
- ← Philip's routes
- ← Peter and John's routes
- ← Peter's routes

4. Peter meets with Cornelius

4. Philip settles in Caesarea Maritima

3. Peter raises Tabitha (Dorcas) to life

1. Philip preaches throughout Samaria

1. Peter and John are sent to investigate claims that Samaritans are receiving the gospel preached by Philip

2. Peter heals Aeneas, a paralytic

3. Philip preaches in Azotus

Peter and John are arrested

Stephen is stoned to death

2. Philip baptizes an Ethiopian official and explains the words of Isaiah

MEDITERRANEAN SEA

Ptolemais (Acco)

LOWER GALILEE

Capernaum

GAULANITIS

Jotapata

Sepphoris

Sea of Galilee

Mt. Carmel

Esdraelon Valley

Nazareth

Mt. Tabor

Yarmuk R.

Jordan R.

Caesarea Maritima

SAMARIA

Scythopolis (Beth-shan)

Pella

DECAPOLIS

Sebaste (Samaria)

Mt. Ebal

Sychar

Neapolis (Shechem)

Mt. Gerizim

Jabbok R.

Apollonia

Yarkon R.

Antipatris (Aphek)

Lebonah

PEREA

Joppa

Lydda

Gophna

32 N

Jamnia

Emmaus

Jericho

Mt. Nebo

Azotus (Ashdod)

Jerusalem

Judean Wilderness

Qumran

JUDEA

Bethlehem

Ascalon (Ashkelon)

Betogabris (Beth-guvrin)

Marisa (Mareshah)

Hebron

DEAD SEA

Anthedon Neapolis

Gaza

En-gedi

Arnon R.

N. Besor

IDUMEA

Masada

Beer-sheba

NABATEA

0   10   20 Miles

0   10   20 Kilometers

35 E

³Saul,ᵃ however, was ravaging the church. He would enter house after house, drag off men and women, and put them in prison.ᵇ

Philip in Samaria

⁴So those who were scattered went on their way preaching the message of good news. ⁵Philip went down to aᴬ city in Samaria and proclaimed the •Messiah to them.ᶜ ⁶The crowds paid attention with one mind to what Philip said, as they heard and saw the signs he was performing. ⁷For •unclean spirits, crying out with a loud voice, came out of many who were possessed, and many who were paralyzed and lame were healed.ᵈ ⁸So there was great joy in that city.

The Response of Simon

⁹A man named Simon had previously practiced sorcery in that city and astounded the •Samaritan people, while claiming to be somebody great.ᵉ ¹⁰They all paid attention to him, from the least of them to the greatest, and they said, "This man is called the Great Power of God!"ᴮ,ᶠ ¹¹They were attentive to him because he had astounded them with his sorceries for a long time. ¹²But when they believed Philip, as he preached the good news about the kingdom of God and the name of Jesus Christ, both men and women were baptized.ᵍ ¹³Then even Simon himself believed. And after he was baptized, he went around constantly withᶜ Philip and was astounded as he observed the signs and great miraclesʰ that were being performed.

Simon's Sin

¹⁴When the apostles who were at Jerusalem heard that Samaria had welcomed God's message, they sent Peter and John to them.ⁱ ¹⁵After they went down there, they prayed for them, so the Samaritans might receive the Holy Spirit. ¹⁶For He had not yet come down onᴰ any of them; they had only been baptized in the name of the Lord Jesus.ʲ ¹⁷Then Peter and John laid their hands on them, and they received the Holy Spirit.

¹⁸When Simon saw that the Holyᴱ Spirit was given through the laying on of the apostles' hands, he offered them money, ¹⁹saying, "Give me this power too, so that anyone I lay hands on may receive the Holy Spirit."

²⁰But Peter told him, "May your silver be destroyed with you, because you thought the gift of God could be obtained with money!ᵏ ²¹You have no part or share in this matter, because your heart is not right before God.ˡ ²²Therefore repent of this wickedness of yours, and pray to the Lord that the intent of your heart may be forgiven you. ²³For I see you are poisoned by bitterness and bound by iniquity."ᵐ

²⁴"Please prayᶠ to the Lord for me," Simon replied, "so that nothing you have said may happen to me."ⁿ

²⁵Then, after they had testified and spoken the message of the Lord, they traveled back to Jerusalem, evangelizing many villages of the Samaritans.

ᵃ 8:3 Ac 7:58; 22:20
ᵇ Ac 22:4,19; 26:10; 1Co 15:9; Gl 1:13; Php 3:6; 1Tm 1:13
ᶜ 8:4-5 Ac 6:5; 15:35
ᵈ 8:7 Mt 4:24; Mk 16:17
ᵉ 8:9 Ac 5:36; 13:6
ᶠ 8:10 Ac 14:11; 28:6
ᵍ 8:12 Ac 1:3; 2:38
ʰ 8:13 Ac 8:6; 19:11
ⁱ 8:14 Lk 22:8; Ac 8:1
ʲ 8:16 Mt 28:19; Ac 2:38; 10:48; 19:2
ᵏ 8:20 2Kg 5:16; Is 55:1; Dn 5:17; Mt 10:8; Ac 2:38
ˡ 8:21 2Kg 10:15; Ps 78:37
ᵐ 8:22-23 Is 55:6-7; Dn 4:27; 2Tm 2:25; Heb 12:15
ⁿ 8:24 Gn 20:7; Ex 8:8; Nm 21:7; Jms 5:16

that it came about after Stephen's death suggest that the persecution focused primarily on Hellenistic Jewish Christians, although the entire church was affected.

8:3 Paul, or **Saul**, seems to have become lead persecutor. His reputation as a destructive force in Jerusalem (**ravaging the church**), and possibly elsewhere, seems to have preceded him to Damascus (9:13).

8:5 Among those who scattered with the heightened persecution was **Philip**, who went to a **city in Samaria**. This territory near Judea was made up of those who had not left under the Assyrian exile and had intermarried with non-Jews. Jews generally looked down on Samaria; ministry here was a significant step for the church, for it indicated that old biases had no place in Christianity.

8:6-7 The **signs** that accompanied Philip's message about Jesus, including the casting out of **unclean spirits** and the healing of **many who were paralyzed and lame**, ensured that the audience **paid attention with one mind**. God was vouching for Philip's preaching.

8:9 This Simon the magician (Simon Magus), who **practiced sorcery** in Samaria, was well-known in post-apostolic Christianity as a heretic and proto-Gnostic.

8:10 The term **Great Power of God** reflects pagan language.

8:13 Even Simon was one of those who **believed** the good news presented by Philip. The authenticity of his belief is doubtful. He seems to have been fixated on the **signs** and **miracles** that accompanied Philip's preaching, not the person of Jesus Christ.

8:17 Early converts received the Holy Spirit at the laying on of hands by apostles or evangelists. Some suggest that this was God's plan to ensure that new believers received trustworthy instruction and got connected to God's chosen apostolic leaders.

8:18-19 Here we see Simon's true heart. He was used to impressing the crowds with magic; now he wanted to impress them with his ability to impart the **Holy Spirit**.

8:20-22 By saying that Simon had **no part or share in this matter**, Peter confirmed that Simon had not truly converted to Christianity. His **heart** (meaning his will, affections, allegiance) was still **not right before God**.

8:25 After several episodes in Samaria, Peter, Philip, and any other apostles traveling with them returned to **Jerusalem**. They evangelized **many villages of the Samaritans**

The Conversion of the Ethiopian Official

[26]An angel of the Lord spoke to Philip: "Get up and go south to the road that goes down from Jerusalem to Gaza." (This is the desert road.)[A,a] [27]So he got up and went. There was an Ethiopian man, a eunuch[b] and high official of Candace, queen of the Ethiopians,[B] who was in charge of her entire treasury. He had come to worship in Jerusalem[c] [28]and was sitting in his chariot on his way home, reading the prophet Isaiah aloud.

[29]The Spirit told Philip, "Go and join that chariot."[d]

[30]When Philip ran up to it, he heard him reading the prophet Isaiah, and said, "Do you understand what you're reading?"

[31]"How can I," he said, "unless someone guides me?" So he invited Philip to come up and sit with him. [32]Now the Scripture passage he was reading was this:

He was led like a sheep
    to the slaughter,
and as a lamb is silent
    before its shearer,
so He does not open His mouth.
[33] In His humiliation justice
    was denied Him.
Who will describe His generation?
For His life is taken from the earth.[C,e]

[34]The eunuch replied to Philip, "I ask you, who is the prophet saying this about—himself

or another person?" [35]So Philip proceeded[D] to tell him the good news about Jesus, beginning from that Scripture.[f]

[36]As they were traveling down the road, they came to some water. The eunuch said, "Look, there's water! What would keep me from being baptized?" [[37]And Philip said, "If you believe with all your heart you may." And he replied, "I believe that Jesus Christ is the Son of God."][E] [38]Then he ordered the chariot to stop, and both Philip and the eunuch went down into the water, and he baptized him. [39]When they came up out of the water, the Spirit of the Lord[g] carried Philip away, and the eunuch did not see him any longer. But he went on his way rejoicing. [40]Philip appeared in[F] Azotus,[G] and he was traveling and evangelizing all the towns until he came to Caesarea.[h]

The Damascus Road

9 Meanwhile, Saul was still breathing threats and murder against the disciples[i] of the Lord. He went to the high priest[j] [2]and requested letters[k] from him to the *synagogues in Damascus, so that if he found any men or women who belonged to the Way,[l] he might bring them as prisoners to Jerusalem. [3]As[m] he traveled and was nearing Damascus, a light from heaven suddenly flashed around him. [4]Falling to the ground, he heard a voice saying to him, "Saul, Saul, why are you persecuting Me?"

[5]"Who are You, Lord?" he said.

---

[a]8:26 Ac 5:19; 8:29
[b]8:27 Ps 68:31; 87:4; Is 56:3; Zph 3:10
[c]1Kg 8:41; Jn 12:20
[d]8:29 Ac 10:19; 11:12; 13:2; 20:23; 21:11
[e]8:32-33 Is 53:7-8; Php 2:8
[f]8:35 Lk 24:27; Ac 17:2; 18:28
[g]8:39 1Kg 18:12; 2Kg 2:16; Ezk 3:12,14; 8:3; 11:1,24; 43:5
[h]8:40 Ac 10:1,24; 12:19; 21:8,16; 23:23,33; 25:1,4,6,13
[i]9:1 Mt 9:10; Mk 10:10; Lk 6:1; Jn 6:3; Ac 6:1
[j]Ac 8:3; 9:13,21
[k]9:2 Ac 15:30; 22:5; 23:25,33
[l]Ac 19:9,23; 22:4; 24:14,22
[m]9:3-8 Ac 22:6-11; 26:12-18; 1Co 15:8

[A]8:26 Or *is a desert place*   [B]8:27 = Nubia   [C]8:32-33 Is 53:7-8   [D]8:35 Lit *Philip opened his mouth*   [E]8:37 Other mss omit bracketed text   [F]8:40 Or *Philip was found at*, or *Philip found himself in*   [G]8:40 Or Ashdod

---

along the way, tearing down ethnic barriers with the global gospel of Jesus Christ.

8:26-39 Through the agency of **an angel of the Lord**, God arranged for Philip to stand in a place that would bring him into contact with an important **Ethiopian man** who would listen, believe, and in turn spread the gospel to other lands.

8:30-31 Philip's question and the Ethiopian's response imply that the OT passage the eunuch was reading (Is 53:7-8) required interpretation in light of what God had done in Jesus of Nazareth.

8:32-34 The Ethiopian was reading Is 53:7-8, apparently from the Greek text. It is likely that he was reading the entire Suffering Servant section of Isaiah (52:13–53:12). The eunuch's question, **who is the prophet saying this about**, allowed Philip to explain Jesus as the subject of the passage. It is Jesus, not Isaiah, who suffered for the sins of humanity (Is 53:6). From the earliest days of the church, the Suffering Servant section has been seen as an ideal starting place for explaining the gospel.

8:35 The phrase, **beginning from that Scripture**, may indicate that Philip went on to explain other relevant OT passages besides those in Isaiah.

8:38-40 The Ethiopian requested and was granted baptism

just as soon as he believed (see note at 10:47-48). That they went **into the water** and then came **up out of the water** apparently indicates baptism by immersion. A miracle is indicated by **carried Philip away**, for **the eunuch** came "up out of the water" and found himself alone. The Holy Spirit had taken Philip to his next appointment, a place called **Azotus**.

9:1 The narrative returns to **Saul**, or Paul. His anger with Jesus' followers continued unabated, to the point that he was threatening to **murder** them. Paul later acknowledged his zeal in persecuting Christians (Php 3:6), and this is how he was known by others (e.g., Ananias, Ac 9:13).

9:2 That Saul was authorized to travel to **Damascus** with warrants from the high priest to imprison people of **the Way** (a common name for early Christians; 19:9,23; 22:4) indicates his high standing among Jewish religious leaders. He planned to bring them back to **Jerusalem** since this city was the center of Judaism.

9:3-4 **Nearing Damascus** and no doubt thinking that his acts there would help halt the spread of Christianity, Saul instead saw **a light from heaven** that changed his life and, eventually, world history.

9:5 It is doubtful that Saul immediately recognized the voice as that of Jesus. His use of **Lord** was probably honorific

"I am Jesus, the One you are persecuting," He replied. ⁶"But get up and go into the city, and you will be told what you must do."

⁷The men who were traveling with him stood speechless, hearing the sound but seeing no one.ᵃ ⁸Then Saul got up from the ground, and though his eyes were open, he could see nothing. So they took him by the hand and led him into Damascus. ⁹He was unable to see for three days and did not eat or drink.

Saul's Baptism

¹⁰There was a disciple in Damascus named Ananias. And the Lord said to him in a vision, "Ananias!"

"Here I am, Lord!" he said.ᵇ

¹¹"Get up and go to the street called Straight," the Lord said to him, "to the house of Judas, and ask for a man from Tarsusᶜ named Saul, since he is praying there. ¹²In a visionᴬ he has seen a man named Ananias coming in and placing his hands on him so he can regain his sight."ᵈ

¹³"Lord," Ananias answered, "I have heard from many people about this man, how much harm he has done to Your •saints in Jerusalem.ᵉ ¹⁴And he has authority here from the •chief priests to arrest all who call on Your name."ᶠ

¹⁵But the Lord said to him, "Go! For this man is My chosen instrumentᵍ to take My name to Gentiles,ʰ kings, and the Israelites.ⁱ

¹⁶I will show him how much he must suffer for My name!"ʲ

¹⁷So Ananias left and entered the house. Then he placed his hands on him and said, "Brother Saul, the Lord Jesus, who appeared to you on the road you were traveling, has sent me so that you can regain your sight and be filled with the Holy Spirit."ᵏ ¹⁸At once something like scales fell from his eyes, and he regained his sight. Then he got up and was baptized. ¹⁹And after taking some food, he regained his strength.ˡ

Saul Proclaiming the Messiah

Saul was with the disciples in Damascus for some days. ²⁰Immediately he began proclaiming Jesus in the synagogues: "He is the Son of God."ᵐ

²¹But all who heard him were astounded and said, "Isn't this the man who, in Jerusalem, was destroying those who called on this name and then came here for the purpose of taking them as prisoners to the chief priests?"ⁿ ²²But Saul grew more capable and kept confounding the Jews who lived in Damascus by proving that this One is the •Messiah.

²³After many days had passed, the Jews conspired to kill him, ²⁴but their plot became known to Saul. So they were watching the gates day and night intending to kill him,ᵒ ²⁵but his disciples took him by night and lowered him in a large basket through an opening in the wall.ᵖ

ᵃ9:7 Dn 10:7; Jn 12:29; Ac 22:9
ᵇ9:10 Ac 10:3,17,19; 22:12
ᶜ9:11 Ac 9:30; 11:25; 21:39; 22:3
ᵈ9:12 Mk 5:23; Ac 9:17
ᵉ9:13 Ac 8:3; 9:32; Rm 1:7; 15:25-26,31; 16:2,15
ᶠ9:14 Ac 7:59; 1Co 1:2; 2Tm 2:22
ᵍ9:15 Ac 13:2; Rm 1:1; Gl 1:15
ʰMt 28:19; Rm 1:5; Gl 1:16
ⁱAc 25:22; 26:1
ʲ9:16 Ac 20:23; 21:4,11; 2Co 6:4-5; 11:23-27; 1Th 3:3
ᵏ9:17 Ac 6:6; 22:13
ˡ9:19 Ac 11:26; 26:20
ᵐ9:21 Mt 4:3; Ac 13:5,14
ⁿ9:21 Ac 8:3; 9:13-14; Gl 1:13,23
ᵒ9:24 Ac 20:3, 19; 23:12,30; 25:3; 2Co 11:26
ᵖ9:25 Jos 2:15; 1Sm 19:12; 2Co 11:33

ᴬ9:12 Other mss omit *In a vision*

(equivalent to "sir") rather than recognition of divinity. Hence the voice said, **I am Jesus**.

9:6 Saul was not told at this point what his mission or purpose was. That was reserved for when he encountered Ananias later in the city of Damascus. This stepwise introduction to his future kept him from being overwhelmed all at once with the changes Jesus had initiated in his life, and it also allowed the Christians in Damascus to meet and accept the one whom they feared.

9:7 This is the first of three accounts of Saul's conversion that appear in the book of Acts (22:6-11; 26:12-18). Here it appears that Saul's traveling companions heard a noise but did not recognize the words that were spoken. The comments, it seems, were intended only for Saul.

9:10 We are not told how **Ananias** came to be a Christian. A possible scenario is that he or someone he knew had been in Jerusalem at Pentecost. There they would have seen and heard wondrous signs as God sent the Holy Spirit, and possibly accepted the message preached by the apostles. The pilgrims would then have taken their newfound faith back to Damascus, establishing the church that Saul now came to persecute.

9:13-14 Ananias's fear of Saul was such that he dared to question God's judgment. Saul's reputation as an enemy of the church was well earned, built as it was on the testimony of **many people**.

9:15-16 God revealed His purpose for Saul to Ananias first. This ensured that Saul would have a support network in place once he learned of his new purpose in life. Otherwise, imagine Saul coming to Ananias and delivering the news. Ananias would have scoffed, assuming he let Saul close enough to speak.

9:17-18 The ordering of events in Saul's conversion may have been altered from the standard pattern so that baptism rather than the filling of the Holy Spirit was the final event. The process may have been extended over several days rather than occurring all at once. But the result was the same: Saul became a follower of Jesus Christ.

9:19-20 Saul stayed **in Damascus for some days**, likely becoming oriented to basic Christianity even as **he began proclaiming Jesus in the synagogues**. He gave priority to the synagogues throughout his ministry, starting there before being forced to take the message elsewhere.

9:21-22 Understandably, the initial response to Saul was skeptical amazement, but as he **grew more capable** he was able to confound unbelieving Jews, **proving** that Jesus is **the Messiah**. Apparently, he was able to explain the messianic connections between the OT and Jesus so clearly that the Jews in Damascus could not refute him.

9:23-25 After many days pictures Saul dutifully preaching Jesus as Messiah for long enough to become the uppermost enemy of unbelieving Jews in Damascus. He had

Saul in Jerusalem

²⁶When he arrived in Jerusalem,ᵃ he tried to associate with the disciples, but they were all afraid of him, since they did not believe he was a disciple. ²⁷Barnabas, however, took him and brought him to the apostles and explained to them how Saul had seen the Lord on the road and that He had talked to him, and how in Damascus he had spoken boldlyᵇ in the name of Jesus.ᶜ ²⁸Saul was coming and going with them in Jerusalem, speaking boldly in the name of the Lord. ²⁹He conversed and debated with the Hellenistic Jews,ᴬ but they attempted to kill him.ᵈ ³⁰When the •brothers found out, they took him down to Caesarea and sent him off to Tarsus.ᵉ

³¹So the churchᶠ throughout all Judea, Galilee, and Samaria had peace, being built up and walking in the •fear of the Lord and in the encouragement of the Holy Spirit, and it increased in numbers.

The Healing of Aeneas

³²As Peter was traveling from place to place,ᴮ he also came down to the saintsᵍ who lived in Lydda.ʰ ³³There he found a man named Aeneas, who was paralyzed and had been bedridden for eight years. ³⁴Peter said to him, "Aeneas, Jesus Christ heals you. Get up and make your bed,"ᶜ and immediately he got up.ⁱ ³⁵So

all who lived in Lydda and Sharonʲ saw him and turned to the Lord.

Dorcas Restored to Life

³⁶In Joppaᵏ there was a disciple named Tabitha, which is translated Dorcas.ᴰ She was always doing good worksˡ and acts of charity. ³⁷In those days she became sick and died. After washing her, they placed her in a room upstairs. ³⁸Since Lydda was near Joppa, the disciples heard that Peter was there and sent two men to him who begged him, "Don't delay in coming with us." ³⁹So Peter got up and went with them. When he arrived, they led him to the room upstairs. And all the widows approached him, weeping and showing him the robes and clothes that Dorcas had made while she was with them. ⁴⁰Then Peter sent them all out of the room. He knelt down, prayed, and turning toward the body said, "Tabitha, get up!" She opened her eyes, saw Peter, and sat up.ᵐ ⁴¹He gave her his hand and helped her stand up. Then he called the saints and widows and presented her alive. ⁴²This became known throughout Joppa, and many believed in the Lord. ⁴³And Peter stayed on many days in Joppa with Simon,ⁿ a leather tanner.ᴱ

Cornelius's Vision

10 There was a man in Caesarea named Cornelius, a •centurion of what was

ᵃ9:26 Ac 22:17; 26:20; Gl 1:17
ᵇ9:27 Ac 13:46; 14:3; 18:26; 19:8; 26:26; Eph 6:20; 1Th 2:2
ᶜAc 4:36; 9:3-6,20,22
ᵈ9:29 Ac 6:1; 2Co 11:26
ᵉ9:30 Ac 8:40; Gl 1:21
ᶠ9:31 Mt 16:18; 1Co 14:4; Rv 1:4
ᵍ9:32 Rm 1:7; Eph 5:3; 6:18
ʰ1Ch 8:12; Ezr 2:23; Neh 7:37; 11:35
ⁱ9:34 Ac 3:6,16; 4:10
ʲ9:35 1Ch 5:16; 27:29; Sg 2:1; Is 33:9; 35:2; 65:10
ᵏ9:36 Jos 19:46; 2Ch 2:16; Ezr 3:7; Jnh 1:3; Ac 10:5
ˡ1Tm 2:10; Ti 3:8
ᵐ9:40 Mt 9:25; Mk 5:41; Lk 22:41; Jn 11:43; Ac 7:60
ⁿ9:43 Ac 10:6,17,32

ᴬ9:29 Lit *Hellenists*; that is, Gk-speaking Jews   ᴮ9:32 Lit *Peter was passing through all*   ᶜ9:34 Or *and get ready to eat*
ᴰ9:36 = Gazelle   ᴱ9:43 Tanners were considered ritually •unclean because of their occupation.

---

come to help their struggle against the growing Christian movement, but now he had become the chief cause of its growth. Thus they **conspired to kill him**. Unable to leave via the city gates, Saul escaped in a most undignified but effective manner: he was placed in a **large basket** and shoved **through an opening in the wall** (lit "through the wall").

9:26 Among believers in **Jerusalem**, Saul's reputation as a persecutor of the church was unchanged. Either news had not come from Damascus, or else **the disciples** in Jerusalem took a "wait and see" attitude. Perhaps they even suspected his conversion was just a ruse to infiltrate the fledgling Christian movement and destroy it from within. See note at 22:17-21.

9:27 Barnabas was convinced of the genuineness of Saul's conversion, apparently because he **had talked to him**.

9:28-30 Saul . . . conversed and debated with the Hellenistic Jews, some of whom may have been involved with him in Stephen's stoning (7:57-60). A Hellenistic Jew himself, Paul had been born in **Tarsus** and spoke Greek as his primary language. Seeing one of their own, a former persecutor of the church no less, argue on behalf of Christianity was more than they could bear. They **attempted to kill** Saul, with the result that he was whisked away to his hometown.

9:31 This verse marks a significant point in the development of the early church (see note at 1:8). The church, having been forced by persecution to scatter outward from Jerusalem, was at **peace** in **Judea, Galilee, and Samaria**. This

set the church up for a second stage of growth, which would see the gospel boldly taken outside Israel.

9:32 The saints at **Lydda** may have been there since Pentecost and the time of persecution that had scattered believers throughout Judea (8:1). It is also possible that they traced their origins to Philip's ministry (8:40).

9:33-35 Again we see that the apostles never hesitated to give all credit for healing miracles to **Jesus Christ** (3:6). Indirect evidence for this is found in the fact that the people in **Lydda and Sharon** turned in faith **to the Lord** rather than His apostolic messengers when they witnessed the healing of **Aeneas**.

9:36 Tabitha (Gk **Dorcas**, lit *gazelle*) is called a disciple. She was not one of the twelve apostles, but she was clearly an active follower of Jesus.

9:37-38 So powerfully had God worked wonders through Peter and the other apostles that even when Dorcas **died** and had been ceremonially washed and **placed . . . in a room upstairs** for viewing, Christians in **Joppa** did not give up hope but instead sent for **Peter**.

9:43 Tanners were often considered impure because of their contact with dead animals. This indicates that either Jewish law on this practice had relaxed by this era, or else that Peter was already enjoying freedom from the Jewish law because of his liberty in Christ (10:6,32).

10:1 Philip had preached in **Caesarea** (8:40), so there would

called the Italian *Regiment.[a] [2] He was a devout man and feared God along with his whole household. He did many charitable deeds for the Jewish people and always prayed to God.[b] [3] About three in the afternoon[A] he distinctly saw in a vision an angel of God who came in and said to him, "Cornelius!"[c]

[4] Looking intently at him, he became afraid and said, "What is it, lord?"

The angel told him, "Your prayers and your acts of charity have come up as a memorial offering before God.[d] [5] Now send men to Joppa and call for Simon, who is also named Peter. [6] He is lodging with Simon, a tanner, whose house is by the sea."[e]

[7] When the angel who spoke to him had gone, he called two of his household slaves and a devout soldier, who was one of those who attended him. [8] After explaining everything to them, he sent them to Joppa.

Peter's Vision

[9] The[f] next day, as they were traveling and nearing the city, Peter went up to pray on the housetop[g] about noon.[B] [10] Then he became hungry and wanted to eat, but while they were preparing something, he went into a visionary state. [11] He saw heaven opened[h] and an object that resembled a large sheet coming down, being lowered by its four corners to the

earth. [12] In it were all the four-footed animals and reptiles of the earth, and the birds of the sky. [13] Then a voice said to him, "Get up, Peter; kill and eat!"

[14] "No, Lord!" Peter said. "For I have never eaten anything common[c] and ritually *unclean!"[i]

[15] Again, a second time, a voice said to him, "What God has made *clean, you must not call common."[j] [16] This happened three times, and then the object was taken up into heaven.

Peter Visits Cornelius

[17] While Peter was deeply perplexed about what the vision he had seen might mean, the men who had been sent by Cornelius, having asked directions to Simon's house, stood at the gate. [18] They called out, asking if Simon, who was also named Peter, was lodging there.

[19] While Peter was thinking about the vision, the Spirit told him, "Three men are here looking for you.[k] [20] Get up, go downstairs, and accompany them with no doubts at all, because I have sent them."[l]

[21] Then Peter went down to the men and said, "Here I am, the one you're looking for. What is the reason you're here?"

[22] They said, "Cornelius, a centurion, an upright and God-fearing man, who has a good reputation with the whole Jewish nation, was

Cross references (center column)

a 10:1 Mt 27:27; Mk 15:16; Jn 18:3,12; Ac 8:40
b 10:2 Ac 10:22, 35; 13:16,26
c 10:3 Ac 3:1; 5:19; 9:10; 10:17,19
d 10:4 Ac 9:43; 11:14
e 10:6 Lk 16:13; Rm 14:4; 1Pt 2:18
f 10:9-32 Ac 11:5-14
g 10:9 Ps 55:17; Jr 19:13; 32:29; Zph 1:5; Mt 24:17
h 10:10-11 Jn 1:51; Ac 22:17
i 10:14 Lv 11:4; 20:25; Dt 4:4-20; Ezk 4:14; Dn 1:8; Ac 9:5
j 10:15 Mt 15:11; Mk 7:19; Rm 14:14; 1Co 10:25; 1Tm 4:4; Ti 1:15
k 10:19 Ac 8:29; 10:3
l 10:20 Ac 15:7-9

A 10:3 Lit *About the ninth hour*   B 10:9 Lit *about the sixth hour*   C 10:14 Perhaps *profane*, or *non-sacred*; Jews ate distinctive food according to OT law and their traditions, similar to modern kosher or non-kosher foods.

---

have been knowledge of Christianity there before this incident with Cornelius. Centurions were essential parts of the Roman army who were distinguished by their abilities to lead men. The **Italian Regiment** was probably an auxiliary force of local soldiers (not Italians or Romans), although the original group may have consisted of Italian soldiers. Roman soldiers

did not have a great reputation since they were often involved in extortion and brutalization of the local population.

10:2 God-fearers respected Jewish beliefs and customs (including food laws and special days). They often associated with the Jews, but they were unwilling to become full-fledged proselytes since this required that they be circumcised and observe other Jewish rituals.

10:4 Fear and bewilderment are common reactions to God's voice or appearance in biblical accounts (9:4). Cornelius's **prayers** and **acts of charity** prompted God's further revelation to him through Peter (vv. 5-6).

10:9-10 Meanwhile, Peter was still in Joppa. It was common to **pray** on the **housetop**. By going at **about noon** (lit "the sixth hour"), Peter was in the heat of the day. But the series of interconnected events in both Peter and Cornelius's lives show that Peter's **visionary state** was far more than a hunger-induced, natural experience. It was a message from God.

10:11-16 Peter's lifelong adherence to the Jewish food laws collided with the Lord's command to **kill and eat** unclean animals. Peter had this vision three times; the repetition served to confirm the shocking message and emphasize its significance.

10:19-20 Whereas an angel had communicated with Cornelius, it was the Holy **Spirit** who spoke to Peter after the Lord had granted him the vision. Alternation between the Spirit and an angel as communicative agents occurs elsewhere (8:26,29).

---

ekstasis

Greek Pronunciation	[EHK stah sihss]
HCSB Translation	visionary state
Uses in Acts	4
Uses in the NT	7
Focus passage	Acts 10:10

The English words *ecstasy* and *ecstatic* come from the Greek noun *ekstasis*, which literally means *to stand out from*. The term refers to a situation in which a person experiences a kind of displacement from reality. Such feelings of displacement are of two kinds in the NT. The term is used four times to describe the astonishment of a crowd that witnessed a miracle: Jesus forgiving and healing a paralytic (Lk 5:26); Jesus raising Jairus's daughter from the dead (Mk 5:42); Jesus' resurrection (Mk 16:8); and Peter healing a lame man (Ac 3:10). The other three uses of *ekstasis* refer to a *revelatory trance*. Through a *trance*, God showed Peter that there is to be no distinction between the clean and the unclean, between Jew and Gentile (Ac 10:10; 11:5). In this same way, Jesus showed Paul that he should leave Jerusalem because of the Jews' unbelief (Ac 22:17-18).

divinely directed by a holy angel to call you to his house and to hear a message from you."[a] 23 Peter then invited them in and gave them lodging.

The next day he got up and set out with them, and some of the brothers from Joppa went with him.[b] 24 The following day he entered Caesarea. Now Cornelius was expecting them and had called together his relatives and close friends. 25 When Peter entered, Cornelius met him, fell at his feet, and worshiped him.

26 But Peter helped him up and said, "Stand up! I myself am also a man."[c] 27 While talking with him, he went on in and found that many had come together there. 28 Peter said to them, "You know it's forbidden for a Jewish man to associate with or visit a foreigner.[d] But God has shown me that I must not call any person common or unclean.[e] 29 That's why I came without any objection when I was sent for. So I ask: Why did you send for me?"

30 Cornelius replied, "Four days ago at this hour, at three in the afternoon,[A] I was[B] praying in my house. Just then a man in a dazzling robe stood before me[f] 31 and said, 'Cornelius, your prayer has been heard, and your acts of charity have been remembered in God's sight. 32 Therefore send someone to Joppa and invite Simon here, who is also named Peter. He is lodging in Simon the tanner's house by the sea.'[C] 33 Therefore I immediately sent for you, and you did the right thing in coming. So we are all present before God, to hear everything you have been commanded by the Lord."

Good News for Gentiles

34 Then Peter began to speak: "Now I really understand that God doesn't show favoritism,[g] 35 but in every nation the person who fears Him and does righteousness is acceptable to Him. 36 He sent the message to the Israelites, proclaiming the good news of peace through Jesus Christ—He is Lord of all.[h] 37 You know the events[D] that took place throughout Judea, beginning from Galilee after the baptism that John preached: 38 how God anointed Jesus of Nazareth with the Holy Spirit and with power, and how He went about doing good and healing all who were under the tyranny of the Devil, because God was with Him.[i] 39 We ourselves are witnesses of everything He did in both the Judean country and in Jerusalem, yet they killed Him by hanging Him on a tree.[j] 40 God raised up this man on the third day and permitted Him to be seen, 41 not by all the people, but by us, witnesses appointed beforehand by God, who ate and drank with Him after He rose from the dead.[k] 42 He commanded us to preach to the people and to solemnly testify that He is the One appointed by God to be the Judge of the living and the dead.[l] 43 All the prophets testify[m] about Him that through His name[n] everyone who believes in Him will receive forgiveness of sins."[o]

Gentile Conversion and Baptism

44 While Peter was still speaking these words, the Holy Spirit came down[p] on all those who heard the message. 45 The circumcised believers[E] who had come with Peter were astounded because the gift of the Holy Spirit had been poured out on the Gentiles also.[q] 46 For they heard them speaking in other •languages and declaring the greatness of[F] God.

Then Peter responded, 47 "Can anyone withhold water and prevent these people from

[a] 10:22 Mk 8:38; Ac 10:2; 11:14
[b] 10:23 Ac 10:45; 11:12
[c] 10:26 Ac 14:15; Rv 19:10; 22:8
[d] 10:28 Jn 4:9; 18:28; Ac 11:3
[e] Ac 10:14-15,35; 15:8-9
[f] 10:30 Ac 1:10; 3:1
[g] 10:34 Dt 10:17; 2Ch 19:7; Rm 2:11; Gl 2:6; Eph 6:9; Col 3:25; 1Pt 1:17
[h] 10:36 Mt 28:18; Ac 2:36; 13:32; Rm 10:12; Eph 2:17; Rv 17:14
[i] 10:38 Mt 4:23; Lk 4:18; Jn 3:2; Ac 4:26
[j] 10:39 Lk 24:48; Ac 2:32; 5:30
[k] 10:41 Lk 24:43; Jn 14:17,22
[l] 10:42 Jn 5:22; Ac 17:31; Rm 14:9; 2Co 5:10; 2Tm 4:1; 1Pt 4:5
[m] 10:43 Is 53:11; Jr 31:34
[n] 1Jn 2:12; 3:23
[o] Lk 24:47; Ac 15:9; Rm 10:11; Gl 3:22
[p] 10:44 Ac 11:15; 15:8
[q] 10:45 Ac 2:33, 38; 10:23; 11:18

[A] 10:30 Lit *at the ninth hour* [B] 10:30 Other mss add *fasting and* [C] 10:32 Other mss add *When he arrives, he will speak to you.*
[D] 10:37 Or *word*; lit *thing* [E] 10:45 Jewish Christians who stressed circumcision; Ac 11:2; 15:5; Gl 2:12; Col 4:11; Ti 1:10
[F] 10:46 Or *and magnifying*

10:24 When God moves powerfully in a person's life, one natural response is to call **relatives and close friends** together and share the experience with them. In this case, it helped to multiply the impact of Peter's radical message of hope.

10:25-26 When Cornelius **fell at** Peter's **feet, and worshiped him**, Peter protested that he too was merely **a man**. The apostles always sought to glorify God, not themselves.

10:28 The vision God gave Peter taught him that cleanliness standards barring Jews from associating with Gentiles had become obsolete. It is hard to overestimate the seismic change this represented for Peter's worldview.

10:33 By saying they had all gathered **before God, to hear everything** God **commanded** Peter to say or do, Cornelius showed the childlike openness Jesus asked of His disciples (Lk 18:15-17).

10:34-35 Due to the vision, Peter now understood that **God doesn't show favoritism**. This does not mean God accepts all people no matter their response to Him or that people who fear Him are **acceptable to Him** and do not need Christ. Rather, it means that God does not restrict any nation or ethnicity from the offer of salvation.

10:37-41 You know the events indicates that the basic biography of Jesus was widely known by now. It was still necessary, however, that **witnesses** to Jesus' life come and fill in any knowledge gaps and call unbelievers to saving faith.

10:42-43 Jesus Himself told the apostles that **He is the One appointed by God** to judge all humans. Backing this claim is the testimony of **all the prophets** (Lk 24:44).

10:44-46 Faith, the coming of the **Holy Spirit**, and believer's baptism are again all components of conversion, although again in a different order. Since the Gentile converts spoke in **other languages** and declared **the greatness of God** just as the Jewish believers had done at Pentecost (2:4-11), the **circumcised believers** who were **with Peter were astounded**.

10:47-48 Again we see prompt baptism in response to new faith (8:36-39).

being baptized, who have received the Holy Spirit just as we have?"[a] [48] And he commanded them to be baptized in the name of Jesus Christ.[b] Then they asked him to stay for a few days.

Gentile Salvation Defended

11 The apostles and the ·brothers who were throughout Judea heard that the Gentiles had welcomed God's message also. [2] When Peter went up to Jerusalem, those who stressed circumcision[A] argued with him,[c] [3] saying, "You visited uncircumcised men and ate with them!"[d]

[4] Peter began to explain to them in an orderly sequence, saying: [5] "I[e] was in the town of Joppa praying, and I saw, in a visionary state, an object that resembled a large sheet coming down, being lowered by its four corners from heaven, and it came to me. [6] When I looked closely and considered it, I saw the four-footed animals of the earth, the wild beasts, the reptiles, and the birds of the sky. [7] Then I also heard a voice telling me, 'Get up, Peter; kill and eat!'

[8] "'No, Lord!' I said. 'For nothing common or ritually ·unclean has ever entered my mouth!' [9] But a voice answered from heaven a second time, 'What God has made ·clean, you must not call common.'

[10] "Now this happened three times, and then everything was drawn up again into heaven. [11] At that very moment, three men who had been sent to me from Caesarea arrived at the house where we were. [12] Then the Spirit told me to accompany them with no doubts at all. These six brothers accompanied me, and we went into the man's house.[f] [13] He reported to us how he had seen the angel standing in his

house and saying, 'Send[B] to Joppa, and call for Simon, who is also named Peter. [14] He will speak a message[C] to you that you and all your household[g] will be saved by.'

[15] "As I began to speak, the Holy Spirit came down on them, just as on us at the beginning.[h] [16] Then I remembered the word of the Lord, how He said, 'John baptized with water, but you will be baptized with the Holy Spirit.'[i] [17] Therefore, if God gave them the same gift that He also gave to us when we believed on the Lord Jesus Christ, how could I possibly hinder God?"[j]

[18] When they heard this they became silent. Then they glorified God, saying, "So God has granted repentance resulting in life[D] even to the Gentiles!"[k]

The Church in Antioch

[19] Those who had been scattered as a result of the persecution that started because of Stephen made their way as far as Phoenicia, Cyprus, and Antioch,[l] speaking the message to no one except Jews. [20] But there were some of them, Cypriot and Cyrenian men, who came to Antioch and began speaking to the Hellenists,[E,F] proclaiming the good news about the Lord Jesus.[m] [21] The Lord's hand was with them, and a large number who believed turned to the Lord.[n] [22] Then the report about them was heard by the church that was at Jerusalem, and they sent out Barnabas to travel[G] as far as Antioch. [23] When he arrived and saw the grace of God, he was glad and encouraged all of them to remain true to the Lord with a firm resolve of the heart,[o] [24] for he was a good man, full of the Holy Spirit[p] and of faith. And large numbers of people were added[q] to the Lord. [25] Then he[H] went to Tarsus to search for Saul, [26] and when

Cross references

a 10:47 Ac 2:4; 8:36; 11:17; 15:8
b 10:48 Ac 2:38; 8:16; 1Co 1:14-17
c 11:2 Ac 10:45; Col 4:11; 1Tm 1:10
d 11:3 Ac 10:28; Gl 2:12
e 11:5-14 Ac 10:9-32
f 11:12 Ac 8:29; 10:23; 15:9
g 11:14 Jn 4:53; Ac 10:2; 16:15,31-34; 18:8; 1Co 1:16
h 11:15 Ac 2:4; 10:44
i 11:16 Mt 3:11; Mk 1:8; Lk 3:16; Jn 1:33; Ac 1:5
j 11:17 Ac 5:39; 10:45,47
k 11:18 Rm 10:12-13; 2Co 7:10
l 11:19 Ac 6:5; 13:1; 14:26; 15:22-23,30,35; 18:22; Gl 2:11
m 11:20 Mt 27:32; Ac 4:36
n 11:21 Lk 1:66; Ac 2:47; 9:35
o 11:23 Ac 13:43; 14:26; 15:40; 20:24,32
p 11:24 Lk 4:1; Ac 6:5; 7:55
q Ac 2:41,47; 5:14

A 11:2 Lit *those of the circumcision*   B 11:13 Other mss add *men*   C 11:14 Lit *speak words*   D 11:18 Or *repentance to life*
E 11:20 Other mss read *Greeks*   F 11:20 In this context, a non-Jewish person who spoke Gk   G 11:22 Other mss omit *to travel*
H 11:25 Other mss read *Barnabas*

11:1-3 News that **Gentiles had welcomed God's message** spread quickly because it was so controversial. Jews who **stressed circumcision** felt Peter had compromised God's laws. This was a recurring source of conflict in the early church, but, informed as he was by the vision from God, Peter corrected those who argued against inclusion of uncircumcised Gentiles (vv. 4-18).

11:14-17 The parallel between what happened on Pentecost and among Cornelius's family proved that God was bestowing the same gifts on Jewish and Gentile believers. In this light, Peter rightly asks, **How could I possibly hinder God?**

11:18 They became silent indicates initial caution. These Jewish believers were having to process the same shocking revelation that had come to Peter at Joppa and then Caesarea (10:9-16,44-48). Eventually, however, **they glorified God** for what He had done.

11:19 The Christian mission continued to spread much fur-

ther afield, including areas well beyond Judea (**Phoenicia, Cyprus, and Antioch**).

11:20-21 The evangelization of **Antioch** was carried out by **Cypriot** and **Cyrenian** believers. As a result, Antioch became the center of the Gentile mission and the church that sent Paul out as a missionary (see chaps. 13 and following).

11:22-24 The spiritual qualities of **Barnabas** were obvious to the Jerusalem church (4:36-37; 9:27). No wonder they sent him to **Antioch**. He was probably sent to determine the genuineness of the conversions taking place there and encourage them to **remain true to the Lord**.

11:25 Saul (soon to be Paul, 13:9) had faded from the picture while the evangelization of Antioch moved forward. Once again Barnabas played a central role in involving Paul in ministry (see note at 9:27). On **Tarsus,** see note at 9:28-30.

11:26 The term **Christians** probably came from Romans who labeled Jesus' followers in **Antioch** "little Christs."

he found him he brought him to Antioch. For a whole year they met with the church and taught large numbers. The disciples[a] were first called Christians at Antioch.[b]

Famine Relief

[27] In those days some prophets came down from Jerusalem to Antioch.[c] [28] Then one of them, named Agabus, stood up and predicted by the Spirit that there would be a severe famine throughout the Roman world.[A] This took place during the time of Claudius.[B,d] [29] So each of the disciples, according to his ability, determined to send relief to the brothers who lived in Judea.[e] [30] They did this, sending it to the elders[f] by means of Barnabas and Saul.

James Martyred and Peter Jailed

12 About that time King •Herod cruelly attacked some who belonged to the church, [2] and he killed James,[g] John's brother, with the sword. [3] When he saw that it pleased the Jews, he proceeded to arrest Peter too, during the days of •Unleavened Bread.[h] [4] After the arrest, he put him in prison and assigned four squads of four soldiers each to guard him, intending to bring him out to the people after the •Passover. [5] So Peter was kept in prison, but prayer was being made earnestly to God for him by the church.

Peter Rescued

[6] On the night before Herod was to bring him out for execution, Peter, bound with two chains, was sleeping between two soldiers, while the sentries in front of the door guarded the prison. [7] Suddenly an angel of the Lord[i] appeared, and a light shone in the cell. Striking Peter on the side, he woke him up and said, "Quick, get up!" Then the chains fell off his wrists.[j] [8] "Get dressed," the angel told him, "and put on your sandals." And he did so. "Wrap your cloak around you," he told him, "and follow me." [9] So he went out and followed, and he did not know that what took place through the angel was real, but thought he was seeing a vision.[k] [10] After they passed the first and second guard posts, they came to the iron gate that leads into the city, which opened to them by itself. They went outside and passed one street, and immediately the angel left him.[l]

[11] Then Peter came to himself and said, "Now I know for certain that the Lord has sent His angel and rescued me from Herod's grasp and from all that the Jewish people expected."[m] [12] When he realized this, he went to the house of Mary, the mother of John Mark,[C,n] where many had assembled and were praying. [13] He knocked at the door in the gateway, and a

Cross references (center column)

a11:26 Ac 6:1; 9:1; 13:52; 14:20; 15:10; 16:1; 19:1
bAc 26:28; 1Pt 4:16
c11:27 Ac 13:1; 15:32; 1Co 12:28; Eph 4:11
d11:28 Mt 24:14; Ac 18:2; 21:10; Gl 2:2
e11:29 Rm 15:26; 2Co 9:1-2; Gl 2:10
f11:30 Ac 14:23; 15:2; 16:4; 20:17; 21:18; 1Tm 5:17,19; Jms 5:14; 2Jn 1
g12:2 Mt 4:21; 20:23
h12:3 Ex 12:15; 23:15; Ac 12:5; 20:6; 24:27; 25:9; 2Co 1:11; Eph 6:18
i12:7 Lk 1:11; Col 4:1; Jd 5
jLk 2:9; 5:19; 16:26; 24:4
k12:9 Ps 126:1; Ac 9:10
l12:10 Ac 5:19; 16:26
m12:11 Ps 33:18-19; 34:7; Dn 3:28; 6:22; Lk 15:17; 2Co 1:10
m12:12 Ac 12:25; 15:37,39; Col 4:10; 2Tm 4:11; Phm 24; 1Pt 5:13

A11:28 Or the whole world   B11:28 Emperor A.D. 41–54; there was a famine A.D. 47–48.   C12:12 Lit John who was called Mark

---

Though it was likely intended as an offense, the label is actually an honor insomuch as it indicates disciples are living Christlike lives.

11:28 Agabus was a prophet from Jerusalem who reappears in 21:10. The reign of **Claudius** (A.D. 41–54) was marked with numerous famines in various parts of the Roman Empire. The famine referred to here may have occurred around 46–47, with the effects of the famine lasting for a number of years after that.

11:29 The church at Antioch determined to provide relief for the believers in **Judea**. In so doing, they gave back to the churches and believers who had brought the gospel to Antioch and abroad in the first place.

11:30 Some object that the early church was loosely organized and dependent on the Spirit and did not have offices such as elders and deacons at this early date. However, there is abundant evidence that formal offices existed even in the earliest stages of the church (14:23; 15:2,4,6,22-23; 16:4; 20:17; 21:18; Php 1:1; 1Tm 3:1-13; 4:14; 5:17,19; Ti 1:5-9). There is nothing contradictory between the early church being filled with the Spirit and having leaders appointed to various responsibilities. The ministry of Paul was characterized by such a balance.

12:1 This **King Herod** was Herod Agrippa I, who ruled in Palestine from A.D. 37 to 44. His attack apparently focused on the apostles in Jerusalem.

12:2 The **James** whom Herod executed was one of the "Sons of Thunder" (Mk 3:17).

12:6-10 Peter was again rescued from prison by an **angel of the Lord** (see note at 5:19-20), though this time he initially thought he was only seeing a vision.

12:11 Jesus too was once rescued from **Herod's grasp**, though it was a different king Herod (Mt 2:13-15).

12:12-16 Knowing that everyone inside was praying for Peter, **Rhoda** rushed back in to tell them that God had answered their prayers, not bothering to let Peter in first! Remarkably,

Christianos box

Christianos

Greek Pronunciation	[krihss tee ah NAHSS]
HCSB Translation	Christian
Uses in Acts	2
Uses in the NT	3
Focus passage	Acts 11:26

From the Greek noun *Christos* (Christ or Messiah) comes the word *Christianos*, meaning *belonging to Christ*. The term occurs in only three places in the NT. Acts 11:26 explains that it was in Antioch that the disciples were "first called *Christians*." The famine mentioned in the following verses occurred in A.D. 46 and indicates the term's usage entered sacred vocabulary about that time. Since this new word for followers of Christ was coined in Antioch rather than Israel, it may indicate that the *Christian* movement was being recognized among Gentiles as something distinct from Judaism and not just another Jewish sect. In Acts 26:28, Agrippa referred to Paul's attempt to persuade the king to become a *Christian*—an attempt Paul admitted applied not only to Agrippa but to everyone who was listening to his words of testimony (v. 29). Peter used the term in reference to suffering "as a Christian" (1Pt 4:16).

servant named Rhoda came to answer. ¹⁴She recognized Peter's voice, and because of her joy, she did not open the gate but ran in and announced that Peter was standing at the gateway.

¹⁵"You're crazy!" they told her. But she kept insisting that it was true. Then they said, "It's his angel!"ᵃ ¹⁶Peter, however, kept on knocking, and when they opened the door and saw him, they were astounded.

¹⁷Motioning to them with his handᵇ to be silent, he explained to them how the Lord had brought him out of the prison. "Report these things to JamesᴬᶜᶜA,c and the •brothers," he said. Then he departed and went to a different place.

¹⁸At daylight, there was a great commotionᴮ among the soldiers as to what could have become of Peter. ¹⁹After Herod had searched and did not find him, he interrogated the guards and ordered their execution. Then Herod went down from Judea to Caesarea and stayed there.ᵈ

Herod's Death

²⁰He had been very angry with the Tyrians and Sidonians.ᶜ Together they presented themselves before him. They won over Blastus, who was in charge of the king's bedroom, and through him they asked for peace, be-

ᵃ12:13-15 Mt 18:10; Lk 24:21
ᵇ12:17 Ac 13:16; 19:33; 21:40
ᶜAc 15:13; 21:18; Gl 1:19; 2:9,12
ᵈ12:19 Ac 8:40; 16:27; 27:42
ᵉ12:20 1Kg 5:11; Ezr 3:7; Ezk 27:17; Mt 11:21
ᶠ12:23 Lk 1:11; Col 4:1; Jd 5
ᵍ1Sm 25:38; 2Sm 24:16-17; Ps 115:1
ʰ12:24 Ac 6:7; 19:20
ⁱ12:25 Ac 4:36; 11:30; 12:12
ʲ13:1 Mt 14:1; Ac 4:36; 11:19,22,27; 1Co 12:28
ᵏ13:2 Ac 8:29; 9:15; Rm 1:1; Gl 1:15
ˡ13:3 Ac 6:6; 14:26

cause their country was supplied with food from the king's country.ᵉ ²¹So on an appointed day, dressed in royal robes and seated on the throne, Herod delivered a public address to them. ²²The assembled people began to shout, "It's the voice of a god and not of a man!" ²³At once an angel of the Lordᶠ struck him because he did not give the glory to God, and he became infected with worms and died.ᵍ ²⁴Then God's message flourished and multiplied.ʰ ²⁵After they had completed their relief mission, Barnabas and Saul returned toᴰ Jerusalem, taking along John who is called Mark.ⁱ

Preparing for the Mission Field

13 In the church that was at Antioch there were prophets and teachers: Barnabas, Simeon who was called Niger, Lucius the Cyrenian, Manaen, a close friend of •Herod the tetrarch,ʲ and Saul.

²As they were ministering toᴱ the Lord and fasting, the Holy Spirit said, "Set apart for Me Barnabas and Saul for the work I have called them to."ᵏ ³Then after they had fasted, prayed, and laid hands on them, they sent them off.ˡ

The Mission to Cyprus

⁴Being sent out by the Holy Spirit, they came down to Seleucia, and from there they

---

ᴬ12:17 This was James, the Lord's brother; Mk 6:3. This was not James the apostle; Ac 12:2. ᴮ12:18 Or *was no small disturbance* ᶜ12:20 The people of the area of modern Lebanon ᴰ12:25 Other mss read *from* ᴱ13:2 Or *were worshiping*

---

they disbelieved her and suggested it was Peter's **angel**. This reflected the common Jewish belief in guardian angels. It also shows how serious the persecutions had become, for it was believed that your guardian angel would sometimes appear shortly after your death. Thus it seems the crowd of believers was better prepared to believe Peter had been executed than that he had been released.

12:17 Peter **went to a different place** most likely in an attempt to throw Herod and the Jewish authorities off his trail. God had freed him miraculously, but this did not mean Peter could flaunt his freedom or act imprudently. Peter instructed those present to **report** his freedom to **James**, Jesus' brother, mentioned here for the first time in Acts. James, apparently not a follower of Jesus until after the resurrection, emerged as a leader in the Jerusalem church (Gl 1:19).

12:20-22 On an appointed day Herod arranged to receive praise from his subjects, but God had other plans (v. 23).

12:23 Herod **died** because he claimed for himself the honor and **glory** that belongs only to God. There have been various speculations about the immediate cause of Herod's death, including appendicitis, poisoning, and intestinal blockage.

12:24 With Herod out of the way, there were fewer hindrances to the spread of the good news, which **flourished and multiplied**.

12:25 **Barnabas and Saul** returned to Jerusalem after their relief mission. Here again we see the vital role Barnabas played in assimilating Saul into leadership of the early church.

13:1 Prophets and teachers apparently refer to functions and (possibly) offices within the early church. The teachers continued the apostolic function of transmitting Jesus' message (see note at 6:2-4), while prophets conveyed divine revelation via interpreting the OT or giving new insights (11:27). This is the only reference in Acts to teachers, although the function of teacher is described elsewhere in the NT (1Co 12:28-29; Eph 4:11; 1Tm 1:7; 2:7; 3:2; 2Tm 1:11; 2:24). The group of prophets and teachers was diverse, including people from Africa and Cyrene, and at least one person (**Manaen**) who was connected to Herod's household.

13:2-3 The routine of the prophets and teachers included **ministering to the Lord and fasting**. This helps to account for their openness to the Holy Spirit, who directed them to set aside **Barnabas and Saul** for a work to which the Spirit had called them. Barnabas and Saul were confirmed in their calling after a process of fasting, praying, and laying on of hands. This commissioning marks an important turning point in the history of the church, as Saul and Barnabas were selected to extend the gospel message beyond Judea and surrounding regions.

13:4 This verse describes the beginning of the first of Paul's three missionary journeys. This journey included the island of **Cyprus** and a part of Asia Minor. The first two journeys began and ended in Antioch, which had become a center for world Christianity, committed to evangelizing Gentiles. Paul's third journey ended in Jerusalem because he was arrested there before he could make his way to Antioch (see chap. 21).

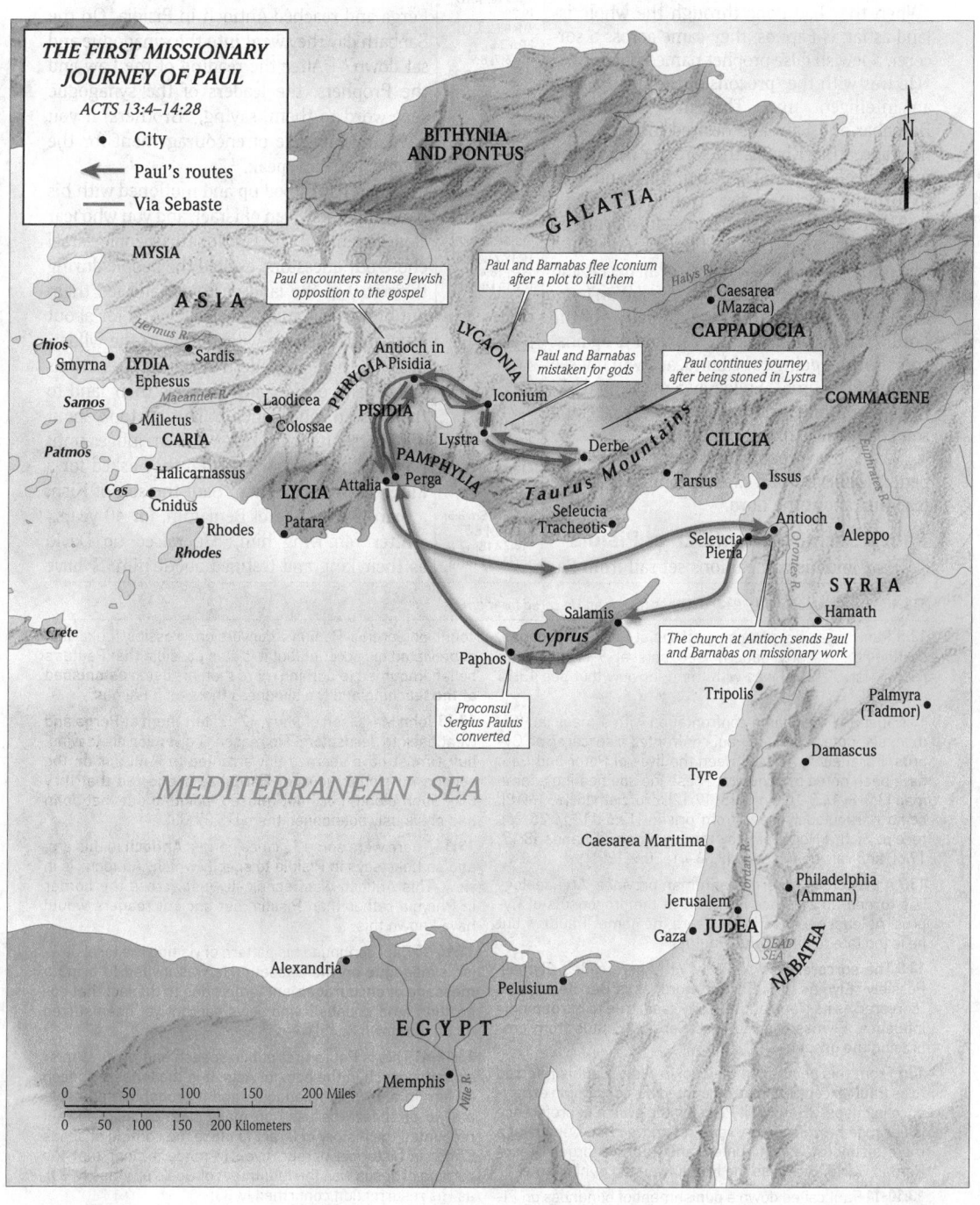

THE FIRST MISSIONARY JOURNEY OF PAUL

ACTS 13:4–14:28

- • City
- ← Paul's routes
- — Via Sebaste

N

BITHYNIA AND PONTUS

GALATIA

MYSIA

ASIA

Hermus R.

Chios

Smyrna

LYDIA

Sardis

Ephesus

Maeander R.

Laodicea

Samos

Miletus

Colossae

CARIA

Patmos

Halicarnassus

Cos

LYCIA

Cnidus

Rhodes

Rhodes

Patara

Attalia

Perga

PAMPHYLIA

PHRYGIA

PISIDIA

Antioch in Pisidia

LYCAONIA

Iconium

Lystra

Derbe

Taurus Mountains

CILICIA

Tarsus

Seleucia Tracheotis

CAPPADOCIA

Caesarea (Mazaca)

Halys R.

COMMAGENE

Euphrates R.

Issus

Seleucia Pieria

Antioch

Aleppo

Orontes R.

SYRIA

Hamath

Salamis

Cyprus

Paphos

Tripolis

Palmyra (Tadmor)

Damascus

Tyre

Jordan R.

Caesarea Maritima

Philadelphia (Amman)

Jerusalem

Gaza

JUDEA

DEAD SEA

NABATEA

Crete

MEDITERRANEAN SEA

Alexandria

Pelusium

EGYPT

Memphis

Nile R.

> Paul encounters intense Jewish opposition to the gospel

> Paul and Barnabas flee Iconium after a plot to kill them

> Paul and Barnabas mistaken for gods

> Paul continues journey after being stoned in Lystra

> The church at Antioch sends Paul and Barnabas on missionary work

> Proconsul Sergius Paulus converted

0   50   100   150   200 Miles

0   50   100 150   200 Kilometers

sailed to Cyprus. 5 Arriving in Salamis, they
proclaimed God's message in the Jewish •syna-
gogues. They also had John as their assistant.[a]
6 When they had gone through the whole island as far as Paphos, they came across a sorcerer, a Jewish false prophet named Bar-Jesus.[b]
7 He was with the •proconsul, Sergius Paulus,
an intelligent man. This man summoned
Barnabas and Saul and desired to hear God's
message.[c] 8 But Elymas the sorcerer (this is the
meaning of his name) opposed[d] them and tried
to turn the proconsul away from the faith.[e]
9 Then Saul—also called Paul—filled with the
Holy Spirit, stared straight at the sorcerer 10 and
said, "You son of the Devil,[f] full of all deceit and
all fraud, enemy of all righteousness! Won't you
ever stop perverting the straight paths[g] of the
Lord? 11 Now, look! The Lord's hand is against
you.[h] You are going to be blind, and will not see
the sun for a time." Suddenly a mist and darkness fell on him, and he went around seeking
someone to lead him by the hand.
12 Then the proconsul, seeing what happened, believed and was astonished at the
teaching about the Lord.[i]

Paul's Sermon in Antioch of Pisidia

13 Paul and his companions set sail from Paphos and came to Perga in Pamphylia. John,
however, left them and went back to Jerusalem.[j] 14 They continued their journey from
Perga and reached Antioch in Pisidia. On the
Sabbath day they went into the synagogue and
sat down.[k] 15 After the reading of the Law and
the Prophets, the leaders of the synagogue
sent word to them, saying, "Brothers, if you
have any message of encouragement for the
people, you can speak."[l]
16 Then Paul stood up and motioned with his
hand and said: "Men of Israel, and you who fear
God, listen![m] 17 The God of this people Israel
chose our ancestors, exalted the people during
their stay in the land of Egypt, and led them
out of it with a mighty[A] arm.[n] 18 And for about
40 years He put up with them[B] in the wilderness;[o] 19 then after destroying seven nations
in the land of Canaan,[p] He gave their land to
them as an inheritance. 20 This all took about
450 years. After this, He gave them judges until
Samuel the prophet.[q] 21 Then they asked for a
king, so God gave them Saul the son of Kish,
a man of the tribe of Benjamin, for 40 years.[r]
22 After removing him,[s] He raised up David
as their king and testified about him: **'I have**

[a] 13:5 Ac 9:20; 12:12
[b] 13:6 Mt 7:15; Ac 8:9
[c] 13:7 Ac 18:12; 19:38
[d] 13:8 Ex 7:11; 2Tm 3:8
[e] Ac 6:7; 8:9
[f] 13:10 Mt 13:38; Jn 8:44
[g] Hs 14:9; 2Pt 2:15
[h] 13:11 Ex 9:3; 1Sm 5:6-7; Ps 32:4; Heb 10:31
[i] 13:12 Ac 13:49; 15:35-36
[j] 13:13 Ac 12:12; 13:6; 15:38
[k] 13:14 Ac 9:20; 14:19,21; 16:3; 17:2; 18:4
[l] 13:15 Mk 5:22; Ac 15:21
[m] 13:16 Ac 10:2; 12:17
[n] 13:17 Ex 1:6; 6:6; Dt 7:6-8; Ac 7:17
[o] 13:18 Dt 1:31; Ac 7:36
[p] 13:19 Dt 7:1; Jos 14:1; 19:51; Ps 78:55; Ac 7:45
[q] 13:20 Jdg 2:16; 1Sm 3:20; Ac 3:24
[r] 13:21 1Sm 8:5; 9:1; 10:1
[s] 13:22 1Sm 15:23,26; 16:13

[A] 13:17 Lit *with an uplifted* [B] 13:18 Other mss read *He cared for them*

13:5 Paul began his preaching efforts at local **synagogues**, continuing his early pattern (see note at 9:19-20). **John** ("John Mark," 12:25) was with them for now (but see 13:13 and note).

13:6 Just as Peter had a confrontation with a magician (Simon; see note at 8:9), so Paul confronted a **sorcerer** on Cyprus. Parallels in Acts between the lives of Peter and Paul have been noted by scholars. These include healing a lame man (3:2-8; 14:8-10; cp. 5:15; 19:12), exorcism (5:16; 16:18), being miraculously freed from prison (12:6-11; 16:25-26), receipt of the Holy Spirit by the laying on of hands (8:17; 19:6), and raising the dead (9:36-41; 20:9-12).

13:7 A **proconsul** governed a Roman province. Archaeology has turned up evidence for many of the proconsuls of Cyprus. At least one inscription bears the name "Paulus," but he is too late to be **Sergius Paulus**.

13:8 The **sorcerer** Bar-Jesus (v. 6) is here called **Elymas**. Possibly "Elymas" is a Semitic word, as is Bar-Jesus, and "sorcerer" is its translation. In any case, true to his demonic influence, Elymas tried to keep Sergius Paulus from embracing the gospel.

13:9 From this point on in the book of Acts, Saul is referred to as **Paul** (except when he recounted his conversion experience in chaps. 22 and 26). Perhaps the switch in preference is because his missionary ventures moved him outside of a more distinctly Jewish context and into the larger Greco-Roman world. Paul was the Roman version of his name.

13:10-11 Paul called down a punishment of blindness on Elymas **for a time**. Hence the judgment was not permanent, giving Elymas the chance to repent and believe.

13:12 The signs normally associated with conversion in Acts (baptism, reception of the Spirit) do not appear in this account of Sergius Paulus's conversion. Possibly Luke just abbreviated his account, but it is also possible that Paulus's belief amounted to nothing more than his being **astonished at the teaching** and the blindness that befell Elymas.

13:13 John Mark (son of Mary, 12:12) **left them** at **Perga** and went back to **Jerusalem**. No reason is given for his leaving, but it must have seemed unwarranted to Paul, for on the second missionary journey Barnabas suggested that they take John along, but Paul refused, pointing out that John had previously abandoned them (15:37-38).

13:14 There were some 16 cities named **Antioch** in this era, and so Luke says **in Pisidia** to specify which "Antioch" is in view. This Antioch was technically just across the border in Phrygia rather than Pisidia, but ancient readers would have known this.

13:14-15 Paul continued his pattern of visiting the local Jewish **synagogue** on the Sabbath. He was invited to bring a **message of encouragement** largely due to the fact that opposition among unbelieving Jews had not yet been stirred up on that town (v. 45).

13:16-41 This is Paul's first public speech and his first missionary speech in the book of Acts. It is the longest speech by him in a Jewish synagogue, and it probably represents a style of speech he used on many such occasions. Paul recounted the history of Israel to place the coming of Jesus Christ in historical perspective. He made it clear that the coming of Jesus was the fulfillment of God's promise (v. 23), as His resurrection confirmed (v. 33).

13:22-23 According to the promise refers to 2Sm 7:12-16, where God promised through the prophet Nathan that He would raise up from David a descendant whose throne would be established "forever."

found David the son of Jesse, **a man loyal to Me,**[A,a] who will carry out all My will.'

[23]"From this man's descendants, according to the promise, God brought the Savior, Jesus,[B] to Israel.[b] [24]Before He came to public attention,[c] John had previously proclaimed a baptism of repentance to all the people of Israel.[c] [25]Then as John was completing his life's work, he said, 'Who do you think I am? I am not the One. But look! Someone is coming after me, and I am not worthy to untie the sandals on His feet.'[d]

[26]"Brothers, sons of Abraham's race, and those among you who fear God, the message of this salvation has been sent to us.[e] [27]For the residents of Jerusalem and their rulers, since they did not recognize Him or the voices of the prophets that are read every Sabbath, have fulfilled their words[D] by condemning Him.[f] [28]Though they found no grounds for the death penalty, they asked 'Pilate to have Him killed.[g] [29]When they had fulfilled all that had been written about Him, they took Him down from the tree and put Him in a tomb.[h] [30]But God raised Him from the dead,[i] [31]and He appeared for many days to those who came with Him from Galilee to Jerusalem, who are now His witnesses to the people.[j] [32]And we ourselves proclaim to you the good news of the promise that was made to our ancestors.[k] [33]God has fulfilled this for us, their children, by raising up Jesus, as it is written in the second Psalm:

> **You are My Son;**
> **today I have become Your Father.**[E,F,l]

[34]Since He raised Him from the dead, never to return to decay, He has spoken in this way, **I will grant you the faithful covenant blessings**[G]

made to David.[H,m] [35]Therefore He also says in another passage, **You will not allow Your Holy One to see decay.**[I,n] [36]For David, after serving his own generation in God's plan, fell 'asleep,[o] was buried with his fathers, and decayed.[p] [37]But the One God raised up did not decay. [38]Therefore, let it be known to you, brothers, that through this man forgiveness of sins is being proclaimed to you,[q] [39]and everyone who believes in Him is 'justified from everything that you could not be justified from through the law of Moses.[r] [40]So beware that what is said in the prophets does not happen to you:

[41]> **Look, you scoffers,**
> **marvel and vanish away,**
> **because I am doing a work**
> **in your days,**
> **a work that you will never believe,**
> **even if someone were to explain it**
> **to you.**"[J,s]

Paul and Barnabas in Antioch

[42]As they[K] were leaving, the people[L] begged that these matters be presented to them the following Sabbath. [43]After the synagogue had been dismissed, many of the Jews and devout 'proselytes followed Paul and Barnabas, who were speaking with them and persuading them to continue in the grace of God.[t]

[44]The following Sabbath almost the whole town assembled to hear the message of the Lord.[M] [45]But when the Jews saw the crowds, they were filled with jealousy and began to oppose what Paul was saying by insulting him.[u]

[46]Then Paul and Barnabas boldly said: "It was necessary that God's message be spoken to you first. But since you reject it and consider yourselves unworthy of eternal life, we

---

Cross references (center column):

[a]13:22 1Sm 13:14; Ps 89:20
[b]13:23 Ps 132:1; Mt 1:1; Lk 2:11; Ac 13:32
[c]13:24 Mt 3:1; Mk 1:4; Lk 3:3; Ac 1:22; 19:4
[d]13:25 Mt 3:11; Mk 1:7; Lk 3:16; Jn 1:20,27; Ac 20:24
[e]13:26 Ac 4:12; 5:20
[f]13:27 Lk 24:27; Ac 3:17
[g]13:28 Mt 27:22-23; Ac 3:14
[h]13:29 Mt 27:59; Lk 23:53; Ac 5:30
[i]13:30 Mt 28:6; Ac 2:24
[j]13:31 Mt 28:16; Lk 24:48; Ac 1:3
[k]13:32 Ac 5:42; 26:6; Rm 4:13; 9:4
[l]13:33 Ps 2:7; Heb 1:5; 5:5
[m]13:34 Is 55:3; Ac 13:30,37
[n]13:35 Ps 16:10; Ac 2:27
[o]13:36 Ac 7:60; 1Co 11:30; 15:6,18,20,51; 1Th 4:13-15
[p]1Kg 2:10; Ac 2:29; 13:22; 20:27
[q]13:38 Lk 24:47; Ac 2:38
[r]13:39 Rm 3:28; 10:4
[s]13:41 Is 29:14; Hab 1:5
[t]13:43 Ac 11:23; 14:22
[u]13:45 Ac 18:6; 1Th 2:16; 1Pt 4:4; Jd 10

A13:22 1Sm 13:14; Ps 89:20   **B**13:23 Other mss read *brought salvation*   **C**13:24 Lit *Before the face of His entrance*   **D**13:27 Lit *fulfilled them*   **E**13:33 Or *I have begotten You*   **F**13:33 Ps 2:7   **G**13:34 Lit *faithful holy things*   **H**13:34 Is 55:3   **I**13:35 Ps 16:10   **J**13:41 Hab 1:5   **K**13:42 Paul and Barnabas   **L**13:42 Other mss read *they were leaving the synagogue of the Jews, the Gentiles*   **M**13:44 Other mss read *of God*

13:27 Though the **prophets** were read in synagogues **every Sabbath**, those in Jerusalem did not recognize that these words were fulfilled in Jesus. They instead condemned Him, their only hope.

13:30-31 The resurrection of Jesus was confirmed by **witnesses** who had followed Him **from Galilee to Jerusalem.** Luke frequently emphasizes the role of eyewitnesses (1:3; Lk 1:1-4).

13:33 Jesus' resurrection confirmed that God had fulfilled His promise (citing Ps 2:7).

13:34-35 Others who had been raised from the dead would **return to decay**, for they were still subject to death. Not Jesus. He destroyed "the one holding the power of death" (Heb 2:14).

13:38-39 Through Jesus is offered **forgiveness of sins**, something **the law of Moses** can never accomplish (Rm 3:20).

13:41 Paul cited Hab 1:5 as a fitting conclusion to his speech. This passage from the prophet referred to the work that God was doing and recognized that some people would scoff and refuse to believe what God was doing, even if it was explained to them.

13:42-43 Whether due to the speech's novelty or their genuine spiritual hunger, the people wanted to hear more. It was probably in the "downtime" outside the synagogues, in small groups or individual meetings, that Paul and Barnabas accomplished their most effective teaching.

13:44-45 Keen interest sprang up over the gospel message everywhere Paul and Barnabas went, whether for or against. Jesus foretold the opposition the evangelists would face (Mk 13:13).

13:46-47 The NT consistently says the gospel message came first to the Jews (e.g., Mk 7:27), though the Gentiles were

now turn to the Gentiles!ᵃ ⁴⁷For this is what the Lord has commanded us:

> **I have made you
> a light for the Gentiles
> to bring salvation
> to the ends**ᴬ **of the earth."**ᴮ,ᵇ

⁴⁸When the Gentiles heard this, they rejoiced and glorified the message of the Lord, and all who had been appointed to eternal life believed. ⁴⁹So the message of the Lord spread through the whole region. ⁵⁰But the Jews incited the prominent women, who worshiped God, and the leading men of the city. They stirred up persecution against Paul and Barnabas and expelled them from their district.ᶜ ⁵¹But they shook the dust off their feetᵈ against themᵉ and went to Iconium. ⁵²And the disciples were filled with joy and the Holy Spirit.ᶠ

Growth and Persecution in Iconium

14 The same thing happened in Iconium; they entered the Jewish •synagogue and spoke in such a way that a great number of both Jews and Greeks believed.ᵍ ²But the Jews who refused to believe stirred up and poisoned the minds of the Gentiles against the brothers.ʰ ³So they stayed there for some time and spoke boldly in reliance on the Lord, who testified to the message of His grace by granting that signs and wonders be performed through them.ⁱ ⁴But the people of the city were divided, some

siding with the Jews and some with the apostles.ʲ ⁵When an attempt was made by both the Gentiles and Jews, with their rulers, to assault and stone them, ⁶they found out about it and fled to the Lycaonian towns called Lystra and Derbe, and to the surrounding countryside.ᵏ ⁷And there they kept evangelizing.ˡ

Mistaken for Gods in Lystra

⁸In Lystra a man without strength in his feet, lame from birth,ᶜ and who had never walked, sat ⁹and heard Paul speaking. After observing him closely and seeing that he had faith to be healed, ¹⁰Paul said in a loud voice, "Stand upright on your feet!" And he jumped up and started to walk around.ᵐ

¹¹When the crowds saw what Paul had done, they raised their voices, saying in the Lycaonian language, "The gods have come down to us in the form of men!"ⁿ ¹²And they started to call Barnabas, Zeus, and Paul, Hermes, because he was the main speaker. ¹³Then the priest of Zeus, whose temple was just outside the town, brought oxen and garlands to the gates. He, with the crowds, intended to offer sacrifice.

¹⁴The apostles Barnabas and Paul tore their robes when they heard this and rushed into the crowd, shouting:ᵒ ¹⁵"Men! Why are you doing these things? We are men also, with the same nature as you, and we are proclaiming good news to you, that you should turn from these worthless thingsᵖ to the living God, **who**

ᵃ13:46 Mt 21:43; Ac 3:26; 18:6; 22:21; 28:28
ᵇ13:47 Is 42:6; 49:6; Lk 2:32
ᶜ13:50 Ac 14:2,19; 2Tm 3:11
ᵈ13:51 Mt 10:14; Mk 6:11; Lk 9:5; Ac 18:6
ᵉAc 14:1,19,21; 16:2; 2Tm 3:11
ᶠ13:52 Mt 5:12; Jn 16:22; Ac 2:4
ᵍ14:1 Ac 13:5,51; 14:19
ʰ14:2 Jn 3:36; Ac 13:50
ⁱ14:3 Mk 16:20; Jn 4:48; Ac 4:29; 20:32; Heb 2:4
ʲ14:4 Ac 17:4-5; 19:9; 28:24
ᵏ14:6 Mt 10:23; 2Tm 3:11
ˡ14:7 Ac 14:15,21; 16:10
ᵐ14:8-10 Mk 6:56; Php 2:12
ⁿ14:11 Ac 8:10; 28:6
ᵒ14:14 Mt 26:65; Mk 14:63
ᵖ14:15 1Sm 12:21; 1Co 8:4; 1Th 1:9

ᴬ13:47 Lit *the end*   ᴮ13:47 Is 49:6   ᶜ14:8 Lit *from his mother's womb*

---

anticipated as eventual recipients. Acts shows the same pattern. Early in their missions work, Paul and Barnabas recognized that their duty was to bring the good news to the Jews **first**. But Jewish rejection of this message warranted their taking it to the **Gentiles**.

13:48 This verse expresses one of the great enigmatic truths of Scripture: **all who had been appointed to eternal life believed**. This touches both on God's election ("appointed") and the human responsibility to choose ("believed").

13:49 The whole region was predominantly Gentile. Thus those who were historically "outside" God's people were coming to overshadow and redefine God's people.

13:50 Seeing that the gospel was gaining wide acceptance, the Jewish leaders incited both **men** and **women** of status to reject Barnabas and Paul. This was a familiar tactic (Mt 27:20).

13:51 They shook the dust off their feet, obeying Jesus' command to His disciples (Lk 10:11).

13:52 Joy is the outward expression of the work of the **Holy Spirit** within a believer.

14:1 The familiar pattern of evangelization took place in **Iconium**: Barnabas and Paul began in the **synagogue**. A **great number** of **Jews** and **Greeks believed**. The Greeks were likely God-fearers (10:2).

14:2-6 Paul and Barnabas ministered **boldly** until they dis-

covered that **both the Gentiles and Jews** had formed a plot to **stone them**. They left Iconium more from prudence than fear of risk.

14:8-13 Here is another test of what motivated the apostles. The town was set to deify **Paul** and **Barnabas** because of the healing of the man **lame from birth**. Lystra apparently shared in the region's mythological tradition that said the Greek gods **Zeus** and **Hermes** (their Roman counterparts were Jupiter and Mercury) had once visited earth. The city had ongoing devotion to these gods. It is not clear why Barnabas was equated with Zeus and Paul with Hermes. Possibly Paul, who served as the major speaker, was equated with Hermes because Hermes was the messenger god. Another possibility is that Barnabas may have been a more imposing figure than Paul (see 2Co 10:10), and thus was equated with Zeus, leader of the Greek pantheon. In any event, how would they respond to such ego-feeding praise?

14:14 That the apostles **tore their robes** indicates not just refusal to be worshiped as gods, but abject horror at the idea. Did they preach Christ out of selfish motives? Obviously not.

14:15-18 This speech, delivered by both Barnabas and Paul to a pagan audience (rather than to Jews or God-fearers), is Paul's second missionary speech in Acts. It drew upon natural theology, which is knowledge of God that can be derived from creation. This approach was appropriate for a group of pagans who thought of their gods as part of nature. Paul also used this approach in his Areopagus speech

made the heaven, the earth, the sea, and ev-erything in them.[A,a] [16] In past generations He allowed all the nations[b] to go their own way, [17] although He did not leave Himself without a witness,[c] since He did what is good by giv-ing you rain from heaven and fruitful seasons[d] and satisfying your[B] hearts with food and hap-piness." [18] Even though they said these things, they barely stopped the crowds from sacrific-ing to them.

[19] Then some Jews came from Antioch and Iconium, and when they had won over the crowds and stoned Paul, they dragged him out of the city, thinking he was dead.[e] [20] After the disciples surrounded him, he got up and went into the town. The next day he left with Barnabas for Derbe.[f]

Church Planting

[21] After they had evangelized that town and made many disciples, they returned to Lystra, to Iconium, and to Antioch,[g] [22] strengthening the[c] disciples by encouraging them to con-tinue in the faith[h] and by telling them, "It is necessary to pass through many troubles[i] on our way into the kingdom of God."

[23] When they had appointed elders[j] in every church and prayed with fasting, they com-mitted them to the Lord in whom they had

believed. [24] Then they passed through Pisidia and came to Pamphylia. [25] After they spoke the message in Perga, they went down to At-talia. [26] From there they sailed back to Antioch where they had been entrusted to the grace of God for the work they had now completed.[k] [27] After they arrived and gathered the church together, they reported everything God had done with them[l] and that He had opened the door[m] of faith to the Gentiles. [28] And they spent a considerable time[D] with the disciples.

Dispute in Antioch

15 Some men[n] came down from Judea and began to teach the brothers: "Unless you are circumcised[o] according to the custom prescribed by Moses,[p] you cannot be saved!" [2] But after Paul and Barnabas had engaged them in serious argument and debate, the church arranged for Paul and Barnabas and some others of them to go up to the apostles and elders in Jerusalem concerning this con-troversy.[q] [3] When they had been sent on their way by the church,[r] they passed through both Phoenicia and Samaria, explaining in detail the conversion of the Gentiles, and they cre-ated great joy among all the brothers. [4] When they arrived at Jerusalem, they were

[a]14:15 Gn 1:1; Ex 20:11; Ps 146:6; Jr 14:22; Rv 14:7
[b]14:16 Ps 81:2; Mc 4:5; Ac 17:30; 1Pt 4:3
[c]14:17 Ac 17:26-27; Rm 1:19-20
[d]Lv 26:4; Dt 11:14; 28:12; Jb 5:10; Ps 65:10; 147:8; Ezk 34:26; Jl 2:23
[e]14:19 Ac 13:45,51; 2Co 11:25; 2Tm 3:11
[f]14:20 Ac 11:26; 14:22,28
[g]14:21 Mt 28:19; Ac 13:51
[h]14:22 Ac 11:23; 13:43
[i]Lk 22:48; Jn 15:20; 16:33; Ac 9:16; Rm 8:17; 1Th 3:3; 2Tm 3:12
[j]14:23 Ac 11:30; 13:3; 20:32; Ti 1:5
[k]14:26 Ac 11:19; 13:3
[l]14:27 Ac 15:12; 21:19
[m]1Co 16:9; 2Co 2:12; Col 4:3; Rv 3:8
[n]15:1 Ac 15:24; Gl 2:12
[o]Ac 15:5; 16:3; 21:21; 1Co 7:18; Gl 5:2
[p]Lv 12:3; Ac 6:14
[q]15:2 Ac 11:30; 16:4; Gl 2:1-2
[r]15:3 Ac 11:18; 21:5; Rm 15:24; 1Co 16:6,11; 2Co 1:16; Ti 3:13; 3Jn 6

[A]14:15 Ex 20:11; Ps 146:6   [B]14:17 Other mss read *our*   [C]14:22 Lit *the souls of the*   [D]14:28 Or *spent no little time*

(17:16-32) with an audience of pagan philosophers, and in Rm 1:18-32.

14:15 Paul and Barnabas cited Ex 20:11 and Ps 146:6 about God creating **heaven . . . earth**, the **sea**, and **everything in them**. This placed the natural order within the realm of God's creative power.

14:17 God's constant witness occurs in the working of na-ture, including the rain cycle, weather, and the production of **food**.

14:19 Having refused the people's worship, the apostles soon tasted their wrath instead. Agitators traveled from **An-tioch** (about 100 miles away) and **Iconium** to catalyze the about-face at Lystra. So seriously did unbelieving Jews take the threat from Christian growth that they followed Paul from town to town, seeking to thwart his missions work (see note at 17:13). In this case, they **stoned Paul** to death. Or so they believed.

14:20 Did Paul literally rise from the dead? Probably not, since Luke does not explicitly say so. The mob apparently jumped to conclusions once Paul fell under the hail of stones (v. 19). Paul recovered and reentered Lystra, presumably without being spotted. He left the next day but returned to Lystra soon afterward (v. 21). This was likely made possible by the Jews from Antioch and Iconium returning home.

14:21-22 After evangelizing Derbe (v. 20), Paul and Barnabas began their return journey to their home base of Antioch of Syria, stopping by each of the towns they had visited along the way (**Lystra . . . Iconium**, and **Antioch** of Pisidia). Their purpose was to strengthen the hearts of **the disciples** and be sure that they understood that **many troubles** come to those

who seek **the kingdom of God**. Paul himself bore witness to this truth (2Co 11:23-27). All the churches Paul and Barna-bas founded on this first missionary journey were in the Ro-man province of Galatia. These were probably the churches to whom Paul addressed his letter to the Galatians.

14:23 **Elders** in these early Pauline churches were appar-ently **appointed** by Paul and Barnabas to establish the first stages of church leadership (see note at 11:30). These prac-ticed official oversight and responsibility within the church (see note at 20:17).

15:1 After arriving back in Antioch, Paul and Barnabas re-ported on what God had done in Asia on the first missionary journey, especially the evangelizing of the Gentiles (14:27). **Some men came down from Judea** and attempted to mod-ify Paul's approach to non-Jews. By insisting that Gentiles be circumcised, they made observance of Jewish ritual a requirement for salvation.

15:2 Unable to reach an agreement, Paul and Barnabas were sent to the **elders in Jerusalem**, a sign that the Je-rusalem church, with its **apostles** and elders, was still the center of the Christian movement. If Paul failed to convince the Lord's apostles, the church would not support him.

15:3 On the way to Jerusalem, Paul and Barnabas wisely shared details about **the conversion of the Gentiles** with believers in **Phoenicia and Samaria**, creating **great joy** among the brothers.

15:4-5 Though the **Pharisees** (including Paul) had opposed Jesus bitterly, some had become **believers** (6:7). In this case a group of them failed to understand the freedoms Christ had won for believers.

welcomed by the church, the apostles, and the elders, and they reported all that God had done with them.ᵃ ⁵But some of the believers from the party of the •Pharisees stood up and said, "It is necessary to circumcise them and to command them to keep the law of Moses!"

The Jerusalem Council

⁶Then the apostles and the elders assembled to consider this matter. ⁷After there had been much debate, Peter stood up and said to them: "Brothers, you are aware that in the early days God made a choice among you,ᴬ that by my mouth the Gentiles would hear the gospel message and believe. ⁸And God, who knows the heart, testified to them by givingᴮ the Holy Spirit, just as He also did to us.ᵇ ⁹He made no distinction between us and them,ᶜ cleansing their hearts by faith.ᵈ ¹⁰Now then, why are you testing God by putting a yoke on the disciples' necksᵉ that neither our ancestors nor we have been able to bear? ¹¹On the contrary, we believe we are saved through the graceᶠ of the Lord Jesus in the same way they are."

¹²Then the whole assembly fell silent and listened to Barnabas and Paul describing all the signs and wonders God had done through them among the Gentiles.ᵍ ¹³After they stopped speaking, James responded: "Brothers, listen to me! ¹⁴Simeonᶜ has reported how God first intervened to take from the Gentiles a people for His name.ʰ ¹⁵And the words of the prophets agree with this, as it is written:

¹⁶ **After these things I will return
    and rebuild David's fallen tent.
    I will rebuild its ruins
    and set it up again,**
¹⁷ **so the rest of humanity
    may seek the Lord—
    even all the Gentiles
    who are called by My name,
    declares the Lord who does
        these things,**
¹⁸ **known from long ago.**ᴰ·ᴱ·ⁱ

¹⁹Therefore, in my judgment, we should not cause difficulties for those among the Gentiles who turn to God, ²⁰but instead we should write to them to abstain from things polluted by idols, from sexual immorality,ʲ from eating anything that has been strangled, and from blood. ²¹For since ancient times, Moses has had those who proclaim him in every city, and every Sabbath day he is read aloud in the •synagogues."ᵏ

The Letter to the Gentile Believers

²²Then the apostles and the elders, with the whole church, decided to select men who were among them and to send them to Antioch with Paul and Barnabas: Judas, called Barsabbas, and Silas,ˡ both leading men among the

ᵃ15:4 Ac 14:27; 15:12   ᵇ15:8 Ac 1:24; 10:44,47   ᶜ15:9 Ac 10:28, 34; 11:12   ᵈAc 10:43; 1Pt 1:22   ᵉ15:10 Mt 23:4; Gl 5:1   ᶠ15:11 Rm 3:24; Eph 2:5-8; Ti 2:11   ᵍ15:12 Jn 4:48; Ac 14:27; 15:4   ʰ15:13-14 Ac 12:17; 15:7   ⁱ15:16-18 Is 45:21; Jr 14:9; Dn 9:19; Am 9:11-12   ʲ15:20 1Co 8:7,13; 10:7-8,14-28; Rv 2:14,20   ᵏ15:21 Ac 13:15; 2Co 3:14   ˡ15:22 Ac 1:23; 15:2; 1Pt 5:12

ᴬ15:7 Other mss read us   ᴮ15:8 Other mss add them   ᶜ15:14 Simon (Peter)   ᴰ15:17-18 Other mss read says the Lord who does all these things. Known to God from long ago are all His works.   ᴱ15:16-18 Am 9:11-12; Is 45:21

15:6 The central issue of the Jerusalem Council was whether Gentile Christians had to be circumcised and keep the law of Moses. Given the Jewish roots of Christianity, it is understandable that the church had to grapple with this issue in an era of transition.

15:7-9 Peter reminded his hearers of four things: (1) God had chosen him to proclaim the gospel to the Gentiles (10:1-43). (2) The Gentiles believed Peter's message. (3) When the Gentiles believed, they received the Holy Spirit (10:44-46). (4) The pattern of Gentile conversion was the same as for Jewish believers. God was making no ethnic distinctions in building the church.

15:10 In light of the above points (see note at vv. 7-9), the believers from the "party of the Pharisees" (v. 5) were **testing God** and putting on Gentile converts a burden that neither Jewish **ancestors** nor contemporary Jews were **able to bear**.

15:11 Having mentioned the inability of Jews and Gentiles alike to fulfill the law perfectly, Peter insisted that salvation is **through the grace of the Lord Jesus**, which means it is a free gift. Rituals such as circumcision cannot save anyone.

15:14 As leader of the Jerusalem church, James, the brother of Jesus, assessed the claims and counterclaims. He began his address by recalling how **Simeon** (Peter) had reported God's plan to **take from the Gentiles**, which had occasioned controversy of its own (11:2ff).

15:15-18 James cited the prophets Amos (Am 9:11-12) and Isaiah (Is 45:21) to show that God had long ago foretold that Gentiles would be called by His name.

15:19 James's position as the first among equals in the Jerusalem church is seen in his summarizing conclusion to the debate. In his **judgment**, Jewish believers **should not cause difficulties** for those turning to God from **among the Gentiles**.

15:20 Despite the common basis of salvation for Jews and Gentiles, a number of restrictions were required (v. 29; 21:25). Some scholars think these may have been introduced as a way for Jews and Gentiles within the church to have a common basis for contact. But it is more likely that these were designed to elevate the moral standards of the Gentiles by prohibiting them from engaging in a number of practices that were associated with pagan temple rites such as animal sacrifice, **sexual immorality**, and idolatry.

15:21 James's reason for invoking **Moses** and the widespread proclamation of the law is not entirely clear. He may have meant that Jewish people who spread throughout the world via the Diaspora had made Moses' law known among Gentiles through their public reading of Scripture. Alternatively, he may have been saying that the standards he demanded of Gentiles in verse 20 reflected universal moral laws that were enshrined in the law of Moses.

15:22-23a **Judas** and **Silas**, both **leading men among the brothers** in Jerusalem, accompanied Paul and Barnabas

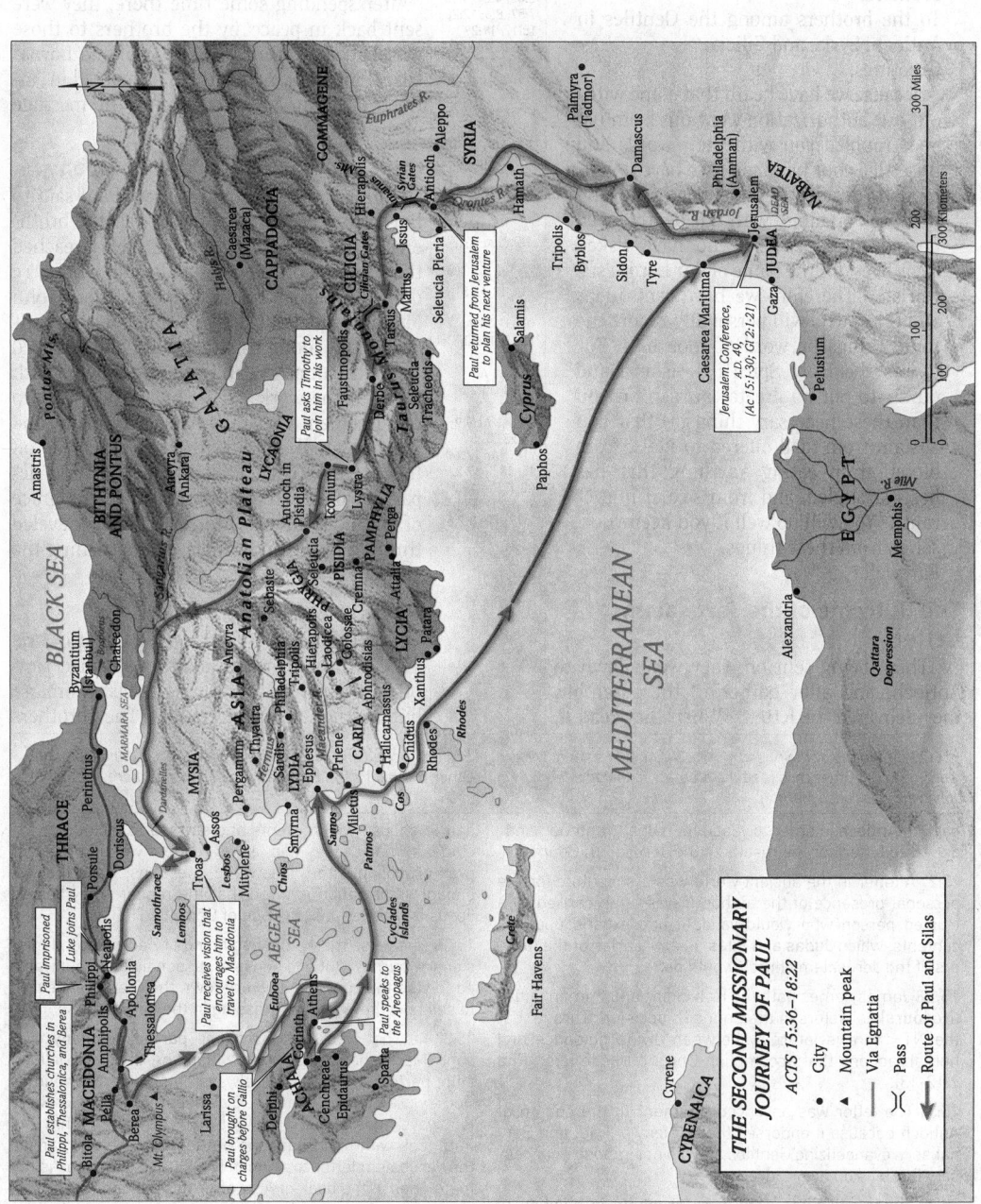

brothers. [23]They wrote this letter to be delivered by them:[A]

From the apostles and the elders, your brothers,
To the brothers among the Gentiles in Antioch, Syria, and Cilicia:[a]
Greetings.
[24]Because we have heard that some without our authorization went out from us[b] and troubled you with their words and unsettled your hearts,[B,c] [25]we have unanimously[d] decided to select men and send them to you along with our dearly loved Barnabas and Paul, [26]who have risked their lives[e] for the name of our Lord Jesus Christ. [27]Therefore we have sent Judas and Silas, who will personally report the same things by word of mouth.[C] [28]For it was the Holy Spirit's decision—and ours—to put no greater burden on you than these necessary things:[f] [29]that you abstain from food offered to idols, from blood, from eating anything that has been strangled, and from sexual immorality.[g] You will do well if you keep yourselves from these things.
Farewell.

The Outcome of the Jerusalem Letter

[30]Then, being sent off, they went down to Antioch, and after gathering the assembly, they delivered the letter. [31]When they read it, they rejoiced because of its encouragement. [32]Both Judas and Silas, who were also prophets themselves, encouraged the *brothers and strengthened them with a long message.[h] [33]After spending some time there, they were sent back in peace[i] by the brothers to those who had sent them.[D,E] [35]But Paul and Barnabas, along with many others, remained in Antioch teaching and proclaiming the message of the Lord.[j]

Paul and Barnabas Part Company

[36]After some time had passed, Paul said to Barnabas, "Let's go back and visit the brothers in every town[k] where we have preached the message of the Lord and see how they're doing." [37]Barnabas wanted to take along John Mark.[F] [38]But Paul did not think it appropriate to take along this man who had deserted them in Pamphylia and had not gone on with them to the work. [39]There was such a sharp disagreement that they parted company, and Barnabas took Mark[l] with him and sailed off to Cyprus. [40]Then Paul chose Silas and departed, after being commended to the grace of the Lord by the brothers.[m] [41]He traveled through Syria[n] and Cilicia, strengthening the churches.

Paul Selects Timothy

16 Then he went on to Derbe and Lystra, where there was a disciple named Timothy,[o] the son of a believing Jewish woman,[p] but his father was a Greek. [2]The *brothers

Cross references (center column):
[a]15:23 Ac 15:1; 23:26; Jms 1:1
[b]15:24 Gl 2:4; 5:12; Ti 1:10
[c]Gl 1:7; 5:10
[d]15:25 Ac 1:14; 2:46; 4:24; 5:12; 7:57; 8:6; 12:20; 18:12; 19:29
[e]15:26 Ac 9:23-25; 14:19
[f]15:28 Ac 5:32; 15:8
[g]15:29 Ac 15:20; 21:25; Rv 2:14,20
[h]15:32 Ac 14:22; 15:1
[i]15:33 Mk 5:34; Ac 16:36; 1Co 16:11; Heb 11:31
[j]15:35 Ac 8:4; 13:1
[k]15:36 Ac 13:4,13-14,51; 14:6,24
[l]15:37-39 Ac 12:12; 13:13; Col 4:10
[m]15:40 Ac 11:23; 14:26; 15:22
[n]15:41 Ac 6:9; 15:23; 16:5
[o]16:1 Ac 17:14-15; 18:5; 19:22; 20:4; Rm 16:21; 1Co 4:17; Php 2:19; 1Th 3:2,6
[p]2Tm 1:5; 3:15

[A]15:23 Lit *Writing by their hand:*   [B]15:24 Other mss add *by saying, "Be circumcised and keep the law,"*   [C]15:27 Lit *things through word*   [D]15:33 Other mss read *the brothers to the apostles*   [E]15:33 Other mss add v. 34: *But Silas decided to stay there.*   [F]15:37 Lit *John who was called Mark*

---

back to **Antioch** in order to vouch (personally and via hand-delivered letter) for the results of the Jerusalem Council.

15:27 A letter in the ancient world was a substitute for the personal presence of the author. It was often carried by a trusted person who would validate and expand upon its contents, which **Judas and Silas** as emissaries of the leaders of the Jerusalem church would do.

15:28 James names both the Holy Spirit and human initiative (**ours**) as factors in the Council's decision. Throughout the NT, there is interplay between divine guidance and human actions that accomplish God's purpose (e.g., Php 2:12-13).

15:31 The letter was an **encouragement** to the church at Antioch because it endorsed the strategy of Paul and Barnabas in evangelizing Gentiles and did not impose unnecessary burdens on new converts.

15:32 **Judas** and **Silas**, who were **prophets** in addition to being leading figures from the Jerusalem church, **encouraged** and **strengthened** the believers in Antioch with a **long message** that Scripture nowhere records. We are reminded yet again that many great speeches and vital events went unreported by the Bible's authors (Jn 20:30; see note at Jn 21:25). Under the guidance of the Holy Spirit, each author

had to choose which events and sayings to include or exclude. In many cases this leaves readers wanting more or even grappling with unanswered questions. Nevertheless, enough information is given that the reader "may believe Jesus is the Messiah, the Son of God" (Jn 20:31).

15:36 This verse marks the beginning of Paul's second missionary journey. Out of a sense of responsibility, Paul wanted to **visit** the converts in **every town** they had evangelized to see how they were progressing in the faith.

15:37-40 That Paul and Barnabas **parted company** over John Mark shows that even within the apostolic fellowship, perfect unity was not always obtainable. Sometimes God's workers have to agree to go separate ways, but there is always hope for reunion (Col 4:10; 2Tm 4:11; Phm 24). Paul took with him **Silas**, one of the men who had carried the Jerusalem letter to Antioch (vv. 23-34). Barnabas is not mentioned in the book of Acts after this incident.

15:41 Rather than going to Cyprus to strengthen the believers there, Paul and Silas went to **Syria** and the region of **Cilicia**, entering the province of Asia Minor.

16:1-3 Paul and Silas continued to retrace the first missionary journey by reentering Galatia. At Lystra, Paul invited a young **disciple named Timothy**—son of a Jewish woman

at Lystra and Iconium spoke highly of him.[a]
[3]Paul wanted Timothy[A] to go with him, so he
took him and circumcised[b] him because of
the Jews who were in those places, since they
all knew that his father was a Greek. [4]As they
traveled through the towns, they delivered the
decisions reached by the apostles and elders
at Jerusalem for them to observe.[c] [5]So the
churches were strengthened in the faith and
increased in number daily.[d]

Evangelization of Europe

[6]They went through the region of Phrygia
and Galatia and were prevented by the Holy
Spirit from speaking the message in •Asia.[e]
[7]When they came to Mysia, they tried to go
into Bithynia, but the Spirit of Jesus[f] did not
allow them. [8]So, bypassing Mysia, they came
down to Troas.[g] [9]During the night a vision appeared to Paul: A Macedonian man was standing and pleading with him, "Cross over to
Macedonia and help us!"[h] [10]After[i] he had seen

the vision, we[B] immediately made efforts to
set out for Macedonia, concluding that God
had called us to evangelize them.

Lydia's Conversion

[11]Then, setting sail from Troas, we ran a
straight course to Samothrace, the next day
to Neapolis, [12]and from there to Philippi,[j] a
Roman colony, which is a leading city of that
district of Macedonia. We stayed in that city
for a number of days. [13]On the Sabbath day we
went outside the city gate by the river, where
we thought there was a place of prayer. We sat
down and spoke to the women gathered there.
[14]A woman named Lydia, a dealer in purple
cloth from the city of Thyatira, who worshiped
God, was listening. The Lord opened her heart
to pay attention to what was spoken by Paul.[k]
[15]After she and her household were baptized,
she urged us, "If you consider me a believer
in the Lord, come and stay at my house."[l] And
she persuaded us.

Cross-references

[a]16:2 Ac 13:51; 16:40 [b]16:3 Gl 2:3 [c]16:4 Ac 11:30; 15:2,28 [d]16:5 Ac 2:47; 9:31; 15:41 [e]16:6 Ac 2:9; 18:23; Gl 1:2; 3:1 [f]16:7 Ac 8:29; Rm 8:9; Gl 4:6; Php 1:19; 1Pt 1:11 [g]16:8 Ac 16:11; 20:5-6; 2Co 2:12; 2Tm 4:13 [h]16:9 Ac 9:10; 20:1,3 [i]16:10-17 Ac 20:5-15; 21:1-18; 27:1-28:16 [j]16:12 Ac 20:6; Php 1:1; 1Th 2:2 [k]16:14 Lk 24:45; Ac 18:7; Rv 1:11 [l]16:15 Gn 19:3; Lk 24:29; Ac 11:14

[A]16:3 Lit wanted this one   [B]16:10 The use of we in this passage probably indicates that the author Luke is joining Paul's missionary team here.

and Greek man—to join him. Paul **circumcised** Timothy not because he was caving in to pressure from "believers from the party of the Pharisees" (15:5), but rather to show respect for Jewish law and identity given the fact that Timothy was half-Jewish. If Timothy had remained uncircumcised, it would seem to many Jews that he had rejected not just Mosaic law but also Jewish ethnicity. Paul's continuing mentorship of Timothy throughout his ministry resulted in, among other things, the writing of two NT letters for his instruction (see 1Tm and 2Tm).

16:4 Besides evangelizing, Paul and his ministry partners conveyed the **decisions** of the **apostles and elders** in Jerusalem about circumcision and Gentile converts (see note at 15:19). Paul wanted to make clear that Gentiles could believe in Jesus without adhering to Jewish rites.

16:5 No doubt one of the reasons **the churches** in this Gentile-dominated region were **strengthened in the faith** and grew **in number daily** was that the Jerusalem Council had decided to minimize the burden imposed on Gentile believers (see notes at 15:19 and 15:20).

16:6-8 Paul and his companions passed through the region of **Galatia** (probably visiting Iconium and Antioch), and were **prevented by the Holy Spirit** from preaching **the message in Asia**. They were also prevented by the **Spirit of Jesus** (i.e., Holy Spirit) from turning north **into Bithynia**. So they passed through **Mysia** and arrived at the coastal city of **Troas** in Asia. Luke did not indicate why the Spirit constrained Paul's plans or by what method He made known the restrictions. The reader is left with questions, but see verse 9 and note; also see note at 15:32.

16:9 God gave Paul a **vision** to communicate His will for the direction his ministry should take, just as He had done with Peter (chap. 10). Paul saw a **Macedonian** man plead with him to cross over the Aegean Sea to Europe and **help** them. Thus it seems Paul was restricted from preaching in other places because God planned for him to "evangelize" (v. 10) in Macedonia.

16:10 This is the beginning of the first "we" section in the book of Acts. It extends until verse 17. The "we" passages are 16:10-17; 20:5-15; 21:1-18; 27:1-37; 28:1-16. The **we** likely indicates that Luke joined Paul's journey at these points. When connected together, the "we" passages form a continuous geographically joined narrative. This indicates a single unified source for these narratives, most likely Luke's own memory or the notes he took.

16:12 Philippi was a leading city of **Macedonia** but not the capital (Thessalonica). It was a **Roman colony** where a number of military veterans lived after completing their service. As a result, Roman law was in effect in Philippi.

16:13 The **place of prayer** refers to the place where Jews of the city gathered. Philippi apparently did not have a synagogue, since only **women** and no men are mentioned. The establishment of a synagogue required the participation of at least ten Jewish men. Paul and his companions met with this group of women on the **Sabbath**, following the pattern of evangelization he had practiced on his first missionary journey.

16:14 The name **Lydia** may have been a personal name or it could merely indicate that this woman was from the city of Lydia. She is the only woman named in this passage (vv. 11-14). She was likely a prominent woman since Luke singled her out for her responsiveness to Paul's message. The **purple cloth** she sold had important uses in the Roman Empire. Luke combined both human and divine initiative in the description of Lydia's response. The Lord **opened her heart**, but she paid **attention** to what Paul said.

16:15 Household baptism is mentioned several times in the book of Acts (vv. 31-34; 18:8; cp. 11:14). It is never stated who exactly was involved in such baptisms. If the leader of a household converted, perhaps others of the household (children, servants, spouse, etc.) were persuaded to respond in the same way. It is assumed on the basis of Lydia's response (16:14) and her question to Paul after her baptism (**if you consider me a believer in the Lord**) that her confession of faith preceded her baptism. This suggests that only

Paul and Silas in Prison

[16] Once, as we were on our way to prayer, a *slave girl met us who had a spirit of prediction.[A,a] She made a large profit for her owners by fortune-telling. [17] As she followed Paul and us she cried out, "These men, who are proclaiming to you[B] the way of salvation, are the slaves of the Most High God." [18] And she did this for many days.

But Paul was greatly aggravated and turning to the spirit, said, "I command you in the name of Jesus Christ to come out of her!" And it came out right away.[C,b]

[19] When her owners saw that their hope of profit was gone, they seized Paul and Silas[c] and dragged them into the marketplace to the authorities. [20] Bringing them before the chief magistrates, they said, "These men are seriously disturbing our city. They are Jews [21] and are promoting customs that are not legal for us as Romans to adopt or practice."[d]

[22] Then the mob joined in the attack against them, and the chief magistrates stripped off their clothes and ordered them to be beaten with rods.[e] [23] After they had inflicted many blows on them, they threw them in jail, ordering the jailer to keep them securely guarded. [24] Receiving such an order, he put them into

the inner prison and secured their feet in the stocks.[f]

A Midnight Deliverance

[25] About midnight Paul and Silas were praying and singing hymns to God, and the prisoners were listening to them. [26] Suddenly there was such a violent earthquake that the foundations of the jail were shaken, and immediately all the doors were opened, and everyone's chains came loose.[g] [27] When the jailer woke up and saw the doors of the prison open, he drew his sword and was going to kill himself, since he thought the prisoners had escaped.

[28] But Paul called out in a loud voice, "Don't harm yourself, because all of us are here!"

[29] Then the jailer called for lights, rushed in, and fell down trembling before Paul and Silas. [30] Then he escorted them out and said, "Sirs, what must I do to be saved?"[h]

[31] So they said, "Believe on the Lord Jesus, and you will be saved—you and your household."[i] [32] Then they spoke the message of the Lord to him along with everyone in his house. [33] He took them the same hour of the night and washed their wounds. Right away he and all his family were baptized. [34] He brought them into his house, set a meal before them,

a16:16 Lv 19:31; Dt 18:11; 1Sm 28:3,7
b16:17-18 Mk 5:7; 16:17
c16:19 Mt 10:18; Ac 8:3; 15:22; 17:6-8; 19:25-26; 21:30; Jms 2:6
d16:21 Est 3:8; Ac 16:12
e16:22 2Co 6:5; 11:25; 1Th 2:2
f16:24 Jb 13:27; 33:11; Jr 20:2-3; 29:26
g16:26 Ac 4:31; 5:19; 12:7,10
h16:30 Ac 2:37; 22:10
i16:31 Mk 16:16; Ac 11:14

A16:16 Or *a spirit by which she predicted the future*   B16:17 Other mss read *us*   C16:18 Lit *out this hour*

---

those of the household who were mature enough to make their own positive response to the gospel would have been baptized.

16:16 That the **slave girl** had a **spirit of prediction** implies demonic possession. The ancients were very interested in oracles and prophecies, hence the girl earned income for her owners.

16:17-18 Though the girl **cried out** truth about Paul and his companions, Paul **was greatly aggravated**. Luke does not say why, but presumably Paul was irritated at the wild and distracting manner in which the girl carried on. Her manner would repel rather than attract crowds.

16:19 Paul and Silas were arrested for cutting off the revenue from this girl's fortune-telling, not for a religious violation.

16:20-21 Paul and Silas were accused of causing civil disorder and **promoting customs** that were **not legal** among **Romans**. The practice of variant religion was not illegal in the Roman Empire, but any activity (religious or otherwise) that risked sparking civil unrest was frowned upon.

16:22-24 The chief magistrates acted rashly under the influence of **the mob**. Paul and Silas were **stripped . . . beaten**, and thrown into **jail** before the charges against them were investigated.

16:25 Rather than being depressed or plotting escape, **Paul and Silas** displayed confidence in what God had in store for them. This was a powerful testimony to the other **prisoners**.

16:26 Luke does not say so, but clearly the **violent earth-**

quake was an act of God in response to the prayers and praises of Paul and Silas. The jailer understood this (v. 29).

16:27 If prisoners escaped, their Roman guards or jailers were forced to serve their sentences. Believing his **prisoners had escaped**, the Philippian jailer preferred a quick death over imprisonment or execution.

16:29-30 The jailer **fell down trembling** because he realized the earthquake was supernatural. This prompted him to ask the most important question in the book of Acts: **What must I do to be saved?** He was spared from death in the quake, spared from suicide by the discovery that the prisoners had not fled, and now wanted to be spared from God's future judgment.

16:31 Paul and Silas had a direct answer for his straightforward question: **Believe on the Lord Jesus, and you will be saved—you and your household**. On household baptism, see note at verse 15.

16:32 Paul's initial response to the jailer was succinct and to the point. That Paul then **spoke the message of the Lord** may indicate that he followed his initial answer, which was aimed at bringing the jailer to saving faith, with a more detailed explanation aimed at building the new disciple's understanding of God and the Christian life.

16:33 Baptism for the jailer and **all his family** followed almost immediately upon their profession of faith in the Lord. On household baptism, see note at verse 15.

16:34 The jailer's joy is palpable. What looked like a life-threatening disaster became the joyous beginning of his new life in Christ. He and his family became part of the growing church at Philippi, a church that was dear to Paul. When Paul later wrote that he thanked God every time he

and rejoiced because he had believed God with his entire household.[a]

An Official Apology

[35] When daylight came, the chief magistrates sent the police to say, "Release those men!"

[36] The jailer reported these words to Paul: "The magistrates have sent orders for you to be released. So come out now and go in peace."[b]

[37] But Paul said to them, "They beat us in public without a trial, although we are Roman citizens, and threw us in jail. And now are they going to smuggle us out secretly? Certainly not! On the contrary, let them come themselves and escort us out!"[c]

[38] Then the police reported these words to the magistrates. They were afraid when they heard that Paul and Silas were Roman citizens. [39] So they came and apologized to them, and escorting them out, they urged them to leave town. [40] After leaving the jail, they came to Lydia's house where they saw and encouraged the brothers, and departed.[d]

A Short Ministry in Thessalonica

17 Then they traveled through Amphipolis and Apollonia and came to Thessa-

lonica,[e] where there was a Jewish •synagogue. [2] As usual, Paul went to the synagogue, and on three Sabbath days reasoned with them from the Scriptures,[f] [3] explaining and showing that the •Messiah had to suffer and rise from the dead: "This Jesus I am proclaiming to you is the Messiah."[g] [4] Then some of them were persuaded and joined Paul and Silas, including a great number of God-fearing Greeks, as well as a number[A] of the leading women.[h]

Riot in the City

[5] But the Jews became jealous, and they brought together some scoundrels from the marketplace, formed a mob, and started a riot in the city. Attacking Jason's house, they searched for them to bring them out to the public assembly.[i] [6] When they did not find them, they dragged Jason and some of the •brothers before the city officials, shouting, "These men who have turned the world upside down have come here too, [7] and Jason has received them as guests! They are all acting contrary to Caesar's decrees,[j] saying that there is another king—Jesus!"[k] [8] The Jews stirred up the crowd and the city officials who heard these things. [9] So taking a security bond from Jason and the others, they released them.

A 17:4 Lit *as well as not a few*

Cross references

a 16:34 Ac 11:14; 16:15
b 16:36 Ac 15:33; 16:27
c 16:37 Ac 22:25-29
d 16:39-40 Mt 8:34; Ac 16:14
e 17:1 Ac 20:4; Php 4:16; 1Th 1:1; 2Tm 4:10
f 17:2 Ac 8:35; 9:20; 13:13-14
g 17:3 Lk 24:26; Jn 20:9; Ac 3:18; 9:22; 18:28
h 17:4 Jn 7:35; Ac 14:4; 15:22
i 17:5 Ac 17:13; Rm 16:21; 1Th 2:14-16
j 17:7 Lk 2:1; Rm 1:32; Eph 2:15
k Lk 23:2; Jn 19:12

---

remembered the Philippians, this man and his family may have come to mind (Php 1:3).

16:35 At dawn the **chief magistrates** ordered that Paul and Silas be released. Some scholars claim verse 35 would be a suitable continuation of verse 24, and that this and other "jailbreak" episodes are part of a body of mythical literature in which God rules over natural phenomena on behalf of His people. Hence they claim verses 25-34 are fictional additions. Among several problems with this conclusion are the following: First, it is possible that the magistrates ordered Paul and Silas released because they realized that they had overreacted in jailing them in the first place. Second, it is very likely that the magistrates experienced the earthquake and were told about the events at the jail, thus prompting them to fear God's judgment.

16:37 Paul knew the laws regulating punishment of Roman citizens. Having been illegally beaten and denied **trial**, he refused to be released and pretend nothing had happened. Paul's Roman citizenship is mentioned here for the first time in Acts (see 22:25-29; 23:27; 25:11). Roman citizens were exempt from certain kinds of punishment (e.g., crucifixion) and were entitled to due process prior to punishment. The question arises as to how Paul would have proven his citizenship. There probably was a register in Tarsus that recorded his citizenship, but citizens also often carried small wooden tablets (some of which have been found), something like a modern passport, that they used to prove their citizenship. Perhaps Paul carried such a document.

16:38 The fear of the magistrates is understandable. Philippi was a Roman colony that followed Roman law. Many people in the town would have known about the rights of a Roman citizen.

16:39 Though not obligated to do so, Paul and Silas chose to count the apology as amends for the wrongs they had suffered. Many times it is best for the Christian to forego demanding full justice.

17:1 The next major stop on this second missionary journey was **Thessalonica**, where once again Paul began by visiting the local **synagogue**. He did this for three weeks (v. 2).

17:2-3 These verses give us insight into what Paul did when he visited synagogues. He **reasoned . . . from the Scriptures**, identifying Jesus as **Messiah** and explaining the necessity of His death and resurrection. Among Jews, who revered the OT as God's Word, Paul used the Scriptures as the basis for his argumentation.

17:4-5 The conversion of **a great number of God-fearing Greeks** and **leading women** prompted jealousy among unbelieving **Jews**. Paul had encountered resistance before, but this was an orchestrated movement involving the roundup of **scoundrels from the marketplace**. Jason was apparently one of the Thessalonians who had become a believer. He had welcomed Paul into his home (v. 7), so the **mob** attacked his house.

17:6 The phrase **these men who have turned the world upside down** may indicate that the Christians were mistaken for Jewish nationalists who had caused riots throughout the Roman Empire, but more likely it is an exaggerated reference to the unrest caused from town to town by Jews who opposed the Christian message.

17:7 Declaring that there was another king besides Caesar was a serious crime in the Roman Empire. This same false charge was used to condemn Jesus before Pilate (Lk 23:2).

The Bereans Search the Scriptures

[10] As soon as it was night, the brothers sent Paul and Silas off to Berea.[a] On arrival, they went into the synagogue of the Jews. [11] The people here were more open-minded than those in Thessalonica, since they welcomed the message with eagerness and examined the Scriptures[b] daily to see if these things were so. [12] Consequently, many of them believed, including a number of the prominent Greek women as well as men. [13] But when the Jews from Thessalonica found out that God's message had been proclaimed by Paul at Berea, they came there too, agitating and disturbing[A] the crowds. [14] Then the brothers immediately sent Paul away to go to the sea, but Silas and Timothy[c] stayed on there. [15] Those who escorted Paul brought him as far as Athens, and after receiving instructions for Silas and Timothy to come to him as quickly as possible, they departed.[d]

Paul in Athens

[16] While Paul was waiting for them in Athens, his spirit was troubled within him when he saw that the city was full of idols. [17] So he reasoned in the synagogue with the Jews and with those who worshiped God and in the marketplace every day with those who happened to be there.[e] [18] Then also, some of the Epicurean and Stoic philosophers argued with him. Some said, "What is this pseudo-intellectual[B] trying to say?"

Others replied, "He seems to be a preacher of foreign deities"—because he was telling the good news about Jesus and the Resurrection.[C,f]

[19] They took him and brought him to the Areopagus,[D] and said, "May we learn about this new teaching you're speaking of?[g] [20] For what you say sounds strange to us, and we want to know what these ideas mean." [21] Now all the Athenians and the foreigners residing there spent their time on nothing else but telling or hearing something new.

The Areopagus Address

[22] Then Paul stood in the middle of the Areopagus and said: "Men of Athens! I see that you are extremely religious in every respect. [23] For as I was passing through and observing the objects of your worship, I even found an altar on which was inscribed:

TO AN UNKNOWN GOD.

Therefore, what you worship in ignorance, this I proclaim to you. [24] The God who made the world and everything in it[h]—He is Lord of

---

Cross references:
[a] 17:10 Ac 17:13-14; 20:4
[b] 17:11 Is 34:16; Lk 16:29; Jn 5:39
[c] 17:14 Mt 10:23; Ac 15:22; 16:1
[d] 17:15 Ac 18:1,5; 1Th 3:1
[e] 17:16-17 Ac 9:20; 2Pt 2:8
[f] 17:18 Ac 4:2; 17:31-32
[g] 17:19 Mk 1:27; Ac 17:22
[h] 17:24 Is 42:5; Ac 14:15

A 17:13 Other mss omit *and disturbing*   B 17:18 Lit *this seed picker*; = one who picks up scraps   C 17:18 = Gk *Anastasis*   D 17:19 Or *Mars Hill*, the oldest and most famous court in Athens with jurisdiction in moral, religious, and civil matters

---

17:10 Paul and Silas were sent out of town at **night**, most likely in order to conceal their departure. Rather than deciding to play it safe from this point on, they traveled to **Berea** and made straight for **the synagogue of the Jews**. Would they be persecuted here also?

17:11 The Bereans exemplify the ideal stance of disciples: They were **open-minded** to biblical instruction and **examined the Scriptures daily** to see if the teachings were true.

17:12 Note again the international appeal of the gospel as **Greek women** and **men** came to faith.

17:13 Just as the appeal of Christ knows no borders (both Jews and Gentiles follow Him), so too opposition to Christ knows no borders. Agitators from **Thessalonica** were unwilling to let faith flourish in **Berea**, and so **they came there too**, intent on thwarting the missionaries.

17:14 **Paul** set sail for Athens, while **Silas** and **Timothy** stayed behind and braved the opposition in Berea. This seems to indicate that Paul had become the focal point of Jewish opposition to the Christian message.

17:16 While waiting for Silas and Timothy to arrive from Berea, Paul observed **Athens** closely. He saw that it was **full of idols**. Athens was a beautiful city with many magnificent buildings and other monuments, many of them related to pagan worship (e.g., the Parthenon). The city was also a center of intellectual, philosophical, and religious discussion. All of this **troubled** Paul as a person who knew the one true God and His Son Jesus Christ.

17:17 Paul followed his custom and **reasoned in the synagogue**, but also expanded his audience even before the onset of trouble from the **Jews**, by taking the gospel to **the marketplace** and engaging whoever was there, likely including philosophers, rhetoricians, and teachers.

17:18 **Epicurean and Stoic philosophers** comprised two of the best-known philosophical schools of thought. They attracted many followers who gathered in various parts of the city to discuss the leading issues of the day. In their arrogance, some of them depicted Paul as a **pseudo-intellectual**. This was actually a slang term that meant "seed-picker." Others misunderstood what Paul was saying and confused his discussion of the **Resurrection** with the description of a new god they had not yet heard about (cp. v. 32).

17:19 By this era, the Athenian court did not have the same kind of jurisdiction it once held. But **the Areopagus** still hosted gatherings where philosophical and religious ideas were debated.

17:22-31 This is Paul's third and final missionary speech in the book of Acts. He appealed to the Athenians' religious inclinations, drew upon observable data from nature to discuss the attributes of **God**, marshaled insights from pagan poets, and identified God and the need for humans to **repent** in preparation for the **day** in which God will **judge the world in righteousness** through Jesus Christ, whom God vindicated by raising Him **from the dead**.

17:23 As an example of Athenian superstition, Paul noted the altar erected **TO AN UNKNOWN GOD**. No such inscription has been found, but it is no surprise that such an altar existed. Doubtless it was erected to ensure that no gods

heaven and earth[a] and does not live in shrines made by hands.[b] [25]Neither is He served by human hands, as though He needed anything,[c] since He Himself gives everyone life and breath and all things.[d] [26]From one man[A] He has made every nationality to live over the whole earth and has determined their appointed times and the boundaries of where they live.[e] [27]He did this so they might seek God, and perhaps they might reach out and find Him, though He is not far from each one of us.[f] [28]For in Him we live and move and exist, as even some of your own poets have said, 'For we are also His offspring.'[B,g] [29]Being God's offspring then, we shouldn't think that the divine nature is like gold or silver or stone, an image fashioned by human art and imagination.[h]

[30]"Therefore, having overlooked[i] the times of ignorance, God now commands all people everywhere to repent, [31]because He has set a day when He is going to judge the world in righteousness by the Man He has appointed. He has provided proof of this to everyone by raising Him from the dead."[j]

[32]When they heard about resurrection of the dead, some began to ridicule him. But others said, "We'd like to hear from you again about this." [33]Then Paul left their presence. [34]However, some men joined him and believed, including Dionysius the Areopagite, a woman named Damaris, and others with them.

Founding the Corinthian Church

18 After this, he[c] left Athens and went to Corinth,[k] [2]where he found a Jewish man named Aquila,[l] a native of Pontus, who had recently come from Italy with his wife Priscilla because Claudius[D] had ordered all the Jews to leave Rome. Paul came to them, [3]and being of the same occupation, stayed with them and worked, for they were tentmakers[E] by trade.[m] [4]He reasoned in the *synagogue every Sabbath and tried to persuade both Jews and Greeks.[n]

[5]When Silas and Timothy came down from Macedonia, Paul was occupied with preaching the message[F] and solemnly testified to the Jews that Jesus is the *Messiah.[o] [6]But when they resisted and blasphemed,[p] he shook his robe[G,q] and told them, "Your blood is on your

Cross references
[a]17:24 Dt 10:14; Ps 115:16; Mt 11:25
[b]Ac 7:48
[c]17:25 Jb 22:2; Ps 50:10-12
[d]Gn 2:7; Jb 27:3; 33:4; Zch 12:1
[e]17:26 Dt 32:8; Jb 12:23; Mal 2:10
[f]17:27 Dt 4:7; Jr 23:23-24; Ac 14:17
[g]17:28 Jb 12:10; Dn 5:23; Ti 1:12
[h]17:29 Is 40:18-19; Rm 1:23
[i]17:30 Lk 24:47; Ac 14:16; Rm 3:25; Ti 2:11-12; 1Pt 1:14; 4:3
[j]17:31 Ps 9:8; 98:9; Mt 10:15; Ac 2:24; Rm 2:16
[k]18:1 Ac 17:15; 19:1; 1Co 1:2; 2Co 1:1,23; 2Tm 4:20
[l]18:2 Ac 18:18, 26; Rm 16:3-5; 1Co 16:19; 2Tm 4:19
[m]18:3 Ac 20:34; 1Co 4:12; 9:15; 2Co 11:7; 12:13; 1Th 2:9; 2Th 3:8
[n]18:4 Ac 9:20; 13:14; 14:1; 18:19
[o]18:5 Jb 32:18; Ac 15:22; 16:1,9; 17:3,14-15; 18:28; 1Th 3:6
[p]18:6 Ac 13:45; Rm 3:8; 1Co 4:13; Ti 3:2
[q]Neh 5:13; Mt 10:14; Ac 13:51

[A]17:26 Other mss read *one blood* [B]17:28 This citation is from Aratus, a third-century B.C. Gk poet. [C]18:1 Other mss read *Paul* [D]18:2 Roman emperor A.D. 41–54; he expelled all Jews from Rome in A.D. 49. [E]18:3 Or *leatherworkers*, or less likely *manufacturers of theatrical properties* [F]18:5 Other mss read *was urged by the Spirit* [G]18:6 A symbolic display of protest; Mt 10:14; Ac 13:51

---

were overlooked (and thus angered) in the people's devotion.

17:24-29 Paul's argument from nature included a basic natural theology: God is Creator of all things; God is beyond the human realm (transcendent); God is not obligated to any human; God is sovereign over all peoples; God as Creator is quantitatively different from His creation.

17:27 Paul did not believe a person could achieve salvation through his own search for God (v. 30), but he did believe God is near to each person and that people through their own reasoning and observation of nature can achieve rudimentary knowledge of who God is. Special revelation from God is necessary for fuller understanding and salvation (see note at Rm 10:14-15).

17:30-31 Paul built upon his argument from natural theology by introducing an eschatological dimension. God had **overlooked the times of ignorance**, but now commanded humanity to acknowledge its evil ways and turn from them (**repent**). He has established a day of judgment on which the world will be held accountable to the righteous standard set by Jesus, whom God raised **from the dead**.

17:32 Neither Stoics nor Epicureans believed in the possibility of bodily **resurrection**, though the Stoics did believe the human spirit continued to exist after bodily death. In any event, Paul's talk about bodily resurrection earned him **ridicule** but also a measure of curiosity.

17:34 Paul's missionary efforts in Athens were not as successful as they were elsewhere since he founded no church there. But there were a number of converts. These included a member of the Areopagus, **Dionysius**, a man of distinction because of this prestigious membership. **Damaris** may also have been a woman of distinction since Luke bothered to name her (vv. 4-5).

18:1 Corinth was another leading city of Greece (Achaia). Its two harbors made it a center of trade for the Mediterranean area.

18:2 It appears that in A.D. 41 emperor Claudius prohibited Jews from gathering together in Rome. Then in A.D. 49 he expelled them altogether, probably because the earlier measures did not work. Presumably **Aquila** and **Priscilla** were expelled at this time. That they had **recently** arrived from **Italy** suggests that Paul arrived in Corinth in about A.D. 50.

18:3 Tentmakers refers to people who worked in leather, possibly related to working in the goat hair cloth that was made in Cilicia, Paul's home region. Later rabbinic tradition confirmed the importance of teachers having a trade to help support themselves.

18:4 As was his custom, Paul **reasoned in the synagogue**, attempting to persuade **both Jews and Greeks**. The Greeks were likely God-fearers he encountered at the synagogue, but possibly outside as well. An inscription has been found in Corinth that attests to a "synagogue of the Hebrews." The date of the inscription is debated, but it probably postdates Paul.

18:5 When **Silas** and **Timothy** finally caught up with Paul in Corinth, he was engaged in what he did best—**preaching** the word and bearing witness to the Jews that Jesus was the **Messiah**.

18:6 Shook his robe symbolized that Paul was finished giving priority to Jewish evangelism, as if he were shaking the

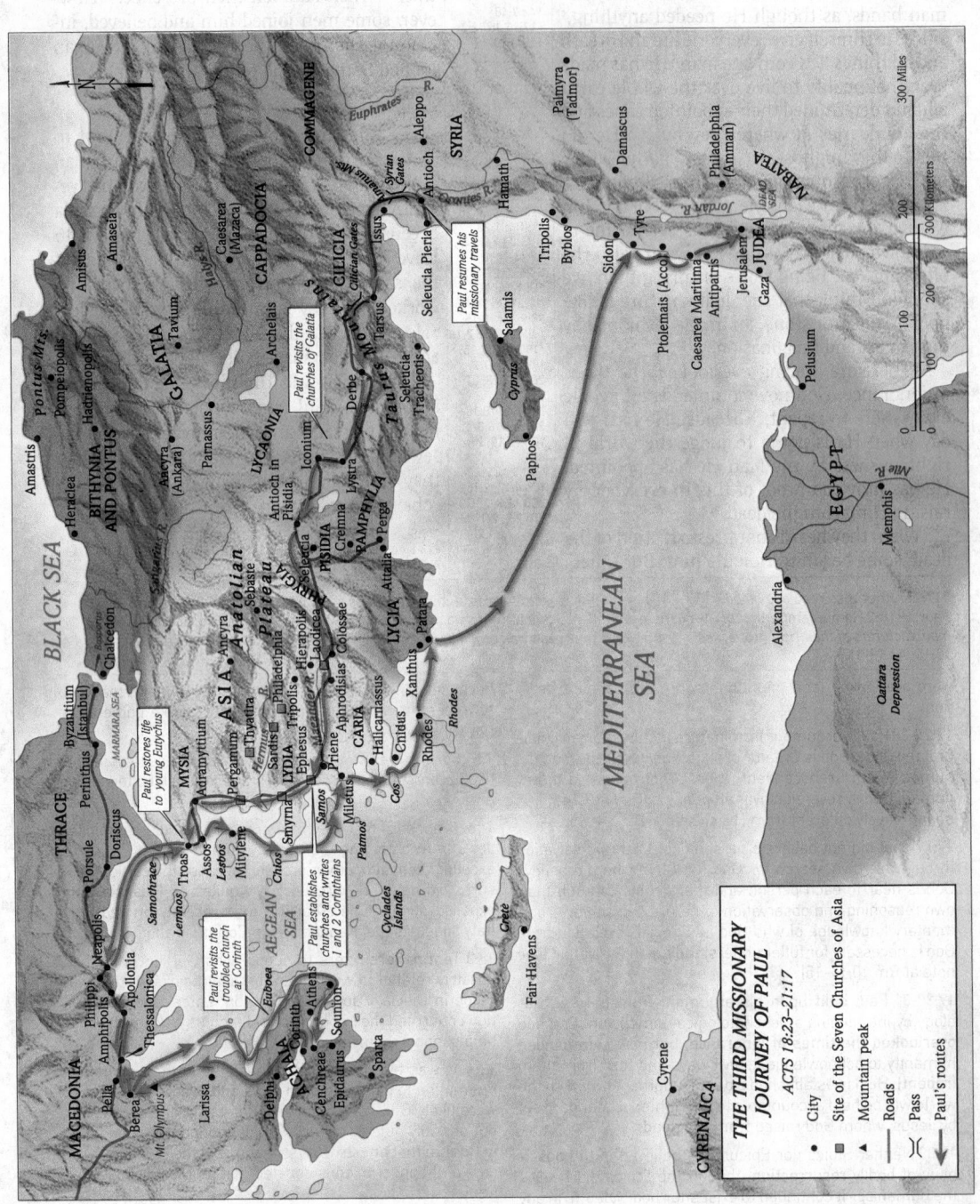

THE THIRD MISSIONARY
JOURNEY OF PAUL

ACTS 18:23–21:17

• City
▪ Site of the Seven Churches of Asia
▲ Mountain peak
)(Pass
— Roads
↓ Paul's routes

Paul revisits the churches of Galatia

Paul resumes his missionary travels

Paul restores life to young Eutychus

Paul establishes churches and writes 1 and 2 Corinthians

Paul revisits the troubled church at Corinth

own heads!ª I am innocent.ᴬ From now on I will go to the Gentiles."ᵇ ⁷So he left there and went to the house of a man named Titius Justus, a worshiper of God, whose house was next door to the synagogue. ⁸Crispus, the leader of the synagogue, believed the Lord, along with his whole household.ᶜ Many of the Corinthians, when they heard, believed and were baptized.

⁹Then the Lord said to Paul in a night vision, "Don't be afraid, but keep on speaking and don't be silent. ¹⁰For I am with you, and no one will lay a hand on you to hurt you, because I have many people in this city."ᵈ ¹¹And he stayed there a year and six months, teaching the word of God among them.

¹²While Gallio was •proconsul of Achaia, the Jews made a united attack against Paul and brought him to the judge's bench.ᵉ ¹³"This man," they said, "persuades people to worship God contrary to the law!"

¹⁴As Paul was about to open his mouth, Gallio said to the Jews, "If it were a matter of a crime or of moral evil, it would be reasonable for me to put up with you Jews. ¹⁵But if these are questions about words, names, and your own law, see to it yourselves. I don't want to be a judge of such things."ᶠ ¹⁶So he drove them

from the judge's bench. ¹⁷Then they allᴮ seized Sosthenes,ᵍ the leader of the synagogue, and beat him in front of the judge's bench. But none of these things concerned Gallio.

The Return Trip to Antioch

¹⁸So Paul, having stayed on for many days, said good-bye to the •brothers and sailed away to Syria. Priscilla and Aquila were with him. He shaved his head at Cenchreae because he had taken a vow.ʰ ¹⁹When they reached Ephesusⁱ he left them there, but he himself entered the synagogue and engaged in discussion withᶜ the Jews. ²⁰And though they asked him to stay for a longer time, he declined, ²¹but he said good-bye and stated,ᴰ "I'll come back to you again, if God wills."ʲ Then he set sail from Ephesus.

²²On landing at Caesarea, he went up and greeted the churchᴱ and went down to Antioch.ᵏ ²³And after spending some time there, he set out, traveling through one place after another in the Galatian territory and Phrygia, strengthening all the disciples.ˡ

The Eloquent Apollos

²⁴A Jew named Apollos,ᵐ a native Alexandrian, an eloquent man who was powerful in

Cross references (center column):
ª18:6 2Sm 1:16; Ezk 18:13; 33:4; Mt 27:25
ᵇEzk 3:18; Ac 13:46
ᶜ18:8 Mk 5:22; Ac 11:14; 1Co 1:14
ᵈ18:9-10 Mt 28:20; Ac 23:11
ᵉ18:12 Ac 13:7; 18:27
ᶠ18:15 Ac 23:29; 25:11,19
ᵍ18:17 1Co 1:1
ʰ18:18 Nm 6:2,5,9,18; Ac 21:24; Rm 16:1
ⁱ18:19 Ac 19:1; 20:16; 1Co 15:32; 1Tm 1:3; 2Tm 1:18
ʲ18:21 Rm 1:10; 1Co 4:19; 16:7; Heb 6:3; Jms 4:15; 1Pt 3:17
ᵏ18:22 Ac 8:40; 11:19
ˡ18:23 Ac 14:22; 16:6
ᵐ18:24 Ac 19:1; 1Co 1:12; 3:5; 4:6; 16:12; Ti 3:13

ᴬ18:6 Lit •clean   ᴮ18:17 Other mss read Then all the Greeks   ᶜ18:19 Or and addressed   ᴰ18:21 Other mss add "By all means it is necessary to keep the coming festival in Jerusalem. But   ᴱ18:22 The church in Jerusalem

---

dust from the folds of his garment. He would concentrate on the more fruitful harvest among the **Gentiles**. Similarly, in 13:46 Paul and Barnabas responded to persistent Jewish rejection of the gospel by saying they would "turn to the Gentiles."

18:7-8 Paul's vow in verse 6 did not mean no one from the synagogue had accepted his message, as the conversion of **Crispus** and **his whole household** indicates. Also, since **Titius Justus** (a Gentile) was said to be **a worshiper of God**, he almost certainly had been a member of **the synagogue** that was right **next door** to his home.

18:9-11 Paul had experienced trouble in previous towns, including Philippi, Thessalonica, and Berea. But the Lord assured him that he would have a productive ministry in Corinth, which explains why he stayed for **a year and six months**.

18:12 The time when **Gallio was proconsul of Achaia**, of which Corinth was the capital, is a relatively firm date in NT chronology. An inscription found at Delphi says Gallio was installed as proconsul in early A.D. 51. Paul appeared before him later that year.

18:13 For another instance in which Paul was accused of persuading people to **worship God** in ways **contrary to the law**, see 16:20-21 and the note there.

18:14-17 **Gallio** seemed both perceptive (**I don't want to be a judge of such things**) and negligent (the beating of **Sosthenes** did not concern him). Keeping order in a multi-ethnic provincial town, heavily involved in trade and travel, was not easy. Gallio preferred the hands-off approach.

18:18 It is not clear that **Paul** was the one who **shaved his head** at **Cenchreae**. It may have been **Aquila**. The Greek syntax seems to indicate the latter, but it is uncertain. The vow may have been a Nazirite vow. If Paul was the person who made the vow, his going up to Jerusalem to visit "the church" (v. 22) may have included a stop at the temple to complete the vow and make an offering of his hair. Such activity was unusual for Paul, especially outside of Judea (cp. 21:26), but would have been consistent with his Jewish identity.

18:19-20 Paul's stop at **Ephesus** must have been very short since he apparently did not encounter Apollos (vv. 24-28) or the misguided teaching that he countered in his later, extended visit to Ephesus (chap. 19).

18:21 Paul promises to come back to Ephesus **if God wills**, as indeed He did (19:1). Paul saw his ministry and indeed his whole life as being in God's service and control (see note at Rm 1:1).

18:22 We know it was the Jerusalem church that Paul greeted since he went **down** from there (Jerusalem is at a higher elevation) to **Antioch**. His arrival back in Antioch marks the completion of his second missionary journey.

18:23 This marks the beginning of Paul's third missionary journey. Like the first two, this one began from Antioch and retraced his steps through Asia Minor, particularly the Phrygian region of the province of Galatia.

18:24-25 **Apollos** was from Alexandria, Egypt, the most learned city in the Greco-Roman world. Since Apollos had been **instructed in the way of the Lord**, we know that Christianity had reached Egypt by this time. However, his

the use of the Scriptures, arrived in Ephesus. [25]This man had been instructed in the way of the Lord; and being fervent in spirit,[A] he spoke and taught the things about Jesus accurately, although he knew only John's baptism.[a] [26]He began to speak boldly in the synagogue. After Priscilla and Aquila heard him, they took him home[B] and explained the way of God to him more accurately.[b] [27]When he wanted to cross over to Achaia, the brothers wrote to the disciples urging them to welcome him. After he arrived, he greatly helped those who had believed through grace.[c] [28]For he vigorously refuted the Jews in public, demonstrating through the Scriptures that Jesus is the Messiah.[d]

Twelve Disciples of John the Baptist

19 While Apollos was in Corinth, Paul traveled through the interior regions and came to Ephesus. He found some disciples[e] [2]and asked them, "Did you receive the Holy Spirit when you believed?"

"No," they told him, "we haven't even heard that there is a Holy Spirit."[f]

[3]"Then what baptism were you baptized with?" he asked them.

"With John's baptism," they replied.

[4]Paul said, "John baptized with a baptism of repentance, telling the people that they should believe in the One who would come after him, that is, in Jesus."[g]

[5]When they heard this, they were baptized in the name of the Lord Jesus. [6]And when Paul had laid his hands on[h] them, the Holy Spirit came on them, and they began to speak in other *languages and to prophesy.[i] [7]Now there were about 12 men in all.

In the Lecture Hall of Tyrannus

[8]Then he entered the *synagogue and spoke boldly over a period of three months, engaging in discussion and trying to persuade them about the things of the kingdom of God.[j] [9]But when some became hardened and would not believe, slandering the Way in front of the crowd, he withdrew from them and met separately with the disciples, conducting discussions every day in the lecture hall of Tyrannus.[k] [10]And this went on for two years, so that

Cross references:
[a]18:25 Lk 7:29; Ac 9:2; 19:3; Rm 12:11
[b]18:26 Mt 2:8; Lk 1:3; Ac 18:25; 23:15,20; 24:22; Eph 5:15; 1Th 5:2
[c]18:27 Ac 18:12,18; 1Co 3:6
[d]18:28 Ac 9:22; 17:2-3; 18:5
[e]19:1 Ac 18:1,24; 1Co 1:12; 3:5-6
[f]19:2 Jn 7:39; Ac 8:16; 11:16
[g]19:4 Mt 3:11; Jn 1:7,27; Ac 13:24-25
[h]19:6 Ac 6:6; 8:17
[i]Mk 16:17; Ac 2:4; 10:46
[j]19:8 Ac 1:3; 9:20; 28:23
[k]19:9 Ac 9:2; 11:26; 14:4; 19:23,30

A18:25 Or *in the Spirit*   **B**18:26 Lit *they received him*

knowledge of Christianity was deficient since he **knew only** the **baptism** of John the Baptist. Nonetheless, some take **fervent in spirit** to mean that Apollos was already filled with the Holy Spirit. However, it is more likely that Apollos was serious about his dawning faith in Christ but had not yet received the baptism of the Holy Spirit.

18:26 We see here that speaking **boldly** about Jesus is not enough. One must also **accurately** understand the faith. **Priscilla and Aquila** did both Apollos and the kingdom a favor by taking time to instruct him.

18:27-28 Once Apollos's rhetorical skills were coupled with

epistamai

Greek Pronunciation	[eh PIH stah migh]
HCSB Translation	know
Uses in Acts	9
Uses in the NT	14
Focus passage	Acts 18:25

The Greek verb *epistamai* literally means *to stand upon* and is a compound word from the preposition *epi*, meaning *upon*, and the verb *histemi*, meaning *to stand*. The term means *to know* in a different sense than the more common words *ginosko* and *oida*, which emphasize intellectual knowledge and/or knowledge gained through experience. Both *ginosko* and *oida* are commonly used for *knowing* persons, including God, with varying degrees of intimacy. The word *epistamai*, on the other hand, is rarely used for *knowing* people and never for *knowing* God. The main idea behind *epistamai* is a thorough *knowledge* of facts, and often understanding the significance of such information, is implied.

The difference between *ginosko* and *epistamai* is best demonstrated in the only verse where both verbs occur. In Acts 19:13-17, would-be exorcists attempted to cast out an evil spirit but were rebuked, "I *know* [*ginosko*] Jesus, and I *recognize* [*epistamai*] Paul—but who are you?" (v. 15).

accurate understanding of the Christian faith, he left Ephesus and went to **Achaia** (Corinth; 19:1). He **vigorously refuted the Jews** using apologetic and instructional techniques similar to Paul's. None of this would have been possible if not for the faithfulness of Priscilla and Aquila.

19:1-6 The **disciples** whom **Paul** encountered in **Ephesus** had never heard of the **Holy Spirit** or **baptism** into Christ (cp.18:25). This is one of the most difficult NT passages to interpret. The basic question is whether these disciples were genuine Christians when Paul first met them. Some argue that they were not since they had neither received the Holy Spirit nor been baptized into Christ. Others insist that they were genuine Christians who had not yet received full knowledge of the faith. Numerous incomplete forms of Christianity were being spread in the early years of the church. The apostles obviously felt that it was important to check the progress of such strains and correct them, bringing the full and complete gospel message to would-be disciples.

19:4 By John's own confession his baptism was incomplete. He urged those whom he baptized **to believe in the One who would come after him** (see Mt 3:11 and note).

19:5-6 The order of conversion here follows the typical pattern in Acts except for the laying on of **hands** and the mention of **other languages** and the ability to prophesy as immediate results of the Spirit's coming.

19:8 Paul apparently encountered the Ephesian disciples (vv. 1-7) before he had a chance to visit the **synagogue**. His **discussion** there marks only the second time that Paul mentioned **the kingdom of God** in his preaching in Acts (14:22).

19:9 Paul **withdrew** from the synagogue when **the Way** was slandered and it became obvious that the crowd would not believe. His choice seems in keeping with Jesus' teachings (see Mt 7:6; Lk 9:3-5). **Tyrannus** either owned the **lecture hall** or taught there regularly. Inscriptions bearing his name

all the inhabitants of ˙Asia, both Jews and Greeks, heard the message about the Lord.[a]

Demonism Defeated at Ephesus

[11]God was performing extraordinary miracles by Paul's hands, [12]so that even facecloths or work aprons[A] that had touched his skin were brought to the sick, and the diseases left them, and the evil spirits came out of them.[b] [13]Then some of the itinerant Jewish exorcists attempted to pronounce the name of the Lord Jesus over those who had evil spirits, saying, "I command you by the Jesus that Paul preaches!"[c] [14]Seven sons of Sceva, a Jewish ˙chief priest, were doing this. [15]The evil spirit answered them, "I know Jesus, and I recognize Paul—but who are you?" [16]Then the man who had the evil spirit leaped on them, overpowered them all, and prevailed against them, so that they ran out of that house naked and wounded. [17]This became known to everyone who lived in Ephesus, both Jews and Greeks. Then fear fell on all of them, and the name of the Lord Jesus was magnified.[d] [18]And many who had become believers came confessing and disclosing their practices, [19]while many of those who had practiced magic collected their books and burned them in front of everyone. So they calculated their value and found it to be 50,000 pieces of silver. [20]In this way the Lord's message flourished and prevailed.[e]

The Riot in Ephesus

[21]When these events were over, Paul resolved in the Spirit to pass through Macedonia and Achaia and go to Jerusalem. "After I've been there," he said, "I must see Rome as well!"[f] [22]So after sending two of those who assisted him, Timothy and Erastus, to Macedonia, he himself stayed in Asia for a while.[g]

[23]During that time there was a major[B] disturbance about the Way.[h] [24]For a person named Demetrius, a silversmith who made silver shrines of Artemis,[C] provided a great deal of[D] business for the craftsmen. [25]When he had assembled them, as well as the workers engaged in this type of business, he said: "Men, you know that our prosperity is derived from this business. [26]You both see and hear that not only in Ephesus, but in almost all of Asia, this man Paul has persuaded and misled a considerable number of people by saying that gods made by hand are not gods![i] [27]So not only do we run a risk that our business may be discredited, but also that the temple of the great goddess Artemis may be despised and her magnificence come to the verge of ruin—the very one all of Asia and the world adore."

[a]19:10 Ac 19:8,22,26-27; 20:31
[b]19:11-12 Ac 5:15; 8:13
[c]19:13 Mt 12:27; Mk 9:38; Lk 11:19
[d]19:17 Ac 5:5,11; 18:19
[e]19:20 Ac 6:6-7; 12:24
[f]19:21 Ac 16:9; 18:12; 20:16,22; Rm 15:24-25,28
[g]19:22 Ac 13:5; 16:1,23; 19:10; 2Tm 4:20
[h]19:23 Ac 9:2; 2Co 1:8
[i]19:26 Dt 4:28; Ps 115:4; Is 44:10-20; Jr 10:3; Ac 17:29; 1Co 8:4; Rv 9:20

have been found in Ephesus, dating to this time. The actual lecture hall has not been discovered.

19:10 After three months of speaking in the synagogue (v. 8), Paul spent another **two years** teaching in Ephesus, making a significant impact on the province of **Asia**. A number of other events recorded elsewhere about Paul's life may have occurred during this time. These included imprisonments and beatings (2Co 1:8-10; 11:23-25).

19:11-12 God's power through faith was at work in these healings (see note at 5:15-16; see also Lk 8:44). That **Paul's** personal items (**facecloths . . . work aprons**) were involved demonstrates his identity as an apostle.

19:13 **Itinerant Jewish exorcists** attempted to use Jesus' **name** to command evil spirits. Ancient magic traditions often involved the invocation of divine names.

19:14 Numerous ancient Jewish nonbiblical texts attest to the interplay of magic and Judaism.

19:15 It takes more than the invocation of powerful names to gain the upper hand over demonic forces. The **evil spirit** knew that the exorcists did not share in Christ's authority through faith.

19:16 The consequences of frivolously invoking Jesus' name were severe. That the men fled **naked** was especially humiliating since Jews shunned nudity.

19:17-18 The **name of the Lord Jesus**, rather than being abused, was **magnified** when people realized the power of the Lord was not available for just anyone to control and manipulate.

19:19-20 Books were expensive in ancient times. **50,000 pieces of silver** represents a large but believable sum.

19:21 Paul intended to return to the places he had evangelized earlier on his second missionary trip and then go to **Jerusalem** before traveling further west. As he stated in his letter to the Romans (Rm 15:23-29), he believed his missionary work in the east was finished. After taking the collection to Jerusalem, he planned to proceed to Rome and then further west to Spain.

19:22 Some believe the **Erastus** mentioned here is the same as in Rm 16:23, while others dispute this. It is also possible that the Erastus of Rm 16:23 is mentioned in a Corinthian inscription. The name was popular during this time.

19:23-25 The cult of **Artemis** at Ephesus was part of a larger Greek cult of Artemis, the "Great Mother." As with many ancient cults, artisans like **Demetrius** made their living by fashioning cultic items such as idols. Paul's preaching jeopardized this vocation (vv. 25-26).

19:26-27 Paul's reputation had spread throughout **Asia**, making him a threat to the beliefs and lifestyle for **a considerable number of people**. The Ephesian **temple** of Artemis, whose foundations went back to the eighth century B.C., was one of the seven wonders of the ancient world. Demetrius foresaw that it would fall into disrepute and **ruin** if Paul persuaded enough people that **gods made by hand are not gods**. In fact, this is exactly what happened. The ruins of the temple were discovered in the nineteenth century, and the altar was uncovered in 1965.

28 When they had heard this, they were filled with rage and began to cry out, "Great is Artemis of the Ephesians!" 29 So the city was filled with confusion, and they rushed all together into the amphitheater, dragging along Gaius[a] and Aristarchus,[b] Macedonians who were Paul's traveling companions. 30 Though Paul wanted to go in before the people, the disciples did not let him. 31 Even some of the provincial officials of Asia, who were his friends, sent word to him, pleading with him not to take a chance by going[A] into the amphitheater. 32 Meanwhile, some were shouting one thing and some another, because the assembly was in confusion, and most of them did not know why they had come together. 33 Then some of the crowd gave Alexander advice when the Jews pushed him to the front. So motioning with his hand, Alexander wanted to make his defense to the people.[c] 34 But when they recognized that he was a Jew, a united cry went up from all of them for about two hours: "Great is Artemis of the Ephesians!"

35 However, when the city clerk had calmed the crowd down, he said, "Men of Ephesus! What man is there who doesn't know that the city of the Ephesians is the temple guardian of the great[B] Artemis, and of the image that fell from heaven? 36 Therefore, since these things are undeniable, you must keep calm and not do anything rash. 37 For you have brought these men here who are not temple robbers or blasphemers of our[c] goddess. 38 So if Demetrius and the craftsmen who are with him have a case against anyone, the courts are in session, and there are ·proconsuls. Let them bring charges against one another.[d] 39 But if you want something else, it must be decided in a legal assembly. 40 In fact, we run a risk of being charged with rioting for what happened today, since there is no ·justification that we can give as a reason for this disorderly gathering." 41 After saying this, he dismissed the assembly.

Paul in Macedonia

20 After the uproar was over, Paul sent for the disciples, encouraged them, and after saying good-bye, departed to go to Macedonia.[e] 2 And when he had passed through those areas and exhorted them at length, he came to Greece 3 and stayed three months. When he was about to set sail for Syria, a plot was devised against him by the Jews, so a decision was made to go back through Macedonia.[f] 4 He was accompanied[D] by Sopater son of Pyrrhus[E] from Berea, Aristarchus and Secundus from Thessalonica, Gaius from Derbe, Timothy,[g] and Tychicus[h] and Trophimus[i] from ·Asia. 5 These men went on ahead and waited for us in Troas,[j] 6 but we sailed away from Philippi after the days of ·Unleavened Bread.[k]

a 19:29 Rm 16:23; 1Co 1:14
b Ac 20:4; 27:2; Col 4:10; Phm 24
c 19:32-33 Ac 12:17; 21:34
d 19:37-38 Ac 13:7; Rm 2:22
e 20:1 Ac 11:26; 16:9; 19:21; 2Co 2:12-13
f 20:3 Ac 9:23; 20:19; 23:12; 25:3; 2Co 11:26
g 20:4 Ac 14:6; 16:1; 17:1; 19:29
h Eph 6:21; Col 4:7; 2Tm 4:12; Ti 3:12
i Ac 21:29; 2Tm 4:20
j 20:5 Ac 16:8,10; 20:6-8,13-15
k 20:6 Ex 12:14-15; 23:15

A 19:31 Lit not to give himself   B 19:35 Other mss add goddess   C 19:37 Other mss read your   D 20:4 Other mss add to Asia   E 20:4 Other mss omit son of Pyrrhus

19:28 Demetrius played to the crowd's worst fears effectively. Fear of loss is often a choice weapon against God's truth and the life of discipleship.

19:29-31 The Ephesian **amphitheater** seated 24,000 people and was thoroughly remodeled in the first century. The **disciples** wisely kept **Paul** from joining his **traveling companions**. It would have been a senseless self-sacrifice to enter into the clutches of such a hostile mob. That some of the **provincial officials** also pleaded with Paul to stay away shows that he had come to be well regarded by some leaders in the province.

19:32 True to mob mentality, **most of them** had no idea why they had gathered in the amphitheater.

19:33-34 The Jews of the city understandably wanted to distance themselves from the controversy caused by Paul and his followers. They shoved forward one of their own, **Alexander**, a Hellenistic Jew (as indicated by his name), to offer an apology on their behalf. Ironically, the Jews would have had the same view of the Artemis cult as Paul and his followers, but in this case they did not want to be lumped in with them. As for the Ephesian mob, they disallowed such a distinction. They knew that anyone whose religious roots were Jewish represented opposition to Artemis.

19:35 The **image that fell from heaven** may indicate that the Artemis cult was inspired by a meteorite that fell to earth.

Alternatively, this could be a way of saying that the cult was thought to originate with the gods.

19:37-39 In their rush to condemn Jesus and the Christian movement, Jews and Gentiles alike often violated civil and judicial procedures (18:14-15; Mt 26:60). In this case, the city clerk made it clear that the actions of Demetrius were against the law and did not follow due process.

19:40-41 Fear of Roman reprisal was a common motivator for clearing up civil unrest. There is no mention of further legal action taken. This shows that Paul and his followers had broken no laws. They were simply upsetting those who profited from the Artemis cult.

20:1 Paul took one last occasion to gather the believers in Ephesus before going to **Macedonia**.

20:2-3 Paul probably went to Philippi and Thessalonica in Macedonia before going to **Greece** (Achaia), where he stayed for **three months**, possibly in Athens and Corinth. The **plot** by some of Paul's Jewish opponents apparently caused him to change his travel plans. He decided to travel overland from Greece to Macedonia, where he caught a ship at Philippi.

20:4 A number of Paul's companions hailed from cities he had visited during his missionary journeys.

20:5 The "we" narrative resumes and continues through verse 15 (see note at 16:10).

In five days we reached them at Troas, where we spent seven days.

Eutychus Revived at Troas

[7] On the first day of the week, we[A] assembled to break bread.[a] Paul spoke to them, and since he was about to depart the next day, he extended his message until midnight. [8] There were many lamps in the room upstairs where we were assembled, [9] and a young man named Eutychus was sitting on a window sill and sank into a deep sleep as Paul kept on speaking. When he was overcome by sleep, he fell down from the third story and was picked up dead. [10] But Paul went down, fell on him, embraced him, and said, "Don't be alarmed, for his •life is in him!"[b] [11] After going upstairs, breaking the bread, and eating, Paul conversed a considerable time until dawn. Then he left. [12] They brought the boy home alive and were greatly comforted.

From Troas to Miletus

[13] Then we went on ahead to the ship and sailed for Assos, intending to take Paul on board there. For these were his instructions, since he himself was going by land. [14] When he met us at Assos, we took him on board and came to Mitylene. [15] Sailing from there, the next day we arrived off Chios. The following day we crossed over to Samos, and[B] the day after, we came to Miletus.[c] [16] For Paul had decided to sail past Ephesus so he would not have to spend time in Asia, because he was hurrying to be in Jerusalem, if possible, for the day of Pentecost.[d]

Farewell Address to the Ephesian Elders

[17] Now from Miletus, he sent to Ephesus and called for the elders of the church. [18] And when they came to him, he said to them: "You know, from the first day I set foot in Asia, how I was with you the whole time[e]— [19] serving the Lord with all humility, with tears, and with the trials that came to me through the plots of the Jews[f]— [20] and that I did not shrink back from proclaiming to you anything that was profitable or from teaching it to you in public and from house to house. [21] I testified to both Jews and Greeks about repentance toward God[g] and faith in our Lord Jesus.[h]

[22] "And now I am on my way to Jerusalem, bound in my spirit,[c] not knowing what I will encounter there,[i] [23] except that in town after town the Holy Spirit testifies to me that chains and afflictions are waiting for me.[j] [24] But I count my life of no value to myself, so that I may finish my course[D] and the ministry[k] I

Cross references
a 20:7 Ac 2:42; 1Co 10:16
b 20:10 1Kg 17:21; 2Kg 4:34; Mt 9:23-24; Mk 5:39
c 20:15 Ac 20:17; 2Tm 4:20
d 20:16 Ac 2:1; 18:19; 19:21; 1Co 16:8
e 20:18 Ac 18:19; 19:1,10
f 20:19-20 Ac 20:3,27
g 20:21 Mk 1:15; Ac 2:38; 18:5
h Ac 24:24; 26:18; Eph 1:15; Col 2:5; Phm 5
i 20:22 Ac 17:16; 20:16
j 20:23 Ac 9:16; 21:4,11; 1Th 3:3
k 20:24 Ac 1:17; 21:13; 2Co 4:1; 2Tm 4:7

A 20:7 Other mss read *the disciples*   B 20:15 Other mss add *after staying at Trogyllium*   C 20:22 Or *in the Spirit*   D 20:24 Other mss add *with joy*

20:6 When Paul reached **Philippi**, he sailed after the days of Unleavened Bread (Passover week) for **Troas**, where he stayed **seven days**.

20:7 On the first day of the week, Paul gathered with other believers to **break bread**, a tradition that apparently began soon after the resurrection and ascension of Christ. Because he was leaving the next day (this event occurred at the end of his week in Troas), Paul spoke **until midnight**.

20:9-10 Peter raised a disciple named Tabitha from the dead (9:36-41), and now Paul ostensibly did the same for **Eutychus**. It is not clear, however, whether Eutychus was actually dead or just unconscious. Paul's statement that **his life is in him** most naturally suggests Eutychus was alive. In that case **picked up dead** would mean he was unconscious and appeared dead.

20:11 Despite the drama with Eutychus, the crowd went upstairs to break **bread**, eat together, and talk **until dawn** before Paul departed.

20:13 The narrative follows the events of those in the "we" group (see note at 16:10), who sailed from Troas to Assos, where they met Paul, who had traveled by **land**.

20:15 The group met in Assos, where Paul joined the ship, stopping at several ports before its arrival in **Miletus**. This verse ends the **we** section (see note at 16:10).

20:16 Paul appears to have consciously decided to **sail past Ephesus** in his hurry to get to Jerusalem for Pentecost. He may have wanted to avoid Ephesus because of the possibility that his presence would cause unrest (cp. 19:23-41).

Also, he had close ties with the Ephesian church, and it might have been difficult to take leave of them if he had stopped in the city.

20:17 In this verse the leaders of the church in Ephesus are called **elders**, but they are referred to as "overseers" in verse 28. These terms designate a functional and formal title of church leadership. The Ephesian church appears to have had a formal leadership structure.

20:18-35 This speech differs from Paul's others in Acts. It is the only one delivered to a group of believers, and it has several parallels with themes in the Pauline letters—reference to his serving the Lord, his persecution, his not shrinking from teaching, his ministry to both Jews and Greeks, the need for repentance, counting his **life** expendable, and finishing the course.

20:20 The mark of a truly faithful teacher of the gospel is that he or she does **not shrink back** from topics that, though unpopular or personally difficult, are **profitable** for disciples.

20:21 Paul's message to both **Jews and Greeks** called for **repentance** toward God for one's sins and **faith** in the Lord Jesus. This is an excellent summary of the mission of the church.

20:22-23 Paul was undaunted by the God-given knowledge that **chains and afflictions** awaited him. His persistence in teaching despite this is a model for all Christian disciples.

20:24 Paul put his trials in perspective by declaring that he counted his life of **no value**. What was important was that he would **finish** the **course** that had been set for him by the

received from the Lord Jesus,[a] to testify to the gospel of God's grace.

[25]"And now I know that none of you will ever see my face again—everyone I went about preaching the kingdom to. [26]Therefore I testify to you this day that I am innocent[A] of everyone's blood,[b] [27]for I did not shrink back from declaring to you the whole plan of God.[c] [28]Be on guard for yourselves and for all the flock[d] that the Holy Spirit has appointed you to as •overseers,[e] to shepherd the church of God,[B] which He purchased with His own blood.[f] [29]I know that after my departure savage wolves will come in among you, not sparing the flock. [30]And men will rise up from your own number with deviant doctrines to lure the disciples into following them.[g] [31]Therefore be on the alert, remembering that night and day for three years I did not stop warning each one of you with tears.[h]

[32]"And now[c] I commit you to God and to the message of His grace,[i] which is able to build you up and to give you an inheritance[j] among all who are •sanctified. [33]I have not coveted anyone's silver or gold or clothing.[k]

[34]You yourselves know that these hands have provided for my needs and for those who were with me.[l] [35]In every way I've shown you that by laboring like this, it is necessary to help the weak and to keep in mind the words of the Lord Jesus, for He said, 'It is more blessed to give than to receive.'"

[36]After he said this, he knelt down and prayed with all of them.[m] [37]There was a great deal of weeping by everyone. They embraced Paul and kissed him, [38]grieving most of all over his statement that they would never see his face again. Then they escorted him to the ship.[n]

Warnings on the Journey to Jerusalem

21 After[o] we tore ourselves away from them and set sail, we came by a direct route to Cos, the next day to Rhodes, and from there to Patara. [2]Finding a ship crossing over to Phoenicia, we boarded and set sail. [3]After we sighted Cyprus, leaving it on the left, we sailed on to Syria and arrived at Tyre, because the ship was to unload its cargo there. [4]So we

[a] 20:24 Gl 1:1; Ti 1:3
[b] 20:25-26 Ac 18:6; 20:38; 28:31
[c] 20:27 Lk 7:30; Ac 20:20; Eph 1:11
[d] 20:28 Lk 12:32; Jn 10:16; 1Co 9:7; 1Pt 5:2-3
[e] Php 1:1; 1Tm 3:2; Ti 1:7; 1Pt 2:25
[f] Eph 1:7,14; Heb 9:12; 1Pt 1:19; Rv 5:9
[g] 20:30 Ac 11:26; 1Tm 1:20; 1Jn 2:19
[h] 20:31 Ac 19:10; 20:19
[i] 20:32 Ac 14:23; Heb 13:9
[j] Ac 26:18; Eph 1:14; Col 1:12; 3:24; Heb 9:15; 1Pt 1:4
[k] 20:33 1Sm 12:3; 1Co 9:12; 2Co 7:2; 11:9; 12:17
[l] 20:34 Ac 18:3; 19:22
[m] 20:36 Lk 22:41; Ac 7:60; 21:5
[n] 20:37-38 Ac 15:3; 20:25
[o] 21:1 Ac 16:10-11

A 20:26 Lit •clean   B 20:28 Other mss read *church of the Lord*; other mss read *church of the Lord and God*   C 20:32 Other mss add *brothers,*

Lord Jesus, which involved testifying to the good news of **God's grace**.

20:25 Either Paul realized that things might go badly for him in Jerusalem, or he had no intention of returning to this part of the Mediterranean. His intention after visiting Jerusalem was to head to Rome and beyond. This is why he declared to the Ephesian elders that he would not see any of them again (cp. v. 38).

20:26-27 Paul declared that he was **innocent of everyone's**

boule

Greek Pronunciation	[boo LAY]
HCSB Translation	plan
Uses in Acts	7
Uses in the NT	12
Focus passage	Acts 20:27

The Greek noun *boule* can mean *counsel, will, plan,* or *purpose*. The related verb *boulomai* occurs 37 times in the NT (14 in Acts) and can mean *to will, purpose, plan,* or *come to a decision*. In Greek religion the term *boule* often referred to the *will* or *plan* of the gods.

In the Greek OT, *boule* normally refers to human *plans* or desires that may or may not occur, and is often advice given to royalty (2Sm 15:31,34; 16:20,23; 1Kg 12:8; 2Ch 22:5). But it can also refer to God's *purpose* that cannot be thwarted (Jb 12:13; Ps 33:11; Pr 19:21; Is 19:17; 46:10; Jr 50:45; see Pr 21:30) and that guides His people (Ps 73:24).

The NT usage of *boule* is very similar to that of the Greek OT. Humans may or may not see their *plans* realized (Lk 7:30; 23:51; Ac 5:38; 27:12,42), but God's *plans* and *purposes* will not fail (Ac 2:23; 4:28; 13:36; Eph 1:11; Heb 6:17).

blood because he had declared the **whole plan of God** to them. This means he had been faithful to proclaim the plan of salvation, including the coming judgment. Thus no one could accuse him of failing to warn them.

20:28 Paul used the language of shepherding to describe the responsibility of the leaders of the Ephesian church. Here they are called **overseers** rather than elders (see note at v. 17), appointed by the Holy Spirit for their task. Reference here to redemption through the **blood** of Jesus is unique in Acts, but the language reflects Paul's statements elsewhere (Rm 3:25; 5:9; Eph 2:13).

20:29-30 Paul clearly did not regard incorrect doctrine as unimportant. He called false teachers **savage wolves** because eternity hangs in the balance of rightly understanding the gospel.

20:31 Paul described his **three years** of active ministry in Ephesus as times of constant vigilance, **warning**, and deep concern. The events recorded in Acts fit this description well.

20:32 Paul committed the Ephesian Christians to God's **grace**, which strengthens disciples in their earthly tasks and provides eternal inheritance to the **sanctified**—those made holy by God.

20:33-35 Paul was never motivated by money or renown, as proven by his labors that **provided for** his own **needs** and those who accompanied him. Jesus' saying, **It is more blessed to give than to receive**, is found only here. It resembles some of Jesus' sayings elsewhere (Lk 6:38). Jesus obviously said much more than is recorded in the Gospels (Jn 20:30-31; 21:25).

21:1 The shipboard journey continued from Ephesus by way of **Cos** to **Rhodes** and **Patara**. This is the third "we" section in Acts (see note at 16:10). It extends through 21:18.

found some disciples and stayed there seven days. Through the Spirit they told Paul not to go to Jerusalem.[a] [5] When our days there were over, we left to continue our journey, while all of them, with their wives and children, escorted us out of the city. After kneeling down on the beach to pray, [6] we said good-bye to one another. Then we boarded the ship, and they returned home.

[7] When we completed our voyage from Tyre, we reached Ptolemais, where we greeted the *brothers and stayed with them one day.[b] [8] The next day we left and came to Caesarea, where we entered the house of Philip[c] the evangelist,[d] who was one of the Seven, and stayed with him. [9] This man had four virgin daughters who prophesied.[e]

[10] While we were staying there many days, a prophet named Agabus came down from Judea. [11] He came to us, took Paul's belt, tied his own feet and hands, and said, "This is what the Holy Spirit says: 'In this way the Jews in Jerusalem will bind the man who owns this belt and deliver him into Gentile hands.'"[f] [12] When we heard this, both we and the local people begged him not to go up to Jerusalem.

[13] Then Paul replied, "What are you doing, weeping and breaking my heart? For I am ready not only to be bound but also to die in Jerusalem for the name of the Lord Jesus."[g]

[14] Since he would not be persuaded, we stopped talking and simply said, "The Lord's will be done!"[h]

Conflict over the Gentile Mission

[15] After these days we got ready and went up to Jerusalem. [16] Some of the disciples from Caesarea also went with us and brought us to Mnason, a Cypriot and an early disciple, with whom we were to stay.[i]

[17] When we reached Jerusalem, the brothers welcomed us gladly.[j] [18] The following day Paul went in with us to James, and all the elders were present.[k] [19] After greeting them, he related in detail what God did among the Gentiles through his ministry.[l]

[20] When they heard it, they glorified God and said, "You see, brother, how many thousands of Jews there are who have believed, and they are all zealous[m] for the law. [21] But they have been told about you that you teach all the Jews who are among the Gentiles to abandon

a 21:4 Ac 11:26; 20:23; 21:11
b 21:7 Jn 21:23; Ac 12:20
c 21:8 Ac 6:5; 8:5
d Eph 4:11; 2Tm 4:5
e 21:9 Lk 2:36; Ac 2:7; 13:1; 1Co 11:5
f 21:11 1Kg 22:11; Jr 13:1-11; Mt 20:19; Ac 20:23; 21:33
g 21:13 Ac 5:41; 9:16; 20:24
h 21:14 Mt 6:10; Lk 22:42
i 21:16 Ac 8:40; 21:3-4
j 21:17 Ac 15:4; 21:7
k 21:18 Ac 11:30; 12:17; 15:13
l 21:19 Ac 1:17; 14:27; Rm 15:18-19
m 21:20 Ac 22:3; Rm 10:12; Gl 1:14

21:3 The most common vessels sailing the Mediterranean were grain ships from Egypt, heading to the rest of the Roman Empire (but especially Rome).

21:4 Some Christians in Tyre had received from the Holy Spirit the same message that Paul disclosed in Ephesus: Trouble awaited Paul in **Jerusalem** (20:22-23).

21:5-6 The departure from the Christians at Tyre resembled the departure from Miletus and the Ephesian elders (20:37-38). They knew Paul was heading for his deepest trouble yet.

21:8 **Philip the evangelist** was probably so called to distinguish him from other Philips. He was one of those selected to serve in the church in Jerusalem (see note at 6:5-6). Philip eventually settled with his daughters in **Caesarea**. Some believe he may have been one of the original Twelve (Mt 10:3; Mk 3:18; Lk 6:14). But he is distinctly identified as **one of the Seven** (6:3).

21:9 The word **virgin** means Philip's daughters were young and unmarried.

21:10-11 **Agabus** (see note at 11:28) explicitly stated that Paul would fall into hostile hands in Jerusalem. As it turned out (21:30-36), Paul was delivered by Gentiles out of Jewish hands, but then remained in Gentile hands throughout the rest of the book of Acts.

21:12 With such an explicit prophecy, it is not surprising that Paul's traveling companions and the locals **begged** him not to go on to **Jerusalem**.

21:13 Paul had already thought about the cost of obedience and decided it was worthwhile.

21:14 Ultimately, the only appropriate response for a believer is the one that Paul's companions stated: **The Lord's will be done**. One of the major themes of the book of Acts is

the simultaneous reality of human choice and the sovereign divine will (4:24-28; see note at 2:23).

21:16 **Mnason** was a **Cypriot** believer who had probably been saved during the first missionary journey. Mnason may be a Hellenized form of a Jewish name, or he may have been a Gentile.

21:17 The **brothers** who **welcomed** Paul and his friends were probably Mnason and his companions.

21:18 **James** is singled out as the leader of the church in Jerusalem, along with a group of **elders**. It is not clear how many of the original apostles would have still been in Jerusalem, but they do not appear in the following events. This verse marks the end of this "we" section.

21:19 As Paul did in his last major meeting in Jerusalem (15:4), he told James and the church elders what God had been doing **among the Gentiles** through his ministry. This was an appropriate follow-up to the original Jerusalem Council (see note at 15:2).

21:20 Having listened to Paul's report about what God had done "among the Gentiles" (v. 19), the Jerusalem leadership rejoiced but also answered back with something like one-upmanship. Mention of **many thousands of Jews** converting in Jerusalem was perhaps exaggeration, for the city had a population between 25,000 and 50,000. At issue in the back-and-forth between Jerusalem leaders and Paul (minister to the Gentiles) is the role of the law in Christian faith; thus the emphasis on Jewish believers being **zealous for the law**. Perhaps this response also represented an attempt by believers in Jerusalem to strengthen their position as they saw the center of the church shift to Gentile Christians.

21:21 Rumor said Paul was teaching Jews who were dispersed among Gentiles to disregard Mosaic law and

Moses, by telling them not to circumcise their children or to walk in our customs.ᵃ ²²So what is to be done?ᴬ They will certainly hear that you've come. ²³Therefore do what we tell you: We have four men who have obligated themselves with a vow. ²⁴Take these men, purify yourself along with them, and pay for them to get their heads shaved. Then everyone will know that what they were told about you amounts to nothing, but that you yourself are also careful about observing the law.ᵇ ²⁵With regard to the Gentiles who have believed, we have written a letter containing our decision thatᴮ they should keep themselves from food sacrificed to idols, from blood, from what is strangled, and from sexual immorality."

The Riot in the Temple Complex

²⁶Then the next day, Paul took the men, having purified himself along with them, and entered the temple, announcing the completion of the purification days when the offering for each of them would be made.ᶜ ²⁷As the seven days were about to end, the Jews from ˙Asia saw him in the ˙temple complex, stirred up the whole crowd, and seized him,ᵈ ²⁸shouting, "Men of Israel, help! This is the man who teaches everyone everywhere against our people, our law, and this place. What's more, he also brought Greeks into the temple and has profaned this holy place."ᵉ ²⁹For they had previously seen Trophimus the Ephesian in the city with him, and they supposed that Paul had brought him into the temple complex.ᶜ,ᶠ

³⁰The whole city was stirred up, and the people rushed together. They seized Paul, dragged him out of the temple complex, and at once the gates were shut.ᵍ ³¹As they were trying to kill him, word went up to the commander of the ˙regiment that all Jerusalem was in chaos. ³²Taking along soldiers and ˙centurions, he immediately ran down to them. Seeing the commander and the soldiers, they stopped beating Paul. ³³Then the commander came up, took him into custody, and ordered him to be bound with two chains.ʰ He asked who he was and what he had done. ³⁴Some in the mob were shouting one thing and some another. Since he was not able to get reliable information because of the uproar, he ordered him to be taken into the barracks.ⁱ ³⁵When Paul got to the steps, he had to be carried by the soldiers because of the mob's violence, ³⁶for the mass of people followed, yelling, "Take him away!"ʲ

Paul's Defense before the Jerusalem Mob

³⁷As he was about to be brought into the barracks, Paul said to the commander, "Am I allowed to say something to you?"

He replied, "Do you know Greek? ³⁸Aren't you the Egyptian who raised a rebellion some time ago and led 4,000 Assassinsᴰ,ᴱ into the wilderness?"ᵏ

³⁹Paul said, "I am a Jewish man from Tarsus of Cilicia,ˡ a citizen of an important city.ᶠ Now I ask you, let me speak to the people."

ᵃ21:21 Ac 6:14; 15:19-20; 21:28; 1Co 7:18
ᵇ21:24 Jn 11:55; Ac 18:18; 21:26; 24:18
ᶜ21:26 Nm 6:13; Ac 24:18
ᵈ21:27 Ac 24:18; 26:21
ᵉ21:28 Mt 24:15; Ac 24:6
ᶠ21:29 Ac 18:19; 20:4
ᵍ21:30 2Kg 11:15; Ac 16:19; 26:21
ʰ21:33 Ac 12:6; 20:23; 21:11; Eph 6:20; 2Tm 1:16; 2:9
ⁱ21:34 Ac 19:32; 23:10
ʲ21:36 Lk 23:18; Jn 19:15; Ac 22:22
ᵏ21:38 Mt 24:26; Ac 5:36
ˡ21:39 Ac 9:11; 22:3

ᴬ21:22 Other mss add *A multitude has to come together, since*   ᴮ21:25 Other mss add *they should observe no such thing, except that*   ᶜ21:29 The inner temple court for Jewish men   ᴰ21:38 Lit *4,000 men of the Assassins*   ᴱ21:38 In Lat, the word *Sicarii* is similar to the Eng word "cut-throats."   ᶠ21:39 Lit *of no insignificant city*

---

traditional Jewish rituals such as circumcision. To dismiss these fears, the brothers proposed a solution that would absolve Paul of the charges (vv. 23-24).

21:23-24 This proposal does not in any way imply that works of the law are necessary for salvation, which would fundamentally contradict Paul's preaching of the gospel (Rm 3:20).

21:25 On the Jerusalem Council, see notes at 15:21 and 15:22-23a. The issue of the **letter** had been solved much earlier, and what Paul had or had not encouraged Jews living among Gentiles to do would not be clarified by the proposal of verses 23-24. James was apparently succumbing to pressures from the Jewish believers in Jerusalem. Ultimately his proposal backfired (v. 27).

21:26 It is somewhat surprising that Paul agreed to perform the ritual of **purification**. Perhaps he sensed this was part of God's overall plan, to which he was partially privy (vv. 10-11; 20:22-23).

21:27 There is no indication that the **Jews** from **Asia** were Christians.

21:28-29 Trophimus, an Ephesian, accompanied Paul to Jerusalem (20:4). It is unlikely that Paul ever brought Trophimus into the temple. After all, Paul was in the process of

fulfilling the Jewish law, not ignoring or flaunting it. Even if the accusation was true, it would be Trophimus, not Paul, who would have been guilty according to the law as stated in temple inscriptions.

21:30 Paul was **seized** and **dragged** out of the temple complex, the **gates** were closed behind him, and he was left in the outermost area of the temple.

21:31-32 Once the crowd had isolated Paul, they tried **to kill him**. Roman soldiers were stationed in the Antonia Fortress on the northwest side of the temple mount. One of their chief jobs was to put down disturbances such as this.

21:34-36 Even with the soldiers protecting him, Paul **had to be carried** as the mob pressed in for the kill. Fortunately the **barracks** were nearby.

21:37-38 Paul asked permission to speak. His use of **Greek** surprised the Roman **commander** ("Claudius Lysias," 23:26). Lysias mistook Paul for an **Egyptian** rebel. The Jewish historian Josephus said this rebel, a messianic pretender, had gathered a number of people at the Mount of Olives to attack Jerusalem in A.D. 54. The group was routed by the Romans, but the leader escaped. Lysias initially suspected that Paul marked the return of this man.

⁴⁰After he had given permission, Paul stood on the steps and motioned with his hand to the people. When there was a great hush, he addressed them in the •Hebrew language:ᵃ

22 ¹"Brothers and fathers, listen now to my defense before you." ²When they heard that he was addressing them in the Hebrew language, they became even quieter.ᵇ ³Heᶜ continued, "I am a Jewish man, born in Tarsus of Cilicia but brought up in this cityᴬ at the feet of Gamalielᵈ and educated according to the strict view of our patriarchal law. Being zealous for God, just as all of you are today,ᵉ ⁴I persecuted this Wayᶠ to the death, binding and putting both men and women in jail,ᵍ ⁵as both the high priest and the whole council of elders can testify about me. After I received letters from them to the brothers, I traveled to Damascus to bring those who were prisoners there to be punished in Jerusalem.ʰ

Paul's Testimony

⁶"Asⁱ I was traveling and near Damascus, about noon an intense light from heaven suddenly flashed around me. ⁷I fell to the ground and heard a voice saying to me, 'Saul, Saul, why are you persecuting Me?'

⁸"I answered, 'Who are You, Lord?'

"He said to me, 'I am Jesus the •Nazarene, the One you are persecuting!' ⁹Now those who were with me saw the light,ᴮ but they did not hear the voice of the One who was speaking to me.ʲ

¹⁰"Then I said, 'What should I do, Lord?'

"And the Lord told me, 'Get up and go into Damascus, and there you will be told about everything that is assigned for you to do.'

¹¹"Since I couldn't see because of the brightness of that light, I was led by the hand by those who were with me, and came into Damascus.ᵏ ¹²Someone named Ananias, a devout man according to the law, having a good reputation with all the Jews residing there,ˡ ¹³came and stood by me and said, 'Brother Saul, regain your sight.' And in that very hour I looked up and saw him. ¹⁴Then he said, 'The God of our fathers has appointedᵐ you to know His will, to seeⁿ the Righteous One,ᵒ and to hear the sound of His voice.ᶜ ¹⁵For you will be a witness for Him to all people of what you have seen and heard.ᵖ ¹⁶And now, why delay? Get up and be baptized, and wash away your sinsᑫ by calling on His name.'ʳ

¹⁷"After I came back to Jerusalem and was praying in the •temple complex, I went into a visionary stateˢ ¹⁸and saw Him telling me, 'Hurry and get out of Jerusalem quickly, because they will not accept your testimony about Me!'

¹⁹"But I said, 'Lord, they know that in •synagogue after synagogue I had those who believed in You imprisoned and beaten.ᵗ ²⁰And when the blood of Your witness Stephen was being shed, I was standing by and approving,ᴰ and I guarded the clothes of those who killed him.'ᵘ

²¹"Then He said to me, 'Go, because I will send you far away to the Gentiles.'"ᵛ

Paul's Roman Protection

²²They listened to him up to this word. Then they raised their voices, shouting, "Wipe this person off the earth—it's a disgrace for him to live!"ʷ

ᵃ21:40 Jn 5:2; Ac 12:17
ᵇ22:1-2 Ac 7:2; 21:40
ᶜ22:3-16 Ac 9:1-22; 26:9-18
ᵈ22:3 Dt 33:3; Ac 5:34; 9:11; 21:39; 2Co 11:22; Php 3:5
ᵉAc 26:5; Rm 10:2; Php 3:6
ᶠ22:4 Ac 9:2; 24:14,22
ᵍAc 8:3; 22:19-20; 26:10
ʰ22:5 Lk 22:66; Ac 13:26; 1Tm 4:14
ⁱ22:6-11 Ac 9:3-8; 26:12-18
ʲ22:9 Dn 10:7; Ac 9:7; 26:13
ᵏ22:10-11 Ac 9:8; 16:30
ˡ22:12 Ac 9:10,17; 10:22
ᵐ22:14 Ac 3:13; 9:15; 26:16
ⁿ1Co 9:1; 15:8
ᵒAc 3:14; 7:52
ᵖ22:15 Ac 23:11; 26:16
ᑫ22:16 Ac 2:38; 1Co 6:11; Heb 10:22
ʳAc 9:14; Rm 10:13
ˢ22:17 Ac 9:26; 10:10
ᵗ22:19 Mt 10:17; Ac 8:3; 22:4
ᵘ22:20 Ac 7:58; 8:1; Rm 1:32
ᵛ22:21 Ac 9:15; 13:46
ʷ22:22 Ac 21:36; 25:24

ᴬ22:3 Probably Jerusalem, but others think Tarsus   ᴮ22:9 Other mss add *and were afraid*   ᶜ22:14 Lit *to hear a voice from His mouth*   ᴰ22:20 Other mss add *of his murder*

21:39 That **Paul** was a citizen of **Tarsus**, a city of importance in the Greco-Roman world, accounted for his knowledge of Greek.

21:40 Though the text says **Hebrew**, Paul probably spoke Aramaic to the crowd in order to communicate clearly with them. Aramaic became the new Hebrew, so to speak, among the Jewish people after the exile. In Paul's day Hebrew was used only by the religious elite.

22:1 Paul labeled his address a **defense** or an apology. This is his first apologetic speech in Acts.

22:3 Paul offered a number of important facts about himself. It appears that Paul spent his youth up to the age of 13 or so in Tarsus where he was probably educated in the first stage of Greek schooling. Then he went to Jerusalem (**this city**) and finished his education under Gamaliel. Elsewhere in Acts Paul indicated that much of his youth was spent in Jerusalem (26:4), and that he had relatives there (23:16).

22:4 Paul's admission that he **persecuted this Way to the death** indicates that he was more than a passive participant in events such as the stoning death of Stephen (7:58).

22:5-21 This is the second account of Paul's conversion in the book of Acts (9:7; 26:12-18).

22:9 According to 9:7, Paul's traveling companions heard the voice that spoke to him on the road to Damascus, but they did not see anyone. In this verse Paul himself said that they **did not hear the voice** of the One who was speaking to him. The grammar here supports the idea that Paul's traveling companions may have heard the voice but they did not understand it, or at least they did not understand it as the voice of the Lord.

22:17-21 Only this account of Paul's conversion mentions the **temple** vision. In his answer to the Lord (**But I said**), newly converted Paul seemed to expect his dramatic reversal from persecutor to advocate for Christianity would make his testimony powerful among Christian Jews in Jerusalem, but the Lord knew at this point they would **not accept** him. On early skepticism about Paul's conversion, see note at 9:26. On the execution of **Stephen**, see notes at verse 4 and 7:58.

22:22 Paul's mention of his commission to the Gentiles struck at the heart of Jewish nationalism.

²³As they were yelling and flinging aside their robes and throwing dust into the air,^a ²⁴the commander ordered him to be brought into the barracks, directing that he be examined with the scourge, so he could discover the reason they were shouting against him like this. ²⁵As they stretched him out for the lash, Paul said to the •centurion standing by, "Is it legal for you to scourge a man who is a Roman citizen and is uncondemned?"^b

²⁶When the centurion heard this, he went and reported to the commander, saying, "What are you going to do? For this man is a Roman citizen."

²⁷The commander came and said to him, "Tell me—are you a Roman citizen?"

"Yes," he said.

²⁸The commander replied, "I bought this citizenship for a large amount of money."

"But I was born a citizen," Paul said.

²⁹Therefore, those who were about to examine him withdrew from him at once. The commander too was alarmed when he realized Paul was a Roman citizen and he had bound him.^c

Paul before the Sanhedrin

³⁰The next day, since he wanted to find out exactly why Paul was being accused by the Jews, he released him^A and instructed the •chief priests and all the •Sanhedrin to convene.^d Then he brought Paul down and placed 23 him before them. ¹Paul looked intently at the •Sanhedrin and said, "Brothers, I have lived my life before God in all good conscience^e until this day." ²But the high

priest Ananias ordered those who were standing next to him to strike him on the mouth.^f ³Then Paul said to him, "God is going to strike you, you whitewashed wall! You are sitting there judging me according to the law, and in violation of the law are you ordering me to be struck?"^g

⁴And those standing nearby said, "Do you dare revile God's high priest?"

⁵"I did not know, brothers, that he was the high priest," replied Paul. "For it is written, **You must not speak evil of a ruler of your people.**"^{B,h} ⁶When Paul realized that one part of them were •Sadducees and the other part were •Pharisees, he cried out in the Sanhedrin, "Brothers, I am a Pharisee, a son of Pharisees!ⁱ I am being judged because of the hope of the resurrection of the dead!"^j ⁷When he said this, a dispute broke out between the Pharisees and the Sadducees, and the assembly was divided. ⁸For the Sadducees say there is no resurrection,^k and no angel or spirit, but the Pharisees affirm them all.

⁹The shouting grew loud, and some of the •scribes of the Pharisees'^l party got up and argued vehemently: "We find nothing evil in this man.^m What if a spirit or an angel has spoken to him?"^{C,n} ¹⁰When the dispute became violent, the commander feared that Paul might be torn apart by them and ordered the troops to go down, rescue him from them, and bring him into the barracks.^o

The Plot against Paul

¹¹The following night, the Lord stood by him and said, "Have courage! For as you have

Cross references (center column)

^a22:23 2Sm 16:13; Ac 7:58
^b22:24-25 Ac 16:37; 21:34; 22:29
^c22:29 Ac 16:38; 21:33
^d22:30 Mt 5:22; Ac 23:3-8
^e23:1 Ac 24:16; 1Co 4:4; 1Tm 3:9; 2Tm 1:5; Heb 13:18; 1Pt 3:16
^f23:2 1Kg 22:24; Jn 18:22; Ac 24:1
^g23:3 Lv 19:15; Dt 25:1-2; Mt 23:27; Jn 7:51
^h23:5 Ex 22:28; Ac 24:17
ⁱ23:6 Ac 26:5; Php 3:5
^jAc 24:15,21; 26:6-8; 28:20
^k23:8 Mt 22:23; Mk 12:18; Lk 20:27
^l23:9 Mk 2:16; Lk 5:30
^mAc 23:29; 25:25; 26:31
ⁿJn 12:29; Ac 22:7,17-18
^o23:10 Ac 21:34; 23:16,32

A22:30 Other mss add *from his chains*   B23:5 Ex 22:28   C23:9 Other mss add *Let us not fight God.*

22:24 The Roman **commander** knew that Paul spoke Greek, but he also knew that he was a Jew. Thus he assumed it was legal to scourge him as the first step in the interrogation.

22:25 Paul knew it was illegal to **scourge** an uncondemned **Roman citizen**; see note at 16:37.

22:28 Roman citizenship could be obtained by paying bribes (equal to as much as a year's wages) to appropriate officials. Sometimes citizenship was granted to entire cities or to individuals who performed meritorious service for the Empire. One of Paul's ancestors may have performed noteworthy service to Rome, including serving in the army or providing supplies for the army, such as making tents. Whatever the origin, Paul had inherited his Roman citizenship.

22:29 The significance of Roman citizenship is made clear, just as it was in Philippi (16:37). Stiff penalties could be handed down for mistreating a **Roman citizen** in this way.

22:30 Paul was either **released** from his chains or released from Roman imprisonment while the **Sanhedrin** convened to try him on charges related to the Jewish law. During this time he remained under the protection of the Roman soldiers.

23:2-3 The high priest ordered Paul struck on the mouth because he thought Paul was lying about having a "good conscience" before God (v. 1). Paul's accusation that the priest was a **whitewashed wall** meant the priest practiced outward piety but was inwardly corrupt.

23:4-5 Paul claimed not to have recognized the **high priest**, but most likely he was only being ironical. In this way he highlighted the high priest's inappropriate behavior.

23:6 Paul deflected the attention of the Sanhedrin by dividing his accusers over the doctrine of **resurrection**. The **Pharisees**, like Paul, believed in resurrection, while the **Sadducees**, of which the high priest Ananias was a member, did not. The ensuing debate led some of the scribes, who were associated with the Pharisees, to find no basis for charging Paul (v. 9).

23:10 Once again Roman intervention saves Paul's life; see 21:34-36 and note.

23:11 Again we see God's sovereign guidance of Paul's mission; see 22:17-21 and note.

testified about Me in Jerusalem, so you must also testify in Rome."[a]

[12] When it was day, the Jews formed a conspiracy and bound themselves under a curse: neither to eat nor to drink until they had killed Paul.[b] [13] There were more than 40 who had formed this plot. [14] These men went to the •chief priests and elders and said, "We have bound ourselves under a solemn curse that we won't eat anything until we have killed Paul. [15] So now you, along with the Sanhedrin, make a request to the commander that he bring him down to you[A] as if you were going to investigate his case more thoroughly. However, before he gets near, we are ready to kill him."[c]

[16] But the son of Paul's sister, hearing about their ambush, came and entered the barracks and reported it to Paul. [17] Then Paul called one of the •centurions and said, "Take this young man to the commander, because he has something to report to him."

[18] So he took him, brought him to the commander, and said, "The prisoner Paul called me and asked me to bring this young man to you, because he has something to tell you."

[19] Then the commander took him by the hand, led him aside, and inquired privately, "What is it you have to report to me?"

[20] "The Jews," he said, "have agreed to ask you to bring Paul down to the Sanhedrin tomorrow, as though they are going to hold a somewhat more careful inquiry about him. [21] Don't let them persuade you, because there are more than 40 of them arranging to ambush him, men who have bound themselves under a curse not to eat or drink until they

[a] 23:11 Ac 18:9; 19:21; 27:23
[b] 23:12 Ac 23:14,21,30; 25:3
[c] 23:15 Ac 22:30; 23:1
[d] 23:21 Lk 11:54; Ac 23:12,14
[e] 23:23 Ac 8:40; 23:33
[f] 23:26 Lk 1:3; Ac 15:23; 24:3; 26:25
[g] 23:27 Ac 21:32-33; 22:25-29
[h] 23:29 Ac 18:15; 25:19
[i] Ac 25:25; 26:31
[j] 23:30 Ac 9:24; 23:12,20
[k] Ac 24:19; 25:16

kill him. Now they are ready, waiting for a commitment from you."[d]

[22] So the commander dismissed the young man and instructed him, "Don't tell anyone that you have informed me about this."

To Caesarea by Night

[23] He summoned two of his centurions and said, "Get 200 soldiers ready with 70 cavalry and 200 spearmen to go to Caesarea at nine tonight.[B] [24] Also provide mounts so they can put Paul on them and bring him safely to Felix the governor."

[25] He wrote a letter of this kind:

[26] Claudius Lysias,
To the most excellent governor Felix: Greetings.[f]
[27] When this man had been seized by the Jews and was about to be killed by them, I arrived with my troops and rescued him because I learned that he is a Roman citizen.[g] [28] Wanting to know the charge they were accusing him of, I brought him down before their Sanhedrin. [29] I found out that the accusations were about disputed matters in their law,[h] and that there was no charge that merited death or chains.[i] [30] When I was informed that there was a plot against the man,[C,j] I sent him to you right away. I also ordered his accusers[k] to state their case against him in your presence.[D]

[31] Therefore, the soldiers took Paul during the night and brought him to Antipatris as they were ordered. [32] The next day, they returned to the barracks, allowing the cavalry

---

[A] 23:15 Other mss add *tomorrow*   [B] 23:23 Lit *at the third hour tonight*   [C] 23:30 Other mss add *by the Jews*   [D] 23:30 Other mss add *Farewell*

23:16 **Paul's** nephew reported the murder plot (vv. 12-15). It is unclear how many of Paul's family members were in Jerusalem (see vv. 17,22). Most likely Paul's sister lived in Jerusalem, perhaps indicating that his entire family had moved there after Paul's childhood in Tarsus. The Greek of this verse suggests Paul's nephew was in his late teens. It is not stated how he came to know of the plot, but certainly the air was ripe for such a plot.

23:23 The commander acted decisively to get Paul out of harm's way. **Caesarea** was the headquarters for the province. Here Paul would be under the protection of the procurator, Felix.

23:24 Originally a slave, **Felix** became procurator of Judea in A.D. 52. He was removed from office around A.D. 59 for mishandling conflicts between Jews and Gentiles in Caesarea.

23:25-30 The letter from **Claudius Lysias**, the commander, followed the standard letter form of the time, with a greeting, the body of the letter, and a closing. Possibly Luke reconstructed it from Paul's recollection, but it is also pos-

sible that Luke himself heard it read in front of Felix and Paul in Caesarea.

23:27 Though in English translation this verse appears to say the commander learned that Paul was a **Roman citizen** before he **rescued** him, the Greek grammar indicates that the commander rescued Paul and then learned that he was a Roman citizen, which is exactly what happened (chaps. 21-22).

23:29-30 Lysias interpreted the conflict as a dispute over Jewish law, which meant the charge against Paul did not merit **death** or imprisonment under Roman law. His sending Paul to Felix might seem to imply otherwise, but this move was aimed at protecting Paul and allowing the Jewish authorities a chance to formally present their **case** before the Roman governor.

23:31-33 The distance from Jerusalem to **Antipatris** was approximately 35 miles along the Roman road. The trip from Antipatris to **Caesarea** was along the coast and did not require such a large guard to ensure Paul's safety.

to go on with him. ³³When these men entered Caesarea and delivered the letter to the governor, they also presented Paul to him.ᵃ ³⁴After heᴬ read it, he asked what province he was from. So when he learned he was from Cilicia,ᵇ ³⁵he said, "I will give you a hearing whenever your accusers get here too." And he ordered that he be kept under guard in •Herod's •palace.ᶜ

The Accusation against Paul

24 After five days Ananias the high priest came down with some elders and a lawyerᴮ named Tertullus. These men presented their case against Paul to the governor.ᵈ ²When he was called in, Tertullus began to accuse him and said: "Since we enjoy great peace because of you, and reforms are taking place for the benefit of this nation by your foresight, ³we acknowledge this in every way and everywhere, most excellentᵉ Felix, with utmost gratitude. ⁴However, so that I will not burden you any further, I beg you in your graciousness to give us a brief hearing. ⁵For we have found this man to be a plague,ᶠ an agitatorᵍ among all the Jews throughout the Ro-

man world, and a ringleader of the sect of the •Nazarenes! ⁶He even tried to desecrate the temple, so we apprehended him [and wanted to judge him according to our law. ⁷But Lysias the commander came and took him from our hands with great force, ⁸commanding his accusers to come to you.]ᶜ By examining him yourself you will be able to discern all these things we are accusing him of." ⁹The Jews also joined in the attack, alleging that these things were so.

Paul's Defense before Felix

¹⁰When the governor motioned to him to speak, Paul replied: "Because I know you have been a judge of this nation for many years, I am glad to offer my defense in what concerns me.ʰ ¹¹You are able to determine that it is no more than 12 days since I went up to worship in Jerusalem.ⁱ ¹²They didn't find me disputing with anyone or causing a disturbance among the crowd, either in the •temple complex or in the •synagogues or anywhere in the city.ʲ ¹³Neither can they provide evidence to you of what they now bring against me. ¹⁴But I confess this to you: I worship my fathers' God

a23:33 Ac 8:40; 23:23-24,26
b23:34 Ac 6:9; 21:39; 25:1
c23:35 Mt 27:27; Ac 24:27; 25:16
d24:1 Ac 21:27; 23:2,24,30
e24:3 Lk 1:3; Ac 23:26; 26:25
f24:5 Ac 16:20; 17:6
g24:9 Ac 21:28; 26:5; 28:22
h24:9-10 Ac 23:24; 1Th 2:16
i24:11 Ac 21:27; 24:1
j24:12 Ac 25:8; 28:17

ᴬ23:34 Other mss read *the governor*   ᴮ24:1 In Gk, the word *rhetor* is similar to the Eng "rhetoric." In this situation, a rhetorician who was skilled in public speaking in the Gk language was needed.   ᶜ24:6-8 Other mss omit bracketed text

23:34-35 Felix could have sent Paul to the governor of Syria, but decided to try the case himself, perhaps because he realized how flimsy the evidence against Paul was and wished to settle the case as quickly as possible. Paul was kept in custody in the procurator's **palace**, originally built by Herod the Great.

24:1 Luke's reporting of the case against Paul reflects standard Roman legal procedure, including the prosecution brought by a *rhetor* (lawyer). Tertullus was a common Roman name, but he may have been a Jew (v. 6), although he refers to the Jews objectively in verse 5.

apologeomai

Greek Pronunciation	[ah pah lah GEH ah migh]
HCSB Translation	offer defense
Uses in Acts	6
Uses in the NT	10
Focus passage	Acts 24:10

The Greek verb *apologeomai* means *to speak in defense, to defend oneself*. The English word *apology* comes directly from the related Greek noun *apologia*. The term *apologia* in Greek means *defense*, not *apology*. Plato's famous work, *The Apology*, is a *defense* of Socrates, not an attempt to apologize for him.

In the NT, *apologia* can refer to a *defense* given through conduct (2Co 7:11) or by speech (Php 1:7,16; 1Pt 3:15)—often in a legal setting (Ac 22:1; 25:16; 2Tm 4:16)—or in written form (1Co 9:3). Similarly, the verb *apologeomai* normally refers to a verbal *defense* (Ac 19:33)—often also in a legal setting (Lk 12:11; 21:14; Ac 24:10; 25:8; 26:1-2,24)—though Paul used it once of the conscience *defending* itself (Rm 2:15) and once of a written *defense* (2Co 12:19).

24:2-3 Tertullus began with a *captatio benevolentiae*, the standard opening of a Greco-Roman speech designed to curry the favor of the listener, **Felix**.

24:5-7 Paul was accused by Tertullus of far more than just bringing a Gentile into the temple (**desecrate the temple**). Although the charge of desecrating the temple would perhaps make Felix suspicious of Paul, the charges of being an **agitator** and **ringleader** would have genuinely alarmed him since it implied Paul was a threat to Roman rule. Tertullus also said the Jewish authorities in Jerusalem would have been able to handle the situation if **Lysias** had not interfered. Clearly the Jews felt they should be left to do with Paul whatever they wished.

24:8 Tertullus finished with another compliment toward Felix, this time expressing confidence in his abilities to rightly judge the case against Paul.

24:10 When Felix asked Paul to **speak**, Paul offered a less flattering *captatio benevolentiae* (see note at vv. 2-3). Instead of offering hyperbole, he recognized that Felix was an experienced governor of **many years** before whom he would gladly offer his **defense**. This is Paul's second apologetic or defensive speech in Acts; see 22:1 and note for the first.

24:11-13 The **12 days** that Paul referred to did not include the time he had spent in Caesarea, but only time spent in **Jerusalem**. This was a sufficient amount of time for Paul's enemies to gather **evidence** that he was a troublemaker, and yet they were unable to **provide** any.

24:14 The phrase **the Way** is used throughout Acts as a self-designation by Christians (v. 22; 9:2; 19:9,23). At this early date, Christianity was considered a sect of Judaism. It became independent over time as it spread to Gentiles, and as Jews continued to reject it in large numbers. Paul

according to the Way,[a] which they call a sect, believing all the things that are written in the Law and in the Prophets.[b] [15] And I have a hope in God, which these men themselves also accept, that there is going to be a resurrection,[A,c] both of the righteous and the unrighteous.[d] [16] I always do my best to have a clear conscience[e] toward God and men. [17] After many years, I came to bring charitable gifts and offerings to my nation,[f] [18] and while I was doing this, some Jews from *Asia found me ritually purified in the temple, without a crowd and without any uproar.[g] [19] It is they who ought to be here before you to bring charges, if they have anything against me. [20] Either let these men here state what wrongdoing they found in me when I stood before the *Sanhedrin, [21] or about this one statement I cried out while standing among them, 'Today I am being judged before you concerning the resurrection of the dead.'"

The Verdict Postponed

[22] Since Felix was accurately informed about the Way,[h] he adjourned the hearing, saying, "When Lysias the commander comes down, I will decide your case." [23] He ordered that the *centurion keep Paul[B] under guard, though he could have some freedom, and that he should not prevent any of his friends from serving[c] him.[i]

[24] After some days, when Felix came with his

wife Drusilla, who was Jewish, he sent for Paul and listened to him on the subject of faith in Christ Jesus. [25] Now as he spoke about righteousness, self-control, and the judgment to come,[j] Felix became afraid and replied, "Leave for now, but when I find time I'll call for you." [26] At the same time he was also hoping that money would be given to him by Paul.[D] For this reason he sent for him quite often and conversed with him.

[27] After two years had passed, Felix received a successor, Porcius Festus,[k] and because he wished to do a favor for the Jews,[l] Felix left Paul in prison.[m]

Appeal to Caesar

25 Three days after Festus arrived in the province, he went up to Jerusalem from Caesarea.[n] [2] Then the *chief priests and the leaders of the Jews presented their case against Paul to him; and they appealed,[o] [3] asking him to do them a favor against Paul,[E] that he might summon him to Jerusalem. They were preparing an ambush along the road to kill him. [4] However, Festus answered that Paul should be kept at Caesarea, and that he himself was about to go there shortly.[p] [5] "Therefore," he said, "let the men of authority among you go down with me and accuse him, if there is any wrong in this man."

[6] When he had spent not more than eight or

[a]24:14 Ac 9:2; 22:4; 24:22
[b]Ac 3:13; 26:22; 28:23
[c]24:15 Ac 23:6; 28:20
[d]Dn 12:2; Jn 5:28-29
[e]24:16 Ac 23:1; 1Co 4:4; 1Tm 3:9; 2Tm 1:5; Heb 13:18; 1Pt 3:16
[f]24:17 Ac 11:29; Rm 15:25-28; 1Co 16:1-3; 2Co 8:1-4; Gl 2:10
[g]24:18 Ac 21:26-27; 26:21
[h]24:22 Ac 9:2; 22:4; 24:14
[i]24:23 Ac 23:35; 27:3; 28:16
[j]24:25 Gl 5:23; Ti 2:12; 2Pt 1:6
[k]24:27 Ac 25:1, 4,9; 26:24
[l]Ac 12:3; 25:9
[m]Ac 23:35; 25:14
[n]25:1 Ac 8:40; 23:34
[o]25:2 Ac 24:1; 25:15
[p]25:3-4 Ac 9:24; 24:23

A24:15 Other mss add *of the dead*　　**B**24:23 Lit *him*　　**C**24:23 Other mss add *or visiting*　　**D**24:26 Other mss add *so that he might release him*　　**E**25:3 Lit *asking a favor against him*

---

saw Christianity as continuous with, and the fulfillment of, ancient Judaism. Thus Paul and other believers worshiped their **fathers' God**.

24:15 Paul's belief in the **resurrection**—of the **righteous** to their reward, and the **unrighteous** to their punishment—aligned him with the Pharisees and against the Sadducees (23:6-9).

24:17 Paul came to Jerusalem **to bring charitable gifts and offerings** he had collected to aid the church there. This collection is mentioned in Paul's letters (Rm 15:25-26; 1Co 16:3; 2Co 8:1-9:15; cp. Gl 2:10), but is not emphasized in Acts.

24:18-19 Paul emphasized his state (**ritually purified**) and the state of the crowd (**without any uproar**) when **Jews from Asia** came across him and stirred up trouble.

24:20-21 Paul justly demanded that the **Sanhedrin** representatives charge him with things they had personally witnessed or heard from him (including talk about **resurrection of the dead**).

24:22 Felix was familiar with **the Way**. Some have speculated that he learned of Christianity through his wife, Drusilla, the daughter of Herod Agrippa (v. 24). As procurator for more than five years, he would have had numerous chances to learn this new movement. Felix seemed to acknowledge that Tertullus had not been a faithful conveyor of the facts surrounding Paul's arrest when he stated that he would wait for the arrival of Claudius **Lysias** before deciding the case.

24:23 The circumstances of Paul's imprisonment in Caesarea allowed visits by **friends** and colleagues. This privilege was likely made possible by his Roman citizenship.

24:24 Felix was interested enough in Christianity that he brought his wife, **Drusilla**, who was **Jewish**, to hear Paul.

24:25 Paul may have tailored his comments specifically for Felix, whose morals were publicly questioned. For instance, he took Drusilla from her first husband Azizus. Feeling the threat of divine judgment, **Felix became afraid** and sent Paul away.

24:26 Whatever hope Paul may have held for Felix's conversion, Felix's hidden motive for their ongoing discussions was base, illegal, and indicative of spiritual destitution.

24:27 Felix's immorality is on further display in the fact that he kept Paul imprisoned for **two years** even though he did not find that Paul had committed any punishable offense, and then left him in this state when **Festus** became the new proconsul (ca A.D. 59).

25:1-3 The new governor, **Festus**, went up from his palace in **Caesarea** to **Jerusalem**, probably to get a sense of the most important Jewish city in the realm. Hoping to seize on his unfamiliarity with the case, the Jewish leaders tried to coax him into sending Paul to Jerusalem, giving them a chance to renew their plans for **ambush**.

25:6-8 Having sinned neither against **Caesar** nor **Jewish**

10 days among them, he went down to Caesarea. The next day, seated at the judge's bench, he commanded Paul to be brought in.[a] [7]When he arrived, the Jews who had come down from Jerusalem stood around him and brought many serious charges that they were not able to prove,[b] [8]while Paul made the defense that, "Neither against the Jewish law,[c] nor against the temple, nor against Caesar have I sinned at all."

[9]Then Festus, wanting to do a favor for the Jews,[d] replied to Paul, "Are you willing to go up to Jerusalem, there to be tried before me on these charges?"

[10]But Paul said: "I am standing at Caesar's tribunal, where I ought to be tried. I have done no wrong to the Jews, as even you can see very well. [11]If then I am doing wrong, or have done anything deserving of death, I do not refuse to die, but if there is nothing to what these men accuse me of, no one can give me up to them. I appeal to Caesar!"[e]

[12]After Festus conferred with his council, he replied, "You have appealed to Caesar; to Caesar you will go!"

King Agrippa and Bernice Visit Festus

[13]After some days had passed, King Agrippa[A] and Bernice arrived in Caesarea and paid a courtesy call on Festus. [14]Since they stayed there many days, Festus presented Paul's case to the king, saying, "There's a man who was left as a prisoner by Felix. [15]When I was in Jerusalem, the chief priests and the elders of the Jews presented their case and asked for a judgment against him.[f] [16]I answered them that it's not the Romans' custom to give any man up[B] before the accused confronts the accusers face to face and has an opportunity to give a defense concerning the charges.[g] [17]Therefore, when they had assembled here, I did not delay. The next day I sat at the judge's bench and ordered the man to be brought in. [18]Concerning him, the accusers stood up and brought no charge of the sort I was expecting. [19]Instead they had some disagreements[h] with him about their own religion and about a certain Jesus, a dead man Paul claimed to be alive. [20]Since I was at a loss in a dispute over such things, I asked him if he wished to go to Jerusalem and be tried there concerning these matters. [21]But when Paul appealed to be held for trial by the Emperor, I ordered him to be kept in custody until I could send him to Caesar."

[22]Then Agrippa said to Festus, "I would like to hear the man myself."

"Tomorrow you will hear him," he replied.[i]

Paul before Agrippa

[23]So the next day, Agrippa and Bernice[j] came with great pomp and entered the auditorium with the commanders and prominent men of the city. When Festus gave the command, Paul was brought in. [24]Then Festus said: "King Agrippa and all men present with us, you see this man about whom the whole Jewish community has appealed to me, both in Jerusalem and here, shouting that he should not live any longer.[k] [25]Now I realized that he had not done anything deserving of death, but when he himself appealed to the Emperor, I decided to send him.[l] [26]I have nothing definite to write to my lord about him. Therefore, I have brought him before all of you, and especially before you, King Agrippa, so that after this examination is over, I may have something to write. [27]For it seems unreasonable to me to send a prisoner and not to indicate the charges against him."

a 25:6 Mt 27:19; Ac 25:10,17
b 25:7 Mk 15:3; Lk 23:2,10; Ac 24:5,13
c 25:8 Ac 6:13; 24:12; 28:17
d 25:9 Ac 24:27; 25:20
e 25:11 Ac 25:21,25; 26:32; 28:19
f 25:14-15 Ac 24:27; 25:2
g 25:16 Ac 23:30; 24:4-5
h 25:19 Ac 18:15; 23:29
i 25:20-22 Ac 9:15; 25:9,11
j 25:23 Ac 25:13; 26:30
k 25:24 Ac 22:22; 25:2,7
l 25:25 Ac 23:29; 25:11-12

A 25:13 Herod Agrippa II ruled Palestine A.D. 52–ca 95.   B 25:16 Other mss add *to destruction*

---

law, Paul was a victim of a smear campaign aimed to snuff out Christianity.

25:9-11 Likely aware of the ongoing plan to murder him, Paul avoided **Jerusalem** by invoking his right as a Roman citizen to **appeal** directly to **Caesar**. Not all such appeals were granted by local governors, but Festus was glad to shift this case to another jurisdiction and free himself of the pressure to appease the Jews (see note at 26:32).

25:13 Herod **Agrippa** II visited Caesarea with his sister **Bernice**, who had a checkered sexual and marital history. Herod was the last of the Herodian rulers. Festus was sly to bring Herod into the controversy over Paul, for Herod had responsibility for the temple and appointing the Jewish high priest. Thus he had an interest in the charges that Paul had violated the temple.

25:18-19 Festus had expected a more serious charge, like fomenting insurrection and revolution. He came to understand that the major issue was whether Jesus, who had died, was now **alive**.

25:20 Realizing that the theological debate was beyond him, Festus attempted to put a good spin on the push for Paul to **go to Jerusalem** for trial.

25:23 The entrance of **Agrippa and Bernice** must have been quite an occasion, with the honored guests and other people forming an elaborate entourage.

25:25 Festus had not previously made it known publicly that he thought Paul was innocent. Since Paul had made his appeal to Caesar, Festus was now free to admit, without repercussion, that he believed the charges were groundless (see note at 26:31).

25:26-27 Festus found the case not only groundless but perplexing. He hoped **Agrippa** would be able to help him think of a way to specify to the Emperor the **charges** laid against Paul.

Paul's Defense before Agrippa

26 Agrippa said to Paul, "It is permitted for you to speak for yourself."

Then Paul stretched out his hand and began his defense: ²"I consider myself fortunate, King Agrippa, that today I am going to make a defense before you about everything I am accused of by the Jews, ³especially since you are an expert in all the Jewish customs and controversies. Therefore I beg you to listen to me patiently.

⁴"All the Jews know my way of life from my youth, which was spent from the beginning among my own nation and in Jerusalem.ᵃ ⁵They had previously known me for quite some time, if they were willing to testify, that according to the strictest party of our religion I lived as a •Pharisee.ᵇ ⁶And now I stand on trial for the hopeᶜ of the promiseᵈ made by God to our fathers, ⁷the promise our 12 tribes hope to attain as they earnestly serve Him night and day. King Agrippa, I am being accused by the Jews because of this hope.ᵉ ⁸Why is it considered incredible by any of you that God raises the dead? ⁹In fact, I myself supposed it was necessary to do many things in opposition to the name of Jesus the •Nazarene.ᶠ ¹⁰I actually did this in Jerusalem, and I locked up many of the •saints in prison, since I had received authority for that from the •chief priests. When they were put to death, I cast my vote against them.ᵍ ¹¹In all the •synagogues I often tried to make them blaspheme by punishing them.ʰ I even pursued them to foreign cities since I was greatly enraged at them.

Paul's Account of His Conversion and Commission

¹²"I was traveling to Damascus underⁱ these circumstances with authority and a commission from the chief priests. ¹³King Agrippa, while on the road at midday, I saw a light from heaven brighter than the sun, shining around me and those traveling with me. ¹⁴We all fell to the ground, and I heard a voice speaking to me in the •Hebrew language, 'Saul, Saul, why are you persecuting Me? It is hard for you to kick against the goads.'ᴬʲ

¹⁵"Then I said, 'Who are You, Lord?'

"And the Lord replied: 'I am Jesus, the One you are persecuting. ¹⁶But get up and stand on your feet. For I have appeared to you for this purpose, to appoint you as a servant and a witness of what you have seenᴮ and of what I will reveal to you.ᵏ ¹⁷I will rescue you from the people and from the Gentiles. I now send you to themˡ ¹⁸to open their eyesᵐ so they may turn from darkness to light and from the power of Satan to God, that by faith in Me they may receive forgiveness of sins and a share among those who are •sanctified.'ⁿ

¹⁹"Therefore, King Agrippa, I was not disobedient to the heavenly vision. ²⁰Instead, I preached to those in Damascus first, and to those in Jerusalem and in all the region of Judea, and to the Gentiles, that they should repent and turn to God, and do works worthy of repentance.ᵒ ²¹For this reason the Jews seized me in the •temple complex and were trying to kill me. ²²To this very day, I have obtained help that comes from God, and I stand and

Cross references

ᵃ26:3-4 Ac 6:14; 25:19; Gl 1:13
ᵇ26:5 Ac 22:3; 23:6; Php 3:5
ᶜ26:6 Ac 24:15; 28:20
ᵈAc 13:32; Rm 15:8
ᵉ26:7 Php 3:11; 1Th 3:10; 1Tm 5:5; Jms 1:1
ᶠ26:9 Jn 16:2; 1Tm 1:13
ᵍ26:10 Ac 8:3; 9:13-14,21; 22:5,20
ʰ26:11 Ac 25:21,25; 26:32; 28:19
ⁱ26:12-18 Ac 9:3-8; 22:6-11
ʲ26:14 Ac 9:7; 21:40
ᵏ26:16 Ezk 2:1; Dn 10:11; Ac 22:14-15
ˡ26:17 1Ch 16:35; Jr 1:8,19; Ac 9:15
ᵐ26:18 Is 35:5; 42:7
ⁿAc 20:32; Eph 5:8; Col 1:13; 1Pt 2:9
ᵒ26:20 Mt 3:8; Lk 3:8; Ac 9:19-20,22,26-29; 13:46; 22:17-20

ᴬ**26:14** Sharp sticks used to prod animals, such as oxen in plowing   ᴮ**26:16** Other mss read *things in which you have seen Me*

26:1 This is Paul's third apologetic or defensive speech in Acts; see 22:1; 24:10.

26:2-3 Paul began his *captatio benevolentiae* (see notes at 24:2-3 and 24:10) by flattering Agrippa about how **fortunate** he was to be making his **defense** before an expert in **Jewish customs** and laws.

26:4-5 My youth indicates that Paul had lived **in Jerusalem** since his teens. All this time his **way of life** had been known and seen by others, and he lived **by the strictest party** of Jewish religion, the Pharisees. In this way Paul painted a portrait of his character for Agrippa.

26:6-8 Paul distilled the entire controversy down to his **hope of the promise made by God** to raise the dead. More than a mere tactic to pit Pharisees and Sadducees against one another, this was an accurate assessment of the Jewish complaint against Christianity: that Jesus was raised from the dead and that faith in Him as risen Lord gives eternal life.

26:12-18 This is the third and final account of Paul's conversion in the book of Acts (9:1-7; 22:6-11).

26:14 Only in this account of his conversion did Paul say the voice from heaven spoke to him in the **Hebrew language**. "Hebrew" may literally have been Aramaic, the common

tongue of the first-century Jew (see note at 21:40). **It is hard for you to kick against the goads** probably meant that Paul should not resist the divine force that was moving him in a new direction.

26:16-18 These three verses are not included in the accounts of Paul's conversion in chapters 9 or 22, even though the mention of Paul's ministry to the **Gentiles** was a message given to Ananias in Damascus (9:15; 22:15). Many scholars believe the essence of Paul's mission to the Gentiles was revealed to him at the time of his conversion. Certainly these three verses summarize Paul's ministry to both Jews and Gentiles.

26:19 I was not disobedient is a spectacular understatement in light of Paul's faithfulness to God's calling, even through remarkable hardships.

26:20-21 Paul's faithfulness to "the heavenly vision" (v. 19) was the very reason **the Jews seized** him and wanted him dead. Thus Paul's stance is reminiscent of the one taken by "Peter and the apostles" in 5:29, where they said, "We must obey God rather than men." This is living out the principle Jesus taught in Mt 10:28.

26:22-23 Paul emphasized that the message of Christ's

testify to both small and great, saying nothing else than what the prophets and Moses said would take place[a]— [23]that the •Messiah must suffer, and that as the first to rise from the dead, He would proclaim light to our people and to the Gentiles."[b]

Not Quite Persuaded

[24]As he was making his defense this way, Festus exclaimed in a loud voice, "You're out of your mind,[c] Paul! Too much study is driving you mad!"

[25]But Paul replied, "I'm not out of my mind, most excellent Festus. On the contrary, I'm speaking words of truth and good judgment.[d] [26]For the king knows about these matters. It is to him I am actually speaking boldly. For I am convinced that none of these things escapes his notice, since this was not done in a corner. [27]King Agrippa, do you believe the prophets? I know you believe."

[28]Then Agrippa said to Paul, "Are you going to persuade me to become a Christian so easily?"

[29]"I wish before God," replied Paul, "that whether easily or with difficulty, not only you but all who listen to me today might become as I am—except for these chains."[e]

[30]So the king, the governor, Bernice, and those sitting with them got up, [31]and when

a 26:22 Lk 24:27;
Ac 10:43; 24:14
b 26:23 Lk 24:26;
1Co 15:20,23;
Col 1:18; Rv 1:5
c 26:24 2Kg 9:11;
Jn 10:20; 1Co
1:23; 2:14; 4:10
d 26:25 Ac 23:26;
24:3
e 26:28-29 Ac
11:26; 21:33;
1Co 7:7
f 26:30-31 Ac
23:9,29; 25:23
g 26:32 Ac 25:11;
28:18
h 27:1 Ac 10:1;
16:10; 25:12,25
i 27:2 Ac 17:1;
19:29
j 27:3 Ac 24:23;
27:43; 28:16
k 27:5 Ac 6:9;
13:13

they had left they talked with each other and said, "This man is doing nothing that deserves death or chains."[f]

[32]Then Agrippa said to Festus, "This man could have been released if he had not appealed to Caesar."[g]

Sailing for Rome

27 When it was decided that we were to sail to Italy, they handed over Paul and some other prisoners to a •centurion named Julius, of the Imperial •Regiment.[h] [2]So when we had boarded a ship of Adramyttium, we put to sea, intending to sail to ports along the coast of •Asia. Aristarchus, a Macedonian of Thessalonica, was with us.[i] [3]The next day we put in at Sidon, and Julius treated Paul kindly and allowed him to go to his friends to receive their care.[j] [4]When we had put out to sea from there, we sailed along the northern coast[A] of Cyprus because the winds were against us. [5]After sailing through the open sea off Cilicia and Pamphylia, we reached Myra in Lycia.[k] [6]There the centurion found an Alexandrian ship sailing for Italy and put us on board. [7]Sailing slowly for many days, we came with difficulty as far as Cnidus. Since the wind did not allow us to approach it, we sailed along the south side[A] of Crete off Salmone. [8]With yet more difficulty we sailed along the coast

---

A 27:4,7 Lit sailed under the lee

suffering, death, and resurrection matched OT teachings. He probably had in mind such prophetic passages as Is 52:13–53:12.

26:24 **Festus** took Paul to be **mad** because of talk about resurrection and Messiah, Jewish beliefs that seemed foolish to the Gentile world.

26:25-26 As evidence for his **good judgment**, Paul pointed out that the major events of Christianity had not taken place **in a corner**, out of sight and scrutiny. Jesus' life, death, and resurrection were all public and could not have escaped King Agrippa's **notice**.

26:27 Paul played to the king's Jewishness. If **Agrippa** was a good Jew, he should have accepted the **prophets** and their message about Jesus.

26:28 Scholars disagree over whether Agrippa's response was sarcastic anger, a jest, or a sign that Paul's logic was close to persuading him.

26:29 Paul's rhetorical skills were at their best as he concluded his speech. His confidence in Christ was such that he wished that **all who listen** could become as him, **except** for the **chains**.

26:31 Objective judgment could lead to only one conclusion: Paul was innocent. But Paul's life was held in the service of the Lord, not the judgments of men.

26:32 The charges against Paul were found to be groundless before both Roman and Jewish authorities. Nevertheless, Paul's appeal to Rome put his case in a special category that must be discharged by Caesar himself.

27:1 This is the fourth **we** section in Acts (see note at 16:10), and it extends to verse 37. The most natural conclusion is that the author of the "we" source was along for the journey. There were a number of people besides Paul and the other prisoners on the ship (e.g., Aristarchus, v. 2).

27:2 **Adramyttium** was in western Asia near the island of Lesbos. Like many ships sailing the Mediterranean Sea, the ship appears to have been a small grain vessel that would have worked its way from Caesarea along the **coast** until it reached Adramyttium.

27:3 There apparently were Christians in **Sidon**, although Acts does not record when the city was evangelized. The Christian presence may have been made possible as a result of citizens traveling to Jerusalem at Pentecost (2:9) or Christians fleeing persecution in Jerusalem (11:19). Paul seemed to have **friends** there who provided for him, possibly friends made during an unrecorded visit as he traveled between Jerusalem and Antioch.

27:4 The route of travel reflects the need to sail close to land and to tack against the **winds**.

27:5-6 The ship from Adramyttium would have taken them out of their way since it was going to follow the coast of the province of Asia. As a result, at **Myra**, on the southern coast of Asia Minor, the centurion found a ship from Alexandria that was going to Rome. The **Alexandrian** ship would have been part of the grain supply trade from Egypt to Rome (see note at v. 38).

27:7-9 The journey was being undertaken at the end of the

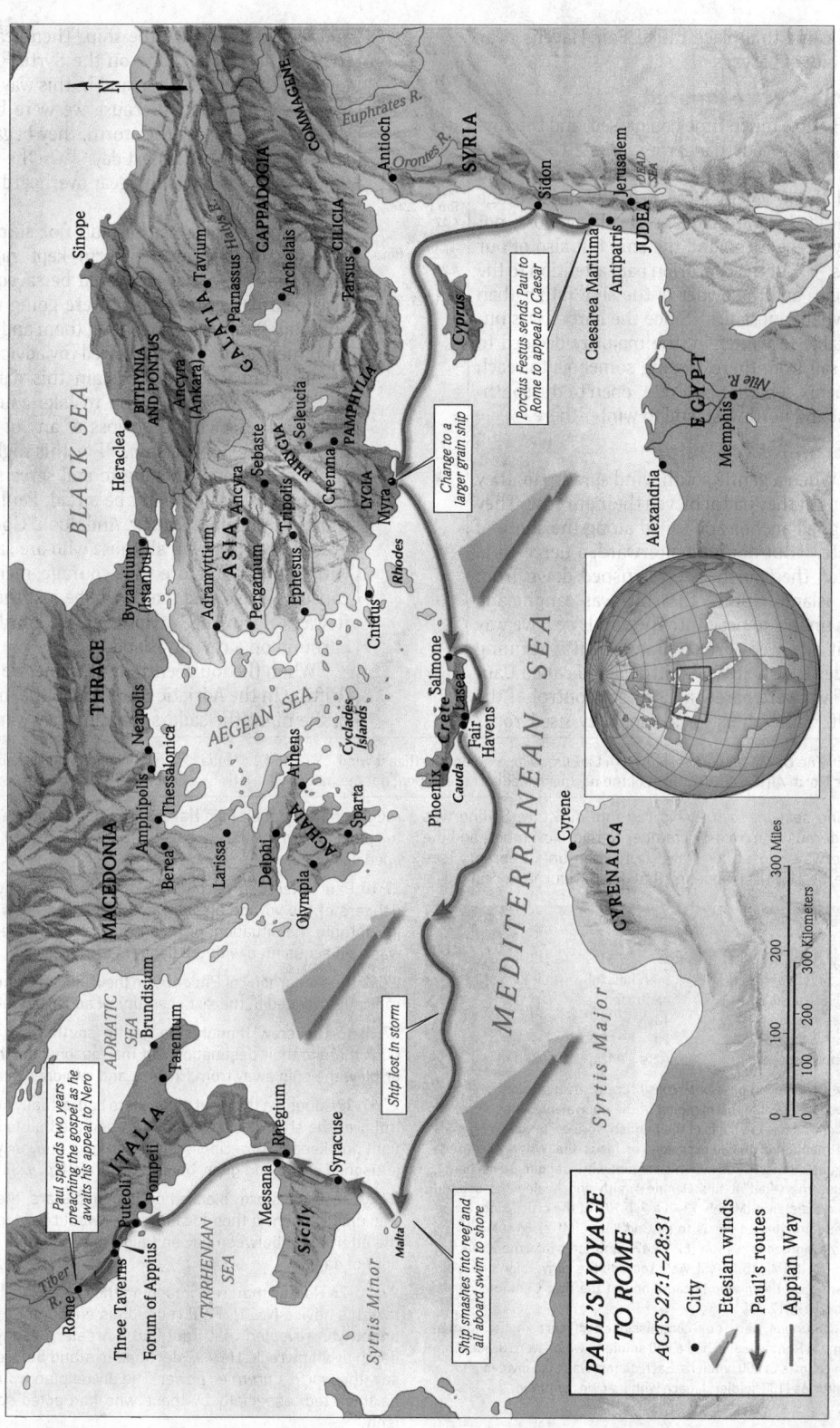

N

Euphrates R.

Sinope

Antioch

Orontes R.

SYRIA

COMMAGENE

CAPPADOCIA

Parnassus Halys R.

Tavium

Archelais

GALATIA

Ancyra
(Ankara)

BITHYNIA
AND PONTUS

Sidon

Jerusalem

DEAD
SEA

JUDEA

Antipatris

Caesarea Maritima

*Porcius Festus sends Paul to
Rome to appeal to Caesar*

Tarsus

CILICIA

Heraclea

BLACK SEA

Byzantium
(Istanbul)

Sebaste

Ancyra

PHRYGIA

Tripolis

Seleucia

Cremna

PAMPHYLIA

LYCIA

Myra

Cyprus

EGYPT

Nile R.

Memphis

Alexandria

THRACE

Adramyttium

Pergamum

ASIA

Ephesus

Cnidus

Rhodes

*Change to a
larger grain ship*

Neapolis

Amphipolis

Thessalonica

MACEDONIA

Berea

Larissa

Delphi

Athens

ACHAIA

Olympia

Sparta

AEGEAN SEA

*Cyclades
Islands*

Phoenix

Cauda

Salmone

Crete

Lasea

Fair
Havens

MEDITERRANEAN SEA

Cyrene

CYRENAICA

Syrtis Major

Ship lost in storm

ADRIATIC
SEA

Brundisium

Tarentum

*Paul spends two years
preaching the gospel as he
awaits his appeal to Nero*

ITALIA

Pompeii

Puteoli

Three Taverns

Forum of Appius

*Tiber
R.*

Rome

Rhegium

Messana

Syracuse

Sicily

*TYRRHENIAN
SEA*

Malta

Sytris Minor

*Ship smashes into reef and
all aboard swim to shore*

0   100   200   300 Miles

0   100   200   300 Kilometers

PAUL'S VOYAGE
TO ROME

ACTS 27:1–28:31

• City

Etesian winds

→ Paul's routes

— Appian Way

and came to a place called Fair Havens near the city of Lasea.

Paul's Advice Ignored

[9] By now much time had passed, and the voyage was already dangerous. Since the Fast[A,a] was already over, Paul gave his advice [10] and told them, "Men, I can see that this voyage is headed toward damage and heavy loss, not only of the cargo and the ship but also of our lives." [11] But the centurion paid attention to the captain and the owner of the ship rather than to what Paul said.[b] [12] Since the harbor was unsuitable to winter in, the majority decided to set sail from there, hoping somehow to reach Phoenix, a harbor on Crete[c] open to the southwest and northwest, and to winter there.

Storm-Tossed Ship

[13] When a gentle south wind sprang up, they thought they had achieved their purpose. They weighed anchor and sailed along the shore of Crete. [14] But not long afterward, a fierce wind called the "northeaster"[B] rushed down from the island. [15] Since the ship was caught and was unable to head into the wind, we gave way to it and were driven along. [16] After running under the shelter of a little island called Cauda,[c] we were barely able to get control of the skiff. [17] After hoisting it up, they used ropes

and tackle and girded the ship. Then, fearing they would run aground on the Syrtis,[D] they lowered the drift-anchor, and in this way they were driven along. [18] Because we were being severely battered by the storm, they began to jettison the cargo the next day.[d] [19] On the third day, they threw the ship's gear overboard with their own hands.

[20] For many days neither sun nor stars appeared, and the severe storm kept raging. Finally all hope that we would be saved was disappearing. [21] Since many were going without food, Paul stood up among them and said, "You men should have followed my advice not to sail from Crete and sustain this damage and loss. [22] Now I urge you to take courage, because there will be no loss of any of your lives, but only of the ship. [23] For this night an angel of the God I belong to and serve stood by me,[e] [24] and said, 'Don't be afraid, Paul. You must stand before Caesar. And, look! God has graciously given you all those who are sailing with you.' [25] Therefore, take courage, men, because I believe God that it will be just the way it was told to me.[f] [26] However, we must run aground on a certain island."[g]

[27] When the fourteenth night came, we were drifting in the Adriatic Sea,[E] and in the middle of the night the sailors thought they were ap-

a 27:9 Lv 16:29-31; 23:27-29; Nm 29:7
b 27:10-11 Ac 27:21; Rv 18:17
c 27:12 Ac 2:11; Ti 1:5
d 27:18 Jnh 1:5; Ac 27:38
e 27:23 Dn 6:16; Ac 18:9; 23:11; Rm 1:9; 2Tm 4:17
f 27:25 Ac 27:22,36; Rm 4:20-21
g 27:26 Ac 27:17,29; 28:1

A 27:9 The Day of Atonement   B 27:14 Lit *Euraquilo*, a violent northeast wind   C 27:16 Or *Clauda*   D 27:17 = sandbanks or sandbars near North Africa   E 27:27 Part of the northern Mediterranean Sea; not the modern Adriatic Sea east of Italy

sailing season, so the ship ran into difficulty. Sailing was dangerous from mid-September to mid-November, and the waterways closed for travel from then until February (see note at 28:11). It appears that Paul's journey occurred in

roughly mid-October. **Fair Havens** was not a suitable place to spend the winter because the harbor was exposed to the open sea (v. 12).

27:10 Paul offered a prophetic-like statement about the dangers of the voyage ahead. He either had divinely given insight into the situation, or as an experienced traveler he was well acquainted with the dangers of seafaring.

27:12 The topography of **Phoenix**, on the island of **Crete**, was radically changed in the sixth century by an earthquake.

27:13-16 The crew thought the **gentle south wind** would push them to their destination, but the seasonal **northeaster** blew the ship away from Phoenix and into open sea.

27:17-19 Caught in the wind, the sailors had virtually no control over the ship. They tied **ropes** around the hull to bind it tight and keep it from ripping apart. To gain buoyancy, they jettisoned **cargo** and **gear**, but not the grain (cp. v. 38).

27:20 Since the storm blacked out **sun** and **stars**, the crew was unable to chart their location. They would have tracked the alternation between day and night by noting the vague light of day.

27:22-26 Rather than reprimanding the crew for failure to take his advice (v. 21), Paul related his encounter with an **angel** who revealed that Paul had a greater destiny than death by shipwreck. He was destined to **stand before Caesar**, the world's premier power. The divine plan would not be thwarted, especially by those who had acted so foolishly.

hekatontarches

Greek Pronunciation	[heh kah tahn TAHR kayss]
HCSB Translation	centurion
Uses in Acts	13
Uses in the NT	20
Focus passage	Acts 27:1,6,11,31,43

The Greek noun *hekatontarches* literally means *leader of a hundred*. This is also the meaning of the equivalent Latin term *centurio*, which is the basis of the English word *centurion*. Centurions are mentioned on two occasions in Jesus' life. When a *centurion* requested that Jesus heal his servant without going to his home, Jesus marveled at this Gentile's faith and healed the servant from a distance (Mt 8:5-13 = Lk 7:1-10). At the crucifixion, a *centurion* proclaimed Jesus to be God's Son (Mt 27:54 = Mk 15:39) and a righteous person (Lk 23:47), and later informed Pilate of His death (Mk 15:44-45). Acts records the conversion of a God-fearing *centurion* who became one of the first Gentile converts (Ac 10:1-8,17-48).

Centurions were non-commissioned officers in the Roman army. A Roman legion had 6,000 soldiers, which were divided into ten cohorts of 600 soldiers. Each cohort was also divided into six centuries (100 soldiers), each with its own *centurion*.

proaching land.[A] [28]They took a sounding and found it to be 120 feet[B] deep; when they had sailed a little farther and sounded again, they found it to be 90 feet[C] deep. [29]Then, fearing we might run aground in some rocky place, they dropped four anchors from the stern and prayed for daylight to come.

[30]Some sailors tried to escape from the ship; they had let down the skiff into the sea, pretending that they were going to put out anchors from the bow. [31]Paul said to the centurion and the soldiers, "Unless these men stay in the ship, you cannot be saved." [32]Then the soldiers cut the ropes holding the skiff and let it drop away.

[33]When it was about daylight, Paul urged them all to take food, saying, "Today is the fourteenth day that you have been waiting and going without food, having eaten nothing. [34]Therefore I urge you to take some food. For this has to do with your survival, since none of you will lose a hair from your head."[a] [35]After he said these things and had taken some bread, he gave thanks to God in the presence of all of them, and when he broke it, he began to eat.[b] [36]They all became encouraged and took food themselves. [37]In all there were 276 of us on the ship.[c] [38]When they had eaten enough, they began to lighten the ship by throwing the grain overboard into the sea.

Shipwreck

[39]When daylight came, they did not recognize the land but sighted a bay with a beach. They planned to run the ship ashore if they could.[d] [40]After casting off the anchors, they left them in the sea, at the same time loosening the ropes that held the rudders. Then they hoisted the foresail to the wind and headed for the beach. [41]But they struck a sandbar and ran the ship aground. The bow jammed fast and remained immovable, while the stern began to break up by the pounding of the waves.

[42]The soldiers' plan was to kill the prisoners so that no one could swim away and escape. [43]But the centurion kept them from carrying out their plan because he wanted to save Paul, so he ordered those who could swim to jump overboard first and get to land. [44]The rest were to follow, some on planks and some on debris from the ship. In this way, everyone safely reached the shore.[e]

Malta's Hospitality

28 Once ashore, we[f] then learned that the island was called Malta.[g] [2]The local people[h] showed us extraordinary kindness, for they lit a fire and took us all in, since it was raining and cold. [3]As Paul gathered a bundle of brushwood and put it on the fire, a viper came out because of the heat and fastened itself to his hand. [4]When the local people saw

Cross references (center column):
[a]27:34 1Kg 1:52; Mt 10:30; Lk 21:18
[b]27:35 Mt 14:19; 15:36
[c]27:37 Ac 2:41; 7:14; Rm 13:1; 1Pt 3:20
[d]27:38-39 Ac 27:18; 28:1
[e]27:41-44 Ac 12:19; 27:3,22; 2Co 11:25
[f]28:1 Ac 16:10; 27:1
[g]Ac 27:26,39
[h]28:2 Rm 1:14; 1Co 14:11; Col 3:11

[A]27:27 Lit *thought there was land approaching them*   [B]27:28 Lit *20 fathoms*   [C]27:28 Lit *15 fathoms*

27:27 The **Adriatic Sea** mentioned here is not the same one that is currently known as the Adriatic Sea between Italy and the former Yugoslavia. It apparently refers instead to the modern day Ionian Sea between Crete, Malta, Italy, and Greece that extends into the Mediterranean Sea.

27:28-29 The sailors took a **sounding** by letting down lengths of weighted rope. They determined that they were approaching land at a fast pace, even though they could not see it. In an effort to slow down the ship, they took the unusual action of lowering **four anchors**, all from the **stern**, rather than dropping anchors from the bow, which would have swung the ship around. Verse 37 ends the fourth "we" section in Acts (see note at 16:10).

27:30-32 The prospect of imminent landfall after being adrift on the stormy sea for two weeks (v. 27) enticed a group of sailors to attempt, selfishly, an escape on the **skiff** (lifeboat). Paul's wisdom in preventing this is seen in the next episode, when all hands were needed (vv. 37ff).

27:33-34 The men had gone **without food** for 14 days, most likely because of severe seasickness brought on by the rough sea.

27:35 Following Jewish custom, Paul **gave thanks** to God for the food they ate.

27:36 Paul's example of steady faith ("he gave thanks to God") and practicality ("he began to eat," v. 35) in the midst of the storm **encouraged** the battered sailors.

27:38 The crew threw out the **grain**, which had been acting as ballast for the ship, so they could run it aground (v. 39).

27:39-40 In light of the damage to the ship and the loss of the lifeboat (vv. 30-32), the only option for reaching shore was to ground the ship.

27:41 With the **bow jammed fast** in the offshore **sandbar**, the ship's **stern** took a beating by the incoming **waves**.

27:42 The soldiers' intention to **kill the prisoners** was probably motivated by the fact that soldiers were held personally responsible for the prisoners whom they guarded. Any soldier whose prisoner escaped would suffer the prisoner's punishment.

27:43 By now the **centurion** recognized that paying attention to **Paul** was a good idea.

27:44 The sea would have been littered with **planks** and **debris** from the shattered ship.

28:1 This is the fifth **we** section in Acts (see note at 16:10), and it extends through verse 16. The shipwreck happened on **Malta**, a small island south of Sicily.

28:3-4 Although there are no poisonous snakes on Malta today, this does not mean there were none in Paul's day. Fauna and flora change over time. The residents of Malta apparently thought **Justice**, a Greek goddess, had singled Paul out because he deserved death (cp. v. 6).

the creature hanging from his hand, they said to one another, "This man is probably a murderer, and though he has escaped the sea, Justice[A] does not allow him to live!"[a] [5]However, he shook the creature off into the fire and suffered no harm.[b] [6]They expected that he would swell up or suddenly drop dead. But after they waited a long time and saw nothing unusual happen to him, they changed their minds and said he was a god.[c]

Ministry in Malta

[7]Now in the area around that place was an estate belonging to the leading man of the island, named Publius, who welcomed us and entertained us hospitably for three days. [8]Publius's father was in bed suffering from fever and dysentery. Paul went to him, and praying and laying his hands on him, he healed him.[d] [9]After this, the rest of those on the island who had diseases also came and were cured. [10]So they heaped many honors on us, and when we sailed, they gave us what we needed.

Rome at Last

[11]After three months we set sail in an Alexandrian ship that had wintered at the island, with the Twin Brothers[B] as its figurehead. [12]Putting in at Syracuse, we stayed three days. [13]From there, after making a circuit along the coast,[c] we reached Rhegium. After one day a south wind sprang up, and the second day we came to Puteoli. [14]There we found believers[D,e]

and were invited to stay with them for seven days.

And so we came to Rome. [15]Now the believers[D] from there had heard the news about us and had come to meet us as far as the Forum of Appius and the Three Taverns. When Paul saw them, he thanked God and took courage. [16]When we entered Rome,[E] Paul was permitted to stay by himself with the soldier who guarded him.[f]

Paul's First Interview with Roman Jews

[17]After three days he called together the leaders of the Jews. When they had gathered he said to them: "Brothers, although I have done nothing against our people or the customs of our ancestors, I was delivered as a prisoner from Jerusalem into the hands of the Romans.[g] [18]After they examined me, they wanted to release me, since I had not committed a capital offense.[h] [19]Because the Jews objected, I was compelled to appeal to Caesar;[i] it was not as though I had any accusation against my nation. [20]For this reason I've asked to see you and speak to you. In fact, it is for the hope of Israel that I'm wearing this chain."[j]

[21]Then they said to him, "We haven't received any letters about you from Judea. None of the brothers has come and reported or spoken anything evil about you. [22]But we would like to hear from you what you think. For

[a]28:4 Lk 13:2,4; Jn 9:2
[b]28:5 Mk 16:18; Lk 10:19
[c]28:6 Ac 8:10; 14:11
[d]28:8 Ac 9:40; Jms 5:14-15
[e]28:14 Jn 21:23; Ac 1:16
[f]28:16 Ac 24:23; 27:3
[g]28:17 Ac 6:14; 25:8
[h]28:18 Ac 22:24; 23:29; 26:31
[i]28:19 Ac 25:11; 26:32
[j]28:20 Ac 21:33; 26:6-7,29; Eph 6:20; 2Tm 1:16

[A]28:4 Gk *Dike*, a goddess of justice   [B]28:11 Gk *Dioscuri*, twin sons of Zeus   [C]28:13 Other mss read *From there, casting off,*   [D]28:14,15 Lit *brothers*   [E]28:16 Other mss add *the centurion turned the prisoners over to the military commander; but*

28:5-6 The superstitious natives of Malta quickly decided Paul was **a god** rather than a "murderer" (v. 4). Paul shrugged off this false praise just as easily as he had shaken off the snake.

28:7 Leading man or "first man" of Malta is a title reflected in inscriptional evidence from the island. **Publius** may have been a leading citizen or political leader.

28:8 Publius's **father** may have suffered from "Malta fever," which is caused by drinking impure goats' milk.

28:10 The **honors** that Paul received may have been monetary rewards or payment. The same word is used elsewhere in Acts to indicate money (5:2-3; 7:16; 19:19).

28:11 The journey aboard the other **Alexandrian ship** probably began in February or shortly thereafter. The **Twin Brothers** were Castor and Pollux (Gemini), sons of Zeus. Sailors regarded them as gods and patrons of seafarers.

28:12 Syracuse was a port on the eastern side of Sicily.

28:13 Puteoli, a major port in southern Italy, was an important shipping harbor for transporting grain from Egypt to Rome.

28:14 It is not known how **believers** came to be in Puteoli, just as it is not known how Christians first came to be in Rome. Perhaps Jews in Puteoli had made contact with Christians from elsewhere who traveled through the seaport.

28:15 Believers from Rome came down the Appian Way to two small towns (**Forum of Appius** and **Three Taverns**) to greet and encourage Paul before his arrival in Rome. J. Polhill suggests these two groups of Christians represented different house churches from Rome (see *Acts*, 537).

28:16 While in Roman custody, Paul appears to have stayed on his own and at his own expense (cp. also vv. 23,30), guarded only by one **soldier**. We know nothing more about his contact with the Roman government or the disposition of his case. This verse is the end of the last **we** section in the book of Acts (see note at 16:10).

28:17 This is the final time in Acts in which Paul began his ministry in a new city. As usual, he started by contacting **the Jews**. Since he was in custody, he invited the Jewish leaders to visit him rather than going to their synagogue.

28:21-22 The Jews in Rome had heard about the **sect** of Christianity (24:14), but they had not received any official word about Paul from Jerusalem. This lack of communication between Jerusalem and Rome may have been caused by winter weather, or it may indicate that the Jewish leaders in Jerusalem had lost interest in Paul's case since he was now out of their sight, beyond their jurisdiction, and unlikely to cause them any more trouble. In any event, the Christians of Jerusalem knew more about Paul's situation than did the unbelieving Jews (see 28:15 and note).

concerning this sect, we are aware that it is spoken against everywhere."[a]

The Response to Paul's Message

[23] After arranging a day with him, many came to him at his lodging. From dawn to dusk he expounded and witnessed about the kingdom of God. He tried to persuade them concerning Jesus from both the Law of Moses and the Prophets.[b] [24] Some were persuaded by what he said, but others did not believe.[c]

[25] Disagreeing among themselves, they began to leave after Paul made one statement: "The Holy Spirit correctly spoke through the prophet Isaiah to your[A] ancestors [26] when He said,

Go to these people and say:
You will listen and listen,
yet never understand;
and you will look and look,
yet never perceive.
[27]   For the hearts of these people

have grown callous,
their ears are hard of hearing,
and they have shut their eyes;
otherwise they might see
    with their eyes
and hear with their ears,
understand with their heart,
and be converted,
and I would heal them.[B,d]

[28] Therefore, let it be known to you that this saving work of God has been sent to the Gentiles; they will listen!"[e] [[29] After he said these things, the Jews departed, while engaging in a prolonged debate among themselves.][C]

Paul's Ministry Unhindered

[30] Then he stayed two whole years in his own rented house. And he welcomed all who visited him, [31] proclaiming the kingdom of God[f] and teaching the things concerning the Lord Jesus Christ with full boldness[g] and without hindrance.

Cross references:
[a] 28:22 Lk 2:34; Ac 24:5; 1Pt 2:12; 4:14
[b] 28:23 Ac 8:35; 17:3; 19:8; 26:22; Phm 22
[c] 28:24 Ac 14:4; 19:9
[d] 28:26-27 Ps 119:70; Is 6:9-10; Mt 13:14-15; Mk 4:12; Lk 8:10; Jn 12:40; Rm 11:8
[e] 28:28 Lk 2:30; Ac 13:26,46; Rm 11:11
[f] 28:31 Mt 4:23; Ac 20:25; 28:23
[g] Ac 4:29,31; 2Tm 2:9

A 28:25 Other mss read *our*   B 28:26-27 Is 6:9-10   C 28:29 Other mss omit bracketed text

---

28:23 Like the risen Christ on the road to Emmaus (Lk 24:13-35), Paul showed how **both the Law of Moses and the Prophets** pointed to Jesus as God's Messiah.

28:25-27 Luke identifies the turning point in the discussion as Paul's provocative **statement** that the Holy Spirit **correctly spoke** about Israel's spiritual stubbornness through Isaiah the prophet. Since Paul said this in response to those who "did not believe" (v. 24) what he was saying about Jesus, his citation of Isaiah clearly implied that the coming of Jesus Christ and His rejection by the Jews were foretold in the OT.

28:28 On God's **saving work** being **sent to the Gentiles**, see notes at 13:46-47 and 18:6.

28:30-31 The book of Acts ends in an unexpectedly open-ended fashion. Paul remained a prisoner **two whole years**. During this time he lived at his own expense and was al-

lowed to have visitors to whom he proclaimed his message boldly and **without hindrance**. Church tradition has long held that Paul was beheaded during the persecution instigated by the Roman emperor Nero (A.D. 64 or 65). It is possible that Paul was executed in Rome after the "two whole years," though church historian Eusebius believed Paul was released from Roman imprisonment, only to be rearrested at a later date, sent to Rome, and executed. The fact that Luke does not write of Paul's execution leads some scholars to conclude that Luke wrote the book of Acts previous to Paul's execution, though it is possible that Luke chose not to discuss the details of Paul's death because his aim was to show that God had fulfilled His purpose in Paul: taking the gospel to the Gentiles. Paul's preaching day and night in the seat of the pagan Roman Empire ensured that Christianity would become an international phenomenon, not just a regional religious anomaly.

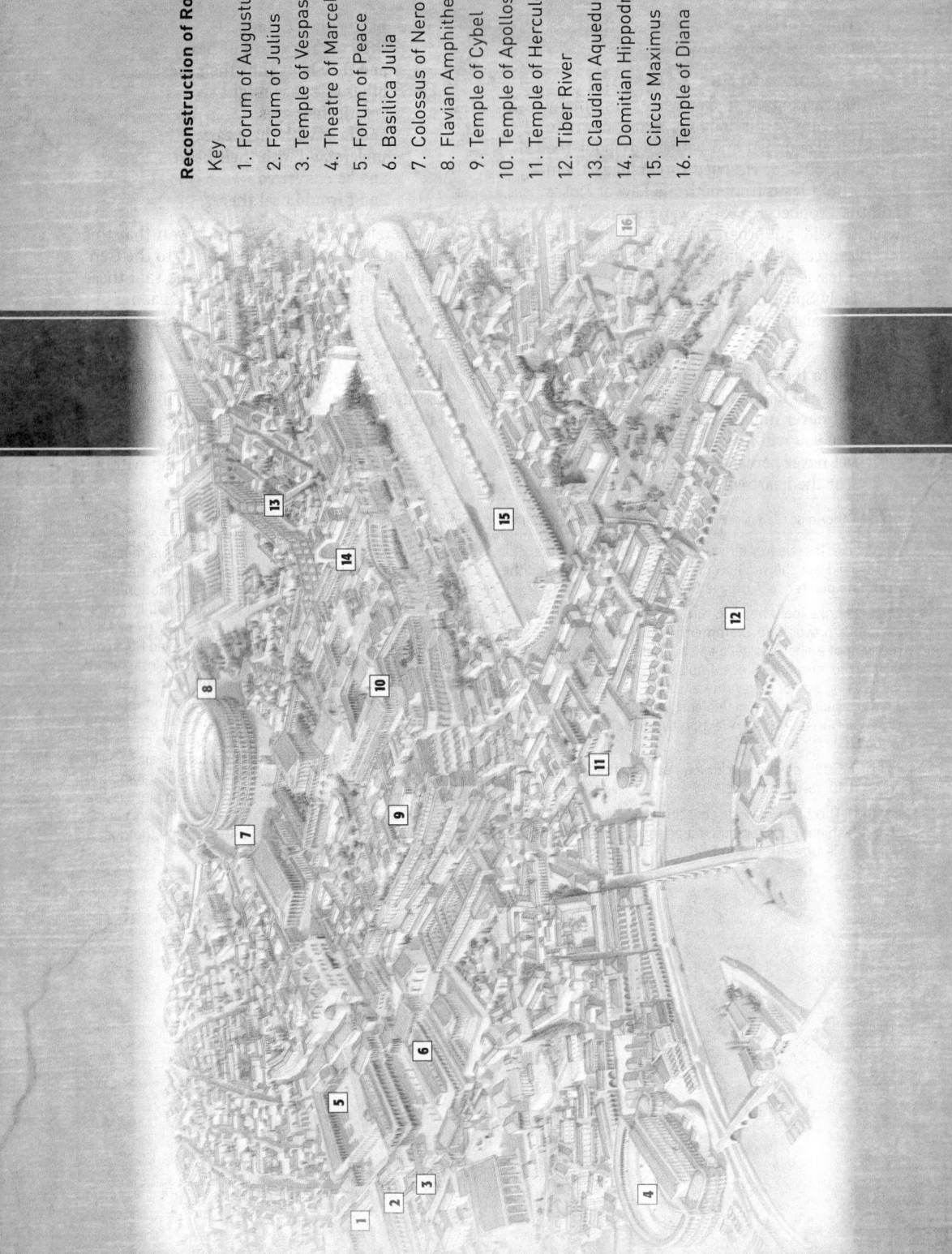

Reconstruction of Rome

Key

1. Forum of Augustus
2. Forum of Julius
3. Temple of Vespasian
4. Theatre of Marcellus
5. Forum of Peace
6. Basilica Julia
7. Colossus of Nero
8. Flavian Amphitheater
9. Temple of Cybel
10. Temple of Apollos
11. Temple of Hercules
12. Tiber River
13. Claudian Aqueduct
14. Domitian Hippodrome
15. Circus Maximus
16. Temple of Diana

Romans

Paul's letter to the Roman house churches has been preeminent among the New Testament writings for its theological and pastoral influence. It focuses on the doctrine of salvation, including the practical implications for believers as they live out the salvation given to them through Jesus Christ.

Full moon rising over the Roman Coliseum, whose construction began in the early 70s by Vespasian. It was completed and opened in A.D. 80 by his son and successor, Titus.

Circumstances of Writing

Author: Paul the apostle is the stated and indisputable author of the book of Romans. From the book of Acts and statements in Romans, we learn that Paul wrote this letter while he was in Corinth and on his way to Jerusalem in the spring of A.D. 57, to deliver an offering from the Gentile churches to poor Jewish Christians (Ac 20:3; Rm 15:25-29).

Background: All of Paul's writings grew out of his missionary/pastoral work and were about the problems and needs of local churches. The book of Romans is also of this genre, but it is the least "local" in the sense that Paul had not yet been to Rome. This letter was his opportunity to expound the good news message (the gospel). He could discuss the essence of sin, the salvation accomplished on the cross, the union of the believer with Christ, how the Spirit works in the Christian to promote holiness, the place of the Jewish people in God's plan, future things, and Christian living or ethics. Though Paul did not write Romans as a systematic theology, his somewhat orderly exposition has been the fountain for the development of that discipline.

The origin of the Roman house churches is unknown. The founding of the Roman church likely goes back to the "visitors from Rome," "both Jews and proselytes" who came to Jerusalem at Pentecost (Ac 2:10). Many of these visitors converted to Christianity (Ac 2:41), some of whom very likely hailed from Rome. In Acts 18:2 Luke mentioned Aquila and Priscilla, who left Rome because emperor Claudius had ordered all Jews to leave the city (A.D. 49). This exodus was caused by strife among Jews over "Chrestus" (Christ). The remaining Christians in Rome would be from a Gentile background. The Jewish-Gentile tensions in Rome had a long history. These tensions are somewhat reflected throughout the letter, most specifically in chapters 2, 11, and 14–15.

Rome was the primary destination of this letter. Yet some manuscripts lack the phrase "in Rome" (1:7), giving some support to the conclusion that Paul intended a wider audience for the book of Romans and sent copies to other churches.

800–450 B.C.

Mythical founding of Rome by Romulus and Remus 753

Rome ruled by seven kings. 753–509

King Tarquin the Proud ousted and the Roman Republic founded. 509

Plebian struggle with patricians results in greater voice in the governance of Rome. 494

Lucius Quinctius Cincinnatus, farmer, general, and consul of Rome from 460–438

450–250 B.C.

A *Decemviri*, committee of ten men, is commissioned to draw up Rome's first code of law, *The Twelve Tables*, binding on both patricians and plebeians. 451

The Via Appia, first of an unparalleled system of roads in the ancient world, is begun by Appius Claudius Caecus running in a southwesterly direction out of Rome. 312

Rome gains control of the entire Italian peninsula as a prelude to far greater expansion and a series of wars with other peoples. 275–272

The Romans begin minting coins. 269

The first recorded gladiatorial games in Rome during the funeral of Junius Brutus. Three pairs of gladiators fought to the death. 264

Message and Purpose

Paul's purpose in writing Romans can be identified from his direct statements in the text and inferred from the content. He expressly wrote that he wanted to impart spiritual strength to the believers at Rome (1:11-12; 16:25-26). He asked for prayer for the difficult task he was undertaking (15:32) and that he might be able to come and see them (15:30). He hoped to enlist the Roman churches to support a mission to the west (15:23-29). The content of the letter shows that the churches experienced tensions between believers from different backgrounds. Paul wanted them to be united and to avoid dissension and false teaching (16:17-18). The content also reveals his exposition of what is essential Christianity and what are matters of indifference.

Contribution to the Bible

What is the gospel? The word *gospel* means "good news." The good news is about Jesus and what He did for us. Most Bible students would say that the gospel is outlined in 1 Corinthians 15:3-5. Romans fills in that outline and clarifies the gospel in relation to the OT promises and the Mosaic law, the role of good works, and the gift of God's righteousness. Paul emphasized righteousness and justification in this letter to a depth and detail not found elsewhere in the Bible. Sin is traced to its core in our union with Adam and the imputation of original sin. Paul also mapped out the spread of human sin and its results in both believers and nonbelievers.

There are three passages in the NT (each one long sentence in the Greek text) that contain the most important theology of the NT: John 1:14 on the incarnation; Ephesians 1:3-14 about the triune purpose and glory of God; and Romans 3:21-26 on justification, redemption, and propitiation. If a Christian understands these three sentences, he has a solid foundation for faith.

Paul in Romans 6–8 gave the most comprehensive development of our union with Christ and the Spirit's work in us. Romans 9–11 (on the role of Israel in God's plan) has been called the key to understanding the Bible. Romans 13 is the classic NT passage on the Christian's relation to and duties to the state. Romans 14–15

250 B.C.–A.D. 30

Romans develop the hypocaust, a central heating system, used in large villas and public baths. 85 B.C.

Julius Caesar is assassinated on March 15, 44 B.C.

Octavian (Augustus), Rome's first emperor 27 B.C.–A.D. 14

The birth of Jesus of Nazareth 5 B.C.

The reign of Tiberius Caesar A.D. 14–37

A.D. 30–80

Jesus' trials, crucifixion, resurrection, and ascension 33

Saul's conversion on the Damascus Road October 34

Paul's letter to the church at Rome written in Corinth 57

Nero blames Christians for the great fire in Rome. 64

Roman Coliseum under construction 70–80

covers how Christians can relate to one another yet have different opinions and convictions on nonessential religious matters.

Structure

Paul wrote 13 of the 21 letters (or "epistles") contained in the NT. The four Gospels, the book of Acts, and the book of Revelation are not classified as letters. Romans is the longest of Paul's letters, and it contains the elements found in a standard letter at that time: salutation (1:1-7); thanksgiving (1:8-17); the main body (1:18–16:18); and a farewell (16:19-24). Some scholars refer to Romans as a tractate (a formal treatise). But it bears all the marks of a real letter, although it is a finely tuned literary composition.

Outline

I. Introduction (1:1-15)
   A. Author and recipients (1:1-7)
   B. Paul and the Roman church (1:8-15)

II. The Universal Need of Righteousness (1:16–3:20)
   A. Guilt of the Gentile world (1:18-32)
   B. Guilt of the Jews (2:1–3:20)

III. Justification: The Imputation of Righteousness (3:21–5:21)
   A. The righteousness of God in justification (3:21-26)
   B. Justification by faith excludes boasting (3:27-31)
   C. Justification and the OT (4:1-25)
   D. Justification involves reconciliation (5:1-11)
   E. The Christ-Adam analogy (5:12-21)

IV. The New Life in Christ (6:1–8:39)
   A. The old man/new man and sin's dominion (6:1-23)
   B. The old man/new man and the Mosaic law (7:1-25)
   C. The old man/new man and the Holy Spirit (8:1-39)

V. The Mystery of Israel (9:1–11:36)
   A. Israel's unbelief and the gospel (9:1-29)
   B. Israel responsible for its blindness (9:30–10:21)
   C. Israel's rejection is not final (11:1-36)

VI. Exhortations about the Christian Life (12:1–15:13)
   A. The living sacrifice (12:1-2)
   B. Spiritual gifts in the body of Christ (12:3-8)
   C. Christians and non-Christians (12:9-21)
   D. The believer's obligation to the state (13:1-7)
   E. The Christian's motivations (13:8-14)
   F. The strong and the weak in the church (14:1–15:13)

VII. Epilogue: Greetings and Travel Plans (15:14–16:27)
   A. Paul's missionary ambitions (15:14-33)
   B. Personal greetings (16:1-24)
   C. Concluding benediction (16:25-27)

God's Good News for Rome

1 Paul, a *slave of Christ Jesus, called as an apostle[A,a] and singled out[b] for God's good news[c]— [2] which He promised long ago[d] through His prophets[e] in the Holy Scriptures— [3] concerning His Son, Jesus Christ our Lord, who was a descendant of David[B,f] according to the flesh[g] [4] and who has been declared to be the powerful[h] Son of God[i] by the resurrection from the dead according to the Spirit of holiness.[C] [5] We have received grace and apostleship[j] through Him to bring about[D] the obedience[k] of faith[E] among all the nations,[F,l] on behalf of His name, [6] including yourselves who also belong to Jesus Christ by calling:[m]

[7] To all who are in Rome, loved by God,[n] called[o] as *saints.[p]

Grace to you and peace from God our Father and the Lord Jesus Christ.

Paul's Desire to Visit Rome

[8] First, I thank my God through Jesus Christ for all of you because the news of your faith[G] is being reported in all the world.[q] [9] For God, whom I serve with my spirit[r] in telling the good news about His Son, is my witness[s] that I constantly mention you,[t] [10] always asking in my prayers that if it is somehow in God's will, I may now at last succeed in coming to you.[u] [11] For I want very much to see you,[v] so I may impart to you some spiritual gift to strengthen you, [12] that is, to be mutually encouraged by each other's faith, both yours and mine.

[13] Now I want you to know,[H,w] *brothers, that I often planned to come to you (but was prevented until now[x]) in order that I might have a fruitful ministry[I] among you,[y] just as among

Cross-references
[a]1:1 1Co 1:1; 9:1; 2Co 1:1;
[b]Ac 9:15; 13:2; Gl 1:15
[c]Mk 1:14
[d]1:2 Ti 1:2
[e]Lk 1:70; Rm 3:21; 16:26
[f]1:3 Mt 1:1
[g]Jn 1:14; Rm 4:1; 9:3,5; 1Co 10:18
[h]1:4 Ac 10:38; 13:33; 17:31; 26:23
[i]Mt 4:3
[j]1:5 Ac 1:25; Gl 1:16
[k]Ac 6:7; Rm 16:26
[l]Ac 9:15
[m]1:6 Jd 1; Rv 17:14
[n]1:7 Rm 5:5; 8:39; 1Th 1:4
[o]Rm 8:28; 1Co 1:24
[p]1Co 1:2-4
[q]1:8 Rm 16:19
[r]1:9 2Tm 1:3
[s]Rm 9:1; 2Co 1:23; 11:31;

Php 1:8; 1Th 2:5,10 [t]Eph 1:16; Php 1:3-5; 1Th 1:2; 2Tm 1:3; Phm 4 [u]1:10 Ac 18:21; Rm 15:32 [v]1:11 Ac 19:21; Rm 15:23 [w]1:13 1Co 10:1; 11:3 [x]Ac 19:21 [y]Jn 4:36; Rm 15:16; Php 1:22; Col 1:6

A1:1 Or *Jesus, a called apostle*   **B**1:3 Lit *was of the seed of David*   **C**1:4 Or *the spirit of holiness*, or *the Holy Spirit*   **D**1:5 Or *Him for*; lit *Him into*   **E**1:5 Or *the obedience that is faith*, or *the faithful obedience*, or *the obedience that comes from faith*; Rm 16:26   **F**1:5 Or *Gentiles*   **G**1:8 Or *because your faith*   **H**1:13 Lit *I don't want you to be unaware*   **I**1:13 Lit *have some fruit*

1:1 Paul calls himself a **slave**. The Greek word *doulos* is mistranslated in most Bibles as "servant" or "bond servant." A slave was owned, was bought for a price, received no wages, and could not quit. A servant could quit, got paid, and was a free person. Jesus Himself took the form of a slave (Php 2:7), and Paul reminded Christians that "you are not your own, for you were bought at a price" (1Co 6:19b-20). Paul was **an apostle** by the call of God. In God's summons of Paul from his previous way of life, He commissioned him as an apostle (Ac 9). "Gospel" is an old English word meaning **God's good news**. Paul had been assigned by God to proclaim and teach this good news about Jesus.

1:2 The good news is the fulfillment of the OT prophecies, and the OT is not correctly understood apart from the NT.

1:3 Jesus is God's **Son** in a different sense than are Christians, who are called "sons" due to spiritual new birth (Jn 3) and adoption into God's family (Rm 8:15). Jesus is God's Son first by being the eternal Son and Second Person of the Trinity (Is 9:6; Gl 4:4), and second by being the virgin-born incarnate Son, conceived as the Spirit came to Mary (Lk 1:35). Jesus was also the messianic Son who came in the family line of David (2Sm 7:12-16; Ps 2:6-7; 89:26-29,36). **Flesh** here means the real human nature of Jesus.

1:4 Jesus in His humiliation was despised and rejected (Is 53:2) and had the form of a slave (Php 2:7). He spoke as the Son of the Father (Jn 5:19-23), but He was persecuted because "He was even calling God His own Father, making Himself equal with God" (Jn 5:18). At the cross, His sonship was called into question (Mt 27:39-43). But the **Spirit of holiness** (another title for the Holy Spirit) raised Jesus from the **dead**. This event set Him apart as God's unique Son exalted over death and Satan, and invested with all power (Mt 28:18).

1:5 The **obedience of faith** (cp. 10:16; 15:18) is best understood as the faith that issues in obedience. Paul's ministry sought to bring **all the nations** to obey Jesus and His Father.

1:6 Christians belong to Jesus **by calling**. This calling is not a bare invitation. It is instead a sovereign summons that results in salvation as people respond in faith to God's summons. By this language Paul reminded the Roman believers that God took the initiative in saving them.

1:7 **Called as saints** does not mean called "to be" saints, as if this is something Christians might become in the future. Neither does it signify an honorary title or an unusually holy person. Rather, all Christians are saints by the sovereign call of God. They have been set apart just as the nation of Israel was set apart (Lv 11:44; 19:2). A Christian is a person who has the forgiveness of sins and is sanctified by faith in Jesus (Ac 26:18) and therefore is a "saint" (1Co 1:2). The Christian belongs to Jesus and is set apart from the world.

1:8 It was common in ancient letters to begin with a prayer. Paul adopted the form, but his prayers were never just formal. As there is joy among the angels at the conversion of one sinner (Lk 15:10), Paul rejoiced over the fact there were house churches in the capital city of the Roman Empire. He was thankful for the spread of the **faith**.

1:9-10 Paul continually prayed for the Roman Christians in his **spirit**. Though too often perceived as otherwise, prayer is just as necessary as teaching or preaching in Christian ministry. Paul had wanted to come to Rome, but God was in control of all his circumstances. The believer must seek God's will in his activities (Jms 4:13-17).

1:11-12 Paul was certain he would bring certain benefits or blessings as he taught among the house churches of Rome. The **spiritual gift** mentioned here was not the special gift(s) in 1Co 12-14 which were given by God (1Co 12:11) but gifts that Christians gave to one another. Paul was certain that the Roman Christians would minister to him since every part of the body of Christ has useful functions in relation to other parts (1Co 12:12-27).

1:13 How is it that the most important city in the world had not yet had a visit from an apostle? Why especially had the "apostle to the Gentiles" not come? Paul **often planned to come**, but these plans had not come to fruition. In the mysterious providence of God it all worked out for the best. After

the rest of the Gentiles. ¹⁴I am obligated both to Greeks and barbarians,^A,a both to the wise and the foolish. ¹⁵So I am eager to preach the good news^b to you also who are in Rome.

The Righteous Will Live by Faith

¹⁶For I am not ashamed of the gospel,^B,c because it is God's power for salvation^d to everyone who believes, first to the Jew,^e and also to the Greek.^f ¹⁷For in it God's righteousness is revealed from faith to faith,^C,g just as it is written: **The righteous will live by faith.**^D,E,h

The Guilt of the Gentile World

¹⁸For God's wrath^i is revealed from heaven against all godlessness and unrighteousness of people who by their unrighteousness suppress the truth,^j ¹⁹since what can be known^F about God is evident among them,^k because God has shown it to them. ²⁰For His invisible attributes, that is, His eternal power and divine nature, have been clearly seen since the creation of the world,^l being understood through what He has made.^m As a result, people are without excuse. ²¹For though they knew God, they did not glorify Him as God or show gratitude. Instead,

^a 1:14 Ac 28:2	
^b 1:15 Rm 15:20; 1Co 9:16	
^c 1:16 2Tm 1:8,12,16	
^d 1Co 1:18,24	
^e Ac 3:26; Rm 2:9	
^f Jn 7:35	
^g 1:17 Rm 3:21; 9:30; Php 3:9	
^h Hab 2:4; Gl 3:11; Heb 10:38	
^i 1:18 Rm 5:9; Eph 5:6; Col 3:6	
^j 2Th 2:6-10	
^k 1:19 Ac 14:17; 17:24-27	
^l 1:20 Mk 10:6	
^m Jb 12:7-9; Ps 19:1-6; Jr 5:21-22	

A 1:14 Or non-Greeks   B 1:16 Other mss add of Christ   C 1:17 Or revealed out of faith into faith   D 1:17 Or The one who is righteous by faith will live   E 1:17 Hab 2:4   F 1:19 Or what is known

all, Paul's delay in fulfilling his trip to Rome caused him to write this wonderful letter. Furthermore, he eventually went to Rome as a prisoner (Ac 25:10–28:14-16), spending two years in the city preaching the gospel "without hindrance" (Ac 28:31). Believers must learn that God works out events in ways we could never imagine (Rm 8:28).

1:14 Paul's conversion placed a special commission and obligation on him (Ac 9:15; 13:47; 1Co 9:16; Gl 2:8-9). The revelations granted to him gave him greater responsibility. His training and Roman citizenship equipped him to reach all varieties of pagans, including the educated and the **barbarians**. These barbarians included people from Spain and Asia Minor (Ac 14:11-18).

1:15 Paul was eager to fulfill his obligation because he expected God to do great things through his ministry.

1:16 Why might someone be **ashamed of the gospel**? On the surface, the gospel seems like a very strange message. It is about a Jewish carpenter and teacher who was put to death on a cross by Pontius Pilate, Roman governor of Judea in A.D. 26–36. The message says that this man Jesus was raised from the dead and is now Lord—the kurios. This title was used of God in the Greek Bible and was applied to the emperor by some Romans. Paul himself wrote that this message seemed foolish to Gentiles (1Co 1:23) and was a

dunamis

Greek Pronunciation	[DOO nah mihss]
HCSB Translation	power
Uses in Romans	8
Uses in the NT	119
Focus passage	Romans 1:16

The English words dynamic and dynamite come directly from the Greek noun dunamis, though dynamite is far removed from the meaning of dunamis. The term dunamis can mean power, might, strength, or ability; the related verb dunamai means to be able (210 uses in the NT), and the adjective dunatos means possible. The synonym exousia means power or authority and usually refers to derived authority, whereas dunamis normally refers to inherent power.

Various kinds of power are described by the term dunamis in Romans. In 1:16 dunamis refers to the gospel that has been infused with God's power so people can be saved. Dunamis is also used to refer to God's omnipotence (1:20), to the Son's power (1:4), and to the Spirit's power (15:13,19). In 8:38 dunamis is used as a way of referring to demons. Finally, dunamis is used as one of the words for miraculous signs and wonders (15:19).

stumbling block to Jews. A crucified Messiah seemed to be a contradiction in terms to the Jews. A crucified **Jew** seemed like foolishness to the Romans, who despised Jews in general. Anyone who was crucified was considered among the lowest members of society. Paul had no confidence in his rhetorical skills to overcome the human objections to the message, but he knew the power of the Spirit to change the lives of people as they heard the good news about Jesus' death and resurrection. People are saved by faith, but faith is not the cause of **salvation**. The cause of salvation is the grace of God, the will of God, and the Spirit's **power** working through the message.

1:17 God's **righteousness** was the core of Paul's message. Luther came to better understand God's grace as he studied this verse in the original Greek rather than in the Latin translation. It forever changed his view of God. God's righteousness can be understood in several ways. First, God always does what is right and can be said to have righteousness as one of His attributes (Dt 32:4; Ps 119:142). Second, since God always does what is right, His actions or activities are sometimes identified as His righteousness (Is 45:8; 46:13; 51:5-6,8; 56:1). Third, God's righteousness is as a gift from Him to us, justifying us in His sight. "Justification" is a courtroom term signifying that a judge declares a person to be "right" or "just." Augustine wrote "the righteousness of God is that righteousness which He imparts in order to make men righteous" (Spirit and the Letter, chap. 16). In the gospel, God reveals His righteousness (His nature, His activity, and His gift of right status) by faith. In the course of this letter, Paul will explain how God is able to declare sinners to be righteous because of Jesus' work on the cross. **From faith to faith** emphasizes that the entire process of being declared righteous comes to us from start to finish by faith.

1:18 All people need the gospel because they are under **God's wrath**, which stems from His holy revulsion to sin. Paul wrote this letter from the Greek city of Corinth—a city full of idolatry and immorality. Mankind originally knew God and fellowshipped with Him (Gn 3:8a). The history of the world and of the OT reveals a subsequent regression and loss of moral knowledge. Since the garden of Eden, people have been unrighteous, and they have suppressed **the truth**.

1:19 God as Creator has disclosed Himself in creation. "The heavens declare the glory of God, and the sky proclaims the work of His hands" (Ps 19:1; cp. Ac 14:15-17). People also have an innate capacity for God as well as a moral conscience. God is at work to show Himself in the world, yet the world is in rebellion against Him.

their thinking became nonsense, and their senseless minds were darkened.[a] [22] Claiming to be wise, they became fools[b] [23] and exchanged the glory of the immortal God for images resembling mortal man, birds, four-footed animals, and reptiles.[c]

[24] Therefore God delivered them over in the cravings of their hearts[d] to sexual impurity, so that their bodies were degraded among themselves. [25] They exchanged the truth of God for a lie,[e] and worshiped and served something created instead of the Creator, who is praised forever.[f] •Amen.

From Idolatry to Depravity

[26] This is why God delivered them over to degrading passions.[g] For even their females exchanged natural sexual relations[A] for unnatural ones. [27] The males in the same way also left natural relations[A] with females and were inflamed in their lust for one another.

Males committed shameless acts with males[h] and received in their own persons[B] the appropriate penalty of their error.

[28] And because they did not think it worthwhile to acknowledge God, God delivered them over to a worthless mind to do what is morally wrong. [29] They are filled with all unrighteousness,[c] evil, greed, and wickedness. They are full of envy, murder, quarrels, deceit, and malice. They are gossips,[i] [30] slanderers, God-haters, arrogant, proud, boastful,[j] inventors of evil, disobedient to parents,[k] [31] undiscerning, untrustworthy, unloving,[D,l] and unmerciful. [32] Although they know full well God's just sentence—that those who practice such things deserve to die[E,m]—they not only do them, but even applaud[F,n] others who practice them.

God's Righteous Judgment

2 Therefore, any one of you[G,o] who judges is without excuse.[p] For when you judge

[a] 1:21 2Kg 17:15; Jr 2:5; Eph 4:17-20
[b] 1:22 Jr 10:14; 1Co 1:20
[c] 1:23 Ps 106:20; Jr 2:11; Ac 17:29
[d] 1:24 Eph 2:3; 4:19
[e] 1:25 Is 44:20; Jr 10:14; 13:25; 16:19
[f] Rm 9:5; 2Co 11:31
[g] 1:26 1Th 4:5
[h] 1:27 Lv 18:22; 20:13; 1Co 6:9
[i] 1:29 2Co 12:20
[j] 1:30 Ps 5:5
[k] 2Tm 3:2
[l] 1:31 2Tm 3:3
[m] 1:32 Rm 6:21
[n] Lk 11:48; Ac 8:1; 22:20
[o] 2:1 Lk 12:14; Rm 9:20
[p] Rm 1:20

[A] 1:26,27 Lit natural use   [B] 1:27 Or in themselves   [C] 1:29 Other mss add sexual immorality   [D] 1:31 Other mss add unforgiving   [E] 1:32 Lit things are worthy of death   [F] 1:32 Lit even take pleasure in   [G] 2:1 Lit Therefore, O man, every one

1:20 Mankind's problem is not that he doesn't know the truth. The history of the human race discloses a determined effort to oppose the will of God. People are **without excuse** for their idolatry and practical atheism.

1:21 Because of human willfulness, people's knowledge of God became clouded and their thinking became **darkened**. Without contact with God, the center of man loses contact with reality, misses the purpose of his existence and becomes ungrateful. People are supposed to **glorify Him as God**, but instead find all sorts of created objects to worship. Part of the wrath of God is revealed in humanity's loss of intelligent **thinking**.

1:22 A classic example of human foolishness is found in Is 44:9-20 where human cleverness ends in stupidity.

1:23 Many people think that the history of religion developed along an evolutionary model. In this view, humanity originally held animistic beliefs and then progressed to polytheism, to tribal deities, and then to a single creator God. From there we progressed to a vague philosophical monotheism in the Enlightenment, and finally we are now embracing atheism in the age of science. But this is not true to the early history of religion. Instead of starting in polytheism, the Bible says humanity started with knowledge of the one true God and then declined into polytheism as humans were separated from God and fractured from one another. Paul warns that loss of knowledge of the true God resulted in the worship of **images resembling mortal man**. Even in the modern age we have seen dictators worshiped as god, and the Bible says this sin will be repeated climactically in the end times (2Th 2:3-12; Rv 13:1-18).

1:24 Because they rejected the truths of God revealed in creation, God punished the Greco-Roman world by delivering them to **the cravings of their hearts**. A similar scenario played out in the life of King Ahab of Israel, who continually rebelled against God (1Kg 16:29-33). As a judgment, God permitted a lying prophetic spirit to deceive Ahab to his doom (1Kg 22:22-23). The ancients were enmeshed in polytheistic idolatry, and in their devotions to their false gods they practiced all sorts of immorality.

1:25 The loss of the knowledge of God in the mind and heart leads to an exchange of **truth** for a **lie**. Something created is served and worshiped rather than the Creator, and judgment is the result (Ps 81:12; Ac 7:42).

1:26-27 Lesbians and homosexuals often argue that this verse only prohibits sexual abuse of children, or else they say that **natural sexual relations** are not violated when men and women who are born with a tendency for homosexual desires (as they claim) practice homosexuality. But Paul clearly says lesbianism is **unnatural**, and the Bible elsewhere strictly prohibits all homosexuality (e.g., Lv 18:22). The Creator intended male and female to be joined in marriage (Gn 2:24). As an example of the sort of sexual perversion Paul would have been aware of in his day, the emperor Nero castrated a boy named Sporus and married him. Such **degrading passions** result in **appropriate penalty**.

1:28-32 In verse 24 God is described as delivering society to impurity, in verse 26 to degrading passions, and in verse 28 to a **worthless mind**. The mind becomes (Gk) *adokimos* (disqualified), an untrustworthy guide in moral choices because people have rejected knowledge of God. Verses 29-31 contain a list of vices similar to ancient vice lists. Pagan moralists often lamented the loss of virtue in their societies. Paul's list of sins was no darker than what other writers of that time reported. All sin is serious. Lesbianism and homosexuality may seem particularly objectionable, but any of the 21 sins listed (cp. Gl 5:19-21) cut people off from the life of God and bring spiritual death. When society applauds **others who practice** these sins, it has lost its moral compass. Ancient philosophers warned about the social effects of popular plays. Murder and immorality were so common on stage that people no longer reacted when they occurred in daily life. Modern entertainments have a similar effect on minds and the values that guide behavior.

2:1 Some interpreters think Paul is speaking about Gentile moralists in verses 1-16, and then Jews beginning at verse 17. The majority of scholars, however, see the Jew as the subject throughout chapter 2. Judgment and condemnation

another,[a] you condemn yourself, since you, the judge, do the same things. [2] We know that God's judgment on those who do such things is based on the truth. [3] Do you really think—anyone of you who judges those who do such things yet do the same—that you will escape God's judgment? [4] Or do you despise the riches of His kindness,[b] restraint,[c] and patience,[d] not recognizing[A] that God's kindness[e] is intended to lead you to repentance? [5] But because of your hardness and unrepentant heart you are storing up wrath[f] for yourself in the day of wrath,[g] when God's righteous judgment is revealed. [6] **He will repay each one according to his works:**[B,h] [7] eternal life[i] to those who by persistence in doing good[j] seek glory, honor,[k] and immortality;[l] [8] but wrath and indignation to those who are self-seeking[m] and disobey the truth[n] but are obeying unrighteousness; [9] affliction and distress[o] for every human being who does evil, first to the Jew, and also to the Greek;[p] [10] but glory, honor, and peace for everyone who does what is good, first to the Jew, and also to the Greek. [11] There is no favoritism with God.[q]

[12] All those who sinned without the law[r] will also perish without the law, and all those who sinned under the law will be judged by the law. [13] For the hearers of the law[s] are not righteous before God, but the doers of the law will be declared righteous.[C] [14] So, when Gentiles, who do not have the law, instinctively[t] do what the law demands, they are a law to themselves even though they do not have the law. [15] They show that the work of the law[D] is written on their hearts.[u] Their consciences confirm this. Their competing thoughts will either accuse or excuse them[E] [16] on the day when God judges[v] what people have kept secret, according to my gospel through Christ Jesus.[w]

---

[a]2:1 2Sm 12:5-7; Mt 7:1; Rm 14:22 [b]2:4 Rm 11:22 [c]Rm 3:25 [d]Ex 34:6; Rm 9:22; 1Tm 1:16; 1Pt 3:20; 2Pt 3:15 [e]2Pt 3:9 [f]2:5 Dt 32:34; Pr 1:18 [g]Ps 110:5; 2Co 5:10; 2Th 1:5; Jd 6 [h]2:6 Ps 62:12; Pr 24:12, Mt 16:27 [i]2:7 1Co 15:42,50,53 [j]Lk 8:15; Heb 10:36 [k]Heb 2:7; 1Pt 1:7 [l]Mt 25:46 [m]2:8 2Co 12:20; Gl 5:20; Php 2:3; Jms 3:14,16 [n]2Th 2:12 [o]2:9 Rm 8:35 [p]Ac 3:26; Rm 1:16; 1Pt 4:17 [q]2:11 Dt 10:17; Ac 10:34 [r]2:12 1Co

[9:21] [s]2:13 Mt 7:21,24; Jn 13:17; Jms 1:22 [t]2:14 Ac 10:35; Rm 1:19 [u]2:15 Rm 2:27 [v]2:16 Ac 10:42; 17:31; Rm 3:6; 14:10 [w]Rm 16:25; 1Co 15:1; Gl 1:11; 1Tm 1:11; 2Tm 2:8

[A]2:4 Or *patience, because you do not recognize* [B]2:6 Ps 62:12; Pr 24:12 [C]2:13 Or *will be justified* or *acquitted* [D]2:15 The code of conduct required by the law [E]2:15 Internal debate, either in a person or among the pagan moralists

---

follow sin as night follows day. Not all people commit the same sins, but all show by their judging and criticism that they do not live up to the moral law they know. No one is without excuse.

2:2 The coming **judgment** will be based on God's **truth**, which no amount of human opinion or protest can alter.

2:3 There will be no **escape** from God's coming **judgment**. Human systems of justice often break down. Stalin killed more than 20 million people and yet died in his own bed at age 74. And yet death offered him no escape from God's justice. All humans, great and small, will be raised to stand before God's judgment (14:10; Rv 20:11-15). The wise course is to settle your case with God before the judgment (Mt 5:25-26).

2:4 Grace should lead people to repent of their sin (2Pt 3:7-13).

---

prasso

Greek Pronunciation	[PRAHSS oh]
HCSB Translation	do
Uses in Romans	10
Uses in the NT	39
Focus passage	Romans 2:1-3

In ancient Greek, the verb *prasso* had a variety of meanings, such as *to practice, effect, transact, negotiate, manage, achieve, accomplish,* and *make.* The term could also mean *to mind one's own affairs or business.* In general, *prasso* meant *to do or to act* and could refer to almost any action. The corresponding noun *praxis* means *deed, action,* or *practice;* the plural form of this term is the first word of the Greek name for the book of Acts (*Praxeis Apostolon,* literally, "Actions of [the] Apostles").

Prasso in the NT ordinarily follows standard Greek usage. The term commonly emphasizes the experience in an action rather than just the action itself. It can refer to *doing good* (Ac 26:20; Rm 2:25; Php 4:9; 1Th 4:11), but most often it refers to habitual evil actions (Lk 22:23; 23:15,41; Jn 3:20; Ac 3:17; 19:19,36; 2Co 12:21; Gl 5:21), especially in Romans (1:32; 2:1-3; 7:15,19; 13:4).

2:5 Like water pooling up behind a dam, people accumulate a debt of **wrath** as they continue to reject God's grace. One day the dam will break, and the flood of divine wrath will sweep up individuals and entire societies.

2:6-10 Cranfield (*Romans,* I:151) outlines 10 different interpretations of this controversial passage. The most likely one is that **works** are the outcome of a person's faith. Christians are declared righteous by faith. At the moment of that declaration, the person is joined to Christ and regenerated by the Holy Spirit, becoming a new creation (2Co 5:17) created for good works (Eph 2:10). As Paul wrote, "What matters is faith working through love" (Gl 5:6). Thus the person of faith who seeks glory, honor, and immortality and continues to do good demonstrates that he is truly regenerate and thus is assured of eternal life. To the person who obeys **unrighteousness** and disobeys **truth**, however, wrath is his destiny.

2:11 No one should think that God's judgment is tainted with **favoritism**. He is a just Judge of both Jews and Gentiles.

2:12 This verse introduces the Mosaic **law** into the discussion of the coming judgment. The law will be considered throughout the remainder of Romans. The Jews saw the Mosaic law as key in the difference between Jews and Gentiles; Paul teaches that the law does not save a person but only reveals sin as people fall short of the law's requirements. Thus in the judgment, the possession of the law will be a basis of condemnation.

2:13 Deuteronomy 6:4 calls Israel to "listen" to the declaration of God's identity, but Dt 6:5 follows up by saying that merely listening is not enough. One must love God with the whole heart, which entails obedience. And yet no one will be **declared righteous** by obeying the law, for no one obeys the law perfectly (3:20,23; Gl 2:16; Jms 2:8-11). The only incorrupt doer of the law was Jesus, the righteous One.

2:14-15 The **Gentiles** do not have the Mosaic law as a moral guide, but they do have an inner **law** that informs their conscience. All humans have this **instinctively** as a component

Jewish Violation of the Law

[17] Now if[A] you call yourself a Jew, and rest in the law,[a] boast in God, [18] know His will, and approve the things that are superior,[b] being instructed from the law, [19] and if you are convinced that you are a guide for the blind, a light to those in darkness, [20] an instructor of the ignorant, a teacher of the immature, having the full expression[B] of knowledge and truth[c] in the law— [21] you then, who teach another,[d] don't you teach yourself? You who preach, "You must not steal"—do you steal? [22] You who say, "You must not commit adultery"—do you commit adultery? You who detest idols, do you rob their temples?[e] [23] You who boast in the law,[f] do you dishonor God by breaking the law? [24] For, as it is written: **The name of God is blasphemed among the Gentiles because of you.**[C,g]

Circumcision of the Heart

[25] For circumcision benefits you if you observe the law, but if you are a lawbreaker, your circumcision has become uncircumcision.[h] [26] Therefore if an uncircumcised[i] man keeps the law's requirements,[j] will his uncircumcision not be counted as circumcision? [27] A man who is physically uncircumcised, but who fulfills the law, will judge you[k] who are a lawbreaker in spite of having the letter of the law and circumcision. [28] For a person is not a Jew who is one outwardly,[l] and true circumcision is not something visible in the flesh. [29] On the contrary, a person is a Jew who is one inwardly,[m] and circumcision is of the heart—by the Spirit, not the letter.[D,n] That man's praise[E] is not from men but from God.[o]

Paul Answers an Objection

3 So what advantage does the Jew have? Or what is the benefit of circumcision? [2] Considerable in every way. First, they were entrusted[p] with the spoken words of God.[q] [3] What then? If some did not believe,[r] will their

*a*2:17 Mc 3:11; Jn 5:45; Rm 9:4 *b*2:18 Php 1:10 *c*2:20 Is 2:1-4; 42:6-7; 49:6 *d*2:21 Mt 23:3-7 *e*2:22 Ac 19:37 *f*2:23 Mc 3:11; Jn 5:45; Rm 9:4 *g*2:24 Is 52:5; Ezk 36:20-23; 2Pt 2:2 *h*2:25 Jr 4:4; 9:25 *i*2:26 Rm 3:30; 1Co 7:19; Eph 2:11 *j*Rm 8:4 *k*2:27 Mt 12:41 *l*2:28 Jn 8:39; Rm 9:6; Gl 6:15 *m*2:29 Php 3:3; Col 2:11 *n*Rm 7:6; 2Co 3:6 *o*Jn 5:44; 12:43; 1Co 4:5; 2Co 10:18 *p*3:2 Dt 4:8; Ps 147:19; Rm 9:4 *q*Ac 7:38 *r*3:3 Rm 10:16; Heb 4:2

A2:17 Other mss read Look— B2:20 Or the embodiment C2:24 Is 52:5 D2:29 Or heart—spiritually, not literally E2:29 In Hb, the words Jew, Judah, and praise are related.

---

of their being created in God's image (Gn 1:26). Kant, the philosopher, spoke of "the starry heavens above and the moral law within." This moral law will **accuse or excuse** daily moral choices, but ultimately demonstrates that all people fall short of God's holiness.

2:16 God knows every **secret**, and Jesus will be the final judge (Jn 5:22-30; Ac 17:31). The coming judgment will be: according to truth, proportional to the rejection of revelation received, according to deeds done, without partiality, and in response to the **gospel**.

2:17-20 Jew was the name given to people who returned to Judea from exile, but later it was extended to cover all Hebrew people (Israelites) wherever they lived. Paul listed eight grounds on which Jews rested their sense of moral superiority over the Gentiles; three times he cited the law as a grounds. The Jews believed that God had granted them special privileges and given them a mission to bring light to the Gentiles (Is 42:6-7). True enough. And yet Jesus taught, "Much will be required of everyone who has been given much. And even more will be expected of the one who has been entrusted with more" (Lk 12:48). Furthermore, Jesus warned the religious leaders, "On the outside you seem righteous to people, but inside you are full of hypocrisy and lawlessness" (Mt 23:28). Mere possession of the law does not win divine favor.

2:21-23 Following Jesus' example, Paul exposed Jewish hypocrisy. He did so with a series of five rhetorical questions that indicted his people for lacking essential righteousness. Paul did not mean that every Jew committed all these sins but that all transgress the law and lack the righteousness to enter God's presence. Jesus taught that even the thought of **adultery** violates the law (Mt 5:27-28). Paul knew from his own experience that his heart was full of covetousness (Rm 7:7-10) and therefore unrighteous. There are examples of all five literal violations from contemporary accounts, including a famous case in Rome of sacrilege. The history of the Jewish nation was full of unrighteous acts. Stephen asked, "Which of the prophets did your fathers not persecute?" (Ac 7:52). The religious leaders of the nation were instrumental in putting Jesus to death, Stephen was stoned by the Sanhedrin, and James the Just (half-brother of Jesus) was killed in the temple area.

2:24 Paul cited Is 52:5 from the Greek OT (the Septuagint, or LXX) as support that Jewish sin resulted in God's name being dishonored among the pagan nations when the Jews were defeated and exiled. To pagan perception, Yahweh seemed powerless since He did not protect His people.

2:25-29 Circumcision was a sign and seal of a covenant that God made with Israel (Ex 12:44-49). The rite went back to Abraham and the covenant God made with him (Gn 17:9-14). Circumcision became a badge of Jewish identity and, it was thought, a guarantee of salvation. Some later rabbis even taught that Abraham sat at the entrance to Gehenna ("hell") and would not permit any uncircumcised Jew to enter there. By implication, the way you lived made no difference. In a similar way, some Christian groups have believed that the rite of baptism saves, and so baptism was delayed until the end of life to make sure all sins were "washed." But Paul declared that circumcision (and by extension, baptism) without obedience is empty. Furthermore, Abraham was a man of faith who was accepted by God long before he was circumcised (Gn 15:1-20). The true Jew is one who has a spiritual **circumcision . . . of the heart**.

3:1 It might seem from chapter 2 that being a Jew and being circumcised conferred no **advantage**, but Paul listed many Jewish advantages in 9:4-5. In our day it is advantageous to have Christian parents, to attend a church, to be baptized, to attend a Christian school, and to read the Bible—but none of these advantages can save us.

3:2 It is a great privilege to be Jewish—**considerable in every way**. They heard God speak the "ten words" or Ten Commandments (Ex 20:1-20) directly to them. Then through a long series of prophets, God's words came to them. No other people on earth had this privilege.

3:3 Even if some of the Jewish people **did not believe**, God will be faithful to His covenant and will bring His promises

unbelief cancel God's faithfulness? [4]Absolutely not![a] God must be true, even if everyone is a liar,[b] as it is written:

> That You may be justified
> in Your words
> and triumph when You judge.[A,c]

[5]But if our unrighteousness highlights[B] God's righteousness,[d] what are we to say?[e] I use a human argument:[C,f] Is God unrighteous to inflict wrath? [6]Absolutely not! Otherwise, how will God judge the world?[g] [7]But if by my lie God's truth is amplified to His glory, why am I also still judged as a sinner?[h] [8]And why not say, just as some people slanderously claim we say, "Let us do what is evil so that good may come"?[i] Their condemnation is deserved!

The Whole World Guilty before God

[9]What then? Are we any better?[D] Not at all! For we have previously charged that both Jews[j] and Gentiles[E,k] are all under sin,[F,l] [10]as it is written:[G]

> There is no one righteous,
> not even one.
> [11]There is no one who understands;
> there is no one who seeks God.
> [12]All have turned away;
> all alike have become useless.
> There is no one who does what is good,
> not even one.[H,m]
> [13]Their throat is an open grave;
> they deceive with their tongues.[I,n]
> Vipers' venom is under their lips.[J,o]
> [14]Their mouth is full of cursing
> and bitterness.[K,p]
> [15]Their feet are swift to shed blood;
> [16]ruin and wretchedness are
> in their paths,
> [17]and the path of peace
> they have not known.[L,q]
> [18]There is no fear of God
> before their eyes.[M,r]

[19]Now we know that whatever the law says[s] speaks to those who are subject to the law,[N,t]

Cross references:
[a]3:4 Lk 20:16; Rm 3:31
[b]Ps 116:11
[c]Ps 51:4
[d]3:5 Rm 5:8; 2Co 6:4; Gl 2:18
[e]Rm 4:1; 7:7; 8:31; 9:14,30
[f]Rm 6:19; 1Co 9:8; 15:32; Gl 3:15
[g]3:6 Rm 2:16
[h]3:7 Rm 9:19
[i]3:8 Rm 6:1
[j]3:9 Rm 2:1-29
[k]Rm 1:18-32
[l]Rm 3:19,23; 11:32; Gl 3:22
[m]3:10-12 Ps 14:1-3; 53:1-3; Ec 7:20
[n]3:13 Ps 5:9
[o]Ps 140:3
[p]3:14 Ps 10:7
[q]3:15-17 Is 59:7-8
[r]3:18 Ps 36:1
[s]3:19 Jn 10:34
[t]Rm 2:12

Footnotes:
[A]3:4 Ps 51:4 [B]3:5 Or *shows*, or *demonstrates* [C]3:5 Lit *I speak as a man* [D]3:9 Are we Jews any better than the Gentiles? [E]3:9 Lit *Greeks* [F]3:9 Under sin's power or dominion [G]3:10 Paul constructs this charge from a chain of OT quotations, mainly from the Psalms. [H]3:10-12 Ps 14:1-3; 53:1-3; Ec 7:20 [I]3:13 Ps 5:9 [J]3:13 Ps 140:3 [K]3:14 Ps 10:7 [L]3:15-17 Is 59:7-8 [M]3:18 Ps 36:1 [N]3:19 Lit *those in the law*

---

to fulfillment. Paul referred particularly to the promises centered in the Messiah, Jesus Christ.

3:4 After he was confronted by the prophet Nathan for his sins surrounding the Bathsheba incident, David confessed in Psalm 51:4 that God is **justified** in His judgments. God **must be true**, for it would be against His infinitely perfect nature to be otherwise.

3:5-8 Paul addressed several implications to which critics mistakenly thought his teachings would lead. For example, if God is shown to be in the right by man's sin and error, then God is honored by our shortcomings. How then can God punish us when we have helped display His righteousness? But Paul answered that as a matter of principle God's judgment of sin is always righteous. People who think otherwise deserve **condemnation**, for their true focus is not on glorifying God but on giving free reign to their sinful desires.

3:9 All the world is **under sin**, and yet sin is considered an archaic topic in our secular society. It is not hard to guess why. Vice is something done against oneself; crime is something done against society or an individual; but sin is against God. Since modern culture is essentially atheistic, "sin" has become a meaningless term.

3:10-18 In these verses Paul linked seven OT passages to demonstrate that all of mankind is under sin's dominion. No one is righteous; no one **understands** (Jn 8:43-44; 1Co 2:14), and **no one . . . seeks God**. Since Adam and Eve's fall, people have hidden from God, but God sent His Son "to seek and to save the lost" (Lk 19:10). All have gone astray (Is 1:2-4; 53:6), and in God's sight none are right. Paul cited Bible passages that show the extent of corruption. As Jesus taught, "from within, out of people's hearts" (Mk 7:21) come all sorts of evil. Man is quick to **shed blood**. During the last century over 39 million people lost their lives in wars. And by conservative estimates, human governments killed an additional 125 million people—led by Lenin, Stalin, Mao, Hitler, and others. The root problem is that humans are often practical atheists even when they profess belief in God. They choose against God's will and show no fear for it.

3:19 Someone may argue that the seven passages cited above are addressed not to Jews but to pagan nations. But everything in the Hebrew Bible is first addressed to the Jews for their instruction so they can learn about sin's power. All people from every nation and ethnicity are sinners, and God will judge **the whole world**. In God's court, everyone is speechless.

3:20 No one can earn justification by obedience to the law's requirements. The law was never intended to be a means of salvation. A primary purpose of the law was to reveal sin in its full scope, thus pointing to man's need for the gift of righteousness.

3:21-26 The phrase **but now** marks a decisive shift in Paul's argument. According to one interpreter, verses 21-26 are the "centre and heart of the whole of Romans 1.16b–15:13" (Cranfield, *Romans*, I:199). This paragraph (one long sentence in the Greek original) is a wonderful compression of theology. It contains three ways of describing Jesus' work on the cross and the benefits that come from the gospel: justification, redemption, and propitiation. Each term pictures the gospel by appealing to a different realm of ancient life. "Justification" is a term from the courts. Sinners stand condemned in God's court, and yet He freely declares "not guilty" anyone who places his faith in Christ. "Redemption" is a term borrowed from the slave market. All people are slaves to sin by their fallen nature, but Christians are purchased by God and freed to new life in Christ. "Propitiation" is a term borrowed from temple rites, where the sacrificial animal figuratively comes under God's wrath as it is killed. Jesus received God's wrath on the cross. By our faith in Christ, God's wrath is counted satisfied and we are no longer under wrath. **God's righteousness** was thus manifested

so that every mouth may be shut and the whole world may become subject to God's judgment.^A,a 20For no one will be *justified^B in His sight by the works of the law,^b because the knowledge of sin comes through the law.^c

God's Righteousness through Faith

21 But now, apart from the law, God's righteousness has been revealed^d—attested by the Law and the Prophets^C,e 22—that is, God's righteousness through faith^f in Jesus Christ,^D,g to all who believe,^h since there is no distinction.^i 23 For all have sinned^j and fall short of the^E glory of God. 24 They are justified freely by His grace^k through the *redemption that is in Christ Jesus.^l 25 God presented Him as a *propitiation^F,m through faith in His blood,^n to demonstrate His righteousness, because in His

restraint God^o passed over the sins previously committed.^p 26 God presented Him to demonstrate His righteousness at the present time, so that He would be righteous and declare righteous^G the one who has faith in Jesus.

Boasting Excluded

27 Where then is boasting?^q It is excluded. By what kind of law?^H,r By one of works? No, on the contrary, by a law^I of faith. 28 For we conclude that a man is justified by faith apart from the works of the law.^s 29 Or is God for Jews only?^t Is He not also for Gentiles? Yes, for Gentiles too, 30 since there is one God^u who will justify the circumcised by faith^v and the

a3:19 Rm 2:9	
b3:20 Ps 143:2; Ac 13:39; Gl 2:16	
cRm 4:15; 5:13,20; 7:7	
d3:21 Rm 1:17; 9:30	
eAc 10:43; Rm 1:2	
f3:22 Rm 4:5	
gAc 3:16; Gl 2:16,20; 3:22; Eph 3:12	
hRm 4:11,16; 10:4	
iRm 10:12; Gl 3:28; Col 3:11	
j3:23 Rm 3:9	
k3:24 Rm 4:4,16; Eph 2:8	
lCo 1:30; Eph 1:7; Col 1:14; Heb 9:15	
m3:25 1Jn 2:2; 4:10	
n1Co 5:7; Heb 9:14,28; 1Pt	

1:19; Rv 1:5   oRm 2:4   pAc 17:30; 14:16   q3:27 Rm 2:17,23; 4:2; 1Co 1:29-31   rRm 9:31   s3:28 Ac 13:39; Rm 9:31; Eph 2:9; Jms 2:20,24,26   t3:29 Ac 10:34; Rm 9:24; 10:12; 15:9; Gl 3:28   u3:30 Rm 10:12   vRm 4:11,16; Gl 3:8

A3:19 Or become guilty before God, or may be accountable to God   B3:20 Or will be declared righteous, or will be acquitted   C3:21 When capitalized, the Law and the Prophets = OT   D3:22 Or through the faithfulness of Jesus Christ   E3:23 Or and lack the   F3:25 Or as a propitiatory sacrifice, or as an offering of atonement, or as a mercy seat; 2Co 5:21; Heb 9:5   G3:26 Or and justify, or and acquit   H3:27 Or what principle?   I3:27 Or a principle

---

and given in the event of the cross. Sinners gain pardon not through their adherence to the law, but through faith in the One who fulfilled all righteousness on our behalf. The **Law and the Prophets** refers to the OT, and the entire OT is correctly understood as a witness to Jesus and His work.

3:22 Jesus is the object of faith and the means of obtaining the gift of **God's righteousness**. The gift is for both Jews and Gentiles who **believe**.

3:23 All have missed the mark that God intended for the human race and have lost the **glory** of the original creation (Ps 8:5). Believing the good news starts the process of the restoration of glory (Rm 8:30; 2Co 3:18).

3:24 Justified means that Christians are declared to be righteous (5:1,9; 8:30; 1Co 1:30; 6:11). The Judge deems believers innocent because of Jesus' work on the cross. **Freely** means that God grants justification not due to any merit in Christians but solely by **His grace**, the undeserved love and mercy of God. **Redemption** is a commercial term that refers to purchasing freedom for slaves. The purchase

price for our freedom was the blood of **Christ Jesus** (see Mk 10:45; 1Pt 1:18-19).

3:25 Propitiation is a term borrowed from the sacrificial system and the temple. The Greek word *hilasterion* was used for the cover of the ark of the covenant. Luther translated it as the "mercy seat" (Heb 9:5). On the Day of Atonement, the high priest would sprinkle blood over the ark to atone for the nation. By this rite sins were deemed expiated; people became reconciled to God and God's wrath was averted. But human sins could not literally be atoned for by the death of animals. "For it is impossible for the blood of bulls and goats to take away sins" (Heb 10:4). Thus Jesus came to accomplish what no priest slaying an animal could ever hope to accomplish: full satisfaction of God's requirements for atonement. God the Father "made the One who did not know sin to be sin for us, so that we might become the righteousness of God in Him" (2Co 5:21). This involves a double imputation. Our sin was imputed to Jesus on the cross, and His **righteousness** was imputed to us. Justification is not a legal fiction; Christians are made righteous by the imputation of God's own righteousness in His Son.

3:26 The **present time** of the cross and preaching of the good news vindicated God, showing that He is just and Justifier of the one **who has faith in Jesus**. It has become fashionable to translate *pisteos Iesou* in verses 22,26 as "Jesus' faithfulness" instead of "faith in Jesus." While the Greek permits this translation, it seems to diminish somewhat Paul's emphasis on faith in Jesus' work on the cross. The HCSB's rendering is to be preferred.

3:27-28 No one can boast in his **works**. No one can boast even in his **faith**. Faith is not the *cause* of justification but the *means* of justification. The cause of salvation is grace and mercy.

3:29-30 There is only one God and only one way to be justified by Him, no matter your ethnic and national identity: **by faith**. The phrase **who will justify** does not mean that justification occurs at a future time (at the last judgment) and is therefore not a present reality for the believer. Rather, it points to the fact that God counts each of us justified as we come to faith. Thus God "will justify" your neighbor tomorrow if he comes to faith.

hilasterion

Greek Pronunciation	[hih lahss TAY ree ahn]
HCSB Translation	propitiation
Uses in Romans	1
Uses in the NT	2
Focus passage	Romans 3:25

The Greek noun *hilasterion* in Rm 3:25 is rich with theological meaning. The only other place this term occurs in the NT is Heb 9:5, which says that the cherubim above the ark of the covenant in the Most Holy Place were "overshadowing the mercy seat." In the OT, the word is used for the lid of the ark of the covenant (traditionally called "the mercy seat"; see Ex 25:17-22; Lv 16:2,13-15). Another related word, *hilasmos*, occurs twice in the NT (1Jn 2:2; 4:10). This word family refers to the turning away of God's wrath against sin by means of a sacrifice. The main ideas of this word group are *mercy* and *satisfactory sacrifice for sin*. The innermost part of the tabernacle was the place where *mercy* was found, but only through the proper sacrifice. Similarly, Jesus' death is the only place one can find *mercy*. God's wrath against sin was turned away by Christ's sacrificial death.

uncircumcised through faith. ³¹ Do we then cancel the law through faith? Absolutely not!^a On the contrary, we uphold the law.^b

Abraham Justified by Faith

4 What then can we say that Abraham, our physical ancestor,^{A,c} has found? ² If Abraham was •justified^B by works,^d he has something to brag about—but not before God.^C ³ For what does the Scripture say?

> **Abraham believed God,**
> **and it was credited to him**
> **for righteousness.**^{D,e}

⁴ Now to the one who works,^f pay is not considered as a gift, but as something owed. ⁵ But to the one who does not work, but believes on Him who declares the ungodly to be righteous,^{E,g} his faith is credited for righteousness.

David Celebrating the Same Truth

⁶ Likewise, David also speaks of the blessing of the man God credits righteousness to apart from works:

⁷ How joyful are those whose lawless
  acts are forgiven
  and whose sins are covered!
⁸ How joyful is the man
  the Lord will never charge
  with sin!^{F,h}

Abraham Justified before Circumcision

⁹ Is this blessing only for the circumcised,ⁱ then? Or is it also for the uncircumcised? For we say, **Faith was credited to Abraham for righteousness.**^{D,j} ¹⁰ In what way then was it credited—while he was circumcised, or uncircumcised? Not while he was circumcised, but uncircumcised. ¹¹ And he received the sign of circumcision^k as a seal of the righteousness that he had by faith^{G,l} while still uncircumcised. This was to make him the father^m of all who believeⁿ but are not circumcised, so that righteousness may be credited to them also. ¹² And he became the father of the circumcised, who are not only circumcised but who also follow in the footsteps of the faith our father Abraham had while he was still uncircumcised.

Cross references

^a3:31 Lk 20:16; Rm 3:4
^bMt 5:17; Rm 4:3; 8:4
^c4:1 Rm 1:3
^d4:2 1Co 1:31
^e4:3 Gn 15:6; Gl 3:6; Jms 2:23
^f4:4 Rm 11:6
^g4:5 Jn 3:33; Rm 3:22
^h4:7-8 Ps 32:1-2; 2Co 5:19
ⁱ4:9 Rm 3:30
^jGn 15:6
^k4:11 Gn 17:10-11
^lJn 3:33
^mLk 19:9
ⁿRm 3:22

Footnotes

^A4:1 Lit *our ancestor according to the flesh*   ^B4:2 Or *was declared righteous*, or *was acquitted*   ^C4:2 He has no reason for boasting in God's presence.   ^D4:3,9 Gn 15:6   ^E4:5 Or *who acquits*, or *who justifies*   ^F4:7-8 Ps 32:1-2   ^G4:11 Lit *righteousness of faith*

3:31 Does the gospel destroy the **law**? To answer this question, Paul considered the case of Abraham in the following chapter.

4:1-25 Abraham was the father of the Hebrew nation (Gn 12:1-3). Jews commonly believed that Abraham kept the whole law before it was given on Mount Sinai (Gn 26:5), so he had something to brag about. Paul refutes this, showing that Abraham was justified by faith and had no grounds to boast.

4:3 Tradition must give way to the clear statements of the **Scripture**. Genesis 15:6 is the text that Paul cited.

4:4-5 Pay and **gift** are as different as works and faith. Paul

logizomai

Greek Pronunciation	[lah GEE zah migh]
HCSB Translation	credit, consider, charge
Uses in Romans	19
Uses in the NT	40
Focus passage	Romans 4:3-11

The Greek verb *logizomai* means *to count* or *to credit to an account*, and thus it was a mathematical term in general and an accounting term in particular. It also had other meanings, such as *to keep a record or list, to think, to consider.* In the NT, *logizomai* means *to credit to one's account* only once outside of Paul's writings (Jms 2:23). The other five non-Pauline occurrences of the term mean *to count* (Lk 22:37), *to consider* (Jn 11:50), *to regard* (Ac 19:27; 1Pt 5:12), or *to reckon* (Heb 11:19). However, the most significant use of *logizomai* is related to salvation. Paul often used the term to explain how a person can be in a right relationship with God. Paul's imagery is that a lost person owes God an infinite debt that he has no ability to pay because of sin. However, Christ's death on the sinner's behalf is the basis of the debt being canceled *(aphiemi)*, with Christ's righteousness being *credited* to the believer's account (Rm 2:26; 4:3-6,10-11,22-24; 2Co 5:19; Gl 3:6).

describes God as having a set of books of the kind an accountant has. God imputed or credited righteousness to Abraham's account because of his faith. **To the one who does not work, but believes on Him who declares the ungodly to be righteous** is a shocking expression. The Reformation focused on this passage. God saves the ungodly, sinners, and His enemies (5:5,8,10). Though Jews took Abraham to be a paragon of virtue, Paul declared that he was just a sinner saved by grace. He was justified by faith, just as any Christian is.

4:6-8 David, Israel's greatest king, sang about the **blessing** that God gave him in the forgiveness of his deliberate **sins**—no works-righteousness here. David understood that, in God's accounting ledger, his sins were wiped out and righteousness was inscribed in their place. Paul's quotation of Ps 32:1-2 clarifies and explains Gn 15:6. Paul similarly links justification and the forgiveness of sin in his synagogue sermon recorded in Ac 13:38-39.

4:9-10 It might seem that God's **blessing** was only for the **circumcised** since David's psalm (Ps 32) was written by a Jew for the Jewish people. Paul returned to his key text in Gn 15:6 and showed that the crediting of righteousness to Abraham took place when he was **uncircumcised**, so God's blessing is also for Gentiles who believe.

4:11 Circumcision was a **sign** and a **seal**. It marked out a man as part of the nation of Israel. It was also to be a seal of the **righteousness** a man had received **by faith**. The timing of Abraham's circumcision enabled him to be the spiritual **father** and model for justification by faith to both circumcised Jews and uncircumcised Gentiles.

4:12 Abraham was the physical **father** of the Hebrew nation, but his greatest legacy was his example of **faith**. Jews and Gentiles alike can **follow in the footsteps** of Abraham's faith.

4:13 The **law** demanded obedience and performance. If the

The Promise Granted through Faith

[13] For the promise to Abraham[a] or to his descendants that he would inherit the world[b] was not through the law, but through the righteousness that comes by faith.[A] [14] If those who are of the law are heirs,[c] faith is made empty and the promise is canceled. [15] For the law produces wrath.[d] And where there is no law,[e] there is no transgression.

[16] This is why the promise is by faith, so that it may be according to grace,[f] to guarantee it to all the descendants[g]—not only to those who are of the law[B] but also to those who are of Abraham's faith. He is the father of us all [17] in God's sight. As it is written: **I have made you the father of many nations.**[C,h] He believed in God, who gives life to the dead[i] and calls[j] things into existence that do not exist.[k] [18] He believed, hoping against hope, so that he became **the father of many nations**[C,l] according to what had been spoken: **So will your descendants be.**[D,m] [19] He considered[E] his own body to be already dead[n] (since he was about 100 years old)[o] and also considered the deadness of Sarah's womb,[p] without weakening in the faith. [20] He did not waver in unbelief at God's promise but was strengthened in his faith and gave glory to God,[q] [21] because he was fully convinced[r] that what He had promised He was also able to perform.[s] [22] Therefore, **it was credited to him for righteousness.**[F,t] [23] Now **it was credited to him** was not written for Abraham alone,[u] [24] but also for us. It will be credited to us who believe in Him[v] who raised Jesus our Lord from the dead.[w] [25] He was delivered up for[G] our trespasses[x] and raised for[G] our justification.[H,y]

Faith Triumphs

[5] Therefore, since we have been declared righteous by faith,[z] we have peace[I] with God through our Lord Jesus Christ.[aa] [2] We have also obtained access through Him[ab] by faith[J]

Cross references

a4:13 Rm 9:8; Gl 3:16; Heb 6:15,17; 7:6; 11:9,17
b Gn 17:4-6; 21:17-18
c4:14 Gl 3:18
d4:15 Rm 7:7,10-25; 1Co 15:56; Gl 3:10
eRm 3:20
f4:16 Rm 3:24
gRm 9:8; 15:8
h4:17 Gn 17:5
iJn 5:21
jIs 48:13; 51:2
k1Co 1:28
l4:18 Gn 17:5
mGn 15:5
n4:19 Heb 11:12
oGn 17:17
pGn 18:11
q4:20 Mt 9:8
r4:21 Rm 14:5
sGn 18:14; Heb 11:19
t4:22 Gn 15:6; Rm 4:3
u4:23 Rm 15:4; 1Co 9:9; 10:11; 2Tm 3:16
v4:24 Rm 10:9; 1Pt 1:21
wAc 2:24
x4:25 Rm 5:6,8; 8:32; Gl 2:20; Eph 5:2
y Rm 5:18; 1Co 15:17; 2Co 5:15
z5:1 Rm 3:28
aaRm 5:11
ab5:2 Eph 2:18; 3:12; Heb 10:19-20; 1Pt 3:18

Text notes

A4:13 Lit righteousness of faith   B4:16 Or not to those who are of the law only   C4:17,18 Gn 17:5   D4:18 Gn 15:5   E4:19 Other mss read He did not consider   F4:22 Gn 15:6   G4:25 Or because of   H4:25 Or acquittal   I5:1 Other mss read faith, let us have peace, which can also be translated faith, let us grasp the fact that we have peace   J5:2 Other mss omit by faith

---

law was violated, wrath resulted. The law was not a system of grace. God's **promise** was one of grace. The promise to Abraham and his seed (Gl 3:16-18) was not through the law but through the **righteousness that comes by faith**.

4:14-15 If the inheritance of the **promise** came by legal obedience, then the way of **faith** is **empty**. Furthermore, no one would inherit the promise since no one could keep the law.

4:16-17 God's **promise is by faith**, so that it may be guaranteed to both Jews and Gentiles who believe. If it were by law, no such guarantee would be possible. To make it certain, therefore, the promise was **according to grace**. **Abraham** was also promised to be the **father** of many nations. Abraham believed in the God who created everything from nothing and **gives life to the dead**.

4:18 It seemed humanly impossible for Abraham to become the **father of many nations** when he was old, but he placed his **hope** in God's promise.

4:19-20 Abraham had a realistic evaluation of his prospects for fatherhood. He was about **100 years old**, and Sarah was childless and long past child-bearing years. Yet Abraham did not doubt **God's promise**, and God strengthened his **faith**.

4:23-24 Everything in Scripture is for our benefit. The experiences of **Abraham** are as relevant to us as they were to him, for we serve the same Creator God who can do the humanly impossible. We are credited as righteous before God in the same manner as Abraham: by faith.

4:25 Jesus was **delivered up for our trespasses** as promised in Is 52:13–53:12. Who delivered up Jesus? Was it Judas? Pilate? The Jewish Sanhedrin? Satan? Certainly all these were causal agents in the crucifixion of Christ, but ultimately it was the sovereign God who brought it to pass in order to fulfill His plan of redemption (Ac 4:27-28). The Father delivered Jesus up for our trespasses, and raised Him so that His righteous Servant would justify many people (Is 53:11).

5:1 Commentators differ over whether chapter 5 belongs thematically to the first major section of Romans or to the Christian life section, chapters 6 through 8. It has connections to both. Paul in 5:1-11 uses "we" and "us" as he explains the benefits that those who are justified possess. Justification is just one of many ways of speaking about salvation. In this division, Paul showed how justification involves reconciliation. Justification speaks to our sound legal status before God while reconciliation describes our repaired relationship to God in more personal terms. We were at war with God, relationally alienated from Him, but He reconciled us by His Son (v. 10). **We have peace** in some manuscripts can be read as "let us grasp the fact that we have peace." This peace is an objective, settled fact because Jesus has accomplished it once and for all.

5:2 Access to God's grace is the privilege of all believers.

---

charis

Greek Pronunciation	[KAH rihss]
HCSB Translation	grace
Uses in Romans	24
Uses in the NT	155
Focus passage	Romans 5:2

The Greek noun charis refers to an unmerited favorable disposition toward someone or something. In the NT, charis is commonly used in relation to salvation, especially in Paul's writings. Paul used charis to explain that salvation comes from God's own choice to show favor in redeeming lost persons through faith in Christ (Rm 5:1; Eph 2:8-9; 2Tm 1:9). However, God's undeserved favor is not toward those who have done nothing offensive; rather, God shows grace toward those who have sinned against Him and are actually His enemies.

In Romans 5, Paul explained that peace with God is an act of God's grace (vv. 1-2). He reminded believers that at one time they were God's enemies (v. 10; see Eph 2:1-16; Col 1:21-22). Therefore, a better NT definition of charis would be unmerited favor toward an enemy—grace toward one who has forfeited any claim on God's favor because of sin and who deserves the opposite—God's judgment (5:9).

into this grace in which we stand,[a] and we rejoice in the hope of the glory of God. [3]And not only that,[b] but we also rejoice in our afflictions,[c] because we know that affliction produces endurance,[d] [4]endurance produces proven character,[e] and proven character produces hope. [5]This hope will not disappoint us,[f] because God's love has been poured out in our hearts[g] through the Holy Spirit who was given to us.

Those Declared Righteous Are Reconciled

[6]For while we were still helpless, at the appointed moment,[h] Christ died for the ungodly. [7]For rarely will someone die for a just person—though for a good person perhaps someone might even dare to die. [8]But God proves[i] His own love for us[j] in that while we were still sinners, Christ died for us! [9]Much more then, since we have now been declared righteous by His blood,[k] we will be saved through Him from wrath.[l] [10]For if, while we were enemies,[m] we were reconciled to God through the death

of His Son, then how much more, having been reconciled, will we be saved by His life![n] [11]And not only that, but we also rejoice in God through our Lord Jesus Christ. We have now received this reconciliation through Him.[o]

Death through Adam and Life through Christ

[12]Therefore, just as sin entered the world through one man,[p] and death through sin,[q] in this way death spread to all men,[r] because all sinned.[A] [13]In fact, sin was in the world before the law, but sin is not charged to a person's account when there is no law.[s] [14]Nevertheless, death reigned from Adam to Moses, even over those who did not sin in the likeness of Adam's transgression.[t] He is a prototype[B] of the Coming One.[u]

[15]But the gift is not like the trespass. For if by the one man's trespass the many died, how much more have the grace of God and the gift overflowed to the many by the grace of the one man,[v] Jesus Christ. [16]And the gift is not like the one man's sin, because from one sin

[a] 5:2 1Co 15:1
[b] 5:3 Rm 5:11; 8:23; 9:10; 2Co 8:19
[c] Mt 5:12; Jms 1:2-3
[d] Lk 21:19
[e] 5:4 Php 2:22; Jms 1:12
[f] 5:5 Ps 119:116; Rm 9:33; Heb 6:18-20
[g] Ac 2:33; 10:45; Gl 4:6; Ti 3:6
[h] 5:6 Gl 4:4
[i] 5:8 Rm 3:5
[j] Jn 3:16; 15:13; Rm 8:39
[k] 5:9 Rm 3:25
[l] Rm 1:18; 1Th 1:10
[m] 5:10 Rm 11:28; 2Co 5:18-20; Eph 2:3; Col 1:21
[n] Rm 8:34; Heb 7:25
[o] 5:11 Rm 11:15; 2Co 5:18-20
[p] 5:12 Gn 2:17; 3:6,19; 1Co 15:21
[q] Rm 6:23; 1Co 15:56; Jms 1:15
[r] Rm 5:19,21; 1Co 15:22
[s] 5:13 Rm 4:15
[t] 5:14 Hs 6:7
[u] 1Co 15:45
[v] 5:15 Ac 15:11

A 5:12 Or have sinned   B 5:14 Or figure, or pattern; = an OT person or thing that prefigures a NT person or thing

We have the freedom to enter His presence at all times. His golden scepter is always extended (cp. Est 4:11–5:2).

5:3-4 Believers can **rejoice** in tough circumstances and **afflictions** because we know that through such things the Father is disciplining us for greater holiness (Heb 12:10).

5:5 The Christian's hope is certain because **God's love** is assured to us by the Holy Spirit's ministry within the core of our being (**our hearts**).

5:6-8 We can be sure of God's love since He did so much for us when we were **helpless**. We were **ungodly**, we were still **sinners**, and we were His enemies (v. 10). Jesus died for that kind of person. The word translated "for" is the Greek preposition huper used in substitution contexts. Jesus **died** in our place. God freely chooses to love us and by doing so confers worth on us through our faith in Him.

5:9 No debt of **wrath** remains for those who **have now been declared righteous** through faith in Christ.

5:10-11 If by the death of Christ **we were reconciled to God**, how much surer must the good news of salvation be now that He has risen and lives forevermore!

5:12-21 In this section, Paul brings his major discussion of justification by faith to a close with a complex, compressed, and controversial analogy. He shows that grace in justification reaches and affects us in Christ much more than sin and death have affected us in Adam.

5:12 Therefore gives this verse a loose connection with the previous section. **Sin** and **death** are almost personified here (cp. v. 21, "sin reigned in death"). **Just as** (Gk hosper) introduces a long and difficult Greek sentence. The main comparisons are clear, but some of the details lead interpreters to different opinions. Paul was thinking of how both the first Adam (Gn 1–3) and the last Adam (Jesus Christ) have a universal significance for humanity. Interpreters are divided over the phrase **because all sinned**. The two major

interpretations are (1) all people commit sin and therefore die, and (2) somehow all humans sinned "in Adam." The second view is more likely and entails either that Adam was the federal head of the race and acted on behalf of us all, or that Adam was the seminal head of the race and we were somehow "in him."

5:13-14 These verses support the second interpretive option for verse 12 (see note there). Sin "reigned" (v. 21) over humanity before the giving of the law even though none had sinned in the way Adam sinned. Adam's sin was a personal, deliberate act that plunged the human race into physical and spiritual death. All humans, including newborn infants and young children who are incapable of judging right and wrong and thus are not deliberate sinners, are under death's domain. All people now are born spiritually dead (Eph 2:1-3). Adam's sin had this broad effect because he was a type (Gk tupos) or prefiguration of Jesus, the **Coming One**, and represented all of humanity just as Jesus would do on the cross.

5:15-16 The works of Adam and Jesus have similar scope but drastically different effect. One **sin** plunged humanity into ruin, but God gave the gift that issued in justification in spite of our many **trespasses**. What was gained through Jesus is far greater than that which was lost through Adam.

5:17 Death took the entire human race into its kingdom. The author of Hebrews portrayed this vividly when he wrote about what Jesus accomplished through His death on the cross: "Through His death He might destroy the one holding the power of death—that is, the Devil—and free those who were held in slavery all their lives by the fear of death" (Heb 2:14-15). Believers, who with the rest of humanity were once slaves in the kingdom of darkness (Col 1:13), were brought into Christ's kingdom as sons to **reign** with Him.

5:18 Adam's sin resulted in **condemnation for everyone**,

came the judgment,[a] resulting in condemnation, but from many trespasses came the gift, resulting in *justification.[A] [17]Since by the one man's trespass, death reigned through that one man, how much more will those who receive the overflow of grace and the gift of righteousness reign in life[b] through the one man, Jesus Christ.

[18]So then, as through one trespass there is condemnation for everyone, so also through one righteous act there is life-giving justification[B,c] for everyone. [19]For just as through one man's disobedience the many were made sinners,[d] so also through the one man's obedience[e] the many will be made righteous. [20]The law came along to multiply the trespass.[f] But where sin multiplied, grace multiplied even more[g] [21]so that, just as sin reigned in death,[h] so also grace will reign[i] through righteous-

ness, resulting in eternal life through Jesus Christ our Lord.

The New Life in Christ

6 What should we say then?[j] Should we continue in sin so that grace may multiply?[k] [2]Absolutely not![l] How can we who died to sin[m] still live in it? [3]Or are you unaware that all of us who were baptized[n] into Christ Jesus were baptized into His death?[o] [4]Therefore we were buried with Him by baptism into death,[p] in order that, just as Christ was raised from the dead[q] by the glory of the Father,[r] so we too may *walk in a new way[c] of life.[s] [5]For if we have been joined with Him in the likeness of His death,[t] we will certainly also be[D] in the likeness of His resurrection. [6]For we know

[a] 5:16 1Co 11:32
[b] 5:17 2Tm 2:12; Rv 22:5
[c] 5:18 Rm 4:25
[d] 5:19 Rm 11:32
[e] Php 2:8
[f] 5:20 Rm 3:20; 7:7; Gl 3:19
[g] Rm 6:1; 1Tm 1:14
[h] 5:21 Rm 5:12,14
[i] Jn 1:17; Rm 6:23
[j] 6:1 Rm 3:5
[k] Rm 3:8; 6:15
[l] 6:2 Lk 20:16
[m] Rm 7:4,6; Gl 2:19; Col 2:20; 3:3; 1Pt 2:24
[n] 6:3 Mt 28:19; 1Co 1:13-17; 12:13; Gl 3:27
[o] Ac 2:38; 8:16; 19:5
[p] 6:4 Col 2:12
[q] Ac 2:24
[r] Jn 11:40;
[s] Rm 7:6; 2Co 5:17; Gl 6:15; Eph 4:23-24; Col 3:10
[t] 6:5 2Co 4:10; Php 3:10; Col 2:12; 3:1
2Co 13:4

[A] 5:16 Or acquittal　[B] 5:18 Lit is justification of life　[C] 6:4 Or in newness　[D] 6:5 Be joined with Him

whereas Christ's substitutionary death made possible **life-giving justification for everyone.**

5:19 The expression **will be made** does not refer to the last judgment, as if our salvation were pending until that time. Rather, it pictures the fact that believers are **made righteous** when they come to faith. Since Paul knew many people were yet to come to faith when he wrote, it was fitting to use future tense.

5:20-21 As in Gl 3:19, Paul describes the **law** as a subordinate player in the drama of redemption. The law was never an end unto itself. Rather, its function was to **multiply the trespass** by bringing the knowledge of **sin**. By this the need for **grace** is highlighted, allowing God to bestow it **even more**. The law also had other functions that Paul does not discuss here.

6:1-23 Can a justified person live the same way as he did before justification? This was a major question in the debates of the Reformation. If as sin abounded, grace super-abounded, why not commit more sin to receive more grace? Some false teachers in church history have actually argued that you can experience more grace by committing more sin. This chapter explains why this is not possible.

6:2 Paul rejected the invalid inference (v. 1) with the strong expression **absolutely not**. Phillips aptly translated it, "What a ghastly thought!" Paul argues that believers have **died to sin**. He does not mean that our sin nature was eliminated at the cross or at the moment of our conversion or baptism. Instead, as he says elsewhere, God "rescued us from the domain of darkness and transferred us into the kingdom of the Son He loves" (Col 1:13). Having experienced such a transfer, dare we go on living in sin?

6:3 In defense of his claim that believers have died to sin, Paul points out that through baptism we were **baptized into Christ Jesus** and His **death**. As R. Mounce put it, "Christ's death for sin becomes our death to sin" (*Romans*, 149).

6:4 Believers are symbolically **buried** with Christ through baptism and **raised** with Him **from the dead** in order that we may **walk in a new way of life**. This makes clear the

absurdity of the idea that we can "continue in sin so that grace may multiply" (v. 1).

6:5 Though believers have not yet experienced resurrection, we are assured this future reality by the fact that Christ, in whose death we share, has been raised from the dead.

6:6 Our old self (Gk *palaios anthropos*; lit "old man") is everything that we were before we became Christians. By contrast, the new self is what we are once we become Christians (Eph 4:22-24; Col 3:9-10). The new self is not perfect. We still sin because we have indwelling sin in our mortal bodies (Rm 7:13-25), but we are in the process of renewal (Eph 4; Col 3). Thus we have the answer to the question about whether a Christian can still live in sin. We cannot live as we once did because the "old self" **was crucified with Him** (Christ). In Christ the believer is a "new creation" (2Co 5:17).

Ancient Byzantine baptistry at Avdat, Israel, showing the importance given baptism by the early church (Rm 6:3-4).

that our old self[A,a] was crucified with Him[b] in order that sin's dominion over the body[B] may be abolished,[c] so that we may no longer be enslaved to sin, [7] since a person who has died[d] is freed[C] from sin's claims.[D] [8] Now if we died with Christ,[e] we believe that we will also live with Him, [9] because we know that Christ, having been raised from the dead,[f] will not die again. Death no longer rules over Him.[g] [10] For in light of the fact that He died, He died to sin once for all; but in light of the fact that He lives, He lives to God. [11] So, you too consider yourselves dead to sin[h] but alive to God in Christ Jesus.[E]

[12] Therefore do not let sin reign in your mortal body, so that you obey[F] its desires. [13] And do not offer any parts[G] of it to sin[i] as weapons for unrighteousness. But as those who are alive from the dead, offer yourselves to God,[j] and all the parts[G] of yourselves to God as weapons for righteousness. [14] For sin will not rule over you, because you are not under law[k] but under grace.[l]

From Slaves of Sin to Slaves of God

[15] What then? Should we sin because we are not under law but under grace?[m] Absolutely not![n] [16] Don't you know that if you offer yourselves to someone[H] as obedient •slaves,[o] you are slaves of that one you obey[p]—either of sin leading to death[q] or of obedience leading to righteousness? [17] But thank God that, although you used to be slaves of sin,[r] you obeyed from the heart that pattern of teaching you were transferred[I] to,[s] [18] and having been liberated from sin,[t] you became enslaved to righteousness. [19] I am using a human analogy[J,u] because of the weakness of your flesh.[K] For just as you offered the parts[G] of yourselves as slaves to moral impurity, and to greater and greater lawlessness, so now offer them as slaves to righteousness, which results in •sanctification. [20] For when you were slaves of sin, you were free from allegiance to righteousness.[L,v] [21] So what fruit was produced[M] then from the

[a]6:6 Eph 4:22; Col 3:9
[b]6:6 Gl 2:20; 5:24; 6:14
[c]Rm 7:24
[d]6:7 1Pt 4:1
[e]6:8 2Co 4:10; 2Tm 2:11
[f]6:9 Ac 2:24
[g]Rv 1:18
[h]6:11 Rm 7:4,6; Gl 2:19; Col 2:20; 3:3; 1Pt 2:24
[i]6:13 Rm 7:5; Col 3:5
[j]Rm 12:1; 2Co 5:14; 1Pt 2:24
[k]6:14 Rm 5:18; 7:4,6; Gl 4:21
[l]Rm 5:17,21
[m]6:15 Rm 6:1
[n]Lk 20:16
[o]6:16 Rm 11:2; 1Co 3:16; 5:6; 6:2-3,9,15-16,19; 9:13,24
[p]Jn 8:34; 2Pt 2:19
[q]Rm 6:23
[r]6:17 Rm 1:8; 2Co 2:14
[s]2Tm 1:3
[t]6:18 Jn 8:32; Rm 8:2
[u]6:19 Rm 3:5   [v]6:20 Mt 6:24

[A]6:6 Lit *man*; = the person before conversion   [B]6:6 Lit *that the body of sin*   [C]6:7 Or *justified*; lit *acquitted*   [D]6:7 Lit *from sin*   [E]6:11 Other mss add *our Lord*   [F]6:12 Other mss add *sin* (lit *it*) *in*   [G]6:13,19 Or *members*   [H]6:16 Lit *that to whom you offer yourselves*   [I]6:17 Or *entrusted*   [J]6:19 Lit *I speak humanly*; Paul is personifying sin and righteousness as slave masters.   [K]6:19 Or *your human nature*   [L]6:20 Lit *free to righteousness*   [M]6:21 Lit *what fruit do you have*

6:7 Sin (personified) has no claim over a dead person and can claim no loyalty from him.

6:8-9 It was because of our sin that death fixed its grip on Jesus, but He arose to live forever. **Death no longer rules** the believer, for we **died with Christ** who no longer dies.

6:10 Jesus went through an irreversible transformation in His death and resurrection. Believers also undergo an irreversible transformation: we die to the "old self" (v. 6) at conversion and thereafter live as new creatures (2Co 5:17). Like Jesus, the believer **lives to God**.

dikaioo

Greek Pronunciation	[dih kigh AH oh]
HCSB Translation	free
Uses in Romans	15
Uses in the NT	39
Focus passage	Romans 6:7

The Greek verb *dikaioo* means *to justify* or *to declare righteous*. Two related words occur quite often in the NT: the noun *dikaiosune*, meaning *righteousness*, and the adjective *dikaios*, meaning *just* or *righteous*. The common thread in this word family is conformity to a standard, and the standard is primarily God's will. In the Greek OT *dikaioo* occurs 30 times, most are in judicial contexts, both divine and human (either God is Judge or man is judge). Human judges are to "declare righteous the righteous" (cp. Dt 25:1; 1Kg 8:32; 2Ch 6:23)—to pronounce the innocent to be so and *free* him legally. The legal aspect of these terms also involves relational concepts, for judges must promote an individual's relation to society by judging fairly.

These two concepts carry over into Paul's letters, especially Romans and Galatians, as he explains how to have a right relationship with God. At the point of faith God declares the believer to be righteous (Rm 3:30-4:9; 5:1; Gl 2:16-17; 3:8,11,24; 5:4), free from the penalty of sin and in a right relationship with God.

6:11 This is the first command in the book of Romans.

6:12-13 The believer, as a member of the new kingdom, must not offer any help to the old king (Satan, sin, death) and his kingdom. We are still slaves, but now we have a new Master. Note that Paul continues the personification of sin as a king (complete with a kingdom and subjects) who seeks to extend his rule. There is a spiritual war between these two kingdoms. We must give ourselves as **weapons** to be used in this warfare on the side of the rightful King. Aiding and abetting the enemy is treason.

6:14 Sin personified has been in view since 5:20-21. Sin is no longer the believer's ruler. Sin gained its power by using the **law**, but the Christian is under the rule of **grace** rather than law.

6:15-23 These verses are another of Paul's extended analogies. People have a choice about which master they will serve.

6:16 Paul used the figure of **slaves**. Whoever you **obey**, you come under his power. Obedience to **sin** brings **death**. Sin pays a wage to his subjects, and it is death (cp. v. 23). Obedience to God brings **righteousness** and the gift of eternal life.

6:17 Paul thanked God for the work of salvation that came to the Roman Christians.

6:18-19 Slavery and redemption are common biblical metaphors for spiritual death and salvation. The Hebrews were once in bondage (literal and spiritual) in Egypt. God broke the bondage so they could come out from Egypt and worship Him (Ex 7:16; 12:29-42). Similarly, the Roman Christians were once in spiritual bondage to false gods, but God liberated them so they could be **slaves to righteousness**.

6:20-23 As **slaves** of God, believers produce **fruit** (see Jn 15:1-8). This is the work of **sanctification** or holiness in their lives, and the final product is eternal life. Lest the figure be misunderstood as a payment for merits earned,

things you are now ashamed of?[a] For the end of those things is death.[b] [22]But now, since you have been liberated from sin and have become enslaved to God,[c] you have your fruit, which results in sanctification[A,d]—and the end is eternal life![e] [23]For the wages of sin is death, but the gift of God is eternal life in Christ Jesus our Lord.[f]

An Illustration from Marriage

7 Since I am speaking to those who understand law, •brothers,[g] are you unaware that the law has authority over someone as long as he lives? [2]For example, a married woman is legally bound to her husband while he lives.[h] But if her husband dies, she is released from the law regarding the husband. [3]So then, if she gives herself to another man while her husband is living, she will be called an adulteress. But if her husband dies, she is free from that law. Then, if she gives herself to another man, she is not an adulteress.

[4]Therefore, my brothers, you also were put to death[i] in relation to the law[j] through the crucified body of the •Messiah,[k] so that you may belong to another—to Him who was raised from the dead—that we may bear fruit for God. [5]For when we were in the flesh,[B,l]

the sinful passions operated through the law in every part of us[C,m] and bore fruit for death. [6]But now we have been released from the law, since we have died to what held us, so that we may serve in the new way[D] of the Spirit[n] and not in the old letter of the law.

Sin's Use of the Law

[7]What should we say then?[o] Is the law sin? Absolutely not![p] On the contrary, I would not have known sin if it were not for the law.[q] For example, I would not have known what it is to covet if the law had not said, **Do not covet.**[E,r] [8]And sin, seizing an opportunity through the commandment,[s] produced in me coveting of every kind. For apart from the law sin is dead.[t] [9]Once I was alive apart from the law, but when the commandment came, sin sprang to life [10]and I died. The commandment that was meant for life[u] resulted in death for me. [11]For sin, seizing an opportunity through the commandment, deceived me,[v] and through it killed me. [12]So then, the law is holy,[w] and the commandment is holy and just and good.

The Problem of Sin in Us

[13] Therefore, did what is good cause my death?[F] Absolutely not![x] On the contrary, sin,

Cross references

a 6:21 Jr 12:13; Ezk 16:63; Rm 7:5
b Rm 1:32; 5:12; 8:6,13; Gl 6:8
c 6:22 1Co 7:22; 1Pt 2:16
d Rm 7:4
e 1Pt 1:9
f 6:23 Mt 25:46; Rm 5:21; 8:39
g 7:1 Rm 1:13
h 7:2 1Co 7:39
i 7:4 Rm 6:2
j Rm 8:2; Gl 2:19; 5:18
k Col 1:22
l 7:5 Rm 8:8-10; 2Co 10:3
m Rm 6:13,21,23
n 7:6 Rm 2:29
o 7:7 Rm 3:5
p Lk 20:16
q Rm 4:15; 5:20
r Ex 20:17
s 7:8 Rm 3:20
t 1Co 15:56
u 7:10 Lv 18:5; Lk 10:28; Rm 10:5; Gl 3:12
v 7:11 Gn 3:13
w 7:12 1Tm 1:8
x 7:13 Lk 20:16

A 6:22 Or *holiness*   B 7:5 = a person's life before accepting Christ   C 7:5 Lit *of our members*   D 7:6 Lit *in newness*   E 7:7 Ex 20:17   F 7:13 Lit *good become death to me?*

---

eternal life is a **gift of God** through Christ. One master (sin) pays an earned wage of death; the other master (God) pays in unearned grace, resulting in eternal life (Jn 17:3).

7:1-6 Roman Christians knew about Roman civil law, and many of them (especially those of a Jewish or proselyte background) knew the Mosaic law. Of course neither law could hold sway over a dead person. Having died with Christ, the believer is not under Mosaic law (6:14).

7:2-3 A married woman, bound by law to her **husband** so long as he lived, was legally free to marry another man if her husband died.

7:4-5 Believers have died to the "old self" (6:2-6) and are free to marry another and **bear fruit for God**. The death of Messiah is the means by which we died to the Mosaic law (Gl 3:13-14; Col 2:14).

7:6 As new creations, believers serve as slaves (Gk *douleuein*) in a **new way** with a new power from the Spirit, not as old men (6:6) laboring vainly under the **letter of the law**.

7:7-8 The law itself is not evil or sinful, but one of its functions is to reveal **sin**. In fact Paul speaks as if sin is an unknown quantity apart from the law when he says, **I would not have known sin if it were not for the law.** Sin, **seizing an opportunity**, uses the law to motivate the flesh (fallen nature) to action. Once again Paul personified sin almost as Satan himself.

7:9-10 The phrase **once I was alive** has been variously interpreted as a reference to (1) Paul before he came to know the law as a young Jewish boy, (2) Paul before his conversion and the conviction brought by the Holy Spirit, (3) Paul speaking as Adam in the garden of Eden before the command

came, or (4) any Hebrew before the giving of the Mosaic law at Mount Sinai. The basic point in each of these interpretations is the same: God's intent in the law was **life**, but sin deceived man by the law and brought **death**.

7:11-12 Though **the law** makes sin known and is in fact used by sin to produce death, it is nevertheless **holy and just and good**, reflecting God's perfect and eternal holiness.

7:13 Did the **good** law cause **death**? The correct understanding is that sin used something good to bring human death.

---

sarx

Greek Pronunciation	[SAHRX]
HCSB Translation	flesh
Uses in Romans	26
Uses in the NT	147
Focus passage	Romans 7:5

The Greek noun *sarx* literally means *flesh*, but it is used figuratively in several different ways. The term normally carries a negative sense, especially in Paul's writings. Jesus sometimes used *sarx* to describe the fallen, sinful aspect of a person (Mt 26:41=Mk 14:38; Jn 6:63), and Paul developed this even more in his writings. Paul used *sarx* to emphasize the ineffectiveness of human effort in spiritual matters (Rm 2:28; 6:19; 8:3). This is particularly the case in Romans and Galatians where the term has a dual connotation: (1) indwelling sin (Rm 7:5; 8:3; 13:14; Gl 5:24) and (2) the desire for a law-based relationship with God (Rm 7:18; Gl 3:3; 6:12-13). Indwelling sin makes a relationship with God based on obedience to the law impossible since no one can meet the law's demands (Rm 3:19-21; 7:25; 8:4; Gl 6:23; see Jms 2:10).

in order to be recognized as sin, was producing death in me through what is good, so that through the commandment, sin might become sinful beyond measure. [14] For we know that the law is spiritual,[a] but I am made out of flesh,[A] sold[b] into sin's power.[c] [15] For I do not understand what I am doing,[d] because I do not practice what I want to do,[e] but I do what I hate. [16] And if I do what I do not want to do, I agree with the law that it is good. [17] So now I am no longer the one doing it, but it is sin living in me. [18] For I know that nothing good lives in me, that is, in my flesh.[f] For the desire to do what is good is with me, but there is no ability to do it. [19] For I do not do the good that I want to do, but I practice the evil that I do not want to do. [20] Now if I do what I do not want, I am no longer the one doing it, but it is the sin that lives in me. [21] So I discover this

principle:[B,g] When I want to do what is good, evil is with me. [22] For in my inner self[C] I joyfully agree with God's law.[h] [23] But I see a different law in the parts of my body,[D,i] waging war against the law of my mind and taking me prisoner to the law of sin in the parts of my body.[D] [24] What a wretched man I am! Who will rescue me from this dying body?[25] I thank God through Jesus Christ our Lord![E,k] So then, with my mind I myself am a slave to the law of God, but with my flesh, to the law of sin.

The Life-Giving Spirit

8 Therefore, no condemnation[l] now exists for those in[m] Christ Jesus,[F,n] [2] because the Spirit's law of life[o] in Christ Jesus has set you[G] free from the law of sin and of death.[p] [3] What the law could not do[q] since it was limited[H] by the flesh,[r] God did. He condemned

Cross references

a 7:14 1Co 3:1
b 1Kg 21:20,25; 2Kg 17:17; Rm 6:6; Gl 4:3
c Rm 3:9
d 7:15 Jn 15:15
e Gl 5:17
f 7:18 Jn 3:6; Rm 8:3
g 7:21 Rm 8:2
h 7:22 2Co 4:16; Eph 3:16; 1Pt 3:4
i 7:23 Rm 6:19; Gl 5:17; Jms 4:1; 1Pt 2:11
j 7:24 Rm 6:6; 8:2; Col 2:11
k 7:25 1Co 15:57
l 8:1 Rm 5:16; 8:34
m Rm 8:9-10
n Rm 8:11,39; 16:3
o 8:2 1Co 15:45
p Jn 8:32,36; Rm 6:14,18; 7:4
q 8:3 Ac 13:39; Heb 10:1-2
r Rm 7:18; Heb 7:18

A 7:14 Other mss read *I am carnal*   B 7:21 Or *law*   C 7:22 Lit *inner man*   D 7:23 Lit *my members*   E 7:25 Or *Thanks be to God—*[it is done] *through Jesus Christ our Lord!*   F 8:1 Other mss add *who do not walk according to the flesh but according to the Spirit*   G 8:2 Other mss read *me*   H 8:3 Or *weak*

God used the law to accomplish His purpose to clarify and to overcome sin.

7:14-25 This section is probably the most difficult and controversial passage in the letter to the Romans. For the most part the Eastern Church has interpreted it as referring to an unregenerate person (e.g., Paul before his conversion). The Western Church has followed Augustine, Luther, and Calvin in thinking it refers to a regenerate person (Paul after his conversion). Some suggest a mediating position. One such view interprets the subject as an OT believer who loves the law (Pss 1; 119) but struggles to perform it. Living before Christ and Pentecost, this person does not have the permanent and empowering gift of the Holy Spirit, as do new covenant believers. Another view holds that the subject is almost converted to Christ and is now under conviction of sin by the law.

The view that the subject of 14-25 is a regenerate person is sometimes modified in the following ways: (1) The subject is saved but has not had "baptism" in the Pentecostal sense or a second work of grace (as held in some types of Wesleyan theology). (2) The subject is an immature believer, not yet equipped for warfare with his fleshly desires. (3) The subject is a believer trying to become sanctified by legalism.

The view outlined here takes the position that the subject is a regenerated believer, most obviously Paul himself but generically every believer. Paul describes the new man in relation to the law of God and is looking at only one aspect of the person. The new man will be considered in relation to the Holy Spirit in the next section where the Holy Spirit is mentioned 21 times. The main reason for the position offered here is a consideration of what this man's problem really is. In verse 14 he is said to be **made out of flesh** (Gk *sarkinos*, not *sarkikos*). Many translations confuse these two Greek words. The first word emphasizes composition while the second emphasizes tendency ("fleshy" vs. "fleshly"). In verse 18 **in my flesh** means the whole fallen nature that needs the resurrection body (Php 3:21). In verse 24 the **wretched man** cries out to be rescued ("out," Gk *ek*) **from this dying body**. As a believer in Christ, Paul longed to be delivered from the fallen human body which still has indwelling sin.

7:14-15 The law is from God and is therefore **spiritual**, but Paul is **made out of flesh** (a metaphorical reference to spiritual fallenness) and thus finds himself conflicted with the heavenly law of God.

7:16-17 Paul agreed with the law and its goodness, but sin is an alien power that has residence within him and causes him to do things he hates.

7:18-19 Even after conversion, there is no part of a person that is sinless, no place without sin's presence, and the believer is unable to keep the whole law. The only **good** in a believer is the presence of the Holy Spirit.

7:20-23 In his **inner self** (Gk *eso anthropos*), in his deepest recesses, the believer delights in God's law, but he finds this alien power living within, waging war with him and taking him **prisoner to the law of sin**.

7:24-25 Many modern commentators and translators try to reorder these verses, but the order makes sense if the interpretation outlined above is followed. In verse 24 the subject cries out for deliverance from the fallen human condition. A cry of thanksgiving is then offered to God because the subject knows that Jesus will deliver him from his body. The believer recognizes that in his mind he wants to serve God's law since it is holy, just, good, and spiritual, but at the same time his fallen nature is in the service of this alien power—sin.

8:1-39 Romans 8 has been called the most wonderful chapter in the Bible. It begins with "no condemnation" (v. 1) and ends with no separation from God (v. 39). Whereas 7:14-25 describes the new man in relation to the law, chapter 8 describes the new man in relation to the Holy Spirit and His work in and through the new man.

8:1 There is **no condemnation** for the believer because he is not under the law (6:14), and he has been released from the law (7:6). He can now serve God in the "new way of the Spirit" (7:6).

8:2-3 The believer's freedom comes from Jesus' incarnation and His work as the **sin offering** and by the Holy Spirit's operation in providing life. The Second Person of the Trinity, the **Son**, took on humanity. He did not cease to be God but

sin in the flesh by sending His own Son in flesh like ours[a] under sin's domain,[A] and as a sin offering,[b 4] in order that the law's requirement would be accomplished[c] in us who do not ˙walk according to the flesh[d] but according to the Spirit. [5] For those who live[B] according to the flesh think about the things of the flesh,[e] but those who live[B] according to the Spirit, about the things of the Spirit. [6] For the mind-set of the flesh[f] is death,[g] but the mind-set of the Spirit is life and peace. [7] For the mind-set of the flesh is hostile[h] to God because it does not submit itself to God's law, for it is unable to do so. [8] Those who are in the flesh[i] cannot please God. [9] You, however, are not in the flesh, but in the Spirit, since[c] the Spirit of God lives in you.[j] But if anyone does not have the Spirit of Christ,[k] he does not belong to Him. [10] Now if Christ is in you,[l] the body is dead[D] because of sin, but the Spirit[E] is life because of righteousness. [11] And if the Spirit of Him who raised Jesus from the dead[m] lives in you, then He who raised Christ from the dead will also bring your

mortal bodies to life through[F] His Spirit who lives in you.

The Holy Spirit's Ministries

[12] So then, ˙brothers, we are not obligated to the flesh to live according to the flesh, [13] for if you live according to the flesh, you are going to die. But if by the Spirit you put to death the deeds of the body,[n] you will live. [14] All those led by God's Spirit[o] are God's sons.[p] [15] For you did not receive a spirit of slavery to fall back into fear,[q] but you received the Spirit of adoption,[r] by whom we cry out, "'*Abba*, Father!'"[s] [16] The Spirit Himself testifies together with our spirit[t] that we are God's children, [17] and if children, also heirs[u]—heirs of God and coheirs with Christ—seeing that[c] we suffer with Him[v] so that we may also be glorified with Him.

From Groans to Glory

[18] For I consider that the sufferings of this present time are not worth comparing[w] with

[a]8:3 Php 2:7; Heb 2:14,17; 4:15
[b]Lv 5:6-7,11; 14:31; Is 53:10
[c]8:4 Lk 1:6; Rm 2:26
[d]Gl 5:16
[e]8:5 Gl 5:19-25
[f]8:6 Gl 6:8
[g]Rm 6:21
[h]8:7 Jms 4:4
[i]8:8 Rm 7:5
[j]8:9 Jn 14:23; 1Co 3:16; 6:19; 2Co 6:16; 2Tm 1:14
[k]Jn 14:17; Gl 4:6; Php 1:19; 1Jn 4:13
[l]8:10 Jn 17:23; Gl 2:20; Eph 3:17; Col 1:27
[m]8:11 Ac 2:24; Rm 6:4
[n]8:13 Col 3:5
[o]8:14 Gl 5:18
[p]Hs 1:10; Mt 5:9; Jn 1:12; Rm 9:8,26; 2Co 6:18; Gl 3:26; 1Jn 3:1; Rv 21:7
[q]8:15 2Tm 1:7; Heb 2:15
[r]Gl 4:5
[s]Mk 14:36;
[t]8:16 Ac 5:32   [u]8:17 Ac 20:32; Gl 3:29; 4:7; Eph 3:6; Ti 3:7; Heb 1:14; Rv 21:7   [v]2Co 1:5,7; Php 3:10; Col 1:24; 2Tm 2:12
[w]8:18 2Co 4:17; 1Pt 4:13

[A]8:3 Lit *in the likeness of sinful flesh*   [B]8:5 Or *those who are*   [C]8:9,17 Or *provided that*   [D]8:10 Or *the body will die*   [E]8:10 Or *spirit*   [F]8:11 Other mss read *because of*

took on a real human nature (without sin) and became the perfect offering. He fulfilled the law's demands in His life and in His death and broke sin's power in a human body on the cross.

8:4 Christians can now live a new way of love. "Love . . . is the fulfillment of the law" (13:10). They can live freely in keeping with the **Spirit**.

8:5 Paul described the two kinds of people: the old man and the new—two different kinds of existence or two "mindsets."

8:6 The outcome of the two ways of thinking are explained: **death** versus **life and peace**.

8:7-8 Unregenerate people (Gk *in sark*; lit "in the flesh") are **hostile to God** and **unable** to **submit** to **God's law** because they lack God's Spirit, which makes submission possible.

8:9-11 Christians are in a new realm, for the **Spirit** indwells them. The Spirit's presence is the mark of Christ's ownership. The Christian's physical body will still die because of sin's effects (unless the Lord returns before death; 1Co 15:50-57). The pledge and promise of the Spirit is that He will raise us as He did Jesus. Now the Spirit provides **life** and **righteousness**.

8:12-13 Freedom brings an obligation. If a person lives to the fallen nature, **death** is his destiny. The Christian is activated by the Holy **Spirit** to stop doing the sinful deeds of the body. He can mortify the flesh and its activities, and he lives.

8:14 The leading of **God's Spirit** is His providential sanctification (Ps 23:3). It is common to all sons, it is constant, and it will bring the believer to glory (Rm 8:17). The leading of the Spirit is not mystical direction or ecstasy. It is the Spirit's empowerment for mortification of fleshly desires (v. 13).

8:15-16 The Holy **Spirit** is not an agent of bondage but is

instead the means of our **adoption** into God's family. By the Spirit we have a consciousness that God is our **Father**. It is the mark of a Christian to cry out to his Father in prayer. The Spirit also gives us assurance of our status and therefore of our salvation.

8:17 All God's **children** are His **heirs** and coheirs with Christ. We are joined to Him in suffering but also in our future destiny. As He is in glory (1Tm 3:16; Heb 1:3; 2:7,9-10) so we will be **glorified with Him**.

8:18 Paul stated the truth of this verse like this: "Our momentary light affliction is producing for us an absolutely incomparable eternal weight of glory" (2Co 4:17).

huiothesia

Greek Pronunciation	[hwee ah theh SEE ah]
HCSB Translation	adoption
Uses in Romans	3
Uses in the NT	5
Focus passages	Romans 8:15,23

The Greek noun *huiothesia* literally means *a son placing* and comes from *huios* (son) and *tithemi* (to place). The term refers to the legal act whereby a child is accepted into a family on an equal basis—including the same rights of inheritance—with any physical offspring of the parents. Although *huiothesia* was quite common in Greek literature and *adoption* was widely practiced in the Greco-Roman world, only Paul used *huiothesia* in the NT, and then only five times. Paul explained that to Israel belonged "*the adoption*" (Rm 9:4), which probably refers to the fact that God called Israel His son on occasion. In the other four passages where Paul used *huiothesia*, the term refers to those who by faith in Christ have been accepted into God's family (Rm 8:15; Gl 4:5), which was His plan before creation (Eph 1:5). Believers do not receive their full inheritance as sons of God until final salvation, "the redemption of our bodies" at the resurrection (Rm 8:23).

the glory[a] that is going to be revealed to us. [19] For the creation eagerly waits with anticipation[b] for God's sons[c] to be revealed. [20] For the creation was subjected[d] to futility[e]—not willingly, but because of Him who subjected it[f]—in the hope [21] that the creation itself[g] will also be set free from the bondage of corruption into the glorious freedom of God's children. [22] For we know that the whole creation has been groaning together with labor pains[h] until now. [23] And not only that,[i] but we ourselves who have the Spirit as the •firstfruits[j]—we also groan within ourselves,[k] eagerly waiting for adoption,[l] the •redemption of our bodies.[m] [24] Now in this hope[n] we were saved, yet hope[o] that is seen is not hope, because who hopes for what he sees? [25] But if we hope for what we do not see,[p] we eagerly wait for it with patience.

[26] In the same way the Spirit also joins to help in our weakness, because we do not know what to pray for as we should,[q] but the Spirit Himself intercedes for us[A,r] with unspoken groanings. [27] And He who searches the hearts[s] knows the Spirit's mind-set, because He intercedes for the •saints according to the will of God.

[28] We know that all things work together[B] for the good[c] of those who love God: those who are called according to His purpose.[t]

[29] For those He foreknew He also predestined[u] to be conformed to the image of His Son,[v] so that He would be the firstborn among many brothers.[w] [30] And those He predestined, He also called; and those He called, He also •justified;[x] and those He justified, He also glorified.[y]

The Believer's Triumph

[31] What then are we to say
about these things?[z]
If God is for us, who is against us?[aa]
[32] He did not even spare His own Son[ab]
but offered Him up for us all;[ac]
how will He not also with Him grant
us everything?
[33] Who can bring an accusation
against God's elect?[ad]
God is the One who justifies.[ae]
[34] Who is the one who condemns?[af]
Christ Jesus is the One who died,[ag]
but even more, has been raised;[ah]
He also is at the right hand of God[ai]
and intercedes for us.[aj]
[35] Who can separate us from the love
of Christ?

[a]8:18 Rm 1:5; Col 3:4; Ti 2:13; 1Pt 5:1　[b]8:19 Php 1:20　[c]1Co 1:7; Col 3:4; 1Pt 1:7,13; 1Jn 3:2　[d]8:20 Gn 3:17-19　[e]Ps 39:5; Ec 1:2　[f]Gn 3:17; 5:29　[g]8:21 Ac 3:21; 2Pt 3:13; Rv 21:1　[h]8:22 Jr 12:4,11　[i]8:23 Rm 5:3　[j]Nm 15:17-21; 1Co 16:15; 2Co 1:22　[k]2Co 5:2,4　[l]Gl 5:5　[m]Rm 7:24　[n]8:24 1Th 5:8; Ti 3:7　[o]Rm 4:18; 2Co 5:7; Heb 11:1　[p]8:25 1Th 1:3　[q]8:26 Mt 20:22; 2Co 12:8　[r]Jn 14:16; Rm 8:15-16; Eph 6:18　[s]8:27 Ps 139:1-5; Lk 16:15; Ac 1:24; Rv 2:23　[t]8:28 Rm 9:24; 11:29; 1Co 1:9; Gl 1:6,15; 5:8; Eph 1:11; 3:11; 2Th 2:14; Heb 9:15; 1Pt 2:9; 3:9　[u]8:29 Rm 9:23; 1Co 2:7; Eph 1:5,11　[v]1Co 15:49; Php 3:21; Col 3:10; 1Jn 3:2　[w]Col 1:18; Heb 1:6　[x]8:30 1Co 6:11　[y]Jn 17:22; Rm 9:23; 1Co 2:7　[z]8:31 Rm 3:5; 4:1　[aa]Ps 118:6; Mt 1:23　[ab]8:32 Jn 3:16; Rm 5:8　[ac]Rm 4:25　[ad]8:33 Lk 18:7　[ae]Is 50:8-9　[af]8:34 Rm 8:1　[ag]Rm 5:6-8　[ah]Ac 2:24　[ai]Mk 16:19　[aj]Heb 7:25; 9:24; 1Jn 2:1

[A]8:26 Some mss omit for us　[B]8:28 Other mss read that God works together in all things　[C]8:28 The ultimate good

---

8:19-21 The created order of this earth was cursed at the fall (Gn 3:17-19), and it will be restored in the regeneration. When we receive our freedom, the entire world will be changed (Is 2:2-4; 11:6-9; Rv 21–22).

8:22-23 Paul describes the **groaning** of **creation**, the groaning of believers, and the groaning of the Holy Spirit (v. 26). Travail gives birth to a new creation. Christians have only the **firstfruits**—the pledge of more to come in our salvation. We groan because of our fallen nature. Our new resurrection bodies will conform us to Jesus' glorified body.

8:24-25 Our salvation is secure, but it is as yet unseen and thus a matter of **hope**. We wait in faith and patience.

8:26-27 In our **weakness** we have the help of the **Spirit**. Jesus is our intercessor in heaven (Heb 7:25), and the Spirit is our intercessor on earth within our hearts. We are limited and ignorant, but the Spirit uses **unspoken groanings** to communicate our needs. This is not "speaking in tongues or languages" (Gk *glossolalia*). It is instead wordless. Our heavenly Father knows what is happening in our lives and within the deep recesses of our personalities (1Sm 16:7; Pr 15:11; Jr 17:10). The Spirit's requests are always **according to the will of God** and are always answered.

8:28 Who are those who **love God**? Paul defines them as **those who are called according to His purpose**. The "called" are all Christians (vv. 29-30). The promise of this verse is that God orders everything for believers so that all of life's experiences **work together** for our ultimate **good**. Not everything is good in and of itself, but God uses everything for our good (vv. 35-36). Jesus taught us that God's sovereign care for and guidance of creation covers even the death of a sparrow and the hairs of our head (Lk 12:6-7,22-34).

8:29-30 God has a plan that spans from eternity past to eternity future. **Those He foreknew** refers to those whom God set His electing love upon in eternity past. **Predestined** means that God planned from eternity that "those [whom] He foreknew" would become like Christ through spiritual rebirth. **Called** is the "effectual" call in which God opens our heart so we can hear His voice (cp. Ac 16:14). "Calling" in Paul's writing never means just an invitation. It is a sovereign summons that draws the sinner from death to life. **Justified** is God's act of declaration that we are "right" in His sight because Jesus paid our penalty and we received His righteousness (2Co 5:21). **Glorified** is the final stage of our salvation. Notice that our future glorification is so certain that it is spoken of in the past tense.

8:31 If God is for us expresses not a hypothetical scenario, but a sure reality: God really is for us. This well summarizes the gospel, and serves as a concise summary of 3:21–8:30 (Cranfield, *Romans*, 1:434). OT believers had the same assurance: "I fear no danger, for You are with me" (Ps 23:4; cp. Ps 27:1). "This I know: God is for me" (Ps 56:9). **Who is against us?** The opposition seems like a lot sometimes—the world, the flesh, Satan, secularists, false religions, our enemies—but God loves us and is sovereign. Yahweh is our Shepherd, Maker of heaven and earth!

8:32 In contrast to Abraham who was permitted to spare his only son, God did not **spare** His Son. If God did the greater (gave His Son), will He not do the lesser and give us all that is necessary for life and godliness? Of course He will.

8:33 Our accusers are numerous, but God the Judge has already pronounced the final verdict.

8:35-36 God's people have always faced persecutions and

Can affliction[a] or anguish
or persecution[b]
or famine or nakedness or danger
or sword?
36 As it is written:
**Because of You
we are being put to death all day long;[c]
we are counted as sheep
to be slaughtered.[A,d]**
37 No, in all these things we are
more than victorious[e]
through Him who loved us.[f]
38 For I am persuaded that not even death
or life,[g]
angels or rulers,[h]
things present or things to come,[i]
hostile powers,
39 height or depth, or any other
created thing
will have the power to separate us
from the love of God[j] that is
in Christ Jesus our Lord![k]

Israel's Rejection of Christ

9 I speak the truth in Christ[l]—I am not
lying; my conscience is testifying to me
with the Holy Spirit[B]— 2 that I have intense
sorrow and continual anguish in my heart.
3 For I could almost wish[m] to be cursed[n] and
cut off[C] from the *Messiah for the benefit of
my *brothers, my own flesh and blood. 4 They
are Israelites,[o] and to them belong the adoption,[p] the glory,[q] the covenants,[r] the giving of
the law,[s] the temple service,[t] and the promises.[u] 5 The ancestors are theirs,[v] and from them,
by physical descent,[D] came the Messiah,[w] who
is God[x] over all,[y] praised forever.[E,z] *Amen.

God's Gracious Election of Israel

6 But it is not as though the word of God
has failed.[aa] For not all who are descended
from Israel are Israel.[ab] 7 Neither are they all

a8:35 Rm 2:9;
2Co 4:8
b1Co 4:11; 2Co
11:26-27
c8:36 Ac 20:24;
1Co 4:9; 15:30-
31; 2Co 1:9; 6:9;
11:23
d1s 53:7; Zch
11:4,7
e8:37 Jn 16:33;
1Co 15:57
fGl 2:20; Eph 5:2;
Rv 1:5
g8:38 1Co 3:22
h1Co 15:24; Eph
1:21; 1Pt 3:22
i1Co 3:22
j8:39 Rm 5:8
kRm 8:1
l9:1 Rm 1:9; 2Co
11:10; Gl 1:20;
1Tm 2:7
m9:3 Ex 32:32
n1Co 12:3; 16:22;
Gl 1:8,9
o9:4 Rm 8:6
pEx 4:22; Rm
8:15
qEx 40:34; 1Kg
8:11; Ezk 1:28;
Heb 9:5
rGn 17:2; Dt
29:14; Lk 1:72;

Ac 3:25; Eph 2:12   sDt 4:13-14; Ps 147:19   tEx 7:6; 14:1; Heb
9:1,6   uAc 2:39; 13:32; Eph 2:12   v9:5 Ac 3:13; Rm 11:28   wMt
1:1-16; Rm 1:3   xJn 1:1; Col 2:9   yCol 1:16-19   zRm 1:25
aa9:6 Nm 23:19   abJn 1:47; Rm 2:28-29; Gl 6:16

A8:36 Ps 44:22   B9:1 Or *testifying with me by the Holy Spirit*   C9:3 Lit *were anathema*   D9:5 Lit *them, according to the flesh*
E9:5 Or *the Messiah, the One who is over all, the God who is blessed forever,* or *Messiah. God, who is over all, be blessed forever*

hardships, as vividly portrayed in the complaints of Ps 44.
Will such things **separate us from the love of Christ?**

8:37 We are **more than victorious** not by our ability but because God **loved us.**

8:38-39 Paul's "grand persuasion" (Gk *pepeismai*) is in the
perfect tense, which indicates a past action that has ongoing
impact. Having been **persuaded** (by God), he stood firm in
the belief that nothing could separate him from the **love of
God.** Jesus conquered death and Satan on the cross, ensuring that nothing can change God's love or purpose for us. We
"are being protected by God's power through faith for a salvation that is ready to be revealed in the last time" (1Pt 1:5).

9-11 Many interpreters have been puzzled by this section
of Romans. Anti-Jewish interpreters argue that God is finished with the Jews (9:1-29), while other interpreters view
these chapters as a digression from Paul's exposition of the
gospel. But K. H. Rengstorff of Germany recognized otherwise in 1949: "During the years of its sufferings, the Confessing Church learnt that Romans 9-11 held the key to the
understanding of the NT."

This is because these chapters help answer tough questions about how Jesus could be the Jewish Messiah and yet
suffer rejection by the majority of Israel. Was the glory of
the Davidic Messiah not supposed to excel the glory of David
himself? Also, the Jewish expectation was that when Messiah came, Israel would be delivered from Gentile oppression and would hold priority over the nations. Since these
things had not happened, many people assumed either that
Jesus was not the promised Messiah or else that God had
broken His promises to Israel. Furthermore, if Jesus really was Messiah and yet God had not delivered Israel, how
could anyone trust Him to keep His gospel promises? And
so the trustworthiness of God seemed to be on the line.

Paul overturned these doubts by answering from three
perspectives: (1) from the viewpoint of divine sovereignty
(chap. 9), (2) from human responsibility (chap. 10), and (3)
from God's final purpose (chap. 11).

9:1-3 Far from being a traitor among the Jews, Paul insisted

that he felt **intense sorrow and continual anguish** over Jewish national unbelief and would willingly forsake his own salvation if it could save his **brothers,** his **own flesh and blood.**

9:4-5 Paul began in 3:1-2 to list Jewish national benefits.
Now he returns to list their privileges, the greatest of which
is the incarnation of God in Jewish flesh.

9:6 It is a basic misunderstanding of the OT promises to
think that all who were in the nation of Israel were guaranteed to receive God's spiritual blessings. Paul provides
examples in the following verses.

9:7 Abraham had children by Hagar and Keturah, but the
promised line was through Sarah's son **Isaac.**

sperma

Greek Pronunciation	[SPUHR mah]
HCSB Translation	descendant, seed
Uses in Romans	9
Uses in the NT	43
Focus passage	Romans 9:7-8

The English word *sperm* comes directly from the Greek noun
sperma, meaning *seed.* The term was often used for the *seeds*
of plants (Mt 13:24-38; Mk 4:31) and sometimes even for *animals*
(referring to reproduction as in humans). The term *sperma* could
refer figuratively to origin but refers more often to *descendants* or
offspring. Paul develops the *descendant/offspring* meaning along
three main lines.

(1) Jesus the Messiah came from the promised *sperma* or family line (Rm 1:3; 2Tm 2:8; see Gl 3:16,19; cp. Jn 8:33; Ac 13:23).

(2) Those who are the *sperma* or *descendants* of Abraham by
physical descent, that is, the Hebrew race (Rm 9:7,29 [translated
"*descendants*"]; 11:1).

(3) Those who are the *sperma* or *descendants* of Abraham by
faith, that is, believers in Christ (Rm 4:13,16,18; 9:7-8 [translated
"*seed*"]; Gl 3:29). Through these various uses of *sperma,* Paul
indicated that actual physical descent from Abraham is neither
necessary nor sufficient for salvation; faith in Christ alone brings
a person into God's family.

children because they are Abraham's descendants.[A,a] On the contrary, **your 'offspring will be traced[B] through Isaac.**[C,b] [8] That is, it is not the children by physical descent[D] who are God's children,[c] but the children of the promise[d] are considered to be the offspring. [9] For this is the statement of the promise: **At this time I will come, and Sarah will have a son.**[E,e] [10] And not only that,[f] but also Rebekah received a promise when she became pregnant[F,g] by one man, our ancestor Isaac. [11] For though her sons had not been born yet or done anything good or bad, so that God's purpose according to election might stand—[h] [12] not from works but from the One who calls—she was told: **The older will serve the younger.**[G,i] [13] As it is written: **I have loved Jacob, but I have hated Esau.**[H,j]

God's Selection Is Just

[14] What should we say then?[k] Is there injustice with God?[l] Absolutely not![m] [15] For He tells Moses:

> **I will show mercy**
> **to whom I will show mercy,**
> **and I will have compassion**
> **on whom I will have compassion.**[l,n]

[16] So then it does not depend on human will or effort[J,o] but on God who shows mercy.[p] [17] For the Scripture tells Pharaoh:

> **I raised you up for this reason**
> **so that I may display My power in you**
> **and that My name may be proclaimed**
> **in all the earth.**[K,q]

[18] So then, He shows mercy to those He wants to, and He hardens those He wants to harden.[r]

[19] You will say to me,[s] therefore, "Why then does He still find fault?[t] For who can resist His will?"[u] [20] But who are you, a mere man, to talk back to God?[v] Will what is formed say to the one who formed it, "Why did you make me like this?"[w] [21] Or has the potter no right over the clay,[x] to make from the same lump one piece of pottery for honor and another for dishonor? [22] And what if God, desiring to display His wrath and to make His power known, endured with much patience[y] objects of wrath

Cross references

a9:7 Jn 8:33,39; Gl 4:23
b Gn 21:12; Heb 11:18
c9:8 Rm 8:14
d Rm 4:13,16; Gl 3:29; 4:28; Heb 11:11
e9:9 Gn 18:10,14
f9:10 Rm 5:3
g Gn 25:21
h9:11 Rm 4:17; 8:28
i9:12 Gn 25:23
j9:13 Mal 1:2-3
k9:14 Rm 3:5
l2Ch 19:7; Rm 2:11
m Lk 20:16
n9:15 Ex 33:19
o9:16 Gl 2:2
p Eph 2:8
q9:17 Ex 9:16
r9:18 Ex 4:21; 7:3; 9:12; 10:20,27; 11:10; 14:4,7; Dt 2:30; Jos 11:20; Jn 12:40; Rm 11:7,25
s9:19 Rm 11:19; 1Co 15:25; Jms 2:18
t Rm 3:7
u2Ch 20:6; Jb 9:12; Dn 4:35
v9:20 Jb 33:13
w Is 29:16; 45:9; 64:8; Jr 18:6; 2Tm 2:20
x9:21 Is 64:8; Jr 18:6
y9:22 Rm 2:4

Translation notes

A9:7 Lit *seed*   B9:7 Lit *called*   C9:7 Gn 21:12   D9:8 Lit *children of the flesh*   E9:9 Gn 18:10,14   F9:10 Or *Rebekah conceived by the one act of sexual intercourse*   G9:12 Gn 25:23   H9:13 Mal 1:2-3   I9:15 Ex 33:19   J9:16 Or *on the one running*; lit *on the one willing*   K9:17 Ex 9:16

9:8-9 Ishmael was a physical son of Abraham, but Isaac was the **physical** son with the spiritual promises.

9:10-11 The case is clearer with **Rebekah** because she had twins. God's choice of the younger twin before their birth showed His gracious **election** and indicated again that God's blessings are His to hand out and that they were not an automatic birthright of all ethnic Jews; see note at verse 6.

9:12-13 The divine purpose was revealed from the beginning of the Hebrew nation when God chose one twin over the other. The prophet Malachi traced God's differing treatment of two nations to this divine choice (Mal 1:1-5). Both nations were punished for their sins, but only one received grace. **I have loved Jacob** means God chose or elected his descendants (the nation of Israel), whereas **I have hated Esau** means that God rejected the nation that stemmed from him (Edom).

9:14-15 **Is there injustice with God?** is a rhetorical question, inspired by the fact that it is difficult to grasp the fact that God does not need to treat all sinners the same in order to be just. Jesus taught the same truth in the parable of the vineyard workers (Mt 20:1-15: "Don't I have the right to do what I want with my business?"). In His first sermon in Nazareth, Jesus pointed out that God gave grace to a widow in Sidon and healed only Naaman the Syrian when there were many needy people in Israel (Lk 4:24-27). His comments enraged the audience, but careful consideration reveals that a just God is perfectly free to make such choices. If you gave money to one beggar but not to another, or if you forgave one debtor but not another, would you be unjust? Of course not. You chose to be gracious to one where you could have justly chosen to be gracious to none. God does not owe **mercy** to anyone. Paul quoted Ex 33:19 to this effect.

9:16 Salvation does not depend on **human will or effort**.

Salvation is based on God's mercy. The situation is not that people want to be saved but cannot be (2Tm 2:25-26), or that they are running after God but cannot find Him. Apart from God's drawing them, none are seeking the one true God—not a single one (Rm 3:11-12).

9:17 God raised up **Pharaoh** as ruler of Egypt and used him as a foil to reveal His name (Yahweh) and His power so the one true God would be known. Pharaoh believed himself to be the epitome of Ra the sun god. He hardened his heart and rejected God's revelation (Ex 7:3; 8:15).

9:18 God hardened Pharaoh in his stubbornness as he progressively rejected the plagues that revealed "the finger of God" (Ex 8:19). Exodus points out that Pharaoh hardened his heart many times before God punished him by hardening him.

9:19 Paul declared that the Judge of the earth is always just. "Will the one who contends with the Almighty correct Him?" (Jb 40:2). Man cannot judge God.

9:20-22 *Adam* (man) is from the *adama* (ground) (Gn 2:7). In pronouncing punishment for Adam and Eve's sin, God said, "For you are dust, and you will return to dust" (Gn 3:19). The image of the village **potter** is common in the OT (Is 41:25; 45:9; Jr 18:1-12) and is used to illustrate different lessons. Here the clay represents fallen humanity. Much as a potter, God works this material into shapes that fulfill His desires (Is 64:6-9). Some pots He chooses to be for **honor**; others He patiently endures until He displays His justified **wrath** against sin.

9:23-24 God desires to display His grace on **objects of mercy**, the ones on whom He has set His redeeming love. These come from both Jewish and Gentile backgrounds.

9:25-26 Drawing from Hosea's marriage, Paul compares

ready for destruction?ᵃ ²³ And what if He did this to make known the riches of His gloryᵇ on objects of mercyᶜ that He prepared beforehand for glory*ᵈ*— ²⁴ on us, the ones He also called,ᵉ not only from the Jews but also from the Gentiles?*ᶠ* ²⁵ As He also says in Hosea:

I will call Not My People, My People,
and she who is Unloved, Beloved.ᴬ,*ᵍ*
²⁶ And it will be in the place where
    they were told,
you are not My people,
there they will be called sons
    of the living God.ᴮ,*ʰ*

²⁷ But Isaiah cries out concerning Israel:

Though the number of Israel's sons
is like the sand of the sea,*ⁱ*
only the remnant will be saved;*ʲ*
²⁸   for the Lord will execute His sentence
completely and decisively
    on the earth.ᶜ,ᴰ,*ᵏ*

²⁹ And just as Isaiah predicted:

If the Lord of ˙Hostsᴱ had not left
    us offspring,*ˡ*
we would have become like Sodom,
and we would have been made
    like Gomorrah.ᶠ,*ᵐ*

Cross references (center column):

ᵃ9:22 Pr 16:4; 1Pt 2:8
ᵇ9:23 Rm 2:4; Eph 3:16
ᶜAc 9:15
ᵈRm 8:29
ᵉ9:24 Rm 8:28
ᶠRm 3:29
ᵍ9:25 Hs 2:23; 1Pt 2:10
ʰ9:26 Hs 1:10; Mt 16:16
ⁱ9:27 Gn 22:17
ʲRm 11:5
ᵏ9:27-28 Is 10:22-23; 28:22
ˡ9:29 Jms 5:4
ᵐDt 29:23; Is 1:9; 13:19; Jr 49:18; 50:40; Am 4:11
ⁿ9:30 Rm 9:14
ᵒRm 1:17; 3:21; 10:6; Gl 2:16; 3:24; Php 3:9; Heb 11:7
ᵖ9:31 Is 51:1; Rm 10:2,20; 11:7
ᑫGl 5:4
ʳ9:32 1Pt 2:6,8
ˢ9:33 Rm 10:11
ᵗIs 8:14; 28:16; Rm 5:5
ᵘ10:2 Ac 21:20
ᵛ10:3 Rm 1:17
ʷ10:4 Rm 7:1-4; Gl 3:24; 4:5

Israel's Present State

³⁰ What should we say then?ⁿ Gentiles, who did not pursue righteousness, have obtained righteousness—namely the righteousness that comes from faith.ᵒ ³¹ But Israel, pursuing the law for righteousness,ᵖ has not achieved the righteousness of the law.ᴳ,ᑫ ³² Why is that? Because they did not pursue it by faith, but as if it were by works.ᴴ They stumbled over the stumbling stone.ʳ ³³ As it is written:

Look! I am putting a stone in ˙Zion
    to stumble over
and a rock to trip over,
yet the one who believes
    on Himˢ
will not be put to shame.ᴵ,ᵗ

Righteousness by Faith Alone

10 ¹Brothers, my heart's desire and prayer to God concerning them*ʲ* is for their salvation! ² I can testify about them that they have zeal for God,ᵘ but not according to knowledge. ³ Because they disregarded the righteousness from Godᵛ and attempted to establish their own righteousness, they have not submitted themselves to God's righteousness. ⁴ For Christ is the endᴷ of the law for righteousnessʷ

ᴬ9:25 Hs 2:23   ᴮ9:26 Hs 1:10   ᶜ9:28 Or *land*   ᴰ9:27-28 Is 10:22-23; 28:22; Hs 1:10   ᴱ9:29 Gk *Sabaoth*; this word is a transliteration of the Hb word for *Hosts*, or *Armies*.   ᶠ9:29 Is 1:9   ᴳ9:31 Other mss read *the law for righteousness*   ᴴ9:32 Other mss add *of the law*   ᴵ9:33 Is 8:14; 28:16   ᴶ10:1 Other mss read *God for Israel*   ᴷ10:4 Or *goal*

Gentile salvation to mercy bestowed on an undeserving adulterous wife (see the book of Hosea).

9:27-29 Paul also cited the words of **Isaiah** to show that God will save a remnant of Israel that He "calls." Unless God had been gracious to the remnant, the whole nation would have been justly wiped out like ancient **Sodom** and **Gomorrah**.

9:30-10:21 Chapter and verse divisions in the Bible are modern inventions made for the convenience of readers. Chapters 9-11 are one unit of thought, and they must be understood together to get a complete picture of Paul's argument.

9:30-33 Gentiles, who were not seeking **righteousness**, were granted it by grace through **faith**. They did not work for it or earn it. But **Israel** missed it by seeking righteousness through the **law** and by their **works**. They stumbled over the Messiah and did not believe in Him (Is 8:14; 28:16). Jesus Himself warned Israel that they missed the "stone" (Mt 21:42-44; see Ps 118:22-23).

10:1 Paul saw no contradiction between election and prayer. Only a sovereign God, who has rights to move unilaterally in the affairs of humanity, can answer **prayer**. Among unbelievers we do not know beforehand who is elect and will come to faith upon hearing the gospel, but we can know that "God our Savior . . . wants everyone to be saved and to come to the knowledge of the truth" (1Tm 2:4). Paul therefore prayed for Jewish **salvation**, and we must be diligent to share the good news of Jesus with everyone. It is never proper to give up on someone as "non-elect."

10:2-3 Both **zeal** and true **knowledge** are necessary if one is truly to know God and serve Him. In his zeal as a non-

Christian Pharisee, Paul (then called Saul; see Ac 7:58 and note there) persecuted the church (Ac 22:3-5). Likewise, zeal among unbelieving Jews led to Jesus' unjust execution. In spiritual blindness they not only missed God's way of **righteousness**, they opposed it.

10:4 Christ is the **end of the law** in being both its fulfillment

telos

Greek Pronunciation	[TEHL ahss]
HCSB Translation	end
Uses in Romans	5
Uses in the NT	40
Focus passage	Romans 10:4

The Greek noun *telos* is related to the verbs *teleo* and *teleioo*, both meaning *to complete, perfect, finish*, and to the adjective *teleion*, meaning *complete, perfect, whole*. The term *telos* refers to the *consummation, completion*, or *fulfillment* of something. In the NT, *telos* is commonly used for the *end* of this life (Mt 10:22; Lk 18:5; 1Co 1:8; Php 3:19; Heb 3:14; 6:11; 7:3; Rv 2:26) or for events related to the *end* times (Mt 24:6,13,14; Mk 13:7,13; Lk 1:33; 21:9; 1Co 10:11; 15:24; 2Co 11:15; 1Pt 4:7,17). In Revelation *telos* occurs twice in the formula "the Beginning and the *End*" as a title for deity (21:6; 22:13). In Romans 10:4 *telos* refers to Christ as "the *end* of the law," which is similar to Paul's statement that believers are no longer "under the law" (Rm 6:14). Christians do not relate to God through the old covenant God made with Israel at Mt. Sinai through Moses, but through the new covenant He made at the cross through Christ's blood (see Jr 31:31-34; Lk 22:20; Heb 8:8-12).

to everyone who believes.[a] [5] For Moses writes about the righteousness that is from the law: **The one who does these things will live by them.**[A,b] [6] But the righteousness that comes from faith[c] speaks like this: **Do not say in your heart, "Who will go up to heaven?"**[B,d] that is, to bring Christ down [7] or, **"Who will go down into the 'abyss?'"**[C,e] that is, to bring Christ up from the dead.[f] [8] On the contrary, what does it say? **The message is near you, in your mouth and in your heart.**[D,g] This is the message of faith that we proclaim: [9] If you confess with your mouth, **"Jesus is Lord,"**[h] and believe in your heart[i] that God raised Him from the dead,[j] you will be saved. [10] One believes with the heart, resulting in righteousness, and one confesses with the mouth, resulting in salvation. [11] Now the Scripture says, **Everyone who believes on Him will not be put to shame,**[E,k] [12] for there is no distinction between Jew and Greek,[l] since the same Lord[m] of all[n] is rich to all who call on Him. [13] For **everyone who calls on the name of the Lord will be saved.**[F,o]

Israel's Rejection of the Message

[14] But how can they call on Him they have not believed in? And how can they believe without hearing about Him?[p] And how can they hear without a preacher?[q] [15] And how can they preach unless they are sent? As it is written: **How beautiful**[G] **are the feet of those**[H] **who announce the gospel of good things!**[I,r] [16] But all did not obey the gospel.[s] For Isaiah says, **Lord, who has believed our message?**[J,t] [17] So faith comes from what is heard,[u] and what is heard comes through the message about Christ.[K,v] [18] But I ask, "Did they not hear?" Yes, they did:

> **Their voice has gone out to all the earth,**
> **and their words to the ends of the inhabited world.**[L,w]

[19] But I ask, "Did Israel not understand?" First, Moses said:

> **I will make you jealous**
> **of those who are not a nation;**[x]
> **I will make you angry by a nation**
> **that lacks understanding.**[M,y]

[20] And Isaiah says boldly:

Cross references

[a]10:4 Rm 3:22
[b]10:5 Lv 18:5; Neh 9:29; Ezk 20:11,13,21; Rm 7:10
[c]10:6 Rm 9:30
[d]Dt 9:4; 30:12
[e]10:7 Dt 30:13; Lk 8:31
[f]Heb 13:20
[g]10:8 Dt 30:14
[h]10:9 Mt 10:32; Lk 12:8; Rm 14:9; 1Co 12:3; Php 2:11
[i]Ac 16:31; Rm 4:24
[j]Ac 2:24
[k]10:11 Is 28:16
[l]10:12 Rm 3:22,29
[m]Ac 10:36
[n]Rm 3:29
[o]10:13 Jl 2:32; Ac 2:21; 7:59
[p]10:14 Eph 2:17; 4:21
[q]Ac 8:31; Ti 1:3
[r]10:15 Is 52:7; Nah 1:15; Rm 1:15; 15:20
[s]10:16 Rm 3:3
[t]Is 53:1; Jn 12:38
[u]10:17 Gl 3:2,5
[v]Col 3:16
[w]10:18 Ps 19:4; Rm 1:8; Col 1:16,23; 1Th 1:8
[x]10:19 Rm 11:11,14
[y]Dt 32:21

Textual notes

[A]10:5 Lv 18:5 [B]10:6 Dt 9:4; 30:12 [C]10:7 Dt 30:13 [D]10:8 Dt 30:14 [E]10:11 Is 28:16 [F]10:13 Jl 2:32 [G]10:15 Or *welcome,* or *timely* [H]10:15 Other mss read *feet of those who announce the gospel of peace, of those* [I]10:15 Is 52:7; Nah 1:15 [J]10:16 Is 53:1 [K]10:17 Other mss read *God* [L]10:18 Ps 19:4 [M]10:19 Dt 32:21

and its termination. Any system of salvation based on performance is excluded.

10:5-7 Paul quoted Moses on both sides of the issue. In Lv 18:5 (cp. Gl 3:12) obedience to the law brings life, but no one can keep the law and gain righteousness (as implied by Paul's citation of Moses in v. 6). Faith-based righteousness is from **Christ**. He is accessible. He died for us and was raised from the **dead**. Moses pointed out that God's revelation was accessible, and Paul quoted his words to show that Christ is accessible.

10:8 The nearness of the message of faith is at the **heart** and **mouth** of people, just as Moses proclaimed the nearness of God's revelation.

10:9-10 **Jesus is Lord** is a confession of faith. "Lord" is the translation of the Greek word *kurios*. This is the regular way of translating the Hebrew name for God (Yahweh) in the Greek OT (the LXX). Jesus is not only the Messiah (Gk *Christ* = Hb *Messiah*), but He is also Yahweh. Not only do we believe that the man Jesus was **raised . . . from the dead**, but we also believe that He shares the same nature with God. This is the start of the understanding of Christ's two natures, as articulated at the Council of Chalcedon (A.D. 451). Jesus is fully human and fully God. Christians by definition believe and confess this truth.

10:11-13 Paul cited biblical support for the universal offer of salvation. Salvation is for both **Jew** and **Greek** (i.e., Gentiles) since the same **Lord** (Gk *kurios,* v. 12) is **rich** in mercy **to all**. The promise is for all who call on the **name of the Lord** (*kurios,* v. 13). As the prophet Joel said, "Everyone who calls on the name of Yahweh will be saved" (Jl 2:32). Jesus is Lord, or Yahweh.

10:14-15 What must occur for someone to call on the name of the Lord? Someone must first be sent to proclaim the gospel message, and then listeners must pay attention and believe. In the absence of any one of these factors, no one can call on the name of the Lord.

10:16-21 Paul quoted several OT passages to show that the conditions described in verses 14-15 had been met for Israel. The gospel message was proclaimed throughout the Roman Empire. The Jews listened and simply did not be-

proginosko

Greek Pronunciation	[prah gih NOH skoh]
HCSB Translation	foreknow
Uses in Romans	2
Uses in the NT	5
Focus passage	Romans 11:2

The Greek verb *proginosko* comes from the preposition *pro* (meaning *before*) and the verb *ginosko* (meaning *to know*); the compound term thus means *to know beforehand*. The related noun *prognosis* means *foreknowledge* and is the basis for the English medical term *prognosis*. On two occasions in the NT, *proginosko* is used for knowledge obtained in advance by human beings (Ac 26:5; 2Pt 3:17). However, when God is the one *foreknowing*, the emphasis is not on prior knowledge but on prior choice. The other three uses of this verb and both uses of the noun indicate that God *foreknows* people, not events. These terms refer to God's choice of His people and of Christ for a redemptive purpose. Since God chose Israel—not the other way around—He did not reject her (Rm 11:2). God chose Christ "*before* the foundation of the world" for the purpose of redemption (1Pt 1:20; see Ac 2:23), and in keeping with this purpose He also chose those whom He would conform "to the image of His Son" (Rm 8:29; see 1Pt 1:2).

I was found
by those who were not looking for Me;
I revealed Myself
to those who were not asking for Me.[A,a]

²¹ But to Israel he says: **All day long I have spread out My hands to a disobedient and defiant people.** [B,b]

Israel's Rejection Not Total

11 I ask, then, has God rejected His people?[c] Absolutely not![d] For I too am an Israelite, a descendant of Abraham,[e] from the tribe of Benjamin. ²God has not rejected His people whom He foreknew.[f] Or don't you know[g] what the Scripture says in the passage about Elijah—how he pleads with God against Israel?

³   **Lord, they have killed Your prophets
and torn down Your altars.
I am the only one left,
and they are trying to take my life!** [C,h]

⁴But what was God's reply to him? **I have left 7,000 men for Myself who have not bowed down to •Baal.** [D,i] ⁵In the same way, then, there is also at the present time a remnant chosen by grace.[j] ⁶Now if by grace,[k] then it is not by works; otherwise grace ceases to be grace.[E]

⁷What then? Israel did not find what it was looking for,[l] but the elect did find it. The rest were hardened,[m] ⁸as it is written:

God gave them a spirit of insensitivity, [F]
**eyes that cannot see
and ears that cannot hear,
to this day.** [G,n]

⁹And David says:

    Let their feasting [H] **become a snare
and a trap,
a pitfall and a retribution to them.**
¹⁰   **Let their eyes be darkened
so they cannot see,
and their backs be bent continually.** [I,o]

Israel's Rejection Not Final

¹¹I ask, then, have they stumbled in order to fall? Absolutely not! On the contrary, by their stumbling,[J] salvation has come to the Gentiles[p] to make Israel jealous. ¹²Now if their stumbling[J] brings riches for the world, and their failure riches for the Gentiles, how much more will their full number bring![q]

¹³Now I am speaking to you Gentiles. In view of the fact that I am an apostle to the Gentiles,[r] I magnify my ministry, ¹⁴if I can somehow make my own people[K,s] jealous and save some of them.[t] ¹⁵For if their rejection brings reconciliation[u] to the world, what will their acceptance mean but life from the dead?[v] ¹⁶Now if the •firstfruits offered up are holy,[w] so is the whole batch. And if the root is holy, so are the branches.

¹⁷Now if some of the branches were broken off,[x] and you, though a wild olive branch, were grafted in among them[y] and have come to share in the rich root[L] of the cultivated olive tree, ¹⁸do not brag that you are better than those branches. But if you do brag—you do not sustain the root, but the root sustains you.[z] ¹⁹Then you will say,[aa] "Branches were

Cross references (center column)

a 10:20 Is 65:1; Rm 9:30
b 10:21 Is 65:2
c 11:1 1Sm 12:22; Jr 33:24-26
d Lk 20:16
e 2Co 11:22;
f 11:2 1Sm 12:22; Ps 94:14; Rm 8:29; 1Pt 1:2
g Rm 6:16
h 11:3 1Kg 19:10,14; 1Th 2:14
i 11:4 1Kg 19:18
j 11:5 2Kg 19:4; Rm 9:27
k 11:6 Rm 4:4
l 11:7 Rm 9:31
m Mk 6:52; Rm 9:18; 11:25; 2Co 2:14
n 11:8 Dt 29:4; Is 29:10; Mt 13:13-14
o 11:9-10 Ps 69:22-23
p 11:11 Ac 28:28
q 11:12 Rm 11:25
r 11:13 Ac 9:15
s 11:14 Gn 29:14; 2Sm 19:12-13; Rm 9:3
t 1Co 1:21; 7:16; 9:22; 1Tm 1:15; 2:4; 2Tm 1:9; Ti 3:5
u 11:15 Rm 5:11
v Lk 15:24,32
w 11:16 Nm 15:17-21; Neh 10:37; Ezk 44:30
x 11:17 Jr 11:16; Jn 15:2
y Eph 2:12-13
z 11:18 Jn 4:22
aa 11:19 Rm 9:19

Translation notes

A 10:20 Is 65:1 B 10:21 Is 65:2 C 11:3 1Kg 19:10,14 D 11:4 1Kg 19:18 E 11:6 Other mss add *But if of works it is no longer grace; otherwise work is no longer work.* F 11:8 Lit *stupification* G 11:8 Dt 29:4; Is 29:10 H 11:9 Lit *table* I 11:9-10 Ps 69:22-23 J 11:11, 12 Or *transgression* K 11:14 Lit *flesh* L 11:17 Other mss read *the root and the richness*

Study notes

lieve. The Gentiles heard too, and many embraced it. Paul's citations show that the Gentile conversion was predicted in the OT. Ultimately, all peoples are **a disobedient and defiant people.** Israel was singled out in this way due to their consistent rejection of God's message and messengers (see Ac 7:51-60).

11:1-4 Paul continued explaining that the unbelief of Israel is no argument against the gospel. Israel's blindness is not total, and God is still working with the nation. In the days of Samuel, the nation rejected God as their king and chose a human king. Yet God continued to work with His people: "The LORD will not abandon His people, because of His great name and because He has determined to make you His own people" (1Sm 12:22). In Paul's time, they had rejected Jesus as King Messiah and their leaders said, "We have no king but Caesar" (Jn 19:15), but God was not finished with them. Paul himself was evidence that God was saving some Jews. God's election of the nation (**whom he foreknew,** v. 2; cp. 8:29) is immutable. Even in times of national apostasy, God saves a remnant.

11:5-6 Grace is by definition unmerited favor. Grace would cease **to be grace** if works played a role in election.

11:7-10 The Jewish nation missed salvation because they sought for it by works. The elect portion was given mercy, but the majority was hardened in unbelief; OT citations are given to show that God has judged His people.

11:11 Like a runner in a race, the Jewish nation had **stumbled,** but they had not totally fallen. Their stumbling had a purpose—to bring **salvation** to the **Gentiles.** Salvation for the Gentiles will eventually provoke the Jews to envy (Ac 13:45-51). In the book of Acts Paul regularly went to preach in the synagogues first, but then would turn to the Gentiles following Jewish rejection. This pattern continued until the end of the book of Acts (cp. 28:26-29).

11:12,15-16 The future reception of Jews by God will result in **world** blessing. If their unbelief brought riches to the Gentiles, their future faith in Jesus as Messiah will enrich the world (cp. Is 2:2-4).

11:16-24 The **olive tree** was a symbol of the nation of Israel. It was used in this section by Paul as an illustration or allegory of God's dealings with Jews and Gentiles. The patriarchs are represented by the **root** of the tree. The Gentiles are a **wild** graft. Pruned off **branches** are the unbelieving Jews. Salvation is by faith, and the Gentiles need to be

broken off so that I might be grafted in." [20] True enough; they were broken off by unbelief, but you stand by faith.[a] Do not be arrogant, but be afraid.[b] [21] For if God did not spare the natural branches, He will not spare you either. [22] Therefore, consider God's kindness and severity: severity toward those who have fallen but God's kindness[c] toward you—if you remain in His kindness.[d] Otherwise you too will be cut off.[e] [23] And even they, if they do not remain in unbelief,[f] will be grafted in, because God has the power to graft them in again. [24] For if you were cut off from your native wild olive and against nature were grafted into a cultivated olive tree, how much more will these—the natural branches—be grafted into their own olive tree?

[25] So that you will not be conceited,[g] •brothers, I do not want you to be unaware[h] of this •mystery:[i] A partial hardening has come to Israel[j] until the full number of the Gentiles has come in.[k] [26] And in this way all[A] Israel will be saved, as it is written:

> The Liberator will come from •Zion;
> He will turn away godlessness
>   from Jacob.
> [27] And this will be My covenant
>   with them[B,l]
> when I take away their sins.[C,m]

[28] Regarding the gospel, they are enemies for your advantage,[n] but regarding election, they are loved because of the patriarchs,[o] [29] since God's gracious gifts and calling[p] are irrevocable.[D,q] [30] As you once disobeyed God, but now have received mercy through their disobedience, [31] so they too have now disobeyed, resulting in mercy to you, so that they also now[E] may receive mercy. [32] For God has imprisoned all in disobedience,[r] so that He may have mercy on all.

A Hymn of Praise

[33] Oh, the depth of the riches[s]
both of the wisdom and the knowledge
    of God![t]
How unsearchable His judgments[u]
and untraceable His ways!
[34] **For who has known the mind
    of the Lord?**[v]
Or who has been His counselor?
[35] **Or who has ever first given to Him,
and has to be repaid?**[F,w]
[36] For from Him and through Him
and to Him are all things.[x]
To Him be the glory forever. •Amen.

A Living Sacrifice

12 Therefore, •brothers, by the mercies of God, I urge you[y] to present your bodies as a living sacrifice,[z] holy and pleasing to God;

Cross references
[a]11:20 Rm 5:2; 1Co 10:12; 2Co 1:24
[b]Rm 12:16; 1Tm 6:17; 1Pt 1:17
[c]11:22 Rm 2:4
[d]1Co 15:2; Heb 3:6,14
[e]Jn 15:2
[f]11:23 2Co 3:16
[g]11:25 Rm 12:16
[h]Rm 1:13
[i]Mt 13:11; Rm 16:25; 1Co 2:7-10; Eph 3:3-5,9
[j]Rm 11:7
[k]Lk 21:24; Jn 10:16
[l]11:26-27 Is 59:20-21
[m]11:27 Jr 31:31-34; Heb 8:10,12
[n]11:28 Rm 5:10
[o]Dt 7:8; 10:15; Rm 9:5
[p]11:29 Rm 8:28; 1Co 1:26; Eph 1:18; 4:1,4; Php 3:14; 2Th 1:11; 2Tm 1:9; Heb 3:1; 2Pt 1:10
[q]Heb 7:21
[r]11:32 Rm 3:9; Gl 3:22-23
[s]11:33 Rm 2:4; Eph 3:8
[t]Col 2:3; Eph 3:10
[u]Jb 5:9; 11:7; 15:8
[v]11:34 Is 40:13-14; 1Co 2:16
[w]11:34-35 Jb 35:7; 41:11; Is 40:13; Jr 23:18
[x]11:36 1Co 8:6; 11:12; Col 1:16; Heb 2:10
[y]12:1 1Co 1:10; 2Co 10:2; Eph 4:1; 1Pt 2:11
[z]Rm 6:13,16,19; 1Co 6:20; Heb 13:15; 1Pt 2:5

[A]11:26 Or *And then all*   [B]11:26-27 Is 59:20-21   [C]11:27 Jr 31:31-34   [D]11:29 Or *are not taken back*   [E]11:31 Other mss omit *now*   [F]11:34-35 Jb 41:11; Is 40:13; Jr 23:18

---

humble about their position. Spiritual pride has no place in salvation by grace. God is able to restore the Jewish people to the place of faith. Salvation is always a miracle. It is no harder for God to save a Jew than a Gentile.

11:25-27 A **mystery** has been revealed by God: (1) A **partial hardening** has come to Israel; (2) this will continue until a **full number of the Gentiles** come in; and (3) then **all Israel will be saved**. "Israel" is the name for the Jewish people. It is used 70 times in the NT of Jews, Hebrews, or Israelites. It is not used as a title for the church. Galatians 6:16 is not an exception; it refers to saved or godly Jews as "the Israel of God." Here in verse 26, "all Israel" means there will be a conversion of the Hebrew nation. It does not mean that every single Jew living will be saved. Salvation is defined in verses 26-27 as the new **covenant** that the Messiah will inaugurate.

11:28-32 Israel's vocation and gifts are **irrevocable**, so their future salvation is certain. God in His mercy gives grace to the disobedient: both to Gentiles and Jews. Both were so **imprisoned** in their **disobedience** that there was no way to escape except by God's **mercy**.

11:33-36 In these verses Paul concludes his line of reasoning that Israel's current unbelief is no argument against the truth of the gospel. He is moved to exclamations of wonder at God's wisdom, power, and plan. Who could have foreseen what God was working out? Paul cites various OT texts to express God's incomprehensible purposes. God is to be honored because He is the Alpha and the Omega—the Creator, the sustainer and ruler, and the goal of all things (cp. Cranfield, *Romans*, 2:591).

12:1-2 Paul commonly used the indicative mode of speech to make statements about what God has done for us before using the imperative mode to outline our proper response (e.g., **Therefore . . . I urge you**). The order of presentation is doctrine first, and then duty. Our **worship** entails offering our **bodies as a living sacrifice**, which means dedication of the total person to living for God's honor. Christians are to be different from non-Christian society. We should experience a progressive transformation of life by **the renewing of our mind**. The mind is changed by prayer, by reading and reflection on God's Word, by worship, and by meditation on God's acts as the Holy Spirit works in us.

12:3-8 As part of a renewed mind, the Christian is to **think** wisely about himself and what his function is to be in the body of Christ (the church; see 1Co 12:12-28). **Measure of faith** may mean a person should measure himself by the gospel. Others see it as different apportionments of faith. Either way, Paul exhorts Christians to be humble and to use what God has given for the good of the body. Based on Rm 12:3; 1Co 12:8-10; Eph 4:11; 1Pt 4:10, Christians are given **gifts** to use for the good of others.

The NT lists at least 17 kinds of gifts. Christians are de-

this is your spiritual worship.[A] [2] Do not be conformed[a] to this age,[b] but be transformed by the renewing of your mind,[c] so that you may discern what is the good, pleasing, and perfect will[d] of God.

Many Gifts but One Body

[3] For by the grace[e] given to me, I tell everyone among you not to think of himself more highly than he should think.[f] Instead, think sensibly, as God has distributed a measure of faith[g] to each one. [4] Now as we have many parts in one body,[h] and all the parts do not have the same function, [5] in the same way we who are many[i] are one body in Christ[j] and individually members of one another. [6] According to the grace given to us, we have different gifts:[k]

> If prophecy,[l]
> use it according to the standard
> of one's[B] faith;
> [7] if service,[m] in service;
> if teaching,[n] in teaching;
> [8] if exhorting,[o] in exhortation;
> giving, with generosity;[p]
> leading,[q] with diligence;
> showing mercy, with cheerfulness.[r]

Christian Ethics

[9] Love must be without hypocrisy.[s] Detest evil;[t] cling to what is good. [10] Show family affection to one another with brotherly love.[u] Outdo one another in showing honor.[v] [11] Do not lack diligence; be fervent in spirit;[w] serve the Lord.[x] [12] Rejoice in hope;[y] be patient in affliction;[z] be persistent in prayer.[aa] [13] Share with the •saints in their needs;[ab] pursue hospitality.[ac] [14] Bless those who persecute you;[ad] bless and do not curse. [15] Rejoice with those who rejoice;[ae] weep with those who weep. [16] Be in agreement with one another.[af] Do not be proud;[ag] instead, associate with the humble. Do not be wise in your own estimation.[ah] [17] Do not repay anyone evil for evil.[ai] Try to do what is honorable[aj] in everyone's eyes. [18] If possible, on your part, live at peace with everyone.[ak] [19] Friends, do not avenge yourselves; instead, leave room for His[C] wrath. For it is written: **Vengeance belongs to Me; I will repay,**[D,al] says the Lord. [20] But

Cross references

a12:2 1Pt 1:14
bMt 13:22; Gl 1:4; 1Jn 2:15
cEph 4:23; Ti 3:5
dEph 5:10,17; Col 1:9
e12:3 Rm 1:5; 15:15; 1Co 3:10; 15:10; Gl 2:9; Eph 3:7-8
fRm 11:20
g1Co 7:17; 2Co 10:13; Eph 4:7; 1Pt 4:11
h12:4 1Co 12:12-14; Eph 4:4,16
i12:5 1Co 10:17,23
j1Co 12:20,27; Eph 4:12,25
k12:6 1Co 7:7; 12:4; 1Pt 4:10-11
l Ac 13:1; 1Co 12:10
m12:7 Ac 6:1; 1Co 12:28
n Ac 13:1; 1Co 14:26
o12:8 Ac 4:36; 11:23; 13:15
p2Co 8:2; 9:11,13
q1Co 12:28; 1Tm 5:17
r2Co 9:7
s12:9 2Co 6:6; 1Tm 1:5
t1Th 5:21-22
u12:10 Jn 13:34; 1Th 4:9; Heb 13:1; 2Pt 1:7
vRm 13:7; Php 2:3;
1Pt 2:17
w12:11 Ac 18:25
xAc 20:19
y12:12 Rm 5:2
zHeb 10:32,36
aaAc 1:14
ab12:13 Rm 15:25; 1Co 16:15; 2Co 9:1; Heb 6:10
acMt 25:35; 1Tm 3:2
ad12:14 Mt 5:44; Lk 6:22; 1Co 4:12
ae12:16 Rm 15:5; 2Co 13:11; Php 2:2; 4:2; 1Pt 3:8
agRm 11:20
ahRm 11:25; Pr 3:7
ai12:17 Pr 20:22; 24:29
aj2Co 8:21
ak12:18 Mk 9:50; Rm 14:19
al12:19 Dt 32:35; Ps 94:1; 1Th 4:6; Heb 10:30

A12:1 Or *your reasonable service*   B12:6 Or *the*   C12:19 Lit *the*   D12:19 Dt 32:35

---

fined not just by their personal faith but also by their inclusion in local faith fellowships that are expressions of the body of Christ (see 1Co 12:12-31). Only some of the gifts are explained in this present passage. **Prophecy** in the NT churches was direct revelation from God before the canon was completed. This gift was to be used and measured in concert with the objective body of Christian truths. **Service** (Gk *diakonia*) is the origin of the word "deacon." A deacon here is not a member of a board of directors but a servant.

nous

Greek Pronunciation	[NOOSS]
HCSB Translation	mind
Uses in Romans	6
Uses in the NT	24
Focus passage	Romans 12:1-2

The Greek noun *nous* was a common term that referred to human intellectual perception and moral judgment, thus the *mind*. The related verb *noeo* means *to think, perceive, understand*. All but three NT occurrences of the word *nous* are in Paul's letters. Luke 24:25 refers to *nous* as the seat of understanding, and Revelation 13:18; 17:9 refer to *nous* as the seat of wisdom. Pauline usage is similar but emphasizes that the *mind* is the seat of the intellect and thus affects the will; that is, the *mind* controls what a person says and does, as can be seen in several passages in Paul's letters (Rm 1:28; 7:23; 14:5; 1Co 14:19; Eph 4:17; Col 2:18; 2Th 2:2; 1Tm 6:5; 2Tm 3:8; Ti 1:15). Paul encouraged believers to be transformed by renewing their *minds*. This transformation comes through the study of God's Word and results in being able to "discern what is the good, pleasing, and perfect will of God" (Rm 12:2).

It describes not a title or office but a gift of ministry. Pastors should have this gift. **Teaching** is an essential gift. Parents teach children, older believers teach younger believers, vocational pastor-teachers are the primary instructors in a church, and elders should be able to teach also. All believers can teach to some level, but those who have a special facility for teaching are responsible to develop and utilize it. **Exhortation** is the gift of motivating and encouraging. This gift is similar to the Holy Spirit's function. **Giving** is to be done with generosity. All can give, but capacities differ. Some delight to give out of very small means (Mk 12:41-44); others give a "reverse tithe"—they give 90 percent and live on 10 percent. **Leading** is a gift of vision and direction that is effective but should not be overbearing. **Mercy** is helping the sick, the poor, and the sorrowful. This gift is to be exercised with cheerfulness. Practical assistance to needy members was a main emphasis of the early churches. This same emphasis should characterize churches today.

12:9-16 Transformed thinking is explained in a series of short exhortations. Paul has expounded divine love in this letter; now he shifts to the disciple's "faith working through love" (Gl 5:6). Christians are one **family**, and they should honor one another and display genuine **affection**. They should be **fervent in spirit** or let the Spirit kindle and motivate their service. They should also **rejoice** in the hope of Jesus' return; **share** what they have, and share the joys and sorrows of the church family. Keep praying—in the afflictions and persecutions of life, members of the body are to support one another. Pride is a great sin and humility is a great virtue. One shouldn't think too much of oneself. "God resists the proud, but gives grace to the humble" (1Pt 5:5).

12:17-21 Christians often suffer hatred and persecution

If your enemy is hungry, feed him.[a]
If he is thirsty, give him something
  to drink.
For in so doing
you will be heaping fiery coals
  on his head.[A,b]

[21] Do not be conquered by evil, but conquer evil with good.

A Christian's Duties to the State

13 Everyone must submit to the governing authorities,[c] for there is no authority except from God,[d] and those that exist are instituted by God. [2] So then, the one who resists the authority is opposing God's command, and those who oppose it will bring judgment on themselves. [3] For rulers are not a terror[e] to good conduct, but to bad. Do you want to be unafraid of the authority? Do what is good, and you will have its approval. [4] For government is God's servant for your good. But if you do wrong, be afraid, because it does not carry the sword for no reason. For government is God's servant, an avenger[f] that brings wrath on the one who does wrong. [5] Therefore, you must submit, not only because of wrath, but also because of your conscience.[g] [6] And for this reason you pay taxes, since the authorities are God's public servants, continually attending to these tasks.[B] [7] Pay your obligations[h] to everyone: taxes to those you owe taxes,[i] tolls to those you owe tolls, respect to those you owe respect,[j] and honor to those you owe honor.

Love, Our Primary Duty

[8] Do not owe anyone anything,[c] except to love one another, for the one who loves another has fulfilled the law.[k] [9] The commandments:

  Do not commit adultery;
  do not murder;
  do not steal;[D]
  do not covet;[E,l]

and whatever other commandment—all are summed up by this: **Love your neighbor as yourself.**[F,m]

[10] Love does no wrong to a neighbor. Love, therefore, is the fulfillment of the law.

Put On Christ

[11] Besides this, knowing the time, it is already the hour[n] for you[G] to wake up from sleep,[o] for

Cross references (center column):

a 12:20 Mt 5:44; Lk 6:27
b 2Kg 6:22; Pr 25:21-22
c 13:1 Ti 3:1; 1Pt 2:13
d Dn 2:21; 4:17; Jn 19:1
e 13:3 1Pt 2:14
f 13:4 1Th 4:6
g 13:5 1Pt 2:13,19
h 13:7 Mt 22:21
i Lk 20:22; 23:2
j Mt 17:25
k 13:8 Mt 7:12; 22:39; Jn 13:34; Rm 12:10; Gl 5:14; Jms 2:8
l 13:9 Ex 20:13-17; Dt 5:17-21
m Lv 19:18; Mt 19:19
n 13:11 1Co 7:29; 10:11; Jms 5:8; 1Pt 4:7; 2Pt 3:9,11; 1Jn 2:18; Rv 1:3; 22:10
o Mk 13:37; 1Co 15:34; Eph 5:14; 1Th 5:6

A 12:20 Pr 25:21-22   B 13:6 Lit *to this very thing*   C 13:8 Or *Leave no debt outstanding to anyone*   D 13:9 Other mss add *you shall not bear false witness*   E 13:9 Ex 20:13-17; Dt 5:17-21   F 13:9 Lv 19:18   G 13:11 Other mss read *for us*

---

from society (1Pt 1:6; 2:11-12; 3:14-17; 4:12-16; 5:9). The normal response is to retaliate, but Christians are called to serve and minister God's grace to a lost and hostile world. Jesus is our model. As much as possible, we are to **live at peace with everyone**. God is the sovereign who can convert even a Saul who persecuted the church. God is the judge and the administrator of wrath. Our role is to display God's grace and love in our lives. God in Jesus conquered evil on the cross. We are not to let **evil** conquer us.

13:1-7 The relation of the church to the state is a matter of perennial controversy. Israel struggled under various world empires and in NT times was under the yoke of Rome. How should God's people relate to ungodly governments? Jesus once addressed this matter by saying, "Give back to Caesar the things that are Caesar's, and to God the things that are God's" (Mt 22:21). Government is an institution ordained by God for man's benefit, but it can be corrupted and twisted out of its proper function. Paul in these few short verses did not address some of the questions that we might ask him, but clearly he wanted Roman Christians to be good citizens. However, that same government put our Lord to death (Jn 19:10-11) and killed both Peter and Paul. This same government is in view again in Revelation 13. Thus the Christian must take care to discern possible cases where obedience to the government entails disobedience to God.

13:1 That **no authority** exists **except from God** indicates God's sovereignty over human affairs. It also shows why unwarranted rebellion against government is de facto rebellion against God (v. 2).

13:2-4 The Jewish nation rebelled against Rome in two costly wars, bringing **judgment** upon themselves at a cost of more than one million lives. Government is ordained by God to reward **good** and punish evil, providing peace and order

for those whom it serves. **The sword** alludes to capital punishment. A government that rewards evil and punishes good will not long survive, for evil is innately destructive. "If a ruler listens to lies, all his officials will be wicked" (Pr 29:12).

13:5-7 Since the civil government is ordained by God and gives us certain benefits, we are to **submit** to it. We are to pay **taxes** to support it, **honor** and **respect** it. Early Christians refused to worship emperor or state, but they showed their respect by praying for the authorities. Paul taught, "I urge that petitions, prayers, intercessions, and thanksgivings be made for everyone, for kings and all those who are in authority" (1Tm 2:1-2).

13:8-10 The Christian is to pay all his obligations, but there is one debt we can never repay. This is the debt of agape **love**. Some have misinterpreted this verse as prohibiting all monetary debt, including having a mortgage on a house or buying a car on an installment plan. It may be wise never to go into monetary debt (cp. "the borrower is a slave to the lender," Pr 22:7), but this verse has little to do with modern methods of finance. It is about fulfilling obligations of all kinds. We can never stop "loving" (agape love) as long as we live. Love fulfills **the law** because if we love our neighbor we will do him no harm. We fulfill the first four commands by loving the Lord and the rest of the law by obeying the prohibitions as we love our **neighbor**.

13:11-14 Christians live between the ages. The old age is passing, and the new is dawning. We long for the new age to fully come, and we recognize that our **salvation** will soon be completed. We have been "rescued . . . from the domain of darkness" (Col 1:13) and from the night of sin into a new realm of **light**. We need to wake up from spiritual lethargy. Paul used the image of taking off the old clothes of sinful behavior and putting on the **Lord Jesus Christ** as our way of

now our salvation is nearer than when we first believed.[a] [12] The night is nearly over, and the daylight is near,[b] so let us discard the deeds of darkness[c] and put on the armor of light.[d] [13] Let us ·walk with decency,[e] as in the daylight: not in carousing and drunkenness;[f] not in sexual impurity and promiscuity; not in quarreling and jealousy. [14] But put on the Lord Jesus Christ,[g] and make no plans to satisfy the fleshly desires.[h]

The Law of Liberty

14 Accept[i] anyone who is weak in faith,[A,j] but don't argue about doubtful issues. [2] One person believes he may eat anything,[k] but one who is weak eats only vegetables. [3] One who eats must not look down on one who does not eat,[l] and one who does not eat must not criticize one who does,[m] because God has accepted him.[n] [4] Who are you to criticize[o] another's household slave? Before his own Lord he stands or falls. And he will stand. For the Lord is able[B] to make him stand.

[5] One person considers one day to be above another day.[p] Someone else considers every day to be the same. Each one must be fully convinced in his own mind.[q] [6] Whoever observes the day, observes it for the honor of the Lord.[c] Whoever eats, eats for the Lord, since he gives thanks to God;[r] and whoever does not eat, it is for the Lord that he does not eat it, yet he thanks God. [7] For none of us lives to himself, and no one dies to himself.[s] [8] If we live, we live for the Lord; and if we die, we die for the Lord. Therefore, whether we live or die, we belong to the Lord.[t] [9] Christ died and came to life[u] for this: that He might rule over both the dead and the living.[v] [10] But you, why do you criticize your brother? Or you, why do you look down on your brother? For we will all stand before the tribunal of God.[D,w] [11] For it is written:

As I live, says the Lord,
every knee will bow to Me,[x]
and every tongue will give praise
to God.[E,y]

[12] So then, each of us will give an account of himself to God.[z]

The Law of Love

[13] Therefore, let us no longer criticize one

Cross-references

[a] 13:11 Ac 19:2; 1Co 3:5; 15:2
[b] 13:12 Heb 10:25; 1Jn 2:8; Rv 1:3; 22:10
[c] Eph 5:11
[d] 2Co 6:7; 10:4; Eph 6:11,13; 1Th 5:8
[e] 13:13 1Th 4:12
[f] Lk 21:34; Gl 5:21; Eph 5:18; 1Pt 4:3
[g] 13:14 Jb 29:14; Gl 3:27; Eph 4:24; Col 3:10,12
[h] Gl 5:16; 1Pt 2:11
[i] 14:1 Ac 28:2; Rm 11:15; 12:3; 15:7
[j] Rm 15:1; 1Co 8:9-11; 9:22
[k] 14:2 Rm 14:14
[l] 14:3 Lk 18:9
[m] Col 2:16
[n] Ac 28:2; Rm 11:15; 15:7
[o] 14:4 Rm 9:20; Jms 4:12
[p] 14:5 Gl 4:10
[q] Lk 1:1; Rm 4:21
[r] 14:6 Mt 14:19; 1Co 10:30; 1Tm 4:3-4
[s] 14:7 Rm 8:38; 2Co 5:15; Gl 2:20; Php 1:20
[t] 14:8 Lk 20:38; Php 1:20; 1Th 5:10; Rv 14:13
[u] 14:9 Rv 1:18; 2:8
[v] Mt 28:18; Jn 12:24; Php 2:11; 1Th 5:10
[w] 14:10 Rm 2:16; 2Co 5:10
[x] 14:11 Php 2:10-11
[y] Is 45:23; 49:18
[z] 14:12 Mt 12:36; 16:27; 1Pt 4:5

A14:1 Or *weak in the Faith*　**B**14:4 Other mss read *For God has the power*　**C**14:6 Other mss add *but whoever does not observe the day, it is to the Lord that he does not observe it*　**D**14:10 Other mss read *of Christ*　**E**14:11 Is 45:23; 49:18

---

life. This passage is famous for bringing Augustine of Hippo to salvation (*Confessions*, 8:12.22).

14:1–15:13 The exact historical background of the problem described in this section is unknown. Christians in Rome had different opinions on certain practices since they came from various backgrounds. If they came from paganism, they may have viewed as tainted the foods and drinks sold in the markets (cp. 1Co 8:1-13; 10:23-33). If they came from certain cults, they could even be vegetarians. Similarly, today people who convert to Christianity from Islam, Judaism, and Hinduism have a history of dietary practices and observation of special days. Food or calendar issues may therefore have special importance to them as matters of conscience. In this passage, most interpreters think the issue came from those who sought to observe (or even enforce) the ceremonial part of OT law. Theologians have called these issues "matters of indifference" (Gk *adiaphora*) since differences of opinion are allowed, but it is easy to see how some believers feel otherwise. The church must strive for tolerance and understanding on such matters, emphasizing the unity of believers, the expression of love for others, and the purity of the gospel message.

14:1 The believer **who is weak in faith** is overly conscientious about matters not regulated by Christian revelation. Paul commanded believers to welcome weak Christians but not to get into arguments about **doubtful issues**.

14:2 Jews were not normally vegetarians, but some were (e.g., Daniel; see Dn 1:8-12).

14:3-4 Mutual toleration is a Christian virtue. God accepts each believer, along with issues stemming from his background and maturity level, and is able to sanctify him. Though we may be used of God to help inform weak believers, we must never **criticize another's household slave**.

14:5 The observing of special days is complicated (cp. Paul's warnings in Gl 4:10 and Col 2:16 about "a sabbath day"). Luther believed Sunday was not the Sabbath but a new day of worship, whereas Calvin believed the Sabbath was changed to Sunday. Some groups believe in Friday/Saturday Sabbath observance. In thinking through this issue, we should consider the implications of Christ's Sunday-morning resurrection and the new covenant.

14:6 Our religious practices are to be done out of conviction before God. How we live and die must come from the conviction that we belong to the Lord.

14:7-9 We are not our own. Christ died and rose to be Lord of all. Luther said paradoxically, "A Christian is a perfectly free lord of all, subject to none. A Christian is a perfectly dutiful servant, subject to all." But most of all, **we belong to the Lord**.

14:10-12 The **tribunal of God** (Gk *beyma*) is elsewhere called the "tribunal of Christ" (2Co 5:10). Many interpreters distinguish this from the great white throne judgment in Rv 20:11-15. The "tribunal of Christ" is where believers will be rewarded or suffer loss of rewards (1Co 3:13) based on their deeds and their stewardship of God-given responsibilities. In distinction to this, the great white throne judgment is the place where unbelievers will be raised for judgment. Believers take part in the first resurrection, and there is no condemnation for them (Rm 8:1; Rv 20:4-6). All people will bow before God and give **an account** of their lives. Christians might think that because they are exempt from the final condemnation they can live any way they want, but Christ the Lord will evaluate His servants.

14:13 Our goal must be to help all believers grow into spiritual maturity and not to hinder their progress.

another.[a] Instead decide never to put a stumbling block or pitfall in your brother's way.[b]
[14] (I know and am persuaded by the Lord Jesus that nothing is *unclean in itself.[c] Still, to someone who considers a thing to be unclean, to that one it is unclean.[d]) [15] For if your brother is hurt by what you eat, you are no longer *walking according to love.[e] Do not destroy that one Christ died for by what you eat.[f] [16] Therefore, do not let your good be slandered,[g] [17] for the kingdom of God is not eating and drinking,[h] but righteousness, peace, and joy[i] in the Holy Spirit. [18] Whoever serves Christ[j] in this way is acceptable to God and approved by men.[k]

[19] So then, we must pursue what promotes peace[l] and what builds up one another.[m] [20] Do not tear down God's work because of food. Everything is *clean, but it is wrong for a man to cause stumbling by what he eats.[n] [21] It is a noble thing not to eat meat, or drink wine, or do anything that makes your brother stumble.[A] [22] Do you have a conviction?[B] Keep it to yourself before God. The man who does not condemn

himself by what he approves is blessed.[o] [23] But whoever doubts stands condemned if he eats,[p] because his eating is not from a conviction,[c] and everything that is not from a conviction[c] is sin.

Pleasing Others, Not Ourselves

15 Now we who are strong have an obligation to bear the weaknesses of those without strength,[q] and not to please ourselves. [2] Each one of us must please his neighbor for his good, to build him up.[r] [3] For even the *Messiah did not please Himself.[s] On the contrary, as it is written, **The insults of those who insult You have fallen on Me.**[D,t] [4] For whatever was written in the past was written for our instruction,[u] so that we may have hope through endurance and through the encouragement from the Scriptures. [5] Now may the God who gives[E] endurance and encouragement[v] allow you to live in harmony with one another,[w] according to the command of Christ Jesus, [6] so that you may glorify the God and Father of our Lord Jesus Christ[x] with a united mind and voice.

Cross references

[a]14:13 Mt 7:1; Rm 14:3
[b]1Co 8:13
[c]14:14 Ac 10:15; Rm 14:2,20
[d]1Co 8:7
[e]14:15 Eph 5:2
[f]1Co 8:11
[g]14:16 1Co 10:30; Ti 2:5
[h]14:17 1Co 8:8
[i]Rm 15:13; Gl 5:22
[j]14:18 Rm 16:18
[k]2Co 8:21; Php 4:8; 1Pt 2:12
[l]14:19 Ps 34:14; Rm 12:18; 1Co 7:15; 2Tm 2:22; Heb 12:14
[m]Rm 15:2; 1Co 10:23; 14:3,26; 2Co 12:19; Eph 4:12,29
[n]14:20 1Co 8:9-13
[o]14:22 1Jn 3:21
[p]14:23 Rm 14:5
[q]15:1 Rm 14:1; Gl 6:2; 1Th 5:14
[r]15:2 1Co 9:22; 10:24,33; 2Co 13:9
[s]15:3 2Co 8:9
[t]Ps 69:9
[u]15:4 Rm 4:23; 2Tm 3:16
[v]15:5 2Co 1:3　[w]Rm 12:16　[x]15:6 Rv 1:6

[A]14:21 Other mss add *or offended or weakened*　[B]14:22 Lit *have faith*　[C]14:23 Or *faith*　[D]15:3 Ps 69:9　[E]15:5 Lit *God of*

14:14 This is one of Paul's most amazing statements. His background as a Pharisee trained him to emphasize the distinction between clean and **unclean**, but Jesus persuaded him that this distinction was no longer valid. Thus Paul adopted a new stance, but he also recognized that some believers, especially those from a Jewish background, had not made this transition. Mature believers should not recklessly push "weak" believers (v. 1) into such a transition.

14:15 A strong Christian must live in love and not violate the conscience of a weak believer. The conscience is the moral faculty of the mind. It can be educated by God through the

Holy Spirit, but we must never teach anyone to go against his conscience. **Do not destroy** means that we can cause a person's spiritual ruin by teaching them to ignore or violate their conscience.

14:16-17 Christian liberty will get a bad name if love does not govern it. Food is never to be a major concern in our lives, but we are to promote **righteousness, peace, and joy** in the churches.

14:18-19 Our actions should serve Christ and help other Christians grow and flourish.

14:20-21 Objectively, **everything is clean** ("everything created by God is good, and nothing should be rejected if it is received with thanksgiving," 1Tm 4:4). Yet some immature believers might stumble over **meat** or **drink** (1Co 8:7-11).

14:22-23 A Christian's sense of freedom in these matters should not translate into public behavior if another believer finds the freedom scandalous. For instance, a Muslim convert who never ate pork or drank wine might stumble if he saw a Christian doing either of these things.

15:1 Why should the **strong** "give in" to the conscience of the weak? The way of love demands it. The strong believer does not forsake his conscience by abstaining from certain of his freedoms, but the weaker believer would have to violate his in order to accommodate the liberties of the strong. Thus the strong should choose in accordance with the weak.

15:2-3 The strong Christian is to follow the example of his Lord, who **did not please Himself**. As foretold in Scripture, Jesus bore the insults and hostility that people had against God (Ps 69:9).

15:4 Far from being irrelevant to Christian faith, the OT writings are for our **instruction** (2Tm 3:16). Not everything in them is applicable to new covenant discipleship, but everything points to Jesus (Lk 24:27).

15:5-6 Paul's prayer is that God will bring these house

hamartia

Greek Pronunciation	[hah mahr TEE ah]
HCSB Translation	sin
Uses in Romans	48
Uses in the NT	173
Focus passage	Romans 14:23

The Greek noun *hamartia* is the most common term in the NT for human violation of God's moral standard. The related verb *hamartano* (43 uses in the NT, 17 in Paul's writings) literally means *to miss the mark*, but the term eventually acquired the additional meanings *to fail* and *to do wrong*. Finally, *hamartano* came to include the idea *to sin*, which is the meaning of the verb in the NT. Both *hamartano* and *hamartia* occur quite frequently in the Greek OT, mainly to translate the most common Hebrew words for *sin*. The root idea here is also *to miss the mark*, picturing human effort *missing the target* of God's standard, His revealed will.

In Romans 14 Paul said, "Everything that is not from a conviction is sin" (v. 23). The essence of *sin* is unbelief, so every violation of God's standard is a lack of faith in Him. God doesn't want superficial obedience to a standard; He wants us to trust Him completely (see Heb 11:6).

Glorifying God Together

[7] Therefore accept one another,[a] just as the Messiah also accepted you, to the glory of God. [8] For I say that the Messiah became a servant of the circumcised[A] on behalf of God's truth,[b] to confirm the promises to the fathers,[c] [9] and so that Gentiles[d] may glorify God for His mercy.[e] As it is written:

**Therefore I will praise You
    among the Gentiles,
and I will sing psalms to Your name.[B,f]**

[10] Again it says: **Rejoice, you Gentiles, with His people![C,g]** [11] And again:

**Praise the Lord, all you Gentiles;
all the peoples should praise Him![D,h]**

[12] And again, Isaiah says:

**The root of Jesse[i] will appear,
the One who rises to rule the Gentiles;
the Gentiles will hope in Him.[E,j]**

[13] Now may the God of hope fill you with all joy and peace as you believe in Him[k] so that you may overflow with hope by the power of the Holy Spirit.[l]

From Jerusalem to Illyricum

[14] My •brothers, I myself am convinced about you that you also are full of goodness,[m] filled with all knowledge,[n] and able to instruct one

another. [15] Nevertheless, I have written to remind you more boldly on some points[F] because of the grace given me by God[o] [16] to be a minister of Christ Jesus to the Gentiles,[p] serving as a priest of God's good news.[q] My purpose is that the offering of the Gentiles may be acceptable,[r] •sanctified by the Holy Spirit. [17] Therefore I have reason to boast in Christ Jesus[s] regarding what pertains to God.[t] [18] For I would not dare say anything except what Christ has accomplished through me[u] to make the Gentiles obedient by word and deed, [19] by the power of miraculous signs and wonders,[v] and by the power of God's Spirit. As a result, I have fully proclaimed the good news about the Messiah from Jerusalem[w] all the way around to Illyricum.[G,x] [20] My aim is to evangelize where Christ has not been named,[y] so that I will not build on someone else's foundation,[z] [21] but, as it is written:

**Those who were not told about Him
    will see,
and those who have not heard
    will understand.[H,aa]**

Paul's Travel Plans

[22] That is why I have been prevented many times from coming to you.[ab] [23] But now I no longer have any work to do in these provinces,[I] and I have strongly desired for many years to come to you[ac] [24] whenever I travel to Spain.[J]

Cross references
[a]15:7 Rm 14:1
[b]15:8 Mt 15:24; Ac 3:26
[c]Rm 4:16; 2Co 1:20
[d]15:9 Rm 3:29; 11:30
[e]Mt 9:8
[f]2Sm 22:50; Ps 18:49
[g]15:10 Dt 32:43
[h]15:11 Ps 117:1
[i]15:12 Rv 5:5; 22:16
[j]Is 11:10; Mt 12:21
[k]15:13 Rm 14:17
[l]1Co 2:4; 1Th 1:5
[m]15:14 Eph 5:9; 2Th 1:11
[n]1Co 1:5; 8:1,7,10; 12:8; 13:2
[o]15:15 Rm 12:3
[p]15:16 Ac 9:15; Rm 11:13
[q]Rm 1:1
[r]Rm 12:1; Eph 5:2; Php 2:17
[s]15:17 Php 3:3
[t]Heb 2:17; 5:1
[u]15:18 Ac 15:12; 21:19; Rm 1:5; 2Co 3:5
[v]15:19 Jn 4:48
[w]Ac 22:17-21
[x]Ac 20:1
[y]15:20 Rm 1:15; 10:15
[z]1Co 3:10; 2Co 10:15-16
[aa]15:21 Is 52:15
[ab]15:22 Rm 1:13; 1Th 2:18
[ac]15:23 Ac 19:21; Rm 1:10

[A]15:8 The Jews   [B]15:9 2Sm 22:50; Ps 18:49   [C]15:10 Dt 32:43   [D]15:11 Ps 117:1   [E]15:12 Is 11:10   [F]15:15 Other mss add *brothers*   [G]15:19 A Roman province northwest of Greece on the eastern shore of the Adriatic Sea   [H]15:21 Is 52:15   [I]15:23 Lit *now, having no longer a place in these parts*   [J]15:24 Other mss add *I will come to you.*

churches of Rome to the place of harmony, love, and unity that will enable them to best honor God.

15:7-8 These verses show that people from Jewish and Gentile backgrounds struggled with accepting one another. Jesus as **the Messiah** was born a Jew and ministered to Israel ("I was sent only to the lost sheep of the house of Israel," Mt 15:24) to fulfill OT **promises** and prophecies. His primary purpose was for Israel, but He also had a design for the nations (Gentiles).

15:9-12 A series of citations from the OT demonstrates God's plans. Quotes from the Law, History, Psalms, and Prophets refer to Gentile reception and praise of God. In Ps 18:49 the Messiah stands among converted Gentiles and offers their praise, along with His own, to the Father. In Dt 32:43 Moses summons the Gentiles to join Israel in joyful praise to God. Psalm 117 is the shortest psalm, and it calls for universal praise from the nations. In Isaiah the Davidic King, the Messiah, is described as the hope not just of Israel but of all the nations (Is 11:10).

15:13 Paul gave a second benediction for the churches with emphasis on hope in God produced by the Holy Spirit's work among them.

15:14-16 Paul was **convinced** that the Roman Christians were gifted by God for effective service and healthy church life. God does not build His church without seeing to these

needs. Yet Paul also knew that God had uniquely called and equipped him as an apostle to the Gentiles. So what he wrote was sure to be useful in helping the Roman house churches grow to maturity. He served as a priest offering the Gentiles to God and wanted this offering to be holy, acceptable, and pleasing to God (12:1-2).

15:17-19 Paul wanted to **boast in Christ Jesus** to the Roman believers about how God had used him to spread the good news all the way from **Jerusalem** to the Roman province of **Illyricum** (modern Albania). God had approved of his ministry by authenticating **signs** and **wonders** and many conversions. The Roman believers would have been comforted by this testimony, for it illustrated the secure basis on which they had rested their hopes for salvation.

15:20-21 In 10 years, God had used Paul as a pioneer church planter in the eastern section of the Roman Empire. Paul felt his ministry was in keeping with OT messianic prophecy (Is 52:15). He was the planter; others would come water the soil, and God would give growth (1Co 3:3-9).

15:22-24 God's **work** for Paul in the eastern half of the Roman Empire had kept him from going to Rome sooner, but now the work was completed and he planned to **pass through** Rome on a mission trip to the western part of the Roman Empire (**Spain**). Scholars are divided on whether Paul ever made it to Spain. The Bible does not record a Spanish mission for Paul.

For I hope to see you when I pass through, and to be assisted by you for my journey there,[a] once I have first enjoyed your company[b] for a while. [25] Right now I am traveling to Jerusalem[c] to serve the •saints,[d] [26] for Macedonia[e] and Achaia[A,f] were pleased to make a contribution for the poor among the saints in Jerusalem. [27] Yes, they were pleased, and indeed are indebted to them. For if the Gentiles have shared in their spiritual benefits,[g] then they are obligated to minister to Jews in material needs. [28] So when I have finished this and safely delivered the funds[B] to them,[h] I will visit you on the way to Spain. [29] I know that when I come to you, I will come in the fullness of the blessing[c] of Christ.

[30] Now I appeal to you, brothers, through our Lord Jesus Christ and through the love of the Spirit,[i] to join with me in fervent prayers to God on my behalf.[j] [31] Pray that I may be rescued from the unbelievers in Judea,[k] that the gift I am bringing to[D] Jerusalem[l] may be acceptable to the saints,[m] [32] and that, by God's will,[n] I may come to you with joy[o] and be refreshed together with you.

[33] The God of peace be with all of you.[p] •Amen.

Paul's Commendation of Phoebe

16 I commend to you[q] our sister Phoebe, who is a servant[E] of the church in Cenchreae.[r] [2] So you should welcome her in the Lord[s] in a manner worthy of the •saints and assist her in whatever matter she may require your help. For indeed she has been a benefactor of many—and of me also.

Greeting to Roman Christians

[3] Give my greetings to Prisca[F] and Aquila,[t] my coworkers in[u] Christ Jesus,[v] [4] who risked their own necks for my

life. Not only do I thank them, but so do all the Gentile churches. [5] Greet also the church that meets in their home.[w] Greet my dear friend Epaenetus, who is the first convert[G,x] to Christ from •Asia.[H,y] [6] Greet Mary,[i] who has worked very hard for you.[j] [7] Greet Andronicus and Junia,[K] my fellow countrymen[z] and fellow prisoners.[aa] They are noteworthy in the eyes of the apostles,[L,M] and they were also in Christ before me. [8] Greet Ampliatus, my dear friend in the Lord. [9] Greet Urbanus, our coworker in Christ, and my dear friend Stachys. [10] Greet Apelles, who is approved in Christ. Greet those who belong to the household of Aristobulus.[ab] [11] Greet Herodion, my fellow countryman. Greet those who belong to the household of Narcissus who are in the Lord. [12] Greet Tryphaena and Tryphosa, who have worked hard in the Lord. Greet my dear friend Persis, who has worked very hard in the Lord. [13] Greet Rufus,[ac] chosen in the Lord; also his mother—and mine. [14] Greet Asyncritus, Phlegon, Hermes, Patrobas, Hermas, and the •brothers who are with them. [15] Greet Philologus and Julia, Nereus and his sister, and Olympas, and all the saints who are with them.[ad] [16] Greet one another with a holy kiss.[ae]

[a]15:24 Ac 15:3 [b]Rm 1:12 [c]15:25 Ac 19:21 [d]Ac 24:17 [e]15:26 Ac 16:9; 1Co 16:5; 2Co 1:16; 2:13; 7:5; 8:1; 9:2,4; 11:9; Php 4:15; 1Th 1:7; 4:10; 1Tm 1:3 [f]Ac 18:12; 19:21 [g]15:27 1Co 9:11 [h]15:28 Jn 3:33 [i]15:30 Gl 5:22; Col 1:8 [j]2Co 1:11; Col 4:12 [k]15:31 2Co 1:10; 2Th 3:2; 2Tm 3:11; 4:17 [l]2Co 8:4; 9:1 [m]Ac 9:13; Rm 15:15 [n]15:32 Ac 18:21; Rm 1:10 [o]Rm 15:23 [p]15:33 Rm 16:20; 2Co 13:11; Php 4:9; 1Th 5:23; 2Th 3:16; Heb 13:20 [q]16:1 2Co 3:1 [r]Ac 18:18 [s]16:2 Php 2:29 [t]16:3 Ac 18:2 [u]Rm 8:11; 2Co 5:17; 12:2; Gl 1:22 [v]Rm 8:1 [w]16:5 1Co 16:19; Col 4:15; Phm 2 [x]1Co 16:15 [y]Ac 16:6 [z]16:7 Rm 9:3; 16:21 [aa]Col 4:10; Phm 23 [ab]16:10 1Co 1:11 [ac]16:13 Mk 15:21 [ad]16:15 Rm 16:2 [ae]16:16 1Co 16:20; 2Co 13:12; 1Th 5:26; 1Pt 5:14

[A]15:26 The churches of these provinces [B]15:28 Lit *delivered this fruit* [C]15:29 Other mss add *of the gospel* [D]15:31 Lit *that my service for* [E]16:1 Others interpret this term in a technical sense: *deacon,* or *deaconess,* or *minister,* or *courier* [F]16:3 Traditionally, *Priscilla,* as in Ac 18:2,18,26 [G]16:5 Lit *the firstfruits* [H]16:5 Other mss read *Achaia* [I]16:6 Or *Maria* [J]16:6 Other mss read *us* [K]16:7 Either a feminine name or "Junias," a masculine name [L]16:7 Or *are outstanding among* [M]16:7 "The apostles" is not always a technical term referring to the 12; cp. 2Co 8:23; Php 2:25 where this word is translated as "messenger."

15:25-29 Paul was on his way to **Jerusalem** to bring a gift from the Gentile churches for the poor of the Jewish church in that city. He planned to come to Rome next. Little did he know he would be taken to Rome in custody (Ac 25:11–28:14,30-31).

15:30-33 Paul made three specific prayer requests: (1) for deliverance from hostile forces, (2) that the gift from Gentile Christians would be welcomed by Jewish Christians, and (3) that he might come to Rome. All three were answered; see Ac 23:10; 21:17-20a; 25:11-12 respectively.

16:1-2 Phoebe was the probable carrier of this letter to Rome. Paul commended her for her service.

16:3-4 Prisca and **Aquila** (Ac 18:1-3,18,26; 2Tm 4:19) were

Paul's coworkers. They had churches in their homes, they instructed Apollos, and they **risked their own necks** to save Paul.

16:5 Epaenetus means "beloved." He was Asia's first convert to Christ.

16:7 The phrase **noteworthy in the eyes of the apostles** is variously translated as "well-known to the apostles" or as "outstanding among the apostles." The word "apostle" can be used in a nontechnical sense, referring to a messenger rather than a commissioned apostle such as Paul.

16:13 Rufus was possibly the same Rufus whose father ("Simon, a Cyrenian") helped carry Jesus' cross to Golgotha (Mk 15:21-22).

All the churches of Christ send you greetings.

Warning against Divisive People

[17] Now I urge you, brothers, to watch out for those who cause dissensions and obstacles contrary to the doctrine you have learned.[a] Avoid them,[b] [18] for such people do not serve our Lord Christ[c] but their own appetites.[A,d] They deceive the hearts of the unsuspecting with smooth talk and flattering words.[e]

Paul's Gracious Conclusion

[19] The report of your obedience has reached everyone.[f] Therefore I rejoice over you. But I want you to be wise about what is good, yet innocent about what is evil.[g] [20] The God of peace[h] will soon crush Satan[i] under your feet. The grace of our Lord Jesus be with you.[j]

[21] Timothy,[k] my coworker, and Lucius,[l] Jason,[m] and Sosipater,[n] my fellow countrymen, greet you.

[22] I Tertius, who wrote this letter,[o] greet you in the Lord.[B]

[23] Gaius,[p] who is host to me and to the whole church, greets you. Erastus,[q] the city treasurer, and our brother Quartus greet you.

[[24] The grace of our Lord Jesus Christ be with you all.][C]

Glory to God

[25] Now to Him who has power to strengthen you[r] according to my gospel and the proclamation about Jesus Christ,[s] according to the revelation of the •mystery kept silent[t] for long ages[u] [26] but now revealed and made known through the prophetic Scriptures,[v] according to the command of the eternal God to advance the obedience of faith[D,w] among all nations— [27] to the only wise God, through Jesus Christ—Him be the glory forever![E,x] •Amen.

[a]16:17 1Tm 1:3; 6:3
[b]Mt 7:15; Gl 1:8-9; 2Th 3:6,14; Ti 3:10; 2Jn 10
[c]16:18 Rm 14:18
[d]Php 3:19
[e]Col 2:4; 2Pt 2:3
[f]16:19 Rm 1:8
[g]Jr 4:22; Mt 10:16; 1Co 14:20
[h]16:20 Rm 15:33
[i]Mt 4:10
[j]1Co 16:23; 2Co 13:13; Gl 6:18; Php 4:23; 1Th 5:28; 2Th 3:18; Rv 22:21
[k]16:21 Ac 16:1
[l]Ac 13:1
[m]Ac 17:5
[n]Ac 20:4
[o]16:22 1Co 16:21; Gl 6:11; Col 4:18; 2Th 3:17; Phm 19
[p]16:23 Ac 20:4; 1Co 1:14
[q]Ac 19:22
[r]16:25 Eph 3:20; Jd 24
[s]Rm 2:16 [t]Mt 13:35; Rm 11:25; 1Co 2:1,7; 4:1; Eph 1:9; 3:3,9; 6:19; Col 1:26; 2:2; 4:3; 1Tm 3:16 [u]2Tm 1:9; Ti 1:2 [v]16:26 Rm 1:2 [w]Rm 1:5 [x]16:27 Rm 11:36

[A]16:18 Lit belly   [B]16:22 Or letter in the Lord, greet you   [C]16:24 Other mss omit bracketed text; cp. v. 20   [D]16:26 Or the obedience that is faith, or the faithful obedience, or the obedience that comes from faith; Rm 1:5   [E]16:25-27 Other mss have these vv. at the end of chap 14 or 15.

16:17-20 **Satan** and false teachers will always assail the church (Ac 20:28-29; 2Co 11:13-15; Gl 5:10-12; Php 3:2,18-20; Col 2:16-19). Paul warned believers at Rome to be alert and **avoid** false teachers. Illustrating the familiar both/and relation between divine sovereignty and human responsibility to choose, we must be diligent in the battle against darkness, but ultimate victory is assured (**The God of peace will soon crush Satan**).

16:22-23 Scholars debate the role of the scribe (in this case, **Tertius**) in ancient writings. Did they typically take dictation word for word, or was their composition taken down in shorthand or perhaps a summary manner? Biblical teaching about divine inspiration of the biblical author commends the first suggestion.

16:24-27 By **my gospel**, Paul did not mean his preaching did not reflect God's direct revelation (see Gl 1:11-12). He meant the gospel as he had faithfully preached it: a gospel of grace for **all nations**. In ages past this gospel was a **mystery kept silent** as God directed history until "the time came to completion" (Gl 4:4). In Christ the "mystery" is revealed to the world.

CORINTH
FIRST-CENTURY

KEY

1. Lechaion Road
2. Propylaia (Entry Gate)
3. Peirene Fountain
4. Peribolos of Apollo
5. Julian Basilica
6. Bema (Judicial Seat)
7. Central Shops
8. South Stoa (market)
9. Bouleuterion (Senate House)
10. Statue of Poseidon and Fountain
11. Northwest shops
12. Archaic Temple (of Apollo)
13. North Market
14. Sanctuary of Athena Chalinitis
15. West Shops
16. Odeion
17. Theater

Paul wrote his letter to the church at Rome in A.D. 57 while he was in Corinth. Paul was staying with Gaius, a leader of the church at Corinth. Phoebe, a servant of the church in Cenchreae, one of Corinth's ports, likely carried the letter to Rome (Rm 16:1-2).

1 Corinthians

Introduction

First Corinthians is the most literary of all of Paul's letters. With a variety of stylistic devices—irony, sarcasm, rhetorical questions, alliteration, antithesis, personification, framing devices, hyperbole, repetition, picturesque words (with local color), double meanings, and other wordplays—Paul attempted to persuade his readers. He wanted to communicate to the Corinthians the necessity of accepting the Lord's authority over their lives.

The site of ancient Corinth at the foot of the 1,886-foot-high Acrocorinth, on top of which was the temple to Aphrodite. In the foreground are the ruins of the Temple of Apollo.

Circumstances of Writing

Author: First Corinthians ascribes Paul as its author (1:1; 16:21). Biblical scholars are almost unanimous that Paul wrote the letter. He wrote it during the last year of his three-year ministry at Ephesus, probably a few weeks before Pentecost in the spring of A.D. 56 (15:32; 16:8; Ac 20:31).

Background: During Paul's second missionary journey, he had a vision at Troas; he heard a man call to him, "Cross over to Macedonia and help us!" (Ac 16:9). That change in plans led Paul to Philippi, Thessalonica, Athens, and ultimately to Corinth (Ac 18:5). Paul ministered in Corinth for at least 18 months (Ac 18:1-18). He left Corinth accompanied by Aquila and Priscilla (Ac 18:18), leaving them at Ephesus where they met and instructed "an eloquent man" named Apollos (Ac 18:24-26). Apollos then went to Corinth and had a powerful ministry there (Ac 18:27–19:1).

First Corinthians is the second letter that Paul wrote to the Corinthian church. He had written them an earlier letter that included an admonition not to mix with the sexually immoral (5:9). The writing of this second letter (1 Corinthians) was prompted by oral reports from Chloe's household about factional strife within the church (1:11). Paul had also received reports about an incestuous relationship among the membership (5:1), factions that arose during observance of the Lord's Supper (11:18), and confusion over the resurrection of the dead (15:12). As a result, Paul addressed these issues in 1 Corinthians. Apparently as he was writing the letter, he received a letter from the Corinthians asking his opinion on various issues (7:1,25; 8:1; 12:1; 16:1). Therefore, he included his replies within this letter to the Corinthian believers.

Message and Purpose

In all of Paul's letters, except Galatians, the main theme of the letter can be identified by the content of the thanksgiving or by the stated reason for his giving thanks. The premise of each of his letters also is usually found in the salutation beginning the letter, as well as in the introductory prayers following the thanksgiving

---

1000–500 B.C.

Corinth founded by Dorian Greeks **1000**

Corinth ruled by Cypselus **(657–627)** and his son Periander **(627–585)**

Periander mints Corinthian coins and constructs the diolkos, a five-foot-wide rock-cut path that ran four miles between two seaports, Lechaion on the Gulf of Corinth and Cenchreae on the Saronic Gulf. **600**

The Isthmian games begin and are held every two years to honor Poseidon, the god of the sea. **582**

Temple of Apollo constructed **550**

500–50 B.C.

Corinth sides with Sparta and prevails against Athens in the Peloponnesian War. **430**

Population of Corinth reaches 100,000. **400**

Phillip II of Macedon conquers Corinth. **338**

After Phillip II's assassination, the Greeks at the Isthmian games choose Phillip's son, Alexander the Great, to lead them in war with Persia. **336**

The Corinthians attempt to resist Roman expansion in Greece and are destroyed by the Roman general Lucius Mummius. **146**

section. Within his prescript and thanksgiving of 1 Corinthians, true to his custom, Paul presented the main theme of his letter—that all believers belong to the Lord (1:2). Jesus is Lord; believers are His possession. For Paul, whatever issue was discussed, the answer to the issue was always addressed with a reminder of the Lord's authority over them (1:2,10). He used more than 75 idioms from first-century slavery to speak about believers' relationship to the Lord, their master. Those who call upon the name of the Lord (1:2) are those who call upon His name as a sign of submission. In 1 Corinthians, "name" (1:2,10,13; 5:4; 6:11) is almost always synonymous with "authority."

Paul's purpose in writing 1 Corinthians was to motivate the Corinthian church to acknowledge the Lord's ownership of them and the implications this had in their lives. Key topics Paul addressed in this overarching theme of the ownership and authority of the Lord include: Christian unity, morality, the role of women, spiritual gifts, and the resurrection.

Contribution to the Bible

First Corinthians contributes greatly to our understanding of the Christian life, ministry, and relationships by showing us how the members of the church—Christ's body—are to function together. Problems can arise in any church because the church is comprised of sinful people (redeemed certainly, but still prone to follow the tug of sin). Paul gave specific solutions to specific problems, but the underlying answer to all these problems is for the church and its members to live Christ-centered lives. It all comes down to living under the lordship and authority of Christ, the head of His body (the church).

Structure

Paul's writing is in the form of a letter, using the standard four parts of a first-century letter: salutation (1:1-3), thanksgiving (1:4-9), the main body (1:10–16:18), and a farewell (16:19-21). It is a pastoral letter, driven by the occasion and the present needs of the recipients.

50 B.C.–A.D. 50

Julius Caesar rebuilds Corinth as a colony of Rome naming it *Colonia Laus Julia Corinthiensis*. 44 B.C.

Augustus Caesar makes Corinth the capital of Achaia. 27 B.C.

Jesus' trials, death, resurrection, and ascension Nisan 14-16 or April 3-5, A.D. 33

Pentecost A.D. 33

Saul's conversion on the Damascus Road October A.D. 34

A.D. 50–57

Paul arrives in Corinth and spends 18 months planting the church. 50–51

Paul's hearing before Corinth's proconsul, Gallio, brother of the Roman philosopher Seneca 51

Paul writes 1 Corinthians from Ephesus. 56

Paul writes 2 Corinthians from Ephesus. 56

Paul spends the winter in Corinth, from where he writes Romans. 57

Perhaps the most noteworthy feature of the way Paul structured his letter was his use of the word "about" to introduce a subject. It is apparent that "about" signals that Paul was responding to items on a list of questions that he had received—perhaps by way of a committee of men (16:17). These questions dealt with males and females in marriage (7:1); virgins (7:25); food offered to idols (8:1); spiritual gifts (12:1); the collection for the saints in Jerusalem (16:1); and Apollos (16:12).

Outline

I. Greetings and Thanksgiving (1:1-9)

II. Problems in the Church (1:10–6:20)
   A. Divisions and factions (1:10–4:21)
   B. Gross immorality (5:1-13)
   C. Litigation before pagan courts (6:1-11)
   D. Fornication with prostitutes (6:12-20)

III. Replies to Questions from the Corinthians (7:1–14:40)
   A. Questions about marriage (7:1-40)
   B. Limitations of Christian liberty (8:1–11:1)
   C. Veiling of women in public worship (11:2-16)
   D. Disorderly behavior at the Lord's Supper (11:17-34)
   E. Exercise of spiritual gifts (12:1–14:40)

IV. The Resurrection of the Body (15:1-58)
   A. Centrality of Christ's resurrection (15:1-20)
   B. Sequence of resurrection events (15:21-28)
   C. The resurrection and suffering (15:29-34)
   D. Nature of the resurrection body (15:35-49)
   E. The believer's victory over death (15:50-58)

V. Conclusion (16:1-24)
   A. Collection for the believers at Jerusalem (16:1-4)
   B. Paul's plans for visiting Corinth (16:5-9)
   C. Exhortations, instructions, and salutations (16:10-24)

Greeting

1 Paul,[a] called as an apostle[b] of Christ Jesus by God's will,[c] and Sosthenes our brother:[d] [2] To God's church at Corinth,[e] to those who are *sanctified[f] in Christ Jesus and called[g] as *saints, with all those in every place who call on the name[h] of Jesus Christ our Lord—both their Lord and ours.

[3] Grace to you and peace from God our Father[i] and the Lord Jesus Christ.

Thanksgiving

[4] I always thank[j] my God for you because of God's grace given to you in Christ Jesus, [5] that by Him you were enriched[k] in everything—in all speech and all knowledge.[l] [6] In this way, the testimony about Christ was confirmed among you,[m] [7] so that you do not lack any spiritual gift as you eagerly wait[n] for the revelation[o] of our Lord Jesus Christ. [8] He will also strengthen you to the end,[p] so that you will be blameless in the day of our Lord Jesus Christ.[q] [9] God is faithful;[r] you were called by Him[s] into fellowship with His Son,[t] Jesus Christ our Lord.

Divisions at Corinth

[10] Now I urge you, *brothers, in the name of our Lord Jesus Christ, that all of you agree in what you say, that there be no divisions among you, and that you be united with the same understanding and the same conviction. [11] For it has been reported to me about you, my brothers, by members of Chloe's household, that there is rivalry[u] among you. [12] What I am saying is this: Each of you says, "I'm with Paul," or "I'm with Apollos,"[v] or "I'm with *Cephas,"[w] or "I'm with Christ."[x] [13] Is Christ divided?[y] Was it Paul who was crucified for you? Or were you baptized in Paul's name? [14] I thank God[A,B] that I baptized none of you except Crispus[z] and Gaius,[aa] [15] so that no one can say you were baptized in my name. [16] I did, in fact, baptize the household[ab] of Stephanas;[ac] beyond that, I don't know if I baptized anyone else. [17] For Christ did not send me to baptize,

a 1:1 Ac 13:9
b Rm 1:1
c 2Co 1:1; Eph 1:1; Col 1:1; 2Tm 1:1
d Ac 18:17
e 1:2 Ac 18:1; 19:1; 2Co 1:1,23; 2Tm 4:20
f Ac 20:32; 26:18; 1Co 6:11; Heb 10:10
g Rm 1:6-7
h Gn 4:26; Ps 79:6; Jn 10:25; Ac 9:14; 15:14; Rv 14:1
i 1:3 Rm 1:7; 2Co 1:2; Gl 1:3; Eph 1:2; Php 1:2; 2Th 1:2; Ti 1:4
j 1:4 Rm 1:8; Php 1:3; Col 1:3; 1Th 1:2; 2Th 1:3; 2Tm 1:3; Phm 4
k 1:5 2Co 8:9; 9:11
l Rm 15:14; 1Co 12:8; 2Co 8:7; 1Jn 2:20
m 1:6 2Th 1:10; 1Tm 2:6; 2Tm 1:8; Rv 1:2
n 1:7 Lk 17:30; Rm 8:19; Php 3:20; Heb 9:28; 2Pt 3:12

o 1Pt 4:13 p 1:8 Php 1:6; 1Th 3:13 q Lk 17:24; 1Co 5:5; 2Co 1:14; Php 2:16; Col 1:22 r 1:9 Dt 7:9; Is 49:7; 1Co 10:13; 2Co 1:18 s Rm 8:28 t Jn 5:19; Heb 1:2; 1Jn 1:3 u Ti 3:9 v 1:12 Ti 3:13 w Jn 1:42 x Mt 23:9-10 y 1:13 1Co 12:5; 2Co 11:4; Eph 4:5 z 1:14 Ac 18:8 aa Rm 16:23 ab 1:16 Rm 16:5 ac 1Co 16:15,17

A 1:14 Other mss omit *God*   B 1:14 Or *I am thankful*

1:1 Paul generally used the designation **as an apostle . . . by God's will** when his apostolic authority was being challenged or when he was writing to correct his readers.

1:2 Paul attached two epithets that identified the church at Corinth: those who were **sanctified in Christ Jesus** and those who were **called as saints**. These epithets and the last qualifying phrase, **with all those in every place who call on the name of Jesus Christ our Lord—both their Lord and ours**, suggests the letter's theme: those who are set apart belong to the Lord and appeal to His authority. Jesus Christ is the "Lord" in every place.

1:3 Paul's standard greeting after the salutation identified two persons of the Trinity, **God** the Father and **the Lord Jesus Christ**. "Lord" recalls "Lord God" of the OT, thus making a clear statement about Jesus' divine identity.

1:4 Paul later used the word **grace** with reference to the Corinthian believers being accepted as blameless at the Lord's appearing (vv. 7-8), and also with reference to their spiritual giftedness that confirmed their relationship with Christ (vv. 6-7). As is only fitting, Paul's chief reason for gratitude toward the Corinthian believers was the gift of grace **God** had given them.

1:5-8 Paul clarified this grace with reference to the gifts given to the Corinthians. Their spiritual giftedness confirmed their reception of the **testimony** of the gospel. Paul declared they **were enriched**, referring not only to gifts that testified to their faith but also to those gifts that were being abused or counterfeited within the congregation. These latter included such gifts as ecstatic speech, a source of pride for the congregation. The Corinthian congregation also was prideful with respect to their possession of special religious knowledge. Despite these problems, their genuine reception of the gospel testimony was **confirmed** by their spiritual giftedness.

1:9 In the introduction to 1 Corinthians, the word **Lord** oc-

curs more than in any other letter introduction of Paul (vv. 2,3,7,8,9). In this transition to the body of the letter, Paul again emphasized his theme—the authority of the Lord over His subjects. He acknowledged the Father's faithfulness to call the Corinthians into a unified fellowship with **His Son, Jesus Christ** who is Lord of the church.

1:10–4:21 The letter includes Paul's responses to two reports. The first was regarding major divisions within the church (1:10–4:21). The second regarded gross sexual immorality (5:1–6:20).

1:10 Paul's appeal to unity is expressed in a first-century idiom translated **agree in what you say**. The added phrase **the same conviction** refers to the shared conviction about the centrality and importance of the gospel message—Christ crucified (v. 17; 1:18–3:4). In Paul's mind, this central conviction was the key to church unity.

1:11-12 Paul disclosed the report from Chloe's household about the quarrelsome, divisive spirit in the church at Corinth. In a vivid, ironic style, he repeated their party slogans which used the stock phrase "I am with so-and-so." Slaves used this expression to identify their master. Also, anyone who slavishly belonged to a factious political party could use this phrase. Even though they said, "I'm with Christ," Corinthian believers who followed mere men exhibited a divisive, slavish spirit contrary to the way of Christ.

1:13-16 Paul answered the rhetorical question **is Christ divided** by illustrating from his own life and ministry two crucial issues related to who he was and what devotion others owed him. In rapid-fire fashion, he asked: **Was it Paul who was crucified for you? Or were you baptized in Paul's name?** The answer to both questions was clearly, "no." Christ died for each of us, and by Christ's authority we are identified with Him in one corporate body that belongs to Christ (12:12-13). Therefore, Christ is the One to whom honor is due.

1:17 Paul did not try to gain a greater faction by baptizing,

but to evangelize—not with clever words, so that the cross[a] of Christ will not be emptied of its effect.

Christ the Power and Wisdom of God

[18] For the message of the cross is foolishness to those who are perishing, but it is God's power to us who are being saved.[b] [19] For it is written:

**I will destroy the wisdom of the wise,
and I will set aside the understanding
of the experts.**[A,c]

[20] Where is the philosopher?[B] Where is the scholar? Where is the debater of this age?[d] Hasn't God made the world's wisdom foolish? [21] For since, in God's wisdom, the *world did not know God through wisdom, God was pleased to save those who believe through the foolishness of the message preached. [22] For the Jews ask for signs[e] and the Greeks seek wisdom, [23] but we preach Christ crucified,[f] a stumbling block to the Jews and foolishness to the Gentiles.[C] [24] Yet to those who are called,[g] both Jews and Greeks, Christ is God's power and God's wisdom, [25] because God's foolishness is wiser than human wisdom, and God's weakness is stronger than human strength.

Boasting Only in the Lord

[26] Brothers, consider your calling: Not many are wise from a human perspective,[D] not many powerful,[h] not many of noble birth. [27] Instead, God has chosen[i] what is foolish in the world to shame the wise, and God has chosen what is weak in the world to shame the strong. [28] God has chosen what is insignificant and despised in the world[j]—what is viewed as nothing—to bring to nothing what is viewed as something, [29] so that no one[E] can boast in His presence.[k] [30] But it is from Him that you are in Christ Jesus, who became God-given wisdom for us—our righteousness,[l] sanctification,[m] and *redemption,[n] [31] in order that, as it is written:[o] **The one who boasts must boast in the Lord.**[F,p]

Paul's Proclamation

2 When I came to you, *brothers, announcing the testimony[G] of God to you, I did not come with brilliance[q] of speech[r] or wisdom. [2] For I didn't think it was a good idea to know anything among you except Jesus Christ and Him crucified.[s] [3] I came to you in weakness,[t] in fear,[u] and in much trembling.[v] [4] My speech[w] and my proclamation were not with persua-

Cross references
a 1:17 Lk 23:26; Php 3:18
b 1:18 Ac 19:11; Rm 1:16; 2Co 13:4
c 1:19 Is 29:14
d 1:20 Lk 16:8
e 1:22 Mt 12:38
f 1:23 Lk 23:26; 1Co 2:2; Gl 3:1; 5:11
g 1:24 Rm 1:6
h 1:26 Ac 25:5
i 1:27 Mt 24:22; Eph 1:4
j 1:28 Lk 18:9
k 1:29 Ac 7:46
l 1:30 Mt 6:33; Rm 1:17; 2Pt 1:1
m 1Th 4:3
n Eph 1:7
o 1:31 Mk 1:2
p Jr 9:23-24
q 2:1 1Tm 2:2
r Col 4:6
s 2:2 1Co 1:23-24; Gl 6:14
t 2:3 2Co 11:30
u Rv 11:11
v Php 2:12
w 2:4 Mt 12:37

A 1:19 Is 29:14   B 1:20 Or *wise*   C 1:23 Other mss read *Greeks*   D 1:26 Lit *wise according to the flesh*   E 1:29 Lit *that not all flesh*
F 1:31 Jr 9:24   G 2:1 Other mss read *mystery*

but rather he preached the gospel, his God-given mission (Ac 9:15). **Not with clever words** emphasizes what the world sees as the gospel's foolishness, that being the message of "Christ crucified" (vv. 18,23; 2:2). The message of **the cross of Christ** should never be diluted in our evangelism, for by such "clever" means we risk voiding it of its power.

1:18-19 The **cross** divides the human race. The division is between **those who are perishing**, to whom the cross is foolishness (lit "stupid folly," "stupidity"), and those **who are being saved**, to whom the cross is wisdom and power. Paul supported this truth by quoting Is 29:14, where God warned the unbelieving leaders of Jerusalem who considered themselves wise. God's judgment will expose all pretensions to human wisdom not anchored in Christ.

1:20-21 Paul introduced God's indictment against those who view themselves as wise in this age. The last question of the series (**Hasn't God made the world's wisdom foolish?**) shows the futility of unbelieving human wisdom. The world takes the gospel and its emphasis on the cross as **foolishness**, but God determined to save people on the basis of their trust in the foolish **message** preached—Christ crucified.

1:22-23 To Jews, the message **Christ crucified** (i.e., "Messiah crucified") signaled weakness, indicating that Jesus was a false messiah. Jews looked instead for signs of Messiah's power (Is 35; 61); thus, the message Christ crucified was a **stumbling block** (Gk *skandalon*; an offense) to their expectations. To the Gentile mind-set, which held no "messianic expectations" but only general conceptions of what deity should be like, the message of "Christ crucified" was foolishness.

1:24 Among the **called** of all nations, **Christ** is **God's power** and **God's wisdom** to save from His judgment (v. 21).

1:25 The **foolishness** (as perceived by the world) of God is **wiser** than the wisdom of man. The term translated "foolishness" (lit "the foolish thing") refers to the foolish content of the message preached—the offensive message of Christ crucified (Gk *kerugma*; cp. v. 21).

1:27-28 Paul gave the rationale for the makeup of God's people. Because the Lord's people embrace the "nothing" message, the world views them as **nothing**. But in the next age God will **shame** the **wise** and the **strong** and bring to nothing the things that in this age are viewed as **something** (2:6; 3:18-20).

1:29 God determined to choose despised ones—those who embrace the foolishness of the cross—so that no one can boast about his human accomplishment or position **in His presence**.

1:30-31 By the Father's doing, believers have an identification in **Christ** (shorthand for "in Christ crucified," cp. vv. 23-24,30; 2:2). Because of this they possess the wisdom of God—Christ crucified, the very essence of wisdom. Through this wisdom, believers have justification at God's court, sanctification that allows their entrance into His presence, and ultimate redemption.

2:1-2 Paul reminded the Corinthian believers that his message was never based on worldly **wisdom**, but on the offensive message of **Christ . . . crucified**.

2:3-5 Paul's preaching was not with **persuasive words of wisdom**, but with **power** as demonstrated by the saving power of the Holy Spirit. **Your faith** refers to all who had embraced the

sive[a] words of wisdom[A] but with a powerful demonstration by the Spirit, [5]so that your faith might not be based on men's wisdom but on God's power.[b]

Spiritual Wisdom

[6] However, we do speak a wisdom among the mature,[c] but not a wisdom of this age, or of the rulers[d] of this age, who are coming to nothing.[e] [7] On the contrary, we speak God's hidden wisdom in a *mystery, a wisdom God predestined[f] before the ages for our glory.[g] [8] None of the rulers of this age knew this wisdom, for if they had known it, they would not have crucified the Lord of glory.[h] [9] But as it is written:

> What eye did not see and ear
>   did not hear,
> and what never entered
>   the human mind—
> God prepared this for those
>   who love Him.[B,i]

[10] Now God has revealed these things to us

by the Spirit, for the Spirit searches everything,[j] even the depths of God.[k] [11] For who among men knows the thoughts[c] of a man except the spirit[l] of the man that is in him? In the same way, no one knows[m] the thoughts[c] of God except the Spirit of God. [12] Now we have not received the spirit of the *world, but the Spirit who comes from God, so that we may understand what has been freely given to us by God. [13] We also speak these things, not in words[n] taught by human wisdom, but in words taught by the Spirit, explaining spiritual things to spiritual people.[D] [14] But the unbeliever[E] does not welcome what comes from God's Spirit, because it is foolishness to him; he is not able to understand it since it is evaluated[F] spiritually. [15] The spiritual person, however, can evaluate[G] everything, yet he himself cannot be evaluated[F] by anyone. [16] For

> who has known the Lord's mind,
>   that he may instruct Him?[H,o]

But we have the mind of Christ.[p]

---

[a]2:4 Php 1:25
[b]2:5 Mk 5:30; Lk 1:35; 6:19; Ac 19:11; 2Co 13:4; 2Tm 1:7; Rv 11:17
[c]2:6 Mt 5:48
[d]Lk 12:58
[e]Heb 2:14
[f]2:7 Eph 1:5
[g]Lk 24:26; 1Pt 5:1,4
[h]2:8 Ps 24:7
[i]2:9 Is 52:15; 64:4; Lk 10:27; 1Jn 4:20
[j]2:10 Ps 17:3; Jn 14:26
[k]Rm 8:39; 11:33; Eph 3:18
[l]2:11 Rm 1:9
[m]1Jn 4:8
[n]2:13 Mt 12:37
[o]2:16 Is 40:13
[p]Col 2:2

[A]2:4 Other mss read *human wisdom*   [B]2:9 Is 52:15; 64:4   [C]2:11 Or *things*   [D]2:13 Or *things with spiritual words*   [E]2:14 Or *unspiritual*; lit *natural*   [F]2:14,15 Or *judged*, or *discerned*   [G]2:15 Or *judge*, or *discern*   [H]2:16 Is 40:13

---

gospel by faith. Their conversion and corporate identity in the body of believers were a result of God's power.

2:6-9 God's supernatural **wisdom** was understood by those who were enabled to see it through the Spirit's illumination.

2:6-7 The phrase **hidden wisdom in a mystery** (Gk *musterion*; lit "a revealed secret") refers to a secret openly revealed by God—the secret being the gospel message that the Lord of glory is truly the Christ crucified.

2:8 The rulers of this age did not recognize Jesus as **the Lord of glory**. Their lack of recognition resulted in His crucifixion, and this in turn became the basis of the gospel. So paradoxically our acceptance was made possible by Christ's rejection.

sophia

Greek Pronunciation	[sah FEE ah]
HCSB Translation	wisdom
Uses in 1 Corinthians	17
Uses in the NT	51
Focus passage	1 Corinthians 2:6

The Greek noun *sophia* means *wisdom, intelligence,* or *knowledge,* but this *intelligence* and *knowledge* pertain more to skill in living than to attainment of facts. Related words are the verb *sophizo,* meaning *to make wise* (2Tm 3:15; 2Pt 1:16), and *sophos,* the adjective meaning *wise* or *clever.*

In the OT, *wisdom* does not refer to intellectual ability but to one who looks to God for instruction. Solomon stated that "the fear of the LORD is the beginning of knowledge" (Pr 1:7), which implies that even a genius who does not fear God is a fool (see Ps 14:1).

Paul understood *sophia* in the light of the OT. He saw worldly *wisdom* and God's *wisdom* as opposites (see 1Co 2:1-9; Col 2:23). The Greeks depended on human mental prowess and insight to unravel the mysteries of life, but Paul relied on God's revelation in Christ (1Co 1:30; Eph 1:8-9,17; 3:8-12). This is why Paul said that God's *wisdom* in Christ is not "of this age" and "the wisdom of this world is foolishness with God" (1Co 2:6; 3:19).

2:9 Paul validated this "revelation of the hidden wisdom" by quoting two OT texts (Is 52:15; 64:4).

2:10 Depths of God refers to the deepest wisdom that God's Spirit reveals to believers. This highest wisdom, as understood from the previous context and throughout the letter, is Jesus Christ, the Lord of glory, "and Him crucified" (v. 2).

2:11 Paul used an analogy of the lesser to the greater. Just as the human **spirit** (Gk *pneuma*) within a man knows what he is thinking, so also **the Spirit** (Gk *pneuma*) **of God** knows the **thoughts** of God.

2:12 Paul declared that with the reception of **the Spirit . . . from God**, a person understands that "Christ and Him crucified" (v. 2) is actually the highest wisdom.

2:13 Spiritual reception is brought about by the Spirit's revelation to **spiritual people** (Gk *pneumatikoi*; lit "spiritual ones"). "Spiritual people" is probably equivalent to "those capable of understanding" (i.e., "mature") in verse 6.

2:14 The **unbeliever** (Gk *psuchikos anthropos*) is identified as a person who does not have the Spirit from God; therefore, he does not welcome (lit "receive," "embrace") **what comes from God's Spirit**. He is not able to know the gospel that "comes from God's Spirit" because he considers it **foolishness**. It is the Spirit who convicts and reveals. Throughout chapters 1–2, "foolishness" is always a reference to "Christ and Him crucified," or the gospel, the wisdom of God.

2:15 The **spiritual person** can discern **everything** with respect to this wisdom; yet he himself is examined by no one. The spiritual person's discernment is an understanding of the deep things of God freely given to the believer. The "spiritual person" is examined by the Lord as Judge to determine how faithful he has been in living and proclaiming the gospel (4:4-5).

2:16 Paul validated his statement in verse 15 by appealing to Is 40:13. When the "spiritual person" is scrutinized by "the natural man" with respect to spiritual things, the

The Problem of Immaturity

3 ¹Brothers, I was not able to speak to you as spiritual people but as people of the flesh, as babies in Christ.ᵃ ²I gave you milk to drink, not solid food, because you were not yet ready for it. In fact, you are still not ready, ³because you are still fleshly. For since there is envyᵇ and strifeᴬ,ᶜ among you, are you not fleshly and living like unbelievers?ᴮ ⁴For whenever someone says, "I'm with Paul," and another, "I'm with Apollos,"ᵈ are you not unspiritual people?ᶜ,ᴰ

The Role of God's Servants

⁵What then is Apollos? And what is Paul?

They are servants through whom you believed, and each has the role the Lord has given. ⁶I planted,ᵉ Apollos watered, but God gave the growth. ⁷So then neither the one who plants nor the one who waters is anything, but only God who gives the growth. ⁸Now the one planting and the one watering are one in purpose, and each will receive his own reward according to his own labor. ⁹For we are God's coworkers.ᴱ You are God's field, God's building.ᶠ ¹⁰According to God's grace that was given to me, I have laid a foundation as a skilled master builder, and another builds on it. But each one must be careful how he builds on it. ¹¹For no one can lay any other foundationᵍ

ᵃ3:1 1Co 14:20; Heb 5:13; 1Pt 2:2
ᵇ3:3 Jms 3:14,16
ᶜTi 3:9
ᵈ3:4 Ti 3:13
ᵉ3:6 Ac 18:4-11; 1Co 4:15; 9:1; 15:1
ᶠ3:9 1Pt 2:5
ᵍ3:11 Is 28:16; Rm 15:20; 2Co 10:16; 11:4; Gl 1:6-9

ᴬ3:3 Other mss add *and divisions* ᴮ3:3 Lit *and walking according to man* ᶜ3:4 Other mss read *are you not carnal* ᴰ3:4 Lit *not just human* ᴱ3:9 Or *are coworkers belonging to God*

natural man does not have the capability to **instruct** those who have the **mind of Christ**. Paul's point from Isaiah is that no natural man can instruct the Lord with respect to God's deep things.

3:1-3b Many of the Corinthians were immature in the Lord. They were not able to receive **solid food** (advanced teaching) because they were full of **envy and strife** ("rivalries"), which marked them as **babies in Christ** who needed **milk** (fundamental Christian instruction) rather than adult fare.

3:3c-4 In a second analogy, this one borrowed from slavery, Paul observed that the Corinthian believers were **living like unbelievers** (lit "walking according to man"), following human masters in a slavish, partisan manner. This has to be one of the most stinging indictments a believer can ever hear. The phrase "according to man" was often an idiom for living like a slave, and "man" (Gk *anthropos*) was commonly used as a pejorative for "slave." This meaning is supported by the servile cries Paul attributed to the Corinthian believers, **I'm with Paul** and **I'm with Apollos**.

misthos

Greek Pronunciation	[mihss THOSS]
HCSB Translation	reward
Uses in 1 Corinthians	4
Uses in the NT	29
Focus passage	1 Corinthians 3:8,14

The Greek noun *misthos* means *pay, wage, reward, recompense*. Other related terms are *misthios* (Lk 15:17,19) and *misthotos* (Mk 1:20; Jn 10:12-13), both meaning *hired hand*; *misthoo* (to *hire someone*, Mt 20:1,7); *misthoma* (*something rented*, Ac 28:30); *misthapodosia* (*reward* in Heb 10:35-36; *penalty* in Heb 2:2); and *misthapodotes* (*rewarder*, Heb 11:6). The main idea in this word family is *compensation* for a task.

The term *misthos* often refers to monetary *payment* but its main use is to describe some aspect of divine evaluation of human activity. Jesus used *misthos* several times in the Sermon on the Mount in reference to *rewards* that the ungodly receive in this life (Mt 5:46; 6:2,5,16; see 2Pt 2:13,15; Jd 11) in contrast to *rewards* that believers will receive in heaven (Mt 5:12; 6:1; see Mk 9:41; Lk 6:23,35; 2Jn 8).

Paul used the term *misthos* four times in 1 Corinthians, and all four refer to the *reward* that comes from Christian ministry. At the day of judgment the Lord will test by fire the purity of everyone's ministry. Some will receive a *reward*, while others will endure loss, though not the loss of salvation (1Co 3:10-15).

3:5-6 Paul made the Corinthian believers aware that both he and Apollos, the founding evangelists of the Corinthian church, were dispatched **servants** (Gk *diakonoi*) through whom they **believed** the message of the gospel. Most scholars understand **planted** to be a reference to Paul's founding of the church and **watered** to refer to Apollos's later ministry after Paul left Corinth.

3:7 The Lord was to receive all the credit for the growth; therefore, the servants were nothing. The reputation of the owner-grower was everything. No servant need establish his own reputation to the detriment of **God who gives the growth**.

3:8-9a Paul and Apollos were equal servants in the gospel work, and each would receive commendation for his labor among the Corinthian believers (i.e., "God's field"; cp. v. 10) when the Lord returned (4:4-5). The word translated **one in purpose** is literally "one" (Gk *hen*). Paul and Apollos were **God's coworkers** who worked His field (the Corinthian congregation).

3:9b-17 Paul identifies **God's building** as the congregation at Corinth (v. 17), but the metaphor is justly extendable to the universal church (1Pt 2:5). The word translated "building" usually designates a structure still under construction (Gk *oikodomey*). This fitting metaphor designates the church as a work both accomplished and ongoing: its foundation of Jesus Christ is secure and permanent (1Co 3:11), but various builders continue the work of adding stones (believers) to the structure.

3:10a-c As a **skilled master builder** (Gk *sophos architekton*; lit "wise architect-builder"), Paul laid a foundation—the message of Christ crucified (v. 11; 2:2). The key word in this context is "skilled," referring to his expertise and wisdom as a builder to construct with "Jesus Christ and Him crucified." The believer who wishes to help spread the gospel must be properly instructed (Ac 18:26). The phrase **another builds on it** refers to later builders who would have a role in building the body of Christ at Corinth (v. 5). These builders included Apollos and others who followed Paul.

3:10d-12 With the word **For** (Gk *gar*; introducing an explanation), Paul explained how future builders must build on the foundation that he had already laid. As a "skilled master builder" (v. 10), Paul issued a warning (as found in construction contracts) to any builder-leader who should follow him to **be careful how he builds**, choosing to use only quality materials, which is symbolic of faithfulness to his God-giv-

than what has been laid down. That foundation is Jesus Christ. [12] If anyone builds on that foundation with gold, silver,[a] costly stones,[b] wood, hay, or straw, [13] each one's work will become obvious, for the day[A] will disclose it, because it will be revealed by fire;[c] the fire will test the quality of each one's work.[d] [14] If anyone's work that he has built survives, he will receive a reward. [15] If anyone's work is burned up, it will be lost, but he will be saved;[e] yet it will be like an escape through fire.[B,f]

[16] Don't you yourselves know that you are God's sanctuary[g] and that the Spirit of God lives in you?[h] [17] If anyone destroys God's sanctuary, God will destroy him;[i] for God's sanctuary is holy,[j] and that is what you are.

The Folly of Human Wisdom

[18] No one should deceive[k] himself. If anyone among you thinks he is wise in this age,[l] he must become foolish[m] so that he can become wise.[n] [19] For the wisdom of this •world is foolishness[o] with God, since it is written:[p] **He catches the wise in their craftiness;**[C,q] [20] and again, **The Lord knows that the reasonings[r] of the wise are meaningless.**[D,s] [21] So no one should boast in human leaders, for everything is yours[t]— [22] whether Paul or Apollos or •Ce-

phas[u] or the world or life[v] or death[w] or things present or things to come[x]—everything is yours, [23] and you belong to Christ,[y] and Christ belongs to God.

The Faithful Manager

4 A person should consider us in this way: as servants[z] of Christ and managers[aa] of God's •mysteries.[ab] [2] In this regard, it is expected of managers that each one of them be found faithful.[ac] [3] It is of little[ad] importance to me that I should be evaluated[ae] by you or by any human court.[E] In fact, I don't even evaluate myself. [4] For I am not conscious of anything against myself, but I am not justified[af] by this. The One who evaluates me is the Lord. [5] Therefore don't judge[ag] anything prematurely, before the Lord comes,[ah] who will both bring to light what is hidden in darkness and reveal the intentions of the hearts. And then praise will come to each one from God.[ai]

The Apostles' Example of Humility

[6] Now, •brothers,[aj] I have applied these things to myself and Apollos[ak] for your benefit, so

a3:12 Jms 5:3
b Rv 17:4
c3:13 2Th 1:8; 1Pt 1:7
d Ps 62:12; Pr 24:12; Mt 16:27; 2Co 5:10; 1Pt 1:17
e3:15 Mt 9:22; Ac 16:30; Eph 2:8
f Jd 23
g3:16 Lk 1:21
h Lv 26:11; Jms 4:5
i3:17 Heb 6:8
j Ps 20:6; 1Co 7:14
k3:18 2Co 11:3
l Lk 16:8
m Mt 5:22
n Is 5:21; Jr 8:8-9; Gl 6:3
o3:19 1Co 1:18
p Ac 15:15; Gl 4:22
q Jb 5:13; Lk 20:23
r3:20 Mt 15:19; 1Tm 2:8
s3:21 Ps 94:11
t Rm 8:32
u3:22 Jn 1:42
v 1Jn 5:12
w Mt 10:21; Jn 8:51; Php 3:10
x Rm 8:38
y3:23 Nm 3:12
z4:1 Jn 18:36
aa Lk 16:1
ab1Co 2:7
ac4:2 Nm 12:7 ad4:3 Mt 5:19 ae1Co 2:14 af4:4 Ac 13:39 ag4:5 Lk 6:37 ah Mk 8:38; 1Pt 5:6 ai2Co 10:18 aj4:6 Ac 9:30 akTi 3:13

en duties as builder of God's church. The urgent reason for this diligence is revealed in verses 13-17.

3:13 Even in the ancient world large buildings were required to be tested and approved. Stipulations within the building contract stated when the inspection day would take place. Paul used the exact words commonly used to refer to this inspection—**the day will disclose it**. Paul was speaking of the eschatological inspection day when God will examine how builders have built the building of God, the body of Christ, on the foundation of the "foolish message" (1:18,23; 2:2,5).

3:14-17 In this section Paul gives three different scenarios describing three different types of subcontractors who were constructing the building of God. He begins each scenario with the expression **if anyone's work . . . if anyone** (vv. 14-15,17; cp. v. 12).

3:14 In the ancient world, a **reward** (Gk *misthos*) was granted to those who constructed the building on time, within budget, and according to specifications.

3:15 Paul warned those who built carelessly that they would suffer loss.

3:16 Paul called on the Corinthians to have self-awareness about the ultimate identity of their corporate body. They were a temple built by God, and the **Spirit of God** resided among them.

3:17 Paul gave stern notice to those who corrupted the church (chap. 15; 2Co 11). In a wordplay on the verb **destroy**, Paul warned that anyone who "destroys" (Gk *phtheiro*; "ruin," "corrupt," "defraud," "destroy") God's temple will, as recompense, be destroyed by God. The word "destroy" was

used in construction contracts to describe building a structure with the intent to defraud. Thus the image here is of a church leader (builder, v. 12) who is willfully negligent.

3:18 Paul's advice to the self-deceived: Let the one who thinks he is wise **in this age** become **foolish** by embracing the message of "foolishness." The "foolish one" who trusted the "foolish message" would be **wise** from God's viewpoint.

3:19-20 God determines what constitutes **foolishness**. These verses are filled with courtroom terminology from OT Wisdom literature (e.g., Jb 5:12-13). Paul affirmed from these witnesses that any disputations (**reasonings**) made before God's bench would be foolish if based on the wisdom of men.

3:21-23 The remedy for divisions in the church is the recognition that all gospel servants—even prominent figures such as **Paul . . . Apollos**, or **Cephas**—are not their own, but **belong to Christ**, who in turn belongs **to God**. In this light, servants must never become a distraction to the church, and believers must never mistake them for the Master.

4:1-2 Paul called on the Corinthians to be aware of the responsibilities of those who manage. The church should view those in leadership as slave-stewards with a responsibility to dispatch the message of Christ.

4:3-4 Paul was aware that the examination of his stewardship with respect to "God's mysteries" (v. 1) came from the Lord (lit "master"), not humans nor even himself. All believers will be tested on how faithful they have been to the foolish message of "Christ and Him crucified" (2:2).

4:6 Paul did not disclose the identity of these misguided, arrogant leaders; he used the names "Apollos" and "Paul"

The Message and Lifestyle of the Apostles

Michael J. Wilkins

The apostles of the New Testament lived through what is arguably the most significant era of human history. They experienced the personal entrance of God into history in the person of Jesus Messiah, and their lives were permanently changed. Their transformation catapulted them into the entire then-known world with the message of what they had experienced—the arrival of the kingdom of God and salvation in Jesus' name.

The term *apostle* has a significantly different meaning than the word *disciple*. "Disciple" is the term used to designate all those who have believed in Jesus and have followed Him as their Savior. The title "apostle" designates those who have been commissioned to be leaders of the church and Jesus' representatives with the gospel message. From out of the large group of His disciples, Jesus chose the Twelve to be sent out as His apostles (Lk 6:13-16).

Therefore, coming from the verb *apostello*, which means "to send someone away to achieve an objective," the noun "apostle" indicates a "sent one" or "messenger." It occurs in the NT in at least four ways.

Four Usages of "Apostle" in the New Testament

First, the term is used especially to refer to the "twelve apostles" who were eyewitnesses of Jesus' earthly ministry. They were first sent out to Israel with the gospel message of the arrival of the kingdom of God (Mt 10:1-7), and after Jesus' death and resurrection they were sent out with the gospel message to make disciples of all nations (Mt 28:18-20). They witnessed Jesus' resurrection appearances, which Luke tells us demonstrated the reality of Jesus' victory over death and the certainty of the kingdom of God in this age (Ac 1:2-3). They were among the first to receive the filling of the Spirit at Pentecost (Ac 2:1-4), and their preaching of the gospel established them as the foundation of the church (Eph 2:20). After Judas Iscariot betrayed Jesus and killed himself, another eyewitness of Jesus' earthly ministry and resurrection, Matthias, was added to the Eleven (Ac 1:21-26).

Second, the term apostle also refers to those who saw the risen Lord and were commissioned by Him for ministry (cp. 1Co 9:1). This is the sense in which Paul identifies himself as an "apostle of Christ Jesus" (1Co 1:1; 2Co 1:1; Col 1:1). He was not one of the Twelve (e.g., 1Co 15:3-11; Gl 1:17-19), but Jesus granted him a unique apostleship to the Gentiles (Gl 2:8-9).

Third, the term apostle can have the more general sense of "missionary." This was the case for Barnabas (Ac 14:4,14), perhaps Timothy and Silvanus (cp. 1Th 1:1; 2:7), and Andronicus and Junia[s] (Rm 16:7). The last may have been a husband-wife team; they were commended by Paul for spreading the gospel along with the other apostles.

Fourth, the term apostle sometimes referred more broadly to "messengers of the churches" who were sent out to perform certain tasks (2Co 8:23). This includes among others, Epaphroditus, who was sent as a messenger to minister to Paul by the church at Philippi (Php 2:25-30).

These different types of apostles had different roles, but what they had in common was either their encounter with Jesus in His earthly ministry or in His risen and ascended ministry, or else their being directly commissioned by one who had met these qualifications. And their transformation in understanding Jesus' identity as God incarnate, offering salvation to the world, became the foundation of their message. The Twelve and Paul are dramatic examples.

Diversity and Unity among the Apostles

The Twelve displayed a remarkable personal diversity. For example, Peter, Andrew, James, and John were partners in a successful fishing business on the Sea of Galilee (Mk 1:16-20; Lk 5:9-11). Matthew was a hated tax collector (Mt 9:9-13), seen as a traitor because he worked for the Roman occupying government extracting as much tax as he could from his own people. Simon the Zealot was a revolutionary who was willing to die for the cause of liberating Israel from Rome. In normal circumstances these men might be ready to stick a knife in each other, but their individual encounters with Jesus transformed them into a cohesive unit dedicated to declaring Jesus to be the only way to eternal life (cp. Jn 6:67-69).

Peter's preaching at Pentecost is an example of his dramatic transformation from one who denied Jesus to one who fearlessly preached to the multitudes in Jerusalem. His message was clear: "Repent . . . and be baptized, each of you, in the name of Jesus Christ for the forgiveness of your sins, and you will receive the gift of the Holy Spirit. . . . Be saved from this corrupt generation!" (Ac 2:38,40). For over 30 years Peter

that you may learn from us the saying: "Nothing beyond what is written."A The purpose is that none of you will be inflated with pride in favor of one person over another. [7] For who makes you so superior? What do you have that you didn't receive? If, in fact, you did receive it, why do you boast as if you hadn't received it? [8] You are already full! You are already rich! You have begun to reign as kings without us—and I wish you did reign, so that we could also reign with you! [9] For I think God has displayed us, the apostles, in last place, like men condemned to die: We have become a spectacle to the world and to angels and to men. [10] We are fools for Christ, but you are wise in

a 4:10 1Pt 5:14
b 4:12 2Jn 8
c Ac 18:3
d 4:13 Is 64:6;
Lm 3:45
e 4:14 1Th 2:11;
Phm 1

Christ![a] We are weak, but you are strong! You are distinguished, but we are dishonored! [11] Up to the present hour we are both hungry and thirsty; we are poorly clothed, roughly treated, homeless; [12] we labor, working[b] with our own hands.[c] When we are reviled, we bless; when we are persecuted, we endure it; [13] when we are slandered, we respond graciously. Even now, we are like the world's garbage, like the dirt everyone scrapes off their sandals.[d]

Paul's Fatherly Care

[14] I'm not writing this to shame you, but to warn you as my dear children.[e] [15] For you can have 10,000 instructors in Christ, but you can't have many fathers. For I became your

---

A 4:6 The words in quotation marks could = the OT, a Jewish maxim, or a popular proverb.

---

as a foil. Paul and Apollos had illustrated dramatically in their foolish message that they did **nothing beyond** what was **written**. Paul had determined to know nothing among the Corinthians "except Jesus Christ and Him crucified" (2:1-2). The church was not to be inflated with **pride** in favor of **one person over another**. They were to boast only in the Lord.

4:7 Paul offered a rhetorical response to those who were claiming superiority in the Corinthian church. He who receives a gift by grace has no grounds for boasting.

4:8 With a strong dose of irony, Paul says the boastful disposition of the Corinthian believers made them **full** and **rich**, as if their glorification was complete and they were already reigning **as kings** in eternity. In part Paul wished all of this were true, for all believers are destined to reign with Christ (2Tm 2:12).

4:9 Paul's mention of a **spectacle** (Gk *theatron*; "theatrical display") refers to the arena where victims (usually criminals) were led in procession before the last public show of the day, and then executed before the eager spectators. But rather than pagan or unbelieving Jewish authorities, Paul

knew that ultimately it was **God** Himself who had chosen to display **the apostles** in a humiliating manner.

4:10 Paul presents an alarming contrast, likely intended as a warning to the Corinthian church. While the apostles were made out to be **fools** as they faithfully dispatched the gospel, the spiritually immature Corinthians were **wise** (Gk *phronimos*) in their escape from ostracism, hardship, and persecution. In short, it seems they were "living like unbelievers" (3:3).

4:11-13 Paul describes the lifestyle and character of apostolic ministry. The world with its human wisdom labeled them as **garbage** and **dirt** (cp. 2Co 2:16), which is "the refuse" (Gk *perikatharma*) of chamber pots and "the offscouring" (Gk *peripsama*) in waste vats and cesspools respectively. The Romans used these terms to describe the dregs of society.

4:14 Paul's warnings were as admonitions from a loving father to his children.

4:15 Paul reminded the Corinthian believers that he was their father **through the gospel**. In contrast to their present **instructors**, he had founded the church in Corinth (Ac 18).

---

traversed the ancient world proclaiming the same message, until finally the Roman government executed him. But Rome couldn't silence the message, for the church continued to proclaim the gospel fearlessly in the face of persecution.

The apostle Paul was a former Pharisee (Php 3:4-6). The Pharisees were well-known critics of Jesus (Mt 12:14), and Paul himself actively persecuted the church as a Pharisee (Ac 22:3-4). But after his encounter with the risen Jesus on the road to Damascus, Paul was radically transformed from an enemy to one who gave the rest of his life as a servant of Jesus. Paul's own testimony of what produced the transformation is found in his letter to Titus. He speaks of his former life of foolishness, malice, envy, and hatred (Ti 3:3), but then says:

"But when the goodness of God and His love for mankind appeared, He saved us—not by works of righteousness that we had done, but according to His mercy, through the washing of regeneration and renewal by the Holy Spirit. He poured out this Spirit on us abundantly through Jesus Christ our Savior, so that having been justified by His grace, we may become heirs with the hope of eternal life" (Ti 3:4-7).

The apostles seem an unlikely group to be used by Jesus to establish the church and proclaim His message of salvation and transformation. But what empowered them was not their own charisma or powerful preaching, nor an ambition to create a movement. Rather, it was the operation of the Spirit that caused their transformation into the image of Jesus, which then impelled them to proclaim Jesus' glorious message of salvation and hope of change to the entire world.

father[a] in Christ Jesus through the gospel. [16] Therefore I urge you to imitate me. [17] This is why I have sent[b] Timothy to you. He is my dearly loved and faithful[c] son in the Lord. He will remind you about my ways in Christ Jesus, just as I teach everywhere in every church. [18] Now some are inflated with pride, as though I were not coming to you. [19] But I will come to you soon,[d] if the Lord wills, and I will know not the talk but the power of those who are inflated with pride. [20] For the kingdom of God is not a matter of talk but of power. [21] What do you want? Should I come to you with a rod,[e] or in love and a spirit of gentleness?[f]

Immoral Church Members

5 It is widely reported that there is sexual immorality[g] among you, and the kind of sexual immorality that is not even tolerated[A] among the Gentiles[h]—a man is living with his father's wife.[i] [2] And you are inflated with pride, instead of filled with grief[j] so that he who has committed this act might be removed from your congregation. [3] For though I am absent in body but present in spirit,[k] I have already decided about the one who has done this thing as though I were present. [4] When you are assembled in the name of our Lord Jesus with my spirit and with the power of our Lord Jesus, [5] turn that one over to Satan for the destruction of the flesh,[l] so that his spirit may be saved in the Day of the Lord.[m]

[6] Your boasting is not good. Don't you know that a little yeast[n] permeates the whole batch of dough?[o] [7] Clean out the old yeast so that you may be a new batch. You are indeed un-

[a]4:15 Gl 4:19; Phm 10
[b]4:17 2Co 9:3; Eph 6:21-22; Col 4:7-8; Phm 12
[c]Nm 12:7
[d]4:19 Ac 19:21; 1Co 16:5; 2Co 1:15-16
[e]4:21 2Co 1:23; 2:1,3; 12:20-21; 13:2,10
[f]Jms 3:13
[g]5:1 1Th 4:3
[h]Gl 1:16
[i]Lv 18:8; Dt 22:30; 27:20
[j]5:2 Lk 6:25
[k]5:3 Col 2:5; 1Th 2:17
[l]5:5 1Jn 5:16
[m]Mt 25:13; Ac 2:20; Php 1:6
[n]5:6 Lk 13:21; Gl 5:9
[o]5:6-8 Lk 13:21

A5:1 Other mss read named

4:16 Paul urged the Corinthian believers to **imitate** him, which entailed being seen as "fools" for the sake of Christ (vv. 10-13; cp. 2:1-2). Thus believers are encouraged to identify with "the world's garbage" (4:13).

4:17 Timothy as a dispatched "son" would **remind** the Corinthians of their father's **ways** (i.e., "fools for Christ," cp. v. 10). Timothy probably had been dispatched from Ephesus before the letter was sent (16:10-11).

4:18-20 Paul would come to examine their teaching from the standpoint of **power**, the standard for all those who were truly teaching the foolishness of Christ crucified—the only wisdom that has the power to save (1:18,22-24).

4:21 Rod pictures a father who is faithful to correct his disobedient children. If the Corinthian believers ignored Paul's rebuke and admonition, they would receive the rod of chastisement upon his arrival. If they repented, however, he would come **in love and a spirit of gentleness**.

5:1-6:20 Paul shifts to discuss specific immoralities that had been reported to him. The key word that joins the two major sections (1:18-4:21 and 5:1-6:20) is the verb translated **you are inflated with pride** (Gk *phusio*; "to have an exaggerated self-conception"; cp. 4:6,18-19; 5:2). The three issues in this section—incest (5:1-13), lawsuits (6:1-11), and prostitution (6:12-20)—all revolve around sexual immorality.

5:1 The phrase **not even tolerated among the Gentiles** refers to Roman law. A son committing incest with his stepmother was a capital crime in a Roman colony, calling for death or banishment.

5:2 Paul connected the problem of ignoring church discipline to arrogance within the corporate body (v. 6). They were so consumed with **inflated...pride** that they had been blinded to the most offensive sins within the church—sins that even pagans in Roman Corinth would not tolerate. They should have **removed** the offender from their fellowship. The purpose of this measure is revealed in verse 5.

5:3 As an apostolic judge, Paul issued a "judicial opinion"—a banishment of the offender but with a view toward ultimate restoration. Taking up the language of a legal trial, he used at least 10 legal idioms in these verses. Beginning with the phrase **I have already decided ... as though I were present** (lit "I have judged as one who is present"), Paul's terms echoed the language from secular courts.

5:4-5 Paul declared that the assembled corporate body was capable of judging the offender in the **name** of their **Lord** (Gk *onoma*; "name," "authority of") because he, as an apostle, had already rendered his legal decision as though he were present. Paul's legal perspective on this case (**with my spirit**) would have supported the church body that possessed the authority of the Lord Jesus to render a decision on this sin. They had the authority to remove him (2:2) from their midst for the **destruction of the flesh**. This may refer to physical judgments such as sickness or even death (11:30). If the person were a true believer, banishment to Satan's domain would cause misery and possibly repentance. Paul expressed hope for the guilty person's ultimate restoration with the legal phrase, **so that his spirit may be saved** on the appointed **Day of the Lord** (Rm 2:6,9).

5:6 Boasting (Gk *kauchama*) within the corporate body gives rise to tolerance of corporate sins (cp. v. 2, "inflated

---

porneia

Greek Pronunciation	[pohr NAY ah]
HCSB Translation	sexual immorality
Uses in 1 Corinthians	5
Uses in the NT	25
Focus passage	1 Corinthians 5:1

The Greek noun *porneia* was a general term for all sexual activity outside marriage, so the term can be translated *fornication* or *sexual immorality*. Related terms include *porneuo*, meaning to *commit sexual immorality* (see 1Co 6:18; 10:18); *porne*, meaning *an immoral woman* or *a female prostitute* (see 6:15-16); and *pornos*, meaning *an immoral person* or *a male prostitute* (5:9-11; 6:9).

Paul condemned a case of incest in the church in Corinth, a sin he called *porneia* (5:1). In chapter 6 he explained that the believer's body is for the Lord and not for *porneia* (v. 13). Then he commanded believers to flee *porneia* (v. 18). On the other hand, sexual union in marriage is commended, partly because it helps believers avoid *porneia* (7:2). It is likely that cult prostitution, in which the Corinthian people could indulge at the temple of Aphrodite, was a major threat to the Corinthian believers' spiritual growth.

leavened, for Christ our *Passover[a] has been sacrificed.[A] [8]Therefore, let us observe the feast, not with old yeast or with the yeast of malice and evil[b] but with the unleavened bread of sincerity and truth.

Church Discipline

[9]I wrote to you in a letter not to associate[c] with sexually immoral people.[d] [10]I did not mean the immoral people of this *world or the greedy[e] and swindlers[f] or idolaters; otherwise you would have to leave the world.[g] [11]But now I am writing[B] you not to associate with anyone who claims to be a believer[C,h] who is sexually immoral or greedy, an idolater or verbally abusive, a drunkard[i] or a swindler. Do not even eat with such a person. [12]For what business is it of mine to judge[j] outsiders? Don't you judge those who are inside? [13]But God judges outsiders. **Put away the evil person from among yourselves.**[D,k]

[a]5:7 Ex 12
[b]5:8 Mk 7:22; Rm 1:29
[c]5:9 2Th 3:14
[d]1Co 6:9; Eph 5:5; 1Tm 1:10; Heb 12:16; 13:4; Rv 21:8; 22:15
[e]5:10 Eph 5:5
[f]Lk 18:11
[g]Jn 17:6
[h]5:11 2Th 3:6
[i]1Co 6:10
[j]5:12 Lk 6:37
[k]5:13 Dt 17:7
[l]6:1 Mt 18:15-17
[m]6:4 Lk 18:9
[n]6:5 1Co 4:14
[o]Ac 9:30
[p]6:6 Lk 12:46
[q]6:7 Rm 11:12
[r]Rv 2:11
[s]Mk 10:19

Lawsuits among Believers

6 If any of you has a legal dispute against another, do you dare go to court[l] before the unrighteous,[E] and not before the *saints? [2]Or don't you know that the saints will judge the *world? And if the world is judged by you, are you unworthy to judge the smallest cases? [3]Don't you know that we will judge angels—not to mention ordinary matters? [4]So if you have cases pertaining to this life, do you select those[F] who have no standing[m] in the church to judge? [5]I say this to your shame![n] Can it be that there is not one wise person among you who is able to arbitrate between his *brothers?[o] [6]Instead, believer[G] goes to court against believer, and that before unbelievers![p]

[7]Therefore, to have legal disputes against one another is already a moral failure for you.[q] Why not rather put up with injustice?[r] Why not rather be cheated?[s] [8]Instead, you

---

[A]5:7 Other mss add *for us*   [B]5:11 Or *now I wrote*   [C]5:11 Lit *anyone named a brother*   [D]5:13 Dt 17:7   [E]6:1 Unbelievers; v. 6
[F]6:4 Or *life, appoint those* (as a command)   [G]6:6-8 Lit *brothers*

---

with pride"). The **yeast** of arrogant hypocrisy had spread throughout the Corinthian **batch of dough**.

5:7-8 With a wordplay on the expression **Christ our Passover**, Paul offered a threefold solution to this corporate arrogance: (1) their recognition of what Christ as their Passover did to deliver them from death; (2) their acknowledgment that Christ as their Passover rendered them clean (**unleavened**) before the Lord; and (3) their remembrance that as they observed Christ as the Passover, they were to purge their household of **malice and evil** to celebrate with **sincerity and truth**.

5:9 Paul's prohibition against associating with **sexually immoral people** was consistent with his warning in a previous **letter**, which is long since lost.

5:10 Paul corrected a mistaken perception that his admonition in the letter (v. 9) had prohibited them from mixing socially with nonbelievers (**the immoral people of this world**). He actually had meant not to mix with "insiders" who lived like "outsiders," believers who live like unbelievers (3:3).

5:11 The Corinthian believers were not to mix with anyone who **claims to be a believer** and yet is **sexually immoral**, but they were also to avoid any professing believer who was **greedy, an idolater or verbally abusive, a drunkard or a swindler**. To **eat** with such people could be taken as a sign of condoning their worldly lifestyle. The Pharisees had this same impression of Jesus but were mistaken (Mk 2:16-17).

6:1 Some Corinthian believers were bringing charges against fellow members before secular judges rather than summoning them before competent arbitrators within the church (v. 5). The phrase **dare go to court before the unrighteous** (Gk *epi ton adikon*) refers to bringing a legal complaint before unbelieving Roman judges at Corinth.

6:2-3 Paul called the church to an awareness of their own authority as a judicial body. He argued their competency to judge cases by drawing from two greater-to-lesser analogies: (1) being qualified to judge **the world** (i.e., nonbelievers) at the end of the age qualified them to judge church members in this age; and (2) being qualified to judge **angels**

at the end of the age qualified them to judge "cases pertaining to this life" (v. 4).

6:4 Paul put forward the issue of legal jurisdiction. The lesser judges (i.e., the unrighteous judges of this age) are unqualified to sit in judgment among those who judge the world. Lesser judges have not been justified, washed, or sanctified (v. 11).

6:7-8 Better to be the victim of wrongdoing (**put up with injustice**) than to be the cause of it (**act unjustly and cheat**) and bring **legal disputes against one another**, which is a **moral failure**. Once again we see the theme of 3:3—believers "living like unbelievers."

krino

Greek Pronunciation	[KRIH noh]
HCSB Translation	judge
Uses in 1 Corinthians	17
Uses in the NT	114
Focus passage	1 Corinthians 6:1-6

The Greek verb *krino* means *to judge* and always involves the process of thinking through a situation and coming to a conclusion. The term could be used in a narrowly judicial sense but it also has several nuances related to *judging* in a more general sense. In nonjudicial contexts, *krino* can mean *to select, prefer, decide, consider.*

In the NT, *krino* most often refers to *judging* something or someone in general. However, *krino* does occur in specific judicial settings several times, and the court can be human (Mt 5:40; Jn 7:51; 18:31; Ac 23:3; 24:21; 25:9-10,20; 26:6; 1Co 6:1,6) or divine (Jn 5:22,30; 12:48; Ac 17:31; Rm 2:16; 3:4-7; 2Tm 4:1; 1Pt 4:5; Rv 20:12-13). In two passages, *krino* is used with the meaning *to rule.* Jesus said that the twelve apostles would *judge* the twelve tribes of Israel "in the Messianic Age" (Mt 19:28), and here *krino* likely means *to rule,* as the verse's reference to sitting on thrones would imply. Similarly, Paul's statement that the saints would *judge* the world and angels (1Co 6:2-3) probably means that believers will *rule* over them both in the future kingdom (cp. Rv 2:26-27).

act unjustly and cheat—and you do this to believers! [9]Don't you know that the unrighteous[a] will not inherit God's kingdom?[b] Do not be deceived: No sexually immoral people, idolaters,[c] adulterers,[d] or anyone practicing homosexuality,[A,e] [10]no thieves,[f] greedy[g] people, drunkards, verbally abusive people,[h] or swindlers[i] will inherit God's kingdom. [11]And some of you used to be like this.[j] But you were *washed, you were *sanctified,[k] you were *justified in the name of the Lord Jesus Christ and by the Spirit of our God.

Glorifying God in Body and Spirit

[12]"Everything is permissible[l] for me,"[B] but not everything is helpful. "Everything is permissible for me," but I will not be brought under the control of anything. [13]"Food[m] for the stomach and the stomach for food," but God will do away with both of them.[C] The body is not for sexual immorality[n] but for the Lord, and the Lord for the body. [14]God raised up the Lord and will also raise us up by His power.[o] [15]Don't you know that your bodies are a part of Christ's body?[p] So should I take a part of Christ's body and make it part of a prostitute? Absolutely not! [16]Don't you know that anyone joined to a prostitute is one body with her?

For Scripture says, **The two will become one flesh.**[D,q] [17]But anyone joined[r] to the Lord is one spirit[s] with Him.

[18]Run[t] from sexual immorality! "Every sin a person can commit is outside the body."[E] On the contrary, the person who is sexually immoral[u] sins against his own body. [19]Don't you know that your body is a sanctuary[v] of the Holy Spirit[w] who is in you,[x] whom you have from God? You are not your own, [20]for you were bought[y] at a price. Therefore glorify God in your body.[F]

Principles of Marriage

7 Now in response to the matters you wrote[G] about: "It is good for a man not to have relations with[H] a woman."[I] [2]But because sexual immorality is so common,[J,z] each man should have his own wife,[aa] and each woman should have her own husband. [3]A husband should fulfill his marital responsibility[ab] to his wife, and likewise a wife to her husband. [4]A wife does not have the right over her own body, but her husband does. In the same way, a husband does not have the right over his own body, but his wife does. [5]Do not deprive[ac] one another sexually—except when you agree for a time, to devote yourselves to[K] prayer. Then

[a]6:9 Lk 16:10
[b]Mk 1:15; Ac 20:25
[c]Eph 5:5
[d]Lk 18:11
[e]Gn 19:5
[f]6:10 Jn 10:1
[g]Eph 5:5
[h]1Co 5:11
[i]Lk 18:11
[j]6:11 Eph 2:2-3; 4:22; 5:8; Ti 3:3
[k]Lk 11:2
[l]6:12 Jn 18:31
[m]6:13 1Tm 6:8
[n]1Th 4:3
[o]6:14 Mk 5:30; Lk 1:35; 6:19; Ac 19:11; 2Co 13:4; Rv 11:17
[p]6:15 Rm 12:5; 1Co 12:27; Eph 5:30
[q]6:16 Gn 2:24
[r]6:17 Jn 11:52
[s]Ps 51:12
[t]6:18 Jms 4:7
[u]1Co 10:8
[v]6:19 Lk 1:21
[w]Rm 8:9,23; 1Co 7:40; 2Co 4:13; Jd 19
[x]Jms 4:5; 1Jn 4:4
[y]6:20 2Pt 2:1
[z]7:2 1Th 4:3
[aa]Mt 1:6; 1Pt 3:1
[ab]7:3 Rm 13:7
[ac]7:5 Mk 10:19

[A]6:9 Lit adulterers, passive homosexual partners, active homosexual partners   [B]6:12-13 The words in quotation marks are most likely slogans used by some Corinthian Christians and corrected by Paul.   [C]6:13 Lit both it and them   [D]6:16 Gn 2:24   [E]6:18 See note at 1Co 6:12–13.   [F]6:20 Other mss add and in your spirit, which belong to God.   [G]7:1 Other mss add to me   [H]7:1 Lit not to touch   [I]7:1 The words in quotation marks are a principle that the Corinthians wrote to Paul about to ask for his view.   [J]7:2 Lit because of immoralities   [K]7:5 Other mss add fasting and to

6:9-11 Believers should not **be deceived** into thinking that unbelieving judges (**the unrighteous**) and their slap-on-the-wrist verdicts about serious sin can render justice in the church. These people have no inheritance in **God's kingdom**. Only believers, who are **washed . . . sanctified**, and **justified**, can rightly judge sins (v. 1). Paul's Corinthian readers would also take this admonition as a cause for asking themselves if their behavior matched that of "the unrighteous" or that of the "washed," the "sanctified," and the "justified."

6:12-20 Paul quotes a slogan apparently put forth by the immature Corinthians (**Everything is permissible for me**) to introduce a series of admonitions emphasizing a dominant theme in this letter: a believer's freedom is to be limited to that which is profitable to the Lord.

6:12-14 Paul's reply to the slogan (v. 12) is that the Corinthian Christians are not their own; they are "bodies" belonging to the Lord (vv. 13,19-20; 1:2; 7:22-23; 10:26). In the Roman world, "body" commonly designated a slave owned by a master, or lord. Making a wordplay of this, Paul said a person's **body** (Gk *soma*) is not for sexual immorality. It is actually a "slave body" (Gk *soma*) for the **Lord** (Gk *kurios*; "master"). God will **do away with** many bodily desires at the resurrection, so why be enslaved to them now?

6:15-17 Paul called the believers at Corinth to remember the oneness and sanctity of their union with Christ. The words **one flesh** in this context refer to becoming one body through sexual relations with a **prostitute**. The implica-

tion in verse 17 is that because Christians are **joined to the Lord**, they should never be joined to a prostitute.

6:18-20 Sexual immorality is unique among sins insomuch as it is sin against the **body**, thus assaulting the sanctity of a believer's sacred oneness with Christ (sealed by **the Holy Spirit who is in you**) and the oneness of holy matrimony (cp. 7:2). The point is that the believer's body is a sacred vessel, **bought at a price** by the Son of God. Believers thus have no business doing anything with the Lord's body that does not **glorify** Him.

7:1 This verse presents a Corinthian position, stated in correspondence previously sent to Paul, that recommended celibacy in marriage. What a divide in the Corinthian church! Some advocated marital celibacy while others were engaged in gross sexual immorality.

7:2-4 Sexual desires, which can readily lead to **sexual immorality**, commend frequent sexual union between husband and wife. The phrase **have the right** in this context refers to sexual relations.

7:5 Paul issues an apostolic ruling: husbands and wives must **not deprive one another sexually** in marriage, **except** when mutually agreed upon for the sake of devotion **to prayer**. Like fasting from food and drink, periods of marital celibacy can hone one's focus on the one great desire: God Himself.

7:6-7 Paul expressed limited agreement to the view stated in verse 1, "It is good for a man not to have relations with a woman." He did think it was "good" if the Corinthians

come together again; otherwise, Satan may tempt you because of your lack of self-control. ⁶ I say the following^A as a concession, not as a command. ⁷ I wish that all people were just like me. But each has his own gift^a from God, one person in this way and another in that way.

A Word to the Unmarried

⁸ I say to the unmarried and to widows:^b It is good for them if they remain as I am. ⁹ But if they do not have self-control,^c they should marry, for it is better to marry^d than to burn with desire.

About Married People

¹⁰ I command the married^e—not I, but the Lord—a wife is not to leave^B her husband. ¹¹ But if she does leave, she must remain unmarried or be reconciled to her husband—and a husband is not to leave his wife.^f ¹² But I (not the Lord)^C say to the rest: If any brother^g has an unbelieving wife and she is willing to live with him, he must not leave her. ¹³ Also, if any woman has an unbelieving husband and he is willing to live with her, she must not leave her husband. ¹⁴ For the unbelieving husband is set apart for God^h by the wife, and the unbelieving wife is set apart for God by the husband.^D

^a7:7 2Co 1:11
^b7:8 Jms 1:27
^c7:9 1Co 9:25
^d1Tm 5:14
^e7:10 1Tm 5:14
^f7:11 Dt 22:19
^g7:12 Ac 9:30
^h7:14 Lk 11:2
^i7:17 Col 3:15
^j7:22 Rm 1:1;
2Tm 2:24
^k7:23 2Pt 2:1

Otherwise your children would be corrupt, but now they are set apart for God. ¹⁵ But if the unbeliever leaves, let him leave. A brother or a sister is not bound in such cases. God has called you^E to live in peace. ¹⁶ For you, wife, how do you know whether you will save your husband? Or you, husband, how do you know whether you will save your wife?

Various Situations of Life

¹⁷ However, each one must live his life in the situation the Lord assigned when God called^i him.^F This is what I command in all the churches. ¹⁸ Was anyone already circumcised when he was called? He should not undo his circumcision. Was anyone called while uncircumcised? He should not get circumcised. ¹⁹ Circumcision does not matter and uncircumcision does not matter, but keeping God's commands does. ²⁰ Each person should remain in the life situation^G in which he was called. ²¹ Were you called while a •slave? It should not be a concern to you. But if you can become free, by all means take the opportunity.^H ²² For he who is called by the Lord as a slave^j is the Lord's freedman.^i Likewise he who is called as a free man^J is Christ's slave. ²³ You were bought^k at a price; do not become slaves

---

^A7:6 Lit *say this*; some interpret the word as referring to v. 2, vv. 2-5, v. 5 (wholly or in part), or v. 6   ^B7:10 Or *separate from*, or *divorce*   ^C7:12 Jesus did not address the situation of a marriage in the Gentile world where only one person is a believer. ^D7:14 Lit *the brother*   ^E7:15 Other mss read *us*   ^F7:17 Lit *called each*   ^G7:20 Lit *in the calling*   ^H7:21 Or *But even though you can become free, make the most of your position as a slave.*   ^I7:22 A former slave   ^J7:22 A man who was never a slave

---

stayed single as he was—but only if they had the **gift** to do so.

7:9 Paul gives another apostolic ruling: unmarried persons who lack self-control should get married. See verse 5 and note there.

7:10 Paul reiterates the Lord's ruling to **the married**, giving an injunction to wives that they must remain in their marriage (Mt 19:1-9; Mk 10:1-12).

7:11 The wife who has separated from her husband has two options: remain apart from him, though celibate, or be **reconciled** to her **husband**. Completing his reiteration of the Lord's instructions for marriage, Paul insisted that **the husband is not to leave his wife**.

7:12-13 The phrase **to the rest** is a reference to mixed marriages—a believer married to an unbeliever. Christians were only to marry "in the Lord" (cp. v. 39). The situation Paul addresses here assumes that both spouses were unbelievers when they married but that one of them thereafter converted to Christianity. Since Jesus did not comment on this situation, Paul gave an apostolic ruling: the believing spouse **must not leave** the unbelieving spouse. One can easily conceive of the self-sacrifice entailed by this ethic. The passage also assumes that the unbeliever agrees that there are benefits to continuing the marital relationship (**is willing to live with** him or her).

7:14 A Christian spouse who remains faithful to his or her unbelieving spouse has a "sanctifying effect" on unbelieving family members. Paul is referring not just to the pos-

sible future salvation of unbelievers in the household, but to their present protection from pagan values through the influence of the Christian member's exemplary morals.

7:15-16 Paul gives a qualification to the above ruling: Do not hinder a nonbeliever's desire to separate. **Peace** in this context refers to being "at peace" if the unbelieving spouse should decide to **leave**, for in this event the believer has done nothing wrong.

7:17-19 Paul issues a "remain-as-you-are" edict and illustrates it with a false dilemma facing a Jewish-born male Christian. Such a man had the option to remain **circumcised** or become uncircumcised (**undo his circumcision**) by undergoing a painful operation, as some secular-minded Jews did in the first century (Josephus, *Ant.* xii. 241). These things are mere distractions. Paul zeroes in on what really matters: keeping the **commands** of God as those who belong to Him.

7:20-23 Paul again states the remain-as-you-are principle and illustrates it with a choice faced by slaves: to willingly remain a **slave** or to seek freedom. The apostle did not condemn slaves to a life of permanent slavery. **By all means take the opportunity** to become free if it presents itself, he said. But on the other hand, the fact of being a slave **should not be a concern**. His logic is thus: whether a Christian was free or a slave when he came to Christ, he owes lifetime obligations to the same master, Jesus Christ. In Roman parlance, a **freedman** was an emancipated slave, whereas a **free man** was one who had never been enslaved.

The Bible and Sexuality

Daniel L. Akin

God created men and women as sexual creatures. Therefore sex should be viewed as a good gift from a great God. Sex as God designed it is to be enjoyed within the covenant of marriage between a man and a woman. It should be good, exciting, intoxicating, powerful, and unifying.

This "one-flesh" relationship (Gn 2:24) is the most intense physical intimacy and the deepest spiritual unity possible between a man and woman. It should remind both partners of the even more remarkable oneness that the human spirit can experience with God in spiritual new birth through faith in Jesus Christ (Jn 3). God approves of sexual relations within marriage alone, where husband and wife are to serve each other and meet each other's physical needs in sexual intercourse (Pr 5:15-21). Paul indicates that sexual problems in marriage can hamper the Christian life, especially prayer (1Co 7:5). Both husband and wife have equal sexual needs which are to be met in marriage (1Co 7:3), and each is to pursue the needs of the other and not his or her own (Php 2:3-5).

Though the Bible is not a book on sex, it does contain a complete theology of sexuality: the purposes for sex, warnings against its misuse, and a beautiful picture of ideal physical intimacy (see especially the Song of Songs). Below are some of the Bible's most important teachings on human sexuality.

God's Purposes for Giving Us the Good Gift of Sex
* Knowledge (Gn 4:1)
* Intimate oneness (Gn 2:24)
* Comfort (Gn 24:67)
* The creation of life (Gn 1:28)
* Play and pleasure (Sg 2:8-17; 4:1-16)
* Avoiding temptation outside marriage (1Co 7:2-5)

God's Commands to the Husband
* He is to find satisfaction in his wife (Pr 5:19)
* He is to find joy in his wife (Ec 9:9)
* He is to concern himself with meeting her unique needs (Dt 24:5; 1Pt 3:7)

God's Commands to the Wife
* She is to be sexually available to her husband (1Co 7:3-5)
* She is to prepare and plan to capture her husband's heart (Sg 4:9-15)
* She is to show sexual interest in her husband (Sg 4:16; 5:2)
* She is to be sensitive to his unique masculine needs (Gn 24:67)

Biblical Principles to Govern Sex
* Sexual relations within marriage are holy and good. God encourages intimate relations and warns against their cessation (1Co 7:5).
* Pleasure in sexual relations is both healthy and expected. The bodies of both parties belong to the other (Pr 5:15-19; 1Co 7:4).
* Sexual pleasure is to be guided by the principle that one's sexuality is to be other-oriented. "Rights" over one's body are given in marriage to our mate (Php 2:3-4).
* Sexual relations are to be regular and normal. No exact number of times per week is prescribed, but the biblical principle is that both parties are to provide adequate sexual satisfaction so that both "burning" (sexual desire) and temptation to find satisfaction outside marriage are avoided (1Co 7:9).
* The principle of satisfaction means that each party is to provide sexual enjoyment (which is "due" him or her in marriage) as frequently as the other party requires. Other biblical principles (moderation, seeking to please another rather than oneself, etc.) also come into play. Consideration of one's mate is to guide one's requests for sexual relations.
* In accordance with the principle of "rights," there is to be no sexual bargaining between married persons ("I'll not have relations unless you . . ."). Neither party has the right to make such bargains. This is a form of "marital prostitution" and must be avoided.
* Sexual relations are equal and reciprocal. The Bible does not give the man superior rights to the woman or the woman superior rights to the man. Mutual service is the goal.
* Whatever is safe, pleasing, enjoyable, and satisfying to both is acceptable. The body of each belongs to the other (1Co 7:4). Neither should demand from the other what is painful, harmful, degrading, or distasteful to him or her.

of men. ²⁴•Brothers, each person should remain with God in whatever situation he was called.

About the Unmarried and Widows

²⁵About virgins: I have no command from the Lord, but I do give an opinion as one who by the Lord's mercy*ᵃ* is trustworthy.*ᵇ* ²⁶Therefore I consider this to be good because of the present distress: It is fine for a man to remain as he is. ²⁷Are you bound to a wife? Do not seek to be loosed. Are you loosed from a wife? Do not seek a wife. ²⁸However, if you do get married,*ᶜ* you have not sinned, and if a virgin marries, she has not sinned. But such people will have trouble in this life,*ᴬ* and I am trying to spare you. ²⁹And I say this, brothers: The time is limited,*ᵈ* so from now on those who have wives should be as though they had none, ³⁰those who weep as though they did not weep, those who rejoice*ᵉ* as though they did not rejoice, those who buy as though they did not possess, ³¹and those who use the world as though they did not make full use of it. For this world in its current form is passing away.*ᶠ*

³²I want you to be without concerns. An unmarried man is concerned about the things of the Lord—how he may please*ᵍ* the Lord. ³³But a married man is concerned about the

things of the world—how he may please his wife— ³⁴and his interests are divided. An unmarried woman or a virgin is concerned about the things of the Lord,*ʰ* so that she may be holy both in body and in spirit. But a married woman is concerned about the things of the world—how she may please her husband. ³⁵Now I am saying this for your own benefit, not to put a restraint on you, but because of what is proper and so that you may be devoted to the Lord without distraction.

³⁶But if any man thinks he is acting improperly toward his virgin,*ᴮ* if she is past marriageable age,*ᶜ* and so it must be, he can do what he wants. He is not sinning; they can get married. ³⁷But he who stands firm in his heart (who is under no compulsion, but has control over his own will*ⁱ*) and has decided in his heart to keep his own virgin, will do well. ³⁸So then he who marries*ᴰ* his virgin does well, but he who does not marry*ᴱ* will do better.

³⁹A wife is bound*ᶠ* as long as her husband is living. But if her husband dies, she is free to be married to anyone she wants—only in the Lord.*ᴳ* ⁴⁰But she is happier if she remains as she is, in my opinion. And I think that I also have the Spirit of God.

Food Offered to Idols

8 About food offered to idols:*ʲ* We know that "we all have knowledge."*ᴴ* Knowledge

*ᵃ*7:25 Mt 5:7; Mk 5:19; Lk 1:50
*ᵇ*Nm 12:7
*ᶜ*7:28 1Tm 5:14
*ᵈ*7:29 Rm 13:11
*ᵉ*7:30 Php 1:18
*ᶠ*7:31 Mk 13:7; 1Jn 2:8
*ᵍ*7:32 1Th 4:1
*ʰ*7:34 1Tm 5:5
*ⁱ*7:37 Jn 1:13
*ʲ*8:1 Ac 15:29; 21:25; 1Co 10:19; Rv 2:14,20

ᴬ7:28 Lit *in the flesh*   **ᴮ**7:36 = a man's fiancée, or his daughter, or his Levirate wife, or a celibate companion   **ᶜ**7:36 Or *virgin, if his passions are strong,*   **ᴰ**7:38 Or *marries off*   **ᴱ**7:38 Or *marry her off*   **ᶠ**7:39 Other mss add *by law*   **ᴳ**7:39 Only a believer   **ᴴ**8:1 See note at 1Co 6:12–13.

7:25-27 The focus of this entire discussion (vv. 25-27) is cast from the male perspective since ancient culture gave males primary responsibility for marital decisions. **About** serves as a marker denoting that Paul is now applying the remain-as-you-are principle (vv. 17-24) to the dilemma facing **virgins**. In this case Paul has **no command from the Lord**, but that does not lessen the impact of his teaching (i.e, **it is fine for a man to remain as he is**) since his **opinion** was made **trustworthy** by the Lord. "Virgins" in this context refers to betrothed, female virgins (cp. "virgins" for "betrothed wives," Lk 1:27; 2Co 11:2). Their dilemma was brought about by an unnamed **present distress** ("impending hardship"), possibly a famine that called the practicality of marital plans into doubt. Paul's talk of being **bound** to or **loosed** from a **wife** in verse 27 can be summarized as follows: (1) the man who was bound by promise to a betrothed virgin (essentially already his wife, given the seriousness of betrothal) was not to seek release from future obligations to consummate the marriage (v. 27a-b), and (2) the man who had already been released from obligation (to a virgin) was not to seek betrothal with another woman (v. 27c-d). In other words, keep your commitments and/or remain as you are.

7:28 Paul does not define **trouble in this life**. Possibly it refers to the responsibilities and hardships that can attend marriage and childrearing. Improperly handled, these can distract us from devotion to God; see verses 32-35.

7:29-31 Regardless of a person's situation, he should live

for the Lord. Two realities should heighten our emphasis on such a lifestyle of devotion: **the time is limited** and **the world . . . is passing away**.

7:32-40 In this section Paul shares his motivation for espousing the remain-as-you-are principle for single men, virgin daughters, their fathers, and widows. It comes down to this: The significant change in life status that would result from these choices, particularly during a time of "present distress" (v. 26), could pose a **distraction** from devotion **to the Lord**.

7:36-38 The identity of **any man** is often misunderstood. Paul is offering special counsel not to engaged bachelors but to fathers of unmarried daughters. They were to use wisdom in giving or withholding their daughters in marriage. The phrase **they can get married** probably refers to the father granting permission. **He who marries** (Gk "he who gives in marriage") refers to the father.

7:39-40 Newly widowed women were free to marry **in the Lord** (i.e., other believers), but Paul reiterates the virtue of the remain-as-you-are principle. Remaining **as she is** offered the widow the possibility of undistracted devotion to the Lord.

8:1a About indicates that Paul is answering a question the Corinthians had asked him in a previous letter (5:9; 7:1). By custom, Corinthians commonly dined in pagan temples (which were centers for civic activity) or else partook of

inflates with pride,[a] but love[b] builds up. [2] If anyone thinks he knows anything, he does not yet know it as he ought to know it.[c] [3] But if anyone loves God,[d] he is known[e] by Him.

[4] About eating food offered to idols, then, we know that "an idol is nothing in the world," and that "there is no God but one."[f] [5] For even if there are so-called gods,[g] whether in heaven or on earth—as there are many "gods" and many "lords"—

[6] yet for us there is one God, the Father.[h]
All things are from Him,[i]
and we exist for Him.
And there is one Lord, Jesus Christ.
All things are through Him,
and we exist through Him.[j]

[7] However, not everyone has this knowledge. In fact, some have been so used to idolatry up until now that when they eat food offered to an idol, their conscience, being weak, is defiled. [8] Food will not make us acceptable to God. We are not inferior if we don't eat, and we are not better if we do eat.[k] [9] But be careful that this right of yours in no way becomes a stumbling block[l] to the weak. [10] For if someone sees you, the one who has this knowledge, dining in an idol's temple, won't his weak conscience be encouraged to eat food offered to idols? [11] Then the weak person, the brother for whom Christ died,[m] is ruined[A,n] by your knowledge.[o] [12] Now when you sin like this against the •brothers

and wound their weak conscience, you are sinning against Christ. [13] Therefore, if food causes my brother to fall, I will never again eat meat,[p] so that I won't cause my brother to fall.

Paul's Example as an Apostle

9 Am I not free? Am I not an apostle? Have I not seen Jesus our Lord? Are you not my work in the Lord? [2] If I am not an apostle to others, at least I am to you, for you are the seal[q] of my apostleship in the Lord. [3] My defense to those who examine me is this: [4] Don't we have the right to eat and drink?[r] [5] Don't we have the right to be accompanied by a Christian wife[B] like the other apostles,[s] the Lord's brothers, and •Cephas?[t] [6] Or do Barnabas[u] and I alone have no right to refrain from working? [7] Who ever goes to war at his own expense?[v] Who plants a vineyard and does not eat its fruit? Or who shepherds a flock and does not drink the milk from the flock? [8] Am I saying this from a human perspective? Doesn't the law also say the same thing? [9] For it is written in the law of Moses, **Do not muzzle an ox[w] while it treads out grain.**[C,x] Is God really concerned with oxen? [10] Or isn't He really saying it for us? Yes, this is written for us,[y] because he who plows ought to plow in hope,[z] and he who threshes should do so in hope of sharing the crop.[aa] [11] If we have sown spiritual things for you, is it too much if we reap material benefits from you? [12] If others have this right to receive benefits from you, don't we even more?

a8:1 1Co 4:6
b1Co 13:1-13
c8:2 1Co 3:18; 13:8-12; 1Tm 6:4
d8:3 Dt 6:5; Lk 10:27
ePr 2:6
f8:4 Dt 6:4
g8:5 2Th 2:4
h8:6 Mt 5:16; 11:27; Lk 11:13; Jn 8:42; Eph 5:20
iPs 104:24; Col 1:16; Rv 3:14
jJn 1:3
k8:8 Rm 14:17
l8:9 Ex 23:33; Rm 14:20
m8:11 Jn 11:51; Rm 5:6,8; 8:34; 14:9,15; 1Co 15:3; Gl 2:21; Eph 5:2; 1Th 5:10
nHeb 6:8
oMt 25:45
p8:13 Dt 12:15
q9:2 Rv 5:1
r9:4 2Th 3:8-9
s9:5 Jd 17
tJn 1:42
u9:6 Ac 4:36
v9:7 Lk 3:14
w9:9 Lk 13:15
xDt 25:4
y9:10 Rm 4:24
zAc 23:6; 1Th 1:3
aa2Tm 2:6

meat portions that had been offered there. The Corinthian Christians wanted to know if it was permissible to eat **food offered to idols** as they reclined "at banquet" in a pagan temple ("dining in an idol's temple," v. 10) or feasted in a household that had received such things.

8:1b-3 Paul offers two guiding principles. First, **knowledge** (of Christian freedom) by itself makes a person arrogant, but **love builds up** believers. Second, it is not by knowledge that we are approved of God, but by our love for God we are **known by Him.** That is the knowledge that counts most. Thus no believer should allow his relatively unimportant knowledge to become a cause of arrogance.

8:4-6 Paul's answer that believers technically have the right to eat **food offered to idols** may surprise us, but the logic is sound: idols are a "non-reality" and **there is no God but one.** But his advice on this matter does not stop here (cp. vv. 7-13; and esp. 10:14-22).

8:7-8 Christian freedom should never be flaunted or wielded carelessly. Believers at Corinth needed to be mindful that some in their fellowship, being **so used to idolatry** and having as yet a **weak . . . conscience,** could be harmed by seeing Christians partake of food associated with idols.

8:8-13 For those who knew that idols were nothing, Paul stated the obvious: Eating food (even food sacrificed to idols) does not make believers unacceptable to God.

8:9 In language reminiscent of Jesus, Paul says the strong are not to be a **stumbling block** to the **weak** (cp. Mt 18:10). When misused, the liberty (Gk exousia; "right") of the strong can destroy a weaker person's allegiance to Christ.

8:10-12 If a **weak person** saw a knowledgeable believer dining in an **idol's temple,** he might attach religious significance to it and become confused about allegiance to Christ.

8:13 Self-limitation by more mature believers safeguards the Christian allegiance of new believers, especially in overtly pagan environments such as Corinth.

9:1-2 Paul offers a rhetorical reply to those who questioned ("examine," v. 3) his apostolic ministry.

9:3-6 Paul's "rights" as an apostle, which were exercised by other apostles, included: (1) the right to be compensated for his apostolic service; (2) the right to take a believing wife; and (3) the right to refrain from outside work, devoting himself entirely to ministry. Paul did not always choose to exercise these rights (e.g., Ac 18:1-3; 20:33-35; Php 4:14-17).

9:8-11 Paul uses a greater-to-lesser argument to justify his right to an allowance. If he has supplied **spiritual things** (the greater) to the Corinthians, surely he ought to receive **material benefits** (the lesser) from them in return.

9:12 Now Paul uses a lesser-to-greater argument to sup-

However, we have not made use of this right; instead we endure everything[a] so that we will not hinder the gospel of Christ. [13] Don't you know that those who perform the temple services eat the food from the temple, and those who serve at the altar[b] share in the offerings of the altar? [14] In the same way, the Lord has commanded that those who preach the gospel should earn their living by the gospel.[c]

[15] But I have used none of these rights, and I have not written this to make it happen that way for me. For it would be better for me to die than for anyone to deprive me of my boast! [16] For if I preach the gospel, I have no reason to boast, because an obligation is placed on me. And woe to me if I do not preach the gospel! [17] For if I do this willingly, I have a reward, but

if unwillingly, I am entrusted[d] with a stewardship. [18] What then is my reward? To preach the gospel and offer it free of charge and not make full use of my authority in the gospel.[e]

[19] Although I am a free man and not anyone's •slave, I have made myself a slave to everyone, in order to win[f] more people. [20] To the Jews I became like a Jew, to win Jews; to those under the law, like one under the law—though I myself am not under the law[A]—to win those under the law.[g] [21] To those who are without that law,[h] like one without the law—not being without God's law but within Christ's law—to win those without the law. [22] To the weak I became weak, in order to win the weak. I have become all things to all people, so that I may by every possible means save some.[i] [23] Now I

Cross references:
[a]9:12 Ac 20:33-35; 2Co 6:3-10; 11:7-12
[b]9:13 Lv 6:16,26; 7:6,31-32; Nm 5:9-10; 18:8-20,31; Dt 18:1
[c]9:14 Mt 10:8-10; Lk 10:7
[d]9:17 Lk 16:11
[e]9:18 2Co 11:7; 12:13
[f]9:19 1Pt 3:1
[g]9:20 Ac 16:3; 21:23-26
[h]9:21 Rm 2:12,14; Gl 2:3; 3:2
[i]9:22 Rm 11:14; 1Co 7:16

[A]9:20 Other mss omit *though I myself am not under law*

port his right to a living wage. If those who presently labored among the Corinthians received wages, how much more should the one who had founded the church? In response to those who said that Paul was illegitimate because the church did not support him (cp. 2Co 10; 12), he declared that he had yielded this right to a wage so he would **not hinder the gospel of Christ**.

9:14 The Lord has commanded may refer to Luke 10:4-8, where among other things Jesus says, "The [gospel] worker is worthy of his wages."

9:16-17 An obligation is placed on me alludes to Paul's commission at Damascus as a "chosen instrument" (Ac 9:15) who had been given a **stewardship** to discharge the message of the gospel to the nations (4:1). Paul had not chosen missions work as a profession. Rather, God chose it for him.

9:18 Though Paul felt bound as Christ's slave to fulfill his

commission (Rm 1:1), his obligation to preach the gospel was rewarding to him. He took such pleasure in it that he could willingly forego his right to compensation.

9:19 Paul as a **free man** (cp. v. 1) put forward his motive for making himself **a slave** (lit "I enslaved myself"). He did it **in order to win more people**.

9:20-22 Paul's "self-imposed slavery" gave him the freedom to accommodate Jews and Gentiles alike and therefore speak the gospel in a forthright manner, unhindered by cultural hang-ups. He exemplified this freedom among Jews when he circumcised Timothy (whose mother was Jewish) to maximize the gospel witness in Jewish areas (Ac 16:3). Among Gentiles who were **without the law**, he yielded his rights in order to maximize the gospel's advance. For example, he would not take a wage if taking a wage would cause those "outside the law" to stumble. The phrase **not being without God's law but within Christ's law** refers to

A training track at Olympia. Paul used athletic training and competition as a picture of the endurance and perseverance of Christians (9:24-27).

do all this because of the gospel, so I may become a partner in its benefits.[A]

[24] Don't you know that the runners in a stadium all race,[a] but only one receives the prize? Run in such a way to win the prize.[b] [25] Now everyone who competes exercises self-control[c] in everything. However, they do it to receive a crown[d] that will fade away,[e] but we a crown that will never fade away. [26] Therefore I do not run like one who runs aimlessly or box like one beating the air. [27] Instead, I discipline my body and bring it under strict control, so that after preaching to others, I myself will not be disqualified.[f]

Warnings from Israel's Past

10 Now I want to know, •brothers, that our fathers[g] were all under the cloud,[h] all passed through the sea,[i] [2] and all were baptized[j] into Moses[k] in the cloud and in the sea. [3] They all ate the same spiritual food,[l] [4] and all drank the same spiritual drink. For they drank from a spiritual rock[m] that followed them, and that rock was Christ.[n] [5] But God was not pleased with most of them, for they were struck down in the wilderness.[o]

[6] Now these things became examples for us, so that we will not desire[p] evil things as they did.[B,q] [7] Don't become idolaters[r] as some of them were; as it is written, **The people sat down to eat and drink, and got up to play.**[C,D,s]

[8] Let us not commit sexual immorality[t] as some of them did,[E] and in a single day 23,000 people fell dead.[u] [9] Let us not test Christ as some of them did[F] and were destroyed by snakes.[v] [10] Nor should we complain[w] as some of them did,[G,x] and were killed by the destroyer.[H,y] [11] Now these things happened to them as examples, and they were written as a warning to us,[z] on whom the ends of the ages[aa] have come.[ab] [12] So, whoever thinks he stands must be careful not to fall.[ac] [13] No temptation has overtaken you except what is common to humanity. God is faithful,[ad] and He will not allow you to be tempted beyond what you are able, but with the temptation He will also provide a way of escape[ae] so that you are able to bear it.

Warning against Idolatry

[14] Therefore, my dear friends, flee from idolatry. [15] I am speaking as to wise people. Judge for yourselves what I say. [16] The cup[af] of blessing[ag] that we give thanks for, is it not a sharing in the blood of Christ? The bread[ah] that we break, is it not a sharing in the body of Christ? [17] Because there is one bread, we who are many are one[ai] body, for all of us share that one bread. [18] Look at the people of Israel.[I] Do not those who eat the sacrifices

Cross-references
a 9:24 Jd 3
b Col 2:18
c 9:25 Gl 5:23
d 1Pt 5:4
e 1Pt 1:18
f 9:27 Heb 6:8
g 10:1 Ps 44:1; Ac 7:11
h Ex 13:21
i Ex 14:29
j 10:2 Ac 22:16
k Ps 77:20; Mt 8:4; Heb 3:2
l 10:3 Ex 16:31
m 10:4 Ex 17:6; Nm 20:7-13
n Jn 4:14; 6:30-35
o 10:5 Jd 5
p 10:6 Mt 27:23; Jms 4:2
q Nm 11:4,33-34; Ps 78:18; 106:14
r 10:7 Eph 5:5
s Ex 32:6
t 10:8 1Co 6:18; Rv 2:14,20; 17:2; 18:3,9
u Nm 25:1-18; Ps 106:29
v 10:9 Nm 21:6
w 10:10 Jn 6:41; Jd 16
x Nm 16:41-50
y Ex 12:23; 2Sm 24:16; 1Ch 21:15; Ps 78:49
z 10:11 Ps 102:18
aa Mk 13:7
ab Mk 10:30
ac 10:12 Pr 24:16; Heb 6:8
ad 10:13 Nm 12:7
ae 2Pt 2:9
af 10:16 Mt 26:27; Mk 14:23; Lk 22:17,20; 1Co 11:25-26
ag Mk 6:41; Gl 3:14
ah Mt 26:26; Mk 14:22; Lk 22:19; Ac 2:42,46; 20:7
ai 10:17 Jn 11:52; Eph 4:4

A 9:23 Lit *partner of it*   B 10:6 Lit *they desired*   C 10:7 Or *to dance*   D 10:7 Ex 32:6   E 10:8 Lit *them committed sexual immorality*   F 10:9 Lit *them tested*   G 10:10 Lit *them complained*   H 10:10 Or *the destroying angel*   I 10:18 Lit *Look at Israel according to the flesh*

---

him as one who had the right under God's law to receive a wage (cp. 9:8-10), yet among Gentiles he yielded that right.

9:24-27 Like hard-driven runners and boxers, Paul had a single-minded focus. His exercise of **self-control** was aimed at keeping him from being **disqualified**. "Disqualified" does not mean loss of salvation, which Paul elsewhere said is impossible (Rm 8:38-39; see also Jn 10:28-30), but rather failure to fulfill his God-given commission to evangelize the nations (Ac 9:15; 13:2; Rm 1:1).

9:24-26a If athletes compete by the rules and master **self-control in everything**, all for the purpose of winning a **crown that will fade away**, how much more should Christians discipline themselves for a **crown that will never fade away**?

9:26b-27 Paul viewed his boxing opponent as his own **body**. When it resisted giving up rights and liberties, he brought it under **strict control** (lit "I enslave it"). Paul had already stated that he endured everything (v. 12), made himself a slave to all (v. 19), and exercised self-control (v. 25) to allow a hearing for the gospel (by not taking a wage).

10:1-5 To make vivid the possibility of disqualification, Paul drew on the exodus (Ex 12ff). Those Hebrews enjoyed unique access to God (**were all under the cloud** of God's presence and **were baptized into Moses**), and yet **most of them . . . were struck down**. The phrase **they all**

ate the same spiritual food points back to God's daily provision for Israel in the wilderness (Dt 8:14-15).

10:6-10 The wilderness generation served as a cautionary example to the Corinthian church, which was on the verge of provoking God. The Corinthians apparently were boasting that they could please the Lord (cp. v. 12) and at the same time partake of food and fellowship at pagan religious clubs (vv. 6,14-22). The Corinthian motto was: "everything is permissible" (v. 23). Paul called them to remember the OT examples. The phrase **now these things** refers to the idolatrous activity of the wilderness generation that provoked God to cut them down (v. 5). The prohibition **don't become idolaters as some of them were** is emphatic in the Greek and becomes the paradigm for three exhortations: (1) do **not commit sexual immorality** (cp. Nm 25:1-18, esp. v. 9); (2) do **not test Christ** (cp. Nm 21:5-6); and (3) do not **complain** (cp. Ex 12:23; Nm 16:41-50). In all three OT examples, God judged and destroyed the people for their sins.

10:11-14 God's judgment on the wilderness generation served as a cautionary tale for any Corinthian believer who thought he was strong enough to participate in pagan religious functions without compromise and escape judgment at **the ends of the ages**. Paul called the Corinthians to recognize their impending accountability before the Lord (1:7-8).

participate in what is offered on the altar?[a] [19] What am I saying then? That food offered to idols is anything, or that an idol is anything? [20] No, but I do say that what they[A] sacrifice, they sacrifice to demons and not to God. I do not want you to participate with demons! [21] You cannot drink the cup of the Lord and the cup of demons. You cannot share in the Lord's table and the table of demons. [22] Or are we provoking the Lord to jealousy? Are we stronger than He?[b]

Christian Liberty

[23] "Everything is permissible,"[B,C] but not everything is helpful. "Everything is permissible,"[C] but not everything builds up. [24] No one should seek his own good, but the good of the other person.[c]

[25] Eat everything that is sold in the meat market, asking no questions for conscience' sake, [26] **for the earth is the Lord's,[d] and all that is in it.**[D,e] [27] If one of the unbelievers invites you over and you want to go, eat everything

[a]10:18 Gn 8:20; Lv 1:5; Nm 3:26; Dt 12:27; 1Sm 2:28; 1Ch 6:49; Ps 26:6; Ezk 8:15; Heb 7:13
[b]10:22 Ec 6:10
[c]10:24 Mk 10:45; Php 2:4
[d]10:26 Mk 13:19
[e]Ps 24:1

A 10:20 Other mss read *Gentiles*   B 10:23 Other mss add *for me*   C 10:23 See note at 1Co 6:12–13.   D 10:26 Ps 24:1

10:16-17 Paul wanted the Corinthians to know that participants at the Lord's Supper represent a unified body that is dependent on the death of Christ. The phrase **because there is one bread, we who are many are one body** refers to the individual members who make up one corporate body, the church (12:12-27). United participation as one body at the Lord's Supper points to unified fellowship brought about by Christ's death as well as each individual believer's union with Christ.

10:18-22 Actual "idolatry" (v. 14) is in view here, not merely partaking of foods offered to idols (8:1-13). Participation in idolatrous rites is a violation of the believer's union with Christ and thus with the one-body relationship that they had with other believers. Therefore, the Lord's Supper and the table of demons are mutually exclusive.

10:18-19 People of Israel (lit "Israel according to the flesh") in the present context refers ultimately to the sinful wilderness generation. Likewise, his reference to **the altar** probably alludes to Ex 32:5-6 (cited in 1Co 10:7), which recounts Aaron's building of an altar in front of the idol, the golden calf.

10:20-21 Paul prohibited participation in pagan ritualistic meals because this involved intimacy with **demons**. He continued to affirm the non-reality of idols as deities (8:4-6), but demons are both real and powerful. He did not want the Corinthians to discount demonic presence at the "idols' table." The word **they** refers back to idolatrous Israel in the wilderness (cp. v. 18, "the people of Israel") when they overlooked demonic presence, just as the Corinthian believers were tempted to do.

10:22 Paul called the Corinthian believers to remember the example of Israel when they provoked the Lord to **jealousy** by their idolatry, which resulted in a plague (Ex 32:33-35).

10:23-11:1 This section concludes the train of thought that began in 8:1, summarizing the principle that believers should limit the exercise of their freedom ("knowledge," 8:1) out of consideration for those who have weak consciences.

10:23-24 The overriding principle of 8:1–11:1 is to seek **the good of the other person**. Believers must conscribe their actions with the aim of benefiting others, especially where this can lead to salvation for nonbelievers (cp. vv. 32-33). All believers should adopt limits on their rights and freedoms.

10:25-26 In what may seem a surprising twist, Paul said seeking "the good of the other person" (v. 24) meant a believer who objected to buying meat that had been sacrificed to idols should not interrogate the meat sellers in order to

The excavations in Corinth show the shops in the Agora. Here in the marketplace, meat that had been offered in the worship of idols was sold. Meat that was sold in this fashion would be bought and then served as a part of a regular family meal. This situation is reflected in Paul's comments in 10:23–11:1. Some of the shops in the Agora used cold, running spring water to keep perishables fresh.

that is set before you, without raising questions of conscience. [28]But if someone says to you, "This is food offered to an idol," do not eat it,[a] out of consideration for the one who told you, and for conscience' sake.[A] [29]I do not mean your own conscience, but the other person's. For why is my freedom judged[b] by another person's conscience? [30]If I partake with thanks,[c] why am I slandered because of something I give thanks for?

[31]Therefore, whether you eat or drink, or whatever you do, do everything for God's glory.[d] [32]Give no offense[e] to the Jews or the Greeks or the church of God, [33]just as I also try to please all people in all things, not seeking my own profit, but the profit of many,[f] so

[a]10:28 Lk 10:8
[b]10:29 Lk 6:37
[c]10:30 Mk 8:6;
Rm 1:8
[d]10:31 Mk
10:37; Lk 9:32;
Jn 17:24; 2Co
3:18; 2Pt 3:18
[e]10:32 Ac 24:16;
Php 1:10
[f]10:33 Mk 10:45
[g]11:1 Php 2:5;
1Pt 2:21
[h]11:2 2Th 2:15;
3:6
[i]Jd 3
[j]11:3 Eph 1:22;
4:15; Col 1:18;
2:10,19
[k]Gn 3:16; Eph
5:23
[l]Co 3:23
[m]11:4 1Pt 3:16
[n]11:5 Dt
21:11-12

11 that they may be saved. [1]Imitate me, as I also imitate Christ.[g]

Instructions about Head Coverings

[2]Now I praise you[B] because you always remember me and keep the traditions[h] just as I delivered[i] them to you. [3]But I want you to know that Christ is the head[j] of every man, and the man is the head of the woman,[C,k] and God is the head of Christ.[l] [4]Every man who prays or prophesies with something on his head dishonors[m] his head. [5]But every woman who prays or prophesies with her head uncovered dishonors her head, since that is one and the same as having her head shaved.[n] [6]So if a woman's head[D] is not covered, her hair should

---

[A]10:28 Other mss add *"For the earth is the Lord's and all that is in it."*   [B]11:2 Other mss add *brothers,*   [C]11:3 Or *the husband is the head of the wife*   [D]11:6 Lit *a woman*

---

certify that the meat had no association with idolatry. Why? Most likely because such questions would seem hostile and alienate the nonbelieving Greeks at Corinth, thus hindering the gospel's advance. Paul offered scriptural support for this position from Ps 24:1: "**The earth is the Lord's, and all that is in it.**" Therefore, partake of the meat out of gratitude and a clear conscience.

10:28-29a Paul prohibited eating meat if someone bothered explicitly to point out that it had been **offered to an idol** (Gk *hierothutos*; "meat devoted to a divinity"). This rare Greek term was used by pagans to designate meat devoted to a particular god. In this situation, the food's history did matter because the person who pointed it out (whether they be a nonbelieving Gentile or a Christian of weak conscience) apparently felt that a Christian eating such meat would be compromising his allegiance to Christ.

10: 29b-30 After a parenthetical interruption that explains an exception to one's freedom (vv. 28-29a), these rhetorical questions introduce the basis for the believer's freedom to

kephale

Greek Pronunciation	[keh fah LAY]
HCSB Translation	head
Uses in 1 Corinthians	10
Uses in the NT	75
Focus passage	1 Corinthians 11:3

The Greek noun *kephale* means *head* and usually refers to that part of the body for humans or animals. In the NT, *kephale* is also used figuratively in several passages, especially in Paul's writings and Revelation.

Paul used the body as a metaphor for the church. In 1Co 12, Paul explained that unity in the church is promoted through mutual dependence and cooperation among the individual members who make up Christ's body (vv. 12-27). This metaphor is modified in Ephesians and Colossians to emphasize the dependence that the body has on its *head*, who is Christ (Eph 1:22; 4:15; 5:23; Col 1:18; 2:19). Paul taught the husband's role as *head* of the home in two passages. Just as Christ is the *Head* of His church, so the husband is the *head* of his wife (Eph 5:23). Divine and human headship are joined in Paul's hierarchy: God is the *head* of Christ; Christ is the *head* of man; man is the *head* of woman (1Co 11:3). A wife's subordination to her husband does not mean that she is inferior to him, for Christ is subordinate to the Father but is also equal with Him (see Jn 5:18; 1Co 15:27-28; Php 2:6).

eat whatever is given them without questions of conscience.

10:31-33 He or she who wishes to **do everything for God's glory** cannot succeed if they act in disregard for others. Paul was always relinquishing his rights for the spiritual **profit** of others—**that they may be saved**.

11:1 Paul's admonition to **imitate** him was justified insomuch as he was an apt imitator of **Christ**.

11:3 Paul issued a principle for application in corporate worship—the principle of voluntary submission to authority. As Christ is the **head** over the church, He certainly has supreme authority over **every man** (cp. 3:23; "you belong to Christ"). The phrase "head of every man" means "authority over" and fits the letter's dominant theme of submission to Christ. **God is the head of Christ** refers to the Father's authority over the incarnate Messiah, who as the God-man voluntarily submitted to God.

11:4 The situation in this verse assumes a public setting where corporate worship was taking place. Paul applied the principle ("Christ is the head of every man") to the praying man. Outward manifestations of piety should not dishonor a believing man's **head** ("Christ"). The phrase **with something on his head** is literally "having down alongside the head." This refers not to a hat but to the Roman practice of pulling down the toga over the head while bowing for pagan worship, to prevent distractions. Because of the association of this practice with pagan worship, a male believer dishonored his true head ("Christ") when he covered his physical head with the toga. By imitating pagan practice, he shamed Christ and himself.

11:5a In the first century, a woman would speak **with her head uncovered** only in private settings. For example, women sometimes led prayer with their "head uncovered" at pagan clubs meeting in private homes. Paul did not give a reason why women in the church at Corinth were uncovered. It may be that they brought into the church religious practices that paralleled habits in the pagan meetings.

11:5b-6 Paul explains why a Corinthian woman's uncovered head dishonored her head. A woman who prayed or prophesied with her head uncovered was **one and the same** with the one **having her head shaved** (Gk *te exureymeney*). Paul equated the shame of a "head uncovered" (imitating the practice in pagan private religious clubs; see note at v. 5a) with the shame of a person who publicly expressed pagan

be cut off. But if it is disgraceful for a woman to have her hair cut off or her head shaved, she should be covered.

[7] A man, in fact, should not cover his head, because he is God's image[a] and glory,[b] but woman is man's glory. [8] For man did not come from woman, but woman came from man.[c] [9] And man was not created for woman, but woman for man. [10] This is why a woman should have a symbol of authority on her head, because of the angels. [11] In the Lord, however, woman is not independent of man, and man is not independent of woman. [12] For just as woman came from man, so man comes through woman, and all things come from God.[d]

[13] Judge[e] for yourselves: Is it proper for a woman to pray to God with her head uncovered? [14] Does not even nature itself teach[f] you that if a man has long hair it is a disgrace[g] to him, [15] but that if a woman has long hair, it is her glory?[h] For her hair is given to her[A] as a covering. [16] But if anyone wants to argue about this, we have no other[B] custom, nor do the churches of God.

The Lord's Supper

[17] Now in giving the following instruction I do not praise you, since you come together not for the better but for the worse. [18] For to

begin with, I hear that when you come together as a church there are divisions among you, and in part I believe it. [19] There must, indeed, be factions[i] among you, so that those who are approved may be recognized among you. [20] Therefore, when you come together, it is not really to eat the Lord's Supper.[j] [21] For at the meal, each one eats his own supper ahead of others. So one person is hungry while another gets drunk! [22] Don't you have houses to eat and drink in? Or do you look down on the church of God and embarrass those who have nothing? What should I say to you? Should I praise you? I do not praise you for this!

[23] For I received from the Lord what I also passed on to you:[k] On the night when He was betrayed, the Lord Jesus took bread, [24] gave thanks, broke it, and said,[C] "This is My body, which is[D] for you. Do this in remembrance of Me."[l]

[25] In the same way, after supper He also took the cup and said, "This cup is the new covenant[m] established by My blood.[n] Do this, as often as you drink it, in remembrance of Me." [26] For as often as you eat this bread and drink the cup, you proclaim the Lord's death[o] until He comes.[p]

Self-Examination

[27] Therefore, whoever eats the bread or

Cross references (center column):
[a]11:7 Gn 1:27
[b]Mk 10:37; Lk 9:32; Jn 17:24; 2Co 3:18; 2Pt 3:18
[c]11:8 Gn 2:21-23; 1Tm 2:13
[d]11:12 Ps 104:24; Rv 3:14
[e]11:13 Jn 5:22-30
[f]11:14 Mt 28:20; Ac 4:2; 2Tm 4:11
[g]2Co 6:8
[h]11:15 Php 3:19
[i]11:19 2Pt 2:1
[j]11:20 Mt 26:26-29; Mk 14:22-25; Lk 22:14-20; 1Co 10:14-22
[k]11:23 Jd 3
[l]11:24 Lk 22:19
[m]11:25 Lk 22:20
[n]Jn 6:54
[o]11:26 Php 2:8; 3:10
[p]Mk 8:38

[A]11:15 Other mss omit *to her* [B]11:16 Or *no such* [C]11:24 Other mss add *"Take, eat.* [D]11:24 Other mss add *broken*

---

dedication (i.e., to have her hair cut off or her head shaved). Pagan women at Corinth sometimes sheared their hair and dedicated their locks as a token of worship or fulfillment of a vow to a god. In the Corinthian setting, the "uncovered head" paralleled practices in pagan clubs and thus blurred the divisions between devotion to the true God and false gods, resulting in dishonor to a believing woman's husband and to Christ.

11:7a A man's uncovered head honored his head because it permitted the immediacy of his reflection of the **image and glory** of God, perhaps especially in light of the fact that man was created first (Gn 1:27; 2:7). Therefore, **he should not cover his head** in imitation of pagan practice, which viewed human creation as an ignoble creation of warring and vain gods.

11:7b-9 Paul's second reason for saying a woman's uncovered head dishonored her head is that the first woman was created from man (Gn 2:21-22). Woman completes man in God's created order in the sense that man mirrors the image of God, and woman reflects **man's glory**. This does not mean woman is inferior to man. She completes God's creation of man as male and female (Gn 1:27), and brings glory to man (Gn 2:23).

11:10 This third reason why a woman's uncovered head dishonored her head is difficult to interpret. Perhaps the church's witness to the angelic hosts would be adversely affected by an uncovered female head. The phrase **authority on her head** seems to refer to an outward symbol that signified to **the angels** her deference to leadership.

11:11-15 These verses are obscure and have yielded various

interpretations. It is best that interpreters remain tentative in their conclusions.

11:17-18 Paul chided the Corinthian believers for their inappropriate, divisive behavior when they came **together as a church** (cp. v. 20). The word "church" refers to their assembly as a unified, corporate body. In the NT, "church" never refers to a building or place of meeting.

11:19 The **approved . . . among you** refers to those who were not the cause of divisions within the body. Their behavior was exemplary during a time of strife.

11:20-22 To the church's shame, the scene Paul describes seems typical of a pagan setting. Instead of coming together in unity, members were focused on their own selfish desires.

11:23-25 **I received from the Lord** most likely means Paul was given a special revelation from Jesus about this matter. For other instances where Paul received such revelation, see Ac 18:9ff; 22:18; 23:11; 27:23-25; 2Co 12:7. Christ's selflessness in giving His life for others stood in stark contrast to the Corinthians' selfishness during the Lord's Supper.

11:26 The phrase **as often as you eat this bread and drink the cup** emphasizes that the solemn remembrance of Christ's death is a corporate declaration of "Jesus Christ and Him crucified" (2:2) **until He comes** again.

11:27 Since the Lord's Supper is a commemoration of Christ's suffering and death on our behalf, to participate in an unworthy manner is to sin **against the body and blood of the Lord**.

drinks the cup of the Lord in an unworthy
way will be •guilty of sin against the body[A] and
blood of the Lord. 28 So a man should examine
himself; in this way he should eat the bread
and drink from the cup. 29 For whoever eats
and drinks without recognizing the body,[B]
eats and drinks judgment[a] on himself. 30 This
is why many are sick and ill among you, and
many have fallen •asleep.[b] 31 If we were properly evaluating ourselves, we would not be
judged, 32 but when we are judged,[c] we are disciplined by the Lord, so that we may not be
condemned[d] with the •world.
33 Therefore, my •brothers, when you come
together to eat, wait for one another. 34 If anyone is hungry, he should eat at home, so that
when you gather together you will not come
under judgment. And I will give instructions
about the other matters whenever I come.[e]

Diversity of Spiritual Gifts

12 Now concerning what comes from the
Spirit:[C] •brothers, I do not want you to
be unaware. 2 You know that when you were
pagans, you used to be led off to the idols[f] that
could not speak.[g] 3 Therefore I am informing
you that no one speaking by the Spirit of God
says, "Jesus is cursed," and no one can say,
"Jesus is Lord," except by the Holy Spirit.
4 Now there are different gifts,[h] but the same
Spirit. 5 There are different ministries, but the
same Lord. 6 And there are different activities,
but the same God activates each gift in each
person.[D] 7 A demonstration of the Spirit is given
to each person[i] to produce what is beneficial:

8 to one[j] is given a message of wisdom[k]
through the Spirit,
to another, a message of knowledge
by the same Spirit,
9 to another, faith by the same Spirit,
to another, gifts of healing[l]
by the one Spirit,
10 to another, the performing of miracles,[m]
to another, prophecy,[n]
to another, distinguishing
between spirits,[o]
to another, different kinds
of •languages,
to another, interpretation
of languages.

11 But one and the same Spirit is active in all
these, distributing to each person as He wills.

Unity Yet Diversity in the Body

12 For as the body is one[p] and has many
parts, and all the parts of that body, though
many, are one body—so also is Christ.[q] 13 For
we were all baptized by[E] one Spirit into one
body—whether Jews or Greeks, whether
•slaves or free—and we were all made to drink
of one Spirit.[r] 14 So the body is not one part

[a] 11:29 Mk 12:40; 1Jn 5:16
[b] 11:30 Jn 11:11; Ac 7:60; 1Th 4:13-15
[c] 11:32 Jn 5:22-30
[d] Mt 12:41; Jn 5:22
[e] 11:34 1Co 4:19
[f] 12:2 1Co 8:4
[g] Ac 8:32; 1Co 14:10; 2Pt 2:16
[h] 12:4 Rm 12:6; 1Co 14:1; Eph 4:8; Heb 2:4; 1Pt 4:10
[i] 12:7 Jms 4:5
[j] 12:8-10 Rm 12:7-8; Eph 4:11; 1Pt 4:11
[k] 12:8 1Co 2:6-7
[l] 12:9 Lk 13:32; Ac 4:22,30; 10:38
[m] 12:10 Ac 19:11
[n] 1Co 13:2
[o] 1Jn 4:1-3
[p] 12:12 Jn 11:52
[q] Eph 4:4
[r] 12:13 Gl 3:28; Eph 2:13-18; Col 3:11

[A] 11:27 Lit *be guilty of the body* [B] 11:29 Other mss read *drinks unworthily, not discerning the Lord's body* [C] 12:1 Or *concerning spiritual things*, or *spiritual gifts* [D] 12:6 Lit *God acts all things in all* [E] 12:13 Or *with*, or *in*

11:28-29 A person must examine himself with respect to Christ's sacrifice for believers and the relationship each believer has within the corporate body. The phrase **whoever eats and drinks without recognizing the body** is a solemn wordplay on the word "body." Believers are to recognize that Jesus selflessly sacrificed His body for others and that this sacrifice was designed to make Christians a selfless corporate body.

11:30-32 If the Corinthian believers judged and examined themselves correctly, this would avert judgment from God within the corporate body. **Asleep** is a term Paul and other biblical authors use for physical death (cp. 15:18; Jn 11:11; Ac 7:60).

11:33-34 By way of a summary, Paul directed the Corinthians to **wait** on the arrival of all the believers before partaking of the Lord's Supper. This act of self-control would prevent unnecessary divisions within the corporate body.

12:1-3 Allegiance to **Jesus** as "exclusive **Lord**" is made possible only through the working of **the Holy Spirit**. Pagan Gentiles **led off to the idols** in ceremonial procession could profess Jesus as one of many deities or else curse Him as a fraud, but never could they abandon their false gods and devote themselves to Jesus unless the **Spirit of God** made it possible.

12:4-11a The Spirit according to His will distributes a diversity of gifts to the body for its common benefit. Verses 4-6 and the beginning of verse 11 have a variety of wordplays that frame this section.

12:4-6. The same triune God brings about a variety of gifts and manifests diverse ministries within the corporate body. The **different gifts . . . ministries**, and **activities** within the unified church reflect the essential unity and unified work of the persons of the Godhead (vv. 6,11,24,27-28)—the same **Spirit**, the same **Lord**, the same **God**.

12:7 Each **demonstration of the Spirit** in a believer **is given** by God for the mutual benefit of the whole body of believers (cp. vv. 12-31). "Demonstration of the Spirit" refers to gifts, ministries, and activities made possible by the Spirit's enabling power. Similar lists of spiritual gifts are given in verse 28; Rm 12:6-8; Eph 4:11; and 1Pt 4:10-11.

12:11 The phrase **one and the same Spirit is active in all these** refers to the Spirit's supernatural working through a diversity of gifted people to produce one cohesive relationship (cp. v. 7, "what is beneficial").

12:12 Christ is compressed language for "the body of Christ," the church (cp. vv. 27-28).

12:13 To illustrate that individual believers become identified as **one body** of Christ (i.e., as the unified church), Paul borrowed imagery from the practice of dying various cloths by immersing them in the same dye vat. **All** believers are **baptized** into one body and are **made to drink of one Spirit**.

but many. ¹⁵If the foot should say, "Because I'm not a hand, I don't belong to the body," in spite of this it still belongs to the body. ¹⁶And if the ear should say, "Because I'm not an eye, I don't belong to the body," in spite of this it still belongs to the body. ¹⁷If the whole body were an eye, where would the hearing be? If the whole body were an ear, where would the sense of smell be? ¹⁸But now God has placed each one of the parts in one body just as He wanted.ᵃ ¹⁹And if they were all the same part, where would the body be? ²⁰Now there are many parts, yet one body.

²¹So the eye cannot say to the hand, "I don't need you!" Or again, the head can't say to the feet, "I don't need you!" ²²But even more, those parts of the body that seem to be weaker are necessary. ²³And those parts of the body that we think to be less honorable,ᵇ we clothe these with greater honor, and our unpresentable parts have a better presentation. ²⁴But our presentable parts have no need of clothing. Instead, God has put the body together, giv-

ing greater honor to the less honorable, ²⁵so that there would be no divisionᶜ in the body, but that the members would have the same concern for each other. ²⁶So if one member suffers, all the members suffer with it; if one member is honored, all the members rejoice with it.

²⁷Now you are the body of Christ,ᵈ and individual members of it. ²⁸And God has placed these in the church:ᵉ

first apostles, second prophets,
    third teachers,ᶠ next miracles,ᵍ
    then gifts of healing,ʰ helping,
    managing, various kinds
        of languages.
²⁹ Are all apostles? Are all prophets?
    Are all teachers? Do all do miracles?
³⁰ Do all have gifts of healing?
    Do all speak in other languages?
    Do all interpret?ⁱ

³¹But desireʲ the greater gifts. And I will show you an even better way.

ᵃ12:18 Ps 143:10; Pr 16:9; Jn 5:30; Gl 1:4; Eph 1:9; 1Jn 2:17
ᵇ12:23 Mk 6:4; 1Pt 2:7
ᶜ12:25 1Co 1:10
ᵈ12:27 Eph 1:23; Col 1:18
ᵉ12:28 Mt 16:18; 1Co 14:4; Rv 1:4
ᶠEph 4:11; Jms 3:1
ᵍMk 13:22
ʰ1Co 12:9
ⁱ12:30 Lk 24:27
ʲ12:31 Nm 25:13; Jms 4:2

12:14-20 Paul tackles the problem of self-deprecation for believers who view themselves as less useful to the corporate body.

12:15-16 Paul personified body parts as speakers to express the absurdity of envy and self-deprecation among members of the physical human body. Some Corinthians apparently fell into grading the gifts, attaching importance to public, showy gifts (such as the gift of utterance), and relative unimportance to less observable gifts.

12:17 A body reduced to just one member would be grotesque and useless.

12:18 The dispersion and diversification of gifts is no accident. God Himself has given them **just as He wanted**.

soma

Greek Pronunciation	[SOH mah]
HCSB Translation	body
Uses in 1 Corinthians	46
Uses in the NT	142
Focus passage	1 Corinthians 12:12-27

The Greek noun *soma* means *body* and usually refers to the physical element of a person's existence. The *soma* needs to be clothed (Mt 6:25), can be killed (Mt 10:28), can be thrown into hell (Mt 5:29-30), can experience resuscitation (Ac 9:40), and will experience resurrection (1Co 15:35-44; see Mt 27:52; Jn 2:19-21). Paul often referred to the *soma* as the vehicle for sinful actions (Rm 1:24; 6:6,12; 8:10,13; 1Co 6:18), but he also used the term figuratively. In Romans 12 the church is "one body in Christ" (v. 5); in 1 Corinthians 12 the church is the *body* of Christ (v. 27); in Ephesians and Colossians, the church is the *body* with Christ as its Head (Eph 1:22-23; 5:23; Col 1:18; 2:19).

The disunity among the believers in Corinth forced Paul to deal with this problem by expounding at length on the *body* metaphor. Believers in the church are the individual parts that make up Christ's *body*. All parts of Christ's *body* must work together for the *body* to function properly.

12:19-20 **Many parts, yet one body** encapsulates our identity as individuals enfolded into the corporate body of Christ.

12:21-22 Counter to Corinthian misperceptions, the **weaker** body parts **are necessary**.

12:23-26 We clothe **unpresentable parts** (private areas) of the human body, which we regard as **less honorable**, thus according them **greater honor**. Similarly, God has arranged the body of Christ in such a way that the "less honorable" members are accorded "greater honor." Humility is a pinnacle value in the kingdom of God (Mt 18:3).

12:27 **Individual members** (Gk *ek merous*; "part by part") becomes key in chapter 13 (cp. *ek merous*, translated "in part" at 13:9; "partial" at 13:10; "in part" at 13:12). It occurs nowhere else in the NT.

12:28 **Church** here refers not just to the local body of believers at Corinth but to the universal church, composed of all believers everywhere and from every age. **God has placed** emphasizes that no one can justly appoint themselves to positions within the body. The appointments are God's prerogative alone. **First . . . second . . . third** gives us a glimpse at the priority of roles during the early church era. All members are equal, but no church would ever have been founded apart from the Lord's appointed **apostles**.

12:29-30 In a series of rhetorical questions, Paul emphasizes that no gift is normative.

12:31a Paul concludes by exhorting the Corinthian church to emphasize the **greater gifts** that have more direct edification for the assembled body.

12:31b-13:3 **And I will show you an even better way** introduces the discussion about the relationship of love to the exercise of gifts within the corporate body. Paul uses three hyperboles to show that gifts without love are pointless.

12:31b Paul established the preeminence of love (13:1-13) when exercising gifts.

Love: The Superior Way

13 If I speak human or angelic •languages
but do not have love,[a]
I am a sounding gong[b]
or a clanging cymbal.

2 If I have the gift of prophecy[c]
and understand all •mysteries
and all knowledge,
and if I have all faith
so that I can move mountains[d]
but do not have love, I am nothing.

3 And if I donate all my goods to feed
the poor,
and if I give my body in order
to boast[A]
but do not have love, I gain nothing.

4 Love is patient,[e] love is kind.
Love does not envy,[f]
is not boastful, is not conceited,[g]

5 does not act improperly,
is not selfish,[h] is not provoked,[i]
and does not keep a record of wrongs.

6 Love finds no joy in unrighteousness
but rejoices in the truth.[j]

7 It bears all things, believes all things,
hopes all things, endures[k] all things.

8 Love never ends.[l]
But as for prophecies,
they will come to an end;
as for languages, they will cease;
as for knowledge, it will come
to an end.

9 For we know in part,

and we prophesy in part.

10 But when the perfect comes,
the partial will come
to an end.

11 When I was a child,
I spoke like a child,
I thought like a child,
I reasoned like a child.
When I became a man,
I put aside childish things.

12 For now we see indistinctly,[B] as
in a mirror,[C]
but then face to face.[m]
Now I know in part,
but then I will know fully,[n]
as I am fully known.[o]

13 Now these three remain:
faith, hope,[p] and love.
But the greatest of these is love.

Prophecy: A Superior Gift

14 Pursue love and desire spiritual gifts,
and above all that you may prophesy.
2 For the person who speaks in another •language[q] is not speaking to men but to God, since no one understands him; however, he speaks •mysteries in the Spirit.[D] 3 But the person who prophesies speaks to people for edification, encouragement, and consolation. 4 The person who speaks in another language builds himself up, but he who prophesies builds up the church. 5 I wish all of you spoke in other languages, but even more that you prophesied. The person who prophesies is greater than the person who speaks in languages, un-

Cross references (center column)

[a]13:1 Jn 13:35; 1Jn 4:7-12
[b]Mt 10:9
[c]13:2 1Co 14:1,3-6,22-39; Eph 4:11; 1Th 5:20
[d]Mt 17:20
[e]13:4 1Th 5:14
[f]Nm 25:13; Gl 4:17
[g]1Co 4:6
[h]13:5 Mk 10:45; Php 2:4
[i]Ac 17:16
[j]13:6 Ps 119:142; Jn 8:14; 14:6
[k]13:7 Jms 1:12
[l]13:8 Mt 7:25,27; Lk 6:49; 11:17; 13:4; 16:17; Ac 15:16; Heb 11:30; Rv 11:13; 16:19
[m]13:12 1Jn 3:2
[n]Pr 2:6; Jn 17:3; 1Jn 4:8
[o]1Co 8:3; Gl 4:9
[p]13:13 1Th 1:3
[q]14:2 1Co 12:10

A13:3 Other mss read *body to be burned*   **B**13:12 Or *indirectly*   **C**13:12 Ancient mirrors were normally made out of polished metals and were not as clear as modern ones.   **D**14:2 Or *in spirit*, or *in his spirit*

13:1 If not accompanied by love, the ability to **speak human or angelic languages** would be unbearable to others, like misused musical instruments.

13:3 Sacrifice of one's life (**give my body**) can be the ultimate act of love (Jn 15:13; Rm 5:6-8), but it is also possible to make such sacrifice **in order to boast** rather than out of love. In this case, **nothing** is gained.

13:4-5 Paul personifies love in order to show its daily character and choices.

13-5-6a The Corinthians would have recognized these faults as taking place among them.

13:6b Contrary to common perception, love is not marked by tolerance for error.

13:7 Love **endures** in this age with a sure expectation of better things to come in the next.

13:8-13 Many aspects of church life will end at the end of this current age, but **love never ends**. This permanence signals love's priority within the church.

13:10 The perfect refers to the next age, the eternal age when Messiah reigns.

13:11 Paul uses the analogy of infancy versus adulthood to

explain the contrast between our present understanding and the understanding we will have in the next age.

13:12 Believers are granted to know truth in this age, but only **indistinctly** so. Our imprecise perception of Christ will be made complete in eternity, where we will know Him **face to face**.

13:13 Of **faith, hope, and love**, love is **greatest** because it continues into the next age. Both faith and hope will be fulfilled in eternity, and so will not remain. This statement concludes a semantic bracket that began in verse 8—"Love never ends."

14:1-4 Paul valued prophecy over uninterpreted **language** (Gk *glossai*; cp. 12:10; "different kinds of languages" implies that these were human languages). Utterance gifts should be exercised only for the edification and exhortation of others. The phrase **no one understands him** refers to the uselessness of uninterpreted language for the corporate body. The phrase **in the Spirit** probably refers to the rational faculties of a person (i.e., "in his spirit") rather than to the Holy Spirit (cp. v. 14).

14:5 Paul discouraged uninterpreted languages within the church by declaring the supremacy of prophecy for the edification of the church.

less he interprets so that the church may be built up.

[6] But now, •brothers, if I come to you speaking in other languages, how will I benefit you unless I speak to you with a revelation[a] or knowledge or prophecy or teaching? [7] Even inanimate things that produce sounds—whether flute or harp[b]—if they don't make a distinction in the notes, how will what is played on the flute or harp be recognized? [8] In fact, if the trumpet makes an unclear sound, who will prepare for battle?[c] [9] In the same way, unless you use your tongue for intelligible speech, how will what is spoken be known? For you will be speaking into the air. [10] There are doubtless many different kinds of languages in the world, and all have meaning.[A] [11] Therefore, if I do not know the meaning of the language, I will be a foreigner[B] to the speaker, and the speaker will be a foreigner to me. [12] So also you—since you are zealous[d] for spiritual gifts,[C,e] seek to excel in building up the church.

[13] Therefore the person who speaks in another language should pray that he can interpret. [14] For if I pray in another language, my spirit[f] prays, but my understanding is unfruitful.[g] [15] What then? I will pray with the spirit,

and I will also pray with my understanding. I will sing with the spirit, and I will also sing with my understanding. [16] Otherwise, if you praise with the spirit,[D] how will the uninformed person[E] say "•Amen"[h] at your giving of thanks, since he does not know what you are saying? [17] For you may very well be giving thanks, but the other person is not being built up. [18] I thank[i] God that I speak in other languages more than all of you; [19] yet in the church I would rather speak five words[j] with my understanding, in order to teach others also, than 10,000 words in another language.

[20] Brothers, don't be childish in your thinking, but be infants in regard to evil and adult in your thinking.[k] [21] It is written in the law:

> **I will speak to these people**
> **by people of other languages**
> **and by the lips of foreigners,**
> **and even then, they will not listen**
> **to Me,**[F,l]

says the Lord. [22] It follows that speaking in other languages is intended as a sign,[G] not for believers but for unbelievers. But prophecy is not for unbelievers but for believers. [23] Therefore, if the whole church assembles together

Cross references

[a] 14:6 1Pt 4:13
[b] 14:7 Rv 5:8; 14:2; 15:2
[c] 14:8 Nm 10:9; Is 58:1; Jr 4:19; Ezk 33:3-6; Jl 2:1
[d] 14:12 Nm 25:13; Gl 1:14
[e] Ps 51:11; Lk 11:34; Jn 1:33; Ac 2:4; Rm 8:9; Gl 5:25; Ti 3:5; 1Jn 4:1; Rv 3:22
[f] 14:14 Ps 51:12
[g] Gl 5:22; Ti 3:14
[h] 14:16 Ps 72:19; Rv 22:21
[i] 14:18 Rm 1:8
[j] 14:19 Mt 12:37
[k] 14:20 Ps 131:2; Is 28:9; Mt 18:3; Rm 16:19; Eph 4:14; Heb 5:12-13
[l] 14:21 Is 28:11-12

A 14:10 Lit *and none is without a sound*   **B** 14:11 Gk *barbaros* = in Eng a *"barbarian."* To a Gk, a *barbaros* was anyone who did not speak Gk.   **C** 14:12 Lit *zealous of spirits*; *spirits* = human spirits, spiritual powers, or the Holy Spirit   **D** 14:16 Or *praise by the Spirit*   **E** 14:16 Lit *the one filling the place of the uninformed*   **F** 14:21 Is 28:11-12   **G** 14:22 Lit *that languages are for a sign*

14:11 Just as a **foreigner** is estranged by those speaking a language he does not know, so too members of the body of Christ become estranged from one another if unintelligible, untranslated languages are spoken in the church.

14:12 Rather than being selfishly ambitious with spiritual gifts, believers must strive for **building up the church**.

14:13-19 This section includes an apostolic ruling in which Paul declares the necessity of intelligible language over untranslated languages for edification of the church body.

14:13-14 Paul bade the person who wanted to speak in **another language** to pray for the ability to **interpret**. Ironically, while praying in an unintelligible language he could not ask God for the power to interpret because he would not know what he was praying.

14:15-17 The legitimacy of a person's speech in the midst of the congregation is measured by the edification it brings the body of Christ. Speeches, prayers of blessing, and expressions of thanksgiving cannot edify the body if they are unintelligible (i.e., if the congregants remain **uninformed**). Paul's statement, **I will pray with the spirit, and I will also pray with my understanding**, means he will pray in a way that is both intelligible to bystanders and drawn his spirit.

14:18 I thank (Gk *eucharisto*) can express either thanksgiving to God ("I give thanks") or prayer ("I pray with thanksgiving"). **More than all of you** indicates that Paul was not merely speaking from theory in his instructions about **other languages** and their proper practice in the church.

14:21-22 Drawing on Is 28:11-12, Paul states that uninterpreted earthly **languages** serve as a **sign** of God's impend-

ing "strange work" of judgment to unbelievers (Is 28:11,21). In Is 28, the leaders of Judah rejected as unintelligible nonsense Isaiah's message that would have given Jerusalem rest from their enemies.

14:23-25 Paul warned the Corinthians that practicing **other languages** carelessly would be harmful to **uninformed** visitors and **unbelievers**. Churchwide **prophesying**, however, would serve to convict and convert visitors. Interpreters

---

glossa

Greek Pronunciation	[GLOH sah]
HCSB Translation	tongue, language
Uses in 1 Corinthians	21
Uses in the NT	50
Focus passage	1 Corinthians 14:2-39

The Greek noun *glossa* can mean *tongue*, and it refers literally to the organ of speech in the mouth. In the NT, *glossa* does occur with the literal meaning *tongue* in several passages (Mk 7:33; Lk 1:64; 16:24; Rm 3:13; Rv 16:10), and the meaning *language* is common also (Ac 2:11; 1Jn 3:18; Rv 5:9; 7:9; 10:11; 11:9; 13:7; 14:6; 17:15).

Glossa is the term used in Acts and 1 Corinthians referring to speaking in *tongues*. Luke explained this phenomenon as the apostles' ability to speak in *languages* spoken by Jews from numerous other countries (Ac 2:4-11; see esp. vv. 6,8,11). These were *languages* that the apostles had not previously learned, which is why those who heard them speak were so surprised (vv. 7-8). In two other passages in Acts, speaking in *tongues* refers to the same supernatural ability as described in chapter 2 (10:46; 19:6).

and all are speaking in other languages and people who are uninformed or unbelievers come in, will they not say that you are out of your minds? [24]But if all are prophesying and some unbeliever or uninformed person comes in, he is convicted by all and is judged by all. [25]The secrets of his heart will be revealed, and as a result he will fall facedown and worship God, proclaiming, "God is really among you."[a]

Order in Church Meetings

[26]What then is the conclusion, brothers? Whenever you come together, each one[A] has a psalm, a teaching, a revelation, another language, or an interpretation.[b] All things must be done for edification. [27]If any person speaks in another language, there should be only two, or at the most three, each in turn, and someone must interpret. [28]But if there is no interpreter, that person should keep silent in the church and speak to himself and to God. [29]Two or three prophets should speak, and the others should evaluate.[c] [30]But if something has been revealed to another person sitting there, the first prophet should be silent. [31]For you can all prophesy one by one, so that everyone may learn and everyone may be encouraged.[d] [32]And the prophets' spirits are under the control of the prophets, [33]since God is not a God of disorder but of peace.

As in all the churches of the •saints,[e] [34]the women[B] should be silent in the churches,[f] for they are not permitted to speak, but should be submissive, as the law also says. [35]And if they want to learn something, they should ask their own husbands[g] at home, for it is disgraceful for a woman to speak in the church

meeting. [36]Did the word of God originate from you, or did it come to you only?

[37]If anyone thinks he is a prophet or spiritual, he should recognize that what I write to you is the Lord's command. [38]But if anyone ignores this, he will be ignored.[C] [39]Therefore, my brothers, be eager[h] to prophesy, and do not forbid speaking in other languages. [40]But everything must be done decently[i] and in order.

Resurrection Essential to the Gospel

15 Now •brothers, I want to clarify[D] for you the gospel I proclaimed to you; you received it and have taken your stand[j] on it. [2]You are also saved by it, if you hold to the message I proclaimed to you—unless you believed for no purpose.[E,k] [3]For I passed on to you[l] as most important what I also received:

that Christ died[m] for our sins
according to the Scriptures,[n]
[4] that He was buried,[o]
that He was raised on the third day[p]
according to the Scriptures,[q]
[5] and that He appeared to •Cephas,[r]
then to the Twelve.[s]
[6] Then He appeared to over 500 brothers
    at one time;[t]
most of them are still alive,
but some have fallen •asleep.
[7] Then He appeared to James,[u]
then to all the apostles.[v]
[8] Last of all, as to one abnormally born,[F,w]
He also appeared to me.[x]

[9]For I am the least of the apostles,[y] unworthy to be called an apostle, because I persecuted[z] the church of God. [10]But by God's grace I am

Cross references (center column):
[a]14:25 Is 45:14; Zch 8:23
[b]14:26 1Co 12:10
[c]14:29 1Jn 4:1
[d]14:31 Lk 16:25
[e]14:33 Eph 6:18
[f]14:34 1Tm 2:11-12; 1Pt 3:1
[g]14:35 Mt 1:19; 1Pt 3:1
[h]14:39 Nm 25:13; Gl 4:17
[i]14:40 Rm 13:13
[j]15:1 Pr 24:16
[k]15:2 Gl 4:11; Heb 6:8
[l]15:3 Jd 3
[m]1Co 8:11 Mt 26:54; 1Pt 1:20
[o]15:4 Mt 27:59-60; Mk 15:46; Lk 23:53; Jn 19:41-42
[p]1Th 4:14
[q]Ps 16:10; Is 53:10; Hs 6:2; Mt 12:40; Jn 2:22; Ac 2:25-32; 13:33-35; 26:22-23
[r]15:5 Lk 24:34
[s]Mk 16:14; Lk 24:36; Jn 20:19,26; Ac 10:41
[t]15:6 Mt 28:10-20
[u]15:7 Jms 1:1
[v]Ac 1:3-11
[w]15:8 1Tm 1:13-16
[x]Ac 9:1-8
[y]15:9 Eph 3:8; 1Tm 1:16-17
[z]Php 3:6

[A]14:26 Other mss add *of you*   [B]14:34 Other mss read *your women*   [C]14:38 Other mss read *he should be ignored*   [D]15:1 Or *I make known*   [E]15:2 Or *believed without careful thought,* or *believed in vain*   [F]15:8 Or *one whose birth was unusual, He*

---

differ over exactly what all was entailed by "prophecy" in NT times, but see verses 29-32 and note.

14:27-28 Again Paul emphasizes the importance of self-restraint for the greater good; see note at 11:33-34.

14:29-32 That Paul instructed people with the gift of prophecy to speak in turn and then await evaluation by others in attendance indicates that the kind of "prophecy" in view here is not predictive or a foretelling of future events.

14:33 God is not the author of **disorder** in a worship service.

14:34-35 During assemblies of the church at Corinth, **women** were **not permitted to speak** in the process of evaluating prophetic utterances (vv. 29-30,37). For the sake of propriety and order, they were to **ask their own husbands** in private at home about what was spoken. These verses should not be taken as a prohibition against women speaking in church. To say otherwise contradicts Paul elsewhere (e.g., 11:5).

14:36 With rhetorical flair Paul reminded the believers at

Corinth of his apostolic authority. He appealed to their own recollection about his role as an apostle who brought them God's authoritative **word**.

14:37-38 Those who were truly prophets would discern that Paul's principles for the orderly exercise of prophetic gifts were consistent with the **Lord's command**. It is unclear exactly what is meant by **will be ignored**. Possibly it means those wishing to conduct services correctly will disregard those clamoring to do otherwise.

15:1-58 This chapter represents the most comprehensive discussion of resurrection in the entire Bible.

15:3-4 These verses recount the basic gospel message as Paul delivered it in town after town.

15:5-11 Early Christian evangelists validated the certainty of Jesus' resurrection by recounting His post-tomb appearances to authoritative eyewitnesses (e.g., Ac 2:32). Paul refers to himself as **one abnormally born** due to his late

what I am, and His grace toward me was not ineffective. However, I worked more than any of them, yet not I, but God's grace that was with me.*[a]* *[11]*Therefore, whether it is I or they, so we proclaim and so you have believed.

Resurrection Essential to the Faith

*[12]*Now if Christ is proclaimed as raised from the dead,*[b]* how can some of you say, "There is no resurrection of the dead"?*[c]* *[13]*But if there is no resurrection of the dead, then Christ has not been raised; *[14]*and if Christ has not been raised, then our proclamation is without foundation, and so is your faith.*[A]* *[15]*In addition, we are found to be false witnesses*[d]* about God, because we have testified*[e]* about God that He raised up Christ—whom He did not raise up if in fact the dead are not raised. *[16]*For if the dead are not raised, Christ has not been raised. *[17]*And if Christ has not been raised, your faith is worthless; you are still in your sins. *[18]*Therefore, those who have fallen asleep in Christ*[f]* have also perished. *[19]*If we have put our hope in Christ for this life only, we should be pitied more than anyone.

Christ's Resurrection Guarantees Ours

*[20]*But now Christ has been raised from the dead, the •firstfruits*[g]* of those who have fallen asleep. *[21]*For since death*[h]* came through a man,*[i]* the resurrection of the dead also comes through a man.*[j]* *[22]*For as in Adam all die, so also in Christ all will be made alive.*[k]* *[23]*But each in his own order:*[l]* Christ, the firstfruits; afterward, at His coming, those who belong to Christ. *[24]*Then comes the end,*[m]* when He hands over the kingdom to God the Father,*[n]* when He abolishes all rule and all authority and power.*[o]* *[25]*For He must reign*[p]* until He puts all His enemies under His feet.*[q]* *[26]*The last enemy to be abolished is death.*[r]* *[27]*For **God has put everything under His feet.**[B,s]* But when it says "everything" is put under Him, it is obvious that He who puts everything under Him is the exception. *[28]*And when everything is subject to Christ, then the Son*[t]* Himself will also be subject to the One who subjected everything to Him, so that God may be all in all.*[u]*

---

*[a]*15:10 2Co 3:5; Php 2:13; Col 1:29
*[b]*15:12 Mt 17:9
*[c]*Mt 22:23; Mk 12:18; Lk 20:27; Ac 23:8; 2Tm 2:18
*[d]*15:15 Mt 26:60
*[e]*Jn 15:26
*[f]*15:18 1Th 4:16; 1Pt 5:14
*[g]*15:20 Ex 23:19; Lv 2:12; Rm 8:23; Col 1:18
*[h]*15:21 Mt 10:21; Jn 8:51; Php 3:10
*[i]*Gn 3:1-7; Rm 5:12-14
*[j]*Mt 28:5-6; Mk 16:6; Lk 24:5-8,34; Jn 11:25; 20:9,15-18
*[k]*15:22 Rm 14:9
*[l]*15:23 1Th 4:17
*[m]*15:24 Mt 24:6; Mk 13:7
*[n]*Mt 5:16; 11:27; Lk 11:13; Jn 8:42; Eph 5:20
*[o]*Ac 8:10; Eph 1:21; 1Pt 3:22
*[p]*15:25 Lk 1:33; Rv 11:15
*[q]*Ps 110:1; Mt 22:44; Eph 1:22
*[r]*15:26 2Co 5:4 *[s]*15:27 Ps 8:6 *[t]*15:28 Jn 5:19; Heb 1:2 *[u]*Ps 104:24; Eph 1:23

---

*[A]*15:14 Or *proclamation is useless, and your faith also is useless*, or *proclamation is empty, and your faith also is empty*   *[B]*15:27 Ps 8:6

---

arrival in the chain of eyewitnesses to Christ's resurrection (Ac 9:1-6).

15:12 Though it is uncertain what caused some Corinthian believers to deny the **resurrection of the dead**, Greeks viewed bodily death as final, with some saying the spirit survived disembodied. This view likely influenced the church at Corinth.

15:13-15 If Christ were not raised, then apostolic preaching of the resurrection was **without foundation**, the Corinthians' **faith** was void, and the apostles were **false witnesses**. "Faith" here refers to the content of the gospel message, and is synonymous with "system of beliefs."

15:16 A restatement, in reverse order, of the implications of the Corinthian skepticism regarding resurrection.

15:19 Christians **should be pitied more than anyone** if there is no resurrection, for in that case we have placed all our hopes in a falsehood. Christianity is fundamentally a resurrection faith.

15:20 Christ's genuine, well-attested resurrection is the guarantee of our future resurrection. **Firstfruits** refers to the guarantee that Christ's resurrection is the first-of-a-kind resurrection that promises others will follow in the end time (cp. Rm 8:23, where "firstfruits" can be translated "guarantee," "first installment"). In this instance the phrase **those who have fallen asleep** refers specifically to those who have died in Christ. For more general usage of "fallen asleep," see note at 11:30-32.

15:21-22 Paul presents a parallel of necessary effects. Through one man, **Adam**, death came to humanity. If this is ever to be reversed, it must be done so through like kind: a man. God has appointed just such a man: Jesus **Christ**, who is fully divine and fully human. Through His resurrection the promise of resurrection comes to a new humanity

"in Christ." The second occurrence of the word **all** refers to all those who are joined to Christ through faith.

15:23 Jesus' resurrection precedes and makes certain the resurrection of **those who belong to Christ** at His coming.

15:24-28 The Son as the resurrected Messiah will conquer and subdue everything, including the last enemy—**death**. By saying **He must reign**, Paul touches on the set-in-stone divine plan that assures us that history will end in just this

aparche

Greek Pronunciation	[ahp ahr KAY]
HCSB Translation	firstfruits
Uses in 1 Corinthians	3
Uses in the NT	8
Focus passage	1 Corinthians 15:20,23

The Greek noun *aparche* comes from the preposition *apo*, meaning *from*, and *arche*, meaning *beginning* or *first*. In ancient Greek, *aparche* was often used in connection with the beginning of an event and was the formal term for *birth certificate*. In the Greek OT, *aparche* was the term for *firstfruits*. The Israelites were to bring the *firstfruits* of their harvest to the priests to be presented before the Lord (Ex 23:16-29; Lv 23:9-14).

In the NT, *aparche* refers figuratively to people as *firstfruits* in seven of eight occurrences (Rm 11:16 excepted). Twice Paul used *aparche* in reference to the believers who were the first converts of a certain province (Rm 16:5; 1Co 16:15). A special group of believers in the end times are also called *firstfruits* (Rv 14:4). Believers receive the Spirit as the *firstfruits* of salvation (Rm 8:23), and this occurs through the power of God's word (Jms 1:18). In discussing the resurrection, Paul referred to Christ as "the *firstfruits* of those who have fallen asleep" (1Co 15:20). Since Christ was the first to arise from the dead (v. 23), His resurrection is the basis for the resurrection of all believers.

Resurrection Supported by Christian Experience

[29] Otherwise what will they do who are being baptized for the dead? If the dead are not raised at all, then why are people baptized for them?[A] [30] Why are we in danger every hour? [31] I affirm by the pride in you that I have in Christ Jesus our Lord: I die every day![a] [32] If I fought wild animals in Ephesus[b] with only human hope,[B] what good did that do me?[C,c] If the dead are not raised, **Let us eat and drink, for tomorrow we die.**[D,d] [33] Do not be deceived: "Bad company corrupts good morals."[E] [34] Come to your senses[F,e] and stop sinning, for some people are ignorant about God. I say this to your shame.[f]

The Nature of the Resurrection Body

[35] But someone will say, "How are the dead raised? What kind of body will they have when they come?" [36] Foolish one! What you sow does not come to life[g] unless it dies. [37] And as for what you sow—you are not sowing the future body, but only a seed,[G] perhaps of wheat or another grain. [38] But God gives it a body as He wants,[h] and to each of the seeds its own body. [39] Not all flesh[i] is the same flesh; there is one flesh for humans, another for animals, another for birds, and another for fish. [40] There are heavenly bodies and earthly bodies, but the splendor[j] of the heavenly bodies is differ-

ent from that of the earthly ones. [41] There is a splendor of the sun, another of the moon, and another of the stars; for one star differs from another star in splendor. [42] So it is with the resurrection of the dead:

> Sown in corruption, raised
> in incorruption;[k]
> [43] sown in dishonor,[l] raised in glory;[m]
> sown in weakness, raised in power;[n]
> [44] sown a natural body, raised
> a spiritual body.

If there is a natural body, there is also a spiritual body. [45] So it is written: **The first man Adam became a living being;**[H,o] the last Adam[p] became a life-giving Spirit. [46] However, the spiritual is not first, but the natural, then the spiritual.

> [47] The first man was from the earth
> and made of dust;[q]
> the second man is[i] from heaven.
> [48] Like the man made of dust,
> so are those who are made
> of dust;
> like the heavenly man,
> so are those who are heavenly.[r]
> [49] And just as we have borne
> the image[s] of the man made of dust,
> we will also bear
> the image of the heavenly man.[t]

a 15:31 Rm 8:36
b 15:32 Eph 1:1
c 1Th 2:19
d Is 22:13
e 15:34 Ti 2:12
f 1Co 4:14
g 15:36 Jn 12:24
h 15:38 Ps 143:10; Pr 16:9; Jn 5:30; Gl 1:4; Eph 1:9; 1Jn 2:17
i 15:39 Php 3:3
j 15:40 Lk 9:31-32; Ac 22:11
k 15:42 Rm 2:7; Eph 6:24; 2Tm 1:10
l 15:43 2Co 6:8
m 1Pt 5:4
n Mk 5:30; Lk 1:35; 6:19; Ac 19:11; 2Co 13:4; Rv 11:17
o 15:45 Gn 2:7
p Rm 8:2
q 15:47 Gn 2:7; 3:19; Ps 90:3
r 15:48 Php 3:20-21
s 15:49 Gn 1:27
t 1Jn 3:2

A 15:29 Other mss read *for the dead*   B 15:32 Lit *Ephesus according to man*   C 15:32 Lit *what to me the profit?*   D 15:32 Is 22:13
E 15:33 A quotation from the poet Menander, *Thais*, 218   F 15:34 Lit *Sober up righteously*   G 15:37 Lit *but a naked seed*
H 15:45 Gn 2:7   I 15:47 Other mss add *the Lord*

way: with God triumphant over all evil and God's people reigning with Christ forever (1Tm 2:12).

15:29 Being baptized for the dead probably refers to the practice, apparently unique to the Corinthian church, of someone undergoing baptism on behalf of a believer who had died without undergoing baptism. Paul was not condoning this practice, and certainly Scripture nowhere directs us to conduct such baptisms. Paul simply pointed out that it was meaningless for the Corinthians to enact such practices if they disbelieved in the resurrection of the dead.

15:32 Wild animals is almost certainly metaphorical for struggles Paul faced from human opponents of the gospel (Ac 19; 2Co 1:8-10).

15:35-38 Paul compares human resurrection to the life-death-life cycle from agriculture. The seed body that **dies** gives rise to a totally different plant body, and yet there is retention of identity. So it is with our present bodies and our future resurrection bodies.

15:42-44 Having reviewed differentiations within the created order (vv. 35-41), Paul turns to differentiations of the resurrected body. It was sown in **corruption** and will be raised in **incorruption**. The body changes from a perishable body (a **natural body**) to an imperishable body (a **spiritual body**), though one that has physical characteristics (e.g., Lk

24:39). It is sown in **dishonor** and **weakness**, and it will be raised a glorious, imperishable body.

15:45 The first man Adam received the breath of life, a life that would become corruptible and perishable. In contrast, the **last Adam** (Jesus) will impart life, granting believers an incorruptible, imperishable, eternal body. Jesus will make believers alive through His **life-giving Spirit** (Gk *pneuma zoopoioun*), a power God alone wields.

15:46 Grammatically, the words **the spiritual** (Gk *pneumatikon*) and **the natural** (Gk *psuchikon*) are in the neuter gender. They refer to two kinds of bodies (cp. v. 44) and not to Adam or Christ. "Spiritual" (*pneumatikon*) here refers to a body brought to life by the last Adam, Christ.

15:47-49 Paul contrasts **the first man** Adam and those who have borne his **image** with the **second man** and those who will bear his image. The first man was made of **earth** (Gk *choikos*; "earthy"), an expression Paul coined in allusion to Gn 2:7. This language emphasizes the transitory nature of those who are related to the first Adam, with bodies that return to dust. The "second man" **from heaven** refers to Jesus in His glorified humanity, as God-man and Messiah, who is coming from heaven to impart imperishable eternal bodies to those who have borne the image of the **man made of dust**.

15:50 Our earthly condition is such (**flesh and blood** and

Victorious Resurrection

[50] Brothers, I tell you this: Flesh[a] and blood[b] cannot inherit the kingdom of God, and corruption cannot inherit incorruption. [51] Listen! I am telling you a *mystery:

We will not all fall asleep,
but we will all be changed,
[52] in a moment, in the blink of an eye,
at the last trumpet.[c]
For the trumpet will sound,
and the dead will be raised incorruptible,
and we will be changed.
[53] For this corruptible must be clothed[d]
with incorruptibility,[e]
and this mortal must be clothed
with immortality.
[54] When this corruptible is clothed
with incorruptibility,
and this mortal is clothed
with immortality,
then the saying that is written
will take place:

Death has been swallowed up[f]
in victory.[A,g]
[55] **Death, where is your victory?**
Death, where is your sting?[B,h]
[56] Now the sting of death is sin,
and the power of sin[i] is the law.[j]
[57] But thanks be to God, who gives us
the victory[k]
through our Lord Jesus Christ!

[58] Therefore, my dear brothers, be steadfast, immovable, always excelling in the Lord's work,[l] knowing that your labor in the Lord is not in vain.

Collection for the Jerusalem Church

16 Now about the collection[m] for the *saints: You should do the same as I instructed the Galatian[n] churches. [2] On the first day of the week,[C,o] each of you is to set something aside and save in keeping with how he prospers, so that no collections will need to be made when I come.[p] [3] When I arrive, I will send with letters[q] those you recommend to carry your gracious gift to Jerusalem.[r] [4] If it is suitable for me to go as well, they can travel with me.

Paul's Travel Plans

[5] I will come to you after I pass through Macedonia[s]—for I will be traveling through Macedonia— [6] and perhaps I will remain with you or even spend the winter, so that you may send me on my way wherever I go. [7] I don't want to see you now just in passing, for I hope to spend some time with you, if the Lord allows.[t] [8] But I will stay in Ephesus[u] until Pentecost,[v] [9] because a wide door[w] for effective ministry has opened for me[D]—yet many oppose me. [10] If Timothy comes, see that he has nothing to fear from you, because he is doing the Lord's work,[x] just as I am. [11] Therefore, no

---

Cross references:

[a]15:50 Php 3:3
[b]Mt 16:17
[c]15:52 Mt 24:31; 1Pt 1:5
[d]15:53 Pr 31:25
[e]1Pt 1:18
[f]15:54 Mt 23:24
[g]Is 25:8
[h]15:55 Hs 13:14
[i]15:56 Rm 4:15
[j]Gl 5:4
[k]15:57 1Jn 5:5
[l]15:58 Mk 14:6; Gl 3:10; Jms 2:14-26
[m]16:1 Ac 11:30; 2Co 8:4
[n]Gl 1:2
[o]16:2 Mt 28:1; Mk 16:9; Lk 24:1; Jn 20:1,19; Ac 20:7
[p]2Co 9:1-5
[q]16:3 2Co 8:16-22
[r]Mt 23:37; Ac 8:1
[s]16:5 Ac 16:9
[t]16:7 Ps 143:10; Pr 16:9; Jn 5:30; Gl 1:4; Eph 1:9; 1Jn 2:17
[u]16:8 Eph 1:1
[v]Ex 34:22
[w]16:9 Col 4:3
[x]16:10 Jn 5:17; 2Jn 8

A15:54 Is 25:8   B15:55 Hs 13:14   C16:2 Or *Each Sunday*   D16:9 Lit *for a door has opened to me, great and effective*

---

corruption, references to our perishable physical nature) that our Adamic bodies cannot inherit the kingdom, implying that they somehow must be changed.

15:51-53 Paul supports the above implication (v. 50) with an apostolic revelation that though not everyone will die (**fall asleep**; see note at v. 20) before Christ's coming, those who are alive when He comes **will all be changed**. No one is transported to the eternal state unchanged.

15:52 In a moment (Gk *atomos*) signifies the smallest possible division of something, in this case time. **Blink of an eye** similarly implies rapidity. Such will be the swiftness of the transformation of the living when **the last trumpet** sounds at Christ's return (1Th 4:16-17).

15:53 The body that bears the image of the man of dust (the first Adam) must inevitably be changed into the **incorruptibility** and **immortality** of the body that bears the image of the man from heaven (the second Adam); see vv. 47-49 and note there.

15:54-55 Paul conflates Isaiah 25:8 and Hosea 13:14 in this citation. The exchange of **corruptible** for **incorruptibility** comes only when death and corruption are **swallowed up** by Jesus Christ. This passage does not teach the doctrine of "soul sleep"—a suspended state for believers between physical death and the change into glorified bodies. Believers are with the Lord immediately after death (e.g., Lk 23:43; Ac 7:55-59; 2Co 5:1-8).

15:56 This verse represents a theological aside that Paul de-

veloped further in a letter he wrote some months after this present one (see Rm 7).

15:58 Most anything we do in this life is vanity (Ec 1:2-3), but **labor in the Lord** has eternal value.

16:1-4 Now about indicates that Paul is responding to a question, expressed to him in a previous letter (see 7:1 and note), about how to organize the **collection** for the Jerusalem church (2Co 8–9). The Corinthians had pleaded for the opportunity to contribute to the collection (2Co 8:4). **Each** person was to **set . . . aside** funds regularly for the collection, based on his ability to give. All the funds were eventually to be collected and sent in care of designated couriers. Paul personally would go with the couriers if it seemed advisable and the circumstances permitted.

16:5-9 Paul planned to go through **Macedonia** to Corinth (on his third missionary journey) and possibly to **spend the winter** at Corinth. He then expected the Corinthians to provide supplies for his journey when he left them. In the meantime, he intended to stay in **Ephesus** until May (the Jewish feast of **Pentecost**) because of the favorable response to the gospel in that city.

16:10-11 Paul gave instructions on how the Corinthian believers should receive **Timothy**. The word **if** (Gk *ean*) here is equivalent to "whenever." Paul was certain Timothy was going to Corinth. **Send him on his way in peace** is idiomatic for "supply him with all he needs for the journey."

one should look down[a] on him. Send him on his way in peace so he can come to me, for I am expecting him with the brothers.[A]

[12]About our brother Apollos:[b] I strongly urged him to come to you with the brothers, but he was not at all willing to come now. However, he will come when he has an opportunity.

Final Exhortation

[13]Be alert, stand firm in the faith,[c] act like a man, be strong. [14]Your every action must be done with love.[d]

[15]*Brothers, you know the household of Stephanas: They are the *firstfruits[e] of Achaia[f] and have devoted themselves to serving the saints. I urge you [16]also to submit to such people, and to everyone who works and labors

with them. [17]I am pleased to have Stephanas, Fortunatus, and Achaicus present, because these men have made up for your absence. [18]For they have refreshed my spirit[g] and yours. Therefore recognize[h] such people.

Conclusion

[19]The churches of *Asia[i] greet you.[j] Aquila and Priscilla[k] greet you warmly in the Lord, along with the church that meets in their home.[l] [20]All the brothers greet you. Greet one another with a holy kiss.[m]

[21]This greeting is in my own hand[B,n]—Paul. [22]If anyone does not love the Lord, a curse be on him. Marana tha that is, Lord, come![C] [23]The grace of the Lord Jesus be with you.[o] [24]My love be with all of you in Christ Jesus.

Cross references

[a]16:11 Lk 18:9
[b]16:12 Ti 3:13
[c]16:13 Jd 3
[d]16:14 1Co 13:1
[e]16:15 Lv 2:12
[f]Ac 18:12
[g]16:18 Ps 51:12
[h]1Th 5:12
[i]16:19 Ac 6:9
[j]16:19-20 Rm 16:3-23; 2Co 13:12; Php 4:21-22; Col 4:10-15; 1Th 5:26; Phm 23-24
[k]16:19 Ac 18:2
[l]Rm 16:5
[m]16:20 2Co 13:12
[n]16:21 2Th 3:17
[o]16:23-24 2Co 13:13; Gl 6:18; Eph 6:23-24; Php 4:23; Col 4:18; 1Th 5:28; 2Th 3:18

[A]16:11 *With the brothers* may connect with Paul or Timothy.   [B]16:21 Paul normally dictated his letters to a secretary, but signed the end of each letter himself; Rm 16:22; Gl 6:11; Col 4:18; 2Th 3:17.   [C]16:22 Or *Maran atha* (an Aram expression transliterated into Gk) = *Our Lord has come!*

16:12 Apollos, whose vital role in growing the Corinthian church Paul readily acknowledged (see 3:5-6 and note), was most likely unwilling **to come now** because of gospel duties elsewhere.

16:13-14 Believers must **be alert** about competing traditions of worldly wisdom and **stand firm** as one body **in the faith.** "Faith" here refers to the content of the gospel—Christ's death and resurrection (15:1-5,14). **Love** confirms our submission to the Lord's authority and to one another.

16:15-16 Paul exhorted the Corinthians to submit to **the household of Stephanas** (1:16). The term **firstfruits** is an honorific title referring to their early reception of the gospel in **Achaia**.

16:17-18 **Stephanas, Fortunatus, and Achaicus** visited Paul and **made up** for the Corinthians' **absence** (lit "these filled up your lack"). Noting their high character and gifts for

ministry, Paul instructed the believers at Corinth to **recognize** them.

16:20 In the context of Paul's letters (Rm 16:16; 2Co 13:12; 1Th 5:26) and the early church, the **holy kiss** was a sign of mutual fellowship within the family of believers.

16:21 Paul concluded the letter in his own handwriting, verifying its authenticity and authority (2Th 3:16-18). By custom Paul spoke his correspondence aloud to a secretary (an amanuensis) who recorded his words on parchment or papyri (Rm 16:22). The signed autographic conclusion probably included verses 21-24.

16:22 The call for judgment on those who were disloyal to the Lord was an uncommon way to end a letter. The Aramaic **Marana tha** can be variously translated. The imperative "Our Lord, come!" seems best.

16:23-24 The letter ends with Paul's formulaic "grace greeting," followed by a personal touch (**My love be with all of you in Christ Jesus**) that is unique to this letter.

2 Corinthians

Introduction

Of all Paul's letters, none is more personally revealing of his heart than 2 Corinthians. At the same time, it is also the most defensive of any New Testament letter. In it Paul mounts a strong argument ("apology" in the positive sense) for his authority and ministry. A number of important doctrines are taught in the epistle, yet its greatest value may be that it reveals the heart and spirit of one of the most effective ministers of all time. We are thus shown that genuine ministry—although it may have to be guarded from attack—is commissioned by Christ and empowered by the Spirit.

Corinth was built adjacent to an isthmus four miles wide with a port on both the east and west of the isthmus. Using 6,000 Judean slaves, Nero attempted to build a canal across the isthmus connecting the port of Lechaion on the Gulf of Corinth and the port of Cenchreae on the Saronic Gulf. Only in the late nineteenth century were engineers able to construct the canal that enables cargo ships to avoid 200 miles of stormy travel around the southern part of the Greek peninsula. In Paul's day, this additional 200 miles was avoided by transporting cargo overland from one port to the other.

Circumstances of Writing

Author: All biblical scholars agree that Paul wrote this letter (1:1; 10:1). It contains more personal informa-tion about him than any other letter, and its Greek style is especially like that of Romans and 1 Corinthians. Proposed chronologies of Paul's life and ministry include a number of variations. Yet for 2 Corinthians, the consensus is that the letter was written about A.D. 56 (from Ephesus during Paul's third missionary journey).

Background: Although Bible students have often disagreed about the sequence of events that led to the writ-ing of 2 Corinthians, the following scenario seems likely.

1. First Corinthians was not well received by the church at Corinth. Timothy had returned to Paul in Eph-esus (1Co 4:17; 16:10). He reported that the church was still greatly troubled. This was partly caused by the arrival in Corinth of "false apostles" (2Co 11:13-15). These were perhaps Judaizers, asking Corinthian believers of Gentile heritage to live according to Mosaic regulations (Gl 2:14).

2. Paul visited Corinth a second time, the first time being his church-planting visit. He described this visit as sorrowful or "painful" (2:1; 13:2). Apparently the false apostles agitated the Corinthians to disown Paul. This second visit, not mentioned in Acts 19, occurred sometime during the apostle's long ministry in Ephesus.

3. Paul then wrote a (now lost) severe letter of stinging rebuke to Corinth from Ephesus (2:3-4,9). He sent this letter by Titus.

4. Titus came to Paul with the news that most of the Corinthian church had repented. They now accepted Paul's authority (7:5-7).

5. Paul decided to write the Corinthians one more time, expressing his relief but still pleading with an un-repentant minority. He promised to come to Corinth a third time (12:14; 13:1). This was fulfilled when

---

A.D. **33–37**

Jesus' trials, death, resurrection, and ascension
Nisan 14–16 or April 3–5, 33

Pentecost 33

Saul's conversion on the Damascus Road
October 34

Paul returns to his native Tarsus. Summer
37–40

Barnabas travels from Antioch of Syria to
find Paul. Summer 40

A.D. **46–50**

Paul, Barnabas, and John Mark make the first
missionary journey. 47–49

Paul and Silas begin second missionary journey by
land through Cilicia, Galatia, and Asia Minor to
Troas. 49–50

Paul, Silas, and Timothy sail from Troas to Macedonia and minister in the Macedonian cities of
Philippi, Thessalonica, and Berea. 50

Paul preaches on Mars Hill in Athens. 50

Paul arrives in Corinth and spends 18 months
planting the church. 50–51

Paul stayed in Corinth while on his way to Jerusalem with the financial collection from many churches (Ac 20:2-3).

Message and Purpose

Paul wrote to the Corinthian Christians mainly to express his joy that the majority had been restored to him, to ask for an offering on behalf of the poor saints in Jerusalem, and to defend his ministry as an apostle to the minority of unrepentant Corinthian believers. His desire was to encourage the majority and to lead the minority to change its mind about the validity of his apostolic ministry.

Important themes Paul developed in 2 Corinthians include the nature of apostolic authority and ministry, the new covenant, the intermediate state (the status of believers between the death of their bodies and the resurrection), and sacrificial giving. The overriding theme is the nature of true ministry. The diversity of these themes was driven by the circumstances that gave rise to the epistle.

The matter of sacrificial giving is the focus of chapters 8–9, the most extensive NT teaching on Christian stewardship. Paul asked the churches he had founded to send a generous offering to the poor believers of Jerusalem. This occupied much of his energy during the last part of his third missionary journey. He mentioned it in his three longest epistles (Rm 15:28; 1Co 16:1-4; 2Co 8–9).

Contribution to the Bible

Second Corinthians contributes to our understanding of ministry. On this subject, we learn four key truths: (1) God was in Christ reconciling the world to Himself and has given to us a ministry of reconciliation; (2) true ministry in Christ's name involves both suffering and victory; (3) serving Christ means ministering in His name to every need of the people; and (4) leaders in ministry need support and trust from those to whom they minister.

A.D. 51–56

A.D. 56–67

Paul meets Aquila and Priscilla, who had come to Corinth when Emperor Claudius expelled the Jews from Rome six years earlier. 51

Paul writes 1 and 2 Thessalonians from Corinth. 51

Paul's hearing before Corinth's proconsul, Gallio, brother of the Roman philosopher Seneca 51

Paul begins his third missionary journey by land through Asia Minor to Ephesus. 53

Paul spends three years in Ephesus. 54–56

Paul writes 1 Corinthians from Ephesus. 56

Paul writes 2 Corinthians from Ephesus. 56

Paul spends the winter in Corinth where he writes the book of Romans. 57

Paul returns to Jerusalem with funds he had collected from Gentile churches to support the poor in the Jerusalem church. 57

Shortly before his death, Emperor Nero brings 6,000 slaves from Judea to build a canal across the Isthmus of Corinth. Following Nero's death the project is abandoned. 67

Structure

This letter follows the standard format found in the other letters bearing Paul's name. The salutation (1:1-2) and thanksgiving (1:3-11) at the beginning are followed by the main body of the letter (1:12–13:10). A final greeting (13:11-13) stands as the conclusion.

The body of 2 Corinthians is the most disjointed of Paul's letters. It is hard to miss Paul's change of tone from chapters 1–9 (which are warm and encouraging) to chapters 10–13 (which are harsh and threatening). Whatever one decides about the original unity of the letter, no doubt the major turning point of 2 Corinthians occurs at 10:1.

Largely because of the change in tone between the first part of the letter and the last part, some interpreters have proposed a different understanding of the original form of 2 Corinthians. They propose that two separate letters of Paul have been joined to make up what is now known as 2 Corinthians. What if, it is asked, chapters 10–13 were in fact the missing severe letter (2:4,9) written after 1 Corinthians but before 2 Corinthians 1–9? The major differences in tone between these chapters would be more readily accounted for if this were true.

However, it seems much more plausible that the letter originated in the form in which we now have it. All the ancient Christian writers knew the letter only in its present form, which is to say unified as one single letter. Surely within a single letter an author may address two different sets of issues (a majority concern and a minority concern) and use two different tones (encouraging and threatening).

Outline

I. Special Greetings (1:1-11)
   A. Salutation (1:1-2)
   B. Expression of thanksgiving (1:3-11)

II. Clarification of Paul's Ministry (1:12–7:16)
   A. Paul's itinerary explained (1:12–2:4)
   B. Forgiveness and recent travel (2:5-13)
   C. True gospel ministry and doctrinal digression (2:14–7:1)
   D. Paul's joy at receiving good news (7:2-16)

III. A Collection for Needy Christians (8:1–9:15)
   A. Encouragement to generous giving (8:1-15)
   B. Management of the collection (8:16–9:5)
   C. Results of cheerful giving (9:6-15)

IV. The Case against False Apostles (10:1–13:10)
   A. Paul's authority from Christ (10:1-18)
   B. False apostles condemned (11:1-15)
   C. Paul's speech as a fool (11:16–12:10)
   D. Signs of a true apostle (12:11-21)
   E. Basis of Paul's authority (13:1-10)

V. Final greetings (13:11-13)

Greeting

1 Paul, an apostle of Christ Jesus by God's will,[a] and Timothy[b] our[A] brother:

To God's church at Corinth,[c] with all the saints who are throughout Achaia.[d]

[2] Grace to you and peace[e] from God our Father[f] and the Lord Jesus Christ.

The God of Comfort

[3] Praise[g] the God and Father of our Lord Jesus Christ, the Father of mercies[h] and the God of all comfort.[i] [4] He comforts us in all our affliction,[B] so that we may be able to comfort those who are in any kind of affliction, through the comfort we ourselves receive from God. [5] For as the sufferings[j] of Christ[k] overflow to us, so through Christ our comfort also overflows.[l] [6] If we are afflicted,[m] it is for your comfort and salvation. If we are comforted, it is for your comfort, which is experienced in your endurance of the same sufferings that we suffer.[n] [7] And our hope[o] for you is firm, because we know that as you share[p] in the sufferings, so you will share in the comfort.

[8] For we don't want you to be unaware, brothers, of our affliction that took place in Asia:[q] we were completely overwhelmed—beyond our strength[r]—so that we even despaired[s] of life. [9] Indeed, we personally had a

death sentence within ourselves, so that we would not trust in ourselves but in God[t] who raises[u] the dead. [10] He has delivered[v] us from such a terrible death,[w] and He will deliver us. We have put our hope in Him that He will deliver us again [11] while you join in helping us by your prayers. Then many will give thanks on our[c] behalf for the gift that came to us through the prayers of many.

A Clear Conscience

[12] For this is our confidence: The testimony[x] of our conscience[y] is that we have conducted ourselves in the world, and especially toward you, with God-given sincerity and purity, not by fleshly[D] wisdom[z] but by God's grace.[aa] [13] Now we are writing nothing to you other than what you can read and also understand. I hope you will understand completely— [14] as you have partially understood us—that we are your reason for pride,[ab] as you are ours,[ac] in the day of our[E] Lord Jesus.[ad]

A Visit Postponed

[15] I planned with this confidence to come to you first,[ae] so you could have a double benefit,[F] [16] and to go on to Macedonia[af] with your help, then come to you again from Macedonia

---

a1:1 1Co 1:1; Eph 1:1; Col 1:1; 2Tm 1:1   b1Th 3:2; 1Tm 1:2   c1Co 1:2   dAc 18:12; Php 1:1   e1:2 Lk 12:51; Rm 1:7; 2Tm 1:2; 3Jn 14   fMt 5:16; 11:27; Lk 11:13; Jn 8:42; Eph 5:20   g1:3 Mk 14:61   hHeb 10:28   iLk 2:25   j1:5 Gl 5:24; Php 3:10   kRm 8:17; 2Co 4:10; Gl 6:17; Php 3:10; Col 1:24   lPhp 1:29   m1:6 Heb 11:37   nPhp 1:29   o1:7 1Th 1:3   pPhm 17   q1:8 Ac 6:9   rAc 8:10; 1Co 15:24; Eph 1:21; 1Pt 3:22   s2Co 4:8   t1:9 Ps 25:2; 26:1; Jr 17:5-7; Lk 18:9   uMk 9:27; Jn 2:19   v1:10 Mt 27:43   wMt 10:21; Jn 8:51; Php 3:10   x1:12 1Tm 2:6   yHeb 13:18   zPr 3:19; 1Co 1:21   aaAc 23:1; 2Co 4:2; 5:12; 1Th 2:10   ab1:14 Rm 2:17; Gl 6:4   ac2Co 9:3; Php 2:16; 4:1; 1Th 2:19-20   adPhp 1:6   ae1:15 Ac 18:1-18; 1Co 4:19   af1:16 Ac 16:9

A1:1 Lit *the*   B1:4 Or *trouble*, or *tribulation*, or *trials*, or *oppression*; the Gk word has a lit meaning of being under pressure. C1:11 Other mss read *your*   D1:12 The word *fleshly* (characterized by flesh) indicates that the wisdom is natural rather than spiritual.   E1:14 Other mss omit *our*   F1:15 Other mss read *a second joy*

1:1 Paul claimed to be an **apostle . . . by God's will**. Only such confidence could provide a foundation sufficient for this high-stakes letter. **Timothy** was perhaps Paul's secretary or scribe who wrote down this letter as it was dictated. **Corinth** was the capital of the Roman province of **Achaia**, the southern part of Greece. Paul recognized that an apostolic letter would be of interest to churches in neighboring cities.

1:2 Grace begins and ends every NT letter that contains Paul's name in the greeting. Without grace from God, a person cannot have **peace** with God. The equality of the **Father** and His Son **Jesus Christ** is implicit. Both are givers of grace and peace.

1:3 Frequently Paul used a form of the verb "thank" at this point in his letters. For this letter and Ephesians, Paul used **praise** (see Eph 1:3). God is praised as the source of all blessings. Jesus had taught that "your Father also is merciful" (Lk 6:36), or kind to the needy. Isaiah 40:1 speaks of God's **comfort** or relief to the sorrowing.

1:4 Believers are to be a channel passing on to others the **comfort** they have received from God. Paradoxically, **affliction**—viewed properly—may be a conduit of blessing to others (v. 6).

1:5 Believers experience none of God's wrath that Christ suffered as our substitute. He is the example of innocent suffering for those who travel "in His steps" (1Pt 2:21). The believers' union with Him means we expect affliction, just as our Lord experienced it (Col 1:24).

1:6-7 In speaking of affliction, Paul probably had in mind the suffering he had endured from the Corinthian church during his painful visit to them (2:1), which was for their **salvation**. He had recently been **comforted** by news from Titus (7:13). The **sufferings** of the Corinthians probably referred to the "fear and trembling" caused by Titus's visit (7:15).

1:8 Paul's **affliction** in **Asia** was a near-death experience during his Ephesian ministry that is not reported in Ac 19. That he **despaired of life** may have prompted his later reflection on what happens to believers at death (5:1-10).

1:9-10 Paul had not died but had been **delivered**. Yet his true hope was in the permanent remedy—the resurrection.

1:11 The phrase **the gift** probably refers to God's gracious sparing of Paul's life for further ministry (Php 1:24-26).

1:12-13 **Sincerity** and **purity** are possible only by **grace**. This letter of 2 Corinthians is a reminder that the Spirit-inspired authors of Scripture intended to write what average believers could **understand**.

1:14 The phrase **partially understood** is a reference to the stormy relations between the church and the apostle. The letter of 2 Corinthians would help return the two parties to mutual **pride** (not arrogance but confidence). The **day of our Lord Jesus** refers to Christ's return, especially to judge believers' works—both Paul's and the Corinthians' (1Co 3:12-13).

1:15-16 First Corinthians had been written while Paul was on reasonably good terms with the church. This is

and be given a start by you[a] on my journey[b] to Judea.[c] [17]So when I planned this, was I irresponsible? Or what I plan, do I plan in a purely human[A,d] way so that I say "Yes, yes" and "No, no" simultaneously? [18]As God is faithful,[e] our message to you is not "Yes and no." [19]For the Son of God,[f] Jesus Christ, who was preached among you by us—by me and Silvanus[B,g] and Timothy—did not become "Yes and no"; on the contrary, a final "Yes" has come in Him.[h] [20]For every one of God's promises[i] is "Yes" in Him. Therefore, the "'Amen"[j] is also spoken through Him by us for God's glory.[k] [21]Now it is God who strengthens us, with you, in Christ and has anointed[l] us. [22]He also has sealed us and given us the Spirit as a down payment[m] in our hearts.[n]

[23]I call on God as a witness,[o] on my life, that it was to spare you that I did not come to Corinth.[p] [24]I do not mean that we have control of[C] your faith, but we are workers with you for your joy, because you stand[q] by faith. [1]In fact, I made up my mind about this:[D] I would not come to you on another painful

Cross references column
a1:16 Ac 20:38
bAc 19:21; 1Co 16:5-7
cLk 1:5
d1:17 Php 3:3; Col 3:22
e1:18 Nm 23:19
f1:19 Jn 5:19; Heb 1:2
g1Th 1:1
hHeb 13:8
i1:20 Gn 12:7
jPs 72:19; Rv 22:21
kMk 10:37; Lk 9:32; Jn 17:24; 2Co 3:18; 2Pt 3:18
l1:21 Lk 4:18; 1Jn 2:20
m1:22 Eph 1:14
nJms 4:5
o1:23 Rm 1:9; Php 1:8; Heb 12:1
p1Co 4:21; 2Co 13:2,10
q1:24 Pr 24:16
r2:3 Php 1:25
s2:5 2Th 3:8
t2:7 Mt 6:12
u2:9 Rm 5:4
vPhp 2:8

visit.[E] [2]For if I cause you pain, then who will cheer me other than the one being hurt by me?[F] [3]I wrote this very thing so that when I came I wouldn't have pain from those who ought to give me joy, because I am confident[r] about all of you that my joy will also be yours. [4]For I wrote to you with many tears out of an extremely troubled and anguished heart—not that you should be hurt, but that you should know the abundant love I have for you.

A Sinner Forgiven

[5]If anyone has caused pain, he has caused pain not so much to me but to some degree—not to exaggerate[s]—to all of you. [6]The punishment inflicted by the majority is sufficient for that person. [7]As a result, you should instead forgive[t] and comfort him. Otherwise, this one may be overwhelmed by excessive grief. [8]Therefore I urge you to reaffirm your love to him. [9]I wrote for this purpose: to test your character[u] to see if you are obedient[v] in everything. [10]If you forgive anyone, I do too. For what I have forgiven—if I have forgiven anything—it is for you in the presence of

---

A1:17 Or a worldly, or a fleshly, or a selfish   B1:19 Or Silas; Ac 15:22-32; 16:19-40; 17:1-16   C1:24 Or we lord it over, or we rule over   D2:1 Lit I decided this for myself   E2:1 Lit not again in sorrow to come to you   F2:2 Lit the one pained

---

demonstrated by his request for them to participate in the collection for Jerusalem (1Co 16:1-3). He had expressed his intent to spend time with them (1Co 16:5-6). Later he had revised this and had **planned . . . to come** twice—once on the way to **Macedonia** (the province north of Achaia), and again on the way south from Macedonia on his way to **Judea** to deliver the offering. Seeing the Corinthians twice would have been a **double benefit** for them.

1:17 Instead of his announced plans, Paul made a brief, painful visit from Ephesus to Corinth, and then returned to Ephesus. Some believers in Corinth accused him of being unreliable and **purely human**. The charge of saying **Yes, yes** one minute and **No, no** the next stung him into reacting defensively.

1:18-19 The apostle's defense against the charge of fickleness was to remind his readers of the unwavering gospel message he had preached. It was no **Yes and no** gospel that he and **Silvanus** (called Silas in Acts) and **Timothy** preached (Ac 18:1,5). The heart of the gospel is that **Jesus** (the human) is God's **Son** and the Messiah promised in the OT.

1:20 Every one of God's promises in Scripture is fulfilled directly or indirectly **in Him** (Rm 1:2; Eph 2:12). **Amen** means "so be it" or "this is true." **God's glory** is displayed in Christ as well as in believers' confession of Him.

1:21-22 This is a Trinitarian text. **God** the Father confirms believers as His own. He initiates the anointing of believers in His Son, **Christ**. He also has **sealed us** with the **Spirit**, guaranteeing our heavenly inheritance (Eph 1:13-14; 4:30).

1:23 The phrase **I call on God as a witness** is a solemn pledge to be telling the truth (Rm 1:9; 1Th 2:5,10). Instead of the visits planned under happier circumstances (2Co 1:15-16), Paul had made a painful visit to Corinth (2:1). He there-

fore cancelled his previously announced itinerary. Time was needed for healing the raw emotions raised on both sides.

1:24 This verse summarizes the relationship between ministers and those under their care. Ministers do not lord it over others but work gently with them.

2:2 Even when a Christian is justified in bringing **pain** to errant believers, it is hardly likely that those **hurt** will be in a position to **cheer** the one who caused the pain. They need to be encouraged after such an incident.

2:3-4 Paul's words **wrote . . . wrote** are probably a reference to the severe letter, now lost, written after his painful visit to Corinth and then sent by Titus (7:6-8), but some Bible students believe the reference is to 1 Corinthians. It is as right for ministers to desire joy in God as it is for them to show costly love to those whom they serve.

2:5 This may refer to the incestuous man of 1Co 5:1-5. More likely the reference is to an episode regarding the false apostles (2Co 11:4), because Paul spoke about a sin that he had personally forgiven (2:10).

2:6-7 Although church discipline is experienced as **punishment**, the intention is redemptive. Upon repentance, believers are to **forgive and comfort**. The congregation is to be careful not to overwhelm a returning sinner with **excessive grief**. The most severe church discipline possible is excommunication (Mt 18:17; 1Co 5:5).

2:8 The phrase **reaffirm your love to him** refers to restoration after repentance.

2:9 On **I wrote**, see note at verses 3-4.

2:10 The first verb (forgive) is in a form implying that forgiveness is a process (Gk present tense); the second verb (have forgiven) implies that forgiveness can be completed (Gk perfect tense).

Christ. ¹¹I have done this so that we may not be taken advantage^a of by Satan. For we are not ignorant of his schemes.

A Trip to Macedonia

¹²When I came to Troas^b to preach the gospel of Christ, the Lord opened a door^c for me. ¹³I had no rest^d in my spirit because I did not find my brother Titus,^{e} but I said good-bye to them and left for Macedonia.^{f}

A Ministry of Life or Death

¹⁴But thanks be to God,^{g} who always puts us on display^A in Christ^B and through us spreads the aroma of the knowledge of Him in every place.^{h} ¹⁵For to God we are the fragrance^i of Christ among those who are being saved^j and among those who are perishing.^{k} ¹⁶To some we are an aroma of death^l leading to death, but to others, an aroma of life^m leading to life. And who is competent for this? ¹⁷For we are not like the many^C who market God's message^n for profit. On the contrary, we speak

with sincerity in Christ, as from God and before God.

Living Letters

3 Are we beginning to commend ourselves again? Or do we need, like some, letters of recommendation to you or from you? ²You yourselves are our letter, written on our hearts, recognized and read by everyone.^{o} ³It is clear that you are Christ's letter,^{p} produced^D by us, not written with ink but with the Spirit of the living God^q—not on stone tablets^r but on tablets that are hearts of flesh.^{s}

Paul's Competence

⁴We have this kind of confidence toward God through Christ. ⁵It is not that we are competent in^E ourselves to consider anything as coming from ourselves, but our competence is from God.^{t} ⁶He has made us competent to be ministers of a new covenant,^{u} not of the letter,^{v} but of the Spirit. For the letter kills, but the Spirit produces life.

^{a}2:11 2Co 12:17	
^{b}2:12 Ac 16:8	
^{c}Col 4:3	
^{d}2:13 2Th 1:7	
^{e}Ti 1:4	
^{f}Ac 16:9	
^{g}2:14 1Co 15:57	
^{h}Jn 17:3; 1Jn 4:8	
^{i}2:15 Eph 5:2; Php 4:18	
^{j}Mt 9:22; Ac 16:30; Eph 2:8	
^{k}Jn 6:27	
^{l}2:16 Mt 10:21; Jn 8:51; Php 3:10	
^{m}1Jn 5:12	
^{n}2:17 Mt 12:36; Mk 4:14; Lk 6:47; 8:21; Jn 1:1; 2:22; 18:32; Ac 17:11; 2Tm 2:15; Heb 4:12	
^{o}3:2 1Co 9:2	
^{p}3:3 Phm 13	
^{q}Dt 5:26	
^{r}Ex 24:12	
^{s}Pr 3:3; 7:3; Jr 17:1; 31:33; Ezk 11:19; 36:26; Heb 8:10	
^{t}3:5 1Co 15:10	
^{u}3:6 Lk 22:20; Heb 7:22	
^{v}Rm 7:6	

^{A}2:14 Or *always leads us in a triumphal procession*, or *always causes us to triumph* ^{B}2:14 Lit *in the Christ*, or *in the Messiah*; 1Co 15:22; Eph 1:10,12,20; 3:11 ^{C}2:17 Other mss read *the rest* ^{D}3:3 Lit *ministered to* ^{E}3:5 Lit *from*

2:11 Behind the sin and discord in the Corinthian church Paul saw **Satan**, the evil one. **His schemes** always include thwarting the unity of believers for which Jesus so fervently prayed (Jn 17).

2:12-13 Troas was a coastal city in the northern part of the province of Asia. Paul went there after the riot in Ephesus (Ac 19:23-41) on his way to **Macedonia** (Ac 20:1-2).**Titus** is not mentioned in Acts. He was Paul's proof that Gentiles could be converted without works of the law such as circumcision (Gl 2:3). That Paul (the Jew) called both Timothy and Titus **brother** (1:1) shows that his primary identity was as a Christian rather than as a Jew. Titus was effective as Paul's ambassador in dealing with the Corinthian crisis. Later he represented the apostle to Christians in Crete (Ti 1:4).

2:14 In antiquity, victorious generals paraded into their

capital city toward the king's palace with human captives and treasure displayed behind them. Sweet incense was offered. The citizens saw and smelled evidence of victory. Here, **Christ** is leading Paul and all other believers into the eternal city where **God** is king.

2:15-16 In these verses two pairs of opposites are crafted so that the inner two elements are negative and the outer two are positive. The same scent produces different results. Those who receive the knowledge of Christ through the gospel message live. All others perish.

2:17 The words **many who market** refer to the false apostles in Corinth whose motive was primarily financial (11:13). Paul's policy was to serve the churches without charge even though he approved of Christians supporting ministers financially (1Co 9:12-15). Accountability for the message lay with the One who was the source of the message.

3:1 The false apostles who had upset the Corinthians had produced **letters of recommendation**. Paul had never felt the need to ask for recommendations, as the implied "No" answers to the two questions asked in this verse make clear.

3:2-3 The spiritual transformation of the Corinthians was endorsement enough for Paul. In their own person, they were spiritual letters, written by **the Spirit** on the tablet of Paul's heart. Literal letters, written with **ink** on paper or even on **stone tablets**, could not compare with changed lives. The reference to stone tablets would remind readers of the Ten Commandments and the old covenant (see note at v. 7; cp. Dt 9:9).

3:4 The **confidence** that Paul described in this verse does not refer to self-confident arrogance or false humility.

3:5 There is no sufficiency for true Christian ministry except **from God**. This verse answers the question at the end of 2:16.

3:6 The word for **ministers** is also translated as "deacons," a broad term that does not refer to a professional class of clergy or priests. The **new covenant** was prophesied in

noema

Greek Pronunciation	[NAH ay mah]
HCSB Translation	intention
Uses in 2 Corinthians	5
Uses in the NT	6
Focus passage	2 Corinthians 2:11

The Greek noun *noema* comes from the verb *noeo*, meaning *to think* or *to understand*. The *-ma* ending indicates the result of thinking, that is, the thought itself, perception, or understanding. Thus, *noema* can mean *mind, thought*, or *intention*. In the NT, the term occurs in a positive sense only in Php 4:7, where Paul stated that the peace of God guards believers' hearts and *minds*. Three times in 2 Corinthians Paul connected the work of Satan with the Christian's *mind (noema)*: believers are not ignorant of Satan's intentions to destroy them (2:11); Satan blinds the *minds* of unbelievers so they cannot be saved (4:4); believers, like Eve, can have their *minds* corrupted by Satan (11:3). Paul's other two uses of *noema* in 2 Corinthians refer to the closed *minds* of the Israelites that keep them from believing in Christ (3:14) and to *thoughts* that keep believers from obeying Christ (10:5).

New Covenant Ministry

[7] Now if the ministry of death, chiseled in letters on stones, came with glory,[a] so that the Israelites were not able to look directly at Moses' face because of the glory from his face—a fading glory— [8] how will the ministry of the Spirit not be more glorious? [9] For if the ministry of condemnation had glory, the ministry of righteousness overflows with even more glory. [10] In fact, what had been glorious is not glorious now by comparison because of the glory that surpasses it. [11] For if what was fading away[b] was glorious, what endures will be even more glorious.

[12] Therefore, having such a hope,[c] we use great boldness. [13] We are not like Moses, who used to put a veil over his face[d] so that the Israelites could not stare at the end of what was fading away, [14] but their minds were closed.[A,e] For to this day, at the reading of the old covenant,[f] the same veil remains; it is not lifted, because it is set aside only in Christ.[g] [15] Even to this day, whenever Moses is read, a veil lies over their hearts, [16] but whenever a person turns[h] to the Lord, the veil is removed.[i] [17] Now the Lord is the Spirit, and where the Spirit of the Lord is, there is freedom. [18] We all, with unveiled faces, are looking as in a mirror[B,j] at the glory of the Lord[k] and are being transformed[l] into the same image[m] from glory to glory;[c] this is from the Lord who is the Spirit.[D]

The Light of the Gospel

[4] Therefore, since we have this ministry because we were shown mercy,[n] we do not give up.[o] [2] Instead, we have renounced shameful secret things, not *walking[p] in deceit or distorting God's message,[q] but commending ourselves to every person's conscience in God's sight by an open display of the truth.[r] [3] But if our gospel is veiled, it is veiled to those who are perishing. [4] In their case, the god of this age[s] has blinded the minds of the unbelievers so they cannot see the light of the gospel of the glory of Christ,[E,t] who is the image of

---

Cross-references column:

[a] 3:7 Ex 34:29-35; Mk 10:37; Lk 9:32; Jn 17:24; 2Co 3:18; 2Pt 3:18
[b] 3:11 Heb 2:14
[c] 3:12 1Th 1:3
[d] 3:13 Ex 34:33
[e] 3:14 Mk 8:17; Heb 3:13
[f] Ac 13:15; 15:21; Heb 7:22
[g] Rm 16:7; 1Pt 5:14
[h] 3:16 1Pt 2:25
[i] Ex 34:34
[j] 3:18 1Co 13:12
[k] Jn 17:24; 2Co 1:20; 4:4-6; 1Tm 1:11,17
[l] Mk 9:2
[m] Gn 1:27; 1Jn 3:2
[n] 4:1 Mt 5:7; Mk 5:19; Lk 1:50
[o] 4:1 2Th 3:13
[p] 2Jn 6
[q] 2Co 2:17; 2Tm 2:15; Heb 4:12
[r] 2Co 5:11-12; 6:7; 7:14
[s] 4:4 Lk 16:8
[t] Mk 10:37

A 3:14 Lit *their thoughts were hardened*   B 3:18 Or *are reflecting*   C 3:18 Progressive glorification or sanctification   D 3:18 Or *from the Spirit of the Lord*, or *from the Lord, the Spirit*   E 4:4 Or *the gospel of the glorious Christ*, or *the glorious gospel of Christ*

Jr 31:31-33, established by Jesus' death in Lk 22:20, and ministered by Paul. **The letter kills** refers to the law of the old covenant, which was not designed to give life. It only revealed sin (Rm 7:7-12). The **Spirit** takes the proclamation of the gospel and creates new **life** by faith (Rm 8:10; 10:17).

3:7 The ministry of death refers to the old covenant made at Mount Sinai. Its effect was condemnation and death, not justification and life. This was not the fault of the old covenant but of sinners who were unable to meet its demands (Rm 7:13). The Ten Commandments were written with **letters on stones** (Ex 31:18). With God as the source of the law, it was right for its human mediator to have something of God's **glory** about him.

3:8-9 The phrases **ministry of righteousness** and **ministry of the Spirit** refer to the new covenant, resulting in righteousness through the indwelling Spirit.

3:10-11 One way in which the old and new covenants contrast is in the degree of **glory** connected with each. In the natural order, the glory of the moon (which wanes every month) is no glory at all in comparison with the unfading sun.

3:13 Paul concluded that the main purpose of Moses' **veil** was to prevent the Israelites from observing the fading of the old-covenant glory. The law was designed by God with a built-in obsolescence (Gl 3:24-25; Heb 8:13).

3:14 Another purpose of a **veil** is to keep the veiled person from seeing outside. Paul implies that the first-century Jews who had not believed the gospel were unable to recognize the fading, temporary nature of **the old covenant**, even when their Scriptures were read.

3:15 The phrase **a veil lies over their hearts** refers not to a literal veil but to a spiritual impairment. One of the great difficulties Jews have had historically in coming to Jesus as Messiah is to acknowledge that He has surpassed the fading old covenant. The words **the veil is removed** refers to the sovereign work of God.

3:17 This is an important Trinitarian text emphasizing the close relationship between the Son and the Spirit. In Rm 8:9 "the Spirit of God" and "the Spirit of Christ" appear to be interchangeable.

3:18 Paul included all believers among the **unveiled**, whose glory, having begun in the new covenant, can never fade. It moves **from glory** (on earth, in regeneration, justification, and sanctification) **to glory** (in heaven, in glorification).

4:1-6 By extension, the first-person plural pronouns in this section may be applied to all true ministers of the gospel (not just professional clergy but all believers).

4:1 Because true **ministry** proceeds only from God's undeserved **mercy**, Paul included with it the strength to persevere despite opposition.

4:2 The false apostles may have pandered to the Corinthians by pretending to have "inside information," like the Jezebel who corrupted the believers of Thyatira with "the deep things of Satan" (Rv 2:24). False teachers are recognized both by wrong motives (**deceit**) and the wrong message (**distorting**). True teachers are recognized by right motives and by "the faith that was delivered to the saints once for all" (Jd 3). There is no secret tier of truth reserved only for those who have been initiated into its secrets.

4:3 On **gospel is veiled**, see note at 3:15. Paul's reference here is to every person (Gentile as well as Jew) who has not responded to the proclamation of the gospel.

4:4 Satan has a role in keeping persons from Christ and the gospel, even though they are accountable for their own souls and cannot blame the Devil. Moreover, Satan cannot prevent the gospel light from penetrating. Without God's enablement, a sinner can no more "see" the gospel than a blind person can see the sun. The foundation and the goal of the **gospel** is that Christ's splendor or **glory** will be dis-

God.[a] [5]For we are not proclaiming ourselves but Jesus Christ as Lord,[b] and ourselves as your •slaves because of Jesus. [6]For God who said, "Let light shine out of darkness,"[c] has shone in our hearts to give the light of the knowledge[d] of God's glory[e] in the face of Jesus Christ.

Treasure in Clay Jars

[7]Now we have this treasure in clay jars, so that this extraordinary power[f] may be from God and not from us. [8]We are pressured in every way but not crushed; we are perplexed but not in despair; [9]we are persecuted but not abandoned; we are struck down but not destroyed. [10]We always carry the death of Jesus[g] in our body, so that the life of Jesus may also be revealed in our body. [11]For we who live are always given over to death[h] because of Jesus, so that Jesus' life may also be revealed in our mortal flesh. [12]So death works in us, but life in you. [13]And since we have the same spirit of faith in keeping with what is written, **I believed, therefore I spoke,**[A,i] we also believe, and therefore speak. [14]We know that the One who raised the Lord Jesus will raise us also with Jesus[j] and present us with you. [15]Indeed, everything is for your benefit, so that grace, extended through more and more people, may cause thanksgiving[k] to increase to God's glory.

[16]Therefore we do not give up.[l] Even though our outer person is being destroyed, our inner person[m] is being renewed day by day. [17]For our momentary light affliction[B,n] is producing for us an absolutely incomparable eternal weight of glory.[o] [18]So we do not focus on what is seen,[p] but on what is unseen. For what is seen is temporary, but what is unseen is eternal.

---

[a]4:4 Gn 1:27
[b]4:5 Php 2:11
[c]4:6 Gn 1:3; Mt 6:23
[d]Php 3:8; 1Jn 4:8
[e]Mk 10:37; Lk 9:32; Jn 17:24; 2Co 3:18; 2Pt 3:18
[f]4:7 Mk 5:30; Lk 1:35; 6:19; Ac 19:11; 2Co 13:4; Rv 11:17
[g]4:10 Lk 9:23; Rm 5:6-8; 6:5-8; 8:34-36; Gl 6:17
[h]4:11 Mt 10:21; Jn 8:51; Php 3:10
[i]4:13 Ps 116:10 LXX
[j]4:14 1Th 4:14
[k]4:15 2Co 9:11
[l]4:16 2Th 3:13
[m]Rm 7:22
[n]4:17 Gl 6:2
[o]Lk 24:26; 1Pt 5:1,4
[p]4:18 Rm 8:24

[A]4:13 Ps 116:10 LXX   [B]4:17 See note at 2Co 1:4.

---

played. Sinners are converted so they may admire and love Him.

4:5 The words **Lord** and **slaves** demonstrate a reciprocal relationship, but here Paul focused on his service to Christ by means of serving other believers.

4:6 The original creation of **light** out of **darkness** (Gn 1:3) provided the paradigm for God's re-creation of spiritual light in a sinner (2Co 5:17). The initiative lies with God **to give the light**. On **the knowledge of God's glory**, compare with note at verse 4. "Light" given by God results in the human response to "gospel/knowledge" which in turn results in "glory of Christ/God's glory" being admired. Coupled with the statement in verse 4 that He is "the image of God," the words **in the face of Jesus Christ** are a strong testimony to

Paul's belief in the deity of Christ, in whose face God's glory is fully displayed (Jn 1:14,18; Heb 1:3).

4:7 Treasure is the unfading glory that accompanies the new covenant (3:8). The **power** to bring this about lies only with God. **Clay jars** is a metaphor for fragile and mortal human bodies. Sometimes the more humble the container, the more glorious its precious contents appear.

4:8-9 These verses contain four pairs of opposites. The first element of each pair characterizes frail humanity, especially humans in service to God. The second element gives evidence of God's power.

4:10-11 In His humanity Jesus was subject to **death**; by God's power He was raised to resurrection **life**. Paul (and indeed all the saints) would follow Jesus' example, although for Paul the resurrection life had already been **revealed in our mortal flesh**. See Eph 2:4-6, where believers are already made alive, raised, and seated with Christ.

4:12 Paul's trials as a minister led ultimately to his experiencing a martyr's bodily **death**; however, his trials were instrumental in bringing spiritual **life** to the Corinthians.

4:13 The Hebrew text of Ps 116:10 is, "I believed, even when I said, 'I am severely afflicted.'" Paul quoted the Septuagint (Gk version). The main point is that trust in the Lord motivates a person to action.

4:14 At Christ's coming, God will raise believers. This must be distinguished from the new spiritual life that Paul enjoyed while still in bodily life (vv. 10-11). The words **us with you** show that the resurrection of the saints is not individualistic. See 11:2 for the other instance of the verb **present** in 2 Corinthians, which also emphasizes the corporate nature of the church (as a bride).

4:15 On **God's glory**, see notes at verses 4 and 6.

4:16 The words **we do not give up** are repeated from verse 1. Between these two statements Paul explains why he was not defeated even in extremely negative circumstances. The apostle is the ideal for all believers.

4:17-18 These verses contain three pairs of opposites. These also contrast the experiences of frail humanity with the evidences of God's power (see note at vv. 8-9).

---

eikon

Greek Pronunciation	[ay KOHN]
HCSB Translation	image
Uses in 2 Corinthians	2
Uses in the NT	23
Focus passage	2 Corinthians 4:4

The English word *icon* comes from the Greek noun *eikon*, which means *image*, *form*, or *statue*. In the NT, *eikon* is used in seven ways. (1) A coin bears the *image* of Caesar (Mt 22:20; Mk 12:16; Lk 20:24). (2) Unbelievers worship *images* of man and animals (Rm 1:23). (3) All humans bear the *image* of Adam (1Co 15:49). (4) Believers bear the *image* of Christ (Rm 8:29; 1Co 15:49). (5) Christ is the *image* of God (2Co 4:4; Col 1:15). (6) The law was a shadowy *image* of what Christ's sacrifice provides (Heb 10:1). (7) The book of Revelation refers to the beast who demands that everyone on earth worship his *image*, and God judges those who do (Rv 13:14-15; 14:9,11; 15:2; 16:2; 19:20; 20:4).

Two main ideas emerge from these uses: representation and manifestation. Caesar is represented by his *image* on a coin, and pagan gods are represented by *images* of themselves. Man was created to represent God and to manifest His presence in the world. However, Christ does not merely represent God; He is the full manifestation of God. Believers are being conformed to Christ's *image* and thus manifest God's presence as well.

Our Future after Death

5 For we know that if our temporary, earthly dwelling[A,a] is destroyed, we have a building from God, an eternal dwelling[B] in the heavens,[b] not made with hands.[c] [2]Indeed, we groan in this body, desiring[d] to put on our dwelling from heaven, [3]since, when we are clothed,[C] we will not be found naked.[e] [4]Indeed, we groan while we are in this tent, burdened as we are, because we do not want to be unclothed but clothed, so that mortality[f] may be swallowed up by life. [5]And the One who prepared us for this very purpose is God, who gave us the Spirit as a down payment.

[6]So, we are always confident and know that while we are at home in the body we are away from the Lord. [7]For we •walk by faith,[g] not by sight,[h] [8]and we are confident and satisfied to be out of the body and at home with the Lord.[i] [9]Therefore, whether we are at home or away, we make it our aim to be pleasing[j] to Him. [10]For we must all appear before the tribunal[k] of Christ,[l] so that each may be repaid[m] for what he has done in the body, whether good or worthless.

[11]Therefore, because we know the •fear of the Lord,[n] we seek to persuade people. We are completely open before God, and I hope we are completely open to your consciences as well. [12]We are not commending ourselves to you again, but giving you an opportunity to be proud of us, so that you may have a reply for those who take pride in the outward appearance[D] rather than in the heart. [13]For if we are out of our mind,[o] it is for God; if we have a sound mind,[p] it is for you. [14]For Christ's love compels[E] us, since we have reached this conclusion: If One died for all,[q] then all died. [15]And He died for all[r] so that those who live should no longer live for themselves,[s] but for the One[t] who died for them and was raised.

The Ministry of Reconciliation

[16]From now on, then, we do not know[F] anyone in a purely human way.[G] Even if we

[a]5:1 2Pt 1:13
[b]Eph 6:9; Php 2:10
[c]Col 2:11
[d]5:2 2Pt 2:2
[e]Mt 25:36; Lk 10:30
[f]5:4 Rm 7:24; 8:23; 1Co 15:26
[g]5:7 Mt 8:10; Ac 3:16; Rm 1:8; 1Co 2:5; Gl 2:16; 1Tm 1:2; Heb 4:2
[h]Lk 3:22
[i]5:8 Php 1:23
[j]5:9 Heb 13:21
[k]5:10 Jn 5:22-30
[l]Mt 25:31-46; Php 1:6; Heb 10:31
[m]Mt 16:27
[n]5:11 Ps 147:11; Pr 1:7; 1Pt 1:17; Rv 14:7
[o]5:13 Ac 10:45
[p]1Pt 4:7
[q]5:14 Jn 11:51; 2Co 4:10
[r]5:15 Lk 20:38; Heb 2:9
[s]Rm 14:7
[t]Lk 20:38

[A]5:1 = our present physical body   [B]5:1 = our future body   [C]5:3 Other mss read *stripped*   [D]5:12 Lit *in face*   [E]5:14 Or *For the love of Christ impels*, or *For the love of Christ controls*   [F]5:16 Or *regard*   [G]5:16 Lit *anyone according to the flesh*

5:1-10 This section, probably motivated by Paul's recent brush with death (1:8-9), contains the most extensive teaching in Scripture on the "intermediate state," or the condition of believers between the death of the body and its resurrection.

5:1 Paul compared our bodily existence to living in a **temporary . . . dwelling**, and the resurrection body to a palace or other grand **building**. The author of the letter to the Hebrews also compared heaven to "the city that has foundations, whose architect and builder is God" (Heb 11:10).

5:2 On **we groan**, see 1:8 and 4:8-9 for examples from Paul's experience. The resurrection will be something like putting on new clothes (**put on our dwelling**).

5:3 The word **naked** is a reference to being disembodied. A human soul or spirit apart from bodily existence—thought of as a desired state in some religious systems—was never considered desirable in the Scriptures. Paul shared this view.

5:4 Paul's preference was for the final state of the resurrection body rather than the intermediate and apparently bodiless situation of the Christian dead.

5:5 Life in the resurrection is impossible without the proper preparation. This verse emphasizes God's sovereignty. On **the Spirit as a down payment**, see 1:22 and Eph 1:14 for the other NT instances of "down payment," always connected with the Spirit. The beginning of salvation is receiving God's person (the Spirit); the goal of salvation is enjoying God's person fully and forever (Rv 22:4).

5:6-8 Paul drew three contrasts between this life and the intermediate state: at home in the body/out of the body; by faith/by sight; and away from the Lord/at home with the Lord. As long as the saints still live in the body, they perceive Christ only by faith. Paul's pattern is to refer to living believers as "in" Christ or the Lord but to dead believers as "with" Christ or the Lord, when faith becomes sight in conscious fellowship with the Lord.

5:9-10 **At home or away** refers to either earthly bodily existence or away from bodily existence (disembodied). The main way in which the righteous dead may be **pleasing to Him** is by receiving a positive verdict before the **tribunal** of Christ. See Rm 14:10 for the other NT instance of "tribunal" (Gk *beyma*) as a future event for believers. The biblical teaching is that Christians are saved by faith, but they will be judged according to the **good or worthless** deeds they have done. This is a judgment to determine rewards, not eternal destination. See especially 1Co 3:10-15.

5:11-12 The **fear of the Lord** is the awe and respect due to Christ as the judge of a believer's works. A prominent OT wisdom theme (Pr 1:7), fear of God may not be forgotten by NT believers (Ac 9:31; Rv 15:4). The Corinthians needed to be reminded of this fear in terms of their treatment of Christ's apostle. Paul's motives were pure, both before the Lord he feared and before the people he served.

5:13-14 Paul's opponents probably had suggested that he was religiously unbalanced (see Ac 26:24). He was "insane" in that **Christ's love** compelled him into vigorous apostolic ministry. On the other hand, his ministry among the Corinthians had never been that of a madman (1Co 2:1-5). Indeed, he had kept his "third heaven" vision private for 14 years until he mentioned it later in this letter (12:1-10). The heart of Paul's message was that the Jewish Messiah **died** on behalf of **all** kinds of sinners (1Co 15:3). Jews as well as Gentiles were included in Jesus' substitutionary death (Rv 7:9). In union with Christ, sinners who believe the gospel have died to sin and have been raised to walk in a new way of life.

5:15 The phrase **those who live** refers to believers who are now spiritually alive (Eph 2:4-6). Christ's death and resurrection ministry have become the pattern for the believer's death and new-life ministry. Paul personally modeled this as well.

5:16 The phrase **in a purely human way** is a good rendering of the Greek text (lit "according to the flesh"). There are always two conflicting perspectives on a situation: the natural

have known[A] Christ in a purely human way,[B] yet now we no longer know[C] Him in this way. [17] Therefore, if anyone is in Christ, he is a new creation;[a] old things have passed away, and look,[b] new things[D] have come.[c] [18] Everything is from God, who reconciled us to Himself through Christ and gave us the ministry of reconciliation:[d] [19] That is, in Christ, God was reconciling the world[e] to Himself,[f] not counting their trespasses against them, and He has committed the message of reconciliation to us. [20] Therefore, we are ambassadors[g] for Christ, certain that God is appealing through us. We plead on Christ's behalf,[h] "Be reconciled to God." [21] He made the One who did not know sin[i] to be sin[E] for us,[j] so that we might become the righteousness of God in Him.

[6] Working together[F] with Him, we also appeal to you, "Don't receive God's grace in vain." [2] For He says:

(cross-references column)
[a]5:17 Jn 1:3; Rv 3:14
[b]Rm 8:24
[c]Is 43:19; 65:17; Rm 6:4; Eph 4:24; Rv 21:5
[d]5:18 Rm 5:11
[e]5:19 2Pt 2:20
[f]Ti 2:11
[g]5:20 Eph 6:20
[h]2Co 12:10; Php 1:29
[i]5:21 1Jn 3:5
[j]Rm 8:3; Gl 3:13; 1Pt 2:24
[k]6:2 Is 49:8
[l]Is 49:8; 55:6; Lk 4:19; Heb 3:13
[m]6:5 Jdg 16:21
[n]6:6 2Co 11:3
[o]Php 3:8; 1Jn 4:8
[p]Ex 34:6; 2Tm 3:10
[q]Rm 2:4; 3:12; 11:22; Gl 5:22; Eph 2:7; Col 3:12; Ti 3:4
[r]1Co 13:1
[s]6:7 2Th 2:10

I heard you in an acceptable time,
and I helped you in the day of salvation.[G,k]

Look, now is the acceptable time; now is the day of salvation.[l]

The Character of Paul's Ministry

[3] We give no opportunity for stumbling to anyone, so that the ministry will not be blamed. [4] But as God's ministers, we commend ourselves in everything:

by great endurance, by afflictions,
by hardship, by difficulties,
[5] by beatings, by imprisonments,[m]
by riots, by labors,
by sleepless nights, by times of hunger,
[6] by purity,[n] by knowledge,[o]
by patience,[p] by kindness,[q]
by the Holy Spirit, by sincere love,[r]
[7] by the message of truth,[s]

[A]5:16 Or have regarded   [B]5:16 Lit Christ according to the flesh   [C]5:16 Or regard   [D]5:17 Other mss read look, all new things   [E]5:21 Or be a sin offering   [F]6:1 Or As we work together   [G]6:2 Is 49:8

---

versus the divine. A natural view of Christ led to His crucifixion and to Paul's persecution of Christ-followers. After the light of divine revelation broke in on Paul on the Damascus road, he could **no longer know Him in this way** (Ac 9).

5:17-18 The words **in Christ** refer to being in union with Him. Genuine conversion begins life transformation, but not by reforming the old nature. The indwelling Spirit creates divine life in believers (Rm 8:8-10), enabling a life of **new things**. Other NT passages communicate this truth by using language such as "born again" or "regeneration" (Jn 3:3-8; Ti 3:5; 1Pt 1:23). Those who were enemies of God have now become friends by being **reconciled** to Him. God's wrath against sin was satisfied in the death of His Son. Sinners—who formerly put self-interest above God's glory (Rm 1:21; 3:23)—have been brought to cherish God as their highest treasure (2Co 4:6). The **ministry of reconciliation**—being an agent of this good news—was Paul's special responsibility, but the task belongs to all who have received this ministry.

katallasso

Greek Pronunciation	[kah tahl LAHSS oh]
HCSB Translation	reconcile
Uses in 2 Corinthians	3
Uses in the NT	6
Focus passage	2 Corinthians 5:18-20

The Greek verb *katallasso* basically means *to change* or *exchange*. It was often used as a monetary term referring to *changing* or *exchanging* money, but in general it referred to *exchanging* one thing for another. A common use of *katallasso* was in reference to changing someone from an enemy into a friend, that is, *bringing together* or *reconciling* two people or parties that are at odds with each other. This is how *katallasso* is used all six times in the NT, as is also the case for all four uses of the related noun *katallage* (meaning *reconciliation*; see 2Co 5:18-19; Rm 5:11; 11:15). These two words are found only in Paul's writings. In 1Co 7:11, Paul used *katallasso* to describe the *reconciliation* of husband and wife. Paul's other five uses of the term explain that unbelievers can be *reconciled* to God through Christ. Because of sin, unbelievers are God's enemies (Rm 5:10), but they can be *reconciled* to God through faith in Christ (2Co 5:18-19).

5:19-21 What **Christ** did, **God** did. Christ's death mainly affected the world, that is, human sinners (rather than evil supernatural beings, for whom no divine provision for reconciliation has been made). Christ's death upholds God's righteousness. Trespasses were placed on **the One who did not know sin**. In return, **the righteousness of God** is credited (imputed) to all who are **in Him**. The **message of reconciliation** is known to others only when **ambassadors for Christ** spread it. The Great Commission is the responsibility of reconciled human beings, not angels (Mt 28:18-20).

6:1 Receiving Paul's apostleship as genuine included receiving his gospel message of **God's grace** as true. The phrase **in vain** may refer to (1) falling away from a profession of faith that was apparent but not genuine and therefore going into eternity apart from Christ (1Jn 2:19); or (2) developing neither Christlike character nor doing good works because of a life of "backsliding" and therefore having one's works burned at the judgment seat of Christ (1Co 3:12-14; 2Co 5:10).

6:2 The larger context of Is 49:8 was God's restoration that would come at last to the covenant people, Israel. Paul's citation shows that he believed this time had now arrived with the incarnation, death, and resurrection of Christ. **Now** and **day of salvation** refer in general to the times between Christ's first and second coming. In particular, they refer to the moment a person hears the good news: there should be no delay in responding.

6:3 The phrase **no opportunity for stumbling** is a reference to Paul's character and actions, which were open to observation. The ministry of reconciliation was worth all the hardship Paul endured. The list in verses 4-13 is not self-commendation (like the false teachers; 3:1) but reflects a survey of Paul's actions as God's appointed minister, demonstrating the character and source of his ministry.

6:4-5 The book of Acts recounts specific instances of Paul's suffering. This part of the list includes experiences that were physically painful. From a human perspective, these were useless and unnecessary—unless the gospel is true.

6:6-7 This part of the list focuses on character traits and spiritual realities perceived only with the eye of faith. On

by the power of God;[a]
through weapons of righteousness
on the right hand and the left,
8 through glory[b] and dishonor,
through slander and good report;
as deceivers yet true;
9 as unknown yet recognized;
as dying and look—we live;
as being disciplined yet not killed;
10 as grieving yet always rejoicing;[c]
as poor yet enriching many;
as having nothing yet
possessing everything.

11 We have spoken openly[A] to you, Corinthians; our heart has been opened wide. 12 You are not limited by us, but you are limited by your own affections. 13 I speak as to my children. As a proper response, you should also be open to us.

Separation to God

14 Do not be mismatched with unbelievers. For what partnership is there between righteousness and lawlessness?[d] Or what fellowship does light[e] have with darkness?[f] 15 What agreement does Christ have with Belial?[B] Or what does a believer have in common with an unbeliever? 16 And what agreement does God's

sanctuary have with idols?[g] For we[c] are the sanctuary of the living God, as God said:

> I will dwell among them[h]
> and walk among them,
> and I will be their God,[i]
> and they will be My people.[D,j]

17 Therefore, come out from among them
and be separate, says the Lord;
do not touch any unclean thing,
and I will welcome you.[E,k]
18 I will be a Father[l] to you,
and you will be sons[m] and daughters
to Me,
says the Lord Almighty.[F,n]

7 Therefore, dear friends, since we have such promises,[o] let us •cleanse ourselves from every impurity of the flesh and spirit,[p] completing our •sanctification[G] in the •fear of God.[q]

Joy and Repentance

2 Accept us.[H] We have wronged no one, corrupted[r] no one, defrauded no one. 3 I don't say this to condemn you, for I have already said that you are in our hearts, to live together and to die together. 4 I have great confidence in you; I have great pride in you. I am filled with

Cross references
a 6:7 Mk 5:30; Lk 1:35; 6:19; Ac 19:11; 2Co 13:4; Rv 11:17
b 6:8 1Pt 5:4
c 6:10 Mt 5:4; Jn 16:22; 2Co 7:4; Php 1:4,25; 2:17-18; 3:1; 4:1,4; Col 1:24; 1Th 1:6; 1Pt 1:6-8
d 6:14 Mt 13:41
e Jn 12:46
f Mt 6:23
g 6:16 Gn 31:19; 1Co 8:4
h Jms 4:5
i Heb 3:6
j Lv 26:12
k 6:17 Is 52:11
l 6:18 Mt 5:16; 11:27; Lk 11:13; Jn 8:42; Eph 5:20
m Mt 5:9
n 2Sm 7:14; Rv 1:8
o 7:1 Gn 12:7
p Ps 51:12
q Ps 147:11; Pr 1:7; Rv 14:7
r 7:2 1Co 3:17; 15:33; 2Co 11:3; Eph 4:22; 2Pt 2:12; Jd 10; Rv 19:2

A 6:11 Lit Our mouths have been open   B 6:15 Or Beliar, a name for the Devil or antichrist in extra-biblical Jewish writings   C 6:16 Other mss read you   D 6:12 Lv 26:12; Jr 31:33; 32:38; Ezk 37:26   E 6:17 Is 52:11   F 6:18 2Sm 7:14; Is 43:6; 49:22; 60:4; Hs 1:10   G 7:1 Or spirit, perfecting holiness   H 7:2 Lit Make room for us

---

weapons of righteousness, see Eph 6:10-20 for a full discussion of spiritual armor.

6:8-10 The paradox of genuine Christian ministry is nowhere better stated than in these verses. Paul noted nine contrasts between frail humanity and the evidence of God's power (see notes at 4:8-9 and 4:17-18).

6:11 Paul's life and teaching were an open book. He had no hidden agenda.

6:12-13 Paul perceived the relationship problem to lie with the Corinthians. The false teachers had strangled the Corinthians' love for Paul. He yearned for them to be as **open** and loving toward him as he had been with them—like a father toward wayward **children**.

6:14 **Mismatched with unbelievers** refers to the false apostles, whom Paul considered to be Satan's servants. The original language pictures two different kinds of animals plowing a field under a single yoke (Dt 22:10). Under such circumstances the objective cannot be reached. **Partnership** has traditionally been translated as "fellowship." Paul emphasized spiritual incompatibility by noting the impossibility of literal light and darkness equally existing, and, in verse 15, the impossibility of Christ and Satan being friends.

6:15 **Belial** is a Hebrew term found elsewhere in an OT phrase, literally "sons of Belial," translated "wicked men" or "perverted men" in the HCSB (Dt 13:13).

6:16a The "we" in **we are the sanctuary** points to the corporate entity of the local congregation (or the body of Christ as a whole) rather than to the individual (for which, see 1Co

6:19). Paul had believers in mind, not literal buildings (1Pt 2:5).

6:16b-18 These verses assemble a number of OT texts. Verse 16b is stated first in Lv 26:12 and repeated in Jr 31:33; 32:38. This was God's promise of His presence to His covenant people, now fulfilled in the new covenant instituted by Christ (Heb 8:7-13). Verse 17 cites Is 52:11, referring to Israel's future holiness when they will be restored to the Lord's favor. Verse 18 is found first in 2Sm 7:14 in God's covenant promise to David, but it is echoed in Is 43:6; 49:22; 60:4; Hs 1:10. In these passages the Lord promised a family relationship between Himself and His people.

7:1 The phrase **dear friends** (lit "beloved") is a statement of Paul's strong affection for these believers, despite the tears they had caused him. **Cleanse ourselves** is not a reference to Christian baptism but to the daily spiritual cleansing that believers are to experience (Jn 13:10). **Completing our sanctification** indicates that growth in holiness is not optional. Believers are to become as mature and Christlike in this lifetime as they can, but the work will be completed only on the day of Christ (Php 1:6). On **fear of God**, see note at 5:11-12.

7:2-3 The false apostles had persuaded some of the Corinthians that Paul had **wronged, corrupted,** and **defrauded** them. He vigorously denied this. He believed he and the Corinthians shared common destinies.

7:4 Paul broke into an exuberant expression of gratitude for the success of Titus's mission to Corinth. Paul's ministry among them had not been in vain but at last had proven to be successful.

encouragement; I am overcome with joy in all our afflictions.

[5] In fact, when we came into Macedonia,[a] we[A] had no rest. Instead, we were troubled in every way: conflicts[b] on the outside, fears[c] inside. [6] But God, who comforts the humble,[d] comforted us by the arrival of Titus, [7] and not only by his arrival, but also by the comfort he received from you. He told us about your deep longing, your sorrow,[B] and your zeal[e] for me, so that I rejoiced even more. [8] For even if I grieved you with my letter,[f] I do not regret it—even though I did regret it since I saw that the letter grieved you, yet only for a little while. [9] Now I rejoice, not because you were grieved, but because your grief led to repentance. For you were grieved as God willed, so that you didn't experience any loss from us. [10] For godly grief produces a repentance not to be regretted and leading to salvation, but worldly grief produces death.[g] [11] For consider how much diligence this very thing—this grieving as God wills—has produced in you: what a desire to clear yourselves, what indignation, what fear, what deep longing, what zeal, what justice! In every way you showed yourselves to be pure[h] in this matter. [12] So even though I wrote to you, it was not because of the one who did wrong, or because of the one who was wronged, but in order that your diligence for us might be made plain to you in the sight of God. [13] For this reason we have been comforted.

In addition to our comfort, we rejoiced even more over the joy Titus[i] had,[C] because his spirit was refreshed by all of you. [14] For if I have made any boast to him about you, I have not been embarrassed; but as I have spoken everything to you in truth,[j] so our boasting to Titus has also turned out to be the truth. [15] And his affection toward you is even greater as he remembers the obedience of all of you, and how you received him with fear and trembling. [16] I rejoice that I have complete confidence in you.

Appeal to Complete the Collection

8 We want you to know, •brothers, about the grace of God granted to the churches[k] of Macedonia:[l] [2] During a severe testing by affliction, their abundance of joy and their deep poverty overflowed into the wealth of their generosity.[m] [3] I testify that, on their own, according to their ability and beyond their ability, [4] they begged us insistently for the privilege of sharing[n] in the ministry to the •saints, [5] and not just as we had hoped. Instead, they gave themselves especially to the Lord, then

---

Cross-references (center column):
[a]7:5 Ac 16:9
[b]Jms 4:1; Ti 3:9
[c]Jn 7:13; Ac 27:29
[d]7:6 Mt 11:29
[e]7:7 Nm 25:13
[f]7:8 2Co 2:2,4
[g]7:10 Mt 10:21; Jn 8:51; Php 3:10
[h]7:11 Php 4:8
[i]7:13 Ti 1:4
[j]7:14 Ps 119:142; Jn 8:14; 14:6; 2Co 11:10; 1Jn 5:20; 3Jn 3
[k]8:1 Mt 16:18; 1Co 14:4; Rv 1:4
[l]Ac 16:9
[m]8:2 Php 4:10
[n]8:4 Ac 24:17; Rm 15:26,31; 2Co 8:19-20; 9:1,12-13

[A]7:5 Lit our flesh   [B]7:7 Or lamentation, or mourning   [C]7:13 Lit the joy of Titus

---

7:5 On **Macedonia**, see notes at 1:15-16 and 2:12-13. Paul was returning to a narration of his travels. Philippi and Thessalonica were prominent Macedonian cities where the apostle had earlier planted churches (Ac 16–17). His **conflicts** and **fears** were not only because of the everyday pressure of ministry but especially because of his anguish over the state of the Corinthian Christians.

lupe

Greek Pronunciation	[LOO pay]
HCSB Translation	grief
Uses in 2 Corinthians	6
Uses in the NT	16
Focus passage	2 Corinthians 7:10

The Greek noun *lupe* means *pain, grief,* or *sorrow.* The related verb *lupeo* means *to cause pain* or *to grieve* and occurs 26 times in the NT (15 of them in Paul's writings; 12 in 2 Corinthians). In ancient Greek both *lupe* and *lupeo* could refer to *pain* experienced by the physical body, but most of the time the terms were used figuratively for mental and emotional *anguish.*

Four times in Paul's writings *lupe* refers in a negative sense to his deep *concern* about spiritual matters, such as Israel's unbelief (Rm 9:2), the attitude of other Christians to his ministry (2Co 2:1,3), and the near death of a fellow worker in the Lord (Php 2:27). Paul also used *lupe* to describe the *grief* caused by sin in the life of a Christian (2Co 2:7) and to explain that Christian giving should not be motivated by *regret [lupe]* but by a cheerful heart (2Co 9:7). In 2Co 7:10 Paul contrasted the false *grief* of the world with the "godly grief" that leads to repentance, warning against the notion that just any form of repentance is genuine.

7:6-7 God uses human agents to bring divine comfort (1:3-7). God's comfort came to Paul through Titus because of the Corinthians' repentance.

7:8 The letter refers to the severe (and now lost) letter written after 1 Corinthians. See note at 2:3-4.

7:11 Paul reminded the Corinthians of the specific occasion, reported to him by Titus, when godly **grieving** had finally broken in on their congregation.

7:12 On **I wrote**, see note at verse 8. Paul was more concerned about the relationship between the Corinthians and himself (as disciples to their spiritual father; see note at 11:2-3) than he was about the troublemaker.

7:13-15 Verses 5-12 describe the effect of the Corinthians' change of heart toward Paul. These verses report the effect on Titus. Paul had predicted that the Corinthians would eventually repent, and Titus had been overjoyed when this turned out to be true.

8:1 The **churches of Macedonia** were congregations in Philippi, Thessalonica, and Berea (Ac 16–17).

8:2-3 These churches had been born in **affliction** (Ac 16–17). Moreover, they were limited in financial resources; yet these factors had not impeded their giving.

8:4 The same word (**ministry**) previously used to describe Christian service (4:1; 5:18; 6:3) is now used to describe Christian giving. Financial stewardship is ministry.

8:5 Here is the key to understanding giving as a ministry. When believers offer **themselves** wholly to **the Lord**, they have no difficulty in offering their wallets to Him.

to us by God's will.[a] [6] So we urged Titus that just as he had begun, so he should also complete this grace to you. [7] Now as you excel in everything—faith, speech, knowledge,[b] and in all diligence, and in your love for us[A]—excel also in this grace.

[8] I am not saying this as a command. Rather, by means of the diligence of others, I am testing the genuineness of your love. [9] For you know the grace of our Lord Jesus Christ: Though He was rich,[c] for your sake He became poor,[d] so that by His poverty you might become rich. [10] Now I am giving an opinion on this because it is profitable for you, who a year ago began not only to do something but also to desire it.[B,e] [11] But now finish the task[c] as well, that just as there was eagerness to desire it, so there may also be a completion from what you have. [12] For if the eagerness is there, it is acceptable according to what one has, not according to what he does not have.[f] [13] It is not that there may be relief for others and hardship for you, but it is a question of equality[D]— [14] at the present time your surplus is available for their need, so their abundance may also become available for our need, so there may be equality. [15] As it has been written:

**The person who gathered much
did not have too much,**

**and the person who
gathered little
did not have too little.**[E,g]

Administration of the Collection

[16] Thanks be to God who put the same concern for you into the heart of Titus. [17] For he accepted our urging and, being very diligent, went out to you by his own choice. [18] We have sent with him the brother[h] who is praised throughout the churches for his gospel ministry.[F] [19] And not only that, but he was also appointed by the churches to accompany us with this gift[G] that is being administered by us for the glory of the Lord Himself and to show our eagerness to help. [20] We are taking this precaution so no one can criticize us about this large sum administered by us. [21] For we are making provision[i] for what is right,[j] not only before the Lord but also before men. [22] We have also sent with them our brother. We have often tested him in many circumstances and found him to be diligent—and now even more diligent because of his great confidence in you. [23] As for Titus, he is my partner[k] and coworker[l] serving you; as for our brothers, they are the messengers[m] of the churches, the glory of Christ.[n] [24] Therefore, show them proof before the churches of your love and of our boasting[o] about you.

---

[a] 8:5 Ps 143:10; Pr 16:9; Jn 5:30; Gl 1:4; Eph 1:9; 1Jn 2:17
[b] 8:7 Php 3:8; 1Jn 4:8
[c] 8:9 Mt 20:28; 2Co 6:10; Php 2:6-7
[d] Php 2:7
[e] 8:10 1Co 16:1-4; 2Co 9:1-2
[f] 8:12 Lk 21:3
[g] 8:15 Ex 16:18
[h] 8:18 2Co 12:18
[i] 8:21 1Tm 5:8
[j] 1Pt 2:12
[k] 8:23 Phm 17
[l] 1Co 3:9
[m] Jn 13:16
[n] Mk 10:37
[o] 8:24 2Co 12:5; Jms 4:16

[A] 8:7 Other mss read *in our love for you*   [B] 8:10 Lit *to will*   [C] 8:11 Lit *finish the doing*   [D] 8:13 Lit *but from equality*   [E] 8:15 Ex 16:18
[F] 8:18 Lit *churches, in the gospel*   [G] 8:19 Or *grace*

8:6 Paul's collection for the Jerusalem Christians had been a long-term project. He had evidently put **Titus** in charge of at least part of it. The Corinthians had "been prepared since last year" (9:2) to give, but had not completed the task. The recent trouble in Corinth, causing Paul's sorrowful visit and the severe letter, had surely been the major factor. Now that the Corinthians were restored, it was time to finish the task, but it would only be done the right way if it was prompted by God's **grace** (v. 1).

8:7 The Corinthians were more affluent than the Macedonians; therefore they could give more generously, and this is what Paul expected to happen (**excel also in this grace**).

8:8 The generosity of the Macedonians set a challenging standard for giving. Only **love** for God by His grace would enable the Corinthians to pass this test.

8:9 Jesus' self-sacrifice is an even higher standard of giving. He willingly exchanged all the wealth of His deity for the **poverty** of the incarnation.

8:10-11 On **finish the task**, see note at verse 6.

8:12 God is more concerned with the quality of giving than with the quantity, as with the widow who gave two coins (Lk 21:1-4).

8:13-14 A congregation that has been generous may later find itself in need of help from others.

8:15 The quotation from Ex 16:18 comes from the Israelites' first experience with gathering daily manna. Paul drew an analogy. **The person who gathered much** was a strong Israelite (like the wealthy Corinthians), while **the person who gathered little** was a weak—sick or aged—Israelite (like the impoverished saints in Jerusalem). Just as there had been an equitable distribution of manna among the Israelites, so there should be a fair sharing of resources among Christians.

8:16-17 **Titus** had volunteered to return to the Corinthians to oversee the collection. **Went out to you** refers to Titus's role as the letter carrier for 2 Corinthians.

8:18 The **brother who is praised** is not named, but it may have been Luke.

8:19 Congregations are to be involved in leadership decisions. Acts 20:4 lists all the church messengers that would **accompany** Paul with this **gift**, with Luke included in Ac 20:5 by the word "we" or "us."

8:20-21 From the beginning of Christianity, a scrupulous concern for integrity in dealing with money has been important. **Before men** implies public accountability.

8:22 Like the **brother** of verse 18, this one is also unnamed but praised.

8:23 On **partner and coworker**, see note at 2:12-13 for more about Titus's credentials. The **messengers** of the churches were literally "apostles." Only those selected by the churches (v. 19) could properly fulfill this function. Just as the gospel itself displays Christ's splendor (see note at 4:4), so do lives transformed by the gospel.

8:24 This verse is another appeal for the Corinthian believers to complete the offering (see note at v. 7).

Motivations for Giving

9 Now concerning the ministry to the ᵃsaints, it is unnecessary for me to write to you. ²For I know your eagerness, and I brag about you to the Macedonians:^A,ᵃ "Achaia^B,ᵇ has been prepared since last year," and your zealᶜ has stirred up most of them.ᵈ ³But I sent the brothers so our boasting about you in the matter would not prove empty, and so you would be prepared just as I said. ⁴For if any Macedonians come with me and find you unprepared, we, not to mention you, would be embarrassed in that situation.ᶜ ⁵Therefore I considered it necessary to urge the brothers to go on ahead to you and arrange in advance the generous giftᵉ you promised, so that it will be ready as a gift and not as an extortion.ᶠ

⁶Remember this:^D The person who sows sparingly will also reap sparingly, and the person who sows generously will also reap generously. ⁷Each person should do as he has decided in his heart—not reluctantly or out of necessity, for God lovesᵍ a cheerful giver. ⁸And God is ableʰ to make every grace

overflow to you, so that in every way, always having everything you need, you may excel in every good work. ⁹As it is written:

> He scattered;ⁱ
> He gave to the poor;
> His righteousness endures forever.^E,ʲ

¹⁰Now the One who provides seed for the sower and bread for food will provide and multiply your seed and increase the harvest of your righteousness.ᵏ ¹¹You will be enrichedˡ in every way for all generosity, which produces thanksgiving to God through us. ¹²For the ministry of this serviceᵐ is not only supplying the needs of the saints, but is also overflowing in many acts of thanksgiving to God. ¹³They will glorify God for your obedience to the confession of^F the gospel of Christ, and for your generosityⁿ in sharing with them and with others through the proof provided by this service. ¹⁴And they will have deep affection for^G you in their prayers on your behalf because of the surpassing grace of God in you. ¹⁵Thanks be to God for His indescribable gift.

ᵃ9:2 Ac 16:9
ᵇAc 18:12
ᶜNm 25:13
ᵈ2Co 8:18; 12:18
ᵉ9:5 Ac 11:30
ᶠEph 5:3
ᵍ9:7 Lk 6:35; Jn 3:16; 12:43; 2Th 2:13; Rv 12:11
ʰ9:8 Eph 3:20
ⁱ9:9 Jn 16:32
ʲPs 112:9; 1Jn 2:17
ᵏ9:10 Is 55:10-11; Hs 10:12
ˡ9:11 1Co 1:5; 2Co 6:10
ᵐ9:12 Heb 8:6
ⁿ9:13 Php 4:10

A9:2 Macedonia was a Roman province in the northern area of modern Greece.   **B**9:2 Achaia was the Roman province, south of Macedonia, where Corinth was located.   **C**9:4 Or *in this confidence*   **D**9:6 Lit *And this*   **E**9:9 Ps 112:9   **F**9:13 Or *your obedient confession to*   **G**9:14 Or *will long for*

9:1-5 This section explains that Paul wanted to spare the Corinthians the embarrassment that would happen if their pledge went unfulfilled and others learned about it.

9:1 On **ministry to the saints**, see note at 8:4.

9:2 The **Macedonians** lived in the province north of **Achaia**, the province in which Corinth was located (see note at 1:1). Evidently what Paul had written in 1Co 16:1-4 had met with an enthusiastic pledge from the Corinthians. He had learned about this and boasted of the Corinthians' **zeal** to the Macedonian churches. This had become a factor in the generous offering for Jerusalem that Paul had already received from Macedonia (8:1-4).

9:4 Paul appealed to the Corinthians' sense of integrity to keep their promise of a generous gift.

9:5 Paul intended to arrive in Corinth after Titus and the two **brothers** arrived, by which time the collection would be **ready** for him to take to Jerusalem. This is in fact what happened, as noted in Rm 15:25-27 (which was written from Corinth). The phrase **a gift and not . . . an extortion** may be translated literally as "a blessing and not a [matter of] greed." In other words, the giving was to be done because this would benefit others, without the givers thinking of getting back something material in return.

9:6-15 These verses contain the most explicit passage in the NT on stewardship. Because no individuals or places are named, the passage is easy to apply broadly.

9:6 The words **sparingly . . . sparingly . . . generously . . . generously** state a principle that is proverbially true, based on common agricultural experience. Here it is applied to financial matters, but see Lk 6:38; Gl 6:7-9.

9:7 Christian stewardship, like other good works, flows ideally from a heart of love for God and others rather than from a sense of duty (Mt 22:37-40).

9:8 A form of the Greek word for "all" is used four times here, translated as **every grace . . . every way . . . everything you need**, and **every good work**. A closely related word is translated **always**.

9:9 This quotation of Ps 112:9 is taken from a song about those who fear the Lord by living lives of righteous obedience to Him, extolling them to give to **the poor**.

9:10-11 These verses return to the agricultural metaphor of verse 6, emphasizing God's sovereignty in providing for the material needs of believers (**seed**) as well as for their spiritual needs (**righteousness**).

9:12-13 The impact of the Corinthians' gift to the poor believers in Jerusalem would go far beyond Jerusalem. Other congregations would learn about it and praise God for the **generosity** of the Corinthians. Christian stewardship is one important way to acknowledge the truth of Christ's **gospel** before others. For other instances of Paul's use of "confess" or **confession**, see Rm 10:9-10; 1Tm 6:12-13.

9:14 An added incentive for giving is that other believers will offer **prayers** for those who give generously, because generous giving is evidence of the **grace of God** already at work in such people.

9:15 **His indescribable gift** refers to God's Son, Jesus. Giving ought to be an expression of appreciation to God for sending Jesus (Jn 3:16).

Paul's Apostolic Authority

10 Now I, Paul, make a personal appeal to you by the gentleness and graciousness of Christ—I who am humble among you in person but bold toward you when absent. [2] I beg you that when I am present I will not need to be bold with the confidence by which I plan to challenge certain people who think we are behaving in an unspiritual way.[A,a] [3] For though we live in the body,[B] we do not wage war in an unspiritual way,[C] [4] since the weapons of our warfare[b] are not worldly,[D] but are powerful[c] through God for the demolition of strongholds. We demolish arguments [5] and every high-minded thing that is raised up against the knowledge[d] of God, taking every thought captive to obey Christ. [6] And we are ready to punish any disobedience, once your obedience has been confirmed.

[7] Look at what is obvious.[E] If anyone is confident that he belongs to Christ,[e] he should remind himself of this: Just as he belongs to Christ, so do we. [8] For if I boast some more about our authority, which the Lord gave for building you up[f] and not for tearing you down, I am not ashamed. [9] I don't want to seem as though I am trying to terrify you with my letters. [10] For it is said, "His letters are weighty and powerful, but his physical presence is weak, and his public speaking is despicable." [11] Such a person should consider this: What we are in the words of our letters when absent, we will be in actions when present.

[12] For we don't dare classify or compare ourselves with some who commend[g] themselves. But in measuring themselves by themselves and comparing themselves to themselves,[h] they lack understanding.[i] [13] We, however, will

Cross references
[a]10:2 Php 3:3
[b]10:4 1Tm 1:18
[c]Ac 25:5
[d]10:5 Jn 17:3; 1Jn 4:8
[e]10:7 1Co 3:23; Gl 5:24
[f]10:8 1Co 14:3
[g]10:12 Gl 2:18
[h]Pr 26:12; 27:2
[i]Mt 13:13

Footnotes
A10:2 Or *are living as a non-Christian*; lit *are walking according to flesh*   **B**10:3 Lit *flesh*   **C**10:3 Lit *war according to flesh*   **D**10:4 Lit *fleshly*   **E**10:7 Or *You are looking at things outwardly*

10:1 These words (**Now I, Paul**) mark the most important transition in the epistle. The only other place he used his own name was in the salutation. The first nine chapters of 2 Corinthians have been warm and encouraging. Here the language dramatically changes to a harsh, threatening tone, because Paul was on the defensive against charges made by the false apostles (11:13).

10:2 Paul planned to **challenge certain people** who had accused him of **behaving in an unspiritual way**—that is, according to human standards. For his earlier discussions of things characteristic of frail humanity versus things that are evidence of God's power, see notes at 4:8-9; 4:17-18; and 6:8-10.

10:4 Paul often used the language of battle and struggle (1Co 14:8; 1Tm 1:18; 4:7), but there is a right way and a wrong way to fight. Christians should resort neither to the

tapeinos

Greek Pronunciation	[tah pay NOSS]
HCSB Translation	humble
Uses in 2 Corinthians	2
Uses in the NT	8
Focus passage	2 Corinthians 10:1

The Greek adjective *tapeinos* means *humble, lowly,* or *downcast*. The related verb *tapeinoo* means *to humiliate, humble,* or *make ashamed,* and occurs 14 times in the NT (four in Paul's writings).

The ancient Greeks so emphasized personal strength and self-sufficiency that *tapeinos* and its related words were almost always used in a negative sense. To be *humble* or *lowly* was considered a vice. However, Jesus elevated *tapeinos* to the status of a virtue when He said, "I am gentle and *humble* in heart" (Mt 11:29), and Paul used *tapeinoo* to describe the incarnation (Php 2:8). Jesus warned that those who promote themselves will be judged by God, but He also said that those who *humble* themselves will be rewarded (Mt 18:4; 23:12; Lk 14:11; 18:14; 2Co 11:7). True *humility* is the opposite of putting self first. *Humility* means that a person does not think of self at all but instead thinks of the needs of others and makes their needs a priority (see Php 2:3-4). God gives grace to those who practice such *humility* (Jms 4:6; 1Pt 5:5).

literal weapons of warfare nor to the rhetorical weapons of sophisticated philosophical reasoning to advance the gospel. Divine, supernatural power is required to defeat Satan's **strongholds**. Believers experience this power by putting on the armor of God (Eph 6:10-18).

10:5 The **high-minded thing** refers to arguments made by false teachers. These would not be defeated by sophisticated reasoning but by the foolishness of the message preached (1Co 1:22). See 1:18-30 for Paul's earlier guidance to the Corinthians on this topic.

10:6 The phrase **your obedience** means the commitment of the Corinthians to Paul's cause in opposing the false apostles. On his intention to deal severely with the troublemakers, see note at 13:2.

10:7 One clique in the Corinthian church—and perhaps the false teachers—had arrogantly claimed, "I'm with **Christ**" (1Co 1:12) to the exclusion of others. Paul had condemned this divisiveness (1Co 1:10-17) because there is no inner circle in Christianity made up of an especially enlightened group.

10:8 Within the church (made up of spiritual equals) Christ has given **authority** and leadership responsibility to certain individuals to use **for building . . . up** believers but never for **tearing . . . down**.

10:9-10 Paul's earlier correspondence caused the Corinthians to be "grieved" (7:8), but it was for their own good and it was not done just to frighten them. The false apostles contrasted the **powerful** impact of his letters with the **weak** impact of his presence and his lack of oratorical skill in his **public speaking** (11:6; 1Co 2:1-4), supposing this was proof of a major defect in the apostle.

10:11 If the situation required, Paul would not hesitate to exercise his God-given authority (13:2).

10:12 The false apostles were good at self-promotion, or commending **themselves**. For people to use themselves as the standard for evaluating their ministry shows that they **lack understanding**.

10:13 Paul's standard of self-evaluation was the extent to which he had obeyed God's call on his life, rather than comparing himself to others. The word **area** suggests either an

not boast beyond measure but according to the measure of the area of ministry that God has assigned[a] to us, which reaches even to you. [14] For we are not overextending ourselves, as if we had not reached you, since we have come to you with the gospel of Christ. [15] We are not bragging beyond measure about other people's labors. But we have the hope[b] that as your faith increases, our area of ministry will be greatly enlarged, [16] so that we may proclaim the good news to the regions beyond you,[c] not boasting about what has already been done in someone else's area of ministry.[d] [17] So **the one who boasts must boast in the Lord.**[A,e] [18] For it is not the one commending himself who is approved, but the one the Lord commends.[f]

Paul and the False Apostles

11 I wish you would put up with a little foolishness[g] from me. Yes, do put up with me.[B] [2] For I am jealous[h] over you with a godly jealousy,[i] because I have promised you in marriage to one husband—to present a pure[j] virgin to Christ. [3] But I fear that, as the serpent[k] deceived[l] Eve[m] by his cunning, your minds may be seduced from a complete and pure[C] devotion to Christ.[n] [4] For if a person comes and preaches another Jesus,[o] whom we did not preach, or you receive a different spirit,[p] which you had not received, or a different gospel,[q] which you had not accepted, you put up with it splendidly!

[5] Now I consider myself in no way inferior to the "super-apostles."[r] [6] Though untrained in public speaking,[s] I am certainly not untrained in knowledge.[t] Indeed, we have always made that clear to you in everything. [7] Or did I commit a sin by humbling[u] myself so that you might be exalted,[v] because I preached the gospel of God to you free of charge?[w] [8] I robbed other churches by taking pay from them to

Cross references (center column)

[a]10:13 Rm 12:3; 1Co 7:17; Heb 7:2
[b]10:15 1Th 1:3
[c]10:16 Ac 19:21
[d]Rm 15:20
[e]10:17 Jr 9:24
[f]10:18 1Th 2:4
[g]11:1 Mk 7:22; 2Co 11:17,21
[h]11:2 Jms 3:16
[i]Nm 25:13; Gl 4:17
[j]Php 4:8
[k]11:3 Gn 3:1; Lk 10:19
[l]Rm 7:11; 16:18; 1Co 3:18; 2Th 2:3; 1Tm 2:14
[m]Gn 3:20
[n]1Th 3:5
[o]11:4 1Co 3:11
[p]1Jn 4:1
[q]Gl 1:6
[r]11:5 Jd 17
[s]11:6 1Co 1:17
[t]Php 3:8; 1Jn 4:8
[u]11:7 Lk 14:11
[v]Lk 1:52
[w]Ac 18:3

[A]10:17 Jr 9:24   [B]11:1 Or *Yes, you are putting up with me*   [C]11:3 Other mss omit *and pure*

agricultural image (a measured-out field to be planted and harvested) or an athletic image (a marked-out lane in which to run; vv. 15-16).

10:14-15 The Corinthians' own conversion experience was proof of Paul's obedience to God's call.

10:16 Paul understood his ministry as essentially that of a pioneer church planter. He may have already been planning to go to Spain, or the **regions beyond** (Rm 15:28).

10:17 The phrase **the one who boasts must boast in the Lord** is a summary of Jr 9:24. Jeremiah 9 prophesied the coming destruction of Judah, a people rich in external appearances but lacking in the true knowledge of God and His holy character. Paul's application to the present situation in Corinth implied that he knew God, but the false apostles did not.

10:18 **The one the Lord commends** refers to the judgment seat of Christ (5:10).

11:1 Paul felt compelled by circumstances to compare himself with those who had usurped his authority in Corinth. He foresaw that this would seem like **foolishness** or madness to some, for which he begged indulgence.

11:2-3 In the marriage analogy in these verses, four parties may be identified: (1) Paul was the spiritual father of the Corinthians, (2) the Corinthians were a **pure virgin** daughter of marriageable age, (3) **Christ** was the bridegroom to whom the Corinthians were to be given **in marriage** (at His return, Rv 19:7-9), and (4) the **serpent** was the Devil working through the false teachers trying to lure the daughter away from **complete and pure devotion** to her bridegroom (vv. 13-14). The reference to the fall (Gn 3) indicates that Paul believed in a historical Adam and Eve (Rm 5:14; 1Co 15:22,45; 1Tm 2:13-14).

11:4 The true, historic, biblical Jesus must be proclaimed carefully. Where the light of truth appears, the spirit of freedom and joy prevail. So adamant was Paul for the one and only **gospel** to be identified and preached that he pronounced a curse on those in Galatia who perverted the message (Gl 1:9).

11:5 The word **super-apostles** is a combination of an adjec-

tive meaning "superior" and the usual NT word for "apostle." The only other place in the NT where this word appears is 12:11. The quotation marks indicate Paul's disdain for such a designation of those who were troubling the Corinthians. It might also be rendered "so-called super-apostles."

11:6 On **untrained in public speaking**, see note at 10:9-10. The "super-apostles" may have received the formal training that Paul had never had. In the battle of style versus substance, Paul claimed to win when it came to **knowledge** of God (see note at 10:17). His ministry concentrated on the clear truth rather than extravagant oratory.

11:7-8 The "super-apostles" obviously expected to be paid (see note at 2:17). They had apparently suggested to the Corinthians that it was a sign of Paul's inferiority that he refused financial support. His derisive refusal of this notion is

gnosis

Greek Pronunciation	[NOH sihss]
HCSB Translation	knowledge
Uses in 2 Corinthians	6
Uses in the NT	29
Focus passage	2 Corinthians 11:6

The Greek noun *gnosis* means *knowledge* or *understanding*, and the related verb *ginosko* means *to know*, *understand*, or *discern*. The verb *ginosko* is much more common than *gnosis* and is prominent in John's writings (57x in John; 25 in 1 John), though Paul used it often as well (50x). The noun *gnosis* never occurs in John's writings and is found primarily in Paul's writings, particularly 1 and 2 Corinthians (16x).

For Paul, *gnosis* refers mainly to the *knowledge* of God and the things of God, so it is a key term for him in describing various aspects of salvation (1Co 1:5; 2Co 2:14; 4:6; 6:6; 8:7; 10:5; Php 3:8; Col 2:3). In 1 Corinthians *gnosis* is listed as a spiritual gift, probably a revelatory one (12:8; 13:2,8; 14:6). Though *knowledge* can cause pride (1Co 8:1), *knowledge* is also essential for Christians to enjoy their liberty in Christ (1Co 8:7,10,11). *Gnosis* in its positive sense is never merely intellectual *knowledge*, it is experiential *knowledge* that changes a person's worldview and lifestyle. Thus, believers must guard against false *knowledge* (1Tm 6:20).

minister to you. ⁹When I was present with you and in need, I did not burden anyone, for the brothers who came from Macedonia*ᵃ* supplied my needs.*ᵇ* I have kept myself, and will keep myself, from burdening you in any way. ¹⁰As the truth of Christ is in me, this boasting of mine will not be stopped*ᴬ* in the regions of Achaia.*ᶜ* ¹¹Why? Because I don't love you? God knows I do!

¹²But I will continue to do what I am doing, in order to deny*ᴮ* the opportunity of those who want an opportunity to be regarded just as our equals in what they boast about. ¹³For such people are false apostles,*ᵈ* deceitful workers, disguising themselves as apostles of Christ. ¹⁴And no wonder! For Satan disguises himself as an angel of light. ¹⁵So it is no great thing if his servants also disguise themselves as servants of righteousness. Their destiny*ᶜ* will be according to their works.*ᵉ*

Paul's Sufferings for Christ

¹⁶I repeat: No one should consider me a fool. But if you do, at least accept me as a fool, so

ᵃ11:9 Ac 16:9
ᵇPhp 4:10
ᶜ11:10 Ac 18:12
ᵈ11:13 Rv 2:2
ᵉ11:15 Gl 3:10
ᶠ11:19 Pr 3:7
ᵍ11:20 Gl 5:15
ʰMt 5:39
ⁱ11:22 Php 3:5
ʲGn 16:15; Gl 3:39

I too may boast a little. ¹⁷What I say in this matter*ᴰ* of boasting, I don't speak as the Lord would, but foolishly. ¹⁸Since many boast in an unspiritual way,*ᴱ* I will also boast. ¹⁹For you, being so wise, gladly put up with fools!*ᶠ* ²⁰In fact, you put up with it if someone enslaves you, if someone devours*ᵍ* you, if someone captures you, if someone dominates you, or if someone hits*ʰ* you in the face. ²¹I say this to our shame: We have been weak.

But in whatever anyone dares to boast—I am talking foolishly—I also dare:

²² Are they Hebrews?*ⁱ* So am I.
Are they Israelites? So am I.
Are they the •seed of Abraham?*ʲ*
So am I.
²³ Are they servants of Christ?
I'm talking like a
madman—I'm a better one:
with far more labors,
many more imprisonments,
far worse beatings, near death*ᶠ*
many times.

ᴬ11:10 Or silenced   ᴮ11:12 Lit cut off   ᶜ11:15 Lit end   ᴰ11:17 Or business, or confidence   ᴱ11:18 Lit boast according to the flesh   ᶠ11:23 Lit and in deaths

---

seen in his exaggerated language. He was neither a sinner nor a robber in his financial habits.

11:9-10 The **brothers** who came from Macedonia were Silas and Timothy (Ac 18:5). After planting Macedonian churches (in Philippi, Thessalonica, and Berea; Ac 16–17), Paul had traveled to Achaia alone. Following a brief stop in Athens, he had settled in Corinth, supporting himself as a tentmaker (Ac 18:1-4). Some time later, his traveling partners Silas and Timothy came with sufficient funds collected from the Macedonian churches, enabling Paul to devote full attention to his ministry. Paul's personal commitment was to serve the churches without pay, underscoring the doctrine that salvation itself is free to the person who believes. On his teaching about Christian financial support for ministers in general, see 1Co 9:12-15. Paul knew that this letter would be read in churches around Corinth (**regions of Achaia**), and they would therefore know about this defense of his ministry.

11:12 I will continue is a reference to preaching without pay, which would sharpen the contrast between Paul and the false teachers. If Paul had received pay for his teaching, this would provide **an opportunity** for them **to be regarded just as our equals** in monetary concerns.

11:13-15 The so-called "super-apostles" were not simply believers who disagreed with Paul in motive or method. They were agents of Satan who had gained a hearing in the church. Verse 13 is the only place in the NT where the phrase **false apostles** occurs, but see Rv 2:2. More frequent is the reference to false prophets, which Jesus predicted (Mt 7:15; 24:11,24).

11:14 Holy angels are sometimes associated with **light** or brightness (Lk 2:9; 24:4; Ac 12:7). No wonder Satan deceives by covering his dark evil with a cloak of light.

11:15 The word behind **servants** is translated as "ministers" in 3:6; 6:4. Jesus taught about the terrible **destiny** awaiting

false prophets in the Sermon on the Mount, noting, "You'll recognize them by their fruit" (Mt 7:16).

11:16–12:10 Bible interpreters have often identified these verses as Paul's "Fool's Speech." In order to defend himself against the false apostles, he boasted about experiences he had had, many of which would usually be considered evidences of shame or humiliation. Yet the false teachers couldn't come close to matching Paul's record.

11:16 The word **fool** is from the Greek *aphronos*, meaning "one who is ignorant or unlearned" (vv. 16,19; 12:6,11; Rm 2:20; 1Co 15:36; Eph 5:17). We might translate it as "ignoramus." The other word translated "fool" is *moros*, meaning "one who is stupid" or "a moron" (1Co 1:25,27; 3:18; 4:10; 2Tm 2:23; Ti 3:9).

11:17 In the Gospels Jesus never spoke the way Paul was about to speak. In 1Co 7:12 Paul also spoke about something Jesus had not addressed.

11:18 The false apostles were as public (**many boast**) about their experiences and achievements as Paul was private.

11:19 Put up with is the same verb as that in 11:4, expressing the same sarcasm. The words **so wise**, *phronimos* in Greek, are the opposite of foolish (see note at v. 16).

11:20-21 Tactics of the false teachers included psychological and physical intimidation. Perhaps Paul used the words **we have been weak** tongue-in-cheek.

11:22 The false apostles and the true apostles were alike in their Jewish heritage. Yet the false apostles were perhaps, like the Judaizers in Galatia (Gl 5:1-6), construing salvation as being based on keeping the law or performing good works.

11:23 Paul did not concede that these false apostles were **servants of Christ**. He had just called them Satan's servants (v. 15). But he granted their claim for the sake of argument.

²⁴ Five times I received 39 lashes
 from Jews.^a
²⁵ Three times I was beaten with rods
 by the Romans.^b
 Once I was stoned by my enemies.^{A,c}
 Three times I was shipwrecked.^d
 I have spent a night and a day
 in the open sea.
²⁶ On frequent journeys, I faced
 dangers from rivers,
 dangers from robbers,^e
 dangers from my own people,^f
 dangers from the Gentiles,
 dangers in the city,
 dangers in the open country,
 dangers on the sea,
 and dangers among false •brothers;
²⁷ labor and hardship,
 many sleepless nights,
  hunger and thirst,
 often without food, cold,
  and lacking clothing.^g

²⁸ Not to mention^B other things, there is the daily pressure on me: my care for all the churches. ²⁹ Who is weak, and I am not weak? Who is made to •stumble,^h and I do not burn with indignation? ³⁰ If boasting is necessary, I will boast about my weaknesses. ³¹ The God

and Fatherⁱ of the Lord Jesus, who is praised forever, knows I am not lying. ³² In Damascus,^j the governor under King Aretas^C guarded the city of the Damascenes in order to arrest me, ³³ so I was let down in a basket through a window in the wall and escaped his hands.^k

Sufficient Grace

12 Boasting is necessary. It is not profitable, but I will move on to visions^l and revelations^m of the Lord. ² I know a man in Christ who was caught upⁿ into the third heaven 14 years ago. Whether he was in the body or out of the body, I don't know, God knows. ³ I know that this man—whether in the body or out of the body I don't know, God knows— ⁴ was caught up into paradise.^o He heard inexpressible words, which a man is not allowed to speak. ⁵ I will boast about this person, but not about myself, except of my weaknesses. ⁶ For if I want to boast, I will not be a fool, because I will be telling the truth.^p But I will spare you, so that no one can credit me with something beyond what he sees in me or hears from me, ⁷ especially because of the extraordinary revelations. Therefore, so that I would not exalt myself, a thorn in the flesh^q was given to me, a messenger^D of Satan^r to torment me so I would not exalt myself.

^a11:24 Dt 25:3
^b11:25 Ac 16:22
^cAc 14:19
^dAc 27:1-44;
1Tm 1:19
^e11:26 Mk 14:48
^fAc 9:23; 13:50;
14:5; 17:5; 18:12;
20:3,19; 21:27;
23:10-12; 25:3
^g11:27 Rm 8:35
^h11:29 Jn 16:1
ⁱ11:31 Mt 5:16;
11:27; Lk 11:13;
Jn 8:42; Eph
5:20
^j11:32 2Sm 8:5
^k11:33 Ac
9:19-25
^l12:1 Lk 1:22
^m1Pt 4:13
ⁿ12:2 1Th 4:17
^o12:4 Lk 23:43
^p12:6 Ps
119:142; Jn 8:14;
14:6; 2Co 11:10;
1Jn 5:20; 3Jn 3
^q12:7 Nm 33:55;
Ezk 28:24; Php
3:3
^rMt 4:1,10; Ac
13:10

^A11:25 A common Jewish method of capital punishment; Ac 14:5   ^B11:28 Lit *Apart from*   ^C11:32 Aretus IV (9 B.C.–A.D. 40), a Nabatean Arab king   ^D12:7 Or *me, an angel*

In any such comparison, Paul had suffered the most for the One they claimed to serve.

11:24-25 The five Jewish beatings (39 lashes; see note at Dt 25:3) and the three Roman beatings were administered during a more brutal era when adults were subjected to corporal punishment by religious or governmental authorities. Of the beatings mentioned here, only the Roman beating at Philippi is reported (Ac 16:22). The stoning occurred in Lystra (Ac 14:19). The shipwreck of Ac 27 occurred after the writing of 2 Corinthians.

11:28 Everything Paul mentioned in verses 23-27 was endured in the course of church planting or evangelism. After converts were made, he faced the task of cultivating these believers in their faith.

11:29 Paul identified emotionally and spiritually with the struggles of his converts.

11:32-33 This episode, Paul's first brush with being persecuted, is also reported in Ac 9:23-25. Luke, the Gentile author of Acts, noted that Jews of **Damascus** initiated the plot, while Paul the Jew remembered this as a plot of the Gentile governor of the city. There was probably a coalition of Jews and Nabateans serving under the governor.

12:1 This verse is a continuation of Paul's boasting as a fool, revealing how great he was in comparison to the false apostles. Paul's conversion came in response to a vision (see Ac 26:19). As an apostle, he received direct **revelations** from Christ (Gl 1:12; Eph 3:3). The **visions** mentioned here are reported nowhere else.

12:2 A **man in Christ** is Paul's euphemism for himself, ex-

pressed in the third person for humility's sake. **Third heaven** is the place of God's dwelling. The first heaven is the atmospheric sky, and the second heaven is the planetary sky. The time period, **14 years ago**, would have been about A.D. 42, assuming 2 Corinthians was written in 56. This vision therefore preceded Paul's missionary travels, and he had evidently never spoken of it until now. He was not sure whether his body (**in the body or out of the body**) was taken to heaven or not during the vision.

12:4 The only other place where Paul used this verb (**caught up**), other than in verse 2, was to refer to the bodily catching up of living believers to meet the Lord in the air at His return, sometimes called the rapture (1Th 4:17). The word **paradise** expresses the same idea as the third heaven of verse 2. It occurs in two other NT passages, where it also means "heaven" (Lk 23:43; Rv 2:7).

12:6 If Paul had wanted to, he could have told more. He declined, however, so the Corinthians could evaluate him on the basis of what they had seen or heard in him.

12:7 Paul did not say what his **thorn in the flesh** was, although the Corinthians probably knew. Uncertainty about the specific identity of the "thorn" has allowed believers down through the ages to apply the concept to their own circumstances. Suggestions about the "thorn" have included physical ailments (poor eyesight or ill health); psychological or spiritual ailments (depression, demonic oppression, or an ongoing temptation from a bodily desire); and opposition to his ministry (enemies both inside and outside the churches).

⁸ Concerning this, I pleaded with the Lord three times to take it away from me. ⁹ But He said to me, "My grace is sufficient for you, for power^(A,a) is perfected in weakness."^b Therefore, I will most gladly boast all the more about my weaknesses, so that Christ's power may reside in me. ¹⁰ So I take pleasure in weaknesses, insults, catastrophes, persecutions, and in pressures, because of Christ.^c For when I am weak, then I am strong.^d

Signs of an Apostle

¹¹ I have become a fool; you forced it on me. I should have been endorsed by you, since I am not in any way inferior to the "super-apostles," even though I am nothing.^e ¹² The signs^f of an apostle^g were performed with great endurance among you—not only signs but also wonders^h and miracles.^i ¹³ So in what way were you treated worse than the other churches,

except that I personally did not burden you? Forgive me this wrong!

Paul's Concern for the Corinthians

¹⁴ Now I am ready to come to you this third time.^j I will not burden you, for I am not seeking what is yours, but you. For children are not obligated to save up for their parents, but parents for their children. ¹⁵ I will most gladly spend and be spent for you.^(B,k) If I love you more, am I to be loved less? ¹⁶ Now granted, I have not burdened^l you; yet sly as I am, I took you in by deceit!^m ¹⁷ Did I take advantage of you by anyone I sent you? ¹⁸ I urged Titus^n to come, and I sent the brother with him. Did Titus take advantage of you? Didn't we •walk in the same spirit° and in the same footsteps?

¹⁹ You have thought all along that we were defending ourselves to you.^C No, in the sight of God we are speaking in Christ, and every-

Cross references

^a 12:9 Mk 5:30; Lk 1:35; 6:19; Ac 19:11; 2Co 13:4; Rv 11:17
^b Is 40:29-31; 1Co 2:5; Php 4:13
^c 12:10 Mt 5:11-12; Rm 5:3; 2Co 13:4
^d Eph 6:10
^e 12:11 Gl 6:3
^f 12:12 Heb 2:4
^g Ac 1:2; Jd 17
^h Mk 13:22
^i Ac 19:11
^j 12:14 Ac 18; 2Co 2:1; 13:1
^k 12:15 2Co 1:6; Php 2:17; Col 1:24; 1Th 2:8; 2Tm 2:10
^l 12:16 1Th 2:7
^m Ps 10:7
^n 12:18 Ti 1:4
^o Ps 51:12

A 12:9 Other mss read *My power*   **B** 12:15 Lit *for your souls,* or *for your lives*   **C** 12:19 Or *Have you thought . . . to you?*

12:8 Paul prayed fervently and repeatedly until he received the Lord's answer. "No" is an answer to prayer as surely as "yes" is.

12:9 The sufficiency of divine **grace** may be easier to grasp intellectually than through experience, especially for those who are naturally inclined to self-reliance. God ensured that Paul never got away from grace (see note at 1:2). God's glorious **power** is more evident when it is displayed in weak vessels (see note at 4:7).

12:10 All of Paul's sufferings—which he recapped here in five short phrases—became occasions for him to be pleased or delighted (Php 4:13).

apokalupsis

Greek Pronunciation	[ah pah KAH loop sihss]
HCSB Translation	revelation
Uses in 2 Corinthians	2
Uses in the NT	18
Focus passage	2 Corinthians 12:7

The Greek noun *apokalupsis* is a compound word from the preposition *apo,* meaning *away from,* and *kalumma,* meaning *veil;* thus, an *unveiling. Kalumma* comes from the verb *kalupto,* which means *to hide;* thus the verb *apokalupto* means *to expose that which was hidden* or *to reveal,* and the noun *apokalupsis* can mean not only an *unveiling* but also a *revelation.*

In the NT, *apokalupsis* always refers to God's *revelation* of Himself in some way. In Lk 2:32, this *revelation* comes in the person of Christ, while in Rm 8:19 it is in His sons. God often *revealed* Himself through supernatural means to apostles and prophets such as Paul (Rm 16:25; 2Co 12:1,7; Gl 1:12; 2:2; Eph 3:3). In the end times, God's judgment will be *revealed* (Rm 2:5), as will Christ (1Co 1:7; 2Th 1:7; 1Pt 1:7,13; 4:13).

The last occurrence of *apokalupsis* in the NT is in Rv 1:1. The first word of the Greek text, it eventually became the name of the book. Only here does *apokalupsis* refer to written *revelation,* that is, Scripture. Revelation 1:1 uses *apokalupsis* in its noblest sense, for it introduces the main theme of the book: "The *revelation* of Jesus Christ."

12:11 On **fool,** see note at 11:16. On **super-apostles,** see note at 11:5.

12:12 The apostles whom Jesus commissioned as His official spokesmen received power from Him to do the same mighty **wonders and miracles** He had done. This authenticated their authority and status (Mk 6:7; 1Th 1:5). Hebrews 2:4 implies that "signs and wonders" were the special prerogative of eyewitnesses of Jesus. Apparently the "super-apostles" lacked these credentials.

12:13 Paul **did not burden** the Corinthian believers because he did not ask for payment for his ministry (see note at 11:7-8). **Forgive me this wrong** is a satirical comment.

12:14 Paul's first visit to the Corinthians was the long church-planting visit, around A.D. 50–51 (Ac 18:11). His second visit was the brief painful experience (2Co 2:1). Earlier in the letter he had promised a **third** visit (see note at 9:5). This was fulfilled, as Rm 15:26 shows. Paul would not burden the Corinthians by asking for money for his personal use. He did, of course, expect them to support the offering for the Jerusalem saints (2Co 8–9). He wanted their hearts and affection, not their money.

12:15 The fatherly **love** Paul felt for the Corinthians resulted in a great sacrifice of time and money (see notes at 6:12-13 and 11:2-3). He yearned for this love to be returned, even though he didn't expect the Corinthians to love him as much as he loved them.

12:16 By the phrase **I took you in by deceit** Paul is either using irony (in which case he meant the opposite) or else he is repeating the slanderous claims made by the false apostles. Their argument may have been along these lines: "Granted, Paul never personally took money from you for his own use, but now he's come up with this elaborate scheme for Jerusalem. He's scamming you and plans to use the money for himself."

12:18 Paul was sending **Titus** and an unnamed **brother** (see 8:6,18,22) along with this letter to oversee the collection for Jerusalem. Paul knew that Titus's behavior in financial matters had been, and would continue to be, above reproach.

12:19 Paul's integrity **in the sight of God** was more important than his reputation with any human group.

thing, dear friends, is for building you up.[a] [20] For I fear that perhaps when I come I will not find you to be what I want, and I may not be found by you to be what you want;[A] there may be quarreling,[b] jealousy,[c] outbursts of anger, selfish ambitions,[d] slander,[e] gossip, arrogance, and disorder.[f] [21] I fear that when I come my God will again[B] humiliate me in your presence, and I will grieve for many who sinned before and have not repented[g] of the moral impurity, sexual immorality,[h] and promiscuity[i] they practiced.

[a]12:19 1Co 14:3-4
[b]12:20 Ti 3:9
[c]Jms 3:14
[d]Rm 2:8
[e]1Pt 2:1
[f]1Co 14:33,40
[g]12:21 Ac 3:19
[h]1Th 4:3
[i]Mk 7:21-22
[j]13:1 2Co 12:14
[k]Dt 17:6; 19:15
[l]13:2 Gl 5:21; 1Th 3:4
[m]13:3 Mt 10:20; 1Co 5:4
[n]13:4 Mt 27:22; Php 2:7-8

Final Warnings and Exhortations

13 This is the third time I am coming to you.[j] **Every fact must be established by the testimony[C] of two or three witnesses.**[D,k] [2] I gave a warning when I was present the second time, and now I give a warning[l] while I am absent to those who sinned before and to all the rest: If I come again, I will not be lenient, [3] since you seek proof of Christ speaking in me.[m] He is not weak toward you, but powerful among you. [4] In fact, He was crucified[n] in weakness, but He

---

[A]12:20 Lit *be as you want*   [B]12:21 Or *come again my God will*   [C]13:1 Lit *mouth*   [D]13:1 Dt 17:6; 19:15

12:20 The phrase **I will not find you to be what I want** is another appeal to the unrepentant minority of Corinthian Christians (see note at 10:1). The eight vices listed in this verse were the "works" of the false apostles, which would result in eternal condemnation (11:15). Paul's other vice lists (1Co 6:9-10; Gl 5:19-21; Eph 5:3-5) also noted that those who practiced such sins were not part of God's family.

12:21 Paul's second visit to Corinth had been devastating because the Corinthians had rejected him (2:1,5). The vices in verse 20 were not sexual, as these were. First Corinthians 5 shows that sexual sins had been longstanding challenges in the Corinthian congregation. The false apostles may have added insult to injury by approving of sexual license.

13:1 On **third time**, see note at 12:14. The quotation from Dt 19:15 (**testimony of two or three witnesses**) established a pattern for verifying the truth of an accusation. Jesus affirmed it in Mt 18:16 as a principle for church discipline (1Tm 5:19). If the Corinthian sinners did not repent voluntarily, Paul would see to it that the congregation exercised the proper disciplinary procedure to expose and expel the evildoers.

13:2 Paul would **not be lenient** on his planned third visit to the Corinthian believers. His sense of apostolic authority is nowhere more evident than in this verse (see note at 1:1).

13:3-4 Paul identified himself with Christ, whose authority he bore. Christ's crucifixion and Paul's own ministry might be taken as proof that they were weak, but the resurrection showed Christ's power, which Paul shared.

The Lechaeum Road at Corinth. Lechaeum was one of two port facilities on either side of the Isthmus of Corinth. Like most ports, Corinth had a well-known reputation for immorality. In 2Co 12:21, Paul warned the Corinthian converts against returning to the "moral impurity, sexual immorality, and promiscuity they practiced."

lives[a] by God's power. For we also are weak in Him,[b] yet toward you we will live[c] with Him by God's power.

[5] Test[d] yourselves to see if you are in the faith. Examine yourselves. Or do you yourselves not recognize that Jesus Christ is in you?—unless you fail the test.[A] [6] And I hope you will recognize that we do not fail the test. [7] Now we pray to God that you do nothing wrong—not that we may appear to pass the test, but that you may do what is right,[e] even though we may appear to fail. [8] For we are not able to do anything against the truth,[f] but only for the truth. [9] In fact, we rejoice when we are weak and you are strong.[g] We also pray that you be-

come fully mature.[B] [10] This is why I am writing these things while absent, that when I am there I will not use severity, in keeping with the authority the Lord gave me for building up[h] and not for tearing down.[i]

[11] Finally, *brothers, rejoice. Become mature, be encouraged, be of the same mind,[j] be at peace,[k] and the God of love[l] and peace will be with you. [12] Greet one another with a holy kiss.[m] All the *saints greet you.

[13] The grace of the Lord Jesus Christ, and the love[n] of God, and the fellowship of the Holy Spirit be with all of you.[C,o]

---

[a]13:4 Rm 14:9; Php 1:21; 1Pt 3:18
[b]2Co 12:10
[c]Rm 6:4,8
[d]13:5 Jms 1:13
[e]13:7 1Pt 2:12
[f]13:8 2Th 2:10
[g]13:9 Ac 25:5
[h]13:10 1Co 14:3
[i]2Co 10:4,8
[j]13:11 Rm 12:16; Php 1:7
[k]Mk 9:50; Rm 16:20; 2Tm 1:2
[l]1Jn 4:16
[m]13:12 Rm 16:16; 1Co 16:20; 1Th 5:26; 1Pt 5:14
[n]13:13 1Co 13:1; 1Jn 4:16
[o]2Th 3:16

[A]13:5 Or *you are disqualified*, or *you are counterfeit* [B]13:9 Or *become complete*, or *be restored* [C]13:12-13 Some translations divide these 2 vv. into 3 vv. so that v. 13 begins with *All the saints . . .* and v. 14 begins with *The grace of . . .*

13:5 These present-tense verbs (**test**, **examine**) could be translated "keep on testing" and "keep on examining." A believer never gets beyond the need for regular self-examination (1Co 11:28; Gl 6:4).

histemi

Greek Pronunciation	[HIHSS tay mee]
HCSB Translation	establish
Uses in 2 Corinthians	2
Uses in the NT	155
Focus passage	2 Corinthians 13:1

The Greek verb *histemi* means *to stand* and has 47 related words that occur in the NT, such as *anistemi* (*to raise* or *stand up*) and *anastasis* (*resurrection*). This gave rise to several figurative meanings referring to that which is *firm, confirmed, established, appointed,* or *ordained.*

For Paul, *histemi* most often served as a term for *standing* by faith (2Co 1:24; Rm 5:2; 11:20; 14:4; 1Co 10:12; 15:1; Eph 6:11,13-14; Col 4:12). In discussing the nature of the law, Paul used *histemi* in teaching that righteousness by faith "*upholds*" [*histemi*], rather than cancels the law, since the law also teaches salvation by faith and not works (Rm 3:31). Similarly, Paul used *histemi* in reference to those who "*establish* their own righteousness" as opposed to those who submit to God's righteousness (Rm 10:3)—another contrast between faith and works as the basis of salvation. Paul also used *histemi* in quoting the Greek OT to *establish* a principle for church discipline that he would apply on his next visit: "Every fact must be *established* by the testimony of two or three witnesses" (2Co 13:1; see Dt 19:15).

13:6-7 *Profession* of faith and *possession* of faith are two different matters. Paul would surely have agreed with the three tests for assurance of salvation identified in 1 John: the doctrinal test (believing the truth about Jesus Christ; 1Jn 2:22-23); the moral test (living according to Christ's commands; 1Jn 2:3-4); and the love test (love for God and for those in God's family; 1Jn 4:7-8).

13:9 The entire letter of 2 Corinthians may be thought of as a celebration of Paul's weakness (see 4:8-9,17-18; 6:8-10; 11:23-27).

13:10 The phrase **when I am there** is a reference to Paul's third visit to the Corinthians. This is the second and last time in the letter that Paul used the term **authority** (10:8). In both cases, he noted that his calling was to build up, not tear down.

13:12 Five NT epistles end with an encouragement for Christians to show appropriate affection with a **holy kiss** (v. 12; Rm 16:16; 1Co 16:20; 1Th 5:26; 1Pt 5:14). The exact expression of this practice will vary from culture to culture. In every case it must be holy and not open to a charge of sexual suggestiveness or insincerity, as in the case of Judas, who betrayed Jesus with a kiss (Mt 26:48-49).

13:13 On **grace**, see note at 1:2. This Trinitarian benediction (**Lord Jesus Christ . . . God . . . Holy Spirit**) has been frequently used to conclude worship services. See 1:21-22 and 3:17 for other references in the letter that point to the Trinity.

Galatians

Galatians, which may be the earliest of Paul's letters, is also his most intense. It gives us a strong presentation of the truth that sinners are justified and live godly lives by trusting in Jesus alone.

The site of ancient Lystra, probably the home of Timothy. In Lystra many who heard and believed Paul's message were turned against him by Judaizers from Antioch and Iconium. If Galatians was written to churches in southern Galatia, the church planted in Lystra would have been one of the recipients of this letter.

Circumstances of Writing

Author: The author's name is "Paul," and he claims to be "an apostle" of Christ (Gl 1:1). The autobiographical information in the letter is consistent with what is known about the apostle Paul from Acts and his other letters. Theologically, everything in Galatians agrees with Paul's views elsewhere, notably in Romans.

Background: It is not certain where the Galatian churches were located or when Paul wrote Galatians. The reason is that, during the NT era, the term *Galatians* was used both ethnically and politically. If "Galatians" is understood ethnically, the founding of the Galatian churches is only implied in the NT. On Paul's second missionary journey, he "went through the region of Phrygia and Galatia" (Ac 16:6) in north central Asia Minor (near the modern capital of Turkey—Ankara). His later visit to the same general area is recorded in Acts 18:23 and 19:1. This is where a group from Gaul (modern France) invaded in the third century B.C., and it became known as Galatia.

Understood politically, "Galatians" can refer to those living in the southern part of the Roman province of Galatia. That region included the cities of Pisidian Antioch, Iconium, Lystra, and Derbe, where Paul worked to plant churches, as recorded in Acts 13:14–14:23.

The view that Galatians was written to the area where the ethnic Galatians lived is called the "North Galatian" theory. The possible dates of writing related to this understanding range from A.D. 52 or 53, if shortly after the second missionary journey, to A.D. 56, if written about the same time as Romans, to which it is similar theologically.

The view that Galatians was sent to churches in the southern portion of the Roman province of Galatia is known as the "South Galatian" theory. Some holding this view date Galatians in the early 50s, but others as early as A.D. 48 or 49, before the Jerusalem Council, which is usually dated to about A.D. 49. If the earlier date here is correct, Galatians is among the earliest of the NT books.

---

300 B.C.–A.D. 33

The Galatians, Celts of European origins, invade Asia Minor. 278 B.C.

Mark Antony and Pompey reward the Galatians with additional territory for supporting Rome in its wars against the Mithridates. 63–36 B.C.

Amyntas, king of Galatia, wills his kingdom to Rome at his death. 25 B.C.

Jesus' trials, death, resurrection, and ascension Nisan 14–16 or April 3–5, A.D. 33

A.D. 34–41

Saul's conversion on the Damascus Road October 34

Paul returns to his native Tarsus. 37–40

Barnabas travels from Antioch of Syria to find Paul. Summer 40

Barnabas and Saul serve together in Antioch. 41

Another key consideration is comparing the basis of contention in Galatians to the topic of debate at the Jerusalem Council. The problem addressed in Galatians is that "the works of the law" of Moses (2:16-17; 3:2; cp. 5:4), notably circumcision (5:2; 6:12-13), were added by some teachers to what was required in being justified before God. This is the same issue that Acts records as the reason why the Jerusalem Council met (Ac 15:1,5), supporting the idea that the existing problem in the Galatian churches was part of the reason for the Jerusalem Council.

If Galatians was written after the Jerusalem Council, it is inconceivable that Paul would not have cited the conclusions of the council, which supported his works-free view of the gospel. This strongly implies that the Jerusalem Council had not yet occurred when Paul wrote Galatians.

Message and Purpose

Galatians was written to clarify and defend "the truth of the gospel" (2:5,16) in the face of a false gospel. This was done by: (1) defending Paul's message and authority as an apostle, (2) considering the OT basis of the gospel message, and (3) demonstrating how the gospel message Paul preached worked practically in daily Christian living. Paul chose this approach to correct those in the Galatian churches in regard to both their faith and practice related to the gospel.

Contribution to the Bible

There is much about the life and movements of the apostle Paul that is only known—or filled in significantly—from Galatians 1:13–2:14 (and the personal glimpse in 4:13-14). Among these factors are Paul's sojourn in "Arabia" (1:17) and descriptions of two trips to Jerusalem (1:18-19; 2:1-10). Paul described a confrontation with Peter (2:11-14) that is mentioned nowhere else in the NT.

In the middle third of Galatians, certain aspects of the gospel's OT background are explained in unique ways. Notable are: (1) the curse related to Jesus being crucified, as cited from Deuteronomy 21:23 (Gl 3:13); (2) Jesus

---

A.D. 41–49

Paul, Barnabas, and John Mark make their first missionary journey. 47–49

From Syrian Antioch, Paul writes his letter to the Galatians, assuming the destination of the letter was the churches of southern Galatia: Iconium, Lystra, and Derbe. 49

Barnabas and Paul travel from Antioch to Jerusalem for the conference dealing with the question of whether Gentiles had to be circumcised in order to be saved. 49

Paul and Barnabas part ways over the question of whether John Mark should be allowed to join them on a second missionary journey. 49

A.D. 49–51

Paul and Silas team up for an overland journey to revisit cities of south Galatia as the first segment of Paul's second missionary journey. 49

Timothy joins Paul and Silas as they travel through north Galatia to Troas. 49

Paul, Silas, and Timothy sail from Troas to Macedonia, planting the first church in Europe in Philippi. 50

Paul and his companions move from Philippi to Thessalonica and Berea. 50

As a result of much persecution, Paul and his companions split up, with Paul going to Corinth by way of Athens. 50–51

fulfilling the prophecy of the singular physical "seed" of Abraham (3:16; see Gn 22:18); (3) the roles of the law as prison (3:22-23) and guardian (3:24-25) until Christ; and (4) the extended allegory of the slave and free sons of Abraham (4:21-31).

Galatians tells us much about the ministry of the Holy Spirit in relation to the Christian life. After the Spirit's role in the ministry of adoption (4:5-6), believers are commanded to "walk by the Spirit" (5:16), be "led by the Spirit" (5:18) and "follow the Spirit" (5:25), as well as "sow to the Spirit" and "reap" the related eternal harvest (6:8). The moment-by-moment outcome of that kind of sensitivity to the ministry of the Holy Spirit is what is meant by "the fruit of the Spirit" (5:22-23).

Structure

The book of Galatians follows the typical pattern for a first-century letter, with the exception of the element of thanksgiving: salutation (1:1-5), the main body (1:6–6:15), and a farewell (6:16-18). Contrasting concepts are prominent in the letter: divine revelation vs. human insight, grace vs. law, justification vs. condemnation, Jerusalem vs. Mount Sinai, sonship vs. slavery, the fruit of the Spirit vs. the works of the flesh, and liberty vs. bondage.

Outline

I. Introduction (1:1-9)
    A. Greeting (1:1-5)
    B. The Galatians' lapse from the gospel (1:6-9)

II. The Authenticity of Paul's Message (1:10–2:21)
    A. Paul's gospel revealed by Christ (1:10-24)
    B. Paul's gospel acknowledged by others (2:1-10)
    C. Paul's gospel vs. Peter's compromise (2:11-21)

III. The Way of Salvation (3:1–4:31)
    A. Salvation is by faith, not works (3:1-14)
    B. Salvation is through promise, not law (3:15-22)
    C. Believers are sons, not slaves (3:23–4:31)

IV. The Path of Freedom (5:1–6:10)
    A. Freedom must not be lost through legalism (5:1-12)
    B. Freedom must not be abused through license (5:13-26)
    C. Freedom must be expressed through service (6:1-10)

V. Conclusion: Sacrificial Living vs. Legalism (6:11-18)

Greeting

1 Paul,ᵃ an apostle—not from men or by man, but by Jesus Christ and God the Fatherᵇ who raised Him from the deadᶜ— ²and all the •brothers who are with me:

To the churches of Galatia.ᴬ,ᵈ

³Grace to you and peace from God the Father and our Lordᴮ Jesus Christ, ⁴who gave Himself for our sinsᵉ to rescue us from this present evil age,ᶠ according to the will of our God and Father.ᵍ ⁵To whom be the glory forever and ever. •Amen.

No Other Gospel

⁶I am amazed that you are so quickly turn-

ing away from Him who calledʰ you by the grace of Christ and are turning to a different gospel— ⁷not that there is another gospel,ⁱ but there are someʲ who are troubling you and want to change the good newsᶜ about the •Messiah. ⁸But even if we or an angelᵏ from heaven should preach to you a gospel other than what we have preached to you,ˡ a curse be on him!ᴰ ⁹As we have said before, I now say again: If anyone preaches to you a gospel contrary to what you received,ᵐ a curse be on him!

¹⁰For am I now trying to win the favor of people, or God?ⁿ Or am I striving to please

ᵃ1:1 Ac 13:9
ᵇMt 5:16; 6:1; 11:27; Jn 8:42
ᶜAc 9:6; 20:24; 22:10-21; 26:16
ᵈ1:2 Ac 16:6; 18:23; 1Co 16:1; 2Tm 4:10; 1Pt 1:1
ᵉ1:4 Rm 6:23; Ti 2:14
ᶠMt 20:28; Rm 4:25; 1Co 15:3; Gl 2:20
ᵍPhp 4:20; 1Th 1:3; 3:11,13; Heb 10:7; 1Pt 3:17; Rv 10:7
ʰ1:6 Col 3:15; 1Pt 1:15
ⁱ1:7 Ac 4:12; 1Co 3:11
ʲJd 4 ᵏ1:8 Gn 16:7; Mt 13:49; Lk 1:11; Ac 5:19; Rv 14:6 ˡRm 15:20 ᵐ1:9 Jd 3 ⁿ1:10 1Th 2:4

ᴬ1:2 A Roman province in what is now Turkey   ᴮ1:3 Other mss read *God our Father and the Lord*   ᶜ1:7 Or *gospel*   ᴰ1:8 Or *you, let him be condemned*, or *you, let him be condemned to hell*; Gk *anathema*

1:1 Paul referred to himself as **an apostle** to assert that his authority for speaking to the problems in the Galatian churches came from **God**, not **men**.

1:2 Paul referred to **all the brothers who are with me** to show that he was hardly alone in the views he expressed in this letter. The phrase **the churches of Galatia** indicates this letter was to be read in multiple congregations, as was Revelation (Rv 1:4,11).

1:3 **Grace** begins and ends every one of Paul's NT letters. **Peace** (Gk *eirene*) translates the traditional Hebrew greeting *shalom*.

1:4 Along with the resurrection, Christ's redemptive death is the heart of the gospel message (1Co 15:1-4). Paul emphasized both the death and resurrection of Christ at the beginning of Galatians (Gl 1:1) to begin to counteract the message they had recently heard which claimed salvation came through "the works of the law" (2:16). **Rescue us from this present evil age** looks ahead to being freed from "slavery" to "the elemental forces of the world" through

Christ (4:3-4), and previews the "new creation" wording in 6:15.

1:5 A key issue between the competing views of the gospel (salvation by grace vs. salvation by works) has to do with who gets the **glory**. Works-salvation provides a basis for a person to "boast" (6:13; Eph 2:9), while appreciation for the undeserved grace of God prompts the believer to give God alone the glory **forever**.

1:6-7 Verse 6 is abrupt. Paul was **amazed** at the Galatians' defection from the **gospel** of grace. To reject the gospel message is the same as rejecting God. After Paul left Galatia, the Galatians thought they had heard and responded to **a different** gospel that was better, but it was actually no true gospel.

1:8-9 The purity of the gospel is so important that even the apostles **or an angel** should be cursed eternally (Gk *anathema*) if they tampered with it.

1:10 The words **win . . . people** and **please people** previews

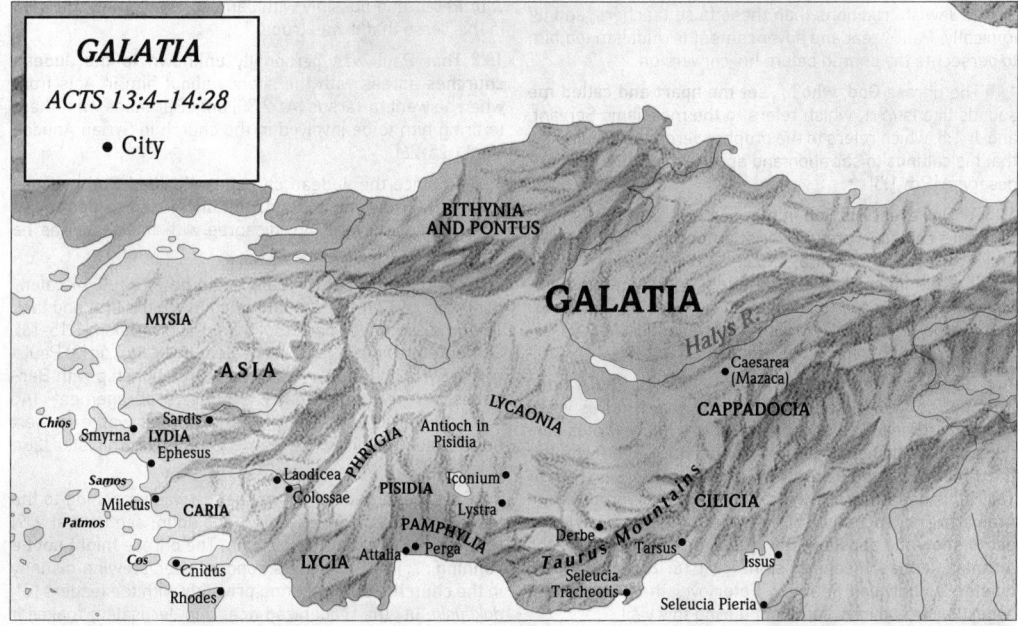

GALATIA
ACTS 13:4–14:28
• City

BITHYNIA AND PONTUS

GALATIA

MYSIA

ASIA

Halys R.

Caesarea (Mazaca)

CAPPADOCIA

Chios
Smyrna Sardis
LYDIA Ephesus

LYCAONIA

Samos
Miletus CARIA
Patmos

Laodicea
Colossae PHRYGIA
PISIDIA

Antioch in Pisidia

Iconium

Lystra

Taurus Mountains

CILICIA

Tarsus

PAMPHYLIA

Derbe

Cos Cnidus
LYCIA Attalia Perga
Rhodes

Seleucia Tracheotis

Issus

Seleucia Pieria

people? If I were still trying to please people, I would not be a •slave of Christ.

Paul Defends His Apostleship

[11] Now I want you to know, brothers, that the gospel preached by me is not based on human thought.[A] [12] For I did not receive it from a human source and I was not taught it, but it came by a revelation[a] from Jesus Christ.[b]

[13] For you have heard about my former way of life[c] in Judaism:[d] I persecuted[e] God's church to an extreme degree and tried to destroy it. [14] I advanced in Judaism beyond many contemporaries among my people, because I was extremely zealous for the traditions of my ancestors.[f] [15] But when God, who from my birth set me apart and called[g] me by His grace, was pleased [16] to reveal His Son[h] in me, so that I could preach Him among the Gentiles, I did not immediately consult with anyone.[B] [17] I did not go up to Jerusalem[i] to those who had become apostles[j] before me; instead I went to Arabia[k] and came back to Damascus.[l]

[18] Then after three years I did go up to Jerusalem[m] to get to know •Cephas,[C,n] and I stayed with him 15 days. [19] But I didn't see any of the other apostles except James,[o] the Lord's brother. [20] Now I am not lying in what I write to you. God is my witness.[D]

[21] Afterward, I went to the regions of Syria[p] and Cilicia.[q] [22] I remained personally unknown to the Judean churches in Christ; [23] they simply kept hearing: "He who formerly persecuted[r] us now preaches the faith[s] he once tried to destroy." [24] And they glorified God because of me.

Paul Defends His Gospel at Jerusalem

2 Then after 14 years I went up again[t] to Jerusalem with Barnabas,[u] taking Titus[v] along also. [2] I went up according to a revelation[w] and presented to them the gospel I preach among the Gentiles—but privately to those recognized as leaders—so that I might not be running, or have run the race, in vain. [3] But not even Titus who was with me, though he was a Greek, was compelled to be circum-

Cross-references

a1:12 1Pt 4:13
b1Co 11:23; 15:3
c1:13 2Pt 3:11
d Ac 8:1–9:2; 26:4; Php 3:5-6
e Php 3:6; 2Tm 3:12
f1:14 Mk 7:3
g1:15 Mt 24:22; Col 3:15
h1:16 Jn 5:19; Heb 1:2
i1:17 Mt 23:37; Ac 8:1
j Jd 17
k Is 21:13; Jr 25:24; Ezk 27:21; Gl 4:25
l 2Sm 8:5
m1:18 Ac 9:26
n Jn 1:42
o1:19 Jd 1
p1:21 Nm 23:7; Lk 2:2
q Ac 9:30; 11:25-26
r1:23 Ac 8:1-3
s Jd 3
t2:1 Ac 15:2-30
u Ac 4:36
v Ti 1:4
w2:2 1Pt 4:13

A 1:11 Lit *not according to man*   **B** 1:16 Lit *flesh and blood*   **C** 1:18 Other mss read *Peter*   **D** 1:20 Lit *Behold, before God*

Peter temporarily "deviating from the truth of the gospel" (2:14) to please a delegation from Jerusalem (2:12).

1:11-12 Paul did not say when his direct **revelation** from **Jesus Christ** came, but "reveal His Son in me" in verse 16 may imply that it was related to his conversion on the Damascus road (Ac 9:1-9; 22:6-10; 26:12-18).

1:13-14 Paul communicated three things to his readers: (1) he had **advanced** much farther in Judaism than those who had distorted the gospel, (2) he was far more **zealous** for the Jewish traditions than these false teachers, and (3) ironically, Paul's zeal and advancement in Judaism led him to persecute the church before his conversion.

1:15 The phrase **God, who . . . set me apart and called me** sounds like Is 49:1, which refers to the messianic Servant, and Jr 1:5, which refers to the prophet Jeremiah. Paul knew that his callings to salvation and apostleship were both undeserved (Rm 1:5).

1:16-17 On **reveal His Son in me**, see note at verses 11-12. On Paul's calling to preach Christ **among the Gentiles**, see Ac 9:15; 26:17-18; Rm 1:5; 16:26. After his conversion (Ac 9:3-9), Paul did not feel any compulsion to travel immediately from Damascus to **Jerusalem** to consult with the authorities on the gospel. He went to **Arabia** (see Ac 9:23-25; 2Co 11:32-33), then back to **Damascus**.

1:18 Because of how time was computed in Paul's time, it cannot be known whether the **three years** in this verse speaks of three full calendar years or one full year plus portions of two additional years. It is also not known whether the three years is figured after: (1) Paul's conversion (vv. 15-16), (2) his departure for Arabia (v. 17), or (3) his return from Arabia to Damascus (v. 17). His trip to Jerusalem was to get to **know** the apostle Peter (the Greek equivalent of the Aramaic **Cephas**, meaning "stone"; Mt 16:18). If there were differences between Paul and Peter over the gospel message, they would have come out during this visit.

1:19 James, the brother of Jesus (Mt 13:55; Jms 1:1), is nowhere else listed as one of the 12 **apostles** (i.e., the 11, without Judas Iscariot, who was replaced by Matthias; Ac 1:23-26). But since he was in the upper room before Pentecost (Ac 1:13-14) and was the senior pastoral figure in the church at Jerusalem (see Ac 15:13; 21:18), James was considered to be virtually an "apostle."

1:20 If anyone in Galatia doubted that Paul had previously had a harmonious discussion about his gospel message with Peter, and possibly with James, he solemnly affirmed in this verse that it was true.

1:22 That Paul was personally **unknown to the Judean churches** agrees with the silence about him in Acts from when he went to Tarsus (Ac 9:30) until Barnabas went there to bring him to be involved in the church in Syrian Antioch (Ac 11:25-26).

1:23-24 Since the Judean churches **glorified God** because Paul was preaching the faith he once tried to **destroy**, it is clear that they did not disagree with the gospel as he preached it.

2:1 This reference to **14 years** could be to a full 14 calendar years or 12 full years and fractions of the first and last. The time could look back to: (1) Paul's conversion (1:15-16), (2) Paul's previous trip to **Jerusalem** (1:18-19), or (3) Paul's trip to Syria and Cilicia (1:21). Paul's relationship with **Barnabas**, whose name means "Son of Encouragement" (Ac 4:36), began in Jerusalem (Ac 9:27). **Titus** was a convert under Paul (Ti 1:4) who became an effective minister (2Co 2:13; 7:13; Ti 1:5).

2:2 Paul **presented . . . the gospel** he was preaching to the **leaders** (at least James, Peter, and John; see note at v. 9) for the sake of helpful discussion. The phrase **might not be running . . . in vain** reflects concern over brewing disunity in the church. Paul's meeting **privately** with the leaders (Gk *dokousin*; lit "the recognized ones") in Jerusalem makes it

cised. [4] This issue arose because of false brothers[a] smuggled in, who came in secretly to spy on the freedom that we have in Christ Jesus, in order to enslave us. [5] But we did not give up and submit to these people for even an hour, so that the truth[b] of the gospel would be preserved for you.

[6] Now from those recognized as important (what they really were makes no difference to me; God does not show favoritism[A,c])—they added nothing to me. [7] On the contrary, they saw that I had been entrusted with the gospel for the uncircumcised,[d] just as Peter[e] was for the circumcised, [8] since the One at work in Peter for an apostleship to the circumcised was also at work in me for the Gentiles. [9] When James,[f] *Cephas,[g] and John,[h] recognized as pillars,[i] acknowledged the grace that had been given to me, they gave the right hand of fellowship to me and Barnabas, agreeing that

we should go to the Gentiles and they to the circumcised. [10] They asked only that we would remember the poor,[j] which I made every effort to do.

Freedom from the Law

[11] But when Cephas[B] came to Antioch, I opposed him to his face because he stood condemned.[C] [12] For he regularly ate with the Gentiles before certain men came from James. However, when they came, he withdrew and separated himself, because he feared those from the circumcision party. [13] Then the rest of the Jews[k] joined his hypocrisy,[l] so that even Barnabas was carried away by their hypocrisy. [14] But when I saw that they were deviating from the truth of the gospel, I told Cephas[B] in front of everyone, "If you, who are a Jew, live like a Gentile[m] and not like a Jew,[n] how can you compel Gentiles to live[o] like Jews?"[D]

a2:4	2Pt 2:1
b2:5	2Th 2:10
c2:6	Dt 16:19
d2:7	Col 3:11
e	Lk 6:14; Ac 10:32
f2:9	Jd 1
g	Jn 1:42
h	Jn 21:7
i1Tm 3:15; Rv 3:12; 10:1
j2:10	Mk 14:7; Rm 15:26
k2:13	Rm 2:28-29
l	Mk 12:15
m2:14	Rm 1:13
n	Rm 14:2
o	Rm 6:2

A2:6 Or *God is not a respecter of persons*; lit *God does not receive the face of man*   B2:11,14 Other mss read *Peter*   C2:11 Or *he was in the wrong*   D2:14 Some translations continue the quotation through v. 16 or v. 21.

unlikely he was talking about the Jerusalem Council, which was larger and more public (Ac 15:6,12).

2:3 To make it clear that he had not adjusted his gospel message during this private conference with the church leadership in Jerusalem, Paul used **Titus** (see note at v. 1) as a test case. Had Paul caved in to the view that had recently been preached in the Galatian churches (that it was necessary for a Gentile to be circumcised and keep the Mosaic law to become a Christian; 2:16; 5:2-3), Titus, a Gentile convert, would have been **compelled to be circumcised**, but he was not, reflecting the fact that Paul's gospel was accepted by the recognized church leaders in Jerusalem.

2:4 False brothers (Gk *pseudadelphoi*) reflects that they were not really Christians. This group heard that Paul was having private discussions about the gospel and the Gentiles, and they found a deceptive way to "crash the party" to try to curtail **freedom . . . in Christ** and enslave Christians to the law, which was happening in the Galatian churches (5:1).

2:5 To maintain the **truth of the gospel**, Paul did not **submit** even momentarily to their argument about circumcision.

2:6 James, Peter, and John were the **recognized** (Gk *doke*) "pillars" of the church (v. 9). **What they really were . . . God does not show favoritism** was not meant as disparaging to them. However, as Paul recounted in verses 11-14, he encountered problems in Syrian Antioch from: (1) those who were claiming authority from James (v. 12), and (2) Peter's hypocritical attempt to appease that group.

2:7-8 Paul was not saying in these verses that there are two different **gospel** messages. Rather, he had been appointed by God as the apostle to **the Gentiles** (Ac 22:21; Rm 11:13), and **Peter** served as an apostle to the Jews. God was **at work** in each ministry.

2:9 The unity of viewpoint between Paul and the leaders of the Jerusalem church was symbolized by the **right hand of fellowship**—a common sign of friendship and agreement.

2:10 To **remember the poor** was the main reason why Paul and Barnabas had made this trip to Jerusalem (Ac 11:28-30).

2:11 Because of the hypocritical behavior of Peter (**Cephas**) in **Antioch**, Paul **opposed him to his face**.

2:12-13 Peter's fear-based hypocrisy was even more flagrant because, besides eating **with the Gentiles** in the church at Syrian Antioch, he had been previously instructed by a vision to fellowship with Cornelius, the Gentile. The words of James at the Jerusalem Council did not reflect that he believed it was necessary for Gentiles to be circumcised in order to be Christians (cp. Ac 15:1-5 with Ac 15:13-21), but James did counsel respect by the Gentiles for traditional Jewish practices (Ac 15:20-21). Peter's hypocrisy swayed **the rest of the Jews** in the church at Antioch, including **Barnabas**.

2:14 As soon as Paul determined that **the truth of the gospel** was hanging in the balance, he confronted Peter (Cephas) **in front of everyone** (i.e., in a church meeting). Peter's behavior, in eating Gentile meals prior to the group

peritome

Greek Pronunciation	[peh ree tah MAY]
HCSB Translation	circumcision
Uses in Galatians	7
Uses in the NT	36
Focus passage	Galatians 2:7-21

The Greek noun *peritome* means *circumcision* and comes from two words that literally mean *a cutting around*. The related verb *peritemno* means *to circumcise* and occurs 17 times in the NT. These two terms refer to the practice of cutting off the foreskin of a male, normally at birth. God chose *circumcision* as a special sign of the relationship between Himself and the covenant people of Israel, starting with Abraham (Gn 17:9-14,22-27).

In Paul's writings, *peritome* is prominently used in relation to salvation. Some Jewish believers claimed that Gentiles must be circumcised and follow the law of Moses to be saved (Ac 15:1-35). Paul explained that this was not true of their father Abraham, for he lived before the law of Moses and was declared righteous before he was circumcised. *Circumcision* made no contribution to Abraham's relationship with God; that relationship was based on faith (Rm 4:9-25). Both the circumcised and the uncircumcised are saved by faith (Rm 3:30; Gl 5:6,11; 6:15).

[15] We who are Jews by birth and not "Gentile sinners" [16] know that no one is *justified by the works of the law[a] but by faith in Jesus Christ.[A] And we have believed in Christ Jesus so that we might be justified by faith in Christ[B] and not by the works of the law, because by the works of the law no human being will[c] be justified. [17] But if we ourselves are also found to be "sinners" while seeking to be justified by Christ,[b] is Christ then a promoter[D,c] of sin? Absolutely not![d] [18] If I rebuild[e] the system[E] I tore down, I show myself to be a lawbreaker.[f] [19] For through the law I have died to the law,[g] so that I might live for God.[h] I have been crucified with Christ[F] [20] and I no longer live, but Christ lives in me.[i] The life I now live in the body,[G] I live by faith in the Son of God,[j] who loved[k] me[l] and gave Himself[m] for me.[n] [21] I do

not set aside the grace of God, for if righteousness comes through the law,[o] then Christ died[p] for nothing.

Justification through Faith

3 You foolish[q] Galatians! Who has hypnotized you,[H] before whose eyes Jesus Christ was vividly portrayed[I] as crucified?[r] [2] I only want to learn this from you: Did you receive the Spirit by the works of the law or by hearing with faith?[J] [3] Are you so foolish? After beginning with the Spirit, are you now going to be made complete by the flesh?[K] [4] Did you suffer[s] so much for nothing—if in fact it was for nothing? [5] So then, does God supply you with the Spirit and work miracles[t] among you by the works of the law or by hearing with faith?[J]

[a]2:16 Rm 3:20; Gl 3:2,5,10
[b]Rm 6:23; 1Tm 1:15
[c]1Co 3:5
[d]2:17 Lk 20:16
[e]2:18 Ac 20:32
[f]Rm 2:25,27; Jms 2:9,11
[g]2:19 Rm 7:4; 1Pt 2:24
[h]Php 1:21
[i]2:20 Mk 10:38; 2Co 13:5
[j]Jn 5:19; Heb 1:2
[k]Jn 3:16
[l]2Th 2:13
[m]Ti 2:14
[n]Lk 20:38; Rm 14:8
[o]2:21 Rm 7:5; 9:31; Gl 5:4; Php 3:6
[p]1Co 8:11; Php 3:10
[q]3:1 Rm 1:14
[r]Mt 27:22
[s]3:4 Php 1:29 [t]3:5 Mk 13:22

[A]2:16 Or by the faithfulness of Jesus Christ   [B]2:16 Or by the faithfulness of Christ   [C]2:16 Lit law all flesh will not   [D]2:17 Or servant   [E]2:18 Lit rebuild those things that   [F]2:19 Other textual traditions place I have been crucified with Christ in v. 20.   [G]2:20 Or flesh   [H]3:1 Other mss add not to obey the truth   [I]3:1 Other mss add among you   [J]3:2,5 Lit by law works or faith hearing or hearing the message   [K]3:3 By human effort

"from James" arriving in Antioch (vv. 11-12), showed he believed it was right to **live like a Gentile** among Gentiles. Thus, his later decision to compel the Gentiles in the church at Antioch to **live like Jews** was seen as inconsistent and hypocritical.

2:15 Theologically, Paul knew all people (not just Gentiles) are sinners (Rm 3:23). He was likely using a phrase (**Gentile sinners**) that his opponents, who were **Jews by birth** and apparently conceited about it, used to describe non-Jews. But because of God's gracious covenant with Israel, the Jews did have certain spiritual advantages (Rm 9:4-5).

2:16 Justification is a legal idea, meaning "to be declared (not *made*) righteous." **Faith** means trusting in the redemptive work of Jesus Christ on the cross. When Paul speaks of the message **we . . . believed**, the plural "we" may refer to: (1) "all the brothers" with Paul at that time (1:2); (2) Paul and the Galatians, who believed when they first heard Paul's preaching (3:2); or (3) both.

2:17 Paul's opponents in Syrian Antioch and Galatia were apparently depicting his message of being **justified** by faith in Jesus **Christ** alone as "lowering" Jews spiritually to the level of being "Gentile **sinners**," which somehow would make **Christ . . . a promoter of sin** (i.e., by making Jews common "sinners"). Paul's response to this preposterous idea was the strongest possible negation—**absolutely not** (Gk *mâ genoito*).

2:18 Having believed a law-free gospel of justification by faith, Paul could not go back and **rebuild** the false gospel message (salvation through "the works of the law"; v. 16) he previously had torn down. If he did this he would be **a lawbreaker** in the sense of sinning against grace.

2:19-20 Paul meant by his statement **through the law I have died to the law** that because Jesus died under the law (3:13), Paul was now separated from the law. "I have died" refers to being **crucified with Christ**, as if the believer died on the cross with Jesus. The Christian continues to live physically, but spiritually this new life is by **faith** in Christ.

2:21 If it were possible to gain God's **righteousness** through keeping **the law**, the death of Christ on the cross would have

been **for nothing**, but since salvation via the law is not possible, the only alternative is justification by faith in Christ.

3:1 Paul's preaching **Christ . . . crucified** to the Galatians was so clear that he asked who had hypnotized them, causing them to lose the certainty they once had about the source of their salvation.

3:2-3 Paul asked questions about: (1) a key aspect of becoming a Christian, and (2) living as a Christian. Paul knew the Galatians would have to admit that the presence of **the Spirit** in their lives began with their **hearing** the gospel and responding with **faith** (Rm 10:17). His second question was whether the Holy Spirit or **the flesh** was God's intended means of sanctification.

3:4 The only other direct reference to suffering (**did you suffer so much**) in Galatians is "being persecuted for the cross of Christ" (6:12). Paul appealed to the fact that whatever suffering the Galatians had gone through for the gospel

nomos

Greek Pronunciation	[NAH mahss]
HCSB Translation	law
Uses in Galatians	32
Uses in the NT	194
Focus passage	Galatians 3:2-26

The Greek noun *nomos* means *custom, ordinance, or law*. In the Greek OT, *nomos* is used to translate the Hebrew term *torah* 247 times, where it normally refers to the *law* of Moses in general or to specific *laws*. Paul was particularly fond of *nomos*, and over half of its occurrences in the NT are in Paul's writings.

In Romans and Galatians, Paul fought the battle over *law* and grace in relation to salvation. Paul's phrase "the works of the *law*" (Gl 3:2) refers to the idea of a salvation based on keeping the *law*. Paul denied that a *law*-based righteousness, which is dependent on human effort instead of God's grace and faith in Christ's work, can save or sustain anyone. The *law* brings the knowledge of sin and makes everyone accountable to God (Rm 3:19-20; Gl 3:15-22). By showing unbelievers their sinfulness, the *law* acts as their guardian until they trust in Christ through faith and become sons of God (Gl 3:23-26).

⁶Just as Abraham **believed God,**[a] **and it was credited to him for righteousness,**[A,b] ⁷then understand that those who have faith are Abraham's sons.[c] ⁸Now the Scripture saw in advance that God would •justify the Gentiles by faith and told the good news ahead of time to Abraham,[d] saying, **All the nations will be blessed through you.**[B,e] ⁹So those who have faith are blessed with Abraham,[f] who had faith.[c]

Law and Promise

¹⁰For all who rely on the works of the law are under a curse,[g] because it is written:[h] **Everyone who does not continue doing everything written in the book of the law is cursed.**[D,i] ¹¹Now it is clear that no one is justified before God by the law, because **the righteous will live**[E,k] **by faith.** ¹²But the law is not based on faith; instead, **the one who does these things will live by them.**[F,l] ¹³Christ has •redeemed us from the curse of the law by becoming a curse for us,[m] because it is written: **Everyone who is hung on a tree is cursed.**[G,n] ¹⁴The purpose was that the blessing of Abraham would come to the Gentiles by Christ Jesus, so that we could receive the promised Spirit through faith.[o]

¹⁵•Brothers, I'm using a human illustration.[H] No one sets aside or makes additions to even a human covenant[I] that has been ratified. ¹⁶Now the promises were spoken to Abraham and to his •seed. He does not say "and to seeds," as though referring to many, but referring to one, **and to your seed,**[J,p] who is Christ. ¹⁷And I say this: The law, which came 430 years later,[q] does not revoke a covenant that was previously ratified by God[K] and cancel the promise. ¹⁸For if the inheritance is from the law, it is no longer from the promise; but God granted it to Abraham through the promise.

The Purpose of the Law

¹⁹Why then was the law given?[r] It was added because of transgressions until the Seed to whom the promise was made would come. The law was put into effect through angels[s] by means of a mediator.[t] ²⁰Now a mediator is not for just one person, but God is one.[u] ²¹Is the law therefore contrary to God's promises? Absolutely not! For if a law had been given that was able to give life, then righteousness would certainly be by the law. ²²But the Scripture has imprisoned everything under sin's power,[L,v] so that the promise by faith in Jesus Christ[w]

---

a3:6 Jn 14:1
bGn 15:6
c3:7 Jn 8:37,39
d3:8 Gn 16:15; Jn 8:37; Heb 2:16
eGn 12:3; 18:18
f3:9 Jn 8:39
g3:10 Jms 3:10
hAc 15:15
iDt 27:26; Rm 4:15
j3:11 Php 1:21
kHab 2:4
l3:12 Lv 18:5
m3:13 1Pt 2:24
nDt 21:23; Ac 5:30
o3:14 Rm 4:16
p3:16 Gn 12:7; 13:15; 17:8; 24:7
q3:17 Gn 15:13; Ex 12:40; Ac 7:6
r3:19 Rm 4:15; 5:20
sGn 16:7; Mt 13:49; Lk 1:11; Ac 5:19; Rv 14:6
tHeb 8:6
u3:20 Dt 6:4
v3:22 Rm 6:23
wRm 3:22

A3:6 Gn 15:6   B3:8 Gn 12:3; 18:18   C3:9 Or *with believing Abraham*   D3:10 Dt 27:26   E3:11 Hab 2:4   F3:12 Lv 18:5   G3:13 Dt 21:23   H3:15 Lit *I speak according to man*   I3:15 Or *will*, or *testament*   J3:16 Gn 12:7; 13:15; 17:8; 24:7   K3:17 Other mss add *in Christ*   L3:22 Lit *under sin*

---

of grace was now wasted. But **if in fact it was for nothing** implies that Paul believed his readers would come to their senses.

3:6 The example of the faith of **Abraham** and the justification that resulted, neutralizes the arguments of those who were teaching justification by the works of the law (2:16).

3:7-9 Those who have faith are Abraham's spiritual **sons** and daughters, whether they are Jewish or Gentile by bloodline. Paul tied the example of Abraham's justification by faith to God's covenant promise to Abraham in Gn 12:3: **All the nations will be blessed through you**. That blessing (being justified by faith) is available to all nations (see Mt 28:19) through the **good news** of Jesus, which the promise to Abraham foretold.

3:10 Not only is it impossible to be justified by the "works of the law" (2:16), but such a perspective actually brings **a curse** on people. According to Dt 27:26, everyone who does not continue observing every detail of the law is cursed.

3:11-12 Paul added Hab 2:4 to the example of Abraham being declared **righteous . . . by faith** (see notes at v. 6; Rm 1:17). Negatively, he quoted Lv 18:5 to show that since Scripture says righteousness is by faith, it is impossible to be righteous by keeping **the law**.

3:13 Since Paul's readers were trying to be justified by the "works of the law" (2:16), they were already under its curse (see note at 3:10). Fortunately, **Christ** had **redeemed** those under such a **curse** by His crucifixion. Paul quoted Dt 21:23 to show that, by His being **hung on a tree** (the cross), Jesus was cursed in our place.

3:14 The Gentiles receive **the blessing of Abraham** through faith (see note at vv. 7-9) in **Christ Jesus**. This

places them in a position to receive the **promised** Holy **Spirit**.

3:15 Paul made his point by using an **illustration** of a last will and testament (**human covenant**). When executed legally, such a document cannot be changed.

3:16-17 The use of the singular **seed** (Gk *sperma*) is Paul's biblical basis for saying that Christ is the one who fulfilled God's **promises . . . to Abraham**. However, the Jews are still the physical seed of Abraham and those in Christ are his spiritual seed (v. 29). Because of the nature of **a covenant** (v. 15), the Mosaic law—and "the works of the law" (2:16)—cannot override the role of Christ in fulfilling the Abrahamic covenant or Abraham's example of justifying faith.

3:18 The exalted position of **the law** with the Jewish teachers who had come to the Galatians did not fit the biblical teaching. God's earlier promise given to **Abraham** was the proper basis for their spiritual **inheritance**.

3:19-20 The divine purpose of **the law** was to clarify sin until Christ (**the Seed**; see note at vv. 16-17) came. Acts 7:38 says that an angel was involved as a **mediator** (a "go-between"), which was needed because the law was a two-party contract, with both **God** and Israel responsible for keeping it. The Abrahamic covenant was a one-party contract, as seen in the way the Lord ratified the covenant as the only active party (Abram was asleep) in Gn 15:9-12. Such a covenant is unconditional.

3:21-23 Paul clarified that the law was never in conflict with **God's promises** to Abraham. The law played the necessary role of convicting people of sin during the almost 1,500 years between Mount Sinai and the gospel of justification by **faith in Jesus Christ**.

might be given to those who believe.[a] [23] Before this faith[b] came, we were confined under the law, imprisoned until the coming faith was revealed.[c] [24] The law, then, was our guardian[A] until Christ,[d] so that we could be justified by faith. [25] But since that faith[e] has come, we are no longer under a guardian, [26] for you are all sons of God through faith in Christ Jesus.

Sons and Heirs

[27] For as many of you as have been baptized into Christ have put on Christ like a garment.[f] [28] There is no Jew or Greek, •slave or free,[g] male or female;[h] for you are all one[i] in Christ Jesus. [29] And if you belong to Christ, then you are Abraham's seed, heirs[j] according to the promise.[k] [1] Now I say that as long as the heir[l] is a child, he differs in no way from a •slave, though he is the owner[m] of everything. [2] Instead, he is under guardians and

stewards until the time set by his father. [3] In the same way we also, when we were children, were in slavery under the elemental forces[B] of the world.[n] [4] When the time came to completion, God sent His Son,[o] born of a woman,[p] born under the law, [5] to •redeem those under the law, so that we might receive adoption as sons.[q] [6] And because you are sons, God has sent the Spirit of His Son[r] into our[C] hearts, crying, "•Abba,[s] Father!"[t] [7] So you are no longer a slave[u] but a son,[v] and if a son, then an heir[w] through God.

Paul's Concern for the Galatians

[8] But in the past, when you didn't know God,[x] you were enslaved to things[D] that by nature are not gods. [9] But now, since you know

Cross references

[a]3:22 Mk 11:24; Jn 3:16; Ac 10:43; Rm 10:9; 1Pt 1:8-10
[b]3:23 Jd 3
[c]Lk 10:21
[d]3:24 Mt 5:17; Col 2:17; Heb 9:10
[e]3:25 Jd 3
[f]3:27 Pr 31:25
[g]3:28 Mt 8:33
[h]Rm 10:12; 1Co 12:13; Gl 5:6
[i]Jn 17:11
[j]3:29 Rm 4:14; 8:17
[k]Rm 4:13
[4:1] Nm 26:52-62
[m]Col 3:22
[n]4:3 Rm 7:6; 2Pt 2:20
[o]4:4 Jn 5:19; Heb 1:2
[p]Gn 3:15; Lk 2:7; Php 2:7
[q]4:5 Dt 14:1; Mt 5:9
[r]4:6 Ac 16:7;

Rm 5:5,20; 8:9,16; 2Co 3:17 [s]Mk 14:36; Rm 8:15 [t]Mt 5:16; 6:1; 11:27; Jn 8:42 [u]4:7 Mt 10:24; Rv 1:1 [v]Dt 14:1; Mt 5:9 [w]Nm 26:52-62; Rm 4:14; 8:17 [x]4:8 Jn 7:28; Php 3:8

[A]3:24 The word translated *guardian* in vv. 24-25 is different from the word in Gl 4:2. In our culture, we do not have a slave who takes a child to and from school, protecting the child from harm or corruption. In Gk the word *paidogogos* described such a slave. This slave was not a teacher.   [B]4:3 Or *spirits*, or *principles*   [C]4:6 Other mss read *your*   [D]4:8 Or *beings*

3:24-25 In verses 22-23, **the law** is pictured as a jail cell. In these present verses, it is portrayed as a **guardian**. A guardian (Gk *paidagogos*) was a slave who took a young pupil for instruction and protected him from harm until he came of age. When the gospel of Christ came on the scene, the guardian role of the law was no longer needed.

3:26 Not only are those who have **faith in Christ Jesus** "Abraham's sons" (v. 7), but they are also adopted **sons of God** (4:5-7; Rm 8:14-17).

3:27 On **baptized into Christ**, see Rm 6:3-4. On **put on Christ**, see Eph 4:20-24; Col 3:9-10. Paul used the image of a person emerging from the water after being baptized to put on new clothes.

3:28 The equality and unity spoken of here is of a spiritual nature—**in Christ**. Paul had just discussed at length that the **Jew** has no spiritual advantage over the **Greek** (Gentile), and now he says the same equality is true for social and gender distinctions. No one people group or gender is to be exalted above others.

3:29 To be **Abraham's seed** is the same thing as being his "sons" (v. 7), but now the additional element of being **heirs** is introduced, previewing 4:7 (Rm 8:15-17).

4:1 In the ancient world, an underage **heir** had no right to his inheritance and was temporarily in the same legal situation as a **slave**, owning nothing.

4:2 Guardians (Gk *epitropoi*) does not refer to the same idea as in 3:24-25 (see note there), where the Greek word is *paidagogos*. In this case, a "guardian" was a slave who protected the underage heir, while **stewards** were trustees responsible for the heir's other needs until he came of age (**the time set by his father**). The analogy was to illustrate that God had everything under control during the period of the Mosaic law, setting things up perfectly for the coming of Christ.

4:3 The **elemental forces of the world** are called "things that by nature are not gods" in verse 8 and "the weak and bankrupt elemental forces" in verse 9. Since these descriptions are linked to the observance of "special days, months, seasons, and years" in verse 10, it appears they are related to religious observances based on the laws and rhythms of nature.

4:4 The Greek word translated **completion** is *pleroma*, indicating that Christ came at the perfect time. Factors that made this such a suitable time included: worldwide peace (*Pax Romana*), an excellent road system, and the dominance of one language all across the empire (Koine Greek). By these means the gospel spread in ways that would not have been possible in earlier times. **God sent His Son, born of a woman** looks back to God's promise in regard to "the seed of the woman" in Gn 3:15, and it may allude to Christ's virgin birth (Is 7:14; Mt 1:18-25). **Born under the law** refers to the fact that Jesus knew what it was like to live under the Mosaic law. This phrase implies that He perfectly kept the whole law, which no other human being could do (see notes at Gl 3:10 and 3:21-23).

4:5-6 One big difference between unbelievers and the un-

huios

Greek Pronunciation	[hwee AHSS]
HCSB Translation	Son, son
Uses in Galatians	13
Uses in the NT	377
Focus passage	Galatians 4:4-7

The Greek noun *huios* means *son*, referring literally to male offspring (Mt 1:21; 20:20). The two most common uses of *huios* in the NT are in titles for Christ and designations for believers. The expressions "*Son*" and "*Son of God*" refer to Christ in His unique and eternal relationship with the Father (Mt 3:17; 8:29; 11:27; Jn 3:16-18,35-36; 5:19-27; 8:36; 14:13; 17:1; Rm 1:3-4; 8:29,32; Heb 1:2,5,8). However, "*Son of God*" is also used many times as a messianic title (Mt 14:33; 16:16; 26:63; Mk 1:1; Jn 1:34,49; 11:27; 20:31), as is "*Son* of David" (Mt 9:27; 12:23; 15:22; 20:30-31; 21:9,15; 22:42,45). Jesus' self-designation "*Son of Man*" is a messianic title taken from Dn 7:13-14 (Mt 8:20; 12:8; 19:28; 24:47; 25:31; 26:64; Jn 1:51). On the basis of Jesus' *Son*-ship, believers are called "*sons*" (Gl 4:6-7) and "*sons of God*" (Mt 5:9; Rm 8:14,19; Gl 3:26). Their adoption (Gk *huiothesia*; lit *a son placing*) into God's family places them in a special relationship to God so that they can call Him "*Abba*, Father" and enjoy an inheritance (Gl 4:4-7).

God,[a] or rather have become known by God, how can you turn back again to the weak and bankrupt[b] elemental forces?[c] Do you want to be enslaved to them all over again? [10] You observe special days, months, seasons, and years.[d] [11] I am fearful for you, that perhaps my labor for you has been wasted.

[12] I beg you, •brothers: Become like me, for I also became like you. You have not wronged me; [13] you know that previously I preached the gospel to you because of a physical illness. [14] You did not despise or reject me though my physical condition was a trial for you.[A] On the contrary, you received me as an angel of God, as Christ Jesus Himself.

[15] What happened to this sense of being blessed you had? For I testify to you that, if possible, you would have torn out your eyes and given them to me. [16] Have I now become your enemy by telling you the truth?[e] [17] They[B] are enthusiastic about you, but not for any good. Instead, they want to isolate you so

you will be enthusiastic about them. [18] Now it is always good to be enthusiastic about good—and not just when I am with you. [19] My children,[f] I am again suffering labor pains[g] for you until Christ is formed in you. [20] I would like to be with you right now and change my tone of voice, because I don't know what to do about you.

Sarah and Hagar: Two Covenants

[21] Tell me, those of you who want to be under the law, don't you hear the law? [22] For it is written that Abraham[h] had two sons, one by a slave[i] and the other by a free woman. [23] But the one by the slave was born according to the impulse of the flesh, while the one by the free woman was born as the result of a promise. [24] These things are illustrations,[C] for the women represent the two covenants. One is from Mount Sinai[j] and bears children into slavery—this is Hagar.[k] [25] Now Hagar is Mount Sinai in Arabia[l] and corresponds to the present

Cross references (center column):
[a]4:9 Pr 2:6; Php 3:8
[b]Mk 14:17; Rm 15:26
[c]Col 2:8
[d]4:10 Rm 14:5; Col 2:16
[e]4:16 Eph 4:15
[f]4:19 1Th 2:11
[g]1Co 4:15; Jms 1:18
[h]4:22 Gn 16:15; Jn 8:37; Heb 2:16
[i]Rm 8:15,21; Heb 2:15
[j]4:24 Ex 16:1
[k]Gn 16:1
[l]4:25 Is 21:13; Jr 25:24; Ezk 27:21; Gl 1:17

A4:14 Other mss read me   B4:17 The false teachers   C4:24 Typology or allegory

---

derage heir of verses 1-2 is that, apart from a relationship with Christ, all people are actually spiritual slaves to sin, which is made clear by **the law**. Thus, it was necessary for Jesus to die; to **redeem** (Gk *exagoraz*; "set free by purchase") sinners out of the slave market. A second great difference is that Christians **receive adoption as sons** instead of being a son of the bloodline. Jesus Christ is the only **Son** naturally related to **God** the Father. All other sons (including females, since "sonship" was a legal status) are by adoption. **Abba** means "Father" in Aramaic, but it has a personal tone, such as "Daddy" or "Papa."

4:7 Paul's appeal to those in the churches in Galatia was that the person who tries to be justified before God by works is a **slave** to the Mosaic law. But he who is justified by faith in Christ is no longer a slave, but **a son**, with full rights as an heir to God's infinite treasures.

4:8-11 Paul's readers had established a true relationship with God through faith in Christ. He asked how they could **turn back again** and be **enslaved** to a viewpoint of justification by works that was as **weak and bankrupt** as the **elemental forces** they had worshiped before (v. 3). The presence of the Jewish teachers in Galatia makes it likely that the **special days** were Sabbath observances, while **months** and **seasons** had to do with longer seasons of the Jewish calendar (e.g., the time from Passover to Pentecost). **Years** would be sabbatical years or the year of Jubilee. Since those in the Galatian churches were back where they started before Paul arrived—enslaved spiritually—he feared that his best efforts had been **wasted**.

4:14-15 It is not known what the exact nature of Paul's **physical condition** was. One theory holds that Paul was stoned and left for dead (Ac 14:19) while in the area on his first missionary journey. That could cause many kinds of injuries, including those related to eyesight. Some think eye problems were Paul's "thorn in the flesh" (2Co 12:7). Others think Paul contracted malaria in the lowlands of southern Asia Minor (Ac 13:13-14).

4:16 Paul was saddened that the Galatians now viewed him

as an **enemy** simply because he told them what they needed to hear (**the truth**), not what they wanted to hear.

4:17-18 Zeal can be deluded (see note at 1:13-14), as it was with the false teachers in Galatia. The only way these teachers could maintain the zeal of the Galatian churches was to **isolate** them from the other Gentile churches who were not trying to be justified by the "works of the law" (2:16).

4:19 Paul wished the Galatians could be "born again" (see Jn 3:3,5-8) a second time, which was not possible (Heb 6:4-6). Emotionally, he felt like a woman in **labor** giving birth to the same baby for the second time (i.e., in trying to bring the Galatians back around to justification by faith, thus ditching the misguided emphasis on works of the law).

4:20 Paul did not enjoy being stern with those whom he cared about, but he didn't know what else to do about their situation since he could not be with them physically.

4:21 **The law** does not refer specifically to the law of Moses, but to the Books of the Law—the Pentateuch (i.e., Genesis–Deuteronomy). Paul's logic was that even the law itself would dispute the view of the false teachers.

4:22-23 Genesis records the births of these **two sons**—Ishmael, born to Hagar, **a slave**, and Isaac, born to Sarah, **a free woman**. Ishmael was born **according to . . . the flesh**, because Sarah and Abraham used Hagar to have a son by their own ingenuity, not through patient trust in God's promise (Gn 16). Isaac was born as God promised (Gn 15:4; 17:16-17; 21:1-3) after many years of waiting by Abraham and Sarah.

4:24-26 Paul declared that he was using **these things** as illustrations in an elaborate allegory (Gk *allēgore*). On one side of the comparison of **covenants** is (a) **Mount Sinai**, where the law of Moses was given, (b) **Hagar**, the mother of Ishmael, and (c) **the present Jerusalem**, from which the false teachers had come to Syrian Antioch (2:11-13) and Galatia. This side of the comparison represents spiritual slavery through the law. On the other side of the comparison is **the Jerusalem above**, a Jewish hope that will be fully

Jerusalem,[a] for she is in slavery with her children. [26]But the Jerusalem above[b] is free, and she is our mother. [27]For it is written:[c]

> Rejoice, childless woman,[d]
> who does not give birth.
> Burst into song and shout,
> you who are not in labor,
> for the children of the desolate
>   are many,
> more numerous than those
>   of the woman who has a husband.[A,e]

[28]Now you, brothers, like Isaac,[f] are children of promise.[g] [29]But just as then the child born according to the flesh persecuted the one born according to the Spirit,[h] so also now.[i] [30]But what does the Scripture say?

> Drive out the slave and her son, for the
> son of the slave will never be a coheir
> with the son of the free woman.[B,j]

[31]Therefore, brothers, we are not children of the slave but of the free woman.[k]

Freedom of the Christian

5 Christ has liberated us to be free. Stand firm[l] then and don't submit again to a yoke of slavery.[m] [2]Take note! I, Paul, tell you that if you get yourselves circumcised, Christ will not benefit you at all. [3]Again I testify to every man who gets himself circumcised that he is obligated to keep the entire law. [4]You who are trying to be •justified by the law are alienated from Christ; you have fallen from grace.[n] [5]For through the Spirit, by faith, we eagerly wait[o] for the hope[p] of righteousness. [6]For in Christ Jesus neither circumcision nor uncircumcision accomplishes anything; what matters is faith[q] working through love.[r]

[7]You were running well. Who prevented you from obeying the truth?[s] [8]This persuasion did not come from the One who called you.[t] [9]A little yeast leavens the whole lump of dough. [10]I have confidence in the Lord you will not accept any other view. But whoever it is that is confusing you will pay the penalty.[u] [11]Now •brothers, if I still preach circumcision, why am I still persecuted? In that case the offense of the cross[v] has been abolished. [12]I wish those who are disturbing you might also get themselves castrated!

[13]For you were called[w] to be free, brothers; only don't use this freedom as an opportunity

---

Cross references

a4:25 Mt 23:37; Ac 8:1
b4:26 Heb 12:22; Rv 3:12; 21:2,10
c4:27 Ac 15:15
dGn 11:30; Lk 1:7
eIs 54:1
f4:28 Ps 105:9; Jms 2:21
gGn 12:7; Rm 9:8; Gl 3:29
h4:29 Ps 51:11; Jn 1:33; Ac 2:4; Rm 8:9; Gl 5:25; Ti 3:5; Rv 3:22
iGn 21:9
j4:30 Gn 21:10
k4:31 1Pt 3:6
l5:1 Rm 14:4; Php 1:27
m4:21–5:1 Gl 4:22
n5:4 2Pt 3:18
o5:5 Jd 21
pRm 8:23–25; 1Th 1:3
q5:6 1Th 1:3
r1Co 13:1; Jms 2:18-22
s5:7 Jn 8:14; 1Jn 5:20
t5:8 Col 3:15; 1Pt 1:15
u5:10 Mk 12:40
v5:11 Lk 9:23
w5:13 Col 3:15

A4:27 Is 54:1   B4:30 Gn 21:10

---

realized only in the new heavens and new earth (Rv 21:2,9–22:5). Interestingly, Sarah is not referred to as the **mother** at this point, but "the Jerusalem above" is.

4:27 The quote from Is 54:1 in this verse deals with the fact that **the children** born after the exile were more fortunate and greater in number than those righteously judged for breaking the law. The implication is that those who still rely on the law are being replaced by the church and its law-free gospel.

4:28-30 Paul assumed that those in the Galatian churches would return to his view and show themselves to be **children of promise** (i.e., Abraham's seed through faith in Christ; 3:29). But, as Ishmael persecuted **Isaac** in Gn 21:9-10, it is to be expected that the Judaizers will persecute true Christians. Paul was confident that eventually his opponents would be exiled from among God's people, while his own view would receive the inheritance.

4:31 Paul placed himself and the Galatians on the side of Isaac and his descendants, the Jews, while his opponents are **children of the slave**, making them non-Jews.

5:1 Paul believed that, even though the Galatians had recently moved toward embracing the false gospel (1:6-7) of being justified by "the works of the law" (2:16), they could still **stand firm** and reject the view. Paul was asking, "If you have been freed from slavery once, why would you go back to it?"

5:2-3 The main issue was whether the Galatians had so completely adopted the Judaizers' perspective that they would now act on this view by being **circumcised** (see note at 2:3). It was probably this dilemma that prompted Paul to bring up earlier that Titus, a Gentile like the Galatians, had not been "compelled to be circumcised" in Jerusalem (2:3), though the Judaizers had applied pressure in that

direction. Paul reminded the Galatians that those who are circumcised are obligated to keep the entire law (see note at 5:11-12).

5:4 Trying to be **justified by the law** was the polar opposite of being justified by God's grace through faith in Christ. **Alienated** (Gk *katargeo*) means "to be cut off from." By being circumcised and seeking justification before God by the law, the Galatians were cutting themselves off from Christ. In this context, **fallen from grace** refers to falling away from, or forfeiting, the perspective of salvation by grace through faith.

5:5-6 Paul stated that **hope** for long-term **righteousness** before God is through living by **faith** in the power of the Holy Spirit.

5:7-10 The Galatians had started **running** the race of the Christian life well, but the Jewish teachers **prevented** them from continuing. The implication of the proverbial statement, **A little yeast leavens the whole lump of dough**, is that, even if the teaching of the Judaizers was initially accepted by only a few in the Galatian churches, it would spread quickly.

5:11-12 Apparently, a rumor from the Jewish teachers claimed that Paul still preached **circumcision** in certain circumstances, evidently a misunderstanding of Paul's actions designed to "become all things to all people, so that I may by every possible means save some" (1Co 9:22). In that spirit, Paul had Timothy circumcised (Ac 16:3). But Timothy was circumcised to become a Jew ethnically so he could minister to Jews. This had nothing to do with becoming a Christian. **Those who are disturbing you** were the Jewish teachers who emphasized circumcision.

5:13-14 Paul expressed concern about the behavioral op-

for the flesh, but serve one another through love. [14] For the entire law is fulfilled[a] in one statement: **Love your neighbor as yourself.**[A,b] [15] But if you bite and devour[c] one another, watch out, or you will be consumed by one another.

The Spirit versus the Flesh

[16] I say then, •walk by the Spirit[d] and you will not carry out the desire of the flesh. [17] For the flesh desires[e] what is against the Spirit, and the Spirit desires what is against the flesh; these are opposed to each other, so that you don't do what you want.[f] [18] But if you are led by the Spirit, you are not under the law.

[19] Now the works of the flesh are obvious:[B,C] sexual immorality,[g] moral impurity,[h] promiscuity,[i] [20] idolatry,[j] sorcery,[k] hatreds,[l] strife,[m] jealousy,[n] outbursts of anger,[o] selfish ambitions,[p] dissensions,[q] factions,[r] [21] envy,[D,s] drunkenness, carousing,[t] and anything similar. I tell you about these things in advance—as I told you before—that those who practice such things will not inherit the kingdom of God.[u]

[22] But the fruit of the Spirit[v] is love,[w] joy,[x] peace, patience,[y] kindness,[z] goodness, faith,[E] [23] gentleness,[aa] self-control.[ab] Against such things there is no law. [24] Now those who belong to Christ Jesus[ac] have crucified the flesh[ad] with its passions and desires.[ae] [25] Since we live[af] by the Spirit, we must also follow the Spirit. [26] We must not become conceited, provoking one another, envying one another.[ag]

Carry One Another's Burdens

[6] •Brothers, if someone is caught in any wrongdoing, you who are spiritual should restore such a person with a gentle[ah] spirit,[ai]

---

a5:14 Mt 1:22 bLv 19:18; Mt 7:12; 19:19; 22:37-40; Jn 13:34 c5:15 Gl 5:20; Php 3:2,20 d5:16 Rm 8:4; 1Tm 3:16; 2Pt 1:4; 2:10 e5:17 1Pt 2:11 fRm 7:15,23; Php 2:13 g5:19 Mk 7:21; 1Th 4:3 h1Th 4:7 iMk 7:22 j5:20 Col 3:5; 1Pt 4:3 kRv 18:23 lRm 8:7 mTi 3:9 nJms 3:4 oRv 14:19 pRm 2:8 qRm 16:17 r2Pt 2:1 s5:21 Rm 1:29 tRm 13:13; 1Pt 4:3 u1Co 6:10; 15:50 v5:22 Mt 7:16-20; Rm 6:21; 7:4; 8:5; Eph 5:9 wJn 15:11; 2Co 6:10 xEx 34:6; 2Tm 3:10 yPs 25:6; 2Co 6:6 zGl 5:22 aa5:23 Jms 3:13 abJms 3:13 ac5:24 Nm 23:10 2Pt 1:4; 2:10 adRm 8:12 ae2Pt 1:4; 2:10 af5:25 Php 1:21; 3:16 ag5:26 Php 2:3 ah6:1 Jms 3:13 aiPs 51:12

A5:14 Lv 19:18   B5:19 Other mss add *adultery*   C5:19 Lit *obvious, which are:*   D5:21 Other mss add *murders*   E5:22 Or *faithfulness*

---

posite of bondage: licentiousness (**an opportunity for the flesh**; see note at vv. 19-21). He also expanded his initial reference to **love** (see note at vv. 5-6). While it is foolish to "submit again to a yoke of slavery" (v. 1) in trying to keep the law, it is right to be servants to other believers "through love." Paul said that to **love your neighbor as yourself** fulfills **the entire law**.

5:15 The phrase **bite and devour one another** probably looks back to "an opportunity for the flesh" (v. 13) and looks forward to parts of the listing of "the works of the flesh" (vv. 19-21). Paul had apparently heard that there was serious dissension in the churches of Galatia. He warned them that such attitudes and behavior would destroy (Gk *analisko;* "to consume, eat up") them.

pneuma

Greek Pronunciation	[NYOO mah]
HCSB Translation	Spirit, spirit
Uses in Galatians	18
Uses in the NT	379
Focus passage	Galatians 5:16-25

The Greek noun *pneuma* comes from the related verb *pneo,* meaning *to blow,* and thus can mean *breath, wind, air, ghost,* or *spirit.* In the NT, *pneuma* is almost always used to mean *spirit* in reference to living beings—humans, angels, demons, and especially the Holy *Spirit* (about 240 times).

Three NT writers emphasized the work of the Holy *Spirit:* Luke, John, and Paul. Luke referred to the filling of the *Spirit* 14 times and each case involves a special work for a specific task, usually proclamation (Lk 1:15-17,41-45,67-79; 4:1-15; Ac 4:8-12; 7:55-60; 13:9-11). John the Baptist (Mt 3:11; Jn 1:33) and Jesus (Ac 1:4-8) promised that the *Spirit* would come to baptize believers, and this was fulfilled on the Day of Pentecost (Ac 2:1-4). Paul explained that the *Spirit* teaches believers to live by faith according to God's grace and thus to overcome the power of sin (Rm 8:1-26; Gl 5:16-26). Paul's expressions *walk by /according to /live by the Spirit* (Rm 8:4; Gl 5:16,25) and *led by the Spirit* (Rm 8:14; Gl 5:18) refer to this sanctifying work of the *Spirit* in the life of the believer.

5:16-18 The Galatian believers were at enmity spiritually. This ongoing struggle of strong **desires** (Gk *epithumia;* "craving, desire") is why it was necessary to consciously **walk by the Spirit** in faith (v. 5). This was the only way not to carry out the **desire of the flesh**. The evidence of the Spirit's leading is "the fruit of the Spirit" (vv. 22-23).

5:19-21 The "flesh" is usually understood as the sinful nature of mankind that continues even after a person becomes a Christian. Some interpreters take it to mean mankind in its unsaved state with its sinful thoughts and behavioral patterns continuing after conversion. When the desire of the flesh has the upper hand, **the works of the flesh** are **obvious** (Gk *phaneros;* "evident, visible"). Some are gross sins, but many are often viewed as "acceptable" behavior. Paul's point is that this type of behavior as a pattern of life (**practice**) is enough to cause a person **not** to inherit **the kingdom of God** (see the list in 1Co 6:9-10). Thus, a legalist cannot be justified by "the works of the law" (Gl 2:16) and a licentious person is excluded from the kingdom of God by the works of the flesh.

5:22-23 The **fruit** illustration calls to mind the vine and the branches which produce fruit (Jn 15:1-5). The mention of **love** first in the list looks back to Gl 5:6,13-14. Such loving behavior comes through the power of the Holy Spirit by faith. **Self-control** (Gk *egkrateia;* "holding in passions and appetites") is placed last in the list for emphasis, because all the works of the flesh reflect lack of self-control. There is no need for prohibitive **law** when people's lives exhibit love and self-control.

5:24-26 Christians belong to **Christ Jesus** and have been crucified with Him (2:20) along with their **passions and desires.** Such crucifixion is followed by resurrection living—**by the Spirit** (2Co 5:17). The logical way to live is to follow the Spirit and not lapse back into the passions and desires of the flesh (Gl 5:19-21).

6:1 A person who falls into sin at a vulnerable point should be spiritually restored in a **gentle** manner (one of "the fruits of the spirit"; 5:23). A danger for those doing such restoration is that they themselves might be pulled into the sin.

watching out for yourselves so you also won't be tempted.[a] [2]Carry one another's burdens; in this way you will fulfill the law of Christ.[b] [3]For if anyone considers himself to be something when he is nothing,[c] he deceives himself. [4]But each person should examine his own work,[d] and then he will have a reason for boasting in himself alone, and not in respect to someone else. [5]For each person will have to carry his own load.

[6]The one who is taught the message must share[e] all his good things with the teacher. [7]Don't be deceived: God is not mocked. For whatever a man sows he will also reap, [8]because the one who sows to his flesh will reap corruption from the flesh, but the one who sows to the Spirit[f] will reap eternal life[g] from the Spirit. [9]So we must not get tired[h] of doing good,[i] for we will reap at the proper time if we don't give up. [10]Therefore, as we have opportunity, we must work[j] for the good[k] of all, especially for those who belong to the household[l] of faith.[m]

[a]6:1 Jms 1:13
[b]6:2 1Co 9:21
[c]6:3 1Co 3:18; 2Co 12:11; Gl 2:6
[d]6:4 Mk 14:6; Gl 3:10; Jms 2:14-26
[e]6:6 Rm 15:27; 1Pt 5:2
[f]6:8 Ps 51:11; Jn 1:33; Ac 2:4; Rm 8:9; Gl 5:25; Ti 3:5; Rv 3:22
[g]Jn 12:25; Ac 13:48
[h]6:9 2Th 3:13
[i]Lk 18:18; Jms 4:17
[j]6:10 2Jn 8
[k]Gn 1:31; 3Jn 11
[l]1Tm 5:8
[m]Jd 3
[n]6:12 Php 3:3
[o]Ac 15:1
[p]2Tm 3:12
[q]Php 3:18
[r]6:13 Lk 11:28
[s]6:15 Col 3:11
[t]Jn 1:3; Rv 3:14
[u]6:16 Lk 3:8
[v]6:17 Php 3:10
[w]6:18 Ps 51:12

Concluding Exhortation

[11]Look at what large letters I use as I write to you in my own handwriting. [12]Those who want to make a good impression in the flesh[n] are the ones who would compel you to be circumcised[o]—but only to avoid being persecuted[p] for the cross[q] of Christ. [13]For even the circumcised don't keep[r] the law themselves; however, they want you to be circumcised in order to boast about your flesh. [14]But as for me, I will never boast about anything except the cross of our Lord Jesus Christ. The •world has been crucified to me through the cross, and I to the world. [15]For[A] both circumcision and uncircumcision[s] mean nothing; what matters instead is a new creation.[t] [16]May peace come to all those who follow this standard, and mercy to the Israel[u] of God!

[17]From now on, let no one cause me trouble, because I bear on my body scars for the cause of Jesus.[v] [18]Brothers, the grace of our Lord Jesus Christ be with your spirit.[w] •Amen.

[A]6:15 Other mss add *in Christ Jesus*

6:2 The person whose life is controlled by the Holy Spirit (v. 1) is to come alongside and help **carry** (Gk *bastazo*; "to bear, endure") the physical, emotional, or spiritual load threatening to crush his fellow believers. The **law of Christ** is "love your neighbor as yourself" (5:14). This is focused somewhat in Jesus' new commandment, "Love one another" (Jn 13:34). It was not possible to keep the entire law of Moses (Gl 3:10,12), but it is possible to fulfill both that law (5:14) and the law of Christ through loving actions.

6:3-5 Anyone who **considers himself** superior to a fallen believer is deceiving himself and risks being tempted also (v. 1). We cannot legitimately compare ourselves to **someone else** because each person is assigned a different **load** (Gk *phortion*; not the same word as in v. 2, but meaning "cargo, capacity") by the Lord.

6:6 The principle that **the one who is taught** the Scriptures should support **the teacher** is also stated elsewhere by Paul (1Co 9:11,14; 1Tm 5:17). In this context it is an application of "carry one another's burdens" (Gl 6:2).

6:8 **Corruption** here may refer to: (1) eternal damnation (5:21) or (2) loss of eternal rewards (1Co 3:12-15). **Eternal life** does not mean earning your salvation since justification before God is through faith (2:16). It refers to life from the Holy Spirit (Rm 6:22).

6:9-10 The Christian life is a marathon race, so **we must not get tired** (i.e., grow weary or lose heart). **Doing good** is not seeking to be justified by works, but living as God has planned for those who have received His gracious salvation through faith (Eph 2:8-10). To "sow to the Spirit" over the long haul means taking the **opportunity** (Gk *kairos*; "opportune or appointed time") that the Lord places before us to **work for the good of all**.

6:11 Paul had dictated the earlier part of the letter to an unnamed amanuensis, or secretary, and now he added a postscript in his own **handwriting**. Some believe that the oversized letters (**large letters**) indicate that Paul was having problems with his eyesight (see note at 4:14-15).

6:12-13 The Jewish teachers who were compelling the Galatians to be **circumcised** were doing so for appearance's sake and to avoid being persecuted by unbelieving Jews for the **cross of Christ**, as Paul had been (Ac 14:19). They had no basis for boasting since they could not **keep the law themselves** (see note at 3:10).

6:14-15 The only basis for believers to boast is in the death of **our Lord Jesus Christ**, which makes us **a new creation** (see 2Co 5:17). On **the world has been crucified to me**, see notes at 2:19-20; 5:24-26 (cp. 1Jn 2:15-17).

6:16 The **Israel of God** may mean: (1) the Gentile church, which through faith has inherited the promise God gave to Abraham (3:29) or (2) more likely, the "remnant" of believing Israel "chosen by grace" (Rm 11:5), as opposed to the "false brothers" among the Jews (Gl 2:4), who were seeking to be justified by "the works of the law" (2:16).

6:17 Paul asked that this letter put an end to the **trouble** he had been facing because of standing against justification by the works of the law and for justification by faith (2:16). Paul's scars were from injuries he had received through persecution (Ac 14:19; 2Co 11:23-25). He considered these far more significant than the "mark" of circumcision (Gl 6:12-13,15).

6:18 Paul ended Galatians on the same note with which he began—**grace** (see note at 1:3). It is also significant that in Paul's last sentence, he addresses the Galatians as **brothers**. Although they have been tempted by "another gospel," Paul ends this letter in the hope that they remain brothers.

Ephesians
Introduction

Paul's letter to the Ephesians is an anthem to the sovereign grace of God displayed toward sinners in Christ. It contains some of the worst news ("you were dead in your trespasses and sins") and best news ("but God . . . made us alive with the Messiah") in all of Scripture. In view of this grace, Paul calls believers to "walk worthy of the calling" we have received.

The ancient city of Ephesus, located in western Asia Minor at the mouth of the Cayster River, was an important seaport. Situated between the Maeander River to the south and the Hermus River to the north, Ephesus had excellent access to both river valleys that allowed it to flourish as a commercial center. Due to the accumulation of silt deposited by the river, the present site of the city is approximately five to six miles inland.

Circumstances of Writing

Author: Paul referred to himself by name as the author of the book of Ephesians in two places (1:1; 3:1). Many regard this book as the crown of all of Paul's writings. Today some scholars think the book contains a writing style, vocabulary, and even some teachings that are not typical of the apostle. If that is the case, then it would mean a disciple of Paul had surpassed him in theological insight and spiritual perception. Of such an erudite disciple the early church has no record. Furthermore, pseudonymity (a writer writing under someone else's name) probably was not practiced by early Christians. We can conclude, in line with the undisputable acceptance of Pauline authorship in the early church, that there is no reason to dispute the Pauline authorship of Ephesians.

Background: Paul penned the letter while in prison (3:1; 4:1; 6:20). Disagreement exists concerning whether Paul was imprisoned in Caesarea (Ac 24:22) around A.D. 57–59 or in Rome (Ac 28:30) in about 60–62 when he wrote this letter. Paul most likely wrote Colossians, Philemon, and Philippians during the same imprisonment. Tradition suggests that Paul wrote the letter from Rome around 60–61, which would have transpired while Paul was under house arrest in guarded rental quarters (Ac 28:30).

Relatively little is known about the recipients of the letter called Ephesians. Some important and early manuscripts do not contain the words "at Ephesus" (1:1). The letter was carried to its destination by Tychicus, who in Ephesians 6:21 and Colossians 4:7 is identified as Paul's emissary. The Ephesian and Colossian letters probably were delivered at the same time since in both letters the apostle noted that Tychicus would inform the churches concerning Paul's situation.

We can suggest the following possible scenario. While Paul was imprisoned in Rome, the need arose to respond to new religious philosophies influencing the Asia Minor area. The impetus to write the letters came to Paul from Epaphras, who informed him of the threats to Christianity in the Lycus Valley. In response, Paul wrote a letter to the church at Colossae. About the same time (either shortly before or shortly thereafter), he

---

1400–450 B.C.

Ephesus first occupied 1400 to 1300

Greeks cross the Aegean Sea and settle in Ephesus. 1000

Croesus, king of Lydia, captures Ephesus. 561

Temple of the moon goddess, Artemis, funded and built by Croesus. 560

Heraclitus of Ephesus, an early philosopher 540–480

450–85 B.C.

Herostratus burns the temple of Artemis to establish his place in history. July 21, 356

A 25,000 seat-stadium built in Ephesus during the reign of Lysimachus. 323–281

Ephesus under the control of the Seleucids and the Ptolemies 280–133

Ephesus comes under Roman control when King Attalus III of Pergamos wills his kingdom to Rome and the Roman province of Asia is created. 133

The Ephesians rebel against Roman taxation looking to Mithridates VI Eupathor, king of Pontus, as liberator. A large number of Italians are killed in the rebellion. 89

penned a more expansive and general letter intended for churches in Asia Minor, including Laodicea (see Col 4:16) and Ephesus.

Message and Purpose

The book hints at several purposes. The apostle taught that Jewish and Gentile believers are one in Christ. This oneness was to be demonstrated by their love one for another. Paul used the noun or verb form of love (*agape*) 19 times (about one-sixth of the total uses in all the Pauline letters). Ephesians begins with love (1:4-6) and ends with love (6:23-24).

Paul implicitly addressed matters raised by the mystery religions in the Lycus Valley. The letter has much to say about redemption (1:7) and the divine intention for the human race (1:3-14). Additional themes include grace (1:2), predestination (1:4-5), reconciliation, and union with Christ (2:1-21).

Central to the message of Ephesians is the re-creation of the human family according to God's original intention for it. The new creation destroys the misguided view that God accepts the Jew and rejects the Gentile. Paul says the distinction was abolished at Christ's sacrificial death. Thus no more hindrance remains to re-uniting all humanity as the people of God, with Christ as the head (1:22-23). The new body, the church, has been endowed by the power of the Holy Spirit to enable them to live out their new lives (1:3—2:10) and put into practice the new standards (4:1—6:9). In sum, we can say that the overall emphasis of Ephesians is on the unity of the church in Christ, through the power of the Spirit.

Contribution to the Bible

The letter to the Ephesians was probably a circular letter, with Ephesus being the primary church addressed. Paul stayed at Ephesus, the capital city of the province of Asia, for almost three years (see Ac 20:31). The fact that it was a circular letter helps explain the absence of personal names of Ephesian believers. From its inception Paul intended for the letter to gain a wider audience than that which would be found in Ephesus alone.

50 B.C.–A.D. 54

Mark Antony and Cleopatra reside in Ephesus. 33–32 B.C.

Ephesus experiences a destructive earthquake. A.D. 17

Paul travels through Ephesus toward the end of his second missionary journey. A.D. 52

Apollos comes to Ephesus and is mentored by Aquila and Priscilla. A.D. 52

Paul returns to Ephesus for a 2 ½ year ministry. A.D. 54

A.D. 55–67

Paul writes 1 Corinthians from Ephesus. 56

Paul writes letter to the Ephesians. 61

Timothy, bishop of Ephesus, receives first letter from Paul. 62

Timothy receives second letter from Paul. 67

Paul's death in Rome 67?

After the Ephesians read it, the letter would have been routed to Colossae, Laodicea, and other churches in the area. Known to be a letter of the apostle Paul, the letter was readily accepted as Scripture by the recipients.

Structure

The salutation and structure of Ephesians are quite similar to Colossians. Many topics are commonly treated in both letters. The message is strikingly similar. Of the 155 verses in Ephesians, over half contain identical expressions with those in Colossians. Colossians, however, is abrupt, argumentative, and seemingly compressed. Ephesians presents a bigger, finished picture that is meditative, instructive, and expansive.

Though Ephesians and Colossians contain many similarities, it is important to observe the distinctives of Ephesians. When the content of Ephesians that is common to Colossians is removed, there remain at least seven units of material unique to Ephesians.

1:3-14	An expanded benediction
2:1-10	A confessional statement on the new life
3:14-21	A prayer to understand the mystery of Christ
4:1-16	An extended exhortation to Christian unity
5:8-14	A section on walking in the light
5:23-32	A theological expansion on the household roles
6:10-17	A unique picture of the Christian's spiritual warfare

Outline

I. Introduction (1:1-14)
   A. Greetings (1:1-2)
   B. God's purposes in Christ (1:3-14)

II. Paul's Prayer of Thanksgiving (1:15-23)

III. Salvation by Grace through Faith (2:1-10)

IV. Unity of God's New People (2:11-22)

V. Revelation of the Divine Mystery (3:1-13)

VI. Paul's Prayer for Strength and Love (3:14-21)

VII. Unity of the Body of Christ (4:1-16)
   A. Exhortation to unity (4:1-6)
   B. The variety of gifts (4:7-10)
   C. The maturity of the church (4:11-16)

VIII. Exhortations to Holy Living (4:17–5:21)

IX. New Relationships (5:22–6:9)
   A. Wives and husbands (5:22-33)
   B. Children and parents (6:1-4)
   C. Slaves and masters (6:5-9)

X. Warfare of the New People (6:10-20)

XI. Conclusion (6:21-24)

Greeting

1 Paul,[a] an apostle of Christ Jesus by God's will:[b]

To the faithful *saints[c] in Christ Jesus at Ephesus.[A,d]

[2] Grace to you and peace from God our Father and the Lord Jesus Christ.

God's Rich Blessings

[3] Praise the God and Father of our Lord Jesus Christ, who has blessed us in Christ with every spiritual blessing in the heavens.[e] [4] For He chose us in Him, before the foundation of the world, to be holy and blameless in His sight.[B,f] In love[c] [5] He predestined us to be adopted through Jesus Christ for Himself, according to His favor and will, [6] to the praise of His glorious grace[g] that He favored us with in the Beloved.[h]

[7] We have *redemption in Him[i] through His blood, the forgiveness[j] of our trespasses, according to the riches of His grace [8] that He

[a]1:1 Ac 13:9
[b]Eph 1:9
[c]Eph 5:2
[d]Ac 18:19-21; 19:9-10; 20:3,17; 1Co 15:32; Rv 2:1
[e]1:3 Eph 1:20; 2:6; 3:10; 6:12
[f]1:4 Jd 24
[g]1:6 Jn 1:14; Rm 5:2; 2Co 4:15
[h]Mt 3:17; Jn 3:35; 10:17; Col 1:13
[i]1:7 Heb 9:12
[j]Ps 25:11; Mt 9:2; Mk 2:5; Lk 24:47

[A]1:1 Other mss omit *at Ephesus*   [B]1:4 Vv. 3-14 are 1 sentence in Gk.   [C]1:4 Or *In His sight in love*

1:1 Paul, the apostle to the Gentiles, wrote the letter to the Ephesians. He may have written it at about the same time as he wrote Colossians and Philemon from prison, most likely in Rome. Paul identified himself as an **apostle**. An apostle was a person whom the resurrected Christ had commissioned and sent on special service, and who was gifted by the Holy Spirit for that service. Paul was carrying out his apostolic commission according to **God's will**. The letter may have been intended for churches throughout Asia Minor, though clearly the more prominent recipients were the **saints** (believers) **at Ephesus**. Ephesus was the most important city in western Asia Minor (present-day Turkey), positioned at an intersection of major trade routes in a significant commercial center. It had a harbor that opened into the Cayster River, which in turn emptied into the Aegean Sea. Ephesus boasted a pagan temple dedicated to the Roman goddess Diana (Ac 19:23-41). The church there apparently flourished for some time, though not without need for additional exhortation (Rv 2:1-7).

1:2 Paul's greeting, though brief, is theologically significant. **Grace** and **peace** are unmerited gifts from God. Paul used the word "grace" 12 times and the word "peace" 8 times. On "grace," see note at 2:4.

1:3-14 Following the greeting in verses 1-2 is a sequence of phrases about the marvelous **spiritual blessing**(s) that belong to the church in Jesus Christ. All of these blessings are assured to each believer, for they flow from God's grace, wisdom, and eternal purpose. These 12 verses form one long sentence in the Greek.

1:3 Praise the God and Father of our Lord Jesus Christ: This section often is called "the doxology" because it recites what God has done and is an expression to Him of worship, praise, and honor. Similar doxologies are found in 2Co 1:3 and 1Pt 1:3. In this majestic section, Paul wrote of the blessings that belong to the church through the Father, Son, and Holy Spirit. God has blessed us with all of the blessings in the heavenly realms. These blessings include our union with Christ; being seated with Him in the heavenlies; and our adoption, redemption, and election. All spiritual gifts and service abilities also flow out of these spiritual blessings that God gives to every believer at the time of salvation.

1:4 He chose us in Him: The idea of divine election flows out of the important theme of spiritual union, for election is "in Christ." The doctrine of election is one of the most central and one of the most misunderstood teachings of the Bible. At its most basic level, election refers to God's plan whereby He accomplishes His will. The meaning of election is best understood as God's Sovereign initiative in bringing persons to faith in Christ, resulting in a special covenant relationship with Him. This theme serves as a foundation to the entire opening section of Ephesians, which includes the phrases: God "chose us" (v. 4); "predestined us" (v. 5); and "predestined according to the purpose" (v. 11). Paul's focus on the Christ-centered character of election is vitally important. God chose us in Christ before the foundation of the world. This indicates the centrality of the gospel in God's plan for history. We are chosen **to be holy and blameless**. Holiness and blamelessness are the results, not the basis, of God's election.

1:5 He predestined us: All of God's blessings are in accord with sovereign predestination, which is purposeful and grounded in love. Predestination refers to the consistent and coherent intention of God's will, an eternal decision rendering certain that which will come to pass. **Adopted through Jesus Christ**: Through God's purposeful love, believers are adopted into God's family. Adoption is the legal declaration that we are God's children with all of the rights, privileges, and duties belonging to believers.

1:6 The ultimate purpose of God's redemption plan is **the praise of His glorious grace**. Grace is God's free favor to the undeserving. Believers are given grace simply because God is gracious.

1:7 Redemption in Him means that believers have been bought with the price of Christ's blood (1Co 6:20; 1Tm 2:6; 1Pt 1:18-19) and have been redeemed from sin, Satan, and the misery of sinful self. The result of redemption is a sending away or banishment of our sin debt, resulting in complete forgiveness.

---

proorizo

Greek Pronunciation	[prah ah RID zoh]
HCSB Translation	predestine
Uses in Ephesians	2
Uses in the NT	6
Focus passage	Ephesians 1:5,11

Proorizo (predestine, predetermine) first appears in Greek literature in the writings of Paul, who may have coined the term. In the NT, this verb consistently refers to God's *predetermined* plan to culminate salvation history in the person of Jesus Christ. For this reason, God the Father is always the subject of this verb in the NT. The early church saw Jesus' sufferings as the *predetermined* plan of God in accordance with OT Scriptures (Ac 4:28). The whole of the Christian salvation experience has been *predestined* by God. Christians have received both their calling and adoption into the rights of Christian sonship because of God's loving *predetermination* (Rm 8:30; Eph 1:5,11). God has *predetermined* those whom He foreknew (see *proginosko*; Rm 11:2) to be ultimately conformed to the image of His Son Jesus (Rm 8:29). Finally, God *predetermined* before the ages His mysterious plan of salvation (1Co 2:7).

Perseverance of the Saints

Daniel B. Wallace

The perseverance of the saints is one of the most vital and precious truths of Scripture. Essentially, this doctrine means two things: (1) those who are genuinely saved will be saved forever, and (2) those who continue in the faith are genuinely saved.

False Security

All who will be saved forever are saved because of Christ's work on the cross and God's power to keep them saved. Known as *eternal security*, this truth is often stated as, "Once saved, always saved." Unfortunately, many people think that simply making a confession at some point in their lives means they are saved even if their lives bear no Christian fruit. Some even think they can live like the Devil and yet be safe because of their earlier confession. But genuine faith requires genuine repentance (Mk 4:12; Ac 2:38; 20:21).

True Security

Genuine believers continue in the faith and good works throughout their lives. One basis for this conclusion is Jesus' parable of the sower (Mt 13:3-23; Mk 4:3-20; Lk 8:4-15). Only the fourth soil type bears fruit even though the second and third types show life (belief) for a short while. The fourth soil symbolizes a genuine believer. The bearing of fruit (continuing in the faith and good works) is also the evidence of genuine belief named in John 15, where Jesus said only the branch that bears fruit is saved (vv. 5-6).

The Source of Security

Believers do not continue in the faith by their own strength. Rather, each member of the Trinity works to preserve them. In the first place our salvation completely depends on Jesus' work, not on our merit (cp. Rm 3:21-26; 4:5-8; 8:1; Eph 2:8-9). Romans 8:30 is to the point: "And those He predestined, He also called; and those He called, He also justified; and those He justified, He also glorified." So sure is our salvation that Paul speaks of our future glorification in the past tense!

Genuine Christians also continue in the faith because they are sealed with the Holy Spirit as a down payment (Eph 1:13-14) of the blessings promised by God, including eternal life. Paul had this in mind when he said: "And don't grieve God's Holy Spirit. You were sealed by Him for the day of redemption" (Eph 4:30). God the Spirit assures us of salvation at the beginning of our spiritual life and keeps us in the faith to the end of our earthly life (Jn 10:27; Rm 8:16; 1Jn 2:20,27; Jd 24).

John 10:27-29 teaches that true believers continue to hear the Lord's voice and *follow* Him, meaning they continue in the faith and in good works. The Lord gives "them eternal life, and they will never perish—ever! No one will snatch them out of My hand. My Father, who has given them to Me, is greater than all. No one will snatch them out of My hand." But can't a believer, of his own free will, choose to wander out of Jesus' protective hand? No. A good shepherd does not allow his sheep to go astray. As our Good Shepherd, Jesus keeps us safe from the thief (Satan) and from ourselves.

lavished on us with all wisdom and understanding. [9]He made known to us the •mystery
of His will,[a] according to His good pleasure
that He planned in Him[b] [10]for the administration[A] of the days of fulfillment[B]—to bring everything together in the •Messiah,[c] both things
in heaven and things on earth[d] in Him.[e]

[11]We have also received an inheritance[C] in
Him, predestined[f] according to the purpose of
the One who works out everything in agreement with the decision of His will, [12]so that
we who had already put our hope[g] in the Messiah might bring praise to His glory.[h]

[13]When you heard the message of truth,[i] the
gospel of your salvation, and when you believed in Him, you were also sealed with the
promised Holy Spirit.[j] [14]He is the down payment[k] of our inheritance, for the redemption
of the possession,[D] to the praise of His glory.

Prayer for Spiritual Insight

[15]This is why, since I heard about your faith

in the Lord Jesus and your love for all the
saints, [16]I never stop giving thanks for you as I
remember you in my prayers. [17]I pray that the
God of our Lord Jesus Christ, the glorious Father,[E] would give you a spirit[F,f] of wisdom and
revelation[m] in the knowledge of Him. [18]I pray
that the perception of your mind[G] may be enlightened so you may know what is the hope[n]
of His calling,[o] what are the glorious riches of
His inheritance among the saints, [19]and what
is the immeasurable greatness of His power[p]
to us who believe, according to the working of
His vast strength.

God's Power in Christ

[20]He demonstrated this power in the Messiah by raising Him from the dead and seating
Him at His right hand[q] in the heavens[r]— [21]far
above every ruler and authority, power and
dominion, and every title given,[H,s] not only in
this age but also in the one to come.[t] [22]And **He
put everything under His feet**[i,u] and appointed

[a]1:9 Rm 11:25;
16:25; Eph 3:3;
Col 1:27
[b]Rm 9:11
[c]1:10 Mt 1:17;
Eph 5:2
[d]Php 2:10
[e]Col 1:16
[f]1:11 Pr 19:21
[g]1:12 1Th 1:3
[h]Mk 10:37
[i]1:13 Col 1:5;
2Th 2:10
[j]Ps 51:11; Jn
1:33; Ac 2:4; Rm
8:9; Gl 5:25; Ti
3:5; Rv 3:22
[k]1:14 Gn 38:17-
18,20; 2Co 1:22;
5:5
[l]1:17 Ps 51:12
[m]1Pt 4:13
[n]1:18 1Th 1:3
[o]Col 3:15
[p]1:19 Ac 4:33
[q]1:20 Php 2:9
[r]Jn 20:17; Eph
1:3; 2:6; 3:10;
6:12; Php 2:10;
1Pt 3:22
[s]1:21 2Tm 2:19
[t]Mk 10:30
[u]1:22 Ps 8:6;
Rm 13:1; 1Co
15:27; 1Pt 3:22

[A]1:10 Or *dispensation*; lit *house law* (Gk *oikonomia*)   [B]1:10 Lit *the fulfillment of times*   [C]1:11 Or *we also were chosen as an
inheritance*, or *we were also made an inheritance*   [D]1:14 The possession could be either man's or God's   [E]1:17 Or *the Father of
glory*   [F]1:17 Or *you the Spirit*   [G]1:18 Lit *the eyes of your heart*   [H]1:21 Lit *every name named*   [I]1:22 Ps 8:6

1:9 God's grace has been lavished upon believers in accordance with **the mystery of His will**. Paul does not mean
that God's will is secret in the way that the mystery religions of Asia Minor taught. The mystery religions held that
the divine expectations were fundamentally hidden from all
but an enlightened few, whereas for Paul "mystery" meant
the revelation of a component of God's plan so that it now
can be understood by all (3:2-13). Specifically the mystery
involved the fulfillment of God's plan to bring everything together in the Messiah.

1:10 Days of fulfillment: The goal of history is based on
God's divine purpose concerning the crucified redeemer,
Jesus the Messiah—for whom, through whom, and in whom
are all things. The goal is to establish a new world order of
which Jesus Christ is the acknowledged Head (v. 22). He is
the head of a reunited universe. He now rules and reigns
from God's right hand; one day He will establish His kingdom and bring in the new heavens and the new earth, fulfilling and finalizing God's redemptive purpose. This is what
is involved in bringing together **things in heaven and things
on earth in Him**.

1:11 Received an inheritance: Paul discusses the end result
of redemption from a standpoint that stretches from eternity
past to eternity future. The recipients of this inheritance are
people whom God has chosen and predestined. They come
to faith in Christ not by chance, coercion, or unaided choice,
but by the enabling of God's Spirit. Building on OT themes,
Paul envisioned those who have received this inheritance as
standing in continuity with the covenant people of OT times.

1:13 Sealed with the promised Holy Spirit: The Holy Spirit
was promised by the prophets and by Jesus (Jl 2:28-29; Jn
14:15-26; 16:5-16). The Spirit is described as both a seal
showing ownership, and as a pledge pointing to future redemption. Though believers have not yet experienced redemption in full, God will bring about final redemption (life
in His immediate presence) for all who have received the
Spirit (Eph 1:14).

1:15 Since I heard about your faith: Most likely Paul wrote
and sent the letters to the Ephesians, the Colossians, and
Philemon at the same time. Philemon 5 indicates that Paul
recently had received word about the faith of the believers
in the region of Asia Minor.

1:16 Never stop giving thanks: Paul particularly was thankful for his readers' faith and love. Faith finds its focus in
Christ and expresses itself in love to others. Such love is the
evidence of genuine faith (Gl 5:6).

1:17 Wisdom and revelation: Paul wanted the Ephesian believers to understand what great spiritual resources were
theirs in Christ. Revelation refers to the insight and the discernment the Spirit brings to the mysteries of divine truth.
Paul wanted his readers to have a spirit of wisdom so that
they might get to know God more completely. God has given
believers wisdom (vv. 8-9), but Paul prayed for the church
not only to understand but to *experience* these blessings.

1:18 The hope of His calling refers to the assurance of eternal life guaranteed by the possession of the Holy Spirit. **The
glorious riches of His inheritance**: Believers will inherit all
of God's blessings (vv. 3,11,14; Rm 8:32). The phrase could
mean either God's inheritance or ours; that is, either the inheritance God receives or the inheritance He bestows. The
OT consistently taught that God's people were His inheritance. Likewise, Paul's words reflect such an understanding pointing to what God will receive by being glorified in
His saints.

1:19 The immeasurable greatness of His power: God's
power alone can bring believers safely to the riches of the
final glory that will be made available in heaven. The extraordinary divine power by which Christ was raised from
the dead is the same power at work in and through believers.

1:20-23 Christ's resurrection was the driving force in Paul's
life. In raising Jesus from the dead, God did not merely reverse the natural process of decay, but transcended it. He

Him as head[a] over everything for the church, [23] which is His body,[b] the fullness[c] of the One who fills all things[d] in every way.

From Death to Life

2 And you were dead[e] in your trespasses and sins [2] in which you previously *walked according to the ways of this world,[f] according to the ruler who exercises authority over the lower heavens,[A,g] the spirit[h] now working in the disobedient.[B] [3] We too all previously lived among them in our fleshly[i] desires, carrying out the inclinations[j] of our flesh and thoughts, and we were by nature children under wrath[k] as the others were also. [4] But God, who is rich in mercy,[l] because of His great love[m] that He had

for us,[C] [5] made us alive[n] with the *Messiah even though we were dead[o] in trespasses. You are saved by grace! [6] Together with Christ Jesus He also raised us up and seated us in the heavens,[p] [7] so that in the coming ages[q] He might display the immeasurable riches[r] of His grace through His kindness[s] to us in Christ Jesus. [8] For you are saved by grace[t] through faith, and this is not from yourselves; it is God's gift— [9] not from works, so that no one can boast. [10] For we are His creation, created[u] in Christ Jesus for good works, which God prepared ahead of time[v] so that we should walk in them.

[a]1:22 Col 2:10
[b]1:23 Eph 4:4
[c]Jn 1:16
[d]Col 3:11
[e]2:1 Jn 5:25
[f]2:2 2Pt 2:20
[g]2Pt 2:10; Jd 8
[h]1Co 2:12; 1Tm 4:1
[i]2:3 Php 3:3
[j]Mt 21:31; Lk 12:47; 23:25; Jn 1:13; 1Co 7:37; 2Pt 1:21
[k]Rm 2:5; Rv 6:16
[l]2:4 Lk 1:50
[m]1Co 13:1; 1Jn 4:16
[n]2:5 Col 2:13; 1Tm 5:6
[o]Jn 5:25
[p]2:6 Eph 1:3,20; 3:10; 6:12;

Php 2:10; 1Pt 3:22   [q]2:7 Mk 10:30   [r]Lk 8:14; 2Co 8:9   [s]Ps 25:6   [t]2:8 Rm 3:24; 6:14; 11:6; Gl 2:21; 2Tm 1:9   [u]2:10 Jn 1:3; Rv 3:14   [v]Rm 9:23

[A]2:2 Lit ruler of the domain of the air   [B]2:2 Lit sons of disobedience   [C]2:4 Lit love with which He loved us

raised Jesus to a completely new life, giving Him a resurrection body. Not only was Jesus raised, but He was also seated at God's right hand, the place of authority from which Christ now reigns. Christ is above all, indicating that He is infinitely superior. The ascension and exaltation completed the resurrection event, providing hope for believers as Jesus Christ became the first fruit for His people.

Paul claimed the church exists and functions only by reason of its vital relationship to its Head, Christ Jesus. As the resurrected and exalted Christ, He is without need and is independent of anything. Yet as Head, He is incomplete without the body, which is the church that fills up Christ. So the body and the Head are one in the truest sense.

2:1-6 Paul's point in these verses was to draw contrasts between the human condition described in verses 1-3 and the new life pictured in verses 4-6.

Old Life (vv. 1-3)	New Life (vv. 4-6)
We were Dead	Now We Are Alive
We were Enslaved	Now We Are Enthroned
We were Objects of Wrath	Now We Are Objects of Grace
We walked Among the Disobedient	Now We Fellowship with Christ
We were Under Satan's Dominion	Now We Are in Union with Christ

2:1 **Dead in your trespasses and sins**: "Trespasses" are lapses; "sins" are shortcomings. Apart from Christ, people are without authentic spiritual life. In this state the most vital part of the human personality is dead; thus people cannot by their own efforts or ingenuity experience fellowship with God or meet His requirements.

2:2 **Walked according to the ways of this world**: "This world" is associated with the realm of Satan. The way of life without Christ is in accordance with Satan's ways.

2:3 **Previously lived among them in our fleshly desires**: The Greek word translated "lived" is a different term from the one in verse 2 translated "previously walked," though the idea is similar. "Lived" means to turn to and fro and behave in accordance with certain principles. Apart from Christ, people are dominated by "fleshly desires," which refers to an orientation away from God toward selfish concerns. The plural suggests multiple unredeemed urges in our life apart from Christ. The unredeemed person is completely at the mercy of the tyrannical self and its lustful impulses. **By nature children under wrath**: The fall into sin described in Genesis 3 was not merely a moral lapse but a

deliberate turning away from God in rejection of Him. Sin's entrance brought about a sinful nature in all humanity. Men and women are "by nature" hostile to God and estranged from Him. While functioning as free moral agents, sin always negatively influences human decisions and actions. People do not genuinely repent or turn to God apart from divine enablement (Eph 2:5).

2:4 **But God**: Over against the human rejection of God, Paul painted a picture of the new life manifested in God's gracious acceptance of sinners because of Christ. The strong contrast points to God's answer to people's dreadful situation. **Rich in mercy**: "Mercy" is God's compassion for the helpless that relieves their situation. While grace involves God giving believers what they do not deserve, mercy means that God does not give what is deserved.

2:5 **Made us alive . . . even though we were dead** is Paul's extension of his thoughts in verse 1, which are viewed in retrospect from the vantage point of redemptive history. Because of God's great love, He "made us alive" **with the Messiah**.

2:6 **Together with Christ Jesus**: God's loving mercy not only makes new life possible, but by it God has made us alive, raised us up, and seated us with Christ. God's great power has enthroned us with Christ in the heavenly places, even as

ergon

Greek Pronunciation	[EHR gahn]
HCSB Translation	work
Uses in Ephesians	4
Uses in the NT	169
Focus passage	Ephesians 2:9-10

Ergon (work) is related to the verbs energeo and ergazomai, both meaning to work or accomplish. Other related terms include katergazomai (to effect or achieve) and energeia (working, action, or activity). Ergon appears several hundred times in the Greek OT and is found in every NT book except Philemon. Paul used ergon in two primary ways in relation to salvation: to deny that works or human effort contribute to salvation (Rm 3:20,27-28; 4:2,6; 11:6; Gl 2:16; 3:2,5,10; 2Tm 1:9) and to affirm that those who are saved will manifest good works (1Co 15:58; 2Co 9:8; Col 1:10; 2Th 2:17; 1Tm 2:10; 6:18; 2Tm 2:21; 3:17; Ti 2:7,14). Salvation is "not from works, so that no one can boast," but God created us "in Christ Jesus for good works, which God prepared ahead of time so that we should walk in them" (Eph 2:9-10).

Unity in Christ

*a*2:11 Gl 6:15
*b*Php 3:3
*c*2:12 Gn 12:7
*d*1Th 1:3; 4:13
*e*2:13 Heb 9:12
*f*2:14 Rm 10:12;
Gl 3:28

11 So then, remember that at one time you were Gentiles in the flesh—called "the uncircumcised" by those called "the circumcised,"*a* which is done in the flesh by human hands.*b* **12** At that time you were without the Messiah, excluded from the citizenship of Israel, and foreigners to the covenants of the promise,*c* without hope*d* and without God in the world. **13** But now in Christ Jesus, you who were far away have been brought near by the blood*e* of the Messiah. **14** For He is our peace, who made both groups one*f* and tore down the dividing wall of hostility. In His flesh, **15** He made of no effect the law consisting of commands and expressed in regulations, so that

---

Christ was exalted to God's right hand following the resurrection.

2:7-10 The work of reconciliation in these verses is described with four key terms:

(1) "kindness"	God's loving tender action;
(2) "grace"	God's free favor toward ill-deserving people (a favorite term of the apostle, used over 100 times in his letters);
(3) "faith"	the instrument that brings us empty-handed to God (see Rm 10:12); and
(4) "saved"	equated with new life, forgiveness of sins, deliverance from the plight described in verses 1-3, liberation, and resurrection

2:7 The salvation of men and women is a display of divine grace. God did all of this in Christ with a single goal in view: to **display the immeasurable riches of His grace**, the exhibition of His divine favor for all of history to see, including angels as well as people (1Pt 1:10-12).

2:8-9 The work of salvation is for God's glory and is not accomplished by human means. The whole process of salvation is not a human achievement, but is an act of God's goodness. The emphasis is always on Christ, the object of faith, not on the amount of faith. Salvation is by God's completely unmerited favor. In the Greek text, the grammatical construction of the entire phrase **by grace through faith** serves as the antecedent of the phrase, **it is God's gift**. We must not portray grace as God's part and faith as our part, for *all* of salvation is a gift from God.

The work of reconciliation is **not from yourselves** and **not from works** so that **no one can boast**. This prevents the slightest self-congratulation or boasting in the believer. God alone saves.

2:10 Created in Christ Jesus for good works: The work of salvation is a display of divine handiwork. Good works are the fruit of our salvation, not the cause of it. Also, good works are not incidental to God's plan; they are instead an essential part of His redemption plan for each believer. Good works are demonstrated in gratitude, character, and actions.

2:11-22 This section of Paul's letter touches on three states of being for the recipients: (1) their former corporate condition apart from Christ (vv. 11-13); (2) their corporate reconciliation in Christ (vv. 14-18); and (3) their new standing as members of God's new humanity (vv. 19-22). The theme of this entire section is reconciliation, which involves bringing fallen humanity out of alienation into a state of peace and harmony with God. Jesus, as Reconciler, heals the separation and brokenness created by sin and restores communion between God and people. Reconciliation is not a process by which people gradually become more acceptable to God but a decisive act (like a legal verdict) by which believers are delivered from estrangement to fellowship with God.

2:11-12 Gentiles in the flesh: Not only were the Gentiles morally separated from God (vv. 1-3), but they were also separated from God's covenant people. They were without any knowledge of Christ. They had no rights in God's family and were not recipients of God's covenants. They were without hope and ultimately without God. Paul did not reproach the Gentiles for their plight; he merely recorded the sad truth of the matter.

2:13 Paul used the strong transitional phrase **But now in Christ Jesus** to point to the Gentiles' new relationship in Christ. The Gentile believers no longer were in their alienated state. They knew Christ, took part in God's covenant blessings, and had hope and fellowship with God. This remarkable turnaround took place "in Christ Jesus." Those who trust in Him have a present salvation and a future hope.

2:14-16 Who made both groups one: This verse emphasizes the centrality of Jesus Christ in bringing Gentiles and Jews together, not only with one another but also with God. Christ is both our **peace** and our Peacemaker. His reconciling death on the cross has made the two—Jews and Gentiles—into one. Gentiles do not become Jews, but the two groups become one at a deeper level than ethnicity, forming Christ's church. The new humanity is greater than the former humanity; God has torn down **the dividing wall of hostility** and removed the hatred forever. By "dividing wall" Paul likely had in mind the area in the Jerusalem temple that separated the court of the Gentiles from the temple. The temple was constructed on an elevated platform. Around it was the court of priests. East of this was the court of Israel. Farther east was the court of women. These three courts

Archaeologists have found one full copy and two fragmentary copies of the inscriptions, in Latin and Greek, designed to warn Gentiles about entering the temple in Jerusalem. The inscription reads: "No foreigner is to go beyond the balustrade and the plaza of the temple zone. Whoever is caught doing so will have himself to blame for his death which will follow."

He might create[a] in Himself one[b] new man from the two, resulting in peace. [16]He did this so that He might reconcile both to God in one body[c] through the cross and put the hostility to death by it.[A] [17]When the Messiah came, He proclaimed the good news[d] of peace to you who were far away and peace to those who were near.[e] [18]For through Him we both have access[f] by one Spirit to the Father.[g] [19]So then you are no longer foreigners and strangers, but fellow citizens with the •saints, and members of God's household, [20]built on the foundation of the apostles and prophets,[h] with Christ Jesus Himself as the cornerstone. [21]The whole building, being put together[i] by Him, grows into a holy sanctuary in the Lord.[j] [22]You also are being built together[k] for God's dwelling[l] in the Spirit.

Paul's Ministry to the Gentiles

3 For this reason, I, Paul, the prisoner[m] of Christ Jesus on behalf of you Gentiles—

[a]2:15 Rv 3:14
[b]Jn 11:52
[c]2:16 Eph 4:4
[d]2:17 Lk 4:18; 1Pt 1:12
[e]Is 57:19
[f]2:18 Jn 10:7-9; Rm 5:2; Eph 3:12
[g]Jn 4:23; 1Co 12:13; Eph 4:4; Col 1:12
[h]2:20 1Co 12:28; Eph 3:5
[i]2:21 Eph 4:16
[j]1Pt 2:5
[k]2:22 Rm 11:18
[l]1Pt 2:5
[m]3:1 2Tm 1:8
[n]3:3 1Pt 4:13
[o]3:4 Col 4:3
[p]3:5 1Co 12:28-29; Eph 2:20
[q]3:6 Gn 12:7
[r]3:7 Mk 5:30; Lk 1:35; 6:19; Ac 19:11; 2Co 13:4; Rv 11:17
[s]3:8 Rm 1:15; 10:12; 11:12; 1Pt 1:12
[t]3:9 Mk 13:19
[u]3:10 Pr 3:19; Rm 11:33; 1Co 1:21,24; Rv 7:12

[2]you have heard, haven't you, about the administration of God's grace that He gave to me for you? [3]The •mystery was made known to me by revelation,[n] as I have briefly written above. [4]By reading this you are able to understand my insight about the mystery of the •Messiah.[o] [5]This was not made known to people[B] in other generations as it is now revealed to His holy apostles and prophets[p] by the Spirit: [6]The Gentiles are coheirs, members of the same body, and partners of the promise[q] in Christ Jesus through the gospel. [7]I was made a servant of this gospel by the gift of God's grace that was given to me by the working of His power.[r]

[8]This grace was given to me—the least of all the •saints—to proclaim to the Gentiles the incalculable riches[s] of the Messiah, [9]and to shed light for all about the administration of the mystery hidden for ages in God who created[t] all things. [10]This is so God's multifaceted wisdom[u] may now be made known

---

[A]2:16 Or *death in Himself*　　[B]3:5 Lit *to the sons of men*

---

were all on the same elevation as the temple. From here a walled platform was five steps away. Fourteen steps away was another wall, which was the outer court of the Gentiles. There was an inscription on this wall warning Gentiles of their ensuing death if they entered the enclosure around the temple. In Christ this dividing wall was broken down, thus banishing the specific commandments that separated Jews from Gentiles because Gentiles did not observe the Jewish law. The burden of the commandments was taken away at the cross in our Lord's crucified body.

2:16 Reconcile both to God: The phrase extends the concept of "peace" and involves the idea of restoration to a unity. The goal was not merely to reconcile two groups but to reconcile them to God. The **one body** is the church, the new humanity, the place of peace. At the cross, everything that caused the disunion was destroyed.

2:18 Access to the Father is available to all who come to Christ. The imagery is of a court official who conducts visitors into the King's presence. Through Christ's reconciling work we have been ushered into God's presence.

2:19 Foreigners means short-term transients, nonresidents with no rights. **Strangers** is a similar word, pointing to resident foreigners who had settled permanently in the country of their choice but who nevertheless had only limited rights. These terms described the Gentiles' position before Christ. **Fellow citizens . . . and members** are terms that picture the Gentiles' new position. Now they enjoy all the privileges of God's **household**, where "household" describes their togetherness and inclusion. Believers are adopted into God's family and are united with the saints of every era—past, present, and future.

2:20 God's new family is not only a new nation, but also a new building with a distinctive foundation. The **apostles and prophets** in their unique relationship to Christ, exemplified by the authoritative teachings they communicated to the church, are the **foundation**. Paul proclaimed Christ Jesus as the **cornerstone** of the foundation. "Cornerstone" refers to a capstone that holds an entire structure together. In ancient structures it was placed at a right angle joining two

walls, with the royal name inscribed on it to signify the ruler who took credit for the building's erection.

2:22 You also are being built together: The description of a building under construction is indicated by the word "grows" (v. 21). It conveys the idea of a dynamic church in the process of expansion. The major theme of union with Christ reappears in Paul's conclusion to this chapter. Paul declared that God's abode is not in the Jerusalem temple but in the church, which is accomplished by the work of the Holy Spirit who indwells the new believing community.

3:1 Paul here initiates a thought that he leaves unfinished until verse 14. The apostle celebrates his present circumstances in light of God's will and calling for his life.

3:2 The administration of God's grace refers to Paul's unique ministry, describing the implementation of a divine strategy. Paul's ministry was not of his own making, but was given to him as a commission from God (Ac 9).

3:3 Mystery points to something that once was hidden or secret and now has been revealed through means impossible by human discovery. The mystery revealed is that God determined through the person and work of Christ to incorporate the Gentiles into one body of the church as equal partners with Israel (v. 6).

3:6 Coheirs shows that believers in Christ are co-inheritors of God's Kingdom. It also characterizes the new community of believers with Christ as head. That the Gentiles would have equal footing with God's covenant people was a new aspect of God's revelation.

3:8 Least of all the saints is a combination of a superlative and a comparative in one Greek term. The unusual term may have been a playful allusion to Paul's name, thus acknowledging that in himself he was insignificant; but in Christ, God had made him a new creature.

3:10 God's intent was that through the church, his **multifaceted wisdom** should be made known. "Multifaceted" means manifold or multicolored like a beautiful jewel. The history of the Christian church and the unfolding drama of redemption

through the church to the rulers and authorities in the heavens.[a] [11] This is according to His eternal purpose[b] accomplished in the Messiah, Jesus our Lord. [12] In Him we have boldness and confident access[c] through faith in Him.[A] [13] So then I ask you not to be discouraged[d] over my afflictions on your behalf, for they are your glory.[e]

Prayer for Spiritual Power

[14] For this reason I kneel[f] before the Father[B] [15] from whom every family in heaven and on earth is named. [16] I pray that He may grant you, according to the riches[g] of His glory,[h] to be strengthened with power[i] in the inner man[j] through His Spirit, [17] and that the Messiah may dwell in your hearts through faith. I pray that you, being rooted and firmly established in love, [18] may be able to comprehend with all the saints what is the length and width, height and depth of God's love,[k] [19] and to know the Messiah's love that surpasses knowledge, so you may be filled with all the fullness of God.

[20] Now to Him who is able[l] to do above and beyond all that we ask or think[m] according to the power[n] that works in us— [21] to Him be glory in the church and in Christ Jesus to all generations, forever and ever. *Amen.[o]

Unity and Diversity in the Body of Christ

[4] Therefore I, the prisoner for the Lord,[p] urge you to *walk worthy of the calling you have received, [2] with all humility[q] and gentleness, with patience,[r] accepting[C,s] one another in love,[t] [3] diligently keeping the unity[u] of the Spirit[v] with the peace[w] that binds us. [4] There is one body and one Spirit[x]—just as you were called to one hope[D,y] at your calling— [5] one Lord,[z] one faith,[aa] one baptism, [6] one God[ab] and Father[ac] of all, who is above all and through all and in all.[ad]

[7] Now grace was given to each one of us[ae] according to the measure of the *Messiah's gift. [8] For it says:

When He ascended[af] on high,
He took prisoners into captivity;[E]
He gave gifts to people.[F,ag]

[9] But what does "He ascended" mean except that He[G] descended to the lower parts of the earth?[H,ah] [10] The One who descended is also the One who ascended far above all the heavens,[ai] that He might fill[I] all things.[aj] [11] And

Cross references

a 3:10 Eph 1:3,20; 2:6; 6:12; Php 2:10
b 3:11 Pr 19:21
c 3:12 Rm 5:2
d 3:13 2Th 3:13
e Jn 5:44; 7:18; Rm 2:7; 1Pt 5:4
f 3:14 Php 2:10
g 3:16 Lk 8:14; 2Co 8:9
h Lk 9:32; Jn 17:24; 2Co 3:18; 2Pt 3:18
i 2Tm 1:7
j Rm 7:22; Php 4:13
k 3:18 Jb 11:7-9; Ps 103:11-14
l 3:20 Rm 16:25; 2Co 9:8; Jd 24
m Mk 14:36
n Rm 15:13; 16:25; 2Tm 1:7; Jd 24
o 3:21 Php 4:20
p 4:1 2Tm 1:8
q 4:2 Col 3:12
r Ex 34:6; 2Tm 3:10
s Heb 13:22
t 1Co 13:1
u 4:3 Eph 4:13
v Ps 51:11; Jn 1:33; Ac 2:4; Rm 8:9; Gl 5:25; Ti 3:5; Rv 3:22
w Lk 12:51; Rm 1:7; 2Tm 1:2; 3Jn 14
x 4:4 Rm 12:4-5; 1Co 10:17; 12:9,12-13; Eph 2:16,18; Col 3:15
y Ac 26:6-7;
z 28:20; Rm 5:2; 8:23-25; Eph 1:18; Col 1:5; 1Th 1:3
aa 4:5 1Co 1:13; 8:6
ab Jd 3
ac 4:6 Dt 6:4
ad Ps 104:24
ae 4:7 1Co 12:7-11
af 4:8 Jn 20:17
ag Ps 68:18
ah 4:9 Jn 3:13; 6:62; Rm 10:6-7; Php 2:6-11
ai 4:10 Jn 3:13; 6:38
aj Eph 1:23; Heb 4:14; 7:26; 9:24

Textual notes

A 3:12 Or through His faithfulness B 3:14 Other mss add of our Lord Jesus Christ C 4:2 Or tolerating D 4:4 Lit called in one hope E 4:8 Or He led the captives F 4:8 Ps 68:18 G 4:9 Other mss add first H 4:9 Or the lower parts, namely, the earth I 4:10 Or fulfill; Eph 1:23

---

is watched with avid interest by the **rulers and authorities in the heavens**, an apparent reference to angels (cp. 1Pt 1:12).

3:11-13 The church is central to God's working in history. The gospel is good news for a new society and new life. Paul described the church as a divine agent and as a divine fellowship with a divine mandate.

3:14 Paul resumed the prayer that he began in verse 1. In this prayer, he asked that believers might be blessed with inner strength, with insightful understanding, and with spiritual excellence.

3:15 This verse involves some difficult translation decisions, but Paul's intent seems to be as follows: the concept and institute of fatherhood (shared with minor variation by all cultures) stems from God's role as Father and Creator of all peoples. It is not only Jews who can "kneel before the Father" (v. 14) and expect to gain audience, but people from every race and nation.

3:16-19 Paul prayed for inner power, which is the result of God dwelling in the hearts of believers. He asked for believers to be **strengthened . . . rooted**, and **filled** via the work of the three Persons of the Trinity: Spirit, Christ, and God the Father.

3:20-21 Paul burst into a grand doxology concerning God's majestic abilities. He prayed that God's glory would be abundantly manifested in the church and in Christ. Even in the eternal state, the church will bring glory to God **forever and ever**.

4:1 This exhortation serves as a major transition in the let-

ter as it moves from the church's belief statement to the church's mission statement. Paul insisted that a believer's behavior must be worthy of their divine calling.

4:3-6 Believers have the responsibility to keep unity in the body of Christ. The seven "ones" enumerated in these verses constitute the foundation on which the Trinitarian God creates a oneness in the church. Paul's plan can be seen from the vantage point of the work of the one Spirit creating one body, the one Lord Jesus Christ creating one hope, faith, and baptism, and the one God the Father bringing about one people of God.

4:6 One God and Father of all reminds believers that God's oneness defines the church's oneness.

4:7 Paul grounds variety within the Church's unity. God has granted a measure of **grace** to each believer as a gift from Christ.

4:8 This verse is an allusion to Ps 68:18. The essence of the Psalm is that a military victor has the right to receive gifts from the people he has conquered and who now are his subjects. Paul suggested that Christ has conquered His enemies (unredeemed sinners) and has given gifts to them, with Paul himself being the perfect example. As Victor over sin and death, Christ gives gifts to His new devoted followers, His captives.

4:9-10 Paul emphasized that the resurrected and exalted Christ now imparts all the fullness of His blessings to the church and to the universe (1:10,19-23; 3:20-21).

4:11 The description here is more about gifted people

He personally gave some to be apostles, some prophets, some evangelists, some pastors and teachers, [12] for the training of the *saints in the work of ministry, to build up the body of Christ,[a] [13] until we all reach unity in the faith and in the knowledge of God's Son,[b] growing into a mature man with a stature[c] measured by Christ's fullness. [14] Then we will no longer be little children, tossed by the waves and blown around by every wind of teaching,[d] by human cunning with cleverness in the techniques of deceit. [15] But speaking the truth in love, let us grow in every way into Him who is the head[e]—Christ. [16] From Him the whole body, fitted and knit together[f] by every supporting ligament, promotes the growth[g] of the body for building up itself in love by the proper working of each individual part.

a4:12 Rm 7:4; 1Co 10:16; 12:27; Col 2:17
b4:13 Jn 5:19; Heb 1:2
cLk 2:52
d4:14 Rm 15:4; Heb 13:9
e4:15 Col 2:10
f4:16 Col 2:2
gCol 2:19
h4:19 1Th 4:17
i4:21 2Th 2:10
j4:22 Rm 13:12
k2Pt 3:11
lRm 6:6; 7:6; 1Co 5:7-8; 2Co 3:14; Col 3:9
m4:23 Ps 51:12
n4:24 Rm 13:12

Living the New Life

[17] Therefore, I say this and testify in the Lord: You should no longer walk as the Gentiles walk, in the futility of their thoughts. [18] They are darkened in their understanding, excluded from the life of God, because of the ignorance that is in them and because of the hardness of their hearts. [19] They became callous and gave themselves over to promiscuity for the practice of every kind of impurity[h] with a desire for more and more.[A]

[20] But that is not how you learned about the Messiah, [21] assuming you heard about Him and were taught by Him, because the truth[i] is in Jesus. [22] You took off[B,j] your former way of life,[k] the old self[c,l] that is corrupted by deceitful desires; [23] you are being renewed[D] in the spirit[m] of your minds; [24] you put on[E,n] the new self, the

A4:19 Lit with greediness　B4:21-22 Or Jesus. This means: take off (as a command)　C4:22 Lit man; = a person before conversion　D4:22-23 Or desires; renew (as a command)　E4:23-24 Or minds; and put on (as a command)

(natural gifts that can be honed and used for the kingdom) than about spiritual gifts (contrast with Paul's meaning in Rm 12; 1Co 12-14). Five groups of gifted people are listed: apostles, prophets, evangelists, pastors and teachers. Apostles and prophets are foundational for the church's work (Eph 3:5; see note at 2:20). The term **apostles** primarily refers to people sent with a divine mission or task. They also served as spokesmen for God, bringing new revelation and understanding to the church. **Prophets** revealed God's will to believers for the present (forthtelling) and predicted the future (foretelling). All apostles were prophets, but not all prophets were apostles.

Evangelists were gifted to spread the gospel and plant churches. Evangelists proclaimed the good news in word and deed and instructed others in evangelism. **Pastors** and **teachers** shared similar responsibilities. Pastors provided oversight, comfort, and guidance as the church's shepherds (Ac 20:28; 1Pt 5:1-4). Teachers instructed and helped apply God's revelation to the life of the church. Teachers were concerned with passing on the church's revealed teachings (1Co 15:3-4) rather than bringing new inspirational insights like the prophets. Teachers are indispensable for building up the church and are necessary to enable believers to distinguish false doctrine from true teaching.

4:12 The purpose of the gifted people is to equip others to minister. Like many other long sentences in Ephesians, verses 11-16 form one long sentence in the Greek text. The term translated **training** was sometimes used to refer to mending or restoring.

4:13 Ministry is intended to move believers toward accomplishing three goals: (1) unity of faith and full knowledge of God's Son, (2) maturity, and (3) the fullness of Christ. Maturity and unity are measured in terms of the relationship of the body to the Head, Christ.

4:14 When the gifted people equip the church, the community of faith will evidence stability in precept and practice.

4:15 Speaking the truth in love can literally be translated "truthing in love." When a church is faithful to speak truth in love, it will have transparent relationships where people edify and benefit one another.

4:16 Ultimately the church will grow up into Christ in all

aspects, with each part fitting together and supporting the other. Each member of the body must function properly if the body is to grow. We get our English word harmony from the Greek term translated **fitted and knit together**.

4:17-19 This section of the letter provides the practical outworking of verse 1. Paul's exhortations denounced the readers' former way of life. The content of the exhortation clearly parallels early Christian baptismal practices of putting off old clothes before putting on new clothes to enter the baptismal waters. The picture is similar to one in Col 3:5-11, except that the Colossians passage contrasts heavenly and earthly life. The Ephesians passage contrasts a person's former lifestyle and the new life in Christ.

4:20-21 Paul pictures the truth totally in terms of the Messiah, who is the way, the truth, and the life (Jn 14:6).

4:22-24 The apostle often described who believers already are, while also pointing to what they should strive to become. The practical paradox is that while freedom from sin's eternal penalty is already ours, freedom from the for-

apolutrosis

Greek Pronunciation	[ah pah LEW troh sihs]
HCSB Translation	redemption
Uses in Ephesians	3
Uses in the NT	10
Focus passage	Ephesians 1:7,14; 4:30

In the NT, *apolutrosis* may refer to present or future *redemption*. When referring to future *redemption*, the term looks to the salvation of the Christian's physical body from the distresses of this world. The Son of Man's return will usher in release from suffering and persecution (Lk 21:28). In Paul's theology, the future *redemption* of our physical bodies will be accompanied both by the church's full adoption into divine sonship and by the creation being set free from decay (Rm 8:18-23). Presently, the Holy Spirit is the down payment guaranteeing the future "*redemption* of the possession" (meaning God will fully redeem His church and/or the church will posses its full inheritance; Eph 1:14; 4:30). Christians have *redemption*, described as the forgiveness of sins (Eph 1:7; Col 1:14). Thus the work of God in Christ ensures both present and future *redemption* for His people.

one created[a] according to God's likeness[b] in righteousness and purity of the truth. [25]Since you put away[c] lying, **Speak the truth, each one to his neighbor,**[A,d] because we are members of one another. [26]**Be angry and do not sin.**[B,e] Don't let the sun go down on your anger, [27]and don't give the Devil an opportunity. [28]The thief must no longer steal. Instead, he must do honest work with his own hands, so that he has something to share[f] with anyone in need. [29]No foul language is to come from your mouth, but only what is good for building up someone in need,[C] so that it gives grace to those who hear. [30]And don't grieve God's Holy Spirit.[g] You were sealed by Him[D] for the day of •redemption.[h] [31]All bitterness, anger and wrath, shouting and slander must be removed from you, along with all malice. [32]And be kind[i] and compassionate[j] to one another, forgiving[k] one another, just as God also forgave you[E] in Christ.

[5] Therefore, be imitators of God, as dearly loved children. [2]And •walk in love, as the •Messiah also loved us and gave Himself for us,[l] a sacrificial and fragrant offering to God. [3]But sexual immorality[m] and any impurity[n] or greed[o] should not even be heard of[F] among you, as is proper for •saints. [4]Coarse and foolish talking or crude joking are not suitable, but rather giving thanks. [5]For know and recognize this: Every sexually immoral[p] or impure[q] or greedy[r] person, who is an idolater,

does not have an inheritance in the kingdom[s] of the Messiah and of God.

Light versus Darkness

[6]Let no one deceive you with empty arguments, for God's wrath[t] is coming on the disobedient because of these things.[G] [7]Therefore, do not become their partners. [8]For you were once darkness, but now you are light[u] in the Lord. Walk as children of light[v]— [9]for the fruit of the light[H] results in all goodness, righteousness, and truth[w]— [10]discerning[x] what is pleasing[y] to the Lord. [11]Don't participate in the fruitless[z] works of darkness, but instead expose them. [12]For it is shameful even to mention what is done by them in secret. [13]Everything exposed by the light is made clear,[aa] [14]for what makes everything clear is light. Therefore it is said:

> Get up, sleeper,[ab] and rise up
> from the dead,[ac]
> and the Messiah will shine on you.[I,ad]

Consistency in the Christian Life

[15]Pay careful attention, then, to how you walk—not as unwise people but as wise— [16]making the most of the time,[J,ae] because the days are evil. [17]So don't be foolish, but understand[af] what the Lord's will[ag] is. [18]And don't get

[a]4:24 Mk 13:19; Jn 1:3; Rv 3:14 [b]Col 3:10; 2Pt 1:4 [c]4:25 Pr 31:25 [d]Zch 8:16 [e]4:26 Ps 4:4; 37:8; Mt 18:21; Jms 1:19-20 [f]4:28 1Tm 2:8; 1Tm 6:18 [g]4:30 Ps 51:11; Jn 1:33; Ac 2:4; Rm 8:9; Gl 5:25; Ti 3:5; Rv 3:22 [h]Php 1:6 [i]4:32 Mt 11:30; Lk 5:39; 6:35; Rm 2:4; 1Co 15:33; 1Pt 2:3 [j]1Pt 3:8 [k]Ps 25:11; Mt 9:2; Mk 2:5; Lk 24:47; Col 3:12-13 [l]5:2 2Th 2:13; Ti 2:14 [m]5:3 1Th 4:3 [n]1Th 4:7 [o]Lk 12:15; Rm 1:29; Eph 4:19; Col 3:5; 1Th 2:5; 2Pt 2:3,14 [p]5:5 1Co 5:9 [q]2Co 6:17 [r]1Co 5:10-11; 6:10 [s]Mk 1:15 [t]5:6 Rm 2:5; Rv 6:16 [u]5:8 Ps 36:9; Jn 12:46 [v]Is 2:5; Lk 16:8; Jn 12:35-36 [w]5:9 Eph 5:17 [x]5:10 Rm 12:2 [y]Lk 18:18 [z]5:11 Gl 5:22; Ti 3:14 [aa]5:13 1Jn 1:2 [ab]5:14 Pr 6:4 [ac]Jn 5:25 [ad]Is 26:19; 51:17; 52:1; 60:1; Mal 4:2; Lk 1:78-79; Rm 13:11 [ae]5:16 Col 4:5 [af]5:17 Jr 31:31-34; Ezk 36:26-27; Rm 12:2; Php 1:9-10; 1Th 5:21 [ag]Ps 143:10; Pr 16:9; Gl 1:4; Eph 1:9

[A]4:25 Zch 8:16 [B]4:26 Ps 4:4 [C]4:29 Lit *for the building up of the need* [D]4:30 Or *Spirit, by whom you were sealed* [E]4:32 Other mss read *us* [F]5:3 Or *be named* [G]5:6 Lit *sons of disobedience* [H]5:9 Other mss read *fruit of the Spirit* [I]5:14 This poem may have been an early Christian hymn based on several passages in Isaiah; Is 9:2; 26:19; 40:1; 51:17; 52:1; 60:1. [J]5:16 Lit *buying back the time*

mer way of life (a life of sin) comes only through our daily quest for obedience and purity. These are lifestyle commitments that every believer is called to make.

4:25-32 Paul offered five examples of what living the new life means in the context of relationship with others. All of the examples include a negative command, a positive command, and a spiritual principle on which the commands are based. At the base of all of Paul's commands is a God-centered spiritual foundation.

4:32 Paul used a play on words to illustrate his point. Believers are urged to be kind (Gk *Chrestos*) because of Christ (Gk *Christos*).

5:1 Believers are challenged to **be imitators of God**. Previously they had been urged to learn about Christ (4:20-21) and not to grieve the Spirit (4:30). Believers cannot imitate God in power, knowledge, or presence, but they can imitate Him in self-sacrifice and in manifesting a forgiving spirit (4:32).

5:3-5 All of God's gifts, including sexuality in the bonds of marriage, are to be subjects for thanksgiving, not of **crude joking**.

5:6-7 Viewed actively, God's **wrath** is His firm, ongoing opposition to evil; He is eternally opposed to everything that

is contrary to His design and His holy nature. God's new community is to reflect the character of God's Kingdom and the character of God's wrath by presenting a witness against evil.

5:10 **Discerning what is pleasing to the Lord** makes duty and Christian living a delight, investing service with joy.

5:11-14 Faithful believers do more than abstain from evil; they denounce the deeds of darkness as unfruitful, shameful, and not worthwhile.

5:15-16 These words provide a solemn warning that Christians should be wise and careful in all things, including their use of time. Our use of time is not neutral; it can be evil if it is not invested for good (Ps 90).

5:17 **Understand what the Lord's will is** summarizes the two philosophies of life described in verses 1-17. The world's lifestyle is characterized by moral and spiritual darkness. The philosophy for godly living is characterized by moral and spiritual light, and its goal is to imitate God and His love.

5:18 Paul's imperatives contrast the differences between being under the influence of wine, which leads to **reckless actions**, and being under the influence of the Spirit, which results in joyful living. The commands are plural, thus the

drunk[a] with wine,[b] which leads to reckless actions, but be filled by the Spirit:[c]

19 speaking to one another
   in psalms, hymns, and spiritual songs,
   singing and making music
   from your heart to the Lord,
20 giving thanks always for everything
   to God the Father
   in the name of our Lord Jesus Christ,
21 submitting to one another
   in the fear of Christ.[d]

Wives and Husbands

22 Wives,[e] submit[A,f] to your own husbands[g] as to the Lord, 23 for the husband is the head of the wife[h] as Christ is the head[i] of the church. He is the Savior of the body.[j] 24 Now as the church submits to Christ, so wives are to submit to their husbands in everything. 25 Husbands,

love your wives,[k] just as Christ loved[l] the church and gave Himself[m] for her 26 to make her holy, cleansing[B] her with the washing of water by the word. 27 He did this to present the church to Himself in splendor, without spot or wrinkle or anything like that, but holy and blameless.[n] 28 In the same way, husbands are to love their wives as their own bodies. He who loves his wife loves himself. 29 For no one ever hates his own flesh but provides and cares for it, just as Christ does for the church, 30 since we are members of His body.[C]

31 **For this reason a man will leave**
   his father and mother
   and be joined to his wife,[o]
   and the two will become one flesh.[D,p]

32 This •mystery[q] is profound, but I am talking about Christ and the church. 33 To sum up,

Cross references

[a] 5:18 Lk 12:45; Jn 2:10; 1Th 5:7; Rv 17:2
[b] Gn 9:21; Dt 7:13; Ps 4:7; Pr 3:10; Lk 5:37
[c] Lk 1:15; Ac 13:52
[d] 5:18-21 Col 3:16-17; 1Pt 1:17
[e] 5:22 1Pt 3:1
[f] Gn 3:16; 1Co 11:3,7-9,11-12; Col 3:18; Ti 2:4-5; 1Pt 3:1-6
[g] 1Pt 3:1
[h] 5:23 1Co 11:3
[i] Col 2:10
[j] Col 3:18-4:1
[k] 5:25 Col 3:19; 1Pt 3:7
[l] Jn 3:16; 1Co 13:1; 2Th 2:13
[m] Ti 2:14
[n] 5:27 Jd 24
[o] 5:31 1Pt 3:1
[p] Gn 2:24
[q] 5:32 1Co 2:7

commands refer not merely to individuals, but to the corporate community of faith.

5:19-21 The Spirit's fullness is demonstrated in spiritual understanding, praise, and thanksgiving that are constant and comprehensive. The church that is filled with the Spirit will be characterized by praise and thanksgiving to God. Beyond that there will be evidence of self-control, mutual encouragement, and mutual submission, which is the opposite of rudeness, haughtiness, and self-assertion.

5:21 This verse serves as a hinge to connect what is prior with what follows. Grammatically, the participial phrase (lit "submitting yourselves") goes with verses 18-20. The content of verses 22-33, however, depends on the principle of submission in verse 21.

5:22 Wives submit directs wives to be submissive to their own (Gk *idios;* "one's own") husbands (cp. Col 3:18-4:1). The distinctive feature here is that the relationship between husband and wife is compared with that between Christ and the church. No verb is in the original language of verse 22. The imperative "submit" is understood from verse 21.

5:22-24 Paul addressed wives first. They were to be voluntarily submissive to their husbands. No external coercion should be involved, nor should submission imply that the wife is a lesser partner in the marital union. The submission is governed by the phrase **as to the Lord.** Christian wives' submission to their husbands is one aspect of their obedience to Christ. Submission is a person's yielding his or her own rights and losing self for another. Submission is patterned after Christ's example (Php 2:5-8) and reflects the essence of the gospel. Submission distinguishes the lifestyle of all Christians.

5:25 Paul turned to the duties of husbands. The society in which Paul wrote recognized the duties of wives to husbands but not necessarily of husbands to wives. As in Col 3:19, Paul exhorted husbands to love their wives, but Ephesians presents Christ's self-sacrificing love for the church as the pattern for the husband's love for his wife.

Husbands are to love their wives continually as Christ loves the church. The tense of the Greek word translated "love" indicates a love that continues. Love is more than family affection or sexual passion. Rather it is a deliberate

attitude leading to action that concerns itself with another's well-being. A husband should love his wife (1) as Christ loved the church (vv. 25-27); (2) as his own body (vv. 28-30); and (3) with a love transcending all other human relationships (vv. 31-33).

5:26-27 Cleansing her with the washing of water: Paul explains more fully the result of Christ's atonement for the church: it makes the church holy and pure. The purpose of Christ's giving himself up for the church is the church's sanctification and cleansing.

5:28 Since **husbands are to love** their wives as Christ loved the church, they give up their personal rights for the good of their wives. It is a solemn picture of covenant love.

5:29-30 On first sight, Paul seems to have descended from the lofty standard of Christ's love to the low standard of self-love when he says **no one ever hates his own flesh,** but he reminded Christian couples of their oneness, the "one-flesh" relationship. For this reason a husband's obligation to cherish his wife as he does his own body is more than a helpful guide. His sacrificial love is an expression of the sacred marital union. True love is evidenced when husbands and wives have this spiritual, emotional, and physical oneness.

5:31-32 Paul appealed to Gn 2:24, which is God's initial statement in the Scriptures regarding marriage. The marriage commitment takes precedence over every other human relationship.

5:31 One flesh means closely joined. It hallows the biblical standard of covenantal heterosexual marital relations and excludes polygamy and adultery. What is primarily a divine ordinance graciously and lovingly is designed for mutual satisfaction and delight.

5:33 Love . . . respect concludes and restates this section's theme. The husband's ultimate responsibility is to love his wife with a Christlike love.

6:1-3 Paul's initial concerns were for **children** to be responsible to their parents. He called for children to be obedient as taught in natural law, in the Mosaic law, and in the gospel. The word for **obey** is different from the term for submission. Obedience involves recognition of authority.

each one of you is to love his wife as himself, and the wife is to respect her husband.

Children and Parents

6 Children, obey[a] your parents as you would the Lord,[A] because this is right. ²**Honor your father and mother**, which is the first commandment[B] with a promise, ³**so that it may go well with you and that you may have a long life in the land.**[C,D,b] ⁴Fathers, don't stir up anger[c] in your children, but bring them up in the training[d] and instruction of the Lord.

Slaves and Masters

⁵•Slaves, obey your human[E] masters[e] with fear and trembling,[f] in the sincerity[g] of your heart, as to Christ. ⁶Don't work only while being watched, in order to please men, but as slaves of Christ, do God's will[h] from your heart.[F] ⁷Serve with a good attitude, as to the Lord and not to men,[i] ⁸knowing that whatever good each one does, slave or free, he will receive this back from the Lord. ⁹And masters, treat your slaves the same way, without threatening[j] them, because you know that both their Master and yours is in heaven, and there is no favoritism[k] with Him.[l]

Christian Warfare

¹⁰Finally, be strengthened by the Lord and by His vast strength.[m] ¹¹Put on[n] the full armor[o] of God so that you can stand against the tactics[G] of the Devil. ¹²For our battle is not against flesh[p] and blood, but against the rulers, against the authorities,[q] against the world powers of this darkness, against the spiritual forces of evil[r] in the heavens.[s] ¹³This is why you must take up the full armor[t] of God, so that you may be able to resist[u] in the evil day, and having prepared everything, to take your stand. ¹⁴Stand,[v] therefore,

with truth[w] like a belt
 around your waist,
righteousness[x] like armor
 on your chest,[y]
¹⁵ and your feet sandaled with readiness
 for the gospel of peace.[H]
¹⁶ In every situation take the shield[z]
 of faith,[aa]
and with it you will be able
 to extinguish
all the flaming arrows of the evil one.[ab]
¹⁷ Take the helmet[ac] of salvation,
 and the sword[ad] of the Spirit,[ae]
 which is God's word.

¹⁸ Pray[af] at all times in the Spirit[ag] with every

a6:1 Pr 1:8; 6:20; 23:22; Col 3:20 b6:2-3 Ex 20:12 c6:4 Rm 10:19 dHeb 12:5 e6:5 Col 3:22; 1Pt 2:18 fPhp 2:12 g2Co 9:11 h6:6 Ps 143:10; Pr 16:9; Gl 1:4; Eph 1:9 i6:7 Col 3:23 j6:9 Ac 4:29; 9:1 kCol 3:25 lCol 4:1 m6:10 Ac 4:33 n6:11 Pr 31:25 oEph 6:11-17 p6:12 Php 3:3 q1Pt 3:22 rMt 6:13; Jn 17:15 sEph 1:3,20; 2:6; 3:10; Php 2:10 t6:13 1Th 5:8 u2Tm 4:15; 1Pt 5:9 v6:14 Pr 24:16; Php 1:27 wJn 14:6; 1Jn 5:20 xMt 6:33; Rm 1:17; 2Pt 1:1 y1Th 5:8 z6:16 Gn 15:1 aaMt 8:10; Ac 3:16; Rm 1:8; 1Co 2:5; Gl 2:16; 1Tm 1:2; Heb 4:2 ab2Th 3:3 ac6:17 1Th 5:8 adMk 14:47 aePs 51:11; Jn 1:33; Ac 2:4; Rm 8:9; Gl 5:25; Ti 3:5; Rv 3:22 af6:18 Mt 5:44; Ac 12:12 agJd 20

A6:1 Lit parents in the Lord   B6:2 Or is a preeminent commandment   C6:3 Or life on the earth   D6:2-3 Ex 20:12   E6:5 Lit according to the flesh   F6:6 Lit from soul   G6:11 Or schemes, or tricks   H6:15 Ready to go tell others about the gospel

---

6:4 Parents have responsibility both to discipline and to instruct their children. Paul indicated that **fathers** are to take the lead in this responsibility. Parents are not to **stir up anger** in their children. Discipline is not to be arbitrary or something done out of anger.

6:5-9 The NT, as well as the OT, includes guidelines for **slaves** and slavery. These guidelines do not condone slavery, but provided ethical guidance for times and places where slavery existed. Paul's claim that slaves and masters are equal before God would have shocked his contemporaries. Where the Roman law unfairly discriminated between master and slave, heavenly law does not. Paul's words in this context provided groundwork for a new sense of brotherhood between races, and were later used to help inspire the anti-slavery movement.

6:10-13 Three times Paul called for believers to **stand** against the Devil's schemes, the spiritual battle that takes place against **the spiritual forces of evil in the heavens**.

6:14-16 The defensive armor that Paul describes in these verses includes five components. Paul called for believers to put on the "full armor" (v. 13), which points to its divine nature more than its completeness.

6:17 The offensive armor included only one weapon, a short **sword** used in close combat. The "sword" symbolized God's word.

6:17 Because of its design, content, and origin, Scripture (**God's word**) can be described as "trustworthy" (2Tm 2:11),

"confirmed" (Heb 2:3; 2Pt 1:19), and "enduring forever" (1Pt 1:24-25).

6:18-20 Each piece of armor must carefully be put on with prayer, drawing upon divine resources. This prayer is

hrema

Greek Pronunciation	[HRAY mah]
HCSB Translation	word
Uses in Ephesians	2
Uses in the NT	68
Focus passage	Ephesians 6:17

Hrema most frequently appears in the narrative literature of the four Gospels and Acts (a total of 52x). In the NT, *hrema (word)* is used with two different senses. The term is first used with the sense of *that which is said or expressed*. Here the word focuses on what is being *communicated*. For example, Jesus speaks of men having to give account for every careless *word* they speak (Mt 12:36). In this sense, *hrema* may also refer to any one of many different types of *communication*. For example, *hrema* can refer to a *prophecy* or *prediction* (e.g., Mk 9:32), to a *speech* or *sermon* (e.g., Rm 10:18), to the *gospel* or a *confessional statement* (e.g., 1Pt 1:25), or to a *commandment* or *order* (e.g., Heb 11:3). However, *hrema* does not always focus on what has been *communicated*. It may refer simply to a *thing, object, matter,* or *event*. For example, Paul speaks of every *word* (i.e., *matter* or *event*) being confirmed on the testimony of two or three witnesses (2Co 13:1), and the angel Gabriel reminds Mary that nothing is impossible with God (Lk 1:37).

prayer and request, and stay alert[a] in this with all perseverance and intercession for all the •saints. [19] Pray also for me, that the message may be given to me when I open my mouth to make known with boldness[b] the •mystery of the gospel. [20] For this I am an ambassador[c] in chains. Pray that I might be bold enough in Him to speak as I should.

Paul's Farewell

[21] Tychicus,[d] our dearly loved brother and

a 6:18 Pr 6:4
b 6:19 2Co 3:12
c 6:20 2Co 5:20
d 6:21 Ti 3:12
e 6:22 Lk 16:25
f Col 4:8
g 6:23 Mt 5:16;
11:27; Lk 11:13;
Jn 8:42

faithful servant[A] in the Lord, will tell you all the news about me so that you may be informed. [22] I am sending him to you for this very reason, to let you know how we are and to encourage[e] your hearts.[f]

[23] Peace to the •brothers, and love with faith, from God the Father[g] and the Lord Jesus Christ. [24] Grace be with all who have undying love for our Lord Jesus Christ.[B,C]

A 6:21 Or deacon   B 6:24 Other mss add Amen.   C 6:24 Lit all who love our Lord Jesus Christ in incorruption

---

Spirit-energized, Spirit-enabled, and Spirit-directed. Praying in the Spirit is an admission of a believer's ignorance and dependence on God.

6:21-24 Paul concluded with greetings that lack the personal references usually present in his letters. Such omissions are hard to explain if the letter was intended only for the church at Ephesus, the place where Paul stayed longer than anywhere else in his ministry (Ac 18:19-21; 19; 20:13-31) and presumably had numerous personal relationships. For this reason many conclude that the letter was intended to circulate more broadly, addressing not just the church at Ephesus but other churches of the region also. Most likely **Tychicus** carried the letter, along with the letter to the Colossian church and the personal letter to Philemon.

Philippians

Philippians is Paul's most warmly personal letter. After initial difficulties in the city of Philippi (Ac 16), a strong bond developed between Paul and the converts there. Paul wrote to thank the church for a gift it had recently sent him in prison and to inform them of his circumstances.

An overview of the Roman colony of Philippi. The great Roman road, the Via Egnatia, visible in the center of the photograph, brought Paul to Philippi from the nearby port city of Neapolis. This was where Paul first preached the gospel in Europe.

Circumstances of Writing

Author: Paul the apostle wrote this short letter, a fact that no scholar seriously questions.

Background: The traditional date for the writing of Philippians is during Paul's first Roman imprisonment (A.D. 60–62); few have challenged this conclusion.

Paul planted the church at Philippi during his second missionary journey (A.D. 51) in response to his "Macedonian vision" (Ac 16:9-10). This was the first church in Europe (Ac 16).

The text of this letter from Paul suggests several characteristics of the church at Philippi. First, Gentiles predominated. Few Jews lived in Philippi, and, apparently, the church had few. Second, women had a significant role (Ac 16:11-15; Php 4:1-2). Third, the church was generous. Fourth, they remained deeply loyal to Paul.

Philippi, the ancient city of Krenides, had a military significance. It was the capital of Alexander the Great, who renamed it for his father Philip of Macedon, and it became the capital of the Greek Empire (332 B.C.). The Romans conquered Greece, and in the civil war after Julius Caesar's death (44 B.C.), Antony and Octavius repopulated Philippi by allowing the defeated armies (Brutus and Cassius) to settle there (800 miles from Rome). They declared the city a Roman colony. It flourished, proud of its history and entrenched in Roman political and social life. In his epistle to the Philippians, Paul alluded to military and political structures as metaphors for the church.

Paul wanted to thank the church for their financial support (4:10-20). He also addressed disunity and the threat of heresy. Disunity threatened the church, spawned by personal conflicts (4:2) and disagreements over theology (3:1-16). The heresy came from radical Jewish teachers. Paul addressed both issues personally and warmly.

The church at Philippi sent Epaphroditus to help Paul in Rome. While there he became ill (2:25-28). The church learned of Epaphroditus's illness, and Paul wished to ease their concern for him. Some people pos-

sibly blamed Epaphroditus for failing his commission, but Paul commended him and sent him home. Perhaps Epaphroditus carried this letter with him.

Message and Purpose

One purpose of this letter was for Paul to explain his situation at Rome (1:12-26). Although he was concerned about the divided Christian community there, his outlook was strengthened by the knowledge that Christ was being magnified. Paul's theology of life formed the basis of his optimism. Whether he lived or died, whether he continued his service to others or went to be in Christ's presence, or whether he was appreciated or not, he wanted Christ to be glorified. Within this explanation are several messages.

Unity: Paul exhorted the church to unity (1:27–2:18). Two factors influenced him. The church at Rome was divided, and he lived with a daily reminder of the effects of disunity. Further, similar disunity threatened the Philippian church as two prominent women differed with each other. Selfishness lay at the heart of the problems at Rome and Philippi. Paul reminded the believers of the humility of Jesus. If they would allow the outlook of Christ to guide their lives, harmony would be restored. The hymn to Christ (2:5-11) dominates the epistle.

Christian unity results when individuals develop the mind of Christ. In more difficult situations, the church collectively solved problems through the involvement of its leadership (4:2-3). Harmony, joy, and peace characterize the church which functions as it should.

Freedom from legalism: Paul warned the church to beware of Jewish legalists (3:2-21). Legalistic Jewish teachers threatened to destroy the vitality of the congregation by calling it to a preoccupation with external religious matters. Paul countered the legalists with a forceful teaching about justification by faith. He chose to express his theology through his personal experience. He had lived their message and found it lacking.

Salvation: Salvation was provided by Christ, who became obedient to death (2:6-8). It was proclaimed by a host of preachers who were anxious to advance the gospel. It was promoted through varying circumstances

A.D. 49–52

Paul, Silas, and Timothy continue through North Galatia to Troas. 49

Paul and his companions arrive in Philippi and plant the first Christian church in Europe. 50

Paul's ministry in the Macedonia cities of Thessalonica and Berea 50

Paul plants the church at Corinth. 50–51

Paul concludes second missionary journey, returning to Antioch of Syria. 52

A.D. 54–62

Paul's third missionary journey takes him to Ephesus. 54

Paul's extended ministry in Ephesus 54–56

Paul likely revisits Philippi collecting funds for the church at Jerusalem. 57

Paul's first imprisonment in Rome 60–62

Paul writes his letter to the church at Philippi. 62

of life—both good and bad—so that the lives of believers became powerful witnesses. Finally, salvation would transform Christians and churches into models of spiritual life.

Stewardship: Paul thanked the Philippian believers for their financial support. The church had sent money and a trusted servant, Epaphroditus, to care for Paul. Their generosity encouraged Paul at a time of personal need, and he took the opportunity to express the rewards of giving and to teach Christian living.

The church at Philippi had reached a maturity regarding material possessions. It knew how to give out of poverty. It knew the value of supporting the gospel and those who proclaim it, and it knew that God could provide for its needs as well. Paul also demonstrated his attitude toward material things. He could maintain spiritual equilibrium in the midst of fluctuating financial circumstances. Christ was his life, and Christ's provisions were all he needed. In everything, Paul's joy was that Christ was glorified in him.

Imitation: The epistle abounds with Christian models for imitation. Most obviously, the church was to imitate Jesus, but other genuine Christians also merited appreciation. Paul, Timothy, and Epaphroditus embodied the selflessness that God desires in His people.

Contribution to the Bible

Paul's letter to the Philippians teaches us much about genuine Christianity. While most of its themes may be found elsewhere in Scripture, it is within this letter that we can see how those themes and messages impact life. Within the NT, Philippians contributes to our understanding of Christian commitment and what it means to be Christlike.

Structure

Philippians can be divided into four primary sections. Paul had definite concerns which he wanted to express, and he also wrote to warn about false teachers who threatened the church. Many of Paul's letters can be divided into theological and practical sections, but Philippians does not follow that pattern. Paul's theological instruction is woven throughout the fabric of a highly personal letter.

Outline

I. Salutation (1:1-2)

II. Explanation of Paul's Concerns (1:3–2:30)
    A. Paul's thanksgiving and prayer (1:3-11)
    B. Paul's joy in the progress of the gospel (1:12-26)
    C. Exhortation to Christlike character (1:27–2:18)
    D. Paul's future plans (2:19-30)

III. Exhortations to Christian Living (3:1–4:9)
    A. Exhortations to avoid false teachers (3:1-21)
    B. Miscellaneous exhortations (4:1-9)

IV. Expression of Thanks and Conclusion (4:10-23)
    A. Repeated thanks (4:10-20)
    B. Greetings and benediction (4:21-23)

Greeting

1 Paul[a] and Timothy,[b] slaves of Christ Jesus:
To all the •saints in Christ Jesus who are in Philippi,[c] including the •overseers[d] and deacons.[e]

[2] Grace to you and peace from God our Father and the Lord Jesus Christ.

Thanksgiving and Prayer

[3] I give thanks to my God for every remembrance of you,[A] [4] always praying with joy for all of you in my every prayer, [5] because of your partnership in the gospel from the first day[f] until now.[g] [6] I am sure of this, that He who started a good work[h] in you[B] will carry it on to completion[i] until the day of Christ Jesus. [7] It is right[j] for me to think this way about all of you, because I have you in my heart,[C] and you are all partners with me in grace, both in my imprisonment[k] and in the defense[l] and establishment of the gospel. [8] For God is my witness,[m] how deeply I miss all of you[n] with the affection of Christ Jesus. [9] And I pray this: that your love[o] will keep on growing[p] in knowledge and every kind of discernment,[q] [10] so that you can approve the things that are superior[r] and can

be pure[s] and blameless[t] in[D] the day of Christ,[u] [11] filled with the fruit[v] of righteousness[w] that comes through Jesus Christ to the glory[x] and praise of God.

Advance of the Gospel

[12] Now I want you to know, •brothers, that what has happened to me has actually resulted in the advance of the gospel,[y] [13] so that it has become known throughout the whole imperial guard,[E] and to everyone else, that my imprisonment is in the cause of Christ. [14] Most of the brothers in the Lord have gained confidence from my imprisonment and dare even more to speak the message[F,z] fearlessly. [15] To be sure, some preach Christ out of envy and strife,[aa] but others out of good will.[G] [16] These do so out of love,[ab] knowing that I am appointed for the defense of the gospel; [17] the others proclaim Christ out of rivalry,[ac] not sincerely, seeking to cause me anxiety in my imprisonment.[H] [18] What does it matter? Just that in every way, whether out of false motives[ad] or true, Christ is proclaimed. And in this I rejoice. Yes,

[a]1:1 Ac 13:9
[b]Ac 16:1; 1Tm 1:2
[c]Ac 16:12-40; 20:3-6; 1Th 2:2
[d]Ac 20:28; Ti 1:7
[e]1Co 3:5
[f]1:5 Ac 16:12-40
[g]1Co 9:15-18; 2Co 11:7-9; Php 4:10,16,18
[h]1:6 2Co 9:8; Gl 3:10
[i]2Co 7:1
[j]1:7 Rm 1:17
[k]Php 1:13-14, 17-20,25,30; 2:17,24; 4:22
[l]Ac 22:1
[m]1:8 Rm 1:9
[n]1Th 3:6
[o]1:9 1Co 13:1
[p]1Co 15:58
[q]Eph 5:17
[r]1:9-10 Rm 12:2
[s]1:10 2Pt 3:1
[t]Ac 24:16; 1Co 10:32
[u]Php 1:6,15
[v]1:11 Mt 3:8; Gl 5:22
[w]Rm 1:17
[x]Lk 9:32; Jn 17:24; 2Co 3:18; 2Pt 3:18
[y]1:12 Mk 13:9; Ac 21-26
[z]1:14 Lk 8:21; Jn 18:32; [aa]1:15 Rm 1:29; Ti 3:9 [ab]1:16 1Co 13:1 [ac]1:17 Rm 2:8 [ad]1:18 1Th 2:5

[A]1:3 Or for your every remembrance of me [B]1:6 Or work among you [C]1:7 Or because you have me in your heart [D]1:10 Or until [E]1:13 Lit praetorium, a Lat word that can also refer to a military headquarters, to the governor's palace, or to Herod's palace. [F]1:14 Other mss add of God [G]1:15 The good will of men, or God's good will or favor [H]1:17 Lit sincerely, intending to raise tribulation to my bonds

---

1:1a Timothy was with Paul and Silas when they planted the church at Philippi (Php 2:19-24; Ac 16). "Slave" (Gk *doulos*) expresses humility.

1:1b Saints are believers. **Overseers** (lit "bishops") and **deacons** (lit "servants") indicate an emerging church structure that became full-blown in later years.

1:2 Grace and **peace**, jointly from **God** and **Jesus Christ**, attest to the deity and coequality of both.

1:5 Partnership (lit "fellowship") expresses participation, including giving (4:10-20) and sending Epaphroditus (2:25). **From the first day** shows Paul's continued joy in these believers, in spite of his initial difficulty in the city of Philippi (Ac 16).

1:9-10 Paul prayed two petitions: a growing love (v. 9) and complete character (v. 10). **Love** (Gk *agape*) is selfless action for another person. **Knowledge** and **discernment** provide the twofold environment that fosters love. "Knowledge" is both intellectual and experiential. "Discernment," unique in the Bible, is moral sensitivity. Love enriched by knowledge and moral discernment leads believers to experience what really matters. The word **pure** emphasizes personal integrity; **blameless** means good character that survives all accusations.

1:11 The phrase **filled with the fruit of righteousness** expresses how a person attains purity and blamelessness. Righteousness is the character of those whom God declares righteous.

1:12 Paul's attitude was that both good and bad promoted **the gospel**. Advancement meant to blaze a trail (e.g., for an

army). Paul's difficult circumstances opened new opportunities for gospel witness.

1:13 The first opportunity (see v. 12 and note) for gospel witness involved the **imperial guard**, an elite military force charged with protecting the Roman emperor and his concerns. As the soldiers rotated shifts, each heard Paul's message. Paul's **imprisonment** was for **Christ** (lit "a prisoner of Christ"). The guard knew that Paul's commitment to Christ had led to his arrest and imprisonment.

1:14-17 The second opportunity for gospel witness involved the church itself. Responding to Paul's imprisonment, Christians divided into those who supported him and those who opposed him. Paul's imprisonment spawned renewed enthusiasm for preaching in both groups, but the group that opposed him preached the gospel out of **envy and strife**. They hoped to cause Paul greater difficulty, perhaps an unfavorable trial verdict. Their motivation was **rivalry**, intending to **cause . . . anxiety** by social turmoil. Paul does not say what drove the rivalry, but apparently they felt Christianity ought to have a different spokesperson than Paul. The group that supported Paul was motivated by **good will** and **love**. They realized Paul was **appointed** (lit "set") by God for defending the gospel, especially to Gentiles. Neither of these groups is identified. Both seem to have held correct doctrine and proclaimed Christ, yet their disparate treatment of Paul indicates that even "correct" believers can behave wrongly.

1:18 Paul accepted the message and work of both groups. Trusting God's sovereignty, he refused to condemn improper motivations as long as, in the end result, **Christ** was **proclaimed**.

and I will rejoice [19]because I know this will lead to my deliverance[A,a] through your prayers and help from the Spirit[b] of Jesus Christ.[c] [20]My eager expectation and hope[d] is that I will not be ashamed about anything, but that now as always, with all boldness, Christ will be highly honored in my body, whether by life[e] or by death.[f]

Living Is Christ

[21]For me, living is Christ[g] and dying is gain.[h] [22]Now if I live on in the flesh, this means fruitful[i] work[j] for me; and I don't know which one I should choose. [23]I am pressed by both. I have the desire to depart and be with Christ[k]—which is far better[l]— [24]but to remain in the flesh is more necessary for you. [25]Since I am persuaded of this, I know that I will remain and continue with all of you for your progress and joy in the faith,[m] [26]so that, because of me, your confidence may grow[n] in Christ Jesus[o] when I come to you again.

[27]Just one thing: Live your life[p] in a manner worthy of the gospel of Christ. Then, whether I come and see you or am absent, I will hear about you that you are standing firm[q] in one[r] spirit, with one mind,[B] working side by side for the faith[s] that comes from the gospel, [28]not being frightened in any way by your opponents.[t] This is a sign of destruction for them,[u] but of your deliverance[v]—and this is from God. [29]For it has been given to you on Christ's behalf not only to believe[w] in Him, but also to suffer for Him, [30]having the same struggle that you saw I had and now hear that I have.

Christian Humility

2 If then there is any encouragement in Christ, if any consolation of love,[x] if any fellowship with the Spirit,[y] if any affection and mercy,[z] [2]fulfill my joy by thinking the same

[a]1:19 Jb 13:16-18
[b]Gl 5:25
[c]Ac 16:7; Rm 8:9; 1Pt 1:11
[d]1:20 Ac 23:6; 1Th 1:3
[e]1Jn 5:12
[f]Jn 8:51
[g]1:21 Rm 14:7-9; Gl 2:19-20; Php 1:11,15; Col 2:6-3:11
[h]Rm 8:38-39; Php 3:7
[i]1:22 Mt 3:8; Rm 1:13; Gl 5:22
[j]Mk 14:6; Gl 3:10; Jms 2:14-26
[k]1:23 Rm 6:8; 2Co 4:14; 13:4-5; 1Th 4:14; 5:9-10
[l]Jn 12:26
[m]1:25 Mt 8:10; Ac 3:16; Rm 1:8; 1Co 2:5; Gl 2:16; 1Tm 1:2; Heb 4:2; Jd 3
[n]1:26 1Co 15:58
[o]Rm 16:7; Eph 2:6; 1Pt 5:14
[p]1:27 Ac 23:1
[q]1Co 16:13; Gl 5:1; Eph 6:13-17; Php 4:1; 2Th 2:15
[r]Jn 11:52
[s]1Tm 3:9; 4:1,6; 5:8; 6:10,21
[t]1:28 1Co 16:9
[u]Mt 7:13; Rm 9:22
[v]Ac 4:12; 2Co 7:10; Heb 5:9
[w]1:29 Mk 11:24; Jn 3:16; Ac 10:43; Rm 10:9; 1Pt 1:8-10
[x]2:1 Rm 5:8; 15:30; 2Th 2:16; 1Jn 3:16; 4:9-10,16
[y]1Co 12:13; 2Co 13:13; Eph 4:3
[z]Col 3:12

A1:19 Or *vindication*   **B**1:27 Lit *soul*

1:19 Paul remained optimistic. **Deliverance** (lit "salvation") may recall Job's attitude (Jb 13:13-18). Paul expected exoneration because Christianity was not illegal throughout the Roman Empire at this time. Paul hoped for **prayers**, the "human" side, and **help**, divine assistance. "Prayers" implies intense intercession. God answers prayers with help (lit "supply"), either something the Holy Spirit provides (a resource), or the presence of the Holy Spirit (the "Comforter"). The grammar of this verse joins "prayers" and "help," indicating Paul's dependence on both working together.

1:20 Ashamed (lit "put to shame") implies cowering, running from battle, or embarrassment. Paul expected that **Christ** would **be highly honored** in his **body**. The physical body symbolizes earthly life. On earth, if Christ is not glorified in the body, He is not glorified at all. Further, Paul hoped Christ would also be glorified in his death.

euangelion

Greek Pronunciation	[yoo ahn GEHL ee ahn]
HCSB Translation	gospel, good news
Uses in Philippians	12
Uses in the NT	76
Focus passage	Philippians 1:27

The Christian *euangelion* (gospel) is the universal message of God's saving grace through faith in Christ, and the message of His kingdom over which Jesus reigns. Jesus preached the *good news* of God's saving grace (Mt 4:23), and substantiated His message by miracles (Mt 9:35). This *good news* of the kingdom's arrival will be preached to the world (Mk 13:10) and is worthy of sacrificial labor (Mk 8:35). Paul believed the *gospel* was an extension of OT promises, where it lay hidden in mystery form (Rm 1:1-3; 16:25-26). Paul's *gospel* encompasses Jesus' entire life: His incarnation, sacrificial death, burial, resurrection, post-resurrection appearances, and ascension (Rm 1:1-6; 1Co 15:1-8; Php 2:9). It is the Spirit-empowered message (1Th 1:5) by which God calls the elect (2Th 2:13-14) and reconciles people to Himself (2Co 5:18-21). Men will one day be judged by it (Rm 2:16; 2Th 1:8).

1:21-24 Living is Christ restates the theme of verse 20. If he carried on living, every aspect of Paul's life would continue to reveal Christ, which would make his life **fruitful** and worthwhile. Likewise, his death would be **gain** since it would usher him into Christ's presence. Paul felt **pressured** (lit "in a dilemma"), acknowledging the benefits of both outcomes. The phrase **is more necessary for you** expresses Paul's servant heart. A selfish outlook would make Paul prefer glorification and reward (via death) over continued life and ministry, but his priority was that Christ be honored and glorified.

1:27-28 Live your life (lit "conduct yourselves as citizens"; cp. Ac 23:1) alludes to Philippi's political history, reminding the church of its higher citizenship (in the kingdom of God). Paul's primary concern, that **you are standing firm in one spirit**, reflected military pride. Roman armies stood ready for combat regardless of the enemy's level of strength and preparedness or the distracting enticements of culture. The church must manifest the same readiness. "One spirit" expresses the believer's unified attitude. **One mind** (lit "same soul") means that believers share "life." Together they prevent divisiveness like Paul witnessed at Rome (vv. 14-17). Standing firm involves **working side by side**. "Working" comes from athletics where teams contended for a prize (cp. 4:3). Harmony, not individualism, achieves God's purposes. Standing also involves not being **frightened . . . by your opponents**. Soldiers used "frightened" to describe horses that might easily be startled.

1:29-30 Given (lit "by grace") indicates that God "graces" Christians to **believe** and **suffer** on **Christ's behalf**. Both contribute to Christ's glory.

2:1-2 Four **if** statements in this verse form the basis of Paul's appeal. These phrases express conditions that are assumed for the sake of argument. Both Paul and his readers will be inclined to believe the truth of these conditions. **Fulfill my joy**, not "make Paul happy," reminded them that their steadfastness completed God's call on his life. Four actions on the Philippians' part explain what Paul meant.

way,[a] having the same love,[b] sharing the same feelings, focusing on one[c] goal. [3]Do nothing out of rivalry[d] or conceit,[e] but in humility[f] consider others as more important[g] than yourselves. [4]Everyone should look out not only for his own interests,[h] but also for the interests of others.[i]

Christ's Humility and Exaltation

[5]Make your own attitude that of Christ Jesus,

[6]   who, existing in the form of God,
      did not consider equality with God[j]
      as something to be used
         for His own advantage.[A]
[7]   Instead He emptied Himself[k]
      by assuming the form of a •slave,[l]
      taking on the likeness of men.[m]
      And when He had come as a man
      in His external form,
[8]   He humbled Himself
         by becoming obedient
      to the point of death—

even to death on a cross.[n]
[9]   For this reason God
         highly exalted Him[o]
      and gave Him the name
      that is above every name,
[10] so that at the name of Jesus
      every knee will bow[p]—
      of those who are in heaven[q]
         and on earth
      and under the earth[r]—
[11] and every tongue[s] should confess
      that Jesus Christ is Lord,[B]
      to the glory[t] of God the Father.

Lights in the World

[12]So then, my dear friends,[u] just as you have always obeyed,[v] not only in my presence, but now even more in my absence, work out your own salvation with fear and trembling. [13]For it is God who is working in you, enabling you

Cross-references (center column):
[a] 2:2 Rm 12:16; 15:5; 2Co 13:11; Php 4:2
[b] 2Th 1:3; 1Jn 3:16
[c] Jn 11:52
[d] 2:3 Rm 2:8
[e] Gl 5:26
[f] Col 3:12
[g] Rm 13:1; Php 3:8; 4:7; 1Pt 2:13
[h] 2:4 Rm 15:1
[i] Lv 19:18; Mk 10:45; 12:31; 1Co 10:24; 13:5; Php 2:21
[j] 2:6 Is 9:6; Jn 1:1,14; 20:28; Rm 9:5; Col 1:15-16; Ti 2:13; Heb 1:2-13; 2Pt 1:1; 1Jn 4:14-15
[k] 2:7 Mk 9:12; 2Co 8:9; 13:4
[l] Is 42:1; 53:12; Mt 20:28; Mk 10:45
[m] Jn 1:14; Rm 8:3; Gl 4:4; 1Tm 2:5; Heb 2:17
[n] 2:8 Lk 23:26; Php 3:10
[o] 2:9 Is 52:13; 53:12; Dn 7:14; Ac 2:32,33; 5:30,31; Eph
1:20-21; Heb 2:9
[p] 2:10 Is 45:23
[q] 2Co 5:1; Eph 1:20; 2:6; 3:10; 6:12; Heb 3:1; 12:22
[r] Mt 28:18; Eph 1:10; Rv 5:13
[s] 2:11 Is 45:23; Rm 10:9; 14:11; 1Co 12:3
[t] Lk 9:32; Jn 17:24; 2Co 3:18; 2Pt 3:18
[u] 2:12 Phm 1
[v] Mk 1:27; Ac 16:14,32,33; Rm 6:12

[A] 2:6 Or to be grasped, or to be held on to   [B] 2:11 Gk kurios = Yahweh; Is 42:8 LXX

Two verbs translate the Greek word *phroneō*—**thinking** and **focusing**. Beyond mere "thinking," this addresses values. The Philippians were to value **the same way** (lit "the same thing") and the **one goal** (lit "a common objective"). Between these two, Paul included shared **love** and **feelings** (lit "the same "soul").

2:3-4 These four habitual actions reveal themselves collectively through another four attributes. **Rivalry or conceit** recalls the problem Paul condemned (1:15,17). **Humility**, the antidote for wrong attitudes, results in considering **others as more important**. Additionally, humility considers the **interests** of others. Proper relationships include the contrast "not only but also." Personal responsibilities demand consideration, but the concerns of others are equally important.

2:5-11 This is one of the most difficult passages in the Bible, prompting various (Gk) *kenosis* (lit "emptying") theories attempting to describe what Jesus gave up in coming to earth. The text illustrates Christian humility. Because of its rhythmic character, it is often considered an early hymn, including two stanzas—verses 6-8 (on Christian humility) and verses 9-11 (on Jesus' ascension).

2:5 The phrase **make your own attitude** ("value"; cp. v. 2) commands the church to value Christ's character as a model.

2:6 The key thought of this verse is that Jesus **did not consider** (cp. v. 3) His own interests, thus allowing them to dominate His actions. **Existing** (lit "existing originally") should be "although existing" since it presents an apparent obstacle for Jesus to overcome in becoming human. **Form** (Gk *morphē*) suggests His complete deity. **Equality with God** indicates His coequality with God and separate personality (the second person of the Trinity). **To be used for His own advantage** is capable of two connotations. It can mean "to grasp" (steal), but because of Jesus' deity it probably means "to clutch" (hang on to at all costs).

2:7-8 The phrase **He emptied** is much debated. Theologians ponder what Jesus emptied Himself of. It is certain that He did not divest Himself of deity or its attributes. Two statements accompany the verb. First, **by assuming the form of a slave** indicates that God the Son became a servant. "Form" (cp. v. 6) indicates true servanthood, as does the word "slave." Second, **the likeness of men** explains both emptying and servanthood. "Likeness" (Gk *schema*; "fashion") differs from "form" (vv. 6-7). Two statements explain the second verb **humbled** (cp. v. 3). First, **when He had come as a man in His external form** provides the time of His humility. "External form" (Gk *scheyma*) contrasts with the form of God (v. 6). Jesus was more than human, though He came to earth in the form of a man. Second, Jesus' humility came through **becoming obedient**. Servants or slaves obey; Jesus obeyed God, even to the point of dying on a cross.

2:9-11 God is described as acting in these verses. Again, two verbs organize the thought. First, **God highly exalted Him** ("super-exalted," occurring only here) suggests that God gave Jesus a new position, although some take it as superlative ("to the highest"). Second, God **gave Him the name**. This name that is **above every name** is Lord (v. 11, *kurios* = *Yahweh*). **Every knee will bow** and **every tongue should confess** state one result of God's exaltation (vv. 10-11). The posture and the confession imply submissive reverence. "Every" includes spatial dimensions: **heaven ... earth**, and **under the earth**. Together they indicate the living and the dead (blessed and condemned). All bring glory to God. This teaches that Jesus mediates between God and humans. He is the focus of worship (Lord) and the administrator of God's will on earth.

2:12-18 Three applications follow in this section: practical Christianity (vv. 12-13), positive steadfastness (vv. 14-16), and personal joy (vv. 17-18).

2:12-13 Obedience is directed to God, not Paul, who hoped his potential death would not dampen Christian enthusiasm. **Work out** means to apply salvation, not to earn it. **Fear and trembling** means to have proper respect in response

both to desire and to work out His good purpose. ¹⁴Do everything without grumbling*a* and arguing,*b* ¹⁵so that you may be blameless*c* and pure,*d* children of God who are faultless*e* in a crooked*f* and perverted*g* generation,*h* among whom you shine like stars in the world. ¹⁶Hold firmly to^A the message*i* of life. Then I can boast*j* in the day of Christ*k* that I didn't run or labor for nothing. ¹⁷But even if I am poured out*l* as a •drink offering*m* on the sacrifice and service of your faith, I am glad and rejoice with all of you. ¹⁸In the same way you should also be glad and rejoice with me.

Timothy and Epaphroditus

¹⁹Now I hope in the Lord Jesus*n* to send Timothy*o* to you soon so that I also may be encouraged when I hear news about you. ²⁰For I have no one else like-minded who will genuinely care about your interests; ²¹all seek their own interests,*p* not those of Jesus Christ.*q* ²²But you know his proven character, because he has served with me in the gospel ministry like a son with a father. ²³Therefore, I hope to send him as soon as I see how things go with me. ²⁴I am convinced in the Lord that I myself will also come quickly.*r*

²⁵But I considered it necessary to send you

Epaphroditus*s*—my brother, coworker, and fellow soldier, as well as your messenger and minister to my need*t*— ²⁶since he has been longing for all of you and was distressed because you heard that he was sick. ²⁷Indeed, he was so sick that he nearly died. However, God had mercy on him, and not only on him but also on me, so that I would not have one grief on top of another. ²⁸For this reason, I am very eager to send him so that you may rejoice when you see him again and I may be less anxious. ²⁹Therefore, welcome him in the Lord with all joy and hold men like him in honor, ³⁰because he came close to death for the work*u* of Christ, risking his life to make up what was lacking in your ministry to me.

Knowing Christ

3 Finally, my •brothers, rejoice*v* in the Lord. To write to you again about this is no trouble for me and is a protection for you.

²Watch out for "dogs,"^B watch out for evil*w* workers, watch out for those who mutilate the flesh. ³For we are the circumcision,*x* the ones who serve by the Spirit*y* of God, boast in Christ Jesus,*z* and do not put confidence in the flesh— ⁴although I once also had confidence in the flesh. If anyone else thinks he

*a*2:14 Jn 7:12; Ac 6:1; 1Pt 4:9
*b*1Tm 2:8
*c*2:15 Lk 1:6
*d*Mt 10:16; Rm 16:19
*e*Jd 24
*f*Lk 3:5; Ac 2:40; 1Pt 2:18
*g*Mt 17:17
*h*Dt 32:5
*i*2:16 Lk 8:21; Jn 18:32; Ac 17:11; Heb 4:12
*j*Rm 2:17; Gl 6:4; Php 1:26
*k*Php 1:6,15
*l*2:17 Php 1:7
*m*Ex 25:29; Nm 28:7
*n*2:19 Lk 24:3
*o*Ac 16:1; 1Tm 1:2
*p*2:21 Rm 15:1; 2Tm 3:2
*q*1Co 10:24; Php 1:15
*r*2:24 Php 1:7
*s*2:25 Php 4:18
*t*Mt 6:8
*u*2:30 Mk 14:6; 2Co 9:8; Gl 3:10; Jms 2:14-26
*v*3:1 Rm 12:12; 2Co 6:10; Php 1:18
*w*3:2 2Co 13:7
*x*3:3 Gl 6:15
*y*Rm 8:4; Gl 5:25; 1Tm 3:16
*z*Rm 16:7; Eph 2:6; Php 1:1,15; 1Pt 5:14

---

^A2:16 Or *Offer*, or *Hold out*   ^B3:2 An expression of contempt for the unclean, those outside the people of God

---

to God's blessing. True obedience comes from reverence, not fright. **God . . . is working** provides the deeper incentive: Christians are recipients of God's initiatives of motivation and empowerment.

2:14-16 Grumbling and arguing come from selfishness and vainglory (1:15,17; cp. Dt 32:5). **Blameless** (complete Christian character) and **pure** (inoffensive living; cp. 1:10) introduce metaphors. First, believers are to be morally **faultless** in a world **crooked and perverted** by its failure to understand the word of God. Believers are straight models for distorted lives. Second, they are to **shine like stars** whose brilliance contrasts with the darkened world.

2:17-18 Drink offering recalls the OT sacrificial system. Paul was the substance being **poured out** for these believers. **Sacrifice** is the offering; **service** performed the ceremony. All of this brought Paul—and the Philippian believers—joy.

2:19-30 Paul in this section expressed his hope to visit some day, but he planned to send Timothy and Epaphroditus to the Philippians immediately.

2:19-24 On **Timothy**, see note at 1:1. **Encouraged** (lit "good souled") means "cheered." **Like-minded** (lit "equal souled") means "soul mate or partner" in service. Paul characterized Timothy three ways: he genuinely cared for their interests (cp. vv. 1-4); he valued the things of Jesus Christ and others; and he had **proven character** (lit "tested by fire"), refined in the demands of the **gospel ministry**.

2:25-30 Epaphroditus shared Paul's ministry (**brother, co-worker, and fellow soldier**) and represented the church. **Messenger** (lit "apostle") and **minister** (lit "religious servant") indicate that the church expected Epaphroditus to care for Paul in Rome. Traveling to Rome, Epaphroditus

suffered a near-fatal illness. He felt he had failed Paul and the church. The words **welcome him** ("appropriately") and **hold . . . him in honor** reveal that Epaphroditus did not fail. He gave his best for the **work of Christ**. The words **what was lacking** refer to the churches' care for Paul. Epaphroditus took it upon himself to make up that lack.

3:2 The Jews hated **dogs**. This word was often used of Gentiles, but in this context it refers to overly zealous Jewish teachers who were ravenous like scavengers. These **evil workers** attempted to gain salvation by keeping the law. **Mutilate the flesh** refers to their "circumcision." Paul used a play on the Greek words for "circumcision" and "mutilation." These "circumcisers" were actually "mutilators" who offered no spiritual benefits.

3:3 Those of **the circumcision**—"true Jews" or Christians—have three characteristics. First, they **serve by the Spirit of God**, not the works of the flesh (Gl 5:16-18). Second, they **boast in Christ Jesus**. "Boast" ("take pride in") means their highest treasure is Jesus. Third, they **do not put confidence in the flesh**. "The flesh" describes the values and activities of humanity unaided by the Holy Spirit.

3:4-6 Paul's fleshly confidence included heredity and accomplishments. On the issue of his heredity, **circumcised the eighth day** (lit "an eighth-day one") placed him in a special group whose parents scrupulously kept the law. A **Hebrew born of Hebrews** means he had impeccable credentials. This countered those who may have assumed otherwise because Paul was from Tarsus. Regarding achievement, he spoke of zeal and the law. **Pharisee** comes from a word meaning "separation," e.g., to honor the OT law. **Zeal**, evidenced by **persecuting the church**, was unnecessary

has grounds for confidence in the flesh, I have
more: 5 circumcised the eighth day;[a] of the
nation of Israel,[b] of the tribe of Benjamin,[c] a
Hebrew born of Hebrews; regarding the law,[d]
a •Pharisee; 6 regarding zeal,[e] persecuting[f] the
church; regarding the righteousness that is in
the law,[g] blameless.[h]
7 But everything that was a gain to me, I
have considered to be a loss because of Christ.
8 More than that, I also consider everything
to be a loss in view of the surpassing value[i]
of knowing Christ[j] Jesus my Lord. Because of
Him I have suffered the loss of all things and
consider them filth, so that I may gain Christ[k]
9 and be found in Him, not having a righteousness of my own from the law,[l] but one that is
through faith in Christ[A]—the righteousness
from God based on faith.[m] 10 My goal is to know
Him and the power of His resurrection and the
fellowship of His sufferings,[n] being conformed
to His death,[o] 11 assuming that I will somehow
reach the resurrection from among the dead.

Reaching Forward to God's Goal

12 Not that I have already reached the goal
or am already fully mature, but I make every
effort to take hold[p] of it because I also have
been taken hold of by Christ Jesus. 13 Brothers,
I do not[B] consider myself to have taken hold of
it. But one thing I do: Forgetting what is behind[q] and reaching forward to what is ahead,
14 I pursue as my goal the prize promised by
God's heavenly[C] call in Christ Jesus.[r] 15 Therefore, all who are mature should think this way.
And if you think differently about anything,
God will reveal[s] this also to you. 16 In any case,
we should live up to whatever truth we have
attained. 17 Join in imitating me, brothers,
and observe those who live according to the
example you have in us. 18 For I have often told
you, and now say again with tears, that many
live as enemies of the cross[t] of Christ. 19 Their
end is destruction; their god is their stomach;
their glory[u] is in their shame. They are focused on earthly things, 20 but our citizenship
is in heaven, from which we also eagerly wait

[a] 3:5 Gn 17:12,25; 21:4; Lv 12:3; Lk 1:59; 2:21 [b] Rm 9:6 [c] Ps 68:27 [d] Ac 5:34; 22:3; Gl 1:14; 5:4 [e] 3:6 Rm 10:2 [f] Ac 22:2-5; 26:9-11; 1Co 15:9; Gl 1:13; 1Tm 1:13; 2Tm 3:12 [g] Rm 3:21; 9:31; 10:4-5; Gl 2:21; 3:21 [h] Lk 1:6; Rm 7:9-10 [i] 3:8 Php 2:3 [j] Jn 17:3; 2Co 4:6; Gl 4:8-9; Php 1:15; Col 2:2; 1Jn 4:8 [k] 1Pt 3:1 [l] 3:9 Rm 10:5 [m] Rm 3:22; 10:4; Gl 2:21; Heb 11:7 [n] 3:10 Rm 8:17; 2Co 1:5-7; Col 1:24; 1Pt 4:13; 5:1,9 [o] Rm 6:5; 8:36; 2Co 4:7-12; 12:9-10; Gl 6:17 [p] 3:12 Jn 1:5; 12:35; Rm 9:30; 1Co 9:24; Eph 3:18 [q] 3:13 Lk 9:62; 17:31 [r] 3:14 Rm 16:7; Eph 2:6; Php 1:1,15; 1Pt 5:14 [s] 3:15 Lk 10:21 [t] 3:18 Lk 23:26; 1Co 1:17; Gl 6:12 [u] 3:19 Lk 14:10; Jn 5:41,44; 8:50,54; 12:43; Rm 9:4; 1Co 11:15; 2Co 6:8; 1Th 2:6

[A] 3:9 Or *through the faithfulness of Christ* [B] 3:13 Other mss read *not yet* [C] 3:14 Or *upward*

even for Pharisees. **Righteousness that is in the law** means that Paul achieved all the law could promise. He had not failed by Jewish standards.

3:7-8 Paul evaluated his former life (vv. 7-8) and expressed his current aspirations (vv. 9-11). **Considered** occurs three times in these verses (cp. 2:5-11). The first (3:7) is a Greek perfect tense (past completed action with continuing results). The others (v. 8) are present, indicating a continuing reaffirmation of the attitude. The word **loss** and a synonym **filth** (lit "garbage" or "dung") are compared with **gain** three times. Paul's loss was for the sake of Christ (v. 7), for the surpassing value of knowing Christ (v. 8), and for gaining Christ (v. 8).

3:9-11 Paul described his new aspirations in three ways: gaining Christ and being found in Him, having a Christian righteousness, and attaining resurrection from the dead. **Found** refers to judgment day. Christ brings a **righteousness** through faith in Christ (imputed), not from works of the law (cp. v. 6). **To know Him** (personally, experientially) parallels and explains "found in him." It involves experiencing the **power of His resurrection**, resulting in Paul's own resurrection from death, and knowing the **fellowship** (lit "participation in") **of His sufferings**. Identification with Christ's suffering brings conformity to Jesus' death through refining obedience, and a believer attains **the resurrection from among the dead**.

3:12-16 These verses contain a call to follow Paul's pattern of living.

3:12-14 Paul acknowledged his imperfection. **Reached the goal** (lit "received") and **fully mature** (lit "been perfected") indicate the need for growth. **Make every effort** recalls the athlete's discipline and focus. Together these reveal that Paul had not yet achieved perfection. **Take hold of it** and **have been taken hold** translate the same Greek word, one active the other passive. Paul aspired to complete salvation through resurrection. **Because** presents the substance of Paul's hope—the perfection of the resurrection. **Pursue** (cp. v. 12), **goal**, and **prize** use athletic imagery of the runner's energy, focus, and reward. "The prize" is **God's heavenly call** (to heaven), like a referee calling a winner to the platform to receive the prize.

3:15-16 Paul exhorted the **mature** (lit "perfect"). The use of the same root word in verse 12 reveals that Paul addressed the false teachers who claimed perfection. **Think this way** is "value" (cp. 2:1-11; 3:15). **Live up to** means to walk in order, in rank like a soldier. **Whatever truth we have attained** is what brought previous success in Christian living.

3:17-21 First, Paul encouraged believers. **Imitating me** reveals his confidence that he lived correctly before God and man. He spoke **with tears** (the only record that Paul cried) because of the damage these false teachers brought to God's work. As **enemies of the cross**, they were inflated with their own spiritual abilities (cp. v. 3) rather than trusting Christ. Paul described them four ways. First, their **end is destruction** (not annihilation but eternal judgment). Second, their **god is their stomach** reflects their preoccupation with Jewish dietary laws. Third, their **glory is in their shame** means focusing inappropriately on the genitals (circumcision). Fourth, they **focused on earthly things**, unable to see beyond the present time.

True believers differ from these false teachers. **Citizenship** was rare and prized, and the Philippians were justifiably proud of their Roman citizenship. "Citizenship" **in heaven** reminded the church of the existence of a greater society and culture. Military images continue with the **Savior** from heaven. Roman citizens called the emperor "savior"; Christians expect their deliverer from heaven. **The body of our humble condition** refers to the body limited by earthiness, finiteness, and sin. Christ will change the body into the **likeness of His glorious body**. Physical bodies will become glorified bodies in the image of Christ. Salvation

for a Savior, the Lord Jesus Christ. [21] He will transform the body of our humble condition into the likeness of His glorious[a] body,[b] by the power that enables Him to subject everything to Himself.

Practical Counsel

4 So then, my *brothers, you are dearly loved and longed for—my joy and crown.[c] In this manner stand firm[d] in the Lord, dear friends. [2] I urge Euodia and I urge Syntyche to agree in the Lord. [3] Yes, I also ask you, true partner,[A] to help these women who have contended for the gospel at my side, along with Clement and the rest of my coworkers whose names are in the book of life. [4] Rejoice in the Lord always. I will say it again: Rejoice! [5] Let your graciousness be known to everyone. The Lord is near.[e] [6] Don't worry about anything, but in everything, through prayer and peti-

[a]3:21 1Pt 5:4
[b]1Co 6:13; 1Jn 3:2
[c]4:1 Rv 12:1
[d]Rm 14:4; 1Co 16:13; Php 1:27; 2:2
[e]4:5 1Co 16:22; Php 1:6; Heb 10:24-25; Jms 5:8; Rv 1:7; 3:11; 22:20
[f]4:7 Php 2:3
[g]Rm 16:7; Eph 2:6; Php 1:1,15; 1Pt 5:14
[h]4:8 Jn 8:14
[i]1Tm 3:8,11; Ti 2:2
[j]Rm 1:17
[k]2Co 7:11; 11:2; 1Tm 5:22; Ti 2:5; Jms 3:17; 1Pt 3:2; 1Jn 3:3
[l]1Pt 2:9; 2Pt 1:3,5
[m]4:9 Jd 3
[n]4:10 Php 1:5
[o]2Co 8:1-2; 11:9

tion with thanksgiving, let your requests be made known to God. [7] And the peace of God, which surpasses[f] every thought, will guard your hearts and minds in Christ Jesus.[g]

[8] Finally brothers, whatever is true,[h] whatever is honorable,[i] whatever is just,[j] whatever is pure,[k] whatever is lovely, whatever is commendable—if there is any moral excellence[l] and if there is any praise—dwell on these things. [9] Do what you have learned and received[m] and heard and seen in me, and the God of peace will be with you.

Appreciation of Support

[10] I rejoiced in the Lord greatly that once again[n] you renewed your care for me.[o] You were, in fact, concerned about me but lacked the opportunity to show it. [11] I don't say this out of need, for I have learned to be content in whatever circumstances I am. [12] I know both

---

A4:3 Or true Syzygus, possibly a person's name

---

has three stages: conversion, moral perfection at death, and the transformation of the body through resurrection at the second coming of Christ.

4:1 **Stand firm** recalls Roman soldiers who never retreated for fear of being killed by their commanders.

4:2 **Euodia** and **Syntyche** were influential, like many women in the Philippian church (Ac 16). There is no evidence that they held offices. **Urge** occurs twice, once with each name, avoiding favoritism. **Agree** translates the Greek word *phroneō*, found so often in this epistle (esp. 2:1-11). This disunity may not have been a significant problem since Paul saved his exhortation for the end of the letter. It was not moral or theological.

4:3 **Ask** is less authoritative than "urge" (v. 2). **True partner** is singular. Someone in authority (the pastor) would be the mediator. "Partner" elsewhere is translated "fellowship." This is the yokefellow, one co-yoked in the work. Paul provided reasons to help these women. First, they **contended**

chairo

Greek Pronunciation	[KIGH roh]
HCSB Translation	rejoice
Uses in Philippians	9
Uses in the NT	74
Focus passage	Philippians 4:4

Chairo means *to enjoy a state of gladness, happiness,* or *well-being.* Scripture records numerous events that result in this joyful state: finding something formerly lost (Mt 18:13; Lk 15:5,32); the hope of reward from God (Mt 5:12 = Lk 6:23; Lk 10:20); Jesus' miracles (Lk 13:17; 19:37); His birth (Lk 1:14); His post-resurrection appearances (Jn 20:20); suffering (Ac 5:41; Col 1:24); the repentance of others (2Co 7:9); the faith of others (Col 2:5); the preaching about Christ (Php 1:18); and many other occasions. This state of *rejoicing* in God is commanded for Christians (Php 3:1; 4:4; 2Co 13:11; 1Th 5:16). *Chairo* also appears as part of a greeting expressing the wish for a person's happiness (Mt 26:49) and commonly appearing in the introduction to a letter (Ac 15:23; 23:26; Jms 1:1). In the context of miraculous encounters with the divine, *chairo* may mean *Rejoice* (Mt 28:9; Lk 1:28).

with Paul (an athletic term). Second, they worked alongside Clement (unknown) and Paul's coworkers. The **book of life**, mentioned rarely in the NT (cp. Rv 3:5; 20:15; 21:27), refers to those listed among the saved.

4:4-9 In this section Paul approached peace from two perspectives—peace within troublesome circumstances (vv. 4-7) and constructing an environment of peace (vv. 8-9).

4:5 **Graciousness** implies selflessness and respect for others (cp. 2:1-4). Seldom mentioned in Paul's writings, graciousness is expected of believers and Christian leaders (cp. 1Tm 3:3; Ti 3:2). **Be known** indicates it is part of the church's reputation. **The Lord is near** reminded the Philippian believers of Christ's unseen presence.

4:6-7 **Worry** is anxiety (Mt 6:25-34). Prayer is the antidote for worry. Three words express different aspects of prayer: **Prayer**, a worshipful attitude; **petition**, a need; and **requests**, the specific concern. **Thanksgiving** shapes prayers with gratitude. In response, **the peace of God** brings power to endure. The peace **surpasses** knowledge, calming a troubling situation when explanations fail. Further, peace guards by keeping anxieties from **hearts** (choices) and **minds** (attitudes).

4:8-9 Seven qualities create an environment of peace. **True** is ethical "truthfulness." **Honorable** is "noble," to be respected. **Just** is giving people what they deserve. **Pure** is holy in relation to God. **Lovely**, mentioned only here in the NT, is attractive. **Commendable**, also used only here in the NT, is praiseworthy. **Excellence** refers to moral excellence. **Praise** is bringing God praise. **The God of peace** complements "the peace of God" (v. 7) in that life with these characteristics encourages God's presence.

4:10 **Once again** indicates that some time had elapsed between the Philippian believers' previous gifts to Paul (cp. 2Co 8) and their sending Epaphroditus to him in Rome (2:25-30). Since Paul had no need, they **lacked the opportunity** to give.

4:11 **Learned** (Greek perfect tense) implies a lesson resulting in better knowledge. **Content** (lit "self-reliant") is self-sufficiency that grows out of trust in Christ.

4:12 **I know** results from evaluating various circumstances.

how to have a little, and I know how to have a lot.*^a* In any and all circumstances I have learned the secret of being content—whether well fed or hungry, whether in abundance or in need. ¹³I am able to do all things through Him^A who strengthens me.*^b* ¹⁴Still, you did well by sharing with me in my hardship.

¹⁵And you Philippians*^c* know that in the early days of the gospel,*^d* when I left Macedonia,*^e* no church shared with me in the matter of giving and receiving except you alone. ¹⁶For even in Thessalonica*^f* you sent gifts for my need*^g* several times. ¹⁷Not that I seek the gift, but I seek the profit^{B,}*^h* that is increasing to your account. ¹⁸But I have received everything in full,*ⁱ* and I have an abundance. I am

fully supplied, having received from Epaphroditus*^j* what you provided—a fragrant offering, an acceptable sacrifice, pleasing*^k* to God. ¹⁹And my God*^l* will supply all your needs according to His riches in glory in Christ Jesus. ²⁰Now to our God and Father*^m* be glory forever and ever.*ⁿ* •Amen.*^o*

Final Greetings

²¹Greet every •saint in Christ Jesus. Those brothers who are with me greet you. ²²All the saints greet you, but especially those from Caesar's*^p* household.*^q* ²³The grace of the Lord Jesus Christ be with your spirit.^{C,}*^r*

*^a*4:12 1Co 15:58
*^b*4:13 2Co 12:9; Eph 3:16; Col 1:11; 1Tm 1:12; 2Tm 4:17
*^c*4:15 Php 1:1
*^d*Ac 16:6-40; Php 1:5
*^e*Ac 16:9
*^f*4:16 Ac 17:1
*^g*Mt 6:8
*^h*4:17 Mt 3:8; Rm 1:13; Gl 5:22
*ⁱ*4:18 Php 1:5
*^j*Php 2:25
*^k*Heb 13:21
*^l*4:19 Mt 27:46; Rm 1:8; Php 1:8
*^m*4:20 Gl 1:4; 1Th 1:3; 3:11,13
*ⁿ*Gl 1:5; 1Tm 1:17; 2Tm 4:18; Heb 13:21
*^o*Rm 11:36; Rv 22:21   *^p*4:22 Mt 22:17; Lk 20:22   *^q*Php 1:7
*^r*4:23 Rm 1:9

---

^A4:13 Other mss read *Christ*   ^B4:17 Lit *fruit*   ^C4:23 Other mss add *Amen.*

The difficult circumstances are **have a little . . . hungry**, and **need**. The contrasting good are **a lot . . . well fed . . . abundance**. Together these taught Paul how to be **content**.

4:13 All things refers to the economic fluctuations of life (v. 12). **Through Him who strengthens me** teaches that Christ empowers believers to live in God's will. Paradoxically, Paul was strong when he was weak; independent only when dependent. Such is the life of a disciple.

4:14 Sharing is the word for "fellowship" (1:5). **Hardship** is "tribulations." Real partners share difficulties.

4:15 The **early days of the gospel** refers to Paul's leaving Philippi to continue witnessing in Europe. **Shared** is, again, "fellowship" (v. 14; 1:5). Others had a one-way relationship, receiving but not giving. **You alone** reveals one reason why Paul loved the Philippian church. They did what others did not.

4:16 Paul entered **Thessalonica** after leaving Philippi, and the Philippian believers' gifts to him began immediately and continued consistently (**several times**).

4:17 With contentment (v. 11) and adaptability (v. 12), Paul did not **seek the gift**. That would abuse his converts and compromise servanthood. With a higher, spiritual motivation, Paul sought **the profit that is increasing to your account**. Using financial terms, Paul declared this "profit" accrued from an action. "Increasing" is the interest it would bear to the account of the Philippian believers. Giving, a physical and material act, is a spiritual transaction.

4:18 Continuing financial language, Paul had **received everything in full**. Any responsibility to him was paid. What Epaphroditus embodied was **an abundance**. Their material support was **a fragrant offering** and an **acceptable sacrifice** because it met Paul's needs and was **pleasing to God** (cp. Rm 12:1-2). Giving always benefits those who give more than those who receive.

4:21-22 Caesar's household indicates there were Christians in Rome related to the Roman emperor. "Household" probably indicates they were not immediate family; they were perhaps members of the civil service.

Colossians

Introduction

Paul's letter to the church at Colossae is one of the prison letters (along with Ephesians, Philippians, and Philemon). Paul's desire with this letter was to correct the false teachings that were cropping up in the church. In doing so, Paul presented a clear picture of Jesus Christ as supreme Lord of the universe, head of the church, and the only One through whom forgiveness is possible.

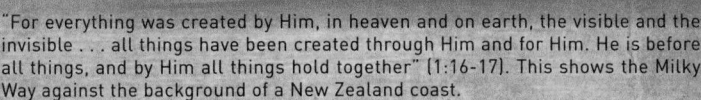

"For everything was created by Him, in heaven and on earth, the visible and the invisible . . . all things have been created through Him and for Him. He is before all things, and by Him all things hold together" (1:16-17). This shows the Milky Way against the background of a New Zealand coast.

Circumstances of Writing

Author: Colossians retains its place among the epistles of Paul, who identified himself as the author (1:1; 4:18). The church fathers unreservedly endorsed Pauline authorship (Irenaeus, *Adv. Haer.*, 3.14.1; Tertullian, *De Praescr. Haer.*, 7; Clement of Alexandria, *Strom.*, 1.1; cp. Justin, *Dialogue*, 85.2; 138.2). A close reading of Colossians reveals a considerable number of lexical, grammatical, and theological similarities with the other Pauline writings (1:9,26; 2:11-14,16,20-21; 3:1,3,5-17). Also favoring the authenticity of Colossians as a letter of Paul is its close connection with Philemon, an epistle widely regarded as Pauline.

Background: During his ministry in Ephesus (Ac 19:10), Paul sent Epaphras to spread the gospel in the Lycus Valley. Epaphras subsequently established the church at Colossae (1:7; 4:12-13). The city's population consisted mostly of Phrygians and Greeks, but it also included a significant number of Jews. The church, likewise, was mostly composed of Gentiles (1:21,27; 2:13), but it also had Jewish members (2:11,16,18,21; 3:11). When Epaphras (Phm 23) informed Paul of certain heretical teachings that had spread there, Paul wrote the letter to the Colossians as a theological antidote.

Paul wrote Colossians during his first Roman imprisonment (4:3,10,18; cp. Ac 28:30-31; Eusebius, *Hist. Eccl.*, 2.22.1) in the early A.D. 60s. Together with Philemon, Philippians, and Ephesians, Colossians is commonly classified as a "prison epistle." All four epistles share several personal links that warrant this conclusion (Col 1:7; 4:7-8,17; Eph 6:21-22; Phm 2,12,23).

Message and Purpose

Paul wrote to counter the "Colossian heresy" that he considered an affront to the gospel of Jesus Christ. The false teaching is identified as a "philosophy" (2:8), presumably drawn from some Hellenistic traditions as indicated by the references to "the fullness" (1:19); the "elemental forces" (Gk *stoicheia*; 2:8,20); "wisdom" (2:3,23); and "ascetic practices" (2:23). In addition, the false teaching contained Jewish elements such as circumcision (2:11; 3:11); "human tradition" (2:8); Sabbath observance, food regulations, festival participation

---

430–190 B.C.

Herodotus describes Colossae as "a great city of Phrygia" strategically located on the main road from Ephesus and Sardis eastward to the Euphrates. **430**

Xenophon describes Colossae as "a populus city, wealthy and large." **400**

Cyrus and his army spend seven days in Colossae as he moves from Sardis east to take the throne of Persia. **400**

Laodicea founded by Antiochus II who named it for his wife, Laodice. **262–246**

The regions of Colossae, Hieropolis, and Laodicea become subject to the Pergamenes after the battle of Magnesia. **190**

130 B.C.–A.D. 18

Hieropolis comes under Roman rule after being established earlier in the second century. **129 B.C.**

A sizeable Jewish population lives in the region of Colossae, Hieropolis, and Laodicea. **62 B.C.**

Laodicea receives from Rome the title of a free city. **10 B.C.**

In his *Geography*, Strabo describes Colossae as a small town. Laodicea was then the growing city in the Lycus Valley because of its location, its banking, and its trade of black sheep wool. **A.D. 7–18**

A destructive earthquake in the region of Colossae, Hieropolis, and Laodicea **A.D. 17**

(2:16); the "worship of angels" together with "access to a visionary realm" (2:18); and harsh human regulations (2:21-23). Paul addressed this syncretistic philosophy by setting forth a proper understanding of the gospel of Jesus Christ and by noting appropriate implications for Christian conduct.

The heresy is not identified, but several characteristics of the heresy are discernible. (1) An inferior view of Christ is combated in 1:15-20. This Christological passage implies that the heretics did not consider Jesus to be fully divine or perhaps did not accept Him as the sole source of redemption. (2) The Colossians were warned to beware of "philosophies" not built on Christ (2:8). (3) The heresy apparently involved the legalistic observance of "traditions," circumcision, and various dietary and festival laws (2:8,11,16,21; 3:11). (4) The worship of angels and lesser spirits was encouraged by the false teachers (2:8,18). (5) Asceticism, the deprivation or harsh treatment of one's "evil" fleshly body, was promoted (2:20-23). (6) Finally, the false teachers claimed to have special insight (perhaps special revelations) which made them (rather than the apostles or the Scriptures) the ultimate source of truth (2:18-19).

Scholars cannot agree on who these false teachers were. Some of the characteristics cited above seem to be Jewish; others sound like gnostic teachings. Some see the teachings of a Greek mystery religion here.

The theology of chapters 1 and 2 is followed by exhortations to live a Christian life in chapters 3 and 4. The commands to "put to death" (3:5) and "now you must also put away" (3:8) the things which will reap the wrath of God (3:5-11) are balanced by the command to "put on" (3:12) those things characteristic of God's chosen people (3:12-17). The changes are far from superficial, however. They stem from the Christian's new nature and submission to the rule of Christ in every area of life (3:9,10,15-17).

Rules for the household appear in 3:18–4:1. The typical first-century household is assumed; thus the passage addresses wives and husbands, fathers and children, masters and slaves. Paul made no comment about the rightness or wrongness of the social structures; he accepted them as givens. Paul's concern was that the structures as they existed should be governed by Christian principles. Submission to the Lord (3:18,20,22; 4:1),

A.D. **33–52**

A.D. **53–64**

Jesus' trials, death, resurrection, and ascension
Nisan 14–16 or April 3–5, 33

Pentecost 33

Saul's conversion on the Damascus Road
October 34

Paul, Barnabas, and John Mark make first
missionary journey. 47–49

Paul and Silas take second missionary journey.
49–52

Paul's third missionary journey 53–57

Paul's ministry in Ephesus becomes the
nucleus of church planting throughout Asia
Minor. 54–56

Paul arrives in Rome. 60

Paul's letter to the Colossians 61

Colossae, Laodicea, and Hieropolis experience
a devastating earthquake. 60 or 64

Christian love (3:19), and the prospect of divine judgment (3:24–4:1) must determine the way people treat one another regardless of their social status. It is this Christian motivation which distinguishes these house rules from those featured in Jewish and pagan sources.

Contribution to the Bible

Colossians provides one of the Bible's fullest expressions of the deity and supremacy of Christ. This is most evident in the magnificent hymn of praise (1:15-20) that sets forth Christ as the image of the invisible God, the Creator and sustainer of the universe, and the head of His body, the church. In Christ are all the "treasures of wisdom and knowledge" (2:3), because in Him "the entire fullness of God's nature dwells bodily" (2:9). The supremacy of Christ also has implication for believers' salvation (2:10,13,20; 3:1,11-12,17) and conduct (3:5–4:6). Colossians contributes to Scripture a high Christology and a presentation of its implications for the believer's conduct.

Structure

Colossians may be divided into two main parts. The first (1:3–2:23) is a polemic against false teachings. The second (3:1–4:17) is made up of exhortations to proper Christian living. This is typical of Paul's approach, presenting a theology position first, a position on which the practical exhortations are built. The introduction (1:1-2) is in the form of a Hellenistic, personal letter.

Notable in the final section are the mention of Onesimus (4:9), which links this letter with Philemon; the mention of a letter at Laodicea (4:16) that may have been Ephesians; and Paul's concluding signature which indicates that the letter was prepared by an amanuensis (secretary; see 4:18).

Outline

I. Greeting and Thanksgiving (1:1-12)

II. God's Work in Christ (1:13-23)
   A. Redemption (1:13-14)
   B. The excellence of Christ (1:15-19)
   C. Reconciliation (1:20-23)

III. Paul's Ministry (1:24–2:3)
   A. Minister of God's mystery (1:24-29)
   B. Sufferer for the Lord (2:1-3)

IV. False Teaching Denounced (2:4-23)
   A. Walking in Christ (2:4-7)
   B. Completeness of Christ's work (2:8-15)
   C. Exhortation against meaningless ritual (2:16-23)

V. The Christian Life (3:1–4:6)
   A. The new and the old (3:1-11)
   B. Exercise of Christian virtues (3:12-17)
   C. Family and social relationships (3:18–4:1)
   D. Exhortation to prayer (4:2-6)

VI. Conclusion (4:7-18)
   A. The mission of Tychicus (4:7-9)
   B. Greetings (4:10-18)

Greeting

1 Paul, an apostle of Christ Jesus by God's will,[a] and Timothy[b] our[A] brother:

[2] To the *saints in Christ at Colossae, who are faithful *brothers.

Grace to you and peace from God our Father.[B]

Thanksgiving

[3] We always thank God, the Father of our Lord Jesus Christ, when we pray for you, [4] for we have heard of your faith in Christ Jesus and of the love you have for all the saints [5] because of the hope reserved for you in heaven. You have already heard about this hope in the message of truth,[c] the gospel [6] that has come to you. It is bearing fruit[d] and growing all over the world,[e] just as it has among you since the day you heard it and recognized God's grace[f] in the truth.[C,g] [7] You learned this from Epaphras,[h] our dearly loved fellow *slave. He is a faithful servant of the *Messiah[i] on your[D] behalf, [8] and he has told us about your love in the Spirit.[j]

Prayer for Spiritual Growth

[9] For this reason also, since the day we heard this, we haven't stopped praying for you. We are asking[k] that you may be filled with the knowledge[l] of His will[m] in all wisdom and spiritual understanding,[E] [10] so that you may *walk worthy of the Lord, fully pleasing to Him, bearing fruit in every good work[n] and growing in the knowledge of God.[o] [11] May you be strengthened[p] with all power,[q] according to His glorious[r] might, for all endurance and patience, with joy [12] giving thanks to the Father, who has enabled you[F] to share in the saints'[G] inheritance in the light.[s] [13] He has rescued[t] us from the domain of darkness and transferred us into the kingdom[u] of the Son[v] He loves.[w] [14] We have *redemption,[H] the forgiveness of sins, in Him.

The Centrality of Christ

[15]   He is the image of the invisible God,[x]
      the firstborn over all creation.[l,y]

[a]1:1 1Co 1:1; 2Co 1:1; Eph 1:1; 2Tm 1:1
[b]Ac 16:1; 1Tm 1:2
[c]1:5 Ps 119:142; Jn 14:6; 2Co 11:10; Eph 1:13; 2Tm 2:15; 3Jn 3
[d]1:6 Mk 4:8
[e]Mt 13:38; 24:14; Rm 3:6; 2Pt 2:20
[f]2Pt 3:18
[g]2Th 2:10
[h]1:7 Col 4:12; Phm 23
[i]Mt 1:17; Eph 5:2
[j]1:8 Ps 51:11; Jn 1:33; Ac 2:4; Rm 8:9; Ti 3:5; Rv 1:10; 3:22
[k]1:9 Jn 14:13; Jms 1:5
[l]Pr 2:6; Col 3:10
[m]Eph 1:9
[n]1:10 2Co 9:8; Gl 3:10
[o]Pr 2:6; Jn 17:3; 2Pt 1:2; 1Jn 4:8
[p]1:11 Php 4:13
[q]Ac 4:33; 2Co 13:4
[r]Lk 9:32; Jn 17:24; 2Co 3:18; 2Pt 3:18
[s]1:12 Ps 36:9; Jn 12:46   [t]1:13 Mt 27:43   [u]Mt 3:2; Mk 1:15; Ac 20:25   [v]Jn 5:19; Heb 1:2   [w]Mt 3:17; Jn 3:16; 15:10; 17:26; 1Jn 4:16   [x]1:15 Php 2:6   [y]Jn 1:3; Rv 3:14

[A]1:1 Lit *the*   [B]1:2 Other mss add *and the Lord Jesus Christ*   [C]1:6 Or *and truly recognized God's grace*   [D]1:7 Other mss read *our* [E]1:9 Or *all spiritual wisdom and understanding*   [F]1:12 Other mss read *us*   [G]1:12 Or *holy ones'*   [H]1:14 Other mss add *through His blood*   [I]1:15 The One who is preeminent over all creation

1:1 Paul followed the customary format for epistolary greetings by introducing himself as the author and by identifying himself as **an apostle** belonging to **Christ Jesus** by God's will.

1:3-8 Paul offered a prayer of thanksgiving for the Colossian believers. In the original Greek, the prayer consists of a single sentence modifying the phrase, "we always thank God" (v. 3).

1:3 Paul's use of **we** probably included Timothy (v. 1) and possibly others (4:7-14). Paul expressed the frequency of his thanksgiving with the adverb **always**.

1:4 The reason for Paul's thanksgiving is rooted in reports he had heard about the Colossians' **faith in Christ Jesus** and **love . . . for all the saints**, which are the hallmarks of genuine Christianity.

1:5-6 The basis of the Colossian believers' faith and love is that they had a **hope** reserved for them in heaven. The triad of faith, love, and hope is a familiar Pauline formula (Rm 5:1-5; Gl 5:5-6; Eph 1:15; 4:2-5; 1Th 1:3; 2Th 1:3; Phm 5). This hope was the result of having heard and received **the message of truth** or more specifically, **the gospel**. Paul emphasized the power and effectiveness of the gospel by tracking its expansion, twice mentioning how the Colossians accepted the truth of the gospel.

1:7-8 Paul did not start the church at Colossae and had not yet visited there, so it was through **Epaphras** that he had learned of their condition. He endorsed Epaphras as a beloved **fellow slave** and a **faithful servant** (cp. 2:1; 4:12-13; Phm 23).

1:9 The opening phrase **for this reason** harks back to Epaphras's good report about the Colossian believers' faith in Christ. The word **filled** (the passive verb indicates God as causal agent) typically conveys the sense of "completeness" in Colossians (vv. 9,19,25; 2:9-10; 4:17). Paul asked

that they receive full **knowledge of His will**. The phrase **in all wisdom and spiritual understanding** expresses the means through which this knowledge comes. This wisdom (v. 28; 2:3,23; 3:16; 4:5) and understanding are spiritual in nature.

1:10-12 The purpose of Paul's prayer was that the believers at Colossae might **walk worthy of the Lord** so that all their conduct would please Him. Christian behavior that pleases the Lord involves the performance of good deeds; continuous spiritual growth; dependence on His power resulting in endurance, patience, and joy; and expressing gratitude for all things because God enables believers to share in the saints' inheritance.

1:13-14 The reference to being **rescued** and **transferred** evokes OT imagery of God delivering His people from the grip of hostile oppressors (Ex 6:6; 14:30; Jdg 6:9; 8:34; Ps 18:19; 79:9; 86:14). Believers have been rescued from the realm of Satan's oppression (**domain of darkness**) by having been transferred to the realm of Christ, which is a kingdom "in the light" (v. 12). The means of this deliverance or exodus was accomplished at their **redemption** through **the forgiveness of sins** because of Christ's atoning work (vv. 15-22).

1:15-23 These verses are a poem or possibly a hymn expressing Christ's supremacy as Creator and redeemer. Paul's high Christology countered the false teaching that had infiltrated the Colossian church.

1:15 The word **image** refers to an exact visible representation of something or someone. Thus, Jesus the Son represented the invisible God of the OT (Jn 1:18). Jesus also represented sinless humanity (Gn 1:26-27). The title **firstborn** does not mean that Jesus was created (v. 16), but indicates His priority of rank as supreme over all the created order.

16 For everything was created by Him,[a]
in heaven and on earth,
the visible and the invisible,
whether thrones or dominions
or rulers or authorities—
all things have been created
    through Him and for Him.[b]

17 He is before all things,[c]
and by Him all things[d] hold together.

18 He is also the head of the body,
    the church;
He is the beginning,[e]
the firstborn from the dead,[f]
so that He might come to have
first place in everything.

19 For God was pleased to have
all His fullness[g] dwell in Him,[h]

20 and through Him to reconcile
everything to Himself
by making peace[i]

through the blood[j] of His cross[A,k]—
whether things on earth or things
    in heaven.

21 Once you were alienated and hostile in your minds because of your evil actions. [22] But now He has reconciled you by His physical body[B] through His death,[l] to present you holy, faultless,[m] and blameless before Him[n]— [23] if indeed you remain grounded and steadfast in the faith[o] and are not shifted away from the hope[p] of the gospel that you heard. This gospel has been proclaimed in all creation[q] under heaven,[r] and I, Paul,[s] have become a servant of it.

Paul's Ministry

24 Now I rejoice in my sufferings[t] for you, and I am completing in my flesh what is lacking

Cross references:
[a] 1:16 Gn 1:1; Mk 13:19
[b] Jn 1:3; Rm 11:36; 1Co 8:6; Eph 1:10,21
[c] 1:17 Jn 1:1-2; 8:58; Heb 1:2-3
[d] Ps 104:24
[e] 1:18 Gn 1:1; Mk 1:1; Jn 1:1; Ac 26:4
[f] Ac 26:23; 1Co 15:20,23; Rv 1:5
[g] 1:19 Ps 72:19; Is 6:3; Jr 23:24; Ezk 43:5; 44:4; Jn 1:14,16; Eph 3:19; Php 2:6; Col 2:9
[h] Dt 12:5
[i] 1:20 Ac 7:26; Eph 2:14
[j] Heb 9:12
[k] Lk 9:23; 23:26
[l] 1:22 Php 2:8
[m] 2Co 4:14
[n] 2Co 4:14
[o] 1:23 Gl 2:16; Jd 3
[p] 1Th 1:3
[q] Rv 3:14
[r] Rm 10:18; Eph 6:9
[s] Ac 13:9
[t] 1:24 2Co 1:4; Php 1:29; 3:10

[A] 1:20 Other mss add *through Him*   [B] 1:22 His body of flesh on the cross

1:16 Christ is supreme over creation because He is the Creator. He is the one who created everything. Paul's mention of **thrones . . . dominions . . . rulers**, and **authorities** may refer to four classes of angelic beings (possibly directing human affairs). This may be a corrective against the false teaching promoting the worship of angels (2:18). Thus Paul asserted the supremacy of Christ over all creation because all things were created **through Him and for Him**.

1:17 **All things** refers to everything created (v. 16). The preposition **before** most likely is a temporal reference to the preexistence of Christ before creation. The phrase **by Him all things hold together** presents Christ as the one who sustains all creation.

1:18 Paul used the word **head** in both a literal and metaphorical sense (2:10,19). Literally, "head" implies authority, rule, and supreme rank. Metaphorically, it plays on the imagery of Christ's relationship to the church as head of the body (1Co 12:12-27; Eph 1:22; 4:15; 5:23). He is the head because He is **the beginning** and **the firstborn from**

the dead. The parallel language to the creation (v. 15) identifies the church as part of the new creation that was inaugurated with the resurrection of Christ. His resurrection resulted in the fulfillment of God's purpose for Christ that **He might come to have first place in everything.**

1:19-20 God was **pleased** that **His fullness**, the entirety of God's being, would **dwell** in the Son. Thus Jesus was fully divine as well as fully human. God took pleasure in this because, through Christ, God would **reconcile** (reestablish a right relationship) all things to Himself on the **cross** (cp. Rm 5:11; 2Co 5:19).

1:21 Paul explained the need for reconciliation to God by appealing to the Colossian believers' spiritual condition before their salvation. Before they heard the gospel they were **alienated** from God. Corrupt thinking results in immoral behavior, which in turn produces more wrong thinking and further estrangement from God.

1:22 Paul contrasted the Colossian believers' former life with their current salvation. The reference to Jesus' **physical body** highlights His humanity, whereas verse 19 expresses His divinity. The purpose of this reconciliation is so that believers may be presented **holy, faultless**, and **blameless** before Him instead of being "hostile in mind" and practicing "evil actions" (v. 21).

1:23 The only way believers will be presented holy, faultless, and blameless is if they do not abandon their **faith** in Christ as presented in the **gospel**. Faith refers to the content of the gospel with Jesus as the object (vv. 4,23; 2:5,7,12). Paul warned the believers at Colossae about their adoption of syncretistic beliefs that perverted the true message of the gospel, subsequently abolishing their **hope** (v. 5).

1:24 Paul rejoiced in his **sufferings** (Rm 8:18; 2Co 1:5; Gl 5:24; Php 3:10) because they benefited the church. By suffering Paul was **completing** in his **flesh** what was **lacking** in **Christ's afflictions**. This enigmatic phrase cannot mean that something was lacking in Christ's atoning work (v. 20). Rather, Paul's sufferings benefited the church by promoting the spread of the gospel.

1:25 God's **administration** (Eph 1:10; 3:2,9) pertains to God's

prototokos

Greek Pronunciation	[proh TAH tah kahs]
HCSB Translation	firstborn
Uses in Colossians	2
Uses in the NT	8
Focus passage	Colossians 1:15,18

Prototokos (firstborn), derived from *protos* (first in time/rank) and *-tikto* (give birth to), appears eight times in the NT. All six occurrences in the singular refer to Jesus, and it is possible that *prototokos* was a title for the incarnate Christ (Heb 1:6). With the exceptions of Lk 2:7 and Heb 11:28, where *prototokos* clearly refers to *firstborn* children, the force of *-tikto* is lost in the NT. The term thus takes on the sense of "preeminence in rank or time." Jesus' preeminent status over His creation is seen in Col 1:15. As Creator "He is before all things" in supremacy (Col 1:17a) and is "the *firstborn* from the dead" (Col 1:18; Rv 1:5): the first to be resurrected and the One having authority over the resurrection of the dead. Additionally, Jesus' post-resurrection transfiguration is a preview of the glorious transfiguration of the saints in the future (Rm 8:29).

in Christ's afflictions for His body,[a] that is, the church. [25] I have become its servant, according to God's administration that was given to me for you, to make God's message fully known, [26] the •mystery hidden for ages and generations but now revealed to His saints. [27] God wanted to make known among the Gentiles the glorious wealth of this mystery, which is Christ[b] in you, the hope[c] of glory. [28] We proclaim Him, warning and teaching everyone with all wisdom, so that we may present everyone mature in Christ. [29] I labor for this, striving[d] with His strength that works powerfully in me.[e]

2 For I want you to know how great a struggle[f] I have for you, for those in Laodicea,[g] and for all who have not seen me in person. [2] I want their hearts to be encouraged[h] and joined together in love, so that they may have all the riches of assured understanding and have the knowledge of God's •mystery[i]—Christ.[A,j] [3] All the treasures of wisdom[k] and knowledge[l] are hidden in Him.

[a]1:24 Eph 4:4
[b]1:27 Col 2:2
[c]1Th 1:3
[d]1:29 Jd 3
[e]1Co 15:10
[f]2:1 2Tm 4:7
[g]Col 4:13-16; Rv 1:11; 3:14
[h]2:2 Lk 16:25; Col 4:8
[i]Php 3:8
[j]Col 1:27
[k]2:3 Pr 3:19; Is 11:2; 45:3; Jr 23:5; Ac 7:22; 1Co 1:21
[l]1Co 14:6
[m]2:5 Ps 51:12; 1Th 2:17
[n]2:6 Jd 3
[o]Eph 3:11
[p]2:7 Eph 2:20
[q]Eph 4:21; Heb 13:9
[r]2:8 Mk 7:3
[s]1Tm 6:20
[t]2:9 Php 2:6; Col 1:19
[u]2:10 1Co 11:3; Eph 1:22; 4:15; 5:23
[v]2:11 Col 1:22; 3:9
[w]Mt 1:17; Eph 5:2

Christ versus the Colossian Heresy

[4] I am saying this so that no one will deceive you with persuasive arguments. [5] For I may be absent in body, but I am with you in spirit,[m] rejoicing to see how well ordered you are and the strength of your faith in Christ.

[6] Therefore, as you have received[n] Christ Jesus the Lord,[o] •walk in Him, [7] rooted and built up in Him[p] and established in the faith, just as you were taught,[q] overflowing with gratitude.

[8] Be careful that no one takes you captive through philosophy and empty deceit based on human tradition,[r] based on the elemental forces of the world, and not based on Christ.[s] [9] For the entire fullness[t] of God's nature[B] dwells bodily[c] in Christ, [10] and you have been filled by Him, who is the head[u] over every ruler and authority. [11] You were also circumcised in Him with a circumcision not done with hands, by putting off the body of flesh,[v] in the circumcision of the •Messiah.[D,w] [12] Having

---

[A]2:2 Other mss read mystery of God, both of the Father and of Christ; other ms variations exist on this v.   [B]2:9 Or of the deity
[C]2:9 Or nature lives in a human body   [D]2:11 = His death

---

plan for Gentiles to receive salvation and to share in the inheritance of God's people. Paul's role was to make this message **fully known** (see note at v. 9).

1:26 The term **mystery** (cp. v. 27; 2:2; 4:3; Rm 11:25; Eph 1:9; 3:3-9) refers to something that was previously **hidden** in God's plan but has now been **revealed**. Here it relates to the inclusion of the Gentiles into the people of God.

1:27 The words **glory** and **wealth** jointly connote the wonder and blessings associated with this mystery. **In you** could mean "among you," or, more likely, refer to Christ's indwelling of believers (Rm 8:10; 2Co 13:5; Gl 2:20; Eph 3:17).

1:28 The words **warning** and **teaching** express the manner of their proclamation, which is further characterized as being in keeping **with all wisdom**. The purpose of this ongoing ministry was to **present everyone mature in Christ** in correspondence with Christ's purpose in reconciliation (v. 22).

1:29 Paul viewed his work along the same lines as Christ's work of purifying and maturing the church. This was not something that Paul accomplished in his own strength but in conjunction with the work of Christ operating in him.

2:1 On **have not seen me in person**, see note at 1:7-8.

2:2 Paul's struggle in the gospel ministry came from his purpose and desire to encourage and join their **hearts** together in **love** and in fully assured **understanding** (see notes at 1:9 and 1:26).

2:3 Christ is the only source required for **wisdom** and **knowledge**; the Colossians did not need to look to any other philosophy. **Hidden** does not mean secretive (1:26) but plays on the word **treasures**. Jewish writers often used this imagery to encourage seekers to dig deep when looking for truth.

2:4 For the first time in the epistle Paul directly stated his opposition to the false teaching. The words **deceive** and **persuasive arguments** imply the use of misleading or faulty

reasoning, which is contrasted with the truth of the gospel (see note at 1:5-6).

2:5 Paul affirmed, **I am with you in spirit** (cp. 1Co 5:3-5), which may refer to the unity of the body of Christ made possible by the Holy Spirit (Eph 4:3).

2:6-7 Paul's primary concern was that believers would grow in spiritual maturity. The basis of their conduct is Christ's lordship (1:15-20) and indwelling (1:27). The command to **walk in Him**, as in 1:10, is followed by expressions of what this involved: (1) being **rooted** (denoting firmness; cp. Eph 3:17); (2) **built up**; (3) **established in the faith** (a legal term meaning "confirmed"); and (4) **overflowing with gratitude** (cp. 1:3,12; 3:15-17; 4:2).

2:8 **Be careful** is a strong warning to watch out so believers are not taken **captive** and enslaved to false doctrines through **philosophy** and **empty deceit**. "Human tradition" implies human origin (whether Jewish or Gentile) as opposed to the divine nature of the gospel. The **elemental forces** were most likely astral deities, spirits, and/or angels commonly associated with pagan worship, astrology, and magical practices.

2:9 On the **fullness** of Christ, see note at 1:19-20.

2:10 **You have been filled** denotes a completed act with ongoing results (see notes at 1:9 and 1:18).

2:11 The reference to **circumcision** indicates the Jewish nature of this false philosophy. Circumcision was established and mandated by God for entrance into the covenant community of His people. But the circumcision of the Messiah was spiritual and associated with "circumcision of the heart" (Dt 10:16; 30:6; Jr 4:4; Ezk 44:7; Rm 2:29). Here the reference is to the death of Christ, not the literal OT practice of circumcision.

2:12 **Baptism** relates to Christ's death and burial (Rm 6:3-8); it is not the NT equivalent of OT circumcision. Believer's baptism symbolizes union with Christ in death and

been buried with Him[a] in baptism, you were also raised with Him[b] through faith in the working of God, who raised Him from the dead.[c] [13] And when you were dead in trespasses and in the uncircumcision of your flesh, He made you alive with Him and forgave us all our trespasses. [14] He erased the certificate of debt, with its obligations, that was against us and opposed to us, and has taken it out of the way by nailing it to the cross.[d] [15] He disarmed the rulers and authorities and disgraced them publicly; He triumphed over them by Him.[A,e]

[16] Therefore, don't let anyone judge[f] you in regard to food and drink[g] or in the matter of a festival or a new moon[h] or a Sabbath day.[B] [17] These are a shadow[i] of what was to come;[j] the substance is[C] the Messiah.[k] [18] Let no one disqualify you,[D,l] insisting on ascetic prac-

tices[m] and the worship of angels, claiming access to a visionary realm and inflated[n] without cause by his unspiritual[E] mind. [19] He doesn't hold on to the head, from whom the whole body,[o] nourished and held together by its ligaments and tendons, develops with growth from God.

[20] If you died with the Messiah[p] to the elemental forces of this world, why do you live as if you still belonged to the world? Why do you submit to regulations: [21] "Don't handle, don't taste, don't touch"? [22] All these regulations refer to what is destroyed by being used up; they are commands and doctrines of men. [23] Although these have a reputation of wisdom[q] by promoting ascetic practices, humility, and severe treatment of the body, they are not of any value in curbing self-indulgence.[F,r]

a2:12 Rm 6:4
bEph 2:6; Col 3:1
cMt 17:9; Jn 5:25; 20:9; 21:14; Ac 2:24
d2:14 Lk 9:23; 23:26
e2:15 Lk 10:18; Jn 12:31; 16:11; Eph 6:12; Heb 2:14
f2:16 Lk 6:37
gJn 6:55; Rm 14:3,17; 1Co 8:4; Heb 9:10
hPs 81:3
i2:17 Heb 8:5; 10:1
jRm 8:38
kGl 3:24; 5:2
l2:18 1Co 9:24; Php 3:14
mCol 3:12
n1Co 4:6
o2:19 1Co 6:13; Eph 4:4
p2:20 Rm 6:8; 1Pt 2:24
q2:23 Ac 7:22　r1Tm 4:8

A2:15 Or *them through it*; = through the cross　B2:16 Or *or sabbaths*　C2:17 Or *substance belongs to*　D2:18 Or *no one cheat us out of your prize*　E2:18 Lit *fleshly*　F2:23 Lit *value against indulgence of the flesh*

complete separation from the former way of life. Likewise, believers are **raised** with Him through faith (1:23; Gl 2:20) according to God's power.

2:13 Prior to their faith in Christ, the Colossians were spiritually **dead in trespasses** (cp. Eph 2:1-3) and cut off from God's people because they were Gentiles (Eph 2:11-12). However, in Christ, God made them **alive** and **forgave** all their sins (Eph 2:4-8).

2:14 The **certificate of debt** may refer to a handwritten document or to the Mosaic law. Paul typically viewed the law's purpose as revealing the guilt of sinners (Dt 27:26; Rm 7:13; 1Co 15:56; Gl 3:10). Some Jewish writings, likewise, speak of God keeping records of people's sins as debts against them. God, however, has abolished those records through Christ's substitutionary atonement that was accomplished when He died on the cross.

2:15 The phrase **disgraced them publicly** relates to God humiliating these spiritual rulers in a public spectacle of shame and defeat. The word **triumphed** (see note at 2Co 2:14) evokes the imagery of a triumphal procession where a victorious general would lead a parade to display the booty and prisoners of war from his conquest.

2:16 Because God has completely reconciled believers to Himself, they are free from condemnation and from practicing customs required for God's covenant people in the past (Rm 8:1). Against this, the Colossian believers were apparently pressured by some in the church to observe Jewish dietary laws and holy days.

2:17 Paul used the words **shadow** and **substance** to contrast the incomplete nature of these former obligations with the fullness brought about by Christ. God instituted the dietary laws and holy days as a means to foreshadow the coming reconciliation in the Messiah. The actual contrast comes from Jewish eschatology (**what was to come**) rather than a Platonic dualism (material vs. immaterial). This is another way of saying that He is the fulfillment of the law (Rm 10:4; Heb 10:1).

2:18 The word **disqualify** comes from the athletic arena where a referee determined that an athlete had violated the rules and was barred from further competition. This

threat of disqualification relates to practicing spiritual disciplines imposed by the false teachers. **Ascetic practices** translates the word "humility," but in the context of the false teaching it most likely refers to harsh treatment of the body (i.e., self-humiliation). The **worship of angels** may be understood as worship improperly rendered to angels, or as worship of God performed by angels. "Ascetic practices" and "worship of angels" are joined, suggesting that through asceticism the participants believed themselves to be partaking in angelic worship. This worship was conducted through entrance into the **visionary realm**. Paul, however, identified these visions as egotistical delusions of a carnal mind.

2:19 On Christ as the **head**, see note at 1:18 (cp. Eph 4:16). Paul's point is that these false teachers had no real authority over the Colossian church.

2:20 Since believers have died with Christ (v. 11) to the **elemental forces** (see note at v. 8) of this world, they are liberated from worldly rules. The word **regulations** means literally "obligation" (v. 14).

2:21 Paul quoted some of the purity and dietary laws imposed by the false teachers, who were judging and disqualifying believers.

2:22 These dietary regulations were merely physical and temporal because once food is consumed it is destroyed. Although the false teachers believed that their obligations promoted spirituality, Paul identified these regulations as human **commands and doctrines** (alluding to Is 29:13; see note at Col 2:8).

2:23 Paul conceded that these regulations had **a reputation of wisdom** in that they appeared to provide enlightened spiritual understanding (1:9), but in reality these practices offered no help in dealing with **self-indulgence**. The term for "self-indulgence" or gratification may play on the word "fullness." This false philosophy promised a fullness of wisdom through severe asceticism, but it failed to achieve its intended goal.

3:1-17 In 2:23, Paul criticized the asceticism of the false teachers by stating that such practices offered no help in curbing sinful fleshly desires. In these verses he offered

The Life of the New Man

3 So if you have been raised with the *Messiah, seek what is above, where the Messiah is, seated at the right hand of God.[a] [2]Set your minds on what is above, not on what is on the earth.[b] [3]For you have died,[c] and your life is hidden with the Messiah in God. [4]When the Messiah, who is your[A] life, is revealed,[d] then you also will be revealed with Him in glory.[e]

[5]Therefore, put to death what belongs to your worldly nature:[B] sexual immorality, impurity,[f] lust,[g] evil desire, and greed,[h] which is idolatry.[i] [6]Because of these, God's wrath[j] comes on the disobedient,[c] [7]and you once *walked in these things when you were living[k] in them. [8]But now you must also put away[l] all the following: anger,[m] wrath,[n] malice,[o] slander,[p] and filthy language from your mouth.[q] [9]Do not lie[r] to one another, since you have put off[s] the old self[D,t] with its practices [10]and have put on[u] the new self. You are being renewed in knowledge according to the image of your[E]

Creator.[v] [11]In Christ[F] there is not Greek and Jew, circumcision and uncircumcision, barbarian, Scythian,[G] *slave and free; but Christ is all and in all.[w]

The Christian Life

[12]Therefore, God's chosen ones, holy and loved,[x] put on heartfelt compassion, kindness,[y] humility,[z] gentleness,[aa] and patience,[ab] [13]accepting one another and forgiving one another if anyone has a complaint against another. Just as the Lord has forgiven you, so you must also forgive.[ac] [14]Above all, put on love—the perfect bond of unity. [15]And let the peace of the Messiah, to which you were also called[ad] in one body, control your hearts. Be thankful. [16]Let the message about the Messiah dwell richly among you, teaching and admonishing one another in all wisdom, and singing psalms, hymns, and spiritual songs, with

[a]3:1 Heb 10:12
[b]3:2 Php 3:19
[c]3:3 Rm 6:8
[d]3:4 2Co 4:11; 1Jn 1:2; 2:28
[e]Lk 9:32; Jn 17:24; 2Co 3:18; 2Pt 3:18
[f]3:5 1Th 4:3,7
[g]Rm 1:26; 1Th 4:5
[h]Eph 5:3
[i]1Co 10:14; Gl 5:20; 1Pt 4:3
[j]3:6 Jms 1:19; Rv 6:16
[k]3:7 Lk 15:13; Rm 6:2
[l]3:8 Rm 13:12
[m]Jms 1:19
[n]Rv 14:19
[o]1Co 14:20
[p]Jn 10:33; Rv 13:6
[q]Eph 4:22-31
[r]3:9 Lv 19:11; 1Tm 2:7
[s]Col 2:15
[t]Eph 4:22
[u]3:10 Pr 31:25
[v]Mk 13:19; Jn 1:3; Rv 3:14
[w]3:11 Eph 1:23
[x]3:12 Jn 3:16; 2Th 2:13; Rv 12:11
[y]2Co 6:6
[z]Ac 20:19; Eph 4:2; Php 2:3; Col 2:18,23; 1Pt 5:5
[aa]Jms 3:13
[ab]2Tm 3:10
[ac]3:13 2Co 2:7,10; 12:13; Eph 4:32
[ad]3:15 Jn 14:27; 1Co 7:15; Php 4:7

[A]3:4 Other mss read our   [B]3:5 Lit death the members on the earth   [C]3:6 Other mss omit on the disobedient   [D]3:9 Lit man; = a person before conversion   [E]3:10 Lit his   [F]3:11 Lit Where   [G]3:11 A term for a savage

---

positive advice on true spiritual living that effectively remedies sinful cravings of the flesh.

3:1-2 So if resumes the implications of believers' identification with Christ begun in 2:20. It signals a shift in the epistle from doctrinal instruction (chaps. 1–2) to practical application (3:1–4:6). The objects of believers' efforts and thoughts are the heavenly places where Christ dwells (Ps 110:1). These commands contrast true spiritual living with the false spirituality promoted by earthly "philosophy."

3:3 The basis for the commands (vv. 1–2) lies in believers' union with Christ. **Hidden** connotes that God fully completed the action in the past with permanent results.

3:4 At present Christ dwells at God's right hand in heaven and is hidden from the view of those living on earth. At some future point He will be **revealed** in the fullness of His glory. When this occurs, believers will also be gloriously revealed with Christ.

3:5 The command to **put to death** (2:20; Mt 5:29-30; Rm 8:13) refers to the practical outworking of seeking and thinking about heavenly things. Paul offered a fivefold catalog of vices explaining what he meant by **what belongs to your worldly nature**. These vices are listed moving from specific outward behavior to general inward inclinations and thoughts.

3:6 God's wrath indicates the severe consequences for these sins.

3:7 Once walked emphasizes the discontinuity between believers' new and former ways of life.

3:8 Put away literally means to "take off" or "remove" something and may evoke the familiar Pauline metaphor of changing clothes (Rm 13:12; Eph 4:22). All the vices listed relate to behaviors that disrupt interpersonal relationships.

3:9-10 The metaphor of changing clothes pertains to an actual observable change of behavior. The new self replaces

the old but is also continuously being **renewed** to reflect the image of God. The reference to the **new self** applies to individuals but also carries corporate connotations relating to the body of Christ (1:15-20).

3:11 The old order was characterized by ethnic and social division, but the new order obliterates those distinctions in the body of Christ. The phrase **Christ is all and in all** refers to His supremacy (1:17) and indwelling presence in believers (1:27).

3:12 After commanding believers to "put away" worldly behaviors, Paul offered a series of positive commands to **put on** or to "clothe yourselves" (Rm 13:14) with behavior fitted for God's people. The adjectives **chosen** (Is 43:20; 65:9; Rm 8:33; 2Tm 2:10; Ti 1:1; 1Pt 1:1; 2:4,6,9), **holy** (Mk 1:24; Lk 4:34; Jn 6:69; 1Pt 2:9), and **loved** (Mt 3:17; Eph 1:6; 1Th 1:4; 2Th 2:13) were all applied to Israel, Jesus, and the church. The five virtues are just the opposite of the vices listed in verses 5 and 8.

3:13 The words **accepting** (cp. Rm 15:7; Eph 4:2) and **forgiving** (cp. Eph 4:32) express the habitual manner in which believers exhibit the stated virtues. Both verbs pertain to interpersonal relationships in the body of Christ. **Just as the Lord has forgiven** echoes Jesus' injunction to forgive because believers are forgiven (Mt 6:12,14-15; 18:23-35; Lk 7:42).

3:14 The imagery here suggests that the final and most important new article of clothing for God's people is **love**, the **perfect bond of unity**, that binds believers together in complete oneness (Eph 4:3).

3:15 The **peace** brought by Christ should control believers' hearts (Rm 8:6; 15:13; 2Co 13:11; Gl 5:22; Eph 2:14; Php 4:7; 2Th 3:16). **Be thankful** harks back to 1:3,12; 2:7 (cp. 3:17; 4:2).

3:16 The words **teaching** and **admonishing** express the means of how the gospel is to dwell among believers. **Wisdom . . . singing**, and **gratitude** characterize the manner of this teaching and admonishing.

gratitude in your hearts to God. ¹⁷And whatever you do, in word or in deed, do everything in the name^a of the Lord Jesus, giving thanks to God the Father through Him.

Christ in Your Home

¹⁸Wives, be submissive to your husbands, as is fitting in the Lord.^b
¹⁹Husbands,^c love your wives^d and don't be bitter^e toward them.
²⁰Children,^f obey your parents in everything, for this pleases the Lord.
²¹Fathers,^g do not exasperate^h your children, so they won't become discouraged.
²²Slaves, obey your human^i masters in everything. Don't work only while being watched, in order to please men, but work wholeheartedly, fearing the Lord.^j
²³Whatever you do, do it

enthusiastically,^A as something done for the Lord and not for men,^k ²⁴knowing that you will receive the reward of an inheritance from the Lord. You serve the Lord Christ. ²⁵For the wrongdoer^l will be paid back for whatever wrong he has done, and there is no favoritism.

4 Masters,^m supply your •slaves with what is right and fair, since you know that you too have a Master in heaven.

Speaking to God and Others

²Devote yourselves^n to prayer; stay alert in it with thanksgiving. ³At the same time, pray also for us that God may open a door^o to us for the message, to speak the •mystery of the •Messiah,^p for which I am in prison,^q ⁴so that I may reveal it as I am required to speak. ⁵Act

---

^a3:17 Jn 14:13; Php 2:10 ^b3:18–4:1 Eph 5:22–6:9 ^c3:19 1Pt 3:1 ^dEph 5:25; 1Pt 3:1 ^eRv 8:11; 10:9-10 ^f3:20 Gn 3:16; Lv 10:14; Dt 31:12; Ps 37:25; Pr 20:7; Lk 1:7; Ac 2:39; Heb 2:13 ^g3:21 Ps 103:13; Eph 6:4; Heb 11:23 ^h2Co 9:2 ^i3:22 Rm 1:3; 4:1; 8:4-5,12-13; 9:3,5; 1Co 1:26; 10:18; 2Co 1:17; 5:16; 10:2-3; 11:18; Gl 4:23,29; Eph 6:5 ^jPr 1:7; Rv 14:7 ^k3:23 Eph 6:7 ^l3:25 Rv 2:11 ^m4:1 Col 3:22 ^n4:2 Rm 12:12 ^o4:3 Ac 14:27; 1Co 16:9; 2Co 2:12 ^p1Co 2:7; Eph 3:4; 5:2 ^qAc 27:2; 28:16,30; Eph 6:18-20

---

^A3:23 Lit do it from the soul

3:18–4:1 Paul in this section showed how doing everything in the name of the Lord applies to every member of a household. Early Christians adopted and modified this format for describing appropriate behavior of members in a Christian household (Eph 5:21–6:9; Ti 2:2-10; 1Pt 2:18–3:7).

3:18 Paul exhorted **wives** to be **submissive** to their husbands (Eph 5:21-24). Paul always used this verb in the context of authority relationships (Rm 8:7; 10:3; 13:1,5; 1Co 14:34; 15:27-28; 16:16; Php 3:21; Ti 2:5,9; 3:1). This submission is not subservience but voluntary subordination. This disposition is based on the wife's relationship with Christ and her role within the family (**as is fitting in the Lord**) rather than on a false notion of inferiority (1Co 11:3,7-9; see note at Eph 5:22-24).

3:19 Coupled with his exhortation for wives, Paul admonished **husbands** to **love your wives**, with the additional warning not to become **bitter toward them**. "Love" refers to selfless sacrificial concern and care for the welfare of an-

other person (Eph 5:25-33). "Bitterness" pertains to harsh treatment and could be translated as "to cause bitter feelings." Husbands must always care for their wives and never deal harshly with them (1Pt 3:7).

3:20 The word **obey** lacks the voluntary sense found in the command to be submissive. Children must be obedient to their parents (Ex 20:12; Dt 5:16; Eph 6:1-3); this is how they please the Lord. This obedience does not include immoral or idolatrous demands from a parent, because this is not behavior pleasing to the Lord.

3:21 Although the term **Fathers** could include both parents (Heb 11:23), fathers in particular are warned to **not exasperate** their children (Eph 6:4). "Exasperate" means to cause or provoke someone to harbor feelings of resentment. The reason for this injunction is so that children do not become **discouraged** or disheartened. Fathers must avoid dealing harshly with them.

3:22-25 Some interpreters believe slaves in the ancient world might have been habitually lazy since they did not profit personally from their labor. Why work hard when you gain nothing personally? Paul offered an extensive rationale for exhorting Christian **slaves** to **obey** their earthly masters in **everything**: (1) slaves are to **work** even when unsupervised, because they are ultimately serving the Lord rather than a human master; (2) their service to the Lord will be gloriously rewarded in eternity; and (3) God does not discriminate when it comes to punishing bad behavior.

4:1 Paul exhorted **masters** to deal justly with their **slaves** because they themselves are slaves of God.

4:2 Stay alert or "staying awake" refers to the mental attitude of expectancy and watchfulness.

4:3 An "open door" was a common expression for an opportunity for someone to do something (Ac 14:27; 1Co 16:9; 2Co 2:12). Paul asked believers to intercede for him so he could continue to spread the gospel. On **mystery**, see note at 1:26.

4:5-6 Paul's final exhortation to the Colossians was that they would use wisdom in their interaction with unbelievers (1:9-10). The phrase **making the most** comes from a verb meaning "to buy up," as if finding a bargain. Here it

---

kleronomia

Greek Pronunciation	[klay rah nah MEE ah]
HCSB Translation	inheritance
Uses in Colossians	1
Uses in the NT	14
Focus passage	Colossians 3:24

Kleronomia (inheritance) occasionally refers to promised possessions (Ac 7:5) or to the inheritance legally due an heir (Lk 12:13). More frequently, however, NT authors employ the term inheritance in a religious, spiritual sense to refer to the future, heavenly, imperishable, eternal salvation of which the saints will one day partake in the kingdom of God (Eph 1:14; Col 3:24; Heb 9:15; 1Pt 1:4). Jesus, in His Parable of the Wicked Tenants (Mt 21:38 = Mk 12:7 = Lk 20:14), loads the term with this deeper, spiritual referent, interpreting the inheritance as the kingdom of God (Mt 21:43). Paul speaks of inheritance only in this religious sense. Christians, as heirs of God through faith (Gl 3:26), have sole rights to this future inheritance (Eph 5:5). The sealing of the Holy Spirit upon believers is the Father's guarantee that He will grant His children their promised inheritance (Eph 1:13-14,18).

wisely toward outsiders, making the most of the time.[a] [6] Your speech should always be gracious, seasoned with salt,[b] so that you may know how you should answer each person.[c]

Christian Greetings

[7] Tychicus,[d] our dearly loved brother, faithful[e] servant, and fellow slave in the Lord, will tell you all the news about me. [8] I have sent him to you for this very purpose, so that you may know how we are[A] and so that he may encourage[f] your hearts.[g] [9] He is with Onesimus,[h] a faithful and dearly loved brother, who is one of you. They will tell you about everything here.

[10] Aristarchus, my fellow prisoner, greets you, as does Mark,[i] Barnabas's[j] cousin (concerning whom you have received instructions: if he comes to you, welcome him), [11] and so does Jesus who is called Justus. These alone of the circumcision are my coworkers for the

kingdom of God, and they have been a comfort to me. [12] Epaphras,[k] who is one of you, a slave of Christ Jesus, greets you. He is always contending[l] for you in his prayers, so that you can stand mature and fully assured[B] in everything God wills.[m] [13] For I testify about him that he works hard[C,n] for you, for those in Laodicea,[o] and for those in Hierapolis. [14] Luke, the dearly loved physician, and Demas[p] greet you. [15] Give my greetings to the •brothers in Laodicea, and to Nympha and the church in her home.[q] [16] When this letter has been read among you, have it read also in the church of the Laodiceans; and see that you also read the letter from Laodicea. [17] And tell Archippus,[r] "Pay attention to the ministry you have received in the Lord, so that you can accomplish it."[s]

[18] This greeting is in my own hand—Paul. Remember my imprisonment.[t] Grace be with you.[D,u]

[a]4:5 Eph 5:15-17
[b]4:6 Mk 9:50; Lk 14:34
[c]1Pt 3:15
[d]4:7 Ac 20:4; Ti 3:12
[e]Nm 23:19
[f]4:8 Lk 16:25
[g]Eph 6:21-22; Col 2:2
[h]4:9 Phm 10,16
[i]4:10 Phm 24
[j]Ac 4:36
[k]4:12 Col 1:7; Phm 23
[l]Jd 3
[m]Gl 1:4; Eph 1:9
[n]4:13 Jd 3
[o]Col 2:1
[p]4:14 2Tm 4:10
[q]4:15 Ac 12:12; Rm 16:5
[r]4:17 Phm 2
[s]2Tm 4:5
[t]4:18 Php 1:7
[u]1Tm 6:21; 2Tm 4:22; Ti 3:15

[A]4:8 Other mss read *that he may know how you are*   [B]4:12 Other mss read *and complete*   [C]4:13 Other mss read *he has a great zeal*   [D]4:18 Other mss add *Amen.*

---

conveys the idea of making the most of one's time spent with unbelievers.

4:7-8 Tychicus, a native of Asia, first joined Paul in Ac 20:4 and continued to serve alongside him (Eph 6:21; 2Tm 4:12; Ti 3:12). He may also have been the person who delivered this letter to the Colossians as well as the letter to the Laodiceans (see note at Col 4:16).

4:9 Onesimus, a native of Colossae, was a runaway slave (Phm 10). His name means "useful."

4:10-11 Aristarchus, a native of Thessalonica, was one of Paul's companions and his fellow prisoner (Ac 19:29; 20:4). John **Mark**, the Gospel writer, joined Paul and Barnabas on their first missionary journey (Ac 12:12,25). Paul and Barnabas parted ways because Paul did not want Mark along for their second journey (Ac 15:37-39). These verses provide evidence that at some point Paul became convinced again of Mark's usefulness. **Jesus** called **Justus** was a fellow Jewish believer.

4:12-13 On **Epaphras**, see note at 1:7-8.

4:14 This is the only place in the NT where Luke's profession is identified. **Demas**, one of Paul's companions, later abandoned the gospel ministry because of his love for the world (2Tm 4:10).

4:15 Laodicea, 10 miles from Colossae, also had a fledgling congregation of believers. Paul specifically mentioned **Nympha**, who hosted the believers in her house (a common practice in the early church).

4:16 Once this letter had been read among the Colossian believers, they were to send it or a copy of it to Laodicea. Paul apparently wrote a letter to the Laodiceans that was also to be read in Colossae. The epistle to the Laodiceans was either another of Paul's epistles (Ephesians?) or a letter that has not been preserved.

4:17 On **Archippus**, compare Philemon 2.

4:18 Although Paul probably used a secretary to write this epistle (Rm 16:22), he often signed his letters himself as a mark of their authenticity and his affection for the recipients (1Co 16:21; Gl 6:11; 2Th 3:17; Phm 19).

1 Thessalonians

Paul spent a very short time in the city of Thessalonica, but he was able to establish a church during his stay. There may have been little time for instruction of the new converts, so it is not surprising that Paul wrote a letter to address some questions.

The famed Arch of Galerius in Thessaloniki built in A.D. 305, celebrating Emperor Galerius's victory over the Persians in A.D. 297. It's located beside the Via Egnatia, one of the famous Roman roads used by Paul in his travels to spread the gospel.

Circumstances of Writing

Author: No serious objections have been made to dispute that Paul was the author of 1 Thessalonians (1:1). The greeting also mentions Silvanus and Timothy. Sometimes Paul wrote from the team perspective, but he was the primary author (2:18; 3:2).

Background: About A.D. 50 the missionary team led by Paul and Silas left Philippi and traveled westward on the Roman road known as the *Via Egnatia*. They proceeded toward the strategic capital city of the Roman province of Macedonia—Thessalonica.

Thessalonica was a large port city on the Aegean Sea in modern-day Greece, with a population of about 200,000. The city was filled with pagan worshipers of idols, the full pantheon of Greek and Roman gods, and was well known for its emperor worship. Thessalonica was loyal to Caesar, and he had granted its citizens many privileges.

As was his custom, Paul found the local Jewish synagogue and started teaching there. For three Sabbaths he reasoned with the Jews from the Scriptures. He explained and demonstrated that the promised Messiah had to suffer and rise from the dead. After explaining the life, death, and resurrection of Jesus, he then stated boldly, "This Jesus I am proclaiming to you is the Messiah" (Ac 17:3). Some of the Jews were persuaded, along with some of the devout Greeks who were worshipers at the synagogue, and some of the prominent women. They joined Paul and Silas, and the church in Thessalonica was born.

There were Jews in the city who were not persuaded, and they became jealous of what Paul and Silas had done. They incited the people into an uproar and attacked Jason's house where the missionary team had been staying. Wanting to drag Paul and Silas out before the crowd, they found only Jason and some new believers. They dragged these out before the city authorities. The rulers, not wanting more unrest, forced Jason and the rest of the brothers to make a financial payment of security to ensure that there would not be a repeat of such a

2300–150 B.C.

- Prehistoric settlement on the site of Thessalonica 2300

- Founding of Therme at the head of the Thermaic Gulf 600

- Cassander, king of Macedon, establishes Thessalonica at the site where Therme had existed, naming the new city in honor of his wife. 316

- The Romans gain control of Thessalonica when Perseus, king of Macedonia, is defeated at Pydna. 168

- First Jewish community in Thessalonica, emigrants from Alexandria 168–103

149–42 B.C.

- Construction of the Macedonian leg of the Egnatian Way, a Roman military road connecting Thessalonica with the Adriatic Sea in the west and with Neapolis in the east 147–120

- Thessalonica becomes the capital of the Roman province of Macedonia and is referred to as "the Mother of Macedonia." 146

- The Roman statesman Cicero spends six months of his self-imposed exile in Thessalonica. 58

- Many Roman officials flee Rome and take up residence in Thessalonica during the Roman civil war. 49–48

- Augustus declares Thessalonica a free city following the battle of Philippi. 42

disturbance. That very night the Thessalonian believers sent Paul and Silas away to Berea, where they could continue their ministry (Ac 17:1-9).

From Berea Paul went to Athens. He wanted to see the Thessalonians again. When he could endure the separation no longer, he sent Timothy to encourage the Thessalonian believers (1Th 3:2). Timothy came back with an encouraging report about the Thessalonian church (3:6). Paul wrote to them from Corinth in response to Timothy's report. Based on the archaeological evidence of a dated inscription mentioning Gallio, proconsul of Achaia, by name (Ac 18:12) and correlating this with Paul's visit to Corinth when Gallio was there, 1 Thessalonians can be reliably dated at A.D. 50 or 51. This would make 1 Thessalonians the earliest of Paul's letters with the probable exception of the book of Galatians.

Message and Purpose

Timothy reported to Paul that although the church at Thessalonica was suffering affliction, they were holding fast to the faith. And though they had some doctrinal misunderstandings, they were laboring for the Lord out of love, and patiently hoping for the return of Christ. Paul wrote to encourage the church in their faith, to remind them that sanctification was God's will for them, and to correct misunderstandings about end-time events. First Thessalonians presents four major themes.

Paul's conduct of his ministry: Paul's ministry centered on two aspects—the impartation of the word of God and the sharing of his life (2:8). The gospel did not come in word only, but in power and deed as well. Paul's motives were to please God (2:4; 4:1) and to express his concern for the Thessalonians' welfare (2:8). His message didn't come in error, uncleanness, and deceit but in purity and truth (2:3,10). Also, Paul didn't use his ministry as a cloak for covetousness (2:5). This was demonstrated by his working to provide for his material needs (2:9).

Persecution: The Thessalonian church was founded in the midst of persecution. Paul had to leave the city for

A.D. 33–44	A.D. 47–53
Tiberius Caesar takes away Thessalonica's status as a free city when her citizens protest increased taxation. 15	Paul, Barnabas, and John Mark make first missionary journey. 47–49
Jesus' trials, death, resurrection, and ascension Nisan 14–16 or April 3–5, 33	Paul and Silas begin second missionary journey. 49
Pentecost 33	Paul, Silas, and Timothy preach in Thessalonica. 50
Saul's conversion on the Damascus Road October 34	Paul writes 1 Thessalonians several months after his ministry among the Thessalonians. 51
Claudius Caesar restores Thessalonica's status as a free city. 44	Paul concludes his second missionary journey and arrives in Antioch of Syria. 52

that reason, and the church continued after he left (1:6; 2:14-15). Paul encouraged the believers there not to be shaken by these afflictions because Christians are certain to suffer (3:3-4).

Sanctification: Salvation isn't finished once a person believes in Christ and receives forgiveness of sins. Paul's prayer for the believers at Thessalonica in 3:13 was that God would establish their hearts blameless in holiness before God. He pointed out that God's will for them was to abstain from sexual immorality and to love one another (4:1-12). Paul used his example of work to encourage them in their own work so they would not be unnecessarily dependent on anyone (4:10-12; 5:14).

The second coming of Christ: Jesus' return is mentioned in every chapter of 1 Thessalonians. Specific attitudes, events, and encouragements about the "Day of the Lord" are given with the assurance that Christians are not appointed to God's wrath (5:9).

Contribution to the Bible

First Thessalonians contributes to our understanding of the second coming of Christ. Paul wrote to correct some misunderstandings of this doctrine, and in the process he showed us that Christ's return gives us true hope. First Thessalonians and 1 Corinthians (chap. 15) are the only books that explicitly mention that Christians who are alive at Christ's return will be changed and will meet Christ in the air without dying.

Structure

First Thessalonians follows the standard form for a first-century letter: greeting (1:1), thanksgiving (1:2-4), body (1:5–5:22), and farewell (5:23-28). The body of the letter does not follow Paul's typical structure of presenting doctrine first, followed by practical exhortation based on that doctrine. Instead, 1 Thessalonians moves back and forth between the doctrinal and the practical.

Outline

I. Greeting (1:1)

II. Commendation for the Thessalonians (1:2-10)
   A. Their work in the gospel (1:2-4)
   B. Their reception of the gospel (1:5-10)

III. Conduct in Ministry (2:1-16)
   A. The missionaries' visit and example (2:1-12)
   B. Mixed responses to God's message (2:13-16)

IV. Concern for the Thessalonians (2:17–3:13)

V. Call to Sanctification (4:1-12)
   A. Abstain from sexual immorality (4:1-8)
   B. Practice brotherly love (4:9-12)

VI. Christ's Second Coming (4:13–5:11)
   A. The rapture of the saints (4:13-18)
   B. The Day of the Lord (5:1-11)

VII. Concluding Exhortations and Blessings (5:12-28)

Greeting

1 Paul, Silvanus,[A,a] and Timothy:[b]
To the church of the Thessalonians[c] in God the Father and the Lord Jesus Christ. Grace to you and peace.[B]

Thanksgiving

[2]We always thank God for all of you, remembering you constantly in our prayers. [3]We recall, in the presence of our God and Father,[d] your work of faith,[e] labor of love, and endurance of hope in our Lord Jesus Christ,[f] [4]knowing your election,[g] •brothers loved[h] by God.[i] [5]For our gospel did not come to you in word only, but also in power, in the Holy Spirit,[j] and with much assurance. You know what kind of men we were among you[k] for your benefit, [6]and you became imitators of us and of the Lord when, in spite of severe persecution, you welcomed the message[l] with joy from the Holy Spirit. [7]As a result, you became an example to all the believers in Macedonia[m] and Achaia.[n] [8]For the Lord's message rang out from you, not only in Macedonia and Achaia, but in every place that your faith[C,o] in God has gone out. Therefore, we don't need to say anything, [9]for they themselves report[D] what kind of reception[p] we had from you: how you turned[q] to God from idols[r] to serve the living[s] and true[t] God [10]and to wait[u] for His Son[v] from heaven, whom He raised from the dead[w]—Jesus, who rescues us[x] from the coming wrath.[y]

Paul's Conduct

2 For you yourselves know, •brothers, that our visit[z] with you was not without result. [2]On the contrary, after we had previously

a1:1 Ac 15:22; 2Co 1:19; 2Th 1:1; 1Pt 5:12
b Ac 16:1; 1Tm 1:2
c Ac 17:1
d1:3 Php 4:20
e Rm 3:28; 9:32; Gl 2:16; 5:6; 2Th 1:11; Heb 6:1; Jms 2:14-26; Rv 2:19
f Ac 15:26
g1:4 Mt 24:22; Eph 1:4
h Jn 3:16; Rv 12:11
i Dt 33:12; 2Th 2:13
j1:5 Jn 1:33; Ac 2:4; Rm 8:9; 1Co 2:4; Gl 5:25; Ti 3:5; Rv 3:22
k Ac 20:18; 1Th 2:10
l1:6 Heb 4:12
m1:7 Ac 16:9
n Ac 18:12
o1:8 Gl 2:16
p1:9 Ac 17:1-9
q1Pt 2:25   r Gn 31:19; 1Co 8:4   s Dt 5:26   t Jd 21   u1:10 Jd 21
v Heb 1:2   w Mt 17:9; Jn 5:25   x Mt 27:43   y Rm 2:5; 1Th 5:9; Rv 6:16   z2:1 Ac 17:1-9

1:1 Paul used the Latin version **Silvanus** (2Co 1:19; 2Th 1:1) for the person whom Luke referred to using the Greek name Silas (Ac 15:22). Silas was chosen by Paul to accompany him on his second missionary journey, replacing Barnabas (Ac 15:40). Silas participated in the work of planting the Thessalonian church (Ac 17:4) and was with Paul in Corinth at the time of the writing of this letter. Paul may have encountered **Timothy** at Lystra on his first missionary journey (Ac 14:8-18). On the second visit Timothy is described as a disciple who was ready to assist Paul in the missionary efforts after he was circumcised (Ac 16:1-3). Timothy is not explicitly mentioned as participating in the founding of the Thessalonian church (Ac 17:1-9), but Paul sent him from Athens to assist the newly formed and persecuted church when Paul realized he could not return to the Thessalonians (1Th 3:1-2). Timothy's encouraging report on the state of the Thessalonian church prompted Paul to write this epistle (3:6). The reference to **church** (Gk *ekklesia*) in NT times could refer generically to any gathering or assembly, but Paul specified it here as the local assembly at Thessalonica **in God the Father and the Lord Jesus Christ.**

1:2 In his epistles Paul normally thanked God for those people to whom he was sending the letter and mentioned that they were in his **prayers** or offered a prayer for them. The only exception to this is Galatians, where he issued a strong rebuke.

1:3 Paul commended the Thessalonians for their work of **faith**, labor of **love**, and endurance of **hope**. He later singled out these three virtues as having special prominence for the Christian community (1Co 13:13). Their **work** and **labor** were evident in that the gospel had gone throughout not only their province of Macedonia but into the neighboring province of Achaia (vv. 7-8). **Endurance** would have been especially needed in the midst of persecution.

1:4 While the Thessalonians were commended for their work, Paul reminded them that God was the One who had brought about their **election** and that they were **loved** by Him. Election (Gk *eklogon*) carries the idea of God's choice or selection.

1:5-6 The **gospel** is more than a message of words. It is a message that comes in **power** and in the **Holy Spirit**. The basic meaning of gospel (Gk *euangelion*) is "good news." Paul often further specified that it was not just any good news but the good news that came from God (2:2,8,13). Even though the church at Thessalonica was founded in the midst of **severe persecution**, the message was warmly received with **joy** that came from the Holy Spirit. That God was working there was also evident since Paul and Silas were able to stay only for a short time before they were forced to leave and yet the church started and flourished anyway (Ac 17:1-9). **What kind of men we were among you** is further explained in 2:1-12.

1:7-9 The Thessalonians' faith and gospel message spread throughout **Macedonia** and **Achaia**. These two Roman provinces—Macedonia in the north and Achaia in the south—make up a large part of modern-day Greece. In NT times, these provinces included major cities such as Philippi, Athens, and Corinth. Thessalonica was the capital of Macedonia. It appears that Paul's missionary strategy worked. He evangelized the major cities with the expectation that the gospel would spread from there into the surrounding areas. The Thessalonians' predominantly Gentile background is evident from the false worship of lifeless **idols**, from which they turned to serve **the living and true God**.

1:10 While the Thessalonians were enduring persecution, they were also waiting for the coming Son from heaven—**Jesus, who rescues us from the coming wrath**. The "coming wrath" was not a persecution that Paul and the Thessalonians were experiencing or would experience from the unbelieving world, but a future time of God's wrath against the unbelieving world. Christians will be rescued from this (5:9). Paul introduced the fact of Jesus' resurrection here and later expressed the hope of the resurrection for Christians who had died (4:16).

2:1 **Brothers** (Gk *adelphoi*; vv. 9,14,17; 3:7; 4:1,10; 5:1,4,12,26) literally means "from the same womb." In this context it is an inclusive term referring to both men and women of the Christian faith. Christians have a new spiritual family relationship based on their common faith (Mt 12:46-50).

2:2 At **Philippi** Paul and Silas were beaten and imprisoned for casting a demon out of a slave girl. As Paul stated at

suffered,[a] and we were treated outrageously in Philippi,[b] as you know, we were emboldened by our God to speak the gospel of God to you in spite of great opposition. [3] For our exhortation didn't come from error or impurity[c] or an intent to deceive.[d] [4] Instead, just as we have been approved by God to be entrusted[e] with the gospel,[f] so we speak, not to please men, but rather God,[g] who examines our hearts.[h] [5] For we never used flattering speech, as you know, or had greedy[i] motives[j]—God is our witness[k]— [6] and we didn't seek glory[l] from people, either from you or from others. [7] Although we could have been a burden as Christ's apostles,[m] instead we were gentle[A] among you, as a nursing mother nurtures her own children. [8] We cared so much for you that we were pleased to share with you not only the gospel of God but also our own lives, because you had become dear to us. [9] For you remember our labor and hardship, brothers. Working[n] night and day so that we would not burden any of you, we preached God's gospel to you. [10] You are witnesses,[o] and so is God, of how devoutly, righteously,[p] and blamelessly[q] we conducted ourselves with you believers. [11] As you know, like a father with his own children,[r] [12] we encouraged, comforted, and implored each one of you to *walk worthy of God,[s] who calls you into His own kingdom[t] and glory.[u]

Reception and Opposition to the Message

[13] This is why we constantly thank God, because when you received the message about God that you heard from us, you welcomed it not as a human message, but as it truly is,[v] the message of God,[w] which also works effectively in you believers. [14] For you, brothers, became imitators of God's churches in Christ Jesus that are in Judea,[x] since you have also suffered[y] the same things from people of your own country,[z] just as they did from the Jews [15] who killed both the Lord Jesus[aa] and the prophets and persecuted us;[ab] they displease God and are hostile to everyone, [16] hindering us from speaking to the Gentiles so that they may be saved. As a result, they are always completing the number of their sins,[ac] and wrath has overtaken them at last.[B]

Paul's Desire to See Them

[17] But as for us, brothers, after we were forced to leave you for a short time (in person, not in heart[ad]), we greatly desired and made every effort to return[ae] and see you face to face. [18] So we wanted to come to you—even I, Paul, time and again—but Satan[af] hindered us. [19] For who is our hope or joy[ag] or crown[ah] of boasting[ai] in the presence of our Lord[aj] Jesus

a 2:2 Ac 16:19-24
b Php 1:1
c 2:3 1Th 4:7
d Ps 10:7
e 2:4 Lk 16:11
f Ac 15:7; Gl 2:7; 1Tm 1:11
g Jn 5:44; 12:43; 1Co 4:5; 2Co 10:18; Gl 1:10; Php 3:19; 1Th 2:15; 1Pt 3:4
h Ps 17:3; Pr 21:2; Rm 8:27
i 2:5 Eph 5:3
j Mk 12:40; Lk 20:47; Jn 15:22; Ac 27:30; Php 1:18
k Rm 1:9
l 2:6 Php 3:19
m 2:7 Ac 1:2; Jd 17
n 2:9 2Jn 8
o 2:10 Rm 1:9
p Ti 2:12
q 1Th 5:23
r 2:11 1Co 4:14; Gl 4:19; 1Tm 1:2; Phm 10
s 2:12 3Jn 6
t Mk 1:15; Ac 20:25
u Lk 9:32; 24:26; Jn 17:24; 2Co 3:18; 1Pt 5:1; 2Pt 3:18
v 2:13 2Th 3:1
w Lk 8:21
x 2:14 Lk 1:5
y Php 1:29
z Ac 17:5
aa 2:15 Lk 24:20
ab Rm 11:3
ac 2:16 Mt 23:30-32
ad 2:17 Col 2:5
ae 1Th 3:10
af 2:18 Mt 4:1,10; Ac 13:10   ag 2:19 Jn 15:11; 2Co 6:10   ah Rv 12:1
ai 2Co 12:5; Jms 4:16   aj Rv 11:8

A 2:7 Other mss read *infants*   B 2:16 Or *to the end*

---

that time, it was illegal to punish Roman citizens like this without a trial (Ac 16:16-40). Paul's statement also indicates that along with Paul, Silas was a Roman citizen. In spite of **great opposition**, which continued into Thessalonica, the **gospel of God** was faithfully proclaimed.

2:3 Paul's motives for ministry were to proclaim truth and to please God.

2:8 Paul's method of ministry was not only the impartation of the gospel but the sharing of his own life as well.

2:9 Paul **preached God's gospel** to the Thessalonians, not taking any financial support but working not to **burden** them. It was clear that Paul was not in the ministry for the money, and this helped testify to the truth of his message. Paul was a tentmaker by trade (Ac 18:3).

2:14 Though the Thessalonian church was founded in the midst of persecution, Paul pointed out that their sufferings were not unique. Starting with the crucifixion of Jesus and continuing into the churches of Judea, persecution was ever present in the early church. Persecution was usually initiated by hostile Jews trying to use the Roman authorities to help them. It was not until the later reign of Nero, following the great fire that burned Rome (A.D. 64), that the first major empire-wide persecution of Christians began as an official Roman policy.

2:15 **They** refers to the Jews of verse 14. This is the only place in Paul's writings where he identified those who were responsible for Jesus' death. **Prophets** appears to

be a reference to the OT prophets who also suffered persecution at the hands of their countrymen (Ac 7:52). The pattern is clear—rejection of the message first, then persecution of the messenger.

2:16 Some Jews objected to offering the message of the gospel to **Gentiles** (Ac 13:46-50; 14:2; 17:5,13). **Completing the number of their sins** is literally "to fill up their sins." This phrase implies that God will tolerate only a certain number of sins before His judgment falls.

2:17-18 The intensity of Paul's desire to see the Thessalonians again is evident by these emphatic descriptions: **greatly desired . . . made every effort . . . even I, Paul . . . time and again**. The phrase **Satan hindered us** probably refers to the persecution Paul was experiencing or possibly an illness (2Co 12:7). Perhaps the security bond that Jason gave to the city officials to calm things down after persecution broke out in Thessalonica ensured that Paul himself would not return. In any case the Thessalonian believers had to send Paul and Silas quickly away at night (Ac 17:8-10). The name Satan means "adversary," as one who is opposed to God, His plan, and His people.

2:19 The reference to a "crown" carries the image of a laurel wreath worn on the head in reward for victory at a Greek athletic contest. Paul viewed the Thessalonian church as his **crown of boasting**, which would be evident at Jesus' coming.

at His coming?[a] Is it not you?[b] [20] For you are our glory[c] and joy!

Anxiety in Athens

3 Therefore, when we could no longer stand it, we thought it was better to be left alone in Athens.[d] [2] And we sent Timothy,[e] our brother and God's coworker[A] in the gospel of Christ,[f] to strengthen and encourage you concerning your faith, [3] so that no one will be shaken by these persecutions. For you yourselves know that we are appointed to[B] this. [4] In fact, when we were with you, we told you previously that we were going to suffer persecution, and as you know, it happened. [5] For this reason, when I could no longer stand it, I also sent him to find out about your faith, fearing that the tempter had tempted you and that our labor might be for nothing.

Encouraged by Timothy

[6] But now Timothy has come to us[g] from you and brought us good news about your faith and love and reported that you always have good memories of us, wanting to see us, as we also want to see you.[h] [7] Therefore, *brothers, in all our distress and persecution, we were encouraged about you through your faith. [8] For now

we live, if you stand firm[i] in the Lord. [9] How can we thank God for you in return for all the joy[j] we experience before our God because of you, [10] as we pray very earnestly night and day to see you face to face[k] and to complete what is lacking in your faith?[l]

Prayer for the Church

[11] Now may our God and Father[m] Himself, and our Lord Jesus,[n] direct our way to you. [12] And may the Lord cause you to increase and overflow with love[o] for one another[p] and for everyone, just as we also do for you. [13] May He make your hearts blameless[q] in holiness[r] before our God and Father at the coming[s] of our Lord[t] Jesus with all His *saints. *Amen.[C]

The Call to Sanctification

4 Finally then, *brothers, we ask and encourage you in the Lord Jesus, that as you have received from us how you must *walk and please God—as you are doing[D]—do so even more. [2] For you know what commands we gave you through the Lord Jesus.

[3] For this is God's will,[u] your *sanctification:[v] that you abstain[w] from sexual immorality, [4] so that each of you knows how to control his own body[E] in sanctification and honor, [5] not

Cross references

a 2:19 1Th 1:10; 1Jn 2:28
b 1Co 15:31; 2Co 1:14; Php 4:1; 2Th 1:4
c 2:20 Jn 12:43; Php 3:19
d 3:1 Ac 17:15
e 3:2 Ac 16:1; 1Tm 1:2
f Php 1:27
g 3:6 Ac 18:5
h 1Co 11:2; Php 1:8
i 3:8 Rm 14:4; 1Co 16:13; Php 1:27
j 3:9 Jn 15:11; 2Co 6:10; Php 1:18
k 3:10 1Th 2:17
l Col 1:24
m 3:11 Jn 8:42; Php 4:20
n Ac 20:21
o 3:12 Lk 7:42
p Rm 13:8
q 3:13 Lk 1:6
r Rm 1:4; 1Co 7:14; 2Co 7:1
s 1Th 1:10; 1Jn 2:28
t Rv 11:8
u 4:3 1Th 5:18
v Rm 6:19,22; 1Co 1:30; 2Th 2:13; 1Tm 2:15; Heb 12:14; 1Pt 1:2
w Tm 4:3

A 3:2 Other mss read *servant*   **B** 3:3 Or *are destined for*   **C** 3:13 Other mss omit *Amen.*   **D** 4:1 Lit *walking*   **E** 4:4 Or *to acquire his own wife*; lit *to possess his own vessel*

3:1-2 Sent from **Athens** to help the Thessalonian church, **Timothy** could help these believers grow in the faith but not be as conspicuous as Paul or Silas. They were the prominent members of the missionary team and were well known by the hostile Jews and city officials.

3:3-4 Christians should not be **shaken** by persecution, because Paul stated **we are appointed to this** in God's

plan. Jesus taught His disciples that if people persecuted Him, they as His followers would be persecuted as well (Jn 15:20). In Paul's case the persecution kept him moving from city to city. As a result many cities were able to hear the gospel from Paul's mouth. This would not have happened had Paul been warmly received among the Jews. Hence God allowed persecution to serve as a means of accomplishing His will.

3:5 For this reason refers back to the persecution of the Thessalonians mentioned in verse 4. **Tempter** is another reference to Satan as one who entices people to sin (Mt 4:1-11).

3:10-13 Paul was praying to see the Thessalonian believers in person in order to complete what was lacking in their faith. Verses 11-13 contain a prayer expressing just that desire. The prayer's request that the church **overflow with love for one another** and be **blameless in holiness** is an expression of desire for the Thessalonians' brotherly love and sanctification specifically addressed in the following two paragraphs (4:1-8,9-12).

4:3 Sanctification (Gk *hagiasmos*) could also be translated "holiness." Here it refers to the consecration of the believer to God in holy and proper behavior in regard to sexual purity. God's will is clear—**to abstain from sexual immorality**. The passage does not say to abstain from sex practiced in the context of marriage but sex that deviates from God's standards. This would include premarital sex, incest, homosexuality, bestiality, and adultery.

4:4 The phrase **control his own body** probably refers to the idea of controlling the body's lustful sexual desires that

stephanos

Greek Pronunciation	[STEH fah nahs]
HCSB Translation	crown
Uses in 1 Thessalonians	1
Uses in the NT	18
Focus passage	1 Thessalonians 2:19

In the Gospels, *stephanos (crown)* refers exclusively to the thorny *crown* worn by Jesus during His Passion (Mt 27:29; Mk 15:17; Jn 19:2,5). Paul consistently exhorts the saints by using the promise of a *crown* as their future reward. Believers should run the Christian race to obtain an imperishable *crown*, even as athletes run for a perishable *wreath* (1Co 9:25; cp. Rv 3:11), and a *crown* of righteousness belongs to all who love the Lord's appearing (2Tm 4:8). Certain congregations are the *crown* with which Paul will appear before the Lord at His return (Php 4:1; 1Th 2:19). James speaks of a *crown* of life given to those who, despite persecution, maintain their love for God (Jms 1:12; cp. Rv 2:10), and an unfading *crown* of glory awaits elders who lovingly shepherd their congregations (1Pt 5:4). *Crown* appears frequently in the apocalyptic imagery of Revelation. There it is usually associated with pictures of authority, rule, dominion, power, and/or enablement for a task.

with lustful desires,[a] like the Gentiles who don't know God. [6]This means one must not transgress against and defraud[b] his brother in this matter, because the Lord is an avenger of all these offenses,[A] as we also previously told and warned you. [7]For God has not called us to impurity[c] but to sanctification. [8]Therefore, the person who rejects this does not reject man, but God, who also gives you His Holy Spirit.[d]

Loving and Working

[9]About brotherly love: You don't need me to write you because you yourselves are taught by God[e] to love one another.[f] [10]In fact, you are doing this toward all the brothers in the entire region of Macedonia.[g] But we encourage you, brothers, to do so even more, [11]to seek to lead a quiet life,[h] to mind your own business,[B] and to work[i] with your own hands, as we commanded you, [12]so that you may walk

properly[C,j] in the presence of outsiders[D] and not be dependent on anyone.[E,k]

The Comfort of Christ's Coming

[13]We do not want you to be uninformed, brothers, concerning those who are ˙asleep, so that you will not grieve like the rest, who have no hope.[l] [14]Since we believe that Jesus died and rose[m] again,[n] in the same way God will bring with Him those who have fallen asleep through[F] Jesus.[o] [15]For we say this to you by a revelation from the Lord:[G,p] We who are still alive at the Lord's coming[q] will certainly have no advantage over[H] those who have fallen asleep.[r] [16]For the Lord Himself will descend from heaven with a shout,[l,s] with the archangel's[t] voice, and with the trumpet of God, and the dead in Christ[u] will rise first. [17]Then[v] we who are still alive will be caught up

a4:5 2Pt 1:4; 2:10
b4:6 2Co 12:17
c4:7 Mt 23:27; 2Co 12:21; Gl 5:19; Eph 4:19; 5:3; Col 3:5; 1Th 2:3
d4:8 Ps 51:11; Jn 1:33; Ac 2:4; Rm 8:9; Gl 5:25; Ti 3:5; 1Jn 5:8; Rv 3:22
e4:9 Jn 6:45
f1Jn 3:11
g4:10 Ac 16:9
h4:11 Lk 14:4; 23:56; Ac 11:18; 21:14
i2Th 3:12; 2Jn 8
j4:12 Rm 13:13; 1Co 14:40
kEph 4:28
l4:13 Jr 14:19; Eph 2:12; 1Th 1:3
m4:14 Lk 18:33
nRm 14:9,15; 1Co 8:11; 15:3-4; 2Co 5:15
oJn 14:19; Rm 8:11; 1Co 6:14; 15:18-20;

2Co 4:14; Php 1:23   p4:15 2Pt 1:21; Rv 11:8   q1Jn 2:28   r1Co 15:51   s4:16 Jn 5:25   tJd 9   uRm 16:7; 1Co 15:18; 1Pt 5:14; Rv 14:13; 20:5   v4:17 1Co 15:23,51-52

A4:6 Lit things   B4:11 Lit to practice one's own things   C4:12 Or may live respectably   D4:12 Non-Christians   E4:12 Or not need anything, or not be in need   F4:14 Or in   G4:15 Or a word of the Lord   H4:15 Or certainly not precede   I4:16 Or command

might lead a Christian to sin. An alternate but less likely view is that it refers to obtaining a wife.

4:6-8 When a person commits a sexual sin, the result is to **transgress against** and **defraud** one's brother. **Brother** in this context probably means a fellow Christian. A sexual transgression defrauds one's brother in the sense that sexual sin is a form of theft: you take something that does not belong to you. It defrauds both the partner of the illicit relationship as well as a spouse or future spouse who alone has rights in sexual matters. **In this matter** points back to the discussion of sexual purity in verses 3-5. Paul gave two reasons for Christians to abstain from sexual immorality. First is that **the Lord is an avenger** who will judge the offense. Second is that sexual impurity violates God's call to **sanctification**. The implication of God's giving us **His Holy Spirit** is that a person should not mix human sexual impurity with God's holy nature in the Holy Spirit, who dwells within the Christian (1Co 6:19).

4:9-12 The reference to **brotherly love** (Gk *philadelphia*) seems to govern the content of these verses in encouraging fellow Christians to **lead a quiet life**, mind one's **own business**, and **work** with one's **hands**. To do otherwise places a burden of dependence on the community of faith and gives a poor testimony to outsiders (5:14; 2Th 3:7-12). Paul demonstrated this work ethic by providing for his own needs (1Th 2:9).

4:13 The term **asleep** in this context is a metaphorical reference to Christians who have died. This metaphor is particularly appropriate because of the future resurrection of the body. Just as a sleeping person expects to rise up in the morning, Christians who have died will experience a bodily resurrection and will rise up once again (v. 16, Jn 11:11). Until this happened for deceased believers, to be out of the body is to be at home with the Lord (2Co 5:8). Apparently the cause of the Thessalonians' grief was related to the misunderstanding that dead Christians would miss the events and subsequent blessings associated with the Lord's coming. Paul corrected this misunderstanding by teaching that the dead in Christ will rise first (1Th 4:16). In contrast to

unbelievers who grieve over the loss of loved ones, Christians who grieve over a fellow believer can do so with **hope** because of the future glorious resurrection.

4:14 Jesus' resurrection revealed what resurrection will be like for those who have **fallen asleep through Jesus**. We can partially understand the nature of our bodily resurrection by reading about His (Lk 24:36-43).

4:15-17 The **revelation** (lit "word") that Paul received relates to what has been called the rapture. It refers to the event when believers who are alive at the Lord's coming are **caught up** (Gk *harpazo*) in the clouds **to meet the Lord in the air**. The term "rapture" is derived from *rapturo*, the Latin translation of the Greek term. The Greek term means "to snatch or take away suddenly." Paul referred to this event as a mystery (some truth previously hidden but now known) in 1Co 15:51-52 and said it will happen in the twinkling of

harpazo

Greek Pronunciation	[hahr PAH zoh]
HCSB Translation	caught up
Uses in 1 Thessalonians	1
Uses in the NT	14
Focus passage	1 Thessalonians 4:17

Harpazo (catch up, snatch up) is often invested with the idea of force. In this sense, *harpazo* refers to an arrest (Ac 23:10) and to the near forceful capture of Jesus by a crowd (Jn 6:15). The term is not limited to the physical realm. The Evil One *snatches away* the message of the kingdom sown upon men's hearts (Mt 13:19), Jude exhorts believers to *snatch* some men from the fire (Jd 23), and no one is able to forcefully *carry off* the sheep belonging to the Good Shepherd (Jn 10:11,28-29). Elsewhere, the term is used of supernatural phenomena and does not carry the concept of force. Paul received glorious revelation after being *caught up* into paradise (2Co 12:2,4). The Holy Spirit *carries* Philip away and transports him to Azotus (Ac 8:39). Believers will one day be *caught up* to meet their returning Lord (1Th 4:17).

together with them in the clouds[a] to meet the Lord in the air and so we will always be with the Lord. [18]Therefore encourage[A] one another with these words.

The Day of the Lord

5 About the times and the seasons:[b] •Brothers, you do not need anything to be written to you. [2]For you yourselves know very well that the Day of the Lord[c] will come just like a thief[d] in the night. [3]When they say, "Peace and security," then sudden destruction[e] comes on them, like labor pains come on a pregnant woman, and they will not escape. [4]But you, brothers, are not in the dark, for this day to overtake you like a thief.[f] [5]For you are all sons of light and sons of the day. We do not belong to the night or the darkness.[g] [6]So then, we must not sleep, like the rest, but we must stay awake and be serious. [7]For those who sleep, sleep at night, and those who get drunk are drunk at night. [8]But since we belong to the day, we must be serious[h] and put the armor[i] of faith and love on our chests, and put on a helmet[j] of the hope of salvation. [9]For God did not appoint us to wrath, but to obtain salvation through our Lord[k] Jesus Christ,[l] [10]who died for us,[m] so that whether we are awake or •asleep,[n] we will live together with Him.[o]

[11]Therefore encourage one another and build each other up as you are already doing.

Exhortations and Blessings

[12]Now we ask you, brothers, to give recognition[p] to those who labor among you and lead you in the Lord and admonish you, [13]and to regard them very highly in love because of their work. Be at peace[q] among yourselves. [14]And we exhort you, brothers:[r] warn those who are irresponsible,[B] comfort the discouraged, help the weak, be patient[s] with everyone. [15]See to it that no one repays evil for evil[t] to anyone,[u] but always pursue what is good for one another and for all.[v]

[16]   Rejoice[w] always!
[17]   Pray constantly.
[18]   Give thanks in everything,
         for this is God's will[x] for you
             in Christ Jesus.
[19]   Don't stifle the Spirit.
[20]   Don't despise prophecies,
[21]   but test all things.[y]
         Hold on to what is good.
[22]   Stay away[z] from every kind
             of evil.

Cross references

[a]4:17 Mt 26:64
[b]5:1 Dn 2:21; Ac 1:7
[c]5:2 Jl 2:1; Mt 25:13; Ac 2:20; Php 1:6
[d]Jn 10:1
[e]2Th 1:9
[f]5:4 Jb 24:13-17
[g]5:5 Col 1:13
[h]5:8 1Pt 5:8
[i]Eph 6:14; Rv 9:9,17
[j]1Sm 17:5,38; Ps 60:7; 108:8; Is 59:17; Eph 6:17
[k]5:9 Rv 11:8
[l]Ac 15:26
[m]5:10 Jn 11:51; Rm 14:9; 1Co 8:11; Gl 1:4
[n]1Th 5:6
[o]Lk 20:38; Php 1:23
[p]5:12 1Co 16:18; Php 2:29
[q]5:13 Mk 9:50
[r]5:14 2Th 3:15
[s]Mt 18:26,29; Lk 18:7; 1Co 13:4; Heb 6:15; Jms 5:7-8; 2Pt 3:9
[t]5:15 Mt 5:44; Rm 12:17; 1Pt 3:9
[u]Lk 7:47
[v]5:15 Rm 12:9; Gl 6:10; 1Th 5:21
[w]5:16 2Co 6:10; Php 1:18
[x]5:18 Eph 6:6; 1Th 4:3; 1Pt 2:15; 4:2; 1Jn 2:17
[y]5:21 Eph 5:17
[z]5:22 1Tm 4:3

[A]4:18 Or comfort   [B]5:14 Or who are disorderly, or who are undisciplined

---

an eye. **We who are still alive** implies that Paul thought the rapture could occur at any moment, even during his lifetime. The "archangel" or chief angel is probably a reference to Michael (Dn 10:13; Jd 9).

5:1 Times and **seasons** mentioned together refers to the end times (Ac 1:7).

5:2 The phrase **Day of the Lord** often signifies a time of God's wrath and judgment poured out in an uncommon way. Here the Day of the Lord refers specifically to the end-time period of God's judgment on the unbelieving world known as the great tribulation (Mal 4:5; Ac 2:20; 2Th 2:2; 2Pt 3:10). The description of the Day of the Lord coming as **a thief in the night** emphasizes that it will come unexpectedly (5:4; 2Pt 3:10).

5:3 It is notable that peace and security are what are often cited as currently needed in the world and especially in the modern state of Israel. Just before the Day of the Lord when people think they have this peace, **sudden destruction** will come upon them. The comparison of this destruction to the **labor pains** of a pregnant woman speaks of the increasing intensity of God's judgment and the certainty of its coming (Mt 24:8).

5:4-6 Paul contrasted **brothers** in the faith who are **sons of light** and **day** with the rest of the world who are of **the night** and **darkness**. Physical sleeping and drunkenness normally occur at night while it is dark, so Paul issued an encouragement for Christians as sons of light to be **awake**, meaning alert and morally ready. One's readiness is described with the military analogy of a soldier who prepares himself for war.

5:6-7 The Greek word for **sleep** in these verses (see also v. 10) is different than that in 4:13-15. In 5:6-7, "sleep" refers to moral lethargy. Some interpreters take "sleep" in verse 10 as a euphemism for death, but a good case can be made that the same Greek word in this context refers to moral lethargy as well. Thus Paul is saying in verse 10 that whether believers are alert or not for the Day of the Lord, we will still "live together" with the Lord.

5:9 Paul reminded the Thessalonians that as Christians they were not appointed to God's **wrath** but to **salvation**. The Day of the Lord will be a great outpouring of God's wrath from the very start (Rv 6:17), and Christians will be kept out of this worldwide hour of testing (Rv 3:10).

5:12-13 To **give recognition** means respect for the authority and work of church leaders.

5:15 Not to repay **evil for evil** but to **pursue what is good** reflects back on Jesus' teaching not to follow a retaliatory "eye for eye" ethic but to give a blessing instead (Mt 5:38-42).

5:17 To **pray constantly** does not mean continuous, uninterrupted prayer but frequent and regular prayers for a consistent prayer life.

5:19 One can **stifle** (lit "quench") **the Spirit** by not submitting to the Holy Spirit's leading or by committing other sins that would grieve the Spirit. In this context Paul may have had in mind listening to or allowing for prophecies (v. 20) that were not Spirit-given.

5:21 Test all things probably refers to the content of the prophecies that had to be evaluated with God's known truth as expressed by the OT, Jesus, and the apostles (1Jn 4:1-3).

23 Now may the God of peace[a] Himself ⸰sanctify you completely. And may your spirit,[b] soul, and body be kept sound and blameless for the coming[c] of our Lord[d] Jesus Christ.[e] 24 He who calls[f] you[g] is faithful, who also will

do it. 25 Brothers, pray for us also. 26 Greet all the brothers with a holy kiss. 27 I charge you by the Lord that this letter be read to all the brothers.[h] 28 The grace of our Lord Jesus Christ be with you.

a 5:23 Rm 15:33
b Ps 51:12
c 1Th 1:10
d Rv 11:8
e 1Jn 2:8
f 5:24 Col 3:15
g 1Pt 1:15
h 5:27 Col 4:16

5:23 The prayer for **spirit, soul, and body** to be kept sound and blameless teaches that God sees the whole person as important in living a life pleasing to God.

5:26 Greeting one another with **a holy kiss**, probably on the cheek, was a common first-century greeting that expressed love similar to a modern handshake (Rm 16:16). This ancient custom is still widely practiced in the Middle East.

2 Thessalonians

Following up on his first letter to the Thessalonians, Paul wrote to give further clarification on how to live the Christian life in light of the coming return of Christ. The Thessalonians were called to stand firm and live useful lives, because the return of Christ might be in the distant future.

Seagulls in Thermaikos Bay, Thessaloniki

Circumstances of Writing

Author: Paul is stated to be the author of 2 Thessalonians (1:1). The greeting also mentions Silvanus and Timothy, but Paul was the primary author (3:17).

Background: See discussion under Introduction to 1 Thessalonians. While there are few indicators about the date and place of writing of 2 Thessalonians, it was probably written from Corinth around A.D. 50–51 shortly after 1 Thessalonians. The mention of Paul, Silvanus, and Timothy together in the salutation, as was the case with 1 Thessalonians (1Th 1:1), supports this conclusion. An additional support for this view is the mention of a previous letter, which was probably 1 Thessalonians (2Th 2:15).

Message and Purpose

Paul wrote in part to encourage the Thessalonian believers to stand firm for the truth in the midst of persecution and to assure them that God would judge those who were afflicting them (1:6-9; 2:13-15). Apparently the Thessalonians thought they were already in the Day of the Lord (2:2). Paul assured them that they were not, since certain end-time events had not yet taken place and one was currently restraining the "lawless one" from appearing (2:6-7). This appears to be the primary impetus for the letter. The fact that some people in the Thessalonian church had stopped working may suggest that their incorrect view was leading to lethargy and laziness (3:10-11).

The letter is not long, and it does not give us a definitive outline of the entire Christian faith. Paul wrote to meet a present need, and the arrangement of his letter focused on local circumstances.

The greatness of God: God loves people like the Thessalonians and has brought them into the church (1:4). He has elected them (2:13), called them (1:11; 2:14), and saved them. His purpose will continue to the end when they will be brought to their climax with the return of Christ and judgment. It is interesting to see so clearly expressed in this early letter these great doctrines of election and call, which meant so much to Paul.

2300–150 B.C.

- Prehistoric settlement on the site of Thessalonica **2300**

- Founding of Therme at the head of the Thermaic Gulf **600**

- Cassander, king of Macedon, establishes Thessalonica at the site where Therme had existed, naming the new city in honor of his wife. **316**

- The Romans gain control of Thessalonica when Perseus, king of Macedonia, is defeated at Pydna. **168**

- First Jewish community in Thessalonica, emigrants from Alexandria **168–103**

149–42 B.C.

- Construction of the Macedonian leg of the Egnatian Way, a Roman military road connecting Thessalonica with the Adriatic Sea in the west and with Neapolis in the east **147–120**

- Thessalonica becomes the capital of the Roman province of Macedonia and is referred to as "the Mother of Macedonia." **146**

- The Roman statesman Cicero spends six months of his self-imposed exile in Thessalonica. **58**

- Many Roman officials flee Rome and take up residence in Thessalonica during the Roman civil war. **49–48**

- Augustus declares Thessalonica a free city following the battle of Philippi. **42**

We also see his doctrine of justification behind the references to God counting the believers worthy (1:5,11) and, of course, in his teaching on faith (1:3-4, 11; 2:13; 3:2).

Salvation in Christ: Salvation in Christ is proclaimed in the gospel and will be consummated when Christ comes again to overthrow all evil and bring rest and glory to His own. This great God loves His people, and He has given them comfort and hope—two important qualities for persecuted people (2:16). The apostle prayed that the hearts of his converts would be directed to "God's love" (3:5), which may mean God's love for them or their love for God. Probably it is God's love for them that was the primary thought, but Paul also noted a mutual love from the new believers. There are repeated references to the revelation (1:7; 2:6,8). While the term is not used in quite the same way as in some other places, it reminds us that God has not left us to our own devices. He has revealed what is necessary and has further revelations for the last days.

The second coming: The second coming is seen here in terms of the overthrow of all evil, especially the "man of lawlessness." Paul made it clear that Christ's coming will be majestic, that it will mean punishment for people who refuse to know God and who reject the gospel, and that it will bring rest and glory to believers (1:7-10). In the end God and righteousness, not Satan and evil, will be triumphant.

Paul made it clear that the Day of the Lord had not yet occurred. Several things must happen first—for example, "the apostasy" that occurs and the revelation of "the man of lawlessness" (2:3). Paul did not explain either. He was probably referring to what he had told the Thessalonians while he had been among them. Unfortunately, we do not know what he said then, so we are left to do some guessing. That a rebellion against the faith will precede the Lord's return is a well-known part of Christian teaching (Mt 24:10-14; 1Tm 4:1-3; 2Tm 3:1-9; 4:3-4).

Life and work: Paul had a good deal to say about people he called "disorderly" and who appeared to be idle, not working at all (3:6-12). This may have been because they thought the Lord's coming was so close there was no point in working, or perhaps they were so "spiritual-minded" that they concentrated on higher things and

---

5 B.C.–A.D. 33

Jesus' birth 5 B.C.

Paul born in Tarsus of Cilicia A.D. 5

Paul studies with Gamaliel in Jerusalem A.D. 15–20

Tiberius takes away Thessalonica's status as a free city when opposition to increased taxation is expressed. A.D. 15

Jesus' trials, death, resurrection, and ascension Nisan 14–16 or April 3–5, A.D. 33

Pentecost A.D. 33

A.D. 34–56

Saul's conversion on the Damascus Road October 34

Paul, Timothy, and Silas minister in Thessalonica, one of the earliest churches planted in Europe. 50

Paul writes 1 Thessalonians a few months after being forced to leave Thessalonica. 51

Paul soon follows up with a second letter to the Thessalonian believers. 51

Paul likely revisits the Thessalonian Christians as he visits the churches planted in Macedonia. 56

let other people provide for their needs. Paul counseled everyone to work for their living (3:12). No doctrinal emphasis, not even that of Christ's return, should lead Christians away from work. People able to work should earn their daily bread. Believers are to work for their living and not grow weary in doing good.

Contribution to the Bible

Second Thessalonians continues and further amplifies some of the same themes as 1 Thessalonians: persecution, sanctification, and end-time events associated with the second coming of Christ. One important difference is that 2 Thessalonians describes the "man of lawlessness" who will be revealed in the end times and what restrains him from being revealed (2:1-12). The book also contains a lengthy discourse on the need for believers to have a proper work ethic to provide for their own needs (3:6-15).

Structure

The tone of Paul's second letter to the Thessalonians is markedly "cooler" than his first letter. In his first letter, Paul was enthusiastic about the Thessalonians' progress in the gospel, and he offered calm advice about congregational life (1Th 5:12-22). In this second letter, though, Paul expressed grave concern about the spiritual state of the Thessalonian believers. He gave them a sharp rebuke about congregational life (2Th 3:6-15). His style is typical of his other letters—a doctrinal section followed by practical exhortation.

Outline

I. Introduction (1:1-12)
    A. Salutation (1:1-2)
    B. Thanksgiving (1:3-10)
    C. Intercession (1:11-12)

II. Instruction of the Thessalonians (2:1-17)
    A. Correction of a misconception (2:1-2)
    B. Revelation of the man of lawlessness (2:3-10)
    C. Judgment of unbelievers (2:11-12)
    D. Thanksgiving and prayer (2:13-17)

III. Injunctions to the Thessalonians (3:1-16)
    A. Call to prayer (3:1-5)
    B. Warning against irresponsible behavior (3:6-15)
    C. Concluding prayer (3:16)

IV. Conclusion (3:17-18)

Greeting

1 Paul, Silvanus,[A,a] and Timothy:[b] To the church of the Thessalonians[c] in God our Father and the Lord Jesus Christ.
[2] Grace to you and peace from God our Father and the Lord Jesus Christ.

God's Judgment and Glory

[3] We must always thank God for you, •brothers. This is right, since your faith is flourishing and the love[d] each one of you has for one another[e] is increasing.[f] [4] Therefore, we ourselves boast[g] about you among God's churches—about your endurance and faith in all the persecutions and afflictions you endure. [5] It is a clear evidence of God's righteous[h] judgment[i] that you will be counted worthy of God's kingdom, for which you also are suffering,[j] [6] since it is righteous for God to repay with affliction those who afflict you [7] and to reward with rest you who are afflicted, along with us. This will take place at the revelation of the Lord Jesus from heaven with His powerful angels, [8] taking vengeance with flaming fire[k] on those who don't know God[l] and on those who don't obey the gospel of our Lord Jesus.[m] [9] These will pay the penalty of eternal destruction[n] from the Lord's presence[o] and from His glorious

strength[p] [10] in that day when He comes[q] to be glorified[r] by His •saints[s] and to be admired by all those who have believed, because our testimony among you was believed. [11] And in view of this, we always pray for you that our God will consider you worthy of His calling,[t] and will, by His power, fulfill every desire for goodness and the work of faith,[u] [12] so that the name[v] of our Lord Jesus will be glorified[w] by you, and you by Him,[x] according to the grace of our God and the Lord Jesus Christ.

The Man of Lawlessness

2 Now concerning the coming[y] of our Lord[z] Jesus Christ and our being gathered to Him: We ask you, •brothers, [2] not to be easily upset in mind or troubled, either by a spirit[aa] or by a message or by a letter as if from us, alleging that the Day of the Lord[B,ab] has come.[ac] [3] Don't let anyone deceive you in any way. For that day will not come unless the apostasy[c] comes first and the man of lawlessness[D] is revealed, the son of destruction. [4] He opposes and exalts himself above every so-called god[ad] or object of worship,[ae] so that he sits[E] in God's sanctuary,[F] publicizing that he himself is God.

[a]1:1 Ac 15:22; 2Co 1:19; 1Th 1:1; 1Pt 5:12 [b]Ac 16:1; 1Tm 1:2 [c]Ac 17:1 [d]1:3 1Co 13:1; 1Jn 4:16 [e]Php 2:2 [f]1Th 4:10 [g]1:4 2Co 12:5 [h]1:5 1Jn 1:9 [i]Mt 12:41; Jn 5:22,27,30; 8:16; 16:11; Heb 9:27; Jms 2:13; 2Pt 3:7; Rv 14:7; 16:7; 19:2 [j]Php 1:29 [k]1:8 1Co 3:13; Heb 10:27; 12:29; 2Pt 3:7; Rv 14:10 [l]Ps 79:6; Is 66:15; Jr 10:25 [m]Pt 4:17 [n]1:9 1Tm 6:9 [o]Gn 4:14 [p]Is 2:10,19,21 [q]1:10 Mk 8:38 [r]Jn 17:10; Rm 8:17 [s]Eph 5:3; 6:18 [t]1:11 Eph 4:1; Col 3:15 [u]Gl 2:16; 1Th 1:3 [v]1:12 Jn 14:13; Ac 3:16; 15:14; Php 2:10 [w]Is 24:15; 49:3; 66:5; Mal 1:11; 2Co 8:23 [x]Jn 13:31

[y]2:1 1Th 1:10; 1Jn 2:28 [z]Rv 11:8 [aa]2:2 1Jn 4:1 [ab]Mt 25:13; Ac 2:20; Php 1:6 [ac]2Tm 2:18; 1Jn 2:28 [ad]2:4 1Co 8:5 [ae]Is 14:12-15; Ezk 28:2; Ac 17:23

A 1:1 Or *Silas*; Ac 15:22-32; 16:19-40; 17:1-16   B 2:2 Other mss read *Christ*   C 2:3 Or *rebellion*   D 2:3 Other mss read *man of sin*   E 2:4 Other mss add *as God*   F 2:4 Or *temple*

1:1 On **Silvanus** and **Timothy**, see note at 1Th 1:1.

1:6-7 God will reward His people with rest and repay those who oppose Him at the future **revelation** of the Lord Jesus from **heaven**. Until then the believer must trust that God in His time will handle current situations that are unjust. Angels are often presented as participating in executing God's awesome judgments and thus are described as **powerful** (cp. Mt 25:31; Mk 8:38).

1:8 The phrase **those who don't know God** is a reference to unbelieving Gentiles (1Th 4:5). **Those who don't obey the gospel** is probably a reference to many Jews who had an opportunity to hear Jesus or the gospel through the ministry of the apostles but rejected it.

1:9 The **penalty of eternal destruction** is described as being away from **the Lord's presence**. The word "destruction" does not imply ceasing to exist or annihilation but separation from God in a miserable state. This is why it is described as eternal. There will be a time when God throws all His enemies into the lake of fire to be eternally judged (Rv 20:11-15).

1:10 The **saints** are the holy people of God. This term refers to all of those called in God's plan of salvation (1Co 1:2; 2Co 1:1).

2:1 Our being gathered to Him probably refers to the gathering of believers at the time of the rapture (1Th 4:13-18).

2:2 Paul taught the Thessalonians that they should not be **troubled** by a false message that they were in the **Day of the**

Lord. That period of time would not come until two events occurred—the "apostasy" and the revealing of the "man of lawlessness" (v. 3).

2:3 The word **apostasy** (Gk *apostasia*) can also be translated "rebellion." It carries the idea of defection or departure from true religion. It probably refers to the widespread religious defection from worship of the true God that will intensify during the Day of the Lord through the workings of the man of lawlessness and Satan (vv. 3-9). An alternate view is that "apostasy" refers to an altogether different kind of departure: the departure of the church from the earth known as the rapture, which will take place before the Day of the Lord begins. The **man of lawlessness** is probably the end-time manifestation of God's enemy known as the antichrist (1Jn 2:18) or the beast from the sea (Rv 13:1-10). This particular title emphasizes that he is opposed to God and His law. He is the **son of destruction** or perdition in the sense that he is destined to be destroyed (v. 8).

2:4 The man of lawlessness (or "man of sin") is so blasphemous that he takes a seat in God's sanctuary, declaring that he himself is **God** and demanding worship (see Rv 13:4 where the beast from the sea is worshiped). This act appears to be what Daniel termed the "abomination of desolation" and what Jesus said would occur during the tribulation period (Mt 24:15; see also Dn 9:27). The reference to **God's sanctuary** or temple suggests that a future rebuilt temple will exist during this time in Jerusalem (Rv 11:1-2). The Greek word used here *(naos)* often refers to the inner sanctuary of the temple precincts.

⁵Don't you remember that when I was still with you I told you about this? ⁶And you know what currently restrains him, so that he will be revealed in his time.ᵃ ⁷For the •mystery of lawlessnessᵇ is already at work, but the one now restraining will do so until he is out of the way, ⁸and then the lawless one will be revealed. The Lord Jesus will destroy him with the breath of His mouthᶜ and will bring him to nothing with the brightness of His coming. ⁹The coming of the lawless one is based on Satan's working, with all kinds of false miracles, signs, and wonders,ᵈ ¹⁰and with every unrighteous deception among those who are perishing. They perish because they did not accept the love of the truth in order to be saved.ᵉ ¹¹For this reason God sends them a strong delusion so that they will believe what is false, ¹²so that all will be condemnedᶠ—those who did not believeᵍ the truth but enjoyed unrighteousness.

ᵃ2:6 Lk 21:8
ᵇ2:7 Mt 13:41
ᶜ2:8 Is 11:4; 30:28
ᵈ2:9 Mt 24:24; Mk 13:22; Rv 13:13
ᵉ2:10 Ac 16:30; Eph 2:8
ᶠ2:12 Jn 5:22-30
ᵍJn 6:64
ʰ2:13 Rm 9:11; 11:5; Eph 1:4; 1Th 1:4
ⁱRm 6:19; 1Co 1:30; 1Th 4:3; 1Tm 2:15; Heb 12:14; 1Pt 1:2
ʲ2:14 Lk 9:32; Jn 17:24; 2Co 3:18; 1Pt 5:1,4; 2Pt 3:18
ᵏ2:15 Rm 14:4; 1Co 16:13; Php 1:27
ˡMk 7:3; 1Tm 4:11; Jd 3
ᵐ2:16 Jn 3:16; Rv 12:11

Stand Firm

¹³But we must always thank God for you, brothers loved by the Lord, because from the beginningᴬ God has chosenʰ you for salvation through •sanctificationⁱ by the Spirit and through belief in the truth. ¹⁴He called you to this through our gospel, so that you might obtain the gloryʲ of our Lord Jesus Christ. ¹⁵Therefore, brothers, stand firmᵏ and hold to the traditions you were taught,ˡ either by our message or by our letter.

¹⁶May our Lord Jesus Christ Himself and God our Father, who has lovedᵐ us and given us eternal encouragement and good hope by grace, ¹⁷encourage your hearts and strengthen you in every good work and word.

Pray for Us

3 Finally, •brothers, pray for us that the Lord's message may spread rapidly and be

---

ᴬ2:13 Other mss read *because as a firstfruit*

2:5 Paul reminded the Thessalonians that he taught about these things when he was with them (Ac 17:1-13). Since Paul was with the Thessalonians for a relatively short time after he and the missionary team planted the church, this emphasizes the importance Paul placed on teaching about end-time events.

2:6-7 The identity of this restrainer has puzzled Bible interpreters for centuries. In verse 6 **what . . . restrains him** is in the neuter in Greek while in verse 7 **the one . . . restraining** is in the masculine. Some things are clear. First, the restrainer is holding back the actual manifestation of the man of lawlessness. Second, at some point the restrainer will cease this activity and the man of lawlessness will be revealed. One common view is that the neuter form refers to government, perhaps the Romans or possibly a future government, while the masculine refers to the leader of that government, perhaps an emperor. Paul elsewhere taught that one of the purposes of government is to promote the common good by restraining wrong (Rm 13:1-5). Possibly the restrainer is a future government and its leader. But

parousia

Greek Pronunciation	[pah roo SEE ah]
HCSB Translation	coming, presence
Uses in 2 Thessalonians	3
Uses in the NT	24
Focus passage	2 Thessalonians 2:8

Parousia means *presence* or *coming*. In the sense of *presence*, it refers to physical proximity. Paul speaks of the obedience of the Philippian church during both his *presence* and absence (Php 2:12) and of the *presence* of his fellow laborers (1Co 16:17). Elsewhere, *parousia* refers to the *coming* or *arrival* of men or events. Paul mentions the *coming* of Titus (2Co 7:6-7), and he hopes to *come* again to the Philippians (Php 1:26). *Parousia* occurs most often in relation to the *coming* of the Lord Jesus as human history moves to closure. His *coming* will be preceded by the *coming* of the "lawless one," the antichrist (2Th 2:8-9). The glorious *coming* of Jesus will be accompanied by the destruction of all His enemies, a resurrection of the dead in Christ, and a gathering of the saints still living (1Co 15:23-25; 1Th 4:15-16; 2Th 2:1).

since the lawless one's action and power stem from Satan's power (2Th 2:9), God's power and sovereignty are strongly suggested as playing a more direct role in the restraining force. A more appealing solution is to see the restrainer as God's Holy Spirit. The Greek word for Spirit (*pneuma*) is neuter, but since the Spirit is a person in Greek, He can be referred to in either the neuter or masculine. Also in verse 6 the reference could be to the restraining force of the Holy Spirit while verse 7 may refer to His personage. Either of these solutions could explain the shift in gender from verses 6 to 7. Another possible variation of this view is that the restrainer is the Holy Spirit working through the church. The phrase **until he is out of the way** would be a removal of the restraining force of the Holy Spirit through the rapture of the church prior to the Day of the Lord.

2:7 In Paul's writings, "mystery" refers to something not previously revealed but now made known. Paul taught that though the man of lawlessness is not currently revealed, the **mystery of lawlessness is already at work**. Satan's program of opposition to God and His standards of righteousness is a current and ongoing reality.

2:9 Miracles, signs, and wonders are not necessarily evidence of God's acts. Satan has the power to perform deceptive supernatural acts. We must examine the source of the act and the content of the message being promoted in order to avoid deception.

2:10-12 Satan's activities will result in wide-scale **deception** of the unbelieving world. First, however, Paul pointed out that unbelievers reject the truth that would save them. Therefore God will send them this **strong delusion** after they have already turned Him away. Their condemnation is based on the fact that they did not believe the **truth**.

2:15 The word **traditions** refers to God's truths passed on to the Thessalonians by Paul (1Th 4:1-2). **Our letter** refers to 1 Thessalonians.

3:2-3 Paul reminded the Thessalonians that **the Lord is faithful** even if **wicked and evil men** were troubling them.

3:6 It is irresponsible behavior for capable people not to work and expect the church to feed them. The view by some people in the Thessalonian church that they were in the Day

honored, just as it was with you,[a] [2] and that we may be delivered[b] from wicked and evil men, for not all have faith.[A] [3] But the Lord is faithful; He will strengthen and guard you from the evil one.[c] [4] We have confidence in the Lord about you, that you are doing and will do what we command. [5] May the Lord direct your hearts to God's love and Christ's endurance.[d]

Warning against Irresponsible Behavior

[6] Now we command you, brothers, in the name[e] of our Lord Jesus Christ, to keep away from every brother[f] who 'walks irresponsibly and not according to the tradition[g] received[h] from us. [7] For you yourselves know how you must imitate[i] us: We were not irresponsible among you; [8] we did not eat[j] anyone's food[B] free of charge;[k] instead, we labored[l] and struggled,[m] working[n] night and day, so that we would not be a burden[o] to any of you. [9] It is not that we don't have the right[p] to support, but we did it to make ourselves an example to you so that you would imitate[q] us. [10] In fact, when we were with you, this is what we com-

manded you: "If anyone isn't willing to work, he should not eat."[r] [11] For we hear that there are some among you who walk irresponsibly, not working at all, but interfering with the work of others.[s] [12] Now we command and exhort such people by the Lord Jesus Christ that quietly working, they may eat their own food.[B] [13] Brothers, do not grow weary[t] in doing good.

[14] And if anyone does not obey our instruction in this letter, take note of that person; don't associate with him, so that he may be ashamed. [15] Yet don't treat him as an enemy, but warn him as a brother.

Final Greetings

[16] May the Lord of peace[u] Himself give you peace always in every way.[v] The Lord be with all of you.[w] [17] This greeting is in my own hand—Paul. This is a sign in every letter; this is how I write. [18] The grace of our Lord Jesus Christ be with all of you.

[a] 3:1 1Th 2:13
[b] 3:2 Mt 27:43; Rm 15:31
[c] 3:3 Mt 5:37; 6:13; 13:19,38; Jn 17:15; Eph 6:16; 1Jn 2:13-14; 3:12; 5:18-19
[d] 3:5 Rm 15:5; Rv 13:10
[e] 3:6 Jn 14:13; Ac 3:16; 15:14; Php 2:10
[f] Mt 18:17; 1Co 5:11; 2Tm 3:5; 2Jn 10
[g] Mk 7:3
[h] Jd 3
[i] 3:7 3Jn 11
[j] 3:8 1Co 10:25
[k] 1Th 2:7
[l] Rv 14:13
[m] 2Co 11:27; 1Th 2:9
[n] Ac 18:3; Eph 4:28; 2Jn 8
[o] 2Co 2:5; 1Th 2:9
[p] 3:9 Mk 1:22; Ac 9:14; Rm 13:1; 1Co 9:4-14
[q] Heb 8:5
[r] 3:10 1Th 4:11
[s] 3:11 1Tm 5:13
[t] 3:13 Lk 18:1; 2Co 4:1,16; Gl 6:9; Eph 3:13
[u] 3:16 1Th 5:23
[v] Nm 6:26; Eph 6:23
[w] Rm 15:33; 1Co 16:24; 2Co 13:13; Ti 3:15; Heb 13:25
[x] 3:17 1Co 16:21

[A] 3:2 Or for the faith is not in everyone　[B] 3:8,12 Or bread

of the Lord and thus Jesus was coming very soon (2:2) may have led them to stop their normal work activities. Or, this may have just been ordinary lazy behavior (1Th 5:14).

3:7-8 Paul had the right to receive financial support while working in evangelism and teaching, but he set an example for the Thessalonians by **working** to provide for his own needs so he did not **burden** them.

3:10 Whatever the reason for this behavior, Paul commanded, **If anyone isn't willing to work, he should not eat** (see Gn 3:18-19). Christian charity is to be directed at true need, not artificial need created by irresponsibility.

3:11 To compound the problem, not only did some Thessalonians not work, but they were **interfering with the work of others**, perhaps encouraging them not to work in order to focus on the Day of the Lord (see note at v. 6).

3:14-15 Paul wanted the Thessalonian church to not **associate with** this type of person and to **warn him as a brother**, with a view toward correcting the problem.

3:16 Paul referred to the Lord as the **Lord of peace** and prayed for God's granting of peace to them **in every way**. This was particularly important for a church under persecution.

3:17 The final **greeting** was written in Paul's **own hand**. This indicates a common ancient practice. The rest of the letter was written with the help of a skilled scribe, called an amanuensis, who was writing as Paul directed him.

THE SECOND MISSIONARY
JOURNEY OF PAUL

ACTS 15:36–18:22

- • City
- ▲ Mountain peak
- — Via Egnatia
- ✕ Pass
- ← Route of Paul and Silas

Paul establishes churches in Philippi, Thessalonica, and Berea

Luke joins Paul

Paul imprisoned

Paul receives vision that encourages him to travel to Macedonia

Paul brought on charges before Gallio

Paul speaks to the Areopagus

Paul asks Timothy to join him in his work

Paul returned from Jerusalem to plan his next venture

Jerusalem Conference, A.D. 49, (Ac 15:1-30; Gl 2:1-21)

A native of Lystra, Timothy may have been converted on Paul's first missionary journey (Ac 14:6-23). Paul was instrumenta
in Timothy's conversion. When Paul came to Lystra on his second journey, Timothy was a disciple who was well respected b
the believers (Ac 16:1-2). Paul asked Timothy to accompany him. Timothy not only accompanied Paul but also was sent o
many crucial missions by Paul (Ac 17:14-15; 18:5; 19:22; 20:4; Rm 16:21; 1Co 16:10; 2Co 1:19; 1Th 3:2,6).

1 Timothy

Introduction

First Timothy, 2 Timothy, and Titus have been referred to as the "Pastoral Epistles" since the eighteenth century. It is reasonable to consider these letters together since they have striking similarities in style, vocabulary, and setting. These letters stand apart from the other Pauline letters in that they were the only ones written to Paul's gospel coworkers. The Pastoral Epistles deal with church structure issues and, unlike Paul's other letters, were addressed to men serving in pastoral roles rather than to churches. But we must also recognize that these are separate letters with their own distinctives. They were not written primarily to describe church structure or pastoral ministry (contrary to popular opinion), but to teach Christian living in response to the gospel.

Remains of the Basilica of St. John at Ephesus. When Paul left Ephesus for Macedonia, he left Timothy as pastor of the church at Ephesus and charged him to instruct certain people who were teaching false doctrines.

Circumstances of Writing

Author: As stated in the opening of each letter, these letters were written by Paul (1Tm 1:1; 2Tm 1:1; Ti 1:1). However, many scholars today assume that Paul did not write them. This opinion is based on the differences from his other letters in vocabulary and style, alleged differences in theology, and uncertainties about where these letters fit chronologically in the life of the apostle. But the differences in style and vocabulary are not troublesome when one considers that authors often use different vocabulary when addressing different groups and situations. Rather than addressing churches in these letters, Paul was writing to coworkers who were in unique ministry settings. Hence we would expect different vocabulary. Also, the traditional view of the historical situation in which Paul wrote these letters is reasonable and defensible. Therefore, in spite of significant opposition by some scholars, there is a solid basis for accepting the Pastoral Epistles as Pauline.

Background: Paul most likely wrote these letters after the time covered in the book of Acts. Acts closes with Paul in prison. Traditionally it has been believed that Paul was released from this imprisonment, then continued his work around the Mediterranean, perhaps even reaching Spain (Rm 15:22-29). During this time, he visited Crete and other places. First Timothy and Titus were written during this period of further mission work. Timothy had been left in Ephesus to handle some problems with false teaching there (1Tm 1:3-4). Titus had been left in Crete after the initial work to set up the church there (Ti 1:5). Eventually Paul was imprisoned again, and this led to his execution. During this final imprisonment, Paul wrote 2 Timothy to request another visit from Timothy and to give final exhortations as he anticipated his martyrdom.

Message and Purpose

In each of these letters, Paul instructed one of his younger coworkers in living out his faith and teaching others to do the same. Each letter is concerned significantly with false teaching and its harmful effects in the

---

A.D. 5–50

Paul born in Tarsus of Cilicia 5

Paul's conversion to Christ as he travels to Damascus 34

Paul takes Titus and Barnabas from Antioch to Jerusalem for the Jerusalem Council. 49

Paul and Silas return to Lystra and take Timothy with them as they travel through Asia Minor to Troas. 50

Timothy ministers with Paul and Silas in Philippi, Thessalonica, and Berea. 50

A.D. 51–56

Paul has to flee Berea; he leaves Timothy and Silas to continue the work. 51

Timothy rejoins Paul in Athens and brings word of the work in Macedonia. 51

Timothy returns to Thessalonica to encourage the new believers. 51–52

Timothy joins Paul in his ministry in Corinth, bringing word of progress in Thessalonica. 52

Timothy comes to Ephesus to work with Paul during Paul's three-year ministry. 54–56

church. In each letter Paul wrote to affirm his representative before the church, to hold up the standard of right doctrine, and to show that right doctrine must result in proper living.

In 1 Timothy Paul directed Timothy to actively oppose false teaching. He also gave instruction on the type of behavior that should characterize those in the church. The letter to Titus shows a similar purpose, albeit briefer in scope. As Paul addressed the character of church members, he presented it in light of the work of Christ. The message in 2 Timothy, Paul's final letter, is quite different. It is much more personal, a letter from one friend to another. Paul was preparing Timothy to carry on the work of ministry after he was gone. Several themes are found in these letters:

The gospel: Paul expressed a concern for the truth of the gospel. The terms that Paul used in describing the gospel in the Pastoral Epistles are not common in his other writings, but they are not unique to these letters. He referred to the gospel as "the faith" (1Tm 3:9; 2Tm 4:7; Ti 1:13); "the truth" (1Tm 4:3; 2Tm 2:25; Ti 1:1); sound or healthy teaching (1Tm 1:10; 2Tm 1:13; 4:3; Ti 1:9; 2:1); and godliness or sound religion (1Tm 3:16; 6:3; Ti 1:1). Paul may have used these terms because they represent the phrases used by his opponents. As he used them, however, he renovated them for his purposes by attaching new meaning to them.

The Christian life: Paul emphasized the importance of a response of holiness to God's act of salvation (1Tm 2:15; 4:12; 5:10; 2Tm 1:9; Ti 2:12). Holiness calls for behavior that is both positive (Ti 3:8) and negative (2Tm 2:19) in emphasis.

Church government: The church is presented as a united family ministering to its constituency and organized for service. The church is the family of God (1Tm 3:5,15), and believers are brothers and sisters (1Tm 4:6; 5:1-2; 6:2; 2Tm 4:21). Paul charged the church with a responsibility to minister to the poor (1Tm 5:16) and to serve as a foundation of doctrinal and ethical truth (1Tm 3:15). Leaders of the church are known as overseers or elders (1Tm 3:1-7; 5:17-19; Ti 1:5-9), and they are assisted by deacons (1Tm 3:8-13).

A.D. 56–62

Paul sends Timothy with the 1 Corinthians letter to the troubled church in Corinth. 56

While ministering in Ephesus, Paul sends Titus to mediate the conflict between Paul and the church at Corinth. 56

Paul comes to Corinth in person and from there he and Timothy write the letter to the Romans. 57

Timothy is with Paul during Paul's first imprisonment in Rome. 60–62

Upon his release from his first imprisonment, Paul goes to Ephesus and appoints Timothy as chief pastor. 62

A.D. 62–67

Paul writes 1 Timothy and Titus. 62–64

Paul commissions Titus to train leaders for the young Christian congregations on Crete. 62–64

Major persecution of the Christians in Rome begins following the great fire. July 18–24, 64

Paul returns to Rome, is arrested, and writes 2 Timothy from the Mamertine Prison. 67 ?

Paul's martyrdom in Rome 67 ?

Contribution to the Bible

These letters are rich theologically and ethically. One of their key contributions is the clear way they show the connection between doctrine and ethics, belief and behavior.

While these letters were not intended to provide a detailed account of church government, they do provide some significant insights on this topic. The lists of characteristics for overseers (1Tm 3:1-7; Ti 1:5-9) and deacons (1Tm 3:8-13) are the only such lists in the NT.

Structure

All three letters follow the typical pattern of a Greek epistle. While there are some lexical differences with many of Paul's other letters, keep in mind that these letters were written to specific individuals. One thing unique to the structure of these letters is the focus on church leadership.

Outline of 1 Timothy

I. Greetings (1:1-2)

II. Introductory Remarks (1:3-20)
   A. The situation at Ephesus (1:3-17)
   B. Charge to Timothy (1:18-20)

III. Worship of the Church (2:1-15)
   A. Prayers (2:1-7)
   B. Conduct of men and women (2:8-15)

IV. Qualifications of Church Leaders (3:1-13)
   A. Overseers (3:1-7)
   B. Deacons (3:8-13)

V. The Minister's Job in Tough Times (3:14–4:16)
   A. Stay focused on the gospel (3:14-16)
   B. Combat false teachings (4:1-5)
   C. Set the example in service (4:6-16)

VI. Duties Toward Others (5:1–6:2)
   A. Relationships with various groups (5:1-2)
   B. Responsibility toward widows (5:3-16)
   C. Instructions for elders (5:17-25)
   D. Instructions for slaves (6:1-2)

VII. Conclusion (6:3-21)
   A. Motives of false teachers (6:3-5)
   B. Warning against materialism (6:6-19)
   C. Final charge to Timothy (6:20-21)

Greeting

1 Paul,[a] an apostle of Christ Jesus by the command[b] of God our Savior[c] and of Christ Jesus our hope:[d]

[2] To Timothy,[e] my true son in the faith.

Grace, mercy, and peace from God the[A] Father and Christ Jesus our Lord.

False Doctrine and Misuse of the Law

[3] As I urged you when I went to Macedonia,[f] remain in Ephesus[g] so that you may instruct certain people[h] not to teach different doctrine [4] or to pay attention to myths[i] and endless genealogies. These promote empty speculations rather than God's plan,[j] which operates by faith. [5] Now the goal of our instruction is love[k] that comes from a pure heart,[l] a good conscience,[m] and a sincere faith.[n] [6] Some have deviated from these and turned aside to fruitless discussion. [7] They want to be teachers of the law, although they don't understand what they are saying or what they are insisting on. [8] But we know that the law is good,[o] provided one uses it legitimately. [9] We know that the law is not meant for a righteous person, but for the lawless and rebellious,[p] for the ungodly and sinful, for the unholy and irreverent, for those who kill their fathers and mothers, for

murderers, [10] for the sexually immoral[q] and homosexuals,[r] for kidnappers,[B] liars,[s] perjurers, and for whatever else is contrary to the sound teaching[t] [11] based on the glorious gospel[u] of the blessed God,[v] which was entrusted to me.[w]

Paul's Testimony

[12] I give thanks to Christ Jesus our Lord who has strengthened[x] me, because He considered me faithful, appointing me to the ministry— [13] one who was formerly a blasphemer,[y] a persecutor,[z] and an arrogant man.[aa] But I received mercy because I acted out of ignorance in unbelief. [14] And the grace of our Lord overflowed, along with the faith and love that are in Christ Jesus. [15] This saying is trustworthy[ab] and deserving of full acceptance: "Christ Jesus came into the world[ac] to save sinners"[ad]—and I am the worst of them.[ae] [16] But I received mercy[af] for this reason, so that in me, the worst of them, Christ Jesus might demonstrate His extraordinary patience[ag] as an example to those who would believe in Him for eternal life.[ah] [17] Now to the King[ai] eternal,[aj] immortal,[ak] invisible, the

[a]1:1 Ac 13:9
[b]Rm 16:26; Ti 1:3
[c]1Tm 2:3; Ti 1:3; 2:10; 3:4; Jd 25
[d]1Co 15:19; Col 1:27; 1Th 1:3; 1Pt 1:3,13
[e]1:2 Ac 16:1; 20:4; 1Co 4:17; 16:10
[f]1:3 Ac 16:9
[g]Eph 1:1
[h]Jd 4
[i]1:4 1Tm 4:7; 2Tm 4:4; Ti 1:14; 2Pt 1:16
[j]Eph 1:10; 3:2,9; Col 1:25
[k]1:5 Rm 13:10
[l]Ps 24:4; 2Tm 2:22; 1Pt 1:22
[m]Ac 23:1; 24:16; Rm 9:1; 2Co 1:12; 1Tm 1:19; 3:9; Heb 10:22; 1Pt 3:21
[n]2Tm 1:5
[o]1:8 Rm 7:12,16
[p]1:9 Ti 1:6,10; Heb 2:8
[q]1:10 1Co 5:9
[r]Gn 19:5; Rm 1:27; 1Co 6:9
[s]Jn 8:44
[t]1Tm 6:3; 2Tm 1:13; Ti 1:9; 2:1
[u]1:11 2Co 4:4
[v]1Tm 6:15
[w]Lv 6:4; Lk 12:48; 1Co 9:17; Gl 2:7; 1Th 2:4; 1Tm 1:11; 6:20; 2Tm 1:12,14;

Ti 1:3   [x]1:12 Ac 9:22; Php 4:13   [y]1:13 Ac 6:11; 2Tm 3:2; 2Pt 2:11   [z]Php 3:6   [aa]1Co 15:8   [ab]1:15 1Tm 3:1; 4:9; 2Tm 2:11; Ti 3:8   [ac]Jn 3:17; 12:46; 18:37; 1Jn 4:9   [ad]Mk 2:17; Lk 19:10; Rm 11:4   [ae]1Co 15:9   [af]1:16 Lk 1:50   [ag]Ex 34:6; Rm 2:4   [ah]Jn 12:25; Ac 13:48   [ai]1:17 Ps 47:7   [aj]Ps 90:2   [ak]1Co 9:25

[A]1:2 Other mss read *our*   [B]1:10 Or *slave traders*

1:1 The fact that this letter clearly claims to be written by **Paul** is an important point. If a person denies that Paul wrote 1 Timothy, this raises significant issues for his view of the reliability of the Scriptures.

1:2 Paul's normal greeting in his letters was **grace** and **peace**. Some interpreters wonder at the addition of **mercy** here, but Paul often introduced topics in the opening of his letters that he would refer to later on. The reference to "mercy" prepares for the discussion of Paul receiving mercy in verses 13,16.

1:3 At least one of Timothy's purposes in **Ephesus** was to address the false teaching that was troubling the church. We are not given enough information to determine exactly what the false teaching was. The concern here is not so much the identity of the false teaching but its effect— "empty speculations" (v. 4) and "fruitless discussion" (v. 6). This is in direct contrast to the goal of apostolic instruction in verse 5.

1:4 **Myths** is a negative term used to characterize something as fanciful or untrue. Thus it is used here (and elsewhere in the Pastoral Epistles; 2Tm 4:4; Ti 1:14) to critique false teaching as the stuff of "fairy tales." **Genealogies** seems to refer to speculative interpretations of the OT.

1:8 There is an important contrast here. The false teachers did not know what they were talking about (v. 7), but Paul and his coworkers (**we**) did know the truth about the law. Many Christians today think of the law as bad, but Paul clearly stated here that **the law is good**. Some have certainly misused the law (as the false teachers did), but the law itself was a gracious gift of God to Israel (Ps 119).

1:9-10 Paul stated that the law is not the basis for Christian living; rather, it works to expose sin. This is similar to his argument in Galatians 5.

1:11 Sound doctrine is what flows out of the **gospel** itself.

1:12 Having just mentioned being entrusted with the gospel (v. 11), Paul gave **thanks** because Christ was willing to appoint him to service in spite of his past sins. Paul marveled that God considered him worthy of His trust, even though he had previously been unbelieving and untrusting (v. 13).

1:13 Paul's **ignorance** was not the reason he had been shown mercy, as if ignorance excused sin or warranted mercy. The point is that his salvation was undeserved. He probably made this point to contrast with the false teachers. When Paul opposed Christ and persecuted the church in the past, he had not yet professed faith. These false teachers professed to follow Christ but still acted to undermine His influence. They were coming dangerously close to being cut off from God's mercy (Mt 12:31-32; Mk 3:28-30; Lk 12:10; 1Jn 5:16).

1:15-16 The designation of certain sayings as **trustworthy** is a particular distinctive of 1 Timothy, 2 Timothy, and Titus. Paul used this designation for emphasis. The apostle's earlier statements may sound as if his salvation was due to his own faithfulness or his ignorance, but these two verses make it clear that Paul marveled at his conversion since he knew himself to be so bad. He was an example of what true instruction was supposed to accomplish. He was the sort of person for whom the law was intended (1Tm 1:9-10). The result of the gospel in his life was not idle speculation but transformation.

only^A God,^a be honor^b and glory^c forever and ever. *Amen.^d

Engage in Battle

^18Timothy, my son, I am giving you this instruction in keeping with the prophecies^e previously made about you, so that by them you may strongly engage in battle, ^19having faith^f and a good conscience.^g Some^h have rejected these and have suffered the shipwreck of their faith. ^20Hymenaeus^i and Alexander^j are among them, and I have delivered them to Satan,^k so that they may be taught not to blaspheme.

Instructions on Prayer

2 First of all, then, I urge that petitions, prayers, intercessions, and thanksgivings be made for everyone, ^2for kings and all those who are in authority,^l so that we may lead a tranquil and quiet life in all godliness^m and dignity.^n ^3This is good, and it pleases God our Savior,^o ^4who wants everyone^p to be saved^q and to come to the knowledge of the truth.^r

^5 For there is one God^s
    and one mediator^t between God
    and humanity,

Christ Jesus, Himself human,^u
^6 who gave Himself—a ransom
    for all,^v
    a testimony at the proper time.

^7For this I was appointed a herald, an apostle^w (I am telling the truth;^B I am not lying), and a teacher of the Gentiles^x in faith and truth.

Instructions to Men and Women

^8Therefore, I want the men in every place to pray, lifting up holy hands without anger or argument.^y ^9Also, the women are to dress themselves in modest clothing,^z with decency and good sense, not with elaborate hairstyles, gold,^aa pearls, or expensive apparel, ^10but with good works,^ab as is proper for women who affirm that they worship God. ^11A woman should learn in silence with full submission.^ac ^12I do not allow a woman to teach or to have authority over a man; instead, she is to be silent. ^13For Adam was created first, then Eve.^ad

a 1:17 Jn 5:44; 1Co 8:6; Eph 4:6; 1Tm 2:5; 6:15; Jd 25
b 2Pt 1:17; Rv 5:12
c Mk 10:37
d Php 4:20; 1Tm 6:16; Rv 22:21
e 1:18 1Co 13:2; 1Tm 4:14; 2Tm 1:6
f 1:19 Eph 3:12; 6:16; Col 1:23; 2:5; 1Th 5:8; 1Tm 3:13; 6:12; 2Tm 4:7; 1Jn 5:4
g Heb 10:22
i 1:20 2Tm 2:17
j 2Tm 4:14
k 1Co 5:5
l 2:2 Ezr 6:10; Rm 13:1; 1Co 2:1
m 2Pt 1:3
n 1Tm 3:4; Ti 2:7
o 2:3 1Tm 1:1
p 2:4 Ti 2:11
q Ezk 18:23,32; Jn 3:17; 1Tm 4:10; Ti 2:11; 2Pt 3:9
r Jn 14:6,17
s 2:5 Dt 6:4; Gl 3:20;
t Heb 8:6
u Jn 1:14; Php 2:7; 3:3; 1Jn

4:2; 5:20 v 2:6 Mt 20:28; Gl 1:4 w 2:7 Eph 3:7-8; 1Tm 1:11; 2Tm 1:11 x Ac 9:15 y 2:8 Mk 7:21; Lk 9:46-47; 24:38; Rm 14:1; Php 2:14 z 2:9 1Pt 3:3 aa Rv 3:18 ab 2:10 2Co 9:8; Gl 3:10 ac 2:11 1Co 14:34; Ti 2:5 ad 2:13 Gn 2:7,22; 3:16; 1Co 11:8-12

---

^A1:17 Other mss add *wise*   ^B2:7 Other mss add *in Christ*

1:18 The point here is that God had spoken through others to set Timothy aside for the task of ministry. The purpose of this assurance of divine call was to strengthen Timothy for the work (see note at 4:14).

1:19 The phrase **shipwreck of their faith** is strong language. It refers to someone who once professed faith but has now destroyed it, showing they were never truly converted.

1:20 **Delivered . . . to Satan** is a typical way of referring to excommunication, or being put out of the church (1Co 5:5). This language highlights the importance and protection of church membership since being put out of the fellowship makes a person more vulnerable to Satan.

2:1 **Petitions, prayers, intercessions, and thanksgivings** are several different terms for prayer. Paul was referring to "all sorts of prayer."

2:4 **Come to the knowledge of the truth** is a way of referring to being converted. "The truth" is often used in 1 and 2 Timothy and Titus as a synonym for the gospel.

2:5-6 These verses provide the theological basis for the preceding statement that God wants people to be saved.

2:8-9 The word **therefore** resumes the call to prayer from verse 1. **Lifting up . . . hands** was a typical posture for prayer in the Bible (Ex 9:29; 1Kg 8:22; Ps 28:2; 63:4; Is 1:15; Lk 24:50). With the words **I want the men . . . also, the women**, Paul addressed specific concerns in regard to each gender.

2:12 The phrase **I do not allow** is not simply a statement of Paul's personal wishes, but the statement of an authoritative position. He wrote with the authority of an apostle (1Th 4:1; 2Th 3:6). When Paul called for the women to be **silent**, he contrasted this with teaching. First Corinthians 11:5 assumes women do speak in the church assembly. This verse prohibits women from providing public teaching for men,

but it does not prevent women from speaking in other circumstances.

2:13 The word **for** introduces the biblical basis for the preceding prohibition in regards to women. The order of creation was more significant in the mind of Paul than it is to most people today (1Co 11:8-9). Rooting the command in the order of creation makes this an abiding command

Bust of Nero, Roman emperor, A.D. 54–68, during whose reign both Paul and Peter were martyred. Paul instructed Timothy to pray "for kings and all those who are in authority" (2:1-2).

¹⁴And Adam was not deceived, but the woman was deceived and transgressed.ᵃ ¹⁵But she will be saved through childbearing, if she continuesᴬ in faith, love, and holiness,ᵇ with good judgment.

Qualifications of Church Leaders

3 This saying is trustworthy:ᴮ·ᶜ "If anyone aspires to be an •overseer,ᵈ he desires a noble work." ²An overseer,ᵉ therefore, must be above reproach, the husband of one wife, self-controlled, sensible,ᶠ respectable, hospitable,ᵍ an able teacher,ᶜ ³not addicted to wine, not a bully but gentle, not quarrelsome, not greedyʰ— ⁴one who manages his own household competently, having his children under control with all dignity. ⁵(If anyone does not know how to manage his own household, how will he take care of God's church?) ⁶He must not be a new convert, or he might become conceited and fall into the condemnation of the Devil.ⁱ ⁷Furthermore, he must have a good reputation among outsiders, so that he does not fall into disgrace and the Devil'sʲ trap.

⁸Deacons,ᵏ likewise, should be worthy of respect, not hypocritical, not drinking a lot of wine, not greedy for money, ⁹holding the •mystery of the faithˡ with a clear conscience.ᵐ ¹⁰And they must also be tested first; if they prove blameless, then they can serve as deacons. ¹¹Wives,ⁿ too, must be worthy of respect, not slanderers, self-controlled,ᵒ faithful in everything. ¹²Deacons must be husbands of one wife, managing their children and their own households competently. ¹³For those who have served well as deacons acquire a good standing for themselves, and great boldness in the faith that is in Christ Jesus.

The Mystery of Godliness

¹⁴I write these things to you, hoping to

Cross references (center column):
ᵃ2:14 Gn 3:6,13; 2Co 11:3;
ᵇ2:15 1Th 3:12–4:10
ᶜ3:1 1Tm 1:15; 4:9
ᵈAc 20:28; Php 1:1; Ti 1:7
ᵉ3:2-4 Ti 1:6-8
ᶠ3:2 Ti 2:2,5
ᵍLv 19:34; 1Pt 4:9; 2Jn 10
ʰ3:3 1Tm 6:10
ⁱ3:6 1Tm 5:12; 2Pt 2:3; Rv 20:1-15
ʲ3:7 Ac 13:10
ᵏ3:8 Php 1:1
ˡ3:9 Php 1:27; 1Tm 1:2,19; Jd 3
ᵐHeb 13:18
ⁿ3:11 1Pt 3:1-6
ᵒTi 2:2

rather than something that held only for Paul's culture and Paul's era. Gender roles are not the result of the fall but are rooted in creation and God's original purposes.

2:14 When Paul declared that **Adam was not deceived**, he did not excuse him for his sin. The point here is not blame but deception. That Adam sinned and bore the primary responsibility for the fall of humanity is clear in Rm 5:12-14.

2:15 This is a difficult verse. Paul did not believe people can earn salvation **through childbearing** or any other means. The verse is probably best understood as an affirmation of roles particular to women in contrast to the role prohibited to them in verses 11-14. People are saved as they persevere in the faith. This persevering is expounded here for women as including noble roles unique to them (such as childbearing).

3:1 The terms **overseer**, "elder," and "pastor" are all used in the NT to refer to the same office. "Overseer" emphasizes the task of watching over the congregation (Heb 13:17).

3:2-7 These verses do not give a job description for the pastor. They describe the character of a person who would serve in this office. The list is not intended to be exhaustive, but it envisions a person of mature Christian character.

3:2 The meaning of **husband of one wife** is widely debated. It probably does not refer to the issue of divorce. It could be a prohibition of polygamy, but most likely it refers to marital faithfulness in general. **An able teacher** is the one requirement in this list that is not necessarily required of all believers. It is also not required of deacons. Thus, it is a distinguishing mark of the pastor (Ti 1:9).

3:4-5 The management of one's own **household** is highlighted by the greater amount of discussion given to it. The home is the proving ground of Christian character. This complements the picture of the church as "God's household" (v. 15).

3:6 The point of this verse is not that **new** believers tend to be more proud, but that quickly elevating a new convert to a leadership position might result in sinful pride.

3:8 Deacons are the other office of the NT church, in addition to the pastor or elder. **Likewise** suggests a link between the lists of qualifications. There are striking similarities between the qualifications for pastor/overseer and for deacons. One key distinction is that deacons are not required to be able to teach.

3:9 The word **mystery** (Gk *musterion*) is a common Pauline word. It refers to the gospel (1Co 2:7; 4:1; 15:51; Col 1:25-26; 2:2; 4:3; Eph 3:4-13).

3:10 The testing described here would presumably be done by the church under the leadership of the overseers.

3:11 The Greek word behind **wives** here can mean "women" or "wives." Context (e.g., v. 2) suggests "wives" is the proper translation choice.

3:12 On **husbands of one wife**, see note at verse 2.

3:13 This verse highlights the value and importance of the office of deacon by stating two results of good service in this role. **Good standing** refers to respect and appreciation from the church toward those who serve the church in this

diakonos

Greek Pronunciation	[dee AH kah nahs]
HCSB Translation	deacon, servant
Uses in 1 Timothy	3
Uses in the NT	29
Focus passage	1 Timothy 3:8,12

Diakonos frequently refers to a *servant* who attends to others' needs. Those responsible for serving a meal (Jn 2:5,9) and the attendants of a king are *servants* (Mt 22:13). The person desiring a position of greatness must become a *servant* (Mk 10:43). One can also serve a spiritual power. False apostles are called *servants* of Satan (2Co 11:15), and Paul is a *servant* of the gospel (Eph 3:7). Governing authorities are *servants* of God, for they dispense justice (Rm 13:4). Elsewhere, *diakonos* retains the idea of *service*, while adopting the more technical sense of a church leadership position (i.e., *deacon*). Paul may use this technical sense when he calls Phoebe a *servant* of the church in Cenchreae (Rm 16:1). In 1Tm 3:8-13, Paul delineates the qualifications for holding the diaconate. Lastly, *diakonos* may refer to a *promoter*. Paul rhetorically asks if Christ is one who *promotes* sin (Gl 2:17).

come^a to you soon. ^{15} But if I should be delayed, I have written so that you will know how people ought to act in God's household,^{b} which is the church of the living God,^{c} the pillar and foundation of the truth.^{d} ^{16} And most certainly, the mystery of godliness^e is great:

> He^A was manifested
> in the flesh,^{f}
> vindicated in the Spirit,^{g}
> seen by angels,
> preached among the nations,
> believed^h on in the world,
> taken up in glory.^{i}

Demonic Influence

4 Now the Spirit^j explicitly says that in later times^k some will depart from the faith,^{l} paying attention to deceitful spirits^m and the teachings of demons,^{n} ^{2} through the hypocrisy^o of liars whose consciences^p are seared. ^{3} They forbid marriage^q and demand abstinence^r from foods that God created^s to be received with gratitude by those who believe and know the truth. ^{4} For everything created by God is good,^{t} and nothing should be rejected if it is received with thanksgiving,^{u} ^{5} since it is sanctified by the word of God^v and by prayer.

A Good Servant of Jesus Christ

^{6} If you point these things out to the •brothers, you will be a good servant of Christ Jesus, nourished by the words of the faith^w and the good teaching that you have followed.^{x} ^{7} But have nothing to do with irreverent and silly myths.^{y} Rather, train yourself in godliness,^{z} ^{8} for

the training of the body has
a limited benefit,^{aa}
but godliness is beneficial in every way,
since it holds promise
for the present life
and also for the life to come.^{ab}

^{9} This saying is trustworthy and deserves full acceptance.^{ac} ^{10} In fact, we labor and strive^B for this, because we have put our hope in the living God,^{ad} who is the Savior^{ae} of everyone,^{af} especially of those who believe.

Instructions for Ministry

^{11} Command and teach these things. ^{12} Let no one despise your youth; instead, you should be an example to the believers in speech,^{ag} in conduct,^{ah} in love,^{C,ai} in faith, in purity.^{aj} ^{13} Until I come,^{ak} give your attention to public reading, exhortation, and teaching. ^{14} Do not neglect the gift that is in you; it was given to you through prophecy,^{al} with the laying on of hands^{am} by the council of elders. ^{15} Practice these things; be committed to them, so that your progress may be evident to all. ^{16} Pay close attention to your life and your teaching; persevere in these things, for by doing this you will save^{an} both yourself and your hearers.^{ao}

5 Do not rebuke an older man, but exhort him as a father, younger men as brothers, ^{2} older women as mothers, and with all propriety, the younger women as sisters.

^{a}3:14 1Tm 4:13
^{b}3:15 1Co 3:16; 2Co 6:16; Eph 2:21-22; 1Pt 2:5; 4:17
^{c}Mt 16:16; 1Tm 4:10
^{d}Ps 119:142; 2Co 11:10; 2Th 2:10
^{e}3:16 2Pt 1:3
^{f}Jn 1:14; Php 2:7; 1Jn 4:2; 5:20
^{g}Rm 1:3-4; 2:28-29; 7:5-6; 8:4; 1Co 5:5; 6:16-17; Gl 3:3; 4:29; 5:16-24; 6:8; Php 3:3; Col 2:5; Rv 1:10
^{h}Mt 11:24; Jn 3:16; Ac 10:43; Rm 10:9; 1Pt 1:8-10
^{i}Mk 16:19; Jn 20:17; 1Pt 3:22
^{j}4:1 Jn 14:17; 16:13; Ac 20:23; 21:11; 1Co 2:10-11
^{k}2Th 2:3-9; 2Tm 3:1; 2Pt 3:3; Jd 18
^{l}Php 1:27; 1Tm 1:2; Jd 3
^{m}Mt 7:15; 1Jn 4:6
^{n}Jms 3:15
^{o}4:2 Mk 12:15
^{p}Heb 13:18
^{q}4:3 1Tm 5:14; Heb 13:4
^{r}Rm 14:6; Col 2:16,23; 1Th 4:3; 5:22; 1Pt 2:11
^{s}Gn 1:29; 9:3
^{t}4:4 Gn 1:31
^{u}Ac 10:15
^{v}4:5 Lk 8:21; 1Tm 2:1; Heb 4:12
^{w}4:6 Php 1:27; 1Tm 1:2; Jd 3
^{x}2Tm 3:10-15
^{y}4:7 1Tm 1:4;

^{aa}4:8 Col 2:23
^{ab}Ps 37:9,11; Pr 19:23; 22:4; Mt 6:33; Mk 10:30; Jn 12:25; Ac 13:48; 1Pt 3:9
^{ac}4:9 1Tm 1:15; 3:1; 2Tm 2:11
^{ad}4:10 Dt 5:26; Jos 3:10; 1Sm 17:26; Ps 42:2; Jr 10:10; Dn 6:20; Ac 14:15; 1Tm 3:15
^{ae}1Tm 1:1
^{af}1Tm 2:4; Ti 2:11
^{ag}4:12 Pr 12:6
^{ah}2Pt 3:11
^{ai}1Co 13:1
^{aj}1Tm 5:2
^{ak}4:13 1Tm 3:14
^{al}4:14 1Co 13:2; 1Tm 1:18; 2Tm 1:6
^{am}1Tm 5:22
^{an}4:16 Eph 2:8; Jd 23
^{ao}Ezk 33:9; Ac 20:28; Rm 11:14

---

^{A}3:16 Other mss read *God* ^{B}4:10 Other mss read *and suffer reproach* ^{C}4:12 Other mss add *in spirit*

---

way. **Great boldness** probably refers to the increase in confidence in the faith that comes from serving and seeing the truths of the gospel proven in ministry.

3:15 This is a significant verse in the letter. It states Paul's reason for writing and provides a threefold description of the church's identity and mission. **Household** refers to the church as God's family with reference to the governing of the family. The phrase **church of the living God** highlights the church as the gathering where God most clearly shows His presence. The church as **the pillar and foundation of the truth** means that God has entrusted to the church the task of promoting and protecting the gospel.

3:16 Again, the word **mystery** refers to the gospel (v. 9). This verse contains a poetic exposition of the gospel.

4:1 Just how the **Spirit explicitly says** is not made clear here. It is probably a reference to a prophecy (perhaps Paul's prediction in Ac 20:29-30). The **later times** in view here included Timothy's day. The last days are considered to have begun with the work of Christ.

4:10 The statement that Jesus is the **Savior of everyone, especially of those who believe** may seem to teach universalism, the belief that every person will eventually go to heaven regardless of whether they accept Christ. But the rest of Scripture clearly denies this idea. The Greek word translated here as "especially" expresses the sense of "particularly." The point is not that Jesus saves everybody and then saves believers even more. Rather, Jesus is the Savior for all—all who believe. Further, "everyone" pictures the transnational scope of the gospel. Thus Christ is the "Savior" of people from every race and nation.

4:13 Public reading refers to the reading of Scripture in corporate worship (Ac 13:15; 2Co 3:14).

4:14 Gift probably refers to Timothy's calling and gifting for ministry indicated by God (**through prophecy**) and recognized by the church (laying on of hands by the **elders**).

4:15 These things that Paul called on Timothy to **practice** and **be committed to** are the things commanded in verses 12-13. These encompassed his behavior and teaching.

5:1-2 The church is described in these verses in family terms (3:4-5,15). Verse 1 does not prohibit the correcting of older men but speaks of the respectful manner in which this should be done.

The Support of Widows

[3]Support[A] widows[a] who are genuinely widows. [4]But if any widow has children or grandchildren, they must learn to practice godliness toward their own family first and to repay their parents, for this pleases God. [5]The real widow, left all alone, has put her hope in God[b] and continues night and day in her petitions and prayers; [6]however, she who is self-indulgent is dead even while she lives.[c] [7]Command this also, so they won't be blamed. [8]But if anyone does not provide[d] for his own, that is his own household, he has denied the faith[e] and is worse than an unbeliever.

[9]No widow should be placed on the official support list[B] unless she is at least 60 years old, has been the wife of one husband, [10]and is well known for good works[f]—that is, if she has brought up children, shown hospitality,[g] washed the 'saints' feet,[h] helped the afflicted,[i] and devoted herself to every good work.[j] [11]But refuse to enroll younger widows, for when they are drawn away from Christ by desire, they want to marry[k] [12]and will therefore receive condemnation[l] because they have renounced their original pledge. [13]At the same time, they also learn to be idle, going from house to house; they are not only idle, but are

also gossips[m] and busybodies, saying things they shouldn't say. [14]Therefore, I want younger women to marry,[n] have children, manage their households, and give the adversary no opportunity to accuse us.[o] [15]For some have already turned away[p] to follow Satan. [16]If any[c] believing woman has widows in her family, she should help them, and the church should not be burdened, so that it can help those who are genuinely widows.

Honoring the Elders

[17]The elders who are good leaders should be considered worthy of an ample honorarium,[D] especially those who work hard[q] at preaching and teaching. [18]For the Scripture says:

**Do not muzzle an ox
while it is treading out the grain,[E,r]**
and,
the worker is worthy of his wages.[s]

[19]Don't accept an accusation against an elder unless it is supported by two or three witnesses.[t] [20]Publicly rebuke those who sin, so that the rest will also be afraid. [21]I solemnly charge you before God and Christ Jesus and the elect angels to observe[u] these things without prejudice, doing nothing out of favoritism.

Cross references (center column)

[a]5:3 Ex 22:22; Jms 1:27
[b]5:5 1Co 7:34
[c]5:6 Lk 15:24; Eph 2:1,5; 5:14; Rv 3:1
[d]5:8 Rm 12:17; 2Co 8:21
[e]Mt 10:33; Php 1:27; 1Tm 1:2; 2Pt 2:1; Jd 4; Rv 2:13
[f]5:10 Mk 14:6; 2Co 9:8; Gl 3:10; Jms 2:14-26
[g]2Jn 10
[h]Lk 7:44; Jn 13:5-14
[i]Heb 11:37
[j]2Co 9:8
[k]5:11 1Tm 5:14
[l]5:12 Mk 12:40
[m]5:13 Pr 17:9; 3Jn 10
[n]5:14 Gn 2:18-25; 1Co 7:9-10; 1Tm 4:3; 5:11
[o]Ti 2:4-5
[p]5:15 Heb 12:13
[q]5:17 1Th 5:12
[r]5:18 Dt 25:4; 1Co 9:9
[s]Lv 19:13; Dt 24:14-15; Mt 10:10; Lk 10:7; 1Co 9:4-14; 2Pt 2:13
[t]5:19 Dt 19:15
[u]5:21 Lk 11:28

[A]5:3 Lit Honor   [B]5:9 Lit be enrolled   [C]5:16 Other mss add believing man or   [D]5:17 Or of respect and remuneration; lit of double honor   [E]5:18 Dt 25:4

5:8 The strong language in this verse indicates that provision for one's **own household** is a spiritual responsibility.

5:9 The phrase **wife of one husband** probably refers to marital faithfulness (see note at 3:2). If it forbids remarriage after the death of a husband (which seems unlikely), then Paul's advice in verse 14 would make those women ineligible.

5:10 This list (along with the last phrase of the previous verse) reviews the deeds of godly older women. These are examples to which younger women should aspire.

5:12-16 The issue in these verses is either that these **widows** who were being supported by the church had pledged to remain unmarried or that these **younger widows** might be tempted by their desires to marry unbelievers, thus turning away from the faith. Since these concerns were prompted by the fact that **some have already turned away to follow Satan**, Paul must have seen this as an important matter. It seems likely that his concern was over remarriage to an unbeliever, with the wife adopting the religion of her husband, as was a common custom in that era.

5:17 The phrase **good leaders** can also be translated as "those who rule well." The role of elder (pastor) involved authority, particularly in **preaching and teaching**. These elders were to be **considered worthy** of "double honor." The exact identify of this double honor is not clear, but plainly extra respect is due those who work hard in leading the church through preaching and teaching.

5:18 The command **not** to **muzzle an ox** is a quote from Dt 25:4. An owner was commanded to allow his ox to eat of the grain it was grinding. The idea is that a person who works for something should be able to benefit from it. **The worker is worthy of his wages** is a direct quote from Lk 10:7. This indicates that Paul was already referring to the recorded statements of Jesus as authoritative Scripture.

5:20 The people to be **publicly** rebuked were elders who sinned. **The rest** who would fear to sin as a result of this rebuke included the rest of the elders and probably the rest of the congregation as well.

---

soter

Greek Pronunciation	[soh TAYR]
HCSB Translation	Savior
Uses in 1 Timothy	3
Uses in the NT	24
Focus passage	1 Timothy 4:10

Outside the NT, the title soter (savior, deliverer) was applied to deserving men, leading officials, rulers, or deities (e.g., of Roman emperors Julius Caesar, Nero, and Vespasian). The term had connotations of "protector," "deliverer," "preserver," or "savior." In the NT, soter refers exclusively to Jesus Christ and to God the Father, with a focus on their saving, delivering character as expressed through their actions. As Savior, Christ grants repentance and forgiveness of sin (Ac 5:31), protects and saves the church (Eph 5:23), will come again to deliver His people from this world (Php 3:20), has made possible the outpouring of the Spirit (Ti 3:6), has abolished death (2Tm 1:10), and has authority in His kingdom (2Pt 1:11). God is "the Savior of everyone, especially of those who believe" (1Tm 4:10), and "wants everyone to be saved" (1Tm 2:4). He manifested His love in His saving acts toward the church (Ti 3:4), He poured out the Holy Spirit (Ti 3:6), and He deserves praise and adoration (Jd 25).

22 Don't be too quick to appoint[A,a] anyone as an elder, and don't share in the sins of others. Keep yourself pure.[b] **23** Don't continue drinking only water, but use a little wine because of your stomach and your frequent illnesses. **24** Some people's sins are obvious, going before them to judgment,[c] but the sins of others surface[B] later. **25** Likewise, good works are obvious, and those that are not obvious cannot remain hidden.

Honoring Masters

6 All who are under the yoke as •slaves must regard their own masters[c] to be worthy of all respect, so that God's name[d] and His teaching will not be blasphemed. **2** Those who have believing masters should not be disrespectful to them because they are •brothers, but should serve them better, since those who benefit from their service are believers and dearly loved.[e]

False Doctrine and Human Greed

Teach and encourage these things. **3** If anyone teaches other doctrine and does not agree with the sound teaching of our Lord[f] Jesus Christ and with the teaching that promotes godliness,[g] **4** he is conceited, understanding nothing, but has a sick interest in disputes and arguments over words.[h] From these come envy,[i] quarreling,[j] slander,[k] evil suspicions, **5** and constant disagreement among people whose minds are depraved and deprived of the truth, who imagine that godliness[D] is a way to material gain.[E,l] **6** But godliness with contentment is a great gain.[m]

7 For we brought nothing into the world, and[F] we can take nothing out.[n] **8** But if we have food and clothing,[G] we will be content with these.

9 But those who want to be rich fall into temptation, a trap, and many foolish and harmful desires, which plunge people into ruin and destruction. **10** For the love of money is a root[H] of all kinds of evil, and by craving it, some have wandered away from the faith[o] and pierced themselves with many pains.

Fight the Good Fight

11 But you, man of God, run
     from these things,
     and pursue righteousness,
       godliness, faith,
     love,[p] endurance,[q] and gentleness.
12 Fight the good fight[r] for the faith;
     take hold of eternal life[s]
     that you were called to
     and have made a good confession about
     in the presence of many witnesses.

13 In the presence of God, who gives life to all,[t] and of Christ Jesus, who gave a good confession before Pontius •Pilate,[u] I charge you **14** to keep the command without fault or failure until the appearing[v] of our Lord[w] Jesus Christ. **15** God will bring this about in His own time.[x] He is

     the blessed and only[y] Sovereign,
     the King of kings,[z]
     and the Lord of lords,[aa]
16   the only One who has immortality,

Cross-references (center column):

a5:22 Ex 29:10; Lv 4:15; Lk 4:40; Ac 6:6; 28:8; 1Tm 4:14; Heb 6:2
b Php 4:8
c5:24 Mt 12:41; Jn 5:22-30; Heb 9:27
d6:1 Jn 10:25; Ac 15:14; Rv 14:1
e6:2 2Th 2:12; 1Jn 4:16
f6:3 Rv 11:8
g2Pt 1:3
h6:4 2Tm 2:14,23; Ti 3:9
i Ps 37:1
j Ti 3:9
k Rv 13:6
l6:5 Eph 4:22; 2Tm 3:8; Ti 1:11,15
m6:6 Ps 37:16; Pr 15:16; 16:8; Php 4:11; Heb 13:5
n6:7 Jb 1:21; Ps 49:17; Ec 5:15
o6:10 Php 1:27; 1Tm 1:2; Jd 3
p6:11 1Co 13:1
q Rv 13:10
r6:12 2Tm 4:7; Jd 3
s1Jn 5:12
t6:13 Mk 13:19; Rm 1:25
u Mt 27:11-14
v6:14 Ti 2:13; 1Jn 2:28
w Rv 11:8
x6:15 Lk 21:8
y Rm 16:27
z Rv 17:14
aa Dt 10:17; Ps 136:2-3; Rv 17:14; 19:16

A5:22 Lit *to lay hands on* = to ordain   B5:24 Lit *follow*   C6:1 Or *owners*   D6:5 Referring to religion as a means of financial gain E6:5 Other mss add *From such people withdraw yourself.*   F6:7 Other mss add *it is clear that*   G6:8 Or *food and shelter*   H6:10 Or *is the root*

5:23 How this verse connects to the rest of the paragraph is not clear. It appears to be a qualification to the call for purity in verses 22 and 24, clarifying that there would be nothing wrong with Timothy using **a little wine**.

5:24-25 After the aside of verse 23, Paul returned to the issue of appointing elders to serve the church. These verses illustrate why it is wise to be patient and thorough in assessing potential elders.

6:2 The chief motive for service, even for a person who is a slave, is love.

6:9-10 What is condemned here is **harmful desires**, not the possession of things. The warning is not simply that **love of money** can be harmful, but that this **craving** has led some people to deny the faith and show themselves to be unbelievers.

6:11-12 Fleeing sin is paired with chasing down virtue. The picture is of a vigorous pursuit of virtue. This corresponds to the call to **fight . . . for the faith** and to **take hold of eternal life**.

6:13 The appearance of **Pontius Pilate** here may seem odd.

epiphaneia

Greek Pronunciation	[epih FAH nay ah]
HCSB Translation	appearing
Uses in 1 Timothy	1
Uses in the NT	6
Focus passage	1 Timothy 6:14

Outside of the NT, the term *epiphaneia* (appearing, manifestation) was often used as a religious technical term to denote the visible *manifestation* of a deity. This divine *manifestation* occurred either in the form of a personal appearance or by some work of power. Within the NT, *epiphaneia* appears exclusively in Pauline literature. Paul employs this religious technical sense of the word to refer to the *appearing* or *manifestation* of Jesus Christ. This *appearing* of Jesus can refer to His first coming to earth (2Tm 1:10). More frequently, however, Paul refers to the second *appearing* of Jesus, at which time He will come to destroy the antichrist and dispense righteous judgment (2Th 2:8; 2Tm 4:1,8). It is this second *appearing* of the Lord Jesus that is the "blessed hope" of the believer (Ti 2:13).

dwelling in unapproachable light;[a] no one has seen or can see Him,[b] to Him be honor and eternal might.[c] *Amen.[d]

Instructions to the Rich

[17]Instruct those who are rich in the present age not to be arrogant[e] or to set their hope on the uncertainty of wealth, but on God,[A] who richly provides us with all things[f] to enjoy. [18]Instruct them to do what is good, to be rich in good works,[g] to be generous, willing to share,[h] [19]storing up for themselves a good

reserve[B] for the age to come,[i] so that they may take hold of life that is real.

Guard the Heritage

[20]Timothy, guard what has been entrusted to you,[j] avoiding[k] irreverent, empty speech and contradictions from the "knowledge" that falsely bears that name.[l] [21]By professing it, some[m] people have deviated from the faith.[n] Grace be with all of you.

[a]6:16 Ps 36:9; 104:2; Jn 12:46 [b]Ex 33:20; Jn 1:18 [c]Jd 25 [d]1Tm 1:17; Rv 22:21 [e]6:17 1Sm 2:3; Ec 7:8; Rm 11:20; 12:16 [f]Ac 17:25 [g]6:18 Mk 14:6; Gl 3:10; Jms 2:14-26; 1Pt 2:12 [h]Rm 12:8,13; Eph 4:28 [i]6:19 Mt 6:20 [j]6:20 1Tm 1:11;

[j]2Tm 1:12,14; Ti 1:3 [k]Heb 12:13 [l]Col 2:8; 2Tm 2:16; 4:4; Ti 1:14 [m]6:21 2Tm 2:18 [n]Php 1:27; 1Tm 1:2

[A]6:17 Other mss read *on the living God*   [B]6:19 Or *foundation*

He appears as a backdrop for Jesus' **good confession**, which is the model for the "good confession" of believers (v. 12).

6:20 The phrase **what has been entrusted to you** refers to the gospel. The **knowledge that falsely bears that name** refers to the false teaching addressed elsewhere in the letter.

The magnificent theater in Ephesus had a seating capacity of 25,000. It was first constructed during the reign of Lysimachus, one of Alexander the Great's generals who succeeded him. It was enlarged during the Roman period. Paul's life was endangered by a riot in this theater. This theater bears witness to the wealth of Ephesus during the years that Paul planted the church there. Paul had left Timothy as pastor of the church at Ephesus. In this first letter to Timothy, Paul charges Timothy to "instruct those who are rich in the present age not to be arrogant or to set their hope on the uncertainty of wealth but on God, who richly provides us with all things to enjoy" (6:17).

2 Timothy

Introduction

See the Introduction to the Pastoral Epistles before 1 Timothy.

Outline of 2 Timothy

Interior of the Mamertine Prison in Rome. The stairs descend to a lower level called the Tullianum. According to tradition, this is the site where Paul may have been imprisoned in the weeks preceding his death. From here Paul would have written 2 Timothy.

Greeting

1 Paul,[a] an apostle of Christ Jesus by God's will,[b] for the promise of life[c] in Christ Jesus:

[2] To Timothy, my dearly loved son.

Grace, mercy, and peace[d] from God the Father and Christ Jesus our Lord.

Thanksgiving

[3] I thank God, whom I serve with a clear conscience[e] as my ancestors did, when I constantly remember you in my prayers night and day.[f] [4] Remembering your tears, I long to see you so that I may be filled with joy, [5] clearly recalling your sincere faith[g] that first lived in your grandmother Lois, then in your mother Eunice,[h] and that I am convinced is in you also.

[6] Therefore, I remind you to keep ablaze[A] the gift of God that is in you through the laying on of my hands.[i] [7] For God has not given us a spirit[B] of fearfulness,[j] but one of power,[k] love,[l] and sound judgment.

Not Ashamed of the Gospel

[8] So don't be ashamed[m] of the testimony about our Lord,[n] or of me His prisoner.[o] Instead, share in suffering for the gospel, relying on the power[p] of God.

[9] He has saved us and called us
with a holy calling,[q]
not according to our works,[r]
but according to His own purpose[s]
and grace,
which was given to us in Christ Jesus
before time began.
[10] This has now been made evident
through the appearing[t] of our Savior
Christ Jesus,
who has abolished death[u]
and has brought life[v] and immortality
to light
through the gospel.

[11] For this gospel I was appointed[w] a herald, apostle, and teacher,[C] [12] and that is why I suffer[x] these things. But I am not ashamed, because I know the One I have believed in and am persuaded that He is able to guard what has been entrusted to me[D,y] until that day.[z]

Be Loyal to the Faith

[13] Hold on to the pattern of sound teaching[aa] that you have heard from me,[ab] in the faith and love that are in Christ Jesus. [14] Guard, through

Cross references

[a]1:1 Ac 13:9
[b]1Co 1:1; Eph 1:1; Col 1:1
[c]1Jn 2:25; 5:12
[d]1:2 1Tm 1:2; 2Jn 3
[e]1:3 Ac 23:1; 24:16; Rm 9:1; 2Co 1:12; 1Tm 1:19; 3:9; Heb 10:22; 1Pt 3:21
[f]Eph 1:6
[g]1:5 1Tm 1:5
[h]Ac 16:1
[i]1:6 1Tm 4:14; 5:22
[j]1:7 Jn 7:13; 14:27; Rm 8:15
[k]Lk 1:35; 4:14; 24:49; Ac 1:8; 4:33; Rm 15:13,19; 1Co 2:4; Eph 3:16,20; 1Th 1:5
[l]1Co 13:1
[m]1:8 Mk 8:38; Rm 1:16; 2Tm 1:12,16
[n]Ac 4:33; 1Co 1:6; Rv 1:2,9; 12:17; 19:10; 20:4
[o]Eph 3:1; 4:1; Phm 1,9
[p]Lk 1:35; 2Co 13:4
[q]1:9 Rm 8:28; 11:14,29; Heb 3:1
[r]Eph 2:9
[s]Pr 19:21; Is 42:6; 46:10; Ac 2:23; 4:28;
[t]1:10 Lk 21:8; 2Tm 4:1; 1Jn 2:28
[u]Jn 8:51; Php 3:10
[v]1Jn 5:12
[w]1:11 1Tm 2:7
[x]1:12 Php 1:29; 2Tm 2:9
[y]1Tm 1:11; 6:20; Ti 1:3
[z]Php 1:6; 2Tm 4:8
[aa]1:13 1Tm 1:10; 6:3; Ti 1:9; 2:1
[ab]2Tm 2:2; 3:14

[A]1:6 Or to rekindle   [B]1:7 Or us the Spirit   [C]1:11 Other mss add of the Gentiles   [D]1:12 Or guard what I have entrusted to Him, or guard my deposit

---

1:1 As Paul wrote, awaiting death, he reminded Timothy that the purpose of his apostleship had been to proclaim the gospel, **the promise of life**.

1:3-5 Paul and Timothy both had a heritage of faith. When Paul said he prayed for Timothy continually **night and day**, he used a common expression for continual prayer. Timothy was on his mind and in his prayers throughout each day.

1:6 The phrase **keep ablaze the gift of God** did not mean that Timothy had "let the fire go out." It was a call to action lest sluggishness set in. On "gift of God," see note at 1Tm 4:14. The **laying on of . . . hands** probably refers to Timothy's ordination (1Tm 4:14). This passage focuses on Paul's part in the event while 1Tm 4:14 focuses on the involvement of the full group of elders.

1:7 Spirit here probably refers to the Holy Spirit. The Greek word translated **fearfulness** is used in extrabiblical literature to refer to a person who fled from battle. It is a strong term for cowardice. Boldness, not cowardice, is a mark of the Holy Spirit (Pr 28:1; Ac 4:31).

1:9-10 These verses summarize the gospel for which believers suffer. They serve as a reminder of the power of God on whom we rely. The use of exalted language suggests that Paul was also arguing that so glorious a message was worth suffering for.

1:12 The phrase **these things** refers to Paul's imprisonment and impending death. He was confident that God would protect either the gospel (**what has been entrusted to me**) or his own soul ("what I have entrusted to Him"; lit "my entrustment"). Either way, it was this confidence in

God that prevented Paul from being **ashamed**. His boldness came not from self-confidence but from God-confidence.

1:14 That good thing entrusted to you was the gospel.

1:15 Asia was the name of the Roman province in which Ephesus was located. Key people who could have supported Paul had failed to do so. We know nothing about **Phygelus** and **Hermogenes**. This highlights the bleak situation in

aphtharsia

Greek Pronunciation	[ahf thahr SEE ah]
HCSB Translation	immortality
Uses in 2 Timothy	1
Uses in the NT	7
Focus passage	2 Timothy 1:10

The apostle Paul uses *aphtharsia* (incorruption, immortality) in reference to two concepts: physical state and temporal aspect. With respect to physical state, *aphtharsia* refers to the state of not being subject to perishing or decay (i.e., *incorruption*). For example, in 1Co 15, Paul uses *aphtharsia* four times to refer to the resurrection body. So, the Christian's corruptible, earthly body will be changed into *incorruption* (i.e., the state of being imperishable) through resurrection from the dead (1Co 15:42,50,53-54). Naturally, that which is *incorruptible* is also *immortal*. The relationship of these two concepts provides the bridge to the temporal aspect of *aphtharsia*, in which the term refers to a continuous state or process (*immortality*). Christ Jesus abolished death and brought life and *immortality* (i.e., continuous life) to light through the gospel (2Tm 1:10).

the Holy Spirit who lives in us, that good thing entrusted to you. [15]This you know: All those in •Asia[a] have turned away from me,[b] including Phygelus and Hermogenes. [16]May the Lord grant mercy[c] to the household of Onesiphorus,[d] because he often refreshed me[e] and was not ashamed of my chains.[f] [17]On the contrary, when he was in Rome,[g] he diligently searched for me and found me. [18]May the Lord grant that he obtain mercy[h] from Him on that day.

And you know very well how much he ministered at Ephesus.[i]

Be Strong in Grace

2 You, therefore, my son, be strong in the grace[j] that is in Christ Jesus. [2]And what you have heard from me[k] in the presence of many witnesses, commit to faithful[l] men who will be able to teach others also.

a 1:15 Ac 6:9; 16:6
b 2Tm 4:10-16
c 1:16 Lk 1:50
d 2Tm 4:19
e Phm 7,20
f Ac 16:26; 20:23; 21:33; 23:29; 26:29; Eph 6:20; Phm 10
g 1:17 Rm 1:7
h 1:18 Lk 1:50
i Eph 1:1
j 2:1 Gl 1:6; 2Pt 3:18
k 2:2 2Tm 1:13 l Nm 12:7

which Paul found himself. Perhaps this is one reason why Timothy, the faithful one, was such a source of joy for Paul at this time.

1:16-18 Onesiphorus was also an example of faithfulness, in contrast to those who had abandoned Paul. Verse 18 is

an expression of Paul's desire that Onesiphorus persevere, continuing in faithfulness, not being pulled away by the false ways of others.

2:1 This verse is a continuation of the call to Spirit-empowered boldness which began in 1:6.

The Bible and Women

Mary A. Kassian

The Bible highly esteems women. It teaches that they are co-bearers of the image of God—that He crowned them with honor and glory, and gave them charge to exercise dominion over the earth. Women, along with men, have the enormous dignity, privilege, and responsibility to put the glory of God on display (Is 43:6-7). The Bible highly esteems women, but unfortunately, women do not always highly esteem the Bible. Some disregard it—they are apathetic and lackadaisical, unwilling to exert the effort to sharpen their Bible study habits, and unconcerned about applying the word of God to their lives. Others disrespect it—they think that they have the right to choose which parts are or are not applicable to women today. Others deride it—claiming that since the writers were exclusively men, Scripture is flawed and insufficient for women. The tendency for women to disrespect and deride the Bible is particularly prevalent in our post-feminist society, even amongst those who claim to follow Christ.

Two women who had an enormous respect for the Bible were Eunice and Lois, Timothy's mother and grandmother. Paul credits them with Timothy's conversion (2Tm 1:5). He also credits them with carefully teaching Timothy Scripture and doctrine. Timothy's father was not a believer, so he didn't contribute to Timothy's spiritual training (Ac 16:1). It was Eunice and Lois that acquainted Timothy with "the sacred Scriptures," taught him what they meant, instructed him in the ways of the Lord, and ensured that he received instruction for salvation through faith in Christ Jesus (2Tm 3:14-15).

Paul reminds Timothy about his mother's and grandmother's attitude toward Scripture and their skill in studying, understanding, and applying it. He wrote the well-known verses about all Scripture being inspired by God and "profitable for teaching, for rebuking, for correcting, for training in righteousness," to make us competent and equipped for every good work, in the context of the outstanding job that Eunice and Lois did equipping Timothy (2Tm 3:14-17). These two women did not disregard, disrespect, or deride the Bible. They held it in highest esteem.

In order to influence for Christ those who are in our relational sphere, women need to have the same regard for Scripture that Eunice and Lois had. We need to be students of the Bible and diligently study it, so we can correctly teach the word of truth (2Tm 2:15). "Correctly teaching" (Gk *orthotomounta*; "cutting straight, holding a straight course, doing right, rightly dividing") suggests the imagery of a farmer cutting a straight furrow, a builder cutting a stone, or a tentmaker cutting the cloth. Precise, faultless workmanship is indicated. Women have a responsibility to develop their ability to handle Scripture correctly. Those who fail to do this are susceptible to error (2Tm 3:6). Women who highly esteem the Bible and have a good grasp of doctrine will be able to "teach what is good" and will have a tremendous impact in mentoring their children and friends in the ways of the Lord (Ti 2:3-4).

³Share in suffering as a good soldier of Christ Jesus.ᵃ ⁴No one serving as a soldier gets entangled in the concerns of civilian life; he seeks to please the recruiter. ⁵Also, if anyone competes as an athlete, he is not crowned unless he competes according to the rules. ⁶The hardworking farmer ought to be the first to get a share of the crops.ᵇ ⁷Consider what I say, for the Lord will give you understanding in everything.

⁸Keep your attention on Jesus Christ as risen from the deadᶜ and descended from David. This is according to my gospel. ⁹I suffer for it to the point of being bound like a criminal, but God's message is not bound. ¹⁰This is why I endureᵈ all things for the elect:ᵉ so that they also may obtain salvation, which is in Christ Jesus, with eternal glory.ᶠ ¹¹This saying is trustworthy:ᵍ

For if we have died with Him,ʰ
    we will also live with Him;
¹² if we endure,
    we will also reignⁱ with Him;
    if we deny Him, He will also deny us;
¹³ if we are faithless, He remains faithful,
    for He cannot deny Himself.

An Approved Worker

¹⁴Remind them of these things, charging them before GodᴬAnd to fight about words;ʲ this is in no way profitable and leads to the ruin of the hearers. ¹⁵Be diligent to present yourself approved to God, a worker who doesn't need to be ashamed, correctly teaching the word of truth.ᵏ ¹⁶But avoid irreverent, empty speech, for this will produce an even greater measure of godlessness.ˡ ¹⁷And their word will spread like gangrene; Hymenaeusᵐ and Philetus are

---

Cross-references (center column):

ᵃ2:3 1Tm 1:18
ᵇ2:6 1Co 9:10
ᶜ2:8 Mt 17:9; Jn 21:14
ᵈ2:10 Jms 1:12
ᵉMt 24:22
ᶠLk 9:32; 24:26; Jn 17:24; 2Co 3:18; 1Pt 5:1,4; 2Pt 3:18
ᵍ2:11 1Tm 1:15; 3:1; 4:9; Ti 3:8
ʰJn 8:51
ⁱ2:12 Rv 20:4
ʲ2:14 1Tm 6:4
ᵏ2:15 Eph 1:13; Col 1:5; Jms 1:18
ˡ2:16 Jd 18
ᵐ2:17 1Tm 1:20

ᴬ2:14 Other mss read *before the Lord*

2:4-6 In these three analogies, Paul expounded the call to service and suffering. Verse 4 calls for single-minded desire to please God. Verse 5 declares that a person must obey God's rules in order to succeed. Verse 6 encourages hard work by holding out the promise of blessing.

2:7 This verse is a call to contemplation of what has been written, not a promise of complete knowledge or **understanding**.

2:8 The phrase **descended from David** is a reminder of Jesus' messianic credentials.

2:11-13 The **trustworthy** statement moves from comfort to challenge and back to comfort. Verse 12 is a clear statement on the necessity of perseverance. As Jesus said, only the person who endures will be saved (Mt 10:22). Verse 13 is a reminder of God's preserving power and faithfulness. In this context, to **deny Him** envisions a more serious offense than being **faithless**. To "deny Him" envisions apostasy, whereas "faithless" refers to a lapse in trust, which is something every believer does at some point.

2:14 It is clear that Paul was willing to confront people when the gospel was at stake. For example, he opposed Peter to his face (Gl 2:11). What he had in mind here was meaningless argument.

Interior of the Mamertine Prison. This second imprisonment was far more severe than the house arrest Paul experienced when he first came to Rome (Ac 28:30-31). Some of his friends deserted him at this time (2Tm 4:10). Onesiphorus was not ashamed of Paul's chains. He searched him out, came to the prison, and ministered to Paul (1:13-18).

among them. [18] They have deviated from the truth, saying that the resurrection has already taken place,[a] and are overturning the faith of some.[b] [19] Nevertheless, God's solid foundation stands firm, having this inscription:[c]

> **The Lord knows those**
> **who are His,**[A,d] and
> Everyone who names the name[e]
> of the Lord
> must turn away from unrighteousness.[f]

[20] Now in a large house there are not only gold and silver bowls,[g] but also those of wood and clay, some for honorable[B] use, some for dishonorable.[C,h] [21] So if anyone purifies himself from anything dishonorable,[D] he will be a special[E] instrument, set apart, useful to the Master, prepared for every good work.[i]

[22] Flee[j] from youthful passions, and pursue righteousness, faith, love, and peace,[k] along with those who call on the Lord[l] from a pure heart. [23] But reject foolish and ignorant disputes, knowing that they breed quarrels. [24] The Lord's[m] •slave must not quarrel,[n] but must be gentle to everyone, able to teach,[F] and patient, [25] instructing his opponents with gentleness.[o] Perhaps God will grant them repentance[p] leading them to the knowledge of the truth. [26] Then they may come to their senses and escape the Devil's trap,[q] having been captured by him to do his will.[r]

Difficult Times Ahead

3 But know this: Difficult times will come in the last days.[s] [2] For people will be lovers of self,[t] lovers of money,[u] boastful, proud,[v] blasphemers, disobedient to parents, ungrateful, unholy,[w] [3] unloving, irreconcilable, slanderers,[x] without self-control, brutal, without love for what is good,[y] [4] traitors,[z] reckless,[aa] conceited,[ab] lovers of pleasure[ac] rather than lovers of God, [5] holding to the form of godliness but denying its power.[ad] Avoid these people![ae]

[6] For among them are those who worm their way into households and capture idle women burdened down with sins, led along by a variety of passions,[af] [7] always learning and never able to come to a knowledge of the truth.[ag] [8] Just as Jannes and Jambres[ah] resisted Moses,[ai] so these also resist the truth, men who are corrupt in mind,[aj] worthless[ak] in regard to the faith. [9] But they will not make further progress, for their lack of understanding will be clear to all, as theirs[G] was also.

Struggles in the Christian Life

[10] But you have followed my teaching, conduct, purpose,[al] faith, patience, love,[am] and endurance, [11] along with the persecutions and

Cross references

a 2:18 Ac 17:32; 1Co 15:12-17; 2Th 2:1-2
b 1Tm 1:19; 6:21
c 2:19 Jos 23:7; Est 9:4; Is 26:13; Rm 15:20; Eph 1:21
d Nm 16:5; Pr 2:6; Jn 10:14,27; 1Co 8:3
e Ac 15:14
f Lv 24:11,16; Nm 16:26-27; Jos 23:7; Ps 6:9; 33:15; Pr 3:4; Is 26:13; 52:11; Jr 20:9
g 2:20 Rm 9:21
h Rm 9:21
i 2:21 2Co 9:8; Gl 3:10; 1Tm 5:10
j 2:22 1Tm 4:12; 6:11; Jms 4:7
k Lk 12:51; 2Tm 1:2; Heb 12:14; 3Jn 14
l Gn 13:4
m 2:24 Rv 11:8
n Jn 6:52; Ac 7:26; Jms 4:2
o 2:25 Jms 3:13
p Ac 26:20; Rm 2:4; 2Co 7:9-10
q 2:26 1Tm 3:7
r Jn 1:13
s 3:1 Jn 6:39; Php 1:6; 1Pt 1:5; 2Pt 3:3; Jd 18
t 3:2 Php 2:21; 1Tm 6:4
u Lk 16:14; 1Tm 3:3; 6:10
v Pr 16:18; Lk 1:51; Rm 1:30
w 1Tm 1:9
x 3:3 Jn 14:6
y Ti 1:8
z 3:4 Lk 6:16; Ac 7:52
aa Ac 19:36
ab 1Tm 3:6; 6:4
ac Php 3:19
ad 3:5 1Co 4:20; 2Co 13:4; Ti 1:16
ae Mt 7:15; 2Th 3:6
af 3:6 2Pt 1:4; 2:10
ag 3:7 2Co 11:10; 1Tm 2:4; 2Tm 2:25; Ti 1:1
ah 3:8 Ex 7:11-12; 8:18; 9:11
ai Ps 77:20; Mt 8:4; Heb 3:2
aj 1Co 14:14; Php 4:7
ak 2Co 13:5-7
al 3:10 Pr 19:21; Ac 11:23
am 1Co 13:1; 1Jn 4:16

Footnotes

A 2:19 Nm 16:5   B 2:20 Or *special*   C 2:20 Or *ordinary*   D 2:21 Lit *from these*   E 2:21 Or *an honorable*   F 2:24 Or *everyone, skillful in teaching*   G 3:9 = Jannes and Jambres

Study notes

2:15 **Be diligent** could also be translated, "Be zealous." Paul had in mind a zealous pursuit of God's approval. One way to do this is to make sure we handle Scripture correctly.

2:17 **Hymenaeus** was mentioned as a false teacher previously in 1Tm 1:20, but **Philetus** is not mentioned elsewhere.

2:18 The idea that **the resurrection has already taken place** is similar to what Paul discussed in 1 Corinthians 15. Apparently some people were teaching that believers had already entered the glorified post-resurrection state. We do not know much about this heresy.

2:19 In spite of the work of these evildoers and evil teachers, God's church still **stands firm**. The **inscription** emphasizes both divine sovereignty (preserving) and human responsibility (persevering).

2:22 The word **passions** in this context refers to sinful desires in general. The desires that are particularly characteristic of youth could include sexual desires, the longing for novelty, or perhaps even impulsiveness (v. 24). It is significant that fleeing wrong is combined with pursuing right. Also, the pursuit of right is not to be done alone but **along with** other believers.

2:23 On **ignorant disputes**, see note at verse 14.

2:24 With the word **slave**, Paul referred to those who preached the gospel, e.g., Paul himself (Rm 1:1; Gl 1:10; Ti 1:1) and Epaphras (Col 4:12).

2:25 The **knowledge of the truth** is salvation.

2:26 Paul often described humanity as enslaved by the **Devil** and in need of rescue (2Co 4:4).

3:1 The words **last days** are more than a prediction. They are also an assessment of what was happening in Paul's time (1Tm 4:1).

3:5 These false teachers had the external trappings of **godliness** but not the real essence.

3:6 Because of their guilt from their past, these **women burdened down with sins** were particularly susceptible to the asceticism and legalism of these false teachers.

3:8 **Jannes** and **Jambres** were the names given in early Jewish nonbiblical writings to the Egyptian magicians who opposed Moses (Ex 7:8-13). Though the names do not appear in the Hebrew Bible, they would have been familiar to Timothy from Jewish writings about Moses.

3:10 The words **but you** set verses 1-9 in contrast with verses 10-17. The false teachers lived and taught one way, but Paul provided a totally different model for Timothy.

3:11 **Antioch, Iconium**, and **Lystra** were the cities that Paul visited on his first missionary journey. Thus, when looking for examples of his sufferings Paul referred to his earliest mission work. Some have questioned why he would refer so far back, especially since this would have been before Timothy joined Paul. But Lystra was Timothy's hometown,

sufferings[a] that came to me in Antioch,[b] Iconium,[c] and Lystra.[d] What persecutions I endured! Yet the Lord rescued me from them all. [12] In fact, all those who want to live a godly life in Christ Jesus will be persecuted.[e] [13] Evil people and impostors will become worse, deceiving[f] and being deceived. [14] But as for you, continue in what you have learned and firmly believed. You know those who taught you,[g] [15] and you know that from childhood you have known the sacred Scriptures,[h] which are able to give you wisdom for salvation[i] through faith in Christ Jesus. [16] All Scripture is inspired by God[A,j] and is profitable for teaching, for rebuking, for correcting, for training in righteousness, [17] so that the man of God may be complete, equipped for every good work.[k]

Fulfill Your Ministry

4 I solemnly charge you before God and Christ Jesus, who is going to judge[l] the living and the dead,[m] and because of His appearing and His kingdom:[n] [2] Proclaim the message; persist in it whether convenient or not; rebuke, correct, and encourage with great patience and teaching. [3] For the time will come when they will not tolerate sound doctrine,[o] but according to their own desires, will multiply teachers for themselves because they have an itch to hear something new.[B] [4] They will turn away from hearing the truth and will turn aside to myths.[p] [5] But as for you, be serious about everything, endure hardship, do the work of an evangelist,[q] fulfill your ministry.

[6] For I am already being poured out as a •drink offering,[r] and the time for my departure is close. [7] I have fought the good fight, I have finished the race, I have kept the faith. [8] There is reserved for me in the future the crown[s] of righteousness, which the Lord, the righteous Judge,[t] will give me on that day, and not only to me, but to all those who have loved His appearing.[u]

Final Instructions

[9] Make every effort to come to me soon,[v] [10] for Demas[w] has deserted me,[x] because he loved this present world, and has gone to Thessalonica.[y]

[a] 3:11 Gl 5:24; Php 3:10
[b] Ac 13:14; 14:19,21
[c] Ac 13:51; 16:2
[d] Ac 14:6,8; 27:5
[e] 3:12 Jn 15:20; Ac 14:22; 2Co 4:9-10
[f] 3:13 Rv 20:10
[g] 3:14 2Tm 1:13
[h] 3:15 Mt 26:54; 2Pt 1:20-21
[i] Ac 4:12; 2Co 7:10; Heb 5:9
[j] 3:16 2Pt 1:20-21
[k] 3:17 2Co 9:8; Gl 3:10; 1Tm 5:10; 2Tm 2:21
[A] 4:1 Jn 5:22-30; Rm 5:18; 1Pt 4:5
[m] Jn 5:25; Rm 14:9; 1Pt 4:5; Rv 18:8; 19:11
[n] Mk 1:15; Ac 20:25
[o] 4:3 Rm 15:4
[p] 4:4 1Tm 1:4; 4:7; Ti 1:14; 2Pt 1:16
[q] 4:5 Ac 21:8; Eph 4:11
[r] 4:6 Gn 35:14; Php 2:17
[s] 4:8 Jm 15:17; Rv 12:1
[t] Lk 18:2,6; Jn 5:22-30; Ac 10:42; Heb 12:23
[u] Ti 2:13; 1Jn 2:28
[v] 4:9 Ti 3:12
[w] 4:10 Col 4:14; Phm 24
[x] 2Tm 1:15
[y] Ac 17:1

[A] 3:16 Lit *breathed out by God*; the Scripture is the product of God's Spirit working through men; 2Pt 1:20-21.   [B] 4:3 Or *to hear what they want to hear*; lit *themselves, itching in the hearing*

so he was probably aware of what had happened to Paul there. In effect Paul is saying: "Timothy, you have known from your earliest awareness of me that suffering is a part of the gospel work."

3:14 The phrase **those who taught you** probably refers to Timothy's mother and grandmother (1:5), especially since verse 15 mentions the teaching he received in childhood.

3:15 The phrase **give you wisdom for salvation** means that Scripture could lead Timothy to the "knowledge of the truth" (2:25; 1Tm 2:4). Scripture has the power to bring people to faith.

3:16-17 Inspired means "breathed out by God" (see textual footnote on 3:16). Because Scripture comes from God Himself, it is profitable in many ways, ultimately leading us to **righteousness**, maturity, and service. **All Scripture** refers to the OT, but by implication to the writings of the NT as well (1Tm 5:18; 2Pt 3:15-16).

4:1-8 These verses flow naturally out of 3:10-17. The strong statements about the saving and edifying power of Scripture in 3:15-17 lead to the command to proclaim this Word (4:1-4).

4:1 The solemnity of the charge is heightened by references to living before the gaze of God, to the fact that this God is judge, to Christ's second coming (**appearing**), and to the reality of His present reign over **His Kingdom**.

4:3 Since Paul exhorted Timothy in how to respond when these things occurred, it is apparent that he did not refer only to some time in the distant future, but to a situation he expected Timothy to face or was already facing.

4:4 The word **myths** does not refer to the content of the false teaching. It characterizes the teaching as fanciful and without a serious basis (1Tm 1:4).

4:6 By referring to a **drink offering**, Paul used OT sacrificial language to refer to his own death (Gn 35:14; Ex 29:40-41; Lv 23:13; Nm 15:5-10). This suggests he saw himself as laying down his life for the sake of the gospel.

4:8 Crown of righteousness probably means "the crown which consists of righteousness," referring to the final righteous state of believers. Thus, it will be given not only to Paul but to **all those who have loved His appearing**, a reference to all believers.

4:10 Paul persevered in spite of suffering (1:11-12; 2:8-13) because he had an eternal perspective (4:6-8), but **Demas** abandoned Paul because **he loved this present world**.

4:11 In spite of his earlier disapproval of Mark (Ac 15:36-

epitimao

Greek Pronunciation	[eh pee tih MAH oh]
HCSB Translation	rebuke, warn
Uses in 2 Timothy	1
Uses in the NT	29
Focus passage	2 Timothy 4:2

Epitimao (to rebuke) appears almost exclusively in the Gospels (27x) and typically refers to a *threatening command* or *rebuke* with negative implications for the one *rebuked*. Jesus *rebuked* the wind and sea (Mt 8:26), a fever (Lk 4:39), and demons (Mt 17:18 = Mk 9:25; Lk 4:35,41). He *rebuked* James, John (Lk 9:55), and Peter (Mk 8:33). However, *epitimao* may have positive implications for the one *rebuked* when that *rebuke* is intended to prevent improper behavior. In such cases, it may be translated *to rebuke, warn*, or *correct*. Jesus commanded His disciples to *rebuke* a sinning brother (Lk 17:3), and *warned* them to keep His identity secret (Mt 12:16; Lk 9:21). Peter inappropriately *rebuked* Jesus (Mt 16:22 = Mk 8:32). The disciples *rebuked* those bringing their children to obtain Jesus' blessing (Mt 19:13 = Mk 10:13 = Lk 18:15). Outside the Gospels, *rebuking* is part of the pastoral role (2Tm 4:2).

Crescens has gone to Galatia,[a] Titus[b] to Dalmatia. [11] Only Luke[c] is with me. Bring Mark[d] with you, for he is useful to me in the ministry. [12] I have sent Tychicus[e] to Ephesus. [13] When you come, bring the cloak I left in Troas[f] with Carpus, as well as the scrolls, especially the parchments. [14] Alexander[g] the coppersmith did great harm to me. The Lord will repay him according to his works. [15] Watch out[h] for him yourself because he strongly opposed our words.

[16] At my first defense, no one stood by me, but everyone deserted me.[i] May it not be counted against them. [17] But the Lord stood with me and strengthened me, so that the proclamation might be fully made through

me and all the Gentiles might hear. So I was rescued from the lion's mouth. [18] The Lord will rescue me from every evil work and will bring me safely into His heavenly kingdom.[j] To Him be the glory forever and ever! *Amen.

Benediction

[19] Greet Prisca and Aquila,[k] and the household of Onesiphorus.[l] [20] Erastus[m] has remained at Corinth; I left Trophimus[n] sick at Miletus.[o] [21] Make every effort to come before winter. Eubulus greets you, as do Pudens, Linus, Claudia, and all the *brothers.

[22] The Lord be with your spirit. Grace be with you.

a4:10 Gl 1:2
bTi 1:4
c4:11 Col 4:14; Phm 24
dAc 15:37-39
e4:12 Ac 20:4; Ti 3:12
f4:13 Ac 16:8
g4:14 1Tm 1:20
h4:15 2Tm 1:14; 2Pt 3:17
i4:16 2Tm 1:15
j4:18 Mk 1:15; Ac 20:25
k4:19 Ac 18:2
l2Tm 1:16
m4:20 Ac 19:22; Rm 16:23
nAc 20:4; 21:29
oAc 20:15,17

40), Paul now desired Mark's presence and considered him **useful . . . in the ministry**.

4:14 The **Alexander** mentioned here cannot be identified with certainty. Paul mentioned an Alexander in 1Tm 1:20 as a person who had been excommunicated. He may have still been in Ephesus causing trouble. Or, since he is identified as a **coppersmith**, and there is evidence of a guild of coppersmiths in Troas, this may refer to a different man living in Troas. This would explain his appearance here after Paul asked Timothy to visit Troas.

4:16 In his forgiveness of others, Paul followed the teaching and model of Jesus (Lk 23:34), the practice of Stephen whom Paul saw die (Ac 7:60), and his own teaching (1Co 13:5).

4:17 Deliverance from a **lion's mouth** was a common bibli-

cal metaphor for rescue from great danger (Ps 22:21).

4:19 Prisca is a variant of Priscilla. This is a reference to the Priscilla and **Aquila** often mentioned in connection with Paul (e.g., Rm 16:3; 1Co 16:19).

4:21 This verse repeats the essence of verse 9. Travel in the Mediterranean area was usually suspended during **winter** because the weather resulted in dangerous conditions on land and sea. Therefore, if the trip were not completed by then, Timothy would be delayed and not be able to come "soon" (v. 9).

4:22 Paul used the phrase **be with your spirit** also in his closing in Gl 6:18, Php 4:23, and Phm 25. There does not appear to be any significant difference in meaning from his more common "be with you" (Rm 16:20; 1Co 16:23; 2Co 13:13; 2Th 3:18).

Titus

Introduction

See Introduction to the Pastoral Epistles before 1 Timothy.

Outline of Titus

I. Greeting (1:1-4)

II. Titus's Ministry in Crete (1:5-16)
  A. Qualifications for elders (1:5-9)
  B. Warnings against the Judaizers (1:10-16)

III. Sound Teaching (2:1-15)
  A. Moral responsibilities of believers (2:1-10)
  B. Salvation and Christian behavior (2:11-15)

IV. The Importance of Good Works (3:1-11)
  A. Christian conduct in the world (3:1-7)
  B. Dealing with difficult people (3:8-11)

V. Final Instructions and Conclusion (3:12-15)

Agios Pavlos is a small village on the southern coast of Crete. Paul left his protégé Titus on Crete to "set right what was left undone" and to appoint elders in every town" (Ti 1:5).

Greeting

1 Paul,[a] a *slave of God[b] and an apostle of Jesus Christ, to build up[A] the faith of God's elect[c] and their knowledge of the truth[d] that leads[B] to godliness,[e] ²in the hope of eternal life[f] that God, who cannot lie,[g] promised before time began.[h] ³In His own time He has revealed[i] His message[j] in the proclamation that I was entrusted[k] with by the command[l] of God our Savior:[m]

⁴To Titus,[n] my true son[o] in our common faith.

Grace and peace from God the Father and Christ Jesus our Savior.[p]

Titus's Ministry in Crete

⁵The reason I left you in Crete[q] was to set right what was left undone and, as I directed you, to appoint elders[r] in every town: ⁶one[s] who is blameless,[t] the husband of one wife, having faithful[C] children not accused of wildness or rebellion. ⁷For an *overseer,[u] as God's administrator, must be blameless, not arrogant, not hot-tempered, not addicted to wine, not a bully, not greedy for money, ⁸but hos-

pitable, loving what is good, sensible, righteous, holy, self-controlled, ⁹holding to the faithful message as taught,[v] so that he will be able both to encourage with sound teaching[w] and to refute those who contradict it.

¹⁰For there are also many rebellious people, full of empty talk and deception, especially those from Judaism.[D] ¹¹It is necessary to silence them; they overthrow whole households by teaching what they shouldn't in order to get money dishonestly. ¹²One of their very own prophets said,

Cretans are always liars, evil beasts, lazy gluttons.[E]

¹³This testimony is true.[x] So, rebuke them sharply,[y] that they may be sound in the faith ¹⁴and may not pay attention to Jewish myths[z] and the commands of men who reject the truth.[aa]

¹⁵To the pure, everything is pure, but to

a1:1 Ac 13:9
bAc 16:17; Rm 1:1; Eph 6:6; Jms 1:1; 1Pt 2:16; Rv 1:1
cMt 22:14; 24:22; Lk 18:7; Rm 8:33; Col 3:12; 1Co 1:27-28; 1Th 1:4; Jms 2:5
d1Tm 2:4; 2Tm 3:7
e1Tm 6:3
f1:2 1Co 15:19; Ti 3:7; Heb 9:15
gNm 23:19; Heb 6:18
hRm 1:2; 2Tm 1:9
i1:3 Jn 21:1; 2Co 4:11; 1Pt 5:4; 1Jn 1:2
jJn 1:1; 2:22; 2Tm 2:15; Heb 4:12
k1Tm 1:11; 6:20; 2Tm 1:12,14
l1Tm 1:1
m1Tm 1:1; 2:3; Ti 2:10; 3:4; Jd 25
n1:4 2Co 2:13; 7:6,13-14; 8:6,16,23; 12:18; Gl 2:1,3; 2Tm 4:10
o1Tm 1:2
pRm 1:7; 1Co 1:3
qAc 27:7,12-13
r1Tm 3:1-7; 5:17
s1:6-8 1Tm 3:2-4
t1:6 Col 1:22
u1:7 Ac 20:28; Php 1:1; 1Pt 2:25
v1:9 Ac 2:42
w1Tm 1:10; 6:3; 2Tm 1:13; Ti 2:1
x1:13 Jn 8:14
y2Co 13:10
z1:14 1Tm 1:4; 4:7; 2Tm 4:4; 2Pt 1:16
aa2Tm 4:4

A1:1 Or *according to*   B1:1 Or *corresponds*   C1:6 Or *believing*   D1:10 Lit *the circumcision*   E1:12 This saying is from the Cretan poet Epimenides (6th century B.C.).

1:1 Slave is sometimes translated "servant," but the stronger word used here is better. The stark terminology is intentional. Paul often used this term as a designation for himself (Rm 1:1; Gl 1:10; Php 1:1) and other Christians (1Co 7:22; Eph 6:6; Col 4:12; see also 2Pt 1:1; Jd 1; Rv 2:20). This terminology is common for leaders in the OT as well. **To build up** translates a difficult phrase. The idea is that the purpose of Paul's apostleship was to see people come to **faith** and grow in faith and **knowledge of the truth**. The word "truth" refers to the gospel specifically, and this gospel leads to **godliness**.

1:5 On **elders**, see notes at 1Tm 3:1 and 3:2-7.

1:6 On **husband of one wife**, see note at 1Tm 3:2. **Having faithful children** assumes, but does not require, that such men will likely have children at home still under their authority. The word "faithful" can also be translated "believing." This raises an important question about whether pastors are required to have Christian children or children who are more generally "faithful" or obedient. This word and its related forms in 1 Timothy, 2 Timothy, and Titus most often refer to having saving faith and not merely to being "faithful." But context is the primary issue in understanding which nuance of the word is intended. The emphasis of the context here is on a man fulfilling his duties well. No father can guarantee the conversion of his own children. He can better insure that they act in a "faithful" way while they live under his supervision. Also, the parallel passage in 1 Timothy 3 speaks only to the children being well behaved, not to their conversion. Thus, Paul was requiring pastors to govern the behavior of their children, not allowing them to be characterized by **wildness or rebellion**.

1:9 It was common for ancient authors to emphasize one item in a list by placing it at the beginning or end and

then giving it significantly longer treatment than the other items. This is what Paul does here. While he spent only a few words on the items in verses 6-9, his treatment of this last subject is both long and grammatically complex. By this means he emphasized the importance of an "overseer" (v. 7) being able to teach. The reason for this is clear from what follows (vv. 10-16).

1:12 Crete was known in the ancient world for its moral decadence. The ancient historian Polybius wrote that it was "almost impossible to find . . . personal conduct more treacherous or public policy more unjust than in Crete" (*Histories*, 6.47). Cicero also stated, "Moral principles are so divergent

episkopos

Greek Pronunciation	[eh PIHS kah pahs]
HCSB Translation	overseer
Uses in Titus	1
Uses in the NT	5
Focus passage	Titus 1:7

By the time of the NT, *episkopos* already enjoyed a long history of usage, referring to deities or community officials, rulers, or leaders. In the NT, however, the term takes on a clearly religious overtone, appearing as a title meaning an *overseer* (apparently synonymous with *presbuteros* [*elder*]; Ac 20:28; Ti 1:7). In the early church, the Holy Spirit commissioned each *overseer* through apostolic selection and appointment (Ac 14:23, 20:28; Ti 1:7). The *overseer* held a vital service role within the congregation (1Tm 3:1). This necessitated high moral standards and management skills (1Tm 3:2-7; Ti 1:7-9). Several *overseers* were responsible for shepherding and managing the affairs of their local congregation (Ac 20:28; Php 1:1; Ti 1:7). Jesus, to whom belongs the church, is the "shepherd and guardian" par excellence (1Pt 2:25).

those who are defiled and unbelieving nothing is pure; in fact, both their mind and conscience[a] are defiled. [16]They profess to know God,[b] but they deny Him by their works.[c] They are detestable, disobedient, and disqualified for any good work.[d]

Sound Teaching and Christian Living

2 But you must say the things that are consistent with sound teaching.[e] [2]Older men[f] are to be level headed, worthy of respect, sensible, and sound in faith, love,[g] and endurance. [3]In the same way, older women[h] are to be reverent in behavior, not slanderers, not addicted to much wine. They are to teach what is good, [4]so they may encourage the young women to love their husbands and to love their children, [5]to be self-controlled, pure, homemakers, kind, and submissive[i] to their husbands, so that God's message[j] will not be slandered.

[6]In the same way, encourage the young men[k] to be self-controlled [7]in everything. Make yourself an example of good works with integrity and dignity[A] in your teaching. [8]Your message is to be sound beyond reproach,[l] so

that the opponent will be ashamed, having nothing bad to say about us.

[9]•Slaves are to be submissive to their masters[m] in everything, and to be well-pleasing,[n] not talking back [10]or stealing, but demonstrating utter faithfulness, so that they may adorn the teaching of God our Savior[o] in everything.

[11]For the grace of God has appeared with salvation[B] for all people,[p] [12]instructing us to deny godlessness[q] and worldly lusts[r] and to live in a sensible, righteous,[s] and godly[t] way in the present age, [13]while we wait for the blessed hope[u] and appearing of the glory[v] of our great God and Savior, Jesus Christ. [14]He gave Himself for us[w] to •redeem us from all lawlessness and to cleanse for Himself a people for His own possession,[x] eager to do good works.

[15]Say these things, and encourage and rebuke with all authority. Let no one disregard[C] you.

[a]1:15 Heb 13:18
[b]1:16 Jn 7:28
[c]Mk 14:6; 2Co 9:8; Gl 3:10; Jms 2:14-26
[d]2Co 9:8
[e]2:1 Ti 1:9
[f]2:2 1Tm 5:1
[g]1Co 13:1; 1Jn 4:16
[h]2:3 1Tm 5:2
[i]2:5 Lk 10:17; Eph 5:22
[j]Lk 8:21; 2Tm 2:15; Heb 4:12
[k]2:6 1Tm 5:1; 1Pt 5:5; 1Jn 2:13-14
[l]2:8 1Tm 2:2
[m]2:9 Eph 6:5-9; Col 3:22; 1Tm 6:1; 1Pt 2:18; Jd 4
[n]Heb 13:21
[o]2:10 1Tm 1:1; 2:3; Ti 1:3; 3:4; Jd 25
[p]2:11 Ac 1:8; Rm 10:14; 2Co 5:18-21; 1Tm 2:4; 4:10; 2Pt 3:9
[q]2:12 Jd 18
[r]2Tm 4:10; 2Pt 1:4; 2:10
[s]Lk 23:41; 1Co 15:34;

1Th 2:10; 1Pt 2:24 [t]2Tm 3:12 [u]2:13 Ac 23:6; 1Th 1:3 [v]Lk 9:32; Jn 17:1,24; 2Co 3:18; 2Pt 3:18 [w]2:14 Mt 20:28; Mk 10:45; Rm 8:32; Gl 1:4; 2:20; Eph 5:2,25; 1Tm 2:6 [x]Ex 19:5; Lk 1:68

[A]2:7 Other mss add *incorruptibility* [B]2:11 Or *appeared, bringing salvation*; or *appeared with saving power* [C]2:15 Or *despise*

that the Cretans . . . consider highway robbery honorable" (*Republic*, 3.9.15).

1:14 On **myths**, see note at 1Tm 1:4. The specific content of the "myths" and **command** Paul had in mind in the present verse is unstated, but the false teaching in Titus is more explicitly tied to a **Jewish** background (v. 10) than that referenced in 1 and 2 Timothy.

1:15 This statement echoes Jesus' teaching (Lk 11:41) and Paul's earlier writing (Rm 14:20). In light of the Jewish origin of the false teaching and contexts of the earlier use of similar wording by Jesus and Paul, the issue here was probably Jewish food laws. The false teachers seemed to be concerned with this ritual purity, but were nevertheless defiled by their own unbelief and sin.

1:16 The actions (**works**) of these people proved conclusively that they were unbelievers, although they claimed to **know God**. Paul was not hesitant to make such a judgment. The three descriptors at the end of the verse summarize the behavior that proved they did not know God.

2:1 The intentional contrast **but you** must not be missed. While some people's deeds disprove their claim to know God, Titus in contrast was to teach the people to live in a way **consistent with sound teaching**—in a way that would affirm rather than deny their claim to know God. The instruction addressed typical groups within the family structure (older men, older women, younger women, younger men, and slaves).

2:3-5 The teaching in these verses is practical and focuses on the domestic sphere. Paul emphasizes that **older women** can help model for **young women** what it means to be a wife and mother.

2:5,8,10 In each of these verses important statements are made about the desired result of "gospel living." Such living keeps us from providing a basis for the gospel (**God's message**) to be **slandered**. Such living also highlights the attractiveness of the gospel.

2:11-14 This paragraph provides the theological basis for the lifestyle commended in verses 1-10. Christians should live sanctified lives because the grace of God that saves us also instructs us to live in a new way. A person cannot claim to be a recipient of God's saving grace if he is not also a trainee in the lifestyle made possible by grace.

2:11 This verse has sometimes been misunderstood as saying that all people will be saved. However, such a reading is not made necessary by the words here, and it flatly contradicts other portions of Scripture. The force of **all people** is to emphasize the universal offer of the gospel. The offer of salvation is proclaimed not just to one group but to all peoples.

2:12 **Godlessness** refers to behavior that is not in accordance with God's ways. **Lusts** refer not only to sexual desires but to sinful desires in general.

2:13 The verb used here for **wait** often carries a connotation of eagerness. The eager expectation of the return of Christ mentioned here is not just the time of the instruction of grace ("while we wait"); it is also the way grace teaches us to renounce sin and live in a "godly way" (v. 12). Setting our minds on the truth of Christ's return impels us to holiness (1Jn 3:2-3). The **blessed hope** is the **appearing of . . . Christ**. The reference to Jesus as **God** and **Savior** is a strong affirmation of His deity.

2:14 The phrase **people for His own possession** translates an unusual phrase with intentional echoes from the OT (Ex 19:5; Mal 3:17). The phrase expresses the sense of "prized, treasured possession" (1Pt 2:9).

2:15 This verse is an unmistakable call for authoritative teaching in the church.

Christian Living among Outsiders

3 Remind them to be submissive[a] to rulers and authorities, to obey, to be ready for every good work, [2]to slander no one, to avoid fighting, and to be kind, always showing gentleness[b] to all people. [3]For we too were once foolish, disobedient, deceived, enslaved by various passions[c] and pleasures,[d] living in malice and envy, hateful, detesting one another.

[4] But when the goodness of God
    and His love
    for mankind appeared,[e]
[5] He saved us[f]—
    not by works of righteousness
        that we had done,[g]
    but according to His mercy,[h]
    through the washing of regeneration[i]
    and renewal by the Holy Spirit.[j]
[6] He poured out this Spirit
        on us abundantly[k]
    through Jesus Christ our Savior,
[7] so that having been •justified
        by His grace,[l]
    we may become heirs with the hope
        of eternal life.[m]

[8]This saying is trustworthy.[n] I want you to insist on these things, so that those who have believed God might be careful to devote themselves to good works. These are good and profitable for everyone. [9]But avoid foolish debates,[o] genealogies,[p] quarrels,[q] and disputes about the law, for they are unprofitable and worthless. [10]Reject a divisive[r] person after a first and second warning,[s] [11]knowing that such a person is perverted and sins, being self-condemned.

Final Instructions and Closing

[12] When I send Artemas or Tychicus to you,[t] make every effort to come to me[u] in Nicopolis, for I have decided to spend the winter there. [13]Diligently help Zenas the lawyer and Apollos[v] on their journey, so that they will lack[w] nothing.

[14] And our people must also learn to devote themselves to good works for cases of urgent need, so that they will not be unfruitful.[x] [15]All those who are with me greet you. Greet those who love us in the faith. Grace be with all of you.[y]

---

[a]3:1 Rm 13:1-7; 1Pt 2:13-14
[b]3:2 Jms 3:13
[c]3:3 2Pt 1:4; 2:10
[d]Jms 4:1
[e]3:4 1Tm 1:1; 2:3; Ti 1:3; 2:10; Jd 25
[f]3:5 Rm 11:14; 2Tm 1:9
[g]Eph 2:9
[h]Eph 2:4; 1Pt 1:3
[i]n 3:5; Eph 5:26; 1Pt 3:21
[j]Rm 12:2
[k]3:6 Jl 2:28; Ac 2:33; 10:45; Rm 5:5
[l]3:7 Ac 13:43; 15:11; 1Co 8:1; Gl 1:6; 1Pt 4:10
[m]Ti 1:2
[n]3:8 1Tm 1:15; 3:1; 4:9; 2Tm 2:11
[o]3:9 1Tm 6:4
[p]1Tm 1:4
[q]Rm 1:29; 13:13; 1Co 1:11; 3:3; 2Co 12:20; Gl 5:20; Php 1:15; 1Tm 6:4
[r]3:10 1Tm 1:9
[s]Mt 18:15; 2Th 3:15
[t]3:12 Ac 20:4; Eph 6:21; Col 4:7; 2Tm 4:12
[u]Lk 14:26; 2Tm 4:9
[v]3:13 Ac 18:24; 19:1; 1Co 1:12; 3:4-6,22; 4:6; 16:12
[w]Jms 2:15
[x]3:14 Mt 13:22; Mk 4:19; 1Co 14:14; Gl 5:22; Eph 5:11; 2Pt 1:8; Jd 12
[y]3:15 Col 4:18; 2Th 3:16

3:1 The phrase **ready for every good work** refers back to 1:16 and 2:14. The false teachers were "disqualified for any good work" (1:16). One of the purposes of the cross was to create a people "eager to do good works" (2:14). And here, in contrast to the false teachers, Titus was to teach the people to be "ready for every good work." The qualities encouraged here (vv. 1-3) are in contrast to the description of the false teachers in 1:10-16.

3:3-7 These verses provide the doctrinal basis for the teaching in verses 1-2.

3:4 The words **goodness of God and His love for mankind** stand in stark contrast to the description of lost humanity in verse 3. The difference is due to the appearance of God our Savior, Jesus Christ.

3:5 Salvation comes **not by works** but through the washing of **regeneration** and **renewal** by the **Holy Spirit**. Some interpreters have understood this as saying that baptism ("the washing") causes salvation, but in the context human deeds are clearly downplayed and the emphasis is on divine action and initiative. The **washing** described here is the spiritual cleansing that is symbolized outwardly by water baptism.

3:8 The command **to insist on these things** is similar to 2:15. Note the emphasis on **good works** as a mark of believers (v. 1; 1:16; 2:14).

3:9 As elsewhere in the letters to Timothy and Titus, the exact nature of these **debates** and **quarrels** is not clear (e.g., 1:10-14). The point is that these **disputes** were **worthless**.

3:10-11 As the marginal readings for these verses indicate, this is a reference to the final stage of church discipline. A divisive person who refused to repent and change after being confronted showed himself to be twisted by sin; thus, he was **self-condemned**.

3:14 Having emphasized the importance of **good works** throughout the letter and having just called for the assistance of fellow laborers (v. 13), Paul paused once more to emphasize the importance of good works. The opportunity to assist Zenas and Apollos was another example of how Titus could be involved in "good works."

3:15 The plural greeting **grace be with all of you** appears odd in a letter addressed to an audience of one (Titus), but it shows Paul's awareness (and likely his intention) that the letter, though written primarily to Titus, would be read to the entire congregation.

Philemon

Philemon is Paul's only letter of a private nature. It concerns a runaway slave, Onesimus, who had robbed his master, Philemon, and escaped from Colossae to Rome. There Onesimus met the imprisoned apostle Paul. Paul wrote to Philemon concerning Onesimus. Paul sent both the letter and Onesimus back to Colossae. By comparison to Paul's other letters, Philemon is little more than a postcard, but it comes from the tender heart of a friend writing as a friend rather than as an apostle exercising his authority.

The Lycus River Valley as seen from Colossae. Philemon came to faith in Christ when Paul was in Ephesus. At the time this letter was written, the church at Colossae met in the home of Philemon, his wife, Apphia, and their son, Archippus.

Circumstances of Writing

Author: During Paul's two-year imprisonment in Rome (Ac 28:30), probably during A.D. 60–61, he wrote four "prison epistles," one of which was Philemon (the others were Colossians, Ephesians, and Philippians).

Background: References to Paul's being in prison at the time of writing are found in verses 1,9-10,13, and perhaps 23. Paul was kept under house arrest—what the Romans called "free custody"—in his own rented house as he awaited trial (Ac 28:30).

Although Paul addresses the letter to Apphia, Archippus, and the church that meets in Philemon's house (vv. 1-2), the main addressee is Philemon himself, for "you" or "your" (vv. 2,4-21,23) is singular and refers to Philemon. Apparently he was a prosperous businessman living in Colossae (implied in Col 4:9) whose household included several slaves and whose house was large enough to accommodate meetings of the young church. He had been converted through Paul's ministry, perhaps by Paul himself (vv. 10,19), and had become Paul's "dear friend and coworker" (v. 1) and "partner" (v. 17) in the gospel service. Although the letter is basically Paul's personal appeal to Philemon, the plural "you" (vv. 3,22) and "your" (vv. 22,25) indicate that the whole church would have listened to its reading and thus been witnesses of Philemon's response to Paul's requests.

Onesimus had apparently run away and taken with him some of his master's money or possessions (vv. 15,18). Perhaps attracted by the anonymity of a large, distant city, he traveled to Rome seeking a life of freedom. His path crossed Paul's, and he became a Christian (vv. 10,16) and a useful helper to Paul (v. 11).

An alternative view denies that Onesimus was a runaway looking for freedom. It instead suggests that he left Philemon and looked for Paul so that Paul could become his advocate regarding some serious loss Philemon had experienced. All along Onesimus had intended to return to his master's household. Paul was therefore not guilty of harboring a fugitive slave. But on this view we would expect Paul to reassure Philemon that Onesimus had always intended to return.

Prehistory–1500 B.C.	1500–132 B.C.
Slavery comes with the development of agriculture in Mesopotamia. **10,000**	References to slavery during China's Shang dynasty **1500–1066**
References to slavery in the Code of Hammurabi **1750**	Economies of the Greek city states are dependent on slavery. **500–400**
Egyptians make slaves of the Israelites. **1600**	The Greek city–state of Athens has some 70,000 slaves. **430**
Hittite Code of Nesilim provides for the humane treatment of slaves. **1650–1500**	In his *Politics*, Aristotle writes on the nature of the master–slave relationship. **330**
Hebrew laws contain provisions pertaining to slaves and slavery. **1445**	First Roman slave revolt in Sicily **134–132**

Message and Purpose: This letter has served as an inspiration for the liberation of slaves. Paul's clear preference was to keep Onesimus with him (v. 13), but he recognized that Philemon was his legal owner and decided to send him back (v. 12) so Philemon could either reinstate him as a slave who was now also a Christian brother (vv. 15-16) or else set him free for further service to Paul back in Rome (vv. 13,20-21). Onesimus returned to his master with this letter, knowing that Paul was confident of Philemon's "obedience" (v. 21) but also knowing that neither forgiveness nor reinstatement nor emancipation was guaranteed.

Contribution to the Bible: Although it is the shortest and most personal of Paul's letters, Philemon was included in the New Testament canon for several reasons.

First, it illustrates the breaking down of social and cultural barriers that occurred between Christians (see Gl 3:28). Paul, a highly educated Roman citizen, takes up the cause of a poor runaway slave whose life was in danger because of his theft and flight (Phm 18). Social and cultural barriers are eliminated in Christian fellowship.

Second, it reflects early Christian attitudes towards slavery. Although Paul accepts (but does not endorse) slavery as an existing social condition and as a legal fact (see v. 12), he emphasizes Onesimus's higher identity as a Christian brother and sets the master–slave relationship on a new footing (v. 16) and so ultimately undermines the institution of slavery. This contrasts with dominant views of the ancient world. For instance, Aristotle defined a slave as "a living tool, just as a tool is an inanimate slave" (*Nicomachean Ethics* viii. 11. 6).

Third, it shows a skillful pastor at work: Paul gives up his apostolic right to issue commands (vv. 8-9) and prefers to appeal to Philemon's free choice (vv. 10,14) to follow his Christian conscience in deciding how his love should be expressed (vv. 5,7); he identifies with Onesimus, his spiritual son (v. 10), calling him "a part of myself" (v. 12) and guaranteeing to repay his debts (vv. 18-19); and he gives his requests to Philemon in the hearing of the whole local church (vv. 1-3,22-25).

---

104 B.C.–A.D. 54

A.D. 60–407

Second Roman slave revolt in Sicily 104–101 B.C.

Third Roman slave revolt led by the gladiator Spartacus 73–71 B.C.

By the time Augustus becomes Roman emperor, there are some 3 million slaves out of a total population of 7.5 million Romans. A.D. 63

In his *Geographia*, Strabo says there are more than 1,000 temple slaves—prostitutes—in the temple of Aphrodite in 6th century B.C. Corinth. A.D. 20

Roman Emperor Claudius rules that a slave who was old or sick and abandoned by his master would be considered free. A.D. 41–54

Paul arrives in Rome. 60

Paul encounters Onesimus, a runaway slave from Colossae. 61

Paul writes his letter to Philemon and sends it and the Letter to the Colossians, by Tychicus and Onesimus. 61

During Nero's rule, slaves gain the right to complain against their masters in court. 54–68

Gregory of Nyssa (d. 395) and Chrysostom (347–407) oppose slavery based on Christian theology.

Fourth, it pictures the heart of the gospel (vv. 16-19). When we come to God in repentance and faith, He gives us a new status and welcomes us as if we were Christ. What we owe God, He has debited to Christ's account. Christ assumed personal responsibility for the full repayment of our debt to God.

Outline

I. Address and Greetings (vv. 1-3)

II. Thanksgiving for Philemon's Faith and Love (vv. 4-7)

III. Paul's Appeal for Onesimus (vv. 8-20)

IV. Plans and Hopes for a Visit (vv. 21-22)

V. Final Greeting (vv. 23-25)

The Bible and Civil Rights

Kevin L. Smith

The Bible was central to the thought, rhetoric, and development of the Civil Rights Movement. This was influenced by the essential role of black churches and preachers in the organization of the movement. Not only was the movement characterized by meetings in churches and the singing of Negro spirituals, it was also marked by biblical themes and biblical rhetoric.

A prime example of popular civil rights rhetoric is Martin Luther King, Jr.'s "I Have a Dream" speech delivered on August 28, 1963. The speech reflected King's criticisms and hopes for America set in the language of the prophets of the Old Testament. For example, he said satisfaction would not come until "justice rolls down like waters, and righteousness like a mighty stream" (Am 5:24). This was familiar language in the Bible-literate America of that day. In the conclusion as King soars into describing his dream, he dreams of a day when "every valley shall be exalted, and every hill and mountain shall be made low, the rough places will be made plain, and the crooked places will be made straight; and the glory of the LORD shall be revealed and all flesh shall see it together" (Is 40:4-5). It should not be taken for granted that the celebrated leader of the Civil Rights Movement was a black Baptist preacher.

The central intellectual strain behind the movement focused on the issue of the equality of all humans, since they were "created . . . in the image of God" (Gn 1:27), whether black or white. Throughout the black freedom struggle in American history, the biblical teachings on creation and human dignity were foundational to the arguments being put forth, both by scholars and by everyday people. Even those who were illiterate knew from the rhetoric of the movement that God had created all people from one man (Ac 17:26).

In his famous "Letter from Birmingham Jail" written April 16, 1963, Dr. King resorts to biblical examples as a defense when he is accused of being an extremist for participating in demonstrations, sit-ins, and boycotts. He asked whether Jesus was an extremist when He said "love your enemies and pray for those who persecute you" (Mt 5:44). He also cites the prophet Amos and the apostle Paul, asking whether their words and actions were not also "extreme." Finally, reflecting on Jesus' death on Calvary, he wrote that "Jesus was an extremist for love, truth, and goodness." In his appeal to white ministers for support, King commonly cited biblical texts and the examples of Christ.

The Bible was central to the energy of the Civil Rights Movement. In planning meetings, preachers and laypersons read from its pages. In public disputes, everyday people quoted its promises and its truth regarding the dignity of all humanity, regardless of skin color. It would not be a stretch to suggest that the Civil Rights Movement would have lacked moral fiber (and one might further say divine blessing) without the underlying truth claims drawn from the Bible.

Greeting

Paul,[a] a prisoner[b] of Christ Jesus,[c] and Timothy[d] our brother:

To Philemon our dear friend and coworker, [2]to Apphia our sister,[A] to Archippus[e] our fellow soldier,[f] and to the church that meets in your home.[g]

[3]Grace to you and peace from God our Father and the Lord Jesus Christ.

Philemon's Love and Faith

[4]I always thank my God when I mention you in my prayers, [5]because I hear of your love[h] and faith toward[B] the Lord Jesus and for all the •saints. [6]I pray that your participation in the faith may become effective[i] through knowing every good thing[j] that is in us[C] for the glory of Christ. [7]For I have great joy and encouragement from your love, because the hearts of the saints have been refreshed[k] through you, brother.

An Appeal for Onesimus

[8]For this reason, although I have great boldness in Christ to command you to do what is right, [9]I appeal to you, instead, on the basis of love. I, Paul, as an elderly man[D] and now also as a prisoner[l] of Christ Jesus, [10]appeal to you for my son,[m] Onesimus.[E,n] I fathered[F,o] him while I was in chains. [11]Once he was useless to you, but now he is useful both to you and to me. [12]I am sending him back to you as a part of myself.[G,H] [13]I wanted to keep him with me, so that in my imprisonment for the gospel he might serve me in your place. [14]But I didn't want to do anything without your consent, so that your good deed might not be out of obligation, but of your own free will. [15]For perhaps this is why he was separated from you for a brief time, so that you might get him back permanently, [16]no longer as a •slave, but more than a slave—as a dearly loved brother. He is especially so to me, but even more to you, both in the flesh[p] and in the Lord.[l,q]

[17]So if you consider me a partner, accept[r] him as you would me. [18]And if he has wronged you in any way, or owes you anything, charge that to my account.[s] [19]I, Paul, write this with my own hand:[t] I will repay it—not to mention to you that you owe me even your own self. [20]Yes, brother, may I have joy from you in

[a]1 Ac 13:9
[b]2Tm 1:8; Heb 13:3
[c]Rm 1:1
[d]Ac 16:1; 1Tm 1:2
[e]2 Col 4:17
[f]Php 2:25
[g]Ac 12:12; Rm 16:5
[h]5 Dt 6:5; Mt 22:37; Gl 5:6,22; Eph 6:23; 1Th 1:3; 3:6; 5:8; 1Tm 1:14; 1Jn 4:20
[i]6 Gl 5:6
[j]Gn 1:31; 18:18; 3Jn 11
[k]7 Lk 12:19; 2Tm 1:16
[l]9 2Tm 1:8; Heb 13:3
[m]10 1Th 2:11
[n]Col 4:9
[o]1Co 4:15
[p]16 Php 3:3
[q]1Co 16:19; Rv 11:8
[r]17 Rm 14:1
[s]18 Rm 5:13
[t]19 1Co 16:21

[A]2 Other mss read *our beloved*   [B]5 Lit *faith that you have toward*   [C]6 Other mss read *in you*   [D]9 Or *an ambassador*   [E]10 In Gk, Onesimus means useful.   [F]10 Referring to the fact that Paul led him to Christ; 1Co 4:15   [G]12 Other mss read *him back. Receive him as a part of myself.*   [H]12 Lit *you—that is, my inward parts*   [I]16 Both physically and spiritually

---

1 On **prisoner**, see Introduction. In the phrase **of Christ Jesus**, "of" may mean "belonging to," "for the sake of," or "because of [my service for]." Or perhaps all three senses are involved. **Timothy** is associated with Paul as co-author or co-sender, but the letter is primarily Paul's own intercession with Philemon on behalf of Onesimus, for only the singular "I" (not "we") is found in verses 4-22.

2 Apphia was probably Philemon's wife and **Archippus** their son. There is no evidence of special buildings being used for church activities until the third century. Until that time houses served as meeting places. NT references to house churches and their hosts are: Gaius at Corinth (Rm 16:23); Aquila and Priscilla at Ephesus (1Co 16:19) and at Rome (Rm 16:3,5); Lydia at Philippi (Ac 16:15,40); Nympha at Laodicea (Col 4:15); Philemon at Colossae (Phm 2); and probably Mary at Jerusalem (Ac 12:12) and Jason at Thessalonica (Ac 17:5-6).

4 Paul's letters usually begin with prayers of thanksgiving for his readers' spiritual life and progress (e.g., Rm 1:8; 1Co 1:4-7; Php 1:3-5).

5 Because believers do not have **faith . . . for all the saints**, the word-order may be a literary technique called "chiasm" where words or phrases correspond to one another crosswise (A-B-B-A), like the Greek letter *chi* (X). Thus the verse means, "your love for all the saints and faith toward the Lord Jesus."

love \ / faith

the Lord Jesus   all the saints

11 Through the conversion power of the gospel (see "my son" in v. 10), a person who had previously been **useless** (Gk *achrestos*) had become **useful** (Gk *euchrestos*), now living up to his name (Onesimus means "useful" in Greek).

12 A runaway slave who was returned to his rightful owner could face a variety of punishments, including flogging, branding, chains, or even crucifixion.

15-16 Whatever his personal hope (see vv. 11-12), Paul seriously reckons with the possibility that Philemon might decide to retain the services of Onesimus as a slave **permanently**. Paul implies (v. 15) that Onesimus's separation from Philemon, which was caused by the slave's unlawful departure, was encompassed within the gracious, providential will of God. Upon his return, Onesimus would be even dearer to Philemon than he was to Paul because their dual relation as slave and master (**in the flesh**) and as Christian brothers (**in the Lord**) would be experienced within the intimacy of a single household.

18 The wrong that Onesimus had done may have been some misconduct before he ran away, a theft when he disappeared, or the loss Philemon suffered by Onesimus's unlawful absence.

19 Unlike his usual practice of dictating his letters to a scribe (see Rm 16:22), Paul may have written this short and intensely personal letter by his own hand. In any case, Paul here is giving a promissory note, a signed statement of indebtedness (Gk *cheirographon* in Col 2:14), by which he formally and legally assumes all of Onesimus's indebtedness toward Philemon. This is a remarkable promise when we remember that Paul was poor (2Co 6:10).

the Lord; refresh my heart in Christ. ²¹ Since I am confident of your obedience, I am writing to you, knowing that you will do even more than I say. ²² But meanwhile, also prepare a guest room for me, for I hope that through your prayers I will be restored to you.

Final Greetings

²³ Epaphras,^a my fellow prisoner in Christ

Jesus, greets you, and so do ²⁴ Mark,^b Aristarchus,^c Demas, and Luke,^d my coworkers.

²⁵ The grace of the Lord^{A,e} Jesus Christ be with your spirit.^f

^a 23 Col 1:7; 4:12
^b 24 Ac 12:12,25; 15:37,39; Col 4:10; 2Tm 4:11; 1Pt 5:13
^c Ac 19:29
^d Col 4:14; 2Tm 4:10-11
^e 25 2Th 3:18; Rv 11:8
^f Ps 51:12

---

^A 25 Other mss read *our Lord*

21 By **your obedience**, Paul could have meant obedience to God's will, obedience to his own requests as a friend and "prisoner of Christ Jesus" (v. 1), or obedience to "what is right" (v. 8). The undefined and climactic **you will do even more** could refer to the forgiveness of Onesimus and his reinstatement as a slave in Philemon's household. More probably it refers to the setting free (manumission) of Onesimus, allowing him to enter Christian service there at Colossae or at Rome with Paul.

22 The request for **a guest room** suggests Paul expected to be released from prison and pay Philemon a visit to see how

his letter had impacted the relationship between Philemon and Onesimus.

23-24 For these names, see Col 4:10,12,14.

25 All of Paul's letters begin and end with a reference to **grace** (Gk *charis*), God's unsought and undeserved favor, His free and unmerited saving action. Salvation and all its associated blessings were brought by Christ (2Co 8:9; 12:9). Although in Paul's benedictions Christ is the sole source of *charis*, in his salutations (as in Phm 3) God the Father and Christ are generally mentioned as the joint and unified source of *charis*.

Hebrews

Introduction

The epistle to the Hebrews is a tribute to the incomparable Son of God and an encouragement to the author's persecuted fellow believers. The author feared that his Christian readers were wavering in their endurance. The writer had a twofold approach: (1) He exalted Jesus Christ, who is addressed as both "God" and "the Son of Man," and is thus the only One who can serve as mediator between God and man; and (2) he exhorted his fellow Christians, "Let us go on to maturity," and live "by faith."

Representatives of the Greek city states had competed in the Olympic Games (*Olympiakoi Agones*) for nearly 850 years when the book of Hebrews was written. The writer of Hebrews had likely seen these kinds of competitions and drew on his readers' experiences of such events when he encouraged them to recall the large cloud of witnesses surrounding them as they ran. He urged them to "lay aside every weight and the sin that so easily ensnares us. Let us run with endurance the race that lies before us, keeping our eyes on Jesus" (12:1-2).

Circumstances of Writing

Author: The text of Hebrews does not identify its author. What we do know is that the author was a second-generation Christian, for he said he received the confirmed message of Christ from "those who heard" Jesus Himself (2:3). Because Paul claimed his gospel was revealed directly by the Lord (1Co 15:8; Gl 1:12), it is doubtful that he was the author of Hebrews. The author was familiar with Timothy, but he referred to him as "our brother" (13:23), rather than as "my true son in the faith," as Paul did (1Tm 1:2).

Scholars have also proposed the following persons as authors: Luke, Clement of Rome, Barnabas, Apollos, Timothy, Philip, Peter, Silas, Jude, and Aristion. Ultimately it does not matter that the identity of the author is now lost. We should be satisfied with the fact that early Christians received the letter as inspired and authoritative Scripture and that its value for Christian discipleship is unquestioned.

Background: The author of Hebrews knew his recipients well since he called them "brothers" (3:12; 7:5; 10:19; 13:22) and "dear friends" (6:9). Like the writer, they were converts who had heard the gospel through the earliest followers of Christ (2:3). Scholars have speculated that those to whom the book was written were a breakaway group such as a house church that had separated from the main church. Another theory holds that the recipients were former Jewish priests who had converted to Christianity, and that they were considering a return to Judaism (at least in conformity to certain practices) in order to avoid persecution from fellow Jews. Another theory holds that the group was not necessarily Jewish since Gentile Christians also revered the OT as Scripture.

Regarding when the book was written, it is clear that the fall of Jerusalem (A.D. 70) had not yet occurred. The destruction of the temple would have been mentioned if it had already occurred, for it would have strengthened the letter's argument about Christ's sacrifice spelling the end of the temple sacrificial system. The public persecution mentioned in 10:32-34 implies one of two possibilities for dating the book. We know that the

---

Prehistory–1900 B.C.

Abel offers a better sacrifice than Cain.

Abram moves from Haran to Canaan. 2091

Sarah conceives at age 90. 2066

Abraham offers up Isaac in obedience to God's command. 2046?

Isaac blesses Jacob and Esau. 1930?

1900–1445 B.C.

Jacob blesses Joseph's sons, Ephraim and Manasseh. 1859

Birth of Moses 1526

Exodus from Egypt and defeat of Pharaoh at the Red Sea 1446

God's awesome manifestation and covenant with Israel at Sinai 1446

Tabernacle is built and dedicated. 1445

Roman emperors Nero and Domitian in (A.D. 64–68 and 81–82 respectively) persecuted Christians. Most likely Hebrews was written during the persecution under Nero, perhaps just before the destruction of the temple.

Message and Purpose

The author of Hebrews wanted to exalt Jesus Christ. A verbal indication of this desire is the consistent and repetitive usage of the Greek word *kreitton*, which means "more excellent," "superior," or "better." This word is the common thread that binds together the complex and subtle theological argumentation of the book. In comparison to everything else in the divine plan for creation and redemption, Jesus Christ is superior. The author described the superiority of the new covenant to the old covenant because he wanted his readers to remember that Jesus Christ is the fulfillment of the law and God's promises in the OT. In this light, readers should be careful about "recrucifying the Son of God and holding Him up to contempt" (6:6). The author wanted to move these believers from their arrested state of development into a pattern of growth in their relationship with Jesus Christ.

Contribution to the Bible

No other book in the NT ties together OT history and practices with the life of Jesus Christ as thoroughly as the book of Hebrews. Just as Jesus Christ taught that the OT was fulfilled in Himself (Mt 5:17-18; Lk 24:27), so the author of Hebrews taught that the old covenant was brought to completion in the new covenant (7:20–8:13). Hebrews also shows that because the old covenant has been fulfilled in the new covenant, the new covenant is actually "better" (7:22). The new covenant was made superior by the ministry of Jesus Christ.

Structure

In concluding the book of Hebrews, the author wrote, "Brothers, I urge you to receive this message of exhortation, for I have written to you briefly" (13:22). If the literary style of Hebrews indicates anything, it is that it is a written theological sermon. It is not so much a letter—although it certainly ends like one—because it has no

1445–1125 B.C.	1125 B.C.–A.D. 95
Israel wanders in the wilderness. 1445–1407	Samson 1120–1060 B.C.?
Rahab supports the conquest of Jericho. 1406	Samuel 1105–1025 B.C.?
Deborah and Barak defeat the Canaanites. 1320?	David 1050–970 B.C.
Gideon 1250–1175?	Jesus' death, resurrection, and ascension A.D. 33
Jephthah 1200–1150?	Hebrews first quoted by Clement of Rome in his letter to the Corinthians A.D. 95

opening subscription, as was the norm with ancient letters. Hebrews instead begins with an introductory essay about the superiority of Jesus Christ (1:1-4). However, its capacity to encounter the reader's soul indicates it is more than just a literary essay. Indeed, it has a definite sermonic character since it expounds the Scriptures at length in order to challenge the reader to faith and faithfulness. The sustained development of a complex, holistic theology of covenant indicates that Hebrews is a written theological sermon that discloses the broad sweep of God's grand redemptive plan for humanity.

Outline

I. The Superiority of the Son of God (1:1–2:18)
  A. The exaltation of Jesus Christ (1:1-4)
  B. The divine nature of the Son (1:5-14)
  C. The human nature of the Son (2:1-18)

II. The Superiority of the Son's Faithfulness (3:1–4:16)
  A. The faithfulness of the Son (3:1-6)
  B. A warning (3:7-19)
  C. The way forward (4:1-16)

III. The Superiority of the Son's Work (5:1–6:20)
  A. The work of the Son (5:1-10)
  B. The call to maturity (5:11–6:3)
  C. The way forward (6:4-20)

IV. The Superiority of the Son's Priesthood (7:1–10:39)
  A. The superiority of His order (7:1-19)
  B. The superiority of His covenant (7:20–8:13)
  C. The superiority of His ministry (9:1-28)
  D. The superiority of His sacrifice (10:1-18)
  E. The way forward (10:19-39)

V. The Superiority of the Christian Faith (11:1–12:2)
  A. The hall of heroes (11:1-40)
  B. The way forward (12:1-2)

VI. The Superiority of the Father's Way (12:3-29)
  A. The work of God (12:3-13)
  B. The way forward (12:14-29)

VII. The Superiority of the Christian Life in the Church (13:1-25)
  A. The way forward (13:1-19)
  B. A blessing from the author (13:20-25)

The Nature of the Son

1 Long ago God spoke[a] to the fathers by the prophets[b] at different times and in different ways.[c] [2] In these last days,[d] He has spoken to us by His Son. God has appointed Him heir of all things and made the universe[A,e] through Him. [3] The Son is the radiance[B] of God's glory and the exact expression[C] of His nature, sustaining all things by His powerful word. After making purification for sins,[D] He sat down at the right hand of the Majesty on high.[E,f] [4] So He became higher in rank than the angels, just as the name He inherited is superior to theirs.[g]

The Son Superior to Angels

[5] For to which of the angels did He ever say,

You are My Son; today I have become Your Father,[F,G] or again, **I will be His Father, and He will be My Son?**[H,h] [6] When He again[i] brings His firstborn into the world,[i] He says, **And all God's angels must worship Him.**[J,j] [7] And about the angels He says:

He makes His angels winds,[K]
and His servants[L] **a fiery flame,**[M,k]

[8] but to[N] the Son:

Your throne, God,
is forever and ever,
and the scepter of Your kingdom

is a scepter of justice.[l]
[9] **You have loved righteousness**
and hated lawlessness;
this is why God, Your God,
has anointed You
with the oil of joy[m]
rather than Your companions.[O,P]

[10] And:

In the beginning, Lord,
You established the earth,
and the heavens are the works
of Your hands;[n]
[11] **they will perish, but You remain.**
They will all wear out like clothing;[o]
[12] **You will roll them up like a cloak,**[Q]
and they will be changed like a robe.
But You are the same,
and Your years will never end.[R,p]

[13] Now to which of the angels has He ever said:

Sit at My right hand
until I make Your enemies
Your footstool?[S,T,q]

[14] Are they not all ministering spirits sent out to serve those who are going to inherit salvation?[r]

A1:2 Lit ages   B1:3 Or reflection   C1:3 Or representation, or copy, or reproduction   D1:3 Other mss read for our sins by Himself
E1:3 Or He sat down on high at the right hand of the Majesty   F1:5 Or have begotten You   G1:5 Ps 2:7   H1:5 2Sm 7:14; 1Ch 17:13
I1:6 Or And again, when He   J1:6 Dt 32:43 LXX; Ps 97:7   K1:7 Or spirits   L1:7 Or ministers   M1:7 Ps 104:4   N1:8 Or about
O1:9 Or associates   P1:8-9 Ps 45:6-7   Q1:12 Other mss omit like a cloak   R1:10-12 Ps 102:25-27   S1:13 Or enemies a footstool
for Your feet   T1:13 Ps 110:1

1:1–2:18 Everything in creation and everything in redemption history is centered in Jesus Christ, the Son of God and the Son of Man. The author was convinced that Jesus was the focal point of all that God had done and, therefore, that He was the focal point of the faith of the church. Jesus Christ is the agent of creation, the height of revelation, the mediator of redemption, and the judge of history.

1:1–2a These verses relate the revelation of Jesus Christ to God's previous revelation to the OT prophets. God spoke in past ages **by the prophets** in a variety of ways and times, but He has now progressed past this former revelation and spoken directly to mankind **by His Son.** The doctrine of progressive revelation recognizes the prophets' words as divine revelation, but their words pointed ahead to the promise of a Messiah. This Messiah has now come—Jesus Christ.

1:2b–4 Seven praises start the letter's argument that Jesus Christ and everything connected with Him is superior to all that had come before and all that will come after Him. (1) Jesus Christ is the **heir** of creation for whom all things have been made. (2) He is the Creator through whom all things have come into existence. (3) He is the **radiance** of the divine glory toward which all of creation looks for fulfillment. (4) He is the **exact expression** (Gk charakteyr) of the "nature" (Gk hupostaseos) of God the Father. This means the Son participates in the divine nature with the Father. (5) He is the "Word" of God, the only prophet of God who is also God Himself. (6) He is the priest of God who has provided the

perfect sacrifice for all human sins. (7) He is the king who sits on the throne at the **right hand** of the Father. Jesus is, therefore, **higher in rank** and **superior** to those high beings of creation known as **angels.**

1:5–14 The author teaches his readers about the divine and human natures of the Son of God by establishing His superiority to the angels and to Moses. It would have shocked the typical Jewish reader to hear that a man was higher in rank than angels. Jesus Christ was fully human, but He was fully divine. This makes Him superior to the angels.

Drawing on a series of OT quotations attributed to God, the author demonstrated how God the Father had addressed His Son as divine. God the Father addressed Him uniquely as **My Son** (2Sm 7:14; 1Ch 17:13; Ps 2:7), "God" (Ps 45:6-7), and "Lord" (Ps 102:22). Moreover, God the Father attributed divine activities to His Son. He is the **firstborn** and "begotten" Son who was brought into the world so that all the angels **must worship Him** (Dt 32:43; Ps 97:7). He is the Son who made the angels **His angels** and **His servants** (Ps 104:4). He is the Son who sits on the divine **throne** and rules with the divine attribute of **righteousness** (Ps 45:6-7). He is the Son who created heaven and earth **in the beginning,** and who will remain the same when creation is consummated, because He shares in the divine attribute of eternal (Ps 102:25-27). These examples show that God the Father declared Jesus Christ, the promised Messiah, to be the eternally begotten Son of God.

Warning against Neglect

2 We must, therefore, pay even more attention to what we have heard, so that we will not drift away. [2]For if the message spoken through angels was legally binding[A,a] and every transgression and disobedience received a just punishment,[b] [3]how will we escape if we neglect such a great salvation? It was first spoken by the Lord and was confirmed to us by those who heard Him.[c] [4]At the same time, God also testified by signs and wonders, various miracles, and distributions of gifts from the Holy Spirit according to His will.[d]

Jesus and Humanity

[5]For He has not subjected to angels the world to come that we are talking about. [6]But one has somewhere testified:

What is man that You remember him,
or the son of man that You care
for him?
[7] You made him lower than the angels

for a short time;
You crowned him with glory
and honor[B]
[8] and subjected everything
under his feet.[c]

For in **subjecting everything** to him, He left nothing that is not subject to him. As it is, we do not yet see **everything subjected** to him.[e] [9]But we do see Jesus—**made lower than the angels for a short time** so that by God's grace He might taste death for everyone—crowned with glory and honor[f] because of His suffering in death.[g]

[10]For in bringing many sons to glory, it was entirely appropriate that God—all things exist for Him and through Him—should make the source[D] of their salvation perfect through sufferings.[h] [11]For the One who *sanctifies and those who are sanctified all have one Father.[E] That is why Jesus is not ashamed to call them *brothers,[i] [12]saying:

---

a 2:2 Dt 33:2; Ac 7:53; Heb 1:1
b Nm 15:30; Heb 10:28
c 2:3 Lk 1:2; Heb 1:2; 10:29
d 2:4 Jn 4:48; Ac 2:22; 1Co 12:4; Eph 1:5
e 2:6–8 Jb 7:17; Ps 8:4-6; 1Co 15:25
f 2:9 Ac 2:33; 3:13
g Jn 3:16; 2Co 5:15; Php 2:9
h 2:10 Lk 13:32; 24:26; Rm 11:36; Heb 7:28
i 2:11 Mt 28:10; Jn 20:17; Ac 17:28; Heb 10:10

A 2:2 Or *valid*, or *reliable*　B 2:7 Other mss add *and set him over the works of your hands*　C 2:6-8 Ps 8:5-7 LXX　D 2:10 Or *pioneer*, or *leader*　E 2:11 Or *father*, or *origin*, or *all are of one*

2:1-18 In this chapter the author turned to the consideration of Jesus as a human being. He is the Son of Man just as surely as He is the Son of God. Believers err if they emphasize one reality to the neglect of the other. The author uses the fact that the law was **binding** to introduce the first of several strong exhortations in the book (3:7-19; 5:11–6:3; 10:26-31; 12:1-2,14-29). He warned his readers about the danger of drifting away from participating in the gospel mission by standing on the sidelines as God's plan for history moves forward. The gospel was verified to its first hearers by **signs** and **wonders, various miracles**, and **distributions of gifts** from the **Holy Spirit** as the church was in its foundational stages. The Word of God is now verified by the internal testimony of the Holy Spirit, so there seems no further need for such spectacular acts of verification.

2:5-9 The author demonstrated that the eternal Son entered creation to become a man and thereby temporarily became **lower than the angels**. Psalm 8, on one level taken to be a reference to mankind and the dominion conferred on him by God, also applies to the **son of man** as Jesus Christ. Psalm 8 is a look backward to Genesis as well as a look forward to events disclosed in the book of Revelation, where God subjects all things to humanity by subjecting them to Jesus. Jesus was **crowned with glory and honor** by God because He suffered death for **everyone**. Like Paul, the author noted that the coronation of Jesus Christ as King of kings followed His humiliating crucifixion in obedience to the Father (Php 2:8-9).

2:10-18 In these verses the author showed why it was necessary that the eternal Son became a man. First, it was **appropriate** that the Son should have a ministry completed in suffering, which all humans experience, so that he might identify with us and bring **many sons** into the presence of God. People who have accepted Christ's sacrifice on their behalf can be referred to as "children" of God because the Son of God has made them His **brothers**. The author quoted three OT verses to show that the Son is present in the

gathered church (Ps 22:22), that the Son trusts the Father (Is 8:17), and that the church can come before the Father because it is united with Christ (Is 8:18). Second, the Son became a man and suffered death so that He could **destroy the one holding the power of death—that is, the Devil**. It is by virtue of Christ's death on our behalf that we are freed from the fear of death. Third, the Son became a man and suffered death so that He could serve as a **faithful high priest** in service to God. The only person who can serve as a mediator between God and man is the One who is both God and man. It is by reason of His faithfulness as a man who was **tested** and **suffered** that He could make **propitiation** for the **sins of the people**. Not only did He suffer divine

---

teleioo

Greek Pronunciation	[teh lay AH oh]
HCSB Translation	perfect
Uses in Hebrews	9
Uses in the NT	23
Focus passage	Hebrews 2:10

The verb *teleioo* (perfect) has several meanings in the NT. In certain texts, *teleioo* sometimes means to *complete*, *finish*, or *accomplish* in the sense of fulfilling a task by bringing it to a desired end. In this sense, Jesus was sent *to finish* the works of His Father (Jn 4:34), a task He faithfully *completed* (Jn 17:4). Paul, in his speech to the Ephesian elders, expressed a desire *to accomplish* the ministry he had received from God (Ac 20:24). In other texts, *teleioo* speaks of *bringing something to an end* or *perfecting something*. In this sense, *teleioo* refers to the process or action of overcoming an imperfect or incomplete state with a more *perfect* or *complete* one. By virtue of His earthly sufferings, Jesus *has been perfected* (qualified, brought to His goal) to minister as high priest forever (Heb 2:10; 5:9; 7:28). Abraham's faith *was perfected* by means of his works (Jms 2:22). The old covenant law could never *perfect* the worshipers who continually offered sacrifices (Heb 7:19; 10:1).

I will proclaim Your name
  to My brothers;
I will sing hymns to You
  in the congregation.[A,a]

[13] Again, **I will trust in Him.**[B] And again, **Here I am with the children God gave Me.**[C,b] [14] Now since the children have flesh and blood in common, Jesus also shared in these, so that through His death He might destroy the one holding the power of death—that is, the Devil[c]— [15] and free those who were held in slavery all their lives by the fear of death.[d] [16] For it is clear that He does not reach out to help angels, but to help Abraham's offspring. [17] Therefore, He had to be like His brothers in every way, so that He could become a merciful and faithful high priest in service[D] to God, to make •propitiation[e] for the sins of the people.[f] [18] For since He Himself was tested and has suffered, He is able to help those who are tested.

Our Apostle and High Priest

3 Therefore, holy •brothers and companions in a heavenly calling, consider Jesus, the apostle and high priest of our confession;[g] [2] He was faithful to the One who appointed Him, just as Moses was in all God's household. [3] For Jesus is considered worthy of more glory than Moses, just as the builder has more honor than the house. [4] Now every house is built by someone, but the One who built everything is God.[h] [5] Moses was faithful as a servant[i] in all God's household, as a testimony to what would be said in the future. [6] But Christ was faithful as a Son over His household. And we are that household if we hold on to the courage and the confidence of our hope.[E,j]

a2:12 Ps 22:22; Heb 12:23
b2:13 Ps 18:2; Is 8:17-18; 12:2; Jn 10:29
c2:14 Jn 1:14; 1Co 15:54-56; Col 2:15; 2Tm 1:10; 1Jn 3:8
d2:15 Rm 8:15; 2Tm 1:7
e2:17 2Co 5:21
fPhp 2:7; Heb 4:15; 5:1-2; 7:26-28
g3:1 Rm 15:8; Php 3:14; Heb 2:11,17; 4:14-15
h3:4 Eph 2:10; 3:9
i3:5 Ex 14:31; Nm 12:7; Dt 18:19
j3:6 Mt 10:22; Rm 5:2; 11:22; 1Co 3:16; Heb 1:2
k3:7-11 Ps 95:7-11; Ac 7:36; Heb 4:3,5
l3:13 Eph 4:22; Heb 10:24
m3:14 1Co 15:2; Heb 3:6; 10:23; 11:1
n3:15 Ps 95:7-8
o3:16 Nm 14:2; Dt 1:35-38
p3:17 Nm 14:29; Ps 106:26

Warning against Unbelief

[7] Therefore, as the Holy Spirit says:

Today, if you hear His voice,
[8]   do not harden your hearts
    as in the rebellion,
on the day of testing
  in the wilderness,
[9] where your fathers tested Me, tried Me,
and saw My works [10] for 40 years.
Therefore I was provoked
  with that generation
and said, "They always go astray
  in their hearts,
and they have not known My ways."
[11] So I swore in My anger,
"They will not enter My rest."[F,k]

[12] Watch out, brothers, so that there won't be in any of you an evil, unbelieving heart that departs from the living God. [13] But encourage each other daily, while it is still called **today**, so that none of you is hardened by sin's deception.[l] [14] For we have become companions of the •Messiah if we hold firmly until the end the reality[G] that we had at the start.[m] [15] As it is said:

Today, if you hear His voice,
  do not harden your hearts
    as in the rebellion.[H,n]

[16] For who heard and rebelled? Wasn't it really all who came out of Egypt under Moses?[o] [17] And who was He provoked with for 40 years? Was it not with those who sinned, whose bodies fell in the wilderness?[p] [18] And who did He swear to that they would not enter His rest, if not those who disobeyed? [19] So we see that they were unable to enter because of unbelief.

A2:12 Ps 22:22   B2:13 2Sm 22:3 LXX; Is 8:17 LXX; 12:2 LXX   C2:13 Is 8:18 LXX   D2:17 Lit *things*   E3:6 Other mss add *firm to the end*   F3:7-11 Ps 95:7-11   G3:14 Or *confidence*   H3:15 Ps 95:7-8

retribution on our behalf, but He is able to help us because He is **like his brothers** in every way except sin.

3:1-4:16 In these chapters the author turned from demonstrating the Son's superiority over the angels to demonstrating that the Son is superior to Moses, the mediator of the law, and Joshua, the conqueror of the promised land. The common thread through these chapters is faithfulness. By explaining that Jesus **was faithful** (3:2), the author hoped to persuade the readers to **hold fast** (4:14) until the end.

3:1-6 The author appealed to his commonality with the readers, addressing them as **holy brothers** and **companions** who had received the same calling from God as he. He asked them to turn their minds and hearts toward the Savior and **consider Jesus**. God had identified Moses as the one who was uniquely **faithful . . . in all God's household** (see Nm 12:7). His faithfulness was for the sake of showing the superiority of the faithfulness of Christ, since Christ was faithful as **a Son over His household**. Jesus was

faithful "over" the "household" of which Moses was a part. Although Moses was faithful in relaying God's law, his appointed role was to point toward the coming Son of God. Jesus, who was faithful in His role of bringing the gospel to those under the condemnation of the law, is therefore **worthy of more glory**.

3:7-19 Having established the superiority of the gospel of Christ to the law of Moses, the author proceeded to explain the meaning of Psalm 95. His purpose was to warn his readers that if the punishment for disobedience of the law was severe, then punishment for faithlessness to the gospel would be far worse. The judgment of God is described in Ps 95:7-11 on the disobedient Israelites in the wilderness. God did not allow that faithless generation to enter the promised land because they hardened their hearts against Him. The lesson is that those who **hear** the **voice** of God should not harden their hearts against God's Word and disobey His commands. The result of such unbelief is divine judgment. They would **not enter** God's **rest**.

The Promised Rest

4 Therefore, while the promise to enter His rest remains, let us fear that none of you should miss it.[A] [2]For we also have received the good news just as they did; but the message they heard did not benefit them, since they were not united with those who heard it in faith[B,a] [3](for we who have believed enter the rest), in keeping with what[c] He has said:

> So I swore in My anger,
> **they will not enter My rest.**[D,b]

And yet His works have been finished since the foundation of the world, [4]for somewhere He has spoken about the seventh day in this way:

> **And on the seventh day**
> **God rested from all His works.**[E,c]

[5]Again, in that passage He says, **They will never enter My rest.**[D] [6]Since it remains for some to enter it, and those who formerly received the good news did not enter because of disobedience,[d] [7]again, He specifies a certain day—**today**—speaking through David after such a long time, as previously stated:

> **Today, if you hear His voice,**
> **do not harden your hearts.**[F,e]

[8]For if Joshua[f] had given them rest, God would not have spoken later about another day. [9]Therefore, a Sabbath rest remains for God's people. [10]For the person who has entered His rest has rested from his own works, just as God did from His.[g] [11]Let us then make every effort to enter that rest, so that no one will fall into the same pattern of disobedience.

[12]For the word of God is living and effective[h] and sharper than any double-edged sword,[i] penetrating as far as the separation of soul and spirit, joints and marrow. It is able to judge the ideas and thoughts of the heart.[j] [13]No creature is hidden from Him, but all things are naked and exposed to the eyes of Him[k] to whom we must give an account.

Our Great High Priest

[14]Therefore, since we have a great high priest who has passed through the heavens—Jesus the Son of God—let us hold fast to the confession.[l] [15]For we do not have a high priest who is unable to sympathize with our weaknesses, but One who has been tested in every way as we are,[m] yet without sin.[n] [16]Therefore let us approach the throne of grace with boldness, so that we may receive mercy and find grace to help us at the proper time.

The Messiah, a High Priest

5 For every high priest taken from men is appointed in service[G] to God for the peo-

Cross references (center column)

a 4:1-2 1Th 2:13; Heb 12:15
b 4:3 Ps 95:11; Heb 3:11
c 4:4 Gn 2:2; Ex 20:11
d 4:5-6 Ps 95:11; Heb 3:19
e 4:7 Ps 95:7-8; Heb 3:7
f 4:8 Jos 22:4
g 4:10 Heb 4:4; Rv 14:13
h 4:12 Jr 23:29; 1Pt 1:23
i Is 49:2; Eph 6:17; Rv 1:16; 2:12
j 1Co 14:24-25
k 4:13 2Ch 16:9; Jb 26:6; 34:21; Ps 33:15-15
l 4:14 Heb 3:1; 6:20; 10:23
m 4:15 Is 53:3; Heb 2:18
n 2Co 5:21; 1Pt 2:22

A 4:1 Or that any of you might seem to have missed it   B 4:2 Other mss read since it was not united by faith in those who heard
C 4:3 Or rest), just as   D 4:3,5 Ps 95:11   E 4:4 Gn 2:2   F 4:7 Ps 95:7-8   G 5:1 Lit things

---

4:1-16 The author now drew the readers into examining their own personal faith as the Word of God shines its penetrating light upon the inner man. Faithfulness begins with a proper internal disposition. The **living and effec-**tive Word of God probes into the deepest part of a person like a surgeon's knife to discern his innermost **ideas and thoughts**. God's Word reveals to him both his ingrained wickedness and the saving way of faith. At that critical point, when the divine judge reveals Himself through His Word, the hearer must **make every effort** to enter the divine **rest** by believing.

If the result of unbelief and disobedience to God is exclusion from divine rest, then the result of true faith and faithfulness to God is entrance into everlasting divine rest. Such a rest was not available through the ministry of Joshua in the OT since it was reserved for the ministry of the NT "Joshua." The name "Jesus" is a Greek derivative of the Hebrew name Joshua, which means "the Lord is salvation." The ministry of Joshua did not bring people **Sabbath rest**. Only through the superior ministry of Jesus the Son of God may a person enter divine rest. Only through the **great high priest**, who has come from heaven and identified with man in his weakness, may we approach the **throne of grace** with **boldness**.

5:1–6:20 In these chapters the author established the superiority of Jesus as priest over Aaron as priest. The Son's superior work as a high priest serves as the basis for a call to Christian maturity.

5:1-10 Aaron was the high priest of Israel who had been **called by God**, thus establishing his authority. His purpose as a priest was to offer to God **sacrifices for sins** on behalf

katapausis

Greek Pronunciation	[kah TAH pow sis]
HCSB Translation	rest
Uses in Hebrews	8
Uses in the NT	9
Focus passage	Hebrews 4:1,3,5,10,11

In the NT, *katapausis* (rest) has multiple referents. Luke makes reference to a temple for God, the place where He would *rest* and live (Ac 7:49). Hebrews refers to *rest* as the Christian's future destination, the place of God's blessing. That *rest* is available to every generation of saints, but its realization comes only through obedience (Heb 4:2,6,11). God's *rest* at creation (Heb 4:4) points past Joshua and David (4:7-8) to this final *rest* for believers (Heb 4:9). For Moses and his generation, that *rest* was the Promised Land, the place of God's blessing (Heb 3:11,16-19). Unfortunately, that generation missed it (Heb 3:19). For the Christian, *rest* is the final place of God's heavenly blessing, which they will receive if they hold fast their confession (Heb 4:14). The author of Hebrews strongly exhorts his audience to strive in obedience and perseverance to ensure they attain that future *rest* (Heb 4:1,11).

ple, to offer both gifts and sacrifices for sins. [2]He is able to deal gently with those who are ignorant and are going astray, since he is also subject to weakness.[a] [3]Because of this, he must make a sin offering for himself as well as for the people.[b] [4]No one takes this honor on himself; instead, a person is called by God, just as Aaron was.[c] [5]In the same way, the •Messiah did not exalt Himself to become a high priest, but the One who said to Him, **You are My Son; today I have become Your Father,**[A,d] [6]also said in another passage, **You are a priest forever in the order of Melchizedek.**[B,e]

[7]During His earthly life,[c] He offered prayers and appeals[f] with loud cries and tears[g] to the One who was able to save Him from death, and He was heard because of His reverence. [8]Though He was God's Son, He learned obedience through what He suffered.[h] [9]After He was perfected, He became the source of eternal salvation for all who obey Him, [10]and He was declared by God a high priest in the order of Melchizedek.

*a*5:2 Heb 2:18; 4:15; 7:28
*b*5:3 Lv 4:3; 9:7; Heb 9:7
*c*5:4 Ex 28:1; 1Ch 23:18
*d*5:5 Php 2:7; Jn 8:54; Heb 1:1
*e*5:6 Ps 110:4; Heb 7:17
*f*5:7 Mt 26:39; Mk 14:36
*g*Ps 22:1; Mt 27:46,50; Mk 15:34,37; Lk 23:46
*h*5:8 Php 2:7-8; Heb 1:2
*i*5:12 1Co 3:2; Heb 6:1; 1Pt 2:21
*j*5:14 Is 7:15; 1Co 2:6
*k*6:1 Php 3:13; Heb 5:12; 9:14
*l*6:2 Jn 3:25; Ac 6:6; 17:31-32; 19:4-6

The Problem of Immaturity

[11]We have a great deal to say about this, and it's difficult to explain, since you have become too lazy to understand. [12]Although by this time you ought to be teachers, you need someone to teach you the basic principles of God's revelation again. You need milk, not solid food.[i] [13]Now everyone who lives on milk is inexperienced with the message about righteousness, because he is an infant. [14]But solid food is for the mature—for those whose senses have been trained to distinguish between good and evil.[j]

Warning against Regression

6 Therefore, leaving the elementary message about the •Messiah, let us go on to maturity, not laying again the foundation of repentance from dead works, faith in God,[k] [2]teaching about ritual washings,[D] laying on of hands, the resurrection of the dead, and eternal judgment.[l] [3]And we will do this if God permits.

[4]For it is impossible to renew to repentance

*A*5:7 Ps 2:7   *B*5:6 Gn 14:18-20; Ps 110:4   *C*5:7 Lit *In the days of His flesh*   *D*6:2 Or *about baptisms*

of the people, and to **deal gently** with the ignorance and waywardness of the people on behalf of God. The problem with Aaron's priesthood was Aaron himself; since he was a sinner, he had to make a sin offering for **himself** as well as for **the people**.

Like Aaron, Jesus was called by God, but according to Ps 110:4, God gave Him a unique calling as **a high priest in the order of Melchizedek**. Christ's priesthood was on an entirely different level than that of Aaron. Like Aaron, he offered **prayers and appeals**, but unlike Aaron, Christ was heard **because of His reverence**. Unlike Aaron, Christ learned **obedience** through suffering. Unlike Aaron, the salvation that Christ brought was eternal.

archiereus

Greek Pronunciation	[ahr kee eh ROOS]
HCSB Translation	high priest
Uses in Hebrews	17
Uses in the NT	122
Focus passage	Hebrews 5:10

In the Gospels and Acts, *archiereus* refers to the Jewish *high priest*, who served as president of the Sanhedrin, the Jewish supreme court (Mt 26:3,57; Ac 24:1). The plural *(chief priests)* indicates members of the priestly aristocracy from which the *high priest* was chosen. These *priests* were key figures in the Sanhedrin and belonged to the Sadducean party (Mk 14:55; Ac 5:17). In Hebrews, *archiereus* refers primarily to Christ's priestly ministry, which came from God (Heb 5:5,10) and was superior to that of any earthly *priest* (Heb 7:27-28). Christ is *high priest* of the new covenant, having accomplished the ultimate sacrifice (Heb 8:1-6). He passed through the heavens, entered the true sanctuary, offered Himself as the one final sacrifice, and sat down at God's right hand (Heb 4:14; 6:20; 7:27; 8:1-2; 9:12). Jesus is able to deal mercifully with His people because He was fully human (Heb 2:17; 4:15; 5:1-10).

5:11–6:3 In this section the author paused to consider the theological and moral state of his readers. He expressed concern that they might not understand the **difficult** doctrines he was explaining (5:11). Because of their immaturity, they needed to be warned about failure and encouraged toward maturity. The author listed six basic principles of the elementary message about the Messiah that serve as the foundation of the Christian faith and life. These principles may be divided into three groups of two each. (1) **Repentance** from sinful actions and **faith** toward God (6:1) are the two sides of conversion that begin the Christian life. (2) The baptism of new believers who have received the gospel and **laying on of hands** for Christian leaders (6:2) to proclaim the gospel are fundamental components of church life. (3) The good news of the **resurrection** and the prospect of **eternal judgment** (6:2) are essential components in the gospel that the church preaches.

6:4-20 Verses 6-9 have been the subject of much debate. There are several possible interpretations regarding the author's intentions and the identity of those **who have fallen away**. First, some say those who had "fallen away" were genuine Christians who had forsaken Jesus and reverted to Judaism. A second view says they were hearers who had understood the gospel but had not become true believers. A third interpretation identifies the **things connected with salvation** as sanctification rather than justification. A fourth interpretation holds that the writer is speaking about apostasy as a possibility rather than a reality.

The first interpretation neglects the author's claim that he was speaking in a rhetorical way and was **confident of the better things** regarding his readers. The second interpretation must overcome the language of conversion (**those who were once enlightened, who tasted the heavenly gift, became companions with the Holy Spirit**, and **who tasted God's good word and the powers of the coming age**). These phrases indicate something beyond a mere hearing of the gospel. The third interpretation does not adequately deal

those who were once enlightened, who tasted the heavenly gift, became companions with the Holy Spirit,[a] [5]tasted God's good word and the powers of the coming age, [6]and who have fallen away, because,[A] to their own harm, they are recrucifying the Son of God and holding Him up to contempt.[b] [7]For ground that has drunk the rain that has often fallen on it and that produces vegetation useful to those it is cultivated for receives a blessing from God. [8]But if it produces thorns and thistles, it is worthless and about to be cursed, and will be burned at the end.[c]

[9]Even though we are speaking this way, dear friends, in your case we are confident of the better things connected with salvation. [10]For God is not unjust; He will not forget your work and the love[B] you showed for His name when you served the •saints—and you continue to serve them.[d] [11]Now we want each of you to demonstrate the same diligence for the final realization of your hope, [12]so that you won't become lazy but will be imitators of those who inherit the promises through faith and perseverance.[e]

Inheriting the Promise

[13]For when God made a promise to Abraham, since He had no one greater to swear by, He swore by Himself:

[14]   **I will indeed bless you,**
         and I will greatly multiply you.[C,f]

[15]And so, after waiting patiently, Abraham[D] ob-

tained the promise. [16]For men swear by something greater than themselves, and for them a confirming oath ends every dispute. [17]Because God wanted to show His unchangeable purpose even more clearly to the heirs of the promise, He guaranteed it with an oath,[g] [18]so that through two unchangeable things, in which it is impossible for God to lie, we who have fled for refuge might have strong encouragement to seize the hope set before us.[h] [19]We have this hope as an anchor for our lives, safe and secure. It enters the inner sanctuary behind the curtain.[i] [20]Jesus has entered there on our behalf as a forerunner,[j] because He has become a high priest forever in the order of Melchizedek.[k]

The Greatness of Melchizedek

7 For this Melchizedek—

     King of Salem, priest of the Most
         High God,
     who met Abraham and blessed him
     as he returned from defeating the kings,
[2] and Abraham gave him a tenth
         of everything;
     first, his name means
         king of righteousness,
     then also, king of Salem,
     meaning king of peace;
[3] without father, mother, or genealogy,
     having neither beginning of days
         nor end of life,
     but resembling the Son of God[l]—
     remains a priest forever.

a6:4 Gl 3:3; Eph 2:8; Heb 10:32
b6:6 Heb 10:29; 2Pt 2:21; 1Jn 5:16
c6:7-8 Gn 3:17-18; Ps 65:10; Is 5:6
d6:10 Pr 19:17; Mt 10:42; 25:40; 2Co 8:4; 1Th 1:3; 2Tm 1:18
e6:12 Heb 10:36; 13:7
f6:13-15 Gn 21:5; 22:16-17; Lk 1:73
g6:16-17 Ex 22:11; Heb 11:9
h6:18 Ti 1:2; Heb 12:1
i6:19 Lv 16:2,15; Heb 9:7
j6:20 Heb 4:14; 8:1; 9:24
k Heb 5:6,10; 7:17
l7:1-3 Gn 14:18-20; Mt 4:3; Mk 5:7; Heb 7:6

with the fact that the apostate cannot renew his repentance once he has chosen the way of faithlessness.

Because of problems with the first three views, the fourth interpretation—that the author was speaking of an unfulfilled possibility rather than a concrete reality—seems most acceptable. Indeed, he used the warning against apostasy as a rhetorical means to call his readers to **demonstrate the same diligence** they had shown before. He was confident of something better than apostasy in their lives because he saw their prior love for Christ and faithful service in His name. The author was not detailing a doctrine of apostasy; he was calling his readers to progress toward maturity. Every succeeding statement promotes this goal. Like Abraham, who obtained the promise of God **after waiting patiently**, the readers should **seize the hope** before them because God has **guaranteed** His promise with an **oath**. And because Jesus has entered the **inner sanctuary** of God's presence, the Christian has a sure and firm **anchor** for the soul. There is not a hint of wavering in the author's voice about either God's will or the final outcome for his "dear friends."

7:1–10:39 These chapters are an extended discourse on the superiority of the priesthood of Christ as demonstrated by the superiority of His order, His covenant, His ministry, and His sacrifice.

7:1–19 The Levitical priesthood of the Jews was grounded in the **order of Aaron**, but the priesthood of Jesus Christ

is grounded in the **order of Melchizedek**. The mysterious Melchizedek appeared in Gn 14:18-20 and was not mentioned again until the messianic promise was made in Psalm 110. The author of Hebrews drew from the OT

apator

Greek Pronunciation	[ah PAH tohr]
HCSB Translation	without father
Uses in Hebrews	1
Uses in the NT	1
Focus passage	Hebrews 7:3

Apator means without father and appears once in the NT (Heb 7:3), in reference to the genealogy of Melchizedek, Salem's king. In Classical Greek, apator generally meant one without a father. It could refer to a deity who had no father (Orphicha, Hymni 10.10), the fatherless or orphans as those separated from a father (Sophocles, Trachiniae 300), or one who is disowned by a father (Plato, Leges 929a). Elsewhere, apator referred to a person of unknown father (Plutarchus, Moralia 2.288e) or of illegitimate birth. In the latter case, apator was followed by the mother's name (e.g., "the illegitimate (apator) daughter of Tanephremmis"). In Hebrews, apator is followed by ametor (without mother), highlighting that Melchizedek was not born illegitimately but that he had no traceable genealogical origin! The OT lists no genealogy for Melchizedek (Gn 14:18-20; Ps 110:4), who, as a type of Christ, remains a priest forever (Heb 7:3).

[4] Now consider how great this man was—even Abraham the patriarch[a] gave a tenth of the plunder to him! [5] The sons of Levi who receive the priestly office have a command according to the law to collect a tenth from the people[b]—that is, from their •brothers—though they have also descended from Abraham.[A] [6] But one without this[B] lineage collected tenths from Abraham and blessed the one who had the promises.[c] [7] Without a doubt,[c] the inferior is blessed by the superior. [8] In the one case, men who will die receive tenths, but in the other case, Scripture testifies that he lives.[d] [9] And in a sense Levi himself, who receives tenths, has paid tenths through Abraham, [10] for he was still within his ancestor[D] when Melchizedek met him.

A Superior Priesthood

[11] If then, perfection came through the Levitical priesthood (for under it the people received the law[e]), what further need was there for another priest to appear, said to be in the order of Melchizedek and not in the order of Aaron?[f] [12] For when there is a change of the priesthood, there must be a change of law as well. [13] For the One these things are spoken about belonged to a different tribe. No one from it has served at the altar. [14] Now it is evident that our Lord came from Judah,[g] and Moses said nothing about that tribe concerning priests.

[15] And this becomes clearer if another priest like Melchizedek appears, [16] who did not become a priest based on a legal command concerning physical[E] descent but based on the power of an indestructible life. [17] For it has been testified:

**You are a priest forever
in the order of Melchizedek.**[F,h]

[18] So the previous command is annulled because it was weak and unprofitable[i] [19] (for the law perfected[j] nothing), but a better hope is introduced, through which we draw near to God.[k]

[20] None of this happened without an oath. For others became priests without an oath, [21] but He became a priest with an oath made by the One who said to Him:

**The Lord has sworn,
and He will not change His mind,
You are a priest forever.**[F,l]

[22] So Jesus has also become the guarantee of a better covenant.[m]

[23] Now many have become Levitical priests, since they are prevented by death from remaining in office. [24] But because He remains forever, He holds His priesthood permanently. [25] Therefore, He is always able to save[G] those who come to God through Him, since He always lives to intercede[n] for them.

[26] For this is the kind of high priest we need: holy, innocent, undefiled, separated from sinners, and exalted above the heavens.[o] [27] He doesn't need to offer sacrifices every day, as high priests do—first for their own sins, then for those of the people. He did this once for all when He offered Himself.[p] [28] For the law appoints as high priests men who are weak, but the promise of the oath, which came after the law, appoints a Son,[q] who has been perfected[r] forever.

A Heavenly Priesthood

8 Now the main point of what is being said is this: We have this kind of high priest, who sat down at the right hand of the throne of the Majesty in the heavens,[s] [2] a minister of the sanctuary and the true tabernacle that was set up by the Lord and not man.[t] [3] For every high priest is appointed to offer gifts[u] and sacrifices; therefore it was necessary for this priest also to have something to offer. [4] Now if He were on earth, He wouldn't be a priest, since there are those[H] offering the gifts prescribed by the law. [5] These serve as a copy and shadow[v] of the heavenly things, as Moses

Cross references
a 7:4 Gn 14:20; Ac 2:29; 7:8-9
b 7:5 Nm 18:21,26; 2Ch 31:4-5
c 7:6 Gn 14:19; Rm 4:13
d 7:8 Heb 5:6; 6:20
e 7:11 Gl 2:21; Heb 7:18-19; 8:7
f 7:14 Is 11:1; Mc 5:2; Mt 1:3; Lk 3:33; Rv 5:5
h 7:17 Ps 110:4; Heb 5:6; 6:20; 7:21
i 7:18 Rm 8:3; Gl 4:9
j 7:19 Ac 13:39; Rm 3:20; Heb 9:9
k Heb 4:16; 6:18
l 7:21 1Sm 15:29; Ps 110:4
m 7:22 Heb 8:6-10; 9:15; 12:24; 13:20
n 7:25 Rm 8:34; Heb 9:24
o 7:26 2Co 5:21; Heb 4:15
p 7:27 Eph 5:2; Heb 5:1,3; 9:12,28
q 7:28 Heb 1:2; 2:10; 5:2,9
r Php 3:12; Heb 10:14; 11:40
s 8:1 Col 3:1; Heb 2:17
t 8:2 Ex 33:7; Heb 9:11,24
u 8:3 Eph 5:2; Heb 5:1; 9:14
v 8:5 Col 2:17; Heb 9:23; 10:1

Textual notes
A 7:5 Lit have come out of Abraham's loins B 7:6 Lit their C 7:7 Or Beyond any dispute D 7:10 Lit still in his father's loins E 7:16 Or fleshly F 7:17,21 Ps 110:4 G 7:25 Or He is able to save completely H 8:4 Other mss read priests

witness to show that the order of Melchizedek was eternal in origin and scope. Melchizedek participated in the divine attributes of eternity, righteousness, peace, and sovereignty. His eternality is evident in that he was a **priest forever**—without beginning or end. His righteousness is evident in His name since Melchizedek is Hebrew for "king of righteousness." His peace is evident in the fact that he was also declared to be the **King of Salem**, which means "king of peace."

Finally, Melchizedek's sovereignty was recognized by **Abraham**, who paid this priest-king a tithe of all he had when he returned victorious from war. If Abraham rec-

ognized Melchizedek's superiority by paying him a tithe, then Israel must, too. The author argued that the Levitical priesthood was inferior to that of Melchizedek because **the inferior is blessed by the superior.** The sovereignty of Melchizedek is reflected in the sovereignty of the Son of God, because while the Levitical priesthood was authorized by **a legal command**, the priesthood of Christ was authorized by the power of an indestructible life.

7:20–8:13 The author addressed next the authorizing sources of the two priesthoods. Typically, authority was granted to an agreement or a covenant through the confirmation of an oath. Citing Jr 31:31-34, the author noted

was warned when he was about to complete the tabernacle. For God said, **Be careful that you make everything according to the pattern that was shown to you on the mountain.**[A,a] [6] But Jesus has now obtained a superior ministry, and to that degree He is the mediator[b] of a better covenant,[c] which has been legally enacted on better promises.[d]

A Superior Covenant

[7] For if that first covenant had been faultless, there would have been no occasion for a second one. [8] But finding fault with His people,[B] He says:[C]

Look, the days are coming,
    says the Lord,
when I will make a new covenant
with the house of Israel
and with the house of Judah—
[9] not like the covenant
that I made with their ancestors
on the day I took them by their hands
to lead them out of the land of Egypt.
I disregarded them, says the Lord,
because they did not continue
    in My covenant.
[10] But this is the covenant
that I will make with the house
    of Israel
after those days, says the Lord:
I will put My laws into their minds
and write them on their hearts.

[a]8:5 Ex 25:40; Heb 11:7; 12:25
[b]8:6 Jb 33:23; Is 29:1; Gl 3:19-20; 1Tm 2:5; Heb 9:15; 12:24
[c]Heb 7:22; 9:15; 12:24; 13:20
[d]Lk 22:20; 2Co 3:6,8
[e]8:10 Zch 8:8; 2Co 3:3; Heb 10:16
[f]8:11 Is 54:13; Jn 6:45; 1Jn 2:27
[g]8:12 Jr 31:31-34; Rm 11:27; Heb 10:17
[h]8:13 2Co 5:17
[i]9:2 Ex 25:8-9, 23-39; 26:1; Lv 24:5-8
[j]9:3 Ex 26:31-33; 40:3
[k]9:4 Ex 16:33; 25:10,16; 30:1-5; Nm 17:10; Dt 10:2

I will be their God,
    and they will be My people.[e]
[11] And each person will not teach
    his fellow citizen,[D]
and each his brother, saying,
    "Know the Lord,"
because they will all know Me,
from the least to the greatest
    of them.[f]
[12] For I will be merciful
    to their wrongdoing,
and I will never again remember
    their sins.[E,F,g]

[13] By saying, **a new covenant**, He has declared that the first is old. And what is old and aging is about to disappear.[h]

Old Covenant Ministry

9 Now the first covenant also had regulations for ministry and an earthly sanctuary. [2] For a tabernacle was set up, and in the first room, which is called the holy place, were the lampstand, the table, and the presentation loaves.[i] [3] Behind the second curtain, the tabernacle was called the most holy place.[j] [4] It contained the gold altar of incense and the ark of the covenant, covered with gold on all sides, in which there was a gold jar containing the manna, Aaron's staff that budded, and the tablets of the covenant.[k] [5] The •cherubim of glory were above it overshadowing the •mercy seat.

A8:5 Ex 25:40   B8:8 Lit *with them*   C8:8 Other mss read *finding fault, He says to them*   D8:11 Other mss read *neighbor*
E8:12 Other mss add *and their lawless deeds*   F8:8-12 Jr 31:31-34

the old covenant between God and Israel was dependent on the oath of man; unfortunately, **they did not continue** in this covenant. But the new covenant promised through Jeremiah was different, because the oath here was made entirely by God. Because God swore to the new covenant, it was eternally guaranteed. He said He would be merciful to them and place His laws in their minds and hearts. Because of the divine oath, the new covenant is **a better covenant**. The first covenant is **old and aging** and **about to disappear**.

The priesthood based on the old covenant was filled with priests who could not remain in office because they died, but the new covenant priest **always lives to intercede**. The old covenant priesthood was filled with priests who were weak (7:28), but the new covenant priest was **perfected forever** through Jesus' obedient suffering. The old covenant priest had to **offer sacrifices every day**, but the new covenant priest offered a sacrifice **once for all**. The old covenant priest sacrificed for both himself and his people, but the new covenant priest, being sinless, **offered Himself** on behalf of the people.

9:1-28 The author turned his attention to a comparison of the ministries of the old and new priesthoods. The **regulations for ministry** given through the old covenant were for an **earthly sanctuary** that represented the transcendence of God insomuch as the people could not enter the **holy**

place in the tabernacle. Only the high priest could enter the **most holy place**, and he did so only once per year. The sacrificial ministry of the old priesthood was unable to **perfect**

diatheke

Greek Pronunciation	[dee ah THAY kay]
HCSB Translation	covenant
Uses in Hebrews	17
Uses in the NT	33
Focus passage	Hebrews 9:4

A *covenant (diatheke)* is a legal arrangement between two parties (Gl 3:15) or a document transferring property from the deceased to an heir (Heb 9:16). The Greek OT influenced the use of *diatheke* in the NT, where the *covenant* was an agreement by which God's people related to Him. The NT frequently mentions three OT *covenants*: (1) the Abrahamic *covenant* (Gn 12:1-3; 15:1-21; 17:1-27), (2) the Mosaic *covenant* (Ex 20:1–24:8), and (3) the new *covenant* (Jr 31:31-34), and it often focuses on the relationship between the Mosaic and new *covenants* (e.g., 2Co 3:6,14). Over half of the occurrences of *diatheke* occur in Hebrews, where Jesus is portrayed as mediator of the new *covenant*, a *covenant* superior to the Mosaic *covenant* (Heb 7:22; 8:6,8-10; 9:15). As the Mosaic *covenant* was inaugurated with blood, so the new *covenant* was inaugurated with Jesus' blood (Heb 10:18-28; 13:20; cp. Mt 26:28; 1Co 11:25).

It is not possible to speak about these things in detail right now.[a]

[6] With these things set up this way, the priests enter the first room repeatedly, performing their ministry.[b] [7] But the high priest alone enters the second room, and he does that only once a year, and never without blood, which he offers for himself and for the sins of the people committed in ignorance.[c]

[8] The Holy Spirit was making it clear that the way into the most holy place had not yet been disclosed while the first tabernacle was still standing.[d] [9] This is a symbol for the present time, during which gifts and sacrifices are offered that cannot perfect the worshiper's conscience.[e] [10] They are physical regulations and only deal with food, drink, and various washings imposed until the time of restoration.[f]

a9:5 Ex 25:18-19; Lv 16:2
b9:6 Nm 28:3
c9:7 Ex 30:10; Lv 16:15,34; Heb 5:3
d9:8 Jn 14:6; Heb 10:19-20
e9:9 Heb 5:1; 7:19
f9:10 Lv 11:2-3; Col 2:16

---

the worshiper's conscience. While the old priesthood was incomplete, the sacrificial ministry of the Messiah is able to **cleanse our consciences**. This perfect cleansing enables the followers of the Messiah to engage in works that serve the living God.

The ministry of the Messiah is that of a new covenant mediator. His ministry is superior because He does not enter an earthly sanctuary, but into **heaven itself**, and thus into the very presence of God. Unlike the high priest who entered annually into the most holy place, the Messiah entered into the most holy place **once for all**. Unlike the old covenant that was inaugurated by the death of animals that had no choice in the matter, the new covenant was inaugurated by the Messiah's voluntary death. Unlike the old

---

Jesus and Atonement in the Old Testament

Eugene H. Merrill

The word "atonement" occurs frequently in the Old Testament (OT) and represents a key concept of OT theology. Christians maintain that Jesus is the fulfillment of the OT, especially the human need for atonement from sins. But what is atonement, and what does Jesus have to do with it?

Many Christians think atonement in the OT originated with the Mosaic law, but in reality humans recognized their need for atonement long before the time of Moses. When Adam and Eve committed the first sin, they hid from God because they were ashamed (Gn 3:8). Rather than giving them up as hopeless, God initiated a plan of atonement whereby the ruptured fellowship between Himself and humanity could be restored. Our English word "atonement" (at-one-ment) explains well the theology behind such restoration, for it suggests that God and humanity can relationally be "at one" again.

How does atonement work? The first (indirect) OT reference to atonement occurs when God provided animal skins to cover Adam and Eve's nakedness, an act necessitating the death of a sinless animal and hence the shedding of its blood on their behalf (Gn 3:21). This introduces a theme that runs throughout the Bible: atonement involves an innocent party taking the punishment that was due to a guilty party.

The Hebrew word translated "atonement" is *kaphar*, meaning "to cover." This suggests that through the act of atonement sin is covered so that God no longer sees it. Throughout the OT the covering is achieved, ostensibly at least, with the blood of an innocent animal whose innocence renders the repentant sinner innocent as well (Lv 1:4-5; 17:11). The New Testament (NT) term *hilasterion*, "propitiation," continues this OT concept, again in contexts of blood sacrifice (Rm 3:25).

What does any of this have to do with Jesus? While animals served as provisional sacrifices for human sins during the OT era, they could not ultimately atone for humans (Heb 4:10). Humanity needed one of their own, one who knew no sin, to stand in and take the punishment that is due to all sinners. Genesis 3:15 gives the first prophetic glimpse at God's final solution to this need and hints at the central role Jesus plays in that solution. Speaking ultimately of Jesus and His role in redemption, it asserts that the seed of the woman would be crushed, but that He would in turn crush the head of the serpent (the Devil), achieving victory over sin and death. The crushing mentioned here is reminiscent of the crushing experienced by the Suffering Servant in Isaiah 52:13–53:12, a passage that has atonement as its central theme. Jesus Christ is both the subject and fulfillment of Isaiah's prophecy. In the events that unfolded during His trial, crucifixion, and resurrection, Jesus was the Suffering Servant on our behalf. Though innocent of all sin, Jesus stood in our place to take our punishment, shedding His blood to atone for us. "He entered the most holy place once for all, not by the blood of goats and calves, but by His own blood, having obtained eternal redemption" (Heb 9:12). "By the sacrifice of Himself" (Heb 9:26) Jesus satisfied God's wrath against sin.

That OT atonement finds its culmination in Jesus Christ is put beyond question by John the Baptist who, seeing Jesus, proclaimed, "Here is the Lamb of God, who takes away the sin of the world!" (Jn 1:29).

New Covenant Ministry

[11] But the *Messiah has appeared, high priest of the good things that have come.[A] In the greater and more perfect tabernacle not made with hands (that is, not of this creation[a]), [12] He entered the most holy place once for all, not by the blood of goats and calves, but by His own blood, having obtained eternal *redemption.[b] [13] For if the blood of goats and bulls and the ashes of a young cow, sprinkling those who are defiled, sanctify for the purification of the flesh,[c] [14] how much more will the blood of the Messiah, who through the eternal Spirit[d] offered Himself without blemish to God, cleanse our[B] consciences from dead works to serve the living God?[e]

[15] Therefore, He is the mediator[f] of a new covenant,[C,g] so that those who are called might receive the promise[h] of the eternal inheritance, because a death has taken place for redemption from the transgressions committed under the first covenant.[i] [16] Where a will exists, the death of the one who made it must be established. [17] For a will is valid only when people die, since it is never in force while the one who made it is living. [18] That is why even the first covenant was inaugurated with blood. [19] For when every command had been proclaimed by Moses to all the people according to the law, he took the blood of calves and goats, along with water, scarlet wool, and hyssop, and sprinkled the scroll itself and all the people,[j] [20] saying, **This is the blood of the covenant that God has commanded for you.**[D,k] [21] In the same way, he sprinkled the tabernacle and all the articles of worship with blood.[l] [22] According to the law almost everything is purified with blood, and without the shedding of blood there is no forgiveness.[m]

[23] Therefore it was necessary for the copies of the things in the heavens to be purified with these sacrifices, but the heavenly things themselves to be purified with better sacrifices than these.[n] [24] For the Messiah did not enter a sanctuary made with hands (only a model[E] of the true one) but into heaven itself, so that He might now appear in the presence of God for us.[o] [25] He did not do this to offer Himself many times, as the high priest enters the sanctuary yearly with the blood of another.[p] [26] Otherwise, He would have had to suffer many times since the foundation of the world. But now He has appeared one time, at the end of the ages,[q] for the removal of sin by the sacrifice of Himself.[r] [27] And just as it is appointed for people to die once—and after this, judgment[s]— [28] so also the Messiah, having been offered once to bear the sins of many,[t] will appear a second time,[u] not to bear sin, but[F] to bring salvation to those who are waiting for Him.[v]

The Perfect Sacrifice

10 Since the law has only a shadow of the good things[w] to come, and not the actual form of those realities, it can never perfect the worshipers by the same sacrifices they continually offer year after year. [2] Otherwise, wouldn't they have stopped being offered, since the worshipers, once purified, would no longer have any consciousness of sins? [3] But in the sacrifices there is a reminder of sins every year. [4] For it is impossible for the blood of bulls and goats to take away sins.

[5] Therefore, as He was coming into the world, He said:

Cross references (center column)
a 9:11 Heb 2:17; 8:2; 10:1
b 9:12 Dn 9:24; Heb 7:27; 10:4
c 9:13 Lv 16:14-15; Nm 19:2,9,17-18
d 9:14 1Pt 3:18; 1Jn 1:7
e Ti 2:14; Heb 6:1; 10:2,22
f 9:15 1Tm 2:5; Heb 8:6; 12:24
g Jr 31:31-34; 1Co 11:25; 2Co 3:6; Heb 7:22; 8:8; 13:20
h Gn 12:7; Rm 8:28; Gl 3:19; Heb 4:1
i Rm 3:25; 5:6
j 9:19 Ex 24:6-8; Lv 14:4-6
k 9:20 Ex 24:8; Mt 26:28
l 9:21 Ex 29:12; Lv 8:15
m 9:22 Lv 17:11
n 9:23 Heb 8:5
o 9:24 Rm 8:34; Heb 7:25; 8:2
p 9:25 Heb 9:7; 10:19
q 9:26 Mt 24:3; 28:20; 1Co 10:11
r Heb 4:3; 7:27
s 9:27 Gn 3:19; 2Co 5:10
t 9:28 Is 53:12; 1Pt 2:24
u Mk 8:38; 1Th 4:16
v Mt 26:28; 1Co 1:7; Ti 2:13
w 10:1 Col 2:17; Heb 8:5; 9:11

Footnotes
A 9:11 Other mss read *that are to come*　B 9:14 Other mss read *your*　C 9:15 The Gk word used here and in vv. 15-18 can be translated covenant, will, or testament.　D 9:20 Ex 24:8　E 9:24 Or *antitype*, or *figure*　F 9:28 Lit *time, apart from sin,*

---

priesthood that offered the blood of animals, the Messiah offered **His own blood**. Unlike the old priesthood that offered sacrifices continually without effect, the blood of the Messiah obtained eternal redemption.

10:1-18 Bringing his comparison of the new and old priesthoods to an end, the author in these verses focused on the superiority of the sacrifice of Christ. The old sacrifices were only a **shadow** of the **actual form** of the blessed realities that come from the personal sacrifice of the Messiah. Citing Ps 40:6-8, the author demonstrated that God was no longer interested in the **whole burnt offerings** and **sin offerings** of the old covenant. The old sacrifices had to be offered continually, and they did not accomplish anything beyond ritual purification because they could not **take away sins**. This is why it was prophesied that the Messiah would come to do God's will. Jesus the Messiah offered **one sacrifice for sins forever** by offering Himself. Afterwards, He sat down at the throne of God. By His blood atonement, He has **perfected forever**

hagiazo

Greek Pronunciation	[hah gee AH dzoh]
HCSB Translation	to sanctify
Uses in Hebrews	7
Uses in the NT	28
Focus passage	Hebrews 10:10,14,29

In the NT, *hagiazo* has three distinct shades of meaning. First, it may indicate the action of dedicating something to the service of God (*consecrate, set aside as holy*). This may involve the *consecration* of objects (Mt 23:19; 1Tm 4:5) or persons (Ac 20:32; 26:18; 1Co 6:11; 7:14; Eph 5:26; Heb 9:13; 10:14) for holy service unto God. Second, *hagiazo* may mean *to treat as holy*. Jesus prays that the Father's name *be honored as holy* (Mt 6:9), and Peter urges believers *to set apart* Messiah as Lord in their hearts (1Pt 3:15). Third, *hagiazo* may mean *to purify* or *make someone holy*, in the sense of causing someone to have the quality of *holiness*. Paul prays that God would *sanctify* the Thessalonian believers (1Th 5:23), and John closes his apocalypse with the heavenly exhortation that the *holy* should go on *being made holy* (Rv 22:11).

**You did not want sacrifice and offering,
but You prepared a body for Me.**
6　**You did not delight
in whole burnt offerings
and sin offerings.**
7　Then I said, "See—
it is written about Me
in the volume of the scroll—
I have come to do Your will, God!"[A,a]

[8] After He says above, **You did not want or delight in sacrifices and offerings, whole burnt offerings and sin offerings** (which are offered according to the law[b]), [9] He then says, **See, I have come to do Your will.**[B] He takes away the first to establish the second. [10] By this will of God, we have been •sanctified through the offering of the body of Jesus Christ once and for all.[c]

[11] Every priest stands day after day ministering and offering the same sacrifices time after time, which can never take away sins.[d] [12] But this man, after offering one sacrifice for sins

forever, sat down at the right hand of God.[e] [13] He is now waiting until His enemies are made His footstool.[f] [14] For by one offering He has perfected forever those who are sanctified. [15] The Holy Spirit also testifies to us about this. For after He says:

16　**This is the covenant I will make
with them
after those days, says the Lord:
I will put My laws on their hearts
and write them on their minds,**

[17] He adds:

**I will never again remember
their sins and their lawless acts.**[C,g]

[18] Now where there is forgiveness of these, there is no longer an offering for sin.

Exhortations to Godliness

[19] Therefore, •brothers, since we have boldness to enter the sanctuary through the blood of Jesus,[h] [20] by a new and living way He has opened for us through the curtain (that is, His

---

Margin cross-references:
[a]10:5-7 Ps 40:6-8; Jr 36:2; Heb 1:6
[b]10:8 Mk 12:33; Heb 10:5-6
[c]10:10 Jn 17:19; Heb 7:27; 9:12
[d]10:11 Nm 28:3; Heb 5:1
[e]10:12 Rm 8:34; Eph 1:20; Col 3:1; Heb 1:3; 8:1; 12:2; 1Pt 3:22
[f]10:13 Ps 110:1; Mt 22:44; Mk 12:36; Lk 20:43; Ac 2:34-35; 1Co 15:25; Heb 1:13
[g]10:16-17 Jr 31:33-34; Heb 8:10,12
[h]10:19 Eph 2:18; Heb 9:25

A10:5-7 Ps 40:6-8　　B10:9 Other mss add *God*　　C10:16-17 Jr 31:33-34

---

those who are sanctified. The old sacrifices are no longer necessary because He offered the perfect sacrifice that perfects believers.

10:19-39 The author again exhorted his **brothers** to faithfulness (see 6:4-20 and note there). This exhortation contains commands, a warning, an encouraging reminder,

The temple veil is a curtain that separated the most holy place from the holy place (2Chr 3:14). Only the high priest was allowed to pass through the veil and then only on the Day of Atonement (Lv 16:2). At Jesus' death the temple veil was ripped from top to bottom, illustrating that in Christ, God had abolished the barrier separating humanity from the presence of God (Mt 27:51; Mk 15:38; cp. Lk 23:45). Hebrews 10:20 uses the tabernacle veil, not as the image of a barrier, but of access. Access to God is gained through the flesh of the historical Jesus (cp. Jn 10:7).

flesh*ᵃ*), ²¹and since we have a great high priest over the house of God,*ᵇ* ²²let us draw near with a true heart in full assurance of faith, our hearts sprinkled ⋅clean from an evil conscience and our bodies washed in pure water.*ᶜ* ²³Let us hold on to the confession of our hope without wavering, for He who promised is faithful.*ᵈ* ²⁴And let us be concerned about one another in order to promote love and good works, ²⁵not staying away from our worship meetings, as some habitually do, but encouraging each other,*ᵉ* and all the more as you see the day drawing near.

Warning against Deliberate Sin

²⁶For if we deliberately sin after receiving the knowledge of the truth, there no longer remains a sacrifice for sins,*ᶠ* ²⁷but a terrifying expectation of judgment and the fury of a fire about to consume the adversaries.*ᵍ* ²⁸If anyone disregards Moses' law, he dies without mercy, based on the testimony of two or three witnesses.*ʰ* ²⁹How much worse punishment do you think one will deserve who has trampled on the Son of God, regarded as profane*ᴬ* the blood of the covenant by which he was sanctified, and insulted the Spirit of grace?*ⁱ* ³⁰For we know the One who has said, **Vengeance belongs to Me, I will repay,**ᴮ·ᶜ and again, **The Lord will judge His people.**ᴰ·ʲ ³¹It is a terrifying thing to fall into the hands of the living God!*ᵏ*

³²Remember the earlier days when, after you had been enlightened, you endured a hard struggle with sufferings.*ˡ* ³³Sometimes you were publicly exposed to taunts and afflictions, and at other times you were companions of those who were treated that way.*ᵐ* ³⁴For you sympathized with the prisoners*ᴱ* and accepted

with joy the confiscation of your possessions, knowing that you yourselves have a better and enduring possession.ᶠ·ⁿ ³⁵So don't throw away your confidence, which has a great reward.*ᵒ* ³⁶For you need endurance, so that after you have done God's will, you may receive what was promised.*ᵖ*

³⁷   For yet in **a very little while,**
        the Coming One will come
           and not delay.
³⁸   **But My righteous one**ᴳ **will live by faith;**
        and if he draws back,
        I have no pleasure in him.ᴴ·*q*

³⁹But we are not those who draw back and are destroyed, but those who have faith and obtain life.

Heroes of Faith

11 Now faith is the reality*ⁱ* of what is hoped for, the proof*ʲ* of what is not seen.*ʳ* ²For our ancestors won God's approval by it. ³By faith we understand that the universe wasᴷ created by God's command,ᴸ·*s* so that what is seen has been made from things that are not visible.

⁴By faith Abel offered to God a better sacrifice than Cain did. By faith he was approved as a righteous man, because God approved his gifts, and even though he is dead, he still speaks through his faith.*ᵗ*

⁵By faith Enoch was taken away so he did not experience death, and **he was not to be found because God took him away.**ᴹ For prior to his removal he was approved, since he had pleased God.*ᵘ* ⁶Now without faith it is impossible to please God, for the one who draws

Cross references (center column)

*ᵃ*10:20 Jn 10:9; Heb 9:3,8
*ᵇ*10:21 Heb 2:17; 4:14
*ᶜ*10:22 Ezk 36:25; Heb 9:14
*ᵈ*10:23 1Co 1:9; Heb 3:6
*ᵉ*10:25 Ac 2:42; Rm 13:11; Heb 3:13
*ᶠ*10:26 Nm 15:30; Dt 17:12; Heb 6:4; 2Pt 2:20-21; 1Jn 5:16
*ᵍ*10:27 Is 26:11; Zph 1:18; 2Th 1:8
*ʰ*10:28 Dt 17:6; Heb 2:2
*ⁱ*10:29 Mt 12:31-32; Eph 4:30; Heb 6:6
*ʲ*10:30 Dt 32:35-36; Ps 135:14; Rm 12:19
*ᵏ*10:31 Mt 16:16; Lk 12:5
*ˡ*10:32 Php 1:29-30; Heb 6:4
*ᵐ*10:33 1Co 4:9; Php 4:14; 1Th 2:14
*ⁿ*10:34 Mt 5:12; 1Pt 1:4-5
*ᵒ*10:35 Heb 2:2; 11:26
*ᵖ*10:36 Lk 21:19; Heb 12:1
*ᑫ*10:37-38 Hab 2:3-4; Lk 18:8; Rm 1:17; Gl 3:11; Rv 22:20
*ʳ*11:1 Rm 8:24; 2Co 4:18
*ˢ*11:3 Gn 1:1; Jn 1:3; 2Pt 3:5
*ᵗ*11:4 Gn 4:4; 1Jn 3:12
*ᵘ*11:5 Gn 5:21-24; 2Kg 2:11

ᴬ10:29 Or *ordinary*   ᴮ10:30 Other mss add *says the Lord*   ᶜ10:30 Dt 32:35   ᴰ10:30 Dt 32:36   ᴱ10:34 Other mss read *sympathized with my imprisonment*   ᶠ10:34 Other mss add *in heaven*   ᴳ10:38 Other mss read *the righteous one*   ᴴ10:37-38 Is 26:20 LXX; Hab 2:3-4   ⁱ11:1 Or *assurance*   ʲ11:1 Or *conviction*   ᴷ11:3 Or *the worlds were,* or *the ages were*   ᴸ11:3 Or *word*   ᴹ11:5 Gn 5:21-24

a promise, and an expression of confidence. Due to the **boldness** that believers have to enter the divine presence through the perfect sacrifice of Christ, he commanded his brothers to (1) **draw near** to God with assurance; (2) **hold on** to their confession without wavering; and (3) **be concerned** for one another and not forsake the gathering of the church. The warning is a reminder that there is no effective sacrifice for sin apart from that provided by Christ. If Christians turn their backs on Jesus, they have no hope—only the expectation of terror.

11:1-40 This chapter compares the faith of the OT fathers with the faith exercised by Christian believers. Faith is defined as **the reality of what is hoped for** and **the proof of what is not seen.** The Greek word for "reality" is *hypostasis.* It has been used previously to describe the relationship of Christ to God (1:3) and the firm confidence that believers possess (3:14). Faith is not fleeting but substantial enough to generate confidence. The Greek word for "proof" is *elegchos,* indicating an inner conviction that is not based on visible matters. Divine approval is the primary consequence of faith. Other results of faith are the declaration

pistis

Greek Pronunciation	[PIS tis]
HCSB Translation	faith
Uses in Hebrews	32 (24 in Heb 11)
Uses in the NT	243
Focus passage	Hebrews 11:6

Pistis carries a spectrum of meanings in the NT. It can refer to something completely *trustworthy.* Christ's resurrection is the *proof* (i.e., *trustworthy evidence*) that God will one day judge the world (Ac 17:31). *Pistis* may also refer to a *solemn promise* (1Tm 5:12). It sometimes means the state of *being faithful* or *trustworthy.* God's *faithfulness* ensures He will fulfill His promises (Rm 3:3). *Pistis* may express belief with complete *trust.* The NT refers to the *faith* of OT characters (Rm 4:9,11-13,16; Heb 11:4-33,39) and of Christians (Heb 6:1; 10:39). In the Gospels, *faith* is often expressed as reliance on the Lord's power over nature, illness, and spiritual powers (Mt 8:10; Mk 2:5; Lk 8:25). Christian piety involves *faith* accompanied by works (Jms 2:14,17, etc.). Finally, *pistis* may refer to the doctrine one believes. Christians should contend for the *faith* (i.e., the body of apostolic doctrine) delivered to them (Jd 3,20).

Salvation in the Old Testament

Paige Patterson

The concept of salvation in the Old Testament (OT) features a variety of applications, including deliverance, rescue, safety, and even welfare. In Exodus 14:30, Yahweh "saved" Israel from the hand of the Egyptians. This usage of the term is typical of the times when salvation focuses on physical deliverance from a specific danger. Another nuance involves forensic or legal rescue, which is observed in passages like Deuteronomy 22:27 where a woman who is the subject of sexual attack in a field has no one to rescue her. But the most significant use of the concept and the one most commonly perceived is the soteriological emphasis in which the fallen spiritual nature of humankind stands in need of salvation or redemption by God.

Implicit in all uses of "salvation" are the perceptions of need and even inability. As often as not, God is featured as the only One who can effect a rescue or bring salvation, which is especially true of the eternal salvation of the individual. Passages such as Isaiah 51:8 contrast the ephemeral nature of physical realities with a salvation that is for all generations. In the famous passage magnifying the beauty of those who bring good news and proclaim salvation, the rescue in view seems to be spiritual and eternal (Is 52:7). Isaiah 59:17 employs language later invoked by New Testament authors such as Paul, who speaks of "righteousness like armor on your chest" and "the helmet of salvation" (Eph 6:14,17). In Jonah's prayer from the belly of the great fish, he declares that "salvation is from the LORD!" (Jnh 2:9). While it could be argued that the prophet's thought is only about his abysmal physical circumstance, most would see a more profound avowal, anticipating God's sovereign redemption of the soul.

Salvation in the OT is also linked with other concepts such as redemption, atonement, and righteousness. Such ideas express the means of salvation (atonement), the goal of salvation (righteousness), or the nature of salvation (redemption). For example, the Passover was designed not only to depict the exodus from Egypt but also to remind the Israelites of the more profound significance of the role of sacrifice in salvation. A lamb dies and its blood is sprinkled on the doorposts so that the death angel will pass over, sparing the life of the firstborn (Ex 12:1-14). The rituals associated with the Day of Atonement also focused on a vicarious, substitutionary atonement for the sins of the people (Lv 16:1-34).

Isaiah 53 conveys the message of a sacrificial act on the part of the Suffering Servant, who made His life an offering for sin that would "justify many" (v. 11). By His stripes we are healed and the iniquity of us all was laid on Him as He was struck by God for the transgressions of us all.

God is the sole author of salvation. The human family, horribly marred by sin, cannot effect salvation even by the keeping of the law. This raises the question of how salvation is appropriated in the OT. Genesis 15:6 declares that "Abram believed the LORD, and He credited it to him as righteousness." Paul makes this passage central to his whole argument in Romans 1–8. "For what does the Scripture say? Abraham believed God, and it was credited to him for righteousness" (Rm 4:3).

While there seems to be general recognition among Christians that righteousness and holiness are required to stand before God, many erroneously believe that salvation was attained in the OT by the keeping of the law. Both Genesis and Romans agree in declaring that salvation may be attained only through faith (believing God). As the sacrificial system perpetually illustrated, atonement must be made. Isaiah 53 presented the Suffering Servant as the One who would ultimately make that atonement. Paul demonstrates explicitly what is always implicit in the OT—the law could save no one. Salvation is extended in any era on the basis of God's grace appropriated by the faith of human beings.

near to Him must believe that He exists and rewards those who seek Him.

7 By faith Noah, after he was warned about what was not yet seen and motivated by godly fear, built an ark to deliver his family. By faith he condemned the world and became an heir of the righteousness that comes by faith.[a]

8 By faith Abraham, when he was called, obeyed and went out to a place he was going to receive as an inheritance. He went out, not knowing where he was going.[b] 9 By faith he stayed as a foreigner in the land of promise, living in tents with Isaac and Jacob, coheirs of the same promise.[c] 10 For he was looking forward to the city that has foundations, whose architect and builder is God.[d]

11 By faith even Sarah herself, when she was unable to have children, received power to conceive offspring, even though she was past the age, since she[A] considered that the One who had promised was faithful.[e] 12 Therefore from one man—in fact, from one as good as dead—came offspring as numerous as the stars of heaven and as innumerable as the grains of sand by the seashore.[f]

13 These all died in faith without having received the promises, but they saw them from a distance,[g] greeted them, and confessed that they were foreigners and temporary residents on the earth.[h] 14 Now those who say such things make it clear that they are seeking a homeland. 15 If they were thinking about where they came from, they would have had an opportunity to return. 16 But they now desire a better place—a heavenly one. Therefore God is not ashamed to be called their God, for He has prepared a city for them.[i]

17 By faith Abraham, when he was tested, offered up Isaac.[j] He received the promises and he was offering his unique son, 18 the one it had been said about, **Your ·seed will be traced**[B] **through Isaac.**[C,k] 19 He considered God to be able even to raise someone from the dead,[l] and as an illustration,[D] he received him back.

20 By faith Isaac blessed Jacob and Esau[m] concerning things to come. 21 By faith Jacob, when he was dying, blessed each of the sons

of Joseph, and **he worshiped, leaning on the top of his staff.**[E,n] 22 By faith Joseph, as he was nearing the end of his life, mentioned the exodus of the Israelites and gave instructions concerning his bones.[o]

23 By faith, after Moses was born, he was hidden by his parents for three months, because they saw that the child was beautiful, and they didn't fear the king's edict.[p] 24 By faith Moses, when he had grown up, refused to be called the son of Pharaoh's daughter 25 and chose to suffer with the people of God rather than to enjoy the short-lived pleasure of sin.[q] 26 For he considered the reproach because of the ·Messiah to be greater wealth than the treasures of Egypt, since his attention was on the reward.[r]

27 By faith he left Egypt behind, not being afraid of the king's anger, for Moses persevered as one who sees Him who is invisible.[s] 28 By faith he instituted the ·Passover and the sprinkling of the blood, so that the destroyer of the firstborn might not touch the Israelites. 29 By faith they crossed the Red Sea as though they were on dry land. When the Egyptians attempted to do this, they were drowned.[t]

30 By faith the walls of Jericho fell down after being encircled by the Israelites for seven days. 31 By faith Rahab the prostitute received the spies in peace and didn't perish with those who disobeyed.[u]

32 And what more can I say? Time is too short for me to tell about Gideon, Barak, Samson, Jephthah,[v] David, Samuel, and the prophets,[w] 33 who by faith conquered kingdoms,[x] administered justice, obtained promises, shut the mouths of lions,[y] 34 quenched the raging of fire, escaped the edge of the sword, gained strength after being weak, became mighty in battle, and put foreign armies to flight.[z] 35 Women received their dead—they were raised to life again. Some men were tortured, not accepting release, so that they might gain a better resurrection, 36 and others experienced mockings and scourgings, as well as bonds and imprisonment.[aa] 37 They were stoned,[F,ab] they were sawed in two, they

---

a 11:7 Gn 6:13-22; 1Pt 3:20
b 11:8 Gn 12:1-4,7; Ac 7:2-4
c 11:9 Gn 12:8; 18:1; Ac 7:5; Heb 6:17
d 11:10 Heb 12:22; 13:14; Rv 21:2,10,14
e 11:11 Gn 17:19; 18:11-14; 21:2
f 11:12 Gn 22:17; Rm 4:19
g 11:13 Mt 13:17; Jn 8:56; Heb 11:39
h Gn 23:4; 1Ch 29:15; Ps 39:12; 1Pt 1:17
i 11:16 Ex 3:6,15; Mk 8:38; 2Tm 4:18; Heb 13:14
j 11:17 Gn 22:1-10; Jms 2:21
k 11:18 Gn 21:12; Rm 9:7
l 11:19 Rm 4:17
m 11:20 Gn 25:25; 27:26-40
n 11:21 Gn 47:31; 48:1,5,16,20
o 11:22 Gn 50:24-25; Ex 13:19
p 11:23 Ex 1:16,22; 2:2
q 11:24-25 Ex 2:10-11; Ps 84:10
r 11:26 Heb 10:35; 13:13
s 11:27 Rm 1:20; Col 1:15-16; 1Tm 1:17
t 11:29 Ex 14:22-30
u 11:31 Jos 2:1; 6:23
v 11:32 Jdg 4:6; 11:1; 13:24
w 1Sm 1:20; 16:1,13
x 11:33 2Sm 7:11; 8:1-3
y Jdg 14:5-6; 1Sm 17:34-37; Dn 6:22
z 11:34 Jdg 15:8; 2Kg 20:7; Dn 3:25
aa 11:36 Gn 39:20; Jr 20:2
ab 11:37 1Kg 21:13; 2Ch 24:20-21

A 11:11 Or *By faith Abraham, even though he was past age—and Sarah herself was barren—received the ability to procreate since he* B 11:18 Lit *called* C 11:18 Gn 21:12 D 11:19 Or *a foreshadowing*, or *a parable*, or *a type* E 11:21 Gn 47:31 F 11:37 Other mss add *they were tempted*

---

of righteousness, the ability to look forward to the heavenly city of God, the ability to understand that faith is possible only because God is faithful, the ability to accomplish great things in the world, and the ability to see that even when believers are persecuted and murdered, beyond this world is a better resurrection.

Throughout the chapter, the author provided examples of people in the OT who exercised faith. He focused most

heavily on **Abraham** and **Moses**. To complete the list with a crescendo, he recounted an inspiring litany of the fruit of faith displayed in the virtuous life, faithful death, and anticipated resurrection of numerous OT heroes. However, although their faith was **approved**, they did not receive what God had **promised**. The purpose of this delay was to ensure that they would not be perfected apart from Jesus Christ.

died by the sword, they wandered about in sheepskins, in goatskins,[a] destitute, afflicted, and mistreated. [38] The *world was not worthy of them. They wandered in deserts and on mountains, hiding in caves and holes in the ground.

[39] All these were approved through their faith, but they did not receive what was promised, [40] since God had provided something better for us, so that they would not be made perfect without us.[b]

The Call to Endurance

12 Therefore, since we also have such a large cloud of witnesses[c] surrounding us, let us lay aside every weight and the sin that so easily ensnares us. Let us run with endurance[d] the race that lies before us, [2] keeping our eyes on Jesus,[A] the source and perfecter[B] of our faith, who for the joy that lay before Him[C] endured a cross and despised the shame[e] and has sat down at the right hand of God's throne.

Fatherly Discipline

[3] For consider Him who endured such hostility from sinners against Himself, so that you won't grow weary and lose heart.[f] [4] In struggling against sin, you have not yet resisted to the point of shedding your blood. [5] And you have forgotten the exhortation that addresses you as sons:

> My son, do not take the Lord's
>   discipline lightly
> or faint when you are
>   reproved by Him,
> [6]   for the Lord disciplines the one
>   He loves

(center column references)

a11:37 1Kg 19:10; 2Kg 1:8
b11:40 Heb 11:16; Rv 6:11
c12:1 Heb 11:2,4-5,39
d1Co 9:24; Heb 10:36
e12:2 Lk 24:26; Php 2:8-9; Heb 13:13
f12:3 Mt 10:24; Gl 6:9
g12:5-6 Jb 5:17; Ps 94:12; Pr 3:11-12; Rv 3:16
h12:7-8 Dt 8:5; 1Pt 5:9
i12:9 Nm 16:22; Is 38:16
j12:10 Lv 11:44; 2Pt 1:4
k12:11 Is 32:17; Jms 3:17-18
l1Pt 1:6
m12:12 Jb 4:3-4; Is 35:3
n12:13 Pr 4:26; Gl 6:1
o12:14 Rm 6:22; 14:19
pMt 5:8; 2Co 7:1
q12:15 2Co 6:1; Gl 5:4; Heb 3:12; 10:39
r12:16 1Tm 1:9; 4:7; 6:20; 2Tm 2:16
sGn 25:33
t12:17 Gn 27:34-38

**and punishes every son
He receives.[D,g]**

[7] Endure suffering as discipline: God is dealing with you as sons. For what son is there that a father does not discipline? [8] But if you are without discipline—which all[E] receive[F]—then you are illegitimate children and not sons.[h] [9] Furthermore, we had natural fathers discipline us, and we respected them. Shouldn't we submit even more to the Father of spirits and live?[i] [10] For they disciplined us for a short time based on what seemed good to them, but He does it for our benefit, so that we can share His holiness.[j] [11] No discipline seems enjoyable at the time, but painful. Later on, however, it yields the fruit of peace[k] and righteousness to those who have been trained by it.[l]

[12] Therefore strengthen your tired hands and weakened knees,[m] [13] and make straight paths for your feet, so that what is lame may not be dislocated[G] but healed instead.[n]

Warning against Rejecting God's Grace

[14] Pursue peace with everyone, and holiness[o]—without it no one will see the Lord.[p] [15] Make sure that no one falls short of the grace of God and that no root of bitterness springs up, causing trouble and by it, defiling many.[q] [16] And make sure that there isn't any immoral or irreverent[r] person like Esau, who sold his birthright in exchange for one meal.[s] [17] For you know that later, when he wanted to inherit the blessing, he was rejected because he didn't find any opportunity for repentance, though he sought it with tears.[t]

[18] For you have not come to what could be touched, to a blazing fire, to darkness, gloom,

---

A12:2 Or *us, looking to Jesus*   B12:2 Or *the founder and completer*   C12:2 Or *who instead of the joy lying before Him*; that is, the joy of heaven   D12:6 Pr 3:11-12   E12:8 = Christians   F12:8 Lit *discipline, of which all have become participants*   G12:13 Or *so that the lame will not be turned aside*

12:1-2 Because Jesus Christ is the **source and perfecter** of the Christian faith, the author called on Christians to keep their eyes on Jesus. The Christian who has faith will **lay aside** every sinful weight and **run** toward Christ. Just as Jesus **endured a cross** and **despised the shame** in order to attain the joy of rejoining the Father on His throne, so should Christians run their race with **endurance**.

12:3-29 In these verses the author encouraged his readers not to lose heart, but to consider Jesus and His example. They should struggle against sin and run toward heaven even if they must do so through intense persecution.

12:3-13 Familial language appears throughout the book of Hebrews. The First Person of the Trinity is God the Father, and the Second Person of the Trinity is His Son. The Son became a human being in order to unite Himself with His believing "brothers." The Son can then bring His brothers into the presence of the Father, who will consider them His "sons." Citing Pr 3:11-12, the author argued that because

believers in Christ are sons of God, they have a superior source of comfort. They are more than mere servants; God addresses them as sons. And yet, a father displays his love for his sons by disciplining them. Just as the readers have accepted discipline from their **natural fathers**, so too should they receive discipline from the **Father of spirits**. God does not discipline His sons to harm them, but to bless them. The benefit of the Father's discipline is fellowship in His **holiness** and receiving His **peace** and **righteousness**.

12:14-29 The sovereign grace of the Father displayed in discipline is the source from which the Christian finds strength to move forward. Salvation is by grace, but it demands a human response. Loving discipline is evidence of the Father's grace, and His children should **hold on to grace**. Christians should move toward peace and holiness, and they should warn one another against falling short of God's grace or allowing a **root of bitterness** to spring up within them. The church does not exist on Mount Sinai with its **terrifying** law that commands and condemns. Rather, the church

and storm, [19] to the blast of a trumpet, and the sound of words. (Those who heard it begged that not another word be spoken to them, [20] for they could not bear what was commanded: **And if even an animal touches the mountain, it must be stoned!**[A,a] [21] The appearance was so terrifying that Moses said, **I am terrified and trembling.**[B,b]) [22] Instead, you have come to Mount •Zion, to the city of the living God (the heavenly Jerusalem), to myriads of angels in festive gathering,[c] [23] to the assembly of the firstborn whose names have been written[c] in heaven, to God who is the Judge of all, to the spirits of righteous people made perfect,[d] [24] to Jesus (mediator[e] of a new covenant[f]), and to the sprinkled blood, which says better things than the blood of Abel.[g]

[25] Make sure that you do not reject the One who speaks. For if they did not escape when they rejected Him who warned them on earth, even less will we if we turn away from Him who warns us from heaven.[h] [26] His voice shook the earth at that time, but now He has promised, **Yet once more I will shake not only the earth but also heaven.**[D,i] [27] This expression, "Yet once more," indicates the removal of what can be shaken[j]—that is, created things—so that what is not shaken might remain. [28] Therefore, since we are receiving a kingdom that cannot be shaken, let us hold on to grace.[E] By it, we may serve God acceptably, with reverence and awe,[k] [29] for our God is a consuming fire.[l]

Final Exhortations

13 Let brotherly love[m] continue. [2] Don't neglect to show hospitality, for by do-

ing this some have welcomed angels as guests without knowing it.[n] [3] Remember the prisoners, as though you were in prison with them, and the mistreated, as though you yourselves were suffering bodily.[F] [4] Marriage must be respected by all, and the marriage bed kept undefiled, because God will judge immoral people and adulterers.[o] [5] Your life should be free from the love of money. Be satisfied with what you have, for He Himself has said, **I will never leave you or forsake you.**[G,p] [6] Therefore, we may boldly say:

> **The Lord is my helper;**
> **I will not be afraid.**
> **What can man do to me?**[H,q]

[7] Remember your leaders who have spoken God's word to you. As you carefully observe the outcome of their lives, imitate their faith.[r] [8] Jesus Christ is the same yesterday, today, and forever.[s] [9] Don't be led astray by various kinds of strange teachings; for it is good for the heart to be established by grace and not by foods, since those involved in them have not benefited.[t] [10] We have an altar from which those who serve the tabernacle do not have a right to eat.[u] [11] For the bodies of those animals whose blood is brought into the most holy place by the high priest[v] as a sin offering are burned outside the camp.[w] [12] Therefore Jesus also suffered outside the gate,[x] so that He might •sanctify[i] the people by His own blood. [13] Let us then go to Him outside the camp, bearing His disgrace.[y] [14] For we do not have an enduring city here; instead, we seek the one to come.[z] [15] Therefore, through Him let us con-

Cross references (center column)

[a] 12:18-20 Ex 19:12-13,18; 20:18-21; Dt 4:11; 5:5,25
[b] 12:21 Dt 9:19
[c] 12:22 Gl 4:26; Heb 11:10
[d] 12:23 Ps 94:2; Lk 10:20; Php 3:12
[e] 12:24 1Tm 2:5; Heb 7:22; 8:6; 9:15
[f] 1Co 11:25; 2Co 3:6; Heb 13:20
[g] Gn 4:10; Heb 11:4
[h] 12:25 Heb 2:2-4; 8:5; 11:7
[i] 12:26 Ex 19:18; Hg 2:6
[j] 12:27 1Co 7:31; 2Pt 3:10
[k] 12:28 Dn 2:44; Heb 13:15
[l] 12:29 Dt 4:24; 2Th 1:8
[m] 13:1 Rm 12:10; 1Pt 1:22
[n] 13:2 Gn 18:3; Mt 25:35
[o] 13:3-4 Mt 25:36; 1Co 6:9
[p] 13:5 Dt 31:6,8; Jos 1:5; Php 4:11
[q] 13:6 Ps 27:1; 56:4,11; 118:6
[r] 13:7 Heb 6:12; 13:17,24
[s] 13:8 Jn 8:58; Heb 1:12
[t] 13:9 Eph 4:14; Col 2:16
[u] 13:10 1Co 9:13; 10:18
[v] 13:11 1Co 9:13; 10:18
[w] Ex 29:14; Lv 16:27
[x] 13:12 Jn 19:17; Ac 7:58
[y] 13:13 Heb 11:26; 1Pt 4:14
[z] 13:14 Mc 3:10; Heb 12:22

Footnotes

[A] 12:20 Ex 19:12   [B] 12:21 Dt 9:19   [C] 12:23 Or *registered*   [D] 12:26 Hg 2:6   [E] 12:28 Or *let us give thanks*, or *let us have grace*
[F] 13:3 Or *mistreated, since you are also in a body*   [G] 13:5 Dt 31:6   [H] 13:6 Ps 118:6   [I] 13:12 Or *set apart*, or *consecrate*

---

epouranios

Greek Pronunciation	[eh poo RAH nee ahs]
HCSB Translation	heavenly
Uses in Hebrews	6
Uses in the NT	19
Focus passage	Hebrews 12:22

Epouranios (heavenly) can refer to objects in the sky. Paul speaks of *heavenly* bodies like the sun, moon, and stars (1Co 15:40-41). *Epouranios* also refers to things related to or located in the spiritual realm. God dwells in the *heavenly* Jerusalem (Heb 12:22), and Christ is seated at God's right hand in *the heavens* (Eph 1:20). Other spiritual beings are located in *the heavens* (Eph 3:10). Paul mentions spiritual forces of evil that battle in *the heavens* (Eph 6:12). All spiritual forces *in heaven* will pay homage to Jesus (Php 2:10). Positionally, believers are seated in *the heavens* with Jesus (Eph 2:6). Hebrews speaks of *heavenly* realities, after which the earthly sacrificial system was modeled (Heb 8:5; 9:23). The saints of old aspired to a *heavenly* homeland (11:16). Additionally, *epouranios* may refer to things originating from God. Thus, Christians share in a *heavenly* calling (3:1).

is moving toward **Mount Zion** where it should dwell in the presence of God, Jesus, angels, and the righteous people who have been perfected by the **sprinkled blood** of Christ.

13:1-25 In the final chapter of the book, the author addressed the benefits and responsibilities of life lived in the church.

13:1-6 Under the general theme of allowing **brotherly love** to reign within the church, the author addressed five specific activities in which Christians should engage: (1) show "hospitality" toward strangers, (2) visit prisoners, (3) minister to the mistreated, (4) honor marriage, and (5) free themselves from the love of money.

13:7-19 The author addressed seven specific ways in which Christians should revere church leaders. (1) Christians should **observe** the lives of their leaders and imitate their faith. (2) Christians should remember that Christ is always the same and judge every teaching according to the gospel. (3) Christians should recognize their church may not be appreciated by the world because the Christian community is gathered to worship their Lord, whom the world despises. (4) Christians should continually offer their own **sacrifice of**

tinually offer up to God a sacrifice of praise, that is, the fruit of our lips that confess His name.*ᵃ ¹⁶Don't neglect to do what is good and to share, for God is pleased with such sacrifices.ᵇ ¹⁷Obey your leadersᴬ and submit to them, for they keep watchᶜ over your souls as those who will give an account, so that they can do this with joy and not with grief, for that would be unprofitable for you. ¹⁸Pray for us; for we are convinced that we have a clear conscience, wanting to conduct ourselves honorably in everything.ᵈ ¹⁹And I especially urge you to prayᴮ that I may be restored to you very soon.

Benediction and Farewell

²⁰Now may the God of peace, who brought

up from the dead our Lord Jesus—the great Shepherd of the sheepᵉ—with the blood of the everlasting covenant,ᶠ ²¹equipᶜ you with all that is good to do His will, working in us what is pleasing in His sight, through Jesus Christ. Glory belongs to Him forever and ever.ᴰ,ᵍ •Amen.

²²•Brothers, I urge you to receive this message of exhortation, for I have written to you briefly. ²³Be aware that our brother Timothy has been released. If he comes soon enough, he will be with me when I see you. ²⁴Greet all your leaders and all the •saints. Those who are from Italy greet you. ²⁵Grace be with all of you.ʰ

ᵃ13:15 Lv 7:12; Hs 14:2; Eph 5:20
ᵇ13:16 Rm 12:13; Php 4:18
ᶜ13:17 Is 62:6; Ezk 3:17; Ac 20:28
ᵈ13:18 Ac 23:1; 1Th 5:25
ᵉ13:20 Jn 10:11; Ac 2:24; Rm 15:33
ᶠZch 9:11; Heb 7:22; 8:6-10; 9:15; 12:24
ᵍ13:21 Rm 11:36; Php 2:13; 1Pt 5:10
ʰ13:22-25 Ac 16:1; Col 4:18; 1Th 3:2; Heb 13:7,17; 1Pt 5:12

ᴬ13:17 Or *rulers*   ᴮ13:19 Lit *to do this*   ᶜ13:21 Or *perfect*   ᴰ13:21 Other mss omit *and ever*

---

praise in appreciation for the sacrifice of Christ by confessing His name. (5) The church should be active in doing good works and sharing with one another. (6) Christians should **obey** their leaders and **submit** to them, because they are accountable to God for caring for Christian souls. (7) Christians should **pray** for their leaders to have clear consciences, conducting themselves with honor in everything.

13:20-25 The author prayed for his brothers in the church to be blessed. Recounting the sacrificial work of Christ, he prayed that God would **equip** them to do His will. He asked them to receive **this message of exhortation**, meaning this theological sermon (the book of Hebrews) that he had written for their benefit. After bringing greetings from the Italian community and news about Timothy, he ended with a blessing, **Grace be with all of you**.

thusia

Greek Pronunciation	[thew SEE ah]
HCSB Translation	sacrifice
Uses in Hebrews	15
Uses in the NT	28
Focus passage	Hebrews 13:15

Thusia (sacrifice) refers to what is *sacrificially* offered up on an altar to God. As prescribed under the Law, Joseph and Mary offered a *sacrifice* to dedicate their firstborn son Jesus (Lk 2:24). Under the OT sacrificial system, God was not impressed with outward *sacrifice* when such acts excluded inward obedience (Mt 9:13; 12:7; Mk 12:33). Christ offered Himself on a cross to God as the perfect and final *sacrifice* for sin (Eph 5:2; Heb 9:26; 10:12). In a figurative sense, *thusia* refers to the spiritual act of *offering* something unto God. Paul speaks of himself as a drink *offering* being poured out upon the *sacrifice* of the faith of the Philippians (Php 2:17). The financial gifts of the Philippian church to Paul are called a *sacrifice* (Php 4:18). Both verbal confession of praise to God and Christian acts of kindness are referred to as *sacrifices* (Heb 13:15-16).

"Now may the God of peace, who brought up from the dead our Lord Jesus—the great Shepherd of the sheep—with the blood of the everlasting covenant, equip you with all that is good to do His will, working in us what is pleasing in His sight, through Jesus Christ" (13:20-21).

James

Introduction

The book of James is a wonderful companion piece to the teachings of Jesus as recorded in the four Gospels. James has a strong ethical emphasis that is consistent with the moral teachings Jesus gave to His disciples. James also mirrors the sometimes harsh denunciations that Jesus spoke against religious hypocrisy. Like Jesus' teachings, the book of James is both a source of exhortation and comfort, reproof and encouragement. Finally, James is known for being extremely practical, yet it contains some of the most profound theological truths of the New Testament.

"Though the tongue is a small part of the body, it boasts great things. Consider how large a forest a small fire ignites. And the tongue is a fire . . . It pollutes the whole body, sets the course of life on fire" (3:5-6).

Circumstances of Writing

Author: James is named as the author in 1:1. A number of NT personalities were named James, but only three are candidates for the authorship of this book. James the son of Zebedee died in A.D. 44, too early to have been the author. No tradition names James the son of Alphaeus (Mk 3:18) as the author. This leaves James the brother of Jesus, also called James the Just (Mk 6:3; Ac 1:14; 12:17; 15:13; 21:18; 1Co 15:7; Gl 2:9,12), as the most likely candidate.

This James is identified as the brother of Jesus in Mt 13:55; Mk 6:3; and Gl 1:19. Though he was not a follower of Christ during His earthly ministry (Jn 7:3-5), a post-resurrection appearance convinced James that Jesus is indeed the Christ (Ac 1:14; 1Co 15:7). James later led the Jerusalem church (Gl 2:9,12), exercising great influence there (Ac 1:14; 12:17; 15:13; 21:18; 1Co 15:7; Gl 2:9,12).

Background: James was probably written between A.D. 48 and 52, though nothing in the epistle suggests a more precise date. James's death in A.D. 62 or 66 means the epistle was written before this time. Similarities to Gospel traditions and Pauline themes are suggestive. If Mark was written around A.D. 65 and time is allowed for the events of Acts 15 and 21 to have occurred between Paul's first and second missionary journeys, a date between A.D. 48 and 52 seems most likely.

The reference to "the 12 tribes in the Dispersion" (1:1) suggests the letter was written to Jewish Christians living in or around Palestine. James led the Jerusalem church, so it is likely that the audience lived in that area (including Antioch). The reference to a synagogue in 2:2 also suggests that his audience were Jewish Christians. References to their circumstances (e.g., oppression by wealthy landowners; 5:1-6) could refer to congregations anywhere in the Roman Empire. However, Semitic word order, quotations from the Septuagint, and the overall dependence of the epistle on the Jewish wisdom tradition suggest a specifically Jewish Christian audience.

2100–900 B.C.

Job 2100–1900?

Abraham 2166–1991

The Mosaic Law at Sinai 1446

Rahab supports the conquest of Jericho. 1406

Proverbs written 970–931

900 B.C.–A.D. 33

Elijah's ministry 862–852 B.C.

The Book of Wisdom 220–50 B.C.?

The deutero-canonical book of Ecclesiasticus 180 B.C.

Jesus' trials, death, resurrection, and ascension Nisan 14–16 or April 3–5, A.D. 33

Following His resurrection, Jesus appears to James, His brother. A.D. 33

Message and Purpose

As a general epistle, James was addressed to a broad audience (Jewish Christians) rather than a specific audience (e.g., Christians at Ephesus only). There is an obvious concern to address internal and external difficulties being faced by Jewish Christian congregations. Externally they were facing trials (1:2), particularly oppression of various sorts exerted by wealthy landowners. It does not appear that the oppression was religious in nature. Internally it appears that dissension was caused by a lack of self-control (1:13-17), uncontrolled speech, and false teachings that led to a misunderstanding of true religion (1:19-27; 2:1-4; 3:1-8), favoritism toward the wealthy (2:1-13), and selfish ambition that led to murder and criticism (4:1-12).

James addressed these issues primarily through the application of principles defined by the OT wisdom tradition. The solutions he named reflected the wisdom from above that comes from the "Father of lights" (1:17) who gives wisdom generously to those who ask for it. Wisdom is required for proper speech in worship and in determining who ought to teach (1:19-27; 3:1-8). Wisdom is also needed to avoid internal conflicts that create dissension within congregations (3:13-18; 4:1-12). The theme of faith in action is also important (1:19-27; 2:14-26); James demonstrated that faith that does not express itself in good works is useless. Another theme of the epistle is ethics, especially social justice (2:1-13; 4:1-12; 5:1-12).

Contribution to the Bible

James continually called for obedience to the law of God. He never referred to the ceremonial law, but to the moral law. While some people think James is at odds with Paul about the Christian's relationship to the law, both authors actually combine to give us a solid understanding of the OT law. Paul showed believers that Christ met the demands of the law and, thus, brings us to salvation. James showed believers that their obedience to God's moral standards is an indication of a living faith, which is a life lived in step with the One who met the demands of the law. Some choose to oversimplify the distinctions between the OT and the NT and say

A.D. 33–44

A.D. 44–330

Pentecost 33

Saul's conversion on the Damascus Road
October 34

Paul meets with Peter and James
on his first visit to Jerusalem
following his conversion. 37?

James becomes leader of the church at
Jerusalem. 44

Execution of James, son of Zebedee, by
Herod Agrippa 44

The Letter of James 48–52

James stoned to death. 62

Destruction of Jerusalem 70

Origen quotes James in his commentary
on the Gospel of John. 230

Eusebius refers to the Letter of James
as Scripture. 330

the OT is grounded in works and the NT is grounded in faith, but James brings both testaments together to show that faith and works are integrally related in both the old and new covenants.

Structure

The book of James is a letter (an epistle), though only the greeting conforms to the ancient Greek form exemplified in Paul's letters, especially Galatians. The greeting identifies the author as James, includes a title demonstrating the source of his authority ("a slave of God and of the Lord Jesus Christ"), names the recipients ("the 12 tribes in the Dispersion"), and conveys "Greetings" (1:1). Epistles were often used as a means of spurring the recipients to a change in behavior or belief based on the authoritative word and guidance of the sender.

The book of James has been compared to OT Wisdom literature. While there are wisdom elements in James, such as comparing the wisdom of the world with the wisdom that comes from God, it also contains exhortations and prophetic elements not common to Wisdom literature.

Outline

I. Salutation (1:1)

II. Surviving Trials and Temptation (1:2-18)
    A. Facing trials (1:2-12)
    B. God and temptation (1:13-15)
    C. Demonstrate God's good gifts (1:16-18)

III. Authentic Religion (1:19–2:26)
    A. Show maturity of character (1:19-21)
    B. Put faith into action (1:22-27)
    C. Shun partiality and favoritism (2:1-13)
    D. Practice good works (2:14-26)

IV. The Need for Wise Teachers (3:1-18)
    A. Teachers and control of the tongue (3:1-12)
    B. Teachers and wisdom from above (3:13-18)

V. Peace with God and One Another (4:1-17)
    A. Pride and humility (4:1-12)
    B. Our will and God's will (4:13-17)

VI. Discipline in the Christian Life (5:1-20)
    A. The hazards of wealth (5:1-6)
    B. Persevere under trial (5:7-11)
    C. Avoid swearing (5:12)
    D. Reach out to God in prayer (5:13-18)
    E. Minister to the wayward (5:19-20)

Greeting

1 James,[a] a •slave of God[b] and of the Lord Jesus Christ:

To the 12 tribes[c] in the Dispersion.[A,d] Greetings.[e]

Trials and Maturity

[2] Consider it a great joy, my •brothers, whenever you experience various trials,[f] [3] knowing that the testing of your faith produces endurance. [4] But endurance must do its complete work, so that you may be mature and complete, lacking nothing.

[5] Now if any of you lacks wisdom, he should ask God, who gives to all generously and without criticizing, and it will be given to him.[g] [6] But let him ask in faith without doubting. For the doubter is like the surging sea, driven and tossed by the wind. [7] That person should not expect to receive anything from the Lord. [8] An indecisive[B] man is unstable in all his ways.[h]

[9] The brother of humble circumstances should boast in his exaltation, [10] but the one who is rich should boast in his humiliation because he will pass away like a flower of the field.[i] [11] For the sun rises with its scorching heat and dries up the grass; its flower falls off, and its beautiful appearance is destroyed. In the same way, the rich man will wither away while pursuing his activities.[j]

[12] A man who endures trials[c] is blessed, because when he passes the test he will receive the crown[k] of life that God[D] has promised to those who love Him.[l]

[13] No one undergoing a trial should say, "I am being tempted by God." For God is not tempted by evil,[E] and He Himself doesn't tempt anyone. [14] But each person is tempted when he is drawn away and enticed by his own evil desires.[m] [15] Then after desire has conceived, it gives birth to sin, and when sin is fully grown, it gives birth to death.[n]

[16] Don't be deceived, my dearly loved brothers.[o] [17] Every generous act and every perfect gift is from above, coming down from the Father of lights; with Him there is no variation or shadow cast by turning.[p] [18] By His own choice, He gave us a new birth by the message of truth[F] so that we would be the •firstfruits of His creatures.[q]

Cross-references (center column):

[a]1:1 Mt 13:55; Mk 6:3; Ac 12:17; 15:13; 21:18; Gl 1:19; 2:9,12; Jd 1
[b]Ac 16:17; Rm 1:1; Eph 6:6; Jms 1:1; 1Pt 2:16; Rv 1:1
[c]Gn 49:28; Ex 24:4; Ezk 47:13; Mt 19:28; Ac 26:7; Rv 21:12
[d]Jn 7:35; 1Pt 1:1
[e]Ti 1:1
[f]1:2 Mt 5:12; 1Pt 1:6
[g]1:5 1Kg 3:9; Pr 2:3-6; Mt 7:7
[h]1:8 Jms 4:8; 2Pt 2:14
[i]1:10 1Co 7:31; 1Pt 1:24
[j]1:11 Ps 102:4,11; Is 40:7
[k]1:12 1Co 9:25; 2Tm 4:8; 1Pt 5:4; Rv 2:10; 3:11
[l]Mt 10:22; Jms 2:5
[m]1:14 Pr 7:6-23
[n]1:15 Jb 15:35; Ps 7:14; Is 59:4; Rm 6:23
[o]1:16 1Co 6:9; Jms 1:19
[p]1:17 Nm 23:19; Mal 3:6; Jn 3:27; 1Jn 1:5
[q]1:18 Jn 1:13; Eph 1:12

[A]1:1 Jewish people scattered throughout Gentile lands who spoke Gk and were influenced by Gk culture   [B]1:8 Or *A doubting*, or *A double-minded*   [C]1:12 Lit *trial*, used as a collective   [D]1:12 Other mss read *that the Lord*   [E]1:13 Or *evil persons*, or *evil things*   [F]1:18 = the gospel

---

1:1 The use of **slave** indicates James's humility and total devotion in service to his Lord. As a "slave" **of God and of the Lord Jesus Christ**, James's words bear authority, for he does his master's bidding and speaks as His representative (2Pt 1:20-21). **The 12 tribes in the Dispersion** refers symbolically to Jewish Christians scattered abroad (see note at 1Pt 1:1-2).

1:2 The phrase **whenever you experience various trials** assumes that trials are a normal part of the Christian life. In fact, trials are a given for a faithful disciple (2Tm 3:12). The Jewish wisdom tradition held that the experience of "trials" was proof of a person's faithfulness. **Joy** suggests an eschatological (end times) hope of deliverance from trials. The joy with which a believer endures trials in the present is a sign of their hope for future relief.

1:3 Knowing (or "because you know") modifies "consider" in verse 2. Knowledge **that the testing of your faith produces endurance** is the basis for joy. "Endurance" is the ability to persevere through increasing levels of testing or suffering.

1:4 Endurance indicates that further **work** must be done for the purpose of making the believer **mature and complete, lacking nothing**. Immaturity and incompletion are not acceptable long-term states for the Christian disciple.

1:5 The world's harsh treatment tempts us to withdraw and refuse to expose our lack of wisdom for fear of being shamed by our peers, but God **gives to all generously and without criticizing**. Thus he who **lacks wisdom** should **ask God** freely.

1:6-8 A person should ask for wisdom **in faith without doubting**. The basis for confidence here is not just the fact that we exercise faith, but the person in whom we place our faith—God.

1:9-11 James offered two illustrations of people facing trials: **the brother of humble circumstances** (the poor) and **one who is rich**. In relation to eternity, neither the poor nor the wealthy have anything to boast about; they are equals before God.

1:12 Blessed reflects the understanding that a person who walks in the paths set by the Lord sees his plight in terms of the eschatological hope that awaits him. Set within this context, his current troubles seem fleeting.

1:13-18 The term **trial** (v. 13) connects this group of verses to the preceding section (vv. 2-12). God's relationship to temptation is made clear by two kinds of statements. On the one hand, there are assertions that clarify what God is not or does not do: **God is not tempted . . . and He Himself doesn't tempt**. On the other hand, there are assertions as to what things do come from God: **every generous act and every perfect gift**.

1:13-14 The twofold negative stance (**God is not tempted** and **He Himself doesn't tempt anyone**) emphatically denies that God leads people into temptation. The source of temptation is one's **own evil desires**. "Desires" focuses on the immediacy that carnal desire creates, spurring a person to act, to be **drawn away and enticed** like a fish is baited to bite a hook and is then pulled from the water.

1:17 Father of lights refers to God (v. 5), who created the lights that rule days and seasons (Gn 1:14-19). **No variation or shadow cast by turning** alludes to the fact that God's nature is unchanging and that His promises are secure.

1:18 Message of truth refers to the gospel, by which **new birth** comes. **Firstfruits** refers to the best that the harvest produces. God gives good gifts that yield wondrous fruit, not temptation that leads to death through wayward desires.

Hearing and Doing the Word

[19] My dearly loved brothers, understand this: Everyone must be quick to hear, slow to speak, and slow to anger,[a] [20] for man's anger does not accomplish God's righteousness. [21] Therefore, ridding yourselves of all moral filth and evil,[A] humbly receive the implanted word, which is able to save you.[B,b]

[22] But[c] be doers of the word and not hearers only, deceiving yourselves. [23] Because if anyone is a hearer of the word and not a doer, he is like a man looking at his own face[C] in a mirror. [24] For he looks at himself, goes away, and immediately forgets what kind of man he was. [25] But the one who looks intently into the perfect law of freedom and perseveres in it, and is not a forgetful hearer but one who does good works—this person will be blessed in what he does.[d]

[26] If anyone[D] thinks he is religious without controlling his tongue,[e] then his religion is useless and he deceives himself. [27] Pure and undefiled religion before our[E] God and Father is this: to look after orphans and widows[f] in their distress and to keep oneself unstained by the •world.[g]

The Sin of Favoritism

2 My •brothers, do not show favoritism as you hold on to the faith in our glorious Lord Jesus Christ.[h] [2] For example, a man comes into your meeting wearing a gold ring and dressed in fine clothes, and a poor man dressed in dirty clothes also comes in. [3] If you look with favor on the man wearing the fine clothes and say, "Sit here in a good place," and yet you say to the poor man, "Stand over there," or, "Sit here on the floor by my footstool," [4] haven't you discriminated among yourselves and become judges with evil thoughts?

[5] Listen, my dear brothers: Didn't God choose the poor in this world[i] to be rich in faith[j] and heirs[k] of the kingdom that He has promised to those who love Him? [6] Yet you dishonored that poor man.[l] Don't the rich oppress you and drag[m] you into the courts? [7] Don't they blaspheme the noble name that was pronounced over you at your baptism?[n]

[8] Indeed, if you keep the royal law prescribed in the Scripture, **Love your neighbor as yourself**,[F,o] you are doing well. [9] But if you show favoritism,[p] you commit sin and are convicted

Cross references (center column)

a 1:19 Pr 10:19; 17:27; Ec 5:1-2
b 1:21 Eph 1:13; 4:22; Col 3:8
c 1:22-25 Mt 7:24-27; Rm 2:13; Jms 2:14-20
d 1:25 Jn 13:17; Jms 2:12
e 1:26 Ps 34:13; 39:1; 141:3; Jms 3:2-3; 1Pt 3:10
f 1:27 Jb 31:17; Is 1:17,23; Mt 25:36
g Rm 12:2; 1Jn 5:18
h 2:1 Lv 19:15; Dt 1:17; Ac 10:34; Rm 2:11; Eph 6:9; Col 3:25
i 2:5 Jb 34:19; 1Co 1:27
j Lk 12:21; Rv 2:9
k Rm 4:13-14; 8:17; Gl 3:29; 4:7; Ti 3:7; Heb 1:2; 11:7
l 2:6 1Co 11:22
m Ac 8:3; 17:6; 18:12
n 2:7 Is 63:19; 65:1; Am 9:12; Ac 15:17
o 2:8 Lv 19:18; Mt 22:39
p 2:9 Lv 19:15; Dt 1:17; Ac 10:34; Rm 2:11; Eph 6:9; Col 3:25

A 1:21 Lit *evil excess*   B 1:21 Lit *save your souls*   C 1:23 Lit *at the face of his birth*   D 1:26 Other mss add *among you*   E 1:27 Or *before the*   F 2:8 Lv 19:18

1:19-27 The focus of this section is on proper Christian conduct, especially regarding use of the **tongue**.

1:21 Implanted word refers to the gospel as received by the believer.

1:22 The presence of the "implanted word" should produce more than idle listening. True worship leads to putting gospel exhortations into action.

1:23-25 In the contrast between the **hearer of the word** who looks at **his own face in a mirror** and yet **forgets**, and the **doer** of the word **who looks intently into the perfect law of freedom** and perseveres, the distinction is found in whether the one who looks allows "the perfect law of freedom" (the gospel) to shape his life's course. The person who hears and does "the word" puts faith into action and is **blessed**; his worship influences his life.

1:26-27 James made an observation about true religion. Just as the hearer looks in a mirror and forgets his own face, so the person who refuses to hold his **tongue** is deceived about his faith. He hears and talks, but he does not act on what he has heard. James's definition of **pure and undefiled religion** is based on action, not heedless hearing and meaningless lip service.

2:1-26 In this chapter James discussed worship in the synagogue. References to the treatment of the wealthy versus the poor are reminiscent of 1:9-11. The focus on the ethics of true spirituality is linked closely with chapter 1.

2:1 The phrase **show favoritism** is addressed four times in the NT (cp. Rm 2:11; Eph 6:9; Col 3:25), each time indicating that God does not show favoritism. When we sin by showing "favoritism" we imply that God did not make all men and

women equal. Thus anyone who shows favoritism is guilty of having "evil thoughts" (Jms 2:4).

2:2-3 James portrayed favoritism by illustrating contrasting attitudes toward a wealthy man and a poor man who enter the **meeting** (Gk *sunagogeyn*). The attendance of a wealthy man promises financial advantage since his tithes and offerings may be large, thus the people in the assembly **look with favor** on him. "Look with favor" is related in meaning to "showing favoritism" in verse 1.

2:4 James condemned favoritism with a rhetorical question (**haven't you discriminated among yourselves and become judges with evil thoughts?**), to which his audience could only answer, "Yes." The word "discriminated" suggests that pandering had created divisions within the fellowship of the synagogue. Probably neither the wealthy man nor the poor man was a member of the synagogue.

2:5 God's choice of **the poor** here is not favoritism because the choice was not based on bias. Discrimination occurs when one ignores the fact that the "law of freedom" (1:25) applies to all people, obligating us to treat everyone equally.

2:7 The noble name refers to Jesus Christ. **Blaspheme** means that the wealthy blaspheme either by speaking against Christ directly or through their actions against members of the assembly.

2:8-11 Attitudes among Christians should be based on the **royal law**, which says **Love your neighbor as yourself** (Lv 19:18; Mt 19:19; 22:39; Mk 12:31; Rm 13:9; Gl 5:14). Favoritism violates this command, thus convicting those guilty of its practice as **transgressors** of the law.

by the law as transgressors. [10] For whoever keeps the entire law, yet fails in one point, is ⋅guilty of breaking it all.[a] [11] For He who said, **Do not commit adultery,**[A] also said, **Do not murder.**[B,b] So if you do not commit adultery, but you do murder, you are a lawbreaker.

[12] Speak and act as those who will be judged by the law of freedom.[c] [13] For judgment is without mercy to the one who hasn't shown mercy.[d] Mercy triumphs over judgment.

[a]2:10 Mt 5:10; Gl 3:10
[b]2:11 Ex 20:13-14; Dt 5:17-18
[c]2:12 Mt 7:12,24-29; 19:17-21; 22:36-40; 28:20
[d]2:13 Jb 22:6; Pr 21:13; Mt 5:7; 18:32-35
[e]2:14-16 Mt 25:35-36; Lk 3:11; 1Jn 3:16-18

Faith and Works

[14] What good is it, my brothers, if someone says he has faith but does not have works? Can his faith[c] save him?

[15] If a brother or sister is without clothes and lacks daily food [16] and one of you says to them, "Go in peace, keep warm, and eat well," but you don't give them what the body needs, what good is it?[e] [17] In the same way faith, if it doesn't have works, is dead by itself.

[A]2:11 Ex 20:14; Dt 5:18   [B]2:11 Ex 20:13; Dt 5:17   [C]2:14 Or Can faith, or Can that faith, or Can such faith

---

2:12-13 James exhorted his readers to have proper attitudes. The phrase **speak and act** refers to "hearing and doing" and tempered speech, as in 1:19-27. The **law of freedom**, or the gospel, will serve as the basis for eschatological judgment (1:2-12).

2:14-26 In this section James continues with the theme of

"being hearers and doers of the word" (1:19-27) by focusing on the relationship between faith and works.

2:14 Can his faith save him should be understood to mean, "Can a faith that does not express itself in good works be a saving faith?" The answer is no.

2:15-17 Giving a blessing to someone in need without

Faith and Works

Mark DeVine

Whenever "faith" is set beside "works" it recalls the theological conflicts that shaped the Reformation of the sixteenth century. To this day these conflicts largely account for the division of the western church between Roman Catholic and Protestant. Martin Luther's rediscovery of the gospel included a recovery of the apostle Paul's insistence that "no one will be justified in His [God's] sight by the works of the law" (Rm 3:20). Instead, "you are saved by grace through faith, and this is not from yourselves; it is God's gift—not from works, so that no one can boast" (Eph 2:8-9).

The faith that saves, Luther realized from his study of the Bible, is not mere historical faith (Gk *fides*), a bare belief that what the Bible declares as true is in fact true, a faith that, according to John Calvin, merely "flits in the brain" and saves no one. Of such faith James could say: "The demons also believe—and they shudder" (Jms 2:19). No, the faith that saves the soul is trusting faith (Gk *fiducia*), so that salvation comes by grace alone through faith alone in Christ alone. This trusting faith is the "faith in His [Christ's] blood" (Rm 3:25) of which Paul spoke; faith that relies upon the death of Jesus Christ on the cross in the place of sinners. There Jesus bore the punishment of sinners upon Himself so that now God promises to treat as righteous those who believe in His name. Just as "Abraham believed God, and it was credited to him for righteousness" (Rm 4:3), so now all who repent of their sins, abandon hope of being made right with God on the basis of their own good works, and trust only in the mercy of God offered in the death of Jesus Christ in their place, will be saved.

Then what of good works? Have they no place in the Christian life? James anticipates and answers this question: "But someone will say, 'You have faith, and I have works.' Show me your faith without works, and I will show you faith from my works" (Jms 2:18). While God's salvation is all of grace, including the faith that saves, which "is not from yourselves; it is God's gift—not from works so that no one can boast" (Eph 2:8-9), Paul follows this assertion with a word about works: "For we are His [God's] creation, created in Christ Jesus for good works, which God prepared ahead of time so that we should walk in them" (Eph 2:10). So good works follow saving faith. Salvation is not gained through works but rather good works are the fruit of saving faith in Jesus Christ.

Sinners saved by grace through faith rest their confidence before God neither in their works nor their faith, as if faith itself were a source of pride. Faith derives its saving power from its object, Jesus Christ. A believer's good works are no grounds for boasting, for the works stem from Christ Himself. The apostle Paul described this mystery as follows: "I have been crucified with Christ and I no longer live, but Christ lives in me" (Gl 2:19-20). Good works are performed by believers due to Christ working in them. Thus a believer's confidence in their salvation is based on Christ, not their performance of good works. With the apostle Paul believers long to "be found in Him [Christ], not having a righteousness of my own from the law, but one that is through faith in Christ—the righteousness from God based on faith" (Php 3:9). They know that "without faith it is impossible to please God" (Heb 11:6).

¹⁸But someone will say, "You have faith, and I have works."^A Show me your faith without works, and I will show you faith from my works.^{B,a} ¹⁹You believe that God is one; you do well. The demons also believe—and they shudder.^b

²⁰Foolish man! Are you willing to learn that faith without works is useless? ²¹Wasn't Abraham our father •justified by works when he offered Isaac his son on the altar? ²²You see that faith was active together with his works, and by works, faith was perfected.^c ²³So the Scripture was fulfilled that says, **Abraham believed God, and it was credited to him for righteousness,**^{C,d} and he was called God's friend.^e ²⁴You see that a man is justified by works and not by faith alone. ²⁵And in the same way, wasn't Rahab the prostitute also justified by works when she received the messengers and sent them out by a different route?^f ²⁶For just as the body without the spirit is dead, so also faith without works is dead.

Controlling the Tongue

3 Not many should become teachers, my •brothers, knowing that we will receive a stricter judgment,^g ²for we all stumble in many ways.^h If anyone does not stumble in what he says,^D he is a mature man who is also able to control his whole body.^{E,i}

³Now when we put bits into the mouths of horses to make them obey us,^j we also guide the whole animal.^F ⁴And consider ships: Though very large and driven by fierce winds, they are guided by a very small rudder wherever the will of the pilot directs. ⁵So too, though the tongue is a small part of the body, it boasts great things.^k Consider how large a forest a small fire ignites. ⁶And the tongue is a fire. The tongue, a world of unrighteousness, is placed among the parts of our bodies. It pollutes the whole body,^l sets the course of life on fire, and is set on fire by •hell.

⁷Every sea creature, reptile, bird, or animal is tamed and has been tamed by man, ⁸but no

^a2:18 Rm 3:28; Heb 11:33; Jms 3:13
^b2:19 Dt 6:4; Mt 8:29; Lk 4:34
^c2:21-22 Gn 22:9; 1Th 1:3; Heb 11:17
^d2:23 Gn 15:6; Rm 4:3; Gl 3:6
^e2Ch 20:7; Is 41:8
^f2:25 Jos 2:4,6,15; Heb 11:31
^g3:1 Mt 23:8; Rm 2:20-21; 1Tm 1:7
^h3:2 1Kg 8:46; Pr 20:9; Jms 2:10
ⁱMt 12:37; Jms 1:26; 1Pt 3:10
^j3:3 Ps 32:9; 39:1
^k3:5 Ps 12:3-4; 73:8-9
^l3:6 Ps 120:2-3; Pr 16:27; Mt 15:11,18

---

^A2:18 The quotation may end here or after v. 18b or v. 19. ^B2:18 Other mss read *Show me your faith from your works, and from my works I will show you my faith.* ^C2:23 Gn 15:6 ^D3:2 Lit *in word* ^E3:2 Lit *to bridle the whole body* ^F3:3 Lit *whole body*

---

offering tangible aid is useless. If faith is not accompanied by works, it is **dead by itself**.

2:18 The argument turns to the relationship between faith and works. Beginning in this verse James answered a "straw man" argument (**but someone will say**) against his assertion that faith without works is dead.

2:19-20 The demons also believe—and they shudder is an answer to the mistaken assertion that belief in God by itself is sufficient for salvation. Demons believe, but it is impossible for them to be saved. Saving faith entails more than mere knowledge. It includes trust and obedience, for **faith without works is useless**.

2:21-23 The example of Abraham and his offer of Isaac as a sacrifice (Gn 22:1-19) affirms James's teachings about faith. What exactly a biblical author means by **justified** depends on the context in which he uses it. For instance, Paul (Rm 4:1-5; Gl 3:6-14) argued that "works of the law" cannot make one "justified" because he wished to make clear that salvation is a gift given only through faith. Abraham believed God, and his trust in God was counted as righteousness (Gn 15:6; Gl 3:6). James focuses more on the role good works play in proving faith genuine. Abraham's faith was proven genuine by his obedience to God's command. His faith made his good works possible.

2:24-26 James's declaration that **man is justified by works and not by faith alone** may seem to contradict Rm 3:28, but note that Paul was writing about "works of the law," meaning the Mosaic law, whereas James spoke only of "works," which has in view good deeds. James's references to law are to "the law of freedom" (the gospel; see 2:12) and to "the royal law" (v. 8; Lv 19:18), both of which affirm his assertion that true faith is expressed through good works.

3:1-12 In this section James continued to address the issue of misguided speech (2:16-18). The focus is on how errant teaching might adversely affect the congregation.

3:1 Many people desire to be **teachers** because this is an important role in the church. Yet the proliferation of untrained teachers can allow false teachings to arise within congregations, leading some astray. Teachers receive **a stricter judgment** and should not be appointed carelessly.

3:2 The most difficult thing for a teacher to control is the tongue. **Body** (Gk *soma*) carries a dual meaning here. It refers to the physical body and the role the tongue plays in it, but it also refers to the body of believers in the synagogue and the influence that teachers have in it.

3:3-6 Like horse **bits** and ship rudders, the size of **the tongue** is disproportionate to the influence it holds. False teaching (expressed by "the tongue") is **a world of unrighteousness**. It pollutes the **whole body** (an individual or a congregation) and determines the destiny of all who follow it.

---

prautes

Greek Pronunciation	[prah OO tays]
HCSB Translation	gentleness
Uses in James	2
Uses in the NT	11
Focus passage	James 3:13

Prautes (gentleness, humility) always appears as a positive quality in the NT. Christians are encouraged to receive with *submission* (a humble attitude toward) the implanted word able to save their lives (Jms 1:21). This inward attitude of *gentleness* always manifests itself outwardly. There is no such thing as a gentle attitude that does not express itself in *gentleness* with relation to others. Therefore, good conduct should operate in the *gentleness* that wisdom requires (Jms 3:13). *Gentleness* is a fruit of the Spirit (Gl 5:23). Christians are to clothe themselves with *gentleness* not only toward one another (Col 3:12) but also toward all people (Ti 3:2). Sinners are to be restored in a spirit of *gentleness* (Gl 6:1). The servant of God is not to quarrel even with his opponents. Rather, he is to instruct them in *gentleness* with a view to their repentance (2Tm 2:24-25; cp. 1Pt 3:16).

man can tame the tongue. It is a restless evil, full of deadly poison.[a] [9]We praise our[A] Lord and Father with it, and we curse men who are made in God's likeness with it.[b] [10]Praising and cursing come out of the same mouth. My brothers, these things should not be this way. [11]Does a spring pour out sweet and bitter water from the same opening? [12]Can a fig tree produce olives, my brothers, or a grapevine produce figs? Neither can a saltwater spring yield fresh water.

The Wisdom from Above

[13]Who is wise and has understanding among you? He should show his works by good conduct with wisdom's gentleness.[c] [14]But if you have bitter envy and selfish ambition in your heart, don't brag and deny the truth.[d] [15]Such wisdom does not come from above but is earthly, unspiritual, demonic.[e] [16]For where envy and selfish ambition exist, there is disorder and every kind of evil. [17]But the wisdom from above is first pure, then peaceloving, gentle, compliant, full of mercy and

[a]3:8 Ps 140:3; Ec 10:11; Rm 3:13
[b]3:9 Gn 1:26; 1Co 11:7
[c]3:13 Jms 1:21; 2:18
[d]3:14 Rm 2:8; 13:13; 2Co 12:20
[e]3:15 2Th 2:2; 1Tm 4:1; Jms 1:17; Rv 2:24
[f]3:17 Lk 6:36; Rm 12:9; 1Co 2:6; Heb 12:11; Jms 2:4
[g]3:18 Pr 11:18; Is 32:17; Hs 10:12; Am 6:12; Gl 6:8; Php 1:11
[h]4:1 Rm 7:23; Ti 3:9
[i]4:3 Ps 18:41; 1Jn 3:22; 5:14
[j]4:4 Jn 15:19; Jms 1:27; 1Jn 2:15
[k]4:5 1Co 6:19; 2Co 6:16
[l]4:6 Ps 138:6; Pr 3:34; Mt 23:12

good fruits, without favoritism and hypocrisy.[f] [18]And the fruit of righteousness[g] is sown in peace by those who cultivate peace.

Proud or Humble

4 What is the source of wars and fights among you? Don't they come from the cravings[h] that are at war within you?[B] [2]You desire and do not have. You murder and covet and cannot obtain. You fight and war. You do not have because you do not ask. [3]You ask and don't receive because you ask with wrong motives, so that you may spend it on your evil desires.[i]

[4]Adulteresses![C,D] Don't you know that friendship with the •world is hostility toward God? So whoever wants to be the world's friend becomes God's enemy.[j] [5]Or do you think it's without reason the Scripture says that the Spirit who lives in us yearns jealously?[E,k]

[6]But He gives greater grace. Therefore He says:

**God resists the proud,
but gives grace to the humble.**[F,l]

[A]3:9 Or praise the   [B]4:1 Lit war in your members   [C]4:4 Other mss read Adulterers and adulteresses   [D]4:4 Or Unfaithful people!   [E]4:5 Or He who caused the Spirit to live in us yearns jealously, or the spirit He caused to live in us yearns jealously, or He jealously yearns for the Spirit He made to live in us   [F]4:6 Pr 3:34

3:9-12 James pointed out the contradictory nature of the tongue. Out of the same mouth comes blessing of God and cursing of fellow humans who are made in God's likeness, a violation of the "royal law" (2:8).

3:13-18 In these verses James continued addressing the role of teachers, particularly their spiritual maturity. Speech plays a role here (**don't brag and deny the truth**), but the larger issues are **envy and selfish ambition**. Far from being minor character flaws, these traits are **earthly, unspiritual,** and **demonic.**

3:13 The wise teacher should **show his works** (see note at 2:18). As faith is demonstrated by works, so also wisdom is demonstrated by **good conduct** and **gentleness.**

3:14-15 The phrase **bitter envy and selfish ambition** contrasts with "good conduct and wisdom's gentleness" in verse 13. Denial of **truth** is a constant threat in churches that tolerate false teachings.

3:16-18 James contrasted the two types of wisdom in terms of their sources. Teachers who teach on the basis of "earthly" wisdom produce **disorder and every kind of evil.** Teachers who possess **wisdom from above** produce virtues that fulfill the "royal law" (2:8) and promote unity within the congregation.

4:1 While pride and selfishness are natural to fallen humanity and often serve as a basis for advancement in worldly rank, James names them as the **source of wars and fights** within the congregation. "Wars and fights" indicates physical conflict among members and/or factions within the congregation. The source of conflict was the **cravings . . . at war within you.** "Cravings" refers to the pleasures of life, the pursuit of which leads to conflicts.

4:2-3 Two statements distinguished by paired opposites (**desire . . . do not have** and **murder and covet . . . cannot obtain**) and two direct assertions (**fight and war** and **do**

not have because you do not ask) describe the problem to which the circumstances had led. People were actually killing one another to appease their misplaced desires! Their desires were unappeased because they were asking with **wrong motives.** The source of conflict was selfish desire and envy run amok (3:13-18).

4:4-5 Adulteresses refers to the congregation's unfaithfulness to God. Self-centeredness is cast as diametric opposition (**hostility**) to God. The phrase **the Spirit who lives in us yearns jealously** plays off "the cravings . . . at war within you" in verse 1, demonstrating the difference in attitude between a Spirit-filled life and one enslaved by selfish cravings.

4:6 The phrase **but He gives greater grace** introduces the

huperephanos

Greek Pronunciation	[hoo pehr AY fah nahs]
HCSB Translation	proud
Uses in James	1
Uses in the NT	5
Focus passage	James 4:6

In the NT, *huperephanos* appears exclusively in an unfavorable sense, referring to one who is *haughty* or *arrogant,* always in relation to other people. Thus, men show their *pride* by foolishly refusing to submit to God and authorities. Consequently, God opposes them (Lk 1:51; Jms 4:6). God is opposed to the *proud* believer who resists those in authority and acts arrogantly toward his fellow brothers and sisters (1Pt 5:5). Thus, *huperephanos* represents a *pride* of heart that manifests itself through a state of demeaning others. Paul's use of *huperephanos* supports this conclusion. Twice he lists the term in a vice-list (Rm 1:30; 2Tm 3:2). From the list in Rm 1:30, the range of meaning of *huperephanos* appears to overlap with that of *hubristas* (a violent, insolent man) and *alazones* (an empty boaster) such that the term appears to be a link between empty verbal boasting and violent action.

7 Therefore, submit to God. But resist the Devil, and he will flee from you.*ᵃ* 8 Draw near to God, and He will draw near to you. Cleanse your hands, sinners, and purify your hearts, double-minded people!*ᵇ* 9 Be miserable and mourn and weep. Your laughter must change to mourning and your joy to sorrow.*ᶜ* 10 Humble yourselves before the Lord, and He will exalt you.

11 Don't criticize one another, •brothers. He who criticizes a brother or judges his brother criticizes the law and judges the law. But if you judge the law, you are not a doer of the law but a judge.*ᵈ* 12 There is one lawgiver and judge^A who is able to save and to destroy. But who are you to judge your neighbor?*ᵉ*

Our Will and His Will

13 Come now, you who say, "Today or tomorrow we will travel to such and such a city and spend a year there and do business and make a profit."*ᶠ* 14 You don't even know what tomorrow will bring—what your life will be! For you are like smoke that appears for a little while, then vanishes.*ᵍ*

15 Instead, you should say, "If the Lord wills,

we will live and do this or that." 16 But as it is, you boast in your arrogance. All such boasting is evil.*ʰ* 17 So it is a sin for the person who knows to do what is good and doesn't do it.*ⁱ*

Warning to the Rich

5 Come now, you rich*ʲ* people! Weep and wail over the miseries that are coming on you. 2 Your wealth is ruined and your clothes are moth-eaten.*ᵏ* 3 Your silver and gold are corroded, and their corrosion will be a witness against you and will eat your flesh like fire. You stored up treasure in the last days!*ˡ* Look! 4 The pay that you withheld from the workers*ᵐ* who reaped your fields cries out, and the outcry of the harvesters has reached the ears of the Lord of •Hosts.^B,*ⁿ* 5 You have lived luxuriously on the land and have indulged yourselves. You have fattened your hearts*ᵒ* for^C the day of slaughter.*ᵖ* 6 You have condemned—you have murdered—the righteous man; he does not resist you.*ᑫ*

Waiting for the Lord

7 Therefore, •brothers, be patient until the

*ᵃ*4:7 Eph 4:27; 6:11; 1Pt 5:8-9
*ᵇ*4:8 2Ch 15:2; Is 1:16; Jms 1:8
*ᶜ*4:9 Mt 5:4; Lk 6:25
*ᵈ*4:11 Mt 7:1; Jms 1:22; 1Pt 2:1
*ᵉ*4:12 Mt 10:28; Rm 14:4
*ᶠ*4:13 Pr 27:1; Lk 12:18-20
*ᵍ*4:14 Jb 7:7; Ps 102:3
*ʰ*4:15-16 Ac 18:21; 1Co 5:6
*ⁱ*4:17 Lk 12:47-48; Jn 9:41; 2Pt 2:21
*ʲ*5:1 Pr 11:28; Lk 6:24
*ᵏ*5:2 Jb 13:28; Is 50:9; Mt 6:19-20
*ˡ*5:3 Rm 2:5; Jms 5:8
*ᵐ*5:4 Lv 19:13; Jb 24:10-11; Jr 22:13; Mal 3:5
*ⁿ*Dt 24:15; Rm 9:29
*ᵒ*5:5 Jb 21:13; Am 6:1
*ᵖ*Jr 12:3; 25:34
*ᑫ*5:6 Heb 10:38; Jms 4:2

^A4:12 Other mss omit *and judge*   ^B5:4 Gk *Sabaoth*; this word is a transliteration of the Hb word for *Hosts*, or *Armies*.   ^C5:5 Or *hearts in*

main point—God's grace is able to overcome unfaithfulness. The exhortation to repent is backed by a stark reality expressed in Pr 3:34 and quoted here by James: **God resists the proud.** "Resist" is a military term used to describe an army arrayed for battle. To remain in sinful pride is to invite God's battle array against you. In contrast to this, God **gives grace to the humble** (1:17).

4:7-9 James issued ten commands needed to resolve the conflict within the congregation. The theme is repentance and forgiveness. The use of imperatives followed by **and** suggests that the result of each command is conditioned by the response to it, which yields the idea, "if you do X, then Y results." **Submit to God** carries the idea of self-humbling; **resist the Devil** suggests an active resistance against temptation. **Sinners** and **double-minded people** are parallel ideas that characterize both the teachers and the congregation. "Double-minded" recalls the doubter of 1:8.

4:10 The words **humble yourselves . . . and He will exalt you** summarize the path to having forgiveness from God as well as reconciliation among members of the congregation.

4:11-12 Criticism is malicious, judgmental speech toward others. It violates the "royal law" (2:8) and by extension the Mosaic law. Since the One who gave the law also judges according to it, there are never grounds for critical speech directed toward another member of the congregation.

4:13-17 In this section the issue is boastful speech that indicates arrogance. It is unclear whether the merchants of verse 17 were all Christians, but verse 15 suggests that some were.

4:13-14 In a hypothetical but realistic scenario, James accused a merchant who had big designs on making a profit of leaving God out of his plans. Neglecting to entrust our hopes and plans to God and His counsel is paramount to arrogance and unbelief. If He is really the Lord of our lives,

we see all things as coming from His hands and we speak of plans and outcomes accordingly.

4:15-16 The phrase **you should say** and what follows indicate that it is God's will that conditions the course of life. The merchants did not recognize this; they were **boasting**, but such boasting is **arrogance** and **evil**.

5:1-6 Oppressive landowners and people who put their trust in riches were commonly addressed in prophetic and apocalyptic speech, including by Jesus Himself (e.g., Lk 6:24). People who use their wealth to oppress others may seem to go unpunished in this lifetime, but James warns that **miseries** are **coming** in the future judgment.

5:2-3 Wealth is often measured in terms of quality foods, clothes, and silver and gold. Besides referring to **moth-eaten** clothing, the phrase **wealth is ruined** could indicate that food is perishable and thus not a measure of lasting wealth. Technically speaking, **silver and gold** do not corrode; James's statement about them corroding is paradoxical, emphasizing that even "incorruptible" commodities are destined to perish. **Last days** emphasizes the eschatological nature of the pronouncement against greed. **Stored up** (or hoarded) wealth will become the undoing of greedy persons.

5:4 In ancient times payment for work performed was due at the end of the workday. Greed motivated some landowners to withhold these wages. **Withheld** could be translated "defrauded." **Lord of Hosts** is an OT reference to God as a warrior (1Ch 11:4-9; Is 2:12ff). The plight of the poor and oppressed worker is known to God.

5:6 Condemned is a legal term suggesting that the wealthy took land and wages through decisions rendered in dishonest courts. **He does not resist you** (see 4:6) indicates the helplessness of the poor.

5:7-8 In light of the certainty of God's coming judgment on

Lord's coming. See how the farmer waits for the precious fruit of the earth and is patient with it until it receives the early and the late rains.[a] [8]You also must be patient. Strengthen your hearts, because the Lord's coming is near.[b]

[9]Brothers, do not complain about one another, so that you will not be judged. Look, the judge stands at the door![c]

[10]Brothers, take the prophets who spoke in the Lord's name as an example of suffering and patience. [11]See, we count as blessed those who have endured.[A] You have heard of Job's endurance[d] and have seen the outcome from the Lord. The Lord is very compassionate and merciful.[e]

Truthful Speech

[12]Now above all, my brothers, do not swear, either by heaven or by earth or with any other oath.[f] Your "yes" must be "yes," and your "no" must be "no," so that you won't fall under judgment.[B]

Effective Prayer

[13]Is anyone among you suffering? He should pray. Is anyone cheerful? He should sing praises.[g] [14]Is anyone among you sick? He should call for the elders of the church, and they should pray over him after anointing him with olive oil in the name of the Lord.[h] [15]The prayer of faith will save the sick person, and the Lord will restore him to health; if he has committed sins, he will be forgiven.[i] [16]Therefore, confess your sins to one another and pray for one another, so that you may be healed. The urgent request of a righteous person is very powerful in its effect.[j] [17]Elijah was a man with a nature like ours; yet he prayed earnestly that it would not rain, and for three years and six months it did not rain on the land.[k] [18]Then he prayed again, and the sky gave rain and the land produced its fruit.[l]

[19]My brothers, if any among you strays from the truth,[m] and someone turns him back,[n] [20]let him know that whoever turns a sinner from the error of his way will save his •life from death and cover a multitude of sins.[o]

Cross references (center column):
a 5:7 Dt 11:14; Jr 5:24; Hos 6:3
b 5:8 Rm 13:11; Php 4:5; 1Pt 4:7
c 5:9 Mt 24:33; 1Co 4:5; Jms 4:12; 1Pt 4:5
d 5:11 Jb 1:21-22; 2:10; 42:10-12
e Ex 34:6; Nm 14:18; Mt 5:10
f 5:12 Mt 5:33-37; 23:16-22; Mk 7:9-13
g 5:13 Ps 50:15; Col 3:16
h 5:14 Mk 6:13; 16:18
i 5:15 Is 33:24; Mt 9:2; Mk 2:5; Lk 24:47
j 5:16 Nm 11:2; Mt 3:6; Jn 9:31; 1Pt 2:24
k 5:17 1Kg 17:1; 18:1; Lk 4:25; Ac 14:15
l 5:18 1Kg 18:41-45; Jms 3:17-18
m 5:19 Mt 18:15; Gl 6:1; Jms 3:14
n Ps 51:13; Dn 12:3; Mal 2:6; Lk 1:16
o 5:20 Pr 10:12; Rm 11:14; 1Pt 4:8

A5:11 Or *have persevered*   B5:12 Other mss read *fall into hypocrisy*

---

their oppressors, James encouraged his audience to **be patient** and to await **the Lord's coming**. The phrase **strengthen your hearts** is an expansion on "be patient," signifying firm resolve in light of the coming of the Lord and in spite of trying circumstances.

5:9 To **complain about one another** constitutes being judgmental, already prohibited in 4:11-12. The immediacy of the Lord's return brings judgment to the person who judges, just as it does for the oppressors.

5:12 Do not swear is an exhortation to truthfulness, not a universal prohibition against oath-making (see Rm 1:9; 2Co 1:23; Gl 1:20; Php 1:8; 1Th 2:5,10, where Paul used oaths; cp. Mt 5:33-37).

5:13-14 James used a series of questions followed by commands as an effective way of exhorting the congregation to prayer and worship. **Suffering** in verse 13 is not a reference to physical illness; it is instead a spiritual burden caused by misfortune or poor choices. **Elders,** who functioned in various capacities in the early church, should anoint any **sick** person with **olive oil** and **pray over him**. Olive oil was considered a cure-all ointment in the ancient world, but for James the real healing power is in prayer.

5:15 The prayer of faith echoes 1:5-8. **Save** refers to physical healing (as in Mk 5:23,28,34; 10:52; Jn 11:12). **The Lord will restore him to health** does not indicate that death is at hand (v. 14), but that once healed by the power of God the sick person could get up and walk (Mt 9:5-7; Mk 1:31; 2:9-12; 9:27; Ac 3:7). **He will be forgiven** indicates that perhaps the illness was connected with sin, and the prayers of the elders could bring spiritual healing as well.

5:16 Pray for one another echoes the prayers of the elders, and these should lead to both physical and spiritual healing (i.e., forgiveness). Prayer is not a magical incantation or a guarantee of healing, but when offered fervently by a righteous person, God will respond in a way that best fits His good purposes.

5:17-18 James cited a biblical personality, **Elijah,** who **prayed** effectively. The illustration is intended to encourage his audience that their prayers could lead to similar results.

5:19-20 James turned to the priority of reclaiming those who had strayed from the faith. **Someone turns** and **whoever turns** both reflect an effort to bring a straying believer back to an authentic Christian faith and lifestyle.

1 Peter

Introduction

First Peter is considered one of the General Epistles. This epistle provided encouragement to suffering believers living in northern Asia Minor who faced intense persecution. The letter encourages faithfulness while under oppression. Specifically, God's holy people should lead distinctive lifestyles as temporary residents in a foreign land. Although they will suffer for Christ while in this non-Christian world, they should remember that heaven is their future homeland.

Nevsehir is the capital of the region of Cappadocia where some of the recipients of Peter's first letter lived. From Acts 2:9 we know that Jews from Cappadocia were in Jerusalem when Peter preached at Pentecost. Those converted to Christianity that day must have given a good witness when they returned home. Cappadocians lived in a harsh environment as is evident from this photo. Three prominent fourth-century theologians were Cappadocians. Basil, his brother, Gregory of Nyssa, and their friend, Gregory of Nazianzus, made substantial contributions to the development of the doctrine of the Trinity.

Circumstances of Writing

Author: The author of 1 Peter identified himself as "Peter, an apostle of Jesus Christ" (1:1). He viewed himself as a divinely ordained, directly commissioned, authoritative representative of the Lord Jesus Himself. Several statements in the letter indicate that the Peter who plays a prominent role in the Gospels is the author. For example, he called himself an "elder and witness" to Christ's sufferings (5:1). Further, he described Christ's crucifixion with an intimate knowledge that only a disciple would have of that event (2:21-24).

Several expressions in 1 Peter reflect Peter's experiences with Jesus. For example, the exhortation for elders to "shepherd God's flock" (5:2) evokes the charge that Jesus gave Peter in Jn 21:15-17. Moreover, the command to "clothe yourselves with humility" (5:5) may recall the episode in Jn 13:2-17 where Jesus washed the disciples' feet.

Several themes in 1 Peter can also be found in Peter's sermons in the book of Acts. For example, God is "the One who judges impartially" (1:17; cp. Ac 10:34) and who raised Christ from the dead and gave Him glory (1:21; cp. Ac 2:32-36). Christ is "the stone that the builders rejected" (2:7-8; cp. Ac 4:10-11).

Objections to the letter's authorship by Peter are inconclusive and cannot be proven. The claim that someone wrote this letter using the apostle's name as a pseudonym cannot be sustained. A number of early church leaders—e.g., Irenaeus, Tertullian, and Clement of Alexandria—accepted the letter as authentic. Further, the early church soundly rejected the practice of writing under an apostolic pseudonym as forgery. In light of the above, the epistle should be accepted as genuinely written by the apostle Peter. Silvanus may have in some fashion helped Peter write the letter while serving as his secretary (Gk *amanuensis*), but more likely he was merely the letter carrier (5:12).

Background: The recipients of 1 Peter are identified in 1:1. Peter wrote to "the temporary residents dispersed in Pontus, Galatia, Cappadocia, Asia, and Bithynia." These were Roman provinces located in the northern part of what is now modern Turkey, unless Galatia includes the Galatia in the southern region of Asia Minor.

A.D. 1–29	A.D. 30–33
Simon Peter born in Galilee, probably in the village of Bethsaida 1?	Jesus heals Simon Peter's mother-in-law. 30
Simon, a fisherman by trade, moves to Capernaum. 20?	Peter's confession at Caesarea Philippi that Jesus is the Messiah 32
Simon's brother, Andrew, introduces him to Jesus. 29	Peter, James, and John witness Jesus' transfiguration. 32
Jesus calls Simon Peter "the rock." 29	Peter vows to die with Jesus. 33
Jesus calls Peter to be one of His 12 disciples. 29	Peter denies Jesus in the courtyard of Annas. 33

These people were likely persecuted Gentile Christians. They had earlier been involved in idolatry (4:3), were ignorant (1:14) and "empty" (1:18) before they came to Christ, and formerly were "not a people" but now were "God's people" (2:9-10).

The reference in 1 Peter 5:13—"The church in Babylon, also chosen, sends you greetings"—suggests Rome as the place of the letter's origin. "Babylon" was used cryptically to refer to a place of exile, but specifically for Rome. Other possibilities for Babylon include the cities of Babylon in Mesopotamia and Egypt, but these places are highly unlikely because we have no record of Peter ever being in those places.

First Peter was probably written sometime between A.D. 62–64. While Paul was under house arrest from A.D. 60–62, he did not refer to Peter in Rome. Peter likewise did not mention Paul as being in Rome; only Silvanus and Mark were his companions (5:12-13). These facts suggest that Peter wrote 1 Peter some time after A.D. 62 and before the writing of 2 Peter.

The theme of suffering appears throughout 1 Peter. The recipients of the letter are the sufferers in four of its five chapters. Given a composition date of about A.D. 62–64, 1 Peter was written during the persecution of Christians under Nero's reign. The persecution arose in Rome and was spreading into Asia Minor.

Message and Purpose

Peter wrote to encourage suffering believers in Asia Minor to stand firm for Christ in the midst of persecution. He urged them to do so by focusing on their spiritual privileges and, more specifically, the place where their rights and privileges lay: the next life. Believers in Jesus are "temporary residents" (Gk *parepid emoi*; 1:1; 2:11) and "strangers" (Gk *paroikoi*; 2:11) in this world, a land of sojourn where they have no real rights or privileges. Inheritance rights, privileges, and justice for Christians really belong to another realm to which God has delivered believers—heaven, their ultimate home.

First Peter emphasizes that suffering is normal for believers because they are temporary residents in this

A.D. 33–40

Following His resurrection, Jesus appears to Peter and recommissions him. 33

Three thousand persons respond to Peter's sermon at the feast of Pentecost. 33

Saul's conversion on the Damascus Road October 34

Paul meets with Peter and James on his first visit to Jerusalem following his conversion. 37?

Peter bears witness to and baptizes Cornelius and his family at Caesarea Maritima. 40

A.D. 40–114

Peter, James, John, Paul, Barnabas, and Titus meet in Jerusalem to deal with the question of whether Gentiles had to be circumcised to become Christians. 49

At Antioch, Paul confronts Peter's refusal to share meals with Gentile believers. 49

Destruction of Jerusalem 70

Peter's martyrdom in Rome during Nero's persecution of Christians 66

Polycarp's *Letter to Philippians* shows dependence on 1 Peter. 112–114

world. As such, they lack rights and receive no justice in this foreign land. Though suffering occurs on earth for temporary residents, their inheritance and exaltation await them in their eternal homeland.

Contribution to the Bible

Peter's intent in writing was to strengthen believers in the midst of the suffering and persecution they were facing. His message to them continues to speak to modern believers, reminding us of our heavenly hope and eternal inheritance in the midst of our sufferings. We are called to holiness and a life of love. We are also called to glorify God in our daily lives and to imitate Christ.

Structure

The structure of 1 Peter has been the subject of discussion from the earliest history of the church. The diversity of outlines illustrates that the task of exegesis is not merely a science but also an art. Peter wrote this letter with a typical opening for a letter (1:1-2) and then began the next major section (1:3–2:10) with a blessing (1:3). The two succeeding sections are marked by "dear friends" (Gk *agap etoi*, 2:11; 4:12), and as noted earlier the segment from 2:11–4:11 concludes with a doxology and "amen." The fourth section of the letter also ends with a doxology and "amen" (5:11) before the closing.

Outline

   I. Opening (1:1-2)

  II. Called to Salvation as Exiles (1:3–2:10)
     A. Praise for salvation (1:3-12)
     B. The future inheritance an incentive to holiness (1:13-21)
     C. Living as the new people of God (1:22–2:10)

  III. Living as Strangers in a Hostile World (2:11–4:11)
     A. The Christian life as a battle and witness (2:11-12)
     B. Testifying to the gospel in the social order (2:13–3:12)
     C. Responding in a godly way to suffering (3:13–4:11)

  IV. Persevering in Suffering (4:12–5:11)
     A. Suffer joyfully in accord with God's will (4:12-19)
     B. Exhortations to elders and the community (5:1-11)

  V. Concluding Words (5:12-14)

Greeting

1 Peter,[a] an apostle of Jesus Christ:
To the temporary residents[b] dispersed[A,c] in Pontus, Galatia, Cappadocia, •Asia, and Bithynia,[d] chosen[e] [2]according to the foreknowledge[f] of God the Father and set apart by the Spirit[g] for obedience[h] and for sprinkling with the blood[i] of Jesus Christ.
May grace and peace be multiplied to you.

A Living Hope

[3]Praise the God and Father of our Lord Jesus Christ.[j] According to His great mercy,[k] He has given us a new birth[l] into a living hope[m] through the resurrection of Jesus Christ from the dead[n] [4]and into an inheritance that is imperishable,[o] uncorrupted, and unfading, kept in heaven[p] for you. [5]You are being protected by God's power[q] through faith for a salvation that is ready to be revealed in the last time.[r] [6]You rejoice in this,[B] though now for a short time you have had to struggle in various trials[s] [7]so that the genuineness of your faith[t]—more valuable than gold, which perishes though refined by fire[u]—may result[v] in[C] praise, glory, and honor[w] at the revelation of Jesus Christ.[x] [8]You love Him,[y] though you have not seen[z] Him. And though not seeing Him now, you believe in Him and rejoice[aa] with inexpressible and glorious joy, [9]because you are receiving the goal of your[D] faith, the salvation of your souls.[E]

[10]Concerning this salvation, the prophets[ab] who prophesied about the grace that would come to you searched and carefully investigated. [11]They inquired into what time or what circumstances[F] the Spirit of Christ[ac] within them was indicating when He testified in advance[ad] to the messianic sufferings[G,ae] and the glories[af] that would follow.[H] [12]It was revealed to them that they were not serving themselves but you. These things have now been announced to you through those who preached the gospel to you[ag] by the Holy Spirit sent from heaven.[ah] Angels desire to look into these things.

A Call to Holy Living

[13]Therefore, with your minds ready for action,[I,ai] be serious[aj] and set your hope[ak] completely on the grace to be brought to you at the revelation[al] of Jesus Christ. [14]As obedient

Cross References

a1:1 Lk 6:14; Ac 10:32
b Gn 23:4; Ps 39:12; Heb 11:9,13; 1Pt 2:11
c Jn 7:35; Jms 1:1
d Ac 2:9; 6:9; 16:6-7; Gl 1:2
e Mt 22:14; 24:22; Ti 1:1
f 1:2 Rm 8:29; 1Pt 1:20
g 2Th 2:13
h 1Pt 1:14,22
i Heb 9:12; 10:22; 12:24
j 1:3 2Co 1:3; Eph 1:3
k Gl 6:16; Ti 3:5
l Jn 1:13; 3:3,7; Jms 1:18; 1Pt 1:23
m Ac 23:6; 1Th 1:3
n 1Co 15:20; 1Pt 3:21
o 1:4 Ac 20:32; Rm 8:17; Col 3:24
p 2Tm 4:8
q 1:5 Jn 10:28; Php 4:7
r Rm 8:18; 2Co 4:17; Heb 12:11; 1Pt 4:13; 5:1,10; Rv 15:1; 21:9
s 1:6 Jms 1:2; 1Pt 4:12
t 1:7 Jms 1:3
u Is 48:10; Zch 13:9; Mal 3:3;

1Co 3:13 v 2Co 5:3; Php 3:9; Rv 14:5 w Rm 2:7,10,29; 1Co 4:5 x Lk 17:30 y 1:8 1Jn 4:20 z Ex 33:20; Rm 8:24 aa Jn 15:11; 2Co 6:10 ab 1:10 Lk 1:70; 10:24; 16:16,29; 18:31; 24:25,27,44 ac 1:11 Rm 8:9 ad Mt 26:24 ae Mk 8:31; Lk 24:26; Php 3:10 af Lk 24:26 ag 1:12 Mk 16:15; 1Co 9:14; 2Co 10:16 ah Jn 14:26; 15:26; Ac 1:8; 2:2-4; 13:4 ai 1:13 Ex 12:11 aj 1Pt 5:8 ak Mt 12:21; Rm 8:24; 1Th 1:3 al 1Pt 4:13; 5:4

Footnotes

A1:1 Jewish people scattered throughout Gentile lands who spoke Gk and were influenced by Gk culture   B1:6 Or In this fact rejoice   C1:7 Lit may be found for   D1:9 Other mss read our, or they omit the possessive pronoun   E1:9 Or your lives   F1:11 Or inquired about the person or time   G1:11 Or the sufferings of Christ   H1:11 Lit the glories after that   I1:13 Lit Therefore, when you have the loins of your mind girded

---

1:1-2 Peter identified himself as **an apostle of Jesus Christ**. The apostles were Christ's divinely ordained, directly commissioned, authoritative representatives in the early church. The recipients to whom Peter wrote were **the temporary residents dispersed**. The term "temporary residents" (Gk *parepideyēmois*; v. 1; 2:11) refers to people living in a region that is not their permanent place of residence—in this case, the five Roman provinces located in what is now modern Turkey. Heaven is the true home of believers. The "Dispersion" means a "scattering" and usually refers to God's people scattered outside of their homeland. Divine **foreknowledge** is the basis on which a believer is **chosen** (i.e., "elect"). It is more than just God's prior knowledge of everything; it also includes His predetermination. **Set apart by the Spirit** is the means by which being "chosen" is made a reality. The phrase **for obedience and for sprinkling with the blood of Jesus Christ** describes the aim and purpose of election (Ex 24:3-8). Christians were chosen by God to have a covenant relationship with Him that is characterized by obedience; Christ's blood brings believers into this relationship.

1:3-12 This section begins with praise to God for the privileges He has bestowed on believers. Peter encouraged his readers by reminding them that through the resurrection of Christ, God had caused them to be born again. The result of this new birth is that they have acquired an eternal inheritance reserved in heaven. Believers will be delivered to heaven, their eternal home, through their faith in the gospel.

1:3-5 Peter informed his readers that God rebirthed (Gk *anagennao*) them to an inheritance that will never perish, be defiled, or fade—indeed a sure salvation.

1:6-9 Peter further encouraged his readers with the fact that Christians can **rejoice** in this imperishable inheritance and sure salvation, though they are tested by persecution and suffering while in this world.

1:10-12 The OT people of God did not specifically know Christ or the gospel, but they did believe the promises of God that pointed to Christ (Heb 11:13). Peter conveyed to his readers that the good news of salvation that the **prophets** sought and looked forward to had now been **revealed**. Salvation in Christ is so great and the blessings so tremendous that **angels desire to look into these things**. The gospel excites their interest so much that they want to study it intently.

1:13-2:10 In this section Peter informed his readers that they were always to fix their hope on the "grace" that would be theirs at the second coming of Christ.

1:13-21 As resident aliens sojourning in this world, Christians are to live distinctively as those who belong to God.

1:13 The **grace to be brought to you at the revelation of Jesus Christ** refers to the culmination of God's redemptive activity in Jesus that will occur at His return (v. 5).

1:14 The phrase **former ignorance** means "without knowledge of God" and suggests that the recipients of this letter were mostly Gentiles who, before coming to Christ, practiced pagan religions.

children,[a] do not be conformed to the desires of your former ignorance. [15]But as the One who called you[b] is holy,[c] you also are to be holy in all your conduct; [16]for it is written, **Be holy, because I am holy.**[A,d]

[17]And if you address as Father the One who judges impartially[e] based on each one's work,[f] you are to conduct yourselves in fear[g] during the time of your temporary residence. [18]For you know that you were •redeemed from your empty way of life[h] inherited from the fathers, not with perishable things like silver or gold,[i] [19]but with the precious blood of Christ,[j] like that of a lamb[k] without defect or blemish. [20]He was chosen[B,l] before the foundation of the world but was revealed at the end of the times[m] for you [21]who through Him are believers in God,[n] who raised Him from the dead[o] and gave Him glory,[p] so that your faith and hope are in God.

[22]By obedience to the truth,[C] having purified yourselves[D] for sincere love of the •brothers, love one another[q] earnestly[E] from a pure[F] heart,[r] [23]since you have been born again[s]—not of perishable seed[t] but of imperishable—through the living and enduring word of God.[u] [24]For

> **All flesh is like grass,**
> **and all its glory[v] like a flower**
> **of the grass.**

The grass withers, and the flower falls,
[25]**but the word of the Lord**
endures forever.[G,w]

And this is the word that was preached as the gospel to you.

The Living Stone and a Holy People

2 So rid yourselves of[x] all malice, all deceit, hypocrisy, envy, and all slander.[y] [2]Like newborn infants, desire the pure spiritual milk,[z] so that you may grow by it for your salvation,[H] [3]since **you have tasted**[aa] **that the Lord is good.**[l,ab] [4]Coming to Him, a living stone—rejected by men but chosen and valuable to God— [5]you yourselves, as living stones, are being built into a spiritual house for a holy priesthood to offer spiritual sacrifices acceptable to God[ac] through Jesus Christ. [6]For it is contained in Scripture:

> **Look! I lay a stone in •Zion,**[ad]
> **a chosen and honored[J] cornerstone,**[K,ae]
> **and the one who believes in Him**
> **will never be put to shame!**[L,M,af]

[7]So honor will come to you who believe, but for the unbelieving,

Cross references (center column):

a1:14 Heb 2:13
b1:15 Gl 1:6; 5:8; 1Th 2:12; 5:24; 1Pt 5:10
cLk 1:49; 1Co 7:14
d1:16 Lv 11:44-45; 19:2; 20:7
e1:17 Ac 10:34; Rm 2:11; Gl 2:6; Eph 6:9
f1Co 3:12
gAc 9:31; Rm 3:18; 2Co 5:11; 7:1; Eph 5:21; Php 2:12
h1:18 2Pt 3:11
iIs 52:3; 1Co 6:20; Ti 2:14; Heb 9:12
j1:19 Jn 6:53; Ac 20:28; 1Co 10:16; Eph 2:13; Heb 10:19
kEx 12:5; Lv 4:32; Is 53:7; Jn 1:29
l1:20 Ac 2:23; Eph 1:4; 1Pt 1:2; Rv 13:8
m2Pt 3:3; Jd 18
n1:21 Ac 10:45; Rm 4:24; 10:9; Eph 1:1; 1Tm 4:12; 6:2
oAc 2:24; Rm 10:9
pJn 17:5,24; 1Tm 3:16; Heb 2:9
q1:22 Zch 7:9; Jn 13:34; Rm 12:10; 1Th 4:9; 1Jn 4:7
rTm 1:5
s1:23 1Pt 1:3
tJn 3:9
uLk 8:21; Heb

v1:24 1Pt 5:4   w1:24-25 Is 40:6-8; Lk 21:33; Jms 1:10-11; 1Jn 2:17   x2:1 Rm 13:12   y2Co 12:20   z2:2 1Co 3:2; 9:7; Heb 5:12-13   aa2:3 Heb 6:4-5   abPs 34:8; Ti 3:4   ac2:5 Rm 12:1; Heb 13:15   ad2:6 Ps 9:11; Heb 12:22   aeEph 2:20   af1Is 28:16; Rm 9:33; 10:11

A1:16 Lv 11:44-45; 19:2; 20:7   B1:20 Or foreknown   C1:22 Other mss add through the Spirit   D1:22 Or purified your souls   E1:22 Or intensely   F1:22 Other mss omit pure   G1:24-25 Is 40:6-8   H2:2 Other mss omit in your salvation   I2:3 Ps 34:8   J2:6 Or valuable   K2:6 Lit head of the corner   L2:6 Or be disappointed   M2:6 Is 28:16 LXX

1:15-16 God is the Christian's standard for holy living (Lv 11:44-45; 19:2; 20:7).

1:19 The metaphor of **a lamb without defect or blemish** points to Christ's sinlessness (Lv 22:19-25). He is the sacrificial Lamb of God (Jn 1:29; Rv 5).

1:20 The plan for Christ's sacrifice on behalf of sinners was fixed in eternity past, a sure reality set to unfold at a divinely appointed time in history (Gl 4:4).

1:22-25 Peter exhorted his readers to love their **brothers** (i.e., other believers; v. 22) as those who are born again through the **living and enduring word of God**, the gospel.

2:1-3 As **newborn infants**, believers are to avoid acts of dissention and feed on the **spiritual milk** of the word. "Spiritual milk" is a metaphor that refers to the divine sustenance drawn from the gospel. The statement **you have tasted that the Lord is good** (cp. Ps 34:8) means they had found God to be gracious. This realization begins at conversion.

2:4-10 Jesus is called the **living stone** and the **cornerstone**, but also the **rejected** stone and the **stone to stumble over**. Peter taught his readers that they are God's valuable possession, but like Jesus believers will be rejected by men. Believers are living stones **built into a spiritual house**. They are part of a living temple that is the corporate people of God, His unique possession. **A chosen race** (v. 9; cp. vv. 4,6; Is 43:20) seems to refer to the corporate unity of believers. In Christ, believers of all races are unified. They are also **a royal priesthood**—a collective company of priests—who offer up spiritual sacrifices to God (v. 5).

---

hierateuma

Greek Pronunciation	[hee eh RAH tyoo mah]
HCSB Translation	priesthood
Uses in 1 Peter	2
Uses in the NT	2
Focus passage	1 Peter 2:5,9

Hierateuma (priesthood) first appears in written literature in the Greek OT (Ex 19:6; 23:22), where the translators of that document used it. If Israel obeyed God, she would be His treasured possession (Ex 23:22) and would function as a royal *priesthood* through which God would dispense His blessing to the whole earth (Ex 19:5-6; 23:22). In the NT, Peter makes direct reference to Ex 19:6 and 23:22 and applies the fulfillment of this OT concept of *royal priesthood* to the church (1Pt 2:9), which now exists to serve God through worship with her words and deeds. She is being built into a spiritual temple where believers perform the role of a holy *priesthood* by offering "spiritual sacrifices acceptable to God through Jesus Christ" (1Pt 2:5). The church also serves God through the proclamation of the praises that belong to Him (1Pt 2:9).

The stone that the builders rejected—
this One has become
   the cornerstone,[A,a]

[8]and

A stone to stumble over,[B]
and a rock to trip over.[C,D,b]

They stumble because they disobey the message; they were destined[c] for this.

[9]   But you are a **chosen race,**[E,F,d]
   a royal priesthood,[G,e]
   a holy nation,[H,f] a people
      for His possession,[I,g]
   so that you may proclaim
      the praises[J,K,h]
   of the One who called you
      out of darkness
   into His marvelous light.[i]
[10]   Once you were not a people,
   but now you are God's people;
   you had not received mercy,[j]
   but now you have received mercy.

A Call to Good Works

[11]Dear friends, I urge you as strangers and temporary residents[k] to abstain[l] from fleshly[m] desires that war against you.[L,n] [12]Conduct[o] yourselves honorably among the Gentiles,[M] so that in a case where they speak against you as those who do what is evil, they will, by observing your good works, glorify God on the day of visitation.[N,p]

[13]Submit[q] to every human authority[o] because of the Lord, whether to the Emperor[P] as the supreme authority[r] [14]or to governors as those sent out by him to punish those who do what is evil and to praise those who do what is good. [15]For it is God's will[s] that you silence the ignorance[t] of foolish people by doing good. [16]As God's •slaves,[u] live as free people, but don't use your freedom as a way to con-

ceal evil.[v] [17]Honor everyone. Love[w] the brotherhood.[x] Fear God.[y] Honor the Emperor.[P]

Submission of Slaves to Masters

[18]Household slaves, submit with all fear[z] to your masters,[aa] not only to the good and gentle but also to the cruel.[Q,ab] [19]For it brings favor[R] if, mindful of God's will,[S,T] someone endures grief from suffering unjustly. [20]For what credit is there if you sin and are punished, and you endure it? But when you do what is good and suffer,[ac] if you endure it, this brings favor with God.

[21]   For you were called to this,
   because Christ also suffered[ad] for you,
   leaving you an example,[ae]
   so that you should follow[af]
      in His steps.
[22]   He **did not commit sin,**[ag]
   and no deceit[ah] **was found**
      in His mouth;[U,ai]
[23]   when He was reviled,
   He did not revile in return;
   when He was suffering,
   He did not threaten
   but entrusted Himself to the One
      who judges[aj] justly.
[24]   He Himself bore our sins[ak]
   in His body[al] on the tree,[am]
   so that, having died to sins,[an]
   we might live for righteousness;[ao]
   you have been healed
      by His wounds.[V,ap]
[25]   For you **were like sheep**
      going astray,[W,aq]
   but you have now returned
   to the Shepherd[ar] and Guardian[X]
      of your souls.

[a]2:7 Ps 118:22; Mt 21:42; Lk 20:17; Ac 4:11
[b]2:8 Is 8:14; Rm 9:33; 14:20
[c]Ac 2:23; 4:27-28; Rm 9:22; 11:7; Jd 4
[d]2:9 Dt 7:6; 10:15; Is 43:20
[e]Is 61:6; Rv 1:6; 5:10; 20:6
[f]Ex 19:6
[g]Ex 34:9; Dt 7:6; Ps 33:12; Is 43:21; Ti 2:14
[h]Is 42:12; 43:21
[i]Is 9:2; Ac 26:18; Eph 5:8; Col 1:12-13
[j]2:10 Mt 5:7; Mk 5:19; Lk 1:50
[k]2:11 1Pt 1:1
[l]1Tm 4:3
[m]Rm 7:23; Php 3:3
[n]Gl 5:17; Jms 4:1
[o]2:12 2Pt 3:11
[p]Is 10:3; Jr 6:15; 8:12; 10:15; Lk 1:68; 7:16; 19:44
[q]2:13-14 Rm 13:1-7; Ti 3:1
[r]2:13 Rm 13:1
[s]2:15 Gl 1:4; Eph 1:9
[t]1Pt 3:16
[u]2:16 Rm 1:1; Ti 1:1; Rv 2:20
[v]1Co 14:20
[w]2:17 Rm 12:11
[x]Heb 13:1; 1Pt 5:9
[y]Pr 1:7; 24:21; Ac 10:2; Rv 14:7
[z]2:18 Rm 13:3,7
[aa]Eph 6:5; Col 3:22; Ti 2:9; Jd 4
[ab]Php 2:15
[ac]2:20 1Pt 4:14
[ad]2:21 Mk 8:31; 1Pt 3:18; 1Jn 3:16
[ae]Jn 13:15
[af]Jn 8:12
[ag]2:22 1Pt 4:1; 1Jn 3:5
[ah]2Pt 2:1
[ai]Is 53:9
[aj]2:23 Rv 18:8; 19:1
[ak]2:24 Heb 7:27-28; 9:27-28 [al]Is 53:4-5,12; Jn 2:21 [am]Ac 5:30; 10:39; 13:29; Gl 3:13 [an]Rm 6:2,8-11; 7:6; Gl 2:19; Col 2:20; 3:3 [ao]Rm 6:2,11; Ti 2:12 [ap]Is 53:5; Mt 13:15; Jn 12:40; Ac 28:27 [aq]2:25 Ps 119:176; Is 53:6 [ar]Gn 48:15; 49:24; Ps 23:1; Jr 31:10

[A]2:7 Ps 118:22   [B]2:8 Or a stone causing stumbling   [C]2:8 Or a rock to trip over   [D]2:8 Is 8:14   [E]2:9 Or generation, or nation
[F]2:9 Dt 7:6; 10:15; Is 43:20 LXX   [G]2:9 Ex 19:6; 23:22 LXX; Is 61:6   [H]2:9 Ex 19:6; 23:22 LXX   [I]2:9 Ex 19:5; 23:22 LXX; Dt 4:20; 7:6;
Is 43:21 LXX   [J]2:9 Or the mighty deeds   [K]2:9 Is 42:12; 43:21   [L]2:11 Or against the soul   [M]2:12 Or among the nations, or
among the pagans   [N]2:12 The day when God intervenes in human history, either in grace or in judgment   [O]2:13 Or creature
[P]2:13,17 Lit king   [Q]2:18 Or unscrupulous; lit crooked   [R]2:19 Other mss add with God   [S]2:19 Other mss read if, because of a good
conscience   [T]2:19 Lit if, because of conscience toward God   [U]2:22 Is 53:9   [V]2:24 Is 53:5   [W]2:25 Is 53:6   [X]2:25 Or Overseer

2:11-4:19 In this section Peter explained further how his readers might maintain their distinctiveness as holy aliens and temporary residents in this fallen world.

2:11-12 Peter commanded his readers to live honorably as holy **strangers** or **temporary residents** so that even hostile Gentile residents of the earth might come to glorify God.

2:13-17 Peter exhorted his readers to be subordinate and respectful to **every human authority because of the Lord.** He commanded them to submit to governmental and civil

authority, acting as free people. The **foolish people** refers to the Gentiles mentioned in verse 12.

2:18-25 Peter commanded **household slaves** to submit to their **masters** by doing good, even though they might suffer unjustly. Such behavior **brings favor with God.** While doing so they are to remember Christ's example, who suffered unjustly while submitting to God's will. The phrase **by His wounds** (cp. Is 53:5; sometimes translated elsewhere as "stripes") refers to the death of Christ and not to the flogging He suffered at the hands of Roman soldiers (Jn 19:1). By His death believers are **healed** spiritually.

Wives and Husbands

3 In the same way, wives,[a] submit yourselves to your own husbands so that, even if some disobey the Christian message,[b] they may be won over[A,c] without a message by the way their wives live[d] [2]when they observe your pure, reverent lives.[e] [3]Your beauty should not consist of outward things like elaborate hairstyles and the wearing of gold ornaments[B] or fine clothes.[f] [4]Instead, it should consist of what is inside[C] the heart[g] with the imperishable quality of a gentle[h] and quiet[i] spirit, which is very valuable in God's eyes. [5]For in the past, the holy[j] women who put their hope[k] in God also beautified themselves in this way, submitting to their own husbands, [6]just as Sarah[l] obeyed Abraham, calling him lord. You have become her children when you do what is good and are not frightened by anything alarming.[m]

[7]Husbands,[n] in the same way, live with your wives with an understanding of their weaker nature[D,o] yet showing them honor as coheirs of the grace of life, so that your prayers will not be hindered.

Do No Evil

[8]Now finally, all of you should be like-minded and sympathetic, should love believers,[E,p] and be compassionate[q] and humble,[F] [9]not paying back evil for evil[r] or insult for insult but, on the contrary, giving a blessing,[s] since you were called for this, so that you can inherit a blessing.

[10] For the[t] one who wants to love life
and to see good days
must keep his tongue from evil[u]
and his lips from speaking deceit,[v]
[11] and he must turn away[w] from evil
and do what is good.
He must seek peace[x] and pursue it,
[12] because the eyes of the Lord are
on the righteous
and His ears are open
to their request.
But the face of the Lord is against
those who do what is evil.[G]

Undeserved Suffering

[13]And who will harm[H] you if you are deeply committed to what is good?[I] [14]But even if you should suffer for righteousness,[y] you are blessed. **Do not fear what they fear[z] or be disturbed,[J,aa] [15]**but honor[K] the •Messiah[L] as Lord in your hearts. Always be ready to give a defense to anyone who asks you for a reason[M] for the hope that is in you.[ab] [16]However, do this with gentleness and respect, keeping your conscience clear,[N,O,ac] so that when you are accused,[P] those who denounce your Christian life[Q] will be put to shame. [17]For it is better to suffer[ad] for doing good, if that should be God's will,[R] than for doing evil.

[18] For Christ also suffered[ae] for sins
once for all,[S,af]

Cross-reference notes (center column)

a3:1 Eph 5:22-33; Col 3:18-19; 1Tm 3:11
b1Co 7:16
c1Co 9:19-22; Php 3:8
d2Pt 3:11
e3:2 Ti 2:5
f3:3 Is 3:18-24; 1Tm 2:9
g3:4 Rm 2:29; 7:22
hMt 5:5
i1Tm 2:2
j3:5 Ps 20:6; 1Co 7:14
k1Tm 5:5; 1Pt 1:3
l3:6 Gn 17:15-21; 18:6-15; Heb 11:11
m Pr 3:25
n3:7 Mt 1:19; 1Co 14:35; Eph 5:22-28; Col 3:18-19; Ti 2:4-5
o1Th 4:4
p3:8 Heb 13:1
qEph 4:32
r3:9 Rm 12:17
sLk 6:28; Rm 12:14; 1Co 4:12
t3:10-12 Ps 34:12-16
u3:10 Jms 1:26
vRm 3:13; Jms 3:5-8
w3:11 Ps 37:27
xLk 12:51; 2Tm 1:2; Heb 12:14; 3Jn 14
y3:14 Mt 6:33; Rm 1:17; 2Pt 1:1
zJn 6:20; 7:13
aa3:14-15 Is 8:12-13
ab3:15 1Jn 4:4
ac3:16 Ac 23:1; 24:16; Rm 9:1; 2Co 1:12; 1Tm 1:5,19; 3:9; Heb 10:22;

1Pt 3:21 ad3:17 Php 1:29; 1Pt 2:19 ae3:18 Mk 8:31; Rm 5:8 af Rm 6:10; Heb 9:28; 10:10; 1Pt 2:21; 4:1

Footnotes

A3:1 Lit may be gained B3:3 Lit and of putting around of gold items C3:4 Lit Instead, the hidden man of D3:7 Lit understanding as the weaker vessel E3:8 Lit sympathetic, loving the brothers F3:8 Other mss read courteous G3:10-12 Ps 34:12-16 H3:13 Or mistreat, or do evil to I3:13 Or you are partisans for the good; lit you are zealots J3:14 Is 8:12 K3:15 Or sanctify; lit set apart L3:15 Other mss read set God M3:15 Or who demands of you an accounting N3:16 Lit good O3:16 Or keeping a clear conscience P3:16 Other mss read when they speak against you as evildoers Q3:16 Lit your good behavior in Christ R3:17 Lit if the will of God should will S3:18 Other mss read died for sins on our behalf; other mss read died for our sins; other mss read died for sins on your behalf

Study notes

3:1-6 Peter instructed **wives** to **submit** to their **husbands** because they bear distinctive witness to them through their God-honoring lifestyles. The statement **you have become her children** means that Christian wives in essence show themselves to be Sarah's spiritual children when they **do . . . good** and **are not frightened by anything alarming**.

3:7 Peter commanded **husbands** to live in harmony with their **wives** and to show them **honor as coheirs of the grace of life**, or to treat them as fellow inheritors of salvation and its privileges. **Weaker nature** denotes physical weakness and should not be taken to mean that wives are morally or intellectually inferior to their husbands. Husbands are typically stronger physically.

3:8-12 In climactic fashion, Peter commanded Christians ("temporary residents," 1:1) not to return **evil for evil** so they could receive God's blessing. The apostle's teaching here (v. 9) reflects that of Christ elsewhere (Mt 5:43-44; Lk 6:27-28).

3:13-4:19 Believers are commanded in this section to distinguish themselves by doing good, even when faced with pagan hostility, because God will vindicate the righteous.

3:13-17 Believers are commanded to suffer only for the doing of good and not for evil among those who call this world their home.

3:13-14 Doing **what is good** will harm no one, though believers may suffer for it—in which case they should count it a privilege to suffer for a lifestyle that pleases God (Jms 1:2).

3:15 Honor . . . in your hearts means "to acknowledge as holy" from the center of one's being. This inner reverence for Christ should lead believers to **always be ready**, especially in the midst of persecution and suffering, to give a frank defense of the **hope** within them. On "hope," cp. v. 5; 1:3,21.

3:18-22 Peter pointed to Christ's example of innocent suffering at the hands of this world's citizens. Jesus' innocent suffering, death, and resurrection/exaltation are the foundation for the salvation and vindication of believers.

the righteous for the unrighteous,[A] that He might bring you[B] to God,[a] after being put to death in the fleshly realm,[C,b] but made alive in the spiritual realm.[D]

[19] In that state[E] He also went and made a proclamation to the spirits[c] in prison[F] [20] who in the past were disobedient, when God patiently waited in the days of Noah[d] while an ark was being prepared. In it a few—that is, eight people[G,e]—were saved through water. [21] Baptism, which corresponds to this, now saves you (not the removal of the filth of the flesh,[f] but the pledge[H] of a good conscience toward God) through the resurrection of Jesus Christ.[g] [22] Now that He has gone into heaven,[h] He is at God's right hand[i] with angels, authorities, and powers subject to Him.[j]

Following Christ

4 Therefore, since Christ suffered[i] in the flesh,[J] equip[k] yourselves also with the

same resolve[L]—because the one who suffered in the flesh has finished[k] with sin[M]— [2] in order to live the remaining time in the flesh, no longer for human desires,[N] but for God's will.[l] [3] For there has already been enough time spent in doing what the pagans choose to do:[O] carrying on in unrestrained behavior, evil desires,[m] drunkenness, orgies,[n] carousing, and lawless idolatry. [4] So they are surprised that you don't plunge with them into the same flood[P] of wild living—and they slander you. [5] They will give an account to the One who stands ready to judge the living and the dead.[o] [6] For this reason the gospel was also preached to those who are now dead,[p] so that, although they might be judged by men in the fleshly[q] realm,[Q] they might live[r] by God in the spiritual realm.[R]

End-Time Ethics

[7] Now the end of all things is near;[s] therefore, be serious and disciplined[t] for prayer.

Cross references:
[a]3:18 Rm 5:2 [b]Eph 2:14 [c]3:19 1Jn 4:1 [d]3:20 Gn 5:29 [e]Gn 5:32; 6:18; 7:7,13; 8:16,18 [f]3:21 Heb 9:14; 10:22 [g]1Pt 1:3 [h]3:22 Ac 1:10,12; 1Tm 3:16; Heb 4:14; 6:20 [i]Ps 110:1; Mk 16:19; Ac 2:33-34; Rm 8:34; Heb 10:12 [j]Eph 1:20-22 [k]4:1 Rm 6:10; Heb 4:15; 7:26; 9:28 [l]4:2 Mk 3:35; Rm 6:11; 12:2 [m]4:3 Mk 7:22 [n]Rm 13:13; Gl 5:21 [o]4:5 Ac 10:42; Rm 14:9; 2Tm 4:1 [p]4:6 Jn 5:25 [q]1Pt 3:18 [r]Php 1:21 [s]4:7 Rm 13:11-12; Heb 9:26; Jms 5:8; 1Jn 2:18; Rv 1:3 [t]1Pt 5:8

Footnotes:
[A]3:18 Or the Righteous One in the place of the unrighteous many [B]3:18 Other mss read us [C]3:18 Or in the flesh [D]3:18 Or in the spirit, or in the Spirit [E]3:19 Or In whom, or At that time, or In which [F]3:19 Perhaps fallen supernatural beings or angels; 2Pt 2:4; Jd 6 [G]3:20 Lit souls [H]3:21 Or the appeal [I]4:1 Other mss read suffered for us [J]4:1 The phrase "in the flesh" probably means in human experience. [K]4:1 Or arm [L]4:1 Or perspective, or attitude [M]4:1 Or the one who has suffered in the flesh has ceased from sin [N]4:2 Lit for desires of human beings [O]4:3 Or Gentiles [P]4:4 Lit you don't run with them into the same pouring out [Q]4:6 Or in the flesh [R]4:6 Or in the spirit

3:19-20a The statement that Christ **made a proclamation to the spirits in prison who in the past were disobedient** is extremely difficult to interpret. According to one plausible view, the term "spirits" refers to the souls of people who died in the great flood (Gn 6-7). The "proclamation" was made by the pre-incarnate Christ through Noah's preaching to his disobedient contemporaries. This preaching of repentance occurred while Noah made preparations for the flood. Peter could refer to Noah's contemporaries as the "spirits in prison" because when he wrote this letter they had long

been dead, were incorporeal spirits, and were under confinement awaiting God's final judgment. The position taken in the text of the HCSB is that Christ after His death and resurrection made a proclamation of victory over the demonic spirits. In this view the "spirits" are evil angels.

3:20b-21 Noah and his family were **saved through water**, or brought safely through the floodwaters, whereas the wicked were destroyed (Gn 7:22-23). Baptism in the NT corresponds to this OT event in that both involve breaks from past lives and a fresh start and entrance into new life. Water cannot save, but **baptism** with water does symbolically depict the changed life of a person whose conscience is at peace with God through faith in Christ. That the act of "baptism" is viewed symbolically and does not actually save us is explained by Peter in the latter half of verse 21 with the words **not the removal of the filth of the flesh**.

4:1-6 Peter commanded believers as temporary residents who looked to Christ as their example to suffer and separate themselves from the practices of those who slandered them. God will condemn the slanderers and vindicate believers in heaven's court.

4:5 The living and the dead means anyone who has ever lived, or people of all generations.

4:6 Those who are now dead seems to refer to deceased believers in Christ. When they were alive, the gospel was preached to them. While on earth they were **judged by men in the fleshly realm**, or condemned and martyred on account of the gospel. But they now **live by God in the spiritual realm**, heaven.

4:7-11 Peter commanded believers to maintain their unity while doing everything to God's glory.

---

makrothumia

Greek Pronunciation	[ma krah thew MEE ah]
HCSB Translation	patience
Uses in 1 Peter	1
Uses in the NT	14
Focus passage	1 Peter 3:20

Makrothumia refers to *patient perseverance* in withstanding a difficult situation. The *patience* of the faithful witnesses and martyrs of old is an example for present day believers (Heb 6:12; Jms 5:10). Paul prayed that the Colossian church would be strengthened for all *patience* (Col 1:11). Elsewhere, *makrothumia* speaks of *patience* within the context of personal relationships, referring to the *patience* of people toward one another or of God toward humanity. Paul exhorts Timothy to encourage his congregation with *patience* (2Tm 4:2), and believers should demonstrate *patience* toward each other (Col 3:12). In reference to God, *makrothumia* always indicates His slowness in bringing about judgment. God's *patience* waited while Noah prepared an ark (1Pt 3:20), and God's *patience* in bringing judgment provides present opportunity for repentance (Rm 2:4). Similarly, the *patience* of Jesus in bringing judgment should be considered as a present opportunity for salvation (2Pt 3:15).

[8] Above all, maintain an intense love[a] for each other, since **love covers a multitude of sins.**[A,b] [9] Be hospitable[c] to one another without complaining. [10] Based on the gift each one has received, use it to serve others,[d] as good managers of the varied grace of God. [11] If anyone speaks, it should be as one who speaks God's words; if anyone serves, it should be from the strength God provides,[e] so that God may be glorified through Jesus Christ in everything. To Him belong the glory and the power forever and ever. •Amen.

Christian Suffering

[12] Dear friends, don't be surprised when the fiery ordeal[B] comes among you to test you as if something unusual were happening to you.[f] [13] Instead, rejoice as you share in the sufferings of the •Messiah,[g] so that you may also rejoice with great joy at the revelation[h] of His glory. [14] If you are ridiculed for the name of Christ,[i] you are blessed, because the Spirit[j] of glory and of God rests on you.[C] [15] None of you, however, should suffer as a murderer, a thief, an evildoer, or a meddler.[D] [16] But if anyone suffers as a "Christian," he should not be ashamed but should glorify God in having that name. [17] For the time has come for judgment[k] to begin with God's household,[l] and if it

begins with us, what will the outcome be for those who disobey the gospel of God?

[18] And **if a righteous person is saved with difficulty, what will become of the ungodly and the sinner?**[E,m]

[19] So those who suffer according to God's will should, while doing what is good, entrust themselves[n] to a faithful Creator.

About the Elders

[5] Therefore, as a fellow elder and witness[o] to the sufferings of the •Messiah and also a participant in the glory about to be revealed,[p] I exhort the elders among you: [2] Shepherd God's flock among you,[q] not overseeing[F] out of compulsion but freely, according to God's will;[G] not for the money but eagerly; [3] not lording it over those entrusted to you, but being examples to the flock. [4] And when the chief Shepherd[r] appears, you will receive the unfading crown[s] of glory.

[5] In the same way, you younger men, be subject to the elders. And all of you clothe yourselves with[H] humility toward one another, because

God resists the proud but gives grace to the humble.[I,t]

Cross references (center column):

a 4:8 1Pt 1:22
b Pr 10:12; Jms 5:20
c 4:9 1Tm 3:2; Ti 1:8
d 4:10 1Co 12:7
e 4:11 Rm 12:6-8; 1Co 15:58
f 4:12 1Pt 1:6-7
g 4:13 Gl 5:24; Php 3:10
h 1Co 1:7; Eph 1:17; 2Th 1:7; 1Pt 1:7,13
i 4:14 Ps 89:50-51; Ac 5:41; 1Pt 2:20
j Ac 4:33; Rv 3:22
k 4:17 Mk 12:40; Jn 5:22; Heb 10:27; 13:4
l Gl 6:10; Eph 2:19; 1Tm 3:15; Heb 3:2
m 4:18 Pr 11:31
n 4:19 Ps 10:14; 2Co 1:9
o 5:1 Ac 4:20
p Rm 8:18; Col 3:4
q 5:2 Jr 3:15; 23:1; Jn 21:16; Ac 20:28
r 5:4 Jn 10:11,14; 21:15-17; Heb 13:20; 1Pt 2:25
s 1Co 9:25; Rv 12:1
t 5:5 Pr 3:34; Jms 4:6

A 4:8 Pr 10:12　B 4:12 Lit the burning　C 4:14 Other mss add *He is blasphemed because of them, but He is glorified because of you.*　D 4:15 Or *as one who defrauds others*　E 4:18 Pr 11:31 LXX　F 5:2 Other mss omit *overseeing*　G 5:2 Other mss omit *according to God's will*　H 5:5 Lit *you tie around yourselves*　I 5:5 Pr 3:34 LXX

4:8 The phrase **love covers a multitude of sins** means that love repeatedly forgives (Pr 10:12).

4:9 When being persecuted, it is easy to snipe and complain even at other believers; thus Peter's command to **be hospitable to one another**.

4:10 The words **based on the gift each one has received** refer to a spiritual gift. Spiritual gifts are divine endowments that God entrusts to believers as stewards.

4:11 Christians should manage and use their spiritual gifts to God's glory, just as God intends.

4:12-19 Peter declared that believers are to rejoice in the test that suffering brings for being members of God's household. Suffering for Christ in this world characterizes believers as strangers, with heaven as their future place of eternal residence.

4:15-16 Peter encouraged his readers to live in such a way that their sufferings were caused by their devotion to Christ and not by any evil acts; they would **glorify God** by doing so.

4:17 If even believers in Christ will be judged, then what terrible punishment must surely await unbelievers, who pay no heed to the gospel of Christ?

4:18 Because Christians suffer (v. 16) and will be judged (v. 17), they live out their salvation **with difficulty** (cp. Pr 11:31).

5:1-11 In this closing exhortation, Peter encouraged his readers who were suffering to be responsible. The word

therefore in verse 1 shows that what follows in this section grows out of the preceding verses.

5:1-4 Peter encouraged elders to be exemplary, responsible servants. The term "elders" refers to the office of pastoral leaders in the church. The word appears to be used interchangeably here with "shepherds/pastors" and elsewhere with "overseers" (Ti 1:5,7). Peter's appeal was based on the fact that he was a **fellow elder** and **witness** to Christ's suf-

hupsoo

Greek Pronunciation	[hoo PSAH oh]
HCSB Translation	exalt, lift up
Uses in 1 Peter	1
Uses in the NT	20
Focus passage	1 Peter 5:6

Hupsoo refers to *lifting* something to a higher location. As Moses *lifted up* the serpent in the wilderness, Christ was *lifted up* on the cross (Jn 3:14). This concept of *lifting up* is figuratively extended to mean to *exalt* or *honor* (raising something to a position of higher status). In the example above, the *lifting up* of Jesus referred to His crucifixion (cp. Jn 8:28) but also to His *exaltation* (cp. Jn 12:32). The One who possesses higher authority must do any real *exaltation* to a higher status. Hence, God is often the One who *exalts* others (Lk 1:52; Ac 2:33; Jms 4:10; 1Pt 5:6). He *exalted* (*made great* in number and power) the people of Israel in Egypt (Ac 13:17), and He *exalts* the humble (Mt 23:12 = Lk 14:11; Lk 18:14). Elsewhere, Paul humbled himself so that those in the Corinthian church might be *honored* (2Co 11:7).

[6]Humble[a] yourselves, therefore, under the mighty hand[b] of God, so that He may exalt you at the proper time,[A] [7]casting all your care on Him, because He cares about you.[c]

Conclusion

[8]Be serious![d] Be alert![e] Your adversary the Devil[f] is prowling around like a roaring lion, looking for anyone he can devour. [9]Resist him[g] and be firm in the faith, knowing that the same sufferings are being experienced by your fellow believers throughout the world. [10]Now the God of all grace, who called you to His eternal glory[h] in Christ Jesus, will person-

ally[B] restore, establish, strengthen, and support you after you have suffered a little.[C] [11]The dominion[D] belongs to Him forever.[E] •Amen.

[12]I have written you this brief letter through Silvanus[F,i] (I know him to be a faithful brother) to encourage you and to testify that this is the true grace of God. Take your stand in it! [13]The church in Babylon,[G,j] also chosen, sends you greetings, as does Mark, my son. [14]Greet one another with a kiss of love.[k] Peace[l] to all of you who are in Christ.[H]

[a]5:6 Lk 14:11	
[b]1Kg 8:42; 2Ch 6:32; Dn 9:15	
[c]5:7 Ps 55:22	
[d]5:8 1Th 5:6,8; 2Tm 4:5; 1Pt 1:13; 4:7	
[e]Rv 16:15	
[f]Mt 4:1,10; Ac 13:10	
[g]5:9 Eph 6:13-14; Jms 4:7	
[h]5:10 1Pt 5:1,4; 2Pt 3:18	
[i]5:12 Ac 15:22; 1Th 1:1; 2Th 1:1	
[j]5:13 Rv 14:8; 16:19; 17:5,18; 18:2,10,21	
[k]5:14 Rm 16:16; 1Co 16:20;	2Co 13:12; 1Th 5:26 [l]Eph 6:23

[A]5:6 Lit *in time* [B]5:10 Lit *Himself* [C]5:10 Or *a little while*, or *to a small extent* [D]5:11 Other mss read *dominion and glory*; other mss read *glory and dominion* [E]5:11 Other mss read *forever and ever* [F]5:12 Or *Silas*; Ac 15:22-32; 16:19-40; 17:1-16 [G]5:13 Probably refers to Rome [H]5:14 Other mss read *Christ Jesus. Amen.*

ferings. This helped him identify fully with the "elders" he was addressing and gave added support for his plea. He commanded them to be shepherds of **God's flock**. In other words, they were to nurture, lead, and protect God's people without **lording it over** them. Elders who have served faithfully, despite suffering while on earth, will receive glory in heaven from Christ, **the chief Shepherd**.

5:5a Here the term **elders** may refer to age, not office.

5:5b-7 Peter encouraged all believers to practice **humility** and trust God with their cares. Humility commends us to God and fellow humans, which is the opposite effect of arrogance and conceit.

5:8-9 Peter warned believers to be aware of Satan's deceitful practices and to **resist** him firmly. Such behavior is fitting for temporary residents of this world. Peter strength-

ened his readers with the knowledge that other Christians were also suffering.

5:10-11 God will **strengthen** and honor in heaven those who endure suffering for their faith while on earth.

5:12-14 Silvanus (Silas, v. 12) may have helped Peter write this letter as his secretary (amanuensis), but more likely he was the letter carrier. Peter conveyed greetings to his readers from the church in Rome, i.e., from **the church in Babylon**, and also from **Mark, my son**—Peter's son in the faith, not his biological son. The **kiss of love** was a customary form of greeting in the first-century church. **Peace** is the sense of well-being and blessedness that believers have because of their relationship with Christ. This benediction is an appropriate ending to the letter because when Christians are being persecuted on earth, heaven's peace cannot be taken from them.

2 Peter

Introduction

Second Peter, one of the General Epistles, emphasizes practical Christian living. To this end, Peter wrote to warn against false teachers and the negative influence they can have on moral living. The letter emphasizes true knowledge of God while facing false teaching and encourages readers to maintain Christian virtue in the midst of the world's vice.

First century A.D. ruins outside the synagogue (fourth century A.D.) at Capernaum with Peter's memorial in the background. The memorial is built on what may have been Peter's house.

Circumstances of Writing

Author: The author of 2 Peter plainly identified himself as the apostle Peter (1:1). He called himself "Simeon Peter" (1:1), a name not generally used of the apostle (elsewhere only in Ac 15:14). The spelling is Semitic and lends a sense of authenticity to Peter's letter. Moreover, it was natural for Peter, as a Semite, to use the original form of his name. Peter designated himself as "a slave and an apostle of Jesus Christ." He viewed himself as a servant submitted to Christ's lordship and as a divinely ordained, directly commissioned, authoritative representative of the Lord Jesus Himself.

The letter contains several personal allusions to Peter's life. He mentioned that his death was close (1:14), described himself as an eyewitness of the transfiguration of Jesus (1:16-18), quoted the words of the voice from heaven at this event (1:17), indicated that he had previously written to the letter's recipients (whom he called "dear friends" in 3:1), and also called Paul "our dear brother" (3:15). This suggests that the author was close to Paul. Such references point to Peter as the author.

Many contemporary scholars, however, reject Peter as the author of this letter. They argue, for example, that (1) the personal references to Peter's life are a literary device used by someone who wrote under the apostle's name in order to create the appearance of authenticity; (2) the style of Greek in 2 Peter is different from that of 1 Peter; (3) the reference to Paul's letters as a collection (3:15-16) points to a date later than Peter's lifetime; and (4) 2 Peter was dependent upon Jude. If this is true, Peter's authorship is problematic.

In response to these objections, one should consider that (1) the early church soundly rejected the practice of writing under an apostolic pseudonym, regarding it as outright forgery; (2) Peter may have had help in writing 1 Peter (1Pt 5:12) and not in writing 2 Peter, which would lead to different styles in his Greek; (3) rather than the whole collection, Peter may have referred only to those Pauline letters that were known at the time of writing; and (4) Peter may have borrowed some from Jude, or both may have used a common source. All of these evidences suggest that 2 Peter should be accepted as authentic.

Prehistory–A.D. 29

Noah, his family, and the animal kingdom are spared in the great flood.

God rescues Lot from the complete destruction of Sodom and Gomorrah. 2085 B.C.?

Israel killed every male, including Balaam, in their war against Midian. 1407 B.C.

Jesus calls Simon Peter "the Rock." A.D. 29

Jesus calls Peter to be one of His 12 disciples. A.D. 29

A.D. 30–33

Jesus heals Simon Peter's mother-in-law. 30

Peter's confession at Caesarea Philippi that Jesus is the Messiah 32

Peter, James, and John witness Jesus' transfiguration. 32

Peter vows to die with Jesus. 33

Peter denies Jesus in the courtyard of Annas. 33

Background: Unlike 1 Peter, 2 Peter does not mention specific recipients or refer to an exact destination. The apostle referred to his epistle as the "second letter" he had written to his readers (3:1). If the letter written prior to 2 Peter is 1 Peter, then he wrote to the same recipients ("the temporary residents dispersed in Pontus, Galatia, Cappadocia, Asia, and Bithynia"; 1Pt 1:1). But if the previous letter is a reference to some other epistle that is now unknown, we cannot determine with certainty to whom or to where 2 Peter was written.

Peter likely wrote 2 Peter from Rome, where church tradition placed the apostle in his latter days. Because he mentioned that his death was near (1:14), it seems the letter was written just before his death. Tradition places the date of Peter's martyrdom at about A.D. 67 during Nero's reign (ruled A.D. 54–68).

Second Peter's literary relationship with Jude is debated. What one decides about this issue inevitably affects the authorship and date of each letter. Both epistles are strikingly similar in content. Thus, if 2 Peter borrowed from Jude and the latter book was written somewhere between A.D. 65 and 80, the apostle Peter could not have been the author of 2 Peter. The use of 2 Peter by Jude, however, poses no problem for authorship or dating. Jude may have borrowed from 2 Peter, or both authors may have used a common source.

Peter wrote this letter shortly before he died (1:14) and though not mentioned, possibly while in prison. He wrote to Christian friends confronted with the threat of false teachers who were denying Christ's saving work and second coming. As an eyewitness of Jesus' life (1:16-18), Peter sought to affirm for his readers the reality of Christ's return and to remind them of truths they might otherwise forget (3:1).

Message and Purpose

Peter cautioned believers to beware of false teachers with their bogus doctrines and licentious lifestyles. The temptation to a sinful lifestyle so concerned Peter that shortly after his first letter, he followed up with this one. Peter also warned against denials of Christ's return with its accompanying judgment. He urged his readers to make every effort to grow in the knowledge and practice of the Christian faith.

A.D. 33–40	A.D. 50–Second Century
Following His resurrection, Jesus appears to Peter and recommissions him. 33	Peter, James, John, Paul, Barnabas, and Titus meet in Jerusalem to deal with the question of whether Gentiles had to be circumcised to become Christians. 49
3,000 persons respond to Peter's sermon at the feast of Pentecost. 33	At Antioch, Paul confronts Peter's refusal to share meals with Gentile believers. 49
Saul's conversion on the Damascus Road October 34	Peter's martyrdom in Rome during Nero's persecution of Christians 66
Paul meets with Peter and James on his first visit to Jerusalem following his conversion. 37?	Destruction of Jerusalem 70
Peter bears witness to and baptizes Cornelius and his family at Caesarea Maritima. 40	Allusions to 2 Peter may exist in a number of second-century documents, including 1, 2 Clement, Barnabas, Shepherd of Hermas, the letters of Ignatius of Antioch, and the Martyrdom of Polycarp.

Contribution to the Bible

Peter made strong connections with the OT and challenged his audience to live authentic Christian lives. Peter had been with Jesus when Jesus first spoke of His return (Mt 24–25), and he gave emphasis to the surety of the second coming.

It is the word of God that holds the forefront of this short letter. Peter does this in chapter 1 by emphasizing knowledge (vv. 3,5,6,8,12,20-21) and its divine origin; in chapter 2 by showing its historicity (vv. 4-8); and in chapter 3 by indicating Paul's letters are equal with "the rest of the Scriptures" (vv. 15-16). Peter insisted on the importance of Scripture for guiding and preserving our faith.

Structure

Second Peter is a general letter with the typical features of a salutation, main body, and farewell. What is missing is an expression of thanksgiving. Its style is that of a pastoral letter, driven by the needs of the recipients, rather than some type of formal treatise.

Outline

I. Greeting (1:1-2)

II. Building on Faith with Godly Qualities (1:3-11)

III. The Apostle Peter's Testimony (1:12-21)

IV. Warning Against False Teachers (2:1-22)

V. Certainty of Christ's Return (3:1-10)

VI. Christ's Return Impels Us to Holy Living (3:11-18)

Greeting

1 Simeon[A] Peter,[a] a •slave and an apostle[b] of Jesus Christ:

To those who have obtained a faith of equal privilege with ours[B] through the righteousness[c] of our God and Savior[d] Jesus Christ.

[2] May grace and peace be multiplied to you through the knowledge of God[e] and of Jesus our Lord.

Growth in the Faith

[3] His[C] divine power[f] has given us everything required for life and godliness through the knowledge[g] of Him who called[h] us by[D] His own glory and goodness. [4] By these He has given us very great and precious promises,[i] so that through them you may share in the divine nature,[j] escaping the corruption that is in the world because of evil desires. [5] For this very reason, make every effort to supplement your faith with goodness, goodness with

knowledge, [6] knowledge with self-control,[k] self-control with endurance, endurance with godliness, [7] godliness with brotherly affection,[l] and brotherly affection with love. [8] For if these qualities are yours and are increasing, they will keep you from being useless[m] or unfruitful[n] in the knowledge of our Lord Jesus Christ. [9] The person who lacks these things is blind and shortsighted and has forgotten the cleansing from his past sins. [10] Therefore, •brothers, make every effort to confirm your calling and election,[o] because if you do these things you will never stumble. [11] For in this way, entry into the eternal kingdom[p] of our Lord and Savior Jesus Christ will be richly supplied to you.

[12] Therefore I will always remind you about these things, even though you know them and are established in the truth[q] you have.

[a]1:1 Mt 16:17; Lk 6:14; Ac 10:32; 15:14
[b]Rm 1:1; Ti 1:1
[c]Rm 5:17,21; Php 1:11
[d]Ti 2:13
[e]1:2 Jn 17:3; Php 3:8; 2Pt 1:3,8; 2:20; 3:18
[f]1:3 1Pt 1:5
[g]Jn 17:3; Php 3:8; 2Pt 1:2,8; 2:20; 3:18
[h]1Th 2:12; 2Th 2:14; 1Pt 5:10
[i]1:4 Jos 21:45; 1Kg 8:56; Is 38:16; Jr 33:14; Rm 9:4; 15:8; 2Co 7:1
[j]Eph 4:24; Heb 12:10; 1Jn 3:2
[k]1:6 Ac 24:25; Gl 5:23
[l]1:7 Rm 12:10; Heb 13:1; 1Pt 1:22
[m]1:8 Jms 2:20
[n]Mt 7:16-21; Gl 5:22; Ti 3:14
[o]1:10 Mt 22:14;
Rm 11:29; 2Pt 1:3   [p]1:11 Col 1:13; 2Tm 4:18   [q]1:12 2Co 11:10; Col 1:5-6; 2Jn 2; 3Jn 3-4

[A]1:1 Other mss read *Simon*   [B]1:1 Or *obtained a faith of the same kind as ours*   [C]1:3 Lit *As His*   [D]1:3 Or *to*

1:1-2 Peter called himself **Simeon Peter**, a name not generally used of him (elsewhere only in Ac 15:14). The spelling is Semitic and may have lent authenticity to his letter. Moreover, it was more natural for Peter to use the original form of his name rather than a later form. He further identified himself as **a slave and an apostle of Jesus Christ**. He saw himself as a servant submitted to Christ's lordship. As an "apostle," he was one of Christ's divinely ordained, appointed, authoritative representatives in the early church. Though he surely had a specific group of people in mind, Peter named neither specific recipients in his letter nor their precise geographic location. The recipients are described simply as **those who have obtained a faith of equal privilege with ours.**

The reason for this equality of privilege between Peter's readers and the apostles is **the righteousness of our God and Savior Jesus Christ**. Through the righteousness that finds its source in Jesus, all believers have equal standing and share the same blessings. Peter described Jesus as both "God and Savior," which is not surprising since elsewhere Jesus is called God (Jn 1:1,18; 20:28; Rm 9:5; Ti 2:13; Heb 1:8). The description of Jesus as "God" in no way denies the Trinity, as if Peter meant to say Jesus is both Father and Son. Peter wished his readers multiplied **grace and peace**. "Grace" is God's unmerited favor displayed toward sinners who trust Christ for salvation. "Peace" is the sense of well-being and the attendant blessings that a person enjoys because of a right relationship with Christ. Peter emphasized **the knowledge of God and of Jesus our Lord** to remind his readers that a person experiences grace and peace only through knowing Christ.

1:3-4 Peter next reminded his readers of the resources they had through knowing Christ. He provides believers everything they need for **life and godliness**. "Life" (Gk *zoe*) is eternal life, whereas "godliness" (Gk *eusebeia*) is godly living; the latter cannot be obtained without the former. The divine call of believers served as a foundation for Peter's appeal for godly living. Christ calls to Himself those whom God has saved, and this calling is brought about by His own **glory and goodness**. Christ's "glory" (Gk *doxa*) and "goodness" (Gk *arete*) combine and seem to refer to the moral

excellence of Christ. **By these**—by Christ's glory and goodness—**He has given us very great and precious promises**. The content of these great promises includes sharing in the **divine nature**. Peter did not mean that believers become gods or that they share in the divine nature of God in every way. He meant that they participate in God's moral excellence and will one day be morally perfected. Participation in the divine nature is possible only after escaping the **corruption** in the world because of **evil desires**. Jesus Christ offers the only way of escape from the rebellion of this evil world system that is opposed to and alienated from God.

1:5-7 Because of God's generous provision in Christ, Peter encouraged his readers to build upon their foundation of **faith**—their initial acceptance of God's love—with the Christian virtues of **goodness . . . knowledge . . . self-control . . . endurance . . . godliness . . . brotherly affection**, and **love**. These graces, sometimes called the "ladder of faith," are the fruit of sharing in the divine nature. Each successive quality seems to spring from the previous one.

1:8-9 Useful and fruitful Christians have an abundance of the qualities mentioned in verses 5-7. On the other hand, those who lack them are **blind and shortsighted** because they have forgotten the cleansing from their **past sins**; they deliberately forget the background from which God delivered them. "Past sins" refers to sins committed before professing faith in Christ.

1:10-11 Because of God's grace, gifts, and the knowledge of Christ (vv. 3-9), Peter commanded his readers to **make every effort** to prove the reality of their **calling and election** to salvation; they would do so by godly living (vv. 5-7). Two results follow: (1) they **will never stumble**, or they "will be spared a disastrous coming to grief" (Green, *2 Peter & Jude*, 83); (2) they will receive a glorious entry into the **eternal kingdom** of our Lord and Savior Jesus Christ.

1:12-13 On the basis of the future hope of entry into the eternal kingdom, Peter determined always to **remind** his readers of teachings that they might otherwise lay aside despite his conviction that they were well-grounded in the truths they had been taught. Though they were established Christians,

The Historical Reliability of the New Testament

Craig L. Blomberg

The New Testament (NT) contains four biographies of Jesus (the Gospels), one history book of the early church (Acts), twenty-one letters (Romans to Jude), and an apocalypse (Revelation). While the letters and the apocalypse contain references to historical events, the Gospels and Acts are written as straightforward historical narratives. These are the NT books about which it makes particularly good sense to ask the question, "Are they historically reliable?" Twelve lines of evidence converge to suggest strongly that the answer is "yes."

First, we have over 5,700 Greek manuscripts representing all, or part, of the NT. By examining these manuscripts, over 99 percent of the original text can be reconstructed beyond reasonable doubt. We also discover that no Christian doctrine or ethic depends solely on one of the doubted texts. These facts do not prove that the NT is true, but it does mean we know what the original writers wrote. Without this assurance, the question of historical reliability is pointless.

Second, the authors of the Gospels and Acts were in an excellent position to report reliable information. Matthew and John were among the twelve disciples Jesus Himself chose; Mark was a close companion of Peter and Luke (who also wrote Acts) and traveled extensively with Paul. Even critical scholars who doubt the traditional attributions of authorship agree that these five books were written by followers of Matthew, Mark, Luke, and John, which still puts them in a good place to tell the stories accurately.

Third, these five books were almost certainly written in the first century, within sixty to seventy years of Jesus' death (most likely in A.D. 30). Conservatives typically date Matthew, Mark, and Luke-Acts to the 60s and John to the 80s or 90s. Liberals suggest slightly later dates, typically placing Mark in the 60s or 70s, Matthew and Luke-Acts in the 80s, and John in the 90s. Even if one accepts the later dates, the amount of time separating the historical events and the composition of the five books is very short as compared to most ancient historical and biographical accounts, where many centuries could intervene between events and the books that narrated them.

Fourth, ancient Jews and Greeks meticulously cultivated the art of memorization, committing complex oral traditions to memory. Even before the Gospels or any other written sources about Jesus were compiled, Jesus' followers were carefully passing on accounts of His teachings and mighty works by word of mouth. This kept the historical events alive until the time they were written down.

Fifth, the ancient memorization and transference of sacred tradition allowed for some freedoms in retelling the stories. Guardians of the tradition could abbreviate, paraphrase, prioritize, and provide commentary on the subject matter as long as they were true to the gist or meaning of the accounts they passed on. This goes a long way to explaining both the similarities and the differences among the four Gospels. All four authors were true to the gist of Jesus' life, yet they exercised reasonable freedom to shape the accounts in ways they saw fit.

Sixth, the fact that these writers had distinct ideological or theological emphases does not mean they distorted history, as is often alleged. Oftentimes the very cause that a historian or biographer supports requires them to write their accounts accurately, for they know that their cause will be undermined if they are charged with bias or distortion. The first Christians had the uphill battle of promoting a crucified Messiah and His bodily resurrection. Had they been known to have falsified the details of their accounts to any significant degree, their movement would have been squelched from the outset.

Seventh, Luke's prologue (Lk 1:1-4) closely parallels the form and content of other works of generally reliable historians and biographers of antiquity, most notably Josephus, Herodotus, and Thucydides. The Gospel writers clearly believed that they were writing historically accurate works, not fiction or embellished history.

Eighth, the so-called hard sayings of Jesus support their authenticity. If the Gospel writers felt free to distort what Jesus originally said in order to increase the attractiveness of Christianity, why would they preserve unmodified His difficult and easily misunderstood teachings about hating family members (Lk 14:26) or not knowing when He would return (Mk 13:32)? The fact that they let these teachings stand indicates their faithfulness to recount true history.

Ninth, the fact that the NT does not record Jesus speaking about many of the topics that arose after His earthly life, during the time of the early church, supports its historical accuracy. For instance, early Christians were divided over how or whether the laws of Moses applied to Gentile converts (Ac 15). The easiest way to settle the controversy would be to cite Jesus' teachings on the matter, but the Gospels record

¹³I consider it right, as long as I am in this bodily tent,^{A,a} to wake you up with a reminder, ¹⁴knowing that I will soon lay aside my tent, as our Lord Jesus Christ has also shown me.^b ¹⁵And I will also make every effort that you may be able to recall these things at any time after my departure.^B

The Trustworthy Prophetic Word

¹⁶For we did not follow cleverly contrived myths when we made known to you the power and coming of our Lord Jesus Christ;^c instead, we were eyewitnesses of His majesty.^d ¹⁷For when He received honor and glory from God the Father, a voice came to Him from the Majestic Glory:

This is My beloved Son.^C
I take delight in Him!^{D,e}

¹⁸And we heard this voice when it came from heaven while we were with Him on the holy mountain.^f ¹⁹So we have the prophetic word strongly confirmed. You will do well to pay attention to it, as to a lamp shining in a dismal place,^g until the day dawns^h and the morning starⁱ rises in your hearts. ²⁰First of all, you should know this: No prophecy of Scripture comes from one's own interpretation, ²¹because no prophecy ever came by the will of man;^j instead, men spoke from God as they were moved by the Holy Spirit.^k

The Judgment of False Teachers

2 But there were also false prophets^l among the people, just as there will be false teachers^m among you. They will secretly bring in destructive heresies, even denying the Master who boughtⁿ them, and will bring swift destruction on themselves. ²Many will follow their unrestrained ways, and the way of truth will be blasphemed because of them.^o ³They will exploit^p you in their greed^q with deceptive words. Their condemnation,^r pronounced

^a1:13 2Co 5:1-4
^b1:14 Jn 21:18-23
^c1:16 Mk 13:26; 14:62; 1Th 2:19
^dMt 17:1-6
^e1:17 Is 42:1; Mt 3:17; 17:5; Mk 1:11; 9:7; Lk 3:22
^f1:18 Ps 2:6; Mt 17:1; Mk 9:2; Lk 9:28
^g1:19 Ps 119:105
^hMal 4:2; Rm 13:12; 2Pt 3:18
ⁱNm 24:17; Rv 22:16
^j1:21 Jr 23:26; 2Tm 3:16
^k2Sm 23:2; Lk 1:70; Ac 1:16; 3:18; 1Pt 1:11
^l2:1 Dt 13:1-5; Mt 7:15
^mAc 20:29; 2Co 11:13-15; Gl 2:4; 1Tm 4:1; 2Tm 4:3
ⁿ1Co 6:20; 7:23
^o2:2 Rm 2:24
^p2:3 Jms 4:13
^qEph 5:3
^rMt 12:41; 23:33; Rm 3:8

^A1:13 = Peter's body   ^B1:15 Or *my death*   ^C1:17 Other mss read *My Son, My Beloved*   ^D1:17 = Christ's transfiguration; Mt 17:5

their lifestyles apparently left much to be desired. As long as he was **in this bodily tent**—alive in the human body, a temporary dwelling place for this life—Peter determined to continue stimulating his readers by way of reminder.

1:14-15 The apostle knew that his death was near, and he committed to make **every effort** to arrange that his readers would be **able to recall** his teachings **at any time**. This seems to refer to a written witness since it could be consulted "at any time." Peter might have been referring to Mark's Gospel. In the early second century, Papias called Mark "Peter's interpreter" (cp. Eusebius, *Hist. eccl.*, 3.39.15), meaning Mark's Gospel was based on eyewitness information given by Peter.

1:16-18 Peter's words were not based on **cleverly contrived myths**. He emphasized that he had been an eyewitness of Jesus' transfiguration (Mt 17:1-7; Mk 9:2-9; Lk 9:28-36).

1:19-21 Peter argued that the prophetic Scriptures affirmed the apostolic witness. In essence he was saying, "If you don't believe me, go to the Scriptures." The metaphor of the prophetic Scriptures as **a lamp shining in a dismal place** means that they act as a torch that shines in this dark world, exposing the dirt and defilement of sin and making it possible to get rid of it. Believers live by Scripture's torchlight **until the day dawns and the morning star rises**, which seems to refer to Christ's return. **In your hearts** may refer to the glowing hope that occurs in believers' hearts when they see clear signs of the Lord's return. Peter further explained that Scripture is trustworthy because it has a divine origin; men **moved by the Holy Spirit** wrote the prophetic statements of the OT.

2:1-3 Not only were Spirit-moved men of God present in OT Israel, but **false prophets** (Gk *pseudoprophetai*) also arose

no such teachings. This silence suggests that the Gospel writers did not feel free to play fast and loose with history by putting on the lips of Jesus teachings that could solve early church controversies.

Tenth, the testimony of non-Christian writers supports the details of the Gospels and Acts. About a dozen ancient Jewish, Greek, and Roman writers mention Jesus. Taken together, their writings attest to the basic contours of Jesus' life. Many names of people and places, as well as the exploits of first-century political and religious leaders, are attested in other writings of the day.

Eleventh, archaeology regularly confirms details about geography, topography, customs, artifacts, buildings, tombs, inscriptions, and graffiti that are mentioned in NT—the Gospels and Acts in particular.

Twelfth, the portions of the NT that were written before the completion of the Gospels and Acts confirm the historicity of these five books. For instance, Paul, James, and Peter show multiple signs of quoting or alluding to teachings and actions of Jesus in letters they wrote before the Gospels were written. Their quotes and allusions agree with what we find in the Gospels. This indicates that the Gospels are in tune with the very earliest writings about Jesus—the NT epistles. These earliest writings were in turn dependent on the authoritative oral traditions that were passed on by eyewitnesses to Jesus' life. Paul expresses this in 1Co 15:3-8, where he lists the beliefs he had "received" from these eyewitnesses when he became a Christian no more than two years after Jesus' death and resurrection. These are no late, slowly developing legends he is reporting!

long ago, is not idle, and their destruction does not sleep.

[4]"For if God didn't spare[a] the angels who sinned but threw them down into Tartarus[A,b] and delivered them to be kept in chains[B] of darkness until judgment;[c] [5]and if He didn't spare the ancient world, but protected Noah,[d] a preacher of righteousness, and seven others,[C,e] when He brought a flood on the world of the ungodly; [6]and if He reduced the cities of Sodom and Gomorrah[f] to ashes and condemned them to ruin,[D] making them an example to those who were going to be ungodly;[E,g] [7]and if He rescued righteous Lot, distressed by the unrestrained behavior of the immoral [8](for as he lived among them, that righteous man tormented himself day by day with the lawless deeds he saw and heard')— [9]then the Lord knows how to rescue[j] the godly from trials and to keep the unrighteous under punishment until the day of judgment,[k] [10]es-

pecially those who follow the polluting desires of the flesh and despise authority.[l]

Bold, arrogant people! They do not tremble when they blaspheme the glorious ones; [11]however, angels, who are greater in might and power, do not bring a slanderous charge against them before the Lord.[F] [12]But these people, like irrational animals—creatures of instinct born to be caught and destroyed—speak blasphemies about things they don't understand, and in their destruction they too will be destroyed, [13]suffering harm as the payment for unrighteousness. They consider it a pleasure to carouse in the daytime. They are spots and blemishes, delighting in their deceptions[G] as they feast with you. [14]They have eyes full of adultery[m] and are always looking for sin. They seduce unstable people and have hearts trained in greed. Children under a curse![n] [15]They have gone astray by abandoning the straight path[o] and have followed the path of Balaam,[p] the son

[a]2:4 Rm 8:32; Jd 6
[b]Rv 20:2-3,10
[c]Mt 25:41
[d]2:5 Gn 5:29
[e]1Pt 3:20
[f]2:6 Gn 19:24; Jd 7
[g]Is 1:9; Jd 15
[h]2:7 Gn 19:16
[i]2:8 Ps 119:136,158; Ezk 9:4
[j]2:9 1Co 10:13
[k]Mt 10:15; Jd 6
[l]2:10-13 Jd 8-12
[m]2:14 Mt 5:27-28
[n]Jr 23:14; Hs 4:2; Eph 2:3; Heb 2:13
[o]2:15 Ac 13:10
[p]Nm 22:5-7; Dt 23:4; Neh 13:2; Jd 11; Rv 2:14

[A]2:4 = Gk name for a place of divine punishment in the underworld. [B]2:4 Other mss read in pits [C]2:5 Lit righteousness, as the eighth [D]2:6 Other mss omit to ruin [E]2:6 Other mss read an example of what is going to happen to the ungodly [F]2:11 Other mss read them from the Lord [G]2:13 Other mss read delighting in the love feasts

---

among the people, just as **false teachers** (Gk *pseudodidaskaloi*) were even now present among Peter's readers. Peter's warning describes these "false teachers" as those who spread **destructive heresies**, or teachings destructive to the faith. The effect of their teaching was so far-reaching that they even denied **the Master** ("sovereign Lord"; Gk *despotes*) who bought them. Though many followed the heretics' shameful immorality and the **way of truth** was **blasphemed**, little did the false teachers realize that denying the Lord would **bring swift destruction on themselves** (cp. v. 3). Driven by greed, the false teachers invented deceptive stories (the exact opposite of Peter in 1:16) with which they exploited their listeners.

2:4-10a In order to warn his readers and urge them to action, Peter recalled three examples of God's judgment and

tartaroo

Greek Pronunciation	[tahr tah RAH oh]
HCSB Translation	throw down into Tartarus
Uses in 2 Peter	1
Uses in the NT	1
Focus passage	2 Peter 2:4

The verb *tartaroo* means to *throw down into Tartarus*. Its only NT occurrence (2Pt 2:4) refers to God casting disobedient angels into *Tartarus*, an idea with a Homeric parallel. Well before NT times, Homer (ca 8th c. B.C.) spoke of *Tartarus* as a subterranean place of punishment where Zeus banished the Titans (a family of ruling gods; Hom. *Il.* 14.279). Hesiod (ca 8th c. B.C.) remarked that "a brazen anvil falling from earth nine nights and days would reach Tartarus upon the tenth" (Hes. *Theog.* 724-5). It is a dark, dank place "under misty gloom," surrounded by a bronze fence—a place "which even the gods abhor" (Hes. *Theog.* 730, 739). Eventually, *tartaroo* made its way into Jewish apocalyptic literature, retaining the idea of a place of punishment. It appears closely equivalent to Jewish *gehenna* [hell] (Syb. *Or.* 4:186), that supplies the Jewish background alluded to in 2Pt 2:4.

deliverance: (1) God judged **the angels who sinned** (cp. Gn 6:1-4). **Tartarus** is a Greek name that means a subterranean place of punishment lower than Hades and reserved for the wicked. (2) God also judged the ancient world at the time of the flood (cp. Gn 7:17-23), but protected **Noah** and **seven others** (cp. Gn 7:13-16). (3) He judged the immoral cities of **Sodom** and **Gomorrah** (cp. Gn 19:23-29), yet rescued **righteous Lot**, who was distressed and tormented by the immoral behavior of the ungodly (cp. Gn 19:29). Peter then pointed out to his readers that God was capable of delivering them, **the godly**, from the destructive false teachings of heretics in their midst. Peter further assured his readers that despite the false teachers' immorality, the unrighteous, especially those who followed the **polluting desires** of the flesh and despised **authority**, would not escape God's sovereignty or punishment.

2:10b-22 Peter further described the false teachers. They were rash, **arrogant**, and, in contrast to the behavior of the more powerful angels, slanderously insolent. They were brute-like and **irrational** in their understanding, blasphemous, and ruled by lust and greed. Peter compared the false teachers to **Balaam** (Nm 22–24). Like Balaam, these false teachers had abandoned the straight path, were consumed by greed, and would receive the wages of their unrighteousness; Balaam's donkey showed more moral sense than Balaam did. The false teachers are described as **springs without water** and **mists driven by a whirlwind**. In other words they were unsatisfactory and unstable. As punishment, **the gloom of darkness** was reserved for them. With their empty boastful words, and despite their promises of freedom to others, these false teachers led their hearers into the same spiritual slavery and corruption to which they themselves were enslaved. Although these heretics had once claimed to know Christ and even experienced some freedom from sin, they returned to their old practices and became **entangled** again. They were worse off in the end with their rejection of Christ than they were at the beginning when in a state of ignorance; indeed, it would be better for them **not to have known** the way of **righteousness**. Just

of Bosor,[A] who loved the wages of unrighteousness[a] [16] but received a rebuke for his transgression: A donkey that could not talk spoke with a human voice and restrained the prophet's irrationality.[b]

[17] These people are springs without water, mists driven by a whirlwind. The gloom of darkness has been reserved for them.[c] [18] For by uttering boastful, empty words,[d] they seduce, with fleshly desires and debauchery, people who have barely escaped[B] from those who live in error. [19] They promise them freedom, but they themselves are •slaves of corruption, since people are enslaved to whatever defeats them.[e] [20] For if, having escaped the world's impurity through the knowledge of our Lord and Savior Jesus Christ,[f] they are again entangled in these things and defeated, the last state is worse for them than the first.[g] [21] For it would have been better for them not to have known the way of righteousness[h] than, after knowing it, to turn back from the holy command[i] delivered[j] to them.[k] [22] It has happened to them according to the true proverb: **A dog returns to its own vomit,** [C,l] and, "a sow, after washing itself, wallows in the mud."

The Day of the Lord

3 Dear friends, this is now the second letter[m] I have written to you; in both letters, I want to develop a genuine[n] understanding with a reminder, [2] so that you can remember the words previously spoken by the holy prophets and the command of our Lord and Savior given through your apostles. [3] First, be aware of this: Scoffers will come in the last days[o] to scoff, living according to their own desires, [4] saying, "Where is the promise of His coming?[p] Ever since the fathers fell •asleep,[q] all things continue as they have been since the beginning of creation." [5] They willfully ignore this: Long ago the heavens and the earth were brought about from water and through water[r] by the word of God.[s] [6] Through these waters the world of that time perished when it was flooded.[t] [7] But by the same word,[u] the present heavens and earth are stored up for fire, being kept until the day of judgment[v] and destruction of ungodly men.

[8] Dear friends, don't let this one thing escape you: With the Lord one day is like a thousand years, and a thousand years like one day.[w] [9] The Lord does not delay His promise,[x] as some understand delay, but is patient with you, not wanting any[y] to perish[z] but all to come to repentance.[aa]

[10] But the Day of the Lord[ab] will come like a thief;[D,ac] on that day the heavens will pass away[ad] with a loud noise, the elements will burn and be dissolved,[ae] and the earth and

Cross references:

[a]2:15 Hs 9:1; Mc 1:7; Ac 1:18
[b]2:16 Nm 22:22-35
[c]2:17 Jd 13
[d]2:18 Jd 16
[e]2:19 Jn 8:34; Rm 6:16; 7:5
[f]2:20 2Pt 1:2
[g]Mt 12:45; Lk 11:26
[h]2:21 Pr 8:20; 12:28; 16:31; 21:21; Mt 21:32
[i]Rm 7:12; 1Tm 6:14
[j]Jd 3
[k]Ezk 18:1-32; Heb 6:4-6; 10:26-27
[l]2:22 Pr 26:11
[m]3:1 1Pt 1:1
[n]Php 1:10
[o]3:3 2Tm 3:1; Heb 1:2; Jms 5:3; 1Pt 1:20
[p]3:4 1Th 2:19; 2Pt 3:12
[q]Ac 7:60
[r]3:5 Ps 24:1-2; 33:6-7; 136:5-6; Pr 8:24-29
[s]Gn 1:3-30; Ps 148:5; Jn 1:1-3; Heb 4:12; 11:3
[t]3:6 2Pt 2:5
[u]3:7 Is 66:15-16; Ezk 38:22; Am 7:4; Zph 1:18; Mal 4:1
[v]Php 1:6; 2Th 1:5; 1Jn 4:17
[w]3:8 Ps 90:4
[x]3:9 Hab 2:3
[y]Ti 2:11
[z]Ezk 18:23,32; 33:11; 1Tm 2:4
[aa]Jl 2:12-13; Jnh 3:10; 4:2; Ac 17:31; Rm 2:4
[ab]3:10 Php 1:6
[ac]Mt 24:43; Lk 12:39; 1Th 5:2
[ad]Mt 5:18; 24:35; Rv 21:1
[ae]Is 24:19; Mc 1:4

A2:15 Other mss read *Beor*　**B**2:18 Or *people who are barely escaping*　**C**2:22 Pr 26:11　**D**3:10 Other mss add *in the night*

---

as a **dog returns to its own vomit** and a pig returns to wallow in the mud, so also these false teachers reverted to the immoral lifestyles they preferred by nature. The immoral behavior of the false teachers shows that they had never been genuinely converted.

3:1-2 Peter referred to his epistle as the **second letter** he had written to his readers. Presumably the previous letter was 1 Peter (see Introduction). In both letters Peter reminded his readers not to forget the teachings they had received through the prophets and apostles. **The command** may refer to the revelation of God in Christ through the apostles, or possibly to specific warnings about false teachers.

3:3-4 The teaching of which Peter spoke included accepting Christ's return, which had been rejected by the false teachers. The apostles expected the presence of scoffers and their activities, and Peter warned his readers that **scoffers will come in the last days to scoff.** They were on the scene in Peter's day; they would also be present in the future. The "last days" refers to the period of time between Christ's incarnation and His return. The scoffers mocked Christ's return because many years had passed and it had not yet occurred. **Ever since the fathers fell asleep, all things continue as they have been since the beginning of creation.** "The fathers" probably refers to the OT patriarchs given the mention of "the beginning of creation." Because the false teachers distorted the OT Scriptures, Peter countered them by alluding to the OT.

3:5-7 The heretics argued that the world was unchanging, that it would remain so, and thus that the Lord would

not return. To counter this charge, Peter took his readers' thoughts back to creation to show them that the world had not always been orderly and that the source of the world's order was God. Peter appeared to speak of water as the element out from which God formed the earth. **By the word** means "by God's decree"—He spoke and it happened. To counter the false teachers' claims, Peter also reminded his readers of the great flood that took place in Noah's day when the earth was destroyed. So God does demonstrate His power and intervene in judgment in a world that otherwise seems unchanging. **By the same word**, He will do it again when Christ returns.

3:8 What seems like a delay makes the Lord's return no less certain. Peter noted that God views time differently than human beings do. Christ will return in accordance with the divine timetable, not ours. **Dear friends** recalls the recipients of the letter (1:1).

3:9 The Lord has not yet returned, says Peter, because He **is patient with you, not wanting any to perish.** "You" is variously interpreted as a reference to the letter's Christian recipients (identified in 1:1) or else more broadly as all people. In chapter 1 "you" and "your" both refer back to the recipients identified in 1:1 (see 1:2,4,5,8,10,11,12,13,15,16,19,20). Peter's later use of "dear friends," (3:1,8,14,17) seems also to point back to those identified in 1:1.

3:10 God's patience toward sinners is not inexhaustible. The **Day of the Lord** will be sudden and will catch many people

the works on it will be disclosed.[A] [11]Since all these things are to be destroyed in this way, it is clear what sort of people you should be in holy conduct and godliness [12]as you wait for and earnestly desire the coming[B] of the day of God.[a] The heavens will be on fire and be dissolved because of it, and the elements will melt with the heat. [13]But based on His promise, we wait for the new heavens and a new earth,[b] where righteousness will dwell.[c]

Conclusion

[14]Therefore, dear friends, while you wait for these things, make every effort to be found at peace with Him without spot or blemish.[d] [15]Also, regard the patience of our Lord as an

opportunity for salvation, just as our dear brother Paul has written to you according to the wisdom given to him.[e] [16]He speaks about these things in all his letters in which there are some matters that are hard to understand. The untaught and unstable twist them to their own destruction,[f] as they also do with the rest of the Scriptures.

[17]Therefore, dear friends, since you know this in advance, be on your guard,[g] so that you are not led away by the error of lawless people and fall from your own stability. [18]But grow in the grace and knowledge[h] of our Lord and Savior Jesus Christ. To Him be the glory both now and to the day of eternity.[C,i] •Amen.[D]

---

[a]3:12 Lk 12:36; 1Co 1:7; 1Th 1:10; Ti 2:13; Jd 21
[b]3:13 Is 65:17; 66:22; Mt 19:28; Rm 8:21; Rv 21:1
[c]Is 32:16; Rm 14:17
[d]3:14 Php 2:15; 1Th 5:23; 1Tm 6:14; Jms 1:27
[e]3:15 Ac 9:17; 15:25; 2Pt 3:2
[f]3:16 Heb 5:11; 2Pt 2:14
[g]3:17 Lk 12:15; 2Tm 1:14; 4:15
[h]3:18 2Pt 1:2
[i]Rm 11:36; 2Tm 4:18; Rv 1:6

A3:10 Other mss read *will be burned up*   **B**3:12 Or *and speed the coming*   **C**3:18 Or *now and forever*   **D**3:18 Other mss omit *Amen.*

---

unprepared, as when a burglar sneaks in and robs a house (cp. Mt 24:43-44; Lk 12:39-40).

3:11-14 Peter insisted that the anticipation of the Lord's return and its accompanying events of judgment should rouse Christians to **holy** living. Evil will be completely destroyed when Christ returns, and **righteousness** will permanently dwell in **the new heavens and a new earth** (cp. Is 32:16).

3:15-16 Peter notes that the teaching in Paul's letters said that the Lord's **patience** provided opportunities for salvation (Rm 2:4). Peter grouped Paul's letters together with **the rest of the Scriptures**. This reference does not necessar-

ily mean that Paul's letters were already circulating as a complete collection. Peter may simply have been referring to the Pauline letters that were widely known and accepted as Scripture at the time he wrote 2 Peter. In any event, Peter clearly affirms the God-given authority of Paul's writings (1:20-21; see note at 1:19-21).

3:17-18 Since Peter's readers had now been warned about the false teachers in their midst, he instructed them to be on their guard and not be led astray. He also encouraged them to grow in the **grace and knowledge** of Jesus Christ (cp. 1:2-11). He closed with a doxology in which he ascribed **glory** to Christ both now and forever.

1 John

Introduction

John's first letter addresses a setting in which some people in the local church had departed the fellowship (2:19), apparently because their doctrine, ethics, devotion, or some combination of these conflicted with those of the church. John wrote in part to stabilize the situation. He reaffirmed and enlarged on key theological truths, particularly the doctrine of Christ. He extolled love and emphasized the necessity for belief to be matched by action. A personal relationship with Christ is the foundation of the Christian life, and out from this grows obedience to divine commands. True faith, proactive ethics, fervent love for God and people—most of the epistle revolves around one or more of these three emphases as the author instructed, admonished, and encouraged his readers.

An ancient baptistry in Ephesus, the city in which John ministered late in the first century.

Circumstances of Writing

Author: Ancient manuscripts are unanimous in naming "John" as the author of 1 John. This was understood to be John the son of Zebedee, the "beloved disciple" who was also the author of the Fourth Gospel. The style and vocabulary of 1, 2, and 3 John are so close to that of John's Gospel that they beg to be understood as arising from the same person. Some contemporary scholars theorize that an "elder John" (see 2Jn 1; 3Jn 1), not the apostle, may have written the letters. Others speak of a "Johannine school" or "circle" as the originators of the epistles of John (and perhaps Revelation too). But the view with the best support is that Jesus' disciple John was the author.

Background: Second-century sources reported that around A.D. 70, the year the Romans destroyed Jerusalem and the temple, John left Jerusalem where he was a church leader and relocated to Ephesus. He continued his pastoral work in that region and lived until nearly A.D. 100. Ephesus is probably the place where John wrote the three NT letters that bear his name. They could have been composed at any time in the last quarter of the first century.

Message and Purpose

John made four purpose statements. First, he wrote to promote his readers' fellowship and joy. "We are writing these things so that our joy may be complete" (1:4).

Second, he wrote to help readers avoid the pitfalls of sin, yet find forgiveness when they stumbled. "My little children, I am writing you these things so that you may not sin" (2:1).

Third, he wrote to protect believers from false teachers. "I have written these things to you about those who are trying to deceive you" (2:26).

Finally, he wrote so they might know they had eternal life. "I have written these things to you who believe in

---

A.D. 4–33

- John the apostle, son of Zebedee and Salome is born. 8?

- John and his brother James are part of their father's fishing business in Capernaum, on the Sea of Galilee. 25

- Jesus calls James and John to be two of His 12 disciples. 29

- Peter, James, and John witness Jesus' transfiguration. 32

- John and Peter are asked to prepare the Passover meal Jesus shares with His disciples. 33

A.D. 33–44

- Peter, James, and John are with Jesus as He prays in Gethsemane. 33

- As He dies, Jesus gives the care of His mother, Mary, to John. 33

- John may be the first of the 12 disciples to believe that Jesus rose from death. 33

- Following Pentecost, John and Peter show great courage in Jerusalem by bearing witness to Jesus' acts. 33

- John's brother, James, is the first of the 12 disciples to die a martyr's death. 44

the name of the Son of God, so that you may know that you have eternal life" (5:13). This last purpose statement governs the other three and brings them together in a unifying theme.

In summary, 1 John was written to confirm Christians in true apostolic Christianity by helping them avoid the destructive beliefs and behaviors to which some had fallen prey.

Contribution to the Bible

First John maps out the three main components of saving knowledge of God: (1) faith in Jesus Christ, (2) obedient response to God's commands, and (3) love for God and others from the heart. This epistle shows how Jesus expects His followers to honor Him in practical church life and wherever God calls His people to go and serve.

Structure

It is widely agreed that 1 John does not logically, methodically, or rigorously set forth and develop its arguments. For this reason scholars are divided on the best way to structurally outline the letter. It is the least letter-like of the three Johannine epistles because of its lack of identification of the sender and the recipient. It is more like an unsystematic treatise. It often makes assertions along thematic lines, moves to related or contrasting themes, and then returns to the earlier topic, or perhaps takes up a different subject altogether.

Outline

I. **The Truth About Christ (1:1-4)**
   A. **An affirmation about the person of Christ (1:1)**
   B. **An affirmation about the author of the letter (1:2-4)**

A.D. 45–65	A.D. 66–Late Second Century
John is among the pillars of the Jerusalem church who meet with Paul, Barnabas, and Titus in Jerusalem to deal with the question of whether Gentiles had to be circumcised to become Christians. 49	The Jewish War is started by zealots who drive the Romans out of Jerusalem temporarily. 66
	John leaves Jerusalem for Ephesus. 66–70 ?
Paul travels through Ephesus toward the end of his second missionary journey. 52	The Romans crush the Jewish rebellion and destroy Jerusalem and the temple. 70
Apollos comes to Ephesus and is mentored by Aquila and Priscilla. 52	John is spiritual leader of the church at Ephesus. 70–100
Paul returns to Ephesus for a 2 1/2 year ministry. 54	Irenaeus (140–202) affirms that the body of John's writings was composed in Ephesus.
Timothy, elder of Ephesus, receives the first letter from Paul. 62	

II. The Believer's Lifestyle (1:5–2:14)
   A. Fellowship with God (1:5-7)
   B. Confession of sin (1:8-10)
   C. Obeying the commands of Christ (2:1-6)
   D. Maintaining relationships with other believers (2:7-14)

III. The Believer's Relationship to the World (2:15-27)
   A. Do not love the world (2:15-17)
   B. Beware of antichrists (2:18-27)

IV. A Message for God's Children (2:28–4:21)
   A. They will one day be like Christ (2:28–3:3)
   B. They are not to continue in sin (3:4-6)
   C. They must not be led astray by evil (3:7-10)
   D. They are to love one another (3:11-24)
   E. They are to "test the spirits" (4:1-3)
   F. They are to overcome the world (4:4-6)
   G. They are to reflect God's character (4:7-21)

V. Final Exhortations (5:1-21)
   A. Obedient love is proof of faith (5:1-5)
   B. Christ brings us eternal life (5:6-15)
   C. God's children do not continue to sin (5:16-21)

Prologue: Our Declaration

1 What was from the beginning,[a]
  what we have heard,
  what we have seen with our eyes,
  what we have observed
  and have touched
    with our hands,
  concerning the Word[b] of life—
2   that life was revealed,[c]
  and we have seen it
  and we testify and declare to you
  the eternal life that was
    with the Father
  and was revealed to us[d]—
3 what we have seen and heard
  we also declare to you,
  so that you may have fellowship[e]
    along with us;
  and indeed our fellowship is
    with the Father[f]
  and with His Son Jesus Christ.
4 We are writing these things[A]
  so that our[B] joy[g] may be complete.

Fellowship with God

[5] Now this is the message we have heard from Him and declare to you: God is light,[h] and there is absolutely no darkness in Him.[i] [6] If we say, "We have fellowship[j] with Him," yet we •walk in darkness,[k] we are lying and are not practicing[c] the truth.[l] [7] But if we walk in the light[m] as He Himself is in the light, we have fellowship with one another, and the blood of Jesus[n] His Son cleanses us from all sin. [8] If we say, "We have no sin,"[o] we are deceiving ourselves, and the truth is not in us. [9] If we confess our sins, He is faithful and righteous to forgive[p] us our sins and to cleanse us from all unrighteousness. [10] If we say, "We don't have any sin," we make Him a liar, and His word[q] is not in us.[r]

2 My little children, I am writing you these things so that you may not sin. But if anyone does sin, we have an •advocate[s] with the Father—Jesus Christ the Righteous One.

Cross references (center column):

[a]1:1 Jn 1:1; 1Jn 2:13-14
[b]Ps 119:25; Jn 1:1,4; 5:24; Php 2:16
[c]1:2 Jn 1:31; 21:1,14; Col 3:4; 1Pt 5:4; 1Jn 2:28; 3:5,8
[d]1Jn 5:20
[e]1:3 Php 3:10
[f]Mt 11:27
[g]1:4 2Co 2:3; Php 1:4,25; 2:18
[h]1:5 Ps 27:1; 36:9; Jn 12:46; 1Tm 6:16
[i]1Jn 2:5
[j]1:6 2Co 8:4
[k]Pr 2:13; Is 9:2; 50:10; Jn 8:12; 12:35; 1Jn 2:11
[l]Jn 14:6; 2Co 11:10; 3Jn 3
[m]1:7 Eph 5:8-14; Col 1:12-14; Php 2:15; 1Th 5:5
[n]Heb 10:19; 12:24; 1Pt 1:2,19; Rv 1:5
[o]1:8 Pr 20:9; Jn 2:35; Rm 3:9-23; Jms 3:2
[p]1:9 Ps 103:3; Jr 31:34;

Mt 9:6; 26:28; Col 1:14; Jms 5:15; [q]1:10 Lk 8:21; Heb 4:12; [r]Jn 8:37; [s]2:1 Jn 14:26

[A]1:4 Other mss add *to you*   [B]1:4 Other mss read *your*   [C]1:6 Or *not living according to*

1:1 The words **what was from the beginning** echo both Gn 1:1 and Jn 1:1. God's purpose in His Son has an eternal dimension. John wrote as an eyewitness. Christ was not just a spiritual vision but an actual human being. Christ is the **Word** made flesh (Jn 1:14) who gives eternal **life** to all who believe in Him.

1:2 God made Christ known. Human hearts and minds require God's aid to see His truth (Mt 16:17; Jn 3:3). The Son, the second Person of the Trinity, has always existed alongside the Father.

1:3 The phrase **we also declare to you** shows that John passed on faithfully to his readers what the apostolic generation had received. **Fellowship** refers to the close ties of kinship that God extends to His people.

1:4 A major reason why John wrote this epistle was so **our joy may be complete**. There is great happiness in knowing the forgiveness of sins and pursuing the will of God. God is the One who acts to complete a believer's joy.

1:5 John had divine guidance in **the message** he related. As an apostle he actually lived alongside the Son of God. Darkness had crept in among the readers whom John addressed. To dispel it John testified to Him who is **light**. God sent the light of the world, Jesus (Jn 8:12).

1:6 The words **if we say** may indicate that John was paraphrasing false views that needed to be exposed and corrected. To **walk in darkness** is to persist in sin. Since God is light (v. 5), His people are called and enabled to live by the light of His wisdom, truth, and love.

1:7 To **walk in the light** is to live consistent with God's commands and character. **Fellowship**, the shared knowledge of God's light and love, is one of life's deepest satisfactions. With the phrase **the blood of Jesus**, John identified the focal point of Christ's saving work in the cross.

1:8 In both Scripture and church history, people have excused their wrongful deeds by claiming to be right with God. John diagnosed an ancient and recurrent human tendency.

1:9 Confessing **our sins** does not mean a shallow reciting of misdeeds. It means owning up to wrongdoing and bringing our lives into line with God's goodness and commands. God can **forgive** and **cleanse** us from terrible transgressions.

1:10 Since God is light and there is no darkness in Him (v. 5), to claim to be without sin is to claim to be on par with God, but God says there is no one like Him (Is 45:18). If **His word is not in us**, the saving message of Christ has not taken root. There may be surface knowledge of Christian religion, but the heart has not been transformed.

2:1 Jesus' death was not the end of His ministry but the move to a new phase. Now He serves as our **advocate** or helper and mediator at the Father's right hand.

---

koinonia

Greek Pronunciation	[koy noh NEE ah]
HCSB Translation	fellowship
Uses in 1 John	4
Uses in the NT	19
Focus passage	1 John 1:3,6,7

Koinonia most often carries the sense of *communion* or *fellowship*, referring to an association involving close mutual relations. This idea of mutual involvement is seen in extrabiblical usage, where *koinonia* can refer to *marriage* (3Macc 4:6). Because of a common Spirit, Christians have *fellowship* with God and one another (1Jn 1:3,6,7). This kind of intimate *fellowship* was displayed among the sharing community of the early church (Ac 2:42). *Koinonia* may also refer to the way in which this *fellowship* is portrayed, namely, through *sharing*, *generosity*, or *participatory-feeling*. Paul speaks of the Corinthian church's generosity in *sharing* a financial gift (2Co 9:13). By extension, *koinonia* may refer to the financial *contribution* itself (Rm 15:26). It may also express *participation* or *common fellowship* in a task or cause. Thus, believers have a common *participation* in the faith (Phm 6) and in Christ's body and blood (1Co 10:16).

[2] He Himself is the •propitiation[a] for our sins, and not only for ours, but also for those of the whole world.[b]

God's Commands

[3] This is how we are sure[c] that we have come to know Him: by keeping His commands.[d] [4] The one who says, "I have come to know Him," yet doesn't keep His commands, is a liar, and the truth is not in him. [5] But whoever keeps His word,[e] truly in him the love of God is perfected.[A] This is how we know we are in Him:[f] [6] The one who says he remains in Him[g] should •walk just as He walked.

[7] Dear friends, I am not writing you a new command[h] but an old command that you have had from the beginning. The old command is the message[i] you have heard. [8] Yet I am writing you a new command, which is true in Him and in you, because the darkness is passing away[j] and the true light[k] is already shining.[l]

[9] The one who says he is in the light but hates his brother[m] is in the darkness until now. [10] The one who loves his brother[n] remains in the light, and there is no cause for stumbling in him.[B] [11] But the one who hates his brother[o] is in the darkness, walks in the darkness,[p] and doesn't know where he's going,[q] because the darkness has blinded his eyes.

Reasons for Writing

[12]   I am writing to you, little children,
        because your sins have been forgiven

        because of Jesus' name.[r]
[13]   I am writing to you, fathers,
        because you have come to know
        the One who is from the beginning.[s]
    I am writing to you, young men,
        because you have had victory
         over the evil one.[t]
[14]   I have written to you, children,
        because you have come to know
        the Father.
    I have written to you, fathers,
        because you have come to know
        the One who is from the beginning.
    I have written to you, young men,
        because you are strong,
        God's word[u] remains in you,
        and you have had victory
         over the evil one.

A Warning about the World

[15] Do not love the •world[v] or the things that belong to[c] the world. If anyone loves the world, love for the Father is not in him. [16] For everything that belongs to[D] the world—the lust of the flesh,[w] the lust of the eyes,[x] and the pride[y] in one's lifestyle—is not from the Father, but is from the world. [17] And the world with its lust is passing away,[z] but the one who does God's will[aa] remains forever.[ab]

Cross-references (center column):

[a] 2:2 Rm 3:25; 2Co 5:21; Heb 2:17; 1Jn 4:10
[b] Mt 26:13; 28:19-20; Mk 14:9; Rm 1:8
[c] 2:3 Jn 13:35; 1Jn 2:5; 3:19,24; 4:2,6,13; 5:2
[d] Jn 14:15; 15:10
[e] 2:5 Jn 14:23
[f] Jn 6:56; 14:20; 15:1-7; Rm 8:1; 2Co 5:17; Eph 2:10; Php 1:1
[g] 2:6 Jn 15:4-7; 1Jn 2:24,27-28; 3:6,24; 4:13,15-16
[h] 2:7 Mk 7:8; Jn 13:34; 2Jn 5
[i] Lk 6:47; Jn 1:1
[j] 2:8 Rm 13:12; 1Co 7:31; 1Jn 2:17
[k] Jn 1:9; 3:19-21; 8:12; 12:46
[l] Jn 1:5; 12:35-36; Rv 22:5
[m] 2:9 1Jn 2:11; 3:15; 4:20
[n] 2:10 Rm 12:10; 1Th 4:9; Heb 13:1; 1Pt 1:22; 1Jn 3:10,14-17; 4:20-21
[o] 2:11 Lv 19:17; 1Jn 3:15; 4:20
[p] 1Jn 1:6
[q] Jn 14:6
[r] 2:12 Ps 25:11; Lk 24:47; Ac 2:38; 10:43
[s] 2:13 1Jn 1:1
[Jn 16:33; 17:15; Eph 6:10; 1Jn 2:14; 4:4; 5:4-5; Rv 2:7]
[u] 2:14 1Jn 1:10
[v] 2:16 Jn 15:19; 17:16; Rm 12:2; Jms 1:27; 4:4; [w] Rm 13:14; Eph 2:3; 1Pt 4:2; 2Pt 2:18; [x] Gn 3:6; Pr 27:20; [y] Jms 4:16 [z] 2:17 1Jn 2:8; [aa] Mk 3:35; Eph 6:6; 1Th 4:3; 1Pt 2:15 [ab] Jn 8:35; 12:34; 2Co 9:9; 1Pt 1:25

[A] 2:5 Or truly completed   [B] 2:10 Or in it   [C] 2:15 Lit things in   [D] 2:16 Lit that is in

---

2:2 Jesus' perfect obedience and sacrificial death satisfied God's just demand for sin to be punished (**propitiation**). But His punishment was for others, not for Himself. The phrase **for those of the whole world** does not mean the salvation of all people. It does mean that, in keeping with God's promise to bless all the nations through Abraham and his descendants (Gn 12:3), Jesus' saving death extends the offer of salvation to all nations.

2:3 John taught an understanding of Christian faith that includes profound assurance, not just the "maybe" of spiritual optimism.

2:4 The words **His commands** mean the same thing as "His word" in verse 5 and Jesus' example in verse 6 ("just as He walked"). The true follower of Jesus is not just a talker but a doer (Jms 1:22).

2:7 **Dear friends** is literally "Beloved." This was a favorite term of address for John (3:2,21; 4:1,7,11). It is a reminder that Christians are what they are—"beloved"—because God has loved them (4:10). The love **command** was intensified and perfected in its expression by Jesus. Yet it is **old**, rooted in God's love and His commands in the OT (Lv 19:18; Dt 6:5).

2:8 God is light (1:5), and Christ has come into the world. This means the gloom of present evil and sin is giving way as the **true light** is **already shining**.

2:9-11 Relationships with fellow believers are key indicators of whether one is walking in the **light** or in **darkness**.

Walks, here and elsewhere in 1 John, is a metaphor for the course of a person's life.

2:12-14 While 1 John lacks a formal personal address in its opening lines, the author used two terms of endearment in these verses (**little children**, v. 12; **children**, v. 14). Then he included all readers with the inclusive terms **fathers** and **young men**.

2:13 The **One who is from the beginning** could refer to either the Father or the Son. They share the attribute of eternality (Jn 1:1; 17:5).

2:14 Believers are strong not in themselves but because of the One in whom they have placed their trust. God's word refers to the saving gospel message that Christ brought, now embodied in the Bible.

2:15 **Things that belong to the world** are not just material objects. They are things that absorb human **love for the Father** to an undue degree, even to the point of supplanting God (see John's warning about idols in 5:21 and note there).

2:16 John warned against what the body desires, what the eyes itch to see, and what people work hard to acquire. These are **not from the Father** but **from the world.**

2:17 Like the darkness in verse 8, **the world with its lust is passing away** because of the coming of Christ. This opens the way for doing **God's will** and establishing fellowship with Him forever.

The Last Hour

[18] Children, it is the last hour.[a] And as you have heard, "Antichrist[b] is coming," even now many antichrists have come. We know from this that it is the last hour. [19] They went out from us, but they did not belong to us; for if they had belonged to us, they would have remained with us. However, they went out so that it might be made clear that none of them belongs to us.

[20] But you have an anointing[c] from the Holy One,[d] and all of you have knowledge.[A] [21] I have not written to you because you don't know the truth, but because you do know it, and because no lie comes from the truth. [22] Who is the liar, if not the one who denies that Jesus is the •Messiah?[e] This one is the antichrist: the one who denies the Father and the Son. [23] No one who denies the Son can have the Father;[f] he who confesses the Son has the Father as well.[g]

Remaining with God

[24] What you have heard from the beginning must remain in you. If what you have heard from the beginning remains in you, then you will remain in the Son[h] and in the Father.[i] [25] And this is the promise that He Himself made to us: eternal life.[j] [26] I have written these things to you about those who are trying to deceive you.

[27] The anointing you received from Him remains in you, and you don't need anyone to teach you. Instead, His anointing teaches you about all things[k] and is true and is not a lie; just as He has taught you, remain in Him.[l]

God's Children

[28] So now, little children, remain in Him, so that when He appears[m] we may have boldness and not be ashamed before Him at His coming.[n] [29] If you know that He is righteous, you know this as well: Everyone who does what is right[o] has been born of Him.[p]

[3] [1] Look at how great a love[B] the Father has given us that we should be called God's children. And we are! The reason the •world does not know us is that it didn't know Him. [2] Dear friends, we are God's children now, and what we will be has not yet been revealed.[q] We know that when He appears, we will be like Him[r] because we will see Him as He is.[s] [3] And everyone who has this hope[t] in Him purifies himself just as He is pure.[u]

[4] Everyone who commits sin also breaks the law;[C] sin is the breaking of law. [5] You know that He was revealed so that He might take away sins,[D,v] and there is no sin in Him.[w] [6] Everyone who remains in Him[x] does not sin;[E,y] everyone who[F] sins has not seen Him or known Him.

Cross references

[a]2:18 Jn 2:4; 1Pt 4:7
[b]Mt 24:5,24; 1Jn 2:22; 4:3; 2Jn 7
[c]2:20 2Co 1:21
[d]Ps 89:18; Mk 1:24; Ac 10:38
[e]2:22 Jn 20:31; Ac 18:5; Eph 5:2; 1Jn 5:1
[f]2:23 Jn 5:23
[g]Jn 8:19; 16:3; 17:3; 1Jn 4:15; 5:1; 2Jn 9
[h]2:24 Jn 15:4-7; 1Jn 2:6,27-28; 3:6,24; 4:13,15-16
[i]Jn 10:38; Col 3:3; 1Th 1:1; 1Jn 4:15-16
[j]2:25 Jn 4:14; 1Tm 4:8; 2Tm 1:1; Ti 1:2
[k]2:27 Jn 14:26
[l]Jn 15:4-7; 1Jn 2:6; 3:6,24; 4:13,15-16
[m]2:28 Lk 17:30; Col 3:4; 1Jn 3:2
[n]1Th 2:19
[o]2:29 Gn 18:19; Dt 6:18; 1Jn 3:7,10
[p]Jn 1:12-13; 3:3-7; 8:41; 1Jn 3:9; 4:7; 5:1,4,18
[q]3:2 2Co 4:11; 1Pt 5:4; 1Jn 2:28
[r]Rm 8:29; 1Co 15:49; 2Co 3:18; Php 3:21; 2Pt 1:4
[s]1Co 13:12; Heb 12:14; Rv 22:4
[t]3:3 Ac 23:6; 1Th 1:3
[u]Php 4:8;
[v]3:5 Jn 1:29; 1Co 15:3; Heb 10:4; 1Pt 2:24;
[w]2Co 5:21; Heb 4:15; 7:26; 1Pt 2:21-22; 3:18; 1Jn 3:5
[x]3:6 Jn 15:4-7; 1Jn 2:6,24,27-28; 3:24; 4:13,15-16;
[y]Rm 6:11-12; 1Jn 2:29; 5:18

[A]2:20 Other mss read *and you know all things* [B]3:1 Or *at what sort of love* [C]3:4 Or *also commits iniquity* [D]3:5 Other mss read *our sins* [E]3:6 Or *not keep on sinning* [F]3:6 Or *who keeps on sinning*

2:18 John warned against many antichrists. This is probably a reference to misguided or diabolical individuals who were guilty of the sins that he described and condemned. They opposed and sought to replace the true Christ.

2:19 The phrase **they went out from us** shows there had been a division among the church members to whom John wrote. But not all who were in the church were authentic believers. Their departure from the fellowship and the apostolic truth was proof of this.

2:20 The **anointing** in this verse could be the Holy Spirit, but it more likely refers to the gospel or the saving message—the teaching that believers had received.

2:21 A mark of those who truly **know** is the ability to admit their lack of knowledge and their desire to learn more. True believers are always "disciples" (learners).

2:22 The error John referred to here was not ethical but theological—false teaching about **the Father** and **the Son**.

2:23 This verse affirms the unity and identity of God **the Father** and **the Son**. Yet it also affirms their distinctiveness.

2:24 The phrase **from the beginning** refers to the earliest exposure of John's readers to gospel teaching. There is a direct tie between what they have **heard** and the status of their souls as residing (or not residing) in **the Son** and in **the Father**.

2:25 Despite John's earlier ethical warnings to remain faithful, salvation is a matter of God's faithfulness, not human achievement.

2:26 God's people cannot always avoid conflict; usurpers and destroyers arise, **trying to deceive**.

2:27 On **anointing**, see note at verse 20. John was content to entrust his readers to the powerful message they had received.

2:28 **Ashamed** refers to the guilt and terror of judgment by God. Those who **remain in Him** avoid this grim prospect.

2:29 The doctrinal knowledge of John's **if** statement sets up the ethical response implied by **does what is right**, but the response is a function of spiritual rebirth (**born of Him**) and not human effort.

3:1 John marveled at God's **love** because of its effect—sinners can be called **God's children**.

3:2 The world may think little of God's children **now**, but at Christ's return things will change. Believers will be transformed because they will **see Him as He is**.

3:3 Knowing that the Lord will return is a strong incentive for believers to live in ways that are pleasing to Him.

3:4 **Sin** is a grave matter because God has revealed His moral character in His holy law, and sin is the **breaking of law**. It is a personal offense against God.

3:6 John was aware that Christians sin (2:1). They can receive forgiveness through Jesus' death (1:7) as they confess

⁷ Little children, let no one deceive you! The one who does what is right is righteous, just as He is righteous. ⁸ The one who commits[A] sin is of the Devil, for the Devil has sinned from the beginning. The Son of God[a] was revealed[b] for this purpose: to destroy the Devil's works. ⁹ Everyone who has been born of God[c] does not sin,[B] because His[c] seed[d] remains in him; he is not able to sin,[D] because he has been born of God. ¹⁰ This is how God's children—and the Devil's children—are made evident.

The Command to Love

Whoever does not do what is right is not of God, especially the one who does not love his brother.[e] ¹¹ For this is the message you have heard from the beginning: We should love one another, ¹² unlike Cain,[f] who was of the evil one[g] and murdered[E] his brother. And why did he murder him? Because his works were evil, and his brother's were righteous. ¹³ Do not be surprised, ˙brothers, if the world hates[h] you. ¹⁴ We know that we have passed from death to life because we love our brothers. The one who does not love remains in death.[i] ¹⁵ Everyone who hates his brother[j] is a murderer,[k] and you know that no murderer has eternal life residing in him.

Love in Action

¹⁶ This is how we have come to know love: He laid down His life[l] for us.[m] We should also lay down our lives for our brothers.[n] ¹⁷ If anyone has this world's goods[o] and sees his brother in need[p] but closes his eyes[q] to his need—how can God's love reside in him?[r]

¹⁸ Little children, we must not love with word or speech, but with truth and action.[s] ¹⁹ This is how we will know we belong to the truth[t] and will convince our conscience in His presence, ²⁰ even if our conscience condemns us, that God is greater than our conscience, and He knows all things.[u]

²¹ Dear friends, if our conscience doesn't condemn us, we have confidence before God ²² and can receive whatever we ask from Him because we keep His commands[v] and do what is pleasing in His sight. ²³ Now this is His command: that we believe in the name[w] of His Son Jesus Christ, and love one another as He commanded us. ²⁴ The one who keeps His commands remains in Him,[x] and He in him. And the way we know that He remains in us[y] is from the Spirit[z] He has given us.

The Spirit of Truth and the Spirit of Error

4 Dear friends, do not believe every spirit, but test the spirits[aa] to determine if they

Cross references

ᵃ3:8 Mk 1:11
ᵇJn 21:1; 2Co 4:11; 1Pt 5:4; 1Jn 5:20
ᶜ3:9 1Jn 2:29
ᵈ1Pt 1:23
ᵉ3:10 1Jn 2:10; 3:14-17; 4:20-21
ᶠ3:12 Gn 4:1; Jd 11
ᵍ2Th 3:3
ʰ3:13 Jn 17:14
ⁱ3:14 Jn 8:51
ʲ3:15 1Jn 2:9,11; 4:20
ᵏMt 5:21-22; Jn 8:44
ˡ3:16 Jn 10:11,14,17-18; 13:37-38; 15:13
ᵐIs 53:10; Mk 10:45
ⁿMk 8:34-35; 1Co 11:1; Php 2:5-8
ᵒ3:17 Mk 12:44; Lk 15:12; 1Jn 2:16
ᵖAc 2:45
ۊ2Co 7:15
ʳJms 2:15-16; 1Jn 2:5
ˢ3:18 Mt 7:21; Jn 13:34-35; 15:12-17; Jms 1:22-25; 2:14-17
ᵗ3:19 Jn 14:6; 2Co 11:10; 3Jn 3
ᵘ3:20 Ps 139:6; Pr 2:6; Jn 14:28
ᵛ3:22 Mk 7:8; Jn 14:15; 1Jn 2:3; 5:2
ʷ3:23 Ps 33:21; Is 50:10; Jn 1:12; 3:18; 1Jn 5:13;
ˣ3:24 Lk 11:13; Jn 15:4-7; Ac 5:32; 15:8;
ʸJn 6:56;
ᶻRm 8:9-16;
ᵃᵃ4:1 1Th 5:21

[A]3:8 Or practices   [B]3:9 Or not practice sin   [C]3:9 God's   [D]3:9 Or to keep on sinning   [E]3:12 Or slaughtered

---

their sins (1:9). By **everyone who sins has not seen Him or known Him**, John had in mind flagrant sin by false "believers" whose confession of Jesus was false (2:23), whose love was set on the world rather than God (2:15), and whose obedience was lacking (2:4). Jesus Himself warned about people who called Him "Lord" and did great things in His name, but ultimately were not genuine disciples (Mt 7:21-23).

3:7 Satan continually seeks to subvert and deceive God's people. We must be vigilant always.

3:8 When believers forsake **sin**, they thwart the Devil's aims and further God's kingdom.

3:9-10 On **does not sin**, see note at verse 6. God's **seed** is the gospel message. Believers are **born of God** by the work of His word, and this makes them able to do "what is right" (v. 7). **Not able to sin** means freedom from bondage to breaking God's law and freedom to live as **God's children**. John spoke of what spiritual rebirth makes **evident**—not sinless perfection but a life surrendered fully to God.

3:11 Apostolic preaching emphasized that faith in a God of love moved believers to become people who **love one another**.

3:12 On **Cain**, see Gn 4:1-16. John assumed his readers were familiar with this grim OT account.

3:13 The phrase **if the world hates you** shows that the division in 2:19 (see note there) may have left hard feelings. Jesus foretold that His followers would not always be well received (Jn 16:2).

3:14 Our assurance of salvation rests in part on the love that

God gives us for **our brothers** (meaning "fellow believers"). If we have this love, it is a sign of our salvation. If not, we are warned to examine our hearts before God.

3:15 There is no middle ground. Love is the gospel mandate (Jn 13:35). The person who neglects to love **hates his brother**. This signals absence of **eternal life**.

3:16 Jesus' death is not only the source of forgiveness of sin (1:7); it is also the yardstick by which believers gauge their own love for other believers (**our brothers**).

3:17 Selfishness and God's love are mutually exclusive.

3:18 With the phrase **with truth and action**, John declared that faith which is only talk is false faith.

3:19 **In His presence** refers to God's observation of our lives. Faithful living results in confident hearts rather than guilt, evasion, or fear.

3:20 Human hearts can be self-deceived, but God who **knows all things** can grant assurance.

3:22 We will receive **whatever we ask** in prayer if our prayer is within God's will (5:14). If we **keep His commands**, we will have no desire to request what God does not wish.

3:23 **His command** and faith in **His Son Jesus Christ** are not different things but two aspects of a single, undivided love of God.

3:24 The role of the Holy **Spirit** has been assumed all along in this epistle, but He is mentioned outright here for the first time.

4:1 God gives the Spirit (3:24), but there are counterfeits in

are from God, because many false prophets have gone out into the world.

²This is how you know the Spirit of God: Every spirit who confesses that Jesus Christ has^A come in the flesh^a is from God.^b ³But every spirit who does not confess Jesus^B is not from God. This is the spirit of the antichrist;^c you have heard that he is coming, and he is already in the world now.

⁴You are from God, little children, and you have conquered them, because the One who is in you^d is greater than the one who is in the world.^e ⁵They are from the •world.^f Therefore what they say is from the world, and the world listens to them. ⁶We are from God. Anyone who knows God listens to us;^g anyone who is not from God does not listen to us. From this we know the Spirit of truth and the spirit of deception.^h

Knowing God through Love

⁷Dear friends, let us love one another, because love is from God, and everyone who loves has been born of God^i and knows God. ⁸The one who does not love does not know

God, because God is love. ⁹God's love was revealed among us in this way:^c God sent^j His •One and Only Son^k into the world so that we might live^l through Him. ¹⁰Love consists in this: not that we loved God, but that He loved us^m and sent His Son to be the^D •propitiation^n for our sins. ¹¹Dear friends, if God loved us in this way, we also must love one another.^o ¹²No one has ever seen God.^E,p If we love one another, God remains in^F us and His love is perfected in us.

¹³This is how we know that we remain in Him^q and He in us: He has given assurance to us from His Spirit.^r ¹⁴And we have seen and we testify that the Father has sent His Son^s as the world's Savior. ¹⁵Whoever confesses^G,t that Jesus is the Son of God—God remains in him and he in God. ¹⁶And we have come to know and to believe the love that God has for us. God is love, and the one who remains in love remains in God, and God remains in him.

¹⁷In this, love is perfected with us so that we may have confidence in the day of judgment,^v

Cross references (center column)

^a4:2 Jn 1:14; Php 2:7; 3:3
^b1Co 12:3
^c4:3 1Jn 2:18,22; 2Jn 7
^d4:4 Rm 8:31; Col 1:27; 1Jn 3:20
^eJn 12:31
^f4:5 Jn 17:6; 2Pt 2:20
^g4:6 Jn 8:47
^hMk 13:5-6; 1Co 2:12; 1Tm 4:1
^i4:7 1Jn 2:29
^j4:9 Mk 9:37
^kJn 1:14,18; 3:16,18
^lJn 10:28
^m4:10 Jn 3:16
^n 2Co 5:21; 1Jn 2:2
^o4:11 Jn 13:14; 15:12; Rm 13:8; 1Th 4:9; 1Pt 1:22
^p4:12 Ex 33:20
^q4:13 Jn 15:4-7; 1Jn 2:6,24,27-28; 3:6,24; 4:15-16
^r Rv 3:22
^s4:14 Rm 1:3
^t4:15 Jn 9:22; Php 2:6
^v4:17 Mt 10:15; 11:22,24; 12:36; 2Pt 2:9; 3:7; Jd 6

---

^A4:2 Or confesses Jesus to be the Christ   ^B4:3 Other mss read confess that Jesus has come in the flesh   ^C4:9 Or revealed in us   ^D4:10 Or a   ^E4:12 Since God is an infinite being, no one can see Him in His absolute essential nature; Ex 33:18-23.   ^F4:12 Or remains among   ^G4:15 Or acknowledges

---

the form of **many false prophets**. Discernment is a critical characteristic for Christian disciples.

4:2 God's **Spirit** does not condone false doctrine. By the end of the first century a view of Christ arose that denied His true humanity. In this view, the Son of God assumed human form for a time, but the divine Christ departed from the earthly Jesus before the crucifixion. John insisted that Christ had **come in the flesh**. God was truly and fully incarnate in Jesus of Nazareth.

4:3 The words **spirit who does not confess Jesus** show that John was aware of people speaking by the power of spirits other than the Holy Spirit.

homologeo

Greek Pronunciation	[hah mah lah GEH oh]
HCSB Translation	confess
Uses in 1 John	5
Uses in the NT	26
Focus passage	1 John 4:2-3,15

Homologeo (to confess) functions in a number of ways in the NT, and it plays an important part in John's theology (nearly 40 percent of its occurrences appear in John's writings). Most often, *homologeo* means *to assert, confess* or *declare publicly* (Mt 7:23; Mt 10:32 = Lk 12:8; Jn 9:22; 12:42; Ac 23:8). This outward *confession* is viewed as a window into the person's actual beliefs (Rm 10:10). In this sense, *homologeo* may refer to a *public declaration* of agreement with some religious *confession* or set of doctrines (Jn 1:20; Ac 24:14; Rm 10:9,10; 1Tm 6:12; Ti 1:16). The *confession* spoken of in 1Jn 1:9 appears to be private but does not exclude public *confession*. Elsewhere, *homologeo* stresses the idea of an *agreement* or *acknowledgment* about something (Heb 11:13), and it may mean *to assure* or *promise* (Mt 14:7; Ac 7:17) and also *to praise* (Heb 13:15).

4:4 The **one who is in the world** probably refers to the Devil, whether in person or as represented by his spiritual and human servants.

4:5 Spiritual deception is more attractive and plausible to non-Christians than the truth of the gospel message.

4:8 **God is love** does not mean that love is God. Love is an attribute of God, like righteousness and goodness. Those who truly know Him share in this attribute.

4:9 The phrase **live through Him** means not just biological existence, but the spiritual high road of eternal life.

4:10 On **propitiation**, see note at 2:2. The standard of love is not what humans feel but what God has revealed in Christ's life and death on the cross.

4:11 The phrase **God loved us in this way** means that Jesus was obedient to the point of death.

4:12 John used the phrase **no one has ever seen God** to refer to God the Father in His heavenly splendor, but God the Son makes the invisible Father clearly known (Jn 1:18).

4:13 **His Spirit** plays a crucial role in assuring and convincing believers. That is why it is so important not to tolerate the presence of false spirits (v. 1).

4:14 Like the "we" of the opening verses of 1 John, this **we** refers to John and other apostles. Few if any of John's readers would have actually **seen** Jesus in the flesh.

4:15 Confession of the truth about **the Son** is a condition for a relationship with **God** the Father.

4:16 In some verses John emphasized the ethical side of saving faith; in others he stressed doctrinal fidelity. Here his emphasis is on the devotion of the passions and heart—**love**.

4:17 The "He" in **we are as He is** could refer to either Jesus or God the Father. If the reference is to Jesus, John was

for we are as He is in this world.[a] [18]There is no fear in love; instead, perfect love drives out fear,[b] because fear involves punishment.[A] So the one who fears has not reached perfection in love.[c] [19]We love[B] because He first loved us.[d]

Keeping God's Commands

[20]If anyone says, "I love God," yet hates his brother,[e] he is a liar.[f] For the person who does not love his brother[g] he has seen cannot love the God he has not seen.[C] [21]And we have this command from Him: The one who loves God must also love his brother.

5 Everyone who believes that Jesus is the •Messiah has been born of God,[h] and everyone who loves the Father also loves the one born of Him. [2]This is how we know that we love God's children when we love God and obey[D] His commands. [3]For this is what love for God is: to keep His commands. Now His commands are not a burden,[i] [4]because whatever has been born of God conquers the •world. This is the victory that has conquered the world: our faith. [5]And who is the one who conquers the world[j] but the one who believes that Jesus is the Son of God?[k]

The Certainty of God's Testimony

[6]Jesus Christ—He is the One who came by water and blood, not by water only, but by water[l] and by blood.[m] And the Spirit is the One

who testifies,[n] because the Spirit is the truth. [7]For there are three that testify:[E,o] [8]the Spirit,[p] the water, and the blood[q]—and these three are in agreement. [9]If we accept the testimony of men, God's testimony[r] is greater, because it is God's testimony that He has given about His Son. [10](The one who believes in the Son of God has this testimony within him. The one who does not believe God has made Him a liar,[s] because he has not believed in the testimony God has given about His Son.) [11]And this is the testimony: God has given us eternal life, and this life is in His Son.

[12]The one who has the Son has life.[t] The one who doesn't have the Son of God does not have life. [13]I have written these things to you who believe in the name[u] of the Son of God, so that you may know that you have eternal life.

Effective Prayer

[14]Now this is the confidence we have before Him: Whenever we ask[v] anything according to His will, He hears us.[w] [15]And if we know that He hears whatever we ask,[x] we know that we have what we have asked Him for.[y]

[16]If anyone sees his brother committing a sin that does not bring death, he should ask, and God[F] will give life to him—to those who commit sin that doesn't bring death. There is sin[G] that brings death. I am not saying he should

Cross references (center column)

[a]4:17 Jn 14:10-11; 15:9-10; 17:11,15,18
[b]4:18 Rm 8:15
[c]Eph 4:11-16
[d]4:19 2Th 2:13
[e]4:20 1Jn 2:9,11; 3:15
[f]1Jn 1:10
[g]1Jn 2:10; 3:10,14-17
[h]5:1 1Jn 2:29
[i]5:3 Dt 30:11; Mt 11:30; 23:4,23
[j]5:5 1Co 15:57; 2Pt 2:20
[k]Jn 5:19; 14:1; Heb 1:2
[l]5:6 Mk 1:11; Jn 1:34
[m]Jn 17:1; 1Jn 1:7; 4:10
[n]Jn 15:26; Ac 26:5
[o]5:7 Dt 19:15; Mt 18:16; Jn 8:17-18
[p]5:8 Jn 1:32; 19:30; 20:22
[q]Jn 19:34
[r]5:9 Jn 5:36-37; 8:18
[s]5:10 Gn 3:4
[t]5:12 Jn 3:15,36; 5:24; 6:40,47
[u]5:13 1Jn 3:23
[v]5:14 Mt 7:7; Jn 14:13; 1Jn 3:22
[w]Mt 7:8; Jn 9:31; 11:22
[x]5:15 Jms 1:5
[y]Jn 11:22; 16:24

saying that as the Son lived in this world, loved others, and pleased God, so can His followers. If the "He" refers to the Father, John meant that as God dwells with His people and moves them to reflect His love, they have complete confidence in view of the coming judgment.

4:18 With the words **no fear**, John was speaking of the terror of final judgment (v. 17) and eternal **punishment**. He was not rejecting the healthy "fear of the Lord" that other biblical writers commend (e.g., Pr 1:7).

4:19 Because God **first loved us**, our wills and affections are transformed so that love replaces our selfishness.

4:20-21 Followers of Christ love God and love others—or they are not true disciples of Christ.

5:1-21 The previous chapter emphasized love. John affirmed in this chapter that the road to love is paved with faith.

5:3 **Love for God** is not separate from keeping **His commands**. God's commands teach His people how to do what God accepts as pleasing (Rm 12:1-2). Knowledge of God transforms the human will, making what was once **a burden** light and easy to carry (Mt 11:30).

5:4 **Whatever has been born** refers to people transformed and made new through **faith**.

5:6 The words **came by water and blood** probably refer to Jesus' baptism and His death. **The Spirit . . . testifies** through John's witness to the meaning of these events in

Jesus' life. John was present at both the baptism and the crucifixion of Jesus. Moreover, Jesus promised the Holy Spirit to John and other believers to aid their understanding (Jn 16:13).

5:9 Both Jewish and Roman law depended on witnesses who bore clear **testimony** to establish the facts of a legal case.

5:10 By speaking of **the testimony God has given**, after writing that it is the Spirit who testifies (vv. 6,8), John affirmed that the Holy Spirit is God.

5:11 John spoke of **the testimony** that is in the believer (v. 10). Believers have growing conviction of the gift they have received (**eternal life**) and its source (**His Son**).

5:12 There is no salvation outside of faith in Christ.

5:13 Assurance was one of John's major goals in writing this epistle.

5:14-15 The deepest answer to prayer is to know that **He hears us**. To know this is to **have what we have asked Him for**. For believers, prayer seeks communion with the Father more than the acquisition of favors or the satisfaction of desires.

5:16 A **sin that does not bring death** (cp. v. 17) is a sin for which forgiveness is possible (1:9). **Sin that brings death** may be the flagrant offenses against God that so much of 1 John warns against. John may have been speaking

pray about that. [17]All unrighteousness is sin, and there is sin that does not bring death.

Conclusion

[18]We know that everyone who has been born of God does not sin, but the One[A] who is born of God keeps him,[B,C,a] and the evil one does not touch him.

[19]We know that we are of God, and the whole world is under the sway of the evil one.

[20]And we know that the Son of God has come[b] and has given us understanding so that we may know the true One.[D] We are in the true One—that is, in His Son Jesus Christ.[c] He is the true God and eternal life.

[21]Little children, guard yourselves from idols.

a 5:18 Jn 17:12; 1Pt 1:5; Jd 24; Rv 3:10 b 5:20 Jn 1:14; 8:42; 1Jn 1:2; 3:5,8 c Jn 10:38; 15:9; 17:21; 1Th 1:1; 1Jn 2:23-24

A 5:18 Jesus Christ   B 5:18 Other mss read *himself*   C 5:18 Or *the one who is born of God keeps himself*   D 5:20 Other mss read *the true God*

about apostasy (falling away from Jesus; denying the apostolic truth). John called on his readers to leave these offenses and offenders in God's hands rather than agonizing in prayer about them. "Death" means spiritual death and eternal separation from God.

5:18 On **does not sin**, see note at 3:6.

5:19 We know refers both to apostles like John and to his readers. The **whole world** is **under the sway** of Satan, but his reign is fleeting and fading (2:8,17).

5:20 With the phrase **He is the true God**, John clearly affirmed the full divinity of Christ.

5:21 This closing verse of the epistle has puzzled interpreters for centuries. **Idols** may be John's shorthand for all the lies, errors, hate, and rebellion that his letter warned against—in the hope that his readers would satisfy their souls with true knowledge of Christ.

eidolon

Greek Pronunciation	[AY doh lahn]
HCSB Translation	idol
Uses in 1 John	1
Uses in the NT	11
Focus passage	1 John 5:21

In the Greek OT, *eidolon* (idol) refers to the physical representation of a god (Ex 20:4, Dt 5:8). By extension, it points not only to that physical representation, but to the supposed existing god behind that form. The worship of these *idols* was evidence of that fact (Ex 20:5, Nm 25:2, Dt 5:9) and some were even understood to have demonic powers (Dt 32:17). This usage provides the background for the NT use of *eidolon*. Paul regards *idols* as false gods, powerless compared to the true God (1Th 1:9). He acknowledges the existence of demonic powers behind *idols* but understands them to have no real power over the Christian, who knows that *idols* are but false gods (1Co 8:4-7; 10:19-21). Christians are exhorted to abstain from association with *idols* and the false gods they represent (Ac 15:20; 1Jn 5:21), for there is only one God (1Co 8:7).

Ephesus, the fourth largest city in the world in the late first century, is probably the city from which John wrote his three letters. The carved paving stone from ancient Ephesus was probably an advertisement for a brothel. As John wrote to young Christians he reminded them that "everything that belongs to the world—the lust of the flesh, the lust of the eyes, and the pride in one's lifestyle—is not from the Father, but is from the world. And the world with its lust is passing away, but the one who does God's will remains forever" (2:16-17).

2 John

The second epistle of John advises "the elect lady" (either a reference to a congregation or to a woman who owned a house where the congregation met) to be fervent in Christian love (v. 5) and watchful of deceivers (vv. 7-8). The writer planned to visit the congregation soon (v. 12).

The harbor at Kusadasi, Turkey, the gateway to Ephesus.

Circumstances of Writing

Author: "The Elder" (v. 1) is a title that the apostle John applied to himself late in life. (The apostle Peter referred to himself the same way; 1Pt 5:1.) No one other than the apostle John was ever suggested by the early church as the writer of 1 John. Since there are so many similarities between 1 and 2 John, it is generally accepted that John also wrote the second letter.

Background: Second John likely was written during the last two decades of the first century. During this era, John gave pastoral leadership to churches in the area of Ephesus. We have no way of precisely dating 2 John, but it is reasonable that it was written around the same time as 1 John or slightly afterwards. Its tone reveals it to be a highly personal letter that reflects John's affection for these believers and his deep concern for their welfare.

Message and Purpose

Like Jesus, who wept over Jerusalem (Lk 19:41), and Paul, who wrote of "the daily pressure" of his "care for all the churches" (2Co 11:28), John was concerned about this congregation. Would they neglect to embody God's love for one another? Would they fall prey to false teachers? Second John was apparently written to help readers follow through on their commitment to follow Christ.

John used six key words to tie together this epistle. He repeatedly used the words "trust" (five times), "love" (four times), "commandment" (four times), "walk" (three times), "teaching" (three times), and "children" (three times). John's message is clear: He told his children to (1) walk in the truth, (2) obey God's commandments, (3) love one another, and (4) guard the teachings of Christ and they would not be deceived by the antichrist. John confirmed the spiritual safety of the believing community with a beginning and ending reference to their election by God (vv. 1,13).

A.D. 17–61

A.D. 62–67

Ephesus experiences a destructive earthquake. 17

Timothy, elder of Ephesus, receives first letter from Paul, 1 Timothy. 62

Paul travels through Ephesus toward the end of his second missionary journey. 52

Peter's first letter from Rome to Christians in Pontus, Galatia, Cappadocia, Asia, and Bithynia 64

Apollos comes to Ephesus and is mentored by Aquila and Priscilla. 52

Peter's second letter from Rome 66

Paul returns to Ephesus for a 2 ½ year ministry. 54

The Jewish War is started by zealots who drive the Romans out of Jerusalem temporarily. 66

Paul writes the letter to the Ephesians. 61

Timothy receives second letter from Paul, 2 Timothy. 67?

Contribution to the Bible

It is easy for congregations to get off track. Second John reminds readers of the high priority of the most basic Christian outlook and activity—mutual love. Yet another priority is no less critical—true Christian teaching. This epistle strikes a short but strong blow for steadfastness, assuring that attentive readers would take the right steps to "receive a full reward" (v. 8).

Structure

Second John is an excellent example of hortatory or exhortation discourse, which has the intent of moving readers to action. It follows the normal NT pattern for a letter with an opening, main body, and closing. There are only two commands in this short letter: a call to "watch yourselves" (v. 8) and the command, "do not receive" those who plant false teaching (v. 10). There is the reminder to "love one another" in verse 5. This bears the force of an imperative, in part because of the close proximity of the word "command," which occurs four times in verses 4-6.

Outline

  I.   Greeting and Blessing (vv. 1-3)

 II.   Exhortation to Christian Love (vv. 4-6)

III.   Warnings About False Teachers (vv. 7-11)

 IV.   Impending Visit and Blessing (vv. 12-13)

A.D. 67–70s

Peter and Paul's death in Rome 64-67?

John leaves Jerusalem for Ephesus. 66–70 ?

The Romans crush the Jewish rebellion and destroy Jerusalem and the temple. 70

John is spiritual leader of the church at Ephesus. 70–100

John's Gospel written 70s

A.D. 80s–100

John's first letter (1 John) to the churches of Asia Minor 80s

John's letter to the elect lady (2 John) 80s

John's letter to Gaius (3 John) 80s

John is exiled to Patmos and writes the book of Revelation. 95

Ephesus becomes one of the world's largest cities with a population approaching 500,000. 100

Greeting

The Elder:[A]

To the elect[a] lady[B] and her children: I love all of you in the truth—and not only I, but also all who have come to know the truth[b]— [2] because of the truth that remains in us[c] and will be with us forever.

[3] Grace, mercy, and peace[d] will be with us from God the Father and from Jesus Christ, the Son[e] of the Father, in truth and love.[f]

Truth and Deception

[4] I was very glad to find some of your children •walking in the truth,[g] in keeping with a command we have received from the Father. [5] So now I urge you, dear lady—not as if I were writing you a new command, but one we have had from the beginning—that we love one another.[h] [6] And this is love:[i] that we walk according to His commands.[j] This is the command as you have heard it from the beginning: you must walk in love.[C]

[7] Many deceivers have gone out into the world; they do not confess the coming of Jesus Christ in the flesh.[D,k] This is the deceiver and the antichrist.[l] [8] Watch yourselves so you don't lose what we[E] have worked for, but that you may receive a full reward.[m] [9] Anyone who does not remain in Christ's teaching[n] but goes beyond it, does not have God.[o] The one who remains[p] in that teaching, this one has both the Father[q] and the Son.[r] [10] If anyone comes to you and does not bring this teaching, do not receive[s] him into your home, and don't say, "Welcome," to him; [11] for the one who says, "Welcome," to him shares[t] in his evil works.[u]

Farewell

[12] Though I have many things to write to you,[v] I don't want to do so with paper and ink. Instead, I hope to be with you and talk face to face[F] so that our joy[w] may be complete.

[13] The children of your elect sister send you greetings.

---

[a]1 Rm 16:13; 1Pt 5:13; 2Jn 13
[b]Jn 8:32; 14:6; 1Tm 2:4
[c]2 1Jn 1:8
[d]3 1Tm 1:2; 2Tm 1:2
[e]Heb 1:2
[f]1Jn 4:12
[g]4 3Jn 3-4
[h]5 1Jn 3:11
[i]6 1Jn 2:5; 5:3
[j]Ps 103:18; Mk 7:8; Jn 14:15,21,23; 15:10
[k]7 Php 3:3
[l]1Jn 2:18,22; 4:3
[m]8 2Pt 2:13
[n]9 Jn 8:31-32; 1Jn 2:21-23,27
[o]Jn 5:12; 8:41; 1Jn 2:23
[p]Jn 15:4-16
[q]Mt 11:27
[r]Heb 1:2; 1Jn 2:23
[s]10 Jn 1:12; 6:21; 13:20
[t]11 1Tm 5:22
[u]Eph 5:11; 1Tm 5:22; Jd 23
[v]12 3Jn 13
[w]Jn 15:11

[A]1 Or *Presbyter*   [B]1 Or *Kyria*, a proper name; probably a literary figure for a local church known to John; the children would be its members.   [C]6 Lit *in it*   [D]7 Or *confess Jesus Christ as coming in the flesh*   [E]8 Other mss read *you*   [F]12 Lit *mouth to mouth*

---

1 The Elder is the self-designation of the aged apostle John. Elders were pastoral leaders of local churches (Ac 11:30; 14:23). John may have had regional oversight, like Titus did under Paul (Ti 1:5). **Elect lady** is an unusual term of address. It probably refers to a congregation since John often addressed his readers in the plural form (vv. 6,8,10,12; see Introduction). When he used the singular (vv. 1,4,5,13), he was speaking collectively. Early Christians knew themselves to be "elect" or "chosen" by the Lord (Rm 16:13; 1Pt 1:1; 2:9).

2 Truth is a favorite word in John's Gospel (used more than two dozen times) and his epistles (used about 20 times). In John's epistles, "truth" frequently refers to the gospel of Jesus Christ and the realm of eternal life that believers have entered through their trust in Him.

3 John was confident of the presence of **grace, mercy, and peace** as tokens of God's favor. John did not mention the Holy Spirit in the opening of this epistle, and yet he elsewhere makes clear the Spirit's divinity and His role of calling attention to the Son, **Jesus Christ** (see Jn 15:26).

4 John had heard good things about the members (**children**) of this congregation. "Children of God" as a title for Christians is rare elsewhere in the NT but appears in John's writings (Jn 1:12; 11:52).

5 Just as it takes effort to keep love fresh in a marriage, **love** in a congregation must be nurtured and protected (**now I urge you**). Jesus declared that love among believers is a primary means of their witness to the world (Jn 13:35).

6 For John, **love** was not sentimental affection but an ethical expectation. The definition and standard for love is found in Scripture's teaching, not personal attraction or preference.

7 In Greek this verse begins with the conjunction *gar* ("because"). Love and obedience are critical *because* **deceivers** always stand ready to mislead and disrupt congregations that grow slack or rebellious. Jesus assumed human form and nature to the full (**in the flesh**). Some early false teachers taught that Jesus was fully divine but not fully human. John declared in his first letter that many antichrists had gone into the world (1Jn 2:18). They sought to sow seeds of confusion about Jesus' full divinity and full humanity.

8 It is dangerous to become lethargic in Christian living or to take God's favor for granted. Assurance should look like diligence, not presumption.

9 There are always new ways to apply **Christ's teaching**, but the foundations were established by His coming and the instruction He gave to His followers. John called for dynamic love and creative faithfulness while warning against perverting the apostolic teachings about Jesus.

10 In 3Jn 5-8, John encouraged support for traveling Christian ministers, but this assumed their teachings were true. If they taught falsity, believers were called to discernment and instructed to withhold support from their destructive mission.

11 The believer is not to "condemn himself by what he approves" (Rm 14:22). To give hospitality to false teachers is to approve of them (**shares in his evil works**).

12 On **don't want to do so with paper and ink**, see note at 3Jn 13.

13 The phrase **children of your elect sister** probably refers to the congregation in which John served when he wrote this epistle to a "sister" congregation.

3 John

The shortest book in the New Testament, 3 John is a
letter with a kind but business-like tone. "The Elder"
sought to encourage Gaius, who was perhaps a pastor
under his oversight. The epistle gives mostly positive
counsel but also warns against a power-hungry leader
named Diotrephes. Truth, love, and the goodness of God
are predominate themes.

Temple of Hadrian in Ephesus. This structure was built in the generation after John's
death. It was built by P. Quintilius and dedicated to the Emperor Hadrian.

Circumstances of Writing

Author: Same as the author of 1 and 2 John (see Introductions there).

Background: Same as 2 John (see Introduction there). The two short epistles of 2 and 3 John are often described as "twin epistles," though they should be viewed as fraternal and not identical. There are some significant similarities worth noting. In both epistles the author described himself as "the Elder" (2Jn 1; 3Jn 1), and the recipients were those whom he loved "in truth" (2Jn 1; 3Jn 1). The recipients were a cause for great rejoicing by John (2Jn 4; 3Jn 3). They were "walking in the truth" (2Jn 4; 3Jn 3), and the elder has received good reports about them (2Jn 4; 3Jn 3,5). Both letters contain a warning (2Jn 8; 3Jn 9-11), and the Elder desired to see the recipients face-to-face (2Jn 12; 3Jn 14). Finally, both letters convey greetings from others (2Jn 13; 3Jn 14).

Message and Purpose

Third John is a personal letter that revolves around three individuals: (1) Gaius, the recipient of the letter; (2) Diotrephes, the one causing trouble; and (3) Demetrius, who was probably the bearer of the letter. The purpose was to give a word of exhortation to Gaius and encourage him not to imitate the bad example of Diotrephes. Instead, Gaius was to continue the good work he was doing in receiving and supporting the traveling teachers or missionaries.

Contribution to the Bible

This brief letter of apostolic instruction underscores certain central Christian convictions: love, truth, faithfulness, the church, and witness. It also testifies to the God-centeredness of apostolic faith (vv. 7,11). Jesus and the Spirit are not mentioned specifically (unless "the truth itself" in v. 12 refers to Jesus; see Jn 14:6; 1Jn 5:20). But in the writer's view, Jesus and the Spirit were undoubtedly included in the reference to "God" whose "truth" this epistle appeals to so frequently (3Jn 1,3,4,8,12).

A.D. 17–61

Ephesus experiences a destructive earthquake. **17**

Paul travels through Ephesus toward the end of his second missionary journey. **52**

Apollos comes to Ephesus and is mentored by Aquila and Priscilla. **52**

Paul returns to Ephesus for a 2 ½ year ministry. **54**

Paul writes the letter to the Ephesians. **61**

A.D. 62–67

Timothy, elder of Ephesus, receives first letter from Paul, 1 Timothy. **62**

Peter's first letter from Rome to Christians in Pontus, Galatia, Cappadocia, Asia, and Bithynia **64**

Peter's second letter from Rome **66**

The Jewish War is started by zealots who drive the Romans out of Jerusalem temporarily. **66**

Timothy receives second letter from Paul, 2 Timothy. **67?**

Structure

The letter follows the basic epistolary pattern with an introduction (vv. 1-4), body (vv. 5-12), and a conclusion (vv. 13-14). Though verses 1-4 clearly function as the salutation, it is also possible to outline the letter around the four personalities of the book. Verses 1-8 contain a multifold commendation of Gaius. Verses 9-10 condemn the highhanded and malicious autocracy of Diotrephes. Verses 11-12, taken as a unit, praise the godly Demetrius. Verses 13-14 close with a glimpse into the heart of the Elder. Four men and their reputations (growing out of their behavior) are the sum and substance of 3 John's subject matter. John constructed this letter with the building blocks of key-word repetition: "dear friend" (vv. 1,2,5,11); "truth" or "true" (vv. 1,3,4,8,12). Third John provides insight into a personality conflict that arose at the end of the first century and the strategy adopted by the Elder to resolve it.

Outline

I. Greeting to Gaius (vv. 1-2)

II. Joy at Seeing Christians Demonstrate the Truth (vv. 3-4)

III. Pressing Issues (vv. 5-12)
   A. Support for traveling ministers (vv. 5-8)
   B. The problem of Diotrephes (vv. 9-10)
   C. Commendation of Demetrius (vv. 11-12)

IV. Impending Visit and Blessing (vv. 13-14)

A.D. 67–70s	A.D. 80s–100
Peter and Paul's death in Rome 64-67?	John's first letter (1 John) to churches of Asia Minor 80s
John leaves Jerusalem for Ephesus. 66–70?	
The Romans crush the Jewish rebellion and destroy Jerusalem and the temple. 70	John's letter to the elect lady (2 John) 80s
	John's letter to Gaius (3 John) 80s
John is spiritual leader of the church at Ephesus 70–100	John is exiled to Patmos and writes the book of Revelation. 95
John's Gospel written 70s	Ephesus becomes one of the world's largest cities with a population approaching 500,000. 100

Greeting

The Elder:[a]

To my dear friend[A] Gaius: I love you in the truth.[b]

[2] Dear friend,[B] I pray that you may prosper in every way and be in good health physically[c] just as you are spiritually.[C] [3] For I was very glad when some *brothers came and testified[d] to your faithfulness to the truth—how you are *walking in the truth.[e] [4] I have no greater joy[f] than this: to hear that my children[g] are walking in the truth.

Gaius Commended

[5] Dear friend,[B] you are showing faithfulness[D] by whatever you do for the brothers, especially when they are strangers. [6] They have testified to your love in front of the church.[h] You will do well to send them on their journey[i] in a manner worthy of God,[j] [7] since they set out for the sake of the Name,[k] accepting nothing from pagans.[l] [8] Therefore, we ought to support such men so that we can be coworkers with[E] the truth.

Diotrephes and Demetrius

[9] I wrote something to the church, but Diotrephes, who loves to have first place among them,[m] does not receive us.[n] [10] This is why, if I come, I will remind him of the works he is doing, slandering[o] us with malicious words. And he is not satisfied with that! He not only refuses to welcome the brothers himself, but he even stops those who want to do so and expels them from the church.

[11] Dear friend,[B] do not imitate what is evil,[p] but what is good. The one who does good is of God;[q] the one who does evil has not seen God.[r] [12] Demetrius has a good testimony from everyone, and from the truth itself. And we also testify for him, and you know[s] that our testimony is true.[t]

Farewell

[13] I have many things to write you, but I don't want to write to you with pen and ink. [14] I hope to see you soon, and we will talk face to face.[F]

Peace be with you. The friends send you greetings. Greet the friends by name.

---

[a]1 2Jn 1
[b]Jn 14:6; 1Jn 5:20
[c]2 1Tm 1:10
[d]3 Jn 15:26; Ac 26:5
[e]2Jn 4
[f]4 Jn 15:11
[g]1Co 4:14; Gl 4:19; Php 2:22
[h]6 Mt 16:18; 1Co 14:4; Rv 1:4
[i]Ac 15:3; 20:38; 21:5; Rm 15:24; 1Co 16:6; 2Co 1:16; Ti 3:13
[j]1Co 10:31; 1Th 2:12
[k]7 Jn 10:25; Ac 15:14; Rv 14:1
[l]1Co 9:15-18
[m]9 Mt 20:25-28; 23:5-12; Col 1:18; 1Pt 5:2-3; 2Jn 9
[n]Ac 18:27; Rm 16:1-2; 2Co 3:1
[o]10 1Tm 5:13
[p]11 1Pt 3:17
[q]1Jn 4:4
[r]Ex 33:20
[s]12 1Jn 2:20-21
[t]Jn 21:24

[A]1 Or my beloved   [B]2,5,11 Or Beloved   [C]2 Lit as your soul prospers   [D]5 Lit are doing a faithful thing   [E]8 Or coworkers for   [F]14 Lit mouth to mouth

---

1 **Dear friend** is literally "beloved." Because God has set his affection on believers, believers are to care deeply for one another (1Jn 4:11). Nothing certain is known about **Gaius**. The name was common in Roman times, and he was probably not one of the persons by that name mentioned elsewhere in the NT (Ac 19:29; 20:4; 1Co 1:14).

2 On **dear friend**, see note at verse 1. **Good health** is valued in every age, but in ancient times it was even more valued since medical care could be ineffective and life expectancy was low. Letters surviving from the period commonly contain this practical good wish, which John reinforced with the words **I pray**.

3 Joy is a feature of the opening of all John's letters (1Jn 1:4; 2Jn 4). John's concerns did not rob him of his delight in Christian faith.

4 On **joy**, see note at verse 3. **My children** may point to the fruit of John's patient and faithful pastoral labors. These may have been converts, or they may have been believers who were encouraged by his ministry. **Walking in the truth** means living in a way that honors and pleases God. It could even refer to living "in Christ" since He is "the truth" (Jn 14:6; 1Jn 5:20).

5 On **dear friend**, see note at verse 1. Faith is not merely mental but is demonstrated by how believers live. Jesus taught that His followers should be gracious to everyone, including **strangers**, and not just to their friends and relatives (Mt 5:43-48).

6 **Send them on their journey** includes physical and monetary provision, not just verbal good wishes. These laborers for the Lord deserved to be supported in a manner **worthy of God** because they were doing God's work (Mt 10:10).

7 **The Name** could refer either to God Himself or to Jesus. Jesus taught that to believe in Him is to believe in the One who sent Him (Jn 12:44). These workers relied on the Lord and His people, the church, not on **pagans**, or nonbelievers, for their support.

8 A privilege of Christian identity is to be **coworkers with the truth**—in sync with what God is doing as well as with fellow servants who are giving their all to do God's bidding.

9 **Wrote something** probably refers to a letter that has not been preserved, although some think it could refer to 1 John. There have always been struggles for power and status in the church (Mk 10:37). **Diotrephes** should have deferred to the authority of the apostle John.

10 The phrase **refuses to welcome the brothers** contrasts with those who did great things "for the brothers" in verse 5. Diotrephes must have been a person with some power in his congregation.

11 On **dear friend**, see note at verse 1. John did not want Gaius to be like Diotrephes (**do not imitate what is evil**). A person like Diotrephes might profess Christian faith, but the profession can be bogus (Mt 7:21-23).

12 Possibly **Demetrius** was supposed to deliver this epistle, so John assured Gaius of his character.

13 With the words **don't want to write**, John indicated that this epistle was a stopgap measure until he could pay a personal visit to his readers.

14 **Peace** harks back to the Hebrew word *shalom*, indicating God's living presence and blessing. **Greetings** and **greet . . . by name** are reminders that one of the great joys of the household of God is the fellowship of shared commitment to Jesus Christ.

Jude

The letter of Jude, one of the General Epistles, is very short. Until recently scholars neglected it more than any other New Testament book. Jude sought to protect Christian truth and strongly opposed heretics who threatened the faith. The letter's message is relevant to any age because believers should defend the gospel vigorously. Jude bears an obvious similarity in content with 2 Peter, a book that also deals firmly with false teachers who were infiltrating the church.

"These are the ones who are like dangerous reefs at your love feasts. They feast with you, nurturing only themselves without fear. They are waterless clouds carried along by winds; trees in late autumn—fruitless, twice dead, pulled out by the roots; wild waves of the sea, foaming up their shameful deeds; wandering stars for whom the blackness of darkness is reserved forever!" (Jd 12-13)

Circumstances of Writing

Author: Jude called himself "a slave of Jesus Christ and a brother of James" (v. 1). The James to whom Jude referred is not the son of Zebedee. He can be ruled out of consideration because he was martyred at an early date (Ac 12:1-2). The James to whom Jude refers is surely the well-known leader of the Jerusalem church (Ac 15:13-21; Gl 2:9). This is significant, for this James was the brother of Jesus (Mk 6:3). If Jude was a brother of James, then he was also a brother of Jesus. Rather than call himself Jesus' brother outright, Jude chose humbly to designate himself as Christ's slave.

Background: Jude wrote to those who are "the called, loved by God the Father and kept by Jesus Christ" (v. 1). This designation is general enough to apply to Christian believers anywhere. But Jude clearly had a specific group in mind because he called them "dear friends" (vv. 3,17,20) and addressed a situation that affected them. The readers were probably Jewish Christians because of Jude's several references to Hebrew history. Beyond this information we do not know exactly who the recipients of the letter were.

Jude is difficult to date precisely. If Jude the brother of Jesus was the author, the letter must be dated sometime within his lifetime. Any date for the letter's writing must also allow time for the false teachings to have developed. Jude may be dated reasonably somewhere between A.D. 65 to 80. Nothing in the letter points to a date of writing beyond this time. A date within Jude's lifetime rules out the viewpoint that the false teaching in question was second-century Gnosticism.

Message and Purpose

Jude had originally meant to write a letter on salvation to his friends. But he changed his plans when he learned of false teachers who had infiltrated the church (vv. 3-4). Because of their influence he instead urged his readers to contend for the faith (v. 3). Jude reminded his readers that they shared a common salvation and alerted them to the need for vigilance in contending for the faith. The reason the church must contend for the faith is that intruders were troubling the church.

2085–1406 B.C.	250 B.C.–A.D. 50
Destruction of Sodom and Gomorrah 2085?	Pseudepigraphal books of Enoch written 250 B.C.–A.D. 50
The Exodus 1446	*The Assumption of Moses* written 4 B.C.–A.D. 30
Korah's Rebellion 1420?	Jesus' birth Winter 5 B.C.
Balaam's error 1409?	Birth of Jude, half-brother of Jesus A.D. 5
Moses' death 1406	Jesus' trials, death, resurrection, and ascension Nisan 14-16 or April 3-5, A.D. 33

In verse 4, Jude introduced his readers to the opponents, pronounced judgment upon them, and outlined their vices. Verses 5-16 provide the evidence for what is said in verse 4. Three examples of God's judgment in the past are relayed in verses 5-7, and in verses 8-10 Jude stated that the opponents deserved judgment because of their lifestyle. In verse 11 the opponents are compared to three men who went astray in the past: Cain, Balaam, and Korah. Verses 12-13 clarify that the character of the opponents placed them in the same category as these infamous figures. Jude closed this section with the prophecy of Enoch, which promises judgment on the ungodly (vv. 14-15). Jude correlated the lives of the adversaries with those who would experience judgment (v. 16).

Contribution to the Bible

Jude is often overlooked because of its brevity. The book is also neglected because of unexpected features such as its quotation of 1 Enoch and its allusion to the *Assumption of Moses*. Some readers wonder how a canonical book could cite noninspired, nonbiblical writings. Furthermore, the message of Jude is alien to many in today's world because Jude emphasized that the Lord will judge evil intruders who are attempting to corrupt the church. The message of judgment strikes many people today as intolerant, unloving, and contrary to the message of love proclaimed elsewhere in the NT.

Nevertheless, some of the Bible's most beautiful statements about God's sustaining grace are found in Jude (vv. 1,24-25), and they shine with a greater brilliance when contrasted with the false teachers who had departed from the Christian faith.

The message of judgment is especially relevant to people today. Jude's letter reminds us that errant teaching and promiscuous living have dire consequences. Jude was written so believers would contend for the faith that was transmitted to them (v. 3) and so they would not abandon God's love at a crucial time in the life of the church.

A.D. 33-62

A.D. 62-180

Pentecost 33

Saul's conversion on the Damascus Road
October 34

James becomes leader of the church at
Jerusalem. 44

The letter of James written 48-52

James stoned to death. 62

The letter of Jude written 66

Jewish War 66-70

Destruction of Jerusalem 70

Jude's grandsons appear before Emperor
Domitian. 96

Muratorian Canon includes Jude as
Scripture. 180

Jude's connection with 2 Peter is debated. What one decides about this issue inevitably affects one's beliefs about the authorship and dating of each letter. They are strikingly similar in content. Thus, if 2 Peter used Jude and the latter book was written somewhere between A.D. 65 and 80, the apostle Peter could not have been the author of 2 Peter. But the use of 2 Peter by Jude poses no such problem, allowing 2 Peter to fit within Peter's lifetime. It seems best to conclude that Jude borrowed from 2 Peter or that both used a common source.

Structure

The epistle of Jude is a vigorous and pointed piece of writing. Scholars have often remarked that its Greek is quite good and that Jude used imagery effectively. The letter bears the marks of a careful and disciplined structure and was directed to specific circumstances in the life of the church. Jude was steeped in the OT and Jewish tradition, and he regularly applied OT types and texts to the false teachers who had invaded the church (vv. 8,12,16).

Pseudepigraphal writings are noncanonical books not written by their purported authors. Jude cited from the pseudepigraphal book of 1 Enoch (1:9) in Jude 14-15. He likely also referred to an event found in the *Assumption of Moses* (Jd 9). But this does not mean that Jude viewed these noncanonical books as authoritative Scripture. Under the inspiration of the Holy Spirit, he simply used them as illustrations.

Outline

I. Greeting and Purpose (vv. 1-4)

II. Description of the False Teachers (vv. 5-19)

III. Exhortation to Faithfulness (vv. 20-23)

IV. Doxology (vv. 24-25)

Greeting

Jude,[a] a •slave of Jesus Christ and a brother of James:

To those who are the called,[b] loved[A,c] by God the Father and kept by Jesus Christ.[d]

[2]May mercy, peace, and love be multiplied to you.[e]

Jude's Purpose in Writing

[3]Dear friends, although I was eager to write you about the salvation we share,[f] I found it necessary to write and exhort you to contend for the faith[g] that was delivered[h] to the •saints once for all. [4]For some men, who were designated for this judgment long ago,[i] have come in by stealth;[j] they are ungodly,[k] turning the grace of our God into promiscuity and denying[l] Jesus Christ, our only Master and Lord.

Apostates: Past and Present

[5]Now I want to remind you, though you know all these things: The Lord[B] first[C] saved

a people out of Egypt and later destroyed those who did not believe;[m] [6]and He has kept, with eternal chains in darkness for the judgment of the great day, the angels[n] who did not keep their own position but deserted their proper dwelling. [7]In the same way, Sodom and Gomorrah[o] and the cities around them committed sexual immorality and practiced perversions,[D] just as angels did, and serve as an example by undergoing the punishment of eternal fire.[p]

[8]Nevertheless, these dreamers likewise defile their flesh, reject authority, and blaspheme glorious ones.[q] [9]Yet Michael[r] the archangel,[s] when he was disputing with the Devil[t] in a debate about Moses'[u] body, did not dare bring an abusive condemnation against him but said, "The Lord rebuke you!" [10]But these people blaspheme anything they don't understand. What they know by instinct like unreasoning animals—they destroy themselves with these

Cross references

[a] 1 Mt 13:55; Mk 6:3
[b] Rm 1:7; 1Co 1:24
[c] 1Th 1:4; 2Th 2:13
[d] Jn 17:11, 15; 1Th 5:23; 1Pt 1:5
[e] 2Pt 1:2; 2Pt 1:2
[f] 3Ti 1:4
[g] 1Tm 6:12; 2Tm 4:7
[h] 2Pt 2:21
[i] 4 1Pt 2:8
[j] Gl 2:4; 2Tm 3:6
[k] Mk 7:22; Rm 5:6
[l] Ti 1:16; 2Pt 2:1; 1Jn 2:22
[m] 5 1Co 10:1-11
[n] 6 Gn 6:1-4; 2Pt 2:4
[o] 7 2Pt 2:6
[p] 2Th 1:8
[q] 8 2Pt 2:10
[r] 9 Dn 10:13,21; 12:1; Rv 12:7
[s] Lk 1:19; 1Th 4:16
[t] Mt 4:1,10; Ac 13:10
[u] Ps 77:20; Mt 8:4; Heb 3:2

A 1 Other mss read *sanctified*   **B** 5 Other mss read *Jesus/Joshua*, *God*, or *God Christ*   **C** 5 Other mss place *first* after *remind you*
D 7 Lit *and went after other flesh*

---

1 Jude called himself **a slave of Jesus Christ and a brother of James**. The James named here was surely the well-known leader of the Jerusalem church (Ac 15:13-21; Gl 2:9; see Introduction). This James was the brother of Jesus (Mk 6:3). Jude humbly designated himself as Christ's slave rather than mention that he was related to Jesus. The **called** are those who respond in faith to God's initiative in salvation. **Loved by God the Father** is a result of being called. The expression **kept by Jesus Christ** means that believers are kept safe or preserved by Jesus until their salvation is consummated at His return.

2 **Mercy** is God's kindness and compassion toward His people. **Peace** is the well-being that results from this relationship. **Love** is (Gk) *agape*, a godly volitional love which has the best interests of other persons in mind whether or not they love in return. The word may refer to God's love for man and to man's love for God and other people.

despotes

Greek Pronunciation	[dehs PAH tays]
HCSB Translation	Master
Uses in Jude	1
Uses in the NT	10
Focus passage	Jude 4

Despotes (*Master*) refers to one who holds authority and power over the life and affairs of another person. Most frequently, *despotes* appears as a title for God or Christ. The term emphasizes God's sovereignty, variously highlighting His right to create, judge, or save. Three times the saints use *despotes* when prayerfully entreating their Sovereign (Lk 2:29; Ac 4:24; Rv 6:10). Paul emphasizes God's sovereign right as *Master* to use His people as He chooses (2Tm 2:21). Likewise, Christ is Sovereign and Lord over salvation, worthy of the saints' obedience (Jd 4), and He is the *Master* who purchased men with His own blood (2Pt 2:1). Elsewhere, *despotes* may refer to an earthly *master* with a slave in the service of his household. In Christian ethic, slaves are exhorted to respect their *masters* (1Tm 6:1-2) and to submit to them in everything (Ti 2:9; 1Pt 2:18).

3-4 Jude originally meant to write a letter about salvation to his friends, but he changed his plans when he learned about false teachers who had secretly made their way into the church. Because of the influence of false teachers he urged his readers to **contend for the faith** entrusted to them **once for all**. Contending for the faith is not just a vigorous defense of the Christian faith but an advancement of the gospel as well. These actions must be accompanied by an obedient lifestyle (cp. vv. 20-23). The **faith . . . delivered** once for all refers to the Christian revelation, or the body of fixed, authoritative, orthodox apostolic teaching that has been handed down to believers.

5-7 Jude pointed out that the false teachers deserved divine judgment and would receive it in the future. He wanted to **remind** his readers that God had acted decisively in the past against those who opposed Him. He mentioned three examples of God's judgment: (1) the judgment of unbelieving Israel in the wilderness after being delivered **out of Egypt** (Nm 32:10-12); (2) the **angels** who fell (cp. 1 Enoch 6:19); and (3) the destruction of **Sodom and Gomorrah** for **sexual immorality** (Gn 19:24-29).

8 The false teachers' sins were like those mentioned in verses 5-7. They pursued empty dreams and arrogantly committed sexual immorality, rebelled against authority, and blasphemed **glorious ones** (Gk *doxas*). The latter term frequently refers to angels.

9 Jude contrasted the heretics' blasphemy of angels with the restraint that **Michael the archangel** showed when **disputing with the Devil in a debate about Moses' body**. Scholars generally agree that this story was taken from the *Assumption of Moses*, an apocryphal book. In the story, Michael sought to bury Moses' body. The Devil opposed the burial with the claim that he was lord over matter and Moses was a murderer. Rather than assuming the right to condemn Satan for his slander, Michael called on the **Lord** to judge.

10 Jude described the false teachers as slandering what they did not understand. He compared them to **unreasoning**

things. ¹¹Woe to them! For they have traveled in the way of Cain,^a have abandoned themselves to the error of Balaam^b for profit, and have perished in Korah's rebellion.^c

The Apostates' Doom

¹²These are the ones who are like dangerous reefs^A at your love feasts.^d They feast with you, nurturing only themselves without fear. They are waterless clouds carried along by winds;^e trees in late autumn—fruitless, twice dead, pulled out by the roots; ¹³wild waves of the sea, foaming up their shameful deeds; wandering stars^f for whom the blackness of darkness^g is reserved forever!^h

¹⁴And Enoch,ⁱ in the seventh generation from Adam, prophesied about them:

> Look! The Lord comes^B
> with thousands of His holy ones^j
> ¹⁵ to execute judgment on all
> and to convict them^C
> of all their ungodly^k acts
> that they have done in an ungodly way,
> and of all the harsh things
>   ungodly sinners
> have said against Him.

¹⁶These people are discontented grumblers,

'walking according to their desires;^l their mouths utter arrogant words, flattering^m people for their own advantage.

¹⁷But you, dear friends, remember what was predicted by the apostles of our Lord Jesus Christ; ¹⁸they told you, "In the end timeⁿ there will be scoffers^o walking according to their own ungodly desires." ¹⁹These people create divisions and are unbelievers,^{D,p} not having the Spirit.

Exhortation and Benediction

²⁰But you, dear friends, as you build yourselves up in your most holy faith and pray in the Holy Spirit,^{q 21} keep yourselves in the love of God,^r expecting the mercy of our Lord Jesus Christ for eternal life. ²²Have mercy on those who doubt; ²³save others by snatching them from the fire;^s have mercy on others but with fear,^t hating^u even the garment^v defiled by the flesh.

²⁴Now to Him^w who is able to protect you from stumbling^x and to make you stand in the presence of His glory, blameless^y and with great joy, ²⁵to the only^z God our Savior, through Jesus Christ our Lord,^E be glory, majesty, power, and authority before all time,^F now and forever. 'Amen.

^a11 Gn 4:1-17,24-25; Heb 11:4; 1Jn 3:12
^bNm 22:5; 2Pt 2:15
^cNm 16:1
^d12 1Co 11:17-22; 2Pt 2:13
^ePr 25:14
^f13 Is 14:12-15; Rv 1:16; 8:10; 9:1
^gMt 6:23; Jd 6
^h2Pt 2:17
ⁱ14 Gn 5:18
^jDt 33:2; Dn 7:10; Mk 8:38; 1Th 3:13; 2Th 1:7; Heb 12:22
^k15 2Pt 2:5-6
^l16 2Pt 2:10
^mLv 19:15; Dt 10:17; 2Ch 19:7; Pr 28:21
ⁿ18 1Tm 4:1; 2Tm 3:1; 1Pt 1:5,20
^o2Pt 3:3
^p19 Rm 8:9; Php 3:3
^q20 Rm 8:15-16,26-27; Eph 6:18
^r21 Jn 15:9-10; 1Jn 4:16
^s23 1Co 3:15; 2Th 1:8
^tRv 11:11
^uPr 6:16-19
^vZch 3:3-4
^w24 Rm 16:25; Eph 3:20
^xJn 17:12
^yEph 1:4; 5:27; Php 2:15; Col 1:22   ^z25 Jn 5:44; Rm 16:27

---

^A12 Or *like spots*   ^B14 Or *came*   ^C15 Lit *convict all*   ^D19 Or *natural*   ^E25 Other mss omit *through Jesus Christ our Lord*
^F25 Other mss omit *before all time*

---

animals that would **destroy themselves** by the things they instinctively pursued.

11 Jude also compared the heretics to **Cain** (Gn 4:4-5,8-9), **Balaam** (Nm 31:16), and **Korah** (Nm 16:1-35). These men deceived others and were known for their hatred, greed, and rebellion.

12-13 To demonstrate further that the false teachers were like those mentioned earlier (v. 11), Jude portrayed them with several metaphors. He described them as **dangerous reefs at your love feasts**. This means the false teachers were like submerged rocks, unseen by sailors, that could wreck a ship. Love feasts were fellowship meals at which the Lord's Supper was observed. These heretics were shepherds who fed **only themselves** without any concern for others. They were useless and full of empty promises like **waterless clouds carried along by winds**. Jude portrayed them as barren fruit trees and **wild waves of the sea** that deposited their refuse of shameful deeds on the shore of people's lives. The heretics were also like **wandering stars** for whom the **blackness of darkness** was reserved forever. Some scholars hold that Jude was influenced here by 1 Enoch 18:13-16. In this text the rebellion of heavenly beings caused the planets to wander. Or, Jude was possibly thinking of the angels who fell earlier (Jd 6). Angels falling from heaven were sometimes pictured as falling stars (cp. Is 14:12-15; Rv 9:1). Like disobedient angels destined for eternal punishment, heretics are heading for eternal darkness.

14-15 Jude emphasized that the heretics would suffer divine retribution. He pictured this judgment by quoting a proph-

ecy from 1 Enoch 1:9. Their punishment would take place when **the Lord** returns to judge the wicked.

16 In the previous verse, Jude warned that the heretics would be judged for their deeds and words. In this verse he focused more on their words. The false teachers were self-indulgent, **discontented** complainers. They uttered **arrogant words**, flattering people in order to take what they wanted from them.

17-19 Jude urged his readers to **remember** that these false teachers were nothing new because the apostles had foretold of such people who scoffed at those who refused to follow them. Jude may have referred to warnings like those in Ac 20:29-30 and 1Tm 4:1-3. The heretics created **divisions** and followed their **ungodly desires**. As people who were **unbelievers**, they did not have **the Spirit**.

20-23 After primarily describing the false teachers up to this point, Jude now exhorted his readers on how to contend for the faith (cp. v. 3). They were to show **mercy** to those who were wavering, reach out to those who had already been taken in and needed to be snatched from **the fire** (cp. Am 4:11; Zch 3:2), and show concern for the wayward heretics, all at the same time. But believers were to be careful lest they also became defiled.

24-25 Jude ended his letter with a doxology that served as a reminder of the divine power available to believers as they contend against heretics. He praised God because He was **able to protect** them from falling into the sinful practices of the false teachers and grant them entrance into His glorious presence.

Revelation

Introduction

The resurrected, glorified Son of Man (Jesus Christ) revealed Himself to the apostle John, who had been imprisoned "on the island called Patmos" (1:9). Christ's twofold purpose was (1) to "unveil" a spiritual diagnosis for seven of the churches in Asia Minor with which John was familiar (chaps. 2–3), and (2) to reveal to John a series of visions setting forth events and factors related to the end times (chaps. 4–22).

Sunrise on Patmos, the small island in the Aegean Sea where John received the Revelation from the risen Christ. The early church historian Eusebius (A.D. 260–340) wrote that John was sent to Patmos by Emperor Domitian in A.D. 95 and released after one and a half years.

Circumstances of Writing

Author: The traditional view holds that the author of Revelation is the apostle John, who wrote the Fourth Gospel and the three letters of John. Evidences for this view include: (1) the writer referred to himself as "John" (1:4,9; 22:8); (2) he had personal relationships with the seven churches of Asia Minor (1:4,11; chaps. 2–3); (3) his circumstances at the time of writing (1:9) matched those of John the apostle (who was placed in Asia Minor from about A.D. 70 to 100 by reliable historical sources from the second century A.D.); and (4) the saturation of the book with OT imagery and echoes implies a Jewish writer, like John, operating in overwhelmingly Gentile Asia Minor.

Background: The initial audience that received the book of Revelation was a group of seven local churches in southwest Asia Minor (1:11; chaps. 2–3). Some of these congregations were experiencing persecution (2:9-10,13), probably under the Roman emperor Domitian (ruled A.D. 81–96). Others had doctrinal and practical problems (2:6,13-15,20-23). Also behind these surface problems was the backdrop of unseen but powerful spiritual warfare (2:10,14,24; 3:9).

Though some scholars have dated the book later and a few have dated it earlier, commonly held dates of Revelation among evangelical scholars are the mid-90s and the late 60s of the first century A.D. The mid-90s view is the stronger view, and it is held by majority opinion. Each view gives a different account of the persecution portrayed in the letters to the churches (2:9-10,13). Substantial historical evidence shows that some of the churches were persecuted intensely by Nero in the late 60s. But the reference in 17:10 to seven kings, five of whom have fallen, supports a date in the mid-90s, during the reign of Domitian.

While a case can be made for a late-60s date based on the Nero-related inferences and a possible reference to the Jerusalem temple in 11:1-2 (which may imply that the temple had not yet been destroyed, as it was by the Romans in A.D. 70), all other factors favor a date of about A.D. 95. Most notable among these factors is the tradi-

---

Prehistory   2166–586 B.C.

Creation   Abraham 2166–1991

The Fall   Moses 1526–1406

Noah   David 1050?–970

Tower of Babylon   Divided Kingdom 931

                                  Israel defeated and taken into exile by
                                    the Assyrians 722

                                  Judah destroyed and taken into exile by
                                    the Babylonians 586

tion that John the apostle was exiled to Patmos during a period of intensifying local persecution of Christians by the Emperor Domitian (ruled A.D. 81–96).

Message and Purpose

Much of the book of Revelation focuses on events at the end of the age (eschatology), more so than any other book in the Bible. But it also focuses on practical choices that believers and unbelievers must make in the course of their lives that have far-reaching consequences at the end.

Contribution to the Bible

The book of Revelation provides an almost complete overview of theology. There is much in this book about Christ, mankind and sin, the people of God (both the church and Israel), holy angels, and Satan and the demons. There is important material on God's power and tri-unity (i.e., Trinity), plus aspects of the work of the Holy Spirit and the nature of Scripture.

Structure

The book of Revelation previews its sequential structure in 1:19: "Therefore write what you have seen, what is, and what will take place after this." From the apostle John's vantage point in being commanded to "write," he had already seen the vision of the exalted Son of Man (chap. 1). Next, he was told to "write" letters to the seven churches, telling each the state of their spiritual health (chaps. 2–3). Lastly comes the body of the book (4:1–22:5), which covers all the events that would "take place after this."

Outline

I. Introduction: "What You Have Seen" (1:1-20)
   A. Prologue (1:1-3)
   B. Salutation and doxology (1:4-8)
   C. The Son of Man and the churches (1:9-20)

539–5 B.C.   A.D. 33–100

Persian hegemony 539–331

Exiles return to Jerusalem 538

Greek hegemony 331–63

Roman hegemony 63 B.C.–A.D. 476

Jesus' birth 5 B.C.

Jesus' trials, death, resurrection, and
   ascension Nisan 14-16 or April 3-5, 33

Pentecost 33

Saul's conversion on the Damascus Road
   October 34

Fall of Jerusalem to the Romans 70

John is spiritual leader of the church at
   Ephesus. 70–100

II. Letters to the Churches of Asia: "What Is" (2:1–3:22)
    A. The church in Ephesus (2:1-7)
    B. The church in Smyrna (2:8-11)
    C. The church in Pergamum (2:12-17)
    D. The church in Thyatira (2:18-29)
    E. The church in Sardis (3:1-6)
    F. The church in Philadelphia (3:7-13)
    G. The church in Laodicea (3:14-22)

III. Visions of the End Times: "What Will Take Place After This" (4:1–22:5)
    A. The heavenly throne room (4:1–5:14)
    B. The opening of the seven seals (6:1–8:1)
    C. The sounding of the seven trumpets (8:2–11:19)
    D. The signs before God's final wrath (12:1–14:20)
    E. The seven bowls of God's wrath (15:1–19:5)
    F. The reign of the King of kings (19:6–20:15)
    G. The new Jerusalem (21:1–22:5)

IV. Conclusion (22:6-21)
    A. The command not to seal the scroll (22:6-13)
    B. Washing robes and the water of life (22:14-17)
    C. Warning about adding to the prophecy (22:18-19)
    D. Closing assurance and benediction (22:20-21)

Prologue

1 The revelation of[A] Jesus Christ that God gave Him to show His •slaves[a] what must quickly[B] take place.[b] He sent it and signified it[C] through His angel[c] to His slave John,[d] [2] who testified to God's word and to the testimony[D] about Jesus Christ,[e] in all he saw.[E] [3] The one who reads this is blessed,[f] and those who hear the words of this prophecy and keep[F] what is written in it are blessed, because the time is near!

[4] John:

To the seven churches in •Asia.

Grace and peace[g] to you from[G] the One who is, who was, and who is coming;[h] from the seven spirits[H,i] before His throne; [5] and from Jesus Christ, the faithful witness, the first-born from the dead and the ruler of the kings of the earth.

To Him who loves us and has set us free[I] from our sins by His blood, [6] and made us a kingdom,[J] priests[K,j] to His God and Father—the glory and dominion are His forever and ever. •Amen.

[7]   **Look! He is coming with the clouds,[k]
        and every eye will see Him,
        including those who pierced[L] Him.
        And all the families of the earth[M,N,l]
        will mourn over Him.[O,P,m]**
        This is certain. Amen.

[8] "I am the •Alpha and the Omega,"[n] says the

---

[a]1:1 Ac 2:18; Rm 6:19; 1Pt 2:16; Rv 22:6
[b]Dn 2:28-29,45; Rv 22:6
[c]Gn 2:28 word; Mt 1:24; Ac 12:11
[d]Jn 21:7; Rv 22:8
[e]1:2 1Co 1:6; Rv 12:17; 19:10; 20:4
[f]1:3 Rv 14:13; 16:15; 19:9; 20:6; 22:7,14
[g]1:4 Ti 1:4
[h]Rv 1:8,17; 4:8; 16:5
[i]Rv 3:1; 4:5; 5:6
[j]1:6 Ex 19:6
[k]1:7 Is 19:1; Zch 12:10; Jn 19:34-37
[l]Gn 12:3; 28:14; Zch 14:17
[m]1:7 Dn 7:13; Zch 12:10
[n]1:8 Is 44:6; Rv 21:6; 22:13

[A]1:1 Or Revelation of, or A revelation of   [B]1:1 Or soon   [C]1:1 Made it known through symbols   [D]1:2 Or witness   [E]1:2 Lit as many as he saw   [F]1:3 Or follow, or obey   [G]1:4 Other mss add God   [H]1:4 Or the sevenfold Spirit   [I]1:5 Other mss read has washed us   [J]1:6 Other mss read kings and   [K]1:6 Or made us into (or to be) a kingdom of priests; Ex 19:6   [L]1:7 Or impaled   [M]1:7 Or all the tribes of the land   [N]1:7 Gn 12:3; 28:14; Zch 14:17   [O]1:7 Or will wail because of Him   [P]1:7 Dn 7:13; Zch 12:10

1:1 Revelation, which means "unveiling," translates the Greek word *apokalypsis*. Its use here indicates that the book of Revelation is apocalyptic literature, like Daniel in the OT. The revelation of **Jesus Christ** could mean the unveiling *about* Jesus, the unveiling *by* Him, or both. **His slaves** refers to all Christians.

1:2 Standing true to **God's word and to the testimony about Jesus Christ** caused John to be exiled to the island of Patmos (v. 9). Christians have been persecuted throughout church history for their fidelity to Christ. Only by failing to stand do we escape persecution.

1:1,3 Must quickly take place and **the time is near** have been used by critics to claim that Revelation's prophecies have failed since they have not been fulfilled in the 1,900+ years since the book was written. However, Christ's imminent return does not carry with it a timetable but communicates a sense of urgency that is an integral part of the NT message as expressed by John the Baptist, Jesus, and the apostles. Christ's first coming marked the time when history entered its last phase before eternity. Paul expressed the urgency this entails: "Look, now is the acceptable time; now is the day of salvation" (2Co 6:2).

1:3 The reading of this prophecy carries with it a promise of blessing. The reading in view is not just mental. The reader must also **keep** (i.e., "take to heart" and apply) **what is written**. This is the first of seven significant "blessing" statements or beatitudes in the book of Revelation (14:13; 16:15; 19:9; 20:6; 22:7,14). *Seven*, the number of perfection, will recur throughout this book.

1:4 The naming of the author and audience, plus a characteristic greeting (**grace and peace**), indicate that Revelation has similar form as other letters of the NT. It is not some exotic, otherworldly work that cannot readily be understood. **The One who is, who was, and who is coming** (v. 8) means that God not only exists now, but always has existed and always will. The **seven spirits before His throne** may refer to: (1) "the angels of the seven churches" (v. 20; chaps. 2–3), (2) other angels seen in the book (e.g., 8:2), or (3) the fullness of the Holy Spirit described in Is 11:2.

1:5-6 Jesus is **the faithful witness** (*martus*, the Gk word from which we get *martyr*). The **firstborn from the dead**

looks back to His resurrection, the guarantee of the future resurrection of all believers and unbelievers (20:4-5; 1Co 15:20,23). Though Christ has all the authority to be universal **ruler** now (Mt 28:18), He will not fully exert it until His second coming (Rv 19:11-21). **Set us free from our sins by His blood** does not mean we are automatically saved by Christ's death on the cross, as if all humanity is saved regardless of their beliefs. Revelation stresses the need for repentance (9:20-21) and a faith-response to the gospel (14:6-7). The wording here may mean that believers are already a **kingdom** and **priests** in this lifetime (1Pt 2:9).

1:7 This collage of Scripture from Dn 7:13 and Zch 12:10 expresses the theme for Revelation. The reference to **mourn** is sometimes understood as the response of those for whom it is too late to be saved. But the context of Zch 12:10 indicates the mourning will be true saving repentance, even for **those who pierced Him** (i.e., the Jews; see notes at Rv 7:4-8 and 11:13).

1:8 Alpha and **Omega** are the first and last letters of the

---

pantokrator

Greek Pronunciation	[pahn tah KRAH tohr]
HCSB Translation	Almighty
Uses in Revelation	9
Uses in the NT	10
Focus passage	Revelation 1:8

Pantokrator means *almighty, omnipotent, all-powerful*. In the Greek OT, the word frequently translates the Hb *Yahweh tseva'ot* (Lord of Hosts), which stresses God's power over forces opposed to Him and His people. *Pantokrator* also translates Hb *Shaddai* (the Almighty), a term emphasizing God's power and authority over all things. In every instance in the OT, the one true God is in view.

In the NT, every occurrence of *pantokrator* refers to God the Father. In the book of Revelation, it occurs with the expressions *Lord God* (1:8; 4:8; 11:17; 15:3; 16:7; 19:6; 21:22), *God* (16:14; 19:15), and variations of the phrase "the One who is, who was, and who is coming" (1:8; 4:8; 11:17). John uses these epithets (along with many others) to describe the supremacy of God over all things including human history. God *Almighty* is actively working to bring everything into conformity with His will.

Lord God, "the One who is, who was, and who is coming, the Almighty."

John's Vision of the Risen Lord

[9]I, John, your brother and partner in the tribulation, kingdom, and endurance that are in Jesus, was on the island called Patmos because of God's word and the testimony about Jesus.[A,a] [10]I was in the Spirit[B,C,b] on the Lord's day,[D] and I heard a loud voice behind me like a trumpet [11]saying, "Write on a scroll[E] what you see and send it to the seven churches: Ephesus, Smyrna, Pergamum, Thyatira, Sardis, Philadelphia, and Laodicea."

[12]I turned to see whose voice[c] it was that spoke to me. When I turned I saw seven gold lampstands, [13]and among the lampstands was One like the *Son of Man,[F,d] dressed in a long robe and with a gold sash wrapped around His chest. [14]His head and hair were white like wool—white as snow—and His eyes like a fiery flame. [15]His feet were like fine bronze as it is fired in a furnace, and His voice like the sound of cascading[G] waters.[e] [16]He had seven stars in His right hand; a sharp double-edged sword came from His mouth,[f] and His face was shining like the sun at midday.[H]

[17]When I saw Him, I fell at His feet like a dead man. He laid His right hand on me and said, "Don't be afraid! I am the First and the Last,[g] [18]and the Living One. I was dead, but look—I am alive forever and ever, and I hold the keys of death and *Hades. [19]Therefore write what you have seen, what is, and what will take place after this. [20]The *secret of the seven stars you saw in My right hand and of the seven gold lampstands is this: The seven stars are the angels[i] of the seven churches, and the seven lampstands[j] are the seven churches.

*a*1:9 Rv 1:2; 6:9; 12:17; 19:10; 20:4
*b*1:10 Rv 4:2; 17:3; 21:10
*c*1:12 Ex 20:18
*d*1:13 Dn 7:13
*e*1:15 Ezk 1:24; 43:2; Rv 14:2; 19:6
*f*1:16 Is 49:2; Heb 4:12; Rv 2:12,16; 19:15
*g*1:17 Is 41:4; 44:6; 48:12; Rv 2:8; 22:13

A1:9 Lit the witness of Jesus   B1:10 Or in spirit; lit I became in the Spirit   C1:10 John was brought by God's Spirit into a realm of spiritual vision.   D1:10 Sunday   E1:11 Or book   F1:13 Or like a son of man   G1:15 Lit many   H1:16 Lit like the sun shines in its power   I1:20 Or messengers   J1:20 Other mss add that you saw

---

Greek alphabet, emphasizing that God is the beginning and the end. On **the One who is . . . and who is coming,** see note at verse 4.

1:9 Tradition indicates the apostle **John** was exiled by the Roman emperor Domitian to a penal colony on the **island called Patmos**, about 40 miles southwest of Ephesus in the Aegean Sea, in about A.D. 95. He was released sometime after Domitian's death in 96. John emphasized being a **partner** in **tribulation** (i.e., "suffering, distress"; see 2:9). This is not a reference to the unparalleled time of difficulty just before the second coming of Christ.

1:10 In the Spirit refers to the exalted spiritual state that John was in as he received the visions of the Apocalypse. **The Lord's day** is likely a phrase referring to the first day of the week—Sunday, the day of resurrection—which had become the day of worship for Christians (Ac 20:7; 1Co 16:2).

1:11 Some interpreters believe that Revelation was written as a "book" (i.e., in a codex format), but it is much more likely that the Greek word here (biblion) should be translated **scroll.** The **seven** local **churches** (see note at 2:1–3:22) addressed in Revelation were chosen from among all the churches in Asia Minor to serve as examples of the kinds of realities playing out in church life. These seven were obvious choices since they were located on the roads of a circular postal route, giving them prominence due to their ease of access.

1:12 The **seven gold lampstands** are the seven churches (v. 11; chaps. 2–3).

1:13-18 John had seen Jesus Christ in a similar glorified state on the Mount of Transfiguration (Mt 17:2). He had also seen His resurrection body after He was raised (Jn 20; Ac 1:2-11). John was also acquainted with the rich OT images of the glorified Son of Man (see Dn 7:13) that this vision on Patmos recalled.

1:14 The similes of the Son of Man's head and hair being **white like wool,** depicting wisdom and purity, and His eyes being **like a fiery flame,** picturing piercing holiness, fuse the vision of the Ancient of Days (Dn 7:9) and Jesus' appearance on the Mount of Transfiguration (Mt 17:2).

1:15 Unlike the **feet** of the statue in Dn 2:33-35, which crumbled, the description **like fine bronze . . . fired in a furnace** speaks of strength and stability. A **voice like the sound of cascading waters** would have riveted John's attention as he was imprisoned on an island where powerful waves crashed ashore.

1:16 The **seven stars** are the angels of the seven churches (v. 20). The **sharp double-edged sword** that **came from His mouth** symbolizes the power of the Word of God to judge (Heb 4:12). The Son of Man's **face . . . shining like the sun** was another reminder to John of what he saw with his own eyes on the Mount of Transfiguration (Mt 17:2).

1:17 That John **fell at His feet** was an act of fear and awe at the Lord revealing Himself so profoundly to mankind (Dn 8:17). John's reaction shows he experienced the glory of Christ more fully here than on the Mount of Transfiguration or in His post-resurrection appearances.

1:18 Christ's authority over **the keys of death and Hades** was stated in His declaration that He would found the church (Mt 16:18). This will be exercised when death and Hades are emptied and then destroyed at the great white throne judgment (Rv 20:11-15).

1:19 The risen Christ here commanded John to **write,** just as in verse 11. **What you have seen** is the vision of verses 12-18. **What is** refers to the present state of affairs in the churches in chapters 2–3. **What will take place after this** refers to the body of the book (chaps. 4–22), which begins with "after this" (4:1).

1:20 The Greek word translated **secret** is musterion, which speaks of something formerly unknown which has now been revealed. The overwhelming usage of the Greek word aggeloi in the book of Revelation is in reference to spirit beings and not human messengers (v. 1; 5:2). Perhaps the **angels of the seven churches** spoken of here functioned like so-called guardian angels for members of those churches (Heb 1:14).

The Letters to the Seven Churches

The Letter to Ephesus

2 "Write to the angel[A] of the church in Ephesus:

"The One who holds the seven stars in His right hand and who walks among the seven gold lampstands says: [2]I know your works, your labor, and your endurance, and that you cannot tolerate evil. You have tested those who call themselves apostles and are not, and

---

[A]**2:1** Or *messenger* here and elsewhere

2:1–3:22 It is likely that these seven churches were chosen to receive letters because of the lessons they provided for "all the churches" (2:23), not because they represent seven stages in church history as is held by some interpreters. Yet in any one historical period, it could be that the majority of churches reflect realities found in one of the seven churches. In general, each letter includes: (1) a *characteristic* of the risen Christ drawn from the vision in 1:12-18, (2) *commendation* of the church (though not the churches at Sardis and Laodicea), (3) *criticism* of the church's shortcomings (though not of the churches at Smyrna and Philadelphia) and how to correct them, (4) a *command* to "listen to what the Spirit says to the churches," and (5) a *commitment* to the persevering spiritual "victor" (Gk *nikao*; "to win, conquer").

2:1 On **the angel of the church**, see note at 1:20. **Ephesus** was one of the largest and most powerful cities in the Roman Empire. It was devoted to the worship of Artemis (Lat *Diana*; Ac 19:28), the fertility goddess, and the emperor of Rome, who was considered a god. The church at Ephesus was apparently planted by Priscilla and Aquila around A.D. 52. Paul ministered there for two or three years (Ac 20:31), and used the city as a home base for the evangelization of the region (Ac 19:8-10). This is almost certainly how the other six churches in Revelation 2–3 were planted. On the **seven stars** and the **seven gold lampstands**, see 1:20.

2:2-4 The church at Ephesus **abandoned the love** they **had at first**, meaning their love for God. The greatest

The Seven Churches of the Revelation

you have found them to be liars. ³You also possess endurance and have tolerated many things because of My name and have not grown weary. ⁴But I have this against you: You have abandoned the love you had at first. ⁵Remember then how far you have fallen; repent, and do the works you did at first. Otherwise, I will come to you[A] and remove your lampstand from its place—unless you repent. ⁶Yet you do have this: You hate the practices of the Nicolaitans, which I also hate.

⁷"Anyone who has an ear should listen to what the Spirit says to the churches. I will give the victor[a] the right to eat from the tree of life, which is in[B] God's paradise.[b]

The Letter to Smyrna

⁸"Write to the angel of the church in Smyrna:

"The First and the Last, the One who was dead and came to life, says: ⁹I know your[C] af-

fliction and poverty, yet you are rich. I know the slander of those who say they are Jews and are not, but are a *synagogue of Satan. ¹⁰Don't be afraid of what you are about to suffer. Look, the Devil is about to throw some of you into prison to test you, and you will have affliction for 10 days. Be faithful until death, and I will give you the crown[D] of life.

¹¹"Anyone who has an ear should listen to what the Spirit says to the churches. The victor will never be harmed by the second death.[c]

The Letter to Pergamum

¹²"Write to the angel of the church in Pergamum:

"The One who has the sharp, double-edged sword[d] says: ¹³I know[E] where you live—where Satan's throne is! And you are holding on to My name and did not deny your faith in Me,[F] even in the days of Antipas, My faithful wit-

ᵃ2:7 1Jn 5:4-5
ᵇGn 2:8-9; Lk 23:43; 2Co 12:4; Rv 22:2,14,19
ᶜ2:11 Rv 20:6,14; 21:8
ᵈ2:12 Is 49:2; Heb 4:12; Rv 1:16; 2:16; 19:15

A2:5 Other mss add *quickly*   B2:7 Other mss read *in the midst of*   C2:9 Other mss add *works and*   D2:10 Or *wreath*   E2:13 Other mss add *your works and*   F2:13 Or *deny My faith*

---

commandment is to love the Lord with all one's being (Dt 6:5; Mt 22:36-38).

2:5 Having **fallen** does not mean losing your salvation, though ceasing to love God is a serious spiritual matter requiring soul-searching repentance (i.e., a change of mind and heart, implying a related change of behavior). If they did not **repent**, Christ would cause the church to close (**remove your lampstand**).

2:6 The **practices of the Nicolaitans** are explained in the letter to the church at Pergamum (vv. 14-15). Their "practices" bore resemblance to the problem in the church at Thyatira (vv. 20-21,24).

2:7 Anyone who has an ear should listen echoes Jesus' warning to His hearers at the end of the parable of the sower (Mt 13:9). Most likely **victor** refers to faithful and obedient believers. In this context, failure to be a victor means losing

nikao

Greek Pronunciation	[nih KAH oh]
HCSB Translation	be victorious, conquer
Uses in Revelation	17
Uses in the NT	28
Focus passage	Revelation 2:7

Nikao means *to be victorious* or *to conquer*, and the related noun *nike* means *victory*, usually in a military sense but also in a judicial context (Rm 3:4). Outside of John's writings, *nikao* occurs only four times (Lk 11:22; Rm 3:4; 12:21). In John's theology, Christ has already *conquered* the forces of evil (Jn 16:33; Rv 5:5). Even though these forces may gain temporary, provisional *victories* over the saints (Rv 11:7; 13:7), it is Christ who has won the definitive *victory* over evil, and those whom He has enlisted in the fight will *conquer* with Him (3:21; 15:2; 17:14). Each of the messages to the Asia Minor churches ends with a promise to *the victor* (2:7,11,17,26-27; 3:5,12,21), to those who overcome evil not through human effort but through solidarity with Christ (Jn 5:4-5; 1Jn 4:4; 5:5; Rv 12:11). These *victors* will inherit the new heaven and new earth (21:7).

spiritual rewards, not losing salvation. Adam and Eve were driven out of the garden of Eden so they could not **eat** from **the tree of life** (Gn 3:22-24) and thereby live there forever in sin. The tree of life in view here will be in the new heavens and earth (Rv 22:2), which is what is meant by **God's paradise**.

2:8 On **the angel of the church**, see note at 1:20. Like Ephesus, **Smyrna**, 35 miles to the north, was a harbor city. Its large Jewish population bitterly opposed Christianity. When Domitian issued an edict declaring emperor worship mandatory for all inhabitants of the Roman Empire, he exempted the Jews from this requirement. The Jews did not want this religious freedom extended to Christians. The **church in Smyrna** was likely founded during Paul's third missionary journey (Ac 19). On **the First and the Last** and **the One who was dead and came to life**, see notes at 1:5-6 and 1:8.

2:9-10 The church at Smyrna, against whom Christ voiced no criticism, was suffering through spiritual warfare. A local **synagogue** of Jews was engaged in **slander** that resulted in church members being jailed for a short time (**10 days**). All of this represented a **test** of their faith. The phrase **those who say they are Jews and are not** does not deny the Jewish bloodlines of the persecutors. Rather, it mirrors Paul's assertion that, ultimately, Jewishness is not just outward but inward, related to the "circumcision is of the heart" by faith (Rm 2:28-29). The **crown of life** is also referred to in Jms 1:12, where it is received by those who love the Lord and endure trials, probably at "the judgment seat of Christ" (2Co 5:10).

2:11 On **anyone who has an ear**, see note at verse 7. The **second death** is the lake of fire (20:14), the place of eternal torment for the Devil, the beast, the false prophet (20:10), and all the non-elect (20:15). On the meaning of **victor**, see note at 2:7.

2:12-13 On the **angel of the church**, see note at 1:20. In the first century A.D., the city of **Pergamum**, 50 miles north of Smyrna, was the leading religious center of Asia Minor. Like Smyrna, Pergamum was a center of emperor worship, and Christians were persecuted harshly for their refusal to

ness who was killed among you, where Satan lives. [14]But I have a few things against you. You have some there who hold to the teaching of Balaam, who taught Balak to place a stumbling block[A] in front of the Israelites: to eat meat sacrificed to idols and to commit sexual immorality.[B] [15]In the same way, you also have those who hold to the teaching of the Nicolaitans.[C] [16]Therefore repent! Otherwise, I will come to you quickly and fight against them with the sword of My mouth.

[17]"Anyone who has an ear should listen to what the Spirit says to the churches. I will give the victor some of the hidden manna.[D,a] I will also give him a white stone, and on the stone a new name[b] is inscribed that no one knows except the one who receives it.

The Letter to Thyatira

[18]"Write to the angel of the church in Thyatira:

"The Son of God, the One whose eyes are

a 2:17 Ex 16:32-34
b Is 55:13; 56:5; 62:2
c 2:23 Ezk 33:27

like a fiery flame and whose feet are like fine bronze,[E] says: [19]I know your works—your love, faithfulness,[F] service, and endurance. Your last works are greater than the first. [20]But I have this against you: You tolerate the woman Jezebel, who calls herself a prophetess and teaches and deceives My •slaves to commit sexual immorality[G] and to eat meat sacrificed to idols. [21]I gave her time to repent, but she does not want to repent of her sexual immorality.[H] [22]Look! I will throw her into a sickbed and those who commit adultery with her into great tribulation, unless they repent of her[I] practices. [23]I will kill her children with the plague.[J,c] Then all the churches will know that I am the One who examines minds[K] and hearts, and I will give to each of you according to your works. [24]I say to the rest of you in Thyatira, who do not hold this teaching, who haven't known the deep things[L] of Satan—as they say—I do not put any other burden on you. [25]But hold on to what you have until I

A 2:14 Or to place a trap   B 2:14 Or commit fornication   C 2:15 Other mss add which I hate   D 2:17 Other mss add to eat
E 2:18 Probably gleaming white hot; Rv 1:15   F 2:19 Or faith   G 2:20 Or commit fornication   H 2:21 Or her fornication
I 2:22 Other mss read their   J 2:23 Or I will surely kill her children   K 2:23 Lit kidneys   L 2:24 Or the secret things

---

engage in such worship. This refusal was deemed disloyal and unpatriotic by non-Christians. This is why Jesus called Pergamum the place **where Satan's throne is**. The situation for Christians in Pergamum was even worse than at Smyrna. A faithful man named **Antipas** had already been **killed**. On the **sharp, double-edged sword**, see note at 1:16.

2:14-15 A viewpoint resembling **the teaching of Balaam** in the OT (Nm 22–25), which is probably linked to **the teaching of the Nicolaitans**, had a strong foothold in the church.

2:16 The **sword of My mouth** is the sword of verse 12. The clear-cut duty of the church at Pergamum was to combat the false viewpoints in their midst (vv. 14-15) or else they would be judged by the Lord Jesus.

2:17 On **anyone who has an ear** see note at verse 7. The reference to the **victor** (see note at v. 7) receiving **hidden manna** is intended to remind readers that Israel's sin in eating food sacrificed to idols in Numbers 25 was that much worse because God was still giving them manna, even as He was still caring for His church in Pergamum. The **white stone** and **new name** may be related to: (1) victory in the ancient Greek athletic games, which allowed an athlete to retire permanently, or (2) entrance to a community feast.

2:18 On **the angel of the church**, see note at 1:20. **Thyatira** was 30 miles southeast of Pergamum on the Lycus River. Each of its trade guilds was devoted to a patron god or goddess, and social events centered on their worship. The pressure for Christians to participate in this idolatrous lifestyle, both for economic and social reasons, was great. The letter to Thyatira is the longest of the seven messages and the centerpiece of all seven. This is odd, considering that Thyatira was the smallest and least consequential city of the group. Also, closer study shows that the spiritual battle being waged at Thyatira is parallel to the battle to be waged

in the end times (Rv 14–18). Christ, for the only time in Revelation, is called the **Son of God**. On **eyes ... like a fiery flame** and **feet ... like fine bronze**, see notes at 1:14 and 1:15.

2:19 Unlike the church at Ephesus, the church at Thyatira was not guilty of a lack of **love**. Significant spiritual growth was taking place.

2:20 **Jezebel** involved her followers in the same sins as those that infected the church at Pergamum—**sexual immorality** and eating **meat sacrificed to idols**. These sins are mentioned in reverse order from the letter to the church at Pergamum (v. 14). This reversal is a literary device that calls even more attention to the connection between the two. "Jezebel" was likely a nickname recalling the idolatrous queen of the northern king of Israel in 1 and 2 Kings.

2:21-23 **Great tribulation** (Gk thlipsis megaley) is used here not for the time of unparalleled suffering just before Christ's second coming, as in Rv 7:14 (Dn 12:1; Mt 24:21), but for a time of intense affliction of an unknown nature. Its use foreshadows the time of great affliction to come upon the entire earth (Rv 3:10; 7:14). The **children** of Jezebel are not her literal children, but spiritual "children" who have committed themselves to her false teaching. This group will be killed with the **plague**, a foreshadowing of widespread death by plague later in the book (e.g., 6:8). The strong parallels between Jezebel and Babylon, the great harlot of the latter part of the book (16:17–19:5), as well as the startling usage of "great tribulation," suggests Jezebel was a first-century preview of Babylon the Great.

2:24 The viewpoint and lifestyle associated with Jezebel (v. 20) are now unmasked as the **deep things of Satan**, meaning that this false belief and behavior originated with the Devil.

2:25 The other members of the church at Thyatira not in league with Jezebel were asked to **hold on** to the faithful acts Christ had commended in verse 19.

come.*a* *26* The one who is victorious and keeps My works to the end: I will give him authority over the nations—

27 **and he will shepherd**[A],*b* **them**
with an iron scepter;
he will shatter them like pottery [B],*c*—

just as I have received this from My Father. *28* I will also give him the morning star.*d*

29 "Anyone who has an ear should listen to what the Spirit says to the churches.

The Letter to Sardis

3 "Write to the angel of the church in Sardis:

"The One who has the seven spirits of God*e* and the seven stars says: I know your works; you have a reputation*c* for being alive, but you are dead. *2* Be alert and strengthen[D] what re-

mains, which is about to die, for I have not found your works complete before My God. *3* Remember, therefore, what you have received and heard; keep it, and repent. But if you are not alert, I will come[E] like a thief, and you have no idea at what hour I will come against you.[F] *4* But you have a few people[G] in Sardis who have not defiled[H] their clothes, and they will walk with Me in white, because they are worthy. *5* In the same way, the victor will be dressed in white clothes, and I will never erase his name from the book of life*f* but will acknowledge his name before My Father and before His angels.

6 "Anyone who has an ear should listen to what the Spirit says to the churches.

The Letter to Philadelphia

7 "Write to the angel of the church in Philadelphia:

*a*2:25 Rv 3:11
*b*2:27 Rv 19:15
*c*Ps 2:9
*d*2:28 Is 14:12; 2Pt 1:19; Rv 22:1
*e*3:1 Rv 1:4; 4:5; 5:6
*f*3:5 Rv 13:8; 17:8; 20:12,15; 21:27

[A]2:27 Or *rule*; see 19:15　　[B]2:27 Ps 2:9　　[C]3:1 Lit *have a name*　　[D]3:2 Other mss read *guard*　　[E]3:3 Other mss add *upon you*
[F]3:3 Or *upon you*　　[G]3:4 Lit *few names*　　[H]3:4 Or *soiled*

2:26-27 By use of a messianic prophecy from Ps 2:9, Christ promises that the victor will have **authority over the nations**, which means ruling with Him after His second coming (20:4,6).

2:28 The **morning star** is a symbol of the Messiah in Nm 24:17. Christ calls Himself the Bright Morning Star in Rv 22:16.

3:1 On **the angel of the church**, see note at 1:20. **Sardis**, 30 miles southeast of Thyatira, was one of the most ancient cities in Asia Minor, founded around 1200 B.C. In A.D. 17 an earthquake destroyed Sardis (and Philadelphia; see note at v. 7), but it was later rebuilt with the help of Emperor Augustus. The people of Sardis were fascinated with death and immortality, observing the fertility cycles of nature and the worship of Artemis, the fertility goddess. On the **seven spirits of God**, see note at 1:4. On the **seven stars**, see note at 1:16. There is no praise for the church in Sardis, and the Lord's criticism is haunting. Spiritually they were as good as **dead**.

3:2 This letter is intended by the Lord as an urgent spiritual wake-up call. If the church at Sardis did not **strengthen** what remained spiritually, they would **die**, because they had not followed through on the **works** that honored God.

3:3 If the church at Sardis did not **remember** God's blessings and **repent** of their failures, Christ would **come like a thief** in swift and severe judgment. Twice in the city's history, it had been captured because it failed to watch out for its enemies.

3:4-5 A remnant of **a few people in Sardis** had remained faithful to the Lord. To be dressed **in white** was to don the garb of the **victor** (see note at 2:7) whose lifestyle was **worthy** both of heaven (7:9) and of returning with Christ at His second coming (19:14). The **book of life** contains the **name** of each person who is eternally elect (13:8; 20:15). These will prove themselves victors, and Christ will never erase their names from the book of life.

3:6 On **anyone who has an ear**, see note at 2:7.

3:7 On the **angel of the church**, see note at 1:20. **Philadelphia**, 40 miles southeast of Sardis, suffered long-term effects from the earthquake of A.D. 17. Thus, the people planned for the future with earthquakes in mind. Although

Ruins of Roman arches at Laodicea, a city of Asia well known for its wealth. In A.D. 60, Laodicea experienced a devastating earthquake and was able to rebuild without relying on financial assistance from Rome. Lydia, one of the original members of the church at Philippi, was a businesswoman from Laodicea. The risen Christ knew Laodicea well. He reminded them of their spiritual poverty and called on them to repent (3:14-22).

"The Holy One, the True One, the One who has the key of David, who opens and no one will close, and closes and no one opens[a] says: [8]I know your works. Because you have limited strength, have kept My word, and have not denied My name, look, I have placed before you an open door that no one is able to close. [9]Take note! I will make those from the •synagogue of Satan, who claim to be Jews and are not, but are lying—note this—I will make them come and bow down at your feet, and they will know that I have loved you.[b] [10]Because you have kept My command to endure,[A] I will also keep you from the hour of testing that is going to come over the whole world to test those who live on the earth. [11]I am coming quickly. Hold on to what you have,[c] so that no one takes your crown. [12]The victor: I will make him a pillar in the sanctuary of My God,

and he will never go out again. I will write on him the name of My God and the name of the city of My God—the new Jerusalem, which comes down out of heaven from My God—and My new name.[d]

[13]"Anyone who has an ear should listen to what the Spirit says to the churches.

The Letter to Laodicea

[14]"Write to the angel of the church in Laodicea:

"The •Amen, the faithful and true Witness, the Originator[B,e] of God's creation says: [15]I know your works, that you are neither cold nor hot. I wish that you were cold or hot. [16]So, because you are lukewarm, and neither hot nor cold, I am going to vomit[c] you out of My mouth. [17]Because you say, 'I'm rich; I have become wealthy and need nothing,' and

---

*a*3:7 Is 22:22
*b*3:9 Is 45:14; 60:14
*c*3:11 Rv 2:25
*d*3:12 Rv 2:17
*e*3:14 Col 1:18; Jn 1:1-5

[A]3:10 Lit *My word of endurance*   [B]3:14 Or *Ruler*, or *Source*, or *Beginning*   [C]3:16 Or *spit*

---

there is little extrabiblical evidence for a Jewish community in the city, the letter indicates a situation similar to that of Smyrna. Nothing is known of the origin of the church, but there was a connection with Paul's ministry in Ephesus, like the other six local churches. The phrases **the key of David** and **no one opens** echo Is 22:22 and speak of Christ's authority in the household of God.

3:8 Christ commended the faithful **works** of this small congregation, in spite of their **limited strength**. The **open door that no one is able to close** opens to heaven and God's kingdom (Col 4:3-4).

3:9 On **synagogue of Satan** and **who claim to be Jews and are not**, see note at 2:9-10. These phrases are in reverse order from 2:9, implying there is a key point of comparison in the two letters. It is likely that the brief and local "tribulation" faced by the church at Smyrna (2:10) contrasts with the promise to the church at Philadelphia that it would be kept from the worldwide "hour of testing" (3:10).

3:10 The **hour of testing** refers to "the great tribulation" (7:14). Though the wording may sound like a reference to all who will inhabit the world at that time, **those who live on the earth** ("earth dwellers" from this point on in the notes) is a phrase used repeatedly in Revelation (6:10; 8:13; 11:10; 13:8), speaking of the non-elect, "whose names have not been written in the book of life" (17:8). To "keep . . . from the hour of testing" has been taken to mean: (1) removed *before* the time of tribulation, or (2) supernaturally protected *within* the tribulation. Since the word "hour" suggests a period of time, and the purpose of the hour of testing is to test the non-elect "earth dwellers" rather than believers, it seems more likely that believers will be removed before the hour of great tribulation begins.

3:11 On **coming quickly**, see note at 1:1,3. To **hold on to what you have** appears to refer to the faithfulness of the church, described in verse 8.

3:12 The **victor** (see note at 2:7) is promised a permanent place in the **sanctuary** in God's eternal city, **the new Jerusalem**. This "sanctuary" is actually the Lord Himself and the Lamb (21:2,22). Christ's **new name** may refer to "a name . . . that no one knows except Himself" (19:12).

3:13 On **anyone who has an ear** see note at 2:7.

3:14 On the **angel of the church**, see note at 1:20. **Laodicea**, 45 miles southeast of Philadelphia and 90 miles east of Ephesus, was an important trade center. Like Philadelphia, it lay in a region prone to earthquakes. The city had to bring in its water supply through an aqueduct. This made it vulnerable to drought and disruption by enemies. The Laodicean church was probably planted by Epaphras (Col 1:7), along with the churches of Hierapolis and Colossae, during Paul's three-year ministry at Ephesus (Ac 19:8-10; 20:31). **Amen** is a transliteration of the Hebrew word for "truth." Being the **Originator of God's creation** means Jesus was the member of the Trinity who was the agent of creation (Jn 1:3; Col 1:16).

3:15-16 Because the water in Laodicea was piped in, it was neither **cold** and refreshing nor **hot** and therapeutic. The **lukewarm** water was thus not useful. The spiritual worthlessness of the church in Laodicea was nauseating to Christ (**I am going to vomit you out of My mouth**).

3:17-19 Because many believers in the Laodicean church were **rich** and arrogant, they were completely **blind** to the fact that they were spiritually **wretched** and **naked**. The only

---

arche

Greek Pronunciation	[ahr KAY]
HCSB Translation	Originator, beginning
Uses in Revelation	3
Uses in the NT	55
Focus passage	Revelation 3:14

Arche indicates the *chief position*, either in time (*beginning, commencement*), rank/position (*ruler, governor, originator*), or location (*corner*; Ac 10:11). It can also refer to the domain of someone's authority (i.e., their *rule*; Lk 20:20; 1Co 15:24). Other related terms include the verb *archo* (to rule), *archomai* (to begin), and the noun *archon* (ruler). In John's writings, *arche* always refers to sequential priority, such as the *beginning* of the world (Jn 1:1,2; 1Jn 1:1; 2:13-14), of some aspect of Jesus' ministry (Jn 2:11; 6:64; 8:25; 15:27; 16:4), of Satan's rebellion against God (Jn 8:44; 1Jn 3:8), and of Christian witness (1Jn 2:7,24; 3:11; 2Jn 5,6). In Revelation, Jesus is called the "Originator of God's creation" (Rv 3:14) as well as "the *Beginning* and the End" (22:13), a title shared by God the Father (21:6), indicating that God started everything and will end everything.

you don't know that you are wretched, pitiful, poor, blind, and naked, [18]I advise you to buy from Me gold refined in the fire so that you may be rich, white clothes so that you may be dressed and your shameful nakedness not be exposed, and ointment to spread on your eyes so that you may see. [19]As many as I love, I rebuke and discipline. So be committed[A] and repent. [20]Listen! I stand at the door and knock. If anyone hears My voice and opens the door, I will come in to him and have dinner with him, and he with Me. [21]The victor: I will give him the right to sit with Me on My throne, just as I also won the victory and sat down with My Father on His throne.

[22]"Anyone who has an ear should listen to what the Spirit says to the churches."

The Throne Room of Heaven

4 After this I looked, and there in heaven was an open door. The first voice that I

had heard speaking to me like a trumpet said, "Come up here, and I will show you what must take place after this."

[2]Immediately I was in the Spirit,[B,a] and a throne was set there in heaven.[b] One was seated on the throne, [3]and the One seated[c] looked like jasper[D] and carnelian[E] stone. A rainbow that looked like an emerald surrounded the throne. [4]Around that throne were 24 thrones, and on the thrones sat 24 elders dressed in white clothes, with gold crowns on their heads. [5]Flashes of lightning and rumblings of thunder came from the throne. Seven fiery torches were burning before the throne, which are the seven spirits of God.[c] [6]Something like a sea of glass, similar to crystal, was also before the throne. Four living creatures[d] covered with eyes in front and in back were in the middle[F] and around the throne. [7]The first living creature was like a lion; the second living creature was like a calf; the third living

a4:2 Rv 1:10; 17:3; 21:10　bDn 7:9　c4:5 Rv 1:4; 3:1; 5:6　d4:6 Is 6:2-3; Ezk 1:5-28; 10:20

A3:19 Or be zealous　B4:2 Or in spirit; lit I became in the Spirit　C4:3 Other mss omit and the One seated　D4:3 A precious stone
E4:3 A translucent red gem　F4:6 Lit In the middle of the throne

---

way Christ would give them spiritual sight and make them spiritually rich and properly **dressed** was for them to **repent** (see note at 2:5) and be **committed** to Him, no longer going through the motions spiritually (i.e., being lukewarm). **As many as I love, I . . . discipline** echoes Pr 3:11-12, which is cited in Heb 12:6.

3:20 The Lord had been pushed to the outside of the church at Laodicea, and He was now seeking to reenter through their repentance (**opens the door**). The phrases **I stand at the door and knock** and **if anyone . . . opens the door, I will come in** may be interpreted one of three ways: (1) if all members of the congregation were actually unbelievers, this would be an evangelistic invitation; (2) if all members were believers, it serves as a call to renewed fellowship with Christ (i.e., pictured by a shared fellowship meal: **have dinner with Him**); or (3) if the congregation was mixed, this is a picturesque way of expressing both kinds of invitations (to salvation and restored fellowship).

3:21 On **victor**, see note at 2:7. The right to **sit** with Christ on His **throne** goes beyond His promise to the apostles in Mt 19:28 and looks to His reign on earth in Rv 20:4-6. The phrase **sat down with My Father on His throne** looks ahead to the heavenly throne room in chapters 4–5.

3:22 On **anyone who has an ear**, see note at 2:7.

4:1-2 The phrases **after this** and **what must take place after this** signal the beginning of the body of the book (4:1–22:5) spoken of in 1:19, in the wording, "what will take place after this." Even though John was told to **come up here**, it is not clear whether: (1) he was actually taken up into **heaven** (with the same command in 11:12 the two witnesses were taken to heaven), or (2) he was still "in the Spirit" (see note at 1:10) on the isle of Patmos (1:9-10). What he saw of the heavenly throne room in chapters 4–5 is trustworthy either way, since the vision came from the Lord.

4:3-4 Jasper is an opaque jewel also mentioned in the description of the new Jerusalem (21:11,19). **Carnelian stone** is a vivid red color. A **rainbow** is God's covenant sign that He will never again judge the earth by a flood destroying

all humanity (Gn 9:8-17). The Apocalypse tells of God's just judgment of the world by other means. The **24 elders** could refer to angels, but since there were elders as leaders in both Israel (Nm 11:16) and the church (Ti 1:5), it is more likely that 12 of the 24 represent the tribes of Israel and the other 12 the apostles of Christ, previewing the reference to the 12 tribes and 12 apostles in the new Jerusalem (21:12,14). Elsewhere in Revelation, **white clothes** and **gold crowns** make up the attire of victorious believers (3:5; 6:11; 7:9; 19:8,14).

4:5 Flashes of lightning . . . and thunder coming from God (**the throne**) represent the first mention in Revelation of phenomena that intensify and spill over from heaven to earth as part of God's just judgment (8:5; 11:19; 16:18,21). On the **seven spirits of God**, see note at 1:4.

4:6-7 The **four living creatures** resemble the cherubim in Ezekiel 1 and 10, though there are differences as well. **Cov-**

hagios

Greek Pronunciation	[HAH gee ahss]
HCSB Translation	holy
Uses in Revelation	25
Uses in the NT	233
Focus passage	Revelation 4:8

Hagios (holy) frequently refers to that which is dedicated or set apart to God's service, describing things that have a derived holiness. This includes the church (1Co 3:17; Eph 5:26; 1Pt 2:9), as well as individual Christians (Rm 12:1). Indeed, hagios may be translated "saints" in reference to believers, who are set apart by God for His service (Mt 27:52; Ac 9:13; Rm 1:7; 1Co 1:2; Rv 5:8). The word also describes Jerusalem (Mt 4:5; Rv 21:2,10; 22:19), the various parts of the sanctuary (Mt 24:15; Heb 9:1-3), angels (Mk 8:38), OT prophets (Lk 1:70), Christian apostles and prophets (Eph 3:5), divine revelation (Rm 1:2; 2Pt 2:21), and various geographical locations (Ac 7:33; 2Pt 1:18). Additionally, hagios may describe what is holy by nature, namely, God the Father (Jn 17:11; 1Pt 1:15; Rv 4:8), Jesus Christ (Mk 1:24; Ac 3:14), and the Spirit (Mt 3:11; Ac 1:5).

creature had a face like a man; and the fourth living creature was like a flying eagle. [8]Each of the four living creatures had six wings;[a] they were covered with eyes around and inside. Day and night they never stop,[A] saying:

> Holy, holy, holy,[B]
> Lord God, the Almighty,
> who was, who is, and who is coming.

[9]Whenever the living creatures give glory, honor, and thanks to the One seated on the throne, the One who lives forever and ever, [10]the 24 elders fall down before the One seated on the throne, worship the One who lives forever and ever, cast their crowns before the throne, and say:

> [11] Our Lord and God,[C]
> You are worthy to receive
> glory and honor and power,
> because You have created all things,
> and because of Your will
> they exist and were created.

The Lamb Takes the Scroll

5 Then I saw in the right hand of the One seated on the throne a scroll with writing on the inside and on the back,[b] sealed with seven seals. [2]I also saw a mighty angel proclaiming in a loud voice, "Who is worthy to open the scroll and break its seals?" [3]But no one in heaven or on earth or under the earth was able to open the scroll or even to look in it. [4]And I cried and cried because no one was found worthy to open[D] the scroll or even to look in it.

[5]Then one of the elders said to me, "Stop crying. Look! The Lion from the tribe of Judah,[c] the Root of David,[d] has been victorious[e] so that He may open the scroll and[E] its seven seals." [6]Then I saw One like a slaughtered lamb standing between[F] the throne and the four living creatures and among the elders. He had seven horns and seven eyes, which are the seven spirits of God[f] sent into all the earth. [7]He came and took the scroll[G] out of the right hand of the One seated on the throne.

The Lamb Is Worthy

[8]When He took the scroll, the four living creatures and the 24 elders fell down before the Lamb. Each one had a harp and gold bowls filled with incense, which are the prayers of the •saints. [9]And they sang a new song:[g]

> You are worthy to take the scroll
> and to open its seals,
> because You were slaughtered,
> and You •redeemed[H] people[I]
> for God by Your blood

[a]4:8 Is 6:2
[b]5:1 Ezk 2:9-10
[c]5:5 Gn 49:9
[d]Is 11:1,10; Rv 22:16
[e]Jn 16:33
[f]5:6 Rv 1:4
[g]5:9 Ps 40:3; 96:1; 98:1; 149:1; Is 42:10; Rv 14:3

[A]4:8 Or they never rest   [B]4:8 Other mss read holy 9 times   [C]4:11 Other mss add the Holy One; other mss read Lord   [D]5:4 Other mss add and read   [E]5:5 Other mss add loose   [F]5:6 Or standing in the middle of   [G]5:7 Other mss include the scroll   [H]5:9 Or purchased   [I]5:9 Other mss read us

---

ered with eyes means that very few things escape the notice of these watchful angelic creatures. The imagery of the lion, calf, man, and eagle has strong linkage to Ezk 1:5-10 and may represent animate creation.

4:8 The mention of the creatures having six wings and the words holy, holy, holy echo the description of the seraphim in the heavenly throne room in Is 6:1-3. On who was, who is, and who is coming, see note at 1:4.

4:9-10 The heavenly throne room is characterized by unceasing joyful praise, thanksgiving, and worship toward the Lord by the four living creatures and the 24 elders.

4:11 The beginning point of worship is to recognize that God is completely worthy to be recognized for His unrivaled glory and honor and power, and His work as Creator and Sustainer of all things.

5:1 The right hand of God symbolizes power and authority. The phrase with writing on the inside and on the back echoes Ezk 2:9-10, where God showed the prophet a scroll with words written "on the front and back . . . of lamentation, mourning, and woe." The scroll John saw foretold woe (8:13; 9:12; 11:14), but it also disclosed God's perfect plan (symbolized by the seven seals) of judgment and the redemption of His creation, which will culminate in the end times. Because the outer edge of the scroll was sealed, the contents could only be seen when all seven seals were removed. Thus, as the seals are opened in chapter 6, what takes place is not the content of the entire scroll, but only those judgments that precede it being fully opened.

5:2-4 The apostle John was emotionally distraught because no one in heaven or on earth or under the earth was found worthy to open the scroll and read the destiny of the world.

5:5-7 Speaking of Jesus as the Lion from the tribe of Judah echoes the messianic prophecy in Gn 49:9-10. Christ was able to open the scroll and its seven seals on the basis of an accomplished fact—His death on the cross like a slaughtered lamb (Is 53:7; Jn 1:29). On the four living creatures, see note at 4:6-7. On the elders, see note at 4:3-4. In the apocalyptic book of Daniel, horns stand for power and authority (Dn 7:8,20,24). On the seven spirits of God, see note at 1:4. God's sending of the seven spirits immediately after the description of the redemptive work of the Lamb (5:6) may preview "the eternal gospel" being preached climactically to the entire world in 14:6-7. The Lamb taking the scroll out of the right hand of the Father signifies a transfer of authority, allowing the Lamb to fulfill the contents of the scroll (i.e., the judgments and other events of the rest of the Apocalypse). For a parallel account, see Dn 7:13-14.

5:8 Believers' prayers are described as filling gold bowls before the throne of God. The "gold" emphasizes their reality and exceeding value to God. The word saints (Gk hagioi) means "holy ones." These are not elite and exceptional Christians. Instead, the NT uses this term for all believers in Christ (Rm 1:7).

5:9-10 The new song sung in heaven about Christ is inspired by His redemptive work, the shedding of His blood on the cross. The target group for redemption (described as

from every tribe and language
and people and nation.*a*
10   You made them a kingdom[A]
and priests to our God,*b*
and they will reign on the earth.

¹¹Then I looked and heard the voice of many angels around the throne, and also of the living creatures and of the elders. Their number was countless thousands, plus thousands of thousands. ¹²They said with a loud voice:

The Lamb who was slaughtered
is worthy
to receive power and riches
and wisdom and strength
and honor and glory and blessing!

¹³I heard every creature in heaven, on earth, under the earth, on the sea, and everything in them say:

Blessing and honor and glory
and dominion
to the One seated on the throne,
and to the Lamb, forever and ever!

*a*5:9 Ex 19:5
*b*5:10 Ex 19:6;
Rv 1:5-6
*c*6:2 Zch 6:1-3
*d*6:4 Mt 10:34

¹⁴The four living creatures said, "'Amen," and the elders fell down and worshiped.

The First Seal on the Scroll

6 Then I saw[B] the Lamb open one of the seven[C] seals, and I heard one of the four living creatures say with a voice like thunder, "Come!"[D,E] ²I looked, and there was a white horse.[c] The horseman on it had a bow; a crown was given to him, and he went out as a victor to conquer.[F]

The Second Seal

³When He opened the second seal, I heard the second living creature say, "Come!"[D,E] ⁴Then another horse went out, a fiery red one, and its horseman was empowered[G] to take peace from the earth, so that people would slaughter one another. And a large sword was given to him.*d*

The Third Seal

⁵When He opened the third seal, I heard the third living creature say, "Come!"[D,E] And I looked, and there was a black horse. The

---

[A]5:10 Other mss read *them kings*   [B]6:1 Lit *saw when*   [C]6:1 Other mss omit *seven*   [D]6:1,3,5 Other mss add *and see*   [E]6:1,3,5 Or *Go!*   [F]6:2 Lit *went out conquering and in order to conquer*   [G]6:4 Or *was granted*; lit *was given*

---

every tribe . . . nation; cp. 7:9; 10:11; 11:9; 13:7; 14:6; 17:15, where the same terms are used in differing order) is the same group that is identified in the Great Commission: "all nations" (Mt 28:19). The reference to Christ's shed blood and the phrase **a kingdom and priests** echo Rv 1:5-6 and may be partially fulfilled in heaven in 7:15. The promise that **they will reign on the earth** is fulfilled in 20:6.

5:11-14 On the **living creatures**, see note at 4:6-7. On **the elders**, see note at 4:3-4. This scene looks ahead to the time when "every knee will bow . . . and every tongue should confess that Jesus Christ is Lord, to the glory of God the Father" (Php 2:10-11).

6:1-8:1 Some interpreters believe that the description of the unsealing of the scroll (5:1) is the beginning of the tribulation period. However, the scroll in the Lamb's hand (5:7) is not open for viewing until all seven seals have been removed. Six of the seals are removed in chapter 6. The two scenes in chapter 7 (7:1-8; 7:9-17) form an interlude prior to the removal of the seventh seal (8:1). Extensive parallelism exists between this section and Jesus' Olivet Discourse (Mt 24:4-14) describing "the beginning of birth pains" (a woman's early or false labor). If both passages refer to the same events and timing, it appears that the "unsealing" sequence in Rv 6:1-8:1 occurs *before* the tribulation period.

6:1-8 The lifting of the first four seals is portrayed in this section as four horsemen, an image likely drawn from Zch 1:7-11, though the colors of the horses are different. There is debate about whether any, or all, of what is pictured here has already taken place. However, no catastrophe has devastated "a fourth of the earth" since the time this prophecy was given (Rv 6:8).

6:1,3,5,7 It appears that the command "Come!" from each of **the four living creatures** sets in motion the dramatic effects unleashed by removing each of the seals.

6:2 Some have taken the **horseman** here as a description of Christ because of its similarity to Him at the second coming (19:11). All that can be said with certainty is that the **bow** indicates the horseman is a warrior and the **crown** shows that he is a king or ruler and that the description parallels Mt 24:5-6. The word for crown (Gk *stephanos*) differs from the many crowns (Gk *diademata*) of Jesus in Rv 19:12.

6:4 The description here strongly parallels Mt 24:6-7, with "wars and rumors of wars" and nations and kingdoms rising up against one another.

6:5-6 The apparent descriptions of famine conditions here would naturally follow the state of war portrayed in verses 2,4. A **quart** of **wheat** or **barley** was enough food for a person

sphragis

Greek Pronunciation	[sfrah GIHSS]
HCSB Translation	seal
Uses in Revelation	13
Uses in the NT	16
Focus passage	Revelation 6:1

Sphragis (seal) could refer to an instrument used to apply a *seal* (7:2) or to the *seal* (5:1,2,5) or *inscription* (2Tm 2:19) itself. The related verb *sphragizo* means *to mark with a seal,* in order to secure (Mt 27:66; Rv 20:3) or hide something (10:4; 22:10). The person who owns the stamp enjoys authority over what is *sealed.* This authority indicates ownership, protection, and approval, themes that predominate in Revelation (7:3-5,8; 9:4). The seven-*sealed* scroll belongs to God, and only the Lamb is worthy to break the *seals* to reveal the scroll's contents (chaps. 5-6; 8:1).

Metaphorically, a *seal* could indicate official authentication or confirmation of a truth, and in this sense Paul speaks of circumcision as the *seal* (i.e., *authentication,* Rm 4:11) of Abraham's faith-based righteousness. Similarly, the Corinthian church was the *seal* (i.e., *confirmation;* 1Co 9:2) of Paul's apostleship.

horseman on it had a set of scales in his hand. [a] [b] ⁶Then I heard something like a voice among the four living creatures say, "A quart of wheat for a •denarius, and three quarts of barley for a denarius—but do not harm the olive oil and the wine."

The Fourth Seal

⁷When He opened the fourth seal, I heard the voice of the fourth living creature say, "Come!"[A,B] ⁸And I looked, and there was a pale green[C] horse. The horseman on it was named Death, and •Hades was following after him. Authority was given to them[D,a] over a fourth of the earth, to kill by the sword, by famine, by plague, and by the wild animals of the earth.

The Fifth Seal

⁹When He opened the fifth seal, I saw under the altar the people[E] slaughtered because of God's word and the testimony they had.[F,b] ¹⁰They cried out with a loud voice: "Lord,[G] the One who is holy and true, how long until You judge and avenge our blood from those who live on the earth?" ¹¹So a white robe was given to each of them, and they were told to rest a little while longer until the number would be completed of their fellow slaves and their •brothers, who were going to be killed just as they had been.

The Sixth Seal

¹²Then I saw Him open[H] the sixth seal. A violent earthquake occurred; the sun turned black like •sackcloth[c] made of goat hair; the entire moon[I] became like blood; ¹³the stars[J] of heaven fell to the earth as a fig tree drops its unripe figs when shaken by a high wind; ¹⁴the sky separated like a scroll being rolled up; and every mountain and island was moved from its place.

¹⁵Then the kings of the earth, the nobles, the military commanders, the rich, the powerful, and every •slave and free person hid in the caves and among the rocks of the mountains.[d] ¹⁶And they said to the mountains and to the rocks, "Fall on us and hide us[e] from the face of the One seated on the throne and from the wrath of the Lamb, ¹⁷because the great day of Their[K] wrath has come! And who is able to stand?"[f]

The Sealed of Israel

7 After this I saw four angels standing at the four corners of the earth,[g] restraining the four winds of the earth so that no wind could blow on the earth or on the sea or on any tree. ²Then I saw another angel, who had the seal of the living God rise up from the east. He cried out in a loud voice to the four angels who were empowered[L] to harm the earth and the sea: ³"Don't harm the earth or the sea or

a 6:8 Mt 10:1; 28:18; Rv 9:3
b 6:9 Rv 1:2,9; 12:17; 19:10; 20:4
c 6:12 Is 50:3
d 6:15 Is 2:10
e 6:16 Hs 10:8
f 6:17 Mal 3:2
g 7:1 Is 11:12; Ezk 7:2; Rv 20:7-8

A 6:7 Other mss add *and see*   B 6:7 Or *Go!*   C 6:8 Or *a greenish gray*   D 6:8 Other mss read *him*   E 6:9 Lit *souls*   F 6:9 Other mss add *about the Lamb*   G 6:10 Or *Master*   H 6:12 Lit *I saw when He opened*   I 6:12 Or *the full moon*   J 6:13 Perhaps meteors   K 6:17 Other mss read *His*   L 7:2 Lit *angels to whom it was given*

for one day. A **denarius** was a day's wage for the average worker (Mt 20:2). Thus, the greatly inflated cost of these necessities indicates a severe drought, though **olive oil** and **wine** are plentiful.

6:8 Hades was popularly known as the grave and resting place after **Death** (see note at 20:11-15). The text does not say that **a fourth** of the population of the earth was killed, but only that **authority** was given to "Death" and "Hades" over this proportion of the world, allowing them to kill freely.

6:9-11 The phrase **under the altar** and the mention of **blood** recall the sacrificial blood poured at the base of the altar in Ex 29:12. The **people slaughtered** may refer to believers killed during the removal of the first four seals (6:2,4,8) or generally to "the blood of prophets and saints, and of all those slaughtered on earth" (18:24). Their being killed because of **God's word** and their **testimony** for Christ is the same reason given for John's imprisonment on the island of Patmos (1:9). Since the "hour of testing" (i.e., the tribulation period; 3:10) is focused on the "earth dwellers," the delay here (**rest a little while longer**) implies the "hour of testing" has not yet begun. The Lord's just vengeance (Rm 12:19) for the martyrs begins in earnest in Rv 16:4-7 and is not completed until 19:2. On **white robe**, see note at 3:4-5. It is not known when the **number** of their fellow martyrs is **completed**.

6:12-17 The effects when the sixth seal is lifted from the

scroll (**sun turned black** and **moon became like blood**) are very similar to those in Jl 2:28-31, which are said to occur just before the Day of the Lord (Jl 2:31). This is the same as the **great day** of the **wrath** of God the Father and **the Lamb** (vv. 16-17; Zph 1:14-15). Some think this is the time of the second coming of Christ because of the similarity in wording between certain aspects of the sixth seal and Mt 24:29-31. Because the exact same Greek word and form for **come** *(elthen)* is used in regard to the prophecy in Jd 14, which has a futuristic meaning, it is best to translate it here as "the great day of their wrath is (about to) come." The question **and who is able to stand** is answered in chapter 7.

7:1-17 Two visions make up this interlude between the opening of the sixth (6:12) and seventh (8:1) seals—(1) the sealing of the 144,000 servants of God on earth (7:1-8), and (2) the innumerable multitude arriving in heaven (7:9-17). The answer to the question "And who is able to stand?" (6:17) is that the 144,000 servants are able to stand on earth, protected by God's seal (7:2-4), while the vast multitude stands triumphantly before the throne in heaven (7:9-10). The calming of winds on the earth (7:1-3) and the half hour of silence in heaven (8:1) form an eye-of-the-hurricane "bookends" effect around chapter 7.

7:1-3 While there is no mention of damaging wind in relation to the removal of the sixth seal (6:12-17), the great earthquake (6:12), with mountains and islands moving (6:14), certainly reflects extensive harm to the **earth** and the **sea** and the **trees**, which begins again as soon as the trumpet

the trees until we seal the •slaves of our God on their foreheads." ⁴And I heard the number of those who were sealed:

144,000 sealed from every tribe
    of the Israelites:
⁵ 12,000 sealed from the tribe of Judah,
  12,000ᴬ from the tribe of Reuben,
  12,000 from the tribe of Gad,
⁶ 12,000 from the tribe of Asher,
  12,000 from the tribe of Naphtali,
  12,000 from the tribe of Manasseh,
⁷ 12,000 from the tribe of Simeon,
  12,000 from the tribe of Levi,
  12,000 from the tribe of Issachar,
⁸ 12,000 from the tribe of Zebulun,
  12,000 from the tribe of Joseph,
  12,000 sealed from the tribe
    of Benjamin.

A Multitude from the Great Tribulation

⁹After this I looked, and there was a vast multitude from every nation, tribe, people, and language, which no one could number, standing before the throne and before the Lamb. They were robed in white with palm branches in their hands. ¹⁰And they cried out in a loud voice:

Salvation belongs to our God,
  who is seated on the throne,
  and to the Lamb!

¹¹All the angels stood around the throne, the elders, and the four living creatures, and they fell facedown before the throne and worshiped God, ¹²saying:

•Amen! Blessing and glory and wisdom
  and thanksgiving and honor
  and power and strength
  be to our God forever and ever. Amen.

¹³Then one of the elders asked me, "Who are these people robed in white, and where did they come from?"

ᴬ7:5-8 Other mss add *sealed* after each number

---

judgments start (e.g., 8:7-8). The "calm in the midst of the storm" calls attention to the **seal of the living God** being applied to the **foreheads** of the **slaves of . . . God**. In the ancient world, seals were signs of ownership (5:1) or authority (Mt 27:66). These servants of the Lord are sealed just before the scroll is completely *unsealed* (Rv 8:1). A truth intended for the reader's reflection is that "the mark" of the beast is placed on the right hand or forehead of all who follow the beast (13:16).

7:4-8 The identity of the **144,000** has been variously interpreted. (1) Jehovah's Witnesses falsely maintain this is the total number of the anointed who will dwell in heaven with Jehovah and rule over the inhabitants of a purified earth. (2) Since all Christians are sealed by the Holy Spirit (2Co 1:22; Eph 4:30), and the 144,000 are called "the slaves of . . . God" in Rv 7:3, the seal of verses 2-4 may be placed on all Christians, and this host is generically representative of them. (3) The most literal interpretation is highly plausible. The 144,000 represent Israel following a future conversion of the nation. The Spirit indwelled Israel in the vision of the valley of dry bones (Ezk 37:14), in which Israel was viewed as "a vast army" (Ezk 37:10), and the 144,000 from **every tribe of the Israelites** appear to be arranged in military formation, as was Israel in the wilderness (Nm 2:2-34). Revelation 7:4-8 could reflect the point at which the "firstfruits" of Jews (14:4) come under the new covenant (Ezk 36:24-28; cp. Jr 31:31-34) during the Apocalypse.

7:5-8 The **tribe of Judah** is mentioned first because it was the royal tribe of Israel (Gn 49:9-10) into which Jesus was born (Rv 5:5). **Reuben** is next because he was Jacob's firstborn (Gn 49:3). The tribes of Dan and Ephraim are omitted from the listing, perhaps because of their instances of gross idolatry (Jdg 17–18). They are replaced by **Joseph** and **Levi**, neither of which was included in the military encampment of tribes in Nm 2.

7:9-12 In 5:9, the Lamb's worthiness to open the scroll is based on the shedding of His redemptive blood for "every tribe and language and people and nation." In 7:9,

this group arrives in heaven. Since "every nation" is listed first, this scene is at least a partial fulfillment of the Great Commission—where Christ's disciples are commanded to reach "all nations" with the gospel by "the end of the age" (Mt 28:19-20). The **vast multitude** wearing white robes links them to the martyrs (6:11) and, in the only other context in Revelation where the phrase "vast multitude" is found (19:1,6), to the bride and the armies of the Lamb (19:8,14). Some interpreters understand the vast multitude to be all martyrs, who arrive in heaven over a period of time. Others see this as the time when the church is raptured, with some who are dead and some who are still alive all arriving at the same time (1Th 4:14-17).

7:13-14 The **robes** of the vast multitude (v. 9) being made **white** in the **blood of the Lamb** likely refers to the redemptive work of Christ (1:5; 5:9). If so, the multitude **coming out of the great tribulation** (Dn 12:1; Mt 24:21; and "the hour of testing" in Rv 3:10) may refer to the rapture of the church

---

phule

Greek Pronunciation	[foo LAY]
HCSB Translation	tribe
Uses in Revelation	21
Uses in the NT	31
Focus passage	Revelation 7:4-9

Phule can refer to a group of people united along socio-political lines (i.e., a *nation*) or to a subgroup within a nation, characterized by a distinctive bloodline (i.e., a *tribe*). Outside of the book of Revelation, *phule* normally refers to one or more of Israel's twelve *tribes* (Mt 19:28; Lk 2:36; 22:30; Ac 13:21; Rm 11:1; Php 3:5; Heb 7:13-14), a usage less frequently attested in the book of Revelation (5:5; 7:4-8; 21:12). *Phule* occurs 21 times in Revelation, where John speaks of *tribes* among the Gentile nations (1:7; 5:9; 7:9; 11:9; 13:7; 14:6; this broader sphere of *tribes* may also be in view in Mt 24:30 and Jms 1:1). In this latter sense, *phule* has some semantic overlap with the Gk terms *genos* (nation, race) and *ethnos* (foreigners, nations).

¹⁴I said to him, "Sir,ᴬ you know."
Then he told me:

These are the ones coming out
of the great tribulation.
They washed their robes
and made them whiteᵃ
in the blood of the Lamb.
¹⁵ For this reason they are
before the throne of God,
and they serve Him day and night
in His sanctuary.
The One seated on the throne
will shelterᴮ them:
¹⁶ They will no longer hunger;
they will no longer thirst;
the sun will no longer
strike them,
nor will any heat.ᵇ
¹⁷ For the Lamb who is at the center
of the throne
will shepherd them;ᶜ
He will guide them to springs
of living waters,ᵈ
and God will wipe away every tear
from their eyes.ᵉ

The Seventh Seal

8 When He opened the seventh seal, there was silence in heaven for about half an hour. ²Then I saw the seven angels who stand in the presence of God; seven trumpets were given to them. ³Another angel, with a gold incense burner, came and stood at the altar. He was given a large amount of incense to offer with the prayers of all the •saints on the gold altar in front of the throne. ⁴The smoke of the incense, with the prayers of the saints, went up in the presence of God from the angel's hand. ⁵The angel took the incense burner, filled it with fire from the altar, and hurled it to the earth; there were rumblings of thunder, flashes of lightning, and an earthquake. ⁶And the seven angels who had the seven trumpets prepared to blow them.

The First Trumpet

⁷The first angelᶜ blew his trumpet, and hail and fire, mixed with blood, were hurled to the earth. So a third of the earth was burned up, a third of the trees were burned up, and all the green grass was burned up.

The Second Trumpet

⁸The second angel blew his trumpet, and something like a great mountain ablaze with fire was hurled into the sea.ᶠ So a third of the sea became blood, ⁹a third of the living creatures in the sea died, and a third of the ships were destroyed.

ᵃ7:14 Ps 51:7; Is 1:18; 43:25; 44:22 ᵇ7:16 Is 49:10 ᶜ7:17 Ps 23:1; Ezk 34:23 ᵈPs 23:2; Is 49:10; Jr 2:13 ᵉIs 25:8; Rv 21:4 ᶠ8:8 Jr 51:25

ᴬ7:14 Lit My lord ᴮ7:15 Or will spread His tent over ᶜ8:7 Other mss include angel

before the great tribulation, if that period does not begin until the events in the scroll are released by the lifting of the seventh seal (8:1). However 3:10 is understood, 7:14 should be taken the same way since both have the Gk preposition *ek* ("from, out from") and a time period (i.e., "the hour of testing" in 3:10 and "the great tribulation" in 7:14).

7:15-17 The vast multitude's priestly service in heaven is a partial fulfillment of the promises in 1:6 and 5:10. The mention of the sanctuary looks ahead to the equating of the vast multitude with the "heaven dwellers" in 12:12 and 13:6.

The Colosseum at Rome, one of the most impressive structures of the Roman Empire. It was originally called the Flavian Amphitheater and was under construction from A.D. 72 to 80. Large numbers of Christians were martyred in the Colosseum.

8:1 When **the seventh seal** is lifted, the scroll is finally opened (5:1), so that its contents can be released. The **half an hour** of **silence in heaven** echoes Zph 1:7: "Be silent in the presence of the Lord God, for the Day of the Lᴏʀᴅ is near." This implies that the Day of the Lord (see note at Rv 6:12-17) begins with the trumpet judgments. The half hour of silence appears to serve as a literary break in the action before everything moves full speed ahead toward the final judgment.

8:2-6 This pause while **the saints** pray implies that God's answer to the prayers for the avenging of the blood of the martyrs (6:10) upon the "earth dwellers," who are the focus of the "hour of testing" (3:10), begins with the judgment of the **seven trumpets**. The phenomena around the throne in heaven in 4:5 is intensified in 8:5 and poured out in the trumpet judgments.

8:7-12 The first four trumpet judgments in this section mirror the plagues upon Egypt in Ex 7–11. The trumpets are stronger than all the effects of the seals being lifted, except for the sixth seal (Rv 6:12-17). Even the scope of the fourth seal (6:7-8)—in which "a fourth of the earth" is selectively impacted but not totally destroyed—is less extensive than the early trumpet judgments.

8:7 The effects of the **first . . . trumpet** are **hail . . . fire**, and **blood**, which combines what happened in the first (Ex 7:19-20) and seventh (Ex 9:22-25) plagues on Egypt.

8:8-9 The description of the **second . . . trumpet** sounds like the eruption of a great island volcano. A **third of the sea** becoming **blood** and a third of the **living creatures** in it dying is similar to what happened to the Nile River and its fish in the first plague on Egypt (Ex 7:17-21), but on a global scale.

The Third Trumpet

[10]The third angel blew his trumpet, and a great star, blazing like a torch, fell from heaven.[a] It fell on a third of the rivers and springs of water. [11]The name of the star is Wormwood, and a third of the waters became *wormwood. So, many of the people died from the waters, because they had been made bitter.

The Fourth Trumpet

[12]The fourth angel blew his trumpet, and a third of the sun was struck, a third of the moon, and a third of the stars, so that a third of them were darkened. A third of the day was without light, and the night as well.[b]

[13]I looked again and heard an eagle[A] flying high overhead, crying out in a loud voice, "Woe![c] Woe! Woe to those who live on the earth, because of the remaining trumpet blasts that the three angels are about to sound!"

The Fifth Trumpet

9 The fifth angel blew his trumpet, and I saw a star that had fallen from heaven to earth.[d] The key to the shaft of the *abyss[e] was given to him. [2]He opened the shaft of the

a 8:10 Is 14:12; Rv 9:1
b 8:12 Am 8:9
c 8:13 Rv 9:12; 11:14; 12:12
d 9:1 Rv 8:10
e Lk 8:31; Rm 10:7; Rv 9:11; 11:7; 17:8; 20:1-3
f 9:3 Mt 10:1; 28:18; Rv 6:8
g 9:7 Jl 2:4
h 9:8 Jl 1:6

abyss, and smoke came up out of the shaft like smoke from a great[B] furnace so that the sun and the air were darkened by the smoke from the shaft. [3]Then locusts came out of the smoke on to the earth, and power[c] was given to them[f] like the power that scorpions have on the earth. [4]They were told not to harm the grass of the earth, or any green plant, or any tree, but only people who do not have God's seal on their foreheads. [5]They were not permitted to kill them but were to torment them for five months; their torment is like the torment caused by a scorpion when it strikes a man. [6]In those days people will seek death and will not find it; they will long to die, but death will flee from them.

[7]The appearance of the locusts was like horses equipped for battle.[g] Something like gold crowns was on their heads; their faces were like men's faces; [8]they had hair like women's hair; their teeth were like lions' teeth;[h] [9]they had chests like iron breastplates; the sound of their wings was like the sound of chariots with many horses rushing into battle; [10]and they had tails with stingers like scorpions, so that with their tails they had

---

[A]8:13 Other mss read *angel* [B]9:2 Other mss omit *great* [C]9:3 Or *authority*

8:10-11 The effects of the **third . . . trumpet** are like a meteorite (i.e., a falling **star**) hitting the earth and causing toxic **water** pollution, killing many people. **Wormwood** is a nonpoisonous but bitter plant common to the Middle East. Biblical authors use it as an analogy for bitterness, sorrow, injustice, etc. (e.g., Jr 23:15; Lm 3:15; Am 5:7).

8:12 It is difficult to understand the exact effects of the **fourth . . . trumpet**, though it clearly echoes the ninth plague on Egypt (Ex 10:21-23). For the **sun . . . moon**, and **stars** to be darkened by **a third** could mean that: (1) these

heavenly bodies are visible for "a third" less time than is normal, or (2) the intensity of their light is reduced by "a third," as if by the recent cosmic disturbances (see notes on the first three trumpets at vv. 7,8-9,10-11).

8:13 The remaining three trumpet judgments will maximize the **woe** upon the "earth dwellers," whom God has previously spotlighted for judgment and vengeance for spilling the martyrs' blood (6:10) during the "hour of testing" (the tribulation period; 3:10).

9:1 The judgment of the **fifth . . . trumpet** recalls both the eighth plague on Egypt in Ex 10:12-15 and the plague of locusts in Jl 1:2-4; 2:25, which was a foreshadowing of the Day of the Lord (Jl 1:15). The **star** here may refer to: (1) the demon mentioned in verse 11, (2) Satan (see notes at 12:4 and 12:7-10), or (3) the angel who has the **key** to the **abyss** (the bottomless pit) in 20:1. The last option is the most likely.

9:2-10 Clouds of **locusts** (or grasshoppers) as thick as **smoke** come up out of **the abyss** (see note at v. 1). Their origin from the abyss, plus the fact that, unlike regular locusts, these are not allowed to harm any **plant** or **tree** on the earth, makes it clear that these creatures are demonic. They target **people** who do not have **God's seal on their foreheads**, apparently meaning everyone still alive on earth besides the 144,000 of Israel who were sealed by the Lord in 7:2-4 (although by this point it is possible that they had numerous converts, who might also be protected from the demonic locusts). Some hold that the span of the torment for all the unbelievers is **five months** because that is the life span of a locust, while others think it has to do with the time of the year when locust plagues occur with devastating impact—from mid-spring to late summer. It is not known how the Lord will prevent the **death** wish of so many people from being carried out.

---

katoikeo

Greek Pronunciation	[kah toi KEH oh]
HCSB Translation	live, dwell
Uses in Revelation	13
Uses in the NT	44
Focus passage	Revelation 8:13

Outside of the book of Revelation, *katoikeo* (*to live, dwell*) mainly refers to *residing* in a city (Mt 2:23; Lk 13:4; Ac 2:5,14; 9:22,32; 19:17) or a region (Ac 2:9; 11:29; 19:10), though the term is used on occasion to describe spiritual realities: unclean spirits *residing* in a man (Mt 12:45 = Lk 11:26); God *dwelling* in His sanctuary (Mt 23:21; cp. Ac 7:48; 17:24); Christ *living* in believers' hearts (Eph 3:17); God's fullness *dwelling* in Christ (Col 1:19; 2:9); and righteousness *dwelling* in the new heavens and new earth (2Pt 3:11).

In Revelation, *katoikeo* always appears in a negative sense. Twelve of its thirteen occurrences (2:13 being the exception) appear in the phrase "those who *live on* the earth" (3:10; 6:10; 8:13; 11:10; 13:8,12,14; 17:2,8). This phrase always focuses upon unbelievers, envisioned as those who serve the beast and persecute believers, thus constituting themselves as God's enemies.

the power[A] to harm people for five months. [11] They had as their king[B] the angel of the abyss; his name in Hebrew is ˙Abaddon,[C] and in Greek he has the name Apollyon.[D] [12] The first woe has passed. There are still two more woes to come after this.

The Sixth Trumpet

[13] The sixth angel blew his trumpet. From the four[E] horns of the gold altar[a] that is before God, I heard a voice [14] say to the sixth angel who had the trumpet, "Release the four angels bound at the great river Euphrates." [15] So the four angels who were prepared for the hour, day, month, and year were released to kill a third of the human race. [16] The number of mounted troops was 200 million;[F] I heard their number. [17] This is how I saw the horses in my vision: The horsemen had breastplates that were fiery red, hyacinth blue, and sulfur yellow. The heads of the horses were like li-

ons' heads, and from their mouths came fire, smoke, and sulfur. [18] A third of the human race was killed by these three plagues—by the fire, the smoke, and the sulfur that came from their mouths. [19] For the power of the horses is in their mouths and in their tails, for their tails, which resemble snakes, have heads, and they inflict injury with them.

[20] The rest of the people, who were not killed by these plagues, did not repent of the works of their hands to stop worshiping demons[b] and idols of gold, silver, bronze, stone, and wood, which are not able to see, hear, or walk.[c] [21] And they did not repent of their murders, their sorceries,[G] their sexual immorality, or their thefts.

The Mighty Angel and the Small Scroll

10 Then I saw another mighty angel[d] coming down from heaven, surrounded by

[a]9:13 Ex 39:38; 40:5 [b]9:20 1Co 10:20 [c]Ps 115:4-7; 135:15-17; Dn 5:23 [d]10:1 Rv 5:2; 18:21

[A]9:10 Or *authority*   [B]9:11 Or *as king over them*   [C]9:11 Or *destruction*   [D]9:11 Or *destroyer*   [E]9:13 Other mss omit *four*
[F]9:16 Other mss read *100 million*   [G]9:21 Or *magic potions*, or *drugs*; Gk *pharmakon*

9:11 The **king** of these demonic creatures is called **Abaddon** (Hb) and **Apollyon** (Gk), which means "destruction" in both languages. It is ironic that unrepentant unbelievers, who worship demons (v. 20), are tormented by the very beings they worship during the judgment of the fifth trumpet.

9:12 The **first woe** predicted in 8:13 has now **passed** with the fifth trumpet (vv. 1-11). The **two** remaining woes are the sixth trumpet (11:14) and the seventh trumpet (11:15-19), which telescopes all the way to the second coming of Christ (19:11-16).

9:13 When the **sixth . . . trumpet** sounds, the authority of the **voice** from the **altar . . . before God** strongly suggests that this is the Lamb (Christ), not the martyrs related to the altar earlier (6:9-10), or even the angel whose actions led into the trumpet judgment (8:3-5).

9:14-16 The **four angels** are apparently demons in positions of authority over the demonic army, like Apollyon (v. 11). The **river Euphrates** was the eastern boundary of the land promised

to Abraham (Gn 15:18) and was crossed by the Assyrian and Babylonian empires on their way to invade Israel. That these demons are **prepared for the hour, day, month, and year** indicates that all these events are according to God's sovereign plan and timing (Dn 9:24-27). An army of **200 million** is large enough to accomplish such a horrific slaughter as killing **a third** (the same proportion of damage as in earlier trumpet judgments in Rv 8:7,9,10,11,12) **of the human race**. Some believe this army is human, but more likely it is demonic, as was the locust plague of the fifth trumpet judgment (vv. 2-11). It may not be either/or but both/and. On the heels of the judgment of the fifth trumpet, in which nobody was allowed to die (vv. 5-6)—which gives them the opportunity to repent before the Lord and be saved (vv. 20-21)—a third of the world's population that survived the earlier judgments (6:2,4,8,12-17; 8:9,11) is now slaughtered by this demonic army.

9:17-19 The term **plagues** (Gk *plege*) is used to echo God's plagues on Egypt in Exodus 7–11. It is also the first of many uses of *plege* in Revelation, speaking of God's judgment in the end times (11:6; 15:1,6,8; 16:9,21; 18:4,8). The statement that the **power** of the horses is in their **tails** and that they are like lions resembles what was said of the demonic locusts (v. 10). But it is unlikely that this refers to the same group since the locusts were not allowed to kill anyone (vv. 5-6).

9:20-21 The only way for anyone who survives the "plagues" of the trumpet judgments to be saved is to **repent** of their sins (Lk 24:47; Ac 26:20) and come to saving faith in Jesus Christ (Ac 16:31). But since the names of the "earth dwellers," upon whom the fifth and sixth trumpet judgments fall (Rv 8:13), are not written in the Lamb's book of life (13:8; 17:8), they will not repent. They give the same hard-hearted response Pharaoh gave when confronted with the plagues (Ex 7:22; 9:7; see also Rm 9:17-18 and notes there). The words **worshiping demons and idols**, as well as **sorceries** and **sexual immorality**, recall violence in the churches at Pergamum and Thyatira (2:13-14,20-21) and point forward to the multiplied sins of Babylon the Great (18:2,3,5,9).

10:1–11:14 This is a second interlude in the book of Revelation (the first is 7:1-17), falling between the sixth and

abussos	
Greek Pronunciation	[AH boos sahss]
HCSB Translation	abyss
Uses in Revelation	7
Uses in the NT	9
Focus passage	Revelation 9:11

Abussos (abyss) was originally an adjective describing something *unfathomable* with no apparent depth or bottom. In the Greek OT, *abussos* envisions the *fathomless* ocean depths (*watery depths*, Gn 1:2; 7:11; 8:2; Is 51:10) and possibly the realm of the dead (*depths of the earth*; Ps 63:9; 71:20). In the few centuries preceding Christ, *abussos* evolved to refer to the place of imprisonment for disobedient angelic spirits. This highly developed meaning carries into the NT, where *abussos* typically refers to the place of punishment in which demonic spirits (including the Devil) are held (Lk 8:31; Rv 9:1-2,11; 20:3), and the place from which the beast originates (11:7-8). *Abussos* may also refer to the present realm of the dead (Rm 10:7), a concept similar to that of the Greek term *hades* and the Hebrew term *sheol* (cp. Ps 16:10; Ac 2:27).

a cloud, with a rainbow[a] over his head.[A] His face was like the sun, his legs[B] were like fiery pillars,[b] [2]and he had a little scroll opened in his hand. He put his right foot on the sea, his left on the land, [3]and he cried out with a loud voice like a roaring lion. When he cried out, the seven thunders spoke with their voices. [4]And when the seven thunders spoke, I was about to write. Then I heard a voice from heaven, saying, "Seal up what the seven thunders said,[c] and do not write it down!"

[5]Then the angel that I had seen standing on the sea and on the land raised his right hand to heaven. [6]He swore an oath by the One who lives forever and ever,[d] who created heaven and what is in it, the earth and what is in it, and the sea and what is in it: "There will no longer be an interval of time,[c] [7]but in the days of the sound of the seventh angel,[e] when he will blow his trumpet, then God's •hidden

plan[f] will be completed, as He announced to His servants[D] the prophets."[g]

[8]Now the voice that I heard from heaven spoke to me again and said, "Go, take the scroll that lies open in the hand of the angel who is standing on the sea and on the land."

[9]So I went to the angel and asked him to give me the little scroll. He said to me, "Take and eat it; it will be bitter in your stomach, but it will be as sweet as honey in your mouth."[h]

[10]Then I took the little scroll from the angel's hand and ate it. It was as sweet as honey in my mouth, but when I ate it, my stomach became bitter.[i] [11]And I was told,[E] "You must prophesy again about[F] many peoples, nations, languages, and kings."[j]

The Two Witnesses

11 Then I was given a measuring reed[k] like a rod,[G] with these words: "Go[H] and mea-

---

a 10:1 Rv 4:3
b Rv 3:12
c 10:4 Dn 8:26; 12:4,9
d 10:6 Dn 12:7
e 10:7 Rv 11:15; 16:17
f Rv 1:20; 17:5,7
g 2 Kg 9:7; 17:23; Ezk 38:17; Am 3:7; Zch 1:6; 1Pt 2:10-12
h 10:9 Ps 119:103; Jr 15:16; Ezk 2:8-3:3
i 10:10 Nm 5:24; Ezk 3:1-3
j 10:11 Dn 3:4,7; 4:1; 5:19; 7:14; Rv 5:9; 7:9; 11:9
k 11:1 Ezk 40:3,5; 42:15-19; Rv 21:15

A 10:1 Or *a halo on his head*   B 10:1 Or *feet*   C 10:6 Or *be a delay*   D 10:7 Or *slaves*   E 10:11 Lit *And they said to me*   F 10:11 Or *prophesy again against*   G 11:1 Other mss add *and the angel stood up*   H 11:1 Lit *Arise*

---

seventh trumpets. Some interpreters think of chapters 12–14 as a third interlude, though these are actually a prelude to the bowl judgments (15:1–19:5).

10:1 The **mighty angel** could be: (1) the angel introduced in 5:2, (2) the angel seen in 18:1, or (3) **another** angel altogether. In spite of his impressive appearance and the similarity to the vision of the Son of Man (i.e., the glorified Christ) in 1:13-16, it is unlikely this is Christ. Christ is never called an angel elsewhere in the NT.

10:2 The **little scroll** (Gk *biblaridion*) may be (1) a second scroll in the Apocalypse, or (2) since it is opened, the scroll which was finally **opened** for viewing in 8:1. Perhaps the scroll in this verse appears small because the angel holding it is so huge (his **right foot** being on **the sea** and his **left** foot being on **the land**).

10:3-4 In 1Pt 5:8, the Devil is said to be like a **roaring lion**. In this case, the angel's lion-like voice may be because he is speaking for the Lion of Judah (5:5), the glorified Christ.

---

phone

Greek Pronunciation	[foh NAY]
HCSB Translation	voice, sound
Uses in Revelation	55
Uses in the NT	139
Focus passage	Revelation 10:3-4,7-8

In classical Greek, *phone* normally refers to *verbal sounds*, including a battle *cry*, the *noise* of an animal, or a human *language* or dialect. Similarly, the related verb *phoneo* means *to produce a sound* or *tone*. In the NT, *phoneo* occurs 43 times, 42 in the Gospels and Acts, with the dominant meanings *to call, call out,* or *summon,* but it also refers to a rooster's *crowing* (e.g., Mt 26:34,74-75). *Phone* most commonly refers to *the voice* (Mt 2:18; Jn 1:23; Rv 10:3-4,7-8), but it also has other uses, such as the *sound* of the wind (Jn 3:8; Ac 2:6), the *sound* of musical instruments (1Co 14:7-8; Heb 12:19; Rv 8:13; 18:22), and human *language* (1Co 14:10-11). In Revelation, *phone* sometimes refers to the *rumblings* of thunder, signifying God's presence and power (4:5; 8:5; 11:19; 14:2; 16:18; 19:6).

The **seven thunders** may be an allusion to Psalm 29. The number seven stands for completeness in Revelation. So these thunders may look forward to the completion of God's judgment in the rest of the book. The proper perspective on the sealed writing is: "The hidden things belong to the LORD our God" (Dt 29:29).

10:5-7 On the **angel . . . standing on the sea**, see note at verse 1. The pace of divine judgment is about to quicken and **be completed**, with the sounding of the seventh trumpet (11:15-19), which telescopes all the way to the second coming of Christ (see note at 11:15-19). God's **hidden plan** (Gk *musterion*) is truth that has not been previously revealed or fulfilled, but is being revealed now (Eph 3:9). The phrase **His servants the prophets** echoes the same wording in Am 3:7, but it probably refers to both OT and NT (Eph 2:20; 4:11) prophets in this passage.

10:8-11 John taking the **open** scroll from **the hand of the angel** represents delegated authority, even as it did when the Lamb (Christ) took the unopened scroll from God the Father in 5:7. For John to **eat** the scroll recalls Ezekiel being commanded to do the same thing (Ezk 3:1-3). This turned out to be a bitter ministry for Ezekiel (3:14). In John's case, while the eating was **as sweet as honey**, the digesting was **bitter**. The implication here is that the ministry of the Word of God is bittersweet because, while the intake and preaching of Scripture (i.e., John's command to **prophesy**) is sweet, the calloused rejection of the hearers is bitter indeed.

11:1-2 The mention of a **measuring reed** like a **rod** and the command to **go and measure God's sanctuary and the altar** calls to mind Ezk 40:3,5. The phrase **count those who worship there** appears to speak of God's people, while the **courtyard outside the sanctuary** was the court of the Gentiles (**the nations**). It is not necessary for the second temple to have still been standing in Jerusalem for John to see a vision of the sanctuary and its court. It is possible that he saw a rebuilt end-times temple in Jerusalem since that seems to be assumed by 2Th 2:4. The statement that the Gentiles will **trample the holy city** (Jerusalem) echoes Jesus' statement about "the times of the Gentiles" (Lk 21:24) just before the second coming of Christ.

sure God's sanctuary and the altar, and count those who worship there. ²But exclude the courtyard outside the sanctuary. Don't measure it, because it is given to the nations,ᴬ and they will trample the holy city for 42 months. ³I will empowerᴮ my two witnesses, and they will prophesy for 1,260 days,ᶜ·ᵃ dressed in •sackcloth."ᴰ ⁴These are the two olive trees and the two lampstands that stand before the Lordᴱ of the earth.ᵇ ⁵If anyone wants to harm them, fire comes from their mouths and consumes their enemies;ᶜ if anyone wants to harm them, he must be killed in this way. ⁶These men have the power to close up the sky so that it does not rain during the days of their prophecy.ᵈ They also have power over the waters to turn them into bloodᵉ and to strike the earth with every plague whenever they want.

ᵃ11:3 Dn 12:11; Rv 12:6,14; 13:5
ᵇ11:4 Zch 4:3, 11-14
ᶜ11:5 Jr 5:14
ᵈ11:6 1Kg 17:1
ᵉEx 7:17-21
ᶠ11:7 Rv 13:1,11; 17:8
ᵍ11:8 Is 66:24
ʰ11:9 Rv 5:9; 7:9; 10:11
ⁱ11:11 Gn 2:7; 6:17; 7:15,22; Ezk 37:5

The Witnesses Martyred

⁷When they finish their testimony, the beastᶠ·ᶠ that comes up out of the •abyss will make war with them, conquer them, and kill them. ⁸Their dead bodiesᴳ·ᵍ will lie in the public squareᴴ of the great city, which prophetically ⁱ is called Sodom and Egypt, where also their Lord was crucified. ⁹And representatives fromᴶ the peoples, tribes, languages, and nationsʰ will view their bodies for three and a half days and not permit their bodies to be put into a tomb. ¹⁰Those who live on the earth will gloat over them and celebrate and send gifts to one another because these two prophets brought judgment to those who live on the earth.

The Witnesses Resurrected

¹¹But after 3½ days, the breathᴷ of lifeⁱ from

ᴬ11:2 Or *Gentiles*   ᴮ11:3 Lit *I will give to*   ᶜ11:3 = 3 1/2 years of 30-day months   ᴰ11:3 Mourning garment of coarse, often black, material   ᴱ11:4 Other mss read *God*   ᶠ11:7 Or *wild animal*   ᴳ11:8 Lit *Their corpse*   ᴴ11:8 Or *lie on the broad street*   ⁱ11:8 Or *spiritually, or symbolically*   ᴶ11:9 Lit *And from*   ᴷ11:11 Or *spirit*

11:3-4 The **1,260 days**, in which **two** unnamed **witnesses . . . prophesy** for the Lord, is in stark contrast to the "42 months" of 11:2 and 13:5. Since no one can harm the witnesses until "they finish their testimony" (11:7), and since they die in Jerusalem (see note at vv. 8-10)—apparently having ministered there—this period of 1,260 days cannot be the same three-and-one-half-year period as the reign of the beast (13:5). The 1,260 days precede the beast's reign, because part of his rise to worldwide prominence is based on killing the two witnesses (11:7). These witnesses are **dressed in sackcloth**, the garb of mourning and repentance (Jl 1:13; Jnh 3:5-6). The **two olive trees** and the **two lampstands** are imagery from Zechariah 4, where the two figures appear to be Zerubbabel the governor and Joshua the high priest, and the task at hand was the rebuilding of the temple. Perhaps John used this imagery to recall the crucial spiritual principle articulated in that chapter: "'Not

therion

Greek Pronunciation	[thay REE ahn]
HCSB Translation	beast
Uses in Revelation	39
Uses in the NT	46
Focus passage	Revelation 11:7

Therion (beast, animal) was used to refer to any living creature excluding man, but usually wild, *undomesticated animals*. In mythological imagery, *therion* could describe supernatural *creatures* such as the griffin, the hydra, or a huge dragon.

In the NT, *therion* normally refers to *undomesticated animals* in general (Mk 1:13; Ac 11:6; Ti 1:12; Heb 12:20; Jms 3:7), including a snake (Ac 28:4-5) and particularly dangerous animals (Rv 6:8). However, Daniel 7 and most of the occurrences of *therion* in Revelation (6:8; 18:2 excepted) reflect the more metaphorical, mythological imagery. *Therion* occurs ten times in the Greek OT of Daniel 7, where four *creatures* arise from the sea, understood as four Gentile empires (7:17). Similarly, Revelation uses *therion* as (1) a vivid personification of an ungodly Gentile empire (Rv 17:3-5), (2) the antichrist (11:7,17; 13:1-4; 17:7-8; 19:19), or (3) the false prophet (13:11).

by strength or by might, but by My Spirit,' says the Lᴏʀᴅ of Hosts" (Zch 4:6).

11:5-6 Besides being invulnerable to physical **harm**, the ministry of the two witnesses echoes the great miracles of the ministries of Elijah and Moses (who had appeared together on the Mount of Transfiguration; Mt 17:3). **Fire** that **consumes their enemies** looks back to Elijah's ministry in 2Kg 1:10-12. No **rain during the days of their prophecy** (which is three-and-one-half years long; v. 3) echoes the three-year drought that Elijah prophesied (1Kg 17:1; 18:1). Power over the waters **to turn them into blood** and **to strike the earth with every plague** recalls Moses' ministry in Egypt (Ex 7–11).

11:7 The **beast**, the great antichrist figure prophesied elsewhere (Dn 7:20-21,25; 2Th 2:9-11; 1Jn 2:18), and the satanically-inspired world ruler in Revelation 13 and 17, now makes his initial appearance. His origin is said to be **the abyss**, from which the demonic locusts came (9:1-10), and where Satan will be imprisoned (20:1-3). It is only because their three-and-one-half-year period of ministry is completed that the beast is able to **make war** with the two witnesses and kill them. The irony of using the word **conquer** to speak of the death of the witnesses is that, while it may seem that the beast is victorious (vv. 7-10), these witnesses, as martyrs, come back to life (vv. 11-12).

11:8-10 **The great city** is the usual way of referring to Babylon the Great in Revelation (17:18; 18:10), as well as **Sodom** (infamous for its sexual immorality) and **Egypt** (where God's people had been slaves). This depicts the wickedness of Jerusalem's inhabitants at this time. The brutal death of the two witnesses, the sacrilege of not giving them a proper burial, and the glee of the non-elect "earth dwellers" (see notes at 13:8 and 17:7-8) at their deaths, demonstrate that wickedness. That the witnesses are also called **prophets** in the context of their death at the hands of the beast places them in the category of other prophets who had died for their faith and who are honored in Revelation (v. 18; 16:6; 18:20,24).

11:11-12 The phrase **after 3½ days** is intended to be compared with Jesus being resurrected on the third day (1Co

God entered them, and they stood on their feet. So great fear fell on those who saw them. [12]Then they heard[A] a loud voice from heaven saying to them, "Come up here." They went up to heaven in a cloud, while their enemies watched them.[a] [13]At that moment a violent earthquake took place,[b] a tenth of the city fell, and 7,000 people were killed in the earthquake. The survivors were terrified and gave glory to the God of heaven. [14]The second woe has passed. Take note: The third woe is coming quickly!

The Seventh Trumpet

[15]The seventh angel blew his trumpet,[d] and there were loud voices in heaven saying:

The kingdom of the *world has become
    the kingdom
of our Lord and of His *Messiah,
and He will reign forever
    and ever![e]

[16]The 24 elders, who were seated before God on their thrones, fell facedown and worshiped God, [17]saying:

We thank You, Lord God, the Almighty,
    who is and who was,[B,f]
because You have taken Your great power
    and have begun to reign.[g]
[18]   The nations were angry,[h]
but Your wrath has come.
The time has come
for the dead to be judged
and to give the reward
to Your servants the prophets,[i]
to the *saints, and to those who fear
    Your name,
both small and great,[j]
and the time has come to destroy
    those who destroy the earth.

[19]God's sanctuary in heaven was opened, and the ark of His covenant[c] appeared in His sanctu-

Cross references:
[a]11:12 2Kg 2:1; Mk 16:19; Lk 24:51; Ac 1:9-10
[b]11:13 Is 29:6; Ezk 38:19
[c]11:14 Rv 8:13; 9:12
[d]11:15 Is 27:13
[e]2Sm 7:16; Is 37:16; Dn 7:14,18; Lk 1:32-33
[f]11:17 Rv 1:4,8; 4:8; 16:5
[g]Lk 1:33; 1Co 15:25; Rv 19:6
[h]11:18 Ps 2:1
[i]Rv 10:7
[j]2Kg 23:2; Ps 115:13; Rv 19:5

[A]11:12 Other mss read *Then I heard*   [B]11:17 Other mss add *and who is to come*   [C]11:19 Other mss read *ark of the covenant of the Lord*

15:4). The **breath of life** probably echoes the spiritual resuscitation of Israel pictured in the "valley of dry bones" in Ezk 37:5,10 and sets the stage for the widespread conversion of Israel in Rv 11:13. **Great fear** can be a positive thing since "the fear of the LORD" is the beginning of wisdom (Pr 1:7). The phrase **come up here** is understood by some interpreters to speak of the rapture of the church at the middle of the tribulation, though this passage refers to only two people.

11:13 Everything changes in one **moment**, from rejoicing at the death of the two witnesses (vv. 7-10) to shock at their resurrection, then hanging on for dear life in the devastation of **a violent earthquake**. In the midst of the widespread damage and death, fear turns into faith with many who saw the resurrection and ascension of the two witnesses. The proper response to the "eternal gospel" to be preached to everyone still alive on the earth in 14:6-7 is to "fear God and give Him glory." Since this takes place in Jerusalem, where most people present would be Jewish, this could be the fulfillment of Paul's prophecy that "all Israel will be saved" (Rm 11:25). Others view this as nothing more than a "foxhole conversion," in which there is a momentary acknowledgment of the Lord but no authentic faith.

11:14 The **second woe** of the three predicted in 8:13 has now passed. Since **the third woe is coming quickly**, it apparently is closely related to the seventh trumpet (vv. 15-19; see note there).

11:15-19 The sense of finality in the wording of the **seventh . . . trumpet** has caused some interpreters to think this is the point of the second coming of Christ and that the following chapters double back and retrace the same ground from a different perspective. In a full-blown "recapitulation" view, it is held that the seals, trumpets, and bowls all speak of the same judgments from different perspectives. Such an approach is not necessary, however, since the seventh trumpet overarches the seven bowls of wrath, with the seventh bowl telescoping all the way to the preparation for the second coming of Christ. This perspective is supported by the fact that the phenomena (lightning, rumblings, thunder,

an earthquake, and severe hail) ready to be poured out on the earth related to the seventh trumpet (v. 19) are not actually poured out until the seventh bowl (16:18,21).

11:15 The phrase **the kingdom of this world has become the kingdom of our Lord and of His Messiah** can be understood as (1) the earthly reign of Christ (20:4-6) has already begun at this point, and chapters 12-19 is a *déjà vu* of the first half of the book, until the narrative arrives at another description of "the kingdom of our Lord over this world," in 20:4-6; (2) the past tense "has become" speaks of certainty so strong that the future is spoken of in the past tense (i.e., "will certainly become"); (3) what is already true in heaven will come true on earth ("Your kingdom come, Your will be done on earth as it is in heaven," Mt 6:10); or (4) the timeless perspective of heaven is different from that of this world (e.g., from the standpoint of heaven, "every creature" in the universe blesses God and the Lamb in Rv 5:13, long before "every knee should bow . . . and every tongue should confess that Jesus Christ is Lord, to the glory of God the Father" [Php 2:10-11] at the final judgment [Rv 20:11-15]). Any of the last three explanations is more likely than the first.

11:16-18 On the **24 elders**, see note at 4:3-4. **Lord God . . . who is and who was** means the One who not only exists but has existed eternally. **You . . . have begun to reign** may mean that (1) the kingdom of God already exists in this world in some sense (1:9), or (2) God's power to reign in heaven is about to come to earth in the wake of His climactic **wrath** being displayed in the pouring out of the bowls of wrath (15:1-19:5), immediately after the prelude to that section (chaps. 12-14). The **time . . . for the dead to be judged . . . to give the reward** to God's people (2Co 5:10), and **to destroy those who destroy the earth** (probably the "earth dwellers" at 3:10; 6:9-11; and 8:13) comes after Christ's return (20:11-15).

11:19 The **ark** of the **covenant** had been in the "holy of holies" in the tabernacle (Ex 40:3) and the temple (1Kg 6:19), which was destroyed by the invading Babylonian army (2Ch 36:19). Now it is seen in the heavenly "holy of holies."

ary. There were flashes of lightning, rumblings of thunder,[a] an earthquake,[A] and severe hail.

The Woman, the Child, and the Dragon

12 A great sign[B] appeared in heaven: a woman clothed with the sun, with the moon under her feet and a crown of 12 stars on her head.[b] [2]She was pregnant and cried out in labor and agony as she was about to give birth. [3]Then another sign[c] appeared in heaven: There was a great fiery red dragon having seven heads and 10 horns,[c] and on his heads were seven diadems.[D] [4]His tail swept away a third of the stars in heaven and hurled them to the earth.[d] And the dragon stood in front of the woman who was about to give birth, so that when she did give birth he might devour her child. [5]But she gave birth to a Son—a male who is going to shepherd[E] all nations with an iron scepter[e]—and her child was caught up to God and to His throne. [6]The woman fled into the wilderness, where she had a place prepared by God,[f] to be fed there[F] for 1,260 days.[g]

[a]11:19 Rv 4:5; 8:5
[b]12:1 Gn 37:9-10
[c]12:3 Dn 7:7
[d]12:4 Dn 8:10
[e]12:5 Ps 2:7-9; Rv 19:15
[f]12:6 1Kg 19:3-8
[g]Dn 12:11; Rv 11:3; 12:14; 13:5
[h]12:7 Dn 10:13,21; 12:1
[i]12:9 Gn 3:1
[j]Lk 10:18; Rm 16:20; Rv 2:9; 3:9; 20:2,7
[k]1Tm 5:15
[l]12:10 Jb 1:9-11; Zch 3:1
[m]12:11 Jn 12:25

The Dragon Thrown Out of Heaven

[7]Then war broke out in heaven: Michael[h] and his angels fought against the dragon. The dragon and his angels also fought, [8]but he could not prevail, and there was no place for them in heaven any longer. [9]So the great dragon was thrown out—the ancient serpent,[i] who is called the Devil[G] and Satan,[H,j] the one who deceives the whole world.[k] He was thrown to earth, and his angels with him.

[10]Then I heard a loud voice in heaven say:

The salvation and the power
and the kingdom of our God
and the authority of His •Messiah
have now come,
because the accuser[l] of our •brothers
has been thrown out:
the one who accuses them
before our God day and night.
[11] They conquered him
by the blood of the Lamb
and by the word of their testimony,
for they did not love their lives
in the face of death.[m]

A11:19 Other mss omit *an earthquake*   B12:1 Or *great symbolic display*; see Rv 12:3   C12:3 Or *another symbolic display*   D12:3 Or *crowns*   E12:5 Or *rule*   F12:6 Lit *God, that they might feed her there*   G12:9 In Gk, *diabolos* means slanderer.   H12:9 In Hb, Satan means adversary.

12:1–14:20 This section functions as a prelude to the bowls-of-wrath sequence (15:1–19:5). During a "time-out" from the progress of the narrative, it provides a midstream orientation to some characters and content that are crucial to understanding the second half of the Apocalypse.

12:1-2 John used an important term he had used in the Fourth Gospel (Jn 20:30)—**sign** (Gk *semeion*). It is first used for imagery that echoes Joseph's vision in Gn 37:9, speaking of the people of Israel. More likely this sign refers to ethnic Israel or a believing remnant of Jews. The woman being **pregnant** and **in labor and agony** recalls Gn 3:15-16. The prophecy of the virgin birth (Is 7:14) of Christ may also be in view.

12:3 The second **sign** (see note at v. 1), a **great . . . dragon**, is interpreted in v. 9 as referring to the Devil and Satan. The description of the dragon having **seven heads** and **10 horns** is similar to that of the beast in 13:1, but different enough ("10 horns and seven heads") to make clear that the two are separate characters.

12:4 It is possible that **a third of the stars in heaven** being **swept away** is related to the destruction of one-third during several of the trumpet judgments (8:7,8,9,10,12; 9:15,18), but since the **dragon** symbolizes Satan, these **stars** may stand for fallen angels who followed Satan in his rebellion (Mt 25:41). The phrase **the dragon stood in front of the woman . . . so that . . . he might devour her child** indicates that the attempt of King Herod the Great to kill the baby Jesus (Mt 2:1-16) was satanically inspired.

12:5 The words **Son . . . all nations**, and **with an iron scepter** are allusions to Psalm 2, which is filled with messianic prophecy. The word **shepherd** may be a reflection that, as Christ will tenderly shepherd His people, there is another side to that role—shepherding the unbelievers among the

nations with an **iron scepter**. The narrative then leaps ahead all the way from the birth of Christ to His ascension (see Ac 1:9-11 and note there).

12:6 Some time after the ascension of the Son, **the woman** is supernaturally cared for by the Lord for **1,260 days** (three and one-half years)—the exact words that describe the period of protection of the two witnesses (11:3). This probably takes place shortly after the two witnesses have ascended, near the beginning of the second half of a seven-year tribulation period. The woman fleeing likely is representative of Jewish converts who feared God (11:18) and glorified Him (11:13) after the witnesses were resurrected and ascended (11:11-13). The imagery of the woman is a continuation from the faithful remnant of Israel, including Mary, the mother of Jesus. The **wilderness** was the setting where the nation of Israel was protected by the Lord from Pharaoh's army and was miraculously fed manna and quail (Ex 16).

12:7-10 Because it is mentioned immediately after the woman fleeing into the wilderness (v. 6) and because its outcome immediately affects the earth at the end of the age (vv. 12-13), the **war . . . in heaven** probably also takes place just after the midpoint of the tribulation period. Some interpreters hold that the cosmic war pictured here occurred after Satan's original fall (Is 14:12-15; Ezk 28:11-17) or during the events surrounding Christ's crucifixion (Col 2:14-15). The sense that the "woman" in Rv 12:6 is a believing remnant of Israel (see notes at 11:13 and 12:6) is strengthened by the clash of the **dragon** (identified as **the Devil and Satan**) with **Michael** the archangel (Jd 9), who is assigned to protect Israel (Dn 12:1).

12:11 Sometimes what looks like defeat is victory, as when believers die for their faith. Satan has killed them, but they are the ultimate victors because of the **blood of the Lamb**

12 Therefore rejoice, you heavens,
　and you who dwell in them!
Woe to the earth and the sea,
　for the Devil has come down to you
　with great fury,
because he knows he has a short time.

The Woman Persecuted

[13]When the dragon saw that he had been thrown to earth, he persecuted the woman who gave birth to the male child. [14]The woman was given two wings of a great eagle, so that she could fly from the serpent's presence to her place in the wilderness, where she was fed for a time, times, and half a time.[A,a] [15]From his mouth the serpent spewed water like a river flowing after the woman, to sweep her away in a torrent. [16]But the earth helped the woman. The earth opened its mouth and swallowed up the river that the dragon had spewed from his mouth. [17]So the dragon was furious with the

woman and left to wage war[b] against the rest of her offspring[B]—those who keep God's commands and have the testimony about Jesus.[c] [18]He[c] stood on the sand of the sea.[D]

The Beast from the Sea

13 And I saw a beast coming up out of the sea.[d] He[E] had 10 horns and seven heads. On his horns were 10 diadems,[e] and on his heads were blasphemous names.[F,f] [2]The beast I saw was like a leopard, his feet were like a bear's, and his mouth was like a lion's mouth.[g] The dragon gave him his power, his throne, and great authority. [3]One of his heads appeared to be fatally wounded,[G] but his fatal wound was healed. The whole earth was amazed and followed the beast.[H,h] [4]They worshiped the dragon[i] because he gave authority to the beast. And they worshiped the beast, saying, "Who is like the beast?[j] Who is able to wage war against him?"

Cross references (center column)

a 12:14 Dn 7:25; 12:7; Rv 11:2; 13:5
b 12:17 Rv 11:7; 13:7
c Rv 1:2,9; 19:10; 20:4
d 13:1 Dn 7:3
e Rv 12:3
f Rv 17:3
g 13:2 Dn 7:4-6
h 13:3 Rv 17:8
i 13:4 Rv 12:3
j Ex 15:11; Is 46:5

A 12:14 This expression, occurring in Dn 7:25; 12:7, = 3 1/2 years or 42 months (Rv 11:2; 13:5) or 1,260 days (Rv 11:3).　**B** 12:17 Or *seed*　**C** 12:18 Other mss read *I*. "He" is apparently a reference to the dragon.　**D** 12:18 Some translations put Rv 12:18 either in Rv 12:17 or Rv 13:1.　**E** 13:1 The beasts in Rv 13:1,11 are customarily referred to as "he" or "him" rather than "it." The Gk word for a beast (*therion*) is grammatically neuter.　**F** 13:1 Other mss read *heads was a blasphemous name*　**G** 13:3 Lit *be slain to death*　**H** 13:3 Lit *amazed after the beast*

(Christ's death on the cross) and **the word of their testimony**.

12:12 Because Satan has been banned from heaven (vv. 7-9), the **heavens** and those **who dwell in them** can **rejoice**. The "heaven dwellers" are the counterpart group in Revelation to the "earth dwellers" (3:10; 6:9-11; 8:13; 11:8-10; 13:8). **The Devil**, having been cast down to earth, is enraged and will take out his great fury on **the earth and the sea**, because **he knows** his time (Gk *kairos*, "occasion, opportunity") is **short**.

hexakosioi hexekonta hex

Greek Pronunciation	[heks uh KAH see oi heks AY kahn tah HEX]
HCSB Translation	666
Uses in Revelation	1
Uses in the NT	1
Focus passage	Revelation 13:18

No biblical number has received as much attention as 666. Much that is said about this mysterious number in popular literature is misleading, but reasonable explanations exist. One explanation applies *Gematria*. This practice of representing words by numerical equivalents was found in extrabiblical religious sources and was based upon the fact that Hebrew and Greek attached a numerical value to each alphabetical letter. Thus every word could be assigned a numerical value by summing the values of its letters. Thus the beast's name could be deduced from his number (Rv 13:18; 15:2). Others believe 666 is one example of John's normal figurative use of numbers (cp. 5:11; 7:4,9; 9:15; 20:8), none of which were ever intended to be calculated. In this view, the number six indicates incompleteness and serves as a contrastive counterpart to the occurrences of seven (signifying completeness) in the book of Revelation. Triple repetition of six would indicate the absolute sinful imperfection of the beast.

12:13-14 Out of frustration for being cast out of heaven and **thrown to earth** (vv. 7-9), the dragon (Satan), also symbolized as the serpent in this passage, persecuted **the woman** (believing Israel) for a period of three and one-half years. The phrase **time, times, and half a time** is a year, two years, and half a year—three and one-half years total. This phrase is taken from Dn 7:25 and 12:7, where it speaks of a period in which "the holy ones" are persecuted in the end times. That the woman was given **two wings of a great eagle** is the same imagery used of Israel escaping the Egyptian army in the wilderness (Ex 19:4).

12:15-16 There is no way of knowing if the onslaught of the **serpent . . . dragon** (Satan; see note at vv. 7-10) against the woman (believing Israel; see notes at v. 6 and 11:13), as well as the description of the Lord's protection (**the earth . . . swallowed up the river**), is meant to be taken literally. Perhaps a metaphorical interpretation is intended.

12:17 Unable to get at the woman, the Devil (**the dragon**) turns aside to **wage war** against (i.e., kill; 11:7) the Gentile "saints" (13:7). The Gentiles are called **the rest of her offspring** because they are Christ's "other sheep that are not of this [Jewish] fold" (Jn 10:16). The other offspring, like John (Rv 1:9) and the martyrs seen under the heavenly altar (6:9), have kept **God's commands** and **the testimony about Jesus**.

13:1-3 The **beast coming up out of the sea** (the so-called sea of humanity), first mentioned in 11:7 (where his origin was the abyss), is described in similar terms (**leopard . . . bear's . . . feet . . . lion's mouth**) to (1) the beasts (esp. the fourth one) in the vision of Daniel 7, (2) the dragon in Rv 12:3 (**10 horns, seven heads, 10 diadems**), and (3) Satan, who now gave him **his power** and **great authority**. Since the beast was embarrassed by the resurrection and ascension of the two witnesses (11:11-12), 13:3 appears to describe either an actual resurrection or a nearly fatal wound.

[5]A mouth was given to him to speak boasts and blasphemies.[a] He was also given authority to act[A,B] for 42 months.[b] [6]He began to speak[c] blasphemies against God: to blaspheme His name and His dwelling—those who dwell in heaven. [7]And he was permitted to wage war against the •saints and to conquer them. He was also given authority over every tribe, people, language, and nation.[c] [8]All those who live on the earth will worship him, everyone whose name was not written from the foundation of the world in the book[D] of life[d] of the Lamb who was slaughtered.[E,e]

[9]If anyone has an ear, he should listen:[f]

[10] If anyone is destined for captivity,
    into captivity he goes.
    If anyone is to be killed[F] with a sword,
    with a sword he will be killed.[g]

This demands the perseverance[G] and faith of the saints.[h]

The Beast from the Earth

[11]Then I saw another beast coming up out of the earth; he had two horns like a lamb,[H,i] but he sounded like a dragon. [12]He exercises all the authority of the first beast on his be-

half and compels the earth and those who live on it to worship the first beast, whose fatal wound was healed. [13]He also performs great signs, even causing fire to come down from heaven to earth in front of people. [14]He deceives those who live on the earth[j] because of the signs that he is permitted to perform on behalf of the beast,[k] telling those who live on the earth to make an image[l] of the beast who had the sword wound and yet lived. [15]He was permitted to give a spirit[J] to the image of the beast, so that the image of the beast could both speak and cause whoever would not worship the image of the beast to be killed. [16]And he requires everyone—small and great, rich and poor, free and •slave—to be given a mark[K] on his right hand or on his forehead,[l] [17]so that no one can buy or sell unless he has the mark: the beast's name or the number of his name.

[18]Here is wisdom:[L,m] The one who has understanding must calculate[M] the number of the beast, because it is the number of a man.[N] His number is 666.[O]

The Lamb and the 144,000

14 Then I looked, and there on Mount •Zion stood the Lamb, and with Him

Cross references (center column)

[a]13:5 Dn 7:8,11,20
[b]13:5 Rv 11:2
[c]13:7 Rv 5:9; 7:9; 11:9; 14:6
[d]13:8 Ex 32:32-33; Ps 69:28; Php 4:3; Rv 3:5; 17:8; 20:12,15; 21:27
[e]1Pt 1:19-20
[f]13:9 Rv 2:7
[g]13:10 Jr 15:2
[h]Rv 14:12
[i]13:11 Dn 8:3
[j]13:14 Rv 12:9
[k]2Th 2:9-12
[l]13:16 Rv 14:1
[m]13:18 Rv 17:9

[A]13:5 Other mss read *wage war*   [B]13:5 Or *to rule*   [C]13:6 Lit *He opened his mouth in*   [D]13:8 Or *scroll*   [E]13:8 Or *written in the book of life of the Lamb who was slaughtered from the foundation of the world*   [F]13:10 Other mss read *anyone kills*   [G]13:10 Lit *Here is the perseverance*   [H]13:11 Or *ram*   [I]13:14 Or *statue*, or *likeness*   [J]13:15 Or *give breath*, or *give life*   [K]13:16 Or *stamp*, or *brand*   [L]13:18 Or *This calls for wisdom*   [M]13:18 Or *count*, or *figure out*   [N]13:18 Or *is a man's number*, or *is the number of a person*   [O]13:18 Other Gk mss read *616*

13:5-7 The Lord allows the beast to **speak. . . against God** as well as the **authority** to conduct his worldwide reign of terror against Gentile believers (**the saints**; see note at 12:17). This blasphemy takes place for the remaining three and one-half years (**42 months**) of the tribulation period, after the witnesses complete their ministry and are taken to heaven (11:3,7,11-12). This is the same 42 months spoken of in 11:2. The use of *skeyney* (Gk, "tent, tabernacle, dwelling place") as the word for **dwelling** equates "the saints" with the "vast multitude from every nation" in 7:9 (see note at 7:9-12), of whom it was said that God "will shelter them" (Gk *skeynoo;* "to live in a tent, dwell with," 7:15). In the wording "vast multitude," these "heaven dwellers" are seen later in the book praising God for His just judgment (19:1) and for the Lamb's marriage to His bride (19:7), just before the second coming of Christ (19:11-16).

13:8 This verse explains why the "earth dwellers" (see notes at 3:10; 6:9-11; 8:13) **worship** the beast—the absence of their names from **the book of life of the Lamb**, which contains the names of all those who will be spared the lake of fire at the last judgment (20:12,15).

13:9-10 The phrase **if anyone has an ear** functions as a call to **perseverance** and the **faith of the saints** (see notes at 13:5-7; 18:20; and 18:24), even unto death if necessary. Some are **destined** by God for **captivity** and some to be martyrs.

13:11 A second beast (**another** of the same kind; Gk *allos*) that arises is apparently a religious leader because he is called "the false prophet" in 16:13; 19:20; 20:10. Outwardly,

he seems gentle like Christ (**like a lamb**), but his prophecies are the voice of Satan (**like a dragon**).

13:12-13 The second beast has full delegated **authority** from **the first beast** to complete his mission—worldwide **worship** of the first beast. Causing **fire** to come down from **heaven** sounds like a mimicking of one of the miracles performed by the two witnesses (11:5).

13:14-15 The second beast shows his likeness to Satan as he **deceives** (12:9) the "earth dwellers" through the spectacular **signs** he can perform (see 2Th 2:9). He persuades the "earth dwellers" to erect an **image** of the first beast to worship. This sort of thing was common to John's original readers, who had been exposed to images of the Greco-Roman gods and Roman emperors, but this image comes to life.

13:16-18 The **mark** of the beast, apparently a sort of tattoo or brand of the beast's **name** or its numerical equivalent, is required for anyone to conduct business in that day. The mark is clearly contrasted with the seal (7:3-4) and the name of the Lamb and the Father (14:1) on the foreheads of the 144,000. The **number** (666) reflects the fact that the number 6 is just short of the number of perfection, which is 7. So the number 666 intensifies the sense that the beast does not possess the perfection of divinity. But the validity of such calculations will become fully clear only as the end-time events unfold.

14:1-5 The **144,000**, first seen on earth in 7:4-8 (see note there), are now seen on the heavenly **Mount Zion** with Christ, the **Lamb**. The beast cannot touch them, even

were 144,000 who had His name and His Father's name written on their foreheads.[a] [2]I heard a sound[A] from heaven like the sound of cascading waters[b] and like the rumbling of loud thunder. The sound I heard was also like harpists playing on their harps.[c] [3]They sang[B] a new song[d] before the throne and before the four living creatures and the elders,[e] but no one could learn the song except the 144,000 who had been *redeemed[c] from the earth. [4]These are the ones not defiled with women, for they have kept their virginity.[f] These are the ones who follow the Lamb wherever He goes. They were redeemed[C,D] from the human race as the *firstfruits[g] for God and the Lamb. [5]No lie was found in their mouths; they are blameless.[h]

The Proclamation of Three Angels

[6]Then I saw another angel flying high overhead,[i] having the eternal gospel to announce to the inhabitants of the earth—to every nation, tribe, language, and people.[j] [7]He spoke with a loud voice: "Fear God and give Him glory, because the hour of His judgment has come. Worship the Maker of heaven and earth, the sea and springs of water."

[8]A second angel[E] followed, saying: "It has fallen, Babylon the Great has fallen,[F] who made all nations drink the wine of her sexual immorality,[G] which brings wrath."[k]

a14:1 Rv 3:12; 7:3; 13:16
b14:2 Ezk 1:24; 43:2; Rv 1:15; 19:6
cRv 5:8
d14:3 Rv 5:9
eRv 4:4,6
f14:4 1Sm 21:4-5
gEx 23:19
h14:5 Zph 3:13
i14:6 Rv 8:13
jRv 5:9; 7:9; 11:9; 13:7
k14:8 Is 21:9; Jr 51:7-8,49; Rv 18:2
l14:10 Ps 75:8; Is 51:17; Jr 25:15-17
mLk 17:29; Rv 20:10; 21:8
n14:11 Is 1:31; 34:10; 66:24; Rv 19:3
o14:12 Rv 13:10
p14:13 Rv 1:3; 16:15; 19:9; 20:6; 22:7,14
q14:14 Dn 7:13; Lk 21:27; Rv 1:13
r14:15 Jl 3:13

[9]And a third angel[H] followed them and spoke with a loud voice: "If anyone worships the beast and his image and receives a mark on his forehead or on his hand, [10]he will also drink the wine of God's wrath, which is mixed full strength in the cup of His anger.[l] He will be tormented with fire and sulfur[m] in the sight of the holy angels and in the sight of the Lamb, [11]and the smoke of their torment will go up forever and ever.[n] There is no rest[I] day or night for those who worship the beast and his image, or anyone who receives the mark of his name. [12]This demands the perseverance[J] of the *saints,[o] who keep God's commands and their faith in Jesus."[K]

[13]Then I heard a voice from heaven saying, "Write: The dead who die in the Lord from now on are blessed."[p]

"Yes," says the Spirit, "let them rest from their labors, for their works follow them!"

Reaping the Earth's Harvest

[14]Then I looked, and there was a white cloud, and One like the Son of Man[L,q] was seated on the cloud, with a gold crown on His head and a sharp sickle in His hand. [15]Another angel came out of the sanctuary, crying out in a loud voice to the One who was seated on the cloud, "Use your sickle and reap, for the time to reap has come, since the harvest of the earth is ripe."[r] [16]So the One seated on the

---

A14:2 Or voice   B14:3 Other mss add as it were   C14:3,4 Or purchased   D14:4 Other mss add by Jesus   E14:8 Lit Another angel, a second   F14:8 Other mss omit the second has fallen   G14:8 Or wine of her passionate immorality   H14:9 Lit Another angel, a third   I14:11 Lit They have no rest   J14:12 Lit Here is the perseverance   K14:12 Or and faith in Jesus, or and faithfulness to Jesus   L14:14 Or like a son of man

---

though they do not have his mark (13:16-17), because they have the name of Christ and the **Father** on their **foreheads**. The **new song** cannot be the same as the one in 5:9-10 because this one can only be learned by the 144,000. On the **four living creatures**, see note at 4:6-7. On **the elders**, see note at 4:3-4. In their spiritual purity, they are fitting **firstfruits** (either the first produce to be harvested, the best of the harvest, or both) of the Lord's final harvest (vv. 14-20). This wording implies that many others are yet to come into the gospel "harvest" (i.e., to saving faith; see vv. 6-7).

14:6-7 Some interpreters think **the . . . gospel** is not expressed in Revelation. However, the Greek word translated "gospel" (*euangelion*) is present, and the climactic preaching calls us to (1) **fear God** and (2) **give Him glory**, recognizing the certainty of **judgment** if one does otherwise.

14:8-11 The fall of **Babylon** and God's **wrath** will be expanded in 16:17-21 and 18:1-19:3. The mention of **sexual immorality** recalls the same problem in the churches at Pergamum and Thyatira (2:14,20-21). While those who die in the Lord will find "rest" (14:13), there will be **no rest day or night** for anyone who worships **the beast** and has his **mark**.

14:12-13 Blessed marks the second beatitude in Revelation (see notes at 1:3; 16:15; 19:9; 20:4-6; 22:6-7; and 22:14-15,17). Believers (**the saints**) who persevere in keep-

ing God's **commands** and **faith in Jesus** will be blessed with the reward of their godly works (20:12; 2Co 5:10).

14:14-20 Some believe that the **One like the Son of Man** in this section must be an **angel** because of the unlikelihood of Christ receiving the command from another angel to **reap . . . the harvest**. But the Son of Man associated with a **cloud** is a clear allusion to Dn 7:13, where the Messiah (Christ) is definitely in view. This section visualizes the "harvest . . . at the end of the age" (Mt 13:38-43), when the "good seed" and the "weeds" are separated to their eternal destinies. The wheat harvest apparently gleans those responding positively to the climactic preaching of the gospel (see notes at Rv 14:6-7 and 15:2-4). A recent view holds that 14:14-16 is the point at which the church is raptured. This is highly unlikely. The harvest of grapes leads to the judgment pictured here as **the great winepress of God's wrath**. Since the winepress imagery related to divine wrath is seen in connection with the second coming of Christ (19:15), the events of 14:17-20 must occur at that point. If taken literally, when the "grapes of wrath" are **trampled** in Christ's winepress (19:15) outside **the city** (Jerusalem, apparently), the **blood** (from the climactic battle at His second coming in 19:19,21) rises to the height of **horses' bridles** for some **180 miles**. This is roughly the length of Israel from north to south. Some view this horrific description as symbolic of

cloud swung His sickle over the earth, and the earth was harvested.

[17] Then another angel who also had a sharp sickle came out of the sanctuary in heaven. [18] Yet another angel, who had authority over fire, came from the altar, and he called with a loud voice to the one who had the sharp sickle, "Use your sharp sickle and gather the clusters of grapes from earth's vineyard, because its grapes have ripened." [19] So the angel swung his sickle toward earth and gathered the grapes from earth's vineyard, and he threw them into the great winepress of God's wrath.[a] [20] Then the press was trampled outside the city, and blood flowed out of the press up to the horses' bridles for about 180 miles.[A,b]

Preparation for the Bowl Judgments

15 Then I saw another great and awe-inspiring sign[B] in heaven:[c] seven angels with the seven last plagues, for with them, God's wrath will be completed.[d] [2] I also saw something like a sea of glass[e] mixed with fire, and those who had won the victory over the beast, his image,[c] and the number of his name, were standing on the sea of glass with harps from God.[D,f] [3] They sang the song of God's servant Moses[g] and the song of the Lamb:

Great and awe-inspiring are
　Your works,
Lord God, the Almighty;

[a]14:19 Rv 16:19; 19:15
[b]14:20 Is 63:1-6
[c]15:1 Rv 12:3
[d]Rv 16:17
[e]15:2 Rv 4:6
[f]Rv 5:8; 14:2
[g]15:3 Ex 15:1; Dt 31:22
[h]15:5 Ex 38:21; Nm 17:7; 18:2
[i]Rv 11:19
[j]15:8 Is 6:4
[k]16:2 Ex 9:9-11

righteous and true are Your ways,
King of the Nations.[E]
[4] Lord, who will not fear
and glorify Your name?
Because You alone are holy,
for all the nations will come
and worship before You
because Your righteous acts
have been revealed.

[5] After this I looked, and the heavenly sanctuary—the tabernacle of testimony[h]—was opened.[i] [6] Out of the sanctuary came the seven angels with the seven plagues, dressed in •clean, bright linen, with gold sashes wrapped around their chests. [7] One of the four living creatures gave the seven angels seven gold bowls filled with the wrath of God who lives forever and ever. [8] Then the sanctuary was filled with smoke from God's glory and from His power,[j] and no one could enter the sanctuary until the seven plagues of the seven angels were completed.

The First Bowl

16 Then I heard a loud voice from the sanctuary saying to the seven angels, "Go and pour out the seven[F] bowls of God's wrath on the earth." [2] The first went and poured out his bowl on the earth, and severely painful sores[G,k] broke out on the people who had the mark of the beast and who worshiped his image.

[A]14:20 Lit *1,600 stadia*　[B]15:1 Or *and awesome symbolic display*　[C]15:2 Other mss add *his mark*　[D]15:2 Or *harps of God*; = harps belonging to the service of God　[E]15:3 Other mss read *ages*　[F]16:1 Other mss omit *seven*　[G]16:2 Lit *and a severely painful sore*

God's righteous judgment resulting in the deaths of many of the unrepentant.

15:1 This is the third **sign** (Gk *semeion*) in the Apocalypse. It differs from the first two (12:1,3)—**seven angels** and their corresponding **plagues** (Gk *pleygey*, calling to mind the judgment of the plagues on Egypt). They are called the "last plagues" because they bring **God's wrath** to completion. Since the seventh bowl of wrath (16:17,21) fulfills exactly what appears about to take place in 11:19, the bowls-of-wrath sequence (15:1–19:6) spans from the end of the trumpets sequence all the way to the second coming of Christ (19:11-16).

15:2-4 Mixed with fire may preview the fire with which Babylon the Great, the climactic focus of the bowl judgments (16:17-21), burns (18:8-9,18). Those who had **won the victory over the beast** are martyrs (12:11) who responded properly to the preaching of the "eternal gospel" (14:6-7; see note there) by fearing, glorifying, and worshiping God. The **song of God's servant Moses** appears in Exodus 15. Israel sang it when they had escaped their Egyptian pursuers, reaching safety on the other side of the Red Sea. Calling Rv 15:3-4 the song of "Moses and the song of the Lamb" infers that these martyrs are spiritually "safe on the other side," meaning heaven.

15:5-8 The **heavenly sanctuary** was last seen in 11:19,

in connection with the sounding of the last trumpet. The previous uses of **tabernacle** (Gk *skeyney*) in the book refer to the "heaven dwellers" (7:15; 13:6). The **angels** with the **plagues** are dressed in the garb of OT priests. The mention of **gold bowls** calls to mind "the prayers of the saints," which are in gold bowls (5:8) before the Lord, especially the martyrs' prayer to avenge their blood on the "earth dwellers" (6:10). The wording of the third bowl of **wrath** (16:4-7), especially the mention of a voice coming from "the altar" (16:7), may link "the prayers of the saints" to the seven gold bowls **filled with the wrath of God**. The sanctuary being **filled with smoke from God's glory** recalls the cloud and the glory of God filling the tabernacle in the wilderness (Ex 40:34), indicating God was present with His people and guiding them.

16:1 The **loud voice** from the sanctuary is probably that of the Lord since it is **God's wrath** that is being poured out **on the earth**.

16:2 Since 6:9-11 and 8:13 (see notes there), it has been expected that the brunt of God's judgment would be focused on the "earth dwellers" at some point. But as the final cycle of judgment (15:1) begins, the **first . . . bowl** is poured out on those who have the **mark of the beast** and who worship his image. They are struck with **painful sores**. This recalls the sixth plague on Egypt (Ex 9:8-11).

The Second Bowl

[3] The second[A] poured out his bowl into the sea. It turned to blood like a dead man's, and all life[B] in the sea died.[a]

The Third Bowl

[4] The third[A] poured out his bowl into the rivers and the springs of water, and they became blood.[b] [5] I heard the angel of the waters say:

You are righteous,
who is and who was,[c]
    the Holy One,
for You have decided these things.
[6] Because they poured out
    the blood of the •saints
        and the prophets,
You also gave them blood to drink;
    they deserve it![d]

[7] Then I heard someone from the altar say:

Yes, Lord God, the Almighty,
    true and righteous are
    Your judgments.[e]

The Fourth Bowl

[8] The fourth[A] poured out his bowl on the

sun. He[C] was given the power[D] to burn people with fire, [9] and people were burned by the intense heat. So they blasphemed the name of God,[f] who had the power[D] over these plagues, and they did not repent and give Him glory.

The Fifth Bowl

[10] The fifth[A] poured out his bowl on the throne of the beast,[g] and his kingdom was plunged into darkness.[h] People[E] gnawed their tongues because of their pain [11] and blasphemed the God of heaven[i] because of their pains and their sores, yet they did not repent of their actions.

The Sixth Bowl

[12] The sixth[A] poured out his bowl on the great river Euphrates,[j] and its water was dried up to prepare the way for the kings from the east. [13] Then I saw three unclean spirits like frogs[k] coming from the dragon's mouth,[l] from the beast's mouth,[m] and from the mouth of the false prophet.[n] [14] For they are spirits of demons performing signs,[o] who travel to the kings of the whole world to assemble them for the battle of the great day of God, the Almighty.[p]

---

[a] 16:3 Rv 8:8-9
[b] 16:4 Ex 7:19-21
[c] 16:5 Rv 11:17
[d] 16:6 Is 49:26
[e] 16:7 Ps 19:9; Rv 19:2
[f] 16:9 Rv 13:6
[g] 16:10 Rv 2:13; 13:2
[h] Ex 10:21
[i] 16:11 Rv 13:6
[j] 16:12 Rv 9:14
[k] 16:13 Ex 8:2-14; Lv 11:9-12,41-47
[l] Rv 12:9
[m] Rv 13:1
[n] Rv 13:11-17
[o] 16:14 2Th 2:9-10
[p] Jl 2:11; 3:2; Rv 19:11-21

[A] 16:3,4,8,10,12 Other mss add *angel*   [B] 16:3 Lit *and every soul of life*   [C] 16:8 Or *It*   [D] 16:8,9 Or *authority*   [E] 16:10 Lit *They*

16:3 The effects of the **second . . . bowl** are like the second trumpet judgment (8:8-9). But only a third of the sea became blood and a third of sea life was killed then, while all the **sea** and **all life in the sea** are affected by this bowl of God's wrath. This echoes the first plague on Egypt (Ex 7:14-21).

16:4-7 The **third . . . bowl** is like the third trumpet judgment (8:10-11) since it impacts the fresh water sources. On the description of God as **who is and who was**, see note at 11:16-18. The significance of turning the water into blood is now clarified. Those who worshiped the beast (16:2) are being judged in divine **righteousness** for the **blood** (6:10)

axios

Greek Pronunciation	[AH ksee ahss]
HCSB Translation	deserve
Uses in Revelation	7
Uses in the NT	41
Focus passage	Revelation 16:6

The adjective *axios* describes something that is of *comparable* value or worth to something else *(comparable, worthy)*, or something that is appropriate to a particular person or activity *(corresponding to, deserving of)*. In the NT, *axios* occurs several times in reference to those receiving a punishment of death (i.e., the punishment corresponds to the crime; Lk 23:15,41; Ac 23:29; 25:11,25; 26:31; Rm 1:32). In the Gospels, *axios* occasionally describes truths about salvation and discipleship (Mt 3:8; 10:37-38; Lk 12:48), and Paul does the same in Rm 8:18 (the related verb *axioo* occurs in 2Th 1:11; 1Tm 5:17, and the adverb *axios* occurs in Eph 4:1; Php 1:27; Col 1:10; 1Th 2:12). In Revelation, the redeemed are found *worthy* of their particular reward (Rv 3:4); God is *worthy* of glory, honor, and power (4:11); and the Lamb is *worthy* to break the seals of the scroll (5:2,4,9,12).

of the martyred **saints** (see note at 5:8) and **prophets** (see note at 10:5-7). Since such vengeance was predicted for the "earth dwellers" (6:10-11), the beast worshipers and the "earth dwellers" must be the same group.

16:8-9 While the fourth trumpet judgment (8:12-13) greatly dimmed the light of the **sun**, moon, and stars, **the fourth . . . bowl** causes people to be burned with **fire** and **intense heat**. Instead of crying out for mercy from God, though, the response of the beast worshipers (v. 2) was to blaspheme the Lord, like the beast himself (13:5) refusing to **repent** (see note at 9:20-21). They also **did not . . . give Him glory**, indicating that they rejected the preaching of the gospel in 14:6-7.

16:10-11 The **fifth . . . bowl** is also like the fourth trumpet (8:12-13) in that the sun, moon, and stars are darkened, but only by "a third." People may have **gnawed their tongues** in **pain** due to (1) extreme cold caused by the ongoing darkness, (2) the sores from the first bowl judgment (v. 2), (3) the severe burns related to the fourth bowl (vv. 8-9), or (4) all three of these factors. That this bowl was poured out on the **throne of the beast** and his **kingdom** was to show that his worldwide authority (13:7) was about to end. On the people's blasphemy and refusal to **repent**, see note at 9:20-21.

16:12-14 The **sixth . . . bowl** of wrath is the preparation for the battle of Armagedon (v. 16). The sixth trumpet judgment also mentioned the **great river Euphrates** (see note at 9:14-16). It is possible that the phrase, **its water was dried up**, is intended to recall the parting of the Red Sea since both concern armies (here, armies of **the kings from the east** side of the Euphrates). These armies are moving to join the kings of the **whole world** for the battle of the great day of **God, the Almighty** (the Day of the Lord; see note at 6:12-17) to war against God (see note at 16:16). The **three unclean spirits**

[15] "Look, I am coming like a thief. The one who is alert and remains clothed[A,a] so that he may not go around naked and people see his shame[b] is blessed."[c]

[16] So they assembled them at the place called in Hebrew, Armagedon.[B,C,d]

The Seventh Bowl

[17] Then the seventh[D] poured out his bowl into the air,[E] and a loud voice came out of the sanctuary[F,e] from the throne, saying, "It is done!" [18] There were flashes of lightning and rumblings of thunder. And a severe earthquake occurred like no other since man has been on the earth—so great was the quake.[f] [19] The great city[g] split into three parts, and the cities of the nations[G] fell. Babylon the Great was remembered in God's presence; He gave her the cup filled with the wine of His fierce anger.[h] [20] Every island fled, and the mountains disappeared.[H,i] [21] Enormous hailstones, each weighing about 100 pounds,[I] fell from the sky on people, and they blasphemed God[j] for the plague of hail because that plague was extremely severe.[k]

The Woman and the Scarlet Beast

17 Then one of the seven angels who had the seven bowls[I] came and spoke with me: "Come, I will show you the judgment of the notorious prostitute[J] who sits on many[K] waters.[m] [2] The kings of the earth committed sexual immorality with her, and those who live on the earth became drunk on the wine of her sexual immorality."[n] [3] So he carried me away in the Spirit[L,o] to a desert. I saw a woman sitting on a scarlet beast that was covered[M] with blasphemous names and had seven

Cross references (center column):

a16:15 Lk 12:35-40; 1Th 5:2,6-8
bRv 3:18
c Rv 1:3; 14:13; 19:9; 20:6; 22:7,14
d16:16 Jdg 5:19; 2Kg 9:27; Ezk 38:8
e16:17 Is 66:6
f16:18 Ex 19:16-19; Rv 4:5; 8:5; 11:19
g16:19 Rv 18:10, 16,18,19,21
hRv 14:19; 19:15
i16:20 Ezk 38:20; Rv 6:14
j16:21 Rv 16:9,11
k Jos 10:11; Ezk 38:22
l17:1 Rv 21:9
mJr 51:13
n17:2 Is 23:16-17; Nah 3:4; Rv 14:8; 18:3
o17:3 Rv 1:10; 4:2; 21:10

Textual notes:

[A]16:15 Or *and guards his clothes* [B]16:16 Other mss read *Armageddon*; other mss read *Harmegedon*; other mss read *Mageddon*; other mss read *Magedon* [C]16:16 Traditionally *the hill of Megiddo*, a great city that guarded the pass between the coast and the valley of Jezreel or Esdraelon; Jdg 5:19; 2Kg 9:27 [D]16:17 Other mss add *angel* [E]16:17 Or *on the air* [F]16:17 Other mss add *of heaven* [G]16:19 Or *the Gentile cities* [H]16:20 Lit *mountains were not found* [I]16:21 Lit *about a talent*; talents varied in weight upwards from 75 pounds [J]17:1 Traditionally translated *the great whore* [K]17:1 Or *by many* [L]17:3 Or *in spirit* [M]17:3 Lit *was filled*

are **demons**, performing deceiving **signs** to influence these kings (see Dn 10:13,20) to do the will of Satan (the dragon; see note at 12:7-10).

16:15 In the midst of the description of the lead-up to Armagedon (see note at v. 16) is the third blessing statement of the Apocalypse (1:3; 14:13; 19:9; 20:6; 22:7,14), warning readers always to be spiritually **alert**. Coming **like a thief** echoes Jesus' parable in Mt 24:43-44 and His earlier threat to the church at Sardis (Rv 3:3). Spiritual nakedness was one of Christ's indictments of the church at Laodicea (3:17-18).

16:16 Many explanations have been offered for the **place called . . . Armagedon**. In Hebrew, it appears to mean "hill or mount of Megiddo." Since there are no full-sized mountains in Israel other than Mount Hermon, referring to a hill overlooking the Valley of Megiddo (the site of some of the most important military battles in world history) as a mount is similar to the references to the hill known as "Mount Moriah" or "Mount Zion." Others think Armagedon is not an actual place but a symbol for the concluding battle between good and evil.

16:17-21 The **seventh . . . bowl** of wrath is focused on **Babylon the Great**, introduced in 14:8. The phrase **it is done** echoes Jesus' declaration on the cross: "It is finished." The work of judgment is now completed, just as Christ's redemptive work was finished. The phenomena poured out in judgment (**lightning . . . rumblings . . . thunder . . . earthquake . . . hailstones**) have been "on hold" since being spotlighted in heaven in 11:19. The **great city** here is not Jerusalem, as in 11:8, but Babylon. The mixing of references closely aligns the ungodly aspects of both cities. In 14:10, the beast worshipers were told they would "drink the wine of God's wrath . . . in the cup of His anger." Now, Babylon receives the cup filled with the **wine** of His **fierce anger**. Thus, each is being equally punished, and it is the punishment that was expected to come upon the "earth dwellers" (see notes at 6:9-11; 8:13). The phrase "Babylon the Great" is taken from Nebuchadnezzar's boast in Dn 4:30. It could speak of a rebuilt end-time city, though Jr 51:26 makes that unlikely. It could be a code name for Rome, or it could picture any proud society, with the Tower of Babel (Gn 11:1-9) and Babylon under Nebuchadnezzar being classic examples.

17:1-19:5 This section is a postscript to the bowls of wrath, expanding the reader's understanding of Babylon the Great, her relationship with the beast, and the scope of her just and final judgment.

17:1-2 On the **seven angels** and **seven bowls**, see note at 15:1. The **notorious prostitute** is Babylon the Great, who in verse 5 is called "the Mother of Prostitutes," apparently underlining the long existence of this Babylon. The **many waters** are explained as "peoples, multitudes, nations, and languages" in verse 15. Babylon has essentially the same relationship of **sexual immorality** with the **kings of the earth** and the "earth dwellers" (v. 2) as "Jezebel" did with the sinners in the church at Thyatira (2:20).

17:3-6 On **in the Spirit**, see note at 1:10. The word translated **desert** (Gk *eremon*) is rendered "wilderness" in 12:6,14. The

bdelugma

Greek Pronunciation	[BDEHL oog mah]
HCSB Translation	vile
Uses in Revelation	3
Uses in the NT	6
Focus passage	Revelation 17:4-5

The noun *bdelugma* (abomination, vile thing), the adjective *bdeluktos* (detestable, vile) and the verb *bdelusso* (to make detestable; Ex 5:21; *bdelussomai*, to abhor, detest, or be detested) occur only rarely in the NT (*bdelugma* 6x; *bdeluktos* 1x; *bdelusso* 2x), though they appear frequently in the Greek OT. In the Mosaic law and the Prophets, *bdelugma* describes things which are ceremonially unclean (Lv 5:2; 7:21; 11:10-13,20,23,41-42), as well as pagan idolatrous practices abhorrent to God (Dt 7:25-26; Jr 4:1; 7:10; Ezk 5:11), including human sacrifice (Dt 12:31), homosexuality (Lv 18:22; 20:13), and occultic rites (Dt 18:9-12). In the NT, Jesus used *bdelugma* to describe the antichrist, who will establish himself in God's sanctuary ("*abomination* that causes desolation"; Mt 24:15 = Mk 13:14; Dn 9:27; 11:31; 12:11; cp. 2Th 2:4). In Revelation, *bdelugma* describes Babylon (Rv 17:4).

heads and 10 horns.[a] [4]The woman was dressed in purple and scarlet, adorned with gold, precious stones, and pearls. She had a gold cup in her hand filled with everything vile[b] and with the impurities of her[A] prostitution. [5]On her forehead a cryptic name[c] was written:

**BABYLON THE GREAT
THE MOTHER OF PROSTITUTES
AND OF THE VILE THINGS
OF THE EARTH.**

[6]Then I saw that the woman was drunk on the blood of the •saints and on the blood of the witnesses to Jesus. When I saw her, I was greatly astonished.

The Meaning of the Woman and of the Beast

[7]Then the angel said to me, "Why are you astonished? I will tell you the •secret meaning of the woman and of the beast, with the seven heads and the 10 horns, that carries her. [8]The beast that you saw was, and is not, and is about to come up from the •abyss[d] and go to destruction.[e] Those who live on the earth whose names have not been written in the book of life from the foundation of the world[f]

will be astonished when they see the beast that was, and is not, and will be present again.[g]

[9]"Here is the mind with wisdom:[B,h] The seven heads are seven mountains on which the woman is seated. [10]They are also seven kings:[C] Five have fallen, one is, the other has not yet come, and when he comes, he must remain for a little while. [11]The beast that was and is not, is himself an eighth king, yet he belongs to the seven and is going to destruction. [12]The 10 horns you saw are 10 kings who have not yet received a kingdom, but they will receive authority as kings with the beast for one hour. [13]These have one purpose, and they give their power and authority to the beast. [14]These will make war against the Lamb, but the Lamb will conquer them because He is Lord of lords and King of kings.[i] Those with Him are called, chosen, and faithful."

[15]He also said to me, "The waters you saw, where the prostitute was seated, are peoples, multitudes, nations, and languages.[j] [16]The 10 horns you saw, and the beast, will hate the prostitute.[k] They will make her desolate and naked, devour her flesh, and burn her up with fire.[l] [17]For God has put it into their hearts to carry out His plan by having one purpose[m]

a 17:3 Rv 13:1
b 17:4 Mt 24:15; Mk 13:14; Lk 16:15; Rv 21:27
c 17:5 Rv 14:1
d 17:8 Rv 11:7
e Rv 1:18; 2:8
f Ps 69:28; Is 4:3; Rv 3:5; 13:8; 20:12,15; 21:27
g Rv 13:3,12,14
h 17:9 Rv 13:18
i 17:14 Dt 10:17; Ps 136:2-3; Dn 2:47
j 17:15 Rv 5:9; 7:9; 10:11; 11:9; 13:7; 14:6
k 17:16 2Sm 13:15-20; Ezk 23:22-35
l Lv 20:14; 21:9
m 17:17 Gn 50:20

A 17:4 Other mss read *of earth's*   B 17:9 Or *This calls for the mind with wisdom*   C 17:10 Some editors or translators put *They are also seven kings:* in v. 9.

---

woman, Babylon, also has a very close relationship with the beast (on the **blasphemous names . . . seven heads . . . and 10 horns**, see note at 13:1-3). To the casual outward observer, Babylon has all the trappings of wealth and royalty, but in actuality, she is characterized by **everything vile** and the **impurities of her prostitution**. The **name** on her **forehead** may imply that Babylon serves the beast (see note at 13:16-18), though it is not the name or number of the beast. The wider "mystery" (**cryptic name**) of Babylon has to do with her being the source of harlotry (**MOTHER OF PROSTITUTES**) and moral abominations (**THE VILE THINGS OF THE EARTH**), and killing throughout history.

17:7-8 Another aspect of **the secret meaning** (Gk *musterion*) of Babylon (**the woman**) and the beast is their hold on the "earth dwellers." It is because their **names** were **not . . . written** in the **book of life** (see note at 13:8). On the **seven heads and the 10 horns**, see note at 13:1-3. It is not clear when the beast could have been manifest before in human history.

17:9 The **seven heads** of the beast (vv. 3,7) are **seven mountains** (or hills; the Gk *oros* can mean either). This seems to be a reference to Rome, which was known in antiquity as "the city on seven hills." But since the woman (Babylon) is seated on the seven mountains, and the seven heads are identified as seven kings (v. 10), it is unwise to be dogmatic on this point.

17:10 The identity of the **seven kings** is highly disputed. Some interpreters understand this to refer to seven historic Roman emperors, but more hold that it refers to seven successive world empires (e.g., Egypt, Assyria, Babylon, Medo-Persia, Greece, Rome, and a yet future empire). The phrase

a little while would refer to the beast's unrivaled reign of "42 months" (13:5).

17:11 On **the beast that was and is not**, see note at verses 7-8. The phrase that the beast is an **eighth king** yet **belongs to the seven** is difficult to interpret. Some in the early church thought this referred to Nero coming back to life. The best explanation, though, seems to be that, even though the physical body remains the same, the beast is two different personalities at "before-and-after" points in his career. This dramatic change could happen either (1) when the beast initially comes to prominence by killing the two witnesses (11:7) or (2) after his "resurrection" from a presumed fatal wound (13:3,12,14). That the beast is **going to destruction** refers to eternal torment in the lake of fire (19:20; 20:10).

17:12-13 The **10 horns** of Dn 7:7,20,24 (see Rv 17:3,7) are **10 kings** who will rule alongside the beast during his unrivaled reign of 42 months (13:5). This period is referred to here as **one hour**, much as the tribulation period is called "the hour of testing" (3:10).

17:14 The battle here takes place at the second coming of Christ (**the Lamb . . . Lord of lords and King of kings**; note the reversed wording from "King of kings and Lord of lords," 19:16). This verse clarifies that the armies following the Lamb in 19:14 are believers since the combined terms **called . . . chosen . . . and faithful** are never used of angels.

17:15-17 The **prostitute** (Babylon the Great) has ingratiated herself to the remaining world population (**peoples . . . languages**). The irony here is that, in the end, the very rulers (**the 10 horns . . . and the beast**) with which the pseudo-queen (v. 4; 18:7), Babylon the Great, has acted immorally (17:2), will turn on her and destroy her. Most amazing is

and to give their kingdom[A] to the beast until God's words are accomplished. [18]And the woman you saw is the great city that has an empire[B] over the kings of the earth."

The Fall of Babylon the Great

18 After this I saw another angel with great authority coming down from heaven, and the earth was illuminated by his splendor. [2]He cried in a mighty voice:

It has fallen,[C]
Babylon the Great has fallen![a]
She has become a dwelling for demons,
a haunt for every •unclean spirit,
a haunt for every unclean bird,
and a haunt[D] for every unclean
    and despicable beast.[E,b]
[3] For all the nations have drunk[F]
the wine of her sexual immorality,
which brings wrath.[c]
The kings of the earth
have committed sexual immorality
    with her,
and the merchants of the earth
have grown wealthy
    from her excessive luxury.

[4]Then I heard another voice from heaven:

Come out of her, My people,
so that you will not share in her sins[d]
or receive any of her plagues.
[5] For her sins are piled up[G] to heaven,[e]
and God has remembered her crimes.
[6] Pay her back the way she also paid,[f]

a18:2 Is 21:9; Rv 14:8
b18:3 Is 13:20-22
c18:3 Rv 14:8; 17:2
d18:4 Is 52:11; Jr 50:8; 51:6,9,45; 2Co 6:17
e18:5 Jr 51:9
f18:6 Jr 50:29
g18:6 Is 40:2; Jr 16:18; 17:18
hRv 14:8
i18:7 Is 47:7-8

and double it according to her works.[g]
In the cup in which she mixed,[h]
mix a double portion for her.
[7] As much as she glorified herself
    and lived luxuriously,
give her that much torment and grief,
for she says in her heart,
"I sit as a queen;
I am not a widow,
and I will never see grief."[i]
[8] For this reason her plagues will come
    in one day[H]—
death and grief and famine.
She will be burned up with fire,
because the Lord God who judges her
    is mighty.

The World Mourns Babylon's Fall

[9]The kings of the earth who have committed sexual immorality and lived luxuriously with her will weep and mourn over her when they see the smoke of her burning. [10]They will stand far off in fear of her torment, saying:

Woe, woe, the great city,
Babylon, the mighty city!
For in a single hour[H]
your judgment has come.

[11]The merchants of the earth will also weep and mourn over her, because no one buys their merchandise any longer— [12]merchandise of gold, silver, precious stones, and pearls; fine fabrics of linen, purple, silk, and scarlet; all kinds of fragrant wood products; objects of ivory; objects of expensive

---

A17:17 Or *sovereignty*   B17:18 Or *has sovereignty* or *rulership*   C18:2 Other mss omit *It has fallen*   D18:2 Or *prison*   E18:2 Other mss omit the words *and a haunt for every unclean beast.* The words *and despicable* then refer to the *bird* of the previous line.   F18:3 Some mss read *have collapsed*; other mss read *have fallen*   G18:5 Or *sins have reached up*   H18:8,10 Suddenly

---

that, ultimately, this will take place according to God's **purpose** and sovereign **plan**.

17:18–18:3 The woman (Babylon the Great; 17:5) is now pictured as the **great city** (see note at 16:17-21), which has secured political influence over the **kings of the earth** (17:18) by sexual immorality (17:2). Babylon could include an actual city in the end times, but the "lament" in Revelation 18 is modeled after Jeremiah 51, which says that the Babylonian Empire and the city of Babylon will "never rise again" (Jr 51:64). It is thus more likely that **Babylon the Great** (18:2) is the world system (1Jn 2:15-17) organized in arrogant rebellion against God throughout history, with the Tower of Babel, the Babylonian Empire, Rome—and even Jerusalem (Rv 11:8)—being classic expressions of this rebellion.

18:4 The insight into the dark demonic "heart" of Babylon the Great (v. 2) causes the Lord (**another voice from heaven**) to command His people to **come out** of Babylon or be caught up in His judgment for **her sins**. A few interpreters understand the rapture of the church to take place at this point.

18:5-8 The reason Babylon the Great was **remembered** in the presence of God in regard to the seventh bowl of wrath

(16:19) is now explained: **her sins** and **crimes** are **piled up to heaven** like a growing refuse heap, the stench of which finally became unbearable. God will **pay . . . back** (Rm 12:19) Babylon for **her works** in full measure and more so. Babylon may arrogantly **sit as a queen**, with a false sense of security, but the judgment for her mountain of sins, including self-glorification and lavish living, is certain and will be strong and swift.

18:9-10 The words **woe, woe** may indicate that the destruction of Babylon is the focus of the third woe predicted in 8:13, which was supposed to come upon the "earth dwellers." If so, it would be either (1) the "earth dwellers" and Babylon the Great are the same entity, or (2) as a result of their stubborn lack of repentance before the Lord (9:20-21), the "earth dwellers" are eventually merged into the Babylonian world system.

18:11-14 The **merchants of the earth** grew wealthy (v. 3) from their relationship with Babylon the Great. They **weep and mourn** at her demise because of their loss of business. The inventory of about 30 items of merchandise is similar to the list in Ezekiel 27. All these **splendid and glamorous things** will disappear.

wood, brass,[A] iron, and marble; [13] cinnamon, spice,[B,C] incense, myrrh,[D] and frankincense; wine, olive oil, fine wheat flour, and grain; cattle and sheep; horses and carriages; and slaves[E] and human lives.[F,a]

[14] The fruit you craved has left you.
All your splendid and glamorous things
    are gone;
they will never find them again.

[15] The merchants of these things, who became rich from her, will stand far off in fear of her torment, weeping and mourning, [16] saying:

Woe, woe, the great city,
    dressed in fine linen, purple,
        and scarlet,
    adorned with gold, precious stones,
        and pearls,
[17] for in a single hour[G]
    such fabulous wealth was destroyed!

And every shipmaster, seafarer, the sailors, and all who do business by sea, stood far off [18] as they watched the smoke from her burning and kept crying out: "Who is like the great city?"[b] [19] They threw dust on their heads and kept crying out, weeping, and mourning:[c]

Woe, woe, the great city,[d]
    where all those who have ships
        on the sea
    became rich from her wealth,

[a]18:13 Gn 36:6; Nm 31:32-35; 1Ch 5:21; Ezk 27:13
[b]18:18 Ezk 27:32
[c]18:19 Ezk 27:30
[d]Rv 18:10,16
[e]18:20 Rv 12:12
[f]18:21 Rv 5:2; 10:1
[g]Jr 51:59-64
[h]Rv 16:20; 18:11,14,22-23
[i]18:22 Is 24:8
[j]18:23 Jr 25:10

for in a single hour[G] she was destroyed.
[20] Rejoice over her, heaven,
    and you •saints, apostles,
        and prophets,[e]
    because God has executed
        your judgment on her![H]

The Finality of Babylon's Fall

[21] Then a mighty angel[f] picked up a stone like a large millstone and threw it into the sea, saying:

In this way, Babylon the great city
    will be thrown down violently[g]
    and never be found again.[h]
[22] The sound of harpists, musicians,
    flutists, and trumpeters
    will never be heard in you again;[i]
no craftsman of any trade
    will ever be found in you again;
the sound of a mill
    will never be heard in you again;
[23] the light of a lamp
    will never shine in you again;
and the voice of a groom and bride
    will never be heard in you again.[j]
All this will happen
    because your merchants
    were the nobility of the earth,
    because all the nations were deceived
        by your sorcery,[l]
[24] and the blood of prophets and saints,

[A]18:12 Or bronze, or copper   [B]18:13 Other mss omit spice   [C]18:13 Or amomum, an aromatic plant   [D]18:13 Or perfume   [E]18:13 Or bodies   [F]18:13 Slaves; "bodies" was the Gk way of referring to slaves; "souls of men" was the Hb way.   [G]18:17,19 Suddenly   [H]18:20 Or God pronounced on her the judgment she passed on you; see Rv 18:6   [l]18:23 Ancient sorcery or witchcraft often used spells and drugs. Here the term may be non-literal, that is, Babylon drugged the nations with her beauty and power.

18:17-19 The next group to lament the loss of Babylon the Great is all whose business has to do with the sea. Their weeping and mourning grows out of the fact that they had become rich through her trade. On **woe, woe,** see note at verses 9-10.

18:20 In stark contrast to the self-centered mourning of the sinful accomplices (v. 3) of Babylon the Great (vv. 9-19), the martyrs in heaven (**saints, apostles, and prophets**) are urged to rejoice because God has judged Babylon, largely because of their shed blood (**your judgment** means "judgment on your behalf"; 6:9-11; 17:6). Among the martyrs by this time were the apostles James (Ac 12:2) as well as Paul and Peter according to credible extrabiblical tradition.

18:21 On **mighty angel**, see note at 10:1. A **large millstone** could weigh several tons.

18:22-23 Throughout Scripture, beautiful aspects of life (e.g., **the voice of a groom and bride**) and culture (e.g., **the sound of . . . musicians**, craftsmen of every trade) have either been used in praise of God (Ps 150:3-5) or in arrogant rebellion against Him (Gn 4:21-22). After the judgment of Babylon the Great, such perversion of God's intention for beauty will **never** happen **again**. The lack of repentance of the "earth dwellers" during the trumpet judgments (Rv 9:21) was caused by the deceptive **sorcery** of Babylon the Great.

18:24 What is seen in Revelation is the end-time manifesta-

planao

Greek Pronunciation	[plah NAH oh]
HCSB Translation	deceive
Uses in Revelation	8
Uses in the NT	39
Focus passage	Revelation 18:23

Planao literally means to wander about (Heb 11:38). This connotation of wandering can be seen in the related nouns planes/planetes (wanderer), from which English word planet ultimately derives. Indeed, the planets often appeared to the ancients as "wandering" across the sky among the seemingly fixed stars. By figurative extension, planao could also mean to go astray (Mt 18:12-13; Heb 3:10; 5:2; Jms 5:19) or to be deceived or misled (Mt 22:29 = Mk 12:24; Jn 7:12,47; 1Co 6:9; Gl 6:7; 2Tm 3:13; Jms 1:16; 1Jn 1:8; 2:26; 3:7). Planao may also mean to mislead someone (Mt 24:4-5 = Mk 13:5-6; Jn 7:12) and this is how the word tends to function in Revelation, where John warns about the deceivers "Jezebel" (Rv 2:20), the false prophet (13:14; 19:20), Babylon (Rv 18:23), and Satan—the archdeceiver (12:9; 20:3,8,10).

and of all those slaughtered on earth,
was found in you.[A,a]

Celebration in Heaven

19 After this I heard something like the loud voice of a vast multitude in heaven, saying:

•Hallelujah![b]
Salvation, glory, and power belong
  to our God,
[2] because His judgments are true[B]
  and righteous,[c]
because He has judged
  the notorious prostitute
who corrupted the earth
  with her sexual immorality;
and He has avenged the blood
  of His •slaves
that was on her hands.[d]

[3]A second time they said:

Hallelujah!
Her smoke ascends
  forever and ever![e]

[4]Then the 24 elders and the four living creatures fell down and worshiped God,[f] who is seated on the throne, saying:

•Amen! Hallelujah![g]

[5]A voice came from the throne, saying:

Praise our God,

all His slaves, who fear Him,
  both small and great![h]

Marriage of the Lamb Announced

[6]Then I heard something like the voice of a vast multitude, like the sound of cascading waters,[i] and like the rumbling of loud thunder, saying:

Hallelujah, because our Lord God,
  the Almighty,
has begun to reign!
[7] Let us be glad, rejoice,
  and give Him glory,[j]
because the marriage of the Lamb
  has come,
and His wife has prepared herself.
[8] She was given fine linen to wear, bright
  and pure.[k]

For the fine linen represents the righteous acts of the •saints.[l]

[9]Then he[C] said to me,[m] "Write: Those invited to the marriage feast[n] of the Lamb are fortunate!" He also said to me, "These words of God are true." [10]Then I fell at his feet to worship him, but he said to me, "Don't do that! I am a fellow slave with you and your •brothers who have the testimony about[D] Jesus.[o] Worship God, because the testimony about Jesus is the spirit of prophecy."[E]

The Rider on a White Horse

[11]Then I saw heaven opened,[p] and there was

Cross references (center column):

[a]18:24 Rv 6:10; 16:6
[b]19:1 Ps 104:35; 105:45
[c]19:2 Jn 8:16; 19:35; Rv 16:7; 15:3
[d]Dt 32:43; 2Kg 9:7; Rv 6:10; 16:6; 17:6; 18:24
[e]19:3 Is 34:8-10; Rv 14:11
[f]19:4 Rv 5:8
[g]Ps 106:48
[h]19:5 Ps 115:13
[i]19:6 Ezk 1:24; 43:2; Rv 1:15; 14:2
[j]19:7 Mt 5:12
[k]19:8 Rv 15:6; 19:14
[l]Eph 2:10
[m]19:9 Rv 17:1; 22:8-9
[n]Is 25:6-8; Lk 13:29
[o]19:10 Rv 1:2,9; 12:17; 20:4
[p]19:11 Rv 4:1; 11:19; 15:5

[A]18:24 Lit in her   [B]19:2 Valid; Jn 8:16; 19:35   [C]19:9 Probably an angel; Rv 17:1; 22:8-9   [D]19:10 Or to   [E]19:10 Or the Spirit

---

tion of Babylon the Great since she is held guilty of the blood of not just **prophets and saints**, but all martyrs **slaughtered on earth** throughout history.

19:1-4 The **vast multitude** pictured as a choir singing the heavenly "Hallelujah Chorus" (vv. 1,3,4,6) was taken to heaven in 7:9 and are identified as the "heaven dwellers" by comparing 7:15 and 13:6. They now praise God for (1) their **salvation** and (2) His righteous judgments upon Babylon, the **notorious prostitute** (17:1), thus avenging the **blood** of His servants, the martyrs (see note at 6:9-11). On the **24 elders**, see note at 4:3-4. On the **four living creatures**, see note at 4:6-7.

19:6-8 The praise of the **vast multitude** (see note at vv. 1-4) as a heavenly choir now turns to (1) the coming reign of the Lord and (2) the joyful **marriage of the Lamb**. The wife of the Lamb (Christ) is the church (Eph 5:31-32), those redeemed from all nations (Rv 5:9-10; 7:9) by His blood (1:5-6; 5:9-10). Since these descriptions are equally true of the vast multitude (7:9; 19:1,6) and the "heaven dwellers" (12:12; 13:6), it appears that there is a shift in imagery from the same group of people being portrayed as a choir to being the wife of the Lamb.

19:9 The fourth beatitude of the Apocalypse has a twist: If a person accepts the "invitation" and goes to **the marriage feast of the Lamb**, his faith will make him part of the wife (the church). It is called a "feast" because it endures, beginning on the evening of the wedding and continuing for days.

19:10 Near the beginning of the Ten Commandments, God's people are prohibited from the **worship** of any being other than God (Ex 20:3-6). Nevertheless, in sheer amazement, John fell prostrate to worship the angel. The angel immediately corrected him. The phrase **the testimony about Jesus is the spirit of prophecy** apparently means that all biblical prophecy either directly or indirectly testifies about Jesus, the Messiah (Lk 24:27,44-48; 1Pt 1:11-12).

19:11-13 John had previously seen **heaven opened** in 4:1. This **rider** on a **white horse** is not the same as the one in 6:2 (see note there). He **judges and makes war in righteousness**, not in the boastful and blasphemous way that the beast does (13:5-7). This is why He is called **Faithful and True**. On **eyes . . . like a fiery flame**, see note at 1:14. **Many crowns** shows that Christ has more power to rule than Satan (12:3) or the beast (13:1). A **name . . . that no one knows except Himself** reminds readers that the Lord has not revealed everything about Himself and His plan (Dt 29:29; see note at Rv 10:3-4). A **robe stained with blood** looks backwards at Jesus' redemptive death (7:9) and forward to His treading the winepress of God's wrath (19:15; Is 63:1-6). In both the Gospel of John (1:1,14) and 1 John (1:1), John began by referring to Jesus as **the Word** (Gk logos).

a white horse. Its rider is called Faithful and True,[a] and He judges and makes war in righteousness.[b] [12]His eyes were like a fiery flame, and many crowns[A] were on His head. He had a name written that no one knows except Himself.[c] [13]He wore a robe stained with blood,[B,d] and His name is the Word of God.[e] [14]The armies that were in heaven followed Him on white horses, wearing pure white linen. [15]A sharp[c] sword[f] came from His mouth, so that He might strike the nations with it.[g] He will shepherd[D] them with an iron scepter.[h] He will also trample the winepress of the fierce anger of God,[i] the Almighty. [16]And He has a name written on His robe and on His thigh:

**KING OF KINGS
AND LORD OF LORDS.[E,j]**

The Beast and His Armies Defeated

[17]Then I saw an angel standing on[F] the sun, and he cried out in a loud voice, saying to all the birds flying high overhead, "Come, gather together for the great supper of God, [18]so that you may eat the flesh of kings, the flesh of commanders, the flesh of mighty men, the flesh of horses and of their riders, and the

flesh of everyone, both free and slave, small and great."[k]

[19]Then I saw the beast, the kings of the earth, and their armies[l] gathered together to wage war against the rider on the horse and against His army. [20]But the beast was taken prisoner, and along with him the false prophet, who had performed the signs in his presence. He deceived those who accepted the mark of the beast and those who worshiped his image with these signs.[m] Both of them were thrown alive into the lake of fire that burns with sulfur.[n] [21]The rest were killed with the sword that came from the mouth of the rider on the horse, and all the birds were filled with their flesh.

Satan Bound

20 Then I saw an angel coming down from heaven with the key to the *abyss[o] and a great chain in his hand. [2]He seized the dragon, that ancient serpent who is the Devil and Satan,[G,p] and bound[q] him for 1,000 years. [3]He threw him into the abyss, closed it, and put a seal on it[r] so that he would no longer deceive the nations[s] until the 1,000 years were completed. After that, he must be released for a short time.

Cross-reference column

[a]19:11 Rv 3:14
[b]Ps 9:8; 96:13; Rv 16:7; 19:2
[c]19:12 Rv 2:17; 3:12
[d]19:13 Is 63:1-6
[e]Jn 1:1-5; Heb 4:12
[f]19:15 Is 49:2; Heb 4:12; Rv 1:16; 2:12,16
[g]Is 11:4; 2Th 2:8; Rv 1:16; 2:12
[h]Ps 2:9; Rv 12:5
[i]Rv 16:19; 14:19-20
[j]19:16 Dt 10:17; Dn 2:47; 1Tm 6:15; Rv 17:14
[k]19:18 Ezk 39:17-20
[l]19:19 Rv 16:13-14
[m]19:20 Rv 13:13-17
[n]Mt 5:22; Mk 9:43; Rv 20:10,14; 21:8
[o]20:1 Lk 8:31; Rv 9:1
[p]20:2 Rv 12:9
[q]Is 24:22
[r]20:3 Dn 6:17; Mt 27:66
[s]Rv 12:9

[A]19:12 Or *diadems*   [B]19:13 Or *a robe dipped in*   [C]19:15 Other mss add *double-edged*   [D]19:15 Or *rule*   [E]19:16 Dt 10:17; Dn 2:47; 1Tm 6:15; Rv 17:14   [F]19:17 Or *in*   [G]20:2 Other mss add *who deceives the whole world*

19:14 Since **the armies** accompanying the Lord are wearing **pure white linen**, as did the Lamb's wife (v. 8), this is another image for the same group elsewhere called the "vast multitude" (vv. 1,6; 7:9) and the "heaven dwellers" (12:12; 13:6). On why these are not angels, see note at 17:14. **White horses** implies that Christ allows His people to participate in the climactic victory, as they later reign with Him (20:6).

19:15-16 God's word pictured as **a sharp sword** looks back to the description of the Son of Man in 1:13-16. **Strike the**

nations sounds like wording from Psalm 2, but there the striking is done with "a rod of iron." **Shepherd . . . with an iron scepter** is the end-time fulfillment of what was predicted of the newborn Son in 12:5. On **the winepress of the fierce anger of God**, see note at 14:14-20.

19:17-19,21 The great **armies** of the earth, led by **the beast** and **the kings of the earth**, assemble to make war against the Lamb (apparently at Armagedon; see notes at 16:12-14 and 16:16). But they end up being killed by the **sword** that comes out of the **mouth** of the rider on the white horse (Christ) and fed to the birds at the **great supper** of God.

19:20 The **beast** (see note at 13:1-3) and the **false prophet** (see note at 13:11) are captured and **thrown alive** into the **lake of fire**, apparently the first to be sentenced there (Mt 25:41). They are not destroyed, but will suffer torment forever (Rv 20:10).

20:1-3 On the **angel . . . with the key to the abyss**, see note at 9:1. The **great chain** is used to bind **the dragon** (Satan) in the abyss. Some hold that the wording **1,000 years** (vv. 2,3,4,5,6,7) is figurative for a long period of time. Others think it speaks of a literal period of 1,000 years. Others think John saw a vision of 1,000 years, but it is impossible to know how the apocalyptic image here will be fulfilled. In regard to Satan not being able to **deceive the nations** (see note at 12:7-10) **until the 1,000 years were completed**, a traditional view has been that Satan is limited (i.e., chained) during the new covenant era, though the apparent upsurge in demonic influence and spiritual warfare in modern times has seriously weakened this view. On Satan being **released**, see note at verses 7-10.

poimaino

Greek Pronunciation	[poy MIGH noh]
HCSB Translation	shepherd
Uses in Revelation	4
Uses in the NT	11
Focus passage	Revelation 19:15

Poimaino (to shepherd) basically means *to tend* or *nurture* sheep (Lk 17:7), and the related noun *poimen* was the common term for *shepherd*. However, *poimaino* was typically used in the more metaphorical sense of *to rule* or *govern*, typically with positive results but occasionally with negative ones (Rv 2:27; 12:5; 19:15). These last three references contain an allusion to Ps 2:9, which indicates that the Lord's anointed will *rule* or *govern* (*poimaino* in the Greek OT) the nations "with a rod of iron." In the NT, *poimaino* typically retains the literal image of a *shepherd* tending sheep, while applying this metaphorically to those who take care of the Father's "flock" (Mt 2:6; Jn 21:16; Ac 20:28; 1Pt 5:2; Rv 7:17). The use of *poimaino* in Rv 7:17 involves a mixed metaphor, in that "the Lamb" is going to "shepherd" the redeemed.

The Saints Reign with the Messiah

[4] Then I saw thrones, and people seated on them who were given authority to judge.[a] I also saw the people[A,b] who had been beheaded[B] because of their testimony about Jesus[c] and because of God's word, who had not worshiped the beast or his image, and who had not accepted the mark on their foreheads or their hands.[d] They came to life[e] and reigned with the •Messiah for 1,000 years. [5] The rest of the dead did not come to life until the 1,000 years were completed. This is the first resurrection. [6] Blessed[f] and holy is the one who shares in the first resurrection! The second death[g] has no power[C] over them, but they will be priests of God and of the Messiah, and they will reign with Him for 1,000 years.[h]

Satanic Rebellion Crushed

[7] When the 1,000 years are completed, Satan will be released from his prison [8] and will go out to deceive the nations at the four corners of the earth,[i] Gog and Magog, to gather them for battle.[j] Their number is like the sand of the sea. [9] They came up over the surface of the earth and surrounded the encampment of the •saints, the beloved city. Then fire came down from heaven[D] and consumed them.[k] [10] The Devil who deceived them was thrown into the lake of fire and sulfur where the beast

a 20:4 Dn 7:22; Mt 19:28; 1Co 6:2-3; Rv 3:21; 6:9
b Rv 6:9
c Rv 1:2,9; 12:17; 19:10
d Rv 13:12-16
e Is 25:6-8; Mt 9:18; 26:29; Lk 13:29; Rv 2:8; 13:14
f 20:6 Rv 1:3; 14:13; 16:15; 19:9; 22:7,14
g Rv 20:14; 21:8
h Rv 1:6; 5:10
i 20:8 Is 11:12; Ezk 7:2; Rv 7:1
j Ezk 38-39
k 20:9 2Kg 1:10,12; Ezk 38:22; 39:6; Lk 9:54
l 20:10 Rv 19:20
m Mt 25:41
n 20:11 Is 51:6; Mt 24:35; 2Pt 3:10; Rv 18:21
o 20:12 Dn 7:10
p Is 4:3; 34:16; Dn 12:1; Rv 3:5; 13:8; 17:8; 20:15; 21:27
q Ps 62:12; Jr 17:10; Rm 2:6; 1Pt 1:17
r 20:13 Rv 1:18; 6:8
s 20:14 Is 25:7-8; 1Co 15:26
t 21:1 Is 65:17; 66:22; 2Pt 3:13
u Rv 13:1
v 21:2 Gl 4:26; Heb 11:10; Rv 3:12; w Is 61:10; Rv 19:7

and the false prophet are,[l] and they will be tormented day and night forever and ever.[m]

The Great White Throne Judgment

[11] Then I saw a great white throne and One seated on it. Earth and heaven fled from His presence, and no place was found for them.[n] [12] I also saw the dead, the great and the small, standing before the throne, and books were opened.[o] Another book was opened, which is the book of life,[p] and the dead were judged according to their works[q] by what was written in the books. [13] Then the sea gave up its dead, and Death and •Hades[r] gave up their dead; all[E] were judged according to their works. [14] Death and Hades were thrown into the lake of fire.[s] This is the second death, the lake of fire.[F] [15] And anyone not found written in the book of life was thrown into the lake of fire.

The New Creation

21 Then I saw a new heaven and a new earth,[t] for the first heaven and the first earth had passed away, and the sea no longer existed.[u] [2] I also saw the Holy City, new Jerusalem, coming down out of heaven from God,[v] prepared like a bride adorned for her husband.[w]

A 20:4 Lit souls   B 20:4 All who had given their lives for their faith in Christ   C 20:6 Or authority   D 20:9 Other mss add from God
E 20:13 Lit each   F 20:14 Other mss omit the lake of fire

20:4-6 Those who sit on the **thrones** and have **authority to judge** are God's people (Dn 7:18,27; 1Co 6:2). The resurrection of martyrs before Christ's earthly reign is called **the first resurrection**. Since "first resurrection" implies a *second* resurrection will follow, some interpreters take the first resurrection to be spiritual only (e.g., being "born again") in order to maintain the concept of a general bodily resurrection at the end of time. The fifth beatitude (**blessed**) of the book recognizes the holiness of those in the first resurrection. On the **second death**, see verse 14 and note at verses 11-15. *Premillennialists* follow the natural order of this passage, taking the 1,000 years as falling after the second coming of Christ. Others believe it is a "flashback" (recapitulation) of the time before the second advent, viewing it from a different perspective. Among those who take the recapitulation approach, *Amillennialists* believe the reign of Christ is being accomplished spiritually even now through the church. This view takes the 1,000 years figuratively, stretching over the entire church era. *Postmillennialists* believe the preaching of the gospel will at some future date bring about virtual worldwide conversion and a golden era of biblical values lasting 1,000 years (a time taken literally by some, figuratively by others).

20:7-10 Satan's release from the abyss (v. 3) is related to the well-known **Gog and Magog** prophecy in Ezekiel 38-39. This incident will serve as final proof that, even after an extended, unrivaled reign of Christ (Rv 20:4-6), mankind (those born during the 1,000 years) will still follow **the Devil**. When the rebellion surrounding **the beloved city** (probably

Jerusalem, "renovated" for Christ's reign of 1,000 years) is put down by fire from heaven, as in Ezekiel 39:6, the Devil is thrown into the lake of fire, to join **the beast and the false prophet** (see note at 19:20) for eternity.

20:11-15 The phrase **great white throne** emphasizes God's purity and holiness in judging and His sovereign right to both rule and judge the earth. The phrases **earth and heaven fled** and **no place was found for them** apparently refer to "the first heaven and the first earth" giving way at the final judgment to "a new heaven and a new earth" (21:1). **The dead . . . standing before the throne** come to life in the "second resurrection" (implied in v. 5). There are two sets of books at this judgment. The names of all believers are in the **book of life**. The names of the "earth dwellers" are not in the book of life (13:8; 17:8). They are **judged according to their works**, which are recorded in the other books. No one can ever be saved by works, because that would leave room for human boasting (Eph 2:8-9). The eternal dwelling place of all unbelievers is the **lake of fire**. As part of the present creation, **Death and Hades** (see note at 1:18) are also thrown into the lake of fire.

21:1 While like the present creation in some ways, the **new heaven and a new earth** will be much different. For example, there will be no **sea**. However, some believe that "sea" is symbolic for the wickedness of the current created order.

21:2 The **bride** of the Lamb, introduced in 19:7-9, is now pictured as **the Holy City, new Jerusalem** (see note at

³Then I heard a loud voice from the throne:[A]

Look! God's dwelling[B] is with humanity,
and He will live with them.
They will be His people,[a]
and God Himself will be with them
and be their God.[c]
⁴ He will wipe away every tear
from their eyes.[b]
Death will no longer exist;[c]
grief, crying, and pain will exist
no longer,[d]
because the previous things[D]
have passed away.[e]

⁵Then the One seated on the throne said, "Look! I am making everything new." He also said, "Write, because these words[E] are faithful and true."[f] ⁶And He said to me, "It is done![g] I am the *Alpha and the Omega,[h] the Beginning and the End.[i] I will give water as a gift to the thirsty[j] from the spring of life.[k] ⁷The victor[l] will inherit these things, and I will be his God, and he will be My son.[m] ⁸But the cowards, unbelievers,[F] vile, murderers, sexually immoral, sorcerers, idolaters, and all liars—their share will be in the lake that burns with fire and sulfur,[n] which is the second death."

The New Jerusalem

⁹Then one of the seven angels, who had held the seven bowls filled with the seven last plagues,[o] came and spoke with me: "Come, I will show you the bride, the wife of the Lamb." ¹⁰He then carried me away in the Spirit[G,p] to a great and high mountain[q] and showed me the holy city, Jerusalem, coming down out of heaven from God, ¹¹arrayed with God's glory.[r] Her radiance was like a very precious stone, like a jasper stone, bright as crystal. ¹²The city had a massive high wall, with 12 gates. Twelve angels were at the gates; the names of the 12 tribes of Israel's sons were inscribed on the gates. ¹³There were three gates on the east, three gates on the north, three gates on the south, and three gates on the west.[s] ¹⁴The city wall had 12 foundations, and the 12 names of the Lamb's 12 apostles were on the foundations.

¹⁵The one who spoke with me had a gold measuring rod[t] to measure the city, its gates, and its wall.[u] ¹⁶The city is laid out in a square; its length and width are the same. He measured the city with the rod at 12,000 *stadia*.[H] Its length, width, and height are equal. ¹⁷Then he measured its wall, 144 *cubits according to human measurement, which the angel used.

Cross references:
a 21:3 Lv 26:11-12; Jr 31:33; Ezk 37:27; Zch 8:8
b 21:4 Is 25:8; 30:19; 51:11; Rv 7:17
c Hs 13:14; 1Co 15:54
d Is 35:10; 60:20; 65:19
e Is 42:9
f 21:5 Rv 22:6
g 21:6 Rv 16:17
h Rv 1:8; 22:13
i Is 44:6; 48:12
j Ps 42:1-2; Is 41:17; 44:3; 55:1; Jn 4:14; 7:37
k Ps 36:9; Jr 2:13; Jn 4:14
l 21:7 Rv 2:7
m 2Sm 7:14
n 21:8 Rv 19:20
o 21:9 Rv 16:1
p 21:10 Rv 1:10; 4:2; 17:3
q Ezk 40:2
r 21:11 Is 60:1-2
s 21:13 Ezk 48:30-34
t 21:15 Rv 11:1
u Ezk 40:3

A 21:3 Other mss read *from heaven* **B** 21:3 Or *tent,* or *tabernacle* **C** 21:3 Other mss omit *and be their God* **D** 21:4 Or *the first things* **E** 21:5 Other mss add *of God* **F** 21:8 Other mss add *the sinful* **G** 21:10 Or *in spirit* **H** 21:16 A *stadion* (sg) = about 600 feet; 12,000 *stadia* = 1,400 miles.

---

vv. 9-11a). The expression **coming down out of heaven** is used in all three references to the new Jerusalem (see note at 3:12). This has been taken to imply that the new Jerusalem will be suspended in the air, slightly above the new earth. **Prepared . . . adorned** may mean that the bride will be just as beautiful—and will be for eternity—as she was during the wedding festivities (19:7-8).

21:3-4 God's presence (**dwelling . . . with humanity**) will do away with all **death . . . grief, crying, and pain**.

alpha

Greek Pronunciation	[AL fah]
HCSB Translation	Alpha
Uses in Revelation	3
Uses in the NT	3
Focus passage	Revelation 21:6

Alpha is the first letter in the Greek alphabet, and *omega* is the last. In the NT, these two letters occur together three times in the phrase "the *Alpha* and the Omega," twice of God the Father (Rv 1:8; 21:6) and once of God the Son (Rv 22:13), indicating the close mutual unity between the Father and Son (cp. Jn 10:38; 14:10-11). "The *Alpha* and the Omega" appears in juxtaposition to "the One who is, who was, and who is to come" (Rv 1:8; cp. 1:4), as well as to "the Beginning and the End" (21:6) and "the First and the Last" (22:13). The phrase sums up the entirety of God's sovereign power over all things, specifically His control over all human history. "The *Alpha* and the Omega" has the power to begin and end all things in accordance with His decree, and the phrase provides strong affirmation of Jesus' deity and messianic lordship.

21:5-8 In the present creation, a Christian is a "new creation" spiritually (2Co 5:17), but in the new heaven and new earth, the Lord will make **everything new**. The written Word of God is faithful and true (2Tm 3:16), and the living Word of God is also faithful and true (Rv 19:11). On **it is done**, see note at 16:17-21. On **the Alpha and the Omega**, see note at 1:8. Living water (22:17) will always be available **as a gift**, and this pictures the word of grace, received through saving faith, that offers eternal life even in the present.

21:9-11a The angel's offer to show John **the bride, the wife of the Lamb**, parallels the angel's offer to show him the judgment of Babylon in 17:1. When Jesus was tempted by the Devil, He was taken up on a high mountain and shown the splendor of the world's kingdoms (Mt 4:8), but it was nothing in comparison to John's view of the new Jerusalem. On **in the Spirit**, see note at 1:10. On **coming down out of heaven**, see note at verse 2.

21:11b-14,21 On **a jasper stone**, see note at 4:3-4. The **12 gates** (each made of a massive single pearl) in the great wall of the new Jerusalem have written on them the names of the **12 tribes** of Israel. The **12 foundations** of the city wall have the **12 names** of the **apostles** of Christ. This strongly implies that the unified people of God will in some sense maintain the distinct covenant promises to Israel and the church eternally.

21:15-20 The mention of the **measuring rod** is an allusion to Ezekiel 40–41 (see note at Rv 11:1-2). For a city to be 1,400 miles square (**12,000 stadia**) with walls over 200 feet thick (**144 cubits**) is mind-boggling, as are the materials of

[18]The building material of its wall was jasper, and the city was pure gold like clear glass.

[19]The foundations of the city wall were adorned with every kind of precious stone:[a]

the first foundation jasper,
the second sapphire,
the third chalcedony,
the fourth emerald,
[20]   the fifth sardonyx,
the sixth carnelian,
the seventh chrysolite,
the eighth beryl,
the ninth topaz,
the tenth chrysoprase,
the eleventh jacinth,
the twelfth amethyst.

[21]The 12 gates are 12 pearls; each individual gate was made of a single pearl. The broad street[A] of the city was pure gold, like transparent glass.

[22]I did not see a sanctuary in it, because the Lord God the Almighty and the Lamb are its sanctuary. [23]The city does not need the sun or the moon to shine on it, because God's glory illuminates it, and its lamp is the Lamb.[b] [24]The nations[B] will walk in its light,[c] and the kings of the earth will bring their glory into it.[C,d] [25]Each day its gates will never close because

it will never be night there. [26]They will bring the glory and honor of the nations into it.[D,e] [27]Nothing profane will ever enter it:[f] no one who does what is vile or false, but only those written in the Lamb's book of life.[g]

The Source of Life

22 Then he showed me the river[E] of living water, sparkling like crystal, flowing from the throne of God and of the Lamb[h] [2]down the middle of the broad street of the city. The tree of life[F] was on both sides of the river, bearing 12 kinds of fruit, producing its fruit every month.[i] The leaves of the tree are for healing the nations, [3]and there will no longer be any curse.[j] The throne of God and of the Lamb will be in the city,[G] and His •slaves will serve Him. [4]They will see His face,[k] and His name will be on their foreheads.[l] [5]Night will no longer exist,[m] and people will not need lamplight or sunlight, because the Lord God will give them light. And they will reign forever and ever.

The Time Is Near

[6]Then he said to me, "These words are faithful and true.[n] And the Lord, the God of the spirits of the prophets,[H] has sent His angel to show His slaves what must quickly take place."[I,o]

a21:19 Ex 28:15-21; Is 54:11
b21:23 Is 24:23; 30:26; 60:19-20; Zch 14:6-7; Rv 22:5
c21:24 Is 42:6; 49:6; 60:3,5
d1s 49:7,23; 60:10
e21:26 Is 60:11
f21:27 Is 35:8; 52:1
gRv 3:5; 13:8; 17:8; 20:12,15
h22:1 Ezk 47:1-2; Jl 3:18
i22:2 Gn 2:9; 3:22
j22:3 Gn 3:14-19; Zch 14:11
k22:4 Ex 33:20; Ps 17:15; Mt 5:8
l Rv 7:3; 9:4; 13:16; 14:1,9; 17:5; 20:4
m22:5 Zch 14:7; Rv 21:25
n22:6 Rv 3:14; 19:11; 21:5
o Dn 2:28-29,45; Rv 1:1

A21:21 Or *The public square*   B21:24 Other mss add *of those who are saved*   C21:24 Other mss read *will bring to Him the nations'*
glory and honor   D21:26 Other mss add *in order that they might go in*   E22:1 Other mss read *pure river*   F22:2 Or *was a tree of life*,
or *was a tree that gives life*   G22:3 Lit *in it*   H22:6 Other mss read *God of the holy prophets*   I22:6 Or *soon*

the wall—**jasper** stone and **gold**. The **foundations of the city** are named for the 12 apostles. It is unknown which precious stone stands for which apostle.

21:22-27 No temple is needed in the new Jerusalem. God the Father (**the Almighty**) and **the Lamb** (Christ) are its **sanctuary**. Also, as there was light from the Lord before the creation of the physical light sources of the universe (Gn 1:3,14-15), there is no need for light (**sun or the moon**) in the new Jerusalem because **God's glory illuminates it**. There apparently will be national distinctions (**the nations**) and human rulers (**the kings of the earth**) in the eternal state, but since all who will be there are included in the Lamb's book of life (excluding the **profane . . . vile**, and **false**; see note at 3:4-5), there is no need for security, and there can be no sin.

22:1-5 The **river of living water** looks back to Ezekiel 47, as well as to Jesus' promise about the Holy Spirit flowing as "streams of living water" (Jn 7:37-39) from those who believe in Him. The **tree of life** was in the center of the garden of Eden (Gn 2:9; 3:3). After the fall of mankind into sin, God denied humanity access to the tree (Gn 3:24). Ezekiel 47:12 speaks of trees that bear fruit with medicinal value. The wording here pictures the new Jerusalem as the new and permanent "Eden," where **there will no longer be any curse** (see Gn 3:14-19). As Adam and Eve walked with the Lord periodically in the garden, His presence will be constant. All inhabitants will have **His name** on **their foreheads**, as was the case with the 144,000 (14:1). On **night will no longer exist**, see note at 21:22-27.

22:6-7 The sixth beatitude of the book (**blessed**) repeats the emphases on the imminence of the events in Revelation and the need for application of its prophecies seen in the first beatitude in 1:3 (see note there), but here those elements are in reverse order.

metopon

Greek Pronunciation	[MEH toh pahn]
HCSB Translation	forehead
Uses in Revelation	8
Uses in the NT	8
Focus passage	Revelation 22:4

In the ancient world, a mark on the *forehead (metopon)* normally involved a master/slave relationship (cp. word study on *seal*, Gk *sphragis*). Such markings were used to signify (1) tribal identity, (2) ownership, or (3) loyalty to a deity (closely related to ownership), as well as (4) to punish runaway slaves.

In the NT, *metopon* occurs in Revelation, where a mark on the *forehead* is always in view. On four occasions God claims ownership of His slaves by applying His name to their *foreheads*, protecting them from His judgment (7:3; 9:4; 14:1; 22:4). Three times God's enemies receive the mark of the beast (perhaps his name or 666) on their right hand or *forehead* (13:16; 14:9; 20:4). This represents a satanic counterpart to God's sealing. Elsewhere, the prostitute riding the scarlet beast bears a cryptic name on her *forehead* (17:5), perhaps an allusion to the ancient practice of Roman prostitutes placing their names on headbands.

7 "Look, I am coming quickly![a] The one
who keeps the prophetic words of this book
is blessed."[b]
8 I, John, am the one who heard and saw
these things. When I heard and saw them, I fell
down to worship at the feet of the angel who
had shown them to me. 9 But he said to me,
"Don't do that! I am a fellow slave with you,
your •brothers the prophets, and those who
keep the words of this book. Worship God."[c]
10 He also said to me, "Don't seal the prophetic
words of this book, because the time is near.[d]
11 Let the unrighteous go on in unrighteousness; let the filthy go on being made filthy; let
the righteous go on in righteousness; and let
the holy go on being made holy."[e]
12 "Look! I am coming quickly, and My reward is with Me[f] to repay each person according to what he has done.[g] 13 I am the •Alpha
and the Omega,[h] the First and the Last,[i] the
Beginning and the End.[j]
14 "Blessed[k] are those who wash their robes,[A]
so that they may have the right to the tree of
life and may enter the city by the gates. 15 Outside are the dogs, the sorcerers, the sexually
immoral, the murderers, the idolaters, and
everyone who loves and practices lying.[l]
16 "I, Jesus, have sent My angel to attest
these things to you[B] for the churches. I am
the Root[m] and the Offspring of David,[n] the
Bright Morning Star."[o]
17 Both the Spirit and the bride say, "Come!"
Anyone who hears should say, "Come!" And
the one who is thirsty should come. Whoever
desires should take the living water as a gift.[p]
18 I testify to everyone who hears the prophetic words of this book: If anyone adds to
them, God will add to him the plagues that
are written in this book. 19 And if anyone takes
away from the words of this prophetic book,
God will take away his share of the tree of life
and the holy city, written in this book.[q]
20 He who testifies about these things[r] says,
"Yes, I am coming quickly."
•Amen! Come, Lord Jesus![s]
21 The grace of the Lord Jesus[C] be with all
the •saints.[D] Amen.[E]

[a]22:7 Rv 3:11 [b]Rv 1:3; 14:13; 19:9; 20:6; 22:14 [c]22:9 Rv 19:10 [d]22:10 Dn 12:4; Rv 1:3; 10:4 [e]22:11 Ezk 3:27; Dn 12:10 [f]22:12 Is 40:10; 62:11 [g]Is 59:18; Jr 17:10; 25:14 [h]22:13 Rv 1:8 [i]Rv 1:17 [j]Rv 21:6 [k]22:14 Rv 1:3; 14:13; 16:15; 19:9; 20:6; 22:7 [l]22:15 Rv 21:8 [m]22:16 Rv 5:5 [n]Is 11:1,10; Rm 1:3 [o]Nm 24:17; Rv 2:28 [p]22:17 Rv 21:6 [q]22:19 Dt 4:2; 12:32 [r]22:20 Rv 1:2 [s]1Co 16:22

[A]22:14 Other mss read *who keep His commands* [B]22:16 In Gk, you is pl [C]22:21 Other mss add *Christ* [D]22:21 Other mss omit *the saints* [E]22:21 Other mss omit *Amen.*

22:8-9 John repeats his mistake of false worship of an angel (see 19:10 and note there). Apparently the reader is to understand that worship of angels (who are majestic) is an easy mistake to make, even for a mature Christian like John.

22:10-12 The book of Daniel was "sealed until the time of the end" (Dn 12:9) to conceal its contents. In clear contrast, and in light of the imminence of the events (**the time is near**) portrayed in Revelation, John was commanded not to **seal the prophetic words of this book**. Until the events of the book are fulfilled, people will continue to act in keeping with their fallen spiritual nature (**unrighteous . . . filthy** or **righteous . . . holy**), but when the Lord comes, He will render to each person according to his deeds (20:12; 2Co 5:10).

22:13 On **the Alpha and the Omega**, see note at 1:8.

22:14-15,17 The final beatitude (**blessed**) of the Apocalypse is an elegant presentation of the gospel, using the imagery of the "new Eden" ("the tree of life") and the eternal city (**enter the city by the gates**). **Wash their robes** means faith in the shed blood of Christ. **The right to the tree of life** is what Adam and Eve were cut off from by their sin. The gates of the city and access to the tree of life are made available to those who believe in Jesus, but all unbelievers, with their various sinful lifestyles, are excluded. With the repeated invitation to **come** and **take the living water as a gift** (i.e., free grace; see Eph 2:8-9), Revelation ends with passionate evangelistic appeal. Though Jews referred to Gentiles as **dogs**, in this case it more likely refers to false teachers, whatever their ethnicity, as in Php 3:2.

22:16 Jesus is the **Offspring of David** in the sense of being a blood descendant of King David. This also serves as a messianic title (see Mt 1:1 and the family tree in Lk 3:23-31). On **the Bright Morning Star**, see note at Rv 2:28.

22:18-19 It is doubtful the wording here directly refers to closing the canon of the Bible (**this book**). The book (Gk *biblion*; "scroll") that is not to be tampered with is the book of Revelation, but the wording does imply that all Scripture should be guarded as sacred, never tampered with. The immediate context in Revelation is of a "new Eden" (vv. 1-5). Also, in Genesis 3, Eve *added to* the Word of God (Gn 3:3) and the Serpent *took away from* what the Lord had said (Gn 3:4). As a result, this "biblical bookends" effect of Rv 22:18-19 and Gn 3:3-4 infers that, just as Genesis is the first book in the Bible, Revelation is the last.

22:20 Jesus promised that He is **coming quickly** (see note at 1:1,3), but it has been well over 1,900 years since He uttered these words. John prayed for Jesus to come soon. God's patience toward the unbelieving world is a cause of Jesus' delay.

22:21 The book of Revelation, though made up largely of apocalyptic (1:1) and prophetic (1:3) literary forms, begins (1:4) and ends (with its concluding **grace**) like a letter. In spite of all the works of the Devil and the judgment and wrath of God detailed in between, the Apocalypse starts with grace and ends with grace, making a full circle from grace to grace. This is a fitting symmetry for a book that foretells the ultimate victory of "the God of all grace" (1Pt 5:10).

HCSB Bullet Notes

The HCSB Bullet Notes are one of the unique features of the Holman Christian Standard Bible®. These notes explain frequently used biblical words or terms. These "bullet" words (for example: •abyss) are marked with a bullet only on their first occurrence in a chapter of the biblical text. Other frequently used words, like •gate, are marked with bullets only where the use of the word fits the definitions given below.

Abaddon	A Hebrew word for either the grave or the realm of the dead
Abba	The Aramaic word for father
abyss	The bottomless pit or the depths (of the sea); it is the prison for Satan and the demons.
acrostic	A device in Hebrew poetry in which each verse begins with a successive letter of the Hebrew alphabet
advocate	The Greek word *parakletos* means one called alongside to help, counsel, or protect; it is used of the Holy Spirit in Jn and 1Jn.
Almighty	The Hebrew phrase is *El Shaddai*; *El* means God, but the meaning of *Shaddai* is disputed; traditionally it is translated "Almighty."
Alpha and Omega	The first and last letters of the Greek alphabet; it is used to refer to God the Father in Rv 1:8 and 21:6 and to Jesus, God the Son, in Rv 22:13.
Amen	The transliteration of a Hebrew word signifying that something is certain, valid, truthful, or faithful; it is often used at the end of biblical songs, hymns, and prayers.
annihilate(d)	During periods of war in Canaan and its neighboring countries, this was the destruction of a city, its inhabitants, and their possessions, including livestock.
Arabah	The section of the Great Rift in Palestine, extending from the Jordan Valley and the Dead Sea to the Gulf of Aqabah; the Hebrew word can also be translated as "plain," referring to any plain or to any part of the Arabah.
Asaph	A musician appointed by David to oversee the music used in worship at the Temple; 12 psalms are attributed to Asaph.
Asherah(s)/ Asherah pole(s)	A Canaanite fertility goddess who was the mother of the god Baal; also the wooden poles associated with the worship of her
Ashtoreth(s)	A Canaanite goddess of fertility, love, and war, who was the daughter of Asherah and consort of Baal; the plural form of her name in Hebrew is *Ashtaroth*.
Asia	A Roman province that is now part of modern Turkey; it did not refer to the modern continent of Asia.
asleep	A term used in reference to believers who have died
atone/ atonement	A theological term for God's provision to deal with human sin; in the OT, it primarily means purification. In some contexts forgiveness, pardon, expiation, propitiation, or reconciliation is included. The basis of atonement is substitutionary sacrifice offered in faith. The OT sacrifices were types and shadows of the great and final sacrifice of Jesus on the cross.
Baal	A fertility god who was the main god of the Canaanite religion and the god of rain and thunderstorms; it is also the Hebrew word meaning "lord," "master," "owner," or "husband."
Beelzebul	A term of slander, which was variously interpreted "lord of flies," "lord of dung," or "ruler of demons"
Bread of the Presence	Bread that was offered in Yahweh's presence, that is, in the holy place, not out on the altar (Lv 24:5-9)
brother(s)	The Greek word *adelphoi* can be used as a reference to males only or to groups that include both males and females. It is the context of each usage that determines the proper meaning.

burnt offering(s) Or *holocaust*; an offering completely burned to ashes; it was used in connection with worship, seeking God's favor, expiating sin, or averting judgment.

cause(s) the downfall of/ cause(s) to sin The Greek word *skandalizo* has a root meaning of snare or trap but has no real English counterpart.

centurion A Roman officer who commanded about 100 soldiers

Cephas The Aramaic word for rock; it is parallel to the Greek word *petros* from which the English name Peter is derived.

cherub(im) A class of winged angels, associated with the throne of God, who function as guardians and who prevented Adam and Eve from returning to the garden of Eden

chief priest(s) A group of Jewish temple officers that included the high priest, captain of the temple, temple overseers, and treasurers

clean When something is clean, it is holy or acceptable to God. When it is unclean, it is unholy (such as an unclean spirit). The term can be used in a ritual sense to apply to moral standards for living.

company Or *cohort*; a Roman military unit that numbered as many as 600 men

completely destroy During periods of war in Canaan and its neighboring countries, this was the destruction of a city, its inhabitants, and their possessions, including livestock.

Counselor The Greek word *parakletos* means one called alongside to help, counsel, or protect; it is used of the Holy Spirit in Jn and 1Jn.

cubit(s) An OT measurement of distance that equaled about 18 inches

Cush/Cushite The lands of the Nile in southern Egypt, including Nubia and Northern Sudan; also the people who lived in that region

Decapolis Originally, it referred to a federation of 10 Gentile towns east of the Jordan River.

denarius/ denarii A small silver Roman coin, which was equal to a day's wage for a common laborer

divination An attempt to foresee future events or discover hidden knowledge by means of physical objects such as water, arrows, flying birds, or animal livers

drink offering(s) An offering of a specified amount of wine or beer given along with animal sacrifices; it was poured over the sacrifice before it was burned.

engaged Jewish engagement was a binding agreement that could only be broken by divorce.

ephod A vest-like garment, extending below the waist and worn under the breastpiece; it was used both by the priests and by the high priest.

everyone Literally *sons of man* or *sons of Adam*

family redeemer A family member who had certain obligations of marriage, redeeming an estate, and punishment of a wrongdoer

fear(s) God or the LORD/ fear of the LORD No single English word conveys every aspect of the word *fear* in this phrase. The meaning includes worshipful submission, reverential awe, and obedient respect to the covenant-keeping God of Israel.

fellowship sacrifice(s) or offering(s) An animal offering was given to maintain and strengthen a person's relationship with God. It was not required as a remedy for impurity or sin but was an expression of thanksgiving for various blessings. An important function of this sacrifice was to provide meat for the priests and the participants in the sacrifice; also called the peace offering or the sacrifice of well-being.

firstfruits The agricultural products harvested first and given to God as an offering with more products to come in later harvests; it is also used as a metaphor for the first people to come to faith, for Jesus, the first person to rise from the dead, or for the Spirit, who is given to believers as the first portion (or down payment) of our salvation with more to come in eternity.

gate(s)	The site of community discussions, political meetings, and trying of court cases
Gittith	Perhaps an instrument, musical term, tune from Gath, or song for the grape harvest
God Almighty	The Hebrew phrase is *El Shaddai*; *El* means God, but the meaning of *Shaddai* is disputed; traditionally it is translated "Almighty."
grain offering(s)	An offering given along with animal sacrifices or given by itself; a portion was burnt and the priests and participant ate the remainder.
guilt/guilty	The liability to be punished for a fault, a sin, an act, or an omission unless there is forgiveness or atonement; the term normally concerns an objective fact, not a subjective feeling.
Hades	The Greek word for the place of the dead; it corresponds to the Hebrew word *Sheol*.
Hallelujah!	Or *Praise the LORD!*; it literally means *Praise Yah!* (a shortened form of *Yahweh*).
headquarters	The Latin word *Praetorium* was used by Greek writers for the residence of the Roman governor; it may also refer to military headquarters, the imperial court, or the emperor's guard.
Hebrew	Or *Aramaic*; the translation of this word is debated since some claim Aramaic was commonly spoken in Palestine during NT times. More recently others claim that Hebrew was the spoken language.
hell/hellfire	The Greek word is *gehenna*; it is the Aramaic term for the Valley of Hinnom on the south side of Jerusalem; formerly, it was a place of human sacrifice, and in NT times, a place for the burning of garbage; it is the place of final judgment for those rejecting Christ.

Herod	Name of the Idumean family ruling Palestine from 37 B.C. to A.D. 95; the main rulers from this family mentioned in the NT are:
Herod I	(37 B.C.–4 B.C.) He was also known as Herod the Great; he built the great temple in Jerusalem and massacred the male babies in Bethlehem.
Herod Antipas	(4 B.C.–A.D. 39) The son of Herod the Great; he ruled one-fourth of his father's kingdom (Galilee and Perea); he killed John the Baptist and mocked Jesus.
Herod Agrippa I	(A.D. 37–44) The grandson of Herod the Great; he beheaded James the apostle and imprisoned Peter.
Herod Agrippa II	(A.D. 52–ca 95) The great-grandson of Herod the Great; he heard Paul's defense.
Herodians	They were the political supporters of Herod the Great and his family.
hidden plan	Translation of the Greek word *mysterion*; it is a secret that was hidden in the past but now revealed.
Higgaion	Term used for a musical notation, for a device denoting a pause in an instrumental interlude, or for a murmuring harp tone
high place(s)	An ancient place of worship most often associated with pagan religions; it was usually built on an elevated location.
horn	A symbol of power based on the strength of animal horns
Hosanna	A term of praise derived from the Hebrew word for save
Host(s)	Military forces consisting of God's angels, sometimes including the sun, moon, and stars, and occasionally Israel
human race	Literally *sons of man* or *sons of Adam*
I assure you	This is a phrase used only by Jesus to testify to the certainty and importance of His words; in Mt, Mk, and Lk it is literally *Amen, I say to you*; in Jn it is literally *Amen, amen, I say to you*.

in this way   The Greek word *houtos*, commonly translated in Jn 3:16 as "so" or "so much," occurs over 200 times in the NT. Almost without exception it is an adverb of manner, not degree (for example, see Mt 1:18). It only means "so much" when modifying an adjective (see Gl 3:3; Rv 16:18). Manner seems primarily in view in Jn 3:16, which explains the HCSB's rendering.

Jews   In John, the term Jews usually indicates those in Israel who were opposed to Jesus, particularly the Jewish authorities in Jerusalem who led the nation.

justification/ justify/ justified   The act of God as judge that declares sinners (who were in the wrong) to be right or righteous in His sight. God is just in doing this because Jesus died on the cross to take away their sins and to give them His own righteousness (2Co 5:21). The sinner receives this justification by faith and by grace when he trusts Christ's work.

language(s)   The Greek word *glossa* can refer to the tongue as the organ of speech (see Mk 7:33) or to language the tongue produces. In certain NT passages, scholars differ on whether the term refers to human languages or to ecstatic speech capable only of divine interpretation ("speaking in tongues").

Leviathan   Or *twisting one*; a mythological sea serpent or dragon associated with the chaos at creation; sometimes it is applied to an animal such as a crocodile.

life/lives   The same Greek word *(psyche)* can be translated life or soul.

mankind   Literally *sons of man* or *sons of Adam*

Mary Magdalene   Or *Mary of Magdala*; Magdala was probably a town on the western shore of the Sea of Galilee, north of Tiberias.

Maskil   It is from a Hebrew word meaning *to be prudent* or *to have insight*; it could also mean a contemplative, instructive, or wisdom psalm.

men   Literally *sons of man* or *sons of Adam*

mercy seat   Or *place of atonement*; it was the gold lid on the ark of the covenant that was first used in the tabernacle and later in the temple.

Messiah   Or *the Christ*; the Greek word is *Christos* and means *the anointed one*. Where the NT emphasizes *Christos* as a name of our Lord or has a Gentile context, "Christ" is used. Where the NT *Christos* has a Jewish context, the title "Messiah" is used.

Miktam   A musical term of uncertain meaning; it possibly denotes a plaintive style.

Milcom   An Ammonite god who was the equivalent of Baal, the Canaanite storm god

Molech   A Canaanite god associated with death and the underworld; the worship ritual of passing someone through the fire is connected with him. This ritual could have been either fire-walking or child sacrifice.

Most High   The Hebrew word is *Elyon*; it is often used with other names of God, such as Hebrew *El (God)* or *Yahweh (Lord)*; it is used to refer to God as the supreme being.

Mount of Olives   A mountain east of Jerusalem across the Kidron Valley

mystery   Translation of the Greek word *mysterion*; it is a secret that was hidden in the past but now revealed.

Nazarene   A person from Nazareth; growing up in Nazareth was an aspect of the Messiah's humble beginnings.

Negev   An arid region in the southern part of Israel; the Hebrew word means south.

offend(ed)   The Greek word *skandalizo* has a root meaning of snare or trap but has no real English counterpart.

offspring   This term is used literally or metaphorically to refer to plants or grain, sowing or harvest, male reproductive seed, human children or physical descendants, and also to spiritual children or to Christ (Gl 3:16).

One and Only | Or *one of a kind*, or *incomparable*, or *only begotten*; the Greek word can refer to someone's only child as in Lk 7:12; 8:42; 9:38. It can also refer to someone's special child as in Heb 11:17.

oracle | A prophetic speech of a threatening or menacing character; it was often against the nations.

overseer(s) | Or *elder(s)*, or *bishop(s)*

palace | The Latin word *Praetorium* was used by Greek writers for the residence of the Roman governor; it may also refer to military headquarters, the imperial court, or the emperor's guard.

Passover | The Israelite festival celebrated on the fourteenth day of the first month, in the early spring; it was a celebration of the deliverance of the Israelites from Egypt, commemorating the final plague on Egypt when the firstborn were killed.

people | Literally *sons of man*, or *sons of Adam*

perverted men | Literally *sons of Belial*; in Hebrew, the basic meaning of Belial is worthless.

Pharisee(s) | A religious sect of Judaism that followed the whole written and oral law

Pilate | Pontius Pilate was governor of the province of Judea A.D. 26–36.

Pit | A term for either the grave or the realm of the dead

proconsul | The chief Roman government official in a senatorial province, who presided over Roman court hearings

propitiation | The removal of divine wrath; Jesus' death is the means that turns God's wrath from the sinner.

proselyte(s) | A person from another race or religion who went through a prescribed ritual to become a Jew

Rabbi | The Hebrew word means *my great one*; it is used for a recognized teacher of the Scriptures.

Rabshakeh | The title of a high-ranking Assyrian official who was the chief cupbearer to the king

Rahab | Or *boisterous one*; it is the name of a mythological sea serpent or dragon defeated at the time of creation. Scripture sometimes uses the name metaphorically to describe Egypt.

redemption/ redeemed | The deliverance from bondage by a payment or ransom (Mk 10:45; 1Pt 1:18-19)

Red Sea | Literally *Sea of Reeds*

regiment | Or *cohort*; a Roman military unit that numbered as many as 600 men

restitution offering(s) | An offering that was a penalty for unintentional sins, primarily committed in relation to the tabernacle or temple; it is traditionally translated *trespass* or *guilt offering*.

sackcloth | A garment made of poor quality material and worn as a sign of grief and mourning

sacred bread | Literally *bread of presentation*; these were 12 loaves of bread, representing the 12 tribes of Israel and put on the table in the holy place in the tabernacle and later in the temple. The priests ate the previous week's loaves.

Sadducee(s) | A religious sect of Judaism that mainly followed the first 5 books of the OT (the Torah or Pentateuch)

saint(s)/ sanctification/ sanctify/ sanctified | The work of the Holy Spirit that separates believers in Jesus from the world; at the time of saving faith in Jesus, the believer is made a saint; therefore, all believers are saints. The believer participates with the Spirit in a process of transformation that continues until glorification. The goal of sanctification is progressive conformity to the image of Jesus Christ.

Samaritan(s) | A people of mixed, Gentile/Jewish ancestry who lived between Galilee and Judea and were hated by the Jews

Sanhedrin	The supreme council of Judaism; it had 70 members and was patterned after Moses' 70 elders.
scribe(s)	A professional group in Judaism that copied the law of Moses and interpreted it, especially in legal cases
secret	Translation of the Greek word *mysterion*; it is a secret that was hidden in the past but now revealed.
seed	This term is used literally or metaphorically to refer to plants or grain, sowing or harvest, male reproductive seed, human children or physical descendants, and also to spiritual children or to Christ (Gl 3:16).
Selah	A Hebrew word whose meaning is uncertain; various interpretations include: (1) a musical notation, (2) a pause for silence, (3) a signal for worshipers to fall prostrate on the ground, (4) a term for the worshipers to call out, and (5) a word meaning forever.
set apart for destruction	During periods of war in Canaan and its neighboring countries, this was the destruction of a city, its inhabitants, and their possessions, including livestock.
shekel(s)	In the OT the *shekel* is a measurement of weight that came to be used as money, either gold or silver.
Sheminith	A musical term meaning *instruments* or *on the instrument of eight strings*
Sheol	A Hebrew word for either the grave or the realm of the dead
Shinar	A land in Mesopotamia, including ancient Sumer and Babylon; it is modern Iraq.
sin offering(s)	Or *purification offering*; it was the most important OT sacrifice for cleansing from impurities. It provided purification from sin and certain forms of ceremonial uncleanness.
slave(s)	The strong Greek word *doulos* cannot be accurately translated in English as servant or bond servant; the HCSB translates this word as slave, not out of insensitivity to the legitimate concerns of modern English speakers, but out of a commitment to accurately convey the brutal reality of the Roman empire's inhumane institution as well as the ownership called for by Christ.
Son of Man	The title that Jesus most frequently used for Himself (Dn 7:13; Mt 8:20)
song of ascents	A term that probably refers to the songs pilgrims sang as they traveled the roads going up to worship in Jerusalem (Pss 120–134)
soul	The same Greek word *(psyche)* can be translated life or soul.
stumble	The Greek word *skandalizo* has a root meaning of snare or trap but has no real English counterpart.
synagogue	A place where the Jewish people met for prayer, worship, and teaching of the Scriptures
tabernacle	Or *tent*, or *shelter*; a term used for temporary housing
take offense	The Greek word *skandalizo* has a root meaning of snare or trap but has no real English counterpart.
tassel	Fringe put on the clothing of devout Jews to remind them to keep the law
temple complex	In the Jerusalem temple, the complex included the sanctuary (the holy place and the holy of holies), at least 4 courtyards (for priests, Jews, women, and Gentiles), numerous gates, and several covered walkways.
testimony	A reference either to the Mosaic law in general or to a specific section of the law, the Ten Commandments, which were written on stone tablets and placed in the ark of the covenant (also called the ark of the testimony)

Topheth	A place of human sacrifice that was located outside Jerusalem in the Hinnom Valley (Jr 7:31-32)	woman	When used in direct address, "Woman" was not a term of disrespect but of honor.
unclean	When something is clean, it is holy or acceptable to God. When it is unclean, it is unholy (such as an unclean spirit). The term can be used in a ritual sense to apply to moral standards for living.	world	The organized Satanic system that is opposed to God and hostile to Jesus and His followers; it also refers to the non-Christian culture including governments, educational systems, and businesses.
Unleavened Bread	A seven-day festival celebrated in conjunction with the Passover (Ex 12:1-20)	wormwood	A small shrub that was used as a medicinal herb and noted for its bitter taste
Urim & Thummim	Two objects used by Israelite priests to determine God's will	Yah/Yahweh	A translation of the Hebrew letters YHWH, traditionally translated *the* LORD; "Yah" is the shortened form. The translation "Yahweh" is used in the HCSB in places where the personal name of God is discussed (Ps 68:4) or in places of His self-identification (Is 42:8).
wadi	A valley, ravine, or stream that is dry except in the rainy season		
walk(ed)/ walking	A term often used in a figurative way to mean "way of life" or "behavior"		
wicked men	Literally *sons of Belial*; in Hebrew, the basic meaning of Belial is worthless.	Zion	Originally a term for the fortified section of Jerusalem and then, by extension, used for the temple and the city of Jerusalem both in the present time and in the future
wise men	The Greek word is *magoi*; the English word "magi" is based on a Persian word. They were eastern sages who observed the heavens for signs and omens.		

Table of Weights and Measures

Weights

Biblical Unit	Language	Biblical Measure	U.S. Equivalent	Metric Equivalent	Various Translations
Gerah	Hebrew	1/20 shekel	1/50 ounce	.6 gram	gerah; oboli
Bekah	Hebrew	1/2 shekel or 10 gerahs	1/5 ounce	5.7 grams	bekah; half a shekel; quarter ounce; fifty cents
Pim	Hebrew	2/3 shekel	1/3 ounce	7.6 grams	2/3 of a shekel; quarter
Shekel	Hebrew	2 bekahs	2/5 ounce	11.5 grams	shekel; piece; dollar; fifty dollars
Litra (pound)	Greco-Roman	30 shekels	12 ounces	.4 kilogram	pound; pounds
Mina	Hebrew/Greek	50 shekels	1¼ pounds	.6 kilogram	mina; pound
Talent	Hebrew/Greek	3,000 shekels or 60 minas	75 pounds/ 88 pounds	34 kilograms/ 40 kilograms	talent/talents; 100 pounds

Length

Biblical Unit	Language	Biblical Measure	U.S. Equivalent	Metric Equivalent	Various Translations
Handbreadth	Hebrew	1/6 cubit or 1/3 span	3 inches	8 centimeters	handbreadth; three inches; four inches
Span	Hebrew	1/2 cubit or 3 handbreadths	9 inches	23 centimeters	span
Cubit/Pechys	Hebrew/Greek	2 spans	18 inches	.5 meter	cubit/cubits; yard; half a yard; foot
Fathom	Greco-Roman	4 cubits	2 yards	2 meters	fathom; six feet
Kalamos	Greco-Roman	6 cubits	3 yards	3 meters	rod; reed; measuring rod
Stadion	Greco-Roman	1/8 milion or 400 cubits	1/8 mile	185 meters	miles; furlongs; race
Milion	Greco-Roman	8 stadia	1,620 yards	1.5 kilometers	mile

Dry Measure

Biblical Unit	Language	Biblical Measure	U.S. Equivalent	Metric Equivalent	Various Translations
Xestes	Greco-Roman	1/2 cab	1⅙ pints	.5 liter	pots; pitchers; kettles; copper pots; copper bowls; vessels of bronze
Cab	Hebrew	1/18 ephah	1 quart	1 liter	cab; kab
Choinix	Greco-Roman	1/18 ephah	1 quart	1 liter	measure; quart
Omer	Hebrew	1/10 ephah	2 quarts	2 liters	omer; tenth of a deal; tenth of an ephah; six pints

Dry Measure

Biblical Unit	Language	Biblical Measure	U.S. Equivalent	Metric Equivalent	Various Translations
Seah/Saton	Hebrew/Greek	⅓ ephah	7 quarts	7.3 liters	measures; pecks; large amounts
Modios	Greco-Roman	4 omers	1 peck or ¼ bushel	9 liters	bushel; bowl; peck
Ephah [Bath]	Hebrew	10 omers	⅗ bushel	22 liters	bushel; peck; deal; part; measure; six pints; seven pints
Lethek	Hebrew	5 ephahs	3 bushels	110 liters	half homer; half sack
Kor [Homer]/ Koros	Hebrew/Greek	10 ephahs	6 bushels or 200 quarts	220 liters/ 525 liters	cor; homer; sack; measures; bushels

Liquid Measure

Biblical Unit	Language	Biblical Measure	U.S. Equivalent	Metric Equivalent	Various Translations
Log	Hebrew	1/72 bath	⅓ quart	.3 liter	log; pint; cotulus
Xestes	Greco-Roman	⅛ hin	1⅙ pints	.5 liter	pots; pitchers; kettles; copper bowls; vessels of bronze
Hin	Hebrew	⅙ bath	1 gallon or 4 quarts	4 liters	hin; pints
Bath/Batos	Hebrew/Greek	1 ephah	6 gallons	22 liters	gallon(s); barrels; liquid measures
Metretes	Greco-Roman	10 hins	10 gallons	39 liters	firkins; gallons

A Topical Concordance to the Holman Christian Standard Bible

A

Ability
From God. 1Pt 4:11.
Giving according to. Ezr 2:69; Ac 11:29.
Greater, promised. Jn 14:12.
Limited only by faith. Mk 9:23.
Measured by one's readiness. 2Co 8:12.
Spiritual, assigned by God. Rm 12:3-8.
Spiritual, inspired by the Spirit. 1Co 12:4-11.
Talents given according to. Mt 25:15.

Abstinence
From sexual immorality. 1Co 6:18-20; Gl 5:19-21;
Eph 5:3-5; 1Th 4:3-5; Rv 22:14-15.

Acceptance
By the grace of God. Rm 5:17; Eph 1:6.
Of prayers. Gn 19:21.
Of sacrifices. Ps 119:108.
Of sinners. Ezk 20:40-41; 36:23-29.

Affections
Of believers, supremely set on God. Ps 42:1; 73:25;
119:10.
Blessedness of making God the object of. Ps 91:14.
Christ claims the first place in. Mt 10:37; Lk 14:26.
False teachers seek to captivate. Gl 1:10; 4:17;
2Tm 3:6; 2Pt 2:3,18; Rv 2:14,20.
Kindled by communion with Christ and Scripture.
Lk 24:32.
Should be set:
Upon the commandments of God. Ps 19:8-10;
119:20,97,103,167.
Upon God supremely. Dt 6:5; 12:30.
Upon heavenly things. Col 3:1-2.
Upon the people of God. Ps 16:3; Rm 12:10;
2Co 7:13-15; 1Th 2:8.
Should be zealously engaged for God. Ps 69:9;
119:139; Gl 4:18.
Should not grow cold. Ps 106:12-13; Mt 24:12;
Gl 4:15; Rv 2:4.
Of the wicked, not sincerely set on God. Is 58:1-2;
Ezk 33:31-32; Lk 8:13.
Worldly, crucified in believers. Rm 6:6; Gl 5:24.
Worldly, should be put to death. Rm 8:13; 13:14;
1Co 9:27; Col 3:5; 1Th 4:5.

Afflictions
Always less than we deserve. Ezr 9:13; Ps 103:10.
Are consequences of the fall. Gn 3:16-19.
Believers appointed to. 1Th 3:3.
Believers are to expect. Jn 16:33; Ac 14:22.
Of believers, but temporary. Ps 30:5; 103:9;
Is 54:7-8; Jn 16:20; 1Pt 1:6; 5:10.
Of believers, comparatively light. Ac 20:23-24;
Rm 8:18; 2Co 4:17.
Of believers, end in joy and blessedness.
Ps 126:5-6; Is 61:2-3; Mt 5:4; 1Pt 4:13-14.
Believers have joy under. Jb 5:17; Jms 5:11.
Frequently result in good. Gn 50:20; Ex 1:11-12;
Dt 8:15-16; Jr 24:5-6; Ezk 20:37.
God appoints. 2Kg 6:33; Jb 5:6, 17; Ps 66:11;
Am 3:6; Mc 6:9.
God determines the continuance of. Gn 15:13-14;
Nm 14:33; Is 10:25; Jr 29:10.
God dispenses, as He will. Jb 11:10; Is 10:15; 45:7.
God regulates the measure of. Ps 80:5; Is 9:1;
Jr 46:28.
Man is born to. Jb 5:6-7; 14:1.
Often arise from being the followers of Jesus
Christ. Mt 24:9; Jn 15:21; 2Tm 3:11-12.
Sin produces. Jb 4:8; 20:11; Pr 1:31.
Sin visited with. 2Sm 12:14; Ps 89:30-32; Is 57:17;
Ac 13:10-11.
Tempered with mercy. Ps 78:38-39; 106:43-46;
Is 30:18-21; Lm 3:32; Mc 7:7-9; Nah 1:12.

Afflictions, Made beneficial
In convincing us of sin. Jb 36:8-9; Ps 119:67;
Lk 15:16-18.
In exercising our patience. Ps 40:1; Rm 5:3;
Jms 1:3; 1Pt 2:20.
In exhibiting the power and faithfulness of God.
Ps 34:19-20; 2Co 4:8-11.
In furthering the gospel. Ac 8:3-4; 11:19-21;
Php 1:12; 2Tm 2:9-10; 4:16-17.
In humbling us. Dt 8:3,16; 2Ch 7:13-14;
Lm 3:19-20; 2Co 12:7.
In keeping us from again departing from God.
Jb 34:31-32; Is 10:20; Ezk 14:10-11.
In leading us to confession of sin. Nm 21:7;
Ps 32:5; 51:35.
In leading us to seek God in prayer. Jdg 4:3;
Jr 31:18; Lm 2:17-19; Hs 5:14-15; Jnh 2:1.
In promoting the glory of God. Jn 9:1-3; 11:3-4;
21:18-19.

In purifying us. Ec 7:2-3; Is 1:25-26; 48:10;
    Jr 9:6-7; Zch 13:9; Mal 3:2-3.

In testing and exhibiting our sincerity. Jb 23:10;
    Ps 66:10; Pr 17:3.

In trying our faith and obedience. Gn 22:1-2;
    Ex 15:23-25; Dt 8:2,16; Heb 11:17; 1Pt 1:7;
    Rv 2:10.

In turning us to God. Dt 4:30-31; Neh 1:8-9;
    Ps 78:34; Is 10:20-21; Hs 2:6-7.

Afflictions, Ministry to those experiencing
Bear them in mind. Heb 13:3.
Comfort them. Jb 16:5; 29:25; 2Cor 1:4; 1Th 4:18.
Have compassion on them. Jb 6:14.
Pray for them. Ac 12:5; Php 1:16,19; Jms 5:14-16.
Protect them. Ps 82:3; Pr 22:22; 31:5.
Relieve them. Jb 31:19-20; Is 58:10; Php 4:14.
Sympathize with them. Rm 12:15; Gl 6:2.
Visit them. Jms 1:27.

Afflictions, Prayer in the midst of
For deliverance. Ps 25:17,22; 39:10; Is 64:9-12;
    Jr 17:14.
For divine comfort. Ps 4:6; 119:76.
For divine teaching and direction. Jb 34:32;
    Ps 27:11; 143:10.
Encouragement to. Jms 5:13-16.
For increase of faith. Mk 9:24.
For mercy. Ps 6:2; Hab 3:2.
For pardon and deliverance from sin. Ps 39:8, 51:1;
    79:8.
For the presence and support of God. Ps 10:1;
    102:2.
For protection and preservation from enemies.
    2Kg 19:19; 2Ch 20:12; Ps 17:8-9.
For restoration to joy. Ps 51:8,12; 69:29; 90:14-15.
That we may be taught the uncertainty of life.
    Ps 39:4.
That we may be turned to God. Ps 80:7; 85:4-6;
    Jr 31:18.
That we may know the causes of our trouble.
    Jb 6:24; 10:2; 13:23-24.

Angels
Announced the ascension and second coming of
    Christ. Ac 1:11.
Birth of Christ. Lk 2:10-12.
Conception of Christ. Mt 1:20-21; Lk 1:31.
Conception of John the Baptist. Lk 1:13,36.
Resurrection of Christ. Mt 28:5-7; Lk 24:23.
Are ministering spirits. 1Kg 19:5; Ps 68:17; 104:4;
    Lk 16:22; Ac 12:7-11; 27:23; Heb 1:7,14.
Not to be worshiped. Col 2:18; Rv 19:10; 22:9.

Subject to Christ. Eph 1:21; Col 1:16; 2:10;
    1Pt 3:22.
Wise. 2Sm 14:20.
Celebrate the praises of God. Jb 38:7; Ps 148:2;
    Is 6:3; Lk 2:13-14; Rv 5:11-12; 7:11-12.
Execute the judgments of God. 2Sm 24:16; 2Kg
    19:35; Ps 35:6; Ac 12:23; Rv 16:1.
Execute the purposes of God. Nm 22:22; Ps 103:21;
    Mt 13:39-42; 28:2; Jn 5:4; Rv 5:2.
Have charge over the children of God. Ps 34:7;
    91:11-12.
Know and delight in the gospel of Christ.
    Eph 3:9-10.
The law given by. Ps 68:17; Ac 7:53; Heb 2:2.
Rejoice over every repentant sinner. Luke 15:7,10.
Will attend Christ at His second coming. Mt 16:27;
    25:31; Mk 8:38; 2Th 1:7.

Anger
Be slow to. Pr 15:18; 16:32; 19:11; Ti 1:7; Jms 1:19.
Characteristic of fools. Pr 12:16; 14:29; 27:3.
Children should not be stirred up to. Eph 6:4;
    Col 3:21.
Pray without. 1Tm 2:8.
A work of sinful nature. Gl 5:20.

Anxiety
The cure for. Mt 6:25-34; Php 2:28; 1Pt 5:7.
Prevented. Ps 121:4; 1Pt 5:7.

Appearance
Can be deceiving. Mt 23:27-28.
Do not judge by. Jms 2:2-4.
Inner versus outward. 1Sm 16:7; 1Pt 3:1-6.

Assurance
Abundant in the understanding of the gospel.
    Col 2:2; 1Th 1:5.
Confirmed by love. 1Jn 3:14,19; 4:18.
Eternal life. Rm 8:28-39; 1Th 1:5; 1Jn 5:13.
Give diligence to attain. 2Pt 1:10-11.
In Christ. Jn 6:39; 17:12; 18:9.
Made full by hope. Heb 6:19.
Produced by faith. Eph 3:12; 2Tm 1:12; Heb 10:22.

B

Baptism
Jesus was baptized. Mt 3:13-16.
Believers were baptized at Pentecost. Ac 2:41.
The Ethiopian eunuch. Ac 8:36.
Paul was baptized. Ac 9:18.
A sign of repentance and sins forgiven. Mk 1:4;
    Ac 2:38.
Shows identification with Jesus Christ. Rm 6:3-8.
A command for all believers. Mt 28:18-20.

Belief

In Christ. Jn 3:16; 14:1; 20:31; Ac 8:37.
In God required. 2Ch 20:20.
Making all things possible. Mk 9:23.
Of devils. Jms 2:19.
Producing healing. Mt 9:22.

Bible

Inspired by God. Jr 36:1-2; 2Tm 3:14-17.
Inspired by the Holy Spirit. Ac 1:16; 2Pt 1:21.
Points to Christ. Jn 5:39; Ac 18:28.
Learn about salvation from. 2Tm 3:15.
An unerring guide. 2Pt 1:19.
Sharp as a sword. Eph 6:17; Heb 4:12.
Hearing is not enough. Jms 1:22.
Received message, not from men, but from God.
    1Th 2:13.
Everything should be tested against. Is 8:20;
    Ac 17:11.
Warning against those who add to or take from.
    Dt 4:2; Rv 22:18-19.

Body

Is the temple of Holy Spirit. 1Co 6:19.
Will be resurrected. 1Co 15:12-58.

C

Capital Punishment

For adultery. Lv 20:10; Jn 8:3-11.
For murder. Gn 9:5-6; Ex 21:12; Nm 35:33.
For violating the Sabbath. Ex 31:14.
Warning against putting innocent to death.
    Ex 23:7.

Celibacy

Jesus' teaching concerning. Mt 19:10-12.
Paul's teaching concerning. 1Co 7:1-9,25-26,32-39.
Wrongly insisted on. 1Tm 4:1-3.

Children

Christ taught. Mk 10:13-16.
Gifts from God. Gn 33:5; Ps 127:3.
Should honor the aged. Lv 19:32; 1Pt 5:5.
Should obey parents. Ex 20:12; Pr 6:20; Eph 6:1.
Should take care of parents. 1Tm 5:4.
Should be treated with respect. Eph 6:4.

Christ

Preexistence. Jn 1:1-18.
Genealogy traced through Joseph. Mt 1:1-17.
Genealogy traced through Mary. Lk 3:23-38.
Birth of. Mt 1:18-25; Lk 2:1-20.
Circumcision and naming of. Lk 2:21.
Childhood. Lk 2:41-52.
Baptism. Mt 3:13-17.

Tempted by Satan. Mt 4:1-11; Mk 1:12-13;
    Lk 4:1-13.
Calls His first disciples. Jn 1:35-51.
Mission. Lk 4:16-21.
Manner of relating to people. Mt 12:18-21.
Sinless. Jn 8:46; 2Co 5:21; Heb 4:14-16.
Forgives sins. Col 3:13; Mk 2:7,10-11.
One with the Father. Jn 10:30,38; 12:45; 14:7-10;
    17:10.
Fully God. Col 2:9; Heb 1:3.
Eternally the same. Heb 1:12; 13:8.
Fully human. Jn 1:14; Heb 2:14.
The only mediator between God and man. 1Tm 2:5.

Church

Christ will build. Mt 16:18.
Commission of. Mt 28:18-20.
Is the bride of Christ. Rv 19:7-8.
Christ is the head. Col 1:18.
Is like a body. 1Co 12:12-13.

Circumcision

Abolished by the gospel. Gl 2:3-5; Eph 2:11,15;
    Php 3:3; Col 2:11; 3:11.
Described. Gn 17:9-11; Ex 4:25.

Civil rights

Exercised by Paul. Ac 16:35-40; 22:24-29.

Contentment

With wages and possessions. Lk 3:14; Heb 13:5.
With food and clothing. 1Tm 6:8.
With godliness is great gain. Ps 37:16; 1Tm 6:6.

Counselor

Necessary for victory. Pr 11:14; 24:6.
A title of Christ. Is 9:6.
A role of the Spirit. Jn 14:16,26; 15:26; 16:7.

Courage

Commanded. Dt 31:6; Jos 1:7; Is 41:10.

Covenant

Abraham's. Gn 12:1-3; 15:7-18; 17:2-14; 1Ch 16:16-
    17; Lk 1:72-75; Ac 3:25; Gl 3:16.
David's. 2Sm 23:5; Ps 89:3- 4.
Isaac's. Gn 17:19,21; 26:3- 4.
Jacob's. Gn 28:13-14.
Israel's. Ex 6:4; Ac 3:25.
New. Jr 31:31-33; Rm 11:27; Heb 8:8-10,13.

Creation

By Christ. Jn 1:3,10; Col 1:16.
By God. Gn 1:1; 2:4-5; Pr 26:10.
For God's pleasure. Pr 16:4; Rv 4:11.
Glorifies God. Neh 9:6; Ps 19:1; 136:3-9; 145:10;
    148:5.

Crown
A reward. 1Co 9:25; 2Tm 2:5; 4:8; Jms 1:12;
    1Pt 5:4; Rv 3:11.
Symbolic. Rv 4:4,10; 6:2; 9:7; 12:1,3; 13:1; 14:14;
    19:12.
Of thorns. Mt 27:29; Jn 19:5.

Crucifixion
Of Christ. Mt 27:32-56.
Symbolic. Rm 6:6; Gl 2:20.

D

Dancing
Praising God with. Ex 15:20; 2Sm 6:14; Ps 150:4.
Example of sinful. Ex 32:19,25; Mt 14:6.

Death
A consequence of sin. Gn 2:17; Rm 5:12-14; 6:23.
Christ delivers from the fear of. Heb 2:15.
Conquered by Christ. Rm 6:9; Rv 1:18.
Described as sleep. Dt 31:16; Jn 11:11-14;
    Ac 7:59-60; 13:36; 1Co 15:6.
Everyone will experience. Jb 30:23; 1Co 15:22;
    1Tm 6:7; Heb 9:27.
For believers, a passage to God. 2Co 5:1-8;
    Php 1:21-24.
For believers, a place of rest. Jb 3:17; Lk 16:22,25;
    Php 1:23; Rv 14:13.
Precious in God's sight. Ps 116:15.

Debt
Borrower is slave of lender. Pr 22:7.
Owe no one anything. Rm 13:8.

Demons
Jesus casts out. Mt 17:14-21; Lk 4:31-36.
Disciples cast out. Mk 16:17; Lk 10:17-20; Ac 5:16.
Paul casts out. Ac 16:16-18; 19:12.

Devil
Assumes the form of an angel of light. 2Co 11:14.
Believers should resist. Jms 4:7; 1Pt 5:9.
Ultimately defeated. Gn 3:15; 2Pt 2:4; Jd 6;
    Rv 20:10.
Is our adversary. Jb 1:6-12; Zch 3:1; 1Th 2:18.
Subtle. 2Co 11:3,13.

Discipleship
Cost of. Mt 16:24-28.
Tests of. Mt 10:32-39; Lk 14:26-27,33; Jn 21:15-19.

Discipling
Commanded. Dt 6:6-7; Mt 28:18-20; 2Tm 2:2.

Disease (see also *Healing*)
Relationship to sin. Ps 107:17; Mt 9:1-8; Mk 2:1-12;
    Ac 12:20-25; Rm 1:26-27; 1Co 11:27-34;
    Jms 5:14-16.

Divorce
Jesus' teaching concerning. Mt 19:1-10;
    Mk 10:2-12.

Doubt (see also *Assurance*)
God's help in. Ps 73:13-17; Is 40:27-28.
Jesus' response to. Mt 11:1-19; Mk 9:14-29;
    Jn 20:24-29.

Drugs
Honor God with body. Rm 12:1; 1Co 6:19-20.
Mind should stay alert. Eph 5:18; 1Pt 1:13; 1Th 5:6.

Drunkenness
Avoid those given to. Pr 23:20; 1Co 5:11.
To be avoided. Pr 23:29-35; Lk 21:34; Rm 13:13;
    Eph 5:18.
Results in punishment. Is 28:1-3; Mt 24:49-51;
    1Co 6:10; Gl 5:21.

E

Earth
Believers will inherit. Ps 25:13; Mt 5:5.
Is the Lord's. 1Co 10:26.
Not to be flooded again. 2Pt 3:6-7.
To be renewed. 2Pt 3:13.
Eagerly longs for redemption. Rm 8:19-22.

Edification
All to be done for. 2Co 12:19; Eph 4:29.
Described. Eph 4:12-16.
Exhortation to. Jd 20-21.
Gospel as the instrument of. Ac 20:32.
Love leads to. 1Co 8:1.

Education
Of children in God's Word. Dt 6:7; Eph 6:4;
    2Tm 3:15-16.
From nature. Pr 6:6.
In the pastoral ministry. 1Tm 4:11.
From personal experience. Ps 78:1-8.

Election
Of Israel. Dt 7:6; Is 45:4.
Of believers. Ps 65:4; Is 65:9; Jn 6:44; 13:18;
    Ac 13:48; 22:14; Rm 8:28-30; 9:11-16; Eph 1:4-
    6,11; 2:10; 1Th 1:4; 2Th 2:13; 1Pt 1:2.
Should be evidenced by diligence. 2Pt 1:10.
Should lead to godliness. Col 3:12.

Encouragement
Exhorted. 1Th 4:18; 5:11; Ti 2:15; Heb 3:13; 10:25.

Through fellow believers. Ac 14:22; 15:31-32; Rm 1:12.

Through God's Word. Rm 15:4.

Through the Spirit. Ac 9:31.

Endurance

God gives. Rm 15:5.

Enemies

Should be loved. Mt 5:44.

Should be prayed for. Ac 7:60.

Christ forgave. Lk 23:34.

God delivers from. Dt 32:35; Ps 18:48; 61:3.

Equality

Among believers. Gn 13:8; Mt 23:8.

In Christ. Gl 3:28.

Under God. Pr 22:2.

In justice. Pr 24:23.

In salvation. Jn 3:16; Rm 5:18-21.

In sin and guilt. Rm 3:10-19; 5:12-21.

Eternal life

May have assurance of. 1Jn 5:13.

To know God and Christ is. Jn 17:3.

To those who believe in Christ. Jn 3:15-16; 6:40,47.

Euthanasia

May lead to devaluing of life. Gn 1:27.

Violates God's command. Ex 20:13.

Evangelism

Commanded by Christ. Mt 28:18-20.

Evolution

Contrary to the consistent teaching of Scripture. Gn 1–2; Jb 38–39; Jn 1:1-3; Col 1:16-17; Heb 11:3.

Excuses

Adam and Eve to the Lord. Gn 3:12-13.

A disciple to Jesus. Mt 8:21.

Elisha to Elijah. 1Kg 19:19-21.

Felix to Paul. Ac 24:25.

Humanity to God. Rm 1:20.

Moses to the Lord. Ex 4:1-14.

Saul to the Lord. 1Sm 15:13-15.

F

Fairness

God's. 2Ch 19:7; Ps 98:9; 99:4; Ezk 18:29; Rm 3:3-6.

In business. Lv 19:36; Dt 25:15; Pr 11:1; 1Tm 5:18.

In legal judgment. Ex 23:3; Dt 1:17; 16:19; Pr 29:14.

In treatment of slaves. Col 4:1.

Through wisdom. Pr 8:15.

Lacking. Ps 82:2- 4; Is 59:9-11; Mc 3:9; Hab 1:4.

Faith

Demonstrated by a pagan soldier. Lk 7:1-10.

All things should be done in. Rm 14:22; Heb 11:6.

Have full assurance of. 2Tm 1:12; Heb 10:22.

The gift of God. Rm 12:3; Eph 2:8; 6:23; Php 1:29.

Christ the source and perfecter of. Heb 12:2.

Proof of things not seen. Heb 11:1.

Examine whether you are in. 2Co 13:5.

A gift of the Holy Spirit. 1Co 12:9.

Right with God by. Gn 15:6; Rm 4:16.

Necessary in prayer. Mt 21:22; Jms 1:6.

Produces confidence. 1Pt 2:6.

Scripture designed to produce. Jn 20:31; 2Tm 3:14-16.

The wicked often profess. Ac 8:9-24.

Family

Believers' families blessed. Ps 128:3-6.

Honoring God in. Dt 6:6-7; Jos 24:15; Eph 5:22–6:9.

Jesus' family. Mk 3:31-35.

Paul's family. Ac 23:16.

Timothy's family. 2Tm 1:5.

Church leaders' families. 1Tm 3:1-13.

Fasting

Expected of Christians. Mt 6:16; 9:15.

Along with prayer, when seeking God's grace. 1Sm 7:5-6; Neh 1:4; Dn 9:3; Ac 13:3; 14:23.

Wrong way and right way compared. Is 58:3-12; Zch 7:5-10; Mt 6:16-18.

Father

God in heaven. Mt 6:9; 23:9.

Duties of godly. Dt 6:6-7; Eph 6:4.

To be honored. Ex 20:12; Pr 23:22; Eph 6:2; Col 3:17.

Fear

Of God, advantages of. Pr 9:10; 15:16; 19:23; 2Co 7:1.

Godly delivered from. Ps 27:1; Pr 1:33; 1Jn 4:16-18.

Fellowship

Blessings of. 1Jn 1:7.

In Christ. Mt 18:20; 1Co 1:9; Rv 3:20.

In the Holy Spirit. 2Co 13:14.

Flattery

Beware of. Ps 5:9; 12:3; Pr 29:5; Rm 16:18; Jd 16.

Flood

Noah's. Gn 6–8.

Came suddenly and unexpectedly. Mt 24:38-39.

Whole earth affected by. Gn 7:23; 2Pt 3:5-6.

Noah warned of. Gn 6:13; Heb 11:7.

Wicked warned of. 1Pt 3:19-20; 2Pt 2:5.

Forgiveness
Of sins, from God. Ex 34:6-7; Ps 103:1-4; Dn 9:9.
Of sins, through Christ. Ac 4:11-12; 1Jn 2:12.
Of each other. Mt 6:14-15; 18:21-35; Mk 11:25;
Eph 4:32; Jms 2:13.

Freedom
Of God. Ac 4:24-28.
Result of truth. Jn 8:32.
From condemnation. Rm 8:1,33-39.
From sin's power. Rm 8:2-4; Rv 1:5.

Friends
Constancy of. Pr 17:17; 18:24.
David and Jonathan. 1Sm 18:1-4; 20:1-29.
Jesus called His disciples. Jn 15:13-15.

G

Gambling
Can result in destructive life-style. 1Tm 6:9.
Harms the poor and families. Pr 14:23; 1Tm 5:8.
Poor example for those who may become addicted.
1Co 8:13; Rm 14:21.
Practiced by those who crucified Jesus. Mk 12:30.
Stems from covetousness. Lk 12:15; 1Tm 6:10.

Genders, Relationship between (see also Women in Roles of Responsibility)
Be subject to one another. Eph 5:21.
Male and female in image of God. Gn 1:26-27;
5:1-2.
Men and women equal as regards salvation.
Ac 10:34; Rm 2:9-11; Gl 3:28.
One flesh in marriage. Gn 2:24.
Partnership in childrearing. Pr 1:8; Eph 6:1-4;
Col 3:20.
Woman a suitable helper of man. Gn 2:18.

Genealogies
Of Patriarchs. Gn 4:16-22; 5; 10; 11:10-32; 22:20-
24; 25:1-4,12-16; 35:23-26; 36; Ru 4:18-20;
1Ch 1–9.
Of Christ. Mt 1:1-17; Lk 3:23-38.
No spiritual value. Mt 3:9; 1Tm 1:4; Ti 3:9.

Giving
Blessings connected with. Ps 41:1; Pr 22:9; 28:27;
Ec 11:1-2; Is 58:10; Ac 20:35.
Encouraged. Lk 6:38; 2Co 8:1-12.
Toward enemies. Pr 25:21.

God
Is all knowing. Is 55:9; Dn 2:20; Rm 11:33.
Is all powerful. Jr 32:27; Lk 1:37; Rv 1:8.

Is faithful. Ps 89:24,33; Is 49:7; Lm 3:23; 1Co 1:9;
1Th 5:24; 2Th 3:3; 2Tm 2:13.
Is good. Ps 25:8; 119:68.
Is holy. 1Sm 2:2; Is 57:15; 1Pt 1:15-16.
Is judge. Ps 9:7; Jms 4:12.
Is just. Dt 32:4; Ezk 18:25; Rm 3:26; 9:14.
Is kind. Rm 2:4.
Is knowable. Jr 31:34; Eph 1:17.
Is love. Dt 7:8; Jr 31:3; Hs 11:4; 1Jn 4:16.
Is our Father. Hs 1:10; Mt 6:9; Rm 8:15.
Is sovereign. Ex 18:11; Dt 10:14; 2Kg 19:15;
Ps 24:1; 115:3; 135:6; 146:10; Is 40:23; 45:23;
Lm 3:37; Dn 4:35; Rm 9:16; Col 2:13.
Is spirit. Jn 4:24.
Is to be glorified. 1Ch 16:28-29; Is 42:12; Dn 5:23;
Rm 1:21; 1Co 6:20.
Is unchanging. Ps 102:26-27; Jms 1:17.

Gospel
Predicted. Is 41:27; 52:7; 61:1-3.
Described. 1Co 15:1-4.
Brings peace. Lk 2:10-14.
Veiled to the lost. 2Co 4:3.
There is only one. Gl 1:8.
Must be believed. Mk 1:15; Heb 4:2.
The power of God for salvation. Rm 1:16; 1Co 1:18;
1Th 1:5.
Produces hope. 1Co 1:23.

Grace
Came by Christ. Jn 1:17; Rm 5:15.
Believers should grow in. 2Pt 3:18.
God's work completed in believers by. 2Th 1:11-12.
Justifies sinners. Ps 51:1-12; Rm 5:1-21.
Not to be abused. Rm 3:8; 6:1,15; 2Co 6:1; Jd 4.
Salvation by. Ac 15:11; Eph 2:1-10; Ti 2:11.

Guidance
Of believers. Ps 32:8; Jn 10:3.

H

Hate
Embitters life. Pr 15:17.
Of neighbors, prohibited. Lv 19:17; 1Jn 3:15.
Of evil, condoned. Ps 97:10; 119:104; 139:21;
Pr 8:13.
Believers should expect. Mt 10:22; Jn 15:18-19.
Return good for. Mt 5:44.

Healing
Comes from God. Ex 15:26; Ps 103:3.
Proof that Jesus is the Messiah. Mt 11:5.
Son of a royal official. Jn 4:46-54.

Heaven
Believers rewarded in. Is 65:17-25; Mt 5:12; 1Pt 1:4; Rv 21:1-7.
Jesus entered. Ac 3:21; Heb 6:20.
God's dwelling place. Ps 11:4; 115:3; Is 66:1; Mt 6:9.
Believers names are written in. Lk 10:20; Heb 12:23.
Wicked are excluded from. Gl 5:21; Eph 5:5; Rv 22:15.

Hell
The beast, false prophet, and the Devil thrown into. Rv 19:20; 20:10.
Body suffers in. Mt 5:29; 10:28.
Described as everlasting fire. Is 1:28-31; 66:24; Mt 3:12; 25:41,46.
Destruction, away from God's presence. 2Th 1:9.
Strive to keep others from. Mt 18:14; Jd 23.

Holiness
God's, as standard. Lv 19:2; Eph 5:1.
Believers called to. Lv 11:45; 20:7; Lk 1:74-75; Rm 6:13,19; 8:29; 12:1; Eph 1:4; 5:8; 1Th 4:7; Heb 12:14; 1Pt 1:14-16.

Holy Spirit
Believers receive. 1Jn 2:20.
Guides into all truth. Is 30:21; Ezk 36:27; Jn 16:13; 1Jn 2:27.
Baptism of, through Christ. Ti 3:6.
Communicates joy. Rm 14:17; Gl 5:22; 1Th 1:6.
Given by the Father. Neh 9:20; Ezk 36:27; Jl 2:28; Jn 14:15-18.
Gives the new birth. Jn 3:5-6.
Called God. Ac 5:3-4.
Convinces of sin. Neh 9:30; Mc 3:8; Jn 16:8-11.
Lives in believers. Is 59:21; Hg 2:5; Jn 14:16-17; 1Co 3:16; 6:19; Eph 5:18; 1Pt 4:14.
Blasphemy against is unpardonable. Zch 7:12-13; Mt 12:31-32; 1Jn 5:16.
Can be grieved. Is 63:10; Eph 4:30; 1Th 5:19.
Believers sealed by. 2Co 1:22; Eph 1:13; 4:30.

Homosexuality
Prohibited. Lv 18:22; 20:13.
Condemned. Gn 18:20-21; 19:4-7; Rm 1:26-27; 1Co 6:9; 1Tm 1:8-10.

Honesty
Commanded. Dt 25:13; Lv 19:35; Pr 11:1; 12:22; Am 8:4-7; Zch 8:16; 2Co 4:2.
Necessary in speaking. Ps 101:7; Pr 12:19; 17:20; Mt 5:33-37; Eph 4:25; Rv 22:15.

Hope
In God. Ps 39:7; Ti 1:2; 1Pt 1:21.
Be ready to give a reason for your. 1Pt 3:15.
Believers enjoy. Rm 5:2; 12:12; Ti 2:13.
Leads to patience. Rm 8:25; 1Th 1:3.

Hospitality
Commanded. Rm 12:13; 1Tm 3:2; 5:10; Ti 1:8; 1Pt 4:9.
To enemies. 2Kg 6:22-23; Rm 12:20.
To the poor. Is 58:7; Lk 14:13-14.
To strangers. Heb 13:2.

Humility
Afflictions intended to produce. Lv 26:41; Dt 8:3.
Averts punishment. 2Ch 7:14; 12:6-7.
Before honor. Pr 15:33.
Brings wisdom. Pr 11:2; Mt 11:25.
Christ's example. Mt 11:29; Jn 13:14-15; Php 2:5-8.
In believers. Mc 6:8; Rm 12:16; Eph 4:1-2; Php 2:3; Col 3:12; 1Pt 5:5.

Husband
To love wife. Gn 2:23-24; Eph 5:25-30; Col 3:19.
To respect wife. 1Pt 3:7.
Should have only one wife. Mt 19:3-9; Mk 10:6-8; 1Co 7:2-4; 1Tm 3:12.

I

Idolatry, Idols
Forbidden by the law. Ex 20:4-5; Dt 4:15-19.
Provokes God. Dt 31:20; Is 65:3; Jr 25:6.
Ridiculed. Is 44:10-20; 45:20; Jr 10:3-5; Hab 2:18-19; 1Co 12:2.
Not gods. Jr 5:7; Gl 4:8.
Nothing. Is 41:24; 1Co 8:4.
Believers should avoid. Ex 34:16; Dt 7:3-5,26; Ac 14:15; 1Co 10:14,19-21.

Image of God
Man created in. Gn 1:26-27; 5:1; 9:5; Jms 3:9.
Christ as. Col 1:15; Heb 1:3.

Immortality
David's hope. 2Sm 12:23.
Jesus' promise of. Jn 6:39-58.

Incest
Forbidden. Lv 18:6-18; 1Co 5:1.
Amnon and Tamar. 2Sm 13:14.
Herod. Mt 14:3-4.
Judah and Tamar. Gn 38:16-18.
Lot's daughters. Gn 19:31-36.

Integrity
Required. Dt 6:5.

Characterizes righteous men. Nm 16:15; Jb 27:5;
Ps 25:21; 26:11; Pr 11:3.

Intercession
Should be made for everyone. 1Tm 2:1; Eph 6:18.
Christ's example. Jn 17:1-26; Rm 8:34; Heb 7:25;
1Jn 2:1.
Holy Spirit's example. Rm 8:26.
Job's example. Jb 42:8-10.
Moses' example. Nm 14:19.
Stephen's example. Ac 7:60.

Intolerance, Religious
Proper. Ex 22:20; Dt 13; 17:1-7; 1Kg 18:40;
2Kg 10:18-30; 2Ch 15:12-13.
Improper. Nm 11:24-30; Mk 9:38-39; Ac 4:1-3;
13:50; 17:5; 18:13; 21:28-31; 22:22.

J

Jealousy
God's righteous. Ex 20:5; 1Kg 14:22; Ps 78:58;
1Co 10:22.
Consequences of man's. Gn 4:4-8; 37:4-8,18,28;
Mt 2:16-18.

Jesus the Christ
Pre-existence. Jn 1:1-18; Col 1:16; Heb 1:2.
Genealogy traced through Joseph. Mt 1:1-17.
Genealogy traced through Mary. Lk 3:23-38.
Birth of. Mt 1:18-25; Lk 2:1-20.
Circumcision and naming of. Lk 2:21.
Childhood. Lk 2:41-52.
Baptism. Mt 3:13-17.
Tempted by Satan. Mt 4:1-11; Mk 1:12-13;
Lk 4:1-13.
Calls His first disciples. Jn 1:35-51.
Mission. Lk 4:16-21.
Manner of relating to people. Mt 12:18-21.
Sinless. Jn 8:46; 2Co 5:21; Heb 4:14-16.
Forgives sins. Col 3:13; Mk 2:7,10-11.
One with the Father. Jn 10:30,38; 12:45; 14:7-10;
17:10.
Fully God. Col 2:9; Heb 1:3.
Eternally the same. Heb 1:12; 13:8.
Fully human. Jn 1:14; Heb 2:14.
Humility of attitude rewarded. Php 2:5-11.
The only mediator between God and man. 1Tm 2:5.

Joy
Commanded of believers. Ps 32:11; Zch 9:9;
Php 3:1.
Despite difficulties. Hab 3:17-18; Mt 5:11-12;
Jms 1:2; 1Pt 1:6.
Over sinners who repent. Lk 15:1-32.
In answer to prayer. Jn 16:24.

In fellowship. 2Tm 1:4; 1Jn 1:3-4; 2Jn 12.
A fruit of the Spirit. Gl 5:22.

Judgment
By God for words spoken. Nm 14:29; Mt 12:36.
Of Christians. Rm 14:10; 2Co 5:10; Jms 2:12-13.
After death. Heb 9:27.
Not by outward appearances. Jn 7:24.
Will be in righteousness. Neh 9:33; Ps 98:9;
Dn 9:14; Ac 17:31.

Justice
Rewarded. Dt 16:20; Ps 119:121; Pr 21:15; Is 33:15-
16; 56:1; Jr 7:5,7; Ezk 18:8-9.

K

Kindness
An attribute of God. Ru 2:20; Hs 11:4; Eph 2:7;
Ti 3:4-7.
A quality of believers. Col 3:12; 2Pt 1:7; 1Co 13:4.

Knowledge
Fear of the Lord is the beginning of. Pr 1:7.
Of God among all human beings. Rm 1:20.
Jesus' disciples have. Lk 8:10; Col 2:2-3.
Every disciple's goal. Php 3:10; Col 1:9; 2Pt 3:18.
Of salvation. Lk 1:77; 1Jn 5:13.
Needed to guide zeal. Rm 10:2-3.

L

Law
1. Ceremonial: Israel's worship. Lv 7:37-38;
Heb 9:1-7.
2. Civil: Israel's justice. Ex 21:1.
3. Moral: universal, timeless. Ex 20:1-17; Dt 6:5;
Mt 22:37-39.
Jesus fulfills. Mt 5:17-20; Gl 3:24-25.
Jesus' interpretation of. Mt 12:9-14; Mk 2:23-28.
Man's sinful nature and the law. Rm 7:7-25.

Lawsuits
Symbolic, of God. Pr 23:11; Is 3:14; Jr 2:9; 25:31;
Hs 4:1; Mc 6:2.
To be avoided. Pr 25:8-10; Mt 5:25-26; 1Co 6:1-8.

Laziness
Characteristics of. Pr 18:9; 26:13-16.
Consequences of. Pr 6:6-9; 10:26; 12:24; 15:19;
19:15; 20:4; 21:25; 24:30-34; Ec 10:18.
Contrasted with diligence. Pr 13:4.

Love
Covers sin. Pr 10:12.
For God. Dt 6:5; Mt 22:36-40.
Described. 1Co 13:4-7.
Fulfills the law. Rm 13:8; Gl 5:6.

God is. 1Jn 4:7-8,16.
Marks the child of God. Jn 13:35; 1Jn 2:15; 4:7.

Lust

Condemned. Pr 5:15-20; Php 4:8.
Must be controlled by God. Rm 13:14; Gl 5:17.
Same as committing adultery. Jb 31:1; Mt 5:27-28.
Leads to trouble. 2Sm 11:2-5; Pr 5:3-5; 6:25-35;
    Jms 1:14-15.
Results in perverted sexual behavior. 2Sm 13:1-18;
    Rm 1:26-27.

Lying

A characteristic of unbelief. 1Th 2:9; 1Tm 4:2; 1Jn
    2:4.
The Devil is the father of. Jn 8:44.
Forbidden. Lv 19:11; Pr 12:22; Zch 1:16; Col 3:9.
Punished. Ps 5:6; 120:3- 4; Pr 19:5; Rv 21:8.

M

Male and Female

Equally saved in Christ. Gl 3:28.
Mutual love. 1Co 7:3-4; Col 3:19; Ti 2:4.
Different roles. Gn 3:16-19; 1Co 14:34-35;
    Eph 5:22-33; Col 3:18-19; 1Tm 2:11; Ti 2:2-5;
    1Pt 3:1-7.

Mankind

Made in God's image. Gn 1:26-27; Jms 3:9.
More valuable than animals. Gn 1:28; 9:3-6;
    Ps 8:4-8; Mt 10:31; 12:11-12.
Object of God's love. Jn 3:16.

Marriage

Jesus blesses. Jn 2:1-11.
Honorable for all. 1Tm 4:3; Heb 13:4.
Not believer with unbeliever. Dt 7:3-4; 1Co 7:39;
    2Co 6:14.
Should be permanent. Pr 5:15-19; Mal 2:14;
    Mt 19:6; 1Co 7:39.
Illustrates Christ and the church. Eph 5:22-32.

Materialism

More to life than. Lk 12:15.
Root of all evil. 1Tm 6:10.
Makes entry into God's kingdom difficult.
    Mk 10:23-25.
Can't provide what humans need most.
    1Pt 1:18-19.

Meditation

Characterizes the godly person. Ps 1:1-2.
On the Lord. Ps 63:6-7; 119:148; 143:5.
On what is good. Php 4:8.

Mercy

Blessedness of showing. Pr 14:21; Mt 5:7.

Denunciations against those lacking. Mt 18:23-35;
    Jms 2:13.
Encouraged. 2Kg 6:21-23; Lk 6:36; Rm 12:20-21.

Mind

Love God with. Mt 22:36-40.
Renewed, key to spirituality. Rm 12:2; Eph 4:23.
To be prepared before taking action. 1Pt 1:13.
God puts law in believer's. Heb 8:10.
Have a sound. 2Tm 1:7.
Use while praying or singing. 1Co 14:15-16.

Miracles

Purpose is to encourage belief. Ex 4:1-5; Mk 16:20;
    Jn 20:30-31.
Insufficient to produce conversion. Ps 106:7;
    Lk 16:31.
Jesus proved to be the Messiah by. Mt 11:4-6;
    Lk 7:20-22; Jn 5:36.
Performed by false prophets. Ex 7:12; Dt 13:1-3;
    Mt 24:24; 2Th 2:9; Rv 19:20.

Missions

All believers are called to. Mt 28:18-20; Mk 16:15.
Principle of. 2Co 5:14-15.
Obligations to engage in. Lk 10:2; Ac 4:19-20;
    Rm 1:13-15; 10:14-15; 1Co 9:16.

Money

Must choose between God or money. Mt 6:24.
Cannot rescue. Pr 11:4; Ezk 7:19; Zph 1:18.
Use your money to benefit others. Lk 16:9.
Test of repentance. Lk 3:10-14.
Love of is root of all evil. 1Tm 6:9-10.

Monotheism

There is only one God. Dt 4:39; 6:4; 1Co 8:4,6;
    Eph 4:5-6.
Christ and His Father are one. Jn 10:30.
The Holy Spirit is the Spirit of God and of Christ.
    Rm 8:9,14; 1Co 3:16.

Morality

Exalts a nation. Pr 14:34.
Sermon on the Mount. Mt 5–7.
Ten Commandments. Ex 20:1-17.
The heart of religion. Am 5:21,24; Mc 6:6-8; Ti 2:7;
    1Jn 2:29.

Mother

To be honored and cared for. Pr 23:22; Jn 19:27;
    Eph 6:2.

Motives

Key to sin. Mt 5:21-30.
Right, required. Mt 6:1-18; 2Co 9:7; Eph 6:5-6;
    Heb 11:6.

Murder

Hatred is. Mt 5:21-22; 1Jn 3:15.

God despises. Gn 4:11; 9:6; Ex 20:13; Pr 6:16-17.

Punished by death. Gn 9:5-6; Ex 21:12; Nm 35:16,30.

Music

Used in the temple. 1Ch 16:4-6; 23:5-6; 25:1; 2Ch 29:25.

Used by Christians. Eph 5:19.

N

Name

God's, not taken in vain. Ex 20:7.

God's, restored. Ezk 20:9,14,22,44.

Importance of good. Pr 22:1; Ec 7:1.

Neighbor

Care for. Pr 3:28-29; Mt 25:34-46.

Love as you love yourself. Lv 19:18; Lk 10:25-37; Rm 13:8-10; Gl 5:13-15; Jms 2:8.

New Birth

Prophesied. Ezk 11:19; 36:26.

All believers partake of. Jn 3:3-9; 1Pt 1:23; 1Jn 2:29; 3:9; 4:7; 5:1,4,18.

New Creation

Christ brings about. Rm 6:4; 2Co 5:14-17; Gl 6:14-15.

Will transform the entire universe. Rm 8:18-21; 2Pt 3:7-13; Rv 21:1-8.

O

Oaths

Permitted. Is 65:16; Jr 12:16; Heb 6:16.

False, condemned. Lv 6:3; Zch 5:4; Mal 3:5.

Forbidden in the name of idol or created thing. Jos 23:7; Mt 5:34-36; Jms 5:12.

Occult

Denounced by God. Lv 19:26,31; Dt 18:9-14.

Severe punishment for. Ex 22:18; Lv 20:27; Dt 13:5; Gl 5:20-21.

Saul and the medium. 1Sm 28:7-25.

P

Pain

None in heaven. Rv 21:4.

Presence in hell. Lk 16:24; Rv 16:10.

Parables

Why Jesus spoke in. Mt 13:10-17.

Paradise

The place of the glorified spirits. Lk 23:43; 2Co 12:4; Rv 2:7.

Patience

Waiting for God. Ps 37:7; 40:1.

Believers receive from God. Col 1:11.

Exercise, toward all. 1Th 5:14.

Running the race with. Heb 12:1.

Peace

Takes the place of worry. Php 4:6-7.

Believers have. Ps 85:8; Is 26:3; 53:5; Rm 5:1; Jn 14:27; Col 1:19-20.

Believers will have forever. Is 57:2; Ezk 34:25.

Wicked do not know. Is 48:22; 59:8; Jr 6:14; Rm 3:17.

Persecution

Christ's followers will have. Mt 16:21-26; 2Tm 3:12.

God will deliver from. Dn 3:25,28; 2Co 1:10; 4:9; 2Tm 3:11.

Poor

Jesus preached to. Lk 4:18.

God cares for. 1Sm 2:8; Ps 35:10; 68:10; Is 41:17.

Do not despise. Dt 15:7; Pr 14:21,31; Jms 2:2-17.

Praise (see also Worship)

Offered continually. Ps 35:28; 71:6.

Christ is worthy of. Rv 5:1-14.

Prayer

Jesus' way. Mt 6:5-13.

Acceptable through Christ. Jn 14:13-14.

Husband and wife relationship important for. 1Pt 3:7.

At all times. Ps 88:1; 1Th 5:17; 1Tm 5:5.

Regarding everything. Php 4:6.

For others. 1Tm 2:1; Jms 5:13-18; 1Jn 5:16.

Preaching

Purpose of. 2Tm 4:1-4.

Predestination

Of the crucifixion. Acts 4:28.

Of salvation. Rm 8:28-33; 9:11-29; 11:5-8; 1Co 2:7; Eph 1:5,11.

Pride

Warnings against. 1Sm 2:3; Pr 21:4; 1Co 8:1-2; 10:12.

God sees and judges. Is 2:12; Zph 2:10-11; Lk 1:51.

Prophecy

Blessing for those who listen. 1Th 5:20; Rv 1:3; 22:7.

Does not come by human will. Jr 1:5; Am 7:14-15; 2Pt 1:20-21.

Purity
Demanded. Rm 13:13; Eph 5:5-6; Php 4:8; Col 3:5;
   Heb 13:4.

Q

Quiet
Achievement of. Is 32:17.
Power of. Is 30:15.
Value of. Ec 4:6.

R

Racism
Rejected since all are from one man. Gn 9:18-19;
   Ac 17:26.
No racial distinction in the law. Lv 24:22; Dt 24:17.
No racial distinction in Christ. Gl 3:28-29;
   Eph 2:19; Rv 5:9-10.

Rape
Forbidden. Dt 22:25-28.

Redemption
Is by the blood of Christ. Heb 9:12; 1Pt 1:18-19;
   Rv 5:9.

Repentance
Given by God. Ac 11:18; 2Tm 2:25.
Godly grief produces. Ezr 9:6-9; Jr 31:19;
   Zch 12:10; 2Co 7:10.
Commanded. Ezk 18:30-32; Mk 1:15; Ac 17:30.
Results are changed attitudes and behavior.
   2Ch 6:26; Lk 3:7-14; 2Co 7:11.

Resurrection
OT doctrine of. Jb 19:26; Ps 16:10; 49:15; Is 26:19;
   Dn 12:2; Hs 13:14.
Of Jesus, the historical event. Mt 28:5-10.
Preached by the apostles. Ac 4:2.
Of the body. Is 26:19; 1Co 15:42-45.
First principle of the gospel. 1Co 15:1-19.

Revenge
Law of. Ex 21:23-25.
Prohibited. Lv 19:18; Rm 12:17-19; 1Th 5:15;
   1Pt 3:9.
Alternatives to. Pr 20:22; Mt 5:38-42; Rm 12:14.

Righteousness
Our own does not save. Ti 3:5.
God gives. Ps 24:5; Is 61:10.
Given through Christ. Rm 3:21-26; Php 3:4-11.

S

Sabbath
Grounds of its institution. Gn 2:2-3; Ex 20:11.
Made for man. Mk 2:27.

Observance of, perpetual. Ex 31:16-17; Mt 5:17-18.
Works of mercy lawful on. Mt 12:12; Lk 13:16;
   Jn 9:14.

Salvation
From God. Ps 3:8; Is 45:21-22; Jr 3:23.
In Jesus alone. Ac 4:11-12; Rm 10:9.
Gospel is power of God to. Rm 1:16; 1Co 1:21.

Sanctification
Through Christ. Rm 8:29-30; 1Co 1:2,30;
   Heb 10:10; 13:12.
Through the Word of God. Jn 17:17,19; Eph 5:26.

Second Coming of Christ
Jesus predicted. Mt 25:31; Jn 14:3.
In same way as He ascended into heaven. Dn 7:13;
   Ac 1:9-11.
Will complete salvation of believers. Heb 9:28.
Time of, unknown and sudden. Mt 24:36,44;
   Mk 13:32-37; Lk 12:40; 1Th 5:1-11; 2Th 1:3-12;
   2Pt 3:10-13.

Self-esteem
Cautions regarding. Rm 12:3; 2Co 10:7-13;
   Gl 6:1-3; Php 2:3.
Self-confidence in Christ. Rm 8:1; 2Co 3:5;
   Php 3:4-7; 4:13.

Sex (see also Abstinence; Homosexuality; Lust;
   Marriage; Rape)
Prohibited outside marriage. Sg 2:7; 1Co 6:15-20;
   Heb 13:4.
Blessed within marriage. Sg 4:1–5:1.
Not to be withheld in marriage. 1Co 7:3-5.

Sin
Begins in the mind. Mt 5:27-28; Jms 1:14-15.
All have committed. Rm 3:23.
Confession of followed by forgiveness. 2Sm 12:13;
   Ps 32:5; 1Jn 1:9.
God helps believers resist. Ps 119:11; 1Co 10:13.
Christ's blood removes. Mt 26:28; Eph 1:7; 1Jn 1:7.

Singing (see also Worship)
Commanded. 1Ch 16:9; Ps 100:2; Eph 5:19; Col
   3:16; Jms 5:13.
From God. Ps 40:3.

Stealing
Prohibited. Ex 20:15.
From the poor, especially forbidden. Pr 22:22.
Do honest work instead. Eph 4:28.

T

Talent (Ability)
Differs in different individuals. Mt 25:15.

Given by God. 1Co 12:4.
To be used. 1Tm 4:14; Rm 12:6.

Tax
Jesus paid. Mt 17:24-27.

Thankfulness
Commanded. Ps 50:14; Php 4:6.
Accompanies prayer. Php 4:6; Col 4:2.
In all things. Eph 5:20; 1Th 5:18; 1Tm 4:4-5.

Tithe
Preceded law. Gn 14:20; Heb 7:6.
Given to the Levites for their services. Nm
    18:21,24; Neh 10:37.
Punishment for withholding. Mal 3:8.

Trinity
Reference to. Rm 8:9; 1Co 12:3-6; Eph 4:4-6;
    2Th 2:13-14; Ti 3:4-6; 1Pt 1:2; Jd 20-21.
Evident at Jesus' baptism. Mt 3:16-17.
To be baptized in the name of. Mt 28:18-20.
The apostolic benediction. 2Co 13:13.

Truth
Leaders should be men of. Ex 18:21; Pr 20:28.
The Holy Spirit guides believers into. Jn 14:17;
    16:13.
The Word of God is. Dn 10:21; Jn 17:17.

U

Unbelief
Is sin. Jn 16:8-11.
Questions truthfulness of God. 2Kg 17:13-15;
    Ps 106:24; 1Jn 5:10.

Unity
The early church a picture of. Ac 4:32.
Paul's urging believers toward. Rm 12:16; 14:19;
    15:5; Php 2:2; 3:16-17.

V

Vegetarianism
In Creation. Gn 2:16; Is 11:7; 65:25.
Tolerance for. Rm 14:1-3.

Voyeurism
Abstain from. Jb 31:1.
David and Bathsheba. 2Sm 11:2.
Same as adultery. Mt 5:28.

W

Widows
Cared for. Dt 10:18; Ps 68:5; Ac 6:1.

Allowed to marry again. Rm 7:3; 1Co 7:39.
Paul's commandments concerning. 1Co 7:8-9;
    1Tm 5:3-16.

Wife
A helper to complement man. Gn 2:18-23.
A capable. Pr 31:10-31.
A blessing to her husband. Pr 12:4; 31:10,12.
Submissive to her husband. 1Co 11:3-12;
    Eph 5:22-33.
Win unbelieving husband by her life. 1Pt 3:1-2.

Women in Roles of Responsibility
Deborah. Jdg 4–5.
Huldah. 2Kg 22:12-20.
Virtuous woman. Pr 31:10-31.
Mary. Mt 28:1-10.
Miriam. Ex 15:20; Mc 6:4.
Phoebe. Rm 16:1.
Priscilla. Rm 16:3-4.

Work
Believers should. Pr 10:4; 13:4,11; Eph 6:5-8;
    2Th 3:10-12.

Works
Do not save. Rm 3:20; Gl 2:16; Eph 2:8-9; 2Tm 1:9;
    Ti 3:5.
Are the fruit of true faith. Mt 3:8; Eph 2:10;
    Jms 2:14-26.

Worship
With fear and reverence. Ps 5:7; 96:9; Is 6:1-7.
With music. Ps 57:7-8; 150.
With a new song. Ps 33:3; 96:1; 98:1; 149:1;
    Is 42:10; Rv 5:9; 14:3.
With dance. 2Sm 6:14-16; Ps 149:3.
Bowing down. 1Ch 29:20; Ps 95:6; Mt 2:11.
Authentic. Jn 4:19-26.

Y

Youth
Examples of. 1Sm 2:11; 17:1-54.
Should be an example. 1Tm 4:12.

Z

Zeal
Sometimes not according to knowledge. Ac 21:20;
    Rm 10:2; Gl 1:14.
Sometimes wrongly directed. 2Sm 21:2; Ac 22:3- 4;
    Php 3:6.
Stimulates others to do good. 2Co 9:2.

Bible Reading Plans

The *HCSB Study Bible* offers two plans for reading through the Bible. The first plan developed by Heather Collins Grattan is structured to take a person through the Bible in three years. This plan may appeal to busy persons who have a limited amount of time each day to read the Scriptures. Reading a smaller portion each day may enable the person to spend more time reading, studying, and meditating on the passage for the day.

The second plan was developed by the late Robert Murray M'Cheyne. This plan takes the reader to four portions of Scripture each day from various parts of the Bible. Following this plan, a person will read through the Old Testament once and the New Testament twice within a year.

Approaching the Bible

In reading and studying the Bible, we draw on the same knowledge, skills, and competencies we use in reading other documents. However, with the Bible there is an added dimension. The Bible was written by human beings but the ultimate Author who worked through a variety of human authors is God Himself. In what may have been his last written words to Timothy, Paul reminded his protégé that all Scripture is inspired by God. For this reason, John Wesley said that Scripture can only be understood with the help of the Spirit who inspired these 66 books. Therefore, as believers come to read and study Scripture, they need to remember the Author of Scripture and ask for the Spirit's help in understanding what they read.

As you read the Scriptures daily, you will find help in George Guthrie's article, "How to Read and Study the Bible" on pp. xlvii–lv of the *HCSB Study Bible*.

- Come to the Bible expecting to grow. It is like both milk (1Pt 2:2) and solid food (Hb 5:14) providing nourishment for both the young and those more mature.
- Come to the Bible for understanding and direction. It is like a counselor (Ps 119:24) and provides light for your journey (Ps 119:105,130).
- Come to the Bible for correction and purification. It is like:
  - a mirror in which the believer sees himself and the changes that God requires,
  - fire and a hammer (Jr 23:29),
  - a scalpel by which God performs spiritual surgery on the heart (Hb 4:12),
  - water that washes and purifies (Eph 5:26)
- Come to the Bible for pleasure. God's Word is like honey (Ps 19:9; 119:103).

Come daily to the Bible with these attitudes and expectations, and you will be changed. This is God's multifaceted instrument for conforming you to the image of His Son.

Three-Year Bible Reading Plan

Edited by Heather Collins Grattan

YEAR ONE

JANUARY

Genesis 1:1-26	1st
Genesis 1:27–2:25	2nd
Genesis 3:1-24	3rd
Genesis 4:1-26	4th
Genesis 5:1-32	5th
Genesis 6:1–7:10	6th
Genesis 7:11–8:22	7th
Genesis 9:1-29	8th
Genesis 10:1-32	9th
Genesis 11:1–12:9	10th
Genesis 12:10–13:18	11th
Genesis 14:1-24	12th
Genesis 15:1–16:16	13th
Genesis 17:1-27	14th
Genesis 18:1-15	15th
Genesis 18:16-33	16th
Genesis 19:1-29	17th
Genesis 19:30–20:18	18th
Genesis 21:1-34	19th
Genesis 22:1-24	20th
Genesis 23:1–24:14	21st
Genesis 24:15-44	22nd
Genesis 24:45-67	23rd
Genesis 25:1-18	24th
Genesis 25:19-34	25th
Genesis 26:1-25	26th
Genesis 26:26–27:20	27th
Genesis 27:21-46	28th
Genesis 28:1–29:12	29th
Genesis 29:13–30:11	30th
Genesis 30:12-43	31st

FEBRUARY

Genesis 31:1-35	1st
Genesis 31:36-55	2nd
Genesis 32:1-32	3rd
Genesis 33:1-20	4th
Genesis 34:1-31	5th
Genesis 35:1–36:8	6th
Genesis 36:9-43	7th
Genesis 37:1-36	8th
Genesis 38:1-30	9th
Genesis 39:1-23	10th
Genesis 40:1–41:14	11th
Genesis 41:15-49	12th
Genesis 41:50–42:26	13th
Genesis 42:27–43:14	14th
Genesis 43:15-34	15th
Genesis 44:1-34	16th
Genesis 45:1-28	17th
Genesis 46:1-34	18th
Genesis 47:1-31	19th
Genesis 48:1-22	20th
Genesis 49:1-28	21st
Genesis 49:29–50:26	22nd
Exodus 1:1-22	23rd
Exodus 2:1-25	24th
Exodus 3:1-22	25th
Exodus 4:1-31	26th
Exodus 5:1–6:13	27th
Exodus 6:14–7:13	28th

MARCH

Exodus 7:14–8:19	1st
Exodus 8:20–9:12	2nd
Exodus 9:13-35	3rd
Exodus 10:1-20	4th
Exodus 10:21–11:10	5th
Exodus 12:1-28	6th
Exodus 12:29–13:16	7th
Exodus 13:17–14:31	8th
Exodus 15:1-27	9th
Exodus 16:1-36	10th
Exodus 17:1-16	11th
Exodus 18:1-27	12th
Exodus 19:1-25	13th
Exodus 20:1-26	14th
Exodus 21:1-36	15th
Exodus 22:1-31	16th
Exodus 23:1-33	17th
Exodus 24:1–25:9	18th
Exodus 25:10-40	19th
Exodus 26:1-37	20th
Exodus 27:1–28:14	21st
Exodus 28:15-43	22nd
Exodus 29:1-34	23rd
Exodus 29:35–30:21	24th
Exodus 30:22–31:18	25th
Exodus 32:1-35	26th
Exodus 33:1–34:9	27th
Exodus 34:10-35	28th
Exodus 35:1–36:1	29th
Exodus 36:2-38	30th
Exodus 37:1-24	31st

APRIL

Exodus 37:25–38:20	1st
Exodus 38:21–39:7	2nd
Exodus 39:8-43	3rd
Exodus 40:1-38	4th
Leviticus 1:1–2:16	5th
Leviticus 3:1–4:12	6th
Leviticus 4:13-35	7th
Leviticus 5:1–6:7	8th
Leviticus 6:8–7:10	9th
Leviticus 7:11-38	10th
Leviticus 8:1-36	11th
Leviticus 9:1-24	12th
Leviticus 10:1–11:8	13th
Leviticus 11:9-40	14th
Leviticus 11:41–13:8	15th
Leviticus 13:9-39	16th
Leviticus 13:40-59	17th
Leviticus 14:1-32	18th
Leviticus 14:33-57	19th
Leviticus 15:1-33	20th
Leviticus 16:1-34	21st
Leviticus 17:1-16	22nd
Leviticus 18:1-30	23rd
Leviticus 19:1-37	24th
Leviticus 20:1-27	25th
Leviticus 21:1–22:16	26th
Leviticus 22:17–23:8	27th
Leviticus 23:9-32	28th
Leviticus 23:33–24:23	29th
Leviticus 25:1-17	30th

MAY

Leviticus 25:18-46	1st
Leviticus 25:47–26:13	2nd
Leviticus 26:14-46	3rd
Leviticus 27:1-34	4th
Numbers 1:1-31	5th
Numbers 1:32-54	6th
Numbers 2:1-34	7th
Numbers 3:1-39	8th
Numbers 3:40–4:20	9th
Numbers 4:21-49	10th
Numbers 5:1-31	11th
Numbers 6:1-27	12th
Numbers 7:1-35	13th
Numbers 7:36-65	14th
Numbers 7:66–8:4	15th
Numbers 8:5-26	16th
Numbers 9:1-23	17th
Numbers 10:1-36	18th
Numbers 11:1-30	19th
Numbers 11:31–13:16	20th
Numbers 13:17–14:10	21st
Numbers 14:11-38	22nd
Numbers 14:39–15:21	23rd
Numbers 15:22-41	24th
Numbers 16:1-24	25th
Numbers 16:25-50	26th
Numbers 17:1–18:7	27th
Numbers 18:8-32	28th
Numbers 19:1-22	29th
Numbers 20:1-29	30th
Numbers 21:1-20	31st

JUNE

Numbers 21:21-35	1st
Numbers 22:1-21	2nd
Numbers 22:22–23:12	3rd
Numbers 23:13–24:14	4th
Numbers 24:15–25:18	5th
Numbers 26:1-37	6th
Numbers 26:38-65	7th
Numbers 27:1–28:8	8th
Numbers 28:9–29:6	9th
Numbers 29:7-40	10th
Numbers 30:1–31:24	11th
Numbers 31:25-54	12th
Numbers 32:1-42	13th
Numbers 33:1-49	14th
Numbers 33:50–34:29	15th
Numbers 35:1-34	16th
Numbers 36:1-13	17th
Deuteronomy 1:1-25	18th
Deuteronomy 1:26-46	19th
Deuteronomy 2:1-23	20th
Deuteronomy 2:24–3:20	21st
Deuteronomy 3:21–4:14	22nd
Deuteronomy 4:15-49	23rd
Deuteronomy 5:1-33	24th
Deuteronomy 6:1-25	25th
Deuteronomy 7:1-26	26th
Deuteronomy 8:1–9:6	27th
Deuteronomy 9:7–10:11	28th
Deuteronomy 10:12–11:7	29th
Deuteronomy 11:8-32	30th

JULY

Deuteronomy 12:1-32	1st
Deuteronomy 13:1–14:21	2nd
Deuteronomy 14:22–15:23	3rd
Deuteronomy 16:1–17:7	4th
Deuteronomy 17:8–18:22	5th
Deuteronomy 19:1-21	6th
Deuteronomy 20:1–21:14	7th
Deuteronomy 21:15–22:21	8th
Deuteronomy 22:22–23:25	9th
Deuteronomy 24:1–25:4	10th
Deuteronomy 25:5–26:15	11th
Deuteronomy 26:16–27:26	12th
Deuteronomy 28:1-35	13th
Deuteronomy 28:36-68	14th
Deuteronomy 29:1-29	15th
Deuteronomy 30:1–31:8	16th
Deuteronomy 31:9-29	17th
Deuteronomy 31:30–32:25	18th
Deuteronomy 32:26-52	19th
Deuteronomy 33:1-19	20th
Deuteronomy 33:20–34:12	21st
Joshua 1:1-18	22nd
Joshua 2:1-24	23rd
Joshua 3:1-17	24th
Joshua 4:1-5:9	25th
Joshua 5:10–6:21	26th
Joshua 6:22–7:15	27th
Joshua 7:16–8:23	28th
Joshua 8:24–9:15	29th
Joshua 9:16–10:15	30th
Joshua 10:16-43	31st

AUGUST

Joshua 11:1-23	1st
Joshua 12:1–13:7	2nd
Joshua 13:8–14:5	3rd
Joshua 14:6–15:19	4th
Joshua 15:20–16:4	5th
Joshua 16:5–17:18	6th
Joshua 18:1-28	7th
Joshua 19:1-39	8th
Joshua 19:40–21:8	9th
Joshua 21:9-42	10th
Joshua 21:43–22:20	11th
Joshua 22:21–23:16	12th
Joshua 24:1-33	13th
Judges 1:1-36	14th
Judges 2:1-23	15th
Judges 3:1-31	16th
Judges 4:1–5:5	17th
Judges 5:6-31	18th
Judges 6:1-24	19th
Judges 6:25-40	20th
Judges 7:1-25	21st
Judges 8:1-35	22nd
Judges 9:1-21	23rd
Judges 9:22-57	24th
Judges 10:1–11:11	25th
Judges 11:12-40	26th
Judges 12:1-15	27th
Judges 13:1-25	28th
Judges 14:1-20	29th
Judges 15:1-20	30th
Judges 16:1-22	31st

SEPTEMBER

Judges 16:23–17:13	1st
Judges 18:1-31	2nd
Judges 19:1-30	3rd
Judges 20:1-18	4th
Judges 20:19-48	5th
Judges 21:1-25	6th
Ruth 1:1-22	7th
Ruth 2:1-23	8th
Ruth 3:1-18	9th
Ruth 4:1-22	10th
1 Samuel 1:1-28	11th
1 Samuel 2:1-26	12th
1 Samuel 2:27–3:18	13th
1 Samuel 3:19–5:5	14th
1 Samuel 5:6–6:18	15th
1 Samuel 6:19–8:9	16th
1 Samuel 8:10–9:17	17th
1 Samuel 9:18–10:16	18th
1 Samuel 10:17–11:15	19th
1 Samuel 12:1-25	20th
1 Samuel 13:1-22	21st
1 Samuel 13:23–14:30	22nd
1 Samuel 14:31-52	23rd
1 Samuel 15:1-35	24th
1 Samuel 16:1-23	25th
1 Samuel 17:1-37	26th
1 Samuel 17:38-58	27th
1 Samuel 18:1-30	28th
1 Samuel 19:1-24	29th
1 Samuel 20:1-34	30th

OCTOBER

1 Samuel 20:35–22:5	1st
1 Samuel 22:6–23:6	2nd
1 Samuel 23:7-29	3rd
1 Samuel 24:1–25:13	4th
1 Samuel 25:14-44	5th
1 Samuel 26:1–27:4	6th
1 Samuel 27:5–28:25	7th
1 Samuel 29:1–30:20	8th
1 Samuel 30:21–31:13	9th
2 Samuel 1:1-27	10th
2 Samuel 2:1–3:5	11th
2 Samuel 3:6-39	12th
2 Samuel 4:1–5:16	13th
2 Samuel 5:17–6:23	14th
2 Samuel 7:1-29	15th
2 Samuel 8:1–9:13	16th
2 Samuel 10:1-19	17th
2 Samuel 11:1-27	18th
2 Samuel 12:1-31	19th
2 Samuel 13:1-27	20th
2 Samuel 13:28–14:17	21st
2 Samuel 14:18–15:12	22nd
2 Samuel 15:13–16:4	23rd
2 Samuel 16:5-22	24th
2 Samuel 16:23–17:29	25th
2 Samuel 18:1-27	26th
2 Samuel 18:28–19:23	27th
2 Samuel 19:24–20:10	28th
2 Samuel 20:11–21:14	29th
2 Samuel 21:15–22:24	30th
2 Samuel 22:25–23:7	31st

NOVEMBER

2 Samuel 23:8-39	1st
2 Samuel 24:1-25	2nd
1 Kings 1:1-31	3rd
1 Kings 1:32–2:12	4th
1 Kings 2:13-38	5th
1 Kings 2:39–3:28	6th
1 Kings 4:1-34	7th
1 Kings 5:1-18	8th
1 Kings 6:1-38	9th
1 Kings 7:1-26	10th

1 Kings 7:27-51	11th
1 Kings 8:1-26	12th
1 Kings 8:27-43	13th
1 Kings 8:44-66	14th
1 Kings 9:1-28	15th
1 Kings 10:1-29	16th
1 Kings 11:1-25	17th
1 Kings 11:26–12:11	18th
1 Kings 12:12-33	19th
1 Kings 13:1-34	20th
1 Kings 14:1-31	21st
1 Kings 15:1-32	22nd
1 Kings 15:33–16:28	23rd
1 Kings 16:29–17:24	24th
1 Kings 18:1-35	25th
1 Kings 18:36–19:18	26th
1 Kings 19:19–20:28	27th
1 Kings 20:29–21:10	28th

JANUARY

1 Chronicles 2:42–3:16	1st
1 Chronicles 3:17–4:23	2nd
1 Chronicles 4:24–5:10	3rd
1 Chronicles 5:11–6:15	4th
1 Chronicles 6:16-53	5th
1 Chronicles 6:54-81	6th
1 Chronicles 7:1-29	7th
1 Chronicles 7:30–8:40	8th
1 Chronicles 9:1-34	9th
1 Chronicles 9:35–11:9	10th
1 Chronicles 11:10-47	11th
1 Chronicles 12:1-37	12th
1 Chronicles 12:38–14:17	13th
1 Chronicles 15:1–16:6	14th
1 Chronicles 16:7-43	15th
1 Chronicles 17:1-27	16th
1 Chronicles 18:1-17	17th
1 Chronicles 19:1–20:8	18th
1 Chronicles 21:1–22:1	19th
1 Chronicles 22:2–23:14	20th
1 Chronicles 23:15–24:19	21st
1 Chronicles 24:20–25:31	22nd
1 Chronicles 26:1-32	23rd
1 Chronicles 27:1-34	24th
1 Chronicles 28:1-21	25th
1 Chronicles 29:1-30	26th
2 Chronicles 1:1–2:10	27th
2 Chronicles 2:11–3:17	28th
2 Chronicles 4:1–5:1	29th
2 Chronicles 5:2–6:11	30th
2 Chronicles 6:12-31	31st

FEBRUARY

2 Chronicles 6:32–7:11	1st
2 Chronicles 7:12–8:18	2nd

1 Kings 21:11-29	29th
1 Kings 22:1-28	30th

DECEMBER

1 Kings 22:29-53	1st
2 Kings 1:1-18	2nd
2 Kings 2:1-25	3rd
2 Kings 3:1–4:7	4th
2 Kings 4:8-44	5th
2 Kings 5:1-27	6th
2 Kings 6:1-33	7th
2 Kings 7:1-20	8th
2 Kings 8:1-29	9th
2 Kings 9:1-29	10th
2 Kings 9:30–10:17	11th
2 Kings 10:18-36	12th
2 Kings 11:1-20	13th

YEAR TWO

2 Chronicles 9:1-31	3rd
2 Chronicles 10:1–11:4	4th
2 Chronicles 11:5–12:16	5th
2 Chronicles 13:1–14:1	6th
2 Chronicles 14:2–15:19	7th
2 Chronicles 16:1–17:19	8th
2 Chronicles 18:1-27	9th
2 Chronicles 18:28–19:11	10th
2 Chronicles 20:1-30	11th
2 Chronicles 20:31–21:20	12th
2 Chronicles 22:1–23:15	13th
2 Chronicles 23:16–24:22	14th
2 Chronicles 24:23–25:16	15th
2 Chronicles 25:17–26:10	16th
2 Chronicles 26:11–28:8	17th
2 Chronicles 28:9–29:11	18th
2 Chronicles 29:12-36	19th
2 Chronicles 30:1–31:1	20th
2 Chronicles 31:2-21	21st
2 Chronicles 32:1-31	22nd
2 Chronicles 32:32–33:25	23rd
2 Chronicles 34:1-28	24th
2 Chronicles 34:29–35:19	25th
2 Chronicles 35:20–36:8	26th
2 Chronicles 36:9-23	27th
Ezra 1:1–2:42	28th

MARCH

Ezra 2:43–3:7	1st
Ezra 3:8–4:16	2nd
Ezra 4:17–5:17	3rd
Ezra 6:1-22	4th
Ezra 7:1-28	5th
Ezra 8:1-30	6th
Ezra 8:31–9:15	7th
Ezra 10:1-17	8th
Ezra 10:18-44	9th

2 Kings 11:21–12:21	14th
2 Kings 13:1-25	15th
2 Kings 14:1-29	16th
2 Kings 15:1-31	17th
2 Kings 15:32–17:6	18th
2 Kings 17:7-33	19th
2 Kings 17:34-18:18	20th
2 Kings 18:19-37	21st
2 Kings 19:1-28	22nd
2 Kings 19:29–20:21	23rd
2 Kings 21:1-26	24th
2 Kings 22:1–23:3	25th
2 Kings 23:4-27	26th
2 Kings 23:28–24:20	27th
2 Kings 25:1-30	28th
1 Chronicles 1:1-31	29th
1 Chronicles 1:32–2:9	30th
1 Chronicles 2:10-41	31st

Nehemiah 1:1–2:10	10th
Nehemiah 2:11–3:19	11th
Nehemiah 3:20–4:14	12th
Nehemiah 4:15–5:19	13th
Nehemiah 6:1-7:3	14th
Nehemiah 7:4-60	15th
Nehemiah 7:61–8:12	16th
Nehemiah 8:13–9:18	17th
Nehemiah 9:19-37	18th
Nehemiah 9:38–10:39	19th
Nehemiah 11:1-36	20th
Nehemiah 12:1-26	21st
Nehemiah 12:27–13:5	22nd
Nehemiah 13:6-31	23rd
Esther 1:1-22	24th
Esther 2:1-23	25th
Esther 3:1–4:17	26th
Esther 5:1–6:14	27th
Esther 7:1–8:17	28th
Esther 9:1-17	29th
Esther 9:18–10:3	30th
Job 1:1–2:10	31st

APRIL

Job 2:11–4:11	1st
Job 4:12–5:27	2nd
Job 6:1-30	3rd
Job 7:1-21	4th
Job 8:1-22	5th
Job 9:1-35	6th
Job 10:1-22	7th
Job 11:1-20	8th
Job 12:1–13:19	9th
Job 13:20–14:22	10th
Job 15:1-35	11th
Job 16:1–17:16	12th
Job 18:1–19:20	13th

Job 19:21–20:29	14th	Psalms 61:1–63:11	7th	**AUGUST**	
Job 21:1-34	15th	Psalms 64:1–65:13	8th		
Job 22:1-30	16th	Psalms 66:1–67:7	9th	Proverbs 5:1–6:19	1st
Job 23:1-17	17th	Psalm 68:1-27	10th	Proverbs 6:20–7:27	2nd
Job 24:1–25:6	18th	Psalms 68:28–69:21	11th	Proverbs 8:1-36	3rd
Job 26:1–27:23	19th	Psalms 69:22–71:16	12th	Proverbs 9:1-18	4th
Job 28:1-28	20th	Psalms 71:17–72:20	13th	Proverbs 10:1-32	5th
Job 29:1-25	21st	Psalm 73:1-28	14th	Proverbs 11:1-31	6th
Job 30:1-31	22nd	Psalms 74:1–75:10	15th	Proverbs 12:1-28	7th
Job 31:1-40	23rd	Psalms 76:1–77:20	16th	Proverbs 13:1-25	8th
Job 32:1-22	24th	Psalm 78:1-39	17th	Proverbs 14:1-35	9th
Job 33:1-33	25th	Psalm 78:40-72	18th	Proverbs 15:1-33	10th
Job 34:1-37	26th	Psalms 79:1–80:19	19th	Proverbs 16:1-33	11th
Job 35:1-16	27th	Psalms 81:1–82:8	20th	Proverbs 17:1-28	12th
Job 36:1-33	28th	Psalms 83:1–84:12	21st	Proverbs 18:1-24	13th
Job 37:1-24	29th	Psalms 85:1–86:17	22nd	Proverbs 19:1-29	14th
Job 38:1-41	30th	Psalms 87:1–88:18	23rd	Proverbs 20:1-30	15th
		Psalm 89:1-18	24th	Proverbs 21:1-31	16th
MAY		Psalm 89:19-52	25th	Proverbs 22:1-29	17th
		Psalms 90:1–91:16	26th	Proverbs 23:1-35	18th
Job 39:1-30	1st	Psalms 92:1–94:23	27th	Proverbs 24:1-34	19th
Job 40:1-24	2nd	Psalms 95:1–97:12	28th	Proverbs 25:1-28	20th
Job 41:1-34	3rd	Psalms 98:1–99:9	29th	Proverbs 26:1-28	21st
Job 42:1-17	4th	Psalms 100:1–102:17	30th	Proverbs 27:1-27	22nd
Psalms 1:1–3:8	5th			Proverbs 28:1-28	23rd
Psalms 4:1–6:10	6th	**JULY**		Proverbs 29:1-27	24th
Psalms 7:1–8:9	7th			Proverbs 30:1-33	25th
Psalm 9:1-20	8th	Psalms 102:18–103:22	1st	Proverbs 31:1-31	26th
Psalm 10:1-18	9th	Psalm 104:1-35	2nd	Ecclesiastes 1:1-18	27th
Psalms 11:1–13:6	10th	Psalm 105:1-45	3rd	Ecclesiastes 2:1-26	28th
Psalms 14:1–16:11	11th	Psalm 106:1-39	4th	Ecclesiastes 3:1-22	29th
Psalms 17:1–18:15	12th	Psalms 106:40–107:22	5th	Ecclesiastes 4:1-16	30th
Psalm 18:16-50	13th	Psalms 107:23–108:13	6th	Ecclesiastes 5:1–6:12	31st
Psalms 19:1–21:7	14th	Psalm 109:1-31	7th		
Psalms 21:8–22:26	15th	Psalms 110:1–112:10	8th	**SEPTEMBER**	
Psalms 22:27–24:10	16th	Psalms 113:1–115:18	9th		
Psalm 25:1-22	17th	Psalms 116:1–117:2	10th	Ecclesiastes 7:1-29	1st
Psalms 26:1–27:14	18th	Psalm 118:1-29	11th	Ecclesiastes 8:1–9:10	2nd
Psalms 28:1–30:12	19th	Psalm 119:1-48	12th	Ecclesiastes 9:11–10:20	3rd
Psalm 31:1-24	20th	Psalm 119:49-88	13th	Ecclesiastes 11:1–12:14	4th
Psalms 32:1–33:22	21st	Psalm 119:89-136	14th	Song of Songs 1:1–2:7	5th
Psalm 34:1-22	22nd	Psalms 119:137–120:7	15th	Song of Songs 2:8–3:11	6th
Psalm 35:1-28	23rd	Psalms 121:1–124:8	16th	Song of Songs 4:1–5:2	7th
Psalms 36:1–37:20	24th	Psalms 125:1–129:8	17th	Song of Songs 5:3–6:13	8th
Psalms 37:21–38:12	25th	Psalms 130:1–134:3	18th	Song of Songs 7:1–8:14	9th
Psalms 38:13–40:10	26th	Psalms 135:1–136:26	19th	Isaiah 1:1-20	10th
Psalms 40:11–42:4	27th	Psalms 137:1–138:8	20th	Isaiah 1:21–2:11	11th
Psalms 42:5–44:16	28th	Psalm 139:1-24	21st	Isaiah 2:12–3:15	12th
Psalms 44:17–46:3	29th	Psalms 140:1–141:10	22nd	Isaiah 3:16–5:7	13th
Psalms 46:4–48:14	30th	Psalms 142:1–143:12	23rd	Isaiah 5:8-30	14th
Psalm 49:1-20	31st	Psalm 144:1-15	24th	Isaiah 6:1–7:9	15th
		Psalm 145:1-21	25th	Isaiah 7:10–8:10	16th
JUNE		Psalms 146:1–147:20	26th	Isaiah 8:11–9:7	17th
		Psalms 148:1–150:6	27th	Isaiah 9:8–10:4	18th
Psalm 50:1-23	1st	Proverbs 1:1-33	28th	Isaiah 10:5-26	19th
Psalm 51:1-19	2nd	Proverbs 2:1-22	29th	Isaiah 10:27–11:16	20th
Psalms 52:1–54:7	3rd	Proverbs 3:1-35	30th	Isaiah 12:1–13:22	21st
Psalms 55:1–56:13	4th	Proverbs 4:1-27	31st	Isaiah 14:1-27	22nd
Psalms 57:1–58:11	5th			Isaiah 14:28–15:9	23rd
Psalms 59:1–60:12	6th			Isaiah 16:1-14	24th

Isaiah 17:1–18:7	25th
Isaiah 19:1–20:6	26th
Isaiah 21:1-17	27th
Isaiah 22:1-25	28th
Isaiah 23:1-18	29th
Isaiah 24:1-23	30th

OCTOBER

Isaiah 25:1-12	1st
Isaiah 26:1-21	2nd
Isaiah 27:1-13	3rd
Isaiah 28:1-22	4th
Isaiah 28:23–29:12	5th
Isaiah 29:13-30:7	6th
Isaiah 30:8-33	7th
Isaiah 31:1–32:20	8th
Isaiah 33:1-24	9th
Isaiah 34:1–35:3	10th
Isaiah 35:4–36:22	11th
Isaiah 37:1-20	12th
Isaiah 37:21-38	13th
Isaiah 38:1–39:8	14th
Isaiah 40:1-26	15th
Isaiah 40:27–41:16	16th
Isaiah 41:17–42:9	17th
Isaiah 42:10–43:7	18th
Isaiah 43:8–44:5	19th
Isaiah 44:6-23	20th
Isaiah 44:24–45:17	21st
Isaiah 45:18–46:13	22nd
Isaiah 47:1-15	23rd
Isaiah 48:1-22	24th
Isaiah 49:1-21	25th
Isaiah 49:22–51:3	26th
Isaiah 51:4-23	27th

Isaiah 52:1-15	28th
Isaiah 53:1-12	29th
Isaiah 54:1–55:5	30th
Isaiah 55:6–56:12	31st

NOVEMBER

Isaiah 57:1-21	1st
Isaiah 58:1-14	2nd
Isaiah 59:1-21	3rd
Isaiah 60:1-22	4th
Isaiah 61:1–62:12	5th
Isaiah 63:1-19	6th
Isaiah 64:1–65:7	7th
Isaiah 65:8–66:4	8th
Isaiah 66:5-24	9th
Jeremiah 1:1–2:3	10th
Jeremiah 2:4-25	11th
Jeremiah 2:26–3:13	12th
Jeremiah 3:14-4:4	13th
Jeremiah 4:5-31	14th
Jeremiah 5:1-19	15th
Jeremiah 5:20–6:12	16th
Jeremiah 6:13-30	17th
Jeremiah 7:1-34	18th
Jeremiah 8:1-22	19th
Jeremiah 9:1-22	20th
Jeremiah 9:23–10:18	21st
Jeremiah 10:19–11:23	22nd
Jeremiah 12:1-17	23rd
Jeremiah 13:1-27	24th
Jeremiah 14:1-22	25th
Jeremiah 15:1-21	26th
Jeremiah 16:1-21	27th
Jeremiah 17:1-27	28th
Jeremiah 18:1-23	29th

Jeremiah 19:1–20:6	30th

DECEMBER

Jeremiah 20:7–21:14	1st
Jeremiah 22:1-23	2nd
Jeremiah 22:24–23:17	3rd
Jeremiah 23:18–24:10	4th
Jeremiah 25:1-31	5th
Jeremiah 25:32–26:24	6th
Jeremiah 27:1-22	7th
Jeremiah 28:1-17	8th
Jeremiah 29:1-32	9th
Jeremiah 30:1-24	10th
Jeremiah 31:1-22	11th
Jeremiah 31:23-40	12th
Jeremiah 32:1-25	13th
Jeremiah 32:26–33:9	14th
Jeremiah 33:10–34:7	15th
Jeremiah 34:8–35:19	16th
Jeremiah 36:1-32	17th
Jeremiah 37:1–38:13	18th
Jeremiah 38:14–39:18	19th
Jeremiah 40:1–41:10	20th
Jeremiah 41:11–42:22	21st
Jeremiah 43:1–44:6	22nd
Jeremiah 44:7-30	23rd
Jeremiah 45:1–46:19	24th
Jeremiah 46:20–47:7	25th
Jeremiah 48:1-25	26th
Jeremiah 48:26-47	27th
Jeremiah 49:1-22	28th
Jeremiah 49:23-39	29th
Jeremiah 50:1-16	30th
Jeremiah 50:17-32	31st

YEAR THREE

JANUARY

Jeremiah 50:33–51:10	1st
Jeremiah 51:11-32	2nd
Jeremiah 51:33-48	3rd
Jeremiah 51:49-64	4th
Jeremiah 52:1-34	5th
Lamentations 1:1-15	6th
Lamentations 1:16–2:9	7th
Lamentations 2:10–3:9	8th
Lamentations 3:10-57	9th
Lamentations 3:58–4:15	10th
Lamentations 4:16–5:22	11th
Ezekiel 1:1-28	12th
Ezekiel 2:1–3:27	13th
Ezekiel 4:1–5:17	14th
Ezekiel 6:1–7:9	15th
Ezekiel 7:10-27	16th
Ezekiel 8:1–9:11	17th
Ezekiel 10:1–11:15	18th
Ezekiel 11:16–12:28	19th

Ezekiel 13:1–14:11	20th
Ezekiel 14:12–16:14	21st
Ezekiel 16:15-43	22nd
Ezekiel 16:44-63	23rd
Ezekiel 17:1-24	24th
Ezekiel 18:1-32	25th
Ezekiel 19:1-14	26th
Ezekiel 20:1-31	27th
Ezekiel 20:32–21:13	28th
Ezekiel 21:14-32	29th
Ezekiel 22:1-31	30th
Ezekiel 23:1-34	31st

FEBRUARY

Ezekiel 23:35–24:14	1st
Ezekiel 24:15–25:17	2nd
Ezekiel 26:1-21	3rd
Ezekiel 27:1-27	4th
Ezekiel 27:28–28:10	5th
Ezekiel 28:11-26	6th

Ezekiel 29:1-21	7th
Ezekiel 30:1-26	8th
Ezekiel 31:1–32:6	9th
Ezekiel 32:7-28	10th
Ezekiel 32:29–33:20	11th
Ezekiel 33:21–34:19	12th
Ezekiel 34:20–35:15	13th
Ezekiel 36:1-32	14th
Ezekiel 36:33–37:28	15th
Ezekiel 38:1-23	16th
Ezekiel 39:1–40:4	17th
Ezekiel 40:5-37	18th
Ezekiel 40:38–41:12	19th
Ezekiel 41:13–42:20	20th
Ezekiel 43:1-27	21st
Ezekiel 44:1-31	22nd
Ezekiel 45:1-25	23rd
Ezekiel 46:1-24	24th
Ezekiel 47:1-23	25th
Ezekiel 48:1-35	26th

Daniel 1:1–2:16	27th	Zechariah 11:1–12:14	22nd	Luke 1:39-80	15th
Daniel 2:17-49	28th	Zechariah 13:1–14:21	23rd	Luke 2:1-40	16th
		Malachi 1:1-14	24th	Luke 2:41–3:20	17th
MARCH		Malachi 2:1–3:6	25th	Luke 3:21–4:13	18th
		Malachi 3:7–4:6	26th	Luke 4:14-44	19th
Daniel 3:1-30	1st	Matthew 1:1–2:6	27th	Luke 5:1-39	20th
Daniel 4:1-27	2nd	Matthew 2:7–3:17	28th	Luke 6:1-36	21st
Daniel 4:28–5:16	3rd	Matthew 4:1–5:12	29th	Luke 6:37–7:17	22nd
Daniel 5:17–6:18	4th	Matthew 5:13–6:4	30th	Luke 7:18-50	23rd
Daniel 6:19–7:14	5th			Luke 8:1-25	24th
Daniel 7:15–8:22	6th	**MAY**		Luke 8:26-56	25th
Daniel 8:23–9:19	7th			Luke 9:1-36	26th
Daniel 9:20–11:4	8th	Matthew 6:5–7:12	1st	Luke 9:37-62	27th
Daniel 11:5-35	9th	Matthew 7:13–8:27	2nd	Luke 10:1-37	28th
Daniel 11:36–12:13	10th	Matthew 8:28–9:34	3rd	Luke 10:38–11:28	29th
Hosea 1:1–2:13	11th	Matthew 9:35–10:31	4th	Luke 11:29-54	30th
Hosea 2:14–4:11	12th	Matthew 10:32–11:30	5th		
Hosea 4:12–5:15	13th	Matthew 12:1-37	6th	**JULY**	
Hosea 6:1–7:16	14th	Matthew 12:38–13:23	7th		
Hosea 8:1–9:9	15th	Matthew 13:24-58	8th	Luke 12:1-34	1st
Hosea 9:10–10:15	16th	Matthew 14:1-36	9th	Luke 12:35-59	2nd
Hosea 11:1–12:14	17th	Matthew 15:1-39	10th	Luke 13:1-30	3rd
Hosea 13:1–14:9	18th	Matthew 16:1–17:13	11th	Luke 13:31–14:24	4th
Joel 1:1-20	19th	Matthew 17:14–18:20	12th	Luke 14:25–15:32	5th
Joel 2:1-17	20th	Matthew 18:21–19:15	13th	Luke 16:1-31	6th
Joel 2:18-32	21st	Matthew 19:16–20:19	14th	Luke 17:1-37	7th
Joel 3:1-21	22nd	Matthew 20:20–21:22	15th	Luke 18:1-34	8th
Amos 1:1–2:5	23rd	Matthew 21:23-46	16th	Luke 18:35–19:27	9th
Amos 2:6–3:15	24th	Matthew 22:1-46	17th	Luke 19:28-48	10th
Amos 4:1-13	25th	Matthew 23:1-39	18th	Luke 20:1-26	11th
Amos 5:1-27	26th	Matthew 24:1-35	19th	Luke 20:27–21:4	12th
Amos 6:1-7:9	27th	Matthew 24:36–25:30	20th	Luke 21:5-38	13th
Amos 7:10–8:14	28th	Matthew 25:31–26:25	21st	Luke 22:1-38	14th
Amos 9:1-15	29th	Matthew 26:26-68	22nd	Luke 22:39-65	15th
Obadiah	30th	Matthew 26:69–27:26	23rd	Luke 22:66–23:25	16th
Jonah 1:1–2:10	31st	Matthew 27:27-56	24th	Luke 23:26–24:12	17th
		Matthew 27:57–28:20	25th	Luke 24:13-53	18th
APRIL		Mark 1:1-39	26th	John 1:1-34	19th
		Mark 1:40–2:22	27th	John 1:35–2:12	20th
Jonah 3:1–4:11	1st	Mark 2:23–3:35	28th	John 2:13–3:21	21st
Micah 1:1–2:5	2nd	Mark 4:1-41	29th	John 3:22–4:26	22nd
Micah 2:6–4:2	3rd	Mark 5:1-43	30th	John 4:27-54	23rd
Micah 4:3–5:9	4th	Mark 6:1-29	31st	John 5:1-30	24th
Micah 5:10–6:16	5th			John 5:31–6:24	25th
Micah 7:1-20	6th	**JUNE**		John 6:25-71	26th
Nahum 1:1–2:10	7th			John 7:1-44	27th
Micah 2:11–3:19	8th	Mark 6:30-56	1st	John 7:45–8:29	28th
Habakkuk 1:1-17	9th	Mark 7:1-37	2nd	John 8:30-59	29th
Habakkuk 2:1-20	10th	Mark 8:1–9:1	3rd	John 9:1-41	30th
Habakkuk 3:1-19	11th	Mark 9:2-37	4th	John 10:1-42	31st
Zephaniah 1:1-18	12th	Mark 9:38–10:22	5th		
Zephaniah 2:1-15	13th	Mark 10:23–11:11	6th	**AUGUST**	
Zephaniah 3:1-20	14th	Mark 11:12–12:17	7th		
Haggai 1:1-15	15th	Mark 12:18-44	8th	John 11:1-44	1st
Haggai 2:1-23	16th	Mark 13:1-37	9th	John 11:45–12:19	2nd
Zechariah 1:1–2:13	17th	Mark 14:1-31	10th	John 12:20-50	3rd
Zechariah 3:1–5:11	18th	Mark 14:32-72	11th	John 13:1-38	4th
Zechariah 6:1–7:14	19th	Mark 15:1-41	12th	John 14:1-31	5th
Zechariah 8:1–9:8	20th	Mark 15:42–16:20	13th	John 15:1–16:4	6th
Zechariah 9:9–10:12	21st	Luke 1:1-38	14th	John 16:5-33	7th

John 17:1-26	8th
John 18:1-24	9th
John 18:25-40	10th
John 19:1-27	11th
John 19:28–20:18	12th
John 20:19–21:14	13th
John 21:15-25	14th
Acts 1:1–2:13	15th
Acts 2:14-40	16th
Acts 2:41–3:26	17th
Acts 4:1-31	18th
Acts 4:32–5:16	19th
Acts 5:17–6:7	20th
Acts 6:8–7:22	21st
Acts 7:23-53	22nd
Acts 7:54–8:25	23rd
Acts 8:26–9:9	24th
Acts 9:10-43	25th
Acts 10:1-43	26th
Acts 10:44–11:30	27th
Acts 12:1–13:3	28th
Acts 13:4-41	29th
Acts 13:42–14:7	30th
Acts 14:8-28	31st

SEPTEMBER

Acts 15:1-35	1st
Acts 15:36–16:15	2nd
Acts 16:16-40	3rd
Acts 17:1-34	4th
Acts 18:1–19:7	5th
Acts 19:8-41	6th
Acts 20:1-38	7th
Acts 21:1-36	8th
Acts 21:37–22:21	9th
Acts 22:22–23:10	10th
Acts 23:11-35	11th
Acts 24:1-27	12th
Acts 25:1-27	13th
Acts 26:1-32	14th
Acts 27:1-26	15th
Acts 27:27–28:10	16th
Acts 28:11-31	17th
Romans 1:1-32	18th
Romans 2:1-29	19th
Romans 3:1-31	20th
Romans 4:1-25	21st
Romans 5:1–6:14	22nd
Romans 6:15–7:25	23rd
Romans 8:1-39	24th
Romans 9:1-33	25th
Romans 10:1–11:10	26th

Romans 11:11-36	27th
Romans 12:1–13:14	28th
Romans 14:1–15:13	29th
Romans 15:14-33	30th

OCTOBER

Romans 16:1-27	1st
1 Corinthians 1:1–2:5	2nd
1 Corinthians 2:6–3:23	3rd
1 Corinthians 4:1–5:13	4th
1 Corinthians 6:1-20	5th
1 Corinthians 7:1-40	6th
1 Corinthians 8:1–9:27	7th
1 Corinthians 10:1–11:1	8th
1 Corinthians 11:2-34	9th
1 Corinthians 12:1–13:13	10th
1 Corinthians 14:1-40	11th
1 Corinthians 15:1-34	12th
1 Corinthians 15:35-58	13th
1 Corinthians 16:1-24	14th
2 Corinthians 1:1-2:4	15th
2 Corinthians 2:5–3:18	16th
2 Corinthians 4:1–5:15	17th
2 Corinthians 5:16–7:1	18th
2 Corinthians 7:2–8:15	19th
2 Corinthians 8:16–9:15	20th
2 Corinthians 10:1–11:15	21st
2 Corinthians 11:16–12:10	22nd
2 Corinthians 12:11–13:13	23rd
Galatians 1:1–2:10	24th
Galatians 2:11–3:26	25th
Galatians 3:27–4:31	26th
Galatians 5:1–6:18	27th
Ephesians 1:1–2:10	28th
Ephesians 2:11–3:21	29th
Ephesians 4:1–5:14	30th
Ephesians 5:15–6:24	31st

NOVEMBER

Philippians 1:1–2:11	1st
Philippians 2:12–3:11	2nd
Philippians 3:12–4:23	3rd
Colossians 1:1–2:3	4th
Colossians 2:4–3:17	5th
Colossians 3:18–4:18	6th
1 Thessalonians 1:1–2:16	7th
1 Thessalonians 2:17–4:12	8th
1 Thessalonians 4:13–5:28	9th
2 Thessalonians 1:1–2:12	10th
2 Thessalonians 2:13–3:18	11th
1 Timothy 1:1–2:15	12th

1 Timothy 3:1–5:2	13th
1 Timothy 5:3-25	14th
1 Timothy 6:1-21	15th
2 Timothy 1:1–2:13	16th
2 Timothy 2:14–3:9	17th
2 Timothy 3:10–4:22	18th
Titus 1:1–2:15	19th
Titus 3:1-15	20th
Philemon	21st
Hebrews 1:1–2:4	22nd
Hebrews 2:5–3:19	23rd
Hebrews 4:1–5:10	24th
Hebrews 5:11–7:10	25th
Hebrews 7:11–8:13	26th
Hebrews 9:1-28	27th
Hebrews 10:1-39	28th
Hebrews 11:1-40	29th
Hebrews 12:1-29	30th

DECEMBER

Hebrews 13:1-25	1st
James 1:1–2:13	2nd
James 2:14–3:18	3rd
James 4:1–5:20	4th
1 Peter 1:1-25	5th
1 Peter 2:1–3:7	6th
1 Peter 3:8–4:11	7th
1 Peter 4:12–5:14	8th
2 Peter 1:1-21	9th
2 Peter 2:1-22	10th
2 Peter 3:1-18	11th
1 John 1:1–2:17	12th
1 John 2:18–3:24	13th
1 John 4:1–5:21	14th
2 John–3 John	15th
Jude	16th
Revelation 1:1-2:7	17th
Revelation 2:8–3:6	18th
Revelation 3:7–4:11	19th
Revelation 5:1–6:11	20th
Revelation 6:12–8:6	21st
Revelation 8:7–9:21	22nd
Revelation 10:1–11:19	23rd
Revelation 12:1–13:10	24th
Revelation 13:11–14:20	25th
Revelation 15:1–16:16	26th
Revelation 16:17–17:18	27th
Revelation 18:1-24	28th
Revelation 19:1–20:6	29th
Revelation 20:7–21:27	30th
Revelation 22:1-21	31st

Daily Bread
The Word of God in a Year

Compiled by the late Rev. Robert Murray M'Cheyne, M.A.

JANUARY

This is My beloved Son. I take delight in Him. Listen to Him (Mt 17:5)!

Genesis 1	Matthew 1	1st	Ezra 1	Acts 1
Genesis 2	Matthew 2	2nd	Ezra 2	Acts 2
Genesis 3	Matthew 3	3rd	Ezra 3	Acts 3
Genesis 4	Matthew 4	4th	Ezra 4	Acts 4
Genesis 5	Matthew 5	5th	Ezra 5	Acts 5
Genesis 6	Matthew 6	6th	Ezra 6	Acts 6
Genesis 7	Matthew 7	7th	Ezra 7	Acts 7
Genesis 8	Matthew 8	8th	Ezra 8	Acts 8
Genesis 9–10	Matthew 9	9th	Ezra 9	Acts 9
Genesis 11	Matthew 10	10th	Ezra 10	Acts 10
Genesis 12	Matthew 11	11th	Nehemiah 1	Acts 11
Genesis 13	Matthew 12	12th	Nehemiah 2	Acts 12
Genesis 14	Matthew 13	13th	Nehemiah 3	Acts 13
Genesis 15	Matthew 14	14th	Nehemiah 4	Acts 14
Genesis 16	Matthew 15	15th	Nehemiah 5	Acts 15
Genesis 17	Matthew 16	16th	Nehemiah 6	Acts 16
Genesis 18	Matthew 17	17th	Nehemiah 7	Acts 17
Genesis 19	Matthew 18	18th	Nehemiah 8	Acts 18
Genesis 20	Matthew 19	19th	Nehemiah 9	Acts 19
Genesis 21	Matthew 20	20th	Nehemiah 10	Acts 20
Genesis 22	Matthew 21	21st	Nehemiah 11	Acts 21
Genesis 23	Matthew 22	22nd	Nehemiah 12	Acts 22
Genesis 24	Matthew 23	23rd	Nehemiah 13	Acts 23
Genesis 25	Matthew 24	24th	Esther 1	Acts 24
Genesis 26	Matthew 25	25th	Esther 2	Acts 25
Genesis 27	Matthew 26	26th	Esther 3	Acts 26
Genesis 28	Matthew 27	27th	Esther 4	Acts 27
Genesis 29	Matthew 28	28th	Esther 5	Acts 28
Genesis 30	Mark 1	29th	Esther 6	Romans 1
Genesis 31	Mark 2	30th	Esther 7	Romans 2
Genesis 32	Mark 3	31st	Esther 8	Romans 3

FEBRUARY

I have treasured the words of His mouth more than my daily food (Jb 23:12).

Genesis 33	Mark 4	1st	Esther 9–10	Romans 4
Genesis 34	Mark 5	2nd	Job 1	Romans 5
Genesis 35–36	Mark 6	3rd	Job 2	Romans 6
Genesis 37	Mark 7	4th	Job 3	Romans 7
Genesis 38	Mark 8	5th	Job 4	Romans 8
Genesis 39	Mark 9	6th	Job 5	Romans 9
Genesis 40	Mark 10	7th	Job 6	Romans 10
Genesis 41	Mark 11	8th	Job 7	Romans 11
Genesis 42	Mark 12	9th	Job 8	Romans 12
Genesis 43	Mark 13	10th	Job 9	Romans 13
Genesis 44	Mark 14	11th	Job 10	Romans 14
Genesis 45	Mark 15	12th	Job 11	Romans 15
Genesis 46	Mark 16	13th	Job 12	Romans 16

Genesis 47	Luke 1:1-38	14th	Job 13	1 Corinthians 1
Genesis 48	Luke 1:39-80	15th	Job 14	1 Corinthians 2
Genesis 49	Luke 2	16th	Job 15	1 Corinthians 3
Genesis 50	Luke 3	17th	Job 16–17	1 Corinthians 4
Exodus 1	Luke 4	18th	Job 18	1 Corinthians 5
Exodus 2	Luke 5	19th	Job 19	1 Corinthians 6
Exodus 3	Luke 6	20th	Job 20	1 Corinthians 7
Exodus 4	Luke 7	21st	Job 21	1 Corinthians 8
Exodus 5	Luke 8	22nd	Job 22	1 Corinthians 9
Exodus 6	Luke 9	23rd	Job 23	1 Corinthians 10
Exodus 7	Luke 10	24th	Job 24	1 Corinthians 11
Exodus 8	Luke 11	25th	Job 25–26	1 Corinthians 12
Exodus 9	Luke 12	26th	Job 27	1 Corinthians 13
Exodus 10	Luke 13	27th	Job 28	1 Corinthians 14
Exodus 11–12:21	Luke 14	28th	Job 29	1 Corinthians 15

MARCH

Mary was treasuring up all these things in her heart and meditating on them (Lk 2:19).

Exodus 12:22ff	Luke 15	1st	Job 30	1 Corinthians 16
Exodus 13	Luke 16	2nd	Job 31	2 Corinthians 1
Exodus 14	Luke 17	3rd	Job 32	2 Corinthians 2
Exodus 15	Luke 18	4th	Job 33	2 Corinthians 3
Exodus 16	Luke 19	5th	Job 34	2 Corinthians 4
Exodus 17	Luke 20	6th	Job 35	2 Corinthians 5
Exodus 18	Luke 21	7th	Job 36	2 Corinthians 6
Exodus 19	Luke 22	8th	Job 37	2 Corinthians 7
Exodus 20	Luke 23	9th	Job 38	2 Corinthians 8
Exodus 21	Luke 24	10th	Job 39	2 Corinthians 9
Exodus 22	John 1	11th	Job 40	2 Corinthians 10
Exodus 23	John 2	12th	Job 41	2 Corinthians 11
Exodus 24	John 3	13th	Job 42	2 Corinthians 12
Exodus 25	John 4	14th	Proverbs 1	2 Corinthians 13
Exodus 26	John 5	15th	Proverbs 2	Galatians 1
Exodus 27	John 6	16th	Proverbs 3	Galatians 2
Exodus 28	John 7	17th	Proverbs 4	Galatians 3
Exodus 29	John 8	18th	Proverbs 5	Galatians 4
Exodus 30	John 9	19th	Proverbs 6	Galatians 5
Exodus 31	John 10	20th	Proverbs 7	Galatians 6
Exodus 32	John 11	21st	Proverbs 8	Ephesians 1
Exodus 33	John 12	22nd	Proverbs 9	Ephesians 2
Exodus 34	John 13	23rd	Proverbs 10	Ephesians 3
Exodus 35	John 14	24th	Proverbs 11	Ephesians 4
Exodus 36	John 15	25th	Proverbs 12	Ephesians 5
Exodus 37	John 16	26th	Proverbs 13	Ephesians 6
Exodus 38	John 17	27th	Proverbs 14	Philippians 1
Exodus 39	John 18	28th	Proverbs 15	Philippians 2
Exodus 40	John 19	29th	Proverbs 16	Philippians 3
Leviticus 1	John 20	30th	Proverbs 17	Philippians 4
Leviticus 2–3	John 21	31st	Proverbs 18	Colossians 1

APRIL

Send Your light and Your truth; let them lead me (Ps 43:3).

Leviticus 4	Psalms 1–2	1st	Proverbs 19	Colossians 2
Leviticus 5	Psalms 3–4	2nd	Proverbs 20	Colossians 3
Leviticus 6	Psalms 5–6	3rd	Proverbs 21	Colossians 4
Leviticus 7	Psalms 7–8	4th	Proverbs 22	1 Thessalonians 1

Leviticus 8	Psalm 9	5th	Proverbs 23	1 Thessalonians 2
Leviticus 9	Psalm 10	6th	Proverbs 24	1 Thessalonians 3
Leviticus 10	Psalms 11–12	7th	Proverbs 25	1 Thessalonians 4
Leviticus 11–12	Psalms 13–14	8th	Proverbs 26	1 Thessalonians 5
Leviticus 13	Psalms 15–16	9th	Proverbs 27	2 Thessalonians 1
Leviticus 14	Psalm 17	10th	Proverbs 28	2 Thessalonians 2
Leviticus 15	Psalm 18	11th	Proverbs 29	2 Thessalonians 3
Leviticus 16	Psalm 19	12th	Proverbs 30	1 Timothy 1
Leviticus 17	Psalms 20–21	13th	Proverbs 31	1 Timothy 2
Leviticus 18	Psalm 22	14th	Ecclesiastes 1	1 Timothy 3
Leviticus 19	Psalms 23–24	15th	Ecclesiastes 2	1 Timothy 4
Leviticus 20	Psalm 25	16th	Ecclesiastes 3	1 Timothy 5
Leviticus 21	Psalms 26–27	17th	Ecclesiastes 4	1 Timothy 6
Leviticus 22	Psalms 28–29	18th	Ecclesiastes 5	2 Timothy 1
Leviticus 23	Psalm 30	19th	Ecclesiastes 6	2 Timothy 2
Leviticus 24	Psalm 31	20th	Ecclesiastes 7	2 Timothy 3
Leviticus 25	Psalm 32	21st	Ecclesiastes 8	2 Timothy 4
Leviticus 26	Psalm 33	22nd	Ecclesiastes 9	Titus 1
Leviticus 27	Psalm 34	23rd	Ecclesiastes 10	Titus 2
Numbers 1	Psalm 35	24th	Ecclesiastes 11	Titus 3
Numbers 2	Psalm 36	25th	Ecclesiastes 12	Philemon
Numbers 3	Psalm 37	26th	Song of Songs 1	Hebrews 1
Numbers 4	Psalm 38	27th	Song of Songs 2	Hebrews 2
Numbers 5	Psalm 39	28th	Song of Songs 3	Hebrews 3
Numbers 6	Psalms 40–41	29th	Song of Songs 4	Hebrews 4
Numbers 7	Psalms 42–43	30th	Song of Songs 5	Hebrews 5

MAY

From childhood you have known the sacred Scriptures (2Tm 3:15).

Numbers 8	Psalm 44	1st	Song of Songs 6	Hebrews 6
Numbers 9	Psalm 45	2nd	Song of Songs 7	Hebrews 7
Numbers 10	Psalms 46–47	3rd	Song of Songs 8	Hebrews 8
Numbers 11	Psalm 48	4th	Isaiah 1	Hebrews 9
Numbers 12-13	Psalm 49	5th	Isaiah 2	Hebrews 10
Numbers 14	Psalm 50	6th	Isaiah 3–4	Hebrews 11
Numbers 15	Psalm 51	7th	Isaiah 5	Hebrews 12
Numbers 16	Psalms 52–54	8th	Isaiah 6	Hebrews 13
Numbers 17–18	Psalm 55	9th	Isaiah 7	James 1
Numbers 19	Psalms 56–57	10th	Isaiah 8:9:7	James 2
Numbers 20	Psalms 58–59	11th	Isaiah 9:8–10:4	James 3
Numbers 21	Psalms 60–61	12th	Isaiah 10:5ff	James 4
Numbers 22	Psalms 62–63	13th	Isaiah 11–12	James 5
Numbers 23	Psalms 64–65	14th	Isaiah 13	1 Peter 1
Numbers 24	Psalms 66–67	15th	Isaiah 14	1 Peter 2
Numbers 25	Psalm 68	16th	Isaiah 15	1 Peter 3
Numbers 26	Psalm 69	17th	Isaiah 16	1 Peter 4
Numbers 27	Psalms 70–71	18th	Isaiah 17–18	1 Peter 5
Numbers 28	Psalm 72	19th	Isaiah 19–20	2 Peter 1
Numbers 29	Psalm 73	20th	Isaiah 21	2 Peter 2
Numbers 30	Psalm 74	21st	Isaiah 22	2 Peter 3
Numbers 31	Psalms 75–76	22nd	Isaiah 23	1 John 1
Numbers 32	Psalm 77	23rd	Isaiah 24	1 John 2
Numbers 33	Psalm 78:1-37	24th	Isaiah 25	1 John 3
Numbers 34	Psalm 78:38ff	25th	Isaiah 26	1 John 4
Numbers 35	Psalm 79	26th	Isaiah 27	1 John 5
Numbers 36	Psalm 80	27th	Isaiah 28	2 John

Deuteronomy 1	Psalms 81–82	28th	Isaiah 29	3 John
Deuteronomy 2	Psalms 83–84	29th	Isaiah 30	Jude
Deuteronomy 3	Psalm 85	30th	Isaiah 31	Revelation 1
Deuteronomy 4	Psalms 86–87	31st	Isaiah 32	Revelation 2

JUNE

The one who reads this is blessed, and those who hear the words of this prophecy and keep what is written in it are blessed (Rv 1:3).

Deuteronomy 5	Psalm 88	1st	Isaiah 33	Revelation 3
Deuteronomy 6	Psalm 89	2nd	Isaiah 34	Revelation 4
Deuteronomy 7	Psalm 90	3rd	Isaiah 35	Revelation 5
Deuteronomy 8	Psalm 91	4th	Isaiah 36	Revelation 6
Deuteronomy 9	Psalms 92–93	5th	Isaiah 37	Revelation 7
Deuteronomy 10	Psalm 94	6th	Isaiah 38	Revelation 8
Deuteronomy 11	Psalms 95–96	7th	Isaiah 39	Revelation 9
Deuteronomy 12	Psalms 97–98	8th	Isaiah 40	Revelation 10
Deuteronomy 13–14	Psalms 99–101	9th	Isaiah 41	Revelation 11
Deuteronomy 15	Psalm 102	10th	Isaiah 42	Revelation 12
Deuteronomy 16	Psalm 103	11th	Isaiah 43	Revelation 13
Deuteronomy 17	Psalm 104	12th	Isaiah 44	Revelation 14
Deuteronomy 18	Psalm 105	13th	Isaiah 45	Revelation 15
Deuteronomy 19	Psalm 106	14th	Isaiah 46	Revelation 16
Deuteronomy 20	Psalm 107	15th	Isaiah 47	Revelation 17
Deuteronomy 21	Psalms 108–109	16th	Isaiah 48	Revelation 18
Deuteronomy 22	Psalms 110–111	17th	Isaiah 49	Revelation 19
Deuteronomy 23	Psalms 112–113	18th	Isaiah 50	Revelation 20
Deuteronomy 24	Psalms 114–115	19th	Isaiah 51	Revelation 21
Deuteronomy 25	Psalm 116	20th	Isaiah 52	Revelation 22
Deuteronomy 26	Psalms 117–118	21st	Isaiah 53	Matthew 1
Deuteronomy 27–28:19	Psalm 119:1-24	22nd	Isaiah 54	Matthew 2
Deuteronomy 28:20ff	Psalm 119:25-48	23rd	Isaiah 55	Matthew 3
Deuteronomy 29	Psalm 119:49-72	24th	Isaiah 56	Matthew 4
Deuteronomy 30	Psalm 119:73-96	25th	Isaiah 57	Matthew 5
Deuteronomy 31	Psalm 119:97-120	26th	Isaiah 58	Matthew 6
Deuteronomy 32	Psalm 119:121-144	27th	Isaiah 59	Matthew 7
Deuteronomy 33–34	Psalm 119:145-176	28th	Isaiah 60	Matthew 8
Joshua 1	Psalms 120–122	29th	Isaiah 61	Matthew 9
Joshua 2	Psalms 123–125	30th	Isaiah 62	Matthew 10

JULY

They welcomed the message with eagerness and examined the Scriptures daily to see if these things were so (Ac 17:11).

Joshua 3	Psalms 126–128	1st	Isaiah 63	Matthew 11
Joshua 4	Psalms 129–131	2nd	Isaiah 64	Matthew 12
Joshua 5–6:5	Psalms 132–134	3rd	Isaiah 65	Matthew 13
Joshua 6:6ff	Psalms 135–136	4th	Isaiah 66	Matthew 14
Joshua 7	Psalms 137–138	5th	Jeremiah 1	Matthew 15
Joshua 8	Psalm 139	6th	Jeremiah 2	Matthew 16
Joshua 9	Psalms 140–141	7th	Jeremiah 3	Matthew 17
Joshua 10	Psalms 142–143	8th	Jeremiah 4	Matthew 18
Joshua 11	Psalm 144	9th	Jeremiah 5	Matthew 19
Joshua 12–13	Psalm 145	10th	Jeremiah 6	Matthew 20
Joshua 14–15	Psalms 146–147	11th	Jeremiah 7	Matthew 21
Joshua 16–17	Psalm 148	12th	Jeremiah 8	Matthew 22
Joshua 18–19	Psalms 149–150	13th	Jeremiah 9	Matthew 23
Joshua 20–21	Acts 1	14th	Jeremiah 10	Matthew 24

Joshua 22	Acts 2	15th	Jeremiah 11	Matthew 25
Joshua 23	Acts 3	16th	Jeremiah 12	Matthew 26
Joshua 24	Acts 4	17th	Jeremiah 13	Matthew 27
Judges 1	Acts 5	18th	Jeremiah 14	Matthew 28
Judges 2	Acts 6	19th	Jeremiah 15	Mark 1
Judges 3	Acts 7	20th	Jeremiah 16	Mark 2
Judges 4	Acts 8	21st	Jeremiah 17	Mark 3
Judges 5	Acts 9	22nd	Jeremiah 18	Mark 4
Judges 6	Acts 10	23rd	Jeremiah 19	Mark 5
Judges 7	Acts 11	24th	Jeremiah 20	Mark 6
Judges 8	Acts 12	25th	Jeremiah 21	Mark 7
Judges 9	Acts 13	26th	Jeremiah 22	Mark 8
Judges 10–11:11	Acts 14	27th	Jeremiah 23	Mark 9
Judges 11:12ff	Acts 15	28th	Jeremiah 24	Mark 10
Judges 12	Acts 16	29th	Jeremiah 25	Mark 11
Judges 13	Acts 17	30th	Jeremiah 26	Mark 12
Judges 14	Acts 18	31st	Jeremiah 27	Mark 13

AUGUST

"Speak, for Your servant is listening" (1Sm 3:10).

Judges 15	Acts 19	1st	Jeremiah 28	Mark 14
Judges 16	Acts 20	2nd	Jeremiah 29	Mark 15
Judges 17	Acts 21	3rd	Jeremiah 30–31	Mark 16
Judges 18	Acts 22	4th	Jeremiah 32	Psalms 1–2
Judges 19	Acts 23	5th	Jeremiah 33	Psalms 3–4
Judges 20	Acts 24	6th	Jeremiah 34	Psalms 5–6
Judges 21	Acts 25	7th	Jeremiah 35	Psalms 7–8
Ruth 1	Acts 26	8th	Jeremiah 36	Psalm 9
Ruth 2	Acts 27	9th	Jeremiah 37	Psalm 10
Ruth 3–4	Acts 28	10th	Jeremiah 38	Psalms 11–12
1 Samuel 1	Romans 1	11th	Jeremiah 39	Psalms 13–14
1 Samuel 2	Romans 2	12th	Jeremiah 40	Psalms 15–16
1 Samuel 3	Romans 3	13th	Jeremiah 41	Psalm 17
1 Samuel 4	Romans 4	14th	Jeremiah 42	Psalm 18
1 Samuel 5–6	Romans 5	15th	Jeremiah 43	Psalm 19
1 Samuel 7–8	Romans 6	16th	Jeremiah 44	Psalms 20–21
1 Samuel 9	Romans 7	17th	Jeremiah 46	Psalm 22
1 Samuel 10	Romans 8	18th	Jeremiah 47	Psalms 23–24
1 Samuel 11	Romans 9	19th	Jeremiah 48	Psalm 25
1 Samuel 12	Romans 10	20th	Jeremiah 49	Psalms 26–27
1 Samuel 13	Romans 11	21st	Jeremiah 50	Psalms 28–29
1 Samuel 14	Romans 12	22nd	Jeremiah 51	Psalm 30
1 Samuel 15	Romans 13	23rd	Jeremiah 52	Psalm 31
1 Samuel 16	Romans 14	24th	Lamentations 1	Psalm 32
1 Samuel 17	Romans 15	25th	Lamentations 2	Psalm 33
1 Samuel 18	Romans 16	26th	Lamentations 3	Psalm 34
1 Samuel 19	1 Corinthians 1	27th	Lamentations 4	Psalm 35
1 Samuel 20	1 Corinthians 2	28th	Lamentations 5	Psalm 36
1 Samuel 21–22	1 Corinthians 3	29th	Ezekiel 1	Psalm 37
1 Samuel 23	1 Corinthians 4	30th	Ezekiel 2	Psalm 38
1 Samuel 24	1 Corinthians 5	31st	Ezekiel 3	Psalm 39

SEPTEMBER

The instruction of the LORD is perfect, renewing one's life (Ps 19:7).

| 1 Samuel 25 | 1 Corinthians 6 | 1st | Ezekiel 4 | Psalms 40–41 |
| 1 Samuel 26 | 1 Corinthians 7 | 2nd | Ezekiel 5 | Psalms 42–43 |

1 Samuel 27	1 Corinthians 8	3rd	Ezekiel 6	Psalm 44
1 Samuel 28	1 Corinthians 9	4th	Ezekiel 7	Psalm 45
1 Samuel 29–30	1 Corinthians 10	5th	Ezekiel 8	Psalms 46–47
1 Samuel 31	1 Corinthians 11	6th	Ezekiel 9	Psalm 48
2 Samuel 1	1 Corinthians 12	7th	Ezekiel 10	Psalm 49
2 Samuel 2	1 Corinthians 13	8th	Ezekiel 11	Psalm 50
2 Samuel 3	1 Corinthians 14	9th	Ezekiel 12	Psalm 51
2 Samuel 4–5	1 Corinthians 15	10th	Ezekiel 13	Psalms 52–54
2 Samuel 6	1 Corinthians 16	11th	Ezekiel 14	Psalm 55
2 Samuel 7	2 Corinthians 1	12th	Ezekiel 15	Psalms 56–57
2 Samuel 8–9	2 Corinthians 2	13th	Ezekiel 16	Psalms 58–59
2 Samuel 10	2 Corinthians 3	14th	Ezekiel 17	Psalms 60–61
2 Samuel 11	2 Corinthians 4	15th	Ezekiel 18	Psalms 62–63
2 Samuel 12	2 Corinthians 5	16th	Ezekiel 19	Psalms 64–65
2 Samuel 13	2 Corinthians 6	17th	Ezekiel 20	Psalms 66–67
2 Samuel 14	2 Corinthians 7	18th	Ezekiel 21	Psalm 68
2 Samuel 15	2 Corinthians 8	19th	Ezekiel 22	Psalm 69
2 Samuel 16	2 Corinthians 9	20th	Ezekiel 23	Psalms 70–71
2 Samuel 17	2 Corinthians 10	21st	Ezekiel 24	Psalm 72
2 Samuel 18	2 Corinthians 11	22nd	Ezekiel 25	Psalm 73
2 Samuel 19	2 Corinthians 12	23rd	Ezekiel 26	Psalm 74
2 Samuel 20	2 Corinthians 13	24th	Ezekiel 27	Psalms 75–76
2 Samuel 21	Galatians 1	25th	Ezekiel 28	Psalm 77
2 Samuel 22	Galatians 2	26th	Ezekiel 29	Psalm 78:1-37
2 Samuel 23	Galatians 3	27th	Ezekiel 30	Psalm 78:38ff
2 Samuel 24	Galatians 4	28th	Ezekiel 31	Psalm 79
1 Kings 1	Galatians 5	29th	Ezekiel 32	Psalm 80
1 Kings 2	Galatians 6	30th	Ezekiel 33	Psalms 81–82

OCTOBER

How I love Your instruction! It is my meditation all day long (Ps 119:97).

1 Kings 3	Ephesians 1	1st	Ezekiel 34	Psalms 83–84
1 Kings 4–5	Ephesians 2	2nd	Ezekiel 35	Psalm 85
1 Kings 6	Ephesians 3	3rd	Ezekiel 36	Psalm 86
1 Kings 7	Ephesians 4	4th	Ezekiel 37	Psalms 87–88
1 Kings 8	Ephesians 5	5th	Ezekiel 38	Psalm 89
1 Kings 9	Ephesians 6	6th	Ezekiel 39	Psalm 90
1 Kings 10	Philippians 1	7th	Ezekiel 40	Psalm 91
1 Kings 11	Philippians 2	8th	Ezekiel 41	Psalms 92–93
1 Kings 12	Philippians 3	9th	Ezekiel 42	Psalm 94
1 Kings 13	Philippians 4	10th	Ezekiel 43	Psalms 95–96
1 Kings 14	Colossians 1	11th	Ezekiel 44	Psalms 97–98
1 Kings 15	Colossians 2	12th	Ezekiel 45	Psalms 99–101
1 Kings 16	Colossians 3	13th	Ezekiel 46	Psalm 102
1 Kings 17	Colossians 4	14th	Ezekiel 47	Psalm 103
1 Kings 18	1 Thessalonians 1	15th	Ezekiel 48	Psalm 104
1 Kings 19	1 Thessalonians 2	16th	Daniel 1	Psalm 105
1 Kings 20	1 Thessalonians 3	17th	Daniel 2	Psalm 106
1 Kings 21	1 Thessalonians 4	18th	Daniel 3	Psalm 107
1 Kings 22	1 Thessalonians 5	19th	Daniel 4	Psalms 108–109
2 Kings 1	2 Thessalonians 1	20th	Daniel 5	Psalms 110–111
2 Kings 2	2 Thessalonians 2	21st	Daniel 6	Psalms 112–113
2 Kings 3	2 Thessalonians 3	22nd	Daniel 7	Psalms 114–115
2 Kings 4	1 Timothy 1	23rd	Daniel 8	Psalm 116
2 Kings 5	1 Timothy 2	24th	Daniel 9	Psalms 117–118
2 Kings 6	1 Timothy 3	25th	Daniel 10	Psalm 119:1-24

2 Kings 7	1 Timothy 4	26th	Daniel 11	Psalm 119:25-48
2 Kings 8	1 Timothy 5	27th	Daniel 12	Psalm 119:49-72
2 Kings 9	1 Timothy 6	28th	Hosea 1	Psalm 119:73-96
2 Kings 10	2 Timothy 1	29th	Hosea 2	Psalm 119:97-120
2 Kings 11–12	2 Timothy 2	30th	Hosea 3–4	Psalm 119:121-144
2 Kings 13	2 Timothy 3	31st	Hosea 5–6	Psalm 119:145-176

NOVEMBER

Like newborn infants, desire the pure spiritual milk, so that you may grow by it for your salvation (1Pt 2:2).

2 Kings 14	2 Timothy 4	1st	Hosea 7	Psalms 120–122
2 Kings 15	Titus 1	2nd	Hosea 8	Psalms 123–125
2 Kings 16	Titus 2	3rd	Hosea 9	Psalms 126–128
2 Kings 17	Titus 3	4th	Hosea 10	Psalms 129–131
2 Kings 18	Philemon 1	5th	Hosea 11	Psalms 132–134
2 Kings 19	Hebrews 1	6th	Hosea 12	Psalms 135–136
2 Kings 20	Hebrews 2	7th	Hosea 13	Psalms 137–138
2 Kings 21	Hebrews 3	8th	Hosea 14	Psalm 139
2 Kings 22	Hebrews 4	9th	Joel 1	Psalms 140–141
2 Kings 23	Hebrews 5	10th	Joel 2	Psalm 142
2 Kings 24	Hebrews 6	11th	Joel 3	Psalm 143
2 Kings 25	Hebrews 7	12th	Amos 1	Psalm 144
1 Chronicles 1–2	Hebrews 8	13th	Amos 2	Psalm 145
1 Chronicles 3–4	Hebrews 9	14th	Amos 3	Psalms 146–147
1 Chronicles 5–6	Hebrews 10	15th	Amos 4	Psalms 148–150
1 Chronicles 7–8	Hebrews 11	16th	Amos 5	Luke 1:1-38
1 Chronicles 9–10	Hebrews 12	17th	Amos 6	Luke 1:39ff
1 Chronicles 11–12	Hebrews 13	18th	Amos 7	Luke 2
1 Chronicles 13–14	James 1	19th	Amos 8	Luke 3
1 Chronicles 15	James 2	20th	Amos 9	Luke 4
1 Chronicles 16	James 3	21st	Obadiah	Luke 5
1 Chronicles 17	James 4	22nd	Jonah 1	Luke 6
1 Chronicles 18	James 5	23rd	Jonah 2	Luke 7
1 Chronicles 19–20	1 Peter 1	24th	Jonah 3	Luke 8
1 Chronicles 21	1 Peter 2	25th	Jonah 4	Luke 9
1 Chronicles 22	1 Peter 3	26th	Micah 1	Luke 10
1 Chronicles 23	1 Peter 4	27th	Micah 2	Luke 11
1 Chronicles 24–25	1 Peter 5	28th	Micah 3	Luke 12
1 Chronicles 26–27	2 Peter 1	29th	Micah 4	Luke 13
1 Chronicles 28	2 Peter 2	30th	Micah 5	Luke 14

DECEMBER

The instruction of his God is in his heart; his steps do not falter (Ps 37:31).

1 Chronicles 29	2 Peter 3	1st	Micah 6	Luke 15
2 Chronicles 1	1 John 1	2nd	Micah 7	Luke 16
2 Chronicles 2	1 John 2	3rd	Nahum 1	Luke 17
2 Chronicles 3–4	1 John 3	4th	Nahum 2	Luke 18
2 Chronicles 5–6:11	1 John 4	5th	Nahum 3	Luke 19
2 Chronicles 6:12ff	1 John 5	6th	Habakkuk 1	Luke 20
2 Chronicles 7	2 John	7th	Habakkuk 2	Luke 21
2 Chronicles 8	3 John	8th	Habakkuk 3	Luke 22
2 Chronicles 9	Jude	9th	Zephaniah 1	Luke 23
2 Chronicles 10	Revelation 1	10th	Zephaniah 2	Luke 24
2 Chronicles 11–12	Revelation 2	11th	Zephaniah 3	John 1
2 Chronicles 13	Revelation 3	12th	Haggai 1	John 2
2 Chronicles 14–15	Revelation 4	13th	Haggai 2	John 3
2 Chronicles 16	Revelation 5	14th	Zechariah 1	John 4

2 Chronicles 17	Revelation 6	15th	Zechariah 2	John 5
2 Chronicles 18	Revelation 7	16th	Zechariah 3	John 6
2 Chronicles 19–20	Revelation 8	17th	Zechariah 4	John 7
2 Chronicles 21	Revelation 9	18th	Zechariah 5	John 8
2 Chronicles 22–23	Revelation 10	19th	Zechariah 6	John 9
2 Chronicles 24	Revelation 11	20th	Zechariah 7	John 10
2 Chronicles 25	Revelation 12	21st	Zechariah 8	John 11
2 Chronicles 26	Revelation 13	22nd	Zechariah 9	John 12
2 Chronicles 27–28	Revelation 14	23rd	Zechariah 10	John 13
2 Chronicles 29	Revelation 15	24th	Zechariah 11	John 14
2 Chronicles 30	Revelation 16	25th	Zechariah 12–13:1	John 15
2 Chronicles 31	Revelation 17	26th	Zechariah 13:2ff	John 16
2 Chronicles 32	Revelation 18	27th	Zechariah 14	John 17
2 Chronicles 33	Revelation 19	28th	Malachi 1	John 18
2 Chronicles 34	Revelation 20	29th	Malachi 2	John 19
2 Chronicles 35	Revelation 21	30th	Malachi 3	John 20
2 Chronicles 36	Revelation 22	31st	Malachi 4	John 21

52-Week Scripture Memory Plan

If you were walking down an old country road at night would you prefer to be carrying a penlight, a flashlight, or a floodlight?

Most of us would choose the floodlight. We want to see the most we can with the hope of avoiding danger. The more light we have, the better off we will be on that dark road. The same is true of God's Word. As we navigate the dark roads of life, we can carry a penlight (10 or so Bible verses), a flashlight (100 or so Bible verses) or a floodlight (1,000 Bible verses). Each verse we memorize will add to the strength of the light we have to guide our steps in this world. We need those words.

Human beings live on words. Words are the fuel that sustains and shapes us as creatures made in God's image. The words we ingest and live by have great consequences in our life on earth and beyond. That's why that cunning serpent in the Garden of Eden focused on God's words to Adam and Eve when he talked with Eve.

"Did God really say, 'You can't eat from any tree in the garden'?", asked the serpent. Up until that moment God's clear word governed the first couple's choices and behavior. The serpent's question had the effect of neutralizing God's word to Adam and Eve. We know the consequences.

Fast forward. Jesus had just been baptized and is about to begin His public ministry. The tempter who came to Eden approached Jesus in the wilderness of Judea with three attractive temptations. With each temptation, Jesus responded with sacred words that had He had memorized and that shaped His thoughts, His affections, and His decision making. We know and are eternally grateful for the consequences.

Dallas Willard, who has written extensively on spiritual disciplines, says that "Bible memorization is absolutely fundamental to spiritual formation. If I had to choose between all the disciplines of the spiritual life, I would choose Bible memorization, because it is a fundamental way of filling our mind with what it needs."

Here is a 52-week plan of Bible memorization. Two Scriptures on the same topic are suggested for each week. The plan begins with some major theological truths. It then takes the participant on a chronological journey ranging from Abraham through the Hebrew prophets. The plan then moves back into a more topical orientation designed to set forth God's way of reconciling human beings to Himself, creating His body (the church), and then guiding believers into an ever-growing likeness of God's Son, Jesus Christ. Each week's passage set is also identified by a Biblical Concept. These 15 Biblical Concepts serve as a tool for categorizing the major truths presented in the Bible. All dated Bible study curriculum developed by LifeWay Christian Resources is built upon these 15 Biblical Concepts. If you are using LifeWay Bible study resources, this 52-Week memory plan supports the lessons you will be studying through the year.

Topic	Basic	Challenge	Biblical Concept
1. God the Creator	Genesis 1:1	John 1:1-5	God
2. Human Beings	Genesis 1:26-28	Psalm 8	Humanity/Self
3. Sin	Genesis 3:6-7	James 1:12-15	Rebellion and Sin
4. Sin's Consequences	Romans 6:23	John 8:34-35	Rebellion and Sin
5. Jesus Christ	John 14:6	Matthew 1:21-23	Jesus
6. The Scriptures	2 Timothy 3:16-17	Romans 15:4	Revelation and Authority/Bible
7. God's Revelation: Creation	Romans 1:20	Psalm 19:1-6	Creation, Sovereignty, and Providence
8. God's Revelation: Law	Psalm 119:13-16	Psalm 19:7-14	Revelation and Authority/Bible
9. Scripture: Jesus' View	Matthew 5:17-20	Luke 24:44-45	Revelation and Authority/Bible
10. Abraham: Father of a Multitude	Genesis 12:1-3	Genesis 15:1	Creation, Sovereignty, and Providence
11. God's Grace to Jacob/Israel	Genesis 28:14-15	Genesis 48:16	Creation, Sovereignty, and Providence
12. Joseph: Man of Character	Genesis 50:19-21	Hebrews 11:22	Creation, Sovereignty, and Providence
13. Moses: Servant of Yahweh	Exodus 3:14-15	Hebrews 11:22-26	God
14. Moses: Remember	Deuteronomy 6:4-9	Deuteronomy 8:2-3	Discipleship and the Christian Life
15. Joshua's Charge	Joshua 1:6-9	Joshua 24:14-15	Discipleship and the Christian Life

Topic	Basic	Challenge	Biblical Concept
16. Retreat to Idolatry	Judges 1:11-13	Judges 21:25	Rebellion and Sin
17. Faithfulness: Human and Divine	Ruth 1:16-17	Ruth 4:14-16	Family
18. Samuel: Israel's Intercessor	1 Samuel 3:10	1 Samuel 12:23-25	Discipleship and the Christian Life
19. David's Reign and Dynasty	2 Samuel 5:4-5	2 Samuel 7:12-13	Creation, Sovereignty, and Providence
20. Psalms of David	Psalm 23	Psalm 32:1-2	Salvation
21. Solomon's Prayer/God's Answer	1 Kings 3:7-9	1 Kings 3:10-14	Reason and Faith
22. Wisdom's Source	Proverbs 1:7	Proverbs 3:1-12	Reason and Faith
23. Hollow Worship	Isaiah 29:13-14	Isaiah 29:15-16	Rebellion and Sin
24. Eternal God	Isaiah 40:6-8	Isaiah 40:27-31	God
25. Judgment	John 3:19-21	Luke 16:15	Rebellion and Sin
26. A New Heart	Ezekiel 36:26-27	Ezekiel 37:14	Salvation
27. God's Gift	Romans 3:23-26	1 Peter 3:18	Salvation
28. Jesus Christ: Our Substitute	Isaiah 53:4-6	Hebrews 9:11-14	Jesus
29. New Birth	John 3:5-8	John 3:14-17	Salvation
30. Peace	Romans 5:1-5	Hebrews 13:20-21	Discipleship and the Christian Life
31. Repent	Mark 1:15	Acts 17:30	Salvation
32. Baptism	Acts 2:38-40	Romans 6:4-5	Discipleship and the Christian Life
33. The Comforter	John 14:16	John 16:8-11	Holy Spirit
34. The Body of Christ	Acts 2:41-43	Ephesians 4:15-16	Church and Kingdom
35. Serving Others	James 2:15-17	Matthew 25:37-40	Church and Kingdom
36. Prayer	Matthew 6:5-8	Romans 8:26-27	Discipleship and the Christian Life
37. Building Well	Ecclesiastes 12:13-14	Matthew 7:24-27	Discipleship and the Christian Life
38. Anger	Matthew 5:21-22	Proverbs 22:24	Ethics and Morality
39. Lust	Matthew 5:27-30	Proverbs 5:18	Ethics and Morality
40. Enemies	Matthew 5:43-48	Ephesians 6:10-18	Discipleship and the Christian Life
41. Jealousy	Ecclesiastes 4:4	James 3:13-18	Reason and Faith
42. Sloth	Proverbs 18:9	2 Thessalonians 3:10	Ethics and Morality
43. Greed	Hebrews 13:5	Malachi 3:8-12	Discipleship and the Christian Life
44. Pride	Ezekiel 16:49	Jeremiah 13:15-17	Rebellion and Sin
45. Depression	Psalm 42:5	Isaiah 26:3	Discipleship and the Christian Life
46. Priorities	Philippians 3:13-14	Matthew 6:33-34	Discipleship and the Christian Life
47. Influence	Matthew 5:13-16	Matthew 18:6	Community and World
48. Witness	Matthew 28:18-20	1 Peter 3:14-16	Discipleship and the Christian Life
49. Marriage: God's Design	Genesis 2:22-24	Song of Songs 8:6-7	Family
50. Husbands/Wives	Ephesians 5:25-26	Ephesians 5:22-24	Family
51. Resurrection	1 Corinthians 15:3-8	1 Corinthians 15:20-22	Time and Eternity
52. Glory	Revelation 21:1-4	Revelation 22:17-21	Time and Eternity

Art Credits

B&H Publishing Group is grateful to the following persons and institutions for use of the graphics in the HCSB Study Bible. Where we have inadvertently failed to give proper credit for any graphic in the Bible, please contact us (bhcustomerservice@lifeway.com) and we will make the required correction on the next printing. We gratefully acknowledge the contributions of G.B. Howell, Jr., Brent Bruce, James McLemore, and the staff of the *Biblical Illustrator* for their counsel. A significant percentage of the photos, illustrations, and reconstructions are from the archives of the *Biblical Illustrator*. Steve Gateley, Sue Woodside, and Virginia Copelin of Dargan Research Library facilitated the considerable research required for the *HCSB Study Bible*.

PHOTOGRAPHS

Museum Abbreviations

IAM = Istanbul Archaeological Museum
JAC = Joseph A. Calloway Archaeological Museum, The Southern Baptist Theological Seminary, Louisville, Kentucky
JAM = Jordan Archaeological Museum
MFB = Museum of Fine Arts, Boston
MNY = Metropolitan Museum, New York, New York

Photographers

Biblical Illustrator, Nashville, Tennessee: pp. 283, 751, 778, 799, 903, 1008, 1091, 1429, 1453, 1457, 1531, 2086, 2209.

Biblical Illustrator (James McLemore, photographer), Nashville, Tennessee: pp. 337, 732, 975, 1320, 1486, 1698, 1758.

Biblical Illustrator (David Rogers, photographer), Nashville, Tennessee: pp.761 (JAC), 911 (MNY), 1050 (JAC), 1064 (JAC), 1237, 1459 (MFB), 1473, 1478, 2081, 2145, 2177.

Biblical Illustrator (Bob Schatz, photographer), Nashville, Tennessee: pp. 25, 95, 131, 217, 382, 403, 441, 505, 541, 664, 889, 1079 (JAM), 1231, 1401, 1507, 1723, 2009, 2031 (IAM), 2081, 2091, 2096, 2157, 2202.

Biblical Illustrator (Ken Touchton, photographer), Nashville, Tennessee: pp. 296, 350, 600, 877, 1109, 1670.

Biblical Illustrator (Jerry Vardaman, photographer), Nashville, Tennessee: p. 429.

Bolen, Todd: pp. 385, 1083, 1824.

Brisco, Thomas V., Dean and Professor of Biblical Background and Archaeology, Logsdon School of Theology, Hardin-Simmons University, Abilene, Texas: pp. 167, 1396, 1398, 1675, 2039, 2183.

Cape Canaveral, http://www.geocities.come/CapeCanaveral/Lab/6529/M45clor.JPG: p. 870., http://www.geocities.come/CapeCanaveral/Lab/6529/OrionX.JPG (Photographer, Jim Pennington): p. 871.

Illustrated World of the Bible: pp. 22, 35, 1520.

iStock: pp. 93, 647, 803, 1333, 1479, 1489, 1521, 1543, 1553, 1561, 1587, 1603, 1797, 1855, 1921, 1955, 1987, 2023, 2051, 2063, 2073, 2111, 2131, 2179, 2187, 2193.

Jenkins, Ferrell: p. 831.

Langston, Scott, Texas Christian University: p. 1975.

McColgan, John, Bureau of Land Management, Alaska Fire Service: p. 2133.

Radovan, Zev: p. 339.

Ritzema, Elliot: p. 2167.

Scofield Collection, E.C. Dargan Research Library, LifeWay Christian Resources, Nashville, Tennessee: pp. 1266, 1830.

Smith, Marsha A. Ellis: p.: 1935.
Stephens, Bill: pp. 748, 1038, 1488.
Stephens, Ken: p. 853.
Tolar, William B., Retired Distinguished Professor of Biblical Backgrounds, Southwestern Baptist
    Theological Seminary, Fort Worth, TX: pp. 1393, 1513, 1535, 2105.
Wikimedia Commons: pp. 24, 495, 647 (James Emery), 1349 (Jasmine N. Walthall, U.S. Army), 1569,
    1645, 1973, 2093, 2101.

ILLUSTRATIONS AND RECONSTRUCTIONS

Biblical Illustrator, Linden Artists, London: pp. 147, 1434, 1920.
Goolsby, Abe, Principal, Officina Abrahae, Nashville, TN: pp. 20, 145, 224, 412, 645, 698, 706, 781, 1183,
    1727, 1784-85.
Latta, Bill, Latta Art Services, Mt. Juliet, TN: pp. 142, 1501, 1634, 1954, 2125.

CHARTS

Pippert, Wesley G., Proverbs Topical Chart, derived from *Words from the Wise: An Arrangement by Word
    and Theme of the Entire Book of the Proverbs*, copyright 2003 by Wesley G. Pippert and published
    by Xulon Press (www.XulonPress.com): pp. 1025–30.
Powell, Doug, pp. lviii, lxi, 1597.

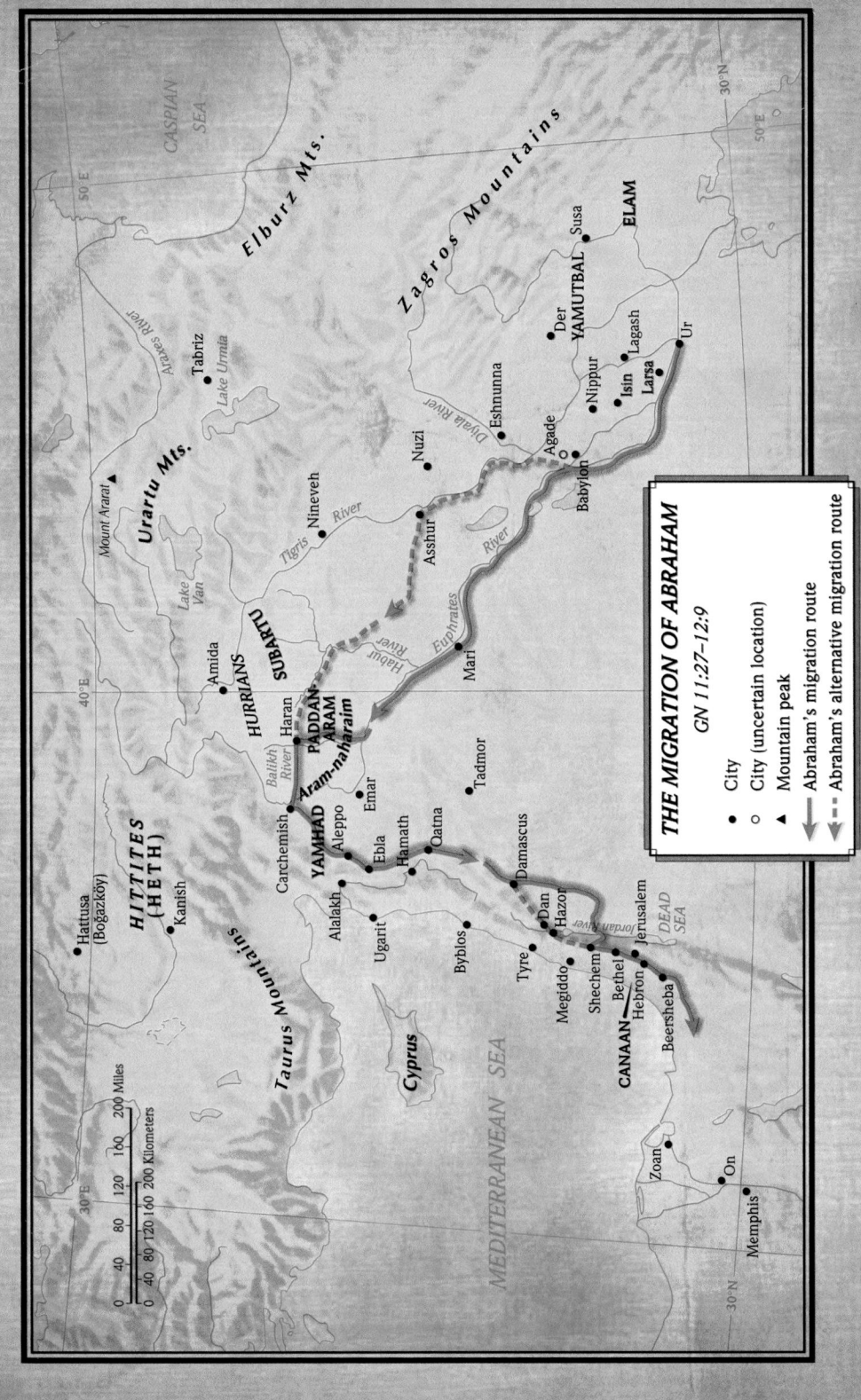

THE MIGRATION OF ABRAHAM

GN 11:27–12:9

• City
○ City (uncertain location)
▲ Mountain peak
→ Abraham's migration route
--→ Abraham's alternative migration route

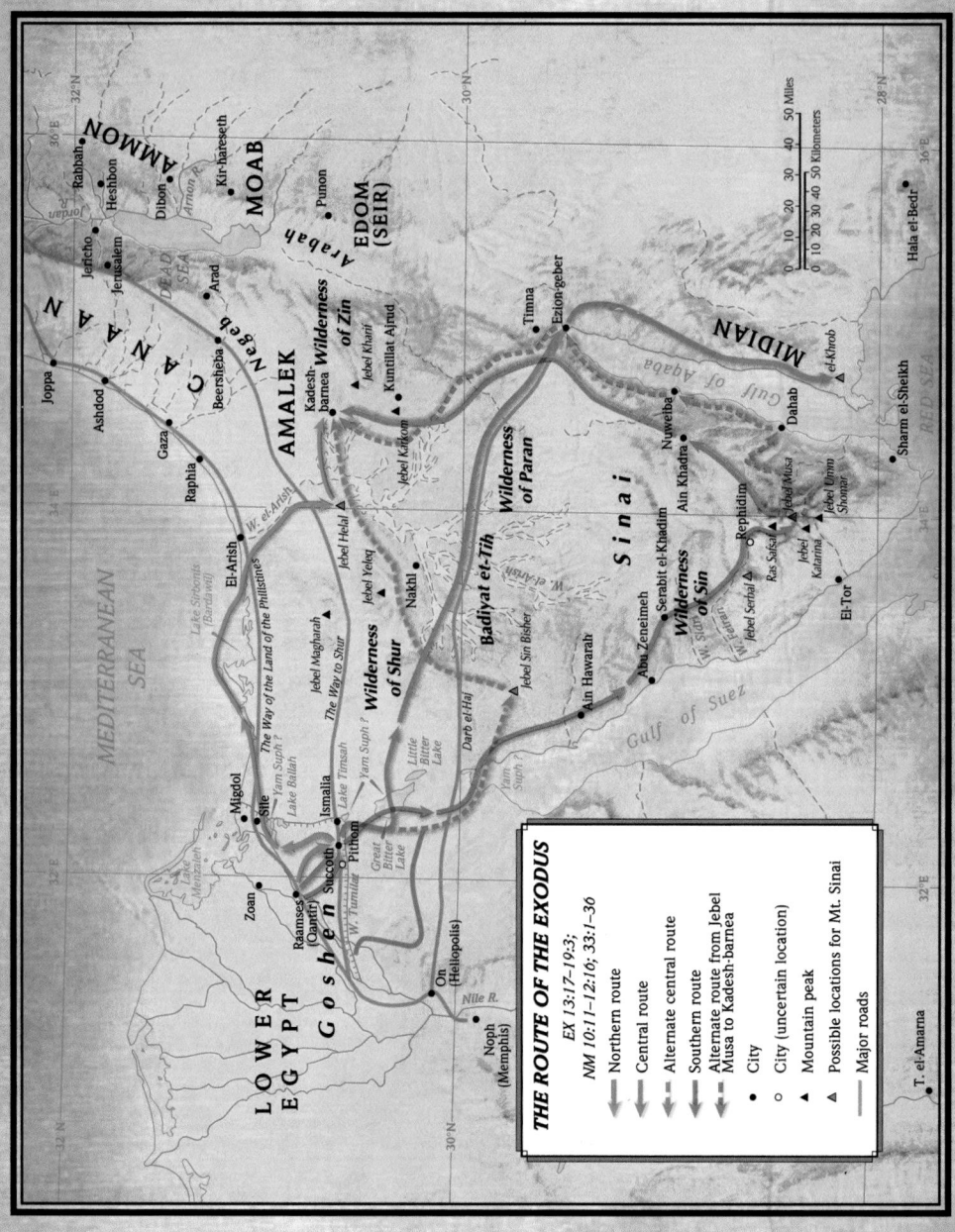

THE ROUTE OF THE EXODUS

EX 13:17–19:3;
NM 10:11–12:16; 33:1–36

Northern route
Central route
Alternate central route
Southern route
Alternate route from Jebel
Musa to Kadesh-barnea

• City
○ City (uncertain location)
▲ Mountain peak
▲ Possible locations for Mt. Sinai
— Major roads

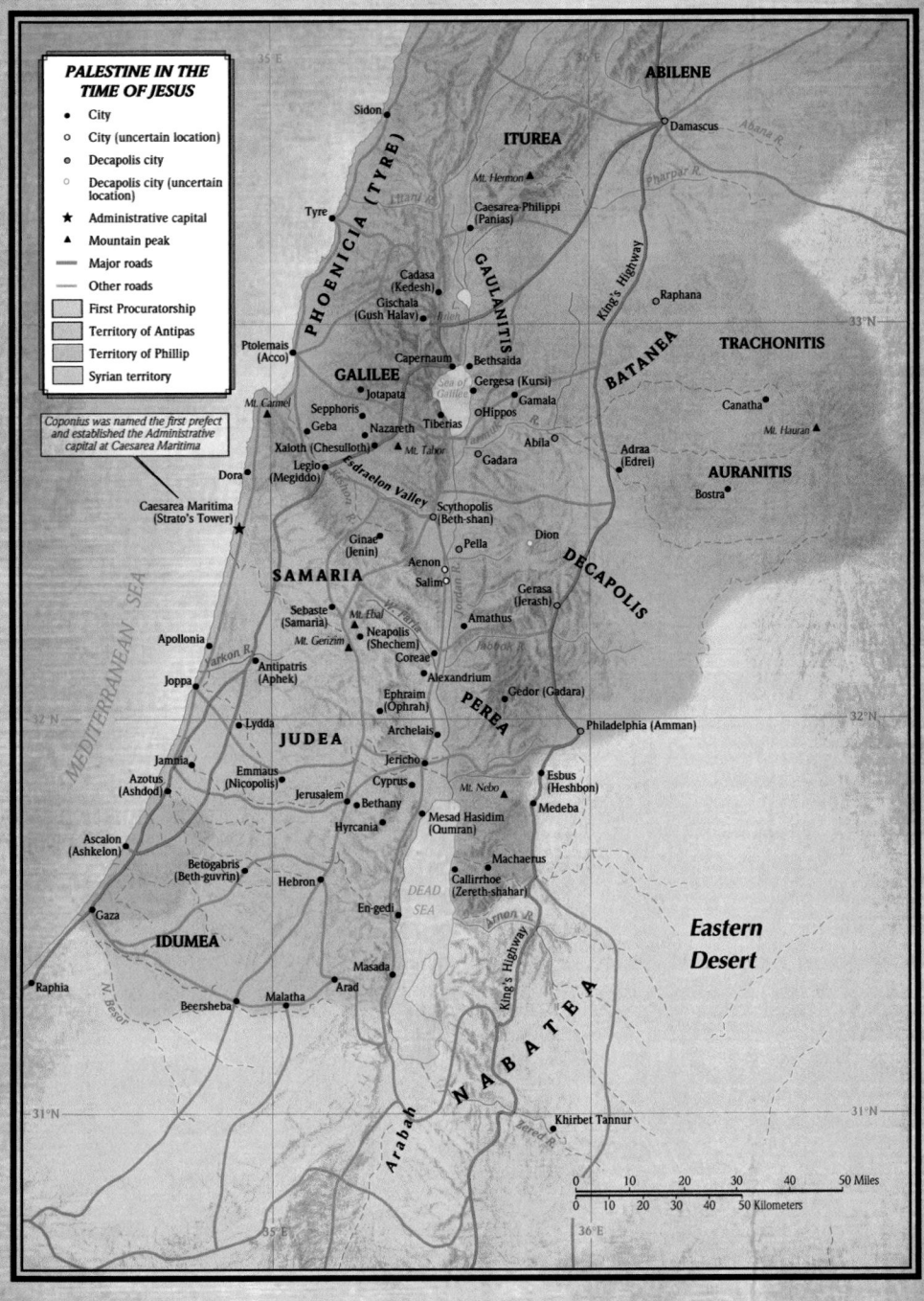

PALESTINE IN THE TIME OF JESUS

- • City
- ○ City (uncertain location)
- ◉ Decapolis city
- ○ Decapolis city (uncertain location)
- ★ Administrative capital
- ▲ Mountain peak
- — Major roads
- — Other roads
- ▢ First Procuratorship
- ▢ Territory of Antipas
- ▢ Territory of Phillip
- ▢ Syrian territory

Coponius was named the first prefect and established the Administrative capital at Caesarea Maritima

35°E
36°E

ABILENE

Sidon

ITUREA

Damascus

Mt. Hermon ▲

Caesarea-Philippi (Panias)

Abana R.

Pharpar R.

Tyre

PHOENICIA (TYRE)

Litani R.

GAULANITIS

King's Highway

Raphana

33°N

Cadasa (Kedesh)

Gischala (Gush Halav)

TRACHONITIS

BATANEA

Ptolemais (Acco)

Capernaum

Bethsaida

GALILEE

Gergesa (Kursi)

Sea of Galilee

Jotapata

Gamala

Canatha

Mt. Carmel ▲

Sepphoris

Tiberias

○Hippos

Mt. Hauran ▲

Geba

Nazareth

Abila ◉

Adraa (Edrei)

Xaloth (Chesulloth)

Mt. Tabor ▲

Gadara

AURANITIS

Dora

Legio (Megiddo)

Esdraelon Valley

Bostra

Scythopolis (Beth-shan)

DECAPOLIS

Caesarea Maritima (Strato's Tower) ★

Ginae (Jenin)

Dion ◉

Pella

SAMARIA

Aenon

Salim

MEDITERRANEAN SEA

Sebaste (Samaria)

Mt. Ebal ▲

Gerasa (Jerash)

Apollonia

Mt. Gerizim ▲

Neapolis (Shechem)

Amathus

Coreae

Jabbok R.

Yarkon R.

Antipatris (Aphek)

Alexandrium

Joppa

Ephraim (Ophrah)

Gedor (Gadara)

PEREA

32°N

Lydda

Archelais

Philadelphia (Amman)

JUDEA

Jericho

Jamnia

Emmaus (Nicopolis)

Cyprus

Mt. Nebo ▲

Esbus (Heshbon)

Azotus (Ashdod)

Jerusalem

Bethany

Medeba

Hyrcania

Mesad Hasidim (Qumran)

Ascalon (Ashkelon)

Betogabris (Beth-guvrin)

Machaerus

DEAD SEA

Callirrhoe (Zereth-shahar)

Hebron

Gaza

En-gedi

Arnon R.

Eastern Desert

IDUMEA

Masada

King's Highway

Raphia

N. Besor

Malatha

Arad

NABATEA

Beersheba

Arabah

Jered R.

Khirbet Tannur

31°N

35°E
36°E

0 10 20 30 40 50 Miles

0 10 20 30 40 50 Kilometers

THE MINISTRY OF JESUS
AROUND THE SEA OF GALILEE

MATTHEW 5–7; 9:1–9
MARK 1:21–34; 2:1–14; 4:–41; 5:1–20; 6:45–52
LUKE 7:1–10; 9:12–17
JOHN 6:1–25

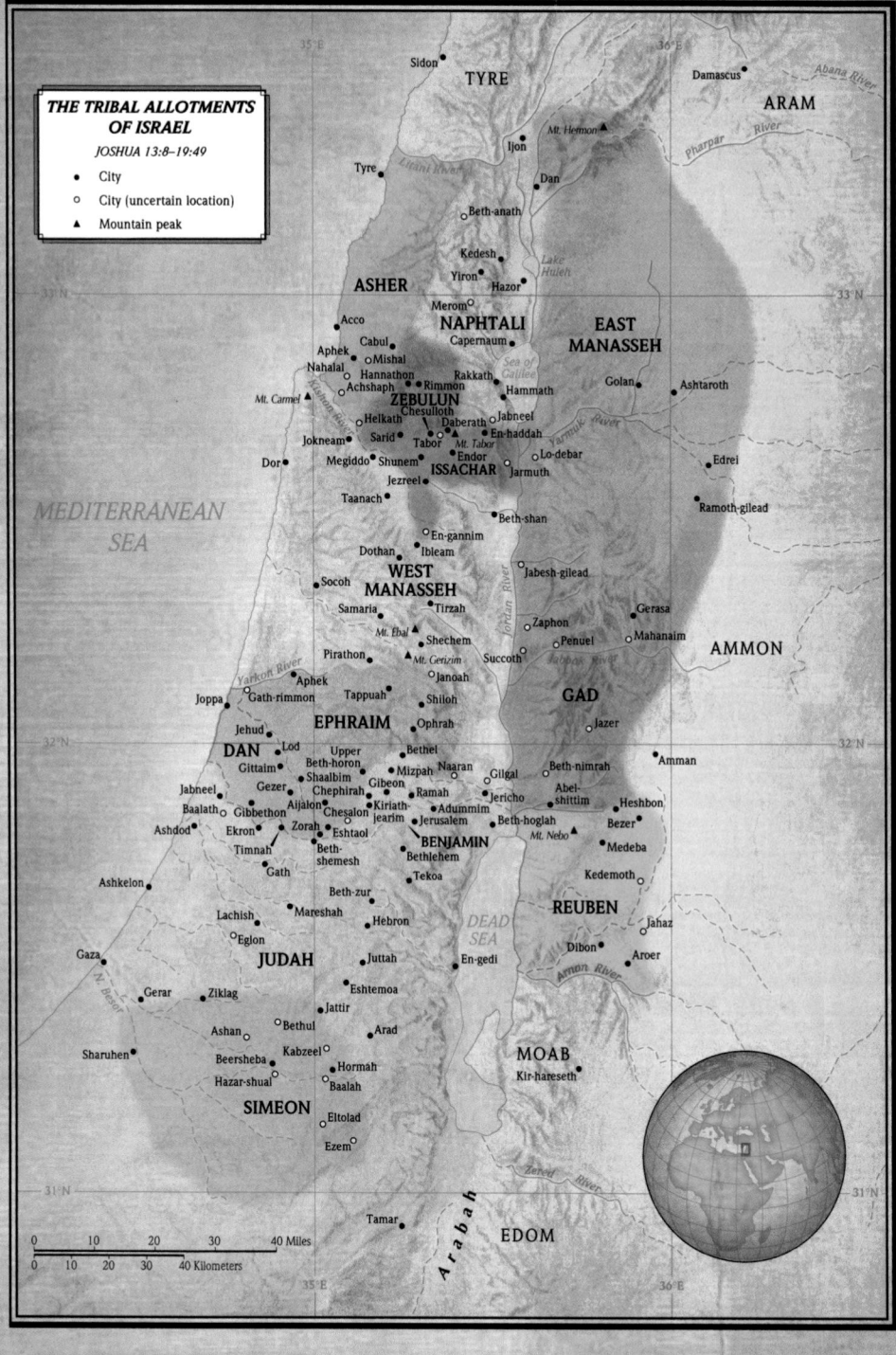

THE TRIBAL ALLOTMENTS
OF ISRAEL

JOSHUA 13:8–19:49

- • City
- ○ City (uncertain location)
- ▲ Mountain peak

MEDITERRANEAN
SEA

DEAD
SEA

Sidon
TYRE
Damascus
ARAM
Abana River

Tyre
Litani River
Ijon
Mt. Hermon ▲
Dan
Pharpar River

Beth-anath

Kedesh
Lake
Huleh
Yiron
Hazor
ASHER
Merom
NAPHTALI
EAST
MANASSEH

Acco
Capernaum
Cabul
Mishal
Aphek
Nahalal
Hannathon
Rakkath
Sea of
Galilee
Golan
Ashtaroth
Achshaph
Rimmon
Hammath
ZEBULUN
Mt. Carmel ▲
Helkath
Chesulloth
Daberath
Jabneel
Yarmuk River
Joknean
Sarid
Tabor
En-haddah
Lo-debar
Edrei
Dor
Megiddo
Shunem
Mt. Tabor
Endor
Jarmuth
Ramoth-gilead
Taanach
Jezreel
ISSACHAR

En-gannim
Beth-shan

Dothan
Ibleam
Jabesh-gilead
Socoh
WEST
MANASSEH
Samaria
Tirzah
Zaphon
Gerasa
Mt. Ebal ▲
Shechem
Penuel
Mahanaim
Pirathon
▲ Mt. Gerizim
Succoth
AMMON
Janoah
Jabbok River
Aphek
Tappuah
Shiloh
GAD
Joppa
Gath-rimmon
Ophrah
Jehud
EPHRAIM
Jazer
Lod
Upper
Bethel
DAN
Gittaim
Beth-horon
Naaran
Beth-nimrah
Amman
Shaalbim
Mizpah
Gilgal
Jabneel
Gezer
Chephirah
Gibeon
Jericho
Abel-
Baalath
Aijalon
Ramah
Adummim
shittim
Heshbon
Ashdod
Gibbethon
Chesalon
Kiriath-
Jerusalem
Beth-hoglah
Bezer
Ekron
Zorah
jearim
Mt. Nebo ▲
Medeba
Timnah
Eshtaol
BENJAMIN
Beth-
Gath
shemesh
Bethlehem
Kedemoth
Tekoa
Beth-zur
REUBEN
Ashkelon
Beth-shemesh
Jahaz
Lachish
Mareshah
Hebron
Dibon
Aroer
Gaza
Eglon
Juttah
En-gedi
Amnon River
Gerar
JUDAH
Eshtemoa
Ziklag
Jattir
Ashan
Bethul
Arad
Sharuhen
Beersheba
Kabzeel
MOAB
Hazar-shual
Hormah
Kir-hareseth
Baalah
SIMEON
Eltolad
Ezem

Tamar
Arabah
EDOM
Zered River

0 10 20 30 40 Miles
0 10 20 30 40 Kilometers

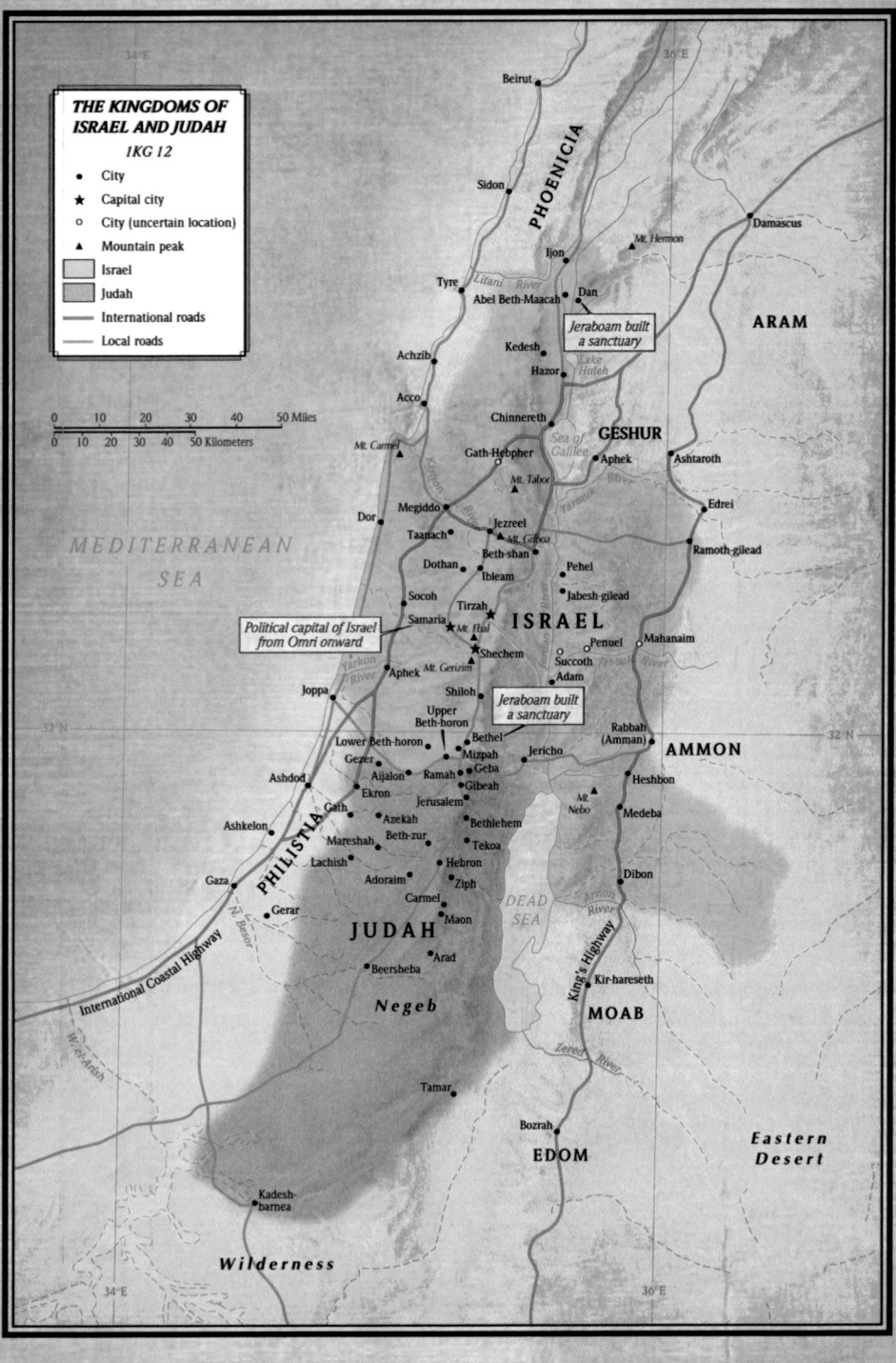

THE KINGDOMS OF
ISRAEL AND JUDAH
1KG 12

- City
★ Capital city
○ City (uncertain location)
▲ Mountain peak
Israel
Judah
International roads
Local roads

0   10   20   30   40   50 Miles
0 10 20 30 40 50 Kilometers

Beirut

PHOENICIA

Sidon

Mt. Hermon

Damascus

Tyre
Abel Beth-Maacah
Ijon
Dan
Jeraboam built a sanctuary

ARAM

Achzib
Kedesh
Hazor
Lake Huleh

Acco
Chinnereth
Sea of Galilee
GESHUR
Aphek
Ashtaroth

Mt. Carmel
Gath-Hepher
Mt. Tabor
Edrei

MEDITERRANEAN
SEA

Dor
Megiddo
Jezreel
Mt. Gilboa
Ramoth-gilead

Taanach
Beth-shan
Pehel

Dothan
Ibleam
Jabesh-gilead

Socoh
Tirzah
ISRAEL

Political capital of Israel from Omri onward
Samaria
Mt. Ebal
Shechem
Penuel
Mahanaim
Succoth
Adam

Yarkon River
Aphek
Mt. Gerizim

Joppa
Shiloh
Jeraboam built a sanctuary

Upper Beth-horon
Bethel
Rabbah (Amman)

Lower Beth-horon
Mizpah
Jericho
AMMON

Ashdod
Gezer
Geba
Heshbon

Ekron
Aijalon
Ramah
Gibeah

Ashkelon
Gath
Jerusalem
Mt. Nebo
Medeba

Mareshah
Azekah
Beth-zur
Bethlehem

Lachish
Tekoa

Gaza
PHILISTIA
Adoraim
Hebron
Ziph
Dibon

Gerar
Carmel
Maon
DEAD
SEA
Arnon River

JUDAH
King's Highway
Kir-hareseth

Beersheba
Arad
MOAB

Negeb
Zered River

Tamar

Wadi el-Arish

Bozrah
Eastern
Desert

EDOM

Kadesh-barnea

Wilderness

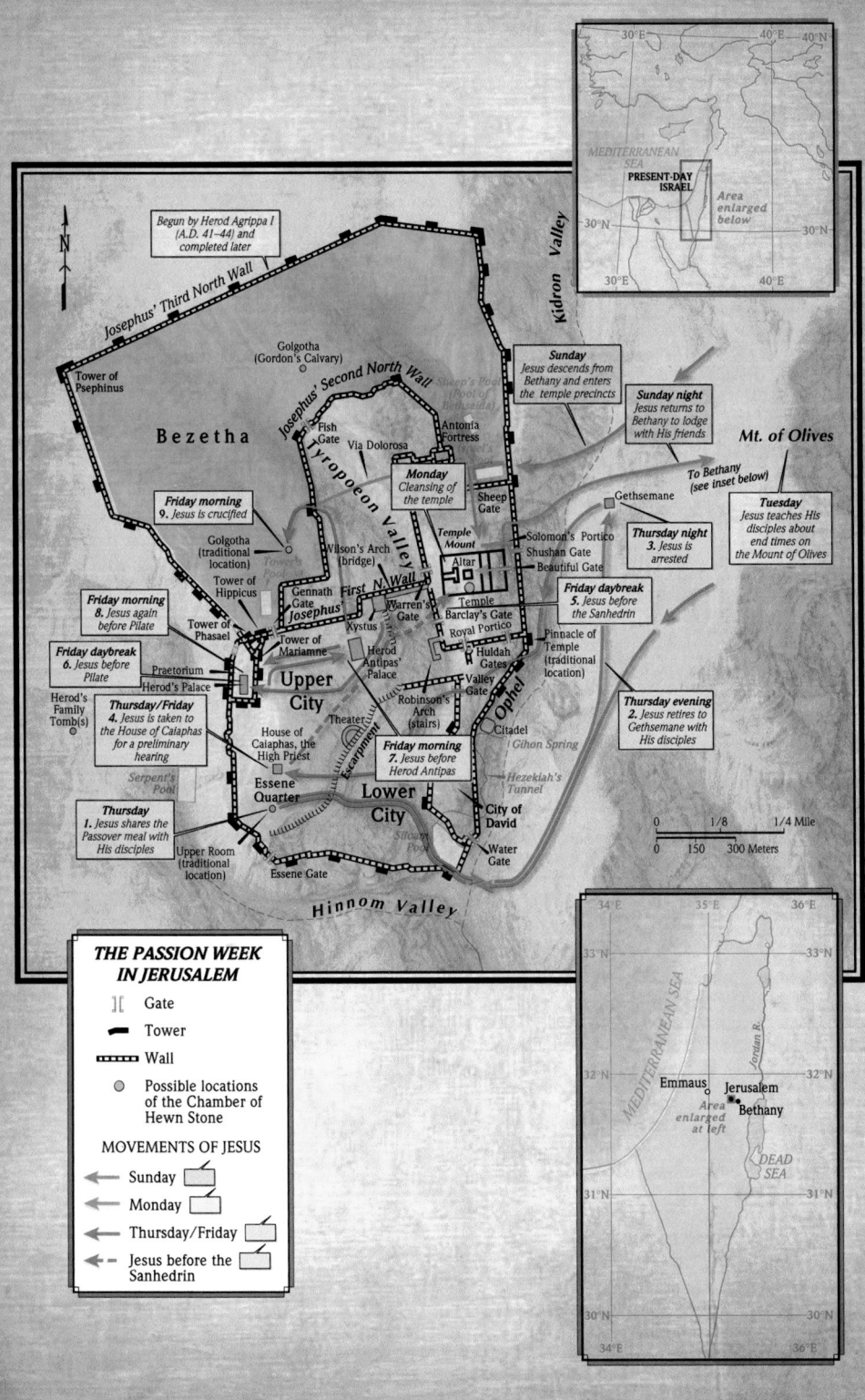

Begun by Herod Agrippa I
(A.D. 41–44) and
completed later

Josephus' Third North Wall

N

Tower of
Psephinus

Golgotha
(Gordon's Calvary)

Bezetha

Josephus' Second North Wall

Fish
Gate

Via Dolorosa

Sheep's Pool
(Pool of
Bethesda)

Antonia
Fortress

Kidron Valley

Sunday
*Jesus descends from
Bethany and enters
the temple precincts*

Sunday night
*Jesus returns to
Bethany to lodge
with His friends*

Mt. of Olives

Monday
*Cleansing of
the temple*

Sheep
Gate

To Bethany
(see inset below)

Gethsemane

Tuesday
*Jesus teaches His
disciples about
end times on
the Mount of Olives*

Tyropoeon Valley

Friday morning
9. Jesus is crucified

Golgotha
(traditional
location)

Wilson's Arch
(bridge)

Tower of Hippicus

Gennath
Gate

Josephus'
First N. Wall

Kystus

Tower of
Mariamne

Tower of
Phasael

Upper City

Friday morning
*8. Jesus again
before Pilate*

Friday daybreak
*6. Jesus before
Pilate*

Praetorium
Herod's Palace

Herod's
Family
Tomb(s)

Thursday/Friday
*4. Jesus is taken to
the House of Caiaphas
for a preliminary
hearing*

Serpent's
Pool

House of
Caiaphas, the
High Priest

Theater

Escarpment

Essene
Quarter

Thursday
*1. Jesus shares the
Passover meal with
His disciples*

Upper Room
(traditional
location)

Essene Gate

**Lower
City**

Friday morning
*7. Jesus before
Herod Antipas*

Robinson's
Arch
(stairs)

Valley
Gate

Herod
Antipas'
Palace

Warren's
Gate

**Temple
Mount**

Altar

Temple

Barclay's Gate
Royal Portico

Huldah
Gates

Solomon's Portico
Shushan Gate
Beautiful Gate

Thursday night
*3. Jesus is
arrested*

Friday daybreak
*5. Jesus before
the Sanhedrin*

Pinnacle of
Temple
(traditional
location)

Ophel

Citadel
Gihon Spring

Hezekiah's
Tunnel

City of
David

Water
Gate

Siloam
Pool

Thursday evening
*2. Jesus retires to
Gethsemane with
His disciples*

Hinnom Valley

| 0 | 1/8 | 1/4 Mile |
| 0 | 150 | 300 Meters |

THE PASSION WEEK
IN JERUSALEM

][Gate

Tower

Wall

○ Possible locations
of the Chamber of
Hewn Stone

MOVEMENTS OF JESUS

← Sunday

← Monday

← Thursday/Friday

←-- Jesus before the
Sanhedrin

30°E   40°E   40°N

MEDITERRANEAN
SEA

**PRESENT-DAY
ISRAEL**

*Area
enlarged
below*

30°N   30°N

30°E   40°E

34°E   35°E   36°E

33°N   33°N

MEDITERRANEAN SEA

Jordan R.

32°N   Emmaus Jerusalem   32°N
                Bethany
        *Area
        enlarged
        at left*

31°N   31°N

DEAD
SEA

30°N   30°N

34°E   35°E   36°E

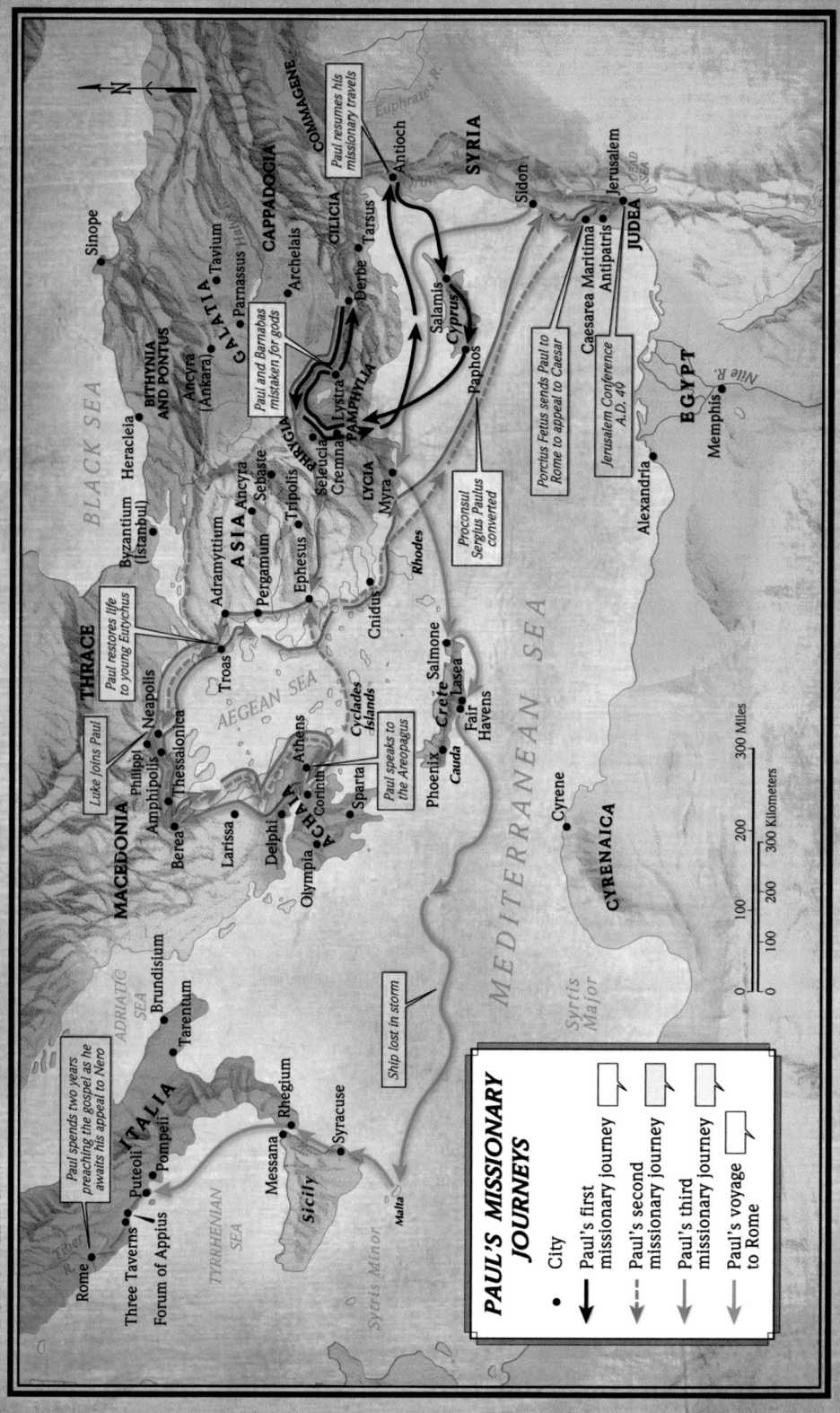

PAUL'S MISSIONARY JOURNEYS

- City
- Paul's first missionary journey
- Paul's second missionary journey
- Paul's third missionary journey
- Paul's voyage to Rome

Paul resumes his missionary travels

Paul and Barnabas mistaken for gods

Porcius Festus sends Paul to Rome to appeal to Caesar

Jerusalem Conference A.D. 49

Proconsul Sergius Paulus converted

Paul restores life to young Eutychus

Luke joins Paul

Paul speaks to the Areopagus

Ship lost in storm

Paul spends two years preaching the gospel as he awaits his appeal to Nero

SYRIA

COMMAGENE

CAPPADOCIA

GALATIA

BITHYNIA AND PONTUS

CILICIA

ASIA

PHRYGIA

PAMPHYLIA

LYCIA

JUDEA

EGYPT

CYRENAICA

THRACE

MACEDONIA

ACHAIA

ITALIA

Antioch
Sidon
Jerusalem
Caesarea Maritima
Antipatris
Tarsus
Derbe
Lystra
Iconium
Salamis
Cyprus
Paphos
Sinope
Tavium
Parnassus Halys
Ancyra (Ankara)
Archelais
Heraclea
Byzantium (Istanbul)
Ancyra
Sebaste
Tripolis
Seleucia
Cnemna
Ephesus
Pergamum
Adramyttium
Myra
Rhodes
Cnidus
Salmone
Lasea
Fair Havens
Crete
Phoenix
Cauda
Athens
Corinth
Sparta
Delphi
Olympia
Larissa
Berea
Thessalonica
Amphipolis
Philippi
Neapolis
Troas
Sidon
Memphis
Alexandria
Cyrene
Brundisium
Tarentum
Rhegium
Messana
Syracuse
Sicily
Pompeii
Puteoli
Three Taverns
Forum of Appius
Rome
Malta

BLACK SEA

AEGEAN SEA

MEDITERRANEAN SEA

ADRIATIC SEA

TYRRHENIAN SEA

Euphrates R.

Nile R.

Tiber

Syrtis Major

Syrtis Minor

Cyclades Islands

300 Miles

100   200   300 Kilometers

0   100   200